The Almanac of American Politics
★ 2010 ★

THE **Senators,** THE **Representatives**

AND THE **Governors:**

THEIR **Records** AND **Election Results,**

THEIR **States** AND **Districts**

Michael Barone
Richard E. Cohen

National
Journal
— GROUP —

Washington, D.C.

© 2009 by National Journal Group. All rights reserved.

Printed in the United States of America by United Book Press. Composition by Data-Stream Content Solutions Inc. Distributed to the trade by the University of Chicago Press.

Cover design by Chris Donovan; original cover concept by Adrian O. Constantyn. Photographs by Liz Lynch and Richard A. Bloom. For information regarding photographs, contact: National Journal, 600 New Hampshire Ave., N.W., Washington, D.C. 20037; 202-739-8400. All rights reserved.

The Almanac of American politics. —1972- —

    v.: i ll. ; 24cm.

    Biennial
    Published by Gambit 1972– ; by National Journal 1988–

ISSN: 0362-076X
ISBN: 978-0-89234-119-1 (2010)
ISBN: 978-0-89234-120-7 (pbk. : 2010)

1. United States. Congress—Biography. 2. United States. Congress—Committees. 3. Election districts—United States—Handbooks, manuals, etc. I. Barone, Michael. II. Ujifusa, Grant. III. Matthews, Douglas.

JK1012 .A44
328.73/005   70-160417

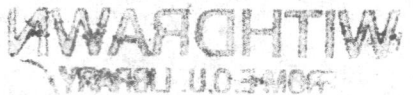

THE ALMANAC OF AMERICAN POLITICS 2010

Author
Michael Barone

Co-Author
Richard E. Cohen

Editor
Jackie Koszczuk

Managing Editor	Karl Eisenhower
Contributing Writers	Kevin Craft, Cameron Joseph, Jessica Taylor
Research Director	Jessica Taylor
Researchers	Jonathan Cannon, Kevin Craft, Zachary Farber, Cameron Joseph
Associate Editors	Jim Humes, Kitry Krause, JoAnne Moncrief, S. Scott Rohrer, Gregg Sangillo, Malorie Sellers, Bob Somerville, Monica C. Sullivan, Margo Zaneski
Information Technology Editor	Marc Lavallee
Photo Editor	Liz Lynch
Election Results, Demographics, Maps	Polidata
Interns	Niraj Chokshi, McRae Dunbar, Elizabeth McNamara, Paula Shulman, Nicole Stempak

TABLE OF CONTENTS

Contents   7

8 Contents

GUIDE TO USAGE

The following guide provides a brief description of the tabular material in the book and the sources from which the information was derived. Much of the material was generated for *The Almanac of American Politics* by Polidata, a Virginia-based political statistics and demographics firm. Other sources include the United States Census Bureau, the staff of National Journal, and the The Cook Political Report. *The 2010 Almanac* uses the latest available data and offers significant updates from the last edition of the book, published in 2007. Figures released by the Census Bureau may vary slightly from those used by *The Almanac* due to different methods of data aggregation or tabulation.

Biography

This section lists the date each governor, senator and representative was elected or appointed, the date and place of birth, current hometown, college education and degrees earned, religion, marital status and, if applicable, spouse's name and number of children. The number of terms listed reflects full, elected terms. Also provided is a brief outline of the subject's past elected offices, professional career and military service and office addresses, telephone numbers and websites. Committee and subcommittee assignments are current as of July 2008. (Note: On many committees, the chairman and ranking minority member are ex officio members of subcommittees.)

Vote Ratings

Group Ratings: The congressional ratings by 10 interest groups provide an idea of a legislator's general ideology and the degree to which he or she reflects a group's point of view. Some of the groups are single-issue organizations, such as environmental groups; others represent a particular sector or industry (e.g., business or technology). More liberal-leaning groups are on the left side of the page and more conservative groups are on the right. Some organizations provided just one rating for the two-year congressional session. Here is a general description of the groups:

ADA Americans for Democratic Action
Liberal: Since its founding in 1947, ADA members have pushed for legislation to curtail defense spending, prevent encroachments on civil liberties and promote international human rights. The ADA used 20 votes during the 110th Congress based on a broad spectrum of issues for its vote analysis.

ACLU American Civil Liberties Union
Pro-individual liberties: ACLU seeks to protect individuals from what it views as legal, executive and congressional infringement on basic rights guaranteed by the Bill of Rights. The ACLU ratings are published once every Congress. The 2008 ratings include the years 2007 and 2008.

AFS American Federation of State, County and Municipal Employees (AFSCME)
Liberal labor: As the nation's largest public service employees union, representing more than 1.6 million members, AFSCME is committed to improving working conditions through collective bargaining. The AFSCME voting records are based on a representative sample of roll call votes from the 110th Congress (2007-08).

LCV League of Conservation Voters
Environmental: Formed in 1970, LCV is the national, non-partisan arm of the environmental movement. LCV works to elect pro-environmental protection candidates to Congress. LCV ratings are based on key votes on energy, environment and natural resource issues.

ITIC Information Technology Industry Council
High-tech industry: ITIC represents the leading U.S. providers of information technology products and services. ITIC's mission is to help shape policies that advance electronic commerce, open new markets, rely on market-based solutions, and foster innovation. The 2008 ratings include the years 2007 and 2008.

NTU National Taxpayers Union

Pro-taxpayer rights: The NTU is the nation's oldest taxpayers' rights group, representing 362,000 members in all 50 states. NTU analyzed every roll call vote taken during both sessions of the 110th Congress that significantly affected federal taxes, spending, debt or level of regulation.

COC Chamber of Commerce of the United States

Pro-business: Founded in 1912 as a voice for organized business, COC represents local, regional and state chambers of commerce in addition to trade and professional organizations.

ACU American Conservative Union

Conservative: Since 1971, ACU ratings have provided a means of gauging the conservatism of members of Congress. Foreign policy, social and budget issues are analyzed.

CFG Club for Growth

Pro-tax limitation: CFG supports limited government, lower taxes and policies that support economic growth. CFG ratings are based on key votes that deal with taxes, trade and the economy.

FRC Family Research Council

Conservative: Founded in 1980, the FRC promotes marriage and family as the bedrocks of society and advocates policies that uphold Judeo-Christian values. FRC ratings are based on legislation dealing with abortion and family issues. The 2008 ratings include the years 2007 and 2008.

National Journal Ratings

National Journal's rating system is an objective method of analyzing congressional voting. A panel of the magazine's editors and writers compiled a list of congressional roll call votes and classified them as either economic, social or foreign policy-related. The votes in each issue area were subjected to a principal-components analysis, a statistical procedure designed to determine the degree to which each vote resembled other votes in the same category (the same members tending to vote together). The analysis also revealed which yea votes correlated with which nay votes within each issue area (members voting yea on certain issues tended to vote nay on others). The yea and nay positions on each roll call were then identified as conservative or liberal. Each roll call vote was assigned a weight from 1 (lowest) to 3 (highest), based on the degree to which it correlated with other votes in the same issue area. A higher weight meant that vote was more strongly correlated with other votes and was therefore a better test of economic, social or foreign-policy ideology. All members of Congress who participated in at least half of the votes in each area received ratings. Those who missed more that half the votes were not scored (shown as *). Absences and abstentions were not counted.

Members of Congress were then ranked according to relative liberalism and conservatism. Finally, they were assigned percentiles showing their rank relative to others in the chamber. The liberal percentage score means that the member voted more liberal than that percentage of his or her colleagues in that issue area in 2008. The conservative score means that the member voted more conservative than that percentage of his or her colleagues. The composite score is an average of a member's six issue-based scores.

Key Votes

The key votes section illustrates a legislator's stance on important votes on national issues. Typically, months of debate, persuasion and compromise go into a final floor vote, which is not reflected in a simple yea or nay vote. However, the voting record remains the best indication of a member's general ideologies and positions on issues. Following is a list of key votes from the 110th Congress (2007-08) selected by *The Almanac* staff. A member who was absent, voted present, or who was not in office at the time of a particular vote receives an *. Roll-call data were obtained from the clerk of the House and the secretary of the Senate.

House Votes:

1. **Increase minimum wage:** (House Vote 18/HR 2) Increase the minimum wage to $7.25 per hour in two years from $5.15 per hour. January 10, 2007. (315-116) (D: 233-0; R: 82-116)
2. **Expand SCHIP:** (House Vote 906/HR 976) Reauthorize and expand the State Children's Health Insurance Program. September 25, 2007. (265-159) (D: 220-8; R: 45-151)
3. **Raise CAFE standards:** (House Vote 1140/HR 6) Increase fuel-efficiency standards to 35 miles per gallon by 2020, shift energy tax incentives, and require electric utilities to use renewable energy sources for 15% of their electricity by 2020. December 6, 2007. (235-181) (D: 221-7; R: 14-174)
4. **Bail out financial markets:** (House Vote 681/HR 1424) Agree to a $700 billion government bailout of the financial industry, and approve extension of expiring tax provisions. October 3, 2008. (263-171) (D: 172-63; R: 91-108)
5. **Share immigration data:** (House Vote 485/HR 2638) Bar funds to state or local governments that refuse to share information on immigrant status with the Immigration and Customs Enforcement Bureau. June 15, 2007. (234-189) (D: 49-180; R: 185-9)
6. **Foreign aid abortion ban:** (House Vote 534/HR 2764) Retain the "Mexico City" policy that bars abortions in certain foreign aid programs. June 21, 2007. (205-218) (D: 25-206; R-180-12)
7. **Ban gay bias in workplace:** (House Vote 1057/HR 3685) Prohibit job discrimination on the basis of a person's sexual orientation. November 7. 2007. (235-184) (D: 200-25; R: 35-159)
8. **Repeal D.C. gun law:** (House Vote 600/HR 6842) Repeal the District of Columbia's local laws that prohibit possession of firearms. September 17, 2008. (260-160) (D: 82-151; R: 178-9)
9. **Withdraw troops 8/08:** (House Vote 186/HR 1591) Require the withdrawal of all U.S. combat troops from Iraq by August 2008. March 23, 2007. (218-212) (D: 216-14; R: 2-198)
10. **No operations in Iran:** (House Vote 364/1585) Bar the use of military funds for contingency operations in Iran. May 16, 2007. (202-216) (D: 196-29; R: 6-187)
11. **Free trade with Peru:** (House Vote 1060/HR 3688) Implement the free trade agreement between the United States and Peru. November 8, 2007. (285-132) (D: 109-116; R: 176-16)
12. **Overhaul FISA:** (House Vote 437/HR 6304) Overhaul the Foreign Intelligence Surveillance Act, including retroactive legal immunity for telecommunications firms that assisted with surveillance of people in the United States. June 20, 2008. (293-129) (D: 105-128; R: 188-1)

Senate Votes:

1. **Raise CAFE standards:** (Senate Vote 225/HR 6) Limit debate on an energy bill setting higher fuel standards for vehicles. June 21, 2007. (62-32; 60 votes required to end filibuster) (D: 41-6; R: 19-26; I: 2-0)
2. **Expand SCHIP:** (Senate Vote 307/HR 976) Reauthorize and expand the State Children's Health Insurance Program. August 2, 2007. (68-31) (D: 48-0; R: 18-31; I: 2-0)
3. **Cap greenhouse gases:** (Senate Vote 145/S 3036) Limit debate on a bill setting up a cap and trade system to curb climate change. June 6, 2008. (48-36; 60 votes required end filibuster) (D: 39-4; R-7-32; I: 2-0)
4. **Bail out financial markets:** (Senate Vote 213/HR 1424) Agree to a $700 billion government bailout of the financial industry, and approve extension of expiring tax provisions. October 1, 2008. (74-25) (D: 39-9; R: 34-15; I: 1-1)
5. **Make English official language:** (Senate vote 198/S 1348) Make English the official language of the United States. June 6, 2007. (64-33) (D: 17-30; R: 47-1; I: 0-2)
6. **Path to citizenship:** (Senate Vote 235/S 1639) Limit debate on the immigration reform bill. June 28, 2007. (46-53; 60 votes to end filibuster) (D: 33-15; R: 12-37; I: 1-1)
7. **Fetus is unborn child:** (Senate Vote 302/HR 976) Define a fetus as an "unborn child." August 2, 2007. (49-50) (D: 5-43; R: 44-5; I: 0-2)
8. **Prosecute hate crimes:** (Senate Vote 350/HR 1585) Limit debate on a measure funding the prosecution of hate crimes. September 27, 2007. (60-39; 60 votes required to end filibuster) (D: 49-0; R: 9-39; I: 2-0)
9. **Withdraw troops 3/08:** (Senate Vote 147/HR 1591) Require the withdrawal of most U.S. troops from Iraq by March 2008. April 26, 2007. (51-46) (D: 48-0; R: 2-45; I: 1-1)
10. **Iran guard is terrorist group:** (Senate Vote 349/HR 1585) Express the sense of the Senate that the Iranian revolutionary guard should be designated as a terrorist organization. September 26, 2007. (76-22) (D: 29-19; R: 46-2; I: 1-1)
11. **Increase missile defense $:** (Senate Vote 198/S 3001) Increase federal funding for missile defense programs. September 10, 2008. (39-57) (D: 1-45; R: 38-10; I: 0-2)
12. **Overhaul FISA:** (Senate Vote 168/HR 6304) Overhaul the Foreign Intelligence Surveillance Act, including retroactive legal immunity for telecommunications companies. July 9, 2008. (69-28) (D: 21-27; R: 47-0; I: 1-1)

Election Results

Listed for each member of the House are results of the 2008 general, runoff and primary elections, as well as any special elections held since November 2006. Most-recent gubernatorial and senatorial results are presented in a like manner. Votes and percentages are included, indicating the margin of victory. Due to rounding up and rounding down, some totals may equal more or less than 100%. Candidates in primaries receiving less than 5% of the total vote were excluded. Candidates in general elections receiving less than 2% of the total vote were excluded. Election returns were collected from the individual states.

Prior winning percentage: This feature provides winning percentage of the vote in past elections. If no percentage is provided for an election year, it indicates that the member lost or did not run for reelection that year; generally this will occur where there has been a gap in service. Two elections in the same year indicate a special and a general election.

Presidential vote: Results were compiled from state and local election authorities; caucus results are not provided. The presidential vote by congressional district is estimated by Polidata, from information collected from state and local election offices. Only a handful of states provide district-level presidential vote data. By necessity, other results are aggregated from precinct-level returns. Voting data from districts with split precincts and centrally counted absentee votes thus should be considered estimates; the allocation of these unassigned votes is determined by Polidata. While estimates of votes are included in each district, the percentage values generally provide reliable information. The total of the congressional district votes may not add up to the total state vote, because some votes (overseas, military and some absentee and early votes) are not assigned to a congressional district and because county election office reports sometimes conflict with reports from state election authorities.

Campaign finance: All data were derived from candidates' campaign finance reports and party reports available from the Federal Election Commission. The dollar figure, in parentheses to the right of the election results, represents the candidates' net expenditures for the period from January 1, 2007 to December 31, 2008. *These figures do not include corrections or amendments filed with the FEC after May 2008.*

Demographics and Politics (Boxed)

Population: All population figures are from the Census Bureau's 2005-07 American Community Survey (ACS), unless otherwise noted. Census estimates are as of July 1, 2008. The estimates are used for voting age population in the states and for the population of congressional districts.

Urban/rural population: The percentage of total population living in areas defined by the Bureau as urban or as rural. Urban/rural figures for the states are from the ACS; urban/rural figures for congressional districts are from the 2000 census.

Native of state: People born in a state of residence as a percentage of total population.

Not a citizen: People who are foreign born and not a citizen as a percentage of the total.

Area size: Area size is in square miles, including water, and is taken from the 2000 census.

Most populous cities: City population figures are from the 2005-07 ACS where available. Where not available, the Bureau's July 1, 2007 estimates are used.

Household income: Household income as a percentage of all households.

Home value: Refers to self-estimated market value of owner-occupied units.

Work sector: A classification of worker by economic sector. The figure is the percentage of employed persons 16 years and older. *Private* refers to people employed by private for-profit or not-for-profit organizations on a wage or salary basis; *Government* refers to federal, state and local government employees.

Unemployment: Unemployed, non-military people 16 years and older as a percentage of the labor force.

Poverty status: The percentage of people 16 years and older for whom poverty status has been determined and who fall below the poverty line, which in 2007 was defined by the federal government as a family of four living on about $21,000 or less a year.

Occupation ("collar"): The figure is the percentage of employed persons 16 years and older. *White collar* refers to managerial, professional, sales and administrative occupations. *Blue collar* refers to construction, production and transportation occupations. *Khaki collar* refers to active-duty military personnel. *Other* refers to the balance of employed people not classified as white collar, blue collar or military, such as those in the farming, fishing and forestry industries or in health care, protective service, food preparation and personal care occupations.

Race/ethnicity: As defined by the Census Bureau, race reflects an individual respondent's perception of his or her racial identity and does not reflect any biological or anthropological definitions. The racial categories are: American-Indian or Alaska Native (designated as *Native Am.*); Asian; Native Hawaiian or other Pacific Islander (*Hawaiian*); black or African-American; white; two or more races (*Two + races*); Other non-Hispanic people (*Other*). Hispanic origin is defined as an ethnicity, and includes those who classified themselves in one of three specific Hispanic categories (Cuban, Mexican, or Puerto Rican) or as of "other Spanish/Hispanic origin." Persons of Latino or Hispanic origin may be of any race for Census purposes, but *The Almanac* includes only non-Hispanic blacks in the black population category and only non-Hispanic whites in the white population category, so that the percentages add up to 100%. The numbers provided for each racial or ethnic group represent a percentage of all people in a state or a congressional district.

Ancestry: Ethnic origin or descent. With this category, the Census Bureau intended to provide data for groups that were not included in the Hispanic origin and race questions; thus, it does not reflect diversity within Hispanic and Asian subgroups. To arrive at the percentages for each category, the bureau used the average number of responses to estimate the percentage of the population that shares the ancestry characteristic. NOTE: The *USA* designation refers to "American" as a unique ethnicity if it was cited alone as a response, in the absence of any other ethnicity. *Subsaharan* refers to the census category of "Subsaharan African." *West Indian* excludes Hispanic groups.

Language: The percentage of households speaking a certain language. The abbreviation *Other Eur.* refers to other Indo-European languages.

Education: *H.S. grad* refers to people with a high school diploma or higher and *college grad* refers to people with a bachelor's degree or higher, both as a percentage of people 25 years and older.

Military veterans: People who were in the Armed Forces as a percentage of voting-age population.

Registered voters: The number of registered voters by party, as close as possible to the November 2008 election. The individual states' election bureaus or political parties provide these figures. Some states have no voter registration. *D* refers to Democrat; *R* refers to Republican; *other* refers to independent voters or those from minor parties.

Turnout: The share of the total voting age population that cast a vote for president in the 2008 election. Other measures could be used to calculate turnout, but many of these measures were not available for all of the states or all of the congressional districts. Basing calculations on voting age population and presidential vote permits comparisons across states and across districts, but it does not account for voting age persons who are not eligible to vote due to the status of their residency and citizenship, for example. Furthermore, voting age population figures for states are taken from July 1, 2008 census estimates, while voting age population figures for congressional districts are taken from the 2005-07 ACS (census estimates are not available for congressional districts). There is likely to be some overstatement of the rate by district because the turnout calculations do not reflect increases in population since the ACS.

State information: Each legislature is referred to according to its proper name, followed by a breakdown of membership by party affiliation. Partisan composition figures are drawn from the National Conference of State Legislatures and are current as of July 2008.

Cook Partisan Voting Index: Developed in 1997 by Charlie Cook, a leading national political handicapper, the partisan voting index (PVI) is designed to provide a quick, overall assessment of a state or district's generic partisan strength. The PVI measures a state or district's recent partisan performance at the presidential level (district value) against that of the nation as a whole (national value). For this volume, the calculations are based on an average of 2004 and 2008 presidential election data for each district as provided by the political statistical analysis firm Polidata. Both years carry equal weight. Only votes for major party nominees are considered. The national Democratic value is 51.2 (an average of John Kerry's 48.8% share and Barack Obama's 53.7% share) and the national Republican value is 48.8. Thus, if Kerry and Obama won an average of 56.2% of the two-party vote in a given district, the district's PVI would be D+5, because it voted five percentage points more Democratic than the national average. A PVI value of "even" indicates an evenly balanced district.

Abbreviations

ACLU	American Civil Liberties Union
ACU	American Conservative Union
ADA	Americans for Democratic Action
AFDC	Aid to Families with Dependent Children
AFL-CIO	American Federation of Labor and Congress of Industrial Organizations
AFS	American Federation of State, County & Municipal Employees (AFSCME)
AID	Agency for International Development
AMI	American Independent (CA)
ANWR	Arctic National Wildlife Refuge
BL	Better Life Party
C	Conservative Party (NY)
CAFE	Corporate Average Fuel Economy
CAFTA	Central America Free Trade Agreement
CFL	Connecticut for Lieberman
CHOB	Cannon House Office Building
CIA	Central Intelligence Agency
CNP	Constitution Party
CPF	Constitution Party of Florida
COC	Chamber of Commerce of the United States
COLA	Cost of Living Adjustment
DCCC	Democratic Congressional Campaign Committee
DFL	Democratic-Farmer-Labor Party (MN)
DLC	Democratic Leadership Council
DNC	Democratic National Committee
DSCC	Democratic Senatorial Campaign Committee
DSOB	Dirksen Senate Office Building
EMILY	EMILY's List (Early Money is Like Yeast)
ERISA	Employee Retirement Income Security Act
FEC	Federal Election Commission
FERC	Federal Energy Regulatory Commission
Green	Green Party
H	Capitol Building Room-House side
HSOB	Hart Senate Office Building
I	Independent
IC	Independent Conservative
ID	Independent Democrat
IG	Independent Green
IMC	Independent Maine Course
Ind	Independence Party
IAP	Independent American Party (NV)
IVP	Independent Voters Party
L	Liberal Party
LCV	League of Conservation Voters
LHOB	Longworth House Office Building
Lib	Libertarian Party
Mod	Moderate Party
NAFTA	North American Free Trade Agreement
NARAL	NARAL Pro-Choice America
NFIB	National Federation of Independent Business
NL	Natural Law Party
NP	Non-Partisan
NPA	No Party Affiliation
NRCC	National Republican Congressional Committee
NRSC	National Republican Senatorial Committee
NSA	National Security Agency
NTU	National Taxpayers Union
PDP	Popular Democratic Party (PR)
PF	Peace and Freedom Party
PJ	Peace and Justice Party (NY)
POP	Populist Party
PRG	Progressive Party
Ref	Reform Party
RHOB	Rayburn House Office Building
RMM	Ranking Minority Member
RNC	Republican National Committee
RSOB	Russell Senate Office Building
RTL	Right-to-Life Party
S	Capitol Building Room, Senate side
SOC	Socialist Party
SW	Socialist Workers Party
UAW	United Auto Workers
WF	Working Families
WI	Write In

Obama's America

By Michael Barone

On November 4, 2008, Barack Obama was elected president of the United States by 53% to 46%, the biggest presidential victory since the election of George H.W. Bush 20 years earlier. The achievement was his but also his political party's. Democrats won the popular vote for the House of Representatives by 53% to 44% and expanded their majority to 257-178. It was the first time since 1988 that either major party had hit 53%. In the Senate, the Democrats initially captured seven seats, which put them within reach of a 60-vote majority impervious to the threat of filibusters. The results of the 2008 election signaled the end of a long period during which both parties appealed to approximately equal segments of the American electorate. After the cliff-hanger 2000 election, *The Almanac of American Politics* described America as a 49% nation. After the 2008 election, it appears that this is, at least for the moment and possibly for a long time, Obama's nation.

The 2008 campaign was the first since 1952 in which neither a president nor a vice president was a candidate. It produced a dramatic expansion in the size of the electorate from George W. Bush's first election in 2000. The only comparable eight-year growth spurt occurred between 1944 and 1952, when the GI generation first voted in large numbers. After many years in which political analysts bemoaned low voter turnout, the presidential electorate grew from 105 million in 2000 to 131 million in 2008, a 25% increase during a period of 8% population growth. About 60% of eligible voters participated in the 2008 presidential election, a level exceeded only rarely in modern times: in 1952, 1960, 1964, and 1968. America elected its first black president with about the same high level of involvement that it displayed in choosing its first Catholic president in 1960, Democrat John F. Kennedy.

Turnout did not rise evenly across the country. It went up more in target states, those places that were seriously contested by the presidential campaigns, and less elsewhere, although it rose by at least 10% in every state and the District of Columbia. In Pennsylvania and Ohio, the increase in turnout from 2000 to 2008 was 22%, while population growth was only 1%. Uncontested California and Texas experienced surges in political participation of 24% and 26%, respectively, driven only partly by population increases of 8.5% and 17%. Nationally, this rush of political adrenaline was fueled by a combination of interest in the candidates and the organizational heft of the two campaigns. Collective enthusiasm worked to the advantage of Republicans in the 2002 midterms and in the 2004 presidential election, but in 2006 and 2008, it worked to the advantage of Democrats even more. Both parties made a concentrated effort to boost turnout, but the Obama campaign's organizing overshadowed Republican operations. In the 2004 exit poll, 26% of people said they were contacted by Democratic nominee John Kerry's campaign and 24% heard from Republican Bush's campaign. In the 2008 exit poll, 26% reported contacts by the Democrats and only 18% by the Republicans.

The fact that Obama won in 2008 with nearly the same 7.7-percentage-point margin that gave George H.W. Bush his victory in 1988 has been cited by some scholars as further evidence that the Republican era that began in the 1980s has been superseded by a Democratic era that solidified some time during George W. Bush's second term. Compelling arguments can be made for this view, and Democrats looking forward from 2008 seem to have more reason than Republicans did in 1988 to believe that their party is on its way to an enduring majority. But the 1988 election and the 2008 election happened in markedly different political periods. In the last quarter century, the United States experienced relatively long periods of trench warfare politics, during which the divisions between the parties were stable and the political battles were fought along familiar lines. There were relatively brief periods of open field politics, in which highly unstable voting behavior produced unlikely electoral outcomes. The period between 1983 and 1991 was one of trench warfare politics: Americans voted Republican for president and Democratic for Congress to the point that political scientists said the former had a lock on the presidency and political commentators did not even bother to calculate the odds of a Republican majority in Congress.

Then came a period of highly unstable, open field politics from 1991 to 1995, in which the unthinkable happened. Third-party candidates led in polls for the presidency—Ross Perot in 1992, Colin Powell in 1995—and a Republican president who presided over a successful war was defeated soundly by a young Democrat with no experience in national office. Then, two years later, voters elected a Republican House and a Republican Senate for the first time in 42 years. The turn of events was so dramatic that the term "Republican revolution" was coined to describe the change in control of Congress.

There followed, from 1995 to 2005, another period of trench warfare politics. This time, the nation was almost evenly divided between the two parties. Democratic President Bill Clinton was re-elected with 49% of the vote in 1996. And in the next two presidential elections, the popular vote was divided 48% to 48%, and 51% to 48%. In five successive House elections, from 1996 to 2004, Republicans won between 47% and 50% of the popular vote while Democrats won between 45% and 49%. Then, starting in 2005, after the public began to sour on the Iraq war, after Hurricane Katrina presented tests that nearly everyone on the political front lines failed, and after Congress wrapped itself in bribery and corruption scandals, Republican Party identification fell, as often happens to the party in power. Democrats won majorities in both chambers of Congress in 2006. The popular vote in House elections was 53% to 45% in favor of Democrats, almost a precise reversal of the Republicans' 52% to 46% in their breakthrough year of 1994. In 2008, Democrats won both the House popular vote and the presidency by almost the same numbers.

But the course of the 2008 campaign suggests that these results were not inevitable. In the first place, the two parties' nominations were not won in the usual way. From 1972, when the parties began selecting most of their delegates in primaries, through 2004, contested nominations were won by the candidate who swept the primaries. This was not so in 2008. Sen. John McCain of Arizona won the Republican nomination by winning narrow pluralities in early primaries—by 5 percentage points in New Hampshire, 3 percentage points in South Carolina, 5 percentage points in Florida, 1 percentage point in Missouri, and 7 percentage points in California. Thanks to Republican winner-take-all delegate allocation rules, he was able to convert those squeaker victories into an insuperable lead by early February. A shift of just 3 percentage points from McCain to former Massachusetts Gov. Mitt Romney in all of the primaries up to that point would have left the two of them virtually tied in delegates, with Romney in better financial shape. The Republican contests showed a party splintered into various warring groups. Former Arkansas Gov. Mike Huckabee carried evangelical Christians, Romney tended to carry affluent suburbanites, and McCain won those betwixt and between. Up through the same-day contests on Super Tuesday, February 5, McCain won 50% of the vote only in New Jersey, New York, and Connecticut—hardly the base of the party these days.

On the Democratic side, Sen. Hillary Rodham Clinton of New York actually won more popular votes and more delegates than Obama in the primaries (if you include the results in Florida and Michigan, which were only partially counted by the Democratic National Committee after a dispute with the states over their decision to move up their primary dates). But the Democrats' proportional representation delegate allocation rules left her with fewer delegates than Obama was able to win in his mostly lopsided victories in 12 of the 13 caucus states. That narrow delegate lead persuaded most of the Democrats' numerous superdelegates to endorse Obama. Party officeholders and insiders were not about to deny the nomination to an African-American candidate who, after a spectacular February and a dreary March and April, clung to a narrow but precious lead in pledged (i.e., won in primaries and caucuses) delegates. Without its superior organizational efforts, the Obama campaign might not have prevailed. The Democratic Party was divided along demographic lines. Clinton consistently carried older voters, downscale voters, Latino voters, and older Jewish voters. And she got her largest majorities in the Appalachian territory stretching from western Pennsylvania southwest through the mountains and west to Arkansas and Oklahoma. Obama consistently won younger voters, upscale voters, and African-American voters. The result was an odd-looking political map, with Clinton carrying most of the northeast and southwest quadrants of the country and Obama winning most of the southeast and northwest quadrants.

A Well-Run Campaign

In the general election campaign, Obama started with great advantages. The Republican president had low job-approval ratings, the Republican Party identification had sharply declined since 2004, and Democrats had a greater share of voter enthusiasm. Despite his protracted battle with Clinton in the primaries, Obama was able to minimize defections in November. The exit poll showed that only 16% of Clinton's primary voters moved to McCain. The Obama campaign made brilliant use of the Internet to create and mobilize communities of Obama supporters. And it raised enormous and unprecedented sums of money—so much money that it would have been an act of folly for Obama not to break his pledge to accept federal financing in the fall.

Still, there was some movement in opinion over the course of the campaign. About 14% of voters shifted between candidates in the 12 months before the election, with 9% switching from McCain to Obama and 5% from Obama to McCain, according to a series of AP/Ipsos polls. During the campaign year, opinion moved against the Democrats on two major issues. The perceived success of President Bush's troop surge strategy in Iraq eliminated a major Republican negative, and $4-a-gallon gasoline stirred most Americans to favor offshore oil drilling and energy exploration in the Arctic National Wildlife Refuge. For most of 2008, Obama led McCain in the polls, often by significant margins. But coming out of the party conventions in September, McCain led Obama for about two weeks. That lead may have just been an unsustainable post-convention bounce or, possibly, a sustainable change in alignment. But events intervened.

The collapse of Lehman Brothers on September 15 led to the crisis in the financial services industry and the subsequent $700 billion government bailout. On September 18, Obama overtook McCain in the RealClearPolitics website's average of recent polls. Obama's cool demeanor in response to the crisis contrasted with McCain's relatively impulsive decision to abandon campaigning and return to Washington. McCain's choice of Alaska Gov. Sarah Palin as his vice presidential nominee, initially an asset because of the enthusiasm she aroused among conservatives long indifferent to him, came to seem, through the lens of the financial crisis, as more evidence of impulsiveness. Opinion shifted little after that, and most pre-election polls were very close to the actual results.

Obama carried the electoral vote by 365 to 173. The big spread is testimony to the organizational strength of his campaign and the shrewdness of his strategists. Without the four states he carried with 50 or 51% of the vote—Florida, Indiana, North Carolina, and Ohio—he would have had 292 electoral votes, just 22 more than the needed majority. He carried all 19 states (plus the District of Columbia) that Kerry won in 2004 and he prevailed in two that had been furiously contested in 2000 and 2004—Florida and Ohio—with only 51% of the vote. He captured nine states that had gone for Bush in 2004. In Nevada and New Mexico, his campaign did a superb job of registering and turning out newcomers and Latinos, and he won 55% and 57%, respectively, in what had been exquisitely close states in 2000 and 2004. In Iowa, where the state Democratic Party has had great organizational success and where Obama campaigned extensively before the caucuses, he won 54%. He also won 54% in Colorado. He received 53% in Virginia, where the elections of Mark Warner as governor in 2001 and Tim Kaine in 2005 led to a Democratic resurgence, especially in the Washington suburbs of Northern Virginia.

Obama carried two states that had seemed far out of reach on the basis of the 2004 results. Indiana, a 60% to 39% Bush state in 2004, went for Obama 50% to 49%, with the biggest Democratic gains in metro Indianapolis. North Carolina, a 56% to 44% Bush state even with home-state Sen. John Edwards on the Democratic ticket in 2004, experienced a 10-percentage-point increase in voter turnout, the biggest in the nation and enough to produce a 49.7% to 49.4% victory for Obama. The Democrat barely missed, by only 3,903 votes, adding Missouri's 11 electoral votes to his tally. In metro Omaha, Neb., he did just well enough to carry the single electoral vote of the 2nd Congressional District.

A comparison of Obama's state percentages with those of Kerry's yields more evidence of his campaign's skill in targeting and turning out voters. The Democratic share of the vote rose 11 percentage points in Indiana; 8 percentage points in New Mexico; 7 percentage points in Colorado, Nevada, and Virginia; 6 percentage points in North Carolina; and 5 percentage points in Iowa. It was up 9 percentage points in Montana and North Dakota, states that Bush had won and that Obama targeted. Obama's percentage was below Kerry's in Arkansas, Louisiana, Oklahoma, Tennessee, and West Virginia, as well as in Appalachian counties in western Pennsylvania. Some might be tempted to blame racism, but there is countervailing evidence: In 1989, southwestern Virginia counties voted for a black governor, Douglas Wilder. Turnout in these areas changed only negligibly from 2004 to 2008, suggesting a lack of enthusiasm for both candidates in 2008.

Building Blocs

Several interesting things can be said about the Obama majority coalition. First, he benefited from increased turnout by African-American voters, who were 13% of the electorate in 2008, up from 11% in 2004. They voted 95% for Obama, up 7 percentage points from the level of support they gave Kerry. The Obama campaign seems to have done an excellent job of increasing black turnout, not only in central cities but also in rural counties in Virginia and North Carolina. In addition, black turnout surged in Georgia, which played a role in reducing overall support for the Republican candidate from 58% in 2004 to 52% in 2008. Overall, Obama's bigger African-American majorities, not to mention his greater support from nonblack voters who were attracted to him in part because of his race, seem to have offset any losses from people who would have voted for a Democrat but not a black Democrat.

The very small percentages of votes cast for Obama by whites in Deep South states, such as Mississippi and Alabama, seem to reflect mostly partisan sentiments. White Democratic candidates in statewide elections there have not done much better among whites in recent years. And the public opinion polls taken before the primary and general election were not wildly out of sync with the election results, as was arguably the case in the 1982 and 1989 gubernatorial races in California and Virginia, which featured black candidates and pre-election polls showing the black candidates with more support than they actually got.

Obama also ran well with Latinos and Asians. The exit poll showed that 9% of voters were Latinos, up from 8% in 2004, and that they voted 67% to 31% for Obama. That was a huge increase for the Democrats from 2004, when the split in their favor was 53% to 44%. Bush ran nearly even with Hispanics in Texas and carried them in Florida. McCain lost Hispanics in both states, and that switch alone could account for Obama's 51% to 48% victory in Florida. Latinos' lopsided votes for Clinton in the primaries seem not to have represented an aversion to Obama, or, as some suggested, the perception of a rivalry between blacks and Latinos. And McCain's advocacy of a bill to give illegal immigrants a shot at citizenship seems to have won him little of the warm feelings that Latinos had for Bush in some states. Hispanic voters have been especially vulnerable in the real estate bust. The four states with the highest foreclosure rates in 2008 were all states with large Latino populations: Arizona, California, Florida, and Nevada.

Asian voters, heavily concentrated in a few heavily Democratic states, voted 62% for Obama. They cast 2% of all votes, the same as in 2004. White voters were 74% of the electorate, and they voted 43% for Obama, 2 percentage points more than for Kerry. It's safe to assume that switches among whites accounted for about one-third of Obama's 2-percentage-point gain over Kerry, while blacks, Latinos and Asians accounted for about two-thirds of it.

Second, Obama created a top-and-bottom coalition. He carried voters with household incomes under $50,000 and those with household incomes over $200,000, while narrowly losing the 56% of voters with incomes in between. Fully 26% of voters reported incomes over $100,000, and they were split 49% to 49%, an astonishing result for those of us old enough to remember when high earners voted heavily Republican. In the 1980s and early 1990s, high earners' opposition to tax increases led them to vote Republican by large margins. By the mid-1990s, cultural issues led many of them to vote Democratic. There was no sign in 2008 that Obama's promise to raise taxes on households earning more than $250,000 caused him political damage. Obama's 52% support among $200,000-plus voters was a huge increase over Kerry's 35%. There is irony here. As the party that typically decries economic inequality, Democrats did well by it electorally in 2008 by carrying the expanding number (at least in this election) of voters from the two income extremes.

Similarly, taking education levels into account, Obama attracted people at the bottom and the top; among those in the middle, he did less well. He won 63% of voters who did not graduate from high school, many of them older blacks, and 58% of voters with postgraduate degrees. Among the 79% in the middle, Obama won a comparatively modest but sufficient 51% of the vote. Among white voters, he won 47% of college graduates and just 40% of non-college graduates—the best proxy for the white working class of all the exit poll demographics. At the Democratic National Convention in August, speaker after speaker talked about the party being in touch with ordinary working families. That message was evidently not entirely persuasive. But white noncollege graduates, once a clear majority of the American electorate, accounted for only 39% of all voters, a percentage that is likely to keep declining. They are almost outnumbered already by the 35% who are white college graduates and who voted 51% to 47% for McCain.

The third thing that is striking about the Obama majority coalition is that it is heavily weighted toward the young. Voters age 30 and older favored Obama by only 50% to 49%. Voters 18 to 29 voted 66% (16 percentage points more than their elders) to 32% for Obama. This is the biggest difference between the young and the old since the exit poll began in 1972. That year, Republican Richard Nixon carried the under-30 group by 52% to 46%, and the 30-and-older group by 66% to 33%. In 2004, voters under 30 preferred Kerry, but only by 54% to 45%. Put another way, Obama got about 22% of his support from young voters and McCain only about 13%.

At the same time, there was no unusually large surge in the young voter turnout. Nationally, young voters made up 17% of the electorate in 2004 and 18% in 2008. An examination of county election returns suggests that the Obama campaign did a splendid job of registering and turning out young voters in university towns and in singles' apartment neighborhoods in metropolitan areas. This success is particularly apparent in Indiana, New Mexico, North Carolina, and Virginia—all Bush 2004 states that Obama carried in 2008. Still, young people participated less than their elders. They accounted for 22% of the voting-age population but just 18% of the electorate. Gallup polls in May 2009 showed that among voters younger than 35, Democrats had a 10-to-18-percentage-point advantage in party identification, similar to the 12-to-16-percentage-point Democratic advantage in party identification among people 55 to 64, the older half of the Baby Boom Generation. In their youth, Boomers accounted for the unusually high percentages of voters who favored anti-war Democrat George McGovern in 1972. Overall, according to the 2009 Gallup results, the Democratic advantage in party identification was 8 percentage points among seniors (ages 64-85), 10 percentage points among Baby Boomers (45-63), 7 percentage points among Generation X-ers (30-44), and 14 percentage points among what Gallup calls Generation Y and others call the Millennial Generation (18-29).

Trends Favor Democrats

Straight-line extrapolations from the 2008 election results reveal an America in which the Obama majority coalition is slated to grow. Millennial Generation voters will be an increasing part of the electorate, as will, most likely, relatively affluent and highly educated voters, and Latino and Asian voters. African-American turnout and Democratic percentages may, however, have peaked in 2008 (though they could be high again in 2012 if Obama seeks re-election), just as the Democratic percentage among Catholics peaked in 1960 at 78% when Kennedy ran for president. McCain carried young voters in only eight states, with 51 electoral votes between them; he did not carry black, Latino, or Asian voters in any state.

Some countervailing data favor the Republicans, but not as strongly. White evangelical Protestants continue to form one-quarter of the electorate. Their numbers were actually up from 23% in 2004 to 26% in 2008, and they continued to vote Republican by 3-to-1. The trend in evangelical churches to take up anti-poverty and environmental protection causes, symbolized by the Rev. Rick Warren of the Saddleback Church in Lake Forest, Calif. (he delivered the invocation at Obama's inauguration), has not yet modified evangelical voting behavior in a major way. And young voters who have no religious commitment may develop one, as members of earlier generations did as they grew older and took on more family obligations.

The fastest growing parts of the country still voted Republican in 2008, though less so than in 2004. McCain carried 86 of the 100 fastest growing counties with populations over 10,000 in 2008. Bush won 97 of the fastest growing counties in 2004. McCain lost three of the five fastest growing—Kendall County, Ill.; Flagler County, Fla.; and Loudoun County, Va. And he lost the three largest fast growing counties—Riverside County, Calif.; Clark County, Nev.; and Wake County, N.C. While there is no doubt that party identification changed to the detriment of Republicans—in 2004, 37% of voters were Republicans and 37% were Democrats, versus 32% Republican and 39% Democratic in 2008—there has also been a shift of attitude among self-identified independents, who tended to resemble Democrats on many issues in the last years of the Bush presidency. In the first months of the Obama presidency, independents tended to resemble Republicans on some issues, for example, by opposing the massive government bailouts of the financial services industry and the domestic automakers.

Whether the country's period of open field politics continues or the 2006 and 2008 election results turn out to be the beginning of another period of trench warfare politics (this time with a small but decisive Democratic majority) is not yet clear. The nation faces new and unfamiliar issues. The continuing troubles of the financial system are unlike anything Americans have experienced since the 1930s, and anyone who was an adult then is older than 90 now. Unprecedented government intervention in the economy has provoked dissatisfaction. The 2008 exit poll showed that 56% of respondents opposed the $700 billion bailout for the financial services industry voted by Congress in October 2008, while 39% supported it. Continued government infusions of vast sums into banks, mortgage lenders Fannie Mae and Freddie Mac, Detroit's automobile companies, and insurance firms raise questions of propriety and favoritism. And Obama's 2010 budget asks Americans to support or reject a vastly larger and more intrusive government. Moreover, the costly Obama programs to provide government health insurance and to regulate carbon dioxide emissions affect different regions of the country differently, in ways that split both parties' constituencies and potential constituencies.

Voters in November 2008 believed, by 47% to 23%, that the economy would get better in the coming year, according to the exit poll. Within a few months, those expectations seemed antiquated. Against the backdrop of fast-changing conditions, public opinion can shift quickly, as it did after September 11, 2001. The United States continues to face major challenges in the world, and in early 2009, Obama decided to continue military operations in Iraq and to step them up in Afghanistan, to the consternation of some on the Democratic left who were so enthusiastic about his candidacy. He decided to continue holding unlawful combatants indefinitely and to try them in military tribunals, both controversial policies with Democrats and some independents during the preceding Bush administration. Obama faces the continuing challenge of dealing with the vicious mullah-cracy of Iran, which has been bent on obtaining nuclear weapons to threaten Israel. The Iranian problem is one that neither the diplomacy nor the aggressive military posture of the previous administration was able to address effectively. Obama also faces a truculent Russia, which seems disinclined to cooperate on any issue from missile defense to the Iranian nuclear program, and a stern China, which provides the United States with a bounty of consumer goods and helps finance its government debt but may not care to do so indefinitely. Any of these challenges could erupt into crisis, with unpredictable repercussions in American public opinion.

The most volatile factor in our politics in the first decade of the 21st century is the balance of enthusiasm. Voter turnout has generally been rising, but the balance of enthusiasm seems to determine which party's supporters increase their turnout most. In 2002 and 2004, that balance favored the Republicans somewhat, and in 2006 and 2008, it favored the Democrats somewhat more. The question for Republican strategists is how they can excite potential voters. The question for Democratic strategists is how to maintain the level of enthusiasm apparent in the 2008 election results. Off-year and special elections provide some clues. Democratic victories in special elections for House seats in 2007 and 2008 in Illinois, Louisiana, and Mississippi showed the balance of enthusiasm working in the party's favor. Special elections in Georgia, Louisiana, and Virginia from December 2008 to February 2009 showed a bigger drop-off in turnout among Democrats than among Republicans. The 2010 midterm congressional elections will provide more clues.

A Turning Point?

Obama's election and his reform program raise the question of whether America has reached another inflection point in the balance of opinion on the relationship between government and markets. Such inflection points are rare, and seem to have come at 40-year intervals. To oversimplify much, the economic distress of the 1930s, symbolized by the breadlines of the Great Depression, convinced most Americans that markets didn't work very well and that government did. The economic distress of the 1970s, symbolized by the gas lines of the stagflation era, convinced most Americans that government didn't work very well and that markets did. In this view (with many exceptions and caveats), the 1930s produced a natural Democratic majority for a long generation, and the 1970s produced a natural Republican majority for a long generation, which may now have come to an end. It may be time for another inflection point, for Americans to decide that markets don't work very well and that government does.

But the picture is incomplete. For the change in the balance of opinion owed much not only to the economic distress of the 1930s and 1970s but also to the success, both in economic policy and in America's position in the world, of the 1940s and 1980s. In the 1940s, the United States was the incredibly productive arsenal of democracy in World War II, and then, in the postwar years, it was the engine of world economic growth. In the 1980s, the United States won an almost entirely bloodless victory in the Cold War and embarked on a quarter century of low-inflation economic growth—"It's morning in America," as Ronald Reagan's 1984 ad proclaimed. Franklin Roosevelt and Reagan both seemed to turn the American economy around, although economists are still arguing to what extent and in what respects. They led the nation to magnificent victories over the fascism of Nazi Germany and the Communism of the Soviet Union. Those triumphs fortified the opinion of the American people that the nation was both great and good.

It is possible to imagine that the American economy may recover sharply and resume its bounteous productivity in another quarter century of low-inflation economic growth, thanks to, or in spite of, Obama's economic policies. It is more difficult to imagine how the United States can emerge as brilliantly successful against the Islamist terrorists and Iranian mullahs who wish our destruction as it was against Germany and Japan in 1945 and during the fall of the Berlin Wall in 1989. But one must remember that it was difficult to imagine those outcomes when the United States under Roosevelt was aiding a lonely Britain against the alliance of Nazi Germany and Soviet Russia in 1940, and when Reagan was proclaiming to the disdain of almost all supposedly enlightened opinion in 1983 that communism would end up on the "ash heap of history." America has had great leaders, but they have had a great country to work with. Maybe this will prove true again.

2008 PRESIDENTIAL ELECTION

States Won by Democrat Barack Obama: 28

California, Colorado, Connecticut, Delaware, Florida, Hawaii, Illinois, Indiana, Iowa, Maine, Maryland, Massachusetts, Michigan, Minnesota, Nevada, New Hampshire, New Jersey, New Mexico, New York, North Carolina, Ohio, Oregon, Pennsylvania, Rhode Island, Vermont, Virginia, Washington, Wisconsin

States Won by Republican John McCain: 22

Alabama, Alaska, Arizona, Arkansas, Georgia, Idaho, Kansas, Kentucky, Louisiana, Mississippi, Missouri, Montana, Nebraska, North Dakota, Oklahoma, South Carolina, South Dakota, Tennessee, Texas, Utah, West Virginia, Wyoming

Top Obama District:		**Top McCain District:**	
NY-16 (Serrano)	95%	AL-6 (Bachus)	77%

McCain Victories in Kerry Districts

Districts that Republican John McCain won in 2008 that were carried by Democrat John Kerry in 2004

Representative	District	McCain %	Bush %
John Murtha (D)	PA-12	49	49

Obama Victories in Bush Districts

Districts that Democrat Barack Obama won in 2008 that were carried by Republican George W. Bush in 2004

Representative	District	Obama %	Kerry %
Dan Lungren (R)	CA-3	49	41
Jerry McNerney (D)	CA-11	54	45
Dennis Cardoza (D)	CA-18	59	49
Elton Gallegly (R)	CA-24	51	43
Buck McKeon (R)	CA-25	49	40
David Dreier (R)	CA-26	51	44
Ken Calvert (R)	CA-44	50	40
Mary Bono Mack (R)	CA-45	52	43
Loretta Sanchez (D)	CA-47	60	49
John Campbell (R)	CA-48	49	40
Brian Bilbray (R)	CA-50	51	44
Alan Grayson (D)	FL-8	52	45
Bill Young (R)	FL-10	52	49
Ileana Ros-Lehtinen (R)	FL-18	51	46
Sanford Bishop (D)	GA-2	54	50
John Barrow (D)	GA-12	55	49
Peter Roskam (R)	IL-6	56	47
Melissa Bean (D)	IL-8	56	44
Debbie Halvorson (D)	IL-11	53	46
Judy Biggert (R)	IL-13	54	45
Bill Foster (D)	IL-14	55	44

Representative	District	Obama %	Kerry %
Don Manzullo (R)	IL-16	53	44
Joe Donnelly (D)	IN-2	54	43
Leonard Boswell (D)	IA-3	54	50
Tom Latham (R)	IA-4	53	48
Dennis Moore (D)	KS-3	51	44
Bart Stupak (D)	MI-1	50	46
Dave Camp (R)	MI-4	50	44
Fred Upton (R)	MI-6	54	46
Mark Schauer (D)	MI-7	52	45
Mike Rogers (R)	MI-8	53	45
Gary Peters (D)	MI-9	56	49
Thaddeus McCotter	MI-11	54	47
Tim Walz (D)	MN-1	51	47
Erik Paulsen (R)	MN-3	52	48
Lee Terry (R)	NE-2	50	39
Dina Titus (D)	NV-3	55	49
Carol Shea-Porter (D)	NH-1	53	48
Frank LoBiondo (R)	NJ-2	54	49
John Adler (D)	NJ-3	52	49
Leonard Lance (R)	NJ-7	50	47
Tim Bishop (D)	NY-1	51	49
John Hall (D)	NY-19	51	45
Patrick Murphy (D)	NY-20	51	46
John McHugh (R)	NY-23	52	47
Michael Arcuri (D)	NY-24	50	47
Bob Etheridge (D)	NC-2	52	46
Larry Kissell (D)	NC-8	52	45
Steve Driehaus (D)	OH-1	55	50
Pat Tiberi (R)	OH-12	54	49
Mary Jo Kilroy (D)	OH-15	54	50
Kurt Schrader (D)	OR-5	54	49
Rubén Hinojosa (D)	TX-15	60	49
Ciro Rodriguez (D)	TX-23	51	43
Solomon Ortiz (D)	TX-27	53	45
Henry Cuellar (D)	TX-28	56	46
Glenn Nye (D)	VA-2	50	42
Randy Forbes (R)	VA-4	50	43
Frank Wolf (R)	VA-10	53	44
Gerald Connolly (D)	VA-11	57	49
Brian Baird (D)	WA-3	53	48
Paul Ryan (R)	WI-1	51	46
Tom Petri (R)	WI-6	50	43
Steve Kagen (D)	WI-8	53	44

Democratic Districts that Voted for McCain

Democrats whose districts were carried by Republican candidate John McCain

Representative	District	McCain %	Obama %
Bobby Bright	AL-2	63	37
Parker Griffith	AL-5	61	38
Ann Kirkpatrick	AZ-1	54	44
Harry Mitchell	AZ-5	51	47
Gabrielle Giffords	AZ-8	52	46
Marion Berry	AR-1	59	38
Vic Snyder	AR-2	54	44
Mike Ross	AR-4	58	39
John Salazar	CO-3	50	48
Betsy Markey	CO-4	50	49
Allen Boyd	FL-2	54	45
Suzanne Kosmas	FL-24	51	49
Jim Marshall	GA-8	56	43
Walt Minnick	ID-1	62	36
Brad Ellsworth	IN-8	51	47
Baron Hill	IN-9	50	48
Ben Chandler	KY-6	55	43
Charlie Melancon	LA-3	61	37
Frank Kratovil	MD-1	59	40
Collin Peterson	MN-7	50	47
Travis Childers	MS-1	62	37
Gene Taylor	MS-4	67	32
Ike Skelton	MO-4	60	38
Harry Teague	NM-2	50	49
Michael McMahon	NY-13	51	49
Eric Massa	NY-29	50	48
Mike McIntyre	NC-7	52	47
Heath Shuler	NC-11	52	47
Earl Pomeroy	ND-AL	53	45
Charlie Wilson	OH-6	50	48
John Boccieri	OH-16	50	48
Zack Space	OH-18	53	45
Dan Boren	OK-2	66	35
Kathy Dahlkemper	PA-3	49	49
Jason Altmire	PA-4	55	44
Christopher Carney	PA-10	53	45
John Murtha	PA-12	49	49
Tim Holden	PA-17	51	48
John Spratt	SC-5	53	46
Stephanie Herseth Sandlin	SD-AL	53	45
Lincoln Davis	TN-4	64	34
Bart Gordon	TN-6	62	37
John Tanner	TN-8	56	43
Chet Edwards	TX-17	67	32
Jim Matheson	UT-2	58	40
Tom Perriello	VA-5	51	48
Rick Boucher	VA-9	59	40
Alan Mollohan	WV-1	57	42
Nick Rahall	WV-3	56	42

Republican Districts that Voted for Obama

Republicans whose districts were carried by President Barack Obama

Representative	District	Obama %	McCain %
Dan Lungren	CA-3	49	49
Elton Gallegly	CA-24	51	48
Buck McKeon	CA-25	49	48
David Dreier	CA-26	51	47
Ken Calvert	CA-44	50	49
Mary Bono Mack	CA-45	52	47
John Campbell	CA-48	49	49
Brian Bilbray	CA-50	51	47
Michael Castle	DE-AL	62	37
Bill Young	FL-10	52	47
Ileana Ros-Lehtinen	FL-18	51	49
Peter Roskam	IL-6	56	43
Mark Kirk	IL-10	61	38
Judy Biggert	IL-13	54	44
Don Manzullo	IL-16	53	46
Tom Latham	IA-4	53	45
Joseph Cao	LA-2	75	23
Dave Camp	MI-4	50	48
Fred Upton	MI-6	54	44
Mike Rogers	MI-8	53	46
Thaddeus McCotter	MI-11	54	45
Erik Paulsen	MN-3	52	46
Lee Terry	NE-2	50	49
Frank LoBiondo	NJ-2	54	45
Leonard Lance	NJ-7	50	49
John McHugh	NY-23	52	47
Pat Tiberi	OH-12	54	45
Jim Gerlach	PA-6	58	41
Charlie Dent	PA-15	56	43
Randy Forbes	VA-4	50	49
Frank Wolf	VA-10	53	46
Dave Reichert	WA-8	57	42
Paul Ryan	WI-1	51	47
Tom Petri	WI-6	50	49

President

Barack Obama (D)

Elected 2008, term expires Jan. 2013, 1st term; b. Aug. 4, 1961, Honolulu, HI; home, Chicago, IL; Attended Occidental College, 1979–81, Columbia U., B.A. 1983, Harvard U., J.D. 1991; Protestant; married (Michelle); 2 children.

Elected Office: IL Senate, 1996–2004; U.S. Senate, 2005–08.

Professional Career: Dir., Illinois Project Vote!, 1992; Practicing atty.; Lecturer, U. of Chicago, 1993–2004.

Vice President

Joe Biden (D)

Elected 2008, term expires Jan. 2013, 1st term; b. Nov. 20, 1942, Scranton, PA; home, Wilmington, DE; U. of DE, B.A. 1965, Syracuse U., J.D. 1968; Catholic; married (Jill); 3 children.

Elected Office: New Castle Cnty. Cncl., 1970–72; U.S. Senate, 1973–2009.

Professional Career: Practicing atty., 1968–72.

Population		Household Income		Work	
Pop. 2007:	298,757,310	Under $15k:	13.4%	Private:	78.5%
Change since 2000:	Up 6.1%	$15k to $50k:	36.7%	Government:	14.5%
Urban:	79.0%	$50k to $100k:	30.9%	Self-employed:	6.8%
Rural:	21.0%	$100k to $150k:	11.4%	Unemployment (3-yr. average):	4.2%
Native of state:	58.9%	Over $150k:	7.6%	Poverty:	13.3%
Not a citizen:	7.3%	Median income:	$50,007	Blue collar:	22.7%
Area size:	3,794,083 sq. mi.			White collar:	59.9%
Most populous cities		**Home Value**		Khaki collar:	0.4%
1. New York	8,246,310	Under $100k:	24.4%	Other:	17.3%
2. Los Angeles	3,770,590	$100k to $300k:	45.9%	**Age**	
3. Chicago	2,740,224	$300k to $500k:	16.7%	Median age:	36.4 yrs.
4. Houston	2,034,749	$500k to $1 mil:	10.7%	More than 65 yrs:	12.5%
		Over $1 million:	2.4%	Less than 18 yrs:	24.7%
		Median:	$181,800		

Race/Ethnicity				Military Veterans		Registered Voters in 2008	
White:	66.3%	*Language*		% of Pop:	10.4%	Voter turnout:	131,312,554
Black:	12.2%	English:	80.5%	*Veterans by Period*		Turnout as % of	
Hispanic:	14.7%	Spanish:	12.1%	WWII and before:	14.0%	voting age:	57.1%
Asian:	4.3%	Asian:	2.9%	Korea:	13.4%		
Native Am.:	0.7%	Other		Vietnam:	33.2%		
Hawaiian:	0.1%	European	3.7%	Gulf (pre-2001):	7.2%		
Two+ races:	1.5%	**Education**		Gulf (post-2001):	14.3%		
Ancestry		H.S. grad:	84.0%	Peace time:	17.9%		
German:	16.9%	College grad:	27.0%				
Irish:	12.0%	Grad degree:	9.9%				
English:	9.4%						

2008 Presidential Vote			2004 Presidential Vote		
Obama (D)	69,498,215	(53%)	Bush (R)	62,040,606	(51%)
McCain (R)	59,948,240	(46%)	Kerry (D)	59,028,109	(48%)

★ ALABAMA ★

Alabama had its beginnings in two surges of settlement. One was from the north, when Jacksonian farmers from Tennessee swept into the red clay hills from which their hero, Andrew Jackson, had expelled the Creek and other Indians. You can see their early Greek Revival buildings in historic Huntsville, surrounded by the boomtown that has grown up around the Marshall Space Center, but Jacksonian Alabama was anything but civil and classical. The settlers brought the fighting faith of the Scots-Irish, a hot-spirited willingness to fight to the death against any perceived insult or threat. The other surge of settlement into Alabama came a few years later, as entrepreneurial Southern planters brought slaves in to pick cotton in the fertile Black Belt (so named for its soil) east and west of Montgomery in the middle of the state. The interplay between the offspring of these two streams of settlers has been the stuff of Alabama politics ever since. The Jacksonians' fighting spirit led them to join the planters to support secession. The first Confederate Congress convened, and Jefferson Davis took the oath of office as president of the Confederacy, in the Alabama Capitol in February 1861.

After the Civil War, Alabama, like other Southern states, became solidly Democratic, with an angry populist accent. Birmingham, with its solid-iron Red Mountain, became the South's first steel producer in the 1880s. Alabama politics in the first half of the 20th century was a struggle between plantation owners of the Black Belt and populists who favored New Deal government spending to help the little guy—Senator and Supreme Court Justice Hugo Black, Sens. Lister Hill and John Sparkman, Gov. "Kissin' Jim" Folsom, and the local economic potentates they called the "Big Mules."

Alabama went on to become, kicking and screaming, one of the birthplaces of the civil-rights movement. Down the hill from the capitol is the Dexter Avenue Baptist Church, where in December 1956 the 27-year-old Martin Luther King Jr. led the boycott that began when Montgomery seamstress Rosa Parks refused to move to the back of the bus. A hundred miles north in Birmingham, while King was held in jail, Birmingham Police Commissioner Bull Connor, then Alabama's Democratic National Committeeman, ordered police dogs and fire hoses to be turned on peaceful demonstrators in May 1963. Four months later, four girls were killed when a bomb exploded in Birmingham's 16th Street Baptist Church. (The bombers were convicted in 1977, 2001, and 2002.) In March 1965, a civil-rights marcher was murdered in Montgomery two weeks after police beat dozens of people at Selma's Edmund Pettis Bridge; another activist was shot and killed in Lowndes County that August. These events had reverberations far beyond Alabama. In June 1963 President Kennedy endorsed what would become the Civil Rights Act of 1964, and in March 1965, Congress passed the Voting Rights Act.

While Alabamians like Parks were leading the nation toward civil rights, Alabama's most prominent politician of the time, George Wallace, was pulling the other way. Elected governor in 1962, he made national news in June 1963 by standing in a schoolhouse door to defy a federal court desegregation order. In 1964, Wallace ran in Northern Democratic presidential primaries against Lyndon Johnson. In 1968, he ran for president as a third-party candidate and won 13.5% of the vote. He ran in the Democratic primaries again in 1972, and was partially paralyzed by a gunshot wound while campaigning in May. He took delegates to the national convention, and did not lose his force as a national politician until Jimmy Carter beat him in the March 1976 Florida primary. But he remained the key figure in Alabama for three decades, running his first wife to succeed him in 1966 (she died midterm), regaining the governorship in 1970 and again in 1974, then running and winning one last time in 1982. He spent his last sad years apologizing for his acts, meeting with the student he tried to block in the schoolhouse door, and proclaiming, "The South has changed, and for the better." He died in September 1998.

It was during Wallace's last term as governor, in 1983, that the state government started publishing a black heritage guide. Today, heritage tourism commemorating the civil-rights movement is one of the fastest-growing segments of the tourism industry, and Alabama is leading the way. Montgomery boasts artist Maya Lin's circular Civil Rights Memorial, Troy University's Rosa Parks Museum, the Dexter Parsonage, and the end point of the Selma-to-Montgomery trail. The Edmund Pettis Bridge in Selma, the Selma-to-Montgomery interpretive center in Lowndes County, and the Tuskegee Airmen National Historic Site all are on the Alabama Civil Rights Museum Trail. In 2007, the Legislature passed a resolution apologizing for slavery. And in early 2009, Democratic Rep. Artur Davis, who is black, launched a serious campaign for governor. As Davis told the *Birmingham News* in 2008: "Voters put on a different lens when they are assessing presidential races in the South than they do when they are assessing races involving people you've gotten to know."

Economically, Alabama in recent years has been gaining ground lost in the Wallace years. Then, while Atlanta was peacefully desegregating and beginning decades of vibrant white-collar growth, Birmingham was violently resisting the civil-rights movement, only to see the shrinkage of its once-substantial blue-collar base in the steel industry and an outflow of talented people of all races. But Alabama's economy has been moving ahead recently and started growing faster than the nation's as a whole. Autos have played a part, and not just at the Talladega NASCAR racetrack or the Porsche Sport Driving School

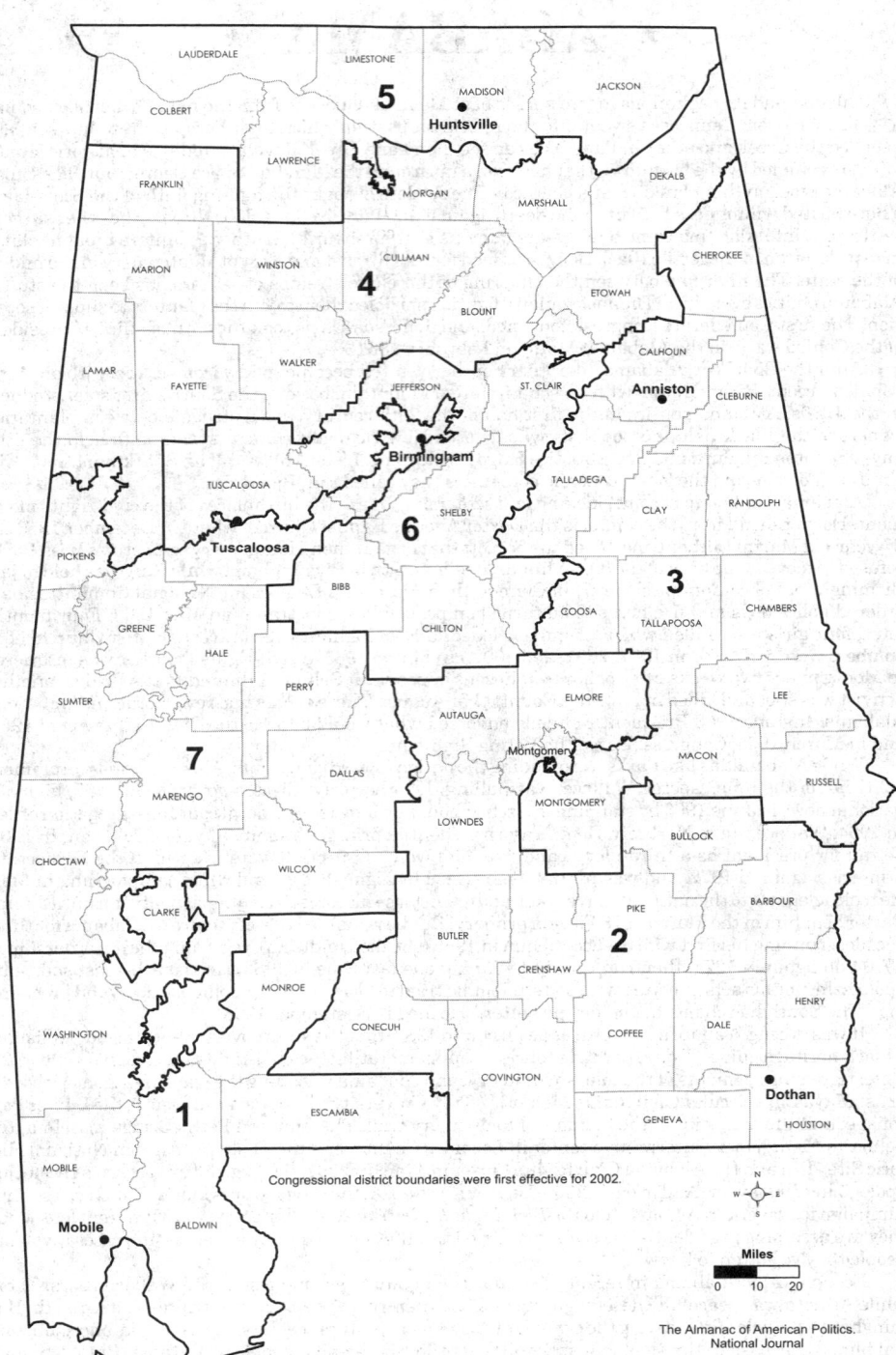

Congressional district boundaries were first effective for 2002.

Miles
0   10   20

near Leeds. Big new automobile manufacturing plants have opened starting in 1997, with Mercedes in Tuscaloosa, Honda in Talladega County, and Hyundai in Montgomery. Unions have tried to organize them without success. Alabama produced 739,000 vehicles in 2007, and the auto companies and suppliers generated 48,000 jobs. Some 2,700 more will be coming when ThyssenKrupp finishes building its $3.7 billion steel-processing facility near Mobile in 2010. Unemployment has risen since it reached a historic low, 3.1%, in October 2007, but income levels have been rising toward the national average, and people are moving in, not out, with higher rates of in-migration in 2007–08 than either Florida or Virginia.

George Wallace delayed for a generation Alabama's move toward the Republican Party. But in the quarter-century since he last appeared on the ballot, Alabama has developed two-party politics and, in presidential elections, has completed its transformation from one of the nation's most Democratic states to one of its most Republican. But state politics remain competitive. On one side of this political conflict are the Democrats. Their voting base is Alabama's large black minority, and the institutional base is the state's well-organized teachers' unions and trial lawyers. On the other side are the Republicans. Their voting base is white evangelical Protestants, and their institutional base is small-business owners and the affluent young families filling the fast-growing suburban areas outside Birmingham, Montgomery, Mobile, and Huntsville. The Republicans have tended to prevail, by large margins in presidential and Senate and state Supreme Court elections, and by narrow margins in races for governor and in statewide down-ballot contests. But the Democrats have fought back hard, holding on to the Legislature and, since Wallace left office, bringing ethics charges against one Republican governor that led to his conviction and removal from office—Guy Hunt in 1993—and defeating another, Fob James, in 1998.

The 2002 race for governor between Democrat Don Siegelman and Republican Rep. Bob Riley showed the close division between the two Alabamas. Siegelman carried the central cities, the Black Belt, and many of the poor, white rural counties in the north. This was the coalition of blacks and poor whites the political scientist V.O. Key Jr. longed for in his midcentury classic, *Southern Politics*. But it was not enough to win. Riley carried by big margins the suburban counties around Birmingham, Mobile, Montgomery, and Huntsville and the smaller, robustly growing counties along the interstate highways. Alabama politics have continued to run into turbulence. One controversy raged over state Chief Justice Roy Moore's installation in 2001 of a huge monument with the Ten Commandments in the Supreme Court building. In 2002, a federal judge ruled the monument unconstitutional, and an appeals court affirmed the judgment and ordered him to remove it in 2003. Moore refused, but the other eight justices complied. The Alabama Court of the Judiciary removed Moore in November 2003, and the U.S. Supreme Court declined to hear his appeal in 2004. Another controversy came when Gov. Riley put on the ballot a referendum on a $1.2 billion tax increase. Riley argued that his changes would reduce taxes on low-income people and that such a move was in line with Christian morality. Alabama's Jacksonians did not buy it. The proposition was defeated 67%-33%, and won by unimpressive margins in black-majority counties and the state capital. It won only 14% in Winston County, an independent-minded hill county that seceded from secessionist Alabama during the Civil War.

Population		Household Income		Work	
Pop. 2007:	4,585,900	Under $15k:	18.7%	Private:	77.5%
State rank:	23rd of 50	$15k to $50k:	40.7%	Government:	16.1%
Change since 2000:	Up 3.1%	$50k to $100k:	27.7%	Self-employed:	6.2%
Urban:	54.8%	$100k to $150k:	10.8%	Unemployment (3-yr. average):	4.2%
Rural:	45.2%	Over $150k:	2.1%	Poverty:	16.8%
Native of state:	71.1%	Median income:	$40,052	Blue collar:	27.9%
Not a citizen:	2.0%	**Home Value**		White collar:	56.0%
Area size:	52,419 sq. mi.	Under $100k:	47.0%	Khaki collar:	0.3%
Most populous cities		$100k to $300k:	43.9%	Other:	15.7%
1. Birmingham	218,090	$300k to $500k:	6.3%	**Age**	
2. Montgomery	200,993	$500k to $1 mil:	2.2%	Median age:	37.1 yrs.
3. Mobile	194,091	Over $1 million:	0.6%	More than 65 yrs:	13.4%
4. Huntsville	166,550	Median:	$106,800	Less than 18 yrs:	24.4%

Race/Ethnicity				Military Veterans		Registered Voters in 2008	
White:	68.8%	*Language*		% of Pop:	11.8%	No party registration	
Black:	26.2%	English:	95.8%	*Veterans by Period*		Voter turnout:	2,099,819
Hispanic:	2.5%	Spanish:	2.5%	WWII and before:	10.0%	Turnout as % of	
Asian:	0.9%	Asian:	0.7%	Korea:	11.7%	voting age:	59.3%
Native Am.:	0.5%	Other		Vietnam:	31.3%	**Legislature**	
Hawaiian:	0.0%	European	0.9%	Gulf (pre-2001):	13.3%	Senate:	19 D 13 R 3 V
Two+ races:	1.0%	**Education**		Gulf (post-2001):	8.7%	House:	62 D 43 R
Ancestry		H.S. grad:	80.0%	Peace time:	25.0%		
USA:	12.5%	College grad:	21.1%				
Irish:	9.3%	Grad degree:	7.8%				
English:	9.2%						

Sparks threatened to flare again in the 2006 Republican primary when Moore ran against Riley, but Riley won, 67%-33%. Moore evidently struck even many of those who had voted against Riley's tax increase as too extreme. Almost as many Alabamians voted in that Republican primary, 460,000, as in the Democratic primary, 467,000, on the same day—a stark contrast with 20 years before, when George Wallace was the retiring incumbent and turnout in the Democratic primary, 830,000, dwarfed that in the Republican primary, 25,000. Riley won the general election by a solid 57%-42%. Democrat Jim Folsom Jr. was narrowly elected lieutenant governor, and Democrat Sue Bell Cobb beat Chief Justice Ryan Nabers, who had beaten a Moore ally in the Republican primary. Republicans won most other statewide offices.

Presidential politics   Alabama has become a solidly Republican state in presidential politics. George W. Bush carried it twice by wide margins. John McCain carried it 60%-39%, his best showing in all but four other states—Oklahoma, Wyoming, Utah, and Idaho. There was clear polarization by race, with McCain carrying whites 88%-10% and Barack Obama carrying blacks 98%-2%. Obama carried the Black Belt, Montgomery County, and Birmingham's Jefferson County, the first time it had gone Democratic since 1952, as whites have moved out to suburbs. McCain carried everything else. But this was not just a vote on race. Here as elsewhere Obama ran poorly among voters with Jacksonian roots.

Alabama's presidential primary for years was held in June, too late to count for much. It might have counted for something in 2008 if the Legislature had left it there. But in 2006, it moved the contest to February 5, Super Tuesday, in the hope of getting some national attention. It didn't work. Ala-

2008 Presidential Vote		
McCain (R)	1,266,546	(60%)
Obama (D)	813,479	(39%)
2008 Democratic Presidential Primary		
Obama (D)	300,319	(56%)
Clinton (D)	223,089	(42%)
2008 Republican Presidential Primary		
Huckabee (R)	227,766	(41%)
McCain (R)	204,867	(37%)
Romney (R)	98,019	(18%)
2004 Presidential Vote		
Bush (R)	1,176,394	(62%)
Kerry (D)	693,933	(37%)

bama was overshadowed by big states such as New York and California that had also joined Super Tuesday. For the first time, more Alabamians voted in the Republican presidential primary, 552,000, than in the Democratic presidential primary, 537,000. Polls showed four different Republicans leading at some point in the cycle, but Mike Huckabee ended up edging McCain 41%-37%, with Mitt Romney at 18%. McCain carried the Black Belt, and the race was very close in the counties including Birmingham and Montgomery. Huckabee ran up big margins in northern, Jacksonian counties. On the Democratic side, blacks mostly voted for Barack Obama and whites mostly for Hillary Rodham Clinton, and Obama won, 56%-42%. A June primary might have turned out differently. The Republican contest would have been over by then, and with no party registration, more whites might have opted for the Democratic primary and boosted Clinton's total.

Congressional districting   In drawing the boundaries of the state's seven congressional districts, the Democrats in control of redistricting in Alabama in 2002 did a pretty good job of helping their party. They marginally strengthened Democratic Rep. Bud Cramer in the 5th District and made the 3rd District significantly more Democratic by subtracting fast-growing St. Clair County east of Birmingham and raising the black percentage from 25% to 32%, the second highest in the state. Rep. Mike Rogers kept the 3rd District Republican, but the redistricting changes helped Democrats hold the 5th District when it came open in 2008. Democrat Bobby Bright, mayor of Montgomery, was able to capture the 2nd District, Republican since 1964, when it came open the same year. Alabama is not expected to gain or lose House seats in the 2010 census.

111th Congress Lineup	
4 R	3 D
110th Congress Lineup	
5 R	2 D

Governor

Bob Riley (R)

Elected 2002, term expires Jan. 2011, 2nd term; b. Oct. 3, 1944, Ashland; home, Ashland; U. of AL, B.A. 1965; Baptist; married (Patsy); 5 children (1 deceased).

Elected Office: Ashland City Cncl., 1972–76; U.S. House of Reps., 1996–2002.

Professional Career: Owner, egg & poultry co.; Rancher; Owner, Midway Transit, 1965–present.

Office: Alabama State Capitol, 600 Dexter Ave., Montgomery, 36130, 334-242-7100; Fax: 334-353-0004; Web site: www.governor.state.al.us.

Election Results

2006 general	Bob Riley (R)	718,327	(57%)
	Lucy Baxley (D)	519,827	(42%)
2006 primary	Bob Riley (R)	306,665	(67%)
	Roy Moore (R)	153,354	(33%)

Republican Bob Riley was elected governor of Alabama in 2002. He grew up in Clay County, east of Birmingham, where his family had lived for seven generations. Riley attended the University of Alabama while it was being desegregated in 1963 and earned a business degree. He and his brother started selling eggs door-to-door, a business they ultimately grew into a large egg-and-poultry company. He also ran a grocery store, owned an airport and a pharmacy and sold real estate. He ended up with a car dealership (Midway Ford and Chrysler), a trucking company (Midway Transit), half a shopping center and a cattle farm. He got into politics as a member of the Ashland City Council.

In 1996, when the 3rd District's Democratic incumbent ran unsuccessfully for the Senate, Riley ran for the House. He started off little known outside Clay County, but he was a strong and energetic campaigner and an ardent conservative. He supported school prayer, term limits, tax cuts, and a balanced-budget amendment. He opposed abortion rights, gun control, and racial quotas. Riley won 50%-47%, a key victory in keeping the House Republican that year. In the House, Riley had a solidly conservative voting record and a reputation as a fierce Republican partisan. He attracted serious competition in 1998 from former Democratic state Chairman Joe Turnham, but he spent $845,000 of his own money and won 58%-42%. In 2002, he ran for governor.

The incumbent was Don Siegelman, a Democrat elected by 58%-42% in 1998 over embattled incumbent Republican Fob James. Siegelman's main proposal was a lottery to fund education, but in 1999 referendum voters rejected the idea. Siegelman had success in attracting automakers Honda and Hyundai to the state and persuaded voters to approve a ballot proposition for $425 million in bonds to fund road and bridge building. But his administration was marred by scandal, including a joint state-federal investigation of his personal finances.

In the June primary, Riley beat Lt. Gov. Steve Windom 74%-18%. In the general election, one of the main issues was financing education. Having failed to sell his lottery plan, Siegelman called for a special session of the Legislature to consider raising taxes on businesses. Riley opposed tax increases and called for limiting spending to the prior year's level. He also focused on ethics, charging that under Siegelman state government was "sinking into a quicksand of corruption and fraud." In late summer, Riley was running ahead in polls, but in September, he made a few blunders and his standing fell. In one instance, Riley stumped with National Rifle Association President Charlton Heston, but the following day it was revealed that the NRA had endorsed Siegelman based on his opposition to gun control. This turned out to be the closest gubernatorial race in the nation in 2002. Riley won by a 3,120-vote margin. Siegelman won overwhelmingly among African-American voters, and his denunciations of corporations that opposed his business tax increase probably helped him carry heavily white rural counties in northwestern Alabama. Riley won big victories in fast-growing suburban counties. On Election Night, a clerical error in heavily Republican Baldwin County credited Siegelman with 7,000 more votes than he actually received, which put him ahead statewide. Both Riley and Siegelman proclaimed themselves winners. Siegelman refused to recognize the error and called for a recount, but conceded two weeks later.

Facing a $675 million budget shortfall and a Democratic legislature, Riley came up with a broad-based proposal to transform state finances. He called for cutting spending but also raising state and local taxes by $1.2 billion. In return for support from the Alabama Education Association's head Paul Hubbert—a candidate for governor in 1990 and a key player in Alabama politics before and since—Riley agreed to maintain spending on teacher pay and to put the increased revenue into an Alabama Excellence

Initiative. Why did a politician who was elected on a no-tax-increase program back such a plan? Riley said he was influenced by North Carolina, which had increased education spending in the 1960s and was experiencing much higher test scores than Alabama. And Riley said he considered it a matter of Christian obligation. "When I read the New Testament, there are three things we're asked to do: That's love God, love each other and take care of the least among us," he said.

Supporting him were Hubbert and the AEA, the state Democratic party, and some leaders of the insurance, banking, utility and consumer-products industries. Opposing him were the state Republican party, timber companies, the state Christian Coalition and national organizations like Americans for Tax Reform. As state Republican Chairman Marty Connors described the situation, "We've got a conservative, evangelical Christian Republican governor, trying to get a massive turnout of black voters to pass a tax increase so he can raise taxes on Republican constituents." Turnout for the September 2003 referendum was high—only 6% below that in the November 2002 general election. The result was unambiguous. Riley's proposal was rejected 67%-33%. It was approved in only 12 Black Belt counties and lost by more than 3-to-1 in most small counties in north Alabama.

For 2004, Riley proposed more spending cuts and forswore broad-based tax increases. Instead, he increased the cigarette tax, some fees and oil and gas severance taxes. As revenues increased, the state ended the fiscal year with a $150 million surplus. In 2005, Riley responded to Hurricane Katrina by scouring the state's public resources—state parks, closed mental hospitals and dormitories at closed military bases—to find accommodations for 10,000 evacuees. He was criticized for requiring criminal background checks on hurricane evacuees and blocking those with records of sexual and drug crimes, but he stuck to his decision.

After the unpopularity of his 2003 tax increase plan, Riley focused on economic development and education. Improving state revenues also helped, allowing him to propose tax cuts and more spending. He reduced taxes on lower- and middle-income people, gave state employees a 5% pay raise, increased pensions for retired state employees and boosted spending for many state services. Riley also signed a bill that increased the income thresholds at which families began paying state income taxes. And he signed the Rosa Parks Act, which allowed people convicted under Jim Crow laws to apply for a pardon.

In his 2006 bid for re-election, he faced Republican primary opposition from former Alabama Chief Justice Roy Moore, who won national attention by defying courts and keeping a monument of the Ten Commandments in the state judicial building; he was removed from office in 2003 as a result. Riley invoked his own religious faith. "Some say they can no longer acknowledge God in government. I think that's sad, because I acknowledge him every day, in speeches, in the office, in meetings, schools and churches," he said. In the June primary, Riley defeated Moore by a 2-to-1 margin. In the general election, Riley faced Democratic Lt. Gov. Lucy Baxley. Riley ran an ad calling Baxley "just too liberal," and he picked up a string of 18 newspaper endorsements around the state that praised his effectiveness and clean administration. He outspent Baxley $13 million to $4 million and won a second term 57%-42%.

In his second term, Riley worked with the Legislature on two major incentive packages, including one for $400 million, to lure German steelmaker ThyssenKrupp to the state. The company chose a site near Mobile, over a competing site in Louisiana, for a $3.7 billion steel-processing facility that is slated to employ 2,700 workers at an average salary of $42,000 a year. Riley then proposed $850 million for school construction and technology spending, a 7% teacher pay raise, another middle-class tax cut, and tax credits for worker training. The AEA opposed his tax-relief proposals, fearing a loss in revenues dedicated to education spending. Riley wound up with an accord with the Legislature that jettisoned the tax cuts but approved a $1 billion bond for general school construction and the teacher pay raise.

After the 2007 legislative session ended, Riley demonstrated political ingenuity in challenging Hubbert and the AEA on an issue that cut to the heart of the group's traditionally strong influence on state politics. Riley sought to ban state legislators from simultaneously working for two-year state colleges. Critics argued that the double-dipping encouraged corruption, a contention supported in 2006, when former State Rep. Bryant Melton pleaded guilty to abusing his position at Shelton State Community College. Ending double-dipping would also affect Democratic power in the Legislature, since more Democratic legislators held jobs in the state school system than Republicans. Hubbert and the AEA strongly opposed the ban, and it had little chance of getting through the Democratic Legislature. So Riley appointed fellow Republican Bradley Byrne as chancellor of the two-year college system, and Byrne introduced a ban on double-dipping to the state board of education, which ratified it on a 6-to-1 vote. The AEA sued to stop implementation, and the group and Riley fought the issue all the way to the state Supreme Court, which was expected to hear the case in 2009.

As the economy worsened in 2008, Riley touted a plan to expand pre-kindergarten programs while urging legislators to eliminate $400 million from the education budget, with four-year colleges bearing the brunt of the cuts. The Legislature reduced the size of the budget cuts, but largely went along. Riley also sought to raise taxes on oil companies after ExxonMobil figured out how to legally deduct enough expenses to offset virtually all of its gas taxes. Riley responded by proposing to change the state severance tax on natural gas wells in a way that would result in doubling the taxes that companies paid on their wells. When that idea was rejected in committee in the Legislature, Riley proposed levying a temporary 6% tax on the companies' gross proceeds. The House Appropriations Committee approved the tax, but the bill bogged down in the full House. As state funds continued to dry up, Riley threw his support behind a state constitutional amendment to increase the Rainy Day fund for education and establish a second reserve fund for other state operations, both of which were ratified by voters on Nov. 4, 2008.

Riley's string of successes suffered a setback with the 2008 election. In developing a new statewide voter-registration system, Riley's legal team had classified more than 400 of Alabama's 575 felony crimes—including relatively minor offenses such as disrupting a funeral and shoplifting—as grounds to disqualify offenders from voting until their rights were formally restored. Previously, just 70 felonies, including rape and murder, had resulted in a suspension of voting rights. Many voters in 2008 were deemed ineligible, including former Republican Gov. Guy Hunt, whose felony conviction on ethics violation for the misuse of inauguration funds temporarily revoked his right to vote. Alabama Democrats worried that thousands of eligible voters would be denied the right to vote, and the American Civil Liberties Union filed suit on behalf of three ex-felons who wanted to vote that November. The lawsuit went nowhere, but the issue continued to draw negative attention to the Riley administration.

For a time, Riley was included among possible Republican vice presidential candidates in 2008. He is prohibited by term limits from running again for governor in 2010 and said in December that he would retire from politics when his term expires. Former Phoenix Suns basketball player Charles Barkley, who had considered running for governor in 1998 as a Republican, said in 2006 he was considering a 2010 gubernatorial bid as a Democrat, but a 2009 drunk-driving conviction probably ended his chances. Democratic Rep. Artur Davis announced his bid to become Alabama's first black governor. Greenville businessman Tim James, a Republican and the son of former Alabama Gov. Fob James, was investing $2 million in personal funds in his quest for the GOP nomination.

Senior Senator

Richard Shelby (R)

Elected 1986, term expires 2010, 4th term; b. May 6, 1934, Birmingham; home, Tuscaloosa; U. of AL, B.A. 1957, LL.B. 1963; Presbyterian; married (Annette Nevin); 2 children.

Elected Office: AL Senate, 1970–78; U.S. House of Reps., 1979–87.

Professional Career: Practicing atty., 1963–78; City prosecutor, Tuscaloosa, 1963–71; U.S. magistrate 1966–70; Spec. asst. to Alabama atty. gen., 1969–71.

DC Office: 304 RSOB, 20510, 202-224-5744; Fax: 202-224-3416; Web site: shelby.senate.gov.

State Offices: Birmingham, 205-731-1384; Huntsville, 256-772-0460; Mobile, 251-694-4164; Montgomery, 334-223-7303; Tuscaloosa, 205-759-5047.

Committees: *Aging (Special)* (2nd of 7 R). *Appropriations* (4th of 12 R): Commerce, Justice, Science & Related Agencies (RMM); Defense; Energy & Water Development; Homeland Security; Labor, Health and Human Services, Education & Related Agencies; Transportation, Housing and Urban Development & Related Agencies. *Banking, Housing & Urban Affairs* (RMM of 10 R).

Group Ratings

	ADA	ACLU	AFS	LCV	ITIC	NTU	COC	ACU	CFG	FRC
2008	15	21	0	18	80	63	75	84	81	100
2007	20	—	0	7	—	65	73	88	69	—

National Journal Ratings

	2007 LIB	—	2007 CONS	2008 LIB	—	2008 CONS
Economic	24%	—	75%	21%	—	78%
Social	22%	—	76%	30%	—	68%
Foreign	16%	—	79%	24%	—	71%
Composite	22%	—	78%	26%	—	74%

Key Votes of the 110th Congress

1. Raise CAFE standards	N	5. Make English official language	Y	9. Withdraw troops 3/08	N
2. Expand SCHIP	N	6. Path to citizenship	N	10. Iran guard is terrorist group	Y
3. Cap greenhouse gases	N	7. Fetus is unborn child	Y	11. Increase missile defense $	Y
4. Bail out financial markets	N	8. Prosecute hate crimes	N	12. Overhaul FISA	Y

Election Results

2004 general	Richard Shelby (R)	1,242,200	(68%)	($1,922,646)
	Wayne Sowell (D)	595,018	(32%)	($4,869)
2004 primary	Richard Shelby (R)	.... unopposed		

Prior Winning Percentages: 1998 (63%); 1992 (65%); 1986 (50%); 1984 House (97%); 1982 House (97%); 1980 House (73%); 1978 House (94%)

Alabama senior Sen. Richard Shelby's political career spans nearly 40 years. He grew up in Birmingham, the son of a steelworker. After earning two degrees from the University of Alabama, he stayed in Tuscaloosa and practiced law with Walter Flowers, who was later a conservative Democratic representative. Shelby, also a Democrat at that time, was elected to the state Senate in 1970 at age 36. When Flowers ran, unsuccessfully, for the U.S. Senate in 1978, Shelby ran for his House seat. The critical contest was the Democratic runoff against Chris McNair, an African-American state legislator whose daughter Denise was one of the four young girls killed in the 1963 Birmingham church bombing. Although the district had the highest black percentage in Alabama at the time, Shelby won 59%-41%. In the House, Shelby had a conservative voting record, opposing the Voting Rights Act extension and the Martin Luther King Holiday. He ran for the Senate in 1986 and won the Democratic primary with 51% of the vote after Alabama's then-Secretary of State (and later governor) Don Siegelman withdrew. In the general election, he ran ads against incumbent Republican Jeremiah Denton, a retired admiral who had been a prisoner of war in Vietnam, for voting to cut Social Security and for owning two Mercedes-Benz cars (not a likely negative now, with the Mercedes plant in Tuscaloosa). Shelby won by 7,000 votes.

As one of a half-dozen or so conservative Southern Democrats in the Senate in the mid-1980s, Shelby at first attracted little notice. He voted for the confirmation of Clarence Thomas to the Supreme Court in the wake of sexual-harassment claims against Thomas by a former colleague. And Shelby voted for the 1991 resolution to go to war in the Persian Gulf after Iraq invaded Kuwait. In 1992, he was re-elected 65%-33%, breaking a jinx on a seat that, before Shelby's election in 1986, had had four different occupants in 10 years.

Soon after President Clinton took office in 1993, Shelby broke ranks with the Democratic Party. At a meeting with Vice President Gore, he turned to the assembled Alabama television cameras and opposed the Clinton program as "high on taxes, low on spending cuts." In response, the administration announced that a multimillion-dollar space facility would be built not in Alabama but in Texas (although it eventually was built in Alabama). The more he defied Clinton, the better Shelby's favorable ratings were at home. He lined up with the Republicans and against the administration on vote after vote on almost every partisan issue. The day after Republicans regained control of the Senate in 1994, Shelby announced he was switching parties, increasing the GOP majority to 53-47. Republicans happily allowed him to keep his seniority on the Banking Committee and gave him seats on Appropriations and its Defense Subcommittee. He got a seat on the Senate Select Intelligence Committee as well, putting him on a course to assume the chairmanship of Intelligence in 1997.

By the time of the September 11 attacks, the Senate was back in Democratic hands, but Shelby, as the ranking Republican on the Intelligence panel, was an important player in the ensuing weeks and months. He had adopted an adversarial posture toward the intelligence agencies during the Clinton years and in the Bush years as well. Soon after September 11, Shelby stopped just short of calling for the resignation of Central Intelligence Agency Director George Tenet, who was appointed by Clinton and retained by Bush. He was negatively impressed when, after India conducted three underground nuclear tests in 1998, Tenet told him, "We didn't have a clue." He also was critical of the lack of information about the February 1993 World Trade Center bombing, the 1998 attacks on the embassies in Kenya and Tanzania, and the 2000 attack on the USS *Cole*. In June 2004, when Tenet announced his resignation, Shelby said, "What was a surprise was that he held on to the job as long as he did."

Shelby was mostly supportive of the Bush administration's conduct of the war on terrorism. In December 2001, he was one of 10 senators to sign a letter saying, "It is imperative that we plan to eliminate the threat from Iraq." But he clashed with the two Intelligence Committee chairmen, Sen. Bob Graham, D-Fla., and Rep. Porter Goss, R-Fla., in the joint investigations of the intelligence community. He helped push aside their choice as staff director and installed his own candidate. At first, he opposed the appointment of an independent September 11 commission as unnecessary, but relented in 2002. He was out front in calling for the creation of a director of National Intelligence after the intelligence agencies, in his view, were unable to work together and to share information. That position was later upheld by the 9/11 commission and adopted in the intelligence reorganization bill approved by Congress in 2004. That bill included a Shelby proposal to give the DNI ombudsman access to all intelligence for analytical reviews, but he was displeased that the new director would not be a Cabinet member.

On domestic issues, Shelby has compiled a conservative record. But he is not a free-market purist. Despite his party switch, he has remained friendly with trial lawyers, who usually support Democrats in Alabama. He opposed Alabama colleague Sen. Jeff Sessions's amendment to cap lawyers' fees in tobacco cases, and insisted tort reform was a state issue. He voted against a 2004 bill to protect gun manufacturers from liability for actions of users of their products. He was the only Senate Republican to vote against financial services deregulation in 1999, and he opposed allowing federally insured banks to sell real estate or insurance.

Since January 2003, Shelby has been either the chairman or the ranking minority member of the Banking, Housing, and Urban Affairs Committee, and from that perch, he has been at the center of congressional attempts to stem problems in the mortgage and insurance industries. On a hotly lobbied issue in 2003, he supported defining stock options as expenses, a measure opposed by the high-technology industry. The same year, he presciently quizzed Federal Reserve Chairman Alan Greenspan about the increasing number of home loans to borrowers with weak credit histories, a trend that sent the home mortgage market into a tailspin by 2008.

In July 2005, the committee voted along party lines for Shelby's legislation to impose tighter limits on Fannie Mae's and Freddie Mac's portfolios, but it contained no affordable-housing fund and was killed by Senate Democrats. In 2008, Democratic Chairman Christopher Dodd of Connecticut pushed a compromise housing bill that would allow bankruptcy judges to restructure mortgages and another proposal to refinance mortgages for millions of homeowners at risk of defaulting. Consumer groups pushed for both, but could not get by Shelby. The government, he said, should not engage in a "taxpayer-funded bailout of investors or homeowners." He later reached agreement with Dodd on a bill to allow Fannie Mae and Freddie Mac to fund the refinancing of home mortgages, but he also got a provision increasing capital requirements for the two quasi-public mortgage giants.

Shelby opposed the $700 billion bailout of the financial markets in September 2008, though President Bush was pushing the package. "What troubles me most is that we have been given no credible assurances that this plan will work. We could very well spend $700 billion and not resolve the crisis," Shelby said. Two months later, he opposed a massive government loan for domestic automakers as well, which he called "dinosaurs." He said, "These companies are going to have to downsize. They're going to have to be innovative. They're going to have to change their whole model, and the government at the end of the day . . . should not choose which companies are going to survive or not survive. We should let the market work." After the automakers presented their plan for recovery in December 2008, he said, "I wouldn't loan them any money. They're either failed or failing." He threatened a filibuster, and the bill did not pass the Senate. When he was criticized on the grounds he was defending foreign automakers with plants in Alabama, he pointed out that he had voted against an earlier bailout of Chrysler long before the plants were built.

In 2006, Shelby pushed through to enactment a bill to direct the Securities and Exchange Commission to designate ratings agencies as Nationally Recognized Statistical Ratings Organizations if they meet certain standards over three years. The SEC had been enforcing a 1975 rule that prevented many ratings agencies from qualifying, and that left 80% of the business in the hands of Moody's and Standard & Poor's. "The dominant rating agencies failed millions of investors by neglecting to lower their ratings on Enron, WorldCom, and other companies headed for bankruptcy. The absence of timely downgrades in these cases was the product of an industry that was beset by conflicts of interest and a lack of competition," Shelby said.

Shelby looks out for Alabama's interests on the Appropriations Committee. When the sock industry in DeKalb County—which calls itself the "sock capital of the world"—stood to be hurt by a 2002 free-trade bill, he held up the bill to get protection from socks mended in the Caribbean, and in 2004 he got country-of-origin labeling for imported and domestic socks. He has obtained some $70 million for buildings at the University of Alabama at Birmingham medical campus, one of which is named for him, and funds for refurbishing the Vulcan statue on Birmingham's Red Mountain—a favorite target of Sen. John McCain, the Arizona Republican and 2008 presidential candidate who crusades against earmarks, the special provisions tucked into spending bills by individual lawmakers.

In 2007, Shelby voted for a measure to force senators to disclose their earmarks, but he was the only Republican senator to oppose a bill to allow the president to send back individual spending items for up-or-down votes in Congress. Shelby sponsored earmarks totaling $203 million in 2006 and $191 million in 2007. In 2008, he sponsored $940,000 for the Southern Research Institute, $235,000 for McWane Science Center, and $392,000 for the Birmingham Intermodal Transit Facility. He registers near the top of the annual list of wasteful-spending earmarks compiled by the watchdog group Citizens Against Government Waste. That's a stark contrast to his Republican colleague in the Senate, Sessions, who was lauded by CAGW in 2007 for his work on the budget to reduce earmarks.

Shelby strongly supported the bid of Airbus and Northrop Grumman to assemble a new Air Force tanker in a plant to be built at Mobile's Brookley Field Industrial Complex. He demanded an apology when an executive at rival company Boeing said that there was a higher risk in Mobile than in Seattle, where Boeing has significant operations, because the region lacked experience in aircraft manufacturing. Airbus was awarded the contract in February 2008, but the Government Accountability Office then sustained Boeing's challenge to the award in July. Shelby lobbied Defense Secretary Robert Gates to award the contract to Airbus.

Shelby's party switch caused him no trouble in increasingly Republican Alabama. In 1998, he was re-elected 63%-37% over a retired ironworker who mortgaged his pickup truck to pay the $2,672 filing fee. For the 2004 election, he accumulated some $11 million, more than any incumbent other than New York's Charles Schumer, a Democrat. His Democratic opponent was Wayne Sowell, Alabama's first black Senate nominee and a telephone claims representative for the Social Security Administration in Birmingham. Shelby spent only $2.3 million of his money, and won 68%-32%, running behind in only nine black-majority counties in the Black Belt. In 2009, he was a heavy favorite to win re-election in 2010.

Junior Senator

Jeff Sessions (R)

Elected 1996, term expires 2014, 3rd term; b. Dec. 24, 1946, Hybart; home, Mobile; Huntingdon Col., B.A. 1969, U. of AL, J.D. 1973; Methodist; married (Mary); 3 children.

Military Career: Army Reserves, 1973–86.

Elected Office: AL atty. gen., 1994–96.

Professional Career: Practicing atty., 1973–75, 1977–81, 1993–94; Asst. U.S. atty., 1975–77; U.S. atty., 1981–93.

DC Office: 335 RSOB, 20510, 202-224-4124; Fax: 202-224-3149; Web site: sessions.senate.gov.

State Offices: Birmingham, 205-731-1500; Huntsville, 256-533-0979; Mobile, 251-414-3083; Montgomery, 334-244-7017.

Committees: *Armed Services* (3rd of 11 R): Airland; Seapower; Strategic Forces. *Budget* (4th of 10 R). *Energy & Natural Resources* (9th of 10 R): Energy; Public Lands & Forests; Water & Power. *Judiciary* (RMM of 7 R): Administrative Oversight & the Courts (RMM); Crime & Drugs; Immigration, Refugees & Border Security; Terrorism & Homeland Security.

Group Ratings

	ADA	ACLU	AFS	LCV	ITIC	NTU	COC	ACU	CFG	FRC
2008	20	23	0	18	80	74	50	84	84	100
2007	10	—	0	13	—	74	40	83	70	—

National Journal Ratings

	2007 LIB	—	2007 CONS	2008 LIB	—	2008 CONS
Economic	26%	—	72%	8%	—	91%
Social	0%	—	91%	27%	—	72%
Foreign	9%	—	87%	24%	—	71%
Composite	14%	—	86%	21%	—	79%

Key Votes of the 110th Congress

1. Raise CAFE standards	N	5. Make English official language Y	9. Withdraw troops 3/08	N
2. Expand SCHIP	N	6. Path to citizenship	N	10. Iran guard is terrorist group	Y
3. Cap greenhouse gases	N	7. Fetus is unborn child	Y	11. Increase missile defense $	N
4. Bail out financial markets	N	8. Prosecute hate crimes	N	12. Overhaul FISA	*

Election Results

2008 general	Jeff Sessions (R)	1,305,383	(63%)	($3,240,151)
	Vivian Figures (D)	752,391	(37%)	($332,007)
2008 primary	Jeff Sessions (R)	199,690	(92%)	
	Earl Gavin (R)	16,718	(8%)	

Prior Winning Percentages: 2002 (59%); 1996 (52%)

Republican Jeff Sessions, Alabama's junior senator, is the ranking Republican on the Judiciary Committee. He grew up in the state's Black Belt, is the son of a country-store owner, and recalls walking to school barefoot. He graduated from Huntingdon College and the University of Alabama Law School, then practiced law in a small town near the Tennessee Valley and later in Mobile. He was appointed U.S. attorney in Mobile in 1981, at age 35, and became known as a tough, aggressive prosecutor over the next dozen years. In 1985, he was nominated for a federal judgeship but was attacked by liberals for "gross insensitivity" in racial matters when he prosecuted vote fraud cases. With Alabama's Democratic Sen. Howell Heflin voting against him in the Judiciary Committee, his nomination never went to the Senate floor. In 1994, Sessions challenged state Attorney General Jimmy Evans, a Democrat who had successfully prosecuted Republican Gov. Guy Hunt the year before, and won 57%-43%. In March 1995, when Heflin announced his retirement, Sessions started running for his seat.

In the contested GOP primary, Sessions relied on his base in southern Alabama, territory that not long ago cast almost no Republican primary votes. Long-distance carrier executive Sid McDonald spent more than $1 million on his campaign. From Birmingham north, the primary was a close race: McDonald led by 30%-29%. But in the rest of the state, Sessions led 48%-12%, for a 38%-22% statewide victory. In the runoff, McDonald extended his lead north from Birmingham, 54%-46%. But almost half the total votes were cast farther south, and there Sessions led 73%-27%, for a 59%-41% win. The Democratic nominee, trial lawyer and state Sen. Roger Bedford, was financed by trial lawyers and endorsed by key public employee unions and African-American organizations—the heart of today's Alabama Democratic Party.

In the past, Democratic primaries had turnouts of nearly 1 million, with the advantage going to moderate or conservative candidates like Glen Browder, the 3rd District representative running in the Senate primary. But only 315,000 people voted in the Democratic primary, about half of them black; Bedford led Browder 45%-29%. In the runoff, Bedford had more money and won 62%-38%. In the general election, Bedford was competitive in fundraising and seemed the better campaigner. He opposed abortion rights, gun control, and gays in the military. Sessions avoided debates and attacked the Democrat as a "Ted Kennedy" supporter, a reference to the Massachusetts liberal senator who suggested Bedford was too far to the left for Alabama. Sessions also emphasized Bedford's role in leading a battle against tort law changes in the Alabama Senate in 1996. Sessions won 52%-45%, running best in the suburban counties around Alabama's cities. Bedford carried the Black Belt and other rural counties.

Sessions has a very conservative voting record in the Senate. He serves on the Judiciary Committee that once rejected his nomination for a judgeship, and in 2003 complained, "I'm angry and passionate about the way the Democrats refused to let the Senate vote on these judgeships." But Sessions also has taken on some atypical causes for a conservative. With none other than Sen. Edward Kennedy, the Massachusetts liberal, he co-sponsored a bill to combat sexual assault in prisons. And he has co-sponsored bills to reduce mandatory minimum sentences for minor players in drug offenses. "I believe as a matter of law enforcement and good public policy that crack cocaine sentences are too heavy and can't be justified," he said. He has not always toed a partisan line on Judiciary. In 2007, he asked Attorney General Alberto Gonzales to make public a memo giving two of his aides power to hire and fire federal prosecutors, and he grilled Gonzales sternly on department policy on election-related crimes.

In 2006, Sessions emerged as one of the most vocal opponents of the bipartisan immigration bill sponsored by Kennedy and Sen. John McCain, R-Ariz. He staunchly opposed granting immigrants who had entered the country illegally a process to achieve citizenship, which the bill established. Over the next two years, as Congress debated changes in immigration policy, Sessions was a major roadblock to proposals easing immigration restrictions. In January 2007, he got the Senate to pass a bill banning federal contracts for 10 years to contractors who do not use the e-verify system and hire illegal immigrants. Later in the year, he fought a bill that came to the floor that created a guest-worker program for illegal immigrants. He objected to a provision that 30% of immigrants be admitted on the basis of marketable skills, saying the percentage should be much higher, and he also said that immigrants with temporary legal status should be ineligible for the Earned Income Tax Credit. "The American people have been clear that they want us to restore the rule of law to our immigration system before legalization programs are considered," Sessions said. In March 2008, he succeeded in getting passed an amendment to the budget to fund completion of a fence along the border with Mexico, to impose mandatory prison terms for illegal border crossers, and to deport illegal immigrants convicted of a felony.

Although Sessions has sponsored few major bills, he has had considerable success in inserting into other legislation provisions he favors that set new federal policy. He typically targets bills that are likely to pass, an effective strategy. When the Medicare prescription drug bill came to the floor in 2003, Sessions inserted a provision for higher Medicare reimbursement for rural hospitals and threatened to vote against the final version of the bill unless it contained his provision. It did, sending $738 million to Alabama, more than any other states except Texas and Florida. The 2004 special-education bill included a Sessions provision giving school districts the authority to establish uniform discipline policies for all schools. With the retirement of New Mexico Republican Pete Domenici in 2008, Sessions may be the Senate's leading advocate of nuclear power. "Nuclear does all four: It's all-American, it creates high-paying American jobs, it emits no CO_2, and it's cost-effective," he told the *Birmingham News*.

On the Armed Services Committee, Sessions has been a big advocate for missile defense and has also focused on building up defense installations in Alabama. He supported the Bush administration on the Iraq war, and was one of nine senators voting against an amendment banning "cruel, inhuman, or degrading treatment" of prisoners. Along with Republicans Tom Coburn of Oklahoma and Jim DeMint of South Carolina, he is one of the Senate's biggest critics of earmarks, the special provisions inserted into spending bills by lawmakers for their districts or states. Nevertheless, on Armed Services Sessions supports major projects with an impact on Alabama.

During the fight in Congress in late 2008 over government bailouts of private industries, Sessions opposed the $700 billion bill for the ailing financial markets. In November 2008, he complained in a letter to President Bush that Treasury Secretary Henry Paulson "is acting as a Wall Street investment banker, allocating hundreds of billions of dollars in taxpayer money, with no oversight and no state plan." He opposed as well a multibillion-dollar government loan for General Motors, Chrysler, and Ford, citing the fact that the foreign manufacturers with plants in Alabama weren't seeking similar treatment. "It strikes me as unfair to our auto industry," Sessions said. "They propose taxing Alabama's healthy auto industry to subsidize a sick one in Detroit."

In 2002 Sessions was opposed by Democrat Susan Parker, the state auditor and a fundraiser for colleges. She had the support of teachers' unions, but Sessions outspent her 4-to-1 and won 59%-40%. Parker carried two Tennessee River counties in the north and 12 Black Belt counties in the center of the state, but Sessions won everything else. He raised early money in advance of the 2008 election, warding off possible challenges by prominent Democrats Artur Davis, a House member, and Ron Sparks, the state agriculture commissioner. His opponent was state Sen. Vivian Davis Figures of Mobile. Sessions raised $6.4 million and spent $3.2 million, while Figures spent $332,000. Sessions won 63%-37%.

FIRST DISTRICT

Jo Bonner (R)

Elected 2002, 4th term; b. Nov. 19, 1959, Selma; home, Mobile; U. of AL, B.A. 1982, U. of AL, J.D. 1988; Episcopalian; married (Janee).

Professional Career: Sr. aide, U.S. Rep. Sonny Callahan, 1984-2002.

DC Office: 2236 RHOB, 20515, 202-225-4931; Fax: 202-225-0562; Web site: www.bonner.house.gov.

State Offices: Foley, 251-943-2073; Mobile, 251-690-2811.

Committees: *Appropriations* (21st of 23 R): Commerce, Justice, Science & Related Agencies; Labor, HHS, Education & Related Agencies. *Standards of Official Conduct* (RMM of 5 R).

Group Ratings

	ADA	ACLU	AFS	LCV	ITIC	NTU	COC	ACU	CFG	FRC
2008	15	18	14	0	100	60	94	83	70	76
2007	15	—	18	10	—	70	85	83	74	—

National Journal Ratings

	2007 LIB	—	2007 CONS	2008 LIB	—	2008 CONS
Economic	21%	—	78%	17%	—	83%
Social	17%	—	81%	16%	—	82%
Foreign	0%	—	72%	19%	—	79%
Composite	18%	—	82%	18%	—	82%

Key Votes of the 110th Congress

1. Increase minimum wage	Y	5. Share immigration data	*	9. Withdraw troops 8/08	N
2. Expand SCHIP	N	6. Foreign aid abortion ban	*	10. No operations in Iran	N
3. Raise CAFE standards	N	7. Ban gay bias in workplace	N	11. Free trade with Peru	Y
4. Bail out financial markets	Y	8. Repeal D.C. gun law	Y	12. Overhaul FISA	Y

Election Results

2008 general	Jo Bonner (R)	210,652	(98%)	($736,705)
2008 primary	Jo Bonner (R)	unopposed		

Prior Winning Percentages: 2006 (68%); 2004 (63%); 2002 (60%)

Population		Race/Ethnicity		Work	
Pop. 2007:	661,098	White:	67.3%	Private:	79.8%
Change since 2000:	Up 4.1%	Black:	27.9%	Government:	13.8%
Urban:	64.4%	Hispanic:	1.7%	Self-employed:	6.1%
Rural:	35.6%	Asian:	1.3%	Blue collar:	26.4%
Area size:	7,182 sq. mi.	Native Am.:	0.8%	White collar:	56.1%
		Hawaiian:	0.0%	Khaki collar:	0.2%
Age		Two+ races:	0.9%	Other:	17.4%
Median age:	37.1 yrs.	*Ancestry*		Median income:	$39,940
More than 65 yrs:	13.7%	USA:	12.3%	Median home value:	$115,000
Less than 18 yrs:	25.5%	Irish:	9.5%	Poverty:	18.1%
Education		English:	7.7%	**Military Veterans**	
H.S. grad:	82.1%			% of Pop:	12.7%
College grad:	20.1%				
Grad degree:	7.0%				

Mobile, the port where the Tombigbee and Alabama rivers flow into the Gulf of Mexico, was a strategic point on the American frontier. Spanish after the Revolutionary War, it was wrested away by threats of war from Secretary of State John Quincy Adams. During the Civil War, it was one of the major Confederate ports. In 1864, Admiral David Farragut, while steaming into the harbor lashed to his mast, cried, "Damn the torpedoes! Full speed ahead." Today, Mobile is full of graceful signs of its exotic

2008 Presidential Vote		
McCain (R)	185,579	(61%)
Obama (D)	116,904	(38%)
2004 Presidential Vote		
Bush (R)	168,817	(64%)
Kerry (D)	91,832	(35%)
Cook Partisan Voting Index:	R + 14	

past. Behind the docks and rail lines are downtown buildings and old houses with Spanish motifs, French accents, or tropical Art Deco lines. Further inland are neighborhoods with spacious houses, often with double porches, overhung by huge live oaks graced with Spanish moss. Mobile is a Gulf Coast version of Charleston or a smaller, more comfortable New Orleans, with a taste for shellfish and spicy food and an even older Mardi Gras, which the locals have been celebrating since 1703. As befits a frontier city with a martial past, Mobile is bristling with arms: One of the city's proudest possessions is the battleship USS *Alabama*, moored at the head of Mobile Bay, with its guns aimed out toward the Gulf. Mobile's economy was based originally on docks and shipyards, factories and terminals but with a determination to impose touches of beauty on its hot, flat landscape. Its economy has been thriving at the shipyards, chemical plants, and a cruise ship terminal. The capital improvements include Mobile's State Docks, which serves Alabama's booming Mercedes, Honda, and Hyundai auto factories. ThyssenKrupp has a new $4.2 billion steel-processing plant in Calvert to supply the auto companies, and Mobile's $300 million container terminal opened in 2008, and immediately more than doubled annual shipments.

In August 2005, Hurricane Katrina struck Mobile and its beaches with Category 4 intensity. On Dauphin Island, the 15-mile spit of land south of Mobile Bay, 300 homes were swept away, and a one-mile gash created a new island. Elsewhere in Mobile and Baldwin counties, Katrina caused major damage to pecan, peanut, and cotton crops. Although the damage received far less national attention than did the devastation in Louisiana and Mississippi, the government authorized $970 million of post-Katrina assistance to Alabama, though it took until 2008 for many of the 2,000 displaced residents to get repairs or new homes.

Mobile is the focus of Alabama's 1st Congressional District, which extends north along the usually lazy Tombigbee and Alabama rivers, with their old forts and mansions. Monroeville was the home of great writers— Winston Groom, author of *Forrest Gump*; Truman Capote, who wrote *In Cold Blood*; and his childhood playmate, Harper Lee, whose classic *To Kill a Mockingbird* is set here. In 2007, President Bush awarded Lee the Presidential Medal of Freedom, saying her book "has influenced the character of our country for the better." There are also surviving backcountry settlements of blacks and Cajuns (who may or may not be descended from Louisiana Cajuns) and Creek Indians. Once cotton fields, this is now timberland, a major contributor to Alabama's economy, though the housing downturn suspended many operations. East of Mobile Bay, along the shores of the Gulf of Mexico, are condominium communities in Baldwin County, one of the two fastest-growing counties in Alabama. The area hosts the annual National Shrimp Festival, and its glorious Gulf beaches are one of the South's best-kept secrets. For years, this southern seaboard of the Confederacy has been one of the most hawkish parts of America, and today it is solidly Republican in national elections. But in September 2005, in elections held after Katrina, Mobile elected its first African-American mayor, Sam Jones; a liberal Democrat who served with John McCain during the Vietnam War.

The congressman from the 1st District is Jo Bonner, a Republican elected in 2002. Bonner was born in Selma and is just a little too young to remember when it was the focus of the civil-rights movement. He grew up in Camden, where his father, who died when Jo was 13, was a probate judge. In college, Bonner majored in journalism and graduated in 1982. Two years later, he started working as a campaign press secretary for Rep. Sonny Callahan, a gregarious nine-term Republican who rose to become an Appropriations subcommittee chairman, one of the so-called "cardinals" of the House. In 1989, Bonner was promoted to chief of staff and later moved his family back to Mobile and continued his staff work for Callahan there. That background left Bonner well positioned when Callahan announced his retirement three months before the 2002 primary. Bonner's strongest opponent in the seven-candidate Republican primary had a similar background: Tom Young had been the chief of staff to Republican Sen. Richard Shelby for 12 years. Like Bonner, Young had his former boss's endorsement and showed a knack for campaign fundraising. The two raised more than $2 million between them, including lots of money from Washington lobbyists. Young contrasted his experience on intelligence and defense policy with Bonner's focus on more mundane constituent-service work. Bonner argued that Young had more connections in Washington than in southern Alabama; he jibed that Young should have been welcomed at a luncheon for "new Mobilians." Young outspent Bonner by $300,000 and was helped by ads from the anti-tax group Club for Growth, but Bonner led the primary 40%-20%. In the runoff, Bonner was endorsed by the other Republicans who ran. He won 62%-38%. In a district held by Republicans since 1964, when Barry Goldwater swept Alabama, Bonner easily won in November, and has been re-elected easily ever since.

In the House, Bonner has a solidly conservative voting record. After Hurricane Katrina, he reassessed his support for repeal of the estate and gift taxes, worried about the bill for reconstruction in hardhit Gulf states like his own. He secured $7.5 million for improved shelter space at the fairgrounds in Baldwin County. In 2006, he voted against renewal of the Voting Rights Act, saying that it was time to give the South "an opportunity to come out from under the burden of crawling to the U.S. Justice Department, on bended knee, and asking for its blessing to continue on the march for equality."

From the moment he arrived in Congress, he lobbied GOP leaders to get Callahan's old seat on the Appropriations Committee, which controls the government purse strings. He finally succeeded in February 2008, when Republicans gave him the seat that had belonged to Rep. Roger Wicker, R-Miss., who was moving up to the Senate to replace the retiring Republican Trent Lott. Although regional identity helped Bonner, he also pledged to Minority Leader John Boehner of Ohio that he would limit spending earmarks, the special provisions tucked into appropriations bills that had tarred the GOP's reputation for thriftiness. Boehner said that with Bonner's appointment, "the old model is broken." Bonner said, "Since we helped create this mess, it should be up to us—House Republicans—to help fix the problem." Bonner also served on the four-member Ethics Committee panel that reviewed the personal finances of Democratic Rep. Charles Rangel of New York, the chairman of the House Ways and Means Committee. In 2009, he became the ranking Republican on the Ethics Committee.

In a rematch against Belk in 2004, Bonner won, 63%-37%. Two years later, he defeated former Mobile County Treasurer Vivian Beckerle 68%-32%. Bonner seems likely to have a lengthy tenure in this safe Republican seat. In February 2009, he decided against a run for governor in 2010.

SECOND DISTRICT

Bobby Bright (D)

Elected 2008, 1st term; b. July 21, 1952, Dale County; home, Montgomery; Auburn U., B.A. 1975; Troy U., M.A., 1977; Faulkner U., J.D. 1982; Baptist; married (Lynne); 3 children.

Elected Office: Montgomery mayor, 1999–2008.

Professional Career: Practicing atty.

DC Office: 1205 LHOB, 20515, 202-225-2901; Fax: 202-225-8913; Web site: bright.house.gov.

State Offices: Dothan, 334-794-9680; Montgomery, 334-277-9113.

Committees: *Agriculture* (19th of 28 D): Conservation, Credit, Energy & Research; Rural Development, Biotechnology, Specialty Crops, and Foreign Agriculture. *Armed Services* (34th of 36 D): Air & Land Forces; Readiness; Terrorism, Unconventional Threats & Capabilities. *Small Business* (15th of 17 D): Regulations & Healthcare; Rural Development, Entrepreneurship & Trade.

Group Ratings and Key Votes: Newly Elected

Election Results

2008 general	Bobby Bright (D)	144,368	(50%)	($1,193,166)
	Jay Love (R)	142,578	(50%)	($2,444,627)
2008 primary	Bobby Bright (D)	19,456	(67%)	
	Cendie Crawley (D)	5,110	(18%)	
	Cheryl Sabel (D)	4,631	(16%)	

Population		Race/Ethnicity		Work	
Pop. 2007:	647,670	White:	65.2%	Private:	73.3%
Change since 2000:	Up 1.9%	Black:	30.8%	Government:	19.7%
Urban:	50.1%	Hispanic:	1.9%	Self-employed:	6.8%
Rural:	49.9%	Asian:	0.8%	Blue collar:	29.2%
Area size:	10,608 sq. mi.	Native Am.:	0.4%	White collar:	53.8%
Age		Hawaiian:	0.0%	Khaki collar:	1.1%
Median age:	36.9 yrs.	Two+ races:	1.0%	Other:	15.9%
More than 65 yrs:	13.6%	*Ancestry*		Median income:	$38,221
Less than 18 yrs:	24.9%	USA:	14.2%	Median home value:	$94,900
Education		Irish:	8.0%	Poverty:	17.3%
H.S. grad:	78.6%	English:	7.6%	**Military Veterans**	
College grad:	18.9%			% of Pop:	13.5%
Grad degree:	6.8%				

Thick green countryside blankets southern Alabama. Even in Montgomery, the stone and brick buildings of the downtown district do not mask the contours of the hills or hide the lush foliage. One can look downhill from the restored Greek Revival capitol toward Dexter Avenue Baptist Church, where the young Martin Luther King Jr. was pastor in the 1950s, or out past the impressive Carolyn Blount Theater, host of the Alabama Shakespeare Festival, toward new subdivisions and shopping malls,

2008 Presidential Vote		
McCain (R)	182,618	(63%)
Obama (D)	107,669	(37%)
2004 Presidential Vote		
Bush (R)	170,427	(67%)
Kerry (D)	84,043	(33%)
Cook Partisan Voting Index:	R + 16	

and easily imagine when this land was covered with cotton fields and pine trees. The atmosphere is even more rural in southeast Alabama's Wiregrass region, named for the stiff native grass. There is the fishing town of Eufaula, along the Chattahoochee River; the Army's Fort Rucker, the home of Army aviation flight training; and Enterprise, site of the Boll Weevil Monument that commemorates the insect that destroyed two-thirds of the cotton crop in 1915 and then spread throughout the South. Timber is an important resource here, and peanuts are now the main crop in the area surrounding Dothan. The region ranks second in the nation in acres harvested for peanuts. But the area is diversifying: Hyundai built its first U.S. assembly plant in southwest Montgomery County, with about 3,000 local jobs.

The 2nd Congressional District covers the southeast corner of the state. It includes most of the city of Montgomery but only a small part of Montgomery County. Democratic redistricters put the rest, including the capitol and many black precincts, into the 3rd District in an attempt to make that seat more Democratic. The result was to make the 2nd District strongly Republican. The Montgomery County precincts, plus suburban Elmore and Autauga counties, vote heavily Republican, as does the area around Dothan and Houston County in the Wiregrass region. The area outvotes by a large number the district's "black belt" counties—Lowndes, Bullock, with a large black majority, and Barbour on the Georgia border, which was George Wallace's home base. It would be a mistake to see these preferences as purely racial, however. African-Americans here tend to support a larger and more generous government, and hence vote Democratic. Alabama whites tend to take a hard line on defense and crime and want government to promote traditional cultural values, and hence vote Republican.

The new congressman from the 2nd District is Democrat Bobby Bright, elected in 2008 to succeed retiring Republican Rep. Terry Everett. He is the first Democrat to represent the district since 1964.

Bright is a fourth-generation Alabamian and the 13th of 14 children. Born in the district's Wiregrass region, Bright spent the first 11 years of his life on the farm where his father worked as a sharecropper. During those years, harvesting crops was the family's priority, and the late-summer cotton harvest often caused him to miss the first week of school. His family moved off the farm when he was 11, and Bright started working full-time at his older brother's sheet-metal business for one dollar per day. He continued attending school and received a partial scholarship to play football at the University of West Alabama. But Bright could not afford to pay the tuition that was not covered by the scholarship, so he attended Enterprise-Ozark Community College for two years. He went on to attend Auburn University, where he earned an undergraduate degree in political science. After college, Bright worked as a prison guard before earning a master's degree in criminal justice from Troy University and a law degree from the Jones School of Law at Faulkner University.

As a newly minted lawyer in 1982, Bright opened a practice in Montgomery specializing in defending doctors and nurses. In 1999, the lack of economic opportunity for many city residents spurred him to run for mayor. He faced 21-year incumbent Emory Folmar, a white politician whose unpopularity among the city's African-American population was partially responsible for Montgomery's polarization. City law required the mayor's office be occupied by a nonpartisan, so Bright ran as an independent and defeated Folmar 54%-46%. As mayor, Bright invested heavily in urban development and, symbolically, moved his home from the city's eastern suburbs to a downtown loft apartment. He also focused on unifying Montgomery's population, alleviating some of the lingering racial tensions by appointing the city's first African-American chief of police and its first black fire chief. Bright easily won re-election in 2003 and 2007.

When Everett announced his retirement in 2007, Bright ran in the primary as a Democrat and won the nomination with 67% of the vote. In the general election, Bright faced businessman and Republican state Rep. Jay Love. Both men served as deacons at the First Baptist Church in Montgomery, and they espoused nearly identical political views, including opposition to abortion rights and support for giving the president the line-item veto. Bright touted his conservative beliefs and independence from Democratic leaders, while Love attempted to associate Bright with national Democrats. He criticized Bright for accepting campaign donations from Democratic House Speaker Nancy Pelosi of California and claimed Bright would support Pelosi's liberal agenda. Love embraced the Republican Party and was the first congressional candidate to feature Republican vice presidential nominee Sarah Palin in a televised campaign ad.

Everett tried to help Love by promoting the notion that Bright would have little influence as a member of the "Blue Dog" Coalition, a conservative Democratic group in the House that Bright said he would join. To counter those claims, Blue Dog leaders John Tanner of Tennessee and Allen Boyd of Florida stumped for Bright in the district. He also was endorsed by two prominent local Republicans, including Love's chief opponent in the Republican primary. Love had the upper hand financially, pouring just under $1 million of personal money into the race and outspending Bright 2-to-1. But Bright's name recognition as Montgomery mayor helped him throughout the district. He defeated Love by 1,790 votes—less than a single percentage point. His better-than-expected showing in the district's Wiregrass area, the most conservative part of the district, swung the election in his favor.

In the House, Bright got seats on the Agriculture, Armed Services, and Small Business committees. In his first month on the job, he was one of only two Democrats to vote against a Democratic initiative to greatly expand the State Children's Health Insurance Program. He also joined 10 other House Democrats in voting against President Obama's economic stimulus bill.

THIRD DISTRICT

Mike Rogers (R)

Elected 2002, 4th term; b. July 16, 1958, Hammond, IN; home, Anniston; Jacksonville St. U., B.A. 1981, M.P.A. 1984, Birmingham Schl. of Law, J.D. 1991; Baptist; married (Beth); 3 children.

Elected Office: Calhoun Cnty. Commission, 1986–90; AL House of Reps., 1994–2002, Min. ldr., 1998–2000.

Professional Career: Practicing atty., 1991–2002.

DC Office: 324 CHOB, 20515, 202-225-3261; Fax: 202-226-8485; Web site: www.house.gov/mike-rogers/.

State Offices: Anniston, 256-236-5655; Montgomery, 334-277-4210; Opelika, 334-745-6221.

Committees: *Agriculture* (6th of 17 R): Conservation, Credit, Energy & Research; Livestock, Dairy & Poultry. *Armed Services* (13th of 25 R): Oversight & Investigations; Readiness; Strategic Forces. *Homeland Security* (5th of 13 R): Border, Maritime & Global Counterterrorism; Emergency Communications, Preparedness & Response (RMM).

Group Ratings

	ADA	ACLU	AFS	LCV	ITIC	NTU	COC	ACU	CFG	FRC
2008	50	18	57	31	71	38	89	50	34	100
2007	20	—	9	15	—	60	90	80	52	—

National Journal Ratings

	2007 LIB	—	2007 CONS		2008 LIB	—	2008 CONS
Economic	31%	—	69%		40%	—	60%
Social	9%	—	85%		20%	—	74%
Foreign	0%	—	72%		34%	—	65%
Composite	19%	—	81%		33%	—	68%

Key Votes of the 110th Congress

1. Increase minimum wage	Y	5. Share immigration data	Y	9. Withdraw troops 8/08	N
2. Expand SCHIP	N	6. Foreign aid abortion ban	Y	10. No operations in Iran	N
3. Raise CAFE standards	N	7. Ban gay bias in workplace	N	11. Free trade with Peru	Y
4. Bail out financial markets	Y	8. Repeal D.C. gun law	Y	12. Overhaul FISA	Y

Election Results

2008 general	Mike Rogers (R)	150,819	(53%)	($2,056,912)
	Joshua Segall (D)	131,299	(46%)	($1,089,890)
2008 primary	Mike Rogers (R)	unopposed		

Prior Winning Percentages: 2006 (59%); 2004 (61%); 2002 (50%)

Population		Race/Ethnicity		Work	
Pop. 2007:	648,915	White:	63.9%	Private:	75.4%
Change since 2000:	Up 2.1%	Black:	32.0%	Government:	18.8%
Urban:	53.3%	Hispanic:	1.6%	Self-employed:	5.6%
Rural:	46.7%	Asian:	0.9%	Blue collar:	30.5%
Area size:	7,988 sq. mi.	Native Am.:	0.3%	White collar:	52.5%
		Hawaiian:	0.0%	Khaki collar:	0.6%
Age		Two+ races:	1.1%	Other:	16.4%
Median age:	36.0 yrs.			Median income:	$36,708
More than 65 yrs:	13.2%	*Ancestry*		Median home value:	$93,400
Less than 18 yrs:	23.7%	USA:	11.3%	Poverty:	18.7%
		English:	9.1%		
Education		Irish:	8.7%	**Military Veterans**	
H.S. grad:	77.2%			% of Pop:	11.8%
College grad:	18.9%				
Grad degree:	8.1%				

Forty years ago, Lineville, Alabama, in the red hills of Clay County, was Ku Klux Klan country, with whites determined to resist race-mixing and blacks under constant threat of violence. More recently in Lineville, integrated crowds regularly cheer mixed black and white high school teams, and people of all races work together, though they tend to pray separately on Sundays. Lineville's progress perhaps echoes that of America's most integrated institution, the military, for the small town produced more

2008 Presidential Vote		
McCain (R)	161,154	(56%)
Obama (D)	124,973	(43%)

2004 Presidential Vote		
Bush (R)	146,380	(58%)
Kerry (D)	103,456	(41%)

Cook Partisan Voting Index: R+ 9

men and women per capita for Operation Desert Storm than any other community in the nation. When the United States invaded Iraq in 2003, Alabama was the nation's top contributor of National Guard personnel. Clay County has one of the highest concentrations of Guard enlistments and reservists in the state.

The 3rd Congressional District of Alabama is centered geographically and philosophically in Lineville. The military presence is unmistakable: Calhoun County is home to the Anniston Army Depot and formerly home to Fort McClellan, which closed in 1999. Horseshoe Bend is where Andrew Jackson won a climactic battle against the Upper Creek Indians. Fort Mitchell, a 19th-century frontier military outpost, is the site of a national military cemetery sometimes referred to as the "Arlington of the South." Phenix City, across the Chattahoochie River from Georgia's Fort Benning, served as a "sin city" in the 1940s and 1950s, with virtually every imaginable vice for pleasure-seeking soldiers, a place so sleazy that Gen. George Patton threatened to level it with his tanks. Today, the huge military installation plays a more constructive role in the local economy. There are other places of distinction in the district: Tuskegee is the home of Booker T. Washington's Tuskegee Institute, the training ground for the Tuskegee Airmen, the first black pilots trained to fly for the U.S. military. Auburn is the home of Auburn University and its renowned sports teams and veterinary school. Talladega, the site of the Alabama Institute for the Deaf and Blind, is perhaps America's most user-friendly city for the disabled. NASCAR fans know it as the home of a famed speedway and for the International Motorsports Hall of Fame—the Cooperstown of auto racing. This looks and feels like rural country, though few people here make a living off their farms. Rather, they work at Tyson Foods or Wal-Mart or in dozens of small or medium-sized factories. An economy once dependent on cotton mills is more diverse, and interstates have brought in new businesses, including a huge Honda assembly plant in Talladega County, where good wages boosted local personal income by 22% in the three years after it opened. In Montgomery, state government is the largest employer.

Politically, this was long one of the heartlands of the Democratic Party, the home of conservative white Democrats who are patriotic supporters of the military and cautious supporters of some domestic programs. There is also a large population of African-American descendants of slaves from plantations. But the area has become Republican, except for Tuskegee's Macon County and portions of Montgomery County added by the 2002 redistricting in an attempt by Democrats to make this district competitive. Democrats have remained competitive in some state elections. George Bush won 52% here in 2000, and 58% in 2004. Barack Obama increased the black turnout, but John McCain won 56% here in 2008.

The congressman from the 3rd District is Mike Rogers, a Republican elected in 2002. He is a fifth-generation resident of Calhoun County who, at the age of 28 in 1986, was the first Republican elected to the county commission. In 1994, he won a seat in the Alabama House, and in his second term he became minority leader. In 2002, after Republican Bob Riley gave up the 3rd District seat to run for governor, Rogers easily won the GOP nomination to succeed him. But in the general election, he had stiff competition from Democrat Joe Turnham Jr., who served three years as state party chairman and challenged Riley unsuccessfully in 1998. Turnham and Rogers tried to "out-bubba" each other, with Turnham calling for a congressional auto racing caucus and demanding that Rogers prove he had hunting and fishing licenses. Rogers touted his working-class values and support from the National Rifle Association. He also emphasized his opposition to abortion rights and support for a constitutional amendment for prayer in the public schools. Though both national parties targeted the district, Turnham did not risk bringing in national Democrats to campaign for him in this socially conservative district, while Rogers got frequent visits from national Republican leaders. Speaker Dennis Hastert of Illinois promised him a seat on the Armed Services Committee. The contrast in national party support was evident in Rogers's big fundraising advantage. Still, Rogers won by only 50%-48%. He did well in his base, Calhoun County, where he got 60% of the vote. In contrast, Turnham lost Lee County, his home, by 52%-46%, and carried the district's portion of Montgomery County by only 57%-42%.

Rogers is one of two Republicans of the same name in the House; the other is from the 8th District of Michigan. Alabama's Mike Rogers has a conservative voting record, though he is more centrist on economic issues. He bucked the Bush administration and won local praise by opposing the free-trade agreement with Morocco on the grounds that it would reduce local textile and apparel jobs. On the Armed Services Committee, he won House passage of a bill to ensure that universities provide access to their facilities for military recruiters and ROTC personnel. As chairman of the Homeland Security Subcommittee on Management, Investigations, and Oversight, Rogers spotlighted in 2005 the defective equipment in a $239 million camera system installed on the borders with Mexico and Canada. He also secured $47 million for an Anniston-based consortium that develops antiterrorism training for emergency responders. In 2008, he added a provision to the defense bill that required the Pentagon to move toward buying only American-bred dogs for bomb-sniffing and related tasks. On the farm bill in 2007, he passed an amendment to require arbitration to settle conflicts between poultry growers and the companies to which they sell.

In this ancestrally Democratic district, Rogers has worked hard to entrench himself and raise money to discourage strong Democratic opposition. In his first two re-election campaigns, his Democratic challengers were inadequately funded and never posed serious threats. But in 2008, Rogers faced a serious contest with Josh Segall, a 29-year-old Montgomery bankruptcy lawyer who stuck with Democratic doctrine on most issues except gay rights and gun control, spent over $1 million, and had the support of the Democratic Congressional Campaign Committee. He attacked Rogers for backing the $700 billion bailout of the financial markets, and also accused him of harming the local textile industry with his support of the Central America Free Trade Agreement. Rogers attacked Segall for his "Hollywood and New York" campaign contributions, and his liberal views that "don't reflect east Alabama's conservative values." Segall took Montgomery County 62%-38% and three nearby counties, but Rogers won 53%-46% overall. The outcome invites a possible serious challenge to Rogers in 2010.

FOURTH DISTRICT

Robert Aderholt (R)

Elected 1996, 7th term; b. July 22, 1965, Haleyville; home, Haleyville; Birmingham-Southern Col., B.A. 1987, Samford U., J.D. 1990; Congregationalist; married (Caroline); 2 children.

Professional Career: Haleyville Municipal Judge, 1992–96; Asst. legal advisor, Gov. Fob James, 1995–96.

DC Office: 1433 LHOB, 20515, 202-225-4876; Fax: 202-225-5587; Web site: www.aderholt.house.gov.

State Offices: Cullman, 256-734-6043; Decatur, 256-350-4093; Gadsden, 256-546-0201; Jasper, 205-221-2310.

Committees: *Appropriations* (10th of 23 R): Commerce, Justice, Science & Related Agencies; Legislative Branch (RMM). *Budget* (11th of 14 R).

Group Ratings

	ADA	ACLU	AFS	LCV	ITIC	NTU	COC	ACU	CFG	FRC
2008	25	18	29	0	43	65	82	92	74	100
2007	20	—	9	10	—	64	79	84	59	—

National Journal Ratings

	2007 LIB	—	2007 CONS		2008 LIB	—	2008 CONS
Economic	29%	—	71%		26%	—	74%
Social	21%	—	75%		9%	—	85%
Foreign	28%	—	71%		31%	—	69%
Composite	27%	—	73%		23%	—	77%

Key Votes of the 110th Congress

1. Increase minimum wage	Y	5. Share immigration data	Y	9. Withdraw troops 8/08	N
2. Expand SCHIP	N	6. Foreign aid abortion ban	Y	10. No operations in Iran	N
3. Raise CAFE standards	N	7. Ban gay bias in workplace	N	11. Free trade with Peru	N
4. Bail out financial markets	N	8. Repeal D.C. gun law	Y	12. Overhaul FISA	Y

Election Results

2008 general	Robert Aderholt (R)...196,741	(75%)	($688,864)
	Nicholas Sparks (D)...66,077	(25%)	($22,701)
2008 primary	Robert Aderholt (R)....................................unopposed		

Prior Winning Percentages: 2006 (70%); 2004 (75%); 2002 (87%); 2000 (61%); 1998 (56%); 1996 (50%)

Population		Race/Ethnicity		Work	
Pop. 2007:	643,595	White:	88.3%	Private:	79.3%
Change since 2000:	Up 1.3%	Black:	5.1%	Government:	12.9%
Urban:	26.5%	Hispanic:	4.6%	Self-employed:	7.4%
Rural:	73.5%	Asian:	0.4%	Blue collar:	36.7%
Area size:	8,524 sq. mi.	Native Am.:	0.5%	White collar:	47.3%
		Hawaiian:	0.0%	Khaki collar:	0.1%
Age		Two+ races:	1.1%	Other:	16.0%
Median age:	38.8 yrs.	*Ancestry*		Median income:	$35,683
More than 65 yrs:	15.2%	USA:	14.9%	Median home value:	$87,200
Less than 18 yrs:	23.5%	Irish:	12.2%	Poverty:	16.8%
Education		English:	11.2%	**Military Veterans**	
H.S. grad:	73.6%			% of Pop:	10.8%
College grad:	12.6%				
Grad degree:	5.0%				

The Appalachian Mountains' corduroy ridges, dividing the Atlantic coast from the interior, are America's coal-and-steel industrial spine, from the black coal country of western Pennsylvania to the red hill country of northern Alabama. Here rose America's two premier steel cities, Pittsburgh and Birmingham. Around both, and for many miles in between them, is countryside settled by feisty Scots-Irish farmers in the years between the Revolution and the Civil War. In valley land accessible to rail-

2008 Presidential Vote		
McCain (R).............................205,362	(76%)
Obama (D) 60,207	(22%)

2004 Presidential Vote		
Bush (R).................................186,509	(71%)
Kerry (D).................................73,504	(28%)

Cook Partisan Voting Index: R + 26

roads, great steel factories were built in the 80 years after the Civil War, along with smaller factories that produced underwear and tires, glass and chemicals, socks and butchered chickens. Northern Alabama was solidly Democratic through the 1950s. It was populist on economics, conservative on cultural issues. Since then, the region has moved toward the Republicans, even though it has benefited from massive federal public works programs. The movement is most pronounced in counties close to Birmingham and along the interstates.

Alabama's 4th Congressional District is a collection of small towns—Cullman, Jasper, Russellville, Fort Payne, and Albertville. The last is the home of a military helicopter plant and other aerospace facilities. Gritty Gadsden (pop. 37,000) is the biggest city, with a large Goodyear tire plant built in 1929. Sandwiched between Huntsville to the north and Birmingham to the south, the 4th District crosses the state and the Appalachian ridges, from the Georgia state line to the Mississippi state line. Decades of coal mining scarred 150 square miles of landscape, about one-fourth of which has been reclaimed. This is Alabama's premier Scots-Irish district, with the lowest African-American percentage of the state's seven congressional districts. Though family income is low and poverty above national averages, high marriage rates give some social stability. There are few vestiges of its Democratic heritage. George Bush won here with 71% in 2004. John McCain won many of these counties with over 70% of the vote in 2008.

The congressman from the 4th District is Robert Aderholt, a Republican first elected in 1996 to replace 30-year Democratic Rep. Tom Bevill, a longtime senior appropriator and federal benefactor for the region. Aderholt is from Winston County, the one ancestrally Republican county in north Alabama, which opposed secession in the Civil War and declared itself the Free State of Winston. His father was a circuit judge for more than 30 years; his wife's father was a state senator and state commissioner of Agriculture and Industry. In 1992, Aderholt was appointed Haleyville municipal judge. Three years later, he became a top aide to Republican Gov. Fob James. With that pedigree, he decided to run for Congress when Bevill retired. As the Republican nominee, he faced state Sen. Bob Wilson Jr., who called himself a Democrat "in the Tom Bevill tradition." In this culturally conservative district, Aderholt didn't hedge on cultural issues, opposing abortion rights, gun control, and same-sex marriage, and supporting school prayer. "We want to go to Washington to deliver a message, and that is, don't mess with our traditional family values," he said. He also attacked Wilson for his support from labor unions and trial lawyers. This was a nationally targeted race, seriously contested, and Aderholt won 50%-48%.

Aderholt's voting record is generally conservative. But he supported quotas on steel imports and sponsored a bill assessing additional antidumping duties on foreign steel. He also reached out to industrial unions with his vote against normalizing trade relations with China. After George W. Bush was elected—and after Aderholt got protection for the local sock industry—he voted to give the president more authority to negotiate trade deals. But his votes on trade tend to still be tied to regional imperatives. He opposed free-trade agreements with Chile, Morocco, and Singapore, but in 2005 he was a crucial vote for the Central American Free Trade Agreement after he got a last-minute letter from President Bush delaying the phaseout of tariffs on socks. Still, the agreement ultimately proved devastating for Fort Payne, which once had 150 plants and proclaimed itself the Sock Capital of the World. By 2007, sock imports from Central America and China closed more than 100 of those mills. Aderholt said that he was "disappointed" that the administration failed to give the mills more time to adjust. He opposed temporary extension of the Andean Trade Promotion Act because he feared more job losses.

Recognizing Aderholt's electoral vulnerability, Republican leaders put him on the Appropriations Committee, where he has been able to secure more highway and sewer money than most of his GOP colleagues. In 2009, Aderholt became ranking Republican on the Legislative Branch Subcommittee at Appropriations.

And he hasn't forgotten the social issues. When Alabama's chief justice Judge Roy Moore called for a new law to prevent federal judges from interfering with public displays of the Ten Commandments, Aderholt sponsored legislation toward that goal. "The acknowledgment of God is not a legitimate subject of review by the federal courts," Aderholt said. He was the only House member from Alabama in 2008 to vote against the $700 billion bailout of the financial markets. He cited public "discontent" with the bailout plan, and the need for a more market-based approach.

Aderholt faced serious challenges in his first two re-elections, but has won easily since. In 2006, former Millport Mayor Barbara Bobo, his Democratic challenger, said "We need checks and balances, not this bobblehead Congress." But Aderholt won 70%-30%. Benefiting from shifts in national politics, he appears to have established a grip on what used to be a swing seat.

FIFTH DISTRICT

Parker Griffith (D)

Elected 2008, 1st term; b. Aug. 6, 1942, Shreveport, LA; home, Huntsville; LA St. U., B.A. 1966; LA St. U., M.D. 1970.; Episcopalian; married (Virginia); 5 children.

Military Career: VA Army Reserves, 1970–73.

Elected Office: AL Sen., 2007–08.

Professional Career: Radiation oncologist, 1975–1992; small business owner, 1975–present.

DC Office: 417 CHOB, 20515, 202-225-4801; Fax: 225-4392; Web site: griffith.house.gov.

State Offices: Decatur, 256-355-9400; Huntsville, 256-551-0190; Shoals, 256-381-3450.

Committees: *Science & Technology* (14th of 26 D): Research & Science Education; Space & Aeronautics. *Small Business* (16th of 17 D): Contracting & Technology; Investigations & Oversight; Regulations & Healthcare. *Transportation & Infrastructure* (40th of 44 D): Aviation; Economic Development, Public Buildings & Emergency Management; Water Resources & Environment.

Group Ratings and Key Votes: Newly Elected

Election Results

2008 general	Parker Griffith (D)	156,642	(51%)	($1,786,989)
	Wayne Parker (R)	147,314	(48%)	($1,276,538)
2008 primary	Parker Griffith (D)	34,543	(90%)	
	David Maker (D)	3,874	(10%)	

Population		Race/Ethnicity		Work	
Pop. 2007:	670,698	White:	76.0%	Private:	76.8%
Change since 2000:	Up 5.6%	Black:	17.3%	Government:	17.1%
Urban:	59.4%	Hispanic:	2.8%	Self-employed:	5.9%
Rural:	40.6%	Asian:	1.2%	Blue collar:	26.2%
Area size:	4,689 sq. mi.	Native Am.:	0.7%	White collar:	59.5%
		Hawaiian:	0.0%	Khaki collar:	0.2%
Age		Two+ races:	1.9%	Other:	14.1%
Median age:	38.1 yrs.	*Ancestry*		Median income:	$44,249
More than 65 yrs:	13.3%			Median home value:	$113,400
Less than 18 yrs:	23.7%	USA:	14.1%	Poverty:	14.1%
		Irish:	10.1%		
Education		English:	9.7%	**Military Veterans**	
H.S. grad:	81.7%			% of Pop:	12.6%
College grad:	26.0%				
Grad degree:	8.9%				

The federal government long has had a hand in shaping the destiny of northern Alabama. In 1933, it created the Tennessee Valley Authority, which took the World War I federal munitions plant at Muscle Shoals on the unnavigable Tennessee River and built a series of dams to control flooding and to produce cheap hydroelectric power. This was backward country then. Poor white farmers scratched an existence out of hardscrabble land, were housed in shacks without electricity or running water, and lived off a diet that produced pellagra and rickets. The TVA was intended to showcase what an enlightened, generous federal government could do.

2008 Presidential Vote
McCain (R)............................190,225   (61%)
Obama (D) 117,838   (38%)

2004 Presidential Vote
Bush (R)................................167,552   (60%)
Kerry (D)...............................110,633   (39%)

Cook Partisan Voting Index: R + 12

Then, after the Soviets put up Sputnik in 1957, the Redstone Arsenal in Huntsville became the nation's foremost missile development center. Huntsville, then a sleepy town huddled around a well-preserved, early-19th-century settlement, grew to become Alabama's fourth-largest city. The first of the large U.S. ballistic missiles were developed here. On the grounds of Redstone, NASA built its Marshall Space Flight Center in the 1960s, and the Huntsville-Decatur area soon achieved high-tech critical mass. With leadership from Werner von Braun and other German engineers, Redstone and Marshall built Explorer 1, the first American orbiting satellite; the Mercury-Redstone vehicle that boosted astronaut Alan Shepard into suborbital flight; and the Saturn V rocket that sent man to the moon. In the 1970s, Marshall produced Skylab and developed the space shuttle's main engines and solid-rocket boosters. The Boeing research center here has been a prime contractor for the space station. In 1990, it helped launch the Hubble Space Telescope. Boeing produces the Delta IV booster at its factory in Decatur. With the approaching retirement of the space shuttle, NASA expects that Marshall will help to prepare the next generation of space vehicles, including the Ares I rocket, which will launch future space missions into orbit. Recently, space-related jobs have evolved with a broader defense focus. In 2005, the Pentagon base-closing commission moved 1,800 jobs in the Missile Defense Agency from northern Virginia to Redstone. Huntsville also was the beneficiary of 1,600 jobs with the Army's Materiel Command.

The 5th Congressional District of Alabama takes in most of the state's TVA and space counties. TVA and the space program were primarily Democratic projects, and for years most voters here were staunch New Deal Democrats, liberal on economics and not much interested in race issues, like longtime Sen. John Sparkman, the party's vice presidential nominee in 1952. But professional and technical people in the space business tend to combine high-tech and traditional values, and this made much of northern Alabama marginal-to-Republican country in the 1990s. The district has voted Republican for president since 1980, and has never elected a Republican to Congress. In 2008, John McCain won this district, 61%-38%.

The new congressman from the 5th District is Parker Griffith, a Democrat elected in 2008 after nine-term Democratic Rep. Bud Cramer retired. Griffith graduated from Louisiana State University's medical school in 1970 and became a radiation oncologist in northern Alabama. He practiced medicine at Huntsville Hospital and later founded a cancer treatment center. Griffith retired from medicine in 1992 and undertook several business projects. He also founded the Parker Griffith Family Foundation, which provides grants to local schools and other community organizations.

In 2004, Griffith ran for mayor of Huntsville, citing a decline in population and a lack of vision for the city. In a nonpartisan race, he forced incumbent Loretta Spencer into a runoff but lost by about 4,000 votes. Griffith ran for the state Senate two years later. He spent $400,000 of personal money, focused his campaign on providing better health insurance, and defeated attorney and Republican nominee Cheryl Guthrie. In the state Senate, Griffith sponsored a bill to establish a statewide trauma center, which passed in 2007.

Cramer announced his retirement in March 2008, leaving Democrats vulnerable in a district that has grown increasingly conservative. Griffith got into the race two weeks later, and the Democratic Party quickly coalesced around his candidacy. He defeated a single opponent in the Democratic primary, and the Democratic Congressional Campaign Committee helped him with $678,000 in media in the general election. His opponent was Wayne Parker, a businessman who had twice unsuccessfully challenged Cramer in the 1990s. Griffith entered the race with better name recognition and more cash on hand than Parker, who had endured a tougher primary.

But Parker ran a tough campaign. The race turned into one of the most bitterly fought in the nation. Parker raised questions about Griffith's professional credentials by disclosing documents from a 1987 peer review that accused Griffith's cancer center of underdosing patients with radiation to protract their treatment and collect more in fees. Griffith called Parker's attacks "a total distortion of the facts," and said the negative peer review was revenge by hospital officials unhappy that Griffith had opened a competing cancer treatment center. Griffith accused Parker of becoming a Washington lobbyist to trade on the influence of his father-in-law, former Rep. Bill Archer of Texas, at the height of Archer's power as the chairman of the tax-writing Ways and Means Committee in the late 1990s. He referred to Parker in ads as "the lobbyist."

Griffith narrowly prevailed 51%-48%. Over 10,000 ballots cast in the 5th District failed to select a candidate in this race or voted for a write-in candidate, a trend that some analysts said reflected voters' unhappiness with the campaign's nasty tone.

In Washington, Griffith was given seats on the Transportation and Infrastructure Committee, the Committee on Science and Technology, and the Small Business Committee.

SIXTH DISTRICT

Spencer Bachus (R)

Elected 1992, 9th term; b. Dec. 28, 1947, Birmingham; home, Columbus; Auburn U., B.A. 1969, U. of AL, J.D. 1972; Baptist; married (Linda); 3 children.

Military Career: Natl. Guard, 1969–71.

Elected Office: AL Senate, 1983–84; AL House of Reps., 1984–87.

Professional Career: Owner, Lumber Co.; Practicing atty., 1972–92; AL Repub. Party chmn., 1991–92.

DC Office: 1431 LHOB, 20515, 202-225-4921; Fax: 202-225-2082; Web site: www.house.gov/bachus.

State Offices: Birmingham, 205-969-2296; Clanton, 205-280-0704.

Committees: *Financial Services* (RMM of 29 R).

Group Ratings

	ADA	ACLU	AFS	LCV	ITIC	NTU	COC	ACU	CFG	FRC
2008	20	18	14	15	71	56	94	84	71	100
2007	10	—	9	5	—	76	79	92	78	—

National Journal Ratings

	2007 LIB	—	2007 CONS		2008 LIB	—	2008 CONS
Economic	22%	—	77%		25%	—	75%
Social	16%	—	83%		20%	—	74%
Foreign	0%	—	72%		38%	—	62%
Composite	18%	—	82%		29%	—	71%

Key Votes of the 110th Congress

1. Increase minimum wage	Y	5. Share immigration data	Y	9. Withdraw troops 8/08	N
2. Expand SCHIP	N	6. Foreign aid abortion ban	Y	10. No operations in Iran	N
3. Raise CAFE standards	N	7. Ban gay bias in workplace	N	11. Free trade with Peru	Y
4. Bail out financial markets	Y	8. Repeal D.C. gun law	Y	12. Overhaul FISA	Y

Election Results

2008 general	Spencer Bachus (R)..	280,902	(98%)	($1,414,799)
2008 primary	Spencer Bachus (R).................................... unopposed			

Prior Winning Percentages: 2006 (100%); 2004 (100%); 2002 (90%); 2000 (88%); 1998 (72%); 1996 (71%); 1994 (79%); 1992 (52%)

Population		Race/Ethnicity		Work	
Pop. 2007:	708,377	White:	84.5%	Private:	80.2%
Change since 2000:	Up 11.5%	Black:	10.7%	Government:	13.0%
Urban:	62.1%	Hispanic:	2.5%	Self-employed:	6.5%
Rural:	37.9%	Asian:	1.4%	Blue collar:	21.1%
Area size:	4,649 sq. mi.	Native Am.:	0.2%	White collar:	67.4%
		Hawaiian:	0.0%	Khaki collar:	0.1%
Age		Two+ races:	0.7%	Other:	11.4%
Median age:	37.6 yrs.	*Ancestry*		Median income:	$56,277
More than 65 yrs:	12.4%	USA:	13.3%	Median home value:	$163,200
Less than 18 yrs:	24.4%	English:	12.8%	Poverty:	8.2%
Education		Irish:	10.7%	**Military Veterans**	
H.S. grad:	87.3%			% of Pop:	11.0%
College grad:	32.8%				
Grad degree:	12.2%				

Birmingham, once one of America's booming industrial cities, was better known in the latter half of the last century as a bastion of white resistance to the civil-rights movement. It has more hopeful prospects in the 21st century. This is a new city by Southern standards. Before the Civil War, there was nothing here but a few creeks running below Red Mountain. But Red Mountain is almost pure iron ore, and by 1890, Birmingham had the South's largest steel mills. In the early 20th century, as the

2008 Presidential Vote		
McCain (R)	268,791	(77%)
Obama (D)	78,150	(22%)
2004 Presidential Vote		
Bush (R)	248,095	(78%)
Kerry (D)	69,449	(22%)
Cook Partisan Voting Index:	R+29	

statue of Vulcan, the Roman god of fire and metalworking, looked out over the smokestack-filled valley, Birmingham seemed the most progressive city in the South. But the worldwide overcapacity of steel and technological obsolescence at home sent the American steel industry into long-term decline starting in the 1950s. Meanwhile, Birmingham's political leaders plotted to avoid desegregation, and the city's violent reaction to civil rights made a vivid impression on the rest of the country, watching it unfold on the relatively new medium of television. Police Commissioner (and Democratic National Committeeman at the time) Bull Connor set dogs and fire hoses against peaceful demonstrators, and Ku Klux Klansmen bombed the 16th Street Baptist Church, killing four young girls in 1963. Those images haunted Birmingham for a generation.

In recent years, Birmingham has worked to improve race relations and has developed a new economic base. Health care is a major industry. The city has some of the largest and most advanced medical care centers in the South, and is especially renowned for its sports medicine facilities and specialists who tend to the ailments of famous athletes. Banking is also important. While Atlanta's banks foundered and were acquired by outsiders, Birmingham became the largest Southern banking center outside Charlotte, N.C. But city leaders worry that the viability of the downtown area and white movement to newer suburbs have arguably caused an uptick in racial polarization. The city's population has declined by 100,000 since 1960 and was 74% black in 2000. Whites have been moving out of Birmingham's Jefferson County southeast to Shelby County, which grew 44% in the 1990s and 26% from 2000 to 2007—the fastest growth in the state. (However, the migration to Shelby has not been entirely white flight. Its African-American population increased significantly as well.) Jefferson County, once more Republican than most of Alabama, votes Democratic in close statewide elections, while Shelby County is one of the most Republican counties in the state. Metropolitan planners project an 85% population increase for Shelby County from 2005 to 2035, but only a 2% increase for Jefferson, whose development growth is limited by its hills.

The 6th Congressional District of Alabama, which once included all of Birmingham and most of Jefferson County, is now the suburban Birmingham-area district and strongly Republican. It includes parts of Jefferson County, such as prosperous Mountain Brook, and stretches southwest to Tuscaloosa and south along Interstate 65 halfway to Montgomery. In 2002, the Democratic line-drawers made it even more Republican by removing the last part of Birmingham and some black precincts in Tuscaloosa, and adding most of fast-growing St. Clair County north of Shelby County. Today, this is one of the most Republican districts in the nation. It voted 74% for George W. Bush in 2000—his second-best district outside of Texas—and four years later, gave Bush 78%. In 2008, John McCain won this district, 77%-22%.

The congressman from the 6th District is Republican Spencer Bachus. A Birmingham native, he owned a sawmill company and for two decades was a trial lawyer. Bachus (*BACK-us*) was the first Republican elected to the state school board in more than 100 years. He won a seat in the state Legislature in 1982, and was also the campaign manager to Guy Hunt when Hunt was elected governor in 1986. After running unsuccessfully for attorney general in 1990, Bachus became Republican state chairman. When the 6th District was radically redrawn in 1992, he won a Republican runoff and defeated incumbent Ben Erdreich, a moderate Democrat.

Bachus has a conservative voting record and has been an aggressive lawmaker. As the top Republican on the House Financial Services Committee, he has also been at the eye of the storm during the recent housing foreclosure crisis and the insurance and financial-markets failure. On what became a $700 billion bailout of the financial industry, he was the only House Republican to participate in the initial September 2008 discussions, and he entered into a tentative agreement with Democrats. But the move angered House GOP leaders, who opposed the deal as it stood and wanted modifications to satisfy Republican conservatives. As a result, Bachus was replaced by then-Minority Whip Roy Blunt during the final negotiations on the bailout. Bachus called the result "very frustrating." The other senior Republican in the negotiations was Sen. Richard Shelby of Alabama, who was unalterably opposed to a deal. Having lost the confidence of Minority Leader John Boehner, who felt Bachus was too quick to compromise with the Democrats, he was at risk of being ousted from his leadership role on the committee, and speculation swirled about who would succeed him. But he showed skill as a survivor, which included promising to toe the party line in the future. He also rallied other influential Republicans to his side, including Virginia Republican Eric Cantor, who replaced Blunt as whip.

Bachus was in the thick of other major legislative battles. He angered Republicans in 2007 on a bill to ban predatory actions on mortgage lending when he cut a deal with committee Chairman Barney Frank, D-Mass., to reduce fraud and abuse. He also cooperated with Democrats on a bill to deter abuses by credit card companies.

In the 1990s, Bachus was an able investigator on the committee. He discovered that the Community Development Financial Institute, which President Clinton established in 1994, directed $11 million in loans to four banks with ties to then-first lady Hillary Rodham Clinton without proper documentation. The two top CDFI officials resigned as a consequence. Bachus was an early critic of then-Securities and Exchange Commission Chairman Harvey Pitt after the Enron corporate accounting scandal broke. He also helped to enact changes in the Fair Credit Reporting Act, which provided consumers additional access to their credit reports and cut back on identity theft. In 2006, he pushed enactment of the controversial ban on Internet gambling.

Bachus has also been something of a maverick on foreign policy. He has been an unlikely crusader for international debt relief for poor Third World nations, and he criticized the Bush administration's dealings with the genocidal regime in Sudan. In 2007, he joined a bipartisan one-day fast to promote international debt relief.

Bachus beat out fellow Republican Richard Baker of Louisiana for the top spot on Financial Services after the 2006 election. He contended that he worked better with colleagues and interest groups than Baker. He once said, "Barney Frank and I represent very different political philosophies, but when we disagree, we do so amicably." He also was helped by his more generous campaign contributions to other Republicans, more than $800,000. And he benefited from his early support for Boehner in Boehner's contest with Blunt for majority leader in 2006; Baker had backed Blunt. Bachus won the top committee slot on a 22-7 vote of the leadership-dominated Republican Steering Committee. Baker quit the House a year later to run a financial-industry trade group.

Bachus has not had a Democratic challenger since 1998. He has voiced interest in a statewide race.

SEVENTH DISTRICT

Artur Davis (D)

Elected 2002, 4th term; b. Oct. 9, 1967, Montgomery; home, Birmingham; Harvard U., B.A. 1990, J.D. 1993; Lutheran; married (Tara Johnson).

Professional Career: Asst. U.S. atty., 1994–1998, Practicing atty., 1998–2002

DC Office: 208 CHOB, 20515, 202-225-2665; Fax: 202-226-9567; Web site: www.house.gov/arturdavis/.

State Offices: Birmingham, 205-254-1960; Demopolis, 334-287-0860; Livingston, 205-652-5834; Selma, 334-877-4414; Tuscaloosa, 205-752-5380.

Committees: *House Administration* (6th of 6 D): Elections. *Ways & Means* (21st of 26 D): Income Security & Family Support; Oversight.

Group Ratings

	ADA	ACLU	AFS	LCV	ITIC	NTU	COC	ACU	CFG	FRC
2008	85	73	100	92	100	9	67	12	9	29
2007	90	—	100	80	—	5	70	4	12	—

National Journal Ratings

	2007 LIB — 2007 CONS		2008 LIB — 2008 CONS	
Economic	73% —	24%	57% —	41%
Social	56% —	44%	54% —	42%
Foreign	53% —	46%	50% —	48%
Composite	61% —	39%	55% —	45%

Key Votes of the 110th Congress

1. Increase minimum wage	Y	5. Share immigration data	N	9. Withdraw troops 8/08	Y
2. Expand SCHIP	Y	6. Foreign aid abortion ban	N	10. No operations in Iran	Y
3. Raise CAFE standards	Y	7. Ban gay bias in workplace	N	11. Free trade with Peru	Y
4. Bail out financial markets	Y	8. Repeal D.C. gun law	Y	12. Overhaul FISA	Y

Election Results

2008 general	Artur Davis (D) 228,518	(99%)	($820,467)
2008 primary	Artur Davis (D) .... unopposed		

Prior Winning Percentages: 2006 (100%); 2004 (75%); 2002 (92%)

Population		Race/Ethnicity		Work	
Pop. 2007:	605,547	White:	32.8%	Private:	77.0%
Change since 2000:	Down 4.7%	Black:	63.6%	Government:	18.0%
Urban:	72.2%	Hispanic:	2.1%	Self-employed:	4.9%
Rural:	27.8%	Asian:	0.6%	Blue collar:	27.6%
Area size:	8,780 sq. mi.	Native Am.:	0.2%	White collar:	52.0%
		Hawaiian:	0.0%	Khaki collar:	0.1%
Age		Two+ races:	0.7%	Other:	20.3%
Median age:	34.8 yrs.	*Ancestry*		Median income:	$30,332
More than 65 yrs:	12.5%	USA:	6.6%	Median home value:	$84,500
Less than 18 yrs:	24.9%	Irish:	5.1%	Poverty:	26.2%
Education		English:	4.9%	**Military Veterans**	
H.S. grad:	78.3%			% of Pop:	9.7%
College grad:	16.7%				
Grad degree:	6.0%				

Alabama has learned to celebrate its black heritage, building striking memorials to the civil-rights movement in Montgomery and Birmingham, acknowledging its history as ground zero of white resistance to the empowerment of blacks in the 1950s and 1960s. Blacks first came here as slaves. The last slave ship to the United States, the *Clotilde*, docked in Mobile in 1859, where its cargo was then set free. Blacks were part of the great migration into the cotton lands after the Jacksonians swept the Indians

2008 Presidential Vote

Obama (D)	207,732	(74%)
McCain (R)	72,801	(26%)

2004 Presidential Vote

Kerry (D)	160,875	(64%)
Bush (R)	88,433	(35%)

Cook Partisan Voting Index: D + 18

out of the Southeast and sent them on their Trail of Tears to what is now Oklahoma. Today, Alabama's rural African-Americans are still clustered in the Black Belt of fertile dark soil across the center of the state. In Selma, founded by Alabama's one vice president, William Rufus King, Sheriff Jim Clark's troops beat up peaceful marchers on the Edmund Pettis Bridge in demonstrations that led to the march on Montgomery and the 1965 Voting Rights Act. All 10 of Alabama's majority-black counties are in the rich farm country of the Black Belt, but most Alabama blacks now live in urban areas—one-quarter in metropolitan Birmingham.

The 7th Congressional District of Alabama was created in 1992 as a majority-African-American district. It includes Black Belt counties where the Alabama and Tombigbee rivers flow past old plantations and the catfish industry has thrived, plus part of Tuscaloosa, home of the University of Alabama, and nearby Vance, site of a Mercedes factory. Most of its people are in Birmingham and surrounding Jefferson County. It is 64% African-American, and solidly Democratic. John Kerry won 64%-35% here in 2004, one of his best showings in the Deep South. In 2008, Barack Obama swept each of the Black Belt counties by large margins, including 87%-13% in Macon County, which is in the 3rd District. Overall, he won this district, 74%-26%.

The congressman from the 7th District is Artur Davis, first elected in 2002. Davis grew up in Montgomery. His parents divorced when he was a boy, and he was raised by his mother, a schoolteacher, and his grandmother. A gifted student, he was admitted to Harvard University, where he graduated magna cum laude, and went on to Harvard Law School. Davis interned at the Southern Poverty Law Center and clerked for federal Judge Myron Thompson, then served four years as an assistant U.S. attorney. Later, he practiced law in Birmingham. In 2000, he challenged 7th District incumbent Earl Hilliard in the Democratic primary. He criticized Hilliard's controversial trip to Libya, which he took despite a State Department ban on travel to the then-terrorist state, and argued that Hilliard failed to aid his financially pressed district. Davis ran a vigorous campaign, but lost 58%-34%.

In 2002, Davis came back for a rematch, raising $1.5 million. The contest split the local African-American political establishment, with some leaders disapproving of Davis's challenge to another black officeholder. Campaign surrogates for Hilliard questioned whether Davis was "black enough" to represent the district. Referring to Davis's background as a federal prosecutor, Hilliard claimed that, "the only thing [Davis] has done for black people is put them in jail." Davis framed the debate as a generational battle between old-style black machine politics and a fresher, more effective approach. One key to Davis's victory appeared to be strong financial backing from supporters of Israel. Hilliard was one of only 21 House members to vote against a resolution supporting Israel's fight against terrorism, just weeks after Palestinian suicide bombers killed hundreds of Israelis. In the primary, Hilliard led Davis by only 46%-43% and was forced into a runoff. Several Congressional Black Caucus members, plus activist Al Sharpton, came in to campaign for Hilliard. Davis accused Hilliard of being divisive and called for "healing." Outspending Hilliard by nearly $180,000, Davis won the runoff 56%-44%. He had no trouble winning in November, or since then.

In the House, Davis quickly reached out to other Black Caucus members, though some tensions remained with Hilliard's allies. Davis has a moderate voting record for House Democrats, and has become a bigger player than Hilliard was in the Democratic caucus. He focused on rural issues and led successful fights to reverse funding cuts for minority land-grant colleges and the HOPE program to revitalize public housing. He helped to win approval of a new interstate highway through Black Belt counties. With Christopher Smith, a New Jersey Republican, he sponsored a bill to increase the availability of umbilical-cord blood and bone marrow for patients in need of a transplant; President Bush signed their bill in 2006. Working with a bipartisan coalition, he called for trade protection to level the playing field with China. His particular concerns were the steel and catfish industries. Following the 2006 election, when Democrats took control of the chamber, he was rewarded with a seat on the powerful, tax-writing Ways and Means Committee.

Davis represents a new generation of African-American political leadership and has told local audiences that blacks must move beyond a preoccupation with race. He also criticized national Democrats—including John Kerry's presidential campaign—for calling on black lawmakers only to rally black voters. Democratic Congressional Campaign Committee Chairman Chris Van Hollen, a Maryland Democrat, appointed Davis as a vice chair and gave him the role of mentoring Democratic candidates for the House. He also is active in the centrist New Democrats. Davis was an early backer of Barack Obama, whom he had met in law school at Harvard, and Davis became one of Obama's closest confidants on Capitol Hill. During the general election, he warned Democrats not to engage in "anti-religious bigotry" in their criticism of Republican vice presidential nominee Sarah Palin, the Alaska governor. "There is a space in my party for conservative-leaning evangelicals," he wrote during the campaign.

In February 2009, Davis launched his campaign for governor in 2010, when Republican Gov. Bob Riley is term-limited. In a statewide race, he hoped to be bolstered by his moderate voting record and style, not to mention Alabama's 26% black population. In 2008, he worked closely with Democratic candidate Bobby Bright and was encouraged by his win in the conservative 2nd District. Davis says his polling shows that whites in Alabama are ready to vote for a black candidate who shares their social values. "Alabama today is looking more like Tennessee or North Carolina," he says. The fact that Obama lost the state 60%-39% has not discouraged Davis since Obama made no effort in the state.

★ ALASKA ★

A laska, America's 49th state, has now celebrated the 50th anniversary of its admission to the union. With 16% of the nation's land area and just .23% of its population, Alaska is a state created by a federal government that it now often resents, and it is an individualistic society that has responded to its unique situation in creative ways. Alaska would not be American at all but for the expansive dream of Secretary of State William Seward, who took advantage of a fleeting opportunity to create an American Pacific empire by purchasing the region from Russia in 1867 for $7.2 million. (The Russian Orthodox Church still claims 30,000 members in Alaska, many of them Alaska Natives.) The Alaska Territory owed most of its early growth to decisions made by the federal government. It started growing feverishly with the Klondike gold rush in 1897, just as President McKinley reaffirmed the gold standard. Anchorage, the largest city, had its beginnings in 1913 as the chief worksite of the federal government's Alaska Railroad, completed in 1923. The Army built the Alcan Highway, connecting Alaska to the lower 48 states, in the grim war days of 1942, when the Aleutian Islands off the Alaska Peninsula were invaded by the Japanese, the only part of the United States occupied by a foreign enemy since the War of 1812. By 1943, 152,000 U.S. troops were stationed here, in a territory whose prewar population was only 72,000. Alaska is the only state abutting Russia, across the Bering Strait and over the North Pole, and even today Alaska remains strategic. The military remains a major presence at Fort Richardson and Elmendorf Air Force Base near Anchorage and at Fort Wainwright and Eielson Air Force Base near Fairbanks. The Pentagon in 2004 installed interceptors for the national missile defense system at Fort Greely.

Alaska's size remains hard for Americans to comprehend. If superimposed on the lower 48, the state would stretch from Florida to California. The westernmost Aleutians are closer to Tokyo than to Juneau and farther west than Wellington, New Zealand. One-third of Alaskans have no access to state roads and are reachable only by boat or airplane. Alaska has, per capita, six times the number of pilots and 16 times the number of aircraft as the rest of the nation, as well as 722 registered airports. The wild is always nearby. Moose walk around residential neighborhoods in Anchorage, and a much higher rate of people go missing here than in the lower 48, or simply "Outside" as Alaskans say. Only 686,000 people live in Alaska, with 61% in Anchorage and (by Alaska standards) the nearby Kenai Peninsula and Matanuska-Susitna Valley. This is the fastest-growing part of Alaska, with a dynamic private-sector economy. Fairbanks, with 13% of the population, is a pipeline and mineral service center deep in the interior, unprotected from Arctic winds in winter and giant clouds of mosquitoes in the brief but hot summer. The Panhandle, with 11% of the people, is the old Alaska, with towns settled by Russians and the old state capital of Juneau built up against steep mountains on inlets from the Pacific. The other 15% live in the bush, scattered in small towns and the oil port of Valdez, in Native settlements and on hundreds of lakes. About half the people here are Alaska Natives. They are greatly outnumbered and outvoted on many issues, and yet are the object of awed respect for their achievement in building viable civilizations with impressive art traditions in such a forbidding environment. Considering its remoteness, Alaska has impressive racial diversity. Its population is 4% black, 13% Native, 5% Asian, and 6% Hispanic.

Alaska won statehood in January 1959, after a valiant campaign. But statehood did not end federal decision-making power over Alaska—or the widespread resentment of it. Alaska's economy depended on fishing, oil production in Cook Inlet around Anchorage, and the military—all federally regulated or controlled. Less than a decade later, however, Alaska's economy and public life were reshaped by the discovery of North Slope oil. It began suddenly, accidentally. On the day after Christmas 1967, at Prudhoe Bay on the Arctic coast, a tremendous roar as loud as four jumbo jets drew a crowd of 40 men, heavily clothed against the 30-below weather, to an oil rig. A natural-gas flare shot 30 feet straight up. This was the great 12 billion-barrel North Slope oil field. Earlier, oil companies had drilled seven dry wells on Prudhoe Bay, and Arco chief executive Robert Anderson wouldn't have ordered this last try, except that he had a drilling rig nearby. This was the greatest oil strike in U.S. history and the beginning of much of today's Alaska.

Finding oil in Prudhoe Bay was somewhat akin to finding it on the moon. It was not clear in 1967 who owned the oil or how it could be taken out. The Statehood Act of 1959 gave the state the right to choose its own public lands, but only after settling Native land claims. The only feasible way to get the oil out—the Arctic Ocean ice breaks up in late July for only six weeks—was a pipeline. But environmentalists opposed that option for fear it would destroy the delicate permafrost and interfere with caribou migrations. Development-minded Alaskans got a pipeline bill through Congress in 1973, by just a one-vote margin in the Senate, but the pipeline had to be built on stilts and wasn't opened until 1977. Then in 1980, after astute lobbying by environmentalists, Congress passed—over the objections of Alaska's two senators and Rep.-at-Large Don Young—the Alaska Lands Act, which set aside 159 million acres as national parks, national monuments, or wilderness: One-third of the state was protected (or barred) from development. Much, if not all of this, turned out to be for the best. The pipeline came on line just as oil prices were approaching a peak, thus generating maximum revenues to the state, which gets 100% of the

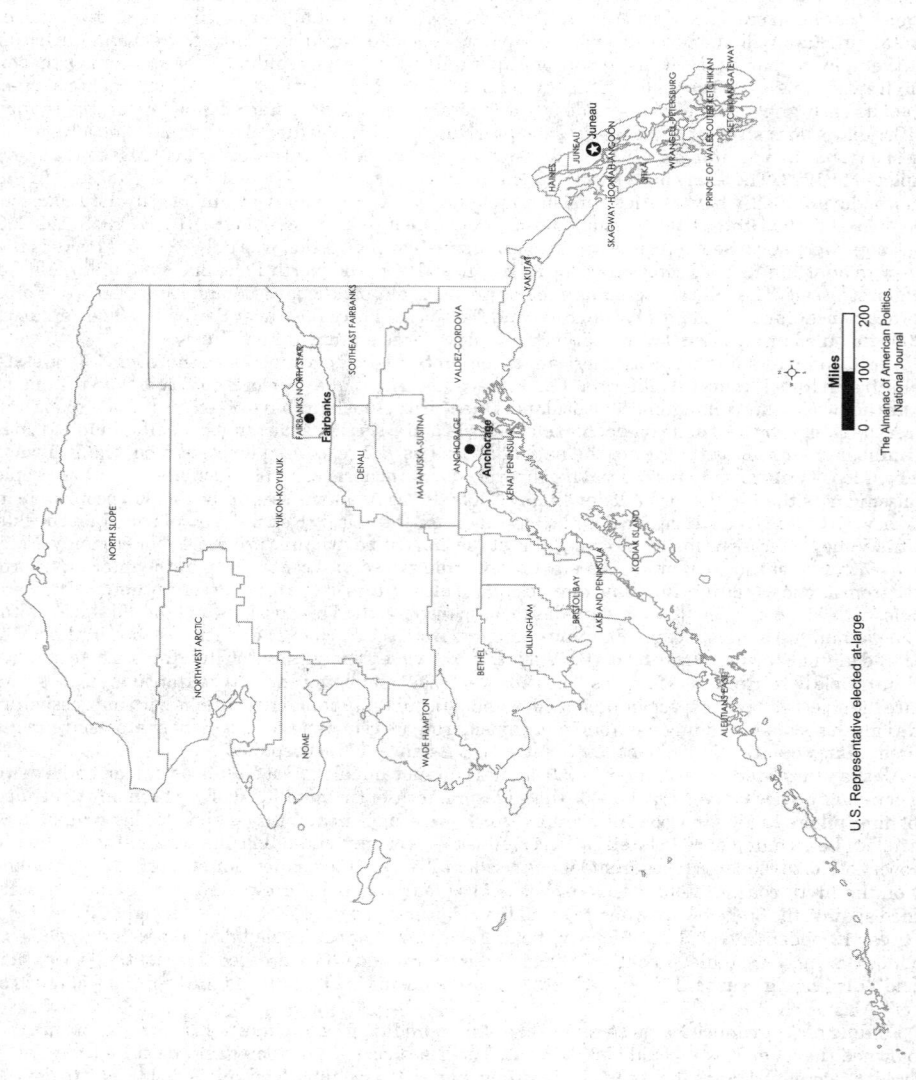

U.S. Representative elected at-large.

royalties. The environment was protected much better than it would have been without the environmentalists' safeguards—although a corroded transmission line caused a major oil spill in March 2006. The caribou herd has risen from 3,000 animals to 32,000, and Native Alaskans got more autonomy than the non-Native majority of Alaskans would have given them. With oil providing some 85% of its revenue, the state government abolished its income tax in 1980 and created a low-tax regime that has helped Alaska to grow even as oil revenues and military spending declined.

Wisely, Alaska did not squander its windfall. In 1976, Republican Gov. Jay Hammond persuaded the Legislature to establish a Permanent Fund for most of the oil revenues. Each year, it presents every resident with a dividend of 20% of the average of profits for the preceding five years—$2,069 in 2008. Even though $14.3 billion has been paid in dividends, most of the money has been invested. The North Slope is producing less than half as much oil as in the late 1980s, but the Permanent Fund's market value was $28 billion in April 2009, and most of its income now comes from investments rather than oil. Some speculated that Alaska voters would pressure legislators for bigger payouts. But Alaskans have acted like investors. They want their dividend checks not just now but in the future. The Legislature and the voters have rejected proposals to spend Permanent Fund earnings, and no one has dared to suggest tapping the capital.

Similarly, 12 regional Native corporations created by the Alaska Native Claims Act have proved to be successful not just in providing income for Natives but in helping them preserve Native traditions and adapt to Alaska's market economy at their own pace. On Indian reservations in the lower 48, all land is held by the tribe and supervised by the government; elections held on the political model have produced a winner-take-all politics that is often corrupt and incapable of pursuing long-range strategies. The corporate model, on the other hand, allows more continuity in office for the Alaska Native corporations' managers—although some have made bad decisions and been thrown out. But the cumulative voting method, by which a minority can get a seat on the board, has produced management that is sensitive to all opinions. Huge windfalls are avoided because 70% of profits from mineral sales are shared by all corporations. The corporation itself, not a distant federal bureaucracy, is left with the choice of how much ancestral land to retain and how much to exploit economically. Individual Natives can make the transition from their traditional communal economy, living on subsistence fishing and hunting, or make their way in the market economy: 43% of Natives now live in Anchorage, Fairbanks, Juneau, Matanuska-Susitna, or the Kenai Peninsula. In 2004, the 42 regional and village Native corporations had revenues of $4.5 billion and employed 13,000 Alaskans. But not all is rosy. Native villages in the bush have little in the way of a private-sector economy, and alcoholism and suicide rates remain high.

The federal government continues to make decisions that shape Alaska's economy—and not always in Alaska's favor, despite the clout of the long-serving Alaska delegation: Sen. Ted Stevens, who was in office from 1968 until he lost re-election in 2008; GOP Sen. Lisa Murkowski, the daughter of former Sen. Frank Murkowski (1981–2002) and Young, in office since 1973. All three are Republicans. They failed to get approval of oil drilling in a sliver of the Arctic National Wildlife Refuge—an area the size of Washington's Dulles International Airport in an area the size of Delaware—although it was on the verge of being approved in 1989, when the *Exxon Valdez* ran aground in Prince William Sound in March 1989. Environmental groups have made ANWR oil drilling one of their main issues in their direct-mail fundraising even though ANWR is estimated to have 9 billion to 16 billion barrels of oil, the most by far in any untapped U.S. oil field. In 2005 and 2006, the Senate approved ANWR drilling as part of its budget resolution, but that was stricken by the House when liberal Republicans threatened to withhold their votes. The Democratic takeover of both chambers in the 2006 elections probably killed the issue in Congress.

Although the North Slope's oil has been pumped out through the pipeline since 1977, there has been no way to get its vast quantities of natural gas out. So it's been burned off at the wellhead or pumped back into the ground. An estimated 30 trillion cubic feet is in Prudhoe Bay and another 70 trillion cubic feet is elsewhere on the Slope. In October 2004, after years of effort, Stevens and Republican Sen. Lisa Murkowski got an 80% federal loan guarantee for a gas pipeline through Congress. That left the ball in the state government's court. Then-Gov. Frank Murkowski accepted two proposals—one from the three North Slope oil companies and another from a pipeline company with Native corporations involved—to build the pipeline, and he urged that the state take an equity interest in the project. But Sarah Palin, then-mayor of Wasilla, and others argued that this was a giveaway to the oil companies. It became the issue that enabled Palin to defeat Murkowski 51%-19% in the August 2006 Republican primary, with 30% going to a third candidate. She went on to defeat former Democratic Gov. Tony Knowles in November, and, working with the Legislature, enacted the Alaska Gasline Inducement Act, which offers up to $500 million in seed money to help build the natural-gas pipeline as well as freeze production taxes for 10 years. The state received five applications to build a gas pipeline, none of them from the North Slope oil producers, and in August 2008, Alaska approved a bid from Calgary-based TransCanada. It was a major victory for Palin.

Alaska's economy is also dependent on fishing, long its largest private employer. Alaska produces half of America's seafood, and the salmon fisheries here, unlike so many elsewhere, have not been dangerously depleted. Tourism, the No. 2 private employer, is on the rise, with over 1.5 million tourists a year, many arriving on cruise ships from which they view glaciers in the southeast, troop into Russian-settled

Sitka, and make side trips to Denali National Park and Mount McKinley. In August 2006, voters by just 52%-48% approved a $50 per passenger cruise ship tax; the ballot proposition also taxed gambling revenues in Alaskan waters and required environmental observers to monitor the ships. The Anchorage airport, near the top of the world, is seven hours from New York City, Tokyo, and London, and it is a major cargo transfer point for UPS, FedEx, Northwest Airlines, and the U.S. Postal Service. More wide-bodied, all-cargo aircraft move through it than any other U.S. airport.

Sarah Palin's election in 2006 was one of several earthquakes that reshaped Alaska's political landscape. That year, three state legislators were convicted of bribery. Bill Allen, head of the oil field services company VECO, was handing out $100 bills to legislators to get them to vote against higher taxes on oil companies. The scandals didn't stop there. In 2007, Rep. Young was revealed to be the target of an investigation involving Rick Smith, the former head of VECO and a major Young contributor. In June 2007, *The New York Times* reported that a Young aide altered the 2005 transportation bill with a $10 million addition for roadwork on Interstate 75 near Naples, Fla., that would help real estate developer Daniel Aronoff, who had raised $40,000 for Young. After yet another federal probe, Sen. Stevens was indicted on charges of concealing $250,000 in gifts from VECO and Allen, including extensive renovations on his home. But his conviction was thrown out in March 2009 because prosecutors had withheld key evidence from Stevens's defense attorneys.

Going into the 2008 election, Stevens and Young had 75 years of seniority in Congress and spent much of that time bringing money back to Alaska. In the 1970s, Stevens had done yeoman work in shaping the Alaska Native Claims Act and as a senior Republican on the Appropriations Committee, he had sponsored construction, highway, sewer, and harbor projects on the state, to the point where federal dollars became known in Alaska as "Stevens money." Anchorage airport was named for him. Young, from his positions as chairman of the Resources Committee (1995–2001) and Transportation Committee (2001–07), fought for oil and gas exploration and sponsored countless infrastructure projects. Most famous, not just in Alaska but nationally, was the "Bridge to Nowhere," as critics called it, between Ketchikan and Gravina Island (pop. 50, plus the local airport), to the tune of some $250 million in the 2005 transportation bill. More than anything else, the "Bridge to Nowhere" tarnished the Republican Congress with a reputation for out-of-control pork-barrel spending and contributed to the Democratic takeover in 2006.

Young managed, barely, to survive the 2008 election, narrowly winning in the August primary over Lt. Gov. Sean Parnell, 45.5%-45.2%. Then, despite trailing in the polls, he defeated Democrat Ethan Berkowitz 50%-45% in November. Stevens did not fare as well. In November, he lost 48%-47% to Anchorage Mayor Mark Begich, a Democrat. His defeat at age 84 marked the end of an era in Alaska, leaving the state with two of the most junior senators, Begich and Republican Lisa Murkowski. Young remained in the House, but not with the clout he once had.

In partisan terms, Alaska is pretty Republican. Begich is the first Alaska Democrat elected to the Senate since 1974. His father, Nick Begich, who died in a plane crash with House Majority Leader Hale

Population		Household Income		Work	
Pop. 2007:	676,778	Under $15k:	9.5%	Private:	64.0%
State rank:	47th of 50	$15k to $50k:	30.3%	Government:	28.4%
Change since 2000:	Up 8.0%	$50k to $100k:	35.1%	Self-employed:	7.4%
Urban:	65.2%	$100k to $150k:	21.8%	Unemployment (3-yr. average):	6.3%
Rural:	34.8%	Over $150k:	3.4%	Poverty:	10.4%
Native of state:	38.9%	Median income:	$61,766	Blue collar:	22.6%
Not a citizen:	3.4%			White collar:	57.3%
Area size:	663,267 sq. mi.	**Home Value**		Khaki collar:	2.4%
		Under $100k:	14.3%	Other:	17.6%
Most populous cities		$100k to $300k:	60.8%		
1. Anchorage	278,735	$300k to $500k:	19.7%	**Age**	
2. Fairbanks	33,593	$500k to $1 mil:	4.7%	Median age:	33.4 yrs.
3. Juneau	30,850	Over $1 million:	0.6%	More than 65 yrs:	6.7%
4. Wasilla	9,780	Median:	$213,400	Less than 18 yrs:	27.0%

Race/Ethnicity				Military Veterans		Registered Voters in 2008	
White:	66.1%	*Language*		% of Pop:	15.0%	D:	77,342 (15.5%)
Black:	3.6%	English:	84.7%	*Veterans by Period*		R:	128,582 (25.8%)
Hispanic:	5.5%	Spanish:	3.5%	WWII and before:	3.9%	Other:	291,758 (58.6%)
Asian:	4.5%	Asian:	4.3%	Korea:	5.8%	Voter turnout:	326,197
Native Am.:	13.1%	Other		Vietnam:	34.7%	Turnout as % of	
Hawaiian:	0.5%	European	2.2%	Gulf (pre-2001):	16.2%	voting age:	64.4%
Two+ races:	6.4%			Gulf (post-2001):	18.0%	**Legislature**	
Ancestry		**Education**		Peace time:	21.4%	Senate:	10 D 10 R
German:	14.7%	H.S. grad:	90.2%			House:	18 D 22 R
Irish:	9.5%	College grad:	26.2%				
English:	8.2%	Grad degree:	9.7%				

Cook Partisan Voting Index: R+13

Boggs in 1972, was the last Alaska Democrat elected to the House. Yet in the Legislature, divisions are not always along party lines. Palin worked more with Democrats than with Republican leaders on the natural-gas pipeline and tougher ethics laws. And, anyway, Alaska is quirky. During the 2008 presidential campaign, liberal commentators portrayed Palin as a religious zealot. But Alaska has the lowest church attendance in the nation and a libertarian streak—people don't move all the way there to let other people tell them how to live their lives. As a candidate and public official, Palin has never pressed for restrictions on abortion rights or for banning same-sex marriage. Oil company workers in their two-week stints on the North Slope are not allowed to have alcohol, illegal drugs, or guns. But don't try to take those things away from Alaskans when they're back home. Arguments that seem so consuming in the lower 48 seem beside the point in Alaska, where the wilderness is always nearby and the possibilities for the future seem limitless.

Presidential politics   When Alaska and Hawaii were admitted to the union in 1959, it was expected that Alaska would vote Democratic and Hawaii Republican. It has turned out to be pretty much the other way around. Alaska voted near the national average in the close elections of 1960 and 1968. Since then, it has voted primarily on Alaska issues, which means against the national Democrats. In 1980, the year of the Alaska Lands Act, it gave only 26% of its votes to Democratic presidential candidate Jimmy Carter, who in some places ran behind Libertarian Ed Clark. In 1992, third-party candidate Ross Perot won 28% here, his second-best showing in the country. In 2000, George W. Bush won 59%-28%, but Ralph Nader got 10% of the vote, Nader's best showing. In 2004, Bush got 61% and John Kerry improved on Al Gore's showing with 36%.

2008 Presidential Vote		
McCain (R)	193,841	(59%)
Obama (D)	123,594	(38%)
2004 Presidential Vote		
Bush (R)	190,889	(61%)
Kerry (D)	111,025	(36%)

So critics scoffed when Democratic National Chairman Howard Dean included Alaska in his 50-state strategy and, on a visit to Anchorage, encouraged the state Democratic Party to hire more than one staffer. But Dean turned out to have a point, even if no presidential candidates showed up in the state before the February 5 caucuses on Super Tuesday. Some 8,900 voters turned out for the Democratic caucuses—not many fewer than the 11,600 who turned out for Republican caucuses, and a whole lot more than the 700 who showed up in 2004. Barack Obama, whose campaign opened an Anchorage office in December 2007, beat Hillary Rodham Clinton by 75%-25%. On the Republican side, Mitt Romney, whose son, Josh, did visit Alaska, won with 44% of the vote to 22% for Mike Huckabee, 17% for Ron Paul (that libertarian streak again), and 16% for John McCain—not coincidentally, the only Republican opposed to oil drilling in ANWR. Mike Gravel, who was elected one of Alaska's senators in 1968 and 1974, didn't show up in the state and raised only $1,476 there.

In the general election campaign, the Obama campaign shrewdly targeted Alaska, and he ran about even with McCain in spring and early-summer polls. It was the first race since 1968 in which the oil-drilling issue did not work heavily in favor of the Republican nominee. By August, Obama had 60 paid staffers in Alaska and his volunteers were busy canvassing voters in the long hours of summer daylight. But McCain's selection of Palin as his vice presidential nominee switched Alaska back to the Republican side. Even as Stevens and Young were battling for re-election after 40 and 35 years in Congress, respectively, McCain—their adversary on ANWR—was running well ahead in September and October. Despite Palin's presence on the ticket and despite the close Senate and House races, turnout was up only 4% over 2004 in Alaska. McCain won 59%-38%, his sixth-biggest-percentage margin in the nation. He carried 32 of Alaska's 40 legislative districts, losing only blue-collar areas in Anchorage and Fairbanks, the trendy quarter (such as it is) of Anchorage, state-employee-heavy Juneau, and two heavily Native areas in the bush.

Governor

Sean Parnell (R)

Assumed office July 2009, term expires Dec. 2010, 1st term; b. Nov. 19, 1962, Hanford, CA; home, Anchorage; Pacific Lutheran U., B.B.A. 1984; U. of Puget Sound, J.D. 1987; Christian; married (Sandy); 2 children.

Elected Office: AK House of Reps., 1992–96; AK Senate, 1996–2000; Lt. gov., 2006–09.

Professional Career: Practicing atty., 1987-present; ConocoPhillips, atty. & lobbyist; Deputy dir., AK Div. of Oil & Gas.

Office: P.O. Box 110001, Juneau, 99811-0001, 907-465-3500; Fax: 907-465-3532; Web site: www.gov.state.ak.us.

Election Results

2006 general	Sarah Palin (R)	114,697	(48%)
	Tony Knowles (D)	97,238	(41%)
	Andrew Halcro (I)	22,443	(9%)
2006 primary	Sarah Palin (R)	51,443	(51%)
	John Binkley (R)	30,349	(30%)
	Frank Murkowski (R)	19,412	(19%)

Republican Sean Parnell was poised to take over as governor of Alaska on July 26, 2009, after Gov. Sarah Palin unexpectedly resigned with 18 months left in her term. Parnell had been elected lieutenant governor in 2006 on a Republican ticket with Palin, who later was swept into the swirl of the 2008 presidential campaign as GOP nominee John McCain's running mate. Although she connected well with party conservatives, Palin's stumbling performance on the national stage raised doubts about her suitability for vice president. She cited residual negative attention from the presidential campaign in announcing her resignation as governor in early July.

Parnell was born in Hanford, Calif., just south of Fresno. His father, Pat, was stationed at the Army's Fort Richardson in Anchorage and fell in love with Alaska. He moved his family there in 1973, when Sean was 10 years old. The elder Parnell opened a law practice in Anchorage and got involved in politics. He served in the Anchorage Assembly and in Alaska's House of Representatives as a Democrat. In 1980, Pat Parnell unsuccessfully challenged Republican Don Young for the state's lone congressional seat. Even then, Alaska tilted heavily Republican, and Young won with 74% of the vote.

Meanwhile, Sean Parnell attended college and law school in Washington state. Following his father's career path, he returned to Anchorage, opened a legal practice, and ran for office. But, unlike his father, he ran as a Republican. In 1992, at age 29, he was elected to the state House, where he served two terms. In 1996, he was elected to the state Senate. Parnell championed legislation to toughen domestic violence penalties, citing the effect his grandfather's alcoholism and physical abuse had on his own family. In the state Senate, he rose to become co-chairman of the powerful Finance Committee, where he worked to increase state oil revenues and to balance the state budget.

In 2000, citing a desire to spend more time with his family, Parnell announced that he would not seek a second Senate term. He returned to work as a commercial contract lawyer in Anchorage, and later took a job with ConocoPhillips as an attorney and lobbyist. In 2003, then-Gov. Frank Murkowski, a Republican, appointed him as deputy director of Alaska's Division of Oil and Gas, a post that got him deeply involved in negotiations over the state's proposed natural-gas pipeline. Two years later, Parnell parlayed his knowledge of energy issues into a job at the Anchorage branch of the Washington, D.C.-based law firm Patton Boggs, which handled such high-profile cases as the defense of what is now ExxonMobil in the 1989 Exxon Valdez oil spill in Alaska's Prince William Sound.

Parnell returned to politics in 2006 with his successful campaign for lieutenant governor. His primary opponent was state Sen. Jerry Ward, who accused Parnell of being too cozy with oil companies. But Ward had his own record to defend—he had been arrested on a burglary charge, which was later dropped, and he had served probation for a gun conviction. Ward had run for lieutenant governor several times and lost. Still, polls showed the two in a tight race, although Parnell ultimately won 57%-43%. After his victory, Parnell joined with Palin, who had won the Republican gubernatorial nomination by defeating the scandal-scarred incumbent, Murkowski. Palin and Parnell faced a Democratic ticket led by former Gov. Tony Knowles, with state Rep. Ethan Berkowitz as his running mate. Knowles entered the race late but campaigned on his considerable experience. He argued that he was the best candidate to negotiate a pipeline deal that could deliver Alaska's great natural-gas reserves to market. Palin started off trailing in the polls and with plenty of political enemies in her own party. But in an election year in which the national mood seemed to be running against incumbent Republicans, Palin's outsider status was an asset to the party. On Election Day, Palin and Parnell defeated Knowles and Berkowitz, 48%-41%, with 9% going to Andrew Halcro, a former Republican legislator running as an independent.

Throughout the first two years of their administration, Parnell was a loyal Palin ally. He supported her tax increase on oil companies and her plan to give Alaskans $100-a-month debit cards to use for gasoline as part of an energy relief plan. But in March 2008, he shocked much of Alaska's political establishment when he announced a primary challenge to Young, hoping to oust the 17-term congressman who had defeated his father 28 years earlier. Young had been tainted by scandals involving appropriations earmarks favoring a Florida company that had been a substantial donor to his campaigns. Parnell ran as a fiscal conservative and pointed to his budgetary experience in the state Legislature as a contrast to Young's decades-long history of effusive earmarking. Parnell called for a one-year freeze on earmarks, which budget hawks have attacked in recent years as wasteful, pork-barrel spending. Palin endorsed her lieutenant over Young, and early polls showed Parnell leading the incumbent. Young forcefully attacked Parnell as inexperienced. On Alaska Public Radio, he called Parnell "Captain Zero," and Young told his challenger during the GOP state convention, "I beat your dad, and I'm going to beat you." Parnell had strong support from the national anti-tax group Club for Growth and was also endorsed by the conservative *National Review*. On the night of the August 26 primary, Young had a narrow lead of 152 votes; after absentee ballots were counted, he prevailed by 304 votes. Parnell decided against requesting a recount, saying that the cost to the state could not be justified. Young went on to defeat Democrat Berkowitz in November.

For his part, Parnell was still the lieutenant governor, and, as it turned out, his responsibilities would multiplied rapidly. After McCain chose Palin as his running mate in August 2008, Parnell took over many of the day-to-day duties of governor while Palin was on the road campaigning. He was thrust into the top job by Palin's sudden decision to step down in midterm. Parnell said he learned he would be taking over as governor only two days before Palin's hastily arranged press conference on July 3 at her Wasilla home on Alaska's Lake Lucille. Palin cited numerous reasons for her premature departure, including not wanting to be a lame-duck governor, frustration with media scrutiny of her family, and state and personal resources that had been spent battling ethics claims against her. "We know we can effect positive change outside government at this moment in time, on another scale, and actually make a difference for our priorities. And so we will, for Alaskans and for Americans," she told a small crowd of neighbors and local reporters.

Palin also praised Parnell's capability as her successor, saying he would carry out their "good, positive agenda for Alaska." Parnell, who was at the press conference, said, "I profoundly respect your decision for I know the depth of character and integrity from which it springs. . . . I believe history will look back on Sarah Palin as one of Alaska's great gifts to all peoples."

Parnell signaled that he planned to continue many of Palin's policies, including pursuing a natural-gas pipeline for the state. He has also said he intends to seek a full term in 2010, although other Alaska Republicans have indicated they plan to run for the nomination. In recent years, Parnell has come under fire from some fellow Republicans for being too close to Palin and her positions. Halcro, the former state House member who ran for governor in 2006, said on his blog, "Having served with Parnell when I was in the Legislature, he was a strong and consistent voice against the tax-and-spend ways of government. However, under Palin, he has stood faithfully beside her while supporting larger budgets and advocating for questionable economic policies."

Senior Senator

Lisa Murkowski (R)

Appointed Dec. 2002, term expires 2010, 1st full term; b. May 22, 1957, Ketchikan; home, Anchorage; Willamette U., 1975–77, Georgetown U., B.A. 1980, Willamette U., J.D. 1985; Catholic; married (Verne Martell); 2 children.

Elected Office: AK House of Reps., 1998–02.

Professional Career: Anchorage Dist. Court Clerk's Office, atty., 1987–89; Practicing atty., 1989–98.

DC Office: 709 HSOB, 20510, 202-224-6665; Fax: 202-224-5301; Web site: murkowski.senate.gov.

State Offices: Anchorage, 907-271-3735; Fairbanks, 907-456-0233; Ketchikan, 907-225-6880; MatSu, 907-456-0233.

Committees: *Republican Conference Secretary. Appropriations* (12th of 12 R): Commerce, Justice, Science & Related Agencies; Homeland Security; Interior, Environment & Related Agencies; Legislative Branch (RMM); Military Construction, Veterans Affairs & Related Agencies. *Energy & Natural Resources* (RMM of 10 R). *Health, Education, Labor & Pensions* (8th of 10 R). *Indian Affairs* (3rd of 6 R).

Group Ratings

	ADA	ACLU	AFS	LCV	ITIC	NTU	COC	ACU	CFG	FRC
2008	25	29	22	9	100	50	86	58	57	55
2007	30	—	14	40	—	50	91	67	47	—

National Journal Ratings

	2007 LIB	—	2007 CONS		2008 LIB	—	2008 CONS
Economic	40%	—	59%		39%	—	60%
Social	41%	—	58%		43%	—	55%
Foreign	21%	—	73%		42%	—	56%
Composite	35%	—	65%		42%	—	58%

Key Votes of the 110th Congress

1. Raise CAFE standards	Y	5. Make English official language	Y	9. Withdraw troops 3/08	N
2. Expand SCHIP	Y	6. Path to citizenship	N	10. Iran guard is terrorist group	Y
3. Cap greenhouse gases	*	7. Fetus is unborn child	N	11. Increase missile defense $	N
4. Bail out financial markets	Y	8. Prosecute hate crimes	N	12. Overhaul FISA	Y

Election Results

2004 general	Lisa Murkowski (R)	149,773	(49%)	($5,465,098)
	Tony Knowles (D)	140,424	(46%)	($5,768,963)
2004 primary	Lisa Murkowski (R)	45,710	(58%)	
	Mike Miller (R)	29,313	(37%)	

Lisa Murkowski is a Republican who was appointed to the Senate in December 2002 by her father, then Alaska Gov. Frank Murkowski, to fill the vacancy caused by his own resignation from the Senate to become governor. The appointment was assailed by critics in both major parties as nepotism. But once in office, Lisa Murkowski performed ably for the final two years of her father's term, and then won a full term in her own right in 2004. She became the first woman elected to Congress from Alaska. She is up for re-election in 2010.

The second of six children, Murkowski grew up in Ketchikan in Alaska's Panhandle and in Fairbanks. In her senior year of high school, she worked for five weeks as an intern in Republican Sen. Ted Stevens's Washington office. She attended Willamette University in Salem, Oregon, and graduated from Georgetown in 1980, the year her father was first elected to the Senate. Murkowski went on to get a degree from Willamette law school in 1985. She served as an Anchorage District Court attorney, worked for an Anchorage law firm for eight years, and then established her own law practice. In 1998, she was elected to the state House from a north Anchorage district that included her neighborhood of Government Hill.

Alaska's state government depends heavily on revenues from North Slope oil and in early 2002 was facing a budget shortfall of $1.1 billion. Murkowski was one of the leaders of the bipartisan Fiscal Policy Caucus, which sought tax increases—a position opposite to that of her father, who was running for governor on a platform of no new taxes. Murkowski pushed hard for increasing the alcohol tax from 3 cents a drink to 10 cents, and her bill was enacted, giving Alaska the nation's highest alcohol tax. Some conservatives referred to her and her allies as RIMs, "Republican invertebrate moderates." She also angered conservatives when she voted against a bill restricting publicly funded abortions. She said, "I may have a very short-lived political future here. But you know, I've got great kids and a great husband, and I'm going to have a good heart, and I'm going to stand up for the women of the state of Alaska, and I'm going to vote no." But she has also said that abortion should be legal only when a mother's life is in danger or in cases of rape or incest. In March 2003, she said she favored a ban on partial-birth abortion. Still, Alaska Right to Life opposed her in 1998, claiming, "She is not pro-life." She had a tough fight for re-election in 2002 against conservative Nancy Dahlstrom, who attacked her for favoring tax increases and tapping the state's Permanent Fund to pay its bills. Murkowski won by only 57 votes. After the election, she was chosen state House majority leader.

That same year, her father, with two years left in his U.S. Senate term, was elected governor. (Republican state legislators saw to it that he, and not outgoing Democratic Gov. Tony Knowles, appointed a successor. Earlier in the year, they passed, over Knowles's veto, a law barring a governor from appointing a successor until five days after the vacancy occurred.) Murkowski said he was looking for someone with legislative experience who was young enough to serve many years and who shared his views on Alaska issues. He unveiled a short list of 26 potential nominees that included Gen. Joseph Ralston, NATO's Supreme Allied Commander in Europe; retired Gen. Mark Hamilton, president of the University of Alaska; Jerry Hood, secretary-treasurer of Teamsters Local 959 and a Republican; Francis Hurley, the retired

Catholic Archbishop of Anchorage; state Senate Majority Leader Ben Stevens, son of Ted Stevens; and finally, his daughter.

On Dec. 20, 2002, he announced that he had decided to appoint Lisa Murkowski. It was the first time a governor had appointed his or her child to the Senate. Most Republicans and many Democrats praised Murkowski's abilities, but others called it a case of nepotism that would undermine public trust in the office. For her part, Murkowski maintained that she and her father kept their political lives separate. "We have always maintained very separate identities, at least for the time I have been in the legislature," she said. "I haven't called him for counseling, and typically he doesn't offer."

As she served the remaining two years of her father's term, Murkowski was acutely aware that she would be closely watched by her critics for signs that she was not up to the job. She proved not only competent, but with help from powerful fellow Senate Republicans, she exceeded expectations for a freshman senator. She got seats on the Energy, Environment, Veterans and Indian Affairs committees, putting her at the center of most issues important to Alaska. Longtime family friend Ted Stevens took her under his wing. As a senior member of the Appropriations Committee, he was then one of the most influential members of Congress. Her biggest success came in October 2004, when she sponsored a measure creating federal loan guarantees for a 3,500-mile pipeline to bring natural gas from the North Slope to the lower 48, a major economic venture for the state. Her pipeline bill, with the guiding hand of Sen. Stevens, passed as part of the appropriations for military construction projects that year. Murkowski also got out front on efforts to pass legislation opening the Arctic National Wildlife Refuge to oil and gas exploration, an idea popular in Alaska but long opposed by environmental and wilderness groups, which have blocked its passage. Stevens praised the work of his former intern, saying that Murkowski "is a hell of a lot better senator than her dad ever was." (She returned his loyalty in 2009, when she asked President Bush to pardon Stevens after his conviction for concealing $250,000 in gifts from an oil executive. Bush declined, but the conviction was later thrown out after it was revealed that prosecutors had allegedly withheld evidence from Stevens's defense lawyers.)

No Alaska Republican senator had ever been defeated for re-election, but Murkowski entered the 2004 campaign in weak condition. She had primary opposition from conservative former legislator Mike Miller, who attacked her stands on abortion, gun rights and taxes. Miller was even supported by her father's lieutenant governor, Loren Leman. But Murkowski was better financed and had the support of Stevens and Rep.-at-Large Don Young. She won the primary 58%-37%.

Her opponent in the general election was former Gov. Ted Knowles, the most successful Alaska Democrat in recent times. A Vietnam veteran and Yale classmate and friend of George W. Bush, Knowles ran a restaurant in Anchorage and had been twice elected the city's mayor in the 1980s. In 1994, he had been elected governor in a multi-candidate field with 41% of the vote; in 1998, he won a second term. Knowles strongly supported ANWR drilling and said that, as a Democrat, he would have a better chance of attracting votes for it. National Republicans responded with an ad featuring Democratic presidential candidate John Kerry and saying he "wouldn't know a caribou if it dropped in for a bowl of Boston clam chowder." Knowles criticized Murkowski for not supporting more spending for veterans' health care. In her defense, Stevens said that Murkowski had supported over $1 billion for veterans' health. Knowles said that, knowing what he did in 2004, he would not have voted for the Iraq war resolution two years earlier; Murkowski said she would have.

Looming over the campaign was the nepotism issue. Knowles's pollster said that 54% of people found it a convincing reason to vote against Murkowski, and she trailed, usually by narrow margins, in most polls during the campaign. Organizers obtained 50,000 signatures for a ballot measure to ban governors from appointing new senators, which later passed with 56% of the vote. Against this, Republicans raised the issue of party and seniority. Stevens said Alaska would be hurt if Democrats gained a majority that year in the Senate and made the point that Murkowski, at age 47, would have a chance of amassing more seniority than would 61-year-old Knowles.

This was one of the national Democrats' best chances to pick up a Republican seat in 2004, but this red state ended up giving its GOP junior senator a full term, by 49%-46%. Like her father in the 2002 governor's race, Murkowski ran behind by a wide margin in the bush and by a lesser margin in the panhandle. In historically Republican Anchorage and Fairbanks, she ran only narrowly ahead. Her winning margins came in south-central Alaska, in the fast-growing arc around Anchorage.

Murkowski has established a moderate voting record, considerably closer to the middle of the road than her father's. She assumed a much larger role in the Senate on Alaska-centric issues after Stevens lost his bid for re-election in 2008 amid the corruption scandal. By 2009, she had won the respect of many of her colleagues and was moving up the ladder. She secured a seat on the Appropriations Committee, where Stevens had been so successful securing federal largesse for Alaska. Luck broke her way with another big promotion: She rose to become the ranking member of the Senate Energy and Natural Resources Committee after three Republicans with more seniority were suddenly off the committee. (Craig Thomas of Wyoming died of leukemia, Larry Craig of Idaho left the Senate after being arrested in a homosexual-sex sting, and Pete Domenici of New Mexico retired.) The move gave Murkowski the top job for the minority party on a committee vital to Alaska's energy interests.

But her first full term was also marred by an ethics controversy. In late 2006, Murkowski and her husband purchased an acre of waterfront land on Alaska's Kenai River from developer Bob Penney, a friend of Stevens. An ethics watchdog group charged that the $179,500 the couple paid for the lot was well below the market value of approximately $350,000. Penney told local newspaper reporters that he had sold Murkowski the land, next to property he owned on the river, for the assessed value. However, in early 2007, just weeks after the sale, the assessed value on the lot went up to $215,000. In July 2007, Murkowski called the deal "nothing nefarious or underhanded" but said she had decided to sell the land back to Penney for the purchase price of $179,500

In the Senate, she continued to pursue the Alaska delegation's longstanding goal of opening up ANWR to drilling, though she had not succeeded as of late spring 2009. She tried a new tack in 2008, promoting a bill that would automatically open the area to drilling if world oil prices topped $125 a barrel for five days, a strategy designed to take advantage of pressure Congress was feeling from soaring consumer prices at the pump.

Murkowski's independence and centrist positions put her in the center of high-profile national debates. In 2005 she came under pressure from conservatives to support the "nuclear option," a proposed change in Senate rules that would have blocked Democrats from using a filibuster to block nominations of conservative judges. Murkowski said she supported up-or-down votes on judicial nominations but did not reveal her position on the controversial rules change. And she did not join the "Gang of 14" senators who met to resolve the issue. Suspicious of her abortion stance, the conservative Christian group Focus on the Family called her a "squishy Republican" and ran radio and newspaper ads in the state that said she was likely to support Democratic obstruction of nominees.

When Bush asked Congress to reauthorize the USA PATRIOT Act, Murkowski was one of four Republican senators to insist the anti-terrorism bill include more civil liberties protections. Their decision to join a Democratic filibuster forced the White House to accept a short-term extension in December 2005 and to return the next year to negotiate a longer reauthorization. A pet issue of Murkowski's is child nutrition. She teamed with Iowa Democratic Sen. Tom Harkin in 2007 on an amendment to the farm bill to raise nutritional standards for food and beverages sold in school vending machines and cafeterias.

Murkowski has been aggressive on Alaska issues. In June 2008, she sponsored an amendment to a Senate tax bill that would have eased the tax burden on plaintiffs sharing $2.5 billion in punitive damages in the *Exxon Valdez* oil-spill case. The more than 32,000 plaintiffs would be allowed to pay their taxes on damage awards over three years rather than in one year. However, the Senate tax bill did not pass. She is also the leading advocate in the Senate for joining the Convention on the Law of the Sea, an international treaty that sets policy for ocean resources, including vast untapped supplies of oil in the Arctic. Some 155 countries, including Russia, have ratified the treaty, but American conservatives have long argued that the United States needs no such document to assert its claims over the Arctic and its natural resources.

Murkowski fought along with Stevens against Pentagon plans to downgrade Eielson Air Force Base during the 2005 base-closure round. They backed a bill that would have halted the base-closing process until the Pentagon met a number of requirements, including the return of most U.S. troops from Iraq. And she criticized the Defense Department when it delayed declassification of information that would have helped the state make its case for keeping the base. The base commission voted 7-0 to keep Eielson open by allowing 18 F-16 fighter jets to remain there, although it approved the transfer of 18 A-10 aircraft. Murkowski also sponsored bills to grant federal recognition and land to five landless native Alaskan communities. Conservationists opposed the recognition out of fear it could lead to logging of environmentally sensitive lands.

And in 2006, not to be out-Alaska'ed by anyone, she bested eight other senators during a Kenai River conservation fundraiser by catching a 63-pound king salmon.

Junior Senator

Mark Begich (D)

Elected 2008, term expires 2014, 1st term; b. March 30, 1962, Anchorage; home, Anchorage; Steller H.S. (Anchorage), 1980.; Catholic; married (Deborah Bonito); 1 child.

Elected Office: Anchorage Assembly, 1988—98; Anchorage mayor, 2003–08.

DC Office: 114 RSOB, 20510, 202-224-3004; Fax: 202-224-2354; Web site: begich.senate.gov.

State Offices: Anchorage, 907-271-5915; Fairbanks, 907-456-0261.

Committees: *Armed Services* (14th of 15 D): Airland; Personnel; Strategic Forces. *Commerce, Science & Transportation* (14th of 14 D): Aviation Operations, Safety & Security; Communications, Technology & the Internet; Competitiveness, Innovation & Export Promotion; Oceans, Atmosphere & Coast Guard; Surface Transportation & Merchant Marine Infrastructure, Safety & Security. *Veterans' Affairs* (8th of 10 D).

Group Ratings and Key Votes: Newly Elected

Election Results

2008 general	Mark Begich (D)	151,767	(48%)	($4,453,292)
	Ted Stevens (R)	147,814	(47%)	($4,050,791)
	Bob Bird (Ind)	13,197	(4%)	($33,019)
2008 primary	Mark Begich (D)	63,747	(84%)	
	Ray Metcalfe (D)	5,480	(7%)	
	Bob Bird (D)	4,216	(6%)	

Mark Begich, Alaska's junior senator, was born five years after his parents moved to the Alaska Territory in 1957 to teach school. His father, Nick Begich, was a major figure in the state's political history. Nick Begich was elected to the Alaska Senate, and in 1970, was elected Alaska's at-large representative to Congress. He defeated Republican Frank Murkowski, who would later become a U.S. senator and governor. In October 1972, Nick Begich was killed along with U.S. House Majority Leader Hale Boggs of Louisiana as they were flying to a campaign fundraiser. Their plane disappeared over the Gulf of Alaska. Mark Begich was only 10 at the time.

Mark was something of a political prodigy, appointed by the mayor to the youth commission at age 17, and then landing a spot in the city health department. (Showing his entrepreneurial side at age 16, Begich opened a teen nightclub called the Motherlode.) When he was 20, he was hired as the personal assistant to Mayor Tony Knowles, who would later become governor. A few years later, Begich followed in his father's footsteps by winning election to the Anchorage Assembly, becoming the city governing board's youngest member ever. He served for 10 years and was chosen chairman.

Begich's quest for higher office took some time. He ran for mayor in 1994, but lost with 42% of the vote. He ran again in 2000 and lost with 48%. In his third attempt in 2003, Begich beat incumbent George Wuerch. During his five years leading Alaska's largest city, he was able to raise the city's bond ratings while lowering property taxes for most taxpayers. He was easily re-elected to a second term in 2006. As mayor, Begich claimed credit for getting voters to twice pass bond issues, for holding down property taxes, for hiring 65 additional police officers, and for setting up a multi-agency anti-gang initiative.

In late 2007, national Democratic leaders began courting Begich for a possible challenge to U.S. Sen. Ted Stevens, a six-term incumbent who was vulnerable as a result of a federal corruption investigation into his relationship with Bill Allen, the former chief executive officer of the VECO oil services company. Stevens was later indicted for failing to report on his Senate financial disclosure forms thousands of dollars in renovation work that VECO employees did on his home. Stevens had represented the state for four decades and had won re-election by wide margins; in one race he carried every precinct in the state. He could claim credit for landmark legislation that allowed the building of the Alaska oil pipeline and that established Alaska Native corporations. As a senior member of the Appropriations Committee, he funneled vast sums of money into Alaska, and stayed in touch with virtually every civic and political group in the state.

Encouraged by Democratic Senatorial Campaign Committee Chairman Charles Schumer of New York, Begich set up an exploratory committee in February 2008. Having never held office outside Anchorage, Begich made visits to Fairbanks, Bethel, Ketchikan, and Sitka. He announced he was running in April. "We've seen here in Alaska the ultimate result of unfettered greed—grainy videotapes of state legislators in hotel rooms laughing at the citizens of our great state," he said. "And we've seen in Washington the ultimate result of special influence and legislative indifference." He issued an "Alaska Ethics Pledge" in which he vowed to make public both his and his wife's finances "to the dollar" and to disclose the beneficiary of his congressional earmarks, the special spending provisions tucked into appropriations bills by individual lawmakers. He called for a citizens ethics board in the Senate and for Internet disclosure of all meetings of senators with lobbyists. He was careful not to attack the revered Stevens personally, and he paid tribute to Stevens's long service to the state. But the message was not lost on voters.

Begich also emphasized Alaska issues. He called for increased spending for rural health care, an important matter for many Alaskan natives, and for loans for energy-efficient community buildings. He advocated repeal of the Bush-era No Child Left Behind Act, with its mandates tying federal funds to students' test performance. He said that the national Democratic Party was "wrong" on gun rights, which he supports, and wrong in opposing drilling in the Arctic National Wildlife Refuge. With help from Schumer and the DSSC, he proved to be a solid fundraiser, nearly matching Stevens. Begich spent $4.4 million to Stevens's $5.7 million. National Democrats ran ads showing federal agents raiding Stevens's house. National Republicans ran ads accusing Begich of rezoning downtown Anchorage land to aid two developers, and highlighting $16,000 in tax liens on his businesses in the 1990s.

On July 29, 2008, Stevens was indicted in the U.S. District Court in Washington, D.C., for failing to report on his Senate forms the value of gifts from Allen and the VECO company in the renovation of his house. The news was dynamite in Alaska. Stevens protested his innocence and his determination to run for re-election. Polls showed the incumbent running a bit behind or no better than even with Begich. In the August Democratic primary, Begich got 84% of the vote over four opponents. In the GOP primary, Stevens beat David Cuddy, a businessman who had run against him 12 years before, 64%-27%. Stevens got slightly more votes than Begich, but could hardly count on those who had voted against him in the primary. Some national Republicans expressed hope that Stevens would resign and let Alaska Republicans pick a new, untarnished candidate. But Stevens refused to quit even though he spent much of October on trial in a D.C. courtroom.

On October 27, 2008, Stevens was convicted on all seven counts. "I am innocent," he declared. "This verdict is the result of the unconscionable manner in which the Justice Department lawyers conducted this trial. I ask that Alaskans and my Senate colleagues stand with me as I pursue my rights. I remain a candidate for the United States Senate." But it was not clear whether Stevens could have kept his seat even if he was re-elected. Senate Republican Leader Mitch McConnell called on Stevens to resign. Stevens would certainly have had to face a Senate Ethics Committee investigation and perhaps expulsion. Some Republicans urged a vote for Stevens on the grounds that, if he was re-elected and then left the Senate, GOP Gov. Sarah Palin could appoint another Republican to fill the vacancy. Stevens may have helped his re-election chances with a two-minute television ad he ran just before the election recounting what he had done for Alaska for 40 years. Last-minute polls showed a dead heat.

The Election Night returns showed Stevens ahead 48%-46% but the race was too close to call. But Barack Obama's superb organization in Alaska had ensured that many Democrats cast early votes or absentee votes, and as they were counted, Begich kept gaining ground. By November 12, Begich was ahead, and on November 18, he led by more than the number of votes left to count. He became the first Democratic senator elected in Alaska since Mike Gravel was re-elected in 1974.

In December 2008, the Senate held a session for colleagues to praise Stevens on his service and accomplishments; little was said about the result of the trial. In the new Congress, Begich sought a seat on the Appropriations Committee on which Stevens had served for so long. Freshman rarely get appointed to the committee, and Democratic leaders instead gave him seats on the Commerce, Science and Transportation Committee and the Armed Services Committee.

Representative-At-Large

Don Young (R)

Elected Mar. 1973, 18th full term; b. June 9, 1933, Meridian, CA; home, Fort Yukon; Yuba Jr. Col., A.A. 1952, Chico St. Col., B.A. 1958; Episcopalian; married (Lu); 2 children.

Military Career: Army, 1955–57.

Elected Office: Fort Yukon City Cncl., 1960–64; Fort Yukon mayor, 1964–68; AK House of Reps., 1966–70; AK Senate, 1970–73.

Professional Career: School teacher, Fort Yukon, 1960–68; Riverboat captain, 1960–68.

DC Office: 2111 RHOB, 20515, 202-225-5765; Fax: 202-225-0425; Web site: donyoung.house.gov.

State Offices: Anchorage, 907-271-5978; Fairbanks, 907-456-0210; Juneau, 907-586-7400; Kenai, 907-283-5808; Ketchikan, 907-225-6880; Wasilla, 907-376-7665.

Committees: *Natural Resources* (2nd of 20 R): Energy & Mineral Resources; Insular Affairs, Oceans & Wildlife; National Parks, Forests & Public Lands. *Transportation & Infrastructure* (2nd of 30 R): Coast Guard & Maritime Transportation; Highways & Transit; Water Resources & Environment.

Group Ratings

	ADA	ACLU	AFS	LCV	ITIC	NTU	COC	ACU	CFG	FRC
2008	55	38	80	23	60	50	73	71	49	76
2007	30	—	45	10	—	55	88	65	48	—

National Journal Ratings

	2007 LIB	—	2007 CONS		2008 LIB	—	2008 CONS
Economic	33%	—	67%		39%	—	61%
Social	33%	—	66%		40%	—	60%
Foreign	41%	—	59%		31%	—	69%
Composite	36%	—	64%		37%	—	63%

Key Votes of the 110th Congress

1. Increase minimum wage	Y	5. Share immigration data	Y	9. Withdraw troops 8/08	N
2. Expand SCHIP	Y	6. Foreign aid abortion ban	Y	10. No operations in Iran	N
3. Raise CAFE standards	*	7. Ban gay bias in workplace	N	11. Free trade with Peru	Y
4. Bail out financial markets	N	8. Repeal D.C. gun law	Y	12. Overhaul FISA	Y

Election Results

2008 general	Don Young (R)..	158,939	(50%)	($3,213,537)
	Ethan Berkowitz (D)..	142,560	(45%)	($1,634,984)
	Don Wright (Ind)...	14,274	(5%)	
2008 primary	Don Young (R)...	48,195	(45%)	
	Sean Parnell (R)...	47,891	(45%)	
	Gabrielle Ledoux (R)...	9,901	(9%)	

Prior Winning Percentages: 2006 (57%); 2004 (71%); 2002 (75%); 2000 (70%); 1998 (63%); 1996 (59%); 1994 (57%); 1992 (47%); 1990 (52%); 1988 (63%); 1986 (57%); 1984 (55%); 1982 (71%); 1980 (74%); 1978 (55%); 1976 (71%); 1974 (54%); 1973 (51%)

Don Young has been Alaska's congressman-at-large since 1973 and is now the second-most-senior Republican in the House, after Bill Young of Florida. But his long political career was nearly destroyed by a recent influence-peddling scandal involving Young's legislative favors for a political fundraiser. He only narrowly survived challenges in the Republican primary and the general election of 2008.

Young grew up on his family's farm in the Sacramento Valley of California, served in the Army, and graduated from college. He had a thirst for adventure and the rugged outdoors—he remembers that *The Call of the Wild* by Jack London was a favorite book growing up. He moved to Alaska in 1959, the year that the vast, untamed U.S. territory became a state. Young worked in construction, fishing, trapping, and gold prospecting. He taught elementary school to indigenous Alaskan children in Fort Yukon, pop. 700. After spring thaws, he worked as a tugboat captain on the Yukon. He is the only licensed mariner in Congress and, in his words, is definitely "not one of these smooth, namby-pamby politicians." He is temperamental and salty-tongued, given to tough talk; to critics who once proposed shifting money for Alaska bridges to Hurricane Katrina recovery efforts, he said, "They can kiss my ear." Young was elected mayor of Fort Yukon in 1964, to the state House in 1966, and to the state Senate in 1970. He ran for Congress in 1972. His opponent, incumbent Democrat Nick Begich, was killed in a plane crash in October and was re-elected posthumously. Young won the March 1973 special election to succeed him. Young is not a free-market conservative and has recently voted with liberals on some cultural issues. But he is a consistent, fierce advocate for Alaska's interests.

Soon after taking his seat in the House, Young voted for building the Alaska pipeline. But he often found that his aggressive pursuit of economic development for his state conflicted with the environmental lobby and its interest in preserving wildlife. On what was then the Interior Committee, he called his critics a "self-centered bunch, the waffle-stomping, Harvard-graduating, intellectual idiots." During the 12 years of Republican control of Congress, Young occupied power positions that allowed him to work around his adversaries. He led the Resources Committee from 1995 to 2001 and the Transportation and Infrastructure Committee from 2001 to 2007. He steered to passage in the House bills allowing oil drilling in the Arctic National Wildlife Refuge in 1995, 2001, and 2006, only to see them defeated or bottled up in the Senate. His attempts to roll back some environmental rulings, such as allowing logging in the Tongass National Forest, were frustrated in the 1990s by Democratic President Clinton, or by adverse votes cast by Republicans from the Northeast, Arizona, and Florida. In May 2006, the House voted 237-181 to prohibit road-building in the forest, virtually wiping out the logging business there. But on both committees, Young also proved capable of forging bipartisan consensus. In 2000, he got the House to pass the Conservation and Reinvestment Act to dedicate royalties from offshore oil and gas wells to state purchases of land. A scaled-down version passed the Senate.

After the 2000 election, Young took over the Transportation and Infrastructure Committee, arguably the most bipartisan panel in the House because its chairmen traditionally larded their bills to make sure every cooperating committee member received plenty of highway or mass transit projects for his or her district. In 2003, Young proposed a surface transportation bill with $375 billion in spending, financed with a gas-tax increase. But the Bush administration and the House Republican leadership were stoutly opposed to any such hike. And the administration set a spending limit of $256 billion. In March 2004, the committee approved Young's bill by voice vote. But the House approved a $275 billion bill, without Young's gas-tax increase. A House-Senate conference committee agreed to $284 billion, a number the administration threatened to veto. The bill languished as members of the House and Senate bickered over funding formulas that granted states a certain share of gas-tax revenues. The conference deadlocked, and no bill passed when Congress adjourned in 2004. Young's proposal for a gas-tax increase was dead.

In 2005, he tried again and got the House to pass a $284 billion bill in March. But there was mounting criticism of the bill's earmarks—special projects for certain lawmakers—particularly of two bridges in Alaska. One was from Anchorage to the largely uninhabited land across the Knik Arm; the other was from the town of Ketchikan (pop. 14,000) to the island of Gravina (pop. 50) with its airport, which could already be reached by local ferry. They were derisively dubbed the "bridges to nowhere." Negotiations with the Senate and the Bush administration continued, and in July, both chambers passed by near-unanimous votes a $286 billion bill with more than 6,300 earmarks. They included $230 million for the Knik Arm bridge and $220 million for the Ketchikan-Gravina bridge. All told, the bill contained about $941 million for Young's Alaska, more than any other state except California, Illinois, and New York. Young's reaction was serene. "It is much-needed legislation that will move our country toward a stronger economy." As for the earmarks, he said, "If I hadn't done fairly well for our state, I'd be ashamed of myself."

That likely would have been the end of the earmark controversy, except that Hurricane Katrina struck the Gulf Coast in August. Suddenly, there were demands that money be shifted from Alaska's "bridges to nowhere" to New Orleans and other parts of the devastated region. "That is the dumbest thing I ever heard," Young said. But for the next year, criticism of earmarks and the bridges continued. Conservative Republicans as well as Democrats chimed in, and profligate spending, symbolized by the two spans, emerged as an issue in the 2006 election. It was among the factors that helped wipe out the Republican majorities that year.

For an incumbent who has been around as long as he has, Young has had a bumpy history with Alaska voters and drew serious challengers in 1978, 1984, 1986, 1990, and 1992. He looked safe for a period in the early 2000s, but in 2006, he again ran into trouble. His Democratic opponent, Diane Benson, a Green Party candidate for governor in 2002, attracted attention as the mother of a soldier who lost both legs in an explosion in Iraq, and she called for a graceful exit strategy from that conflict. Then, the *Anchorage Daily News* (the "Daily Screw," as Young calls it) ran a story detailing Young's receipt of $20,000 in campaign contributions from Indian tribes that were clients of disgraced lobbyist Jack Abramoff; his use of Abramoff's skybox at MCI Center (now Verizon Center) to hold two fundraisers; and his behind-the-scenes work pressuring a government agency to give preferential treatment to tribes on proposals to redevelop Washington's Old Post Office. Young spent nearly $2 million on heavy advertising while avoiding joint appearances with Benson. She spent only $197,000 and did not tape her first television ad until late October. Young appeared upbeat and predicted in October that Republicans would lose no seats in the House. Ultimately, Young won but by the considerably reduced ratio of 57%-40%.

His problems had just begun. In April 2007, a former Young aide pleaded guilty to accepting cash from Abramoff in exchange for inside government information. Records released in April 2008 showed 120 contacts between Young and his staff with Abramoff and his clients. In May 2007, Rick Smith, an associate of Young's and a former lobbyist with the oil-services firm VECO, a major Young contributor since 1989, pleaded guilty to bribing Alaska state legislators. In July, *The Wall Street Journal* reported that the investigation had expanded to include Young. *The New York Times* published a story about a Young staffer altering the 2005 transportation bill to add $10 million for an interstate interchange in Florida that would help real estate developer Daniel Aronoff, who had raised $40,000 for the lawmaker. Young dismissed the allegations, telling the *Anchorage Daily News* that it was just "a recycled story." Plus, he said, Florida Gulf Coast University supported the Coconut Road interchange. In April 2008, Democratic Speaker Nancy Pelosi ordered an investigation, and the Senate voted 64-28 and the House 358-51 for a U.S. Justice Department inquiry. Young used $25,000 in campaign funds to retain a Washington law firm, and he eventually spent more than $1.1 million in campaign money on legal fees.

Young consistently maintained he was innocent of any wrongdoing and said he was barred from commenting by government investigators and his own attorneys. Defenders of Wildlife, a longtime Young opponent, started running ads against him in October 2007. Former Alaska House Minority Leader Ethan Berkowitz, a Democrat, lined up to run against him in the general election in 2008, and Republican Lt. Gov. Sean Parnell announced he would challenge Young in the primary. Parnell was endorsed by GOP Gov. Sarah Palin.

Polls in the summer of 2008 showed Young trailing both Parnell and Berkowitz, but he professed to be unfazed. "Go back to the 19 races I've run and just tell me how many of them were easy races. . . . Most of them are doggone interesting races," Young said in the *Anchorage Daily News*. Later, during a debate with Parnell, he said: "I've been accused of being arrogant, being a bully, and sometimes I'll plead to being both of those. Most of the time and every time I've done that is because I'm fighting for this state." On Alaska Public Radio, he called Parnell "Captain Zero," and an Alaska TV station reported that Young told Parnell during the GOP state convention: "I beat your dad, and I'm going to beat you." Pat Parnell was the Democratic nominee against Young in 1980. Sean Parnell spent $572,000, with strong support from the anti-tax Club for Growth. "We're tired of being the nation's symbol of excess and greed," Parnell said in an August debate, after the indictment of Republican Sen. Ted Stevens in an influence-peddling case. Young beat Parnell by just 304 votes, 45.47% to 45.19%. Only when the last 350 votes were counted on September 17 was it clear that Young had won.

His battle was far from over, however. Gearing up for the general election, Berkowitz was well funded, with $1.6 million, while Young's resources were being steadily depleted by legal fees in the ongoing investigation and by the primary contest. Plus, the Democratic Congressional Campaign Committee spent $1.4 million on ads charging that Young was the subject of four investigations, basing its claim on allegations by Citizens for Responsibility and Ethics in Washington. Berkowitz and Young were not far apart on the issues. Rather than cater to hard-line anti-war Democrats on Iraq, Berkowitz told a primary-debate audience, "Our soldiers and sailors and airmen and marines have fought hard, and fought valiantly, and they've won a victory." While Young had been at odds with Palin, Berkowitz noted that he had been on friendly terms with the governor and was her ally on state ethics issues.

Berkowitz framed the choice as one of style. "If you want to be persuasive, you cannot just confront people who you disagree with, you cannot bully and intimidate them into agreeing with you. You need to find common ground, you need to find consensus," he said. He strongly backed oil drilling in the Arctic National Wildlife Refuge and said he could do more as a Democrat to promote it than Young could in the minority party. He said he would seek earmarks if communities and citizens asked for them, but not for lobbyists. Young responded during a debate, tongue in cheek, that he is "one of the nicest, kindest persons in the world." He added, "But when you mess with the state, you're messing with me."

In October, polls showed Young trailing Berkowitz. But either most polls were wrong or public opinion changed in the final days. Perhaps Alaskans feared losing the clout of both Young and Stevens, who that month had been convicted on corruption charges. Young defeated Berkowitz 50% to 45%. Young ran only even in usually Republican Anchorage and carried the Fairbanks area 50%-44%, thanks largely to support from his hometown of Fort Yukon. But he held Berkowitz's margins down in the Panhandle, carrying Ketchikan, and he won the Matanuska-Susitna area 62%-33%. Most important, he carried the Bush 49%-45%, even as Stevens was losing it to Democratic challenger Mark Begich 54%-41%. Berkowitz conceded on November 18 and noted he had received more votes running against Young than any other Democrat had.

Young returned to Washington, but he was under a cloud. In November, he lost his seat on the Republican Steering Committee to Mike Simpson of Idaho; in December, he lost the ranking minority member position on Resources, the committee on which he had served for 36 years, to Washington state Rep. Doc Hastings. Young issued a press release saying he would regain the post when "my name is cleared." In early 2009, nearly two years into their investigation of Young's Abramoff connections and the Coconut Road interchange, federal prosecutors had not brought an indictment.

★ ARIZONA ★

Arizona is both old and young: It is the home of indigenous America's oldest continuous community and also is one of America's two fastest-growing states. The Hopi Indians, who thrived as shepherds on the plateaus east of the Grand Canyon, have been rooted in northeastern Arizona for more than 900 years. They have spurned Christianity since 1680, when they killed the local Franciscan priests and burned their churches. More recently, they have been involved in land disputes with the more numerous Navajo tribe. The Hopi are the oldest Arizonans, and the newest are moving in every day, into subdivisions rising from the empty desert east, north, and west of Phoenix, hemmed in only by dry riverbeds, upcroppings of mountains, and Indian reservation boundaries.

In the 2000s, Arizona has been one of the nation's boom states. Its population grew 27% between 2000 and 2008, at a faster rate than any other state except Nevada (and in fact more rapidly than Nevada in the years from 2004 to 2008). Arizona started off the decade as the nation's 20th largest state, but surpassed Indiana in 2007 and Massachusetts in 2008, to the rank of 14th, just behind Washington state. Maricopa County, where Phoenix is located, has 61% of the state's people and is the fourth-most-populous county in the nation. Some 934,000 people moved into the state from 2000 to 2008, one-quarter of them immigrants. That is a bigger influx than any state except Texas and Florida.

When it was admitted to the Union in 1912, just about no one would have envisioned the Arizona of today. For decades, its growth was attributable to the five Cs, memorialized in the state seal. The first C was copper: The dome of the state capitol is encased in copper, and one of Arizona's leading public figures was Lewis Douglas—copper heir, congressman, Franklin D. Roosevelt's first budget director, and Harry Truman's ambassador to Britain. The second C was cattle: As late as the mid-1960s, a dozen or so cattlemen ran the state Legislature. The third C was cotton: Carl Hayden, a Democratic senator from 1927 to 1969, concentrated on bringing public works to Arizona; his signal achievement was the Central Arizona Project, a massive irrigation program that brought cotton farms to the flatlands around Phoenix. The water also helped with the fourth C: citrus. The fifth C was climate, which kept people out of Arizona for many years.

Then came air conditioning. In the years after World War II, Arizona became less dependent on federal largesse, except for its military bases and defense contracts. Businessmen, lawyers, developers, and water companies, notably the Salt River Project, built Arizona based on the opposite of New Deal principles: with minimal government and precious little regulation of business, a welcoming of new technological ideas, and a shunning of cultural liberalism. Their political champion was Barry Goldwater, Phoenix City Council member and senator and the nation's most recognizable conservative for much of the 1950s and 1960s. He helped to make Arizona solidly Republican, the only state to vote Republican for president in every election from 1952 to 1992.

Modern Arizona grew phenomenally, from 700,000 people immediately after the war to 3.6 million in 1990 and 6.5 million in 2008. For years, its growth was based on high technology and low taxes. Contrary to popular perception, this was not growth based on an influx of elderly retirees. Arizona may have Sun City, but just 13% of its residents are over 65, compared to 12% nationally. Neither was it based on subsidized farming, since cotton farms have been bought out by subdivision developers. The Valley around Phoenix lost nearly half its farmland between 1975 and 2000. It is explained partly, but only partly, by immigration. Arizona has attracted immigrants from Mexico and Latin America eager for entry-level jobs, so eager that many cross the lightly guarded border in the desert at the risk of death. Arizona still produces two-thirds of the nation's copper. But more than anything else, the engine of Arizona's growth was technology. Phoenix started attracting high-tech industries when Motorola built a research center for military electronics there in 1948. Big employers included Honeywell, Raytheon, Motorola, Intel, Avnet, and Northrop Grumman. Defense industries are important here. Arizona ranked No. 6 in Defense Department contracts in 2006. The state counts two Air Force bases and a Marine air station plus the huge Barry M. Goldwater Range, where many of America's pilots have been trained. In Phoenix and Tucson, another major engine of growth was real estate. In the early 1990s, Arizona's 10 biggest employers included four high-tech firms and four financial firms. In 2008, the largest employers included only two high-tech firms, while Wal-Mart and Banner Health led the list. But as housing prices started crashing in 2008, Arizona's sizzling growth rate, second in the nation in 2006, fell to 22nd in 2007 and was 46th in August 2008.

In recent years, Arizona has become the focal point of illegal immigration. With stronger border enforcement in Texas and a fence going up near San Diego, the hilly Arizona desert in Cochise and Santa Cruz counties became a major entry point for illegal immigrants. Thousands streamed in over ranchlands, heading north to Phoenix or west to California. Locals formed a Minuteman organization, reporting illegal border crossings to authorities and demanding stronger enforcement by the federal government. Anger at the flood of illegal immigrants contributed to the passage of ballot propositions: Proposition 200 in 2004 denied certain welfare benefits and required government employees to report illegal

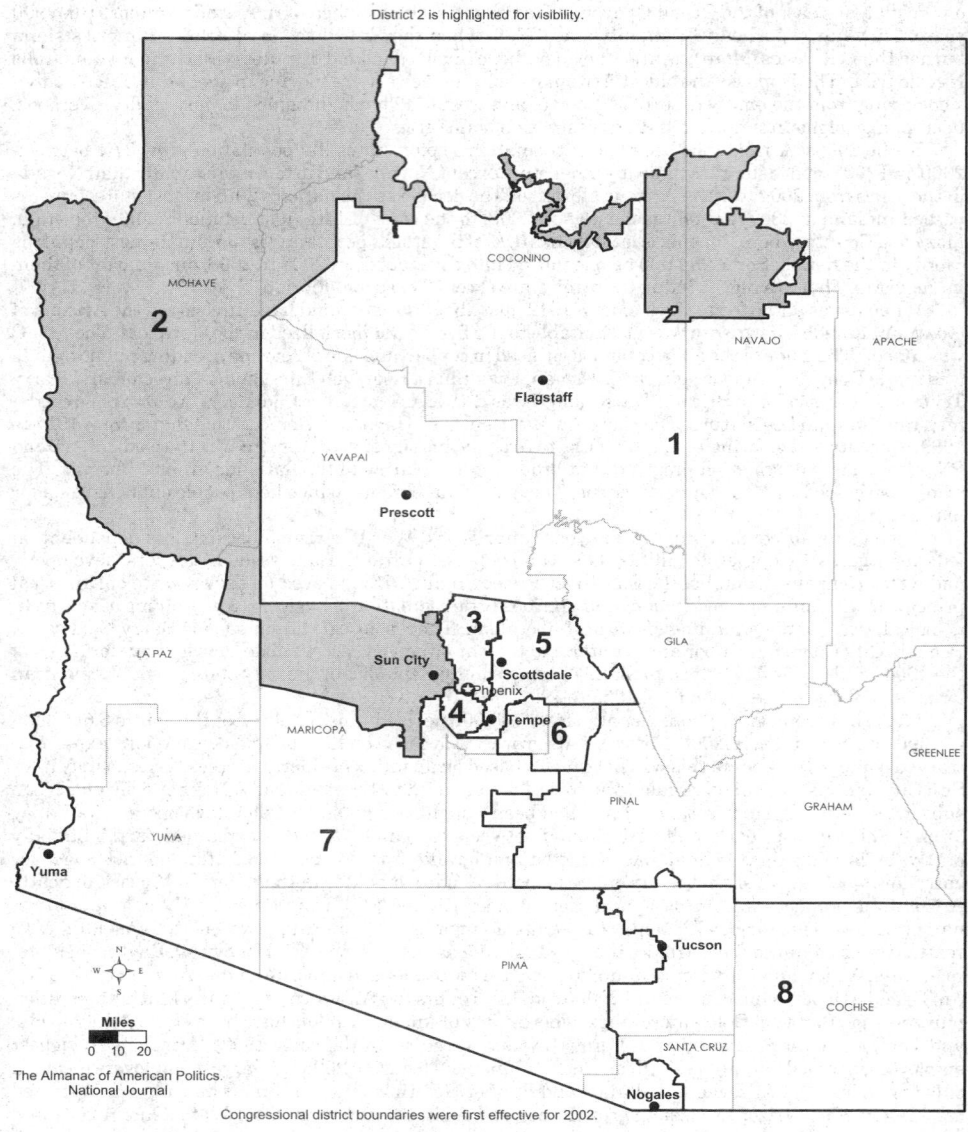

District 2 is highlighted for visibility.

The Almanac of American Politics.
National Journal

Congressional district boundaries were first effective for 2002.

residents, and Proposition 102 in 2006 denied punitive damages to illegal immigrants. Other ballot measures declared English Arizona's official language and denied illegal residents in-state tuition at state colleges. These were characterized by some as signs of bigotry, but they were supported by at least 40% of Hispanics as well as majorities of Anglo whites.

Arizona's congressional delegation was split on the remedy for illegal immigration. In 2007, Republican Sens. John McCain and Jon Kyl favored a comprehensive immigration bill creating a guest-worker program and a path to citizenship for the country's 12 million illegal residents, along with imposing tougher enforcement measures. But others in the delegation opposed it. When Congress failed to pass a bill that year, the Arizona Legislature stepped in and passed a law punishing employers who hire illegal immigrants, unless they used the federal E-Verify system to try to weed out illegal workers. Business licenses could be suspended for a first violation and revoked for a second. Democratic Gov. Janet Napolitano signed the bill in July 2007. It resulted in no prosecutions, but was upheld by the federal courts and, as Napolitano said, "Its benefit has been more on the deterrent side than the actual case side." Fast-food franchisees put on the November 2008 ballot a proposition to effectively repeal the law, but it was defeated 59%-41%, and lost in every county. Meanwhile, Maricopa County Sheriff Joe Arpaio continued to arrest illegal immigrants picked up in traffic stops and to work with federal immigration agents on deportation actions. Citizenship applications spiked upward, but there was also evidence that many illegal residents were leaving the state, as the number of construction jobs plummeted and the threat of punishment for employers began to have an impact. The Census Bureau reported a sharp drop in immigration in July 2008.

The collapse of the housing market and worsening national economy threaten Arizona's long-standing experiment with a robustly free-market economy. State taxes were slashed in the 1990s and remain relatively low. Arizona has had a profusion of charter schools, and is the home of the for-profit University of Phoenix. Many towns use private covenants rather than public zoning to regulate who can move where. For example, children are banned in Youngtown, near Phoenix. The Salt River District allocates precious water. Phoenix is the No. 3 metropolitan area for women business owners per capita, and there is a burgeoning number of Latino-owned businesses. But there is a downside. Arizona also has one of the highest percentages of people without health insurance, and there is a wide income and education gap between affluent native newcomers and poor immigrants.

This wide-openness is reflected in its politics. Arizona has had women governors since September 1997, when Jane Hull succeeded Fife Symington. In 1998, Arizona became the first state to elect women to all of its top five statewide down-ballot offices. When Napolitano, elected governor in 2002 and 2006, resigned in January 2009 to become President Obama's Homeland Security secretary, she was succeeded by Arizona Secretary of State Jan Brewer. It is one of the relatively few states with more registered Republicans than Democrats. Still, Democrats have become increasingly competitive. Bill Clinton carried Arizona in 1996, and Obama had hopes of doing so had the Republican nominee been anyone but native-son McCain. He and Kyl remain politically safe, but a majority of Arizona's U.S. House members are Democrats. The Legislature seems solidly Republican—the state House has been in GOP hands since 1966. But Democrats have won the governorship in four of the last eight elections, though Brewer's elevation has restored it to the Republicans.

Arizona's 1912 constitution authorized ballot initiatives, and as on immigration, the voters have made important policy decisions for the state. A 1998 initiative bars the Legislature from cavalierly overturning them. Sometimes they are not what one might predict from the generally conservative bent of the electorate. In November 2006, Arizona became the first state to reject a constitutional amendment barring same-sex marriage, apparently because the initiative also banned benefits for domestic partners. In November 2008, a similar measure, shorn of the partner-benefits clause, passed, but only by 56% to 44%—not much more than California's Proposition 8, which passed 52%-48%. And Arizona is, understandably, open to increased reliance on solar energy. It has long prided itself on its Wild West atmo-

Population		Household Income		Work	
Pop. 2007:	6,152,175	Under $15k:	12.1%	Private:	78.8%
State rank:	14th of 50	$15k to $50k:	39.2%	Government:	14.7%
Change since 2000:	Up 19.9%	$50k to $100k:	31.3%	Self-employed:	6.2%
Urban:	82.1%	$100k to $150k:	14.2%	Unemployment (3-yr. average):	3.6%
Rural:	17.9%	Over $150k:	3.2%	Poverty:	14.2%
Native of state:	35.4%	Median income:	$48,609	Blue collar:	22.2%
Not a citizen:	10.5%	**Home Value**		White collar:	59.3%
Area size:	113,998 sq. mi.	Under $100k:	16.1%	Khaki collar:	0.3%
Most populous cities		$100k to $300k:	51.6%	Other:	18.2%
1. Phoenix	1,440,018	$300k to $500k:	20.4%		
2. Tucson	520,482	$500k to $1 mil:	10.0%	**Age**	
3. Mesa	478,014	Over $1 million:	1.9%	Median age:	34.8 yrs.
4. Glendale	239,178	Median:	$221,800	More than 65 yrs:	12.8%
				Less than 18 yrs:	26.4%

Race/Ethnicity				Military Veterans		Registered Voters in 2008	
White:	59.6%	*Language*		% of Pop:	12.3%	D:	1,022,252 (34.2%)
Black:	3.3%	English:	72.1%	*Veterans by Period*		R:	1,118,587 (37.4%)
Hispanic:	29.0%	Spanish:	21.7%	WWII and before:	13.4%	Other:	846,612 (28.3%)
Asian:	2.3%	Asian:	1.5%	Korea:	13.1%	Voter turnout:	2,293,475
Native Am.:	4.1%	Other		Vietnam:	30.9%	Turnout as % of	
Hawaiian:	0.1%	European	2.1%	Gulf (pre-2001):	11.6%	voting age:	47.9%
Two+ races:	1.4%	**Education**		Gulf (post-2001):	6.9%	**Legislature**	
Ancestry		H.S. grad:	83.5%	Peace time:	24.0%	Senate:	12 D 18 R
German:	13.3%	College grad:	25.2%			House:	25 D 35 R
Irish:	8.7%	Grad degree:	9.2%				
English:	8.3%						

sphere, but Scottsdale politicians recently have pondered tearing down their "World's Most Western Town" signs.

Presidential politics   Arizona has tried every so often to make itself another Iowa or New Hampshire in presidential politics, with little success. In 1972, it had an early Democratic primary, and the improbable winner was Republican-turned-Democrat New York Mayor John Lindsay. His campaign went nowhere from there. In 1996, Arizona tried to set its primary on the same date as New Hampshire's; when that failed, the state set it one week later. The intended beneficiary was Texas Republican Sen. Phil Gramm, a conservative running with the support of John McCain. But Gramm pulled out of the race a week before New Hampshire, and Arizona became a battleground between Kansas Sen. Bob Dole, who now had McCain's support; conservative pundit Pat Buchanan, who urged his followers to "mount up and ride" after his narrow victory in New Hampshire; and magazine publisher Steve Forbes, who peppered the state with ads boosting his flat tax and attacking Washington politicians. The sight of Buchanan campaigning in a gunslinger costume with a black hat was a bit much, and he finished third, with 27%, and it was clear he had no chance to win the nomination. Dole finished second with 30%. Forbes won 33% and all the delegates, after which his campaign, like that of his fellow Easterner Lindsay a quarter-century before, went nowhere.

2008 Presidential Vote
McCain (R)...........................1,230,111   (54%)
Obama (D) 1,034,707   (45%)

2008 Democratic Presidential Primary
Clinton (D) 229,501   (50%)
Obama (D) 193,126   (42%)

2008 Republican Presidential Primary
McCain (R)..............................255,197   (47%)
Romney (R) 186,838   (34%)
Huckabee (R) 48,849   (9%)

2004 Presidential Vote
Bush (R)...............................1,104,294   (55%)
Kerry (D)................................893,524   (44%)

In 2000, Arizona tried again. McCain had irritated local Republicans enough that Gov. Jane Hull and other party leaders endorsed George W. Bush. McCain, however, won a solid victory in his home state in the February primary, but it was overshadowed by his victory the same day in Michigan. Arizona Democrats ran and paid for their own primary in March, because the state's February date was outside the "window" permitted by national Democratic Party rules. They allowed voting via the Internet, and about 35,000 Arizonans mouse-clicked their choices, another 20,000 voted by mail, and still others voted by computer or paper ballot at the polls. But the Internet voting was not flawless, and the primary didn't matter because Al Gore had already clinched the nomination. In 2004, a regular primary was held one week after New Hampshire, on February 3, the same day as contests in Delaware, Missouri, New Mexico, North Dakota, Oklahoma, and South Carolina. Democrats John Kerry and Wesley Clark were the only candidates who targeted the state, and Kerry got 43% of the vote to Clark's 26%. Only 603,000 voted in a state of 5.6 million people. In 2006, Arizona Democrats made a bid to have their state designated as the site for a caucus election soon after Iowa. But in August of that year, the Democratic National Committee picked Nevada instead.

So in 2008, Arizona settled for being another Super Tuesday state. The Republican primary was conceded to McCain, but having aroused the lasting hostility of some conservatives, he beat Mitt Romney by only 47% to 34%. Romney carried the 6th Congressional District (Mesa, Chandler) and rural Graham County, both with large Mormon populations. On the Democratic side, Hillary Rodham Clinton, with heavy support from Latinos, beat Barack Obama 50%–42%. Obama carried the upscale 5th Congressional District (Scottsdale, Tempe) and Coconino and Yavapai counties.

Native-son Barry Goldwater, born when Arizona was still a territory, carried the state in 1964, and it voted Republican in every presidential election from 1952 to 1992. But it has become more seriously contested since. Bill Clinton was competitive in 1992 and, with increased support in Phoenix and other metro areas, carried it 47%–44% in 1996. George W. Bush won here by only 51%–45%. He increased that victory to 55%–44% in 2004, as Kerry's campaign thought about targeting Arizona and then thought better of it. In 2008, Obama's campaign conceded the state to McCain, but he won by just 54%-45%, suggesting that Arizona, with its increasing number of Latino voters, could be a target state in 2012.

Congressional districting

111th Congress Lineup	
5 D	3 R
110th Congress Lineup	
4 D	4 R

Arizona gained two House seats in the 2000 census, after gaining one each in the censuses of 1960, 1970, 1980, and 1990. It is projected to gain two more in the 2010 census, though if growth slows in 2009 and 2010, it may gain just one. In any case, it will have gone from two seats to nine or 10 seats in 50 years. After the 2000 census, redistricting was done not by the Legislature but by a five-member Arizona Independent Redistricting Commission, a body created by ballot proposition in 2000. Two Republican and two Democratic legislators appoint four members, and the fifth, to be neither a Democrat nor a Republican, is picked by the other four. The commission held 66 hearings and meetings, and in October 2001 approved a plan. Democrats were disappointed because it didn't create a competitive seat in the Phoenix area, but commissioners said such a district could be created only by drawing grotesque lines that, in their view, would be gerrymandering. Democrats challenged the plan in court for not creating enough competitive seats, and the case bounced around the courts for years. As it turned out, there were more competitive congressional districts than the Democrats, or the Republicans, had thought. Democrats captured the 5th and 8th districts in 2006 and the 1st District in 2008, and now have a majority of the Arizona delegation for the first time since 1966. The commission will redistrict the House districts again after the 2010 census. Tucson's Pima County will be entitled to about 1.5 districts, a little more than it has now. Maricopa County will be entitled to six districts if Arizona gets a total of 10, and 5.5 if it gets a total of nine, compared to essentially five today.

Arizona's redistricting issues often also involve its two major Indian tribes. The Hopi have had disputes for many years with the far more numerous Navajo, whose reservation surrounds theirs. The 2000 redistricting commission decided that the Hopi should have a U.S. representative who doesn't also represent the Navajo. (Confusingly, most of the Hopi Reservation is in Navajo County and most of the Navajo Reservation is in Apache County.)

Governor

Jan Brewer (R)

Assumed office Jan. 2009, term expires Jan. 2011, 1st term; b. Sept. 26, 1944, Hollywood, CA; home, Glendale; Lutheran; married (John); 3 children (1 deceased).

Elected Office: AZ House, 1983–86; AZ Senate, 1987–96; Maricopa Co. Bd. of Supervisors, 1996–2002; AZ sec. of st., 2002–09.

Office: State Capitol, 1700 W. Washington, Phoenix, 85007, 602-542-4331; Fax: 602-542-1381; Web site: governor.state.az.us.

Election Results

2006 general	Janet Napolitano (D)	959,830	(63%)
	Len Munsil (R)	543,528	(35%)
2006 primary	Janet Napolitano (D)	unopposed	

Jan Brewer, a Republican, is the new governor of Arizona. She had been the secretary of state, but ascended to governor on Jan. 21, 2009, after Democratic Gov. Janet Napolitano resigned to become President Obama's secretary of Homeland Security. Brewer is the fifth secretary of state to succeed a governor—Arizona has no lieutenant governor—in state history. Brewer grew up in Los Angeles. Her father died of lung cancer when she was 11, and her mother started a small dress shop, where Brewer cleaned dressing rooms and worked the cash register. She got a degree in radiology from a California community college. In 1970, she married physician John Brewer and moved to Glendale in the West Valley near Phoenix. As a stay-at-home mom, she started attending school board meetings in 1981 and thought about running for the school board herself. Instead, a seat in the state Legislature opened, and she successfully ran for a House seat in 1982. She was re-elected in 1984 and then in 1986, won a seat in the state Senate, to which she was re-elected four times. In 1993, she became majority whip. She is a conservative who advocated tax cuts and voted against a Martin Luther King state holiday. She also opposed the 1988 impeachment of Republican Gov. Evan Mecham, who was charged with obstruction of justice and misuse of government funds. She backed charter schools and Arizona's open-enrollment law, which allows students to attend any public school of their choice. She sponsored the first living-will statute in the nation.

In 1996, residents of Sun City were incensed when the Maricopa County Board of Supervisors approved a .25% sales tax to build the Bank One Ballpark. Brewer decided to run for the West Valley seat on the board, was elected, and went on to become chairman. She helped persuade voters to support a .2% sales tax increase to build and upgrade county jails. Maricopa County is the fourth-largest county in the United States, and in 1996, it had serious financial problems, issuing $165 million in bonds to maintain cash flow. Brewer was regarded as a fiscal hawk, and by 2002 *Governing* magazine called Maricopa "one of the two best-managed large counties in the United States." Brewer also took the lead in planning a homeless shelter campus in downtown Phoenix, preserving open space in the West Valley mountains, and keeping new subdivisions away from Luke Air Force Base. In February 2002, she resigned to run for secretary of state. "I always wanted to be secretary of state," she said.

Brewer had two opponents in the Republican primary: Sal DiCiccio, a former Phoenix councilman, and Sharon Collins, an aide to Republican Gov. Jane Hull. DiCiccio criticized Brewer for not paying dues to a homeowners' association in Mexico, where she and her husband had a house. Brewer contested that assertion and criticized DiCiccio for filing late and inaccurate financial reports in a congressional race. Collins called for conducting elections entirely through mail-in ballots, as in Oregon. Brewer called for eliminating punch cards in the nine rural counties where they were used and using optical-scan ballots instead. Brewer won with 45% of the votes, to 34% for DiCiccio and 21% for Collins. The Democratic nominee was state Sen. Chris Cummiskey, who promised a summer academy for high school students and cooperation with colleges and universities to encourage young people to vote. This was a close election year in Arizona: Democratic Attorney General Janet Napolitano beat former GOP Rep. Matt Salmon for governor 46%-45%; Democrat Terry Goddard, a former mayor of Phoenix and a 1990 and 1994 gubernatorial nominee, was elected attorney general by 52%-45%; and Brewer beat Cummiskey 49%-46%.

Relations between Napolitano and Brewer were sometimes testy; Brewer battled to keep her Tucson office open in 2003 after Napolitano took over the space and gave her a conference room. In 2004, Democrats criticized Brewer for serving as state co-chairman of the Bush-Cheney campaign and for attending the 2004 Republican National Convention when Arizona was conducting its primary election on September 2. Brewer replied, "I did not give up my First Amendment rights when I was elected." Democrats were also critical of Brewer's defense and implementation of Proposition 200, passed by voters in 2004, which required voters to show identification and proof of citizenship to vote. In 2005, she and Goddard agreed that showing one piece of photo identification or two pieces of non-photo identification was sufficient. She was successful in getting optical-scan ballots in all counties, with special touch screens to enable the handicapped to vote unassisted, and in allowing ballots from military personnel overseas to be faxed in. When she was attacked by demonstrators for buying Diebold voting machines, which they argued are vulnerable to hacking, she called them "conspiracy theorists." She was re-elected in 2006 by a comfortable 57%-39%, while Napolitano was re-elected by 63%-35% and Goddard by 60%-40%.

In Arizona, the secretary of state is the designated successor of the governor and has gubernatorial powers when the incumbent is out of state. That produced tension in July 2005, when Napolitano vacationed in Russia. Brewer herself wrote in an opinion article in the *Arizona Republic* in 1994 that the duties of the office "do little to prepare that officeholder for the statewide leadership role required of a governor." The Brewers also suffered a personal tragedy in 2007, when they lost the middle of their three sons, John, to cancer.

As secretary of state, Brewer strove to avoid becoming isolated in the job. She continued to have a listed telephone number and drove to work in a convertible with the top down playing her favorite music, songs by ABBA in the musical *Mamma Mia*. Her ascent to the governorship came after the defeat of fellow Arizonan John McCain in the 2008 presidential race. President-elect Obama was impressed with Napolitano's experience as a prosecutor and border-state governor, and on Dec. 1, 2008, he announced that he would nominate Napolitano for the Homeland Security post. Some Democrats were perturbed because Brewer's elevation would give Republicans control of state government, and others feared that she would approve restrictions on gun ownership and on abortion that Napolitano had blocked. They also were concerned that she would have Arizona recede from the Western Climate Initiative, which Napolitano had supported. Brewer, referring to the fights between Napolitano and Republican legislative leaders, said, "I will reach out to both sides of the aisle and hope that we don't have that kind of fallout that we've seen in the past." She added, "I'm not on a mission to go in and do an across-the-board procedure of removing everyone from office. Certainly I want people who will be good for Arizona. People that will work with me. People that can find solutions, because we are in a situation in Arizona that is not real promising at this time."

Arizona, the nation's fastest or second fastest growing states for two decades, had experienced a real estate bubble as a result, and the bubble burst in 2007 as the recession set in. The considerable share of its economy in construction had severe problems. Napolitano prepared a final budget, which showed a $4.6 billion budget shortfall in the remaining 18 months of the biennium, a huge amount considering that the annual general fund is $9.9 billion. Shortly after taking office, Brewer told the *Arizona Daily Star* : "First I was worried, then I was concerned, and now I'm just angry to see what has happened and the irresponsible management that has led us to the brink of bankruptcy." She said raising taxes would have to be an option. Brewer quickly named former state Senate President Ken Bennett to fill her old job as secretary of state. And at her inauguration as governor, she said: "We must make sure that beleaguered businesses in California and other such overtaxed places hear the music of our commerce and our culture and see brighter prospects in the cities and towns across Arizona."

On January 30, after consulting with Brewer, Republican legislative appropriators approved a $1.6 billion reduction in spending, cutting $300 million from K-12 and higher education, eliminating emergency dental care and adult speech therapy, cutting $18 million intended for private-prison beds, and placing a one-year moratorium on scheduled bond sales of nearly $1 billion to finance improvements at the state's three public universities. They also restored the $1.6 million for Maricopa Sheriff Joe Arpaio that Napolitano, angry about his program targeting illegal aliens, had canceled. Early in 2009, Brewer also proposed a spring special election to approve a 1% increase in the 5.6% sales tax and expressed the hope that she could allow the state property tax to expire as scheduled in 2010.

Brewer assumed the governorship 22 months before the 2010 general election. Of the five secretaries of state who have ascended to the governorship in Arizona, only one, Hull in 1998, was elected governor in her own right. In early 2009, several Republicans were mentioned as possible primary challengers: former U.S. Transportation Secretary Mary Peters, state Treasurer Dean Martin, and former Arizona Republican state chairman John Munger. On the Democratic side, a possible challenger is Attorney General Goddard, the former Phoenix mayor and gubernatorial nominee who lost to Republican Fife Symington by only 52%-48% in 1990.

Senior Senator

John McCain (R)

Elected 1986, term expires 2010, 4th term; b. Aug. 29, 1936, Panama Canal Zone; home, Phoenix; U.S. Naval Academy, B.S. 1958, Natl. War Col., 1973–74; Episcopalian; married (Cindy); 7 children.

Military Career: Navy, 1958–80 (Vietnam).

Elected Office: U.S. House of Reps., 1982–86.

Professional Career: Dir., Navy Senate Liaison Ofc., 1977–81.

DC Office: 241 RSOB, 20510, 202-224-2235; Fax: 202-228-2862; Web site: mccain.senate.gov.

State Offices: Phoenix, 602-952-2410; Tempe, 480-897-6289; Tucson, 520-670-6334.

Committees: *Armed Services* (RMM of 11 R). *Energy & Natural Resources* (6th of 10 R): National Parks; Public Lands & Forests; Water & Power. *Health, Education, Labor & Pensions* (6th of 10 R). *Homeland Security & Governmental Affairs* (3rd of 6 R): Contracting Oversight; Federal Financial Management, Government Information, Federal Services & International Security (RMM); Investigations (Permanent). *Indian Affairs* (2nd of 6 R).

Group Ratings

	ADA	ACLU	AFS	LCV	ITIC	NTU	COC	ACU	CFG	FRC
2008	5	17	0	0	100	—	100	63	54	44
2007	10	—	0	0	—	—	100	80	94	—

National Journal Ratings

	2007 LIB — 2007 CONS		2008 LIB — 2008 CONS	
Economic	*%	—	*%	*%	—	*%
Social	40%	—	59%	*%	—	*%
Foreign	*%	—	*%	*%	—	*%
Composite	*%	—	*%	*%	—	*%

Key Votes of the 110th Congress

1. Raise CAFE standards	*	5. Make English official language	Y	9. Withdraw troops 3/08	*
2. Expand SCHIP	N	6. Path to citizenship	Y	10. Iran guard is terrorist group	*
3. Cap greenhouse gases	*	7. Fetus is unborn child	Y	11. Increase missile defense $	*
4. Bail out financial markets	Y	8. Prosecute hate crimes	*	12. Overhaul FISA	*

Election Results

2004 general	John McCain (R)	1,505,372	(77%)	($2,140,807)
	Stuart Starky (D)	404,507	(21%)	($12,716)
2004 primary	John McCain (R)	unopposed		

Prior Winning Percentages: 1998 (69%); 1992 (56%); 1986 (60%); 1984 House (78%); 1982 House (66%)

John McCain, Arizona's senior senator, is the 26th person to be nominated for the presidency by the Republican Party. McCain was born in the Canal Zone, the son and grandson of Navy admirals. (His married-to-the-military mother, Roberta McCain, at age 96, was one of his hardest-working campaign supporters; she danced at the podium at the Republican National Convention celebrating his nomination.) McCain graduated from the Naval Academy, fifth from the bottom of his class academically but high in demerits, and trained to be a fighter pilot. He volunteered for service in Vietnam, and flew ground-attack aircraft from carriers at sea. In July 1967, he was severely injured in a flight-deck explosion on the carrier USS *Forrestal*. McCain could have returned home, but refused. He continued to fly bombing runs over North Vietnam. That October, on his 23rd bombing mission, his A-4E Skyhawk was shot down by a missile, and McCain ejected from the plane, breaking both of his arms and a leg in a fall into Truc Back Lake near Hanoi. After pulling him from the water, his North Vietnamese "rescuers" crushed one of his shoulders with a rifle butt, bayoneted him, and then refused McCain medical treatment during his stay at a prison dubbed by U.S. soldiers the Hanoi Hilton. He spent the next five and a half years in prisoner-of-war camps, most of it in suffering as a result of repeated torture by his Communist captors. He spent two of those years in solitary confinement. That chapter of McCain's life is recounted in Robert Timberg's *The Nightingale's Song*, and in McCain's 1999 best-seller *Faith of My Fathers*. When he was offered release because of his father's rank, he refused to be let out ahead of those who had been imprisoned longer, and he returned to the United States only in March 1973 with other POWs.

McCain recovered in military hospitals, and despite intensive physical therapy, suffered permanent injuries, including restricted movement of his arms. On top of the many medals and commendations he received, his heroism was rewarded with a final assignment in a high-profile, noncombat role as the Navy's liaison to the Senate in 1977. McCain says the job launched his career in politics. He became close to several senators, including Republicans John Tower of Texas and William Cohen of Maine and Democrat Gary Hart of Colorado. On the personal front, McCain's first marriage failed. In 1980, he was remarried, to Cindy Lou Hensley, the wealthy daughter of a beer distributor from Phoenix. Two years later, he ran for an open House seat in Arizona. Attacked as an outsider, he responded, "The longest place I ever lived in was Hanoi." He won a four-way primary 32%-26%, and then the general election in November. In 1986, he easily defeated former Arizona state legislator Democrat Richard Kimball to win the Senate seat of conservative icon Barry Goldwater, who was retiring.

In Congress, McCain established a conservative voting record and, at first, a low profile. He was a strong supporter of the Reagan administration, and surprised some by opposing the president's dispatch of troops to Lebanon in 1982, arguing they were too few to be effective and too vulnerable to attack. Later, he backed President George H.W. Bush's war in the Persian Gulf in 1990, and his decision not to oust Iraqi Leader Saddam Hussein. In the 1990s, he worked with Massachusetts Sen. John Kerry, a Democrat and also a decorated Vietnam veteran, to end the trade embargo on Vietnam, and pressed for establishing diplomatic relations. He supported air strikes in Kosovo in 1999, but criticized the Clinton administration for ruling out ground troops in Bosnia and for not using "all necessary force" in Kosovo.

McCain strongly supported President Bush in the war on terrorism after September 11, and in his later decision to go to war with Iraq. McCain repeatedly pushed for more ground troops in Afghanistan and signed a letter urging that Iraq be the next target. He called for a special commission to investigate intelligence failures before the terrorist attacks. The final version of the law provided, at the insistence of relatives of 9/11 casualties, that McCain and Richard Shelby of Alabama get a veto over appointees to the commission. When Bush decided to invade Iraq in 2003, McCain continually pushed for a larger army and more troops to get the job done. He clashed frequently with Defense Secretary Donald Rumsfeld.

McCain finally concluded that the administration's handling of the war "will go down as one of the worst" mistakes in U.S. military history. He dismissed the recommendations of the Iraq Study Group in December 2006 and called for the surge of troops that Bush ordered in January 2007. To those who said the troops were already overextended, he replied, "There's only one thing worse than an overstressed Army and Marine Corps, and that's a defeated Army and Marine Corps." He strongly opposed Democratic calls for a troop withdrawal. When critics speculated that his support for the war would hurt his chances to become president, McCain said, "I would much rather lose an election than lose a war."

McCain's other locus of legislative activity has been the Commerce, Science, and Transportation Committee, which handles heavily lobbied regulatory issues and sets policy for just about every major industry in the nation. He tended to support deregulation, but he took little part in shaping the Telecommunications Act of 1996 and voted against it, arguing that it did not effectively ensure competition. As chairman of the committee from 2003 to 2005, he showed distaste for the political logrolling common on Capitol Hill, perhaps because his willingness to engage in business as usual once nearly ended McCain's career.

In the mid-1980s, McCain was one of the Keating Five senators investigated for allegedly pressuring regulators on behalf of Charles Keating's Arizona savings and loan. Ultimately, he was cited for exercising bad judgment for attempting to influence regulators overseeing Keating's thrift. Vindicated by his re-election in 1992, McCain launched himself as a reformer. When Republicans won control of Congress two years later, McCain sought out Democrat Russ Feingold of Wisconsin, who had a bill to clamp down on campaign finance abuses. For the next several years, the McCain-Feingold bills went through several transformations. Key features included prohibitions on soft money—the large, unregulated contributions to political parties that were ripe for abuse—and limits on issue advertising by independent organizations within 60 days of an election. The changes were fiercely opposed as an infringement on free speech and as a threat to the Republican Party by the powerful Mitch McConnell of Kentucky, who used threats of filibusters to prevent the bill from coming to a vote.

In early 2001, McCain threatened to tie up the Senate unless Majority Leader Trent Lott, R-Miss., set aside time for debate on the issue. In March 2001, after two weeks of civilized but spirited debate, during which McCain and Feingold fended off several poison-pill amendments, the legislation passed April 2 by a 59-41 vote. An amendment by Fred Thompson, R-Tenn., and Dianne Feinstein, D-Calif., was passed to raise limits on individual contributions from $1,000 to $2,000, but the bill retained the soft-money ban and the limit on issue ads prior to the election, which some senators felt would be struck down by the courts as an unconstitutional ban of free speech. The House passed its version of the bill in February 2002, and the bill became law in March 2002. Most of it has since been upheld by the U.S. Supreme Court.

McCain seems to believe that elected officials should act, like military officers, out of a sense of honor and duty, without regard for how it affects their electoral prospects or the interests of their constituents. Another of his legislative crusades has been his war on earmarks, the practice among lawmakers of slipping special, often high-dollar projects into spending bills to benefit a particular congressional district or state. In 2001, McCain was the only Republican to vote against a water projects bill, charging that it contained $1.2 billion in wasteful earmarks. Each year, McCain highlighted the pork-barrel spending he found in the appropriations bills, to the growing irritation of his colleagues in both parties, who were accustomed to using earmarks to score points with constituents at election time. But eventually McCain's lonely campaign was joined by conservatives in the House, and the issue was a factor in the 2006 and 2008 elections.

McCain's generally conservative voting record has as many quirks as the man himself. He supported funding of embryonic-stem-cell research, in opposition to most other Republicans. With liberal Democrat Kerry, he proposed fuel-efficiency standards of 36 miles per gallon for cars and light trucks by 2015. And with independent Sen. Joseph Lieberman of Connecticut, he co-authored a bill to reduce carbon dioxide emissions. McCain opposed the constitutional amendment to ban same-sex marriage as "antithetical in every way to the core philosophy of Republicans. It usurps from the states a fundamental authority they have always possessed and imposes a federal remedy for a problem that most states believe does not confront them."

His biggest act of ideological heresy in recent years came on the issue of immigration. "The truth is, border enforcement alone does not work," McCain said, as most conservatives were pursuing tougher enforcement strategies. McCain sponsored a guest-worker law, which would provide six-year temporary-worker visas and three-year visas for those who are here illegally now. He also co-sponsored with fellow Arizona Republican Jon Kyl a bill to fund border-security measures. He opposed Arizona's Proposition 200, which would cut off public benefits to illegal immigrants, arguing that it would "delay, possibly derail, the search for a solution." In 2005, McCain and liberal Sen. Edward Kennedy of Massachusetts sponsored an immigration bill that gave illegals a path to legalization, allowing them to obtain two three-year visas and then "get in the back of the line" of legal immigrants. "Some Americans believe we must find all these millions, round them up, and send them back to the countries they came from. I don't know how you do that. And I don't know why you would want to," McCain said. But a comprehensive bill failed in 2006 and again in June 2007.

McCain's quest for the presidency began with the 2000 election. In 1999, he decided to skip the caucuses in dovish and ethanol-enthusiastic Iowa (McCain had long denounced ethanol subsidies as pork-barrel spending) to concentrate on New Hampshire, where he traveled around in his "Straight Talk Express" bus. At first, only a few reporters traveled with him and crowds were sparse. But McCain was striking a chord. To increasingly larger and more enthusiastic crowds, he told his personal story in self-deprecating terms, and pledged, "I will never tell you a lie." He talked about defense and foreign-policy issues—the only candidate to spend much time doing so—and invariably called for campaign finance regulation. On the campaign bus, McCain was always available to answer reporters' questions and banter with the press while making fun of his aides. McCain did not have much support from his colleagues. Only four fellow senators endorsed him. Back home, Republican Gov. Jane Hull, who had had her fill of McCain's sometimes abrasive treatment, endorsed Texas Gov. George W. Bush, and the *Arizona Republic* wrote editorials warning of McCain's "volcanic" temper. But the strength of feeling among his ever-larger crowds was real, and on Feb. 1, McCain beat Bush by an impressive 49%-31%. Suddenly he became, if not the front-runner, at least the front-runner's most serious opponent.

From there, the "Straight Talk Express" had mixed success. It went to South Carolina, where both the Republican establishment and Christian conservatives lined up with Bush. The campaigning got negative, but what hurt even more was McCain's failure to win over self-identified Republicans. His emphasis on campaign finance regulation and his criticisms of Bush's tax plan for giving too much to the rich helped with independents, but sounded like enemy talk to Republicans. On Feb. 18, Bush won 53%-42% in South Carolina, in what turned out to be a decisive victory. The race continued, with McCain running about even with Bush among self-identified Republicans, way ahead among self-identified independents, but way behind among Republicans in Southern states. McCain's most striking win was in Michigan that February, where he prevailed 50%-43%, among an atypical electorate: 17% of Republican primary voters were self-identified Democrats, 35% were independents, and only a minority were Republicans.

McCain might have done better had he emphasized other issues on which he had consistently taken stands in line with most Republicans' thinking, such as national defense, tax cuts (he had a tax-cut plan himself, but he spent less time on it than on attacking Bush's), abortion rights, and Social Security individual investment accounts. Instead, after South Carolina, he gave a speech in Virginia Beach attacking the religious right, and in an offhand comment on the bus, called Pat Robertson and Jerry Falwell "forces of evil." McCain lost in Virginia and Washington on February 29. On Super Tuesday, March 7, McCain won in Massachusetts, Connecticut, Rhode Island, and Vermont. But he lost decisively in New York, Ohio, and California. He suspended his campaign in March, and two months later, grudgingly endorsed Bush.

Four years later, as Bush headed into his 2004 re-election campaign, McCain was a major national figure, with high positives among Republicans and very low negatives among Democrats. Always enchanted with him, the press gave McCain plenteous coverage. As Kerry, his fellow Vietnam veteran, clinched the Democratic nomination in March 2004, there was speculation that he would ask McCain to be his vice presidential nominee. Polls showed Kerry-McCain running far ahead of Bush-Cheney. After some days of speculation and some talks with Kerry, McCain firmly rejected the idea. "I am a pro-life, deficit-hawk, free-trade Republican," he said. Subsequently, the Bush and McCain camps made peace. In June 2004, McCain appeared with Bush at a campaign stop in Nevada and strongly endorsed him. When the Swift Boat Veterans for Truth ads appeared against Kerry, McCain called them "dishonorable" and said they should be dropped from the air. When Bush declined to join that demand, he didn't press the issue further, and said that he had advised Kerry against mentioning the war, as he had done in his 2000 campaign, and to let others do it. In August, he asked Kerry to stop running an ad showing him criticizing Bush in 2000, and Kerry did. At the Republican National Convention, McCain delivered another eloquent speech unequivocally endorsing Bush. "He has been tested and has risen to the most important challenge of our time, and I salute him," McCain said.

In the 2006 election season, McCain traveled around the country to support Republican candidates, raising more than $10 million for them. In May 2006, he delivered identical commencement speeches at Liberty University, where he was welcomed by Falwell, and The New School, where he was welcomed by former Democratic colleague Bob Kerrey of Nebraska. His long derision of pork-barrel spending by then had become a national issue. McCain voiced more frequently and fervently his long-standing opposition to abortion rights. Even so, many conservatives were not enthusiastic about McCain, given his stands on campaign finance, immigration, and carbon dioxide emissions.

The skepticism among the conservative GOP base doomed McCain's early strategy in 2007, which was to campaign as the next-in-line Republican for the presidential nomination in 2008. By early 2007, he was behind New York's Rudolph Giuliani in the polls, and he fell far short of his fundraising goals, raising just $13.6 million in the first quarter of 2007, behind Giuliani and Massachusetts' Mitt Romney. By late June, the McCain campaign was broke. Its opulent headquarters was closed, and the campaign's top managers were fired, replaced with McCain stalwart Rick Davis and Bush-Cheney veteran Steve Schmidt. Backed into a corner, McCain adopted the campaign strategy that some of the best consultants rely on—campaign on what you believe in. And, he had a backup strategy that even the worst consultants are ashamed to advance—wait for all the other candidates' strategies to fail.

They both worked. After a spring trip to Iraq, McCain commented in July 2007 that he was convinced the troop surge strategy was working and praised the outcome despite near-universal skepticism in the press. In September, he launched his "No Surrender" tour. In the GOP primary debates, McCain was treated respectfully and uncritically by his opponents, while he was quick to jab at any who expressed skepticism about the surge. Meanwhile, his opponents' strategies started to fail. Romney's poll numbers were stalled at about 30%. Tennessee's Fred Thompson took months to announce he was running, then seemed strangely unenergetic. Judging that the field was stacked against him in early contests, New York's Rudy Giuliani decided to wait until the Florida primary. Only Mike Huckabee, the former minister and Arkansas governor, exceeded expectations, running second in the Iowa straw poll in August 2007 and first, ahead of the free-spending Romney, in the Iowa caucuses on Jan. 3, 2008.

As in 2000, McCain had written off dovish Iowa. He focused on the New Hampshire primary, and campaigned hard in that state. On January 8, he beat Romney, who owned a vacation home in New Hampshire, 37%-32%. "Mac is back," chanted the crowd on Election Night.

Next up was Michigan, where Romney had grown up and where his father was governor 40 years before. Romney promised to bring back jobs in the state's important automobile industry, while McCain stated bluntly that many jobs would never return. With fewer crossovers than in 2000, Michigan gave Romney 39% and McCain 30%. From Michigan, it was on to South Carolina, where McCain had lost decisively in 2000. This was the one real four-way Republican contest in 2008. McCain, with 33%, came out ahead of Huckabee, with 30%. Thompson undoubtedly took votes away from fellow Southerner Huckabee and got 16%. Romney was fourth with 15%.

In critical and always baffling Florida on January 29, GOP Gov. Charlie Crist delivered a surprise endorsement of McCain. Meanwhile, support was draining from Giuliani, who was depending so heavily on the state. That was especially true among Miami's Cuban-Americans, who were going to McCain. The result was a 36%-31% victory for McCain over Romney. A few days later on Super Tuesday, February 5, McCain effectively sewed up the nomination, winning absolute majorities (his first) in New York, New Jersey, and Connecticut and winning a 1% victory over Huckabee in Missouri. He racked up victories in states as diverse as California, Illinois, Oklahoma, and Delaware. Two days later, Romney withdrew. Huckabee stayed in the race for another month.

The Republican Party's winner-take-all delegate allocation rules allowed McCain to cinch the nomination with narrow pluralities—5% in New Hampshire, 3% in South Carolina, 5% in Florida, 1% in Missouri, and 7% in California. This gave Republicans a nominee out of sync with the party's base supporters on some important issues. Yet, at the same time, he was admired by some hard-core conservatives for his support of the troop surge and for enduring his increasingly negative treatment by the national press. By late spring, McCain had consolidated the Republican base, but it was smaller than in 2004, and not sufficiently motivated to come anywhere close to matching the fundraising feats of Democrat Barack Obama. Working against McCain were Bush's low job rating, an increasing Democratic advantage in party identification, doubts about the course of the economy, the continuing unpopularity of the war in Iraq, and the enthusiasm among young and black voters for Obama. Another factor was McCain's own campaign finance law. Obama eschewed federal funding and was able to massively outspend McCain, who had little choice but to take public financing.

In these circumstances, what is perhaps surprising is that McCain made a contest of it and that he was actually leading during part of the fall campaign. He sought to portray himself, more than Obama, as an agent of change. After Obama chose 36-year Senate veteran Joe Biden of Delaware as his running mate, McCain chose the two-year governor of Alaska, Sarah Palin. Her initial appearance in Ohio and her speech before the Republican National Convention sparked huge enthusiasm among the Republican base and, for the first time, enabled the McCain campaign to muster volunteer and fundraising efforts competitive with Obama's. Palin's record of defeating powerful Republicans in Alaska underlined McCain's message of change and reform, and polls after the convention showed a sharp narrowing of the race in states like Washington, Oregon, North Dakota, Minnesota, Wisconsin, and Michigan. For about two weeks, the McCain-Palin ticket actually led Obama-Biden by narrow margins.

Whether this was a sustainable lead or just a temporary post-convention bounce cannot be conclusively established. On September 15, Lehman Brothers went into bankruptcy, and a financial crisis ensued. The same day, McCain said, "The fundamentals of our economy are strong." Four days later, Treasury Secretary Henry Paulson and Federal Reserve Chairman Ben Bernanke called for a $700 billion bailout of the financial markets. Obama overtook McCain and never relinquished his lead after that. On September 24, McCain announced he was suspending his campaign, pulling his television ads, and returning to the Capitol to work on the financial industry bill. He said he might not appear at the first presidential debate scheduled two days later. Obama coolly said that the president had to tend to more than one thing at a time, and the debate went off. When the House rejected the financial bailout on September 29, McCain was blamed for not bringing along a sufficient number of House Republicans. He received precious little credit when revised legislation passed the Senate on October 1 and the House on October 3.

In the rhetoric war, McCain attacked Obama sharply on taxes, energy, and other issues in October, but modulated his attacks on October 10, saying, "I want to be president of the United States and obviously I do not want Senator Obama to be, but I have to tell you, I have to tell you he is a decent person, and a person that you do not have to be scared of as president of the United States." He criticized Obama for saying he wanted to "spread the wealth around," but when asked in a debate about the economy, McCain fell back on his determination to stop spending on earmarks, which could hardly be viewed as a comprehensive economic agenda. McCain refused to allow his campaign to use as a campaign tactic Obama's 20-year relationship with the Rev. Jeremiah Wright of Chicago, who had made controversial, racially loaded remarks during the campaign.

In the final days of the campaign, Obama avoided mistakes. He won 53%-46%, the best Democratic percentage since 1964. Obama got 95% support from African-American voters, and he won 66%-32% among voters under age 30. Among those older than 30, McCain lost by only 50%-49%. On Election Night, McCain made a gracious concession speech, saying, "Senator Obama has achieved a great thing for himself and for his country."

After the election, McCain continued to weigh in on major issues, even as the spotlight moved decisively to the new Obama administration. And he seemed unlikely to draw a serious primary challenge in 2010. General elections in 1992, 1998, and 2004 were no problem for him, but his 54%-45% presidential victory in Arizona in 2008, and his relatively low showing among the state's growing number of Latinos (whom he lost 56%-41%), suggest that he might have more serious competition in 2010. The appointment of Gov. Janet Napolitano as secretary of Homeland Security, however, presumably removes the state's most formidable Democrat from the race.

Junior Senator

Jon Kyl (R)

Elected 1994, term expires 2012, 3rd term; b. April 25, 1942, Oakland, NE; home, Phoenix; U. of AZ, B.A. 1964, L.L.B. 1966; Presbyterian; married (Caryll); 2 children.

Elected Office: U.S. House of Reps., 1986–94.

Professional Career: Practicing atty., 1966–86; Chmn., Phoenix Chamber of Commerce, 1984–85.

DC Office: 730 HSOB, 20510, 202-224-4521; Fax: 202-224-2207; Web site: kyl.senate.gov.

State Offices: Phoenix, 602-840-1891; Tucson, 520-575-8633.

Committees: *Assistant Minority Leader & Whip. Finance* (4th of 10 R): Health Care; Social Security, Pensions & Family Policy; Taxation, IRS Oversight & Long-Term Growth (RMM). *Judiciary* (4th of 7 R): Administrative Oversight & the Courts; Constitution; Immigration, Refugees & Border Security; Terrorism & Homeland Security (RMM).

Group Ratings

	ADA	ACLU	AFS	LCV	ITIC	NTU	COC	ACU	CFG	FRC
2008	0	14	0	18	40	79	63	96	90	100
2007	5	—	0	13	—	86	60	100	92	—

National Journal Ratings

	2007 LIB	—	2007 CONS		2008 LIB	—	2008 CONS
Economic	0%	—	97%		0%	—	96%
Social	26%	—	72%		0%	—	79%
Foreign	21%	—	73%		0%	—	84%
Composite	18%	—	83%		7%	—	93%

Key Votes of the 110th Congress

1. Raise CAFE standards	N	5. Make English official language Y	9. Withdraw troops 3/08	N
2. Expand SCHIP	N	6. Path to citizenship Y	10. Iran guard is terrorist group Y
3. Cap greenhouse gases	N	7. Fetus is unborn child Y	11. Increase missile defense $ Y
4. Bail out financial markets	Y	8. Prosecute hate crimes N	12. Overhaul FISA Y

Election Results

2006 general	Jon Kyl (R)	814,398	(53%)	($15,571,727)
	Jim Pederson (D)	664,141	(43%)	($14,709,241)
2006 primary	Jon Kyl (R)	unopposed		

Prior Winning Percentages: 2000 (79%); 1994 (54%); 1992 House (59%); 1990 House (61%); 1988 House (87%); 1986 House (65%)

Jon Kyl is Arizona's junior senator, and although he's often overshadowed by Arizona's John McCain, Kyl is a political force in his own right. He was the unanimous choice of his colleagues in late 2007 for minority whip, the No. 2 ranking post in the Senate Republican leadership. Kyl (*KILE*) was born in Nebraska, but his family moved to Iowa when he was young. His father was a school principal who went on to become active in politics and was elected to the U.S. House in 1958 and again in 1966. He encouraged his son's interest in politics and brought him to Washington with him during the summers. Kyl fell in love with Arizona when he did his undergraduate work at the University of Arizona, and then stayed to get his law degree there. He settled in Phoenix and practiced law while also working on Republican campaigns and heading that city's Chamber of Commerce. Kyl won the heavily Republican 4th District seat in the U.S. House in 1986. In the decisive GOP primary, he defeated former Rep. John Conlan (1973–77), who had support from the Religious Right, 60%-28%. While in the House, Kyl had a solidly conservative voting record and developed expertise in missile defense systems. He was a vocal critic of fellow members who had overdrafts at the House bank, which grew into a major scandal in 1992, and that helped him establish credibility as a reformer. He was well positioned two years later to run for the Senate seat of Dennis DeConcini, a three-term Democrat who was retiring after being named one of the "Keating Five" senators accused of pressuring regulators on behalf of a shady savings and loan owner. Kyl had no primary opposition. His Democratic opponent was one-term Rep. Sam Coppersmith. With far more money, Kyl ran ads with a home-movie flavor showing him traveling through the Arizona desert, dressed in jeans and working on ranches, and talking about how he and his wife fell in love with the state.

(He has climbed Camelback Mountain "more than 1,000 times.") Coppersmith stressed his support for abortion rights. Kyl won easily, 54%-40%.

In the Senate, the unassuming Kyl quietly built a reputation for hard work, for his knowledge of the nuances of policy, and for his ability to play the inside game. *Time* magazine named him one of the 10 best senators in a 2006 feature story; *Washingtonian* magazine, after surveying congressional aides, said in 2008 that he was considered one of the smartest, most hardworking members of Congress. In December 2007, GOP senators unanimously chose Kyl to be minority whip, making him the chamber's highest-ranking Republican after Minority Leader Mitch McConnell of Kentucky. Kyl also sits on the influential Finance Committee, where he is the senior Republican on the Subcommittee on Taxation and Internal Revenue Service Oversight. He started his rise in the leadership as chairman of the Republican Steering Committee in 2001. He became Republican Policy Committee chairman in 2003, and chairman of the Republican Conference, the third-ranking post, in 2007. (For a fairly reserved conservative, Kyl has a racy side: He is a big fan of fast cars and has been seen spotted driving the lead car around the track in warm-up laps at Phoenix International Raceway.)

In the leadership, Kyl did his share to promote President Bush's agenda in Congress, but he sometimes took principled stands in opposition to the Republican president. In 2007, he was harshly critical of the administration's ouster of eight U.S. attorneys around the country, which many viewed as retribution for their failure to aggressively prosecute Democratic officeholders. Kyl called the firings "ham-fisted" and told *The Arizona Republic:* "Everybody acknowledges that the attorney general and the president had the absolute right to dismiss any of these individuals. But the fact that they had the right to do that doesn't necessarily make it a good idea." Kyl's generally positive reviews in the press took a negative turn in 2007 when he used Senate prerogatives to hold up a bipartisan bill to end the sometimes years-long delays in obtaining government information under freedom of information laws. Kyl said he was concerned that the law could force the release of sensitive Justice Department information about ongoing litigation or criminal cases. The Society of Professional Journalists dubbed him "Senator Secrecy."

Kyl is a major player on defense policy. He was one of the staunchest congressional champions of a missile defense system to protect the United States from nuclear attack. In 1997, he and Republican Sen. Jesse Helms of North Carolina led the losing fight against the Chemical Weapons Convention. Learning from that experience, Kyl organized the winning battle to reject the Comprehensive Test Ban Treaty, an international agreement to halt all underground nuclear tests with a maximum force equal to 150,000 tons of TNT. President Clinton sent the treaty to the Senate for ratification in 1997. Kyl studied the details and convinced Republican colleagues that compliance by other nuclear-armed countries would not be verifiable and the terms of the treaty not enforceable.

Kyl told then-Republican Majority Leader Trent Lott that he had 34 solid votes against the test-ban treaty, enough to prevent ratification. Unaware of Kyl's efforts, Democrats wrote Helms, the Foreign Relations Committee chairman, in July 1999 demanding that the treaty be brought to the floor for a vote. Democrat Byron Dorgan of North Dakota even famously promised to "plant myself on the floor like a potted plant" until the CTBT was considered. The Democrats believed that 25 Republicans could be persuaded to vote for the treaty, and concurred when Lott promised to bring it up in October. Only then did Senate Democrats and the Clinton White House discover that Kyl had done his work well: The CTBT did not even get a majority of votes, much less the two-thirds required for ratification, and was defeated 48-51.

Kyl strongly supported the Bush administration on the wars in Afghanistan and Iraq, and defended Bush when no weapons of mass destruction were found in Iraq. "The reality is, no one was duped," Kyl said. We were all working off the same data. Reasonable people reached different conclusions about what to do based on a commonly understood set of facts." He is the ranking Republican on the Judiciary Committee's Terrorism, and Homeland Security Subcommittee. Before September 11, he and Democratic Sen. Dianne Feinstein of California co-sponsored a bill to prepare U.S. defenses for attacks by terrorists with chemical and biological weapons; in November 2001, they introduced a bill to establish a comprehensive lookout database that would combine information from the Central Intelligence Agency, the Federal Bureau of Investigation, and the State Department. In that period, Kyl continually pointed up problems with lax State Department visa policies—notably the Visa Express program in Saudi Arabia, which delegated visa issuance to travel agents and enabled most of the September 11 hijackers to enter the United States.

Immigration is Kyl's other big focus on Judiciary, and it has brought him both success and great political pain. For years, Kyl was on the side of many Arizonans who favored a beefed-up Border Patrol, better tracking of legal immigrants, and reimbursements to states and localities for the costs of hospitalizing and incarcerating illegal aliens. He and his constituents took a generally dim view of bipartisan bills in recent years that attempted to address illegals already in the county by allowing them into guest-worker programs and giving them a path to citizenship. He was often at odds with his powerful home-state colleague, John McCain, who sponsored a bipartisan bill with liberal Democratic Sen. Edward Kennedy of Massachusetts. Kyl favored a guest-worker program only if it required immigrants to first return home and apply for work permits before seeking jobs in the United States. That proposal failed, but Kyl did succeed in attaching an amendment to a defense spending bill that provided $1.8 billion for 370 miles of fencing along the U.S.-Mexico border. In 2006, President Bush signed into law a bill that allowed construction to begin on a 700-mile border fence but provided no new money for the project.

Once he reached the upper echelon of leadership, Kyl came under increased pressure to find a compromise on immigration. In 2007, he surprised his supporters by backing a compromise immigration bill that established a temporary guest-worker program and a path to legalization for millions of undocumented workers. The bill ultimately died in Congress, but not before Kyl took a thumping. Fellow Republicans accused him of supporting "amnesty" for illegal immigrants, and one state senator said that the legislation would foster an "invasion by illegal aliens." Another Republican state senator told *The Arizona Republic* that the bill had destroyed the party's volunteer recruitment efforts. Describing the reaction back home in May 2007, Kyl said, "Yes, I have learned some new words from some of my constituents."

Water is one of the most sensitive issues in Arizona. For years Kyl had worked mostly behind the scenes on settling American Indian claims to Colorado and Gila river water and an ongoing intergovernmental dispute about how much money Arizona should pay the federal government for the Central Arizona Project, completed in 1993 at a cost of $3.6 billion. With McCain as co-sponsor and with the support of the Arizona House delegation, Kyl succeeded in passing the Arizona Water Settlement Act in 2004, which resolved Indian lawsuits against Arizona and New Mexico and set Arizona's reimbursement to the federal government at $1.65 billion. It was the most far-reaching Indian water settlement in history.

Kyl was the lead Senate sponsor of an Internet gambling ban and a bill prohibiting credit card companies from processing online wagers. The House in July 2006 overwhelmingly passed a similar bill, and later that year Bush signed legislation that included a ban on interstate and international online gambling transactions. (A group of hopping-mad poker players started an online fundraising drive to support Kyl's 2006 re-election opponent.)

Kyl had no difficulty winning re-election in 2000: No Democrat filed to run against him, and he won 79% of the vote. His opponent in 2006 was former state Democratic Chairman Jim Pederson, a wealthy real estate developer who had revitalized the state party by pouring millions of dollars of his personal wealth into it.

Kyl portrayed Pederson as inexperienced and ran ads accusing him of attempting to buy the Senate seat and of supporting amnesty for illegal immigrants because he favored a guest-worker program. Pederson painted Kyl as a Washington insider and part of its "special-interest" culture, while also tying him to the unpopular president. Pederson called for the resignation of Defense Secretary Donald Rumsfeld and for conditions to bring U.S. troops home from Iraq. Surveys showed Kyl leading Pederson throughout the campaign but polling less than 50%. Pederson spent nearly $15 million on the race, $11 million of it his own money; Kyl spent slightly more. Five days before the election, the Democratic Senatorial Campaign Committee poured $1 million into the state to boost Pederson. Kyl won 53%-43%, carrying all but four counties and the Phoenix metro area. He lost Flagstaff's Coconino County and Tucson's Pima County. Pederson won the Latino vote, but by only 54%-41%, and the African-American vote by only 53%-40%.

Kyl had signaled early in the 2006 election season that he would run for a third term, breaking a campaign promise to serve no more than two terms.

FIRST DISTRICT

Ann Kirkpatrick (D)

Elected 2008, 1st term; b. March 14, 1950, McNary; home, Flagstaff; U. of AZ, B.A. 1972, J.D. 1979.; Catholic; married (Roger Curley); 2 children.

Elected Office: AZ House, 2004–07.

Professional Career: Coconino dep. co. atty., 1980–81; Pima Co. dep. atty., 1981–85; Practicing atty., 1985–1990; Sedona city atty., 1990–91; Instructor, Coconino Comm. Col., 2005.

DC Office: 1123 LHOB, 20515, 202-225-2315; Fax: 202-226-9739; Web site: kirkpatrick.house.gov.

State Offices: Prescott, 928-445-3434.

Committees: *Homeland Security* (12th of 20 D): Border, Maritime & Global Counterterrorism; Intelligence, Information Sharing & Terrorism Risk Assessment; Transportation Security & Infrastructure Protection. *Small Business* (6th of 17 D): Finance & Tax; Rural Development, Entrepreneurship & Trade. *Veterans' Affairs* (17th of 18 D): Disability Assistance & Memorial Affairs; Economic Opportunity.

Group Ratings and Key Votes: Newly Elected

Election Results

2008 general	Ann Kirkpatrick (D)	155,791	(56%)	($1,997,089)
	Sydney Hay (R)	109,924	(39%)	($675,723)
	Brent Maupin (I)	9,394	(3%)	($30,467)
2008 primary	Ann Kirkpatrick (D)	26,734	(47%)	
	Mary Titla (D)	18,428	(33%)	
	Howard Shanker (D)	8,056	(14%)	
	Jeffrey Brown (D)	3,376	(6%)	

Population		Race/Ethnicity		Work	
Pop. 2007:	724,275	White:	57.9%	Private:	69.5%
Change since 2000:	Up 12.9%	Black:	1.3%	Government:	23.3%
Urban:	55.5%	Hispanic:	18.3%	Self-employed:	6.9%
Rural:	44.5%	Asian:	0.6%	Blue collar:	25.7%
Area size:	58,714 sq. mi.	Native Am.:	20.2%	White collar:	52.5%
		Hawaiian:	0.1%	Khaki collar:	0.1%
Age		Two+ races:	1.4%	Other:	21.7%
Median age:	36.1 yrs.	*Ancestry*		Median income:	$40,448
More than 65 yrs:	14.6%	German:	12.4%	Median home value:	$163,100
Less than 18 yrs:	25.2%	English:	9.5%	Poverty:	19.1%
Education		Irish:	8.5%		
H.S. grad:	81.6%			**Military Veterans**	
College grad:	19.3%			% of Pop:	13.2%
Grad degree:	7.6%				

Beyond Phoenix, Arizona is a vast state of stunning beauty: the awe-inspiring Grand Canyon, the subtle pastel hues of the Painted Desert, the sheer cliff walls of Canyon de Chelly, the still waters of Lake Powell, the mountainous pine forests around Flagstaff, and the rust-and-rosy red rocks of Sedona. It is also has man-made landmarks: The celebrated U.S. 66, now mostly superseded by Interstate 40, the old gold mining camp of Prescott, home since 1888 of America's oldest annual rodeo. Jerome, a mining town built improbably on hillside stilts, has been reborn as an artist colony. There are old copper mining towns like Globe.

2008 Presidential Vote		
McCain (R)	157,160	(54%)
Obama (D)	127,790	(44%)

2004 Presidential Vote		
Bush (R)	139,221	(54%)
Kerry (D)	117,673	(46%)

Cook Partisan Voting Index: R + 6

All of these places are in the 1st Congressional District of Arizona, which includes over half the state and is larger than Pennsylvania. It covers most of northern Arizona, except for Mohave County and the Hopi Indian Reservation and a narrow band of land connecting them. It reaches south to the northern edges of the Phoenix and Tucson metro areas. The 1st is the home of the nation's largest Indian population, and a full 20% of its residents identify themselves as American Indians. There are several reservations here—Fort Apache, San Carlos, Zuni—but by far the largest is the Navajo Nation. (The Hopi are excluded because they have a long and angry boundary dispute with the Navajo and agreed to be part of the 2nd District). Most of the Navajo are in Apache County, with the rest in Navajo and Coconino counties. They have a history of fiercely contested tribal elections and considerable social problems. Unemployment has run close to 50%, nearly 60% of dwellings are without phone service, and 30% are without running water or electricity. Alcoholism and drug abuse remain rampant, and there is little economic development.

The 1st District was designed to be closely divided between the two parties, but today is solidly Republican in presidential elections. The copper mining counties of Greenlee, Graham, and Gila are historically Democratic and still register that way, but they tend to vote Republican. Apache County, with its Navajo majority, is heavily Democratic. Coconino County includes the college town and growing retirement mecca of Flagstaff, part of the Navajo Reservation, and Sedona, where the Army drove the Apaches off the land in the 1870s after gold was discovered; it is increasingly Democratic. Yavapai County is heavily Republican. It includes Prescott, where conservative icon Barry Goldwater always began his Arizona campaigns. President Bush won the district easily in 2004 with 54% of the vote, and Arizona native son John McCain won it similarly with 54% in 2008.

The congresswoman from the 1st District is Democrat Ann Kirkpatrick, whose 2008 election came after the fall from grace of incumbent Republican Rick Renzi, who was indicted in an alleged extortion scheme.

Kirkpatrick was born on the White Mountain Apache Nation reservation in eastern Arizona and grew up speaking both Apache and English. After earning a law degree from the University of Arizona, she worked as a prosecutor for the Coconino County attorney's office, specializing in drug crime cases. She later served as the city attorney of Sedona. In 2004, Kirkpatrick ran for the Arizona House of Representatives in state District 2. At the time, conventional wisdom held that a non-Native American could not be elected in the district, where two-thirds of the registered voters were Native Americans. But this did not deter Kirkpatrick from challenging incumbent Rep. Sylvia Laughter, a Navajo and political independent. Kirkpatrick campaigned door-to-door and took advantage of Arizona's Clean Elections law, which provides candidates with public money if they agree to limit contributions from private donors. Voters responded to her efforts. In her two terms, Kirkpatrick worked to provide Indian tribes with money to build communications infrastructure and lobbied the U.S. Justice Department to rescind state election laws that she contended disenfranchised Native Americans.

When allegations of misconduct by Renzi surfaced in early 2007, the Democratic Congressional Campaign Committee identified the seat as one of its top targets. Kirkpatrick saw an opportunity. She resigned from the Legislature in July 2007 and began campaigning for the Democratic nomination. Renzi opted not to seek re-election and was eventually indicted for extortion and other charges relating to a land deal that allegedly benefited one of his former business partners.

In addition to help from the DCCC, Kirkpatrick was endorsed by the national fundraising group EMILY's List. The fundraising prowess that she demonstrated in two state elections and her appeal among rural voters made her a formidable candidate. She won a four-way Democratic primary with 47% of the vote, and the DCCC reserved $1.7 million for advertising for the fall campaign.

On the Republican side, the national and state parties were unable to convince former state Senate President Ken Bennett or state Rep. Bill Konopnicki to get into the race. Anti-tax activist Sydney Hay became the frontrunner for the nomination, but she barely defeated former State Department employee Sandra Livingstone in the Republican primary. The Arizona GOP opted not to aid Hay's campaign. In the general election campaign, Kirkpatrick outspent her 3-to-1. In a swing district that voted for both President Bush and Democratic Gov. Janet Napolitano, Kirkpatrick's more moderate views resonated with voters. She carried six of the district's eight counties and soundly defeated Hay 56% to 39%.

In the House, Kirkpatrick got seats on the Homeland Security, Veterans Affairs, and Small Business committees. She said her priority is improving infrastructure in her district, including expanding basic services such as electricity, running water, telephone and Internet access.

SECOND DISTRICT

Trent Franks (R)

Elected 2002, 4th term; b. June 19, 1957, Uravan, CO; home, Glendale; Ottawa University, 1989–90; Baptist; married (Josie); 2 children.

Elected Office: AZ House of Reps., 1984–86.

Professional Career: Director, AZ Governor's Office for Children, 1987–88; Exec. director, AZ Family Research Institute, 1989–93; Writer-commentator, AZ radio station KTKP; Co-owner, Franks Brothers Independent Drilling; Pres.-CEO, Liberty Petroleum Corp.

DC Office: 2435 RHOB, 20515, 202-225-4576; Fax: 202-225-6328; Web site: house.gov/franks.

State Offices: Glendale, 623-776-7911.

Committees: *Armed Services* (14th of 25 R): Oversight & Investigations; Readiness; Strategic Forces. *Judiciary* (10th of 16 R): Commercial & Administrative Law (RMM); Constitution, Civil Rights & Civil Liberties.

Group Ratings

	ADA	ACLU	AFS	LCV	ITIC	NTU	COC	ACU	CFG	FRC
2008	0	18	0	0	29	93	76	100	100	100
2007	0	—	0	5	—	93	70	100	94	—

National Journal Ratings

	2007 LIB — 2007 CONS		2008 LIB — 2008 CONS	
Economic	0%	— 97%	0%	— 98%
Social	0%	— 91%	0%	— 91%
Foreign	0%	— 72%	0%	— 95%
Composite	7%	— 93%	3%	— 97%

Key Votes of the 110th Congress

1. Increase minimum wage	N	5. Share immigration data	Y	9. Withdraw troops 8/08	N
2. Expand SCHIP	N	6. Foreign aid abortion ban	Y	10. No operations in Iran	N
3. Raise CAFE standards	N	7. Ban gay bias in workplace	N	11. Free trade with Peru	Y
4. Bail out financial markets	N	8. Repeal D.C. gun law	Y	12. Overhaul FISA	Y

Election Results

2008 general	Trent Franks (R)	200,914	(59%)	($442,232)
	John Thrasher (D)	125,611	(37%)	($37,187)
	Powell Gammill (Lib)	7,882	(2%)	
2008 primary	Trent Franks (R)	unopposed		

Prior Winning Percentages: 2006 (59%); 2004 (59%); 2002 (60%)

Population		Race/Ethnicity		Work	
Pop. 2007:	896,194	White:	72.0%	Private:	79.0%
Change since 2000:	Up 39.7%	Black:	3.1%	Government:	14.4%
Urban:	89.0%	Hispanic:	19.2%	Self-employed:	6.5%
Rural:	11.0%	Asian:	2.1%	Blue collar:	22.3%
Area size:	20,391 sq. mi.	Native Am.:	1.7%	White collar:	60.0%
Age		Hawaiian:	0.1%	Khaki collar:	0.4%
Median age:	38.7 yrs.	Two+ races:	1.5%	Other:	17.3%
More than 65 yrs:	17.8%	**Ancestry**		Median income:	$51,284
Less than 18 yrs:	25.0%	German:	15.8%	Median home value:	$229,200
Education		Irish:	9.7%	Poverty:	10.7%
H.S. grad:	86.3%	English:	9.3%	**Military Veterans**	
College grad:	21.0%			% of Pop:	16.0%
Grad degree:	7.2%				

Beyond the cities of Phoenix and Tucson, much of Arizona looks as it did a century ago. Some is intentionally preserved in its natural state, such as the sere uplands of the Hopi Indian Reservation. Other places maintain a timeless Western look, like Wickenburg, the oldest Arizona town north of Tucson. Still others preserve antiquated ways of life, such as the polygamist community of Colorado City, just south of Utah. In some cases, nature and settlement juxtapose jarringly: The real London Bridge has been transplanted to Lake Havasu City, a retirement community on the Colorado River.

2008 Presidential Vote

McCain (R)	220,667	(61%)
Obama (D)	138,275	(38%)

2004 Presidential Vote

Bush (R)	182,326	(61%)
Kerry (D)	112,620	(38%)

Cook Partisan Voting Index: R + 13

All of these areas are part of the 2nd Congressional District of Arizona, which stretches from the Hoover Dam and Lake Mead in the northwest corner of the state to the western suburbs of Phoenix, where 80% of its voters live. Astride Grand Avenue, the only diagonal street in the rigorous grid of metro Phoenix, is the mushrooming suburb of Glendale, not so long ago just a crossroads but now home to 253,000. The Phoenix Coyotes hockey stadium went up in Glendale in 2003, followed in 2006 by the University of Phoenix Stadium, where Super Bowl XLII was played in February 2008, and a new baseball facility where the Los Angeles Dodgers and Chicago White Sox set up spring training in 2009. The nearby Westgate City Center is now one of several edge cities in Phoenix's Valley of the Sun. Just west in the former desert are Peoria, as Middle American as its namesake in Illinois, and the huge retirement community of Sun City, started in the 1950s. This had been a growth area, but the mid-2000s housing boom was followed by a bust, with median housing values in the Phoenix area down 33% from October 2007 to October 2008.

The 2nd District also includes the fast-growing corridor along the Interstate 10 Papago Freeway, taking in Luke Air Force Base, which has the largest fighter training wing in the Air Force and the only active-duty F-16 training base in the United States. It extends to the once-open spaces of Goodyear and Buckeye and Mohave County, with its growing Las Vegas suburbs, and the Hopi Indian Reservation, connected to the rest of the district by a narrow, oddly shaped corridor that runs along the bottom of the Grand Canyon.

This is Republican territory. The retirees here remember the culturally conservative, Ozzie-and-Harriet lifestyle of the 1950s, and the upwardly striving, family-oriented young migrants who have populated new towns in the desert are trying to replicate it. Culture, more than affluence, which by national standards is not all that striking here, accounts for their political conservatism. Republicans also dominate the new cities along the Colorado River.

The congressman from the 2nd District is Trent Franks, a Republican first elected in 2002. He grew up in Colorado, attended college only briefly, and started his own oil-and-gas exploration business. His political career began when he won a single term in the Arizona House in 1984. There, he was known for wearing a tie tack in the shape of the feet of a fetus, as a constant reminder of his anti-abortion-rights views. In 1987, he was the director of the Governor's Office for Children under Evan Mecham, a conservative Republican who was later impeached. In 1989, he became executive director of the Arizona Family Research Institute, an organization associated with James Dobson's Focus on the Family, and he was a consultant to conservative Pat Buchanan's presidential campaign. Franks sought unsuccessfully for a

1992 ballot initiative to limit abortion rights. He designed the state's 1997 scholarship tax credit legislation, a much-litigated measure that ultimately was upheld by the U.S. Supreme Court. The plan provides tax credits for donations to nonprofit organizations to help families pay for private education. In 1994, he ran for an open U.S. House seat but lost to John Shadegg in the Republican primary, 43%-30%.

In 2002, Republican Rep. Bob Stump announced he was retiring and endorsed Lisa Atkins, his chief of staff throughout his 26-year congressional career. When the campaign started, Franks was not in the top tier of candidates. But his base of Christian conservatives and abortion opponents, plus an infusion into his campaign of $300,000 of his own money, made him a contender. Franks spent heavily on radio ads, and he benefited from the distribution of a voter guide by the Center for Arizona Policy, which described itself as "the only organization in Arizona actively fighting in the Legislature and media for conservative, traditional views on gambling, homosexuality, and pornography." Franks called for overturning the Supreme Court's *Roe v. Wade* decision legalizing abortion, and for constitutional protection for fetuses. He endorsed a flat tax as a step toward eliminating the federal income tax, supported individual investment accounts in Social Security, and called for tougher enforcement of immigration laws. His base of activists made the difference. He finished first with 28% of the vote, only 797 votes ahead of Atkins, who got 26%. In November, he won 60%-37%.

In the House, Franks has a solidly conservative record. He has sought co-sponsors for his Children's Hope Act, which was based on his 1997 state scholarship tax credit. And he wrote an anti-child-pornography bill. In the 110th Congress (2007–08), he opposed expansion of the State Children's Health Insurance Program, and sought to deny eligibility for the program to illegal immigrants. He proved his outsider stripes by proposing that service on the Appropriations Committee be limited to a maximum of three terms in 10 years. And he said he had no interest in serving on the committee, which controls the government purse strings and is ground zero for earmarks, the special spending provisions inserted into appropriations bills by individual lawmakers. But he succumbed to pressure from Republican leaders and earned their gratitude in December 2003 by switching his vote to support the Medicare prescription drug bill during a tension-filled, three-hour roll-call vote. Many conservatives opposed the massive expansion of the program to pay for prescription drugs for senior citizens.

On the Armed Services Committee, Franks worked to secure $27 million for Arizona to buy land adjacent to Luke Air Force Base in order to curtail housing development, and he worked to locate the new F-35 joint strike fighter planes at Luke. He has strongly supported missile defense and Boeing's bid to build the new Air Force tanker. From 2007 until 2009, he was the ranking Republican on the Constitution subcommittee of Judiciary where worked to promote building a fence along the U.S. borders to stem illegal immigration. Also in 2007, his amendment to require the Pentagon to inform Congress of weapons provided by Iran to the Taliban passed by voice vote. Franks, who has had multiple surgeries in his cleft palate, has encouraged public awareness of the facial deformity. In 2009, Franks became the ranking Republican on the Commercial and Administrative Law Subcommittee of the Judiciary Committee.

In his first bid for re-election in 2004, Franks faced a competitive primary against Rick Murphy, a free-spending radio station owner, who criticized Franks for supporting the prescription drug bill. Murphy was endorsed by several local Republican officials who complained about their lack of contact with Franks. Murphy also attacked Franks for abandoning his promise not to take money from political action committees. Franks won 64%-36%, a good showing but less than what safe incumbents usually get over primary challengers. He narrowly lost Mohave County, but he took 68% in Maricopa, which cast 76% of the total vote. In November Franks won 59%-39%, a downtick from 2002.

He had no primary opposition in 2006 or 2008, and won both general elections with 59% of the vote. In the early maneuvering for the 2008 GOP presidential nomination, Franks backed Duncan Hunter, the top Republican on the Armed Services Committee, as "an unequivocal social conservative and fiscal conservative" over home-state favorite Sen. John McCain of Arizona. In November 2008, he called newly elected President Obama "the most dangerous president the country has ever had."

THIRD DISTRICT

John Shadegg (R)

Elected 1994, 8th term; b. Oct. 22, 1949, Phoenix; home, Phoenix; U. of AZ, B.A. 1972, J.D. 1975; Episcopalian; married (Shirley); 2 children.

Military Career: Air Natl. Guard, 1969–75.

Professional Career: Practicing atty., 1975–94; U.S. spec. asst. atty. gen., 1983–90; Spec. cnsl., AZ House Republican Caucus, 1991–92; Cnsl., AZ Wildlife Conservation, 1992.

DC Office: 436 CHOB, 20515, 202-225-3361; Fax: 202-225-3462; Web site: johnshadegg.house.gov.

State Offices: Phoenix, 602-263-5300.

Committees: *Energy & Commerce* (8th of 23 R): Communications, Technology & the Internet; Energy & Environment; Health.

Group Ratings

	ADA	ACLU	AFS	LCV	ITIC	NTU	COC	ACU	CFG	FRC
2008	0	18	0	0	43	84	83	96	92	94
2007	0	—	0	5	—	92	70	100	97	—

National Journal Ratings

	2007 LIB — 2007 CONS		2008 LIB — 2008 CONS	
Economic	0% —	97%	2% —	97%
Social	0% —	91%	0% —	91%
Foreign	0% —	72%	5% —	93%
Composite	7% —	93%	4% —	96%

Key Votes of the 110th Congress

1. Increase minimum wage	N	5. Share immigration data	Y	9. Withdraw troops 8/08	N
2. Expand SCHIP	N	6. Foreign aid abortion ban	Y	10. No operations in Iran	N
3. Raise CAFE standards	N	7. Ban gay bias in workplace	N	11. Free trade with Peru	Y
4. Bail out financial markets	Y	8. Repeal D.C. gun law	Y	12. Overhaul FISA	Y

Election Results

2008 general	John Shadegg (R)	148,800	(54%)	($2,911,880)
	Bob Lord (D)	115,759	(42%)	($1,813,648)
	Michael Shoen (Lib)	10,602	(4%)	
2008 primary	John Shadegg (R)	unopposed		

Prior Winning Percentages: 2006 (59%); 2004 (80%); 2002 (67%); 2000 (64%); 1998 (65%); 1996 (67%); 1994 (60%)

Population		Race/Ethnicity		Work	
Pop. 2007:	696,295	White:	72.2%	Private:	83.0%
Change since 2000:	Up 8.6%	Black:	2.9%	Government:	9.9%
Urban:	96.5%	Hispanic:	19.3%	Self-employed:	7.0%
Rural:	3.5%	Asian:	2.7%	Blue collar:	16.8%
Area size:	599 sq. mi.	Native Am.:	1.4%	White collar:	67.0%
Age		Hawaiian:	0.1%	Khaki collar:	0.1%
Median age:	36.3 yrs.	Two+ races:	1.1%	Other:	16.1%
More than 65 yrs:	10.6%	*Ancestry*		Median income:	$55,568
Less than 18 yrs:	24.5%	German:	15.2%	Median home value:	$291,400
Education		Irish:	10.2%	Poverty:	10.7%
H.S. grad:	88.1%	English:	8.4%	**Military Veterans**	
College grad:	31.2%			% of Pop:	11.0%
Grad degree:	10.9%				

In May 1998, conservative trailblazer Barry Goldwater died at his home in the Phoenix suburb of Paradise Valley. His life had spanned almost the whole history of Arizona. He was born on New Year's Day, 1909, when Arizona was still a territory, and he could remember when it was the "baby state," with fewer people than any state except Delaware, Wyoming, and Nevada. When he returned from service in World War II, Paradise Valley was still undeveloped, and Phoenix—founded after the Civil War as

2008 Presidential Vote

McCain (R)	162,724	(56%)
Obama (D)	121,996	(42%)

2004 Presidential Vote

Bush (R)	150,511	(58%)
Kerry (D)	107,881	(41%)

Cook Partisan Voting Index: R+ 9

a hay market for cavalry horses at Fort McDowell—was not much more than a tiny outpost of American civilization, a metropolitan area of fewer than 300,000 in a sizzling desert. By 2008, Arizona had 6.5 million people, with more than 4 million in metropolitan Phoenix. The city had been transformed from a frontier outpost to a diversified high-tech center, an example of how creativity and ingenuity can build a sophisticated city even in the most unwelcoming desert environs.

Like Los Angeles and San Francisco, Phoenix is dotted with mountains that rise grandly from the plains and are preserved as undeveloped parkland. Some, such as Shaw Butte, contain archeological evidence that Indians used them as a base for sophisticated astronomical observations. From Camelback Mountain, 1,800 feet above Phoenix and Paradise Valley, one can get with equal awe a sense of what the land was originally like and an understanding of how impressively Phoenix has grown. East of Camelback, subdivisions were often built with grass and greenery. In the affluent areas north of Camelback and spreading out Scottsdale Road and the Black Canyon Freeway, the natural desert look is more common. The master-planned community of Anthem, 35 miles north of downtown and established in 1998, already has about 40,000 residents. Grass is discouraged, and often banned by subdivision covenant;

planting anything but desert flora is frowned upon. The architecture of the houses tends toward unadorned stucco with picture windows facing away from the sun. The idea is to suggest that there is a horse corral over in the next lot, and sometimes, especially in the northern edges of Phoenix, there is.

The 3rd Congressional District of Arizona includes the northern part of Phoenix plus Paradise Valley, bounded on the south by a zigzag line that approximates the Arizona Canal. The 3rd also includes the communities of New River, Cave Creek, and Carefree, so named in 1955 by developers who hoped to lure snowbird retirees. Here the stores are more likely to feature horse feed than designer clothes, but that is changing fast as metro Phoenix moves inexorably north, bringing with it more-upscale malls. This is an affluent, and largely Republican, district.

The congressman from the 3d District is John Shadegg, first elected in 1994, with a fine Arizona Republican pedigree. His father, Stephen Shadegg, managed Barry Goldwater's first campaign for the Senate in 1952, when Goldwater upset Democrat Ernest McFarland, the Senate majority leader. In those days before faxes and e-mail, the older Shadegg helped deliver campaign press releases. The younger Shadegg is a lawyer who served as special assistant to the state attorney general and as a special counsel to the Arizona House Republican caucus. When then-Rep. Jon Kyl ran for the Senate in 1994, Shadegg ran for his House seat and won 43% in the GOP primary, to 30% for Trent Franks (now the 2nd District representative). Shadegg won the general election easily, 60%-36%.

In the House, Shadegg has been a consistent conservative who has stuck to principle. As one of the firebrand 1994 Republican freshmen, he held firm against President Clinton's policies and often rebelled against his own party's leadership. He refused to back the balanced-budget amendment without a three-fifths supermajority for tax increases, in defiance of Republican Speaker Newt Gingrich of Georgia. When he chaired the House Republican Study Committee in 2001 and 2002, Shadegg agreed to support the annual budget resolution but insisted, with occasional success, that free-spending appropriators comply with budget limits. He voted against President Bush's No Child Left Behind education act in 2001 though it was a signature bill for the new Republican president. His independence cost him a seat on the powerful House Ways and Means Committee in 1997. But he got a seat on also influential Energy and Commerce Committee, where, at the direction of GOP Speaker Dennis Hastert of Illinois, he often worked on health care policy. In 2003, Shadegg was one of only two Republicans serving on the committee who refused to support the Republicans' Medicare prescription drug bill. The energy bill enacted in 2005 reflected Shadegg's efforts to promote hydroelectric power.

In January 2005, Shadegg ran unopposed to replace Rep. Christopher Cox of California as chairman of the Republican Policy Committee. Both wings of the party praised him as open to ideas, and he organized a series of "unity dinners" to try to find common ground on immigration legislation. In January 2006, he gave up that post to run for majority leader after Texas Rep. Tom DeLay was forced to step down amid an ethics and fundraising scandal. Shadegg finished a distant third to Missouri Rep. Roy Blunt and Ohio Rep. John Boehner, with 40 votes, and withdrew after the first ballot. His candidacy may have prevented a first-ballot win by Blunt, and most of his supporters went to Boehner, who won the contest. In November 2006, he ran against Blunt for minority whip in what was widely expected to be a close contest. But Shadegg lost, 137-57. In contrast to other contenders, he did not actively raise money for GOP candidates, which is one of the best ways to curry favor in a leadership contest.

After leaving the leadership, Shadegg said he had no regrets about losing his seat at the table and returning to his role as a reformer. In March 2007, he criticized fellow lawmakers for including pork-barrel projects in the Iraq war spending bill. He opposed the Republican-backed immigration bill, but favored a stand-alone agricultural guest-worker law. He voted against the January 2008 economic stimulus bill sent to Congress by the Bush administration. When Democratic Speaker Nancy Pelosi of California adjourned the House in August 2008 without allowing a vote on opening up more coastal areas to offshore oil drilling, Shadegg led Republican members into the empty chamber, where they spoke for days urging Pelosi to call a vote, a tactic Shadegg called "a modern-day Boston Tea Party." He voted against the $700 billion bailout for the financial markets on Sept. 29, 2008, but after new provisions were added, including a higher limit on Federal Deposit Insurance Corporation (FDIC) insurance and relaxation of market-to-market rules, voted for the bill. Later in October, he accused Treasury Secretary Henry Paulson of trying to bully Congress into passing the bill with little time for review. He has been an outspoken critic of earmarks and has sought none for his district.

Shadegg has exercised his independence at home, too. In 2004, he opposed a tax increase for Phoenix-area transportation (which passed anyway), but he supported higher taxes on business to pay for full-day kindergarten for Arizona children. In 2008, he supported Proposition 101, which protected a citizen's right to choose any health insurance.

From 1996 to 2004, Shadegg won re-election every two years with at least 64% of the vote against weak opponents. Then in 2006, he won by only 59%-38% against Democrat Herb Paine, a former United Way executive. During that campaign, he warned that his party was no longer aggressive enough and risked losing its majority. He cited the failure to strip pension rights from lawmakers convicted of crimes and its reluctance to overhaul the rules for Indian gambling facilities to prevent further abuses after the Jack Abramoff lobbying scandal ensnared several high-ranking GOP lawmakers.

On Feb. 11, 2008, Shadegg announced he would not run for re-election. But 145 Republican congressional colleagues and 33 leaders of conservative organizations signed petitions urging him to reconsider—an unusual outpouring of support for a rank-and-file lawmaker. A few days later, he reversed his decision and decided to run again. Democratic lawyer Bob Lord had started campaigning for the seat in April 2007, and by the summer before the election had raised $1.1 million. Inspired by the defeat of conservative Rep. J. D. Hayworth in the neighboring 5th District in 2006, national Democrats targeted the seat. Lord ultimately raised $1.5 million, and the Democratic Congressional Campaign Committee put in another $1.8 million. They ran ads picturing Shadegg morphing into by-then-unpopular President Bush, and Lord's own ads accused Shadegg of voting for a congressional pay raise while voting against a pay raise for U.S. troops fighting in Iraq. Shadegg won 54%-42%, a solid victory but his lowest re-election numbers to date.

FOURTH DISTRICT

Ed Pastor (D)

Elected Sept. 1991, 9th full term; b. June 28, 1943, Claypool; home, Phoenix; AZ St. U., B.A. 1966, J.D. 1974; Catholic; married (Verma); 2 children.

Elected Office: Maricopa Cnty. Bd. of Supervisors, 1976–91.

Professional Career: High schl. teacher, 1966–69; Asst., AZ Gov. Castro, 1975.

DC Office: 2465 RHOB, 20515, 202-225-4065; Fax: 202-225-1655; Web site: www.pastor.house.gov.

State Offices: Phoenix, 602-256-0551.

Committees: *Chief Deputy Whip. Appropriations* (12th of 37 D): Energy & Water Development; Interior, Environment & Related Agencies; Transportation, HUD & Related Agencies.

Group Ratings

	ADA	ACLU	AFS	LCV	ITIC	NTU	COC	ACU	CFG	FRC
2008	100	100	100	92	50	10	50	4	0	0
2007	95	—	100	90	—	2	47	0	0	—

National Journal Ratings

	2007 LIB	—	2007 CONS	2008 LIB	—	2008 CONS
Economic	62%	—	38%	85%	—	0%
Social	77%	—	17%	82%	—	0%
Foreign	84%	—	16%	78%	—	17%
Composite	75%	—	25%	88%	—	12%

Key Votes of the 110th Congress

1. Increase minimum wage	Y	5. Share immigration data	N	9. Withdraw troops 8/08	Y
2. Expand SCHIP	Y	6. Foreign aid abortion ban	N	10. No operations in Iran	Y
3. Raise CAFE standards	Y	7. Ban gay bias in workplace	Y	11. Free trade with Peru	N
4. Bail out financial markets	Y	8. Repeal D.C. gun law	N	12. Overhaul FISA	N

Election Results

2008 general	Ed Pastor (D)	89,721	(72%)	($815,864)
	Don Karg (R)	26,435	(21%)	
	Rebecca DeWitt (Green)	4,464	(4%)	
	Joe Cobb (Lib)	3,807	(3%)	
2008 primary	Ed Pastor (D)	unopposed		

Prior Winning Percentages: 2006 (73%); 2004 (70%); 2002 (67%); 2000 (69%); 1998 (68%); 1996 (65%); 1994 (62%); 1992 (66%); 1991 (56%)

Population		Race/Ethnicity		Work	
Pop. 2007:	708,649	White:	21.9%	Private:	84.9%
Change since 2000:	Up 10.5%	Black:	7.2%	Government:	9.7%
Urban:	99.5%	Hispanic:	66.5%	Self-employed:	5.3%
Rural:	0.5%	Asian:	1.2%	Blue collar:	38.2%
Area size:	199 sq. mi.	Native Am.:	2.1%	White collar:	40.1%
		Hawaiian:	0.2%	Khaki collar:	0.0%
Age		Two+ races:	0.9%	Other:	21.7%
Median age:	28.0 yrs.			Median income:	$36,257
More than 65 yrs:	5.7%	*Ancestry*		Median home value:	$170,900
Less than 18 yrs:	33.4%	German:	5.0%	Poverty:	25.5%
		Irish:	3.9%		
Education		English:	3.0%	**Military Veterans**	
H.S. grad:	62.6%			% of Pop:	6.5%
College grad:	12.6%				
Grad degree:	4.4%				

Phoenix is a relatively new American metropolis; it's grown to big-city size just in the past generation. Yet it is also an ancient city, or built on top of one. The Arizona Canal, several miles north of downtown Phoenix, runs along the route of a canal built about 600 years ago by the Hohokam aboriginal people. They distributed irrigated water diverted from the Salt River in its wet moments to farmers in what today is called the Valley of the Sun, and they made sophisticated astronomical observations

2008 Presidential Vote
Obama (D) ....86,815　(65%)
McCain (R)..............................43,610　(33%)

2004 Presidential Vote
Kerry (D)...................................71,805　(62%)
Bush (R)...................................43,967　(38%)

Cook Partisan Voting Index:　D + 13

from the mountains that jut up from the plains. This society disappeared for reasons unknown less than half a century before the Spaniards arrived in North America. So today's Phoenix is the second civilization to prosper in this desert region. Phoenix and Maricopa County had 331,000 people in 1950 and more than 4 million by 2008. Half a century ago, Phoenix spread six miles north, west, and east of the downtown and only a few miles south. Downtown was its only office district and its main shopping area, and people blew fans over boxes of ice to cool off. Today, the view from downtown Phoenix's office towers seems to stretch as far as the eye can see, toward groupings of other office towers to the north, northeast, and northwest.

The 4th Congressional District of Arizona is centered in downtown Phoenix and is based entirely in Maricopa County. It covers the capitol, in a rundown neighborhood a couple of miles to the west, and busy Sky Harbor International Airport, situated in an industrial corridor several miles east. It includes most of southern Phoenix, and its boundaries follow approximately the southern and western city limits. It extends as far north as Bethany Home Road and Northern Avenue. It stretches south into Guadalupe and northwest into Glendale. Geographically, it covers most of the land between South Mountain and Camelback Mountain. The district is one of Arizona's two Hispanic districts; its population by the mid-2000s was 69% Hispanic. Most are Mexican, but there has been an influx of Guatemalans. The typical Latino neighborhood here is a collection of 1940s and 1950s bungalows. Habitat for Humanity built South Ranch, its largest low-income subdivision, in the district, with the idea of clustering poor homeowners together and encouraging them to stave off neighborhood decline collectively. Politically, this is a solidly Democratic district, the most Democratic in Arizona.

The congressman from the 4th District is Ed Pastor, a Democrat who won a 1991 special election to replace Morris (Mo) Udall, the revered, 14-term liberal who championed environmental causes. (At the time, the district's boundaries were different.) Pastor grew up in Claypool, a mining town in Gila County. He has spent his entire career in politics, but has a much lower profile than his predecessor in the seat. After teaching high school, Pastor got a law degree at Arizona State University. He was an assistant to Democratic Gov. Raul Castro, the first Hispanic governor of Arizona, in 1975. He was elected in 1976 to the Maricopa County Board of Supervisors, where he served until his election to Congress. In 1991, he defeated Republican Pat Connor, 56%-44%. He has not faced serious competition since.

Pastor has been a faithful follower of the Democratic leadership and has a mostly liberal voting record. He supported the North American Free Trade Agreement of 1993 despite strong labor opposition, but he opposed normal trade relations with China and the free-trade agreement with Central America. He vigorously opposed Arizona's English Only law and supports bilingual ballots. In 2002, he sponsored legislation to provide amnesty to immigrants who were in the United States prior to January 2000. After a 2002 trip to Cuba, where he met with President Fidel Castro for three hours, he urged the immediate end of the trade embargo. In 2004, he narrowly lost a vote in the Appropriations Committee on his proposal to allow banks to accept the Mexican *matricula consular* cards for identification. Pastor serves in the Democratic leadership as a chief deputy whip, and is also active in the Hispanic Caucus.

Much of Pastor's work has been on the Appropriations Committee, where he has often earmarked funds for local projects. He has evolved into the "go-to guy" for federal funds for Arizona because he is the only House or Senate appropriator from Arizona, and because most influential fellow Arizonans, like GOP Sen. John McCain and Republican Reps. Jeff Flake and John Shadegg, ideologically oppose earmarks. When money is needed, said a Maricopa County supervisor, "you go to Ed." In early 2009, Pastor took temporary control of the chairmanship of the Subcommittee on Energy and Water after Chairman Peter Visclosky of Indiana stepped aside for the duration of a grand jury probe into possible corruption in the appropriations process. The arrangement put Pastor at the helm of a $30 billion energy and water projects bill that year. Visclosky was under investigation for his ties to the lobbying firm PMA Group, which secured tens of millions of dollars for its clients with Visclosky's help.

Pastor also drew unfavorable publicity for his work on appropriation bills. *The Arizona Republic* reported in June 2007 that Pastor had significantly increased from $200,000 to $333,000 the federal grant money to a Maricopa Community Colleges scholarship program after his daughter Laura was hired to help run it. She had less experience than other applicants. Pastor said that he had supported the program long before his daughter was hired in 2005.

FIFTH DISTRICT

Harry Mitchell (D)

Elected 2006, 2nd term; b. July 18, 1940, Phoenix; home, Tempe; AZ St. U., B.A. 1962, M.P.A. 1980; Catholic; married (Marianne); 2 children.

Elected Office: Tempe City Cncl., 1970–78; Mayor, 1978–94; AZ Senate, 1998–2006.

Professional Career: High school teacher, 1964–1992.

DC Office: 1410 LHOB, 20515, 202-225-2190; Fax: 202-225-0096; Web site: mitchell.house.gov.

State Offices: Scottsdale, 480-946-2411.

Committees: *Science & Technology* (21st of 26 D): Technology & Innovation. *Transportation & Infrastructure* (27th of 44 D): Aviation; Highways & Transit; Water Resources & Environment. *Veterans' Affairs* (6th of 18 D): Oversight & Investigations (Chmn).

Group Ratings

	ADA	ACLU	AFS	LCV	ITIC	NTU	COC	ACU	CFG	FRC
2008	75	82	86	77	100	31	67	32	18	11
2007	80	—	91	100	—	18	60	8	22	—

National Journal Ratings

	2007 LIB — 2007 CONS		2008 LIB — 2008 CONS	
Economic	53%	— 46%	51%	— 49%
Social	52%	— 48%	48%	— 50%
Foreign	56%	— 43%	58%	— 42%
Composite	54%	— 46%	53%	— 47%

Key Votes of the 110th Congress

1. Increase minimum wage	Y	5. Share immigration data	Y	9. Withdraw troops 8/08	Y
2. Expand SCHIP	Y	6. Foreign aid abortion ban	N	10. No operations in Iran	N
3. Raise CAFE standards	Y	7. Ban gay bias in workplace	Y	11. Free trade with Peru	Y
4. Bail out financial markets	Y	8. Repeal D.C. gun law	Y	12. Overhaul FISA	Y

Election Results

2008 general	Harry Mitchell (D)	149,033	(53%)	($2,324,598)
	David Schweikert (R)	122,165	(44%)	($1,416,883)
	Warren Severin (Lib)	9,158	(3%)	
2008 primary	Harry Mitchell (D)	unopposed		

Prior Winning Percentages: 2006 (50%)

Population		Race/Ethnicity		Work	
Pop. 2007:	679,980	White:	72.0%	Private:	82.5%
Change since 2000:	Up 6.0%	Black:	3.1%	Government:	11.1%
Urban:	97.2%	Hispanic:	16.5%	Self-employed:	6.3%
Rural:	2.8%	Asian:	4.4%	Blue collar:	14.1%
Area size:	1,423 sq. mi.	Native Am.:	2.2%	White collar:	70.4%
		Hawaiian:	0.2%	Khaki collar:	0.0%
Age		Two+ races:	1.5%	Other:	15.5%
Median age:	35.7 yrs.			Median income:	$59,158
More than 65 yrs:	11.2%	*Ancestry*		Median home value:	$333,500
Less than 18 yrs:	21.8%	German:	14.8%	Poverty:	9.9%
		Irish:	10.3%		
Education		English:	9.1%	**Military Veterans**	
H.S. grad:	91.5%			% of Pop:	10.0%
College grad:	40.8%				
Grad degree:	15.4%				

As metropolitan Phoenix has expanded in the Valley of the Sun, it has absorbed the crossroads towns that were separate and distinct 50 years ago. Two such towns are Tempe and Scottsdale. Tempe is east of downtown Phoenix, south of the Arizona Canal. It was founded in 1871 as Hayden's Ferry, by the father of the future Democratic Sen. Carl Hayden (1927–1969), and was renamed in 1879 for an ancient Greek vale. The old town centered on Arizona State University, and both the town and the

2008 Presidential Vote		
McCain (R)	153,736	(51%)
Obama (D)	140,287	(47%)

2004 Presidential Vote		
Bush (R)	152,576	(54%)
Kerry (D)	127,811	(45%)

Cook Partisan Voting Index: R + 5

university have expanded greatly. The university sits astride a rise with a fine view of much of metropolitan Phoenix. Tempe is relatively affluent and still growing, with 174,000 people in 2007, up from 7,600 in 1950. It has eight stations along Phoenix's new 20-mile light-rail system and new high-rises in its downtown. Scottsdale is east of the affluent part of Phoenix and north of Tempe and the Salt River Indian Reservation; it encompasses Frank Lloyd Wright's Taliesin West, which was beyond the reach of electricity and telephone lines when it was built in the 1940s. Scottsdale features luxury shopping malls and resorts, lots of nightlife, the Buffalo Bill Historical Center, and the WestWorld equestrian center. Local politicians argue over whether Scottsdale should keep marketing itself as a Western town or emphasize its new live-work downtown. It had 236,000 people in 2007, compared to 2,000 in the 1950 census.

The 5th Congressional District of Arizona includes Tempe, Scottsdale, and the northeast corner of Maricopa County—Fountain Hills, the Salt River and Fort McDowell Indian Reservations, and part of the Tonto National Forest. Politically, this has been a Republican district, though less so than a dozen years ago. The 5th has the highest percentage of college graduates and high-income households of any district in Arizona, and some affluent people here, like those on both coasts, have been attracted to the Democrats by their stands on cultural issues. This was the only Arizona district to vote for Barack Obama over Hillary Rodham Clinton in the Democratic presidential primary.

The congressman from the 5th District is Harry Mitchell, a Democrat elected in 2006 who was, at 66, the oldest freshman of the 110th Congress (2007–08). Mitchell grew up in Tempe when it was still a small town, and earned two degrees from Arizona State University. For 28 years, he taught American government and economics at his alma mater, Tempe High School, and was also an adjunct professor at ASU. In 1970, he was elected, at age 30, to the Tempe City Council and served eight years before becoming mayor in 1978. He held that job for 16 years, leading efforts to revitalize the downtown area and expand mass transit, and setting in motion the Rio Salado Project and Tempe Town Lake. After he left office in 1994, the city erected a 35-foot steel statue of Mitchell and renamed its government center for him. In 1998, he was elected to the state Senate, where he focused on education issues and job creation and was assistant minority leader.

In 2006, Mitchell challenged 5th District incumbent J.D. Hayworth, a 12-year incumbent. There was a stark difference in tone between Hayworth, a combative conservative partisan whose rhetoric particularly on immigration irritated Democrats, and Mitchell, who had spent most of his political career in nonpartisan city government seeking to build consensus. *The Arizona Republic*'s endorsement of Mitchell ran under the headline, "Mitchell Over the Bully." That editorial encouraged the Democratic Congressional Campaign Committee to put more money into the race to support Mitchell. Immigration was a major issue. Hayworth said Mitchell supported "amnesty" and Social Security benefits for illegal immigrants. Mitchell supported the 2006 immigration bill debate in the Senate, which provided a path to legalization for illegals and created a guest-worker program. He criticized Hayworth for doing little on the issue other than writing a book titled, *Whatever It Takes* .

Mitchell said he agreed with 3rd District Republican Rep. John Shadegg that "divisive and emotional rhetoric is not helpful to [the immigration] debate." Hayworth said that "enforcement is a proven strategy" and that Mitchell did not favor strict measures to secure the border. Mitchell focused heavily on Hayworth's ties to GOP House Leader Tom DeLay of Texas and disgraced lobbyist Jack Abramoff, whose Indian tribal clients contributed about $100,000 to Hayworth. Mitchell appealed to affluent voters who took moderate positions on cultural issues. He won 50%-46%.

In the House, Mitchell took moderate stands on issues. He was one of 13 Democrats who voted against the Democratic budget resolution in 2007, and in November 2007 he voted against a bill raising taxes on private equity firms and hedge funds. With Republican Chris Shays of Connecticut in 2007, he sponsored a bill to reduce capital-gains and estate taxes. He was one of two Democrats who provided the margin of victory for the Democratic leadership in its battle against a GOP amendment barring housing aid to illegal immigrants. With Republican Rep. Ron Paul of Texas, Mitchell co-sponsored a resolution in January 2008 to block the annual pay raise for members of Congress. When that failed, he donated his raise to local charities. He voted against the $700 billion bailout for the financial markets in 2008, which he called "fundamentally flawed" and with "no oversight, no protection for taxpayers, and little accountability."

The Democratic leadership made Mitchell the chairman of the Oversight and Investigations Subcommittee of the Veterans' Affairs Committee, which was a hot seat after the *Washington Post* published a series about poor conditions at the Walter Reed Army Medical Center. Mitchell presided over hearings about Walter Reed and other veterans' facilities and led the first congressional trip that followed the trail of injured soldiers from battlefields in Iraq and Afghanistan to military hospitals in Germany and on to veterans' care facilities in the United States. He co-sponsored a version of the new G.I. Bill similar to that sponsored by Virginia Democratic Sen. Jim Webb, which passed both houses and was signed into law in 2008. Unlike prominent members of the Arizona delegation such as Republican Sen. John McCain and GOP Reps. Jeff Flake and John Shadegg, Mitchell supports congressional earmarks, and obtained $200,000 for the SkySong research center, $1.3 million for Williams Gateway Airport in Mesa, and $90 million for the Valley Metro light-rail system.

In 2008, national Republicans targeted Mitchell, but there was a fractious six-candidate Republican primary, in which Susan Bitter Smith charged the front-runner, former Maricopa Treasurer David Schweikert, with mismanagement and said he was responsible for the bankruptcy of two local school districts. Schweikert won the September primary by only a narrow margin, 29%-27%, over Bitter Smith. In the general election campaign, Mitchell spent $2 million and got yet more financial support from the Democratic Congressional Campaign Committee. Mitchell's campaign attacked Schweikert for supporting a national sales tax. Schweikert emphasized his support of offshore oil drilling, but Mitchell had cast votes in favor of it as well. Mitchell emphasized his work on veterans' issues and local projects. He won 53%-44%.

SIXTH DISTRICT

Jeff Flake (R)

Elected 2000, 5th term; b. Dec. 31, 1962, Snowflake; home, Mesa; Brigham Young U., B.A. 1986, M.A. 1987; Mormon; married (Cheryl); 5 children.

Professional Career: Pub. plcy. exec., Shipley, Smoak & Henry, 1987–89; Exec. dir., Fndt. for Democracy (Namibia), 1989–90; Owner, Interface Pub. Affairs, 1990–92; Exec. dir., The Goldwater Inst., 1992–99.

DC Office: 240 CHOB, 20515, 202-225-2635; Fax: 202-226-4386; Web site: flake.house.gov.

State Offices: Mesa, 480-833-0092.

Committees: *Foreign Affairs* (9th of 19 R): Asia, the Pacific & the Global Environment; Africa & Global Health. *Natural Resources* (5th of 19 R): Insular Affairs, Oceans & Wildlife; National Parks, Forests & Public Lands. *Oversight & Government Reform* (12th of 16 R): Government Management, Organization & Procurement; National Security & Foreign Affairs (RMM).

Group Ratings

	ADA	ACLU	AFS	LCV	ITIC	NTU	COC	ACU	CFG	FRC
2008	0	9	0	8	29	98	61	100	100	94
2007	5	—	0	15	—	96	68	100	100	—

National Journal Ratings

	2007 LIB — 2007 CONS		2008 LIB — 2008 CONS	
Economic	4%	95%	0%	98%
Social	38%	60%	0%	91%
Foreign	39%	61%	22%	74%
Composite	28%	73%	10%	90%

Key Votes of the 110th Congress

1. Increase minimum wage	N	5. Share immigration data	Y	9. Withdraw troops 8/08	N
2. Expand SCHIP	N	6. Foreign aid abortion ban	Y	10. No operations in Iran	N
3. Raise CAFE standards	N	7. Ban gay bias in workplace	Y	11. Free trade with Peru	Y
4. Bail out financial markets	N	8. Repeal D.C. gun law	Y	12. Overhaul FISA	Y

Election Results

2008 general	Jeff Flake (R)..208,582	(62%)	($845,005)
	Rebecca Schneider (D)....................................115,457	(35%)	($4,478)
	Rick Biondi (Lib)..10,137	(3%)	
2008 primary	Jeff Flake (R).. unopposed		

Prior Winning Percentages: 2006 (75%); 2004 (79%); 2002 (66%); 2000 (54%)

Population		Race/Ethnicity		Work	
Pop. 2007:	932,094	White:	71.6%	Private:	83.0%
Change since 2000:	Up 45.3%	Black:	2.5%	Government:	11.3%
Urban:	96.8%	Hispanic:	20.1%	Self-employed:	5.5%
Rural:	3.2%	Asian:	3.0%	Blue collar:	20.9%
Area size:	724 sq. mi.	Native Am.:	0.9%	White collar:	63.8%
		Hawaiian:	0.2%	Khaki collar:	0.1%
Age		Two+ races:	1.5%	Other:	15.2%
Median age:	34.1 yrs.	*Ancestry*		Median income:	$58,350
More than 65 yrs:	12.6%	German:	15.5%	Median home value:	$246,400
Less than 18 yrs:	28.7%	English:	10.4%	Poverty:	8.4%
Education		Irish:	9.9%	**Military Veterans**	
H.S. grad:	87.8%			% of Pop:	12.2%
College grad:	27.1%				
Grad degree:	8.8%				

The city of Phoenix is exceedingly young. Conservative trailblazer Barry Goldwater, born in 1909, grew up knowing people who remembered when the Valley of the Sun—or the Valley, as most people say—was virtually empty, with a few parched settlements set above the dry riverbed. As late as 1950, only 106,000 people lived in Phoenix and 331,000 in all of Maricopa County. But the air conditioner and military technology transformed Phoenix from a sleepy whistle-stop to today's high-rise-studded

2008 Presidential Vote

McCain (R)............................220,718	(61%)
Obama (D) 135,178	(37%)

2004 Presidential Vote

Bush (R)................................188,372	(64%)
Kerry (D)..............................102,902	(35%)

Cook Partisan Voting Index: R + 15

metropolis, with 1.5 million city dwellers and nearly 4 million people in Maricopa County. From 2000 to 2007, Maricopa posted the largest numerical gain of any county in the nation. This is not, as some people think, a giant retirement village, nor is it overrun by crooked land salesmen and fast-buck artists, though Phoenix has attracted its share of each.

The second-largest city in Maricopa County is Mesa, south of the Salt River and east of Phoenix. It was founded by Mormons in 1878 on a square mile, and was laid out Salt Lake City-style on broad streets with large lots. A gleaming white Mormon temple was built in 1927, one of the few in the United States then. In 1950, Mesa had 17,000 people, enough to make it Arizona's third-largest city. In 2007, it had 453,000 people, more than Minneapolis or Pittsburgh. Mesa has been making plans to grow even more. A former Air Force base is now Phoenix-Mesa Gateway Airport, with plans for it to become a major multimodal center for passengers and freight. Nearby is the site of a proposed giant hotel and conference center on the former GM Desert Proving Ground. Next door is Arizona State University's Polytechnic campus.

The 6th Congressional District of Arizona is made up of the southeast suburbs of Phoenix, with distinct incorporated towns like Mesa, Chandler, Gilbert, and Queen Creek. It crosses the Pinal County line and includes fast-growing Apache Junction, Gold Camp, and Sun Lakes. For years growth has been constant here: In 2007, Chandler and Gilbert had populations of 246,000 and 208,000, respectively. But with the collapse of the local housing market and the departure of many Latinos after Arizona adopted tough enforcement policies on illegal immigrants, growth is slowing considerably. The 6th includes some high-income precincts, and Asians lead whites in income in Chandler and Gilbert. But the district's cultural tone is resolutely middle class and churchgoing. By most measures, it is the most Republican district in Arizona.

The congressman from the 6th District is Jeff Flake, a Republican first elected in 2000 and known in his party as a maverick. A fifth-generation Arizonan, he is a Mormon who was born and raised on a ranch in Snowflake, a town named after his great-great-grandfather. The fifth of 11 children, Flake graduated with a degree in international studies from Brigham Young University and did missionary work in South Africa and Zimbabwe. In 1989, he moved to Namibia to become executive director of the Foundation for Democracy, which monitored democratic progress in that country. After Namibia gained independence in 1990, Flake returned to Arizona and became executive director of the Goldwater Institute, where he led the fight for Arizona's charter-school law. In 2000, when conservative Republican Matt Salmon kept his pledge to serve only three terms in Congress, he hand-picked Flake to succeed him. Flake faced four opponents in a hard-fought September primary, in which he ran as the most conservative candidate. He had the support of several prominent Republican state leaders and was bolstered by more than $200,000 from the anti-tax organization Club for Growth. Flake won with 32% to 24% for Phoenix Councilman Sal DiCiccio. In the general election, Flake won 54%-42% over Democrat David Mendoza, a longtime lobbyist for public employees.

Flake promised to serve no more than three terms and to "continue to rock the boat" as Salmon had as a principled conservative who often bucked the Republican leadership. In his first year in the House, as Congress debated the first round of Bush-era tax cuts, Flake said that it would be a mistake for the Republican president to limit his proposed tax cut to the "easy things," such as repeal of the marriage penalty, and estate and gift taxes. He called for replacing the income tax with a national sales tax, a proposal that never got off the ground. Flake has a habit of taking lonely stands. He was one of two members who voted against a bill to punish Sudan for its human-rights abuses. Flake said he had seen in Africa the adverse impact of economic sanctions on poor nations. He was one of 33 Republicans who voted against final passage of Bush's No Child Left Behind education bill in 2001, and one of 25 Republicans who opposed the GOP's Medicare prescription drug bill in 2003.

Perhaps his loneliest stand has been his battle against congressional earmarks, the special spending provisions slipped into bills by lawmakers to benefit their individual districts or states. The federal projects are then touted by their sponsors at election time, and due to its political value, earmarking is a widespread practice in Congress. From the beginning of his service in the House, Flake vowed never to ask members of the Appropriations Committee for earmarks. He has sponsored numerous amendments to delete specific earmarks, and in 2004 he began naming an "Egregious Earmark of the Week." Almost all of his amendments have been overwhelmingly defeated. He got an average of 68 votes for them in 2006 and 85 votes in 2007. Flake finally won a round in June 2007, when he targeted $129,000 requested for the Home of the Perfect Christmas Tree sought by North Carolina Republican Patrick McHenry. Democrats, irritated by McHenry's pugnacious conservatism, provided most of the votes for passage. In July 2007, Flake sought to block fellow Arizona Rep. Ed Pastor's earmark for a Maricopa Community Colleges project after *The Arizona Republic* reported that MCC had hired Pastor's daughter to run the program. When appropriators once tried to call him out for hypocrisy by publicizing his requests to them for military spending projects, Flake responded that earmarks solely for national defense were legitimate.

Immigration is a big issue in Arizona, which shares a border with Mexico, and Flake has joined with Republican Sen. John McCain of Arizona in backing comprehensive bills with legalization and guest-worker programs as well as enforcement provisions. He warned that Republicans faced negative political consequences from Latino voters if they failed to pursue legislation that went beyond simply punishing illegal immigrants. In March 2007, he and Illinois Rep. Luis Gutierrez, a liberal Democrat, introduced such a bill requiring illegal immigrants to pay fines and back taxes and return to their countries before being granted legal status. With Democrats in the majority, Flake said "the planets were aligned" for the legislation, but it failed to pass the Senate in June and July of 2007, and the House leadership never brought it to the floor for a vote. Flake also organized the bipartisan Cuba Working Group to review the U.S. embargo of Cuba, and he has pushed repeatedly to lift restrictions on travel by U.S. citizens to Cuba, with occasional victories on the House floor. He has made five trips to Cuba and has continued to work, most recently with Democrat Bill Delahunt of Massachusetts, to end the U.S. embargo on trade.

Flake has paid a price for his independence. In January 2007, the Republican leadership took away his seat on the Judiciary Committee, though six other members had less seniority than he did. In January 2008, after Republican Rep. Roger Wicker of Mississippi was appointed to the Senate and resigned from the House, Flake sought his seat on Appropriations—ground zero for earmarks. The seat went instead to Alabama Republican Jo Bonner, who had been chief of staff to longtime Appropriations member Sonny Callahan before being elected to take Callahan's place. In November 2008, Flake once again sought a seat on Appropriations but seemed to realize that his chances were nil. So that month, he called for the replacement of the Republican leadership.

Flake gave some thought to challenging McCain in the 2004 Senate primary but decided against it. Instead he faced a serious primary challenge himself. Former state Sen. Stan Barnes called Flake "fringe, libertarian, and just a bit kooky," and attacked him for his stance on immigration. Flake won 59%-41%, an unimpressive showing for an incumbent. But he had no Democratic opponent in November. Just days after the election, he announced that he would abandon his term-limit pledge. "As much as I hate to admit making a mistake, I made a big one here," he said, repeating a theme often invoked by lawmakers who find they like being in Washington more than they though they would.

In 2006, Flake had no opposition in the primary and no Democratic opponent in the general election. Unlike some Arizona Republicans, he supported McCain for president early on, and campaigned for him in New Hampshire, an early primary state, when McCain's chances appeared slight. In 2008, Flake had a Democratic opponent, but won 62%-35%. The day after the election, he wrote words of advice to the Republican Party, which he published on the Web: "I suggest that we return to first principles. At the top of that list has to be a recommitment to limited government. After eight years of profligate spending and soaring deficits, voters can be forgiven for not knowing that limited government has long been the first article of faith for Republicans.

SEVENTH DISTRICT

Raul Grijalva (D)

Elected 2002, 4th term; b. Feb. 19, 1948, Tucson; home, Tucson; U. of AZ, B.A. 1985; Catholic; married (Ramona); 3 children.

Elected Office: Tucson Unified Schl. Dist. Governing Bd., 1974–86; Pima Cnty. Bd. of Supervisors, 1988–2002.

Professional Career: Asst. dean of Hisp. Affairs, U. of AZ., 1987.

DC Office: 1440 LHOB, 20515, 202-225-2435; Fax: 202-225-1541; Web site: www.house.gov/grijalva.

State Offices: Tucson, 520-622-6788; Yuma, 928-343-7933.

Committees: *Education & Labor* (14th of 29 D): Early Childhood, Elementary & Secondary Education; Workforce Protections. *Natural Resources* (8th of 29 D): National Parks, Forests & Public Lands (Chmn); Water & Power.

Group Ratings

	ADA	ACLU	AFS	LCV	ITIC	NTU	COC	ACU	CFG	FRC
2008	100	100	100	85	43	15	44	8	8	0
2007	100	—	100	90	—	3	50	0	0	—

National Journal Ratings

	2007 LIB	—	2007 CONS		2008 LIB	—	2008 CONS
Economic	82%	—	0%		85%	—	0%
Social	89%	—	8%		82%	—	0%
Foreign	86%	—	14%		92%	—	0%
Composite	89%	—	11%		93%	—	7%

Key Votes of the 110th Congress

1. Increase minimum wage	Y	5. Share immigration data	N	9. Withdraw troops 8/08	Y
2. Expand SCHIP	Y	6. Foreign aid abortion ban	N	10. No operations in Iran	Y
3. Raise CAFE standards	Y	7. Ban gay bias in workplace	Y	11. Free trade with Peru	N
4. Bail out financial markets	N	8. Repeal D.C. gun law	N	12. Overhaul FISA	N

Election Results

2008 general	Raul Grijalva (D)	124,304	(63%)	($720,896)
	Joseph Sweeney (R)	64,425	(33%)	
	Raymond Petrulsky (Lib)	7,755	(4%)	
2008 primary	Raul Grijalva (D)	unopposed		

Prior Winning Percentages: 2006 (61%); 2004 (62%); 2002 (59%)

Population		Race/Ethnicity		Work	
Pop. 2007:	785,959	White:	34.3%	Private:	74.0%
Change since 2000:	Up 22.6%	Black:	3.0%	Government:	19.8%
Urban:	83.6%	Hispanic:	54.5%	Self-employed:	6.0%
Rural:	16.4%	Asian:	1.7%	Blue collar:	27.4%
Area size:	22,891 sq. mi.	Native Am.:	5.0%	White collar:	49.7%
		Hawaiian:	0.1%	Khaki collar:	0.5%
Age		Two+ races:	1.2%	Other:	22.3%
Median age:	31.1 yrs.			Median income:	$38,660
More than 65 yrs:	11.2%	*Ancestry*		Median home value:	$145,400
Less than 18 yrs:	29.4%	German:	8.9%	Poverty:	20.8%
		Irish:	5.9%		
Education		English:	5.2%	**Military Veterans**	
H.S. grad:	73.6%			% of Pop:	10.8%
College grad:	15.0%				
Grad degree:	5.3%				

Southern Arizona, though technically part of Mexico for hundreds of years, was never a home to Latin American civilization as northern New Mexico was. Here the hot desert land was inhabited mainly by Native American tribes such as the Apache and Cocopah. They kept their culture and language alive in the region until they were uprooted by English-speaking whites who came in on cavalry horses and in miners' wagons and railroad cars in the late 19th century. In 1854, the Gadsden Purchase—$10 million to Mexico for 30,000 square miles of desert—cleared the way for a southern transcontinental railroad.

2008 Presidential Vote		
Obama (D)	123,202	(57%)
McCain (R)	89,725	(42%)
2004 Presidential Vote		
Kerry (D)	105,532	(57%)
Bush (R)	79,674	(43%)
Cook Partisan Voting Index:	D + 6	

Today's Hispanic Arizonans are mostly descendants of later immigrants from Mexico, some of whom came over the border in the sleepier days before World War II, when *la frontera* was scarcely patrolled. Many more have come since the 1980s to partake in the dazzling economic growth in the region over a quarter-century. That immigration pattern has slowed considerably in recent years, with the collapse of the real estate market in Arizona and stronger law enforcement against illegal aliens.

The 7th Congressional District of Arizona was newly created in 2002 and is the state's second Hispanic-majority district, with a population in 2000 that was 51% Hispanic. It is geographically a giant of a district—larger than Rhode Island, Delaware, Hawaii, Connecticut, and New Jersey put together—and shares 300 miles of border with Mexico. The district is a collection of four distant communities connected by many square miles of uninhabited Sonoran desert. One is the suburb of Tolleson just west of downtown Phoenix. The second is the heavily Latino west and south sides of Tucson. The largest employer in southern Arizona is the University of Arizona in Tucson. The third community is Yuma, located at a Colorado River crossing in an irrigated agricultural valley, often the hottest place in the country. The lower Colorado produces much of the nation's lettuce and in the winter is one of the nation's biggest RV centers. The fourth is the Mexican border town of Nogales, which is 94% Hispanic and located near many maquiladora plants, long an entry point for the drug trade and the scene of many illegal border crossings in recent years. The twin smuggling tides—drugs and people—have inflicted damage on the fragile desert ecosystem. In an interesting example of international cooperation, the sister cities of Nogales, Arizona, and Nogales, Sonora, have signed an agreement to respond jointly to fire and hazardous-materials emergencies.

Out in the desert there is the Organ Pipe Cactus National Monument, the Tohono O'odham Indian Reservation, and the Barry M. Goldwater Air Force Range, the largest aerial gunnery range after Nevada's Nellis Air Force Range. It is twice the size of Delaware. However, 95% of it is not used for target practice in order to protect the habitat of the endangered Sonoran pronghorn antelope. Near Nogales, other unique forms of wildlife are found in the Tumacacori Highlands, including endangered species such as the jaguar, peregrine falcon, Chiricahua leopard frog, and Mexican spotted owl. With its brutal desert heat, the Baboquivari trail that runs north to the Tohono O'odham nation has been the deadliest immigrant crossing in the nation. Trash left behind by illegal crossers has caused growing environmental problems. The 7th District, home to seven Indian tribes, is one of two overwhelmingly Democratic districts in Arizona.

The congressman from the 7th District is Raul Grijalva, a Democrat first elected in 2002. He grew up in Tucson, the son of a bracero, or, guest worker, who emigrated from Mexico in 1945. He graduated from the University of Arizona and has lived in the city all of his life; he has deep roots in the immigrant community on the city's southwest side. He was director of El Pueblo Neighborhood Center and assistant dean for Hispanic student affairs at the university. In 1974, he was elected to the Tucson school board and served 12 years. In 1988, he was elected a Pima County supervisor and served 14 years. As supervisor, he backed an effort to extend medical and dental benefits to same-sex domestic partners of county employees and focused on affordable health care, family and children services, and economic growth. Developers and builders helped elect him to office, but his support for planned growth and impact fees later alienated them.

When the district was created in 2002, the Democratic primary in effect determined who would get the seat. Grijalva entered with a home-court advantage: 64% of the primary votes were cast in Pima County. His chief opponent was state Sen. Elaine Richardson, who was endorsed by the women's fundraising group EMILY's List and spent more than $500,000 on ads. She criticized Grijalva for wasting taxpayer money on a $3.8 million contract to survey all the manholes in Pima County. Although outspent nearly 3-1, Grijalva had a well-organized grassroots effort and endorsements from labor unions, teachers' unions, and the Sierra Club. Mocking his opponent's national funding, Grijalva created "Adelita's List," invoking a name alluding to the independent women who fought in the Mexican Revolution. He opposed the partial privatization of Social Security and a proposed increase in the retirement age, and he supported amnesty for illegal immigrants. He won the primary with 41% to Richardson's 21%. In Pima County, Grijalva got 54% of the vote. He won easily in November and his daughter, Adelita, won a seat on the school board.

In the House, Grijalva's voting record is strongly liberal. On the Education and Labor Committee, he urged full funding of the Bush administration's 2001 No Child Left Behind law, which tied federal funding to student performance on standardized tests. Grijalva and other liberals complained the program was too underfinanced to be effective; he derisively dubbed it the "No Child Left Untested" law. Much of his effort has been focused on immigration policy. He has co-sponsored bills to raise the number of low-skill visas from 5,000 to 400,000 and to allow legalization for some illegal immigrants, provided they pay a $500 civil fine. He has worked to expedite citizenship for members of the U.S. military and to do away with per-country limits on green cards.

Another strong area of interest for him is his work as chairman of the Subcommittee on National Parks, Forests and Public Lands, which is a part of the Natural Resources Committee. He has worked to stop uranium mining in the Kaibab National Forest and on federal lands near the Grand Canyon. He also has sought wilderness designation for the Tumacacori Highlands, to prevent mining claims in the Coronado National Forest, and, more generally, to prevent oil and gas drilling without environmental review on public lands where it is currently allowed. He and Tucson-area colleague Democratic Rep. Gabrielle Giffords got the House to vote in favor of creation of a Santa Cruz Valley National Heritage Area in October 2007. He has opposed the 4,000-acre Rosemont copper mine on U.S. Forest Service land southeast of Tucson, and has sought to protect Tumamoc Hill from development by trading federal lands with the developer. He has worked to create a Sonoran Desert conservation system, which would protect 3.3 million acres and 56 miles of trails in Arizona.

In 2008, Grijalva was widely mentioned as a possible nominee for Interior secretary, and was supported by several national Hispanic organizations and by Natural Resources Chairman Nick Rahall, D-W.V. But in December, Obama announced then-Sen. Ken Salazar, D-Colo., as his choice. "The problem was, I didn't have anybody on the inside promoting me on the transition team," Grijalva told reporters. "We are a little more assertive about some of the issues than others. That possibly played a role." The same month, he turned down an offer of a seat on the Ways and Means Committee, saying he preferred to stay on Natural Resources. "You come to Congress for the things that you care about—resources, education, and labor," he said. "Ways and Means is prestigious and powerful. It ain't my cup of tea."

Grivalja is on the far left in the Democratic Caucus. In December 2007, he joined 22 other Democrats in the move to impeach Dick Cheney. In November 2008, he was elected co-chair with Rep. Lynn Woolsey, D-Calif., of the 75-member Congressional Progressive Caucus. He endorsed former North Carolina Sen. John Edwards for president but switched to Obama shortly before Edwards's withdrawal. But Hillary Rodham Clinton carried Arizona and the 7th District in the Super Tuesday primary. In the general election, Grijalva campaigned for Obama among Hispanic voters in Arizona, Colorado, and New Mexico. He has been re-elected by wide margins.

EIGHTH DISTRICT

Gabrielle Giffords (D)

Elected 2006, 2nd term; b. June 8, 1970, Tucson; home, Tucson; Scripps Col., B.A. 1993, Cornell U., M.S. 1996; Jewish; married (Mark Kelly); 2 children.

Elected Office: AZ House of Reps., 2000–02; AZ Senate, 2002–05.

Professional Career: Price Waterhouse Coopers, 1996–97; CEO and pres., El Campo Tire, 1997–2000.

DC Office: 1728 LHOB, 20515, 202-225-2542; Fax: 202-225-0378; Web site: giffords.house.gov.

State Offices: Sierra Vista, 520-459-3115; Tucson, 520-881-3588.

Committees: *Armed Services* (26th of 35 D): Air & Land Forces; Readiness. *Foreign Affairs* (27th of 28 D): Western Hemisphere. *Science & Technology* (9th of 26 D): Energy & Environment; Space & Aeronautics (Chmn).

Group Ratings

	ADA	ACLU	AFS	LCV	ITIC	NTU	COC	ACU	CFG	FRC
2008	80	91	86	77	100	19	67	20	12	5
2007	80	—	91	95	—	9	61	4	14	—

National Journal Ratings

	2007 LIB	—	2007 CONS	2008 LIB	—	2008 CONS
Economic	62%	—	37%	52%	—	48%
Social	53%	—	46%	48%	—	50%
Foreign	54%	—	45%	55%	—	43%
Composite	57%	—	43%	52%	—	48%

Key Votes of the 110th Congress

1. Increase minimum wage	Y	5. Share immigration data	Y	9. Withdraw troops 8/08	Y
2. Expand SCHIP	Y	6. Foreign aid abortion ban	N	10. No operations in Iran	Y
3. Raise CAFE standards	Y	7. Ban gay bias in workplace	*	11. Free trade with Peru	*
4. Bail out financial markets	Y	8. Repeal D.C. gun law	Y	12. Overhaul FISA	Y

Election Results

2008 general	Gabrielle Giffords (D) 179,629	(55%)	($2,775,313)
	Tim Bee (R) 140,553	(43%)	($1,932,103)
	Paul Davis (Lib) 8,081	(2%)	
2008 primary	Gabrielle Giffords (D) .... unopposed		

Prior Winning Percentages: 2006 (54%)

Population		Race/Ethnicity		Work	
Pop. 2007:	728,729	White:	71.0%	Private:	71.9%
Change since 2000:	Up 13.6%	Black:	3.3%	Government:	21.3%
Urban:	87.3%	Hispanic:	20.3%	Self-employed:	6.6%
Rural:	12.7%	Asian:	2.5%	Blue collar:	15.9%
Area size:	9,057 sq. mi.	Native Am.:	0.7%	White collar:	64.8%
Age		Hawaiian:	0.1%	Khaki collar:	1.5%
Median age:	41.0 yrs.	Two+ races:	1.8%	Other:	17.8%
More than 65 yrs:	17.5%	*Ancestry*		Median income:	$48,586
Less than 18 yrs:	22.2%	German:	15.9%	Median home value:	$214,700
Education		Irish:	10.2%	Poverty:	10.7%
H.S. grad:	90.9%	English:	9.9%	**Military Veterans**	
College grad:	33.8%			% of Pop:	17.0%
Grad degree:	13.5%				

Arizona's first frontier was just south of today's Tucson, where Franciscan friars built San Xavier del Bac mission in the 18th century. To the east, the late-19th-century mining towns of Tombstone and Bisbee sprang up on mountainsides, where miners dug up gold and silver and much of America's copper. Cochise County, where Tombstone and Bisbee are located, was the most populous county when Arizona became the 48th state in 1912. Here the white man finally quashed the rebellion of the land-starved American Indian, when the Apache leader Geronimo faced the U.S. Army in 1900. In the last decade, Cochise County has been an active frontier again. After the Border Patrol reduced illegal crossings in California and Texas, Mexicans wishing to enter the United States came to Agua Prieta, just across the border from the town of Douglas. There they fan out, cross the border, and use the area's numerous roads, mountain trails, and ranch lands to get to Tucson and Phoenix. The Border Patrol's Tucson sector has become the most active on the border, with nearly half the total border apprehensions and illegal drugs seized in 2008. More-intensive border enforcement has resulted in decreases in these metrics since 2004, but many bodies are still found in the mountains and in the desert.

2008 Presidential Vote

McCain (R)	181,771	(52%)
Obama (D)	161,164	(46%)

2004 Presidential Vote

Bush (R)	167,647	(53%)
Kerry (D)	147,300	(46%)

Cook Partisan Voting Index: R + 4

One immigrant destination is Tucson itself, Arizona's second metropolis. It is much smaller, more rough-hewn, and politically less conservative than Phoenix. Tucson is a high-tech city and home of the University of Arizona. It is also a tourist destination, with famed resorts. For nearly 40 years, Tucson was the political base of the brothers Udall: Stewart, a representative in the 1950s and the Interior secretary in the 1960s; and Morris, a representative for 30 years and pioneering environmentalist who retired in 1991 because of Parkinson's disease and died in 1998. Now their sons, Tom and Mark Udall, represent New Mexico and Colorado in the Senate; a cousin, Stephen Udall, finished second in the 2002 Democratic primary in Arizona's 1st District.

The 8th Congressional District of Arizona includes all of Tucson, except the Latino-dominated west and south sides, which are in the 7th District. The 8th also includes the eastern half of surrounding Pima County and much southeastern Arizona desert real estate: all of Cochise County, Douglas, and Sierra Vista near Fort Huachuca, which is the site of the Army Military Intelligence Center, where military interrogators are trained. It also takes in small portions of Santa Cruz and Pinal counties. Politically it is closely divided, voting narrowly for George W. Bush in 2000 and 2004 and for John McCain in 2008.

The congresswoman from the 8th District is Gabrielle Giffords, a Democrat elected in 2006. Giffords grew up in Tucson, a third-generation southern Arizonan. She attended Scripps College in California, won a William Fulbright scholarship to study in Mexico, and graduated from Cornell University in 1996 with a master's degree in regional planning. After working briefly in New York, Giffords returned home to Tucson to take over for her father at the family tire business. Giffords was elected to the state House in 2000, and two years later, at age 32, became the youngest woman ever elected to the state Senate. While in the Legislature, she was a managing partner for a commercial property management business.

When 11-term Republican Rep. Jim Kolbe announced his retirement in November 2005, Giffords was a serious contender for the swing district. Kolbe, the House's only openly gay Republican, had been a leader on free trade, Social Security restructuring, and immigration. Except for a close race in 1998, the moderate Kolbe had little trouble winning re-election, but he faced tougher competition in the 2004 Republican primary. Then-state Rep. Randy Graf criticized Kolbe for his support of an immigrant guest-worker program and held the incumbent to 57%.

Giffords resigned her seat in the state Senate to campaign. In the Democratic primary, she faced local television news anchor Patty Weiss. Giffords was supported by labor unions, the women's fundraising group EMILY's List, and the Sierra Club. She had a nearly 3-to-1 fundraising advantage. She won the six-candidate September primary 54%-31%. The Republican primary was a battle between Graf, supported by the Minuteman Project border patrol group, moderate state Rep. Steve Huffman, and former state Republican Chairman Mike Hellon. Huffman and Hellon split the moderate vote. Graf beat Huffman, 42%-38%, with 13% for Hellon. After the primary, national Republicans ran ads against Giffords but by October gave up the contest and canceled the airtime it had reserved. Kolbe pointedly refused to endorse Graf. Giffords portrayed herself as a pro-business moderate who could work across party lines and publicized her experience running the family tire store. Giffords won 54%-42%, even carrying Cochise County, where the Minuteman Project was active.

Giffords has shown a flair for attracting attention. Her campaign featured photos of her with her motorcycle and with her fiancé, Discovery astronaut Mark Kelly (they were married in November 2007). Her ambition has also drawn notice. National Public Radio shadowed her as a freshman throughout 2007, reporting on her early days in Congress. She made 340 appearances in the district in her first term and sent out more franked mail than any other House member in 2007. "I wouldn't be surprised if she's the first or second female president of the United States," said former Labor Secretary Robert Reich, a Giffords mentor, in 2007. The Democratic leadership, mindful of the two large military bases in the district, gave her a seat on the Armed Services Committee. She was the first freshman to travel to the Iraq war zone in February 2007 and vocally opposed the Bush administration's troop surge to try to regain control of the country. "A surge can temporarily drive out insurgents or drive them underground. It's not a long-term solution," she said. But in May 2007, Giffords voted for the war supplemental spending bill with no timetable for withdrawal, as some Democrats were demanding. After a trip to Iraq in November 2007, she conceded that the surge had resulted in some progress. She spent four days in Afghanistan and Pakistan in April 2008, then called for a phased withdrawal from Iraq and greater attention to Afghanistan.

Giffords favored an immigration bill with a guest-worker program and creating a path to legalization as well as enforcement provisions. The Tucson sector of the border is the only sector without a permanent interior checkpoint. Residents in towns along Interstate 19 south of Tucson feared that one would cause illegal immigrants to cross their property, and Kolbe had used his seat on the powerful Appropriations Committee to prevent the Border Patrol from building one. In 2007, the Border Patrol opened a checkpoint north of Tubac. Giffords convened a legislative working group on the subject, which voted against a permanent checkpoint. The Border Patrol went ahead anyway, prompting Giffords to host several raucous community meetings in the area. She got the agency to reduce the size of the checkpoint south of Green Valley, and the agency offered to build only an interim checkpoint and to study making it permanent. Giffords called for a doubling of the number of H-1B visas for high-tech workers, and extension of the E-Verify system, which allows employers to check the immigration status of new hires. With 7th District Rep. Raul Grijalva, a Democrat, she sought $5 billion in the stimulus package to renovate ports of entry on the border.

She has backed funding for solar energy, and called for Arizona to be the Silicon Valley of solar. Giffords said that she opposed earmarking, the practice among lawmakers of inserting pet spending items into appropriations bills, but that she would actively seek and disclose earmarks as long as they are allowed under House rules. She asked for $326 million in earmarks in 2007, mostly for projects in Fort Huachuca and the Davis-Monthan Air Force Base, and for $120 million in 2008, including $4 million for advanced research on Silver Fox and Manta unmanned aerial systems.

Both major political parties made the 8th District a priority in 2008. The Service Employees International Union began running ads for Giffords as early as July 2007, and she raised $1.2 million by October 2007. Her Republican opponent was state Senate President Tim Bee, a popular moderate. He and Giffords were schoolmates in northeast Tucson from kindergarten through high school, and were both first elected to the Legislature in 2000. Bee criticized Giffords for voting to sideline the Colombia Free Trade Agreement in April 2008, and criticized her for seeking earmarks and opposing offshore oil drilling. In July 2008, Kolbe withdrew his support of Bee after he cast the deciding vote to put on the ballot a state prohibition on same-sex marriage. In September, Giffords voted against the $700 billion bailout of the financial markets, but in October, she voted in favor of an amended bill. Bee opposed both and criticized her for switching. She said she did so because the October bill included an extension of the solar-energy tax credit. She won 55%-43%, narrowly carrying Cochise County and winning solidly in Pima County.

★ ARKANSAS ★

Jutting out over the banks of the Arkansas River, in Little Rock's Market District, is the William J. Clinton Presidential Center, home of the nation's largest presidential library. It is a monument to the nation's 42nd president, the most talented and accomplished politician produced by a small state that has produced more than its share of them. Bill Clinton's presidential library is the first with electronic records as well as paper documents. In its alcoves are exhibits and electronic connections to what Clinton considers his greatest achievements, along with a treatment of "the politics of persecution," his take on his impeachment. Clinton, a notoriously hearty eater, decreed that planners set aside space on the grounds for picnics and cookouts. He may not have returned to live in Arkansas after his presidency ended (eight other presidents also chose not to return to their home states), but he is clearly regarded here and elsewhere as an Arkansan, a man whose eloquence and earthiness, outsized ambitions and overly visible faults, are redolent of the state from which he began his unlikely ascent to prominence. That rise has been on the whole a source of pride to Arkansans. For many of them, Clinton's success wiped away the stain of Gov. Orval Faubus, whose disobedience of an order desegregating Little Rock's Central High School prompted President Eisenhower to dispatch federal troops to enforce it in 1957.

Arkansas, like Clinton, began life without many advantages. In area, it's the smallest state between the Mississippi River and the Pacific Ocean. In population, it's the smallest state in the South. It has not been blessed with any great natural resources, unless you count flame-retarding bromine, of which the state produces half the world supply. And it's home to no major industry. Arkansas is the land left over when Louisiana and Missouri were carved out of the Louisiana Purchase and what is now Oklahoma was fenced off as Indian Territory. Its first two senators could not agree on how to pronounce the state's name, but since 1881 it's been illegal to call it *ar-KAN-sas*. Settled by poor farmers with large families, few slaves, and little cash, Arkansas has had no Atlanta or Dallas or even Memphis as a focal point of growth. Arkansas consistently has the second- or third-lowest income levels and percentage of college graduates of any state. However, its economy is far more vibrant and productive than it was in the Faubus years half a century ago. Northwest Arkansas, around Bentonville and Fayetteville, is a boom area, housing the headquarters of Wal-Mart, Tyson Foods, and J.B. Hunt trucking. Population growth has been rapid, with Wal-Mart leading the way. Food processing is a big business; so is the manufacturing of auto parts and medical and construction equipment, and the growing of federally subsidized rice and cotton. Oil is yet another source of wealth: In southern Arkansas, Murphy Oil promises to pay for college for graduates of El Dorado public schools.

Culturally, Arkansas is Jacksonian and religious, settled more by dirt farmers than plantation owners, people who are proud of their independence and willing to fight to maintain it. It is the birthplace of Pentecostal denominations. The Church of God in Christ was started in Little Rock in 1907, and the Assembly of God (now headquartered in Springfield, Mo.) in Hot Springs in 1914. The state has the highest married rate after heavily Mormon Utah and Idaho, but also a high divorce rate, as highlighted in 2005 when Gov. Mike Huckabee, a former Baptist minister, declared "a state of marital emergency" in Arkansas. Huckabee, who, like Clinton, grew up in Hope, was a Republican candidate for president in 2008.

As the late political scientist Diane Blair noted, Arkansas never had a power elite of great plantation owners or economic robber barons. That has left it a heritage without honored traditions or tight standards, but it has also made Arkansas a place of great opportunities, where talented people can move up fast and amass huge fortunes with breakthrough ideas. Sam Walton believed that rural and small-town America would support a chain of giant discount stores that, through tough bargaining with vendors and ultraquick distribution, could undersell competitors. Walton was the richest American when he died in April 1992, and Wal-Mart today is the largest private employer in the world, with a payroll of 1.8 million people. Jack Stephens and his brother, Witt, both now deceased, started an investment banking house in Little Rock specializing in underwriting municipal bonds and investing in businesses that are a mix of private enterprise, government subsidies, and public regulation. They amassed a billion-dollar fortune. Don Tyson took his father's chicken business and made it one of the biggest food producers in America. J.B. Hunt established his trucking empire in Arkansas. These business giants have cultivated a down-home, laid-back style, but they have also skillfully united their interests with those of the state's politicians.

Politically, Arkansas was long solidly Democratic, with Republican pockets in the mountains of the northwest. For years, it produced Democratic politicians who accumulated great seniority and power in Washington—longtime House Ways and Means Chairman Wilbur Mills; Sens. John McClellan and William Fulbright, who represented the state for a total of 65 years from the 1940s to the 1970s; and Sens. Dale Bumpers and David Pryor, who served a total of 42 years from the 1970s to the 1990s. The state's current 5-1 Democratic congressional delegation started off in the late 1990s with little seniority, but it has the potential to prosper in Washington. Republicans have won top races occasionally: Winthrop

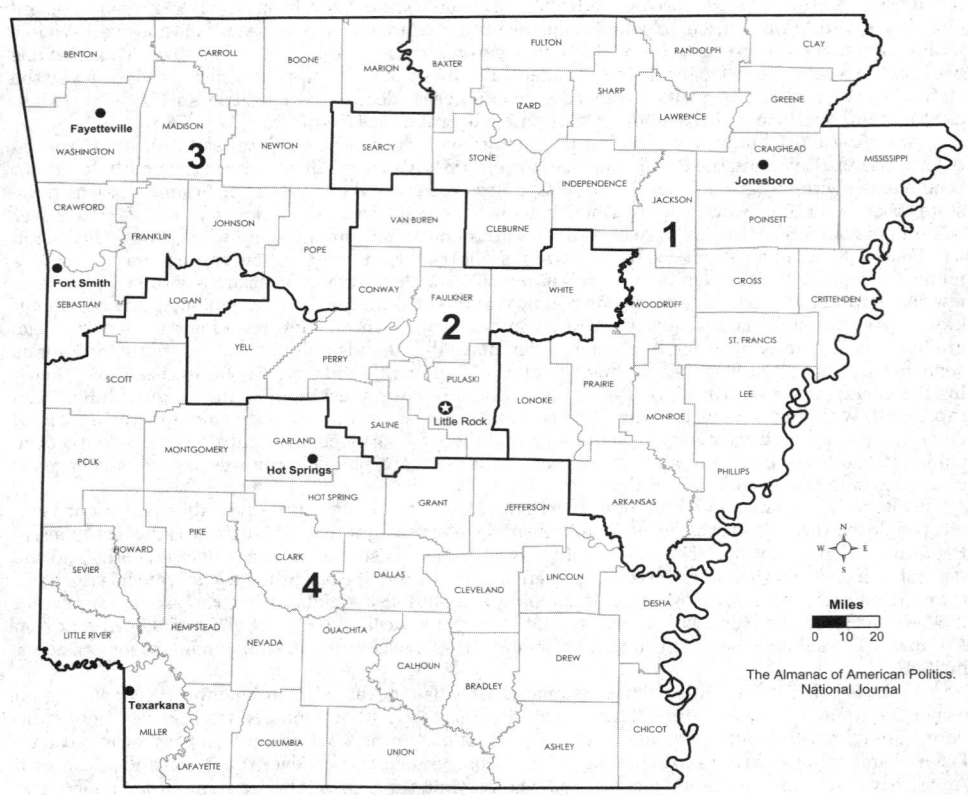

Congressional district boundaries were first effective for 2002.

Population		Household Income		Work	
Pop. 2007:	2,805,353	Under $15k:	18.8%	Private:	76.1%
State rank:	32nd of 50	$15k to $50k:	44.2%	Government:	16.4%
Change since 2000:	Up 4.9%	$50k to $100k:	26.8%	Self-employed:	7.3%
Urban:	52.3%	$100k to $150k:	8.6%	Unemployment (3-yr. average):	4.5%
Rural:	47.7%	Over $150k:	1.6%	Poverty:	17.5%
Native of state:	61.3%	Median income:	$37,555	Blue collar:	28.4%
Not a citizen:	2.9%	**Home Value**		White collar:	54.0%
Area size:	53,179 sq. mi.	Under $100k:	53.7%	Khaki collar:	0.2%
Most populous cities		$100k to $300k:	40.0%	Other:	17.3%
1. Little Rock	190,142	$300k to $500k:	4.3%	**Age**	
2. Fort Smith	83,575	$500k to $1 mil:	1.7%	Median age:	36.8 yrs.
3. Fayetteville	69,000	Over $1 million:	0.3%	More than 65 yrs:	13.9%
4. Springdale	63,837	Median:	$93,700	Less than 18 yrs:	24.8%

Race/Ethnicity				Military Veterans		Registered Voters in 2008	
White:	76.3%	*Language*		% of Pop:	12.2%	No party registration	
Black:	15.5%	English:	93.9%	*Veterans by Period*		Voter turnout:	1,086,617
Hispanic:	5.0%	Spanish:	4.4%	WWII and before:	12.0%	Turnout as % of	
Asian:	1.0%	Asian:	0.8%	Korea:	11.6%	voting age:	50.5%
Native Am.:	0.7%	Other		Vietnam:	32.3%	**General Assembly**	
Hawaiian:	0.1%	European	0.8%	Gulf (pre-2001):	12.0%	Senate:	27 D 8 R
Two+ races:	1.4%	**Education**		Gulf (post-2001):	7.1%	House:	71 D 28 R 1 I
Ancestry		H.S. grad:	80.6%	Peace time:	25.0%		
Irish:	11.2%	College grad:	18.7%				
German:	10.6%	Grad degree:	6.3%				
USA:	10.1%						

Rockefeller Sr., was elected governor in 1966 and 1968, following Faubus, and Frank White beat Clinton in 1980. Huckabee took over as governor after Democrat Jim Guy Tucker was convicted and forced from office in 1996. Huckabee was re-elected in 1998 and 2002. But none founded a political dynasty, and each was replaced by a Democrat. Booming northwest Arkansas, heavily Republican, tends to dominate that party's primaries. So Arkansas, which gave George W. Bush solid majorities in 2000 and 2004 and John McCain one of his best showings in 2008, remains at the state and congressional level one of the most Democratic states.

Presidential politics   Arkansas voted for the winners of nine consecutive elections, then for the loser in 2008. It voted 53% for Bill Clinton in 1992 and 54% for him in 1996. Without Clinton at the top of the ticket, it voted less Democratic in subsequent years—46% for Al Gore in 2008, 44% for John Kerry in 2004, and 39% for Barack Obama in 2008. Arkansas, like other states with Jacksonian roots, seemed unenchanted with Obama. At the same time, it showed genuine affection for Hillary Rodham Clinton, notwithstanding her relocation to New York. She trounced Obama in Arkansas's presidential primary on Super Tuesday, 70%-26%, her best margin of victory in any state contest. Polls looking ahead to the general election suggested that Clinton might well have won Arkansas against John McCain or any other Republican candidate, except perhaps former Arkansas Gov. Mike Huckabee, who captured the state's 2008 Republican presidential primary easily.

2008 Presidential Vote
McCain (R)..........................638,017   (59%)
Obama (D) 422,310   (39%)

2008 Democratic Presidential Primary
Clinton (D)..........................220,136   (70%)
Obama (D) 82,476   (26%)

2008 Republican Presidential Primary
Huckabee (R)........................138,557   (60%)
McCain (R)............................46,343   (20%)
Romney (R) 30,804   (14%)

2004 Presidential Vote
Bush (R)..............................572,898   (54%)
Kerry (D)..............................469,953   (45%)

Arkansas's presidential primary used to be in May, and it attracted little attention. The Legislature in 2005 voted to hold it on February 5, which in 2008 came on Super Tuesday. Arkansas Democrats tried to get the Democratic National Committee to make it one of the first four states to vote, but the national Democrats instead chose South Carolina because of its higher African-American percentage and its tradition of early Republican primaries.

Congressional districting

111th Congress Lineup	
3 D	1 R
110th Congress Lineup	
3 D	1 R

In April 2001, the Democratic Legislature slightly adjusted the boundaries of Arkansas's four congressional districts to meet the equal-population standard. Because it didn't split counties, the Legislature's plan had the highest population difference in the nation between the districts—6,698 people—but it also contained a backup provision: If a court found the plan invalid, it would be repealed and 4,400 voters would be shifted between districts. A court challenge never materialized, however. Republican Gov. Mike Huckabee, lacking the votes to prevent an override of his veto, let the plan become law without his signature. Arkansas is expected to retain its four districts in the reapportionment following the 2010 census, and because the Legislature is likely to remain overwhelmingly Democratic, there seems little prospect for much change in district boundaries beyond what is required by the equal-population standard.

Governor

Mike Beebe (D)

Elected 2006, term expires Jan. 2011, 1st term; b. Dec. 28, 1946, Amagon; home, Searcy; AR St. U., B.A. 1968, U. of AR, J.D. 1972; Episcopalian; married (Ginger); 3 children.

Military Career: Army Reserve, 1968–74.

Elected Office: AR Senate, 1982–2002; AR atty. gen., 2002–06.

Professional Career: Practicing atty., 1972–2002.

Office: State Capitol, Rm. 250, Little Rock, 72201, 501-682-2345; Fax: 501-682-1382; Web site: www.governor.arkansas.gov.

Election Results

2006 general	Mike Beebe (D)	430,765	(56%)
	Asa Hutchinson (R)	315,040	(41%)
2006 primary	Mike Beebe (D)	unopposed	

Democrat Mike Beebe (*BEE-bee*) was elected governor of Arkansas in 2006. He was born to a single mother in his great-grandmother's country shack outside of tiny Amagon. As a child he moved frequently—St. Louis, Detroit, Houston, and Alamogordo, N.M.—as his mother worked through a succession of waitressing jobs and marriages. He never met his father and recalls going to five different schools in the fifth grade alone. "It taught me to adapt, to be resilient, and it taught me to make friends fast," he told the *Arkansas Democrat-Gazette.* His mother returned to Arkansas in time for him to enroll in high school and to put down roots in the state. Beebe studied political science at Arkansas State University, earned a law degree at the University of Arkansas at Fayetteville and served in the U.S. Army Reserves. He excelled as a trial lawyer, and he continued to practice during his years in the state Legislature.

In 1982, Beebe won election to the state Senate, where he served for two decades and developed a reputation as a consensus builder. He helped write laws setting a uniform property-tax rate for school funding and creating a $300 homestead property-tax exemption. In 2002, Beebe, who had run unopposed in every election, considered running for governor against Republican Gov. Mike Huckabee, but he lacked statewide name recognition. So he ran instead for attorney general. Unopposed again, he became attorney general.

Term limits prevented Huckabee from running again in 2006, leaving no incumbent governor on the ballot for the first time since a young Bill Clinton won the office in 1978. The governor's office was the next logical move for Beebe, who told the *Democrat-Gazette* that he was unlikely to run for another office if he lost the race. "I'm not running for governor because I want to run for something else. I'm running for governor because that's what I want to be, nothing else, and for a very good reason: You can do a whole lot to lead your state," he said. Beebe had no opposition in the Democratic primary. At first it appeared Republicans would have a contested primary between former Rep. Asa Hutchinson and Lt. Gov. Win Rockefeller, the billionaire heir to the Standard Oil fortune. But Rockefeller suffered from a rare blood ailment and dropped out of race in July 2005. He died a year later. Hutchinson, who had run unsuccessfully for Senate and for attorney general, had won three terms in Congress before resigning the seat to head the Drug Enforcement Agency. He later became a Homeland Security undersecretary.

In the general election contest against Hutchinson, Beebe reminded voters of his humble upbringing and campaigned on expanded pre-kindergarten programs, comprehensive health care, a $50 million discretionary fund to help attract business investment and phasing out the state's 6-cent grocery tax. Hutchinson questioned Beebe's commitment to tax relief; Beebe suggested Hutchinson chose to run for governor because President Bush had not promoted him to secretary of the Homeland Security Department. The two candidates argued over how best to combat illegal immigration, debated Hutchinson's record at Homeland Security, and sparred over past gun-control votes. Hutchinson attacked Beebe for standing on the sidelines as attorney general after the state Supreme Court struck down a state rule that prevented gay foster parenting. He also tried to link Beebe to state Sen. Nick Wilson, who went to prison in 1999 for tax evasion and conspiracy. Although Beebe and Wilson had served together in the state Senate, they were in opposing factions and often disagreed. In the last two weeks of the campaign, one Hutchinson television spot featured children describing a politician as a "backslapper" and a "flip-flopper" and saying that politicians "tell voters what they want to hear." A girl concludes: "Just like Mike Beebe." Beebe called the ad shameful; Hutchinson maintained it was meant to be lighthearted. Beebe had a big financial advantage: $6.3 million to Hutchinson's $3.3 million. And Bill Clinton campaigned for Beebe, while Bush stumped for Hutchinson. On Election Day, Beebe won 56%-41% and helped sweep six other Democrats into statewide offices.

With the help of a Democratic Legislature, Beebe moved quickly in his first months to make good on campaign promises and had the good fortune to inherit an estimated $919 million budget surplus. Beebe's years in the Legislature and his hands-on approach to governing helped him avoid public battles with the lawmakers and allowed him to advance much of his legislative agenda, including a bill that halved the state grocery sales tax, from 6% to 3%. The grocery-tax cut accounted for about $122 million of $197.5 million in total tax relief passed by the Legislature; it also included an increase in the homestead property-tax credit to $350, the elimination of state income tax for people with incomes below the poverty level, and a reduction in the sales-tax rate that manufacturers paid for natural gas and electricity. Legislators also approved $456 million to build and improve public school buildings and gave the governor discretion to spend nearly $188 million on other projects.

Beebe kept a low profile on a Republican proposal banning gays from serving as foster parents, and the proposal died in committee. The Legislature also fell short of passing campaign finance and ethics changes, animal-cruelty legislation and limits on payday lending practices. Lawmakers wrapped up work in 86 days, making for the Legislature's shortest session since Bill Clinton was governor.

In 2008 and 2009, the state-revenue picture grew bleaker as the effects of the national recession kicked in. Beebe's agenda became less ambitious, but he managed to win an $86 million increase in the cigarette and tobacco tax, over the objections of some lawmakers and cigarette manufacturers. The proceeds of the tax hike were to pay for Beebe's plan to expand health care programs, including state-of-the-art improvements in emergency care, an expansion of Medicaid health insurance for children, and community health centers. He also worked with the Legislature to establish a state lottery, which was approved by voters in November and was to be used to fund college scholarships. Beebe also hoped to reduce the grocery sales tax by another 1%, bringing it to 2%. The reduction would cut state revenues by $30 million, but Beebe has long argued that the tax is regressive and unfair to lower income workers.

With the passage of time since his election, Beebe sought to mend relationships with Republicans in the Legislature. Republican state Sen. Gilbert Baker, the influential chairman of the Joint Budget Committee, reached out to Beebe for a meeting. In 2006, Baker had been chairman of the state Republican Party, which had helped pay for the ads trying to connect Beebe to Wilson. The ad said: "Nick Wilson stole millions from Arkansas taxpayers. Mike Beebe let it happen."

Senior Senator

Blanche Lincoln (D)

Elected 1998, term expires 2010, 2nd term; b. Sept. 30, 1960, Helena; home, Little Rock; U. of AR, 1979–80, Randolph-Macon Woman's Col., B.S. 1982; Episcopalian; married (Steve); 2 children.

Elected Office: US House of Reps., 1992–96.

Professional Career: Staff asst., U.S. Rep. Bill Alexander, 1982–84; Lobbyist & govt. affairs rep., 1985–91.

DC Office: 355 DSOB, 20510, 202-224-4843; Fax: 202-228-1371; Web site: lincoln.senate.gov.

State Offices: Dumas, 870-382-1023; Fayetteville, 479-251-1224; Jonesboro, 870-910-6896; Little Rock, 501-375-2993; Texarkana, 870-774-3106.

Committees: *Aging (Special)* (3rd of 12 D). *Agriculture, Nutrition & Forestry* (5th of 12 D). *Energy & Natural Resources* (8th of 13 D): National Parks; Public Lands & Forests; Water & Power. *Finance* (6th of 13 D): Energy, Natural Resources & Infrastructure; Health Care; Social Security, Pensions & Family Policy (Chmn).

Group Ratings

	ADA	ACLU	AFS	LCV	ITIC	NTU	COC	ACU	CFG	FRC
2008	80	46	78	91	100	13	75	8	17	11
2007	90	—	86	67	—	9	55	10	6	—

National Journal Ratings

	2007 LIB	—	2007 CONS	2008 LIB	—	2008 CONS
Economic	66%	—	30%	55%	—	43%
Social	62%	—	37%	60%	—	38%
Foreign	56%	—	43%	65%	—	6%
Composite	62%	—	38%	66%	—	35%

Key Votes of the 110th Congress

1. Raise CAFE standards	Y	5. Make English official language	Y	9. Withdraw troops 3/08	Y
2. Expand SCHIP	Y	6. Path to citizenship	Y	10. Iran guard is terrorist group	N
3. Cap greenhouse gases	Y	7. Fetus is unborn child	N	11. Increase missile defense $	N
4. Bail out financial markets	Y	8. Prosecute hate crimes	Y	12. Overhaul FISA	Y

Election Results

2004 general	Blanche Lincoln (D)	580,973	(56%)	($5,816,913)
	Jim Holt (R)	458,036	(44%)	($148,682)
2004 primary	Blanche Lincoln (D)	231,037	(83%)	
	Lisa Burks (D)	47,010	(17%)	

Prior Winning Percentages: 1998 (55%); 1994 House (53%); 1992 House (70%)

Blanche Lambert Lincoln, the senior senator from Arkansas, is a Democrat who was elected to the Senate in 1998, when she was just 38 years old. She is the youngest woman ever elected to the Senate and only the second woman to win a U.S. Senate seat from Arkansas. The first was Hattie Caraway, in 1932. Lincoln grew up in Helena, on the flat rice lands of eastern Arkansas, where her father and brother are the sixth and seventh generations running a farm raising rice, wheat, soybeans, and cotton. She got her bachelor's degree from Randolph-Macon Woman's College in Virginia, and then went to work in 1982 as an aide to 1st District Rep. Bill Alexander, a Democrat. She also was a lobbyist in Washington, D.C., for a brief period. In 1992, she moved back to Arkansas and ran against Alexander, sensing he was in trouble. Her former boss had lost a leadership race in 1986, was named in a lawsuit for a $308,000 debt and had 487 overdrafts totaling $208,000 at the House bank, a practice among lawmakers that was developing into a national scandal. "I'll promise you one thing," ' the 31-year-old challenger said, "I can sure enough balance my checkbook." She won the primary 61%-39%, carrying 23 of 25 counties.

In the House, Lincoln compiled a moderate voting record. She supported much of the Republicans' Contract with America in 1995. But when the moratorium on regulations threatened duck-hunting season and national wildlife refuges were closed, she got laws changed to ensure it wouldn't happen again. (Lincoln likes to both duck-hunt and fish.) She was re-elected in 1994 by only 53%-47%, but she seemed positioned to hold the seat when, in January 1996, she announced that she was pregnant with twin boys and would not run for re-election because of the strain of campaigning in an Arkansas summer during a difficult pregnancy. She and her husband, Steve, are the parents of twin boys, Reece and Bennett.

When Democratic Sen. Dale Bumpers announced he would not run for re-election in 1998, Lincoln got into the race. She flashed snapshots of her twins and ran ads showing her overseeing mealtime, balancing one twin on her lap, bouncing the other on her knee, laying her head on her husband's shoulder. "Daughter, wife, mother, congresswoman . . . Living our rock-solid Arkansas values," the announcer said. In the May primary, she faced Attorney General Winston Bryant, the Democratic nominee in the 1996 Senate race. She led by an impressive 45%-27%, getting 64% in her old 1st District, which cast nearly one-third of the votes. She won the June runoff 62%-38%.

In the general election, Lincoln stanched a Republican tide that had been rising since President Clinton left the state. The Republican nominee was Fay Boozman, an ophthalmologist from Rogers, in northwest Arkansas. Boozman said he had had a profound religious experience in 1992, sold his medical practice, and ran for the state Senate, where he was the champion of a ban on partial-birth abortion. He said the Bible dictated his anti-tax philosophy. But he made a serious gaffe when he said it is rare for women to get pregnant by rape because fear triggers a hormonal change that blocks conception. Lincoln won 55%-42%. Boozman carried the northwest corner of the state and little else.

Lincoln's voting record is to the left of the midpoint of the Senate. In 2000, she was among a group of senators who formed a centrist group called the Third Way. Working with her 1st District successor, Democratic Rep. Marion Berry, she promoted farm exports and strongly supported ending the Cuba trade embargo. She voted for the partial-birth abortion ban, saying it was "always a difficult vote." In February 2001, Lincoln got a seat on the Finance Committee and played an important role in some key votes in the closely divided Senate. She and other moderates negotiated with Republican Chairman Charles Grassley on legislation to make the child-care tax refundable to those who pay no income tax and to create a new

10% income bracket, both of which ultimately passed. She was one of 12 Democrats to vote for President Bush's massive tax cut in 2001.

In 2005, she opposed Republican attempts in the Finance Committee to reduce the growth of Medicare and Medicaid spending, and in 2006 she successfully fought for funding in the budget to combat methamphetamine. Lincoln has also proposed numerous changes in tax law: legislation making it easier for disabled veterans to claim tax refunds, a bill permitting individuals to contribute $5,000 annually to tax-free accounts for long-term care, expanding the use of the "rehab tax credit" for the revitalization of older neighborhoods and low-income areas, and providing tax incentives for landowners who protect endangered species on their properties. In 2008, she pushed legislation to give tax credits to small businesses that pay at least 60% of the cost of their employees' health insurance. It didn't pass, but it was a top priority for Lincoln heading into the 111th Congress (2009-10).

As a centrist, Lincoln often goes her own way. She supported the Iraq War but later criticized the Bush administration for mismanaging the war and its aftermath. She was the only Arkansas Democrat to vote for the 2003 Republican plan to create a prescription-drug benefit as part of the Medicare program. "I thought the good outweighed the bad," she said. But in 2004 she co-sponsored a bill to authorize the government to negotiate drug prices with pharmaceutical companies, a provision expressly left out of the original bill because many Republicans opposed it, as did the powerful pharmaceutical industry. While she joined other Democrats in filibustering the nomination of Miguel Estrada and other appeals court nominees, Lincoln supported the nomination of Arkansan Leon Holmes even after he was criticized for years-earlier comments on abortion. He was confirmed 51-46. Lincoln voted for John Roberts as chief justice of the Supreme Court, but she opposed the nomination of Samuel Alito to the court.

Never far from her mind are the rice farmers of Arkansas's Delta. She was one of two Democrats to vote against the farm bill in February 2002, because she said it was not generous enough to cotton and rice farmers. She fought unsuccessfully against limits on farm subsidies. Three rice farms in Stuttgart and Helena were among the top five recipients of farm subsidies in the country. She has supported the $16 million Grand Prairie irrigation project, to replace water that rice farmers get from the nearly depleted alluvial aquifer. And in 2006, she supported disaster relief assistance for farmers hurt by drought and fuel costs.

After Democrats won control of Congress in 2006, Lincoln earned a seat on the Energy and Natural Resources Committee, a position that allows her to promote incentives for biofuels and biodiesel producers. She was expected to focus on energy policy in the new Congress, building on the work she and a group of bipartisan senators began in 2008. The group, which includes fellow Arkansas Sen. Mark Pryor, a Democrat, is aimed at coming up with strategies to end U.S. reliance on oil for energy.

National Republicans, anticipating a Bush victory in Arkansas in 2004, hoped to target Lincoln. But in August 2003, GOP Gov. Mike Huckabee said he wouldn't run against her, and former Rep. Asa Hutchinson made no move to leave his No. 2 post in the Department of Homeland Security. That left the Republican nomination to state Sen. Jim Holt, who raised only $106,000. Lincoln raised $6.4 million. Holt emphasized his opposition to same-sex marriage, which that year Arkansans voted 74%-26% to prohibit, and Lincoln's vote against the federal Family Marriage Amendment. Lincoln ran 11% ahead of Democratic presidential nominee John Kerry and won 56%-44%, losing 20 of Arkansas's 75 counties, mostly in the northwest.

Junior Senator

Mark Pryor (D)

Elected 2002, term expires 2014, 2nd term; b. Jan. 10, 1963, Fayetteville; home, Little Rock; U. of AR, B.A. 1985, J.D. 1988; Christian; married (Jill); 2 children.

Elected Office: AR House of Reps., 1990–94; AR atty. gen., 1998–02.

Professional Career: Practicing atty., 1988–96.

DC Office: 255 DSOB, 20510, 202-224-2353; Fax: 202-228-0908; Web site: pryor.senate.gov.

State Offices: Little Rock, 501-324-6336.

Committees: *Appropriations* (16th of 18 D): Agriculture, Rural Development, Food and Drug Administration & Related Agencies; Commerce, Justice, Science & Related Agencies; Labor, Health and Human Services, Education & Related Agencies; Legislative Branch; Military Construction, Veterans Affairs & Related Agencies. *Commerce, Science & Transportation* (9th of 14 D): Aviation Operations, Safety & Security; Communications, Technology & the Internet; Consumer Protection, Product Safety & Insurance (Chmn); Science & Space; Surface Transportation & Merchant Marine Infrastructure, Safety & Security. *Ethics (Select)* (2nd of 3 D). *Homeland Security & Governmental Affairs* (5th of 10 D): Contracting Oversight; Federal Financial Management, Government Information, Federal Services & International Security; Investigations (Permanent); State, Local & Private Sector Preparedness & Integration (Chmn). *Rules & Administration* (9th of 11 D). *Small Business & Entrepreneurship* (8th of 11 D).

Group Ratings

	ADA	ACLU	AFS	LCV	ITIC	NTU	COC	ACU	CFG	FRC
2008	85	50	100	91	100	6	75	4	8	22
2007	70	—	86	60	—	7	45	12	13	—

National Journal Ratings

	2007 LIB	—	2007 CONS		2008 LIB	—	2008 CONS
Economic	63%	—	35%		61%	—	36%
Social	53%	—	46%		48%	—	48%
Foreign	47%	—	52%		56%	—	40%
Composite	55%	—	45%		57%	—	43%

Key Votes of the 110th Congress

1. Raise CAFE standards	N	5. Make English official language Y	9. Withdraw troops 3/08	Y
2. Expand SCHIP	Y	6. Path to citizenship	N	10. Iran guard is terrorist group Y
3. Cap greenhouse gases	Y	7. Fetus is unborn child	N	11. Increase missile defense $	N
4. Bail out financial markets	Y	8. Prosecute hate crimes	Y	12. Overhaul FISA	Y

Election Results

2008 general	Mark Pryor (D)..	804,678	(80%)	($3,284,632)
	Rebekah Kennedy (Green)................................	207,076	(20%)	($13,392)
2008 primary	Mark Pryor (D)... unopposed			

Prior Winning Percentages: 2002 (54%)

Mark Pryor, the Democratic junior senator from Arkansas elected in 2002, is among the state's most popular politicians. He was the only U.S. senator in 2008 who did not draw a major-party challenge to his re-election, and he coasted to a second term with more than 79% of the vote. Pryor is the son of former Democratic Sen. David Pryor and is one of five children of former senators now serving in the Senate. (The others are Christopher Dodd of Connecticut, Robert Bennett of Utah, Evan Bayh of Indiana and Lisa Murkowski of Alaska.) Mark Pryor grew up in southern Arkansas, the Washington area and Little Rock, the latest in several generations of politically active Pryors in Arkansas. His grandmother, Susie Newton Pryor, was the first woman in Arkansas to run for office after women won the right to vote. His father was elected to the U.S. House in 1966, elected governor in 1974, and then senator in 1978. Mark Pryor graduated from the University of Arkansas and its law school in the 1980s. He practiced law in Little Rock and was elected to the Arkansas House in 1990 and 1992. He became the state attorney general at age 35, the youngest attorney general in the nation (but not in Arkansas history: Bill Clinton won the office at 30). In 1995, he was diagnosed with clear-cell sarcoma, a rare form of cancer. He underwent tendon transplant surgery in his left heel in 1996; the cancer has not returned.

As attorney general, Pryor implemented the state's "Do Not Call Registry." He also pushed for legislation to increase penalties for nursing home accidents and to strengthen background checks for long-term care employees. He worked to reduce utility rates and to remove unsafe baby products from day care centers. In July 2001, Pryor announced that he would run against Sen. Tim Hutchinson, the first Republican to win an Arkansas Senate seat since 1879. A Baptist minister, radio station owner and founder of a Christian school in Rogers, Hutchinson represented that conservative area in the Legislature from 1984 and then for two terms as 3rd District representative in the House. Hutchinson's conservative voting record would ordinarily have made him a favorite for re-election. But in June 1999, Hutchinson filed for divorce from his wife of 29 years, and in August 2000, he married a former member of his staff. For some senators, this would not have hurt politically. But for a Christian conservative, who criticized President Clinton strongly during the impeachment crisis, it was a handicap.

Pryor never mentioned Hutchinson's divorce and remarriage, but a recurrent theme in his campaign was "Tim Hutchinson has changed"—even though Hutchinson's positions on issues had not changed much, if at all. However, one of Pryor's earlier positions had changed, rather dramatically. Running for attorney general in 1998, Pryor had called himself a "pro-choice" candidate. But in the Senate contest, he emphasized his belief that abortion was wrong except in cases of rape, incest, or to save the life of the mother. He avoided saying whether or not the *Roe v. Wade* Supreme Court ruling legalizing abortion should be overturned. Pryor also campaigned on his support for gun rights, increased military spending, and for the Iraq war resolution. He accused Hutchinson of working for special interests, especially the pharmaceutical companies, and for supporting plans that would risk Social Security benefits. Pryor called Hutchinson "way too conservative" for Arkansas.

Pryor's ads were some of the most artful of the 2002 cycle. One showed him, his wife and their two children saying grace before a meal. Then Pryor, holding a Bible, said, "The most important lessons in life are in this book right here." The Pryors belonged to an evangelical church in Little Rock and sent their children to a private Christian school. He turned down an invitation to appear with Hutchinson on the *Meet the Press* news program, explaining that voters wouldn't be able to watch "because they're in church Sunday morning." Another ad invoked the name of his politically popular father. "You know me as Arkansas Attorney General, but I'm also my father's son," Pryor says in the spot. Hutchinson's ads were pedestrian by contrast. President Bush made visits to Arkansas to campaign for him, but the strategy did not succeed in nationalizing the race. Pryor pulled ahead in polls in mid-year and never really fell behind. He won 54%-46%, a solid victory in a year when Democrats lost their majority in the Senate. A survey by pollster John Zogby showed that 12% said Hutchinson's divorce affected their vote—enough by itself to explain his drop from 53% in 1996 to 46% in 2002. Hutchinson's losses were particularly great in his home area. In 1996, he had won 65%-35% in the 3rd Congressional District; in 2002, he carried the district by 56%-44%.

In the Senate, Pryor established a conservative voting record for a Democrat. He backed Bush on efforts to weaken Clinton-era environmental controls (although he later voted against oil drilling in the Arctic National Wildlife Refuge). In March 2003 he voted for the ban on partial-birth abortion and supported an amendment, which failed, granting an exception if the mother's physical health was at risk. He also voted against a resolution supporting *Roe v. Wade,* and in 2006, Pryor voted with Republicans for a bill that would make it a crime to help a minor avoid parental notification laws by traveling to another state for an abortion. He voted against a constitutional amendment barring same-sex marriages, saying the issue should be left to the states, and then supported a state ballot measure in 2004 banning same-sex marriage in Arkansas.

In 2003, Pryor voted against the omnibus appropriations bill that contained $300 million for Arkansas projects and against the $350 billion Bush tax cut. "I just can't support these budgets that send our deficits and national debt soaring out of control," he said. He'll have greater opportunities to rein in spending now that he is a member of the powerful Senate Appropriations Committee, an appointment he secured in early 2009.

The crowning achievement of Pryor's first term was a bill imposing sweeping changes on the Consumer Product Safety Commission. Passed in 2008, the legislation mandated that products be tested by independent laboratories, restricted levels of lead allowed in children's toys, and increased the budget for consumer safety to $105 million from $80 million. His success with that legislation, and his position as chairman of the Commerce Subcommittee on Consumer Protection, Product Safety, and Insurance, gave Pryor a leading role in the Obama administration's efforts to add teeth to the federal regulation of financial markets in the aftermath of the major company failures in 2008 that rocked the economy. Pryor also was poised to be a player on energy policy in the 111th Congress (2009–10). He and a group of nine other senators from both major parties began meeting in 2008 to come up with proposals for moving the United States away from its reliance on oil-based energy. The economic crisis at the end of the year interrupted the group's work. Pryor has also advocated stronger parental controls for the Internet, and has encouraged movie rental chains and retailers to put up signs warning parents about the content of video games.

Pryor prides himself on his ability to work across party lines. "I've checked my party label at the door, and it works," he said in a 2008 interview. He has led successful efforts on legislation to prevent price gouging in the oil supply chain, to make the national "Do Not Call" list permanent, and to require employers to use the federal e-verify system to curb hiring of illegal immigrants.

His centrist voting record has put him in the center of the several high-profile debates. While Pryor opposed Bush's troop "surge" plan to send more combat troops to Iraq, he also opposed a Democratic resolution in 2007 setting a public timetable for withdrawing U.S. troops from Iraq. (He said he favors a deadline but that the timetable should remain classified to prevent terrorists from using it as a planning tool.) In 2005, he was one of the "Gang of 14" senators that brokered the compromise that allowed Bush's judicial nominees to advance through the process while preventing GOP leaders from taking away the Democratic minority's right to filibuster nominees. In 2006, he voted to allow the nomination of the Supreme Court Justice Samuel Alito to advance, but then voted against his confirmation.

Republicans initially planned to target Pryor in 2008, when he was up for re-election for the first time, but they failed to field a prominent candidate to take him on. Their strongest challenger would have been Mike Huckabee, the former 10-year Republican governor, and Huckabee had been encouraged by some Republicans to drop his 2008 presidential bid and run against Pryor. He declined. Meanwhile, Pryor built a $5.5 million war chest. His only opponent was Green Party candidate Rebekah Kennedy, a 30-year-old Quitman attorney with no political experience. He barely campaigned and was easily re-elected.

FIRST DISTRICT

Marion Berry (D)

Elected 1996, 7th term; b. Aug. 27, 1942, Bayou Meto; home, Gillett; U. of AR, B.S. 1965; Methodist; married (Carolyn); 2 children.

Professional Career: Pharmacist, 1965–67; Farmer, 1968–present; AR Soil & Water Conservation Comm., 1986–94, chmn. 1992; Special asst. to the pres., Domestic Policy Cncl., White House, 1993–96.

DC Office: 2305 RHOB, 20515, 202-225-4076; Fax: 202-225-5602; Web site: www.house.gov/berry.

State Offices: Cabot, 501-843-3043; Jonesboro, 870-972-4600; Mountain Home, 870-425-3510.

Committees: *Appropriations* (25th of 37 D): Energy & Water Development; Military Construction, Veterans Affairs & Related Agencies; Transportation, HUD & Related Agencies. *Budget* (7th of 24 D).

Group Ratings

	ADA	ACLU	AFS	LCV	ITIC	NTU	COC	ACU	CFG	FRC
2008	75	82	86	77	71	6	56	13	0	29
2007	90	—	100	70	—	8	55	8	6	—

National Journal Ratings

	2007 LIB	—	2007 CONS		2008 LIB	—	2008 CONS
Economic	53%	—	46%		48%	—	52%
Social	57%	—	42%		62%	—	34%
Foreign	69%	—	29%		65%	—	32%
Composite	60%	—	40%		60%	—	41%

Key Votes of the 110th Congress

1. Increase minimum wage	Y	5. Share immigration data	N	9. Withdraw troops 8/08	Y
2. Expand SCHIP	Y	6. Foreign aid abortion ban	N	10. No operations in Iran	Y
3. Raise CAFE standards	Y	7. Ban gay bias in workplace	N	11. Free trade with Peru	Y
4. Bail out financial markets	Y	8. Repeal D.C. gun law	Y	12. Overhaul FISA	Y

Election Results

2008 general	Marion Berry (D)	.... unopposed	($848,992)
2008 primary	Marion Berry (D)	.... unopposed	

Prior Winning Percentages: 2006 (69%); 2004 (67%); 2002 (67%); 2000 (60%); 1998 (100%); 1996 (53%)

Population		Race/Ethnicity		Work	
Pop. 2007:	671,885	White:	79.5%	Private:	75.1%
Change since 2000:	Up 0.5%	Black:	16.5%	Government:	16.0%
Urban:	44.5%	Hispanic:	1.9%	Self-employed:	8.6%
Rural:	55.5%	Asian:	0.5%	Blue collar:	31.4%
Area size:	17,521 sq. mi.	Native Am.:	0.4%	White collar:	50.1%
Age		Hawaiian:	0.0%	Khaki collar:	0.1%
Median age:	37.9 yrs.	Two+ races:	1.1%	Other:	18.4%
More than 65 yrs:	15.3%	*Ancestry*		Median income:	$33,183
Less than 18 yrs:	24.6%	Irish:	11.8%	Median home value:	$78,300
Education		USA:	11.5%	Poverty:	20.6%
H.S. grad:	76.6%	German:	10.3%	**Military Veterans**	
College grad:	13.2%			% of Pop:	12.0%
Grad degree:	4.2%				

The Mississippi Delta, the flat, mucky, river-crossed lowland on both sides of the great river, was some of the country's first industrial farmland. This land was uncultivated in most of the 19th century, when plows were still pulled by mules and muddy flatlands were impassable. Then, big landowners used machines to drain the marshlands and persuaded poor blacks to move here to tend fields of cotton, rice, and later, soybeans. The results were bountiful agriculture and impoverished people.

2008 Presidential Vote

McCain (R)	145,340	(59%)
Obama (D)	95,102	(38%)

2004 Presidential Vote

Bush (R)	127,179	(52%)
Kerry (D)	115,994	(47%)

Cook Partisan Voting Index: R+ 8

Around 1940, the Delta began to slowly change: the first minimum-wage and war-industry jobs up North drew young people out of the Delta, and the introduction of the mechanical cotton picker idled many farm workers.

But this land—stretching flat as far as the eye can see, along ribbons of asphalt that shimmer in the heat—remains poor by national standards. The people are undereducated, and the area has substantial pockets of unemployment. Local rice farmers are among the largest recipients of federal farm subsidies: The congressional district ranked fifth in the nation, pulling in $5.2 billion from 1995 to 2006. Riceland Foods, in the town of Stuttgart, is the world's largest rice miller and marketer and the largest recipient of subsidies in the United States, having received $554 million from 1995 to 2006. The rice producer has attracted an unusual partner in recent years, Colusa Biomass, which hopes to make ethanol out of rice hulls and plans to move its corporate headquarters to Stuttgart in 2009. The local rice fields also attract ducks, helping put Arkansas on the map as the most productive state for mallard hunters. Several big auto-parts plants have been built in Marion, across the Mississippi River from Memphis. But in 2007, when Toyota chose a site for its seventh North American plant, Marion lost out to Tupelo, Miss., in part because of local air-quality problems. The 2007 closure of the Addison Shoe Co. plant in Wynne brought additional economic woes to the area, idling about 174 workers.

The 1st Congressional District of Arkansas includes most of the state's Delta lands and stretches west to the cool, green Ozarks. The largest city in the district is Jonesboro, whose cheap labor and flat land have made it an industrial hub for food-processing companies like Nestle and Frito-Lay. In 2008, the StarTek call center brought a few hundred more jobs to the area. The district's natural beauty draws outdoorsmen to the sleepy Ozark town of Mountain Home, named *Outdoor Life* magazine's best place to live in 2008. The Delta, with its large black population, is the most Democratic part of Arkansas. Some of the hill counties are ancestrally Republican, and there is a Republican trend in Jonesboro and in Lonoke County, which is part of the Little Rock metro area. The result is that the district is closely divided in national politics. It voted 50%-48% for Democrat Al Gore in 2000 but 52%-47% for Republican George W. Bush in 2004. In 2008, the district voted 59% for Republican John McCain.

The congressman from the 1st District is Marion Berry, a Democrat who was first elected in 1996. He is the type of folksy, small-town Southern Democrat who has been prominent in Congress: "a pharmacist and a farmer, the owner of a loud laugh," as the *Arkansas Democrat-Gazette* described him. Berry grew up in the town of Bayou Meto near DeWitt in Arkansas County. After his first year of college, his rice-farming father suggested that he study something besides farming, so he earned a pharmacy degree from the University of Arkansas at Little Rock. He spent a lot of time at Bruice Drugstore, a small pharmacy run by family friend George Wimberly, who later became the mayor of Little Rock. Berry developed an interest in politics through his friendship with Wimberly. "All the political horsepower came and went through that drugstore," he recalls.

In 1968, he returned to Arkansas County to farm with his brothers and participated in politics on the side. Berry was a farmer in some capacity until 2005. During that time, he accumulated a net worth of more than $1 million. In 2006, the *Arkansas Democrat-Gazette* reported that since 1994, Berry had received more than $800,000 in federal farm subsidies through a corporate structure, of which he owned 50%. The other 50 percent was divided equally between Berry's son, Mitchell, and a family friend, Danny Sloate. Berry said in a 2008 interview that he is not involved in the day-to-day management of the corporation and does not receive a salary.

Berry began to move into the political realm in 1986, when Democratic Gov. Bill Clinton, advocating changes in the state's water policy, appointed him to the Arkansas Soil & Water Conservation Commission. Berry later made the transition to Washington after attending a Clinton political party: "I made a comment that I thought it'd be fun to come here [to Washington] and work with a new administration." Not expecting anything to come of his offhand remark, Berry received a call from the Clinton administration three days later and an appointment as White House liaison to the Agriculture Department. Berry returned to Arkansas in 1996 to run for the U.S. House after Rep. Blanche Lincoln, pregnant with twins, did not pursue re-election. (Lincoln later won the Senate seat of retiring Democrat Dale Bumpers.) Berry had tough opposition for the seat in Tom Donaldson, a 28-year-old deputy prosecutor in Crittenden County who spent little money but ran rural radio ads criticizing Berry for accepting farm subsidies. Berry won the primary runoff by only 52%-48%. In the general election, Berry faced Republican Warren Dupwe, a former Jonesboro city attorney. They sparred over Medicare, both candidates opposed abortion rights and gun control, and both favored a balanced budget. Berry outspent Dupwe nearly 2-to-1 and, in a district that has never elected a Republican, won 53%-44%.

Berry's cooperation with Democratic leaders earned him a seat on leadership-run legislative task forces and a slot on the Appropriations Committee. His voting record is mostly moderate but a bit more liberal on foreign policy. A Blue Dog Democrat, he supported the balanced-budget amendment and said he wanted to pay off the national debt. He voted against Republican tax cuts because they are "just borrowing money from our children and grandchildren." He visited Cuba twice to promote an end to the trade embargo, so that Arkansas farmers could sell rice and feed products there. He also has a personal interest in the country. In 1958, his father was in Cuba working to organize a rice farm there, and while he was home for Christmas, Castro took power, ending the plan.

With his background as a pharmacist, Berry was a natural choice to be out front in the Democratic opposition to the GOP prescription-drug bill in 2003. He was one of three House Democrats appointed to the House-Senate conference committee, all of whom complained of being shut out of the negotiations over creating the first drug benefit in the Medicare program. The final bill was "the sorriest piece of legislation" that Congress ever enacted, Berry said. "It is nothing but an expedited way to make it legal to cheat and steal from old people," he said. His partisan instincts got the best of him during a 2005 House floor debate on the budget, when he called the boyish-looking, redheaded Adam Putnam, a Florida Republican, "a Howdy Doody-looking nimrod." After Democrats won a majority in 2006, Berry became a leading sponsor of legislation that would allow the federal government to negotiate prescription-drug prices with drug companies under Medicare, an element expressly left out of the 2003 bill because of strong objections from the pharmaceutical industry.

Berry also got a seat on the Budget Committee, making him one of only a handful of representatives to serve on both the budget and appropriations committees. As a member of the Blue Dogs, he is an advocate on the budget panel for sticking to the "pay go" rule, which requires new spending or tax cuts to be offset elsewhere in the budget. "If it's not paid for, I won't vote for it," Berry told the *Arkansas Democrat-Gazette*. But on the appropriations committee, he has also been an advocate for federal spending in his hard-pressed district. He told the newspaper, "Being an appropriator, I like earmarks, make no apologies for them." Berry can also be a tough critic of federal agencies that fall short of his expectations. After severe storms struck Arkansas in April 2006, Berry, with his usual blunt rhetoric, call the Federal Emergency Management Agency "an incompetent bunch of nincompoops who can't run their agency." He has been re-elected easily and in 2008 was unopposed.

SECOND DISTRICT

Vic Snyder (D)

Elected 1996, 7th term; b. Sept. 27, 1947, Medford, OR; home, Little Rock; Willamette U., B.A. 1975, U. of OR, M.D. 1979, U. of AR, J.D. 1988; Methodist; married (Betsy Singleton); 4 children.

Military Career: Marine Corps, 1967–69 (Vietnam).

Elected Office: AR Senate, 1990–96.

Professional Career: Practicing physician, 1982–present.

DC Office: 2210 RHOB, 20515, 202-225-2506; Fax: 202-225-5903; Web site: www.house.gov/snyder.

State Offices: Little Rock, 501-324-5941.

Committees: Joint Economic Committee (6th of 6 D). *Armed Services* (7th of 37 D): Military Personnel; Oversight & Investigations (Chmn). *Veterans' Affairs* (3rd of 18 D): Health.

Group Ratings

	ADA	ACLU	AFS	LCV	ITIC	NTU	COC	ACU	CFG	FRC
2008	90	70	100	92	100	7	67	5	0	5
2007	85	—	100	85	—	5	60	4	12	—

National Journal Ratings

	2007 LIB	—	2007 CONS		2008 LIB	—	2008 CONS
Economic	69%	—	28%		61%	—	39%
Social	62%	—	37%		74%	—	25%
Foreign	51%	—	48%		52%	—	46%
Composite	62%	—	39%		63%	—	37%

Key Votes of the 110th Congress

1. Increase minimum wage	Y	5. Share immigration data	N	9. Withdraw troops 8/08	Y
2. Expand SCHIP	Y	6. Foreign aid abortion ban	N	10. No operations in Iran	Y
3. Raise CAFE standards	Y	7. Ban gay bias in workplace	Y	11. Free trade with Peru	Y
4. Bail out financial markets	Y	8. Repeal D.C. gun law	N	12. Overhaul FISA	Y

Election Results

2008 general	Vic Snyder (D)	212,303	(77%)	($307,060)
	Deb McFarland (Green)	65,063	(24%)	
2008 primary	Vic Snyder (D)	unopposed		

Prior Winning Percentages: 2006 (61%); 2004 (58%); 2002 (93%); 2000 (58%); 1998 (58%); 1996 (52%)

Population		Race/Ethnicity		Work	
Pop. 2007:	708,433	White:	72.7%	Private:	74.5%
Change since 2000:	Up 6.4%	Black:	20.6%	Government:	19.1%
Urban:	66.2%	Hispanic:	3.6%	Self-employed:	6.1%
Rural:	33.8%	Asian:	1.2%	Blue collar:	22.3%
Area size:	6,045 sq. mi.	Native Am.:	0.4%	White collar:	61.2%
Age		Hawaiian:	0.1%	Khaki collar:	0.4%
Median age:	36.1 yrs.	Two+ races:	1.4%	Other:	16.1%
More than 65 yrs:	12.4%	*Ancestry*		Median income:	$43,081
Less than 18 yrs:	24.9%	German:	11.0%	Median home value:	$110,900
Education		Irish:	10.7%	Poverty:	14.4%
H.S. grad:	85.8%	USA:	8.9%	**Military Veterans**	
College grad:	25.7%			% of Pop:	12.7%
Grad degree:	9.2%				

Little Rock has been the capital of Arkansas and also its largest city for more than a century. It is at the geographic center of an otherwise rural state, and it is home to the presidential library of Bill Clinton, the former Arkansas governor. The city is best known for its role at the dawn of the civil rights movement. In September 1957, Democratic Gov. Orval Faubus sent in the National Guard to block a desegregation order at Central High School. President Eisenhower sent in U.S. troops and federalized

2008 Presidential Vote
McCain (R).............................161,540   (54%)
Obama (D) 131,891   (44%)

2004 Presidential Vote
Bush (R).................................145,392   (51%)
Kerry (D)................................134,478   (48%)

Cook Partisan Voting Index: R + 5

the National Guard to enforce the order, and Little Rock became a synonym for bigotry around the world. Forty years later, the Little Rock Nine who had integrated the high school returned for an anniversary commemoration with then President Clinton. "It was Little Rock that made racial equality a driving obsession in my life," he said. Today, Little Rock is still the political center of Arkansas, setting the tone of the public life of its state as do only a few other state capitals—Boston, Providence, Atlanta, Denver, and Honolulu. It is home to the *Arkansas Democrat-Gazette*, the feisty, conservative paper whose editor Paul Greenberg christened Clinton "Slick Willie." On the banks of the Arkansas River is the Clinton Presidential Center and Park, opened in 2004 and designed to promote local economic revitalization and with architecture evocative of a "bridge to the 21st century."

The 2nd Congressional District of Arkansas includes Little Rock and North Little Rock, a kind of industrial suburb across the Arkansas River and known informally for years as Dog Town. The district takes in Saline (named for its early salt works) and Faulkner (named for fiddle player Sanford C. Faulkner, the original Arkansas Traveler) counties, which have grown rapidly as people move farther out on the freeways. This is the seat once held by legendary Ways and Means chairman Wilbur Mills, who retired in 1976. In 2004, the district favored President Bush 51%-48%—the same as in the national popular vote. In 2008, John McCain defeated Barack Obama, 54%-44%.

The congressman from the 2nd District is Vic Snyder, a Democrat first elected in 1996. Snyder is an unusual politician, "an inveterately private man in a public profession, quite content to be all alone," wrote the *Arkansas Democrat-Gazette*. Snyder was raised by his mother in Medford, Ore., after his parents divorced when he was a toddler. He dropped out of Willamette University at age 20 to join the Marine Corps during the Vietnam War. After his service, he returned to Oregon, finished college and went on to medical school on the G.I. bill. He did his residency in Little Rock and settled there as a family doctor. But he also volunteered for medical missions in Thailand, Honduras, Sierra Leone, and Sudan. While practicing medicine, he got a law degree, but never practiced law. In 1990, he was elected to the state Senate and made news when he called for repeal of Arkansas's anti-sodomy law and when he refused to accept a government pension. When the seat in Congress opened in 1996, Snyder decided to run. He campaigned as a reformer, promising not to accept a congressional pension until an equitable system was established for federal employees. His main Democratic opponents had more political backgrounds. But in a 51%-49% upset, Snyder won the runoff against Pulaski County prosecutor Mark Stodola, who was a strong Clinton supporter. Snyder sounded reform themes in the general election against Republican lawyer Bud Cummins and also outspent Cummins. He won narrowly, 52%-48%.

Snyder's voting record is close to the center of House Democrats, but he is the most liberal in the Arkansas delegation and an occasional maverick. He voted for needle exchanges to prevent the spread of AIDS and against the partial-birth abortion ban. In 2004, he opposed a state constitutional amendment to ban same-sex marriage; the ballot measure passed 75%-25%. Snyder also has supported Republican tax cuts. He helped to organize the bipartisan Cuba working group to push the House to end the trade embargo and the ban on travel there; Cuba is seen as a potential new market for Arkansas rice farmers.

He focuses on military and veterans issues on the Armed Services Committee, where he is chairman of the Oversight and Investigations Subcommittee. He was the only Arkansas House member to vote against the use of military force against Iraq. After the war began, he visited Iraq and called for more support for U.S. troops, and he criticized the Pentagon for failing to inform Congress of prison abuses. In 2004, he sponsored legislation establishing separate medals for service in Afghanistan and Iraq, and it was signed into law by Bush. The House unanimously passed his bill to improve health care for soldiers wounded overseas, and he sought to provide members of the National Guard and Reserves the same G.I. benefits that go to active duty personnel. In early 2008, Snyder held hearings to highlight an element of Bush's longstanding power struggle with the legislative branch. At issue were "signing statements" the president attached to a military authorization in which he objected to provisions that he said would limit his executive powers, including one that protected whistle-blowers who expose abuses by defense contractors in Iraq and another that established a legislative commission to investigate contracting irregularities in Iraq.

Snyder has been active on internal House issues. He unsuccessfully sought changes in Democratic rules to spread committee assignments more equitably among members. And, he challenged as a possible violation of the House's anti-bribery rule the practice of interest groups notifying members that they will include an upcoming vote in their legislative scorecard.

Since his initial tight election, Snyder has been re-elected with at least 58% of the vote. In 2004, Republican challenger Marvin Parks aligned himself with President Bush and criticized Snyder for being out of touch with local views, especially on issues such as abortion and gay marriage. Although he raised more than $500,000, Parks had little national Republican support. Parks carried Saline and Faulkner counties, but Snyder won 58%-42%. In endorsing Snyder, the *Democrat-Gazette* wrote, "While we may abhor some of his political stances, there is no doubting the sincerity with which he takes them. Or his patriotism. . .We're endorsing an honorable opponent today, not his politics."

In 2008, Snyder had no Republican opponent. His personal life offered plenty of excitement, however. In 2003, after a life of bachelorhood, Snyder married the Rev. Betsy Singleton, pastor of the United Methodist Church in Little Rock. A son, Penn, was born in 2006, and in December 2008, when Snyder was 61 and his wife 47, they became the parents of triplet boys. Singleton took an indefinite leave of absence from the ministry beginning Easter 2009.

THIRD DISTRICT

John Boozman (R)

Elected Nov. 2001, 4th full term; b. Dec. 10, 1950, Shreveport, LA; home, Rogers; U. of AR, 1969–72, Southern Col. of Optometry, O.D. 1977; Baptist; married (Cathy); 2 children.

Elected Office: Rogers School Bd., 1994–2001.

Professional Career: Optometrist, 1977–2001

DC Office: 1519 LHOB, 20515, 202-225-4301; Fax: 202-225-5713; Web site: www.boozman.house.gov.

State Offices: Ft. Smith, 479-782-7787; Harrison, 870-741-6900; Lowell, 479-725-0400.

Committees: *Foreign Affairs* (12th of 19 R): Europe; Foreign Affairs & Global Health; Terrorism, Nonproliferation & Trade. *Transportation & Infrastructure* (15th of 30 R): Aviation; Highways & Transit; Water Resources & Environment (RMM). *Veterans' Affairs* (6th of 11 R): Economic Opportunity (RMM); Health.

Group Ratings

	ADA	ACLU	AFS	LCV	ITIC	NTU	COC	ACU	CFG	FRC
2008	25	18	14	8	71	53	94	84	61	100
2007	15	—	9	10	—	69	90	92	73	—

National Journal Ratings

	2007 LIB	—	2007 CONS	2008 LIB	—	2008 CONS
Economic	26%	—	73%	26%	—	74%
Social	21%	—	75%	20%	—	74%
Foreign	30%	—	69%	22%	—	74%
Composite	27%	—	73%	24%	—	76%

Key Votes of the 110th Congress

1. Increase minimum wage	Y	5. Share immigration data	Y	9. Withdraw troops 8/08	N
2. Expand SCHIP	N	6. Foreign aid abortion ban	Y	10. No operations in Iran	N
3. Raise CAFE standards	N	7. Ban gay bias in workplace	N	11. Free trade with Peru	Y
4. Bail out financial markets	Y	8. Repeal D.C. gun law	Y	12. Overhaul FISA	Y

Election Results

2008 general	John Boozman (R)	215,196	(79%)	($325,926)
	Abel Tomlinson (Green)	58,850	(21%)	($7,131)
2008 primary	John Boozman (R)	unopposed		

Prior Winning Percentages: 2006 (62%); 2004 (59%); 2002 (99%); 2001 (56%)

Population		Race/Ethnicity		Work	
Pop. 2007:	766,757	White:	82.6%	Private:	80.1%
Change since 2000:	Up 14.0%	Black:	2.4%	Government:	12.2%
Urban:	54.4%	Hispanic:	9.8%	Self-employed:	7.5%
Rural:	45.6%	Asian:	1.8%	Blue collar:	29.5%
Area size:	8,661 sq. mi.	Native Am.:	1.2%	White collar:	54.4%
Age		Hawaiian:	0.2%	Khaki collar:	0.1%
Median age:	35.1 yrs.	Two+ races:	1.8%	Other:	16.0%
More than 65 yrs:	12.5%	*Ancestry*		Median income:	$40,689
Less than 18 yrs:	25.8%	German:	12.5%	Median home value:	$120,400
Education		Irish:	11.1%	Poverty:	15.3%
H.S. grad:	80.8%	English:	10.3%	**Military Veterans**	
College grad:	20.5%			% of Pop:	11.9%
Grad degree:	6.8%				

In the mid-2000s, the northwest corner of Arkansas became one of America's boom areas, with major corporate headquarters and dozens of small factories, tourist attractions and retirement developments in the Ozarks. The Fayetteville-Springdale-Rogers metropolitan region grew by nearly 7% in 2005, outpacing the rest of the state. The region also had a rapidly growing population of Hispanics, who make up more than 20% of the population of Springdale and Rogers. Driving the local economy are three major employer anchors: Wal-Mart Stores, J.B. Hunt Transport Services and Tysons Foods. This is also home to the handsome University of Arkansas in Fayetteville, where young lawyers Bill Clinton and Hillary Rodham married in the living room of a brick bungalow, and the mountain-bound resort town of Eureka Springs.

2008 Presidential Vote

McCain (R)	185,055	(64%)
Obama (D)	96,485	(34%)

2004 Presidential Vote

Bush (R)	171,853	(62%)
Kerry (D)	100,656	(36%)

Cook Partisan Voting Index: R + 16

For most of the 20th century, the rounded green mountains and pleasant wide valleys, farmhouses and small towns of northwest Arkansas seemed left behind. But the friendly atmosphere and strong religious faith of these communities have proved to be assets, not liabilities, conducive to economic creativity and personal serenity. There have also been touches of genius. Sam Walton, who opened his first Wal-Mart on the town square of Bentonville (it's now a small museum), had the inspiration to build a retail chain in tradition-minded small towns and rural areas using sophisticated computerized management. It made him the richest man in America, though he still drove a pickup truck and kept the corporate headquarters in a deliberately unglitzy building in Bentonville. Don Tyson built Tyson Foods, with headquarters outside Springdale, into the world's leading chicken producer and processor. In 2007, Tyson Foods announced it would invest $150 million to build the first plant to refine animal and vegetable fats into fuel. Other firms have flocked in, especially to do business with Wal-Mart, now the world's largest food retailer.

The 3rd Congressional District covers northwest Arkansas, including Bentonville, Fayetteville and Springdale, plus Fort Smith on the Oklahoma line. It extends as far east as Marion County, home to Ranger Boats, the renowned manufacturer of tournament-quality fishing boats. Its population rose 30% in the 1990s and another 14% from 2000 to 2007—more than Arkansas's other three districts. Politically, this area has been the most Republican part of Arkansas since the Civil War. John Paul Hammerschmidt was elected to the U.S. House in 1966 as one of the first Republican congressmen from the South. He was strong enough even in Democratic 1974 to beat Bill Clinton, then 28, in Clinton's first election, though Clinton did get an impressive 48% of the vote. Lately, this area has become even more Republican, as Christian conservatives have entered politics and new migrants and millionaires have voted heavily Republican. After voting narrowly for Clinton in 1992 and narrowly against him in 1996, the 3rd twice voted strongly for George W. Bush and gave John McCain 64% in 2008.

The congressman from the 3rd District is John Boozman (*BOZ-man*), a Republican who won a special election in November 2001. He replaced Asa Hutchinson, who had resigned to head the Drug Enforcement Administration. A graduate of the University of Arkansas, where he was an offensive guard for the football team, Boozman became an optometrist in Rogers, part of rapidly growing Benton County. He served two terms on the local school board. To win the House seat, Boozman prevailed in three close contests in two months, even though he was outspent in each. In the primary, Boozman had the endorsement of

GOP Gov. Mike Huckabee. His initial chief opponent, former state Rep. Jim Hendren, was damaged by revelations that he had had an extramarital affair. Boozman faced a runoff against state Sen. Gunner DeLay, a Republican who raised few funds but had name recognition as a cousin of then Majority Whip Tom DeLay of Texas. With a stronger grass-roots organization, Boozman won 57%-43%. His opponent in the general election was state Rep. Mike Hathorn, a 28-year-old lawyer who local Democrats hoped could prevail with his Clinton-like personality. But the national party did little to help his campaign, and Boozman won 56%-42%.

His voting record has been reliably conservative. But he sometimes showed his independence from the Bush White House, as in his votes to remove the embargo on trade with Cuba and to import U.S.-made prescription drugs from Canada. He also opposed Bush's immigration proposal as amnesty for illegal aliens. Boozman sponsored bills to abolish the tax code and to display the Ten Commandments in the House and Senate chambers, and he voted against renewal of the Voting Rights Act, saying the South had made racial progress. An evangelical Christian, Boozman advocates weakening restrictions on churches' political activities. In 2007, he was a sponsor of legislation making English the country's official language. He said, "This bill will allow new citizens to create a foundation based on English, which will allow them to better realize the promise of the American dream."

He is the ranking Republican on the Veterans Affairs' Economic Opportunity Subcommittee. With Democrat Tammy Baldwin of Wisconsin, he sponsored the Veteran Vision Equity Act to improve benefits for veterans with impaired vision. In 2008, the House passed a veterans bill with a couple of minor provisions sponsored by Boozman. One would authorize the Department of Veterans Affairs to air television and radio commercials to advertise benefits available to veterans, and the other directs the department to conduct a 20-year study on the vocational rehabilitation and education programs it administers.

On the Transportation Committee, Boozman caused a stir in 2005 when he sponsored, but then withdrew, a bill that would have had the effect of making the maximum workday for truckers 16 hours, up from the current limit of 14 hours. Wal-Mart, with a huge trucking component to its business, favored the change, but critics called it the "sweatshop on wheels" amendment and said it would jeopardize safety. On local issues, Boozman is working to have U.S. 71 designated an interstate and to connect Interstate 540 from Fort Smith to Bentonville with interstates running north to Kansas City and south to Texarkana and New Orleans.

In the 2004 campaign, he was opposed by surprisingly well-funded Democratic state Rep. Janice Judy, the owner of a Fayetteville pizza restaurant. Boozman criticized her opposition to a constitutional amendment to ban same-sex marriage and civil unions in Arkansas. He won 59%-38%. He faced modest opposition in the tougher climate of 2006 and won 62%-38%. After the election, in which Democrats swept every statewide office, Boozman was left as the highest ranking Republican in Arkansas and the only one in the congressional delegation. In 2008, he had no Democratic opposition.

FOURTH DISTRICT

Mike Ross (D)

Elected 2000, 5th term; b. Aug. 2, 1961, Texarkana; home, Prescott; U. of AR, B.A. 1987; Methodist; married (Holly); 2 children.

Elected Office: Nevada County Quorum Court, 1983–85; AR Senate, 1990–2000.

Professional Career: Chief of staff, AR Lt. Gov. Winston Bryant, 1984–89; Owner, Holly's Health Mart, 1993–2007.

DC Office: 2436 RHOB, 20515, 202-225-3772; Fax: 202-225-1314; Web site: ross.house.gov.

State Offices: El Dorado, 870-881-0681; Hot Springs, 501-520-5892; Pine Bluff, 870-536-3376; Prescott, 870-887-6787.

Committees: *Energy & Commerce* (20th of 36 D): Energy & Environment; Health; Oversight & Investigations. *Foreign Affairs* (22nd of 28 D): Asia, the Pacific & the Global Environment; Middle East & South Asia.

Group Ratings

	ADA	ACLU	AFS	LCV	ITIC	NTU	COC	ACU	CFG	FRC
2008	85	64	100	77	100	7	67	12	0	29
2007	85	—	100	60	—	6	70	28	6	—

National Journal Ratings

	2007 LIB — 2007 CONS		2008 LIB — 2008 CONS	
Economic	53% —	46%	48% —	50%
Social	51% —	49%	62% —	34%
Foreign	56% —	43%	55% —	43%
Composite	54% —	46%	56% —	44%

Key Votes of the 110th Congress

1. Increase minimum wage	Y	5. Share immigration data	Y	9. Withdraw troops 8/08	Y
2. Expand SCHIP	Y	6. Foreign aid abortion ban	N	10. No operations in Iran	Y
3. Raise CAFE standards	Y	7. Ban gay bias in workplace	N	11. Free trade with Peru	Y
4. Bail out financial markets	Y	8. Repeal D.C. gun law	Y	12. Overhaul FISA	Y

Election Results

2008 general	Mike Ross (D)...203,178	(86%)	($1,722,151)
	Joshua Drake (Green)..32,603	(14%)	
2008 primary	Mike Ross (D).. unopposed		

Prior Winning Percentages: 2006 (75%); 2004 (100%); 2002 (61%); 2000 (51%)

Population		Race/Ethnicity		Work	
Pop. 2007:	658,278	White:	69.5%	Private:	73.6%
Change since 2000:	Down 1.2%	Black:	24.3%	Government:	19.0%
Urban:	44.7%	Hispanic:	3.9%	Self-employed:	7.0%
Rural:	55.3%	Asian:	0.6%	Blue collar:	31.5%
Area size:	20,951 sq. mi.	Native Am.:	0.6%	White collar:	48.8%
Age		Hawaiian:	0.0%	Khaki collar:	0.2%
Median age:	38.9 yrs.	Two+ races:	1.1%	Other:	19.5%
More than 65 yrs:	15.8%	*Ancestry*		Median income:	$33,327
Less than 18 yrs:	23.8%	Irish:	11.2%	Median home value:	$72,300
Education		USA:	10.3%	Poverty:	20.4%
H.S. grad:	79.1%	German:	8.3%	**Military Veterans**	
College grad:	14.7%			% of Pop:	12.2%
Grad degree:	4.8%				

West from the Delta flatlands along the Mississippi River, where the water-soaked fields produce America's largest rice crop, are small cities like Pine Bluff and El Dorado and the Ouachita Mountains. Southern Arkansas might well be called the northwest corner of the Deep South. It includes the state's largest African-American population, a reminder that parts of southern Arkansas were once plantation country. There is also oil production, and the broiler-chicken industry looms large in these parts.

2008 Presidential Vote

McCain (R)..............................146,082	(58%)
Obama (D) 98,832	(39%)

2004 Presidential Vote

Bush (R)................................128,474	(51%)
Kerry (D)...............................118,825	(48%)

Cook Partisan Voting Index: R+ 7

The accent is clearly Arkansan: El Dorado, Nevada and Lafayette are all pronounced with long a's and accents on the penultimate syllable, and Ouachita, with a bow to the original French rendition of the Indian name, is *wa-SHEE-ta*. The district includes the little railroad-crossing county-seat town of Hope, where former President Clinton and his first White House Chief of Staff Mack McLarty were classmates in Miss Mary's kindergarten and where Gov. Mike Huckabee grew up a decade later. (The region is also home to Crater of Diamonds State Park, the source of the 4.24 carat Kahn canary diamond that Hillary Rodham Clinton wore to her husband's second inauguration as president.) Hot Springs is the spa resort and gambling haven where Clinton's stepfather sold Buicks, his mother bet on the horses, and he excelled in high school as he began his climb from southern Arkansas obscurity to world prominence.

The 4th Congressional District occupies almost all of the southern half of Arkansas, from the Mississippi River to Texarkana. It is historically a Democratic district, and one that for most of the 20th century elected young men to the House and kept them there for years, to cut deals with the Democratic leadership and bring home the bacon. During the 1990s, it had a very different congressional politics: bipartisan, with rancorous debates on national issues, followed by narrow election victories.

The congressman from the 4th District is Mike Ross, a Democrat who in 2000 defeated Republican Jay Dickey, the only House Republican outside California to be defeated that year. A fifth-generation Arkansan, Ross was born in Texarkana. He graduated from Hope High School and from the University of Arkansas at Little Rock. He got his start in local politics in 1982 as a travel aide to Bill Clinton during his successful bid for governor. While in college, Ross was on the staff of Lt. Gov. Winston Bryant and was executive director of the Arkansas Youth Suicide Prevention Commission. Later, Ross sold insurance and worked as a sales manager for a pharmaceutical company. He and his wife, who is a pharmacist, ran Holly's Health Mart in rural Prescott until they sold the business in 2007. Ross was elected to the state Senate in 1990. When term limits forced him out a decade later, he ran for Congress. This was perhaps the only district in the nation where impeachment played a pivotal role in 2000. Dickey, representing Clinton's boyhood homes, had voted for impeachment, angering the White House. Although Dickey often was a thorn to Republican leaders, Ross tied him to them and argued that "the real Jay Dickey" voted to cut Medicare and Social Security benefits to fund tax cuts for the rich. Dickey responded that Ross was getting his script from "his liberal masters in Washington." Clinton had an impact. He helped bring in $300,000 for Ross at fundraisers, orchestrated endorsements from administration officials with Arkansas roots, and campaigned for Ross in Pine Bluff on the Sunday before the election. There were plenty of independent expenditures as well, by pharmaceutical groups that were against Ross and by labor unions that were against Dickey. Ross won, 51%-49%.

In the House, Ross joined the conservative Blue Dog Democrats and became a vocal proponent of prescription-drug legislation, often citing his experiences as a small-town pharmacist. He cultivates a "country boy" image, regularly shooting skeet from the back of his pickup truck. In 2002 he won approval of his proposal to remove Arkansas's constitutional limit on interest rates, which local bankers and consumer groups agreed had made financing difficult. His action won wide support from political leaders in Arkansas, the only remaining state to mandate such terms. On the Energy and Commerce Committee, he said that he hoped to fix the "flawed Medicare prescription-drug bill" passed by the GOP in 2003. He also introduced legislation in 2008 to open the Arctic National Wildlife Refuge in Alaska and the outer continental shelf to oil drilling.

Although Ross voted for the use of force in Iraq in 2002, he later questioned whether the United States should finance reconstruction after the ouster of Iraqi leader Saddam Hussein. He also said he regretted his 2002 vote. "Had I known that the information the president shared with me on Sept. 26, 2002, was not accurate, I would have never given him the authority to use force in Iraq. At worst, the president misled us, and at best, our intelligence failed us."

In 2006, Ross was a lieutenant to Illinois Democrat Rahm Emanuel, who as chairman of the Democratic Congressional Campaign Committee helped orchestrate the party's successful campaigns that year. Ross warned against moving the party to the left: "We didn't defeat the Republicans with liberal Democrats." In the 110th Congress (2007–08), he was one of three co-chairs of the Blue Dogs, the group of roughly 50 conservative Democrats in the House. "We're in the middle, where the American people are," said Ross, who handled communications and message for the faction.

Dickey decided to run again in 2002. Both candidates again raised substantial sums, but the Republican's campaign stumbled from the start. Dickey refused, as he had in the past, to accept funds from political action committees, but the Republicans' campaign committee got him to back down. He constantly reminded voters that he had delivered federal money to the district from his Appropriations Committee seat and had secured a pledge from GOP Speaker Dennis Hastert that he would get back his seat on the committee. Ross won by a convincing 61%-39% margin. That seems to have made the 4th a safe Democratic district again, after more than a decade of fierce partisan contests. Ross had no Republican opposition in 2004, and Dickey became a Washington lobbyist. Ross has been re-elected easily since.

★ CALIFORNIA ★

C alifornia is America's largest state, a nation-state really, with an economy larger than all but seven nations. It is the site of the world's most advanced technology, yet it is a place with plenty of Third World neighborhoods. And it greeted the 21st century with Third World-like rolling blackouts of electricity. The state's growth has been extraordinary. The Census Bureau estimated that California had a population of nearly 37 million in 2008, far ahead of second-place Texas, with 24 million people. Metro Los Angeles had 13 million people, second only to metro New York City's 19 million; the San Francisco Bay Area had more than 7 million, not so far behind Chicagoland's 9.6 million. The Central Valley and mountain counties had 7 million people, which equates to only 19% of the total state population. San Diego County, with 3 million people, was the sixth-largest county in the United States. California owes its preeminence not only to its natural advantages, including its vast geographic area, but also to its human ingenuity. Los Angeles, despite having little in the way of natural resources and no natural harbor, is the nation's leading port and biggest manufacturer, as well as the world's entertainment center. The Bay Area, which once made its living by exporting food, is now the global leader in computers and high technology. But the state is not without contradictions. California loves its physical environment, but it also has the largest urban sprawl in the United States. It likes to think of itself as cutting edge, even as it watched the electricity flicker early in the decade. It likes to see itself as the nation's political leader, but it is well to the left of America's ideological center. In the half-century after World War II, California was a magnet for migrants, a promised land where dreams could be realized. But from 2000 to 2008, some 1.4 million Americans left California for places east and north, even as 1.8 million foreign immigrants moved in. In 2007, nearly half of the state's people were ethnic in origin: 36% were Hispanic and 12% were Asian.

Most of all, California is a place that is always changing: Its economy has been transformed several times over, its population has been transformed by one group of newcomers after another, and its politics are periodically transformed with the suddenness of an earthquake. If other states have changed gradually over time on an analog scale, California has changed sharply on a digital scale. So it has been from the beginning. In 1848, when California passed from Mexico to the United States by the Treaty of Guadalupe Hidalgo, it was sparsely populated, inhabited by a few thousand Indians and Mexicans and by a few hundred U.S. soldiers and men on the make. Then in 1849, gold was found in Sutter's Mill and thousands of people arrived in the Gold Rush. Within months, San Francisco became one of America's 25 largest cities. The big money was made not by the miners but by the grocers and dry-goods merchants and transportation entrepreneurs who provisioned them, such as the Big Four—Crocker, Hopkins, Huntington, Stanford—who built the Central and Southern Pacific Railroads. Many of the laborers were Chinese, and California whites, angry at low-wage competition and fearful of an Asian tidal wave, were the impetus behind the aptly-named Chinese Exclusion Act of 1882, which suspended legal Chinese immigration and was not fully repealed until 1965.

The railroads sold off vast chunks of the Central Valley to large farming operations and enticed settlers with low fares to newly platted suburbs in the Los Angeles Basin. Engineers built great aqueducts that stretched hundreds of miles, from Yosemite to San Francisco and from the Owens River to Los Angeles. Without a water supply, the cities would not exist. Early-20th-century California was affluent and cultured, containing great universities such as the University of California (Berkeley) and Stanford and fine museums and libraries. It was America's window on the Pacific, alert to developments in China and Japan, Hawaii and the Philippines, and it was eager to extend America's economic reach and military strength. Nevertheless, as author Carey McWilliams wrote, California was an "island" separated from the rest of the country. Then in World War II, California became one of the great defense industry states, building ships and airplanes by the thousands. Millions of Americans came and millions stayed. The population rose from 7 million in 1940 to 17 million in 1963, when California passed New York as the nation's most populous state.

The heads of the big units of government and business planned California's future—leaders such as President Franklin D. Roosevelt and industrial mogul Henry J. Kaiser, who constructed vast shipyards and steel and aluminum factories. Republican Gov. Earl Warren husbanded tax monies to build schools and freeways in the years after the war. Educators Robert Sproul and Clark Kerr transformed the University of California into what Kerr called "the multiversity," and Democratic Gov. Pat Brown completed the vast system of canals and aqueducts that brought water from the wet north to the dry south. But the real engine of growth was the little people who took advantage of this infrastructure and built a humming economy. When California's defense plants closed down after World War II, government and civic leaders imagined that hundreds of thousands would head back east. Instead, as urbanologist Jane Jacobs pointed out, one-eighth of all the new jobs in the nation in the late 1940s were created in metro Los Angeles. This small-scale growth, multiplied thousands of times over, helped make California the nation's largest state.

The infusion of migrants transformed California politically. Before the war, this was a Republican state, with progressive leanings. Political struggles took place inside the Republican Party. The in-rush

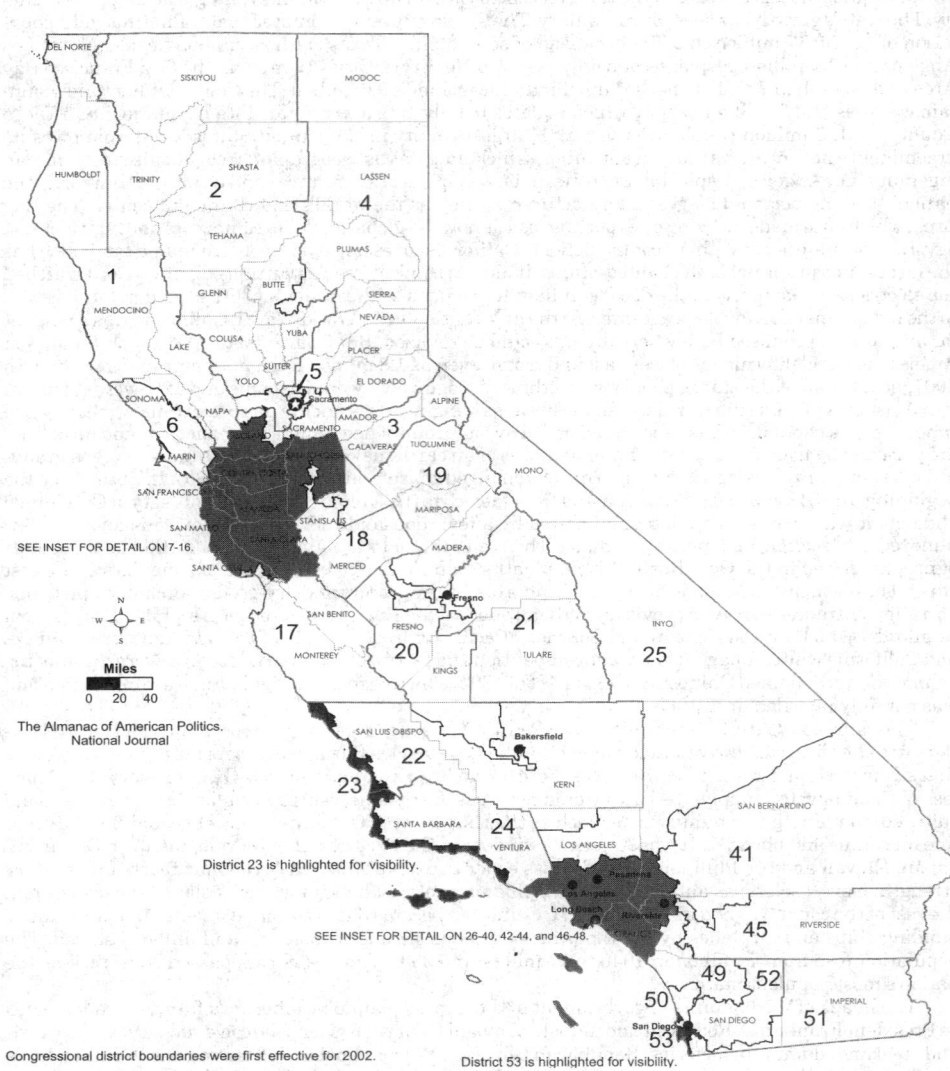

SEE INSET FOR DETAIL ON 7-16.

Miles

0   20   40

The Almanac of American Politics.
National Journal

District 23 is highlighted for visibility.

SEE INSET FOR DETAIL ON 26-40, 42-44, and 46-48.

Congressional district boundaries were first effective for 2002.

District 53 is highlighted for visibility.

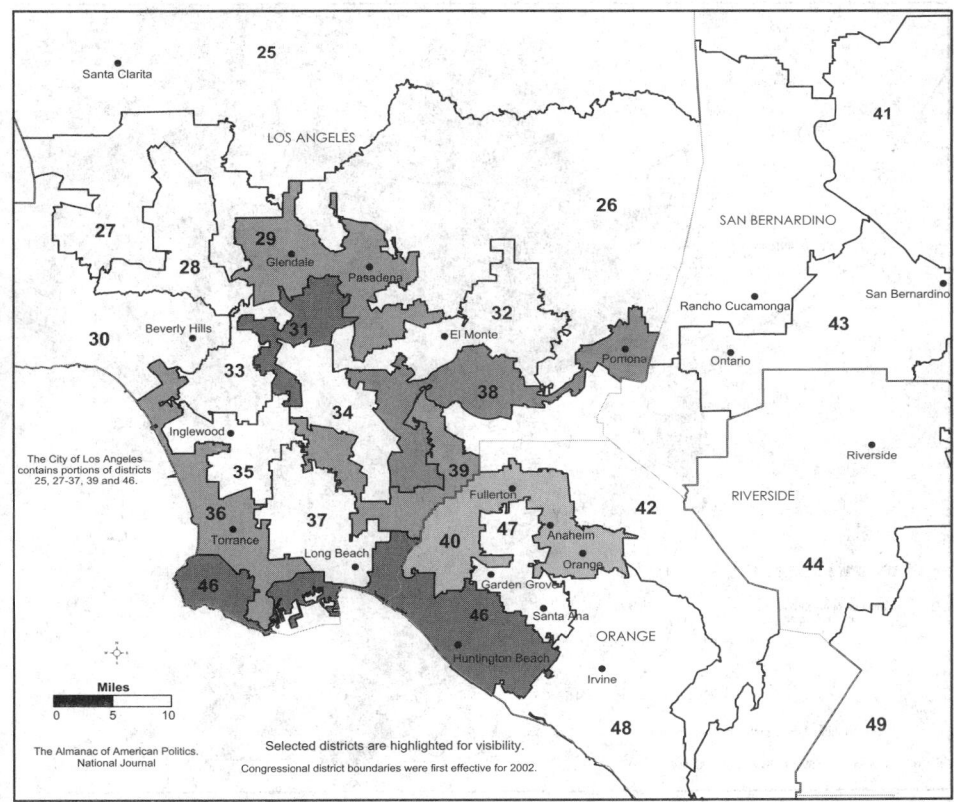

The City of Los Angeles contains portions of districts 25, 27-37, 39 and 46.

Miles
0   5   10

The Almanac of American Politics. National Journal

Selected districts are highlighted for visibility.

Congressional district boundaries were first effective for 2002.

of the GI generation, with its allegiance to the New Deal, and the building of auto and steel factories, which unionized their workforces, transformed California into a two-party state. These new migrants were middle and working class, family men and women enjoying a life in suburbs in the lovely California climate. Warren's progressive Republicans remained dominant through the mid-1950s, but with Brown's election as governor in 1958, a group of talented liberal Democrats took over. Things turned sour in the mid-1960s, when student rebellions starting at Berkeley and the Watts riot upset the New Deal order. Californians responded by calling in a disillusioned New Dealer espousing the conformist cultural conservatism of the GI generation, Ronald Reagan. California was a harbinger: It showed the nation where it would go next in the 1980s.

In 1974, California elected Democrat Jerry Brown as governor, entranced for a time by his fresh vision of Baby Boomer liberalism. California's laid-back lifestyles became a magnet for highly educated Boomers, lawyers, scientists, techies, and show-biz types. Nearly 40 years later, they remain a force, although, like the Reaganites before them, not the *only* force in the state's politics. California voted Republican in every presidential election from 1968 to 1988. Brown's administration was not wholly successful on policy. Voters froze property taxes by passing Proposition 13 in 1978, rejected Brown's bid for the U.S. Senate in 1982, and ousted three of his state Supreme Court justices in 1986. Republicans followed Brown in the governorship: George Deukmejian, elected in 1982 and 1986, and Pete Wilson, elected in 1990 and 1994.

In the 1980s, California's defense industry boomed and Silicon Valley flowered south of San Francisco. Immigration continued, in vast numbers, with newcomers living in the dirty stucco bungalows and garden apartments that white blue-collar workers left behind in neighborhoods south and east of downtown Los Angeles. Large swaths of the San Fernando Valley became mostly Latino. Public policy increasingly was set by Willie Brown, speaker of the California Assembly from 1980 to 1995 and later by the Democratic Legislature. In the 1990s, disaster struck in several forms. Defense industry cutbacks hit the Los Angeles area hard, costing hundreds of thousands of jobs and sending housing values plummeting. Television screens were filled with news of floods and earthquakes, of riots and trials. California government responded competently to the natural disasters, less well to those that were man-made. *Official Negligence*, the definitive story of the Rodney King case, is a story of public-sector incompetence as dis-

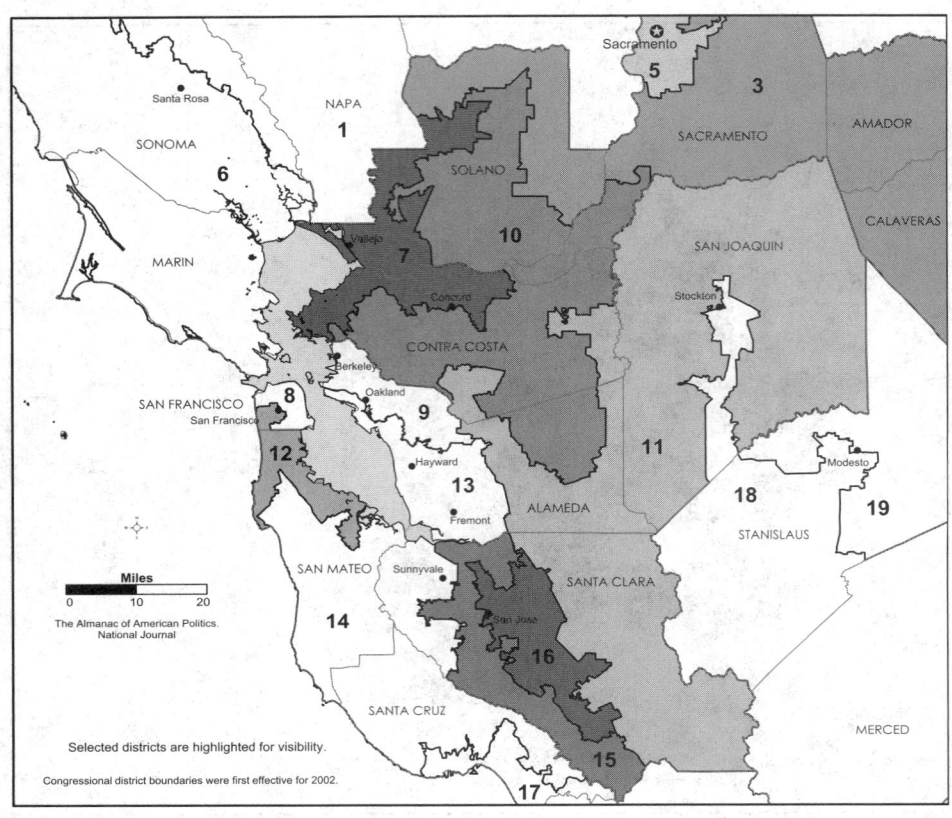

Selected districts are highlighted for visibility.

Congressional district boundaries were first effective for 2002.

maying as that spotlighted for the nation in the O.J. Simpson murder trial. In the 1990s, California also lost many of its trademark big businesses to mergers and relocations.

In the past two decades, California's current demographic and political trends were set. Since 1990, California has had an outflow of people to other states offset by an even larger inflow of people from other countries. In the first half of the 1990s, about 2 million Californians, mostly white and affluent, left for other Western states or moved east, while immigrants kept arriving. The Census Bureau reported that California's Hispanic population rose from 16% in 1980 to 32% in 2000 and to 36% in 2007. The Asian percentage was 5% in 1980, 11% in 2000, and 12% in 2007. The pace accelerated from 2000 to 2007, when domestic out-migration was 1.4 million and foreign in-migration was 1.8 million. Los Angeles County is what New York City was 100 years ago: the great entry point in the United States. The county has the world's largest numbers of Mexicans, Iranians, Samoans, Filipinos, Salvadorans, Armenians, Guatemalans, Koreans, and Thais outside their native lands. Even far Northern California is 15% Hispanic. The farmlands of Imperial County are three-quarters Hispanic. Asians make up half the population of the west side of San Francisco and Los Angeles County's San Gabriel Valley, and more than one-third in the south end of San Francisco Bay, from Palo Alto and Fremont south to San Jose.

Perhaps the first politician to intuit how the combination of Baby Boom liberals—or "gentry liberals," as California political analyst Joel Kotkin calls them—and immigrants would come to dominate California politics was Bill Clinton. After carrying California 46%-33% in the 1992 general election, at a time when the state was presumed to be part of a Republican "lock" on the presidency, he assiduously returned again and again, courting Silicon Valley entrepreneurs, Hollywood celebrities, feminist icons, Asian contributors, and Latino politicians. The Democratic trend was helped along by the response to Proposition 187, which denied non-emergency government spending on illegal immigrants and their children and became a central issue in state politics in 1994. Gov. Wilson, trailing state Treasurer Kathleen Brown (Jerry Brown's sister) in polls and concerned about fast-rising state spending on illegal immigrants, supported Prop 187; although he was careful to differentiate between illegal and legal immigrants, he also ran ads showing Mexicans sprinting across the border and stating in ominous tones, "They keep coming." Voters made that distinction, too: 59% of all voters and about one-third of Hispanics voted for the proposition. Wilson won a decisive victory, 55%-41%, but one that came with considerable collateral damage to his party. In 1996, Clinton carried California and Republicans lost their briefly held majority in the state Assembly. Republican George W. Bush's courtship of Hispanics enabled him to run with 29% and 34% of the Latino vote in 2000 and 2004 respectively, but GOP nominee John McCain's share fell to 23% in 2008. Asians, who seemed to rally to Republicans when predominately black rioters looted Los Angeles's "Koreatown" in 1992, went with Democrat Al Gore in 2000 (remember his visit to the Buddhist temple in Hacienda Heights?), and cast nearly two-thirds of their votes for the Democratic presidential tickets in 2000, 2004, and 2008.

The gentry liberals provided the other building block for California's Democratic majorities. They were repelled by the Republican Party of U.S. House Speaker Newt Gingrich and President George W. Bush, of Christian conservatives and gun-rights activists. They were similarly repelled by the conservative brand of California Republican, who habitually denounced immigration and championed opposition to abortion rights. As a result, Democrat Gray Davis was elected governor by 58%-38% in 1998, and Gore carried the state by 53%-42% in 2000, even though Bush spent $20 million on California media and Gore not a penny. In 2002, Davis, with low job ratings after the 2001 electricity crisis, was re-elected by only 47%-42%, but Democrats won every statewide office for the first time since 1882.

Those results seemed to establish California as a solidly Democratic state. And the cataclysmic event of 2003—the recall of Gov. Davis and the election of Republican Arnold Schwarzenegger to replace him—seemed to be a major exception. But in the end, the exception has proved to be the rule. The recall was a response not so much to Davis, who had been trying to hold down the Democratic Legislature's spending, as to a political governing class that had insulated itself largely from public control. The California Legislature adopted redistricting plans that seemed to provide zero chance of change in party control. The collapse of revenues after the dot-com bust of 2000 and the collapse of the electricity deregulation system made Davis vulnerable, although he had little to do with either one. The feckless effort of a few conservatives in early 2003 to gather signatures for recall petitions fizzled until U.S. Rep. Darrell Issa, a wealthy Republican businessman, revived it with a large infusion of his own money and Davis unwittingly stimulated it by signing a bill authorizing driver's licenses for illegal aliens and by unilaterally raising the license-plate fee. By July, it was apparent that Davis's foes would obtain enough petition signatures to force a recall election, which would also allow voters to choose a successor to Davis if the recall passed. Relatively few signatures are needed to get on the ballot, and only a plurality is needed to win. The election was scheduled for October. Conservatives Issa and Tom McClintock got their names on the ballot. Prominent Democrats pledged to support Davis. Then in August, Schwarzenegger went on NBC's *Tonight Show* and surprised his political advisers by announcing he would run. Dejected but realistic, Issa got off the ballot. Democratic Lt. Gov. Cruz Bustamante got on, while saying he wanted Davis to stay in office.

In October 2003, the recall of Gov. Davis won 55%-45%, and on the replacement ballot, Schwarzenegger won 49% of the vote to 32% for Bustamante and 13% for McClintock. A solid majority in this Democratic state had voted for Republicans. Turnout was way up from 2002—from 7.5 million to 9 million—and Schwarzenegger received more votes in 2003, 4.2 million, than Davis had in 2002, 3.5 million. Schwarzenegger's election seemed to mean the end of insider politics in California and the beginning of plebiscitary politics. Television stations rushed to set up news bureaus in Sacramento, and newspapers headlined state government news. Schwarzenegger was the first governor since Brown to get such news coverage. Taking advantage of it, he got busy, ordering an audit of state government, forcing the Legislature to repeal driver's licenses for illegal immigrants, and pushing through changes in workmen's compensation laws. He put two bond issues on the March 2004 ballot, campaigned for them vigorously, and saw them passed with 63% and 71% of the vote. He forced the Legislature to accept his budget by using his star power and threatening to take the issue to the people. California voters seemed to be in line with their new Republican governor.

But it was a different story in 2005. Schwarzenegger planned a frontal attack on the power structure in Sacramento. That year, he put on the November ballot measures that would give the governor new powers to cut spending, to increase the number of years it took teachers to get tenure, and to create a commission to redistrict the Legislature and the California delegation in the U.S. House. He got strong opposition this time. Public employees spent more than $100 million on anti-Schwarzenegger TV ads. One ad featured members of the nurses' union saying they were not, as he had said, "special interests." His job rating sunk to under 50%, and the three ballot propositions failed.

These results proved decisive in governance—and in proving California's strong Democratic allegiance. Schwarzenegger promptly hired one of Davis's top aides as his chief of staff and swapped Republican advisers for Democrats. He worked closely with Democratic legislative leaders to put $37 billion of bonds on the November ballot, for highways, housing, school construction, and flood control: shades of Pat Brown. The governor and Legislature even reached early agreement on a budget in 2006 and came close to passing a state health insurance plan. All of Schwarzenegger's bond proposals passed this time, and he won re-election with 56% of the vote. In 2009, when tax revenues came crashing down as the housing crisis and then the recession hit California, Schwarzenegger, like Davis, found himself accepting substantial spending increases and acquiescing in raising the taxes that, in 2003 and 2005, he had said were driving businesses out of the state. He even accepted an increase in the car tax, while much of his energy was devoted to keeping the Bush administration from denying a waiver to California's carbon-emissions law, signed by Davis in 2002.

Once upon a time, people used to analyze California politics by distinguishing between Northern California and Southern California. Northern California—the Central Valley and the North Coast as well as the San Francisco Bay Area—tended to vote for John F. Kennedy, Hubert Humphrey, Jimmy Carter, and other Democrats. Southern California—Los Angeles County as well as the smaller suburban and desert counties—tended to vote for Richard Nixon, Gerald Ford, and other Republicans. Today the geographic divisions run the other way. The two sides are coastal California and interior California. Coastal California is defined as all of the counties that touch the coast or San Francisco Bay, plus tiny Napa and the Lake and San Benito counties. From 2000 to 2007, coastal California had an immigrant inflow of 6% and a domestic outflow of 9%. That's a lot of people: 1.4 million immigrants moving in, 1.8 million Americans moving out. The latter moved to places with lower housing prices and more middle-class accommodations: to the Central Valley, to Arizona, Nevada, Texas, and the Rocky Mountain states. Interior California from 2000 to 2007 saw quite different movements—an immigrant inflow of 3% overshadowed by a domestic inflow of 9%. The result was that coastal California grew 4% in those years, less than the national average of 6%, while interior California grew by 17%, more than any state except Nevada and Arizona.

The huge immigrant inflow and domestic outflow from coastal California is making the region an increasingly two-tiered society economically. There is the very affluent elite in the professions, entertainment business, science, and high tech, who live in houses costing millions. And there is a very large body of immigrants, mostly Central Americans living in the modest stucco houses built for middle-income Americans in the 1950s and 1960s, who work double shifts on and off the books in the hopes of making it to a more comfortable suburb. Low-growth policies have limited population growth; coastal California, as a result, grew only 3% from 2000 to 2008. Those policies boosted housing values in affluent areas to astronomical levels, and the subprime mortgage crisis is presumably widening the already wide wealth gap here. Some immigrants thus may be heading home. Nonetheless, affluent elites and low-income immigrants remain united in voting Democratic. Coastal California voted 65%-33% for Barack Obama over John McCain for president in 2008, a higher percentage than in any other state except Obama's native Hawaii and tiny Vermont. The transformation of coastal California over the last generation can be measured another way: Reagan in 1984 lost the Bay Area 51%-48%; McCain in 2008 lost it 74%-24%. The Democratic trend is even apparent in the far south coast. Orange County and San Diego County voted 75%-24% and 65%-33%, respectively, for Reagan. McCain carried Orange County by only 50%-48% and lost San Diego County by 54%-44%.

Interior California is a very different kind of place, with twice as many native-born Americans moving in as immigrants. The income gap is not nearly as wide as in coastal California, and low-income immigrants enjoy at least a somewhat lower cost of living—no Neiman Marcuses here and not so many swap-meets; instead, the area has more Wal-Marts and more Targets. Since 2000, population growth has been vibrant, even frenetic. Interior California grew 18% between 2000 and '08, accounting for two-thirds of the statewide population growth. But the explosion has had negative consequences. The Inland Empire and large parts of the Central Valley from Bakersfield to Sacramento were subprime mortgage territory. Lending institutions granted immigrants with little income no-down-payment mortgages on $450,000 houses, and blue-collar families fleeing the pricey Bay Area got risky alt-A mortgages on $650,000 tract homes in Stanislaus and San Joaquin counties. In 2004, interior California voted 57%-42% for President Bush, a result similar to that in fast-growing Georgia or North Carolina, and not much inferior to Reagan's 61%-38% in the same territory in 1984. But the collapse of the housing market hit hard here, and the Inland Empire and the Central Valley had some of the highest foreclosure rates in the country. Interior California trended Democratic in 2008. The swing here was much greater than in coastal California, where political attitudes seem pretty firmly set, and Obama actually carried the interior 50%-48%.

Clearly, coastal California—and the Democratic Party it so heavily favors—is dominant politically. Obama carried the state with 61% of the vote, far above John Kerry's 54% in 2004. Democrats gained seats in the Legislature, leaving them one vote short in the Senate and three short in the House of the two-thirds majorities needed to pass a budget or to override a Schwarzenegger veto. For a dozen years or more, the majority coalition of ethnic minorities and gentry liberals, financed by Hollywood and Silicon Valley and by the public employee unions, determined public policy. Schwarzenegger's drive to put policy on a different path crashed and burned in 2005. But there were troubling signs for the ruling coalition. California's sales tax is the highest in the nation, and its income tax nearly so. The exodus of businesses continues, and in early 2009, the state came close to leading the nation in unemployment. Public employee unions' success in negotiating salaries and benefits has sent some municipalities hurtling toward bankruptcy. Amazingly, California's Internet usage by individuals and in schools was lower than the national average. Recent data indicate that the state lost more college graduates than it gained in the first half of the decade. Suddenly it looks as if California has some of the same problems as North Dakota or Nebraska.

The dominant political class's commitment to environmental causes has a powerful basis in experience. Air pollution, which reached horrifying levels during Reagan's years as governor, has been vastly reduced by laws pioneered by California that impose tougher restrictions on auto emissions than does the federal government—a huge success in public policy. But some successful policies can have unintended consequences, putting the state at a disadvantage. California's determination to reduce carbon dioxide emissions, which in the short run are relatively benign, threaten to impose huge costs on the state. The slow-growth policies of coastal California, together with the subprime mortgage abuses prevalent in interior California, have left residents with housing prices in urban areas well above the average person's reach. A judge's decision to protect the 3-inch delta smelt by blocking the pumping of all federal and most state water from the Sacramento delta southward, threatens to leave farmland in the most productive agricultural state in the world parched. Traffic continues to worsen, as coastal Californians resist new highways and vote instead for higher taxes to finance mass transit. Meanwhile, California politicians occupy themselves with banning trans fats and blocking new fast-food restaurants in South Central Los Angeles, in hopes of improving the eating habits of city residents, and banning landlords from ascertaining renters' immigration status even as the state struggles to keep up with services for illegal transplants.

There are also some fragile aspects to California's governing coalition of affluent white Boomers and struggling immigrants. In 2008, liberals prevailed in the fight to defeat Proposition 4, which would have required parental notification of minors' abortions. Narrow majorities of African-Americans, Latinos, and Asians voted for it, while whites, with lower birthrates and higher ages themselves, rejected it. In another revealing outcome at the polls, voters approved Proposition 8 banning same-sex marriages. Whites and Asians, perhaps with many gay and lesbian friends and relatives, voted narrowly against it. But blacks, whose turnout increased thanks to the Obama candidacy, voted 70% in favor of it, as did 53% of Latinos. In any case, the results from the ballot issues suggest that the state's majority coalition, especially in coastal California, is unstable. And it raises the question of whether it can be maintained if analyst Kotkin is right when he writes, "Today our Golden State appears headed, if not for imminent disaster, then toward an unanticipated, maddening, and largely unnecessary mediocrity."

Population		Household Income		Work	
Pop. 2007:	36,264,467	Under $15k:	10.8%	Private:	76.5%
State rank:	1st of 50	$15k to $50k:	32.4%	Government:	14.5%
Change since 2000:	Up 7.1%	$50k to $100k:	30.8%	Self-employed:	8.8%
Urban:	92.7%	$100k to $150k:	20.1%	Unemployment (3-yr. average):	4.5%
Rural:	7.3%	Over $150k:	5.8%	Poverty:	13.0%
Native of state:	52.3%	Median income:	$58,361	Blue collar:	21.0%
Not a citizen:	15.5%	**Home Value**		White collar:	60.6%
Area size:	163,696 sq. mi.	Under $100k:	5.3%	Khaki collar:	0.4%
Most populous cities		$100k to $300k:	14.3%	Other:	18.0%
1. Los Angeles	3,770,590	$300k to $500k:	28.9%	**Age**	
2. San Diego	1,264,263	$500k to $1 mil:	41.5%	Median age:	34.5 yrs.
3. San Jose	898,901	Over $1 million:	10.0%	More than 65 yrs:	10.8%
4. San Francisco	757,604	Median:	$513,200	Less than 18 yrs:	25.9%

Race/Ethnicity				Military Veterans		Registered Voters in 2008	
White:	43.0%	*Language*		% of Pop:	8.0%	D:	7,653,495 (44.4%)
Black:	6.1%	English:	57.7%	*Veterans by Period*		R:	5,428,052 (31.4%)
Hispanic:	35.7%	Spanish:	28.3%	WWII and before:	13.7%	Other:	4,192,544 (24.2%)
Asian:	12.0%	Asian:	9.0%	Korea:	12.2%	Voting Age:	26,861,968 (74.1%)
Native Am.:	0.5%	Other		Vietnam:	32.1%	Voter turnout:	13,561,900
Hawaiian:	0.3%	European	4.2%	Gulf (pre-2001):	10.3%	Turnout as % of	
Two+ races:	2.0%	**Education**		Gulf (post-2001):	7.1%	voting age:	49.5%
Ancestry		H.S. grad:	80.0%	Peace time:	24.6%	**Legislature**	
German:	8.4%	College grad:	29.1%			Senate:	26 D 14 R
Irish:	6.6%	Grad degree:	10.4%			Assembly:	51 D 29 R
English:	5.9%						

Presidential politics   California has 55 electoral votes, substantially more than any other state. (Texas has the next highest number, with 34.) And that fact supposedly gave Republicans a lock on the presidency from 1968 to 1988. Then, from 1992 to 2008, California gave the Democrats, if not a lock on the presidency, then at least a way to be competitive at the presidential level. The state's percentages for Democratic presidential candidates have been on an upward trajectory—46% in 1992, 51% in 1996, 53% in 2000, 54% in 2004, and 61% in 2008. In 2000, George W. Bush's chief strategist, Karl Rove, spent $20 million ads in California media. Democrat Al Gore's campaign, coolly assessing the polls, put in nothing at all, and he won the state 53%-42%. In 2004, Rove and Bush campaign manager Ken Mehlman kept a close eye on California but never saw evidence that the state was in play. In 2008, Republican John McCain's strategists didn't seem to give California a second thought.

2008 Presidential Vote		
Obama (D)	8,274,473	(61%)
McCain (R)	5,011,781	(37%)

2008 Democratic Presidential Primary		
Clinton (D)	2,608,184	(51%)
Obama (D)	2,186,662	(43%)

2008 Republican Presidential Primary		
McCain (R)	1,238,988	(42%)
Romney (R)	1,013,471	(35%)
Huckabee (R)	340,669	(12%)
Giuliani (R)	128,681	(4%)
Paul (R)	125,365	(4%)

2004 Presidential Vote		
Kerry (D)	6,745,485	(54%)
Bush (R)	5,509,826	(44%)

Even so, the size of Obama's victory merits examination. Obama won California with 61% of the vote to McCain's 37%. He did better than favorite-son Reagan in 1984 and Democrat Lyndon Johnson in 1964, and he received a higher percentage of votes than any presidential candidate since Franklin Roosevelt won 67% in California in 1936. The exit poll provides some insight. Ten percent of California voters were black—lower than in any of the other 10 large states but significantly higher than blacks' 7% share of the U.S. population. They voted 94% for Obama. Another 18% of the voters were self-identified Latinos, and they voted for Obama 74%-25%. About 6% of the voters were Asian, and they went 64%-35% for Obama. These three groups, amounting to 34% of the electorate, accounted for about 13% of Obama's 24-percentage-point margin of victory.

Another large quantum of the Obama vote came from the group that California political analyst Joel Kotkin dubbed the "gentry liberals." That's not an exit-poll category, of course, but some exit-poll categories do provide useful proxies. White college graduates voted 57% for Obama, more than white nongraduates, and voters with incomes above $200,000 voted 58% for Obama. But perhaps the most illuminating group is the 50- to 64-year-old age group, which is roughly congruent with the Baby Boom Generation. It includes relatively few Hispanics and Asians (because immigrants tend to be younger than average). This cohort voted conspicuously out of line with adjacent age groups: 62% of them voted for Obama, compared with 55% of Obama voters in their 40s (roughly congruent with Generation X) and 48% of Obama voters age 65 and over. (McCain won the latter group 50%-48%.) The elderly are by and large the Californians who came to the state before the 1970s, when the influx to California was primarily from Middle America—the people for whom Reagan, with his timeless moral precepts, struck a chord.

When the Baby Boom voters are added to the ethnic minorities and the sum is adjusted for overlap, this group accounts for almost the entire Obama margin. Pretty much all the rest can be attributed to vote-switchers in the mortgage-crisis epicenters in interior California. Is it an enduring majority? Quite possibly, although the shakeout from the mortgage crisis might impel marginalized immigrants, more than cranky conservatives, to move out of the state. And in time, the Baby Boom Generation will diminish in numbers and may fade into political irrelevance. But voters under 30 cast 76% of their votes for Obama, as did 83% of first-time voters. If these young voters have a future in the state—which will depend in part on its economic course—California could remain the Left Coast for some time.

A few old-timers can still recall when California's June primary was the national tiebreaker. In 1964, the state was the center of national attention when Nelson Rockefeller lost here to Barry Goldwater in the Republican primary. California returned to the limelight in 1968, when Robert Kennedy and Eugene McCarthy slugged it out in the Democratic primary (Kennedy won but was assassinated by Palestinian terrorist Sirhan Sirhan on primary night) and once again in 1972, when George McGovern edged Hubert Humphrey in the Democratic primary. California was all the more important because it was still winner-take-all in both parties.

California waned in importance following two developments—Democrats got rid of winner-take-all primaries after the 1972 election, and in the next five election years, both parties' nominations were clinched long before California voted. For the 1996 campaign, California moved its presidential primary from the first week in June to March 26, which was still too late to make a difference. So in 2000 and 2004, California held its primary in the first week of March, and it became one of several states that clinched nominations for Bush in 2000 and Democrat Kerry in 2004. In 2008, California joined other major states, including New York and New Jersey, in holding its primary on February 5, Super Tuesday.

As it turned out, both parties' races were still competitive when Californians voted. But the state's leverage in the Democratic race was limited because all but 11 of its delegates were allotted by proportional representation within each of the 53 congressional districts. The enthusiasm for Obama in Silicon

Valley and Hollywood, and his endorsement by Schwarzenegger's wife, Maria Shriver, a Kennedy clan member, were not reflected in the results. Turnout was enormous—5 million, compared with 3 million in 2004. Hillary Rodham Clinton won 51%-43%. Obama narrowly lost the San Francisco Bay Area 46% to 48%, while Clinton won 55% in Los Angeles County and Southern California generally. She took the Central Valley as well. Obama carried six congressional districts in Northern California, one of two coastal Santa Barbara districts, one San Diego beachfront district, and the three Los Angeles County districts that have African-American House members.

In enormous California, the organizational edge that Obama enjoyed in caucus states made little difference. Voting ran more along ethnic lines. Obama won among African-Americans, but Clinton carried Latinos, who outnumber blacks in the electorate by about 4-to-1, by 67%-32%. She carried Asians 71%-25%. Obama's advantage among upscale liberals was minimal because Jewish voters, as in New York and Florida, preferred Clinton. Clinton carried 42 congressional districts to Obama's 11, but proportional representation limited her delegate advantage to 204-166. If the Republican winner-take-all rules had been in force, she would have led 279-91, perhaps enough to have given her the delegate lead and put her in the favor of superdelegates in the months to come.

The Republican primary attracted far fewer voters—2.9 million, only slightly more than the 2.8 million who voted in 2000. Far fewer dollars were spent by Republican candidates than by Democratic candidates, and there was far less in the way of GOP organizing efforts. Polling showed a close race between McCain and Mitt Romney, with Mike Huckabee not a serious factor. McCain won 42%-35%. McCain's margin was widest, 53%-28%, among the relatively few Republican voters in the San Francisco Bay Area. (Three times as many Democrats as Republicans voted in the Bay Area.) McCain led 44%-35% in Los Angeles County and by a narrow 40%-37% in the rest of Southern California. The race was closest in the Central Valley and mountains, where McCain led 39%-35%.

But McCain's 7-point margin enabled him to carry 48 of the 53 congressional districts. He lost in only one Central Valley district and in four in Orange and San Diego counties. Republican winner-take-all rules gave McCain a 155-15 delegate lead in the 53 congressional districts, an outcome that left Romney so far behind in delegates that he had little choice but to fold his campaign.

Congressional districting

111th Congress Lineup		
32 D	19 R	2 V
110th Congress Lineup		
34 D	19 R	

California has gained House seats in every census going back to 1850, when it became a state, going from just two to its present 53, far more than any other state. But this tradition may be ending. According to the research of statistical firm Polidata, which performed a straight-line extrapolation to 2010 of the Census Bureau's estimates of 2000–08 population growth, California for the first time in its history will gain no House seats after the 2010 census. One projection in 2008 even showed California just 18 people shy of losing a seat in the House. The days are gone when California gained eight seats at a time, as it did after the 1960 census.

The tradition of partisan redistricting in California goes way back. Republicans drew the lines to their advantage in the 1940s and 1950s, Democrats from the 1960s to the 1980s. The great genius of redistricting was U.S. Rep. Phillip Burton, a Democrat who dominated the line-drawing for congressional seats and for the state Senate and Assembly seats. His 1982 plan left Democrats in secure control of the delegation. In the 1990s, neither party had full control of the Legislature. Republican Gov. Pete Wilson, after hard-nosed bargaining with Democratic legislators, persuaded the state Supreme Court to adopt a plan drawn by his appointed commission in 1992. It was a relatively evenhanded plan, with generally regular boundaries. The fact that Democrats had a 32-20 edge (California had 52 districts then) in the congressional delegation after the 2000 election reflected the party's strength in most parts of the state, not any acuity in drawing district lines.

The assumption after the 2000 election was that California would produce a Democratic redistricting plan. Democrats held the governorship and controlled the state Senate 26-14 and the Assembly 50-30. But that is not what happened. For the second decade in a row, California ended up with a plan that gave neither party a great advantage. Democrats protected all incumbents and took the new seat created by reapportionment; Republicans were able to protect 19 of 20 incumbents. Long Beach Republican Steve Horn was sacrificed to create a new Hispanic Democratic seat, and Republicans got a new seat in the Central Valley.

Many journalists and political scientists condemned the plan for protecting incumbents and reducing competition. Schwarzenegger has sought to take redistricting out of the Legislature's hands. In 2005, his ballot proposition setting up an independent commission of retired judges to draw redistricting plans was defeated. In December 2006, he came up with a new way to create a commission: State officials would draw up a pool of 60 Democrats, Republicans, and independents. Eight people would be chosen at random from the list—three Democrats, three Republicans, and two independents. That group would then choose six more members from the list, two in each category. The final commission would have until September 2011 to draw up the Senate and Assembly boundaries.

In 2007, Assembly Speaker Fabian Nunez said he would support putting such a commission on the ballot for the Assembly and Senate, but he hesitated at having it cover congressional districts too. U.S.

House Speaker Nancy Pelosi, a Democrat from San Francisco, opposed giving the line-drawing authority for congressional districts to a commission. The 33-member California Democratic delegation provided critical support in her race to become party leader and in capturing the House majority in 2006. Pelosi prevailed, and Proposition 11 on the November 2008 ballot covered only state legislative districts. It was approved 51%-49%, with most Democrats opposed and most Republicans in favor.

It's not clear that this change will make a major difference in governance. Coastal California from Los Angeles north is now so heavily Democratic that it is very hard to create Republican districts. A few forlorn Republican enclaves don't add up to even an Assembly district. Politically neutral redistricters aren't likely to create many Republican or even marginal districts in coastal California. The 2008 referendum requirement that congressional districts be compact and not tend divide neighborhoods will reinforce this tendency. But they are likely to create Democratic districts in Interior California and in the coastal counties of Orange and San Diego, if they follow the prevailing interpretation of the Voting Rights Act, which requires maximizing the number of districts that are 50% Hispanic. (It's difficult to draw a 50% black district in California, except perhaps in a few select urban areas like Oakland.)

As legislators watch the commission draw their new districts, they will still be able to redistrict California's congressional districts. Term limits already give them an incentive to draw boundaries that will help them get elected to Congress. The prospect that the commission may alter their current districts will only enhance that incentive. Pelosi and the Democrats' leader on redistricting, U.S. Rep. Zoe Lofgren, a Democrat representing the 16th District, will undoubtedly plead for maintaining the California Democratic delegation's impressive seniority and clout, and may seek to squeeze out a few Republicans as well. But demographics will push in the other direction. Interior California, now with about 15 districts, will be entitled to about 16 and a half districts in a delegation of 53. Everyone assumes that Democrats will maintain large majorities in the Legislature in 2010, but competing pressures could still produce a deadlock on congressional redistricting. Ultimately a court may step in to finish the job, as in the 1990s.

Governor

Arnold Schwarzenegger (R)

Elected Oct. 2003, term expires Jan. 2011, 1st full term; b. July 30, 1947, Thal, Austria; home, Los Angeles; U. of WI-Superior, B.A. 1979; Catholic; married (Maria Shriver); 4 children.

Military Career: Austrian Army, 1965–66.

Professional Career: Bodybuilder, 1965–80; Chairman, President's Council on Physical Fitness and Sports, 1990–93; Actor, 1970–2003.

Office: State Capitol Bldg., Sacramento, 95814, 916-445-2841; Fax: 916-445-4633; Web site: gov.ca.gov.

Election Results

2006 general	Arnold Schwarzenegger (R)	4,850,157	(56%)
	Phil Angelides (D)	3,376,732	(39%)
2006 primary	Arnold Schwarzenegger (R)	1,724,281	(90%)

Arnold Schwarzenegger, bodybuilder, movie actor, and entrepreneur, was elected governor of California in October 2003 and re-elected in November 2006. He grew up in Graz, Austria, where his father was a police officer. At age 13, he told his parents, "I want to be the best-built man in the world." He started training and at 17 competed in his first bodybuilding contest. Getting drafted into the Austrian army slowed him down but not much. He left base without permission one day to compete in the Mr. Europe Junior contest in Stuttgart, Germany, which he won. But his superiors put him in the brig. In 1966, at age 19, he won the Mr. Europe competition in London. There were three organizations holding Mr. Universe contests, and by 1970 he had won them all. In 1970, he won the Mr. Olympia contest for the first of seven times and was generally hailed as the strongest man in the world.

In the course of these competitions, Schwarzenegger visited California in September 1968. The presidential contest between Republican Richard Nixon and Democrat Hubert Humphrey was dominating the news, and he decided he preferred the Republican. He also liked Nixon's home state. Schwarzenegger started buying commercial properties in Santa Monica. In 1970, he got a bit part in a movie called *Hercules in New York*, which opened the door to more acting opportunities. In 1982, he starred in *Conan the Barbarian*, the first in a string of box-office hits that included *The Terminator*, *Predator*, *Total Recall*, and *True Lies*. He also continued his quest for self-improvement, earning a business degree from the University of Wisconsin at Superior in 1979.

In the decade of the 1980s, Schwarzenegger's interest in politics and public service grew, an interest no doubt fostered by the woman he married in 1986, television journalist Maria Shriver, the daughter of Sargent Shriver, first head of the Peace Corps and the Great Society's anti-poverty program, and Eunice Kennedy Shriver, founder of Special Olympics. Schwarzenegger got involved in promoting physical fitness among underprivileged children. From 1990 to 1993, he was chairman of President George H. W. Bush's Council on Physical Fitness and Sports, and in 1995 he established the National Inner City Games Foundation. In 2002, he sponsored a California ballot proposition to establish a publicly supported after-school program. Proposition 49 passed 57%-43%, with roughly even support in all regions of the state.

There was speculation that Schwarzenegger might run for governor in 2006, but many thought his liberal positions on cultural issues—pro-abortion rights, pro-gun control, pro-civil unions for gays and lesbians—would make it hard for him to win a Republican primary. But there turned out to be another path to the governorship when California fell on hard times. In early 2003, the state deficit was projected at as much as $35 billion, California had just undergone crippling electricity shortages, and its economic morale was still recovering from the dot.com bust. Against this backdrop, Democratic Gov. Gray Davis mulled tax increases. Conservative activist Ted Costa started a movement to recall Davis. California law provides that a recall election must be called if petitions are filed with signatures amounting to 12% of the votes most recently cast for the office. Because of the low voter turnout in the state in the 2002 election, that meant 897,000 signatures. In March and April, the drive seemed to falter as polls showed most voters critical of Davis but opposed to recall. Then in May 2003, U.S. Rep. Darrell Issa, R-Calif., who made millions of dollars in a car-alarm business, started pumping $1.7 million into the recall effort. After the July 4 weekend, organizers said they had 1.2 million signatures, and the recall election was set for October 7.

The ballot allowed voters to decide whether to recall Davis and to choose from a list of replacement candidates. Anyone could file as a replacement candidate by paying a $3,500 fee and providing 65 signatures. Speculation turned to a possible run by Schwarzenegger, but he said he was busy promoting his new movie, *Terminator 3,* and would only decide after that. In early August, Davis sued to try to get the recall delayed or called off. State Democratic leaders threatened that anyone who went on the replacement ballot would kill his or her chances for the nomination to succeed Davis in 2006. On August 5, Sen. Dianne Feinstein, whom some Democrats wanted as a backup to hold the governorship if Davis was recalled, announced she would not run. That afternoon, Schwarzenegger went to Burbank to tape *The Tonight Show.* His political consultants believed he would announce he was not running. He shocked them when he said he was. A few hours later, Lt. Gov. Cruz Bustamante broke ranks with other Democrats by saying he was running on the replacement ballot. Within 24 hours, Issa withdrew from the race. In all, 135 candidates qualified for the replacement ballot. But the ranks of serious candidates soon dwindled. By mid-September it was clear that there were three serious candidates on the replacement ballot: Schwarzenegger, Bustamante, and state Sen. Tom McClintock, a fiscal and cultural conservative who had lost the 2002 race for state controller by only 45.4%-45.1%. On September 15, a three-judge panel of the Ninth Circuit federal appeals court postponed the election, but a full 11-judge panel ordered the recall to go ahead on October 7.

Throughout the campaign, Schwarzenegger made few specific proposals but said that Davis must be removed, taxes must not be increased, and spending must be reduced. His campaign organized monster rallies that attracted thousands of people, but where he spoke only briefly and did not mingle with the crowd. Davis rallies were sparsely attended, mainly by Democratic activists and union officials. Bustamante, who announced his candidacy by fax, scarcely campaigned at all, though he did back driver's licenses for illegal immigrants. On October 2, the *Los Angeles Times* ran a story alleging that Schwarzenegger had groped various women some years ago. He admitted that he had "behaved badly sometimes" and apologized. But the stories failed to stop the tide. Davis, elected 58%-38% in 1998 and re-elected 47%-42% in 2002, was recalled 55%-45%. On the replacement ballot Schwarzenegger won 49% of the vote, Bustamante 32%, and McClintock 13%. The San Francisco Bay Area voted 64%-36% against recall, but Los Angeles County rejected it by only 51%-49%. Southern California voted 69% for recall, and the rest of the state voted 64% in favor of recall. Schwarzenegger trailed Bustamante 46%-33% in the Bay Area, but in coastal California from Los Angeles north equaled him 40%-40%, and led 61%-20% in the South Coast and 56%-23% in interior California.

Democrats were bitter over losing control of state government in this generally Democratic state, and some even threatened to recall Schwarzenegger in 2004. But Davis conceded graciously and ordered his appointees to cooperate with the new administration. On November 17, Schwarzenegger became governor. He ordered a performance review of state government and plunged into the business of drafting a budget. He pressed the Legislature for repeal of the law Davis signed providing driver's licenses for illegal immigrants. He also repealed Davis's car tax increase and approved appropriations to help local governments. They agreed to give up $1.3 billion in each of the next two years in return for a constitutional amendment making it harder for the state to take over local revenues. He got two constitutional amendments put on the March 2004 primary ballot, one to authorize $15 billion of debt to cover the current budget deficit and another to require a balanced budget in the out-years. Both trailed in the polls, but after Schwarzenegger started campaigning for them, the first passed with 63% of the vote and the second with 71%. In April 2004, by threatening to take the issue to the voters, he got the Legislature to make changes in workers' compensation laws without the rate regulation Democrats were seeking. In May 2004, Schwarzenegger released a $99 billion budget with deficits that seemed likely to be $8 billion over two years. It called for higher payments from Indian casinos and cuts in pay and benefits for state employees. Unlike his Republican predecessors Ronald Reagan and Pete Wilson, he refused to support a tax increase in the budget crisis. California requires budgets to be approved by two-thirds votes in the Legislature, so they always represent something of a consensus. After negotiations broke down, Schwarzenegger signed a $105 billion budget on July 31.

Schwarzenegger tried to better his odds in the Legislature by campaigning for Republican legislative candidates in the fall of 2004, but none won. But he had his successes in November 2004 referenda. A measure he backed promising $3 billion for stem-cell research passed 59%-41%. His measure to protect local government revenues from state takeover was approved 84%-16%. A measure to limit tort actions passed 59%-41%. Indian tribes' attempts to augment their casino businesses were rejected by voters. Proposals for a telephone tax for emergency medical funding and to mandate health insurance coverage for small businesses also failed. California voters seemed to be falling in line with their new Republican governor.

In early 2005 Schwarzenegger proposed a $111 billion budget, with cuts in scheduled increases in health care, transportation, and school aid. And he went on the offensive, attacking the heart of Democratic institutional power in the state. He demanded action on four issues and, again, threatened to take them to the people in November. He demanded a nonpartisan board of retired judges to redistrict California's congressional and legislative districts, automatic across-the-board spending cuts if spending grew faster than revenues, merit pay for teachers, and defined-contribution 401(k)-like pensions for state employees. Schwarzenegger said, "We're going right where all the evil is, and we're going to fix it." Redistricting would presumably put more Democrats (and some Republicans) at risk of losing their seats. Across-the-board spending cuts would give the governor huge leverage in budget negotiations. Merit pay for teachers, furiously opposed by teacher unions, would reduce the power of one of the Democrats' key allies. Defined-contribution pension plans would reduce, over time, the power of CalPERS, which invests California's pension money and is one of the biggest institutional investors in the country, and Democrats had dominated CalPERS. The Democratically controlled Legislature seemed certain to reject those measures, so in June, Schwarzenegger called a November 2005 special election to get voters to approve them. Three of his favored measures qualified for the ballot: One would give the governor new authority to cut spending, another called for an increase in the service required before teachers could receive tenure, and a third would create a nonpartisan board of retired judges with the authority to redistrict state legislative boundaries. Schwarzenegger dropped his initiative to overhaul the state employee pension system and got rid of the merit pay proposal.

Schwarzenegger's attempt at plebiscitary government failed. Democrats and labor unions spent over $100 million on television ads against the Schwarzenegger proposals. In 2004, Schwarzenegger had referred to the nurses' union as a "special interest" and said its leaders disliked him "because I am always kicking butts." Now television viewers saw a pleasant-looking woman in a nurse's uniform quote these words back at him. Unaccountably, Schwarzenegger's political advisers did not respond with a campaign of their own, until the last two months before the November election. Evidently the Governator believed he could still get direct access to voters through the TV cameras always stalking him. But local television news was tired of the Arnold story. Schwarzenegger's job rating dropped. And on Election Day, all of his proposals lost. Ironically, the highest percentage of votes, 47%, went to a proposition put together by others and only lukewarmly supported by Schwarzenegger, a ban on public employee unions spending dues money on politics without members' permission.

Schwarzenegger's response to this shattering defeat was an almost immediate U-turn. As he later put it, "The people sent a very clear message. They said, 'Hey, don't come to us. We sent you to Sacramento. Work with them up there. That's what we expect you to do.'" He hired a new chief of staff, Susan Kennedy, a top aide to Gray Davis. He cultivated Assembly Speaker Fabian Nunez and Senate President Don Perata and in the spring of 2006 agreed with them on a "Let's Rebuild California" program, which would issue billions of dollars in bonds for transportation, housing, school construction, and flood control. Schwarzenegger also reached agreement with Nunez and Perata on a $131 billion budget earlier than in the preceding six years; most Republican legislators voted against it. This was made easier by the appearance of an $8 billion tax windfall, of the sort that California's progressive tax system tends to produce in times of economic growth. Schwarzenegger also signed bills increasing the hourly minimum wage and purporting to cut drug prices. He signed several bills supported by gay-rights groups, but he vetoed same-sex marriage.

His signature issue in this period was reducing carbon emissions. For more than 50 years, California has had an exemption from federal clean-air legislation. It is authorized to pass more-stringent legislation, for the very good reason that the Los Angeles Basin and other mountain-surrounded valleys in California are subject to inversion, which holds pollution in. California started regulating its air in the 1940s. Smog peaked around 1970, when Schwarzenegger had just come to California. As governor, he called the Bush administration's position on reducing emissions "embarrassing" and urged California to fill "the vacuum" on carbon emissions policy. In July 2006, he signed an agreement with British Prime Minister

Tony Blair to trade scientific and economic research. In March 2007, he signed a cap-and-trade system for reducing carbon emissions with four Western state governors. He went to Detroit to urge automakers to produce cleaner-running cars. In September 2006, he signed a Global Warming Solutions Act, requiring a 25% cut in carbon dioxide emissions by 2020 and a 40% cut by 2050. Only one Republican legislator voted for it. "What we're basically saying to the federal government is, 'Look, we don't need Washington.' And so let us create the partnerships and let the world know that America is actually fighting global warming," Schwarzenegger said. Leaders of some environmental groups still charged that his programs relied too much on markets. But on this issue, as on many others, voters were faced in 2006 with a very different Arnold Schwarzenegger than the one they repudiated in 2005.

And they responded very differently. Democrats had two serious choices in the Democratic primary: Controller Steve Westly, a Silicon Valley multimillionaire who campaigned as a "new Democrat," and state Treasurer Phil Angelides, a Sacramento-area real estate developer and former state party chairman. He campaigned as a vitriolic critic of George W. Bush. Angelides won the June primary 48%-43%. But he was not able to raise the large sums he had hoped for, and his angry criticisms went largely unheard as Schwarzenegger traveled the state with top Democrats in the Legislature for bipartisan support of the bond ballot propositions. In November 2006, Schwarzenegger won re-election 56%-39%. He had little in the way of coattails for Republicans. Democrat John Garamendi beat McClintock for lieutenant governor 49%-45%, and Secretary of State Bruce McPherson, a Schwarzenegger appointee, was beaten by Democrat Debra Bowen 48%-45%. Former Democratic Gov. Jerry Brown was elected attorney general 56%-38%. One Republican, Silicon Valley millionaire Steve Poizner, beat Bustamante for insurance commissioner, 51%-39%. Schwarzenegger did better on the ballot propositions. His four bond issues won majorities ranging from 57% to 64%.

After his victory, Schwarzenegger proclaimed an era of "post-partisanship" and called 2007 the year of health care. He kept Republican legislators at arm's length and worked closely with Democratic Speaker Nunez. But agreement proved difficult. Democrats rejected a proposal to require everyone to buy health insurance as a burden on the poor, despite proposals for offsetting tax breaks. Republicans opposed requiring employers to offer health insurance or pay into a state fund as an undue burden on business. Through the fall, the governor and Legislature struggled to no avail to settle on a plan that could pass the Assembly and the Senate. With the start of a new year, Schwarzenegger proclaimed 2008 to be the year of education, and in March he presented a proposal for longer hours for day care, expanded English as a Second Language programs, and a school inspection system.

But that went nowhere as the fiscal crisis took precedence. California was one of the epicenters of subprime mortgage lending, with reduced standards or outright fraud in providing financing for marginal buyers, a large percentage of them Latino. Housing prices peaked in 2006, and soon many borrowers found themselves under water, with more debt than their houses were worth. Foreclosures skyrocketed; construction plummeted, and revenues, thanks to California's progressive taxes, fell far below projections. The robust spending increases that Schwarzenegger, like Davis, had allowed became unsustainable. Schwarzenegger signed a $145 billion budget, with a 10% spending increase, in August 2007, but by the end of the year, he faced a budget shortfall of $18 billion. During the fat years, state salaries grew by 37%, with nearly 1,000 state employees earning over $200,000 a year. The number of state employees per resident grew 8%. By May 2008, Schwarzenegger was calling for borrowing against future lottery receipts and, absent that, instituting a "temporary" 1% sales tax increase. Democrats balked at that, while Republicans opposed any tax increases. In August, Schwarzenegger tried to pressure legislators by cutting state wages to the minimum wage and laying off 10,000 state employees. Only in September was agreement reached on a budget. In October 2008, he told Treasury Secretary Henry Paulson that California might have to borrow $7 billion from the federal government. In November, facing a $40 billion shortfall, he signed a bill to borrow $5 billion against future lottery receipts, but it still needed approval from the voters. In February 2009, after three months of furious argument, including a plan to furlough state employees two days a month, Schwarzenegger got the required number of Republican votes to pass a $41 billion package, with about $14 billion in tax increases, $16 billion in spending cuts, and $11 billion in borrowing. Ironically, it included an increase in the car tax—a measure that was the political breaking point for Gray Davis. It also authorized referenda on two constitutional amendments: One was Schwarzenegger's proposal to cap future state spending, and the other was to create an open primary system (the price for the crucial vote of Republican state Senator Abel Maldonado).

Despite the state's fiscal straits, Schwarzenegger continued his activist ways as governor. In September 2008, he signed a bill to require local planners to develop goals for reducing carbon emissions and containing sprawl in their regions, and he unsuccessfully sought a ballot initiative to borrow $9 billion for water projects. He succeeded in placing on the ballot a proposal to borrow $10 billion to establish a high-speed rail line between Los Angeles and San Francisco, which, despite dubious economic prospects, was approved 53%-47% in 2008. Also passed, by a 51%-49% margin, was his proposal for a bipartisan commission to draw district lines for the state Senate and Assembly—but not, at the insistence of U.S. House Speaker Nancy Pelosi of California, congressional districts. Schwarzenegger promoted his green policies nationally, but had less of a profile in presidential politics than he had had in 2004. He endorsed Republican John McCain for president in January 2008, but did little campaigning for him.

During the 2008-09 budget struggle, Schwarzenegger's job rating fell to well below 50%, and he had long since brushed aside speculation that he run against Democratic Sen. Barbara Boxer in 2010. He is of course constitutionally ineligible to run for president, about which he has said, "You will never hear me complain that I can't run for president. I look at the things that I was able to do rather than the things I am not able to do. I am very, very happy about how America has received me and the kind of things I was able to accomplish here."

Senior Senator

Dianne Feinstein (D)

Elected Nov. 1992, term expires 2012, 3rd full term; b. June 22, 1933, San Francisco; home, San Francisco; Stanford U., B.A. 1955; Jewish; married (Richard C. Blum); 4 children.

Elected Office: San Francisco Bd. of Supervisors, 1970–78, Pres., 1970–71, 1974–75, 1978; San Francisco mayor, 1978–88.

Professional Career: CA Women's Parole Bd., 1960–66.

DC Office: 331 HSOB, 20510, 202-224-3841; Fax: 202-228-3954; Web site: feinstein.senate.gov.

State Offices: Fresno, 559-485-7430; Los Angeles, 310-914-7300; San Diego, 619-231-9712; San Francisco, 415-393-0707.

Committees: *Appropriations* (9th of 18 D): Agriculture, Rural Development, Food and Drug Administration & Related Agencies; Commerce, Justice, Science & Related Agencies; Defense; Energy & Water Development; Interior, Environment & Related Agencies (Chmn); Transportation, Housing and Urban Development & Related Agencies. *Intelligence (Select)* (Chmn of 10 D). *Judiciary* (3rd of 12 D): Administrative Oversight & the Courts; Constitution; Crime & Drugs; Immigration, Refugees & Border Security; Terrorism & Homeland Security. *Rules & Administration* (5th of 11 D).

Group Ratings

	ADA	ACLU	AFS	LCV	ITIC	NTU	COC	ACU	CFG	FRC
2008	100	57	100	100	100	3	63	4	3	11
2007	90	—	86	87	—	7	45	0	13	—

National Journal Ratings

	2007 LIB — 2007 CONS		2008 LIB — 2008 CONS	
Economic	77%	— 21%	91%	— 0%
Social	61%	— 38%	67%	— 31%
Foreign	73%	— 26%	65%	— 6%
Composite	71%	— 29%	81%	— 19%

Key Votes of the 110th Congress

1. Raise CAFE standards	Y	5. Make English official language N	9. Withdraw troops 3/08	Y
2. Expand SCHIP	Y	6. Path to citizenship	Y	10. Iran guard is terrorist group Y
3. Cap greenhouse gases	Y	7. Fetus is unborn child	N	11. Increase missile defense $	N
4. Bail out financial markets	Y	8. Prosecute hate crimes	Y	12. Overhaul FISA	Y

Election Results

2006 general	Dianne Feinstein (D)	5,076,289	(59%)	($8,030,489)
	Dick Mountjoy (R)	2,990,822	(35%)	($195,265)
2006 primary	Dianne Feinstein (D)	2,176,829	(87%)	
	Colleen Fernald (D)	199,170	(8%)	
	Martin Luther Church (D)	127,291	(5%)	

Prior Winning Percentages: 2000 (56%); 1994 (47%); 1992 (54%)

Dianne Feinstein, California's senior senator, is a Democrat first elected in 1992. Feinstein (*FINE-stine*) grew up in San Francisco in lush Presidio Heights, the daughter of a doctor who hoped she would follow him into the profession. In her first semester at Stanford University, Feinstein got a D in genetics and decided she did not have the aptitude for medicine. But she did love a class she took on American political thought. She graduated with a degree in criminology and then, while doing an internship, wrote a paper about post-conviction phases of the justice system that she thought contained valuable ideas for the state of California. Feinstein sent her paper to Gov. Pat Brown. Despite her youth—she was just 27—the governor appointed her to the California Women's Board of Terms and Parole. A few years later, in 1969, she won her first election, to the San Francisco County Board of Supervisors. Feinstein went on to become president of the board and in 1978, was suddenly catapulted to mayor when Mayor George Moscone and Supervisor Harvey Milk were shot to death by former Supervisor Dan White. Feinstein discovered Moscone's body and in the subsequent weeks, displayed a steadiness and a sense of command that calmed the city. She was elected to full terms in 1979 and 1983. In 1984, Democratic presidential candidate Walter Mondale seriously considered her for vice president, but passed over her for Geraldine Ferraro because of qualms about the business dealings of Feinstein's husband, Richard Blum. She presided gracefully that year over the Democratic National Convention in San Francisco, while ironically, Ferraro juggled questions about *her* family's business dealings.

Ineligible for a third full term, Feinstein left the mayor's office in 1987 and ran for governor in 1990. She won the Democratic primary impressively, then lost 49%-46% to Republican Pete Wilson. When Wilson appointed Orange County state Sen. John Seymour—an unknown and bland choice—to replace him in the Senate, Feinstein quickly announced for the seat. She had primary competition from Gray Davis, then state controller, who ran an ad against her campaign finance practices and compared her to haughty New York billionaire Leona Helmsley, who went to jail for tax evasion. Feinstein won 58%-33%, and after that, her relations with Davis, elected governor in 1998 and 2002, were never warm. Davis was forced out of office in a 2003 recall election. In the 1992 general election, nothing worked for the hapless Seymour, the appointed GOP incumbent—not his switch from having opposed abortion rights to favoring them, not his attempt to play on fears of illegal immigration and not his attacks on Feinstein's arguably tricky financing of her 1990 gubernatorial campaign, which resulted in a $190,000 fine. Feinstein won 54%-38%, coming close even in Seymour's Southern California base.

In the Senate, Feinstein kept a distance from the Clinton administration, negotiating for changes before voting for its 1993 budget, voting against the North American Free Trade Agreement, and withdrawing her support of the Clinton health care plan in 1994. She was also critical of the Democratic president after he was caught lying about having a sexual relationship with a White House intern. Feinstein had two significant legislative achievements in her first two years. One was a ban on assault weapons in 1994. When Idaho Republican Larry Craig argued that her definition of assault weapons was not rigorous enough and challenged her knowledge of firearms, she stopped the argument in its tracks by reminding the Senate of the horrific tragedy earlier in her political career. "I know something about what firearms can do," Feinstein said. "I came to be mayor of San Francisco as a product of assassination." (In 2000, she sponsored an unsuccessful bill to require licensing of all guns and in 2004, pressed fervently for reauthorization of the 1994 assault-weapons ban. The act expired in September 2004.) Her other achievement in her early Senate years was the California Desert Protection Act, which had long been held up by the state's Republican senators as too restrictive.

Feinstein has had a moderate to liberal voting record and has differed on some issues from her colleague and Bay Area neighbor, Democratic Sen. Barbara Boxer. Feinstein voted to repeal the marriage penalty and the estate tax. She supported the Bush tax cut in 2001 and the Iraq War resolution in 2002, although two years later she said she had been misled into voting for the war by an exaggeration of the threat and regretted her vote. Feinstein supported the GOP's Medicare prescription-drug bill in 2003 as well. She supported the death penalty and took a tough stance on fighting terrorism after September 11. With Republican Jon Kyl of Arizona, she co-sponsored a bill to bar entry to the United States for people from nations that sponsor terrorism, plus other measures that were more stringent than a similar bill sponsored by Massachusetts Democrat Edward Kennedy and Kansas Republican Sam Brownback. The two versions were melded and signed into law in 2002.

On the Judiciary Committee, Feinstein took an active role in the immigration debate in recent years. She pressed in 2005 for reauthorization of the federal program reimbursing state and local governments for the cost of detaining illegal immigrants. In the debate on immigration in 2006, she opposed guest-worker proposals, and she and Boxer proposed a 20-year sentence for people caught building or financing underground cross-border tunnels, which became part of the border-fence bill that passed both houses in September. On other issues in the Judiciary Committee, Feinstein joined with Utah Republican Orrin Hatch to get 54 senators to sign a letter calling for more embryonic-stem-cell research, which uses excess embryos from in vitro fertilization. She supported Pennsylvania Republican Arlen Specter's bill establishing a compensation fund for asbestos victims and won passage of an amendment requiring that the sickest claimants be paid first. But the bill came up two votes short of the needed 60 in 2006. In 2005, Feinstein said she did not believe that the USA PATRIOT Act, the Bush administration's centerpiece anti-terrorism law, had led to violations of civil liberties, a statement cited by President Bush in pressing for renewal of the act. She also was the only Democrat on the committee to vote in 2006 for the amendment authorizing prosecutions for flag desecration.

Feinstein was less bipartisan in the war over some of President Bush's judicial nominees, but she also was frequently willing to compromise in the end. With other Judiciary Democrats, she opposed several nominees to the federal appeals court. But then, with Boxer, she made an arrangement with the Bush administration to set up six-member panels to decide on the potential merits of federal trial judges in California. Three members were appointed by each side, and four votes were required to approve a nominee. This bypassed the senior Republicans in the House delegation. In May 2005, Feinstein voted against the nomination of conservative nominee Priscilla Owen, but declined to take the harsher step of a filibuster. After an interview with Supreme Court nominee John Roberts in July 2005, she called him "very impressive" but opposed his confirmation nonetheless, out of concern that he might overturn the *Roe v. Wade* decision legalizing abortion. After Harriet Miers's nomination for the high court was withdrawn in October 2005, Feinstein said, "I don't believe they would have attacked a man the way she was attacked." In 2007, Feinstein and New York's Charles Schumer were the only Judiciary Committee Democrats to vote to confirm Michael Mukasey as attorney general. But she was not so gentle with the administration when it came to the abrupt firing of seven U.S. attorneys, including Carol Lam in San Diego, in a purge that was assailed as politically motivated. Feinstein questioned whether Lam's firing was related to the criminal investigation of California Rep. Randy (Duke) Cunningham, a Republican who pleaded guilty to accepting bribes.

In January 2009, Feinstein became chairman of the Senate Intelligence Committee and indicated she wanted to clean house at the intelligence agencies. "My view is that it's time for a new start," she said. "I want to see the Senate Intelligence Committee with much closer oversight and a much closer relationship with the intelligence community." When former Clinton White House chief of staff Leon Panetta was announced as Obama's choice for director of the Central Intelligence Agency, she said that she thought Obama should have appointed "an intelligence professional." But after Vice President Joseph Biden said it was a mistake not to have informed her in advance of the appointment, she was conciliatory, saying, "I'm very respectful of the president's authority, and if this is the man he wants, then that means a lot to me."

Feinstein doesn't hesitate to go her own way on the committee, no matter what her party's preferences. She had called for a single national intelligence director in 2002, long before the 9/11 Commission recommended one. In 2007, she supported immunity for telecommunications companies that had allowed the government to listen in on telephone calls from suspected terrorists abroad to persons in the United States. Many Democrats opposed immunity for the companies. Feinstein attached amendments to the 2007 and 2008 intelligence authorization bills to require that all government interrogations be conducted under the rules of the Army Field Manual, and she attempted to apply that standard to government contractors as well. In January 2009, she called for closing the detention camp at Guantanamo, which she called a "failed experiment." In February 2009, she was criticized for saying that Predator drones directed at extremists near the Pakistan-Afghanistan border were launched from bases in Pakistan. A Feinstein aide said that the fact had been revealed in the *Washington Post* months earlier.

On the Senate Rules Committee, Feinstein has worked on institutional reforms. She co-sponsored a requirement that earmarks added to spending bills be posted on the Internet for at least 24 hours. She was in the spotlight in January 2009, when former Illinois Attorney General Roland Burris, a Democrat, was appointed by Gov. Rod Blagojevich to fill Obama's Senate seat. Democratic leaders initially said they would refuse to seat him because his appointment was tainted by allegations that Blagojevich had demanded personal and political favors in exchange. Feinstein argued that Burris should be seated, and she prevailed. She said: "The question, really, is one, in my view, of law. And that is, does the governor have the power to make the appointment? And the answer is yes. Is the governor discredited? And the answer is yes. Does that affect his appointment power? And the answer is no, until certain things happen." Burris, after being turned back at the door of the Capitol, was seated. As Rules chairman in the 110th Congress, Feinstein also presided over the presidential inauguration ceremonies on January 20.

With a seat on the powerful Appropriations Committee and on the Energy and Water Development Subcommittee, Feinstein has worked for several years to revive the CALFED program, which attempts to resolve water-scarcity issues in California. In 2003 and 2004, she worked with House Resources Chairman Richard Pombo, a California Republican, to reauthorize CALFED and to protect water quality in San Francisco Bay and the Sacramento Delta. And in 2006, when the delta levees were threatened by severe flood, she and Boxer backed spending $22 million to repair 29 levee sites. Feinstein also has sought public and private funding to protect old-growth redwoods in the Headwaters Forest and salt ponds in the San Francisco Bay area.

She is more accommodating of trade ties with China than her powerful home-state ally, U.S. House Speaker Nancy Pelosi. Feinstein has supported trade with China since she established a sister-city relationship in 1990 between San Francisco and Shanghai, then led by Jiang Zemin. She opposed Pelosi's efforts to impose penalties on China because of its human rights violations. In 2005, Feinstein called on China to crack down on piracy of intellectual property and to revalue its currency, but she opposed a bill sponsored by Lindsey Graham, R-S.C., and Schumer to impose 27.5% tariffs on Chinese goods if it did not revalue.

Feinstein has had only one serious challenge since she was elected to the Senate, in the Republican year of 1994. U.S. Rep. Michael Huffington spent $30 million of his own money running against her and pulled even in the polls in September. Feinstein was clearly frustrated that she could not count on outspending him. Huffington slipped when it was revealed that he and his wife, Arianna Huffington, employed an illegal alien as a nanny. (Arianna Huffington now runs the liberal *Huffington Post* blog.) On the Thursday before the election, it was revealed that Feinstein, despite her earlier denials, had employed a woman whose work permit had expired. The media ran stories casting doubt on assertions that the woman was an illegal alien. That probably made the difference. Feinstein won 47%-45%. She carried Los Angeles County 52%-40% and the San Francisco Bay Area 63%-30%, offsetting Huffington's margins in Southern California and the rest of the state.

Since then, Feinstein has enjoyed positive poll ratings. In 2000, Republican U.S. Rep. Tom Campbell, a libertarian Stanford Law professor, challenged her. Campbell had also tried to run against Boxer in 1992, but failed to get the nomination. This time, Feinstein far outspent her opponent, $10.3 million to $4.4 million. She won 56%-37%, carrying all of the major regions of the state. In her 2006 re-election contest, Republicans nominated conservative state Sen. Richard Mountjoy. Feinstein spent $8 million on her campaign, while Mountjoy spent just $195,000. She won 59%-35%.

In July 2007, Feinstein endorsed Hillary Rodham Clinton for president in her primary contest with Barack Obama and backed her strongly in the California primary. But in May 2008, after Clinton lost badly in North Carolina and won only narrowly in Indiana, Feinstein said, "I think the race is reaching the point now where there are negative dividends in it, in terms of strife within the party." On June 5, two days after the last primaries, Feinstein hosted a meeting between Clinton and Obama in her Washington home. While the two talked for an hour, she worked upstairs. After Clinton's withdrawal from the race, Feinstein pushed her for the vice presidential nomination.

In late 2008 and early 2009, Feinstein was being mentioned as a possible candidate for governor in 2010, when Republican Arnold Schwarzenegger will reach the end of his second term. Polls showed her ahead in a theoretical Democratic primary and general election. In early 2009, as other Democrats jockeyed for the nomination, she said there was still plenty of time for her to decide whether to run. Her Senate seat comes up for re-election in 2012.

Junior Senator

Barbara Boxer (D)

Elected 1992, term expires 2010, 3rd term; b. Nov. 11, 1940, Brooklyn, NY; home, Rancho Mirage; Brooklyn Col., B.A. 1962; Jewish; married (Stewart); 2 children.

Elected Office: Marin Cnty. Bd. of Supervisors, 1976–82; U.S. House of Reps., 1982–92.

Professional Career: Stockbroker & researcher, 1962–65; Journalist, *Pacific Sun*, 1972–74; Dist. aide, U.S. Rep. John Burton, 1974–76.

DC Office: 112 HSOB, 20510, 202-224-3553; Fax: 202-224-0454; Web site: boxer.senate.gov.

State Offices: Fresno, 559-497-5109; Los Angeles, 213-894-5000; Sacramento, 916-448-2787; San Diego, 619-239-3884; San Francisco, 415-403-0100; San Bernardino 909-888-8525

Committees: *Commerce, Science & Transportation* (5th of 14 D): Aviation Operations, Safety & Security; Consumer Protection, Product Safety & Insurance; Oceans, Atmosphere & Coast Guard; Science & Space; Surface Transportation & Merchant Marine Infrastructure, Safety & Security. *Environment & Public Works* (Chmn of 12 D). *Ethics (Select)* (Chmn of 3 D). *Foreign Relations* (4th of 11 D): East Asian & Pacific Affairs; International Development & Foreign Assistance, Economic Affairs & International Environmental Protection; International Operations & Organizations, Democracy & Global Women's Issues (Chmn); Near Eastern & South & Central Asian Affairs.

Group Ratings

	ADA	ACLU	AFS	LCV	ITIC	NTU	COC	ACU	CFG	FRC
2008	95	85	100	100	80	3	57	4	3	0
2007	80	—	100	80	—	7	33	4	8	—

National Journal Ratings

	2007 LIB — 2007 CONS		2008 LIB — 2008 CONS	
Economic	88%	11%	91%	0%
Social	87%	12%	91%	0%
Foreign	93%	6%	65%	6%
Composite	90%	10%	90%	10%

Key Votes of the 110th Congress

1. Raise CAFE standards	*	5. Make English official language N	9. Withdraw troops 3/08 Y
2. Expand SCHIP	Y	6. Path to citizenship Y	10. Iran guard is terrorist group N
3. Cap greenhouse gases	Y	7. Fetus is unborn child N	11. Increase missile defense $ N
4. Bail out financial markets	Y	8. Prosecute hate crimes Y	12. Overhaul FISA N

Election Results

2004 general	Barbara Boxer (D)	6,955,728	(58%)	($14,886,426)
	Bill Jones (R)	4,555,922	(38%)	($7,802,657)
2004 primary	Barbara Boxer (D)	unopposed		

Prior Winning Percentages: 1998 (53%); 1992 (48%); 1990 House (68%); 1988 House (73%); 1986 House (74%); 1984 House (68%); 1982 House (52%)

Barbara Boxer, California's junior senator, is a Democrat first elected to the House in 1982 and a decade later to the Senate. She is the chairman of the Environment and Public Works Committee. Boxer grew up in Brooklyn. In 1962, she graduated from Brooklyn College, where she met her husband, Stewart. The couple moved to Marin County in 1968. Boxer, a stockbroker, volunteered for Eugene McCarthy's presidential campaign that year. In 1970, she and some neighbors formed the Marin Alternative to oppose the Vietnam War. Marin County was only on its way to being trendy then; the overall political tone was liberal Republican, but heading left. In 1972, Boxer ran for the Board of Supervisors and lost to an incumbent Republican. She then went to work as an aide to Democratic U.S. Rep. John Burton. In 1976, she ran again for the county board and won. When Burton retired unexpectedly in 1982, Boxer ran for the House seat and was easily elected. In the House, she was known for her aggressive investigation into wasteful spending, unearthing the Air Force's $7,622 coffee pot in 1984, and for her vocal opposition to the Gulf War in the early 1990s. She also led a group of women House members in a march to the steps of the Senate to demand hearings into law professor Anita Hill's sexual-harassment allegations against Clarence Thomas, who was in the process of being confirmed for appointment to the Supreme Court.

In 1992, Boxer ran for the Senate. She started off as neither the best-known nor the best-financed candidate, but 1992 turned out to be the "Year of the Woman," in which the enthusiasm of the feminist left helped produce important victories for Democratic candidates. Boxer won the June primary with 44% of the vote, to 31% for Lt. Gov. Leo McCarthy and 22% for U.S. Rep. Mel Levine. In the general election, her opponent was Bruce Herschensohn, a Los Angeles television and radio commentator. The Boxer-Herschensohn race was a battle of opposites, the far left versus the far right of the ideological spectrum. Herschensohn opposed abortion rights and advocated a flat tax and offshore oil drilling. Boxer's positions were precisely the opposite. Her bid was helped by the poor showing of President George H.W. Bush's campaign in California and by the revelation late in the campaign that Herschensohn had frequented nightclubs that featured nude dancers. She won with 48% of the vote.

Boxer's voting record is among the most liberal in the Senate. She is one of the strongest proponents of abortion rights in Congress and a prime sponsor of the Freedom of Choice Act, which would nullify all state restrictions on abortion. Boxer has pulled back when she has sensed she doesn't have the votes. In 2005, she declined to bring forward a bill blocking a law that allowed health care providers to refuse to perform abortions, and the following year, she declined to filibuster a bill penalizing those who transport minors across state lines to get abortions.

She was a staunch defender of President Bill Clinton during the impeachment proceedings in 1998, when the president was accused of lying about an extramarital affair with a White House intern. In 2001, Boxer supported the use of force in Afghanistan. But in October 2002, she voted against the use of force in Iraq, and she later cast votes against funding for the war. In January 2005, as the electoral vote count was read out to a joint session of Congress, she was the one senator to protest the awarding of Ohio's electoral votes to Republican President George W. Bush. She recalled that four years earlier, no senator had protested the Florida vote in the bitterly contested presidential contest of 2000, and Boxer said she regretted not having protested then. Her protest triggered the dissolution of the joint session and a debate in each of the two chambers. The Senate voted 74-1 to accept the Ohio count, with Boxer as the lone dissenter, and the House voted 267-31 on the same question. "I hate inconveniencing my friends, but I think it's worth a couple of hours to shine some light on these issues," Boxer said. In January 2005, Boxer engaged in a stinging denunciation of Condoleezza Rice during a Foreign Relations Committee hearing on Rice's nomination as secretary of state. Rice's "loyalty to the mission," Boxer said, "overwhelmed your respect for the truth." Speaking of the troops, she said, "You sent them in there because of weapons of mass destruction. Later the mission changed when there were none." Rice responded, "I really hope you will refrain from impugning my integrity. I really hope that you will not imply that I take the truth lightly."

Boxer has supported gun control and has sponsored amendments to require childproof safety locks on all handguns and to ban sales of guns to people who are intoxicated. But in summer 2002, she and Kentucky Republican Sen. Jim Bunning emerged as the Senate's leading advocates of allowing airline pilots to carry guns. Boxer argued that pilots could be trusted with that responsibility and that they could protect passengers against terrorists. The measure passed in both the House and Senate. In 2003, Boxer warned of the danger to airliners from shoulder-fired missiles and called for installation of anti-missile devices on all airliners.

During the Clinton years, Boxer was frustrated when Republicans held up nominations to the Ninth Circuit Court of Appeals, long the most liberal in the country. During the Bush years, she held up nominations of judges she considered too conservative. In 2001, she opposed the nomination of Rep. Christopher

Cox of California to the Ninth Circuit. When Democratic Sen. Dianne Feinstein said she might oppose him too, Cox withdrew. In 2005, Boxer said she would "use all the parliamentary tools I've been given as a U.S. senator" to delay a vote on the confirmation of John Roberts to the Supreme Court, and she voted against both Roberts and Samuel Alito. It was a case of life imitating art, or perhaps the other way around: Later in 2005, Boxer's novel *A Time to Run* was published. It is tale about a liberal woman senator from California opposing a conservative Supreme Court nominee.

In recent years, Boxer has concentrated on environmental issues. As the ranking minority member on the Environment and Public Works Committee during the years of Republican control of Congress, she sparred continually with conservative Chairman James Inhofe of Oklahoma over the issue of reducing carbon emissions to combat global warming. Inhofe famously said that the theory of human-caused global warming was a "hoax." The committee's emphasis changed abruptly when Democrats won the Senate majority in 2006. Boxer made addressing the causes of global warming her top legislative priority and assigned herself the chairmanship of the subcommittee on Public Sector Solutions to Global Warming, Oversight, Children's Health Protection and Nuclear Safety. "I really have two major goals," she said on becoming chairman. "They are to protect the health of the American people. And the second is to make the environment a bipartisan issue again on Capitol Hill."

But her aggressive style did not always foster bipartisanship. In December 2007, she harshly criticized Environmental Protection Agency chief Stephen Johnson for refusing to grant a waiver allowing California's tough carbon-emissions law to go into effect. She sought access to an EPA staff document recommending a waiver and accused Johnson of lying. She fumed during the summer and fall of 2008 when he refused to appear before the committee and testify. Inhofe boycotted the hearings as well.

Boxer's primary goal is to enact a cap-and-trade system to reduce carbon emissions, which she has called "the greatest challenge of our generation." Such a system would allow companies to trade emissions "credits," depending on the amount of pollution they generate. Boxer called former Vice President Al Gore to testify in a highly publicized hearing in March 2007, showering him with praise for his campaign to spur action on global warming. One of her great allies on the issue has been Connecticut Sen. Joe Lieberman, an independent who co-sponsored cap-and-trade bills with Republican Sens. John McCain of Arizona and John Warner of Virginia. In July 2006, when Lieberman was opposed by anti-Iraq War candidate Ned Lamont in the Democratic primary, Boxer traveled to Connecticut to campaign for Lieberman, telling his antiwar critics, "Senator Lieberman has been one of my staunchest allies on the environment and choice, two issues very important to me."

In 2007, Boxer's subcommittee took up the Lieberman-Warner cap-and-trade bill, and in nearly 10 hours of hearings, she fended off more-restrictive amendments from independent Vermont Sen. Bernie Sanders and less-restrictive amendments from others. In May 2008, she advanced a version with changes she hoped would increase support. In early June, her bill attracted only 48 votes in the Senate, well short of the 60 needed to proceed. The measure died, but in November 2008, Boxer said she was preparing a revised bill. In the new Congress (2009–2010), senators from some states that are heavily dependent on coal-generated electricity wanted to stop any cap-and-trade bill that would put their states at a competitive disadvantage, but during the first weeks of the Obama administration in 2009, Boxer continued to push the legislation.

Boxer did pursue some bipartisan initiatives, working in 2007 with the Bush White House to increase the energy efficiency of federal buildings and sponsoring, with Republican Sen. Lamar Alexander of Tennessee, a bill to use the Capitol's power plant as a demonstration site for carbon-capture technologies. She also sought to have the federal government limit perchlorates (from rocket fuels) in drinking water. She continued to oppose offshore oil drilling in the Pacific Ocean as well as in Alaska's Arctic National Wildlife Refuge. And she opposed amendments to the 2008 farm bill that would have weakened prohibitions on pesticides and wetland development.

Boxer also co-sponsored, with Republican John Ensign of Nevada, a bill to reduce the tax on corporate profits earned abroad if they were invested in creating American jobs. This was uncharacteristic enough to attract some notice. As Boxer told the *Los Angeles Times*: "I do not stand here every day and endorse tax breaks." She and Ensign estimated the 10-year revenue loss as $18 billion. But after Congress' Joint Committee on Taxation pegged the revenue loss at $28 billion, the measure was not included in the president's February 2009 economic stimulus bill.

Boxer had more success with public works legislation. The water-projects bill she assembled in May 2007 had $1.4 billion for California projects—about the same as California's proportionate share by population—including improvements to the Folsom Dam, levee construction in the Sacramento-San Joaquin delta and auxiliary spillways to prevent flooding in high-risk Sacramento. The water bill passed the Senate 81-12 in September 2007. President George W. Bush vetoed the legislation, but was overridden 79-14 in November.

In 2007 and 2008, Boxer was entrusted with considerable institutional responsibilities when Majority Leader Harry Reid appointed her to temporarily replace the disabled Tim Johnson of South Dakota as chairman of the Senate Ethics Committee. (Johnson suffered a brain hemorrhage in late 2006 but recovered.) In February 2008, she led the committee in admonishing Republican Larry Craig of Idaho for attempting to withdraw his guilty plea following his arrest in a homosexual sex sting in a Minneapolis airport men's room. He had pleaded guilty to a disorderly conduct charge, a misdemeanor, and later, after the incident was publicized, tried to change the plea. Under Boxer, the panel also admonished New Mexico Republican Pete Domenici for contacting a federal prosecutor who was investigating state Democrats in a corruption case. In June 2008, after public revelations that Democrats Christopher Dodd of Connecticut and Kent Conrad of North Dakota had received favorable terms on home mortgages, committee members voted unanimously to require more disclosure of members' mortgage terms.

During her first three years in the Senate, Boxer's job ratings were among the Senate's lowest. But California, with its large metropolitan areas, trended sharply toward the Democrats in the mid-1990s. From about 1997 on, Boxer generally has had positive job ratings, though they are somewhat lower than those of her more centrist colleague Feinstein. In 1998, Boxer was challenged by Republican state Treasurer Matt Fong. Boxer raised $15 million and ran ads attacking Fong for what she called his ambiguous stances on issues like abortion rights. Fong attacked her for what he called the hypocrisy of her support for Clinton, and Boxer guarded herself from reporters to avoid questions about the impeachment case against Clinton. The president's brother-in-law, Tony Rodham, married Boxer's daughter. But Fong spoke haltingly and for the most part unconvincingly in the sound bytes that are a staple of California politics and never succeeded in raising much money. Boxer won 53%-43%. She won 61% of the vote in Los Angeles County and 63% in the San Francisco Bay Area, and was not far behind in Southern California and the rest of the state—an impressive performance for a Democrat dismissed a few years before as too left-wing for much of the state.

When she was up for re-election in 2004, Boxer raised impressive amounts of money early, and well-known Republicans declined to make the race against her. Her opponent was Bill Jones, who had been elected secretary of state by narrow margins in 1994 and 1998 and was not well known outside his home base in Fresno County. Boxer spent $16 million to Jones's $7 million. She won with 58% of the vote to Jones' 38%. In coastal California from Los Angeles north Boxer won 67%-29%. She ran essentially even in the rest of the state, carrying the South Coast 48%-47% and losing the rest of the state 47%-45%.

In September 2007, Boxer said she would definitely run for re-election in 2010. Two months later, Republican Gov. Arnold Schwarzenegger said he had no interest in challenging her, and polls in early 2009 showed him running far behind her if he did. Boxer did not take a major role in the 2008 presidential race. In July 2007, when Feinstein endorsed New York Democratic Sen. Hillary Rodham Clinton, Boxer refused to make an endorsement, telling the *San Francisco Chronicle* : "No, I won't, because I have so many dear friends, so many brothers and sisters running. I've known them for so long." Boxer did endorse Clinton after she won the California primary on February 5.

FIRST DISTRICT

Mike Thompson (D)

Elected 1998, 6th term; b. Jan. 24, 1951, St. Helena; home, St. Helena; CA St. U., B. A. 1982, M. A. 1996.; Catholic; married (Janet); 2 children.

Military Career: Army, 1969–73 (Vietnam).

Elected Office: CA Senate, 1990–98.

Professional Career: Supervisor, Beringer Winery; CA Assembly fellow, 1982–83; Chief of staff, CA Assemblyman Lou Papan, 1984–87; Chief of staff, CA Assemblywoman Jackie Speier, 1987–90.

DC Office: 231 CHOB, 20515, 202-225-3311; Fax: 202-225-4335; Web site: mikethompson.house.gov.

State Offices: Eureka, 707-269-9595; Fort Bragg, 707-962-0933; Napa, 707-226-9898; Woodland, 530-662-5272.

Committees: *Intelligence (Select)* (7th of 13 D): Terrorism, Human Intelligence, Analysis & Counterintelligence (Chmn.); Oversight & Investigations. *Ways & Means* (11th of 26 D): Health; Select Revenue Measures.

Group Ratings

	ADA	ACLU	AFS	LCV	ITIC	NTU	COC	ACU	CFG	FRC
2008	90	100	100	92	100	13	56	8	2	5
2007	90	—	100	90	—	4	55	0	12	—

National Journal Ratings

	2007 LIB	—	2007 CONS	2008 LIB	—	2008 CONS
Economic	67%	—	33%	62%	—	37%
Social	77%	—	17%	75%	—	18%
Foreign	80%	—	19%	78%	—	17%
Composite	76%	—	24%	74%	—	26%

Key Votes of the 110th Congress

1. Increase minimum wage	Y	5. Share immigration data	N	9. Withdraw troops 8/08	Y
2. Expand SCHIP	Y	6. Foreign aid abortion ban	N	10. No operations in Iran	Y
3. Raise CAFE standards	Y	7. Ban gay bias in workplace	Y	11. Free trade with Peru	Y
4. Bail out financial markets	Y	8. Repeal D.C. gun law	Y	12. Overhaul FISA	N

Election Results

2008 general	Mike Thompson (D) 197,812	(68%)	($1,391,605)
	Zane Starkewolf (R) 67,853	(23%)	
	Carol Wolman (Green) 24,793	(9%)	($6,428)
2008 primary	Mike Thompson (D) 69,622	(88%)	
	Mitchell Clogg (D) 9,752	(12%)	

Prior Winning Percentages: 2006 (66%); 2004 (67%); 2002 (64%); 2000 (65%); 1998 (62%)

Population		Race/Ethnicity		Work	
Pop. 2007:	682,712	White:	66.9%	Private:	67.6%
Change since 2000:	Up 6.8%	Black:	1.6%	Government:	20.0%
Urban:	76.0%	Hispanic:	20.9%	Self-employed:	11.9%
Rural:	24.0%	Asian:	5.3%	Blue collar:	20.0%
Area size:	12,195 sq. mi.	Native Am.:	2.2%	White collar:	57.2%
Age		Hawaiian:	0.3%	Khaki collar:	0.0%
Median age:	36.0 yrs.	Two+ races:	2.5%	Other:	22.7%
More than 65 yrs:	12.8%	*Ancestry*		Median income:	$49,677
Less than 18 yrs:	22.3%	German:	11.9%	Median home value:	$440,900
Education		Irish:	9.7%	Poverty:	14.9%
H.S. grad:	84.7%	English:	9.1%	**Military Veterans**	
College grad:	28.1%			% of Pop:	10.1%
Grad degree:	11.0%				

The North Coast of California is unlike any other place in America. It is the only part of the lower 48 states first settled by Russians, who built Fort Ross in 1812. They sold it in 1841 to a Swiss named John Augustus Sutter, whose discovery of gold near Sacramento eight years later started the Gold Rush. It is the only part of the world with large numbers of redwood trees, shooting up hundreds of feet in the drizzly air. It is wet country, and for years it was one of America's prime lumbering areas. Eureka and

2008 Presidential Vote

Obama (D) 199,835	(66%)
McCain (R)..............................96,530	(32%)

2004 Presidential Vote

Kerry (D)...............................173,926	(60%)
Bush (R) 111,754	(38%)

Cook Partisan Voting Index: D + 13

smaller lumber towns are filled with filigreed Victorian houses and old mills, but also art galleries, hiking trails, pubs, and waterfront hotels. The region has moved on to other crops. In sunny valleys sealed off from the Coast Range, some of the nation's premium wine grapes are grown on ridges. Humboldt County is known for its quality marijuana fields, and the local economy relies heavily on the product, as depicted in the 2008 movie *Humboldt County*. Local voters that year in next-door Mendocino County pulled back from the nation's most liberal marijuana law by falling in line with the state limit of six plants per resident—instead of 24, which had been the county law since 2000—because of concern about nonmedical abuses of the crop. Thirty years ago, there were only 20 wineries in Napa Valley. Today, there are several hundred, with more just west of the ridges in Sonoma County. Wineries were a favorite investment for Silicon Valley millionaires until the recession caused production cutbacks and thousands of job layoffs in 2008. Olive trees are also grown here. Some of California's earliest literary haunts were in the valleys. Robert Louis Stevenson took his honeymoon near Calistoga in Napa, and Jack London owned a giant house in Sonoma that mysteriously burned down in 1913. Along the coast, a 2006 law designated 273,000 acres of wilderness and restored the rights of commercial fishermen to drive trucks on the beaches of the Redwood National Park.

The 1st Congressional District of California consists of the North Coast from Mendocino County to the Oregon border. To the south, it includes Napa County and the eastern edge of Sonoma County—Healdsburg, the Alexander Valley, and part of Sonoma Valley—plus part of the Yolo County flatlands, including the University of California at Davis and industrial West Sacramento. The North Coast lumbering area, from Mendocino on north, was once filled with rough-hewn working men, and was historically Democratic. But the timber business was hurt in the 1980s by environmental protections for the northern spotted owl, and the local backlash prompted more interest in Republican politics. Now, the focus is on sustainable forestry. And the area remains largely Democratic. The Pacific Lumber Company, the longtime landlord of the town of Scotia, one of the last company-owned towns in the United States, sold all of its 275 houses in 2008 and planned to continue limited timber production. Inland, the wine-growing country around Healdsburg and in Napa County, was Republican in the 1970s, but now partakes of the San Francisco Bay Area's liberal consensus. This district changed partisan hands four times during the 1990s, thanks largely to splits among Democrats, but redistricting in 2001 made it solidly Democratic.

The congressman from the 1st District is Mike Thompson, a Democrat first elected in 1998. Thompson grew up in the Napa Valley town of St. Helena, dropped out of high school, served in the Army in Vietnam, and earned a Purple Heart. Later, he got a bachelor's and master's degree from what is now California State University at Chico. He owned a vineyard and worked as a maintenance supervisor for Beringer, a big winery in the valley. From 1984 to 1990, he was the chief of staff to two Bay Area Assembly members. In 1990, he was elected to the state Senate, where he chaired the Budget Committee. In 1998, he ran for the U.S. House seat of Republican Frank Riggs, who planned to challenge Democratic Sen. Barbara Boxer that year. Thompson faced only weak opposition and had support from almost every interest group that matters in the district: unions, medical providers, vintners, oil and timber interests, environmental advocates, law enforcement groups, and fishermen. His issue stands—opposition to oil drilling off the California coast, support of abortion rights and the death penalty—were broadly popular. He won the primary 78%-22% and the general election 62%-33%. He has not been seriously challenged since then.

In the House, Thompson is a moderate Democrat whose voting record is among the least liberal of coastal Californians. He joined both the New Democrats and the Blue Dog Coalition of conservative Democrats. With Republican Rep. George Radanovich of California, he started the Congressional Wine Caucus. The group lost a battle with conservative senators, allied with beer and alcohol wholesalers, on a bill giving states new power to restrict sales over the Internet. He joined California GOP Rep. Jerry Lewis on a proposal to create a $1 billion fund for making buildings more resistant to earthquakes. After a massive fish kill caused by flooding of the Klamath River in 2002, he won $60 million in emergency aid for fishermen and businesses. And his legislation for a salmon recovery plan in California and Oregon passed the House in December 2006.

Thompson has been a close ally of House Speaker Nancy Pelosi, D-Calif., which gives him influence among House Democrats. But his ambition to head the Democratic Congressional Campaign Committee after the 2002 election was dashed by an ill-timed visit to Iraq. Thompson traveled to Baghdad in 2002, before the United States went to war with Iraq, with Reps. David Bonior, D-Mich., and Jim McDermott, D-Wash. While there, Bonior criticized President Bush, and McDermott suggested that Iraqi Leader Saddam Hussein was more credible than Bush—statements that could be deemed impolitic with tensions running high on the sensitive issue of Iraq's possible possession of weapons of mass destruction. Although Thompson did not make controversial comments and later conceded it was a bad idea to criticize the president from Iraq, the trip dashed his chances of assuming a high-profile party role at that time.

As consolation, Thompson was asked to lead the DCCC's incumbent protection program, and got a seat on the House Ways and Means Committee. On the powerful panel, he was able to enact a tax break for landowners who place their land under conservation easements, a way to preserve farmland. In 2007, Thompson sponsored the Airline Passenger Bill of Rights, which requires airlines to provide basic necessities, like food, water, and well-ventilated facilities, when flights are delayed for long periods. The House passed his bill in 2007 when it reauthorized the Federal Aviation Administration.

Thompson also chairs the Intelligence Subcommittee on Terrorism, Human Intelligence, Analysis, and Counterintelligence. The 2008 defense bill contained his provision cracking down on abuses of private contractors in Iraq and expanded the authority of a special inspector general. Thompson said that inspectors had found that "contractors in Iraq charged $45 per case of soda and $100 per 15-pound bag of laundry. . . . $8.8 billion was handed over to Iraqi ministries with virtually no tracking of what it was spent on."

Following the 2008 election, he was mentioned as a contender for Interior secretary in the Obama administration, a position that ultimately went to then-Sen. Ken Salazar, D-Colo.

SECOND DISTRICT

Wally Herger (R)

Elected 1986, 12th term; b. May 20, 1945, Yuba City; home, Chico; American River Comm. Col., A.A. 1967, CA St. U., 1968–69; Mormon; married (Pamela); 9 children.

Elected Office: CA Assembly, 1980–86.

Professional Career: Rancher; Owner, Herger Gas Inc., 1969–present.

DC Office: 242 CHOB, 20515, 202-225-3076; Fax: 202-226-0852; Web site: www.house.gov/herger.

State Offices: Chico, 530-893-8363; Redding, 530-223-5898.

Committees: *Ways & Means* (2nd of 15 R): Health (RMM); Trade. *Joint Committee on Taxation.*

Group Ratings

	ADA	ACLU	AFS	LCV	ITIC	NTU	COC	ACU	CFG	FRC
2008	10	18	0	0	71	67	89	88	82	100
2007	5	—	0	0	—	80	80	96	91	—

National Journal Ratings

	2007 LIB	—	2007 CONS		2008 LIB	—	2008 CONS
Economic	8%	—	92%		3%	—	95%
Social	27%	—	72%		0%	—	91%
Foreign	31%	—	69%		17%	—	83%
Composite	22%	—	78%		9%	—	92%

Key Votes of the 110th Congress

1. Increase minimum wage	N	5. Share immigration data	N	9. Withdraw troops 8/08	N
2. Expand SCHIP	*	6. Foreign aid abortion ban	Y	10. No operations in Iran	N
3. Raise CAFE standards	N	7. Ban gay bias in workplace	N	11. Free trade with Peru	Y
4. Bail out financial markets	Y	8. Repeal D.C. gun law	Y	12. Overhaul FISA	Y

Election Results

2008 general	Wally Herger (R)	163,459	(58%)	($1,256,602)
	Jeff Morris (D)	118,878	(42%)	($33,371)
2008 primary	Wally Herger (R)	unopposed		

Prior Winning Percentages: 2006 (64%); 2004 (67%); 2002 (66%); 2000 (66%); 1998 (63%); 1996 (61%); 1994 (64%); 1992 (65%); 1990 (64%); 1988 (59%); 1986 (58%)

Population		Race/Ethnicity		Work	
Pop. 2007:	699,360	White:	73.0%	Private:	69.0%
Change since 2000:	Up 9.4%	Black:	1.1%	Government:	19.2%
Urban:	67.7%	Hispanic:	16.7%	Self-employed:	11.4%
Rural:	32.3%	Asian:	4.0%	Blue collar:	22.7%
Area size:	21,977 sq. mi.	Native Am.:	1.4%	White collar:	54.3%
		Hawaiian:	0.2%	Khaki collar:	0.4%
Age		Two+ races:	3.2%	Other:	22.5%
Median age:	35.9 yrs.			Median income:	$42,297
More than 65 yrs:	14.1%	*Ancestry*		Median home value:	$274,900
Less than 18 yrs:	23.6%	German:	13.8%	Poverty:	15.5%
		Irish:	10.7%		
Education		English:	9.2%	**Military Veterans**	
H.S. grad:	83.5%			% of Pop:	12.4%
College grad:	19.1%				
Grad degree:	6.0%				

Rising 14,000 feet over low foothills and the Central Valley, visible for 100 miles, is the snow-capped volcanic cone of Mount Shasta, one of a string of (supposedly) burnt-out volcanoes up and down the Pacific Coast states. This is the far northern end of California, where truck traffic on Interstate 5 is the only reminder of the choked metropolitan areas where most of the state's people live. This is lumber country mostly, where the mountains that rise on all sides—the Coast Range to the west, the Sierra

2008 Presidential Vote

McCain (R)	161,636	(55%)
Obama (D)	125,291	(43%)

2004 Presidential Vote

Bush (R)	173,528	(62%)
Kerry (D)	102,254	(37%)

Cook Partisan Voting Index: R + 11

Nevada to the east, the scattered mountains sealing off the Central Valley north of Redding—are carpeted with trees. It's rugged, flannel-shirt, two-lane-road country that was left behind economically when Los Angeles and San Francisco boomed after World War II. North of Shasta, the tiny town of Weed became a logging center and a noted locale for racial integration a half-century ago, but the loss of jobs has led younger blacks and whites to move out. Farther south are the flat farm fields of the Sacramento Valley, spread across the 50 miles between the Sierra Nevada and the Coast Range. Since the 1980s, this northern end of California has been attracting people, mostly young families who come here to raise their children in a small-town environment, but also retirees looking for a calm atmosphere and low cost of living.

The 2nd Congressional District of California covers most of this area. The district has three major population areas. One is Redding, south of Mount Shasta, where increased high-altitude snowfall has allowed the Whitney Glacier to defy global warming trends by growing in the past century, the only glacier to do so. The second is farther south, at the edge of the Sierra foothills, around the Butte County communities of Paradise and Chico, home to a state university campus and Sierra Nevada Pale Ale. In 2008, surrounding areas suffered devastating forest fires. Still farther south are the farm counties of Colusa, Yuba, and Sutter, not far north of Sacramento. The locally cultivated rice hybrids from Colusa County, the leading rice-producing county in the nation, are a lucrative export. From 2000 to 2007, the district had a 9% population increase, with Hispanics increasing from 14% to 17%. The region has a Democratic heritage but is culturally conservative, angry at the "diktats" of urban environmentalists. Until 1980, it elected rough-and-ready Democrats who pulled strings in Sacramento and Washington to build roads and dams. Since then, it has elected abstemious Republicans who have solidly conservative voting records and tend to local needs. George W. Bush won 62% of the vote here in 2004, and John McCain won 55% in 2008, their best showings in a northern California district.

The congressman from the 2nd District is Wally Herger, a Republican first elected in 1986. He grew up in the farm country north of Sacramento, where he was a local farmer and rancher. He also owned a propane gas company. Herger married young, and his first marriage did not last. Then he met his present wife, Pamela, a nurse who like him was a Mormon who wanted a large family. The couple had three children from their first marriages and together had six more, although they mourned the loss of one child who died as a toddler. In 1980, he was elected to the California Assembly. Six years later, Herger was elected to the U.S. House after winning solid margins over the mayor of Redding in the primary and beating a Shasta County supervisor in the general.

Herger has a solidly conservative voting record and has served quietly on the Ways and Means Committee, voting for balanced budgets and lower taxes. When federal budget deficits disappeared in the late 1990s, Herger was a leader of the battle to create "lockboxes" to shield the surpluses in the Social Security and Medicare trust funds. That debate became moot with the return of big deficits. As chairman of the Human Resources Subcommittee, he helped write the Republican welfare law in 1996, which increased work requirements for recipients and incentives for states to reduce caseloads.

His advancement on the committee, however, has been slowed by more aggressive and charismatic Republicans. More junior lawmakers have twice leapfrogged him to take the top Republican post on the committee. In 2007, Rep. Jim McCrery of Louisiana jumped over him, with the leadership's blessing, to become the ranking Republican. When McCrery retired two years later, Dave Camp of Michigan, a more aggressive party spokesman and campaign contributor, ascended to the top minority slot, with the support of Minority Leader John Boehner of Ohio. In 2009, Herger did become the ranking Republican on one of the most important subcommittees, the one responsible for health care policy. He has pledged to make health care more affordable for all Americans, and to keep medical decisions with patients and their doctors.

On local issues, Herger has tended to water projects and called for exemption of flood control programs from the Endangered Species Act. With Republican Rep. Greg Walden of Oregon he proposed full compensation of farmers and related businesses that suffered damages from the Klamath River flooding, but he rejected environmentalists' calls for management controls of the fisheries, which he called part of "an anti-agriculture agenda." He helped to enact a program to aid about 750 counties that have suffered from a loss of revenue from timber sales.

Herger had been easily re-elected every two years, with more than 60% of the vote, until 2008, when he was held to a 58%-42% win by Democrat Jeff Morris, the Trinity County supervisor. Herger lost by 87 votes in Butte, the largest county, which has been growing with urban refugees. Democrat Morris criticized Herger's depiction of environmentalists as "radical."

THIRD DISTRICT

Dan Lungren (R)

Elected 2004, 8th term; b. Sept. 22, 1946, Long Beach; home, Folsom; Notre Dame U., A.B. 1968, Georgetown U., J.D. 1971; Catholic; married (Bobbi); 3 children.

Elected Office: U.S. House of Reps.1978–88; CA Atty. Gen. 1990–98.

Professional Career: Staff, U.S. Sen. George Murphy, 1969–70; Staff, U.S. Sen. Bill Brock, 1971; Spec. asst. RNC, 1971–72; Practicing atty., 1973–78.

DC Office: 2262 RHOB, 20515, 202-225-5716; Fax: 202-226-1298; Web site: lungren.house.gov.

State Offices: Gold River, 916-859-9906.

Committees: *Homeland Security* (4th of 13 R): Emerging Threats, Cybersecurity & Science and Technology (RMM); Management, Investigations & Oversight; Transportation Security & Infrastructure Protection. *House Administration* (RMM of 3 R): Capitol Security (RMM). *Judiciary* (6th of 16 R): Crime, Terrorism & Homeland Security; Immigration, Citizenship, Border Security & International Law.

Group Ratings

	ADA	ACLU	AFS	LCV	ITIC	NTU	COC	ACU	CFG	FRC
2008	5	18	14	0	83	65	94	88	76	94
2007	0	—	0	5	—	80	83	96	86	—

National Journal Ratings

	2007 LIB — 2007 CONS		2008 LIB — 2008 CONS	
Economic	16% —	83%	13% —	86%
Social	9% —	85%	0% —	91%
Foreign	0% —	72%	22% —	74%
Composite	14% —	86%	14% —	86%

Key Votes of the 110th Congress

1. Increase minimum wage	N	5. Share immigration data	Y	9. Withdraw troops 8/08	N
2. Expand SCHIP	N	6. Foreign aid abortion ban	Y	10. No operations in Iran	N
3. Raise CAFE standards	N	7. Ban gay bias in workplace	N	11. Free trade with Peru	*
4. Bail out financial markets	Y	8. Repeal D.C. gun law	Y	12. Overhaul FISA	Y

Election Results

2008 general	Dan Lungren (R)	155,424	(49%)	($1,325,036)
	Bill Durston (D)	137,971	(44%)	($731,513)
	Dina Padilla (PF)	13,378	(4%)	
	Douglas Tuma (Lib)	7,273	(2%)	($553)
2008 primary	Dan Lungren (R)	unopposed		

Prior Winning Percentages: 2006 (59%); 2004 (62%); 1986 (73%); 1984 (73%); 1982 (69%); 1980 (72%); 1978 (54%)

Population		Race/Ethnicity		Work	
Pop. 2007:	772,720	White:	66.7%	Private:	71.6%
Change since 2000:	Up 20.9%	Black:	5.7%	Government:	20.3%
Urban:	86.4%	Hispanic:	13.3%	Self-employed:	7.9%
Rural:	13.6%	Asian:	10.2%	Blue collar:	17.1%
Area size:	3,422 sq. mi.	Native Am.:	0.8%	White collar:	67.4%
		Hawaiian:	0.4%	Khaki collar:	0.1%
Age		Two+ races:	2.5%	Other:	15.4%
Median age:	36.3 yrs.	*Ancestry*		Median income:	$64,887
More than 65 yrs:	11.8%	German:	12.7%	Median home value:	$412,000
Less than 18 yrs:	26.1%	Irish:	9.8%	Poverty:	8.6%
Education		English:	8.7%		
H.S. grad:	89.3%			**Military Veterans**	
College grad:	28.7%			% of Pop:	12.1%
Grad degree:	9.1%				

Until recently, Sacramento was chiefly the metropolis of a fertile valley that produced a marvelous variety of crops: rice, plums, almonds, olives, asparagus, pears, hops, beans, celery, onions, potatoes, plus caviar-yielding sturgeon in pools of filtered water. The farmlands remain, and the capital city flourishes as a center of government. Until recessionary forces struck in 2007, greater Sacramento was one of the fastest-growing metro areas in the country. Almost all the growth has been away from

2008 Presidential Vote

Obama (D)	165,617	(49%)
McCain (R)	164,025	(49%)

2004 Presidential Vote

Bush (R)	176,512	(58%)
Kerry (D)	123,671	(41%)

Cook Partisan Voting Index: R+6

the floodplain of the Sacramento River, in the higher land east of the city that eventually turns into hills rising toward the Sierra Nevadas. But home sales plunged and foreclosures soared in 2007, which led to service cutbacks in Sacramento County. Amador and Calaveras counties are Mother Lode Country, which filled up with people in the gold rush days, when Mark Twain was inspired to write his story about the famous jumping frog of Calaveras County. In rapidly growing Rancho Cordova, local leaders created a "new urbanist" development plan with a new downtown in place of aging strip malls. But some things have not changed. When an animal-rights group tried to cancel the annual Jumping Frog Jubilee, a local official said that the frogs are not tortured and that the jubilee would continue.

The 3rd Congressional District of California includes much of suburban Sacramento, some territory in Solano County and some of the Mother Lode Country to the east. The district reaches over the Sierras to Alpine County, the smallest county in California (1,145 people in 2007), with the state's highest mountain ridgeline. The district stops at the Nevada line. Population in the district grew 21% from 2000 to 2007. More than 80% of the people in the district live in Sacramento County, in suburbs like Carmichael, Citrus

Heights, Arden-Arcade, and the old town of Folsom, where Intel has a campus of about 6,000 employees and created a prosperous company town. Historically, Sacramento was Democratic. But Sacramento County, with its rapid growth, continues to shift politically. The district voted 58% for George W. Bush in 2004, but Barack Obama prevailed over John McCain, 49.3%-48.8%, in 2008.

The congressman from the 3rd District is Dan Lungren, elected in 2004 after an earlier decade as representative to the 42nd District. Lungren grew up in Long Beach, and his father was President Nixon's personal physician. Young Dan worked on the staffs of Sens. George Murphy of California and Bill Brock of Tennessee, both Republicans. After a few years of law practice in Long Beach, he unsuccessfully challenged Democratic "Watergate baby" Mark Hannaford in the U.S. House in 1976, then came back and won rather easily in 1978 with a boost from the anti-tax Proposition 13. He entered a freshman class that included Reps. Dick Cheney and Newt Gingrich, as well as Jerry Lewis and Bill Thomas of California. During his initial years in Congress, Lungren focused on criminal-code reform on the Judiciary Committee.

Lungren was also a member of the Conservative Opportunity Society, the influential group of young House conservatives organized by Gingrich, who went on to lead Republicans to capture majority control of the house in 1994. He played a key role on major immigration legislation in 1986, which made it illegal to knowingly hire illegal immigrants. He left the House in 1989 after he was nominated to be California state treasurer, but he was deemed too partisan and was not confirmed by the state Senate. In 1990, he was elected to the first of two terms as California attorney general. After losing 58%-38% to Democrat Gray Davis in the 1998 race for governor, Lungren worked in the Sacramento area as a visiting professor and radio talk-show host. He joined a Washington-based law firm.

In 2004, 3rd District incumbent Republican Doug Ose honored his pledge to retire after serving three terms, and Lungren ran for the seat. His toughest competition was in the Republican primary, in which he faced Mary Ose, the incumbent's sister, and state Sen. Rico Oller. Ose, a real estate developer, raised more than $2 million, much of it from her own pocket. Despite an almost 2-to-1 fundraising advantage over the others, she won only 23% of the votes. Oller, with a geographic base in Amador and Calaveras counties, attacked Lungren as soft on immigration. Lungren ran an ad with praise from Gingrich for his work on the 1986 immigration bill, and beat Oller 39%-36%, winning 42%-32% in Sacramento County, which cast 82% of the total vote. In the GOP-leaning district, Lungren easily won the general election over Democrat Bill Lockyer, 62%-35%. He returned to Congress representing a district nearly 400 miles north of his old one.

Lungren quickly resumed his status as an influential Republican player and usually voted with conservatives. He got credit for his previous service and gained senior positions on the Judiciary Committee and the Homeland Security Committee, though he lost a bid in September 2005 to chair Homeland Security. Subsequently, he worked with Rep. Jane Harman, D-Calif., to enact a bill enhancing port security, including requirements to scan cargo containers for radioactive materials.

On Judiciary, he opposed restrictions on the USA PATRIOT Act as "compromising our ability to investigate terrorist cases," and helped to write the House-passed bill for warrantless surveillance, which has been controversial with civil-liberties groups. Lungren sided with most House Republicans in 2006 in opposing the Senate-passed immigration bill that included a guest-worker program. He emphasized the need to "get control of our border." He also was a sponsor of a proposed constitutional amendment to ban gay marriage.

Sometimes a maverick, Lungren criticized his party for the huge growth of spending earmarks during the years they controlled the majority. That may be one of the reasons his leadership ambitions have been stymied. In November 2006, he ran fourth of four candidates to become chairman of the Republican Conference, the third-ranking post. And he ran a seemingly futile last-minute challenge to Minority Leader John Boehner of Ohio in November 2008. Lungren cited the need for the party to adopt more fiscally conservative policies. In 2009, Boehner tapped him as the ranking Republican on the House Administration Committee, the housekeeping panel that controls perks for fellow members.

In 2006, Lungren was re-elected 59%-38% against Bill Durston, an emergency-room physician who served with the Marines in Vietnam and was endorsed by a national group that funded candidates who backed the impeachment of President Bush. He had an unexpectedly close rematch with Durston in 2008. Durston tried to connect Lungren to special interests in Washington, and Lungren accused him of "McCarthyism on the left." Lungren this time won by only 49%-44%, and he could draw another tough challenge in 2010.

FOURTH DISTRICT

Tom McClintock (R)

Elected 2008, 1st term; b. July 10, 1956, Bronxville, NY; home, Granite Bay; U.C.L.A., B.A. 1978.; Baptist; married (Lori); 2 children.

Elected Office: CA Assembly, 1982–92, 1996–2000; CA Senate 2000–08.

Professional Career: Newspaper columnist, journalist.

DC Office: 508 CHOB, 20515, 202-225-2511; Fax: 202-225-5444; Web site: mcclintock.house.gov.

State Offices: Granite Bay, 916-786-5560.

Committees: *Education & Labor* (16th of 19 R): Early Childhood, Elementary & Secondary Education; Health, Employment, Labor & Pensions. *Natural Resources* (19th of 20 R): National Parks, Forests & Public Lands; Water & Power.

Group Ratings and Key Votes: Newly Elected

Election Results

2008 general	Tom McClintock (R)	185,790	(50%)	($3,532,595)
	Charlie Brown (D)	183,990	(50%)	($2,598,080)
2008 primary	Tom McClintock (R)	51,655	(53%)	
	Doug Ose (R)	37,802	(39%)	
	Suzanne Jones (R)	4,920	(5%)	
	Theodore Terbolizard (R)	2,249	(2%)	

Population		Race/Ethnicity		Work	
Pop. 2007:	739,001	White:	80.2%	Private:	71.9%
Change since 2000:	Up 15.6%	Black:	1.5%	Government:	16.5%
Urban:	67.4%	Hispanic:	10.7%	Self-employed:	11.3%
Rural:	32.6%	Asian:	3.9%	Blue collar:	19.0%
Area size:	17,159 sq. mi.	Native Am.:	1.0%	White collar:	62.9%
		Hawaiian:	0.1%	Khaki collar:	0.1%
Age		Two+ races:	2.3%	Other:	18.0%
Median age:	39.3 yrs.			Median income:	$61,219
More than 65 yrs:	14.1%	*Ancestry*		Median home value:	$459,800
Less than 18 yrs:	21.8%	German:	14.8%	Poverty:	7.9%
		English:	11.4%		
Education		Irish:	11.3%	**Military Veterans**	
H.S. grad:	90.1%			% of Pop:	13.0%
College grad:	29.0%				
Grad degree:	9.0%				

California sprang into existence with the Gold Rush of 1849. Statehood and the creation of the first 27 counties followed in 1850. The new state's first boom area was the Mother Lode Country in the foothills of the Sierra Mountains above Sacramento. Mining camps the size of Eastern cities grew up almost overnight in vacant valleys locked amid steep hills, with thousands of would-be millionaires gathered to find gold, though most of those who actually got rich did so by providing goods and services

2008 Presidential Vote		
McCain (R)	206,385	(54%)
Obama (D)	167,604	(44%)

2004 Presidential Vote		
Bush (R)	216,838	(61%)
Kerry (D)	132,267	(37%)

Cook Partisan Voting Index: R + 10

that catered to miners' needs. In Placerville, John Studebaker had a buggy shop, Phillip Armour ran a butcher shop, and Mark Hopkins had a dry goods store. The biggest mine in California was in Grass Valley in 1857 and was worked for half a century. But long before that, most of the Mother Lode Country emptied out, leaving ghost towns and villages with hundreds of deserted houses, an antique vacation country left behind in time.

When local residents celebrated the sesquicentennial, the area had been resurrected as a booming exurban and tourist mecca. "The American River near Coloma becomes a virtual freeway of whooping rafters on summer weekends," wrote *USA Today*. "The Mother Lode also offers modern-day prospectors an intriguing pastiche of bed-and-breakfast inns, musty antique stores and such blink-and-you'll-miss-'em outposts as Volcano, Fiddletown, Rough and Ready." Thousands of Californians—many of them families from smog-filled, middle-class suburbs of the Los Angeles Basin and the San Francisco Bay Area—went looking for a more pleasant, small-town, orderly environment, and found it along fast-flowing creeks where the '49ers camped. Placer County, which includes Sacramento suburbs and part of the Mother Lode Country, grew 34% from 2000 to 2007 and was among the fastest-growing counties in California. It also has the highest percentage of registered Republicans in the state and ranks among its most wealthy counties. On Lake Tahoe, Truckee has grown with the development of ski resorts. Politically, this growth has changed the Mother Lode Country from Democratic to Republican. In 1976, nine Mother Lode counties from Sierra to Mariposa cast 118,000 votes and voted 50%-47% for Jimmy Carter over Gerald Ford. In 2004, they cast 370,000 votes and voted 61% for George W. Bush, and in 2008, they cast 445,000 votes and backed John McCain over Barack Obama, 54%-44%. California as a whole favored Obama over McCain 61%-37%. The culture here could not be more different from that of the Bay Area, less than 50 miles away.

The 4th Congressional District of California consists of the northern half of the Mother Lode Country and the Placer County suburbs of Sacramento, plus a small slice of Sacramento County. It extends north through thinly populated mountain counties like Modoc, site of a World War II detention facility for Japanese-Americans. Modoc County shares a border with Oregon and Nevada. Most residents live within the Interstate 80 corridor, clustered near Sacramento in suburbs like Roseville, the district's most populous city, which grew 34% from 2000 to 2006 and has plans to build a large private university. Some 33% of district residents live in areas classified as rural, the largest percentage of the state's 53 districts.

The new congressman from the 4th District is Republican Tom McClintock. He spent his early childhood in White Plains, N.Y., where he lived until he was 9. His earliest exposure to politics came at a young age, when his mother took him to a campaign rally with Dwight Eisenhower and Richard Nixon at a local airport in 1960. After graduating from the University of California at Los Angeles, he worked briefly as a political columnist and a state Senate aide before leaping into elected office at age 26 with a successful run for the California Assembly in 1982. From his earliest days in the Legislature, McClintock established himself as perhaps its most vocal, if not the most effective, budget hawk, railing against tax increases and high spending under Democratic and Republican administrations alike. Supporters saw an eloquent champion of conservative ideas, a policy wonk with a penchant for quoting Abraham Lincoln. Detractors viewed him as an ideological obstructionist with few legislative accomplishments.

McClintock tested the limits of his appeal in a liberal state through a relentless effort to win higher office. His name has appeared on a ballot in California in every state election since 1982. He ran twice for a U.S. House seat in Southern California, dropping out of the 1986 race during the Republican primary and losing the 1992 race to Democrat Rep. Anthony C. Beilenson. He ran for state controller in 1994 and again in 2002, narrowly losing both times. In 2006, he was unsuccessful as his party's nominee for lieutenant governor, even as Republican Gov. Arnold Schwarzenegger sailed to re-election. But no race elevated McClintock's profile in the state as much as his quixotic campaign for governor in the 2003 recall election. As star-struck Republicans lined up behind former actor Schwarzenegger, McClintock forged ahead unbowed, presenting himself as the true Republican in a field of hopefuls that at one point included political commentator Arianna Huffington and actor Gary Coleman. McClintock emphasized his decades-long opposition to the state's car tax. (Increases in the vehicle registration fee during Democrat Gray Davis's tenure were at the heart of the embattled governor's unpopularity.) He finished with 13.5%.

Opportunity struck yet again for McClintock in 2008. In February, after nine-term Republican Rep. John Doolittle announced he would step down amid a federal probe of disgraced Republican lobbyist Jack Abramoff, several Republicans in the district urged McClintock to get into the race. Barred by term limits from seeking re-election, McClintock got in and faced an intense, three-month primary campaign against former Rep. Doug Ose, a Republican moderate who held the neighboring 3rd District seat from 1999 to 2005. Ose attacked McClintock as a career politician and carpetbagger, although Ose also lived outside the district. McClintock, who noted that he had lived in the district's Sacramento suburbs while serving in the Legislature, ran ads branding Ose as a liberal who had voted to raise taxes and had earmarked millions of dollars for federal projects in his district. McClintock won the primary 54%-39% over Ose.

In the general election, McClintock faced Democrat Charlie Brown, a retired Air Force officer who came within 10,000 votes of beating Doolittle in 2006. Brown, who raised his family in the Sacramento suburb of Roseville, renewed criticism of McClintock as an opportunist who didn't live in the district. McClintock ran ads calling attention to Brown's attendance at a 2005 protest by Code Pink, the fiercely anti-war group, and asserted that Brown supported gay marriage but not the troops in Iraq. He portrayed Brown as a clone of Speaker Nancy Pelosi, a liberal Democrat. McClintock's expected easy victory actually took weeks to unfold. He won by precisely 1,800 votes, 50.2%-49.8%, and took six of the nine counties. McClintock said he had turned back "a liberal wave that swept over America and lapped at the edge of this district."

In the House, McClintock got seats on the Education and Labor Committee and the Natural Resources Committee. He promised to eschew earmarks, the funding requests that members often tack on to major spending bills for special projects in their districts. He faces the prospect of a tough re-election race in 2010.

FIFTH DISTRICT

Doris Matsui (D)

Elected March 2005, 2nd full term; b. Sept. 25, 1944, Poston, AZ; home, Sacramento; U. of CA, B.A. 1966; United Methodist; widowed; 1 child.

Professional Career: Transition team, President-elect Bill Clinton, 1992–93; Dep. asst. to the pres., dep. dir. of public liaison, White House, 1993–98; Lobbyist, 1998–2005.

DC Office: 222 CHOB, 20515, 202-225-7163; Fax: 202-225-0566; Web site: www.house.gov/matsui.

State Offices: Sacramento, 916-498-5600.

Committees: *Energy & Commerce* (27th of 36 D): Commerce, Trade & Consumer Protections; Communications, Technology & the Internet; Energy & Environment. *Rules* (4th of 9 D): Rules & Organization of the House.

Group Ratings

	ADA	ACLU	AFS	LCV	ITIC	NTU	COC	ACU	CFG	FRC
2008	100	100	100	92	100	6	56	0	0	0
2007	95	—	100	95	—	5	55	0	11	—

National Journal Ratings

	2007 LIB	—	2007 CONS	2008 LIB	—	2008 CONS
Economic	78%	—	18%	81%	—	15%
Social	89%	—	8%	82%	—	0%
Foreign	86%	—	11%	78%	—	17%
Composite	86%	—	14%	85%	—	15%

Key Votes of the 110th Congress

1. Increase minimum wage	Y	5. Share immigration data	N	9. Withdraw troops 8/08	Y
2. Expand SCHIP	Y	6. Foreign aid abortion ban	N	10. No operations in Iran	Y
3. Raise CAFE standards	Y	7. Ban gay bias in workplace	Y	11. Free trade with Peru	Y
4. Bail out financial markets	Y	8. Repeal D.C. gun law	N	12. Overhaul FISA	N

Election Results

2008 general	Doris Matsui (D)	164,242	(74%)	($889,113)
	Paul Smith (R)	46,002	(21%)	($3,605)
	L. R. Roberts (PF)	10,731	(5%)	
2008 primary	Doris Matsui (D)	unopposed		

Prior Winning Percentages: 2006 (71%)

Population		Race/Ethnicity		Work	
Pop. 2007:	666,646	White:	39.8%	Private:	71.6%
Change since 2000:	Up 4.3%	Black:	13.9%	Government:	22.2%
Urban:	99.7%	Hispanic:	25.4%	Self-employed:	6.1%
Rural:	0.3%	Asian:	15.3%	Blue collar:	20.6%
Area size:	150 sq. mi.	Native Am.:	0.8%	White collar:	60.1%
Age		Hawaiian:	1.0%	Khaki collar:	0.1%
Median age:	32.7 yrs.	Two+ races:	3.4%	Other:	19.2%
More than 65 yrs:	10.9%	*Ancestry*		Median income:	$46,313
Less than 18 yrs:	25.6%	German:	8.1%	Median home value:	$334,200
Education		Irish:	6.9%	Poverty:	16.9%
H.S. grad:	79.6%	English:	5.5%	**Military Veterans**	
College grad:	24.7%			% of Pop:	9.3%
Grad degree:	8.0%				

Sacramento, capital of the nation's largest state, is the focus of California's third-largest media market, is home to a national sports franchise (the NBA's Sacramento Kings), and has an 18-mile light-rail system. It is no longer just a small city with a lot of civil servants and a vegetable-packing economy. It is a vibrant metropolis, with some of the nation's highest job growth. Sacramento started as a river port on the sluggish waters of the Sacramento and American rivers. It was the destination of many

2008 Presidential Vote		
Obama (D)	165,776	(70%)
McCain (R)	67,625	(28%)
2004 Presidential Vote		
Kerry (D)	125,378	(61%)
Bush (R)	77,788	(38%)
Cook Partisan Voting Index:	D + 15	

overland migrants, the site of Sutter's Fort, where John Augustus Sutter found the gold that set off the Gold Rush of 1848, and the western terminus of the Pony Express in 1860. This was the natural choice at the time to be California's capital, halfway between the San Francisco Bay and the Mother Lode Country in the foothills of the Sierras, and in the middle of California's vast valley. Agriculture continues to be important today in Sacratomato, as some call it. It has the world's largest almond processing plant. A growing local concern is the city's location in a floodplain, inadequately protected by levees, which has occasionally resulted in heavy flooding.

In the old days, government was not a big business. Just a few lobbyists hung out in saloons on K or J streets, the governor's mansion was a musty antique, and the summers of 100-plus degrees emptied out what there was of the city. But air conditioning has replaced awnings, and freeways and shopping malls have followed the city's growth east and north toward the Sierra foothills. Today, Sacramento is one of America's higher-income metropolitan areas. In the 1980s, metropolitan Sacramento grew by 35% and in the 1990s by 22%, so that it now has 2 million people, about the same as metro Cincinnati or Orlando. Some high-tech firms have moved east from Silicon Valley, with Intel and Hewlett-Packard maintaining large campuses. Bay Area refugees have welcomed less expensive and more comfortable living standards. The increase has continued in recent years, but at a slower pace due to housing shortages and the nationwide recession.

Government expanded, too; platoons of lobbyists, lawyers and consultants have set up permanent shop, and new hotels have been built to serve them. Today, 1,000 registered lobbyists prowl the halls of the capitol. As Sacramento has grown, this once-Democratic, working-class bastion has become closer to an upscale Sun Belt boomtown. In 1966, Sacramento was just about the only part of California beyond the Bay Area that stuck with Pat Brown over challenger Ronald Reagan. But when John Kerry carried California 54%-44% in 2004, he carried Sacramento County by only 49.6%-49.3%. In the 2003 recall election, 60% of county voters voted to remove Gray Davis, and Schwarzenegger won 52% of the vote on the replacement ballot. In 2008, Barack Obama won the county 58%-39%.

The 5th Congressional District of California consists of all of the city of Sacramento and some of its close-in suburbs. It contains affluent neighborhoods and scattered low-income black and Latino neighborhoods, plus new condominiums north of the American River and middle-class subdivisions south of downtown. This is a true majority-minority district. In 2007, 66% of the population was Hispanic, Asian, African-American, or "some other race." According to the Public Policy Institute of California, Sacramento's neighborhoods are more ethnically diverse than those of any other big city in California. They are home to, among others, recent Hmong refugees from Laos, Vietnamese, and since the late 1980s, Russians and Ukrainians. This is the solidly Democratic part of metro Sacramento, and the 5th is the most Democratic district in the great valley from Bakersfield north to Oregon.

The congresswoman from the 5th District is Doris Matsui, who won a special election in March 2005 to replace her late husband, Democrat Robert Matsui. She was born in an Arizona internment camp and was a well-known political figure during her husband's career in Congress. She grew up in Dinuba in Fresno County and graduated from the University of California at Berkeley. In Sacramento, she chaired the board of the local public television station and participated in many civic organizations. After working on Bill Clinton's presidential campaign, she joined his transition team and then served as deputy director of public liaison, where she worked on economic and budget issues. When she left the White House in 1998, she became a senior adviser at a Washington law firm. Robert Matsui died of complications from a rare blood disorder in January 2005, after serving 13 terms. He was a senior member of the House Ways and Means Committee and a confidant to then-Minority Leader Nancy Pelosi. He and his family were among the Japanese-Americans forced into internment camps in 1942, when he was an infant; he was one of the lead sponsors of the 1988 Japanese-American redress law that apologized for the internment policy and provided monetary compensation for every survivor of the camps and for so-called "voluntary evacuees."

A few days after the Washington and Sacramento memorial services for her husband, Doris Matsui announced that she would run in the special election. "People lose their spouses every day and make decisions about what they'll do next. I'm no different than anyone else," she said. With her strong support from Pelosi, other prominent Sacramento Democrats decided not to run. None of Matsui's 10 opponents in the nonpartisan contest had significant political experience or name recognition. Matsui emphasized her support for local water projects and her opposition to President Bush's proposal for personal retirement accounts in Social Security. She also opposed the war in Iraq. Her investment in a partnership with a longtime friend who was a Sacramento land developer sparked a brief flurry of criticism, but she emphasized that her husband had nothing to do with the deal while he was in office, and that there was no conflict of interest. Some called the contest a "coronation," but the lack of competition surely reflected the respect the Matsuis had won over the years. She won the all-party primary with 68% of the vote to 9% for the runner-up.

In the House, she has a reliably liberal voting record. From her seat on the Transportation and Infrastructure Committee, she tended to the many highway and water-resource needs of her district. Working with former Rep. John Doolittle, R-Calif., she expedited funding for flood control in flood-prone Sacramento, an issue with increased urgency following the devastation that Hurricane Katrina caused in New Orleans in 2005. In 2007, she got House approval of a plan to improve the flood-protection plan of the Folsom Dam. She opposed a renewed push for the Auburn Dam as "not a politically viable option."

Matsui has taken on leadership assignments and fought for party priorities such as federal funding for embryonic-stem-cell research, reduced prescription drug prices, and opposition to the Central American Free Trade deal. She cited her family's experience in internment camps to warn of potential civil-liberties abuses in the USA PATRIOT Act and with detainees at Guantanamo. In 2008, she became the sixth California Democrat to get a seat on the Energy and Commerce Committee.

Matsui has been re-elected easily. In 2008, she chaired the Asian-American voter outreach campaign for Democratic candidate Hillary Rodham Clinton.

SIXTH DISTRICT

Lynn Woolsey (D)

Elected 1992, 9th term; b. Nov. 3, 1937, Seattle, WA; home, Petaluma; U. of San Francisco, B.S. 1981; Presbyterian; divorced; 4 children.

Elected Office: Petaluma City Cncl., 1985–92, Vice Mayor, 1986, 1991.

Professional Career: Human Resources Mgr., Harris Digital Telephone, 1969–80; Owner, Woolsey Personnel Svc., 1980–92.

DC Office: 2263 RHOB, 20515, 202-225-5161; Fax: 202-225-5163; Web site: woolsey.house.gov.

State Offices: San Rafael, 415-507-9554; Santa Rosa, 707-542-7182.

Committees: *Education & Labor* (6th of 30 D): Early Childhood, Elementary & Secondary Education; Workforce Protections (Chmn). *Foreign Affairs* (17th of 28 D): Africa & Global Health. *Science & Technology* (4th of 27 D): Energy & Environment.

Group Ratings

	ADA	ACLU	AFS	LCV	ITIC	NTU	COC	ACU	CFG	FRC
2008	80	100	100	92	75	16	56	4	7	5
2007	80	—	91	95	—	6	40	0	7	—

National Journal Ratings

	2007 LIB	—	2007 CONS	2008 LIB	—	2008 CONS
Economic	82%	—	0%	66%	—	33%
Social	92%	—	0%	66%	—	33%
Foreign	71%	—	28%	69%	—	31%
Composite	86%	—	14%	67%	—	33%

Key Votes of the 110th Congress

1. Increase minimum wage	Y	5. Share immigration data	N	9. Withdraw troops 8/08	N
2. Expand SCHIP	Y	6. Foreign aid abortion ban	N	10. No operations in Iran	Y
3. Raise CAFE standards	Y	7. Ban gay bias in workplace	Y	11. Free trade with Peru	N
4. Bail out financial markets	Y	8. Repeal D.C. gun law	N	12. Overhaul FISA	N

Election Results

2008 general	Lynn Woolsey (D)	229,672	(72%)	($686,383)
	Mike Halliwell (R)	77,073	(24%)	($49,657)
	Joel Smolen (Lib)	13,617	(4%)	
2008 primary	Lynn Woolsey (D)	unopposed		

Prior Winning Percentages: 2006 (70%); 2004 (73%); 2002 (67%); 2000 (64%); 1998 (68%); 1996 (62%); 1994 (58%); 1992 (65%)

Population		Race/Ethnicity		Work	
Pop. 2007:	637,575	White:	71.7%	Private:	74.3%
Change since 2000:	Down 0.2%	Black:	2.1%	Government:	11.4%
Urban:	89.8%	Hispanic:	18.3%	Self-employed:	14.0%
Rural:	10.2%	Asian:	4.6%	Blue collar:	16.7%
Area size:	2,119 sq. mi.	Native Am.:	0.5%	White collar:	64.7%
Age		Hawaiian:	0.2%	Khaki collar:	0.2%
Median age:	40.9 yrs.	Two+ races:	2.4%	Other:	18.4%
More than 65 yrs:	13.4%	*Ancestry*		Median income:	$68,010
Less than 18 yrs:	21.4%	German:	12.3%	Median home value:	$697,000
Education		Irish:	10.9%	Poverty:	8.7%
H.S. grad:	88.4%	English:	9.7%	**Military Veterans**	
College grad:	39.8%			% of Pop:	9.5%
Grad degree:	15.3%				

When the Golden Gate Bridge was opened in 1937, San Francisco was one of the nation's best-known cities, but few knew much about the land beyond the bridge's north pier head. There were fewer than 50,000 people in Marin County then and another 65,000 just to the north in Sonoma County. For San Franciscans, Marin was known for the ferry terminus in Sausalito, a fishing village and art colony, and as the beginning of the Redwood Empire, with its giant trees in Muir Woods that grow taller than

2008 Presidential Vote
Obama (D) 253,087 (76%)
McCain (R)..............................73,345 (22%)

2004 Presidential Vote
Kerry (D)...............................226,051 (70%)
Bush (R)..................................90,432 (28%)

Cook Partisan Voting Index: D + 23

any others in the world (the largest is more than 300 feet tall and 30 feet in diameter), and with a dense concentration of spotted owls that demand quiet during the mating season. Near the Bay and adjacent to the Interstate 580 bridge is the state prison at San Quentin, one of the oldest in the nation, with its famous gas chamber and crowded death row. Plans in 2007 for a $337 million overhaul of the facility were sidetracked, and led to local calls to demolish it and use the valuable land for more commercial enterprises. Inverness has old wooden storefronts and attracts weekenders escaping city life. Farther north is the Point Reyes peninsula with its organic farming and recreational activities, and the wine country of Sonoma County, sunny valleys protected from the fog by the Coast Range. In one such valley is Santa Rosa, which was destroyed by the 1906 earthquake and later the site of agronomist Luther Burbank's laboratory, a town that looked Middle American enough to be the set for dozens of movies. Politically, the area was then typical of the nation: traditionally Republican, but favoring Franklin D. Roosevelt in the 1930s.

Today, this part of California is far more populous, with 248,000 people in Marin County and 464,000 in Sonoma, and is affluent beyond the dreams of post-World War II Americans. It is struggling to keep up with the pace of growth, as witnessed by the 2008 leaking into the bay of more than 5 million gallons of sewage from aging pipes. The area is also extreme in its cultural attitudes, with relatively few racial minorities compared to other counties in the Bay Area. Until it was surpassed by the Silicon Valley in the late 1990s, it was the nation's most expensive housing market. Santa Rosa is thriving, thanks to the wine and telecommunications industries. Trendy Marin became a national caricature: economically affluent, culturally liberal. When the war in Iraq began, "many of the same people who marched against the Vietnam War have held nightly peace vigils," *The Washington Post* reported. They included a group of feminists who "bared witness" by using their nude bodies to spell out "PEACE." After a while, such an image feeds on itself. Marin attracts affluent people who share its values, while those who don't go elsewhere—in the Bay Area to the more conservative San Ramon Valley, beyond the mountains east of Oakland. Indeed the Bay Area as a whole seems to attract liberals and repel conservatives, just as the Dallas-Fort Worth Metroplex does the opposite. Marin and Sonoma attract the most liberal of the liberal—averse to traditional religious denominations, indifferent to traditional sexual and marriage mores, and viscerally anti-military.

The 6th Congressional District of California includes all of Marin County and all of Sonoma County except for its rural eastern border. These counties have been transformed politically over the past generation. In 1980, they voted for Ronald Reagan over Jimmy Carter 47%-36%. Then they moved left and voted in 1988 for Michael Dukakis over George H. W. Bush by 57%-41%. Now Republicans seem almost an endangered species here. In 2004, the district voted for John Kerry over George W. Bush by 70%-28%. Barack Obama's 2008 victory over John McCain in Marin and Sonoma was a stunning 76%-22%.

The congresswoman from the 6th District is Lynn Woolsey, a Democrat first elected in 1992. Woolsey grew up in the Pacific Northwest, moved to Marin, and was a stay-at-home mother with three children under age six when her marriage ended in 1968. She went on welfare, got a low-paying job, and left her children with 13 different babysitters in a year. Deliverance appeared in the form of a job with a high-tech start-up firm, where she rose to become a top executive. She remarried and moved to a house in

Petaluma where her mother could live in and look after the kids. She put herself through business school at night, earned a degree in human resources, and started her own personnel service. In 1984, Woolsey won a seat on the Petaluma Council. In 1992, she won the U.S. House seat in a nine-candidate primary with 26%, well ahead of 19% for the runner-up. In the general, she faced liberal Republican Assemblyman Bill Filante. He was prevented from campaigning when he fell ill and had to have surgery for a brain tumor. She won 65%-34%.

An apt representative of her district, Woolsey has one of the most liberal voting records in the House. As the first former welfare recipient in Congress, she opposed the 1996 welfare overhaul and supports easing work requirements and providing more child care. She says she thinks a parent ought to be at home until children reach age 11. She lobbied against banning gays in the military, accompanied by her son, who is gay. Republicans sought to embarrass Democrats by calling for a vote on Woolsey's bill to revoke the federal charter for the Boy Scouts because the group excludes gays, and her bill was defeated 362-12. On the Science and Technology Committee, Woolsey has worked to promote energy efficiency and increase support for alternative-energy sources. She is an unabashed liberal who told *National Journal* after the 2008 election that it would be a mistake for President Obama to take Democratic House Speaker Nancy Pelosi's advice that "the country must be governed from the middle."

With Reps. Barbara Lee and Maxine Waters, fellow California Democrats, she created the Out of Iraq Caucus in 2005, and anti-war groups called it "the conscience" of the Democratic Caucus. For President Bush's State of the Union message in 2006, she gave a gallery ticket to anti-war protestor Cindy Sheehan, who was arrested during the speech. As co-chair of the Progressive Caucus in 2007, Woolsey called for withdrawing U.S. troops from Iraq in six months, even as Speaker Pelosi was pushing for a 2008 deadline. Woolsey lamented that many of her liberal colleagues eventually backed long-term funding for the war because "they can't hold up under the pressure," and she called for primary challenges to Democratic moderates. She wants "a complete re-evaluation of U.S. national security policy." In September 2008, Woolsey was one of 13 Democrats who voted against House passage of a bill to lift the moratorium on offshore drilling. She wrote that the plan "continues the myth . . . that we can drill our way out of our nation's energy crisis." With her occasionally fractious relationship with Pelosi, she has failed in her quest to win a seat on the influential Appropriations Committee, holding spots on Education and Labor as well as Science and Technology.

But Woolsey did manage to get the House to authorize $15 million to renovate the immigration complex on Angel Island, where countless Chinese arrivals were detained in deplorable conditions. She has been easily re-elected. She was challenged in the 2002 primary by Santa Rosa Mayor Mike Martini, the founder of a winery in Sebastopol, who criticized her for lack of leadership, excessively liberal votes, and failure to bring sufficient funds to the district. Woolsey responded that she had delivered $430 million since 1997, and defended her record on civil-liberties grounds. She won 80%-20%. In the 2008 Democratic presidential primary contest, she endorsed Sen. Hillary Rodham Clinton, though Woolsey said that her own views were closer to those of Rep. Dennis Kucinich, the liberal Ohio Democrat who was a long-shot candidate in the race.

SEVENTH DISTRICT

George Miller (D)

Elected 1974, 18th term; b. May 17, 1945, Richmond; home, Martinez; San Francisco St. U., B.A. 1968, U. of CA at Davis, J.D. 1972; Catholic; married (Cynthia); 2 children.

Professional Career: Legis. aide, CA Senate Majority Ldr., 1969–74; Practicing atty., 1972–74.

DC Office: 2205 RHOB, 20515, 202-225-2095; Fax: 202-225-5609; Web site: georgemiller.house.gov.

State Offices: Concord, 925-602-1880; Richmond, 510-262-6500; Vallejo, 707-645-1888.

Committees: *Democratic Steering Committee Co-Chair. Education & Labor* (Chmn of 30 D): Healthy Families & Communities. *Natural Resources* (14th of 29 D): Water & Power.

Group Ratings

	ADA	ACLU	AFS	LCV	ITIC	NTU	COC	ACU	CFG	FRC
2008	95	100	100	92	86	6	50	0	0	0
2007	100	—	100	95	—	4	42	0	1	—

National Journal Ratings

	2007 LIB	—	2007 CONS		2008 LIB	—	2008 CONS
Economic	78%	—	18%		85%	—	0%
Social	73%	—	26%		82%	—	0%
Foreign	86%	—	11%		92%	—	0%
Composite	80%	—	20%		93%	—	7%

Key Votes of the 110th Congress

1. Increase minimum wage	Y	5. Share immigration data	*	9. Withdraw troops 8/08	Y
2. Expand SCHIP	Y	6. Foreign aid abortion ban	N	10. No operations in Iran	Y
3. Raise CAFE standards	Y	7. Ban gay bias in workplace	Y	11. Free trade with Peru	N
4. Bail out financial markets	Y	8. Repeal D.C. gun law	N	12. Overhaul FISA	N

Election Results

2008 general	George Miller (D)	170,962	(73%)	($948,684)
	Roger Petersen (R)	51,166	(22%)	($13,167)
	Bill Callison (PF)	6,695	(3%)	
	Camden McConnell (Lib)	5,950	(3%)	
2008 primary	George Miller (D)	unopposed		

Prior Winning Percentages: 2006 (84%); 2004 (76%); 2002 (71%); 2000 (76%); 1998 (77%); 1996 (72%); 1994 (70%); 1992 (70%); 1990 (61%); 1988 (68%); 1986 (67%); 1984 (66%); 1982 (67%); 1980 (63%); 1978 (63%); 1976 (75%); 1974 (56%)

Population		**Race/Ethnicity**		**Work**	
Pop. 2007:	645,488	White:	39.6%	Private:	74.7%
Change since 2000:	Up 1.0%	Black:	15.4%	Government:	17.5%
Urban:	98.7%	Hispanic:	25.4%	Self-employed:	7.6%
Rural:	1.3%	Asian:	15.0%	Blue collar:	22.2%
Area size:	443 sq. mi.	Native Am.:	0.4%	White collar:	58.8%
Age		Hawaiian:	0.6%	Khaki collar:	0.5%
Median age:	36.3 yrs.	Two+ races:	3.0%	Other:	18.5%
More than 65 yrs:	10.7%	*Ancestry*		Median income:	$62,951
Less than 18 yrs:	24.7%	German:	8.2%	Median home value:	$492,300
Education		Irish:	6.5%	Poverty:	11.0%
H.S. grad:	83.2%	English:	5.5%	**Military Veterans**	
College grad:	24.6%			% of Pop:	9.8%
Grad degree:	7.2%				

The journey inward from the Pacific Ocean to the vast flatness of California's Central Valley passes through a wondrous variety of terrain. The traveler starts at the Golden Gate Bridge, with the lush green Presidio on one side and the bluffs of mountains in Marin County on the other. The journey continues through the San Francisco Bay, through the narrow Carquinez Strait to Suisun Bay, with its sloughs and marshes and ships ready for scrap, and finally past the mountains, to the flat, fertile ex-

2008 Presidential Vote

Obama (D)	179,037	(72%)
McCain (R)	66,272	(27%)

2004 Presidential Vote

Kerry (D)	153,988	(67%)
Bush (R)	72,994	(32%)

Cook Partisan Voting Index: D + 19

panse of California's great interior. This is not a journey most tourists make, but it was a familiar route to the first Americans in California, and it passes by much of the industrial base of the Bay Area. On the east side of the bay is Richmond, developed almost instantaneously during World War II when Henry J. Kaiser built a shipyard in its deep-water port and 91,000 people from all over the country were put to work building ships for the Pacific theater. What became known as Rosie the Riveter Memorial Park is now a national park. The city is attracting high-tech spin-offs, despite a downtown that has seen better days. Chevron, with its local refinery, pays one-third of the city's revenues.

Across Carquinez Strait is Vallejo, named for a Mexican general and member of the first California Senate, the site from 1853 to 1996 of the giant Mare Island Naval Shipyard, where 41,000 worked during World War II. In May 2008, the city filed for bankruptcy, which was caused in part by the closing of the shipyard and in part by huge public employee salaries and pensions—292 of 411 city workers earned more than $100,000 a year. Farther up the bay, to the south, is Concord, the largest city in Contra Costa County, whose city officials were unique in that they lobbied the Pentagon to close the mostly unused Concord Naval Weapons Station. They wanted to use the land for business and residential development, which is banned beyond the urban limit that county voters imposed in 1990. The Defense Department complied and included about half of the site on the 2005 base-closure list, with plans under way for mixed-use development near a rapid-transit station. This is the industrial part of the Bay Area, with tank farms and refineries. The towns are among the most ethnically diverse in the country, with large percentages of African-Americans, Hispanics, Asians, and Filipinos.

The 7th Congressional District includes most of this territory, from Richmond to Vallejo, Hercules, Martinez, and Pittsburg. It also proceeds inland through the mountain interstices of Contra Costa County to include part of Concord. Northeast of Vallejo, it includes Vacaville on flatland beneath Vaca Mountain. Politically, this industrial area was blue-collar Democratic back in the days when San Francisco, with its larger white-collar population, often voted Republican. Today, it remains heavily Democratic, but not as leftist on cultural issues as other San Francisco areas. John Kerry won the district 67%-32% over George W. Bush in 2004, and Barack Obama won it 72%-27% over John McCain in 2008.

The congressman from the 7th District is George Miller, one of three remaining Democrats of the Watergate class of 1974, who came to power in the backlash over the Nixon-era scandal. (The others are James Oberstar of Minnesota and Henry Waxman of California.) Miller is the chairman of the Education and Labor Committee, and a trusted confidant of House Speaker Nancy Pelosi.

Miller is heir to a tradition of Bay Area working-class politics. His father was chairman of the state Senate Finance Committee. When his father died in 1969, Miller lost the race to succeed him, but became a staffer for Senate Leader George Moscone, who was later the mayor of San Francisco. Miller was a protégé of Rep. Phillip Burton, D-Calif., who helped establish liberal hegemony in the U.S. House in the 1970s. Miller has one of the most liberal voting records in the House, and he brings a zest for political combat reminiscent of Burton. He is a strong backer of protecting the environment against what he sees as greedy private-sector operators, and of furthering the causes of labor unions. Like Burton, Miller has grasped for top party leadership posts but hasn't made it. But he has learned a legislator's virtues of patience, timing, and creativity. Now, his close alliance with Burton's successor—Speaker Pelosi—places him among the most powerful people in Congress.

Pelosi relies on Miller for his advice, judgment, and protection from potential adversaries within the Democratic Caucus. "She is the leader that I've been waiting for for 30 years," Miller said in a 2005 interview with *National Journal*. "She is the complete package. She understands policy, politics, and has a core of values that is clear and solid. She is a rare breed." Pelosi named Miller chairman of the Democratic Policy Committee, where he was instrumental in preparing the "New Direction" agenda for the 2006 campaign. His longtime staff director became Pelosi's chief of staff in 2005. Because Miller rarely does anything that runs contrary to Pelosi's views or interests, his early support for Californian Henry Waxman's ultimately successful bid to oust John Dingell of Michigan as chairman of the Energy and Commerce Committee in November 2008 was a strong signal of Pelosi's otherwise unstated view: She preferred Waxman for the job.

As chairman of the Education and Labor Committee, a priority for him is an overhaul of the Bush-era No Child Left Behind Act, with increased funding and incentives for improved teacher quality. Bush's opposition to additional funding led Miller to defer renewal of the act until the inauguration of a new president in 2009. In the 110th Congress (2007–08), Miller focused on higher-education programs and efforts to help more students pay for college and to foster loan-forgiveness programs for graduates who work as teachers. His bill, enacted in May 2008, increased the amounts that students could borrow to pay for college. Dependent undergraduates could borrow up to $31,000, and independent undergraduates could borrow up to $57,500 over the course of getting their degree.

Miller doesn't always follow the dictates of the teachers' unions, especially if he thinks they are getting in the way of improving public schools. He has long advocated more spending on education, but he has also wanted more-rigorous standards, with measurable consequences. When he was in the minority, he worked with then-committee Chairman John Boehner, R-Ohio, to write No Child Left Behind, and Bush praised Miller for his contributions at the bill signing in January 2002. Though he thinks the act's mandates were underfunded by the Republicans, Miller also has lauded its impact on test scores for minority and poor students.

On labor issues, Miller in 2007 won enactment of an increase in the hourly minimum wage from $5.15 to $7.25. He has pressed for enactment of the card-check bill, which would require an employer to recognize a union if it persuaded a majority of workers to sign union authorization cards. Secret-ballot elections would be held only if requested by unions, which would have little incentive to do so. His agenda on behalf of organized labor also included a bill mandating new safety features in mines and stepped-up oversight of mine safety, which passed the House in 2008. The legislation was a response to the Crandall Canyon Mine disaster, in which six miners died in Utah in 2007 after a cave-in blocked all exits.

In response to the recession and steep drop in the stock market in 2008, Miller explored changes in 401(k) retirement plans and suggestions for a guaranteed retirement account for every worker. "We can't allow the promise of a secure retirement for workers to become a casualty of this financial crisis," he told the *Contra Costa Times* in October 2008.

As a longtime member of the Natural Resources Committee, Miller has long crusaded against water reclamation projects that provided cheap water to farmers. In 1992, during a California drought, he passed a Central Valley Project law that raised farmers' prices closer to those of urban users and imposed environmental restrictions, over the fierce opposition of Central Valley politicians and Republican Gov.

Pete Wilson. When Republicans were in the majority, Miller was a major obstacle to attempts to scale back the reach of environmental regulations and the Endangered Species Act, and to GOP efforts to open up the Arctic National Wildlife Refuge to oil drilling and the Tongass National Forest to more logging.

Miller played an important role in early 2009 in shaping the initial direction of the Obama presidency. His strong support influenced the tilt toward huge education spending in the economic stimulus bill that Democrats enacted in February 2009.

EIGHTH DISTRICT

Nancy Pelosi (D)

Elected June 1987, 11th full term; b. March 26, 1940, Baltimore, MD; home, San Francisco; Trinity Col., B.A. 1962; Catholic; married (Paul); 5 children.

Professional Career: CA Dem. party, Northern chmn., 1977–81, St. chmn., 1981–83; DSCC finance chmn., 1985–87; PR exec., Ogilvy & Mather, 1986–87.

DC Office: 235 CHOB, 20515, 202-225-4965; Fax: 202-225-8259; Web site: www.house.gov/pelosi; www.speaker.gov.

State Offices: San Francisco, 415-556-4862.

Committees: *Speaker of the House.*

Group Ratings and Key Votes: *As speaker, did not usually vote.*

Election Results

2008 general	Nancy Pelosi (D)	204,996	(72%)	($2,727,177)
	Cindy Sheehan (I)	46,118	(16%)	($628,411)
	Dana Walsh (R)	27,614	(10%)	($637,731)
	Philip Berg (Lib)	6,504	(2%)	
2008 primary	Nancy Pelosi (D)	83,510	(89%)	
	Shirley Golub (D)	10,105	(11%)	

Prior Winning Percentages: 2006 (80%); 2004 (83%); 2002 (80%); 2000 (85%); 1998 (86%); 1996 (84%); 1994 (82%); 1992 (82%); 1990 (77%); 1988 (76%); 1987 (63%)

Population		Race/Ethnicity		Work	
Pop. 2007:	617,277	White:	44.3%	Private:	78.1%
Change since 2000:	Down 3.4%	Black:	7.8%	Government:	12.0%
Urban:	100.0%	Hispanic:	15.9%	Self-employed:	9.6%
Rural:	0.0%	Asian:	28.9%	Blue collar:	11.0%
Area size:	114 sq. mi.	Native Am.:	0.2%	White collar:	72.0%
Age		Hawaiian:	0.4%	Khaki collar:	0.0%
Median age:	39.0 yrs.	Two+ races:	2.2%	Other:	16.9%
More than 65 yrs:	14.1%	*Ancestry*		Median income:	$62,333
Less than 18 yrs:	13.7%	German:	7.1%	Median home value:	$763,100
Education		Irish:	7.0%	Poverty:	12.8%
H.S. grad:	83.9%	English:	5.6%	**Military Veterans**	
College grad:	48.5%			% of Pop:	5.1%
Grad degree:	18.2%				

On Feb. 20, 1915, a crowd of 150,000 gathered on the grounds of the Panama-Pacific International Exposition to see the Spanish-Italian baroque-style structure built on reclaimed land in what was to become San Francisco's Marina district. The Exposition ostensibly celebrated the completion of the Panama Canal, but it was clearly intended to show off San Francisco's recovery from the 1906 earthquake. It also spotlighted the city as the central focus of America's efforts to open an economic door

2008 Presidential Vote		
Obama (D)	266,210	(85%)
McCain (R)	38,665	(12%)
2004 Presidential Vote		
Kerry (D)	244,009	(85%)
Bush (R)	40,558	(14%)
Cook Partisan Voting Index:	D + 35	

to the eastern part of the world, especially in light of the acquisition of Hawaii and the Philippines and of its interest in an open-door policy with China and trade with Japan. The Exposition established the physical style of San Francisco, encouraging the use of Mediterranean color, accent and detail that characterizes most of the post-Victorian houses and commercial structures in The City, as the *San Francisco Examiner* called it for years. It set the tone for the picturesque Marina district, whose old buildings had been among those damaged in the 1989 earthquake, and for Fisherman's Wharf and Ghirardelli Square. On a sunny day, San Francisco looks almost tropical, with brown mountains baking in the sun and light shining off the pastel stucco buildings. When the clouds scud in from the Pacific, it can look sinister, full of dark corners where a private detective's partner might be ambushed by a pretty woman. The buildings can be majestic, like the monumental Beaux Arts City Hall, or tawdry, like the hotels of the Tenderloin district. It is a city that at first looks exotic but, when you look closely, can only be American.

San Francisco has been a dynamic city. It grew from nothing to a major city in the single year of 1850, an instant product of the California Gold Rush. Within just a few years, culture was flourishing in the city, and San Francisco developed a parochial pride in the great writers who worked there—Jack London, Ambrose Bierce, Frank Norris—and in giving birth to the Arts and Crafts movement. Later, San Francisco newspaper scribe Herb Caen coined the term "beatnik" to describe the youthful penchant for freedom in the 1950s and wrote definitively about the hippies who thronged Haight-Ashbury in 1967. In the 1970s, the city was among the first to embrace the gay movement, in the Castro district (although lately, gays have been moving to the suburbs and straights have been moving in). Over the years, the city's booming economy-based initially on food processing, but now on finance, high-tech and clothing (Levi Strauss, the Gap)–attracted talented newcomers, though its population is increasingly polarized between high-income and low-income. The dot.com crash in 2000 took a brutal toll, but the city rallied in mid-decade, as new high-rise office buildings and condominiums sprang up on the waterfront and south of Market. Google and other Silicon Valley firms started leasing office space for their young, hip employees. The housing bust in 2008 did not hit as hard here as in California's Central Valley subdivisions, where many modest-income Bay Area residents had been fleeing. San Francisco has the lowest percentage of children (16%) of any major city, and only a little more than half the number of African-Americans it had in 1970. The population on the west side is nearly half Asian. But overall, proudly tolerant San Francisco is one of California's whitest cities.

Politically, San Francisco was a progressive Republican town, like the two men who led the way into the Exposition: Mayor "Sunny Jim" Rolph and California Gov. Hiram Johnson. The sour-tempered Johnson made his name as a reformer, throwing out crooked city politicians. His administration gave California primary elections, referenda and recall, and strong civil-service laws. Rolph, mayor from 1911–30 and then governor, built the civic center, parks, schools, streetcars and the Hetch Hetchy aqueduct—the antique infrastructure of San Francisco today (though the water quality is terrific). Sympathetic to the conservation movement, willing to deal with organized labor in a union town that had America's only general strike in 1934 and tolerant of California's diversity, these progressive Republicans were the recognizable ancestors of, though certainly not identical to, the latter-day San Franciscans who became increasingly liberal.

The city has elected strong liberal politicians, notably Mayor George Moscone and the first openly gay supervisor, Harvey Milk; both were shot to death in 1978 by a political opponent, who was later acquitted of murder by a jury on the theory that he had been crazed by junk food. Over the next decade, the city's cultural liberalism was tempered by Democratic Mayor Dianne Feinstein, who vetoed a domestic-partnership ordinance and opposed commercial rent control. In 1995, Willie Brown, ousted after 15 years as speaker of the state Assembly, returned home and was elected mayor. Brown's political flair was always in evidence, but high taxes and an increasing homeless population drove out middle-class families and immigrants. As his successor, San Francisco installed Gavin Newsom, who in February 2004 started issuing marriage licenses to same-sex couples, although California voters had outlawed same-sex marriage. The state Supreme Court ordered him to stop and voided the marriages. In 2008, Newsom was vindicated when the state Supreme Court declared same-sex marriages legal. But his victory statement— "This door's wide open, it's going to happen, whether you like it or not" —was featured in ads for proponents of Proposition 8, which by a 52%-48% vote reversed the court's decision. In April 2009, Newsom announced his candidacy for governor in 2010.

The 8th Congressional District of California takes in four-fifths of San Francisco, all but the southwest corner. It includes all of San Francisco's high-rise downtown, the crowded and bustling Chinatown, Telegraph Hill, Nob Hill and Russian Hill, North Beach, Pacific Heights, and the Marina District (which does not have a very big marina). In the valleys are the mostly black Fillmore and Western Addition areas. The district is 8% African-American, 16% Hispanic and 29% Asian. The 8th also has Noe Valley; the Castro, which is still mainly gay; Haight-Ashbury, once the bedraggled center of hippie culture and now another gentrifying San Francisco neighborhood; and Portrero Hill, with its restored houses overlooking downtown. Farther south are the old residential areas overlooking Interstate 280, with pastel houses strewn along grid streets that hug the steep hills. The district is overwhelmingly Democratic and voted 85%-12% for Democratic presidential nominee Barack Obama in 2008.

The 8th District is represented by Nancy Pelosi, the first female speaker of the House. Elected in June 1987, she has the energy and shrewdness of one who has handled the most delicate of political chores, and the charm and unflappability of one who is the mother of five and grandmother of seven. Pelosi grew up on Albemarle Street in Baltimore's Little Italy, just east of downtown. Her father, Thomas D'Alesandro

Jr., served in the House from 1939–47 and was mayor of Baltimore for 12 years after that. Her mother, Annunciata D'Alesandro, was an indefatigable political organizer, and her brother, Thomas, was mayor from 1967–71. Pelosi says of her parents, "What I got from them was about economic fairness. That was the difference between Democrats and Republicans all those years ago." She graduated from Trinity University in Washington, D.C., where she met her husband. After marrying, they moved to his hometown of San Francisco. There he became a successful real estate investor, and she raised their children and got into local Democratic politics.

At first, Pelosi impressed rough-hewn U.S. Rep. John Burton of California as just another stylish hostess in a city that had many of them. But she soon got Burton's attention and that of his older brother, U.S. Rep. Phillip Burton, the de facto liberal leader of the House, who lost his race for majority leader to Texas Democrat Jim Wright by one vote in 1976. That year, Pelosi returned East to run the Maryland campaign of presidential candidate Jerry Brown, the quirky liberal governor of California. She was able to relate both to "Governor Moonbeam," as Brown was dubbed, and to the practical-minded politicians she had met through her parents. In 1977, she became chairman of the Northern California Democratic Party, and four years later, she became chairman of the California Democratic Party. The positions required a considerable amount of diplomacy. Assembly Majority Leader Howard Berman of Los Angeles was attempting to oust Assembly Speaker Leo McCarthy of San Francisco, a protracted struggle out of which Democrat Willie Brown of San Francisco emerged with the speakership. Pelosi managed to remain on good terms with all of them and to help Democrats hold majorities in the Legislature.

Then John Burton declined to run for re-election in a new Marin-and-San-Francisco-based district. Some Democrats sounded out Pelosi, whose Presidio Heights home was in the district, but she declined to run, and the seat went instead to Marin-based Democrat Barbara Boxer. In the next few years, Pelosi worked with Mayor Feinstein to land the 1984 Democratic National Convention for San Francisco. In 1985, she ran for Democratic National Chairman, but lost to Paul Kirk. Technically, Pelosi was still a stay-at-home mother, but she was dealing with politicians of the first order of magnitude or soon to become so. Gov. Brown was a presidential candidate in 1976 and 1992, Phil Burton was a major power in the House, and John Burton was later president of the California Senate. Berman was elected to Congress and now chairs the Foreign Affairs Committee, McCarthy became lieutenant governor, Willie Brown remained speaker for 15 years, and Feinstein is now a U.S. senator. This was a fast political track. In April 1983, Phil Burton, who chain-smoked Pall Malls and drank vodka from tumbler glasses, dropped dead at 57. Elected to succeed him was his widow, Sala Burton, who idolized his record and whose political instincts were as shrewd as his own. But her health failed too. In 1987, as she was dying of cancer, she told her friends whom she wanted to succeed her: Nancy Pelosi.

Only two years before, Pelosi had told the press, "I won't be running for office." Her children were not yet grown, her husband's business interests kept him mostly in California, and their net worth was not yet such that she could afford to self-finance a campaign. (The couple eventually became extremely wealthy, with houses in San Francisco, a vineyard in the Napa Valley, a townhome in the Sierras and a condominium in Washington.) But she ran, moving her residence from Presidio Heights to a Pacific Heights rental apartment (Presidio Heights is back in her district now). Her chief opponent in the Democratic primary was San Francisco Supervisor Harry Britt, who had succeeded Milk after the assassination. San Francisco's gay community at that time was not as mainstream as it is now, but Britt, who was gay, had a good record in office, and Pelosi had to work hard to beat him 35%-31%.

There seemed to be no clue in Pelosi's early work in the House that she would seek a leadership position as Phil Burton had. Instead she took the lead on important issues of local sensitivity. One was the Presidio. Burton had inserted into legislation a provision that transferred the Presidio from the military to the Interior Department. The problem was that it was so expensive to maintain, it threatened to exceed the National Park Service's budget for it. Through several Congresses, Pelosi worked to get bipartisan support for a funding source, and in 1997 created the Presidio Trust, with a declining appropriation scheduled to be phased out in 2012. Another sensitive issue was human rights, especially in China. After the Tiananmen Square massacre, she sponsored an amendment to give Chinese students the right to remain in the United States. President George H. W. Bush vetoed it. In 1991, she became the lead sponsor of the bill to make China's most-favored-nation status conditional on human rights reforms. The House overrode Bush's veto, but it was upheld in the Senate. After that, Pelosi led the annual fight against normalizing trade relations with China.

She did all this at some political risk. Pelosi's position was by no means universally popular with Asian-Americans in her district; many thought that the United States should trade and negotiate quietly with China. One of her chief adversaries was her San Francisco neighbor, Sen. Feinstein; for many years, they lived in houses just a few blocks apart in Presidio Heights. Pelosi courted support from people on the opposite end of the ideological spectrum, especially religious conservatives in the Republican caucus who also wanted to remain vigilant on China's human rights record. At the time of the September 11 attacks, Pelosi was the senior Democrat on the Intelligence Committee, where she cooperated with Republican Chairman Porter Goss of Florida. She joined in the committee's conclusion that, while the intelligence community did not have specific evidence in advance, it did have information that was relevant to the attacks. On other issues, Pelosi maintained an almost perfectly liberal voting record and established herself as a leader in encouraging family planning and environmental protection overseas.

Her move into the leadership was persistent, shrewd and well-organized. In 1997, as a member of the Committee on Standards of Official Conduct, she doggedly pursued ethics charges against Republican Speaker Newt Gingrich and worked with Minority Whip David Bonior in using scorched-earth tactics against him. (Gingrich had used a nearly identical strategy to weaken former Democratic Speaker Jim Wright of Texas, who ultimately stepped down amid an ethics investigation.) In 1999, she launched a campaign for majority whip, anticipating that Democrats would win a majority in 2000, which they nearly did. Her opponent was Democrat Steny Hoyer of Maryland. They were old acquaintances, having served as interns for Sen. Daniel Brewster of Maryland in the 1960s, but not confreres: There were considerable stylistic and ideological differences. Many of the Democratic women in the House felt there should be a woman in the leadership. Pelosi, who raised $3 million for Democratic candidates that cycle, said she was not running as a woman, but "the fact that I am a woman is an enhancement, because we absolutely must have diversity in the leadership." But in 2000, Republicans held on to their majority, and the race for majority whip was moot. Not for long though. Michigan's Republican Legislature, in drawing new congressional districts, put Bonior in a district it was plain he could not win, and he decided to run for governor. He resigned as minority whip, and Pelosi was off and running against Hoyer. Pelosi said that Democrats needed to refocus on grassroots organization, money and message. Some supporters played up her potential to become a celebrity— "a glamorous grandmother who knocks people off their feet," as Hawaii's Rep. Neil Abercrombie put it. With nearly unanimous support from the 32 California Democrats and from most female members, Pelosi started off with a strong base. Her support also crossed ideological lines. She was nominated by John Murtha, a mostly hawkish and culturally conservative Vietnam veteran from the coal country of western Pennsylvania, with a following among old-line Democrats. Pelosi and Murtha formed an alliance similar to that between Phil Burton and the hard-bitten conservative Wayne Hays from the coal country of eastern Ohio a quarter-century earlier. In October 2001, Pelosi won by a convincing 118-95.

As whip, Pelosi moved quickly to assert herself, sometimes independently from then Minority Leader Dick Gephardt of Missouri. She sparked a controversy when she contributed $10,000 to Rep. Lynn Rivers in a redistricting-forced Michigan primary against John Dingell, the powerful ranking Democrat on the Energy and Commerce Committee who had been a strong supporter of Hoyer for whip. Normally, party leaders do not take sides in such primaries. Dingell won handily. Pelosi's biggest conflict came in the fall of 2002, when she actively encouraged opponents of the resolution authorizing the use of force in Iraq, which Gephardt had enthusiastically endorsed. Pelosi contended that supporters had not made the case for using force and that she had seen no evidence that Iraq "poses an imminent threat to our nation." To the surprise of many, her efforts helped win 126 Democratic votes against the resolution, while only 81 backed Gephardt's pro-invasion position. In retrospect, the split signaled a transition in the caucus. Once the disappointing 2002 election results were in and Gephardt said that he was stepping down, Pelosi had all but locked up the support of a majority of the caucus. Rep. Martin Frost of Texas announced his candidacy with warnings that the selection of Pelosi might create a "permanent minority party." He withdrew from the contest a day later, conceding that he could not win. Harold Ford of Tennessee made a belated, quixotic bid designed to appeal to a combination of blacks and New Democrats, but Pelosi won 177-29.

As the Democratic leader in the House, she brought a burst of energy—and favorable press coverage—to a party that badly needed it. She showed hands-on management in selecting members for House committee vacancies and in developing a Democratic message highlighting the shortcomings of the Bush agenda. There were bruised feelings over some committee assignments, but even allies of Hoyer and Frost credited her with bringing a breath of fresh air and enthusiasm to party deliberations. As Republicans pressed their agenda, Pelosi declared that Democrats would take "a party position" in opposition to the Republican Medicare prescription-drug bill. But 16 Democrats voted for the final deal in November 2003, providing the critical margin for passage. She was largely silent about the renegades, many of whom were responding to local pressures. It was a painful lesson for Pelosi in the limited power of the minority leader in the House.

In 2004, Pelosi traveled the country raising money and boosting local candidates. If she became speaker, Pelosi pledged, she would reform the House to give a greater voice to all members and to assure fairness. She cited Democratic gains of open seats in Kentucky and South Dakota in special elections in early 2004 as proof that the political tide was turning their way. But the three-seat loss in the November election that year turned out to be yet another disappointment for House Democrats, though Pelosi noted correctly that they won a net gain apart from the effects of the 2003 Texas redistricting. She also cast some of the blame on the presidential campaign of John Kerry.

In early 2005, she firmly insisted that House Democrats would not sit down with Republicans on a plan for overhauling Social Security until they removed President Bush's proposal to introduce private investment accounts into the program. Bush's declining job approval ratings and the rising prospects of Democrats in the 2006 election helped Pelosi maintain party discipline. She saluted her longtime supporter Murtha for a November 2005 speech calling for a redeployment of troops out of Iraq, and she suggested without saying so that it would be the party's position. "A vote on the war is an individual vote. It may be viewed as the position of the party; it is not. But I do know that a majority of House Democrats will support Mr. Murtha," she said. Hoyer was adamantly opposed to withdrawing from Iraq, which he said would be a "disaster."

In the summer of 2006, Hoyer, whatever his private feelings, declared that he had no intention of challenging Pelosi if once again Democrats failed to win a majority that fall. "If we lose, it will not be Nancy Pelosi's fault. She's done everything she possibly can. Win, lose or draw, she's going to be our leader." Just days later, Murtha announced he would run for majority leader if Democrats won, presumably against Hoyer, and said that Pelosi had neither encouraged nor discouraged him from saying so. For months, House Democrats struggled to come up with a platform to run on in 2006 and after many postponements, emerged with a "Six for '06" program of increasing the minimum wage and enacting the remaining recommendations of the 9/11 Commission. Pelosi campaigned tirelessly across the country and was rewarded with a Democratic majority on November 7.

"I understand my role as leader of the Democrats. And I very, very much respect that I will be the Speaker of the House, not of the Democrats," Pelosi said when it was clear Democrats had won a majority. It was not an accurate forecast, perhaps, and a bit of boilerplate, yet it seemed to represent some sincere hope in her, as it had in her Republican and Democratic predecessors. She said the resignation of Bush Defense Secretary Donald Rumsfeld was "a fresh start toward a new policy in Iraq, signaling a willingness on the part of the president to work with the Congress to devise a better way forward." And she told Fox News that Iraq was "a problem to be solved, not a war to be won." She made some missteps along the way, as new leaders often do. She vigorously supported Murtha for majority leader. Hoyer was supported by most of the conservative Blue Dog Democrats, by most freshmen and by senior incoming committee chairmen like Dingell and Henry Waxman of California. Hoyer won 149-86, putting him in the No. 2 spot in the leadership, just after Pelosi. Whether they liked it or not, Pelosi and Hoyer were a team.

Pelosi finessed Democratic Congressional Campaign Committee Chairman Rahm Emanuel of Illinois, who wanted to serve as majority whip as a reward for his role in capturing the House, by persuading him to take the caucus chairmanship with new responsibilities. That paved the way for the whip position to go to the well-liked James Clyburn of South Carolina, an African-American who brought some racial diversity to the top ranks of the new leadership. Pelosi had long been at odds with California's Jane Harman, the ranking Democrat on Intelligence, who had voted for the Iraq resolution, and Pelosi was determined not to allow her to chair the committee. But the next Democrat in seniority, Alcee Hastings of Florida, although bright and charming, had been impeached and removed from his office as federal judge earlier in his career. After an embarrassing interval, the position went to Silvestre Reyes of Texas.

As she assumed the office that put her third in line for the presidency on Jan. 4, 2007, Pelosi said, "This is an historic moment, for Congress, and for the women of this country. It is a moment for which we have waited more than 200 years. For our daughters and granddaughters, today we have broken the marble ceiling. To our daughters and granddaughters, the sky is the limit." Minority Leader John Boehner of Ohio echoed the sentiment, saying, "In a few moments, I'll have the high privilege of handing the gavel of the House of Representatives to a woman for the first time in history. Whether you're a Republican, a Democrat or an independent, this is a cause for celebration."

There was some awkwardness in Pelosi's first months as speaker. The 100 hours to pass the "Six for '06" program turned out to be 100 legislative hours, stretched over a couple of weeks. A request for a military plane to fly her to her district seemed an extravagant request, although the previous speaker, Republican Dennis Hastert, had had use of military planes to travel to his Illinois district, and Pelosi, not unreasonably, wanted an aircraft that could fly nonstop to San Francisco. Beneath the velvet glove, Pelosi continued to operate with an iron fist. One of her key issues is reducing carbon dioxide emissions to curb global warming. So she announced the creation of a Select Committee on Energy Independence and Global Warming, to be headed by Energy and Commerce member Edward Markey of Massachusetts. When her old nemesis, Energy and Commerce Chairman Dingell, protested that he was being sidelined, Pelosi promised him that the special committee would have no legislative power.

She had some early impressive legislative successes. But there were also disappointments, especially when Democratic leaders in the closely divided Senate failed to rally the 60 votes needed to pass bills sent over from the House. The minimum wage was finally raised after many years, and an ethics reform bill that banned lobbyists' gifts and required public disclosure of the identity of lawmakers sponsoring spending earmarks was enacted. Her greatest frustration was being unable to end military involvement in Iraq. The House passed measures with timetables for withdrawal, but they failed in the Senate. She disappointed antiwar liberals by bringing to the floor war-funding bills she opposed because, as she said, she had promised to protect the troops. In July 2007, she settled for a measure prohibiting permanent U.S. military bases in Iraq. A couple months later, Gen. David Petraeus testified about the success of Bush's troop "surge" strategy, and by then, the public pressure for withdrawal from Iraq diminished. Pelosi conceded that she had underestimated the Republicans' willingness to stick with the president on the war, a position at odds with statements they had made to her privately and also at odds with the public mood in some GOP districts. In all, the 110th Congress (2008–09) voted $352 billion to fund the war, and in early 2009, Bush's successor, Democratic President Barack Obama, decided to keep troops there another 19 months.

On other foreign policy issues, Pelosi attracted attention in February 2007 when she said that Bush lacked authority to invade Iran and in April 2007 when she and five other lawmakers met in Damascus with Syrian President Bashar al-Assad. Speaking to reporters, Pelosi said she delivered a message to Assad that Israeli Prime Minister Ehud Ohlmert was ready to negotiate for peace. But Ohlmert issued a clarification saying that although Israel was interested in peace, Syria was still part of "the axis of evil."

On domestic policy, Pelosi and her Democratic leadership ran a tight ship and were largely successful, at least in the House. She held back on the issue of addressing illegal immigration, about which many Democrats were skittish, and watched as the Senate failed to act. The Democrats' bill to expand the State Children's Health Insurance Program was passed by both chambers, but Bush vetoed it. Pelosi then went along with abandoning the pay-go rule, which requires that tax cuts be paid for by spending cuts, in order to finance a fix of the Alternative Minimum Tax, which otherwise threatened to hit many middle-income earners. In April 2008, she prevailed when she ignored the law giving the president broad authority over trade and refused to bring the Colombia Free Trade Agreement to the floor. When gasoline hit $4 a gallon in 2008 and public opinion began to favor more offshore oil drilling, Pelosi refused to allow a roll call vote. "I'm trying to save the planet," she said. Republicans screamed foul, and during the August recess, though Congress had technically gone home, they made speeches to curious tourists in the House chamber urging a vote. Pelosi ordered the lights turned out. But Democrats too were coming under pressure to act on gas prices, and on August 16, Pelosi agreed to allow a vote on a bill that gave the individual states a role in offshore-drilling decisions.

In September 2008, the House was confronted with a request by Treasury Secretary Henry Paulson and Federal Reserve Chairman Ben Bernanke for $700 billion to bail out financial firms on the brink of collapse in the weakening economy. Pelosi, with Financial Services Committee Chairman Barney Frank of Massachusetts, decided to grant the request. But a few days later, it became clear that Democrats with serious political challengers were unwilling to vote for it. Pelosi announced she would bring Democrats along if 100 Republicans supported it as well. But when the bill came to a vote on September 29, it was defeated 225-208. Republicans blamed Pelosi for speaking harshly about Bush administration economic policies. The Senate changed some of the terms of the bill, and it passed on October 1. The House took up the Senate version and, with some vote switches prompted by Pelosi, passed it. Next on the agenda was the threatened bankruptcy of the big Detroit automakers. Pelosi resisted proposals to use $25 billion previously approved for developing fuel-efficient cars to keep the companies afloat. But she yielded on that point in December. However, the Senate could not pass the bill, and Bush approved loans for the auto companies out of the $700 billion intended to bail out the financial markets.

Pelosi remained neutral in the 2008 race for the Democratic presidential nomination, noting that as speaker she would preside over the party's convention. But in March 2008, after a month of consecutive victories for Obama over rival Hillary Rodham Clinton of New York, she said, "If the votes of the superdelegates overturn what's happened in the elections, it would be harmful to the Democratic party" —a statement that obviously favored Obama.

Democrats gained 21 House seats in the election, and Pelosi entered the 111th Congress in 2009 as the leader of 257 Democrats (up from 236)—the biggest majority a speaker has enjoyed since Democrat Thomas Foley of Washington in 1993–94. In December, Pelosi told Emanuel, as he was preparing to leave the House to become Obama's White House chief of staff, that she expected the administration to work through her and not make side deals with conservative Democratic factions, much less the Republicans. In January, Pelosi pushed through the House rules changes repealing the six-year term-limit on committee chairmen that Republicans imposed in 1995, and placing restrictions on motions to recommit, which Republicans had used frequently to delay or stop legislation. As the unions pressed for a card-check bill effectively abolishing the secret ballot in unionization elections, Pelosi let it be known that the Senate would have to act before she would ask Democrats in the House to cast what for some would be a politically dangerous vote. She said, "A country must be governed from the middle." Still, in early 2009, she worked with Appropriations Chairman David Obey of Wisconsin to put forward an $819 billion economic-stimulus bill that not a single Republican voted for. Then, House Democrats bristled, but went along, when Senate Democrats cut aid to state governments and school-construction funds to get the three Republican votes needed to pass the bill.

Back home, Pelosi was re-elected with 80% or more of the vote from 1992 to 2006. In 2008, antiwar protester Cindy Sheehan ran against her as an independent. Pelosi refused to debate or acknowledge Sheehan, who wound up getting 16% of the vote, more than the Republican nominee's 10%. Pelosi got 72%. It was her lowest percentage since the 1987 special election when she first won the seat. But the numbers are relevant only as a metric of the far left constituency of San Francisco and not as an indication of any political peril for Pelosi.

NINTH DISTRICT

Barbara Lee (D)

Elected April 1998, 6th full term; b. July 16, 1946, El Paso, TX; home, Oakland; Mills Col., B.A. 1973, U. of CA-Berkeley, M.S.W. 1975; no religious affiliation; divorced; 2 children.

Elected Office: CA Assembly, 1990–96; CA Senate, 1996–98.

Professional Career: Chief of staff, U.S. Rep. Ron Dellums, 1975–87.

DC Office: 2444 RHOB, 20515, 202-225-2661; Fax: 202-225-9817; Web site: lee.house.gov.

State Offices: Oakland, 510-763-0370.

Committees: *Appropriations* (26th of 37 D): Financial Services & General Government; Labor, HHS, Education & Related Agencies; State, Foreign Operations & Related Programs. *Foreign Affairs* (19th of 28 D): Africa & Global Health; Western Hemisphere.

Group Ratings

	ADA	ACLU	AFS	LCV	ITIC	NTU	COC	ACU	CFG	FRC
2008	100	100	100	100	86	14	41	4	0	5
2007	90	—	91	95	—	8	45	0	6	—

National Journal Ratings

	2007 LIB	—	2007 CONS	2008 LIB	—	2008 CONS
Economic	82%	—	0%	85%	—	0%
Social	92%	—	0%	67%	—	28%
Foreign	65%	—	33%	85%	—	8%
Composite	84%	—	16%	84%	—	17%

Key Votes of the 110th Congress

1. Increase minimum wage	Y	5. Share immigration data	N	9. Withdraw troops 8/08	N
2. Expand SCHIP	Y	6. Foreign aid abortion ban	N	10. No operations in Iran	Y
3. Raise CAFE standards	Y	7. Ban gay bias in workplace	Y	11. Free trade with Peru	N
4. Bail out financial markets	Y	8. Repeal D.C. gun law	N	12. Overhaul FISA	N

Election Results

2008 general	Barbara Lee (D)	238,915	(86%)	($1,048,228)
	Charles Hargrave (R)	26,917	(10%)	
	James Eyer (Lib)	11,704	(4%)	
2008 primary	Barbara Lee (D)	unopposed		

Prior Winning Percentages: 2006 (86%); 2004 (85%); 2002 (81%); 2000 (85%); 1998 (83%); 1998 (67%)

Population		Race/Ethnicity		Work	
Pop. 2007:	617,090	White:	36.0%	Private:	72.4%
Change since 2000:	Down 3.4%	Black:	22.1%	Government:	16.5%
Urban:	99.9%	Hispanic:	21.5%	Self-employed:	10.8%
Rural:	0.1%	Asian:	16.2%	Blue collar:	17.2%
Area size:	152 sq. mi.	Native Am.:	0.3%	White collar:	67.1%
Age		Hawaiian:	0.5%	Khaki collar:	0.1%
Median age:	36.5 yrs.	Two+ races:	2.7%	Other:	15.7%
More than 65 yrs:	11.1%	*Ancestry*		Median income:	$51,777
Less than 18 yrs:	21.7%	German:	6.1%	Median home value:	$616,500
Education		Irish:	5.3%	Poverty:	16.6%
H.S. grad:	82.8%	English:	5.0%	**Military Veterans**	
College grad:	40.7%			% of Pop:	6.2%
Grad degree:	18.8%				

On the East Bay opposite San Francisco, Oakland and Berkeley stand today on one of the lushest sites in America, overlooking the San Francisco-Oakland Bay Bridge and the Golden Gate Bridge and basking in the sunshine that is more common here than across the bay. Both cities host great institutions, but in different ways they are also museum pieces, antiques from a moment in the 1960s when both, especially Berkeley, gained identities that became hard to shake.

Berkeley was founded as a university town, named after the 18th-century Irish philosopher Bishop George Berkeley for his proclamation, "Westward the course of empire takes its way." Famous for years as the home of first-rate scholarship at the University of California, Berkeley became famous politically in 1964 as ground zero of student rebellion when an administrator's refusal to let students set up a table to sign up volunteers for Democrat Lyndon Johnson's presidential campaign led to months of riots, student strikes, and classroom confrontation. In 1969, students led protests at "People's Park," a lot owned by the university, and Republican Gov. Ronald Reagan sent in the National Guard to protect state property: an episode in which both sides relished the confrontation. Berkeley gave birth to a street culture that still exists. Its denizens made common cause with the quasi-political Black Panthers from nearby Oakland, and smoked marijuana with the Hell's Angels motorcycle gang. With its view of the bay, the campus is beautiful, and old buildings like the shingled Claremont Hotel are grand, although construction of new offices and apartment buildings created a more modern feel by 2008. All of those yoga classes, bean sprouts, and healthy lifestyles led in 2007 to a life expectancy in Berkeley of 83 years, five years longer than the national average.

Oakland has a different history, centered on commerce and building its own civic institutions. (Gertrude Stein was wrong: There is a there there.) It became the western terminus of the transcontinental railroad in 1870 and was connected by ferry to San Francisco. It has always had heavy industry, and its port today is the busiest on the bay. The docks attracted young roustabouts like the writer Jack London, after whom a downtown square is named. Civic affairs were run by the local elite, like the Knowland family who owned the *Oakland Tribune*. With the Bay Area's largest black community, Oakland spawned the Black Panthers. African-American leaders began to dominate city government in the 1970s and the *Tribune* in the 1980s. Then Jerry Brown came on the scene. Governor of California 20 years earlier and an unsuccessful presidential candidate several times over, he ran an unorthodox campaign for mayor, and won. Brown irritated local factions by firing department heads and ignoring long-standing alliances, but he seemed to take seriously his mission of propelling Oakland to prominence. With his tough talk on crime and advocacy of big commercial-development projects that drove up rents, he sounded like a conservative. He even set up a military high school. Crime rates dropped, and the local economy thrived, partly with the growth of middle-income refugees from the exorbitant housing costs of San Francisco. But many longtime residents, especially African-Americans, complained about rising costs, and they in turn moved to the outskirts. The black population fell from 47% in 1980 to about 30% in 2007. In 2006, Brown was elected state attorney general. His successor as mayor was former Democratic U.S. Rep. Ron Dellums.

The 9th Congressional District of California consists of Oakland and Berkeley, plus Castro Valley. It has the largest African-American percentage of any northern California district (22.1% in 2007), and also has high percentages of Hispanics (21.5%) and Asians (16.2%). Politically, it may be the most left-wing district in the nation. It voted 86%-13% for John Kerry in 2004 and 88%-10% for Barack Obama in 2008.

The congresswoman from the 9th District is Barbara Lee, a Democrat who won an April 1998 special election. Lee spent her childhood in Texas and says her political thinking was shaped by her early exposure to race discrimination. While in labor with her, Lee's mother was at first denied treatment at an El Paso hospital. Lee attended a segregated school in that city until her parents sent their children to a Catholic school. In 1960, the family moved to Southern California, where Lee was the first black cheerleader in her high school, a distinction she won after enlisting the help of the local chapter of the NAACP. In 2008, Lee authored a memoir, *Renegade for Peace and Justice,* in which she discussed her experiences as a single welfare mother raising two children while attending college, and her early days of social advocacy. "In order to go the policy front, I had to do the personal," she said. Lee graduated from Mills College in Oakland and got a degree in social work at the University of California at Berkeley. She started a community mental health center in Berkeley and then worked as a staffer for 12 years for Rep. Dellums, who chaired the House Armed Services Committee. She was elected to the California Assembly in 1990 and to the Senate in 1996. After Dellums announced he was resigning, he endorsed Lee as his successor, and she won the special election with 67% of the vote.

In the House, Lee is at the far left of the ideological spectrum. She wants to reduce the nation's weapons stockpiles and cut Pentagon spending sharply. She supports increased funding for international AIDS programs, and after a visit to Cuba, called for steps to end the 40-year trade embargo; the House accepted her amendment to lift restrictions on education travel to Cuba. As co-chair of the Progressive Caucus, she laid out an agenda with three priorities: economic justice and security, protection of civil rights and liberties, and promotion of global peace. She was a founder of the Out of Iraq Caucus, a group of the most vocal anti-war House members.

Lee has consistently opposed military action to the point of being a lonely but principled voice. She criticized President Clinton's bombing of Iraq in 1998. As most Democrats voted to authorize bombing of Serbia in 1999, Lee was the only House member to oppose a resolution supporting U.S. troops. In September 2001, she was the only member of Congress to vote against the resolution authorizing the use of force in response to the terrorist attacks. "If we rush to launch a counterattack, we run too great a risk that women, children, and other noncombatants will be caught in the crossfire," she said at the time. Her vote brought a torrent of national attention. Lee received threats of violence, and the Capitol police provided her with 24-hour protection. But there were supportive rallies in her district. During debate in October 2002 to authorize the use of force in Iraq, Lee offered an alternative calling for diplomatic action; it was defeated 355-72.

In 2008, Lee became chair of the Congressional Black Caucus, with plans to "really continue to be the conscience of the Congress." In February 2009, she criticized Senate cuts in the House-passed version of President Obama's economic stimulus bill. When Obama named conservative Republican Sen. Judd Gregg of New Hampshire as Commerce secretary, Lee was among the African-American leaders who complained about his past failure to support a full census count, especially of racial minorities. Gregg later withdrew as a nominee.

In 2007, House Speaker Nancy Pelosi gave Lee a seat on the powerful Appropriations Committee. She was the only Democrat on the panel to vote against the withdrawal timetable assembled by Democratic leaders; then she was one of 14 Democrats to vote against the funding bill on the House floor. "My conscience is that we can't put up more money to fund this war," said Lee, who supported what she called "a fully funded withdrawal." In July 2008, the House passed, 399-24, Lee's bill to prevent permanent U.S. military bases in Iraq or U.S. control of Iraqi oil. The House also passed her bill to encourage states to divest from companies that do business in Sudan, as a protest of the genocide in the Darfur region.

TENTH DISTRICT
Vacant

Election Results

2008 general	Ellen Tauscher (D)	192,226	(65%)	($1,049,777)
	Nicholas Gerber (R)	91,877	(31%)	($104,128)
	Eugene Ruyle (PF)	11,062	(4%)	
2008 primary	Ellen Tauscher (D)	unopposed		

Population		Race/Ethnicity		Work	
Pop. 2007:	690,534	White:	57.2%	Private:	75.2%
Change since 2000:	Up 8.0%	Black:	7.2%	Government:	15.8%
Urban:	96.5%	Hispanic:	19.6%	Self-employed:	8.9%
Rural:	3.5%	Asian:	11.7%	Blue collar:	17.5%
Area size:	1,085 sq. mi.	Native Am.:	0.3%	White collar:	67.5%
Age		Hawaiian:	0.3%	Khaki collar:	0.5%
Median age:	37.5 yrs.	Two+ races:	3.2%	Other:	14.5%
More than 65 yrs:	12.0%	*Ancestry*		Median income:	$77,937
Less than 18 yrs:	25.5%	German:	10.8%	Median home value:	$620,800
		Irish:	8.6%	Poverty:	7.8%
Education		English:	8.2%		
H.S. grad:	90.1%			**Military Veterans**	
College grad:	38.3%			% of Pop:	9.7%
Grad degree:	14.5%				

In the 1950s, when San Francisco and Oakland were already thriving cities, the rolling grasslands east of the mountain ridges were still mostly empty. In the years since, they have filled up. Freeways took the first commuters through the Caldecott Tunnel to the woodsy, trail-like roads of Orinda and Lafayette. Interstate 580 brought people east from the southern East Bay towns to the Amador Valley and Livermore, site of the Lawrence Livermore National Laboratory, which conducts nuclear warhead research. Interstate 680 running north-south provided a spine for businesses and shopping centers up

2008 Presidential Vote

Obama (D)	204,138	(65%)
McCain (R)	104,628	(33%)

2004 Presidential Vote

Kerry (D)	169,373	(59%)
Bush (R)	117,037	(40%)

Cook Partisan Voting Index: D + 11

and down the San Ramon Valley, from burgeoning Concord to Walnut Creek in Contra Costa County to points south. BART stations in Walnut Creek and Orinda took commuters to downtown San Francisco. Not all of the inhabitable areas are filled up yet, and local voters have passed measures to set limits on growth. But what has evolved in this sunny land, shielded by the mountains from the ocean fogs and rains, is a civilization of highly skilled and educated people. They are affluent and generally less culturally liberal than San Francisco, but they are concerned about preserving a physical environment that is one of America's most pleasant.

This territory is the heart of the 10th Congressional District of California. Redistricting in 2001 removed the San Ramon Valley south of Walnut Creek and added part of the Sacramento River Delta and parts of booming Solano County to the north. Fairfield is the largest city in the 10th, but suffered a big drop in residential property values when the recession hit in 2008. Travis Air Force Base, with its C-17 cargo haulers and constant traffic to and from Iraq, adds $1.4 billion annually to the local economy. From 2000 to 2007, about three-fourths of the population growth was attributable to Hispanics, who increased from 15% to 20% of the total. The district is largely Democratic. In 2004, Democratic presidential nominee John Kerry carried it 59%-40%, and in 2008, Democrat Barack Obama won it 65%-33%.

The 10th District has been represented since 1997 by Democrat Ellen Tauscher. In early 2009, President Barack Obama selected Tauscher to be undersecretary of State for arms control and international security. She was confirmed by the U.S. Senate on June 25, 2009. At *The Almanac's* press time, Republican Gov. Arnold Schwarzenegger had not yet scheduled a special election to choose a successor.

Prominent Democrats were jockeying for an anticipated competitive primary. State Sen. Mark DeSaulnier was the early front-runner, with endorsements from organized labor, Tauscher, and neighboring 7th District Rep. George Miller, a prominent California Democrat. A first-term senator, DeSaulnier previously chaired the California Assembly's Transportation Committee and served on the Contra Costa Board of Supervisors. First-term Assemblywoman Joan Buchanan also entered the contest, with encouragement from national women's groups. Democratic Lt. Gov. John Garamendi joined the field after abandoning his plan to run for governor in 2010. With the 10th District's Democratic tilt, a Republican candidate would have an uphill climb. Perhaps the best-known among local Republicans was Contra Costa Sheriff Warren Rupf. In the all-party primary, a candidate who gets 50% of the vote would win outright. If no one gets that amount, the top vote-getter from each party would compete in a runoff.

In the House, Tauscher chaired the Armed Committee's Strategic Forces Subcommittee—useful background for her State Department post. She supported the use of force in Iraq in 2002, but called for repeal of the resolution in 2007. She criticized the failure of the Pentagon to provide intelligence on Iraq. She also worked to stop the spread of nuclear, chemical and biological weapons, and to shift research from nuclear to conventional weapons.

ELEVENTH DISTRICT

Jerry McNerney (D)

Elected 2006, 2nd term; b. June 18, 1951, Albuquerque, NM; home, Pleasanton; Attended U.S. Military Academy, 1969–71, U. of NM, B.S. 1973, M.S. 1975, Ph.D. 1981; Catholic; married (Mary); 3 children.

Professional Career: National security contractor, Sandia National Laboratories, 1979–85; Engineer, U.S. Windpower, Kenetech, 1985–94; Energy consultant, 1994–99; CEO, start-up wind turbine manufacturer, 2000–06.

DC Office: 312 CHOB, 20515, 202-225-1947; Fax: 202-225-4060; Web site: mcnerney.house.gov.

State Offices: Pleasanton, 925-737-0727; Stockton, 209-476-8552.

Committees: *Energy & Commerce* (33rd of 36 D): Communications, Technology & the Internet; Energy & Environment. *Veterans' Affairs* (13th of 18 D): Health.

Group Ratings

	ADA	ACLU	AFS	LCV	ITIC	NTU	COC	ACU	CFG	FRC
2008	85	91	100	77	86	9	61	13	0	5
2007	95	—	91	90	—	9	50	4	7	—

National Journal Ratings

	2007 LIB	— 2007 CONS	2008 LIB	— 2008 CONS
Economic	78%	— 18%	55%	— 44%
Social	55%	— 45%	48%	— 50%
Foreign	75%	— 24%	59%	— 37%
Composite	70%	— 30%	55%	— 45%

Key Votes of the 110th Congress

1. Increase minimum wage	Y	5. Share immigration data	N	9. Withdraw troops 8/08	Y
2. Expand SCHIP	Y	6. Foreign aid abortion ban	N	10. No operations in Iran	Y
3. Raise CAFE standards	Y	7. Ban gay bias in workplace	Y	11. Free trade with Peru	N
4. Bail out financial markets	Y	8. Repeal D.C. gun law	Y	12. Overhaul FISA	Y

Election Results

2008 general	Jerry McNerney (D)..164,500	(55%)	($2,957,100)
	Dean Andal (R) 133,104	(45%)	($1,406,404)
2008 primary	Jerry McNerney (D)................................. unopposed		

Prior Winning Percentages: 2006 (53%)

Population		Race/Ethnicity		Work	
Pop. 2007:	763,111	White:	55.3%	Private:	77.0%
Change since 2000:	Up 19.4%	Black:	4.8%	Government:	14.9%
Urban:	90.1%	Hispanic:	23.3%	Self-employed:	7.9%
Rural:	9.9%	Asian:	12.6%	Blue collar:	18.8%
Area size:	2,316 sq. mi.	Native Am.:	0.5%	White collar:	66.2%
		Hawaiian:	0.4%	Khaki collar:	0.1%
Age		Two+ races:	2.8%	Other:	15.0%
Median age:	35.3 yrs.			Median income:	$76,465
More than 65 yrs:	9.9%	*Ancestry*		Median home value:	$579,000
Less than 18 yrs:	28.0%	German:	11.9%	Poverty:	8.2%
		Irish:	8.4%		
Education		English:	7.0%	**Military Veterans**	
H.S. grad:	86.5%			% of Pop:	8.9%
College grad:	31.3%				
Grad degree:	10.2%				

California is often defined by its cosmopolitan cities, its gorgeous Pacific coastline, and its world-class vineyards, but beyond Beverly Hills and Nob Hill, there is another California that likes to get its hands dirty. This is an old part of the state, settled in the 1840s beginning with the Gold Rush. When the fortune seekers departed, the land was left to a determined population of farmers. Crisscrossed with railroads and canals, the Central Valley became one

2008 Presidential Vote		
Obama (D) 169,183	(54%)
McCain (R)...............................139,863	(44%)
2004 Presidential Vote		
Bush (R) 151,397	(54%)
Kerry (D)...................................127,102	(45%)
Cook Partisan Voting Index: R + 1		

of the world's greatest agricultural regions. The San Joaquin River channel was deepened to 37 feet, and Stockton today is the Central Valley's ocean port. (The city is named after Robert Stockton, the second U.S. military governor of California, who captured Santa Barbara and Los Angeles from Mexico and proclaimed California U.S. territory.) The rich land attracted immigrants from all over: Mexicans came up Route 99 and joined North Dakotans flocking to the town of Lodi. Italian and Yugoslav immigrants brought their Old World crops. Yankees and Okies brought their distinct churches and beliefs. Later, Southeast Asian refugees crowded into the older streets of Stockton.

More recently, Stockton has positioned itself to take advantage of the region's economic strength by turning into a warehouse and distribution center for Northern California. This growth came even though the farm economy was threatened by actions to reduce water subsidies, the growing difficulty of attracting migrant workers for harvests, and a devastating drought that began in 2007 and has reduced the acreage of useable land. Many of the valley's crops, especially fruits and vegetables, are not subject to the vagaries of federal controls, though the area is still a big cotton producer. And the Central Valley has also become a suburban zone. Because of the high cost of living in San Francisco, Bay Area workers with modest incomes are increasingly buying lower-priced houses around Tracy and Stockton and commuting to work on Interstate 580, past the windmills of Altamont. While the Bay Area's population rose only 1% from 2000 to 2007, the population in Stockton's San Joaquin County increased 18%. In that period, Hispanics grew from 30% of the population to 36%. Stockton, now a growing urban center, is in the midst of a $125 million waterfront renovation project. The city's diversity led to its selection as a site for early testing of methods for the 2010 census.

The 11th Congressional District of California includes much of this area plus the Bay Area suburbs of San Ramon Valley in Contra Costa County. The central part of Stockton is in the 18th District, connected by a thin corridor to the valley further south. But the 11th does include northwest Stockton and most of the rest of San Joaquin County—Tracy, Lodi, and the almond center of Manteca. It also takes in the adjacent town of Brentwood in Contra Costa County, the fastest-growing city in the Bay Area in the 1990s and early 2000s. Brentwood nearly doubled in population from 2000 to 2006, but growth slowed considerably after the housing bust in 2007. The farm town of Morgan Hill anchors the far southern edge of the 11th in Santa Clara County. The San Ramon Valley towns—Danville and San Ramon in Contra Costa County, and Dublin and Pleasanton in Alameda County—are much more affluent than the Central Valley parts of the district. The district has moved cautiously toward Republicans on cultural issues and on the strength of farmers' hostility to environmental restrictions that impede their livelihoods. The San Ramon Valley is the most Republican part of the Bay Area, but that is not very Republican by national standards; it is fairly liberal on cultural issues and conservative on economic issues. This district, whose odd lines were drawn by Republicans in 2001 as their only Bay Area district, voted 54% for President George W. Bush in 2004. But Democrat Barack Obama carried it with 54% in 2008.

The congressman from the 11th District is Jerry McNerney, a Democrat who won in one of the most hard-fought contests of 2006. McNerney's father was a union organizer in the 1930s and later worked for the U.S. Geological Survey in Albuquerque, where Jerry McNerney was born. Along with his twin brother, McNerney was sent to a military boarding school in Hays, Kan., and he later won an appointment to the U.S. Military Academy. He left West Point after two years because he opposed the war in Vietnam and transferred to the University of New Mexico, where he eventually earned a doctoral degree in differential geometry. He spent several years as a contractor for Sandia National Laboratories, working on national security programs. In 1985, he moved to the private sector with U.S. Windpower. He later consulted for several utility companies that built windmills in the Altamont Pass. He became chief executive of a firm that planned to manufacture wind turbines. McNerney, who named his daughter Windy, claimed that his work contributed to saving the equivalent of 8.3 million tons of carbon dioxide. Before running for Congress, he had never held elected office.

McNerney was an unlikely winner against Republican Rep. Richard Pombo, a local rancher in an area where he was so well known, it was dubbed "Pombo Country." As the chairman of the House Resources Committee when the chamber was controlled by Republicans, Pombo was the leader of the property-rights movement backed by ranchers and farmers. When McNerney first challenged Pombo in 2004, he was crushed, 61%-39%. In the 2006 primary, the Democratic Congressional Campaign Committee endorsed another candidate because party officials didn't think McNerney could win. The DCCC unsuccessfully urged local legislators to run and then endorsed Steve Filson, an airline pilot and political neophyte who turned out to be a disappointment. McNerney, endorsed by the state party and by local organized labor, soundly defeated Filson, 53%-28%.

In the general election, Pombo outspent McNerney by nearly 2-to-1. McNerney managed nevertheless to turn the election into a referendum on the controversial seven-term incumbent. Pombo had attracted a withering assault from national environmental groups, which referred to him as an "eco-thug" and "Wildlife Enemy No. 1." The campaign contributions he received from disgraced lobbyist Jack Abramoff also came under close scrutiny. Over the summer, McNerney captured the imagination of liberal Internet activists and got a boost from the Net-roots. Democracy for America, a political action committee inspired by 2004 Democratic presidential candidate Howard Dean, endorsed him, triggering a wave of campaign contributions from around the country. As McNerney inched closer to Pombo in the polls, the DCCC began to air ads against the Republican. McNerney emphasized his background as an energy consultant and focused his attacks on Pombo's environmental voting record. The two candidates disagreed on virtually every issue, including the Iraq war, the partial privatization of Social Security, and oil exploration in Alaska. But Pombo was running against a strong anti-Republican wind. McNerney won 53%-47%. In San Joaquin County, which cast a bit more than half of the vote, Pombo led 51%-49%. But McNerney won comfortably in counties closer to the Bay Area, with 54% in Contra Costa, 63% in Alameda, and 61% in Santa Clara.

In the House, McNerney established a moderate voting record, especially on cultural issues. Democratic leaders gave him an early opportunity to sponsor a bill that won House passage—a pilot program to help communities with endangered water supplies to find alternative sources. In the 2007 energy bill, he added a provision to promote research and development of geothermal energy. And in 2009, with crucial help from Bay Area neighbor Nancy Pelosi, the Democratic House speaker, McNerney got a coveted slot on the influential Energy and Commerce Committee.

In February 2007, he joined senior Democrats seeking an August 2008 deadline to withdraw U.S. troops from Iraq, but he made liberal activists unhappy by saying he was willing to compromise with Republicans on the timing of a troop withdrawal mandate.

Widely viewed as one of the rare vulnerable Democrats in 2008, McNerney worked the district aggressively with "Congress at Your Corner" events and citizen advisory panels for issues such as agriculture, health care, and small business. He was also able to tout the $15 million for asparagus growers that he inserted in the final version of the 2008 farm bill, an earmark of great interest to Central Valley's asparagus farmers. Pombo announced in May 2007 that he would not try to win back the seat, and California Assemblyman Dean Andal became the Republican nominee. The GOP sought to tie McNerney to the more-liberal Pelosi, calling him a "Pelosi clone." Andal's campaign highlighted his reputation as a budget hawk in the Assembly, including his opposition to tax increases. He said he supported opening up more protected areas to oil drilling and that he would not support the effort in Congress to give illegal immigrants a path to citizenship.

But some Republicans said that Andal's campaign was poorly-financed and disorganized. Democrats criticized his conservative record in the Assembly, including his opposition to a bill that would have prevented employers from requiring women to wear dresses to work. Andal said the bill was a government intrusion on business, but Democrats dubbed him "Radical Andal." McNerney wound up winning re-election handily, 55%-45%. He led in each of the four counties. The closest outcome was in San Joaquin, where McNerney won 52%-48%. If he wins re-election in 2010, Democrats likely would seek to give McNerney more friendly district lines in the 2011 redrawing of the congressional map.

TWELFTH DISTRICT

Jackie Speier (D)

Elected April 2008, 1st full term; b. May 14, 1950, San Francisco; home, Hillsborough; U. of CA-Davis, B.A., 1972, U of CA-Hastings Col. of Law, J.D., 1976.; Catholic; married (Barry Dennis); 2 children.

Elected Office: San Mateo Cnty. Bd. of Supervisors, 1980–86, CA Assembly, 1986–96, CA Senate, 1998–2006.

Professional Career: Staff aide, Rep. Leo Ryan, 1973–78, Dir. government affairs, Community Gatepath, 1996–98, Dir. government affairs, Electronic Arts, 1996–98, attorney, 2007–08.

DC Office: 211 CHOB, 20515, 202-225-3531; Fax: 202-226-4183; Web site: speier.house.gov.

State Offices: San Mateo, 650-342-0300.

Committees: *Financial Services* (32nd of 42 D): Capital Markets, Insurance & Government Sponsored Enterprises; Financial Institutions & Consumer Credit; Oversight & Investigations. *Oversight & Government Reform* (23rd of 24 D): Government Management, Organization & Procurement.

Group Ratings

	ADA	ACLU	AFS	LCV	ITIC	NTU	COC	ACU	CFG	FRC
2008	60	100	100	89	100	7	43	0	5	0
2007	—	—	—	—	—	—	—	—	—	—

National Journal Ratings

	2007 LIB	—	2007 CONS	2008 LIB	—	2008 CONS
Economic	*%	—	*%	85%	—	0%
Social	*%	—	*%	82%	—	0%
Foreign	*%	—	*%	92%	—	0%
Composite	*%	—	*%	93%	—	7%

Key Votes of the 110th Congress

1. Increase minimum wage	*	5. Share immigration data	*	9. Withdraw troops 8/08	*
2. Expand SCHIP	*	6. Foreign aid abortion ban	*	10. No operations in Iran	*
3. Raise CAFE standards	*	7. Ban gay bias in workplace	*	11. Free trade with Peru	*
4. Bail out financial markets	Y	8. Repeal D.C. gun law	N	12. Overhaul FISA	N

Election Results

2008 general	Jackie Speier (D)	200,442	(75%)	($893,615)
	Greg Conlon (R)	49,258	(18%)	($103,889)
	Nathalie Hrizi (PF)	5,793	(2%)	
	Barry Hermanson (Green)	5,776	(2%)	($26,378)
	Kevin Peterson (Lib)	5,584	(2%)	
2008 primary	Jackie Speier (D)	60,393	(90%)	
	Michelle McMurry (D)	3,827	(6%)	
2008 spec. election	Jackie Speier (D)	66,279	(77%)	
	Greg Conlon (R)	7,990	(9%)	
	Michelle McMurry (D)	4,546	(5%)	
	Mike Moloney (R)	4,517	(5%)	

Population		Race/Ethnicity		Work	
Pop. 2007:	642,330	White:	44.6%	Private:	76.0%
Change since 2000:	Up 0.5%	Black:	2.3%	Government:	14.2%
Urban:	99.9%	Hispanic:	16.0%	Self-employed:	9.6%
Rural:	0.1%	Asian:	32.5%	Blue collar:	13.8%
Area size:	363 sq. mi.	Native Am.:	0.3%	White collar:	71.7%
		Hawaiian:	1.0%	Khaki collar:	0.0%
Age		Two+ races:	2.6%	Other:	14.5%
Median age:	40.7 yrs.			Median income:	$82,203
More than 65 yrs:	14.1%	*Ancestry*		Median home value:	$795,700
Less than 18 yrs:	20.2%	Irish:	8.0%	Poverty:	6.0%
		German:	7.3%		
Education		Italian:	6.0%	**Military Veterans**	
H.S. grad:	89.4%			% of Pop:	7.0%
College grad:	45.7%				
Grad degree:	15.9%				

The city of San Francisco sits at the tip of the San Francisco Peninsula on the California coast. This is geologically interesting, and active, country. The San Andreas Fault runs just east of the Coast Range, underneath the reservoirs that store San Francisco's water supply. To the west are green mountains running down to the ocean. To the east is a zone of flat land between mountain and bay, an unbroken chain of suburbs and urban settlement, with light industry and salt flats along the bay front,

2008 Presidential Vote
Obama (D) 214,850   (74%)
McCain (R)...............................69,029   (24%)

2004 Presidential Vote
Kerry (D)................................193,689   (72%)
Bush (R) 73,740   (27%)

Cook Partisan Voting Index: D + 23

and some residential neighborhoods and commercial strips. Daly City and Pacifica on the ocean are a kind of extension of San Francisco's old working-class districts, with boxy houses on streets looking out on the ocean or the freeway. Today, these neighborhoods are home to many of the Bay Area's Asian immigrants. Pacific Islanders are prominent, too. The nation's biggest concentration of Samoans is in Daly City, and the biggest concentration of Tongans is in San Bruno. On the Bay side is South San Francisco, where Herb Boyer and Bob Swanson sketched on a napkin their plans for the first biotechnology company, Genentech. They bought space in an old warehouse on the waterfront near a Bethlehem Steel plant. In March 2009, Genentech was purchased by the Swiss pharmaceutical firm Roche and had a market capitalization exceeding $100 billion, though the recession set back its growth. The area is one large biotech campus overlooking the Bay, with lawns, parkways, and earth-toned office complexes, the center of the industry. *YouTube,* the 2005 start-up that today is second to corporate parent Google as an Internet search provider, is headquartered in San Bruno, a few miles from the San Francisco airport. Farther south, between the Bayshore Freeway and Interstate 280, are middle-class suburbs that grew up to be cities with office complexes—Millbrae, Burlingame, San Mateo, and San Carlos.

The 12th Congressional District of California consists of these northern peninsula suburbs plus the southwest quadrant of the city of San Francisco, the middle-income Sunset district, with older houses on curving hills that were once sand dunes. It is an ethnically and racially diverse, economically productive part of America; 33% of its residents are Asian, one of the highest ratios among congressional districts, and another 16% are Hispanic. The economic orientation here was historically toward San Francisco, then later south toward the Silicon Valley, but now the district has its own burgeoning biotech industry. Income levels are among the highest in the state, very far above average. Politically, the peninsula was long a bastion of progressive Republicanism, a lively force in California from the election of Gov. Hiram Johnson in 1910 until the liberal Democratic breakthrough in 1958. But that tradition is only a memory now. In national and state elections, the 12th District votes overwhelmingly Democratic.

The congresswoman from the 12th is Jackie Speier *(SPEER),* a Democrat who won a special election in April 2008 to succeed Tom Lantos, the chairman of the House Foreign Affairs Committee who died during his 14th term in office. Born in San Francisco's Sunset district, she graduated from the University of California at Davis and got her law degree at U.C.'s Hastings College of Law. While an undergraduate, she interned in Sacramento for Democratic Assemblyman Leo Ryan and later joined his staff after he was elected to Congress. In November 1978, Speier accompanied third-term Rep. Ryan on a trip to Jonestown, Guyana, to investigate claims that some of Ryan's constituents, who were members of a church called the Peoples Temple, were being held against their will by the Rev. Jim Jones of San Francisco. Some defectors from the church joined Ryan's entourage for the journey home, but the group made it only as far as the airport. Four assassins sent by Jones opened fire on the defenseless group. Ryan and four others, including two journalists, were killed. Speier was shot five times and left for dead on the airstrip, where she waited 15 hours before the Guyana police rescued her. In the meantime, Jones, back at his jungle camp, set in motion events that shocked the world. He forced his cult followers to commit "revolutionary suicide" by drinking poison-laced punch, which resulted in the deaths of more than 900 followers, some of them babies and children.

Once back in California, Speier underwent 10 surgeries, including skin grafts. Despite her injuries, she ran in the special election to succeed Ryan, but she got only 15% of the total vote and finished third among Democrats in the primary. She returned to the Bay Area and built her political career, starting on the San Mateo County Board of Supervisors and then serving 18 years in the Legislature. Her pinnacle achievement was legislation protecting consumers' privacy from invasive practices by banks and insurance companies. In 2006, she unsuccessfully sought the nomination for lieutenant governor.

Before Lantos died, Speier explored running for his House seat in 2008, when Lantos would turn 80 years old. But Lantos, the only Holocaust survivor to serve in Congress, announced his retirement in early January, endorsed Speier as his successor, and died in February of complications from cancer of the esophagus. Speier immediately became the front-runner to succeed him. Stanford University law professor Larry Lessig, who has crusaded against the influence of money in politics, briefly considered a challenge, but decided not to run and candidly conceded that he would probably have lost to Speier. She won the all-party election with 75% of the vote against four little-known opponents.

In the House, Speier quickly established her mark as an ardent and sometimes outspoken liberal. Immediately after she took her oath of office, she caused an unusual ruckus when she launched a sharp partisan attack on President George W. Bush's handling of the war in Iraq. "History will not judge us kindly if we sacrifice four generations of Americans because of the folly of one," she declared. Her remarks triggered a volley of boos among Republican members on the House floor and prompted Republican Rep. Darrell Issa of California to walk out of the chamber. "Her conduct was inappropriate and violated House rules," Issa later said. Speier responded that she had been "forthright," and she called the Republicans' reaction "childlike and inappropriate in their treatment of a new member."

In September 2008, Speier got a bill passed renaming the San Mateo post office in honor of Leo Ryan. In other highlights of her first term, she called for a national speed limit of 60 miles per hour on freeways in urban areas to reduce gasoline consumption. As a member of the Financial Services Committee, she sponsored proposals to regulate credit agencies and to raise federal housing-loan limits in high-cost areas. Her opposition scuttled a bipartisan 2008 proposal to create an office of insurance information in the Treasury Department. She objected that the measure could pre-empt state laws that limit rate increases. In February 2009, Speier joined 20 mostly moderate House Democrats who voted against the omnibus spending bill. In particular, she criticized the approval of a slew of earmarks for individual lawmakers' districts "without spending enough time to fully examine where the money is going." She created her own citizens' panel to review congressional earmarks and chose Lessig to chair it.

THIRTEENTH DISTRICT

Pete Stark (D)

Elected 1972, 19th term; b. Nov. 11, 1931, Milwaukee, WI; home, Fremont; MIT, B.S. 1953, U. of CA, M.B.A. 1960; Unitarian; married (Deborah); 7 children.

Military Career: Air Force, 1955–57.

Professional Career: Founder, Beacon Savings & Loan Assn., 1961; Founder & pres., Security Natl. Bank, Walnut Creek, 1963–72.

DC Office: 239 CHOB, 20515, 202-225-5065; Fax: 202-226-3805; Web site: www.house.gov/stark.

State Offices: Fremont, 510-494-1388.

Committees: *Ways & Means* (2nd of 26 D): Health (Chmn); Income Security & Family Support. *Joint Committee on Taxation* (2nd of 3 D).

Group Ratings

	ADA	ACLU	AFS	LCV	ITIC	NTU	COC	ACU	CFG	FRC
2008	90	100	100	100	71	27	47	13	23	11
2007	80	—	100	100	—	10	47	4	13	—

National Journal Ratings

	2007 LIB	—	2007 CONS		2008 LIB	—	2008 CONS
Economic	67%	—	31%		68%	—	31%
Social	92%	—	0%		67%	—	33%
Foreign	61%	—	38%		83%	—	17%
Composite	75%	—	25%		73%	—	27%

Key Votes of the 110th Congress

1. Increase minimum wage	Y	5. Share immigration data	N	9. Withdraw troops 8/08	*
2. Expand SCHIP	Y	6. Foreign aid abortion ban	N	10. No operations in Iran	Y
3. Raise CAFE standards	Y	7. Ban gay bias in workplace	Y	11. Free trade with Peru	N
4. Bail out financial markets	N	8. Repeal D.C. gun law	N	12. Overhaul FISA	*

Election Results

2008 general	Pete Stark (D) 166,829	(76%)	($659,570)
	Raymond Chui (R) 51,447	(24%)	
2008 primary	Pete Stark (D) .... unopposed		

Prior Winning Percentages: 2006 (75%); 2004 (72%); 2002 (71%); 2000 (70%); 1998 (71%); 1996 (65%); 1994 (65%); 1992 (60%); 1990 (58%); 1988 (73%); 1986 (70%); 1984 (70%); 1982 (61%); 1980 (55%); 1978 (65%); 1976 (71%); 1974 (71%); 1972 (53%)

Population		Race/Ethnicity		Work	
Pop. 2007:	648,716	White:	31.2%	Private:	81.4%
Change since 2000:	Up 1.5%	Black:	7.0%	Government:	12.1%
Urban:	99.3%	Hispanic:	22.8%	Self-employed:	6.3%
Rural:	0.7%	Asian:	34.7%	Blue collar:	20.4%
Area size:	281 sq. mi.	Native Am.:	0.3%	White collar:	65.6%
		Hawaiian:	0.9%	Khaki collar:	0.2%
Age		Two+ races:	2.6%	Other:	13.8%
Median age:	36.7 yrs.			Median income:	$73,482
More than 65 yrs:	10.9%	*Ancestry*		Median home value:	$616,900
Less than 18 yrs:	24.5%	German:	6.0%	Poverty:	8.5%
		Irish:	4.9%		
Education		English:	4.6%	**Military Veterans**	
H.S. grad:	85.9%			% of Pop:	6.9%
College grad:	36.1%				
Grad degree:	12.6%				

The East Bay is the workaday, unglamorous side of the San Francisco Bay Area—a narrow strip of land between the bay and the surprisingly high mountains that rise just to the east. The shoreline is not picturesque, with its closed-down Navy bases and its docks, airports, and salt evaporators. The Bay Bridge, bisected by Yerba Buena Island, cuts an inspiring figure, though it requires constant patching; work is under way to add a new span, with completion scheduled in 2013. The San Mateo Bridge to the

2008 Presidential Vote		
Obama (D) 175,838	(74%)
McCain (R) 56,299	(24%)
2004 Presidential Vote		
Kerry (D) 153,598	(71%)
Bush (R) 60,559	(28%)
Cook Partisan Voting Index:	D + 22	

south of Oakland was still largely uninhabited farm fields. After the war, the area filled up, south along old Route 17: San Leandro, originally settled by Portuguese; Hayward with its California State University campus and seafood industry; Union City with its rail yards; Fremont, home of a General Motors/Toyota joint-venture auto plant; and Newark, with dozens of industrial plants ranging from salt processing to computer network servers. Hit hard by the dot-com bust, the East Bay revived with biotech, construction, and health care. Underneath the East Bay is the Hayward Fault, not as famous as the San Andreas, but just as dangerous. An earthquake there in 1868 registered about 7.0 on the Richter scale.

The 13th Congressional District of California is made up of this string of East Bay towns in Alameda County. The district is racially and ethnically mixed in the California manner. Fremont is home to the Little Kabul neighborhood of Afghans. Koreans and other Asians have moved in large numbers to Fremont and Hayward. In 2007, the district was 35% Asian, 23% Hispanic, and 7% African-American. This has long been a Democratic area. Democrat John Kerry got 71% of the vote here in 2004, and Democrat Barack Obama won it with 74% in 2008.

The congressman from the 13th District is Pete Stark, a liberal Democrat first elected in 1972. Stark grew up in Wisconsin, served in the Air Force, got an engineering degree at the Massachusetts Institute of Technology and a master's degree in business administration from the University of California at Berkeley. In 1963, he started a bank in Walnut Creek, which he later sold. An early opponent of the Vietnam War, he attracted attention, and accounts, all over the Bay Area when he put a giant peace symbol atop his bank headquarters and peace symbols on all of the checks. In 1972, he ran for Congress, spending his own money freely and beating 81-year-old incumbent George Miller in the primary 56%-22%. Stark held on in the George McGovern undertow that year to win the general election with 53% of the vote. By his third term, he had a safe seat and was on the powerful Ways and Means Committee, where he is now the second-ranking Democrat, and chairs the Health Subcommittee, which has a large role in setting health care policy.

In the House, Stark is a vocal advocate for the liberal wing of his party. For many years, his major focus has been using the power of the federal government to make health care more affordable and more broadly available. His record of legislative success is mixed. He has been effective in expanding Medicare benefits and making sure younger workers have continued coverage under COBRA health insurance plans. His major achievement was the Catastrophic Health Care Act of 1988, which created a new benefit for Medicare recipients. But it was overwhelmingly repealed in 1989 after an outpouring of protest from the elderly, who didn't like its tax on high-income seniors and thought that the benefits were insufficiently generous. He has supported universal health insurance bills in various forms.

During a dozen years in the minority, Stark mostly criticized Republican policies, found few areas of agreement with the opposing party, and had testy personal dealings with his GOP counterparts. He was one of two House members to vote against the 1996 Kennedy-Kassebaum bill, on the grounds that it did not include mental health coverage and extended patent protection for a drug. Much later, when President George W. Bush presented his proposal for prescription drug coverage for seniors, Stark countered with a plan that would guarantee affordable and comprehensive coverage for all seniors under Medicare. But other than voicing criticism from the sidelines, he had little role in the debate on the Medicare prescription drug bill in 2003. When the projected 10-year cost of providing the new benefit ballooned to $720 billion, Stark sniffed, "I told you so. We can't trust numbers provided by administration officials." He continued to push for the importation of U.S. prescription drugs from other countries, where they are sold more cheaply, and opposed trade agreements with nations that wouldn't allow the practice. When AARP, the venerable advocacy group for the elderly, offered its own prescription drug plan, he attacked the group for seeking to "leverage a trusting membership of America's seniors to pass legislation that you know will do little more than line your own pocket."

Once Democrats gained the majority, Stark in 2007 played a central role in pushing the bill to expand the State Children's Health Insurance Program. After Congress failed to override Bush's veto of the legislation, Barack Obama in early 2009 enacted the SCHIP legislation with his first signature as president. And Stark went to work on a bill to provide universal health insurance in the United States, which he predicted would become law during Obama's first term.

Stark has a distinct maverick streak. He was one of two House members, for example, to vote against repeal of the 3% telephone excise tax. His willingness to go his own way extended to cultural issues when he was one of three House members who opposed the resolution denouncing the 9th Circuit Court of Appeals decision that declared the Pledge of Allegiance unconstitutional. In 2003, he called the bombing of Iraq "an act of extreme terrorism." Stark co-sponsored a plan to reinstate the military draft as a way of criticizing what he viewed as the disproportionate burden the war placed on the poor and minorities. The House defeated the measure 402-2. During the debate on SCHIP, he harshly chided Republicans who opposed the bill, saying they preferred to spend government money "to blow up innocent people if we can get enough kids to grow old enough for you to send to Iraq, to get their heads blown off for the president's amusement." Angry Republicans filed a resolution to censure Stark, which 173 House members, including five freshman Democrats, supported; Stark apologized.

Known for his incendiary debating style, he concedes that his remarks are sometimes "unnecessary." At a 2001 Ways and Means subcommittee hearing, he referred to Rep. J.C. Watts of Oklahoma, who is African-American, as the "current Republican Conference chairman, whose children were all born out of wedlock." In 1995, he called mild-mannered Republican Rep. Nancy Johnson of Connecticut a "whore for the insurance industry." And after Rep. Scott McInnis, R-Colo., told him to "shut up" in 2003, Stark replied, "You think you are big enough to make me, you little wimp. Come over here and make me, I dare you. You little fruitcake." The *San Francisco Chronicle* then reported "rumblings that it might be time for the veteran congressman to retire." But Stark said he had no intention of leaving Congress. "I've got to keep running," he said. "I've got 2-year-old twins and I've got to get them through college. Our retirement plan is good, but it ain't that good."

In March 2007, he again attracted attention for describing his religious affiliation as "a Unitarian who does not believe in a supreme being." Atheist groups then claimed that Stark was the first member of Congress and the highest-ranking American politician to say he does not believe in God.

Stark is next in line to head Ways and Means after current Chairman Charles Rangel of New York. Some have speculated that if Rangel retires, another committee Democrat might challenge Stark for the chairmanship. It seems more likely that House Speaker Nancy Pelosi would protect her Bay Area colleague but also keep a tight leash on him. Despite occasional talk of a serious primary challenge against Stark, well-known local politicians have shown no interest in running.

FOURTEENTH DISTRICT

Anna Eshoo (D)

Elected 1992, 9th term; b. Dec. 13, 1942, New Britain, CT; home, Atherton; Canada Col., A.A. 1975; Catholic; divorced; 2 children.

Elected Office: San Mateo Cnty. Bd. of Supervisors, 1982–92, pres., 1986.

Professional Career: Chmn., San Mateo Cnty. Dem. Party, 1980; Chief of staff, CA Assembly speaker, 1981.

DC Office: 205 CHOB, 20515, 202-225-8104; Fax: 202-225-8890; Web site: www.eshoo.house.gov.

State Offices: Palo Alto, 650-323-2984.

Committees: *Energy & Commerce* (8th of 36 D): Communications, Technology & the Internet; Health. *Intelligence (Select)* (3rd of 13 D): Intelligence Community Management (Chmn.).

Group Ratings

	ADA	ACLU	AFS	LCV	ITIC	NTU	COC	ACU	CFG	FRC
2008	90	100	100	100	100	8	61	0	4	5
2007	95	—	100	90	—	6	55	0	12	—

National Journal Ratings

	2007 LIB	—	2007 CONS	2008 LIB	—	2008 CONS
Economic	69%	—	28%	71%	—	25%
Social	77%	—	17%	82%	—	0%
Foreign	81%	—	16%	85%	—	8%
Composite	78%	—	22%	84%	—	16%

Key Votes of the 110th Congress

1. Increase minimum wage	Y	5. Share immigration data	N	9. Withdraw troops 8/08	Y
2. Expand SCHIP	Y	6. Foreign aid abortion ban	N	10. No operations in Iran	Y
3. Raise CAFE standards	Y	7. Ban gay bias in workplace	Y	11. Free trade with Peru	Y
4. Bail out financial markets	Y	8. Repeal D.C. gun law	N	12. Overhaul FISA	N

Election Results

2008 general	Anna Eshoo (D)	190,301	(70%)	($1,476,279)
	Ronny Santana (R)	60,610	(22%)	
	Brian Holtz (Lib)	11,929	(4%)	
	Carol Brouillet (Green)	9,926	(4%)	
2008 primary	Anna Eshoo (D)	unopposed		

Prior Winning Percentages: 2006 (71%); 2004 (70%); 2002 (68%); 2000 (70%); 1998 (69%); 1996 (65%); 1994 (61%); 1992 (57%)

Population		Race/Ethnicity		Work	
Pop. 2007:	645,252	White:	55.3%	Private:	80.9%
Change since 2000:	Up 1.0%	Black:	2.8%	Government:	8.8%
Urban:	93.6%	Hispanic:	18.9%	Self-employed:	10.1%
Rural:	6.4%	Asian:	19.2%	Blue collar:	10.9%
Area size:	1,030 sq. mi.	Native Am.:	0.2%	White collar:	75.2%
		Hawaiian:	0.7%	Khaki collar:	0.0%
Age		Two+ races:	2.5%	Other:	13.9%
Median age:	38.6 yrs.			Median income:	$90,905
More than 65 yrs:	12.2%	*Ancestry*		Median home value:	$591,700
Less than 18 yrs:	23.1%	German:	9.5%	Poverty:	7.3%
		English:	8.2%		
Education		Irish:	7.2%	**Military Veterans**	
H.S. grad:	90.5%			% of Pop:	6.9%
College grad:	56.0%				
Grad degree:	27.9%				

Silicon Valley is a place and a state of mind, an area that had no distinctive identity three decades ago but that people all over the world today recognize and imitate. In the 1980s and '90s, Silicon Valley emerged as the center of America's computer industry, a place where creative minds develop products that large corporations never thought would sell. Its beginnings can be traced back to 1939, when William Hewlett and David Packard started their electronics firm in a Palo Alto garage, or perhaps even

2008 Presidential Vote		
Obama (D) 213,671	(73%)
McCain (R)..............................72,707	(25%)
2004 Presidential Vote		
Kerry (D)...............................188,864	(68%)
Bush (R) 83,326	(30%)
Cook Partisan Voting Index:	D + 21	

to 1891, when Stanford University was founded on the estate of a California governor and senator. Not every aspect of the computer business is centered here. Microsoft, routinely disparaged in every Palo Alto espresso shop and bar, is in Redmond, Wash., and the downsized IBM is in Armonk, N.Y., But Silicon Valley is where most of the giants and much of the creativity of the high-tech business—as well as many dot-coms—have been based.

How did Silicon Valley come to be where it is? One factor is Stanford, the students it attracts and produces, and its tradition of encouraging faculty members to pursue profit-making activity. Another key component is venture capital, widely available from innovation-minded old San Francisco money, dispensed mostly from nondescript office buildings on Sand Hill Road on the reclaimed flatlands along San Francisco Bay. A third ingredient is the presence of smart young innovators, attracted to the Valley's lifestyle. Elite law and medical school graduates head to the prestigious, high-salary jobs of central cities. But techies are free to live in this pleasant, healthy environment. Sheltered by hills from coastal fogs and rains, Silicon Valley boasts a sunny climate with perceptible but gentle seasons, perfect for year-round outdoor sports. There may well be more jogging trails and bicycle paths here than anywhere else in the country. These communities were rustic but never poor, rural but not small-minded, country-like but still easily accessible to urban luxuries. People here were ahead of the rest of the nation in fighting for the environment, in favoring natural over processed foods, and in incorporating regular exercise into busy lives.

And the area has been quick to adapt to change. In the 1980s, in the face of threats from Japanese firms, Silicon Valley shifted to microprocessors and personal computers. In the 1990s, when PCs became a low-profit commodity business, Silicon Valley shifted to the Internet. Yahoo and Hotmail reportedly were conceived at Buck's restaurant, the networking nexus in Woodside. When the Internet bubble burst in 2000, however, Silicon Valley fell on hard times. By one estimate, the area lost 220,000 jobs, nearly two-thirds of the 350,000 created during the dot-com boom. Stock prices plummeted and real estate prices did too, though they are still among the highest in the nation. The area actually lost population from 2000 to 2003. Billions of dollars in paper wealth disappeared, and technology exports from California fell. The question became whether Silicon Valley still had the ability to adapt. Before the 2008 recession, the Valley was in an upturn, with rising profits and a net gain of jobs, including increased research and investment in clean energy. But the recession took a toll in home values and start-up businesses. More than 140,000 jobs at Silicon Valley companies were lost in 2008, according to one local estimate.

The 14th Congressional District of California includes much of Silicon Valley, along with Menlo Park, Palo Alto, and most of Redwood City. Further south along El Camino Real are Mountain View and the several thousand employees of Google. Sunnyvale is the district's largest city. There are some ultra-wealthy enclaves here: Woodside, with its mansions dotting the hills, and Portola Valley and Los Altos Hills, with stark contemporary homes overlooking San Francisco Bay. Over the mountains, the district takes in the little town of Half Moon Bay, with its pumpkin farms rising over the ocean. Imposing redwoods grow within 5 miles of spectacular beaches. The 14th's political heritage is progressive, with a sort of environmentalist, dovish, culturally liberal but entrepreneurial Republicanism, typified by former Reps. Pete McCloskey, Ed Zschau, and Tom Campbell, each of whom quit the House to run unsuccessfully for the Senate between 1982 and 2000. But this kind of Republican is now virtually extinct, and Silicon Valley has become Democratic. In 2008, Barack Obama won this district 73%-25%.

The congresswoman from the 14th District is Anna Eshoo, a Democrat first elected in 1992. Born in Connecticut, Eshoo *(EH-shoo)* is the only member of Congress of Assyrian descent. Her father, a jeweler and an FDR Democrat, sparked her interest in politics at a young age by taking her to political rallies. The family moved to California. Eshoo married and had two children, and for a while was a stay-at-home mother working on a degree in English literature. (She later divorced.) Eshoo was active in civic groups, then chaired the San Mateo County Democratic Party and in 1982 was elected to the San Mateo Board of Supervisors. In 1988, she ran for the U.S. House against incumbent Republican Tom Campbell. The two spent a total of $2.5 million, and Eshoo was the first congressional candidate to distribute videotapes to voters. Campbell won 52%-46%. In 1992, Campbell gave up his seat to run for the Senate, and Eshoo ran for his House seat. In the primary, she beat Assemblyman Ted Lempert, who had strong backing from environmentalists but lost ground by making unsubstantiated attacks against Eshoo. She prevailed 40%-36%. In the general election, Eshoo had a tough contest against Republican Tom Huening, the San

Mateo supervisor who was backed by David Packard and other Silicon Valley business leaders. But Eshoo won by a convincing 57%-39%. She has not had a serious challenge for re-election.

In the House, Eshoo's voting record has been mostly liberal with more-moderate inclinations on issues such as taxes that affect high-income earners in her district. She was not enthusiastic about supporting President Clinton's 1993 budget and tax bill. She joined Republicans and high-tech interests in votes on securities litigation and normalizing trade relations with China. Despite local pressure, she voted against granting President George W. Bush broad authority to negotiate trade deals and against the Central American Free Trade Agreement. She opposed a proposal to charge stock options against earnings, which would have hit hard in Silicon Valley. Eshoo also fought telecommunications legislation that would have allowed Internet carriers to have a two-tier pricing system, contending that it would disadvantage start-up firms.

As a senior member of the Energy and Commerce Committee, Eshoo was instrumental in preparing the party's Innovation Agenda, which calls for energy independence within a decade. She has also been active on health technology issues. In 2008, the House passed her bill to increase research and support services for arthritis victims, and she also sponsored a bill to reduce the volume of television commercials. Eshoo's other legislative work includes enactment of bills to increase Internet access for schools, allow the use of electronic signatures in business transactions, and improve access to treatment for low-income women with breast and cervical cancer. Another of her bills required insurance companies to pay for reconstructive surgery for cancer patients.

Eshoo is a member of House Speaker Nancy Pelosi's inner circle. The two women have been close friends and confidants since they met at a Democratic event in the Bay Area in the early 1970s, and their families have spent time together. Eshoo is a fierce and loyal advocate for Pelosi.

FIFTEENTH DISTRICT

Mike Honda (D)

Elected 2000, 5th term; b. June 27, 1941, Walnut Creek; home, San Jose; San Jose St. U., B.S. 1969, B.A. 1970, M.A. 1973; Protestant; widowed; 2 children.

Elected Office: San Jose Unified Sch. Bd., 1981–90; Santa Clara Cnty. Bd. of Supervisors, 1990–96; CA Assembly, 1996–2000.

Professional Career: Peace Corps, 1965–67; Elem. schl. principal, 1978–90.

DC Office: 1713 LHOB, 20515, 202-225-2631; Fax: 202-225-2699; Web site: honda.house.gov.

State Offices: Campbell, 408-558-8085.

Committees: *Appropriations* (28th of 37 D): Commerce, Justice, Science & Related Agencies; Labor, HHS, Education & Related Agencies; Legislative Branch.

Group Ratings

	ADA	ACLU	AFS	LCV	ITIC	NTU	COC	ACU	CFG	FRC
2008	95	100	100	100	100	5	50	0	0	5
2007	95	—	100	90	—	4	58	0	11	—

National Journal Ratings

	2007 LIB	—	2007 CONS	2008 LIB	—	2008 CONS
Economic	82%	—	0%	85%	—	0%
Social	92%	—	0%	82%	—	0%
Foreign	94%	—	4%	85%	—	8%
Composite	94%	—	6%	91%	—	9%

Key Votes of the 110th Congress

1. Increase minimum wage	Y	5. Share immigration data	N	9. Withdraw troops 8/08	Y
2. Expand SCHIP	Y	6. Foreign aid abortion ban	N	10. No operations in Iran	Y
3. Raise CAFE standards	Y	7. Ban gay bias in workplace	Y	11. Free trade with Peru	Y
4. Bail out financial markets	Y	8. Repeal D.C. gun law	N	12. Overhaul FISA	N

Election Results

2008 general	Mike Honda (D)	170,977	(72%)	($833,894)
	Joyce Stoer Cordi (R)	55,489	(23%)	
	Peter Myers (Green)	12,123	(5%)	
2008 primary	Mike Honda (D)	unopposed		

Prior Winning Percentages: 2006 (72%); 2004 (72%); 2002 (66%); 2000 (54%)

Population		Race/Ethnicity		Work	
Pop. 2007:	661,278	White:	41.0%	Private:	83.8%
Change since 2000:	Up 3.5%	Black:	2.3%	Government:	9.2%
Urban:	99.3%	Hispanic:	19.7%	Self-employed:	6.8%
Rural:	0.7%	Asian:	33.6%	Blue collar:	15.0%
Area size:	289 sq. mi.	Native Am.:	0.3%	White collar:	72.1%
Age		Hawaiian:	0.4%	Khaki collar:	0.0%
Median age:	37.0 yrs.	Two+ races:	2.3%	Other:	12.9%
More than 65 yrs:	10.6%	*Ancestry*		Median income:	$83,228
Less than 18 yrs:	23.7%	German:	7.4%	Median home value:	$713,300
Education		Irish:	5.7%	Poverty:	7.7%
H.S. grad:	88.0%	English:	5.5%	**Military Veterans**	
College grad:	44.5%			% of Pop:	6.4%
Grad degree:	18.0%				

A few decades ago, the broad valley of Santa Clara County around San Jose was mostly orchards and vineyards. Sheltered by mountains from the chilly ocean fogs, with soil incredibly fertile once it was irrigated, this valley produced peaches, plums, prunes, apricots, and grapes and made San Jose the nation's biggest fruit-packing center. Today, subdivisions, shopping centers, and office buildings have replaced the orchards, and Santa Clara County has a population of 1.7 million. San Jose, with a growing

2008 Presidential Vote
Obama (D) 174,571   (68%)
McCain (R)...............................75,753   (30%)

2004 Presidential Vote
Kerry (D)................................145,007   (63%)
Bush (R) 82,742   (36%)

Cook Partisan Voting Index: D + 15

downtown, an arena for its National Hockey League team, and 940,000 people, has become a major American city. In 2005, it replaced Detroit on the list of the nation's 10 largest cities. But this has not been a family-friendly increase: a shortage of students has led to the closing of several schools. Despite price declines triggered by the recession, real estate prices in the San Jose metropolitan area were the highest in the nation in 2008.

The 15th Congressional District consists of the central slice of still-growing Santa Clara County, which is the sixth biggest in the state and has large numbers of Chinese, Vietnamese, and Mexican immigrants. Nearly half of the district's population is in San Jose, and the majority of those residents live in the city's affluent neighborhoods. West of San Jose, the district includes the cities of Santa Clara and Cupertino, where Steve Jobs started Apple in a garage in the 1970s and where the company is still headquartered. The district also includes the salt flats of San Jose, now the site of a Great America theme park; the heavily Asian city of Milpitas; and, far to the south, connected by a swath of mountains, Gilroy, the garlic capital of the world. Outside of Hawaii, this district has the highest percentage of Asians in the nation, 34%. In Cupertino, where Asians are nearly a majority, their influence has made them a political force. This area was once marginal political territory but is now heavily Democratic. John Kerry got 63% of the vote here in 2004, and Barack Obama got 68% in 2008.

The congressman from the 15th District is Mike Honda, a Democrat first elected in 2000. Honda's grandparents came to the United States from Japan's Kumamoto Prefecture, which served as the primary battleground for the Seinan Civil War in the 1870s (memorialized in the film *The Last Samurai*). Honda was born in Walnut Creek and spent 14 months during his childhood in a World War II internment camp in Colorado. His wife, Jeanne, who died of cancer in 2004, was born in Hiroshima and survived the atomic attack before immigrating to the United States several years later. Honda received his bachelor's and master's degrees from San Jose State University and served two years in the Peace Corps in El Salvador, where he became fluent in Spanish and gained a passion for teaching.

In 1971, San Jose Mayor Norman Mineta appointed him to the city Planning Commission. Honda worked as a science teacher, and then was a principal at two area elementary schools from 1978 to 1986; during that period, he served on the San Jose Unified School Board. He was then elected to the Santa Clara County Board of Supervisors. In 1996, he was elected to the California Assembly, where he worked to reduce classroom sizes and increase teacher benefits. He also tried to secure an apology from Japan for its wartime atrocities against other Asian nations.

In 2000, Republican Rep. Tom Campbell decided to run against Sen. Dianne Feinstein, D-Calif. At first Honda was reluctant to run for the House, but persuasive telephone calls from several leading House Democrats and, finally, from President Clinton, changed his mind. Honda won the primary over Bill Peacock, a venture capitalist, 67% to 24%. His Republican opponent was Assemblyman Jim Cunneen, a Campbell protégé who was strongly supported by national GOP leaders and many Silicon Valley capitalists. Cunneen favored liberal positions on cultural issues, and he tried to depict the contest as a referendum on the old economy versus the new. Honda, despite his close ties to unions, supported normal trade relations with China, a position strongly backed by the high-tech industry. He won 54%-42%.

Honda has been among the most liberal members of the House. He chairs the Congressional Asian Pacific American Caucus, which advocates for underrepresented groups on issues such as immigration and expanding the State Children's Health Insurance Program. He helped to enact a cyber-security law that funds training and programs to protect computer data and networks. He was a major architect of the Nanotechnology Research and Development Act of 2003 to encourage the development of networked facilities, which involve the manipulation of matter at the atomic level. This has become a booming technology in the Bay Area.

In 2007, with help from House Speaker Nancy Pelosi, he got a seat on the powerful Appropriations Committee, which controls the government purse strings. He has focused on trying to win full funding for education programs, many of which are financed at levels well below what is called for in the enabling legislation.

Honda has also continued his quest to prompt apologies from Japan, publicizing the cause of American POWs in World War II who were transported on "hell ships" to work as slave laborers in Japan. More recently, Honda in 2007 won House passage of a resolution calling on Tokyo to apologize for forcing as many as 200,000 women into sexual slavery during the war. His efforts have generated controversy in Japan, and *The New York Times* referred to Honda as "one of the most famous American congressmen in his ancestral land." In September 2008, Honda called the comments of Republican Jason Chaffetz of Utah "offensive and embarrassing to all Americans" when Chaffetz called for the detention of illegal immigrants in tent cities as part of his campaign for the House.

Honda cast one of the three votes against a resolution condemning a decision by the U.S. Court of Appeals for the 9th Circuit that found the words "under God" in the Pledge of Allegiance unconstitutional. He sponsored a bill stating that military recruiters must have parents' consent to contact their children. Another of his passions is addressing low voter turnout in national elections, a situation he calls a "serious illness." He has a bill to reschedule federal elections for the first full weekend in November. As vice chairman of the Democratic National Committee during the 2008 campaign, Honda criss-crossed the nation to try to spark more participation by Asian-Americans in the election. Larry Gerston, a political scientist at San Jose State University, told the *San Jose Mercury News* that rather than take high-profile leadership roles, Honda prefers to put together coalitions for causes that might not otherwise get attention. "He really puts the K in 'Kumbaya,' " Gerston said.

SIXTEENTH DISTRICT

Zoe Lofgren (D)

Elected 1994, 8th term; b. Dec. 21, 1947, San Mateo; home, San Jose; Stanford U., B.A. 1970, U. of Santa Clara Law Schl., J.D. 1975; Protestant; married (John Collins); 2 children.

Elected Office: Santa Clara Bd. of Supervisors, 1980–94.

Professional Career: Staff Asst., U.S. Rep. Don Edwards, 1970–78; Practicing atty., 1978–80; Prof., U. of Santa Clara Law Schl., 1981–94.

DC Office: 102 CHOB, 20515, 202-225-3072; Fax: 202-225-3336; Web site: lofgren.house.gov.

State Offices: San Jose, 408-271-8700.

Committees: *Homeland Security* (6th of 20 D): Border, Maritime & Global Counterterrorism. *House Administration* (2nd of 6 D): Elections (Chmn). *Judiciary* (7th of 24 D): Commercial & Administrative Law; Crime, Terrorism & Homeland Security; Immigration, Citizenship, Border Security & International Law (Chmn). *Standards of Official Conduct* (Chmn. of 5 D).

Group Ratings

	ADA	ACLU	AFS	LCV	ITIC	NTU	COC	ACU	CFG	FRC
2008	100	100	100	100	100	5	56	0	4	5
2007	95	—	100	100	—	5	55	0	12	—

National Journal Ratings

	2007 LIB — 2007 CONS		2008 LIB — 2008 CONS	
Economic	82%	0%	85%	0%
Social	88%	12%	82%	0%
Foreign	78%	20%	70%	25%
Composite	86%	14%	85%	15%

Key Votes of the 110th Congress

1. Increase minimum wage	Y	5. Share immigration data	N	9. Withdraw troops 8/08	Y
2. Expand SCHIP	Y	6. Foreign aid abortion ban	N	10. No operations in Iran	Y
3. Raise CAFE standards	Y	7. Ban gay bias in workplace	Y	11. Free trade with Peru	Y
4. Bail out financial markets	Y	8. Repeal D.C. gun law	N	12. Overhaul FISA	N

Election Results

2008 general	Zoe Lofgren (D) 146,481	(71%)	($592,974)
	Charel Winston (R) 49,399	(24%)	
	Steven Wells (Lib) 9,447	(5%)	
2008 primary	Zoe Lofgren (D) .... unopposed		

Prior Winning Percentages: 2006 (73%); 2004 (71%); 2002 (67%); 2000 (72%); 1998 (73%); 1996 (66%); 1994 (65%)

Population		Race/Ethnicity		Work	
Pop. 2007:	641,310	White:	28.1%	Private:	82.4%
Change since 2000:	Up 0.3%	Black:	3.1%	Government:	10.2%
Urban:	98.7%	Hispanic:	38.4%	Self-employed:	7.2%
Rural:	1.3%	Asian:	27.5%	Blue collar:	22.5%
Area size:	232 sq. mi.	Native Am.:	0.3%	White collar:	60.4%
Age		Hawaiian:	0.4%	Khaki collar:	0.0%
Median age:	34.5 yrs.	Two+ races:	1.9%	Other:	17.1%
More than 65 yrs:	9.2%	*Ancestry*		Median income:	$73,419
Less than 18 yrs:	25.4%	German:	5.7%	Median home value:	$662,300
Education		Irish:	4.3%	Poverty:	11.4%
H.S. grad:	78.6%	English:	3.9%	**Military Veterans**	
College grad:	31.4%			% of Pop:	5.5%
Grad degree:	10.8%				

With more people than San Francisco, a tradition of high-tech innovation, and a professional sports team, San Jose finally has great claims on national attention and respect. Yet San Jose does not register on the national consciousness as it should. At the southern end of the Bay, it remains in the shadow of the city on the Golden Gate. San Francisco is every tourist's idea of a city: geographically compact, with picturesque public transportation; old and new immigrant groups; an economy historically based on

2008 Presidential Vote
Obama (D) 154,324	(70%)
McCain (R)..............................63,975	(29%)

2004 Presidential Vote
Kerry (D)................................125,415	(63%)
Bush (R) 70,190	(36%)

Cook Partisan Voting Index: D + 16

heavy industry and sea trade; a large city bureaucracy; and a monumental City Hall. San Jose is quite different. It got its start as a farm-market town, with canneries and fruit-packing operations for the produce from the surrounding fertile plains. Farm-labor icon Cesar Chavez settled with his family in the East San Jose barrio of Sal Si Puedes ("get out if you can"). San Jose sits not on the Bay but on the Southern Pacific rail line above the marshes and salt evaporators. Its major transportation arteries are the freeways—U.S. 101, Interstates 280, 680, and 880, California 17—that encircle its revitalized downtown. In August 2008, voters approved a 16-mile extension of the Bay Area Rapid Transit system into Santa Clara County.

Starting in the 1950s, San Jose grew in every direction, with developers hopscotching across the farmland and at times putting up subdivisions faster than the few city employees could update the street maps. Economically, San Jose has been sustained by everything from its traditional agriculture to manufacturing to the high-tech businesses that are centered in Silicon Valley towns just to the west but are omnipresent here: an American city, 21st-century style. Santa Clara County had the highest median household income in the Bay Area, and it held up comparatively well when the recession hit in 2007.

For many years, San Jose has been viewed as a focal point for immigration issues. It has Northern California's largest Mexican-American community, many of whose members are farmworkers. Now there is a diverse immigrant presence, with large numbers from Latin America and East and South Asia. Nearly half of all Santa Clara County residents speak a language other than English at home, mostly Spanish, Vietnamese, or Chinese, and one in three are foreign-born.

The 16th Congressional District of California consists of about two-thirds of San Jose, plus a nearby unincorporated area to the south. More than 90% of its residents live inside the jagged city limits of San Jose. It includes the old and new downtowns and the heavily Mexican-American areas to the east. It has the largest Hispanic share (38%) of any district in the Bay Area, and the largest concentration of Vietnamese in the country. Politically, it is solidly Democratic.

The congresswoman from the 16th District is Zoe Lofgren, a Democrat first elected in 1994. Lofgren grew up in the Bay Area, where her father was a Teamsters truck driver and her mother worked for the Machinists Union. She graduated from Stanford University, and then moved to Washington to work for Democratic Rep. Don Edwards while he was a leader on the Judiciary Committee that voted to impeach President Richard Nixon. She stayed on for eight years as an aide to Edwards. She met her husband, a lawyer, one Election Night. Lofgren returned to California to get a law degree, and then specialized in immigration law. In 1980, she was elected to the Santa Clara County Board of Supervisors. When Edwards retired, Lofgren ran for his House seat. Her chief Democratic opponent, former San Jose Mayor Tom McEnery, was better known. But Lofgren raised almost twice as much money, with support from national women's organizations and women in the California delegation. She gained considerable recognition after she insisted on listing herself as a county supervisor/mother on the ballot. Election officials refused, and the national press covered the ensuing controversy. Lofgren won the primary 45%-42%, and easily won the general election.

Her predecessor never spent a day in the minority during his 32 years in the House, but that's where Lofgren found herself for 12 years. Still, she had some impact, and her voting record, while mostly liberal, includes bipartisan free-market positions responsive to local businesses. Working with Republican David Dreier, a fellow Californian, she won expanded allotments of visas for high-tech workers. She pushed for looser controls on encryption exports, securities litigation limitations, and relaxation of trade restraints on supercomputers, all big Silicon Valley causes. When the House split 210-210 on a proposal to restrict government access to library records, Lofgren was the only House member to vote "present." She said that the amendment went too far in preventing legitimate law enforcement searches.

When Democrats won the majority in 2006, Lofgren, a trusted lieutenant of House Speaker Nancy Pelosi's, did not lack for good committee assignments. She became chairwoman of the Judiciary Subcommittee on Immigration, Citizenship, Refugees, Border Security, and International Law, which deals with issues familiar to her. She hopes to see a major overhaul of immigration policy enacted in 2009, something that has eluded Congress for several years as lawmakers became mired in deep differences in approach: tougher border security versus allowing illegal immigrants already working in the country to attain legal status.

Lofgren also chaired the Election Subcommittee of the House Administration Committee, where she investigated problems with electronic voting machines and reviewed proposals for redistricting reform. In January 2009, Pelosi picked her to chair the House Committee on Standards of Official Conduct, informally known as the Ethics Committee. She took over as a politically sensitive inquiry was under way involving House Ways and Means Chairman Charles Rangel, D-N.Y., and questions were being raised about other senior Democrats' connections to lobbyists. Lofgren's skills as a former staffer and law professor were sure to be tested by these politically combustible cases. In February 2009, Lofgren announced she was returning $7,000 in campaign contributions that she had received from the PMA lobbying firm, which figures in some of the pending cases.

Lofgren usually is a reliable liberal vote in the House Democratic Caucus, although that does not prevent her from pursuing bipartisan compromises. In 2001, the Republicans' energy plan included her proposal to accelerate the development of fusion as an energy source, but she voted against the final bill. When Republicans brought up a measure to make it a separate offense to injure or kill a fetus while committing a crime against a pregnant woman, she offered an alternative to add stiffer penalties for an attack on a pregnant woman without conferring rights to the fetus. But it lost 229-196.

After the 2002 election, she tried to get a foothold in leadership by running for vice chairman of the Democratic Caucus. But Pelosi, who is also from the Bay Area, had already been elected minority leader, and the Congressional Black Caucus pressed to have one of its members in the leadership. Lofgren got 53 votes to 95 for James Clyburn, an African-American from South Carolina, who won the post. As head of the California Democratic delegation, she led efforts to oppose the recall in 2003 of Democratic Gov. Gray Davis.

Lofgren has had no trouble winning re-election every two years.

SEVENTEENTH DISTRICT

Sam Farr (D)

Elected June 1993, 8th full term; b. July 4, 1941, San Francisco; home, Carmel; Willamette U., B.S. 1963; Episcopalian; married (Shary); 1 child.

Elected Office: Monterey Cnty. Bd. of Supervisors, 1975–80, chmn., 1979; CA Assembly, 1980–93.

Professional Career: Peace Corps, Colombia, 1963–65; Staff, CA Assembly, 1965–75.

DC Office: 1126 LHOB, 20515, 202-225-2861; Fax: 202-225-6791; Web site: www.farr.house.gov.

State Offices: Salinas, 831-424-2229; Santa Cruz, 831-429-1976.

Committees: *Appropriations* (18th of 37 D): Agriculture, Rural Development, FDA & Related Agencies; Homeland Security; Military Construction, Veterans Affairs & Related Agencies.

Group Ratings

	ADA	ACLU	AFS	LCV	ITIC	NTU	COC	ACU	CFG	FRC
2008	100	100	100	92	100	5	61	0	2	5
2007	95	—	100	90	—	4	55	0	11	—

National Journal Ratings

	2007 LIB — 2007 CONS		2008 LIB — 2008 CONS	
Economic	82%	0%	69%	29%
Social	92%	0%	82%	0%
Foreign	90%	8%	92%	0%
Composite	93%	7%	86%	14%

Key Votes of the 110th Congress

1. Increase minimum wage	Y	5. Share immigration data	N	9. Withdraw troops 8/08	Y
2. Expand SCHIP	Y	6. Foreign aid abortion ban	N	10. No operations in Iran	Y
3. Raise CAFE standards	Y	7. Ban gay bias in workplace	Y	11. Free trade with Peru	Y
4. Bail out financial markets	Y	8. Repeal D.C. gun law	N	12. Overhaul FISA	N

Election Results

2008 general	Sam Farr (D)	168,907	(74%)	($775,793)
	Jeff Taylor (R)	59,037	(26%)	($41,568)
2008 primary	Sam Farr (D)	unopposed		

Prior Winning Percentages: 2006 (76%); 2004 (67%); 2002 (68%); 2000 (69%); 1998 (65%); 1996 (59%); 1994 (52%); 1993 (52%)

Population		Race/Ethnicity		Work	
Pop. 2007:	642,100	White:	42.4%	Private:	72.8%
Change since 2000:	Up 0.5%	Black:	2.3%	Government:	17.6%
Urban:	90.0%	Hispanic:	46.7%	Self-employed:	9.3%
Rural:	10.0%	Asian:	5.4%	Blue collar:	18.9%
Area size:	5,386 sq. mi.	Native Am.:	0.3%	White collar:	52.7%
		Hawaiian:	0.3%	Khaki collar:	1.0%
Age		Two+ races:	2.2%	Other:	27.4%
Median age:	33.0 yrs.			Median income:	$58,849
More than 65 yrs:	10.1%	*Ancestry*		Median home value:	$676,100
Less than 18 yrs:	26.0%	German:	8.2%	Poverty:	12.3%
		Irish:	6.9%		
Education		English:	6.7%		
H.S. grad:	73.6%			**Military Veterans**	
College grad:	26.7%			% of Pop:	7.9%
Grad degree:	10.2%				

The California coast around Monterey Bay is for many a working definition of paradise. This kernel of California, site of the first state capital, still makes a fine living off the land and sea, as it has for 150 years. The locale for *The Grapes of Wrath* and many other John Steinbeck novels, the fields around Salinas provide much of the nation's lettuce and cauliflower. The area is often referred to as "the salad bowl of the world." Nearby, the farmlands around Castroville supply the country with its arti-

2008 Presidential Vote		
Obama (D)	171,180	(72%)
McCain (R)	61,163	(26%)
2004 Presidential Vote		
Kerry (D)	149,029	(66%)
Bush (R)	75,005	(33%)
Cook Partisan Voting Index:	D + 19	

chokes, and the vast greenhouses around Watsonville produce a goodly portion of its roses. In 2007, Monterey County's agricultural yield grew to $3.8 billion. The fishing fleet and the 18 now-closed canneries of Monterey (the last sardines were canned in 1964) have generated a new industry. Once described by Steinbeck as "a poem, a stink, a grating noise, a quality of light, a tone, a habit, nostalgia, a dream," Cannery Row now is refurbished with upscale shops and hotels. The magnificent Monterey Bay Aquarium is one of California's top tourist destinations, and the National Marine Sanctuary holds more than 400 shipwrecks and ditched aircraft. The Monterey Bay area calls itself the world's language learning capital, with the Defense Language Institute, Language Line Services, and Cal State's Monterey Bay Center for Intensive Language and Culture on the site of Fort Ord, which was closed in 1994. Perhaps the main attraction of the Monterey peninsula is the lush 17-Mile Drive along the Pacific Coast Highway, with Pebble Beach's golf courses, the Del Monte Lodge, and Carmel, whose restrictive laws—no house numbers, no door-to-door mail delivery, no live entertainment, no stoplights, no cutting trees without City Council permission—reflect an effort to maintain the atmosphere of nearly a century ago, when it really was an artists' colony. Not immune to California's propensity for destructive wildfires, the Big Sur area, heavily dependent on tourism, suffered major fire damage in 2008, including the loss of trees on more than 220,000 acres of national park land.

The 17th Congressional District of California includes the entire coast of Monterey Bay and follows the stunning Big Sur coastline south along the steep slopes almost to William Randolph Hearst's castle, San Simeon, taking in some of the most beautiful scenery in America. To the north along Monterey Bay, it runs past Watsonville to Santa Cruz. The district extends inland, into sunny valleys sheltered from ocean mists, and covers some of the nation's richest farmland. Most of the farmworkers are Latino, mainly Mexican, and in the 1990s, the Hispanic population rose from 31% to 43%, the largest increase in any Northern California district; in 2007, the share grew to 47%.

The gap between rich and poor in Monterey County is wide. It has thousands of homes valued at more than $1 million but also usually ranks high in the share of households below the poverty line. Forty years ago, this was a solidly Republican area, dominated politically by the landowners in Salinas and the townspeople who sympathize with them, plus retirees in Santa Cruz and on the Monterey peninsula. But an influx of young people, attracted less by the economy than by the atmosphere, moved the coast to the left. Monterey and Santa Cruz counties have become steadily more Democratic than the nation, and each now exceeds the national Democratic presidential vote by more than 10 percentage points. A district that once consistently voted for Ronald Reagan gave Democratic presidential nominees John Kerry 66% of the vote in 2004 and Barack Obama 72% in 2008.

The congressman from the 17th District is Sam Farr, a Democrat first elected in June 1993. A fifth-generation Californian, he grew up in Monterey County, where his father was a state senator for many years. Farr signed up for the Peace Corps after college, learned Spanish at the Monterey Institute of International Studies, and served two years in Colombia. He was a California Assembly staff member for a decade, became a Monterey County supervisor in 1975, and was elected to the Assembly in 1980. There, he wrote one of the nation's strictest oil-spill liability laws. In 1993, when Democratic Rep. Leon Panetta resigned from the House to become director of the Office of Management and Budget, Farr ran for his seat. He entered the race as the overwhelming favorite, and won 26% of the vote in the all-party primary to defeat two other Democrats. But in the runoff, which came after President Clinton's budget and tax increase had arrived in Congress, he had trouble against Republican Bill McCampbell, whom Panetta had defeated 72%-24% seven months earlier. Farr won, but by just 52%-43%.

In the House, Farr has a solidly liberal voting record. He is a close ally of House Speaker Nancy Pelosi's. On the Appropriations Committee, Farr is a senior member on subcommittees dealing with two major local concerns: farming and military bases. He helped to negotiate the final agreement that conveyed the former Fort Ord to civilian hands, and he took the lead in transferring the lands to local governments and in refusing to permit the Navy to establish a practice bombing range near Big Sur. Working with Democratic Sen. Patrick Leahy of Vermont, he led a successful effort in 2003 to repeal a little-noted provision of an appropriations bill that would have allowed poultry and beef to be raised on non-organic food but still be labeled organic. In 2002, President George W. Bush signed Farr's bill to add 55,000 acres to the Big Sur wilderness area. Farr has pushed a major proposal to overhaul ocean management, with national and regional governance. He helped to write the 2006 law revising rules for offshore fisheries, and he also has a bill to encourage research on sea otters.

After the local spinach crop was affected by an E. coli outbreak in 2006, Farr held a press conference to urge constituents to "go Popeye" and eat spinach. He pushed for $25 million to aid producers, a provision that generated controversy after it was added to the emergency war spending bill, and it was stripped from the measure that passed in April 2007. "It's easy to make fun of spinach," Farr said in defense of the subsidy. "But if we had eaten more of it, we would be a stronger society."

Nationally, Farr gets attention for some of his relatively extreme liberal positions. In 2007, he co-sponsored a resolution calling for the impeachment of Vice President Cheney. While most Democrats had a hearty dislike for Cheney, few thought that impeachment was the solution. At a February 2008 hearing, Farr compared U.S. immigration agents to the Nazi Gestapo, explaining that his constituents had "a very ill will" toward the agents.

Farr has been re-elected easily.

EIGHTEENTH DISTRICT

Dennis Cardoza (D)

Elected 2002, 4th term; b. March 31, 1959, Merced; home, Atwater; U. of MD, B.A. 1982, CA St. U. Stanislaus; Catholic; married (Kathleen McLoughlin); 3 children.

Elected Office: Atwater City Cncl., 1984–86; Merced City Cncl., 1994–95; CA Assembly, 1996–2002.

Professional Career: Agribusiness owner.

DC Office: 1224 LHOB, 20515, 202-225-6131; Fax: 202-225-0819; Web site: www.house.gov/cardoza.

State Offices: Merced, 209-383-4455; Modesto, 209-527-1914; Stockton, 209-946-0361.

Committees: *Agriculture* (6th of 28 D): Horticulture & Organic Agriculture (Chmn); Livestock, Dairy & Poultry. *Rules* (5th of 9 D): Legislative & Budget Process.

Group Ratings

	ADA	ACLU	AFS	LCV	ITIC	NTU	COC	ACU	CFG	FRC
2008	85	91	100	92	100	9	65	8	8	11
2007	90	—	100	65	—	5	63	4	12	—

National Journal Ratings

	2007 LIB	—	2007 CONS		2008 LIB	—	2008 CONS
Economic	67%	—	33%		59%	—	40%
Social	66%	—	33%		54%	—	42%
Foreign	60%	—	39%		59%	—	37%
Composite	65%	—	35%		59%	—	41%

Key Votes of the 110th Congress

1. Increase minimum wage	Y	5. Share immigration data	N	9. Withdraw troops 8/08	Y
2. Expand SCHIP	Y	6. Foreign aid abortion ban	N	10. No operations in Iran	Y
3. Raise CAFE standards	Y	7. Ban gay bias in workplace	Y	11. Free trade with Peru	Y
4. Bail out financial markets	Y	8. Repeal D.C. gun law	Y	12. Overhaul FISA	Y

Election Results

2008 general	Dennis Cardoza (D).....................................	unopposed
2008 primary	Dennis Cardoza (D).....................................	unopposed

Prior Winning Percentages: 2006 (65%); 2004 (68%); 2002 (51%)

Population		Race/Ethnicity		Work	
Pop. 2007:	707,492	White:	32.7%	Private:	79.6%
Change since 2000:	Up 10.7%	Black:	5.2%	Government:	13.3%
Urban:	91.3%	Hispanic:	49.6%	Self-employed:	6.9%
Rural:	8.7%	Asian:	9.3%	Blue collar:	32.5%
Area size:	3,101 sq. mi.	Native Am.:	0.6%	White collar:	44.3%
		Hawaiian:	0.4%	Khaki collar:	0.1%
Age		Two+ races:	1.8%	Other:	23.1%
Median age:	29.5 yrs.	*Ancestry*		Median income:	$42,316
More than 65 yrs:	9.2%	German:	6.2%	Median home value:	$326,300
Less than 18 yrs:	31.0%	Irish:	5.2%	Poverty:	19.9%
		English:	3.7%	**Military Veterans**	
Education				% of Pop:	7.5%
H.S. grad:	66.0%				
College grad:	10.3%				
Grad degree:	2.8%				

The Central Valley of California is a miraculous landscape, an outdoor factory stretching as far as the eye can see. Nature created the vast flatlands, rimmed by mountains rising in the distant haze. In the 20th century, people disciplined the land with a remorseless mile-square grid of roads, the California Aqueduct, and dozens of arrow-straight canals. Pipes fitted with valves and gauges pump water, fertilizer, and pesticides to the fields in measured quantities with industrial precision. The crops grow

2008 Presidential Vote
Obama (D) 104,299   (59%)
McCain (R)...............................68,629   (39%)

2004 Presidential Vote
Bush (R)....................................80,157   (50%)
Kerry (D)..................................79,764   (49%)

Cook Partisan Voting Index: D + 4

in carefully spaced rows. The rich soil and the irrigated water are too precious to waste on decorative fountains or flower gardens. Throughout history, farming here has been a business, not a way of life. In the 19th century, the U.S. government did not give the land to 160-acre homesteaders but rather sold it to large enterprises in thousands-of-acres parcels. Among the most famous local capitalists were the Gallo brothers, Ernest and Julio, who started a winery in Modesto in 1933 with virtually no money. It now covers more than 10,000 acres of vineyards and produces 80 million cases of wine each year.

In recent years, the Central Valley has become one of California's surprise boom areas, not just for crops but also for people. Middle-income employees in the San Francisco Bay area drive east at the end of the day on Interstate 580, past surreal windmills whirling on the bare hills of the Altamont Pass, to modestly priced homes in Modesto, the town immortalized (when it was much smaller) in the 1973 film *American Graffiti*. Warehouses and factories have sprung up on land that for all its farming value is cheaper than industrial land in the Bay Area. With increases in water prices, some croplands have been given over to pasture. Inland California had a 46% increase in jobs from 1990 to 2005, while jobs in coastal California grew by 10% in the same period. But there are costs. Traffic is a problem, air-pollution levels on bad days can be among the worst in the nation, and the pace of life has become more hectic. In 2009, the impact of the national recession on the Central Valley in some ways was more severe than elsewhere in the country. Stockton, pop. 260,000, suffered a higher rate of housing foreclosures than any other city in the United States. By early 2009, the city had knocked Detroit from first place on *Forbes* magazine's list of "most miserable cities" to live. Rural areas were not immune to hardship. A severe drought forced farmers to face a major cutback in water supply.

The 18th Congressional District of California includes a large chunk of the Central Valley from Stockton, south to Modesto, through Merced County, to the fringes of Fresno. The political tradition here had been Democratic: In the 1960s, Democrats in Washington and Democratic Gov. Pat Brown built the irrigation canals and authorized the water subsidies; Democrats owned the McClatchy newspapers, the predominant Central Valley chain; and Democrats staffed the Bank of America, long the dominant financial force here. Signed photographs of Franklin D. Roosevelt and Brown lined the walls of insider law firms. The district produced two U.S. House Democratic whips, John McFall in the late 1970s and Tony Coelho in the late 1980s. The Central Valley has the highest proportion of families and children in California, and many of its local politicians share the natural cultural conservatism that exists here. In the 1980s and 1990s, the Central Valley trended Republican, and even the Latinos here were less solidly Democratic than those in Los Angeles. The 18th District is still modestly Democratic, because of very careful redistricting and because of a recent influx of traditional liberals from the Bay Area. In 2004, Republican President George W. Bush carried the district only narrowly, 50%-49%, and in 2008, Democrat Barack Obama won it 59%-39%. One cause of the voter shift was the increase in the Hispanic population from 42% in 2000 to 50% in 2007, while total population grew by 11%.

The congressman from the 18th District is Dennis Cardoza, a Democrat first elected in a 2002 contest that drew international attention because of the notoriety of his predecessor, Democratic Rep. Gary Condit. Cardoza grew up in Atwater, the son of farmers who raised sweet potatoes and dairy cows. Like many people in the Central Valley, he is descended from Portuguese immigrants from the Azores Islands (as are Democrat Jim Costa of the adjacent 20th District and Republican Devin Nunes of the 21st). Interested in politics a youth, Cardoza attended the University of Maryland just outside of Washington, D.C., and interned on Capitol Hill. In the mid-1980s, he was an aide to Condit, who was then a California assemblyman; he worked on Condit's 1989 special-election campaign and served on his Washington staff. In 1996, Cardoza was elected to the Assembly. He very likely would have remained close to Condit had it not been for the case of Chandra Levy. She was a Modesto resident who was working as an intern in the executive branch when she and Condit began having an affair. She vanished in Washington in April 2001 and was later found murdered in the city's Rock Creek Park. Her disappearance generated saturation media coverage. It was revealed that Condit had an extramarital relationship with her, and Condit was hounded by reporters and photographers. Though Condit had nothing to do with Levy's tragic death (she apparently was the random victim of a sexual predator), the revelations about his personal life destroyed his career. Condit had always portrayed himself as a family man and the son of a preacher. His wife was well known and beloved in the Modesto area. When it turned out that Condit had been living another life in Washington, his loyal base of support in the district evaporated.

National and local Democrats urged Cardoza to enter the contest because they feared that Condit could not survive the general election and that the party would lose the seat to the Republicans. When he did, he received immediate endorsements from Democratic Sens. Dianne Feinstein and Barbara Boxer and many members of the House delegation. Condit stayed in the race despite his tattered reputation, but Cardoza beat him in the primary 53%-39%. In the general election, Republicans nominated state Sen. Dick Monteith, whose seat included 73% of the congressional district. Monteith claimed that Cardoza was too liberal for an agriculture-oriented constituency, but Cardoza cited his business-oriented reputation in the Legislature. In October, Condit's children released a letter that harshly criticized Cardoza and urged a vote against him. But Cardoza won 51%-43%. Stockton made the difference. Cardoza led 67%-27% in San Joaquin County, which gave him a 10,000-vote margin that wiped out Monteith's 2,000-vote lead elsewhere.

In the House, Cardoza, like Condit, established his independence from the liberal Democratic leadership and racked up a centrist voting record. He joined the moderate Democrats' Blue Dog Coalition and emphasized the need for fiscal discipline.

Cardoza naturally gravitated to the issues of agriculture and resources. He bucked environmentalists and worked with Republicans on farmer-friendly revisions to the Endangered Species Act, including changes in designating critical habitat. He advocated solar power and other sources of renewable energy. The father of two adopted children, Cardoza also worked on legislation encouraging placement of more children in foster care.

When Democrats assumed the majority on Capitol Hill in 2007, Cardoza became chairman of the Agriculture Subcommittee on Horticulture and Organic Agriculture, a title that sounds more coastal than Valley, but it gave him a seat at the table in drafting the 2008 farm bill. He pushed for increasing subsidies for "specialty crops," notably the fruits and vegetables that farmers grow in his district, and he helped secure more than $2 billion in new federal spending for those crops. With other Blue Dogs, he pushed for some constraints on overall spending and supported a provision that stops federal payments to farmers with incomes of $1 million a year or more. "This bill threads the needle," Cardoza said. "There is something for everyone to dislike, but everyone got what they needed."

Despite occasional differences with House Speaker Nancy Pelosi, including his public support for Maryland Rep. Steny Hoyer in his pitched battle against Pennsylvania Rep. John Murtha for majority leader in 2007 (Pelosi backed Murtha), she gave him a seat on the leadership-run Rules Committee. He later patched things up with Pelosi by co-chairing the Democratic Congressional Campaign Committee's "Frontline" program to help endangered incumbents.

Cardoza has won re-election handily and with far less attention than in his first race.

NINETEENTH DISTRICT

George Radanovich (R)

Elected 1994, 8th term; b. June 20, 1955, Mariposa; home, Mariposa; CA Polytechnic U., B.S. 1978; Catholic; married (Ethie); 1 child.

Elected Office: Mariposa Cnty. Planning Comm., 1982–86, Chmn., 1985–86; Mariposa Cnty. Bd. of Supervisors, 1989–92.

Professional Career: Farmer; Founder & owner, Radanovich Winery, 1986–2003.

DC Office: 2410 RHOB, 20515, 202-225-4540; Fax: 202-225-3402; Web site: www.radanovich.house.gov.

State Offices: Fresno, 559-449-2490; Modesto, 209-579-5458.

Committees: *Energy & Commerce* (11th of 23 R): Commerce, Trade & Consumer Protection (RMM); Communications, Technology & the Internet; Oversight & Investigations.

Group Ratings

	ADA	ACLU	AFS	LCV	ITIC	NTU	COC	ACU	CFG	FRC
2008	20	22	14	8	71	64	94	87	75	82
2007	0	—	0	0	—	84	68	100	90	—

National Journal Ratings

	2007 LIB — 2007 CONS		2008 LIB — 2008 CONS	
Economic	0%	— 97%	15%	— 85%
Social	29%	— 71%	0%	— 91%
Foreign	0%	— 72%	7%	— 92%
Composite	15%	— 85%	9%	— 91%

Key Votes of the 110th Congress

1. InCRease minimum wage	N	5. Share immigration data	Y	9. Withdraw troops 8/08	N
2. Expand SCHIP	N	6. Foreign aid abortion ban	Y	10. No operations in Iran	N
3. Raise CAFE standards	N	7. Ban gay bias in workplace	N	11. Free trade with Peru	Y
4. Bail out financial markets	Y	8. Repeal D.C. gun law	Y	12. Overhaul FISA	Y

Election Results

2008 general	George Radanovich (R) 179,245	(98%)	($712,277)
2008 primary	George Radanovich (R) .... unopposed		

Prior Winning Percentages: 2006 (61%); 2004 (66%); 2002 (67%); 2000 (65%); 1998 (79%); 1996 (67%); 1994 (57%)

Population		Race/Ethnicity		Work	
Pop. 2007:	727,685	White:	55.0%	Private:	74.4%
Change since 2000:	Up 13.9%	Black:	3.7%	Government:	16.6%
Urban:	80.6%	Hispanic:	33.7%	Self-employed:	8.7%
Rural:	19.4%	Asian:	4.6%	Blue collar:	22.4%
Area size:	6,781 sq. mi.	Native Am.:	0.7%	White collar:	57.0%
Age		Hawaiian:	0.2%	Khaki collar:	0.0%
Median age:	33.6 yrs.	Two+ races:	1.9%	Other:	20.6%
More than 65 yrs:	11.4%	*Ancestry*		Median income:	$52,397
Less than 18 yrs:	26.7%	German:	10.5%	Median home value:	$350,700
Education		Irish:	7.7%	Poverty:	13.0%
H.S. grad:	79.9%	English:	7.1%	**Military Veterans**	
College grad:	20.7%			% of Pop:	9.2%
Grad degree:	6.8%				

The city of Fresno started as a farm-marketing center—one high-income neighborhood is called Fig Garden because that's what it used to be—and as a tourist rest stop on the way to Yosemite National Park. But it has long since grown out north, east, and west from its old downtown, and its economy has diversified. Like all of the Central Valley, Fresno has always been ethnically diverse, with a telephone book that reads like the United Nations directory. It is home to the second-largest Armenian

2008 Presidential Vote
McCain (R).............................141,013   (52%)
Obama (D) 124,533   (46%)

2004 Presidential Vote
Bush (R).................................151,603   (61%)
Kerry (D)................................93,918   (38%)

Cook Partisan Voting Index: R + 9

community in the U.S. (only Los Angeles surpasses it). Its already large Latino population has more than doubled in the past 20 years, and Fresno County was 48% Hispanic in 2007. Asians, including Chinese, Filipinos, Vietnamese, and Hmong, were 9% of the county's population. The city has grown 10% since 2000, despite some serious problems: high unemployment, violent teenage gangs, and air pollution that made the Sierra Nevadas invisible on many days. Fresno has had some success addressing those problems, but the poverty rate remains high. Among the nation's largest cities, it ranks 16th in poverty level. Tighter border patrolling has encouraged illegal Mexican immigrants to remain in Fresno County year-round, even during the off-season for farmwork. Migrants have been crowding into trailers and makeshift homes on formerly vacant farmland. The growing Hispanic presence has increased the popularity of the Spanish *charreadas,* which are part-rodeo and part-fiesta and are not advertised to the general public. Historically, Fresno was a Democratic town, the prime Democratic bastion in the Central Valley south of Sacramento. Since the 1990s, it has moved toward the Republicans. It voted for George W. Bush twice and for Republican gubernatorial candidates in 1998 and 2002. But in 2008, Barack Obama narrowly won the county, 50%-48%.

The 19th Congressional District of California includes nearly half of Fresno, the relatively affluent north side of the city, and the farm towns of Madera County. This area is one of the two heavily populated parts of the district. The other, nearly 100 miles away, is the northern and eastern half of Stanislaus County, including the northern edge of Modesto and towns like Turlock, Riverbank, and Oakdale. These two areas are linked by mountainous Mariposa and Tuolumne counties, which include the Sierra foothills, the peaks of the Sierra Nevadas, and Yosemite National Park.

The congressman from the 19th District is George Radanovich, a Republican first elected in 1994. Radanovich is the son of Croatian immigrants and has relatives all over the Valley. His parents owned a clothing store and ran a small ranch. After college, Radanovich worked on the ranch and, in 1986, after studying local microclimates, opened the first winery in Mariposa County. At one time, the Radanovich Winery shipped 4,000 cases annually of sauvignon blanc, merlot, zinfandel, and cabernet sauvignon. (The business later faltered, and Radanovich closed it in 2003.) He served on the Mariposa County Planning Commission in the 1980s and won a seat on the Board of Supervisors in 1989. In 1992, he ran for Congress, losing the primary 33%-30% to 28-year-old Tal Cloud, who lost the election to Democratic Rep. Richard Lehman. In 1994, Radanovich ran again and was an easy winner in the primary. In the general election campaign, he attacked Lehman for supporting the Clinton administration and California Democratic Rep. George Miller's efforts to raise the price of Central Valley water. Radanovich won 57%-40%.

In the House, Radanovich has been among the most conservative members from California. One of his major interests over the years has been a resolution requiring Turkey to acknowledge the Armenian genocide of 1915. In 1996, his measure passed, but Turkey spurned U.S. aid under such conditions. In 2000, Radanovich secured $90 million in aid for Armenia, one of the largest recipients of U.S. aid. But Republican Speaker Dennis Hastert acceded to President Bill Clinton's appeal to abandon another resolution that recognized the Armenian genocide. In 2004, the House initially approved a similar resolution, but it was dropped from the final version of the foreign aid bill that year. With Democrats in the majority in 2007, the resolution appeared to have better prospects. After the House Foreign Affairs Committee narrowly approved the resolution in October 2007, however, House Speaker Nancy Pelosi pulled the bill from the floor in response to pleas from President Bush and some Democrats.

On the Natural Resources Committee for several years, Radanovich chaired the National Parks Subcommittee. He was able to pass proposals to improve the remote schools serving families that work at Yosemite National Park, but he encountered opposition from conservatives to his plan designating the 318-mile Highway 49 as a National Heritage Corridor. Property owners complained about losing rights to use their land as they pleased, and Radanovich modified the plan. He also is the sponsor of an ambitious plan to restore the San Joaquin River, which began drying up when Friant Dam was built decades ago to irrigate San Joaquin Valley farms. Downstream sections of the river are sometimes completely dry because of the dam. Radanovich and Democratic Sen. Dianne Feinstein have sponsored a bill that would settle a long-standing lawsuit by environmentalists over the decline of the river and its salmon population. New canals would be built to continue to supply water for irrigation, but farmers represented by Republican Rep. Devin Nunes in the adjacent 21st District remain skeptical.

In 2009, Radanovich became the became ranking Republican on the Energy and Commerce Subcommittee on Commerce, Trade, and Consumer Protection, where his priority is legislation to protect privacy and ward off identity theft.

After pledging to serve only 10 years in the House, Radanovich broke the promise in 2004 to stay in Congress, saying he needed "some flexibility" to accomplish his goals. That year he explored challenging Democratic Sen. Barbara Boxer, but decided to hold on to his safe seat in the House. He suffered a black eye in July 2004 when the *Fresno Bee* published a lengthy report about the collapse of his winery, which left several investors short hundreds of thousands of dollars while Radanovich continued to own the land and other assets. The story questioned whether the investors' losses amounted to a gift to Radanovich, which House rules would prohibit. He said that the newspaper was representing the views of "unhappy investors." The controversy has not caused him problems at election time.

TWENTIETH DISTRICT

Jim Costa (D)

Elected 2004, 3rd term; b. April 13, 1952, Fresno; home, Fresno; CA State U. Fresno, B.A. 1974; Catholic; single.

Elected Office: CA Assembly, 1978–94; CA Senate, 1994–2002.

Professional Career: Consultant, 2002–04.

DC Office: 1314 LHOB, 20515, 202-225-3341; Fax: 202-225-9308; Web site: www.costa.house.gov.

State Offices: Bakersfield, 661-869-1620; Fresno, 559-495-1620.

Committees: *Agriculture* (11th of 28 D): Conservation, Credit, Energy & Research; Horticulture & Organic Agriculture; Livestock, Dairy & Poultry. *Foreign Affairs* (25th of 28 D): Europe; Middle East & South Asia. *Natural Resources* (10th of 29 D): Energy & Mineral Resources (Chmn); Water & Power.

Group Ratings

	ADA	ACLU	AFS	LCV	ITIC	NTU	COC	ACU	CFG	FRC
2008	80	82	100	77	100	7	67	9	1	11
2007	90	—	100	75	—	5	65	4	12	—

National Journal Ratings

	2007 LIB	—	2007 CONS		2008 LIB	—	2008 CONS
Economic	59%	—	41%		51%	—	48%
Social	60%	—	40%		54%	—	42%
Foreign	59%	—	40%		50%	—	48%
Composite	60%	—	41%		53%	—	47%

Key Votes of the 110th Congress

1. Increase minimum wage	Y	5. Share immigration data	N	9. Withdraw troops 8/08	Y
2. Expand SCHIP	Y	6. Foreign aid abortion ban	N	10. No operations in Iran	Y
3. Raise CAFE standards	Y	7. Ban gay bias in workplace	Y	11. Free trade with Peru	Y
4. Bail out financial markets	Y	8. Repeal D.C. gun law	Y	12. Overhaul FISA	Y

Election Results

2008 general	Jim Costa (D)	93,023	(74%)	($922,364)
	Jim Lopez (R)	32,118	(26%)	($14,112)
2008 primary	Jim Costa (D)	unopposed		

Prior Winning Percentages: 2006 (100%); 2004 (53%)

Population		Race/Ethnicity		Work	
Pop. 2007:	693,805	White:	19.3%	Private:	75.6%
Change since 2000:	Up 8.6%	Black:	6.3%	Government:	18.3%
Urban:	91.2%	Hispanic:	67.2%	Self-employed:	5.8%
Rural:	8.8%	Asian:	5.3%	Blue collar:	28.6%
Area size:	4,989 sq. mi.	Native Am.:	0.5%	White collar:	35.5%
		Hawaiian:	0.1%	Khaki collar:	1.0%
Age		Two+ races:	1.0%	Other:	34.9%
Median age:	27.6 yrs.			Median income:	$33,256
More than 65 yrs:	7.3%	*Ancestry*		Median home value:	$202,200
Less than 18 yrs:	32.9%	German:	4.2%	Poverty:	29.2%
		Irish:	3.1%		
Education		English:	2.1%	**Military Veterans**	
H.S. grad:	55.1%			% of Pop:	6.1%
College grad:	7.0%				
Grad degree:	1.8%				

By car, California's Central Valley is a monotonous landscape: mile after mile of farmland with mile-square grid roads, intersected by railroads and canals, with an occasional cluster town. The land is hilly and gets more water near the Sierra Nevada Mountains, and this is where the larger cities are. On the other side are the Westlands, where the land is flatter and the water scarcer. Its 600,000 acres are-ethe nation's largest irrigation district. Here the land was always developed and sold in big plots;

2008 Presidential Vote		
Obama (D)	77,158	(60%)
McCain (R)	50,146	(39%)
2004 Presidential Vote		
Kerry (D)	58,534	(51%)
Bush (R)	56,045	(48%)
Cook Partisan Voting Index:	D + 5	

today it has some of the world's largest farming operations.The land produces abundantly: alfalfa, cantaloupes, cotton, grapes, lima beans, olives, peaches, plums, raisins, sugar beets, tomatoes, walnuts, wheat. The landowners are a hardy and politically independent lot, but they have been happy to receive government help over the years, with money for crop price supports (in the case of cotton), agricultural research, irrigation systems, and, most important, subsidized and plentiful water. Landowners have fought hard against liberals' efforts at change, from Democratic Gov. Jerry Brown's encouragement of Cesar Chavez's United Farm Workers in the 1970s to former House Natural Resources Committee Chairman George Miller's 1992 law to draw off more water to the Sacramento delta and charge higher prices for it in the valley. They were also stymied when conservatives controlled Congress, and it deadlocked on expansion of guest-worker programs pushed by valley farmers. Landowners also worry that Los Angeles users might outbid them for scarce water. After suffering several hundred million dollars in drought-related losses in 2008, they are scurrying to restore old wells and find alternative water sources. In the Westlands, several hundred thousand acres have gone fallow.

The 20th District of California includes most of the Westlands of the Central Valley, from Bakersfield to a point northwest of Fresno. Its irregular boundaries were drawn to maximize the Hispanic population and Democratic percentage, so the 20th includes the old downtown neighborhoods of Bakersfield and Fresno but not their more affluent neighborhoods. It includes heavily Latino towns such as Delano, Chavez's old headquarters, and the site of a potentially large natural-gas discovery. Just 36% of Fresno's population is included within the 20th, and just 18% of Bakersfield's. The district's Hispanic population is 67%, about double that of other Central Valley districts. In 60% of homes, the main language is not English. This is the most Democratic valley seat between Sacramento and Los Angeles, although in 2004 George W. Bush won 49% here and in 2006 Republican Gov. Arnold Schwarzenegger won 54%. As in most of California, Democratic presidential candidate Barack Obama won easily here in 2008, 60%-39%.

The congressman from the 20th District is Jim Costa, a Democrat elected in 2004. Born in Fresno, he was raised on his family's dairy farm. He is the grandson of Portuguese immigrants who settled in the San Joaquin Valley near the turn of the 20th century. In 1978, Costa was elected to the state Assembly, where he was known as a moderate Democrat. In 2002, after he was forced to retire that year because of term limits, Costa founded a consulting firm. Two years later, when Democratic Rep. Cal Dooley retired after 14 years, Costa entered the race and started off with solid name recognition—his former state Senate district covered the entire congressional district. But in the March primary, he faced a bruising challenge from Lisa Quigley, Dooley's chief of staff. Quigley grew up in the Central Valley, but she hadn't lived in the district in nearly two decades, not since leaving for the University of California (Berkeley) and a career on Capitol Hill. Costa, a third-generation farmer and a Fresno native, questioned her residency and her agricultural credentials. Quigley, who was endorsed by Dooley and national abortion-rights groups, bashed Costa's legislative record and painted him as a special-interest lobbyist. In the campaign's final days, Quigley ran ads mentioning Costa's 1986 arrest for soliciting a prostitute and a 1994 incident in which police found drug paraphernalia in his home. Costa shrugged off the attacks and won the primary by an unexpectedly large 73%-27%.

In the general election, Costa began as a clear favorite in this Democratic-leaning district. But the Republican nominee, state Sen. Roy Ashburn, ran a formidable campaign. He focused on cultural issues, including his opposition to same-sex marriage, hoping to win Latino votes. He criticized Costa for supporting tax policies that he said hurt low-income families. GOP heavy hitters made appearances for him, including Vice President Cheney, House Speaker Dennis Hastert, and Schwarzenegger. The National Republican Congressional Committee ran $1.5 million in ads saying, "Jim Costa—he's gonna cost ya." But Costa's lengthy legislative record didn't readily lend itself to the "liberal" label. He criticized Ashburn as an "extreme partisan" who would be a tool of the Republican leadership. In a relatively low turnout, Costa won 53%-47%. In Fresno County, which cast 42% of the vote, he won 61%-39%. Costa also carried Bakersfield-centered Kern County, 55%-45%. Ashburn won in the geographically central Kings County, 61%-39%.

In the House, Costa got seats on the Agriculture and the Natural Resources committees, both important to the valley. His voting record is the most conservative among California House Democrats and placed him near the political center of the House as a whole.

As chairman of Natural Resources' Energy and Mineral Resources Subcommittee, Costa supported lifting the ban on oil drilling 50 to 100 miles off the nation's coast, but he sought to maintain the federal ban on drilling within 25 miles of shore and to allow states to decide whether drilling is permitted between 25 and 50 miles off the coast. He has also focused on trying to restore the Chinook salmon population on the San Joaquin River; the fish died off after the Friant Dam was built near Fresno and the river dried out downstream. On the Agriculture, Nutrition, and Forestry Committee, he worked with Rep. Adam Putnam, R-Fla., and with industry groups in 2009 on a bipartisan approach to toughen food safety regulation, including the creation of a foreign supplier quality assurance program, which would hold food imports to the same safety standards as domestic products.

On other issues, Costa co-sponsored a bill that would require states to establish independent commissions to handle redistricting after the 2010 census. The highly partisan process used by many state legislatures after the 2000 census resulted in heavily gerrymandered districts across the country. Costa is also a leader of the Transatlantic Legislators' Dialogue, a biannual meeting between members of Congress and European parliaments to discuss global issues.

After his initial tough contests in 2004, Costa has not faced a significant re-election challenge.

TWENTY-FIRST DISTRICT

Devin Nunes (R)

Elected 2002, 4th term; b. Oct. 1, 1973, Tulare; home, Tulare; Col. of the Sequoias, A.D. 1993, CA Poly. U., B.S. 1995, M.A. 1996; Catholic; married (Elizabeth); 1 child.

Elected Office: Col. of the Sequoias Governing Bd., 1996–2002.

Professional Career: State Dir., USDA Rural Dev., 2001

DC Office: 1013 LHOB, 20515, 202-225-2523; Fax: 202-225-3404; Web site: www.nunes.house.gov/.

State Offices: Clovis, 559-323-5235; Visalia, 559-733-3861.

Committees: *Budget* (10th of 15 R). *Ways & Means* (8th of 15 R): Health; Trade.

Group Ratings

	ADA	ACLU	AFS	LCV	ITIC	NTU	COC	ACU	CFG	FRC
2008	0	18	14	0	71	80	94	100	92	94
2007	5	—	0	0	—	79	79	100	86	—

National Journal Ratings

	2007 LIB	—	2007 CONS	2008 LIB	—	2008 CONS
Economic	15%	—	85%	7%	—	92%
Social	15%	—	84%	27%	—	71%
Foreign	0%	—	72%	16%	—	83%
Composite	15%	—	85%	17%	—	83%

Key Votes of the 110th Congress

1. Increase minimum wage	N	5. Share immigration data	Y	9. Withdraw troops 8/08	N
2. Expand SCHIP	N	6. Foreign aid abortion ban	Y	10. No operations in Iran	N
3. Raise CAFE standards	*	7. Ban gay bias in workplace	N	11. Free trade with Peru	Y
4. Bail out financial markets	N	8. Repeal D.C. gun law	Y	12. Overhaul FISA	Y

Election Results

2008 general	Devin Nunes (R)..	143,498	(68%)	($734,226)
	Larry Johnson (D)...	66,317	(32%)	($33,825)
2008 primary	Devin Nunes (R)... unopposed			

Prior Winning Percentages: 2006 (67%); 2004 (73%); 2002 (70%)

Population		Race/Ethnicity		Work	
Pop. 2007:	739,428	White:	40.9%	Private:	74.6%
Change since 2000:	Up 15.7%	Black:	2.3%	Government:	17.6%
Urban:	79.9%	Hispanic:	47.9%	Self-employed:	7.6%
Rural:	20.1%	Asian:	6.2%	Blue collar:	22.0%
Area size:	8,090 sq. mi.	Native Am.:	0.8%	White collar:	50.6%
Age		Hawaiian:	0.1%	Khaki collar:	0.1%
Median age:	29.8 yrs.	Two+ races:	1.6%	Other:	27.3%
More than 65 yrs:	9.7%	*Ancestry*		Median income:	$45,805
Less than 18 yrs:	30.7%	German:	7.9%	Median home value:	$259,500
Education		Irish:	5.5%	Poverty:	19.6%
H.S. grad:	72.1%	English:	5.3%	**Military Veterans**	
College grad:	16.8%			% of Pop:	7.8%
Grad degree:	5.0%				

In California's Central Valley, between the flat Westlands and the Sierras, is Fresno, a city that is both agricultural and industrial, middle American and ethnically diverse. Although it began as a farm-marketing center, the city has long since grown out to the north, east, and west from its downtown, and its economy has diversified. It is a creation of the Industrial Age and the Central Pacific Railroad. Fresno's city fathers bred the local wine grape, developed the raisin industry, and introduced the

2008 Presidential Vote
McCain (R)..............................125,347   (56%)
Obama (D) 93,578   (42%)

2004 Presidential Vote
Bush (R)................................133,004   (66%)
Kerry (D)................................68,501   (34%)

Cook Partisan Voting Index: R + 13

Smyrna fig. These are among the area's 300-plus crops, which include cotton, lima beans, nectarines, almonds, tomatoes, cantaloupes, plums, peaches, and alfalfa. Dairy, however, is now the biggest commodity. Fresno County produces more farm products in dollar value than any other county in the United States; neighboring Tulare County is close behind. Central Valley agriculture is industrial in its thoroughness and in its ownership by large corporations. The vineyards outside Fresno radiate in mechanical precision, with vines just 10 feet apart and exposed to the relentless summer sun: nothing romantic or quaint about it. Until recently, times were good. The weak dollar boosted farm exports, large citrus groves benefited from losses in hurricane-plagued Florida, and nuts have found new export markets. The recession, plus a serious continuing drought, hit this area hard in 2008. Among the many business setbacks was the decision by the San Joaquin Railroad, which had served farm and food centers, to abandon 39 miles of rail line. Railroad officials said that the line serving Ducor, Exeter, Lindsay, Porterville, Richgrove, Strathmore, and Terra Bella was not economically viable.

The 21st District, the most productive farm district in the nation, covers most of Fresno County east of Fresno and all of Tulare County to the south; 42% of the population is in Fresno County and 58% is in Tulare. Here and there amid the farm fields are small cities, and connecting many of these places is state Route 99, the old Farm-to-Market Corridor that will become Interstate 9. Past Kings Canyon and Sequoia National Parks loom the giant peaks of the Sierra Nevada Mountains, including Mount Whitney, at 14,494 feet, the highest point in the lower 48 states. This part of the Central Valley grew 16% from 2000 to 2007, and it is 48% Hispanic. In 2004, George W. Bush got 66% of the vote, his second-highest percentage in a California district. In 2008, Republican John McCain defeated Democrat Barack Obama here, 56%-42%, McCain's second-highest percentage in the state, after the neighboring 22nd District.

The congressman from the 21st District is Devin Nunes, a Republican first elected in 2002. Nunes *(NEW nez)* is the descendent of Portuguese immigrants from the Azores. His grandfather established the 600-acre-plus dairy farm that his parents ran when he was growing up in Tulare County. He graduated from California Polytechnic State University (San Luis Obispo) with degrees in agriculture, worked on the family farm, and married a local elementary schoolteacher whose family roots are also in Portugal. (Nunes and his wife, Elizabeth, had their first child, Evelyn Rose, in 2007.) In 1998, at age 25, Nunes ran for the U.S. House in the 20th District and finished second in the primary, losing 52%-48%. In 2000, he was the Tulare County campaign chairman for former Republican Rep. Bill Thomas, who chaired the powerful Ways and Means Committee before he retired. In 2001, with Thomas's help, Nunes was appointed California director of rural development for the U.S. Agriculture Department. When California's redistricting plan was unveiled in September 2001, the 21st District was left without an incumbent, and Nunes moved quickly. He was supported by Thomas, whose deep-pocketed campaign contributors in the pharmaceutical and insurance industries agreed to give to Nunes. At home, Nunes won the endorsement of the California Farm Bureau, the state's largest farm organization and a powerful voice in Central Valley politics.

But Nunes had serious primary competition. The best-known candidate was Jim Patterson, Fresno's conservative former mayor, who was well-financed by the national anti-tax group Club for Growth. Another serious candidate was Assembly member Mike Briggs. There were few differences among them on policy. All three said that agriculture was their top priority, and all promised to seek new water sources for farmers about to lose the San Joaquin River as a primary source. Environmentalists were working to restore the river, which for years had been dammed for irrigation purposes. The candidates also called for tax cuts, fewer federal regulations, and expanded guest-worker programs in the pending immigration legislation in Congress. Nunes won with 37% of the vote to 33% for Patterson and 26% for Briggs. In his base of Tulare County, which cast 49% of the Republican votes, Nunes received 46% of the vote. In Fresno County, he finished third with 27%, but his two opponents divided the vote: Patterson got 37% and Briggs 30%. Nunes won easily in November 70%-26%.

Nunes has a mostly conservative voting record, although it tends to be more centrist on social issues. Then-House Speaker Dennis Hastert sought him out as a promising freshman and included him in a group of about a dozen House members who met informally to advise the Republican speaker each week. Legislatively, Nunes dove into the district's most pressing issue: the use of water from the San Joaquin. He got a feasibility study for a new water reservoir near Temperance Flat, which would help farmers if the river was restored to its original flow. But he clashed with Rep. George Radanovich, a Republican from the adjacent, downstream district, over Radanovich's push to increase water flow over the Friant Dam so that salmon could be returned to the parched lower reaches of the San Joaquin River. Nunes contended that the move would drive farmers out of business by fatally weakening the area's water supply for irrigation.

After Rep. Rob Portman, R-Ohio, left the House in 2005 to become U.S. trade representative, Nunes got his seat on the Ways and Means Committee. In 2008, he enacted a bill guaranteeing GI benefits to soldiers who leave the military after a sibling dies in combat. His action was inspired by Jason Hubbard, the surviving brother who returned home from his unit in Iraq after his two brothers died there. Hubbard was denied a number of benefits usually given to honorably discharged soldiers. The incident was reminiscent of the World War II story dramatized in the movie *Saving Private Ryan*. In 2006, Nunes sponsored a bill to open the Arctic National Wildlife Refuge to oil drilling, but he distinguished it from similar proposals by adding a provision creating tax incentives for clean-energy sources, a strategy to draw votes from Democrats otherwise opposed to opening ANWR to energy exploration.

Nunes has been easily re-elected. He was an early backer of GOP Gov. Arnold Schwarzenegger's referendum on a nonpartisan redistricting plan, which had lost handily in the Legislature.

TWENTY-SECOND DISTRICT

Kevin McCarthy (R)

Elected 2006, 2nd term; b. Jan. 26, 1965, Bakersfield; home, Bakersfield; Attended Bakersfield Col., 1984–85, CA St. U., B.S. 1989, M.B.A. 1994; Baptist; married (Judy); 2 children.

Elected Office: Kern Comm. Col. Board, 2000–02, CA Assembly, 2002–06, min. ldr., 2003–06.

Professional Career: Owner, Kevin O's Deli, 1986–87, Mesa Marin Batting Range, 1991–92; Dist. dir., U.S. Rep. Bill Thomas, 1987–2002.

DC Office: 1523 LHOB, 20515, 202-225-2915; Fax: 202-225-2908; Web site: kevinmccarthy.house.gov.

State Offices: Atascadero, 805-461-1034; Bakersfield, 661-327-3611.

Committees: *Chief Deputy Republican Whip. Financial Services* (24th of 29 R): Capital Markets, Insurance & Government Sponsored Enterprises; Financial Institutions & Consumer Credit. *House Administration* (2nd of 3 R): Elections (RMM).

Group Ratings

	ADA	ACLU	AFS	LCV	ITIC	NTU	COC	ACU	CFG	FRC
2008	10	18	14	0	71	77	94	100	86	100
2007	5	—	0	0	—	79	85	100	90	—

National Journal Ratings

	2007 LIB	—	2007 CONS		2008 LIB	—	2008 CONS
Economic	11%	—	88%		15%	—	84%
Social	9%	—	85%		31%	—	62%
Foreign	32%	—	64%		27%	—	72%
Composite	19%	—	81%		26%	—	74%

Key Votes of the 110th Congress

1. Increase minimum wage	N	5. Share immigration data	Y	9. Withdraw troops 8/08	N
2. Expand SCHIP	N	6. Foreign aid abortion ban	Y	10. No operations in Iran	N
3. Raise CAFE standards	N	7. Ban gay bias in workplace	N	11. Free trade with Peru	Y
4. Bail out financial markets	N	8. Repeal D.C. gun law	Y	12. Overhaul FISA	Y

Election Results

2008 general	Kevin McCarthy (R)	unopposed
2008 primary	Kevin McCarthy (R)	unopposed

Prior Winning Percentages: 2006 (71%)

Population		Race/Ethnicity		Work	
Pop. 2007:	744,814	White:	58.5%	Private:	68.4%
Change since 2000:	Up 16.5%	Black:	6.4%	Government:	22.6%
Urban:	82.5%	Hispanic:	28.3%	Self-employed:	8.7%
Rural:	17.5%	Asian:	3.5%	Blue collar:	23.4%
Area size:	10,454 sq. mi.	Native Am.:	0.6%	White collar:	56.0%
Age		Hawaiian:	0.1%	Khaki collar:	0.4%
Median age:	33.5 yrs.	Two+ races:	2.3%	Other:	20.3%
More than 65 yrs:	10.4%	*Ancestry*		Median income:	$52,580
Less than 18 yrs:	27.4%	German:	11.5%	Median home value:	$307,800
		Irish:	9.2%	Poverty:	14.5%
Education		English:	8.2%	**Military Veterans**	
H.S. grad:	81.4%			% of Pop:	11.4%
College grad:	19.8%				
Grad degree:	6.7%				

At the southern end of California's Central Valley is Bakersfield. It has been the focus of great migrations four times—in the gold rush of 1885, in the boomlet that followed the discovery of oil in 1899, in the 1930s flight of Dust Bowl refugees from Oklahoma, Kansas and Texas and in a flood of newcomers in the 1980s and 1990s, when Bakersfield and Kern County grew more rapidly than California's biggest metro areas. The migration that made the deepest imprint was in the 1930s. The Okies

2008 Presidential Vote

McCain (R)	172,792	(60%)
Obama (D)	110,910	(38%)

2004 Presidential Vote

Bush (R)	180,584	(68%)
Kerry (D)	82,356	(31%)

Cook Partisan Voting Index: R + 16

drove over a thousand miles of brown landscape, then through the Tehachapi Pass, and found this vast green valley, with its irrigated fields and its eucalyptus-shaded towns—the richest farming country in the world. The story is told vividly in novelist John Steinbeck's *The Grapes of Wrath* and in Dan Morgan's *Rising in the West*, which explains how the migrants prospered in California.

The area around Bakersfield is one Southern-accented part of California, the home of country singers Buck Owens and Merle Haggard and a thriving country-music scene. People here are culturally conservative with little empathy for Los Angeles-style flamboyant liberalism. But Bakersfield's personality may be diluted as Southern California spreads north. And city officials are intent on expanding its boundaries. Developers are working on Centennial, a master-planned new town of 70,000 scheduled to be under construction in 2011 on land that has been used for cattle grazing for more than a century.

The 22nd Congressional District of California, the southernmost district in the Central Valley, includes most of Bakersfield and Kern County, plus most of the land area of San Luis Obispo County and a slice of northern Los Angeles County, including half the desert town of Lancaster and the tiny desert town of Gorman. At the eastern end, in the Mojave Desert, is Edwards Air Force Base, where Chuck Yeager flew the X-1 and where the Space Shuttle has frequently landed. The 22nd includes oil fields and high-income subdivisions. The rich farmland produces most of the olives grown in the United States and more than 70% of the carrots (this is where the baby carrot was born). Politically, Kern County was Democratic territory, but by the late 1960s, it had become solidly Republican in national politics. The inland portion of San Luis Obispo County has always been Republican. George W. Bush won 68% of the vote in the district in 2004, his best showing in any California district. Republican presidential candidate John McCain won 60% in 2008 to 38% for Democrat Barack Obama, McCain's best district in the state.

The congressman from the 22nd District is Kevin McCarthy, a Republican who won the seat in 2006 without serious competition. McCarthy comes from a fourth-generation Bakersfield family and has a political background that has moved him quickly onto the leadership track in Congress. In college, he was chairman of the California Young Republicans and later headed the national Young Republicans organization. A graduate of California State University in Bakersfield, with an MBA, he started his own deli with $5,000 in winnings from the state lottery and made a success of the business. He sold the business and joined the district office of Republican U.S. Rep. Bill Thomas, the powerful chairman of the House Ways and Means Committee; McCarthy eventually became his district director and local protege. In 2002, McCarthy followed in Thomas's footsteps by winning election to the state Legislature. A mainstream conservative, McCarthy quickly impressed his colleagues and was elected minority leader during his first term. He served on the transition team for newly elected GOP Gov. Arnold Schwarzenegger and then worked closely with the governor on reducing the state's budget deficit, overhauling its workers' compensation system, and crafting a redistricting proposal that drew districts in which no political party had more than a 7% advantage among registered voters.

When Thomas announced his retirement in March 2006, McCarthy was the logical successor. He faced only token opposition in the June primary, a testament both to the strength of his candidacy and to the fact that Thomas announced his retirement just four days before the filing deadline, leaving little time for other prospective challengers to organize for a campaign. In this solidly Republican district, winning the GOP nomination was tantamount to victory. In November, McCarthy won 71%-29%. Yet he raised more than $1 million and traveled the country campaigning for and contributing to other Republican congressional candidates. He doled out at least $80,000, $50,000 of it to the National Republican Congressional Committee and most of the rest to Republican candidates for open seats. His hustle to raise money for the party put McCarthy in good stead with GOP leaders. He was also chosen as the freshman representative to the Republican Steering Committee, the leadership-run panel that hands out all-important committee assignments.

McCarthy caught on quickly in the House. As fellow California Republican Rep. Devin Nunes told the *Los Angeles Times,* McCarthy "lives and breathes politics." He got seats on the Financial Services and House Administration committees, and he occasionally departed from mainstream conservative views. As one of the younger Republican members, he expedited the systematic linking of lawmakers' websites and widely watched YouTube videos. He chaired the Platform Committee at the 2008 Republican National Convention in Minneapolis-St. Paul, winning praise for soliciting a wide spectrum of views and uniting conservatives and moderates.

In 2009, Virginia Republican Eric Cantor, the House Minority Whip, appointed McCarthy as his chief deputy whip, a role that Republicans usually reserve for their brightest up-and-coming star. The appointment gave McCarthy a role in Minority Leader John Boehner's senior leadership team. McCarthy has continued to be a prolific fundraiser for the GOP, and he contributed to nearly 80 House Republican candidates in 2008. As a member of Cantor's Young Guns campaign team, McCarthy took a prominent role in 2009 as the head of recruiting for the National Republican Congressional Committee's 2010 campaign.

At home, McCarthy was re-elected without opposition in 2008.

TWENTY-THIRD DISTRICT
Lois Capps (D)

Elected March 1998, 6th full term; b. Jan. 10, 1938, Ladysmith, WI; home, Santa Barbara; Pacific Lutheran U., B.S. 1959, Yale U., M.A. 1964, U. of CA at Santa Barbara, M.A. 1990; Lutheran; widowed; 3 children (1 deceased).

Professional Career: Staff nurse, Visiting Nurses Assn., 1963–64; Head nurse, Yale New Haven Hospital, 1960–63; Instructor, Santa Barbara City Col., 1983–95; Nurse, Santa Barbara Schl. Dist., 1979–96.

DC Office: 1110 LHOB, 20515, 202-225-3601; Fax: 202-225-5632; Web site: www.house.gov/capps.

State Offices: San Luis Obispo, 805-546-8348; Santa Barbara, 805-730-1710; Ventura County, 805-985-6807.

Committees: *Energy & Commerce* (13th of 36 D): Energy & Environment; Health. *Natural Resources* (21st of 29 D): Insular Affairs, Oceans & Wildlife; National Parks, Forests & Public Lands.

Group Ratings

	ADA	ACLU	AFS	LCV	ITIC	NTU	COC	ACU	CFG	FRC
2008	100	100	100	100	100	6	61	0	2	0
2007	95	—	100	95	—	3	55	0	11	—

National Journal Ratings

	2007 LIB	—	2007 CONS		2008 LIB	—	2008 CONS
Economic	82%	—	0%		71%	—	25%
Social	92%	—	0%		82%	—	0%
Foreign	94%	—	4%		92%	—	0%
Composite	94%	—	6%		87%	—	13%

Key Votes of the 110th Congress

1. Increase minimum wage	Y	5. Share immigration data	N	9. Withdraw troops 8/08	Y
2. Expand SCHIP	Y	6. Foreign aid abortion ban	N	10. No operations in Iran	Y
3. Raise CAFE standards	Y	7. Ban gay bias in workplace	Y	11. Free trade with Peru	Y
4. Bail out financial markets	Y	8. Repeal D.C. gun law	N	12. Overhaul FISA	N

Election Results

2008 general	Lois Capps (D)...171,403	(68%)	($957,695)
	Matt Kokkonen (R)..80,385	(32%)	($61,178)
2008 primary	Lois Capps (D)..unopposed		

Prior Winning Percentages: 2006 (65%); 2004 (63%); 2002 (59%); 2000 (53%); 1998 (55%); 1998 (53%)

Population		Race/Ethnicity		Work	
Pop. 2007:	653,587	White:	45.9%	Private:	74.2%
Change since 2000:	Up 2.3%	Black:	1.8%	Government:	16.6%
Urban:	98.0%	Hispanic:	44.2%	Self-employed:	8.9%
Rural:	2.0%	Asian:	5.6%	Blue collar:	20.3%
Area size:	2,479 sq. mi.	Native Am.:	0.4%	White collar:	55.3%
		Hawaiian:	0.2%	Khaki collar:	0.5%
Age		Two+ races:	1.7%	Other:	23.9%
Median age:	32.2 yrs.	*Ancestry*		Median income:	$53,653
More than 65 yrs:	12.0%	German:	8.8%	Median home value:	$624,000
Less than 18 yrs:	23.3%	Irish:	7.1%	Poverty:	15.7%
Education		English:	7.1%		
H.S. grad:	76.7%			**Military Veterans**	
College grad:	27.5%			% of Pop:	8.9%
Grad degree:	9.8%				

In a state where stunning coastal landscapes and charming small towns are a dime a dozen, Santa Barbara stands out as someplace special. It is a collection of red tile roofs and leafy live oaks, sheltered by towering mountains just above the sea. The impression is a bit misleading, for Santa Barbara has its problems. Most of its quaint white stucco buildings were put up not as part of 18th-century mission settlement, but after a 1925 earthquake leveled much of the town. Like Disneyland, Santa

2008 Presidential Vote		
Obama (D) 172,348	(66%)
McCain (R)..............................85,261	(32%)

2004 Presidential Vote		
Kerry (D)................................147,361	(58%)
Bush (R) 101,817	(40%)

Cook Partisan Voting Index: D + 12

Barbara is not an authentic antique, but rather a bigger, more attractive, cleaner version of a historical artifact, one that is maintained not by a company, but by an architectural review board. Santa Barbara's affluence isn't ersatz. This has long been one of the nation's richest retirement communities, one determined to preserve its pristine environment and serenity. Both features came under threat spectacularly in 1969, when an underwater oil well ruptured, coating the beach with oil. Pictures of the oil slick in the channel, and of volunteers trying to wash oil off grounded birds, helped to launch the 1970s environmental movement. Almost all of the wells are closed now (though some old 19th-century wells still send globs of oil to the beach at nearby Summerland). But the oil spill left a long-lasting residue in Santa Barbara's politics. This was once a mostly Republican community, uninterested in redistribution of wealth, but always concerned about the environment (it has built the nation's largest desalination plant) and having moderate-to-liberal impulses on cultural issues. Like most of coastal California, it has moved decisively to the left in the past decade. But some of the changes have not gone smoothly, as pressure grew to split Santa Barbara into two counties of roughly equal population: a Mission County to the west and north, which would be more conservative, and a Santa Barbara County, which would be more liberal. In June 2006, county voters overwhelmingly rejected the proposal.

The 23rd Congressional District of California is a thin strip of Pacific coastline, two to 12 miles wide, that runs from the industrial ports of Oxnard and Port Hueneme southeast of Santa Barbara to the north end of San Luis Obispo County on the Big Sur coast, just north of William Randolph Hearst's San Simeon. Nearly half of the population lives in upscale Santa Barbara County. But the largest city is Oxnard, in Ventura County, which, with a large number of immigrants, is anything but upscale. Overall, the district is 44% Hispanic. Much of the Santa Barbara coastline is occupied by Vandenberg Air Force Base, which launches unmanned government and commercial satellites into polar orbit. The largest towns in northern Santa Barbara County, like San Luis Obispo to the north, are pleasant, comfortable places, as untrendy as you can find in coastal California. Environmentalists want to extend the Monterey Bay National Marine Sanctuary to cover the waters off San Luis Obispo. In its final working days in January 2009, the Bush Administration proposed opening much of this area to oil and natural gas exploration, which spurred a lively debate here. This was a marginal district, seriously contested several times in the 1990s. But in its current iteration, it is safely Democratic. In 2008, Democrat Barack Obama won the district by a solid 66%-32% over Republican John McCain.

The congresswoman from the 23rd District is Lois Capps, a Democrat first chosen in a March 1998 special election to replace her late husband, Walter Capps. Lois Capps grew up in Wyoming and Montana, the daughter of a Lutheran minister. She graduated from college with a nursing degree and was the head nurse at Yale New Haven Hospital when she met Walter Capps, a student at Yale Divinity School. In 1964, he became a professor at the University of California at Santa Barbara. Lois Capps became the head elementary-school nurse for the Santa Barbara school system, director of the county's teenage pregnancy and parenting project, and a part-time instructor at Santa Barbara City Community College. In 1996, Walter Capps ran for the U.S. House and defeated Andrea Seastrand, a conservative state Assemblywoman. He died of a heart attack in his first year in office, in October 1997.

Lois Capps ran for his seat against Republican Assemblyman Tom Bordonaro, the favorite of Christian conservatives. Bordonaro, a paraplegic since a car accident in college, emphasized his "blue-collar roots and common values." Capps had help from labor unions and environmental groups. In the January 1998 primary, she finished first with 45% to 29% for Bordonaro. In the runoff, Bordonaro was hurt by divisions in the local GOP. Capps won a surprisingly large 53%-45% victory. The same two candidates were on the ballot in November. But national Republicans had little hope of winning by then, and it was not a priority race. Capps won 55%-43%.

She is a solid liberal, but she worked more successfully with Republicans when she was in the minority than the typical California Democrat. Perhaps it is her disposition. A 2006 survey of congressional aides by *Washingtonian* magazine named Capps "the nicest member of Congress."

With her background as a nurse and her seat on Energy and Commerce Committee, Capps has focused on the national nursing shortage, mental health issues and reforming the Medicare program for the elderly and disabled. She won enactment of a bill to attract more students into the nursing profession. In 2007, she became vice chair of the Health Subcommittee of Energy and Commerce, an important perch for shaping the nation's health care policy.

Another of her major interests, in keeping with her district's interests, is environmental policy. In 2004, the House passed her amendment to stop a comprehensive inventory of oil and gas resources beneath the outer continental shelf. She also opposed the Bush administration plan to drill in the Los Padres National Forest and has been outspoken against offshore drilling along the California coast. She called Bush's 11th-hour proposal for offshore drilling "nothing more than a parting gift to his buddies in the oil and gas industry" and predicted it would be shelved by the Obama administration. In 2005, she successfully opposed an attempt by California Republicans to convert part of the Channel Islands into a private recreation area for the military.

Capps has had an up-and-down relationship with her friends in organized labor. After she voted for normalizing trade relations with China, the Teamsters claimed that she'd betrayed them. She later patched things up by opposing the proposal to give President Bush broad authority to negotiate free-trade agreements.

In her first re-election bid, in 2000, Capps had serious competition from moderate Republican Mike Stoker, a former Santa Barbara County Supervisor and California Agricultural Labor Relations Board chairman. She had a big fundraising edge and won 53%-44%. After promising in 1998 to serve only three terms, she abandoned that pledge. Since 2002, she has not been seriously challenged. She has some family ties to the new Obama administration. In July 2007, her daughter, Laura Capps, a Democratic press aide on Capitol Hill, married Obama press aide Bill Burton.

TWENTY-FOURTH DISTRICT

Elton Gallegly (R)

Elected 1986, 12th term; b. March 7, 1944, Huntington Park; home, Simi Valley; Los Angeles St. Col., 1962–63; Protestant; married (Janice); 4 children.

Elected Office: Simi Valley City Cncl., 1979–80; Simi Valley mayor, 1980–86.

Professional Career: Owner, real estate firm.

DC Office: 2309 RHOB, 20515, 202-225-5811; Fax: 202-225-1100; Web site: www.house.gov/gallegly.

State Offices: Solvang, 805-686-2525; Thousand Oaks, 805-497-2224.

Committees: *Foreign Affairs* (4th of 19 R): Europe (RMM); Western Hemisphere. *Judiciary* (4th of 16 R): Immigration, Citizenship, Border Security & International Law. *Natural Resources* (3rd of 19 R): National Parks, Forests & Public Lands. *Intelligence (Select)* (2nd of 9 R).

Group Ratings

	ADA	ACLU	AFS	LCV	ITIC	NTU	COC	ACU	CFG	FRC
2008	15	18	14	0	83	67	89	92	74	100
2007	5	—	9	15	—	74	89	92	77	—

National Journal Ratings

	2007 LIB	—	2007 CONS		2008 LIB	—	2008 CONS
Economic	23%	—	76%		27%	—	73%
Social	0%	—	91%		31%	—	62%
Foreign	0%	—	72%		13%	—	84%
Composite	14%	—	86%		25%	—	75%

Key Votes of the 110th Congress

1. Increase minimum wage	N	5. Share immigration data	Y	9. Withdraw troops 8/08	N
2. Expand SCHIP	N	6. Foreign aid abortion ban	Y	10. No operations in Iran	N
3. Raise CAFE standards	N	7. Ban gay bias in workplace	N	11. Free trade with Peru	Y
4. Bail out financial markets	N	8. Repeal D.C. gun law	Y	12. Overhaul FISA	Y

Election Results

2008 general	Elton Gallegly (R)	174,492	(58%)	($737,060)
	Marta Ann Jorgensen (D)	125,560	(42%)	($11,927)
2008 primary	Elton Gallegly (R)	45,124	(77%)	
	Michael Tenenbaum (R)	13,446	(23%)	

Prior Winning Percentages: 2006 (62%); 2004 (63%); 2002 (65%); 2000 (54%); 1998 (60%); 1996 (60%); 1994 (66%); 1992 (54%); 1990 (58%); 1988 (69%); 1986 (68%)

Population		**Race/Ethnicity**		**Work**	
Pop. 2007:	674,698	White:	63.7%	Private:	74.7%
Change since 2000:	Up 5.6%	Black:	1.4%	Government:	14.7%
Urban:	94.2%	Hispanic:	26.5%	Self-employed:	10.2%
Rural:	5.8%	Asian:	5.5%	Blue collar:	16.3%
Area size:	4,157 sq. mi.	Native Am.:	0.4%	White collar:	66.7%
		Hawaiian:	0.2%	Khaki collar:	0.4%
Age		Two+ races:	1.9%	Other:	16.6%
Median age:	37.7 yrs.			Median income:	$76,982
More than 65 yrs:	12.0%	*Ancestry*		Median home value:	$632,700
Less than 18 yrs:	26.0%	German:	12.1%	Poverty:	7.0%
		Irish:	9.0%		
Education		English:	8.9%	**Military Veterans**	
H.S. grad:	87.7%			% of Pop:	10.2%
College grad:	33.3%				
Grad degree:	12.3%				

The city of Simi Valley is a product of the 1960s, the expansive postwar years when migrants from points across the United States went west to Los Angeles and then spread beyond city and county limits to fill up barren valleys between the mountains. With their work ethic, varied skills, and appreciation of the local environment, they brought a distaste for the crime and civil strife that seemed all too common in Los Angeles during that turbulent decade in U.S. history. The valleys of Ventura County, west of Los Angeles, filled up with people building new communities in what had been orange and lemon groves. Like California overall, the Ventura County population has trended socially liberal and economically conservative. To the south is upscale Thousand Oaks, one of the safest large cities in the nation. Farther west in Pleasant Valley is Camarillo. In the inland valleys still farther west are Santa Paula and Ojai. Academy Award nominee *Sideways*, which dealt with the abundant consumption of local wines by two friends, was filmed in nearby Buellton. Looking out toward these valleys and to the Pacific beyond is the Ronald Reagan Presidential Foundation and Library in Simi Valley. Housed there are 55 million pages of presidential documents and a large piece of the Berlin Wall, which Reagan famously urged Mikhail Gorbachev to tear down.

2008 Presidential Vote

Obama (D)	160,738	(51%)
McCain (R)	151,678	(48%)

2004 Presidential Vote

Bush (R)	165,430	(56%)
Kerry (D)	127,875	(43%)

Cook Partisan Voting Index: R + 4

The 24th Congressional District of California includes the interior of Ventura and Santa Barbara counties (most of their coastlines are in the 23rd District), plus a stretch of the Ventura County coastline and the Point Mugu Naval Weapons Test Center. The Santa Barbara County interior is lightly inhabited. It includes the small towns of Lompoc, Solvang, and Santa Ynez, near Reagan's beloved cabin in the mountains. It shares Vandenberg Air Force Base and the five Channel Islands and their steep cliffs with the 23rd. Most of the population is in eastern Ventura County. Politically, these areas trended Republican, but were more marginal in 2008. The district voted 56% for President George W Bush in 2004, but gave Democrat Barack Obama a 51%-48% edge four years later.

The congressman from the 24th District is Elton Gallegly, a Republican first elected in 1986. Gallegly *(GAL-eh-glee)* grew up in the working-class suburb of Huntington Park in Los Angeles County, the son of Dust Bowl migrants from Oklahoma who resettled in California. He dropped out of college and became a real estate broker, then started his own successful real estate business. In 1979, he was elected to the Simi Valley City Council and a year later became mayor. He built his campaign for the U.S. House on his record on economic development for Simi Valley. In the Republican primary, he ran against Tony Hope, son of comedian and actor Bob Hope, and won. He went on to win the general election overwhelmingly.

Gallegly has a moderate-to-conservative voting record and has played a mostly backstage role on major issues. As a member of the Judiciary Committee, he has been one of the Republican hard-liners on the issue of illegal immigration in recent years. He once proposed that public schools be given the option of turning away the children of illegal immigrants because of the cost of educating them. He also advocated a constitutional amendment to deny citizenship to the children of illegal immigrants, an end to welfare for illegal aliens and a tamperproof identification card for immigrants. In 2007, he sponsored a bill to require the Internal Revenue Service to report people suspected of working illegally in the United States to the Homeland Security Department.

Gallegly passed up several opportunities to chair a Judiciary subcommittee and declined to serve as a House manager during the Senate impeachment trial of President Bill Clinton. He was more interested in becoming chairman of the Natural Resources Committee. But in 2003, Republican leaders passed over Gallegly and other more senior Republicans to give the gavel to Richard Pombo of California, a favorite of Majority Leader Tom DeLay. Gallegly was passed over again in 2009 for the top Republican slot on the committee, which went to Rep. Doc Hastings of Washington state. His treatment by the leadership contributed to Gallegly's decision to retire from the House in 2006. But he was persuaded to stay by contrite Republican leaders, who faced a tough battle for control of the House that year and did not want another open seat to defend.

Gallegly is ranking Republican on the Europe Subcommittee of the Foreign Affairs Committee. In 2004, he was able to pass a resolution calling on the United Nations to respond to the threat that Burma posed to Southeast Asia. Locally, he had helped to save the Point Mugu Navy base, threatened with closure in 1996. He worked to get a wing of 16 E-2 radar planes assigned there, as well as two new C-130s that would be used to fight forest fires.

In 2003, Gallegly spent a few days campaigning for governor in the recall election, but withdrew because he lacked statewide name recognition. In his re-election campaign in 2008, Democratic challenger Marta Jorgensen accused him of ignoring the district, but she spent less than $12,000 compared with Gallegly's $737,000, and he won 58%-42%. His earlier inclination to retire from Congress, plus Democratic aspirations, could make this district a target for redistricters in 2011.

TWENTY-FIFTH DISTRICT

Buck McKeon (R)

Elected 1992, 9th term; b. Sept. 9, 1938, Los Angeles; home, Santa Clarita; Brigham Young U., B.S. 1985; Mormon; married (Patricia); 6 children.

Elected Office: William S. Hart Schl. District Bd., 1979–87; Santa Clarita mayor, 1987–88; Santa Clarita City Cncl., 1988–92.

Professional Career: Small businessman; Owner, Howard & Phil's Western Wear, 1973–00; Chmn., Valencia Natl. Bank, 1987–88.

DC Office: 2184 RHOB, 20515, 202-225-1956; Fax: 202-226-0683; Web site: mckeon.house.gov.

State Offices: Palmdale, 661-274-9688; Santa Clarita, 661-254-2111.

Committees: *Armed Services* (RMM of 25 R): Air & Land Forces; Strategic Forces.

Group Ratings

	ADA	ACLU	AFS	LCV	ITIC	NTU	COC	ACU	CFG	FRC
2008	5	18	0	8	86	67	100	88	78	82
2007	10	—	9	10	—	83	80	96	91	—

National Journal Ratings

	2007 LIB	—	2007 CONS		2008 LIB	—	2008 CONS
Economic	6%	—	93%		17%	—	82%
Social	21%	—	79%		31%	—	62%
Foreign	0%	—	72%		5%	—	93%
Composite	14%	—	86%		19%	—	81%

Key Votes of the 110th Congress

1. Increase minimum wage	N	5. Share immigration data	Y	9. Withdraw troops 8/08	N
2. Expand SCHIP	N	6. Foreign aid abortion ban	Y	10. No operations in Iran	N
3. Raise CAFE standards	N	7. Ban gay bias in workplace	N	11. Free trade with Peru	Y
4. Bail out financial markets	Y	8. Repeal D.C. gun law	Y	12. Overhaul FISA	Y

Election Results

2008 general	Buck McKeon (R)	144,660	(58%)	($903,400)
	Jackie Conaway (D)	105,929	(42%)	($10,486)
2008 primary	Buck McKeon (R)	unopposed		

Prior Winning Percentages: 2006 (60%); 2004 (64%); 2002 (65%); 2000 (62%); 1998 (75%); 1996 (62%); 1994 (65%); 1992 (52%)

Population		Race/Ethnicity		Work	
Pop. 2007:	792,899	White:	45.3%	Private:	74.5%
Change since 2000:	Up 24.1%	Black:	9.4%	Government:	17.2%
Urban:	88.2%	Hispanic:	36.4%	Self-employed:	8.0%
Rural:	11.8%	Asian:	5.0%	Blue collar:	23.8%
Area size:	21,622 sq. mi.	Native Am.:	0.8%	White collar:	57.1%
Age		Hawaiian:	0.3%	Khaki collar:	0.6%
Median age:	31.9 yrs.	Two+ races:	2.5%	Other:	18.5%
More than 65 yrs:	7.9%	*Ancestry*		Median income:	$59,993
Less than 18 yrs:	31.3%	German:	9.7%	Median home value:	$378,500
Education		Irish:	7.3%	Poverty:	14.5%
H.S. grad:	79.9%	English:	6.2%	**Military Veterans**	
College grad:	20.0%			% of Pop:	9.3%
Grad degree:	6.3%				

The settled area of Los Angeles County does not end at the mountains at the northern rim of the San Fernando Valley. It continues along Route 14 past the mountain-surrounded city of Santa Clarita, with 170,000 residents, and the Six Flags Magic Mountain theme park, past the former gold-mining center of Acton, and on to where the mountains stop at the San Andreas Fault and the desert stretches out low and flat. This is Antelope Valley, with huge aerospace plants and military bases around the

2008 Presidential Vote
Obama (D) 134,222 (49%)
McCain (R) 131,201 (48%)

2004 Presidential Vote
Bush (R) 142,052 (59%)
Kerry (D) 96,355 (40%)

Cook Partisan Voting Index: R + 6

fast-growing towns of Palmdale and Lancaster, where more than 285,000 people live. Not far from upscale shopping centers, there has been a resurgence of specialty farm crops such as baby carrots, organic onions, and parsnips. Traffic congestion and incidents of gang crime have supplanted the once rural lifestyle. A new expressway that's under construction will eventually link Antelope and Victor valleys. However, overall transportation services were set back in 2009 when the Palmdale airport closed, two months after United Airlines ended flights to the airport. The adjacent Air Force Plant 42 is home to many defense contractors, with projects that include the B-2 Stealth Bomber, the F-117 Stealth Fighter, and the Joint Strike Fighter. Beyond Antelope Valley, the desert stretches for miles, with clumps of human settlement—Edwards Air Force Base, where Chuck Yeager flew the X-1 and where the Space Shuttle has frequently landed, and the desert towns of Victorville and Barstow.

The 25th Congressional District of California covers these areas, though it shares Edwards AFB with the 22nd District. Geographically, it is vast, the largest in the state. It extends far to the north, across the almost uninhabited Mojave Desert and mountains to include the national parks of Death Valley and Owens Valley. The military occupies hundreds of thousands of acres with its China Lake Naval Air Weapons Station, the Goldstone deep-space communications complex, and the battlefield training center at Fort Irwin. The district then swings north to include mountainous Inyo and Mono counties. Politically, this has been a Republican district, though in the 2008 presidential election, Democrat Barack Obama won 49.4%-48.3%.

The congressman from the 25th District is Howard (Buck) McKeon, a Republican first elected in 1992. McKeon *(mac-KEE-an)* in 2009 became the ranking Republican on the House Armed Services Committee, making him the minority's party's leading voice on defense issues. He grew up in Southern California, graduated from Brigham Young University, and then went to work in the family business, Howard and Phil's Western Wear. He later took over the chain, which at its peak had 52 stores in California, Arizona, Nevada, and Utah. (The business closed in 2000.) McKeon was the first mayor of Santa Clarita, after it was incorporated in 1987. He ran for a new U.S. House seat in 1992 and won the crucial GOP primary 40%-38% over Assemblyman Phil Wyman.

With a voting record that has been reliably conservative, McKeon has long been an influential member of the Education and Labor Committee. He is a former chairman of the committee, and was the ranking Republican until he gave up the post in June 2009 to become the ranking Republican on Armed Services. In 2001, he handled the renewal of the higher-education bill and advocated steps that would penalize hundreds of universities and colleges that have raised tuition much faster than inflation. Many schools and Democrats complained loudly that he was advocating price controls. McKeon responded that he simply was calling for removal of federal aid from schools that push their rates too high. But in the face of opposition from the Bush administration, he abandoned the proposal, claiming that many colleges had moved to rein in tuition hikes. Another of his priorities was a bill granting full Social Security benefits to teachers and other public servants who receive local pensions and take a second job. (In 13 states, these retirees must take cuts in Social Security.)

When Rep. John Boehner of Ohio stepped down as full committee chairman to become majority leader in February 2006, McKeon succeeded him, leapfrogging two more-senior Republicans. In the remaining months of the Republican majority, he completed an overhaul of employment training programs and a sweeping rewrite of pension laws, with the support of Boehner, who had initiated the legislation as chairman.

In 2007, after Republicans lost the majority, McKeon became ranking Republican, a challenging post, with activist chairman Democrat George Miller of California in charge. In 2008, he cooperated with Miller on the renewal of the Higher Education Act, which took steps to control college costs and to increase financial aid for students. Despite strong criticism from the Bush administration, the House overwhelmingly approved the legislation, which established a list of the nation's most expensive colleges and cracked down on the way student loan companies try to gain favor with college officials and get access to students. The legislation also raised the maximum Pell grant, a financial award to needy students, from $4,000 to $8,000 a year. And it prohibited gifts and profit-sharing arrangements between lenders and colleges.

On an issue of great local interest, McKeon in 2008 joined Democratic Sen. Barbara Boxer of California on a proposal to give wilderness protection to 430,000 acres in the Sierra Nevada and San Gabriel mountains. It was enacted in March 2009 as part of a public-lands bill.

McKeon has been re-elected without serious opposition. In 2008, he won his closest-ever re-election, 58%-42%, over Democrat Jackie Conaway, a law-office manager who campaigned on tougher enforcement of immigration laws.

TWENTY-SIXTH DISTRICT

David Dreier (R)

Elected 1980, 15th term; b. July 5, 1952, Kansas City, MO; home, San Dimas; Claremont McKenna Col., B.A. 1975, Claremont Grad. Schl., M.A. 1976; Christian Scientist; single.

Professional Career: Corp. relations dir., Claremont McKenna Col., 1976–78; Mktg. dir., Industrial Hydrocarbons, 1978–80; V.P., Dreier Development Co., 1985–present.

DC Office: 233 CHOB, 20515, 202-225-2305; Fax: 202-225-7018; Web site: dreier.house.gov.

State Offices: San Dimas, 909-575-6226.

Committees: *Rules* (RMM of 4 R): Legislative & Budget Process.

Group Ratings

	ADA	ACLU	AFS	LCV	ITIC	NTU	COC	ACU	CFG	FRC
2008	10	18	14	0	100	63	100	86	70	82
2007	20	—	0	15	—	80	85	88	89	—

National Journal Ratings

	2007 LIB — 2007 CONS		2008 LIB — 2008 CONS	
Economic	18%	— 82%	18%	— 81%
Social	29%	— 69%	39%	— 60%
Foreign	0%	— 72%	35%	— 62%
Composite	21%	— 79%	32%	— 69%

Key Votes of the 110th Congress

1. Increase minimum wage	N	5. Share immigration data	Y	9. Withdraw troops 8/08	N
2. Expand SCHIP	N	6. Foreign aid abortion ban	Y	10. No operations in Iran	N
3. Raise CAFE standards	N	7. Ban gay bias in workplace	Y	11. Free trade with Peru	Y
4. Bail out financial markets	Y	8. Repeal D.C. gun law	*	12. Overhaul FISA	Y

Election Results

2008 general				
	David Dreier (R)	140,615	(53%)	($2,919,351)
	Russ Warner (D)	108,039	(40%)	($1,334,171)
	Ted Brown (Lib)	18,476	(7%)	
2008 primary	David Dreier (R)	29,627	(74%)	
	Sonny Sardo (R)	10,158	(26%)	

Prior Winning Percentages: 2006 (57%); 2004 (54%); 2002 (64%); 2000 (57%); 1998 (58%); 1996 (61%); 1994 (67%); 1992 (58%); 1990 (64%); 1988 (69%); 1986 (72%); 1984 (71%); 1982 (65%); 1980 (52%)

Population		Race/Ethnicity		Work	
Pop. 2007:	690,946	White:	47.4%	Private:	75.1%
Change since 2000:	Up 8.1%	Black:	4.7%	Government:	16.2%
Urban:	98.8%	Hispanic:	27.3%	Self-employed:	8.5%
Rural:	1.2%	Asian:	17.7%	Blue collar:	15.8%
Area size:	755 sq. mi.	Native Am.:	0.3%	White collar:	71.0%
		Hawaiian:	0.3%	Khaki collar:	0.0%
Age		Two+ races:	2.1%	Other:	13.2%
Median age:	37.0 yrs.	*Ancestry*		Median income:	$74,839
More than 65 yrs:	11.5%	German:	9.4%	Median home value:	$585,900
Less than 18 yrs:	25.2%	English:	6.8%	Poverty:	6.5%
Education		Irish:	6.3%	**Military Veterans**	
H.S. grad:	89.1%			% of Pop:	7.8%
College grad:	36.2%				
Grad degree:	13.5%				

It was the great route west to California in the first half of the 20th century: Passengers on the Santa Fe railroad's *Super Chief* or motorists on U.S. 66, after hours and days in barren desert, descended through the Cajon Pass into the Los Angeles Basin, then moved in a stately procession beneath the 10,000-foot snow-capped San Gabriel Mountains, marveling at orange groves and exotic plants. The railroad and highway ran through a line of towns built by Midwestern Protestants as independent

2008 Presidential Vote

Obama (D)	149,249	(51%)
McCain (R)	137,329	(47%)

2004 Presidential Vote

Bush (R)	148,352	(55%)
Kerry (D)	117,532	(44%)

Cook Partisan Voting Index: R+3

communities that today have been transformed into high-income suburbs with their own civic institutions. There is Claremont, home of the academically renowned Claremont Colleges and referred to as "The City of Trees and Ph.D.'s." There are La Verne, Glendora and San Dimas, with its rodeo and horse trails. Arcadia has the Santa Anita racetrack and the Los Angeles County Arboretum. Luxurious San Marino is the home of the Huntington Library, one of the world's great museums and scholarly institutions, with more than 150 acres of botanical gardens.

The 26th Congressional District of California covers these foothill communities in the San Gabriel Valley. It includes, east of Claremont, the newer San Bernardino cities of Upland, Montclair and Rancho Cucamonga, the largest city in the district. It also encompasses the new suburb of Walnut to the south and, far to the west, the mountain-enclosed suburb of La Canada-Flintridge, home of NASA's Jet Propulsion Laboratory, which is vital to the space program. Historically, the towns running east from Los Angeles have been heavily Republican. But the area now has large and growing Hispanic and Asian populations. San Marino, Arcadia, San Dimas and Walnut have sizable Chinese populations. A foreign language is spoken in 36% of homes in the district. And its communities are no longer solidly Republican. President George W. Bush won 55% of the vote here in 2004, but Barack Obama won 51%-47% in 2008.

The congressman from the 26th District is David Dreier, an influential Republican first elected in 1980. Dreier *(DRY-er)* grew up in Kansas City, Mo., the son of a former Marine Corps drill instructor who ran a real-estate investment firm. Dreier spent a decade mostly on the Claremont McKenna campus, first as a student and then as an administrator, before he was elected to Congress. He first ran in 1978, at age 25, and lost to Democratic incumbent Rep. Jim Lloyd. Two years later, he beat Lloyd. Dreier personifies the intellectually rigorous conservatism and free-market economics that have thrived at Claremont, and he maintains a California-style cheerfulness and good humor. He has been a powerful force for Republicans on the Rules Committee, the leadership-driven panel that sets the ground rules for debate on every important bill that comes to the House floor. A procedural rule can mean the difference between success and failure of a bill on the floor. As Rules chairman from 1999 to 2006, he was a top lieutenant of Republican Speaker Dennis Hastert.

In that time, Dreier's committee produced hundreds of rules, and he lost only two fights over them on the House floor. He also led a bipartisan review that reduced the number of standing House rules from 51 to 28. After September 11, he helped establish the Homeland Security Committee. In 2003, he pushed through rules changes to allow the speaker to adjust the number of House members required for a quorum in the case of a catastrophic attack on the capital. Dreier has long maintained that regularly occurring vacancies should be filled by special elections rather than by appointments by governors, as they are in the Senate. After the controversy in 2009 over the potentially tainted appointment of Illinois Sen. Roland Burris by Democratic Gov. Rod Blagojevich, Dreier assembled a bipartisan group to promote a constitutional amendment to require election of senators to all vacancies. Blagojevich was impeached and charged by federal prosecutors with trying to sell the Senate seat.

When Republicans lost the majority in 2006, Dreier became the ranking Republican on Rules. He has frequently clashed with Democratic Chairman Louise Slaughter of New York, and has shown a new zest in challenging the Democrats' procedural moves and occasionally outmaneuvering them.

His voting record is mostly conservative, though it's more centrist on cultural issues. His policy agenda is free trade, promotion of high technology and issues related to diminishing water supplies in the San Gabriel Valley. In the late 1990s, he was the chief advocate of normalizing trade relations with China and led the fight for many months. In 2001 and 2002, he worked to pass a measure giving the president wide authority to negotiate free-trade deals. It was enacted in 2002. On high-tech issues, he was a leading sponsor of legislation increasing the number of visas for high-technology workers from overseas. In 2005, with Judiciary Committee Chairman Jim Sensenbrenner, R-Wis., Dreier won enactment of the "Real ID" bill to prevent states from issuing drivers' licenses to illegal immigrants.

In 2005, after Republican Rep. Tom DeLay of Texas was forced to step down as majority leader amid an ethics scandal, Hastert wanted to name Dreier as acting majority leader. But conservatives objected to Dreier as insufficiently conservative on cultural issues, and Majority Whip Roy Blunt privately urged Hastert to give the position to him. Hastert agreed, and Dreier was given additional duties in coordinating the leadership's outreach to committee chairmen. In February 2006, when Republican John Boehner of Ohio was elected by Republicans to permanently replace DeLay, Dreier was assigned to push lobbying and ethics reforms. The House passed the bill.

Dreier took the lead for California Republicans on redistricting in 2001 and reached an agreement with Democratic redistricter Michael Berman under which 19 of the 20 Republican incumbents got safe districts and the GOP got a newly created seat in return for Republican support in the Legislature. That helped Dreier, whose district was becoming more Hispanic and more Democratic. He supported Republican Arnold Schwarzenegger for governor in the recall election in 2003 and appeared with him at almost every campaign rally. In the six weeks between Schwarzenegger's election and his inauguration, Dreier acted as head of his 65-member transition team in Sacramento.

After decades without a serious re-election contest, Dreier was opposed in the 2004 primary by a conservative who attacked him on the issues of trade and illegal immigration. Dreier won easily. But then two Los Angeles radio talk-show hosts, critical of his moderate positions on illegal immigration, launched a "Fire Dreier" campaign. In September, they held a rally outside Dreier's office with his Democratic opponent, Cynthia Matthews. She spent only $26,000 on her challenge, while Dreier spent $1.3 million. He won, 54%-43%. In a 2006 rematch, he defeated Matthews 57%-38%.

In 2008, businessman Russ Warner was the Democratic challenger and spent over $1.3 million. Republicans sent out flyers citing tax problems in Warner's business dealings. Dreier won 53%-40%, with comfortable margins in each of the district's two counties. Those contests, plus the changing demographics of his district, could embolden Democratic redistricters to force Dreier into new territory in 2012.

TWENTY-SEVENTH DISTRICT

Brad Sherman (D)

Elected 1996, 7th term; b. Oct. 24, 1954, Los Angeles; home, Sherman Oaks; U.C.L.A., B.A. 1974, Harvard U., J.D. 1979; Jewish; married (Lisa); 1 child.

Elected Office: CA St. Board of Equalization, 1990–95, chmn., 1991–95.

Professional Career: Accountant, 1980–90.

DC Office: 2242 RHOB, 20515, 202-225-5911; Fax: 202-225-5879; Web site: www.house.gov/sherman.

State Offices: Sherman Oaks, 818-501-9200.

Committees: *Financial Services* (9th of 42 D): Capital Markets, Insurance & Government Sponsored Enterprises; Domestic Monetary Policy & Technology; Financial Institutions & Consumer Credit. *Foreign Affairs* (5th of 28 D): Asia, the Pacific & the Global Environment; Middle East & South Asia; Terrorism, Nonproliferation & Trade (Chmn). *Judiciary* (17th of 24 D): Commercial & Administrative Law; Constitution, Civil Rights & Civil Liberties; Courts & Competition Policy.

Group Ratings

	ADA	ACLU	AFS	LCV	ITIC	NTU	COC	ACU	CFG	FRC
2008	85	91	100	92	71	17	61	9	13	11
2007	100	—	100	95	—	3	50	0	7	—

National Journal Ratings

	2007 LIB	—	2007 CONS	2008 LIB	—	2008 CONS
Economic	82%	—	0%	77%	—	23%
Social	77%	—	17%	59%	—	38%
Foreign	63%	—	35%	85%	—	15%
Composite	78%	—	22%	74%	—	26%

Key Votes of the 110th Congress

1. Increase minimum wage	Y	5. Share immigration data	N	9. Withdraw troops 8/08	Y
2. Expand SCHIP	Y	6. Foreign aid abortion ban	N	10. No operations in Iran	N
3. Raise CAFE standards	Y	7. Ban gay bias in workplace	Y	11. Free trade with Peru	N
4. Bail out financial markets	N	8. Repeal D.C. gun law	N	12. Overhaul FISA	Y

Election Results

2008 general	Brad Sherman (D)..	145,812	(69%)	($565,838)
	Navraj Singh (R)...	52,852	(25%)	($32,645)
	Tim Denton (Lib)..	14,171	(7%)	
2008 primary	Brad Sherman (D)..	unopposed		

Prior Winning Percentages: 2006 (69%); 2004 (62%); 2002 (62%); 2000 (66%); 1998 (57%); 1996 (49%)

Population		Race/Ethnicity		Work	
Pop. 2007:	669,109	White:	40.7%	Private:	78.2%
Change since 2000:	Up 4.7%	Black:	4.5%	Government:	10.0%
Urban:	99.7%	Hispanic:	40.6%	Self-employed:	11.6%
Rural:	0.3%	Asian:	11.8%	Blue collar:	20.3%
Area size:	152 sq. mi.	Native Am.:	0.3%	White collar:	63.0%
		Hawaiian:	0.1%	Khaki collar:	0.0%
Age		Two+ races:	1.4%	Other:	16.6%
Median age:	35.9 yrs.			Median income:	$57,014
More than 65 yrs:	10.9%	*Ancestry*		Median home value:	$576,600
Less than 18 yrs:	24.9%	German:	5.6%	Poverty:	12.2%
		Irish:	4.6%		
Education		English:	4.2%	**Military Veterans**	
H.S. grad:	79.6%			% of Pop:	5.5%
College grad:	28.9%				
Grad degree:	8.5%				

In the early 20th century, when the movie business was young, the San Fernando Valley was a vast expanse of empty land that had been annexed to Los Angeles in 1915. Moviemakers, looking for filming sites for a western, drove past the vacant lots of Westwood, up narrow roads through the Santa Monica Mountains and over into the vast Valley, sheltered from ocean breezes and rain-bearing clouds by the mountains. Since then, this vast bowl of land has been transformed, first into 1950s

2008 Presidential Vote		
Obama (D)	157,100	(66%)
McCain (R)	75,286	(32%)
2004 Presidential Vote		
Kerry (D)	130,567	(59%)
Bush (R)	86,397	(39%)
Cook Partisan Voting Index:	D+13	

suburbia, and then into a postmodern city of its own, economically vital and yeastily ethnic. Even in its suburban years, the San Fernando Valley was not entirely residential. Big factories provided jobs—the now shuttered General Motors Van Nuys assembly plant, the Anheuser Busch brewery, Rockwell (now Boeing) and Litton (now Northrop Grumman) defense plants. In those years, this was fast-growing, family-friendly territory. And politically, it was turf fought over by Republicans and Democrats.

There is plenty of upscale territory left in the uplands of the Valley, in Granada Hills and Tarzana. The office blocks and mini-malls show unmistakable signs of affluence. In what had been the culturally arid Valley, lounges and bars have become prevalent. Urban planners have revived the planned community of Panorama City, which was the busy center of the Valley during the 1950s. In the inner lowlands of the Valley, new immigrants have moved to the growing communities of Reseda and Van Nuys. Some old neighborhoods have become rough enclaves, with youth gangs and boarded-up houses and apartments. Iranians and Chinese, Mexicans and Koreans, Israelis and Filipinos are keeping other neighborhoods diverse and solidly middle class. Even this multiethnic Valley has been unhappy to be linked with the city of Los Angeles, whose City Council imposes high taxes and irksome regulations. A Valley secession movement arose, and the issue was put on the November 2002 ballot. The Valley voted 51%-49% for it, with stronger support in the western part. But it needed a majority in all of Los Angeles to pass, and so it failed, though some embers of secession interest remain. In 2007, the Valley had 1.76 million residents, more than 40% of them foreign-born. Compared to most Americans and Californians, Valley residents make more money, spend more of it on housing, and endure longer commutes to work, according to the 2007 Valley census report.

The 27th Congressional District of California on the map looks like an inverted "U" over the San Fernando Valley, between the Santa Monica and San Gabriel mountains. On the east it includes part of Burbank, the home of NBC studios and Disney headquarters, and also blue-collar and heavily Hispanic neighborhoods filled with renters. To the north, are Sunland and Tujunga at the base of the San Gabriel Mountains. The larger and more settled parts of the district are west of the 405 Freeway (roughly the dividing line between the East and West valleys), including most of Granada Hills, Northridge, Van Nuys, and Tarzana. This is a diverse district, indeed: 41% of residents are Hispanic, most of them Mexican, and 12% are Asian, roughly half of them Filipino or Korean. The district is comfortably Democratic, and traces of the Valley as the onetime base for President Ronald Reagan long ago disappeared.

The congressman from the 27th District is Brad Sherman, a Democrat first elected in 1996. Sherman grew up in Monterey Park, in the San Gabriel Valley east of Los Angeles. He started working on Democratic campaigns at age 6, licking stamps and stuffing envelopes for U.S. Rep. George Brown. He set up his own stamp-wholesaling firm at age 14. He graduated with high honors from the University of California at Los Angeles, worked as an accountant, then went to Harvard Law School. He came back to the Los Angeles area to practice tax law, and he represented the Philippines in its successful effort to seize the assets of deposed president Ferdinand Marcos.

In 1990, Sherman was elected from Los Angeles County to the state Board of Equalization, which is a sort of tax court. He was known as a stickler for detail, a "tax nerd," as one former staffer said, who used the office with a keen scent for political advantage. He irritated cartoonists with a ruling that exempted artwork from the state tax but not illustrations. They took their revenge by setting up a website, the Sherman Gallery, where they vied in caricaturing the balding and bespectacled Sherman. In 1996, he moved his residence from Santa Monica to Sherman Oaks, where a U.S. House seat had opened. Both he and his Republican opponent, businessman Rich Sybert, were self-financers; Sherman spent $578,000 of his own money. And both stressed their moderation. Sherman ran against then House Speaker Newt Gingrich and the Republican Congress, but he also supported the death penalty, called for phasing out racial quotas and preferences, and favored tough measures on illegal immigration. Sybert stressed his independence from Gingrich as well as his support of abortion rights and environmental protections. Sherman won 49%-44%.

In the House, his voting record has been more moderate than those of most other Los Angeles County Democrats, and he has shown occasional independence from party leaders. In 2002, he voted for the use of force in Iraq, after initially backing a provision to urge more support from the United Nations. The House passed his amendment to require competitive bidding procedures for the procurement of oil from Iraq, but a conference committee later dropped it. He sought to limit the use of franked mailings by House committee chairmen.

On the Foreign Affairs Committee, Sherman chairs the Terrorism, Nonproliferation, and Trade Subcommittee, where his priority is preventing Iran from obtaining nuclear weapons. He has sought tougher economic sanctions on Iran and companies that do business there.

One of the few certified public accountants in Congress, he also serves on the Financial Services Committee, where his experience has been useful in congressional attempts to unravel recent corporate accounting scandals. In 2008, he was an outspoken foe of the bill to bail out the financial-services industry, dubbing it "cash for trash." As the most senior Democrat on the committee to oppose the bill, he criticized the "panic atmosphere" that surrounded the push for passage, which he said was unjustified by the facts. "I understand Wall Street without being part of Wall Street," he said. When domestic-auto-company executives testified in favor of a proposed bailout for that industry in November 2008, Sherman got them to concede that they had all flown separately to Washington in private airplanes, a revelation that sparked a public backlash. In March 2009, he advocated a 70% surtax on all compensation exceeding $1 million for executives of financial institutions receiving large federal bailouts.

Sherman has won re-election easily, even after redistricting following the 2000 census gave him a district that was two-thirds new to him and 37% Hispanic. He has not had serious opposition. The area's growing Hispanic population and ambitious redistricters in Sacramento could place him at risk in 2012, though he is confident in his role as a self-described "trouble maker."

TWENTY-EIGHTH DISTRICT

Howard Berman (D)

Elected 1982, 14th term; b. April 15, 1941, Los Angeles; home, N. Hollywood; U.C.L.A., B.A. 1962, LL.B. 1965; Jewish; married (Janis); 2 children.

Elected Office: CA Assembly, 1973–82, maj. ldr., 1974–79.

Professional Career: Practicing atty., 1967–72.

DC Office: 2221 RHOB, 20515, 202-225-4695; Fax: 202-225-3196; Web site: www.house.gov/berman.

State Offices: Van Nuys, 818-994-7200.

Committees: *Foreign Affairs* (Chmn of 28 D). *Judiciary* (2nd of 24 D): Immigration, Citizenship, Border Security & International Law.

Group Ratings

	ADA	ACLU	AFS	LCV	ITIC	NTU	COC	ACU	CFG	FRC
2008	85	91	100	100	100	7	69	4	4	5
2007	85	—	100	85	—	5	53	4	12	—

National Journal Ratings

	2007 LIB — 2007 CONS		2008 LIB — 2008 CONS	
Economic	82%	0%	77%	22%
Social	92%	0%	75%	18%
Foreign	72%	28%	70%	25%
Composite	86%	14%	76%	24%

Key Votes of the 110th Congress

1. Increase minimum wage	Y	5. Share immigration data	N	9. Withdraw troops 8/08	Y
2. Expand SCHIP	Y	6. Foreign aid abortion ban	N	10. No operations in Iran	Y
3. Raise CAFE standards	Y	7. Ban gay bias in workplace	Y	11. Free trade with Peru	Y
4. Bail out financial markets	Y	8. Repeal D.C. gun law	N	12. Overhaul FISA	Y

Election Results

2008 general	Howard Berman (D)	unopposed
2008 primary	Howard Berman (D)	unopposed

Prior Winning Percentages: 2006 (74%); 2004 (71%); 2002 (71%); 2000 (84%); 1998 (82%); 1996 (66%); 1994 (63%); 1992 (61%); 1990 (61%); 1988 (70%); 1986 (65%); 1984 (63%); 1982 (60%)

Population		**Race/Ethnicity**		**Work**	
Pop. 2007:	655,343	White:	31.4%	Private:	80.4%
Change since 2000:	Up 2.5%	Black:	3.1%	Government:	7.3%
Urban:	99.9%	Hispanic:	57.3%	Self-employed:	12.1%
Rural:	0.1%	Asian:	6.3%	Blue collar:	27.0%
Area size:	78 sq. mi.	Native Am.:	0.2%	White collar:	53.8%
		Hawaiian:	0.1%	Khaki collar:	0.1%
Age		Two+ races:	1.1%	Other:	19.2%
Median age:	33.1 yrs.	*Ancestry*		Median income:	$49,253
More than 65 yrs:	9.6%	German:	3.9%	Median home value:	$579,700
Less than 18 yrs:	26.6%	Irish:	3.6%	Poverty:	16.1%
Education		English:	3.0%		
H.S. grad:	69.7%			**Military Veterans**	
College grad:	25.9%			% of Pop:	4.2%
Grad degree:	8.3%				

A hiker looking north from the crest of the Santa Monica Mountains in 1910 would have seen a valley almost totally empty and barren, 20 miles long and 12 miles wide. Separated by the Cahuenga Pass from rapidly growing Los Angeles and Hollywood, the San Fernando Valley was bought up in massive tracts by civic leaders as they were urging city engineer William Mulholland to build a huge 250-mile aqueduct from the Owens Valley to give Los Angeles water and persuading the city in 1915 to annex 200

2008 Presidential Vote		
Obama (D)	147,958	(76%)
McCain (R)	42,815	(22%)
2004 Presidential Vote		
Kerry (D)	125,351	(71%)
Bush (R)	49,220	(28%)
Cook Partisan Voting Index:	D + 23	

square miles of the Valley. In the years after World War II, this was modern suburbia, filled with *Leave It to Beaver* families. Today the San Fernando Valley is postmodern urban, with Disney headquarters in Burbank and Universal City's CityWalk shopping and entertainment center. The driver topping the crest today sees office towers looming out over slightly hazy air, shopping centers, occasional palm trees, stucco subdivisions, and the squat factory and warehouse buildings that have made Los Angeles County a top manufacturing locale. The Valley has aged, in some ways gracefully. Homeowners in Van Nuys, Sun Valley, and Granada Hills are forming preservation districts, maintaining the antic architecture of the Valley in the 1950s.

The people in the Valley have also changed. The 1950s white Anglo families with stay-at-home moms have been replaced by hard-working Latino families with parents juggling two jobs. But there is continuity: These are communities where people work hard trying to raise children who will have a better chance than they had. Pacoima, at the northern end of the Valley, where Rodney King was pulled over and beaten and arrested, is mostly Latino. Farther south, in Canoga Park, Van Nuys, and Burbank, was the industrial base—the GM plants were mostly shut down in the 1980s, and only one of the defense plants remains open, the old Rocketdyne plant, which is now owned by Pratt and Whitney. But now there are hundreds of small factories and multimedia plants where thousands of jobs have been created. The southern rim of the Valley, around Studio City and North Hollywood, is still heavily Jewish and is attracting new families who often send their kids to religious schools. There is a trendy and lively shopping strip along Ventura Boulevard. People with money cluster near the foot of the mountains around the Valley; those less well off settle on the flatlands beyond. But rich or poor, many of these neighborhoods were hit hard when the housing bubble burst in 2007 and 2008. With its perpetually inflated real estate market, the Valley suffered from a huge wave of foreclosures.

The 28th Congressional District of California consists of about half of the San Fernando Valley and some of the mountains to the south. It includes parts of Van Nuys and several miles of land on either side of the Hollywood Freeway, from the point where it comes through the Cahuenga Pass from Hollywood to the junction with the Golden State Freeway. Much of the northern end of the Valley, including Pacoima and the small city of San Fernando, is in the district. Mulholland Drive, which runs along the crest of the Santa Monica Mountains and the Ventura Freeway, is the southern border, until the district dips south to Hollywood Boulevard. Within these borders are affluent North Hollywood, Studio City, Sherman Oaks, and Encino, with big houses on twisting streets overlooking the Valley and just above the shops of Ventura Boulevard. The population of the district is about 57% Hispanic, mostly concentrated in the central and northern sections. But Hispanics are still not the majority voting bloc here, because many are not citizens, and many are children or young people not yet in the voting stream. The high Democratic percentages here are due as much to Jewish as to Latino voters. The spark of hope that some Republicans saw in this district when George W. Bush's percentage rose from 24% in 2000 to 28% in 2004 was doused when Republican John McCain got only 22% in 2008.

The congressman from the 28th District is Howard Berman, a Democrat first elected in 1982. He has endured as one of the most creative members of the House and one of the most clear-sighted operators in American politics. Berman grew up in Los Angeles in modest circumstances. His father was a Polish immigrant who worked in the textile industry. Berman got interested in politics in high school and went to the University of California at Los Angeles, where he befriended Henry Waxman, who has been an ally in politics ever since. Today, Waxman is an influential House member from California's 30th District. At UCLA law school, Berman got an internship at the California Assembly and was assigned to farm-labor issues with César Chávez's movement. "From then on, I was hooked," Berman said. A few years later, he and Waxman were elected to the California Assembly, Berman by beating the Assembly's Republican leader in a Hollywood Hills district. This was the beginning of the so-called Berman-Waxman political machine—not so much a precinct organization as a group of consultants who raised money, redrew district lines, and endorsed candidates through direct mail. Their core constituency was liberal Westside Jews. A key player was Berman's brother Michael Berman, who became an expert on redistricting and who helped draw the new lines for California after the 2000 census. Howard Berman became Assembly Majority Leader in his first term. In 1980, he tried to unseat Speaker Leo McCarthy, but ultimately they both lost to Willie Brown, who remained in the post for 15 years. Berman's consolation prize was a Valley-based congressional seat in 1982. The machine fell on hard times in the 1990s, as Republicans wrested away control of redistricting and the feminist left became the Democratic Party's driving force. "We don't have a machine anymore, if we ever did," Berman said in 2004. "We just helped some friends." In recent years, Berman has been a political force on his own, with a record that is mostly but not always liberal.

Berman has been an active legislator on all manner of issues, but not one who gets much publicity. On foreign policy, he started off less as a Vietnam War dove than as a backer of Israel. For a decade, he floor-managed foreign-aid authorization bills, defending aid to many countries as well as Israel. With the respected Henry Hyde, an Illinois conservative, Berman wrote the law authorizing embargoes on nations that condone terrorism. In April 1990, he called for sanctions on Iraq, four months before Saddam Hussein invaded Kuwait. Berman also voted for the Gulf War resolution. He played a critical role in winning passage by a wide margin of the Iraq War resolution in October 2002. He strongly supported military action against Iraq, and in September he organized a group of Democrats who shared his views. Berman's discussions led to Minority Leader Richard Gephardt's agreement with the administration on the terms of the resolution—talks that undercut the demands of other senior Democrats, including then Minority Whip Nancy Pelosi and Senate Foreign Relations Chairman Joseph Biden. In June 2006, Berman voted for the Republican resolution to reject a timetable for withdrawal from Iraq.

Berman has been a major player on immigration as well. In 1988, he sponsored the legislation allowing 20,000 immigrant visas for migrants without close relatives in the United States, to be selected randomly by computer— "Berman visa applications," they are called. In 2003, he and Sen. Edward Kennedy, D-Mass., worked out a bipartisan agreement to temporarily legalize farm workers and give them a way to eventually become legal residents. But it was set aside in favor of President George W. Bush's broader guest-worker program, although that legislation failed to be enacted after many months of debate.

Berman also focuses on intellectual-property issues of vital concern to the entertainment and high-tech industries, both with a strong presence in this district. From his seat on the Judiciary Committee, he won passage of an anti-cyber-squatting law to discourage pouncing on website names, a 2003 law creating new judgeships to determine copyright royalty rates and distribution of royalties, and a bipartisan bill creating criminal penalties for mass down-loaders of music and requiring file-sharing software to contain warnings of security risk. Electronics-industry lobbyist John Palafoutas described what it's like being on the opposing side of Berman on an issue: "There are two problems with Howard Berman," he told the *Los Angeles Times*, "One, he's really smart. And two, he knows how to represent his constituents, which in this case is Hollywood."

In 2007, after Democrats won a House majority, Berman moved up to chairman of the Subcommittee on Courts, the Internet and Intellectual Property. He won passage in the House of a major reform of the patent law, creating a new review process and giving legal priority to the "first inventor to file," thereby replacing what some said was the outdated "first to invent" standard. A major beneficiary would have been the technology industry, which had been the target of a slew of nuisance lawsuits for patent-infringement claims. The Senate did not complete action on the bill in the 110th Congress (2007–08), and Berman likely will try again in the new Congress.

From 1997 to 2003, Berman was the ranking Democrat on the House Ethics Committee. During his tenure, few complaints were filed for partisan reasons. After he left the committee in 2003, that no longer was the case. Then in 2006, when Ethics Committee senior Democrat Alan Mollohan of West Virginia resigned the post because of ethics questions raised about him, Pelosi asked Berman to take the post. "This is an honor I could have done without," Berman said. "The ethics committee should be neither a member protection agency nor a forum for deciding partisan and ideological battles. If the committee chooses to pursue either option, then expect my tenure to be even briefer than it is intended to be." He worked amicably with Chairman Doc Hastings, a Washington state Republican, and the committee staff.

After revelations that Florida Republican Mark Foley had sent sexually suggestive emails to Capitol pages but was treated lightly by House leaders, Hastings and Berman formed an investigative subcommittee and promised an expedited probe. Congressional scholar Norman Ornstein of the American Enterprise Institute wrote at the time: "The House Ethics Committee's tattered reputation is on the line, and two words are keeping it from total collapse: Howard Berman." The subcommittee worked late hours throughout October 2006, interviewing Republican House Speaker Dennis Hastert, his top aides and others who had knowledge of Foley's emails and explicit instant messages. The committee issued an exhaustive report on December 8, finding fault with the way House leaders had handled the Foley problem but declining to recommend any disciplinary action.

In February 2008, Berman took over as chairman of the Foreign Affairs Committee following the death of Rep. Tom Lantos, D-Calif. Berman staked out positions concerning several of the world's trouble spots. Despite his more supportive views of the war in Iraq, he avoided proposals that could create conflict with Pelosi and the Democratic Caucus. His own views had evolved by that time, and he now had doubts about the prospects for U.S. success. So he helped craft measurable "benchmarks" for progress in Iraq.

Berman has been a longtime backer of sanctions on Iran to limit the development of its nuclear arsenal, and he focused on Russia as the chief stumbling block to an agreement. His most significant legislative achievement during his first year as chairman was approval of the civilian nuclear agreement with India, despite his earlier concern about proliferation of nuclear weapons. As part of the deal, he insisted on increased congressional oversight, including a requirement that the president notify Congress of new discussions with India. Regarding the Middle East, Berman remained a strong supporter of Israel and of increased military sales to that country. He also has a goal of overhauling the foreign-assistance program after years of Republican policies.

Berman is not the most senior member of the California delegation, but he is the go-to guy on many state issues. One California Assembly lobbyist said of him, "He's the conscience and dad of the delegation. In this era of term limits and turnover, Howard Berman is the constant. He has a vast institutional knowledge of issues in both Congress and the Legislature that is rare these days."

California gained one seat in the 2000 Census, and Democrats controlled the process. Berman's brother, Michael, was hired as redistricting consultant by all U.S. House and state Senate Democrats at $20,000 per member. When the lines were unveiled in August 2001, the biggest controversy came over the San Fernando Valley. Rep. Brad Sherman, the Democrat from the 27th District, claimed that Howard Berman had been given too much of his secure territory and had added a significant number of Hispanics. "Howard Berman stabbed me in the back," Sherman said. Berman agreed to negotiate, adjustments were made in the lines, and Sherman's district ended up 37% Hispanic and Berman's 56%. The Mexican American Legal Defense Fund immediately took the plan to court, arguing that seats in the San Fernando Valley and San Diego tended to reduce Hispanic representation. The court approved the plan in June 2002. Although redistricting outcomes are unpredictable, not least in California, it's possible to imagine a similar battle between Berman and Sherman in 2011. By then, Hispanic lawmakers in Sacramento may have more leverage to protect their community's interests.

Berman may have at least one more big committee move in the House. Although he gave up his Judiciary Committee slot immediately behind Chairman John Conyers, D-Mich., after he took over at Foreign Affairs, he could reclaim it following the departure of Conyers, who is the second most senior House member. The opportunity to be a central player on issues ranging from courts and immigration to the copyright conflicts of the entertainment industry may be an irresistible capstone for this entrepreneurial lawmaker.

TWENTY-NINTH DISTRICT

Adam Schiff (D)

Elected 2000, 5th term; b. June 22, 1960, Framingham, MA; home, Burbank; Stanford U., B.A. 1982; Harvard U., J.D. 1985; Jewish; married (Eve); 2 children.

Elected Office: CA Senate, 1996–00.

Professional Career: Prosecutor, U.S. Atty. Gen. Ofc., L.A., CA 1987–93; Practicing atty., 1986–87, 1995–96.

DC Office: 2447 RHOB, 20515, 202-225-4176; Fax: 202-225-5828; Web site: www.house.gov/schiff.

State Offices: Pasadena, 626-304-2727.

Committees: *Appropriations* (27th of 37 D): Commerce, Justice, Science & Related Agencies; Financial Services & General Government; State, Foreign Operations & Related Programs. *Judiciary* (21st of 24 D). *Intelligence (Select)* (11th of 13 D).

Group Ratings

	ADA	ACLU	AFS	LCV	ITIC	NTU	COC	ACU	CFG	FRC
2008	90	91	100	100	100	13	61	4	4	5
2007	95	—	100	95	—	6	60	0	12	—

National Journal Ratings

	2007 LIB	—	2007 CONS		2008 LIB	—	2008 CONS
Economic	77%	—	23%		71%	—	25%
Social	70%	—	29%		75%	—	18%
Foreign	69%	—	31%		78%	—	17%
Composite	72%	—	28%		77%	—	23%

Key Votes of the 110th Congress

1. Increase minimum wage	Y	5. Share immigration data	N	9. Withdraw troops 8/08	Y
2. Expand SCHIP	Y	6. Foreign aid abortion ban	N	10. No operations in Iran	Y
3. Raise CAFE standards	Y	7. Ban gay bias in workplace	Y	11. Free trade with Peru	Y
4. Bail out financial markets	Y	8. Repeal D.C. gun law	N	12. Overhaul FISA	Y

Election Results

2008 general	Adam Schiff (D)..146,198	(69%)	($909,396)
	Charles Hahn (R)..56,727	(27%)	($76,097)
	Alan Pyeatt (Lib) 9,219	(4%)	
2008 primary	Adam Schiff (D).. unopposed		

Prior Winning Percentages: 2006 (63%); 2004 (65%); 2002 (63%); 2000 (53%)

Population		Race/Ethnicity		Work	
Pop. 2007:	646,921	White:	41.6%	Private:	78.1%
Change since 2000:	Up 1.2%	Black:	5.5%	Government:	12.1%
Urban:	99.4%	Hispanic:	24.4%	Self-employed:	9.7%
Rural:	0.6%	Asian:	26.4%	Blue collar:	14.9%
Area size:	102 sq. mi.	Native Am.:	0.3%	White collar:	69.7%
Age		Hawaiian:	0.1%	Khaki collar:	0.0%
Median age:	39.2 yrs.	Two+ races:	1.4%	Other:	15.4%
More than 65 yrs:	13.9%	*Ancestry*		Median income:	$56,299
Less than 18 yrs:	20.7%	German:	4.8%	Median home value:	$617,300
Education		English:	4.1%	Poverty:	11.5%
H.S. grad:	82.9%	Irish:	3.8%	**Military Veterans**	
College grad:	37.2%			% of Pop:	4.6%
Grad degree:	13.1%				

In the early part of the 20th century, when Los Angeles was growing rapidly and on its way to becoming one of America's major cities, its richest citizens settled not on the beach (too clammy and cold) or on the west side (too dusty and remote), but in communities they built at the base of the San Gabriel Mountains. Their snow-capped peaks, rising 10,000 feet above the city, are visible most of the year. The place to be was Pasadena, home of the Rose Bowl, Cal Tech, and a baroque-domed city hall. Pasadena

2008 Presidential Vote
Obama (D) 159,947 (68%)
McCain (R)...........................71,860 (30%)

2004 Presidential Vote
Kerry (D)...............................136,796 (61%)
Bush (R) 83,448 (37%)

Cook Partisan Voting Index: D + 14

and South Pasadena have carefully preserved their bungalow neighborhoods, and Pasadena preserved and rebuilt the 80-year-old curving Colorado Boulevard Bridge over Arroyo Seco. More middle class is Glendale, north of downtown Los Angeles, site of Forest Lawn Cemetery and DreamWorks Animation. To the west, beneath the Verdugo Mountains, is Burbank, the "media capital of the world" as the headquarters for NBC Studios, ABC Studios, Warner Brothers, and Disney, plus many small entertainment and multimedia companies. With their lower taxes and business-friendly attitude, Glendale and Burbank were booming before the nationwide recession struck in 2007 and 2008. To reduce traffic congestion, planners are exploring a lengthy tunnel to link the freeways in South Pasadena and Pasadena.

The 29th Congressional District of California includes Pasadena, South Pasadena, Glendale, and the eastern half of Burbank. Historically, these were solidly Republican cities, but they have become more Democratic in recent years, for various reasons—Pasadena because of the cultural liberalism of affluent voters and the Democratic preference of the growing black community; Glendale because of large communities of Armenians (the nation's largest), Iranians, Koreans, and Filipinos; and Burbank from the trendiness of show business. The district also includes, south of South Pasadena, cities with large Asian populations: Vietnamese in San Gabriel and Chinese in Alhambra, Temple City, and the northern edge of Monterey Park (which the locals call Little Taipei). This is a polyglot district—24% Hispanic, 26% Asian, 11% Armenian, and 6% African-American. It has become solidly Democratic, casting only 37% of its votes for President Bush in 2004 and 30% for Republican presidential candidate John McCain in 2008.

The congressman from the 29th District is Adam Schiff, a Democrat elected in 2000. Schiff's father was a traveling salesman and later owned a lumberyard. Schiff grew up throughout the country, eventually graduating from high school in Northern California. He went on to Stanford University and Harvard Law School. From 1987 to 1993, he worked in the U.S. attorney's office in Los Angeles. He ran for the California Assembly and lost three times. But in 1996, he was elected to the state Senate, where he became its youngest member. In his first two years, he authored dozens of measures that Republican Gov. Pete Wilson signed into law, including a bill guaranteeing up-to-date textbooks in classrooms and another reforming the child-support system. Schiff also taught political science at Glendale Community College.

Schiff ran for the House in the first election following the impeachment of President Clinton, and the issue became a factor in a number of races in 2000. Schiff challenged incumbent Republican James Rogan, who was a leader in the Judiciary Committee's deliberations and a persuasive voice for the case against Clinton. Rogan had won re-election in 1998 by just 51%-46%, and Clinton pal and entertainment mogul David Geffen was promising to raise millions of dollars to oppose him. The Schiff-Rogan race became a fundraising marathon, and was then the most expensive House race on record. The candidates raised more than $10 million combined, and much more was spent independently by Clinton's supporters as well as his detractors.

In addition to their opposing positions on Clinton's impeachment, the candidates disagreed on health care, abortion rights, gun control, and taxes. Rogan branded his opponent as a traditional tax-and-spend liberal, who would "run naked through the Treasury, spending everything he can." Schiff attacked Rogan for calling abortion a Holocaust for the African-American community. And he said Rogan's focus on Washington led him to ignore local problems. The two also battled for the support of more than 67,000 local Armenians. Rogan was a lead sponsor of a House resolution commemorating Armenians who died in the genocide from 1915 to 1923 by the Ottoman Turks, and Schiff got the state of California to spend $400,000 to produce a documentary about Armenian issues. Schiff won by an unexpectedly large 53%-44% vote, and has been easily re-elected since.

In the House, Schiff's voting record has been moderate, especially on foreign policy. He joined the Blue Dog Coalition of moderate to conservative Democrats, and has sometimes worked across party lines. He was instrumental on bipartisan legislation that was enacted making identity theft a crime. And on a bill to implement recommendations of the 9/11 commission, he was the only Democrat voting with Judiciary Committee Republicans on added immigration restrictions. The final bill included his provisions to establish new penalties for developing a "dirty bomb," and to give new tools to law enforcement to crack down on weapons of mass destruction.

Schiff stirred complaints from liberal constituents when he supported the resolution approving the use of force in Iraq in 2002 and for voting for the USA PATRIOT Act, the Bush administration's anti-terrorism law giving law enforcement broad new powers. But he also has been a solid party activist, contributing to the Democratic Congressional Campaign Committee's re-election efforts by co-chairing a mentoring program for prime candidates. Schiff also took the lead in writing a Democratic resolution in 2007 to urge the resignation of Attorney General Alberto Gonzales after several U.S. attorneys around the country were fired in what critics charged was a political purge. His contribution to congressional ethics reform was a bill, passed by the House in July 2007, preventing lawmakers from placing their spouses on campaign payrolls.

As the co-founder of a Democratic study group on national security, Schiff has focused especially on legislation to secure nuclear materials in the former Soviet Union and elsewhere to keep them out of the hands of terrorists. In 2007, he sponsored a bill creating a worldwide data bank on nuclear material. He has continued to press the cause for recognition of the Armenian genocide as the responsibility of the Ottoman Empire, a move Turkey adamantly opposes. His resolution was approved by the House Foreign Affairs Committee in October 2007, but he agreed to postpone further action after a strong reaction from Turkey. It threatened to deny the U.S. military access to its strategically vital Incirlik Air Base in Turkey. Some of Schiff's legislative allies backed away from their support after Turkey's threat. With seats on both the Intelligence and Appropriations committees, Schiff in July 2008 launched an effort to increase foreign aid to Jordan.

THIRTIETH DISTRICT

Henry Waxman (D)

Elected 1974, 18th term; b. Sept. 12, 1939, Los Angeles; home, Los Angeles; U.C.L.A., B.A. 1961, J.D. 1964; Jewish; married (Janet); 2 children.

Elected Office: CA Assembly, 1968–74.

Professional Career: Practicing atty., 1965–68.

DC Office: 2204 RHOB, 20515, 202-225-3976; Fax: 202-225-4099; Web site: www.house.gov/waxman.

State Offices: Los Angeles, 323-651-1040.

Committees: *Energy & Commerce* (Chmn of 36 D).

Group Ratings

	ADA	ACLU	AFS	LCV	ITIC	NTU	COC	ACU	CFG	FRC
2008	95	100	100	100	100	11	61	4	5	5
2007	90	—	100	95	—	7	53	0	15	—

National Journal Ratings

	2007 LIB	—	2007 CONS		2008 LIB	—	2008 CONS
Economic	78%	—	18%		81%	—	15%
Social	84%	—	15%		82%	—	0%
Foreign	89%	—	11%		77%	—	23%
Composite	85%	—	16%		84%	—	16%

Key Votes of the 110th Congress

1. Increase minimum wage	Y	5. Share immigration data	N	9. Withdraw troops 8/08	Y
2. Expand SCHIP	Y	6. Foreign aid abortion ban	N	10. No operations in Iran	Y
3. Raise CAFE standards	Y	7. Ban gay bias in workplace	Y	11. Free trade with Peru	Y
4. Bail out financial markets	Y	8. Repeal D.C. gun law	N	12. Overhaul FISA	N

Election Results

2008 general	Henry Waxman (D)......................................	unopposed
2008 primary	Henry Waxman (D)......................................	unopposed

Prior Winning Percentages: 2006 (71%); 2004 (71%); 2002 (70%); 2000 (76%); 1998 (74%); 1996 (68%); 1994 (68%); 1992 (61%); 1990 (69%); 1988 (72%); 1986 (88%); 1984 (63%); 1982 (65%); 1980 (64%); 1978 (63%); 1976 (68%); 1974 (64%)

Population		**Race/Ethnicity**		**Work**	
Pop. 2007:	647,145	White:	75.3%	Private:	75.7%
Change since 2000:	Up 1.3%	Black:	2.7%	Government:	9.0%
Urban:	97.5%	Hispanic:	9.1%	Self-employed:	15.0%
Rural:	2.5%	Asian:	10.3%	Blue collar:	5.6%
Area size:	388 sq. mi.	Native Am.:	0.1%	White collar:	84.4%
Age		Hawaiian:	0.1%	Khaki collar:	0.0%
Median age:	40.2 yrs.	Two+ races:	2.0%	Other:	9.9%
More than 65 yrs:	15.0%	*Ancestry*		Median income:	$77,159
Less than 18 yrs:	17.8%	German:	8.4%	Median home value:	$910,400
Education		Irish:	6.9%	Poverty:	8.7%
H.S. grad:	94.4%	English:	6.8%	**Military Veterans**	
College grad:	57.7%			% of Pop:	6.6%
Grad degree:	24.1%				

The Westside: The term was not much used 20 years ago, but is now shorthand for what might be the biggest and flashiest concentration of affluence in the world. It is the heartland of one of America's most productive and creative industries and one of the nation's major exports, show business. The first moviemakers came here looking for a place to shoot silent films where the sunlight was more dependable than in Astoria, Queens, or Englewood, New Jersey. They found it in Hollywood, a suburb

2008 Presidential Vote

Obama (D)	242,022	(70%)
McCain (R)	95,869	(28%)

2004 Presidential Vote

Kerry (D)	220,181	(66%)
Bush (R)	109,014	(33%)

Cook Partisan Voting Index: D + 18

just annexed by burgeoning Los Angeles when the first movie studio was built in 1911. In 1923 came the "Hollywood" sign, overlooking the soon-famous intersection of Hollywood and Vine. By the 1930s, big studio lots were scattered around town, over the mountains in Burbank, or out toward the ocean in Westwood and Culver City. Miraculously, the studio bosses of that era—most of them Jewish immigrants with little ancestral experience of America—created a popular culture that was universally accessible and embodied the American spirit in a way that captured the imagination.

Showbiz still sets the tone for the Westside. It remains tremendously profitable, and not just for the big conglomerate-owned studios. There are thousands of entrepreneurs, actors, writers, and craftsmen who are the best in the world at what they do and who tend to cluster on the Westside because so many of the others they do business with are there. Not everyone is in show business, of course. The Westside is metro Los Angeles's biggest office center, with horrifying traffic inbound in the morning and outbound in the evening. Most office workers can't afford to live anywhere nearby. Los Angeles ranks first in the nation in the percentage of people who work at home.

There are large numbers of singles and gays here. It is the center of the nation's second-largest Jewish community, or actually, communities. The old Fairfax district, where corner delis have long been a hub of political discourse, is now home to many Russian Jewish immigrants. Orthodox Jews are building communities, amid protests of overdevelopment, along Pico Boulevard. Iranian Jews have poured in since 1979, and now make up about one-quarter of the population of Beverly Hills, which elected an Iranian-American mayor in 2007. Beverly Hills and the Westside remain the locus of some of America's most expensive residential real estate, where people buy houses for multiples of $1 million, knock them down, and build something new for many more millions. And it has one of the world's premier high-priced shopping areas—Rodeo Drive.

The 30th Congressional District of California contains most of Westside Los Angeles plus territory to the west. It includes the Fairfax neighborhood east to La Brea Avenue, heavily gay West Hollywood, Beverly Hills, Westwood and UCLA, Bel Air, Brentwood, Santa Monica, and the whole 27 miles of Malibu on the ocean. The district also includes the western end of the San Fernando Valley, with the high-income neighborhoods of Woodland Hills and Chatsworth up against the mountains that rim the Valley. And it includes the high-income suburbs of Hidden Hills, Calabasas, Agoura Hills, and Westlake Village, nestled amid mountains along the Ventura Freeway. By today's definitions it is the least diverse district in metro Los Angeles. Only 3% of its residents are African-American, and only 9% are Hispanic, by a considerable margin the lowest percentage in Southern California. Many Latinos work in the district, but few are interested in paying the prices for housing that have been bid up by rich people who can't imagine living anywhere else. Politically, the 30th District is heavily Democratic, but not as heavily as San Francisco. In 2008, the Westside was torn between Barack Obama and Hillary Rodham Clinton in the Democratic presidential primary, with political reporters writing breathless stories about which studio mogul was defecting from one to the other. (The Westside was also the home of a former president who did not at all exemplify its politics: Ronald Reagan. Before his Alzheimer's disease worsened, he kept his office on the former Fox lot that is now Century City.) The district voted 66%-33% for John Kerry in 2004 and 70%-28% for Barack Obama in 2008.

The congressman from the 30th District is Henry Waxman, a Democrat first elected in 1974, and today one of the ablest members of the House, a shrewd political operator, and an idealistic policy entrepreneur. He is chairman of the Energy and Commerce Committee. There is no Westside glitz about him. The son of Russian immigrants, Waxman grew up over his family's store in Watts. He has never attended the Oscars ceremony. He graduated from the University of California at Los Angeles and its law school, where he met Howard Berman, his longtime political ally and colleague. (Berman is also a House member from California.) They became immersed in the Federation of Young Democrats, based in California, and Waxman chaired the group for a year. He moved up rapidly in politics by spying openings before others did. He ran against Assemblyman Lester McMillan in the mostly Jewish Fairfax area in 1968, at age 28, and won 64% in the primary. From 1971 to 1972, he chaired the Assembly's redistricting committee, a good place to make friends. In 1974, he was elected to Congress. Waxman's biggest break in Congress came after the 1978 election, when he was elected chairman of the Commerce Committee's Health and Environment Subcommittee. This was one of the first times House Democrats decided to ignore seniority in handing out subcommittee chairs. Waxman argued his case on the issues. And in a move quite unprecedented at the time, though common in Sacramento, he made campaign contributions to other Democrats on the full committee. (The practice is all but expected today of anyone trying to get a committee gavel or role in party leadership in Congress.) Waxman won the post, 15-12, over the widely respected Richardson Preyer of North Carolina.

In the 1970s and 1980s, Waxman and Berman built their own political machine in Los Angeles. Its power came not from patronage but from fundraising and savvy. They raised huge sums on the Westside for favored candidates. They put out carefully targeted direct mail, with hundreds of customized letters and endorsement slates sent out to different lists of people. In California, where television advertising is exceedingly expensive and political activists are widely dispersed geographically, this made them critical though not always successful players. But their organization withered over time. Waxman is less active now in Los Angeles-area politics, though he did endorse former Assembly Speaker Antonio Villaraigosa in his successful race against Los Angeles Mayor James Hahn in 2005.

From 1978 to 1994, Waxman was part of the Democratic majority in the House and the chairman of an important subcommittee, making him a major national policy maker, usually from behind the scenes. In 1981 and 1982, he prevented the Reagan administration and Commerce Committee Chairman John Dingell, D-Mich., from revising the Clean Air Act, because he wanted tougher pollution controls. Biding his time, Waxman worked to strengthen the law in its 1990 revision. He also had a hand in legislation addressing chemicals in drinking water, radon abatement, and lead contamination. Another Waxman project was expanding Medicaid for the poor. Between 1984 and 1990, he got coverage for all poor children up to 18, all children under 7, and pregnant women in families under 133% of poverty income. This helped raise Medicaid from 9% to 14% of state spending in the 1980s, and explains why Waxman was unpopular with many governors.

He had less success with overhauling national health care. He supported the 1993 Clinton plan, which significantly increased government's role in the U.S. health care system, but the proposal never got through Congress. Waxman has secured funding for AIDS research, important in a district with a large gay population. In early 1994, in widely publicized hearings, he lined up the chief executive officers of leading tobacco companies and accused them of adding nicotine and other substances to cigarettes and of lying in their testimony. All of this had no immediate legislative result, and when Republican Thomas Bliley of Virginia became Commerce Committee chairman, the hearings stopped. But Waxman brought the tobacco issue into public view, and he helped inspire the lawsuits against tobacco companies that resulted in a massive redistribution of corporate assets—from the tobacco companies to state governments and trial lawyers.

When Republicans took over Congress in 1995, there was no slackening of effort on Waxman's part, though he was largely shut out of the legislative process. In 1996, he gave up the ranking position on the health subcommittee to become the ranking Democrat on the Government Reform Committee, where he concentrated on holding hearings and seeking and publicizing Government Accountability Office reports. "When the Republicans excluded me and other Democrats from legislating, we had to figure out something else to do. So we did our own investigations," he said. Waxman sharply attacked Chairman Dan Burton's investigation of Clinton campaign misdeeds, arguing that Burton had given himself unprecedented subpoena power and was misusing it. He emerged as the House's most articulate defender of President Clinton during the campaign finance scandal. In 2001, with Republican George W. Bush as the new president, Waxman switched from being a defender of the White House to being a critic, frequently writing letters to Burton calling for investigations. He and Dingell instigated a GAO investigation of company executives who had been consulted by Vice President Cheney's energy task force. In February 2002, the GAO brought a lawsuit against Cheney, but a federal judge ruled against the agency.

In January 2003, Virginia Republican Tom Davis took over as committee chairman and promised a more constructive relationship with Waxman. Nevertheless, Waxman indefatigably wrote multipage letters with dozens of footnotes and questions, called for GAO investigations, and invoked the 1920s seven-member rule, which entitles any seven members of the committee to seek information from the executive branch. He assembled a staff of dozens of investigators, squirreled in tiny offices around the Capitol Hill complex. He and Ohio Democratic Rep. Sherrod Brown demanded that 10 pharmaceutical companies reveal how much they paid in consulting fees and stock options to National Institutes of Health scientists, which led to a stricter NIH policy on ethics and disclosure in 2005. Waxman has been a leading critic of Halliburton and other government contractors in Iraq, pointing out relentlessly that Cheney was once Halliburton's chief executive officer. In 2004, he said that State Department documents showed that Halliburton employees tried to extract bribes for fuel contracts. The committee held hearings on contracting in Iraq, for which Waxman commended Davis. They also worked together on investigations on mad-cow disease and D.C. drinking water. But Waxman blistered Davis in a seven-page letter for investigating former Clinton National Security Adviser Sandy Berger in July 2004. Berger said then that he only inadvertently took classified documents out of the National Archives. But in 2005, Davis was more than vindicated when Berger admitted that he took them on purpose.

Democrats took control of the House in 2007, giving Waxman the gavel at the renamed Oversight and Government Reform Committee. When asked whether he would issue a flurry of subpoenas of the Bush administration, Waxman said, "I'd prefer not to. We want to return to civility and bipartisanship. Legislation ought to be based on evidence, not ideology." Davis, who became the ranking minority member, said, "There is no question that life is going to be different for the administration. Henry is going to be tough . . . and he's been waiting a long time to do this." Waxman reduced the number of subcommittees from seven to five and doubled the staff reporting to him. His first hearings were on whether the administration had interfered with the work of climate scientists and on fraud and waste in reconstruction projects in Iraq. Witnesses denied that, as Waxman alleged, there was $10 billion in fraud, but Davis noted that there was "an arcane, ill-suited management structure."

Waxman called secret agent Valerie Plame to the stand to air her complaints that the revealing of her name by an undisclosed, high-level government source had violated national security, which touched off a scandal that ultimately sent Cheney Chief of Staff Lewis (Scooter) Libby to jail for perjury and obstruction of justice. In 2007, Waxman subpoenaed Secretary of State Condoleezza Rice to testify on prewar intelligence in Iraq. He also sought information on White House contacts with disgraced Republican lobbyist Jack Abramoff, calling on incoming Attorney General Michael Mukasey in October 2007 to hand over White House files relating to Abramoff, and threatening Mukasey with contempt of Congress in June 2008. He relented after President Bush claimed executive privilege, but in a December 2008 report, he and Davis called Bush's claim "legally unprecedented" and "inappropriate." Few subjects seemed too far afield for a Waxman investigation: He probed the health effects of uranium mines on Navajo lands, the pricing of government contracts with Sun Microsystems, and steroid use in professional baseball. Probably his most publicized hearing came in February 2008, when baseball pitcher Roger Clemens and his former trainer gave conflicting testimony on drug use. In 2008, Waxman turned his focus to the collapse of major financial institutions as a result of shaky lending practices. He sought information on the compensation of executives of Fannie Mae and Freddie Mac, the government-backed mortgage issuers, and in October 2008 he called former Lehman Brothers chief Richard Fuld to testify.

Amid this flurry of activity, Waxman was looking ahead to the likelihood that a Democratic administration in 2009 would provide fewer targets than the Bush administration. And with a Democratic president (as it turned out), Waxman could achieve more of his policy goals on the Energy and Commerce Committee than on the oversight committee. He remained particularly interested in issues related to air pollution and global warming. He had co-sponsored bills limiting carbon emissions and supported the bill passed by the California Legislature and signed by Republican Gov. Arnold Schwarzenegger in 2006. In addition, he had long been eager to advance national health insurance legislation. All of this suggested that Waxman wanted to be chairman of the Energy and Commerce panel. But there was a hitch. An equally savvy and effective Democrat, Dingell of Michigan, was in line to be chairman. But Dingell was 81 years old and in failing health. Also working against Dingell was his sometimes rocky relationship with Democratic House Speaker Nancy Pelosi, who, by contrast, was a big fan of Waxman's. In 2007, Pelosi created a special committee headed by Massachusetts Democrat Edward Markey to examine global warming. This was seen as an end run around Dingell, who represents a Detroit-area district and whose views on air-pollution regulation had long differed from those of Pelosi, Waxman, and Markey.

The clash that had been brewing finally came after the November 2008 elections. House Democratic rules provided for committee chairmen to be chosen by a vote of the Democratic Caucus, the group of all House Democrats. Waxman had been quietly seeking support and making contributions to Democrats in close elections. When Waxman made it public that he was challenging Dingell for the chair of Energy and Commerce, Dingell was evidently not as well prepared. Majority Leader Steny Hoyer of Maryland tried to bargain a compromise that would have had Dingell agreeing to cede the chair after two years and Waxman promising not to seek it until then. Waxman and Dingell both declined the compromise.

In the past, some Democratic members had retired before they reached the point where they could be humiliated by being deprived of a gavel because they were seen as less competent than a challenger, but this was not the issue here: Both men were regarded as highly competent. On Nov. 19, 2008, the Democratic Steering and Policy Committee voted 25-22 for Waxman. This was seen as a signal that Pelosi was supporting Waxman, though the margin was pretty small. There were signs that President-elect Obama was leaning Waxman's way. Obama had just reiterated his support for tougher carbon emissions legislation and had hired Waxman's longtime chief of staff, Phil Schiliro, as the White House liaison to Congress. The caucus vote was scheduled for November 20. Dingell had the support of many members of the Congressional Black Caucus, of the conservative "Blue Dogs," and of the moderate New Democrats. He also had the backing of lawmakers from industrial and coal states that would be hit hard by carbon emissions legislation. Waxman had the support of most of the 33 Democrats in the California delegation, and of the bulk of the Democratic freshmen. Waxman won 137-122. Dingell was named chairman emeritus and assigned ex officio seats on subcommittees where he was not already a voting member.

As chairman, Waxman is in a position to play a major role on environmental and health care legislation. In early 2009, it seemed unlikely that there would be tension between him and Markey over the latter's non-legislative committee, but the 122 votes cast for Dingell suggested that it would be difficult to hold all Democrats in line for the carbon emissions legislation, which would impose a cap-and-trade system forcing companies to seek credits from "cleaner" companies in order to pollute the air beyond certain government-set levels. When the House voted on the bill in June, 44 Democrats opposed it, but it passed. Also, in December 2008 Waxman and Minnesota Democrat James Oberstar, chairman of the Transportation and Infrastructure Committee, called for expanding the reach of the Clean Water Act. Waxman's committee shares jurisdiction over health care policy with the Ways and Means Committee, but still has considerable influence there.

Waxman has always won re-election easily, and continues to contribute generously, and strategically, to other Democrats' campaigns.

THIRTY-FIRST DISTRICT

Xavier Becerra (D)

Elected 1992, 9th term; b. Jan. 26, 1958, Sacramento; home, Eagle Rock; Stanford U., B.A. 1980, J.D. 1984; Catholic; married (Carolina Reyes); 3 children.

Elected Office: CA Assembly, 1990–92.

Professional Career: Staff atty., Legal Assistance Corp. of Central MA; Dist. dir., CA Sen. Art Torres, 1986; CA dep. atty. gen., 1987–90.

DC Office: 1119 LHOB, 20515, 202-225-6235; Fax: 202-225-2202; Web site: becerra.house.gov.

State Offices: Los Angeles, 213-483-1425.

Committees: *Democratic Caucus Vice Chairman. Budget* (4th of 24 D). *Ways & Means* (8th of 26 D): Health; Oversight; Social Security.

Group Ratings

	ADA	ACLU	AFS	LCV	ITIC	NTU	COC	ACU	CFG	FRC
2008	100	100	100	92	86	13	50	8	8	5
2007	95	—	100	85	—	3	58	0	11	—

National Journal Ratings

	2007 LIB	—	2007 CONS		2008 LIB	—	2008 CONS
Economic	82%	—	0%		85%	—	0%
Social	87%	—	12%		82%	—	0%
Foreign	89%	—	10%		78%	—	17%
Composite	89%	—	11%		88%	—	12%

Key Votes of the 110th Congress

1. Increase minimum wage	Y	5. Share immigration data	N	9. Withdraw troops 8/08	Y
2. Expand SCHIP	Y	6. Foreign aid abortion ban	N	10. No operations in Iran	Y
3. Raise CAFE standards	Y	7. Ban gay bias in workplace	Y	11. Free trade with Peru	Y
4. Bail out financial markets	N	8. Repeal D.C. gun law	N	12. Overhaul FISA	N

Election Results

2008 general	Xavier Becerra (D)	unopposed
2008 primary	Xavier Becerra (D)	unopposed

Prior Winning Percentages: 2006 (100%); 2004 (80%); 2002 (81%); 2000 (83%); 1998 (81%); 1996 (72%); 1994 (66%); 1992 (58%)

Population		Race/Ethnicity		Work	
Pop. 2007:	638,605	White:	10.1%	Private:	81.1%
Change since 2000:	Down 0.1%	Black:	4.2%	Government:	8.2%
Urban:	100.0%	Hispanic:	69.7%	Self-employed:	10.5%
Rural:	0.0%	Asian:	14.4%	Blue collar:	30.3%
Area size:	40 sq. mi.	Native Am.:	0.2%	White collar:	44.5%
		Hawaiian:	0.2%	Khaki collar:	0.1%
Age		Two+ races:	0.8%	Other:	25.2%
Median age:	31.5 yrs.	*Ancestry*		Median income:	$34,169
More than 65 yrs:	8.2%	German:	1.9%	Median home value:	$504,900
Less than 18 yrs:	27.2%	Irish:	1.4%	Poverty:	25.4%
Education		English:	1.1%	**Military Veterans**	
H.S. grad:	58.8%			% of Pop:	2.5%
College grad:	18.1%				
Grad degree:	4.6%				

Surrounding downtown Los Angeles are neighborhoods built in the mid-20th century that are just now starting to take on the patina of the historic. Downtown L.A., with its pink cylinders jutting up to 70 stories from what was once a low-rise business district, has become surprisingly pedestrian-friendly, with attractive plazas like the one around the redesigned Los Angeles Library. But downtown remains detached from the ethnically diverse neighborhoods around it. They seem to change

2008 Presidential Vote
Obama (D) 113,941   (80%)
McCain (R)...............................25,441   (18%)

2004 Presidential Vote
Kerry (D)..................................92,894   (77%)
Bush (R) 26,054   (22%)

Cook Partisan Voting Index: D + 29

character with every new immigration flow. South of downtown is the garment district, with factories in nondescript buildings, an economically vibrant area that has helped make Los Angeles the largest manufacturing city in America today. The anti-sweatshop movement has struggled to maintain new facilities here while attempting to compete with overseas manufacturers. To the north is Lincoln Heights, a heavily Hispanic area centered on the busy shopping street of North Broadway, where residents have been fighting gangs and graffiti. Highland Park and Eagle Rock, which were white middle-class enclaves 30 years ago, are now ethnically mixed middle-class enclaves with large numbers of Latinos and Asians. Eagle Rock is the home of Occidental College, where President Obama attended his first two years of college. West of downtown are Pico Union, an entry point for new immigrants; University Park, which surrounds the University of Southern California campus; and Thai Town, along Hollywood Boulevard between Normandie and Western. Lower Sunset Boulevard and gentrifying Echo Park have become lively shopping strips filled with that rare L.A. commodity: pedestrians. Historic Filipinotown, known locally as Hi-Fi, was settled by Filipinos in the early 1900s and has become more of a polyglot. Hollywood has long had a seedy look—it has not sprouted the office buildings like Burbank or Glendale—but has recently been spiffed up.

Almost all of these areas, centering geographically on Dodger Stadium, are part of California's 31st Congressional District. In Los Angeles's booming 1980s, these neighborhoods were suddenly thronged with immigrants, with small houses and garden apartments full of large families and many children. In the 1990s, the population surge stopped, and this became the slowest-growing district in California, as the newcomers of the decade before moved out to middle-class neighborhoods and incoming immigrants spread more evenly around the Los Angeles Basin. The trend continued between 2000 and 2007, when this was the only Los Angeles-area district to see a slight drop in population. This remains a district of immigrants. In the 2000 census, it ranked first in the nation with its noncitizens (41%) and last in the nation in homes where English is spoken (21%). In 2007, 52% of its residents were foreign-born.

The congressman from the 31st District is Xavier Becerra, a Democrat first elected in 1992. Becerra *(beh-SEH-ra)* grew up in Sacramento. His mother was a Mexican immigrant, and his father, who was born in the United States, supported the family with construction and other jobs. Becerra worked his way through college and law school at Stanford University, becoming the first in his family to get a college degree. He married a Harvard Medical School graduate who became vice president of California's largest health care foundation. Becerra started his career at a legal-services clinic in Massachusetts, doing work for mentally disabled clients. When he returned to California, Becerra was an aide to state Sen. Art Torres and then to Attorney General John Van de Kamp. In 1990, he was elected to the California Assembly. In 1992, when U.S. Rep. Edward Roybal, California's first Latino congressman and a Democrat, announced that he was retiring, Becerra jumped into the race. His main competitor, Leticia Quezada, was a member of the Los Angeles school board. Becerra had the endorsements of Roybal and County Supervisor Gloria Molina. Becerra won the primary with 32% of the vote to 22% for Quezada. He went on to defeat Republican Morry Waksberg in the general election with 58% of the vote.

In the House, Becerra has been a consistent liberal. He has also been successful in moving into the House Democratic leadership. When Democrats won majority control of the House, fellow Californian and House Speaker Nancy Pelosi gave him the newly created position of assistant to the speaker, where he helped to set priorities for the party's agenda and drive legislative decision-making. "A seat at the table has been priceless," he said at the time. In the November 2008 leadership shuffle after Rep. Rahm Emanuel, D-Ill., resigned to become White House chief of staff, Becerra sought to advance by running for one of the elected leadership posts (the assistant's role was appointive). He ran for vice chairman of the Democratic Caucus, and with Pelosi's help, defeated Rep. Marcy Kaptur of Ohio, 175-67.

Becerra was also on the new Obama administration's radar. In December 2008, he was offered the post of U.S. trade representative. But he declined after deciding that trade policy would not be a major White House priority in Obama's early years. Becerra had been Obama's campaign liaison to the Hispanic community.

Becerra is also on the powerful House Ways and Means Committee. And the fact that he is at least nine years younger than any of the members with more seniority could put him in line for committee chairman in another decade or so. He is the committee's first Hispanic member. Becerra has advocated tax changes to curtail the overseas exodus of jobs in the entertainment industry, including a tax credit for labor costs of independent film producers. He supported normalizing trade relations with China and won House approval of his resolution supporting reunification efforts between North and South Korea. His support for free-trade deals with Chile and Singapore led to local protests by union activists, and he demanded improvements in the labor standards in the Central American Free Trade Agreement in return for his support. Becerra also sponsored a bill that would forgive student loans for graduates who work as librarians in poor neighborhoods and another to assist low-income taxpayers in preparing their tax returns while protecting them from predatory loan providers.

In May 2008, Becerra won enactment of a bill establishing a commission to develop a national museum of the American Latino, which would be located on the National Mall and would be part of the Smithsonian Institution.

The one career setback for Becerra in recent years was his failed run for mayor of Los Angeles in 2001. He did not raise enough money to establish name recognition outside his district, and he was overshadowed by former Assembly Speaker Antonio Villaraigosa. In the primary, Becerra finished fifth, with just 6% of the vote, far behind Villaraigosa's 30% and James Hahn's 25%. Hahn won the runoff. Among the 21% of voters who were Hispanic, Villaraigosa led Becerra 62%-17%. Post-election analyses noted that Becerra damaged his standing among Latino leaders with negative campaign telephone calls. Villaraigosa ran again in 2005 and defeated Hahn.

THIRTY-SECOND DISTRICT
Vacant

Election Results

2008 spec. primary	Judy Chu (D)	17,661	(33%)
	Gil Cedillo (D)	12,570	(23%)
	Emanuel Pleitez (D)	7,252	(13%)
	Betty Chu (R)	5,648	(10%)
	Teresa Hernandez (R)	4,581	(8%)
	David Truax (R)	3,303	(6%)
2008 general	Hilda Solis (D)	unopposed	
2008 primary	Hilda Solis (D)	unopposed	

Population		Race/Ethnicity		Work	
Pop. 2007:	656,309	White:	12.2%	Private:	80.7%
Change since 2000:	Up 2.7%	Black:	2.5%	Government:	12.5%
Urban:	100.0%	Hispanic:	63.7%	Self-employed:	6.5%
Rural:	0.0%	Asian:	20.3%	Blue collar:	30.5%
Area size:	93 sq. mi.	Native Am.:	0.2%	White collar:	50.6%
Age		Hawaiian:	0.0%	Khaki collar:	0.0%
Median age:	32.7 yrs.	Two+ races:	0.8%	Other:	18.8%
More than 65 yrs:	10.5%	*Ancestry*		Median income:	$49,771
Less than 18 yrs:	28.0%	German:	2.6%	Median home value:	$452,300
Education		Irish:	1.9%	Poverty:	14.6%
H.S. grad:	66.7%	English:	1.8%	**Military Veterans**	
College grad:	15.9%			% of Pop:	4.5%
Grad degree:	4.3%				

Straight east from downtown Los Angeles on Interstate 10 is a string of suburbs that grew up in the 1940s and 1950s as white middle-class communities and today are a melting pot of immigrant groups that have achieved the American dream of home ownership and decent schools. The stucco houses were once filled with Midwest and East Coast migrants who discovered California during World War II. Now, they are more likely to be occupied by Mexican-American families who spread out

2008 Presidential Vote
Obama (D)	119,726	(68%)
McCain (R)	52,356	(30%)

2004 Presidential Vote
Kerry (D)	99,286	(62%)
Bush (R)	58,341	(37%)

Cook Partisan Voting Index: D + 15

from their original East Los Angeles base to blue-collar suburbs like El Monte, Baldwin Park, Azusa and West Covina. Chinese and other Asians are the majority in Monterey Park and 49% of the population in Rosemead. The late *New York Times* food maven R.W. Apple Jr. described "a memorable week in the gastronomic trenches" of the local Asian restaurant scene, and reported that "it is easier to buy bok choy than iceberg" in Monterey Park. Almost every neighborhood here is mixed, with people whose origins are in different continents and cultures. The relatively recent arrivals have upgraded neighborhoods, bringing in energy and money, the enthusiasm of the young and the community-spiritedness of the homeowner. There are busy shops with new signs, newly painted homes with carefully tended gardens, and neighborhoods filled with children. When blacks and Latinos were rioting in South Central and Hollywood in 1992, East Los Angeles and the San Gabriel Valley were quiet and orderly. East Los Angeles broke through into pop culture in the 1987 film *Born in East L.A* ., about a Mexican-American deported to Mexico. Some local officials of the 129,000-population community in unincorporated Los Angeles County want to incorporate as a city, but the proposal has failed three times.

The 32nd Congressional District of California covers much of this territory. It includes part of East Los Angeles and a small part of Los Angeles, most of Monterey Park and all of Rosemead, El Monte, Baldwin Park, Azusa, West Covina and Covina. It is 64% Hispanic and 20% Asian—the second-highest Asian percentage (after the adjacent 29th District) in southern California. Forty-two percent of its residents are foreign born. Politically, the new Latinos and Asians have been up for grabs. In the early 1990s, Asians, dismayed that civic leaders seemed more interested in the complaints of rioters than in compensating the store owners whose property was destroyed, moved toward the Republicans. In the middle 1990s, Latinos, because of Republican-inspired immigration and welfare laws halting aid to legal immigrants, moved heavily toward the Democrats. Republicans Arnold Schwarzenegger and Tom McClintock together won nearly half of the Latino vote in the 2003 recall of Gray Davis as governor, according to exit polls. George W. Bush got 37% here in the 2004 contest for president and Schwarzenegger got 42% in 2006. In 2008, the vote for Republican presidential nominee John McCain returned to a more conventional 30%, while Democrat Barack Obama cleaned up with 68%.

The district re-elected Democrat Hilda Solis easily in 2008, but then she was chosen to be secretary of Labor in the new Obama administration. At the *Almanac's* press time in early July 2009, Democrat Judy Chu was headed toward victory in a July 14 special election to replace Solis. Chu would be the second Chinese-American member of the House, after Rep. David Wu, D-Ore. She graduated from the University of California at Los Angeles, got her Ph.D. in psychology, and then taught for 13 years at the East Los Angeles Community College. She served for three years on the Garvey School District board and for 12 years as mayor of Monterey Park. In 2000, she was elected to the California Assembly, where she focused on criminal justice and environmental protection issues. As chairman of the Appropriations Committee, she sponsored a tax amnesty program that brought in significant sums for the state. In 2006, she was elected to the state Board of Equalization, where she worked on closing tax loopholes.

After Solis' Cabinet appointment, the contest for the Democratic nomination to replace her quickly settled into a contest between Chu and state Sen. Gil Cedillo. He was the leading Hispanic candidate after state Sen. Gloria Romero decided to focus on her 2010 bid for statewide office. Although many observers viewed the election as an ethnic showdown between an Asian and a Latino, it was more complicated than that. Chu gained the endorsement of much of the Democratic establishment and the state party, including some prominent Hispanics, such as Los Angeles Mayor Anthony Villaraigosa and members of Solis's family. The Los Angeles County Labor Federation, which was impressed by Chu's support for farm workers, supported her, as did EMILY's List, the national advocacy group for pro-choice Democratic women.

Cedillo attracted negative media coverage for spending more than $120,000 in campaign funds for personal travel and shopping. Cedillo maintained that he did nothing illegal, but Chu used the news stories to contrast with her more modest life style. His decade in the Legislature proved to be less of an asset than one would think, given that the Democratic primary was held on the same day that voters overwhelmingly defeated five state referenda on controversial tax and spending policies. A third candidate was also Hispanic and drew votes from likely Cedillo voters: political novice Emanuel Pleitez, a 26-year-old financial analyst who had worked on Obama's presidential campaign and used Internet strategies for fundraising and voter mobilization. In the pre-primary spending report, Chu had raised nearly $1 million, Cedillo more than $700,000, and Pleitez $200,000.

The May 19, 2009 primary drew fewer than 50,000 voters. Chu won with 32%, to 23% for Cedillo and 14% for Pleitez. Because she failed to receive a majority of the total primary vote, she faced a July 14 runoff with Republican Betty Chu, a distant cousin and Monterey Park councilwoman who was little known to most voters. Betty Chu got 10% of the primary vote to 9% for Republican-endorsed Teresa Hernandez. Hispanic groups in Washington lamented the likely loss of a seat in the House.

THIRTY-THIRD DISTRICT

Diane Watson (D)

Elected June 2001, 4th full term; b. Nov. 12, 1933, Los Angeles; home, Los Angeles; U.C.L.A., B.A. 1954, CA State L.A., M.A. 1968, Claremont U., Ph.D. 1987; Catholic; single.

Elected Office: L.A. Bd. of Education, 1975–78; CA Senate, 1978–98.

Professional Career: Teacher & school psychologist, 1954–75; lecturer, CA State L.A. & CA State Long Beach; U.S. ambassador, Micronesia 1999–2001.

DC Office: 2430 RHOB, 20515, 202-225-7084; Fax: 202-225-2422; Web site: www.house.gov/watson.

State Offices: Los Angeles, 323-965-1422.

Committees: *Foreign Affairs* (10th of 28 D): Asia, the Pacific & the Global Environment; Africa & Global Health; Terrorism, Nonproliferation & Trade. *Oversight & Government Reform* (8th of 24 D): Domestic Policy; Government Management, Organization & Procurement (Chmn); Information Policy, Census & National Archives.

Group Ratings

	ADA	ACLU	AFS	LCV	ITIC	NTU	COC	ACU	CFG	FRC
2008	100	100	100	92	57	12	53	4	0	0
2007	95	—	91	90	—	5	47	0	6	—

National Journal Ratings

	2007 LIB — 2007 CONS		2008 LIB — 2008 CONS	
Economic	82%	— 0%	85%	— 0%
Social	92%	— 0%	67%	— 28%
Foreign	76%	— 24%	92%	— 0%
Composite	88%	— 12%	86%	— 14%

Key Votes of the 110th Congress

1. Increase minimum wage	Y	5. Share immigration data	N	9. Withdraw troops 8/08	N
2. Expand SCHIP	*	6. Foreign aid abortion ban	N	10. No operations in Iran	Y
3. Raise CAFE standards	Y	7. Ban gay bias in workplace	Y	11. Free trade with Peru	N
4. Bail out financial markets	Y	8. Repeal D.C. gun law	N	12. Overhaul FISA	N

Election Results

2008 general	Diane Watson (D)	186,924	(88%)	($229,692)
	David Crowley (R)	26,536	(12%)	($5,773)
2008 primary	Diane Watson (D)	44,934	(88%)	
	Felicia Ford (D)	3,738	(7%)	
	Mervin Evans (D)	2,315	(5%)	

Prior Winning Percentages: 2006 (100%); 2004 (89%); 2002 (83%); 2001 (75%)

Population		Race/Ethnicity		Work	
Pop. 2007:	643,104	White:	22.4%	Private:	76.2%
Change since 2000:	Up 0.6%	Black:	26.6%	Government:	11.7%
Urban:	100.0%	Hispanic:	36.7%	Self-employed:	11.9%
Rural:	0.0%	Asian:	11.7%	Blue collar:	17.8%
Area size:	48 sq. mi.	Native Am.:	0.2%	White collar:	60.6%
		Hawaiian:	0.1%	Khaki collar:	0.0%
Age		Two+ races:	1.7%	Other:	21.5%
Median age:	34.4 yrs.	*Ancestry*		Median income:	$40,625
More than 65 yrs:	10.1%	German:	3.3%	Median home value:	$590,900
Less than 18 yrs:	22.3%	Irish:	3.1%	Poverty:	20.3%
		English:	2.7%		
Education				**Military Veterans**	
H.S. grad:	76.9%			% of Pop:	4.3%
College grad:	32.0%				
Grad degree:	10.5%				

Since the Los Angeles riots of 1992 and 1965, the city has had to live down its reputation as being inhospitable to African-Americans, a problem exacerbated by racial tensions in the city's infamous police department. But by other measures—levels of income and degree of residential integration with nonblacks—blacks in Los Angeles are doing better than blacks elsewhere in the United States. The city's black-owned businesses have the highest revenues of any city in the nation. Among states, Cali-

2008 Presidential Vote		
Obama (D)	205,470	(87%)
McCain (R)	27,672	(12%)

2004 Presidential Vote		
Kerry (D)	172,382	(83%)
Bush (R)	33,132	(16%)

Cook Partisan Voting Index: D + 35

fornians have historically shown less prejudice toward African-Americans. And job opportunities in Los Angeles—up to and including the office of mayor for 20 years—have been relatively good for blacks. This is apparent in the hills just west of Crenshaw, an Art Deco neighborhood built in the 1920s and 1930s and the birthplace of West Coast hip-hop music. Here, in Baldwin Hills, where on clear days one can see the snow-capped San Gabriel Mountains, is a high-income African-American neighborhood. Near Windsor Hills along Slauson Avenue are other comfortable black-majority neighborhoods. In the more run-down Crenshaw area, former L.A. Lakers basketball player Magic Johnson built his successful multiplex theaters. On the site of the old Ambassador Hotel, the Los Angeles Unified School District decided to build a school rather than approve retail shops. To the north at Hollywood Boulevard, near the tourist mecca of the famed Grauman's Chinese Theatre, a huge new complex includes the Kodak Theater, which hosts the Oscars and many television and award events, including the finals of the Fox network's *American Idol* program.

These parts of central Los Angeles are the heart of the 33rd Congressional District, which is bisected by the Santa Monica Freeway, and runs from the Golden State Freeway southwest to the economically revived Culver City and almost to Venice on the Pacific Ocean. It includes most of Koreatown, centered on Western Avenue and Olympic Boulevard, which has become a hub for the city's cultural and business life and an investment opportunity for many South Koreans. It takes in some of Hollywood and the affluent Los Feliz neighborhoods. Its population in 2007 was 37% Hispanic, 27% black, and 12% Asian. But many of the district's Latinos are not citizens or registered voters, and a majority of Democratic primary voters are African-American. This is one of the most Democratic districts in the nation: John Kerry got 83% of the vote in 2004, and Barack Obama got 87% in 2008.

The congresswoman from the 33rd District is Diane Watson, a Democrat first elected in a June 2001 special election. She grew up in Los Angeles, the daughter of a police officer and a postal worker. She graduated from the University of California at Los Angeles, and later got her master's degree from California State University and a doctorate degree in educational administration from Claremont. She worked as an elementary school teacher, a school psychologist, and a lecturer at Cal State Los Angeles. Watson began her political career in 1975 as the first black woman elected to the Los Angeles Board of Education, where she worked on school desegregation issues. Three years later, she ran for the state Senate, again becoming the first black woman in that body. She served as chairman of the Health and Human Services Committee for 17 years before term limits forced her to retire in 1998. In 1999, Watson was confirmed as U.S. ambassador to Micronesia.

She returned home to run in the special election to replace Democratic Rep. Julian Dixon, who died in office in December 2000 after 22 years in Congress. Her chief opponents in the primary were state Sen. Kevin Murray and Los Angeles City Councilman Nate Holden. Watson's theme was familiarity. Murray argued that, at age 41, 26 years younger than Watson and 30 years younger than Holden, he could build seniority. Watson countered by campaigning with her 91-year-old mother. Watson got help from the women's fundraising group EMILY's List and an endorsement from Magic Johnson. Murray was endorsed by Dixon's widow, Bettye Dixon, and Los Angeles-area Democratic Reps. Maxine Waters, Henry Waxman, and Howard Berman. Holden was endorsed by outgoing Mayor Richard Riordan. Watson won 33% of the vote, to 26% for Murray and 17% for Holden. On her victory night, she angrily attacked the party leaders who opposed her. In the June runoff, she won 75%-20% over a Republican who spent $709,000 of her own money on the campaign.

Watson has a solidly liberal voting record. Even with Democrats in the majority, Watson had modest committee assignments and legislative output, which perhaps were a residual effect of her rocky start with the senior Democrats she denounced on election night. In 2009, she became chairman of the Oversight and Government Reform Subcommittee on Government Management, Organization, and Procurement, which appeared likely to have a limited agenda with Democrats controlling both Congress and the White House.

In 2007, Watson sought to cut off funds to the Cherokee Nation because of its decision to remove Freedmen slave descendants from tribal membership. Tribal leaders insisted on blood descent for membership. "I do not believe that your or my taxpayer dollars should go to any group that practices discrimination," Watson said in an editorial on the *Huffington Post*. The Indian housing bill enacted in October 2008 included a provision that she backed to bar funds to the Cherokees pending a settlement of federal litigation on the controversy.

Earlier, Watson drew protests from California dentists with a bill to prohibit the use of mercury amalgams in dental fillings, which she said could be a health hazard. She also demanded that Kellogg's stop placing a Spider-Man toy in its cereal boxes because it contained a mercury battery. In November 2004, she gained attention when she claimed that she had tipped off federal agents to an alleged terror plot at an Albany, N.Y., mosque; law enforcement authorities said that they had launched a sting operation months earlier. With a constituency that includes people in the media and entertainment industries, Watson in 2005 won House passage of a resolution urging Russia to protect intellectual-property rights.

THIRTY-FOURTH DISTRICT

Lucille Roybal-Allard (D)

Elected 1992, 9th term; b. June 12, 1941, Los Angeles; home, Los Angeles; CA State L.A., B.A. 1965; Catholic; married (Edward Allard); 4 children.

Elected Office: CA Assembly, 1986–92.

DC Office: 2330 RHOB, 20515, 202-225-1766; Fax: 202-226-0350; Web site: www.house.gov/roybal-allard.

State Offices: Los Angeles, 213-628-9230.

Committees: *Appropriations* (17th of 37 D): Homeland Security; Labor, HHS, Education & Related Agencies; Transportation, HUD & Related Agencies.

Group Ratings

	ADA	ACLU	AFS	LCV	ITIC	NTU	COC	ACU	CFG	FRC
2008	95	100	100	92	71	15	44	8	8	11
2007	100	—	100	85	—	4	55	0	6	—

National Journal Ratings

	2007 LIB	—	2007 CONS	2008 LIB	—	2008 CONS
Economic	82%	—	0%	81%	—	15%
Social	89%	—	8%	82%	—	0%
Foreign	94%	—	4%	92%	—	0%
Composite	92%	—	8%	90%	—	10%

Key Votes of the 110th Congress

1. Increase minimum wage	Y	5. Share immigration data	N	9. Withdraw troops 8/08	Y
2. Expand SCHIP	Y	6. Foreign aid abortion ban	N	10. No operations in Iran	Y
3. Raise CAFE standards	Y	7. Ban gay bias in workplace	Y	11. Free trade with Peru	N
4. Bail out financial markets	N	8. Repeal D.C. gun law	N	12. Overhaul FISA	N

Election Results

2008 general	Lucille Roybal-Allard (D)	98,503	(77%)	($594,045)
	Christopher Balding (R)	29,266	(23%)	($1,849)
2008 primary	Lucille Roybal-Allard (D)	unopposed		

Prior Winning Percentages: 2006 (77%); 2004 (74%); 2002 (74%); 2000 (85%); 1998 (87%); 1996 (82%); 1994 (81%); 1992 (63%)

Population		Race/Ethnicity		Work	
Pop. 2007:	653,913	White:	9.0%	Private:	84.2%
Change since 2000:	Up 2.3%	Black:	4.4%	Government:	9.4%
Urban:	100.0%	Hispanic:	79.5%	Self-employed:	6.2%
Rural:	0.0%	Asian:	5.9%	Blue collar:	37.3%
Area size:	59 sq. mi.	Native Am.:	0.2%	White collar:	44.3%
Age		Hawaiian:	0.1%	Khaki collar:	0.0%
Median age:	29.6 yrs.	Two+ races:	0.5%	Other:	18.4%
More than 65 yrs:	8.0%	*Ancestry*		Median income:	$35,932
Less than 18 yrs:	30.8%	USA:	2.3%	Median home value:	$473,600
Education		German:	1.8%	Poverty:	23.6%
H.S. grad:	54.4%	Irish:	1.2%	**Military Veterans**	
College grad:	10.6%			% of Pop:	3.6%
Grad degree:	2.8%				

A block from the 452-foot trademark white tower of the Los Angeles City Hall is the huge retail shopping street of Broadway. The sidewalks are thronged with Latinos, the signs are mostly in Spanish, and the merchandise is displayed on tables. This could be Mexico City or Lima. It is Latin America transplanted just a short walk from City Hall and the 60- and 70-story post-modern pink cylinders that define downtown L.A. these days. Broadway is neither the geographical nor spiritual

2008 Presidential Vote		
Obama (D)	106,695	(75%)
McCain (R)	33,056	(23%)
2004 Presidential Vote		
Kerry (D)	82,942	(69%)
Bush (R)	35,926	(30%)
Cook Partisan Voting Index: D + 22		

center of Los Angeles's Latino communities, and it is just one of many shopping and dining areas. But it is an emblem of the entry-level Latino neighborhoods of the nation's second-largest city, the places where many immigrants, not only from Mexico but also from Central and South America, come to find a cheap place to live—doubling and tripling up with other families and single newcomers, close enough to drive an old car to work in factories and warehouses that fill the acreage south and east of downtown.

Broadway and many of these entry-level neighborhoods are part of the 34th Congressional District of California. It includes downtown and Boyle Heights, once an entry neighborhood for Irish and Jewish immigrants and for the last 40 years predominantly Mexican-American. Near the Hollywood Freeway is the Cathedral of Our Lady of the Angels, the $190 million center of the nation's largest and most ethnically diverse Roman Catholic archdiocese, which Cardinal Roger Mahony dedicated as an "anchor for the ages." Another new landmark is the Walt Disney Concert Hall, home of the Los Angeles Philharmonic. The commercial revival has helped to reduce crime and spurred residential development in the central business district, with both new housing and renovations. The 34th also includes the giant factories south of downtown along the Southern Pacific Railroad and Santa Ana Freeway. And it takes in part of East Los Angeles.

To the south it includes the garment factories of Vernon and the 1940s working-class suburbs of Huntington Park, with its vibrant shopping strip on the wide Pacific Boulevard, Bell and Bell Gardens, Commerce, Maywood, and Cudahy, all of which are now heavily Latino. City officials have declared Maywood a "sanctuary city" for illegal immigrants. Beyond those areas are the more affluent suburbs of Downey, home of the Boeing (formerly Rockwell) plant that built the space shuttle, and Bellflower, a formerly prime shopping area struggling for a comeback. Bisecting much of the district is the concrete-lined Los Angeles River. City officials plan to clean up the river and return it to a more natural condition, with adjacent parkland, while preserving its flood-control assets.

The 34th District is 80% Hispanic, the highest percentage in any California district, and 80% of the residents speak a language other than English at home. Politically, this area is heavily Democratic. It is not clear what the future political preferences of people here will be, for the large majority of adults here do not vote. In 2008, in a constituency of 654,000 people, only 143,000 voted in the general election, far fewer than the 344,000 who voted in the Westside 30th District or even the 237,000 who voted in the downtown 33rd District.

The congresswoman from the 34th District is Lucille Roybal-Allard, first elected in 1992. She is the first Mexican-American woman to be elected to Congress. Roybal-Allard grew up in the Los Angeles area, the daughter of longtime U.S. Rep. Edward Roybal, who was the first Latino to serve on the Los Angeles City Council. She dreamed of a show business career as a teenager and later worked as a department store clerk and for nonprofit organizations. After raising a family—two of her children are lawyers—she followed her father into politics when she was 45 years old. She was elected to the California Assembly in 1986. Six years later, she ran for a newly created House district that took in much of the Los Angeles area that her father had represented for 30 years. Her father retired in 1992, the year she ran for the House. Roybal-Allard won easily with 75% of the vote in the primary and 63% in the general election.

Roybal-Allard has compiled a solidly liberal voting record. On the Appropriations Committee, she has focused on immigration issues, and she has pushed aggressively for an immigration overhaul bill that would include a path to citizenship for illegal immigrants currently in the country. The bill has not passed despite repeated attempts in recent years by members of both parties. In 2004, the House passed her amendment to prevent the privatizing of services for immigration information officers or investigators. With Reps. Howard Berman, D-Calif., and Lincoln Diaz-Balart, R-Fla., she is the sponsor of the American Dream Act to provide a path to legal immigration for college-bound students. In the past, she also has pushed for in-state college tuition rates for illegal immigrants. Citing recent deaths in three immigration detention facilities, Roybal-Allard sponsored a proposal in February 2009 to compel the Homeland Security Department to set humane standards for people who are detained as part of immigration proceedings.

On local issues on the committee, Roybal-Allard secured $1.5 million for an AIDS clinical trials unit at the University of Southern California's Medical Center and $1.1 million for a parking garage in the Fashion District.

On other issues, she won House passage of an amendment to allow breast-feeding in national parks and museums. As a curb on underage drinking, she has advocated higher taxes on alcohol and restraints on advertising. In 2006, she got the House to adopt more-modest measures in a bill that coordinates federal programs aimed at teen drinking and funds an education campaign about its dangers. In 2007, she co-sponsored with Education and Labor Chairman George Miller, D-Calif., a bill requiring employers to pay for personal protective equipment such as respirators, chemical resistant clothing, safety glasses, and face shields.

One of her recent successes was a bill enacted in 2008 that authorizes federal grants for newborn health screening for congenital, genetic, and metabolic disorders. She called the legislation "a giant step towards ensuring that parents and health providers are knowledgeable about newborn screening, and that babies receive the comprehensive and consistent testing they need."

Unlike several other Democratic women in the California delegation, Roybal-Allard isn't as close to House Speaker Nancy Pelosi and her powerful inner circle, which sometimes limits her leverage in the House. In 2006, Roybal-Allard seconded the nomination Democrat Steny Hoyer of Maryland for majority leader, a public declaration of support for Hoyer against Pelosi's preferred candidate, Democrat John Murtha of Pennsylvania. However, Hoyer won the contest, so Roybal-Allard still has a friend or two in high places.

THIRTY-FIFTH DISTRICT

Maxine Waters (D)

Elected 1990, 10th term; b. Aug. 15, 1938, St. Louis, MO; home, Los Angeles; CA State L.A., B.A. 1970; Christian; married (Sidney Williams); 2 children.

Elected Office: CA Assembly, 1976–90.

Professional Career: Head Start teacher, 1966; Dpty., City Councilman David Cunningham, 1973–76.

DC Office: 2344 RHOB, 20515, 202-225-2201; Fax: 202-225-7854; Web site: www.house.gov/waters.

State Offices: Los Angeles, 323-757-8900; Los Angeles, 310-642-4610.

Committees: *Chief Deputy Whip. Financial Services* (3rd of 42 D): Financial Institutions & Consumer Credit; Housing & Community Opportunity (Chmn); International Monetary Policy & Trade. *Judiciary* (9th of 24 D): Crime, Terrorism & Homeland Security; Immigration, Citizenship, Border Security & International Law.

Group Ratings

	ADA	ACLU	AFS	LCV	ITIC	NTU	COC	ACU	CFG	FRC
2008	95	100	100	100	86	7	47	0	4	5
2007	85	—	91	100	—	7	42	0	6	—

National Journal Ratings

	2007 LIB	—	2007 CONS	2008 LIB	—	2008 CONS
Economic	82%	—	0%	85%	—	0%
Social	92%	—	0%	67%	—	28%
Foreign	65%	—	33%	65%	—	32%
Composite	84%	—	16%	76%	—	24%

Key Votes of the 110th Congress

1. Increase minimum wage	Y	5. Share immigration data	N	9. Withdraw troops 8/08	N
2. Expand SCHIP	Y	6. Foreign aid abortion ban	N	10. No operations in Iran	Y
3. Raise CAFE standards	Y	7. Ban gay bias in workplace	Y	11. Free trade with Peru	N
4. Bail out financial markets	Y	8. Repeal D.C. gun law	N	12. Overhaul FISA	N

Election Results

2008 general	Maxine Waters (D)...150,778	(83%)	($831,984)
	Ted Hayes (R)...24,169	(13%)	($13,282)
	Herb Peters (Lib) 7,632	(4%)	
2008 primary	Maxine Waters (D)....................................... unopposed		

Prior Winning Percentages: 2006 (84%); 2004 (81%); 2002 (78%); 2000 (87%); 1998 (89%); 1996 (86%); 1994 (78%); 1992 (83%); 1990 (79%)

Population		Race/Ethnicity		Work	
Pop. 2007:	674,307	White:	9.3%	Private:	78.1%
Change since 2000:	Up 5.5%	Black:	30.0%	Government:	13.5%
Urban:	100.0%	Hispanic:	53.1%	Self-employed:	8.2%
Rural:	0.0%	Asian:	5.8%	Blue collar:	30.2%
Area size:	55 sq. mi.	Native Am.:	0.2%	White collar:	47.8%
		Hawaiian:	0.1%	Khaki collar:	0.1%
Age		Two+ races:	1.1%	Other:	21.9%
Median age:	30.5 yrs.			Median income:	$39,525
More than 65 yrs:	8.1%	*Ancestry*		Median home value:	$460,000
Less than 18 yrs:	31.0%	USA:	5.4%	Poverty:	22.9%
		German:	1.9%		
Education		Subsaharan:	1.7%	**Military Veterans**	
H.S. grad:	66.8%			% of Pop:	5.0%
College grad:	15.9%				
Grad degree:	4.7%				

In the years just after World War II, Los Angeles was the fastest-growing metropolitan area in America. LAX, today the nation's third-busiest airport, with eight central terminals, was then a small airfield amid open country. The mile-square grids east, north, and south of the airport were just filling up with rapidly multiplying subdivisions. Also north of the airport were the wetlands along Ballona Creek, where Howard Hughes took his Spruce Goose, the largest airplane ever built, up for its one and only

2008 Presidential Vote

Obama (D) 165,761	(84%)
McCain (R)...............................27,789	(14%)

2004 Presidential Vote

Kerry (D)................................130,764	(79%)
Bush (R) 33,110	(20%)

Cook Partisan Voting Index: D + 31

flight. The rapidly growing suburb of Inglewood, just east of the airport around the Hollywood Park racetrack, was filling up with the young families of people who had moved to Los Angeles during the war—workers in the giant aircraft factories or in the small factories that every day were making California less dependent on goods from back East. In Hawthorne, home of a big Northrop Grumman plant, future celebrities were growing up—Sonny Bono and the Beach Boys. Gardena, east of Hawthorne, was known for its legal poker clubs and its Japanese-American residents, back from the wartime internment camps.

East of Gardena is the part of Los Angeles called South Central or, more recently, South Los Angeles, after the City Council in 2003 officially renamed the community to rid it of the stigma of gang wars and race riots. In the days of residential segregation, much of this area was the home of Los Angeles's black community, its numbers greatly expanded by migration from the South during and after the war. In the Central Avenue entertainment district were clubs and theaters hosting Ella Fitzgerald, Sarah Vaughn, Billy Eckstine, Duke Ellington, Louis Armstrong, Count Basie, Dizzy Gillespie, and Charlie Parker. Later, it was the epicenter of L.A.'s two postwar riots, in the Watts district of Los Angeles in 1965 and at the corner of Florence and Normandie in 1992. In the last 20 years, Latinos have been buying houses here, which are among the cheapest in the metropolitan area — only five L.A. zip codes have median prices below $200,000—and new businesses have been cropping up in garages and small factories.

The 35th Congressional District of California today is made up of all these areas, with a landscape and population very different from 60 years ago. At its west and east ends are two of the Los Angeles area's great transportation facilities. One is LAX and the cluster of hotels and office buildings all around (LAX's swooping arches, intended in 1961 to symbolize the jet era, are now a historic landmark). The other is the Alameda Corridor, the 20-mile express rail line connecting the ports of Los Angeles and Long Beach with rail distribution points near downtown Los Angeles. Once mostly white working class and middle class, the district's population in 2007 was 30% African-American and 53% Hispanic. Since the

1992 riot, local businesses have revived, though the district still suffers high crime rates and plenty of mistrust of local police. Politically, this is an overwhelmingly Democratic district.

The congresswoman from the 35th District is Maxine Waters, a Democrat first elected in 1990. She grew up in St. Louis, one of 13 children. She has said, "I know all about welfare. I remember the social workers peeking in the refrigerator and under the beds." She moved to California in 1961, worked in a garment factory, and raised two children. Waters got a sociology degree at California State University in Los Angeles and became an assistant Head Start teacher after the Watts riot of 1965. She likes to call herself "The Organizer" and has shown the capacity to draw big supportive crowds to her protests over the years. From 1973 to 1976, she worked on the staff of a Los Angeles city councilman. In 1976, she won a seat in the California Assembly, where she helped pass legislation divesting state pension funds from South Africa, setting up a child-abuse-prevention training program, and prohibiting police strip searches for nonviolent offenses. When Democratic Rep. Augustus Hawkins retired in 1990 after 28 years in the U.S. House, Waters was the obvious choice for the seat and won it easily. Her husband, a former professional football player and Mercedes Benz salesman, became President Clinton's ambassador to the Bahamas.

Having grown up in poverty and lived under segregation laws, Waters believes with fervor in federal aid for the poor and for racial preferences to help blacks overcome years of slavery, segregation, and discrimination. She has favored drastic reductions in defense spending in favor of domestic spending. She was one of six members who voted against supporting the Gulf War in 1991, asking how urban gang members could be expected to stop fighting when America's own leaders were waging battles. She has been a staunch opponent of the Iraq war. In the summer of 2006, she campaigned in Connecticut for Ned Lamont in his successful primary challenge to then-Democratic Sen. Joseph Lieberman. "I believe this is the most significant election of all the Democrats that are running," she said. In 2007, she lobbied her colleagues against the Iraq supplemental funding bill with a timetable for withdrawal supported by the Democratic leadership. And she played a leading role with the Out of Iraq Caucus. She brings to her work a fury that is almost palpable, and an insistence that she will assert herself regardless of protocol. Her anger is a political weapon she uses shrewdly to get both publicity and results. "I don't have time to be polite," Waters says.

She came to Washington shortly before the 1992 race riots in L.A., which occasioned her best and worst moments. She flew home immediately and roused the Department of Water and Power to restore water to the riot area, and she was effective in gaining provisions to the post-riot emergency act that were eventually signed into law. But she also suggested rioters were morally justified and claimed ominously, "Los Angeles is under siege. . . . The violence could spill over to many other cities in this country."

Waters isn't afraid to step on toes in pursuit of her legislative or political agenda. She has pushed for federal loan guarantees to cities for economic and infrastructure development. In a rare legislative success in the Republican-controlled House, Waters sponsored an amendment to triple spending for the erasure of the debts of poor nations, mostly in Africa. Many Republicans agreed, and it passed 216-211. She has sponsored bills to repeal mandatory minimum sentences for drug crimes, and charges that the war on drugs has created "apartheid." In 2006, she sponsored a bill to provide routine HIV/AIDS testing of federal prison inmates, with an opt-out provision for those who objected. During the Judiciary Committee's 1998 impeachment inquiry of President Clinton, she assailed "trumped-up charges" and accused special prosecutor Kenneth Starr of "raw, unmasked, unbridled hatred and meanness that drives this impeachment coup d'etat."

As a senior member of the Financial Services Committee, Waters moved aggressively in the majority once Democrats gained control of the House in 2007. She sponsored measures to overhaul discredited housing-finance programs, expand affordable-housing programs, and aid local governments to rehabilitate foreclosed homes. She harshly criticized the Federal Reserve Board and big bankers for their financing practices and the tight credit that resulted. In a sarcastic voice, she told a panel of banking executives in February 2009, "To the captains of the universe sitting here before all of us, all of my political life I have been in disagreement with the banking industry."

But in recent years, her personal finances have become the target of watchdogs. In 2005, the liberal-leaning Citizens for Responsibility and Ethics criticized the fact that members of her family have made more than $1 million in eight years doing business with companies, candidates, and causes that she had helped. Her reply: "They do their business and I do mine." In March 2009, news stories raised the issue of whether Waters had urged favorable treatment by federal regulators of a bank in which she and her husband had held stakes. Federal regulators told *The New York Times* that they were taken aback when they learned that a California congresswoman who helped set up a meeting with bankers (in 2008) had family financial ties to a bank whose chief executive asked them for up to $50 million in special bailout funds. Waters defended her actions by saying, "I have been an outspoken advocate for minority communities and businesses in California and nationally for decades."

Waters is a force to be reckoned with in L.A. politics as well. Other politicians are eager to be included on her Progressive Connections slates of candidates that are mailed out to many thousands of black voters. Politicians pay to be included—a common California practice. (City Councilman Mike Feuer, in a contest for city attorney in 2001, paid $10,000 to be on the slate and ran even in African-American areas with Deputy Mayor Rocky Delgadillo. But Feuer wouldn't pay $25,000 to be on the slate for the June runoff. Delgadillo paid $35,000 and got 65% in black areas.)

For mayor in 2001, Waters strongly supported City Attorney James Hahn in his successful campaign against former Assembly Speaker Antonio Villaraigosa. After Hahn won, Waters approached banker and *L.A. Focus* magazine owner Jheryl Busby and insisted he fire columnist Najee Ali, who had backed Villaraigosa. Busby fired Ali in July 2001. Ali sued Busby, and Busby's attorney said Busby "told me he needs a positive relationship with Waters because of her ability to help him with his bank and other business interests." In the March 2005 rematch between Hahn and Villaraigosa, Waters supported Villaraigosa against Hahn. As a footnote, Ali turned up at a 2006 protest meeting organized by Waters, and when she recognized him, Ali said that Waters ordered him not to speak to the media. "I remember her saying she was going to make it rough for me and that she was going to get me," Ali told the *L.A. CityBeat* weekly. "I was stunned that a U.S. congresswoman would threaten me because I wanted to exercise my freedom of speech."

Waters has been re-elected without difficulty. The biggest potential threat to her tenure is the rising Hispanic percentage in the district.

THIRTY-SIXTH DISTRICT

Jane Harman (D)

Elected 2000, 8th term; b. June 28, 1945, New York, NY; home, Venice; Smith Col., B.A. 1966, Harvard U., J.D. 1969; Jewish; married (Sidney); 4 children.

Elected Office: U.S. House of Reps., 1992–98.

Professional Career: Legis. dir., U.S. Sen. John Tunney, 1972–73; Chief cnsl. & staff dir., Senate Judiciary Subcmtee., 1973–77; Dep. cabinet secy., White House, 1977; Defense Dept. special cnsl., 1979; Harman Intl. Industries, corp. secy., 1985–92, Dir., 1990–92; Practicing atty., 1970–72, 1982–92; Regents prof., U.C.L.A., 1999.

DC Office: 2400 RHOB, 20515, 202-225-8220; Fax: 202-226-7290; Web site: www.house.gov/harman.

State Offices: El Segundo, 310-643-3636; Wilmington, 310-549-8282.

Committees: *Energy & Commerce* (15th of 36 D): Energy & Environment; Health. *Homeland Security* (3rd of 20 D): Border, Maritime & Global Counterterrorism; Intelligence, Information Sharing & Terrorism Risk Assessment (Chmn).

Group Ratings

	ADA	ACLU	AFS	LCV	ITIC	NTU	COC	ACU	CFG	FRC
2008	95	91	100	100	100	13	65	0	7	0
2007	95	—	100	90	—	5	56	0	12	—

National Journal Ratings

	2007 LIB	—	2007 CONS	2008 LIB	—	2008 CONS
Economic	82%	—	0%	76%	—	23%
Social	59%	—	40%	75%	—	18%
Foreign	81%	—	16%	76%	—	24%
Composite	78%	—	22%	77%	—	23%

Key Votes of the 110th Congress

1. Increase minimum wage	Y	5. Share immigration data	N	9. Withdraw troops 8/08	Y
2. Expand SCHIP	Y	6. Foreign aid abortion ban	N	10. No operations in Iran	Y
3. Raise CAFE standards	Y	7. Ban gay bias in workplace	Y	11. Free trade with Peru	Y
4. Bail out financial markets	Y	8. Repeal D.C. gun law	N	12. Overhaul FISA	Y

Election Results

2008 general	Jane Harman (D)	171,948	(69%)	($687,693)
	Brian Gibson (R)	78,543	(31%)	($8,988)
2008 primary	Jane Harman (D)	unopposed		

Prior Winning Percentages: 2006 (63%); 2004 (62%); 2002 (61%); 2000 (48%); 1996 (52%); 1994 (48%); 1992 (48%)

Population		Race/Ethnicity		Work	
Pop. 2007:	655,573	White:	46.6%	Private:	78.7%
Change since 2000:	Up 2.6%	Black:	3.7%	Government:	11.0%
Urban:	100.0%	Hispanic:	31.6%	Self-employed:	10.1%
Rural:	0.0%	Asian:	14.8%	Blue collar:	15.0%
Area size:	122 sq. mi.	Native Am.:	0.2%	White collar:	70.5%
Age		Hawaiian:	0.4%	Khaki collar:	0.2%
Median age:	36.8 yrs.	Two+ races:	2.4%	Other:	14.2%
More than 65 yrs:	10.6%	*Ancestry*		Median income:	$65,678
Less than 18 yrs:	23.4%	German:	8.8%	Median home value:	$699,800
Education		Irish:	7.3%	Poverty:	10.5%
H.S. grad:	85.9%	English:	6.2%	**Military Veterans**	
College grad:	41.5%			% of Pop:	7.2%
Grad degree:	15.0%				

For many Southern Californians, there is no better place to be than the beach. It is not a perfect environment: In the morning there may be mists, the winter air is damp and clammy, and even in summer the weather can be chilly. The water is never very warm and is sometimes polluted. But for many this is echt-California, and in this democratic polity, there is a beach to suit the taste of just about everyone, many of them with their unique piers and athletes, especially volleyball. The funkiest of all is

2008 Presidential Vote		
Obama (D)	176,924	(64%)
McCain (R)	92,105	(34%)
2004 Presidential Vote		
Kerry (D)	154,010	(59%)
Bush (R)	103,425	(40%)
Cook Partisan Voting Index:	D + 12	

Venice: "Muscle Beach," with its beach houses and expensive new mansions jammed together, sharing the shoreline with the homeless people in cars and campers who have staked out spots along the beach in recent years. Venice is known for its chaotic boardwalk, where skateboarding got its start and in-line skating sports are de rigueur. The 2005 movie *Lords of Dogtown* is about the group of Venice surfers who revolutionized the skateboarding culture in the 1970s. To the south is Marina Del Rey, with sleek modern apartment complexes and expensive yacht moorings, and south of LAX Airport, El Segundo, named for Chevron's second oil refinery and now with big office buildings. Next is South Bay, with Manhattan Beach, a favorite of the Beach Boys, who grew up a couple of miles inland in Hawthorne. Tiny Hermosa Beach, with tightly packed frame houses originally the homes of elderly retirees, is now filled with the young and the trying-to-stay-young. Many of the beaches enforce no-smoking rules. Farther south are the flower-planted rises of Redondo Beach and the larger city of Torrance, whose vast inland expanse is the home of large Korean and Japanese communities and of the North American headquarters of both Toyota and Honda. Overlooking L.A.'s modern container port are Wilmington and San Pedro, once working class, but moving up as well.

The 36th Congressional District of California includes most of this beach territory, from Venice south to San Pedro (both of which are within the Los Angeles city limits, though the area in between is not). The district is multiethnic: 32% of residents are Hispanic, 15% Asian, and 28% foreign-born. But the beach communities, as if in the 1950s, are still filled mostly with white Anglos. This area is leery of taxes, but culturally it is libertarian—against restrictions or even aspersions on its various lifestyles. This has been one of America's leading defense and aerospace areas, where Howard Hughes built planes half a century ago and where much of the 1980s defense buildup took place. With its many military and space facilities for electronics research and development, Boeing is the largest private employer in the area, including its assembly operation in El Segundo. Nearby, Northrop has been building a robotic patrol plane for the Navy.

The congresswoman from the 36th District is Democrat Jane Harman, who was first elected in 1992 and regained the seat in 2000 after running unsuccessfully for governor in 1998. Born in New York City, she grew up in Los Angeles, the daughter of a Westside physician. She had early exposure to politics: She was a volunteer usher when John F. Kennedy was nominated at the 1960 Democratic convention in Los Angeles. Harman graduated from Smith College and then Harvard Law School, when that was still rare for women. In the 1970s, she worked for California Sen. John Tunney, a Democrat on the Senate Judiciary Committee. She later was a special counsel in the Defense Department and then worked as a lobbyist in Washington. She is one of the wealthiest members of Congress. Her husband, Sidney Harman, is the founder of audio-equipment maker Harman International Industries, and she has spent large amounts of her own money on her campaigns. In 1992, Harman campaigned as "pro-choice and pro-change," defeating a Republican woman who opposed abortion rights 48%-42% in a new district. Harman was twice narrowly re-elected, in 1994 and 1996. She spent more than $20 million running for governor in 1998, including $15 million of her own money, but finished a disappointing third among Democrats, far behind Gray Davis.

Congressional and state Democrats lobbied her hard to reclaim her former House seat, which Republican Steven Kuykendall narrowly won in 1998. Kuykendall supported abortion rights and took liberal stands on environmental issues; many Democrats believed that only Harman could defeat him. She decided to run again in 2000, attacking Kuykendall for failing to support the Democrats' proposal for a prescription drug benefit in Medicare and for voting to repeal the estate tax. She stressed her earlier House record, economically somewhat conservative and culturally liberal. Kuykendall was hurt by the lack of appeal of George W. Bush in coastal California. This was a race targeted by both parties, with each candidate spending nearly $2 million. After more than a week of absentee-ballot counting, Harman won 48%-47%.

Her voting record has been the most conservative of Democrats from Los Angeles, with some support for business causes and energy conservation. After September 11, she began to focus increasingly on national security. With a seat on the Intelligence Committee, she became the ranking Democrat of the Terrorism and Homeland Security Subcommittee. Working closely with Chairman Saxby Chambliss, then a Georgia Republican representative, she criticized the Central Intelligence Agency, the Federal Bureau of Investigation, and the National Security Agency for moving too slowly to share information to respond to terrorism threats. She was an early supporter of creating a Department of Homeland Security and she voted for the use of force in Iraq.

Then-Minority Leader Nancy Pelosi, who was the ranking Democrat on the full Intelligence panel, chose Harman to replace her after the 2002 election, despite a vigorous campaign by Rep. Sanford Bishop, D-Ga. "I live and breathe security 24/7," Harman said. She agreed with the 9/11 commission's recommendations to give more authority to a national intelligence director and to unify intelligence resources. She again established a bipartisan working relationship with the Republican in charge, Intelligence Committee Chairman Pete Hoekstra of Michigan. The two worked with Senate Governmental Affairs Chairman Susan Collins, R-Maine, in getting Congress to complete the intelligence reorganization bill in 2004. The following year, Harman called for a ban on torture by U.S. interrogators and a prohibition on transfer of detainees to countries that engage in torture. She also said that President Bush lacked authority for his domestic surveillance program.

Her bipartisanship and pragmatism occasionally rankled other Democrats on the committee and in the House. In 2006, she had reason to believe that she would chair the Intelligence Committee if Democrats regained the majority in the election. But Pelosi had other ideas. Having earlier promised other lawmakers that Harman would be the top Democrat on the panel for only four years, Pelosi made clear that the position was up for grabs. But the independent-minded Harman did not get the message. And the more she defended her qualifications, stated her intention to remain, and had her allies lobby for her, the more Pelosi was angered by the pressure. Pelosi gave the gavel to Rep. Silvestre Reyes, D-Texas, and Harman got the consolation prize of chairman of the Homeland Security Subcommittee on Intelligence, Information Sharing and Terrorism Risk Assessment: a big title, but less authority. The House in 2008 passed her bills to require the Homeland Security Department to expedite the disclosure of unclassified information, including unclassified versions of intelligence documents. When President Obama took office in 2009, she promised a continued push to reverse Bush-era policies on enemy combatants.

Harman and Pelosi found themselves thrown together in another controversy in April 2009. The Intelligence Committee launched an investigation of news reports that Harman had been wiretapped by the NSA in 2005 and was overheard telling an Israeli agent she would push for the Justice Department to ease espionage charges against two former American Israeli Public Affairs Committee officials. In exchange, the Israeli agent allegedly pledged to lobby Pelosi to appoint Harman to chair the Intelligence panel. Harman denied improper involvement and pushed Justice officials to release the transcript. Pelosi said she was aware in 2005 that Harman was being wiretapped, but expressed her belief that Harman had acted appropriately.

In 2006, Harman survived a primary with Marcy Winograd, president of Progressive Democrats of Los Angeles, who harshly attacked her for supporting the Iraq war and for backing President Bush on intelligence issues. Harman defended her record as independent, and won 62%-38%. She had no re-election problems in 2008.

THIRTY-SEVENTH DISTRICT

Laura Richardson (D)

Elected Aug. 2007, 1st full term; b. April 14, 1962, Los Angeles; home, Long Beach; U.C.L.A., B.A. 1984, U. of S. CA, M.B.A. 1996; Christian; divorced.

Elected Office: Long Beach City Cncl., 2000–06; CA Assembly, 2006–07.

Professional Career: Teacher, 1984–87; Mktg. rep., Xerox Corp., 1987–2001; Field Dpty., Rep. Juanita Millender-McDonald, 1996–98; Southern CA dir., Lt. Gov. Cruz Bustamante, 2001–05.

DC Office: 1725 LHOB, 20515, 202-225-7924; Fax: 202-225-7926; Web site: richardson.house.gov.

State Offices: Long Beach, 562-436-3828.

Committees: *Homeland Security* (11th of 20 D): Emergency Communications, Preparedness & Response; Emerging Threats, Cybersecurity & Science and Technology. *Transportation & Infrastructure* (32nd of 44 D): Aviation; Coast Guard & Maritime Transportation; Highways & Transit; Railroads, Pipelines & Hazardous Materials.

Group Ratings

	ADA	ACLU	AFS	LCV	ITIC	NTU	COC	ACU	CFG	FRC
2008	100	75	100	85	83	6	59	0	0	50
2007	—	—	100	100	—	5	67	0	12	—

National Journal Ratings

	2007 LIB	—	2007 CONS	2008 LIB	—	2008 CONS
Economic	*%	—	*%	67%	—	33%
Social	*%	—	*%	72%	—	28%
Foreign	*%	—	*%	78%	—	17%
Composite	*%	—	*%	73%	—	27%

Key Votes of the 110th Congress

1. Increase minimum wage	*	5. Share immigration data	*	9. Withdraw troops 8/08	*
2. Expand SCHIP	Y	6. Foreign aid abortion ban	*	10. No operations in Iran	*
3. Raise CAFE standards	Y	7. Ban gay bias in workplace	Y	11. Free trade with Peru	N
4. Bail out financial markets	Y	8. Repeal D.C. gun law	N	12. Overhaul FISA	Y

Election Results

2008 general	Laura Richardson (D)	131,342	(75%)	($1,075,767)
	Nicholas Dibs (I)	42,774	(24%)	($64,894)
2008 primary	Laura Richardson (D)	25,713	(74%)	
	Peter Mathews (D)	5,860	(17%)	
	Lee Davis (D)	2,983	(9%)	

Prior Winning Percentages: 2007 (67%)

Population		**Race/Ethnicity**		**Work**	
Pop. 2007:	658,832	White:	14.3%	Private:	79.0%
Change since 2000:	Up 3.1%	Black:	22.4%	Government:	14.6%
Urban:	100.0%	Hispanic:	47.7%	Self-employed:	6.3%
Rural:	0.0%	Asian:	12.1%	Blue collar:	27.8%
Area size:	75 sq. mi.	Native Am.:	0.3%	White collar:	52.2%
		Hawaiian:	1.0%	Khaki collar:	0.1%
Age		Two+ races:	1.7%	Other:	19.9%
Median age:	30.5 yrs.	*Ancestry*		Median income:	$43,629
More than 65 yrs:	7.9%	German:	3.3%	Median home value:	$443,500
Less than 18 yrs:	30.5%	Irish:	2.7%	Poverty:	21.2%
Education		English:	2.3%	**Military Veterans**	
H.S. grad:	70.4%			% of Pop:	6.0%
College grad:	18.8%				
Grad degree:	5.3%				

With 465,000 people, Long Beach would be a major metropolis almost anywhere but in Los Angeles County, where it seems just the largest of many suburbs. But it has an identity of its own. Started as a beach resort 1888, it soon became a port when Los Angeles civic leaders decided that if their town was to be a world-class city, it must have a world-class harbor. Since nature had not provided one, they built it where the Los Angeles River flows into the ocean at the western edge of Long Beach. By

2008 Presidential Vote
Obama (D) 157,219   (80%)
McCain (R)...............................36,940   (19%)

2004 Presidential Vote
Kerry (D)................................126,068   (74%)
Bush (R) 43,160   (25%)

Cook Partisan Voting Index: D + 26

1909, Los Angeles had annexed the harbor towns of San Pedro and Wilmington on the other side of the river. Over the next decades, the two cities persuaded the federal government to dredge channels and build a breakwater and turning basins. Long Beach was developing other businesses as well. It sprouted oil derricks in the 1920s and briefly became one of the nation's big oil producers. It was the site of major aircraft plants in the 1940s and beyond.

Since then, the Los Angeles-Long Beach port has become the nation's largest, the fastest-growing major cargo center in the world, with huge steel-gray container ships pulling quietly up to enormous automated loading facilities—a 21st-century contrast to the rotting docks of New York and San Francisco. The length of three football fields, these ships unload a daily average of 19,900 containers, which accounts for 26% of West Coast shipping. From there, about half of the cargo leaves by rail in 50 daily trains along the $2.4 billion high-speed 20-mile Alameda Corridor to the large rail yards near downtown Los Angeles. But the recession hit these ports hard, and reduced volume by almost a third in early 2009. There also has been a big increase in cargo inspections since September 11, with scanning at the port of all high-risk containers. But with three major highways threading through the port, cargo security remains a major concern. Long Beach's naval station was closed in the 1990s, and there were job losses at the huge McDonnell Douglas aircraft plant. Boeing, the new owner, stopped producing commercial jets here, but it continues to build military planes, although there have been fewer orders for the giant C-17 transport. Small businesses have grown, and Long Beach's beachfront has thrived. The *Queen Mary,* converted into a floating hotel, is a big tourist attraction, and there is a glittering array of high-rises and a huge new aquarium along the beach.

The 37th Congressional District of California includes 80% of the city of Long Beach and Signal Hill, surrounded by Long Beach, where the oil rigs are still pumping. It includes the two industrial suburbs of Compton and Carson. Compton switched from all-white to all-black in the 1960s, and in the 1980s became heavily Latino and economically depressed. Carson, with recent subdivisions amid freeway interchanges, has a multiethnic population. The district includes the south end of South Central Los Angeles, including the Watts tower, where the riot of 1965 broke out. In 2000, the district's population was 22% African-American and 48% Hispanic. But many of the Latinos are not U.S. citizens and were only an estimated 22% of registered voters in 2007. It is a heavily Democratic district.

The new congresswoman from the 37th District is Laura Richardson, a Democrat who won the seat in an August 2007 special election after the death of Rep. Juanita Millender-McDonald, a Democrat who was chair of the House Administration Committee. A former field deputy for Millender-McDonald, Richardson majored in political science at the University of California at Los Angeles, worked as a marketing representative for Xerox, and got an MBA from the University of Southern California. In 2000, she began her career in elected office by winning a seat on the Long Beach City Council and simultaneously served as Southern California director for Democratic Lt. Gov. Cruz Bustamante. In 2006, Richardson ran for an open Assembly seat and won the primary 54% to 46%; she won the general with 68% of the vote.

In the special election, the June primary was the critical test of African-American and Hispanic voting clout in a district where power is shifting from blacks to Hispanics. Seventeen candidates filed for the election, but the front-runners were Richardson, who is African-American, and state Sen. Jenny Oropeza, who is Latina. Both are from Long Beach. Oropeza had served six years in the Assembly, where she chaired the Budget and Transportation committees, and was elected to the state Senate in 2006. Each candidate sought to downplay the racial component of the contest, but Richardson's endorsements came chiefly from African-American leaders, including Rep. Maxine Waters of the adjacent 35th District, and Oropeza got her support mostly from Hispanics, including some Los Angeles-area members of Congress and state legislators. Assembly Speaker Fabian Nunez, however, supported Richardson.

Oropeza and Richardson both called for an end to the war in Iraq and said that they would focus on the needs of the local port, such as additional security. Oropeza got significant financial support for voter-turnout efforts from an Indian tribe in Riverside County. Organized labor's opposition to the tribe's proposed casino led national and county labor federations to back Richardson. In the low-turnout voting, Richardson won 37% to secure the Democratic nomination, while Oropeza got 31%. Valerie McDonald, daughter of the late congresswoman, finished third with 9%. John Kanaley, a Long Beach policeman and Iraq war veteran, finished first among Republicans with 8%. Since none of the candidates received more than 50% of the vote, each party's leading candidate faced an August 21 runoff. But this was a pro forma contest in this solidly Democratic district, with Richardson winning 67% to Kanaley's 25%.

In the House, Richardson has a relatively moderate voting record for a Los Angeles-area Democrat. She joined the locally useful Transportation and Infrastructure Committee and the Homeland Security Committee, where she pledged to educate House members about the "national significance" of her district's transportation infrastructure. In response to a racially charged 2007 incident at a high school in Jena, La., in which six black teens were accused of beating a white high school student, she pushed a resolution to criminalize the use of hanging nooses.

But most of the early attention Richardson drew was unwanted. Her personal finances were a mess, especially her home ownership. Local news reports detailed that she had defaulted on home payments six times in eight years. Her home in Sacramento was foreclosed on by a bank, which sold it but then reversed that action after Richardson objected. She also abandoned her car after failing to pay a repair bill. The liberal-leaning Citizens for Responsibility and Ethics in Washington called her a "deadbeat," and filed an ethics complaint alleging lenders may have given her preferential treatment. Richardson gave little explanation, though she told the *Long Beach Press-Telegram* in October 2008 that "everything is currently in order" with her finances. Her constituents did not seem to mind her personal problems. She was re-elected easily that year.

THIRTY-EIGHTH DISTRICT

Grace Napolitano (D)

Elected 1998, 6th term; b. Dec. 4, 1936, Brownsville, TX; home, Norwalk; Brownsville H.S.; Catholic; married (Frank); 5 children.

Elected Office: Norwalk City Cncl., 1986–92; Norwalk mayor, 1989–92; CA Assembly, 1992–98.

Professional Career: Employee, Ford Motor Co., 1970–1992.

DC Office: 1610 LHOB, 20515, 202-225-5256; Fax: 202-225-0027; Web site: www.napolitano.house.gov.

State Offices: Santa Fe Springs, 562-801-2134.

Committees: *Natural Resources* (6th of 29 D): National Parks, Forests & Public Lands; Water & Power (Chmn). *Transportation & Infrastructure* (20th of 44 D): Highways & Transit; Railroads, Pipelines & Hazardous Materials; Water Resources & Environment.

Group Ratings

	ADA	ACLU	AFS	LCV	ITIC	NTU	COC	ACU	CFG	FRC
2008	95	100	100	92	71	15	44	8	9	11
2007	100	—	100	90	—	3	45	0	1	—

National Journal Ratings

	2007 LIB	—	2007 CONS	2008 LIB	—	2008 CONS
Economic	82%	—	0%	85%	—	0%
Social	89%	—	8%	82%	—	0%
Foreign	90%	—	8%	92%	—	0%
Composite	91%	—	9%	93%	—	7%

Key Votes of the 110th Congress

1. Increase minimum wage	Y	5. Share immigration data	N	9. Withdraw troops 8/08	Y
2. Expand SCHIP	Y	6. Foreign aid abortion ban	N	10. No operations in Iran	Y
3. Raise CAFE standards	Y	7. Ban gay bias in workplace	Y	11. Free trade with Peru	N
4. Bail out financial markets	N	8. Repeal D.C. gun law	N	12. Overhaul FISA	N

Election Results

2008 general	Grace Napolitano (D)	130,211	(82%)	($385,568)
	Christopher Agrella (Lib)	29,113	(18%)	
2008 primary	Grace Napolitano (D)	unopposed		

Prior Winning Percentages: 2006 (75%); 2004 (100%); 2002 (71%); 2000 (71%); 1998 (68%)

Population		Race/Ethnicity		Work	
Pop. 2007:	655,739	White:	10.6%	Private:	80.7%
Change since 2000:	Up 2.6%	Black:	3.2%	Government:	12.6%
Urban:	100.0%	Hispanic:	74.1%	Self-employed:	6.5%
Rural:	0.0%	Asian:	10.8%	Blue collar:	31.8%
Area size:	105 sq. mi.	Native Am.:	0.3%	White collar:	49.7%
		Hawaiian:	0.1%	Khaki collar:	0.2%
Age		Two+ races:	0.6%	Other:	18.4%
Median age:	31.7 yrs.			Median income:	$51,641
More than 65 yrs:	10.0%	*Ancestry*		Median home value:	$443,700
Less than 18 yrs:	29.3%	German:	2.3%	Poverty:	12.5%
		Irish:	2.0%		
Education		English:	1.8%	**Military Veterans**	
H.S. grad:	64.5%			% of Pop:	5.0%
College grad:	13.9%				
Grad degree:	3.8%				

One of the great population trends in the United States is the upward social movement of hundreds of thousands of immigrants in the Los Angeles Basin, from crowded entry-level neighborhoods out on freeways to suburban cul-de-sacs. It is visible east and southeast of Los Angeles, in suburbs that over a generation have changed from solidly white Anglo to largely Latino. Many people here have climbed the economic ladder by working in small smokeless factories along railroad tracks and riv-

2008 Presidential Vote
Obama (D) 130,092 (71%)
McCain (R)...............................48,599 (27%)

2004 Presidential Vote
Kerry (D)................................106,652 (65%)
Bush (R).................................54,869 (34%)

Cook Partisan Voting Index: D + 18

erbeds and beneath roaring freeways, and in small business offices and stores. These workers have made Los Angeles the nation's top metropolitan area for manufacturing, surpassing Chicago. Their values resemble those of working-class Americans of the 1960s: pro-family and traditional (L.A.-area Latinos have lower-than-average divorce rates), patriotic and hardworking (Latino males have the highest workforce participation of any measured group, and the incomes of U.S.-born Los Angeles County Latinos are at the county average).

Many of these relatively new residents live in the 38th Congressional District of California, where the percentage of Hispanics in 2007 was 74%. This is a swath of Los Angeles County anchored by four primarily Hispanic suburbs. To the northwest is Montebello (Italian for "beautiful hill"), a working-class suburb just beyond East Los Angeles and once the site of oil drilling. Heavy traffic on the Union Pacific line from the Long Beach port has led to proposals to place the rails underground to minimize dangers and routine traffic interference. To the east is La Puente, a center of the light manufacturing economy that created thousands of jobs in the Los Angeles Basin. Increasing numbers of its small businesses are owned by Asians, Latinos, and African-Americans. Farther east is the old town of Pomona, the district's largest city and the site of the Los Angeles County Fair. It has been troubled for decades by gang wars. To the south are Norwalk, a rail crossroad astride the Santa Ana Freeway, and Santa Fe Springs.

The congresswoman from the 38th District is Grace Napolitano, a Democrat first elected in 1998. Napolitano grew up in the lower Rio Grande Valley of Texas, married at age 18, and eventually had five children. When she was 23, the family moved to California. She got a job as a secretary at Ford Motor and stayed for 22 years. After her first husband died, she married Frank Napolitano, and in 1980, they started a pizzeria. She served on the Norwalk City Council from 1986 to 1992, and also served one term as mayor, becoming the first Latino to hold the position. In 1992, she was elected to the California Assembly from a district that covered much of her current congressional district.

Term-limited in 1998, she got the opportunity to run for Congress when 16-year Democratic Rep. Esteban Torres announced three days before the filing deadline that he was retiring. Torres's surprise move seemed designed to promote the election of Jamie Casso, his son-in-law and chief of staff, who immediately announced his candidacy. But Napolitano was not deterred. She persuaded the state AFL-CIO to vote an "open endorsement," although the executive board had backed Casso and Torres had been a senior United Auto Workers official in the 1960s. Napolitano and Casso waged a fierce campaign. She criticized him for not living in the district, and he criticized her $180,000 loan to her campaign at an unusual 18% interest rate. Napolitano had the financial backing of national women's organizations, including EMILY's List, plus the benefit of higher name recognition. The two candidates had few differences on major issues. Napolitano signed a pledge to serve only three terms. She won the primary by 618 votes, and her victory in November was assured in this Democratic district.

In the House, Napolitano has a mostly liberal voting record. As chairman of the Congressional Hispanic Caucus in 2005, she urged changes in the Democratic Party's outreach to Hispanic voters and was more consensus-oriented on immigration reform than some caucus members. On the Natural Resources Committee, Napolitano was active in the 2004 reauthorization of the California Bay-Delta water-allocation program, which featured unusual bipartisanship among Californians.

When Democrats took majority control in 2007, she became the chairman of the Natural Resources panel's Water and Power Subcommittee, with a focus on Southern California's acute need for an adequate water supply of good quality. In 2007, she co-founded the bipartisan Congressional Water Caucus to inform Congress of clean-water needs and to monitor the impact of global warming. She helped to enact a bill in 2008 to study more-efficient management of water resources and to cap the costs to consumers of guards at Bureau of Reclamation dams.

Napolitano is also involved in the needs of the mentally ill, an interest that was sparked by a report that one in three Hispanic girls contemplates suicide. "Mental health is treatable. But [the Latino community has] a stigma attached to it," Napolitano said. "We don't want to see it, we don't want to hear it, we don't want to feel it. We hide it." She supports requiring insurers to treat mental health services the same as other medical services in coverage decisions.

Napolitano's work has played well at home. She has not been seriously challenged for re-election and she continued the unusual practice of charging her campaign 18% for her personal loans. In February 2003, she abandoned her earlier pledge to serve only three terms; she ran for a fourth in 2004 and won. In 2007, she was criticized by the watchdog group Citizens for Responsibility and Ethics in Washington for paying her daughter, Yolanda Dyer, and her daughter's consulting firm nearly $53,000 for work on her campaigns between 2002 and 2006. Napolitano said her daughter ran her campaigns and probably should have been paid more for her work.

Local Hispanic leaders undoubtedly will have their eyes on the 38th during redistricting and will be nudging Napolitano, who will be in her mid-70s, to retire. Democrats ought to have no trouble retaining the seat.

THIRTY-NINTH DISTRICT

Linda Sánchez (D)

Elected 2002, 4th term; b. Jan. 28, 1969, Orange; home, Lakewood; U. of CA, B.A. 1991, U.C.L.A., J.D. 1995; Catholic; married (Jim Sullivan); 1 child.

Professional Career: Practicing atty., 1995–98; Exec. secy. treas. of Orange Cnty. AFL-CIO, 2000–02.

DC Office: 1222 LHOB, 20515, 202-225-6676; Fax: 202-226-1012; Web site: lindasanchez.house.gov.

State Offices: Cerritos, 562-860-5050.

Committees: *Judiciary* (22nd of 24 D): Immigration, Citizenship, Border Security & International Law. *Ways & Means* (24th of 26 D): Social Security; Trade.

Group Ratings

	ADA	ACLU	AFS	LCV	ITIC	NTU	COC	ACU	CFG	FRC
2008	100	100	100	100	71	15	50	8	12	5
2007	100	—	100	95	—	3	55	0	1	—

National Journal Ratings

	2007 LIB	—	2007 CONS		2008 LIB	—	2008 CONS
Economic	82%	—	0%		85%	—	0%
Social	92%	—	0%		82%	—	0%
Foreign	96%	—	0%		92%	—	0%
Composite	95%	—	5%		93%	—	7%

Key Votes of the 110th Congress

1. Increase minimum wage	Y	5. Share immigration data	N	9. Withdraw troops 8/08	Y
2. Expand SCHIP	Y	6. Foreign aid abortion ban	N	10. No operations in Iran	Y
3. Raise CAFE standards	Y	7. Ban gay bias in workplace	Y	11. Free trade with Peru	N
4. Bail out financial markets	N	8. Repeal D.C. gun law	N	12. Overhaul FISA	N

Election Results

2008 general	Linda Sánchez (D)	125,289	(70%)	($439,587)
	Diane Lenning (R)	54,533	(30%)	($18,479)
2008 primary	Linda Sánchez (D)	unopposed		

Prior Winning Percentages: 2006 (66%); 2004 (61%); 2002 (55%)

Population		Race/Ethnicity		Work	
Pop. 2007:	674,856	White:	17.3%	Private:	81.2%
Change since 2000:	Up 5.6%	Black:	5.5%	Government:	12.7%
Urban:	100.0%	Hispanic:	65.2%	Self-employed:	6.1%
Rural:	0.0%	Asian:	9.8%	Blue collar:	31.2%
Area size:	65 sq. mi.	Native Am.:	0.3%	White collar:	53.0%
		Hawaiian:	0.5%	Khaki collar:	0.1%
Age		Two+ races:	1.1%	Other:	15.8%
Median age:	30.9 yrs.			Median income:	$53,663
More than 65 yrs:	8.8%	*Ancestry*		Median home value:	$492,500
Less than 18 yrs:	30.5%	German:	3.6%	Poverty:	13.4%
		Irish:	2.7%		
Education		English:	2.6%	**Military Veterans**	
H.S. grad:	67.2%			% of Pop:	5.5%
College grad:	16.3%				
Grad degree:	4.6%				

In the years just after World War II, much of southeast Los Angeles County was farmland—citrus groves and dairy farms. The Zamboni ice-resurfacing machine for skating rinks was invented, not in some frozen Northern clime, but by local businessmen Frank and Lawrence Zamboni, who, in 1949, found an innovative new use for the refrigeration technology they were using to service the local dairy industry. In the next two decades, housing subdivisions were built and new cities incorporated so that

2008 Presidential Vote
Obama (D) 128,579 (66%)
McCain (R)............................63,680 (32%)

2004 Presidential Vote
Kerry (D)................................102,660 (59%)
Bush (R) 70,635 (40%)

Cook Partisan Voting Index: D + 12

what had been a few towns separated by farmland became one continuous swath of suburbia. The towns were different in character. Whittier, founded by Midwestern Quakers, was the hometown of Richard Nixon, a young lawyer thinking about running for Congress in early 1946 who later became president. South Gate and Lynwood, with new auto plants and other factories, filled up with newcomers from the south. Lakewood, just north of Long Beach, used to be an area of lima bean fields. Developers built it up so rapidly in the 1950s that *Life* magazine featured it as one of the first mass-produced suburbs. Other towns were late-bloomers. There were still dairy farms in Cerritos in the 1970s, though few remain now.

The 39th Congressional District of California is made up of a heterogeneous and oddly fashioned collection of these suburbs. It is shaped like a U. Two-thirds of Whittier, all of South and West Whittier, and La Mirada are on the east. The bottom part of the U includes Lakewood, and in former dairy country, Cerritos, Artesia, and Hawaiian Gardens. The west end includes South Gate, Lynwood, Paramount, and the eastern fringe of South Central Los Angeles. These were once working-class white communities, then mostly black, then heavily Latino. The district's population is 65% Hispanic and 10% Asian. More evidence of the 39th's diversity can be found at a local motor vehicles office, where the written exam can be taken in 33 languages. As this area grew in the postwar years, it was pretty closely divided between the parties. But in the 1990s, it trended Democratic. This district in its present form was created in 2001 to be a safe seat for California Democrats. On the presidential level, it voted 59%-40% for Democrat John Kerry in 2004 and 66%-32% for Democrat Barack Obama in 2008.

The congresswoman from the 39th District is Linda Sánchez, a Democrat first elected in 2002 and the junior member of the first pair of sisters ever elected to Congress. Her sister is Loretta Sanchez, who is nine years older and was elected to the House from Orange County in 1996. They are two of the seven children of Mexican immigrant parents Ignacio Sánchez, a machinist, and Maria Macias, a bilingual education aide in an elementary school. Their parents met while trying to organize a union at a tire shop where they worked when they were young. Their mother once took little Linda to a rally to hear famed migrant farmworker organizer César Chávez speak. Linda Sánchez earned her undergraduate and law degrees at the University of California (Los Angeles), working her way through school with jobs as a security guard, nanny, and teacher's aide. She became a civil-rights lawyer and was executive secretary-treasurer of the Orange County Federation of Labor. "She's definitely the more liberal one," Loretta has said. Two of their five siblings are business owners, one is a mortgage broker, another is a securities broker, and the other a civil engineer.

When the district lines were unveiled for this new seat, Linda Sánchez was one of six Democrats who ran for it. Her most important asset was her sister's support. She tapped Loretta's extensive fundraising network, walked precincts with her, and appeared in a television commercial with her. In a Spanish ad, their mother urged voters to send both of her daughters to Capitol Hill. All of this work gave Linda Sánchez an advantage over her two chief opponents, who were better known when the race began: two-term Assemblywoman Sally Havice and South Gate Councilman Hector De La Torre, who had worked several years in Washington as a legislative aide and Labor Department official. The three candidates differed very little on the issues.

Sánchez's ties to labor helped her build a strong voter-turnout operation, and with help from her sister, she won the endorsement of then-House Minority Whip Nancy Pelosi of California. Her opponents noted that no Latino members of Congress endorsed Sánchez, and they charged that she was a political opportunist who changed her name and residence to run in the newly created district. Like her sister, Sánchez had used her non-Latino married name until she started to run for the House. But she won the primary with 33% of the vote; De La Torre received 29% and Havice 19%. This district is not as Democratic as the four other L.A.-based Hispanic-majority districts, and the negative primary campaign may have hurt Sánchez in the general election. Republican Tim Escobar, a financial adviser and former Army helicopter pilot, called her an inexperienced liberal extremist. But Sánchez won 55%-41%, and she has been re-elected easily since then.

Sánchez has a strongly liberal voting record. The first law she sponsored as a member of Congress would have provided federal funds to help stop bullying in schools. She was able to get the proposal into the Justice Department authorization bill, but it died in the Senate. Later, in 2008, Sánchez took the lead in defining "cyberbullying" as electronic communications intended to "coerce, intimidate, harass, or cause substantial emotional distress." She sponsored a bill making it a crime. Her other legislative priorities have included an increase in small-business loan limits from $35,000 to $50,000. She attacked the House Republican proposal to deny driver's licenses to undocumented immigrants for "using national security as a facade to alienate law-abiding and taxpaying immigrants."

With Democrats in the majority in 2007, Sánchez gained more influence as the chairwoman of the Judiciary Committee's Commercial and Administrative Law Subcommittee, where she worked with senior Democrats on hearings to oversee the Bush administration's allegedly politically motivated firings of U.S. attorneys around the country. When senior White House political adviser Karl Rove refused to cooperate, Sánchez initiated a move to find him in contempt of Congress. When Rove capitulated in March 2009, the House dropped its lawsuit against him. In January 2009, Sánchez won a plum assignment to the House Ways and Means Committee. As co-founder of the House Trade Working Group, she pledged tougher review of proposed international trade deals. Liberal Democrats have long maintained that trade deals should be contingent on foreign countries' complying with U.S.-style labor, health, and environmental laws. She also sponsored a bill to permit consumer lawsuits against overseas manufacturers of defective products.

In the 2008 presidential contest, the Sánchez women split. Linda endorsed Barack Obama for the Democratic nomination as "very principled," and Loretta backed Hillary Rodham Clinton and criticized her younger sister for ignoring the gender significance.

On the personal front, Sánchez has won kudos from Washington insiders for her hilarious routines at the D.C. Improv, a professional comedy club that often hosts charity fundraisers featuring members of Congress. One of her jokes is often cited: "Republicans make love like they make war. They lie to get in, and they don't know what to do when they get there." In November 2008, Sánchez announced that she was pregnant with her first child. Sánchez, who was divorced, in April 2009 married boyfriend Jim Sullivan, public-relations consultant, in a quiet ceremony on Capitol Hill. "I don't think that marriage and childbirth are black-and-white," Sánchez told the *Los Angeles Times*. "There are certain instances in which you have to do things in reverse order."

FORTIETH DISTRICT

Ed Royce (R)

Elected 1992, 9th term; b. Oct. 12, 1951, Los Angeles; home, Fullerton; CA State Fullerton, B.A. 1977; Catholic; married (Marie).

Elected Office: CA Senate, 1982–92.

Professional Career: Tax mgr., 1979–82.

DC Office: 2185 RHOB, 20515, 202-225-4111; Fax: 202-226-0335; Web site: www.royce.house.gov.

State Offices: Orange, 714-744-4130.

Committees: *Financial Services* (4th of 29 R): Capital Markets, Insurance & Government Sponsored Enterprises; Financial Institutions & Consumer Credit; International Monetary Policy & Trade. *Foreign Affairs* (7th of 19 R): Asia, the Pacific & the Global Environment; Middle East & South Asia; Terrorism, Nonproliferation & Trade (RMM).

Group Ratings

	ADA	ACLU	AFS	LCV	ITIC	NTU	COC	ACU	CFG	FRC
2008	0	9	0	0	40	88	83	100	98	100
2007	0	—	0	15	—	93	70	100	96	—

National Journal Ratings

	2007 LIB	—	2007 CONS		2008 LIB	—	2008 CONS
Economic	9%	—	90%		0%	—	98%
Social	21%	—	79%		0%	—	91%
Foreign	0%	—	72%		8%	—	89%
Composite	15%	—	85%		5%	—	95%

Key Votes of the 110th Congress

1. Increase minimum wage	N	5. Share immigration data	Y	9. Withdraw troops 8/08	N
2. Expand SCHIP	N	6. Foreign aid abortion ban	Y	10. No operations in Iran	N
3. Raise CAFE standards	N	7. Ban gay bias in workplace	N	11. Free trade with Peru	Y
4. Bail out financial markets	N	8. Repeal D.C. gun law	Y	12. Overhaul FISA	Y

Election Results

2008 general	Ed Royce (R)	144,923	(63%)	($1,172,942)
	Christina Avalos (D)	86,772	(37%)	
2008 primary	Ed Royce (R)	unopposed		

Prior Winning Percentages: 2006 (67%); 2004 (68%); 2002 (68%); 2000 (63%); 1998 (63%); 1996 (63%); 1994 (66%); 1992 (57%)

Population		Race/Ethnicity		Work	
Pop. 2007:	668,766	White:	42.7%	Private:	80.2%
Change since 2000:	Up 4.6%	Black:	2.4%	Government:	11.7%
Urban:	100.0%	Hispanic:	33.7%	Self-employed:	7.7%
Rural:	0.0%	Asian:	18.5%	Blue collar:	21.3%
Area size:	102 sq. mi.	Native Am.:	0.5%	White collar:	63.6%
		Hawaiian:	0.3%	Khaki collar:	0.1%
Age		Two+ races:	1.5%	Other:	15.1%
Median age:	35.2 yrs.			Median income:	$66,233
More than 65 yrs:	11.4%	*Ancestry*		Median home value:	$614,400
Less than 18 yrs:	26.0%	German:	9.3%	Poverty:	9.1%
		Irish:	6.9%		
Education		English:	6.4%	**Military Veterans**	
H.S. grad:	82.4%			% of Pop:	7.6%
College grad:	29.5%				
Grad degree:	9.1%				

Orange County is the fifth-most-populous county in the United States, having grown steadily from 130,000 people in 1940, to nearly 2 million in 1980, to 3 million in 2007. It is now a community with the patina of maturity, and in some places an aging community, fraying around the edges. The county can no longer double its population, as it did for several decades when Disneyland sprung up on empty land and when orange groves and bean fields were transformed into subdivisions, shopping centers

2008 Presidential Vote

McCain (R)	125,066	(51%)
Obama (D)	114,025	(47%)

2004 Presidential Vote

Bush (R)	138,766	(60%)
Kerry (D)	88,631	(39%)

Cook Partisan Voting Index: R+8

and office towers. Although developers have plans for a few more huge projects in the next decade, "We're outta land," a real estate analyst told the *Los Angeles Times* in 2003. "We don't have any dirt left." Ranchers and farmers have given way to aerospace engineers. Until relatively recently, the communities of Orange County were mostly white and middle-class. The area has been transformed by its openness to economic and ethnic change. Its economy has been constantly reshaped by the inevitable upheavals of capitalism, and that pattern continues. Tourism remains key, but there is no single industry that is responsible for Orange County's prosperity. The region was hit hard by the defense spending cutbacks and recession of the early 1990s but it bounced back, fueled by start-ups and small entrepreneurial successes not anticipated by government or corporate planners. Orange County was again rocked by recession in 2008, when the hyperinflation of the local housing market abruptly burst and home values slid as much as 20% from 2007 levels.

Always Republican, Orange County became a symbol of conservatism, first in California and then nationally. This was a solid base for Ronald Reagan in his campaigns for governor and president. In 1988, the district's 317,000-vote plurality for George H.W. Bush was his largest in any county in the nation. Orange County's conservatism reflected a belief in technological progress and traditional values as unyielding as the mile-square grid that the county's founders imposed on most of its land, and a belief in market economies that produced wonders such as the area's advanced military technologies. Over the years, Orange County has become racially and ethnically more diverse. Contrary to the images presented in the television series *The OC,* the all-white Orange County stereotype is now thoroughly out of date, exemplified by the election in 2007 of the county's first Vietnamese-American supervisor. In 2004, Orange County gave George W. Bush a 222,000-vote margin, well below his father's margin 16 years before. The GOP advantage dwindled significantly in 2008, when John McCain prevailed over Barack Obama by only 29,500 votes.

The 40th Congressional District of California is located entirely in Orange County. At the geographic center is Fullerton, with 36,000 students at its own branch of California State University. The campus's business school is the largest in the state. To the southwest are Buena Park, home of Knott's Berry Farm, the earliest theme park (1940), plus Cypress, Los Alamitos, La Palma, Stanton, and parts of Garden Grove and Westminster. Southeast of Fullerton, the district includes most of Placentia, part of eastern Anaheim, and all of Villa Park and Orange, the district's largest city. Overall, the 40th District is 34% Hispanic, 19% Asian (primarily Korean, Vietnamese and Filipino) and 2% African-American.

The congressman from the 40th District is Ed Royce, a Republican first elected in 1992. His lifetime almost precisely spans the area's growth. He grew up in Fullerton and belonged to the conservative Young Americans for Freedom at Cal State Fullerton. He was later the head of Youth for Reagan in California during Reagan's 1976 challenge to Gerald Ford. Royce worked several years as a tax and capital projects manager for a cement company. In 1982, a bunch of conservative state legislators known as the "Cave Men" took him to a Black Angus restaurant—no avocado-and-sprout sandwiches for them—and persuaded him to run for the state Senate. He won at age 31. When the Legislature refused to pass Royce's bill allowing crime victims to object to trial delays, giving grand juries more power, and ending "jury-shopping," he got the measure on the ballot as an initiative and it passed by a wide margin. He also wrote the first law making it a felony to stalk someone, allowing police more latitude to take action. In 1992, Royce ran for the U.S. House. With the blessing of Orange County Republican leaders, he was unopposed in the primary and easily won the general. He has been re-elected by wide margins ever since.

In the House, Royce has a conservative voting record. He co-chaired the group of House "porkbusters," risking other members' wrath by opposing appropriations bills with dubious earmarks for individual lawmaker's districts. In July 2005, he was among eight Republicans, and the only Californian, to vote against a highway bill packed with road, bridge, and dam projects. Royce's proposal to ensure that nonprofit religious organizations have access to all necessary financial resources was a forerunner of President George W. Bush's faith-based initiative. On the Financial Services Committee, he has worked with Rep. Paul Kanjorski, D-Pa., to expand lending authority for credit unions and to put them on an equivalent status with banks. With Rep. Melissa Bean, D-Ill., in 2009, Royce proposed a federal regulator for insurance companies to replace the patchwork state regulatory system.

As chairman of the International Relations Subcommittee on Africa and an ardent free-trader, Royce was instrumental in enacting an Africa free-trade bill, teaming with House Ways and Means Committee senior Democrat Charles Rangel of New York. With legislative creativity, Royce helped steer the bill to enactment. When Congress expanded the president's powers to negotiate free-trade agreements, Royce revised the bill to raise the cap on duty-free apparel imports from Africa. Although he had never set foot in Africa before he became chairman, Royce was widely praised for getting up to speed on issues affecting the continent. His other Africa-focused initiatives have included measures to encourage oil production, promote human rights, and condemn the genocide in Sudan.

In the minority, Royce is the ranking Republican on the Foreign Affairs Subcommittee on Terrorism, Nonproliferation, and Trade, where he has focused on the spread of radical Islam. President Bush signed his bill establishing Radio Free Afghanistan as a tool in the fight against terrorism. In 2006, Royce won enactment of his bill to promote nuclear nonproliferation in North Korea. He has also urged stronger strategic and trade relationships between the United States and India.

FORTY-FIRST DISTRICT

Jerry Lewis (R)

Elected 1978, 16th term; b. Oct. 21, 1934, Seattle, WA; home, Redlands; U.C.L.A., B.A. 1956; Presbyterian; married (Arlene); 7 children.

Elected Office: San Bernardino Sch. Bd., 1964–68; CA Assembly, 1968–78.

Professional Career: Insurance exec., 1959–78; Field rep., U.S. Rep. Jerry Pettis, 1968.

DC Office: 2112 RHOB, 20515, 202-225-5861; Fax: 202-225-6498; Web site: www.house.gov/jerrylewis.

State Offices: Redlands, 909-862-6030.

Committees: *Appropriations* (RMM of 23 R).

Group Ratings

	ADA	ACLU	AFS	LCV	ITIC	NTU	COC	ACU	CFG	FRC
2008	20	18	14	8	57	63	100	84	74	70
2007	10	—	9	15	—	66	80	88	80	—

National Journal Ratings

	2007 LIB	—	2007 CONS	2008 LIB	—	2008 CONS
Economic	19%	—	81%	20%	—	80%
Social	40%	—	59%	20%	—	74%
Foreign	36%	—	64%	22%	—	74%
Composite	32%	—	68%	22%	—	78%

Key Votes of the 110th Congress

1. Increase minimum wage	N	5. Share immigration data	Y	9. Withdraw troops 8/08	N
2. Expand SCHIP	N	6. Foreign aid abortion ban	Y	10. No operations in Iran	N
3. Raise CAFE standards	N	7. Ban gay bias in workplace	N	11. Free trade with Peru	Y
4. Bail out financial markets	Y	8. Repeal D.C. gun law	Y	12. Overhaul FISA	Y

Election Results

2008 general	Jerry Lewis (R)	159,486	(62%)	($1,192,618)
	Tim Prince (D)	99,214	(38%)	($123,655)
2008 primary	Jerry Lewis (R)	36,663	(82%)	
	Eric Stone (R)	4,330	(10%)	
	Pamela Zander (R)	3,455	(8%)	

Prior Winning Percentages: 2006 (67%); 2004 (83%); 2002 (67%); 2000 (80%); 1998 (65%); 1996 (65%); 1994 (71%); 1992 (63%); 1990 (61%); 1988 (70%); 1986 (77%); 1984 (85%); 1982 (68%); 1980 (72%); 1978 (61%)

Population		Race/Ethnicity		Work	
Pop. 2007:	763,801	White:	55.1%	Private:	70.4%
Change since 2000:	Up 19.5%	Black:	5.7%	Government:	21.2%
Urban:	89.4%	Hispanic:	32.0%	Self-employed:	8.3%
Rural:	10.6%	Asian:	4.1%	Blue collar:	25.9%
Area size:	13,350 sq. mi.	Native Am.:	1.0%	White collar:	53.6%
Age		Hawaiian:	0.2%	Khaki collar:	1.7%
Median age:	32.9 yrs.	Two+ races:	1.8%	Other:	18.8%
More than 65 yrs:	12.2%	*Ancestry*		Median income:	$48,979
Less than 18 yrs:	27.8%	German:	11.4%	Median home value:	$317,400
Education		Irish:	9.4%	Poverty:	15.0%
H.S. grad:	81.7%	English:	7.9%	**Military Veterans**	
College grad:	18.6%			% of Pop:	11.8%
Grad degree:	7.5%				

With the Pacific Coast well developed, young families have increasingly moved away from the high-cost, high-crime coast to the sunny, often hot, valleys inland. This impulse has resulted in rapid growth in the Central Valley, the repopulation of the Mother Lode country in the foothills of the Sierra, and the startling growth of the Inland Empire, at the eastern end of the Los Angeles Basin. This Inland Empire, generally defined as San Bernardino and Riverside counties, though other definitions abound—grew from 1.6 million people in 1980 to 3.2 million in 2000 to 4 million in 2007. "The L.A. dream still exists—it just moved east," says author and California political analyst Joel Kotkin.

2008 Presidential Vote

McCain (R)	147,982	(54%)
Obama (D)	119,255	(44%)

2004 Presidential Vote

Bush (R)	149,673	(62%)
Kerry (D)	89,424	(37%)

Cook Partisan Voting Index: R + 10

The 41st Congressional District covers some of the Inland Empire and the desert beyond the San Bernardino Mountains. It includes most of the land area of San Bernardino County, which with 20,052 square miles is the largest county in the United States and more than twice the size of New Jersey. Nearly half its population is concentrated in its southwest corner, in the Inland Empire, including the northern and eastern edges of San Bernardino and all of Loma Linda, Redlands, Highland, and Yucaipa; many of these small towns were founded by Midwesterners at the base of 10,000-foot mountains. The district also includes a number of towns in Riverside County just to the south: Calimesa, Beaumont, Banning, and San Jacinto. East of the mountains is the vast Mojave Desert, mostly uninhabited but with growing clusters of population. In the Victor Valley are Hesperia and Apple Valley, new towns in the desert with 156,000 people between them, and Victorville, another high-growth, high-desert community that was once home to cowboy actors Roy Rogers and Dale Evans. The district includes the mountain country around Lake

Arrowhead and Big Bear Lake; Desert Hot Springs, the rustic town north of posh Palm Springs; and Twentynine Palms and the huge Twentynine Palms Marine Corps Base, the largest Marine base in the world and the Marines' leading live-fire training facility. It also takes in the city of Needles, pop. 5,700, which often has the hottest temperature in the nation. The district has a fast-growing Hispanic population, which grew from 23% of the total in 2000 to 32% in 2007. This fast-growing area is Republican country. It voted 62%-37% for GOP President George W. Bush in 2004 and 54%-44% for Republican nominee John McCain in 2008.

The congressman from the 41st District is Jerry Lewis, a Republican first elected in 1978 and a former chairman of the Appropriations Committee. Lewis grew up in San Bernardino, worked as a lifeguard and graduated from the University of California at Los Angeles. (He maintains his swimming skills and once saved former Speaker Jim Wright off the shore of Hawaii.) He was an insurance agent in Redlands, where he joined civic groups and was elected to the school board in the early 1960s. He won a seat in the California Assembly in 1968, at age 34. A decade later, he was elected to the U.S. House after the incumbent congressman retired. In 1980, Lewis got a seat on the Appropriations Committee, where bipartisan cooperation was the norm, enabling even minority members to confer favors on their districts. With a small-city background and an accommodating attitude toward Democrats, he steadily won leadership positions: chairman of the Republican Research Committee in 1984, chairman of the Republican Policy Committee in 1986, and Republican Conference chairman in 1988. Lewis seemed destined to rise to the minority leader post. But a small group of young conservatives, followers of Rep. Newt Gingrich of Georgia, rebelled against the bipartisan cooperation that Lewis and other more senior Republicans practiced, believing that it would prevent the party from ever gaining a House majority. In March 1989, the minority whip position came open when Rep. Dick Cheney of Wyoming was appointed secretary of Defense. Lewis considered running, but aware of the growing unrest in the GOP conference, declined. Gingrich won on an 87-85 vote. In December 1992, Rep. Dick Armey of Texas, with support from Gingrich, challenged Lewis for the Conference chairmanship and won 88-84. Those two votes put in place the two top leaders of the Republican-controlled Congress in 1995, the first time in 40 years the party had had a House majority.

Lewis recovered from that setback, and when Republicans won the majority in 1994, he became chairman of the Appropriations subcommittee in charge of veterans and housing programs. That made him a member of the so-called "college of cardinals," as the appropriations subcommittee chairmen are known, for their collective power to control government spending. As part of the new majority's call for tighter federal budgets, Lewis made deep cuts in agency spending, including in popular agencies like NASA. In 1999, Lewis became chairman of the Defense Subcommittee on Appropriations, which has the largest share of the federal pie of any of the 13 subcommittees. Under his stewardship, the subcommittee voted unanimously to cut $1.8 billion from the Air Force's costly F-22 program. Funds were restored by the Senate, but the program was cut by $500 million. (Lewis continued to promote the Predator unmanned air vehicle, which was tested in the Mojave Desert in his district; the craft proved to be of prime importance in Afghanistan and Iraq.)

The crafty Lewis, with a nose for a deal, led the subcommittee through several relatively uneventful years of making defense budgets. In November 2002, after the September 11 attacks, the subcommittee acted swiftly on a $317 billion defense appropriation, which was passed by the House. Lewis's job got increasingly difficult during the Iraq War years, as the mounting bill for that protracted military campaign began to arouse opposition among Democrats and some Republicans. In 2003, the House accepted a $368 billion defense spending bill, but Iraq was to be dealt with separately in a supplemental spending bill. In 2004 Lewis warned Defense Secretary Donald Rumsfeld that "people will be targeting our budget in a serious way." But that year he managed to get through the House a $417 billion appropriation that included $25 billion for Iraq. However, Lewis insisted that only $1 billion of the money be available for "flexible" use; the Bush administration had wanted discretion over how the entire amount was spent.

As an appropriator, Lewis has been unapologetic about channeling funds into his district. One special beneficiary has been Loma Linda University, where he has promoted cancer treatment and NASA research. He played a role in converting the former George and Norton Air Force bases into successful airports. Some of his projects are sentimental. He got $1 million to rebuild the Perris Hill Plunge, a WPA-built pool where he had been a lifeguard and taught dozens of children to swim. He helped to get another $1 million for the Jerry Lewis Community Center in his hometown of Highland. But his long tenure as an appropriator also has had a downside. Lewis has been under investigation since 2006 by the U.S. Justice Department, which has looked into his work on earmarks that benefited a lobbying firm led by former Rep. Bill Lowery, R-Calif., a longtime Lewis friend who obtained abundant appropriations earmarks for the defense industry and California communities. Lewis has denied wrongdoing, but has piled up hundreds of thousands of dollars in defense lawyers' bills.

In 2004, when Bill Young of Florida reached the end of his six-year term limit as chairman of the full Appropriations Committee, Lewis was third in seniority among committee Republicans. He sought the chairmanship anyway and had to compete with the more senior Ralph Regula of Ohio, who voted less often with the Republican leadership, and the less senior Hal Rogers of Kentucky. The contest turned on who among them had contributed the most money to fellow Republicans to help the party maintain its House majority, sums that were closely monitored by Republican leaders. Regula had contributed little.

At a pivotal meeting in July 2004, Rogers came forward with a check for $300,000, at which point Lewis stepped forward with a check for $600,000. In all, Lewis contributed $1.35 million to Republicans that election season, and he secured the chairmanship.

Lewis had a rocky two years as chairman. He wanted to streamline the appropriations process and end the growing dependence on omnibus spending bills, which were taking the place of individual spending bills as the House grew more politically polarized and unable to conduct the basic business of funding the government. He failed to achieve either goal. The combination of Iraq War funding and Hurricane Katrina relief and reconstruction added more than $200 billion to the original budget in 2005. The next year, Lewis's committee finished most of its work, but breakdowns in the Republican-controlled Senate meant that most spending decisions were deferred to the Democrats after they won majority control of Congress in 2006.

Once in the minority, Lewis became the ranking Republican on the committee. In 2007, he criticized Democrats for their defense bill that "ties the hands of our commander-in-chief during a time of war, places military decisions in the hands of politicians and attempts to buy votes for its passage, on the left and on the right, by literally promising something for everyone." In 2008, he called the committee's failure to handle most of its bills in the usual manner "an historic dereliction of duty." Democrats blamed the inaction in part on Lewis for pushing votes on controversial proposals, like one to increase drilling off U.S. coasts. Still, like a savvy appropriator, Lewis continued to bring bounty to his district, securing more than $137 million in earmarks in 2007 alone, the fifth highest amount for House members.

Lewis remains popular in his district. In the 1990s, he took note of the rising Hispanic population in his district and took Spanish lessons. House Democrats thought Lewis might be vulnerable in 2008 because of the federal probe of his ties to lobbyists. But they miscalculated. Lewis was re-elected easily, 62%-38%, against Democrat Tim Prince, who had run unsuccessfully in 1997 for mayor of San Bernardino. Rumors of retirement continued to swirl around Lewis, not least because term limits will force him to give up his Appropriations post after 2010.

FORTY-SECOND DISTRICT

Gary Miller (R)

Elected 1998, 6th term; b. Oct. 16, 1948, Huntsville, AR; home, Diamond Bar; Mt. San Antonio Col. 1971, 1988–89; Christian; married (Cathy); 4 children.

Military Career: Army, 1967.

Elected Office: Diamond Bar City Cncl., 1989–95; Diamond Bar Mayor, 1992; CA Assembly, 1995–98.

Professional Career: Businessman, real estate developer, G. Miller Development Co., 1971–98.

DC Office: 2349 RHOB, 20515, 202-225-3201; Fax: 202-226-6962; Web site: www.house.gov/garymiller.

State Offices: Brea, 714-257-1142; Mission Viejo, 949-470-8484.

Committees: *Financial Services* (10th of 29 R): Housing & Community Opportunity; International Monetary Policy & Trade (RMM). *Transportation & Infrastructure* (8th of 30 R): Highways & Transit; Railroads, Pipelines & Hazardous Materials; Water Resources & Environment.

Group Ratings

	ADA	ACLU	AFS	LCV	ITIC	NTU	COC	ACU	CFG	FRC
2008	5	18	17	0	67	65	100	81	70	88
2007	0	—	0	5	—	79	89	100	89	—

National Journal Ratings

	2007 LIB	—	2007 CONS	2008 LIB	—	2008 CONS
Economic	18%	—	82%	25%	—	75%
Social	0%	—	91%	18%	—	81%
Foreign	0%	—	72%	0%	—	95%
Composite	12%	—	88%	15%	—	85%

Key Votes of the 110th Congress

1. Increase minimum wage	*	5. Share immigration data	Y	9. Withdraw troops 8/08	N
2. Expand SCHIP	N	6. Foreign aid abortion ban	Y	10. No operations in Iran	N
3. Raise CAFE standards	*	7. Ban gay bias in workplace	N	11. Free trade with Peru	Y
4. Bail out financial markets	Y	8. Repeal D.C. gun law	Y	12. Overhaul FISA	Y

Election Results

2008 general	Gary Miller (R)	158,404	(60%)	($325,244)
	Edwin Chau (D)	104,909	(40%)	($347,351)
2008 primary	Gary Miller (R)	unopposed		

Prior Winning Percentages: 2006 (100%); 2004 (68%); 2002 (68%); 2000 (59%); 1998 (53%)

Population		Race/Ethnicity		Work	
Pop. 2007:	680,959	White:	49.3%	Private:	78.5%
Change since 2000:	Up 6.6%	Black:	2.5%	Government:	13.4%
Urban:	98.7%	Hispanic:	27.4%	Self-employed:	7.8%
Rural:	1.3%	Asian:	18.6%	Blue collar:	14.2%
Area size:	317 sq. mi.	Native Am.:	0.2%	White collar:	73.9%
		Hawaiian:	0.1%	Khaki collar:	0.1%
Age		Two+ races:	1.6%	Other:	11.8%
Median age:	36.6 yrs.	*Ancestry*		Median income:	$87,051
More than 65 yrs:	9.5%	German:	10.6%	Median home value:	$642,900
Less than 18 yrs:	26.1%	Irish:	8.0%	Poverty:	4.5%
Education		English:	6.9%	**Military Veterans**	
H.S. grad:	89.6%			% of Pop:	7.2%
College grad:	37.9%				
Grad degree:	12.8%				

The fastest growth in the Los Angeles metropolitan area over the past 25 years has been in the Inland Empire, at the eastern end of the Los Angeles Basin. Mostly orange groves and dairy farms a few decades ago, this territory is now the site of a booming economy, personal upward mobility, and ethnic and cultural diversity. The main ingredient of the economic growth has been small entrepreneurial businesses, usually started by people with no particular connections or advantages and often of Asian or Latino immigrant background. California has never been a land of leisure, as stereotype would have it, but rather a place for hard work, where the fertility of the soil and the productivity of the people have led to prosperity and, more recently, relative tolerance toward newcomers. (Anti-Asian sentiment expressed itself in the Chinese Exclusion Act of 1882 and the Japanese-American internment camps of 1942–44. Despite occasional tensions since World War II, this has been one of the more welcoming destinations for immigrants.)

2008 Presidential Vote

McCain (R)	152,256	(53%)
Obama (D)	128,474	(45%)

2004 Presidential Vote

Bush (R)	164,998	(62%)
Kerry (D)	98,108	(37%)

Cook Partisan Voting Index: R + 10

The 42nd Congressional District of California is centered in the Inland Empire where Los Angeles, San Bernardino and Orange counties come together. In San Bernardino County, it includes Chino, site of a large low-security prison and large meat-packing plants, whose smell can carry across the valley on a windy day, and Chino Hills, incorporated in 1991 and full of subdivisions for commuters who battle the heavy traffic on Interstate 5 to Orange and L.A. counties. In Los Angeles County, it includes Diamond Bar, La Habra Heights and the eastern part of Whittier. Nearly two-thirds of the district's population is in Orange County. The county includes Yorba Linda, the birthplace of Richard Nixon and the site of his presidential library. Only 40,000 people lived there in 1913, when Nixon was born; 3 million live there today. Other Orange County towns in the 42nd are Brea and La Habra; the eastern part of Anaheim; and the newer condominium communities of Mission Viejo and Rancho Santa Margarita. The area lost more than 100 homes during wildfires in November 2008.

Ethnically diverse, the district is 27% Hispanic and 19% Asian, and relatively stable socially: It has the highest percentage of married people in the state. It leans Republican. In 2004, George W. Bush won the district with 62% here, and in 2008 John McCain won by 53%-45%.

The congressman from the 42nd District is Gary Miller, a Republican first elected in 1998. He was born in Arkansas, but grew up in Whittier. In his early 20s, he became a home builder and later developed planned communities. He is among the wealthiest members of the House. He began his public service in 1988, when he was appointed to the Diamond Bar Municipal Advisory Council. A year later, after Diamond Bar was incorporated, Miller was elected to the City Council and served as mayor. In 1995, he was elected to the California Assembly in a special election. After chairing the Assembly's Budget Committee, he decided in 1997 to run for the U.S. House against scandal-tarred incumbent Republican Jay Kim. Kim and his wife had pleaded guilty to accepting and concealing $230,000 in illegal campaign contributions. In March 1998, Kim was sentenced to house arrest, confined to the House and his apartment in suburban Virginia, and required to wear an electronic bracelet around his ankle for two months. As a result, he could not campaign back home. Miller emphasized standard Republican themes—lower taxes, tougher penalties for crime, improved local education—and financed his campaign largely with his own money.

Miller won the all-party primary with 48% to 26% for Kim. Democrats did not pose a serious challenge in November.

Since then, Miller has come under scrutiny for questionable ethics himself. Several of his land deals have been investigated by the media and by the Justice Department. One involved Miller's sale of 165 acres to the city of Monrovia, Calif. According to several published reports, he made $10 million on the deal, then avoided paying capital-gains taxes by claiming the land had been threatened by an eminent-domain action by Monrovia. In another case, he got a $1.28 million earmark in an appropriations bill to improve streets in front of development property he co-owned in the town of Diamond Bar. Miller has maintained that he did nothing wrong and that he was the victim of a smear campaign by Democrats.

Miller, who has a conservative voting record in the House, has advanced some original proposals. He sponsored anti-spam legislation in the California Assembly long before spam became a notorious problem. In Congress, he sponsored a bill giving Internet service providers a cause of action against spammers, with $500 per message in penalties. A Civil War buff, Miller sponsored a bill to preserve Civil War battlefields after discovering that nearly 20% of the major battle sites have been lost. He won approval of matching grants for local governments and nonprofit organizations to preserve battle sites .

On the Financial Services Committee, he used his familiarity with development to focus on affordable-housing programs. He also won House passage of amendments for additional funding of brownfield redevelopment. He was active on legislation to address the mortgage crisis and sought to increase the maximum mortgage-loan limits for Fannie Mae and Freddie Mac in high-cost areas such as California. In 2008, he joined a bipartisan effort to revive a program that allowed sellers of properties to provide down-payment assistance to borrowers participating in the federal mortgage-insurance program

Democrats talked about trying to unseat Miller in 2008 in light of his ethics troubles. But they failed to put up much of a fight. Miller won easily, 60%-40%, over Montebello lawyer and school-board member Ed Chau in a low-budget contest. He suffered two personal tragedies in 2007. His 33-year-old daughter died for reasons that were not made public, and the children of one of his sons were abducted by their mother after a bitter custody dispute.

FORTY-THIRD DISTRICT

Joe Baca (D)

Elected Nov. 1999, 5th full term; b. Jan. 23, 1947, Belen, NM; home, Rialto; CA State L.A., B.A., 1971; Catholic; married (Barbara); 4 children.

Military Career: Army, 1966–68.

Elected Office: CA Assembly, 1992–98; CA Senate, 1998–99.

Professional Career: Community affairs rep., General Telephone and Electric, 1974–89; Co-owner, Interstate World Travel, 1989–present.

DC Office: 2245 RHOB, 20515, 202-225-6161; Fax: 202-225-8671; Web site: www.house.gov/baca.

State Offices: San Bernardino, 909-885-2222.

Committees: *Agriculture* (5th of 28 D): Department Operations, Oversight, Nutrition & Forestry (Chmn); Livestock, Dairy & Poultry. *Financial Services* (16th of 42 D): Capital Markets, Insurance & Government Sponsored Enterprises; Financial Institutions & Consumer Credit. *Natural Resources* (23rd of 29 D): Water & Power.

Group Ratings

	ADA	ACLU	AFS	LCV	ITIC	NTU	COC	ACU	CFG	FRC
2008	90	91	100	85	57	11	67	8	1	11
2007	100	—	100	85	—	4	55	0	6	—

National Journal Ratings

	2007 LIB — 2007 CONS		2008 LIB — 2008 CONS	
Economic	82%	— 0%	75%	— 25%
Social	73%	— 27%	58%	— 42%
Foreign	65%	— 33%	59%	— 37%
Composite	77%	— 23%	65%	— 35%

Key Votes of the 110th Congress

1. Increase minimum wage	Y	5. Share immigration data	N	9. Withdraw troops 8/08	Y
2. Expand SCHIP	Y	6. Foreign aid abortion ban	N	10. No operations in Iran	Y
3. Raise CAFE standards	Y	7. Ban gay bias in workplace	Y	11. Free trade with Peru	N
4. Bail out financial markets	Y	8. Repeal D.C. gun law	Y	12. Overhaul FISA	Y

Election Results

2008 general	Joe Baca (D)	108,259	(69%)	($885,963)
	John Roberts (R)	48,312	(31%)	($64,941)
2008 primary	Joe Baca (D)	13,177	(66%)	
	Joanne Gilbert (D)	6,701	(34%)	

Prior Winning Percentages: 2006 (64%); 2004 (66%); 2002 (66%); 2000 (60%); 1999 (51%)

Population		Race/Ethnicity		Work	
Pop. 2007:	722,827	White:	17.0%	Private:	81.7%
Change since 2000:	Up 13.1%	Black:	11.1%	Government:	11.7%
Urban:	99.3%	Hispanic:	66.0%	Self-employed:	6.5%
Rural:	0.7%	Asian:	3.6%	Blue collar:	38.0%
Area size:	193 sq. mi.	Native Am.:	0.2%	White collar:	44.8%
Age		Hawaiian:	0.3%	Khaki collar:	0.0%
Median age:	27.9 yrs.	Two+ races:	1.1%	Other:	17.1%
More than 65 yrs:	6.0%	*Ancestry*		Median income:	$48,555
Less than 18 yrs:	33.0%	German:	4.4%	Median home value:	$358,400
Education		Irish:	3.1%	Poverty:	15.6%
H.S. grad:	65.2%	USA:	2.5%	**Military Veterans**	
College grad:	10.8%			% of Pop:	6.2%
Grad degree:	2.9%				

The gateway to the Los Angeles Basin for decades was San Bernardino. Passengers on the Santa Fe Railroad and motorists on U.S. 66 traveled from the hot and dusty desert, through the twisting, windy Cajon Pass, and wound up in the green, tree-lined Los Angeles Basin. This was an agricultural zone until World War II, when Henry J. Kaiser built the West Coast's first major steel mill between the Santa Fe and Southern Pacific rail lines in Fontana, just west of San Bernardino. Today, these lands

2008 Presidential Vote		
Obama (D)	112,020	(68%)
McCain (R)	49,594	(30%)
2004 Presidential Vote		
Kerry (D)	79,946	(58%)
Bush (R)	55,952	(41%)
Cook Partisan Voting Index:	D + 13	

have largely filled up. The Inland Empire, as it is called, may be where the smog piles up against the mountains, but it also has some of the lowest real estate prices in the Los Angeles Basin and an energetic small-business economy. Business growth has been spurred by huge distribution and warehouse centers that service overseas cargo from the Long Beach port. Within 26 miles of San Bernardino, there are more than 15 Wal-Marts. The area's farmlands and dairy pastures have been reduced substantially, the land sold to developers. From 1990 to 2005, jobs in the county grew from 408,000 to 643,000. But the recession hit hard and early in the Inland Empire, with home foreclosures among the highest in the nation in 2007 and new-home sales in the area down by nearly 60% in 2008.

The 43rd Congressional District of California includes most of San Bernardino and Colton and the towns running west—Rialto, Ontario, and Fontana, where many new businesses have supplanted the steel mill that was closed in 1994 and reassembled in China. San Bernardino's economy turned downward after the closure of Norton Air Force Base and the Santa Fe rail repair yard. But the base has been redeveloped as San Bernardino's airport, the city has built a new baseball stadium, and Northrop Grumman has opened a Missile Engineering Center. Politically this area—and San Bernardino County in general—trended Republican in the 1980s. But as the Latino population grew—the district was 66% Hispanic in 2007—it trended Democratic. Barack Obama's 68% in the 43rd District was his second-best Southern California district outside Los Angeles.

The congressman from the 43rd District is Joe Baca, a Democrat first elected in 1999. He was born in Belen, N.M., the youngest of 15 children. His family moved to Barstow, Calif., in the desert, when he was four years old. His father worked as a laborer for the Santa Fe Railroad. At age 10, Baca went to work, first shining shoes and then selling newspapers and working as a janitor. He served in the Army as a paratrooper during the Vietnam War, but did not see combat. After graduating from California State University at Los Angeles, Baca moved to the San Bernardino area, where he spent 15 years as a community-affairs representative for General Telephone and Electric. He was elected four times to the San Bernardino Community College board. After two unsuccessful campaigns, the persistent Baca was elected to the state Assembly in 1992. He rose to become speaker pro tempore of the Assembly, the first Latino to hold the position. He earned a reputation as a hard worker, introducing many bills, including legislation to to reduce welfare rolls, lower taxes on middle-income earners and increase penalties for drug dealers.

Facing term limits in 1998, he considering running in the primary against incumbent U.S. Rep. George Brown, a Democrat. Instead he ran for the state Senate, spending $2 million to win the seat and raise his profile. His opportunity to run for Congress came in July 1999, when Brown died in his 18th term. His widow, Marta Macias Brown, ran for the seat. Widows of members had won in 35 of the previous 36 such races, but Minority Leader Richard Gephardt refused her request to clear the field, and Baca ran. He won the endorsement of organized labor and had a base among Latino voters. Brown attacked him for receiving the endorsement of the National Rifle Association. Baca won the all-party primary with 32% of the vote to Brown's 30%. He then focused on Republican nominee Elia Pirozzi, a real estate developer. Brown did not endorse Baca, who emphasized his centrist voting record and his support for targeted tax cuts, a minimum-wage increase and abortion rights. In a light turnout, Baca won 51%-45%.

In the House, Baca has one of the more conservative voting records of California Democrats. As a junior member, he was in a hurry to move up, and he lobbied for a seat on the Rules Committee. He then complained that he had been "bypassed" after Gephardt filled two openings with other lawmakers.

He finally achieved a high-profile role in the 110th Congress (2007–08), when he was chosen as chairman of the Congressional Hispanic Caucus. But his tenure was marked by internal discord. In 2007, several women members complained about his handling of the caucus and about allegedly sexist remarks; all but one woman abstained from the vote naming him chairman. A year earlier, when Baca was running the group's political action committee, some members protested when funds were used to support bids for office by two of his sons. As chairman, he urged action on immigration reform, but he failed to accomplish much.

In 2007, he became chairman on the Agriculture Subcommittee on Department Operations, Oversight, Nutrition and Forestry and was the most senior Californian working on the farm bill that year. Dairy production is the chief agricultural business in his district. He focused on greater opportunities for socially disadvantaged farmers and won support for a new program to give minority farmers better access to Agriculture Department services. With a seat as well on the Financial Services Committee, Baca sought relief for people facing home foreclosures. He voted for the second version of the bill bailing out the financial markets in 2008 after securing a commitment for subsequent mortgage-relief legislation.

With redistricting changes, the district became significantly more Democratic and less competitive. In 2006, Baca's two sons lost bids for the state Legislature. But in 2009, son Joe Baca Jr. became the mayor of Rialto. In 2008, Baca Sr.'s competition for re-election was Fontana City Councilman John Roberts; Baca won by his best-ever ratio, 69%-31%.

FORTY-FOURTH DISTRICT

Ken Calvert (R)

Elected 1992, 9th term; b. June 8, 1953, Corona; home, Corona; Chaffey Col., 1972–73; San Diego St. U., B.A. 1975; Protestant; divorced.

Professional Career: Restaurant owner, 1975–80; Real estate broker, 1980–92; Chmn., Riverside Cnty. Repub. Party, 1984–88.

DC Office: 2201 RHOB, 20515, 202-225-1986; Fax: 202-225-2004; Web site: calvert.house.gov.

State Offices: Las Flores, 949-888-8498; Riverside, 951-784-4300.

Committees: *Appropriations* (20th of 23 R): Energy & Water Development; Homeland Security; Interior, Environment & Related Agencies.

Group Ratings

	ADA	ACLU	AFS	LCV	ITIC	NTU	COC	ACU	CFG	FRC
2008	15	18	14	8	71	66	100	83	75	88
2007	15	—	0	0	—	68	89	88	75	—

National Journal Ratings

	2007 LIB	—	2007 CONS		2008 LIB	—	2008 CONS
Economic	21%	—	79%		22%	—	78%
Social	25%	—	74%		20%	—	74%
Foreign	0%	—	72%		5%	—	93%
Composite	20%	—	80%		17%	—	83%

Key Votes of the 110th Congress

1. Increase minimum wage	N	5. Share immigration data	Y	9. Withdraw troops 8/08	N
2. Expand SCHIP	N	6. Foreign aid abortion ban	Y	10. No operations in Iran	N
3. Raise CAFE standards	N	7. Ban gay bias in workplace	N	11. Free trade with Peru	Y
4. Bail out financial markets	Y	8. Repeal D.C. gun law	Y	12. Overhaul FISA	Y

Election Results

2008 general	Ken Calvert (R)..129,937	(51%)	($1,150,432)
	Bill Hedrick (D)..123,890	(49%)	($191,461)
2008 primary	Ken Calvert (R).. unopposed		

Prior Winning Percentages: 2006 (60%); 2004 (62%); 2002 (64%); 2000 (74%); 1998 (56%); 1996 (55%); 1994 (55%); 1992 (47%)

Population		Race/Ethnicity		Work	
Pop. 2007:	806,427	White:	43.7%	Private:	77.6%
Change since 2000:	Up 26.2%	Black:	5.2%	Government:	14.0%
Urban:	97.7%	Hispanic:	41.9%	Self-employed:	8.1%
Rural:	2.3%	Asian:	6.2%	Blue collar:	25.2%
Area size:	549 sq. mi.	Native Am.:	0.4%	White collar:	58.9%
		Hawaiian:	0.2%	Khaki collar:	0.1%
Age		Two+ races:	1.9%	Other:	15.8%
Median age:	30.8 yrs.	*Ancestry*		Median income:	$67,237
More than 65 yrs:	7.9%	German:	9.5%	Median home value:	$497,100
Less than 18 yrs:	28.3%	Irish:	7.3%	Poverty:	10.1%
Education		English:	6.4%		
H.S. grad:	80.2%			**Military Veterans**	
College grad:	24.5%			% of Pop:	7.7%
Grad degree:	8.6%				

Riverside was a sleepy town of 34,000 people, a couple hours' drive from Los Angeles, when Richard and Pat Nixon were married there in 1940 at the Mission Inn, originally built in 1876 and adorned with bell towers, fountains, rotunda, and stained-glass windows. Riverside was not much larger, with 46,000 people, when Ronald and Nancy Reagan spent their honeymoon at the Mission Inn a dozen years later, in 1952. Riverside then was a citrus center, a market town amid orange groves, where the

2008 Presidential Vote		
Obama (D) 133,535	(50%)
McCain (R)............................131,003	(49%)
2004 Presidential Vote		
Bush (R) 139,476	(59%)
Kerry (D).................................94,374	(40%)
Cook Partisan Voting Index: R+6		

local agricultural college developed, among other things, the navel orange. Today the Mission Inn is again doing business, after being closed from 1985 to 1992, but Riverside has changed completely. The city has grown to 294,000 people, and Riverside County, now has over 2 million, more than double its population in 1980. Much of that growth came in the Inland Empire around Riverside, where the flat Los Angeles Basin plains are interrupted by oddly shaped hills and ridges. This has been a boom part of California, where modest-income families found new houses in inexpensive developments and small businesses expanded mightily. After being hit hard by the recession of the early 1990s, it rebounded strongly. Near Moreno Valley, the former March Air Force Base became a business park and regional hub for shipping giant DHL. But the recent recession has halted that progress. The region's unemployment rate in November 2008 was the highest in the nation among large metropolitan areas, and it had a high level of home foreclosures during the housing-credit crisis. DHL announced in 2008 that it was closing its domestic-delivery business and leaving Riverside. On the upside, the University of California announced plans that year for a new medical school in Riverside.

The 44th Congressional District of California, which covers much of this area, has been one of the fastest-growing congressional districts in the nation in the past two decades; from 2000 to 2007, it grew another 26%. Much of the increase was in the Hispanic population, which went from 35% to 42% of the total. Some 40% of district residents live in the city of Riverside and most others in nearby towns like Corona and Norco, the self-proclaimed Horsetown USA and the home of a Naval Surface Warfare Center, which evaluates weapons systems. In 2005, the Pentagon recommended closing the base, which would have resulted in a loss of 3,300 local jobs. But the base-closure commission decided to save the base and build a new lab there. The district includes the eastern edge of Orange County all the way to the ocean, much of it uninhabited mountainsides. But it also takes in San Clemente, where President Nixon lived after he resigned the presidency, and half of San Juan Capistrano, to which the swallows famously return every March. This has been a solidly Republican district, where President George W. Bush won 59%-40% in 2004. However, Democrat Barack Obama did unexpectedly well in 2008, edging out Republican John McCain in the presidential contest, 49.5%-48.6%. Obama won the Riverside portion of the district by more than 13,000 votes, while McCain led in Orange County by nearly 11,000 votes. Local Republicans blamed the shift on the region's high unemployment and foreclosure rates.

The congressman from the 44th District is Ken Calvert, a Republican first elected in 1992. Calvert grew up in Corona. While in college, he was a congressional intern at the Senate Watergate hearings of 1973. Later, he ran the family restaurant back home and in 1980, got into the commercial real estate business. In 1982, at age 29, he ran for Congress in a district that included almost all of Riverside County and lost a nine-candidate primary to Al McCandless by 868 votes. In 1992, he ran in a new district and won the primary with 28% of the vote. His Democratic opponent was Mark Takano, an eighth grade teacher who had the support of teachers' unions and Japanese-Americans. In a district where George H.W. Bush beat Bill Clinton by 797 votes, Calvert beat Takano by 519 votes. Calvert ran into trouble at home soon after he was elected, when the Riverside *Press-Enterprise* reported that he had been stopped by police with a prostitute in his car. Calvert apologized and said that he was upset because his wife had divorced him the month before and his father had recently committed suicide. His opponents in 1994 used the incident against him. Calvert won the primary 51%-49%, with only an 884-vote margin, against business Professor Joseph Khoury. Takano, running again in the general election, ran an ad with the song "The Liar" and accused Calvert of "flagrant womanizing." But with the Republican tide that year, Calvert won 55%-38%.

In the House, Calvert has compiled a moderate-to-conservative voting record. He has usually been a Republican team player. In 2001, Calvert took over as chairman of the Water and Power Subcommittee of the Resources Committee, which distributes public works projects. He focused intensively on building support for reauthorization of the vital water-supply program (CALFED) for California's Central Valley. In the middle of the water fight, Calvert was one of several contenders seeking to chair the Resources Committee in 2003, but he lost to fellow Californian Richard Pombo, who was backed by then powerful Republican Majority Leader Tom DeLay. Calvert kept the Water and Power chairmanship, and with Pombo's help, negotiated a compromise with the Senate and among the competing users, ending up with a plan that called for new levees and recycling projects.

With the water issues largely resolved, in 2005 Calvert became chairman of the Science and Technology Committee's Space and Aeronautics Subcommittee. That year, he enacted a reauthorization of NASA programs, which included the goal of returning a man to the moon by 2020 and incentives for private entrepreneurs to develop space technologies. He aggressively sought spending earmarks for his district, claiming credit for more than $42 million in the 2009 omnibus spending bill alone. He then accused the majority Democrats of increasing spending by "epic and historic proportions."

In 2003, Calvert abandoned his 1992 pledge to serve only 12 years. But he was re-elected easily anyway. In recent years, his ethics have been called into question, which could hurt him in future elections and hurt efforts to move up the ladder in the House. In 2006, the *Los Angeles Times* reported that he and his real estate partner had bought a four-acre tract of land for $550,000, then sold it less than a year later for $985,000, after Calvert secured an $8 million spending earmark for the overhaul and expansion of a nearby freeway interchange. Calvert described the story as "scurrilous" and denied wrongdoing. "They still haven't passed a law that you can't make personal investments," he said. But a year later, when Calvert was tapped to replace the ethically tainted Rep. John Doolittle, R-Calif., on the Appropriations Committee, the story came back to haunt him. Conservative bloggers reacted angrily to his selection in the wake of other Republican ethics scandals. The popular redstate.com blog wrote, "We must scalp one member. That member's name is Ken Calvert." The liberal watchdog group Citizens for Responsibility and Ethics in Washington has Calvert on its list of the 20 "most corrupt members of Congress."

In 2008, Calvert had a close contest against Democrat Bill Hedrick, a Corona-Norco school-board member who was poorly funded and had no national party help. Hedrick seemed to benefit not just from Calvert's ethics problems, but also from Obama's success in the district. Calvert won by only a little more than 6,000 votes, 51.2% to 48.8%. He was rescued by his nearly 15,000 vote lead in the heavily Republican Orange County portion of the district. Calvert's weak showing placed him on the GOP's vulnerable list for 2010. If he survives, shifting demographics could make him a prime target for Democratic redistricters in 2012.

FORTY-FIFTH DISTRICT

Mary Bono Mack (R)

Elected April 1998, 6th full term; b. Oct. 24, 1961, Cleveland, OH; home, Palm Springs; U. of S. CA, B.F.A. 1984; Protestant; married (Connie Mack); 4 children.

Professional Career: Gen. mgr., Bono restaurant, 1986–90.

DC Office: 2300 RHOB, 20515, 202-225-5330; Fax: 202-225-2961; Web site: bonomack.house.gov.

State Offices: Hemet, 951-658-2312; Palm Springs, 760-320-1076.

Committees: *Energy & Commerce* (13th of 23 R): Commerce, Trade & Consumer Protections; Communications, Technology & the Internet; Energy & Environment.

Group Ratings

	ADA	ACLU	AFS	LCV	ITIC	NTU	COC	ACU	CFG	FRC
2008	40	27	43	31	100	44	88	74	50	35
2007	30	—	20	30	—	57	89	65	59	—

National Journal Ratings

	2007 LIB	—	2007 CONS		2008 LIB	—	2008 CONS
Economic	35%	—	65%		35%	—	65%
Social	43%	—	57%		40%	—	60%
Foreign	36%	—	63%		31%	—	69%
Composite	38%	—	62%		35%	—	65%

Key Votes of the 110th Congress

1. Increase minimum wage	Y	5. Share immigration data	Y	9. Withdraw troops 8/08	N
2. Expand SCHIP	Y	6. Foreign aid abortion ban	N	10. No operations in Iran	N
3. Raise CAFE standards	Y	7. Ban gay bias in workplace	Y	11. Free trade with Peru	Y
4. Bail out financial markets	Y	8. Repeal D.C. gun law	Y	12. Overhaul FISA	Y

Election Results

2008 general	Mary Bono Mack (R)	155,166	(58%)	($1,622,511)
	Julie Bornstein (D)	111,026	(42%)	($487,826)
2008 primary	Mary Bono Mack (R)	38,726	(89%)	
	George Pearne (R)	4,618	(11%)	

Prior Winning Percentages: 2006 (61%); 2004 (67%); 2002 (65%); 2000 (59%); 1998 (60%); 1998 (64%)

Population		Race/Ethnicity		Work	
Pop. 2007:	819,869	White:	44.6%	Private:	77.3%
Change since 2000:	Up 28.3%	Black:	6.3%	Government:	13.6%
Urban:	89.9%	Hispanic:	40.5%	Self-employed:	8.9%
Rural:	10.1%	Asian:	4.1%	Blue collar:	24.5%
Area size:	6,062 sq. mi.	Native Am.:	0.5%	White collar:	53.7%
		Hawaiian:	0.3%	Khaki collar:	0.4%
Age		Two+ races:	1.8%	Other:	21.5%
Median age:	33.5 yrs.	*Ancestry*		Median income:	$51,844
More than 65 yrs:	14.6%	German:	9.3%	Median home value:	$374,500
Less than 18 yrs:	27.4%	English:	7.0%	Poverty:	13.0%
Education		Irish:	7.0%	**Military Veterans**	
H.S. grad:	78.3%			% of Pop:	11.1%
College grad:	20.3%				
Grad degree:	6.9%				

From the air three decades ago, a night flight east from Los Angeles flew over the lights of homes of 10 million people and then into almost perfect darkness. The city then was a vast metropolis surrounded by almost uninhabited territory. Today the sprinkled pattern of white lights has spread into the Inland Empire around Riverside and San Bernardino and is multiplying outward into the desert. The Inland Empire has filled up with instant towns like family-oriented Moreno Valley, which did not

2008 Presidential Vote
Obama (D)	142,305	(52%)
McCain (R)	129,664	(47%)

2004 Presidential Vote
Bush (R)	132,288	(56%)
Kerry (D)	101,679	(43%)

Cook Partisan Voting Index: R+3

exist in 1980 but had 189,000 people in 2007. Over the 10,000-foot San Jacinto Mountains, desert communities have boomed: Palm Springs was once the lone winter resort for the stars but now is popular for its retro architecture and as a destination for gays. It is one of a string of communities along Highway 111 and Frank Sinatra and Bob Hope drives. Among rich retirees, the coast's cachet lessened as beach cities filled up with roller bladers and rent-control crusaders. The clean, dry, roomy desert, where the days are almost always crystal clear and the sky usually blue and cloudless, became more attractive and, with the prevalence of air-conditioning, a comfortable year-round home. Two presidents retired to the desert here: Dwight Eisenhower, who wintered in Palm Desert, and Gerald Ford, who resided for 30 years after his presidency in nearby Rancho Mirage. Rancho Mirage is called the "playground of presidents" not for its connection to Ford, but rather for the corporate executives who retire or keep second homes there. The population is nearly 300,000 for the entire desert corridor if the count includes Indio and Coachella, the heavily Latino and fast-growing cities in the agricultural Coachella Valley. The valley has 75% of the country's date palms and features camel races at its annual festival. *Rolling Stone* magazine called the launch of the annual music festival in Coachella one of the 50 greatest moments in rock history.

The 45th Congressional District of California covers almost all of the desert in Riverside County, from Blythe on the Nevada border to Palm Springs. Joshua Tree National Park, with its high-desert sands, is a popular tourist spot (it's shared with the 41st District, though most of it is in the 45th), and real estate values are growing in nearby towns. About half the district's population lives west of the 10,000-foot peak that looms above Palm Springs, in fast-growing Moreno Valley, socially conservative Murrieta and the old town of Hemet. This area has grown 28% since 2000. Hispanics contributed much of that growth and now make up 41% of the district's population. It has tended to vote Republican, but in 2008, Democratic presidential candidate Barack Obama won the district by an unexpectedly comfortable 52%-47%.

The congresswoman from the 45th District is Mary Bono Mack, who won the seat in an April 1998 special election after the death of her husband Sonny Bono, the onetime showbiz celebrity who became a member of the U.S. House. In 2008, she married U.S. Rep. Connie Mack, a Florida Republican, and officially changed her name from Mary Bono to Mary Bono Mack.

Bono Mack grew up as Mary Whitaker in South Pasadena, the daughter of a surgeon and a chemist. She was an accomplished gymnast and remains a fitness buff and a certified personal fitness instructor who has studied karate and Tae Kwan Do. She met Sonny Bono when she was celebrating her college graduation at his Los Angeles restaurant in 1984. They were married two years later. The couple was on a family vacation when he was killed in a skiing accident in South Lake Tahoe, Calif. At the time of his death, she had no political experience and was little known in Washington. House Republican leaders encouraged her to run for her husband's seat, believing she was the only one who could avert a divisive Republican primary. In the special election, Democrats backed actor Ralph Waite, best known as Pa Walton in *The Waltons*. Waite was hurt during the brief campaign because he kept a commitment to play Willy Loman in *Death of a Salesman* six times a week in a New Jersey theater. The campaign's biggest controversy came when Sonny's 83-year-old mother said that her son would have opposed Mary's candidacy, preferring that she care for their children. But it was no contest. Mary Bono won 64%-29%, a bigger margin than Sonny's two victories.

Bono Mack has a moderate voting record, especially on social issues, and is the least conservative of the California Republicans. She helped pass the reauthorization of the Ryan White AIDS research law in 2006, and she supported embryonic-stem-cell research and increases in the federal minimum wage. Her initial legislative priority was passage of Sonny Bono's bill to restore the Salton Sea, an artificial body of water in the desert created when a canal burst in 1905. In recent decades, it has been shrinking, increasing the salinity of the water, and it has been polluted by agricultural runoff. Although some Democrats objected to taking funds from other California projects, Bono Mack initially secured $13 million for what became the Sonny Bono Salton Sea National Wildlife Refuge. In 2007, she got another $30 million in the Water Resources Development bill for the project.

Later, she enacted a bill to establish the Santa Rosa and San Jacinto National Monument in the Palm Springs area. Bono Mack is on the Energy and Commerce Committee, and in 2007, the House passed her legislation to crack down on invasive computer "spyware," which can hijack a computer and tamper with its operations; among other things, it can record key strokes, which allows hackers to gain access to bank accounts. Bono Mack, who collects about $100,000 annually from her late husband's royalties, has opposed legislation to relax controls on digital piracy. During the immigration debate, she supported tougher enforcement at the border as well as an expanded guest-worker program. With Rep. Adam Schiff, D-Calif., she passed a bill in the House in 2007 to establish a national registry of arsonists.

Bono Mack has been easily re-elected. She thought about running for Barbara Boxer's Senate seat in 2004, but declined. In 2008, she was challenged by former Assemblywoman Julie Bornstein, a Democrat who ran an ad depicting Bono Mack as a bobblehead for Bush's policies. A Bono Mack ad alleged that when Bornstein headed an organization called Campaign for Affordable Housing, she took contributions from the federally backed mortgage giants Fannie Mae and Freddie Mac and paid herself a salary of $163,000 and travel expenses of $50,000. Bornstein spent nearly $400,000 and got some attention from national Democrats. But Bono Mack won 58%-42%.

FORTY-SIXTH DISTRICT

Dana Rohrabacher (R)

Elected 1988, 11th term; b. June 21, 1947, Coronado; home, Huntington Beach; Long Beach St. Col. B.A. 1969, U. of S. CA, M.A. 1975; Christian; married (Rhonda); 3 children.

Professional Career: Radio & print journalist, 1970–80; Sr. speechwriter, Special asst. to Pres. Reagan, 1981–88.

DC Office: 2300 RHOB, 20515, 202-225-2415; Fax: 202-225-0145; Web site: www.house.gov/rohrabacher.

State Offices: Huntington Beach, 714-960-6483.

Committees: *Foreign Affairs* (5th of 19 R): Asia, the Pacific & the Global Environment; International Organizations, Human Rights & Oversight (RMM); Middle East & South Asia. *Science & Technology* (4th of 17 R): Space & Aeronautics.

Group Ratings

	ADA	ACLU	AFS	LCV	ITIC	NTU	COC	ACU	CFG	FRC
2008	10	36	14	0	29	82	82	96	91	76
2007	5	—	0	10	—	86	75	96	88	—

National Journal Ratings

	2007 LIB	—	2007 CONS		2008 LIB	—	2008 CONS
Economic	7%	—	92%		13%	—	87%
Social	35%	—	65%		0%	—	91%
Foreign	36%	—	63%		38%	—	61%
Composite	26%	—	74%		19%	—	81%

Key Votes of the 110th Congress

1. Increase minimum wage	N	5. Share immigration data	Y	9. Withdraw troops 8/08	N
2. Expand SCHIP	N	6. Foreign aid abortion ban	Y	10. No operations in Iran	N
3. Raise CAFE standards	N	7. Ban gay bias in workplace	N	11. Free trade with Peru	Y
4. Bail out financial markets	N	8. Repeal D.C. gun law	Y	12. Overhaul FISA	Y

Election Results

2008 general	Dana Rohrabacher (R)	149,818	(53%)	($741,821)
	Debbie Cook (D)	122,891	(43%)	($481,660)
	Thomas Lash (Green)	8,257	(3%)	
	Ernst Gasteiger (Lib)	4,311	(2%)	
2008 primary	Dana Rohrabacher (R)	43,693	(87%)	
	Ronald St. John (R)	6,751	(13%)	

Prior Winning Percentages: 2006 (60%); 2004 (62%); 2002 (62%); 2000 (62%); 1998 (59%); 1996 (61%); 1994 (69%); 1992 (55%); 1990 (59%); 1988 (64%)

Population		Race/Ethnicity		Work	
Pop. 2007:	651,141	White:	58.7%	Private:	77.4%
Change since 2000:	Up 1.9%	Black:	1.7%	Government:	12.7%
Urban:	99.9%	Hispanic:	19.1%	Self-employed:	9.7%
Rural:	0.1%	Asian:	17.6%	Blue collar:	15.1%
Area size:	825 sq. mi.	Native Am.:	0.4%	White collar:	70.6%
		Hawaiian:	0.3%	Khaki collar:	0.2%
Age		Two+ races:	1.9%	Other:	14.2%
Median age:	39.4 yrs.	*Ancestry*		Median income:	$73,511
More than 65 yrs:	14.2%	German:	11.0%	Median home value:	$707,100
Less than 18 yrs:	21.5%	Irish:	8.5%	Poverty:	7.4%
Education		English:	8.4%	**Military Veterans**	
H.S. grad:	88.5%			% of Pop:	8.8%
College grad:	38.9%				
Grad degree:	14.2%				

In the 1950s, when the Beach Boys were at Hawthorne High School, surfers would drive far down the coast to the vast expanse of Huntington Beach in Orange County to catch a wave. This was empty country then, vegetable fields and orange groves mainly, with nary a freeway or shopping center in sight. Today, the 42-mile shoreline of Orange County is pretty much filled in with pricey coastal resorts and other development. Huntington Beach, a city of 193,000, is a mixture of family subdivisions

2008 Presidential Vote		
McCain (R)	150,937	(50%)
Obama (D)	145,393	(48%)
2004 Presidential Vote		
Bush (R)	168,158	(57%)
Kerry (D)	122,991	(42%)
Cook Partisan Voting Index:	R + 6	

and garden apartments and home of the International Surfing Museum. Its eight miles of beach and self-depiction as Surf City make it a tourist draw in the summer. To the north is Westminster, the center of the nation's most prominent Vietnamese-American community, with miles of shops with Vietnamese names and its own Vietnamese-language daily newspaper. Southeast along San Diego Freeway is Fountain Valley, the central focus of many Asian-owned high-technology businesses. Near the coast is Costa Mesa, site of South Coast Plaza's luxury stores and a grand performing arts center.

The 46th Congressional District of California includes all of this beachfront plus the Long Beach Harbor area and the Palos Verdes Peninsula. It also includes inland territory: the eastern end of Long Beach and next-door Seal Beach, areas settled by many retirees; most of Westminster; all of Fountain Valley and Costa Mesa; the southwest corner of Santa Ana; and a tiny slice of Los Angeles. The eastern part of the district is connected to the Palos Verdes Peninsula by a thin strip of beach or the port area. Politically, the two ends of the district are solidly Republican, from high-income Palos Verdes to Westminster. This is no longer the monoracial Orange County of the 1960s: The district's population is 19% Hispanic and 18% Asian (nearly half of whom are Vietnamese). Unlike other coastal California districts, this one has remained Republican. In 2008, GOP presidential candidate John McCain won it, albeit narrowly, 50%-48%.

The congressman from the 46th District is Dana Rohrabacher, a Republican first elected in 1988. He calls himself a surfer Republican and sports an American-flag surfboard on his lapel. He grew up in Southern California, went to college and experimented with drugs, and once had a folk band called the Goldwaters. By the mid-70s, he was on a straighter path as a press aide in Ronald Reagan's 1976 and 1980 presidential campaigns. He wrote editorials for the *Orange County Register* and later was a speechwriter in the Reagan White House. He returned to Southern California in 1988, when Long Beach-based GOP Rep. Dan Lungren was appointed acting state treasurer. With fundraising help from Oliver North, the Reagan White House aide—cum—Iran-Contra-scandal protagonist, Rohrabacher won the primary with 35% of the vote and went on to win the general election easily, with 64% of the vote. In 2004, Rohrabacher, then 56, and his wife, Rhonda, became the parents of triplets.

A self-styled free spirit, Rohrabacher likes to make waves in the House. His website once featured the motto: "Fighting for freedom and having fun." His voting record can be unpredictable, especially on cultural issues. He supported the use of medical marijuana and federal funding for embryonic-stem-cell research.

That helps to explain why this maverick has found himself on second-level committees. But he has made the most of his opportunities. As chairman of the Science Subcommittee on Space and Aeronautics, he worked for the single-stage-to-orbit vehicle. In 2004, President George W. Bush signed his bill to promote the development of the commercial human spaceflight industry. He has supported an obscure NASA program to search for and knock off course asteroids and comets that could slam into Earth. As much as he seems to love science, Rohrabacher has toed the party line on the issue of climate change, which he calls "nonsense" that jeopardizes the nation's freedom and prosperity. In 2007, he lost to the more senior Rep. Ralph Hall, R-Texas, for the ranking minority position on the full Science and Technology Committee.

Rohrabacher's other main focus has been the Foreign Affairs Committee. Soon after the September 11 attacks, he visited the exiled king of Afghanistan in Rome, encouraged him to return to Kabul and promised that the United States would oust the Taliban and help rebuild Afghanistan. Rohrabacher has been a longtime critic of China's rulers and strongly opposed normal trade relations with China and Vietnam. Despite the Bush administration's criticism that it would violate the peace treaty, he won House passage of his amendment to allow World War II prisoners of war to sue Japanese companies for enslaving them.

In 2003, he delayed his support for the Republicans' Medicare prescription-drug bill until Republican leaders, in exchange for his vote, gave him a vote on his bill to require hospitals to report potential illegal immigrants to the Homeland Security Department. He also has led voter initiatives to remove illegal aliens from California's welfare and school rolls, and he successfully urged Bush to grant pardons to two former Border Patrol agents who shot a Mexican drug dealer.

Rohrabacher was routinely re-elected by wide margins. But in 2008, he faced his most competitive challenger: Huntington Beach Mayor Debbie Cook, a Democratic lawyer and environmental activist who claimed he had done little during his time in Congress. With no help from the national party, she raised

$482,000. Rohrabacher criticized Cook's opposition to more oil drilling and her support for the bailout of the financial markets, which he said rewarded "those who acted irresponsibly." Rohrabacher won 53%-43%, leading comfortably in each of the two counties in the district.

FORTY-SEVENTH DISTRICT

Loretta Sanchez (D)

Elected 1996, 7th term; b. Jan. 7, 1960, Lynwood; home, Garden Grove; Chapman U., B.A. 1982, American U., M.B.A. 1984; Catholic; divorced.

Professional Career: Mgr. & financial analyst, Orange Cnty. Transp. Auth., 1984–87; Asst. vice pres., Fieldman, Rolapp & Assoc., 1987–90; Assoc., Booz, Allen & Hamilton, 1990–93; Principal, Amiga Advisors, 1993–96.

DC Office: 1114 LHOB, 20515, 202-225-2965; Fax: 202-225-5859; Web site: www.house.gov/sanchez.

State Offices: Garden Grove, 714-621-0102.

Committees: *Armed Services* (9th of 36 D): Military Personnel; Oversight & Investigations; Strategic Forces. *Homeland Security* (2nd of 20 D): Border, Maritime & Global Counterterrorism (Chmn); Emerging Threats, Cybersecurity & Science and Technology. *Joint Economic Committee.*

Group Ratings

	ADA	ACLU	AFS	LCV	ITIC	NTU	COC	ACU	CFG	FRC
2008	80	91	86	92	60	19	41	8	9	5
2007	100	—	100	90	—	4	60	0	1	—

National Journal Ratings

	2007 LIB	—	2007 CONS	2008 LIB	—	2008 CONS
Economic	77%	—	23%	61%	—	39%
Social	84%	—	15%	58%	—	41%
Foreign	72%	—	28%	65%	—	32%
Composite	78%	—	22%	62%	—	38%

Key Votes of the 110th Congress

1. Increase minimum wage	Y	5. Share immigration data	N	9. Withdraw troops 8/08	Y
2. Expand SCHIP	Y	6. Foreign aid abortion ban	*	10. No operations in Iran	Y
3. Raise CAFE standards	Y	7. Ban gay bias in workplace	Y	11. Free trade with Peru	N
4. Bail out financial markets	N	8. Repeal D.C. gun law	N	12. Overhaul FISA	N

Election Results

2008 general	Loretta Sanchez (D)	85,878	(69%)	($1,258,594)
	Rosemarie Avila (R)	31,432	(25%)	($52,639)
	Robert Lauten (AMI)	6,274	(5%)	
2008 primary	Loretta Sanchez (D)	unopposed		

Prior Winning Percentages: 2006 (62%); 2004 (60%); 2002 (61%); 2000 (60%); 1998 (56%); 1996 (47%)

Population		Race/Ethnicity		Work	
Pop. 2007:	637,958	White:	13.8%	Private:	87.1%
Change since 2000:	Down 0.2%	Black:	1.3%	Government:	6.9%
Urban:	100.0%	Hispanic:	68.6%	Self-employed:	5.9%
Rural:	0.0%	Asian:	14.7%	Blue collar:	36.5%
Area size:	55 sq. mi.	Native Am.:	0.2%	White collar:	40.0%
Age		Hawaiian:	0.4%	Khaki collar:	0.0%
Median age:	29.4 yrs.	Two+ races:	0.6%	Other:	23.4%
More than 65 yrs:	7.1%	*Ancestry*		Median income:	$50,681
Less than 18 yrs:	31.5%	German:	3.1%	Median home value:	$534,500
Education		Irish:	2.4%	Poverty:	16.0%
H.S. grad:	56.1%	English:	2.0%	**Military Veterans**	
College grad:	12.6%			% of Pop:	3.8%
Grad degree:	3.3%				

When Walt Disney began planning Disneyland in the late 1940s, he did not have to drive far from downtown Los Angeles before finding agricultural land. Dairy farms and orange groves covered most of southeast Los Angeles County and adjacent Orange County, which had only 216,000 people in 1950. As Disneyland opened there in 1955 and became a vast success, the area around it—a mass of flat land surrounded by mountains and sea—found itself directly in the path of the most explosively growing metropolitan area in the United States. Now, with 3 million people, Orange County is the nation's fifth-largest county, just a bit ahead of San Diego County.

2008 Presidential Vote		
Obama (D)	77,144	(60%)
McCain (R)	48,461	(38%)
2004 Presidential Vote		
Bush (R)	56,226	(50%)
Kerry (D)	54,623	(49%)
Cook Partisan Voting Index:	D+4	

Just as Orange County was once transformed by newcomers from Los Angeles County and the Midwest, so it is again being transformed by immigrants, from Mexico and other parts of Latin America, and from Vietnam, Taiwan, Korea, and other parts of East Asia. By 2007, the county was 33% Hispanic and 16% Asian. The county seat of Santa Ana is a major arrival point for immigrants from Mexico, and is 80% Hispanic. Others immigrants have moved farther out, like so many Southern Californians before them, working hard jobs, commuting on freeways, and living in stucco subdivisions. There are concentrations in various places—Latinos in Santa Ana and much of Anaheim; Vietnamese in Westminster and Garden Grove, who constitute the largest Vietnamese community in the nation—but many of these new Californians are scattered throughout the county. These demographic changes have made for some political wobble. Until the mid-1990s, Asians were split between the parties, and few Latinos were registered to vote. After the 1994 approval of Proposition 187, which sought to deny most social services to illegal immigrants, many more Latinos began voting, and voting mostly Democratic. Asian voters were less predictable.

The 47th Congressional District of California is the geographic heart of Orange County. About half its people live in Santa Ana. The district includes most of Garden Grove and Anaheim and many Orange County landmarks—Angel Stadium of Anaheim, Disneyland, and Disney's California Adventure. The district's population in 2007 was 69% Hispanic and 15% Asian, primarily Vietnamese. This core area has always been the most Democratic part of Orange County. But it is not overwhelmingly Democratic like most majority-Hispanic districts in Los Angeles County. In 2003, the district voted 62% to recall Democratic Governor Gray Davis. Republican President George W. Bush won the district in 2004, but by only 50%-49% over Democrat John Kerry. In 2008, Barack Obama returned the district to the Democrats—at least, for now—by winning over Republican John McCain 60%-38%.

The congresswoman from the 47th District is Loretta Sanchez, a Democrat first elected in 1996. She and her sister, Linda Sánchez, are the first sisters to serve in Congress. (Linda uses the accent mark with her surname; Loretta does not.) Loretta is nine years older than Linda, who represents California's 39th District. They co-authored a 2008 memoir titled *Dream in Color.*

Sanchez was raised in Anaheim. Her parents were Mexican immigrants, her father a machinist and her mother a secretary who worked to organize a union at the plant where she worked. Sanchez graduated from Chapman University in Orange, and got an M.B.A. from American University in Washington. She worked as a financial analyst, providing advice on municipal finances to public agencies and private businesses, and then started her own firm in the early 1990s. In 1994, she ran for the Anaheim City Council under her married name, Loretta Sanchez-Brixey, and lost. In 1996, she ran for the U.S. House, this time as Loretta Sanchez, against one of the most vocal conservatives, Rep. Robert Dornan. In the primary against three Anglo male Democrats, she won with 35%. That victory attracted little attention, not even from Dornan. But she shrewdly counted on increasing Latino turnout, plus attracting contributions from the many enemies that Dornan had made over a political career that went back to 1976. President Bill Clinton came to Santa Ana late in the campaign to stump for Sanchez, and may have made the difference. She won by 984 votes, 47%-46%. Dornan charged vote fraud, and, using the privileges afforded to former members, he regularly appeared on the House floor trying to convince his former colleagues to call for a special election. But in February 1998, the House Administration Committee upheld Sanchez's victory.

After her election, Sanchez was named general co-chairwoman of the Democratic National Committee to lead a Hispanic voter-registration drive, and Vice President Al Gore tapped her as an honorary chair of his political action committee. But that proved a mixed blessing for both Sanchez and her party. She scheduled a fundraiser during the 2000 Democratic National Convention in Los Angeles at Hugh Hefner's Playboy Mansion, which Gore and many other Democrats said was not good for the party's image. She was urged to choose a new site and was warned that she was jeopardizing her political future. She moved the event to Universal Studio's City Walk. In early 2007, Sanchez was at the center of a controversy at the Congressional Hispanic Caucus. She and other women in the caucus complained that Chairman Joe Baca of California was dismissive of them. Further, she accused Baca of calling her "whore," which he denied.

In the House, Sanchez's voting record has been in the Democratic middle. U.S.-Vietnam relations have been a focus for her. She accompanied Clinton on his 2000 visit there, and met with dissidents to discuss human rights. In 2007, after three times having been denied a visa, she returned to Vietnam and again stirred controversy by attempting to meet with the wives of imprisoned dissidents and criticizing the government's lack of openness. As the senior woman on the Armed Services Committee, she has tried to update the sexual assault crimes in the Uniform Code of Military Justice to comply with the way civilian sexual assault crimes are handled at the federal level. In 2004, the House passed her provision for the Pentagon to study the loss of civilian income by reservists on active duty. She is the No. 2 Democrat on the Homeland Security Committee, where she has focused on port security, including her proposal for a secure, long-range automated vessel-tracking system. She chairs the Border, Maritime and Global Counterterrorism Subcommittee.

Sanchez has been re-elected comfortably. Voters have grown accustomed to her unconventional style, including her quirky Christmas cards, which feature her aging white cat Gretzky, and her monthly cable access show titled *Loretta Live*. Ever ambitious, Sanchez has said that she might like to be a senator someday. For a few days in August 2003, she floated her name as a Democratic candidate in the governor recall election. And in 2009, she was again considering a run for California governor.

FORTY-EIGHTH DISTRICT

John Campbell (R)

Elected Dec. 2005, 2nd full term; b. July 19, 1955, Los Angeles; home, Irvine; U.C.L.A., B.A. 1976, U. of S. CA, M.B.T., 1977; Presbyterian; married (Catherine); 2 children.

Elected Office: CA Assembly, 2000–04; CA Senate, 2004–05.

Professional Career: Tax accountant, 1977–78; Auto dealership executive, 1978–2003.

DC Office: 1507 LHOB, 20515, 202-225-5611; Fax: 202-225-9177; Web site: campbell.house.gov.

State Offices: Newport Beach, 949-756-2244.

Committees: *Budget* (8th of 14 R). *Financial Services* (19th of 29 R): Capital Markets, Insurance & Government Sponsored Enterprises; Financial Institutions & Consumer Credit. *Joint Economic Committee*.

Group Ratings

	ADA	ACLU	AFS	LCV	ITIC	NTU	COC	ACU	CFG	FRC
2008	5	9	0	0	86	81	76	86	84	94
2007	10	—	0	20	—	89	70	92	96	—

National Journal Ratings

	2007 LIB — 2007 CONS		2008 LIB — 2008 CONS	
Economic	16%	— 84%	8%	— 92%
Social	29%	— 69%	0%	— 91%
Foreign	0%	— 72%	21%	— 78%
Composite	20%	— 80%	11%	— 89%

Key Votes of the 110th Congress

1. Increase minimum wage	N	5. Share immigration data	Y	9. Withdraw troops 8/08	N
2. Expand SCHIP	N	6. Foreign aid abortion ban	Y	10. No operations in Iran	N
3. Raise CAFE standards	N	7. Ban gay bias in workplace	Y	11. Free trade with Peru	Y
4. Bail out financial markets	Y	8. Repeal D.C. gun law	Y	12. Overhaul FISA	Y

Election Results

2008 general	John Campbell (R)	171,658	(56%)	($776,452)
	Steve Young (D)	125,537	(41%)	($268,129)
	Don Patterson (Lib)	11,507	(4%)	
2008 primary	John Campbell (R)	unopposed		

Prior Winning Percentages: 2006 (60%); 2005 (44%)

Population		Race/Ethnicity		Work	
Pop. 2007:	693,935	White:	62.4%	Private:	79.4%
Change since 2000:	Up 8.6%	Black:	1.7%	Government:	10.2%
Urban:	99.9%	Hispanic:	16.8%	Self-employed:	10.2%
Rural:	0.1%	Asian:	16.3%	Blue collar:	9.7%
Area size:	301 sq. mi.	Native Am.:	0.2%	White collar:	79.5%
		Hawaiian:	0.2%	Khaki collar:	0.1%
Age		Two+ races:	1.9%	Other:	10.7%
Median age:	38.2 yrs.			Median income:	$85,640
More than 65 yrs:	12.2%	*Ancestry*		Median home value:	$736,700
Less than 18 yrs:	22.8%	German:	11.3%	Poverty:	7.4%
		Irish:	8.7%		
Education		English:	8.5%	**Military Veterans**	
H.S. grad:	93.1%			% of Pop:	8.2%
College grad:	51.6%				
Grad degree:	20.2%				

Forty years ago, the area south of Santa Ana and the John Wayne Airport was open land, a vacant landscape of flat plains and low mountains, all beneath the 4,600-foot Trabuco Peak in the distance. This was the Irvine Ranch, purchased by Gold Rush merchant James Irvine from the Sepulveda and Yorba families and maintained as a ranch until the early 1970s, the last large plot of vacant land in metro Los Angeles. Ten miles along the Pacific Coast and 22 miles inland to the mountains,

2008 Presidential Vote
Obama (D) 163,063   (49%)
McCain (R).............................160,584   (49%)

2004 Presidential Vote
Bush (R) 178,739   (58%)
Kerry (D)................................123,664   (40%)

Cook Partisan Voting Index: R + 6

a traveler on the freeway could still get a sense of what the first American settlers to reach California saw. As Orange County grew up to the limits of the Irvine Ranch, the Irvine family was sitting on some immensely valuable land. In 1959, they donated a site for the University of California at Irvine, which has grown to more than 25,000 students. In the 1970s, they sold the rest to developers. The resulting city of Irvine was a planned community, with eight-lane parkways, huge office parks and shopping malls, and attractive subdivisions and condominiums. Irvine has attracted high-tech and high-growth businesses, highly educated and affluent people, and also Asian immigrants. Its population is 37% Asian, with enough Chinese to support a Chinese supermarket and a Chinese-language library.

Irvine is set amid a raft of affluent communities, except for low-income and 76% Hispanic Santa Ana. To the north is Tustin, an older town built on Irvine land. To the south is Newport Beach, one of California's richest cities, which has resisted the rapid development of Irvine. Newport Harbor is chock-full of expensive boats, and nearby Balboa Island is filled with multimillion-dollar homes. To the east is Lake Forest; the name used to be El Toro, and some residents now complain that it has few lakes or forests. To the southeast on the ocean is Laguna Beach, with its art galleries and cute shops, and more conventionally affluent Dana Point. Inland are Laguna Niguel, Laguna Hills, and the Laguna Woods retirement community. The El Toro Marine Corps Air Station that closed in 1999 is being developed as the Great Park in Irvine, with 1,300 acres of parkland ringed by 2,400 acres of development, 3,600 homes, and 3 million square feet of commercial and industrial space.

The 48th Congressional District of California, entirely contained within Orange County, is centered geographically on the Irvine Ranch lands and includes all of these communities. Politically, this is a conservative area, and for a long time it was one of the most Republican districts in the United States. Since the 1990s, like most of metro Los Angeles, it has trended to the Democrats. In 2007, it was 17% Hispanic and 16% Asian. It is still Republican, but far from the most Republican district in the state. Republican George W. Bush won with 58% here in 2000 and 2004, but Democrat Barack Obama won the district by 2,500 votes in 2008, 49.3% to 48.6% for Republican John McCain.

The congressman from the 48th District is John Campbell, a Republican who won a special election in December 2005. He has deep roots in Southern California. His great-grandfather was a Republican member of the state Assembly in 1860, and his grandfather was the managing editor of the now-defunct *Herald-Examiner*, W.R. Hearst's rival to the *Los Angeles Times*. Campbell's father was an oil field geologist and investor who later edited the *Herald-Examiner* 's financial pages. John Campbell graduated from the University of California at Los Angeles and got a master's degree in business taxation from the University of Southern California. A certified public accountant, he did a stint with Ernst & Young, one of the big accounting firms, and then joined an Orange County automobile dealership group as controller in 1978. Reviewing the company's books, Campbell discovered that the company's management had diverted $500,000 toward personal expenses. He alerted shareholders, including his father. The chief executive officer was fired, and Campbell was given the job. He later declared a no-haggling policy at each of Campbell Automotive's car dealerships. "We want to be the Nordstrom of auto retailing," he told the *Orange County Register* in 1989. In the 1990s, he sold off Campbell Automotive's Mazda, Ford, and Nissan dealerships to focus on its remaining Saab franchises—and on politics. In 2000, Campbell won an Irvine-based seat in the California Assembly, and four years later was elected to the state Senate.

Campbell got his opportunity to run for Congress when President Bush selected Rep. Christopher Cox to chair the Securities and Exchange Commission in June 2005. Campbell was instantly the front-runner in this solidly Republican district. Also in the primary was Marilyn Brewer, a former state Assembly member who supported abortion rights and embryonic-stem-cell research, and drew support from the moderate Republican Main Street Partnership. Campbell was endorsed by Republican Gov. Arnold Schwarzenegger, whom he had worked closely with in Sacramento, and by the state and Orange County Republican parties. With 19 candidates running for the seat in the all-party October 4 special primary, Campbell finished first with 45%, well above Brewer's 17%, to win the Republican nomination. Steve Young was the Democratic nominee after winning 9%. Jim Gilchrist, founder of the anti-illegal-immigrant Minuteman Project, finished third with 15% and was the nominee of the American Independent Party. In the campaign for the December 4 runoff, Gilchrist criticized Campbell for his votes in the Assembly, prompting Campbell to say that he made a mistake in 2001 when he voted to allow illegal immigrants to receive in-state college tuition. Gilchrist's single-issue campaign caught Campbell off guard and turned the contest into a referendum on immigration. Campbell won, though with a surprisingly modest 44% to 28% for Democrat Young and 25% for Gilchrist. Nearly 13,000 more votes were cast in December than October, but Campbell picked up just 4,800 votes over his October performance; the bulk of the other votes went to Young and Gilchrist.

In the House, Campbell's voting record is mostly conservative but more centrist on economic issues. He has seats on the Budget and Financial Services committees. He moved quickly into a leadership role among conservatives as chairman of the budget and spending task force of the Republican Study Committee. He led Republicans angry about Congress's lack of spending restraint, offering a series of amendments designed to embarrass sponsors of questionable spending earmarks. Campbell rarely got many more than 100 votes, but made a point about wasteful spending. He started the *Green Eyeshade* blog on the *Townhall.com* conservative website to explain details of the federal budget. When he learned that Democrats planned to embarrass him by highlighting his support for a $2.5 million water project for his district, he withdrew his support for it. But he parted company with most fiscal conservatives in September 2008 when he backed the bailout of the financial industry, which he said was vital to rescue the economy. With that shift, he abandoned his bid to chair the conservative Republican Study Committee. But he remained an outspoken critic of "big spending."

At home, Campbell has been re-elected easily.

FORTY-NINTH DISTRICT

Darrell Issa (R)

Elected 2000, 5th term; b. Nov. 1, 1953, Cleveland, OH; home, Vista; Sienna Heights U., B.A. 1976; Antioch Orthodox Christian; married (Kathy); 1 child.

Military Career: Army, 1970–72; 1976–80.

Professional Career: Founder & pres., Directed Electronics, 1982–99.

DC Office: 2347 RHOB, 20515, 202-225-3906; Fax: 202-225-3303; Web site: www.issa.house.gov.

State Offices: Temecula, 909-693-2447; Vista, 760-599-5000.

Committees: *Judiciary* (7th of 16 R): Commercial & Administrative Law; Courts & Competition Policy. *Oversight & Government Reform* (RMM of 16 R).

Group Ratings

	ADA	ACLU	AFS	LCV	ITIC	NTU	COC	ACU	CFG	FRC
2008	10	18	0	8	67	81	94	100	97	70
2007	20	—	0	0	—	85	74	88	89	—

National Journal Ratings

	2007 LIB	—	2007 CONS	2008 LIB	—	2008 CONS
Economic	4%	—	95%	10%	—	90%
Social	38%	—	62%	16%	—	82%
Foreign	0%	—	72%	13%	—	84%
Composite	19%	—	81%	14%	—	86%

Key Votes of the 110th Congress

1. Increase minimum wage	N	5. Share immigration data	Y	9. Withdraw troops 8/08	N
2. Expand SCHIP	N	6. Foreign aid abortion ban	Y	10. No operations in Iran	N
3. Raise CAFE standards	N	7. Ban gay bias in workplace	N	11. Free trade with Peru	Y
4. Bail out financial markets	N	8. Repeal D.C. gun law	Y	12. Overhaul FISA	Y

Election Results

2008 general	Darrell Issa (R)	140,300	(58%)	($950,631)
	Robert Hamilton (D)	90,138	(37%)	($63,217)
	Lars Grossmith (Lib)	10,232	(4%)	
2008 primary	Darrell Issa (R)	unopposed		

Prior Winning Percentages: 2006 (63%); 2004 (63%); 2002 (77%); 2000 (61%)

Population		Race/Ethnicity		Work	
Pop. 2007:	748,265	White:	52.7%	Private:	73.1%
Change since 2000:	Up 17.1%	Black:	4.3%	Government:	18.8%
Urban:	90.3%	Hispanic:	34.5%	Self-employed:	7.9%
Rural:	9.7%	Asian:	4.9%	Blue collar:	24.3%
Area size:	1,778 sq. mi.	Native Am.:	0.7%	White collar:	53.6%
		Hawaiian:	0.3%	Khaki collar:	4.3%
Age		Two+ races:	2.2%	Other:	17.8%
Median age:	32.0 yrs.			Median income:	$60,194
More than 65 yrs:	11.3%	*Ancestry*		Median home value:	$460,000
Less than 18 yrs:	28.0%	German:	11.1%	Poverty:	9.9%
		Irish:	8.0%		
Education		English:	6.9%	**Military Veterans**	
H.S. grad:	81.9%			% of Pop:	12.0%
College grad:	23.0%				
Grad degree:	7.5%				

The California coast between Los Angeles and San Diego has never entirely filled up with development—and never will as long as the Marine Corps retains custody of Camp Pendleton, the giant training base just south of the Orange-San Diego County line and the Corps's largest expeditionary training facility on the West Coast. The land along the coast and inland in northern San Diego County, usually referred to as North County, was largely empty territory a half-century ago—never fertile enough to

2008 Presidential Vote

McCain (R)	137,739	(53%)
Obama (D)	117,283	(45%)

2004 Presidential Vote

Bush (R)	149,283	(63%)
Kerry (D)	86,998	(37%)

Cook Partisan Voting Index: R + 10

produce a large farm community, never endowed with much manufacturing, never actively promoted as a retirement community. But North County has been growing rapidly since then. Today about 1 million people live here, and who can blame them? This is one of America's most beautiful and comfortable environments, with ocean and mountain scenery, sunny and warm weather, no rural poverty, and low crime. Amid dry but not desert landscape, there are miles of rolling hills, with occasional sagebrush-like bushes. Mountains rise up not in ridges, but here and there at random. It has attracted thousands of new migrants—many, but by no means all, retirees.

The 49th Congressional District of California occupies the northern part of San Diego County and the southwestern corner of Riverside County. It was the fastest-growing California district in the 1990s, with a population increase of 35%; it grew another 17% between 2000 and 2007. On the coast next to Camp Pendleton is Oceanside, a lower-middle-income town heavily dependent on the base. Oceanside suffered many casualties during the Iraq war. Inland is Vista, a higher-income community that calls itself the "climatic wonderland of the United States," with day after day of blue skies, sunshine, and average high temperatures that range from 68 degrees in January to 82 degrees in July. About 35% of the district's population is in these two areas. About 25% is in small communities in North County, including a small portion of San Diego. Another 40% is in Riverside County in an area with many evangelical Christians and mega-churches.

The district also takes in Temecula, an increasingly congested area with more than 100,000 people, mostly commuters attracted by low-priced homes and a family-oriented lifestyle. The city was hit badly by the recession, with an estimated 15% of its homes in foreclosure in 2008. To the north are the older communities of Lake Elsinore, Canyon Lake and Perris. Politically, this is a heavily Republican area, which rarely elects Democrats to any office. It voted 63% for Republican President George W. Bush in 2004 and 53% for GOP nominee John McCain in 2008.

The congressman from the 49th District is Darrell Issa (*EYE-sah*), a Republican first elected in 2000. He grew up in a working-class section of Cleveland, the son of an X-ray technician. Hampered by dyslexia, Issa found academics difficult, and he dropped out of high school to join the Army. After his service, the military paid for him to finish school, and he graduated from Sienna Heights University in Michigan. A brother's run-ins with the law for car theft spurred Issa's idea for his first business venture. He invested all of his savings, some $7,000, in a car-alarm business in Cleveland, eventually taking it over with his wife, Kathy, and relocating the business to Vista, Calif., north of San Diego. Their Directed Electronics became the nation's largest manufacturer of vehicle security systems, including the popular Viper system, and earned them a fortune estimated at $200 million. Issa became active in the high-technology industry, serving as chairman of the Consumer Electronics Association.

In the early 1990s, he turned to politics, contributing to Republicans and chairing the 1996 campaign to pass Proposition 209, which banned the use of racial quotas and preferences in California. In 1998, he ran for the Republican nomination to challenge Democratic Sen. Barbara Boxer and spent $9.8 million of his own money. But he lost the primary 45%-40% to Matt Fong. In November 1999, when U.S. Rep. Ron Packard announced his retirement, there was a crowded field of 10 for the Republican primary, which in all likelihood would determine the winner given the political lean of the district. The race turned into a bruising two-man contest between Issa and state Sen. Bill Morrow. Mark Dornan, the son of former Republican Rep. Robert Dornan, trailed well behind. Morrow questioned Issa's business practices, and Issa raised questions about Morrow's honesty. On most issues, the candidates took similar positions. They supported streamlining government, opposed abortion rights, and favored rebuilding the military. Issa spent $1.5 million of his own money on the primary, and beat Morrow 46%-30%. In the fall, the Democratic nominee abandoned his campaign after getting little national party support, and Issa won 61%-28%. He has been re-elected easily.

In the House, Issa's voting record has been relatively moderate, especially on the foreign-affairs issues that capture his attention. On the eve of George W. Bush's decision to start military action in Afghanistan, Issa joined Rep. Robert Wexler, D-Fla., in a visit to several Middle East nations to build support for the United States. During that trip, he suggested that he was the victim of racial profiling when he was kept off an Air France flight to Paris; the airline claimed that he was late. Of Lebanese descent, Issa has been vocal in condemning the sponsorship of terrorism by Arab nations while also urging the United States to reach out to build coalitions with friendly Arab nations. That earned him enemies among pro-Israel groups, including extremists on that side of the conflict. Two members of the militant Jewish Defense League were charged with plotting to blow up Issa's office in San Clemente and a Culver City mosque. One of them died in 2002 and the other pleaded guilty to civil-rights and weapons violations in September 2005. In April 2007, Issa joined a delegation to Syria led by Democratic House Speaker Nancy Pelosi, who criticized President Bush's lack of dialogue with Syrian leaders.

On immigration, a big issue in California, Issa has sought to prevent illegal immigrants from getting driver's licenses, and has demanded more vigorous prosecution of smuggling across the border. He also has been active on patent-reform issues. Drawing on his experience as a patent holder (he holds 37 of them), Issa sponsored in 2009 a bipartisan bill to enhance the expertise of district court judges hearing patent cases. Courts would be assigned a clerk with expertise in patent law or with the technical issues arising in patent cases. With Democrat Howard Berman of California, he co-sponsored legislation to create a post-grant review of already-issued patents and to establish an "apportionment rule" for calculating damages in a patent lawsuit. He worked to broker a deal that would satisfy both the drugmakers who oppose the bill and the high-tech firms that support it. The technology industry has led the charge for patent reform, contending it is being held hostage by "patent trolls" who obtain patents solely for the purpose of launching infringement suits to cash in on multibillion-dollar damage awards.

Issa is the senior Republican on the Oversight and Government Reform Committee, where he leads the minority party's oversight of the Obama administration. By hiring aides with investigative backgrounds, Issa hoped to conduct independent investigations in the 111th Congress (2009–10), despite lacking the majority's subpoena power. He also has a strong interest in the 2010 census and redistricting.

Issa became widely known outside his district for his role in the 2003 recall election of California Gov. Gray Davis, which got national attention. He spent $1.7 million of his own money to get the signatures needed for the recall election. Without his money, the partisan effort likely would have failed. He wanted to run for governor on the replacement ballot, but got elbowed out by the celebrity campaign of former actor and bodybuilder Arnold Schwarzenegger. Issa tearfully announced that he would not run. After Schwarzenegger won, Issa was an early supporter of his nonpartisan redistricting proposal and made known his interest in running for lieutenant governor in 2006. But Republicans chose conservative Tom McClintock to run.

FIFTIETH DISTRICT

Brian Bilbray (R)

Elected June 2006, 5th full term; b. Jan. 28, 1951, Coronado; home, Carlsbad. Attended SW Commun. Col., 1970–72, 1974; Catholic; married (Karen); 2 children.

Elected Office: Imperial Beach City Cncl., 1976–78; Imperial Beach Mayor, 1978–84; San Diego Cnty. Bd. of Supervisors, 1984–94; U.S. House of Reps., 1994–2000.

Professional Career: Tax consultant, 1972–present; Lobbyist, 2001–05.

DC Office: 2348 RHOB, 20515, 202-225-0508; Fax: 202-225-2558; Web site: www.house.gov/bilbray.

State Offices: Solana Beach, 858-350-1150.

Committees: *Oversight & Government Reform* (10th of 15 R): Federal Workforce, Postal Service & the District of Columbia; Government Management, Organization & Procurement (RMM). *Science & Technology* (14th of 17 R): Investigations & Oversight; Research & Science Education. *Veterans' Affairs* (7th of 11 R): Disability Assistance & Memorial Affairs; Oversight & Investigations.

Group Ratings

	ADA	ACLU	AFS	LCV	ITIC	NTU	COC	ACU	CFG	FRC
2008	15	18	29	38	43	73	88	92	80	70
2007	10	—	9	25	—	82	80	92	91	—

National Journal Ratings

	2007 LIB	—	2007 CONS		2008 LIB	—	2008 CONS
Economic	16%	—	84%		34%	—	65%
Social	31%	—	67%		16%	—	82%
Foreign	0%	—	72%		13%	—	84%
Composite	21%	—	79%		22%	—	78%

Key Votes of the 110th Congress

1. Increase minimum wage	N	5. Share immigration data	Y	9. Withdraw troops 8/08	N
2. Expand SCHIP	N	6. Foreign aid abortion ban	Y	10. No operations in Iran	N
3. Raise CAFE standards	N	7. Ban gay bias in workplace	N	11. Free trade with Peru	Y
4. Bail out financial markets	N	8. Repeal D.C. gun law	Y	12. Overhaul FISA	Y

Election Results

2008 general	Brian Bilbray (R)	157,502	(50%)	($1,456,454)
	Nick Leibham (D)	141,635	(45%)	($1,284,549)
	Wayne Dunlap (Lib)	14,365	(5%)	
2008 primary	Brian Bilbray (R)	unopposed		

Prior Winning Percentages: 2006 (53%); 2006 (50%); 1998 (49%); 1996 (53%); 1994 (49%)

Population		**Race/Ethnicity**		**Work**	
Pop. 2007:	703,028	White:	61.6%	Private:	76.0%
Change since 2000:	Up 10.0%	Black:	1.6%	Government:	13.9%
Urban:	97.8%	Hispanic:	20.8%	Self-employed:	9.9%
Rural:	2.2%	Asian:	12.8%	Blue collar:	14.2%
Area size:	365 sq. mi.	Native Am.:	0.4%	White collar:	69.1%
		Hawaiian:	0.2%	Khaki collar:	1.5%
Age		Two+ races:	2.3%	Other:	15.2%
Median age:	37.0 yrs.			Median income:	$75,741
More than 65 yrs:	12.2%	*Ancestry*		Median home value:	$635,900
Less than 18 yrs:	25.1%	German:	11.7%	Poverty:	7.5%
		English:	8.8%		
Education		Irish:	8.7%	**Military Veterans**	
H.S. grad:	89.2%			% of Pop:	10.9%
College grad:	44.4%				
Grad degree:	18.0%				

The affluent San Diego neighborhood of La Jolla is spectacularly situated between Soledad Mountain and the Pacific Ocean. A 15-minute drive from the city's downtown, La Jolla (*la-HOY-uh*) is known for its beaches, upscale shopping, and restaurants, but mostly for its physical beauty and temperate climate. La Jolla is also home to the University of California at San Diego and the Scripps Institution of Oceanography. West of La Jolla are several inland communities, such as Escondido and San Marcos,

2008 Presidential Vote		
Obama (D)	172,962	(51%)
McCain (R)	158,845	(47%)
2004 Presidential Vote		
Bush (R)	169,935	(55%)
Kerry (D)	135,007	(44%)
Cook Partisan Voting Index:	R+3	

that are also pleasant and affluent, attractively planned, and many with red tile roofs that contrast with the tan hillsides. Also to the west, beyond the mountain, is the Miramar Marine Corps Air Station.

The 50th Congressional District of California covers much of this part of San Diego County. About 40% of its population is in the city of San Diego, including most of scenic La Jolla, hillside Clairemont, Carmel Valley, University City, Mira Mesa, Rancho Penasquitos, and part of Rancho Bernardo. About 25% lives on or near the coast, from Del Mar to Encinitas and Carlsbad, home of the La Costa resort and a big tourist destination. Just inland is Rancho Santa Fe, one of the wealthiest communities in the nation, with multimillion-dollar mansions set amid rolling hills and lush greenery. About 30% of the district's people are in Escondido and fast-growing San Marcos. Politically, this has been Republican territory but not overwhelmingly so; it is more liberal on the coast and more conservative inland. Democrat Barack Obama prevailed in 2008 with 51% to 47% for Republican John McCain.

The congressman from the 50th District is Brian Bilbray, a Republican who served in Congress from 1995 to 2001 and then returned to win a June 2006 special election. Bilbray grew up in Imperial Beach, south of San Diego. A former lifeguard and an avid surfer, Bilbray owned his own tax preparation business and then at age 25 was elected to the Imperial Beach Council in 1976. Two years later, he became mayor. He made a local splash in 1980 when he mounted a loader and built a berm to keep the sewage-polluted Tijuana River from seeping into the San Diego County beaches. In 1984, he was elected to the San Diego County Board of Supervisors, where he worked on environmental protection and economic development issues. In 1994, Bilbray ousted first-term U.S. Rep. Lynn Schenck, a Democrat who had a moderate voting record but voted for the 1993 Clinton budget and tax increases. Once in office, Bilbray went to the other extreme in his approach to the Clinton administration, voting to impeach the president in 1998. He said at the time that in his politically marginal district (he was then in the 49th Congressional District), the vote might be the issue that "drives a nail through my political coffin." That comment proved prescient as Bilbray lost 50%-46% in 2000 to Democrat Susan Davis, who said that Bilbray "talks moderate in San Diego but votes conservative in Washington."

Bilbary stayed on in Washington as a lobbyist, and stayed involved in issues as the co-chairman of the Federation for American Immigration Reform, which lobbies for limiting immigration levels and toughening border controls. The 50th District House seat opened when Republican Rep. Randy (Duke) Cunningham, a former decorated Navy pilot, pleaded guilty in November 2005 to evading taxes and taking more than $2 million in bribes to help a defense contractor. Bilbray got into the race and was an early front-runner, but he faced competitive contests in both the primary and the special general election. His chief Republican opponents were more conservative. State Sen. Bill Morrow, former Assemblyman Howard Kaloogian and wealthy businessman Eric Roach all criticized Bilbray for becoming a lobbyist and claimed his voting record had been too liberal. Bilbray highlighted his work with FAIR, and won the nomination with 15% of the total vote cast to 14% for Roach, 7% for Kaloogian, and 5% for Morrow.

Spotting an opportunity to take a longtime Republican seat in the wake of the Cunningham scandal, national Democrats invested heavily in Francine Busby, a professor of women's studies and local school board member who had lost two years earlier to Cunningham. The fundraising powerhouse EMILY's List, which had ignored Busby in 2004, became an active supporter. By mid-May, Busby had collected more than $2 million, roughly 10 times the amount she raised two years earlier. And she embraced the theme that the GOP-controlled Congress was mired in a "culture of corruption." Bilbray said that Busby had no ideas of her own to offer on immigration and pollution at the border with Mexico. Then, five days before the June 6 election, Busby made a critical mistake when she told a crowd that "you don't need papers for voting, you don't need to be a registered voter to help." Bilbray and the Republicans seized on the remark as an invitation for illegal aliens to vote, and blitzed the airwaves with a final round of ads. Bilbray won 50%-45%, with anti-immigration sentiment driving his victory.

Once back in the House, Bilbray's voting record became more conservative on social issues. In 2007, he replaced Republican Rep. Tom Tancredo of Colorado as chairman of the Immigration Reform Caucus. Although less of a rhetorical firebrand than Tancredo, he has advocated tough enforcement on the U.S. border and stronger curbs on illegal immigration. With Democratic Rep. Heath Shuler of North Carolina in 2007, he sponsored the Secure America with Verification and Enforcement (SAVE) Act, which requires employers to use the E-Verify program to verify the immigration status of new hires, mandates information-sharing between the Department of Homeland Security, the Social Security Administration and the

IRS, and provides an 8,000-agent increase for the U.S. Border Patrol. Democratic leaders blocked House action on the bill.

Bilbray was re-elected 53%-44% in a rematch with Busby in 2006 . Two years later, he had a close race against attorney Nick Leibham, who raised $1.3 million and criticized Bilbray's opposition to the bailout of the financial markets in 2008. Bilbray won 50%-45%. He could face problems in the future if redistricting in 2010 adds Democratic voters from the neighboring 51st and 53rd districts.

FIFTY-FIRST DISTRICT

Rep. Bob Filner (D)

Elected 1992, 9th term; b. Sept. 4, 1942, Pittsburgh, PA; home, San Diego; Cornell U., B.A. 1963, Ph.D. 1973, U. of DE, M.A. 1969; Jewish; married (Jane Merrill); 2 children.

Elected Office: San Diego Schl. Bd., 1979–83, Pres., 1982–83; San Diego City Cncl., 1987–92, Dpty. mayor, 1991.

Professional Career: Prof., San Diego St. U., 1970–92; Legis. asst., U.S. Sen. Hubert Humphrey, 1974; Legis. asst., U.S. Rep. Don Fraser, 1975; Spec. asst., U.S. Rep. Jim Bates, 1984.

DC Office: 2428 RHOB, 20515, 202-225-8045; Fax: 202-225-9073; Web site: www.house.gov/filner.

State Offices: Chula Vista, 619-422-5963; Imperial, 760-355-8800.

Committees: *Transportation & Infrastructure* (8th of 44 D): Aviation; Highways & Transit; Railroads, Pipelines & Hazardous Materials; Water Resources & Environment. *Veterans' Affairs* (Chmn of 18 D).

Group Ratings

	ADA	ACLU	AFS	LCV	ITIC	NTU	COC	ACU	CFG	FRC
2008	100	100	100	92	71	22	47	12	22	5
2007	90	—	100	90	—	4	45	0	6	—

National Journal Ratings

	2007 LIB	—	2007 CONS	2008 LIB	—	2008 CONS
Economic	82%	—	0%	63%	—	36%
Social	92%	—	0%	58%	—	41%
Foreign	86%	—	11%	85%	—	8%
Composite	92%	—	9%	70%	—	30%

Key Votes of the 110th Congress

1. Increase minimum wage	Y	5. Share immigration data	N	9. Withdraw troops 8/08	Y
2. Expand SCHIP	Y	6. Foreign aid abortion ban	N	10. No operations in Iran	Y
3. Raise CAFE standards	Y	7. Ban gay bias in workplace	Y	11. Free trade with Peru	N
4. Bail out financial markets	N	8. Repeal D.C. gun law	N	12. Overhaul FISA	N

Election Results

2008 general	Bob Filner (D)	148,281	(73%)	($927,615)
	David Joy (R)	49,345	(24%)	
	Dan Litwin (Lib)	6,199	(3%)	
2008 primary	Bob Filner (D)	31,690	(76%)	
	Daniel Ramirez (D)	10,182	(24%)	

Prior Winning Percentages: 2006 (67%); 2004 (62%); 2002 (58%); 2000 (68%); 1998 (99%); 1996 (62%); 1994 (57%); 1992 (57%)

Population		Race/Ethnicity		Work	
Pop. 2007:	698,803	White:	18.2%	Private:	69.5%
Change since 2000:	Up 9.3%	Black:	7.3%	Government:	23.7%
Urban:	95.6%	Hispanic:	59.2%	Self-employed:	6.6%
Rural:	4.4%	Asian:	12.1%	Blue collar:	23.1%
Area size:	4,896 sq. mi.	Native Am.:	0.4%	White collar:	53.7%
Age		Hawaiian:	0.4%	Khaki collar:	1.5%
Median age:	31.7 yrs.	Two+ races:	2.0%	Other:	21.7%
More than 65 yrs:	10.4%	*Ancestry*		Median income:	$49,057
Less than 18 yrs:	29.7%	German:	4.2%	Median home value:	$436,700
Education		Irish:	2.8%	Poverty:	15.3%
H.S. grad:	71.5%	English:	2.4%	**Military Veterans**	
College grad:	16.6%			% of Pop:	9.8%
Grad degree:	4.9%				

Anchoring a corner of the continental United States, San Diego not so long ago was a small Navy town known for its good harbor and splendid weather. It of course now is a major metropolis of 1.3 million people and the center of a county of 3 million. To its occasional discomfort, it is also one of the largest cities directly on an international border, situated between countries with strikingly different economic conditions, political systems, and cultural

2008 Presidential Vote		
Obama (D)	135,960	(63%)
McCain (R)	76,438	(36%)
2004 Presidential Vote		
Kerry (D)	100,062	(53%)
Bush (R)	85,762	(46%)
Cook Partisan Voting Index:	D + 8	

traditions. San Diego sits on the busiest border crossing in the world, and on a daily basis, agents for the Border Patrol play a sometimes-violent cat-and-mouse game with people trying to cross illegally. In 2005, about 127,000 were apprehended in the San Diego area, but many more crossed the border without being captured. In 2006, authorities found a sophisticated tunnel dug under the border for drug running. Recently, tougher enforcement in California shifted some of the illegal crossings to Arizona.

Thousands of legal workers cross the border daily to reach the industrial zone on San Diego's southern edge, on brown hills in Otay Mesa and San Ysidro, and the industrial suburbs of Chula Vista and National City. Many children from Mexico cross daily to attend public and private schools. Latinos pour billions into the San Diego economy and are scattered in various parts of the city, in the southern corridor, and in Encanto and Chollas Park in the eastern section. Oddly, there is not much evidence of Mexican style in San Diego—less than in Los Angeles.

The 51st Congressional District of California covers California's entire border with Mexico, including the southeast corner of San Diego, and also National City and Chula Vista. The district extends east to the Arizona border and includes all of Imperial County, with its string of farms and towns running south from the Salton Sea to Mexicali, Mexico. Water comes from the Colorado River through the All-American Canal. (A project begun in 2007 to line a 23-mile segment of the canal with concrete to decrease the flow of water to farmers in Mexico stirred controversy.) With farmland being turned into moderately priced subdivisions, rapidly growing Imperial County in 2007 had 162,000 people, 76% of them Hispanic. Imperial is also being considered as a site for a new airport. El Centro, the county seat of Imperial, had 22% unemployment in 2009—the highest in the nation—resulting from drought, the decline of the Mexican peso, and the national recession. Hispanics are a majority in the district, which was created to be solidly Democratic. In 2004, Democratic presidential nominee John Kerry won 53% of the district's vote, and in 2008 Democrat Barack Obama won 63%.

The congressman from the 51st District is Bob Filner, a Democrat first elected in 1992. Filner grew up in New York City, and became politically active early in his adult life by joining the civil-rights movement. He was a fundraiser for the Rev. Martin Luther King Jr. and in 1961 joined the Freedom Riders, which were groups of whites and blacks that traveled to the South to ride public transportation and use public facilities to challenge the lack of compliance with Supreme Court rulings outlawing segregation. The protests often sparked violent reactions from local citizens. Filner was arrested in Mississippi while trying to integrate a lunch counter, and was imprisoned for two months. He earned a Ph.D. at Cornell, taught history at San Diego State University, and directed the Lipinsky Institute for Judaic Studies. He worked on Democratic Sen. Hubert Humphrey's staff in the 1970s, and was elected to the San Diego school board in 1979 and to the City Council in 1987. Redistricting in 1992 created a new Democratic seat in San Diego County, and Filner decided to run. He was strongly backed by local activists even though he had better-known rivals in the Democratic primary. Filner won with 26% of the vote, to 23% for Waddie Deddeh, a state senator and assemblyman; 20% for Jim Bates, a four-term congressman defeated in 1990 after being disciplined for sexual harassment; and 19% for Juan Carlos Vargas. Filner went on to win the general election easily in the Democratic district.

Filner is politically savvy, with some original ideas about policy, and he is aggressive in articulating his views. He is also one of the most liberal members of the House, and among the most confrontational. He once got into a heated argument with Republican Rep. Joe Wilson of South Carolina on C-SPAN, and once was reported by immigration officials at a detention facility after demanding a visit to a detainee. In August 2007, he made headlines when he was charged with assault and battery after an altercation with an airline employee at Dulles International Airport. He later paid a $100 fine, but did not plead guilty. He denied physically assaulting the employee, but conceded: "I overreacted, I behaved discourteously, and I shouldn't have." The Committee on Standards of Official Conduct looked into the matter and determined that Filner had shown "poor judgment."

In 2007, Filner became chairman of the Veterans' Affairs Committee following a contest with Rep. Mike Michaud, D-Maine, who criticized Filner for poor working relationships with Republicans and some of the veterans' groups. Filner cited praise from major veterans' organizations, and bolstered by support from House Speaker Nancy Pelosi, with whom he sometimes had a testy relationship, he won the Democratic Caucus vote over Michaud, 112-69.

Filner has long been a vocal advocate of veterans' rights and benefits, a popular cause in a district with many members of the military and military retirees. In 2008, he won enactment of a major overhaul of the GI Bill, which dates to 1944 and has boosted countless veterans to the middle class by paying for college and first homes. Filner's legislation gives veterans the full cost of any public college, up from half the cost in current law, plus an average $1,100-a-month living stipend depending on the local housing market. It is expected to cost $62 billion over a decade. Outraged by the treatment of Filipino veterans, who in the past did not get full benefits, Filner in 2009 got included in the economic stimulus bill lump-sum bonus payments for Filipino veterans. In 2006, he won bipartisan support in the House to improve data security at the Veterans Affairs Department, following reports of a major computer security lapse.

Filner has survived several political challenges at home. In the 1996 primary, he was again opposed by Vargas, by then on the San Diego Council. Filner won, but by just 55%-45%. After redistricting placed heavily Latino parts of San Diego in his district in 2002, he faced Danny Ramirez, an Imperial County businessman. Filner won 70%-30%, despite losing 60%-40% in Imperial County. In 2006, Vargas challenged Filner a third time. The bitter primary contest featured negative campaigning on each side. Vargas, by then a California assemblyman, said that Filner had paid his wife more than $500,000 in campaign funds for her consulting services, which she operated from their condominium in Washington. Filner spotlighted questionable campaign payments by Vargas to his brother-in-law, who was a lobbyist for realtors. Filner benefited from his constituent work in Imperial County, where Vargas was not well known despite his Hispanic ties, and won 51%-43%. "People vote for the person who's going to be the most effective for them, not by their last name," Filner said. He had his usual easy re-election victories since then.

FIFTY-SECOND DISTRICT

Duncan D. Hunter (R)

Elected 2008, 1st term; b. Dec. 7, 1976, San Diego; home, Lakeside; San Diego St. U., B.S. 2000.; Protestant; married (Margaret); 3 children.

Military Career: Marine Corps, 2002–05 (Iraq); Marine Reserves, 05–present (Afghanistan).

Professional Career: Business analyst, Cayenta Inc., 2000–02; Residential developer, 2005–07.

DC Office: 1429 LHOB, 20515, 202-225-5672; Fax: 202-225-0235; Web site: hunter.house.gov.

State Offices: El Cajon, 619-448-5201.

Committees: *Armed Services* (21st of 25 R): Air & Land Forces; Seapower & Expeditionary Forces. *Education & Labor* (17th of 19 R): Early Childhood, Elementary & Secondary Education; Health, Employment, Labor & Pensions.

Group Ratings and Key Votes: Newly Elected

Election Results

2008 general	Duncan D. Hunter (R)	160,724	(56%)	($1,280,755)
	Mike Lumpkin (D)	111,051	(39%)	($482,063)
	Michael Benoit (Lib)	13,316	(5%)	
2008 primary	Duncan D. Hunter (R)	47,930	(72%)	
	Brian Jones (R)	10,862	(16%)	
	Bob Watkins (R)	5,539	(8%)	

Population		Race/Ethnicity		Work	
Pop. 2007:	666,238	White:	66.8%	Private:	73.4%
Change since 2000:	Up 4.2%	Black:	4.3%	Government:	18.2%
Urban:	93.6%	Hispanic:	17.4%	Self-employed:	8.1%
Rural:	6.4%	Asian:	7.4%	Blue collar:	17.0%
Area size:	2,129 sq. mi.	Native Am.:	0.5%	White collar:	66.4%
Age		Hawaiian:	0.4%	Khaki collar:	1.0%
Median age:	36.1 yrs.	Two+ races:	2.9%	Other:	15.5%
More than 65 yrs:	10.8%	*Ancestry*		Median income:	$68,713
Less than 18 yrs:	26.4%	German:	14.0%	Median home value:	$552,900
Education		Irish:	10.0%	Poverty:	8.0%
H.S. grad:	89.8%	English:	8.6%	**Military Veterans**	
College grad:	32.9%			% of Pop:	13.5%
Grad degree:	12.1%				

San Diego began as a port, but today most metropol-itan-area residents live out of sight of the sea, in hill-top neighborhoods that look out over distant ridges and freeways or in warm, sunny valleys amid the mountains that become dense and taller as one travels east from the Pacific Ocean. There is a dis-cernible difference in attitudes and values between those who have settled inland and those who live nearer the ocean, part of the split between coastal California and interior California that has been at

2008 Presidential Vote		
McCain (R)	161,332	(53%)
Obama (D)	135,848	(45%)
2004 Presidential Vote		
Bush (R)	177,055	(61%)
Kerry (D)	108,806	(38%)
Cook Partisan Voting Index:	R + 9	

the heart of the state's political struggles and culture wars. In San Diego, both groups have tended to identify as Republicans. Coastal residents tend to be more affluent, and those who settle inland are more likely to be conventionally religious and to have traditional moral values; they tend to be more supportive of the military and an assertive foreign policy, and they are more dubious about the ability of government to help society's have-nots. They are more conservative and therefore more reliably Republican. Inland San Diego County produced higher percentages for Republican George W. Bush in 2004 than in 2000, while coastal San Diego County did not.

The 52nd Congressional District of California takes in many of the inland San Diego suburbs and most of the mountain and desert interior of San Diego County. It includes the part of San Diego north of Interstate 8 and east of Interstate 15. It has Santee, an East County city of 53,000; and El Cajon, which has the nation's second-largest (after the Detroit area) community of Chaldeans, Catholic Arabs from Iraq. The district also includes high-income Poway, north of San Diego, and more modest La Mesa, east of San Diego. The mountains and the desert to the east are lightly inhabited. In the mountains is tiny Alpine. In the desert is the town of Borrego Springs amid the giant Anza-Borrego Desert State Park. This East County area was swept by horrific fires in October and November 2003, which killed 17 people and destroyed more than 2,400 homes. Subsequent years brought additional wildfires and mass evacuations. Politically, this is a solidly Republican district. Republican presidential candidate John McCain in 2008 posted a smaller win than either of Bush's here, but he still prevailed easily, 53%-45%, over Democrat Barack Obama.

The new congressman from the 52nd District is Duncan D. Hunter, a Republican who was elected to the seat that his father held for 28 years. The senior Duncan Hunter, the longtime chairman of the House Armed Services Committee, gave up the seat to compete for the GOP presidential nomination in 2008.

Hunter grew up in El Cajon and got a degree in business administration from San Diego State Uni-versity. He worked in the computer industry for several years during the technology boom of the late 1990s. He says that the September 11 terrorist attacks prompted him to rethink his career plans. The next day, Hunter quit his job and enlisted in the Marine Corps. After completing officer training, Hunter was commissioned as a lieutenant. He was deployed to Iraq in 2003, served in Baghdad after the fall of the city, and in 2004 fought in the battle of Falluja. In 2006, he was promoted to captain and placed on reserve status. But shortly after announcing his candidacy in March 2007 for his father's House seat, Hunter was again called to active duty, this time in Afghanistan. Hunter was prohibited from any cam-paign activities, including fundraising and planning, and held only one event before leaving. In his ab-sence, the management of his nascent campaign fell to his wife, Margaret Hunter. She took over all ap-pearances and campaign duties in addition to caring for their three young children. When Hunter called home from Afghanistan, it was still illegal for him even to inquire how the campaign was going, and he remained largely in the dark about its status until his duty ended in December 2007. He returned home to resume campaigning full-time.

In the June primary, Hunter faced two competitors, Santee Councilman Brian Jones and San Diego Board of Education President Bob Watkins. Although both were well known locally and campaigned ac-tively, Hunter and his family surrogates effectively ran on the basis of his military credentials. Hunter also benefited from his father's political and congressional connections, raising nearly three times as much money as his Republican challengers, including contributions from the political action committees of members of Congress and a $2,300 contribution from former Secretary of Defense Donald Rumsfeld. Hunter cruised to victory in the June primary with 72% percent of the vote. His closest challenger, Jones, got 16%. In the general election, Hunter faced another military veteran, retired Navy SEAL Commander Mike Lumpkin, a former Republican turned Democrat. He agreed with Hunter on many issues, including gun rights and the need for a fence along the U.S.-Mexico border. But national Democrats paid little attention to the contest, and Hunter prevailed in the predominantly Republican district, 56%-39%.

Hunter shares not only his father's name, but also many of his political beliefs. Both were 31 years old when they were elected to Congress. He followed in his father's footsteps with a seat on the Armed Services Committee, and cites national security as his top priority. "I can tell you what the guys on the ground, the men and women out there fighting, actually need," Hunter said. "We have a whole lot of brass out there at the Pentagon and in the DOD [Department of Defense] who haven't left their offices in six or seven years." Hunter's other interests include tougher immigration laws and finding ways to halt the outflow of jobs overseas.

In one of his first legislative efforts, Hunter in 2009 introduced a bill to bar the transfer of terrorism suspects from the federal prison camp in Guantanamo to San Diego County. He said that the Obama administration's proposal would make the region a bigger target for terrorists crossing the U.S.-Mexico border. "The decision to close the facility was made without any consideration for the security risks and legal consequences that will undoubtedly arise," Hunter told the *San Diego Union-Tribune*, accusing Obama of making a "purely political" decision. "If it weren't, President Obama would have more closely examined the issue before rushing to a decision on his first day in office."

FIFTY-THIRD DISTRICT

Susan Davis (D)

Elected 2000, 5th term; b. April 13, 1944, Cambridge, MA; home, San Diego; U. of CA, B.A. 1964, U. of NC, M.A. 1968; Jewish; married (Steven); 2 children.

Elected Office: San Diego School Bd., 1983–92; CA Assembly, 1994–2000.

Professional Career: Devel. assoc., KPBS Radio, 1980–82.; Exec. dir., Aaron Price Fellows, 1990–94.

DC Office: 1526 LHOB, 20515, 202-225-2040; Fax: 202-225-2948; Web site: www.house.gov/susandavis.

State Offices: San Diego, 619-280-5353.

Committees: *Armed Services* (13th of 35 D): Military Personnel (Chmn); Oversight & Investigations. *Education & Labor* (13th of 29 D): Early Childhood, Elementary & Secondary Education; Higher Education, Lifelong Learning & Competitiveness. *House Administration* (5th of 6 D): Elections.

Group Ratings

	ADA	ACLU	AFS	LCV	ITIC	NTU	COC	ACU	CFG	FRC
2008	95	100	100	100	71	6	56	0	4	5
2007	90	—	100	95	—	6	55	0	12	—

National Journal Ratings

	2007 LIB — 2007 CONS		2008 LIB — 2008 CONS	
Economic	67%	— 31%	81%	— 15%
Social	74%	— 25%	82%	— 0%
Foreign	65%	— 33%	78%	— 17%
Composite	70%	— 31%	85%	— 15%

Key Votes of the 110th Congress

1. Increase minimum wage	Y	5. Share immigration data	N	9. Withdraw troops 8/08	Y
2. Expand SCHIP	Y	6. Foreign aid abortion ban	N	10. No operations in Iran	Y
3. Raise CAFE standards	Y	7. Ban gay bias in workplace	Y	11. Free trade with Peru	Y
4. Bail out financial markets	Y	8. Repeal D.C. gun law	N	12. Overhaul FISA	Y

Election Results

2008 general	Susan Davis (D)	161,315	(68%)	($455,081)
	Michael Crimmins (R)	64,658	(27%)	($23,617)
	Edward Teyssier (Lib)	9,569	(4%)	
2008 primary	Susan Davis (D)	43,171	(88%)	
	Mike Copass (D)	6,113	(12%)	

Prior Winning Percentages: 2006 (68%); 2004 (66%); 2002 (62%); 2000 (50%)

Population		Race/Ethnicity		Work	
Pop. 2007:	634,840	White:	50.8%	Private:	71.2%
Change since 2000:	Down 0.7%	Black:	7.1%	Government:	21.2%
Urban:	99.9%	Hispanic:	30.4%	Self-employed:	7.4%
Rural:	0.1%	Asian:	8.7%	Blue collar:	16.3%
Area size:	251 sq. mi.	Native Am.:	0.4%	White collar:	61.6%
		Hawaiian:	0.4%	Khaki collar:	4.2%
Age		Two+ races:	1.9%	Other:	18.0%
Median age:	31.2 yrs.			Median income:	$48,009
More than 65 yrs:	9.5%	*Ancestry*		Median home value:	$546,000
Less than 18 yrs:	19.3%	German:	9.5%	Poverty:	18.4%
		Irish:	8.0%		
Education		English:	6.5%	**Military Veterans**	
H.S. grad:	84.4%			% of Pop:	10.7%
College grad:	37.2%				
Grad degree:	14.5%				

When the United States was dictating the terms of the Treaty of Guadalupe Hidalgo in 1848, after its successful war with Mexico, it made sure the southern boundary of its new California territory was just south of the port of San Diego. This is one of three splendid natural harbors on the Pacific Coast, and in 1914 the Marine Corps established a base on North Island. This was just the first of many military bases in San Diego, with its mild climate, deep harbor, and plentiful land for aircraft maneuvers.

2008 Presidential Vote
Obama (D) 177,863   (68%)
McCain (R)...............................77,930   (30%)

2004 Presidential Vote
Kerry (D)...............................146,160   (61%)
Bush (R) 89,890   (38%)

Cook Partisan Voting Index: D + 14

This has been the major West Coast U.S. Navy base for more than 50 years, the second-largest Navy port behind Norfolk, and home to about 30,000 active-duty Navy and Marine Corps personnel on shore. Also based here are the retired aircraft carriers *Midway* and *Constellation*, plus the *Ronald Reagan*, which was commissioned in 2003, with a flight deck that covers 4.5 acres.

The port and Navy base in the sheltered harbor remain the central focus of a rapidly growing metropolis that now stretches far inland and to the north. Downtown there are post-modern buildings like the Horton Plaza amid a few well-preserved early-20th-century relics like the Spreckels Theatre. Across the harbor, on the sand spit that guards it against the ocean, is the white frame castle of the Hotel Del Coronado, with its surprisingly dark wooden interior—the U.S.'s largest wooden structure, opened in 1888 and a favored resort of past American presidents; the town of Coronado has long been a favorite retirement mecca for Navy admirals and captains.

San Diego is not all harbor and Navy. To the north, the Pacific waves pound against the beach beneath erose cliffs of unique rock formations along the coast. Located here are some of San Diego's great cultural institutions: the Scripps Institute of Oceanography, the University of California San Diego campus, the Salk Institute, and the Torrey Pines reserve, home of the unique, wide-spreading pine tree. To the south are raffish Mission Beach; Ocean Beach, with its strong rip currents; and Point Loma, overlooking the entrance to the harbor. The weather—a sunny 70 degrees most of the time—lures tourists and new residents. But this also is a working town, a sophisticated high-tech center with growing biotechnology, electronics, software, and telecommunications industries. It is a manufacturing center as well, with maquiladora factories clustering near the Mexican border. The city has had a long-running battle over proposals to expand or move Lindbergh Field, its landlocked airport, with options ranging from a floating airport in the ocean to a site nearly 100 miles away in Imperial County.

The 53rd Congressional District of California—and the only 53rd district in American history—consists of the center of San Diego, the San Diego beaches from Blacks Beach to Ocean Beach, the port, La Jolla beach (but not the neighborhood itself), and Balboa Park. It includes the heavily Latino neighborhoods south and east of downtown; the Gaslamp District, with its glitzy nightlife scene; and the older neighborhoods of University Heights and East San Diego. Altogether, 85% of the district's population is within the city limits. It also includes Coronado and Imperial Beach, just north of the Mexican border, and the inland suburbs of La Presa and Lemon Grove, site of a celebrated school-desegregation case in the 1930s. The district is 30% Hispanic. Historically, this was a Republican district, but with coastal California's trend toward cultural liberalism and with more Democratic areas added in the most recent redistricting, it is now solidly Democratic. In 2004, Democratic nominee John Kerry won the district 61%-38%, and in 2008, Democrat Barack Obama won it 68%-30%.

The congresswoman from the 53rd District is Susan Davis, a Democrat first elected in 2000. She grew up in Richmond, Calif., the daughter of a pediatrician. She graduated from the University of California at Berkeley and got a degree in social work at the University of North Carolina. After she married, she and her husband lived for a time in Japan while he served as an Air Force doctor during the Vietnam War. In 1972, they moved to San Diego. She was a producer for a local television station while also volunteering in civic groups, including as president of the local League of Women Voters. In 1983, she was elected to the San Diego school board. In 1994, she won the first of three terms in the California Assembly, where she chaired the Consumer Protection Committee. Facing term limits, Davis in 2000 challenged U.S. Rep. Brian Bilbray, a Republican who had won three close elections. She portrayed him as too conservative for the district, though he took liberal and moderate positions on abortion rights and environment protection. But Bilbray had voted with conservatives to impeach President Clinton in 1998, and Davis attacked him as well for supporting bills that would deny citizenship to U.S.-born children of illegal immigrants. The AFL-CIO ran so much advertising on her behalf that Davis requested it stop. Davis won 50%-46%, and has been re-elected easily. Bilbray returned to Congress in June 2006 when he won a special election in the neighboring 50th District.

In the House, Davis has a liberal voting record but tends to be more centrist on foreign policy. Assigned to the Armed Services and Education and Labor committees, she set herself priorities that have included higher military pay, increased aid for school districts with a large military presence, increased student loans, and incentives for better teachers. She angered organized labor and some Democratic activists by voting to give President George W. Bush wide authority to negotiate international trade deals, which labor unions opposed. She called the vote "agonizing," but one that served the interests of a city that has been built on trade. Organized labor rescinded its endorsement of her. In 2005, Davis went in a different direction on trade by voting against the Central American Free Trade Agreement.

On Armed Services, she voted against the use of force in Iraq in 2002 and against Bush's troop "surge" strategy in 2007, but Davis stopped short of cutting off funding for the war, which some Democrats advocated. In 2005, she criticized committee Republicans for seeking to limit women from service in combat units in Iraq. She also sponsored a bill to prevent interest from accruing on student loans held by military personnel while they are serving combat tours. And, with Rep. Ginny Brown-Waite, R-Fla., Davis won House passage of a bill to increase the maximum loan amount that the Veterans Administration approves for home mortgages.

Davis also serves on the House Administration Committee, where she proposed allowing universal vote by mail in federal elections. On a major regional controversy, she won enactment in 2007 of a measure that had the effect of killing a proposed Foothill South toll road that would have crossed a coastal nature preserve in southern Orange County.

★ COLORADO ★

With its distinct and variable geography, its sea of Great Plains, and its majestic Rocky Mountains, Colorado has also been at the front edge of economic, cultural, and political change in the West. With vistas of vast emptiness, it is mostly an urban state. More than half of its 5 million people live in metropolitan Denver, and four-fifths of them are in the urban strip paralleling the Front Range, where the Rockies rise suddenly from the mile-high plateau. The state's very ruggedness is inviting more settlement. While the eastern Plains continue to lose population, the valley crevices between the mountains are filling up with second-home condominiums and ranchettes, and the rolling land on three sides of metro Denver is being platted into subdivisions.

Colorado started off with a boom, and its recent history has been one of booms punctuated by pauses of moderate growth. The first boom came after the discovery of gold and silver in the Rocky Mountains. Evidence of this mining boom can still be seen in the opera houses and storefronts of Cripple Creek and Central City, Aspen, and Telluride, built when Denver was just a village on the creek that is the South Platte River. Then Denver grew as a meatpacking, banking, and manufacturing center, and also as the state capital and regional headquarters of the federal government. After that came the 1970s' spike in energy prices, and Colorado's natural gas, oil, and shale sparked a boom. Half a million people moved in and the Denver skyline sprouted buildings overlooking the Capitol's golden dome, while entrepreneurs built premier ski resorts and year-round mountain residences. Colorado's economy sagged during the period of low energy prices in the 1980s, but with an influx of telecommunications and high-tech companies, it rebounded in the 1990s. The visible signs of this boom are all around—in the skyscrapers of downtown Denver, bearing at various times, the names of Qwest and TCI and other high-tech companies; in the retro Coors Field baseball park set amid Denver's LoDo neighborhood, where warehouses have been renovated into restaurants and clubs; in the startling architecture of the Denver International Airport far out in the plains; in the sprawling Denver Tech Center south of the city; and in the fast-growing tracts of subdivisions and office parks in Douglas County on the city's southern rim. Colorado's economy grew robustly in the 1990s, and the state attracted well-educated newcomers from around the country, including many from California. It ranked No. 1 in high-tech workers per capita and third in venture capital financing per capita. Without a doubt, the bursting of the high-tech bubble hit Colorado hard. In 2001 and 2002 the state painfully shed high-tech jobs, and since then has settled back into a pattern of moderate growth.

Although Colorado ranks among the top states in economic development and venture capital, with high salaries and low unemployment, the state's in-migration was not as robust as that of Arizona or Nevada over the past decade. So the housing bubble did not get as big in Denver as it did in Phoenix or Las Vegas; the recession was slow in coming and did not hit as hard as it did in those cities. With its relatively young and highly educated population and its stunning environment, Colorado is also the leanest state, with the lowest incidence of obesity, and arguably the healthiest, with relatively low rates of cancer and heart disease. Coloradans like to ride, jog, bike, and, of course, ski. There are bike paths not only in Denver, but also in the mountains, and Boulder is a national center for bungee jumping, mountain biking, snowshoe running, and hot-air ballooning.

Colorado has been reshaped, economically and politically, by its successive waves of newcomers. The conservative and boosterish Colorado of the 1960s was transformed in the 1970s by a wave of young liberal migrants who swept the state's politics by calling for environmental protections and slow growth. Its national leaders reflected this trend—slow-growth Gov. Dick Lamm, Sen. Gary Hart, Rep. Patricia Schroeder, Rep. Tim Wirth. Democrats controlled the governorship for 24 years but Republicans held on to the Legislature. Then, in the 1990s, a new wave of migrants—tech-savvy, family-oriented cultural conservatives looking for an environment to prosper—moved Colorado's politics to the right. In the 1990s, public school enrollment rose 14%, while private school enrollment was up 33% and the number of home-schooled children tripled. If the spirit of the 1970s newcomers was embodied in Boulder, with its pedestrian mall, outdoor sports shops, and vegetarian restaurants, and was dominated politically by environmentalist liberals, the spirit of the 1990s newcomers was embodied in Colorado Springs, the home of the Air Force Academy, Fort Carson, and the Focus on the Family advocacy organization, and was dominated politically by religious conservatives. Both of these politically divergent communities have some reason to believe that they exemplify the state. Colorado elections can be viewed as contests to determine which one does.

The victories of the liberal Democrats in the 1970s, starting with the 1972 referendum blocking the Winter Olympics from Denver, were followed by a long period in which Republicans held control of the Legislature and the congressional delegation. The victories of the conservative Republicans in the 1990s, starting with the 1990 referendum imposing term limits and the 1992 Taxpayers' Bill of Rights requiring referenda to raise taxes, have been followed by a resurgence of the Democratic Party, led by liberal entrepreneurs such as Jared Polis, now the 2nd District representative. Polis was one of the "Gang of Four,"

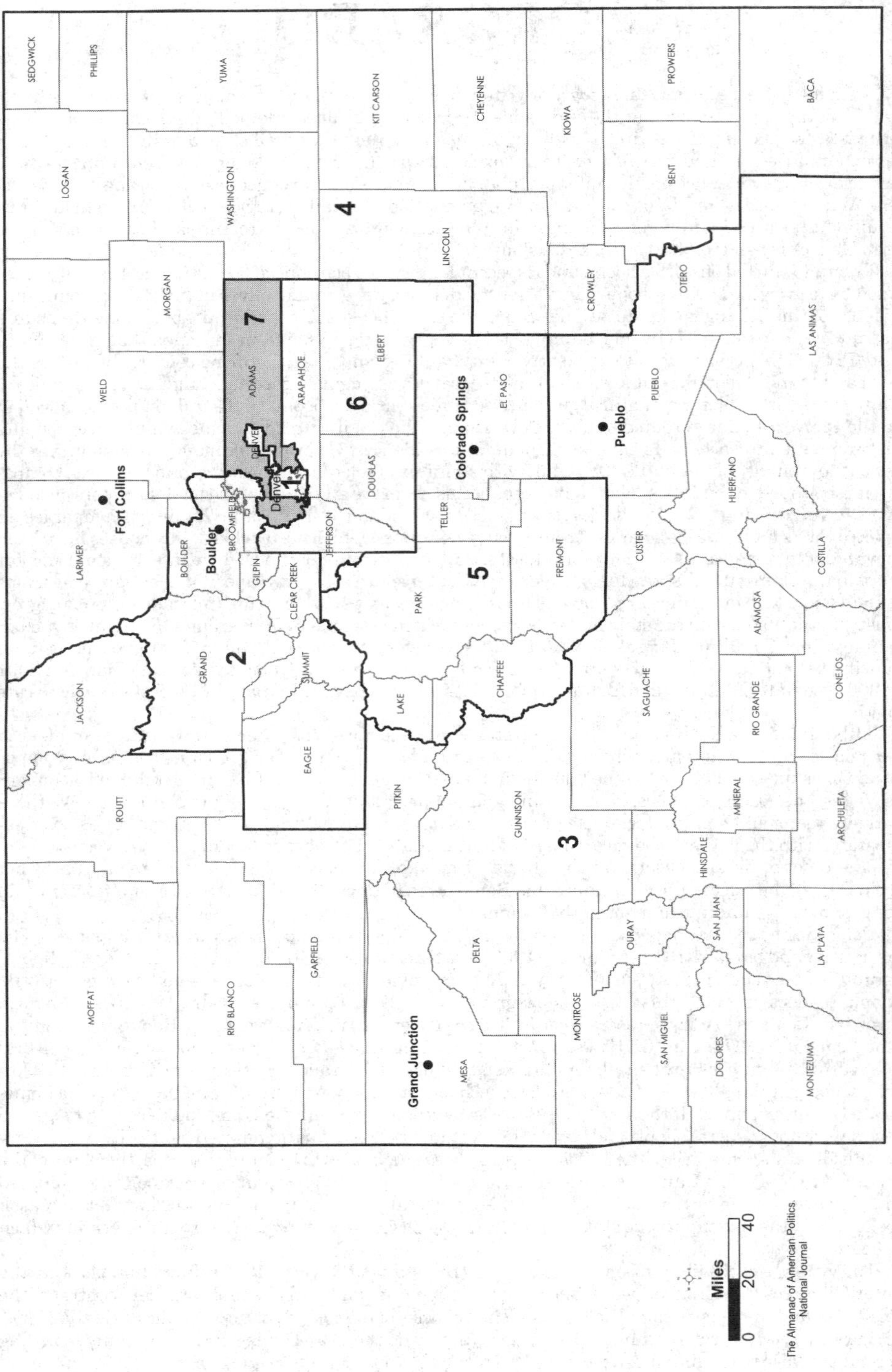

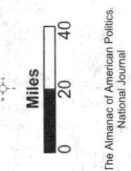

SEDGWICK

PHILLIPS

YUMA

KIT CARSON

CHEYENNE

KIOWA

PROWERS

BACA

LOGAN

WASHINGTON

MORGAN

4

LINCOLN

CROWLEY

BENT

OTERO

WELD

ADAMS

ARAPAHOE

ELBERT

6

Colorado Springs

EL PASO

PUEBLO

LAS ANIMAS

Fort Collins

BROOMFIELD

DENVER

Denver

DOUGLAS

Pueblo

HUERFANO

LARIMER

BOULDER

Boulder

GILPIN

JEFFERSON

TELLER

5

FREMONT

CUSTER

COSTILLA

GRAND

CLEAR CREEK

PARK

ALAMOSA

2

SUMMIT

CHAFFEE

SAGUACHE

RIO GRANDE

CONEJOS

JACKSON

LAKE

ROUTT

EAGLE

PITKIN

GUNNISON

3

MINERAL

ARCHULETA

HINSDALE

GARFIELD

DELTA

OURAY

SAN JUAN

LA PLATA

MOFFAT

RIO BLANCO

MONTROSE

SAN MIGUEL

Grand Junction

MESA

DOLORES

MONTEZUMA

Congressional district boundaries were first effective for 2002.

District 7 is highlighted for visibility.

Miles

0   20   40

The Almanac of American Politics,
National Journal

a group of high-powered political contributors who financed the resurgence of the party. The other three were QuarkXPress founder Tim Gill, medical technology heiress Patricia Stryker, and geophysicist, and MicroMAX software creator Rutt Bridges. The group nurtured a web of liberal activist organizations, framed issues, chose their targets shrewdly, and helped reshape the political landscape. In 2002, when Republicans were dominant, Gov. Bill Owens was re-elected overwhelmingly, the GOP had majorities in both houses of the Legislature, and held both U.S. Senate seats and five of the seven House seats. Today, it's just the other way around. Democratic Gov. Bill Ritter has high job ratings. Democrats have majorities in both houses of the Legislature, and they hold both U.S. Senate seats and five of the seven House seats.

These Democratic gains made Colorado an obvious target state for 2008. The Democratic National Committee had that in mind when it chose to hold the 2008 national convention in Denver, unbothered by the fact that the only previous national convention held there, in 1908, nominated the losing ticket of William Jennings Bryan and John W. Kern. In the Democratic primary, Barack Obama's campaign targeted Colorado early on. He beat Hillary Rodham Clinton 2-to-1 in the state's Super Tuesday Democratic caucuses, which attracted 120,000 people, more than in any other caucus state except Iowa and Minnesota. His campaign worked with the like-minded liberal groups that had sprung up during the decade. Colorado remained a target throughout the general election as well, but Obama beat John McCain by a solid 54%-45%.

Obama was helped by the changing demographics of the state. Colorado has one of the nation's youngest populations, with large university enclaves. Its electorate is more than 10% Latino. People support environmental causes of all kinds, sometimes to the point of endangering their own species. Boulder used to protect the local bears until they killed not only dogs and cats but also a jogger. Denver and Boulder attract young professionals imbued with liberal values; the ski resorts—Telluride, Aspen, Vail, Crested Butte, Steamboat Springs—are inhabited by the wealthy and the people who wait on them in restaurants, and both groups tend to be Democratic in Colorado. But the liberal impulse does not prevail on all issues. In addition to the military families and religious conservatives of Colorado Springs, farm counties in the east and mining counties in the west reject environmental measures that hurt their local economies. Colorado had 14 ballot propositions in the 2008 election, and the Left did not prevail on all of them. Voters rejected 58%-42% an amendment that would have put higher taxes on oil and gas producers; they rejected by only 51%-49% another measure that would have barred the state from using racial quotas and preferences. Voters defeated a right-to-work law opposed by unions 56%-44%.

Population		Household Income		Work	
Pop. 2007:	4,767,161	Under $15k:	11.5%	Private:	77.7%
State rank:	22nd of 50	$15k to $50k:	34.7%	Government:	14.6%
Change since 2000:	Up 10.8%	$50k to $100k:	32.5%	Self-employed:	7.4%
Urban:	80.4%	$100k to $150k:	17.5%	Unemployment (3-yr. average):	4.1%
Rural:	19.6%	Over $150k:	3.9%	Poverty:	11.8%
Native of state:	42.2%	Median income:	$54,262	Blue collar:	20.3%
Not a citizen:	7.0%			White collar:	62.6%
Area size:	104,094 sq. mi.	**Home Value**		Khaki collar:	0.7%
		Under $100k:	9.0%	Other:	16.5%
Most populous cities		$100k to $300k:	59.0%		
1. Denver	576,842	$300k to $500k:	21.4%	**Age**	
2. Colorado Springs	390,397	$500k to $1 mil:	8.6%	Median age:	35.5 yrs.
3. Aurora	296,999	Over $1 million:	1.9%	More than 65 yrs:	10.0%
4. Lakewood	143,157	Median:	$230,400	Less than 18 yrs:	24.7%

Race/Ethnicity				Military Veterans		Registered Voters in 2008	
White:	71.5%	*Language*		% of Pop:	11.6%	D:	1,056,077 (32.9%)
Black:	3.7%	English:	83.0%	*Veterans by Period*		R:	1,065,150 (33.2%)
Hispanic:	19.6%	Spanish:	12.1%	WWII and before:	9.3%	Other:	1,089,022 (33.9%)
Asian:	2.6%	Asian:	1.8%	Korea:	9.4%	Voter turnout:	2,401,361
Native Am.:	0.6%	Other		Vietnam:	33.9%	Turnout as % of	
Hawaiian:	0.1%	European	2.4%	Gulf (pre-2001):	14.9%	voting age:	64.3%
Two+ races:	1.7%	**Education**		Gulf (post-2001):	8.1%	**General Assembly**	
Ancestry		H.S. grad:	88.3%	Peace time:	24.5%	Senate:	21 D 14 R
German:	17.9%	College grad:	34.6%			House:	38 D 27 R
Irish:	9.9%	Grad degree:	12.3%				
English:	9.3%						

Presidential politics   Colorado started the decade as a state that lured Democratic presidential campaigns with a promise of being competitive and seemed likely to end the decade as a state that Republican presidential campaigns consider unwinnable.

In retrospect, Republican George W. Bush's 51%-42% win here in 2000 was misleadingly large: Ralph Nader won 5% in that race, and those votes were likely to go Democratic in the future. In mountain communities and on the rural plains, Democrat Al Gore was hurt in 2000 by the environmental policies of the Clinton administration, which would be forgotten as time went on. In 2004, Democrat John

2008 Presidential Vote		
Obama (D) 1,288,576	(54%)
McCain (R)....................1,073,589	(45%)
2004 Presidential Vote		
Bush (R)........................1,101,255	(52%)
Kerry (D)........................1,001,732	(47%)

Kerry's campaign failed to target Colorado until late in the game but still managed to increase the party's margins by 34,000 votes in Denver and 33,000 in Boulder County, while Bush's margins went up only 17,000 votes in El Paso County and 12,000 in Douglas County. Bush's 52%-47% win over Kerry looked much like taking Nader's percentage in 2000 and adding it to Gore's.

In 2008, the real question was whether Colorado was ever in reach for Republican John McCain. Polling just after the Republican National Convention suggested that it might be, but McCain fell behind significantly after the crisis in the financial markets broke later in September. Liberals were energized and conservatives were dejected. Turnout was up from 2004 by 14% in Denver County and by 8% in Boulder County, where population growth has been low. It also surged well ahead of population growth in the Denver suburbs. Barack Obama's percentage increase over Kerry's in 2004 was biggest in metro Denver and the Front Range from Fort Collins down to Colorado Springs. Obama carried all of the suburban counties except fast-growing Douglas County, where he got a respectable 41% of the vote.

Nebraska and Maine are the only states that split their electoral vote, and as aficionados of politics know, Nebraska's 2nd Congressional District voted for Obama in 2008 and gave him its one electoral vote, while McCain got the state's other four. In 2004, Coloradoans had debated the idea of splitting their state's electoral votes. The proposition was on the ballot that year, and was vociferously opposed by Republicans such as Gov. Owens, who feared that Bush would lose two or three electoral votes if it passed. But as the campaign went on, and Colorado seemed within Kerry's reach, some prominent state Democrats started to oppose the idea too. Support for the measure slipped in the opinion polls from 51% in mid-September to 36% in late October. The proposition was defeated 65%-35%, losing in both Republican and Democratic counties. That defeat may have doomed similar efforts in other states. Partisans on both sides will oppose such a move in a closely divided state, and minority party members in a state will find it hard to muster sufficient votes to pass it.

Colorado has had an early March presidential primary since 1992, when long-shot California Democrat Jerry Brown won it. It has not attracted much attention since. In 2003, to save money, the Legislature voted to eliminate its presidential primary in 2004. Three years later, the Legislature passed a law leaving it to the major parties to decide when to hold 2008 caucuses; both selected February 5. The Democratic caucuses attracted 120,000 voters, the Republican caucuses only 70,000, a sign of the prevailing trend in a state where Republicans four years earlier had 120,000 participants. Enthusiasm for Obama and his campaign's organizational skill gave him a 67%-32% victory over Hillary Rodham Clinton in the primary. Ninety percent of the votes were cast in 13 of the 64 counties, and Obama carried them all except industrial Pueblo. Clinton ran well among Latinos but not among other ethnic groups. The highest turnouts were in Denver and Boulder counties, where Obama won 69% and 74%, respectively. Mitt Romney, the only Republican with much of an organization in Colorado, won the Republican caucuses with 60% of the vote; McCain got only 18%, and Mike Huckabee got 13%.

Congressional districting   Colorado gained a House seat from the 2000 census, just as it had from the 1970 and 1980 censuses. In 2000, Republicans would have controlled the redistricting process if they had not lost control of the state Senate that year. When the Legislature proved unable to reach a compromise, a state court judge selected a Democratic-designed plan. The judge did not make major changes in the existing districts, but Republicans responded angrily. They wanted the new district drawn in the fast-growing Republican counties on the south side of Denver. Instead, the newly created 7th District was anchored in the inner Denver suburbs to the north of the city, making it highly competitive.

111th Congress Lineup	
5 D	2 R
110th Congress Lineup	
4 D	3 R

The Republicans' one-seat takeover of the Senate in 2002 gave them the opportunity to take another crack at the congressional map. They prepared a new plan, and introduced and passed it in late May 2003, in the final days of the legislative session. Then-Attorney General Ken Salazar, a Democrat, sued in the Colorado courts, and in December 2003, the state Supreme Court threw out the new map on the grounds that the state constitution prohibited more than one plan every 10 years.

Colorado's Democratic trend has made obsolete many of the political judgments that influenced redistricting in recent years. The 3rd District went Democratic when Republican Rep. Scott McInnis retired. Likewise, the 7th District went Democratic when GOP Rep. Bob Beauprez ran for governor in 2006. The

4th District went Democratic when Republican Rep. Marilyn Musgrave was defeated by a solid margin in 2008. Only the 5th District (Colorado Springs) and the 6th District (southern Denver suburbs) remained in Republican hands at the end of 2008.

Colorado is not expected to gain a House seat in the 2010 census. If Gov. Ritter is re-elected and Democrats retain their legislative majorities, they will control the redistricting process, and for the first time since the 1970s, a court may not have to draw the lines. Democrats might want to put most of Colorado Springs and Douglas counties into one district and thus reduce the Republicans to one seat, but that strategy could leave too much still-Republican suburban territory in Democratic districts for comfort.

Governor

Bill Ritter (D)

Elected 2006, term expires Jan. 2011, 1st term; b. Sept. 6, 1956, Denver; home, Denver; CO St. U., B.A. 1978; U. of CO, J.D. 1981; Catholic; married (Jeannie); 4 children.

Elected Office: Denver dist. atty., 1993–2004.

Professional Career: Denver chief deputy dist. atty., 1981–87, 1992–93; Catholic missionary to Zambia, 1987–90; Asst. U.S. atty., 1990–92; Practicing atty., 2005–06.

Office: 136 State Capitol, Denver, 80203, 303-866-2471; Fax: 303-866-2003; Web site: www.colorado.gov/governor.

Election Results

2006 general	Bill Ritter (D)	888,095	(57%)
	Bob Beauprez (R)	618,342	(40%)
2006 primary	Bill Ritter (D)	unopposed	

Bill Ritter, a Democrat, was elected governor in 2006. He grew up on a five-acre wheat farm in eastern Arapahoe County, the sixth of 12 children. His father worked the farm and earned extra money as a heavy-equipment operator. An alcoholic, he left the family when Ritter was 13. (The family reconciled in his father's later years.) Ritter's mother applied for welfare and worked as a bookkeeper, while he and his siblings got jobs to support the household. Ritter found work in construction at age 14. He then won a scholarship to a Catholic prep school in San Antonio, but after two years decided to return home. He joined the local pipe-layers union at age 18 and worked his way through Colorado State University and later through law school at the University of Colorado.

After earning his law degree in 1981, Ritter joined the Denver district attorney's office. He rose to chief deputy prosecutor. In 1987, Ritter shocked his colleagues by quitting and moving with his wife, Jeannie, and young son to Zambia, where the couple volunteered for three years as Catholic missionaries to expand a food-distribution and nutrition center. While Ritter was driving slowly through a crowd, a man abruptly stepped in front of the vehicle and was killed. Car accidents were common, and Ritter was cleared of any wrongdoing. But Ritter, who rarely talks of the incident, later told the *Denver Post* he was devastated: "It is a very big tragedy."

In 1990, he returned home to Colorado to work as a prosecutor in the U.S attorney's office, and two years later, he rejoined the Denver district attorney's office. In 1993, after Ritter's boss left for private practice, Democratic Gov. Roy Romer appointed Ritter as his successor. Ritter was elected to the position three times and served until 2004, when he was term limited.

In 2006, term limits also prevented Republican Gov. Bill Owens from seeking a third term. Ritter jumped into the race to succeed him in May 2005, which gave him an early start in organizing a campaign. Party leaders worried about his abortion stance. He was personally opposed to abortion but said he would enforce *Roe v. Wade*, the Supreme Court case that legalized abortion across the country; he also said that if *Roe v. Wade* were overturned, he would sign a law banning abortion except in cases of rape or incest or to save the life of the mother. Some Democrats, worried that he was not supportive enough of abortion rights, urged him to change his position or drop out of the race. But Ritter would not switch, although he did not embrace the term "pro-life" or the anti-abortion-rights agenda. He also picked as his running mate Barbara O'Brien, the head of a children's advocacy group who supported abortion rights. Ritter won the state party's endorsement in May 2006.

Ritter's Republican opponent, two-term Rep. Bob Beauprez, had a much harder time winning his party's nomination, and the primary fight required him to court anti-tax and social conservatives. Beauprez faced former University of Denver President Marc Holtzman, who criticized him for his opposition to a 2005 referendum that amended the 1992 Taxpayer Bill of Rights to allow budget surpluses to be tapped to pay for health care, transportation and education rather than be refunded to taxpayers. Beauprez won the state GOP convention 72%-28%, but Holtzman's criticism of "Both Ways Bob" stuck with Beauprez into the general election campaign. By the end of the summer, a series of gaffes was taking a toll. In a media interview, Beauprez incorrectly suggested that 70% of African-American pregnancies end in abortion. In August, he picked first-term Mesa County Commissioner Janet Rowland as his running mate. She had once ignited controversy by comparing gay marriage to bestiality, saying, "Do we allow a man to marry a sheep?"

By July, Ritter had raised $2 million, nearly matching Beauprez, and had run a solid campaign. He had won friends in the business community with his efforts to keep the Taxpayer Bill of Rights intact. When Beauprez accused Ritter of supporting amnesty for illegal immigrants, Ritter countered that a Republican Congress had failed to address the issue. Then in October, the Federal Bureau of Investigation began a criminal probe into whether a federal agent had illegally supplied Beauprez's campaign with information that was used in an ad attacking Ritter's prosecution of an illegal immigrant. Ritter's campaign quickly cut its own spot asking, "How can we trust him to be governor?" The unpopularity of President Bush and the Iraq war exacerbated Beauprez's difficulty getting traction. Ritter won a lopsided 57%-40% victory, winning 38 of 64 counties. For the first time in 40 years, Democrats had control of the governor's office and both chambers of the Legislature. Ritter lost only Colorado Springs, Douglas County, Grand Junction and the lightly populated eastern plains.

The first governor in three decades not to come out of the Legislature, Ritter had a ready-made agenda. He had campaigned on the "Colorado Promise," a series of policy objectives that included renewable energy, education reform, affordable health care and highway funding. After his election, Ritter named veteran former legislator Norma Anderson, a moderate Republican, to his transition team. In 2008, he severed ties with his campaign manager after learning that the aide had embezzled funds from Ritter's inaugural fund.

Ritter has focused on renewable-energy development, signing a bill requiring utility companies to get 20% of their power from renewable resources by 2020, the first such law in the nation. In April 2008, he signed a bill that established a goal of a 20% reduction in greenhouse gas emissions from Colorado by 2020 and an 80% reduction by 2050. His 2008 budget included $3.5 million to fund bioscience and clean energy, which business leaders praised as the most aggressive initiative in those fields in a decade. Ritter suffered a setback in 2008 when a statewide amendment he had backed to end a tax break for oil companies lost on the ballot by 3-to-2. Oil companies had waged a campaign to keep their tax break. In 2007, Ritter led a trade mission to Japan and China to promote international investment in his state's emerging green-energy and bioscience industries as well as to push for a direct flight from Denver to Tokyo.

His budget for 2008 shifted away from the trend toward "more and bigger prisons" by including the lowest increase in prison funding in years. Ritter instead called for investing $5.9 million in programs aimed at reducing recidivism. As the national economy collapsed in late 2008 and early 2009, he was forced to rework his budget to cover an expected $600 million gap in 2009 and a $385 million one in 2010. He proposed $1 billion in spending cuts, including $125 million from K-12 education, $200 million from health-care programs, and $100 million from higher education. The budget zeroed out funding for two prisons and eliminated a property-tax break for senior citizens and veterans. It also included furloughs for some state workers and canceled pay raises for them in the next year. His decision to suspend the homestead exemption for seniors and disabled veterans was the most controversial move, sparking a battle with Republican legislators.

In February 2007, Ritter angered labor unions by vetoing a bill that would have made it easier for unions to organize nonunion shops. But he sent them an olive branch that November when he issued an executive order giving unions the right to limited collective bargaining. The order was controversial, because it was crafted in secret without input from the GOP or other lawmakers and because union organizing of any sort raised hackles in a state that traditionally has not been union friendly.

In 2008, Ritter opposed a "Personhood Amendment" to the state constitution that would have defined personhood as beginning at the moment of conception, because it made no exceptions for cases of rape or incest or for when the mother's life was in danger. He called the amendment "bad policy, bad medicine, and bad law." Pro-life groups, including the National Right to Life and the Catholic Church, also opposed the bill, because, in the words of the church, "It does not provide a realistic opportunity for ending abortions in Colorado." The amendment lost 3-to-1.

In 2008, Ritter was rumored to be a dark horse candidate as Democratic nominee Barack Obama considered his vice presidential pick. Some columnists suggested Ritter would be a good selection because of his position on abortion and his Catholic beliefs. He is up for re-election in 2010.

Senior Senator

Mark Udall (D)

Elected 2008, term expires 2014, 1st term; b. July 18, 1950, Tucson, AZ; home, Boulder; Williams Col., B.A. 1972; no religious affiliation; married (Maggie L. Fox); 2 children.

Elected Office: CO House of Reps., 1996–98; U.S. House of Reps., 1998–2008.

Professional Career: CO Outward Bound Course dir., 1975–85, Exec. dir., 1985–95.

DC Office: 317 HSOB, 20510, 202-224-5941; Fax: 202-224-6471; Web site: markudall.senate.gov.

State Offices: Denver, 303-650-7820; Grand Junction, 970-245-9553.

Committees: *Aging (Special)* (9th of 12 D). *Armed Services* (12th of 15 D): Emerging Threats & Capabilities; Readiness & Management Support; Strategic Forces. *Energy & Natural Resources* (12th of 13 D): Energy; National Parks (Chmn); Public Lands & Forests.

Group Ratings (House)

	ADA	ACLU	AFS	LCV	ITIC	NTU	COC	ACU	CFG	FRC
2008	80	89	100	92	86	17	61	13	10	5
2007	90	—	100	95	—	5	60	4	12	—

National Journal Ratings (House)

	2007 LIB	—	2007 CONS		2008 LIB	—	2008 CONS
Economic	61%	—	38%		55%	—	44%
Social	60%	—	40%		54%	—	42%
Foreign	59%	—	41%		50%	—	50%
Composite	60%	—	40%		54%	—	46%

Key Votes of the 110th Congress (House)

1. Increase minimum wage	Y	5. Share immigration data	N	9. Withdraw troops 8/08	Y
2. Expand SCHIP	Y	6. Foreign aid abortion ban	N	10. No operations in Iran	Y
3. Raise CAFE standards	Y	7. Ban gay bias in workplace	Y	11. Free trade with Peru	Y
4. Bail out financial markets	N	8. Repeal D.C. gun law	Y	12. Overhaul FISA	Y

Election Results

2008 general	Mark Udall (D)	1,230,994	(53%)	($12,987,562)
	Bob Schaffer (R)	990,755	(42%)	($7,205,644)
	Douglas Campbell (AC)	59,733	(3%)	
	Bob Kinsey (Green)	50,004	(2%)	
2008 primary	Mark Udall (D)	unopposed		

Prior Winning Percentages: 2006 House (68%); 2004 House (67%); 2002 House (60%); 2000 House (55%); 1998 House (50%)

Mark Udall, Colorado's senior senator, is a Democrat first elected to the House in 1998 and to the Senate in 2008. Udall grew up in Tucson, Ariz., in a family with deep political roots in the West. His grandfather, Levi Stewart Udall, a Republican, was a justice on Arizona's Supreme Court from 1947 to 1960. An uncle, Democrat Stewart Udall, was the representative from the Tucson district from 1955 to 1961 and then secretary of the Interior for eight years. Stewart was succeeded in the House by Morris Udall, Mark's father, who served from 1961 until 1991. He was the longtime Democratic chairman of the Interior Committee and an unsuccessful presidential candidate in 1976. As a child, Mark listened in on living room conversations between his father and prominent political figures like Robert Kennedy and Supreme Court Justice William Douglas. In Tucson, the two Udall brothers lived a bike-ride apart, and young Mark used to ride over to see Stewart's son, cousin Tom Udall, who was elected to the Senate from New Mexico in 2008. Mark Udall says he and his cousin have been as close as brothers throughout their lives.

Udall graduated from Williams College in 1972. The same year, he was arrested for possession of marijuana, and after pleading guilty to a misdemeanor, moved to Boulder, Colo., where he worked for the Colorado Outward Bound School and became an accomplished mountaineer. He has climbed Mount Aconcagua, the highest peak in the Western Hemisphere, and Kanchenjunga, the third-highest peak in the world, and he has scaled the north face, though he did not reach the top, of Mount Everest. He was executive director of the school from 1985 to 1995. In 1996, Udall ran for the state House and with his family's connections raised 40% of his money out of state and won. When 2nd District Democratic Rep.

David Skaggs retired in 1998, Udall ran for his seat against Republican Bob Greenlee, the mayor of Boulder. Udall stressed environmental protection, growth management, and education. Greenlee was popular in usually Democratic Boulder. But Udall won Boulder, and he defeated Greenlee 50%-47%.

In the House, Udall compiled a mostly liberal voting record. On environmental issues, he opposed allowing states to designate roads in wilderness areas, but dismayed some local environmental groups by supporting cutbacks in forests to combat infestation by bark beetles and to reduce the threat of wildfires. He worked with Republican Sen. Wayne Allard on a bipartisan project to convert the Rocky Flats nuclear weapons facility in Colorado into a wildlife refuge. In 2004, he championed Colorado's Amendment 37, which imposed a renewable-energy standard on the state, and he helped persuade the U.S. House to pass renewable-energy standards in 2007 energy legislation.

Udall served on the House Armed Services Committee and voted against the Iraq war resolution in October 2002, citing his father's regret over supporting the Tonkin Gulf resolution in 1964. He later voted against $87 billion in funding for the war. In 2005, he led House efforts to seek a redeployment of U.S. troops from Iraq. But by May 2007, he had softened his anti-war stance somewhat, voting in favor of funding for the war and against an amendment that called for troops to be withdrawn within 180 days. "I'm not going to play chicken when it comes to the needs of the soldiers on the ground. . . . We rushed into this war, and we need to withdraw in a phased fashion so we don't leave the Middle East aflame," he told *The Denver Post*. In response, anti-war protesters stormed his Washington office and were arrested. His analysis changed as events did. In 2007, he called President Bush's increase in troop strength in Iraq "a tragic mistake," while on the television news program *Meet the Press* in September 2008, he said, "The surge has helped. There are other factors in Iraq that have been helpful."

Udall was often mentioned as a contender for statewide office. In 2003, he declined to challenge Republican Sen. Ben Nighthorse Campbell, but the following year, when Campbell suddenly announced he would retire, Udall entered the race. Within 24 hours, however, under pressure from Democrats who thought they needed a more moderate candidate, Udall dropped out and endorsed state Attorney General Ken Salazar, who went on to win the Senate seat in 2004. But Udall made it clear he would run for the Senate seat up in 2008, when Republican Sen. Wayne Allard would be at the end of the two terms he had said he would serve.

Udall was unopposed in the Democratic primary. Former Rep. Scott McInnis, considered the front-runner for the Republican nomination, dropped out of the race, which cleared the way for former Rep. Bob Schaffer, who retired from the House in 2002 in line with his pledge to serve only three terms. In 2004, Schaffer ran for the Senate and lost the nomination to beer-company executive Pete Coors. So, two candidates who were passed over in the 2004 Senate race faced each other in 2008.

There was fairly sharp contrast between the candidates' views, underlined by their political rhetoric. Republicans constantly referred to Udall as a "Boulder liberal," while Democrats referred to Schaffer as "Big Oil Bob." Udall emphasized his support of renewable-energy sources, but said he also supported clean-coal development and nuclear power. In July 2008, he came out for allowing additional forms of recreation beyond skiing, including mountain biking and concerts, in ski-permit areas on U.S. Forest Service land. Schaffer, who had earlier in his career attacked conservation programs as infringement on property rights, cited his work after he left Congress on seismic technology, and said he supported renewable-energy sources. The Democratic Senatorial Campaign Committee ran an ad criticizing Schaffer for supporting tax breaks for energy companies and then subsequently earning $800,000 as an oil-company executive.

In May 2008, gas prices hit $4 a gallon, and public opinion shifted in favor of offshore oil drilling. Schaffer attacked Udall for his long opposition to offshore drilling. In August, as Congress was about to adjourn, Udall cast one of the last votes for the Democratic leadership's move to adjourn without, as Republicans demanded, voting on offshore drilling. Then in mid-August he switched and supported proposals for offshore and more domestic drilling, a move that Schaffer derided as a "fig leaf," according to *The Denver Post*.

When the crisis in the financial markets came to a head in September 2008, Schaffer told *The Denver Post* it was "largely the creation of Congress" and called the proposed $700 billion government bailout of big, private financial institutions "a tragic response to an even greater tragedy." Udall said the crisis was "the Reagan revolution coming to its logical conclusion" and said the bailout was a necessary step.

Udall won 53%-42%, while Democratic presidential nominee Barack Obama was carrying the state 54%-45%. Schaffer ran well ahead in Colorado Springs, in exurban Douglas County and the eastern plains, and also in mining areas on the Western Slope. But Udall carried the other Denver suburbs by impressive margins, and his big margins in ski resort areas and Pueblo enabled him to carry the 3rd Congressional District, something many Democrats feared impossible. It was the widest margin for a Democrat in a Colorado Senate race since Gary Hart's victory in 1974.

So Mark Udall joined cousin Tom in the Senate. Another cousin, with whom they were on good terms, Oregon Republican Sen. Gordon Smith, was defeated for re-election. The two Udalls continued to work out in the gym together. Mark Udall told the newspaper *Politico* that he would bring his Outward Bound spirit to his work in the Senate. He said, "I think what I brought was the sense that you have when you're on the mountain, when you're all tied together on a rope, that you don't cut the rope, you don't leave people behind. . . . So I think my attitude is, everybody with whom you're working, assume they're always going to be a part of your team. Clear the air when necessary, find what things that you have in common and then keep trying to reach the goal together." Udall and new Colorado Sen. Michael Bennet, also a Democrat, were part of the Gang of 20 that negotiated the Senate version of the economic stimulus bill in February 2009. That month, Udall also became chairman of the Energy and Natural Resources Committee's National Parks Subcommittee.

When home-state colleague Ken Salazar was confirmed as Interior secretary and resigned from the Senate in 2009, Udall became a senior senator after just 16 days as a junior senator—a vivid contrast to the likes of Delaware's Joe Biden, who served 28 years as junior senator. Bennet, appointed to replace Salazar, is now the junior senator.

Junior Senator

Michael Bennet (D)

Appointed Jan. 2009, term expires 2010, 1st term; b. Nov. 28, 1964, New Delhi, India; home, Denver; Wesleyan U., B.A. 1987; Yale U., J.D. 1993.; No religious affiliation; married (Susan Daggett); 3 children.

Professional Career: Dep. atty. gen., U.S. Dept. of Justice, 1995–97; Managing dir., Anschutz Investment Co., 1997–2003; Chief of Staff, Denver Mayor John Hickenlooper, 2003–05; Superintendent, Denver Public Schl., 2005–09.

DC Office: 702 HSOB, 20510, 202-224-5852; Fax: 202-228-5036; Web site: bennet.senate.gov.

State Offices: Alamosa, 719-587-0096; Colorado Springs, 719-328-1100; Denver, 303-455-7600; Durango, 970-259-1710; Fort Collins, 970-224-2200; Fort Morgan, 970-542-9446; Grand Junction, 970-241-6631; Pueblo, 719-542-7550.

Committees: *Aging (Special)* (11th of 12 D). *Agriculture, Nutrition & Forestry* (11th of 12 D). *Banking, Housing & Urban Affairs* (13th of 13 D): Financial Institutions; Securities, Insurance & Investment; Security & International Trade & Finance. *Homeland Security & Governmental Affairs* (10th of 10 D): Investigations (Permanent); Oversight of Government Management, the Federal Workforce & the District of Columbia.

Group Ratings and Key Votes: Newly Elected

Election Results

2004 general	Ken Salazar (D)	1,081,188	(51%)	($9,886,551)
	Pete Coors (R)	980,668	(47%)	($7,858,598)
2004 primary	Ken Salazar (D)	173,167	(73%)	
	Mike Miles (D)	63,973	(27%)	

Colorado's junior senator is Michael Bennet, a Democrat appointed by Gov. Bill Ritter in January 2009 to succeed Ken Salazar, who'd been named Interior secretary by President Barack Obama. Bennet was born in New Delhi, India, where his father, Douglas Bennet, was an aide to Amb. Chester Bowles. His mother and her family were Jews who'd emigrated from Poland after World War II. Michael grew up and attended private schools in Washington, D.C., while his father pursued his career in public service. Douglas Bennet was a staffer for Vice President Hubert Humphrey, assistant secretary of state in the Carter administration and later president of National Public Radio. The younger Bennet graduated from Wesleyan University, then was a staffer for Democratic Gov. Richard Celeste of Ohio, a family friend. In 1990, Bennet entered Yale Law School, where he was editor-in-chief of the *Yale Law Journal* (the equivalent of Barack Obama's presidency of the *Harvard Law Review*). He then worked as a law clerk for a federal judge in Baltimore, where he met his wife, Susan Daggett, then joined Lloyd Cutler's law firm in Washington. In 1995 he was named counsel to Deputy Attorney General Jamie Gorelick in the Clinton administration and wrote speeches for Attorney General Janet Reno. In 1997, he moved to Denver, where his wife, a natural resources lawyer, went to work for the Sierra Club Legal Defense Fund. Bennett took a job with the investment company headed by billionaire Philip Anschutz, a political conservative. Bennet had never read a balance sheet, and Anschutz told him to attend accounting school at night at his own expense. Eventually, Bennet got such assignments as restructuring $3 billion in debt for several companies, including Forcenergy, Regal Cinemas, United Artists and Edwards Theaters. He also oversaw the consolidation of the three theater chains into Regal Entertainment Group, the world's largest movie-theater company.

In 2003, an old friend from Wesleyan, John Hickenlooper, was elected Denver mayor and asked Bennet to be his chief of staff. Bennet says he gave up millions in stock options to accept "an opportunity that wouldn't come around again." He worked on balancing the budget, mediating a dispute between United and Frontier airlines at Denver International Airport and brokering agreements with public-employee unions. "I have referred to him as the second mayor, the hidden mayor," Hickenlooper told the *Denver Post*. In 2005, the position of Denver Public Schools superintendent came open, and among the 14 top candidates was Bennet—even though he had no experience in education, had himself attended private schools, and was sending his daughter to a private kindergarten. But he had had no relevant experience for his previous two jobs either and said he was passionately committed to helping children learn. In 2005, the board picked him to head a system of 73,000 students, three-quarters of them Latino or African-American and two-thirds of them eligible for the school lunch program. When he closed the predominately minority Manual High School in 2006, black community leaders protested and called Bennet a "dictator." But the school reopened in 2008 with a new emphasis on student achievement, and Bennet had mended fences with the community leaders. He instituted a "Denver Plan," which boosted performance standards in the schools and created workshops to teach principals how to lead schools to reform. An early-childhood education program was put in place, and more than 90% of five-year-olds got full-day kindergarten. By 2008, metrics showed positive results. Enrollment was at its highest point since 1976, in contrast to falling enrollment in many central-city school systems. Test scores rose faster than or at the state average in 140 of 164 schools. Still, Denver schools performed below statewide levels: Only 46% of Denver students showed proficiency in reading and 35% in math, compared to the statewide averages of 68% and 53%, respectively.

When Illinois Sen. Barack Obama was running for president in 2008, Bennet co-hosted a fundraiser for him, and Bennet was included in the Democratic candidate's weekly education conference calls with innovative big-city school heads. After Obama was elected, Bennet was on the short list for secretary of Education, although Obama ultimately chose Chicago schools chief Arne Duncan. But Bennet was not even considered a long shot for U.S. senator after Obama named Ken Salazar his Interior secretary. That left it up to Democratic Gov. Ritter to appoint a replacement to serve until Salazar's Senate seat came up for re-election in 2010. Bennet had taken on national politics just once, in 2004, when he made a speech before a group of business leaders denouncing the Iraq War and President Bush. In Colorado political circles, Bennet was on exactly no one's radar.

The name most often mentioned was outgoing state House Speaker Andrew Romanoff, who had ties to Democratic politicians and activists across the state. Another possibility was Hickenlooper, Bennet's mentor, who was well-known and popular throughout the state. On the list were other seasoned pols, including Democratic Reps. Ed Perlmutter and John Salazar, the new Interior secretary's brother. Latino leaders let it be known they would like another Latino to take Salazar's place. Others called for the appointment of a woman, like former state Senate President Joan FitzGerald. On Jan. 2, 2009, Ritter astonished just about everyone by naming Bennet, saying he was impressed with his record of bringing diverse interests together to solve problems and by his pragmatic approach to turning around troubled public and private enterprises. Republican leaders relished the prospect of taking on a candidate far less formidable electorally than Hickenlooper or Romanoff in 2010. "What the hell?!?" wrote a blogger on ColoradoPols.com.

Bennet flew to Washington to set up a transition with Salazar's staff, then embarked on a four-city tour of Colorado with Ritter, during which he expressed a willingness to listen and an eagerness to learn. He noted that he had before taken on difficult jobs for which he did not have obvious credentials, with Anschutz's investment company, with Hickenlooper's mayoral administration, and with the Denver public schools. On January 22, he was sworn in as a senator. The other Colorado senator, Democrat Mark Udall, had been elected in November 2008, and so, after just 16 days on the job, Udall became the senior senator from Colorado and Bennet the junior senator. (Vice President Joe Biden, who swore Bennet in, served 28 years before he became the senior senator from Delaware). For five days, Bennet, 44, was the Senate's youngest member, until Kirsten Gillibrand of New York, another appointee, was sworn in.

In several media interviews, Bennet called for a phased withdrawal from Iraq and said that although he would not support repealing the Bush tax cuts because of the potential harm to the shaky economy, he would vote to allow them to expire as stated in the enacting legislation. He also said he would advocate putting in their place tax cuts targeted at the middle class. He voted for the February 2009 economic-stimulus bill, even after the Senate version cut almost half the spending for Colorado's state government. On an important state issue, Bennet said he would follow Ritter's and Udall's go-slow approach on oil-shale leasing in western Colorado.

In his early days as senator, Bennet also began setting up a campaign organization heavy with veterans of the Obama campaign, who had helped the new president carry previously Republican Colorado by 54%-45%. Bennet promised to visit all 64 counties. In early 2009, there was speculation that more prominent Colorado Democrats would challenge him in the 2010 primary. And Republican state Chairman Dick Wadhams said he expected several serious Republicans would run.

FIRST DISTRICT

Diana DeGette (D)

Elected 1996, 7th term; b. July 29, 1957, Tachikawa, Japan; home, Denver; CO Col., B.A. 1979, N.Y.U., J.D. 1982; Presbyterian; married (Lino Lipinsky); 2 children.

Elected Office: CO House of Reps., 1992–96, Asst. min. ldr., 1994–95.

Professional Career: Practicing atty., 1982–96.

DC Office: 2335 RHOB, 20515, 202-225-4431; Fax: 202-225-5657; Web site: www.house.gov/degette.

State Offices: Denver, 303-844-4988.

Committees: *Chief Deputy Whip. Energy & Commerce* (12th of 36 D): Commerce, Trade & Consumer Protections; Communications, Technology & the Internet; Health; Oversight & Investigations. *Natural Resources* (19th of 29 D): Insular Affairs, Oceans & Wildlife; National Parks, Forests & Public Lands.

Group Ratings

	ADA	ACLU	AFS	LCV	ITIC	NTU	COC	ACU	CFG	FRC
2008	80	100	100	77	100	7	59	0	0	5
2007	90	—	100	95	—	6	55	0	12	—

National Journal Ratings

	2007 LIB — 2007 CONS		2008 LIB — 2008 CONS	
Economic	76%	— 23%	61%	— 39%
Social	92%	— 0%	82%	— 0%
Foreign	92%	— 7%	76%	— 23%
Composite	88%	— 12%	76%	— 24%

Key Votes of the 110th Congress

1. Increase minimum wage	Y	5. Share immigration data	N	9. Withdraw troops 8/08	Y
2. Expand SCHIP	Y	6. Foreign aid abortion ban	N	10. No operations in Iran	Y
3. Raise CAFE standards	Y	7. Ban gay bias in workplace	Y	11. Free trade with Peru	Y
4. Bail out financial markets	Y	8. Repeal D.C. gun law	N	12. Overhaul FISA	N

Election Results

2008 general	Diana DeGette (D)	203,755	(72%)	($925,776)
	George Lilly (R)	67,345	(24%)	($14,060)
	Martin Buchanan (Lib)	12,135	(4%)	
2008 primary	Diana DeGette (D)	unopposed		

Prior Winning Percentages: 2006 (80%); 2004 (73%); 2002 (66%); 2000 (69%); 1998 (67%); 1996 (57%)

Population		Race/Ethnicity		Work	
Pop. 2007:	636,476	White:	52.2%	Private:	81.1%
Change since 2000:	Up 3.6%	Black:	9.5%	Government:	11.6%
Urban:	100.0%	Hispanic:	32.7%	Self-employed:	7.1%
Rural:	0.0%	Asian:	3.2%	Blue collar:	20.4%
Area size:	173 sq. mi.	Native Am.:	0.6%	White collar:	61.7%
Age		Hawaiian:	0.2%	Khaki collar:	0.1%
Median age:	35.1 yrs.	Two+ races:	1.4%	Other:	17.8%
More than 65 yrs:	10.6%	*Ancestry*		Median income:	$43,519
Less than 18 yrs:	23.9%	German:	12.3%	Median home value:	$233,400
Education		Irish:	8.4%	Poverty:	17.8%
H.S. grad:	82.4%	English:	7.6%	**Military Veterans**	
College grad:	37.6%			% of Pop:	8.9%
Grad degree:	15.1%				

Denver is serious about being the mile-high city: There are three markers on the granite steps of the gold-domed Capitol that proclaim the elevation of 5,280 feet. Denver is situated a few miles from where the High Plains yield to the sharp peaks of the Front Range of the Rockies, with a freshwater supply adequate for a town one-tenth of its size. With 567,000 people, the city for a century has been the economic and cultural capital of the Rocky Mountain region. On top of its Old West heritage

2008 Presidential Vote
Obama (D) 222,009   (74%)
McCain (R).............................72,573   (24%)

2004 Presidential Vote
Kerry (D)...............................180,064   (68%)
Bush (R) 81,265   (31%)

Cook Partisan Voting Index: D + 21

and early-20th-century elegance, Denver has developed an exuberant postmodern style. The National Western Stock Show held here every year and the LoDo entertainment district along the South Platte River evoke the Old West. The Capitol, the spacious parks, the aspens that line the streets, give the city a lush, burnished air, in contrast to the dry high plains and the stark Rocky peaks. Amid its downtown grid, slanted on a 45-degree angle to align with the South Platte and the railroads, are the skyscrapers of the 1970s energy boom and the 1990s high-tech boom, plus the new-old Coors Stadium, the Elitch Gardens amusement park and the expanded Museum of Nature and Science. Rather than losing population as many central cities have, Denver has gained people since 1990. Most of its neighborhoods have vitality, including the African-American neighborhoods of northeastern Denver, filled with neat 1950s bungalows, and the Hispanic quarter northwest of downtown. But more than three-quarters of the metro area's people now live in the suburbs, and Denver has disproportionate numbers of singles and cultural liberals who value an urban and physically active lifestyle in the gentrified areas south of the Capitol.

Denver is the liberal heart of Colorado, heavily Democratic, while the rest of the state has voted mostly Republican over the years. But statewide politics has moved closer to Denver in recent elections. The city remains majority Anglo, but has elected Hispanic and black mayors. In the early 1970s, Denver liberals were hostile to growth and boosterism. Today's Denver, from the wealthy enclave of Cherry Creek to the night life of LoDo, has shown that growth can produce more of the distinctiveness that people here appreciate. Civic pride was rampant during the 2008 Democratic convention in Denver, with an emphasis on its green projects. There was good reason: Denver has been ranked among the nation's top 10 cities in business climate, livability, libraries, and bikeways. In the lower downtown near Coors Field, dilapidated bars have been replaced by art galleries in the past decade. In 2004, voters easily approved a sales-tax increase to pay for the "FasTracks" expansion of commuter rail and bus service across the metro area.

The 1st Congressional District of Colorado includes all of Denver and extends northeast to take in Denver International Airport, encompassing places with warehouses and trucking terminals as well as curved-street subdivisions. The district extends to affluent suburbs, long-settled Englewood and newly settled Cherry Hills Village in Arapahoe County. It counts most of metro Denver's African-Americans and Hispanics, singles and gays; the Hispanic share has grown to 33%. The percentage of households with married couples and children has been among the lowest in America, and was lower in 2000 than in 1990. In an era when cultural attitudes are a better clue to voting behavior than economic status, this district, which last elected a Republican in 1970, is solidly Democratic.

The congresswoman from the 1st District is Diana DeGette, a Democrat elected in 1996. She is a fourth-generation Denverite, though she was born on a military base in Japan. DeGette (*de GET*) went away for law school, returned to practice employment law and became involved in politics. In 1992, at age 35, she was elected to the Colorado House. In 1995, when U.S. Rep. Patricia Schroeder, a pioneer of the feminist left, announced she was retiring after 24 years in the House, DeGette decided to run for the seat. Organizationally adept, legislatively creative and liberal, she has proved a worthy successor.

Until 2007, DeGette had never served in the majority party—either in Denver or Washington. Yet in both the minority and the majority, she has managed to achieve some legislative successes, in the Democratic leadership and on the Energy and Commerce Committee. She has focused especially on health care issues. Teaming with Republican Mike Castle of Delaware, she established a broad, bipartisan coalition to expand federal funds for stem-cell research, which uses excess embryos from in vitro fertilization. President Bush opposed more money for such research, but in 2005, DeGette and Castle won majority support in the House; the Senate passed the bill a year later. "It took four years, hundreds of one-on-one meetings, and a heck of a lot of shoe leather to win," said DeGette. Bush vetoed the bill, his first veto as president, and the House fell 51 votes short of an override. Their efforts achieved a similar result in 2007 when House Speaker Nancy Pelosi included the bill in the new Democratic majority's "first 100 hours" agenda. The House passed the bill again, 253-174, but still 32 votes short of the two-thirds necessary to override. In early 2009, President Barack Obama removed most federal restrictions. DeGette wrote a book on the topic in 2008 called *Sex, Science, and Stem Cells*. She says she was inspired to take on the cause after one of her daughters was diagnosed with diabetes at age 4.

On other health issues, DeGette has been a leading advocate for expanding the State Children's Health Insurance Program. She won enactment in 2008 of a bill to increase funding for organ transplants, and she has worked to give the Food and Drug Administration more authority over food safety.

DeGette has ambitions to be in the House leadership, though she's been on the losing side of some important internal party contests. She backed Maryland's Steny Hoyer in his unsuccessful bid for Democratic whip against Pelosi in 2001. When Hoyer eventually got the job as party whip, in 2002, Hoyer added DeGette to his whip team, and she moved into a role as a party strategist. Once the Democrats gained control of the House in 2007, Hoyer decided to run for majority leader, and DeGette seriously considered running to succeed Hoyer as whip against South Carolina's James Clyburn. She said that she could have won, but decided that it would have been disruptive to have another internal party brawl at a time when Pennsylvania's John Murtha was challenging Hoyer for the leader's job. Clyburn retained DeGette as a chief deputy whip.

In the 110th Congress (2007–08), DeGette was vice chairman of the Energy and Commerce Committee and a key lieutenant to Chairman John Dingell of Michigan, brokering some of the frequent clashes among the panel's Democrats. She had to rebuild some of those relationships after the bitter fight between Dingell and California Rep. Henry Waxman for the chairmanship in late 2008. DeGette backed Dingell, but Waxman won. She also was on the wrong side as an early backer of Hillary Rodham Clinton in the presidential primary fight in 2008.

In 2002, DeGette fared impressively against credible primary and general election opponents. Ramona Martinez, a 15-year member of the Denver City Council and a Democratic National Committeewoman, criticized DeGette for having lost touch with the district. DeGette returned her family to Denver from the Maryland suburbs in 2001 and won by an unexpectedly large 73%-27% split. In November, she faced Republican Ken Chlouber, a rural state senator known for folksy humor and a flame-painted pickup truck. He also had the Teamsters union endorsement; DeGette won 66%-30%. Since then, she has not been seriously challenged.

SECOND DISTRICT

Jared Polis (D)

Elected 2008, 1st term; b. May 12, 1975, Boulder; home, Boulder; Princeton U., B.A. 1996.; Jewish; partner (Marlon Reis).

Military Career: ROTC, 1992–96.

Elected Office: CO Bd. of Education, 2001–07; Chmn., 2004; Vice chmn., 2005–06.

Professional Career: Entrepreneur, 1996–2008.

DC Office: 501 CHOB, 20515, 202-225-2161; Fax: 202-225-7840; Web site: polis.house.gov.

State Offices: Boulder, 303-484-9596.

Committees: *Education & Labor* (25th of 29 D): Early Childhood, Elementary & Secondary Education; Healthy Families & Communities; Higher Education, Lifelong Learning & Competitiveness. *Rules* (9th of 9 D): Legislative & Budget Process.

Group Ratings and Key Votes: Newly Elected

Election Results

2008 general	Jared Polis (D)	215,571	(63%)	($7,323,502)
	Scott Starin (R)	116,591	(34%)	($90,252)
	J. A. Calhoun (Green)	10,026	(3%)	
2008 primary	Jared Polis (D)	20,493	(42%)	
	Joan Fitz-Gerald (D)	18,599	(38%)	
	Will Shafroth (D)	10,075	(20%)	

Population		Race/Ethnicity		Work	
Pop. 2007:	690,953	White:	75.5%	Private:	79.5%
Change since 2000:	Up 12.4%	Black:	1.0%	Government:	13.2%
Urban:	87.3%	Hispanic:	17.8%	Self-employed:	7.0%
Rural:	12.7%	Asian:	3.7%	Blue collar:	19.0%
Area size:	5,664 sq. mi.	Native Am.:	0.5%	White collar:	64.8%
		Hawaiian:	0.0%	Khaki collar:	0.1%
Age		Two+ races:	1.5%	Other:	16.1%
Median age:	34.2 yrs.	*Ancestry*		Median income:	$62,476
More than 65 yrs:	7.2%	German:	18.3%	Median home value:	$262,600
Less than 18 yrs:	24.0%	Irish:	10.2%	Poverty:	9.8%
Education		English:	9.2%		
H.S. grad:	90.6%			**Military Veterans**	
College grad:	41.0%			% of Pop:	9.0%
Grad degree:	14.5%				

Nestled against the Front Range of the Rocky Mountains is Boulder, home of the 29,000-student University of Colorado, once billed by the city as "a combination of lycra-clad athletes, New Age artists, and thoughtful intellectuals sipping cappuccinos." Boulder is one of the nation's leading centers for bungee jumping, mountain biking, snowshoe running, rock and ice climbing, downhill skiing, land surfing, and hot-air ballooning. It has been calledthenation'sNo.1townforoutdoorsportsby*Outdoor* magazine. Marathoners from around the world train in several camps here. It is also the home of the Buddhist Naropa Institute and the Boulder School of Massage Therapy. All have come because of the terrain. The streets of Boulder literally look up at craggy peaks rising to 14,000 feet from a mile-high plain stretching farther east than the eye can see. Five of the 10 counties in the nation with the highest life-expectancy rates are in this district.

2008 Presidential Vote		
Obama (D) 235,165	(64%)
McCain (R) 125,048	(34%)
2004 Presidential Vote		
Kerry (D) 188,538	(58%)
Bush (R) 132,642	(41%)
Cook Partisan Voting Index: D+11		

The 2nd Congressional District is centered in Boulder. It includes most of Boulder County and extends west along Interstate 70 on its awesome course through the mountains as it takes in picturesque Rocky Mountain acreage, including the old mining town of Central City, the nearby casino mecca of Black Hawk, and the lodges and resorts of Vail. There is talk of widening the often congested I-70. Once dependent on mining and agriculture, Vail evolved into an international resort after the 10th Mountain Division ski troops were introduced to the Eagle River Valley in the 1940s. After World War II, a group of Army buddies returned and developed a ski resort. The district also contains some of Denver's northwest suburbs—Northglenn, Federal Heights, Lafayette, and most of Westminster and Thornton. It includes the old Rocky Flats nuclear weapons plant, so toxic that it required a $7 billion cleanup before being transformed into a national wildlife refuge. The plant, where plutonium triggers were once manufactured, housed the notorious Building 771, once known as the "most dangerous building in America" because of its immeasurably high levels of radioactive contamination. More than $2 billion has been paid to workers who were exposed to radiation and toxic chemicals at the site. Politically, the Metro North area is marginal, while Boulder is heavily Democratic. The mountain counties have been trending Democratic. Overall, this remains one of a half-dozen safe Democratic districts in the Rocky Mountain states.

The new congressman from the 2nd District is Jared Polis, an Internet entrepreneur in his early 30s who spent more than $5 million of his own money in the most expensive primary in Colorado history. Despite his large financial advantage, Polis eked out a victory in the Democratic primary by only 1,894 votes. He went on to defeat Republican Scott Starin in the general election, and succeeds Democratic Rep. Mark Udall, who was elected to the Senate in 2008. Polis is the second openly homosexual individual to be elected to Congress as a non-incumbent. Democratic Rep. Tammy Baldwin of Wisconsin was the first. Despite the historic implications of Polis's win, sexual orientation was a relative non-issue on the campaign trail.

Polis was born in Boulder to anti-war parents who took him to rallies against nuclear proliferation. He received a bachelor's degree in politics from Princeton University in 1996, then returned home and founded the online greeting card website Bluemountainarts.com. He also established ProFlowers.com, a website that connected flower vendors with flower buyers. The sale of the two businesses earned him a great deal of money, and Polis developed a robust civic life. He served on the Colorado State Board of Education from 2001 to 2007, where he helped pass a statewide amendment that increased public school funding. In 2000, he established the Jared Polis Foundation, which helped him bankroll two philanthropic projects: the New America School for immigrant students and the Academy of Urban Learning for homeless youth. In 2006, he drew attention for spearheading a coalition that put an amendment on the state ballot banning lobbyists from giving gifts of more than $50 to most elected officials. That coalition spent $150,000 on lobbyists, lawyers, and consultants of its own, and the amendment passed with more than 60% of the vote.

Polis showed his activist roots when he made ending the war in Iraq a central theme of his campaign for the House. In November 2007, he traveled to war zones in Iraq, where he blogged about the misuse of military contractors and held live question-and-answer sessions. He co-authored "A Responsible Plan to End the War in Iraq" and presented the proposal in Washington, D.C., with nine other congressional candidates.

In a district that gave Democrat John Kerry a 17-point advantage over Republican George W. Bush in 2004, the Democratic primary essentially decided the election. Polis announced his candidacy in May 2007 and faced state Senate President Joan Fitz-Gerald and conservationist Will Shafroth in a three-way race. Rank-and-file Democrats backed Fitz-Gerald, who was credited with helping the party regain a majority in the state Senate in 2004. She picked up endorsements from Democratic U.S. Rep. Ed Perlmutter, former Democratic Gov. Roy Romer, and EMILY's list, the liberal women's fundraising group. Shafroth found support from the district's environmentalists and from some politicos who compared him to Udall. Fitz-Gerald and Shafroth each raised more than $1 million, but through July, Polis had outspent each of them by 4-to-1.

Fitz-Gerald accused Polis of trying to buy the race. Polis criticized her for accepting money from political action committees. Shafroth called for a moratorium on self-funding of campaigns. Fitz-Gerald and Shafroth each took advantage of the "millionaire's amendment," which allowed opponents of House candidates who spend more than $350,000 of their own money to accept larger individual contributions than normally permitted under election law. The U.S. Supreme Court overturned the law in June 2008.

The campaign turned negative a few weeks before the August 12 primary, when Colorado Counts, a group funded by four labor unions that backed Fitz-Gerald, aired a television ad attacking Polis's record on education. His campaign responded with an ad implying that Fitz-Gerald's campaign had paid for the attack ad; Fitz-Gerald's campaign manager said that Polis's ad contained false information and thus violated a Colorado statute that makes it illegal to knowingly broadcast false information about a candidate.

On Election Day, voters gave Polis 42% of the vote. Fitz-Gerald got 38%, and Shafroth, who received late endorsements from both of Denver's daily newspapers, got 20%. Polis carried his home county of Boulder and the surrounding counties of Bloomfield and Jefferson, while Fitz-Gerald won big in the rural counties of Grand, Summit, and Clear Creek. But it was Polis's surprise win in blue-collar Adams County, where Fitz-Gerald's support from labor unions and teachers was supposed to help her, that indicated the effectiveness of his campaign.

In the general election, Republican nominee Scott Starin, an engineer, provided little opposition. After the contentious primary, Polis toned down his campaign and ran fewer advertisements. Starin focused on energy production and claimed that Polis would not appeal to the county's blue-collar workers. But he did not get much traction. Raising less than $100,000, Starin could not compete with Polis, who won 63% to 34%, carrying every county except Grand and Weld. When it was all said and done, Polis had spent $7 million; of that, $6 million was his own money.

In his first term, Polis said he wants to influence a rewrite of the Bush-era No Child Left Behind education law, which tied federal funding to student performance on standardized tests, and to direct more federal resources to schools that serve the most-at-risk students. He also supports a government-run "single payer" health care system to give all Americans the "basic level of coverage that our seniors enjoy today."

THIRD DISTRICT

John Salazar (D)

Elected 2004, 3rd term; b. July 21, 1953, Alamosa; home, Manassa; Adams St. Col., B.A. 1981; Catholic; married (Mary Lou); 3 children.

Military Career: Army Criminal Investigations Unit, 1973–76.

Elected Office: CO House, 2002–04.

Professional Career: Farmer.

DC Office: 326 CHOB, 20515, 202-225-4761; Fax: 202-226-9669; Web site: www.house.gov/salazar.

State Offices: Alamosa, 719-587-5105; Durango, 970-259-1012; Grand Junction, 970-245-7107; Pueblo, 719-543-8200.

Committees: *Appropriations* (37th of 37 D): Energy & Water Development; Military Construction, Veterans Affairs & Related Agencies.

Group Ratings

	ADA	ACLU	AFS	LCV	ITIC	NTU	COC	ACU	CFG	FRC
2008	85	73	100	85	80	14	61	12	8	17
2007	90	—	100	70	—	5	60	8	12	—

National Journal Ratings

	2007 LIB	—	2007 CONS		2008 LIB	—	2008 CONS
Economic	61%	—	39%		55%	—	44%
Social	57%	—	43%		62%	—	34%
Foreign	54%	—	46%		50%	—	48%
Composite	57%	—	43%		57%	—	43%

Key Votes of the 110th Congress

1. Increase minimum wage	Y	5. Share immigration data	N	9. Withdraw troops 8/08	Y
2. Expand SCHIP	Y	6. Foreign aid abortion ban	N	10. No operations in Iran	N
3. Raise CAFE standards	Y	7. Ban gay bias in workplace	Y	11. Free trade with Peru	Y
4. Bail out financial markets	N	8. Repeal D.C. gun law	Y	12. Overhaul FISA	Y

Election Results

2008 general	John Salazar (D) 203,455	(62%)	($901,272)
	Wayne Wolf (R) 126,762	(38%)	($21,669)
2008 primary	John Salazar (D) .... unopposed		

Prior Winning Percentages: 2006 (62%); 2004 (51%)

Population		Race/Ethnicity		Work	
Pop. 2007:	672,264	White:	73.3%	Private:	73.0%
Change since 2000:	Up 9.4%	Black:	0.7%	Government:	16.6%
Urban:	61.0%	Hispanic:	22.3%	Self-employed:	10.0%
Rural:	39.0%	Asian:	0.7%	Blue collar:	25.3%
Area size:	54,100 sq. mi.	Native Am.:	1.4%	White collar:	55.1%
		Hawaiian:	0.0%	Khaki collar:	0.0%
Age		Two+ races:	1.4%	Other:	19.6%
Median age:	37.4 yrs.	*Ancestry*		Median income:	$44,290
More than 65 yrs:	13.7%	German:	16.1%	Median home value:	$174,400
Less than 18 yrs:	23.1%	English:	10.1%	Poverty:	14.2%
Education		Irish:	10.0%	**Military Veterans**	
H.S. grad:	86.7%			% of Pop:	12.1%
College grad:	25.6%				
Grad degree:	8.4%				

On a clear night from the air, they look like tiny mottled veins, thickest near Denver. These are the lights of the civilization Americans have built on the Western Slope of the Rockies in Colorado. The lights follow the trails of valley roads and mountainside switchbacks. The nodes mark the dozens of little towns built during mining boom years: the gold rush of the 1870s, the uranium boom of the 1950s, and the oil-shale boomlet of the 1970s. The Western Slope—everything west of the Front Range, with

2008 Presidential Vote
McCain (R) 170,852   (50%)
Obama (D) 162,254   (48%)

2004 Presidential Vote
Bush (R) 171,115   (55%)
Kerry (D) 135,755   (44%)

Cook Partisan Voting Index: R + 5

dozens of peaks over 14,000 feet—has always blocked east-west movement. Except for mining and skiing, few would have followed the Ute Indians and settled here. The miners who tracked gold and silver and lead ores also built Victorian towns with opera houses and gingerbread storefronts in Aspen and Telluride, in valleys and defiles scarcely accessible to the outside world. Now many of these towns have been restored by ski-resort operators and joined by dozens of new condominiums and shopping malls. Cries of overdevelopment have followed. Amid the tourism, some resource development continues, of gas deposits trapped beneath the Roan Plateau. More than half of the area's iconic aspen trees have died in recent years due to fire or natural causes.

The political map of the Western Slope is as diverse as its history. Aspen and Telluride are liberal and Democratic. The former coal-mining center of Crested Butte and Steamboat Springs, today sporting contemporary condominiums and ski lodges, were formerly Republican, but are now Democratic as well. Durango, an old frontier town, has moved in the same direction. Republicans still have a voter-registration edge in surrounding La Plata County. Some areas are still heavily Republican and hostile to environmentalists and others of the liberal ilk: the rough-handed mining area around Grand Junction, where piles of tailings still crackle with radioactivity; Glenwood Springs, with its old hot-springs hotel once visited by President Taft; and the northwest corner of the state, where people remember the oil shale boom with nostalgia. Generally on the Western Slope, the high-income areas, with lots of liberal-minded trustfunders opposed to new oil and gas drilling, are the most Democratic, while modest-income, working-class towns are the most Republican.

The 3rd Congressional District of Colorado is the state's largest—roughly the size of Arkansas—and includes most of the Western Slope. It extends east of the Front Range to include the small industrial city of Pueblo. There, on the banks of the Arkansas River, the Rockefellers built large steel factories before World War I to make barbed wire and rails. Now this blue-collar town has attracted large medical centers and some industrial plants. Pueblo is heavily Democratic, and so are the counties on the plains and in the San Luis Valley to the south. These inhabitants are Hispanic, not Mexican-American: Spanish-speaking people have been living here, as in northern New Mexico, for 350 years. The 3rd District voted for Democrat Bill Clinton in 1992, for Republican Bob Dole in 1996 and for Republican George W. Bush in 2000 and 2004. In 2008, John McCain took 15 counties and Barack Obama won 14 counties here. The two largest counties are resource-heavy Mesa, which McCain took 64%-34%, and Pueblo, which Obama won 56%-42%. On balance, it is a Republican district, but it can be unpredictable. Republican John McCain won the district, 50%-48%.

The congressman from the 3rd District is John Salazar, a Democrat elected in 2004 and the older brother of Interior Secretary Ken Salazar, who was a U.S. senator until President Obama chose him for his Cabinet in 2009. The Salazar brothers grew up on a family ranch without running water or electricity in the San Luis Valley, east of the Front Range just north of the New Mexico border. They hail from a family of Mexican-American farmers who homesteaded in the area in the mid-1800s. His father grew alfalfa and potatoes using a horse-drawn cultivator. John and Ken Salazar shared a single room with three brothers, while their three sisters shared another. After high school, John Salazar served in the Army, including a tour of duty in a criminal investigations unit overseas. After his service, he returned to Colorado and got a business degree from Adams State College. He settled on the ranch, which has been in his family since 1850, and developed a seed-potato operation, growing millions of potatoes in huge fields. He was active in the Colorado Certified Seed Growers and on state farming boards. When a private developer in the mid-1990s tried to buy up water rights in the San Luis Valley to ship it to the Denver area, Salazar organized a citizens' revolt. Younger brother Ken had held high state office from the 1980s and was elected attorney general in 1998; John Salazar did not run for office until 2002, when he was elected to the state House.

When Republican Rep. Scott McInnis announced his retirement in 2003, Salazar moved quickly to run. Rather than emphasizing his Hispanic heritage, he called himself a farmer. And wisely in this district, he cast himself as a pragmatic centrist and a friendly guy, not a partisan Democrat. But he proved to be a good fundraiser too, and he won endorsements from state unions that helped him win 69% of the delegate votes in the May 2004 state party convention. Meanwhile, five candidates battled for the Republican nomination. Former state Department of Natural Resources Director Greg Walcher narrowly beat McInnis's brother-in-law, state Rep. Matt Smith, 32%-31%.

Walcher, considered the most socially conservative of the candidates, was the only one who in 2003 supported Gov. Bill Owens's referendum to authorize $2 billion in bonds for water storage projects, which was defeated 67%-33% statewide and 85%-15% on the Western Slope. Salazar, who was state co-chairman of the anti-referendum campaign, hammered away on the issue. Walcher accused Salazar of being a pro-tax liberal and attempted to tie him to that year's Democratic presidential nominee, John Kerry. But the image wouldn't stick. Though he supports abortion rights and opposes a constitutional amendment banning same-sex marriage, the folksy, cowboy-hat wearing Salazar crafted a moderate image and kept Kerry at a distance. He embraced tax cuts for farmers and ranchers and supported repeal of the estate tax. He also sported an "A" rating from the National Rifle Association. Salazar won 51%-47%, taking 16 of the 29 counties.

In the House, Salazar had a centrist voting record and is a member of the Hispanic Caucus. Following an August 2006 trip to Iraq, he opposed a timetable for withdrawal, which his brother supported in the Senate. But he has kept his focus on district issues. In the 110th Congress (2007–08), he worked on energy issues, opposing big subsidies to oil companies and natural-gas drilling on federal land on the Western Slope's scenic Roan Plateau. Despite the Army's claims that it needed the Pinion Canyon maneuver site for training in the war on terrorism, he successfully opposed an expansion of the site, pointing to opposition by local farmers and ranchers. With a seat on the Transportation and Infrastructure Committee, he got $32 million for his district in the 2005 highway bill, which was among the highest totals for a freshman.

In this ticket-splitting district, Salazar's work for the district and his political savvy have discouraged serious opposition.

FOURTH DISTRICT

Betsy Markey (D)

Elected 2008, 1st term; b. April 27, 1956, Creskill, NJ; home, Ft. Collins; U. of FL, B.S. 1978; American U., M.P.A., 1983.; Christian; married (Jim Kelly); 3 children.

Professional Career: Legis. aide, U.S. Rep. Herb Harris, 1979–1981; President's office, American U., 1981–83; Pres. Mgmt. Fellow, U.S. Dept. of Treasury, 1983; Office of Information Systems Security, U.S. Dept. of State, 1984; CEO and CFO, Syscom Services, Inc., 1988–2005; Regional Dir., U.S. Sen. Ken Salazar, 2005–07.

DC Office: 1229 LHOB, 20515; 202-225-4676; Fax: 202-225-5870; Web site: betsymarkey.house.gov.

State Offices: Ft. Collins, 970-221-7110; Greeley, 970-351-6007.

Committees: *Agriculture* (20th of 28 D): Conservation, Credit, Energy & Research; General Farm Commodities & Risk Management; Livestock, Dairy & Poultry. *Transportation & Infrastructure* (39th of 44 D): Economic Development, Public Buildings & Emergency Management; Railroads, Pipelines & Hazardous Materials.

Group Ratings and Key Votes: Newly Elected

Election Results

2008 general	Betsy Markey (D)..187,347	(56%)	($2,897,153)
	Marilyn Musgrave (R) 146,028	(44%)	($2,876,753)
2008 primary	Betsy Markey (D).. unopposed		

Population		Race/Ethnicity		Work	
Pop. 2007:	695,823	White:	76.3%	Private:	75.7%
Change since 2000:	Up 13.2%	Black:	0.7%	Government:	15.7%
Urban:	75.1%	Hispanic:	19.3%	Self-employed:	8.3%
Rural:	24.9%	Asian:	1.7%	Blue collar:	22.7%
Area size:	31,048 sq. mi.	Native Am.:	0.4%	White collar:	59.6%
		Hawaiian:	0.0%	Khaki collar:	0.1%
Age		Two+ races:	1.3%	Other:	17.6%
Median age:	33.9 yrs.	*Ancestry*		Median income:	$49,766
More than 65 yrs:	10.4%	German:	22.2%	Median home value:	$207,100
Less than 18 yrs:	24.3%	Irish:	9.7%	Poverty:	13.6%
Education		English:	9.1%	**Military Veterans**	
H.S. grad:	87.3%			% of Pop:	10.1%
College grad:	31.2%				
Grad degree:	11.2%				

The High Plains of eastern Colorado are dusty brown, gently rolling grasslands that seem flat but actually slope imperceptibly up toward the Rocky Mountains. The land is fertile, but dry. Rainfall is rare, the rivers are just a trickle most of the year, and in many places, groundwater is scarce. It is fine wheat country when irrigated, and one of the foremost beef-cattle regions. But it has been squeezed in recent decades by declining prices for wheat plus declining demand for beef and increased prices for

2008 Presidential Vote
McCain (R)............................171,981 (50%)
Obama (D) 169,113 (49%)

2004 Presidential Vote
Bush (R).................................180,017 (58%)
Kerry (D)................................128,002 (41%)

Cook Partisan Voting Index: R + 6

water because of high demand in Denver and along the Front Range. Bitter confrontations have erupted over who gets access to the South Platte River, leading to limitations on pumping from the basin. Local farmers are now finding that the value of their water rights to metro Denver far exceeds what they could hope to gain by farming. Their neighbors condemn them for selling out and betraying a way of life that seems destined to decline. The prairie lands and small towns of the High Plains have small reminders of their past: the Pawnee National Grasslands, where antelope, coyotes, and prairie dogs still roam, and Burlington's 1905 carousel, one of the few with the original paint. But the free market that once peopled the High Plains with farmers and ranchers and made it the scene of farm protests and revolts is now causing it to empty out and revert to untamed land, ready again for increasingly numerous buffalo, elk, deer and bighorn sheep.

The 4th Congressional District of Colorado contains almost all of the High Plains plus the medium-sized and fast-growing developments around Greeley, Fort Collins and Loveland—the northern end of the densely populated Front Range, off Interstate 25 as it heads toward Cheyenne, Wyo. It includes all of fast-growing Larimer County east of the mountains and reaches into Boulder County to pick up the city of Longmont. Fort Collins became a center for California transplants seeking a different lifestyle at start-up telecommunications firms. It also is home to a Centers for Disease Control and Prevention lab that conducts cutting-edge research to combat bioterrorism. To the east is Weld County, still mostly rural and more conservative in its politics. By heritage and usually by inclination, this was once reliably Republican territory, but it is getting friendlier to Democrats as liberal and independent-minded Denver residents migrate to northern Colorado for cheaper real estate. The district was evenly split in 1992, though it later gave solid margins to Bob Dole and George W. Bush. In 2008, Barack Obama won Larimer County with 54% of the vote, but McCain won the district, 50%-49%.

The new congresswoman from the 4th District is Democrat Betsy Markey, who defeated three-term Republican Rep. Marilyn Musgrave in a bitterly fought contest in 2008. While Musgrove survived a close 2006 race against state Rep. Angie Paccione by fewer than 6,000 votes, an anti-incumbent year coupled with a Democratic wave was enough to propel the moderate Markey to victory over the stoutly conservative Musgrave. The district had not been won by a Democrat since 1973.

Born in New Jersey, Markey was the sixth of seven children. In her large Irish Catholic family, she was often challenged by her siblings, in everything from ping pong to poker, instilling in her a competitive spirit. Political conversations were not uncommon at the Markey dinner table. Her father, a construction worker who founded his own refrigeration and air-conditioning business, was a staunch Democrat and union member who supported John F. Kennedy for president. Her mother, a lifelong Republican, voted for Richard Nixon. The children learned the value of work from a young age. All were expected to get a high school job to begin saving for college. Markey majored in political science at the University of Florida and after graduation, moved to Washington, D.C., to work for the House Subcommittee on Post Office and Civil Service. Meanwhile, she got a master's degree in public administration from American University. Markey did a fellowship with the Treasury and State departments, then was hired at State to work on cybersecurity and on identifying cyberterrorism threats. When she left the department following the birth of her second daughter, Markey was given its Meritorious Honor Award.

Building on her experience in the emerging technology market, Markey and husband, Jim Kelly, launched their own Internet business called Syscom Services, from their home in the late 1980s. The family moved to Colorado in 1995, and Markey and Kelly purchased Huckleberry's, an ice cream and coffee shop in Fort Collins. They later sold the business. Markey got involved in local politics, founding the Northern Colorado Democratic Business Coalition. In 2002, she was elected chair of the Larimer County Democratic Party. Soon afterward, Markey went to work for Democratic Sen. Ken Salazar as his regional director in the northern part of the state.

When Musgrave proved vulnerable because of her support for conservative social issues, including sponsoring a bill to ban same-sex marriage, Markey in 2007 announced her candidacy for the seat. Other potential candidates declined to make the race, leaving Markey unopposed in the primary. Mindful of the conservative leanings in the 4th District, Markey spent much of the general election promising to work with Republicans as well as Democrats. She also was an adept fundraiser. By the fall, she had pulled nearly even with Musgrave; each of them had about $2.9 million. Markey was also the beneficiary of spending by several interest groups, including the Defenders of Wildlife Action Fund, which spent $1.6 million on anti-Musgrave advertising; she also received independent support from EMILY's List and over $1 million from the Democratic Congressional Campaign Committee.

The race turned negative. Markey criticized Musgrave for co-sponsoring a bill to lower taxes on coins and precious metals investments, which she said would benefit Musgrave and her husband, who have nearly $100,000 invested in coins and metals. Musgrave charged that Markey used her Senate job to obtain government contracts for Syscom; Markey claimed she divested her ownership of the contracts while working for Salazar. On Election Day, Markey prevailed convincingly, winning 56% to Musgrave's 44%. Her 12-point margin of victory was the largest for a Democrat challenging a Republican incumbent in 2008.

FIFTH DISTRICT

Doug Lamborn (R)

Elected 2006, 2nd term; b. May 24, 1954, Leavenworth, KS; home, Colorado Springs; U. of KS, B.S. 1978, J.D. 1986; Christian; married (Jeanie); 5 children.

Elected Office: CO House of Reps., 1994–98; CO Senate, 1998–2006.

Professional Career: Practicing atty., 1987–2007.

DC Office: 437 CHOB, 20515, 202-225-4422; Fax: 202-226-2638; Web site: lamborn.house.gov.

State Offices: Colorado Springs, 719-520-0055.

Committees: *Armed Services* (18th of 25 R): Oversight & Investigations; Readiness; Strategic Forces. *Natural Resources* (11th of 20 R): Energy & Mineral Resources (RMM); Insular Affairs, Oceans & Wildlife. *Veterans' Affairs* (8th of 11 R): Disability Assistance & Memorial Affairs (RMM).

Group Ratings

	ADA	ACLU	AFS	LCV	ITIC	NTU	COC	ACU	CFG	FRC
2008	0	18	0	0	29	90	83	100	100	100
2007	0	—	0	5	—	93	70	100	100	—

National Journal Ratings

	2007 LIB	—	2007 CONS	2008 LIB	—	2008 CONS
Economic	0%	—	97%	3%	—	95%
Social	0%	—	91%	0%	—	91%
Foreign	0%	—	72%	0%	—	95%
Composite	7%	—	93%	4%	—	96%

Key Votes of the 110th Congress

1. Increase minimum wage	N	5. Share immigration data	Y	9. Withdraw troops 8/08	N
2. Expand SCHIP	N	6. Foreign aid abortion ban	Y	10. No operations in Iran	N
3. Raise CAFE standards	N	7. Ban gay bias in workplace	N	11. Free trade with Peru	Y
4. Bail out financial markets	N	8. Repeal D.C. gun law	Y	12. Overhaul FISA	Y

Election Results

2008 general	Doug Lamborn (R)	183,178	(60%)	($593,491)
	Hal Bidlack (D)	113,025	(37%)	($240,798)
	Brian Scott (AC)	8,894	(3%)	
2008 primary	Doug Lamborn (R)	24,995	(44%)	
	Jeff Crank (R)	16,794	(30%)	
	Bentley Rayburn (R)	14,986	(26%)	

Prior Winning Percentages: 2006 (60%)

Population		Race/Ethnicity		Work	
Pop. 2007:	680,137	White:	75.4%	Private:	72.4%
Change since 2000:	Up 10.7%	Black:	5.4%	Government:	20.6%
Urban:	85.7%	Hispanic:	12.8%	Self-employed:	6.8%
Rural:	14.3%	Asian:	2.6%	Blue collar:	18.2%
Area size:	7,732 sq. mi.	Native Am.:	0.7%	White collar:	60.8%
		Hawaiian:	0.2%	Khaki collar:	4.5%
Age		Two+ races:	2.8%	Other:	16.5%
Median age:	35.2 yrs.			Median income:	$52,970
More than 65 yrs:	9.9%	*Ancestry*		Median home value:	$200,800
Less than 18 yrs:	25.1%	German:	18.2%	Poverty:	10.7%
		Irish:	10.3%		
Education		English:	9.7%	**Military Veterans**	
H.S. grad:	90.7%			% of Pop:	17.8%
College grad:	32.0%				
Grad degree:	11.6%				

In 1893, Katherine Lee Bates took the cog railway up from Colorado Springs to the top of 14,110-foot Pikes Peak, and looking out at the purple mountain's majesty above amber waves of grain, she wrote the lines of "America the Beautiful." Pike's Peak, espied by Zebulon Pike in 1806, and Colorado Springs, with the Garden of the Gods and the Broadmoor Hotel, have been tourist attractions for more than 100 years. In the second half of the 20th century, Colorado Springs, safe in the vastness of

2008 Presidential Vote		
McCain (R)	189,498	(59%)
Obama (D)	129,095	(40%)

2004 Presidential Vote		
Bush (R)	190,190	(66%)
Kerry (D)	93,684	(33%)

Cook Partisan Voting Index: R + 14

North America, also became a great American military fortress. During the height of the Cold War in the 1960s, the Pentagon constructed the North American Aerospace Defense Command more than 1,000 feet below Cheyenne Mountain, a fortified bunker theoretically able to survive a nuclear strike from a Soviet missile. The Pentagon, in part because of local traffic congestion, moved NORAD's surveillance operations to nearby Peterson Air Force Base, site of space-based defense research, with the option of a rapid return to secure Cheyenne Mountain in an emergency. Other military installations dominate the landscape as well: rapidly growing Fort Carson, site of the Air Force Academy, and Schriever Air Force Base, named in 1998 for Gen. Bernard A. Schriever, a pioneer in the development of ballistic-missile programs.

Colorado Springs has built a high-tech, innovative economy. And with the arrival of Dr. James Dobson's Focus on the Family in 1994 and other Christian organizations, it has been a center of conservative Christianity, the home of Colorado's young conservatism and the counterpoint to Denver's aging liberalism. This was the birthplace of Colorado's anti-tax initiatives and of Amendment 2, which in 1992 repealed the city's gay-rights ordinances only to be later overturned by the U.S. Supreme Court. It is one of America's most Republican metropolitan areas. In 2004 Colorado Springs's El Paso County cast more votes than Denver County, and its 83,000-vote margin for George W. Bush almost balanced out Denver's 96,000-vote margin for John Kerry. The Democrats regained the advantage in 2008, as Barack Obama made gains among white evangelicals. John McCain won El Paso County by only 59% with 51,000 votes, while Obama took Denver by 135,000 votes.

The 5th Congressional District consists of Colorado Springs and El Paso County, plus all or most of four mountain counties to the west. One of them, Lake County, includes the old mining town of Leadville and usually votes Democratic. But 87% of the district's population is in El Paso County, and in effect, this is the Colorado Springs congressional district. The 5th District is the most Republican district in Colorado and one of the most Republican in the nation.

The congressman from the 5th District is Doug Lamborn, a Republican elected in 2006. The son of a prison guard, Lamborn was born in Leavenworth, Kansas, and studied journalism at the University of Kansas. He said he voted in 1976 for Jimmy Carter, which he calls a mistake, but was then drawn to Republican politics by Ronald Reagan. Lamborn ran unsuccessfully in 1982 as the Republican candidate for a heavily Democratic seat in the Kansas Legislature, then went back to school for a law degree. In 1987, Lamborn moved his family to Colorado Springs, where he practiced business and real estate law and became an avid mountain climber. In 1994, he won the first of two terms in the Colorado House and in 1998, was appointed to a vacant state Senate seat. Lamborn ran unopposed in the next election and later served as state Senate president pro tem. During 12 years in the legislature, Lamborn compiled a reliably conservative record on social and fiscal issues. He opposed abortion rights, sponsoring bills to limit late-term abortions, and advocated tax cuts, including a reduction in state income taxes. He backed legislation that would have ended some benefits to illegal immigrants and increased penalties for illegal-immigrant smugglers.

He ran for the House when Republican Rep. Joel Hefley retired. In the primary, Hefley endorsed Jeff Crank, his former aide. Lamborn had the backing of the anti-tax Club for Growth and the Colorado Christian Coalition. At the May GOP party convention, Crank won the delegate vote 46%-40%, but Lamborn had more than the minimum 30% needed to secure a place on the primary ballot. Lamborn emphasized his conservative voting record and vowed never to raise taxes. The state Christian Coalition sent a mailer suggesting Crank backed the "radical homosexual lobby." In the August primary, Crank won five of the district's six counties and appeared headed to victory. But once absentee ballots were counted, the results flipped and Lamborn won by 892 votes, defeating Crank 27%-25%.

In the general election, Lamborn faced Democrat Jay Fawcett, an Air Force Academy graduate who won a Bronze star during the Gulf War. In most years, the Democratic nominee would not have drawn a second look, because no Democrat had won the seat since it was created in 1972. But the bruising Republican primary and a tough national election environment for Republicans made for an unusually competitive general election. Hefley accused Lamborn of running a "sleazy" primary campaign and refused to endorse him. Fawcett sought to take advantage of the Republican discord, purchasing a newspaper ad featuring the names and photos of three dozen prominent local Republicans who also declined to endorse Lamborn. He tried to appeal to Republicans and unaffiliated voters by emphasizing his military experience, a strong selling point in a military-oriented district. In October, polls showed a dead heat, an alarming result for a district that national Republicans were unaccustomed to worrying about. But on Election Day, voters overcame lingering animosity toward Lamborn and gave him a 60%-40% victory. Asked after the election about Republican defectors, Lamborn said, "Those people represented some whiners and some of the most liberal Republicans."

In the House, Lamborn established a solidly conservative voting record. He tried, but lost overwhelmingly, to pass amendments to eliminate funding for the National Endowment for the Arts and the Corporation for Public Broadcasting, two government-sponsored entities that conservatives consider far too liberal. He also sponsored a bill to prohibit federal funding from going to schools that provide access to emergency contraception services. In October 2007, he got a seat on the Armed Services Committee, a critical committee for his district.

Back home, lingering resentment over the 2006 primary led to a rematch with Crank in 2008. The challenger attacked Lamborn's job performance. This time, Lamborn took all of the counties except Lake, and won the district overall with 44% to 30% for Crank. He won easily in November against token Democratic opposition.

SIXTH DISTRICT

Mike Coffman (R)

Elected 2008, 1st term; b. March 19, 1955, Fort Leonard Wood, MO; home, Aurora; U. of CO, B.A., 1979.; Methodist; married (Cynthia).

Military Career: Army, 1972–79, Marine Corps, 1979–94, 2005–06 (Iraq).

Elected Office: CO House 1988–94; CO Senate, 1994–98; CO treasurer, 1998–05; CO Secy. of st., 2006–08.

Professional Career: Property management firm owner, 1983–2000.

DC Office: 1508 LHOB, 20515, 202-225-7882; Fax: 202-226-4623; Web site: coffman.house.gov.

State Offices: Lone Tree, 720-283.9772.

Committees: *Armed Services* (23rd of 25 R): Air & Land Forces; Seapower & Expeditionary Forces. *Natural Resources* (16th of 20 R): National Parks, Forests & Public Lands; Water & Power. *Small Business* (12th of 12 R): Finance & Tax; Regulations & Healthcare.

Group Ratings and Key Votes: Newly Elected

Election Results

2008 general	Mike Coffman (R)...	250,877	(61%)	($1,325,282)
	Hank Eng (D)..	162,639	(39%)	($270,609)
2008 primary	Mike Coffman (R)...	28,509	(40%)	
	Wil Armstrong (R)...	23,213	(33%)	
	Ted Harvey (R)...	10,886	(15%)	
	Steve Ward (R)...	8,452	(12%)	

Population		Race/Ethnicity		Work	
Pop. 2007:	743,545	White:	83.8%	Private:	80.5%
Change since 2000:	Up 21.0%	Black:	2.7%	Government:	12.2%
Urban:	84.7%	Hispanic:	7.8%	Self-employed:	7.1%
Rural:	15.3%	Asian:	3.5%	Blue collar:	12.5%
Area size:	4,111 sq. mi.	Native Am.:	0.3%	White collar:	75.4%
Age		Hawaiian:	0.0%	Khaki collar:	0.2%
Median age:	37.2 yrs.	Two+ races:	1.6%	Other:	11.9%
More than 65 yrs:	8.0%	*Ancestry*		Median income:	$82,430
Less than 18 yrs:	26.8%	German:	20.2%	Median home value:	$296,200
Education		Irish:	11.4%	Poverty:	4.3%
H.S. grad:	95.4%	English:	10.9%	**Military Veterans**	
College grad:	47.2%			% of Pop:	11.3%
Grad degree:	16.1%				

Two generations ago, most people in metro Denver lived in the city itself. At the city limits, the tree-shaded sidewalks gave way to the empty High Plains. Today, more than three-quarters of metro Denver residents live outside the city, some in long-settled suburbs, some in large new subdivisions raised up in the 1990s and 2000s on rolling land with magnificent views of the Rocky Mountains. Littleton, originally a small, long-settled suburb just south of Denver, now extends to vast new

2008 Presidential Vote

McCain (R).............................	229,791	(53%)
Obama (D)	202,122	(46%)

2004 Presidential Vote

Bush (R).................................	223,156	(60%)
Kerry (D)................................	144,683	(39%)

Cook Partisan Voting Index: R+8

tracts. Just south of Littleton is Douglas County, which until the 1970s was a sparsely populated patch of the High Plains just east of the Front Range. From 2000 to 2008, it grew 51%, making it the fastest growing county in the state, and also largely avoided the housing slump, as young families moved into 35-acre "ranchettes," or to subdivisions around Castle Rock and Parker. There were high-paying telecommunications jobs at local employers Echo Star and AT&T Broadband, now a part of Comcast. Lockheed is attracting scientists to build the Orion space exploration vehicle in Jefferson County. In 2000, Douglas was the nation's most affluent county in median household income ($84,645) and had the smallest percentage of people living in poverty (1.8%). This is Patio Land, as conservative writer David Brooks has described it: an area with a high-tech economy, a highly educated population with relatively conservative cultural values, and families looking for a safe environment for their children, with the serenity, if not the close personal ties, of the traditional small town and the creativity of a metropolis. "The fastest-growing regions of the country tend to have the highest concentrations of children. Young families move away from what they perceive as disorder, vulgarity, and danger and move to places like Douglas County," Brooks wrote in *The New York Times.*

The 6th Congressional District of Colorado is centered on Littleton and Douglas County. To the west, it includes much of Jefferson County, including part of affluent Evergreen in the mountains. To the east, it includes much of Arapahoe County and, southeast, Elbert County, long empty land but now sprouting new subdivisions. After the Colorado Springs-based 5th District, this is the state's second most Republican district. President Bush got 60% of the vote here in 2004, and Republican candidate John McCain won it, 53% to 46%, in 2008.

The new congressman from the 6th District is Mike Coffman, a Republican elected in 2008 to succeed retiring five-term Republican Tom Tancredo, who ran a long-shot race for president that year.

The son of an Army doctor, Coffman enlisted in the Army before he finished high school and completed his diploma in the military. He went to the University of Colorado on the GI Bill, and then officer's school in the Marine Corps. After his active duty service ended, he started several Denver-area property management firms, which he sold in 2000. In 1988, Coffman was elected to the Colorado House of Representatives. Two years later, he was called back to active duty with the Marines to serve in the first Gulf War. His colleagues draped his desk with a Marine Corps flag and yellow ribbons, and read his letters from the front lines on the House floor. After his service, Coffman returned to public life, first as a state senator and then as Colorado treasurer. But military duty called again in 2005. Coffman resigned as treasurer to go to Iraq on a six-month deployment, during which he helped facilitate elections in the Al Anbar Province and establish local governments in the Western Euphrates River Valley. When he got home, he was elected secretary of state, touting his experience with the Iraqi elections and promising to revamp election machines statewide.

During his two-year tenure, Coffman drew criticism for taking several voting machines out of commission because of possible problems with them and not having replacement machines ready as the election approached. County clerks lobbied for an all mail-ballot voting system, but he strongly opposed it, instead supporting paper ballots at polling places. The August 2008 primary was plagued with errors, and many voters did not receive their absentee ballots. After he announced his candidacy for Congress in November 2007, Coffman was the subject of an ethics complaint by Colorado Ethics Watch. The group objected that a consulting firm he hired for his campaign had also worked with the election machine company, Premier Election Solutions, which supplied all of Colorado's election machines.

In the GOP primary, Coffman first had to ward off a challenge from businessman Wil Armstrong, the son of former Republican Sen. Bill Armstrong. Also running were state senators Ted Harvey and Steve Ward. The four were nearly uniformly conservative. All supported the Iraq war and opposed a timeline for withdrawing troops. Like incumbent Tancredo, who waged an unsuccessful bid for president based on his get-tough approach to illegal immigration, all four were staunch opponents of giving citizenship to illegal aliens. But Coffman had the highest name recognition, thanks to his statewide offices, and also outraised his challengers. He won with 40% of the vote, with Armstrong coming in at 33%, a victory that all but assured him the seat in this Republican district.

Amid his campaigning, Coffman had to balance his duty of carrying out the election in a crucial swing state in the presidential race. He was criticized for the alleged purging of thousands of names from voter rolls shortly before the November election because they were suspected of being duplicate or erroneous registrations. He disputed the number of names purged and said their removal was valid. Still, the Advancement Project, a national voting-rights group, sued Coffman over the purged registrations, and a judge four days before the election ordered him to reinstate 146 voters.

The controversy apparently had no effect on Coffman's own election. In the general election, he cruised to victory against Democrat Hank Eng, winning with 61% of the vote. Unlike in the primary, elections around the state proceeded relatively smoothly. Coffman told *The Denver Post* that "People were pretty stressed out, in this office and at the county level, but we managed to pull it off." Despite his victory, Coffman irked many Colorado Republicans for refusing to step down as secretary of state during the campaign. If he had resigned earlier, a special election could have been held on Election Day to replace him. Instead, Democratic Gov. Bill Ritter appointed a Democrat as his replacement after the election.

Once in Congress, Coffman opposed President Obama's sweeping economic stimulus bill. Given his military background, Coffman was a natural to be appointed to the House Armed Services Committee. He was also named to the House Natural Resources Committee, of special importance to his district.

SEVENTH DISTRICT

Ed Perlmutter (D)

Elected 2006, 2nd term; b. May 1, 1953, Denver; home, Golden; U. of CO, B.A. 1975, J.D. 1978; Protestant; divorced; 3 children.

Elected Office: CO Senate, 1994–2002.

Professional Career: Practicing atty., 1979–2006.

DC Office: 415 CHOB, 20515, 202-225-2645; Fax: 202-225-5278; Web site: perlmutter.house.gov.

State Offices: Lakewood, 303-274-7944.

Committees: *Financial Services* (28th of 42 D): Capital Markets, Insurance & Government Sponsored Enterprises; Financial Institutions & Consumer Credit. *Rules* (7th of 9 D): Rules & Organization of the House.

Group Ratings

	ADA	ACLU	AFS	LCV	ITIC	NTU	COC	ACU	CFG	FRC
2008	95	82	100	85	100	7	59	0	0	11
2007	95	—	100	90	—	6	60	4	13	—

National Journal Ratings

	2007 LIB — 2007 CONS		2008 LIB — 2008 CONS	
Economic	77%	22%	54%	45%
Social	62%	37%	59%	38%
Foreign	62%	37%	64%	36%
Composite	68%	33%	60%	40%

Key Votes of the 110th Congress

1. Increase minimum wage	Y	5. Share immigration data	Y	9. Withdraw troops 8/08	Y
2. Expand SCHIP	Y	6. Foreign aid abortion ban	N	10. No operations in Iran	Y
3. Raise CAFE standards	Y	7. Ban gay bias in workplace	Y	11. Free trade with Peru	Y
4. Bail out financial markets	Y	8. Repeal D.C. gun law	N	12. Overhaul FISA	Y

Election Results

2008 general	Ed Perlmutter (D)..	173,931	(63%)	($1,276,238)
	John Lerew (R)...	100,055	(37%)	($37,121)
2008 primary	Ed Perlmutter (D)...................................... unopposed			

Prior Winning Percentages: 2006 (55%)

Population		Race/Ethnicity		Work	
Pop. 2007:	647,963	White:	61.1%	Private:	81.4%
Change since 2000:	Up 5.5%	Black:	6.5%	Government:	12.4%
Urban:	97.7%	Hispanic:	26.7%	Self-employed:	6.0%
Rural:	2.3%	Asian:	2.9%	Blue collar:	25.6%
Area size:	1,265 sq. mi.	Native Am.:	0.6%	White collar:	57.6%
		Hawaiian:	0.1%	Khaki collar:	0.1%
Age		Two+ races:	1.7%	Other:	16.8%
Median age:	35.4 yrs.			Median income:	$50,256
More than 65 yrs:	10.7%	*Ancestry*		Median home value:	$218,600
Less than 18 yrs:	25.1%	German:	16.6%	Poverty:	13.7%
		Irish:	8.7%		
Education		English:	8.2%	**Military Veterans**	
H.S. grad:	84.0%			% of Pop:	11.7%
College grad:	26.4%				
Grad degree:	8.5%				

The inner circle of suburbs around Denver was developed between the 1950s and 1970s. West of Denver, on broad avenues running toward the mountains, is Lakewood, where growth was sparked by the Denver Federal Center. The suburbs are affluent in the south, more marginal near the Denver city limits. Out to the west is the town of Golden, with the old Colorado School of Mines and the Coorsbrewery. To the north are Arvada (which is shared with the 2d District) and Wheat Ridge, mid-

2008 Presidential Vote
Obama (D) 168,819   (59%)
McCain (R)............................113,848   (40%)

2004 Presidential Vote
Kerry (D)................................130,984   (51%)
Bush (R) 122,772   (48%)

Cook Partisan Voting Index: D+4

dle-income suburbs with an increasing number of Latinos. On the other side of Denver, to the east of the now-closed Stapleton Airport, is Aurora, as vast as Lakewood and somewhat newer, with its huge regional mall and an increasing number of middle-class African-Americans. East of Aurora are rolling, empty plains that stretch to the Kansas state line.

The 7th Congressional District of Colorado, newly created for the 2002 election, covers parts of three counties and most of the inner Denver suburbs. The bulk of its land area, but only 15% of its voters, are in Adams County, which includes the industrial zone along the South Platte River and the Rocky Mountain Arsenal National Wildlife Refuge. Adams County has long been the most Democratic of the suburban Denver counties, but its political future cannot be predicted. It is beginning to fill up with new subdivisions. Aurora, partly in Adams County with a larger part in Arapahoe County, has long been Republican. But with more black and Latino residents, it has been trending Democratic. Lakewood is the largest city in the district, and with the other towns in Jefferson County (or Jeffco, as people call it), it is perhaps Colorado's premier political battleground. Denver's new light-rail line extends to Lakewood, which is sparking more growth in technology. Long solidly Republican, Lakewood is now more marginal. And it is crucial here: Jeffco has 62% of the 7th District's voters. The judge who handed down the redistricting plan deliberately chose to make the 7th evenly divided between the parties, and so it has been. In the 2002 House election, this was the most closely divided district in the nation.

The congressman from the 7th District is Ed Perlmutter, a Democrat elected in 2006. He grew up in Jefferson County, walking precincts with his father on Democratic campaigns. He attended the University of Colorado and earned a law degree in 1978, and then went into private practice. In 1994, a bad political year for Democrats, Perlmutter won election to the state Senate from a northern Jefferson County district that had not elected a Democrat in nearly 30 years. In the Legislature, where he gained a reputation as a mediator, he chaired the renewable energy caucus and worked on legislation protecting consumer rights and promoting responsible growth. He won a second term in 1998 and served two years as Senate president pro tem, then retired from the chamber in 2002, when term limits forced him from office. Perlmutter was considered the early frontrunner for the newly created 7th District, but he opted not to run in 2002, citing the time it would take him away from his three daughters. The new district elected Republican Bob Beauprez by just 121 votes. When Beauprez ran for governor in 2006, Democrats immediately touted it as one of their top pickup opportunities. This time, Perlmutter got into the race.

His most significant primary opposition came from Peggy Lamm, a former state representative who used to be the sister-in-law of former Democratic Gov. Richard Lamm. Perlmutter criticized Lamm's ties to the gun lobby and her support for Republican Bill Owens for governor in 2002. At a time when gas prices were nearing $3 a gallon, Lamm pointed to Perlmutter's sponsorship of an oil and gas bill to portray him as beholden to those interests. Perlmutter campaigned in favor of embryonic-stem cell research, and in his first commercial, his oldest daughter talked about how stem-cell research might find a cure for her epilepsy. EMILY's List endorsed Lamm, but she trailed Perlmutter in fundraising. Perlmutter won the primary by a solid 53%-38%.

In the general election, he faced Republican Rick O'Donnell, a rising Republican star who left his post as executive director of the Colorado Higher Education Department to run. At a time of multiple ethics scandals in Congress, O'Donnell argued that Perlmutter's marriage to a Denver lobbyist for a D.C.-based lobbying firm would lead to conflicts of interest, an argument Lamm had also made in the primary. Perlmutter seized on an article that O'Donnell had written 11 years earlier that called for abolishing Social Security. The two candidates also debated illegal immigration: Perlmutter supported a guest-worker program for immigrants, while O'Donnell opposed it. By October the two were closely matched in fundraising, each with well over $2 million. However, the strength of Perlmutter's candidacy, Beau-prez's poor showing in the governor's race, and Bush's unpopularity all worked against O'Donnell. A week before the election, national Republicans redirected funding reserved for him to shore up the re-election of nearby Republican Rep. Marilyn Musgrave. But national Democrats continued to spend heavily on the race, to the tune of $2 million. Perlmutter won by 55%-42%. He carried Jefferson County by nearly 15,000 votes, 55%-43%.

In the House, Perlmutter was the first member of the Colorado delegation to support withdrawing U.S. troops from Iraq by the end of 2008. Inspired by his daughter's struggles with epilepsy, he won passage of a bill creating epilepsy centers for returning combat veterans. In sync with local interests, he sponsored a bill to offer incentives to lenders who create a market for green buildings. On the Financial Services Committee, he also worked to add protections for taxpayers to the $700-billion government bailout of Wall Street and the financial markets.

In 2008, Perlmutter was re-elected easily against political novice John Lerew, with more than 60% in each of the district's three counties. He spent much of his campaign time in 2008 helping Barack Obama and Democratic Rep. Mark Udall, who was running for the Senate from Colorado.

★ CONNECTICUT ★

By many measures, Connecticut is the nation's highest-income state and quite likely its wealthiest. But it's also the state with the greatest rate of increase in inequality between rich and poor. It is high on lists of states competitive in the global knowledge economy, yet it has grown achingly slowly and has not enjoyed an appreciable gain in jobs since the recession of 1990–91. Connecticut has drawn freely on its Yankee heritage of inventiveness and openness to technical innovation. Yet at times it seems headed for a comfortable French-style retirement, as hedge-fund managers on their estates in Greenwich savor life untormented by the travails of low-income workers in Stamford and Norwalk.

Connecticut was founded by Puritans who considered Massachusetts too lenient and backsliding. Connecticut Yankees for years were flintier and more unyielding, more tightfisted and set in their ways than other New Englanders. Yet they were also open to certain reforms. In 1784, Connecticut voted for gradual emancipation of the state's slaves—one of the first societies anywhere to do so. Life here still bears the imprint of the 17th-century settlers, even though most Connecticut residents today are descendants of Catholic immigrants who arrived here between 1840 and 1924. This small chunk of rocky terrain has been an odd duck politically, the last state to back the Federalist Party (in 1816), one of the few to vote to re-elect Herbert Hoover (1932), and one of the last states to impose an income tax (1991).

Connecticut's affluence came not from any windfall but from a knack for tinkering and making good productive use of savings. George Washington called it the "provision state" for the supplies of food and cannon it provided his Revolutionary War forces. Connecticut made clocks, hats, combs, cigars, silk thread, pins, matches, and furniture. It invented and still manufactures Pez candy in the town of Orange, Nivea cream in Norwalk, the Stanley Powerlock tape measure in New Britain, and the Wiffle Ball in Shelton. The quintessential Connecticut Yankee, Eli Whitney, was the inventor not only of the cotton gin but also of rifles with interchangeable parts. The state has been a major arms maker ever since Samuel Colt won a War Department contract to manufacture guns for the Mexican-American War. During President Reagan's defense buildup of the 1980s, Connecticut produced Air Force jets and Army helicopters and, in the Electric Boat Shipyard in New London, most of the Navy's nuclear submarines. These industries, like Connecticut's civilian manufacturers, depend heavily on meticulous work. For years, the state was the center of the brass industry, the nation's main producer of precision instruments. Through decades of immigration, its workers never lost the Yankee knack: Connecticut ranks first in patents per capita. Over the years, the state has accumulated capital and invested shrewdly, with great skill at assessing risk. It is the home of several of the nation's great insurance companies, and its laws are uniquely friendly to creditors and harsh on debtors.

But Connecticut has been finding its success at accumulating wealth hard to sustain. The state has never entirely recovered from the recession of the early 1990s, and has had the slowest rate of job growth of any state since. Its insurance companies were hit by huge casualty losses, and cuts in defense spending cost Connecticut nearly 150,000 manufacturing jobs. Its small central cities—New Haven, Hartford, Bridgeport—have been plagued by crime and have lost manufacturing jobs and people. In 1950, the three cities had 500,000 people in a state of 2 million; in 2007, they had 385,000 in a state of 3.5 million. Connecticut's post-1990 economic growth has been concentrated in two corners of the state, on opposite sides of the invisible divide that separates Yankee fans and Red Sox fans. In the southeast is the state's biggest employer and taxpayer, the Foxwoods Resort Casino, which opened in 1992 and is run by a battery of lawyers and lobbyists and developers working for the 650-member Mashantucket Pequot tribe. Its big competitor is Mohegan Sun, owned by the 1,600-member Mohegans. In the southwest, Stamford and Greenwich have become major financial services centers and the headquarters of the hedge-fund industry. But both were hard hit by the collapse of the financial markets and the recession that began in 2007. The hedge-fund business shed 10,000 employees in 2008 and was predicted to lose another 20,000 in 2009.

It's not clear that Connecticut's top-and-bottom workforce, with many highly educated people and many with little education, is poised to spark growth. In recent years, its 18-to-34-year-old population has declined by about 200,000, the third-fastest rate of any state. An influx of immigrants from Mexico, Peru, the Dominican Republic, and other parts of Latin America has filled jobs that would otherwise go begging. Hispanics are now 11.2% of the state's population, slightly higher than African-Americans, at 9.1%. Its state and local taxes are the eighth-highest in the nation. Small-business growth is inhibited by high taxes, heavy regulation, and requirements that health insurance policies cover every imaginable contingency—a comfortable enough situation for those who are well off, but a "Get out" sign to those who want to move up the ladder. Corruption has been widespread. Mayors of Waterbury and Bridgeport were sent to prison, and the Hartford mayor was arrested on bribery charges in January 2009. Republican Gov. John Rowland went to prison in 2005 for corruption. As former Republican state legislator Kevin Rennie wrote, "Affluence, high scholastic scores, and verdant hills have masked an increasingly corrupt political system that thrives on a complacent public and political elite." The question is whether the

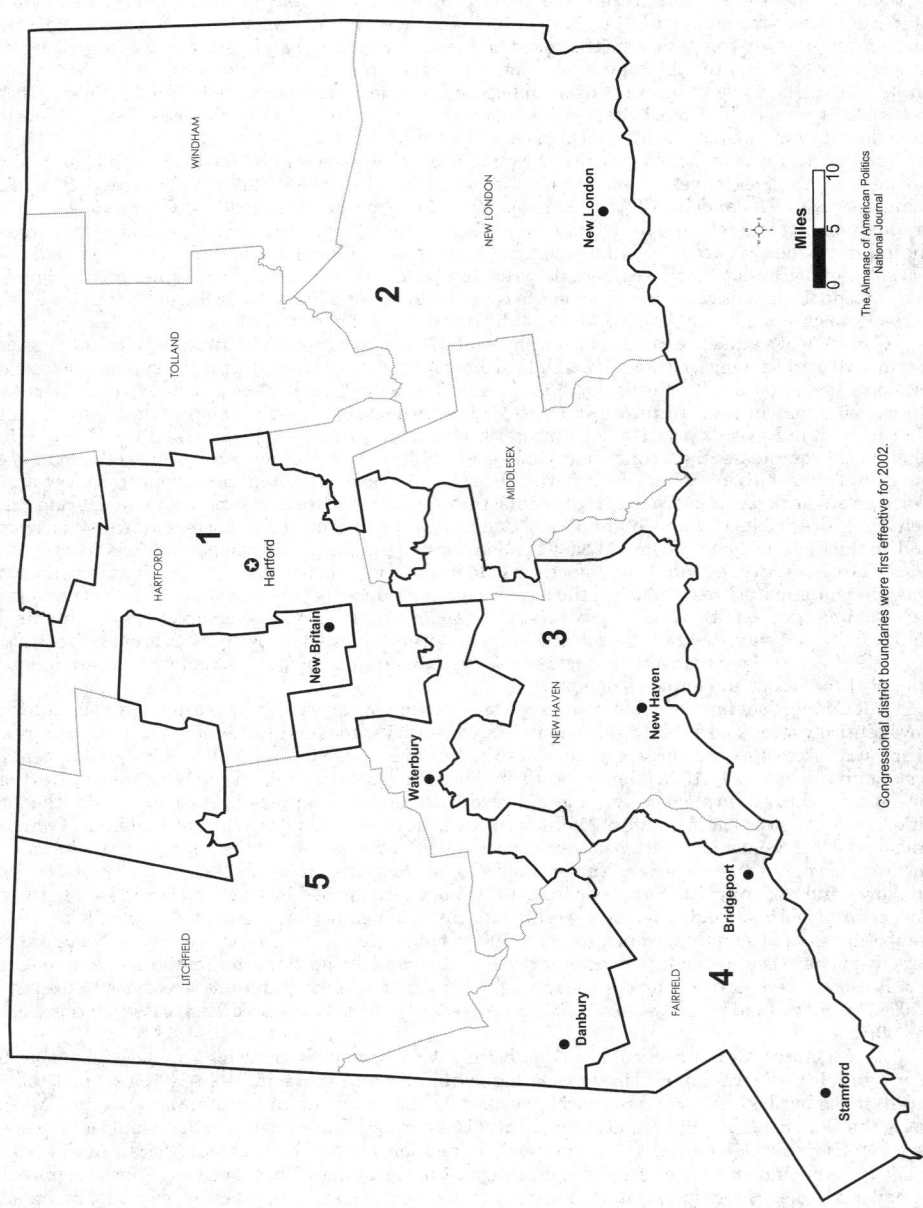

The Almanac of American Politics
National Journal

Congressional district boundaries were first effective for 2002.

achievements of the tinkerers and investors who built this state can be sustained while its new lead industries—gambling and hedge funds—are reeling.

For most of the 20th century, Connecticut politics was an ethnic struggle between Yankee Republicans and Catholic Democrats. Slowly, as Catholic birthrates exceeded Protestants', Democrats gained ground. Their great leader was John Bailey, state party chairman from 1946–75, a master legislative strategist and ticket-balancer, who was one of the first to endorse John F. Kennedy for president. The central cities and Catholic suburbs voted Democratic, and the WASPy suburbs and rural towns Republican. But those days are gone. In the 2004 and 2008 presidential elections, the state's Protestants voted Democratic and its Catholics voted Republican; secular voters went heavily Democratic. Now, the central cities, heavily black and Latino, remain Democratic and are joined by many high-income suburbs—Greenwich voted for Democrat Barack Obama—while old mill towns in the Naugatuck Valley and eastern Connecticut vote Republican. Similar patterns were apparent in the 2006 Senate contest between Democrat Ned Lamont and independent Joe Lieberman, with many historically Republican areas favoring the more liberal, anti-war Lamont, and historically Democratic areas favoring moderate Lieberman, a former Democrat who became an independent after Lamont beat him in the Democratic primary that year.

Cultural issues have played a role in this. The state whose ban on contraceptives produced the U.S. Supreme Court's *Griswold* decision in 1965, the precursor of *Roe v. Wade*, is now solidly for abortion rights, and its Legislature passed a law in 2005 legalizing civil unions for same-sex couples. Connecticut legislators have also voted for in-state college tuition for children of illegal immigrants and, after the Rowland scandal, Connecticut became the third state with public financing of state legislative races. Republican Gov. Jodi Rell, who succeeded Rowland, has either approved or acquiesced in these decisions, and has had some of the highest job-approval ratings in the nation.

Rell's political success has been the exception to the rule that Connecticut has become a mostly Democratic state. All seven of its members of Congress are Democrats, albeit one; Lieberman identifies himself as an "Independent Democrat." The state's only remaining GOP House member, Christopher Shays, was defeated in 2008. The Legislature is solidly Democratic, although Democrats lost their veto-proof majority in the Senate in 2008. But Connecticut's two U.S. senators may be on shaky political ground. Christopher Dodd's job-approval ratings dropped sharply beginning in 2008 after several controversies, including revelations that he had received a favorable mortgage loan from Countrywide Financial. Lieberman had low job ratings from Democrats, who view him as a traitor for his support of Republican John McCain in the 2008 presidential contest. Dodd faces the voters in 2010, Lieberman in 2012.

Population		Household Income		Work	
Pop. 2007:	3,494,851	Under $15k:	9.9%	Private:	79.7%
State rank:	29th of 50	$15k to $50k:	28.5%	Government:	13.2%
Change since 2000:	Up 2.6%	$50k to $100k:	32.3%	Self-employed:	7.0%
Urban:	87.0%	$100k to $150k:	22.0%	Unemployment (3-yr. average):	4.3%
Rural:	13.0%	Over $150k:	7.3%	Poverty:	8.2%
Native of state:	55.9%	Median income:	$65,496	Blue collar:	18.8%
Not a citizen:	6.6%	**Home Value**		White collar:	64.8%
Area size:	5,543 sq. mi.	Under $100k:	3.4%	Khaki collar:	0.3%
Most populous cities		$100k to $300k:	47.8%	Other:	16.1%
1. Bridgeport	130,748	$300k to $500k:	29.2%	**Age**	
2. New Haven	123,507	$500k to $1 mil:	14.7%	Median age:	38.9 yrs.
3. Hartford	118,655	Over $1 million:	4.9%	More than 65 yrs:	13.5%
4. Stamford	118,008	Median:	$294,100	Less than 18 yrs:	23.7%

Race/Ethnicity				Military Veterans		Registered Voters in 2008	
White:	74.6%	*Language*		% of Pop:	9.6%	D:	780,338 (37.2%)
Black:	9.1%	English:	80.6%	*Veterans by Period*		R:	427,110 (20.4%)
Hispanic:	11.2%	Spanish:	9.2%	WWII and before:	16.9%	Other:	891,573 (42.5%)
Asian:	3.2%	Asian:	1.9%	Korea:	13.4%	Voter turnout:	1,646,792
Native Am.:	0.2%	Other		Vietnam:	31.6%	Turnout as % of	
Hawaiian:	0.0%	European	7.7%	Gulf (pre-2001):	7.2%	voting age:	61.2%
Two+ races:	1.3%	**Education**		Gulf (post-2001):	4.5%	**General Assembly**	
Ancestry		H.S. grad:	87.8%	Peace time:	26.4%	Senate:	24 D 12 R
Italian:	14.4%	College grad:	34.3%			House:	114 D 37 R
Irish:	13.3%	Grad degree:	14.8%				
English:	8.0%						

Presidential Politics Why does the nation's highest-income state vote Democratic for president? Because liberal stands on cultural issues have trumped any hunger for tax cuts among most of Connecticut voters and because most of its voters regard themselves as members of ethnic groups with a historic Democratic heritage. The Obama-Biden ticket carried Connecticut 61%-38%, better than Kerry-Edwards' 54%-44% in 2004 or Gore-Lieberman's 56%-38% in 2000.

2008 Presidential Vote		
Obama (D)	997,772	(61%)
McCain (R)	629,428	(38%)
2008 Democratic Presidential Primary		
Obama (D)	179,742	(51%)
Clinton (D)	165,426	(47%)
2008 Republican Presidential Primary		
McCain (R)	78,836	(52%)
Romney (R)	49,891	(33%)
Huckabee (R)	10,607	(7%)
2004 Presidential Vote		
Kerry (D)	857,488	(54%)
Bush (R)	693,826	(44%)

Though it comes fairly early in the calendar, Connecticut's presidential primary has not been quite early enough to make a great difference. Only registered Democrats or Republicans can vote, and here, as in Massachusetts, large pluralities have not registered to vote in either party. Democrats who have won Connecticut's primary include Edward Kennedy in 1980, Gary Hart in 1984, and Jerry Brown in 1992. Republican John McCain won in 2000. But they all ultimately fared no better than the Federalists whom Connecticut favored in 1816. Two recent presidential candidates from Connecticut, Lieberman in 2004 and Dodd in 2008, failed to keep their candidacies alive long enough to contest their home state.

In 2008, Connecticut played a greater role, with its primary set for Super Tuesday, February 5. Thanks to Greenwich and the hedge funds, it was vital in the money primary. By the end of 2007, Democrats Barack Obama and Hillary Rodham Clinton raised $2 million and $1.8 million in the state, respectively. Republicans Mitt Romney and John McCain raised $1.5 million and $1.1 million, respectively. As the numbers indicate, interest was greater on the Democratic side and, with polls showing a close race, Obama held a rally in Hartford on the day before the primary and Clinton had an event at Yale (she had a rally in Hartford the week before). Democratic turnout was 354,539, far more than the past record of 241,000 in 1988. Obama won 51%-47%. Obama carried central cities and affluent suburbs, African-Americans, and secular voters; Clinton carried ethnic areas and mill towns, Latinos, and Catholics. The Republican primary was less seriously contested and attracted only 151,604 voters, less than the record 178,000 in 2000. McCain won 52% of the vote. Romney, though governor of neighboring Massachusetts for four years, won only 33%.

Congressional districting Connecticut has devised a bipartisan process for redistricting. Two Republicans and two Democrats from each chamber of the Legislature meet to draw the lines. If their map is approved by a two-thirds vote in both chambers, it becomes law. Otherwise, a ninth member is chosen by the other eight, and they try to reach consensus. The process worked in 1991, when the Legislature approved a plan that made minimal changes in the congressional district lines. And it worked in 2001,

111th Congress Lineup	
5 D	
110th Congress Lineup	
4 D	1 R

with a nudge from the state Supreme Court, when the task was much harder: Connecticut had lost one of its six seats in the 2000 census, and two incumbents had to be put together in one district. Legislators of both parties said they wanted a district that would set up a "fair fight" between a Republican and a Democrat.

The commission decided to create a new seat out of the 5th District represented by Democrat Jim Maloney and the 6th District represented by Republican Nancy Johnson. The narrow and elongated 5th, the only district that bounded all the others, seemed to many the obvious district to eliminate. But the commissioners haggled over precisely what boundaries would set up a fair fight. Maloney wanted to keep the three biggest cities in the 5th in the new district: Danbury, his hometown, Waterbury, and Meriden. But some Republicans tried to put Danbury into the heavily Republican 4th District. Johnson insisted on keeping her hometown of New Britain, even though it is heavily Democratic and she had not always carried it. The eight-member commission failed to come up with a plan by the September 2001 deadline, and it appointed as its tie-breaker former state House Speaker Nelson Brown, a Republican. The commission ultimately agreed to put some 27,000 of Waterbury's residents into the 3rd District, but otherwise let Maloney keep his three cities. Johnson kept New Britain. Both incumbents said they were satisfied. Johnson ended up winning 54%-43%. But in 2006, she was swept to defeat.

Connecticut is not expected to lose a seat in the reapportionment following the 2010 census, and with all five seats now held by Democrats, redistricting is likely to be much less controversial than it was in 2001.

Governor

M. Jodi Rell (R)

Assumed office July 2004, term expires Jan. 2011, 1st full term; b. June 16, 1946, Norfolk, VA; home, Brookfield; Attended Old Dominion U., Western CT St. U.; Protestant; married (Louis); 2 children.

Elected Office: CT House of Reps., 1984–1994; Lt. gov., 1994–2004.

Office: 210 Capitol Ave., Hartford, 06106, 860-566-4840; Fax: 860-566-4677; Web site: www.state.ct.us/governor.

Election Results

2006 general	M. Jodi Rell (R)	710,048	(63%)
	John DeStefano (D)	398,220	(35%)
2006 primary	M. Jodi Rell (R)	...............unopposed	

M. Jodi Rell, a Republican, became the 87th governor of Connecticut in July 2004 after the resignation of John Rowland, also a Republican. Rell was born Mary Carolyn Reavis and grew up in Norfolk, Va. Her mother died when she was 7 years old. She spent summers with relatives in North Carolina, picking tobacco and driving a truck. A teenage boyfriend nicknamed her Jodi. She attended Old Dominion University but dropped out to marry her husband, Louis Rell, a Navy pilot. After military service, he became a pilot for what was then Trans World Airlines, and the Rells moved to Parsippany, N.J. They later moved to Brookfield, Conn., to a house built in 1843 with views of wild turkeys, deer, and foxes. Rell worked as an office clerk for an investment firm in Danbury. After her children were born, she became a stay-at-home mom, active in the PTA and a volunteer for the local Republican Party. She took classes at Western Connecticut State University but did not graduate. In 1984, Brookfield state Rep. David Smith, an Eastern Airlines pilot, told Rell that he was not running for re-election and thought that she should run for the seat. Connecticut has small legislative districts, and this one was heavily Republican. Rell was elected with 64% of the vote.

In the state House, Rell's maternal manner helped weld the minority Republicans into a solid voting bloc. House Minority Leader Robert Ward said: "When it appeared that most of us were supporting something that was good for the state, a good Republican issue, and, say, 90% of us were behind it, she knew if she could get us to 100% we'd be a more effective voice. That became known as 'Rell's Rule.'" She moved up the leadership ladder to become deputy minority leader. In 1994, Rowland, whom she had met 10 years earlier at a campaign event, was running for governor and asked her to be his lieutenant governor. The Rowland-Rell ticket won a narrow victory in a three-way race, and then was re-elected in 1998 with 63% of the vote and in 2002 with 56%. As lieutenant governor, Rell presided over the state Senate, where she was regarded as businesslike and fair. Rowland named her his chief liaison to municipalities, and she traveled to all 169 Connecticut cities and towns. She continued to live in Brookfield, where she rose each morning at 5:30 and started the day with a two-hour walk. She was known for writing personal notes, baking brownies for her staff, and delivering food to friends when they were sick.

Scandals dominated the headlines during Rowland's last term. In 1999, former state Treasurer Paul Silvester, a Republican appointed by Rowland, pleaded guilty to federal charges involving a scheme to steer state pension funds to investment firms in return for campaign contributions. Rowland was forced to fire his two co-chiefs of staff in connection with the troubled Connecticut Resources Recovery Authority, the state trash-collection agency, and in March 2003, Rowland's former deputy chief of staff pleaded guilty to accepting bribes. Then, in December 2003, charges surfaced that Rowland had accepted gifts from contractors who had received $100 million-plus no-bid contracts. Rowland said he hadn't received gifts, but then admitted he had lied.

Rowland's poll numbers plummeted, and three newspapers called for his resignation. Rell, who by all accounts had not been part of Rowland's inner circle, said, "I feel sick at heart. I'm disappointed, and I'm angry." As the state House geared up for impeachment proceedings, Rowland announced he would resign on July 1, 2004. (He later pleaded guilty to income-tax evasion and served 10 months in a federal prison.) On that day, Rell was sworn in as governor. "Today, we begin to restore faith, integrity, and honor to our government," she said. Rell announced that she would accept no gifts of any kind. She demanded that all appointees submit resignations, and she proceeded to fire four commissioners and accept the resignation of a fifth. She installed an ethics lawyer in the governor's office, ordered a review of contracting provisions, and banned lobbyists from her office. In October, she suspended four transportation managers after contracting irregularities were discovered. In June 2004, her favorable job rating in polls was just 34%. By November, it was at 80%.

In December 2004, Rell received a diagnosis of breast cancer and underwent a mastectomy. A few days later, she delivered a State of the State address at the Capitol as legislators of both parties applauded and wept. She unveiled a budget that raised cigarette, alcohol, and gasoline taxes to close a projected $1.2 billion deficit. Democratic leaders insisted on a "millionaire's tax" on people who earned more than $1 million annually, and Rell said she would go along if Democrats agreed to spending cuts. In June 2005, when the budget deal was hammered out, neither side got exactly what it wanted. The sin and gasoline taxes were not increased and no millionaire's tax was enacted. Rather, the state restored its tax on the transfer of estates valued at $2 million or more. Rell also signed measures that established a 10-year, $100 million plan to fund embryonic-and adult-stem-cell research, increased the minimum wage, and allowed civil unions for same-sex couples. She vetoed a heavily lobbied bill that would have restricted the sale of junk food in schools and mandated at least 20 minutes of recess every day for elementary school children. Rell said it infringed on local control of schools; some school officials were reluctant to give up vending-machine revenues. She also vetoed a major ethics bill, prompted by the Rowland scandal, that was designed to stop corrupt contracting practices. Instead, she issued an executive order with many of the same provisions that gave the governor the power to appoint all five members to a state contracting standards board.

After refusing for a time to say whether she would seek a full term in 2006, Rell announced in October 2005 that she was running. "I want you to believe in me," she said. "I want you to know I'm a different kind of governor." That month, she called a special session of the Legislature to deal with campaign finance reform, which lawmakers had failed to pass in the regular session that ended in June. In December, she signed into law a wide-ranging measure that created a voluntary system of public financing for statewide office, and banned contributions from lobbyists and state contractors. As with many of her other accomplishments, Rell worked with Democrats, who held large majorities in both chambers, to get the law passed.

In 2006, a budget surplus led her to seek elimination of the property tax on noncommercial motor vehicles, which she partially paid for by eliminating the property-tax credit under the state income tax—a credit created by Democrats. All in all, her tax relief proposals totaled about $295 million, pleasing even Republicans who had voted against her budget the year before. Her earnest and pragmatic style kept her riding high in the polls. "She's already at 80 percent," Douglas Schwartz, director of the Quinnipiac University Polling Institute, told the *Connecticut Post* in April 2006. "I don't know if she can get any higher."

On the Democratic side, New Haven Mayor John DeStefano and Stamford Mayor Dannel Malloy battled for the gubernatorial nomination through the summer. With support from labor unions, DeStefano won 51%-49%, but ended up paired with Malloy's designated running mate for lieutenant governor, former Simsbury First Selectman Mary Glassman, who defeated his preferred candidate, West Hartford Mayor Scott Slifka.

Sprawl and job creation were key issues in the general election. Rell campaigned on her record, and used her executive powers to create an Office of Responsible Growth. DeStefano tried to link Rell to Rowland, running an ad with video from the 2002 Republican state convention where she referred to Rowland as "the greatest governor Connecticut has ever had." But with three closely contested U.S. House races and a contentious Senate race involving Sen. Joe Lieberman, the governor's race took a back seat that year. Rell ran a low-key campaign, eschewed negative ads, and raised nearly $4 million without accepting contributions from lobbyists or political action committees. DeStefano, after the hard-fought Democratic primary, struggled to raise money in the final weeks. Rell won 63%-35%, carrying Stamford, Waterbury, and nearly everywhere else outside the bigger cities. DeStefano won Bridgeport 56%-42% and carried New Haven and Hartford with 65% or more, but turnout in those areas was too low to overcome Rell's suburban margins across the state.

In February 2007, Rell shocked both Democrats and Republicans with a two-year, $36 billion budget that called for a $3 billion increase in the state income tax over five years, from 5% to 5.5%, to significantly boost education spending. She told legislators that it was time to invest "in the generations—in this generation and in the generations to come." The increase signaled the first proposal from a Connecticut governor to raise rates since the state income tax cap was instituted in 1991. Her push for more education funding stunned Republicans, and one Democratic lawmaker gleefully told *The Hartford Courant*, "Frankly, you could just put a Democratic head on her shoulders, because it sounded more like a Democratic response to major issues in our state." Democrats supported her emphasis on education, but some questioned whether her motives were aimed at enhancing her résumé for a run for higher office. Democratic House Speaker James Amann, with whom Rell had a testy relationship, told *The Courant* that she "didn't have the guts to tell people" in her 2006 election that she planned to raise taxes.

Democrats countered with a plan supporting some of Rell's education increases while adding more health care funding. Their tax hike affected only couples making more than $190,000. Rell said she would veto the Democratic plan, but with Democrats holding veto-proof majorities in both chambers, she said she was open to negotiations. Republican lawmakers had a "no tax increase" proposal but were mostly sidelined. By May 2007, Rell had shied away from her own tax plan, instead saying that her budget could be passed without the tax hikes thanks to a projected budget surplus of $1.2 billion. However, the Senate and House passed competing plans, both with tax increases and each differing over the tax burden on wealthier taxpayers. The final bill contained Rell's proposed increase in the cigarette tax to $2 per pack, up from $1.51, but her proposals to eliminate personal property taxes on cars and to enact a 3% cap on annual property-tax increases were left out.

With the economy trending downward, Rell took a different approach in 2008. She did not propose raising taxes or increasing the state's spending cap. To spur growth, she proposed cutting business taxes and hiring more state troopers to improve public safety, primarily on roads. But the state's fiscal crisis grew critical—with an $80 million deficit—and legislators agreed to leave the second year of the two-year budget they had passed in 2007 in place. Rell and the Legislature did agree on a mortgage bill to provide lower interest rates to struggling homeowners. Lawmakers also approved an increase in the state's hourly minimum wage, from $7.65 to $8 by 2009 and to $8.25 in 2010. Although she had signed a previous increase, Rell vetoed the bill, citing the weak economy and potential harm to employers. The Legislature narrowly overrode Rell's veto, by a single vote in both the House and Senate. She also vetoed a controversial health care bill that would have allowed municipalities and small businesses to join the state's health insurance plan, promising to work with legislators the following year on a better bill.

Heading into 2009, another budget battle was brewing. In a $19 billion, one-year proposal, Rell promised not to cut municipal aid or raise taxes, although the state faced a deficit of nearly $6 billion over two years in maintaining its current level of service. Detractors said that her revenue estimates were too optimistic. One of her proposals to boost revenues was to allow bars at casinos to stay open 24 hours, but after a Connecticut College student was killed in a drunken-driving accident, Rell said she would rethink that proposal. In the spring of 2009, Rell was widely expected to run for a second full term. Her old nemesis, Amann, who retired from the state House in 2008, had already announced his candidacy for the Democratic nomination. Secretary of State Susan Bysiewicz and Stamford Mayor Malloy were also expected to run in the Democratic primary.

Senior Senator

Christopher Dodd (D)

Elected 1980, term expires 2010, 5th term; b. May 27, 1944, Willimantic; home, East Haddam; Providence Col., B.A. 1966, U. of Louisville, J.D. 1972; Catholic; married (Jackie Clegg); 2 children.

Military Career: Army Reserves, 1969–75.

Elected Office: U.S. House of Reps., 1974–80.

Professional Career: Peace Corps, Dominican Republic, 1966–68; Practicing atty., 1972–74.

DC Office: 448 RSOB, 20510, 202-224-2823; Fax: 202-224-1083; Web site: dodd.senate.gov.

State Offices: Hartford, 860-258-6940.

Committees: *Banking, Housing & Urban Affairs* (Chmn of 13 D). *Foreign Relations* (2nd of 11 D): East Asian & Pacific Affairs; European Affairs; Near Eastern & South & Central Asian Affairs; Western Hemisphere, Peace Corps & Global Narcotics Affairs (Chmn). *Health, Education, Labor & Pensions* (2nd of 13 D). *Rules & Administration* (4th of 11 D).

Group Ratings

	ADA	ACLU	AFS	LCV	ITIC	NTU	COC	ACU	CFG	FRC
2008	100	85	100	100	100	4	50	4	3	0
2007	70	—	100	60	—	4	17	0	9	—

National Journal Ratings

	2007 LIB	—	2007 CONS	2008 LIB	—	2008 CONS
Economic	62%	—	37%	91%	—	0%
Social	94%	—	0%	73%	—	26%
Foreign	71%	—	28%	65%	—	6%
Composite	77%	—	23%	83%	—	17%

Key Votes of the 110th Congress

1. Raise CAFE standards	Y	5. Make English official language	*	9. Withdraw troops 3/08	Y
2. Expand SCHIP	Y	6. Path to citizenship	Y	10. Iran guard is terrorist group	N
3. Cap greenhouse gases	Y	7. Fetus is unborn child	N	11. Increase missile defense $	N
4. Bail out financial markets	Y	8. Prosecute hate crimes	Y	12. Overhaul FISA	N

Election Results

2004 general	Christopher Dodd (D) 945,347	(66%)	($3,938,132)
	Jack Orchulli (R)...457,749	(32%)	($1,462,401)
2004 primary	Christopher Dodd (D) .... unopposed		

Prior Winning Percentages: 1998 (65%); 1992 (59%); 1986 (65%); 1980 (56%); 1978 House (70%); 1976 House (65%); 1974 House (59%)

Democrat Christopher Dodd, the senior senator from Connecticut, competed for the Democratic nomination for president in the early part of the 2008 campaign, but he ended his bid after finishing sixth in the Iowa caucuses. He was born into politics, one of five senators who are children of former senators. (The others are Lisa Murkowski, Mark Pryor, Evan Bayh and Bob Bennett.) His father, Thomas Dodd, was a lead prosecutor for the post-World War II Nuremberg trials and was elected to the House in 1952. The elder Dodd lost a Senate race to Prescott Bush, George W. Bush's grandfather, in 1956, then won a seat in 1958. Christopher Dodd graduated from Providence College in Rhode Island with a degree in English, and served from 1966–68 in the Peace Corps in the Dominican Republic, where he learned to speak fluent Spanish. While he was overseas, the Senate censured his father for misuse of funds. Thomas Dodd ran as an independent in 1970, and his son, back from the Peace Corps, managed his campaign. The senior Dodd finished behind Republican Lowell Weicker and Democrat Joseph Duffey. (Bill Clinton, then a student at Yale Law School, was a volunteer on Duffey's campaign.) Almost immediately after law school, Christopher Dodd ran for the House in the open-seat, eastern Connecticut 2nd District. In the Watergate year of 1974, he won comfortably, and he was easily re-elected in 1976 and 1978. In 1980, he outmaneuvered Toby Moffett, a fellow member of the House's post-Watergate class, to get the Democratic nomination to succeed Democratic Sen. Abraham Ribicoff. He won by a wide margin and became the youngest senator ever elected in Connecticut. Recalling his father's service, Dodd said, "Every time I walk on the Senate floor, I feel he's vindicated."

For many years, Dodd has built on his Peace Corps experience and his Spanish proficiency to play a major role in Congress on Latin American issues. On the Foreign Affairs Committee's Western Hemisphere Subcommittee in the 1980s, he took the lead in opposing U.S. military aid to El Salvador's government and the Nicaraguan Contras. He has long backed freer travel to Cuba and an end to the trade embargo. In contrast to his wariness of U.S. military aid to Central America in the 1980s, Dodd supported the Clinton administration's Plan Colombia, to provide equipment and military training to Colombians fighting the FARC guerrillas. In 2002, he called for international cooperation to disarm Iraqi leader Saddam Hussein but said that, lacking such cooperation, "I don't think we have any choice but to act alone." He voted for the Iraq war resolution in October of that year, but later said he had second thoughts. In 2004, he said of the Iraq war resolution: "There wouldn't have been a vote if we knew then what we know now. Only the threat of weapons of mass destruction caused us to vote as we did." In 2007, he sponsored a bill to prohibit increases in U.S. forces in Iraq without a vote by Congress, but the measure went nowhere. Citing his father's experience at Nuremberg, Dodd has argued that the United States must uphold the rule of law against its enemies, and he sponsored a bill to give habeas corpus protection to anyone, including unlawful combatants, in U.S. custody. In September 2007, he published *Letters From Nuremberg*, excerpts from his father's letters to his mother during the war-crimes trials. The younger Dodd wrote in the book, "For six decades, we learned the lessons of the Nuremberg men and women well. We didn't start wars, we ended them. We didn't commit torture, we condemned it. We didn't turn away from the world, we embraced it. But that has changed in the past few years."

For all of his work on foreign affairs in the early part of his Senate career, Dodd was best known for his colorful personal life. He had a reputation as a party boy and a partner-in-nightlife-crime of Sen. Edward Kennedy of Massachusetts, who was also then a regular on the Washington cocktail circuit. Dodd was married in 1970 and divorced in 1982, and he seemed to enjoy bachelorhood. In those days, he dated actress Carrie Fisher and Bianca Jagger, the ex-wife of Rolling Stones legend Mick Jagger. But in the 1990s, Dodd seemed to settle down to business in the Senate. He was one of the chief sponsors of the 1993 Family and Medical Leave Act, which for the first time entitled Americans to unpaid leave from their jobs to take care of children or elderly relatives. In 1999, he married Jackie Marie Clegg, an official with the Export-Import Bank. The couple has two daughters: Grace, born in 2001, and Christina, born in 2005.

In 1994, Dodd tried to leverage his legislative successes into a leadership role in the Senate. He campaigned among fellow Democrats for the post of minority leader, but lost to Tom Daschle of South Dakota by just 24-23. But Dodd got a place in the national spotlight anyway when President Clinton named him chairman of the Democratic National Committee. He performed ably against then-Republican Chairman Haley Barbour but was embarrassed in October 1996 when he followed White House orders to stonewall charges that a top DNC fundraiser, John Huang, had raised millions in illegal foreign contributions. Dodd left the chairmanship in January 1997.

In 2002, Dodd was the lead Democratic sponsor of the Senate terrorism insurance bill, which proposed to have the government pay for the first $10 billion of terrorism claims outright each year and then 90% of any following claims. The House version of the bill was far less generous to private insurers, providing full coverage of only the first $1 billion of damages and requiring insurers to repay the government. In lengthy negotiations, Dodd managed to get a compromise bill limiting the government's obligation to pay claims to a sliding scale of percentages of premiums and placing a surcharge on all commercial insurance if companies' claims exceeded a designated sliding scale of limits. After the bitterly contested presidential election in 2000, Dodd, then chairman of the Senate Rules Committee, worked with Republican Sen. Mitch McConnell on an elections procedure bill. The House and Senate versions of the measure differed significantly, and Dodd again had a part in crafting a compromise that set aside nearly $4 billion to help states upgrade their voting equipment.

Dodd gave some consideration to running for president in 2004, but in March 2003 he opted out and endorsed his home-state colleague, Joe Lieberman, then a Democrat. After Daschle was defeated for reelection in 2004, Dodd wanted to run for minority leader but bowed out when it became quickly apparent that Harry Reid of Nevada had the votes.

After Democrats won control of both houses of Congress, Dodd became chairman of the Senate Banking, Housing, and Urban Affairs Committee in January 2007. His record shows a generally skeptical view of government's role on economic and regulatory issues: Connecticut, with its big insurance companies, has long been a creditor state that is leery of trial lawyers. Dodd co-sponsored the product-liability bill that Clinton vetoed in 1996, and he supported a 2005 bill to limit class-action lawsuits and require that many such suits be transferred to federal court. He also supported the 2005 bankruptcy bill that included favorable provisions for creditors. However, he criticized card issuers that year for "turning credit cards into nothing less than wallet-sized predatory loans," and called for more disclosure, a ban on finance charges for on-time payments, and a study of fees that banks charge merchants. He also helped write the Sarbanes-Oxley Act of 2002, which tightened controls on corporate accounting. But Dodd staunchly opposed federal regulation of hedge funds, many of which are headquartered in Greenwich. As Banking Committee chairman, Dodd was sensitive to arguments that financial regulation could have enormous negative consequences. He said, "At the end of my tenure on this committee, I want it to be said that the safety and soundness of our financial institutions was not weakened on my watch." Unfortunately for Dodd, that is precisely what happened in 2008, when risky practices in the finance and insurance markets contributed to a near total collapse of the finance services industry.

But in 2007, none of that was yet known, and Dodd had his eye on the promotion of a lifetime. He turned 63 that year and saw the 2008 election as arguably his last chance to run for president. Launching his campaign early, he missed many roll call votes but tried to stay on top of committee business, holding more than 30 hearings. His record was mixed, and the committee failed to act quickly on the unfolding crisis in the credit markets. In March 2007, Dodd accused the Federal Reserve Board and other regulators of causing the crisis in the subprime mortgage market through a "pattern of neglect." The House passed a bill creating a new regulator for government-sponsored mortgage lenders Fannie Mae and Freddie Mac, but Dodd did not get a bill to the Senate floor. The committee did act on flood insurance, student loans, and foreign ownership of U.S. companies, an issue sparked by the Dubai Ports controversy in 2006, but it passed no major housing or financial regulation legislation. As the crisis in home mortgages deepened, Dodd left the campaign trail in Iowa and blamed the housing crisis on unscrupulous lenders. He called for lifting the limits on Fannie's and Freddie's portfolios, but Treasury Secretary Henry Paulson Jr. rejected that proposal in September unless it was coupled with stricter regulation.

In October 2007, Dodd rented a house in Des Moines, Iowa, where he and his wife, Jackie, enrolled their daughter in kindergarten. He had 72 paid staff members in the state and campaigned full time there until the January 2008 caucuses. On January 3, Dodd finished sixth, with less than 1% of the national convention delegate equivalents, and he promptly ended his campaign. On February 26, he endorsed Illinois Sen. Barack Obama, who had a run of victories that month.

Returning to Washington, Dodd dived into crafting a legislative response to the mortgage crisis. In July 2008, he won Senate passage of a sweeping bill aimed at helping homeowners and banks refinance troubled mortgages. It pumped into the market up to $300 billion in federally guarantees for mortgage loans and created a tougher regulator for Fannie and Freddie. Dodd worked with his House counterparts to resolve differences between the two chambers' bills, and President Bush signed the legislation into law. Dodd said he was particularly proud of the provisions that provided mortgage holders direct aid to prevent foreclosures. In fall 2008, Dodd was again at the eye of the storm when Treasury Secretary Paulson asked Congress for $700 billion to buy up troubled mortgage-based securities and underwrite failing financial institutions as a way of trying to reopen the credit pipeline, which had virtually dried up as the economy worsened. Although the committee's ranking Republican, Sen. Richard Shelby of Alabama, was stoutly opposed, Dodd supported the Troubled Asset Relief Program (TARP) that Congress passed in October 2008. Dodd's committee took on an oversight role of the huge new government program.

The election of Sen. Joe Biden of Delaware as vice president left Dodd with a choice of committee chairmanships in January 2009. He quickly decided to turn down the chance to take over the more glamorous Foreign Relations Committee chairmanship to stay at Banking and continue his work on the financial crisis. In December 2008, he said that the government should not release the unallocated $350 billion of TARP funds until Treasury provided better oversight and a better foreclosure procedure. "They have spent the money . . . in an ad hoc and arbitrary manner," Dodd complained. In late January 2009, he unveiled a plan for more-robust oversight and called for a 90-day moratorium on foreclosures. But his emerging image as populist hero of everyday Americans with mortgage problems vanished in the wake of multiplying controversies. Dodd first came under attack in the media, including home-state newspaper *The Hartford Courant*, for accepting a deal on his own mortgages from Countrywide Financial, which had waived fees on mortgages of $506,000 for his Capitol Hill town house and $275,000 for his home in Connecticut. Dodd's name was on an internal list kept by the company called "Friends of Angelo," a reference to chief executive Angelo Mozilo. Dodd said, "I did not seek, nor was I aware of, nor did I at any time try to solicit" a special deal. He promised in June 2008 to release his mortgage documents, but didn't. In early 2009, he allowed reporters to examine some documents in his office, and then in February, announced he was refinancing the properties. *The Hartford Courant* also reported that in 1994 Dodd bought a one-third share in a $160,000 house on the west coast of Ireland with a business associate of Edward Downe, who pleaded guilty to securities fraud in 1992. (Back in January 2001, at Dodd's request, Downe was pardoned by President Clinton.) Just as the imbroglio over his properties was dying down, Dodd was caught in another tempest. After an explosion of public anger over big bonuses paid to executives of insurance giant American International Group, which was being bailed out by taxpayers, Dodd was forced to admit that he had weakened a provision in the economic stimulus bill that would have banned such bonuses. Dodd said he did so at the insistence of the Obama administration, which he said was worried that AIG employees would sue to keep their bonuses.

Dodd had not had a serious challenge to his re-election in a long time, but the negative fallout from the controversies left him with job-approval ratings in Connecticut under 50%, making him vulnerable. In March 2009, former Rep. Rob Simmons, a Republican who lost his seat by 83 votes in the Democratic sweep of 2006, said he would challenge Dodd in 2010. A poll that month showed Simmons and Dodd in a dead heat 43%-42%. "Senator Dodd has disappointed a lot of his supporters up here in Connecticut with his activities over the last several years," Simmons said. Another possible Republican candidate was state Sen. Sam Caligiuri, a past mayor of Waterbury. Some speculated that Democrats might try to persuade Dodd to retire in favor of a candidate such as Democratic Attorney General Richard Blumenthal. In 2004, Dodd won 66%-32%, carrying all but five of Connecticut's 169 cities and towns. In February 2007, he passed the mark of Republican Orville Platt to become the longest-serving Connecticut senator in history.

Junior Senator

Joe Lieberman (I)

Elected 1988, term expires 2012, 4th term; b. Feb. 24, 1942, Stamford; home, Stamford; Yale U., B.A. 1964, LL.B. 1967; Jewish; married (Hadassah); 4 children.

Elected Office: CT Senate, 1970–80, Maj. ldr., 1974–80; CT atty. gen., 1982–88.

Professional Career: Practicing atty., 1967–70, 1980–82.

DC Office: 706 HSOB, 20510, 202-224-4041; Fax: 202-224-9750; Web site: lieberman.senate.gov.

State Offices: Hartford, 860-549-8463.

Committees: *Armed Services* (4th of 15 D): Airland (Chmn); Personnel; Seapower. *Homeland Security & Governmental Affairs* (Chmn of 10 D). *Small Business & Entrepreneurship* (5th of 11 D).

Group Ratings

	ADA	ACLU	AFS	LCV	ITIC	NTU	COC	ACU	CFG	FRC
2008	85	36	100	100	100	6	75	8	9	11
2007	70	—	86	93	—	11	73	8	8	—

National Journal Ratings

	2007 LIB	—	2007 CONS	2008 LIB	—	2008 CONS
Economic	72%	—	23%	68%	—	30%
Social	59%	—	40%	54%	—	45%
Foreign	38%	—	61%	54%	—	45%
Composite	58%	—	43%	59%	—	41%

Key Votes of the 110th Congress

1. Raise CAFE standards	Y	5. Make English official language N	9. Withdraw troops 3/08	N
2. Expand SCHIP	Y	6. Path to citizenship	Y	10. Iran guard is terrorist group Y
3. Cap greenhouse gases	Y	7. Fetus is unborn child	N	11. Increase missile defense $	N
4. Bail out financial markets	Y	8. Prosecute hate crimes	Y	12. Overhaul FISA	Y

Election Results

2006 general	Joe Lieberman (CFL)	564,095	(50%)	($17,210,710)
	Ned Lamont (D)	450,844	(40%)	($20,557,217)
	Alan Schlesinger (R)	109,198	(10%)	($204,113)
2006 primary	Ned Lamont (D)	146,404	(52%)	
	Joe Lieberman (D)	136,490	(48%)	

Prior Winning Percentages: 2000 (63%); 1994 (67%); 1988 (50%)

Joe Lieberman, Connecticut's junior senator, is an independent known for his troubled recent history with the Democratic Party. He was a Democrat until 2006, when he lost in the primary to an anti-war candidate but went on to be re-elected anyway as an independent. He calls himself an Independent Democrat, but the label doesn't mean much given his estrangement from the party, especially after he campaigned for Republican presidential nominee John McCain in 2008.

Lieberman grew up in Stamford, the son of a liquor store owner, and was interested in politics early on. He remembers coming home from school at age 9 eager to watch the televised Kefauver hearings. He graduated from Yale College and Yale Law School, became chairman of the *Yale Daily News,* and worked summers for Sen. Abraham Ribicoff and the Democratic National Committee. Even then, his political ambitions were no secret—other students called him "the Senator." In college he wrote an admiring yet academically solid biography of that quintessential political boss John Bailey, Connecticut Democratic chairman from 1946 to 1975. Still, he was unafraid to challenge the political establishment, founding an anti-war Caucus of Connecticut Democrats. In 1970, he ran for the state Senate in New Haven against state Senate Majority Leader Edward Marcus and won, with help from, among others, a Yale Law student volunteer named Bill Clinton. In 1980, he ran for an open U.S. House seat and lost 52%-46% in a Republican year. In 1982, he was elected Connecticut attorney general.

In 1988, Lieberman challenged Republican Sen. Lowell Weicker, another maverick but of a different sort. Weicker was well to the left of most Republicans on economic and cultural issues; Lieberman was to the right of most Democrats on cultural issues and foreign policy. He ran witty ads, one showing a bear sleeping through work—a takeoff on the growling and erratic Weicker. Lieberman won 50%-49%.

In his first years in the Senate, Lieberman made a mark in foreign policy. He was one of the leaders in favor of the Gulf War resolution in 1991, and without his earnest and vehement support, it might not have passed. Presciently, he called for "final victory" over Iraqi Leader Saddam Hussein. An Orthodox Jew, he is a strong supporter of Israel. After September 11, he avidly supported the war on terrorism in Afghanistan and in December 2001 was one of 10 members who signed a letter urging President Bush to target Iraq next. The following year, he urged the administration to move its putative allies in the Arab world toward political freedom to prevent a "theological iron curtain" behind which terrorism could build.

Lieberman played a key role on homeland security as it developed into a major issue. He initiated the call in Congress for a Department of Homeland Security with a bill in October 2001 that became one of the working documents in the debate over the creation of the department. Bush differed with Lieberman, however, on the side issue of barring unions in certain divisions of the department. Lieberman argued that his version allowed removal on a case-by-case basis if union rights were a threat to national security. But the Bush administration held out for a tougher position on unionization, and Republicans kept the bill from coming to the floor. Lieberman and the Democrats ultimately conceded on the issue.

As the ranking Democrat on Governmental Affairs in 2005 and 2006, Lieberman worked closely with Chairman Susan Collins, a Maine Republican. They threatened to launch an investigation of the base-closing process unless the Pentagon released certain documents, part of Lieberman's successful campaign to prevent the recommended closing of the submarine base at Groton. They investigated the government's response to Hurricane Katrina and recommended the appointment of an inspector general to monitor recovery efforts. In 2006, they called for an independent Office of Public Integrity, in which nonmembers would conduct investigations requiring final approval by the Senate Select Ethics Committee, but the plan was rejected. Lieberman was also part of the "Gang of 14" that promised to prevent the filibuster of judicial nominees except in extreme cases.

Lieberman has spoken out eloquently on moral issues, and has said, "We in government should look to religion as a partner, as I think the founders of our country did." In highly publicized Commerce Committee hearings in September 2000, Lieberman denounced the marketing of violent movies, music, and video games to children. He refused to be a lockstep defender of President Clinton when Clinton was accused of lying about extramarital relations with a White House intern. He called Clinton's behavior "wrong and unacceptable" and said he deserved "some measure of public rebuke and accountability." But he stopped well short of backing impeachment or resignation. Lieberman has long believed, as he said in 2002, that "faith-based groups can help government solve pressing social problems," but he opposed the Bush administration's faith-based charities bill in 2001, calling instead for tax incentives for corporate giving.

Al Gore's decision to make Lieberman his vice presidential nominee in 2000 was history-making. He was the first Jew on a major party ticket. Plus, Lieberman's reputation for probity and his denunciation of Clinton gave the ticket some insulation from the scandals of the Clinton era. Lieberman's moderate record on issues was an asset. He generally supported Democratic policies on economic issues but backed such measures as capital-gains tax cuts for small business. "You can't be pro-jobs and anti-business," he said. Another asset proved to be Lieberman's fervent avowals that religious faith had a rightful place in politics. What might have been resented from a Christian conservative seemed attractive coming from an Orthodox Jew.

His poll ratings were high, and if there was general agreement that Dick Cheney excelled at the October 6 vice presidential debate, Lieberman also performed well. Lieberman's Judaism seems not to have hurt the ticket anywhere, and it probably helped in crucial Florida. He made memorable campaign appearances in heavily Jewish Broward and Palm Beach counties, which together voted 65%-32% for Gore-Lieberman. But there was some tension between positions Lieberman had taken before 2000 and his campaign rhetoric. He had questioned racial quotas and preferences, but declined to say they should be curtailed. He supported publicly funded private-school vouchers for students in the failing District of Columbia schools, but he told teachers' union leaders that overall he wanted to put money into public schools. In the later controversy over the vote count in Florida, the usually temperate Lieberman took what to some was a surprisingly sharp partisan role.

As he contemplated his own bid for the presidency four years later, Lieberman was not a clear choice for the party, especially given widespread doubts about his unswerving support of the Iraq war. He had supported Bush on going into Afghanistan and going into Iraq, not just perfunctorily or after the fact, but fervently, even as many Democrats soured on the war. He stuck to those positions in the summer of 2003, even as Vermont's Howard Dean attracted a mass constituency over the Internet and rose in the polls in part on his stringent criticism of Bush on Iraq. In August 2003 Lieberman said, "I share the anger of my fellow Democrats with George Bush and the wrong direction he has taken our nation. But the answer to his outdated, extremist ideology is not to be found in outdated extremes of our own. That path will not solve the challenges of our time and it could well send us Democrats back to the political wilderness for a long time." He told unions that foreign trade is good for the American economy. He cautioned Democrats not to abandon Clinton-era principles that "made our party once again fiscally responsible, pro-growth, strong on values, for middle-class tax cuts," adding that "Howard Dean is against all of these."

Like other hawkish candidates—Gore in 1988, McCain in 2000—Lieberman decided to avoid dovish Iowa. He was stung in December 2003 when Gore, without notice, endorsed Dean. "I don't have anything to say today about Al Gore's sense of loyalty, I really don't, and I have no regrets about the loyalty that I had to him when I waited until he decided whether he would run [in 2004] to make my decision because that was the right thing to do," he said. While Dean, Kerry, John Edwards, and Dick Gephardt were attracting attention in Iowa, Lieberman spent the month before the January 27 primary living in a basement apartment in New Hampshire, chatting with voters over coffee, speaking to groups wherever he could. But Dean was attracting far more volunteers and far larger crowds, and Kerry, after his come-from-behind victory in Iowa, was also much better organized. "We have JOE-mentum," Lieberman would proclaim cheerfully, but it wasn't enough. He finished fifth in New Hampshire, with 9% of the vote. For another week he persisted in campaigning for the February 3 primaries in six states, but the best he could do was a second-place finish in Delaware, with 11% of the vote, and he ended his campaign.

In 2005, after he delivered his State of the Union address, Bush embraced Lieberman as he was leaving the House floor. Many thought Bush kissed him—and "the kiss" became one of the war cries of Lieberman's critics in the blogosphere. The Democratic leadership was not pleased when he continued to support the Iraq war, voted to confirm Alberto Gonzales as attorney general, and supported faith-based initiatives. Most Connecticut Democrats wouldn't dream of challenging the well-financed Lieberman based on his wayward views, but money was not a problem for Ned Lamont, the great-grandson of J. P. Morgan partner Thomas Lamont and the owner of a successful cable television installation business. He had been a selectman in Greenwich in 1987–89, had lost a race for the state Senate in 1990, and had contributed to many Democratic candidates, including Lieberman in 2000. He recruited Tom Swan, head of the Connecticut Citizen Action Group, to manage his campaign.

At first Lamont's campaign seemed a long shot. To get on the primary ballot, he had to get 15% of the votes at the state party convention in May (or signatures from 2% of registered Democrats, an avenue he didn't pursue). That was not an overwhelming obstacle, given the anti-war views of most Connecticut Democrats, but Lieberman had been deeply involved in Connecticut Democratic politics for 40 years and had built up many close personal relationships. Given his easy re-elections in 1994 and 2000, he seemed certain to keep the seat out of the hands of the Republicans. Lieberman's work on saving the Groton base would pay dividends in eastern Connecticut, and he had support from key Democratic groups, from the state AFL-CIO to the Human Rights Campaign. Also, Lamont was an inexperienced candidate not given to easy repartee, and he made some mistakes along the way—for instance, saying that job losses from free-trade agreements were a necessary "transition cost."

But he had enthusiastic support from Weicker, the man whom Lieberman beat in 1988 and who in 1990 was elected governor as an independent. Video clips championing Lamont's candidacy got wide airing on *YouTube*, and Lieberman was booed at the state Jefferson Jackson Bailey dinner. At the May 19 state convention, Lamont won a third of the delegates. Lieberman emphasized his Democratic credentials and his votes against some of Bush's policies, and said that he hoped troops could be pulled out by the end of the year. He also had some $4 million, which he used on television advertising. At a July debate, while Lamont attacked him on Iraq, Lieberman said, "The people of Connecticut and I have known each other for a long time. We have laughed and cried together. We prayed and dreamed together. And, most of all, we have worked together." But Lamont was also spending liberally, both his own money—he ultimately put in $17 million—and funds raised over the Internet.

It turned out to be a close election. Lamont won 52%-48%. Lieberman won more than 60% in working-class New Haven suburbs, Waterbury, and the industrial Naugatuck Valley. Lieberman won the votes of 61% of Jews and 55% of Catholics, but still lost. John Bailey would have been amazed to learn that you could carry Catholics and Jews in a Democratic primary and still not win. Lamont carried the upscale suburbs, with 68% in Greenwich, and his network of campaigners helped him carry almost all of the small towns, with percentages ranging up to 91% in tony Cornwall.

Lieberman declared that he would run in the general on the "Connecticut for Lieberman" party line, and said he offered "a new politics of unity and purpose." In a tough blow for him, his close friend and fellow home-state senator, Democrat Christopher Dodd, endorsed Lamont and even appeared in a TV spot for him. Most Democrats shunned Lieberman when he returned to Washington in September, and some called for him to drop out of the race. However, five Senate Democrats endorsed Lieberman: Mary Landrieu of Louisiana, Tom Carper of Delaware, Ben Nelson of Nebraska, Mark Pryor of Arkansas, and Ken Salazar of Colorado. Quickly, leading Republicans sent out unmistakable signals that the White House was for Lieberman, discouraging a strong challenge from the GOP side.

Most polls from primary day through November showed Lieberman leading Lamont. Liberal bloggers speculated hopefully that the mostly ignored Republican candidate, Derby Mayor Alan Schlesinger, would surge and take votes from Lieberman, but that never happened. Lamont seemed unprepared for this second struggle, and Swan admitted that 98% of his planning was for the primary. Lieberman researchers revealed that Lamont had missed a vote on increasing property taxes on the Greenwich Board of Selectmen. He also resigned from the Round Hill Club in Greenwich, having discovered after many years that it didn't have many black members. And Swan was quoted as saying that the industrial town of Waterbury was "where the forces of slime meet the forces of evil." This was a reference to crooked local politicians, but it looked like a slur against a working-class, and Democratic, city.

The polls proved to be on point. Lieberman won 50%-40%, with only 10% for the hapless Schlesinger. This time it was Lieberman who carried most of the small towns and cities in the state. Lamont's patches of support in such areas came only from the towns around the University of Connecticut in the east and the tony residences of New York expatriates in the far northwest of Litchfield County. Lamont carried Hartford, New Haven, and Bridgeport, where Democratic party loyalty prevailed. But Lieberman carried most of the suburbs, many by wide margins. Exit polls showed Lieberman winning 70% of Republicans, 54% of Independents, and 33% of Democrats.

Lieberman was welcomed back to the Democratic Caucus by Majority Leader-elect Harry Reid, who said, "We're all family." Senate Democrats—and Republicans—were very much aware that it was Lieberman's vote alone that gave them a Senate majority and that, for all his professions of loyalty to the Democratic Party, the quick withdrawal of that vote would lead them back into the minority. But Lieberman continued his independent ways. He co-sponsored, with Republicans John McCain of Arizona and Lindsey Graham of South Carolina, a resolution opposing the Democrats' calls for withdrawal from Iraq, and he strongly supported President Bush's troop "surge" to try to restore order in the country, which was on the brink of civil war.

As the new Chairman of the Homeland Security and Governmental Affairs Committee, Lieberman declined to initiate investigations of Bush administration policies, prompting North Dakota Sen. Byron Dorgan to use the Democratic Policy Committee to launch a probe of private contractors in Iraq. "We like to do legislation. We don't like investigating," Lieberman said. While continuing to back Democratic stands on most domestic issues, he opposed a vote of no confidence in Gonzales and in November 2007 delivered a stinging speech condemning most Democrats' approach to national security policy.

Then, on Dec. 18, 2007, Lieberman shocked many Democrats when he endorsed McCain for president. They had worked together on many issues over the years, and had often traveled together. "When it comes to leading America to victory against the Islamist terrorists who attacked us on 9/11, there's no one better prepared than John McCain," Lieberman said. Moreover, he campaigned for McCain in New Hampshire, Florida, and other states. There was speculation that McCain might give him the vice presidential nomination, which Lieberman tried to parry. "Been there, done that," Lieberman said in August 2008. But inside the McCain camp, Graham pushed hard for Lieberman, who evidently made McCain's short list before being passed over for Alaska Gov. Sarah Palin. A Lieberman nomination might have caused a nasty floor fight. On the other hand, as one adviser to Democrat Barack Obama told the newspaper *Politico* after the election: "It did have the potential to be a game changer."

In any case, Lieberman, having attended eight Democratic conventions from 1976 to 2004 and having been nominated for vice president at the one in 2000, attended his first Republican National Convention and spoke at the end of Tuesday night's proceedings. He called Obama "a gifted and eloquent young man" —which enraged many Democrats—and said, "When colleagues like Barack Obama were voting to cut off funding for our troops on the battlefield" —the audience started booing— "John McCain had the courage to stand against the tide of public opinion and support the surge. And because of that, today our troops are at last beginning to come home, and they are coming home with honor."

After the speech, Democratic Net-roots groups launched a campaign to have his committee chairmanship stripped in 2009, when it was widely expected that he would no longer hold the 51st vote in determining party control of the Senate. A "Lieberman Must Go" online petition accumulated 47,000 signatures by July 2008. Reid said he was "disappointed" in Lieberman. But two days after the election, Reid and Lieberman conferred for an hour, at which Lieberman reportedly said losing the chairmanship was "unacceptable," and that he might consider joining the Republican Party—a decision that, with the Georgia, Alaska, and Minnesota races then still undecided, would have made it impossible for Democrats to reach a 60-seat filibuster-proof majority. Dodd and others began lobbying colleagues to let Lieberman keep his gavel, and word leaked that the Obama transition team did not want him punished. On Nov. 18, 2008, the Senate Democratic Caucus voted 42-13 to let him remain as chairman of the Homeland Security panel. For his part, Lieberman apologized for some of the things he had said about Obama.

On the committee, Lieberman was the lead sponsor of the bill giving the District of Columbia congressional representation, which passed 61-37 in February 2009 with an amendment repealing most of the District's gun-control laws. Lieberman also worked to gain support for Obama's economic stimulus bill from moderate Republicans. But hard feelings in his former party remained. Democratic Rep. John Larson, who represents Connecticut's 1st District, told the *Hartford Courant*, "I think Joe is on a different roster. He's made a conscious decision to go over to the other side."

Lieberman comes up for re-election in 2012. With most Democrats expressing negative feelings, a February 2009 poll showed him trailing Democratic Attorney General Richard Blumenthal 58%-30%. Connecticut Republicans in 2008 said they would welcome Lieberman into their party, but it was not clear whether the welcome mat might be withdrawn if he continued, as he did in early 2009, to support the Obama administration and the Democratic leadership on most issues.

FIRST DISTRICT

John Larson (D)

Elected 1998, 6th term; b. July 22, 1948, Hartford; home, E. Hartford; Central CT St. U., B.S. 1971; Catholic; married (Leslie); 3 children.

Elected Office: E. Hartford Bd. of Ed., 1977–79; E. Hartford Town Cncl., 1979–83; CT Senate, 1982–95; Pres. pro-tem 1986–95.

Professional Career: H.S. teacher, 1972–77; Insurance broker, 1977–98; Sr. fellow, Yale Bush Ctr., 1995–1998.

DC Office: 106 CHOB, 20515; 202-225-2265; Fax: 202-225-1031; Web site: larson.house.gov.

State Offices: Hartford, 860-278-8888.

Committees: *Democratic Caucus Chairman. Ways & Means* (12th of 26 D): Oversight; Select Revenue Measures.

Group Ratings

	ADA	ACLU	AFS	LCV	ITIC	NTU	COC	ACU	CFG	FRC
2008	95	100	100	85	100	2	65	0	0	5
2007	95	—	100	90	—	4	55	0	5	—

National Journal Ratings

	2007 LIB	—	2007 CONS		2008 LIB	—	2008 CONS
Economic	78%	—	18%		85%	—	0%
Social	77%	—	17%		82%	—	0%
Foreign	81%	—	16%		83%	—	15%
Composite	81%	—	19%		89%	—	11%

Key Votes of the 110th Congress

1. Increase minimum wage	Y	5. Share immigration data	N	9. Withdraw troops 8/08	Y
2. Expand SCHIP	Y	6. Foreign aid abortion ban	N	10. No operations in Iran	Y
3. Raise CAFE standards	Y	7. Ban gay bias in workplace	Y	11. Free trade with Peru	Y
4. Bail out financial markets	Y	8. Repeal D.C. gun law	*	12. Overhaul FISA	N

Election Results

2008 general	John Larson (D-WF)	211,493	(72%)	($1,379,640)
	Joe Visconti (R)	76,860	(26%)	($15,816)
	Stephen Fournier (Green)	7,201	(2%)	
2008 primary	John Larson (D)	unopposed		

Prior Winning Percentages: 2006 (74%); 2004 (73%); 2002 (67%); 2000 (72%); 1998 (58%)

Population		Race/Ethnicity		Work	
Pop. 2007:	693,239	White:	68.2%	Private:	80.1%
Change since 2000:	Up 1.8%	Black:	13.3%	Government:	14.0%
Urban:	93.4%	Hispanic:	13.1%	Self-employed:	5.8%
Rural:	6.6%	Asian:	3.4%	Blue collar:	18.6%
Area size:	673 sq. mi.	Native Am.:	0.2%	White collar:	65.0%
		Hawaiian:	0.0%	Khaki collar:	0.0%
Age		Two+ races:	1.3%	Other:	16.3%
Median age:	39.4 yrs.			Median income:	$60,299
More than 65 yrs:	14.3%	*Ancestry*		Median home value:	$232,600
Less than 18 yrs:	23.2%	Italian:	13.0%	Poverty:	9.9%
		Irish:	11.9%		
Education		Polish:	7.2%	**Military Veterans**	
H.S. grad:	86.2%			% of Pop:	9.6%
College grad:	31.0%				
Grad degree:	12.9%				

In 1871, Mark Twain moved to Hartford to become director of an insurance company, and in time, became the Connecticut capital's most famous citizen. And Hartford became the nation's best-known insurance center. This was not what the Puritans who founded Hartford had in mind, but Connecticut's Yankees turned out to be shrewd businessmen. Hartford is the boyhood home of financier J.P. Morgan and also home to the nation's longest-circulating newspaper, the *Hartford Courant*, established

2008 Presidential Vote		
Obama (D)	218,794	(66%)
McCain (R)	108,572	(33%)
2004 Presidential Vote		
Kerry (D)	187,089	(60%)
Bush (R)	121,263	(39%)
Cook Partisan Voting Index:	D+13	

in 1764. Thanks to the broad Connecticut River, Hartford also became a seaport. Its merchants wrote fire insurance, using the capital they had accumulated in the Napoleonic Wars to finance their ventures. One was Samuel Colt's gun factory just south of downtown Hartford, which became one of the nation's great arms plants.

Although each sector has downsized, insurance and arms are still economic mainstays of Hartford, Connecticut's biggest metropolitan area. Connecticut has the largest concentration of financial and insurance firms in the nation, mostly in the Hartford area. The Hartford Financial Services Group, Aetna, and St. Paul Travelers are the largest employers, with a total of nearly 25,000 employees statewide in 2006. Across the river is the Pratt & Whitney jet engine plant in East Hartford, cornerstone of Connecticut-based United Technologies. Though its local workforce is less than one-fourth its size in 1980, it still builds engines for more than 600 customers around the world. The central core of Hartford is suffering, however, with bedraggled, high-crime neighborhoods filled with abandoned buildings, a school system that's deeply troubled, and downtown landmarks such as the Civic Center and Broadcast House in Constitution Plaza that are in jeopardy. Many words have been written about the sad decline of this once rich city. Where 177,000 people lived in 1950, there were 125,000 in 2006. Its population is 38% African-American and 41% Hispanic, the largest share for a city in the Northeast, and heavily Puerto Rican. Beyond Hartford, the metropolitan area is more affluent but growing slowly.

The 1st Congressional District of Connecticut is centered on Hartford and upscale West Hartford. On the map it looks like a lobster claw. The claw extends west, excluding some affluent suburbs while including small towns and part of Torrington in the north. Southwest of Hartford, the district includes

Bristol, site of the sprawling headquarters of ESPN, the multimedia network that revolutionized sports broadcasting and employs about 3,400 locally. East of the Connecticut River are East Hartford and more affluent suburbs. Politically, the Hartford area has long been more Democratic than the rest of Connecticut. It owes some of its Democratic character to John Bailey, an old-fashioned political boss with a scandal-free career who promoted a raft of first-class candidates. Bailey was state Democratic chairman from 1946 to 1975 and national Democratic chairman from 1961 to 1968.

The congressman from the 1st District is John Larson, a Democrat first elected in 1998 to replace Rep. Barbara Kennelly, John Bailey's daughter, who ran unsuccessfully for governor. One of eight children, Larson grew up in the Mayberry Village public-housing project in East Hartford. His father was a fireman at Pratt & Whitney who worked a second job as an auto mechanic, and his mother worked at the state Capitol. He graduated from Central Connecticut State, taught high school and coached athletics. He also worked in the hometown industry as an insurance agent. His family liked politics. His mother served on the town council, and his brother Timothy was mayor of East Hartford. In 1982, at age 34, John Larson was elected to the state Senate. Four years later he was Senate president. He sponsored one of the nation's first family-medical-leave laws, a prototype for the bill sponsored by Connecticut Sen. Christopher Dodd, a Democrat, and signed into law by President Clinton in 1993.

He seemed headed for the governorship and in 1994 won the party designation at the state convention. But Comptroller Bill Curry built an organization of unionists and liberal activists and beat him 55%-45% in the primary. When Kennelly announced her retirement, Larson decided to try for her seat. In the primary, he faced Secretary of State Miles Rapoport, who led in the polls and fundraising. But Larson raised impressive sums as well, built a local organization, did a lot of door-to-door campaigning, and benefited from the support of Hartford Mayor Mike Peters. He won 46%-43%. In the general election, he competed against Kevin O'Connor, a 31-year-old former law clerk and Securities and Exchange Commission lawyer who was endorsed by the *Hartford Courant*. Larson won 58%-41% and has not been seriously challenged since.

In the House Larson's voting record places him near the center of his party. In 2002, he actively opposed authorizing the use of force in Iraq, saying that unilateral action could unite Arab countries against the United States. In 2004, he added a provision to the defense bill to reimburse soldiers and their families who have purchased body armor before deploying to Iraq. In 2005, Larson secured a seat on the powerful tax-writing Ways and Means Committee. The 2005 energy bill included his provisions expanding tax incentives for fuel-cell technologies. In 2007, he won federal protection for local tax breaks for volunteer firefighters and other emergency first responders. On an important parochial issue in 2008, he won National Historic Landmark status for the original Colt factory and grounds.

In 2003, Larson became the senior Democrat on the House Administration Committee, the congressional housekeeping panel that handles office space and other perks of interest to colleagues. Leadership on the committee can be a stepping-stone to better things. Then-Minority Leader Nancy Pelosi brought Larson into her circle of advisers, and his influence in the Democratic Caucus grew. In 2006, he won a hotly contested race for caucus vice chairman. His competitors were the better-known Jan Schakowsky of Illinois and Joseph Crowley of New York. But Schakowsky finished third on the first ballot and was eliminated. She then threw her support to Larson. With Schakowsky's former supporters, Larson prevailed on the second ballot 116 to 87 over Crowley, who was allied with Maryland's Steny Hoyer, Pelosi's arch rival in leadership. Larson also got help from John Murtha, the powerful senior Democrat of the Defense Appropriations Subcommittee. In 2007, Larson planned to run for caucus chairman, but he stepped aside when it became apparent that Rahm Emanuel of Illinois had broad support for the job. When Emanuel quit the House in November 2008 to become chief of staff to President-elect Obama, Pelosi persuaded Chris Van Hollen, D-Md., to remain as chairman of the Democratic Congressional Campaign Committee, clearing the field for Larson to finally become caucus chairman.

Larson has taken on a number of assignments for Pelosi, including coordinating the Democrats' 2008 initiative against oil speculators and high energy prices. He sought to tamp down party dissidents who complained that Pelosi's Iraq strategy was too accommodating to President Bush. Some Democrats privately dismissed him as a Pelosi cheerleader. Larson discounts the criticism, saying that his "bottom-up, member's member" approach is very different from the aggressive, in-your-face style Emanuel was known for, but it's no less effective. "If you were using generals as analogy, [Rahm] would be Patton. I would be Omar Bradley," he says. Larson says his goal is to spread the limelight to members and groups across the party. His quick move up the leadership ladder left him on the rung behind the top three party leaders, and he is well-positioned to advance further. He retained interest in another run for governor or perhaps for the Senate. Whatever the course, Larson was well-positioned for further advances.

SECOND DISTRICT

Joe Courtney (D)

Elected 2006, 2nd term; b. April 6, 1953, Hartford; home, Vernon; Tufts U., B.A. 1975, U. of CT, J.D. 1978; Catholic; married (Audrey); 2 children.

Elected Office: CT House of Reps., 1986–94.

Professional Career: Practicing atty., 1978–2006; CT coordinator, John Edwards pres. campaign, 2004.

DC Office: 215 CHOB, 20515, 202-225-2076; Fax: 202-225-4977; Web site: courtney.house.gov.

State Offices: Enfield, 860-741-6011; Norwich, 860-886-0139.

Committees: *Armed Services* (23rd of 36 D): Readiness; Seapower & Expeditionary Forces. *Education & Labor* (22nd of 29 D): Health, Employment, Labor & Pensions; Higher Education, Lifelong Learning & Competitiveness.

Group Ratings

	ADA	ACLU	AFS	LCV	ITIC	NTU	COC	ACU	CFG	FRC
2008	95	100	100	100	43	17	50	8	8	11
2007	100	—	100	95	—	5	50	0	6	—

National Journal Ratings

	2007 LIB	—	2007 CONS		2008 LIB	—	2008 CONS
Economic	69%	—	28%		71%	—	25%
Social	66%	—	33%		82%	—	0%
Foreign	81%	—	16%		78%	—	17%
Composite	73%	—	27%		82%	—	19%

Key Votes of the 110th Congress

1. Increase minimum wage	Y	5. Share immigration data	N	9. Withdraw troops 8/08	Y
2. Expand SCHIP	Y	6. Foreign aid abortion ban	N	10. No operations in Iran	Y
3. Raise CAFE standards	Y	7. Ban gay bias in workplace	Y	11. Free trade with Peru	N
4. Bail out financial markets	N	8. Repeal D.C. gun law	N	12. Overhaul FISA	N

Election Results

2008 general	Joe Courtney (D-WF)	212,148	(66%)	($1,792,920)
	Sean Sullivan (R)	104,574	(32%)	($395,207)
2008 primary	Joe Courtney (D)	unopposed		

Prior Winning Percentages: 2006 (50%)

Population

Pop. 2007:	714,144
Change since 2000:	Up 4.8%
Urban:	66.7%
Rural:	33.3%
Area size:	2,143 sq. mi.

Age

Median age:	38.9 yrs.
More than 65 yrs:	12.7%
Less than 18 yrs:	22.7%

Education

H.S. grad:	89.8%
College grad:	31.7%
Grad degree:	13.9%

Race/Ethnicity

White:	86.4%
Black:	3.5%
Hispanic:	5.4%
Asian:	2.5%
Native Am.:	0.3%
Hawaiian:	0.0%
Two+ races:	1.6%

Ancestry

Irish:	14.5%
Italian:	11.2%
English:	10.6%

Work

Private:	76.2%
Government:	17.4%
Self-employed:	6.3%
Blue collar:	19.1%
White collar:	62.5%
Khaki collar:	1.1%
Other:	17.3%
Median income:	$67,434
Median home value:	$252,800
Poverty:	5.9%

Military Veterans

% of Pop:	12.2%

One of the longest-settled parts of the United States, eastern Connecticut has experienced great, and sometimes painful, change in recent years— change comparable to that of the 1640s or 1810s or 1950s. When the Puritan settlers from Massachusetts and England arrived, these flinty hills were the home of small Indian tribes, whose numbers were decimated by warfare and even more by disease. This was never fertile farming country, but

2008 Presidential Vote		
Obama (D) 204,221	(59%)
McCain (R).............................139,945	(40%)

2004 Presidential Vote		
Kerry (D)...............................180,235	(54%)
Bush (R)................................147,819	(44%)

Cook Partisan Voting Index: D + 6

New London and Norwich were among the 13 Colonies' leading workshops and ports. (Norwich was the home of Samuel Huntington, signer of the Declaration of Independence, and the president of the Continental Congress in 1781, when the nation officially was named the United States of America.) Factories developed around mills in little villages on the fast-flowing Quinebaug and Shetucket rivers. Sandbars kept oceangoing ships out of the rivers, but they docked at New London. In the mid-20th century, new technology shaped the area. Four nuclear power plants were built here, more than in any similarly populated part of the United States. In Groton, the "Submarine Capital of the World" across the Thames River from New London, is General Dynamics' Electric Boat Company, which built its first submarines in 1915 and later, nuclear submarines.

In the 1990s, the local economy was in trouble. Nuclear plants were wearing out and being shut down across the country. After the end of the Cold War, many in the Electric Boat workforce were laid off, though some remained to work on the next-generation Virginia-class submarine. About 10,000 are employed at both the Groton and Rhode Island facilities today. Even with the Navy's December 2008 announcement of a $14 billion contract for additional production, the port's long-term survival is in doubt. The area's economic base shifted to entertainment, specifically to gambling. The Foxwoods Casino, built by the 650-member Mashantucket Pequot tribe and opened in 1992, is the largest casino in the world, with hotels, golf courses, and a convention center. In 2008, Foxwoods completed a $700 million expansion. It is now the largest employer in Connecticut. Eight miles away, near Norwich, is the Mohegan Sun casino, the second largest casino in the world, which opened in 1996. Gambling now provides more tax dollars to the state than any insurance or defense company. But competition from nearby states is slowing the growth of gaming in the area. New London has taken steps to become a cruise-ship destination.

The 2nd Congressional District of Connecticut includes most of the eastern part of the state, centering on the small cities of New London and Norwich and including mill towns and the University of Connecticut in Storrs. The northeastern edge of Windham County, long known as Quiet Corner for its small towns and dairy farms, has lured away many Rhode Island and Massachusetts residents looking to escape high taxes and housing prices. The district stretches west to the outskirts of Hartford and to antique-filled small towns like Essex and Old Lyme on Long Island Sound. For many years, this was a politically marginal district, with close battles between Yankee Republicans and Catholic Democrats. More recently, it has trended Democratic and has become volatile.

The congressman from the 2nd District is Joe Courtney, a Democrat elected in 2006. Courtney was raised in West Hartford, the youngest of five boys. He studied at Tufts University, graduated from the University of Connecticut law school and went into private practice. In 1986, he won the first of four terms in the state House, where he served as chairman of the public health and human services committees. He ran unsuccessfully for lieutenant governor in 1998, and then unsuccessfully against Republican Rep. Rob Simmons in 2002. Simmons, who earned two Bronze Stars in Vietnam and later served as a CIA operations officer, had defeated 20-year Democratic Rep. Sam Gejdenson two years earlier. Courtney ran on the Democratic themes of Social Security restructuring, better prescription drug coverage for seniors and opposition to President Bush's tax cuts. The environmental group Friends of the Earth gave Simmons a boost, saying that he had the most pro-environment record of the freshmen Republicans. Courtney gained ground late in the 2002 campaign, but Simmons won 54%-46%. Courtney stepped aside for Democrat Jim Sullivan to take on Simmons in 2004, but Sullivan lost by the same 54%-46% score.

Courtney came back for a rematch with Simmons in 2006, getting his campaign under way early in 2005. Economic uncertainty abounded locally after the Pentagon named the district's submarine base as a candidate for closure. From his seat on the Armed Services Committee, Simmons lobbied the Pentagon hard to keep the base open and held hearings on the need for more submarines. In August 2005, the base-closing commission recommended that the base remain open, which boded well for Simmons's re-election chances. Democrats worked diligently to nationalize the race by exploiting voter anger over the Iraq War and GOP ethics scandals in Congress. Simmons was attacked for donating $1,000 to the legal defense fund for Republican leader Tom DeLay, who was caught up in dual ethics and fundraising investigations. After DeLay left Congress in disgrace, Democrats sought to tether Simmons to the increasingly unpopular Republican president. Courtney called Simmons Bush's "No. 1 supporter in Connecticut," and his television ads portrayed Simmons as aligned with Bush on energy policy, Medicare prescription drug coverage and the war. Simmons touted his independence by pointing to votes he took on partial-birth abortion and same-sex marriage in opposition to the administration's positions, and he criticized Courtney for supporting higher gasoline taxes as a state legislator.

More than 242,000 voters turned out on Election Day, which was 25,000 more than in 2002. Courtney won towns like Old Lyme that he had lost four years earlier, and he posted larger margins in Mansfield, Norwich, New London and Vernon. Simmons did well in smaller towns in Windham County. When the results came in, Courtney held a slim 167-vote lead, a margin that was small enough to trigger an automatic recount. A week later, Courtney's lead was cut in half, but official results gave him a winning margin of 83 votes out of the more than 242,000 cast and made him the survivor of the closest House race of the 2006 elections. The voters in the 2nd District seem to like exciting elections. Gejdenson won re-election in 1994 by just 21 votes.

In the House, Courtney's new colleagues gave him a nickname, "Landslide Joe." But he also got a seat on the prestigious Armed Services Committee, where he could more effectively lobby for more money for the Navy's shipbuilding program at Groton. In 2007, he worked with other Connecticut and Rhode Island lawmakers to successfully secure an extra $588 million in the Defense appropriations bill for submarines, paving the way for the Navy to double its submarine production from one a year to two a year. Democratic leaders were eager to help the rookie representative secure his hold on the district. Courtney was able to get Armed Services Chairman Ike Skelton, D-Mo., and Defense Appropriations Subcommittee Chairman John Murtha, D-Pa., to visit the district, and both of the powerful chairmen backed improvements at Electric Boat. In 2008, Courtney won enactment of a bill giving environmental protection to 25 miles of the Eightmile River, bringing it under the Wild and Scenic Rivers Act. He was the only member of the Connecticut delegation who voted against the $700 billion bailout for financial firms on Wall Street, which he said focused too much on "a square mile of New York City." In a 2007 profile, the *Washington Post* Sunday magazine depicted Courtney as "an Irish fatalist" hustling to keep his seat and hoping to show that delivering more money for Electric Boat would show that he "had acquired savvy and clout in a hurry."

In 2008, Republicans initially touted Sean Sullivan, former commander of the Groton submarine base, in what they said would be a competitive contest. Sullivan called for alternative energy sources, criticized Courtney for supporting tax increases and said that Courtney was a lockstep loyalist for Democratic leaders. Courtney cited his accomplishments and said that voters had elected him to "stand up to Bush's policies." He ran strongly across the district and won 66%-32%, establishing a firm grip on this formerly competitive seat.

THIRD DISTRICT

Rosa DeLauro (D)

Elected 1990, 10th term; b. March 2, 1943, New Haven; home, New Haven; Marymount Col., B.A. 1964, London Sch. of Econ., 1962–63, Columbia U., M.A. 1966; Catholic; married (Stanley Greenberg); 3 children.

Professional Career: Exec. asst., New Haven Mayor Frank Logue, 1976–77; Exec. asst. & develop. admin., City of New Haven, 1977–79; Chief of staff, U.S. Sen. Christopher Dodd, 1980–87; Exec. dir., Countdown '87, 1987–88; Exec. dir., EMILY's List, 1989.

DC Office: 2413 RHOB, 20515, 202-225-3661; Fax: 202-225-4890; Web site: delauro.house.gov.

State Offices: New Haven, 203-562-3718; Stratford, 203-378-9005.

Committees: *Democratic Steering Committee Co-Chair. Appropriations* (9th of 37 D): Agriculture, Rural Development, FDA & Related Agencies (Chmn); Financial Services & General Government; Labor, HHS, Education & Related Agencies. *Budget* (16th of 24 D).

Group Ratings

	ADA	ACLU	AFS	LCV	ITIC	NTU	COC	ACU	CFG	FRC
2008	100	100	100	92	57	6	56	0	0	5
2007	100	—	100	85	—	4	45	0	0	—

National Journal Ratings

	2007 LIB	—	2007 CONS	2008 LIB	—	2008 CONS
Economic	78%	—	18%	81%	—	15%
Social	77%	—	17%	82%	—	0%
Foreign	93%	—	6%	78%	—	17%
Composite	85%	—	16%	85%	—	15%

Key Votes of the 110th Congress

1. Increase minimum wage	Y	5. Share immigration data	N	9. Withdraw troops 8/08	Y
2. Expand SCHIP	Y	6. Foreign aid abortion ban	N	10. No operations in Iran	Y
3. Raise CAFE standards	Y	7. Ban gay bias in workplace	Y	11. Free trade with Peru	N
4. Bail out financial markets	Y	8. Repeal D.C. gun law	N	12. Overhaul FISA	N

Election Results

2008 general	Rosa DeLauro (D-WF)	230,172	(77%)	($1,098,930)
	Bo Itshaky (R)	58,583	(20%)	
	Ralph Ferrucci (Green)	8,613	(3%)	
2008 primary	Rosa DeLauro (D)	unopposed		

Prior Winning Percentages: 2006 (76%); 2004 (72%); 2002 (66%); 2000 (72%); 1998 (71%); 1996 (71%); 1994 (63%); 1992 (66%); 1990 (52%)

Population		Race/Ethnicity		Work	
Pop. 2007:	697,260	White:	72.5%	Private:	80.5%
Change since 2000:	Up 2.4%	Black:	12.2%	Government:	13.3%
Urban:	96.6%	Hispanic:	10.0%	Self-employed:	6.1%
Rural:	3.4%	Asian:	3.5%	Blue collar:	19.7%
Area size:	485 sq. mi.	Native Am.:	0.2%	White collar:	64.1%
		Hawaiian:	0.0%	Khaki collar:	0.1%
Age		Two+ races:	1.3%	Other:	16.1%
Median age:	38.2 yrs.	*Ancestry*		Median income:	$59,726
More than 65 yrs:	13.8%	Italian:	19.4%	Median home value:	$279,600
Less than 18 yrs:	22.6%	Irish:	13.8%	Poverty:	9.3%
Education		German:	6.9%	**Military Veterans**	
H.S. grad:	88.1%			% of Pop:	9.3%
College grad:	31.4%				
Grad degree:	14.9%				

The beginnings of Connecticut's defense industry date to more than two centuries ago, in 1798, when Eli Whitney, a young Yale graduate, won an order from the young United States government to produce 10,000 muskets at $13.40 each. Six years before, Whitney had invented the cotton gin, which revolutionized the South but for years embroiled him in a patent suit. On the musket contract, he was determined to make a profit right off, so he set up a system of interchangeable parts and invented a milling machine and gauges: the birth of standardized American manufacturing. It also launched New Haven, established more than 150 years earlier as a religious haven for strict Puritans, as a manufacturing center; Whitney set up his factory along a small, rapidly flowing river just north of town. For the next 150 years or so, New Haven mass-produced rifles, clocks, locks, hardware and toys—anything its tinkerers and entrepreneurs could fashion. Few factories remain in New Haven, and the state's defense contracts are modest compared to those of the city's heyday. The factory that produced Winchester rifles and guns for 140 years closed in 2006. The Sikorsky plant in Stratford failed to get the contract to produce the new Marine One helicopter. In recent years, southern Connecticut around New Haven discovered a new source of prosperity in scores of small technology and biomedical firms. Minority population grew rapidly in New Haven County from 2000 to 2007, with a 29% increase for Hispanics and a 46% increase for Asians.

2008 Presidential Vote

Obama (D)	201,741	(63%)
McCain (R)	117,114	(36%)

2004 Presidential Vote

Kerry (D)	174,382	(56%)
Bush (R)	128,960	(42%)

Cook Partisan Voting Index: D+9

But the city itself, with significant crime rates and many neighborhoods scarred by abandoned homes, has shrunk in population: It had 164,000 people in 1950 and 124,000 in 2007. Nearly 29% of its children live in poverty. Yale, with its Gothic spires and redbrick halls, has always been the visual focus of New Haven and is now its largest employer. Some local revival has been sparked by a state development program that has turned old retail and office buildings into residences and by $1 billion in investments by biotech firms. New Haven also has a more recent claim on history: It was the birthplace of George W. Bush in 1946, and he lived his first two years on Hillhouse Avenue in a building that now houses the economics department.

The 3rd Congressional District of Connecticut covers the New Haven metropolitan area, which has long since spread beyond the narrow city limits into what were once Yankee villages and countryside. New Haven proper cast only 13% of the district's votes in 2008. For many years, the 3rd was a marginal district, changing partisan hands in the 1980s as well as in the 1940s and 1950s. But it is now a strongly Democratic district. In recent presidential contests, Barack Obama got 63% of the vote here in 2008, and John Kerry won 56% in 2004 against fellow Yale graduate Bush.

The congresswoman from the 3rd District is Rosa DeLauro, first elected in 1990. She is well connected in New Haven and Washington. She grew up in New Haven's Wooster Square. Both her parents were New Haven aldermen. Her mother, Luisa DeLauro, retired from the Board of Aldermen in 1999 after 35 years, the longest tenure in New Haven history. Rosa DeLauro's husband, Stanley Greenberg, was Bill Clinton's chief pollster from 1991 to 1994 and worked for Al Gore's presidential campaign in 2000 and John Kerry's in 2004. Obama White House Chief of Staff Rahm Emanuel lived in the couple's basement apartment on Capitol Hill when Emanuel was a House member commuting between his Illinois district and Washington. (Emanuel dubbed himself "The Hobbit.") Emanuel also officiated at the wedding of Greenburg's daughter Anna, who is a political consultant. DeLauro has been in politics nearly all of her life. She was a development administrator in New Haven in the 1970s, chief of staff to Democratic Sen. Christopher Dodd from 1980 to 1987, then spent a year working to stop U.S. military aid to Nicaraguan contras before going on to become director of EMILY's List, the women's campaign fundraising group. When 3rd District incumbent Bruce Morrison ran for governor in 1990, DeLauro ran for his seat and won, 52%-48%, over anti-tax and anti-abortion rights state Sen. Tom Scott. Her last serious competition came in 1992, when she won a rematch against Scott, 66%-34%.

DeLauro has a consistently liberal voting record, is a close ally of Speaker Nancy Pelosi and is one of the Democratic leadership's most vocal champions in debate. She is an active and ardent supporter of feminist issues. A cancer survivor, she sponsored the law to require that patients and doctors, not insurance companies, decide on 48-hour hospital stays for mastectomies, lobbied for insurance coverage of early-detection tests for cervical cancer, and helped to enact "Johanna's Law" to increase awareness of gynecological cancers. In 2009, Congress passed her bill to reverse a Supreme Court decision that had made it more difficult to ensure that women and men doing the same job are paid the same. DeLauro worked with abortion-rights opponent Tim Ryan, an Ohio Democrat, on a consensus Democratic bill to add more money for family-planning and pregnancy-prevention programs. After a trip to Cuba in 2007, she called for an end to the U.S. trade embargo.

As chairman since 2007 of the Appropriations Subcommittee on Agriculture, Rural Development, the Food and Drug Administration, and Related Agencies, she has taken a keen interest in food safety, which she said should have the same priority as prescription-drug and medical-device safety. Her subcommittee in 2008 increased by $1.8 billion President Bush's funding request for the FDA. Most of the money, DeLauro said, was aimed at reversing Bush-era cuts in consumer-protection spending. She also challenged the "pervasive pattern of failure at the FDA," including the agency's inadequate review of private blood and tissue donors. In July 2008, she called it "unconscionable" that the FDA gave bonuses to "top-level political managers who contribute to the low morale and negative culture at the agency." She successfully demanded release of a list of school districts that might have received contaminated beef.

As a political strategist and advocate of Democratic causes, DeLauro is "a live wire whose words rush out like sparks," as a *New York Times* profile described her. In one memorable stunt, DeLauro in 2002 helped draft the bill creating the Homeland Security Department and embarrassed House Republican leaders by winning a vote to prevent the department from contracting with corporations that move overseas for tax purposes. She has run twice for chairman of the Democratic Caucus and suffered two painfully close losses. In 1998, she lost 108-97 to Rep. Martin Frost of Texas, but then Minority Leader Dick Gephardt named her an assistant leader in charge of the party's message. In 2002, she lost by 104-103 to Rep. Robert Menendez of New Jersey after an intense yearlong contest. DeLauro was an active supporter of Pelosi in her leadership races through the years, which helped cement the bond between the two Italian-American liberal women. Pelosi has leaned on DeLauro for important appointive leadership roles. Pelosi made her co-chair of the Democratic Steering Committee, a powerful internal post that makes committee assignments. In 2007, DeLauro also became a vice chair of the Democratic Congressional Campaign Committee, the House Democrats' fundraising and recruiting arm. She was tasked with encouraging member participation. In 2004, working in close coordination with the John Kerry presidential campaign, DeLauro led the drafting of the Democratic platform.

She has expressed interest in running for the Senate if a Connecticut seat becomes open.

FOURTH DISTRICT

Jim Himes (D)

Elected 2008, 1st term; b. July 5, 1966, Lima, Peru; home, Greenwich; Harvard U., B.A. 1988; Oxford U., M.Phil. 1990.; Presbyterian; married (Mary); 2 children.

Elected Office: Greenwich Bd. of Estimates in Taxation, 2005–07.

Professional Career: Financial analyst and V.P., Goldman Sachs, 1990–2002; V.P., Enterprise Community Partners, 2004–08.

DC Office: 214 CHOB, 20515, 202-225-5541; Fax: 202-225-9629; Web site: himes.house.gov.

State Offices: Bridgeport, 866-453-0028; Stamford, 266-453-0028.

Committees: *Financial Services* (40th of 42 D): Capital Markets, Insurance & Government Sponsored Enterprises; Housing & Community Opportunity. *Homeland Security* (17th of 20 D): Intelligence, Information Sharing & Terrorism Risk Assessment; Transportation Security & Infrastructure Protection.

Group Ratings and Key Votes: Newly Elected

Election Results

2008 general	Jim Himes (D-WF)	158,475	(51%)	($3,909,937)
	Christopher Shays (R)	146,854	(48%)	($3,828,300)
2008 primary	Jim Himes (D)	12,260	(87%)	
	Lee Whitnum (D)	1,840	(13%)	

Population		Race/Ethnicity		Work	
Pop. 2007:	684,558	White:	68.2%	Private:	81.4%
Change since 2000:	Up 0.5%	Black:	11.0%	Government:	8.9%
Urban:	95.9%	Hispanic:	15.0%	Self-employed:	9.6%
Rural:	4.1%	Asian:	4.0%	Blue collar:	15.6%
Area size:	539 sq. mi.	Native Am.:	0.1%	White collar:	69.4%
Age		Hawaiian:	0.0%	Khaki collar:	0.0%
Median age:	38.9 yrs.	Two+ races:	0.8%	Other:	15.0%
More than 65 yrs:	12.9%	*Ancestry*		Median income:	$81,356
Less than 18 yrs:	25.9%	Italian:	13.7%	Median home value:	$582,500
Education		Irish:	12.6%	Poverty:	7.3%
H.S. grad:	88.1%	German:	7.9%	**Military Veterans**	
College grad:	44.8%			% of Pop:	7.5%
Grad degree:	19.5%				

No one in colonial America imagined that the rocky shore of southern Connecticut on Long Island Sound would some day lodge one of the largest concentrations of wealth in the world. The soil was stony, the terrain unaccommodating, the harbors not as convenient as those in New York, Rhode Island, and Massachusetts. For 200 years, this was the home of unnoticed Yankee farmers, sailors, and tinkerers. Then, factories were built on its fast-running stream. In the 19th century, Bridgeport be-

2008 Presidential Vote		
Obama (D)	190,995	(60%)
McCain (R)	126,849	(40%)
2004 Presidential Vote		
Kerry (D)	162,166	(52%)
Bush (R)	143,280	(46%)
Cook Partisan Voting Index:	D + 5	

came famous as the home of P.T. Barnum (the city's mayor before he started his circus), and around that time, rich New Yorkers began taking the train north to country houses in Connecticut. In the 20th century, Greenwich and other Yankee villages clustered around commuter railroad stations became the home of some of New York's elite. Greenwich has beautifully manicured hills, elaborately simple boat docks, carefully casual roads, good manners and dull haircuts. It has over a dozen private clubs and nearly a dozen private schools—and houses that routinely sell at high prices and are then torn down to make way for grander mansions. Many towns report nearly as many demolitions as new homes. Starting in the 1950s, New York City-based executives, eager to minimize their commutes and avoid New York's income taxes, moved their headquarters to Greenwich and farther, including General Electric in Fairfield and several firms in Stamford. Greenwich, sometimes referred to as "Wall Street by the Sea" for its proliferation of hedge fund offices and financial firms, is closest to New York and commands the highest commercial rents of all these places. These firms manage more than $300 billion in assets. Not all of the businesses are gigantic: In Shelton, Wiffle Ball Inc. sells millions of wiffle balls and bats each year.

The 4th Congressional District covers Connecticut along Long Island Sound, from industrial Bridgeport, the state's largest city, to affluent Greenwich. It goes inland to take in Ridgefield, Redding, Monroe, and Oxford. This is the wealthiest district in the nation's wealthiest state. It includes bustling and pricey Stamford, woodsy Darien, modest Norwalk, artsy-craftsy Westport, Fairfield, and then Bridgeport, an odd duck, an industrial and low-income town, though spruced up when the state-financed Harbor Yard sports complex opened for minor league baseball and a major downtown rehabilitation resulted. The basic political balance has been the same since the 1940s, when the heavily affluent suburbs out-voted Bridgeport and elected Republican Clare Boothe Luce to Congress. More than the rest of Connecticut, the 4th is oriented to New York City rather than to Hartford or Boston. People here watch New York television stations. They are Yankees, not Red Sox, fans. Their political attitudes are shaped by what is happening in New York as much as in Hartford. Opposition to high taxes has helped Republicans to win here. In tax year 2004, the 4th District had the third-highest federal individual income tax burden of all congressional districts. But the influence of Christian conservatives in the GOP has repelled Episcopalians and other mainline Protestants, and they have been increasingly voting Democratic. This is the district where George H. W. Bush grew up and one that he carried in 1988 and 1992. But George W. Bush lost it in 2000 and 2004, and Democrat Barack Obama defeated Republican John McCain 60% to 40% in 2008.

The new congressman from the 4th District is Democrat Jim Himes. A former nonprofit organization executive, Himes rode Obama's coattails to victory in 2008, finally sinking moderate Republican Christopher Shays, who had previously made a habit of withstanding challenges to his seat from covetous Democrats. Though he represents one of the wealthiest areas of the country, Himes grew up in different surroundings. Born in Lima, Peru, he spent his early years in Peru and Colombia, where his father worked for the Ford Foundation, the automotive pioneer's international development organization. Around the time of his 10th birthday, after his parents divorced, he came to the United States with his mother and two sisters and settled in Pennington, N.J. His early experience in Latin America had an enduring effect. He speaks fluent Spanish and maintains a deep interest in the region. Himes earned his undergraduate degree from Harvard University and then got a Rhodes scholarship to study at Oxford. When he returned to the United States, he went to work for Goldman Sachs as a financial analyst. He spent 12 years at the powerful investment house, and left the company in 2002 as a vice president. The following year, he joined Enterprise Community Partners, a Columbia, Md.-based nonprofit dedicated to alleviating urban poverty. Beginning in 2004, he managed its offices in the Northeast.

Like many other Wall Street executives, Himes moved in 1998 to the affluent suburb of Greenwich to raise a family with his wife, Mary. He became active in the town Democratic committee after the 2000 presidential election, and served as committee chairman from 2003 to 2007. On Sept. 11, 2001, Himes left his Goldman Sachs office against company orders to provide assistance to victims. In 2006, he worked as a campaign volunteer for Democrat Diane Farrell, who finished roughly 7,000 votes behind Shays in that year's race for the seat. The following April, Himes announced his own campaign against Shays, promising the third competitive race in a row in this Democratic district. He criticized Shays for voting against timelines for withdrawing troops from Iraq, provoking inevitable comparisons to Ned Lamont, the wealthy Greenwich businessman who unseated Sen. Joe Lieberman in the 2006 Democratic primary on an antiwar platform. Lieberman ran in the general election as an independent and won re-election anyway.

Unseating a ten-term incumbent, even a perennially endangered one, is a daunting task, but in the early stages of the race, Himes' determined efforts help him set a torrid fundraising pace, aided in large measure by his connections on Wall Street. The Democratic Congressional Campaign Committee also made him one of its top prospects in 2008. After easily dispatching a minor challenger in the August Democratic primary, Himes returned his focus to Shays and the Bush administration and attempted to link the two over the Iraq war. He held press conferences at the Congress Street Bridge in Bridgeport, a drawbridge that has been frozen in the upright position for more than 10 years, to emphasize what he called Shays' misplaced priorities. The charge so angered Shays that he appeared unannounced at one of the press conferences in August to confront Himes face-to-face. The two met seven more times in October at scheduled debates. Himes embraced the national Democratic establishment, frequently reminding voters that he would appear on the same ticket as presidential nominee Barack Obama of Illinois. In September, House Speaker Nancy Pelosi of California appeared at a fundraiser for Himes in Stamford, and a month later, Obama recorded a radio spot in support of Himes. The efforts of national Democrats helped Himes slightly outraise Shays, and the DCCC further tipped the scales by investing $1.2 million in the race.

Sensitive to his district's politics, Shays made his own overtures to Democrats, running ads that touted him as the candidate with "the hopefulness of Obama" and "the straight talk of McCain." But he made a questionable move in September 2008, when he echoed McCain's claim that the fundamentals of the United States' economy were strong. Himes and the DCCC criticized that assessment, but Shays stuck to it and even reiterated it at a debate in late October. In past years, Shays' moderate record and seniority on Capitol Hill helped him weather even the most severe political storms, including the Democratic wave of 2006. But in 2008, the surge of enthusiasm for Obama's candidacy was too powerful. Himes defeated Shays 51% to 48%, leaving New England without a single Republican House member. Himes won the district's urban regions by substantial margins—in Bridgeport alone, he got 31,286 votes compared to Shays' 7,662 votes—and also managed to stay competitive in the affluent suburbs that tend to break Republican.

Himes promised during the campaign to seek a seat on the Transportation and Infrastructure Committee to explore solutions to the district's traffic problems. But as the country's financial crisis deepened, he explored ways to put his Wall Street background to use in Congress and began seeking a foothold on issues relating to the financial services industry. He earned appointments to the Financial Services Committee and the Committee on Homeland Security.

FIFTH DISTRICT

Chris Murphy (D)

Elected 2006, 2nd term; b. Aug. 3, 1973, White Plains, NY; home, Cheshire; Attended Exeter College (England), 1994–95; Williams Col., B.A. 1996; U. of CT, J.D. 2002; Protestant; married (Cathy Holahan); 1 child.

Elected Office: CT House of Reps., 1998–2002; CT Senate, 2002–06.

Professional Career: Southington zoning commission, 1997–99; Practicing atty., 2002–06.

DC Office: 412 CHOB, 20515, 202-225-4476; Fax: 202-225-5933; Web site: chrismurphy.house.gov.

State Offices: Danbury, 203-798-2072; Meriden, 203-630-0815; New Britain, 860-223-8412; Waterbury, 203-759-7541.

Committees: *Energy & Commerce* (31st of 36 D): Communications, Technology & the Internet; Health. *Oversight & Government Reform* (20th of 24 D): Government Management, Organization & Procurement; National Security & Foreign Affairs.

Group Ratings

	ADA	ACLU	AFS	LCV	ITIC	NTU	COC	ACU	CFG	FRC
2008	95	82	100	100	86	9	61	0	4	5
2007	100	—	100	100	—	6	50	0	1	—

National Journal Ratings

	2007 LIB	—	2007 CONS		2008 LIB	—	2008 CONS
Economic	64%	—	34%		64%	—	35%
Social	69%	—	31%		67%	—	28%
Foreign	69%	—	29%		52%	—	46%
Composite	68%	—	32%		62%	—	38%

Key Votes of the 110th Congress

1. Increase minimum wage	Y	5. Share immigration data	N	9. Withdraw troops 8/08	Y
2. Expand SCHIP	Y	6. Foreign aid abortion ban	N	10. No operations in Iran	Y
3. Raise CAFE standards	Y	7. Ban gay bias in workplace	Y	11. Free trade with Peru	N
4. Bail out financial markets	Y	8. Repeal D.C. gun law	N	12. Overhaul FISA	N

Election Results

2008 general	Chris Murphy (D-WF)	179,327	(59%)	($3,056,641)
	David Cappiello (R)	117,914	(39%)	($1,330,995)
2008 primary	Chris Murphy (D)	unopposed		

Prior Winning Percentages: 2006 (54%)

Population		Race/Ethnicity		Work	
Pop. 2007:	705,650	White:	77.0%	Private:	80.7%
Change since 2000:	Up 3.6%	Black:	5.6%	Government:	11.8%
Urban:	85.9%	Hispanic:	12.7%	Self-employed:	7.4%
Rural:	14.1%	Asian:	2.8%	Blue collar:	20.7%
Area size:	1,282 sq. mi.	Native Am.:	0.1%	White collar:	63.6%
		Hawaiian:	0.0%	Khaki collar:	0.1%
Age		Two+ races:	1.4%	Other:	15.6%
Median age:	39.3 yrs.			Median income:	$63,814
More than 65 yrs:	13.6%	*Ancestry*		Median home value:	$292,600
Less than 18 yrs:	24.0%	Italian:	14.8%	Poverty:	8.8%
		Irish:	13.5%		
Education		German:	8.6%	**Military Veterans**	
H.S. grad:	86.6%			% of Pop:	9.3%
College grad:	32.9%				
Grad degree:	13.3%				

Over the years, Connecticut's stony soil has become home to some of the most affluent people in the nation and the world. This is true even in the hills of northwest Connecticut, off the interstates and far from Connecticut's small urban capital of Hartford and its sometime booming edge city of Stamford. In Litchfield County are exquisite Yankee towns like Washington and Kent, which were prosperous in the post-Revolutionary era, when Connecticut's shipowners accumulated capital and invested it in

2008 Presidential Vote
Obama (D) 182,022   (56%)
McCain (R)............................136,966   (42%)

2004 Presidential Vote
Kerry (D)................................153,616   (49%)
Bush (R) 152,504   (49%)

Cook Partisan Voting Index: D + 2

factories and mills, and now are considered the "anti-Hamptons," a country-home mecca for ultrarich New Yorkers seeking to avoid the glitz of Southampton and East Hampton. Not far away are small industrial cities like New Britain, America's ball-bearing capital for years; Meriden, which turned from making ivory combs, clocks, cutlery, and silver to producing electrical signaling equipment, biotech filters, and nuclear instruments; and Waterbury, once the nation's largest producer of brass, where political corruption and economic malaise resulted in the state taking over its finances in 2001. Danbury, once the nation's leading producer of hats, is now a growing corporate headquarters with an eclectic mix of recent immigrants from South America, the Caribbean and Southeast Asia. Over the hills from Hartford are Avon and Simsbury, booming towns that have become comfortable bedroom communities and home to champion international ice-skaters.

The 5th Congressional District of Connecticut covers much of the western side of the state, dipping down to include the northern towns of Fairfield County. It has two arms that reach into the hills of central Connecticut—one to Democratic Meriden and the other to the affluent and Republican-leaning Farmington Valley suburbs of Hartford. This district was carefully drawn by a bipartisan redistricting commission to provide a "fair fight" between two incumbents forced into the same district after Connecticut lost a House seat in the 2000 census. Until recently, small towns like Kent and Salisbury in Litchfield County were dominated by Republicans, but the influx of newcomers has altered voting patterns. In 2006, the district recorded 17,000 new registered voters; 48% of them were unaffiliated, 34% were Democrats and 17% were Republicans. Barack Obama won this district by 45,056 votes; George W. Bush lost it in 2004 by only 1,112 votes.

The congressman from the 5th District is Chris Murphy, a Democrat elected in 2006. Murphy grew up in Wethersfield, and his father is a prominent member of a Hartford law firm. He graduated from Williams College in 1996 and the same year, at age 22, became the campaign manager for Democrat Charlotte Koskoff, who came 1,587 votes short of ousting veteran Republican Rep. Nancy Johnson. The lessons of that campaign would serve Murphy well in his political career. He won a seat in the state House in 1998, got a law degree in 2002 and later that year won election to the state Senate. He served as co-chairman of the public health committee, where he worked to curb hospital collection practices, ban smoking in workplaces, and increase investment in embryonic-stem-cell research.

In early 2005 Murphy moved into Johnson's 5th District, announcing in April that he planned to challenge her. He was backed by the Democratic establishment and faced no primary opposition. Unlike Connecticut's other two competitive congressional races in 2006, this one did not revolve around the Iraq War and President Bush. Much of the debate focused instead on the Medicare prescription-drug benefit that moderate Republican Johnson had helped design in 2003 as chairwoman of the House Ways and Means Health Subcommittee. The liberal group MoveOn.org ran ads in April 2006 tying Johnson to disgraced former GOP lobbyist Jack Abramoff and to the oil and pharmaceutical industries, spots designed to elevate the competitiveness of what was then viewed as a second-tier race.

Murphy contended that the Republicans' prescription drug program's enrollment deadlines penalized seniors, and he spotlighted drug industry contributions to Johnson to portray her as a shill for the industry. National security issues did not play a major role in the race until the day after the fifth anniversary of the September 11, 2001, terrorist attacks. In a television ad resembling a movie trailer for an espionage thriller, Johnson attacked Murphy for opposing the Bush administration's warrantless wiretapping program. The 30-second spot, which featured a series of rapid images, suggested that seeking a court warrant for surveillance takes too long and could jeopardize national security. The security focus briefly put Murphy on the defensive, and some Democrats feared Murphy was too slow to respond. But he struck back with an ad that implied Johnson was slow to help a mother obtain health coverage to pay for surgery to fix her infant's cleft palate. In October, Johnson used an ad to accuse Murphy of voting to raise taxes 27 times and for being weak on terrorism and soft on drug dealers. But all the negative campaigning may have undermined Johnson's image as a cool-headed, seasoned legislator with a grandmotherly air. Johnson, who collected over $1.2 million from the health care industry alone, outspent Murphy $5 million to $2.5 million. But Murphy won 54%-44%.

In the House, Murphy has established a centrist voting record among Democrats. On the Financial Services Committee, he added an amendment to a mortgage-overhaul bill that restricted "backdoor payments" to mortgage brokers that were often passed along to unwitting borrowers. He took the lead in organizing freshman Democrats for ethics reform, especially the creation of an outside commission to review ethics complaints against House members. Although his proposal failed, the House did create an Office of Congressional Ethics, with independent investigators. In April 2008, the House passed his Government Contractor Accountability Act, requiring disclosure of the names and salaries of top officers of large companies that made most of their money from contracts with the government. "If there are people out there making millions off of governments, we should know about it," he said. In 2009, he won a seat on the influential Energy and Commerce Committee, where he was positioned to work on health care issues, a primary focus of the committee and its chairman, Henry Waxman of California.

The National Republican Congressional Committee initially saw an opportunity when State Sen. David Cappiello challenged Murphy in 2008. Cappiello ran as a John McCain-style maverick, and he criticized the hundreds of thousands of campaign dollars given to Murphy by finance firms as well as his support for the 2008 bailout of financial markets. "Did Chris Murphy shake up Washington, or shake down Wall Street?" he asked in a closing ad. Murphy emphasized the need for sweeping policy change, including a reworking of tax and trade policies that had led to the financial crisis. National party interest waned in the closing weeks as Cappiello failed to gain traction, and Murphy won 59%-39%.

★ DELAWARE ★

Delaware, the first state to ratify the Constitution, the second smallest state in area, and the sixth smallest in population, is a small corner of America but with some considerable claims on U.S. history. The mouth of the Delaware River was explored by Henry Hudson, and the Dutch and Swedes built settlements on the west bank in the 1630s. But the three counties of Delaware owe their separate existence to the politics of the proprietors of William Penn's colony of Pennsylvania, and to Delawareans' own speed in ratifying the Constitution, which made it literally the "First State."

Throughout most of its history, Delaware has been unusually affluent. It had the nation's highest income levels during the early 20th century and still has relatively high income levels. The many members of the du Pont clan occupy beautiful cobblestone mansions in its chateau country. Delaware's racial and ethnic mix is not radically different from the rest of the nation's; it is home to more African-Americans (20%) and fewer Hispanics (6%). It has a mixture of suburbs, old immigrant neighborhoods, urban black neighborhoods, attractive beach towns, and farmlands. Sussex County in southern Delaware is a world of its own. It produces more chickens than any other county in the country—chickens outnumber people 300-to-1 in Delaware—and also thousands of tons of processed chicken dung (or "broiler litter"). Its beach communities are bustling with growth, and there is a move toward historic preservation in the old, inland towns.

For much of the last two centuries, the central focus of Delaware's economy was the business started by Eleuthère Irénée du Pont, the practical-minded son of a dreamy, idealistic French immigrant. He built a gunpowder mill on the banks of Brandywine Creek in 1802, which was the first enterprise of the du Pont family. Over time, it became one of America's great munitions and chemical companies. It switched from gunpowder to dynamite in the 1880s, and the company grew especially rapidly during World War I, generating so much capital that it bought a large share of General Motors stock in the 1920s and controlled GM for 30 years, when GM was the country's largest corporation. DuPont capital also financed what was arguably the world's finest research and development program. In the years on either side of World War II, DuPont prospered by bringing to the consumer and industrial markets new synthetics and plastics such as rayon, nylon, synthetic dyes, cellophane, Lucite, Teflon, and Dacron: "Better Living Through Chemistry."

Business trends in Delaware have had a big impact on national policy. In the late 19th century, the state passed pioneering laws of incorporation, giving more flexibility and power to managers and owners. Most companies in the *Fortune* 500 and on the New York Stock Exchange and the Nasdaq are incorporated in Delaware. Their legal births take place in a federal-style building near the Capitol in Dover, which means that much of the nation's corporate law, especially on mergers and acquisitions, is made in Delaware's Chancery Court. Delaware takes care in choosing judges and writing corporate law to produce a reliable legal environment. Recently, the Chancery Court's jurisdiction has been extended to intellectual property, and the Wilmington bar has been boning up on corporate bankruptcy law. In the quarter-century span starting in the early 1980s, Delaware fostered a new industry: credit cards. In 1981, Gov. Pete du Pont pushed through a law abolishing Delaware's usury laws and lowering its bank franchise tax. Inflation was high, and banks were looking for a state with no limit on interest rates to locate their credit card operations. Although South Dakota abolished its usury law in 1980, the state didn't have a labor force large enough to support many banks. Delaware did. MBNA moved there from Maryland in 1982 and invented the affinity card in 1983. It became the nation's largest credit card issuer; its chief executive officer, Charles Cawley, replaced the du Pont family as Delaware's most visible philanthropist and community leader. Cawley retired in 2003, and Bank of America acquired MBNA in 2005. The 2007 financial crisis hit the credit card business hard, helping to send Delaware into recession, and the troubles in the domestic auto industry reverberated in the state as well. More than 1,000 people lost their jobs when Chrysler closed its Dodge manufacturing plant in Newark at the end of 2008, and another 550 were laid off when General Motors shuttered its Wilmington plant in 2009. Still, DuPont is keeping the state on the cutting edge by developing alternative fuels, and life sciences businesses are growing. AstraZeneca has its U.S. headquarters in Delaware. The state's economy may surge again from the rise of an industry as little anticipated now as the credit card business was in 1980.

One way Delaware thrives is by "exporting taxes." Journalist Jonathan Chait, irritated at the $2 tolls and the traffic jams at the tollbooths on the Delaware Turnpike, wrote in the *New Republic*: "The organizing principle of Delaware government is to subsidize its people at the rest of the country's expense." State government gets 3% of its operating budget from the turnpike tolls, 22% from corporate and franchise taxes, and 8% from slot machines. A 1993 U.S. Supreme Court decision sanctioned Delaware's tax on unclaimed property from other states. Exporting taxes has allowed Delaware to be one of the five states with no sales tax (Maryland's tax is 6%). And it has lowered its income tax several times in recent years, first under du Pont, then under Republican Gov. Michael Castle and Democratic Gov. Thomas Carper. Property taxes are low, with no reassessments since 1974 in Sussex County, since 1983

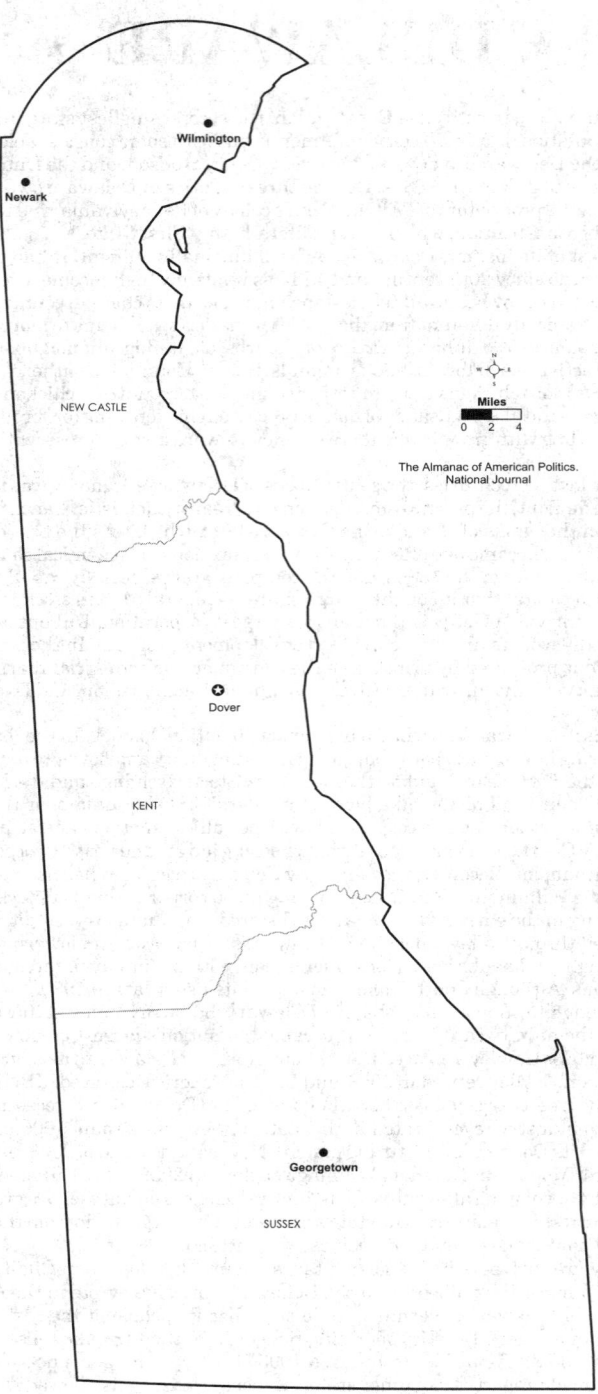

Wilmington

Newark

NEW CASTLE

Miles
0   2   4

The Almanac of American Politics.
National Journal

Dover

KENT

Georgetown

SUSSEX

U.S. Representative elected at-large.

in New Castle County, and since 1987 in Kent County. The Census Bureau reports that Delaware's state government has the fifth-highest revenue per capita of any state, and the Tax Foundation found that Delaware has the fourth-lowest tax burden on its residents. Delaware boosters can argue that its state policies have enabled America's industrial economy to grow robustly, have provided credit to millions of people and businesses, and have led the nation in a virtuous cycle of lowering taxes. Certainly Delaware has done well. Its population grew 18% in the 1990s, and another 12% from 2000 to 2008—faster than any other state in the East or Midwest.

Delaware is on both sides of the Mason-Dixon line. It was a slave state with many emancipation sympathizers. On his Wilmington stop during his train ride to Washington in January 2009, President-elect Obama, joined by Vice President-elect Biden, paid tribute to Delaware's Underground Railroad. They did not mention that Abraham Lincoln, during his 1861 train ride to Washington, decided not to risk a stop in slaveholding Delaware. Delaware also has immigrant communities in the Wilmington area, and it has Southern-accented farmers in Kent and Sussex counties (plus Latino migrants working in its chicken plants). Its New Castle County suburbs range from very affluent to not-so-affluent. Well-preserved 18th-century buildings line the streets of New Castle, the capital from 1704 to 1777. Newark has grown from a country crossroads to a small city as the University of Delaware has expanded.

From the 1950s through the 1980s, the state's considerable variety produced a robust two-party politics in which tiny Delaware's vote mirrored that of the nation's. But in the 1990s, Delaware, like many of America's largest metro areas, trended toward the Democrats. Now it is virtually a one-party state. Democrats hold both U.S. Senate seats: Thomas Carper won his by beating incumbent Republican William Roth in 2000, and Edward Kaufman, a longtime Biden aide, was appointed to Biden's seat in January 2009. After 16 years of Democratic governors, Delaware elected another one. In 2008, Treasurer Jack Markell won 68%-32%, after he defeated Lt. Gov. John Carney in the September primary. Democrats increased their lead in the state Senate to 16-5, while the state House, formerly 22-19 Republican, is now 24-17 Democratic. The major exception to Democratic rule is Republican Rep. Michael Castle, who was elected to the state's lone House seat in 1992 after two terms as governor. He was re-elected 61%-38% in 2008. Delaware's big race in 2010 will be for the remaining four years of Biden's Senate term. A likely candidate is his son, Beau Biden, the state attorney general who as a member of the Delaware National Guard served in Iraq in 2008. The biggest question mark at press time in July 2009 was whether Castle would seek the seat.

Delaware elections are not bitter contests. Thanks to the state's small size, politics remain intimate. Personal campaigning is important, and voters are not at all surprised to run into their senators in the supermarket. Successful Delaware politicians are almost always nice people; they couldn't get elected otherwise. Then there is Delaware's unique custom, dating back to 1792, of "Return Day." On the Thursday after an election, winning and losing candidates go to the Sussex County seat of Georgetown and ride together in carriages to receive the bipartisan cheers of the voters and, literally, bury a hatchet in a box of Lewes Beach sand. Not a bad example for the other 49 states.

Population		Household Income		Work	
Pop. 2007:	852,689	Under $15k:	10.1%	Private:	80.5%
State rank:	45th of 50	$15k to $50k:	34.6%	Government:	14.3%
Change since 2000:	Up 8.8%	$50k to $100k:	33.7%	Self-employed:	5.0%
Urban:	76.4%	$100k to $150k:	18.2%	Unemployment (3-yr. average):	3.8%
Rural:	23.6%	Over $150k:	3.4%	Poverty:	10.6%
Native of state:	46.2%	Median income:	$55,303	Blue collar:	21.0%
Not a citizen:	4.4%	**Home Value**		White collar:	62.5%
Area size:	2,489 sq. mi.	Under $100k:	13.1%	Khaki collar:	0.2%
Most populous cities		$100k to $300k:	55.0%	Other:	16.3%
1. Wilmington	63,619	$300k to $500k:	23.9%	**Age**	
2. Dover	33,796	$500k to $1 mil:	6.6%	Median age:	37.6 yrs.
3. Newark	29,916	Over $1 million:	1.4%	More than 65 yrs:	13.4%
		Median:	$225,200	Less than 18 yrs:	23.9%

Race/Ethnicity		Language		Military Veterans		Registered Voters in 2008	
White:	69.1%	English:	88.1%	% of Pop:	12.3%	D:	281,650 (46.6%)
Black:	20.0%	Spanish:	6.2%	*Veterans by Period*		R:	181,870 (30.1%)
Hispanic:	6.3%	Asian:	1.5%	WWII and before:	12.1%	Other:	140,857 (23.3%)
Asian:	2.7%	Other		Korea:	12.3%	Voter turnout:	412,412
Native Am.:	0.2%	European	3.2%	Vietnam:	31.0%	Turnout as % of	
Hawaiian:	0.0%	**Education**		Gulf (pre-2001):	11.5%	voting age:	61.8%
Two+ races:	1.4%	H.S. grad:	85.9%	Gulf (post-2001):	8.0%	**General Assembly**	
Ancestry		College grad:	26.6%	Peace time:	25.2%	Senate:	16 D 5 R
Irish:	14.5%	Grad degree:	10.6%			House:	24 D 17 R
German:	12.6%						
English:	10.0%			**Cook Partisan Voting Index:** D+7			

Presidential politics   Delaware has been competitive in most presidential elections since the Federalists were battling the Jeffersonians. Until 2000, it could claim to be a presidential bellwether: It had voted for every winner from 1952 to 1996, the longest winning streak of any state. But starting in 2000, this affluent state has been voting significantly more Democratic than the national average. The New Castle County suburbs, like other affluent parts of major metropolitan areas, tilted toward the Democrats and away from the Republicans on cultural issues. Most Delaware voters still see plenty of ads, because in the past three elections all candidates have targeted Pennsylvania and most of the state is in the Philadelphia media market. But it seldom sees presidential or vice presidential candidates, except for Biden, whom voters saw often during his 36 years in the Senate.

In 2004, Delaware scheduled its primary one week after New Hampshire's, on February 3, but it was only one of several states voting that day. Sen. Joe Lieberman of Connecticut, endorsed by Carper, Carney, and Markell, paid several trips to Delaware. Other candidates were scarcer. Sen. John Kerry of Massachusetts won the primary with 50% of the vote; Lieberman ran second with 11%, in what amounted to a tie with John Edwards, Howard Dean, and Wesley Clark.

In 2008, Delaware held its primary on February 5, Super Tuesday. Interest was higher, at least on the Democratic side, as Democratic Party registration surged while Republican registration sagged. Little campaigning occurred until after the Iowa caucuses, and Biden had already withdrawn from the race. On January 31, Michelle Obama appeared at a theater in Wilmington and drew a crowd of 2,600. Encouraged, the Obama campaign scheduled a February rally in Rodney Square, and 10,000 thronged to see the candidate himself. Barack Obama was endorsed by gubernatorial primary rivals Markell and Carney. Hillary Rodham Clinton was endorsed by outgoing Gov. Ruth Ann Minner. The Clinton campaign scheduled a Chelsea Clinton appearance for February 4, but that was not enough. Obama carried the state 53%-42%, winning by a big margin in both black neighborhoods and affluent suburbs in New Castle County. Clinton carried Southern-accented Sussex County.

Some 96,000 Delawareans voted in the Democratic primary, and only 50,000 in the GOP primary. The Republican candidates did little campaigning here. John McCain, endorsed by Castle, won with 45% of the vote, to 33% for Mitt Romney and 15% for Mike Huckabee.

In recent general elections, Democrats Al Gore and John Kerry carried Delaware by decisive margins, 55%-42% and 53%-46%, respectively, in 2000 and 2004. In 2008, with Biden on the ticket—the first Delawarean on a national ticket—Obama carried the state 62%-37%. Regional patterns did emerge in the voting. Obama carried New Castle County—once marginal political ground—by an astonishing 70%-29%, much better than in demographically similar areas in southeast Pennsylvania or southern New Jersey. But Obama carried Kent County by only 54%-45%, and he lost Sussex County by 45%-54%.

2008 Presidential Vote		
Obama (D)	255,459	(62%)
McCain (R)	152,374	(37%)

2008 Democratic Presidential Primary		
Obama (D)	51,124	(53%)
Clinton (D)	40,751	(42%)

2008 Republican Presidential Primary		
McCain (R)	22,626	(45%)
Romney (R)	16,344	(33%)
Huckabee (R)	7,706	(15%)

2004 Presidential Vote		
Kerry (D)	200,152	(53%)
Bush (R)	171,660	(46%)

Governor

Jack Markell (D)

Elected 2008, term expires Jan. 2013, 1st term; b. Nov. 26, 1960, Newark; home, Wilmington; Brown U., B.A. 1981; U. of Chicago, M.B.A. 1985; Jewish; married (Carla); 2 children.

Elected Office: DE treas., 1999–2008.

Professional Career: Officer, First Natl. Bank Chicago, 1982–86; Assoc., McKinsey & Co., Inc., 1986–1988; Sr. v.p., Nextel, 1989–95; V.P., Comcast, 1996–1998.

Office: Tatnall Bldg., Dover, 19901, 302-744-4101; Fax: 302-739-2775; Web site: www.state.de.us/governor.

Election Results

2008 general	Jack Markell (D)	266,861	(68%)
	William Lee (R)	126,662	(32%)
2008 primary	Jack Markell (D)	37,849	(51%)
	John Carney (D)	36,112	(49%)

Jack Markell is the new Democratic governor of Delaware. The state's first Jewish governor, he was elected after upsetting establishment-backed Lt. Gov. John Carney in the Democratic primary in 2008.

Markell (*mar-KEL*) was raised in a split-level house in Newark, Del., the youngest of three children. His father was a professor at the University of Delaware and his mother was a state social worker. Growing up, Markell came to love Delaware's small-town familiarity; he went to kindergarten with his future wife, Carla. His first foray into politics came at age 17, when he was elected president of his high school's student body. The same year, he accompanied his father on an overseas sabbatical, living for half a year in the United Kingdom and for half a year in New Zealand. After graduating from Brown University and earning an M.B.A. from the University of Chicago, Markell set off on a 16-year career in business. He worked briefly in banking and consulting before joining a telecommunications startup called Fleet Call in 1989. Over the next decade, Fleet Call grew into a major cellular service provider and rebranded itself as Nextel, a name Markell coined. He struck up a lasting friendship there with one of Fleet Call's early investors, Mark Warner, the future Democratic governor of Virginia. Following a brief stint as an executive for cable service provider Comcast, Markell defeated Republican state Treasurer Janet Rzewnicki in 1998 in his first campaign for public office.

Markell brought his business acumen to the treasurer's office and played an influential role in shaping the state's finances. Shortly after taking office, he sought to cut state spending by consolidating purchases across agencies. He helped pioneer a program that provides every state employee a detailed health assessment in an effort to provide better care while reducing the state's costs. Markell also brought a didactic touch to his work in the state capital. Believing that most citizens knew relatively little about monetary issues, he sought to improve financial literacy in the state where most of the nation's credit cards are issued. Together with community and church leaders in Wilmington, he led a campaign to encourage eligible families to apply for the Earned Income Tax Credit. He created the Delaware Money School, which offers free classes on a range of personal financial topics. He was re-elected by wide margins in 2002 and 2006.

Markell was a natural to run for governor in 2008, when Democratic Gov. Ruth Ann Minner was barred by term limits from running again. But there was someone of equal political stature ahead of him in line. Carney, the lieutenant governor, was the favorite to succeed her. In a small state where most elected officials are on personal terms with one another, most office seekers defer to the wishes of party elders, who hoped to avoid the first contested Democratic gubernatorial primary since 1992. They urged Markell to run for lieutenant governor instead. But he was steadfast about wanting the top job. Deprived of his anticipated coronation, Carney lined up support from much of the party establishment, including Minner, state legislators, and unions. But Markell campaigned tirelessly across the state and raised more than $4 million, including $725,000 of his own money, a record fundraising haul in a Delaware governor's race. Carney could not keep pace with Markell's fundraising, but enjoyed the backing of the state party's executive committee, which ran ads against Markell. As Minner's popularity flagged after two terms in office, Markell subtly distanced himself from her by campaigning on a theme of change, and in June released a detailed compendium of policy proposals called the "Blueprint for a Better Delaware." Still, Markell's victory in the September primary was nothing short of a stunner. He took 51% of the vote to Carney's 49%, a margin of about 1,700 votes.

The party rallied behind Markell for the general election, where he faced Republican Bill Lee, a retired Superior Court judge making his third straight run for the office. Jeff Brown, a bartender and the founder of the Blue Enigma Party, also qualified for the ballot but never posed a credible threat. On the campaign trail, Markell and Matt Denn, the Democratic candidate for lieutenant governor, touted a plan they claimed would save taxpayers over $100 million while simultaneously balancing a state budget faced with a massive deficit. The 12-page document drew heavily on previous Markell proposals for health care, education, and energy. The Republican Party tried to taint Markell with ads that referenced a 1994 lawsuit alleging that he and other Nextel executives had made false statements to boost the company's stock price. The executives settled the lawsuit for $27 million without admitting wrongdoing.

In the weeks leading up to the general election, few doubted that Markell would keep the governor's mansion in Democratic hands. He entered October with a commanding lead in the polls and 10 times as much money as his opponent. During a debate in late October, Lee pushed Markell to pledge not to levy any new taxes in order to fund his proposed programs. Markell refused, but did not appear to suffer negative fallout. He defeated Lee 68%-32%.

Markell took office at a time of deepening economic uncertainty for the state, whose reliance on the financial services industry for its tax revenue left it disproportionately affected by volatility on Wall Street. He pledged to create 25,000 jobs during his first term, a promise that will not be easy to keep. In October 2008, Chrysler announced that it would close its plant in Newark. The plant is a major area employer. Early in his term, Markell toured the state, engaging citizens in discussions on how to reduce a budget deficit projected to reach $606 million by 2010. Markell took initial steps to reduce state spending, including ending state-funded travel, reducing state-vehicle usage by 20%, and introducing a new energy usage policy for state buildings. On other issues, Markell's election will mean a change from the past. He supports the construction of a wind farm off the Delaware coast, which Minner had opposed.

Senior Senator

Thomas Carper (D)

Elected 2000, term expires 2012, 2nd term; b. Jan. 23, 1947, Beckley, WV; home, Wilmington; OH St. U., B.A. 1968, U. of DE, M.B.A. 1975; Presbyterian; married (Martha); 2 children.

Military Career: Navy, 1968–73 (Vietnam); Naval Reserves, 1973–91.

Elected Office: DE treas., 1976–82; U.S. House of Reps., 1982–92; DE gov. 1992–2000.

Professional Career: Industrial devel. specialist, DE Div. of Econ. Devel., 1975–76.

DC Office: 513 HSOB, 20510, 202-224-2441; Fax: 202-228-2190; Web site: carper.senate.gov.

State Offices: Dover, 302-674-3308; Georgetown, 302-856-7690; Wilmington, 302-573-6291.

Committees: *Environment & Public Works* (3rd of 12 D). *Finance* (13th of 13 D): Energy, Natural Resources & Infrastructure; Health Care; Taxation, IRS Oversight & Long-Term Growth. *Homeland Security & Governmental Affairs* (4th of 10 D): Contracting Oversight; Federal Financial Management, Government Information, Federal Services & International Security (Chmn); Investigations (Permanent).

Group Ratings

	ADA	ACLU	AFS	LCV	ITIC	NTU	COC	ACU	CFG	FRC
2008	85	43	89	100	80	8	63	0	7	0
2007	85	—	100	93	—	10	55	8	13	—

National Journal Ratings

	2007 LIB	—	2007 CONS	2008 LIB	—	2008 CONS
Economic	58%	—	41%	51%	—	48%
Social	60%	—	39%	55%	—	44%
Foreign	59%	—	36%	65%	—	6%
Composite	60%	—	40%	62%	—	38%

Key Votes of the 110th Congress

1. Raise CAFE standards	Y	5. Make English official language Y	9. Withdraw troops 3/08	Y
2. Expand SCHIP	Y	6. Path to citizenship Y	10. Iran guard is terrorist group Y
3. Cap greenhouse gases	Y	7. Fetus is unborn child N	11. Increase missile defense $ N
4. Bail out financial markets	Y	8. Prosecute hate crimes Y	12. Overhaul FISA Y

Election Results

2006 general	Thomas Carper (D)	170,567	(70%)	($2,632,603)
	Jan Ting (R)	69,734	(29%)	($212,765)
2006 primary	Thomas Carper (D)	unopposed		

Prior Winning Percentages: 2000 (56%); 1996 (70%); 1992 (65%); 1990 House (66%); 1988 House (68%); 1986 House (66%); 1984 House (59%); 1982 House (52%)

Democrat Tom Carper, after over three decades in statewide office, is Delaware's senior senator. He grew up in Southside Virginia and Ohio and graduated from Ohio State University. He first came to Delaware as an ensign in the Navy, then returned to get his M.B.A. after service in Southeast Asia, where he was a mission commander piloting submarine-hunting planes. In 1976, he was elected state treasurer, at age 29. He ran for Congress in 1982 and beat a scandal-tarred incumbent. In the House, Carper had a moderate voting record and worked to let banks into the securities business and to prevent ocean sludge dumping, both causes supported by Delaware constituencies. In 1992, when Republican Gov. Mike Castle was term-limited and ran for the House, Carper ran for governor and won the general election with 65% of the vote.

As governor, Carper pursued an agenda in many ways more conservative than liberal. He continued former Republican Gov. Pete du Pont's policy of cutting taxes, reducing income tax rates (about 10%) and also cutting small business and utility taxes. Revenues gushed in from Delaware's strong economy, and he boosted the state's credit rating to a historic high even as state spending rose 40% in eight years. He also signed a bill authorizing charter schools. He was re-elected by 70%-30% over then-Treasurer Janet Rzewnicki. Barred from a third term, he ran in 2000 for the Senate seat held by Republican William Roth since 1970.

This was a battle of positives. Both candidates had very high approval ratings at home, and both were familiar figures to many voters; they brought a combined total of 58 years in statewide office to the race. Roth had a record of achievements that paid direct benefits to people in this generally affluent state: the Kemp-Roth tax cut of 1981, the Roth IRAs enacted in 1997, the reform of the Internal Revenue Service passed in 1998, $2.3 billion for Amtrak capital improvements in 1998. Roth's main problem was that he was 79 years old in 2000. When Carper announced his candidacy in September 1999, a poll showed him ahead 48%-38%. He was careful not to campaign negatively against Roth or to attack him for his age, but his slogan "A Senator for Our Future" spotlighted the contrast between their ages. Carper's 16-hour campaign days contrasted with Roth's approach; he stayed in Washington and made only a few campaign appearances with his trademark St. Bernard dogs. Roth outspent Carper, $4.3 million to $2.5 million, but the Democratic Party spent some $4 million in Delaware, more than evening the score. In October, Roth fainted twice on the campaign trail, once in full view of cameras. Polls showed the race close to even in September and October, but in November, Carper won by a solid 56%-44%.

In the Senate, Carper has had one of the more moderate voting records among Democrats, and is a vice chairman of the moderate-to-conservative Democratic Leadership Council. With five Republicans and five other Democrats, he moved unsuccessfully to condition the Bush tax cut on deficit reduction. In 2001, he and Republican Judd Gregg of New Hampshire got $125 million for public school choice programs and $400 million for charter schools. On Social Security privatization, he said in 2005, "I don't rule out at some point having private accounts." Carper supported President Bush's nomination of John Roberts as Supreme Court Chief Justice but voted against Samuel Alito. In 2007, he voted to fund Bush's plan for a surge of troop strength in Iraq.

Carper has taken a major role in clean air legislation. In his first Senate term, he voted with Independent Jim Jeffords of Vermont to impose Clean Air Act regulations on old power plants. In 2006, he co-sponsored with Republican Lamar Alexander of Tennessee a bill to limit emissions not only of sulphur dioxide, nitrous oxide and mercury, as called for in the Bush Clear Skies bill, but also carbon dioxide. He also supported the so-called cap-and-trade mechanism, which imposes a cap on greenhouse gas emissions but allows companies to buy emissions "credits" from companies that pollute less. In 2007, he co-sponsored the McCain-Lieberman cap-and-trade bill, but later that year, declined to back a bipartisan cap-and-trade bill because it did not include limits on mercury, sulfur dioxide and nitrogen oxide. After a federal appeals court rejected the Environmental Protection Agency's mercury rules in February 2008, he pressed for tougher enforcement of them. On the issue of car emissions, Carper in May 2007 proposed a credit for cars that can run on both gasoline and renewable fuels, and $50 million in financing for advanced battery technology research; he supported a compromise bill that passed in December 2007. He has called for increased use of nuclear energy and was the only Democrat on the Environment and Public Works Committee to support the Bush EPA's decision to deny California a waiver so it could impose more stringent auto emissions regulations.

On the Governmental Affairs Committee, Carper worked with moderate Republican Susan Collins of Maine to pass in December 2006 the first major revision of Postal Service business operations since 1970. (More than half of credit card issuers have operations in Delaware, and that industry provides one-quarter of the Postal Service's mail.) Their bill provided for a streamlined rate-increase procedure and for holding increases below inflation for 10 years; it passed after last-minute compromises with postal unions and retiree groups. He has also called for stepped-up efforts to collect unpaid taxes and to recover sums wrongly paid out by the government. And he has called attention to the government's difficulties in using information technology, notably the Census Bureau's problems developing handheld devices for the 2010 census. And in 2007, he teamed with Alexander to extend the 1998 moratorium on Internet taxation for another four years.

Carper supported the bankruptcy bill long sought by Delaware's credit card industry, but has since responded to criticism of industry practices. In June 2007, he backed an amendment for clearer disclosure of interest rate changes and encouraged the industry to develop a "gold standard" of disclosure.

Delaware is a small state in which unusually large percentages of voters actually meet with their elected representatives in person. It has a unique tradition of Return Day, the day after the election, in which losing candidates along with winners take part in a parade in the town of Georgetown. It is a familiar ritual for Carper, who has been elected to statewide office 12 times, more than anyone else in Delaware history. As might be expected of such a seasoned pol, he has paid attention to local issues. He was quick to complain in 2007 when the Department of Homeland Security issued a rule that would require buyers of more than 7,500 pounds of propane gas to register with the department. The rule was opposed by Delaware's chicken growers; there are about 300 chickens in the state to every person. Working often with Democrat Joe Biden, then the state's senior senator, and Republican Rep. Mike Castle, the state's at-large House member, he has brought federal dollars to the state: $4 million for the University of Delaware at Lewes to study onshore wind, $2.25 million for a fireboat for the Wilmington Fire Department, and $10 million for desert-ready combat jackets from Delaware-based W. L. Gore. In March 2008, after such earmarking of federal funds for local projects became controversial, Carper said he would begin to disclose his earmarks.

In 2006, Carper was re-elected, 70%-29%. Over his long career, he has had ties with just about every Democratic politician. In 2007, he tried to get state Treasurer Jack Markell, who had served in his gubernatorial Cabinet, to run for lieutenant governor, so that Democratic Lt. Gov. John Carney, whom he had recruited for office a decade before, would be unopposed in the primary for governor. But Markell ran for governor anyway, beat Carney in the primary and was elected in November. Carper had supported Biden's unsuccessful presidential candidacy and expressed pleasure when Barack Obama picked him for vice president. Carper and Castle appeared in a film made by Delaware natives called *Jack of Clubs*.

Junior Senator

Ted Kaufman (D)

Appointed Jan. 2009, term expires 2010, 1st term; b. March 15, 1939, Philadelphia, PA; home, Wilmington; Duke U., B.S., 1960; U. of PA, M.B.A., 1966.; Catholic; married (Lynne); 3 children.

Professional Career: DuPont Co., 1966–73; St. dir., U.S. Sen. Joe Biden, 1973–76; Chief of staff, Sen. Biden, 1976–95; Duke Law Schl. Center for Study of Congress, 1995–99; Sr. lecturing fellow, Duke U., 1991–2008; Board mbr., Broadcasting Board of Govs., 1995–2008.

DC Office: 383 RSOB, 20510, 202-224-5042; Fax: 202-228-3075; Web site: kaufman.senate.gov.

State Offices: Milford, 302-424-8090; Wilmington, 302-573-6345.

Committees: *Foreign Relations* (10th of 11 D): African Affairs; European Affairs; International Operations & Organizations, Democracy & Global Women's Issues; Near Eastern & South & Central Asian Affairs. *Judiciary* (10th of 12 D): Administrative Oversight & the Courts; Antitrust, Competition Policy & Consumer Rights; Crime & Drugs; Human Rights & the Law; Terrorism & Homeland Security.

Group Ratings and Key Votes: Newly Elected

Election Results

2008 general	Joseph Biden (D)	257,539	(65%)	($4,907,245)
	Christine O'Donnell (R)	140,595	(35%)	($116,050)
2008 primary	Joseph Biden (D)	unopposed		

Ted Kaufman, Delaware's junior senator, was appointed by Democratic Gov. Ruth Ann Minner in November 2008 to replace his former boss, newly elected Vice President Biden. Kaufman, a Democrat, grew up in Philadelphia, the son of a Jewish father and Catholic mother, attending Mass every Sunday and then lunching on bagels and lox. He received an engineering degree from Duke University and a business degree from the Wharton School at the University of Pennsylvania. In 1966, at age 27, Kaufman moved to Delaware to work for DuPont. In his spare time, he helped out on political campaigns, and in 1971, he set up a meeting between a neighborhood association and a 29-year-old New Castle Council member who was running for U.S. senator named Joe Biden. In early 1972, Valerie Owens, Biden's sister and campaign manager, called Kaufman to recruit him to conduct voter registration. This was a long-shot race against Republican Sen. Caleb Boggs, who had held statewide office since 1947 and was widely liked and admired. But Biden ran a convincing campaign that argued the state needed a fresh face in the Senate and warned that Boggs was ready to retire.

Biden won that race, but soon afterward tragedy struck. His young wife and daughter were killed in an automobile accident in December. Biden nearly resigned but decided to begin his Senate term as planned, and he asked Kaufman to set up his Delaware office. Kaufman took a leave of absence from DuPont for a year. Biden wound up adding to his responsibilities, and Kaufman stayed on. In 1976, he became Biden's chief of staff, serving in that role for nearly two decades. This was in line with the practice of many members of Congress, who are backstopped by a trusted aide who remains with them for many years and is known to reflect the legislator's thinking. Kaufman usually commuted with Biden every night from Washington back to Wilmington, first by car and then by Amtrak train. Kaufman served as treasurer of Biden's presidential campaign in 1987, and he was by his side after the candidate underwent surgery for a near-fatal aneurysm in 1988.

In 1991, Kaufman started teaching a course on government, politics, and public policy in the global economy at Duke Law School and its Sanford Public Policy Institute. When he left Biden's staff in 1995, he was for four years the co-chair of the Duke Law School Center for the Study of Congress. Kaufman also served as a member of the Broadcasting Board of Governors from 1995 to 2008, where he worked on expanding freedom of the press around the world. He opened a political and management consulting business in Wilmington and helped with Biden's 1996 and 2002 re-election campaigns. Kaufman was an adviser to the senator's 2008 presidential campaign and traveled with him after he was nominated for vice president. In November 2008, Biden made him co-chair of his vice presidential transition team.

While sharing the ticket with Democratic presidential nominee Barack Obama, Biden was also on the Delaware ballot seeking a seventh Senate term, a race everyone knew he would win, and at some point he asked Kaufman whether he would accept appointment to the Senate if Obama won the presidency. "He said if I was offered the job I should take it," Kaufman later told the *Wilmington News Journal*. On November 21, as Kaufman and his wife were preparing to fly to London for a family Thanksgiving, he was contacted by outgoing Gov. Minner about the Senate appointment. On November 24, Minner stunned the Delaware political world by announcing that she would appoint Kaufman rather than any of the Democratic state officeholders who were considered likely picks. The governor said she believed that Kaufman had a record of putting the state's interests ahead of his own and that he most closely reflected Biden's views. (The 74-year-old Minner told the *The New York Times* that she didn't appoint herself because "I didn't want to commute, and I didn't want to work.") The vice president-elect praised the appointment, but some Delaware political noses were out of joint. Some had expected Minner to appoint Lt. Gov. John Carney, whom she had endorsed to succeed her and who had lost the September Democratic primary to Treasurer Jack Markell by a close 51%-49%. Democratic state Chairman John Daniello declined to congratulate Kaufman, and his office referred callers to Minner, Biden, and Kaufman.

Kaufman made it clear from the start that he would not run for the seat in 2010, when Biden's six-year term ends. "I do not think Delaware's appointed senator should spend the next two years running for office," he told the Wilmington newspaper. His appointment was seen in Washington and in some quarters of Delaware as a move to keep the seat open for Biden's son, Democrat Beau Biden; Beau had won election as Delaware's attorney general by 53%-47% in 2006, and he did a tour of duty in Iraq with the Delaware National Guard in 2008. Biden says he thinks that his son "would make a great United States senator." Kaufman was compared by some to Benjamin A. Smith II, John Kennedy's college roommate, who in 1960 was appointed to fill his Senate seat so that it would be available to brother Edward Kennedy in 1962 when he reached the constitutional age of 30. But Smith's public service was limited to a term as mayor of Gloucester, nothing like the years of experience Kaufman has had in the Senate.

Responding to criticism that other, more likely candidates had been passed over, Kaufman argued that he was well prepared for the role, given his experience in and knowledge of the Senate and its machinations. And he stressed in the interview with the *News Journal* that he and Biden have much in common: "My mother and his mother are both Irish, both are strong-willed, smart. We just shared a lot of common things. We had common values. We both are strong Catholics. Family is really, really important to us."

Biden resigned on January 15, 2009, having served 12 days of his seventh term. Kaufman was sworn in on January 16 by Vice President Cheney with Biden, no longer a senator, silent by his side. He was assigned seats on Biden's committees, Foreign Relations and Judiciary, and he hired many current and former Biden staffers. He supported the February 2009 economic stimulus bill proposed by Obama, saying he was mainly interested in working on "getting the economy moving." With Connecticut Democrat Patrick Leahy and Iowa Republican Charles Grassley, Kaufman co-sponsored a bill in February 2009 funding federal law enforcement efforts to prosecute financial fraud.

In early 2009, Michael Castle, Delaware's Republican representative-at-large, was on the list of potential Senate contenders.

Representative-At-Large

Michael Castle (R)

Elected 1992, 9th term; b. July 2, 1939, Wilmington; home, Wilmington; Hamilton Col., B.A. 1961, Georgetown U., LL.B. 1964; Catholic; married (Jane).

Elected Office: DE House of Reps., 1966–68; DE Senate, 1968–76, Minority ldr., 1975–76; DE lt. gov., 1980–84; DE gov., 1984–92.

Professional Career: Practicing atty., 1964–80; DE dep. atty. gen., 1965–66.

DC Office: 1233 LHOB, 20515, 202-225-4165; Fax: 202-225-2291; Web site: www.house.Gov/castle.

State Offices: Dover, 302-736-1666; Georgetown, 302-856-3334; Wilmington, 302-428-1902.

Committees: *Education & Labor* (5th of 19 R): Early Childhood, Elementary & Secondary Education (RMM); Higher Education, Lifelong Learning & Competitiveness. *Financial Services* (2nd of 29 R): Capital Markets, Insurance & Government Sponsored Enterprises; Domestic Monetary Policy & Technology; Financial Institutions & Consumer Credit.

Group Ratings

	ADA	ACLU	AFS	LCV	ITIC	NTU	COC	ACU	CFG	FRC
2008	65	55	57	69	71	34	78	28	26	23
2007	50	—	27	95	—	44	75	20	35	—

National Journal Ratings

	2007 LIB — 2007 CONS		2008 LIB — 2008 CONS	
Economic	46% —	53%	45% —	55%
Social	46% —	54%	45% —	54%
Foreign	46% —	54%	45% —	54%
Composite	46% —	54%	45% —	55%

Key Votes of the 110th Congress

1. Increase minimum wage	Y	5. Share immigration data	N	9. Withdraw troops 8/08	N
2. Expand SCHIP	Y	6. Foreign aid abortion ban	N	10. No operations in Iran	N
3. Raise CAFE standards	Y	7. Ban gay bias in workplace	Y	11. Free trade with Peru	Y
4. Bail out financial markets	Y	8. Repeal D.C. gun law	N	12. Overhaul FISA	Y

Election Results

2008 general	Michael Castle (R) 235,437	(61%)	($1,808,076)
	Karen Hartley-Nagle (D)..................................146,434	(38%)	($27,788)
2008 primary	Michael Castle (R) .... unopposed		

Prior Winning Percentages: 2006 (57%); 2004 (69%); 2002 (72%); 2000 (68%); 1998 (66%); 1996 (70%); 1994 (71%); 1992 (55%)

Michael Castle, a Republican first elected in 1992, is Delaware's representative-at-large. A direct descendant of Benjamin Franklin, Castle grew up in Delaware, the son of a DuPont patent lawyer. He graduated from Hamilton College and the law school at Georgetown University, and returned to Delaware, where he became a deputy attorney general. In 1966, at age 27, Castle ran for a Democratically held seat in the state House at the urging of local Republicans; he won. Two years later, he was elected to the state Senate and in time became minority leader. He left the Legislature in 1976 to practice law in Wilmington; he still lives there, in the same house, and commutes to Washington. In 1980, Republican Gov. Pierre (Pete) du Pont asked him to run for lieutenant governor, which he did and won. He was elected governor in 1984 and 1988. Barred from running for re-election by term limits, he pursued Delaware's lone seat in the U.S. House. Castle defeated state Treasurer Janet Rzewnicki, 56%-30%, in the Republican primary and went on to win the general election, 55%-43%, over Democratic Lt. Gov. S.B. Woo.

Castle arrived just a couple of years before the Republican takeover of Congress in 1995 and became a pivotal moderate deal-broker when the new majority pushed a broad, conservative agenda through the House. He was one of 10 Republicans to support Clinton administration positions on most issues, forging compromises on gun control, tax cuts, and education spending. With a voting record at the middle of the House, he has been a leader of the informal Tuesday Group, which meets weekly for lunch, and is a co-founder of the Republican Main Street Partnership. In early 2007, after the GOP had lost its majority, he was one of just three Republicans who voted for all six bills in the Democrats' "first-100-hours" agenda. He backed the 2001 Bush tax cuts with some ambivalence, fearing that they would return the government to chronic deficit spending. He initially opposed the 2003 tax cut but voted for it when it was reduced to $350 billion, with $20 billion in aid to the states.

In 2005, when the conservative Republican leadership pressed for a budget with spending cuts, Castle and the Main Street group resisted, demanding the removal of a provision allowing oil drilling in the Arctic National Wildlife Refuge. The leadership complied, and Castle provided a key vote when the spending plan passed 217-215. In subsequent budgets written by conservatives, Castle and his group held out for fewer cuts in education and health care programs, winning some battles and losing others. When Democrats voted as a bloc to try to stop GOP proposals, Castle and his band of Republican moderates gained leverage with conservative leaders who needed their votes. After Republicans lost their majority in 2007, he found it harder to put his imprint on legislation, especially after several fellow moderates retired or were defeated for re-election.

For six years, Castle chaired the Education Reform Subcommittee, and although he supported spending more on education than other Republicans, he also questioned the worth of programs originally fashioned by Democrats. That was evident in his work on Head Start in 2003. Castle's bill maintained the core program; but citing studies showing that the progress Head Start children make tends to be lost by the third or fourth grade, he added provisions requiring more-rigorous academics and also one allowing eight states to adapt their own programs. Democrats raised a storm of criticism, contending that Castle and the Republicans were gutting a successful program for inner-city children. His bill barely passed the House, 217-216, and died in the Senate. In 2007, Castle worked with then-subcommittee Chairman Dale Kildee, a Michigan Democrat, to pass a Head Start bill that increased spending from $6.9 billion to $7.4 billion and toughened qualification requirements for teachers. Castle has remained a supporter of the Bush-era bill called No Child Left Behind, which requires schools to improve test scores to keep their federal funding. Democrats want to rewrite the law, and Castle is positioned to be a player in those discussions in the 111th Congress (2009–10).

While Republicans still held the majority, Castle considered making a bid for chairman of the full Education and the Workforce Committee. But he had not been a leadership loyalist and had not raised much money for other Republicans—two major strikes against him. In February 2006, when Chairman John Boehner of Ohio was elected GOP majority leader and the chairmanship came open, Castle announced he would not seek it. "The bottom line is, I wouldn't make it," he said. "Let's face it, once you become the head of a committee, you have to totally support the leadership on everything. And that's never been one of my interests. . . . I'd give up my independence if I were a committee chairman. I'd have to worry about committee business instead of what I consider the important issues." But he maintained good relations with the new chairman, California Republican Buck McKeon.

Castle continued to enjoy his independence from the leadership. He opposed President Bush's call for a "surge" of troops in Iraq in 2007. And he was a leader in the explosive debate over expanding federal funding for embryonic-stem-cell research, which Bush, many conservatives, and anti-abortion activists opposed. He argued that the embryos, which are created for fertility treatments but then discarded when there are too many, should be available if donors consent. "There is more potential here than anything that has ever happened in the history of medicine," he said. In 2005, Castle threatened to vote against the Republicans' budget unless he got a vote on a bipartisan bill to expand embryonic-stem-cell funding. The leadership acceded and it passed, 238-194. But the tally was not sufficient to override Bush's veto, the first of his presidency. In January 2007, Democrats brought the bill to the floor as part of their new agenda and it passed, 253-174, still less than the two-thirds required to override a veto. Also that year, Castle, with other moderate Republicans, unsuccessfully sought middle ground to expand the State Children's Health Insurance Program.

Castle serves on the Financial Services Committee, which is of great importance to Delaware. He has supported measures to prevent identity theft and to promote low-income housing programs. In 2008, he opposed passage of a bill by Democratic Rep. Carolyn Maloney of New York to crack down on credit card issuers—a major business in Delaware. During the financial crisis on Wall Street that year, he joined with committee Democrats on a bill to remove legal liability from loan servicers who readjust at-risk mortgages. His pet project on the committee is coins. Castle sponsored the 1997 law establishing commemorative quarters, with different designs for each state. The state quarters have become collector's items and have brought the government a cool $6 billion, the most successful coin program in the nation's history.

He is a strong supporter of Amtrak train service and opposed Bush administration proposals to divide the operation into three units and to spin off control of rails, stations, and infrastructure to the states. In 2008, he said that high-speed rail service could reduce the trip between Washington and New York to two hours, including a stop in Wilmington.

Castle has been re-elected every two years, usually with 65% of the vote or better. He has often been mentioned as a candidate for the Senate. In September 2006, Castle suffered a minor stroke and was off the campaign trail for four weeks. That year, Democrats came on strong against a politically weakened Republican Party, and Castle faced a tough challenge from Democrat Dennis Spivack. After outspending Spivack by $1.1 million to $387,000, Castle won, but by the sharply reduced tally of 57%-39%. In 2008, House Democrats could not find a top-tier challenger. Democrats won the three other statewide contests with at least 62% of the vote, but Castle was re-elected 61%-38%. That led to speculation he would be a top candidate for the open Senate contest in 2010—appointed Democratic Sen. Ted Kaufman has said that he will not seek to complete Joe Biden's six-year term. Biden left the Senate in early 2009 to become vice president. Castle has said he's keeping his options open.

★ DISTRICT OF COLUMBIA ★

The capital of the most powerful and affluent nation in history, Washington is a physically beautiful city of great achievements and astonishing contrasts. It is also a polity that has its hopes pinned on achieving representation in Congress now that there is a Democratic president sympathetic to the cause. That history goes back more than 200 years. In 1787, the Constitution's Framers, familiar with contemporary London and Paris mobs and remembering how unruly crowds had threatened Congress in Philadelphia, purposely gave the new federal government control of the 10-mile-square enclave that came to be called the District of Columbia. (The portion across the Potomac River was retroceded to Virginia in 1846.) Over the years, Congress kept control of the District for its own advantage and, at times, out of distrust of the city's large African-American population. Since the 1790s, blacks have consistently made up one-quarter of the population of Washington and surrounding counties, and the city was a center for free blacks even before the Civil War and emancipation. Radical Republicans gave the District self-government during Reconstruction in 1871, but Gov. Alexander (Boss) Shepherd, in building great public works, spent the District into bankruptcy, and the experiment ended in 1874. Later, Washington's growth spurts, starting with the New Deal and World War II, resulted in the development of large, mostly white suburbs, and African-Americans became a larger percentage of the city's population, reaching a majority in the 1960 census. Amid the 1960s civil-rights revolution, it began to seem absurd to deny the vote to the District of Columbia. So in 1964, after the Constitution was amended, District residents began to cast three electoral votes for president; in 1968 they were allowed to vote for the school board; in 1971 they got to elect a nonvoting delegate to Congress; and in 1974 they got home rule and could vote for a mayor and D.C. council.

For some time, this self-government worked no better than it did in the 1870s. The Boss Shepherd of modern times was Marion Barry, a talented politician but a disastrous mayor who held office 16 of 20 years between 1978 and 1998. Under Barry, the District was a dysfunctional polity, a city with above-average incomes and a vibrant commercial property base, but with a local government so bloated with employees (up to 51,000 at its peak) and so indifferent to its responsibilities that it destroyed one marginal neighborhood after another. Crime flourished despite a 1978 law that essentially outlawed possession of handguns acquired after that date. Barry raised money from public employee unions and real estate developers and increasingly won votes from poor blacks by attacking any critic as racist. In January 1990, he was arrested in a D.C. hotel for using crack cocaine, and was prosecuted and sent to prison. A reform-minded mayor, Sharon Pratt Kelly, was elected that fall but flinched when it came time to cut the payroll. Barry, out of prison and elected to the D.C. Council in 1992, won a fourth term as mayor in 1994.

The District's fiscal crisis after Barry's return led Congress in 1995 to take most of the government from his control. This was not a hostile takeover. House Speaker Newt Gingrich appointed Tom Davis as chairman of the D.C. subcommittee. Davis was a Republican member of Congress from Northern Virginia long sympathetic to the District, and he worked closely with D.C.'s elected delegate, Eleanor Holmes Norton. They got Congress to establish a five-member financial control board in April 1995, and the board's CFO, Anthony Williams, hacked away at the payroll, reformed management practices, and literally cleaned up messes in District government offices. When Barry announced in May 1998 that he wouldn't run again, there was a push, encouraged by *The Washington Post,* to draft Anthony Williams as mayor. An unlikely candidate who was diffident in crowds and could be spotted wearing an unfashionable bow tie, Williams had lived in Washington for only a few years, but he beat council member Kevin Chavous 50%-35% in the Democratic primary and defeated Republican council member Carol Schwartz 66%-30% in the general election. The control board immediately delegated power to the new mayor, and in fall 2000, judges returned control of most District departments to the city.

Over the next decade, the District thrived. Its population has been increasing since 2000, according to revised census estimates. Affluent professionals and eager immigrants flowed in, gentrifying and giving vitality to neighborhoods long given up to decline—Columbia Heights, Logan Circle, Shaw. New apartment buildings sprang up on land left empty for years. In the process, the African-American percentage fell from a peak of 71% in 1970 to 55% in 2007, as whites moved back to the city and middle-income blacks moved to the suburbs, to majority-black Prince George's County and other suburbs, where three-quarters of metro Washington blacks now live. Whites cast approximately half or almost half of the District's votes. But the electorate remains overwhelmingly Democratic. In 2004, John Kerry carried the District over George W. Bush by 89%-9%. In 2008, Barack Obama won it 92%-7%. Whites voted 80% for Kerry and 86% for Obama. The District is the one jurisdiction where Hispanics are more likely than whites to vote Republican.

Under Williams, city services began to improve. Departments were removed from court control, and the city's finances were in excellent shape, as gentrification and rising real estate values swelled revenues. Williams was pleased when in September 2004, Major League Baseball decided to move the Montreal Expos to Washington, and he got the council to agree to build a stadium on a long-neglected site next to the Washington Navy Yard at a cost of $611 million. Williams announced in September 2005 that he would not seek another term, and the front-runner to succeed him was council President Linda Cropp, who had years of experience in city government, going back to the time when her husband was a top aide to Barry. But the winner of the mayoral election was 35-year-old council member Adrian Fenty. The son of a black father and a white mother who grew up over their athletic-shoe store in the diverse Mount Pleasant area, Fenty had an undistinguished record as a practicing lawyer. He did, however, possess a strong ambition for political office. In 2000, Fenty ran for the council seat in Ward 4, an affluent, mostly black area just east of Rock Creek Park. Campaigning relentlessly, he beat a longtime incumbent. On the council, he opposed Williams on closing D.C. General Hospital and building the baseball stadium. He specialized in constituent services, winning a reputation for getting almost instant action from the D.C. bureaucracy. He had little time for the intricacies of legislation. In council meetings, he constantly worked on his BlackBerry.

Fenty started campaigning early and hard. Accompanied often by some of his many volunteers, he knocked on about half the doors in the District of Columbia. He ran less on issues than on energy. "Government, like business, is about follow-through, responsiveness, attention to detail. That's what I do," he said. "Some people say I am too eager. I am very hungry. I want this job more than anybody else." Political reporters interviewing voters heard dozens of stories about how he had solved people's problems, and fast. Every neighborhood in the District sprouted green Fenty signs. By August 2006, Fenty's energetic campaigning had put him ahead in the polls. Cropp had the support of most of the local business community. But Fenty got most of the voters. In the September 12 primary, he trounced Cropp 57%-31%. He carried all eight wards and all 142 precincts in the city. Electoral politics in Washington has often divided voters on lines of race. Fenty did not do so. "There's no question that gives me a tolerance and an appreciation for the views of everyone. I always heard politicians talk about race, but not the people." In the general election, he won 89% of the vote.

In office, Fenty showed as much energy as on the campaign trail. He signaled his new style by literally knocking down walls. His office is in the middle of a large room resembling a Wall Street trading floor, with desks for 33 staffers and two conference areas separated by glass partitions. On the advice of New York City Mayor Michael Bloomberg, he proposed that the mayor's office, and not the elected school board, run the public schools. Williams' proposal for a similar schools takeover had been rejected in 2004, but within days, Fenty got most of the incoming council members to agree with him in principle, and he carried the issue by a 9-2 council vote in April 2007. The District's school system, despite some of the highest spending levels in the nation, has long been considered abysmal, with enrollments declining every year. By 2006, 25% of the students were enrolled in charter schools, one of the highest rates in the country. Fenty installed as his schools superintendent Michelle Rhee, an alumna of the Teach for America program and the founder of the New Teacher Project. An outside-the-mainstream choice who didn't come from a government background, she promptly ordered the closing of 23 schools and indicated support for charter schools. She took on the teachers union in another area: Rhee promised teachers higher pay in return for relinquishing tenure.

Population			Household Income		Work	
Pop. 2007:	585,267		Under $15k:	17.2%	Private:	67.5%
Change since 2000:	Up 2.3%		$15k to $50k:	31.0%	Government:	27.3%
Urban:	100.0%		$50k to $100k:	26.2%	Self-employed:	5.1%
Rural:	0.0%		$100k to $150k:	17.5%	Unemployment (3-yr. average):	6.2%
Native of state:	39.7%		Over $150k:	8.2%	Poverty:	18.8%
Not a citizen:	8.4%		Median income:	$52,187	Blue collar:	8.3%
Area size:	68 sq. mi.		**Home Value**		White collar:	74.4%
			Under $100k:	2.0%	Khaki collar:	1.1%
			$100k to $300k:	26.0%	Other:	16.3%
			$300k to $500k:	32.2%	**Age**	
			$500k to $1 mil:	30.2%	Median age:	35.0 yrs.
			Over $1 million:	9.6%	More than 65 yrs:	11.9%
			Median:	$424,200	Less than 18 yrs:	19.5%

Race/Ethnicity				Military Veterans		Registered Voters in 2008	
White:	31.4%	*Language*		% of Pop:	7.9%	D:	321,027 (75.2%)
Black:	55.0%	English:	84.9%	*Veterans by Period*		R:	30,465 (7.1%)
Hispanic:	8.3%	Spanish:	8.1%	WWII and before:	12.3%	Other:	75,269 (17.6%)
Asian:	3.1%	Asian:	1.7%	Korea:	11.4%	Voter turnout:	265,853
Native Am.:	0.3%	Other		Vietnam:	25.8%	Turnout as % of	
Hawaiian:	0.0%	European	3.9%	Gulf (pre-2001):	9.5%	voting age:	55.4%
Two+ races:	1.3%	**Education**		Gulf (post-2001):	13.8%		
Ancestry		H.S. grad:	84.1%	Peace time:	27.3%		
Irish:	5.6%	College grad:	45.4%				
German:	5.5%	Grad degree:	25.0%				
English:	4.3%						

Other long-standing District programs felt the lash of change. Washington's taxi zone fare system, purportedly imposed by Congress to reduce lawmakers' fares on trips downtown, was abolished with an assist from Sen. Carl Levin, D-Mich., and taxi meters were installed by May 2008. The sale of Greater Southeast Community Hospital was finalized. The baseball stadium was finished in time for Opening Day in March 2008 (capped by a game-winning Nationals' home run), and offices and entertainment facilities started going up in the District's once derelict neighborhoods. High-rise condominiums and rental apartments targeted at singles (only 22% of District households are married-couple families, while 45% of residents have college degrees) were built in what had once been high-crime areas. Congress even included the District in Treasury's quarters program commemorating each state, thanks to

2008 Presidential Vote		
Obama (D)	245,800	(92%)
McCain (R)	17,367	(7%)
2008 Democratic Presidential Primary		
Obama (D)	93,386	(75%)
Clinton (D)	29,470	(24%)
2008 Republican Presidential Primary		
McCain (R)	4,198	(68%)
Huckabee (R)	1,020	(16%)
Paul (R)	494	(8%)
Romney (R)	398	(6%)
2004 Presidential Vote		
Kerry (D)	202,970	(89%)
Bush (R)	21,256	(9%)

Democratic Rep. Jose Serrano of the Bronx, who wanted Puerto Rico in and included the District and the other territories as well.

Fenty's one setback came on the District's handgun ban, passed when he was 7 years old. In March 2007, the U.S. Court of Appeals for the District of Columbia Circuit ruled that the ban violated the Second Amendment. Judge Laurence Silberman's opinion skillfully recounted the recent legal scholarship (liberal as well as conservative) that has concluded the amendment recognizes an individual right to keep and bear arms. The U.S. Supreme Court in June 2008, with an incisive opinion by Justice Antonin Scalia, reached the same conclusion, albeit by a 5-4 vote. The 1978 law, though it was followed by a 10-year decline in gun violence, had not prevented a high rate of gun crime in the 1980s and 1990s, and it required even legal guns to be disassembled when kept at home. Fenty and Norton criticized the decision. Fenty ordered the police department to draw up regulations to register handguns, and District Attorney General Peter Nickles said that the District would have to develop an amnesty program for those who had possessed them in violation of the District law. The D.C. Council prepared legislation imposing various requirements for legal gun possession, and opponents prepared litigation.

The Democratic takeover of Congress in 2006 and the election of Barack Obama as president two years later foreshadowed another milestone in D.C.'s quest for full political rights. After Obama was inaugurated in January 2009, Congress immediately took up the long-languishing legislation to give D.C. a vote in the House of Representatives. In a push led by its long-suffering, nonvoting Rep. Eleanor Holmes Norton, the U.S. Senate passed a bill giving D.C.'s representative a vote, with a filibuster-proof 61 votes for the first time. The bill was a compromise between the two parties. It expanded the House by two seats, one for heavily Democratic D.C. and one for Republican Utah. But the Senate also added a provision to the bill that in effect overturned D.C.'s regulations on guns. The provision was unacceptable to gun control advocates in the House, and the legislation bogged down.

Delegate

Eleanor Holmes Norton (D)

Elected 1990, 10th term; b. June 13, 1937, Washington, D.C.; home, Washington, D.C.; Antioch Col., B.A. 1960, Yale, M.A. 1963, LL.B. 1964; Episcopalian; divorced; 2 children.

Professional Career: Asst. legal dir., ACLU, 1965–70; New York City Human Rights Comm., 1970–77; Equal Empl. Oppor. Comm., 1977–81; Sr. fellow, The Urban Inst., 1981–82; Prof., Georgetown U. Law Ctr., 1982–present.

DC Office: 2136 RHOB, 20515, 202-225-8050; Fax: 202-225-3002; Web site: www.norton.house.gov.

District Offices: SE Washington, D.C., 202-678-8900; NW Washington, D.C., 202-783-5065.

Committees: *Homeland Security* (5th of 21 D): Emergency Communications, Preparedness & Response; Transportation Security & Infrastructure Protection. *Oversight & Government Reform* (14th of 25 D): Federal Workforce, Postal Service & the District of Columbia; Information Policy, Census & National Archives. *Transportation & Infrastructure* (5th of 45 D): Aviation; Economic Development, Public Buildings & Emergency Management (Chmn); Water Resources & Environment.

Election Results

2008 general	Eleanor Holmes Norton (D)	228,376	(92%)	($380,922)
	Maude Hills (SG)	16,693	(7%)	
2008 primary	Eleanor Holmes Norton (D)	38,999	(98%)	

Prior Winning Percentages: 2006 (100%); 2004 (91%); 2002 (93%); 2000 (90%); 1998 (90%); 1996 (90%); 1994 (89%); 1992 (85%); 1990 (62%)

Eleanor Holmes Norton, who was first elected delegate from the District of Columbia in 1990, grew up in Washington. The daughter of a District government employee and a school teacher, she graduated from then-segregated Dunbar High School and went on to get a law degree from Yale University. She worked for the American Civil Liberties Union and the New York City Commission on Human Rights, and was head of the Equal Employment Opportunity Commission in the Carter administration. Afterward, she taught law at Georgetown University. When the delegate seat came open in 1990, she ran for it, and drew criticism because her husband hadn't filed their income taxes for several years. But in the primary, she edged past Council member Betty Anne Kane, 39%-33%. Norton has been re-elected easily since.

In the House, she had the difficult and sometimes vexing task of responding to the fiscal collapse of the District government just as Republicans took over Congress in 1995. But she was seen as hardworking, competent, intellectually honest, able to get along with opponents as well as fellow partisans, and willing to take personal and political risks. She established good relations with Republicans active on District matters. She led the drive to give the D.C. delegate and the four territorial delegates to the House—all of whom were then Democrats—votes on most legislation in the House. In 1995, she worked with Republican Rep. Tom Davis of Virginia and Republican Speaker Newt Gingrich to create the fiscal control board to oversee District finances in the aftermath of the disastrous reign of drug-using Mayor Marion Barry. In 1997, she and Davis came up with the legislation that rescued District finances and removed control over most of the government from Barry. The measure also included tax breaks for downtown and some other neighborhoods. The District subsequently recovered financially and moved past Barry's divisive politics, a process that culminated with the election of Mayor Anthony Williams, the re-establishment of brisk capital investment in the city, and the end of middle-class flight from D.C. neighborhoods.

In spite of lacking a full vote in the House, Norton successfully pushed several local projects, including the Southeast Federal Center Public-Private Development Act that provided a coordinated approach to developing the area around the Washington Navy Yard. She supported the transfer of 200 acres of federal land to the District that passed in 2006 and the decision to place the Coast Guard headquarters on the grounds of St. Elizabeth's Hospital. She protested vigorously when the House voted to repeal the District's ban on handguns. In June 2007, Norton won a House vote to remove the ban on using local tax dollars for an anti-AIDS campaign to provide clean needles to drug addicts.

However, one of Norton's top goals—full voting rights for D.C. in the House of Representatives—was doomed as long as Republicans remained in control of Congress. The ruling party was loathe to grant a vote to a jurisdiction as heavily and wholeheartedly Democratic as Washington. Her luck began to change when Democrats gained control of both chambers of Congress in 2006, and of the White House in 2008. In April 2007, the House passed, 241-177, the D.C. House Voting Rights Act introduced by Norton and Davis, who represented the Northern Virginia suburbs outside of D.C. The legislation established the city as a congressional district with full voting rights in the House. It also included a plan to create an additional district for fast-growing and Republican Utah. But when the bill came up for a vote in the Senate that year, it fell three votes short of the 60 necessary to prevent a filibuster. Minority Leader Mitch McConnell argued that the measure violated the Constitution, and Norton led a mock tea party on the banks of the Potomac to protest. The next year, after further Democratic successes at the polls and Obama's victory, the Senate in February 2009 passed the bill, 61-37. It created voting privileges for the D.C. delegate while adding a concession for Republicans by adding a House seat to heavily Republican Utah. But the Senate also added a provision overturning D.C.'s restrictions on guns, which proved unacceptable to gun control advocates in the House and the bill bogged down in a stalemate over the provision.

★ FLORIDA ★

Florida, the nation's fourth largest state (and closing in on No. 3, New York), is a kind of nation-state, historically Southern, demographically Northeastern and Midwestern, and culturally Latin American. It is economically vibrant but subject to sudden contractions, as in the mid-1920s, the mid-1970s and the late 2000s. It has the nation's largest percentage of elderly citizens, but its exotic past reaches back to Ponce de Leon's quest for the Fountain of Youth. It is the only Atlantic Coast state that was not part of the colonial United States. Through the exertions of John Quincy Adams and Andrew Jackson, then political allies but later bitter political enemies, it was acquired from Spain in 1819. Starting off as a forgotten swamp, Florida has emerged as almost an empire of its own, a prototype in many ways of America's future, with an international flavor and sometimes almost with its own foreign policy. Within the lifespan of the typical octogenarian, it went from 1.5 million people to 18 million. Pivotal was the advent of air conditioning. In 1950, only 20% of Florida houses had it; in 2000, 95% of them did. For many years, Florida was the place millions of retirees looked forward to: sunny, year-round warmth after years of gray skies over factories and office buildings.

Then in the 1980s and 1990s, the percentage of children and young couples as a share of Florida's population grew rapidly as people migrated from the South, from various points north and from Latin America. They were lured by jobs and opportunities in communities that hadn't existed a generation earlier. Some 17% of Florida's population today is over age 65, more than the national average of 13%, but not extraordinarily more. The state's percentage of children under age 18 is 22%, not much below the national average of 25%. For refugees from Cuba and Haiti and for immigrants from the Caribbean and Latin America, Florida has been a land of freedom and security from authoritarian regimes and totalitarian police states. For Americans and foreigners of all kinds—some 80 million of them—Florida is the place to visit, with lively attractions, year-round swimming, and accommodations to suit most pocketbooks. Yet all is not sunny. Crime is down, but still a threat. An economy that sizzled until 2007 was inordinately affected by the recession, which had been fueled by a crisis in the mortgage market and so hit areas of brisk building particularly hard.

Florida is a creation not of America's elite—though a few millionaires, such as Henry Flagler and Marcus Plant, pioneered tourism there—but a place for which ordinary people have voted with their feet. It has been continually replenished with people from out of state, two-thirds of them from the United States, one-third from foreign countries. Miami has long been the economic and commercial capital of Latin America, as well as a mecca for its political exiles. You can fly nonstop from Miami to just about anyplace in Latin America, both English and Spanish are commonly understood, and it has been one place where many Latinos could be sure their money and their persons were safe from government takeover. Recent ructions in their countries have brought thousands of Venezuelans, Bolivians, and Ecuadorans, some affluent and some struggling, to south Florida. Large number of Puerto Ricans have been moving to central Florida's Interstate 4 corridor, and Mexicans to the Tampa Bay area; as a result, Cubans now account for only about a third of Florida's Hispanics.

For almost two decades, Florida had one of America's most buoyant economies, though its economy often seems a mystery to outsiders. That economy is based heavily on small business—98% of businesses have fewer than 100 employees, and in the 1990s Florida ranked No. 1 in small-business starts. There is also a high-tech sector and a substantial amount of international merchandise, which increased from $24 billion in 1987 to $81 billion in 2004. For years, two of the leading sectors of the state's economy were construction and real estate. They prosper and grow during booms but are subject to sudden busts, such as the Miami land boom that ended abruptly when a hurricane struck in 1926. Something like that seems to have happened in 2007. Speculators had been buying up condos in Miami and Cape Coral, Orlando and Port St. Lucie, and then suddenly prices started to fall, even as property taxes and insurance premiums rose. Housing values plummeted by half in some speculator-heavy precincts and by significant amounts just about everywhere. The state's population continued to grow from 2007 to 2008, but at a much slower pace than it did mid-decade. A flood of foreclosures followed, and Florida became one of the "sand states" —the others are Nevada, Arizona and California—which have the nation's highest foreclosure rates by far, accounting for half of all foreclosures in 2007 and 2008. Local tax receipts, heavily dependent on property values and the construction industry, sagged. Unemployment rose from 5.5% in May 2008 to 8.1% in January 2009. Retirees and workers started leaving for Georgia, the Carolinas and elsewhere; in 2007 and 2008 Florida had a net domestic outmigration of 9,000 people, although the state's population still increased by 127,000.

All this was happening in a state with a fragile civil society. Florida can be disorderly and chaotic in the best of times. Most people do not have deep roots in the state—most communities sprang into existence within living memory—and if Florida gives people more freedom and options than elsewhere, it also gives them more disruption and crime than they surely anticipated. Its largest urban focus, Miami, is geographically off to one corner and culturally uniquely Cuban. The rest of the Gold Coast, Broward

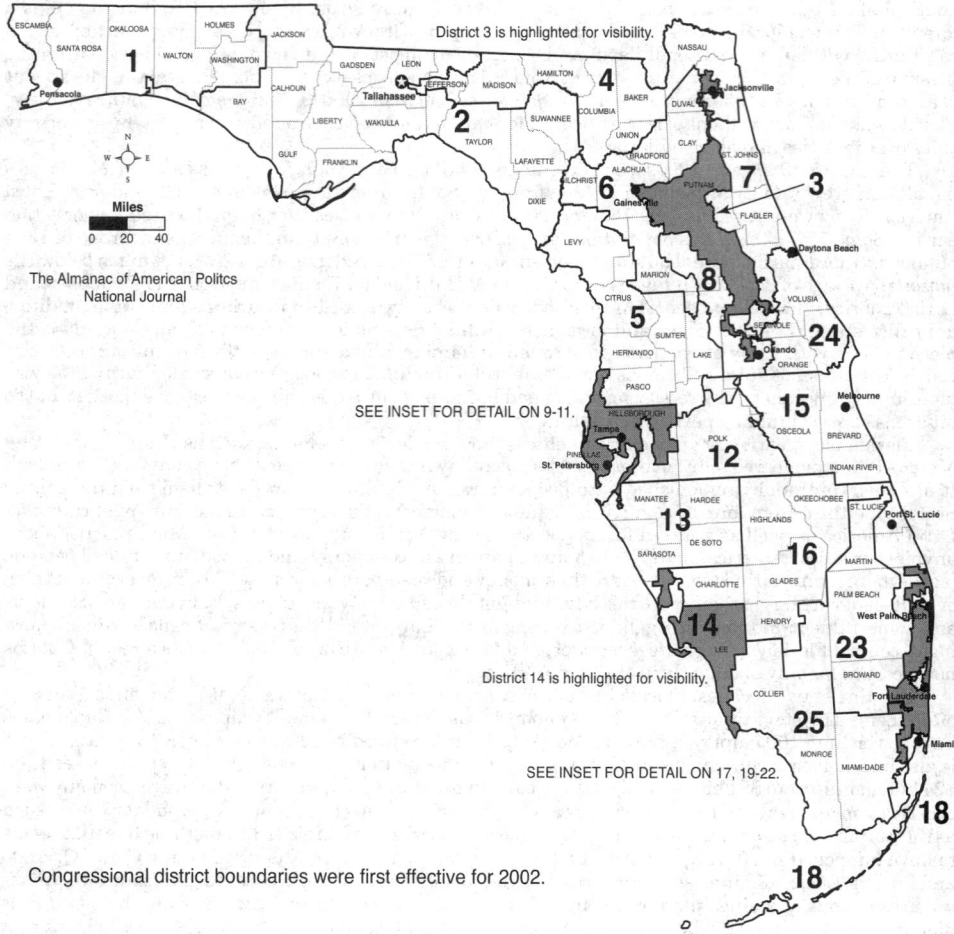

District 3 is highlighted for visibility.

The Almanac of American Politcs
National Journal

Miles
0   20   40

SEE INSET FOR DETAIL ON 9-11.

SEE INSET FOR DETAIL ON 17, 19-22.

District 14 is highlighted for visibility.

Congressional district boundaries were first effective for 2002.

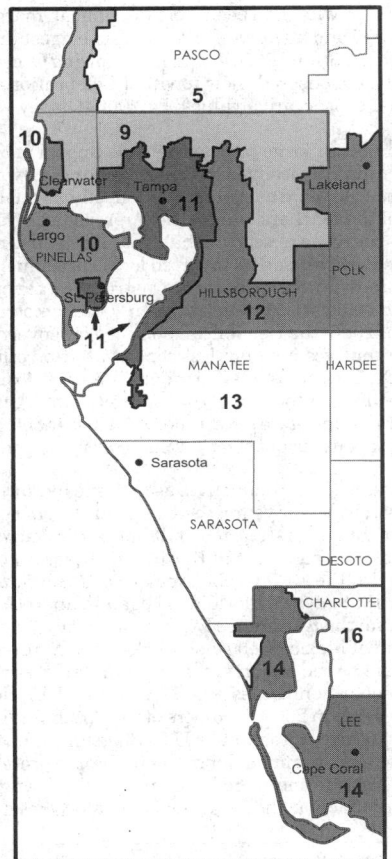

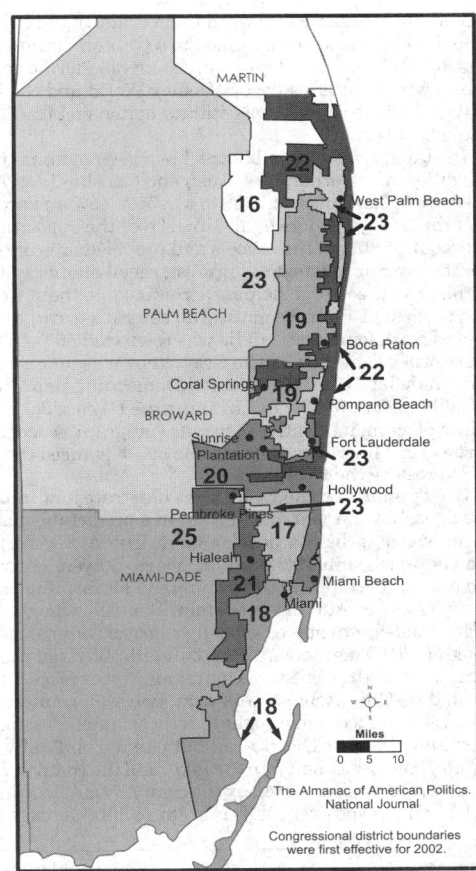

The Almanac of American Politics.
National Journal

Congressional district boundaries
were first effective for 2002.

and Palm Beach counties, with one-sixth of Florida's population, is also atypical, with a population drawn heavily from New York and other Northeastern cities, plus non-Latino migrants from Miami-Dade and large numbers of Jews and retirees. Central Florida—the I-4 corridor from Tampa-St. Petersburg through citrus and tourist country and Orlando—is mostly family, not retiree, country. It thrives on high-tech industries as well as tourism, and is a year-round rather than seasonal megalopolis of 4.8 million people. Most newcomers are from the United States, not from abroad. There is also the Gulf Coast, the affluent and burgeoning communities south of Tampa Bay and the more modest retirement counties to the north. The western Panhandle, the so-called Redneck Riviera around Pensacola and Panama City, is culturally very Southern. State government is headquartered in Tallahassee, chosen because it was midway between the two population centers of Jacksonville and Pensacola at a time when almost no one lived in the Florida peninsula.

Politically, this all adds up to a state that is closely divided between the parties and politically volatile. The trend in Florida politics since the 1990s has been toward the Republicans, who captured the state House in 1994, the state Senate in 1996, and the governorship in 1998 and now hold all the statewide offices and have big majorities in the Legislature: 26-14 in the Senate, 76-44 in the House. They have been helped by term limits and redistricting, which Republicans influenced in 1992 and controlled in 2002: African-American and Jewish areas are concentrated in a few districts. But Democrats have held their own in federal races. Republican George H. W. Bush carried the state 61%-39% in 1988, but Democrat Bill Clinton lost the state by only 41%-39% in 1992 and carried it 48%-42% in 1996. Four years later, Democrat Al Gore lost the state by the excruciating margin of 48.85%-48.84%, determined after the epic 36-day multi-court contest that decided the 2000 presidential election. In 2008, Democrat Barack Obama undertook a massive organizational effort in Florida and won with 51% to Republican John McCain's 48%. In recent years, drops in the crime rates and welfare rolls deprived Republicans of issues in metropolitan areas in Central Florida and on the Gold Coast. Cultural issues like abortion rights and gun control favored Democrats, and the increasing Jewish population in Broward and Palm Beach counties moved the Gold Coast even more toward Democrats. In the I-4 corridor, what had been a big Republican margin for Bush in 1988 was transformed to a Clinton margin in 1996 and a standoff in 2000. The biggest drop in the Republican percentage in any county in Florida between 1988 and 2000 was in fast-growing Osceola County, which contains part of Disney World and the Disney-sponsored "new town" of Celebration. In the 1980s, Disney World was still an epitome of traditional conservative values; by 2000, Disney was hosting Gay Day.

In state politics, Republicans have been dominant, thanks in large part to the wide appeal of two quite different governors, Jeb Bush and Charlie Crist. After initially losing a bid for governor to Lawton Chiles, Bush came back in 1998 to win 55%-45% and proceeded to build a record that made him arguably one of the best governors of his time. Over the opposition of the teachers' unions, he improved the rigor and accountability of the schools and provided alternatives for those in schools that were failing. He cut taxes, he overturned, to great protest, racial quotas and preferences, and he involved local governments and the private sector in helping accommodate the state's rapid growth with new infrastructure. He prepared meticulously for the natural disasters that are part of Florida's natural heritage. In 2002 Democrats targeted Bush for defeat, but he was re-elected 56%-43%. In 2006, the Republican nominee for governor was Attorney General Charlie Crist, known as tough on law enforcement but less conservative on other issues than Jeb Bush. He defeated Democratic Rep. Jim Davis, from the I-4 corridor, 52%-45%, losing the Gold Coast 59%-40% but winning the I-4 corridor 54%-43% and the rest of the state 59%-38%. Crist put into place an innovative insurance program, essentially making state government the insurer of last resort against hurricane damage. He also advanced the idea of buying out the U.S. Sugar Corporation in order to restore the Everglades.

Crist's efforts on the Everglades illustrate how important the environment is as an issue in Florida these days, but one that may not cut in a predictably partisan way. For years, the Everglades were seen as a nuisance, a bar to development. The Army Corps of Engineers started building a dike across Lake Okeechobee in 1930 and for nearly 50 years, worked to straighten the Kissimmee River and to build dikes and channels to reclaim land for farming. But with the 1947 publication of *The Everglades: River of Grass* by Marjory Stoneman Douglas, who died in 1998 at 108, Floridians began to appreciate the Everglades, which is essentially a flow of water south, from the Kissimmee River near Disney World, through Lake Okeechobee down to Florida Bay and the Gulf of Mexico. Jeb Bush worked with national politicians of both parties on a giant, multiyear project to reverse the projects of the past and restore the Everglades. One problem was that two well-connected sugar companies—U.S. Sugar and Florida Crystals—produced cane sugar in critical lands south of the lake. In 2007, members of the South Florida Water Management District, all but one appointed by Gov. Crist, voted to bar U.S. Sugar from back-pumping polluted runoff into the lake, and the company sent two prominent lobbyists to Crist to protest. He responded by offering to buy the company out. In June 2008, he announced his plan to buy U.S. Sugar for $1.75 billion and eventually take its 187,000 acres out of production and let water from Lake Okeecho-

Population		Household Income		Work	
Pop. 2007:	18,014,927	Under $15k:	13.0%	Private:	80.4%
State rank:	4th of 50	$15k to $50k:	40.2%	Government:	13.3%
Change since 2000:	Up 12.7%	$50k to $100k:	30.4%	Self-employed:	6.0%
Urban:	86.1%	$100k to $150k:	13.1%	Unemployment (3-yr. average):	3.7%
Rural:	13.9%	Over $150k:	3.3%	Poverty:	12.6%
Native of state:	33.6%	Median income:	$46,602	Blue collar:	20.9%
Not a citizen:	10.3%	**Home Value**		White collar:	60.0%
Area size:	65,755 sq. mi.	Under $100k:	16.6%	Khaki collar:	0.4%
Most populous cities		$100k to $300k:	50.7%	Other:	18.7%
1. Jacksonville	797,966	$300k to $500k:	21.0%	**Age**	
2. Miami	352,064	$500k to $1 mil:	9.1%	Median age:	39.8 yrs.
3. Tampa	325,265	Over $1 million:	2.6%	More than 65 yrs:	16.9%
4. St. Petersburg	240,507	Median:	$217,800	Less than 18 yrs:	22.3%

Race/Ethnicity				Military Veterans		Registered Voters in 2008	
White:	61.2%	*Language*		% of Pop:	12.4%	D:	4,722,076 (42.0%)
Black:	14.8%	English:	74.4%	*Veterans by Period*		R:	4,064,301 (36.1%)
Hispanic:	20.1%	Spanish:	18.7%	WWII and before:	16.7%	Other:	2,461,257 (21.9%)
Asian:	2.1%	Asian:	1.3%	Korea:	13.7%	Voter turnout:	8,390,744
Native Am.:	0.3%	Other		Vietnam:	28.4%	Turnout as % of	
Hawaiian:	0.1%	European	5.1%	Gulf (pre-2001):	10.7%	voting age:	58.6%
Two+ races:	1.1%	**Education**		Gulf (post-2001):	6.3%	**Legislature**	
Ancestry		H.S. grad:	84.4%	Peace time:	24.3%	Senate:	14 D 26 R
German:	10.4%	College grad:	25.2%			House:	44 D 76 R
Irish:	9.2%	Grad degree:	8.8%				
English:	7.9%						

bee flow through them, restoring the old flow pattern of the Everglades. The water management district approved the plan in December 2008, though negotiations continued over the purchase price, and some questioned whether the state could afford the purchase. In fact, the deal was significantly scaled back in April 2009, with the state slated to buy 72,500 acres for $533 million and getting a 10-year option to purchase the remaining land.

Presidential politics   In the 2004 and 2008 elections, Florida was a target state for both parties. The key in both cases was not so much persuading undecided voters but turning out base supporters at the polls. In the process turnout rose from 6 million in 2000 to 7.6 million in 2004 to 8.4 million in 2008, a 40% increase during a time when population rose 15%. In 2004, President Bush's campaign had out-organized the other side. Its volunteer-rich registration and turnout efforts increased the Bush percentage in almost every county, and Bush beat Democrat John Kerry 52%-47%. In 2008, Illinois Democrat Barack Obama's campaign exceeded those efforts. Spending some $39 million on television ads and organization, and targeting potential supporters early, Obama raised turnout and the Democratic percentage sharply in Orlando and Osceola County, Tampa, Jacksonville and Miami. Over the period from 2000 to 2008, the Democratic percentage rose most in counties with many African-Americans and Hispanics and along the southern Gulf Coast, while the Republican percentage went up markedly in most of north Florida and the smaller counties of central Florida.

2008 Presidential Vote		
Obama (D)	4,282,074	(51%)
McCain (R)	4,045,624	(48%)
2008 Democratic Presidential Primary		
Clinton (D)	870,986	(50%)
Obama (D)	576,214	(33%)
Edwards (D)	251,562	(14%)
2008 Republican Presidential Primary		
McCain (R)	701,761	(36%)
Romney (R)	604,932	(31%)
Giuliani (R)	286,089	(15%)
Huckabee (R)	262,681	(13%)
2004 Presidential Vote		
Bush (R)	3,964,522	(52%)
Kerry (D)	3,583,544	(47%)

Of the 10 largest states, only Florida and Ohio gave their winning presidential candidates margins of less than 5% in each of the three elections from 2000 to 2008, and Florida is far larger, with 27 electoral votes to Ohio's 20. Florida's presidential primary, held from 1988 to 2004 on Super Tuesdays, also produces very large delegations to the two parties' national conventions. But it has not been crucial in determining a nomination since 1976, when Democrat Jimmy Carter defeated George Wallace, ending his national political career.

Determined to give Florida more clout in the 2008 election, the Legislature decided to move the primary to an earlier date. In May 2007, it voted to schedule the primary for January 29, and Crist signed the bill. Democratic legislators protested, because their party's rules forbade the state from voting before February 5, but to no avail. In August 2007, the Democratic National Committee under Chairman Howard Dean voted to strip Florida of its delegates, and in September, all the major Democratic candidates agreed not to campaign in the state. In October 2007, Democratic Sen. Bill Nelson and Rep. Alcee Hastings sued the DNC, but the judge ruled against them in December. Meanwhile, in November, the Republican National Committee took the less onerous step of depriving Florida of half its delegates without a demand that candidates boycott the state. The national parties' decisions had the result of making Florida decisive in the race for the Republican nomination and making it a bone of contention for Democrats until their nominee was decided in June.

For much of 2007, Florida didn't look like much of a contest among Republicans, with New York's Rudolph Giuliani leading in all the polls. But Giuliani's standing began to slip at year's end, and when he failed to win an appreciable number of votes in any state before Florida, his support in the state collapsed, even as he campaigned heavily there in January 2008. Meanwhile, Massachusetts' Mitt Romney here, as elsewhere, outspent the other candidates and campaigned as a mainstream conservative. Arkansas' Mike Huckabee, with little money but considerable charm, struggled to extend his appeal beyond evangelical Christians in a state with eight media markets and a Republican electorate drawn from many parts of the nation. On January 19, 10 days before the Florida primary, Arizona's John McCain beat Huckabee in South Carolina 33%-30%. Tennessee's Fred Thompson won 16% of the votes there, leading some to conclude that Huckabee would have beat McCain if Thompson had not been not in the race. Thompson promptly dropped out, and for 10 days the spotlight was on Florida. On Saturday, January 26, Crist endorsed McCain.

That may have tipped the balance, and presumably affected at least a few votes in a fluid race with a crowded field. Turnout was large: 1.9 million, nearly triple the 690,000 who had voted in the previous GOP presidential primary, in 2000. McCain won with 36% of the votes to 31% for Romney. Giuliani got 15%, and Huckabee 13%. McCain carried metro Tampa, Crist's home area, but his highest percentages were in south Florida. Polls suggest that many original Giuliani supporters there voted for McCain, especially Cuban-Americans. McCain was also endorsed by Miami's three Cuban-American House members and won his highest percentages in their three congressional districts. Romney carried metro Jacksonville and southwest Florida. Under the state Republicans' winner-take-all rules, McCain won all of the state's delegates at stake in the contest. While McCain's Florida victory technically did not clinch the nomination, it put him in position to do so a week later on Super Tuesday, after Romney ended his campaign. Anticlimactically, the Republicans voted in August 2008 to restore all of Florida's delegates.

Democratic candidates mostly kept their promises to not campaign in Florida. Turnout in the primary was 1.75 million, less than in the Republican contest despite impressive gains in Democratic party registration, though still far ahead of the 754,000 who turned out in 2004. New York Sen. Hillary Rodham Clinton won 50% of the vote, Obama 33%, and North Carolina's John Edwards 14%. Obama carried counties with large black populations (Jacksonville, Pensacola, rural north Florida counties) and those with universities or state employees (Gainesville, Tallahassee). He carried six of the 25 congressional districts. Edwards won 11 small counties in north Florida. Clinton won every county south of Gainesville. She carried Latino and Jewish voters 2-to-1. Young voters were evenly split. Clinton, barred from the state during the campaign by her September promise, made an election night appearance to celebrate her victory.

The desire of Florida Democrats to be counted in the nomination process guaranteed continued controversy. It was suggested that Florida could stage another primary, or have a mail-in rerun, but the cost—up to $18 million for a primary, $5 million for a mail-in—was prohibitive for the Florida Democratic party. Plaintive cries went up that Florida Democrats were being disenfranchised by a Republican legislature and a Republican governor, but to no avail. (No similar excuse was available to their confreres from Michigan, which had a Democratic governor and state House.) Democratic legislators filed a lawsuit in May, but it was quickly dismissed. Florida Democrats appealed to the DNC in May to have half the delegation seated, but the Obama campaign, short of clinching the nomination and aware that the proposal would give Clinton a delegate edge, resisted. On May 31, a few days before the last primary, a compromise was reached giving Clinton a 52.5-33.5 delegate edge over Obama (John Edwards got 6.5 delegates), not quite what her showing in the Florida and Michigan primaries would have justified and not enough to change the outcome of the nomination fight as superdelegates moved toward Obama. On August 2, when it no longer mattered, Obama asked that all the Florida delegates be seated, and so they were in Denver.

Obama started the general election campaign in Florida at a disadvantage. In other primary and caucus states, the campaign had been able to start early in assembling its impressive organizations. Nevertheless, trends in party registration were going his way. Many more new voters registered as Democrats than as Republicans, and the fact that more votes were cast in the Republican primary than in the Democratic primary proved to be a misleading indicator. Importantly, by May 2008 registered Democrats for the first time outnumbered registered Republicans among Hispanics. There also was a disparity in spending in the state between the two candidates. The Obama campaign planned to spend about $39 million in Florida and flooded the airwaves from summer on. The McCain campaign, aware that it was behind in other states that had voted more heavily for Bush in 2004, gambled and spent almost no money in Florida. It proved to be correct in assuming that the swing away from the Republican ticket would be far smaller in Florida than it was in states like Virginia, North Carolina, and Indiana. But it proved to be incorrect in assuming that the swing would be too small to allow Obama to win the state's 27 electoral votes.

The Obama campaign did an excellent job of increasing African-American turnout in Miami, Tampa, and Jacksonville. But it also concentrated on increasing Hispanic turnout, especially in the Orlando area, where the many new Puerto Rican voters had little in common with Miami Cubans. Obama's weakness among Jewish voters, evident in the primary results, was transfigured by the nomination of Alaska Gov. Sarah Palin as McCain's running mate. Despite her pro-Israel views, she seemed to tip them heavily against the Republican ticket. Broward and Palm Beach counties delivered huge majorities to Obama, as they had to the Gore-Lieberman ticket in 2000. The Obama campaign neglected no critical angle, running early-voter efforts in black barbershops, getting Creole speakers to call voters in Haitian neighborhoods, and taping comedian Sarah Silverman urging young Jews to tell their grandparents in Florida to vote for Obama. The Republicans held big rallies for their ticket, with 60,000 appearing at The Villages, northwest of Orlando, in sizzling heat to hear Palin speak.

The final results revealed the Florida electorate to be more polarized than ever, with hugely Democratic areas (Broward and Palm Beach Counties) balanced against hugely Republican areas (the Panhandle). White evangelical Protestants voted more than 3-to-1 for McCain; Jews about 3-to-1 for Obama. Cuban-Americans voted 65% for McCain—less than in the past—but young Hispanics voted more than 3-1 for Obama. Here, perhaps, was the biggest difference from the previous election: In 2004, Hispanics voted 56% for Bush; in 2008, despite McCain's support of immigration legislation offering a path to citizenship for illegal immigrants, they voted 57% for Obama. This was one state without much of a gender gap, perhaps because elderly voters, most of them women, voted 53%-45% for McCain (the Social Security issue once again failing to give Democrats a majority). In Florida, as nationally, voters with incomes over $200,000 voted for Obama. Did organization matter? An amazing 29% of voters said they'd been contacted by the Obama campaign, and 20% by the McCain campaign; 14% said they'd been contacted by both, and a majority of them voted for McCain.

Congressional districting

Florida has gained congressional districts after every census since 1930, when it was still the smallest state in the South and elected just four House members. In the 2000 census, it gained two seats, for a total of 25. Then, the redistricting process was controlled by Republicans, who passed a plan in March 2002. Disagreement between the state House and Senate was resolved when senators agreed to create a district tailor-made for Republican House Speaker Tom Feeney; the other

111th Congress Lineup	
15 R	10 D
110th Congress Lineup	
16 R	9 D

new district was tailor-made for Republican Mario Diaz-Balart, chairman of the House Congressional Districting Committee. Democrats filed lawsuits against the plan in state and federal courts, but lost those challenges. The plan was solidly in place by the July 9 filing deadline for 2002 contests.

This was, at least for a time, one of the most successful partisan redistrictings of the 2002 cycle. Feeney and Diaz-Balart were both elected to the House by wide margins. Democratic Rep. Karen Thurman was defeated by Republican state Sen. Ginny Brown-Waite. Two senior Republicans, Bill Young of St. Petersburg and Clay Shaw of Fort Lauderdale, were strengthened. Democrat Allen Boyd, of the 2nd District, was weakened. The seats of the three black Democrats and two Latino Republicans were protected. The 2002 plan produced a delegation of 18 Republicans and 7 Democrats, a lopsided GOP majority in a state that had been evenly divided in the 2000 presidential election.

But, as often happens with partisan redistricting plans, the effects wore off after a while. In 2006, Republican Clay Shaw, in line to become chairman of the House Ways and Means committee, was defeated, and Democrats picked up the 16th District, represented by disgraced Republican incumbent Mark Foley. In 2008, Republicans regained the Foley seat after the Democratic incumbent was caught up in his own scandal, but they lost two seats anchored in Orlando, the part of the state where Obama made his biggest gains over the Democratic showing four years before. The 18-7 Republican edge was reduced over the course of two elections to 15-10.

In early 2009, it seemed likely, though by no means assured, that Republicans would control redistricting in Florida after the 2010 census. Republican margins in the Legislature remained large enough that they seemed unlikely to be reversed. Ballot propositions planned for November 2010 would require legislators to draw compact districts that conformed to political or geographic boundaries. However, those conditions were in tension with the prevailing judicial interpretations of the Voting Rights Act, which required that the number of black- or Hispanic-majority districts be maximized. That result can be obtained in a state with demographics like Florida's only by creating districts that are anything but compact and that cut across many political and geographical boundaries.

Governor

Charlie Crist (R)

Elected 2006, term expires Jan. 2011, 1st term; b. July 24, 1956, Altoona, PA; home, St. Petersburg; Attended Wake Forest U., FL St. U., B.A. 1978, Samford U. Cumberland Schl. of Law, J.D. 1981; Methodist; married (Carole).

Elected Office: FL Senate, 1992–98; FL commissioner of educ., 2000–02; FL atty. gen., 2002–06.

Professional Career: Gen. counsel, Minor League Baseball, 1982–88; Practicing atty., 1988–89; State dir., U.S. Sen. Connie Mack, 1989–91; Dep. sec., FL Dept. of Bus. and Prof. Regulation, 1998–2000.

Office: The Capitol, Tallahassee, 32399, 850-488-4441; Fax: 850-487-0801; Web site: www.flgov.com.

Election Results

2006 general	Charlie Crist (R)	2,519,845	(52%)
	Jim Davis (D)	2,178,289	(45%)
2006 primary	Charlie Crist (R)	630,816	(64%)
	Tom Gallagher (R)	330,165	(33%)

Republican Charlie Crist was elected governor of Florida in 2006. He was born in Altoona, Pa., where his grandfather, a Greek immigrant from Cyprus who arrived in America in 1912, ran a shoe-shine parlor. He moved to Atlanta before his first birthday, when his father, who shortened the family name from Christodoulos to Crist, was accepted to medical school at Emory University. In 1960, the Crists settled in sleepy St. Petersburg. A nearby Greek community and a rising population of retirees made the location a nice fit for a young doctor hoping to build a practice. By the time Charlie was 10, he was campaigning for his father, who was seeking—and won—a seat on the Pinellas County School Board. In high school, he was the starting football quarterback and class president. He was a walk-on player at Wake Forest University, where he studied for two years. He transferred after his sophomore year to Florida State, where he was student body vice president and homecoming king before graduating in 1978. He earned his law degree at Cumberland School of Law in Alabama in 1982 and then worked as general counsel for the minor-league division of Major League Baseball.

Crist's first run for the state Senate in 1986 was unsuccessful. Afterward, he served a stint as state director for U.S. GOP Sen. Connie Mack; he again ran for the state Senate, and this time he won. In the Legislature, he acquired the nickname "Chain Gang Charlie" for taking tough stances on crime. Over the years, he also gained a reputation as an ambitious, media-savvy pol, always sporting a healthy tan and blessed with retail campaigning skills. He has been on the statewide ballot in four of five elections between 1998 and 2006. In 1998, he challenged Democratic Sen. Bob Graham but lost 62%-38%. Two years later, he was elected state education commissioner by a vote of 54%-44%. And in 2002, he won the race for Florida attorney general 53%-47%. Four years later, Crist was elected governor 52%-45%.

As attorney general, Crist surprised some with his attention to civil-rights issues, including landmark civil-rights legislation that Florida enacted in 2003. The legislation enabled the attorney general's office to go after businesses that engage in a pattern or practice of discrimination based on race, sex, or disability. In 2004, he reopened the murder probe into the deaths of Harry and Harriette Moore, Florida civil-rights pioneers killed when their home was bombed in 1951. At a 2006 press conference, Crist declared that four Ku Klux Klansmen (all deceased by that time) had been responsible, although some scholars have raised questions about the findings.

In 2006, with GOP Gov. Jeb Bush term-limited and ineligible to run for re-election, the battle for the Republican nomination was between Crist and Tom Gallagher, Florida's chief financial officer. A former state legislator from Miami, Gallagher was making his fourth try for governor. He had dropped out of the 1982 race, and lost in the 1986 and 1994 primaries. He positioned himself as a social conservative and referred to Crist as a liberal. Gallagher supported adding a gay marriage ban to the state constitution and opposed gay adoption. Crist highlighted his school-reform work as education commissioner and his accomplishments as attorney general, and said gay marriage and adoption are "not a major focus in my campaign." He took another position that did not endear him to religious conservatives, saying he disagreed with President Bush's veto of a bill to expand funding for embryonic-stem-cell research. The contest turned highly negative. When documents from Gallagher's 1979 divorce were leaked to a newspaper, he was forced to admit he had used drugs and committed adultery in the 1970s. Other records leaked to the press revealed that Crist was the subject of an 18-year-old paternity suit. He had denied the claim and had relinquished any parental rights to the child, who had been put up for adoption. The results were not close. Crist won the primary 64%-33%, carrying all but a handful of small counties, mainly in the Panhandle.

The Democratic nominee for governor was Tampa-area Rep. Jim Davis, who started with little statewide name recognition. Crist ran as a fiscal conservative and portrayed Davis as a liberal, "do-nothing congressman" who raised taxes. He pointed out that Davis had attended private schools, contrasting that background with his own and describing himself as a "proud product of Florida's public school system." He also called for doubling homestead tax exemptions. Davis promised $1 billion in property-tax relief and increased salaries for teachers. He criticized Crist's record as attorney general by highlighting Florida's rising murder rate and sought to tie Crist to by-then-unpopular President Bush. Crist outspent Davis $20 million to $7 million and won 52%-45%. It was the fourth time in the last six elections that a Republican had won the Florida governorship. He carried 59 of 67 counties, winning by large margins in the western Panhandle and in the Jacksonville area and carrying central Florida and the I-4 corridor. He lost the Gold Coast (Miami-Dade, Broward, and Palm Beach counties) 59%-40%, the University of Florida's Alachua County, and four counties around Tallahassee. He won 59%-38% among white voters, ran evenly with Latino voters (70%-29% among Cubans; 33%-66% among other Hispanic groups), and got the votes of 18% of blacks, an unusually high figure for a Republican.

Crist brought to the governorship a folksy style and a bipartisan perspective that contrasted with the more cerebral and ideological approach of predecessor Jeb Bush. The first issue he tackled was insurance. Seven hurricanes had slammed Florida in 2004 and 2005, and property-insurance rates had skyrocketed. Crist denounced insurance companies for being stingy about paying claims and expanded the state-owned Citizens Property Insurance until it became the largest wind insurer in Florida. In a special session of the Legislature, he won approval of a bill that made the state the insurer of last resort in natural disasters. Rates did not immediately come down as much as he had predicted, and conservatives charged that a major hurricane could bankrupt the state, but the plan was widely popular.

Fiscally, Crist proved to be as conservative as Jeb Bush had been. He used the line-item veto to cut $459 million from the $70 billion state budget in 2007. He sought no tax increases and froze state salaries. In January 2008, as revenues dropped, he proposed a budget $869 million below the previous year's, taking $1 billion out of the rainy day fund. He cut property taxes, an idea that Florida voters approved 64%-36% in early 2008. In early 2009, Crist used the line-item veto to restore some of the Legislature's budget cuts, including funds for his own version of teacher merit pay and his land-preservation fund. He enthusiastically supported the Obama administration's 2009 economic stimulus bill and proposed using $12 billion in stimulus money for education, transportation projects, and economic development.

Crist's policies appealed to liberals as well as conservatives. He kept a 2006 campaign promise by pushing through a law restoring voting rights to released felons. "I believe in forgiveness and atonement," he told the *National Review*. He sought to reduce automotive emissions by 22% by 2012, and he made a $68 million commitment to combating global warming. He replaced Florida's touch-screen voting machines with devices that provided a paper trail. He appointed a moderate as well as two conservatives to the state Supreme Court. In June 2008, he announced a plan to buy out U.S. Sugar Corp. for $1.75 billion and use its lands to accelerate restoration of the Everglades. The plan was to allow waters from Lake Okeechobee to flow directly over the land into the Everglades. Negotiations continued for months, and it was approved by the South Florida Water Management District, but the plan was significantly scaled back in April 2009, with the state slated to buy 72,500 acres for $533 million and getting a 10-year option to purchase the remaining land.

On cultural issues, Crist struck a moderate course as well. Once "pro-choice" on abortion, by 2008 he was "pro-life," though he did not favor overturning the *Roe v. Wade* Supreme Court decision legalizing abortion. He supported civil unions but backed the November 2008 state constitutional ban on same-sex marriage. The issue is "not top-tier for me," he told the *Orlando Sentinel*. The ban passed 62%-38%.

Crist made frequent appearances throughout the state, visiting small businesses and unemployment offices, exuding optimism even as Florida's economy worsened. "Somebody has to say we're going to get out of this, that there is a future and it's going to be OK," he told the *Miami Herald*. He consulted frequently with Democratic legislators as well as Republicans, even though his own party had large majorities in the Legislature. He also played a role in presidential politics. Three days before Florida's presidential primary, he appeared at an event with Republican Sen. John McCain and, to everyone's surprise, including McCain's, endorsed the Arizonan. It certainly helped, and may have made the difference, in McCain's 36%-31% victory over former Massachusetts Gov. Mitt Romney in the primary. Crist continued to support McCain vigorously and downplayed talk that McCain would choose him for vice president.

Crist's job ratings have been extraordinarily high. Republicans don't rate him as positively as they did Jeb Bush, but majorities of independents and Democrats regularly indicate their approval. After GOP Sen. Mel Martinez announced he would not seek re-election in 2010, Crist said in early 2009 that he would seek the Republican nomination for the Senate. He was immediately endorsed by the National Republican Senatorial Committee over former Florida House Speaker Marco Rubio, who is considered more conservative than Crist.

Senior Senator

Bill Nelson (D)

Elected 2000, term expires 2012, 2nd term; b. Sept. 29, 1942, Miami; home, Orlando; Yale U., B.A. 1965; U. of VA, J.D. 1968; Protestant; married (Grace Cavert); 2 children.

Military Career: U.S. Army, 1968–70; U.S. Army Reserves, 1965–71.

Elected Office: FL House of Reps., 1972–78; U.S. House of Reps., 1978–90; FL treasurer, insurance comm. & fire marshal, 1994–2000.

Professional Career: Practicing atty., 1970–79, 1991–94; Legis. asst., FL Gov. Reubin Askew, 1971; Crew member, Space Shuttle Columbia, 1986.

DC Office: 716 HSOB, 20510, 202-224-5274; Fax: 202-228-2183; Web site: billnelson.senate.gov.

State Offices: Coral Gables, 305-536-5999; Davie, 954-693-4851; Fort Myers, 239-334-7760; Jacksonville, 904-346-4500; Orlando, 407-872-7161; Tallahassee, 850-942-8415; Tampa, 813-225-7040; West Palm Beach, 561-514-0189.

Committees: *Aging (Special)* (5th of 13 D). *Armed Services* (7th of 15 D): Emerging Threats & Capabilities; Seapower; Strategic Forces (Chmn). *Budget* (6th of 13 D). *Commerce, Science & Transportation* (6th of 14 D): Aviation Operations, Safety & Security; Communications, Technology & the Internet; Consumer Protection, Product Safety & Insurance; Science & Space (Chmn). *Finance* (11th of 13 D): Energy, Natural Resources & Infrastructure; Health Care; Social Security, Pensions & Family Policy. *Intelligence (Select)* (7th of 8 D).

Group Ratings

	ADA	ACLU	AFS	LCV	ITIC	NTU	COC	ACU	CFG	FRC
2008	95	43	100	91	80	15	50	8	10	0
2007	90	—	100	100	—	11	45	4	14	—

National Journal Ratings

	2007 LIB	—	2007 CONS		2008 LIB	—	2008 CONS
Economic	79%	—	13%		91%	—	0%
Social	73%	—	25%		62%	—	36%
Foreign	52%	—	47%		65%	—	6%
Composite	70%	—	30%		79%	—	21%

Key Votes of the 110th Congress

1. Raise CAFE standards	Y	5. Make English official language	Y	9. Withdraw troops 3/08	Y
2. Expand SCHIP	Y	6. Path to citizenship	Y	10. Iran guard is terrorist group	Y
3. Cap greenhouse gases	Y	7. Fetus is unborn child	N	11. Increase missile defense $	N
4. Bail out financial markets	N	8. Prosecute hate crimes	Y	12. Overhaul FISA	Y

Election Results

2006 general	Bill Nelson (D)..	2,890,548	(60%)	($16,116,224)
	Katherine Harris (R)	1,826,127	(38%)	($9,334,232)
2006 primary	Bill Nelson (D)..	unopposed		

Prior Winning Percentages: 2000 (51%); 1988 House (61%); 1986 House (73%); 1984 House (61%); 1982 House (71%); 1980 House (70%); 1978 House (61%)

Bill Nelson was first elected to the Senate in 2000. He grew up in Melbourne, Fla. His mother was a schoolteacher, and his father was a lawyer and real estate investor who died when he was 14. Nelson likes to recall that his great-grandfather arrived in Florida from Denmark as a stowaway on a ship. From his family home in Rock Point, Nelson could see rockets blast off in the 1950s and 1960s from what is now the Kennedy Space Center. He was active in student government and has always been something of a straight arrow; he doesn't drink, smoke or swear. He attended the University of Florida for two years, and then graduated from Yale and the University of Virginia law school. After a two-year hitch in the Army, he returned to Melbourne and briefly practiced law and worked on the staff of Democratic Gov. Reubin Askew. In 1972, at age 30, he was elected to the state House of Representatives.

In 1978, when Republican Rep. Louis Frey retired, Nelson ran for the U.S. House in a district that then included the Space Coast's Brevard County and most of Orlando's Orange County. His religious faith and traditional values, his indefatigable campaigning and folksy manner made him popular in an area that was trending Republican. He won the seat 61%-39%; in five succeeding elections, he captured 61% to 73% of the ballots in a district that voted just 29% for Democrat Michael Dukakis in the 1988 presidential race. In the House, he became chairman of the Science Committee's Space Subcommittee, obviously of prime importance to the district. Nelson not only boosted the space program in every possible way but also rode the space shuttle *Columbia* himself, spending six days orbiting the Earth in early 1986. Less than two weeks later, space shuttle *Challenger* exploded as it took off. After the *Columbia* was lost in February 2003, he called for continued manned space flight despite the risks.

In 1989, with the support of leading Florida Democrats, Nelson set out to run against Republican Gov. Bob Martinez, who was not faring well in polls. But in early 1990, some Democrats became antsy about Nelson's prospects and persuaded Lawton Chiles, who had retired from the Senate in 1988 after three terms, to run. Chiles was always far ahead in their race and won the September primary 69%-31%. Nelson returned to his 77-acre oceanfront home in Melbourne, his political career seemingly over. But in 1994, he found an opening when state Insurance Commissioner Tom Gallagher, a Republican, ran for governor. Nelson was elected in November to an office whose full title was treasurer, insurance commissioner, and state fire marshal, and proceeded to compile an activist record.

Nelson was obviously setting himself up to run for higher statewide office, and his chance came in March 1999, when Republican Sen. Connie Mack said he would not run for re-election in 2000. Mack's retirement left a seat up for grabs in a state that, as Election Night 2000 returns would show, was closely divided between the parties. Republicans nominated 20-year, Orlando-based Rep. Bill McCollum, one of the House managers of the impeachment of President Clinton.

Washington observers considered the race a contest about the wisdom of impeachment but mostly it was a battle of competing styles. Running his fourth statewide race in 10 years, Nelson consistently led in polls. His easygoing manner contrasted favorably with McCollum's stiff, often aggressive demeanor. With a long conservative record on abortion rights and gun control, McCollum attempted to moderate his positions but only succeeded in antagonizing his base supporters. His charges that Nelson was a "liberal" and a proponent of "class warfare" proved unconvincing. This was the most expensive Florida Senate race to that point, with the two candidates spending more than $15 million between them. Nelson won 51%-46%. He prevailed 60%-37% in the Gold Coast. In the Interstate 4 corridor, which included McCollum's congressional district and most of the district that Nelson had represented in the House, Nelson won 51%-46%. In the rest of the state, Nelson lost by only 52%-46%, compared with the 55%-42% ratio by which Democratic presidential nominee Al Gore lost there that year. Folksiness and Florida roots counted.

In the Senate, Nelson has been active on national security issues. In October 2002, he sided with President Bush on the Iraq war resolution. But in defiance of the Bush White House, Nelson in December 2006 traveled to Damascus to meet with Syrian President Bashar Assad. He called for aggressive diplomacy with Syria and perhaps Iran, saying: "The costs of failure in Iraq will be catastrophic—in growing threats to us and our allies and in more American and Iraqi lives lost—if we do not awaken to the fact that an aggressive diplomatic effort, not military might, is what is needed to end the sectarian violence in Iraq." In 2007, Nelson voted in the Foreign Relations Committee for the resolution opposing Bush's troop "surge" strategy in Iraq. But he looked with favor on military involvement elsewhere, calling in May 2007 for United Nations peacekeeping troops on both sides of the Sudan-Chad border and a no-fly zone over the area. With two Senate colleagues, he met in 2005 with Venezuela's President Hugo Chavez, who told him he would cooperate in keeping Colombian FARC guerrillas from reaching sanctuary in Venezuela.

Since January 2007, Nelson has been chairman of the Commerce subcommittee with jurisdiction over the space program. After the loss of *Columbia,* he called for accelerated development of a reusable space vehicle to ferry astronauts to the International Space Station. In 2004, Nelson won passage of an amendment calling on NASA to report to Congress on the costs of extending the space shuttle program beyond 2010, but he did not get approval of another amendment requiring NASA to find laid-off shuttle workers similar jobs in the agency. In 2008, he secured an amendment mandating that the agency take no action that would preclude continuing the shuttle program past 2010, in order to leave the decision to the next administration.

After hurricanes hit Florida in August and September 2004, Nelson successfully pushed to get $1 billion for agricultural assistance in the Homeland Security appropriation. Starting in 2005, Nelson worked with Republican colleague Mel Martinez of Florida to block oil and gas exploration in the eastern part of the Gulf of Mexico. In 2007, he and Martinez threatened to block the energy bill unless it barred further seismic exploration off the Florida coast. After Republican Gov. Charlie Crist came out in favor of offshore drilling in June 2008, Nelson continued to oppose it. Then, in September 2008, Nelson said he would back a bipartisan deal allowing some offshore drilling in the Gulf of Mexico, provided it was limited to 125 miles, rather than 50 miles, from the Florida coast.

On other issues important to Florida, Nelson sought a 25% tax credit for home improvements designed to withstand hurricanes. But the bill never gained much traction; neither did one he sponsored to set up a national catastrophe fund to lower insurance costs. In May 2007, his amendment to oppose a $25 per flight surcharge on both commercial airlines and general aviation was defeated 12-11 in committee.

Florida seems to have more than its share of disputes over elections. After the 2006 balloting in Florida's 13th District raised questions about the dependability of electronic voting machines, Nelson introduced a bill requiring voting equipment to produce a paper record. During the 2008 presidential campaign, Nelson objected vigorously when the Democratic National Committee stripped Florida of its national delegates and urged presidential candidates to boycott the state after the Legislature set the state's primary for January 29 rather than the earliest date permitted by party rules, February 5. He and Democratic Rep. Alcee Hastings sued the DNC, but a judge ruled against them. Nelson then pressed for a second primary or a mail-in vote, which the committee refused to pay for, and he tried to have half of the delegates seated, which the DNC resisted. The committee ultimately decided to seat about half of Florida's delegates.

As a Democratic senator from the nation's largest politically marginal state, Nelson was mentioned as a possible vice presidential nominee in 2004 and 2008 but was not on either short list. He was re-elected in 2006 by a margin that was anything but marginal. He positioned himself well, stoutly opposing Bush's plan to partially privatize Social Security. After the Pentagon limited access to military bases for the Boy Scouts, he introduced a resolution supporting the Scouts and embarked on a tour of Florida on their behalf.

In June 2005, two-term Republican Rep. Katherine Harris announced she would challenge Nelson. Polling data indicated that Harris's prominent role as Florida secretary of state during the disputed 2000 presidential election had left her too unpopular to win, but she enjoyed celebrity status among many rank-and-file Republican voters. Efforts to persuade Gov. Jeb Bush, former House Speaker Allen Bense, and former Rep. Joe Scarborough to run failed, and Harris became the nominee. In February 2006, she accumulated additional baggage when a defense contractor who had illegally contributed $32,000 to Harris's 2004 House campaign and had asked her for legislative favors pleaded guilty to bribing former Rep. Randy (Duke) Cunningham, a California Republican. The next month, Harris announced she would use $10 million of her own money on her campaign; she ended up spending a third of that amount. Staff resignations followed, and Harris was notably absent from a Republican "unity tour" after the September primary. Nelson won in a landslide, 60%-38%. He lost in the Panhandle but carried 57 of 67 counties, including Harris's home county of Sarasota.

Junior Senator

Mel Martinez (R)

Elected 2004, term expires 2010, 1st term; b. Oct. 23, 1946, Sagua La Grande, Cuba; home, Orlando; FL St. U., B.A. 1969, J.D. 1973; Catholic; married (Kitty); 3 children.

Elected Office: Orange County chairman, 1998–2001.

Professional Career: Practicing atty., 1973–98; Secy., U.S. Dept. of Housing and Urban Dev., 2001–03.

DC Office: 356 RSOB, 20510, 202-224-3041; Fax: 202-228-5171; Web site: martinez.senate.gov.

State Offices: Coral Gables, 305-444-8332; Jacksonville, 904-398-8586; Naples, 239-774-3367; Orlando, 407-254-2573; Pensacola, 850-433-2603; Tampa, 813-977-6950.

Committees: *Aging (Special)* (RMM of 7 R). *Armed Services* (7th of 11 R): Emerging Threats & Capabilities; Personnel; Seapower (RMM). *Banking, Housing & Urban Affairs* (5th of 10 R): Financial Institutions; Housing, Transportation & Community Development; Securities, Insurance & Investment. *Commerce, Science & Transportation* (10th of 11 R): Aviation Operations, Safety & Security; Communications, Technology & the Internet; Competitiveness, Innovation & Export Promotion (RMM); Oceans, Atmosphere, Fisheries & Coast Guard.

Group Ratings

	ADA	ACLU	AFS	LCV	ITIC	NTU	COC	ACU	CFG	FRC
2008	30	14	11	36	100	40	88	60	43	100
2007	20	—	0	13	—	73	100	80	83	—

National Journal Ratings

	2007 LIB	—	2007 CONS		2008 LIB	—	2008 CONS
Economic	28%	—	70%		36%	—	63%
Social	34%	—	65%		36%	—	60%
Foreign	30%	—	66%		37%	—	61%
Composite	32%	—	68%		38%	—	63%

Key Votes of the 110th Congress

1. Raise CAFE standards	N	5. Make English official language Y	9. Withdraw troops 3/08	N
2. Expand SCHIP	N	6. Path to citizenship	Y	10. Iran guard is terrorist group Y
3. Cap greenhouse gases	Y	7. Fetus is unborn child	Y	11. Increase missile defense $	Y
4. Bail out financial markets	Y	8. Prosecute hate crimes	N	12. Overhaul FISA	Y

Election Results

2004 general	Mel Martinez (R)	3,672,864	(49%)	($12,836,836)
	Betty Castor (D)	3,590,201	(48%)	($11,472,071)
2004 primary	Mel Martinez (R)	522,994	(45%)	
	Bill McCollum (R)	360,474	(31%)	
	Doug Gallagher (R)	158,360	(14%)	
	Johnnie Byrd (R)	68,982	(6%)	

Melquiades (Mel) Martinez, a Republican, was elected Florida's junior senator in 2004. In December 2008, after just four years in the Senate, he surprised many in his party by announcing that he would not seek re-election to a second term in 2010. "My decision is not based on re-election prospects, but on what I want to do with the next eight years of my life," he told the *Sarasota Herald-Tribune,* and said he wanted to spend more time with his family. The announcement came after several polls showed him with some of the lowest approval ratings among senators, a result of positions he has taken that angered both conservatives and moderates in the party and possibly also because of his close association with President Bush.

Martinez grew up in the Cuban countryside, near Sagua La Grande, where his father was a veterinarian. In February 1962, after a 16-year-old neighbor was shot by a firing squad for dealing with the underground, Martinez's parents sent him to the United States. He traveled to Florida under the aegis of Operation Pedro Pan, a Catholic Church program that brought 14,000 unaccompanied children to the United States. He stayed in a camp along the St. John's River west of St. Augustine and then was taken in as a foster child by an Orlando couple; he spoke very little English at the time. Martinez attended Orlando Junior College and worked at a Publix supermarket. His parents were finally able to join him in 1966, and he bought them a used Chevy to drive. He transferred to Florida State, graduated from its college and law school, and practiced law in Orlando with Orlando Mayor Bill Frederick's firm.

A Democrat in college and law school, Martinez became a Republican in 1979. As one of the few bilingual lawyers in town, he attracted many Spanish-speaking clients. He became a wealthy personal-injury plaintiffs attorney and was head of the Florida Academy of Trial Lawyers. He started a law practice with his college roommate, Ken Connor. Connor ran for governor in 1994 as an anti-abortion-rights Republican and asked Martinez to be his running mate. Jeb Bush won the primary with 46% of the vote, and Connor finished fifth with 9%, but Martinez got noticed. In 1998, he ran for chairman of the Orange County government and, in a nonpartisan three-way race, won by a wide margin. In 2000, he co-chaired George W. Bush's Florida campaign, and after the election, Bush appointed him secretary of Housing and Urban Development.

As HUD secretary, Martinez set up a $1.7 billion tax credit program for investors who were building affordable housing and a $1 billion program to help 650,000 low-income families come up with the money for down payments. He increased spending on Section 8 housing vouchers from $12 billion to $18 billion, but his attempt to streamline the closing process for home purchases was unsuccessful. During his tenure, Martinez traveled extensively and was constantly available to Spanish-language media, speaking not only about HUD programs but also in defense of the administration's domestic and foreign policies in general.

When Democratic Sen. Bob Graham came up for re-election in 2004, he announced his plans to run for president. Although he ultimately withdrew from the presidential contest, his decision set off a pitched battle for his Senate seat. Democrats nominated Betty Castor, a former state legislator from Tampa, who was elected state education commissioner in 1986 and 1990 and later president of the University of South Florida. On the Republican side, White House strategist Karl Rove met with Rep. Katherine Harris to discourage her from entering the Senate contest. She was Florida's secretary of state during the 2000 presidential vote recount and had become a lightning rod for the Democrats. Meanwhile, GOP senators were encouraging Martinez to throw his hat in the ring, but he had his eye on running for governor in 2006. It seemed a natural fit for his executive experience. In December 2003, he resigned as HUD secretary and announced he was entering the Senate race. He quickly raised enough money to be competitive.

In the GOP primary, Martinez faced former Rep. Bill McCollum, who had lost a Senate bid to Democratic Sen. Bill Nelson in 2000, and businessman Doug Gallagher, who had his own money but no name recognition. It was a fractious contest, with heavy doses of negative campaigning. McCollum attacked Martinez as a trial lawyer and as a "failed" HUD secretary, and Gallagher spent $6.3 million on ads calling his opponents "the M&M boys" and citing his business accomplishments. Martinez's ads attacked McCollum as "anti-family" because he supported embryonic-stem-cell research and said he was appeasing "the radical homosexual lobby" because he supported a hate crimes bill. In a debate, McCollum called the ads "despicable" and said that Martinez was "unfit" to serve. But Martinez won big, with 45% of the vote. McCollum finished with 31%, and Gallagher with 14%.

In the early fall, polls showed Martinez and Castor locked in a dead heat. There was plenty of contrast between the candidates on issues—the Iraq war, abortion, stem-cell research, Cuba, tax cuts, Social Security, and education. Both sides spent plenty of money: Martinez, $12.8 million; Castor, $11.4 million. But it was a tough environment for getting messages through to the voters. Florida's airwaves filled up with ads from the presidential candidates and from backers and opponents of a medical malpractice ballot measure. Four hurricanes that swept through the state dominated the local newscasts. Martinez accused Castor of going soft on a "terrorist cell" at the University of South Florida and ran an ad featuring a retired immigration agent criticizing her. Castor called the ad "despicable" and depicted herself as independent and Martinez as a rubber stamp for Bush. She also ran ads charging Martinez with ethical improprieties at HUD.

On election night, the returns showed a very close race, and Castor declared that a recount would be needed. The next morning, however, when more of the returns had come in, she conceded. Martinez had won by fewer than 100,000 votes, 49%-48%. Castor led 57%-41% in the Gold Coast, and the Interstate 4 corridor produced a 49%-49% tie. Martinez won 56%-42% in the rest of the state

In the Senate, Martinez sat on the Banking, Housing, and Urban Affairs Committee, where he advocated legislation to overhaul the mortgage process for consumers and implement policies he had backed at HUD. In his maiden Senate speech in February 2005, he defended Attorney General Alberto Gonzalez, who was under fire for the dismissal of U.S. attorneys around the nation. Martinez expressed disappointment that Bush did not use his 2006 State of the Union speech to challenge Cuba for its undemocratic practices, and he introduced a bill that would deny visas to foreign entities that help Cuba develop its oil exploration program. In 2005, he took a lead role on the bill seeking federal judicial review of the case of Terri Schiavo, a severely brain-damaged woman who was at the center of a right-to-die battle among members of her family. But Martinez was embarrassed after he unknowingly handed Sen. Tom Harkin, D-Iowa, a memo, drafted by one of Martinez's staffers, that mentioned the political advantages presented by the case.

Martinez worked with New Mexico Republican Pete Domenici, then-chairman of the Senate Energy and Natural Resources Committee, on a compromise bill to open up a large section of the Gulf of Mexico to offshore oil and gas drilling. Concerned about Florida's beaches and tourism industry, Martinez negotiated a ban on drilling within 125 miles of the Florida Panhandle and 235 miles of Tampa and Naples. In

2007, with Democrats in the majority on Capitol Hill, Martinez teamed with Democrat Bill Nelson, Florida's senior senator, to block the energy bill unless it barred further exploration off the Florida coast. In September 2008, they accepted a bipartisan plan to allow drilling at 125 miles, rather than 50 miles, off the state's coastline. Martinez took some stands against Bush administration policy. He voted to override the president's veto of a water bill that provided $2 billion for Everglades restoration, and he tried to delay a White House proposal to cut $3.9 billion from Medicaid payments to hospitals. He supported other administration policies, including the Republican version of the State Children's Health Insurance Program and the troop surge in Iraq.

As the Senate's only immigrant, Martinez took a lead role on immigration legislation in 2006 and 2007. In 2006, he and Sen. Chuck Hagel, R-Neb., worked out a compromise that established requirements for illegal immigrants to legalize their status depending on the length of time they had been in the U.S. Martinez warned fellow Republicans that they would alienate Hispanic voters with anti-immigrant rhetoric, but conservatives attacked him. Backers of building a fence along the U.S.-Mexican border to keep immigrants out sent bricks to his office. The Senate passed the immigration bill in 2007, but without enforcement provisions that a majority of House members wanted.

Later that year, Martinez and other senators tried to draft a comprehensive bill that would include tougher enforcement of immigration laws, but also provisions for guest workers and a path to citizenship for illegal workers. Opponents went to work trying to weaken the guest-worker elements with proposals to cut the number of allowable visas in half and to sunset the guest-worker program after a certain period. Majority Leader Harry Reid, R-Nev., finally yanked the bill from the floor. In June, Martinez and other bill sponsors brought it back with a tweak that attempted to satisfy the opposition: Illegal immigrants would have to go back to their country of origin before seeking legal status. But the bill got insufficient support and died. Throughout the debate, Martinez came under fire from fierce opponents of the bill. Florida polls showed his approval rating hovering between 42% and 37%—not reassuring numbers for an incumbent.

In January 2007, Bush chose Martinez to chair the Republican National Committee, and he accepted. As chairman, he spoke frequently for Republican positions on Spanish-language media, but he drew repeated criticism on talk radio for his stand on immigration, which opponents derided as "amnesty" for illegal aliens. He also found it difficult to stay in touch with the voters in his large, multi-media-market state. In October 2007, he abruptly resigned the chairmanship. All the while, Martinez continued to raise money for his re-election campaign and in August 2008 published a book, *A Sense of Belonging: From Castro's Cuba to the U.S. Senate: One Man's Pursuit of the American Dream.* His poll numbers remained low, however, and late in the year, he announced his intentions to vacate his Senate seat.

In January 2009, former Gov. Jeb Bush, still enjoying high retrospective poll ratings, said he would not run for the seat. In February 2009, GOP Gov. Charlie Crist entered the contest rather than run for re-election. Another Republican contender was former Florida House speaker Marco Rubio. Among Democrats, U.S. Rep. Kendrick Meek was the early frontrunner.

FIRST DISTRICT

Jeff Miller (R)

Elected Oct. 2001, 4th full term; b. June 27, 1959, St. Petersburg; home, Chumuckla; U. of FL, B.A. 1984; Methodist; married (Vicki); 2 children.

Elected Office: FL House of Reps., 1998–2001.

Professional Career: Real estate broker, Henry Co. homes; Owner, Jeff Miller Real Estate; Deputy sheriff.

DC Office: 2439 RHOB, 20515, 202-225-4136; Fax: 202-225-3414; Web site: jeffmiller.house.gov.

State Offices: Ft. Walton Beach, 850-664-1266; Pensacola, 850-479-1183.

Committees: *Armed Services* (7th of 25 R): Air & Land Forces; Terrorism, Unconventional Threats & Capabilities (RMM). *Veterans' Affairs* (5th of 11 R): Disability Assistance & Memorial Affairs. *Intelligence (Select)* (7th of 9 R): Oversight & Investigations (RMM); Technical & Tactical Intelligence.

Group Ratings

	ADA	ACLU	AFS	LCV	ITIC	NTU	COC	ACU	CFG	FRC
2008	5	20	0	0	33	86	89	100	97	100
2007	10	—	9	10	—	86	58	92	88	—

National Journal Ratings

	2007 LIB	—	2007 CONS		2008 LIB	—	2008 CONS
Economic	24%	—	75%		3%	—	95%
Social	0%	—	91%		0%	—	91%
Foreign	38%	—	61%		0%	—	95%
Composite	23%	—	78%		4%	—	96%

Key Votes of the 110th Congress

1. Increase minimum wage	N	5. Share immigration data	Y	9. Withdraw troops 8/08	N
2. Expand SCHIP	N	6. Foreign aid abortion ban	Y	10. No operations in Iran	*
3. Raise CAFE standards	N	7. Ban gay bias in workplace	N	11. Free trade with Peru	*
4. Bail out financial markets	N	8. Repeal D.C. gun law	Y	12. Overhaul FISA	Y

Election Results

2008 general	Jeff Miller (R)..232,559	(70%)	($458,359)
	James Bryan (D)..98,797	(30%)	($18,358)
2008 primary	Jeff Miller (R).. unopposed		

Prior Winning Percentages: 2006 (69%); 2004 (77%); 2002 (75%); 2001 (66%)

Population		Race/Ethnicity		Work	
Pop. 2007:	690,477	White:	76.1%	Private:	69.2%
Change since 2000:	Up 8.0%	Black:	14.0%	Government:	24.7%
Urban:	77.5%	Hispanic:	4.0%	Self-employed:	5.9%
Rural:	22.5%	Asian:	2.3%	Blue collar:	23.0%
Area size:	5,241 sq. mi.	Native Am.:	0.6%	White collar:	54.4%
		Hawaiian:	0.1%	Khaki collar:	4.7%
Age		Two+ races:	2.7%	Other:	18.0%
Median age:	38.2 yrs.			Median income:	$46,013
More than 65 yrs:	13.4%	*Ancestry*		Median home value:	$159,800
Less than 18 yrs:	22.9%	Irish:	11.1%	Poverty:	13.3%
		German:	11.0%		
Education		USA:	10.4%	**Military Veterans**	
H.S. grad:	85.6%			% of Pop:	19.4%
College grad:	22.6%				
Grad degree:	7.5%				

The "Redneck Riviera" is the affectionate local name for the Gulf Coast beaches of Florida's Panhandle, stretching from Pensacola east to Destin. This has been military country ever since John Quincy Adams persuaded Spain to sell Florida to the United States in 1819 with the goal of getting the port of Pensacola. In October 1861, the Union defeated the Confederates in a battle to control Santa Rosa Island, the outermost spit of land protecting Pensacola Bay. (A quarter century later, the

2008 Presidential Vote

McCain (R)............................234,257	(67%)
Obama (D) 112,726	(32%)

2004 Presidential Vote

Bush (R)................................231,199	(72%)
Kerry (D)................................88,686	(28%)

Cook Partisan Voting Index: R+21

site of that clash, Fort Pickens, became Apache warrior Geronimo's prison.) In the 20th century, the Pensacola Naval Air Station was turned into the nation's first naval-aviation training base, giving birth to carrier aviation. Today, about 20,000 people are employed at Eglin Air Force Base, which spreads over three counties and, with approximately 100,000 square miles of airspace stretching over the Gulf of Mexico to the Florida Keys, is considered the largest air base in the free world. Eglin developed the BLU-82 "Daisy Cutter" bomb that was used in Afghanistan, and it was the test site for the largest conventional bomb in the U.S. arsenal, the 21,000-pound ordnance that is dropped from the rear of a C-130 cargo plane and is referred to as the "Mother of All Bombs." Base realignment was expected to add more than 4,000 troops and 100 F-35 jet fighters to Eglin by 2011.

The western panhandle of Florida is closer to Houston than to Miami, and is culturally part of Dixie. A columnist for the *Pensacola News Journal* once recommended the creation of an independent commonwealth of West Florida. "We don't have much in common with the people inhabiting what I call peninsular Florida," wrote Jerry Maygarden. "I'm convinced that the further south you drive, the further north you get." Until recently, the panhandle was economically backward and heavily dependent on the military. As the South has become more prosperous, the shore has attracted vacationing and retiring Southerners to its vast, fine-grained white sand beaches and its pleasant inlet-dotted bays. It also has become a leading spring-break destination for college students and the site of a large annual gay Memorial Day weekend party. The region has long been culturally and economically conservative, with a strong pro-military bent.

The 1st Congressional District of Florida is so far west, it's in the Central time zone. Pensacola's Escambia County, where about half the district's people live, is the state's westernmost county. The time-zone issue became a sore point in 2000, when television network news announced that Florida's polls had closed at 7 p.m. Eastern time, though they were still open in the Panhandle, and then declared Al Gore the winner of Florida's electoral votes 10 minutes before the Panhandle's polls had closed. In the absence of that misinformation, a few thousand votes might have been cast for George W. Bush here and made the whole Florida recount controversy unnecessary. The district's shoreline runs from Pensacola, adjoining the Alabama border, through Fort Walton Beach to the west side of Destin. Inland, the 1st stretches farther east, taking in rural Walton, Holmes and Washington counties. The population here has grown steadily, with young civilians, not just military retirees, moving in and shifting attention to education and quality-of-life issues. In 2004, four massive hurricanes roared through the region, with devastating effect. In Pensacola alone, 45,000 homes were deemed unlivable. In 2005, Hurricane Katrina also left its mark here. With the most military veterans of any district in the nation, the 1st District is strongly Republican. It voted 69%-31% for George W. Bush in 2000 and 72%-28% in 2004, his best numbers in the state. John McCain, likewise, had his best Florida showing in this district, with a 67%-32% lead over Barack Obama.

The congressman from the 1st District is Jeff Miller, a Republican who won a special election in October 2001. The scion of a pioneer farm family that settled in central Florida in the mid-1800s, Miller grew up in Levy County, where his parents raised cattle. He graduated from the University of Florida and became an aide to the state's longtime agriculture commissioner, Democrat Doyle Conner. In 1998, he moved to Santa Rosa County, his wife's family's home, and began to sell real estate. Also in 1998, a year after he switched to the Republican Party, he ran his first political campaign, challenging a Republican state representative who had received some negative press after an altercation with a state trooper. Miller won 53%-47%. Not long afterward, the 1st District seat came open following the resignation of Republican Rep. Joe Scarborough, who became a talk-show host on the MSNBC cable network. Miller quickly became the favorite of national party leaders. Sensitive to coastal interests, Miller and the other serious contenders all claimed to be ardent environmentalists, an unusual twist in a Republican primary. Miller's best-known opponent was state Rep. Randy Knepper, chief of staff to the district's former representative, Earl Hutto, D-Fla., who retired in 1994. Scarborough endorsed Miller as "a strong voice for northwest Florida." In the six-candidate contest, Miller got 54% to only 15% for Knepper and 16% for businessman Michael Francisco, a decorated combat pilot. National Democrats made no major effort to win this seat that they had held less than seven years earlier, and Miller won the general election, 66%-28%.

In the House, Miller has compiled a mostly conservative record. In contrast to the vocal Scarborough, he gained a reputation for being soft-spoken and a good listener. But he also has a decidedly lower profile. As a more active and outspoken member, Scarborough often got the attention of the Republican leadership. When he arrived in Washington, Miller got seats on the Armed Services and Veterans' Affairs committees, obvious assignments for this district. He made multiple visits to U.S. troops in Afghanistan and Iraq and praised the conduct of the war. He worked to protect local military facilities in the base-closing process. In 2004, when Democrats were seeking to force a House vote on Miller's bill to provide a 100% annuity to surviving military spouses, he persuaded Republican leaders to call up the bill and avoid a partisan conflict; the measure was passed into law. A long-standing foe of oil and gas drilling in the eastern Gulf of Mexico, he relented in 2006, accepting a deal that opened up some offshore drilling but included a bar on drilling rigs in a military training range that extends at least 200 miles south of Fort Walton Beach. An avid gun-rights advocate, he sponsored a bill in 2007 to give hunters in the District of Columbia in-state rates for licenses in the more open spaces of Maryland or Virginia. He also has sponsored a bill to place the face of Ronald Reagan on the half-dollar coin.

When Republicans lost control of the House, Miller became the ranking Republican on the Health Subcommittee on the Veterans' Affairs Committee. In 2008, he secured $54 million for an in-patient center at Eglin Hospital and pushed for a new veterans' hospital near the base to replace one destroyed by Hurricane Katrina in 2005. At the outset of the 111th Congress in 2009, Miller got a promotion, becoming the ranking Republican on the Armed Services Committee's subcommittee on terrorism and unconventional threats.

In the 2002 primary, Miller faced a rematch with special election primary runner-up Francisco, who criticized his lack of military experience. Miller won 64%-36%. Since then, Democrats have run only token challengers against him.

SECOND DISTRICT

Allen Boyd (D)

Elected 1996, 7th term; b. June 6, 1945, Valdosta, GA; home, Monticello; N. FL Jr. Col., A.A. 1966, FL St. U., B.S. 1969; Methodist; married (Cissy); 3 children.

Military Career: Army 1969–71 (Vietnam).

Elected Office: FL House of Reps., 1989–96.

Professional Career: Farmer.

DC Office: 1227 LHOB, 20515, 202-225-5235; Fax: 202-225-5615; Web site: www.house.gov/boyd.

State Offices: Panama City, 850-785-0812; Tallahassee, 850-561-3979.

Committees: *Appropriations* (21st of 37 D): Agriculture, Rural Development, FDA & Related Agencies; Defense; Financial Services & General Government. *Budget* (8th of 24 D).

Group Ratings

	ADA	ACLU	AFS	LCV	ITIC	NTU	COC	ACU	CFG	FRC
2008	75	73	71	85	100	13	67	12	21	5
2007	80	—	82	65	—	8	74	12	14	—

National Journal Ratings

	2007 LIB — 2007 CONS		2008 LIB — 2008 CONS	
Economic	49%	— 50%	48%	— 52%
Social	54%	— 45%	62%	— 34%
Foreign	54%	— 46%	50%	— 48%
Composite	53%	— 47%	54%	— 46%

Key Votes of the 110th Congress

1. Increase minimum wage	Y	5. Share immigration data	N	9. Withdraw troops 8/08	Y
2. Expand SCHIP	Y	6. Foreign aid abortion ban	N	10. No operations in Iran	N
3. Raise CAFE standards	N	7. Ban gay bias in workplace	*	11. Free trade with Peru	Y
4. Bail out financial markets	Y	8. Repeal D.C. gun law	Y	12. Overhaul FISA	Y

Election Results

2008 general	Allen Boyd (D)	216,804	(62%)	($962,421)
	Mark Mulligan (R)	133,404	(38%)	($33,430)
2008 primary	Allen Boyd (D)	unopposed		

Prior Winning Percentages: 2006 (100%); 2004 (62%); 2002 (67%); 2000 (72%); 1998 (100%); 1996 (59%)

Population		Race/Ethnicity		Work	
Pop. 2007:	695,539	White:	70.5%	Private:	65.4%
Change since 2000:	Up 8.8%	Black:	22.0%	Government:	28.6%
Urban:	62.1%	Hispanic:	4.0%	Self-employed:	5.7%
Rural:	37.9%	Asian:	1.5%	Blue collar:	19.2%
Area size:	11,141 sq. mi.	Native Am.:	0.4%	White collar:	60.7%
Age		Hawaiian:	0.0%	Khaki collar:	0.8%
Median age:	36.6 yrs.	Two+ races:	1.4%	Other:	19.3%
More than 65 yrs:	12.7%	**Ancestry**		Median income:	$43,852
Less than 18 yrs:	21.8%	Irish:	10.5%	Median home value:	$160,700
Education		English:	9.9%	Poverty:	17.3%
H.S. grad:	83.6%	German:	9.8%	**Military Veterans**	
College grad:	25.7%			% of Pop:	14.1%
Grad degree:	10.0%				

Tallahassee is a small city in the middle of swampy lowlands, the opposite of the image people have the typical booming Florida city, with endless miles of beach or a Magic Kingdom beckoning vacationing families or snowbirds from elsewhere. So how did Tallahassee become the capital of the nation's fourth-largest state? The answer is, it was chosen back when Florida's modest population lived mostly along the state's northern tier, placing Tallahassee, more or less, at the state's center of gravity. Ralph

2008 Presidential Vote		
McCain (R)	199,661	(54%)
Obama (D)	163,872	(45%)
2004 Presidential Vote		
Bush (R)	181,300	(54%)
Kerry (D)	153,164	(46%)
Cook Partisan Voting Index:	R+6	

Waldo Emerson, visiting Tallahassee in the 19th century, called it a "grotesque place, rapidly settled by public officers, land speculators and desperadoes." Today the countryside around Tallahassee is distinctly Dixie: cotton fields, soft pine stands, catfish farms, small towns with big churches. Until recently, Tallahassee was little more than a Spanish-mossed county seat with a pair of universities and a handsome Creole capitol, built in 1845 and preserved opposite its 1977 skyscraper replacement. Since the 1980s, it has spread out and become a middling-sized city, with a tight-knit and sometimes fractious political and legal elite, bringing a taste of newly urbanized Florida to the state's north. Tallahassee has not yet attained the critical mass of Sacramento, Austin or Albany, but perhaps it is on its way as the state continues to expand and diversify and its Legislature inches closer to professional status. In 2007, Moody's business-vitality index ranked the city 35th among the nation's 379 metro areas.

The 2nd Congressional District of Florida is centered on Tallahassee, and extends along the Gulf coast west to Destin and east to the Suwanee River, which empties into the Gulf in the only part of Florida where the beach is still undeveloped. Inland, the 2nd runs north to the Alabama and Georgia borders, and far enough east to be within an hour's drive of Jacksonville. Historically, this was Democratic country, as in Jeffersonian and segregationist. Today, it is still mostly Democratic, though for different reasons. More than one in three Tallahassee-area jobs are in city and state government, three times the statewide level. The city's African-American population grew from about 25% into the 1990s to 32% in 2007. The district includes Gadsden County, the state's only black-majority county. Growth is spreading south into Wakulla County, which grew 30% from 2000 to 2007. There is similar growth along the beach areas near Destin, which have attracted affluent families to "new urbanist" communities like Seaside and Rosemary Beach. For all this recent growth, this remains the part of Florida with the highest percentage of native Floridians. The town of Panama City Beach (separate from Panama City) is "cheerfully demotic, vulgar even," wrote the *Washington Post* in 2008, and reminiscent of "the old Florida of cheap and tacky fun."

Tallahassee and Leon County have voted solidly for Democratic presidential nominees in recent elections. Beyond Leon County, which casts about 40% of the district's votes, partisan performance is less predictable. Gadsden County is heavily Democratic, while the Gulf beach areas tend to be Republican. The 2d District voted twice for George W. Bush, but in 2002 it gave a hefty margin to Democrat Bill McBride over Republican Gov. Jeb Bush, who was disliked by most public-employee unions, and in 2006, GOP Gov. Charlie Crist also struggled here. He lost only eight of 67 counties statewide, but three of them—Gadsden, Leon and Jefferson—were in the 2nd District. John McCain beat Barack Obama 54%-45% in the district.

The congressman from the 2nd District is Allen Boyd, a Democrat first elected in 1996. A lifelong farmer, Boyd grew up in Monticello in Jefferson County just east of Tallahassee. He graduated from Florida State University and served in the Army during the Vietnam War. His political career began when he won a special election to the state House in 1989. He won his seat in Congress after Rep. Pete Peterson, a moderate Democrat and Vietnam prisoner of war, retired after three terms, saying he believed in term limits. In the Democratic primary, Boyd took 48% of the vote to 26% for Leon County Commissioner Anita Davis. Boyd easily won the runoff 64%-36%. In the general election, Boyd campaigned with Blue Dog conservative Democrats and outspent the Republican by 2-to-1 to win a solid 59%-40% victory.

In the House, Boyd has worked as a behind-the-scenes consensus builder. With one of the chamber's most centrist voting records, he called himself a "moderate Democrat with a social conscience." Soon after Democrats won control of Congress in 2006, Boyd and other Blue Dog leaders met with President Bush to explore possible areas of agreement. "The Blue Dogs believe in partnership, not partisanship," he said. Since then, Boyd has been a leader of the Blue Dogs efforts to impose "pay-go" restrictions on new spending and tax cuts. They had little immediate success, but planned to renew the effort in President Obama's first term. In January 2009, Boyd was one of 11 House Democrats to vote against the initial $787 billion economic-stimulus bill, but he voted in favor of the final version, after a bipartisan Senate group made changes to produce what he called a "smarter" stimulus.

In December 2004, Boyd caused a stir among Democrats when he co-sponsored a bipartisan bill that created private retirement accounts in Social Security and lowered benefits. He said that he would seek additional Democratic supporters, but he ultimately found none in the House. His goal, he said, was "a fair balance between preserving the basic benefit of Social Security while also encouraging individual responsibility." He opposed President Bush's 2001 tax cuts but voted to repeal the Clinton administration's ergonomics regulation. Later, he opposed giving the president more powers to negotiate free-trade agreements, but voted to authorize the use of force in Iraq. In 2003, he was one of 16 House Democrats who voted for the Republicans' bill to create a prescription-drug benefit under Medicare and was taken to the woodshed by Minority Leader Nancy Pelosi as a result. As a member of the defense and agriculture subcommittees of the Appropriations Committee, Boyd has delivered largess to local universities, farmers and military facilities.

He has been easily re-elected. In 2004, he was challenged by Republican state Rep. Bev Kilmer, who raised substantial funds and said she would support Bush's agenda on defense, terrorism, health care and the economy. Boyd countered that he sometimes supported Bush, but said that voters wanted somebody who would be independent. He won handily, 62%-38%. He has been sometimes mentioned as a possible Senate candidate, including when Sen. Mel Martinez, R-Fla., said that he would not seek re-election in 2010. But Boyd said in January 2009 that he would not run because he would have "an even stronger voice" on policy decisions in the House.

THIRD DISTRICT

Corrine Brown (D)

Elected 1992, 9th term; b. Nov. 11, 1946, Jacksonville; home, Jacksonville; FL A&M, B.S. 1969, M.S., 1971; Baptist; single; 1 child.

Elected Office: FL House of Reps., 1982–92.

Professional Career: Prof., FL Commun. Col., 1977–82, Guidance counselor, 1982–92.

DC Office: 2336 RHOB, 20515, 202-225-0123; Fax: 202-225-2256; Web site: www.house.gov/corrinebrown.

State Offices: Jacksonville, 904-354-1652; Orlando, 407-872-0656.

Committees: *Transportation & Infrastructure* (7th of 44 D): Aviation; Coast Guard & Maritime Transportation; Railroads, Pipelines & Hazardous Materials (Chmn); Water Resources & Environment. *Veterans' Affairs* (2nd of 18 D): Health.

Group Ratings

	ADA	ACLU	AFS	LCV	ITIC	NTU	COC	ACU	CFG	FRC
2008	95	91	100	85	100	5	69	0	0	11
2007	90	—	100	85	—	4	60	0	6	—

National Journal Ratings

	2007 LIB	—	2007 CONS	2008 LIB	—	2008 CONS
Economic	63%	—	36%	78%	—	20%
Social	72%	—	27%	75%	—	18%
Foreign	67%	—	33%	69%	—	31%
Composite	68%	—	32%	76%	—	25%

Key Votes of the 110th Congress

1. Increase minimum wage	Y	5. Share immigration data	N	9. Withdraw troops 8/08	Y
2. Expand SCHIP	Y	6. Foreign aid abortion ban	N	10. No operations in Iran	Y
3. Raise CAFE standards	Y	7. Ban gay bias in workplace	Y	11. Free trade with Peru	Y
4. Bail out financial markets	Y	8. Repeal D.C. gun law	N	12. Overhaul FISA	Y

Election Results

2008 general	Corrine Brown (D)	unopposed
2008 primary	Corrine Brown (D)	unopposed

Prior Winning Percentages: 2006 (100%); 2004 (100%); 2002 (59%); 2000 (58%); 1998 (55%); 1996 (61%); 1994 (58%); 1992 (59%)

Population		Race/Ethnicity		Work	
Pop. 2007:	660,058	White:	35.4%	Private:	82.3%
Change since 2000:	Up 3.2%	Black:	50.9%	Government:	13.2%
Urban:	89.7%	Hispanic:	9.9%	Self-employed:	4.4%
Rural:	10.3%	Asian:	1.7%	Blue collar:	26.8%
Area size:	2,097 sq. mi.	Native Am.:	0.4%	White collar:	49.0%
Age		Hawaiian:	0.0%	Khaki collar:	0.2%
Median age:	33.8 yrs.	Two+ races:	1.2%	Other:	24.0%
More than 65 yrs:	11.0%	*Ancestry*		Median income:	$33,876
Less than 18 yrs:	26.7%	German:	5.9%	Median home value:	$123,200
Education		USA:	5.8%	Poverty:	22.0%
H.S. grad:	77.7%	West Indian:	5.6%	**Military Veterans**	
College grad:	14.3%			% of Pop:	11.3%
Grad degree:	4.5%				

Before the Civil War, most of Florida was still an uncharted watery wilderness, festooned with exotic greenery, inhabited by unusual animals, a part of the United States so far out of the experience of most Americans as to seem foreign. As late as 1940, Florida had the smallest population of any Southern state, and most of the people here lived in classic Dixie rural counties with small courthouse towns, where civic affairs were run by the richest white men and African-Americans lived in poorly con-

2008 Presidential Vote
Obama (D) 190,646   (73%)
McCain (R).............................69,099   (27%)

2004 Presidential Vote
Kerry (D)...............................151,466   (65%)
Bush (R) 81,778   (35%)

Cook Partisan Voting Index: D + 18

structed, unpainted shotgun shacks propped up on blocks, with little money and no vote. This was a land of swamps, lakes and orange groves, and of author Marjorie Kinnan Rawlings's Cross Creek, where she wrote the great children's classic *The Yearling*. The broad St. Johns River, one of the few North American rivers that flows (if only sluggishly) north, meanders through orange-grove country to the port of Jacksonville, which was for many years Florida's largest city. In 2008, the port supported nearly 50,000 jobs in the area.

The 3rd Congressional District of Florida occupies much of this swampy terrain. The district was created in 1992 to be north Florida's black-majority seat and has had three sets of boundaries. The district borders five Republican-held districts, each of which was designed to shift as many Democrats as possible to the 3rd to strengthen Republicans elsewhere. In its current form, it follows the St. Johns River upstream from Jacksonville's city center to downtown Orlando, reaching out to pluck additional minority and Democratic voters from Sanford, where Amtrak's Auto Train unloads its Florida-bound travelers, and Gainesville, home of the University of Florida. Along the way, the district takes in smaller black settlements, such as lettuce-producing Zellwood, and Eatonville, home of author Zora Neale Hurston. In time, this relatively unpopulated, lake-filled region may become Florida's next development frontier. After losing population early in the decade, the district grew 3.2% from 2000 to 2007. It is solidly Democratic.

The congresswoman from the 3rd District is Corrine Brown, a Democrat first elected in 1992. She grew up in Jacksonville, taught at the community college, was a guidance counselor and in 1982, was elected to the Florida House. With her Jacksonville base, she was the clear favorite in this new district. In the Democratic primary, she faced white talk-radio host Andy Johnson, who called himself "the blackest candidate in the race." Brown led 43%-31% in the primary and won 64%-36% in the runoff. She won the general election 59%-41%.

Brown has compiled a liberal record on most issues. In her district, many voters work at military bases and she tends to support high defense spending and argues that the military can be a source of opportunity. She hailed the Navy's January 2009 decision to create a home port for a nuclear carrier at Jacksonville's Mayport naval station as a local economic boost and "a decision that will make our country safer." On the Veterans' Affairs Committee, she sought additional veteran's cemeteries for Florida, which is the home to more veterans than any other state except California. New cemeteries were approved for Jacksonville and Sarasota in 2003. On the Transportation and Infrastructure Subcommittee, Brown worked on legislation to strengthen security at the ports. A project of hers in the 111th Congress (2009–10) is a high-speed rail line from Tampa to Orlando and Miami.

Her outspoken, partisan views cause her problems from time to time. In 2004, she criticized Bush administration representatives at a briefing on the Haiti crisis, saying that they were "a bunch of white men" who "all look alike to me." After Rep. Henry Bonilla, R-Texas, called her on her remarks, Brown apologized, but she continued to call the White House policy on Haiti racist. Also in 2004, under parliamentary pressure from fellow members, she rescinded her comment to the House that Republicans "stole the election" in 2000. In a dispute in 2008 over the seating of convention delegates from Florida, Brown, who had endorsed Hillary Rodham Clinton for president, said, "If we are not seated, then nobody is going to be seated." The problem was resolved after Barack Obama became the certain nominee.

Brown has had spirited campaign opposition, resulting largely from personal issues. Her most difficult contest came in 1998 amid charges of questionable ethical conduct. In June of that year, the *St. Petersburg Times* reported that her daughter had been given a $50,000 Lexus car by agents of African millionaire Foutanga Sissoko. He had been imprisoned in Miami on federal charges of paying an illegal gratuity to a Customs Service officer, and Brown worked furiously to get him released, lobbying Attorney General Janet Reno to have him deported to Africa to continue his humanitarian work. The newspaper also reported that she kept a jazz singer on her payroll as a "congressional outreach specialist" and that the singer occasionally visited the district from her New York City home. Brown reacted with fury, filing a criminal contempt charge against the *Times* reporters with the Capitol Police, claiming they "accosted" her and their questions made her cry. The charges went nowhere.

The Republicans found a credible challenger in Bill Randall, an African-American like Brown and a former General Motors manager who had become a minister. He opposed abortion rights and favored local control of schools and government vouchers for private school tuition. He held Brown to 55%, getting 45% of the vote.

A subsequent investigation by the House Committee on Standards of Official conduct found that Brown "demonstrated, at the least, poor judgment and created substantial concerns regarding both the appearance of impropriety and the reputation of the House." But it dropped the case because, the committee said, it was unable to question key witnesses, including Sissoko. But the story continued to have political repercussions for Brown. She faced a vigorous re-election challenge in 2000 from Republican Jennifer Carroll, a retired 20-year Navy officer who criticized Brown for a lack of vision and an inability to work with people. She also outspent her. Brown called Carroll "a zero" and "a Republican puppet." With help from an October campaign rally with President Clinton and a strong grass-roots organization, Brown won 58%-42%. In 2002, Carroll again challenged Brown. But local Republicans were not enthusiastic about her candidacy in this heavily Democratic district. Brown won 59%-41%, again with huge leads in Jacksonville and Orlando. She has been unopposed since then. Barring unexpected problems, she appears secure until the next redistricting.

FOURTH DISTRICT

Ander Crenshaw (R)

Elected 2000, 5th term; b. Sept. 1, 1944, Jacksonville; home, Jacksonville; U. of GA, B.A. 1966, U. of FL, J.D. 1969; Episcopalian; married (Kitty); 2 children.

Elected Office: FL House of Reps., 1972–78; FL Senate 1986–93.

Professional Career: Investment banker, 1980–2000.

DC Office: 440 CHOB, 20515, 202-225-2501; Fax: 202-225-2504; Web site: crenshaw.house.gov.

State Offices: Jacksonville, 904-598-0481; Lake City, 386-365-3316.

Committees: *Appropriations* (16th of 23 R): Financial Services & General Government; Military Construction, Veterans Affairs & Related Agencies; State, Foreign Operations & Related Programs.

Group Ratings

	ADA	ACLU	AFS	LCV	ITIC	NTU	COC	ACU	CFG	FRC
2008	10	22	14	15	67	64	100	90	78	94
2007	15	—	18	5	—	65	87	83	72	—

National Journal Ratings

	2007 LIB	—	2007 CONS	2008 LIB	—	2008 CONS
Economic	27%	—	73%	17%	—	83%
Social	17%	—	81%	20%	—	74%
Foreign	0%	—	72%	*%	—	*%
Composite	20%	—	80%	*%	—	*%

Key Votes of the 110th Congress

1. Increase minimum wage	Y	5. Share immigration data	Y	9. Withdraw troops 8/08	N
2. Expand SCHIP	N	6. Foreign aid abortion ban	Y	10. No operations in Iran	N
3. Raise CAFE standards	N	7. Ban gay bias in workplace	N	11. Free trade with Peru	Y
4. Bail out financial markets	Y	8. Repeal D.C. gun law	Y	12. Overhaul FISA	Y

Election Results

2008 general	Ander Crenshaw (R) 224,112	(65%)	($613,594)
	Jay McGovern (D)...119,330	(35%)	($159,929)
2008 primary	Ander Crenshaw (R) .... unopposed		

Prior Winning Percentages: 2006 (70%); 2004 (100%); 2002 (100%); 2000 (67%)

Population		Race/Ethnicity		Work	
Pop. 2007:	705,530	White:	74.3%	Private:	78.2%
Change since 2000:	Up 10.4%	Black:	14.7%	Government:	16.5%
Urban:	78.2%	Hispanic:	5.9%	Self-employed:	5.2%
Rural:	21.8%	Asian:	3.2%	Blue collar:	21.6%
Area size:	4,368 sq. mi.	Native Am.:	0.3%	White collar:	62.2%
Age		Hawaiian:	0.1%	Khaki collar:	1.0%
Median age:	37.3 yrs.	Two+ races:	1.4%	Other:	15.2%
More than 65 yrs:	11.4%	*Ancestry*		Median income:	$53,053
Less than 18 yrs:	23.9%	Irish:	11.1%	Median home value:	$189,400
Education		German:	11.0%	Poverty:	9.6%
H.S. grad:	87.8%	English:	10.4%	**Military Veterans**	
College grad:	27.0%			% of Pop:	15.0%
Grad degree:	9.1%				

With a metropolitan area of 1.2 million people, Jacksonville has outgrown its reputation as Florida's overlooked city. Not long ago, it was considered a backwater, dominated by insurance and smelly paper mills. It now boasts a National Football League franchise, bold new skyscrapers looming above the St. Johns River, and a shopping mall that overshadows tiny shotgun houses. Wide freeways sidestep primeval wetlands on their way to huge beachfront subdivisions. The harbor has grown as

2008 Presidential Vote		
McCain (R)............................229,996	(62%)	
Obama (D) 136,777	(37%)	

2004 Presidential Vote		
Bush (R)................................227,431	(69%)	
Kerry (D)................................100,414	(31%)	

Cook Partisan Voting Index: R + 17

a destination for cargo and passenger operations. With the Mayport Naval Station and the Naval Air Station, Jacksonville has a significant military employment base; the two are the largest metro area employers. Shrewd marketing has lured big-name private-sector companies. Jacksonville is the headquarters of railway giant CSX and also hosts major operations such as Winn-Dixie supermarkets, UPS, and Bank of America. Business leaders are working to make the area into the "Silicon Valley of Logistics" —building on its land, air, and sea transportation facilities—and they have dredged the port for larger ships. In 2007, Jacksonville passed Indianapolis as the 12th largest city in the nation. In 2008 demographers projected that the area population would double by 2060.

The 4th Congressional District of Florida includes much of Jacksonville, minus the African-American neighborhoods, which are in the 3rd District. It takes in a northern tier of counties along the Georgia border that runs all the way west to Tallahassee. This northern tier is sleepy territory punctuated by small towns like White Springs, Lake City, and Raiford (home to a big state prison). It is crisscrossed by Interstates 10 and 75. Some 70% of the population is in Jacksonville and rapidly growing Nassau County. The boosterish Jacksonville civic culture and significant military presence make the 4th a pro-business, pro-military and pro-Republican district. George W. Bush won 66% of the district's vote in 2000 and 69% in 2004; each was his second highest percentage in Florida. John McCain won 62% in 2008.

The congressman from the 4th District is Ander Crenshaw, a Republican first elected in 2000. He grew up in Jacksonville, where he has family roots dating to the early 20th century. The son of a lawyer, he attended the University of Georgia on a basketball scholarship, then graduated from the University of Florida law school. His wife's father, Claude Kirk, was a Republican elected governor in 1966, then defeated in 1970. Crenshaw was elected to the state House in 1972 and served for six years, before running unsuccessfully for secretary of state. He then became an investment banker. In 1980, he ran for the U.S. Senate and finished third of six in the 1980 Republican primary, which was won by Paula Hawkins. From 1986 until 1993, he served in the state Senate and in 1992, became the first Republican state Senate president in 118 years. He ran for governor in 1994 but finished fourth in the primary, far behind Jeb Bush, who narrowly lost to Lawton Chiles in November. Crenshaw's opportunity to run for the House came in 2000, when Republican Rep. Tillie Fowler announced that she would honor her promise to serve only four terms. Crenshaw was promptly endorsed by local Republican leaders, which discouraged several potential candidates. He won the primary 70%-30% and the general election 67%-31%. He has won re-election easily since then.

In the House, Crenshaw is a reliable conservative. Although his tall frame makes him hard to miss in a crowd, he has not sought the limelight. He says he adheres to former President Reagan's motto:

"There's no limit to what you can do as long as you don't care who gets the credit." He was his freshman class's liaison to the Republican leadership, and he became friends with former Majority Whip Roy Blunt, who later named him to chair a House GOP budget task force. In his second term, Crenshaw won a seat on the Appropriations Committee, where his top priorities are the district's large military and veterans' facilities. He pushed successfully for new veterans' cemeteries in Jacksonville and Sarasota, and he fought for expanded disability coverage for Gulf War veterans.

In 2005, he waged an unsuccessful battle to save the *USS John F. Kennedy*, a carrier ship based in Mayport that was decommissioned by the Pentagon in 2007. But he did manage to slip a provision into the 2008 military construction spending bill telling the Navy to start work on converting Mayport to a nuclear base. In 2009, the Pentagon announced that a carrier would be moved from Norfolk to Mayport by 2014, despite objections by Virginia officials.

Crenshaw made a bid for the senior Republican seat on the Budget Committee, raising nearly $1 million for other Republican candidates in the 2006 election to pay his dues. But the slot went to Paul Ryan of Wisconsin, who had less seniority than Crenshaw. He was not helped by his role in an earlier lobbying scandal that felled former Majority Leader Tom DeLay of Texas: Crenshaw had traveled with DeLay on a trip to South Korea in 2001 that had been paid for by lobbyists close to DeLay. Crenshaw also was on the wrong side of a pitched leadership battle for DeLay's successor; he backed Blunt for the job, but John Boehner of Ohio emerged the winner.

FIFTH DISTRICT

Ginny Brown-Waite (R)

Elected 2002, 4th term; b. Oct. 5, 1943, Albany, NY; home, Brooksville; S.U.N.Y. Albany, B.S. 1976, Russell Sage Col., M.S. 1984; Catholic; widowed; 3 children.

Elected Office: Hernando Cnty. Commissioner, 1990–92; FL Senate, 1992–2002.

Professional Career: Small business owner; Legis. dir., NY Senate, 1972–90.

DC Office: 414 CHOB, 20515, 202-225-1002; Fax: 202-226-6559; Web site: brown-waite.house.gov.

State Offices: Brooksville, 352-799-8354.

Committees: *Ways & Means* (10th of 15 R): Health; Social Security.

Group Ratings

	ADA	ACLU	AFS	LCV	ITIC	NTU	COC	ACU	CFG	FRC
2008	35	22	20	38	57	62	79	77	73	76
2007	20	—	18	20	—	62	90	72	50	—

National Journal Ratings

	2007 LIB — 2007 CONS		2008 LIB — 2008 CONS	
Economic	34%	— 66%	37%	— 63%
Social	31%	— 67%	30%	— 69%
Foreign	32%	— 64%	19%	— 79%
Composite	33%	— 67%	29%	— 71%

Key Votes of the 110th Congress

1. Increase minimum wage	Y	5. Share immigration data	Y	9. Withdraw troops 8/08	N
2. Expand SCHIP	N	6. Foreign aid abortion ban	Y	10. No operations in Iran	N
3. Raise CAFE standards	N	7. Ban gay bias in workplace	N	11. Free trade with Peru	Y
4. Bail out financial markets	N	8. Repeal D.C. gun law	Y	12. Overhaul FISA	*

Election Results

2008 general	Ginny Brown-Waite (R)	265,186	(61%)	($563,685)
	John Russell (D)	168,446	(39%)	($37,220)
2008 primary	Ginny Brown-Waite (R)	49,134	(80%)	
	Jim King (R)	12,232	(20%)	

Prior Winning Percentages: 2006 (60%); 2004 (66%); 2002 (48%)

Population		Race/Ethnicity		Work	
Pop. 2007:	845,555	White:	81.8%	Private:	81.7%
Change since 2000:	Up 32.3%	Black:	5.5%	Government:	12.4%
Urban:	64.5%	Hispanic:	9.3%	Self-employed:	5.7%
Rural:	35.5%	Asian:	1.5%	Blue collar:	23.4%
Area size:	4,801 sq. mi.	Native Am.:	0.3%	White collar:	57.2%
Age		Hawaiian:	0.0%	Khaki collar:	0.2%
Median age:	43.0 yrs.	Two+ races:	1.1%	Other:	19.2%
More than 65 yrs:	22.8%	*Ancestry*		Median income:	$44,164
Less than 18 yrs:	20.2%	German:	14.5%	Median home value:	$167,300
Education		Irish:	12.7%	Poverty:	10.7%
H.S. grad:	84.5%	English:	10.1%	**Military Veterans**	
College grad:	18.3%			% of Pop:	16.7%
Grad degree:	5.8%				

Over the past quarter century, Florida's urban areas have grown in almost every direction, occupying the high ground between the swamps that still take up much of the state's peninsula. The pattern of development is evident in counties to the north and east of St. Petersburg and Tampa, where subdivisions, trailer parks, and shopping centers with Eckerd drugstores and Winn-Dixie supermarkets sprang up in what had been farms and sleepy little towns with low brick buildings baking in the Florida

2008 Presidential Vote
McCain (R)...........................255,714   (56%)
Obama (D) 197,613   (43%)

2004 Presidential Vote
Bush (R)...............................221,259   (58%)
Kerry (D)..............................156,632   (41%)

Cook Partisan Voting Index: R + 9

sun. This area—a haven for manatees, the unusual and beloved sea mammal—has seen suburban development run up the spines of U.S. 19, along the Gulf Coast, and along U.S. 41 and Interstate 75. Though there are plenty of working people here, this is mainly retirement country. Residents are comfortable, though not usually affluent. One of every four residents is over 65, and Citrus and Hernando counties have high percentages of military veterans. Citrus County has the second highest percentage of retirees—33%—in the state. Drawn by the many inland lakes, greenery and the pleasant climate, retirees from Michigan, Indiana and Ohio flocked here by traveling south on Interstate 75 south—a pattern distinct from the retirees who drove Interstate 95 from the Boston-Washington corridor to such destinations as Palm Beach, Fort Lauderdale and Miami. To meet increased demand, the local electric utility plans to open an additional nuclear power plant by 2020.

The 5th Congressional District of Florida occupies much of this rapidly growing area. Between 2000 and 2007 it added 206,000 new residents, more than any other congressional district in the state. The beach areas in Levy, Citrus and Hernando counties are largely undeveloped. The bulk of the population lives inland, in such places as Citrus Springs, Brooksville, Zephyrhills, Land o' Lakes, and Clermont. More than two-thirds of the population is in Pasco, Hernando and Citrus counties. Sumter County, one of the few areas in the Florida peninsula with large tracts of open land, is growing rapidly in part due to a massive "golf cart" retirement community of 75,000 known as "The Villages," which is split between the 5th and 6th Districts. In 2005, the district had 251,000 Social Security recipients, 39% of the population, more than any other district in the country and 65,000 more than any other district in Florida. Politically, this is marginal territory. The district lines were drawn by Republicans in 2002 to make the district more Republican. In 2008, John McCain ran strongly in these counties and won the district 56%-43%.

The congresswoman from the 5th District is Ginny Brown-Waite, a Republican elected in 2002. She grew up in Albany, N.Y. Her mother was a file clerk, and separated from her abusive husband when she was small. Brown-Waite graduated from State University of New York at Albany and from Russell Sage College. She married a state trooper and worked for two decades as a Republican staffer in the New York state Senate. When her husband retired, the couple moved to Spring Hill, Fla., where Brown-Waite worked as a health care consultant. In 1990, she was elected to the Hernando County Commission. After her successful efforts to block a local mining company's controversial plan to burn hazardous waste, she was elected to the state Senate in 1992.

As a member of the Senate congressional redistricting committee, Brown-Waite was well positioned to shape the 5th District boundaries. Republican leaders had asked her to run for the House in 1996, but she didn't think the district was winnable. In 2002, she helped to draw a district that was, and she gave it a try. In the primary, health care consultant Don Gessner said he was the only "true conservative" and criticized Brown-Waite's willingness to vote across party lines. She won 58%-42%. In the general election, she faced incumbent Rep. Karen Thurman, a Democrat who had held the seat since 1993. This was one of the most competitive contests in the country. The issue of abortion rights was a key area of disagreement. Both said they supported abortion rights, but Brown-Waite highlighted Thurman's vote against the partial-birth abortion ban as evidence of Thurman's fealty to the Democratic party line. Thurman outspent Brown-Waite 2-to-1, but Brown-Waite benefited from a late visit by President Bush and the strong showing of his brother, Florida Gov. Jeb Bush, who carried every county in the district. Brown-Waite won 48%-46%. This was an election decided by redistricting: Thurman carried the parts of the district she had previously represented, which cast 49% of the votes, by 52%-43%. Brown-Waite carried the new parts of the district, 53%-41%.

In the House, Brown-Waite has a mostly conservative voting record that is toward the center on some economic issues. Although she styled herself as a fiscal hawk demanding spending restraint, she took a different approach on the Veterans' Affairs Committee, where she stressed her independence and worked hard to expand veterans' benefits. The House passed her proposal to reduce long waits for veterans to get medical treatment, and she helped to broker a deal to permit disabled retirees to receive both their pensions and their full disability benefits. When France opposed military action in Iraq, Brown-Waite proposed removing the remains of World War II veterans buried in France. In 2009, Brown-Waite got a promotion to an A-list committee, gaining a seat on the tax-writing Ways and Means panel, where she says she wants to focus on health care and Social Security. With Rep. Anna Eshoo, a California Democrat, she launched a pancreatic cancer initiative in Congress. Brown-Waite's husband died of pancreatic cancer in 2008.

She takes a hard line on immigration issues. When House Democrats in 2007 removed from a homeland-security spending bill her provision to require cross-checks of employees at nuclear plants with immigrant data banks, she voted against the final version. In 2008, she drew a storm of criticism from Hispanic groups and their Democratic allies after she said that tax-rebate checks from the economic stimulus bill should not go to Puerto Ricans because they are "foreign citizens." Residents of Puerto Rico have been U.S. citizens since 1917. Brown-Waite blamed the stir on "race hustlers" in Orlando.

While many Republicans elsewhere in Florida and the nation struggled in the past two elections, Brown-Waite was returned to Congress easily.

SIXTH DISTRICT

Cliff Stearns (R)

Elected 1988, 11th term; b. April 16, 1941, Washington, DC; home, Ocala; George Washington U., B.S. 1963; Presbyterian; married (Joan); 3 children.

Military Career: Air Force, 1963–67.

Professional Career: Data Control Systems Inc., 1967–68; Negotiator, CBS, 1969–70; Pres., Stearns House Inc., 1972–present.

DC Office: 2370 RHOB, 20515, 202-225-5744; Fax: 202-225-3973; Web site: www.house.gov/stearns.

State Offices: Gainesville, 352-337-0003; Ocala, 352-351-8777; Orange Park, 904-269-3203.

Committees: *Energy & Commerce* (4th of 23 R): Commerce, Trade & Consumer Protections; Communications, Technology & the Internet (RMM); Energy & Environment. *Veterans' Affairs* (2nd of 11 R): Health; Oversight & Investigations.

Group Ratings

	ADA	ACLU	AFS	LCV	ITIC	NTU	COC	ACU	CFG	FRC
2008	15	27	14	0	43	82	89	100	96	100
2007	5	—	9	15	—	79	80	92	81	—

National Journal Ratings

	2007 LIB — 2007 CONS		2008 LIB — 2008 CONS	
Economic	27%	— 73%	16%	— 83%
Social	27%	— 72%	0%	— 91%
Foreign	0%	— 72%	35%	— 62%
Composite	23%	— 77%	19%	— 81%

Key Votes of the 110th Congress

1. Increase minimum wage	Y	5. Share immigration data	Y	9. Withdraw troops 8/08	N
2. Expand SCHIP	N	6. Foreign aid abortion ban	Y	10. No operations in Iran	N
3. Raise CAFE standards	N	7. Ban gay bias in workplace	N	11. Free trade with Peru	Y
4. Bail out financial markets	N	8. Repeal D.C. gun law	Y	12. Overhaul FISA	Y

Election Results

2008 general	Cliff Stearns (R)	228,302	(61%)	($789,774)
	Tim Cunha (D)	146,655	(39%)	($249,754)
2008 primary	Cliff Stearns (R)	unopposed		

Prior Winning Percentages: 2006 (60%); 2004 (64%); 2002 (65%); 2000 (100%); 1998 (100%); 1996 (67%); 1994 (100%); 1992 (65%); 1990 (59%); 1988 (54%)

Population		Race/Ethnicity		Work	
Pop. 2007:	761,612	White:	74.8%	Private:	74.6%
Change since 2000:	Up 19.1%	Black:	13.0%	Government:	19.5%
Urban:	69.4%	Hispanic:	7.1%	Self-employed:	5.6%
Rural:	30.6%	Asian:	2.8%	Blue collar:	21.3%
Area size:	3,026 sq. mi.	Native Am.:	0.4%	White collar:	60.5%
Age		Hawaiian:	0.1%	Khaki collar:	0.5%
Median age:	37.9 yrs.	Two+ races:	1.6%	Other:	17.7%
More than 65 yrs:	16.1%	*Ancestry*		Median income:	$45,428
Less than 18 yrs:	21.4%	German:	12.3%	Median home value:	$161,200
Education		Irish:	10.4%	Poverty:	13.1%
H.S. grad:	86.9%	English:	9.7%	**Military Veterans**	
College grad:	23.6%			% of Pop:	16.5%
Grad degree:	9.4%				

The flat grasslands of central Florida, once by-passed by southbound tourists heading for the coastal resorts and cities, have over the past two decades become a prime growth area in this high-growth state. Central Florida's economy once depended on farming, on tourists getting off the interstate, and on state institutions, most notably the University of Florida in Gainesville. Then retirees began settling in places like the bluegrass country around Ocala, one of America's prime horse-

2008 Presidential Vote
McCain (R)............................226,985   (57%)
Obama (D) 170,173   (43%)

2004 Presidential Vote
Bush (R)................................210,101   (61%)
Kerry (D)................................136,622   (39%)

Cook Partisan Voting Index: R + 10

breeding grounds, and Leesburg, perched on a narrow spit of land between Lake Griffin and Lake Harris. Initially, these areas were studded with trailer parks, but the 1990s brought more-upscale development, albeit nothing approaching the high-rise apartments and gated communities that line the coasts farther south. At the same time, the large citrus groves have been cut back, victims of booming property values and of environmental changes that have resulted in devastating frosts and more diseases. Some of this development is at the intersection of Lake, Marion and Sumter counties in the sprawling "The Villages" retirement community. This part of central Florida grew by 19% from 2000 to 2007.

The 6th Congressional District of Florida includes much of central Florida and also part of the Jacksonville metropolitan area, connected by a strip of lightly populated counties. In the south, it includes parts of Marion and Sumter counties, around Ocala, and a corner of Lake County. In the north, it includes the western part of Jacksonville's Duval County and most of Clay County. In between, it includes most of Alachua County except for Gainesville. On balance, this is a Republican district. Alachua is one of the few Florida counties to regularly vote Democratic, but its most heavily Democratic precincts are located in the 3rd District. The country around Ocala and the Villages in the south is Republican. Western Jacksonville and Clay County, with many military retirees, are even more Republican. In the 2008 presidential race, Republican John McCain won 71% of the vote in Clay County, and 57% in the district.

The congressman from the 6th District is Cliff Stearns, a Republican first elected in 1988. The son of a U.S. Justice Department attorney, Stearns grew up and attended public schools in Washington, D.C. After college, he served in the Air Force, where he was a specialist in satellite reconnaissance. In the early 1970s, he saw potential in land development in Florida and moved to Ocala. He ultimately ended up owning five motels, three restaurants and other properties, while also becoming active in community affairs. In 1988, he beat the favored candidate for the district seat, Democratic state House Speaker Jon Mills, 54%-46%. "I was elected to put the federal government on a diet," Stearns said, and went on to compile a mostly conservative voting record. Since losing a low-level leadership contest in 1994, he has been an occasional maverick. He bucked party leaders on free trade in the 1990s and complained about the growth in the federal deficit under President Bush. "We used to be the party of accountability and fiscal responsibility," he said. Stearns also supports ending automatic cost-of-living increases for members of Congress.

Stearns has been a productive legislator. On the Veterans' Affairs Committee, he sponsored a center to do research on Gulf War syndrome. For his district, he secured expansion of a veterans' hospital in Gainesville and a new national cemetery in Jacksonville. On Energy and Commerce, he has worked on health care and Internet policy. In 2004, he won House passage of a bill to restrict abuses of computer spyware. His Do-Not-Call Implementation Act became law and authorized the Federal Trade Commission to establish a national registry of consumers who opt out of telemarketing calls. He helped to enact the anti-spam law that requires most commercial e-mail to be labeled and to have a valid return address. He was the chief sponsor of the widely debated 2005 legislation that limited lawsuits against the firearms industry when their products are used in crimes. The House also passed a bill with his provision to protect consumers from price-gouging during fuel emergencies. He backed a measure that opened parts of the outer continental shelf to oil and gas leasing, but he opposed new drilling in Florida waters. He held hearings on problems in college athletics, including gambling and recruitment.

But Stearns suffered some setbacks. The House defeated his proposal for a Federal Boxing Commission, with enforcement of uniform standards, and he lost on an amendment to prohibit federal funds for bilingual ballots and language assistance under the Voting Rights Act. With his diminished role under Democratic rule, Stearns has worked to make the Do-Not-Call Registry permanent and to enhance its enforcement. In 2009, he became the ranking Republican on the Subcommittee on Communications, Technology, and the Internet of the Energy and Commerce Committee. He has pressed for additional steps to protect personal privacy as corporations use computers to collect vast amounts of information on people.

In 2008, Stearns won re-election easily, 61%-39%, over Democratic Ocala attorney Tim Cunha. But Alachua, which produced the second largest vote among the counties in the district, backed the Democrat, 52%-48%. That could signal redistricting changes in 2011.

SEVENTH DISTRICT

John Mica (R)

Elected 1992, 9th term; b. Jan. 27, 1943, Binghamton, NY; home, Winter Park; Miami-Dade Commun. Col., A.A. 1965, U. of FL, B.A. 1967; Episcopalian; married (Patricia); 2 children.

Elected Office: FL House of Reps., 1976–80.

Professional Career: Exec. dir., Palm Beach & Orange Cnty. Govt. Charter Study Commissions, 1970–74; Pres., MK Development, 1975–92; A.A., U.S. Sen. Paula Hawkins, 1981–85; Partner, Mica, Dudinsky & Assoc., 1985–92.

DC Office: 2313 RHOB, 20515, 202-225-4035; Fax: 202-226-0821; Web site: www.house.gov/mica.

State Offices: Deltona, 386-860-1499; Maitland, 407-657-8080; Ormond Beach, 386-676-7750; Palatka, 386-328-1622; Palm Coast, 386-246-6042; St. Augustine, 904-810-5048.

Committees: *Oversight & Government Reform* (4th of 16 R): Information Policy, Census & National Archives; National Security & Foreign Affairs. *Transportation & Infrastructure* (RMM of 30 R).

Group Ratings

	ADA	ACLU	AFS	LCV	ITIC	NTU	COC	ACU	CFG	FRC
2008	10	20	0	8	43	79	94	100	94	100
2007	5	—	0	5	—	76	89	100	88	—

National Journal Ratings

	2007 LIB — 2007 CONS		2008 LIB — 2008 CONS	
Economic	6% —	93%	13% —	86%
Social	0% —	91%	9% —	85%
Foreign	0% —	72%	19% —	79%
Composite	8% —	92%	15% —	85%

Key Votes of the 110th Congress

1. Increase minimum wage	N	5. Share immigration data	Y	9. Withdraw troops 8/08	N
2. Expand SCHIP	N	6. Foreign aid abortion ban	Y	10. No operations in Iran	N
3. Raise CAFE standards	N	7. Ban gay bias in workplace	N	11. Free trade with Peru	Y
4. Bail out financial markets	N	8. Repeal D.C. gun law	Y	12. Overhaul FISA	Y

Election Results

2008 general	John Mica (R)..238,721	(62%)	($1,031,911)
	Faye Armitage (D)...146,292	(38%)	($34,241)
2008 primary	John Mica (R).. unopposed		

Prior Winning Percentages: 2006 (63%); 2004 (100%); 2002 (60%); 2000 (63%); 1998 (100%); 1996 (62%); 1994 (73%); 1992 (56%)

Population		Race/Ethnicity		Work	
Pop. 2007:	773,238	White:	76.9%	Private:	82.9%
Change since 2000:	Up 21.0%	Black:	9.3%	Government:	11.3%
Urban:	86.7%	Hispanic:	9.8%	Self-employed:	5.7%
Rural:	13.3%	Asian:	2.2%	Blue collar:	19.4%
Area size:	2,221 sq. mi.	Native Am.:	0.3%	White collar:	62.9%
Age		Hawaiian:	0.0%	Khaki collar:	0.2%
Median age:	40.7 yrs.	Two+ races:	1.3%	Other:	17.5%
More than 65 yrs:	17.0%	*Ancestry*		Median income:	$48,564
Less than 18 yrs:	21.5%	German:	12.7%	Median home value:	$224,500
Education		Irish:	11.6%	Poverty:	10.8%
H.S. grad:	88.2%	English:	10.3%	**Military Veterans**	
College grad:	26.9%			% of Pop:	14.0%
Grad degree:	8.9%				

In 1513, Spanish explorer Ponce de Leon headed to the New World, hoping to discover the Fountain of Youth. Instead, he found Ponte Vedra Beach, located just south of modern-day Jacksonville. A few decades later, Spanish colonists founded St. Augustine, the oldest permanent European settlement in North America—42 years older than Jamestown, Va., and 55 years older than the Plymouth colony in Massachusetts. Much later, John D. Rockefeller wintered in Ormond Beach, and cars have been

2008 Presidential Vote
McCain (R)............................218,858   (54%)
Obama (D)..............................187,417   (46%)

2004 Presidential Vote
Bush (R).................................204,454   (57%)
Kerry (D)................................155,302   (43%)

Cook Partisan Voting Index: R + 7

zooming up and down Daytona's rock-hard beach for decades. Near St. Augustine are a Northrop Grumman aircraft plant and some new communities. St. Johns and Flagler counties, the two coastal counties between Jacksonville and Daytona Beach, were filled with cattle ranches a few decades ago. But St. Johns grew 37% between 2000 and 2007. Flagler County grew 83% from 2000 to 2008, making it the fastest growing county in the nation. In 2008, the recession slowed the growth rate somewhat and increased the supply of vacant housing. Nearby DeLand has a small-town atmosphere centered around the Stetson University campus, while Heathrow, just off Interstate 4, serves as the home base of the American Automobile Association. Other places are much newer, instant cities: the Palm Coast development on the beach in Flagler County, and Deltona, which was built inland on a drained swamp in Volusia County. Although disappearing, some farming and ranching continue to fill gaps between these growing areas.

The 7th Congressional District of Florida covers the Atlantic coast for nearly 100 miles, from Ponte Vedra Beach to Daytona Beach. Inland it includes affluent, Seminole County suburbs of Orlando as well as the timber center of Palatka. Nearly two-thirds of the population is in the south, around Orlando, Deltona, and Daytona Beach. The political tendencies in this area are mixed. Seminole County and St. Augustine's St. Johns County are affluent and heavily Republican. Palm Coast's Flagler County is marginal. Daytona Beach's Volusia County leans Democratic, but about 40% of it is in the 24th District. On balance, this is a Republican district, but not overwhelmingly so.

The congressman from the 7th District is John Mica, a Republican first elected in 1992. Mica (*MY-kah*) grew up in south Florida, in a bipartisan political family originally from upstate New York. His younger brother, Dan Mica, was a Democratic congressman from Palm Beach County from 1978 to 1988, when he lost a primary for U.S. Senate; he then became a credit union lobbyist. Another brother, David Mica, worked for Democratic Gov. Lawton Chiles and became executive director for the Florida Petroleum Council. John Mica made a small fortune in real estate by developing New Smyrna beachfront. He was elected to the state House in 1976 and served four years. He worked on the staff of U.S. Sen. Paula Hawkins, a Republican, from 1981 to 1985, and then became a lobbyist. He ran for the U.S. House when the district was created after the 1990 census. In the GOP primary, his opponents attacked him as an insider representing special interests, to which Mica responded, "Some of the finest folks I've met are lobbyists." He still managed to win the primary 53%-34%. In the general election, against a liberal Democrat, he won 56%-44%.

Mica has been a consistent conservative but also a brash reformer. After taking office, he led the charge to abolish House select committees and to make public the names of lawmakers who sign petitions to discharge legislation, or to bring it to the floor for a vote over the objections of congressional leaders. When Republicans took control of the House in 1995, Mica became chairman of Government Reform's Civil Service Subcommittee. There he helped pass the White House Accountability Act of 1996, imposing on the White House the laws that are imposed on the private sector. His image is that of a fiscal conservative, though with one exception: He was an early backer of the Capitol Visitors Center, whose costs soared dramatically from original estimates. Mica called critics of the project a "chorus of prima donnas" and said the recently completed facility is "absolutely magnificent." On other issues, Mica also has focused on fighting drugs by promoting eradication and interdiction programs. He was the only House member from Florida who voted to lift the moratorium on oil drilling off the coasts of his state.

His chief legislative front has been at the Transportation and Infrastructure Committee. When he took over in 2001 as chairman of the Aviation Subcommittee, he pledged faster building of runways across the nation. But after the September 11 attacks, he focused on security. When congressional leaders moved quickly to pass a bill to aid the airlines, Mica played a major role in designing the next legislation: improved screening at all airports. The Senate passed a bill that federalized the screeners, and Mica and House Republicans sought to preserve some role for the private sector. They reached a deal to allow airports to opt out of the federal system after three years if they met certain standards. A few months later, Mica introduced a bill to permit commercial airline pilots to carry guns in the cockpit. The bill was initially opposed by the Bush administration and the Senate, and airlines worried about the risks. But the House voted 310-113 to allow pilots to carry guns. The Senate agreed 87-6, and Bush bowed to popular will. Since then, Mica has raised alarms about gaps in security.

On local transportation issues, Mica waged a long fight for mass transit in the traffic-clogged Orlando area and ultimately secured a pledge from federal officials of $300 million for a commuter rail project in central Florida. Local officials in 2007 settled on a $615 million system covering 61 miles in Volusia, Seminole, Orange, and Osceola counties. Pending approval by the state legislature, it was scheduled for completion in 2013. "You can only pave over so much of central Florida," Mica said.

In 2006, he was one of several Republicans seeking the chairmanship of the transportation panel in the next Congress. Although he was less senior than adversaries Tom Petri, R-Wis., and John Duncan, R-Tenn., Mica was more of a party regular and won the backroom contest of the leadership-controlled Steering Committee, reportedly by one vote. The prize was less valuable after the GOP lost House control in November that year, but Mica retained some clout because the committee has a history of bipartisanship. And he of course would be in line for the chairmanship if Republicans retake the majority. In 2009, he pledged to cooperate with Democratic Chairman James Oberstar of Minnesota on renewing highway and transit programs. But in January, he complained about the lack of funds for transportation projects in the Democrats' economic stimulus bill, which all House Republicans opposed. "Where's the beef?" he asked Democrats. "I wanna know where the jobs are."

In 2002, Mica faced a serious challenge at home from Democrat Wayne Hogan, a Jacksonville trial lawyer who spent $2.7 million of his own money on his campaign. Hogan, part of the legal team that won Florida's settlement with the tobacco industry, said he would fight for "ordinary families against powerful interests." Mica responded that Hogan was trying to buy the seat and that his pledge not to take contributions from political action committees was like "Rockefeller saying he won't take food stamps." Mica won comfortably, 60%-40%, carrying all six counties. Since then, he has not been seriously challenged.

EIGHTH DISTRICT

Alan Grayson (D)

Elected 2008, 1st term; b. March 13, 1958, New York, NY; home, Orlando; Harvard U., B.A. 1978; J.D., 1983, M.A., 1983.; Jewish; married (Lolita); 5 children.

Professional Career: Pres., IDT Corp., 1990–91; Partner, Grayson & Kubli P.C., 1991–2008.

DC Office: 1605 LHOB, 20515, 202-225-2176; Fax: 202-225-0999; Web site: grayson.house.gov.

State Offices: Orlando, 407-841-1757.

Committees: *Financial Services* (39th of 42 D): Capital Markets, Insurance & Government Sponsored Enterprises; Oversight & Investigations. *Science & Technology* (24th of 26 D): Investigations & Oversight; Space & Aeronautics.

Group Ratings and Key Votes: Newly Elected

Election Results

2008 general	Alan Grayson (D)	172,854	(52%)	($3,210,502)
	Ric Keller (R)	159,490	(48%)	($1,774,992)
2008 primary	Alan Grayson (D)	16,104	(48%)	
	Charlie Stuart (D)	9,146	(28%)	
	Mike Smith (D)	5,727	(17%)	

Population		Race/Ethnicity		Work	
Pop. 2007:	765,160	White:	63.2%	Private:	84.2%
Change since 2000:	Up 19.7%	Black:	9.4%	Government:	10.2%
Urban:	91.7%	Hispanic:	21.5%	Self-employed:	5.4%
Rural:	8.3%	Asian:	3.6%	Blue collar:	19.6%
Area size:	1,158 sq. mi.	Native Am.:	0.2%	White collar:	63.2%
Age		Hawaiian:	0.1%	Khaki collar:	0.1%
Median age:	36.8 yrs.	Two+ races:	1.3%	Other:	17.1%
More than 65 yrs:	12.9%	*Ancestry*		Median income:	$49,952
Less than 18 yrs:	23.9%	German:	11.2%	Median home value:	$226,700
Education		Irish:	9.3%	Poverty:	10.2%
H.S. grad:	87.3%	English:	8.5%	**Military Veterans**	
College grad:	29.3%			% of Pop:	10.9%
Grad degree:	9.5%				

Who would have supposed 40 years ago that the most popular tourist destination in the world would rise amid the swamps and orange groves of central Florida? The answer: Walt Disney, and just about no one else. In the mid-1960s, Disney looked at the map and decided that the intersection of Interstate 4 and Florida's Turnpike, the "crossroads of Florida," just a few miles southwest of Orlando, was the perfect place for the vast theme park he was planning. The spirit of this place was established by a

man who never lived here but created something now taken for granted. Disney conceived the first theme park in Orange County, Calif., in 1955, but he perfected it in the 17,000 acres of Florida swamp that his associates stealthily snapped up and where Walt Disney World opened in 1971. With the invention of the theme park, Disney also pioneered sophisticated communications, utility, and waste-disposal methods—all out of sight and underground. Disney World is not just an engineering marvel. It requires some 56,000 people with know-how and earnest cheerfulness to entertain its 40 million-plus visitors annually. But it is hardly the only site that has made Orlando one of the world's great tourist destinations. Other popular theme parks here include Sea World and Universal Studios; Cape Canaveral is less than 40 miles away. The high-tech economy also has moved into Greater Orlando. Defense contractor Lockheed Martin has a big missile facility southwest of the city, with more than 6,000 employees. Continuing growth—of the downtown skyline and in the expanding metropolitan region—has spurred what may be uphill efforts to control the sprawl and congestion in one of the nation's booming areas.

The 8th Congressional District of Florida includes parts of Orlando and surrounding Orange County and most of the enormous Disney complex, including the Disney new-urbanist town of Celebration. It includes most of the southeast and southwest parts of Orlando and adjoining suburbs. Heavily African-American areas of central Orlando are in the 3rd District. More than three-quarters of the district's residents live in Orange County. The rest live in a ribbon of territory to the northwest, past Lake Apopka, in little market towns like Mount Dora and Umatilla in Lake County, which seem insulated from the booming metro area. Around here, turtles, alligators, and river otters go about their lives underneath cypress trees draped with Spanish moss. Nearby is Silver Springs, where tourists can view the world's largest formation of clear artesian springs from glass-bottomed boats—a theme park from an earlier era. Beyond that is the horse farm country of Marion County, around Ocala. In the 1980s, the Orlando area was heavily Republican, but in the 1990s, it moved perceptibly toward national Democrats. The 8th District was designed to be a Republican district, though it's not comfortably so. Some 21.5% of its residents are Hispanic, most of them not Cubans, but Puerto Ricans and people from elsewhere in Latin America; many work in the tourism industry. They favored Republican Govs. Jeb Bush in 2002 and Charlie Crist in 2006, and trended toward President Bush in 2004, when he got 55% of the vote. Barack Obama beat John McCain 52%-47%.

The new congressman from the 8th District is Democrat Alan Grayson. In 2008, Grayson unseated incumbent Republican Ric Keller, a top Democratic target since reneging on the term-limits pledge he made in 2000.

Grayson had a rough childhood growing up in the Bronx in New York City. A product of public housing, he says a bully threw him in the path of a bus when he was 11, but he survived. Standardized tests in high school identified him as gifted academically, and Grayson was accepted at Harvard University. To help get through financially, he lived modestly and took odd jobs cleaning toilets and working as a night watchman. He ultimately left Harvard with a law degree. Grayson went to work at a law firm, but in 1990 took a break from law to start a telecommunications firm. When he sold it, he became a wealthy man. In recent years, Grayson has worked as a lawyer, taking private defense contractors to court for providing faulty equipment to U.S. soldiers in Iraq. He won a $10 million claim against defense contractor Custer Battles, which was found to have supplied the military with trucks that didn't work properly.

Grayson emphasized his work against corrupt contractors during his campaign against Keller. The incumbent tried to use Grayson's anti-war positions to paint him as an "ultra liberal," and in one ad accused Grayson of advocating cutting off funds to troops in Iraq and of being allied with the Code Pink anti-war protest group. Keller also criticized Grayson for his relationship with law firm partner Victor A. Kubli, who, five years before joining Grayson's firm, pleaded guilty to a felony bribery charge. Grayson claimed he wasn't aware of the conviction. Grayson accused Keller in an ad of being the deciding "no" vote on a bill that would have supplied returning war veterans with replacement limbs. In the ad, Grayson holds an artificial leg in his hand. Keller's opposing vote was on a bill that actually would have funded several veterans' programs.

Despite the mudslinging from both campaigns, Grayson connected with voters angered by Keller's broken term-limit pledge. He was also helped by a surge in Democratic registration, and defeated Keller 52% to 48%. Grayson lost three out of the four counties that comprise the 8th District, but his 22,901 vote advantage in Orange County, which includes Orlando, swung the results in his favor. He was not shy about lending personal money into his campaign. He invested $2.6 million in the race and outspent Keller $3.2 million to $1.8 million. Grayson's personal wealth makes him one of the richest members of Congress.

In his first month in the House, Grayson referred to conservative radio talk show host Rush Limbaugh as a "has-been hypocrite loser." At a congressional hearing, he demanded that a Federal Reserve official explain why the Fed had not made more information regarding which banks received government bailout money available to the public. He sits on the Financial Services Committee and the Committee on Science and Technology.

NINTH DISTRICT

Gus Bilirakis (R)

Elected 2006, 2nd term; b. Feb. 8, 1963, Gainsville; home, Palm Harbor; Attended St. Petersburg Jr. Col., U. of FL, B.A. 1986, Stetson U., J.D. 1989; Greek Orthodox; married (Eva Lialios); 4 children.

Elected Office: FL House of Reps., 1998–2006.

Professional Career: Intern, U.S. Pres. Ronald Reagan, 1983; Intern, NRCC, 1984; Aide, U.S. Rep. Don Sundquist, 1985; Teacher, St. Petersburg Col., 1997–2001; Practicing atty., 1989–2006.

DC Office: 1124 LHOB, 20515, 202-225-5755; Fax: 202-225-4085; Web site: bilirakis.house.gov.

State Offices: Palm Harbor, 727-773-2871; Temple Terrace, 813-985-8541.

Committees: *Foreign Affairs* (19th of 19 R): Europe; Middle East & South Asia; Western Hemisphere. *Homeland Security* (8th of 13 R): Border, Maritime & Global Counterterrorism; Management, Investigations & Oversight (RMM). *Veterans' Affairs* (9th of 11 R): Economic Opportunity; Health.

Group Ratings

	ADA	ACLU	AFS	LCV	ITIC	NTU	COC	ACU	CFG	FRC
2008	30	18	14	38	57	63	83	88	73	100
2007	20	—	18	15	—	61	90	80	60	—

National Journal Ratings

	2007 LIB	—	2007 CONS	2008 LIB	—	2008 CONS
Economic	35%	—	65%	31%	—	69%
Social	9%	—	85%	31%	—	62%
Foreign	0%	—	72%	27%	—	72%
Composite	20%	—	80%	31%	—	69%

Key Votes of the 110th Congress

1. Increase minimum wage	Y	5. Share immigration data	Y	9. Withdraw troops 8/08	N
2. Expand SCHIP	N	6. Foreign aid abortion ban	Y	10. No operations in Iran	N
3. Raise CAFE standards	N	7. Ban gay bias in workplace	N	11. Free trade with Peru	Y
4. Bail out financial markets	N	8. Repeal D.C. gun law	Y	12. Overhaul FISA	Y

Election Results

2008 general	Gus Bilirakis (R)	216,591	(62%)	($1,542,347)
	Bill Mitchell (D)	126,346	(36%)	($394,756)
2008 primary	Gus Bilirakis (R)	unopposed		

Prior Winning Percentages: 2006 (56%)

Population		Race/Ethnicity		Work	
Pop. 2007:	740,463	White:	79.7%	Private:	83.0%
Change since 2000:	Up 15.8%	Black:	4.9%	Government:	11.3%
Urban:	93.8%	Hispanic:	10.8%	Self-employed:	5.5%
Rural:	6.2%	Asian:	2.9%	Blue collar:	15.7%
Area size:	800 sq. mi.	Native Am.:	0.3%	White collar:	68.3%
Age		Hawaiian:	0.1%	Khaki collar:	0.3%
Median age:	41.4 yrs.	Two+ races:	1.1%	Other:	15.7%
More than 65 yrs:	17.5%	*Ancestry*		Median income:	$50,518
Less than 18 yrs:	22.5%	German:	14.3%	Median home value:	$204,800
Education		Irish:	12.8%	Poverty:	9.2%
H.S. grad:	88.4%	English:	9.6%	**Military Veterans**	
College grad:	29.0%			% of Pop:	14.2%
Grad degree:	9.8%				

Half a century ago, the land north of St. Petersburg and Tampa was scarcely inhabited. Behind the barrier island of beaches, the land along the Gulf shore was swampy. Further inland was dense, semitropical forest spotted with lakes. Over the years, development has moved up the coast and inland via the major highways, first to Clearwater and Tarpon Springs in Pinellas County and then up the once-empty coast of Pasco County. Much of this area originally was designed for retirees, offering everything

2008 Presidential Vote
McCain (R).............................190,344   (52%)
Obama (D) 169,897   (47%)

2004 Presidential Vote
Bush (R) 196,837   (57%)
Kerry (D)................................148,694   (43%)

Cook Partisan Voting Index: R + 6

from condominiums to garden apartments to trailer parks. In 2000, Clearwater, in Pinellas County north of St. Petersburg, had a higher percentage of senior citizens than any other city over 100,000. It also has the spiritual headquarters of the Church of Scientology, which has transformed the city's downtown by redeveloping a dozen buildings, transforming five waterfront acres into a luxury condominium complex and building a 384,000-square-foot religious center. There are about 12,000 Scientologists in the city. Before the recession hit in 2007, businesses were sprouting in northern Pinellas County and inland off the Interstate 75 corridor. Nearly half of Pasco County's workers commute to jobs in other counties. The people who settled here in recent decades brought their ancestral political beliefs with them. In the 1950s and 1960s, only white-collar retirees could afford to buy new places in Florida, and they were heavily Republican. As Florida retirements became more feasible for people with modest incomes in the 1970s and 1980s, the partisan balance shifted toward Democrats. In the 1990s, young immigrants with professional and technical backgrounds flooded the area. Their political independence has turned this into one of Florida's most politically marginal areas. In 2004, Republican organizers brought out a lot of new voters, many of them Christian conservatives. Republican President Bush won the district that year with 57%. Four years later, Democrat Barack Obama's campaign worked to increase turnout in this area, which was vital to his statewide win in Florida. In Hillsborough, Obama got nearly 59,000 more votes than Democrat John Kerry had in 2004, while Republican John McCain got 9,000 votes less than Bush in 2004. John McCain narrowly won the district with 52%.

The 9th Congressional District of Florida covers an area north of St. Petersburg and north and east of Tampa. It includes the string of towns on the coast of Pasco County—Holiday, New Port Richey, Bayonet Point, and Hudson. In Pinellas County to the south, the 9th includes Clearwater, Tarpon Springs, an old resort first settled by Greek sponge divers a century ago, the affluent neighborhoods of East Lake, the young commuter families of Oldsmar, and the bayside community of Safety Harbor. The district also includes the northern Tampa suburbs in Hillsborough County and much of the eastern part of the county, including part of strawberry-growing Plant City (named not for plants but for Tampa pioneer Henry B. Plant). The area produces 90% of Florida's strawberry yield. From 2000 to 2007, the geographically confined Pinellas had a net loss of 4,000 people, while the more spacious Hillsborough gained 176,000, up 18%. Also noteworthy, the share of senior citizens in the district dropped from 20.5% to 17.5%. The vote in the district is distributed among Hillsborough, with about 45%, Pinellas, with 30%, and Pasco, with 25%.

The congressman from the 9th District is Gus Bilirakis, a Republican elected in 2006 to succeed his father, 12-term Republican Rep. Michael Bilirakis. Bilirakis (*bil-uh-RACK-iss*) joined Republican Connie Mack and Democrat Kendrick Meek in the Florida delegation as members who followed a parent into Congress. Bilirakis remembers stuffing envelopes at age seven for Republican Louis "Skip" Bafalis, who lost his 1970 bid for governor but was elected to five terms in Congress. In college, Bilirakis interned in the Reagan White House and went on to earn a law degree from Stetson University. He worked for former Rep. Don Sundquist, a Republican who went on to become Tennessee's governor, and later was a probate lawyer and estate planner. In 1998, he was elected to the first of four terms in the Florida House. Bilirakis' career has always been closely tied to his father's. (On Election Day 2002, the two were campaigning together on a street corner when a driver lost control of his car and struck the younger Bilirakis, leaving him with bruises and just missing his father.)

When Michael Bilirakis decided not to seek a 13th term, his son was presumed to be the favorite for the seat and drew only nominal opposition for the Republican nomination. Gus Bilirakis was not shy about running on the family name. He appeared on the ballot as Gus Michael Bilirakis and raised money from many political action committees that supported his father, who had had a seat on the House Energy and Commerce Committee. Bilirakis's campaign website praised his father's patriotism and integrity and declared, "There is no one better suited to carry on the mission than Gus, who has been instilled with these vital attributes."

Democrats recruited Phyllis Busansky, a former 8-year member of the Hillsborough County Commission and the first executive director of the state's welfare-to-work program. Busansky played up her background in health care and senior citizens' issues. Bilirakis pointed to his own credentials as a lawyer who specialized in elder law. In the Legislature, he had also spearheaded legislation supporting community health care centers that treat the uninsured. Bilirakis' soft-spoken style contrasted with Busansky's assertive personality. She ran television ads portraying Bilirakis as a follower and accused him of ducking public debate and relying heavily on his father's reputation. She trailed in the polls for much of the campaign, but gained some momentum in October after criticizing Bilirakis for his "deep and lucrative ties" to GOP leaders who had early knowledge of sexually explicit emails sent by disgraced Republican Rep. Mark Foley of Florida to congressional pages but who had failed to act. The national Republican Party did not leave this race to chance. President Bush, Vice President Dick Cheney and Speaker Dennis Hastert all stumped for Bilirakis and helped him raise money. He outspent Busansky $2.6 million to $1.4 million, and won 56%-44%.

In the House, Bilirakis established a voting record placing him near the center of House Republicans. He distanced himself from partisan fights and focused on his legislative agenda. Soon after taking office, he voted to increase the minimum wage and implement the homeland-security recommendations of the bipartisan 9/11 commission. In 2008, he worked with Rep. Lloyd Doggett, a Texas Democrat, to win House passage of a "silver alert" bill to assist states in finding senior citizens who disappear. Bilirakis was spurred by the case of an 86-year-old Largo woman who was found dead in the Intracoastal Waterway after she disappeared from an assisted-living facility. He was also a lead cosponsor of the Christopher and Dana Reeve Paralysis Act, which was designed to improve treatments for paralyzed people and which passed the House in 2007. Bilirakis is the ranking Republican on the Management, Investigations, and Oversight Subcommittee of the Homeland Security Committee.

He had a surprisingly easy re-election against lawyer and former Naval submarine Officer Bill Mitchell, who criticized Bilirakis' opposition to the bailout of the financial markets and to a bill extending the renewable-energy credit, calling him "a friend of Big Oil." Bilirakis largely ignored the attacks and won handily, 62%-36%.

TENTH DISTRICT

Bill Young (R)

Elected 1970, 20th term; b. Dec. 16, 1930, Harmarville, PA; home, Indian Shores; St. Petersburg H.S.; Methodist; married (Beverly); 6 children.

Military Career: Army Natl. Guard, 1948–57.

Elected Office: FL Senate, 1960–70, Min. ldr., 1966–70.

Professional Career: Aide, U.S. Rep. William Cramer, 1957–60; Insurance executive.

DC Office: 2407 RHOB, 20515, 202-225-5961; Fax: 202-225-9764; Web site: www.house.gov/young.

State Offices: Seminole, 727-394-6950; St. Petersburg, 727-893-3191.

Committees: *Appropriations* (2nd of 23 R): Defense (RMM); Military Construction, Veterans Affairs & Related Agencies.

Group Ratings

	ADA	ACLU	AFS	LCV	ITIC	NTU	COC	ACU	CFG	FRC
2008	25	18	43	38	57	69	83	88	79	88
2007	30	—	18	35	—	50	90	72	46	—

National Journal Ratings

	2007 LIB — 2007 CONS	2008 LIB — 2008 CONS
Economic	38% — 62%	33% — 66%
Social	21% — 79%	31% — 62%
Foreign	32% — 64%	31% — 67%
Composite	31% — 69%	33% — 67%

Key Votes of the 110th Congress

1. Increase minimum wage	Y	5. Share immigration data	Y	9. Withdraw troops 8/08	N
2. Expand SCHIP	Y	6. Foreign aid abortion ban	Y	10. No operations in Iran	N
3. Raise CAFE standards	N	7. Ban gay bias in workplace	N	11. Free trade with Peru	Y
4. Bail out financial markets	N	8. Repeal D.C. gun law	Y	12. Overhaul FISA	Y

Election Results

2008 general	Bill Young (R)...	182,781	(61%)	($969,224)
	Bob Hackworth (D)	118,430	(39%)	($155,590)
2008 primary	Bill Young (R)...	unopposed		

Prior Winning Percentages: 2006 (66%); 2004 (69%); 2002 (100%); 2000 (76%); 1998 (100%); 1996 (67%); 1994 (100%); 1992 (57%); 1990 (100%); 1988 (73%); 1986 (100%); 1984 (80%); 1982 (100%); 1980 (100%); 1978 (79%); 1976 (65%); 1974 (76%); 1972 (76%); 1970 (67%)

Population		Race/Ethnicity		Work	
Pop. 2007:	637,667	White:	83.9%	Private:	82.4%
Change since 2000:	Down 0.3%	Black:	4.9%	Government:	10.9%
Urban:	100.0%	Hispanic:	6.4%	Self-employed:	6.5%
Rural:	0.0%	Asian:	3.2%	Blue collar:	19.1%
Area size:	448 sq. mi.	Native Am.:	0.2%	White collar:	65.2%
		Hawaiian:	0.1%	Khaki collar:	0.2%
Age		Two+ races:	1.2%	Other:	15.5%
Median age:	45.5 yrs.			Median income:	$43,621
More than 65 yrs:	21.4%	*Ancestry*		Median home value:	$190,900
Less than 18 yrs:	18.4%	German:	14.3%	Poverty:	10.8%
		Irish:	13.0%		
Education		English:	10.7%	**Military Veterans**	
H.S. grad:	87.4%			% of Pop:	15.4%
College grad:	26.2%				
Grad degree:	8.7%				

St. Petersburg was first settled in the 1870s, it was reached by railroad in 1888, and it got its name in 1892, when, after a coin toss, builder and railway operator Pyotr Dementyev christened it in memory of his native city in Russia. If his partner had won the toss, it would have been named Detroit. For decades, it was known as the American city with the largest percentage of elderly residents. In the early 1900s, *St. Petersburg Times* editor W. L. Straub sought to reverse the industrialization of the water-

2008 Presidential Vote

Obama (D) 164,148	(52%)
McCain (R).............................150,962	(47%)

2004 Presidential Vote

Bush (R)................................158,082	(51%)
Kerry (D)...............................150,761	(49%)

Cook Partisan Voting Index: R + 1

front, establishing the parks that continue to define the city's character. Starting out on the grid streets facing Tampa Bay, St. Petersburg later spread toward the Gulf Coast as the migration of retirees accelerated. Mostly from the North and modestly affluent, the newcomers adapted easily to a city whose civic tone was set by the *St. Petersburg Times* and its longtime owners Nelson and Henrietta Poynter: Sober, good-humored, supportive of clean government and civil rights. More recently, retirees have come to prefer homes in less urbanized settings, and St. Petersburg has become a more conventional central city, with a larger working population, more families and minorities, and more office buildings and civic attractions, such as the Salvador Dali Museum, the Florida International Museum, and the Museum of Fine Arts. The new balance has brought new politics. In the 1940s and 1950s, white-collar Yankee retirees made St. Petersburg and surrounding Pinellas County the first Republican county in ancestrally Democratic Florida. Then, in the early 1970s, Social Security was vastly increased and indexed to inflation, and St. Petersburg basked in prosperity. More workers could afford a Florida retirement, the affluent moved farther down the Gulf Coast, and in the 1970s and 1980s, St. Petersburg trended Democratic. The whole of St. Petersburg and Pinellas County are now pretty well built up, with new projects replacing old buildings in downtown St. Pete and elsewhere. Except for Monroe County in the Florida Keys, this was the slowest growing large county in the state. In 2008, the area was hit hard by the housing foreclosure crisis.

The 10th Congressional District is the only district in Florida contained entirely within one county. It includes all of Pinellas County south of Clearwater except for heavily African-American precincts in south St. Petersburg, which are part of the Tampa-based 11th District. It includes all the Pinellas County beach communities on the barrier islands facing the Gulf, from Belleair Beach to Mullet Key. North of Clearwater, it includes middle-class Dunedin, pricey Palm Harbor, and the new subdivisions of Largo in the center of the peninsula. In 2004 the district voted 51% for President Bush, but in 2008 it went for Democrat Barack Obama 52%-47%.

The congressman from the 10th District is Bill Young, a Republican first elected in 1970. He is the most senior Republican in the House, and only three Democrats have more seniority than he does. He grew up poor in a Pennsylvania coal town. His first home was a shotgun shack that was swept down a river when he was 6 years old. At 16, he was shot in a hunting accident. The family moved to Florida, and Young dropped out of high school to support his ill mother by hauling concrete blocks and mixing mortar. At age 25, he applied for a job as an insurance salesman and ultimately ran a successful insurance agency. In the 1950s, he worked for St. Petersburg's first Republican congressman, William Cramer, and got the politics bug. Young was elected to the state Senate in 1960, at age 29, and was the lone Republican there. When Cramer ran for the U.S. Senate in 1970, Young ran for his House seat and won.

Young has a moderate to conservative voting record. Early on, he got a seat on Appropriations, where he, like many Republicans, worked closely with the Democratic chairmen through many years in the minority. When Republicans finally won control of the House in 1994, Young did not rise to full committee chairman though he had the seniority to do so. Speaker Newt Gingrich passed over him, as well as two more senior Republicans, for being too accommodating to Democrats. With some reason: After 34 years as a minority-party legislator, Young's instincts were bipartisan. "I came into the majority party with this strong conviction that every member of Congress has been elected by their constituents and should be given respect," he said at the time. "I've tried to deal with anybody on that basis, whether it is a first-term freshman or a 20-year veteran." But he certainly was not left powerless. He assumed the chairmanship of the defense appropriations subcommittee, giving him considerable sway over U.S. defense spending. In that role, he worked to produce bipartisan appropriations out of the spotlight.

In 1998, Young considered retiring, but at the end of the year he finally got the full committee gavel. Three days after the November election, when Republicans suffered stinging losses, Gingrich decided to resign as speaker. In the subsequent leadership reshuffling, Young took over as Appropriations chairman from Bob Livingston of Louisiana. He stayed in the job six years, until 2004, the maximum allowed under GOP rules. During the Bush era, Young was caught between White House demands to hold down spending and the rank and file's enormous appetite for earmarks, the special projects for home districts. For the most part, he came down on the president's side, but he demurred when the administration tried to get him to end earmarking altogether. Always the appropriator at heart, he also chafed at various attempts by the Budget Committee to impose caps on spending. Ever the bipartisan conciliator, he refused repeated demands from the Republican leadership to reduce the amount of projects for Democratic appropriators.

Young by no means ignored his own district or his own self-interest when it came to earmarking. "I try to make sure things that are needed in the whole state of Florida are taken care of," he once said. But he has also not been immune to the ongoing controversy surrounding earmarks, and in 2008, two of his earmarks dinged his reputation for high ethical standards. The *St. Petersburg Times* reported that he had directed $45 million to defense contractor Science Applications International Corp. after the company hired his 20-year-old son, Patrick, as a security administrator, though Patrick had only a GED and scant work experience. The newspaper also reported that Young had directed $28 million over nine years to another company that had employed another son, Billy Young, 23, for almost a year. The senior Young said that the companies got the earmarks on merit, not because they hired his children.

One of Young's special projects has been the bone-marrow donor program, originated by Dr. Robert Good of All Children's Hospital in St. Petersburg. Among his other earmarks in recent years were $20 million for the Florida National Guard, $750,000 for state police athletic leagues, $2 million to help colleges and universities prepare for hurricanes, $100,000 for a waterfront park at St. Petersburg Airport, and $344,000 for research on the interaction of medications and grapefruit juice. As head of the defense subcommittee, he took an avid interest in Florida's many military installations. MacDill Air Force Base in Tampa, across the bay from St. Petersburg, is the headquarters of Central Command and Special Operations Command. Young has pushed through a $25 million intelligence and operations center and $78 million for a conference center for SOCOM, as well as $31 million for more family housing.

He also pays close attention to veteran's issues. In the 1970s, he persuaded Congress and President Ford to build the Bay Pines Veterans Medical Center in St. Petersburg, now the second largest veterans' hospital. Since the Iraq War began in 2003, Young and his wife, Beverly, have visited wounded soldiers almost every week at military hospitals, including Walter Reed Army and Bethesda Naval Hospitals. Sometimes they found care lacking—a soldier sitting in a pool of urine, a sergeant's brain surgery delayed because of malfunctioning equipment—and they regularly complained to Gen. Kevin Kiley at Walter Reed and others officers. In 2007, the *Washington Post* published a series of stories about wretched conditions at the facility, which led to reforms. After the story broke, Young was attacked by Florida Democratic chairwoman Karen Thurman, a former House member, for not reporting the abuses he saw during his visits there. Young accused Thurman of a "personal smear campaign" against his family, and prominent Democrats came to his defense as well. Rep. Neil Abercrombie, D-Hawaii, said that he was "embarrassed" by the partisan criticism of Young, which he called "totally baseless."

The trend toward Democrats in Pinellas County for years had not posed any threat to Young. But Republican redistricters in 2002 made the district more Republican, so that the party could hold it when he retires. Still, Democrats can be expected to target the district. Young's son, Billy, is sometimes mentioned as a possible successor when his father retires.

ELEVENTH DISTRICT

Kathy Castor (D)

Elected 2006, 2nd term; b. Aug. 20, 1966, Miami; home, Tampa; Emory U., B.A. 1988, FL St. U., J.D. 1991; Presbyterian; married (William Lewis); 2 children.

Elected Office: Hillsborough Cnty. Comm., 2002–06.

Professional Career: Asst. gen. counsel, FL Dept. of Community Affairs, 1991–94; Practicing atty., 1994–2000.

DC Office: 317 CHOB, 20515, 202-225-3376; Fax: 202-225-5652; Web site: castor.house.gov.

State Offices: Tampa, 813-871-2817.

Committees: *Energy & Commerce* (29th of 36 D): Commerce, Trade & Consumer Protections; Communications, Technology & the Internet; Health.

Group Ratings

	ADA	ACLU	AFS	LCV	ITIC	NTU	COC	ACU	CFG	FRC
2008	95	90	100	85	86	16	63	9	12	5
2007	95	—	100	95	—	5	55	0	9	—

National Journal Ratings

	2007 LIB — 2007 CONS		2008 LIB — 2008 CONS	
Economic	67%	— 31%	85%	— 0%
Social	75%	— 23%	75%	— 18%
Foreign	72%	— 27%	83%	— 17%
Composite	72%	— 28%	85%	— 15%

Key Votes of the 110th Congress

1. Increase minimum wage	Y	5. Share immigration data	N	9. Withdraw troops 8/08	Y
2. Expand SCHIP	N	6. Foreign aid abortion ban	N	10. No operations in Iran	Y
3. Raise CAFE standards	Y	7. Ban gay bias in workplace	Y	11. Free trade with Peru	Y
4. Bail out financial markets	N	8. Repeal D.C. gun law	N	12. Overhaul FISA	Y

Election Results

2008 general	Kathy Castor (D)..184,106	(72%)	($662,366)
	Eddie Adams (R)...72,825	(28%)	($57,655)
2008 primary	Kathy Castor (D).......................................unopposed		

Prior Winning Percentages: 2006 (70%)

Population		Race/Ethnicity		Work	
Pop. 2007:	665,061	White:	44.0%	Private:	82.8%
Change since 2000:	Up 4.0%	Black:	27.6%	Government:	12.5%
Urban:	99.6%	Hispanic:	24.4%	Self-employed:	4.7%
Rural:	0.4%	Asian:	2.2%	Blue collar:	21.7%
Area size:	460 sq. mi.	Native Am.:	0.2%	White collar:	58.6%
Age		Hawaiian:	0.1%	Khaki collar:	0.3%
Median age:	35.4 yrs.	Two+ races:	1.1%	Other:	19.4%
More than 65 yrs:	11.7%	*Ancestry*		Median income:	$38,982
Less than 18 yrs:	24.2%	German:	8.4%	Median home value:	$172,500
Education		Irish:	7.4%	Poverty:	18.8%
H.S. grad:	80.7%	English:	6.3%	**Military Veterans**	
College grad:	23.2%			% of Pop:	10.6%
Grad degree:	7.5%				

One of America's boomtowns, Tampa has a history that goes back not much more than a century. Its industrial past can be traced to 1886, when Cuban cigar-makers from Key West settled in the city's Latin Quarter, called Ybor City. Then Tampa became the major embarkation port for U.S. troops in the Spanish-American War of 1898. It also became a major citrus distribution center. The old industrial city developed along the waterfront, with distinctive architectural touches like the 13 minarets

2008 Presidential Vote		
Obama (D)	179,523	(66%)
McCain (R)	89,410	(33%)
2004 Presidential Vote		
Kerry (D)	145,831	(58%)
Bush (R)	103,748	(41%)
Cook Partisan Voting Index:	D + 11	

on the Arabian-style Tampa Bay Hotel, built by railroad and real estate tycoon Henry B. Plant in the 1890s. The building is now part of the University of Tampa. For a time, Tampa was Florida's one industrial city. Today, it has a diversified economy: a healthy service sector, an academic sector with two universities, and tourism, led by Busch Gardens. Tampa's subdivisions and condominiums, office towers, and low-rise commercial buildings have spread inland across swamps and lowlands.

Through its history, in contrast to St. Petersburg with its many retirees, Tampa has remained a city of families and young people. Senior citizens account for only about one in eight residents here, an unusually low percentage for Florida. As Tampa expands, its blue-collar character is moving upscale. But as in other parts of Florida, its housing market was hit hard by the recession in 2008. Tampa is an important military center. MacDill Air Force Base, on the south side of the city and jutting into Tampa Bay, is the headquarters of Central Command, which ran the Persian Gulf War and the campaigns in Afghanistan and Iraq. It is also headquarters for Special Operations Command. Both Generals Norman Schwarzkopf and Tommy Franks retired in the same gated community in Tampa.

The 11th Congressional District of Florida is centered on Tampa, but has irregular boundaries. It includes most of the city and close-in suburbs, the east shore of Tampa Bay, plus two areas across Tampa Bay. One is the heavily African-American and lower-income neighborhoods south of Central Avenue in St. Petersburg. The other is a strip of Manatee County bordering Tampa Bay that includes working-class neighborhoods in Memphis, Palmetto, and Bradenton. Connecting them is the distinctive Sunshine Skyway Bridge, a four-mile span completed in 1987 that has come to symbolize the Tampa Bay area. The district has a population that is 27% black and 24% Hispanic, making it the most heavily minority district in Florida outside the Gold Coast and the Jacksonville-to-Orlando 3rd District. While Hillsborough County as a whole voted for Republican George W. Bush in 2000 and 2004, the 11th District cast solid majorities for Democrats Al Gore and John Kerry. In 2008, Barack Obama won the district with 66% of the vote.

The congresswoman from the 11th District is Kathy Castor, a Democrat elected in 2006. Castor studied political science at Emory University, earned her law degree from Florida State University and worked as a land-use attorney. Her parents were heavily involved in public service. Her father, Don Castor, sat on the Hillsborough County court for two decades. Her mother, Betty Castor, served in the state Senate, as state education commissioner and as president of the University of South Florida. In 2004, Betty Castor was the Democratic nominee for U.S. Senate, but lost 49%-48% to Republican Mel Martinez. Kathy Castor herself appeared on the ballot twice, first in 2000, when she ran unsuccessfully for the state Senate, and again in 2002, when she won a four-year term on the Hillsborough County Commission.

When five-term Democratic Rep. Jim Davis decided to run for governor in 2006, opening up a safe Democratic district, Kathy Castor entered the contest, benefiting from the familiarity of the Castor name after her mother's close Senate election. In a district where Democrats enjoy a nearly 2-to-1 advantage over Republicans, Castor faced four opponents in the primary. The most formidable was state Senate Minority Leader Les Miller, a veteran African-American legislator. Although Miller was familiar to voters from his service in the state House and Senate, he proved unable to keep pace with Castor's prolific fundraising. With the support of EMILY's List, Castor raised nearly $1 million before the primary and outspent Miller 3-to-1. Whites make up less than half the district's population, and Miller contended the seat was drawn to elect a minority candidate after the 2000 census, especially since the Tampa-St. Petersburg area has never elected a black representative. Castor trailed Miller in the heavily African-American portion of the Pinellas County, but she defeated him by more than 8,600 votes in Tampa's Hillsborough County. She won 54%-34%.

The outcome of the general election in this comfortably Democratic district was never in doubt. Republican Eddie Adams, an architect, struggled to raise money and was absent from the campaign trail for three weeks in October while recovering from a ruptured appendix. Castor campaigned for expanded health care for low-income families and for stronger ethics and lobbying rules. Both were issues she advocated as a county commissioner. She also advocated a rapid withdrawal of U.S. troops from Iraq. She won the general election 70%-30%.

In the House, Castor has a liberal voting record. From her early days in Congress, she positioned herself for future roles in the Democratic leadership. She asked Democratic Speaker Nancy Pelosi to be appointed as the freshman representative to the Democratic Steering and Policy Committee, which determines committee assignments. Pelosi, surprised because no one had asked her for the position before, promptly gave it to Castor. In 2007, she got choice seats on the Rules and the Armed Services committees. As a member of the leadership-run Rules panel, she was the first freshman to speak on the House floor when Congress took up its first legislative business under the new Democratic majority, which was a change in ethics rules.

But in 2007, she was one of only eight House Democrats to oppose the expansion of the State Children's Health Insurance Program, complaining that Senate revisions to the bill made its benefits less favorable for Florida. Many of her constituents were also opposed to a significant hike in the cigar tax in the legislation. Later, Castor, following her loyalist instincts, voted to override President Bush's veto of the bill. When Republicans pushed in 2008 for increased oil production, she insisted on a permanent offshore drilling ban within 125 miles of the Florida coastline. In 2009, Castor took up the issue of increased trade and travel to Cuba, a popular move with many of her constituents and an idea that was being resurrected by the new Obama administration.

Castor was rewarded in 2009 with a seat on the influential Energy and Commerce Committee, where she wants to work on the issue of making health care more available and affordable.

In a rematch against Republican Eddie Adams in 2008, she increased her share of the vote from 70% to 72%, winning easily.

TWELFTH DISTRICT

Adam Putnam (R)

Elected 2000, 5th term; b. July 31, 1974, Bartow; home, Bartow; U. of FL, B.S. 1995; Episcopalian; married (Melissa); 4 children.

Elected Office: FL House of Reps., 1996–2000.

Professional Career: Rancher, Putnam Groves, Inc.

DC Office: 442 CHOB, 20515, 202-225-1252; Fax: 202-226-0585; Web site: www.adamputnam.house.gov.

State Offices: Bartow, 863-534-3530.

Committees: *Financial Services* (20th of 29 R): Capital Markets, Insurance & Government Sponsored Enterprises; Housing & Community Opportunity.

Group Ratings

	ADA	ACLU	AFS	LCV	ITIC	NTU	COC	ACU	CFG	FRC
2008	15	10	0	8	86	59	94	83	63	94
2007	10	—	0	5	—	78	80	92	87	—

National Journal Ratings

	2007 LIB	—	2007 CONS	2008 LIB	—	2008 CONS
Economic	18%	—	81%	18%	—	82%
Social	0%	—	91%	26%	—	73%
Foreign	0%	—	72%	0%	—	95%
Composite	12%	—	88%	16%	—	84%

Key Votes of the 110th Congress

1. Increase minimum wage	N	5. Share immigration data	Y	9. Withdraw troops 8/08	N
2. Expand SCHIP	N	6. Foreign aid abortion ban	Y	10. No operations in Iran	N
3. Raise CAFE standards	N	7. Ban gay bias in workplace	N	11. Free trade with Peru	Y
4. Bail out financial markets	Y	8. Repeal D.C. gun law	Y	12. Overhaul FISA	Y

Election Results

2008 general	Adam Putnam (R)	185,698	(57%)	($2,054,571)
	Doug Tudor (D)	137,465	(43%)	($121,851)
2008 primary	Adam Putnam (R)	unopposed		

Prior Winning Percentages: 2006 (70%); 2004 (65%); 2002 (100%); 2000 (57%)

Population		Race/Ethnicity		Work	
Pop. 2007:	765,556	White:	64.1%	Private:	82.8%
Change since 2000:	Up 19.7%	Black:	14.2%	Government:	12.2%
Urban:	84.3%	Hispanic:	18.2%	Self-employed:	4.7%
Rural:	15.7%	Asian:	1.5%	Blue collar:	25.1%
Area size:	2,097 sq. mi.	Native Am.:	0.2%	White collar:	56.7%
		Hawaiian:	0.0%	Khaki collar:	0.2%
Age		Two+ races:	1.2%	Other:	18.0%
Median age:	37.2 yrs.			Median income:	$44,786
More than 65 yrs:	15.7%	*Ancestry*		Median home value:	$156,300
Less than 18 yrs:	25.0%	German:	10.6%	Poverty:	12.3%
		USA:	9.5%		
Education		Irish:	9.4%	**Military Veterans**	
H.S. grad:	82.4%			% of Pop:	13.4%
College grad:	19.1%				
Grad degree:	5.9%				

The heart of central Florida is Polk County, filled with lakes and small-to-medium-sized cities: Lakeland, Bartow, Lake Wales, Winter Haven, Frostproof, and Haines City. It is the part of Florida most dependent on agriculture. Strawberries, cattle, and citrus are economic mainstays, although periodic freezes in recent years have persuaded some orange growers to move south or to switch to tomatoes. Still, Polk County remained the largest citrus producer in the state in 2007. Turpentine distilleries,

2008 Presidential Vote

McCain (R)..............................168,501   (50%)
Obama (D) 164,732   (49%)

2004 Presidential Vote

Bush (R) 167,216   (58%)
Kerry (D)................................119,825   (42%)

Cook Partisan Voting Index: R + 6

dependent on the big stands of pine, and phosphate mining businesses can be found as well. Proportionately, there are more manufacturing jobs here than almost anywhere else in Florida (though still not very many). In 1929, retired *Ladies Home Journal* Editor Edward Bok built the most prominent landmarks here: the 205-foot-tall gothic Bok Tower and the surrounding Mountain Lake Sanctuary and gardens. A remnant of old Florida, this area has not become a major retiree haven. Its population grew 19.7% between 2000 and 2007—an impressive rate by national standards but not compared with other parts of Florida.

The 12th Congressional District of Florida includes almost all of Polk County, which holds about 60% of the population. This was the home of Spessard Holland and Lawton Chiles, two legendary Democrats who each served as governor and senator. Even today there are more registered Democrats than Republicans, but Polk County, like most of the Deep South, increasingly votes Republican. In the 2006 governor's race, Republican Charlie Crist won the county with 56% of the vote. The 12th District also includes a sliver of Osceola County and the rapidly growing suburbs east of Tampa in Republican-leaning Hillsborough County—such places as Brandon, home to strip malls and younger, pro-business families. Overall, this district is becoming reliably Republican. It voted 58% for President Bush in 2004. And in the locally hard-fought 2008 campaign, Republican John McCain narrowly beat Democrat Barack Obama 50%-49%.

The congressman from the 12th District is Adam Putnam, a Republican first elected in 2000 at age 26. He grew up in Polk County, a fifth-generation member of a Bartow family that has been prominent in cattle ranching and citrus growing in the area. Interested in politics from childhood, Putnam graduated from the University of Florida, plotting his first political campaign while still in his senior year. In 1996, he was elected to the state House at age 22 and went on to become chairman of the Agriculture Committee. In 2000, when Republican Rep. Charles Canady kept his term-limit pledge, Putnam ran and was unopposed in the Republican primary. He supported most of the Republican agenda: He opposed abortion rights and gun control, he called for lowering the capital-gains tax, and he favored a missile defense system for the United States. In the general election, Putnam had a tough challenger in auto dealer and first-time candidate Michael Stedem, who said Putnam did not have enough life experience for the job. Stedem's message gained some traction; Putnam was ridiculed in the press. "Putnam is 26 and looks as if he's going on 13," *The Tampa Tribune* wrote in October 2000, in a story headlined, "Opie runs for Congress." But he won the seat 57%-43%.

In the House, Putnam has been a star among the chamber's Republicans. When the GOP was in the majority, he rose through the ranks quickly, from subcommittee chairman to the third-ranking post in the leadership. After the party lost its majorities in Congress, Putnam found his influence in the House diminished. In early 2009, Putnam announced he would vacate his House seat in 2010 to run for state agriculture commissioner. Success in that post could become a springboard for his ambition to become Florida's governor.

Except for free-trade legislation, which usually finds him on the protectionist-prone side of the citrus industry, Putnam has been a reliably conservative vote in the House. He also earned a footnote in history on September 11, 2001, when he happened to be with President Bush during a visit to an elementary school in Sarasota. After word of the terrorist attacks reached the president's entourage, Putnam was hustled aboard Air Force One and flown to Barksdale Air Force Base in Louisiana. Bush discussed his options that morning with Putnam and then-Rep. Dan Miller from Florida's 13th District. The two lawmakers then returned to Washington on another plane.

In 2003, Putnam became chairman of the Technology, Information Policy, Intergovernmental Relations, and Census Subcommittee of the Government Reform Committee, making him the youngest subcommittee chair in the post-World War II era. In early 2006, he defeated three other candidates to become chairman of the Republican Policy Committee. House Speaker Dennis Hastert tasked him to develop the GOP's partisan approach on immigration policy, and he helped to broker the deal to permit limited oil drilling off the coast of Florida. Later that year, Putnam defeated three opponents to become chairman of the Republican Conference, the third-ranking leadership position in the minority. In that post, he formed a rapid-response team and assembled a new communications strategy that focused on small media markets. He said his party's challenge was to get noticed against the backdrop of a Democratic majority, a presidential election cycle, and "the historical nature of a woman speaker."

He also stayed in tune with matters of local importance. After hurricanes ravaged parts of Florida in 2004, Putnam worked to secure $500 million in federal disaster relief for the state's agricultural industry. And he has maintained a strong interest in legislation affecting agriculture.

He often went his own way on issues. Putnam pushed for broad immigration reform, including tougher enforcement, and told the Lakeland *Ledger* that constituents had told him the nation was "losing our cultural identity." He also supported Bush's proposal to increase the number of guest workers, based partly on his own family's hiring experiences. In 2007, he was among the early Republicans calling on Attorney General Alberto Gonzales to step down, telling *The Ledger* that his credibility in running the Justice Department had been "severely damaged" after revelations that U.S. attorneys around the country may have been dismissed for political reasons. His outspoken support for the 2008 bailout of the financial markets angered some conservatives.

Putnam is planning to run for Florida agriculture commissioner. The early Democratic frontrunner for the seat was Polk County Elections Supervisor Lori Edwards. On the Republican side, former state lawmaker Dennis Ross also announced in early 2009 that he intends to run.

THIRTEENTH DISTRICT

Vern Buchanan (R)

Elected 2006, 2nd term; b. May 8, 1951, Detroit, MI; home, Longboat Key; Cleary U., B.B.A. 1975, U. of Detroit, M.B.A. 1986; Baptist; married (Sandy); 2 children.

Military Career: MI Air Natl. Guard, 1970–76.

Professional Career: Taekwondo instructor, 1971–74; Marketing representative, Burroughs Corp., 1975–76; Founder, Vern Buchanan and Associates, 1976–78; Founder and CEO, American Speedy Printing Centers, 1976–92; Founder and chmn., Buchanan Automotive Group, 1992–2007; Founder and chmn., Buchanan Enterprises, 1992–2007.

DC Office: 218 CHOB, 20515, 202-225-5015; Fax: 202-226-0828; Web site: buchanan.house.gov.

State Offices: Bradenton, 941-747-9081; Sarasota, 941-951-6643.

Committees: *Small Business* (8th of 12 R): Finance & Tax (RMM); Regulations & Healthcare. *Transportation & Infrastructure* (25th of 30 R): Aviation; Highways & Transit; Railroads, Pipelines & Hazardous Materials. *Veterans' Affairs* (10th of 11 R): Health.

Group Ratings

	ADA	ACLU	AFS	LCV	ITIC	NTU	COC	ACU	CFG	FRC
2008	50	18	43	62	71	43	83	60	36	100
2007	35	—	27	25	—	55	85	84	47	—

National Journal Ratings

	2007 LIB	—	2007 CONS		2008 LIB	—	2008 CONS
Economic	39%	—	60%		40%	—	59%
Social	21%	—	75%		41%	—	58%
Foreign	0%	—	72%		31%	—	67%
Composite	26%	—	75%		38%	—	62%

Key Votes of the 110th Congress

1. Increase minimum wage	Y	5. Share immigration data	Y	9. Withdraw troops 8/08	N
2. Expand SCHIP	Y	6. Foreign aid abortion ban	Y	10. No operations in Iran	N
3. Raise CAFE standards	N	7. Ban gay bias in workplace	N	11. Free trade with Peru	Y
4. Bail out financial markets	Y	8. Repeal D.C. gun law	Y	12. Overhaul FISA	Y

Election Results

2008 general	Vern Buchanan (R)	204,382	(56%)	($4,345,554)
	Christine Jennings (D)	137,967	(37%)	($2,434,002)
	Jan Schneider (NPA)	20,289	(6%)	($50,212)
2008 primary	Vern Buchanan (R)	unopposed		

Prior Winning Percentages: 2006 (50%)

Population		Race/Ethnicity		Work	
Pop. 2007:	731,968	White:	82.0%	Private:	81.9%
Change since 2000:	Up 14.5%	Black:	4.8%	Government:	11.0%
Urban:	89.4%	Hispanic:	10.4%	Self-employed:	6.8%
Rural:	10.6%	Asian:	1.3%	Blue collar:	23.0%
Area size:	2,948 sq. mi.	Native Am.:	0.2%	White collar:	58.5%
Age		Hawaiian:	0.1%	Khaki collar:	0.1%
		Two+ races:	0.9%	Other:	18.5%
Median age:	46.5 yrs.	*Ancestry*		Median income:	$48,073
More than 65 yrs:	26.3%	German:	15.2%	Median home value:	$238,600
Less than 18 yrs:	18.5%	English:	11.5%	Poverty:	9.9%
Education		Irish:	11.4%		
H.S. grad:	86.6%			**Military Veterans**	
College grad:	26.5%			% of Pop:	15.3%
Grad degree:	9.9%				

When the Ringling Brothers made a success of the circus they founded in the 1880s, they needed a place for performers and animals to rest during the winter months. They settled on the bayfront village of Sarasota, located behind a barrier island on the Gulf of Mexico. It was just far enough north to be reachable by railroad and just far enough south to be semitropical so the elephants would stay healthy. Here, on the calm Sarasota Bay, John Ringling established the Ringling Museum of Art,

2008 Presidential Vote

McCain (R)	199,585	(52%)
Obama (D)	178,349	(47%)

2004 Presidential Vote

Bush (R)	200,932	(56%)
Kerry (D)	156,727	(44%)

Cook Partisan Voting Index: R + 6

a huge sculpture garden, and his own Venetian palace, the Ca'd'Zan. Next door, his brother, Charles, built a pair of neoclassical revival mansions in pink Georgia marble, which are now part of New College of Florida. After World War II, the balmy Gulf Coast attracted new settlers—affluent, well-educated Republicans from upper-crust suburbs in the North. The population exploded. Manatee and Sarasota counties grew from 63,000 in 1950 to 732,000 in 2007. This part of Florida is no longer a winter community for snowbirds from the North. It has generated its own economy, one with as much vitality and diversity as the places from which its residents have come. In 2007, *Money* magazine ranked Sarasota as the 7th best city "to retire young."

The 13th Congressional District of Florida runs from just below Tampa Bay to Charlotte Harbor, north of Fort Myers. It includes all of Sarasota County, which accounts for just over half the district's population. It takes in all of lightly populated, rural DeSoto and Hardee counties, most of Manatee County to the north and an adjoining sliver of Charlotte County to the south. Idyllic beachfronts beautify the barrier islands, from sleepy Anna Maria down through pricey Longboat Key and Lido Key to more casual Siesta Key. The bayfront area, along the Intracoastal Waterway, is lined with high-rises and often clogged with traffic from Bradenton to Sarasota. Below that, Venice—established in 1920 as a speculative land venture by the Brotherhood of Locomotive Engineers—sits directly on the Gulf of Mexico. Though some high-tech firms diversify the economy, the district as a whole remains a place of tourists and well-off retirees: 26% of its population is 65 and older, and it has 195,000 Social Security recipients, the second highest level of all congressional districts in Florida. For many years, the 13th District was heavily Republican, and it remains that way in party registration. But like the affluent northern suburbs from which so many of its voters came, it trended toward the Democrats in the 1990s. George W. Bush carried this district, but just 54% of the vote in 2000 and 56% in 2004. In 2008, Republican John McCain won the district, 52%-47%, over Barack Obama.

The congressman from the 13th District is Vern Buchanan, a Republican elected in 2006. Buchanan grew up outside of Detroit, the eldest of six children and the son of a factory foreman. He joined the Michigan Air National Guard and worked his way through college as a tae kwon do instructor. He earned a business degree at Cleary University and later an M.B.A. at the University of Detroit. Buchanan founded American Speedy Printing Centers and made his fortune by selling 700 quick-printing franchises before his 40th birthday. In 1990, he moved his family to Florida, where he found new success as an automobile dealer with franchises throughout the Southeast. Buchanan became active in Republican Party politics, serving as a top fundraiser for Gov. Jeb Bush and Sen. Mel Martinez. In 2002, he wanted to run for the 13th District House seat, but stepped aside for then-Florida Secretary of State Katherine Harris, who had become a national Republican figure after her controversial role in the 2000 presidential vote recount.

Buchanan got his chance in 2006, when Harris ran for the Senate. His party connections and personal finances made him the front-runner. In the primary, he stressed his conservative credentials and challenged his chief rival, former Sarasota Republican Party Chairman Tramm Hudson, for his positions on abortion rights and immigration. Hudson claimed that Buchanan resigned from his printing company just days before it declared bankruptcy. But Hudson stumbled when, in telling a story about his Army days, asserted that black soldiers were poor swimmers. After spending more than $2 million of his own money, Buchanan won 32% victory in the five-way primary. Hudson and moderate state Rep. Nancy Detert finished next with 24% each. The bruising primary left Buchanan little time to recover before the general election.

The Democratic nominee was Christine Jennings, who like Buchanan, was a transplanted Midwesterner and a self-made business success. An Ohio native, she rose from bank teller to bank owner. National Democrats took an interest in the Jennings campaign and pummeled Buchanan through the fall for his business dealings. Buchanan responded by characterizing Jennings as a pro-tax liberal, a charge that was tough to stick on the former Republican with a business background. Despite the Republican advantage in the district, Buchanan was hurt by the attacks on his business dealings, the poor political environment for Republicans and late-breaking revelations about Florida GOP Rep. Mark Foley's sexually explicit e-mails to congressional pages. But he was able to spend over $8 million on his campaign, including $5.5 million of his own money. Jennings spent $3 million, about $2 million out of her own pocket. This was the most expensive House race in 2006.

Buchanan prevailed on Election Day, but Democrats disputed the results for another year. After a recount, Republican election officials certified Buchanan as the winner by 369 votes out of nearly 240,000 votes cast. Jennings filed a lawsuit challenging the results, pointing to more than 18,000 "undervotes" on ballots that registered a vote for other offices but did not indicate a choice in the congressional race. She suggested that a software glitch on touch-screen voting machines in Sarasota County was to blame for the unusually high number of undervotes. But several rounds of testing were inconclusive, and in November 2007, Jennings dropped her lawsuit.

In the House, Buchanan softened his ideological positions. He had the most moderate voting record of all among the 16 Republicans elected in 2006. And he was one of 19 Republicans who supported most of the Democrats' early legislative agenda when they took control of the House in 2007. He voted for raising the minimum wage, cutting subsidies to industries, and allowing the federal government to negotiate lower drug prices with pharmaceutical companies. "I ran as a conservative, but I also ran as someone who is going to be independent," Buchanan told the *Sarasota Herald-Tribune*.

Later in 2007, Buchanan voted to override President Bush's veto of the Democrats' expansion of the State Children's Health Insurance Program. He worked with Democrats on a bill to clean up the Gulf of Mexico, and on other environmental and consumer issues. The former car dealer voted against the bailout of Detroit automakers in 2008 because, he said, the companies "failed to develop viable restructuring proposals." The industry problems led him to sell several of his dealerships. On the Small Business Committee, he became the ranking member on the Finance and Tax Subcommittee.

In 2008, Jennings was back for a rematch. Though not as costly as the 2006 race, the contest was similarly bitter and expensive, with a crossfire of accusations of business fraud, slander, and campaign finance violations. Buchanan sought to emphasize his bipartisanship. With help from EMILY's List and other national Democratic groups, Jennings's campaign ads focused on his earlier corporate dealings. But she may have paid a price for her extended challenge of the 2006 results, and the outcome this time was very different. Buchanan outpolled Republican presidential nominee John McCain, and returned this district to its familiar pattern with a 56%-37% win. A third-party candidate got 6% of the vote.

FOURTEENTH DISTRICT

Connie Mack (R)

Elected 2004, 3rd term; b. Aug. 12, 1967, Fort Myers; home, Fort Myers; U. of FL, B.S. 1993; Catholic; married (Mary Bono Mack); 2 children.

Elected Office: FL House, 2000–03.

Professional Career: Marketing consultant, 1994–2004.

DC Office: 115 CHOB, 20515, 202-225-2536; Fax: 202-226-0439; Web site: mack.house.gov.

State Offices: Cape Coral, 239-573-5837; Naples, 239-252-6225.

Committees: *Budget* (7th of 15 R). *Foreign Affairs* (14th of 19 R): Western Hemisphere (RMM). *Transportation & Infrastructure* (20th of 30 R): Aviation; Highways & Transit; Water Resources & Environment.

Group Ratings

	ADA	ACLU	AFS	LCV	ITIC	NTU	COC	ACU	CFG	FRC
2008	10	27	0	8	29	83	88	100	96	76
2007	5	—	0	5	—	83	79	88	92	—

National Journal Ratings

	2007 LIB — 2007 CONS	2008 LIB — 2008 CONS
Economic	17% — 83%	15% — 85%
Social	33% — 67%	0% — 91%
Foreign	0% — 72%	22% — 78%
Composite	21% — 79%	14% — 86%

Key Votes of the 110th Congress

1. Increase minimum wage	N	5. Share immigration data	Y	9. Withdraw troops 8/08	N
2. Expand SCHIP	N	6. Foreign aid abortion ban	Y	10. No operations in Iran	N
3. Raise CAFE standards	N	7. Ban gay bias in workplace	N	11. Free trade with Peru	Y
4. Bail out financial markets	N	8. Repeal D.C. gun law	Y	12. Overhaul FISA	Y

Election Results

2008 general	Connie Mack (R)	224,602	(59%)	($1,008,108)
	Robert Neeld (D)	93,590	(25%)	($15,252)
	Burt Saunders (NPA)	59,699	(16%)	($165,327)
2008 primary	Connie Mack (R)	unopposed		

Prior Winning Percentages: 2006 (64%); 2004 (68%)

Population		Race/Ethnicity		Work	
Pop. 2007:	806,944	White:	76.8%	Private:	82.2%
Change since 2000:	Up 26.2%	Black:	6.0%	Government:	10.6%
Urban:	90.7%	Hispanic:	15.0%	Self-employed:	6.9%
Rural:	9.3%	Asian:	1.1%	Blue collar:	23.1%
Area size:	1,718 sq. mi.	Native Am.:	0.3%	White collar:	58.0%
		Hawaiian:	0.0%	Khaki collar:	0.0%
Age		Two+ races:	0.6%	Other:	18.8%
Median age:	44.8 yrs.			Median income:	$51,617
More than 65 yrs:	24.9%	*Ancestry*		Median home value:	$283,600
Less than 18 yrs:	19.5%	German:	15.2%	Poverty:	9.0%
		Irish:	11.2%		
Education		English:	9.7%	**Military Veterans**	
H.S. grad:	87.0%			% of Pop:	15.4%
College grad:	26.9%				
Grad degree:	9.9%				

The edge of the tropics, in a physical environment once teeming with disease and inhospitable to advanced civilization, Florida's Gulf Coast has evolved into a model for retirement living. Early on, there were only a few white settlements here. One was Fort Myers, built in 1850 as an Army post to pursue the Seminole Indians; in 1858, the last of the natives were driven out. For a century after that, this corner of Florida was mostly deserted. But in time, it became resort country, thanks to its wide,

2008 Presidential Vote		
McCain (R)	226,818	(57%)
Obama (D)	168,404	(42%)

2004 Presidential Vote		
Bush (R)	222,234	(62%)
Kerry (D)	136,049	(38%)

Cook Partisan Voting Index: R + 11

white-sand beaches with gentle breakers. The inlets and broad estuaries are perfect for boating, and the wetlands are graced with exotic birds. Thomas Edison had his winter home in Fort Myers, Henry Ford used to visit here, and tourists were drawn to beaches thick with seashells on nearby Sanibel and Captiva islands. But the local economy could not support many permanent residents, and at the beginning of World War II, there were only 68,000 people living on the Gulf Coast from Bradenton south to Naples.

By 2007, there were more than 1.7 million. The climate and environment, and the fact that Florida has no state income or inheritance tax, attracted waves of affluent suburbanites from the Midwest and Northeast. Developers such as Barron Collier, who built the Tamiami Trail across the soggy Everglades and designed Naples with the wealthy in mind, were determined to avoid the high-rise canyons that line the Atlantic from Palm Beach to Miami. Their alternative was to construct low-rise, city-style developments such as Cape Coral, a retirement community that was the fourth-fastest-growing city in the nation in 2006. Named for Collier, the county itself grew 20% from 2000 to 2007. It has 409 miles of canals running through most backyards and boutique towns such as Naples, set amid St. Augustine grass and banyan trees. This is very much retirement country—for those who can afford it. Much of this area was damaged by multiple hurricanes over the past few years. But there was no appreciable slowdown in development until the recession took hold in 2008. That year, land values sank and a large inventory of housing went unsold. The area had the nation's greatest number of housing foreclosures, and they accounted for nearly half of the home sales. Exurban Lehigh Acres became an extreme example of the boombust pattern, as housing growth suddenly stopped and the town was plagued by high crime. In February 2009, President Obama spoke at Fort Myers about the need for his economic stimulus plan.

The 14th Congressional District of Florida occupies the southern half of the habitable Gulf Coast below Tampa Bay. Retirees account for more than one in four residents. The 14th includes a small part of Port Charlotte and Charlotte County; all of Lee County; and the coastal strip of Collier County, including Naples and Marco Island. Two-thirds of the district's residents live in Lee County, in Fort Myers and Bonita Springs, and on Sanibel and Captiva islands. In a state where Republican registration rates often understate Republican voting strength, the district in 2008 counted 48% of its electorate as registered Republicans. Just 29% were registered Democrats, the lowest percentage of any Florida congressional district.

The congressman from the 14th District is Connie Mack, a Republican elected in 2004. His father is also Connie Mack; he held the same seat for three terms in the 1980s and then served two terms in the Senate. His great-grandfather and best-known forebear was the owner and manager of baseball's Philadelphia Athletics for 50 years, Cornelius McGillicuddy, who shortened his name to Connie Mack. Rep. Mack graduated from the University of Florida after seven years and worked as a marketing consultant. In 2000, he was elected to the state House from a district in Broward and Palm Beach counties. In Tallahassee, he formed the anti-tax Freedom Caucus, which was against increased state spending and in favor of lower taxes and limits on attorneys' fees in personal injury and malpractice cases.

In 2004, after Republican Rep. Porter Goss left the House to become the Central Intelligence Agency's director, Mack resigned from the state Legislature and moved across the state to Lee County to run for the seat. He raised $1.4 million for the primary, outpacing his nearest Republican rival more than 2-to-1 and blanketing southwestern Florida with television ads. His three GOP opponents, state Rep. Carole Green, Lee County Commissioner Andy Coy, and Naples physician Frank Schwerin, attacked him as a carpetbagger who hadn't lived in the district since he was a teenager. Mack countered that he was the only candidate born and raised in the district. His opponents claimed that he was an inexperienced lightweight, and editorial writers were dismissive of his business credentials. "What a hoot," wrote the *Palm Beach Post,* noting that his marketing consulting included sending scantily clad young women who worked for the Hooters restaurant chain to charity events. The four Republicans differed little on the issues: All of them campaigned as conservatives and all backed President Bush's policies. While he opposed abortion rights, Mack broke with the Bush administration on federal funding of embryonic-stem-cell research, which uses embryos left over from in vitro fertilization. Mack won the primary with 36% of the vote. Green was his closest competitor with 32%. In the November general election, Mack won easily, 68%-32%. Since then, he has not been seriously challenged.

In the House, he has a conservative voting record. But he is more moderate on environmental issues, especially those that threaten his district's tourist trade. He parted with other Florida House members to oppose a compromise to permit oil drilling off the state's coast. Mack sponsored a bill to find the cause of the red tide algae that plagued Gulf Coast beaches, killing dolphins and manatees. He also worked to secure money to widen Interstate 75. But he was drawn into the controversy surrounding Rep. Don Young, an Alaska Republican, who in 2005 included a $10 million earmark for the federal purchase of Fort Myers-area property owned by a campaign contributor to both Young and Mack. Mack angrily said he knew nothing about the deal, which became part of a U.S. Justice Department investigation of Young.

In 2009, Mack became the ranking Republican on the Foreign Affairs Committee's Western Hemisphere Subcommittee, where he has been an outspoken critic of Venezuelan President Hugo Chavez. He introduced a bill calling on the administration to designate Venezuela as a state sponsor of terrorism.

In December 2007, Mack married Rep. Mary Bono, a California Republican and the widow of former pop singer and GOP Rep. Sonny Bono. Local Democrats appeared to get little traction with their criticism that Mack was ignoring the district and spending much of his time with Bono in California.

FIFTEENTH DISTRICT

Bill Posey (R)

Elected 2008, 1st term; b. Dec. 18, 1947, Washington, DC; home, Rockledge; Brevard Comm. Col., A.A. 1969.; Methodist; married (Katie Ingram); 2 children.

Elected Office: Rockledge City Cncl., 1976–86; FL House, 1992–2000; FL Senate, 2000–08.

Professional Career: McDonnell Douglas Astronautics Co., 1966–69; Crawford & Co./Gay & Taylor, 1970–74; Founder, Posey & Co. Realtors, 1974-present.

DC Office: 132 CHOB, 20515, 202-225-3671; Fax: 202-225-3516; Web site: posey.house.gov.

State Offices: Melbourne, 321-632-1776.

Committees: *Financial Services* (25th of 29 R): Capital Markets, Insurance & Government Sponsored Enterprises; Domestic Monetary Policy & Technology.

Group Ratings and Key Votes: Newly Elected

Election Results

2008 general	Bill Posey (R)	192,151	(53%)	($909,257)
	Stephen Blythe (D)	151,951	(42%)	($113,372)
	Frank Zilaitis (NPA)	14,274	(4%)	($38,694)
2008 primary	Bill Posey (R)	40,892	(77%)	
	Alan Bergman (R)	7,809	(15%)	
	Kevin Lehoullier (R)	4,519	(8%)	

Population		**Race/Ethnicity**		**Work**	
Pop. 2007:	763,227	White:	70.8%	Private:	82.0%
Change since 2000:	Up 19.4%	Black:	8.6%	Government:	11.9%
Urban:	89.6%	Hispanic:	16.4%	Self-employed:	5.9%
Rural:	10.4%	Asian:	2.2%	Blue collar:	22.1%
Area size:	3,253 sq. mi.	Native Am.:	0.3%	White collar:	58.1%
		Hawaiian:	0.0%	Khaki collar:	0.2%
Age		Two+ races:	1.3%	Other:	19.6%
Median age:	41.6 yrs.			Median income:	$46,779
More than 65 yrs:	19.1%	*Ancestry*		Median home value:	$214,700
Less than 18 yrs:	21.4%	German:	13.1%	Poverty:	10.5%
		Irish:	11.9%		
Education		English:	9.9%	**Military Veterans**	
H.S. grad:	87.0%			% of Pop:	15.6%
College grad:	24.6%				
Grad degree:	8.5%				

When Cape Canaveral was chosen as the nation's rocket testing site in the 1940s, there were only 20,000 people in all of Brevard County, which stretches along 63 miles of the coast north and south of the Cape. It was reliant economically on fishing and citrus-growing, and chosen because it was on the sunny Atlantic coast. Rockets could be launched eastward so that spent parts fell into the ocean. In 1948, the Brooklyn Dodgers (now the Los Angeles Dodgers) established their spring training home in

2008 Presidential Vote		
McCain (R)	199,604	(51%)
Obama (D)	185,314	(48%)
2004 Presidential Vote		
Bush (R)	195,076	(57%)
Kerry (D)	146,914	(43%)
Cook Partisan Voting Index: R + 6		

Vero Beach, 60 miles south of Canaveral in Indian River County. Their training facilities were affably nicknamed Dodgertown, but Jim Crow segregation laws remained in place through the mid-1950s, until Dodger executives used an ingenious method to flex their economic muscle in the service of integration: They stamped the team's name on 20,000 dollar bills and told players and reporters to spend them freely at local establishments. Local officials got the message, easing off enforcement of segregation, at least when Jackie Robinson and his teammates were in town. Today, the region has come a long way. Brevard County has 536,521 people, and the Kennedy Space Center attracts 1.5 million visitors annually. The county has no city center but plenty of shopping centers along strip highways, with a white-collar, service economy, knitted together by interest in the space program. But the scheduled retirement of the space shuttle in 2010 threatens the local economy, as NASA estimates that as many as 4,500 shuttle-related jobs could be lost at the center. Development in other areas has continued to be strong. Proximity to Disney World has spawned growth in the cruise line business, and Port Canaveral is the second-largest passenger port in the world. And Vero Beach lost the Dodgers. The team held its last spring training there in 2008 before moving to Glendale, Ariz. in 2009.

The 15th Congressional District of Florida includes much, but not all, of the 72-mile Space Coast; the area code here is 321. Its northern end is at Cape Canaveral itself, but most of the space center facilities, including the visitors' center, are in the 24th District. It runs south along the Atlantic Coast and includes 75% of Brevard County and all of Indian River County. Among the bigger towns are Cocoa Beach, Melbourne, Palm Bay, and Vero Beach. To the west, the district includes all but a small piece of Osceola County; the population there is just south of Disney World and concentrated around Kissimmee and St. Cloud. This is the fastest-growing part of the district, with a rapidly increasing Puerto Rican and Latino population. The district also includes the northern tip of Polk County. The population there is a mix of young workers and retirees, plus military families stationed at Patrick Air Force Base, home of the 45th Space Wing.

Politically, the district leans Republican. In 2004, the Bush campaign worked intensively on outreach to the new Latino voters in Osceola County and won the county 52%-47%, after losing it four years earlier. Brevard remains Republican too, but it is becoming less so. Republican Charlie Crist got 54% there in his successful 2006 governor's race . Republican John McCain won the district in 2008 with 51% of the vote to Democrat Barack Obama's 48%.

The new congressman from the 15th District is Bill Posey, a Republican who succeeded seven-term GOP Rep. Dave Weldon in 2008. Posey was born in Washington, D.C., but moved several times due to his father's work in the aircraft business. His family landed in Brevard County in 1956, and after graduating from high school, Posey took a job with McDonnell Douglas Astronautics at the Kennedy Space Center. He worked on the Apollo 11 Launch Team and attended Brevard Community College at night. After Apollo 11 successfully put men on the moon, Posey received a congratulatory letter from the director of NASA, and a month later, was laid off. Despite the turn of events, Posey does not harbor ill will towards NASA. "There's only one thing in this world that the United States is first and foremost respected in right now, and that happens to be space exploration," he says. Posey changed careers and went into real estate. He founded Posey & Co. Realtors in 1974 and is still president of the company. Posey is also an accomplished stock car racer, although an accident at an Orlando speedway in 2004 left him with spinal fractures and he says he has taken a break from racing.

He was the first member of his family to register as a Republican, a decision inspired by a college professor who lauded the Democratic Party's championing of inflation and deficit spending. "He literally was trying to convince the class that inflation was good because you could buy the things you wanted now and finance them later with cheaper money," Posey recalls. He was elected to the Rockledge City Council in 1976 and served until 1986. Four years later, he won a seat in the Florida House of Representatives, and served until 2000, when term limits forced him to resign. He then won a close and contentious state Senate race.

After Weldon announced his retirement in January 2008, Posey decided to run for the seat. He got Weldon's endorsement and that of Florida GOP Chairman Jim Greer, who called for the party to unite behind Posey. Veteran state Rep. Stan Mayfield, who had also announced his candidacy, fell in line, withdrew from the race and endorsed Posey.

Florida Democrats were unable to find a strong candidate after former Brevard County Commissioner Nancy Higgs dropped out of the race in February, and Posey became the clear favorite to win the general election. He won the GOP primary with 77% of the vote, and entered the general election with $230,000 in cash on hand. Stephen Blythe, a Melbourne family physician, won the Democratic primary with 65% of the vote and entered the general election with $8,789 in cash.

Posey made government accountability the central theme of his campaign. In the Florida House, Posey authored legislation that set new standards for state government accountability, and he wrote a book entitled, "Activity Based Total Accountability" detailing his work on the issue. The legislation won praise from the American Legislative Exchange Council. Posey also stressed immigration reform, advocating securing America's borders and deporting all illegal immigrants who are known to have committed a crime.

It was an amiable contest. Both candidates expressed mutual admiration and said that they would vote for each other if they could not vote for themselves. Posey outspent Blythe by almost 9-to-1, and won 53% to 42%. Independent candidate Frank Zilaitis got 4%.

Once in Washington, Posey got a seat on the House Financial Services Committee, the center of the action in the House on the ongoing government bailout of the financial markets. In January 2009, Posey took his first step towards his goal of increasing government transparency when he succeeded in getting the committee to post the results of every committee vote on its website within two days. He said he will not accept the cost-of-living pay raise that House members receive each year, and will return the money to the Treasury or donate it to charity.

SIXTEENTH DISTRICT

Tom Rooney (R)

Elected 2008, 1st term; b. Nov. 21, 1970, Philadelphia, PA; home, Tequesta; Washington & Jefferson Col., B.A., 1993; U. of FL, M.A., 1996; U. of Miami, J.D., 1999.; Catholic; married (Tara); 3 children.

Military Career: Army JAG, 2000–04; Army Reserves, 2004–07.

Professional Career: FL asst. atty. gen., 2004–05; CEO, Children's Place at HomeSafe, 2005–06.

DC Office: 1529 LHOB, 20515, 202-225-5792; Fax: 202-225-3132; Web site: rooney.house.gov.

State Offices: Fort Pierce, 772-461-3933, Punta Gorda, 941-575-9101; Stuart, 772-288-4668.

Committees: *Armed Services* (24th of 25 R): Military Personnel; Seapower & Expeditionary Forces; Terrorism, Unconventional Threats & Capabilities. *Judiciary* (15th of 16 R): Constitution, Civil Rights & Civil Liberties; Crime, Terrorism & Homeland Security.

Group Ratings and Key Votes: Newly Elected

Election Results

2008 general	Tom Rooney (R)	209,874	(60%)	($1,819,259)
	Tim Mahoney (D)	139,373	(40%)	($3,116,453)
2008 primary	Tom Rooney (R)	20,637	(37%)	
	Gayle Harrell (R)	19,626	(35%)	
	Hal Valeche (R)	15,916	(28%)	

Population		Race/Ethnicity		Work	
Pop. 2007:	756,184	White:	75.2%	Private:	81.2%
Change since 2000:	Up 18.3%	Black:	7.7%	Government:	12.5%
Urban:	84.5%	Hispanic:	14.3%	Self-employed:	6.1%
Rural:	15.5%	Asian:	1.4%	Blue collar:	21.9%
Area size:	5,249 sq. mi.	Native Am.:	0.4%	White collar:	56.6%
Age		Hawaiian:	0.0%	Khaki collar:	0.1%
Median age:	43.5 yrs.	Two+ races:	0.8%	Other:	21.4%
More than 65 yrs:	23.1%	*Ancestry*		Median income:	$47,944
Less than 18 yrs:	20.8%	German:	13.4%	Median home value:	$221,200
Education		Irish:	11.2%	Poverty:	10.1%
H.S. grad:	83.7%	English:	9.6%	**Military Veterans**	
College grad:	21.3%			% of Pop:	15.0%
Grad degree:	7.4%				

Urban Florida has fanned far across the swamplands from its original nuclei in beachfront resort
communities. Once, metro Palm Beach was a narrow stretch along Lake Worth; now it runs inland
almost halfway to Lake Okeechobee, spreading out
from its original locus around the posh Breakers
Hotel. Old beach towns such as Hobe Sound have
become the hub of affluent developments that
stretch all the way to Stuart in Martin County. Farther north, near the old town of Fort Pierce, are

2008 Presidential Vote		
McCain (R)	192,453	(52%)
Obama (D)	175,031	(47%)
2004 Presidential Vote		
Bush (R)	183,339	(54%)
Kerry (D)	154,632	(46%)
Cook Partisan Voting Index:	R + 5	

larger but more modest developments like Port St. Lucie, which lost its image as a sleepy bedroom community with the $40 million relocation of the Torrey Pines Institute of Molecular Studies in 2009. But Port
St. Lucie was hit hard during the 2008 mortgage industry meltdown, resulting in more than 10,000 properties in foreclosure and an unemployment rate of over 10%.

The 16th Congressional District of Florida stretches from the Atlantic Ocean almost to the Gulf of
Mexico, and is one of the most oddly designed districts in the nation. On the Atlantic coast, it includes
most of Martin County, with its affluent towns of Stuart and Hobe Sound, and also much of St. Lucie
County. Tequesta is its northernmost beach town. By a thin corridor of land, this coastal area is connected
to rural territory north and west of Lake Okeechobee. There, huge farms produce citrus, tomatoes, and
other vegetables, or support large dairy herds. The only population cluster is around Sebring, with its
automobile racetrack. In recent years, encroaching development, hurricanes, and citrus diseases have
threatened the viability of the citrus industry, and rising land prices have tempted farmers to get out of
the business. The area was hit hard by Hurricane Fay in August 2008, with estimates of $20 million in
damage to citrus crops. This area is connected by the swamps of eastern Charlotte County with the Gulf
Coast towns of Port Charlotte and Punta Gorda, on the wide Peace River where it empties into Port Charlotte and the Gulf of Mexico. In recent presidential elections, the district has voted consistently for Republicans but not by large margins. President Bush won the district with 54% in 2004, and in 2008 McCain
carried it by a similar margin, 52%-47%.

The new congressman from the 16th District is Tom Rooney, a Republican elected in 2008 and the
third person to hold the seat in the past four years. The two occupants before Rooney were forced from
office by scandal. In 2006, Tim Mahoney was able to secure the seat for the Democrats after Republican
incumbent Mark Foley resigned amid allegations that he had sent sexually explicit messages to male
congressional pages. Then in 2008, Mahoney looked to be headed for an easy re-election until ABC News
broke the story that he had paid a former aide $121,000 to keep quiet about their affair after he ended the
relationship and fired her. Rooney's campaign immediately picked up momentum as Mahoney's political
problems deepened, and he became the obvious choice for scandal-fatigued voters in the district.

The grandson of Pittsburgh Steelers founding owner Art Rooney, he was born in Philadelphia and
was a waterboy for the team. When he was 14, his father moved to Palm Beach Gardens, Fla., where his
family owned the Palm Beach Kennel Club, a racetrack and gambling business. Rooney briefly attended
Syracuse University, where he earned a spot as a tight end and deep snapper for the Orangemen. But with
no desire for a professional football career, Rooney transferred to the smaller Washington and Jefferson
College just outside Pittsburgh, where he played both football and golf.

He was a staff assistant for former Republican Sen. Connie Mack of Florida for a brief period, and
then got a law degree from the University of Miami, where he met his wife, Tara. After graduation, Rooney
was a special assistant U.S. attorney at Fort Hood in Texas, and later taught constitutional and criminal
law at the U.S. Military Academy at West Point. When Republican Charlie Crist became the Florida
attorney general, he hired Rooney as an assistant attorney general in 2004. After leaving the attorney
general's office, he headed a home for abused children, and in 2006 entered private law practice in Stuart.

After flirting with a 2006 challenge to Democratic Sen. Ben Nelsen, Rooney decided to challenge
Mahoney in 2008 and began raising money and campaigning nearly a year before the primary. He was
widely considered the GOP favorite, securing endorsements from Mack and Crist, who had since become
governor. The governor's endorsement riled the other two candidates, state Rep. Gayle Harrell and former Palm Beach Gardens City Councilman Hal Valeche, who pointed to the campaign contributions Crist
had received from Rooney's family. Rooney won the primary by only 1,011 votes over Harrell, 36.7%-
34.9%. Harrell won pluralities in Martin and St. Lucie counties, but Rooney's decisive victory in Charlotte
County put him over the top.

In the general election campaign, Rooney portrayed Mahoney as too liberal for the district. But Mahoney far outpaced him in fundraising, and was ahead in most polls throughout the fall. The race changed
course abruptly on Oct. 13, with the news that Mahoney had paid hush money to a former staffer with
whom he'd had an extramarital affair. Mahoney then admitted to "multiple affairs" while in office, including one with a Marin County official he met while she was trying to secure hurricane reimbursements
from the Federal Emergency Management Agency. Nonetheless, Mahoney said he had done nothing to
violate his oath of office. Rooney shot up nearly 25 points in the polls. Still, Mahoney declined to end his

bid for re-election, even after Democratic House Speaker Nancy Pelosi called for an ethics committee investigation into the payment. Mahoney's financial contributions quickly dried up. Rooney won easily won with 60% of the vote.

In the House, Rooney's military and legal experience won him coveted freshman appointments on both the House Armed Services and Judiciary committees. Along with the rest of the Republican caucus, Rooney voted against the economic stimulus bill in January 2009, but his vote made him an early target of Democratic Congressional Campaign Committee ads attacking his position. Rooney also voted against expanding the State Children's Health Insurance Program. His first bill would create a tax-deferred reserve for insurance companies to set aside money for future natural disasters, an idea that was supported by many insurers. Rooney also sponsored a bill that would prevent detainees from Guantanamo Bay from being transferred to nearby Florida.

SEVENTEENTH DISTRICT

Kendrick Meek (D)

Elected 2002, 4th term; b. Sept. 6, 1966, Miami; home, Miami; FL A&M U., B.S. 1989; Baptist; married (Leslie); 2 children.

Elected Office: FL House of Reps., 1994–98; FL Senate, 1998–2002.

DC Office: 1039 LHOB, 20515, 202-225-4506; Fax: 202-226-0777; Web site: http://kendrickmeek.house.gov.

State Offices: Miami Gardens, 305-690-5905; Pembroke Pines, 954-450-6767.

Committees: *Ways & Means* (19th of 26 D): Income Security & Family Support; Select Revenue Measures.

Group Ratings

	ADA	ACLU	AFS	LCV	ITIC	NTU	COC	ACU	CFG	FRC
2008	95	100	100	92	100	5	61	4	0	11
2007	95	—	100	85	—	4	55	0	6	—

National Journal Ratings

	2007 LIB	—	2007 CONS	2008 LIB	—	2008 CONS
Economic	82%	—	0%	85%	—	0%
Social	69%	—	30%	75%	—	18%
Foreign	69%	—	31%	69%	—	31%
Composite	77%	—	24%	80%	—	20%

Key Votes of the 110th Congress

1. Increase minimum wage	Y	5. Share immigration data	N	9. Withdraw troops 8/08	Y
2. Expand SCHIP	Y	6. Foreign aid abortion ban	N	10. No operations in Iran	Y
3. Raise CAFE standards	Y	7. Ban gay bias in workplace	Y	11. Free trade with Peru	Y
4. Bail out financial markets	Y	8. Repeal D.C. gun law	Y	12. Overhaul FISA	N

Election Results

2008 general	Kendrick Meek (D)...................................... unopposed
2008 primary	Kendrick Meek (D)...................................... unopposed

Prior Winning Percentages: 2006 (100%); 2004 (100%); 2002 (100%)

Population		**Race/Ethnicity**		**Work**	
Pop. 2007:	658,996	White:	15.6%	Private:	78.2%
Change since 2000:	Up 3.1%	Black:	56.3%	Government:	15.0%
Urban:	100.0%	Hispanic:	24.6%	Self-employed:	6.7%
Rural:	0.0%	Asian:	2.0%	Blue collar:	24.0%
Area size:	99 sq. mi.	Native Am.:	0.2%	White collar:	49.5%
		Hawaiian:	0.0%	Khaki collar:	0.1%
Age		Two+ races:	1.0%	Other:	26.4%
Median age:	33.8 yrs.			Median income:	$35,372
More than 65 yrs:	11.1%	*Ancestry*		Median home value:	$217,500
Less than 18 yrs:	27.2%	West Indian:	23.1%	Poverty:	21.4%
		USA:	3.1%		
Education		Italian:	2.2%	**Military Veterans**	
H.S. grad:	75.0%			% of Pop:	5.2%
College grad:	16.5%				
Grad degree:	5.1%				

North from downtown Miami, alongside Interstate
95, Miami's main north-south artery, is the city's
largest African-American community. It stretches
from the Miami Arena downtown through Allapat-
tah and Liberty City to the brightly painted minarets and Moorish arches of the city of Opa-Locka.
This has been a kind of frontierland in Miami,
where hostilities between Miami's blacks and its
Cuban-American majority have played out. Many
of Miami's African-Americans have resented the

2008 Presidential Vote		
Obama (D) 209,758	(87%)
McCain (R)..............................29,723	(12%)
2004 Presidential Vote		
Kerry (D)................................178,605	(83%)
Bush (R)..................................35,642	(17%)
Cook Partisan Voting Index: D + 34		

economic upward mobility and political strength of the Cubans. There is also tension between the Cubans
and the Haitians in Little Haiti as a result of federal policies that give Cubans who reach U.S. shores
refugee status while Haitians are treated as any other immigrant group with the potential for deportation
if they're not here legally. This animosity is reflected in partisan politics. Cuban Americans have been
solidly Republican over the years, though somewhat less so recently. South Florida blacks have remained
largely Democratic, as has the growing Haitian-American community.

The 17th Congressional District of Florida covers much of northeast Miami-Dade County, including
Liberty City and Overtown, Opa-Locka, and Miami Gardens (known as Carol City until it was incorporated in 2003), right up to Biscayne Boulevard. It does not include the affluent enclaves facing Biscayne
Bay or the beach towns north of Miami Beach, nor does it include heavily Latino Hialeah to the west.
This is the historic heart of Miami's black community. Some 56% of the district's residents are black, the
highest percentage of any Florida district; 25% are Hispanic. The district also includes part of Hollywood
and other communities in southern Broward County, which are also strongly Democratic.

The congressman from the 17th District is Kendrick Meek, a Democrat first elected in 2002. He is
the son of his predecessor, Carrie Meek, who was first elected when the district was created in 1992. She
is the granddaughter of a slave and was elected to the state Legislature in 1978, when Kendrick Meek
was 12. In July 2002, just two weeks before the filing deadline, Carrie Meek announced that she would
not run again and promised to work "24 hours a day, seven days a week" to elect her son. The election did
not require that much effort. The timing of her announcement left little time for a candidate to emerge
against Kendrick Meek, whose name was familiar in the district, and no Democrat or Republican filed
to run against him, a rare instance of a non-incumbent winning unopposed. The Meeks are not the first
mother and son to be elected to Congress. In 1952 Oliver Bolton, an Ohio Republican, was elected to the
House from a district adjoining the one that had been represented by his mother, Frances Bolton, since
1940 and by his father, Chester Bolton, before that.

Kendrick Meek would have been a formidable candidate even without the succession scheme. He
was a page in the Florida Legislature when his mother was elected. At Florida A&M University in Tallahassee, he was president of state College Young Democrats and a football player. After receiving his degree in criminology, he worked as a captain in the Highway Patrol and became a security aide to Democratic Lt. Gov. Buddy MacKay. In 1994, when he was 28, Meek was elected to the Florida House; four
years later he was elected to the Senate. In each case, he took on longtime, respected incumbents and
waged contentious campaigns to oust them. In January 2000, he staged a 25-hour sit-in at the lieutenant
governor's office to protest Republican Gov. Jeb Bush's "One Florida" executive orders, which called for
ending the use of racial preferences in state contracting and university admissions. Meek failed to change
Bush's mind, but his act of political theater helped spark the largest-ever protest march on the state
Capitol two months later. In 2002, he was well-known as the chief proponent of the ballot initiative to
force the state to decrease school class sizes, which, despite Bush's opposition, was approved.

In Washington, Democratic leaders were impressed by Meek's political and fundraising skills. He
was one of the youngest members of Congress and co-chaired then Democratic Whip Nancy Pelosi's
30-Something Working Group. He and Ohio Democratic Rep. Tim Ryan made sometimes humorous
YouTube videos explaining how Congress works. A lover of cigars, Meek has been featured in *Cigar
Aficionado* and hosts an annual cigar party. But in keeping with the anti-Castro sentiment that runs
strong among the many Cuban-Americans in his district, Meek never smokes Cuban cigars.

There may be hostility on the streets between South Florida blacks and Cubans, but not in the state's
congressional delegation. Meek set out to establish solid working relationships with Republicans, as well
as other Democrats, from South Florida. He has worked hand-in-hand with GOP Rep. Mario Diaz-Balart,
with whom he became close in the Legislature, to try to keep the trade embargo against Cuba. In turn,
Diaz-Balart and Cuban-American Reps. Ileana Ros-Lehtinen and Lincoln Diaz-Balart, Mario's brother,
have come to Meek's aid on other projects. Meek refused to take sides when Democrats ran strong though
ultimately unsuccessful campaigns against the three Cuban-American Republicans in 2008. Meek has
also pushed to give Haitians refugee status and reduce deportations.

In 2007, Meek's House career got a big boost when he landed a seat on the powerful Ways and Means
Committee. He sponsored a bill setting up a mortgage-fraud task force in the Federal Bureau of Investigation, which passed the House in September 2008. He also now has a seat on the leadership's Steering and

Policy Committee, which wields considerable power. The *Miami Herald* said in an October 2006 editorial that Meek "is tireless, creative and willing to work across party lines."

But his star was tarnished a bit later in 2007, when the *Herald* ran critical stories about Boston developer Dennis Stackhouse, who in 2003 had proposed building a $250 million biopharmaceutical center in Liberty City. Stackhouse hired Carrie Meek, then no longer in Congress, and paid her $40,000 to be a consultant. In 2004, Kendrick Meek secured a $72,750 House earmark for the project, and in 2005, he helped get a $1 million grant for Miami Dade College to train workers for the center; the following year, Meek requested $4 million in federal funds for the center, but he didn't get them. Stackhouse and his wife donated $5,000 to Meek's campaign fund. But Poinciana Biopharmaceutical Park was never built, and most of the companies Stackhouse had claimed were interested in locating at the center said they'd never heard of it. Meek responded to the series by donating Stackhouse's campaign contributions to charity and said he had never discussed the project with his mother. He also wrote Miami-Dade County Mayor Carlos Alvarez saying federal dollars should not be used for Poinciana Park.

Meek will try to move up to the Senate in 2010. When Democratic Sen. Mel Martinez announced in early 2009 that he would not seek a second term, Meek announced his candidacy for the seat. Certainly he starts off with a base in South Florida's black community and, given his stands on many issues, in South Florida generally. The African-American vote could be as much as 30% of the total in the primary. Meek hired Steve Hildebrand, a deputy campaign manager for Barack Obama's presidential campaign. Hildebrand specializes in Democratic strategies for winning over moderate and independent voters. This is Meek's first statewide campaign.

The next representative of the 17th District will undoubtedly be chosen in the Democratic primary. In the spring of 2009, three Haitian-Americans were being mentioned as possible candidates: activist Marleine Bastien, former state Rep. Phillip Brutus and state Rep. Yolly Roberson.

EIGHTEENTH DISTRICT

Ileana Ros-Lehtinen (R)

Elected Aug. 1989, 10th full term; b. July 15, 1952, Havana, Cuba; home, Miami; Miami-Dade Comm. Col., A.A. 1972, FL Intl. U., B.A. 1975, M.S. 1986, U. of Miami, Ed.D.. 2004; Episcopalian; married (Dexter); 4 children.

Elected Office: FL House of Reps., 1982–86; FL Senate, 1986–89.

Professional Career: Teacher, principal & owner, Eastern Academy Elem. Schl., 1978–85.

DC Office: 2470 RHOB, 20515, 202-225-3931; Fax: 202-225-5620; Web site: www.house.Gov/ros-lehtinen.

State Offices: Miami, 305-668-2285.

Committees: *Foreign Affairs* (RMM of 19 R).

Group Ratings

	ADA	ACLU	AFS	LCV	ITIC	NTU	COC	ACU	CFG	FRC
2008	65	55	57	69	71	34	78	32	29	76
2007	25	—	20	30	—	51	90	60	61	—

National Journal Ratings

	2007 LIB	—	2007 CONS	2008 LIB	—	2008 CONS
Economic	37%	—	62%	46%	—	54%
Social	50%	—	50%	46%	—	54%
Foreign	32%	—	64%	44%	—	56%
Composite	41%	—	60%	45%	—	55%

Key Votes of the 110th Congress

1. Increase minimum wage	Y	5. Share immigration data	N	9. Withdraw troops 8/08	N
2. Expand SCHIP	N	6. Foreign aid abortion ban	Y	10. No operations in Iran	N
3. Raise CAFE standards	Y	7. Ban gay bias in workplace	N	11. Free trade with Peru	Y
4. Bail out financial markets	Y	8. Repeal D.C. gun law	Y	12. Overhaul FISA	Y

Election Results

2008 general	Ileana Ros-Lehtinen (R)	140,617	(58%)	($2,838,976)
	Annette Taddeo (D)	102,372	(42%)	($1,177,003)
2008 primary	Ileana Ros-Lehtinen (R)	unopposed		

Prior Winning Percentages: 2006 (62%); 2004 (65%); 2002 (69%); 2000 (100%); 1998 (100%); 1996 (100%); 1994 (100%); 1992 (67%); 1990 (60%); 1989 (53%)

Population		Race/Ethnicity		Work	
Pop. 2007:	628,361	White:	27.6%	Private:	78.9%
Change since 2000:	Down 1.7%	Black:	5.4%	Government:	10.2%
Urban:	99.1%	Hispanic:	64.8%	Self-employed:	10.7%
Rural:	0.9%	Asian:	1.2%	Blue collar:	20.3%
Area size:	3,196 sq. mi.	Native Am.:	0.1%	White collar:	59.0%
Age		Hawaiian:	0.1%	Khaki collar:	0.1%
Median age:	41.6 yrs.	Two+ races:	0.6%	Other:	20.6%
More than 65 yrs:	18.2%	*Ancestry*		Median income:	$40,001
Less than 18 yrs:	18.2%	German:	4.3%	Median home value:	$392,100
Education		English:	3.8%	Poverty:	17.7%
H.S. grad:	76.1%	Irish:	3.8%	**Military Veterans**	
College grad:	30.8%			% of Pop:	4.9%
Grad degree:	12.4%				

A century ago, it was a tiny tropical village where the Miami River empties into Biscayne Bay. Today it is a world-class city. The surrealistic high-rises of Brickell Boulevard, the reminders of the 1920s in the pseudo-Spanish Villa Vizcaya, the winding lanes of Coral Gables, and the shimmer of orange and pink neon signs in the hot night air: This is Miami today. It lives on the cusp of two civilizations, North America and Latin America, with different traditions, styles, and sensibilities converging in

2008 Presidential Vote		
Obama (D)	129,145	(51%)
McCain (R)	123,570	(49%)
2004 Presidential Vote		
Bush (R)	127,746	(54%)
Kerry (D)	107,073	(46%)
Cook Partisan Voting Index:	R+3	

this one place, with the strength of both despite some friction. Miami is in many ways the commercial and economic capital of Latin America. From Miami, it is easy to fly directly to any part of Latin America where top business and banking services are available to a sophisticated Spanish-speaking (and usually also English-speaking) clientele. There is an underside to this, portrayed in the 1980s TV program *Miami Vice*. What is striking about Miami though is less its vices than its virtues—the vitality and creativity of its entrepreneurs and artists, the sophistication of people living and prospering in two (or more) cultures, and the successful Americanization of Cubans and other Latinos, with the retention of a cultural flavor that is linked to the past but headed fast into the future. In 2006, a movie version of *Miami Vice* depicted a more modern and glitzy city.

John Quincy Adams believed that Cuba would inevitably become a part of the United States. That never happened, but many of Cuba's people have become U.S. citizens, and the focus of Cuban America has been Miami, ever since the first refugees fled Fidel Castro in 1959. In the 1960s, the tone of Miami civic life was set by the large Jewish community and the liberal voice of the *Miami Herald*. But increasing numbers of Cuban immigrants, implacably opposed to the totalitarian Castro, and estranged by President Kennedy's betrayal of their cause at the Bay of Pigs, entered the voting stream as Republicans. Then, Cubans were a noisy minority in the Miami area. Now, they are a dominant voice in a Latino majority in Miami-Dade County (as Dade County was renamed in 1997). In 2007, the population of Miami-Dade was 61% Hispanic and 20% black, leaving Anglo whites a fading minority. The city has the highest percentage of immigrants of any large city in the world. Most of South Florida's Jewish community has moved north to Broward and Palm Beach counties. Little Havana around Calle Ocho (S.W. 8th Street in English) is now home to many Nicaraguans, Hondurans and Peruvians. Its annual spring carnival has featured the world's largest paella (serving 300,000 people) and the longest conga line (four miles). Latinos in Miami-Dade tend to go to school at Miami Dade College, the nation's largest community college, or Florida International University, then start businesses or join the professions in Miami's vibrant economy.

Politically, Miami-Dade County is sharply divided, with black neighborhoods north of downtown and the remaining heavily Jewish condominium developments in the northeast heavily Democratic, and the Latino districts in the west and south mostly Republican. Once the most Democratic county in Florida, it delivered relatively small margins for Democratic presidential candidates in the last five elections. Cuban-Americans remain Republican, but less monolithically than in the past. Younger Cubans are less focused on overthrowing the Castro regime, and many opposed the Bush administration's restrictions on travel and remittances to Cuba while still favoring the embargo.

The 18th Congressional District of Florida is one of Miami-Dade's three Hispanic-majority districts. It is 65% Hispanic and only 5% African-American. The district includes most of the city of Miami. It follows Calle Ocho west to heavily Hispanic West Miami and Westchester. It includes most of metro Miami's high-income residential areas: Coral Gables, with luxurious streets laid out in the 1920s and Spanish, French-country, and even Chinese-style houses; Cocoplum, a gated community with huge houses for rich Cuban-Americans and docks for their boats; the postmodern apartment buildings and upscale hotels along Brickell Boulevard; and Key Biscayne, with its high-rise apartments owned mostly by Latin American immigrants and their second-generation offspring. The district includes parts of Miami Beach: South

Beach, where old art-deco hotels are home to the glitziest celebrities of North America, Latin America and Europe. It also takes in the high-rises along Collins Avenue facing the ocean, and the Latino neighborhoods around 63rd Street. Miami Beach was the focus of the Florida land boom of 1925 and the bust of 1926, and in the past few years, boom has turned to bust again. Big apartment buildings on Brickell and in downtown Miami stand mostly empty, as speculators default on mortgages. Condo values have plummeted by as much as 40%.

South of Miami, the district is connected to the Florida Keys by U.S. 1. The highway ends in bustling, tropical Key West, the southernmost city in the continental United States. Key West was long accessible only by sea, and treasures from shipwrecks along the miles of coral reefs once provided its residents the highest per capita income in the nation. Key West has attracted famous residents—Ernest Hemingway, Tennessee Williams, Jimmy Buffett—and a large gay population, many living in quaint clapboard bungalows called "conch houses." The gay communities in Key West and Miami Beach are solidly Democratic, and they wield some clout. The 18th was drawn to be a Republican district and voted twice for George W. Bush. But in 2008, it delivered a narrow majority to Barack Obama.

The congresswoman from the 18th District is Ileana Ros-Lehtinen, the first Cuban-American and the first Hispanic woman elected to Congress. She was born in Havana, came to Miami at the age of 8 not knowing English, and graduated from Miami Dade Community College and Florida International University. She became a teacher, then was the owner of a private school. In 2004, she got her doctorate in education from the University of Miami. Her dissertation was on the views of House members regarding national testing for high school students. She was elected to the Florida House in 1982, at age 30, and to the state Senate in 1986. While there, she met her husband, Dexter Lehtinen, who also served in both houses of the Legislature and as U.S. attorney in Miami during the first Bush administration. In 1989, Ros-Lehtinen ran for the U.S. House in the special election after the death of Democrat Claude Pepper, one of the most enduring liberals in American politics and a staunch opponent of Castro. At that time, there were no Republicans and no Cuban-Americans representing Miami or Dade County. Democratic nominee Gerald Richman played on suspicions of Cubans and won the votes of 96% of blacks and 88% of non-Hispanic whites. Ninety percent of Hispanics, almost all of them Cuban, voted for Ros-Lehtinen. That was enough to give her a 53%-47% victory. In the years afterward, the district became more Hispanic, and she had no serious challenges until 2008. That year, the increasing number of non-Cuban Hispanics and the generational changes in attitude among Cuban-Americans provided the basis for a serious Democratic challenge.

Ros-Lehtinen has a mixed voting record: moderate on cultural policy and more conservative on economic and foreign issues. When Republicans took over the House in 1995, she refused to sign the Contract with America and was a harsh critic of Republican attempts to pass English-only legislation, to cut off welfare benefits for legal immigrants—she voted against the 1996 welfare bills—and to reduce the immigration quota for relatives of U.S. citizens. In February 2007, she protested the Bush administration's increase in the permanent-resident fee from $325 to $905, and in the 2007 debate over immigration, she pleaded with Republicans not to alienate the growing Hispanic voting bloc. She has been the chief sponsor of a bill to bar the transport of minors across state lines for abortions. The House passed it, but it died in the Senate. But she opposed the military's ban on openly gay troops and in 2008, she opposed the Florida constitutional amendment banning same-sex marriage.

In 2007, she became the ranking Republican on the House Foreign Affairs Committee. She strongly backed the 1996 Helms-Burton law that tightened sanctions against Castro, and she has opposed farm-state Republicans who have sought to relax the trade embargo on Cuba in effect since 1961. In February 2008, after Castro stepped down as head of state, she called for his indictment for shooting down two Brothers to the Rescue planes in 1996.

Ros-Lehtinen has been a booster of Israel, winning enactment of bills to impose additional economic sanctions on Libya and Iran. In September 2007, after Israel bombed an apparent nuclear installation in Syria, reportedly constructed with help from North Korea, Ros-Lehtinen criticized the Bush administration for its "veil of secrecy" on intelligence about the raid and its willingness to reach agreements with North Korea in light of the Syrian installation. In October, she held a tense meeting with Secretary of State Condoleezza Rice on the subject, and threatened that Congress would not appropriate money for fuel-oil shipments to North Korea if the administration refused to disclose "critical information." Ros-Lehtinen also supported the Israeli shelling of the Gaza strip in December 2008.

Ros-Lehtinen and the committee's Democratic chairman, Howard Berman of California, led the House in 2008 in approving a nuclear agreement with India, but with international oversight of civilian nuclear reactors. Ros-Lehtinen has been a steady supporter of the Iraq War.

As the 2008 election approached, national Democrats thought Ros-Lehtinen and the two other Miami-area Cuban-American Republicans, brothers Lincoln and Mario Diaz-Balart, might be vulnerable. Polls showed that President Bush was unpopular in Miami-Dade County. Younger Cuban-Americans seemed less obdurately opposed to the Castro regime than their elders and more supportive of easing travel restrictions and money transfer to Cuba. Non-Cuban Hispanics leaned Democratic, and Miami Beach and bayfront liberals were hostile to the Iraq war. Democrat Annette Taddeo, owner of the LanguageSpeak translation service, launched a challenge and financed it with $400,000 of her own money. Taddeo, who was born in Colombia to a Colombian mother, favored the embargo but wanted to ease travel restrictions and money transfers. By June 2008, Ros-Lehtinen was issuing press releases detailing her disagreements with the Bush administration. In the early fall, the Democratic Congressional Campaign Committee poured $1.4 million into television ads, and former presidential candidate Hillary Rodham Clinton and U.S. House Speaker Nancy Pelosi campaigned for Taddeo. In their one joint appearance Taddeo criticized Ros-Lehtinen for voting for the $700 billion bailout of the financial markets, but the incumbent noted that the bill had $100 million in tax breaks helpful to the district. Ros-Lehtinen spent $2.8 million, about the same as Taddeo's $1.1 million plus the money spent by the DCCC and other anti-Republican groups.

Ros-Lehtinen won 58%-42%, even though the district voted 51%-49% for Barack Obama. (The other two districts represented by Cuban-Americans voted 51%-49% and 50%-49% for John McCain.) "This could have been the perfect storm," she told the *Miami Herald*. "It had all the makings of me going down. If I can make it in this election, I can make it in any election." Obama even called with congratulations, but Ros-Lehtinen, thinking that one of the local radio stations was pulling a prank, hung up on him. She said, "I thought, 'Why would Obama want to call a little slug on the planet like me?'" When White House Chief of Staff Rahm Emanuel called to explain, she hung up on him too. Then Berman called and persuaded her that the calls were genuine. When she finally took his call, Obama laughed and said he didn't blame her for being skeptical.

NINETEENTH DISTRICT

Robert Wexler (D)

Elected 1996, 7th term; b. Jan. 2, 1961, Queens, NY; home, Boca Raton; U. of FL, B.A. 1982, George Washington U., J.D. 1985; Jewish; married (Laurie); 3 children.

Elected Office: FL Senate, 1990–96.

Professional Career: Practicing atty., 1985–96.

DC Office: 2241 RHOB, 20515, 202-225-3001; Fax: 202-225-5974; Web site: www.wexler.house.gov.

State Offices: Boca Raton, 561-988-6302; Margate, 954-972-6454.

Committees: *Foreign Affairs* (6th of 28 D): Europe (Chmn); International Organizations, Human Rights & Oversight; Middle East & South Asia. *Judiciary* (11th of 24 D): Courts & Competition Policy.

Group Ratings

	ADA	ACLU	AFS	LCV	ITIC	NTU	COC	ACU	CFG	FRC
2008	90	100	100	69	83	6	54	5	3	5
2007	95	—	100	85	—	2	55	0	6	—

National Journal Ratings

	2007 LIB	—	2007 CONS	2008 LIB	—	2008 CONS
Economic	82%	—	0%	67%	—	33%
Social	92%	—	0%	82%	—	0%
Foreign	75%	—	25%	65%	—	32%
Composite	87%	—	13%	75%	—	25%

Key Votes of the 110th Congress

1. Increase minimum wage	Y	5. Share immigration data	N	9. Withdraw troops 8/08	Y
2. Expand SCHIP	Y	6. Foreign aid abortion ban	N	10. No operations in Iran	Y
3. Raise CAFE standards	Y	7. Ban gay bias in workplace	Y	11. Free trade with Peru	N
4. Bail out financial markets	Y	8. Repeal D.C. gun law	N	12. Overhaul FISA	N

Election Results

2008 general	Robert Wexler (D)	202,465	(66%)	($2,372,548)
	Edward Lynch (R)	83,357	(27%)	($61,352)
	Ben Graber (NPA)	20,214	(7%)	($425,784)
2008 primary	Robert Wexler (D)	unopposed		

Prior Winning Percentages: 2006 (100%); 2004 (100%); 2002 (72%); 2000 (72%); 1998 (100%); 1996 (66%)

Population		Race/Ethnicity		Work	
Pop. 2007:	710,825	White:	68.7%	Private:	83.7%
Change since 2000:	Up 11.2%	Black:	9.9%	Government:	10.1%
Urban:	99.6%	Hispanic:	17.1%	Self-employed:	6.1%
Rural:	0.4%	Asian:	2.6%	Blue collar:	17.6%
Area size:	234 sq. mi.	Native Am.:	0.2%	White collar:	63.8%
		Hawaiian:	0.0%	Khaki collar:	0.0%
Age		Two+ races:	0.8%	Other:	18.5%
Median age:	45.5 yrs.	*Ancestry*		Median income:	$48,509
More than 65 yrs:	26.5%	Italian:	9.1%	Median home value:	$242,600
Less than 18 yrs:	19.5%	German:	8.1%	Poverty:	8.4%
Education		Irish:	7.5%	**Military Veterans**	
H.S. grad:	88.0%			% of Pop:	13.0%
College grad:	29.7%				
Grad degree:	10.7%				

When the first millionaires came to Palm Beach in the 1920s to winter in their new Addison Mizner pseudo-Mediterranean mansions, there was virtually nothing man-made between Palm Beach and Miami. In 1920, Dade, Broward, and Palm Beach counties boasted a mere 66,000 residents. In 2008, 5.4 million people lived in the five- to 20-mile strip between the Atlantic Ocean and the protected Everglades. The contrast between then and now is especially striking in Boca Raton, where Mizner built

2008 Presidential Vote
Obama (D) 223,144   (66%)
McCain (R).............................115,719   (34%)

2004 Presidential Vote
Kerry (D)................................210,695   (66%)
Bush (R) 107,348   (34%)

Cook Partisan Voting Index: D + 15

the Boca Raton Resort & Club in 1926. Its azure fountains and red-tiled roofs, its pseudo-Moorish columns and pink stucco walls bespeak a vision of a holiday Florida, a bit mannered and antique to today's eye, but still exuberant and benefiting from tasteful refurbishing. The coast from Boca Raton to Palm Beach is fully built up, and over the past 20 years, the area has become home to one of the nation's largest Jewish populations. There are the "condo commandos," the political activists among elderly Jewish retirees from New York and the Northeast, but also young families and middle-aged businessmen. However, since 2005, growth here has stalled, and the area has been hit by many foreclosures and a loss in construction jobs.

The 19th Congressional District of Florida includes Palm Beach and Broward counties. It does not touch the ocean at all, kept inland by the 22nd and 23rd districts. The boundaries of the 19th District are irregular, obviously drawn with an eye to political advantage. The Republicans who controlled the redistricting process were happy to pack heavily Democratic precincts into the 19th. It extends north from Fort Lauderdale to Okeechobee Boulevard in unglamorous but booming West Palm Beach. The district also takes in Margate, Mission Bay, most of Boca Raton, and parts of Boynton Beach and Delray Beach. The district's Jewish percentage is the one of the largest among the 435 congressional districts. A lot of people here are still voting for the party of Franklin D. Roosevelt, and the 19th is solidly Democratic, although neither John Kerry nor Barack Obama was able to duplicate the 73% of the vote that the ticket of Al Gore and Joe Lieberman received here in 2000.

The congressman from the 19th District is Robert Wexler, a Democrat first elected in 1996. Wexler is one of South Florida's two Queens-born members; the other is Democrat Debbie Wasserman Schultz. He grew up in Florida from age 10 and graduated from the University of Florida and the George Washington Law School. He went into law practice in Boca Raton. In 1987, he ran for county commissioner and lost. In 1990, at age 29, he was elected to the state Senate, beating incumbent Democrat Don Childers, who had supported George Wallace in 1972, a sign of the change in Florida's Democratic party and Palm Beach County politics. In the state Senate, Wexler backed chemical castration of repeat sex offenders at the same time that state Sen. Charlie Crist, now the governor, was backing forced work for convicts; they became known as "Castration Bob" and "Chain Gang Charlie." In 1996, when U.S. Rep. Harry Johnston retired, Wexler was one of three Democratic legislators who jumped into the race. In the primary, he led with 47% to 29% for state Sen. Peter Weinstein. The runoff was bitter, and Wexler won 65%-35%. Weinstein filed a $10 million defamation suit against him, citing an unflattering picture of himself in a Wexler television ad, but the suit was soon dropped. In this heavily Democratic district, Wexler has not faced serious Republican opposition.

With seats on the Foreign Affairs and Judiciary committees, Wexler has a liberal voting record in the House and a flair for gaining attention. In his first years in Congress, he made his greatest mark as an ardent defender of President Bill Clinton during his 1998 impeachment proceedings. Wexler was a fixture on cable news shows, where he brought energy and conviction to his defense of Clinton. He had another round in the cable news spotlight during the Florida presidential recount controversy in 2000. In the next election, in 2004, he demanded that Florida election officials provide paper printouts from touch-screen voting machines to assure a credible paper trail. After losing several court proceedings, he supported Crist's efforts as attorney general and then as governor to switch to machines that left a paper trail.

In 2005, Wexler again became a frequent face on national news shows, this time with a less welcome voice for his party as he introduced his own Social Security bill in response to President Bush's, which would have incorporated private investment in the program. Wexler's plan imposed a 6% tax on income above the existing $90,000 cap. Democratic leaders were unhappy with his defection and sought to isolate him, but Wexler said, "My allegiance to seniors is greater than my allegiance to the Democratic Party." He said he wanted to show that the financial problems of Social Security could be solved without a cut in benefits or privatization.

Wexler has been a strong supporter of Israel. In December 2002, he said that Israel was engaged in full-scale war and that it was time for the United States to force the ouster of terrorist leaders in the Mideast, including Palestinian leader Yassir Arafat and Iraqi leader Saddam Hussein. He voted for the Iraq war resolution, but changed his mind on Iraq and in 2005 called for immediate withdrawal of U.S. troops. In September 2007, he sponsored a resolution supporting Israel's bombing of an apparent nuclear facility in Syria.

In March 2007, Wexler endorsed Democratic presidential candidate Barack Obama, becoming the first Jewish official outside of Illinois to do so. He became Obama's Florida co-chairman, while neighboring Democrats Debbie Wasserman Shultz and Alcee Hastings endorsed Hillary Rodham Clinton. Wexler later said of Obama: "He wanted somebody who had longtime credentials in the Jewish community to be part of his inner circle on Middle East policy." Obama did not carry the 19th district in the primary, but Wexler remained steadfast in his support, representing his campaign at the May 31 Rules and Bylaws meeting, where Florida regained some but not all of its convention representation. Speaking at the Democratic National Convention in Denver in 2008, Wexler proclaimed Obama a supporter of Israel.

In his quest for media exposure, Wexler has sometimes risked embarrassment. In a now infamous July 2006 appearance on *The Colbert Report*, he allowed host Stephen Colbert to get him to say, "I enjoy cocaine because it's a fun thing to do." Opponents seized on this spoof, but to no political effect. In June 2008, Wexler published an autobiography, *Fire Breathing Liberal: How I Learned to Survive (and Thrive) in the Contact Sport of Congress*, which catapulted up the chart on Amazon. In July 2008, Fox News reported that Wexler did not live in his district. Wexler admitted that his family lived in Potomac, Md., a suburb outside Washington, and that his district residence was in fact his in-laws' Delray Beach apartment. He cited an 1879 Florida Supreme Court decision that members of Congress don't lose their residency while "attending to the duties of public office" in Washington. To be on the safe side, he rented an apartment in Boca Raton. There was some political fallout in the district, but not much in the way of a change in attitude. In November, Wexler was re-elected with 66% of the vote.

TWENTIETH DISTRICT

Debbie Wasserman Schultz (D)

Elected 2004, 3rd term; b. Sept. 27, 1966, Forest Hills, NY; home, Weston; U. of FL, B.A. 1988, M.A. 1990; Jewish; married (Steve); 3 children.

Elected Office: FL House, 1992–2000; Min. leader pro tem., 1999–2000; FL Sen., 2000–04.

Professional Career: State legislative aide, 1989–1992.

DC Office: 118 CHOB, 20515, 202-225-7931; Fax: 202-226-2052; Web site: www.house.Gov/schultz.

State Offices: Aventura, 305-936-5724; Pembroke Pines, 954-437-3936.

Committees: *Chief Deputy Whip. Appropriations* (34th of 37 D): Financial Services & General Government; Legislative Branch (Chmn). *Judiciary* (23rd of 24 D): Crime, Terrorism & Homeland Security.

Group Ratings

	ADA	ACLU	AFS	LCV	ITIC	NTU	COC	ACU	CFG	FRC
2008	100	100	100	92	100	5	59	0	0	0
2007	90	—	100	90	—	4	55	0	11	—

National Journal Ratings

	2007 LIB	—	2007 CONS	2008 LIB	—	2008 CONS
Economic	73%	—	27%	85%	—	0%
Social	85%	—	13%	82%	—	0%
Foreign	73%	—	27%	70%	—	25%
Composite	77%	—	23%	85%	—	15%

Key Votes of the 110th Congress

1. Increase minimum wage	Y	5. Share immigration data	N	9. Withdraw troops 8/08	Y
2. Expand SCHIP	Y	6. Foreign aid abortion ban	N	10. No operations in Iran	Y
3. Raise CAFE standards	Y	7. Ban gay bias in workplace	Y	11. Free trade with Peru	Y
4. Bail out financial markets	Y	8. Repeal D.C. gun law	N	12. Overhaul FISA	N

Election Results

2008 general	Debbie Wasserman Schultz (D)........................202,832	(77%)	($1,475,441)
	Margaret Hostetter (NPA)..................................58,958	(23%)	($8,621)
2008 primary	Debbie Wasserman Schultz (D)................... unopposed		

Prior Winning Percentages: 2006 (100%); 2004 (70%)

Population		Race/Ethnicity		Work	
Pop. 2007:	681,265	White:	58.6%	Private:	81.8%
Change since 2000:	Up 6.6%	Black:	9.3%	Government:	11.3%
Urban:	99.7%	Hispanic:	27.3%	Self-employed:	6.5%
Rural:	0.3%	Asian:	2.8%	Blue collar:	15.0%
Area size:	218 sq. mi.	Native Am.:	0.2%	White collar:	69.3%
		Hawaiian:	0.1%	Khaki collar:	0.1%
Age		Two+ races:	1.4%	Other:	15.6%
Median age:	40.7 yrs.	*Ancestry*		Median income:	$54,674
More than 65 yrs:	15.6%	Italian:	8.4%	Median home value:	$309,400
Less than 18 yrs:	22.2%	German:	7.5%	Poverty:	8.8%
Education		Irish:	7.2%	**Military Veterans**	
H.S. grad:	89.4%			% of Pop:	8.9%
College grad:	35.3%				
Grad degree:	13.7%				

Back when Connie Francis made it famous in the 1960 spring-break movie *Where the Boys Are*, Fort Lauderdale was just a small town with a strip of motels along the beach and some nice houses fronting its canals. Now it's the center of a sprawling metropolitan area with resort hotels on the beach but a much larger workaday population inland. It is a center of business and commerce and a major port. In 1950, Fort Lauderdale and Broward County had 183,000 people; in 2008, they had 1.76 million. From

2008 Presidential Vote

Obama (D)	187,054	(63%)
McCain (R)	106,455	(36%)

2004 Presidential Vote

Kerry (D)	183,510	(64%)
Bush (R)	104,039	(36%)

Cook Partisan Voting Index: D + 13

the strip of beach along the Atlantic Ocean, west to the Sawgrass Expressway and the Everglades Wildlife Management Area, the land has filled up with subdivisions, shopping centers, office complexes, warehouses, and trucking terminals. As it has grown, the ethnic composition of Broward County has changed. In the 1950s, it was understood that Jews couldn't buy houses or rent hotel rooms this far north of Miami. But from the 1960s through the 1990s, as Cubans and other Latinos moved into the Miami-Dade County area, many Jews moved north, and Broward County became one of the most heavily Jewish parts of the United States. Nearer the coast, especially in the huge high-rises of Hollywood and Hallandale, most of Broward's Jews were retirees from New York and other Northeastern cities. But inland, in towns like booming Davie, Plantation, and Sunrise, many young Jewish parents raised families in communities that prided themselves on fine schools and high property values.

Now Broward County seems to be changing again. Jewish migration over the past 15 years has gone farther north, to Palm Beach County. Broward's population peaked in 2006, then for the first time in history, it fell, as whites moved out of the county and immigrants moved in. Fort Lauderdale and next-door Wilton Manors have become the home of choice for many gay people, and metro Fort Lauderdale now has a higher percentage of same-sex couples than any other metropolitan area except San Francisco/Oakland and Seattle.

The 20th Congressional District of Florida includes much of southeastern Broward County and the northern Biscayne Bay shoreline in Miami-Dade County. Precinct by precinct, its computer-generated borders are drawn to include heavily Democratic areas. It includes much of Fort Lauderdale, Hollywood and Dania Beach on the coast. But its biggest blocks of territory are inland. In Miami-Dade, it includes the shores of Biscayne Bay, both on the Miami and Miami Beach side, with expensive homes and huge high-rises. This is a strongly Democratic district, though in recent years not quite as strongly as in 2000, when it cast 69% of its vote for Al Gore and Joe Lieberman.

The congresswoman from the 20th District is Debbie Wasserman Schultz, a Democrat elected in 2004. She accomplished the unusual feat of winning her seat in Congress without a primary opponent or a significant general-election foe. Like many of her constituents, she was born in Queens. She grew up on Long Island, where she ran for student council every year and always lost. She got bachelor's and master's degree from the University of Florida. In her last year at school, she sent out 180 resumes to legislators in Florida and New York and got five interviews. Florida State Rep. Peter Deutsch, a Democrat and former New Yorker from Broward County, gave her a summer job, and then appointed her his legislative aide. In 1992, he ran for the 20th District House seat and urged Wasserman Shultz to run for his seat in the Legislature. She did, knocking on doors for six months and finishing far ahead of four opponents in the Democratic primary.

At age 26, she became the state's youngest woman ever elected to the state House. Many of her constituents treated her like a granddaughter. She served eight years in the state House, including two years as minority leader, followed by four years in the state Senate. She calls herself "a pragmatic liberal," and she sponsored a controversial law to require an equal number of men and women on state boards and a bill that failed to pass requiring that dry cleaners and some other businesses charge the same prices for women as for men.

In 2004, when Deutsch ran for the Democratic nomination for Bob Graham's open Senate seat, Wasserman Schultz moved to again replace Deutsch, this time in Congress. She began laying the groundwork early. More than a year before the primary, she had raised $115,000. By February 2004, she had lined up endorsements from Minority Leader Nancy Pelosi and six of Florida's seven House Democrats. Wasserman Schultz ultimately collected more than $1 million for what turned out to be an uncompetitive race, since no one else filed to run in the decisive Democratic primary. In June 2004, she pledged $100,000 to the Democratic Congressional Campaign Committee, a substantial contribution from a nonincumbent. Wasserman Schultz called for repeal of the Bush tax cuts, a reduction in the budget deficit, greater use of diplomacy overseas, improved prescription-drug coverage, gay civil rights, and abortion rights. Against a Republican who attacked the "homosexual agenda" in the public schools, she won 70%-30%.

In the House, she has a mostly liberal voting record, though it's more centrist on foreign policy. Within days of arriving in Congress, she was making an impact. In the debate then raging over whether to intervene to retain the feeding tube for severely brain-damaged Terri Schiavo of Florida, Wassermann Schultz argued that Congress would set a dangerous precedent if it attempted to circumvent the courts. After an insurance company denied her additional life-insurance coverage because she said she might travel to Israel, the House passed her bill barring such denial of coverage, though it allowed increased premiums. She also sponsored a bill, passed by the House in 2007, toughening the Internet Crimes Against Children program by adding hundreds of federal agents at a cost of $1 billion over eight years.

In 2006, after working hard for the DCCC, Wasserman Schultz was appointed co-chairman of its "Red to Blue" effort. Working closely with DCCC chairman Rahm Emanuel, now White House chief of staff, she became a party spokesman and a mentor to Democratic recruits. She helped Ron Klein, a longtime colleague in the state Legislature, upset longtime Republican incumbent Rep. Clay Shaw in the neighboring 22nd District.

When Democrats won House control, she was a prime beneficiary. Majority Whip James Clyburn tapped her as a chief deputy whip. She got a seat on the Appropriations Committee, which controls the government purse strings, and immediately became a "cardinal" as chairman of the Legislative Branch Subcommittee. Working with ranking Republican Zack Wamp of Tennessee, she took charge of the Capitol Visitors Center project, which was plagued by cost overruns, and extracted commitments on costs and completion dates. She pushed successfully for a unionization vote at the Government Accountability Office. She founded the Cuban Democracy Caucus and argued that Cubans, like Jews, extolled the democratic process against the efforts of extremists and totalitarians. In June 2007, she lobbied House members against New York Rep. Jose Serrano's proposal to repeal the ban on travel to Cuba. He angrily dropped the proposal. She also joined the Lesbian, Gay, Bisexual, and Transgender Equality Caucus.

In the 2008 election season, Wasserman Schultz continued working with the DCCC incumbent-retention program. She was criticized by liberal bloggers in March 2007 when she refused to campaign against the three Cuban-American Republican members from South Florida who were facing unusually strong Democratic challenges: Ros-Lehtinen and brothers Lincoln and Mario Diaz-Balart. (All three incumbents were re-elected.) She was Hillary Rodham Clinton's co-chair in Florida and nationally. She protested the decision depriving Florida of its delegation at the national convention and tried all spring to have it reversed.

In late 2008, Wasserman Shultz was interested in becoming vice chairman of the Democratic Caucus if the incumbent, California's Xavier Becerra, a favorite of U.S. House Speaker Nancy Pelosi, was appointed Special Trade Representative, and she was mentioned as a candidate to succeed Maryland's Chris Van Hollen as DCCC chairman. But Becerra did not accept the job, and Van Hollen was reappointed. Wasserman Shultz, who had supported Maryland Rep. Steny Hoyer over Pelosi candidate John Murtha of Pennsylvania for majority leader in 2006, was named vice chair of the DCCC's incumbent-retention program, a challenging assignment now that Democrats have so many more incumbents to protect. She showed no interest in running for the Senate in 2010 after Democratic Sen. Mel Martinez announced his retirement. When asked about her relatively quick success in the House, Wasserman Schultz says she advises other new members to work hard rather than always anticipating the next promotion, because hard work gets rewarded. Her rise seemed all the more impressive when she announced in March 2009 that for much of the previous year she had been battling breast cancer. Although her tumor was in early stages, which would typically require only surgery and radiation, she said that she elected to have a double mastectomy after learning that as an Ashkenazi Jew, she has a greater predisposition to recurrence. The mother of three school-aged children, Wasserman Schultz was diagnosed just after turning 40. She talked about her experience on ABC's *Good Morning America* as a way of educating young women about early diagnosis.

TWENTY-FIRST DISTRICT
Lincoln Diaz-Balart (R)

Elected 1992, 9th term; b. Aug. 13, 1954, Havana, Cuba; home, Miami; New Col. of FL, B.S. 1977, Case Western Reserve U., J.D. 1979; Catholic; married (Cristina); 2 children.

Elected Office: FL House of Reps., 1986–89; FL Senate 1989–92.

Professional Career: Practicing atty., 1979–92; Asst. FL atty., 1983–84.

DC Office: 2244 RHOB, 20515, 202-225-4211; Fax: 202-225-8576; Web site: diaz-balart.house.gov.

State Offices: Miami, 305-470-8555.

Committees: *Rules* (2nd of 4 R): Legislative & Budget Process (RMM).

Group Ratings
	ADA	ACLU	AFS	LCV	ITIC	NTU	COC	ACU	CFG	FRC
2008	55	55	57	31	86	49	82	52	55	82
2007	25	—	18	20	—	56	89	60	61	—

National Journal Ratings
	2007 LIB —	2007 CONS	2008 LIB —	2008 CONS
Economic	35% —	65%	44% —	55%
Social	48% —	52%	43% —	57%
Foreign	32% —	64%	38% —	62%
Composite	39% —	61%	42% —	58%

Key Votes of the 110th Congress
1. Increase minimum wage	Y	5. Share immigration data	N	9. Withdraw troops 8/08	N
2. Expand SCHIP	N	6. Foreign aid abortion ban	Y	10. No operations in Iran	N
3. Raise CAFE standards	N	7. Ban gay bias in workplace	Y	11. Free trade with Peru	Y
4. Bail out financial markets	N	8. Repeal D.C. gun law	Y	12. Overhaul FISA	Y

Election Results
2008 general	Lincoln Diaz-Balart (R)	137,226	(58%)	($3,390,478)
	Raul Martinez (D)	99,776	(42%)	($1,881,108)
2008 primary	Lincoln Diaz-Balart (R)	unopposed		

Prior Winning Percentages: 2006 (59%); 2004 (73%); 2002 (100%); 2000 (100%); 1998 (75%); 1996 (100%); 1994 (100%); 1992 (100%)

Population		Race/Ethnicity		Work	
Pop. 2007:	681,719	White:	16.2%	Private:	81.9%
Change since 2000:	Up 6.6%	Black:	7.5%	Government:	11.4%
Urban:	99.9%	Hispanic:	73.1%	Self-employed:	6.5%
Rural:	0.1%	Asian:	2.3%	Blue collar:	21.7%
Area size:	140 sq. mi.	Native Am.:	0.1%	White collar:	62.3%
		Hawaiian:	0.0%	Khaki collar:	0.2%
Age		Two+ races:	0.6%	Other:	15.8%
Median age:	39.6 yrs.			Median income:	$46,660
More than 65 yrs:	15.1%	**Ancestry**		Median home value:	$316,600
Less than 18 yrs:	23.1%	West Indian:	3.3%	Poverty:	12.8%
Education		Italian:	2.8%		
H.S. grad:	77.6%	USA:	2.6%	**Military Veterans**	
College grad:	27.0%			% of Pop:	3.4%
Grad degree:	9.2%				

Miami's Cuban-American community has been one of America's most dynamic immigrant groups over the past 40 years, growing from 50,000 in 1960, the year after Fidel Castro took over Cuba, to well over 1 million today. Over time, the Cuban-American neighborhoods centered along S.W. 8th Street—Calle Ocho—expanded west to the Florida Turnpike Extension in Weston and Sweetwater, southwest to Kendall and northwest to Hialeah. Starting

2008 Presidential Vote		
McCain (R)............................127,084	(51%)
Obama (D) 121,805	(49%)
2004 Presidential Vote		
Bush (R)................................127,326	(57%)
Kerry (D)................................96,232	(43%)
Cook Partisan Voting Index:	R + 5	

in the 1980s, there was an influx of other Latinos, from Nicaragua, El Salvador, Venezuela, and Colombia. In the process, new communities were built and old ones transformed. Built on swampland, Sweetwater is now probably more Cuban than the old Little Havana on Calle Ocho. Kendall, where the last strawberry field was torn up 30 years ago, is the site of the upscale Dadeland Mall, where Spanish is heard more often than English. Hialeah, famous for its racetrack first opened in 1925, was transformed, as one writer put it, "from redneck to Latino" in just a few years. The racetrack closed in 2001, and Hialeah, always downscale and with a colorful municipal politics, is now 94% Hispanic, the highest percentage in the Miami area.

The 21st Congressional District of Florida is an irregular rectangle about 20 miles long and two to six miles wide in Miami-Dade County and southern Broward County. In Miami-Dade, it includes Kendall, Cutler, Westwood Lakes and Sweetwater. It includes raffish Hialeah and nearby Miami Lakes, a planned town developed in the 1960s by future Democratic Sen. Bob Graham and his brothers. In Broward County, the district includes much of Miramar and Pembroke Pines. It includes Florida International University and Miami International Airport, which ranks third in the nation for international travel and first for overseas freight. The population of the district is 73% Hispanic, the highest of any Florida district, and just under 44% of residents are of Cuban origin. Cuban voters continue to be heavily Republican. Other Latino voters are less so, but by no means overwhelmingly Democratic. Many here do not vote at all: The 21st has the lowest number of registered voters of any Florida district. With relatively few Hispanics, the Broward County portion of the district tends to vote Democratic. Overall, this is a Republican district, but one that sometimes votes for Democrats who support the Cuban community's issues. Some Cuban-Americans—typically, the more recent arrivals—were unhappy with the Bush administration's tightened restrictions on travel and remittances to Cuba, but others supported any steps that kept American dollars from Castro. George W. Bush carried the district twice, but Barack Obama came close to winning it in 2008. He got 48.8% of the vote to John McCains 50.9%.

The congressman from the 21st District is Lincoln Diaz-Balart, a Republican first elected when the district was created in 1992. Diaz-Balart was born in Cuba, where his grandfather, father and uncle served in the Cuban Congress. The family fled Cuba in 1959, shortly after Castro took over and after their house was looted and burned while they were vacationing in Paris. His aunt was briefly the wife of Fidel Castro and the mother of Castro's only recognized child. Diaz-Balart's education included stops in Spain and England. He started his career as a poverty lawyer and a Democrat, but switched parties. He was elected to the state House in 1986, two years before his younger brother, Mario, now the representative from the 25th District, was elected to the same chamber. The Diaz-Balarts are sometimes called the "Cuban Kennedys." Another brother is a television news anchorman for Telemundo and a fourth is an investment banker. In 1989, Jorge Mas Canosa's Cuban American National Foundation persuaded Diaz-Balart not to run against Ileana Ros-Lehtinen in the special election to replace Democratic Rep. Claude Pepper. He instead won her state Senate seat. In 1992, the organization endorsed him in the 21st. State Sen. Javier Souto, also Cuban-born, opposed him in the primary, charging that he was backed by wealthy contributors and was not a lifelong Republican. Diaz-Balart won 69%-31%.

Diaz-Balart has a voting record that is centrist on social issues and occasionally liberal on economics. He was one of three Republican incumbents who refused to sign the Contract with America when Republicans took over the House in 1995, and he voted against the GOP welfare bills because of their provisions denying benefits to legal immigrants. Many older Cubans who have not become U.S. citizens because they hope to return someday to Cuba are dependent on Supplemental Security Income and other aid. He persevered, and his bill to restore SSI benefits to legal immigrants passed. In 2006, he objected to a deal opening areas off the Florida coast to oil drilling, citing the need to protect "environmental treasures."

In 2007, he sponsored a bill to allow two Colombian college students whose parents had brought them illegally into the country at ages 2 and 3 to remain in the United States, and he sought to use their example to promote the DREAM Act, the bill to allow in-state tuition for children of illegal immigrants who graduate from high school and get good grades in college. When Democrats advanced a bill in 2008 to allow housing authorities to buy foreclosed properties and sell them to low-income families, he was one of 11 Republicans to support it.

Diaz-Balart is the second-ranking Republican on the Rules Committee, where he seems destined to play second fiddle to California's David Dreier. Perhaps because of Diaz-Balart's independence on issues, Republican leaders have kept appointing Dreier to the post.

Diaz-Balart hopes that he will return someday to a freed Cuba, where Castro has referred to the Diaz-Balarts as "his most repulsive enemies" and "miserable Judases." Diaz-Balart has strongly favored sanctions against Cuba, and when the Clinton administration announced in 1995 that it would no longer give automatic safe haven to Cuban refugees, Diaz-Balart was arrested while protesting in front of the White House. The next year, he wrote the section of the Helms-Burton Act codifying the embargo against Cuba. During the Elian Gonzalez custody controversy in 2000, Diaz-Balart closely advised the Miami family trying to keep the boy from returning to his father in Cuba and gave the then six-year-old a black Labrador puppy. Diaz-Balart was a prominent spokesman for the local community, which also wanted to keep the boy in the United States, though he was ultimately returned to Cuba. When farm-state Republicans, working with Democrats, got the House to pass bills relaxing the trade embargo on Cuba, Diaz-Balart urged the Bush administration to continue to oppose trade openings. When Congress finally agreed to some trade, he made sure that payments for goods had to be received in advance. He created the House's Cuba Democracy Group as a counterpoint to the trade-opening Cuba Working Group. In 2006, he strongly objected when the Cuban team was permitted to play in the World Baseball Classic, some of which was played in Florida, and he unsuccessfully urged its players to "escape totalitarianism." In 2008, Diaz-Balart objected to allowing a Little League team from Vermont and New Hampshire to travel to a baseball tournament in Cuba.

From 1994 to 2004, Diaz-Balart had little trouble winning re-election and often had no opposition. In 2006, Democrat Frank Gonzalez called the Cuba embargo an "act of war" and supported legalization of drugs. Diaz-Balart won by 59%-41%, and Gonzalez got 57% in the Broward County portion of the district. The outcome was one of the factors that encouraged national Democrats to target the three Cuban-American Republicans from the Miami area in 2008. Another was the growing awareness that younger Cuban-Americans are less obdurately opposed to the Castro regime. Moreover, an increasing number of Latino voters are not of Cuban origin and tend to favor Democrats. In 2008, the Democratic Congressional Campaign Committee found a candidate to run against Diaz-Balart: Raul Martinez, mayor from 1981 to 2005 of heavily Cuban Hialeah, which Diaz-Balart carried 5-to-1 in 2006.

Diaz-Balart began with some advantages. He had made friends by steering federal money to community projects and firms, and he had $900,000 in his campaign treasury. But Martinez campaigned aggressively. "I'm not running for president of Cuba," he said. "Cuban-Americans finally see themselves as part of the wider U.S.A., and they care about other issues." He favored the embargo on Cuba, but called for loosening restrictions on travel and remittances. He aimed much of his campaign at non-Cubans in Broward, and he pressed for union endorsements, though Transport Workers Local 291 spurned the AFL-CIO and came out for Diaz-Balart again. An August poll showed Martinez ahead. National Democrats spent more than $500,000 trying to help him win.

National Republicans retaliated, spending $1.6 million in the district, more than in any other. In August, Diaz-Balart began running negative ads. One referred to Martinez's 1991 conviction on federal racketeering and extortion charges without mentioning that the decision had been reversed on appeal. Another showed the 275-pound Martinez repeatedly slugging a thin 21-year-old butcher in 1999. A third showed a former Hialeah police captain denouncing Martinez as "the most corrupt politician you will ever see in your life." In response, Democrats ran ads referring to "crooks, lobbyists and dirty deals" associated with Diaz-Balart, and Democrats spotlighted claims by an indicted Puerto Rico politician that he had brought a suitcase full of cash to Diaz-Balart in 2006.

Diaz-Balart won 58%-42%, just 1% behind his showing in 2006. In Broward County, he ran behind Martinez by only 16 votes. He carried every precinct but one in Hialeah. He ran well ahead of GOP presidential candidate John McCain, whom he had endorsed early.

TWENTY-SECOND DISTRICT

Ron Klein (D)

Elected 2006, 2nd term; b. July 10, 1957, Cleveland, OH; home, Boca Raton; OH St. U., B.A. 1979, Case Western Reserve U., J.D. 1982; Jewish; married (Dori Dragin); 2 children.

Elected Office: FL House of Reps., 1992–96; FL Senate, 1996–2006; FL Senate min. ldr., 2002–04.

Professional Career: Practicing atty., lobbyist, 1982–2006.

DC Office: 313 CHOB, 20515, 202-225-3026; Fax: 202-225-8398; Web site: klein.house.gov.

State Offices: Boca Raton, 561-544-6910; Ft. Lauderdale, 954-522-4579.

Committees: *Financial Services* (26th of 42 D): Capital Markets, Insurance & Government Sponsored Enterprises; Financial Institutions & Consumer Credit; Oversight & Investigations. *Foreign Affairs* (28th of 28 D): Middle East & South Asia; Terrorism, Nonproliferation & Trade; Western Hemisphere.

Group Ratings

	ADA	ACLU	AFS	LCV	ITIC	NTU	COC	ACU	CFG	FRC
2008	95	90	100	92	100	8	67	4	3	5
2007	95	—	91	75	—	6	67	0	11	—

National Journal Ratings

	2007 LIB	—	2007 CONS		2008 LIB	—	2008 CONS
Economic	62%	—	38%		57%	—	41%
Social	61%	—	39%		59%	—	38%
Foreign	57%	—	43%		59%	—	37%
Composite	60%	—	40%		60%	—	40%

Key Votes of the 110th Congress

1. Increase minimum wage	Y	5. Share immigration data	Y	9. Withdraw troops 8/08	Y
2. Expand SCHIP	Y	6. Foreign aid abortion ban	N	10. No operations in Iran	N
3. Raise CAFE standards	Y	7. Ban gay bias in workplace	Y	11. Free trade with Peru	Y
4. Bail out financial markets	Y	8. Repeal D.C. gun law	N	12. Overhaul FISA	Y

Election Results

2008 general	Ron Klein (D)	169,041	(55%)	($2,372,293)
	Allen West (R)	140,104	(45%)	($555,543)
2008 primary	Ron Klein (D)	20,507	(85%)	
	Paul Renneisen (D)	3,603	(15%)	

Prior Winning Percentages: 2006 (51%)

Population		Race/Ethnicity		Work	
Pop. 2007:	676,914	White:	75.6%	Private:	83.0%
Change since 2000:	Up 5.9%	Black:	5.3%	Government:	9.5%
Urban:	99.2%	Hispanic:	15.3%	Self-employed:	7.3%
Rural:	0.8%	Asian:	2.2%	Blue collar:	15.6%
Area size:	500 sq. mi.	Native Am.:	0.3%	White collar:	68.0%
Age		Hawaiian:	0.1%	Khaki collar:	0.1%
Median age:	44.7 yrs.	Two+ races:	0.9%	Other:	16.4%
More than 65 yrs:	19.9%	*Ancestry*		Median income:	$61,432
Less than 18 yrs:	19.0%	Irish:	11.8%	Median home value:	$382,300
Education		German:	11.4%	Poverty:	7.7%
H.S. grad:	90.1%	Italian:	10.2%	**Military Veterans**	
College grad:	36.5%			% of Pop:	12.0%
Grad degree:	13.1%				

The barrier islands of Florida's Gold Coast have been developed in spasms of land-speculation frenzy, not just as vacation places and retirement homes but as embodiments of dreams and fantasies. Consider Palm Beach, the great beach resort of the 1920s, where rich WASPs would abandon their snow-covered Tudor or Georgian mansions to live in Addison Mizner's pseudo-Mediterranean confections. Or Boca Raton, where Mizner built the Boca Raton Hotel in 1926. Or Fort Lauderdale, a tiny

2008 Presidential Vote

Obama (D)	175,895	(52%)
McCain (R)	162,076	(48%)

2004 Presidential Vote

Kerry (D)	169,161	(53%)
Bush (R)	153,265	(48%)

Cook Partisan Voting Index: D + 1

town when Clyde Beatty brought his circus there for the winter in the 1930s (locals complained about the roaring lions). Back in the 1950s, many of these beachfront communities were "restricted," which meant no Jews were allowed. Starting in the 1970s, high-rise condominiums sprouted up and down the Atlantic coast of Broward and Palm Beach counties. Today, they are home to many Jewish retirees from New York and the Northeast generally. But there are also working-age people here, and plans to attract more. Florida and Palm Beach County have subsidized the Scripps Research Institute's new center in Jupiter, in hopes of attracting biotechnology businesses.

In recent years, the old town centers have been revived. Palm Beach remains, as it has been since the 1920s, the precinct of the very rich. Conservative talk-show host Rush Limbaugh has his South Florida headquarters there, and it was the favorite playground of swindler Bernard Madoff—and many of his now unhappy clients. Boca Raton now sports the stylish Mizner Park, a collection of upscale stores. Downtown Fort Lauderdale, separated from the beach by miles of canals, is the site of new condominiums, the Museum of Art Fort Lauderdale, the Museum of Discovery and Space, the Broward Center for the Performing Arts, and the International Swimming Hall of Fame.

The 22nd Congressional District of Florida covers most of the Atlantic oceanfront in Palm Beach and Broward counties, from Jupiter in Palm Beach County to Fort Lauderdale in Broward County. It is rarely more than a few miles wide, and in some places it is not much wider than the barrier islands separated from the mainland by the Indian River and Lake Worth. But it also has jagged salients that extend several miles inland. The district, a testament to the advances made in redistricting software, was drawn by Republicans in an attempt to provide a safe seat for Republican Rep. Clay Shaw after he barely won re-election in 2000. They removed the Miami-Dade County portion of the district and heavily Democratic Hollywood in Broward County, and they brought in Republican precincts in Plantation and Coral Springs. The resulting district is affluent and elderly, with a large Jewish population that's politically very active in condominium groups. But the intentions of the mapmakers, here as elsewhere, were defeated by changing demographics and changing attitudes. The 22nd District has given Democratic nominees at least 52% of the vote in the last three presidential elections, and in 2006 it ousted Shaw.

The congressman for 22nd District is Ron Klein, a Democrat first elected in 2006. Klein was born in Cleveland, where his father owned a five-and-dime store and his mother was a teacher. He interned in the Ohio House and for Ohio Democratic Rep. Tom Luken. He graduated from Ohio State University and Case Western Reserve Law School, then entered private practice in Ohio. In 1985, he moved to Boca Raton, where he became a name partner at a law firm that also did lobbying. He was elected to the state House in 1992, seven years after arriving in Florida, and to the state Senate in 1996, where he went on to become minority leader. While in the Legislature, Klein worked to pass bills requiring mandatory education about the Holocaust in public schools, trade initiatives that benefited Florida and extended jail time for sexual predators. Klein was a Democratic partisan, but also became a dealmaker in the Republican-controlled state Senate. Term limits barred him from seeking another term in 2006, and he entered the race against Shaw in March 2005, early enough to discourage primary opposition and to raise the large sums needed to challenge a well-funded incumbent.

Shaw, first elected in 1980, was the second-ranking Republican on the House Ways and Means Committee. But in South Florida, he was in some political peril. After he won re-election in 2000 by just 599 votes, Republican-sponsored redistricting changes enabled him to win by fair margins in 2002 and 2004 despite vigorous Democratic challenges. Shaw, who was recovering from lung-cancer surgery in January 2006, touted his seniority, which made him next in line for Ways and Means chairman, even though most insiders considered Republican Rep. Jim McCrery of Louisiana the front-runner. Klein campaigned as a "moderate, pro-business Democrat," but he had liberal stances on social issues, supporting abortion rights and embryonic-stem-cell research and opposing a ban on same-sex marriage. Each courted Jewish voters and pledged their support for Israel. Each offered fixes to bring down hurricane insurance premiums for homeowners and businesses. Shaw proposed a federal fund to back up insurance companies, while Klein proposed a federal income-tax deduction for homeowners who weatherproof their properties.

Shaw slammed Klein as a well-heeled lobbyist with connections to special interests. Klein insisted he had never lobbied state colleagues. And his prodigious fundraising allowed him to counter with ads that charged Shaw had let down the district's large senior population by supporting a Medicare prescription-drug bill that prevented the government from negotiating lower drug prices. Shaw touted his plan to fund private investment accounts in the Social Security program, an idea Klein called fiscally irresponsible. Klein attacked Shaw for supporting the Iraq War and many of President Bush's policies. The race attracted national attention and drew top party leaders. President Bush helped Shaw raise $800,000 during a campaign swing in the district, and First Lady Laura Bush and Vice President Dick Cheney made appearances for him. It was one of the most expensive House contests in 2006. Shaw spent $5.2 million to Klein's $4.2 million. Klein won 51%-47%.

On the Financial Services Committee, Democratic Chairman Barney Frank appointed Klein to lead the panel's efforts on property-insurance legislation. And Klein sponsored a bill to set up a government-sponsored enterprise that would issue low-interest loans directly to states to help them pay off claims after a catastrophe. His bill passed by the House 258-155 in November 2007 but was opposed by the Bush administration. Klein weighed in on other issues of importance to the Florida coast. He sponsored a bill to launch two new weather satellites, at a cost of $2.8 billion, to provide information to the National Hurricane Center in Miami. He voted for the Peru Free Trade Agreement in November 2007.

Klein started fundraising almost immediately after taking office, bringing in nearly $1.3 million in the first half of 2007, the second highest total among Democratic freshmen. Despite a Republican registration advantage in the district, George W. Bush had lost there twice, and the district did not seem any better disposed toward Republicans in 2008. Several local Republican officeholders who would have been serious challengers declined, among them Boca Raton Mayor Steven Abrams. The only Republican candidate was former Army Lieutenant Col. Allen West, who had retired after a 2003 incident in which he fired a gun near the head of an Iraqi detainee in an effort to make him reveal information about plans to attack U.S. troops. West's explanation was that he had "sacrificed" his military career "for the lives of my men." West received little support from the national party but still managed to raise $584,000. Klein raised $4 million and spent just $2.3 million of it to win 55%-45%, a solid margin, but one that suggests the presence of a fairly large Republican minority in the district.

After Republican Sen. Mel Martinez announced in early 2009 that he would not seek re-election in 2010, Klein told the *South Florida Sun Sentinel* that he was taking a look at a possible run and "waiting to just understand what the race is shaping up to be, who's running and just analyzing the logistics of the race." In June 2009, Klein endorsed U.S. Rep. Kendrick Meek.

TWENTY-THIRD DISTRICT

Alcee Hastings (D)

Elected 1992, 9th term; b. Sept. 5, 1936, Altamonte Springs; home, Miramar; Fisk U., B.A. 1958, Howard U., 1958–60, FL A&M, J.D. 1963; Methodist; single; 3 children.

Elected Office: Broward Cnty. Circuit Court judge, 1977–79.

Professional Career: Practicing atty., 1964–77; Federal judge, U.S. District Court, 1979–89.

DC Office: 2353 RHOB, 20515, 202-225-1313; Fax: 202-225-1171; Web site: www.alceehastings.house.gov.

State Offices: Ft. Lauderdale, 954-733-2800; Mangoria Park, 561-881-9618.

Committees: *Rules* (3rd of 9 D): Legislative & Budget Process (Chmn).

Group Ratings

	ADA	ACLU	AFS	LCV	ITIC	NTU	COC	ACU	CFG	FRC
2008	95	91	100	92	83	5	65	0	0	5
2007	90	—	100	90	—	1	50	0	7	—

National Journal Ratings

	2007 LIB — 2007 CONS		2008 LIB — 2008 CONS	
Economic	82%	0%	85%	0%
Social	92%	0%	75%	18%
Foreign	80%	19%	85%	8%
Composite	89%	11%	87%	14%

Key Votes of the 110th Congress

1. Increase minimum wage	Y	5. Share immigration data	N	9. Withdraw troops 8/08	Y
2. Expand SCHIP	Y	6. Foreign aid abortion ban	N	10. No operations in Iran	Y
3. Raise CAFE standards	Y	7. Ban gay bias in workplace	Y	11. Free trade with Peru	N
4. Bail out financial markets	Y	8. Repeal D.C. gun law	N	12. Overhaul FISA	Y

Election Results

2008 general	Alcee Hastings (D)	172,835	(82%)	($671,962)
	Marion Thorpe (R)	37,431	(18%)	($50,970)
2008 primary	Alcee Hastings (D)	31,182	(88%)	
	Ray Sanchez (D)	4,235	(12%)	

Prior Winning Percentages: 2006 (100%); 2004 (100%); 2002 (77%); 2000 (76%); 1998 (100%); 1996 (73%); 1994 (100%); 1992 (59%)

Population		Race/Ethnicity		Work	
Pop. 2007:	680,654	White:	24.9%	Private:	82.8%
Change since 2000:	Up 6.5%	Black:	54.5%	Government:	12.2%
Urban:	97.9%	Hispanic:	17.1%	Self-employed:	4.9%
Rural:	2.1%	Asian:	1.5%	Blue collar:	25.2%
Area size:	3,703 sq. mi.	Native Am.:	0.2%	White collar:	47.8%
Age		Hawaiian:	0.1%	Khaki collar:	0.0%
Median age:	33.3 yrs.	Two+ races:	1.2%	Other:	27.0%
More than 65 yrs:	11.0%	*Ancestry*		Median income:	$38,154
Less than 18 yrs:	27.4%	West Indian:	20.7%	Median home value:	$204,500
Education		Irish:	4.2%	Poverty:	21.5%
H.S. grad:	74.4%	German:	4.1%	**Military Veterans**	
College grad:	15.6%			% of Pop:	6.5%
Grad degree:	4.6%				

In the morning shadow of the high-rise condominiums that line the Atlantic Ocean, behind the quiet waters that separate the barrier islands from the mainland and a few blocks off old U.S. 1, are the African-American neighborhoods of South Florida's Gold Coast. They are gatherings of older stucco homes and commercial storefronts, ranging from upper-middle-class enclaves to rundown slums. These neighborhoods, populated by the working poor and with relatively few seniors, are bypassed by most tourists.

2008 Presidential Vote		
Obama (D)	194,396	(83%)
McCain (R)	39,530	(17%)

2004 Presidential Vote		
Kerry (D)	155,915	(76%)
Bush (R)	50,138	(24%)

Cook Partisan Voting Index: D + 28

The 23rd Congressional District of Florida gathers together many of South Florida's black neighborhoods in a geographically contrived, but demographically coherent, constituency. Geographically, most of the district is in the Everglades, east and south of Lake Okeechobee. This is a land of swamps and drainage canals, with some farms and citrus groves. Some people live in migrant-worker camps, some on the Miccosukee Indian Reservation, and some in places like Southwest Ranches, a new community where residents have opposed roads and street lights. The district has four narrow tentacles that extend east from the Everglades and get close to, but never reach, the Atlantic Ocean. The northernmost stretches into St. Lucie County and takes in black neighborhoods in Fort Pierce. In northern Palm Beach County, a tentacle reaches past high-income Wellington into West Palm Beach, then continues south along the railroad tracks and U.S. 1 to Delray Beach, which was the site of a civil rights showdown in 1956 and now has a large Haitian community. The most populated tentacle reaches east into Broward County to take in African-American areas in Lauderhill, Fort Lauderdale, Pompano Beach, and Deerfield Beach. Farther south in Broward County, a smaller tentacle reaches into parts of fast-growing Miramar and Pembroke Pines, home to upwardly mobile Haitians and also to one of the Century Village communities, the retirement development known for its politically powerful, liberal associations led by "condo commandos." But in some parts of Pembroke Pines and Sunrise, Hispanics from Miami-Dade County are replacing Jews. Overall, the population is 55% black and 17% Hispanic. This is a heavily Democratic district, with incoming Cubans providing the only minor countertrend. But it is not uniformly liberal on all issues. In 2008, African-American voters backed a state constitutional amendment banning same-sex marriage by about 2-to-1, enabling it to carry Broward County despite its large gay population.

The congressman from the 23rd District is Alcee Hastings, a Democrat first elected in 1992 and the only member of Congress ever to have been impeached and removed from office as a federal judge. Hastings had a relatively wide-ranging upbringing in the segregated America of the post-World War II decades. He grew up in a black suburb of Orlando and moved as a child to Jersey City and New York, where his parents worked as domestic servants for a rich Jewish family. He recalls attending a bar mitzvah as a guest. He also attended a Rosenwald school in Altamonte Spring, one of hundreds established for Southern blacks by Sears executive Julius Rosenwald. He graduated from Fisk University in Nashville and from Florida A&M Law School in Tallahassee.

From those beginnings, he made a rapid ascent, practicing law in Fort Lauderdale and finishing fourth in the five-candidate Democratic primary when he ran for the U.S. Senate in 1970, at age 34. He became a state judge in Broward County in 1977 and was appointed a federal judge in 1979. Then his career took a sharp turn downward. He was charged with conspiring with a friend to take a $150,000 bribe and give two convicted swindlers light sentences. A Miami jury acquitted Hastings in 1983, but the friend was convicted. The 11th Circuit Court of Appeals called for impeachment in 1987 and referred the case to Congress. Hastings was impeached by the U.S. House on a vote of 413-3 and convicted by the Senate 69-26. In the House, Democratic Rep. John Conyers of Michigan, senior member of the Congressional Black Caucus, made the case for impeachment. As a footnote, during a 1997 investigation into the Federal Bureau of Investigation crime lab, the Department of Justice found that an agent falsely testified against Hastings. He and Conyers moved to reopen the case, but nothing came of it.

After his removal from the bench, Hastings was unapologetic. In 1990, he ran an abortive campaign for governor, then lost in a primary for secretary of state. When the 23rd District was created in 1992, he led in the primary 28%-27%. In the October runoff, he faced Palm Beach County legislator Lois Frankel, who blasted Hastings for his record. He responded, "The bitch is a racist." Hastings was helped by a ruling by federal Judge Stanley Sporkin that his removal from office was invalid since the full Senate did not hear the charges. The Supreme Court later ruled to the contrary in a case of another convicted federal judge in 1993, but by that time Hastings was in Congress. He won the runoff 58%-42%, with voting closely following racial lines. He won the general election 59%-31%. Since then, he has not had a serious primary or general-election challenge.

In the House, Hastings' voting record has been mostly liberal, but toward the center on foreign policy. He opposed the use of force in Iraq and has been a strong supporter of Israel. He told the *Palm Beach Post* in May 2007: "There is a nexus between Jews and blacks by virtue of the Holocaust and by virtue of slavery which, independent of each other, were horrible events that humankind does not want to happen again."

In 2004, with the support of Republican Speaker Dennis Hastert, he was elected president of the Organization for Security and Cooperation in the pan-European Parliamentary Assembly and served two one-year terms. In 2007, he became chairman of the counterpart U.S. commission. In 2006, the House passed his resolution condemning Iran for hosting a conference on Holocaust denial. The next year, Hastings pressed for the opening of Holocaust archives in Bad Arolsen, Germany, and three weeks later, the archives were opened. He took a nuanced stand on the issue of detaining terrorism suspects at Guantanamo, saying, "Guantanamo has to be closed, over and out, but if Europe isn't prepared to stand up and take their share, I believe they ought to mute some of their criticism." As head of the OSC, he monitored the elections in Georgia in January 2008.

After the 2006 election, he was seriously considered for chairman of the House Intelligence Committee. He had support from the Congressional Black Caucus but was opposed by the Blue Dogs and others who maintained that his controversial past disqualified him from such an assignment. Hastings attacked his critics as "misinformed fools," but Democratic House Speaker Nancy Pelosi nevertheless selected Texas Democrat Silvestre Reyes. Hastings said he was persuaded to step aside during a late-night telephone conversation with former President Bill Clinton. "I am not angry," he told *National Journal* afterward. "At some point along the way, it became too much to explain. That is legitimate politics. But it's unfortunate for me." However, Hastings does have a seat on the Rules Committee, an influential post that gives him a hand in setting the terms for bringing bills to the floor.

Hastings made his mark on some issues of local importance. He sponsored a bill to preserve former stops on the Underground Railroad in Florida and elsewhere. His bill to prevent Haitian illegal immigrants from being routinely deported received little support in September 2008, but when hurricanes hit Haiti, he successfully pressed Homeland Security Secretary Michael Chertoff to delay deportations for two months. He pressed the issue again in January 2009.

Naturally, Hastings' opinion was sought when the subject of impeachment arose, and it was exuberantly given. He saw President Bill Clinton's 1998 impeachment as being driven by prosecutors abusing their powers, like the judges in his own case. "In my case, they nullified a jury. In this case, they are nullifying an election," he said. He moved to impeach Independent Counsel Kenneth Starr, but his motion was voted down 340-71 in the Republican-controlled House. In June 2008, he was consistent with his previous position, when he voted against the resolution to impeach President George W. Bush and Vice President Dick Cheney. He told the *Miami Times* in June 2008: "It would tear this country apart.... This nation is in a gut-wrenching death grip ideologically. To split it, no matter what Cheney and Bush have done, would leave us probably beyond repair in our lifetimes."

On national issues, Hastings, with Democratic Sen. Bill Nelson, filed a lawsuit in 2007 to prevent the Democratic National Committee from refusing to seat the Florida delegation because the Legislature had set the state's primary before Super Tuesday. The lawsuit was dismissed in December. A supporter of Hillary Rodham Clinton for president, Hastings campaigned for her in Florida and in Super Tuesday primary states, even though Barack Obama carried his district in the primary. Taking an original stand, Hastings in June 2008 called for a commission to consider expanding the size of the House beyond 435 members. That number, he pointed out, was established by statute in 1929 and can be changed by an act of Congress. He said there were too many constituents in each district for lawmakers to serve them adequately.

TWENTY-FOURTH DISTRICT

Suzanne Kosmas (D)

Elected 2008, 1st term; b. Feb. 25, 1944, Arlington, VA; home, New Smyrna Beach; Stetson U., B.S. 1998.; Methodist; divorced; 4 children.

Elected Office: FL House, 1997–2004.

Professional Career: Owner, Prestige Properties, 1979–present.

DC Office: 238 CHOB, 20515, 202-225-2706; Fax: 202-226-6299; Web site: kosmas.house.gov.

State Offices: Orlando, 407-208-1106; Port Orange, 386-756-9798.

Committees: *Financial Services* (38th of 42 D): Capital Markets, Insurance & Government Sponsored Enterprises; Domestic Monetary Policy & Technology. *Science & Technology* (25th of 26 D): Space & Aeronautics.

Group Ratings and Key Votes: Newly Elected

Election Results

2008 general	Suzanne Kosmas (D)	211,284	(57%)	($2,083,810)
	Tom Feeney (R)	151,863	(41%)	($2,002,969)
2008 primary	Suzanne Kosmas (D)	18,672	(72%)	
	Clint Curtis (D)	7,137	(28%)	

Population		Race/Ethnicity		Work	
Pop. 2007:	745,228	White:	74.1%	Private:	81.2%
Change since 2000:	Up 16.6%	Black:	7.1%	Government:	13.4%
Urban:	91.2%	Hispanic:	13.9%	Self-employed:	5.1%
Rural:	8.8%	Asian:	3.0%	Blue collar:	18.1%
Area size:	1,915 sq. mi.	Native Am.:	0.2%	White collar:	65.0%
		Hawaiian:	0.1%	Khaki collar:	0.2%
Age		Two+ races:	1.3%	Other:	16.8%
Median age:	38.7 yrs.			Median income:	$52,584
More than 65 yrs:	14.2%	*Ancestry*		Median home value:	$226,600
Less than 18 yrs:	22.0%	German:	12.7%	Poverty:	10.3%
		Irish:	11.2%		
Education		English:	9.9%	**Military Veterans**	
H.S. grad:	89.8%			% of Pop:	14.0%
College grad:	27.8%				
Grad degree:	9.2%				

In 1960, central Florida was a sleepy place. Orlando was a small city surrounded by citrus groves. The Atlantic coast from Cape Canaveral north was a quiet winter-vacation spot, with small motels lining U.S. 1 and the beach. Then two outsiders—President John F. Kennedy and Walt Disney—transformed this part of America, making it in two different ways a leader in the world. Kennedy promised in 1961 to put a man on the moon before the end of the decade, and the Kennedy Space Center was built on an island near Cape Canaveral. The Space Coast was created. In 1971, Disney opened Disney World southwest of Orlando, near the intersection of Interstate 4 and Florida's turnpike. Other theme parks followed, and metro Orlando became the nation's No. 1 tourist destination. In the process, the populations of metro Orlando and the Space Coast have more than quadrupled since 1960. People from all over the United States, and more recently, immigrants from Latin America, have come in large numbers; with the aid of ubiquitous air conditioning, they have transformed sleepy backwaters into vibrant metropolitan areas. This part of Florida has attracted many more young families and people in their working years than retirees. With a diversified economy— "Innovation Way," a high-tech corridor, is being built between the airport and the University of Central Florida, and the university is opening a medical school—and continuing tourism, metro Orlando has been hit less hard by the recession than other parts of Florida. But Brevard County's economy has been lagging, and the shutdown of the Space Shuttle, scheduled for 2010, threatens up to 4,500 jobs.

The 24th Congressional District of Florida has about half its population in the Orlando area, much of it in affluent Orange and Seminole county suburbs north and northeast of Orlando. It takes in all of Oviedo and parts of Maitland and Altamonte Springs. The other half of the district is on the coast. The 24th covers nearly 80 miles of coastline and encompasses the northern half of Brevard County, including the main grounds of the Space Center, the Canaveral National Seashore, and the county seat of Titusville. The 24th also takes in the southern half of Volusia County, including part of Daytona Beach, where NASCAR is a big employer. Also in the district is New Smyrna Beach, founded as a colony by Andrew Turnbull, a Scotch doctor, where you can see the ruins of an 1820s sugar mill. The 24th is as close as Florida gets to a typical suburban district. There are higher than average numbers of homeowners, families with children, working women, and white-collar employees. This was designed by Republican legislators to be a Republican district, but after voting 55% for George W. Bush in 2004, it voted only 51% for John McCain in 2008.

The new congresswoman from the 24th district is Suzanne Kosmas, a Democrat elected in 2008. Kosmas *(KAZ muss)* grew up in the suburbs of Washington, D.C., and attended Penn State University. In 1973, she moved to New Smyrna, Fla., where she raised four children and started a real estate brokerage, Prestige Properties, in 1979. She went back to school late in life and graduated Phi Beta Kappa from Stetson University in 1998. She was active in civic affairs, chairing the Southeast Volusia Zoning Board, volunteering for Friends of Spruce Creek, and working for Habitat for Humanity. At one point, she served on 20 community boards.

In 1996, she was elected to the Florida House of Representatives. When she arrived in Tallahassee, the Republicans had just won a majority in the House, which they've held ever since. She voted for more funding for health care and education, especially pre-kindergarten, and lobbied successfully to change the state policy of refusing Medicaid payments for heart-transplant patients over age 21. She unsuccessfully tried to ban minors from riding in the back of pickup trucks and to abolish the statute of limitations on sexual assaults when there is DNA evidence. She aroused some controversy in 1998, when the Volusia County Cultural Arts Advisory Board recommended buying a sculpture for $25,000, twice as much

2008 Presidential Vote
McCain (R)............................193,808   (51%)
Obama (D) 186,825   (49%)

2004 Presidential Vote
Bush (R).................................188,973   (55%)
Kerry (D)...............................153,130   (45%)

Cook Partisan Voting Index: R+4

as originally planned, from an artist who had contributed to her campaign. The artist later withdrew the piece.

In 2007, Kosmas decided to run against Republican U.S. Rep. Tom Feeney, who had held the seat since it was created in 2002. Feeney had been Jeb Bush's running mate in his nearly successful 1994 campaign for governor. In November 2000, Feeney became the Florida House speaker. In the controversy over Florida's electoral votes in the 2000 presidential contest, he aggressively challenged the rulings of the Florida Supreme Court and was a prominent defender of Republican George W. Bush's position. In Washington, Feeney was an influential and sometimes controversial conservative. He won re-election with solid margins in 2004 and 2006. But in 2007, he was reprimanded by the House Committee on Standards of Official Conduct for having traveled to St. Andrews, Scotland, on a golf trip paid for by disgraced GOP lobbyist Jack Abramoff. He reimbursed the Treasury $5,643 for the trip and announced that he was cooperating with a Justice Department investigation. The liberal watchdog group Citizens for Responsibility and Ethics named Feeney one of the "20 Most Corrupt Members of Congress."

National Democrats targeted Feeney, and with the help of the Democratic Congressional Campaign Committee, Kosmas at the end of the summer of 2008 had $836,000 in cash to Feeney's $804,000. Feeney took the unusual step of running ads and making robocalls before the primary for Democrat Clint Curtis, whom he had beaten 58%-42% in 2006. But Kosmas won the August 26 primary, 72%-28%.

In the general election, Feeney maintained that Kosmas was too liberal for the district, that she had done little in the Legislature, and that she had been involved in a "shady art deal." He charged that a vote she cast on driver's licenses had allowed the September 11 hijackers to obtain Florida licenses, and he highlighted her vote against a ban on partial-birth abortion. Kosmas ads talked about "integrity," while the DCCC emphasized that Feeney had spent $147,000 in campaign funds for legal fees. Kosmas' ads portrayed soldiers criticizing Feeney's record on veterans and called for withdrawal from Iraq.

In late September, after polls showed an even race, Feeney ran an apology ad saying he had made "a rookie mistake." He said, "Five years ago, when I was first elected to Congress, I was invited on a trip to Scotland. I found out later that it was paid for by a corrupt lobbyist. I did everything I could to make it right. I reported it to the Ethics Committee, and I paid the money back. I embarrassed myself and I embarrassed you, and for that I am very sorry. . . . Public service is about being honest even when you make mistakes." The ad seemed to backfire, or perhaps the news of Abramoff's sentencing that month hurt. A Democratic poll taken afterward showed Feeney 23% behind. The final result was not that one-sided, but still decisive. Kosmas won 57%-41%, carrying every county and running 8% ahead of Democratic presidential nominee Barack Obama.

In the House, Kosmas was given a seat on the Financial Services and Science and Technology committees. She announced she would donate the automatic congressional pay increase to charity. And in January 2009, she sponsored an amendment to increase NASA funding in Obama's economic stimulus bill from $600 million to $2 billion.

TWENTY-FIFTH DISTRICT

Mario Diaz-Balart (R)

Elected 2002, 4th term; b. Sept. 25, 1961, Ft. Lauderdale; home, Miami; U. of S. FL; Catholic; married (Tia); 1 child.

Elected Office: FL House of Reps., 1988–92, 2000–02; FL Senate, 1992–00.

Professional Career: A.A., Miami Mayor Xavier Suarez, 1985–88; Public relations executive.

DC Office: 328 CHOB, 20515, 202-225-2778; Fax: 202-226-0346; Web site: mariodiaz-balart.house.gov.

State Offices: Miami, 305-225-6866; Naples, 239-348-1620.

Committees: *Budget* (3rd of 15 R). *Science & Technology* (13th of 17 R): Energy & Environment. *Transportation & Infrastructure* (18th of 30 R): Economic Development, Public Buildings & Emergency Management (RMM); Highways & Transit; Water Resources & Environment.

Group Ratings

	ADA	ACLU	AFS	LCV	ITIC	NTU	COC	ACU	CFG	FRC
2008	55	55	57	38	86	49	83	52	55	82
2007	25	—	18	15	—	58	89	60	63	—

National Journal Ratings

	2007 LIB	—	2007 CONS	2008 LIB	—	2008 CONS
Economic	34%	—	66%	43%	—	56%
Social	48%	—	52%	42%	—	57%
Foreign	36%	—	63%	38%	—	62%
Composite	40%	—	61%	41%	—	59%

Key Votes of the 110th Congress

1. Increase minimum wage	Y	5. Share immigration data	N	9. Withdraw troops 8/08	N
2. Expand SCHIP	N	6. Foreign aid abortion ban	Y	10. No operations in Iran	N
3. Raise CAFE standards	N	7. Ban gay bias in workplace	Y	11. Free trade with Peru	Y
4. Bail out financial markets	N	8. Repeal D.C. gun law	Y	12. Overhaul FISA	Y

Election Results

2008 general	Mario Diaz-Balart (R)	130,891	(53%)	($2,583,098)
	Joe Garcia (D)	115,820	(47%)	($1,787,834)
2008 primary	Mario Diaz-Balart (R)	unopposed		

Prior Winning Percentages: 2006 (58%); 2004 (100%); 2002 (65%)

Population		Race/Ethnicity		Work	
Pop. 2007:	786,726	White:	20.6%	Private:	81.5%
Change since 2000:	Up 23.1%	Black:	9.6%	Government:	11.9%
Urban:	94.4%	Hispanic:	67.0%	Self-employed:	6.4%
Rural:	5.6%	Asian:	1.5%	Blue collar:	21.6%
Area size:	4,724 sq. mi.	Native Am.:	0.1%	White collar:	60.0%
		Hawaiian:	0.0%	Khaki collar:	0.1%
Age		Two+ races:	0.6%	Other:	18.4%
Median age:	35.0 yrs.			Median income:	$52,883
More than 65 yrs:	10.0%	*Ancestry*		Median home value:	$310,600
Less than 18 yrs:	26.6%	USA:	3.8%	Poverty:	12.8%
		West Indian:	3.7%		
Education		German:	3.7%	**Military Veterans**	
H.S. grad:	78.2%			% of Pop:	4.8%
College grad:	23.9%				
Grad degree:	7.7%				

An interconnected sea of wetlands once covered 8.9 million acres of southern Florida, stretching from present-day Orlando to the peninsula's southern tip. It was once a coherent ecosystem, a "river of grass" in which water moved slowly down a gentle slope to the ocean. It buffered plants and animals from meteorological extremes and provided different micro-environments for flora and fauna based on an inch or two of variation in elevation. It was long a dream of Florida's white settlers to make it

2008 Presidential Vote

McCain (R)	130,062	(50%)
Obama (D)	127,910	(49%)

2004 Presidential Vote

Bush (R)	122,342	(56%)
Kerry (D)	95,001	(44%)

Cook Partisan Voting Index: R+5

more useful, but for decades, this goal proved elusive. It took three attempts between 1915 and the late 1920s to build the Tamiami Trail from Miami to Tampa. To this day, it is one of only two roads that cross the South Florida interior from coast to coast. Over time, people managed to reshape the Everglades. In 1948, Congress approved the Central and South Florida Project, which authorized the construction of 1,000 miles of canals and 720 miles of levees to channel and drain the Everglades. Since then, about half of the original ecosystem has been turned over to agriculture and housing, and the amount of water discharged into the ocean has fallen by 70%.

In recent years, Floridians have had second thoughts about taming the Everglades. In 2000, Congress passed a law to restore the land in 16 counties, authorizing $7.8 billion over 30 years. In 2002, President George W. Bush and his brother Jeb Bush, the governor of Florida, signed an agreement to proceed. After a slow start, initial steps have included a huge storage reservoir and a safety valve to protect Lake Okeechobee and its dikes. In December 2008, the South Florida Water Management District approved Republican Gov. Charlie Crist's proposal to buy much of the land owned by U.S. Sugar Corp. around Lake Okeechobee for $1.35 billion, with most farming to be phased out within seven years. That would allow water to pass over land from the lake, through the Everglades, to the Gulf of Mexico. But the recession forced Crist to scale back the project to $533 million, with a 10-year option to buy the remaining acreage.

The 25th Congressional District of Florida sprawls almost all the way across this uninhabitable portion of South Florida, connecting population centers near, but not on, each of Florida's two coasts. About 13% of its residents live in Collier County, in new housing wedged between decidedly upscale and artsy Naples and the wild Everglades, and in the farm town of Immokalee, where an estimated 80% of workers are illegal aliens. The large majority of the district's residents live on the western and southern edges of metropolitan Miami, mostly close to the swamps. Here one can drive out on roads past the subdivisions and find strawberry, tomato, and citrus farms. The trees thin out, and then the road just ends where the Everglades begin.

The towns in the northern part of Miami-Dade are heavily Cuban and Latino—Hialeah Gardens, Tamiami, Kendale Lakes, South Miami Heights and Cutler Ridge. Farther south, the 25th takes in low-income agricultural areas along South Dixie Highway (U.S. 1), like Princeton and Naranja, as well as a few older tourist attractions like the Metrozoo, the Monkey Jungle and Coral Castle. Even further south is Homestead, which was leveled by Hurricane Andrew in 1992 and has since been redeveloped with housing, shops, hospitals, parks and schools, plus a Coast Guard base. NASCAR has an annual race at the speedway. By 2007, Homestead was the fastest-growing town in Florida, with large Mexican and Cuban populations. Politically, this area leans Republican, thanks to the allegiance of its many Cuban Americans, though this is the least Cuban of the three South Florida districts that have Hispanic majorities.

The congressman from the 25th District is Mario Diaz-Balart, a Republican first elected in 2002. The Diaz-Balart family history is intertwined with that of Fidel Castro and the rise of communism on the island nation of Cuba. His father, Rafael Lincoln Diaz-Balart, was the majority leader in pre-revolution Cuba's House of Representatives. His uncle and grandfather also served in the Cuban House. His family is sometimes called the "Cuban Kennedys" and seems to have politics in its blood. The Diaz-Balarts fled Cuba in 1959, shortly after Castro took over and after their house was looted and burned while they were vacationing in Paris. His aunt was briefly Castro's wife and is the mother of his only recognized child. One of Mario's three older brothers is Lincoln Diaz-Balart, the representative from the 21st District, just to the east of the 25th. Mario Diaz-Balart, unlike Lincoln, was born in the United States after the family had resettled. Another brother is a television news anchorman for Telemundo and a fourth is an investment banker.

Diaz-Balart dropped out of the University of South Florida at age 24 to work for former Miami Mayor Xavier Suarez, a Republican. In 1988, he was elected to the Florida House; four years later, at age 31, he became the youngest person ever elected to the state Senate. Diaz-Balart was named chairman of the Senate Ways and Means Committee, where he was a budget hawk. His 1995 call for state agencies to cut spending by 25% earned him the nickname "The Slasher" —a moniker he wore with pride. The eight-year term limit forced him from the state Senate in 2000, so he again ran for the Florida House and was elected.

No ordinary freshman, Diaz-Balart requested and received the chairmanship of the congressional redistricting committee. The resulting plan included a central Florida district tailored to state House Speaker Tom Feeney and a western Miami-Dade district tailored for Diaz-Balart. He coasted to victory over Democratic state Rep. Annie Betancourt, a former social worker and the widow of a Bay of Pigs veteran. Her campaign was underfinanced, and she remained largely unknown. With support from teachers and other unions, Diaz-Balart won 65%-35%.

In the House, his voting record has generally been more conservative than his brother Lincoln's on economic and foreign policy, and he has been a moderate on cultural issues. He told the *Naples Daily News* in July 2008: "I'm not a laissez faire Republican. I don't like government. It's bloated, fat, and doesn't work." He co-sponsored a bill in 2007 to ban disaster-aid spending on puppet shows, dance lessons, yoga on the beach, and other entertainment. He has opposed oil drilling off Florida's coast in the Gulf of Mexico. In 2008, as gas prices skyrocketed, he called for allowing commuters to write off part of the cost of gas to get to work.

Diaz-Balart organized the Congressional Hispanic Conference, a Republican alternative to the Democrats' Congressional Hispanic Caucus. Diaz-Balart vocally opposed the Democratic proposal to expand the State Children's Health Insurance Program because it was to be financed in part with a $3 tax on cigars. He said the tax would hurt South Florida-based cigar producers, an industry, he said, "that is almost entirely Hispanic." With his brother and GOP Rep. Ileana Ros-Lehtinen, also of South Florida, he supported a bill to allow children of illegal immigrants to qualify for college. After the 2007 immigration debate in Congress, he said, "The tone of some Republicans was offensive to the vast majority of Hispanics." Like his older brother, Mario Diaz-Balart favors maintaining the trade embargo on Cuba and the 2004 restrictions on travel and remittances to Cuba.

In 2006, Diaz-Balart was re-elected 58%-42%. Democrats believed that he and the other two Cuban-American Republicans from the Miami area were vulnerable. Younger Cuban-Americans are less focused on Castro, and many oppose the restrictions on travel and remittances. The number of non-Cuban Hispanics in the area also has been increasing, and in 2008, the Republican registration advantage fell almost to zero. In 2008, Diaz-Balart faced a serious challenge from Joe Garcia, the Miami-Dade County Democratic chairman and former executive director of the Cuban American National Foundation. Garcia opposed the restrictions on travel and remittances to Cuba. He criticized the Diaz-Balart brothers for focusing on Cuba rather than on gas prices and the crisis in housing foreclosures. "Their vision is vengeance, not justice," Garcia said. "You've got to do something. We're looking at very scary times."

Diaz-Balart criticized Garcia for appearing at a New York fundraiser sponsored by Democratic Rep. Charles Rangel, an opponent of the Cuba embargo, and called on him to return $14,000 in contributions Rangel had given him. He also ran an ad criticizing Garcia for opposing the Colombia Free Trade Agreement, and he repeatedly accused Garcia of hiding the names of small contributors, though they're not required to be reported. Garcia raised and spent $1.8 million. Diaz-Balart raised $2 million and, drawing on unspent campaign funds, spent $2.6 million.

Diaz-Balart won 53%-47%, the narrowest of the three Cuban-American Republicans' victories. He won 53% in Miami-Dade County and 54% in Collier County. Polling indicated that he carried Cubans as well as Nicaraguans and Venezuelans, who may have been motivated by a dislike of their countries' left-wing governments. "When it comes to Cuban-Americans, it's pretty clear where they are," Diaz-Balart told the *Miami Herald* after the election.

★ GEORGIA ★

The metropolitan area of Atlanta spreads out over the red clay hills of 28 of Georgia's 159 counties, and has been one of America's great boom areas over the last dozen or so years. It has also been the site of the great political transformations of the first decade of the 21st century. From 2000 to 2008, Georgia's population grew by 18%, the fourth-highest growth rate among the states, after Nevada, Arizona, and Utah, ahead of Florida and Texas, and far ahead of California. Georgia was the 10th-largest state in the 2000 census, the first time it had been in the top 10 since the census of 1850. If its growth rate continues at 2007–08 rates, it will pass Michigan and become 8th-largest state in the 2010 census. Atlanta grew by 23% from 2000 to 2007, from 4.3 million to 5.3 million people, a larger actual population growth than any other region of the country. Atlanta and Georgia have been in many ways, for many years, the center of the South, at least since Gen. William Tecumseh Sherman marched here in 1864. This is where John Stith Pemberton invented Coca-Cola, where Margaret Mitchell wrote *Gone With the Wind*, where Martin Luther King Jr. grew up, and where most of the civil-rights organizations that changed America were headquartered. But in population and reputation, Georgia for decades was outdazzled nationally by other parts of the South—by Texas with its oil wells and high-tech industries, by Florida with Miami Beach and Disney World, even by North Carolina with its Research Triangle and college basketball champions.

Neither Atlanta's rise to world eminence nor its role as the "capital" of the South was inevitable. Georgia was the last of the seaboard colonies, founded by James Oglethorpe in 1733 as an "asylum of the unfortunate," reserved for debtors and other outcasts from England. Oglethorpe forbade slavery, but the settlers rebelled and repealed his ban in 1750. Atlanta was only a small, though strategic, railroad crossroads when it was burned by Sherman's Union troops on their "march to the sea." Richmond, Charleston, and New Orleans all had stronger claims to being the central focus of the South a century ago. But in the 20th century, two figures imprinted Atlanta on the national imagination. One was Mitchell, whose 1936 novel inspired the 1939 movie of the same name. The other was King, who was based in Atlanta for most of his career and who ultimately led the civil-rights revolution that changed the South and the nation. Linking the two was Atlanta's business community, notably Robert Woodruff, who headed Coca-Cola from 1932 to 1960 and made Coke a worldwide enterprise. Perhaps aware that a world company could not indefinitely be associated with racial segregation, Woodruff and William Hartsfield, the city's mayor from 1937 to 1961, cooperated with blacks and promoted Atlanta as "the city too busy to hate." Hartsfield's successor, Ivan Allen, elected in 1961 and 1965, supported the Civil Rights Act of 1964, as Peachtree Center and the first atriumed Hyatt Regency were going up in downtown Atlanta. It's fitting that Atlanta's airport, one of the greatest in the world, is named for Hartsfield and Maynard Jackson, Atlanta's first African-American mayor.

This new Atlanta was growing up amid a mostly rural, deeply segregationist Georgia that as late as 1960 cast the second-highest Democratic percentage of any state for president. Hatred of Sherman was still strong 96 years later. Political contests typically matched Atlanta-supported moderates against rural-supported segregationists, and the latter invariably won. Georgia's electoral votes were cast for Barry Goldwater in 1964 and George Wallace in 1968. Then came change in the person of Jimmy Carter, a one-term state senator who was elected governor in 1970 with a rural base as well as conspicuous black support. On taking office, he proclaimed a reconciliation of the races and installed a portrait of King in the state capitol. Carter thus became one of the first politicians from the rural South to celebrate and honor the civil-rights movement, and in the process set himself on the road to being elected president in 1976.

Since then, Georgia and Atlanta have seen an in-migration of African-Americans. The state's population was 30% black in 2008, more than any other states except Mississippi and Louisiana. The presence of nine historically black colleges, and of large numbers of prominent black public officials and businessmen, and the growth of middle- and upper-income predominantly black suburban neighborhoods in DeKalb and Cobb and smaller counties to the southeast and west—all have made metro Atlanta in some sense the capital of black America. Arguably, Georgia has developed what Charles Moskos and John Sibley Butler described in their book on race in the Army, *All We Can Be*, an Anglo-African culture, a merger of traditions that were long associated intimately in private life but rigidly and even violently separated in public. (Interestingly, Georgia has tried to get the Pentagon to headquarter its new Africa Command in a military base in metro Atlanta.) Georgia has four black Democratic representatives, two from non-black-majority districts, and Andrew Young won in a white-majority district as long ago as 1972. Black Democrats Thurbert Baker and Michael Thurmond have been elected attorney general and labor commissioner, respectively, and re-elected despite a strong Republican trend. In 2004, Georgia elected its first black Republican state representative since Reconstruction, and African-Americans came in second in the contests for the Republican nomination for the Senate and the 8th District House seat. Georgia also has been attracting immigrants, and 8% of its residents in 2007 were Hispanic and 3% were

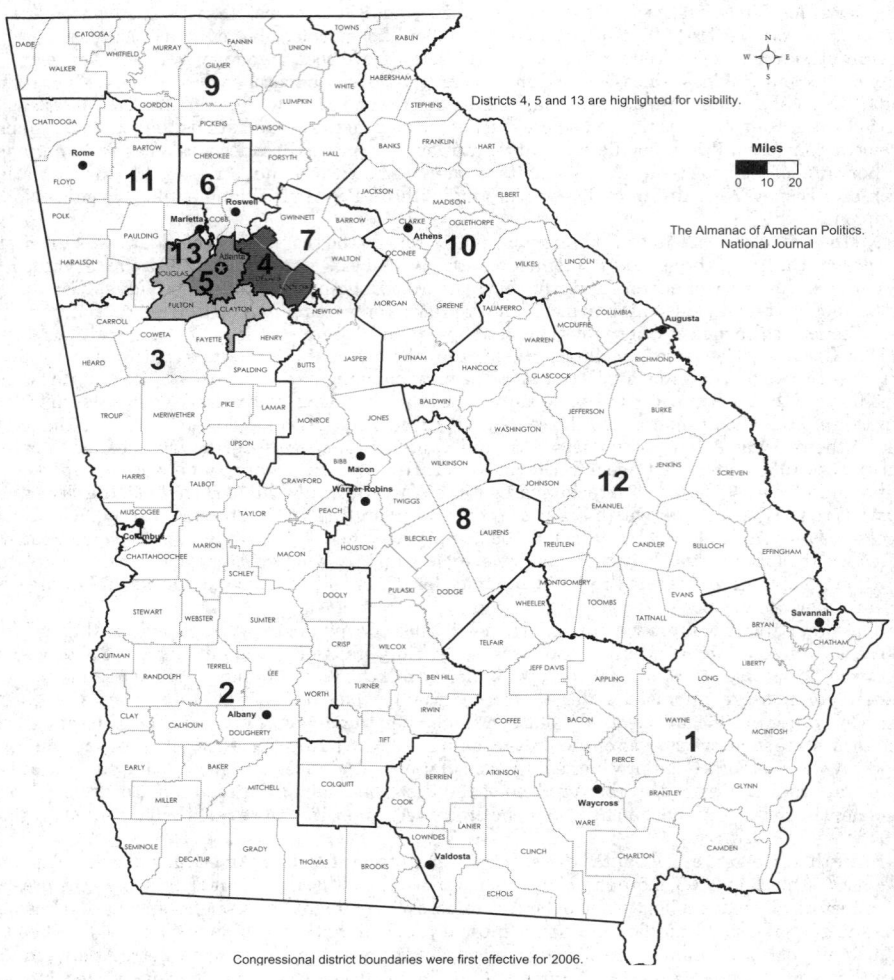

Districts 4, 5 and 13 are highlighted for visibility.

Miles
0   10   20

The Almanac of American Politics.
National Journal

Congressional district boundaries were first effective for 2006.

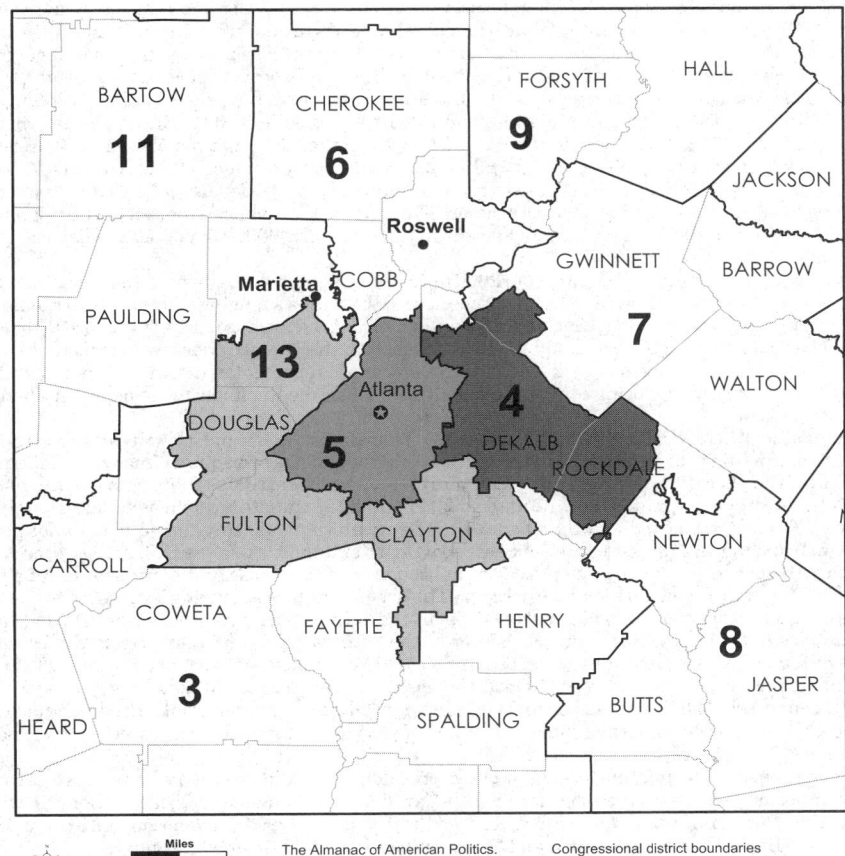

BARTOW
11

CHEROKEE
6

FORSYTH
9

HALL

JACKSON

Roswell

GWINNETT

BARROW

PAULDING

Marietta COBB

7

WALTON

13

Atlanta

4

DOUGLAS

5

DEKALB
ROCKDALE

FULTON

CLAYTON

NEWTON

CARROLL

COWETA

FAYETTE

HENRY

8

JASPER

3

BUTTS

HEARD

SPALDING

Miles   The Almanac of American Politics.   Congressional district boundaries

Asian—quite a change over the past quarter-century. And it has been attracting significant numbers of internal migrants from the United States: Domestic inflow from 2000 to 2008 was 7% of the 2000 population. These newcomers were attracted by Georgia's vibrant private-sector economy. At the same time, few native-born Georgians leave. The proportion of people born in the state who still live there is higher than in any other states but North Carolina and Texas.

Demographic change and economic change in Georgia have been followed by political change, to the point that this once heavily Democratic state now seems to be predominantly Republican. In retrospect, this change was a long time coming. It was delayed by the presence of politically skillful Democrats, from Georgia and other parts of the South, with rural bases: Wallace, who carried the state in 1968; Carter, who sent it in a different direction in 1970 and carried it solidly in 1976 and 1980; Carter's successors as governor, each of whom served for eight years—George Busbee, Joe Frank Harris, and Zell Miller; and Bill Clinton, who carried the state 43.5%-42.9% in 1992 and lost it by only 47%-46% in 1996. The year 2000 signaled a change. George W. Bush carried Georgia by a solid 55%-43%. Bush carried metro Atlanta (which cast 53% of the state's votes) by 52%-45% and the rest of Georgia, historically Democratic, by a resounding 57%-41%. The memory of William Tecumseh Sherman was dead.

The Republican trend continued in 2002, 2004, and 2006. In 2002, incumbent Democratic Gov. Roy Barnes, with a $19 million campaign chest, was beaten by Republican Sonny Perdue, 51%-46%. And incumbent Democratic Sen. Max Cleland, a wounded Vietnam veteran, who had won by 1% six years before, lost to Republican Rep. Saxby Chambliss 53%-46%. These results were driven in part by state Republican Chairman Ralph Reed, former head of the Christian Coalition, who created an on-the-ground organization that ultimately deployed 3,000 volunteers and 500 paid workers to knock on 150,000 doors in 600 precincts. Turnout rose robustly in central Atlanta and in black-majority counties, but it rose even more in the fast-growing suburbs. Demographic growth translated into votes. In the week after the election, four state senators switched parties and gave Republicans control of the state Senate for the first time since Reconstruction.

In 2004, Democratic Sen. Zell Miller, about to retire from office, denounced his party in his book *A National Party No More.* "The modern South and rural America are as foreign to our Democratic leaders as some place in Asia or Africa," he wrote. He endorsed President Bush for re-election and gave a rip-roaring speech at the Republican National Convention. Though Georgia was not a target state, turnout rose 28%, and Bush beat John Kerry 58%-41%. In the Senate contest that year, Republican Johnny Isakson beat Democratic Rep. Denise Majette by an almost identical 58%-40%. Bush won 55% in metro Atlanta, up from 52% in 2000, and he won 62% in the rest of the state, up from 57% in 2000. Kerry won among blacks, who cast 25% of the votes, by 88%-12%. But Bush won among whites, who cast 70% of the votes, by 76%-23%. Republicans increased their majority in the state Senate to 34-22 and transformed the state House from a 102-77 Democratic majority to a 99-80-1 Republican majority. The reign of Tom Murphy, the House speaker for 30 years and the force behind the 2002 Democratic redistricting plan, was over.

The Republican trend was apparent in 2006 even as most other states favored Democrats that year. The new Republican majorities in the Legislature passed the nation's toughest law on illegal immigrants, requiring employers to consult a federal database when hiring, and welfare recipients to prove their legal status. They cut income, corporate, and property taxes. And they passed their own partisan districting plan for Georgia's 13 congressional districts. Two Democratic representatives, Jim Marshall and John Barrow, came very close to losing central Georgia House seats, the Republicans' strongest challenges in the nation in 2006.

But political victory carries with it the perils of responsibility, and rapid growth can strain the capacity of infrastructure. The problem is water: Since 1989, Georgia has been quarreling with Alabama and Florida over the allocation of water from reservoirs created by federal dams that serve Atlanta and that drain into the other two states. Low rainfall in 2006 and 2007 threatened to dry up lakes Lanier and Allatoona. Georgia restricted and then banned outdoor watering, and threatened to cut allotments to commercial and industrial users. Interior Secretary Dirk Kempthorne told the U.S. Army Corps of Engineers to settle the interstate arguments. Georgia brought one court case and Florida and Alabama another. Then Georgia legislators got another idea. The act of Congress admitting Tennessee to the Union set the boundary between Georgia and Tennessee at the 35th parallel, but a surveyor in 1818 placed it several miles to the south. Restoring the border to the 35th parallel would give Georgia access to the waters of the Tennessee River (which a study said could be drained without much harm to Tennessee and Alabama reservoirs), and in April 2008, the Legislature passed a resolution telling Perdue to negotiate with Tennessee Gov. Phil Bredesen to set up a boundary-line commission. But a Bredesen spokesman threw cold water on the idea, saying Bredesen "has no intention of moving Tennessee's border, nor will he give away Tennessee's natural resources."

For many years, Georgia shunned Republican presidential candidates even when states less ravaged by Gen. Sherman's troops, like next-door South Carolina and Alabama, embraced them. It was the second-most-Democratic state for John F. Kennedy in 1960, but it also voted for opponents of the Civil Rights Act—Barry Goldwater in 1964 and George Wallace in 1968. It voted heavily Republican only in 1972, 1984, and 1988. Then, in 2000 and 2004, Georgia, both metro Atlanta and the counties beyond, voted solidly for Bush.

The 2008 elections saw Georgia swinging some distance, but not fully, toward the Democrats. It was not exactly a target state in the presidential election, but Democratic nominee Barack Obama's campaign set up 25 offices in the state and worked, as he did in Virginia and North Carolina, to turn out rural as well as urban blacks. African-American turnout zoomed up from 25% of the total in 2004 to 30% in 2008. Just as Ralph Reed's Republicans and the Bush 2004 campaign increased turnout in rapidly growing white suburban counties, so the Obama campaign increased turnout in rapidly growing black and Latino suburban counties. As a result, Georgia, which has long had one of the nation's lowest voting participation rates, has now moved up toward the national average.

Population		Household Income		Work	
Pop. 2007:	9,331,515	Under $15k:	14.1%	Private:	77.9%
State rank:	9th of 50	$15k to $50k:	37.2%	Government:	15.9%
Change since 2000:	Up 14.0%	$50k to $100k:	30.9%	Self-employed:	6.1%
Urban:	69.6%	$100k to $150k:	14.4%	Unemployment (3-yr. average):	4.8%
Rural:	30.4%	Over $150k:	3.4%	Poverty:	14.5%
Native of state:	55.9%	Median income:	$48,540	Blue collar:	24.3%
Not a citizen:	6.2%			White collar:	59.3%
Area size:	59,425 sq. mi.	**Home Value**		Khaki collar:	0.8%
		Under $100k:	25.3%	Other:	15.6%
Most populous cities		$100k to $300k:	57.4%		
1. Atlanta	439,275	$300k to $500k:	11.5%	**Age**	
2. Augusta	191,991	$500k to $1 mil:	4.7%	Median age:	34.6 yrs.
3. Columbus	189,173	Over $1 million:	1.1%	More than 65 yrs:	9.8%
4. Savannah	127,526	Median:	$156,300	Less than 18 yrs:	26.5%

Race/Ethnicity				Military Veterans		Registered Voters in 2008	
White:	59.0%	*Language*		% of Pop:	10.6%	No party registration	
Black:	29.4%	English:	88.2%	*Veterans by Period*		Voter turnout:	3,924,486
Hispanic:	7.4%	Spanish:	6.9%	WWII and before:	7.6%	Turnout as % of	
Asian:	2.7%	Asian:	1.8%	Korea:	8.8%	voting age:	55.0%
Native Am.:	0.2%	Other		Vietnam:	32.1%	**General Assembly**	
Hawaiian:	0.0%	European	2.4%	Gulf (pre-2001):	16.2%	Senate:	22 D 34 R
Two+ races:	1.0%	**Education**		Gulf (post-2001):	9.6%	House:	75 D 105 R
Ancestry		H.S. grad:	82.2%	Peace time:	25.7%		
USA:	9.9%	College grad:	26.6%				
English:	8.4%	Grad degree:	9.3%				
Irish:	8.3%						

Republican nominee John McCain still carried the state, but by only 52%-47%. Obama carried metro Atlanta 51%-48%. Outside metro Atlanta, McCain won 58%-41%, down only 3% from Bush's showing in 2004, but these 131 counties cast only 43% of the vote, a historic low. Obama carried 98% of black voters, 10% more than Kerry; McCain won 76% of white voters, the same percentage as Bush. The closeness of the race suggests Georgia may be a target state in any reasonably close election. But it will be hard for Democrats to surpass the strong turnout for Obama in 2008. Democratic Senate nominee Jim Martin held Chambliss to a 49.8%-46.8% edge, requiring a runoff. In that December contest, turnout was down 43%, and Chambliss won 57%-43%. In 2010, when Perdue cannot run for re-election and Republican Sen. Isakson's seat is up, the question may be whether November 2008 or December 2008 is the new norm. In early 2009, several prominent Democrats were lining up to run for governor.

Presidential politics Georgia's presidential primary comes early in the cycle and has been of some importance. In 1992, Gov. Miller had it scheduled one week before Super Tuesday in order to help Clinton, and it did: Clinton won solidly to balance losses in Maryland and Colorado the same day. In 1996 and 2000, Georgia was of little importance except as a measure of turnout: Democratic turnout fell from 622,000 in 1988 to 284,000 in 2000, while Republican turnout rose from 400,000 to 643,000. In 2004, Democratic hopeful John Edwards of North Carolina visited Georgia five times after the Iowa caucuses and Kerry only once. But Kerry beat Edwards 47%-41%, making it plain that Edwards had no chance to win the nomination and would be hardpressed to win other Southern states. He withdrew from the race.

For 2008, Georgia moved up its primary to February 5, Super Tuesday. On the Democratic side, it was no contest once black voters swung behind Obama. He beat Hillary Rodham Clinton 66%-31%,

2008 Presidential Vote		
McCain (R)	2,048,759	(52%)
Obama (D)	1,844,123	(47%)
2008 Democratic Presidential Primary		
Obama (D)	704,247	(66%)
Clinton (D)	330,026	(31%)
2008 Republican Presidential Primary		
Huckabee (R)	326,874	(34%)
McCain (R)	304,751	(32%)
Romney (R)	290,707	(30%)
2004 Presidential Vote		
Bush (R)	1,914,254	(58%)
Kerry (D)	1,366,149	(41%)

as turnout rose sharply to over 1 million, by far the highest ever. Turnout was almost as high, 964,000, in the Republican primary, far ahead of the 643,000 who voted in 2000 or the 654,000 in 1996. This was almost a three-way tie. Arkansas's Mike Huckabee won with 34%, carrying rural counties and exurban metro Atlanta counties. McCain finished second with 32%, carrying the Savannah River valley and the southwest corner of the state, both areas with big military bases. Massachusetts' Mitt Romney was third with 30%, carrying most of metro Atlanta, although McCain ran close behind in the inner counties.

Congressional districting After the 1990 and 2000 censuses, Georgia Democrats pushed through convoluted redistricting plans—arguably the most convoluted in the nation each time—to guarantee majorities for their party in the state's U.S. House delegation. Both times they failed. In the 1990s, state House Speaker Thomas Murphy tried to end the career of Republican U.S. Rep. Newt Gingrich and strengthen incumbent Democrats. Instead, what was a 9-1 Democratic delegation in October 1992 was 8-3 Republican in April 1995, and Gingrich was speaker of the House. In 2001, the Democrats tried again, and this time the boundaries were even more convoluted. They had only marginally more success—with some unintended consequences. Then-U.S. Rep. Chambliss, placed in the new 1st District with fellow Republican Jack Kingston, ran for the Senate and beat Cleland. The new 11th and 12th districts, created to elect Democrats, elected Republicans instead. The new 13th District did elect a Democrat, but the delegation remained Republican, 8-5. And Georgia's plan prompted Rep. Tom Davis, R-Va., who headed the House GOP's campaign, to push successfully for a similarly convoluted Republican

111th Congress Lineup	
7 R	6 D
110th Congress Lineup	
7 R	6 D

gerrymander in Pennsylvania, one which netted the Republicans more gains than the Democrats achieved in Georgia.

In March 2004, a court redrew the district lines for the state House and state Senate, which helped the Republicans increase their Senate margin and gain control of the state House in November. In February 2005, Republicans by then in control of the governorship and the state Legislature worked with Republicans in Washington to make redistricting of the U.S. House districts one of their top priorities. Moving more deliberately and facing far less Democratic resistance than Republicans encountered in Texas in 2003, they passed the plan in March with a few Republican defections and with limited Democratic support. It passed the federal review mandatory under the Voting Rights Act and survived a court challenge.

The 2005 Republican plan had much more regularly shaped districts than the 2001 Democratic map, and split many fewer counties (19 rather than 34). It strengthened Republican Phil Gingrey in the 11th District and weakened Democrats Jim Marshall and John Barrow of the 3rd and 12th districts. Republicans quietly worked with some of the African-American congressional Democrats to accommodate their personal concerns with the new districts. Two Atlanta-area districts are 56% and 53% African-American, while three others have black percentages of 48%, 45%, and 41%. In 2007, Republican Gov. Perdue called for the establishment of an independent commission to draw redistricting plans that can be voted up or down by the Legislature. Perdue seemed to be confident that relatively regularly shaped and neutrally drawn districts would leave the party with majorities in Georgia in the 21st century. But the Legislature perhaps did not share that confidence, and in 2008 it failed to adopt his plan.

Georgia is expected to gain one seat from the reapportionment following the 2010 census. Republicans will have control of redistricting if they retain the governorship and majorities in both houses in the 2010 election.

Governor

Sonny Perdue (R)

Elected 2002, term expires Jan. 2011, 2nd term; b. Dec. 20, 1946, Perry; home, Bonaire; U. of GA, D.V.M 1971; Baptist; married (Mary); 4 children.

Military Career: Air Force, 1971–74 (Vietnam).

Elected Office: GA Senate, 1990–2001; Maj. ldr. 1994–97.

Professional Career: Veterinarian; Owner, Houston Fertilizer and Grain; Owner, Perdue Inc.; Owner, AgroStar.

Office: 203 State Capitol, Atlanta, 30334, 404-656-1776; Fax: 404-657-7332; Web site: www.gov.state.ga.us.

Election Results

2006 general	Sonny Perdue (R)	1,229,724	(58%)
	Mark Taylor (D)	811,049	(38%)
	Garrett Hayes (Lib)	81,412	(4%)
2006 primary	Sonny Perdue (R)	370,756	(88%)
	Ray McBerry (R)	48,498	(12%)

Prior Winning Percentages: 2002 (51%)

Sonny Perdue, the first Republican governor of Georgia since Reconstruction, grew up on his family's farm in Bonaire in central Georgia. He was a high school football quarterback and earned a veterinary degree at the University of Georgia, where he was a walk-on football player. He served in the Air Force from 1971 to 1974, practiced as a veterinarian for two years in North Carolina, then returned to Georgia and started a fertilizer and grain business and a trucking firm near Warner Robins. In 1990, he was elected to the state Senate as a Democrat, was easily re-elected and then became majority leader in 1994 and Senate president pro tem in 1997. The following year, he announced that he was switching parties and running for re-election as a Republican. He was stripped of his leadership posts and staff, but was returned to the Legislature with 70% of the vote. In December 2001, after his Senate district was hacked up in redistricting, he resigned and announced his candidacy for governor.

In 2002, Perdue challenged Democratic Gov. Roy Barnes, elected in 1998 by 52%-44% over businessman Guy Millner. Barnes had pushed through an ambitious program that included creation of the Georgia Regional Transportation Authority to serve 20 counties in metro Atlanta and also passage of an education-reform plan that required annual testing and held teachers accountable for results, with bonuses for some and adverse consequences for others; it also ended tenure for newly hired teachers. In January

2001, Barnes persuaded the Legislature to replace the Confederate battle flag that had been chosen as the state flag in 1956; the state seal occupied most of the new design, and the Confederate flag was reduced to just one of five small flags that had once flown over the state capital. Although Barnes accomplished a lot, he had, one by one, antagonized key groups—Confederate-battle-flag lovers, the Georgia Association of Educators, and opponents of the Northern Arc highway he wanted to build north of Atlanta.

Perdue capitalized on that disillusionment with Barnes and called for dismantling the Office of Education Accountability and relying less on yearly tests. He attacked Barnes for the Democrats' highly partisan redistricting of state legislative and U.S. House seats. Touting his roots in central Georgia, he employed a rural strategy. "We're trying to capture the basic voting instincts of the non-metro voter," he said. He also promised a referendum on the state flag. His battle plan worked in tandem with the program of state Republican Chairman Ralph Reed to build Republican organizations and volunteer corps not just in heavily Republican metro Atlanta counties, but also in 70 target counties outside the metro area. With a big turnout and solid majorities outside metro Atlanta, Perdue won the August primary with 51% of the vote, enough to avoid a runoff.

Barnes still had a positive job approval and outspent Perdue $19 million to $3 million. But he was put on the defensive when the Georgia Association of Educators refused to endorse anyone for governor and endorsed Republican Kathy Cox, another opponent of the Barnes education reform, for school superintendent. Barnes also put a hold on the Northern Arc. Still, it was a shock on election night when Perdue beat him 51%-46%. Barnes led narrowly in metro Atlanta, 49%-48%, but Perdue won the rest of the state 55%-43%—just 2% below George W. Bush's 2000 showing there. Key to Perdue's victory was his rural strategy. Barnes carried only 41 of the 159 counties, down from 118 in 1998, and most of the counties he won were either central city or very small and rural. Also key for Perdue was increased turnout, which was up 13% statewide and 15% in metro Atlanta. It was up far more in the heavily Republican fast-growing counties, which gave him a 116,000-vote margin, more than his statewide margin of 104,000 votes.

It turned out to be a Republican victory up and down the line. Within a week of the election, four Democratic state senators switched parties, giving Republicans a 30-26 margin in the Senate. Still, once in office, Perdue was forced to cut some $1.7 billion of projected spending and pushed the Legislature to raise the cigarette tax. With help from former President Jimmy Carter, he proposed a new design for the state flag, with a red, white and blue background similar to the first Confederate flag, but wholly unlike the familiar battle flag. Perdue's design and Barnes's 2001 flag were put on the March 2004 ballot, and voters approved the Carter-Perdue flag 73%-27%. In 2004, Perdue proposed no tax increases, cut spending, and gave teachers a 2% pay increase and tax deductions for purchases of school supplies.

In 2004, as President Bush was carrying the state with 58% of the vote, Republicans raised their majority in the state Senate to 34-22 and transformed a 77-102 deficit in the state House to a 99-80-1 majority. The new Republican-controlled Legislature helped Perdue get his legislation passed. In February, he signed a medical-malpractice bill that capped pain-and-suffering awards and punished frivolous lawsuits. A month later, he signed a bill requiring a 24-hour waiting period for women seeking an abortion and parental notification for minors, measures long blocked by majority Democrats. In May, he signed two bills strengthening ethics rules. He also signed a modest tax deduction for teachers. But he angered some black legislators when he signed a bill requiring voters to show government-issued photo identification at the polls.

As Perdue came up for re-election in 2006, he attended to those who had put him in office. He made plans to dedicate 72% of the state's new revenues to education and to further increase teacher salaries by 4%. He called for funding broadband Internet access in rural areas and for spending $234 million on road and highway improvements in all of Georgia's counties. In March 2006, he announced that South Korean automaker Kia planned to build a manufacturing plant in West Point, which helped cushion the blow of impending Ford and GM auto-plant closings in Atlanta. Perdue also signed into law one of the nation's toughest immigration laws, a wide-ranging measure so restrictive it drew criticism from President Vicente Fox of Mexico.

Perdue kicked off his re-election campaign in May with a 20-stop tour across the state. He was attacked from the right by a little-known "Southern nationalist" challenger, still angry over the Confederate-flag compromise. Perdue ignored him and won the primary with 88%. Democrats had a far more contentious primary, which featured Lt. Gov. Mark Taylor and Secretary of State Cathy Cox, both from southern Georgia. Taylor won 52%-44% but spent more than $4 million, depleting his resources for the general election against Perdue, who had raised more than $10 million by July.

Ethics issues played a role in the campaign. Perdue was dogged by questions surrounding a Florida land purchase from a developer whom he had appointed to the state economic development board. And Taylor claimed Perdue had used the governor's office to enrich himself. "He made more money in four years as Gov. Perdue than he made in 54 years as Sonny Perdue," he said in one debate. Perdue dismissed Taylor's attacks as "wild allegations." In one television ad, Perdue reminded voters of Taylor's role in the bitter Democratic primary by turning to his wife Mary and observing that it would be nice "if we could go the whole campaign without those negative ads like they had in the Democratic primary." Perdue beat Taylor 58%-38%, winning by 2-to-1 margins across much of north Georgia and again winning big majorities in the heavily Republican, fast-growing counties in the Atlanta metro area. Taylor won mainly in counties that were majority black or had high percentages of African-American voters; he also won Clarke County, home to the University of Georgia.

Perdue's victory celebration was short-lived. In April 2007, he vetoed the state's mid-session budget, which included a $142 million property-tax cut and had been passed unanimously by the Legislature amid fights over spending priorities. The Republican-controlled House overrode the veto by an over-whelming margin. Perdue later "rescinded" his veto without restoring the tax rebate. The lawmakers' budget gave Perdue much of what he wanted, including $18 million to promote fishing tourism in Georgia, $81 million to shore up the PeachCare health-insurance program for children, and $1 billion in schools construction. Perdue maintained that the tax rebate would hurt funding for adult literacy, state prosecu-tors and hazardous-waste cleanup. "I believe politics got in the way of doing the right thing," he said.

Lawmakers privately grumbled that Perdue, after being keenly engaged in legislative matters in his first term, seemed conspicuously absent in his second. One of Perdue's harshest critics was his former friend and ally Republican House Speaker Glenn Richardson, who said the governor was "acting like a child" and was just "wrong, wrong, wrong."

The next year saw no improvement in the governor's fractious relationship with the Legislature. The House began the session by voting to override 12 of Perdue's vetoes, and the Legislature pushed for additional tax cuts, including elimination of the state's car-tag tax and further reductions in property taxes. Perdue complained there would have to be draconian cuts in government programs, particularly education. He grudgingly signed a $332 million midyear spending plan. He did get $100 million more in education spending and also managed to use his veto pen to cut several spending earmarks for individual lawmakers. But he also aggravated state Republicans by leaving town for a trip to China during the last week of the legislative session.

Some of the governor's fears about draining the state treasury were borne out in early 2009, when revenues dipped sharply as the economy worsened, leaving a projected budget deficit of over $2 billion. Seemingly resigned to the Legislature's desire for tax cuts, he signed a bill continuing homeowner tax rebates while worrying out loud that the consequence would be damaging cutbacks in education, health-care and public-safety programs. The governor also was the subject of several news stories about his personal finances. A 2009 story in the *Atlanta Journal-Constitution* said that unlike previous Georgia governors, Perdue had declined to put his business affairs into a blind trust and that he had continued to buy and sell real estate and operate his grain-and-fertilizer business while running the state govern-ment. In 2006, the governor reported a net worth of $6 million, an increase of more than 30% during his first term in office. But by early 2009, he was also $21 million in debt, having borrowed money with two agriculture business partners just as the economy soured. The newspaper noted that a farm credit bank based in Perry, Ga., had given them the loan with favorable terms, requiring only 19% in collateral.

As his second term wore on, Perdue seemed happier on the national stage, where he tried to help lead disheartened Republicans in setting out a new agenda. He was elected by his peers around the country to head the Republican Governors Association after Gov. Mitt Romney of Massachusetts left the post to campaign for president in 2007. Perdue began holding meetings in Atlanta with a small group of gover-nors to write new policy positions on energy, conservation, education and health care.

Senior Senator

Saxby Chambliss (R)

Elected 2002, term expires 2014, 2nd term; b. Nov. 10, 1943, Warrenton, NC; home, Moultrie; U. of GA, B.A. 1966, U. of TN, J.D. 1968; Episcopalian; mar-ried (Julianne); 2 children.

Elected Office: U.S. House of Reps., 1994–2002.

Professional Career: Practicing atty., 1968–94.

DC Office: 416 RSOB, 20510, 202-224-3521; Fax: 202-224-0103; Web site: chambliss.senate.gov.

State Offices: Atlanta, 770-763-9090; Augusta, 706-738-0302; Macon, 478-741-1417; Moultrie, 229-985-2112.

Committees: *Agriculture, Nutrition & Forestry* (RMM of 8 R). *Armed Services* (4th of 11 R): Airland; Person-nel; Readiness & Management Support. *Intelligence (Select)* (4th of 7 R). *Rules & Administration* (5th of 8 R).

Group Ratings

	ADA	ACLU	AFS	LCV	ITIC	NTU	COC	ACU	CFG	FRC
2008	25	15	11	9	100	53	100	76	66	100
2007	10	—	0	7	—	75	82	92	81	—

National Journal Ratings

	2007 LIB	—	2007 CONS		2008 LIB	—	2008 CONS
Economic	14%	—	85%		19%	—	79%
Social	9%	—	87%		0%	—	79%
Foreign	21%	—	73%		16%	—	79%
Composite	17%	—	84%		16%	—	84%

Key Votes of the 110th Congress

1. Raise CAFE standards	N	5. Make English official language	Y	9. Withdraw troops 3/08	N
2. Expand SCHIP	N	6. Path to citizenship	N	10. Iran guard is terrorist group	Y
3. Cap greenhouse gases	N	7. Fetus is unborn child	Y	11. Increase missile defense $	Y
4. Bail out financial markets	Y	8. Prosecute hate crimes	N	12. Overhaul FISA	Y

Election Results

2008 runoff	Saxby Chambliss (R)......................................1,228,033	(57%)	
	Jim Martin (D)...909,923	(43%)	
2008 general	Saxby Chambliss (R)......................................1,867,097	(50%)	($15,692,294)
	Jim Martin (D)...1,757,393	(47%)	($7,508,505)
	Allen Buckley (Lib) 127,923	(3%)	($28,666)
2008 primary	Saxby Chambliss (R).................................. unopposed		

Prior Winning Percentages: 2002 (53%); 2000 House (59%); 1998 House (62%); 1996 House (53%); 1994 House (63%)

Saxby Chambliss, the senior senator from Georgia, was elected in 2002 and won his first re-election to the Senate in 2008. He earlier served four terms in the House. Chambliss grew up in Shreveport, La., the son of an Episcopalian minister, and graduated from the University of Georgia. He practiced business and agricultural law in Moultrie starting in 1968. In 1992, he ran for the U.S. House and lost the Republican primary. In 1994, he ran again and was the sole Republican candidate, while Democrats had a multi-candidate contest. The winner was Craig Mathis, the 32-year-old son of Rep. Dawson Mathis (1971–81). Chambliss won 63%-37%. Speaker Newt Gingrich of Georgia saw that Chambliss got the committee assignments he needed most—Armed Services, to look after Robins Air Force Base, and Agriculture, to protect subsidies for peanut farmers.

When then-Budget Chairman John Kasich, R-Ohio, announced his retirement in July 1999, Chambliss started a campaign for the post. In July 2000, after Republican Sen. Paul Coverdell died suddenly, Chambliss considered running in the November election to replace him. House Speaker Dennis Hastert persuaded him to stay in the House, and Chambliss came away feeling he would get the Budget chairmanship. But he had competition from Jim Nussle of Iowa. The Republican leadership ultimately picked Nussle, and as consolation, Chambliss got an Agriculture subcommittee chairmanship. Hastert also made him chairman of the Intelligence Subcommittee on Terrorism and Homeland Security.

Chambliss got a second chance to run for the Senate in 2002. Democratic incumbent Max Cleland had won the seat only narrowly, 49%-48%, in 1996, and Georgia was trending Republican, evident in George W. Bush's 55%-43% victory there in 2000. Chambliss was not an early favorite to win. Cleland had a compelling biography. After college he volunteered for the Army and in 1967 went to Vietnam, where he lost both legs and his right arm in a grenade explosion. He served on the Armed Services Committee and had a moderate voting record. But in 2001 and 2002, he tended to stick with the close-knit Democratic Caucus while his new colleague, Georgia Democratic Sen. Zell Miller, dissented vociferously on issues from the tax cut to the Department of Homeland Security personnel rules. On the Republican side, Chambliss won the August 2002 primary 61%-27%. He set out to convince voters that Cleland was "too liberal for Georgia."

Cleland's two major strengths—his sacrifice in Vietnam and support from the highly popular Miller—seemed formidable. Cleland backers noted that Chambliss had received four student deferments in the 1960s and then was found ineligible for service because of a bad knee. Miller, in ads, told voters of Cleland's "rock-solid Georgia values." But that did not deter Chambliss from sharp attacks. He ran a series of ads mentioning Cleland's opposition to an amendment banning aid for schools that barred the Boy Scouts, his votes against the "partial-birth" abortion ban, and his support of school clinics passing out morning-after pills without parental permission—all ending with an astounded announcer asking, "Why would he do that?"

But probably the most important issue was homeland security. Cleland stood with other Senate Democrats in opposing flexibility in work rules in the new department. The dispute occupied the Senate for much of October 2002 and prevented passage of the bill to create the department. Chambliss ran an ad showing pictures of Al Qaeda leader Osama bin Laden, Iraqi President Saddam Hussein, and Cleland, and saying that Cleland "voted against the president's vital homeland security efforts 11 times." Against this, Cleland's ads attacking Chambliss for opposing an increase in the minimum wage and for cutting student loans were weak stuff. Plus, Cleland's impressive record in Vietnam did not inoculate him against charges that he had given short shrift to homeland security. The tide of opinion, as measured by very late polls, was moving toward Chambliss. Bush visited the state three times on his behalf. Chambliss won

53%-46%, a much bigger victory than just about anyone expected. Chambliss carried metro Atlanta 52%-46%, running ahead of Republican gubernatorial candidate Sonny Perdue, and he carried the rest of Georgia 54%-46%.

In the Senate, Chambliss established a mostly conservative voting record. (He also garnered a reputation for a great golf game. He has been rated the second-best golfer in the Senate behind Nevada Republican John Ensign, with a 6.5 handicap.)

When Republicans were in power, he was the chairman of the immigration subcommittee of Judiciary, and in 2003 succeeded in passing a law modifying some visas so that international companies who bring in foreign employees cannot shop them out to other employers. He continued to be favorable to firms seeking more visas for high-tech foreign employees. Initially, he was favorable to Bush's proposal for a guest-worker program, at least for farmworkers, but he opposed a controversial provision to give illegal workers a process to achieve citizenship.

In the spring of 2007 he and his Georgia GOP colleague Johnny Isakson—who had known each other since their days as classmates at the University of Georgia—worked together in a bipartisan coalition to fashion a comprehensive immigration bill. For that they were booed at the May 2007 Republican state convention. Chambliss argued that Georgia was the No. 1 destination for illegal border crossers and that the state's agricultural industry needed a guest worker program. They got a provision sponsored by Isakson requiring that the border be secured before the guest worker program could begin. When Majority Leader Harry Reid brought the bill to the floor in late June, Chambliss and Isakson opposed allowing the legislation to move forward unless a separate appropriation bill for border security was passed.

On the Armed Services Committee, Chambliss has paid close attention to the needs of Georgia military bases and defense contractors. In 2006, he moved successfully to reverse plans to cut back on procurement of the F-22 Raptor, produced by Lockheed Martin. He worked with Democratic Rep. Jim Marshall of Georgia to get new software facilities for Robins Air Force Base. He also sponsored legislation that reduced the retirement age for National Guard members in proportion with overseas deployments. Chambliss supported the Bush administration on Iraq, but in 2007 he showed his frustration, telling the *Macon Telegraph* there were "a lot of bad decisions" in the war in Iraq. He was one of 14 senators who voted against the nomination of George Casey as Army chief of staff. However, he consistently voted against cutting off funding of Bush's troop surge.

In 2005, Chambliss became chairman of the Agriculture Committee—a remarkable feat considering he'd been in the Senate such a short time. He resisted demands to impose income caps on wealthy farmers and budget cuts in cotton and other commodity programs important to Georgia. When Republicans lost the majority in 2006, he became the ranking Republican on the committee. He worked on the 2008 farm bill with Democratic Chairman Tom Harkin of Iowa, striving to keep programs at existing levels. In bipartisan negotiations in 2006 and 2007, he added incentives to the bill for cellulosic ethanol, made from switchgrass and pine trees that are plentiful in south Georgia. He supported the legislation that passed the Senate in December 2007, and later voted to override Bush's veto of the bill.

In July 2008, as Congress was responding to high gas prices, Chambliss and Democratic Sen. Kent Conrad of North Dakota assembled a group of 10 senators to put together a bipartisan energy bill. Their legislation, unveiled as Congress adjourned in August, included offshore oil drilling from Virginia to Georgia, measures to encourage building of additional nuclear power plants, and more tax credits for biofuels and wind and solar energy. It was attacked by influential conservative radio talk host Rush Limbaugh, but Chambliss persisted.

Georgia Republicans' success this decade convinced many that Chambliss was a shoo-in for re-election in 2008, but he insisted throughout the campaign cycle that he expected a close race. In 2007, DeKalb County Chief Executive Officer Vernon Jones, an African-American Democrat, announced he would run for the seat, as did WSB-TV investigative reporter Dale Cardwell. Democrat Barack Obama's smashing 66%-31% victory in the state's Feb. 5, 2008, presidential primary and the high black turnout convinced many Democratic leaders that they had a chance to win the seat. Conservatives were also disgruntled with Chambliss's stands on immigration and the farm bill. In March 2008, Democrat Jim Martin got into the contest. He was little known but had a long résumé: freshman class president at the University of Georgia, a stint as a military intelligence officer in Vietnam, a member of the state House in the 1980s and 1990s, and head of the state human resources department. He was promptly endorsed by former first lady Rosalynn Carter, former Gov. Roy Barnes, Agriculture Commissioner Tommy Irvin, and state House Minority Leader DuBose Porter. He also raised substantially more money than Jones or Cardwell.

Chambliss was unopposed in the GOP primary. In the July 15 Democratic primary, Jones led with 40% of the vote, but he failed to get 50% to avoid a runoff. Martin was second with 34%, while Cardwell got 16%. In the August 5 runoff, without the presidential contest in play, there was a huge drop-off in turnout, and Martin won 60%-40%. Jones failed to carry his base of DeKalb County. Martin's victory gave national Democrats a plausible nominee, and the Obama campaign's registration and turnout efforts gave Democrats the confidence that African-Americans would be a higher percentage of the electorate than in the past. Martin pounded away at Bush, and linked Chambliss to the by-then-unpopular president's policies. Chambliss took pains to point out that he differed with Bush on immigration, the Medicare prescription drug bill, and the farm bill.

After the financial crisis hit in mid-September, some polls showed the race to be very close, with Chambliss well under 50%. When Chambliss and Sen. Isakson, operating as usual in tandem, voted for the $700 billion bailout of the financial market on October 1, Martin responded with ads denouncing their votes. Chambliss campaigned hard and ultimately outspent Martin, $16 million to $7.5 million, but the Democratic Senatorial Campaign Committee and other Democratic groups made up much of the difference. Georgia law requires a candidate to get 50% of the vote to avoid a runoff. In 1992, the stipulation had prevented incumbent Democratic Sen. Wyche Fowler from winning in November, and he was beaten in the December runoff by Republican Paul Coverdell. That scenario seemed to unfold again as the votes were counted in November. Chambliss led Martin by 110,000 votes, but won just 49.8% of the vote to Martin's 46.8%, falling 9,146 votes short of winning without a runoff.

Some dissatisfaction among conservatives may be inferred from the results: Chambliss ran 182,000 votes behind Republican presidential nominee John McCain; Martin ran 87,000 votes behind Obama. African-Americans, who were 28% of voters (and nearly two-thirds of whom were women) voted 93%-4% for Martin. Whites voted 70%-26% for Chambliss. Chambliss carried young voters 47%-46%, winning young whites by a wide margin. He carried the elderly 50%-48%. The biggest drop-offs in Chambliss's percentages from 2002 were in metro Atlanta counties with rising black populations—Rockdale, Douglas, Clayton, Henry, and Newton—or a growing Latino population, as in Gwinnett County. Chambliss actually increased his percentages in north Georgia, perhaps because former governor and senator Zell Miller, a north Georgia native who supported Cleland in 2002, this time loudly backed Chambliss.

The runoff came four weeks later, on December 2. The national parties and allied groups pumped in at least $5 million. The Obama campaign kept open its 25 field offices and sent 75 more organizers to help Martin. National Republicans sent in operatives to work for Chambliss. National political figures streamed in: McCain, vice presidential nominee Sarah Palin, Arkansas's Mike Huckabee, Massachusetts' Mitt Romney on the Republican side, and former President Clinton, former Vice President Gore, and Democratic television commentator Donna Brazile on the Democratic side. Obama taped a radio ad and robo-calls.

This was a battle of turnout, and the signs for Democrats were ominous. While 35% of early voters before the November election were black, only 23% of early voters for the December runoff were. Overall, turnout in the runoff was only 57% of that for the general election, and all indications were that the drop-off was greater than average among African-Americans, left-leaning students, and other typically Democratic constituencies. Only 2.1 million Georgians voted, far behind the 3.7 million in November, and not much more than the 2 million who voted in the off-year 2002 election. Chambliss won 57%-43%, with percentages 8% to 12% higher than in November in the outer Atlanta suburbs and in north Georgia.

Junior Senator

Johnny Isakson (R)

Elected 2004, term expires 2010, 1st term; b. Dec. 28, 1944, Atlanta; home, Marietta; U. of GA, B.B.A. 1966; Methodist; married (Dianne); 3 children.

Military Career: GA Air Natl. Guard, 1966–72.

Elected Office: GA House of Reps., 1976–90, Repub. ldr., 1983–90; GA Senate, 1993–96; U.S. House of Reps., 1999–2004.

Professional Career: Northside Realty, 1967–99, Pres., 1979–99; Co-chair, Dole GA presidential campaign, 1988, 1996; Chmn., GA Board of Ed., 1997.

DC Office: 120 RSOB, 20510, 202-224-3643; Fax: 202-228-0724; Web site: isakson.senate.gov.

State Offices: Atlanta, 770-661-0999.

Committees: *Commerce, Science & Transportation* (7th of 11 R): Aviation Operations, Safety & Security; Communications, Technology & the Internet; Consumer Protection, Product Safety & Insurance; Oceans, Atmosphere & Coast Guard; Science & Space; Surface Transportation & Merchant Marine Infrastructure, Safety & Security. *Ethics (Select)* (RMM of 3 R). *Foreign Relations* (3rd of 7 R): African Affairs (RMM); East Asian & Pacific Affairs (RMM); Near Eastern & South & Central Asian Affairs; Western Hemisphere, Peace Corps & Global Narcotics Affairs. *Health, Education, Labor & Pensions* (5th of 10 R). *Small Business & Entrepreneurship* (6th of 7 R). *Veterans' Affairs* (2nd of 5 R).

Group Ratings

	ADA	ACLU	AFS	LCV	ITIC	NTU	COC	ACU	CFG	FRC
2008	25	14	0	9	100	50	88	76	63	100
2007	10	—	0	7	—	75	82	96	79	—

National Journal Ratings

	2007 LIB — 2007 CONS			2008 LIB — 2008 CONS		
Economic	7%	—	91%	22%	—	77%
Social	9%	—	87%	21%	—	73%
Foreign	16%	—	79%	16%	—	79%
Composite	13%	—	88%	22%	—	78%

Key Votes of the 110th Congress

1. Raise CAFE standards	N	5. Make English official language Y	9. Withdraw troops 3/08	N
2. Expand SCHIP	N	6. Path to citizenship	N	10. Iran guard is terrorist group Y
3. Cap greenhouse gases	N	7. Fetus is unborn child	Y	11. Increase missile defense $ Y
4. Bail out financial markets	Y	8. Prosecute hate crimes	N	12. Overhaul FISA	Y

Election Results

2004 general	Johnny Isakson (R)	1,864,202	(58%)	($8,038,200)
	Denise Majette (D)	1,287,690	(40%)	($2,391,248)
2004 primary	Johnny Isakson (R)	346,670	(53%)	
	Herman Cain (R)	170,370	(26%)	
	Mac Collins (R)	133,952	(21%)	

Prior Winning Percentages: 2002 House (80%); 2000 House (75%); 1999 House (65%)

Johnny Isakson, a Republican, was elected Georgia's junior senator in 2004. Isakson grew up outside Atlanta, in south Fulton County. His father drove a Greyhound bus, and his parents bought old houses, renovated them, and sold them for a profit. Isakson graduated from the University of Georgia and served in the Air National Guard. He went to work for Northside Realty in 1967 and eventually became president of the firm. He volunteered for Republican Barry Goldwater's presidential campaign in 1964 and for President Nixon's in 1972. In 1974, he ran for the state House and lost. In 1976, he ran again and won, and in 1983 became minority leader. He ran for governor in 1990, losing 53%-45% to Democrat Zell Miller. Two years later, he was elected to the state Senate. In 1996, he ran statewide again and lost the Republican runoff for U.S. senator to self-financing businessman Guy Millner, who lost in November to Democrat Max Cleland 49%-48%. In December 1996, Gov. Miller appointed Isakson head of the state board of education. His partisan political career seemed over, but it was revived by two timely retirements.

In November 1998, Newt Gingrich of Georgia announced that he was stepping down as speaker of the U.S. House and that he would resign his seat in Congress. That opened up a vacancy in the heavily Republican 6th District, which included much of Atlanta's northern suburbs plus the affluent Buckhead neighborhood. Isakson was by far the best-known of the six candidates in the February 1999 nonpartisan election. He raised $1 million and spent $500,000 of his own money. He won the seat with 65% of the vote. In the House, Isakson served on the Transportation and Infrastructure Committee, where he pushed for a rapid-transit line for the overburdened Georgia 400 corridor. On the Education and the Workforce Committee, he took a leading role in negotiations on President Bush's signature education law, the No Child Left Behind Act, which tied federal funds for schools to test performance. He added a provision requiring that 25% of technology funds be used for teacher classroom training.

Isakson passed up a chance to run against Cleland in 2002. But the state's other Senate seat came open in 2004 when Zell Miller, who by then had moved from governor to senator, announced he would retire after just one term. Isakson decided to run for the seat. He had two serious competitors in the Republican primary: Herman Cain, who grew up in a black neighborhood in Atlanta and, starting from low-level jobs, became the owner of Omaha-based Godfather's Pizza; and Rep. Mac Collins, whose district included the southern edge of metro Atlanta. Cain and Collins were both solid conservatives and abortion-rights opponents, and they made abortion a major issue. Isakson also was an opponent of abortion, but he had voted against a law preventing the use of foreign-aid money to fund abortions overseas and had voted for allowing servicewomen to have abortions at their own expense in military hospitals. In the 1996 Senate primary, he had irked religious conservatives by saying, "I will not vote to amend the Constitution to make criminals of women and their doctors. I trust my wife, my daughter, and the women of Georgia to make the right choices." Collins called him "a certified moderate," and Cain, in a television spot, said, "There's a big difference between me and Johnny Isakson. And it's not just the color of our eyes." Cain also backed a consumption tax and private investment accounts in Social Security; Collins criticized Isakson for favoring an extension of the date for the turnover of sovereignty in Iraq. Isakson called for staying the course in Iraq and for tax reform. With his business contacts, Isakson raised $5.5 million for the primary; Cain spent $3 million, much of it his own money, and Collins $1.9 million. Many observers thought the race would end with a runoff. But Isakson got 53% of the vote to 26% for Cain and 21% for Collins. He won 55% in metro Atlanta and 52% in the rest of the state.

This was the first state primary in which more Georgians chose the Republican ballot (650,000) than the Democratic (625,000) one. Democrats had a hard time finding a candidate for a seat held by a Democrat, Miller, albeit one who usually voted with Senate Republicans and supported Bush for re-election.

The Democratic race came down to two late-entering candidates, 4th District Rep. Denise Majette and businessman Cliff Oxford. Majette had served just one term after her upset victory over Cynthia McKinney in the 2002 primary, and she had a solidly liberal voting record. Oxford was accused of spousal abuse by a former wife. He spent $1 million of his own money. In the primary, Majette led 41%-21%, and in the August runoff, she won 59%-41%. In both contests, she had big leads in metro Atlanta but ran behind in the rest of the state, not a good harbinger for November.

In the general election campaign, Isakson ran positive ads. In the last two weeks, he attacked Majette's liberal voting record, including her vote against an $87 billion spending bill for Iraq. Majette criticized Isakson for undercutting Bush's education reforms by not voting to fully fund them. Isakson won 58%-40%, almost the same margin by which Bush beat John Kerry in the state. Majette carried only 19 of 159 counties, including Atlanta's Fulton County and two black-majority counties in metro Atlanta.

Isakson has a conservative voting record in the Senate. On the Health, Education, Labor, and Pensions Committee, he worked actively on pension reform, with the chief goal of advocating the interests of Delta Airlines, which was bankrupt and had huge pension obligations to its workers. Isakson sponsored a proposal to give the airlines additional time beyond the limits set in the bill to make payments to cover the liabilities of their defined-benefit plans. In 2005, the Senate passed a pension-reform measure that included Isakson's amendment to give the airlines 20 additional years to meet their obligations. House Education Committee Chairman John Boehner, R-Ohio, who had been Isakson's ally, countered that he opposed "any industry-specific relief." Negotiations between the House and Senate dragged on until August 2006. The final version gave Delta and Northwest 17 years to amortize their pension payments, while American and Continental got only 10 years. "The winners are tens of thousands of employees in the airline industry," Isakson said, and he received much of the credit for the final deal.

On many issues, Isakson works closely with Georgia colleague Sen. Saxby Chambliss, a Republican whom he has known since their days as classmates at the University of Georgia. Although Isakson opposed the McCain-Kennedy immigration bill in 2006, he and Chambliss worked with a bipartisan group of senators in 2007 on a bill including a path to legalization for illegal workers, a guest worker program, and tougher enforcement. Isakson sponsored a "trigger" provision that would delay legalization measures until enforcement goals were met. Nonetheless, he and Chambliss were booed by anti-illegal-immigration hardliners at the May 2007 Republican state convention. In June, when Democratic Majority Leader Harry Reid brought the bill to the floor, Isakson and Chambliss said they would vote against allowing it to go forward unless a separate appropriation boosting border security was passed.

Isakson supported the Bush administration on Iraq war policy. He voted against the Democrats' proposed expansion of the State Children's Health Insurance Program in August 2007, despite Republican Gov. Sonny Perdue's support because, he said, some states were using the program to insure adults and some planned to extend eligibility up to the $80,000 annual income level. He and Chambliss stood together in September 2008 in supporting the "Gang of 10" bipartisan energy bill that was opposed by many conservatives.

With Massachusetts Democrat John Kerry, he co-sponsored a bill to finance interstate high-speed rail projects, specifically supporting such connections on the route from Birmingham to Washington, which runs through Atlanta. When housing prices sagged in 2007, he recalled the stimulative effect of a $2,000 homebuyers' tax credit in 1975 and proposed a $15,000 tax credit for buyers of homes within a one-year time period. In February 2009, the Senate unanimously passed his $15,000 credit as part of the economic stimulus bill. Also in early 2009, he and Democrat Kent Conrad of North Dakota called for setting up a commission like the 9/11 commission to examine the collapse of the financial system.

In 2008, it was widely reported that Isakson was thinking about running for governor in 2010, when Perdue would be term-limited. But in May 2008, he told his staff that he would seek re-election to the Senate.

FIRST DISTRICT

Jack Kingston (R)

Elected 1992, 9th term; b. April 24, 1955, Bryan, TX; home, Savannah; U. of GA, B.S. 1977; Episcopalian; married (Libby); 4 children.

Elected Office: GA House of Reps., 1984–92.

Professional Career: Insurance agent, 1979–92.

DC Office: 2368 RHOB, 20515, 202-225-5831; Fax: 202-226-2269; Web site: kingston.house.gov.

State Offices: Baxley, 912-367-7403; Brunswick, 912-265-9010; Savannah, 912-352-0101; Valdosta, 229-247-9188.

Committees: *Appropriations* (5th of 23 R): Agriculture, Rural Development, FDA & Related Agencies (RMM); Defense.

Group Ratings

	ADA	ACLU	AFS	LCV	ITIC	NTU	COC	ACU	CFG	FRC
2008	10	18	0	0	43	79	61	96	88	100
2007	10	—	0	0	—	84	65	96	90	—

National Journal Ratings

	2007 LIB	—	2007 CONS		2008 LIB	—	2008 CONS
Economic	9%	—	90%		24%	—	76%
Social	28%	—	72%		0%	—	91%
Foreign	32%	—	64%		26%	—	73%
Composite	24%	—	76%		18%	—	82%

Key Votes of the 110th Congress

1. Increase minimum wage	N	5. Share immigration data	Y	9. Withdraw troops 8/08	N
2. Expand SCHIP	N	6. Foreign aid abortion ban	Y	10. No operations in Iran	N
3. Raise CAFE standards	N	7. Ban gay bias in workplace	N	11. Free trade with Peru	Y
4. Bail out financial markets	N	8. Repeal D.C. gun law	Y	12. Overhaul FISA	Y

Election Results

2008 general	Jack Kingston (R)	165,890	(67%)	($873,385)
	Bill Gillespie (D)	83,444	(33%)	($136,150)
2008 primary	Jack Kingston (R)	unopposed		

Prior Winning Percentages: 2006 (69%); 2004 (100%); 2002 (72%); 2000 (69%); 1998 (100%); 1996 (68%); 1994 (77%); 1992 (58%)

Population		Race/Ethnicity		Work	
Pop. 2007:	666,429	White:	68.4%	Private:	70.2%
Change since 2000:	Up 5.8%	Black:	24.2%	Government:	23.3%
Urban:	57.3%	Hispanic:	4.6%	Self-employed:	6.2%
Rural:	42.7%	Asian:	1.0%	Blue collar:	27.0%
Area size:	12,243 sq. mi.	Native Am.:	0.2%	White collar:	52.6%
Age		Hawaiian:	0.1%	Khaki collar:	2.4%
Median age:	34.0 yrs.	Two+ races:	1.2%	Other:	17.9%
More than 65 yrs:	11.0%	*Ancestry*		Median income:	$41,764
Less than 18 yrs:	26.8%	English:	10.7%	Median home value:	$112,200
Education		USA:	10.2%	Poverty:	16.2%
H.S. grad:	81.3%	Irish:	9.5%	**Military Veterans**	
College grad:	19.6%			% of Pop:	14.5%
Grad degree:	7.3%				

Georgia's south Atlantic coast was settled in the 1730s by Englishman James Oglethorpe as a refuge and reformatory for convicts. But before long, the sea islands and lowlands along the wide rivers and inlets were plantation country. It is here that Gen. William Tecumseh Sherman and his troops famously marched from Atlanta in 1864 and, without supplies or lines of communication, burned plantation houses, destroyed crops, and captured the Confederacy's leader. When their march was complete,

2008 Presidential Vote		
McCain (R)	166,138	(63%)
Obama (D)	95,451	(36%)
2004 Presidential Vote		
Bush (R)	148,806	(66%)
Kerry (D)	75,399	(34%)
Cook Partisan Voting Index:	R + 16	

they left behind memories of property destroyed and slaves freed, which have been handed down as family lore through several generations.

The 1st Congressional District of Georgia includes much of the southeast and south part of the state. It includes the state's southern Atlantic coast and runs west approximately to Interstate 75 at Valdosta, the largest city in the district. It heads toward the center of the state just short of Vidalia and runs from the Ocmulgee and Altamaha Rivers in the north to the Florida border. It takes in almost one-third of Chatham County's population but only a sliver of Savannah, most of which is now in the 12th District. It contains the Sea Islands, with their vibrant resort economy and efforts to preserve the African-American Gullah culture and its eponymous West African-originated Creole language. One of those coastal communities is the historic black settlement of Pin Point, 11 miles southeast of Savannah. Its 300 citizens are mostly descendants of the first slaves in the area. Its most famous son is Supreme Court Justice Clarence Thomas.

It has a few modest-sized cities, like Brunswick, a World War II shipbuilding center that has been revitalized as the gateway to the Sea Islands, and isolated Waycross, a railroad junction and gateway to the Okefenokee Swamp, the largest swamp in North America. Prior to the abolitionist movement, this swamp-filled area was a site of the Underground Railroad, with trails to north Florida. Much of the district is rural, with cotton and tobacco fields and softwood forests inhabited by wild hogs and bears. Appling County and Berrien County are known for their turpentine and bell peppers. Many popular films have been produced in the region, including *Glory* and *Forrest Gump*. Shipping has grown at the Savannah and Brunswick ports, and Savannah is now the country's fourth-busiest port for container cargo.

This was Democratic country for a century after Sherman's troops marched through Georgia, but voters here are solidly conservative on most issues. For two decades, this part of south Georgia voted for national Republicans but Georgia Democrats. Since 2000, it has voted solidly Republican for governor and senator as well. Redistricting changes in 2005 increased the black population and reduced President Bush's vote in 2004 from 68% to 66%. In 2008, Republican John McCain did nearly that well, with 63%.

The congressman from the 1st District is Jack Kingston, a Republican first elected in 1992. The son of a college professor, Kingston grew up in Texas and Georgia, but also spent time in Ethiopia. After college, he moved to Savannah to be a commercial insurance agent. In 1984, at age 29, he was elected to the Georgia House and served eight years. In 1992, when Democratic U.S. Rep. Lindsay Thomas retired, Kingston ran for Congress, against Democrat Barbara Christmas, a school principal. He won decisively, 58%-42%, and has not been seriously challenged since.

In the House, Kingston has a mostly conservative voting record but he is not among the hard-liners in the Georgia delegation. During the Clinton era, he parted company with Republicans on trade issues, notably the North American Free Trade Agreement and normal trade relations with China. But he gave President Bush his vote on the 2005 Central American Free Trade Agreement. During a 2007 visit to Cuba, he softened his opposition to trade with that country, at least where the market for Vidalia onions was concerned.

He is the ranking Republican on the Appropriations Subcommittee on Agriculture, where he has been an advocate of the peanut-warehousing program. He also has a seat on the Defense Appropriations Subcommittee. In 2008, working with House Minority Leader John Boehner, he crafted a proposed moratorium on earmarking while permanent guidelines were set up for the practice, in which individual lawmakers slip pet projects into spending bills. But the proposal hinged on cooperation from the Democratic majority, which was unlikely. In the meantime, Kingston has made it his business to grab his slices of pork. In 2007, he had more earmarks than anyone else in the Georgia delegation, according to taxpayer watchdog groups. "I am convinced there are good earmarks and bad earmarks," he said, while conceding that they got out of control when Republicans ran the House.

Kingston has been a party activist in the House. In 2004, he played a key role in persuading the Republican leadership to back the $10 billion tobacco buyout, which ended the quota system in place since 1938. In 2005, he joined Rep. Eliot Engel, D-N.Y., in a bipartisan initiative to reduce oil consumption by increasing auto fuel efficiency. "The age of cheap oil and gas is over," Kingston said, a view that proved to be prescient in the late 2000s as gas prices soared. As head of the Republicans' "theme team," which coordinates the party's national message, he became a spokesman for the House GOP on television talk shows. He encouraged colleagues to make appearances on Comedy Central and to make more use of blogs. In 2002, he was elected vice chairman of the Republican Conference. But he may have been the victim of a desire for change in 2006, after Republicans lost their majority in the House. Kingston fell short in a bid for chairman of the conference, losing to Adam Putnam of Florida on the third ballot.

On local issues, Kingston has fought for historic preservation and looked after local military facilities. As an appropriator, he has brought millions of dollars home to improve the water flow of the Savannah River and to complete the Sidney Lanier drawbridge in Brunswick. Kingston considered but turned down opportunities to run for the Senate in 2002 and 2004, when less senior Republicans prevailed. He seems comfortable with patiently reaping the benefits of seniority in the House.

SECOND DISTRICT

Sanford Bishop (D)

Elected 1992, 9th term; b. Feb. 4, 1947, Mobile, AL; home, Albany; Morehouse Col., B.A. 1968, Emory U., J.D. 1971; Baptist; married (Vivian Creighton Bishop); 1 child.

Military Career: Army, 1970–71.

Elected Office: GA House of Reps., 1976–90; GA Senate, 1990–92.

Professional Career: Practicing atty., 1971–92.

DC Office: 2429 RHOB, 20515, 202-225-3631; Fax: 202-225-2203; Web site: www.house.gov/bishop.

State Offices: Albany, 229-439-8067; Columbus, 706-320-9477.

Committees: *Appropriations* (24th of 37 D): Agriculture, Rural Development, FDA & Related Agencies; Defense; Military Construction, Veterans Affairs & Related Agencies.

Group Ratings

	ADA	ACLU	AFS	LCV	ITIC	NTU	COC	ACU	CFG	FRC
2008	90	82	100	92	100	5	67	4	0	11
2007	90	—	100	75	—	5	70	4	11	—

National Journal Ratings

	2007 LIB — 2007 CONS	2008 LIB — 2008 CONS
Economic	64% — 34%	78% — 20%
Social	64% — 35%	62% — 34%
Foreign	55% — 44%	59% — 37%
Composite	62% — 38%	68% — 32%

Key Votes of the 110th Congress

1. Increase minimum wage	Y	5. Share immigration data	N	9. Withdraw troops 8/08	Y
2. Expand SCHIP	Y	6. Foreign aid abortion ban	N	10. No operations in Iran	N
3. Raise CAFE standards	Y	7. Ban gay bias in workplace	Y	11. Free trade with Peru	Y
4. Bail out financial markets	Y	8. Repeal D.C. gun law	Y	12. Overhaul FISA	Y

Election Results

2008 general	Sanford Bishop (D)..158,435	(69%)	($1,034,540)
	Lee Ferrell (R)..71,351	(31%)	($10)
2008 primary	Sanford Bishop (D).......................................unopposed		

Prior Winning Percentages: 2006 (68%); 2004 (67%); 2002 (100%); 2000 (54%); 1998 (57%); 1996 (54%); 1994 (66%); 1992 (64%)

Population		Race/Ethnicity		Work	
Pop. 2007:	628,501	White:	47.3%	Private:	69.2%
Change since 2000:	Down 0.2%	Black:	47.5%	Government:	24.9%
Urban:	58.1%	Hispanic:	3.1%	Self-employed:	5.7%
Rural:	41.9%	Asian:	0.6%	Blue collar:	26.8%
Area size:	11,001 sq. mi.	Native Am.:	0.3%	White collar:	48.9%
Age		Hawaiian:	0.1%	Khaki collar:	4.9%
Median age:	34.4 yrs.	Two+ races:	1.0%	Other:	19.3%
More than 65 yrs:	12.0%	*Ancestry*		Median income:	$33,643
Less than 18 yrs:	26.3%	USA:	8.0%	Median home value:	$87,500
		Irish:	7.0%	Poverty:	23.0%
Education		English:	6.1%		
H.S. grad:	75.7%			**Military Veterans**	
College grad:	15.1%			% of Pop:	11.6%
Grad degree:	5.8%				

Before the Civil War, the southwest corner of Georgia was plantation country. This is where the Confederate Army ran the Andersonville military prison, which killed about 13,000 of the 45,000 Union soldiers confined there, through disease, poor sanitation, malnutrition, overcrowding and exposure. They are remembered at the National Prisoner of War Museum at Andersonville, which is dedicated to all Americans who have endured wartime captivity. Today, the military is still a strong presence, and bases in the area have been largely unscathed by several rounds of closings in recent years. Fort Benning is the Army's third largest installation, home of the Army Infantry School and the Army Armor Center and School. Benning can train as many as 16,000 soldiers at a time. As a boost to the otherwise gloomy local economy, its workforce in 2013 is expected to be 41,600, including transfers as a result of the military's overseas downsizing.

But the region is mostly farmland: Cotton and peanuts are major crops, and pecans are also grown here. Near the Florida border is Cairo, the birthplace of baseball's black pioneer Jackie Robinson; Plantation Trace, near Thomasville, is where rich Northerners have come to shoot quail and ducks in winter since the 1880s, a part of Georgia culture memorialized in Tom Wolfe's *A Man in Full*. A bit to the north is Albany, with several factories, a civil rights museum and the site of Martin Luther King Jr.'s least successful civil rights protests in the 1960s. Not far from Albany, between upland pine stands and bottomland habitats, lies the Chickasawhatchee Swamp, one of the Southeast's largest freshwater swamps

2008 Presidential Vote

Obama (D) 131,408	(54%)
McCain (R)............................108,818	(45%)

2004 Presidential Vote

Bush (R)................................104,014	(50%)
Kerry (D)................................103,163	(50%)

Cook Partisan Voting Index: D + 1

and home to rare plant species such as the needle palm and the green fly orchid. Two counties north is the village of Plains, the home since childhood of former President Jimmy Carter, who has said he wants to be buried in his front yard. Plains now has a major biofuels factory. This is still hardscrabble country: As recently as World War II, most rural residents lived in clapboard cabins without power or running water, eking a living out of over-tilled soil.

This is Georgia's 2nd Congressional District. In the 2005 redistricting, it lost virtually all of Valdosta, but increased to two-thirds its share of Columbus and Muscogee County. Eight rural counties between Columbus and Macon were added. The net effect was to raise the African-American population in the district from 45% to 48%. President Bush won here in 2004, but with only 50.02%. In 2008, Barack Obama took Muscogee County 60%-40%, and the district as a whole voted for Obama 54%-45%.

The congressman from the 2nd District is Sanford Bishop, a Democrat first elected in 1992. Bishop grew up in Mobile, Ala., where his father was a college president. He went to Morehouse College in Atlanta, where he was student body president in 1968 and sang at Martin Luther King Jr.'s funeral. He went to Emory Law School, then served in the Army. After a year in New York, he settled in Columbus to practice law. He was elected to the state Legislature in 1976 at age 29. He served there until 1990, when he was elected to the Georgia Senate. In 1992, he ran for the U.S. House against Democratic Rep. Charles Hatcher, who, with more than 800 check overdrafts, was tarred by the House bank scandal that year. Bishop defeated Hatcher in the runoff 53%-47% and won the general election 64%-36%.

Bishop is a moderate Democrat who calls himself a "traditionalist" on cultural issues. His style is nonconfrontational. Along with Rep. Artur Davis, D-Ala., he has a voting record that's among the most conservative in the Congressional Black Caucus. He is also a member of the conservative Blue Dog Democrats and supported a balanced budget, school prayer, a ban on flag burning and a proposed amendment to prohibit same-sex marriage. He was one of 10 House Democrats to vote for President Bush's tax cuts in 2001.

In 2003, Bishop won a long-sought seat on the Appropriations Committee. He has worked to safeguard his district's military facilities and has delivered funds to its military installations. Bishop also has been active on farm programs. He worked with the Republican House majority in 1996 on the Freedom to Farm Act to fashion a "market-oriented, no-net cost" program for peanuts. In 2002, he helped to craft the scaled-back program for peanut support, which was based on phasing out quotas and price guarantees. On the 2008 farm bill, he again was focused on the peanut farmers in his district. He helped design the peanut-rotation program, which he said encourages "a cleaner, greener method of planting while ensuring an affordable and accessible supply to the markets that rely on U.S.-grown peanuts."

After the Democrats won control of the House in 2006, Bishop was considered for the chairmanship of the Intelligence Committee, but it ultimately went to Rep. Silvestre Reyes, D-Texas. Instead, Bishop gained seats on the constituent-friendly Agriculture, Defense and Military Construction subcommittees at Appropriations. In 2007, he got committee approval for $74 million for peanut storage in the Iraq War supplemental spending bill. When Bush objected, Bishop responded that the money would help farmers compete internationally. In 2008, he won passage of an amendment to the defense spending bill that provided 180 days of health care for military members who transition from active to reserve status.

In 2000, Bishop faced serious re-election competition from Dylan Glenn, a former aide to George H.W. Bush on the staff of the Republican National Committee. The contest between two African-Americans in a rural, then majority-white district was unprecedented, but race was not an issue in the campaign. Bishop largely ignored the challenger and ran on his record, while Glenn offered the perspective of a new generation focusing on economic growth. Bishop won 54%-46%. Redistricting changes made a serious challenge less likely. Bishop contemplated a run in 2008 against Sen. Saxby Chambliss, but decided to stay in the House, where his seniority gives him growing influence. He was an early supporter of Democrat Barack Obama for president, though his wife, Vivian Creighton Bishop, who is prominent at home as the municipal court clerk for Muscogee County, actively backed Democrat Hillary Rodham Clinton.

THIRD DISTRICT

Lynn Westmoreland (R)

Elected 2004, 3rd term; b. April 2, 1950, Atlanta; home, Grantville; Attended GA State U., 1969–71; Baptist; married (Joan); 3 children.

Elected Office: GA House of Reps., 1992–2004; Min. ldr. 2000–03.

Professional Career: Real estate developer; Owner, L.A.W. Builders, 1982-present.

DC Office: 1213 LHOB, 20515, 202-225-5901; Fax: 202-225-2515; Web site: http://www.house.gov/westmoreland/.

State Offices: Newnan, 770-683-2033.

Committees: *Oversight & Government Reform* (8th of 15 R): Information Policy, Census & National Archives; National Security & Government Reform. *Small Business* (5th of 12 R): Regulations & Healthcare (RMM). *Transportation & Infrastructure* (21st of 30 R): Aviation; Railroads, Pipelines & Hazardous Materials; Water Resources & Environment.

Group Ratings

	ADA	ACLU	AFS	LCV	ITIC	NTU	COC	ACU	CFG	FRC
2008	0	0	0	8	29	84	72	100	100	82
2007	0	—	0	0	—	90	72	100	92	—

National Journal Ratings

	2007 LIB — 2007 CONS		2008 LIB — 2008 CONS	
Economic	0%	97%	9%	91%
Social	0%	91%	0%	91%
Foreign	0%	72%	13%	84%
Composite	7%	93%	9%	91%

Key Votes of the 110th Congress

1. Increase minimum wage	N	5. Share immigration data	*	9. Withdraw troops 8/08	N
2. Expand SCHIP	N	6. Foreign aid abortion ban	Y	10. No operations in Iran	N
3. Raise CAFE standards	N	7. Ban gay bias in workplace	*	11. Free trade with Peru	Y
4. Bail out financial markets	N	8. Repeal D.C. gun law	Y	12. Overhaul FISA	Y

Election Results

2008 general	Lynn Westmoreland (R)	225,055	(66%)	($920,966)
	Stephen Camp (D)	117,522	(34%)	($54,855)
2008 primary	Lynn Westmoreland (R)	unopposed		

Prior Winning Percentages: 2006 (68%); 2004 (76%)

Population		Race/Ethnicity		Work	
Pop. 2007:	757,344	White:	71.3%	Private:	77.1%
Change since 2000:	Up 20.3%	Black:	22.1%	Government:	16.8%
Urban:	56.4%	Hispanic:	3.5%	Self-employed:	5.8%
Rural:	43.6%	Asian:	1.6%	Blue collar:	25.2%
Area size:	4,180 sq. mi.	Native Am.:	0.2%	White collar:	59.5%
Age		Hawaiian:	0.0%	Khaki collar:	0.5%
Median age:	35.4 yrs.	Two+ races:	1.2%	Other:	14.8%
More than 65 yrs:	10.6%	*Ancestry*		Median income:	$54,553
Less than 18 yrs:	27.3%	USA:	13.7%	Median home value:	$165,200
Education		Irish:	9.8%	Poverty:	11.3%
H.S. grad:	84.3%	English:	9.7%	**Military Veterans**	
College grad:	23.6%			% of Pop:	13.0%
Grad degree:	8.4%				

South of Atlanta, Henry County is among the fastest growing areas in the United States, with a leap in population of 56% from 2000 to 2007. The county's flourishing residential, commercial and industrial development took root near its seven Interstate 75 interchanges and has benefited from the proximity to Hartsfield-Jackson Atlanta International Airport. West of Henry County is the old courthouse town of Fayetteville, whose Holliday-Dorsey-Fife House is thought to have inspired the

2008 Presidential Vote
McCain (R)	233,197	(65%)
Obama (D)	125,087	(35%)

2004 Presidential Vote
Bush (R)	207,252	(70%)
Kerry (D)	86,361	(29%)

Cook Partisan Voting Index: R+19

columned architecture of Tara in author Margaret Mitchell's *Gone With the Wind*. The town is now engulfed by suburban subdivisions spreading out from Atlanta. The city's sprawl has reached Newnan and Carrollton, and spread farther south to Thomaston. In the old textile town of West Point in Troup County, along the Alabama border, South Korean automaker Kia is building a $1.2 billion plant that is expected to bring 4,500 jobs to the area. Production of up to 300,000 cars annually was scheduled to start in late 2009.

Much of this territory is within the 3rd Congressional District of Georgia. In the 2005 redistricting, it replaced the old 8th District. It includes roughly one-third of the small industrial city of Columbus (the rest is in the 2nd District, which also contains most of Fort Benning), but Fayette County is the largest population center. And the ring of five counties that are closest to Atlanta include roughly half of the district's population. From 2000 to 2007, the district grew by 20%. This is conservative country, with young tradition-minded families and a large share of military families. People here are upwardly mobile, but aren't necessarily at the upper end of the income scale. The ancestral politics of most of this area was Democratic, but that is as much a part of history now as Tara. This is one of the most heavily Republican congressional districts in Georgia. President Bush won 70% here in 2004, and Republican candidate John McCain won 65% in 2008.

The congressman from the 3rd District is Lynn Westmoreland, a Republican elected in 2004. Westmoreland grew up in the Atlanta area, left Georgia State University after two years and became a real estate broker and homebuilder in Fayette County. After losing two races for the state Senate, Westmoreland was elected in 1992 to the Georgia House, where he founded the Conservative Policy Caucus, a group of fiscally conservative, anti-tax lawmakers. He got under the skin of the Democratic establishment to say the least; longtime Democratic House Speaker Tom Murphy once called him "a braying jackass." In 2000, he was elected House Minority Leader and in that position refused to agree to tax increases, even when it meant defying newly elected Republican Gov. Sonny Perdue.

In 2004, Republican Rep. Mac Collins ran for the Senate, and Westmoreland faced a choice between staying in Georgia, where he stood to become speaker if Republicans won a majority in the state House, or running for a safe Republican open seat in the U.S. House. He chose the latter and ran on an anti-spending platform. The primary race was a contest between Westmoreland and Dylan Glenn, a former staffer for Perdue and George H.W. Bush. Glenn, an African-American from Columbus, had run twice unsuccessfully in the 2nd District. He was endorsed by former House Speaker Newt Gingrich of Georgia, who argued that a Glenn victory would help the party appeal to black voters. Republican Sen. Saxby Chambliss endorsed Westmoreland. In the primary, he beat Glenn 46%-38%, winning 60% of the vote in his base in Fayette and Coweta counties. Glenn led in the three counties nearest his home base in Columbus. During the three weeks between the primary and the August runoff, Glenn accused Westmoreland of taking excessive gifts from lobbyists, airing an ad that depicted his opponent as a hog. Westmoreland labeled Glenn a "Washington insider" with an inflated resume. Westmoreland won 55%-45%, carrying 12 of the 18 counties.

In the House, Westmoreland has a conservative voting record. Following Hurricane Katrina in 2005, he worked with other conservatives to propose "Operation Offset," an attempt to limit the cost of the relief and reconstruction efforts in Gulf Coast states. In 2008, he helped to organize a month-long protest on the House floor of Speaker Nancy Pelosi's refusal to bring up for a vote energy legislation allowing more oil exploration.

He was outspoken in his opposition to the extension of the Voting Rights Act, citing the "great progress" Georgia made since enactment of the law in 1965 and the fact that many of the local communities with the worst records on voting rights "are controlled by minorities." When the House debated the bill in 2006, he offered an amendment to make it easier for states to opt out of the law's requirements, but lost. He opposed the bill giving the majority-black District of Columbia a full vote in the House, and in 2007 he was one of two House members who voted against a resolution authorizing special divisions in the FBI and U.S. Justice Department focused on investigating murders during the civil rights era. His views have led to rocky relationships with leading African-American politicians. During the 2008 presidential campaign, he called Democratic candidate Barack Obama "uppity," then said he was surprised to learn it was a racially loaded term. Westmoreland was among the House Republicans who demanded that Rep. Charles Rangel, a black Democrat from New York, step down as chairman of the Ways and Means Committee pending the resolution of ethics charges against Rangel.

Shortly after he took office, Westmoreland worked intensively with the new Republican majority in the state Legislature to redraw congressional district lines to create more compact districts, with the not unintended benefit of making a Republican incumbent safer and jeopardizing two incumbent Democrats. In March 2005, the Legislature passed a new congressional map designed by a 23-year-old legislative aide to Westmoreland. He has been re-elected with only token opposition and is considered a possible candidate for governor in 2010.

FOURTH DISTRICT

Hank Johnson (D)

Elected 2006, 2nd term; b. Oct. 2, 1954, Washington, D.C.; home, Lithonia; Clark Atlanta U., B.A. 1976, Texas S. U., J.D. 1979; Buddhist; married (Mereda Davis); 2 children.

Elected Office: DeKalb Cnty. comm., 2001–06.

Professional Career: Practicing atty., 1980–2006; Associate judge, DeKalb Cnty. Magistrate Court, 1989–2006.

DC Office: 1133 LHOB, 20515, 202-225-1605; Fax: 202-226-0691; Web site: hankjohnson.house.gov.

State Offices: Lithonia, 770-987-2291; Tucker, 770-939-2016.

Committees: *Armed Services* (21st of 36 D): Military Personnel; Readiness. *Judiciary* (13th of 24 D): Commercial & Administrative Law; Constitution, Civil Rights & Civil Liberties; Courts & Competition Policy (Chmn).

Group Ratings

	ADA	ACLU	AFS	LCV	ITIC	NTU	COC	ACU	CFG	FRC
2008	100	100	100	92	71	15	47	8	8	5
2007	100	—	100	95	—	3	47	0	0	—

National Journal Ratings

	2007 LIB — 2007 CONS			2008 LIB — 2008 CONS		
Economic	82%	—	0%	85%	—	0%
Social	88%	—	12%	82%	—	0%
Foreign	96%	—	0%	65%	—	32%
Composite	92%	—	8%	83%	—	17%

Key Votes of the 110th Congress

1. Increase minimum wage	Y	5. Share immigration data	N	9. Withdraw troops 8/08	Y
2. Expand SCHIP	Y	6. Foreign aid abortion ban	N	10. No operations in Iran	Y
3. Raise CAFE standards	Y	7. Ban gay bias in workplace	Y	11. Free trade with Peru	N
4. Bail out financial markets	N	8. Repeal D.C. gun law	N	12. Overhaul FISA	N

Election Results

2008 general	Hank Johnson (D) .... unopposed	($381,105)
2008 primary	Hank Johnson (D) .... unopposed	

Prior Winning Percentages: 2006 (75%)

Population		Race/Ethnicity		Work	
Pop. 2007:	673,585	White:	24.7%	Private:	79.8%
Change since 2000:	Up 7.0%	Black:	55.3%	Government:	14.4%
Urban:	98.5%	Hispanic:	13.7%	Self-employed:	5.6%
Rural:	1.5%	Asian:	4.8%	Blue collar:	24.9%
Area size:	333 sq. mi.	Native Am.:	0.1%	White collar:	58.3%
		Hawaiian:	0.1%	Khaki collar:	0.1%
Age		Two+ races:	0.9%	Other:	16.8%
Median age:	34.3 yrs.			Median income:	$47,728
More than 65 yrs:	7.2%	*Ancestry*		Median home value:	$165,300
Less than 18 yrs:	25.9%	English:	4.7%	Poverty:	14.6%
Education		Irish:	4.1%		
H.S. grad:	83.2%	Subsaharan:	3.8%	**Military Veterans**	
College grad:	29.3%			% of Pop:	8.9%
Grad degree:	10.5%				

In 1920, when Gutzom Borglum began sculpting Jefferson Davis, Robert E. Lee, and Stonewall Jackson into the side of Stone Mountain, the huge outcropping of granite—the largest single piece of sculpture in the world—was a day's drive into the country from central Atlanta and was soon to become a rallying point for the Ku Klux Klan. Even when the memorial was completed in 1972, suburban development barely reached this far. But today, after three decades of some of the most explosive

2008 Presidential Vote
Obama (D) 219,046   (79%)
McCain (R)...............................55,378   (20%)

2004 Presidential Vote
Kerry (D)................................167,666   (71%)
Bush (R) 67,040   (28%)

Cook Partisan Voting Index: D + 24

metropolitan growth in the country, DeKalb County is part of the Atlanta metropolitan area, and this monument to the Confederacy sits among one of the most cosmopolitan and liberal constituencies in the South.

In north DeKalb County are affluent suburbs, including much of Atlanta's Jewish community, with voting habits much more liberal than in other suburbs. South DeKalb County has been transformed from mostly rural territory in the 1970s into one of the nation's largest collections of affluent African-American neighborhoods, rivaled only by Prince George's County in Maryland. The county was a prime destination for evacuees from New Orleans following Hurricane Katrina in 2005. DeKalb's population grew by 22% in the 1990s, and by 9% from 2000 to 2007. The demographic changes have moved its politics well to the left. It was a Republican county when rural Georgia was almost all Democratic in the 1960s. Now it is the most heavily Democratic major county in Georgia. In 2004, DeKalb voted 73%-27% for Democrat John Kerry, his best percentage in the state, except for one tiny rural county. In 2008, Democrat Barack Obama won DeKalb, 79%-20%.

The 4th Congressional District of Georgia consists of more than two-thirds of DeKalb County, a corner of the more Republican Gwinnett County and much of Rockdale County, including Conyers. In 2008,

Rockdale elected its first black County Commission chairman. About 75% of the population of the district now is in DeKalb. The 4th and the next-door 5th District, both with African-American majorities, are the most Democratic in Georgia.

The congressman from the 4th District is Hank Johnson, a Democrat who won the seat in 2006. He was born in Washington, D.C., where his father was director of classifications and paroles for the Bureau of Prisons and his mother was a schoolteacher. He practiced law as a civil and criminal litigator, served 12 years as a magistrate judge in DeKalb County and then five years on the DeKalb County Commission. He resigned from the commission to run for Congress. Although his immediate family members are Presbyterians, he has been a Buddhist since the 1970s; he and Rep. Mazie Hirono, D-Hawaii, are the first practicing Buddhists in Congress.

Johnson ousted Democratic Rep. Cynthia McKinney in the primary. McKinney had served five terms in the House before losing her seat to Denise Majette in the 2002 Democratic primary. But she won it back two years later, after Majette decided to run for the Senate. She was a controversial incumbent, once suggesting that President Bush might have had prior knowledge of the September 11 terrorist attacks but did not act on it because a war on terrorism would boost defense stocks held by his father's friends. In 2006, McKinney drew criticism even from within her own party after an altercation with a Capitol Police officer who stopped her at a security checkpoint. Then Democratic Minority Leader Nancy Pelosi said, "I find it hard to see any set of facts that would justify striking a police officer." McKinney apologized on the House floor a week later, but the damage was done. Until that incident, McKinney looked to be beating Johnson for the nomination

In the July 18 primary, McKinney did lead Johnson, 47%-44%, but her failure to break the 50% threshold in the three-candidate field forced a runoff three weeks later between the top two vote-getters. Johnson gained additional momentum after the primary. His fundraising, which had been anemic, suddenly picked up, as donors from both parties, including former Democratic Gov. Roy Barnes, weighed in against McKinney. She responded by criticizing Johnson's past financial troubles, which included declaring bankruptcy in the late 1980s. But in the runoff, turnout was up and Johnson beat McKinney easily, 59%-41%. He carried all three counties, winning 57%-43% in McKinney's stronghold of DeKalb. McKinney was a victim not only of her only mishaps, but also of the changing political and cultural demographics in DeKalb. Johnson breezed to victory in the general election against minor opposition.

In the House, Johnson has established a solidly liberal voting record and a reputation as a thoughtful lawmaker. On the Judiciary Committee, he questioned political hirings and firings at the Justice Department during the Bush administration and sponsored a resolution calling for the impeachment of Vice President Cheney. He also called for an investigation of the use of water boarding, a form of coercion that simulates drowning and had been used on suspected terrorists. He backed relief for people facing housing foreclosures and sought protections against predatory lending. In 2009, he became chairman of the revamped Judiciary Subcommittee on Courts and Competition Policy, and he took a step in the direction of getting on a leadership track by joining the House Democratic whip organization in 2009.

Johnson won re-election without major party opposition, the first such outcome in 52 years in the 4th District. McKinney considered a rematch with Johnson, but then decided to run for president as the nominee of the Green Party.

FIFTH DISTRICT

John Lewis (D)

Elected 1986, 12th term; b. Feb. 21, 1940, Troy, AL; home, Atlanta; Amer. Baptist Theol. Seminary, B.A. 1961, Fisk U., B.A. 1963; Baptist; married (Lillian); 1 child.

Elected Office: Atlanta City Cncl., 1981–86.

Professional Career: Chmn., Student Nonviolent Coord. Cmte., 1963–66; Field Foundation, 1966–67; Community organization dir., Southern Regional Cncl., 1967–70; Exec. dir., Voter Educ. Project, 1970–76; Assoc. dir., ACTION, 1977–80; Community affairs dir., Natl. Coop. Bank, 1980–82.

DC Office: 343 CHOB, 20515, 202-225-3801; Fax: 202-225-0351; Web site: www.house.gov/johnlewis.

State Offices: Atlanta, 404-659-0116.

Committees: *Senior Chief Deputy Whip. Ways & Means* (5th of 26 D): Income Security & Family Support; Oversight (Chmn).

Group Ratings

	ADA	ACLU	AFS	LCV	ITIC	NTU	COC	ACU	CFG	FRC
2008	95	100	100	100	100	13	50	4	0	5
2007	85	—	90	95	—	7	55	0	11	—

National Journal Ratings

	2007 LIB	—	2007 CONS	2008 LIB	—	2008 CONS
Economic	82%	—	0%	85%	—	0%
Social	92%	—	0%	67%	—	28%
Foreign	63%	—	37%	83%	—	15%
Composite	83%	—	17%	82%	—	18%

Key Votes of the 110th Congress

1. Increase minimum wage	Y	5. Share immigration data	N	9. Withdraw troops 8/08	N
2. Expand SCHIP	Y	6. Foreign aid abortion ban	N	10. No operations in Iran	Y
3. Raise CAFE standards	Y	7. Ban gay bias in workplace	Y	11. Free trade with Peru	Y
4. Bail out financial markets	Y	8. Repeal D.C. gun law	N	12. Overhaul FISA	N

Election Results

2008 general	John Lewis (D) .... unopposed		($1,195,117)
2008 primary	John Lewis (D) 36,713	(69%)	
	Markel Hutchins (D)..8,287	(16%)	
	'Able' Mable Thomas (D)..8,185	(15%)	

Prior Winning Percentages: 2006 (100%); 2004 (100%); 2002 (100%); 2000 (77%); 1998 (79%); 1996 (100%); 1994 (69%); 1992 (72%); 1990 (76%); 1988 (78%); 1986 (75%)

Population		Race/Ethnicity		Work	
Pop. 2007:	667,877	White:	37.3%	Private:	80.8%
Change since 2000:	Up 6.1%	Black:	50.8%	Government:	12.7%
Urban:	99.7%	Hispanic:	8.1%	Self-employed:	6.3%
Rural:	0.3%	Asian:	2.5%	Blue collar:	15.8%
Area size:	247 sq. mi.	Native Am.:	0.2%	White collar:	67.2%
Age		Hawaiian:	0.0%	Khaki collar:	0.0%
Median age:	35.1 yrs.	Two+ races:	1.0%	Other:	16.9%
More than 65 yrs:	9.2%	**Ancestry**		Median income:	$45,881
Less than 18 yrs:	21.7%	English:	7.5%	Median home value:	$242,200
Education		German:	5.6%	Poverty:	21.0%
H.S. grad:	83.6%	Irish:	4.8%	**Military Veterans**	
College grad:	41.2%			% of Pop:	7.4%
Grad degree:	16.6%				

Venture out of the quiet of the Ebenezer Baptist Church or the shade of the Rev. Martin Luther King Jr.'s boyhood home two blocks away and into the steamy heat of the Georgia sun, and one can see, a mile away, downtown Atlanta's atrium skyscrapers. They are evidence of the wealth and vibrant growth of the commercial capital of the South, the metropolis that has grown up where there was little more than a railroad junction at the time of the Civil War. But the human achievement that is downtown

2008 Presidential Vote

Obama (D) 231,893	(80%)
McCain (R)...............................57,213	(20%)

2004 Presidential Vote

Kerry (D).................................179,576	(74%)
Bush (R) 62,351	(26%)

Cook Partisan Voting Index: D+26

Atlanta is overshadowed by the revolution started in large part by a man who grew up on Auburn Avenue. Atlanta's white establishment, led by mayors William Hartsfield and Ivan Allen and Coca-Cola's Robert Woodruff, deserve credit for abandoning segregation, but it was King and other civil rights leaders who took the risks that led them to do so. Atlanta's city fathers acted out of good will, but also with an eye for the economic growth of the city, which they knew would be hurt by violent resistance.

Today, Atlanta is the center of the nation's ninth-largest metropolitan area. From Auburn Avenue, it spreads into two dozen counties of northern Georgia. From 2000 to 2007, it was the nation's fastest-growing metropolitan area. Its Hartsfield-Jackson Airport is the busiest in the world, with 90 million passengers in 2008, nearly 1 million takeoffs and landings and an expansion of its international terminal under way. Atlanta also has vibrant office centers, in downtown, midtown, and Buckhead to the north. Stadiums and sports facilities were built for the 1996 Summer Olympics. Coca-Cola's skyscraper headquarters stands as a symbol of Atlanta's most successful worldwide business. In 2006, Coca-Cola donated a $10 million parcel of land near Centennial Park for a $100 million civil rights museum to house the Martin Luther King Jr. papers. Mayor Shirley Franklin had orchestrated a $32 million loan to rescue them from a Sotheby's auction.

The 5th Congressional District of Georgia includes all of the city of Atlanta, down to the suburb of East Point to the south. It occupies most of the land inside the Interstate 285 ring road—the city of

Atlanta, including posh and Republican Buckhead, the westernmost part of DeKalb County, and the northern edge of Clayton County, including the airport. The 5th District is overwhelmingly Democratic.

The congressman from the 5th District is John Lewis, who made history as a leader of the civil rights movement, an experience he recounted in his 1998 autobiography, *Walking With the Wind*. A sharecropper's son from Troy, Ala., he was seized by religious fervor as a child, preaching in the barnyard, determined to be a minister. Lewis was the first in his family to finish high school. He wrote to activist Ralph Abernathy for help in suing for the right to enter Troy State College, and he met King when he was 18. In 1959, at age 19, he helped organize the first lunch-counter sit-in, which was received with open hostility. In 1960, the day after John F. Kennedy was elected president, Lewis sat in the Krystal Diner in Nashville, where a waitress poured cleansing powder down his back and water over his food to get him to leave. The restaurant manager then turned a fumigating machine on him.

In May 1961, he was on the first of the Freedom Rides, in which protesters of segregation rode buses through the South and were attacked as they went. Lewis was viciously beaten in Rock Hill, S.C., and Montgomery, Ala. He spoke at the 1963 March on Washington, criticizing Kennedy liberals for inaction on civil rights and calling for massive help for the poor. In 1964, he helped coordinate the Mississippi Freedom Project. And in March 1965, he led the Selma-to-Montgomery march to petition for voting rights and was beaten by policemen, who fractured his skull. Quietly maintaining his poise and sound judgment under harsh circumstances, Lewis was one of the people who risked their lives to make the civil rights revolution happen. He worked for Robert Kennedy for president in 1968 and was with him in Indianapolis when they heard King had been shot.

Lewis's first foray into electoral politics was unsuccessful. He ran in 1977 to replace Democratic Rep. Andrew Young in the House and was soundly beaten by Democrat Wyche Fowler. After winning a seat on the Atlanta Council in 1981, Lewis ran again for Congress in 1986 and trailed Julian Bond 47%-35% in the primary. Even though Bond won more than 60% of the black vote, Lewis won the runoff by assembling a coalition of poor blacks and affluent whites. "Vote for the tugboat, not the showboat" was his slogan, stressing his hard work on local issues. He has been re-elected easily since.

Lewis has been a strong partisan, with a firmly liberal voting record. Usually quiet, he can speak in the forceful cadences reminiscent of black preachers during the civil rights movement, as he did in opposition to the Gulf War resolution in January 1991 and to the impeachment of President Clinton in December 1998. He is a member of the Democratic leadership, the senior chief deputy whip. He also chairs the Oversight Subcommittee of the House Ways and Means Committee. Only occasionally does he defect from his party, as when he opposed the 1994 crime bill because of his disapproval of capital punishment and when he voted against the Iraq supplemental spending bill in March 2007 because it contained funds for continued military action.

Lewis has worked to commemorate the civil rights revolution in which he played such a large part. He got a federal building in Atlanta named for King and won historic-trail designation for the demonstrators' route from Selma to Montgomery. Since 1998, he has led members of Congress on pilgrimages to civil rights sites. In 2005, Georgia Republican Sen. Saxby Chambliss and Democratic Rep. David Scott sponsored a bill to rename a building at the Martin Luther King Jr. National Historic Site the John Lewis Civil Rights Institute.

Lewis has stoutly defended racial quotas and preferences. He strongly championed the reauthorization of the Voting Rights Act, and his support helped ensure it carried by a large majority over the objections of critics, who claimed it was no longer necessary. In June 2007, he won House passage of his bill authorizing and funding new offices in the FBI and the U.S. Justice Department to investigate old civil rights cases that have languished over the years. In early 2009, the ethics travails of Ways and Means Committee Chairman Charles Rangel, D-N.Y., fueled speculation that Lewis could be an acceptable alternative if Rangel were forced to step down, even though Lewis was only the fifth-ranking Democrat on the panel.

The 2008 presidential campaign was a difficult experience for Lewis. Following extensive pressure from various camps, he endorsed Hillary Rodham Clinton in 2007 as "a strong leader," and he defended her from attacks by other civil rights leaders. When Barack Obama won the Georgia primary, Lewis came under local and national pressure to switch. Some of the pressure came from two challengers in the July primary, which Lewis eventually won, with 69% of the vote. In late February, he endorsed Obama "following a long, hard, difficult struggle" and spoke of Obama's candidacy as a transformational moment. "Something's happening in America, something some of us did not see coming," Lewis said. "It's a movement. It's a spiritual event."

Obama welcomed the switch, and Lewis became an outspoken advocate, sometimes excessively so, as in an October statement when he compared the campaign rhetoric of Republican nominee John McCain to that of former segregationist presidential candidate George Wallace of Alabama. McCain called the comparison "shocking and beyond the pale." At the Democratic convention in August, where he was treated as an iconic hero, Lewis broke down in tears as he spoke of Obama's historic candidacy and the 45th anniversary of King's famous "I Have a Dream" speech. In a dramatic epilogue to Lewis's involvement in the presidential campaign, in February 2009, Elwin Wilson of Rock Hill, S.C., apologized on national television for slugging Lewis in the Freedom Ride attack, saying "I am ashamed." Seated next to him, Lewis embraced the 68-year-old man, and said, "I forgive you." Lewis called the apology "amazing, unreal, unbelievable" and said that it showed the "power of reconciliation."

SIXTH DISTRICT

Tom Price (R)

Elected 2004, 3rd term; b. Oct. 8, 1954, Lansing, MI; home, Roswell; U. of MI, B.A. 1976, M.D. 1979; Presbyterian; married (Betty); 1 child.

Elected Office: GA Senate, 1996–2004; Maj. ldr., 2002–03.

Professional Career: Practicing orthopedic surgeon, 1979–2002; Asst. prof., Emory U., 2002-present.

DC Office: 424 CHOB, 20515, 202-225-4501; Fax: 202-225-4656; Web site: www.house.gov/tomprice.

State Offices: Canton, 678-493-6176; Marietta, 770-565-4990.

Committees: *Education & Labor* (12th of 19 R): Health, Employment, Labor & Pensions; Workforce Protections (RMM). *Financial Services* (17th of 29 R): Capital Markets, Insurance & Government Sponsored Enterprises; Domestic Monetary Policy & Technology; Financial Institutions & Consumer Credit.

Group Ratings

	ADA	ACLU	AFS	LCV	ITIC	NTU	COC	ACU	CFG	FRC
2008	10	9	0	8	71	85	72	100	100	94
2007	0	—	0	10	—	88	80	100	98	—

National Journal Ratings

	2007 LIB	—	2007 CONS		2008 LIB	—	2008 CONS
Economic	6%	—	93%		6%	—	93%
Social	0%	—	91%		0%	—	91%
Foreign	0%	—	72%		0%	—	95%
Composite	8%	—	92%		5%	—	96%

Key Votes of the 110th Congress

1. Increase minimum wage	N	5. Share immigration data	Y	9. Withdraw troops 8/08	N
2. Expand SCHIP	N	6. Foreign aid abortion ban	Y	10. No operations in Iran	N
3. Raise CAFE standards	N	7. Ban gay bias in workplace	N	11. Free trade with Peru	Y
4. Bail out financial markets	N	8. Repeal D.C. gun law	Y	12. Overhaul FISA	Y

Election Results

2008 general	Tom Price (R)	231,520	(68%)	($1,607,716)
	Bill Jones (D)	106,551	(32%)	($640,883)
2008 primary	Tom Price (R)	unopposed		

Prior Winning Percentages: 2006 (72%); 2004 (100%)

Population		Race/Ethnicity		Work	
Pop. 2007:	779,388	White:	74.7%	Private:	84.7%
Change since 2000:	Up 23.8%	Black:	8.6%	Government:	8.2%
Urban:	93.5%	Hispanic:	8.7%	Self-employed:	6.8%
Rural:	6.5%	Asian:	6.0%	Blue collar:	12.0%
Area size:	695 sq. mi.	Native Am.:	0.1%	White collar:	77.3%
Age		Hawaiian:	0.1%	Khaki collar:	0.0%
Median age:	36.5 yrs.	Two+ races:	1.1%	Other:	10.6%
More than 65 yrs:	7.8%	*Ancestry*		Median income:	$79,184
Less than 18 yrs:	27.4%	German:	11.3%	Median home value:	$279,600
Education		English:	10.9%	Poverty:	5.5%
H.S. grad:	93.3%	Irish:	10.2%	**Military Veterans**	
College grad:	52.6%			% of Pop:	9.0%
Grad degree:	17.1%				

In the red clay north of Atlanta, an almost wholly new metropolitan quarter has grown up over the past four decades, as affluent Atlanta has spread out past the Interstate 285 Perimeter into territory that was once farms, small towns, and modest factory cities. Where there were perhaps 100,000 people in the 1950s, there are more than 1 million today. No longer is downtown Atlanta the only focus. The edge cities of Perimeter Center and the area near Cumberland Mall are not just for shopping. They are major office centers, exceeding downtown Atlanta in square footage. Along the usually jammed Georgia 400 highway, in the fast-growing northern part of Fulton County, are the affluent suburbs of Sandy Springs, Roswell, and Alpharetta. At the tip of the county, near the Chattahoochee River, the new cities of Johns Creek and Milton were incorporated in 2006 to free residents of county government. Cobb County is the headquarters of The Weather Channel. Home Depot, the nation's second-largest retailer, is based in Sandy Springs. Farther out in Cherokee County, where the population has more than doubled since 1990, the big issue has been the proposed Northern Arc highway. Commuters on congested roads have ached for relief. For all this economic and demographic change, this Golden Crescent north of the Perimeter and between Interstate 75 in Cobb County and Interstate 85 strives to keep at least some reminders of old rural Georgia. The buildings are tree-shaded, and lush foliage and large-lot requirements have given most of the communities a woodsy look.

2008 Presidential Vote		
McCain (R)	226,456	(65%)
Obama (D)	120,093	(34%)
2004 Presidential Vote		
Bush (R)	215,437	(70%)
Kerry (D)	90,348	(29%)
Cook Partisan Voting Index:	R + 19	

The 6th Congressional District of Georgia occupies a large portion of this suburban area north of Atlanta, including the eastern slice of Cobb County, much of northern Fulton, the northwest tip of DeKalb, and all of Cherokee County. It contains affluent Alpharetta, fast-growing Canton, and historic Roswell. This seat was created after the 1990 census, and its boundaries have twice been reshaped by redistricting. It would surely surprise Georgians a generation or two ago to learn that one of their congressional districts would rank among the nation's richest and most educated. Now the 6th and the 7th districts both do. The 6th is one of several heavily Republican Georgia districts, and the political tension here tends to be between economic and cultural conservatives. In 2004, President Bush defeated Democrat John Kerry 70%-29%. In 2008, Democrat Barack Obama trimmed the Republican lead for John McCain here to 65%-34%.

The congressman from the 6th District is Tom Price, a Republican elected in 2004. Price grew up in Michigan and graduated from the University of Michigan and its medical school. His father and grandfather were both physicians. He did his residency in orthopedic surgery at Emory Medical School and then moved to Roswell, where he was involved in civic affairs and was president of the Rotary Club. Working closely with the Medical Association of Georgia, he campaigned locally against President Clinton's health care plan in the early 1990s. When a seat opened in the state Senate in 1996, he was elected, and quickly moved up the leadership ranks to become majority leader when Republicans captured the Senate in 2002 for the first time since Reconstruction.

When Republican U.S. Rep. Johnny Isakson announced he was running for the Senate seat being vacated by Democrat Zell Miller, the contest for this heavily Republican open seat was hard-fought and big-spending. Three state senators ran—Price from Fulton County, and Robert Lamutt and Chuck Clay from Cobb County. Price spent $499,000 of his own money and contrasted his work in medicine with the legal and business careers of his two main opponents. He highlighted his fiscal conservatism and strong support for limiting jury awards in malpractice suits, a position that won him considerable support from the medical community. Calling the federal income tax "broken," he supported a national retail sales tax. He said that he had "a surgeon's mentality. . . . I get things done." Price led the first round of the primary with 35% of the vote; Lamutt made it into the runoff with 28% (to 21% for Clay). Lamutt, who cited his success in creating an assets-management firm and gave $1.5 million to his campaign, criticized Price as a "special interest" candidate because he raised large sums from fellow doctors. He also attacked Price's 2003 support for a 25-cent tax increase on cigarettes. Price defended his vote as a tool to reduce local property taxes, and claimed Lamutt helped cigarette makers at the expense of everyday people. In the runoff, Price got 79% in Fulton County and held Lamutt to 59% in Cobb. With the small vote in Cherokee County split nearly evenly, Price won 54%-46%.

In 2004, Lamutt was one of two candidates in Georgia runoffs endorsed by former Speaker Newt Gingrich, who once represented this district; both lost. With physician Paul Broun, obstetrician Phil Gingrey and dentist John Linder, Price is the fourth medical professional in the Georgia Republican delegation.

In the House, Price's voting record is among the most conservative. As a member of the Financial Services Committee, he has dealt contentiously on housing issues with liberal Chairman Barney Frank, D-Mass. On health care, he opposed government intervention to negotiate Medicare drug prices, which he said were being reduced by market forces. He joined Wisconsin Democrat Tammy Baldwin on a proposal to increase health insurance coverage by giving the states more authority and flexibility. During debate of the State Children's Health Insurance Program in 2007, he crafted a conservative alternative to the Democratic plans to expand the program. The Democrats wanted to increase the program by $35 billion over five years. Price called for an $11.5 billion increase over five years, with incentives to encourage people to get into the private insurance market. As one of 13 physicians in the House in 2009, he helped to create the Medical and Dental Doctors Caucus to try to establish a unified Republican message on health care.

Price also has been a fierce partisan. In 2009, he became chairman of the Republican Study Committee, which promotes conservative ideas and legislation and includes some of the most conservative House members. He also helped create an "Official Truth Squad" to highlight statements and positions of Democrats that he thinks might be unpopular with the public. *The Washington Post* wrote in 2007: "The bookish physician has transformed himself into a Republican guerrilla warrior, a near-constant presence on the House floor, gumming up the works with parliamentary objections, verbal volleys, and partisan maneuvering." He was a leading organizer of the House Republicans' protest in the House chamber during the August 2008 recess, which was aimed at pressuring Democratic Speaker Nancy Pelosi to bring to the floor a bill allowing offshore oil exploration in America's coastal waters.

Georgia's redistricting in 2005 served the Fulton County-based Price's interest by reducing opportunities for GOP primary challengers from Cobb County. That county is now divided between the 6th, 11th, and 13th districts. He has been re-elected with only minor opposition.

SEVENTH DISTRICT

John Linder (R)

Elected 1992, 9th term; b. Sept. 9, 1942, Deer River, MN; home, Duluth; U. of MN, B.S. 1964, D.D.S., 1967; Presbyterian; married (Lynne); 2 children.

Military Career: Air Force, 1967–69.

Elected Office: GA House of Reps., 1974–80, 1982–90.

Professional Career: Practicing dentist, 1969–82; Founder & pres., Linder Financial Corp., 1977–92.

DC Office: 1026 LHOB, 20515, 202-225-4272; Fax: 202-225-4696; Web site: linder.house.gov.

State Offices: Lawrenceville, 770-232-3005.

Committees: *Ways & Means* (7th of 15 R): Income Security & Family Support (RMM); Oversight; Select Revenue Measures.

Group Ratings

	ADA	ACLU	AFS	LCV	ITIC	NTU	COC	ACU	CFG	FRC
2008	0	9	0	8	29	87	72	100	100	100
2007	0	—	0	0	—	89	75	100	98	—

National Journal Ratings

	2007 LIB — 2007 CONS		2008 LIB — 2008 CONS	
Economic	0%	— 97%	11%	— 88%
Social	0%	— 91%	16%	— 82%
Foreign	0%	— 72%	8%	— 89%
Composite	7%	— 93%	13%	— 87%

Key Votes of the 110th Congress

1. Increase minimum wage	N	5. Share immigration data	Y	9. Withdraw troops 8/08	N
2. Expand SCHIP	N	6. Foreign aid abortion ban	Y	10. No operations in Iran	N
3. Raise CAFE standards	N	7. Ban gay bias in workplace	N	11. Free trade with Peru	Y
4. Bail out financial markets	N	8. Repeal D.C. gun law	Y	12. Overhaul FISA	Y

Election Results

2008 general	John Linder (R)	209,354	(62%)	($375,540)
	Doug Heckman (D)	128,159	(38%)	($174,163)
2008 primary	John Linder (R)	unopposed		

Prior Winning Percentages: 2006 (71%); 2004 (100%); 2002 (79%); 2000 (100%); 1998 (69%); 1996 (64%); 1994 (58%); 1992 (51%)

Population		Race/Ethnicity		Work	
Pop. 2007:	845,418	White:	62.2%	Private:	82.9%
Change since 2000:	Up 34.3%	Black:	18.4%	Government:	10.7%
Urban:	86.8%	Hispanic:	10.5%	Self-employed:	6.2%
Rural:	13.2%	Asian:	7.3%	Blue collar:	20.6%
Area size:	978 sq. mi.	Native Am.:	0.2%	White collar:	67.0%
		Hawaiian:	0.1%	Khaki collar:	0.0%
Age		Two+ races:	1.1%	Other:	12.4%
Median age:	34.0 yrs.			Median income:	$65,284
More than 65 yrs:	6.8%	*Ancestry*		Median home value:	$190,900
Less than 18 yrs:	29.4%	German:	9.1%	Poverty:	8.6%
		Irish:	8.8%		
Education		English:	8.6%	**Military Veterans**	
H.S. grad:	86.9%			% of Pop:	9.2%
College grad:	32.9%				
Grad degree:	10.1%				

In the last two decades, greater Atlanta has grown out in every direction: south past the airport, west over the Chattahoochee River, north past the Perimeter Center, and east and northeast past Stone Mountain. The outer suburbs north of Atlanta have grown fastest of all. Gwinnett County features more-mature neighborhoods of affluent professionals and entrepreneurs. The closer-in portions of Gwinnett, near Interstate 85, with their older shopping districts, have been attracting Georgia's largest concentration of Hispanics and also middle-class blacks. The county's rapidly growing school system boasts that its students speak more than 100 languages. Farther out in Lawrenceville, Duluth, and Buford, downtown Atlanta seems very far away, both physically—it is 30 to 50 miles, and more than an hour of clogged rush-hour driving, to Peachtree Street—and in state of mind. For many, Atlanta is something that whizzes by on the way to Hartsfield-Jackson Atlanta International Airport.

2008 Presidential Vote		
McCain (R)	211,493	(60%)
Obama (D)	139,259	(39%)
2004 Presidential Vote		
Bush (R)	199,492	(70%)
Kerry (D)	85,472	(30%)
Cook Partisan Voting Index:	R + 16	

The growth here and its diversity are hard to overstate. Gwinnett County cast 21,000 votes in 1972 and 291,000 in 2008. By contrast, Fulton County, which includes central Atlanta, cast 405,000, and DeKalb County cast 322,000. Gwinnett's population grew 32% from 2000 to 2007, to 776,000. Like other metro Atlanta counties, the non-Hispanic white population has been dropping in the schools, while the overall numbers soar. There is some international flavor here: Mexicans in Norcross, Koreans in Duluth, and Bosnians in Lawrenceville. Beyond Gwinnett, recent increases have been equally robust, with growth spurts of 37% to 55% in Barrow, Walton, and Newton counties. These were once rural, low-income, and heavily Democratic areas. Now they are full of strivers and achievers, with many religious conservatives and many economic conservatives, and relatively few liberals and Democrats. Concern over excessive growth led Wal-Mart in 2008 to abandon plans for a supercenter in Duluth.

The 7th Congressional District of Georgia owes its existence to the rapid growth here since the early 1990s. Redistricting in 2005 gave it a more compact shape and recentered the district in Gwinnett, which has 78% of the population, compared to 58% previously. In addition to all of Barrow and Walton counties, the 7th includes thin slices of Forsyth and Newton counties. The changes increased the African-American population from 7% to 12% and had the effect of reducing the 2004 vote here for President Bush from 76% to 70%. In 2008, Republican John McCain beat Democrat Barack Obama in the district 60%-39%.

The congressman from the 7th District is John Linder, a Republican first elected in 1992 in the old 4th District. Like others in the Georgia delegation, Linder grew up elsewhere, in his case Minnesota, where he went to college and dental school. After two years in the Air Force, he moved to greater Atlanta and practiced dentistry for 13 years. In 1977, he started Linder Financial Corporation, a lending institution for entrepreneurial ventures in the South. In 1974, at age 32, he was elected to the Georgia House, where he served all but two of the next 16 years. In 1990, he challenged Democratic U.S. Rep. Ben Jones, but lost 52%-48%. In 1992, Linder ran first in a six-candidate primary and won the runoff with 62% of the vote. In the general election, he faced Democratic state Sen. Cathey Steinberg and won 51%-49%. From this tenuous beginning Linder quickly became an important representative. For a time, he was a close ally to House Speaker Newt Gingrich of Georgia. They went back a ways. In 1975 Linder, Gingrich, and Paul Coverdell began meeting to try to build a strong Georgia Republican Party, and in 20 years, they were a representative, speaker, and senator, respectively. Gingrich resigned in 1998 after Republican losses at the polls, and Coverdell died in 2000.

Linder has solidly conservative views, though they're a bit more Wall Street than Main Street. After Republicans won control, Gingrich gave Linder a seat on the House Rules Committee and called on him often to preside over contentious debates. After the 1996 election, Gingrich chose Linder as chairman of the National Republican Congressional Committee to run the GOP's efforts to maintain the majority. He excelled at fundraising, and relentlessly prevailed on incumbents to contribute to Republican challengers. He did a good job of recruiting candidates and shared the assumption of most observers that Republicans would gain seats as the out party in an off-year election. But one of his ads misfired. At the behest of Gingrich, it raised the impeachment issue against Clinton. While it ran in only a few districts, the ad was publicized nationally, and yielded a minimum of gain and a maximum of pain. When Republicans lost five seats, Linder was in deep trouble. He said the problem was the lack of a "strong message," which "was not my responsibility"—a reference to Gingrich. Rep. Tom Davis of Virginia started running to replace Linder at the NRCC, with the support of others in the leadership, and Linder reacted bitterly, saying he was being blamed unfairly for Republican losses. But the rank and file was uninterested in the finger-pointing, and decided to clean house. Two days after the election, Gingrich announced his resignation, and 12 days later, Linder lost to Davis 130-77.

Taking a lower profile, Linder resumed his legislative work and got on well with the new Republican leadership. He turned his attention to the fight for tax reform and his FairTax plan, which would abolish all federal income taxes, including payroll taxes, and replace them with a single 23% national retail sales tax, with no exceptions for food or medical expenses but a monthly rebate for low-income citizens. As Linder explains, "The FairTax gives the American people control over their own lives again by allowing them to keep 100% of their paychecks and shielding their personal information from bureaucrats."

Linder had longed to be chairman of the Rules Committee, but Speaker Hastert in 2005 decided that the six-year limit on committee chairmen did not apply to the Rules Committee, and gave California Rep. David Dreier another term as chairman. Linder left the committee and later that year got a seat on the influential Ways and Means Committee, with jurisdiction over tax policy. With Republicans consumed by Social Security reform and other issues, he made no legislative headway on tax reform. But he continued to try to generate grassroots interest, and in 2005 his *FairTaxBook,* written with radio host Neal Boortz, debuted at No. 1 on the *New York Times* nonfiction best-seller list. When Republicans lost control of Congress in 2007, his proposal lost much of its legislative saliency. He focused more of his attention on the water shortages in the Atlanta metro area, and organized a House caucus to address the "devastating condition."

In 2002, Linder was inconvenienced by the redistricting plan drawn by Georgia Democrats. Although the new 7th appeared tailor-made for him, he found himself in a primary contest with fellow Republican Bob Barr. Most Republicans expected Barr would run in the new 11th District, which contained more of his old area. The race was a contrast of styles, not of voting records. Linder campaigned as a political insider who quietly got things done. Barr, an early advocate of the impeachment of Clinton, campaigned as a champion of conservative principles. Linder had more local financial support, while Barr had contributors across the nation. The campaign grew bitter, but the final result was unambiguous. Linder won 64%-36%. In 2008, he won 62%-38% over Democrat Doug Heckman, a former Army colonel who served in Iraq.

EIGHTH DISTRICT

Jim Marshall (D)

Elected 2002, 4th term; b. March 31, 1948, Ithaca, NY; home, Macon; Princeton U., B.A. 1972, Boston U., J.D. 1977; Catholic; married (Camille); 2 children.

Military Career: Army, 1968–70 (Vietnam).

Elected Office: Macon mayor, 1995–99.

Professional Career: Mercer U. law professor, 1979–95, 1999–2002.

DC Office: 504 CHOB, 20515, 202-225-6531; Fax: 202-225-3013; Web site: www.house.gov/marshall.

State Offices: Dublin, 478-296-2023; Macon, 478-464-0255; Tifton, 229-556-7418.

Committees: *Agriculture* (8th of 28 D): General Farm Commodities & Risk Management; Specialty Crops, Rural Development & Foreign Agriculture. *Armed Services* (17th of 36 D): Air & Land Forces; Readiness; Terrorism, Unconventional Threats & Capabilities.

Group Ratings

	ADA	ACLU	AFS	LCV	ITIC	NTU	COC	ACU	CFG	FRC
2008	70	45	71	69	86	22	67	28	20	88
2007	60	—	60	55	—	29	53	61	16	—

National Journal Ratings

	2007 LIB	—	2007 CONS	2008 LIB	—	2008 CONS
Economic	45%	—	55%	45%	—	55%
Social	44%	—	56%	46%	—	52%
Foreign	41%	—	58%	43%	—	57%
Composite	44%	—	57%	45%	—	55%

Key Votes of the 110th Congress

1. Increase minimum wage	Y	5. Share immigration data	Y	9. Withdraw troops 8/08	N
2. Expand SCHIP	N	6. Foreign aid abortion ban	Y	10. No operations in Iran	N
3. Raise CAFE standards	N	7. Ban gay bias in workplace	N	11. Free trade with Peru	N
4. Bail out financial markets	Y	8. Repeal D.C. gun law	Y	12. Overhaul FISA	Y

Election Results

2008 general	Jim Marshall (D)	157,241	(57%)	($1,736,540)
	Rick Goddard (R)	117,446	(43%)	($1,192,303)
2008 primary	Jim Marshall (D)	44,211	(86%)	
	Robert Nowak (D)	7,396	(14%)	

Prior Winning Percentages: 2006 (51%); 2004 (63%); 2002 (51%)

Population		Race/Ethnicity		Work	
Pop. 2007:	693,757	White:	60.6%	Private:	71.7%
Change since 2000:	Up 10.2%	Black:	33.6%	Government:	22.0%
Urban:	56.6%	Hispanic:	3.6%	Self-employed:	5.8%
Rural:	43.4%	Asian:	1.0%	Blue collar:	27.9%
Area size:	7,239 sq. mi.	Native Am.:	0.2%	White collar:	53.4%
		Hawaiian:	0.0%	Khaki collar:	0.7%
Age		Two+ races:	0.9%	Other:	18.0%
Median age:	35.2 yrs.			Median income:	$41,431
More than 65 yrs:	11.8%	*Ancestry*		Median home value:	$107,100
Less than 18 yrs:	26.5%	USA:	14.4%	Poverty:	18.8%
		English:	8.8%		
Education		Irish:	7.6%	**Military Veterans**	
H.S. grad:	78.5%			% of Pop:	12.6%
College grad:	17.4%				
Grad degree:	6.4%				

The hub of central Georgia, Macon is a city proud of its restored houses and its Japanese cherry trees, which it shows off during its annual International Cherry Blossom Festival. It is the home of music legends Otis Redding, James Brown, Little Richard, and the Allman Brothers, and of the Harriet Tubman Historical and Cultural Museum. Surrounding Macon are the farm and forest lands of central Georgia. Much of this land was the site of Gen. William Tecumseh Sherman's 1864 march

2008 Presidential Vote
McCain (R)	161,027	(56%)
Obama (D)	123,712	(43%)

2004 Presidential Vote
Bush (R)	147,729	(61%)
Kerry (D)	93,875	(39%)

Cook Partisan Voting Index: R + 10

from Atlanta to the sea. Twiggs and Wilkinson counties have been among the world's major sources of kaolin, a clay used for china and ceramics. A short drive north on Interstate 75 is Juliette, an old mill town that's too small for most maps. Many scenes in the movie *Fried Green Tomatoes* were filmed there. In 2008, the area suffered from major job losses in manufacturing and health care services, and construction of a new tire plant was delayed.

The 8th Congressional District of Georgia includes all of Macon and Bibb County and stretches about 200 miles north and south, from fast-growing Newton County in metro Atlanta to Colquitt County nearly at the Florida border. About one-half of its votes are cast in the five-county Macon metro area. From 2000 to 2007, Bibb County had virtually no change in population. With its Air Logistics Center and testing and repair site for the F-22 Raptor, Robins Air Force Base and the surrounding city of Warner Robins have grown significantly in recent years. This was Democratic country from the time of Gen. Sherman's march until the civil-rights revolution of the 1960s. Today the political balance is different. More than 70% of whites usually vote Republican. About 90% of blacks usually vote Democratic. So the political leanings of any district in this part of Georgia depend on the racial percentages. Redistricters in 2005 significantly changed the district with the goal of electing a Republican. It was renumbered from the 3rd to the 8th, and its shape was elongated to add new Republican territory. Slightly more than half of the population was new to the district in the 2006 election, and the new lines reduced the black population from 40% to 33%. President Bush's 2004 performance in this district was 61%, up from 55% four years earlier. In 2008, Republican John McCain won the district 56%-43%.

The congressman from the 8th District is Democrat Jim Marshall, first elected in 2002. The son and grandson of Army generals, he grew up at several Army posts. He graduated from high school in Mobile, Ala., and went on to Princeton University. But he interrupted his education to enlist in the Army and volunteer for infantry combat during the Vietnam War. He served in the elite Airborne Ranger reconnaissance platoon, was wounded in combat, and was awarded two Bronze Stars and a Purple Heart. After his military service, he graduated from Princeton and Boston University Law School. He joined the faculty of Mercer University law school in Macon, practiced business law, and became active in Democratic politics. His wife, Camille, is a federal bankruptcy trustee.

In his first political contest, Marshall was elected mayor of Macon in 1995. He made his first run for Congress in 2000 against Rep. Saxby Chambliss in the old 8th District. He campaigned almost exclusively on making prescription drugs more affordable for seniors, and lost 59%-41%. When Democrats redrew the district, Marshall quickly entered the contest and made his military experience the centerpiece of his 2002 campaign. Against three opponents in the Democratic primary, his toughest competitor was politically connected attorney Chuck Byrd, whose father was a former lieutenant governor. Byrd ran as a conservative in the tradition of former conservative Democratic Sen. Sam Nunn and as an opponent of abortion rights. But Marshall carried Bibb County solidly and won 54% of the vote, enough to avoid a runoff. In the general election, Marshall faced Bibb County Commissioner Calder Clay, an energetic fundraiser who claimed Marshall was too liberal for the district. Marshall emphasized his military record; Clay had not served in the military. Both supported President Bush on Iraq. In one of 2002's closest contests, Marshall won 50.5%-49.5%.

In the House, Marshall's voting record puts him among the most conservative Democrats. In March 2003, on the day after hostilities began in Iraq, Marshall showed up, uninvited, at a press conference convened by a group of anti-war House Democrats. "The time for debate is past," he announced. He then invoked an obscure House rule to cancel a Democratic Caucus meeting organized to debate war alternatives. After a September 2003 visit to Iraq, he criticized news coverage of the war for focusing disproportionately on setbacks. In an *Atlanta Journal-Constitution* opinion article, he urged Democrats to "carefully avoid using the language of failure," which he said could be "unforgivably self-fulfilling." He has made several trips to Iraq to follow the progress of the war. In 2007, he was one of two Democrats to vote against a resolution condemning the military surge in Iraq. He called the proposal "akin to sitting on the sidelines and booing in the middle of our own team's play, because we don't like the coach's call." In 2008, he continued to oppose timetables for withdrawal.

Marshall avidly backed legislation to permit veterans to receive full retirement pay plus disability compensation at the same time. In 2005, he turned his attention to changing another inequity for veterans: an 1891 law that required a dollar-for-dollar offset for those receiving both retirement pay and disability compensation. In 2007, he joined 95 House Republicans and one other Democrat who objected to House action on a bill to allow illegal immigrants to obtain citizenship. And in January 2008, Marshall was the only House Democrat who voted to sustain Bush's veto of a major expansion of the State Children's Health Insurance Program.

In 2004, Marshall turned down pleas from national and state Democrats to run for the Senate seat left open by Democrat Zell Miller's retirement. Instead, he faced a rematch with Calder Clay. In an unexpectedly strong showing, Marshall won 63%-37%. In 2006, Republicans nominated former Rep. Mac Collins, who served six terms before running unsuccessfully in 2004 for the Republican Senate nomination. Marshall, with the advantage of greater name recognition in the Macon area, ran against "extremists on both sides." Collins ran ads criticizing Marshall for support of Democratic policies. The result was one of the closest in the nation and took a week before it became official. Marshall won by 1,752 votes. His margin of victory came in Bibb County, which he took 63%-37%.

In 2007, Senate Democrats encouraged Marshall to challenge Republican Sen. Saxby Chambliss for re-election in 2008, but he declined. In his bid for re-election in 2008, he faced Republican Rick Goddard, the former commander of the Warner Robins Air Logistics Center at Robins Air Force Base, who was heavily recruited by the National Republican Congressional Committee. Goddard ran a conventional Republican campaign in a Democratic-leaning year, with emphasis on more energy production and campaign appearances by Bush and Vice President Cheney. Marshall won by a comfortable 57%-43%.

NINTH DISTRICT

Nathan Deal (R)

Elected 1992, 9th term; b. Aug. 25, 1942, Millen; home, Clermont; Mercer U., B.A. 1964, J.D. 1966; Baptist; married (Sandra); 4 children.

Military Career: Army, 1966–68.

Elected Office: Hall Cnty. Juvenile Court judge, 1971; GA Senate, 1980–92, Pres. pro tem, 1989–90, 1991–92.

Professional Career: Hall Cnty. atty., 1966–70; Asst. dist. atty., NE Judicial Circuit, 1970–71; Practicing atty., 1965–92.

DC Office: 2133 RHOB, 20515, 202-225-5211; Fax: 202-225-8272; Web site: www.house.gov/deal.

State Offices: Dalton, 706-226-5320; Gainesville, 770-535-2592; Lafayette, 706-638-7042.

Committees: *Energy & Commerce* (5th of 23 R): Communications, Technology & the Internet; Health (RMM); Oversight & Investigations.

Group Ratings

	ADA	ACLU	AFS	LCV	ITIC	NTU	COC	ACU	CFG	FRC
2008	5	18	0	8	17	83	83	100	98	100
2007	0	—	0	5	—	90	68	100	92	—

National Journal Ratings

	2007 LIB	—	2007 CONS		2008 LIB	—	2008 CONS
Economic	5%	—	94%		14%	—	86%
Social	0%	—	91%		0%	—	91%
Foreign	0%	—	72%		22%	—	74%
Composite	8%	—	92%		14%	—	86%

Key Votes of the 110th Congress

1. Increase minimum wage	N	5. Share immigration data	Y	9. Withdraw troops 8/08	N
2. Expand SCHIP	N	6. Foreign aid abortion ban	Y	10. No operations in Iran	N
3. Raise CAFE standards	N	7. Ban gay bias in workplace	N	11. Free trade with Peru	Y
4. Bail out financial markets	N	8. Repeal D.C. gun law	Y	12. Overhaul FISA	Y

Election Results

2008 general	Nathan Deal (R)	217,493	(76%)	($898,875)
	Jeff Scott (D)	70,537	(24%)	($23,708)
2008 primary	Nathan Deal (R)	unopposed		

Prior Winning Percentages: 2006 (77%); 2004 (100%); 2002 (100%); 2000 (75%); 1998 (100%); 1996 (66%); 1994 (58%); 1992 (59%)

Population		Race/Ethnicity		Work	
Pop. 2007:	759,233	White:	81.7%	Private:	82.4%
Change since 2000:	Up 20.6%	Black:	3.3%	Government:	10.8%
Urban:	47.3%	Hispanic:	12.4%	Self-employed:	6.5%
Rural:	52.7%	Asian:	1.1%	Blue collar:	33.3%
Area size:	4,418 sq. mi.	Native Am.:	0.3%	White collar:	53.2%
		Hawaiian:	0.0%	Khaki collar:	0.1%
Age		Two+ races:	1.1%	Other:	13.4%
Median age:	34.9 yrs.			Median income:	$47,104
More than 65 yrs:	11.3%	*Ancestry*		Median home value:	$154,800
Less than 18 yrs:	26.5%	USA:	17.6%	Poverty:	12.6%
		Irish:	11.4%		
Education		English:	9.6%	**Military Veterans**	
H.S. grad:	76.2%			% of Pop:	9.8%
College grad:	19.3%				
Grad degree:	6.3%				

At the end of the 20th century, the hills and mountains of north Georgia suddenly became one of the boom areas of the South. It was a sharp turn in the region's history. Since the early 19th century, when settlers drove out the Cherokee Indians, this was poor country, where small farmers scratched out a living on rocky land. Gen. William Tecumseh Sherman's march through Georgia during the Civil War devastated the area, and many of its young men who left to fight for the Confederacy never returned.

2008 Presidential Vote		
McCain (R)	227,063	(75%)
Obama (D)	70,718	(24%)
2004 Presidential Vote		
Bush (R)	196,023	(77%)
Kerry (D)	58,530	(23%)
Cook Partisan Voting Index:	R + 28	

After the war, not much changed for a long time. Most communities lived in isolation. Roads with hairpin curves led to remote hills where moonshine stills were more common than summer cabins. James Dickey's 1970 novel *Deliverance* was a thinly disguised portrait of life along the Coosawattee River in Gilmer and Murray counties (although the movie was filmed on the Chattooga River in Rabun County). Eventually, textile mills began springing up along the railroads; poultry production became a big business around Gainesville; and in Dalton, the traditional craft of tufted bedspread handiwork was transformed into a carpet industry so large that at its height it produced 60% of the world's tufted carpet. But these were low-wage industries populated by poor whites.

Since the 1980s, north Georgia has seen a rush of change. Interstate highways have brought it within easy range of Atlanta. Small manufacturing is thriving, with higher-skill workplaces replacing low-tech mills. Vacation and retirement communities have sprung up in the mountains and around the lakes. Agribusiness remains important, with huge poultry processors in Hall County around Gainesville. The carpet industry, more high-tech now than before, still plays a key economic role because the area is vulnerable to fluctuations in new construction. Once-rural counties are now part of the boom encircling Atlanta. The area around Lake Sidney Lanier, named for the 19th-century poet who wrote "The Song of the Chattahoochee," is filled with vacation houses and second homes (although in 2007 a drought and water demands from Florida left the lake at its lowest level in 50 years). Tens of thousands of Latinos from Mexico and other countries came to the Dalton and Gainesville areas to snap up jobs before the recession of 2008. This area, 1,200 miles from the Mexican border, is now home to almost four times as many Hispanics as blacks, and the surge of illegal immigrants that rescued the carpet industry has strained local services.

The 9th Congressional District covers most of northwest Georgia. Its northern tier of counties borders North Carolina, Tennessee, and Alabama, and those counties are in the Chattanooga media market. The district extends south to the outer reaches of metro Atlanta to include most of Forsyth County, which grew by 61% between 2000 and 2007. Today this region has mostly forgotten its Democratic history, and it is solidly Republican in national and state elections. In the 2004 presidential election, the 9th gave George W. Bush won his biggest margin of victory in the state: He won 77% of the district's support. In 2008, Republican John McCain beat Democrat Barack Obama, 75%-24%.

The congressman from the 9th District is Nathan Deal. He was first elected in 1992 as a Democrat but switched parties and became a Republican in April 1995. Deal grew up in Gainesville, went to Mercer University, and then served in the Army from 1966–68. He returned home to practice "street-level law," always choosing offices located on a ground floor. He was an assistant district attorney, a juvenile court judge, and a county attorney. In 1980, at age 38, he was elected to the state Senate as a Democrat. President Carter was still in office, and the Legislature was overwhelmingly Democratic. It would have been pointless to run as a Republican. A capable legislator, Deal was elected Senate president pro tem twice. In 1992, when "Boll Weevil" Democrat Ed Jenkins retired from the U.S. House, Deal ran for his seat and defeated a Republican by winning 59% of the vote.

In the House, Deal opposed the new Clinton administration's economic policies, voting against the 1993 budget, for the line-item veto, and for the balanced-budget amendment. Many saw Deal as a potential party-switcher, but while he was campaigning in 1994, he said, "If I choose to switch during the term, I think the honest thing to do is resign and have a special election." In early 1995, he worked with other Democrats to offer an alternative to the Republicans' welfare reform package. He expressed unhappiness with his party's opposition to tax cuts and with senior Democrats' criticism of Clean Water Act revisions that he had won on a bipartisan committee vote. On April 10, 1995, back home in Gainesville, Deal announced that he was switching to the Republican Party—but he did not resign and run in a special election. He said the national Democratic Party was unwilling to admit it was "out of touch with mainstream America." Democrats were stunned, and Republican House Speaker Newt Gingrich of Georgia was delighted. Deal's reward was a seat on the Energy and Commerce Committee.

Deal is influential on health care issues in his role as ranking Republican on the Health Subcommittee, a panel he chaired when Republicans were in the majority. In 2007, he sought additional funds for low-income kids in Georgia's PeachCare health insurance system, but he resisted Democrats' attempts to expand the State Children's Health Insurance Program by $35 billion in five years. He insisted that already-eligible persons should receive coverage first and that immigrant children should wait five years. He and other Republicans also wanted to raise the income threshold for family eligibility and thereby reduce the program's enrollment and costs. Deal was a key negotiator at talks with the majority Democrats that ultimately failed to produce a SCHIP bill that year. In 2008, he pressed Congress to require public disclosure of medical costs, saying such transparency is necessary to stop health providers from price-gouging the uninsured, whom they often charge more than they charge people with insurance for the same services.

Deal also worked with subcommittee Chairman Rep. Frank Pallone, D-N.J., to reform the Food and Drug Administration. In 2005, when he chaired the subcommittee, he assembled $11 billion in Medicaid cuts over five years, including elimination of prescription coverage for Viagra. "Taxpayers are willing to pay for somebody's heart medication, but they are not going to buy their beer or their Viagra."

Deal's voting record is mostly conservative, with an occasional deviation on foreign policy. He is the longtime sponsor of unsuccessful legislation to cut congressional salaries as much as 10% when the budget is not balanced. As a member of the Immigration Reform Caucus, he sponsored higher penalties for illegal aliens and proposed ending automatic citizenship for their children born in the United States. Deal made some accommodations for the rapidly growing Hispanic population in his own district by backing increased spending for bilingual education. A majority of school children in Dalton are Hispanic.

Deal has not faced serious primary or general election opposition since he switched parties.

TENTH DISTRICT

Paul Broun (R)

Elected July 2007, 1st full term; b. May 14, 1946, Atlanta; home, Athens; U. of GA, B.S.1967; Medical Col. of GA, M.D. 1971; Baptist; married (Niki Bronson); 3 children.

Military Career: Marine Corps Reserves, 1964–1967; Naval Reserves, 1967–1973; GA Air Natl. Guard, 1972–1973; Air Force Reserves, 1973–1988.

Professional Career: Owner, Travel and Adventure, 1985–92; Practicing physician, 1971-present.

DC Office: 325 CHOB, 20515, 202-225-4101; Fax: 202-226-0776; Web site: broun.house.gov.

State Offices: Athens, 706-549-9588; Augusta/Evans, 706-447-3857; Toccoa, 706-886-1008.

Committees: *Homeland Security* (9th of 13 R): Emerging Threats, Cybersecurity & Science and Technology; Intelligence, Information Sharing & Terrorism Risk Assessment. *Natural Resources* (14th of 20 R): National Parks, Forests & Public Lands. *Science & Technology* (16th of 17 R): Investigations & Oversight (RMM); Technology & Innovation.

Group Ratings

	ADA	ACLU	AFS	LCV	ITIC	NTU	COC	ACU	CFG	FRC
2008	0	0	0	0	29	93	67	100	100	100
2007	—	—	0	0	—	92	64	100	99	—

National Journal Ratings

	2007 LIB	—	2007 CONS		2008 LIB	—	2008 CONS
Economic	*%	—	*%		0%	—	98%
Social	*%	—	*%		0%	—	91%
Foreign	*%	—	*%		0%	—	95%
Composite	*%	—	*%		3%	—	97%

Key Votes of the 110th Congress

1. Increase minimum wage	*	5. Share immigration data	*	9. Withdraw troops 8/08	*
2. Expand SCHIP	N	6. Foreign aid abortion ban	*	10. No operations in Iran	*
3. Raise CAFE standards	N	7. Ban gay bias in workplace	N	11. Free trade with Peru	Y
4. Bail out financial markets	N	8. Repeal D.C. gun law	Y	12. Overhaul FISA	Y

Election Results

2008 general	Paul Broun (R)	177,265	(61%)	($1,800,502)
	Bobby Saxon (D)	114,638	(39%)	($128,894)
2008 primary	Paul Broun (R)	44,956	(71%)	
	Barry Fleming (R)	18,372	(29%)	

Prior Winning Percentages: 2007 (50%)

Population		Race/Ethnicity		Work	
Pop. 2007:	697,417	White:	72.7%	Private:	70.5%
Change since 2000:	Up 10.7%	Black:	19.6%	Government:	22.0%
Urban:	50.4%	Hispanic:	4.2%	Self-employed:	7.3%
Rural:	49.6%	Asian:	1.9%	Blue collar:	26.1%
Area size:	6,061 sq. mi.	Native Am.:	0.2%	White collar:	55.1%
Age		Hawaiian:	0.0%	Khaki collar:	2.1%
Median age:	34.5 yrs.	Two+ races:	1.0%	Other:	16.7%
More than 65 yrs:	12.1%	*Ancestry*		Median income:	$42,092
Less than 18 yrs:	24.1%	USA:	11.9%	Median home value:	$137,800
Education		Irish:	9.7%	Poverty:	16.6%
H.S. grad:	79.8%	English:	9.2%	**Military Veterans**	
College grad:	23.9%			% of Pop:	10.8%
Grad degree:	9.7%				

Northeastern Georgia is a land where the coastal plains and cotton fields yield to gently rolling hills and, near the North Carolina border, to the Appalachian Mountains. For most of its history, this was quiet, rural country, with courthouse towns and a few small cities, mostly forgotten by national elites, bypassed even by Union soldiers on their march to the sea. But in the last two decades, economic growth has radiated outward from Atlanta and spread across much of the region. The effects can be

2008 Presidential Vote
McCain (R)..............................191,401   (62%)
Obama (D) 113,210   (37%)

2004 Presidential Vote
Bush (R)..................................168,831   (65%)
Kerry (D)..................................90,304   (35%)

Cook Partisan Voting Index: R + 15

seen as far away as the old city of Augusta, on the Savannah River across from South Carolina. Founded in 1735, it is rich in history, with an old Cotton Exchange and mansions untouched by Sherman. It is also a center for newer industries that are replacing the paper industry, though the city retains a large share of low-income people. Augusta is best known as the home of the Augusta National Golf Club, the site of the Masters Tournament every year, its entrance barely visible off four-lane Washington Road. The city also houses the Fort Gordon Army base and has become a site for Hollywood film production.

The 10th Congressional District of Georgia takes in much of the northeast corner of the state. It includes about 40% of Augusta in Richmond County, but not the city's heavily black precincts. The 2005 redistricting added Clarke County and the liberal enclave of Athens, home of the University of Georgia, graceful Greek Revival mansions, boxwood gardens, and magnolias—and also, incidentally, rock bands R.E.M. and the B-52s. State planners have discussed a "brain train" to connect Athens to Atlanta. Clarke and Richmond counties are now the two largest population centers here. Columbia County, next to Augusta, and Oconee County, next to Athens, are particularly affluent and also rapidly growing. The Lake Oconee area has more than 100 subdivisions, including gated communities and golf courses that beckon to second-home buyers and retirees. Voters here prefer traditional values: Several counties recently rejected ballot propositions to end a prohibition of alcohol. The redistricting changes increased the African-American population from 14% to 20%, but this remains a solidly Republican district in national politics. In 2008, John McCain led Democrat Barack Obama here, 62%-37%.

The congressman from the 10th District is Paul Broun, a Republican who was the surprise winner of a special election in 2007 after the death of GOP incumbent Charlie Norwood. Born in Atlanta, Broun is a lifelong Georgia resident who got his bachelor's degree from the University of Georgia and his medical degree from the Medical College of Georgia in Augusta. His father, Paul Broun Sr., served as a moderate Democratic state senator from Athens for 38 years. The younger Broun was also active in politics, though he has said that he was "far, far apart on the issues" from his father. He served as president of the Georgia Sport Shooting Association, an affiliate of the National Rifle Association, and as vice president of political action for Safari Club International, a national advocacy group for hunters. He first ran for the House in 1990 against Democratic incumbent Richard Ray in the old 3rd District, which was then based in west-central Georgia. Ray won 63%-37%. After redistricting two years later, Broun ran in the revamped and more Republican 3rd District south of Atlanta, and lost the primary 55%-45% to Mac Collins, who held the seat for 12 years. In 1996, Broun closed his medical practice to campaign full-time for a year for Georgia's open Senate seat. He was vastly outspent, and finished a distant fourth in the primary with an anemic 3%.

There was little doubt that a Republican would succeed Norwood in this conservative district, but few predicted it would be Broun. State Sen. Jim Whitehead was the early front-runner. Whitehead attended the University of Georgia, where he was a star offensive lineman on the football team. He later opened a tire and auto shop in the Augusta area, served seven years on the Columbia County Commission—the final two as chairman—and won a state Senate seat in 2004. He was a close friend of Norwood's, a fact he highlighted while campaigning, and he was endorsed by Norwood's widow, Gloria.

The seat seemed to be his to lose, which is exactly what he did. He avoided debates and committed several gaffes, including remarking, "Iraq has not been a big thing in our district." He also was forced to explain a 2004 comment that dismissed the University of Georgia as a "bunch of liberals" who, except for the football team, ought to be bombed. In the June 19 special election, he won 44%, ahead of Broun's 21%, but not enough to avoid a runoff. Broun finished 198 votes ahead of Democrat James Marlow, a former Yahoo executive, who came in third with 20%. Whitehead got 69% in Columbia County, the district's second-largest county, but he won barely 10% in the largest county, Democratic-leaning Clarke County. This was a sign of trouble for Whitehead in the July 17 runoff as the race turned into a contest between candidates representing the district's two population centers, Augusta, Whitehead's turf, and Athens, Broun's home base.

Broun touted his medical background, claiming he was perhaps the only physician in Georgia who regularly made house calls. "I've got an old-fashioned medical bag," he said. "My office is my GMC Yukon." Broun said he opposed any steps to permit illegal immigrants to gain legal status, highlighted his connections to Christian conservatives on social issues, and also reached out to African-Americans and other Democrats, especially in Athens. Whitehead talked up his Augusta-area roots and complained about his Athens-based opposition. Whitehead had a considerable advantage in campaign dollars. Still, Broun won with 50.4%, just 394 votes ahead of Whitehead, with 49.6%. Broun carried Athens's Clarke County with a remarkable 90%, while holding Whitehead to 73% in Columbia County. He also won 12 other counties.

Hours after he was sworn into the House, Broun expressed his libertarian instincts by voting for an amendment to bar the Justice Department from prosecuting the use of marijuana for medicinal purposes. He called the vote "a constitutional issue pertaining to 'restraining' the federal government from interfering with the rights of the states," and joined 14 other Republicans backing the proposal, which was defeated, 165-262.

In the House, he catered to his religious conservative base. "I wasn't supposed to be here," he told anti-abortion protesters in January 2008. "I believe in my heart the Holy Spirit called me to run for Congress." The first bill he introduced would ban all abortions, and he called for a national sales tax to replace the income tax. He also called for a ban on the sales of *Playboy* and *Penthouse* magazines at military installments, no doubt getting thousands of soldiers stationed at Georgia's bases to snap to attention. With a flourish for colorful quotes, he said this of his opposition to the financial market bailout bill in 2008: "This is a huge cow patty with a piece of marshmallow stuck in the middle of it, and I am not going to eat that cow patty."

After Democrat Barack Obama's historic election as the first African-American president, Broun described Obama's agenda as "Marxist" and criticized Republican nominee John McCain's campaign as "inept." He ultimately backed away from those remarks. But his management of his office seemed to be no smoother than his political discourse. Broun spent almost all of the annual allotment that lawmakers receive to run their offices in the first half of 2008, prompting staff members to quit, *The Atlanta Journal-Constitution* reported.

Broun had another competitive primary in 2008, this time against former state House Majority Whip Barry Fleming, who was Augusta-based and sought to play down tensions with Athens. Fleming criticized Broun's opposition to federal spending for economic development and law enforcement, and he had an early fundraising advantage. But Broun was helped by the endorsement of the anti-tax group Club for Growth and by other Republicans in the Georgia delegation. Fleming made a late-campaign attack against Broun's financial problems, but it had little impact. Broun won the primary with unexpected ease, 71%-29, and leading in every county. In the general election against Bobby Saxon, an Iraq war veteran and gun-rights advocate, Broun won 61%-39%.

ELEVENTH DISTRICT

Phil Gingrey (R)

Elected 2002, 4th term; b. July 10, 1942, Augusta; home, Marietta; GA Inst. of Tech., B.S. 1965, Med. Col. of GA, M.D. 1969; Catholic; married (Billie); 4 children.

Elected Office: Marietta Schl. Bd., 1993–97; GA Senate, 1998–2002.

Professional Career: Practicing obstetrician, 1976-present.

DC Office: 119 CHOB, 20515, 202-225-2931; Fax: 202-225-2944; Web site: www.house.gov/gingrey/.

State Offices: Marietta, 770-429-1776; Rome, 706-290-1776.

Committees: *Energy & Commerce* (22nd of 23 R): Commerce, Trade & Consumer Protections; Health; Oversight & Investigations.

Group Ratings

	ADA	ACLU	AFS	LCV	ITIC	NTU	COC	ACU	CFG	FRC
2008	10	20	0	0	43	77	78	96	92	94
2007	0	—	0	0	—	86	75	100	89	—

National Journal Ratings

	2007 LIB	—	2007 CONS		2008 LIB	—	2008 CONS
Economic	0%	—	97%		9%	—	91%
Social	0%	—	91%		0%	—	91%
Foreign	0%	—	72%		0%	—	95%
Composite	7%	—	93%		5%	—	95%

Key Votes of the 110th Congress

1. Increase minimum wage	N	5. Share immigration data	Y	9. Withdraw troops 8/08	N
2. Expand SCHIP	N	6. Foreign aid abortion ban	Y	10. No operations in Iran	N
3. Raise CAFE standards	N	7. Ban gay bias in workplace	N	11. Free trade with Peru	Y
4. Bail out financial markets	N	8. Repeal D.C. gun law	Y	12. Overhaul FISA	Y

Election Results

2008 general	Phil Gingrey (R)	204,082	(68%)	($1,242,887)
	Hugh Gammon (D)	95,220	(32%)	
2008 primary	Phil Gingrey (R)	unopposed		

Prior Winning Percentages: 2006 (71%); 2004 (57%); 2002 (52%)

Population		Race/Ethnicity		Work	
Pop. 2007:	750,588	White:	75.6%	Private:	81.2%
Change since 2000:	Up 19.2%	Black:	13.5%	Government:	12.7%
Urban:	70.4%	Hispanic:	7.4%	Self-employed:	6.0%
Rural:	29.6%	Asian:	1.8%	Blue collar:	26.7%
Area size:	2,718 sq. mi.	Native Am.:	0.3%	White collar:	58.9%
Age		Hawaiian:	0.0%	Khaki collar:	0.2%
Median age:	34.5 yrs.	Two+ races:	1.1%	Other:	14.2%
More than 65 yrs:	9.6%	*Ancestry*		Median income:	$51,608
Less than 18 yrs:	27.3%	USA:	12.7%	Median home value:	$154,700
Education		Irish:	10.6%	Poverty:	12.4%
H.S. grad:	81.5%	English:	9.7%	**Military Veterans**	
College grad:	23.6%			% of Pop:	10.0%
Grad degree:	7.4%				

Northwest Georgia was long the home of the Cherokee Nation before the tribe was sent west in the 1830s on the Trail of Tears. It has been manufacturing country for the last century. Hundreds of textile mills and dozens of carpet mills once clustered near the supply of natural cotton and along the railroad lines heading southwest at the base of the southern Appalachian chain. The late 19th-century propagandists of the New South hailed factories as the

2008 Presidential Vote

McCain (R)	207,298	(66%)
Obama (D)	102,493	(33%)

2004 Presidential Vote

Bush (R)	183,750	(71%)
Kerry (D)	74,268	(29%)

Cook Partisan Voting Index: R+20

vanguard of technological progress, and in fact the plants produced a higher standard of living than farms on this stubborn land. But the mills put scant premium on education or the cultivation of civic virtues and did little to bring in higher-skilled work. All-white hiring practices maintained racial segregation in mostly white north Georgia. Today, this area is developing a different kind of economy, as metro Atlanta spreads out along highways to the north and to the west. There are sprawling subdivisions in what once were mill towns. Floyd County is home to an auto parts manufacturing cluster, in addition to the carpet mills of Rome, where Latino immigrants have become a major part of the workforce.

The 11th Congressional District of Georgia includes much of this part of the state, taking in small industrial towns, and rural cotton-, poultry-, and cattle-producing areas, plus a cluster of older suburbs around Atlanta. It stretches from Rome in the north to suburban Marietta, which is about 15 miles up Interstate 75 from Atlanta and where Lockheed Martin builds the F-22 Raptor jet fighter and the C-130 cargo plane. (In an attempt to maintain production of the F-22, Lockheed began in 2007 to make overseas sales, with the Pentagon's approval.) West of Atlanta is Carrollton, once the home of an untenured West Georgia College professor who in his third try became a Republican congressman: Newt Gingrich, who went on to become speaker of the House. The 2005 redistricting made the 11th significantly more compact (it is more than 1,000 square miles smaller than the previous version) and more Republican, by moving boundaries to include the northern part of Cobb County, all of exurban Bartow County and all of fast-growing Paulding County, with a 57% increase in population between 2000 and 2007. The changes also shifted many African-American precincts of Cobb County to the 13th District and reduced the black share in the new 11th from 28% to 12% at that time. The result considerably altered the partisan composition, changing this from a somewhat competitive seat to one that seems out of reach for Democrats.

The congressman from the 11th is Republican Phil Gingrey, an obstetrician first elected in 2002. Gingrey grew up in Augusta, graduated from Georgia Tech, and returned home to attend the Medical College of Georgia. After training in Georgia hospitals, he settled in Marietta, where he set up an obstetrics and gynecology practice. He also chaired the local school board. In 1998, he was elected to the state Senate, where he had a reputation as a staunch social conservative who could work with Democrats on other issues. Gingrey says the book that most influenced his political thinking is Barry Goldwater's classic *The Conscience of a Conservative*. In the contest for the U.S. House seat, Gingrey faced tough competition in both the primary and general election. The issue differences were small among the three candidates in the Republican primary. Gingrey, who is Catholic, styled himself as the only native Georgian. Cecil Staton, an ordained Baptist minister, vowed to view all legislation from the perspective of the traditional family. Gingrey won 40% of the vote to 32% for Staton and 28% for Bob Herriott, a pilot for Delta Airlines.

The bitter September runoff revolved around their respective religions and allegations by Staton that Gingrey supported homosexual causes. Voters who knew Gingrey from his state Senate tenure didn't buy it. He won 64%-36%, carrying every county. The Democrats, meanwhile, nominated Roger Kahn, a millionaire beer distributor. In the general election campaign, Kahn accused Gingrey of seeking special favors for cocaine-dealing felons and violent criminals who had assaulted police officers. He spent $2.8 million from his own pocket, and complained that national Democrats did not give him more help. Gingrey spent $600,000 of his own money, and portrayed Kahn as a wealthy liquor distributor posing as a modest farmer. With a boost from the Georgia Republican tide and the National Republican Congressional Committee, Gingrey won 52%-48%.

In the House, Gingrey has a very conservative voting record. So he quite unexpectedly found himself on the wrong side of some of the nation's best known conservatives in 2009 when he told the newspaper *Politico* in offhand remarks: "It's easy if you're Sean Hannity or Rush Limbaugh or even sometimes Newt Gingrich to stand back and throw rocks. You don't have to try to do what's best for your people and your party." His sentiments may have resonated with other office-holders, but he wound up apologizing to the pundits the next day, praising Limbaugh as a "conservative giant," and adding, "I regret those stupid comments."

Insisting that there are "no throwaway lives," Gingrey opposed embryonic-stem-cell research, which uses embryos from in vitro fertilization. After receiving assurances on protection for the textile industry, he voted for the Central American Free Trade Agreement in 2005. Also that year, he sought but failed to get a seat on the powerful Ways and Means Committee. Instead, he got a seat on the Rules Committee, an influential panel that writes the rules for bringing bills to the floor. In February 2006, Gingrey lost a bid for the chairmanship of the Republican Policy Committee, which is part of the GOP leadership.

When Democrats took control of the House in 2007, he had to give up his seat on Rules, and he shifted his focus to the Armed Services Committee, where he has been an avid booster of Lockheed's Marietta plant. After an August 2007 visit to Iraq, Gingrey called for more patience to "give victory a chance." In 2009, he got a seat on the Energy and Commerce Committee, where he can work more effectively on health care issues, including shifting the industry toward electronic record-keeping and limiting damages in medical-malpractice lawsuits. He won House passage in July 2007 of a ban on federal funding for a program giving school-age children a vaccine for sexually transmitted diseases.

Democrats claimed they would seriously contest Gingrey in 2004 but he had an easier than expected re-election. He raised $2.3 million, much of it from the medical community. The campaign of his opponent, conservative Democrat Rick Crawford, failed to impress national Democrats. Gingrey won 57%-43%, and has not had a problem getting re-elected since.

TWELFTH DISTRICT

John Barrow (D)

Elected 2004, 3rd term; b. Oct. 31, 1955, Athens; home, Savannah; U. of GA, B.A. 1976, Harvard U., J.D. 1979; Baptist; married (Victoria); 2 children.

Elected Office: Athens-Clarke City-Co. comm., 1990–2004.

Professional Career: Practicing atty., 1981–2004.

DC Office: 213 CHOB, 20515, 202-225-2823; Fax: 202-225-3377; Web site: www.house.gov/barrow.

State Offices: Augusta, 706-722-4494; Sandersville, 478-553-1923; Savannah, 912-354-7282; Vidalia, 912-537-9301.

Committees: *Energy & Commerce* (25th of 36 D): Commerce, Trade & Consumer Protections; Energy & Environment; Health.

Group Ratings

	ADA	ACLU	AFS	LCV	ITIC	NTU	COC	ACU	CFG	FRC
2008	75	64	86	54	86	28	67	24	10	29
2007	70	—	73	65.	—	17	80	24	25	—

National Journal Ratings

	2007 LIB	—	2007 CONS	2008 LIB	—	2008 CONS
Economic	47%	—	53%	47%	—	53%
Social	45%	—	54%	48%	—	50%
Foreign	45%	—	55%	48%	—	51%
Composite	46%	—	54%	48%	—	52%

Key Votes of the 110th Congress

1. Increase minimum wage	Y	5. Share immigration data	Y	9. Withdraw troops 8/08	N
2. Expand SCHIP	Y	6. Foreign aid abortion ban	N	10. No operations in Iran	N
3. Raise CAFE standards	N	7. Ban gay bias in workplace	N	11. Free trade with Peru	Y
4. Bail out financial markets	N	8. Repeal D.C. gun law	Y	12. Overhaul FISA	Y

Election Results

2008 general	John Barrow (D)	164,562	(66%)	($2,502,783)
	John Stone (R)	84,773	(34%)	($365,140)
2008 primary	John Barrow (D)	45,235	(76%)	
	Regina Thomas (D)	13,955	(24%)	

Prior Winning Percentages: 2006 (50%); 2004 (52%)

Population		Race/Ethnicity		Work	
Pop. 2007:	654,534	White:	50.3%	Private:	73.7%
Change since 2000:	Up 3.9%	Black:	44.0%	Government:	20.1%
Urban:	59.9%	Hispanic:	3.3%	Self-employed:	5.9%
Rural:	40.1%	Asian:	0.9%	Blue collar:	29.0%
Area size:	8,734 sq. mi.	Native Am.:	0.2%	White collar:	49.5%
Age		Hawaiian:	0.1%	Khaki collar:	0.6%
Median age:	33.6 yrs.	Two+ races:	0.9%	Other:	20.9%
More than 65 yrs:	11.5%	*Ancestry*		Median income:	$35,019
Less than 18 yrs:	25.7%	USA:	9.9%	Median home value:	$92,000
Education		Irish:	8.1%	Poverty:	21.4%
H.S. grad:	76.3%	English:	7.3%	**Military Veterans**	
College grad:	15.0%			% of Pop:	11.2%
Grad degree:	5.6%				

In Georgia, the focus is usually on Atlanta. But the state also has some urbane smaller cities with roots deep in the past. One is Savannah, the state's first capital, which by the 1830s was one of America's booming cotton ports. It languished after the Civil War, and lived off paper mills and chemical plants in the 20th century, while impoverished blacks on the islands a few miles offshore still spoke Gullah dialects. Then, a few decades ago, preservationists started restoring houses and churches on a street

2008 Presidential Vote
Obama (D) 145,107 (55%)
McCain (R).............................116,072 (44%)

2004 Presidential Vote
Bush (R) 112,735 (50%)
Kerry (D)................................110,192 (49%)

Cook Partisan Voting Index: D + 1

grid punctuated by 24 squares that James Oglethorpe had laid out more than 200 years before. Today, Savannah is one of the most graciously preserved cities in the country and a major tourism destination thanks to the popularity of John Berendt's *Midnight in the Garden of Good and Evil,* a somewhat fact-based story of eccentricity and murder that was on best-seller lists for four years in the 1990s. In 2007, Savannah acquired a different sort of notoriety when the local Episcopal Church parted ways with the national diocese over the main church's decision to affirm an openly gay bishop. The city actively competes with neighboring, and equally well-preserved, Charleston, S.C., not only for tourists but also for shipping. Another such city is Augusta, upriver on the Savannah. Founded in 1735 as a fur-trading post, it has been home to the Medical College of Georgia since 1835. The city, which has its own Cotton Exchange and Riverwalk, is also the boyhood home of Woodrow Wilson.

The 12th Congressional District of Georgia runs along the Savannah River and comprises almost all of Savannah and some of its suburbs and about 60% of Augusta. It contains the Depression-racked farm country near Augusta that Erskine Caldwell chronicled in his scandalous best-seller, *Tobacco Road.* The titular dirt thoroughfare, which led to a small port on the Savannah River, is now paved and runs through a nondescript mix of residential and commercial areas. In 2008, the district voted for Democrat Barack Obama over Republican John McCain, 55%-44%.

The congressman from the 12th District is Democrat John Barrow, whose family has been rooted in Georgia for seven generations. His father handled school desegregation cases as a lawyer and as a Superior Court judge in the Athens area. A graduate of the University of Georgia and Harvard Law School, Barrow became a trial lawyer and made his name in local politics by winning four terms as an Athens-Clarke city-county commissioner. In 2004, he decided to run against Republican Rep. Max Burns, who had won the 12th District seat in an upset in 2002.

Although most Democratic voters in the district are black, all four candidates in the Democratic primary were white. Barrow raised more than $700,000 and, with the endorsements of former Sen. Max Cleland, the Sierra Club, and the Georgia AFL-CIO, extended his appeal beyond his home base. He won 51% of the vote and all 14 counties, enough to avoid a runoff. In the general election, Barrow distanced himself from Democratic presidential nominee John Kerry and the national party. He focused on Burns's support of a national retail sales tax to replace the income tax. He attacked the proposal as a tax increase that was anti-family and labeled it "the Max Tax." Burns accused Barrow of distorting his proposal and called his opponent a "liberal trial attorney" controlled by "Atlanta party bosses." Burns ran well in rural areas, but Barrow won big margins among African-American voters in the three counties that cast two-thirds of the district's votes—62% in Richmond, 58% in Chatham, and 58% in Clarke. Overall, Barrow won 52%-48%.

In the House, Barrow ranks among the most conservative Democrats. He took a hard line against illegal immigrants and cast votes in 2007 against proposals to limit war funding in Iraq. He sponsored a bill to give tax credits equal to 50% of an employer's health insurance costs. Also in 2007, Democratic leaders gave him a leading role in pushing for an increase in the minimum wage, and he secured a seat on the powerful Energy and Commerce Committee. In 2008, after an explosion at a sugar refinery near Savannah, Barrow won House passage of his bill to force the Occupational Safety and Health Administration to tighten rules on industrial dust.

Barrow's political life was made more difficult by the 2005 redistricting, which moved his Clarke County base into the heavily Republican 10th District. He said he would run in the new district that included the largest part of his former district, which turned out to be the 12th. Barrow moved his residence to Savannah and emphasized his independence. "No boss, no leader, no caucus can tell me how to vote. And none of them has," he declared. Burns ran against him and got fundraising help from national Republicans. The outcome was even closer this time, and Burns waited nine days before conceding. In his 50.3%-49.7% victory, Barrow won only eight of 22 counties, but he captured 62% of the vote in Chatham and 65% in Richmond, the two largest counties.

In 2008, Barrow faced state Sen. Regina Thomas, an African-American, in the July primary. A liberal political action committee ran ads criticizing Barrow for supporting President Bush on tax cuts and the Iraq war. He ran strongly across the district and won 76%-24%. In November, he won re-election easily, losing only two counties en route to a 66%-34% victory over Republican John Stone.

THIRTEENTH DISTRICT

David Scott (D)

Elected 2002, 4th term; b. June 27, 1946, Aynor, SC; home, Atlanta; FL A&M U., B.A. 1967, U. of PA, M.B.A. 1969; Baptist; married (Alfredia); 2 children.

Elected Office: GA House of Reps., 1974–82; GA Senate, 1982–2002.

Professional Career: Founder and pres., Dayn-Mark Advertising, 1979–2002.

DC Office: 225 CHOB, 20515, 202-225-2939; Fax: 202-225-4628; Web site: house.gov/davidscott.

State Offices: Jonesboro, 770-210-5073; Smyrna, 770-432-5405.

Committees: *Agriculture* (7th of 28 D): Livestock, Dairy & Poultry (Chmn). *Financial Services* (19th of 42 D): Capital Markets, Insurance & Government Sponsored Enterprises; Financial Institutions & Consumer Credit. *Foreign Affairs* (24th of 28 D): Europe; Terrorism, Nonproliferation & Trade.

Group Ratings

	ADA	ACLU	AFS	LCV	ITIC	NTU	COC	ACU	CFG	FRC
2008	95	82	100	92	86	9	67	4	0	23
2007	90	—	100	80	—	5	65	4	6	—

National Journal Ratings

	2007 LIB	—	2007 CONS		2008 LIB	—	2008 CONS
Economic	82%	—	0%		85%	—	0%
Social	68%	—	32%		75%	—	18%
Foreign	52%	—	47%		59%	—	37%
Composite	71%	—	30%		77%	—	23%

Key Votes of the 110th Congress

1. Increase minimum wage	Y	5. Share immigration data	N	9. Withdraw troops 8/08	Y
2. Expand SCHIP	Y	6. Foreign aid abortion ban	N	10. No operations in Iran	N
3. Raise CAFE standards	Y	7. Ban gay bias in workplace	Y	11. Free trade with Peru	N
4. Bail out financial markets	Y	8. Repeal D.C. gun law	N	12. Overhaul FISA	Y

Election Results

2008 general	David Scott (D)..205,919	(69%)	($1,433,435)
	Deborah Honeycutt (R).....................................92,320	(31%)	($5,204,670)
2008 primary	David Scott (D)..30,719	(64%)	
	Donzella James (D)...17,526	(36%)	

Prior Winning Percentages: 2006 (69%); 2004 (100%); 2002 (60%)

Population		Race/Ethnicity		Work	
Pop. 2007:	757,444	White:	32.0%	Private:	79.9%
Change since 2000:	Up 20.3%	Black:	52.3%	Government:	15.5%
Urban:	96.6%	Hispanic:	10.6%	Self-employed:	4.6%
Rural:	3.4%	Asian:	3.1%	Blue collar:	25.5%
Area size:	577 sq. mi.	Native Am.:	0.1%	White collar:	58.8%
		Hawaiian:	0.0%	Khaki collar:	0.3%
Age		Two+ races:	1.1%	Other:	15.5%
Median age:	32.6 yrs.			Median income:	$49,535
More than 65 yrs:	7.0%	*Ancestry*		Median home value:	$148,400
Less than 18 yrs:	28.1%	USA:	6.2%	Poverty:	12.6%
		Irish:	4.7%		
Education		English:	4.5%	**Military Veterans**	
H.S. grad:	84.6%			% of Pop:	11.0%
College grad:	24.8%				
Grad degree:	7.8%				

Many of the great landmarks of the civil-rights movement, and the headquarters of many of its leading organizations, are in the central city of Atlanta. The city's cohesive and talented African-American community, more than any other, provided the leadership and inspiration for the struggle that transformed the United States. In the 1960s, Atlanta's blacks were clustered in ghetto neighborhoods on the south and west sides of the city. The north side and the suburbs in every direc-

2008 Presidential Vote
Obama (D) 226,700   (72%)
McCain (R)..............................87,228   (28%)

2004 Presidential Vote
Kerry (D)................................144,870   (60%)
Bush (R) 96,393   (40%)

Cook Partisan Voting Index: D + 15

tion were heavily or entirely white. Today, metro Atlanta's thriving black middle class has moved outward in almost every direction in one of the nation's fastest-growing metro areas—to southern DeKalb County to the east, to Clayton County directly south of the city, to southwest Fulton County, to eastern and southern Cobb and Douglas counties to the west.

The 13th Congressional District of Georgia is a collection of suburban areas that have attracted Atlanta's African-American middle class. It is a majority-black district with a nucleus in Clayton County, which is heavily dependent economically on the airport. The biggest change in the 2005 redistricting was the addition of Cobb County. Cobb and Clayton counties each contain about one-third of the district's population, and the rest is parceled out across DeKalb, Douglas, Fulton, and Henry counties. The district is heavily Democratic.

The congressman from the 13th District is David Scott, a Democrat first elected in 2002. Born in rural South Carolina, Scott is the son of a minister and grandson of a deacon. During his middle-school years, his family moved to tony Scarsdale, N.Y., where his parents took jobs as a chauffeur and housekeeper for a wealthy family. Scott was the only African-American in his otherwise all-white school. He later graduated from Florida A&M University, and then did an internship at the U.S. Labor Department in Washington. There he met George Taylor, an authority in labor-management relations who encouraged the bright young man to apply to the prestigious Wharton School at the University of Pennsylvania, which Scott did, eventually earning his M.B.A. He moved to Atlanta in the early 1970s, and in 1974, he was elected to the Georgia House. In 1982, he won election to the state Senate, where he chaired the

Rules Committee. From 1979 to 2002, he owned Dayn-Mark Advertising, which creates and places radio, television, and print ads. The firm is now operated by his wife and two daughters.

In 2002, Scott made a bid for the newly created 13th District seat. It was obvious that the primary would be decisive in this heavily Democratic district. Four other Democrats ran, the best known of whom was former state party Chairman David Worley, who had nearly defeated Republican Rep. Newt Gingrich in 1990. Scott, however, was familiar to many voters after more than a quarter-century in the state Legislature. And if they didn't know Scott, they certainly knew of his campaign co-chairman: Hank Aaron, the Hall of Fame slugger and Atlanta-area icon, who is Scott's brother-in-law. Scott brought his advertising expertise to the campaign, plastering the interstate highways with eye-catching billboards. His chief competitors, Worley and state Sen. Greg Hecht of Clayton County, both white, ran ads attacking each other. Scott won the primary with 54% of the vote and at least 50% in every county but one. He credited God, saying that "a divine hand worked with us." He won the general election 60%-40%, not a huge ratio but a decisive one.

In the House, Scott's voting record is centrist for a Democrat, especially on foreign-policy issues. He brought to the chamber nearly three decades' experience in representing multiracial, multiethnic constituencies. He joined both the liberal Congressional Black Caucus and the conservative Blue Dog Democrats, and showed no reluctance about going his own way. In 2003, he was one of seven House Democrats to vote for final passage of President Bush's tax cut and one of 16 to vote for the new Republican prescription drug benefit under Medicare. In 2004, he was one of 11 Democrats who angered party leaders by joining Republicans on a procedural vote in support of a measure to buy out tobacco farmers, which Scott helped to write. He split with most of his party by voting for the constitutional amendment to ban same-sex marriage.

On the Financial Services Committee, Scott criticized predatory lenders that exploit would-be homeowners in poor communities, but he was reluctant to pass measures to eliminate favorable interest deals. He spoke out strongly for extension of the Voting Rights Act and against claims by Georgia Republicans that the law had achieved its goals and was no longer necessary. He initially opposed the bailout of the financial markets; but after Chairman Barney Frank, D-Mass., promised to address the Congressional Black Caucus's call for additional protections for homeowners facing foreclosure, Scott switched his vote to support a revised version.

In 2006, Scott faced a primary challenge from Donzella James, who served 10 years in the state Senate and criticized Scott for living outside the district. Scott won 67%-33% and took every county, including 74%-26% in Clayton, which cast the largest vote. In the general election, he was opposed by first-time candidate Deborah Honeycutt, a family physician who surprisingly raised $1.3 million. But she had little name recognition and lost 69%-31%.

Before the 2008 election, Scott was the subject of several unflattering stories about back taxes he owed on his home and business, and about payments out of his campaign fund to family members and Dayn-Mark Advertising. Since his first congressional race in 2002, Scott's campaign had paid a total of $643,000 to his family and to Dayn-Mark and its employees, the newspaper *Politico* reported in 2007. An attorney for Scott said that the transactions were legal under campaign finance law. Nonetheless, Scott attracted both primary and general election challenges in 2008. In the Democratic primary, James again challenged Scott and attacked him for backing President Bush on the war in Iraq, for favoring the GOP prescription drug benefit, and for opposing increases in education funding. Scott won 64%-36%. In a November rematch, Honeycutt upped the stakes considerably by spending $5.2 million to try to defeat Scott, who spent far less, $1.4 million. Despite the negative news stories about his finances and purportedly close polls on the eve of the election, Scott swamped Honeycutt, 69%-31%.

★ HAWAII ★

Hawaii, geographically the most isolated archipelago in the world and geologically some of the youngest land on Earth, is continuing to undergo transformations. Humans settled these islands only about 1,000 years ago, when Polynesians paddled across vast Pacific expanses in small outrigger canoes. When Capt. James Cook arrived in 1776, he found that his Maori interpreter from New Zealand could understand Hawaiian. On this subtropical land, teeming with food and seldom inconvenienced by bad weather, Hawaiians built a fierce yet wondrous civilization of harsh taboos and cannibalism as well as alluring music and dance. The islands were united politically in 1779 by King Kamehameha I, who ate one of his rivals and maintained the old culture. In 1819, within a year of his death, his consort Kaahumanu outlawed the Hawaiian religious taboos and welcomed the American missionary Hiram Bingham. New England missionaries and their trader cousins came, while British and Russian ships occasionally put into port, and established the dominant culture. Starting in the 1850s, laborers from China, Japan, Portugal, and the Philippines streamed in to work the sugar and pineapple plantations. American planters and businesspeople bridled at the caprices of the royal family and, in January 1893, with the help of the U.S. Marines, ousted Queen Liliuokalani from the Iolani Palace and called on the United States to annex Hawaii. President Grover Cleveland demurred, and Hawaii for five years was a republic. President William McKinley annexed it in July 1898. This history is a source of regret for some. An *Onipa'a* ceremony remembering Liliuokalani's overthrow was staged by John Waihee, the first governor of Native Hawaiian descent, in January 1993, with the American flag conspicuously absent. Later that year, Congress passed and President Bill Clinton signed an apology for the overthrow of Liliuokalani 100 years before.

Hawaii created a better life for its citizens than almost any other island or native commonwealth. Its people have not walled themselves off in ethnic blocs but have been mixing for the last century. Each group has made worthy contributions. The Asian migrant laborers brought traditions of hard work, family loyalty, and group solidarity that found expression most vividly in the performance of the 442nd "Go for Broke" Regimental Combat Team, which was made up mostly of sons of Japanese immigrants and became the most decorated unit in U.S. military history. The Yankee spirit has been evident in Hawaii's commercial success and in its attachment to the rule of Anglo-American law. The Hawaiian spirit is apparent in the vitality of the *aloha* ambience, the welcoming of others despite their differences, and a willingness to absorb the teachings of others while maintaining a certain Polynesian attitude toward life. It was Hawaii's tolerance that inspired segregationist Southern Democrats to block its admission to the Union for years. Today's Hawaiians can take pride in their ethnic heritage—or heritages: About half of the married couples in Hawaii are, like President Obama's parents, interracial. In the 2000 census, 18% of Hawaiians identified themselves as being of two races and 7% said three or more. Some 23% described themselves as at least partly Native Hawaiian. There are some 246,000 descendants of the 45,000 Native Hawaiians of the late 19th century, though all but 10,000 are of mixed ancestry. The Census Bureau estimates that in 2007 Hawaiians were, wholly or in combination, 42% white (up from 40% in 2000), 4% black, 8% Hispanic, 56% Asian, and 23% Native Hawaiian and Pacific Islander. Hawaii has many Samoans, including Honolulu Mayor Mufi Hannemann. According to local experts, the Asian population is 18% Japanese, 12% Filipino, and 5% Chinese.

Politically, the Hawaii Territory was Republican. After all, Southern Democrats were blocking statehood and championing racial segregation. John Kennedy carried it in 1960 by just 115 votes. But from 1962 to 2002, its politics was dominated by a Democratic machine that had its beginning in the 1950s. At that time, World War II veterans such as Daniel Inouye, Spark Matsunaga, and George Ariyoshi joined forces with former mainlander John Burns, who as a police officer during the war helped prevent persecution of Japanese-Americans. They allied themselves with the then-powerful International Longshoremen's and Warehousemen's Union, which represented sugar and pineapple plantation hands as well as dock workers, and cemented the allegiance of Japanese-American voters. The Burns-Inouye machine built on the grievances against the *haole* (the Hawaiian word for white) owners of the big companies, and triumphed. Inouye was elected as a Democrat to the U.S. House in 1959 and to the Senate in 1962. Burns was elected governor in 1962, and for 40 years the office was passed down in lineal succession to George Ariyoshi, John Waihee, and Benjamin Cayetano. Over the years, this machine has built a large government. Hawaii has high taxes and by far the highest number of state and local employees per capita. This is centralized government: Hawaii has five counties (and one, Honolulu, has 70% of the population), one school district, and one statewide health care plan. Landholdings are centralized too. Eight public and private entities own 69% of Hawaii's land: The federal government 16%, the state 29%, and six private landowners 24%. The Bishop Estate—founded by descendants of Kamehameha I—now called the Kamehameha Schools Estate, owns 8%.

During the 50 years of Democratic dominance, Hawaii's economy was transformed. By the 1960s, tourism edged out agriculture—mainly pineapples and sugar—as Hawaii's No. 1 industry. (With more

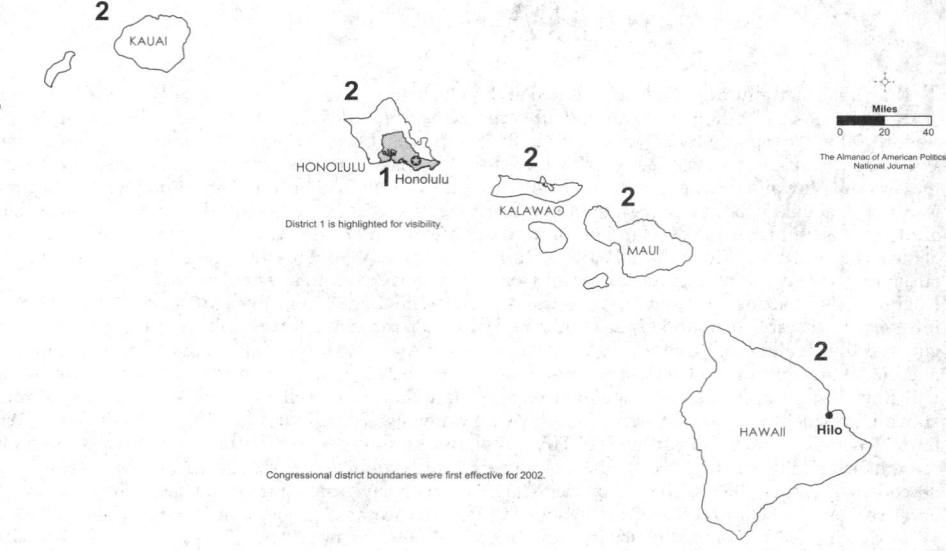

2 KAUAI

2

HONOLULU **1** Honolulu

District 1 is highlighted for visibility.

2

2 KALAWAO

2

MAUI

Miles
0   20   40

*The Almanac of American Politics.
National Journal*

2

HAWAII   Hilo

Congressional district boundaries were first effective for 2002.

than 100 military installations of varying size, the state's No. 2 industry is the military.) Pineapple acreage declined from 77,000 to 10,000, and Del Monte closed its last pineapple operations in 2006. Sugar production declined 67% in the 1990s, and most of the sugar produced is now processed into biofuel. Hawaii's agriculture today is dedicated to specialty crops whose high cost of production can be recovered in local, national, or international markets: flowers, wasabi, macadamia nuts, Kona coffee, bananas, avocados, papayas, and genetically engineered seeds. As big agriculture shriveled, the ILWU has become overshadowed by the 44,000-member Hawaii Government Employees Association. Voting long tended to follow ethnic lines. Japanese Americans, used to working in organizations in unions and government, were the heart of the Democratic Party. Whites, with relatively high incomes, have tended toward Republicans. Filipinos, often in menial jobs, are heavily Democratic, and Chinese, somewhat less so. Native Hawaiians are heavily Democratic but not as likely to be active in politics.

As it changed, Hawaii found its vulnerabilities. It imports 90% of its food, and has only one-week's supply available at any given time. This was a problem when commercial airline flights were cut off after September 11, 2001. Tourism has been vulnerable to slumps in the business cycle. The 1990–91 recession in California and the prolonged 1990s slump in Japan resulted in tourism peaking in 1990 and not reaching that level again until 2000. Then came September 11. Tourism bounced back by 2004 and kept rising through 2007, then plunged some 10% with the recession. The revival of the Japanese economy helped, and a 2007 U.S.-China agreement allows routine entry for Chinese tour groups. But lucrative wedding and honeymoon tourism has declined, and the bankruptcy of Aloha Airlines in 2008 hurt. Housing is expensive, bid up by luxury buyers who have made their money elsewhere. The median home price rose from $272,000 in 2000 to $510,000 in 2008. But Hawaii has a low rate of homeownership and many properties are held on 99-year leases. The combination of high housing prices and an economy that is not generating as many high-paying jobs for young people has prompted more migration of Hawaiians to the mainland. Obama, who has chronicled his anxiety growing up black in the seemingly tolerant Hawaii of the 1970s (and in one of its most elite private schools, Punahou Academy), is the first president born and raised in Hawaii. But he chose to be educated in California, New York, and Massachusetts and to make his career in Illinois.

This economic turbulence has been accompanied by some political turbulence. Hawaii's Democratic machine faced challenges over the years, in primaries and from third-party candidacies, but the most effective challenge came from Missouri-born Republican Linda Lingle, the mayor of Maui. After losing to Gov. Cayetano by only 50%-49% in 1998, she came back to win the governorship four years later, 52%-47%. She proved highly popular, and was re-elected in 2006 with 63%. Union-backed Democrats, however, increased the already large Democratic margins in the Legislature in 2006 and again in 2008. Lingle, term-limited in 2010, seems likely to be succeeded by a Democratic governor.

Hawaii's reputation for tolerance has been marred by controversy over the status of Native Hawaiians and by occasional violence, including attacks on military personnel by Native Hawaiians. A Native Hawaiian protest movement grew in the 1990s, with demonstrations on the anniversaries of the overthrow of Queen Liliuokalani and the U.S. annexation of the islands. A state sovereignty commission sponsored a referendum on electing delegates to create a Native Hawaiian government. All of this raised the issue of just who is a Native Hawaiian, since almost no one is of pure Native ancestry any longer. Advocates of special treatment for Natives argued that they ranked below all other Hawaii ethnic groups (except, "of course," as one said, "the Filipinos") in income and education, and some called for independence from the United States. Native activist Haunani-Kay Trask disagreed: "As a nationalist, I hate the United States of America. But [independence] doesn't live in the political-military world we live in, with 26 military bases in Hawaii and 7 million tourists a year." She has also said, "Our native people have been essentially confined to a servant class."

In February 2000, the U.S. Supreme Court declared unconstitutional the 1978 Hawaii state constitutional amendment setting up Native-Hawaiian-only elections for the Office of Hawaiian Affairs, which administers a $400 million trust fund. That decision casts doubt on other provisions of the 1978 amendment, including the Hawaiian Homes Commission and the recognition of Native gathering rights on private property. Democratic Sen. Daniel Akaka responded with a bill granting Native Hawaiians sovereignty. It would allow a separate sovereign Native Hawaiian government, with apparently no territorial jurisdiction, but with potential custody of the $400 million trust monies held in the Office of Hawaiian Affairs. A version was passed by the U.S. House in 2000, but it was not brought up in the Senate. Akaka finally got it to the floor in June 2006, and Lingle and a delegation of other Hawaiian leaders flew to Washington to lobby for it. But opponents stopped it from going forward. After the 2008 election, Akaka said it would have a better chance with Democratic control of the White House and Congress, and on the campaign trail, Obama said he would sign the bill. Akaka reintroduced the same language in February 2009.

Hawaii, so far removed from any other land, has a particularly fragile ecology, with a profusion of bird and plant species that are vulnerable to invasive predators. Airliners' wheel housings are routinely inspected for the brown tree snakes that have killed off most of the birds in Guam. The oceans around the islands are vulnerable too, and a source of controversy. In 2006, President Bush issued an order dedicating the Northwestern Hawaiian Islands Marine National Monument, which covers an expanse of ocean plus a few uninhabited islands that is 1,400 miles long and 100 miles wide. The area contains 70% of the nation's tropical, shallow-water coral reefs, some 7,000 marine species (one-quarter found nowhere else), the endangered Hawaiian monk seal population, and threatened species of predatory fish (sharks, groupers, jacks). It is the largest marine sanctuary in the world and was supported strongly by Lingle and former U.S. House Speaker Newt Gingrich, R-Ga. But Sens. Inouye and Akaka, apprehensive about the effect on a tiny fishing fleet employing some 20 fishermen and the precedential effect the order would have, were dubious if not hostile to the designation. Concerns were raised on Kauai and Maui when the 866-passenger, 286-vehicle ferry between Oahu and those islands started operating in August 2007. Until then, Hawaii was the world's only archipelago without ferry service. Kauai protesters claimed it would bring heavy traffic, invasive species, and depletion of fish stocks, and the service was stopped. Service to

Population		Household Income		Work	
Pop. 2007:	1,276,534	Under $15k:	9.9%	Private:	67.2%
State rank:	42nd of 50	$15k to $50k:	29.4%	Government:	25.4%
Change since 2000:	Up 5.4%	$50k to $100k:	34.9%	Self-employed:	7.3%
Urban:	90.8%	$100k to $150k:	21.5%	Unemployment (3-yr. average):	2.9%
Rural:	9.2%	Over $150k:	4.3%	Poverty:	9.1%
Native of state:	54.5%	Median income:	$62,543	Blue collar:	18.4%
Not a citizen:	7.4%			White collar:	56.9%
Area size:	10,931 sq. mi.	**Home Value**		Khaki collar:	3.4%
		Under $100k:	2.5%	Other:	21.4%
Most populous cities		$100k to $300k:	18.2%		
1. Honolulu	359,694	$300k to $500k:	28.1%	**Age**	
2. Hilo	50,289	$500k to $1 mil:	42.5%	Median age:	37.7 yrs.
3. Waipahu	36,059	Over $1 million:	8.8%	More than 65 yrs:	14.0%
4. Kailua	35,841	Median:	$510,500	Less than 18 yrs:	22.3%

Race/Ethnicity				Military Veterans		Registered Voters in 2008	
White:	24.5%	*Language*		% of Pop:	12.2%	No party registration	
Black:	2.3%	English:	75.7%			Voter turnout:	453,568
Hispanic:	8.1%	Spanish:	1.9%	*Veterans by Period*		Turnout as % of	
Asian:	38.8%	Asian:	21.0%	WWII and before:	9.8%	voting age:	45.2%
Native Am.:	0.2%	Other		Korea:	10.9%		
Hawaiian:	8.1%	European	1.3%	Vietnam:	30.1%	**Legislature**	
Two+ races:	17.8%	**Education**		Gulf (pre-2001):	10.0%	Senate:	23 D 2 R
Ancestry		H.S. grad:	88.7%	Gulf (post-2001):	17.1%	House:	45 D 6 R
German:	6.0%	College grad:	28.6%	Peace time:	22.1%		
Irish:	4.4%	Grad degree:	9.5%				
English:	4.2%						

Maui resumed in December 2007, with expensive devices to avoid harming whales. Meanwhile, Hawaii, with great potential for wind and geothermal energy, is still 90% dependent on nonrenewable sources, although a 2006 law requires a reduction to 80% by 2020. But nature is not always benign. The Kilauea volcano on the Big Island started erupting in 1983 and hasn't stopped, and it is threatening hundreds of houses insured by a state program instituted in 1993. There is always at least a little trouble in paradise.

Presidential politics   Hawaii's presidential voting over the years has been the product of two some-times countervailing forces. One is the islands' historic preference for the Democratic Party. Thus Hawaii, voted Democratic when few other states did in 1980 and 1988. The other is an inclination to support incumbents in a state that takes patriotism very seriously, in part because the patriotism of so many of its citizens was once unjustly questioned and in part because of the large presence of the military. This helps explain why Hawaii supported Ronald Reagan solidly in 1984 and came close to voting for Gerald Ford in 1976, though it wasn't nearly

2008 Presidential Vote		
Obama (D) 325,871	(72%)
McCain (R).............................120,566	(27%)

2004 Presidential Vote		
Kerry (D)...............................231,708	(54%)
Bush (R)................................194,191	(45%)

enough to help George H.W. Bush in 1992. Ross Perot's military background, and the presence of Hawaiian Orson Swindle among his top leaders, gave him 14% and helped Democrat Bill Clinton carry Hawaii 48%-37%. In 1996 and 2000, as in 1968 and 1980, both those forces were moving in the same direction, and Hawaii voted 57%-32% for Clinton and 56%-37% for Al Gore.

In 2004, the two countervailing forces were in tension. October polls showed the contest a dead heat and suggested that Filipino- and Japanese-Americans, ordinarily Democratic, were leaning toward Bush, the commander-in-chief. Vice President Cheney flew 8,270 miles to appear in Honolulu at 10 p.m. on the Sunday night before the election and left two hours later—the first national nominee to campaign in Hawaii since 1960, when Republican Richard Nixon fulfilled his pledge to campaign in all 50 states (in the first election when there were 50 states). Hawaii's Democratic preference prevailed, and John Kerry won 54%-45%.

In 2008, for the first time in Hawaii's history as a state, no incumbent was running for president or vice president, and the Democratic presidential candidate was, for the first time for any party in America's history, a native of Hawaii. Obama vacationed in Hawaii for a week before the Democratic National Convention, and returned to the state just before the election to see his ailing grandmother, who died two days before the election. Hawaii voted 72%-27% for Barack Obama. Whites voted 70% for him, Asians 68%, and "others" (presumably mostly Native Hawaiians) 80% for him. Obama carried nearly every precinct in the state.

Hawaii chooses presidential delegates by caucus. Sometimes insurgent candidates have been able to swamp thinly attended meetings and win, as Democrat Michael Dukakis and Republican Pat Robertson did in 1988. In 2008, Hawaii Democrats held their caucuses on February 19, and more than 37,000 voters turned out, compared with 4,000 in 2004. The Obama campaign ran television ads in which the candidate stressed his Hawaiian heritage. Hillary Rodham Clinton sent daughter Chelsea in to campaign for a couple of days. Obama's 76%-24% win was one of the string of victories in February that propelled him to the nomination. The Republican caucuses took place on May 17, long after Arizona's John McCain had clinched the party's nomination.

Congressional districting   Hawaii has two congressional districts: The 1st includes urban Honolulu and extends westward to Pearl Harbor and the rural area beyond. The 2nd includes the rest of Oahu and the Neighbor Islands. The 1st District elected a Republican in 1986 and 1988. The 2d District has elected only Democrats since it was created in 1970. Before that, Hawaii elected one Democrat at large in 1959 and 1960 and two Democrats at large from 1962 to 1968. The Democratic Legislature made minor and politically insignificant changes in the district lines in 2002.

111th Congress Lineup
2 D
110th Congress Lineup
2 D

Governor

Linda Lingle (R)

Elected 2002, term expires Dec. 2010, 2nd term; b. June 4, 1953, St. Louis, MO; home, Honolulu; CA St. U. at Northridge, B.A. 1975; Jewish; divorced.

Elected Office: Maui Cnty. Cncl., 1980–90; Mayor, Maui Cnty., 1990–98.

Professional Career: Founder and editor, *Moloka'i Free Press*, 1977–80.

Office: State Capitol, Executive Chambers, Honolulu, 96813, 808-586-0034; Fax: 808-586-0006; Web site: www.hawaii.gov/gov.

Election Results

2006 general	Linda Lingle (R)	215,313	(63%)
	Randy Iwase (D)	121,717	(35%)
2006 primary	Linda Lingle (R)	unopposed	

Prior Winning Percentages: 2002 (52%)

Linda Lingle is the first woman elected governor of Hawaii and the first Republican elected to the post since 1959. She grew up near St. Louis and in Los Angeles's San Fernando Valley. Her home life was difficult. Lingle's mother, Mildred Cutter, suffered from bipolar disorder and sometimes had manic episodes that required she be restrained and hospitalized. Lingle lived with relatives during her teen years, but she and her mother were close until her mother's death in 2008. After graduating from California State University, Northridge, in 1975, Lingle moved to Hawaii, where her father owned a Ford dealership. She worked for the Teamsters and Hotel Workers unions in Honolulu and then founded the *Moloka'i Free Press* on that island, which is part of Maui County. In 1980, she was elected to the Maui Council and represented Molokai for six years; she held an at-large seat for four more. Lingle was elected mayor of Maui in 1990 over House Speaker Elmer Carvalho, and she won re-election in 1994.

In 1998, Lingle ran for governor. She hailed what she called "the Maui miracle" during her tenure as mayor—job growth in at least one part of Hawaii—and said, "It's time for a change, and change is about joining the other 49 states with economic revitalization that is taking place across the country." Lingle led in polls throughout the campaign, but incumbent Ben Cayetano appealed to Hawaii's ethnic groups and Democratic tradition. In August, Lingle accused the Cayetano campaign of spreading the false rumor that she is gay (she is twice divorced). The outcome may have been determined by Lingle's decision to take state matching funds and abide by a $2.7 million spending limit. Cayetano heavily outspent her in the last two weeks, and he won narrowly, 50%-49%.

Lingle immediately set out to run again. She became Republican state chairman, traveled extensively in Hawaii, and built an organization for the 2002 campaign much stronger than what she had in 1998. In 2000, Republicans made notable gains in state House representation. She raised plenty of money, much of it from the mainland, and tried to change the mind-set in Hawaii that Democratic victories were inevitable. In the meantime, Cayetano struggled with budget problems. In 2001, teachers in the state's single public school district went on strike seeking a 22% raise. Prominent Democrats were caught up in scandals. Against this backdrop, Lingle led in the polls from the start. She was by no means conservative on all issues. She called for 20% of energy to come from renewable sources by 2020 and backed Native Hawaiian groups' claims for some form of sovereignty. She favored parental consent for abortions for minors and a ban on partial-birth abortions, but she did not oppose abortion rights altogether. Her campaign's chief theme, however, was change.

Cayetano was prevented by law from seeking a third term. Lt. Gov. Mazie Hirono, part of the ruling Democratic machine and the favorite of the powerful public employees union, won the September 2002 primary with 41% of the vote. Hirono had an appealing life story. She was born in Japan and raised by a single mother who came to Hawaii to escape an abusive husband. She was a legislator from 1980 to 1994 and lieutenant governor from 1994 to 2002; one of her main accomplishments in the latter post was setting up a state-owned workmen's compensation insurer. When Lingle ran an ad highlighting Hawaii's poor test scores, low rate of job creation and growing poverty, Hirono said that Lingle was "always putting our people down." But Democrats remained on the defensive on corruption, and Hirono was far behind Lingle in fundraising. With the Democrats no longer seen as inevitable winners, business interests were no longer ponying up for the party that had held the governorship for 40 years. Ethnic balance for once helped Republicans. They had a ticket with a white Caucasian (Lingle) and a Native Hawaiian (retired state Circuit Judge James "Duke" Aiona), while the Democrats had a ticket with two Japanese-Americans, Hirono and former state Sen. Matt Matsunaga.

Hirono did manage to narrow the gap by appealing to party loyalties and by evoking now ancient memories of the state's Democratic tradition that had rallied late victories for Cayetano in 1998 and Gov. John Waihe'e in 1986. But it wasn't quite enough. Lingle won 52%-47%.

Lingle proclaimed her governorship a "New Beginning" and held a series of talk-story town meetings around the state, where she ate stew and rice with participants and listened to citizens' complaints. With Democrats controlling the state Senate 20-5 and the state House 36-15, the new governor had little leverage. The Legislature overrode Lingle's veto of a raise for 23,000 white-collar state employees and did not act on her calls for changes in workmen's compensation and for reducing business fees. Hawaii has the nation's highest gas prices, and the Legislature passed a law capping wholesale prices. Lingle warned that it would lead to higher prices while diverting attention from the real problem as she saw it—an overdependence on oil. The effective date was postponed until September 2005, but the governor could not persuade the Legislature to repeal the law.

She was determined to change education in Hawaii. Lingle called for the creation of seven local school boards to replace the statewide board, which would require a constitutional amendment, and she called for giving school principals control over 90% of operational money. The Legislature rejected the constitutional amendment, but in April 2004 it passed a bill with a new spending formula and giving principals power to oversee 70% of operational money. Lingle vetoed it, and asked for five changes. The Legislature overrode her veto. She was also able to enact a new junior kindergarten program for children who turn 5 after August 1.

In November 2004, Republicans lost five seats in the state House and after that Lingle took a different approach to governing. She found common ground with Democrats on alternative energy, education, and affordable housing. In 2005, Lingle approved a 9.6% pay raise for public school teachers and a bill appropriating more money to charter schools. She rolled out a plan for building 17,000 units of affordable housing within five years, and the Legislature gave her $100 million in bonding authority. Her budget also included money for shelters and additional services for the homeless. In 2006, with a projected $574 million budget surplus, she proposed $300 million in tax relief but was pleased enough when the Legislature approved $50 million and directed much of the rest of the surplus to education. After gas prices rose in nine of 10 weeks beginning in February 2006, the Legislature suspended the gas cap. Later that year, Lingle signed into law her energy initiative providing financing and tax credits for renewable-energy projects.

Not all of Lingle's stands pleased her few fellow Republicans. She said that Oahu should raise taxes to finance its $2.64 billion light-rail system, and her failure to veto a tax increase for mass transit or increases to the cigarette and real estate conveyance taxes angered conservatives. Still, Lingle's standing in the polls remained strong, and no top-tier challenger emerged when her first term was up in 2006. Democrats sought to crimp her national fundraising by passing in 2005 a campaign finance law that placed limits on mainland donations. The ploy did not work: Lingle ramped up her mainland fundraising before the law took effect in 2006, holding events in Houston, Los Angeles, New York City, and Philadelphia. Her effort put her on a pace to meet her ambitious goal of $6 million. In January 2006, former state Sen. Randall Iwase announced he would seek the Democratic nomination, but he was little known and the party continued to solicit candidates right up until the July filing deadline. By then, Lingle was well financed, the economy was strong, and unemployment was low.

Iwase won the Democratic nomination over two political newcomers. His performance, however, was uninspiring: A quarter of primary voters cast blank votes for governor. In the fall campaign, he argued that Lingle exaggerated her accomplishments and took too much credit for the state economy and the budget surplus. He criticized her for sending Hawaii inmates to mainland prisons, while she touted her crime-fighting efforts against sexual predators. Iwase also seized on the Iraq war issue, calling for a timetable for a troop withdrawal, and he sought to tie Lingle to President Bush. Lingle responded that she had visited Iraq to support the troops but that she would not back a withdrawal timetable. The election wasn't close. Lingle won 63%-35%, impressive enough for a Hawaii Republican, but especially so in the face of a strong Democratic wind both nationally and in Hawaii. In the concurrent Senate race, incumbent Daniel Akaka won re-election 61%-37%. Lingle's victory was built on her appeal to independent voters. Exit polls showed she won them by 66%-29%.

Lingle started out her second term with high hopes of passing tax cuts, including a $1,000 exemption for families with children, deductions for college savings, a reduction in the state's cellphone tax, and a plan to exempt the first $25,000 in income from taxation for people 65 years and older. But the economy softened in Hawaii along with the rest of the country, and the Democratically controlled Legislature balked. Lingle looked to the spending side as state revenues dropped, and in 2008, she eliminated Hawaii's universal health insurance program for children, which cost the state $50,000 a month and was mostly free to recipients. Her substitute plan charged parents $55 a month for each child enrolled. She also tried to stimulate the local economy in December 2008 by speeding up nearly $2 billion in capital improvement projects for highways, schools, public housing, libraries, and college campuses. The Legislature overrode four of her vetoes, including her rejection of a program to import cheaper prescription drugs from abroad and of a bill to limit her ability to suspend state workers' wages. By early 2009, the shortfall in revenues had become acute, and Lingle proposed to cut discretionary spending by 14% and to reduce wages and benefits for state workers. Democratic lawmakers called for raising taxes to help close the gap, but Lingle resisted.

One of the highlights of her second term was a 2008 agreement that Lingle reached with Hawaiian Electric Co. to buy a third of its electricity for Oahu consumers from wind farms on Moloka'I and Lana'i. An undersea cable will carry the electricity to large population centers on Oahu and Maui.

As the Republican governor of a state that produced the Democratic nominee for president in 2008, Lingle was a much-sought-after spokesperson for John McCain's presidential campaign. But she was sharply rebuked by prominent Democratic Hawaiians after she said in October that Barack Obama had been largely unknown in his home state and was indecisive, as demonstrated by his votes of "present" when he was in the Illinois Senate. Lingle introduced running mate Sarah Palin, the Alaska governor, at the Republican National Convention in August. Like Lingle, Palin was the first woman elected governor of her state. After McCain lost, Lingle said that the national party should be less ideological and try to attract more women and ethnic minorities. She told the Associated Press, "If someone looks up and they don't see anybody who looks like them in the party hierarchy or power structure, by nature they are not going to feel attracted there."

Senior Senator

Daniel Inouye (D)

Elected 1962, term expires 2010, 8th term; b. Sept. 7, 1924, Honolulu; home, Honolulu; U. of HI, B.A. 1950, George Washington U., J.D. 1952; United Methodist; married (Irene Hirano); 1 child.

Military Career: Army, 1943–47 (WWII).

Elected Office: HI House of Reps., 1954–58; HI Senate, 1958–59; U.S. House of Reps., 1959–62.

Professional Career: Honolulu dpty. public prosecutor, 1953–54.

DC Office: 722 HSOB, 20510, 202-224-3934; Fax: 202-224-6747; Web site: inouye.senate.gov.

State Offices: Hilo, 808-935-0844; Honolulu, 808-541-2542; Kauai, 808-245-4611; Kona, 808-935-0844; Maui, 808-242-9702; Molokai, 808-642-0203; West Oahu, 808-623-8334.

Committees: *Appropriations* (Chmn of 18 D): Commerce, Justice, Science & Related Agencies; Defense (Chmn); Homeland Security; Labor, Health and Human Services, Education & Related Agencies; Military Construction, Veterans Affairs & Related Agencies; State, Foreign Operations & Related Programs. *Commerce, Science & Transportation* (2nd of 14 D): Aviation Operations, Safety & Security; Communications, Technology & the Internet; Oceans, Atmosphere & Coast Guard; Science & Space; Surface Transportation & Merchant Marine Infrastructure, Safety & Security. *Indian Affairs* (2nd of 9 D). *Rules & Administration* (3rd of 11 D).

Group Ratings

	ADA	ACLU	AFS	LCV	ITIC	NTU	COC	ACU	CFG	FRC
2008	85	43	100	91	100	3	71	0	3	0
2007	90	—	100	80	—	4	45	0	14	—

National Journal Ratings

	2007 LIB	—	2007 CONS		2008 LIB	—	2008 CONS
Economic	70%	—	29%		71%	—	28%
Social	73%	—	25%		57%	—	42%
Foreign	70%	—	29%		65%	—	6%
Composite	72%	—	28%		70%	—	31%

Key Votes of the 110th Congress

1. Raise CAFE standards	Y	5. Make English official language	N	9. Withdraw troops 3/08	Y
2. Expand SCHIP	Y	6. Path to citizenship	Y	10. Iran guard is terrorist group	N
3. Cap greenhouse gases	Y	7. Fetus is unborn child	N	11. Increase missile defense $	N
4. Bail out financial markets	Y	8. Prosecute hate crimes	Y	12. Overhaul FISA	Y

Election Results

2004 general	Daniel Inouye (D)	313,629	(76%)	($1,768,886)
	Cam Cavasso (R)	87,172	(21%)	($57,123)
2004 primary	Daniel Inouye (D)	157,367	(94%)	
	Brian Evans (D)	8,051	(5%)	

Prior Winning Percentages: 1998 (79%); 1992 (57%); 1986 (74%); 1980 (78%); 1974 (83%); 1968 (83%); 1962 (69%); 1960 House (74%); 1959 House (68%)

The largest figure in Hawaii's public life remains Democrat Daniel Inouye, the state's senior senator who has held various elective offices since before Hawaii attained statehood in 1959. The son of Japanese immigrants, Inouye (*in-NO-ay*) grew up in Honolulu. His ambition was to become a surgeon. At age 17, he was teaching a first aid course when Pearl Harbor was attacked. He tended the wounded for a week, and then went on to serve in the 442nd Regimental Combat Team in France and Italy, eventually earning 15 medals and citations. Just as the war was ending, he lost his right arm in combat. Recovering in a Michigan veterans' hospital, he asked a fellow veteran from Kansas, whose right arm had been shattered, what his plans were. The soldier said he planned to go to law school, run for the state legislature, and eventually get elected to Congress. He was Bob Dole, who was also wounded in Italy, exactly one week before Inouye, and who went on to become a senator and the Republican nominee for president in 1996. Inouye and Dole served together for two years in the House and for 28 years in the Senate. Inouye graduated from the University of Hawaii and George Washington University Law School, then became a leader of a group of young veterans who took over Hawaii's creaking Democratic Party. He was elected to the territorial Legislature in 1954, the U.S. House in 1959, and the U.S. Senate in 1962. Inouye is the third-most-senior member of the Senate, after Democrats Robert Byrd of West Virginia and Edward Kennedy of Massachusetts. He was a tenacious member of the Senate Watergate Committee in 1973–74 and the first chairman of the Senate Intelligence Committee in 1976. In 2000, he was awarded the Congressional Medal of Honor for his heroism in World War II.

In 2009, Inouye rose to the chairmanship of the powerful Appropriations Committee. He replaced the chronically ill Byrd, who was pressed by Senate Majority Leader Harry Reid to step down from the demanding job after the 2008 election. Byrd called Inouye a friend and "genuine American hero," and predicted he would be a "skillful and fair" replacement. Democratic Rep. Neal Abercrombie of Hawaii called it "a remarkable story" for their small state: Inouye took over the post just as native-son Barack Obama became the new president. Inouye had an unusually close working relationship with former Republican Appropriations Chairman Ted Stevens of Alaska, who lost re-election in 2008 after being convicted of corruption-related charges. Inouye was a character witness at Stevens's October 2008 trial. The two men had served together since the 1960s representing the two states most recently admitted to the Union and geographically the most distant from other states. They referred to each other as "brother."

Inouye said that he would not alter the committee's handling of lawmakers' pet projects, in spite of recent controversies over congressional earmarks. He has long used his seat on Appropriations to fund projects he finds worthy, from his alma mater of George Washington University to Native Hawaiian education. From 1998 to 2003, he steered $1.4 billion to military projects in Hawaii, which occupies a forward geographical position in the country's national defense. Among them were an Army high-tech intelligence center, the Maui Space Surveillance System, and the Pacific Missile Range Facility on Kauai. He generally is a Pentagon booster. In 2008, his defense spending bill gave nearly full funding to the Bush administration's requests for new combat systems, national missile defense, and shipbuilding.

Inouye chaired the Indian Affairs Committee from 1989–94 and again in 2001–03. He saw many analogies between the condition of mainland American Indians and Native Hawaiians, and generally erred on the side of Native Americans in disputes with the federal government. In 2006, he removed from a lobbying regulation bill a provision that would require Indian tribes to report contributions to the Federal Election Commission. He also sponsored a measure, defeated 6-6, to give tribes the right to appeal a rejection by the states of their bids for casinos. At one point, he refused contact with companies that hired disgraced lobbyist Jack Abramoff, who was accused of swindling tribes. "I took it personally. He was ripping off Indians," Inouye told *The Washington Post*. He was also a co-sponsor of the 1993 bill in which the United States apologized for overthrowing the Hawaiian monarchy. In 2000, he secured funding for Native Hawaiians purchasing property in the Home Lands, the 200,000 acres set aside in 1920 for a permanent homeland for Native Hawaiians. On the heated issue of Native Hawaiian sovereignty, some activists consider him lukewarm, especially in comparison to the junior senator from Hawaii, Daniel Akaka, who has pushed the legislation for years.

On the Commerce, Science, and Transportation Committee, which Inouye chaired in the last Congress (2007–08), he has been deeply involved in communications issues and tends to favor government regulation over markets. He and Stevens co-sponsored a 2005 bill that passed the Senate facilitating the transition from analog broadcasting, and since then he has prodded regulators and the industry to be prepared for the likely confusion, especially among the 20 million American households continuing to rely on over-the-air signals. He was not enthusiastic about Stevens's far-ranging rewrite of the 1996 telecommunications act, and when he took over the chairmanship in 2007, he indicated that he was not interested in such sweeping legislation. Instead he pushed more-modest measures, like one setting criteria for Commerce Department grants to strengthen emergency communications, and a 2008 bill to crack down on online predators. Also that year, Congress passed Inouye's Broadband Data Improvement Act, aimed at identifying areas of the nation that have fallen behind in high-speed Internet access. He opposed a permanent ban on Internet taxes because "we don't know what the future holds."

Over the years, Inouye has taken more-moderate positions on some issues than most Democrats. He was one of the Gang of 14 senators who pledged in 2005 not to filibuster judicial nominees except in extraordinary circumstances. But he voted against the Iraq war resolution in 2002, and was among the 12 Democrats who voted in 2006 to withdraw all combat troops from Iraq by July 2007. Inouye spoke out against the confirmation of Alberto Gonzales as U.S. attorney general in 2005, saying, "I am appalled that he has professed only a 'vague knowledge' of the racial and ethnic disparities in the imposition of the death penalty in federal cases."

Inouye sponsored a 2006 law granting $38 million to research and restore sites where Japanese-Americans were interned during World War II, and in 2007, he sponsored a bill to investigate the cases of people of Japanese origin in Latin America who were deported from countries there and sent to the United States, evidently to be exchanged for American prisoners of war held by Japan. But he objected to House-passed legislation that year to call on Japan to apologize for its use of sex slaves during the war. Six Japanese prime ministers already had apologized, he said, while noting the U.S. government's improper war-time internment of Japanese-Americans.

Inouye is part of the powerful faction of Hawaii's Democratic Party that held the governorship from 1962 to 2002. In 2002, he vigorously supported Lt. Gov. Mazie Hirono in her nearly successful attempt to extend the 40-year string. In early 2007, Inouye endorsed Hillary Rodham Clinton for president, saying native-son Barack Obama needed more experience. He was forced to issue an apology after suggesting during the primaries that Obama attended an elitist high school in Hawaii. "Shame on Danny for trying to pull that stunt," Obama told a local interviewer. "I went to Punahou [school] on a scholarship." Following the death of his wife Margaret in 2006, Inouye in 2008 married Irene Hirano, the president of the Japanese American National Museum in Los Angeles.

He has been re-elected by wide margins. He seems certain not to face much competition when his seat comes up in 2010. Abercrombie, when asked whether Inouye would retire, said, "May that day not come for many years. Someone will take his position, but not his place."

Junior Senator

Daniel Akaka (D)

Appointed May 1990, term expires 2012, 3rd full term; b. Sept. 11, 1924, Honolulu; home, Honolulu; U. of HI, B.Ed. 1952, M.A. 1966; Congregationalist; married (Mary Mildred); 5 children.

Military Career: Army Corps of Engineers, 1945–47 (WWII).

Elected Office: U.S. House of Reps., 1976–90.

Professional Career: Public schl. teacher, principal & admin., 1953–71; Dir., HI Office of Econ. Oppor., 1971–74; Asst., HI Gov. Ariyoshi, 1975–76; Dir., Progressive Neighborhoods Program, 1975–76.

DC Office: 141 HSOB, 20510, 202-224-6361; Fax: 202-224-2126; Web site: akaka.senate.gov.

State Offices: Hilo, 808-935-1114; Honolulu, 808-522-8970.

Committees: *Armed Services* (6th of 15 D): Personnel; Readiness & Management Support; Seapower. *Banking, Housing & Urban Affairs* (7th of 13 D): Financial Institutions; Housing, Transportation & Community Development; Securities, Insurance & Investment. *Homeland Security & Governmental Affairs* (3rd of 10 D): Federal Financial Management, Government Information, Federal Services & International Security; Oversight of Government Management, the Federal Workforce & the District of Columbia (Chmn); State, Local & Private Sector Preparedness & Integration. *Indian Affairs* (4th of 9 D). *Veterans' Affairs* (Chmn of 10 D).

Group Ratings

	ADA	ACLU	AFS	LCV	ITIC	NTU	COC	ACU	CFG	FRC
2008	100	93	100	100	80	3	50	0	3	11
2007	95	—	86	87	—	3	36	0	7	—

National Journal Ratings

	2007 LIB — 2007 CONS		2008 LIB — 2008 CONS	
Economic	66%	30%	91%	0%
Social	70%	28%	80%	9%
Foreign	79%	17%	65%	6%
Composite	73%	27%	87%	13%

Key Votes of the 110th Congress

1. Raise CAFE standards	Y	5. Make English official language	N	9. Withdraw troops 3/08	Y
2. Expand SCHIP	Y	6. Path to citizenship	Y	10. Iran guard is terrorist group	Y
3. Cap greenhouse gases	Y	7. Fetus is unborn child	N	11. Increase missile defense $	N
4. Bail out financial markets	Y	8. Prosecute hate crimes	Y	12. Overhaul FISA	N

Election Results

2006 general	Daniel Akaka (D)	210,330	(61%)	($2,651,026)
	Cynthia Thielen (R)	126,097	(37%)	($356,413)
2006 primary	Daniel Akaka (D)	129,158	(55%)	
	Ed Case (D)	107,163	(45%)	

Prior Winning Percentages: 2000 (73%); 1994 (72%); 1990 (54%); 1988 House (89%); 1986 House (76%); 1984 House (82%); 1982 House (89%); 1980 House (90%); 1978 House (86%); 1976 House (80%)

Democrat Daniel Akaka is the first senator of Native Hawaiian descent. Born four days after fellow Democratic Sen. Daniel Inouye, he served in the Army Corps of Engineers in the 1940s, then became a public school teacher and principal. In 1971, he was the director of the Hawaii anti-poverty program, and in 1975, he became an assistant to Democratic Gov. George Ariyoshi. The next year, when both of Hawaii's representatives ran for the Senate, he was elected to the House, where he served quietly on the Appropriations Committee. In May 1990, after the death of Democratic Sen. Spark Matsunaga, Democratic Gov. John Waihee appointed Akaka to the Senate. He has thus been an integral part of the dominant Democratic organization, and a quiet but diligent worker on Hawaii issues, for more than 30 years. But after all of his time in Congress, Akaka is not well known nationally. "I was taught not to be a show horse but a workhorse," he told *The Honolulu Advertiser* in 2006. "So, in a way, it's been a part of me not to brag."

In 2007, as the new chairman of the Veterans' Affairs Committee, Akaka pledged to secure more health care funding for American military forces returning home from Iraq and Afghanistan. He also wants to reorganize the Department of Veterans Affairs to handle more quickly "invisible wounds" such as post-traumatic stress disorder and brain injuries. He complained that doctors had been barred from some medical information about injured troops, and he got the Pentagon to reverse its policy. He also called for a new GI Bill with expanded education benefits for veterans. With Democratic Sen. Jim Webb of Virginia, Akaka enacted in January 2008 an amendment requiring that the Army report to Congress before fixing Arlington National Cemetery's Tomb of the Unknowns, which has cracks running through the marble monument; he wants to repair the tomb rather than replace it, as some have advocated.

Akaka likely would have become chairman of the more powerful Homeland Security and Governmental Affairs Committee in 2009 if Senate Democrats had been successful in ousting Chairman Joe Lieberman, the Connecticut independent who fell out of favor with Democrats after actively supporting John McCain in the 2008 presidential contest. But Lieberman held on, with support from Obama.

Akaka has waged a lonely and long campaign in the Senate on the issue of Native Hawaiian sovereignty. He was the sponsor of the 1993 Apology Resolution, signed by President Clinton, in which the United States acknowledged as illegal the overthrow of the Kingdom of Hawaii in 1893 and the denial of Native Hawaiians' right to self-determination. Akaka in 2000 introduced a bill that would have recognized Native Hawaiians as an indigenous people with a right to self-determination and would have established a process for formation of a Native Hawaiian governing body that was to have, as many Indian tribes do, a government-to-government relationship with the United States. Many Hawaiians believe they need the law to allow them to negotiate more forcefully with the federal government over land-use issues, a major concern for many residents. A companion bill passed the House that year but died in the Senate. Akaka brought the bill up again in 2001 and it was passed by the Indian Affairs Committee. Akaka had lobbying help from Alaska Native and American Indian groups, but a hold was placed on the bill by a Republican senator after some Native Hawaiians argued against it, saying it would make them wards of the government. (In the Senate, a bill can be stopped indefinitely when a senator declares a "hold".) Akaka brought the bill up again in 2004 with some changes, but it again was subject to a hold, by Republican Sen. Jon Kyl of Arizona, who said: "Persons of different races, who live together in the same society, would be subject to different legal codes. This would not produce racial reconciliation in Hawaii. Instead, it is a recipe of permanent racial conflict."

In 2005, Republican Gov. Linda Lingle traveled to Washington to lobby for Akaka's bill with the White House and Republican senators. But Sen. John Ensign, R-Nev., placed a hold on it, claiming the assertion of native rights could lead to legalized gambling in Hawaii, one of only two states without it, and an expansion of gambling on the mainland. In June 2006, Akaka finally got the Senate to consider whether to bring the bill to the floor. It voted 56-41, which was a majority but still four votes short of the 60 needed to bring it up for passage. Republicans cast all 41 votes. When Democrats took majority control of the Senate in 2007, Akaka stepped up his efforts. The House passed the bill in October 2007, and Akaka secured a commitment from Senate Majority Leader Harry Reid of Nevada to bring the bill to the floor. But Reid failed to do so, and some Democrats defended the decision by citing President Bush's veto threat. Akaka turned his attention to getting an endorsement of his bill added to the 2008 Democratic presidential platform, and said he was "ecstatic" that native-son Barack Obama was supportive. He can be expected to resurrect his efforts in the 111th Congress (2009–10), with Obama in the White House. However, Akaka will still have to contend with resistance from Republicans and perhaps Senate Majority Leader Reid.

Another of Akaka's legislative causes was passage of a law making permanent the waiver of visa requirements from some countries, including Japan, which sends 2 million visitors a year to Hawaii. He took a leading role in passage of the 1989 and 1994 laws to protect government whistle-blowers and with Sen. Susan Collins, R-Maine, has sought to expand those protections to allow federal workers to make classified disclosures to members of Congress and their aides. Akaka was among the nine senators voting against the homeland-security bill of 2002, arguing that it gave the government too much power to compile information about citizens and failed to protect the rights of whistle-blowers. In 2006, he was one of nine Senate Democrats who voted against renewing the USA PATRIOT Act, the Bush administration's antiterrorism law that expanded law enforcement powers.

Akaka has supported oil drilling in the Arctic National Wildlife Refuge, perhaps in part out of solidarity with colleagues from Alaska, who like Hawaiians often feel resentment that policy is made by mainlanders who have little knowledge or understanding of the unique needs of their states. "To some of my colleagues, the debate about the Arctic National Wildlife Refuge is about energy. To others, it is about the environment," Akaka said. "To me, the [issue] is really about whether or not the indigenous people who are directly impacted have a voice about the use of their lands." Akaka and Inouye have been among the few Democrats who have supported deployment of a ballistic missile defense system. Hawaii is much more vulnerable to North Korean missiles than the U.S. mainland.

Since his initial 54%-45% victory in 1990 against Republican Rep. Pat Saiki, Akaka has won re-election by large margins. But in 2006, at the age of 82, he faced a competitive primary challenge from 2nd District Democratic Rep. Ed Case. This was a remarkable election for Hawaii, where the creaky Democratic establishment retains a tight grip on elections and no incumbent member of Congress has ever been defeated for re-election. Akaka was the establishment candidate, strongly supported by labor unions, Inouye, and Hawaii's other Democratic representative, Neil Abercrombie. Case was an archenemy of the establishment after challenging its candidate in the 2002 primary for governor. The 54-year-old Case argued that Hawaii, with its two octogenarian senators, needed to begin preparing for the inevitable transition by electing a more youthful Democrat who could begin accumulating seniority.

In most other states, Case would have had ample ammunition between Akaka's low profile in Washington, the failure of his Native Hawaiian federal recognition bill, and a *Time* magazine article that ranked Akaka as "affectionate and earnest" but one of the five worst senators. But in Hawaii, Akaka is revered for his gentleness and modesty, and there were limits on how far Case could go in criticizing him. Case highlighted his outsider status and noted that Akaka was a "product" of a "culture that perceives any innovation, any advance, any progress, and even any disagreement as a threat to their power." Akaka played up his vote against authorizing the use of force in Iraq and his close relationship with Inouye, and suggested that Case was not a real Democrat. He won 55%-45%. Akaka carried Oahu, where 69% of the votes were cast, 53%-47%; he won larger margins elsewhere, including 64% in Maui. Case said afterward: "This was a clear and convincing victory for the Democratic machine that has been increasingly hanging on to power in Hawaii by their fingernails."

The general election was easier for Akaka. The Republican was state Rep. Cynthia Thielen, a moderate who supports abortion rights. Akaka won easily, but Thielen held him to a 61%-37% victory—his lowest Senate re-election percentage.

FIRST DISTRICT

Neil Abercrombie (D)

Elected 1990, 10th full term; b. June 26, 1938, Buffalo, NY; home, Honolulu; Union Col., B.A. 1959, U. of HI, M.A. 1964, Ph.D. 1974; no religious affiliation; married (Nancie Caraway).

Elected Office: HI House of Reps., 1974–78; HI Senate, 1978–86; U.S. House of Reps., 1986–87; Honolulu City Cncl., 1988–90.

Professional Career: College prof., 1959–63; Probation officer, Marin Cnty., CA, 1964–67; Sociologist, 1967–74; Asst. prof., HI Loa Col., 1979–80; Consultant, 1983–87, 1989–90; Asst., HI Superintendent of Educ., 1987–88.

DC Office: 1502 LHOB, 20515, 202-225-2726; Fax: 202-225-4580; Web site: www.house.gov/abercrombie.

State Offices: Honolulu, 808-541-2570.

Committees: *Armed Services* (5th of 36 D): Air & Land Forces (Chmn); Readiness. *Natural Resources* (4th of 29 D): Insular Affairs, Oceans & Wildlife; National Parks, Forests & Public Lands.

Group Ratings

	ADA	ACLU	AFS	LCV	ITIC	NTU	COC	ACU	CFG	FRC
2008	95	100	100	77	57	9	50	8	0	0
2007	100	—	100	70	—	4	53	4	6	—

National Journal Ratings

	2007 LIB	—	2007 CONS		2008 LIB	—	2008 CONS
Economic	58%	—	41%		85%	—	0%
Social	92%	—	0%		72%	—	26%
Foreign	77%	—	23%		78%	—	17%
Composite	77%	—	23%		82%	—	18%

Key Votes of the 110th Congress

1. Increase minimum wage	*	5. Share immigration data	N	9. Withdraw troops 8/08	Y
2. Expand SCHIP	Y	6. Foreign aid abortion ban	N	10. No operations in Iran	Y
3. Raise CAFE standards	Y	7. Ban gay bias in workplace	Y	11. Free trade with Peru	N
4. Bail out financial markets	Y	8. Repeal D.C. gun law	Y	12. Overhaul FISA	N

Election Results

2008 general	Neil Abercrombie (D)	154,208	(77%)	($2,010,449)
	Steve Tataii (R)	38,115	(19%)	
	Li Zhao (Lib)	7,594	(4%)	
2008 primary	Neil Abercrombie (D)	unopposed		

Prior Winning Percentages: 2006 (69%); 2004 (63%); 2002 (73%); 2000 (69%); 1998 (62%); 1996 (50%); 1994 (54%); 1992 (73%); 1990 (60%); 1986 (30%)

Population		Race/Ethnicity		Work	
Pop. 2007:	625,529	White:	18.6%	Private:	66.5%
Change since 2000:	Up 3.1%	Black:	3.1%	Government:	27.6%
Urban:	99.3%	Hispanic:	5.6%	Self-employed:	5.7%
Rural:	0.7%	Asian:	52.5%	Blue collar:	16.2%
Area size:	326 sq. mi.	Native Am.:	0.2%	White collar:	60.2%
		Hawaiian:	5.7%	Khaki collar:	3.7%
Age		Two+ races:	14.0%	Other:	20.0%
Median age:	39.4 yrs.	*Ancestry*		Median income:	$62,012
More than 65 yrs:	16.1%	German:	4.9%	Median home value:	$517,700
Less than 18 yrs:	20.2%	Irish:	3.4%	Poverty:	8.6%
Education		English:	3.2%		
H.S. grad:	88.3%			**Military Veterans**	
College grad:	31.5%			% of Pop:	12.8%
Grad degree:	10.7%				

The landmarks for visitors to Honolulu are the Hickam Air Force Base, the *Arizona* monument in Pearl Harbor, the downtown area, with its wondrously Victorian Iolani Palace, and, of course, Waikiki, with its 40-story hotels rising within a few feet of each other. This part of Hawaii is tightly packed with people living between the 3,000-foot Koolau Range and the beaches and harbor, where tropical bungalows and garden apartments house Hawaiians of all incomes. Hawaii's largest shopping cen-

2008 Presidential Vote

Obama (D)	152,990	(70%)
McCain (R)	61,116	(28%)

2004 Presidential Vote

Kerry (D)	110,702	(53%)
Bush (R)	99,256	(47%)

Cook Partisan Voting Index: D + 11

ters and its state university are located here. Neighborhoods where the rich overlook the ocean are wedged next to poor enclaves where residents are crammed onto clogged streets. Hawaii's topography jams cars onto just a few freeways and avenues, where traffic slows during rush hour and the aloha spirit is sorely tested. High taxes and high land and utility costs have limited growth. And although tourism remains brisk, the recession hit here early, resulting in declining hotel occupancy. Homelessness grew, and Aloha Airlines went bankrupt, ending its passenger service in March 2008. The military remains an important presence on Oahu. Hickam is home to eight C-17 Air Force cargo carriers that can transport 20-ton armored Stryker vehicles.

All of these areas are in the 1st Congressional District of Hawaii. It is an area of well-established neighborhoods, and with little land left to develop, it is growing less rapidly than the rest of the state. Politically, the neighborhoods around Honolulu's downtown and the university campus are middle and lower income and usually Democratic. To the west, around the harbor, are many military families in modest neighborhoods who may vote for Democrats but can be attracted to Republicans. To the east, past Waikiki, around Diamond Head, and out to the Kahala and Koko Head beach areas, is higher-income territory that often votes Republican. Asians are 59% of the population in Honolulu. Favorite-son Barack Obama, who was photographed bodysurfing at Sandy Beach prior to the Democratic National Convention in August, reigned supreme here in 2008, when he got 70% of the vote in Honolulu County.

The congressman from the 1st District is Democrat Neil Abercrombie. With his graying beard and sometime ponytail, he has been affectionately referred to as the aging hippie of Capitol Hill. But he is also known as the "Gym God" for his ability to bench-press 260 pounds in the House gym, where he is frequently found. (He spearheaded an $8 million renovation for the members-only facility.) He is also known for an aggressive and bombastic debating style that is often tempered by enthusiasm and good humor. After college in upstate New York, Abercrombie taught school, moved to Hawaii, earned a Ph.D. in American studies, and at various times worked as a waiter, custodian, and probation officer. In those years, Abercrombie, now in his 70s, got to know Obama's parents and knew their son as "Little Barry." He was elected to the Hawaii Legislature in 1974 and served 12 years. He first came to Congress in 1986, when he won a special election, and served only three months. He lost the primary for the full term to Democrat Mufi Hannemann (now mayor of Honolulu), who then lost to Republican Pat Saiki. When Saiki ran for the U.S. Senate in 1990, Abercrombie won a three-way primary for her House seat and won the general election easily.

Abercrombie is one of the distinctive figures in the House. His voting record is mostly liberal, though a bit less so on economic issues. He serves on the Armed Services Committee and sees no contradiction between his protests of the Iraq war and his votes for military spending for Hawaii and elsewhere. "I see my work on Armed Services as a fulfillment of my principles and the motivating force of my life," Abercrombie says. "It's not about pro-war or anti-war, but how do you keep the peace." When Republicans controlled Congress, he and Ohio liberal Dennis Kucinich were the lead sponsors of a resolution calling for a date-certain withdrawal of U.S. troops from Iraq. Abercrombie was a vocal opponent of the Bush administration's "surge" proposal for adding more combat troops. "This is the craziest, dumbest plan I've ever seen or heard of in my life," he told Joint Chiefs of Staff Chairman Peter Pace during a 2007 hearing. He said he worried that "endless deployments" jeopardized troop readiness, and that Democratic leaders allowed Iraq to "fall off the table." In October 2007, the House passed the bill he sponsored with Democratic Rep. John Tanner of Tennessee requiring the Bush administration to report every 90 days on its plans to withdraw troops from Iraq; the bill died in the Senate.

Once Democrats took the majority in 2007, Abercrombie chaired the Air and Land Forces Subcommittee. He has worked to assure adequate funding for Micronesia and the Marshall Islands 2,500 miles to the southwest in the Pacific, and he pressed the Army to explain the dumping of 8,000 tons of chemical munitions off Oahu after World War II. In 2007, he backed an $867 million cut in technology-based Future Combat Systems, the Army's main modernization program, after continual delays in testing the new systems. In his usual colorful way, Abercrombie described his frustration with the Army: "The problem with FCS is, they're waiting for Dumbledore or someone to come in and say, 'Harry, this is the magic incantation. Say this and, believe me, the Dark Lord will be vanquished'—the Dark Lord of schedule and testing and delays. They're looking for Harry Potter!" In the 2008 defense bill, Abercrombie added 15 C-17 transports and 20 F-22 fighters that the Pentagon did not request. The watchdog group Citizens Against Government Waste listed him in 2008 as the fourth-highest House recipient of local earmarks, mostly for military projects.

Abercrombie is protective of Hawaii interests but is not always predictable. He voted for a Republican energy bill in 2005 because it included a study for turning sugarcane into ethanol, quite understandably since Hawaii is a major sugar producer. But he angered environmentalists when he joined Republicans on legislation allowing offshore natural-gas drilling, with the receipts shared by states that open their coasts to leasing. In August 2008, he sharply criticized Democratic leaders as "way behind the curve in terms of what people want" for failing to address high gasoline prices. He sponsored another bill to allow businesses to write off the travel costs of spouses on business trips—Hawaii has lots of hotels. But despite Hawaii's strategic location in global trade, he voted against normal trade relations with China and opposed giving the president broad powers to negotiate trade deals. Abercrombie has consistently backed Hawaii Democratic Sen. Daniel Akaka's bill to recognize Native Hawaiians as an indigenous people with a right to self-determination.

The 1st District is usually solidly Democratic, but in 1994 Abercrombie had serious competition from Orson Swindle, a Marine Corps pilot, a Vietnam-era prisoner of war, and a national leader of Ross Perot's United We Stand America. Swindle charged that Abercrombie was too dovish, but Abercrombie outraised him, and won 54%-43%. Swindle ran again in 1996, labeled Abercrombie a far-left hippie, and called for big spending cuts. Abercrombie narrowly outspent him, and won 50%-46%. Since then, he has been re-elected by overwhelming margins. Abercrombie announced in March 2009 he will run for governor in 2010, when Republican Gov. Linda Lingle is term-limited.

SECOND DISTRICT

Mazie Hirono (D)

Elected 2006, 2nd term; b. Nov. 3, 1947, Fukushima, Japan; home, Honolulu; U. of HI, B.A. 1970, Georgetown U., J.D. 1978; Buddhist; married (Leighton Kim Oshima); 1 child.

Elected Office: HI House of Reps., 1980–94, HI lt. gov. 1994–2002.

Professional Career: Dep. atty. gen., 1978–80; Practicing atty., 1984–88.

DC Office: 1524 LHOB, 20515, 202-225-4906; Fax: 202-225-4987; Web site: hirono.house.gov.

State Offices: Honolulu, 808-541-1986.

Committees: *Education & Labor* (18th of 29 D): Early Childhood, Elementary & Secondary Education; Higher Education, Lifelong Learning & Competitiveness. *Transportation & Infrastructure* (22nd of 44 D): Aviation; Highways & Transit; Water Resources & Environment.

Group Ratings

	ADA	ACLU	AFS	LCV	ITIC	NTU	COC	ACU	CFG	FRC
2008	100	100	100	92	57	10	56	4	0	0
2007	100	—	100	90	—	3	45	0	6	—

National Journal Ratings

	2007 LIB	—	2007 CONS		2008 LIB	—	2008 CONS
Economic	82%	—	0%		85%	—	0%
Social	77%	—	17%		82%	—	0%
Foreign	90%	—	8%		78%	—	17%
Composite	87%	—	13%		88%	—	12%

Key Votes of the 110th Congress

1. Increase minimum wage	Y	5. Share immigration data	N	9. Withdraw troops 8/08	Y
2. Expand SCHIP	Y	6. Foreign aid abortion ban	N	10. No operations in Iran	Y
3. Raise CAFE standards	Y	7. Ban gay bias in workplace	Y	11. Free trade with Peru	N
4. Bail out financial markets	Y	8. Repeal D.C. gun law	N	12. Overhaul FISA	N

Election Results

2008 general	Mazie Hirono (D)	165,748	(76%)	($970,819)
	Roger Evans (R)	44,425	(20%)	
2008 primary	Mazie Hirono (D)	unopposed		

Prior Winning Percentages: 2006 (61%)

Population		Race/Ethnicity		Work	
Pop. 2007:	651,005	White:	30.2%	Private:	67.8%
Change since 2000:	Up 7.6%	Black:	1.6%	Government:	23.2%
Urban:	83.8%	Hispanic:	10.5%	Self-employed:	8.8%
Rural:	16.2%	Asian:	25.6%	Blue collar:	20.5%
Area size:	10,605 sq. mi.	Native Am.:	0.3%	White collar:	53.7%
Age		Hawaiian:	10.3%	Khaki collar:	3.0%
Median age:	36.1 yrs.	Two+ races:	21.4%	Other:	22.8%
More than 65 yrs:	12.1%	*Ancestry*		Median income:	$63,249
Less than 18 yrs:	24.3%	German:	7.0%	Median home value:	$503,500
Education		Portuguese:	5.6%	Poverty:	9.6%
H.S. grad:	89.1%	Irish:	5.2%	**Military Veterans**	
College grad:	25.7%			% of Pop:	11.6%
Grad degree:	8.3%				

The 2nd District encompasses all of the islands in the Hawaii archipelago, including most of Oahu's acreage beyond Honolulu, which belongs to the state's other congressional district. It takes in Wheeler Army Airfield and the farmlands north of Pearl Harbor, between two jagged chains of mountains that lift the island out of the sea. Over the mountains to the west on Oahu is the Leeward Coast—calm, sultry, and lightly populated. Over the mountains to the northeast is the Windward

2008 Presidential Vote		
Obama (D)	172,881	(73%)
McCain (R)	59,450	(25%)
2004 Presidential Vote		
Kerry (D)	120,633	(56%)
Bush (R)	94,860	(44%)
Cook Partisan Voting Index:	D + 14	

Coast, with many prosperous, Republican-leaning subdivisions in and around Kaneohe and Kailua. The 137 islands have distinct personalities. Hawaii, the Big Island, is the size of Connecticut and boasts huge cattle ranches; the active volcano Kilauea, which started erupting in 1983 and has not stopped since; and Mauna Kea, the highest mountain in the world if the count begins at its base far under the ocean. Tourists are told that it is bad luck to take pieces of lava home. On the north shore, with heavy rainfall and tropical foliage, is the old port of Hilo and Hawaii's macadamia nut industry; this is a blue-collar Democratic area in a natural wonderland. On the Kona Coast, where there is little rainfall and the landscape is dominated by lava flows, there are retirement condominiums and a higher-income, more Republican population. Even before the recession of 2008, tourism dropped sharply on the island, and tourist officials are encouraging new visitors from China. Energy prices are among the highest in the nation, and "vog" emissions from volcanoes are a growing health concern. The island of Maui, favored more by North American than Asian tourists, has dozens of luxury condominiums and upscale resorts. Workers are employed chiefly in tourism, the military, social services, and agriculture. Kauai, much of which was devastated by Hurricane Iniki in 1992, is the least developed and most agricultural of the main islands. Parts of it have the nation's highest rainfall, while others seldom get wet. Its large farm workforce—a reminder of what most of Hawaii was like a century ago—makes it the most Democratic of the islands. Overall, the district is Democratic. In 2008, voters on the Big Island effectively decriminalized small amounts of marijuana possession by requiring that police make such arrests their lowest priority.

The congresswoman from the 2nd District is Mazie Hirono, a Democrat elected in 2006. Hirono was born in Fukushima, Japan, and immigrated to Hawaii in 1955 just before her eighth birthday with her mother, who fled an abusive husband with alcohol and gambling problems. As a child, she shared a single bed in a boardinghouse room with her mother and older brother, and at age 10 was sent to work to help support the family. These childhood struggles with poverty and the adjustment to a new country shaped her liberal politics. "I know what it feels like to be discriminated against, to feel powerless, to have landlords who threaten to kick you out, and not having a place to go," she told *The Honolulu Advertiser*. Hirono mastered English in the public schools and became a naturalized citizen in 1959, the same year Hawaii became a state. After graduating from the University of Hawaii, she ran for a seat in the state House and lost, then earned a law degree from Georgetown University and worked in the Hawaii attorney general's office. She ran again for the state House in 1980 and won; she held the seat for 14 years. In 1994, she was elected to the first of two terms as lieutenant governor. In 2002, she defeated Democrat Ed Case, who was then a state representative, in the gubernatorial primary. After that, her poorly organized campaign struggled to gain momentum, and she was undermined by Democratic corruption scandals, budget woes, and an acrimonious teachers' strike. She lost the general election 52%-47% to Linda Lingle, the first Republican to win the office since 1959.

Hirono's defeat was a painful setback for her, but not a career-ender. She formed the Patsy Mink political action committee (named for the late Hawaii representative) to assist state-level Democratic women who support abortion rights. When then-U.S. Rep. Case decided to challenge Sen. Daniel Akaka in the Democratic Senate primary in 2006, Hirono was one of 10 Democrats and two Republicans who wanted to succeed him. The field included experienced campaigners such as state Sens. Colleen Hanabusa and Clayton Hee, and former state Sen. Matt Matsunaga, the son of the late U.S. Sen. Spark Matsunaga. Hirono entered the race in April 2006 and was endorsed by the fundraising group EMILY's List. She had more money and name recognition than the other candidates and was considered a front-runner.

She ran radio ads that highlighted her efforts on early-childhood education, land reform, and workers' compensation. Hirono was forced to confront criticism about her record of accomplishment in state government and lingering doubts about the strength of her candidacy in the wake of her 2002 gubernatorial defeat. But Hirono narrowly won the splintered September primary with 22% of the vote and finished 844 votes ahead of Hanabusa, who garnered 21%. Matsunaga was third with 14%. After clinching the Democratic nomination, Hirono had a much easier time winning the general election in a district that had never elected a Republican. Republican state Sen. Bob Hogue, a former sportscaster, struggled to stay competitive with Hirono. Depicting Hirono as too liberal even for Hawaii, Republicans mocked her as a "big-government peacenik" for her support for liberal presidential candidate Dennis Kucinich's proposal to create a federal Department of Peace. Hirono emphasized her experience and raised more money, winning the general election 61%-39%. Though she is no longer an active practitioner, Hirono entered office as one of only two Buddhists ever to serve in Congress. (The other is Hank Johnson of Georgia, also elected in 2006.)

In the House, Hirono has had a solidly liberal voting record and kept a relatively low profile. She worked with Hawaii Democratic Rep. Neil Abercrombie to pass the Native Hawaiian recognition bill in October 2007. On the Education and Labor Committee, she pushed to add $1 billion over five years for preschool education. She backed a phased troop withdrawal from Iraq, and said during a June 2008 visit to the country that military progress should expedite the return home of U.S. forces. The House passed her bill to create a memorial on Kalaupapa Peninsula in Hawaii for the 8,000 people forcibly exiled there with leprosy from 1866 to 1969. In October 2008, she reversed earlier opposition to the $700 billion bailout of the financial and insurance industries after getting a call from Democratic presidential nominee Barack Obama, who was raised in Hawaii. Hirono was re-elected easily in 2008.

★ IDAHO ★

One of the American success stories of the last 20 years has been the state of Idaho. Tucked off near the northwest edge of the country, far from any major metro area, it was ignored by coastal elites except for those who jetted in to Sun Valley. From 1990 to 2007, the state's population grew nearly 50%, from 1 million to 1.5 million, thanks to technological progress and economic creativity. From 2000 to 2007, Idaho had a higher rate of domestic in-migration than all but four other states—Nevada, Arizona, and at different times Florida and Utah. It has spawned some awesomely large businesses. Mining is less important here than potatoes, of which Idaho produces one-third of the nation's total. And it processes them: Back in 1953, J. R. Simplot perfected the process of freezing French fries; his company got a contract with a relatively new enterprise called McDonald's and grew to be one of the biggest potato processors in the world, selling 3 billion pounds a year. Idahoans complain about the Atkins diet, and they bellyached when then-Republican Gov. Dirk Kempthorne put the peregrine falcon and not the potato on the Idaho quarter; the potato business continues to thrive nonetheless. In the 1970s Simplot put up $1 million to finance Micron Technology, which became the state's largest employer and spawned a booming high-tech sector including Hewlett-Packard's laser-jet printers. Idaho produces more patents per worker than any other state and is far above average in per capita research and development and IPOs. In 2008, the state saw the opening of the Idaho Regional Optical Network, which is working to establish a high-performance computing network that can support large-scale research efforts.

Idaho is big: Montpelier, in the southeast, is closer to Farmington, N.M., than to Bonner Springs in the northern panhandle. And the wilderness is never far away. Towering over the state Capitol in Boise is the vast peak of Shafer Butte, and not far away are the impassable mountains of the Frank Church River of No Return Wilderness, the largest U.S. wilderness area outside Alaska, and the Salmon River, at 425 miles the longest undammed river in the lower 48 states. Idaho was the last North American area that European fur traders set eyes on. In the 1840s, New England Yankees led by ministers made their way west on the Oregon Trail through southern Idaho. Idaho's northern panhandle, an extension of Washington's Columbia River Valley, was first settled by miners seeking gold and silver, then by loggers seeking timber. Mormons moved north from Utah and settled in eastern Idaho. Federal water-reclamation projects first authorized in 1894 attracted the most settlers; they transformed the barren Snake River Valley into some of the nation's best volcanic, soil-enriched farmland, which along with warm days and cool nights, proved ideal for the Burbank russet potato and, more recently, for a fledgling wine industry. Still fresh in family lore are the people who pioneered this state, built the first towns and farms, established the first churches and schools and became its community leaders. Some major businesses got their start in Idaho—the Albertsons supermarket chain, the construction giant Morrison-Knudsen, and of course Simplot and Micron. The state is also a national leader in exports.

Idaho's economic vitality has attracted many newcomers over the past 20 years. A few highly publicized liberal entertainment personalities and investment bankers have moved to Sun Valley or over the state line from Jackson Hole, Wyo., and some liberal professionals are appearing in Boise. But a much larger number of conservative engineers and entrepreneurs have come, from California and all over, for a fresh environment and a fresh start, clean air and sparse crowds, and few cumbersome or expensive regulations. As Republican Gov. James Risch said in 2006, "People are coming not because they want to change Idaho, but because they like what they see." As a result, Idaho has been transformed from a state of farms and small towns, where Boise, the pleasant state capital, was just the largest of them. Today, nearly 60% of its people live in just five counties in and around Boise, Idaho Falls, Coeur d'Alene, and Pocatello, and all but the last are growing rapidly. About 40% of Idahoans live in Treasure Valley around Boise, which accounted for nearly 60% of the state's population growth from 2000 to 2007. Large influxes of people have come from California, and from Mexico and other parts of Latin America. Idaho's Hispanic population is now 9.5% of the total. The state gives driver's license exams in English, Spanish, Serbo-Croatian, Russian, Arabic, and Vietnamese. Overall, the political trend has been toward the Republican Party. Most newcomers are from Orange County, not San Francisco, and they seek not cultural liberation, but an environment in which they can raise their children in traditional lifestyles.

Even in the prosperous years before the 2008 recession, small counties that depended on mining and grazing were hurting. But people there see themselves as pioneering entrepreneurs who, rather than seek federal help, want to get a bloated, bossy federal government off their backs. The U.S. government owns 62% of Idaho's land, and most Idahoans strongly opposed the Clinton administration's environmental policies, which blocked road-building on one-third of national forestland, limited grazing on public lands, reintroduced the grey wolf, and proposed to breach dams on the Snake River to protect salmon (in the process, depriving potato farmers of water). Such policies made a Republican state more Republican, and George W. Bush carried it by 67%-28% in 2000 and 68%-30% in 2004. John Kerry carried only one county, the richest by far in the state, where his wife owns a house near Sun Valley. In 2008, John McCain carried the state with 62% to 36% for Barack Obama.

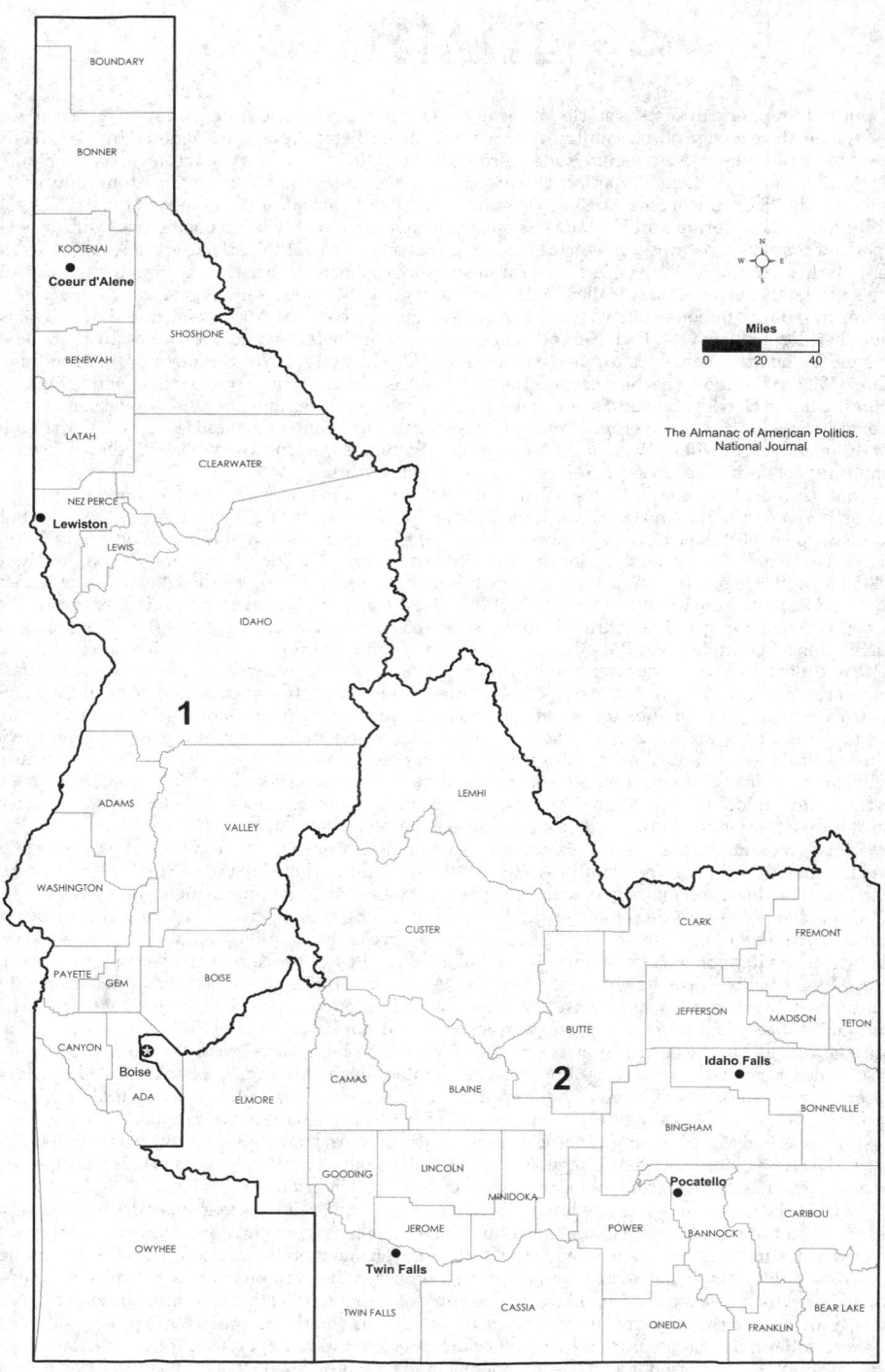

The Almanac of American Politics.
National Journal

Population		Household Income		Work	
Pop. 2007:	1,463,059	Under $15k:	12.7%	Private:	74.8%
State rank:	39th of 50	$15k to $50k:	42.5%	Government:	15.9%
Change since 2000:	Up 13.1%	$50k to $100k:	32.4%	Self-employed:	9.0%
Urban:	64.9%	$100k to $150k:	10.3%	Unemployment (3-yr. average):	3.6%
Rural:	35.1%	Over $150k:	2.0%	Poverty:	13.0%
Native of state:	46.0%	Median income:	$44,901	Blue collar:	24.8%
Not a citizen:	3.7%			White collar:	56.6%
Area size:	83,570 sq. mi.	**Home Value**		Khaki collar:	0.4%
		Under $100k:	23.3%	Other:	18.3%
Most populous cities		$100k to $300k:	59.3%		
1. Boise City	204,777	$300k to $500k:	11.7%	**Age**	
2. Nampa	74,558	$500k to $1 mil:	4.5%	Median age:	34.2 yrs.
3. Meridian	58,254	Over $1 million:	1.3%	More than 65 yrs:	11.6%
4. Idaho Falls	52,590	Median:	$158,600	Less than 18 yrs:	27.3%

Race/Ethnicity				Military Veterans		Registered Voters in 2008	
White:	86.0%	*Language*		% of Pop:	12.6%	No party registration	
Black:	0.6%	English:	90.1%	*Veterans by Period*		Voter turnout:	655,032
Hispanic:	9.5%	Spanish:	7.4%	WWII and before:	12.1%	Turnout as % of	
Asian:	1.1%	Asian:	0.8%	Korea:	11.8%	voting age:	58.9%
Native Am.:	1.0%	Other		Vietnam:	32.3%	**Legislature**	
Hawaiian:	0.1%	European	1.3%	Gulf (pre-2001):	11.8%	Senate:	7 D 28 R
Two+ races:	1.7%	**Education**		Gulf (post-2001):	8.1%	House:	18 D 52 R
Ancestry		H.S. grad:	87.4%	Peace time:	23.9%		
German:	16.6%	College grad:	23.6%				
English:	14.4%	Grad degree:	7.3%				
Irish:	8.8%						

But as memories of the 1990s grow dim, Idaho may have inched a little toward the Democratic Party. Republican Kempthorne was re-elected governor by just 56%-42% in 2002. His successor as governor, Republican James Risch, won the nomination for U.S. senator in 2008 in the open seat that was, prudently, vacated by Larry Craig after the revelation of his arrest on suspicion of soliciting sex in a men's room in the Minneapolis-St. Paul airport. Risch beat former Democratic Rep. Larry LaRocco, 58%-34%. And controversial 1st District Republican Rep. Bill Sali, a narrow winner in 2006, and renominated by only 60%-40%, a sure sign of trouble for an incumbent, lost to Democrat Walt Minnick in 2008 by 51%-49%—the first time a Democrat won a congressional election in Idaho since 1992. But Republicans maintained overwhelming strength in the state Legislature. There were signs, meanwhile, that Idaho's 20-year economic boom was slowing down. Unemployment ballooned from 2% in September 2007 to 5% in September 2008. Idaho did not experience the bubble of speculative housing that burst in Nevada and Arizona, but housing prices declined. Micron laid off workers and state officials reported a drop-off in firms looking to set up operations in the state.

Presidential politics   Idaho is one of the most Republican states in presidential politics. No Democratic nominee has come close to carrying it since 1964, and Bill Clinton came within 1% of finishing third behind third-party candidate Ross Perot and Republican George H.W. Bush in 1992. Despite his victories in both caucuses and primary here, Barack Obama was not in contention in Idaho and carried just three counties, two of them populated by wealthy expatriates from New York and California and one of them the home of the University of Idaho. John McCain carried the state 62%-36%.

Idaho has held its presidential primary in late May, long after the action in most recent presidential contests, and McCain's victory over GOP Rep. Ron Paul here was little noticed. But Democrats decided to select their delegates in caucuses, with the first round held on Super Tuesday, February 5. Few of the presidential campaigns paid much heed, but Obama's team did, setting up a state headquarters and organizing supporters around the state. Some 20,200 Idahoans participated, and Obama led Hillary Rodham Clinton 80% to 17%. This was a far bigger victory than the 56%-38% Obama win in the May 27 primary, in which 42,800 Idahoans voted. Obama's success in this and other caucus states, particularly in the Midwest and West, provided his margin of victory over Clinton, who won more votes and more delegates than her rival in Democratic primaries.

2008 Presidential Vote
McCain (R)............................403,012   (62%)
Obama (D) 236,440   (36%)

2008 Republican Presidential Primary
McCain (R)..............................87,460   (70%)
Paul (R)...................................29,785   (24%)

2004 Presidential Vote
Bush (R)...............................409,235   (68%)
Kerry (D)...............................181,098   (30%)

Some Republicans have tried to limit voting in party primaries to registered Republicans. A bill to that effect passed the state House in early 2008, but the Senate took no action. A lawsuit was filed in April to require closed primaries.

Congressional districting

111th Congress Lineup	
1 R	1 D
110th Congress Lineup	
2 R	

Idaho has two congressional districts, which split Boise between them. After the 2000 census, a bipartisan commission drew new boundaries, moving the dividing line in Boise about a mile to the west, along Cole Road, a minor and uncontroversial change. If Idaho ever gets a third district, redistricting should be a cinch. Most of the Boise area would become one district, and eastern Idaho and northern Idaho would get one each. Absent that, chances are that the boundary will be shifted a few miles again after the 2010 census, unless a Republican Legislature decides to try to make bigger changes to disadvantage Democrat Walt Minnick, who won the 1st District seat in 2008.

Governor

C.L. "Butch" Otter (R)

Elected 2006, term expires Jan. 2011, 1st term; b. May 3, 1942, Caldwell; home, Star; Col. of ID, B.A. 1967; Catholic; married (Lori Easley); 4 children.

Military Career: ID Natl. Guard, 1967–73.

Elected Office: ID House of Reps., 1972–76; ID lt. gov., 1986–2000; U.S. House of Reps., 2000–06.

Professional Career: Rancher; Dir., Food Products Div., Pres., Simplot Livestock, Pres., Simplot Intl., 1963–1993.

Office: P.O. Box 83720, Boise, 83720, 208-334-2100; Fax: 208-334-3454; Web site: http://gov.idaho.gov.

Election Results

2006 general	Butch Otter (R)	237,437	(53%)
	Jerry Brady (D)	198,845	(44%)
2006 primary	Butch Otter (R)	96,045	(70%)
	Dan Adamson (R)	29,093	(21%)
	Jack Johnson (R)	7,652	(6%)

Clement Leroy "Butch" Otter is a Republican elected as governor in 2006. He was the sixth of nine children and the first in his family to get a college degree. His father was a journeyman electrician and carpenter and a lifelong Democrat. After high school, Otter entered an abbey to pursue the priesthood but quickly decided that was not his calling. In 1967, at the age of 25, he graduated from the College of Idaho, now known as Albertson College of Idaho. He went to work for his father-in-law, billionaire J.R. Simplot, at the J.R. Simplot Company, one of the largest potato processors in the world and owner of the largest feedlot in the nation. In 1972, Otter won the first of two terms in the state House. He ran for governor in 1978, finishing third in the Republican primary, and in 1986, he was elected lieutenant governor. His career advancement was temporarily halted by a drunk-driving arrest. Otter unsuccessfully tried to talk the police officer out of charging him by explaining that he had not been drinking, but chewing tobacco soaked in Jack Daniels whiskey. The officer didn't buy it. Otter was convicted in 1993 of drunk driving, dashing his hopes of running for governor the following year. Still, he went on to be re-elected lieutenant governor and held the post longer than anyone in Idaho history. He served under three governors before he was elected to Congress in 2000.

As part of his libertarian political philosophy, Otter is a big supporter of gun ownership and property rights. But he is not the social conservative that other Idaho Republicans have been. (In 1992, he won the "Mr. Tight Jeans" contest at the Rockin' Rodeo bar in Boise.) During his tenure in the state Legislature, Otter voted against an anti-pornography bill by responding "Hell no!" during the roll call. He also questioned the government's right to restrict marijuana use. In Congress, where he served three terms, he sought to check the power of the federal government. Having become a ranch owner after his 1993 divorce, he was well-acquainted with the government's reach. The Environmental Protection Agency had charged him three times with violating the Clean Water Act. In 2001, after fighting the agency for two years, he paid a fine of $50,000 for dredging and filling wetlands without a permit. In Congress, Otter was one of three House Republicans to vote against the USA PATRIOT Act, a tough anti-terrorism enforcement law, because of potential intrusions on privacy and civil liberties. In 2004, he sponsored an amendment with independent Bernie Sanders of Vermont to prevent authorities from using the act to demand information on book buyers or library users. He lost on a tie vote after Republican leaders held the roll call open for 23 extra minutes to turn the outcome their way.

In December 2004, Otter announced his intention to run for governor, giving him an organizational and fundraising head start over then-Lt. Gov. Jim Risch, a Republican who was also considering running. In November 2005, Risch decided to run for re-election as lieutenant governor (later briefly becoming governor when Republican Gov. Dirk Kempthorne left office in 2006 to serve as President Bush's Interior secretary). Without competition from Risch, Otter easily outdistanced three opponents in the May 2006 primary, winning with 70%.

He then faced Democrat Jerry Brady, a former publisher of the Idaho Falls *Post Register* making his second consecutive bid for governor. In heavily Republican Idaho, which hadn't elected a Democratic governor since 1990, Otter began as the front-runner. But Brady, who highlighted environmental issues and compared himself to former Democratic Gov. Cecil Andrus, gained momentum by criticizing Otter's co-sponsorship of a bill that would have sold millions of acres of federal land in Idaho and the western United States to raise money for Hurricane Katrina relief. Otter eventually rescinded his support for the bill in January 2006. Brady also attacked Otter for accepting $6,000 from a company attempting to build a coal-fired power plant in Idaho. Otter countered by highlighting controversial editorials written by Brady's newspaper, the second largest in Idaho, including one that called for breaching Snake River dams to protect endangered salmon.

Otter ran a Rose Garden campaign, avoiding the traditional Idaho public-television debate and initially refusing to take a position on Proposition 2, a controversial property-rights initiative that required state and local governments to compensate property owners when the value of their land was reduced by land-use regulations. Otter later came out against the ballot measure. In August, he found time to get married to a former Miss Idaho, whom he had first met at a Fourth of July parade in 1991.

Brady, the great-grandson of former Idaho Republican Governor James Brady, proved to be the more energetic candidate and remained competitive. Polls taken a week before the election showed him within striking distance. Despite national discontent with the Republican Party and a lackluster campaign, Otter won, 53%-44%. He lost eight of the state's 44 counties, including Boise's Ada County, the state's most populous county, and the counties that included Sun Valley and the University of Idaho. In heavily Mormon eastern Idaho, where Otter's libertarian stands and lifestyle had hurt him in prior statewide elections, he lost just two counties: Bannock, home to Pocatello and Idaho State University, and Teton County, which shares a border with Wyoming's wealthy Teton County, where Jackson Hole and its ski resort are located.

Soon after taking office, Otter caused a minor controversy by halting construction on a $130 million statehouse-expansion project that the Republican-controlled Legislature had approved the previous year. He objected to the project's cost and the fact that it represented an expansion of government. Negotiations with the Legislature produced a compromise that reduced the size of the new addition by half and cut out construction of new offices for legislators, though it was unclear if the changes would lessen the project's total cost.

Otter supported removing gray wolves from the federal government's Endangered Species List and allowing public hunting of the animals in Idaho. In January 2007, he got national media attention when he stood on the Idaho statehouse steps and proclaimed, "I'm prepared to bid for that first ticket to shoot a wolf." He later softened his stance by backing a plan to let the Idaho Department of Fish and Game manage the state's wolf population. Otter had long been opposed to the federal government's decision in the 1990s to reintroduce wolves, a practice that some hunters saw as threat to Idaho's elk and deer populations.

Otter's ability to attract media attention did not translate into legislative success. In 2007, he proposed increasing the state's grocery tax credit for the lowest-income Idahoans to $90 a year. Idaho gives people a credit on their taxes as reimbursement for sales taxes they've paid on their groceries. The Legislature agreed to increase the credit to $40 for all Idahoans and to $60 for senior citizens; Otter vetoed the bill because it didn't target the lowest-income groups. The Legislature did pass a highway bill that approved $250 million in borrowing power—Otter originally wanted $264 million—and gave the Idaho Transportation Board the authority to earmark money for road projects, a practice Otter hoped would take politics out of the earmarking process. He bucked the state Republican Party by refusing to support its proposal that voters register with a political party before being eligible to vote in primary elections.

In 2008, Otter also had difficulty getting many of his proposals through the Legislature, even though he had Republican majorities in both chambers. He proposed an 11% increase in the state's budget, a 5% pay raise for state employees and an increase in vehicle-registration fees to fund road repairs, all of which the Legislature either modified or rejected outright. Otter did not improve his standing with lawmakers when he failed to notify them that he would miss a month of work in the middle of the legislative session to have hip surgery. At the time, Idaho tax revenue was coming up short of projections, prompting lawmakers to decrease Otter's spending proposals. As the session came to a close, he wrote press releases criticizing legislators for rejecting his proposals. They in turn openly expressed their frustration at his refusal to compromise on many issues. Yet during the session, Otter did sign grocery-tax legislation that was similar to the bill he'd vetoed in 2007.

At the beginning of 2009, Otter's priority was providing money for road construction. Despite reservations about increased government spending, he decided to accept $1.2 billion in economic-stimulus money from the federal government.

Senior Senator

Mike Crapo (R)

Elected 1998, term expires 2010, 2nd term; b. May 20, 1951, Idaho Falls; home, Idaho Falls; Brigham Young U., B.A. 1973, Harvard U., J.D. 1977; Mormon; married (Susan); 5 children.

Elected Office: ID Senate, 1984–92, Senate ldr., 1988–92; U.S. House of Reps., 1992–98.

Professional Career: Practicing atty., 1977–92.

DC Office: 239 DSOB, 20510, 202-224-6142; Fax: 202-228-1375; Web site: crapo.senate.gov.

State Offices: Boise, 208-334-1776; Caldwell, 208-455-0360; Coeur D'Alene, 208-664-5490; Idaho Falls, 208-522-9779; Lewiston, 208-743-1492; Pocatello, 208-236-6775; Twin Falls, 208-734-2515.

Committees: *Banking, Housing & Urban Affairs* (4th of 10 R): Financial Institutions (RMM); Housing, Transportation & Community Development; Securities, Insurance & Investment. *Budget* (5th of 9 R). *Environment & Public Works* (5th of 7 R). *Finance* (6th of 10 R): Energy, Natural Resources & Infrastructure; Health Care; International Trade, Customs & Global Competitiveness (RMM). *Indian Affairs* (5th of 6 R).

Group Ratings

	ADA	ACLU	AFS	LCV	ITIC	NTU	COC	ACU	CFG	FRC
2008	15	21	0	18	80	73	75	88	85	100
2007	15	—	0	13	—	68	82	88	70	—

National Journal Ratings

	2007 LIB	—	2007 CONS	2008 LIB	—	2008 CONS
Economic	12%	—	87%	19%	—	79%
Social	22%	—	76%	21%	—	73%
Foreign	9%	—	87%	0%	—	84%
Composite	16%	—	85%	17%	—	83%

Key Votes of the 110th Congress

1. Raise CAFE standards	Y	5. Make English official language Y	9. Withdraw troops 3/08	N
2. Expand SCHIP	N	6. Path to citizenship	N	10. Iran guard is terrorist group	Y
3. Cap greenhouse gases	N	7. Fetus is unborn child	Y	11. Increase missile defense $	Y
4. Bail out financial markets	N	8. Prosecute hate crimes	N	12. Overhaul FISA	Y

Election Results

2004 general	Mike Crapo (R)..499,796	(99%)	($1,031,912)
2004 primary	Mike Crapo (R)... unopposed		

Prior Winning Percentages: 1998 (70%); 1996 House (69%); 1994 House (75%); 1992 House (61%)

Mike Crapo is a Republican first elected to the House in 1992 and to the Senate in 1998. He grew up in Idaho Falls. His father ran the local post office, and his mother stayed home to care for their six children. The couple also farmed on 200 acres, growing potatoes and grain. Crapo (*CRAY-po*) graduated from Brigham Young University and Harvard Law School. A devout Mormon, he was named a bishop in the church at age 31. A former congressional intern, he was elected to the state Senate at 33 in 1984, two years after leukemia took his older brother Terry's life. Terry Crapo had been state House majority leader and a rising star in state politics. The two brothers were close, and Mike Crapo decided to follow his brother's path to the Legislature. He became state Senate leader in 1988. Four years later, he ran for Congress, campaigning against tax increases and in favor of spending cuts, a balanced-budget amendment, and the line-item veto. He won the primary 68%-32%. "Cowboy Democrat" J.D. Williams, the state controller, ran on a "Put America First" platform on industrial policy and trade. Crapo won 61%-35%.

With a self-professed "passion for reform," Crapo became a Republican freshman class leader and championed institutional reforms, advocating more power for rank-and-file members to bring bills to the floor and calling for more open voting, while arguing against closed rules and closed committee meetings. Many of those ideas were adopted after Republicans won control of the House in 1994. Like many Republicans then, Crapo favored hard-and-fast rules in the budget process to force tough decisions: He favored a balanced budget and across-the-board discretionary spending cuts, excluding Social Security. He sponsored the deficit-reduction bill that passed the House in 1995. His overall voting record in the House was very conservative, with some exceptions on economics. He opposed the North American Free Trade Agreement in 1993 but supported normalizing trade relations with China in 2000. He criticized some trade agreements for accepting limits on U.S. agricultural exports as leverage for opening up access for other products.

In 1997, Crapo, who prides himself on returning to Idaho Falls to be with his family every weekend, faced a career choice that many House members would like to face. Republican Gov. Phil Batt announced his retirement, and GOP Sen. Dirk Kempthorne said he would run for governor. Within days, Crapo announced he would run for the Senate seat the following year, and he was unopposed in the Republican primary. His opponent was Bill Mauk, a former Democratic chairman and Boise trial lawyer. Idaho, one-quarter Mormon, had never elected a Mormon to the Senate, but this time it did. Crapo led in polls by a wide margin and won 70%-28%, carrying every county.

In his first years in the Senate, Crapo became chairman of the subcommittee with jurisdiction over the troubled Superfund program and many Environmental Protection Agency efforts. He sponsored the Senate version of the Bush-era Healthy Forests Restoration Act, aimed at cutting dense forest land after widespread fires in 2002. He has worked over the years on altering the Endangered Species Act. With Sen. Blanche Lincoln, an Arkansas Democrat, he has pressed for legislation that would provide tax credits or tax deductions for landowners who sign conservation easements and for more money to improve the habitat for endangered species. They first introduced such a bill in 2006 and again in 2007.

In 2005, Crapo won a seat on the Finance Committee, where he has worked quietly and productively. He secured a permanent tax break for state colleges by attaching it to a pension bill, while separately he headed off a cut in food stamps. Crapo also urged the Internal Revenue Service to implement a tax break that would help the country's short-line railroads, one of the largest of which is used by Idaho farmers to move crops and equipment. From his seat on the Banking Committee, Crapo won passage in 2006 of a bill that would ease outdated regulation of the banking industry. In a bid to protect Boise-based chipmaker Micron Technology, Crapo also sponsored a bill that would limit the type of companies that could receive loans from the Export-Import Bank.

Crapo has developed a reputation for diligence in trying to forge consensus legislation. Oregon Democrat Ron Wyden said, "He is not a showboat. He is somebody who, day in and day out, is always a constructive force for sensible public policy." Crapo opposed reintroduction of grizzly bears to the Bitterroot Mountains, and he wrote a bill to compensate businesses around the Dworshak Reservoir for summer draw-downs to help migrating salmon. He supported the bill allowing gun possession in national parks and wildlife refuges, and a bill to rescind fees in national forests. Crapo has also worked to get compensation for downwinders, residents of Idaho counties subjected to radiation from above-ground nuclear weapons tests in Nevada in the 1950s. In 2007, he and Montana's senators sponsored a bill extending compensation to Idaho and Montana.

From 2001 to 2004, Crapo worked to forge a consensus on the Owyhee Canyonlands wilderness proposal with the Owyhee County Commissioners, landowners, and cattlemen, environmental groups and the Shoshone-Paiute tribe. In November 2004, consensus was reached—199,000 acres formerly off limits would be opened to fence-building and pipelines, with independent review of Bureau of Land Management decisions; 517,000 acres would be set aside as wilderness and 384 miles of rivers would be protected, all of it open to hikers and boaters; and the habitat of the California bighorn sheep and sage grouse would be protected. His measure was included in the lands bill enacted in early 2009.

Crapo and Montana Democrat Max Baucus, chairman of the Finance Committee, have co-sponsored bills to relax restrictions on agricultural sales to Cuba. In 2007, Crapo was named to the Senate Republican task force on earmarks, where he supported increased transparency but not a moratorium on earmarks, the provisions inserted into bills by lawmakers that are often derided as pork-barrel spending. In August 2007, when it was revealed that fellow Idaho Sen. Larry Craig had been arrested at a Minneapolis airport men's room on suspicion of soliciting sex, Minority Leader Mitch McConnell dispatched Crapo to tell Craig that he might face embarrassing hearings unless he voluntarily resigned from the Senate. Craig refused to resign, but on the last day in August, he said he would not run for re-election in 2008.

Though he had expressed interest in a federal District Court judgeship, Crapo sought re-election in 2004. He had no Democratic opponent and won with 99% of the vote. In early 2009, he appeared to be in excellent shape for re-election in 2010.

Junior Senator

James Risch (R)

Elected 2008, term expires 2014, 1st term; b. May 2, 1943, Milwaukee, WI; home, Boise; U. of ID, B.S. 1965, J.D., 1968.; Catholic; married (Vicki); 5 children.

Elected Office: Ada Co. prosecuting atty., 1970–74; ID Senate, 1974–89, 1995–2003; ID lt. gov., 2003–2006, 2007–09; ID gov., 2006.

Professional Career: Partner, Risch, Goss, Insinger, 1975–08; Rancher.

DC Office: 483 RSOB, 20510, 202-224-2752; Fax: 202-224-2573; Web site: risch.senate.gov.

State Offices: Boise, 208-342-7986; Coeur d'Alene, 208-667-6130; Idaho Falls, 208-523-5541; Lewiston, 208-743-0792; Pocatello, 208-236-6817; Twin Falls, 208-734-6780.

Committees: *Energy & Natural Resources* (5th of 10 R): Energy (RMM); Public Lands & Forests; Water & Power. *Ethics (Select)* (3rd of 3 R). *Foreign Relations* (4th of 7 R): African Affairs; European Affairs; Near Eastern & South & Central Asian Affairs (RMM); Western Hemisphere, Peace Corps & Global Narcotics Affairs. *Intelligence (Select)* (7th of 7 R). *Joint Economic Committee.*

Group Ratings and Key Votes: Newly Elected

Election Results

2008 general	James Risch (R)	371,744	(58%)	($3,573,256)
	Larry LaRocco (D)	219,903	(34%)	($1,421,746)
	Rex Rammell (I)	34,510	(5%)	($439,397)
2008 primary	James Risch (R)	80,743	(65%)	
	Scott Syme (R)	16,660	(13%)	
	Richard Phenneger (R)	6,532	(5%)	

James Risch, who has been Idaho's lieutenant governor and governor, was elected to the U.S. Senate in 2008. He succeeded Republican Sen. Larry Craig, who declined to seek re-election after he was arrested the previous year in a solicitation-for-sex sting. Risch (*RISH, like wish*) grew up in Wisconsin and moved to the West to study forestry. He earned a law degree at the University of Idaho. In 1970, at age 27, Risch was elected Ada County prosecutor—a high-profile position in the state's capital and largest city, Boise. He went after the illicit drug trade so aggressively that his enemies tried to plant a bomb in his car. After that incident, Risch and his wife and political confidant, Vicki, put a piece of tape on the hood of their car every night so they could detect any tampering. In 1974, Risch was elected to the state Senate, where he served longer than anyone else in Idaho history. He earned a reputation as an ambitious and determined legislator; he always carried an index card in his back pocket, one side listing bills that he wanted to pass and the other listing bills he was determined to kill. Immediately gunning for a leadership position, he became majority leader after the 1976 election, defeating a young colleague named Larry Craig for the position. Although popular with some of his colleagues, Risch was known as a bully to a number of the younger senators whom he pressured to vote his way.

He was brought back down to earth by a Democratic challenger who beat him in the 1988 election. He ran again in 1990, but this time he was defeated in the GOP primary. Five years later, he was appointed to fill a state Senate vacancy. Less confrontational this time around, Risch moved back into the ranks of leadership as assistant Republican floor leader. He became one of the driving forces in the Idaho Republican Party even as the state elected a string of Democratic governors. In 2002, Risch ran for lieutenant governor and won by a comfortable margin. He served in the shadow of Republican Gov. Dirk Kempthorne for three years and finally assumed the top job when Kempthorne became President Bush's Interior Department secretary. Risch had just seven months in what he considered his dream job, and he was determined to make the most of it. He had vowed not to run against fellow Republican Butch Otter for the GOP nomination for governor in 2006; his plan was to run for a second term as lieutenant governor. Although many political insiders expected him to reconsider after he became governor, Risch kept his word and poured his energy into the period between Kempthorne's departure and the 2006 gubernatorial election.

Within two weeks of taking office, Gov. Risch ordered a reorganization of Idaho's Health and Welfare Department. He created the position of state drug czar to counter the growth in the illicit methamphetamine market in the state. Displeased that the Legislature failed to provide property-tax relief in its regular session, he called the first special session in 14 years. One day in August, the heavily Republican Legislature obediently passed bills cutting local property taxes by $260 million, raising the sales tax from 5% to 6% (which generated $219 million), and cutting state spending by $50 million. The voters approved the tax changes 72%-28%. After wide consultation, he prepared a roadless-areas plan for 9 million acres of national forest that was approved by U.S. Agriculture Secretary Mike Johanns and was generally accepted by environmental groups. Risch moved to protect the Boulder-White Clouds and Owyhee Canyonlands wilderness areas. To prevent mercury contamination, he effectively barred construction of pulverized coal plants in the state.

When November rolled around, Otter was elected governor by an unremarkable margin, besting Democrat Jerry Brady 53%-44%. Risch beat former Democratic Rep. Larry LaRocco for lieutenant governor 58%-39%. But another goal beckoned: the U.S. Senate seat first won by his old rival Craig in 1990. Craig was arrested in a Minneapolis airport men's room in 2007 for soliciting sex from an undercover police officer and pleaded guilty to disorderly conduct; he was under immense pressure, especially from some Senate colleagues, to resign. It was widely speculated that Risch would be Otter's choice to replace Craig if he did. Craig declined to resign but decided not to seek re-election in 2008. Soon afterward, Risch announced his intention to run for the seat.

He had little competition for the Republican nomination. His Democratic opponent was, once again, LaRocco, who had been elected to the House in 1990 and 1992 but was defeated in the Republican sweep of 1994. Another opponent was Democrat Rex Rammell, a rancher who had lost 160 of his elk herd after they escaped from his land and were ordered shot by then-Gov. Risch. Rammell ran as an independent; a Republican lawsuit to remove him from the ballot failed. Risch raised more than twice as much money as LaRocco, and the national Democratic Party never targeted the race. Risch felt free to go out to Iowa and campaign for his erstwhile fellow governor, Mitt Romney, in the January presidential caucuses.

Risch won the election 58%-34%, with 5% for Rammell. LaRocco carried just four counties, two dominated by wealthy residents in the resorts of Sun Valley and Jackson Hole, one dominated by the University of Idaho, and one dominated by old silver-mining towns such as Kellogg. Risch entered the Senate at age 65, after an extensive political career. But he had considerably better prospects for staying in the Senate longer than the only other Idahoan to serve as lieutenant governor, governor, and U.S. senator—Democrat Charles Gossett. When Gossett was governor, he appointed himself to the Senate in 1945, only to be defeated in the 1946 primary.

FIRST DISTRICT

Walt Minnick (D)

Elected 2008, 1st term; b. Sept. 20, 1942, Walla Walla, WA; home, Boise; Whitman Col., B.A. 1964; Harvard U., M.B.A. 1966, J.D. 1969.; Unitarian; married (A.K. Lienhart-Minnick); 4 children.

Military Career: Army, 1970–72

Professional Career: White House OMB, 1973; T.J. International, 1974–95; Founder, SummerWinds Garden Centers, 1998–08.

DC Office: 1517 LHOB, 20515, 202-225-6611; Fax: 202-225-3029; Web site: minnick.house.gov.

State Offices: Coeur d'Alene, 208-667-0127; Lewiston, 208-743-1388; Meridian, 208-888-3188.

Committees: *Agriculture* (28th of 28 D): Conservation, Credit, Energy & Research; Livestock, Dairy & Poultry; Specialty Crops, Rural Development & Foreign Agriculture. *Financial Services* (34th of 42 D): Capital Markets, Insurance & Government Sponsored Enterprises; Financial Institutions & Consumer Credit.

Group Ratings and Key Votes: Newly Elected

Election Results

2008 general	Walt Minnick (D)	175,898	(51%)	($2,649,953)
	Bill Sali (R)	171,687	(49%)	($1,168,536)
2008 primary	Walt Minnick (D)	unopposed		

Population		Race/Ethnicity		Work	
Pop. 2007:	780,377	White:	86.8%	Private:	75.5%
Change since 2000:	Up 20.3%	Black:	0.5%	Government:	14.8%
Urban:	65.8%	Hispanic:	8.4%	Self-employed:	9.3%
Rural:	34.2%	Asian:	1.2%	Blue collar:	25.4%
Area size:	39,972 sq. mi.	Native Am.:	0.9%	White collar:	57.0%
Age		Hawaiian:	0.2%	Khaki collar:	0.2%
Median age:	35.3 yrs.	Two+ races:	1.9%	Other:	17.5%
More than 65 yrs:	11.9%	*Ancestry*		Median income:	$46,461
Less than 18 yrs:	27.1%	German:	17.9%	Median home value:	$175,100
Education		English:	12.0%	Poverty:	12.1%
H.S. grad:	87.6%	Irish:	10.0%	**Military Veterans**	
College grad:	22.4%			% of Pop:	13.3%
Grad degree:	6.6%				

The 1st District of Idaho stretches from the Nevada border to Canada and includes some of usually Republican Boise and all of the panhandle, which is historically Democratic but more recently has been leaning Republican. It encompasses two of Idaho's big growth areas, the western suburbs of Boise and the Coeur d'Alene area in Kootenai County. High-tech businesses and tourism have fueled the economy. Boise is home to Micron Technology, which has led the nation in patents. And in 2007, *Forbes*

2008 Presidential Vote		
McCain (R)............................220,787	(62%)
Obama (D) 128,134	(36%)
2004 Presidential Vote		
Bush (R)................................215,069	(69%)
Kerry (D).................................94,915	(30%)
Cook Partisan Voting Index: R + 18		

named Boise the third-best city in the country for business, citing the region's low unemployment rate. In Nampa—whose population nearly doubled in the 1990s, allowing it to replace Pocatello as Idaho's second-largest city—commercial developers have taken over land that not long ago grew wheat and alfalfa. Subdivisions are being constructed in nearby Meridian, the fastest-growing city in Idaho, with 23,000 new residents since 2000. Valley County, just north of Boise, has also seen a spike in growth, with a 6% increase in population.

The growth is turning these once-rural areas into urban centers, but that has reinforced rather than altered the political landscape. Newcomers routinely say they moved to conservative Idaho to "escape" from places like California. Some old-timers worry that their communities may become new versions of San Jose or Orange County. Politically, the 1st District is overwhelmingly Republican. Kootenai County, once a Democratic stronghold, is now as likely to cast as many Republican votes as conservative Canyon County. Northern mining counties were once the district's Democratic base; now it is the university town of Moscow in Latah County, one of only two in Idaho to vote against a 2006 constitutional amendment outlawing same-sex marriage. Every county in the district voted for George W. Bush in 2000 and 2004. In 2008, Latah County went for Democrat Barack Obama, but the district as a whole voted for Republican John McCain, giving him 62%.

The new congressman from the 1st District is Walt Minnick, a Democrat narrowly elected in 2008. Minnick ousted one-term Republican Bill Sali by capitalizing on Sali's campaign missteps. Minnick is the first Democrat Idahoans have sent to Congress since 1992.

Minnick was born on a wheat farm in Walla Walla, Wash. His father was a small-town lawyer, and his mother was a leader in the local Republican Party. At Whitman College in Washington state, Minnick was president of the College Republicans and earned a business degree. After getting a law degree from Harvard University, he served two years in the Army, then got further immersed in Republican politics by going to work for former President Nixon as an assistant; he helped create the Drug Enforcement Administration. Frustrated by the escalating Watergate scandal, Minnick resigned in protest immediately after the 1973 "Saturday night massacre," in which Nixon fired his attorney general and deputy attorney general in order to remove Archibald Cox as the Watergate special prosecutor. Minnick left Washington in 1974, moved to Idaho to work in the forest industry at T.J. International, a wood-products business, eventually rising to president and chief executive officer. In 1995, he founded SummerWinds Garden Centers, which has stores in California, Missouri, and Arizona.

In the mid-90s, with Newt Gingrich and his followers newly dominant on Capitol Hill, Minnick came to believe his party had drifted too far to the right. He became a Democrat and in 1996, challenged conservative Republican Sen. Larry Craig, who was up for re-election. He held Craig to just 57% of the vote, Craig's lowest Senate re-election percentage. Minnick also pulled nearly even with Craig in fundraising. (Craig later retired from the Senate in 2008 after getting arrested in a homosexual sex sting in a Minneapolis-St. Paul airport bathroom.)

Minnick's fundraising mettle was important in his second try at public office. Although he entered the Democratic primary for Sali's seat relatively late, after two other candidates had announced, Minnick jumped ahead in fundraising and pulled in support from high-ranking Democrats, including former Gov.

Cecil Andrus. The other candidates withdrew, and Minnick was unopposed in the May primary. Meanwhile, Sali had to beat back a primary challenge from Iraq War veteran Matt Salisbury, finally winning with 60% to Salisbury's 40%.

In the general election campaign, Sali also found it difficult to keep pace with Minnick on the money front, raising $1.2 million to Minnick's $2.6 million, which included nearly $900,000 of Minnick's own money. At one point, Sali encouraged his supporters to host "Yard Sales for Sali" and donate their proceeds to his campaign. Sali also had an embarrassing moment when he and members of his staff were caught heckling Minnick's communication director while he was being interviewed by a local television station. Minnick espouses a libertarian political philosophy: He believes government intervention should be limited and so supports abortion rights and opposes an increase in capital gains taxes. He emphasized his support of gun ownership and his business résumé to peel away some of Sali's voters. He ran ads that depicted him hunting and touting the fact that he owns seven guns. Sali tried to discredit those claims by pointing out that he had been endorsed by the National Rifle Association, which had given Minnick a "D+" grade. Sali's ads charged Minnick was too cozy with environmental groups.

In the final weeks, some heavyweights tried to save Sali. The anti-tax group Club for Growth and the National Republican Congressional Committee both funded direct mailings and television ads. The conservative group Freedom's Watch also made calls to voters questioning Minnick's support of traditional family policies. In the end, their influence would not be enough. Even as McCain swept most of the district, Minnick narrowly edged out Sali by a margin of 4,211 votes, 50.6% to 49.4%. Minnick was the beneficiary of ticket-splitting in counties where McCain had prevailed: Ada, Benewah, Bonner, Nez Perce, Shoshone, and Valley.

Once in the House, Minnick was cautious in dealing with the liberal wing of the Democratic Party, joining the moderate Blue Dog Coalition instead. He was appointed to the Financial Services and Agriculture committees. He was one of only 11 Democrats to vote against the January 2009 economic-stimulus package, saying, "I think it's a horrible idea to try to appropriate large sums of taxpayer dollars to programs that have never before been debated or authorized." Minnick introduced his own stimulus bill, which trimmed the plan from $1 trillion to $170 billion by stripping out earmarks and focusing on cutting taxes and investing in infrastructure.

Minnick, who is high on Republican hit lists for 2010, was getting help and advice from the Democratic Congressional Campaign Committee as he prepared for a likely challenge to his re-election. In January 2009, Sali signaled that he was planning a rematch with Minnick when he filed a statement of candidacy with the Federal Election Commission. But if Sali does run, he could face another crowded Republican primary.

SECOND DISTRICT

Mike Simpson (R)

Elected 1998, 6th term; b. Sept. 8, 1950, Burley; home, Blackfoot; UT St. U., 1968–72; Washington U., D.D.S. 1977; Mormon; married (Kathy).

Elected Office: Blackfoot City Cncl., 1980–84; ID House of Reps., 1984–98, Speaker, 1993–98.

Professional Career: Practicing dentist, 1977–98.

DC Office: 2312 RHOB, 20515, 202-225-5531; Fax: 202-225-8216; Web site: www.house.gov/simpson.

State Offices: Boise, 208-334-1953; Idaho Falls, 208-523-6701; Pocatello, 208-233-2222; Twin Falls, 208-734-7219.

Committees: *Appropriations* (13th of 23 R): Energy & Water Development; Interior, Environment & Related Agencies (RMM). *Budget* (5th of 15 R).

Group Ratings

	ADA	ACLU	AFS	LCV	ITIC	NTU	COC	ACU	CFG	FRC
2008	35	20	43	23	100	51	94	80	60	82
2007	20	—	10	5	—	50	84	72	47	—

National Journal Ratings

	2007 LIB	—	2007 CONS	2008 LIB	—	2008 CONS
Economic	36%	—	64%	31%	—	69%
Social	26%	—	74%	31%	—	62%
Foreign	37%	—	62%	22%	—	74%
Composite	33%	—	67%	30%	—	70%

Key Votes of the 110th Congress

1. Increase minimum wage	Y	5. Share immigration data	Y	9. Withdraw troops 8/08	N
2. Expand SCHIP	Y	6. Foreign aid abortion ban	*	10. No operations in Iran	N
3. Raise CAFE standards	N	7. Ban gay bias in workplace	N	11. Free trade with Peru	Y
4. Bail out financial markets	Y	8. Repeal D.C. gun law	Y	12. Overhaul FISA	Y

Election Results

2008 general	Mike Simpson (R)	205,777	(71%)	($649,431)
	Deborah Holmes (D)	83,878	(29%)	($16,765)
2008 primary	Mike Simpson (R)	49,586	(85%)	
	Jack Chappell (R)..	4,900	(8%)	
	Gregory Nemitz (R)...	3,747	(6%)	

Prior Winning Percentages: 2006 (62%); 2004 (71%); 2002 (68%); 2000 (71%); 1998 (53%)

Population		Race/Ethnicity		Work	
Pop. 2007:	682,682	White:	85.0%	Private:	74.0%
Change since 2000:	Up 5.8%	Black:	0.7%	Government:	17.0%
Urban:	67.0%	Hispanic:	10.7%	Self-employed:	8.6%
Rural:	33.0%	Asian:	1.0%	Blue collar:	24.1%
Area size:	43,598 sq. mi.	Native Am.:	1.0%	White collar:	56.2%
Age		Hawaiian:	0.1%	Khaki collar:	0.6%
Median age:	32.8 yrs.	Two+ races:	1.5%	Other:	19.1%
More than 65 yrs:	11.3%	*Ancestry*		Median income:	$43,277
Less than 18 yrs:	27.5%	English:	17.2%	Median home value:	$137,600
Education		German:	15.1%	Poverty:	14.1%
H.S. grad:	87.1%	Irish:	7.4%	**Military Veterans**	
College grad:	25.0%			% of Pop:	11.7%
Grad degree:	8.2%				

The 2nd District of Idaho, from central Boise east to the Wyoming border, is one of America's most picturesque, with thick forests, mountain ranges, broad river valleys, and vacant expanses. It was settled from the east by overland pioneers who stopped in Idaho's farmlands, and from the south by Mormons moving up from Utah to Franklin, Bear Lake, and Caribou counties. It has one of the largest concentrations of Mormons among congressional districts. Pocatello began as a railroad town, with un-

2008 Presidential Vote		
McCain (R).............................	182,225	(61%)
Obama (D)	108,306	(36%)
2004 Presidential Vote		
Bush (R)	194,166	(69%)
Kerry (D).................................	86,183	(30%)
Cook Partisan Voting Index: R + 17		

ionized railroad workers. Fifty miles north on Interstate 15, Idaho Falls serves as the metropolis for a vast region stretching from West Yellowstone, Wyo., to the Salmon River Mountains. Near Idaho Falls, on a windswept, desolate range, is the Idaho National Laboratory, one of the Energy Department's 10 national laboratories. DOE's leading laboratory for civilian nuclear energy research, development, and demonstration, the facility covers 890 square miles and employs more than 8,000 workers, making it the third-largest employer in the state. West of the laboratory campus, amid the mountains, are Sun Valley and the nearby town of Ketchum. Sun Valley was established as a ski resort in 1936 by Averell Harriman before he began his political career. Ketchum attracted writer Ernest Hemingway in 1939, and various movie stars came as well. In recent years, Blaine County, which includes both Sun Valley and Ketchum, has attracted rich expatriates from the East and West coasts, including heiress Teresa Heinz Kerry and her husband, Massachusetts Democratic Sen. John Kerry. The wealthy imports and the people who wait on them at ski resorts have made Blaine County the most Democratic county in Idaho. It stands in vivid contrast to the Idaho Falls area, the Mormon country, and the farmland along the Snake River, which are among the most Republican areas in the nation. The 2nd District also includes the east side of Boise, which leans Republican but has some Democratic precincts.

The congressman from the 2nd District is Mike Simpson, a Republican first elected in 1998. Simpson grew up in Blackfoot, became a dentist, and joined his father's dental practice. He was elected to the City Council in 1980 and to the state House in 1984. He didn't declare himself as a Republican until then, and was opposed by the local Republican party. In 1993, he became speaker of the Idaho House, but he kept up his dental practice as well. In the Legislature, he was known as a moderate in a predominately conservative chamber, affable and able to get differing sides together. When Republican Gov. Phil Batt announced he would retire in 1998, Simpson wanted to run, but GOP Sen. Dirk Kempthorne's decision to seek the office closed that option. GOP Rep. Mike Crapo decided to run for Kempthorne's Senate seat, thus opening up the House race for Simpson.

The seat was hotly contested. In the Republican primary, state Rep. Mark Stubbs called for lower payroll taxes. He had opposed nuclear programs at the INL, while Simpson wanted more work at the facility. But the big issue was term limits. Simpson refused to take a pledge to serve only three terms, while the other candidates did. Term-limit advocates spent large sums against Simpson. Angry at the ads, Batt endorsed Simpson five days before the election. Simpson ran ads against "out-of-state folk" interfering with Idaho's elections. Simpson beat Stubbs 47%-41%. The Democratic nominee was Richard Stallings, a former history professor elected to the House in 1984 and re-elected three times. In 1992, he ran against Kempthorne for the Senate and lost 57%-43%. Stallings emphasized his conservative voting record in the House, called for more education spending, and said he would act to fix falling farm commodity prices. Simpson called for a smaller federal role in education. He favored tax cuts and the creation of personal investment accounts in Social Security. Simpson won 53%-45%, losing the most well-known parts of the district—Pocatello, Sun Valley, Boise—but carrying just about everything else.

In the House, Simpson built a moderate record, particularly for a Western Republican. He has reached out to Democrats on economic and social issues, and he helped establish a bipartisan caucus to talk about the trade-related needs of farmers and ranchers. Simpson voted against the Central American Free Trade Agreement in 2005 because of its potential impact on Idaho's sugar beet industry. "When I came to Congress, I was a free-trader. But we don't live in an ideal world, and I've come to understand that more and more. I'm starting to become one of those people I disagreed with a few years ago," he said in 2007. President Bush signed two of his bills: one to protect hunting rights in the expanded portions of the Craters of the Moon National Monument and Preserve, and the other to overhaul job-training programs for veterans.

In 2003, Simpson showed his skills as a party insider when he got a seat on the Appropriations Committee, a post he used to win funding for the Idaho National Laboratory, the Bureau of Reclamation, and the Army Corps of Engineers. Simpson became a leading defender of appropriations earmarks, the special spending projects inserted into bills for individual lawmakers' districts and states. He opposed restricting earmarks but supported greater transparency in the process. After Democrats took control of the House in 2007, Simpson called incoming Appropriations Chairman David Obey one of Congress's most honest members. "He's the kind of guy I can work with," he said. In 2007, Simpson lost his seat on the Energy and Water Appropriations Subcommittee, which oversees nuclear energy spending. He pleaded with Obey, and Obey obliged by adding one Democratic and one Republican seat—Simpson's—to the subcommittee. Obey said of Simpson, "He works with people on both sides and he's a good, solid legislator." Simpson was the only Idaho member to vote for the State Children's Health Insurance Plan, a Democratic initiative that attracted few Republicans. As a dentist, he said that the addition of dental care for children would save money in the long run. In 2008, Simpson was the only member of the Idaho congressional delegation to support the $700 billion bailout of the financial markets. "We got into this mess because of failure of government oversight," he said. "Consequently, I think there's a role for government to play in trying to get us out of this, as much as I don't like it."

Simpson has said he would "die trying" to create a Boulder-White Cloud Management Area and he has spent seven years negotiating the plan with opposing constituencies. In 2006, he came up with a plan to preserve 312,000 acres in the central Idaho mountains and to transfer federal land in the Sawtooth National Recreation Area, a winter range for elk, to the city of Stanley and to Custer County to bolster their tax bases. To placate motorized-recreation advocates, he included a new 960-acre motorized park south of the Boise airport. To woo environmental groups, which were divided over the plan, Simpson added 630 acres of state land along the Salmon River and proposed to turn over federal land in eastern Idaho for a new state park. Simpson got his bill added to a sure-to-pass tax-cut bill in 2006, and secured a promise from Idaho Sen. Larry Craig, a Republican who opposed it, not to stand in the way. But the bill was dropped in last-minute tinkering by congressional leaders, and Simpson has continued to push versions of it since without success.

Simpson won re-election three times with a better than 2-1 ratios, but his lead slipped to 62%-34% in 2006, when he faced former Democratic state Rep. Jim Hansen, the son of former Republican Rep. Orval Hansen, who represented the district from 1969 to 1975. Simpson was back on his game in 2008, winning re-election with 71% of the vote.

★ ILLINOIS ★

Illinois, the Land of Lincoln, is a land of contradictions. It is a center of American excellence given to spasms of public corruption. Its political culture typically has little use for people who aren't "from here," yet it spawned three presidents who all came from elsewhere. When Abraham Lincoln's father chose to go back to Indiana, Lincoln headed west in Illinois. Ulysses S. Grant grew up in Ohio, lived in Missouri and stayed only briefly in Galena before heading off to war. Barack Obama, whose formative years were spent in Hawaii, arrived after law school to be a community organizer in Chicago. It is a state whose political discourse is ordinarily conducted in language that is coarse at best and yet has offered up the spare eloquence of Lincoln and the inspiring cadences of Obama.

Illinois has come a long way since May 1860, when Abraham Lincoln was nominated at the Republican National Convention in the 10,000-seat Wigwam in Chicago, to November 2008, when Obama celebrated his victory before a crowd of 1 million in Chicago's Grant Park, less than a mile from the old Wigwam site. Chicago had 112,000 people in 1860, and was the nation's boom city in the next three-quarters of a century, growing to a population of 1.4 million by the time it hosted the Columbian Exposition in 1893. "Make no little plans," Chicago architect Daniel Burnham exhorted. And the city made vast plans, building grand parks on the lakefront, erecting America's first downtown of skyscrapers, lining its boulevards with retail palaces, creating a great university from scratch on the Exposition's Midway Plaisance, and housing union agitators as well as corporate leaders. Chicago hosted the Democratic Convention of 1896 that nominated 36-year-old William Jennings Bryan after his "cross of gold" speech, and was the headquarters of the brilliant campaign Mark Hanna waged for William McKinley, who beat Bryan in the fall. Chicago started with the advantage of a great location, where the Great Lakes meet the prairies of the vast Mississippi Valley, and the city's entrepreneurs made it the hub of the nation's railroad network and the center of U.S. trade in lumber, grain, and meat.

A century later, Chicago is the nation's third-largest metropolis and, although often overshadowed by coastal New York and Los Angeles, is still a creative, world-class city, the center of a metropolitan area of 9.7 million people. In commerce, Chicago remains a prime producer and processor of food products, a major manufacturing center, and the strongest white-collar and service economy between the coasts. In finance, it is the home of the world's greatest commodities exchanges and futures markets. O'Hare Airport, promoted and nurtured by longtime Mayor Richard J. Daley (1955–76), the father of the current mayor, is one of the world's busiest airports and one of its great hubs of commerce. Chicago was established not by government but by markets. It has always been a bastion of free enterprise, settled by pioneers from New England and Kentucky, by immigrant Irishmen who dug the first canal connecting Lake Michigan to the Illinois River, and by railroad promoters who saw its potential as the great connecting point between East and West, the Great Lakes and the Mississippi Valley. Its factories were built where iron ore from Great Lakes freighters and coal from inland hills came together. Today, many of the old factories have been closed or demolished, and some of the Chicago area's biggest corporations have had problems. But the city's economy, based on finance and commodities, manufacturing and food, and undergirded by thousands of small firms, continues to thrive. The O'Hare area rivals downtown Chicago in the number of jobs. Central-city neighborhoods north and south of the Loop attract affluent residents, many to houses worth well over $1 million. Latinos are thronging to the Chicago area, adding vitality to tired old neighborhoods. Illinois's population is 15% Hispanic and 15% African-American. In June 2008, Chicago was selected as one of the finalists for the 2016 Olympics.

Illinois produced some crucial votes and important public figures in the 20th century. The list starts with Charles Dawes, a 30-year-old lawyer sent to Chicago by Hanna to manage McKinley's campaign. Dawes later was a World War I general and Calvin Coolidge's vice president. Next comes Chicago lawyer Harold Ickes, who was Franklin Roosevelt's great Interior secretary. Prominent Illinois Republicans have included House Speaker Joseph Cannon, Senate Republican Leader Everett Dirksen, Sen. Charles Percy and House Speaker Dennis Hastert. Prominent Democrats have included Gov. Adlai Stevenson, both Mayor Daleys, and House Ways and Means Chairman Dan Rostenkowski. It did not produce a serious presidential candidate in the half century after Stevenson, but when Obama announced his candidacy in Lincoln's hometown of Springfield in February 2007, he won almost unanimous support from Chicago's civic and financial establishment.

For most of the 20th century, Illinois was a key political battleground, closely divided between Democratic Chicago and Republican downstate. Its mixture of blacks and whites and Hispanics, immigrants and pioneers, city-dwellers and suburbanites and farmers, the affluent and the impoverished, heavy industry and high-technology, long made it a rough proxy for the nation. For a century, Illinois was a political bellwether, voting only twice for losing presidential candidates between 1896 and 1996—in 1916 and 1976, when it went Republican while the nation went Democratic. But in the 1990s, Illinois became steadily more Democratic than the nation. In 2000, it was one of Al Gore's best states. In 2004, it voted a solid 55%-44% for John Kerry, with Kerry leading in metro Chicago 60%-39% and Bush leading downstate

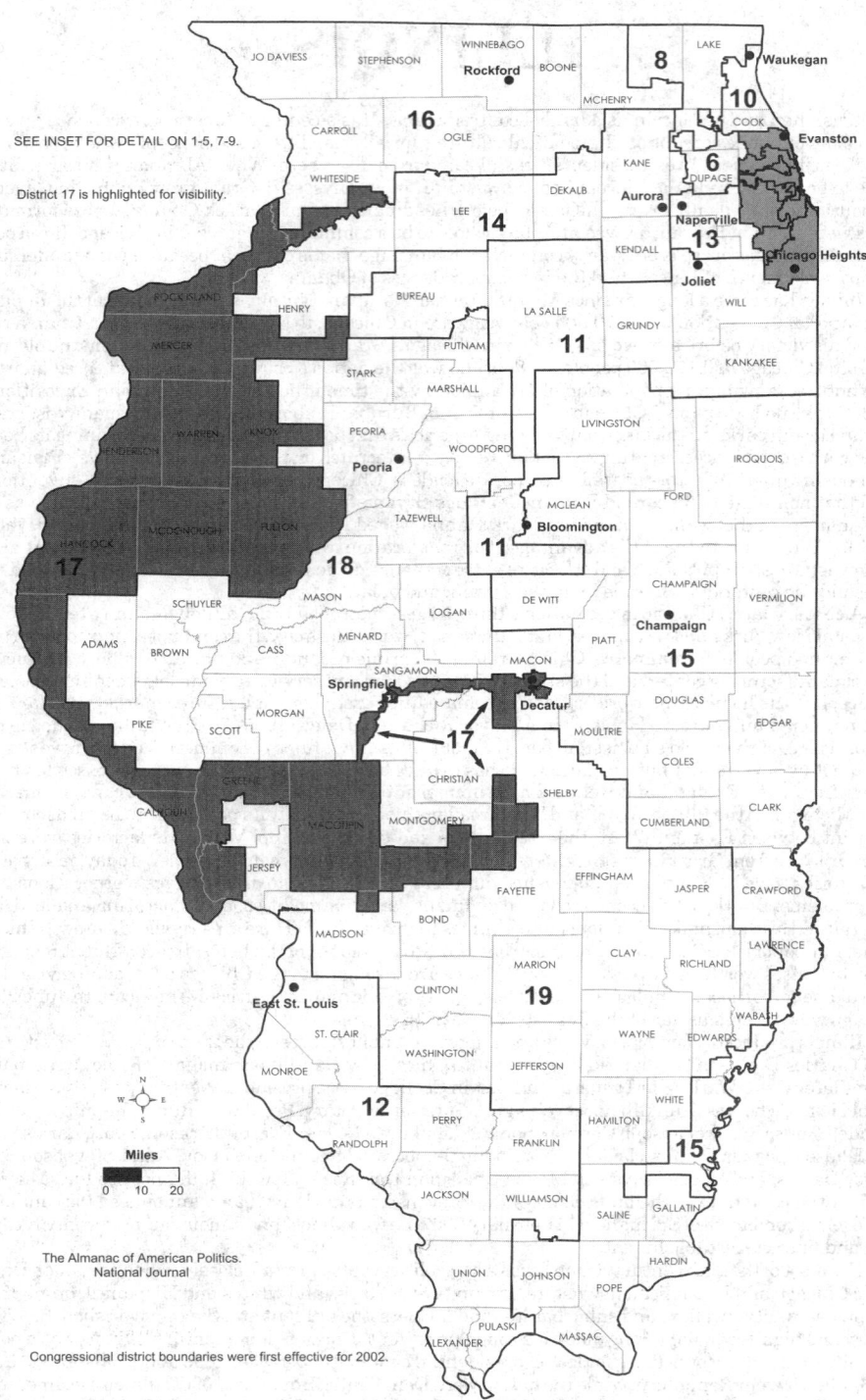

SEE INSET FOR DETAIL ON 1-5, 7-9.

District 17 is highlighted for visibility.

The Almanac of American Politics.
National Journal

Congressional district boundaries were first effective for 2002.

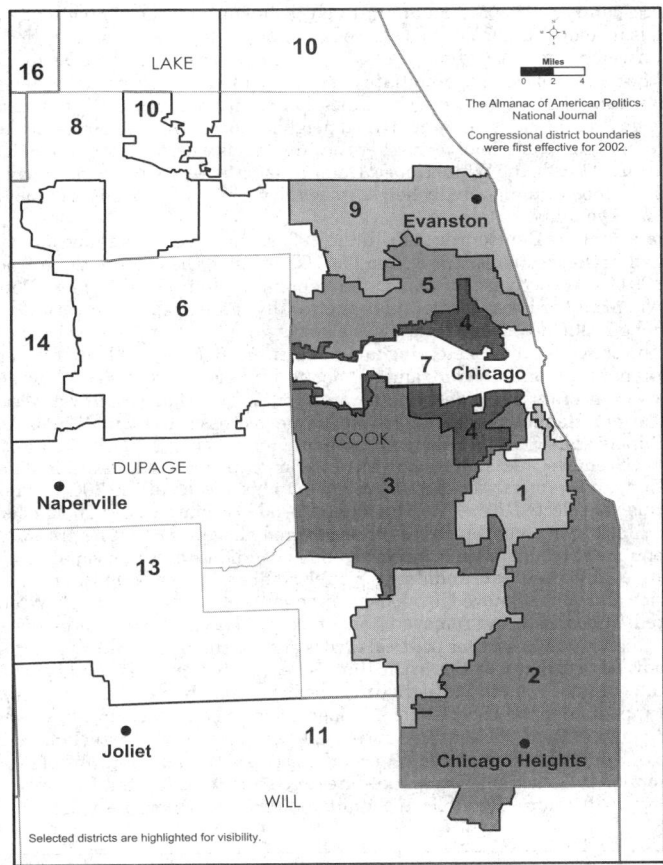

55%-45%. In 2008 with favorite son Obama on the ballot, Illinois was not even close. Obama carried the state 62%-37%, metro Chicago 68%-31%, and he won formerly rock-ribbed Republican DuPage and McHenry Counties, He carried downstate as well by a more modest 51%-47%.

Perhaps more than any other state, Illinois has a history of machine politics and more than occasional political corruption. Lincoln was no stranger to the Republican machine of his day, which rallied thousands of partisans to cheer him at his debates with Stephen Douglas in 1858 and packed the Wigwam convention hall for him in 1860. Machine politics continued through the Gilded Age, as politicians in a closely divided state competed for public jobs and as politicians of both parties courted the immigrants streaming into Chicago. Both the city and downstate had thriving two-party politics in the early 20th century. It was a Republican mayor, Big Bill Thompson, who threatened to punch King George V "in the snoot" if he came to Chicago and who looked the other way as Al Capone's goons controlled the speakeasies. During the Depression, Chicago became reliably Democratic. In the decades that followed, the suburbs, wary of Chicago, became Republican and developed machines of their own.

Starting in the 1950s, Illinois's political trends were set by reactions to the officeholder most visible to the voters, who was not the governor off in remote Springfield and certainly not the senators who have to work "out of town" in Washington, but the mayor of Chicago. It was only through the herculean efforts of mayor and Democratic party boss Richard J. Daley that John F. Kennedy was able to win Illinois by exactly 8,858 votes out of 4.7 million cast. In the 1970s, reaction against Daley was key to the rise of Republican James Thompson, who as U.S. attorney successfully prosecuted machine pols and went on to become governor. For most of the 1980s, the dominant figure was Mayor Harold Washington, the able African-American mayor who was vociferously opposed by white politicians in what became know as the "council wars." Suburbanites, repelled by the hubbub and fearful that Chicago's problems might increase their taxes, voted heavily Republican.

The major figure today is Mayor Richard M. Daley, elected in 1989. Like his father, he seems to know the city block by block and has worked to beautify it, planting thousands of trees, encouraging handsome wrought-iron fences, and creating Millenium Park on the lakefront. The old political machine that his father so ably led is no more, and Daley has steered clear of the scandals that have brought down some of his associates as well as the last two governors, Republican George Ryan and Democrat Rod Blagojevich. He has used the powers of office to propitiate the black politicians who at first seemed to be obdurate opponents and has won solid support from Hispanics, lakefront liberals and the burgeoning numbers of young singles and gays in the city's many gentrified neighborhoods. He has been re-elected five times, by increasingly larger margins each time. He has kept on good terms with presidents of both parties and now presumably has a direct line to the White House. Daley's luster has extended to his party. His example as the state's leading Democrat undoubtedly helped ease the way for suburbanites to move toward Democrats over the past 15 years.

Illinois became a solidly Democratic state in the 1990s, but it took some time for Democrats to take a commanding lead in the elections. Republican Gov. Thompson, the longest-serving governor in state history (1977 to 1991), was succeeded by downstate Republican Jim Edgar. In 1998, Republicans scored a double victory when banker Peter Fitzgerald beat ethically challenged Democratic Sen. Carol Moseley Braun and veteran officeholder George Ryan was elected governor. But Ryan was driven from office by scandal in 2002 and convicted of racketeering and fraud in 2006. Fitzgerald, an independent type, was loathed by most Republican officeholders and did not seek re-election in 2004. Their departures led to the election of two Democrats of decidedly disparate reputations. Blagojevich was elected governor in 2002 by 52%-45% over a Republican with the unfortunate last name of Ryan, Illinois Attorney General Jim Ryan. And Illinois state Sen. Obama got a promotion in 2004 to the U.S. Senate. Obama profited from scandals, which removed his chief Democratic primary opponent and the original Republican nominee from contention, and from the sensational reaction to his speech at the 2004 Democratic National Convention. Obama was elected 70%-27%, the most one-sided Senate victory in Illinois history, after a serious contender, Jack Ryan, was forced to withdraw amid allegations that he pressured his ex-wife to go to sex clubs; Republicans could muster as a replacement candidate only Maryland resident Alan Keyes, a social conservative and perennial candidate for public office who moved to Illinois to run. The career paths of Blagojevich and Obama moved in opposite directions—Obama went to the White House, Blagojevich was arrested, impeached, and removed from office amid accusations that he tried to leverage his power to appoint Obama's successor for political favors and personal reward.

Democrats now have firm majorities in the Illinois Legislature and a 12-7 margin in the state's U.S. House delegation. Looking ahead to 2010, they may be in trouble. Roland Burris, a longtime statewide officeholder, was appointed to the U.S. Senate by Blagojevich on Dec. 30, 2008, but was soon swept up in the "pay to play" scandal. By the following February, it was plain that Burris had given a misleading impression of his contacts with the tainted governor's associates about the terms of his appointment to Obama's seat. Prominent Democrats across the state urged him to resign, but Burris refused. The disarray left an opening in 2010 for a Republican candidate like North Shore Rep. Mark Kirk. On Jan. 29,

Population			Household Income		Work	
Pop. 2007:		12,783,049	Under $15k:	12.3%	Private:	81.9%
State rank:		5th of 50	$15k to $50k:	34.2%	Government:	12.7%
Change since 2000:		Up 2.9%	$50k to $100k:	32.4%	Self-employed:	5.3%
Urban:		86.6%	$100k to $150k:	17.0%	Unemployment (3-yr. average):	5.0%
Rural:		13.4%	Over $150k:	4.1%	Poverty:	12.1%
Native of state:		66.8%	Median income:	$53,745	Blue collar:	22.8%
Not a citizen:		7.7%			White collar:	60.7%
Area size:		57,914 sq. mi.	**Home Value**		Khaki collar:	0.2%
			Under $100k:	21.1%	Other:	16.3%
Most populous cities			$100k to $300k:	50.1%		
1. Chicago		2,740,224	$300k to $500k:	19.6%	**Age**	
2. Aurora		176,413	$500k to $1 mil:	7.8%	Median age:	35.7 yrs.
3. Rockford		147,794	Over $1 million:	1.5%	More than 65 yrs:	12.0%
4. Naperville		143,956	Median:	$198,100	Less than 18 yrs:	25.1%

Race/Ethnicity				Military Veterans		Registered Voters in 2008	
White:	65.3%	*Language*		% of Pop:	8.7%	No party registration	
Black:	14.6%	English:	78.4%	*Veterans by Period*		Voter turnout:	5,522,371
Hispanic:	14.6%	Spanish:	12.6%	WWII and before:	14.8%	Turnout as % of	
Asian:	4.1%	Asian:	2.5%	Korea:	13.0%	voting age:	56.8%
Native Am.:	0.1%	Other		Vietnam:	31.5%	**General Assembly**	
Hawaiian:	0.0%	European	5.7%	Gulf (pre-2001):	9.8%	Senate:	37 D 22 R
Two+ races:	1.0%	**Education**		Gulf (post-2001):	5.9%	House:	70 D 48 R
Ancestry		H.S. grad:	85.2%	Peace time:	25.0%		
German:	16.7%	College grad:	29.0%				
Irish:	10.4%	Grad degree:	10.8%				
Polish:	6.3%						

2009, when the state Senate voted Blagojevich out of office on a 59-0 vote, Democratic Lt. Gov. Pat Quinn became governor.

Presidential politics   Illinois's presidential primary, for years held fittingly on or around St. Patrick's Day, clinched the nominations for Republican victors Gerald Ford in 1976, Ronald Reagan in 1980, and George Bush in 1988, and Democratic victors Jimmy Carter in 1980, Walter Mondale in 1984, and Bill Clinton in 1992. As more states have moved their primaries to earlier dates, Illinois has voted too late to decide a nomination. In January 2007, Speaker Michael Madigan proposed moving the primary to Feb. 5, 2008, to help Barack Obama, and the bill was signed into law in June. Some 2 million people turned out to vote in the Democratic primary, many more than the 1.1 million who voted in 2004 or the record 1.66 million in 1984. Obama beat Hillary Rodham Clinton 65%-33%, losing only a few downstate counties. There was little campaigning on the Republican side, and only 893,000 GOP votes were cast, not many more than in other recent years and well below the record 1.1 million in 1980, when Illinois native Ronald Reagan and Illinois Rep. John Anderson were on the ballot. John McCain won the primary with 47% of the vote, to 29% for Mitt Romney and 16% for Mike Huckabee. Romney did not do well in affluent suburban counties.

2008 Presidential Vote		
Obama (D)	3,419,348	(62%)
McCain (R)	2,031,179	(37%)

2008 Democratic Presidential Primary		
Obama (D)	1,318,234	(65%)
Clinton (D)	667,930	(33%)

2008 Republican Presidential Primary		
McCain (R)	426,777	(47%)
Romney (R)	257,265	(29%)
Huckabee (R)	148,053	(16%)
Paul (R)	45,055	(5%)

2004 Presidential Vote		
Kerry (D)	2,891,550	(55%)
Bush (R)	2,345,946	(44%)

In the 1990s, as Republican margins in the suburban collar counties dwindled, Illinois became a solidly Democratic state in presidential politics. It was not seriously contested in 2000 or 2004, much less in 2008, when favorite son Obama carried it by 62%-37%. A map of the results shows Obama winning in the territory carried by Republican Abraham Lincoln's supporters in the epic 1858 Senate race, while losing in most of the areas carried by the supporters of Democrat Stephen Douglas.

Congressional districting   Illinois lost one of its 20 House seats in the 2000 census, and control of redistricting was split between the Democratic state House and the Republican state Senate and governor. In similar circumstances, the 1980s and 1990s redistricting plans had been drawn by courts, with results that were politically unpredictable and unpalatable to incumbents. In 1992, four incumbents lost their primaries. Things worked differently in 2001. U.S. House Speaker Dennis Hastert of Illinois, a Republican, and 3rd District Democratic Rep. Bill Lipinski started negotiating early to produce an incumbent-protection plan that would pass both houses of the Legislature. Before the census data came in, it was assumed that the 5th District would be eliminated, since Democratic incumbent Blagojevich had announced his bid for governor. But the census figures showed that the 5th District and adjacent districts in Chicago, bursting with new immigrants, had gained population, while rural southern Illinois had lost population. Mayor Daley let it be known that he would not like to see Chicago lose a seat.

111th Congress Lineup	
12 D	7 R
110th Congress Lineup	
10 D	9 R

So Hastert and Lipinski concocted a new plan taking a district away from southern Illinois. The victim was 19th District Democratic Rep. David Phelps, a former professional gospel singer with little seniority and a somewhat conservative voting record. His hometown was connected by a narrow band of land on the eastern edge of the state with the central Illinois 15th District held by Republican Tim Johnson. Phelps had no clout in Congress, and the Hastert-Lipinski plan became law in May 2001. Phelps sued unsuccessfully and then ran, also unsuccessfully, against Republican incumbent John Shimkus in the new 19th District. Why were Lipinski, Daley and Speaker Michael Madigan willing to sacrifice a fellow Democrat and lose their party's 10-10 parity in the House delegation? Because the low-seniority Phelps could do little for them in the House, while Hastert had been generous in using his powers as speaker to aid Daley, Lipinski, and other Chicago Democrats on Chicago issues and projects. Maintaining a Republican majority that would keep Hastert in the speakership was in the interest of Chicago Democrats.

The resulting map is a nightmare for those who believe redistricting plans should have compact and competitive districts. Aside from Phelps and perhaps Shimkus, every other incumbent was strengthened. And the resulting district lines are grotesque. The 17th District, long confined to west-central Illinois, now has a narrow finger extending to downtown Springfield and Decatur. The 15th District in central Illinois has a long, narrow tentacle along the eastern border of the state, then snakes south to the Kentucky border. Hastert's former district, the 14th, extends from the Chicago suburbs to a point six miles from the Iowa border. Incumbents were accommodated in the minutest fashion. A small portion of

Livingston County was added to Republican Jerry Weller's 11th District so his parents could vote for him. Jesse Jackson Jr.'s 2nd District was extended southward to be nearer to Peotone, the site of the proposed third Chicago airport that he has been tirelessly promoting. Lipinski lost a heavily black ward in Chicago and majority-Hispanic Cicero and in return got the white Bridgeport neighborhood and some heavily white suburbs.

In 2005, Rep. Rahm Emanuel, the newly installed chairman of the Democratic Congressional Campaign Committee, sought to revisit the issue of the state's congressional map. The idea was to draw a new map to retaliate for post-2002 Republican redistricting efforts in Colorado, Georgia and Texas. But the Legislature didn't seem to have much interest in drawing new lines, and neither did a majority of the Democratic congressional delegation; the idea was shelved.

Illinois is likely to lose a House seat in the reapportionment following the 2010 census. This time, unless Republicans win the governorship in 2010, Democrats will almost surely control the redistricting process and will probably try to eliminate a Republican seat. They may have a little difficulty. The fastest-growing parts of the state are the still-Republican exurbs, and Democrats will probably want to shore up the incumbents who picked up the 8th, 11th and 14th districts for the party in 2004 and 2008, districts that contain much exurban territory.

Governor

Pat Quinn (D)

Assumed office Jan. 2009, term expires Jan. 2011, 1st term; b. Dec. 16, 1948, Chicago; home, Chicago; Georgetown U., B.A., 1971; Northwestern U., J.D. 1980; Catholic; divorced; 2 children.

Elected Office: Commissioner, Cook Cnty. Bd. of Tax Appeals, 1982–86; IL treasurer, 1991–95; Lt. gov., 2003–09.

Professional Career: Chicago revenue dir., 1986–87; Practicing atty., 1994–2002; Author.

Office: Office of the Governor, 207 State House, Springfield, 62706, 217-782-0244; Fax: 217-524-4049; Web site: http://www.illinois.gov/gov/.

Election Results

2006 general	Rod Blagojevich (D)	1,736,731	(50%)
	Judy Baar Topinka (R)	1,369,315	(39%)
	Rich Whitney (Green)	361,336	(10%)
2006 primary	Rod Blagojevich (D)	669,006	(71%)
	Edwin Eisendrath (D)	275,375	(29%)

Democrat Pat Quinn became governor of Illinois on Jan. 29, 2009, after the impeachment and removal from office of Democratic Gov. Rod Blagojevich. Quinn's grandfather was an Irish immigrant who raised his family above the family grocery store in Chicago. Quinn's father put himself through college on the GI Bill after serving in the Navy during World War II, and rose to become the public-relations director of Catholic Cemeteries in the Chicago archdiocese. Growing up in the comfortable Chicago suburb of Hinsdale, Patrick Quinn attended a parochial elementary school and then Fenwick High School, run by the Dominican Order in suburban Oak Park. He was captain of the school's track team, and wrote about sports for the school newspaper, an interest that has stayed with him through life as a diehard Chicago White Sox fan. Quinn graduated with honors with a degree in international economics from Georgetown University. In 1972, a year out of college, he signed up as a volunteer for the anti-machine Democratic candidate for Illinois governor, Daniel Walker. When Walker won, Quinn got a job in state government, working on patronage appointments and transferring state workplace safety operations to the federal Occupational Safety and Health Administration. In 1975, he left state government to attend Northwestern Law School—and to engage in politics, in his own way.

Walker, defeated for renomination in 1976 and later jailed for defrauding a savings and loan, could be of no help. And in his suburban upbringing, Quinn acquired none of the connections that are usually essential to the rise of Democratic politicians in Illinois. "It's not exactly an easy path I had," he told the *Chicago Tribune* in February 2009. "I had no political patrons or ward committeemen backing me for any job." Young and idealistic, Quinn launched the Coalition for Political Honesty, which operated out of an Oak Park basement, and got enough signatures for a 1976 referendum to stop legislators from collecting their entire salaries on the first day of their terms. In 1980, he got enough signatures for a "cutback" initiative to reduce the size of the state House from 177 to 118 members. Previously each district elected three legislators, with each party allowed only two candidates. This gave minority parties representation, but in some Chicago wards, the nominal Republicans were obedient to Chicago machine politicians. The measure passed, with help from what became a Quinn trademark—Sunday morning press conferences at the Blackstone Hotel, across the street from Chicago's City Hall. Some labeled Quinn a political gadfly; others saw him as a political reformer.

In 1982, Quinn was elected to the Cook County Board of Tax Appeals, which handled property-tax appeals. In 1983, he created the Citizens Utility Board, a group that challenged utility and phone rate increases. Founding the CUB, which became a highly effective consumer organization, established his reputation statewide and helped him shake the label of gadfly. In 1986, he ran for state treasurer and lost in the Democratic primary to Jerome Cosentino. Chicago Mayor Harold Washington appointed him city revenue director, but he lost the job after a falling-out with other officials in the administration and after some internal grumbling about his penchant for seeking publicity. He began practicing law, specializing in property-tax appeals, and wrote a book called *How to Appeal Your Property Taxes Without a Lawyer*. He was also the lead attorney in a case, decided by the U.S. Supreme Court in 1990, that banned political considerations in state and local hiring.

In 1990, Quinn finally was elected state treasurer. He claimed to have made $848 million in investment income for taxpayers, but in the Republican year of 1994, he lost a contest for secretary of state to incumbent George Ryan, who was later elected governor and then jailed on federal corruption charges. Throughout his career in state politics, a reputation for shameless self-promotion followed Quinn from post to post. His successor as treasurer, Republican Judy Baar Topinka, claimed that on taking office, she found "Quinn for Governor" bumper stickers in the desk. In 1996, he ran for U.S. senator and lost in the primary 65%-30% to downstate Rep. Richard Durbin, who went on to be elected in November. In 1998, he ran for lieutenant governor, narrowly losing the Democratic primary to Kane County Coroner Mary Lou Kearns, 50.1%-49.9%, a margin of 1,468 votes out of 781,000 cast. The Democratic ticket lost in November, and Quinn continued to practice law and to attract public attention, notably by walking across Illinois from the Mississippi River to Lake Michigan to highlight the need for decent health care.

In 2002, he ran for lieutenant governor again, and this time won the Democratic primary, with 42% of the vote to 32% for Chicago hospital executive Joyce Washington and 25% for Downstate college teacher Mike Kelleher. He ran 849 votes behind Washington in Cook County, 150 votes ahead of Kelleher downstate, and carried the collar-county suburbs with 50% of the vote, to 28% for Washington and 22% for Kelleher. It was a rare example of a Democrat winning an Illinois primary by sweeping the suburbs. Success in the primary put Quinn on the same ticket in November with Democratic Rep. Rod Blagojevich, whose political career began to thrive after he married the daughter of powerful 33rd Ward Committeeman Richard Mell. Quinn had not been the choice of most Chicago insiders, and his relations with Blagojevich were never warm, but the ticket won 52%-45%, and Quinn accepted more than $48,000 in contributions from Blagojevich crony Tony Rezko, a businessman whose favorable deals for prominent politicians later tarred Barack Obama's presidential campaign. Quinn says he gave the money to charity after Rezko went to jail for fraud and bribery.

Quinn was appointed to several boards, including the Mississippi River Coordinating Council, the Illinois Biofuels Investment and Infrastructure Working Group, and the Broadband Deployment Council. Blagojevich spent most of his time in Chicago, taking the state plane to Springfield when the Legislature was meeting. Quinn lived mostly in Springfield, and frugally, never accepting his $32-a-day meal allowance and paying for his own lodging, proudly showing off his Super 8 preferred customer card. He pushed a military relief act for aid to families of National Guardsmen and reservists called to active duty, and a Let Them Rest in Peace Act, to prevent disruptive protests at service members' funerals. Always a bit of an eccentric, he carried a beat-up, 28-year-old briefcase he called Betsy and eschewed a laptop in favor of scribbling notes on scraps of paper. One of his proud possessions is a bow tie that belonged to longtime Democratic Sen. Paul Simon, who was lieutenant governor under Walker and a Quinn political hero. In 2006, as he and Blagojevich ran for second terms, he supported the incumbent governor without reservation, despite the fact that Blagojevich was under federal investigation. Quinn told the *Tribune* he found the governor to be "an honest person." The Blagojevich-Quinn ticket was re-elected 50%-39%.

In Blagojevich's second term, Quinn became more critical of the governor. He was not alone: Blagojevich was at odds with legislators of both parties, especially Democratic House Speaker Michael Madigan. At one point, the House rejected the governor's budget by a unanimous vote. In March 2007, Quinn opposed Blagojevich's proposed $6 billion business-receipts tax. Later that year, he called on Blagojevich to urge Democratic Senate President Emil Jones (a mentor of his former colleague Obama) to pass an ethics bill. By April 2008, he was telling reporters he was "disappointed" in Blagojevich, blaming him for a "disintegration of comity in Springfield."

Then on Dec. 9, 2008, as Chicago was celebrating election of favorite-son Obama as president, the city was stunned by the news that Blagojevich had been arrested by federal marshals and charged with attempting to trade the appointment of a successor to Obama in the Senate for personal or political favors. Quinn initially called for a special election to fill the Senate seat in the light of the taint of a Blagojevich appointment, but he quickly backed down under pressure from other Democrats who evidently feared a Republican might win such a contest. Quinn called for Blagojevich's resignation, as did several other prominent Illinois Democrats, but the governor proclaimed his innocence and refused to budge. "He disgraced himself, he disgraced the people of Illinois and the proper thing to do is step aside and resign," Quinn said on CBS's *Face the Nation.* On December 30, even as the possibility of impeachment loomed, Blagojevich went forward and appointed former state Attorney General Roland Burris to the Senate. Senate Democrats at first refused to seat him, then acquiesced. In the meantime, the Illinois House voted 114-1 on January 9 to impeach Blagojevich. On January 29, the Illinois Senate voted 59-0 to remove him from office. And erstwhile gadfly Pat Quinn was suddenly governor of Illinois.

Quinn met that day with the other Democratic statewide officials to prepare for a transition. In early February, he started making appointments: A former head of his Citizens Utility Board became head of the Commerce department, the former president of Voice for Illinois Children became his chief of staff, the general counsel of the Illinois Reform Commission was named his general counsel, and a former Blagojevich Commerce head was appointed chief operating officer. On February 20, after Burris admitted he had more contacts with Blagojevich intimates about the Senate appointment than he had disclosed, Quinn said he should resign and allow his seat be filled in a special election, a process untainted by the Blagojevich scandal. On February 26, when he more forcefully said Burris would be forced to resign and to compete in a special election, black Chicago politicians objected. Quinn said he feared a revival of the racially polarizing "Council Wars" of the 1980s, in which African-American Mayor Harold Washington confronted powerful white aldermen. He met with top black officials, who may have reminded him that African-Americans cast 30% of the vote in statewide Democratic primaries, and he backed down on March 2. "My position is well known. I think there should be a special election," Quinn said. "You cannot have a special election unless the incumbent resigns. The incumbent has said he will not resign."

In addition to the political chaos he inherited from the pay-to-play scandal, Quinn faced major fiscal problems. It was estimated that state government needed another $3 billion to get through the fiscal year. State workers' health care bills were delinquent, school districts were scrambling for cash, doctors and hospitals were going unpaid. On Feb. 4, 2009, Comptroller Dan Hynes said the state faced a $9 billion budget deficit. But Quinn declined to rescind Blagojevich's pledge of $150 million should Chicago be awarded the 2016 Olympics. He ordered cuts in travel, contracts, and hiring, but opposed raising highway tolls (a significant expense for Chicago suburbanites). But that was not enough, and in March, he proposed raising the state income tax from 3%, where it has been since 1989, to 4.5%, cushioning the blow by raising the personal exemption from $2,000 to $6,000.

In 2009, Quinn was expected to run for a full term.

Senior Senator

Richard Durbin (D)

Elected 1996, term expires 2014, 3rd term; b. Nov. 21, 1944, E. St. Louis; home, Springfield; Georgetown U., B.S. 1966, J.D. 1969; Catholic; married (Loretta); 3 children (1 deceased).

Elected Office: U.S. House of Reps., 1982–96.

Professional Career: Staff, Lt. Gov. Paul Simon, 1969–72; Legal cnsl., IL Sen. Judiciary Cmte., 1972–82; Prof., S. IL Schl. of Medicine, 1978–82.

DC Office: 309 HSOB, 20510, 202-224-2152; Fax: 202-228-0400; Web site: durbin.senate.gov.

State Offices: Chicago, 312-353-4952; Marion, 618-998-8812; Springfield, 217-492-4062.

Committees: *Assistant Majority Leader & Whip. Appropriations* (10th of 18 D): Agriculture, Rural Development, Food and Drug Administration & Related Agencies; Defense; Financial Services & General Government (Chmn); Labor, Health and Human Services, Education & Related Agencies; State, Foreign Operations & Related Programs; Transportation, Housing and Urban Development & Related Agencies. *Judiciary* (6th of 12 D): Constitution; Crime & Drugs; Human Rights & the Law (Chmn); Immigration, Refugees & Border Security; Terrorism & Homeland Security. *Rules & Administration* (6th of 11 D).

Group Ratings

	ADA	ACLU	AFS	LCV	ITIC	NTU	COC	ACU	CFG	FRC
2008	100	86	100	100	100	4	63	4	3	0
2007	95	—	100	93	—	6	45	0	7	—

National Journal Ratings

	2007 LIB	—	2007 CONS	2008 LIB	—	2008 CONS
Economic	79%	—	13%	77%	—	13%
Social	88%	—	8%	91%	—	0%
Foreign	78%	—	21%	65%	—	6%
Composite	84%	—	16%	86%	—	14%

Key Votes of the 110th Congress

1. Raise CAFE standards	Y	5. Make English official language	N	9. Withdraw troops 3/08	Y
2. Expand SCHIP	Y	6. Path to citizenship	Y	10. Iran guard is terrorist group	Y
3. Cap greenhouse gases	Y	7. Fetus is unborn child	N	11. Increase missile defense $	N
4. Bail out financial markets	Y	8. Prosecute hate crimes	Y	12. Overhaul FISA	N

Election Results

2008 general	Richard Durbin (D)	3,615,844	(68%)	($8,016,455)
	Steve Sauerberg (R)	1,520,621	(29%)	($1,034,454)
	Kathy Cummings (Green)	119,135	(2%)	
2008 primary	Richard Durbin (D)	unopposed		

Prior Winning Percentages: 2002 (60%); 1996 (56%); 1994 House (55%); 1994 House (55%); 1992 House (57%); 1990 House (66%); 1988 House (69%); 1986 House (68%); 1984 House (61%); 1982 House (50%)

The senior senator from Illinois is Richard Durbin, a Democrat first elected to the House in 1982 and the Senate in 1996. He is now the assistant majority leader and Democratic whip, making him the second-ranking leader in the Senate, after Majority Leader Harry Reid. Durbin grew up in East St. Louis, the youngest of three brothers. His father, a railroad night watchman, died of lung cancer when Durbin was 14. He graduated from Georgetown University and its law school, and then returned to Illinois with an ambition for politics. He joined Democrat Paul Simon's staff when Simon was the lieutenant governor (1969–73), then was a state Senate staffer in the 1970s. Durbin lost races for the state Senate in 1976 and for lieutenant governor in 1978, but in 1982, won the nomination to oppose Republican Rep. Paul Findley, who had characterized himself as Palestinian leader Yasser Arafat's best friend in Congress. Durbin had no trouble raising money from well-heeled Israel supporters. Durbin won that race, got a seat on the House Agriculture Committee and then moved to Appropriations, where in 1993, he became chairman of the Agriculture subcommittee. Durbin's centerpiece legislation in the House was the 1988 ban on smoking on domestic airline flights, a battled inspired by the death at a young age of his chain-smoking father. He followed that up by trying to limit tobacco subsidies and to give the Food and Drug Administration authority to regulate tobacco as a health hazard. "I didn't realize it would trigger a change in America," he later said of the airline smoking ban, but indeed it led to smoking bans in many more settings. After his onetime boss, U.S. Sen. Simon, announced his retirement, Durbin won his Senate seat in 1996. Raising more than $1 million, he outspent former state Treasurer (now Governor) Pat Quinn in the March 1996 primary and won 65%-30%. In the general, he faced trial lawyer and abortion opponent Al Salvi and won 56%-41%.

In the Senate, Durbin has compiled a liberal voting record—in 2008 he was in the top 10 most liberal senators, according to *National Journal*'s annual vote analysis—though he has supported welfare reform and the death penalty. He has been an active and dependable Democratic partisan on the floor and on cable news networks, espousing support for farm disaster aid, deductibility of health insurance for the self-employed, reductions in interest rates on student loans and full funding of Pell grants. While serving in the House, Durbin favored restrictions on abortion, but has opposed most legislation to restrict abortion since coming to the Senate. This has had some negative fallout for him among his fellow Catholics. In April 2004, the priest at his home church in Springfield said that he wouldn't give him communion. On other domestic issues, Durbin has had a very strong pro-union voting record, but split with labor on trade, supporting the North American Free Trade Agreement and normal trade relations with China. Illinois is a big exporter. But in 2006, Durbin said he felt "betrayed" by the results of NAFTA and has opposed more recent trade agreements.

In 2001, former Democratic Leader Tom Daschle appointed him assistant Democratic floor leader. After Daschle's defeat in 2004 and the elevation of Reid as minority leader, Durbin became minority whip, and then majority whip in January 2007, after Democrats won control of the Senate.

He serves on the Judiciary Committee and has been a strong opponent of many Bush administration judicial nominees, including Supreme Court nominees John Roberts and Samuel Alito. In his early years in the Senate, he attempted to move his goal of gun control incrementally forward, without success. Durbin took a lead role on asbestos legislation in 2003. He negotiated with Judiciary Committee Chairman Orrin Hatch, a Utah Republican, on a bill backed by Illinois-based businesses that established quick recovery for injured plaintiffs and reduced the burden on businesses only tangentially connected with asbestos. But the two failed to produce a compromise bill. In 2006, he helped defeat the asbestos trust fund sponsored by Pennsylvania Republican Arlen Specter, which would have replaced a multitude of lawsuits against the asbestos industry with a $140 billion trust fund to compensate victims. Durbin strongly opposed taking the matter out of the courts, although he conceded the need for "significant changes in the existing tort system." In 2003, Minority Leader Daschle made Durbin the Democrats' point man on efforts to limit damages in medical malpractice lawsuits, and he successfully blocked action on the legislation.

In more recent legislative battles, Durbin in 2007 sponsored an amendment to the farm bill to create a single agency to monitor the food supply. He was also the chief sponsor of a bill to allow high school graduates who are illegal immigrants to go to U.S. colleges. The outcome was 52-44, short of the 60 votes needed. Throughout 2008 and early 2009, Durbin pushed for his "cram-down" bill allowing bankruptcy judges to modify the terms of distressed mortgages on primary residences in bankruptcy cases. In September 2008, when the Senate was considering the $700-billion bailout of the financial markets, Durbin, echoing the sentiments of many lawmakers, said, "I want to do the right thing. I'm not sure what the right thing is." He decided to support the bill.

Durbin voted against the Gulf War resolution in 1991 and the Iraq war resolution in 2002, though he voted to authorize the use of force in Iraq when President Clinton was president in February 1998. He supported a Senate measure to withdraw troops from Iraq by March 2008. On a trip to Iraq in 2007, he said he saw signs of progress but was more pessimistic than ever. "More than any of my other visits, I felt tragedy," he said. In September 2007, before Gen. David Petraeus's report to Congress, Durbin called it the "Bush-Petraeus report" and said, "By carefully manipulating the statistics, the report will try to convince us the surge is wrong. Even if the statistics are right, the surge is wrong."

In June 2005, Durbin was at the center of a storm over remarks he made from the Senate floor concerning detainees at Guantanamo Bay. Citing an FBI report that described the mistreatment of some prisoners, Durbin likened the American interrogators to "Nazis, Soviets in their gulags, or some mad regime—Pol Pot or others—that had no concern for human beings." His comments dominated the news cycle for days. Durbin at first said he regretted the misunderstanding of his remarks, but after Chicago Mayor Richard M. Daley criticized them, he issued an emotional apology from the Senate floor. In December 2007, Durbin demanded an investigation of the Central Intelligence Agency's destruction of two video-tapes showing agents using extreme interrogation methods.

Durbin's leadership position enables him to work effectively on local issues. He worked with former Speaker Dennis Hastert of Illinois on funding Metra and the CTA mass-transit systems for the Chicago region, on Mississippi River locks and dams, and for O'Hare Airport expansion. He has worked for ethanol tax incentives and pushed for an ethanol research pilot plant at Southern Illinois University at Edwardsville. On the Appropriations Committee, he keeps an eye out for Chicago's commodities exchanges, opposing new fees on the exchanges and in 2008 working behind the scenes to soften the impact of proposed controls on speculators in the oil futures market as gas prices soared. Durbin is also a champion of the $4.6 billion FutureGen clean-coal project in Mattoon, which critics have derisively called "the biggest earmark in history." The Bush Energy Department declined to build FutureGen, but Durbin renewed the push in 2009 with the more supportive Obama administration.

Many senators have tense relationships with home-state colleagues, but Durbin had a warm relationship with Obama after he was elected in 2004. Rather than chafing at Obama's quick rise and celebrity, Durbin in November 2006 urged him to run for president. He endorsed Obama when he announced his candidacy in February 2007. When Obama was elected, Durbin said, "To have a president of the United States who is a close personal friend and has the opportunity to lead this nation and change the world is a dream come true for me in public life." Obama said that Durbin "has been very generous with advice and counsel" and is "a terrific partner."

Durbin did not have a close relationship with Gov. Rod Blagojevich. After Blagojevich's arrest in December 2008 in a "pay to play" scandal, Durbin called on the state Legislature to pass a law ruling that Obama's seat had to be filled by a special election. Blagojevich was caught on investigators' wiretaps apparently trying to benefit politically and personally from his power to name Obama's successor in the Senate. Blagojevich denied wrongdoing and went ahead and appointed former Illinois Attorney General Roland Burris to the Senate in December 2008. By the following February, it was plain that Burris had given a misleading impression of his contacts with the tainted governor's associates about the terms of his appointment to the seat. Durbin urged Burris to resign, but Burris refused.

Durbin was mentioned briefly in 2000 as a possible vice presidential nominee. He was asked to provide information to the Gore campaign in June, but four days later removed his name from consideration. In 2004, he was not much mentioned as a vice presidential nominee and played only a small role, introducing his soon-to-be colleague Obama at the Democratic National Convention. In his 2008 re-election campaign, Durbin was opposed by physician Steven Sauerberg, who loaned his campaign $1.7 million but spent only $1 million, while Durbin spent $13 million. Sauerberg criticized Durbin for his 2005 "Nazis" statement, but the issue proved to have little traction. Durbin won 68%-29%.

Junior Senator

Roland Burris (D)

Appointed Jan. 2009, term expires 2010, 1st term; b. Aug. 3, 1937, Centralia; home, Chicago; S. IL U., B.A. 1969; Howard U., J.D. 1963; Baptist; married (Berlean); 2 children.

Elected Office: IL comptroller, 1979–91; IL atty. gen., 1991–95.

Professional Career: National bank examiner, U.S. Dept. of Treasury, 1963–65; VP, Continental IL Natl. Bank & Trust, 1964–73; Admin. officer, IL gov. cabinet, 1973–77; Practicing atty., 1995–2009

DC Office: 387 RSOB, 20510, 202-224-2854; Fax: 202-228-3333; Web site: burris.senate.gov.

State Offices: Chicago, 312-886-3506; Moline, 217-492-5089; Springfield, 217-492-5089.

Committees: *Armed Services* (15th of 15 D): Airland; Personnel; Readiness & Management Support. *Homeland Security & Governmental Affairs* (9th of 10 D): Disaster Recovery; Federal Financial Management, Government Information, Federal Services & International Security; Oversight of Government Management, the Federal Workforce & the District of Columbia. *Veterans' Affairs* (9th of 10 D).

Group Ratings and Key Votes: Newly Appointed

Election Results

2004 general	Barack Obama (D)	3,595,299	(70%)	($14,532,493)
	Alan Keyes (R)	1,389,850	(27%)	($2,545,325)
2004 primary	Barack Obama (D)	655,923	(53%)	
	Daniel Hynes (D)	294,717	(24%)	
	Blair Hull (D)	134,453	(11%)	
	Maria Pappas (D)	74,987	(6%)	

Roland Burris was named the junior senator from Illinois by then-Democratic Gov. Rod Blagojevich on December 30, 2008, amid a controversy over whether Blagojevich sought favors from candidates for the seat. The taint from the Blagojevich scandal followed Burris to Washington in early 2009, making for an unusually rough transition to the Senate. Then, after a series of damaging revelations about his conversations with people close to Blagojevich prior to his appointment, Burris announced in July 2009 that he would not run for the seat in 2010.

Burris grew up in Centralia, in Southern Illinois just about halfway between Chicago and Mississippi, and a stop on the Illinois Central Railroad's famed City of New Orleans train. Burris's father was a laborer for the IC. In the 1940s and early 1950s, racial segregation prevailed in Centralia, and well before the Rev. Martin Luther King's bus boycott, the young Burris objected to being excluded from Centralia's public swimming pool. On Memorial Day 1953, he showed up for a swim—with his lawyer. Centralia's swimming pool was integrated. At that moment in his life, Burris decided to become a lawyer. In 1959, he graduated from Southern Illinois University at Carbondale, where he documented racial discrimination by merchants in the college town. In 1963, he graduated from Howard University Law School.

Those were the days of civil-rights demonstrations in the South and black political activism in Chicago, but Burris chose a different course. After law school, he worked as a bank examiner for the comptroller of the currency and, in 1964, went to work for Continental Illinois National Bank, then one of the nation's largest banks, in the trust tax and commercial lending departments. He stayed with Continental until 1973. At a time when the streets of Chicago resounded with violent protests against racial bigotry and the Vietnam War, Burris worked in the quiet marble corridors of 231 South LaSalle St. and made loans to minority businesses. In five years, he became a vice president of the bank. He settled in the middle-class Chatham neighborhood on the South Side, around Cottage Grove and 82nd Street, a formerly Jewish neighborhood that had became predominantly African-American. He was active in local community groups and was a Democratic precinct worker.

As an African-American independent of Chicago's machine politics and with banking experience, Burris attracted the attention of Gov. Daniel Walker, who was elected in 1972 as a maverick Democrat. From 1973 to 1977, Burris worked for Walker as the administrative officer in charge of central management services. (Gov. Pat Quinn also served in Walker's administration.) For a short time in 1977, he was executive director of Operation PUSH, an organization founded by the Rev. Jesse Jackson. In 1978, when Michael Bakalis ran for governor, Burris ran for state comptroller again and was slated by the powerful Chicago Democratic Party. He won the primary over state Rep. Richard Luft with 64% of the vote. In the general election, Burris ran against Republican John Castle, whom Gov. James Thompson had appointed as state comptroller. Burris gained an advantage by arguing that the comptroller should be independent of the governor, and he beat Castle only narrowly, 52%-46.5%. The victory made Burris, at age 41, the first black statewide official in Illinois history and a politician who might reasonably believe he had a limitless political future. Heady stuff for a kid from Centralia who half a dozen years earlier was an unknown bank officer.

In his 1982 bid for re-election, Burris had no primary opposition. He won the general election by 1.1 million votes, the third-largest popular-vote margin in Illinois history. Burris's career continued on an upward trajectory. In February 1985, he unseated Gary, Ind., Mayor Richard Hatcher as vice chairman of the Democratic National Committee. Burris's continuing criticism of Thompson's fiscal policies so nettled the governor that he recruited a well-known state senator, Adeline Geo-Karis, to challenge Burris for re-election in 1986. Geo-Karis criticized Burris for working only part-time as a lawyer and for accepting contributions from firms reimbursed by the state; but with strong support in Chicago and downstate, Burris won, 61% to 35%. Burris decided to run for attorney general in 1990, after the Democratic incumbent left the post to run for governor. (Thompson was retiring.) Campaigning as a supporter of abortion rights and gun control, Burris was unopposed for the nomination, thanks to strong support from state House Speaker Michael Madigan. In November, he beat Republican Jim Ryan, the DuPage County state's attorney, 52%-48%. His onetime colleague in the Walker administration, Pat Quinn, was elected state treasurer that year, 56%-44%. As attorney general, Burris was criticized by some liberals for not challenging Republican redistricting plans and for not investigating the validity of a death penalty conviction after the lawyer on the case said the evidence was faulty. Some black political leaders also were miffed when he endorsed Sen. Alan Dixon in the 1992 Democratic primary over challenger Carol Moseley Braun, who won and made history as the first African-American woman elected to the Senate.

Running for governor had long been on Burris's mind, and in the next three elections, in 1994, 1998, and 2002, he did run but without success. There was a common pattern: After many years of holding statewide office, he started off ahead in the polls and then fell behind, losing to three candidates with very different profiles—a lakefront liberal, a downstate moderate, and a Chicago congressman whose father-in-law was a longtime Democratic ward committeeman. Each time, Burris was underfinanced and lost with successively lower percentages of the vote.

On his third try in 2002, Burris once again started out ahead in the polls. "A name you know, a name you trust" was his slogan, and as usual, he called for gun control and more education funding. He was endorsed by U.S. Reps. Danny Davis and Bobby Rush, and also by Jackson and his congressman son, Rep. Jesse Jackson Jr. But Burris met serious competition in Rod Blagojevich, the 5th District representative and the son-in-law of 33rd Ward Democratic committeeman Richard (Dick) Mell. Blagojevich had much more money than Burris. Also in the contest was Paul Vallas, the Chicago Public Schools chief who had a creditable record. The final result: Blagojevich 37%, Vallas 34%, and Burris 29%. "I'm done, and it's very easy to say that," Burris said after the primary. "I'm at peace with myself." He hung out a shingle as a political consultant and retreated from the limelight.

Fast-forward to December 2008. Illinois Sen. Barack Obama was the president-elect of the United States, and Blagojevich was in his second term as governor. On December 9, Blagojevich was arrested, and U.S. Attorney Patrick Fitzgerald released audiotapes in which the governor seems to boast about being in a position to profit personally or politically from his power to appoint a successor to Obama in the Senate. Sen. Dick Durbin and Lt. Gov. Quinn called for the Illinois Legislature to change the law so the seat could be filled in a special election but then backtracked when Democrats feared that a Republican might win. Senate Majority Leader Harry Reid of Nevada announced that a Blagojevich appointment "will not stand," and 50 Democratic U.S. senators signed a letter calling on the governor to refrain from making an appointment. But on December 30, Blagojevich announced Burris as his choice. Burris stood by his side as Democratic Rep. Bobby Rush urged people "not to hang or lynch the appointee as you try to castigate the appointer" and noted that Burris "has not in 40 years had one iota of a taint" of corruption. Blagojevich stated ominously, "I don't think that anyone, any U.S. senator who's sitting in the Senate right now, wants to go on record to deny one African-American from being seated in the U.S. Senate." But others reacted critically. Quinn said Burris "made a mistake in accepting the appointment." Illinois Secretary of State Jesse White refused to sign Blagojevich's certificate appointing Burris.

When Burris arrived in Washington on Monday, January 5, 2009, Majority Leader Reid and Sen. Durbin said they would block him from entering the Senate on Tuesday but would meet with him on Wednesday. On Tuesday, armed guards prevented Burris from entering the Capitol. But there were problems with the Democratic leaders' position. The Supreme Court had ruled in 1967 that the House could not exclude a member from being seated. In that case, the controversial black congressman was Adam Clayton Powell Jr. Just hours after Burris was blocked from entering the Senate floor, Senate Rules Committee Chairman Dianne Feinstein of California said that Burris, having been legally appointed, must be seated. Burris's attorneys argued cogently that White's refusal to sign the certificate was irrelevant; otherwise the secretary of state would have veto power over any gubernatorial appointment. In a visit to Capitol Hill, Obama said, "If Burris has legal standing, and it appears he has, he should be seated as quickly as possible."

On Thursday, Burris told the Illinois House impeachment committee that before the election he had raised the idea of a senatorial appointment with Blagojevich's former chief of staff and that the governor offered him the appointment a few days before Christmas. When asked if there was a quid pro quo, he said, "Absolutely, positively not." Burris also said, "Never once did I doubt their intentions were motivated by anything other than doing what's right for the people of Illinois and what they believe had to be done to protect the Senate as an institution." On January 15, with Durbin led Burris up the aisle and Vice President Dick Cheney swore him in. He was assigned seats on the Armed Services, Homeland Security, and Veterans' Affairs committees, and his maiden speech, in February, was in support of the nomination of Attorney General Eric Holder.

Two weeks after Burris was sworn in, the Illinois Senate voted 59-0 to remove Blagojevich from office, and Quinn became governor. On February 5, Burris filed an affidavit with the House impeachment committee in which he admitted to discussing a possible Senate appointment with three Blagojevich aides at different times, and saying that the governor's brother had asked him to raise money for Blagojevich's re-election—something Burris said he refused to do. On February 16, while making a statewide "goodwill tour," Burris said he had asked about the appointment while raising money for Blagojevich.

After Burris's seemingly contradictory statements, Illinois's Democratic Attorney General Lisa Madigan asked for further investigation and the *Chicago Tribune* called on Burris to resign. On February 24, Durbin called Burris into his office and suggested he consider resigning. The same day, presidential spokesman Robert Gibbs said, "Senator Burris needs to take some time and think about whether he can actually help this country, whether he can serve the constituents of Illinois." Quinn gave Burris an ultimatum: Resign in two weeks, or the Legislature would pass a law requiring a special election to fill the seat. Some African-American leaders felt Quinn had gone too far, and the next day, February 29, Quinn said he feared the return of the racial tensions that sparked Chicago's bitterly divisive "Council Wars" in the 1980s. State Senate Democrats rejected the call for a special election. Meanwhile, Burris set up a legal defense fund and hunkered down to try to hang on to his Senate seat. But he struggled to raise money and several prominent state Democrats were preparing to challenge him if he ran for the seat in 2010. Finally, on July 10, 2009, Burris announced he would not run. His exit improved the Democratic Party's chances of holding on to the Senate seat.

FIRST DISTRICT

Bobby Rush (D)

Elected 1992, 9th term; b. Nov. 23, 1946, Albany, GA; home, Chicago; Roosevelt U., B.A. 1973, U. of IL, M.A. 1994, McCormick Seminary, M.A. 1998; Baptist; married (Carolyn); 6 children (1 deceased).

Military Career: Army, 1963–68.

Elected Office: Chicago city alderman, 1983–92; 2nd ward committeeman, 1984–present.

Professional Career: Member, Student Non–Violent Coord. Cmte., 1966–68; Co–founder, IL Black Panther Party, 1968; Med. clinic dir., 1970–1973; Insurance agent, 1978–83.

DC Office: 2416 RHOB, 20515, 202-225-4372; Fax: 202-226-0333; Web site: www.house.gov/rush.

State Offices: Chicago, 773-224-6500; Midlothian, 708-385-9550.

Committees: *Energy & Commerce* (7th of 36 D): Commerce, Trade & Consumer Protection (Chmn); Communications, Technology & the Internet.

Group Ratings

	ADA	ACLU	AFS	LCV	ITIC	NTU	COC	ACU	CFG	FRC
2008	30	100	100	31	86	20	67	13	0	5
2007	100	—	100	85	—	4	60	0	6	—

National Journal Ratings

	2007 LIB	—	2007 CONS		2008 LIB	—	2008 CONS
Economic	73%	—	24%		*%	—	*%
Social	92%	—	0%		*%	—	*%
Foreign	78%	—	22%		*%	—	*%
Composite	83%	—	17%		*%	—	*%

Key Votes of the 110th Congress

1. Increase minimum wage	Y	5. Share immigration data	N	9. Withdraw troops 8/08	Y
2. Expand SCHIP	Y	6. Foreign aid abortion ban	N	10. No operations in Iran	Y
3. Raise CAFE standards	Y	7. Ban gay bias in workplace	Y	11. Free trade with Peru	N
4. Bail out financial markets	Y	8. Repeal D.C. gun law	N	12. Overhaul FISA	*

Election Results

2008 general	Bobby Rush (D)	233,036	(86%)	($435,961)
	Antoine Members (R)	38,361	(14%)	($422,267)
2008 primary	Bobby Rush (D)	134,343	(87%)	
	William Walls (D)	19,272	(13%)	

Prior Winning Percentages: 2006 (84%); 2004 (85%); 2002 (81%); 2000 (88%); 1998 (87%); 1996 (86%); 1994 (76%); 1992 (83%)

Population		Race/Ethnicity		Work	
Pop. 2007:	637,395	White:	26.0%	Private:	78.3%
Change since 2000:	Down 2.5%	Black:	63.7%	Government:	17.8%
Urban:	100.0%	Hispanic:	7.8%	Self-employed:	3.7%
Rural:	0.0%	Asian:	1.4%	Blue collar:	21.0%
Area size:	99 sq. mi.	Native Am.:	0.1%	White collar:	58.8%
		Hawaiian:	0.0%	Khaki collar:	0.0%
Age		Two+ races:	0.9%	Other:	20.2%
Median age:	35.6 yrs.			Median income:	$41,034
More than 65 yrs:	12.9%	*Ancestry*		Median home value:	$187,900
Less than 18 yrs:	26.6%	Irish:	7.2%	Poverty:	22.5%
		German:	6.3%		
Education		Polish:	4.8%	**Military Veterans**	
H.S. grad:	81.6%			% of Pop:	8.4%
College grad:	20.7%				
Grad degree:	8.2%				

The South Side of Chicago has been the nation's largest urban black community for nearly a century. A hundred years ago, there were just a few blocks where black families from the South could settle. But the ghetto grew rapidly with the first influx of blacks from the Mississippi Delta in the 1910s. By the 1920s, the South Side was well established, a center of black-owned businesses and of music, from blues to jazz. Politically, the South Side was a heavily Republican constituency throughout

2008 Presidential Vote

Obama (D)	251,102	(87%)
McCain (R)	37,472	(13%)

2004 Presidential Vote

Kerry (D)	234,086	(83%)
Bush (R)	47,533	(17%)

Cook Partisan Voting Index: D + 34

those years. The comfortable white Protestants who settled in solid brick houses here believed in the party of Yankee propriety, while the blacks had faith in the party of Lincoln. This was a Republican Party heartland, represented in the House in the 1920s by Appropriations Chairman Martin Madden. After Madden died in the Appropriations Committee room in 1928, the 1st District elected Republican Oscar DePriest, the first African-American elected to the House in the 20th century. Blacks remained faithful to the party of Lincoln even during the Depression, voting for Herbert Hoover and DePriest in 1932.

The New Deal and the racial liberalism of New Dealers like Eleanor Roosevelt and Interior Secretary Harold Ickes, both former Republicans themselves, attracted blacks to the Democratic Party, and black Democrat Arthur Mitchell beat DePriest in 1934. The South Side has been Democratic ever since. For 40 years, it was a cooperative part of Chicago's Democratic machine. Then, after the death of longtime Rep. William Dawson, it rebelled against Mayor Richard J. Daley. The South Side seemed to take over the city when Rep. Harold Washington was elected mayor in 1983 and 1987. After he died in November 1987, other black South Side politicians were bogged down by infighting, though Chicago's black electorate peaked at about 40% black.

The 1st Congressional District of Illinois includes about half of Chicago's African-American community on the South Side, plus many suburbs beyond the city boundaries. The 1st has a northern salient that includes some of Chicago's first black neighborhoods as well as the Gothic spires of the University of Chicago and the mansions of Kenwood, once the home of Chicago's Jewish aristocracy and more recently the headquarters of the Nation of Islam and home of its leader Louis Farrakhan. Bronzeville, once a destination point for thousands of black families from the South, lately has become popular with upscale professionals of diverse backgrounds, who reside in condos and townhouses. The Illinois Institute of Technology has attracted dozens of high-tech growth companies by building a research institute and business center. The district includes most of the South Side, from Stony Island west almost to the city limit and from 60th Street to 95th—miles and miles of bungalow neighborhoods, where single-family houses line arrow-straight streets. For 20 years, Barack Obama attended church at Trinity United

Church of Christ, where the pastor was Jeremiah Wright. Wright's racially inflamed remarks later became controversial during Obama's quest for the White House.

In neighborhoods such as Englewood, once the city's second busiest shopping district before losing half of its population after 1970, thousands of private residential homes have been built with federal support in recent years in hopes of creating a new black middle-class community; some have been placed on vacant land or in abandoned buildings that had housed gangs. In 2007, an entrepreneurial business professor at Northwestern University told the *Chicago Tribune* that Englewood "is about to be revitalized" and gentrified—spurred partly by the new Kennedy-King College, a campus of the City Colleges of Chicago. A narrow neck of urban geography connects the city part of the 1st with a still mostly white collection of suburbs, starting with Blue Island and fanning southwest to Palos Heights, Orland Park, and Oak Forest. The district is overwhelmingly Democratic. Just 17% of people here voted for George W. Bush in 2004. Obama beat McCain in 2008 87% to 13%.

The congressman from the 1st District is Bobby Rush, a man who has gone through several transformations. He grew up on the North Side, a Boy Scout whose mother was a Republican precinct captain. While in the Army, he became involved in the Student Non-Violent Coordinating Committee in the South, then became disillusioned with the military and went AWOL in 1968. That year, he founded the Illinois Black Panthers, with its "Power to the People" slogan, and recruited Fred Hampton, who became chairman of the organization but was later killed by police in a 1969 raid. The next day, police raided Rush's family's apartment, but he wasn't there. Rush served six months in prison for illegal possession of firearms, but also during his time with the Black Panthers, he ran a program providing free breakfasts to children and a medical clinic that developed the nation's first mass sickle-cell-anemia testing program. "I don't repudiate any of my involvement in the Panther party—it was part of my maturing," Rush later said. Lately, he has commemorated the anniversary of the raid by holding a job fair to promote the future. In 1983 he was elected the 2nd Ward alderman on the Chicago City Council and became a strong supporter of Harold Washington, who became mayor. As he built a career in politics, Rush went back to school and earned masters' degrees in political science and theological studies. In 1992, he challenged Democratic Rep. Charles Hayes, an older-generation politician with a union background. Just before the primary, it was revealed that Hayes had 716 overdrafts on the House bank, a practice among lawmakers that blossomed into a national scandal. Rush won 42%-39%.

In the House, Rush has a liberal voting record. His rhetoric has toned down over the years, and his more deliberate style contrasts sharply with his days as a Panther. Gun violence caused great pain to Rush in 1999, when his son Huey Rich, who was born three weeks before the 1969 police raid, was murdered by a man wielding a handgun as he returned to his South Side home with his fiancée. Ordained as a Baptist minister, Rush founded a church in 2002 in the depressed Englewood community, but it struggled financially. Legislatively, he has focused on children's health and the nursing shortage.

In recent years, he has devoted much of his time to the Energy and Commerce Committee, where he is chairman of the Commerce, Trade and Consumer Protection Subcommittee. He has held hearings on dangerous children's toys and betting by a referee in the National Basketball Association. (He was unhappy when Oversight and Government Reform Chairman Henry Waxman of California pre-empted him in 2008 on the issue of steroid use in baseball.) Rush was absent from Capitol Hill during much of 2008, however, after doctors diagnosed a form of salivary cancer and removed a tumor near his jaw. Following surgery and treatment, doctors in August ruled him cancer free.

Rush waged a quixotic mayoral campaign in 1999 against Richard M. Daley, the second Daley to develop an iron grip on the mayor's office. Rush has been a frequent Daley critic, and during the campaign, he attacked the mayor for tolerating police brutality, inadequate mass-transit service and cronyism in city government. Two of his Democratic House colleagues, Jesse Jackson Jr. and Danny Davis, sided with Rush, but only 3 of the 50 aldermen endorsed him. Rush tried to build a multiracial coalition, but for practical purposes, his only chance was with black voters. Daley was popular, and his financial advantage overwhelming. The incumbent won the primary 72%-28%, with nearly 45% of the African-American vote and the support of many prominent black ministers. After that pounding, Rush found himself challenged in his own re-election primary in 2000 by two state senators—Donne Trotter and the then little-known Barack Obama. Obama waged an active campaign, but was attacked for being absent from the Legislature for two months and missing a vote on a gun-control bill. He was on a family trip to Hawaii that was extended after his daughter got sick, he said. (South Side voters may have had little sympathy for a candidate who escaped a Chicago January for Hawaii's sunny climate, even if Obama happened to have been raised in the sunny island state.) "It was a race in which everything that could go wrong did go wrong," Obama later wrote in his book *Audacity of Hope*. Rush was also helped by an endorsement from President Clinton and beat Obama 61%-30%. Surely not by coincidence, redistricting in 2002 shifted Obama's Hyde Park home two blocks outside the new lines and removed the 19th Ward that he had carried. Rush has been routinely re-elected since then.

In the 2004 Senate primary, Rush supported Blair Hull, who finished third, but after the primary, endorsed Obama. During Obama's pitched primary fight with Hillary Rodham Clinton, Rush endorsed Obama, calling it "one of the most difficult decisions I've had to make in politics," Rush endorsed Obama for president, though he criticized Obama for failing to address big issues, including national health care.

He gained national prominence when he joined the December 2008 press conference at which Gov. Rod Blagojevich announced his selection of Roland Burris to fill President-elect Obama's vacant Senate seat. Rush cited the importance of having an African-American serve in the Senate. "I would ask you to not hang or lynch the appointee as you try to castigate the appointer," he said, referring to the scandal surrounding Blagojevich's alleged attempts to profit personally and politically from the appointment of Obama's successor.

SECOND DISTRICT

Jesse Jackson Jr. (D)

Elected Dec. 1995, 7th full term; b. March 11, 1965, Greenville, SC; home, Chicago; NC A&T, B.S. 1987, Chicago Theological Seminary, M.A. 1990, U. of IL, J.D. 1993; Baptist; married (Sandi); 2 children.

Professional Career: Civil rights activist; Pres., Keep Hope Alive PAC, 1989–90; V.P., Operation PUSH, 1991–95; Field dir., Natl. Rainbow Coalition, 1993–95.

DC Office: 2419 RHOB, 20515, 202-225-0773; Fax: 202-225-0899; Web site: www.house.gov/jackson.

State Offices: Chicago, 773-734-9660; Homewood, 708-798-6000.

Committees: *Appropriations* (19th of 37 D): Agriculture, Rural Development, FDA & Related Agencies; Labor, HHS, Education & Related Agencies; State, Foreign Operations & Related Programs.

Group Ratings

	ADA	ACLU	AFS	LCV	ITIC	NTU	COC	ACU	CFG	FRC
2008	100	100	100	92	86	12	61	4	0	0
2007	100	—	100	95	—	5	50	0	1	—

National Journal Ratings

	2007 LIB	—	2007 CONS		2008 LIB	—	2008 CONS
Economic	82%	—	0%		85%	—	0%
Social	85%	—	13%		82%	—	0%
Foreign	90%	—	8%		85%	—	8%
Composite	89%	—	11%		91%	—	9%

Key Votes of the 110th Congress

1. Increase minimum wage	Y	5. Share immigration data	N	9. Withdraw troops 8/08	Y
2. Expand SCHIP	Y	6. Foreign aid abortion ban	N	10. No operations in Iran	Y
3. Raise CAFE standards	Y	7. Ban gay bias in workplace	Y	11. Free trade with Peru	N
4. Bail out financial markets	Y	8. Repeal D.C. gun law	N	12. Overhaul FISA	N

Election Results

2008 general	Jesse Jackson Jr. (D)	251,052	(89%)	($1,673,968)
	Anthony Williams (R)	29,721	(11%)	
2008 primary	Jesse Jackson Jr. (D)	unopposed		

Prior Winning Percentages: 2006 (85%); 2004 (88%); 2002 (82%); 2000 (90%); 1998 (89%); 1996 (94%); 1995 (76%)

Population		Race/Ethnicity		Work	
Pop. 2007:	650,595	White:	18.5%	Private:	78.1%
Change since 2000:	Down 0.5%	Black:	67.4%	Government:	18.2%
Urban:	99.9%	Hispanic:	12.2%	Self-employed:	3.5%
Rural:	0.1%	Asian:	0.6%	Blue collar:	23.2%
Area size:	192 sq. mi.	Native Am.:	0.1%	White collar:	58.1%
Age		Hawaiian:	0.0%	Khaki collar:	0.0%
Median age:	34.9 yrs.	Two+ races:	1.0%	Other:	18.7%
More than 65 yrs:	12.2%	*Ancestry*		Median income:	$44,914
Less than 18 yrs:	29.2%	German:	5.0%	Median home value:	$144,400
Education		Irish:	3.9%	Poverty:	18.9%
H.S. grad:	83.4%	Polish:	3.5%	**Military Veterans**	
College grad:	20.5%			% of Pop:	9.7%
Grad degree:	7.1%				

Chicago is a great center of both commerce and industry, and if its white-collar offices are heavily concentrated in the Loop, its blue-collar heavy industries are most visible on the far South Side. This part of Chicago, diminished in economic importance today, is historically significant and, with the remnants of its great hulking factories around Lake Calumet and the nearby rail yards, has a certain undeniable majesty. Thomas Geoghegan wrote in his book *Which Side Are You On?* of the fights to win

2008 Presidential Vote		
Obama (D)	262,750	(90%)
McCain (R)	28,748	(10%)
2004 Presidential Vote		
Kerry (D)	230,613	(84%)
Bush (R)	43,822	(16%)
Cook Partisan Voting Index:	D+36	

benefits for the workers of shuttered steel mills and of the decline of the labor movement in a place where it got much of its inspiration. This is where the Pullman strike of 1894 was broken by federal troops and where policemen killed 10 union supporters in the Little Steel strike of 1937. Over the years, Chicago grew around the tight ethnic neighborhoods where workers went home at shift break each afternoon or midnight. Today, those workplaces are mostly empty buildings that suburbanites speed past on the Calumet and Dan Ryan expressways. A local historic preservation group has listed the Hulett Iron Ore Unloaders, built in 1912 and resembling a giant preying mantis, as endangered structures.

The 2nd Congressional District of Illinois includes much of Chicago's old South Side industrial area, U.S. Cellular Field, the new home of the White Sox baseball team near the site of the old Comiskey Park, and several Cook County suburbs to the south. The district reaches north to include Jackson Park, where the Columbian Exposition of 1893 was held, and south to take in South Shore, a once heavily Jewish neighborhood and now home to middle-class blacks. The district includes all of Chicago south of 95th Street and east of Interstate 57, including the old industrial area around Lake Calumet. The Chicago portion of the 2nd is overwhelmingly black, though many African-Americans, especially young parents fleeing Chicago public schools, are moving into suburbs directly to the south—Harvey, Dolton, Markham, Hazel Crest, and Lynwood. Farther south are economically revitalized Homewood and Flossmoor, with significant Jewish populations; high-income Olympia Fields; and the still vibrant Park Forest, the post World War planned town where William H. Whyte's *The Organization Man* was set. Also in the district are mixed-income Chicago Heights, the hometown of David Broder, one of the country's premier political reporters for a half century. In the south end of the district is struggling Ford Heights, the nation's leader in single mothers per capita, the vast majority of whom live in public housing. The 2nd District now has more people in the suburbs than in Chicago. Only 40% of the 2008 vote was cast in Chicago precincts. The district remains one of the most Democratic in the nation.

The congressman from the 2nd District is Jesse Jackson Jr., a Democrat first elected at age 30 in 1995 and the son of civil rights leader Jesse Jackson, who ran for president in 1984 and 1988. Jesse Jackson Jr. was born in Greenville, S.C., while his father was marching to Selma. But he spent much of his early life in Washington, D.C., and attended the prestigious St. Albans School. He went to North Carolina A&T, his father's alma mater, earned a master's degree at Chicago Theological Seminary and a law degree at the University of Illinois. He spent his 21st birthday in a Washington, D.C., jail for protesting apartheid at the South African embassy. Jackson worked for his father's Rainbow Coalition and did not run for office until Democratic Rep. Mel Reynolds was driven from office for having sexual relations with a teenage campaign worker. In a 1995 special election, Jackson had serious competition from Democrat Emil Jones, then a state legislator for 23 years and later the state Senate President, who had the support of Mayor Richard M. Daley. Jones emphasized his clout and political experience. Jackson said being his father's son was a lifetime of political experience. He talked of bringing dollars to the South Side and, quoting longtime Illinois Democratic Rep. Dan Rostenkowski, said, "The only way one grows into leadership in Congress is to get elected young enough that you become speaker of the House or chairman of the Ways and Means Committee." Jackson won the primary 46%-37% and easily won the special election in December.

In the House, Jackson has combined liberal advocacy with careful attention to the interests of his constituents and to the steady advancement of his own influence. In 2001, he helped to create the National Center on Minority Health and Health Disparities at the National Institutes of Health. In recent years, he has sponsored few legislative bills, but nine constitutional amendments creating new rights, such as a right to "health care of equal high quality," to "decent, safe, sanitary and affordable housing" and to "full employment and balanced economic growth." He plans to keep introducing his amendments "as long as I am alive and in Congress," he says. None have passed and are unlikely to, even with Democrats in control of Congress. Topping Jackson's list of parochial projects is a long-standing proposal for a third Chicago-area airport in Peotone, 45 miles south of the Loop and just south of the district. The fight pitted him against fellow Democrats, including Daley, whose No. 1 priority has been expansion of O'Hare Airport. Jackson's allies have included Republicans from the northern suburbs who are worried about an increase in noise levels in neighborhoods around O'Hare.

Jackson has had a seat on the powerful Appropriations Committee for nearly a decade and is well positioned to move up to a subcommittee chairmanship. Except for Democratic Rep. Patrick Kennedy of Rhode Island, every committee chairmen with more seniority than Jackson is at least 13 years older.

After years of flirting with a race for mayor of Chicago, he seems content to remain in the House. In 2005, his increasingly sharp criticism of Mayor Richard M. Daley led to speculation that he would mount a challenge in the February 2007 Democratic primary. In September 2006, Jackson said, "It's more likely than not" that he would challenge Daley. But after Democrats took control of the House that year, he decided to stay where he was. Jackson has been careful not to exploit his high degree of name recognition, and, as an early and enthusiastic supporter of Barack Obama for president, he criticized as "reckless" his father's off-color gibes at Obama. The movement of middle-class blacks to the far suburbs continues to diminish his core constituency, but Jackson's connection to the city's politics is still strong. In 2007, his wife Sandi, a deputy political director of the Democratic National Committee, was elected alderman of Chicago's 7th Ward.

After Obama's election in 2008, Jackson was briefly caught up in the behind-the-scenes campaign for Obama's open Senate seat that led to the downfall of Illinois Gov. Rod Blagojevich, who was charged with trying to profit personally and politically from his power to appoint a successor. Jackson was "Senate Candidate Five" in the transcripts of prosecutors' wiretapped conversations, in which fundraising for Blagojevich was discussed. In comments aimed at persuading the public to "give me my name back" Jackson said: "I did not initiate or authorize anyone at any time to promise anything to Governor Blagojevich on my behalf.... I thought, mistakenly, that the process was fair, aboveboard, and on the merits. I thought, mistakenly, that the governor was evaluating me and other Senate hopefuls based upon our credentials and qualifications."

Before the scandal broke, the *Chicago Sun-Times* endorsed Jackson as "a thoughtful, committed legislator" for the seat. But Senate Majority Leader Harry Reid quietly opposed his selection, reportedly because he did not believe Jackson could win a statewide election.

THIRD DISTRICT

Daniel Lipinski (D)

Elected 2004, 3rd term; b. July 15, 1966, Chicago; home, Western Springs; Northwestern U., B.S. 1988, Stanford U., M.A. 1989, Duke U., Ph.D. 1998; Catholic; married (Judy).

Professional Career: Asst. professor, U. of TN, 2001–04.

DC Office: 1717 LHOB, 20515, 202-225-5701; Fax: 202-225-1012; Web site: lipinski.house.gov.

State Offices: Chicago, 312-886-0481; LaGrange, 708-352-0524; Oak Lawn, 708-424-0853.

Committees: *Science & Technology* (8th of 26 D): Energy & Environment; Research & Science Education (Chmn); Technology & Innovation. *Small Business* (10th of 17 D): Regulations & Healthcare. *Transportation & Infrastructure* (21st of 44 D): Aviation; Highways & Transit; Railroads, Pipelines & Hazardous Materials.

Group Ratings

	ADA	ACLU	AFS	LCV	ITIC	NTU	COC	ACU	CFG	FRC
2008	90	82	100	100	43	17	59	8	12	58
2007	85	—	100	90	—	6	55	20	1	—

National Journal Ratings

	2007 LIB	—	2007 CONS		2008 LIB	—	2008 CONS
Economic	60%	—	40%		71%	—	25%
Social	52%	—	48%		75%	—	18%
Foreign	52%	—	48%		55%	—	43%
Composite	55%	—	45%		69%	—	31%

Key Votes of the 110th Congress

1. Increase minimum wage	Y	5. Share immigration data	Y	9. Withdraw troops 8/08	Y
2. Expand SCHIP	Y	6. Foreign aid abortion ban	Y	10. No operations in Iran	Y
3. Raise CAFE standards	Y	7. Ban gay bias in workplace	N	11. Free trade with Peru	N
4. Bail out financial markets	N	8. Repeal D.C. gun law	N	12. Overhaul FISA	Y

Election Results

2008 general	Daniel Lipinski (D)	172,581	(73%)	($553,030)
	Michael Hawkins (R)	50,336	(21%)	
	Jerome Pohlen (Green)	12,607	(5%)	($6,960)
2008 primary	Daniel Lipinski (D)	62,439	(54%)	
	Mark Pera (D)	29,544	(25%)	
	Jim Capparelli (D)	13,312	(11%)	
	Jerry Bennett (D)	10,742	(9%)	

Prior Winning Percentages: 2006 (77%); 2004 (73%)

Population		Race/Ethnicity		Work	
Pop. 2007:	657,526	White:	59.6%	Private:	81.7%
Change since 2000:	Up 0.6%	Black:	6.3%	Government:	13.8%
Urban:	100.0%	Hispanic:	29.6%	Self-employed:	4.3%
Rural:	0.0%	Asian:	3.5%	Blue collar:	27.4%
Area size:	126 sq. mi.	Native Am.:	0.1%	White collar:	55.1%
		Hawaiian:	0.0%	Khaki collar:	0.0%
Age		Two+ races:	0.7%	Other:	17.5%
Median age:	36.7 yrs.			Median income:	$54,140
More than 65 yrs:	12.9%	*Ancestry*		Median home value:	$243,400
Less than 18 yrs:	25.9%	Irish:	13.5%	Poverty:	10.2%
		Polish:	13.2%		
Education		German:	10.8%	**Military Veterans**	
H.S. grad:	80.5%			% of Pop:	7.9%
College grad:	22.3%				
Grad degree:	8.0%				

A century ago, humorist Finley Peter Dunne's fictional Mr. Dooley pontificated on matters political in a saloon on Archery Road. This was Archer Avenue on the South Side of Chicago, one of the radial streets that cut across what was once open prairie near the Loop and along the Chicago River. Archer Avenue was one of the paths of outward migration and upward mobility for the children and grandchildren of Chicago's ethnic and cultural groups, and still is. Even today, in Archer Heights, you can

2008 Presidential Vote

Obama (D)	158,161	(64%)
McCain (R)	86,406	(35%)

2004 Presidential Vote

Kerry (D)	144,657	(59%)
Bush (R)	100,257	(41%)

Cook Partisan Voting Index: D+11

scarcely go a block without hearing someone speaking Polish. Italians from the river wards along the Chicago and Sanitary Ship Canal moved west, the South Side Irish moved west and south along Cicero Avenue toward Oak Lawn, the Bohemians (as they were called then; now Czechs) were heavily concentrated in the neat bungalows of industrial suburbs like Berwyn. Today, Latinos are driving these same avenues, up before dawn to arrive at factory jobs, or taking CTA "El" trains to the Loop or to "edge city" jobs out the expressways. Midway Airport, Chicago's main airport from 1927 until O'Hare Airport opened in 1955, is now a discount-airline hub. It has been renovating and expanding its congested terminals and parking lots, all squeezed into the heart of a busy commercial area on the southwest side.

The 3rd Congressional District of Illinois consists of much of this territory, crisscrossed by grid-pattern streets, the canal, the railroad lines and the switching yards so common in this, the center of the nation's rail network. It is part of Chicago's bungalow belt, with one after another of the ubiquitous peaked brick houses neatly lining every street like Monopoly pieces, the handiwork of Swedish, Italian and Polish masons. The 3rd also includes the far southwest edge of Chicago, most of the suburbs of Berwyn and Riverside, with its early-20th-century prairie-style houses, and a few older affluent suburbs like Western Springs and the more recent and middle-income expanses of Oak Lawn and Palos Hills. In the Archer Avenue city neighborhoods, Poles cling to their heritage, with more than 20 weekend schools teaching Polish to local kids and adults. A narrow corridor extends to the famed Bridgeport neighborhood, the lifetime home of the late Mayor Richard J. Daley, father of the current Mayor Richard M. Daley, and the storied Irish stronghold that produced four other Chicago mayors. In recent years, Bridgeport has diversified, as Hispanics and Asians have moved in. But it still attracts few African-American families, who are perhaps wary of Bridgeport's history of racial hostility and violence. The district's overall Hispanic population increased to 30% in 2007, making it the second largest in the state. Politically, this has been marginal territory: ancestrally Democratic, culturally conservative, multiethnic and viscerally patriotic. Of the seven congressional districts that include parts of Chicago, the 3rd has cast the highest percentages for Republican presidential candidates, though the GOP vote has fallen well short of a majority.

The congressman from the 3rd District is Dan Lipinski, elected in 2004 and the son of Rep. Bill Lipinski, who represented the district for 22 years. Dan Lipinski grew up in Chicago, in the city's 23rd Ward, and first served as a campaign volunteer for his father in 1979. He got engineering degrees from Northwestern and Stanford universities, before switching to political science with his doctorate at Duke. He worked on the staffs of four House Democrats from Illinois, though not on his father's, and was an American Political Science Association congressional fellow for the House Democratic Policy Committee. He wrote his doctoral thesis on the topic of congressional newsletters (*Congressional Communication*, published by the University of Michigan Press). At the beginning of 2004, he was an assistant professor of political science at the University of Tennessee in Knoxville.

The process behind Lipinski's nomination to run for his father's seat is a case study in Chicago's still thriving backroom politics. In the summer of 2004, Bill Lipinski denied widespread rumors that he was going to give up his seat. Then on August 13, he abruptly announced he would not seek re-election in November because "I want to come back to Chicago and spend more time with my wife." (Not *that* much time as it turns out, because he later became a transportation lobbyist.) His announcement came just 13 days before the August 26 deadline to replace a withdrawing candidate. A meeting was scheduled for August 17 for the 19 ward and township Democratic committeemen in the 3rd District. The group was to choose the new nominee by weighted vote and consisted of a *Who's Who* of connected Chicago politicians and their family members: John Daley, the 11th Ward committeeman and brother of the current mayor, Richard M. Daley; Michael Madigan, the 13th Ward committeeman and speaker of the Illinois House; Edward Burke, the 14th Ward committeeman and husband of an Illinois Appeals Court judge; Tom Hynes, the 19th Ward committeeman and father of Illinois Comptroller Dan Hynes; and finally, apparently not feeling the need for a pretense of objectivity, there was Bill Lipinski, the 23rd Ward Committeeman. At the meeting, Lipinski offered for consideration the name of the most qualified person he could think of, his son, Dan, and shortly afterward, Dan Lipinski was nominated without opposition.

The nominee was not briefed quite as well by the political heavyweights in the room as he perhaps should have been. At his first press conference, Lipinski, who had not lived in Illinois for 15 years, made the politically unconscionable assertion that he had for many years been a fan of the Chicago Cubs, Chicago's North Side baseball team. The White Sox is the hands-down favorite team of the 3rd District's South Side neighborhoods and suburbs. A state lawmaker at the back of the room signaled Lipinski to wrap up his remarks before further damage could be done. Luckily for Lipinski, a Democratic nomination, even one decided by a group of old political pals getting together in a room, is tantamount to election in the 3rd District, and he sailed to victory in November. The Republican nominee was Ryan Chlada, a 26-year-old college dropout and bar owner who won the GOP nomination unopposed. He was a political ally of former suburban Cicero Mayor Betty Loren-Maltese, who was serving prison time for racketeering. Chlada avoided publicity, had no website, and filed no reports with the Federal Election Commission, which is legal if a candidate does not raise or spend much money. Lipinski won, 73%-25%.

In the House, Dan Lipinski has kept his pledge to be "not really that different from my father," which was the most conservative Democrat in the Illinois delegation. He opposes same-sex marriage and abortion rights except when the mother's life is at stake. Also like his father, he has focused on local transportation projects, especially helping Midway Airport, which generates more jobs than any other employer in the district, and on improving Chicago's rail infrastructure. In his second term, Lipinski won a seat on the Transportation and Infrastructure Committee. In 2007, he played a key role on two pieces of that year's massive energy bill: cash incentives for progress toward hydrogen-based energy, and a mandate requiring high-efficiency lightbulbs in federal buildings.

Lipinski has drawn primary opposition in both of his re-election bids, and even though he easily survived, it's a sign that he has not locked up this district. In 2006, an observant John Sullivan, an assistant Cook County state's attorney, said that Lipinski got his seat in "a backroom deal" and often had voted in Chicago while living out of state. Financial planner John Kelly used "no tricks, no fix" as a campaign slogan. Lipinski won, 54% to 26% for Kelly and 20% for Sullivan. In the 2008 primary, Lipinski faced Cook County Assistant State's Attorney Mark Pera, an abortion-rights supporter who criticized Lipinski's support for the war in Iraq and questioned his campaign payments to his father for consulting work. And Democratic Rep. Luis Gutierrez, of Illinois' neighboring 4th District, withdrew his endorsement of Lipinski because Lipinski had opposed establishing a path to citizenship for illegal immigrants. Several liberal interest groups, local reformers, and others contributed to Pera, who raised and spent $770,000. But Lipinski prevailed, 54%-25%. Despite the candidacy of favorite-son Barack Obama in the presidential contest that year, Lipinski remained neutral in the Illinois primary.

FOURTH DISTRICT

Luis Gutierrez (D)

Elected 1992, 9th term; b. Dec. 10, 1953, Chicago; home, Chicago; NE IL U., B.A. 1975; Catholic; married (Soraida); 2 children.

Elected Office: Chicago city alderman, 1986–92, Pres. pro tem, 1989–92.

Professional Career: Teacher, Puerto Rico, 1977–78; Social wkr., Chicago Dept. of Children & Family Svcs., 1979–83; Advisor, Chicago Mayor Harold Washington, 1984–86.

DC Office: 2266 RHOB, 20515, 202-225-8203; Fax: 202-225-7810; Web site: luisgutierrez.house.gov.

State Offices: Chicago, 312-342-0774.

Committees: *Financial Services* (5th of 42 D): Financial Institutions & Consumer Credit (Chmn); Housing & Community Opportunity; International Monetary Policy & Trade. *Judiciary* (16th of 24 D): Immigration, Citizenship, Refugees, Border Security & International Law.

Group Ratings

	ADA	ACLU	AFS	LCV	ITIC	NTU	COC	ACU	CFG	FRC
2008	90	91	100	85	86	6	56	0	0	5
2007	100	—	100	80	—	3	44	0	6	—

National Journal Ratings

	2007 LIB — 2007 CONS		2008 LIB — 2008 CONS	
Economic	82% —	0%	85% —	0%
Social	92% —	0%	72% —	26%
Foreign	81% —	19%	69% —	30%
Composite	89% —	11%	78% —	22%

Key Votes of the 110th Congress

1. Increase minimum wage	Y	5. Share immigration data	*	9. Withdraw troops 8/08	Y
2. Expand SCHIP	Y	6. Foreign aid abortion ban	N	10. No operations in Iran	Y
3. Raise CAFE standards	*	7. Ban gay bias in workplace	Y	11. Free trade with Peru	N
4. Bail out financial markets	Y	8. Repeal D.C. gun law	N	12. Overhaul FISA	Y

Election Results

2008 general	Luis Gutierrez (D)	112,529	(81%)	($188,438)
	Daniel Cunningham (R)	16,024	(11%)	
	Omar Lopez (Green)	11,053	(8%)	
2008 primary	Luis Gutierrez (D)	unopposed	

Prior Winning Percentages: 2006 (86%); 2004 (84%); 2002 (80%); 2000 (89%); 1998 (82%); 1996 (94%); 1994 (75%); 1992 (78%)

Population		Race/Ethnicity		Work	
Pop. 2007:	615,311	White:	17.6%	Private:	88.6%
Change since 2000:	Down 5.9%	Black:	5.0%	Government:	7.0%
Urban:	100.0%	Hispanic:	73.8%	Self-employed:	4.3%
Rural:	0.0%	Asian:	2.5%	Blue collar:	36.3%
Area size:	39 sq. mi.	Native Am.:	0.2%	White collar:	42.9%
		Hawaiian:	0.0%	Khaki collar:	0.0%
Age		Two+ races:	0.6%	Other:	20.8%
Median age:	29.4 yrs.			Median income:	$40,471
More than 65 yrs:	6.0%	*Ancestry*		Median home value:	$290,500
Less than 18 yrs:	29.8%	Polish:	4.1%	Poverty:	21.9%
		German:	3.8%		
Education		Irish:	3.3%	**Military Veterans**	
H.S. grad:	60.9%			% of Pop:	2.9%
College grad:	18.4%				
Grad degree:	6.0%				

Just west of the Loop, the Chicago River splits into North and South Branches, both penetrating the heart of old neighborhoods where immigrants got their start. The South Branch is the guts of Chicago, the site of one of Western civilization's astonishing engineering feats. In 1900, the course of the river was reversed so that sewage flowed downstate through a canal rather than out into Lake Michigan. Just blocks away was Maxwell Street, then thronged with market stalls and long the arrival

2008 Presidential Vote		
Obama (D) 126,399	(85%)
McCain (R)..............................19,777	(13%)
2004 Presidential Vote		
Kerry (D)...............................105,419	(79%)
Bush (R) 27,684	(21%)
Cook Partisan Voting Index:	D + 32	

point for Chicago-bound Jews. Not far away, in an Italian-American neighborhood on Halsted Street, was Jane Addams's Hull House, the original settlement house, where social workers instructed new immigrants on adapting to American life. To the south were Pilsen, arrival neighborhood for the Bohemians (Czechs), and the Irish neighborhoods along Archer Avenue. To the north was Milwaukee Avenue, the main street of Polish-Americans and Ukrainian-Americans.

Today, many of these places are arrival neighborhoods again, mostly for Chicago's wide variety of Hispanic immigrants. On the South Side, in the old river wards, is Chicago's Mexican-American community, extending west into Pilsen and into the once Bohemian suburb of Cicero, famous as a haven for Al Capone's mobsters in the 1920s. This is the largest community of Mexican-Americans in the nation outside California. On the gentrifying North Side are many Puerto Ricans and other Hispanics. In the 1990s, Chicago's Hispanic population increased from 545,000 to 754,000, by far the largest Latino concentration north of Texas and Florida and between the two coasts and not all that many fewer than the 1.1 million African-Americans in Chicago. By 2005, the city population was almost 30% Hispanic. Spanish-language radio stations have become a local political force.

The 4th Congressional District of Illinois is a Hispanic-majority district created in 1992. With the South Side Mexican-American areas and the smaller North Side Puerto Rican communities separated by the West Side black ghetto, the solution was the creation of one of the most bizarrely shaped congressional districts in the country. Essentially these two Latino communities, defined by careful boundaries to maximize the Hispanic percentage, are connected by a thin line of territory stretching around the black-majority 7th District to meet at the Cook-DuPage County line. The district is sandwiched between the 5th District to the north and the 3rd District to the south. It is shaped something like a pair of earmuffs. More than 95% of the votes are in Chicago or Cicero. The 2001 redistricting raised the Hispanic share of the district population to 74% (75% of these are Mexican; 10% are Puerto Rican). Even so, because many have not become citizens and some who have do not vote, Latinos may be only a bare majority of the electorate. The community has sought to increase turnout, which is about half that in nearby black-majority or suburban districts.

The congressman from the 4th District is Luis Gutierrez, a Democrat and the first Hispanic member of Congress from Illinois. He has held the seat since its creation in 1992. Gutierrez (*goo-tee-AIR-ez*) is of Puerto Rican descent and grew up in Chicago. As a student at Northeastern Illinois University in the 1970s, he joined a protest of the lack of basic English classes for students from other countries, which ended up with the protesters taking over an administration building. Gutierrez returned for two years to Puerto Rico as a teacher after college. When he came back to Chicago, he worked as a cab driver and social worker. In 1983, he ran for 32nd Ward committeeman against U.S. Rep. Dan Rostenkowski and lost decisively. Then he became a staffer for Mayor Harold Washington, the city's first black mayor. He ran for alderman in 1984 and lost. In 1986, he ran again and won in one of two new Hispanic-majority aldermanic seats. After Washington died, Gutierrez backed Richard M. Daley, the longtime Chicago mayor's son, in the 1989 election to succeed Washington, which Daley won. In the 1992 primary, for the new House seat, rival Alderman Juan Solis called Gutierrez a machine candidate. Gutierrez won, 60%-40%. Since easily winning a rematch in 1994, Gutierrez has not had serious competition.

In the House, Gutierrez has staked out liberal positions, and his feisty, blunt style has produced mixed results. As a freshman, his outspoken opposition to congressional pay raises and his appearance on a *60 Minutes* broadcast—in which he called the House "the belly of the beast" and charged that Democratic leaders had stifled reform and that some freshmen Democrats had "sold out" — was not well received. "I've gotten my rear end kicked around here," Gutierrez told the *Washington Post*. The leadership rezsponded by denying Gutierrez seats on choice committees, and he has stayed on the Financial Services Committee, though he's moved up in seniority over the years. He chairs the Financial Institutions & Consumer Credit Subcommittee. In 2008, he said there was a "need to act immediately" to change the composition of the penny and the nickel because the price of the standard metals had soared. In May, the House passed a bill to change the penny.

One of his major efforts in recent years has been pushing changes in immigration policy. As a member of the Hispanic Caucus, Gutierrez chaired the immigration task force, where he pushed efforts to restore food-stamp eligibility and other benefits to legal immigrants. He sponsored other bills to grant automatic citizenship to immigrants in military combat and legal status to immigrants without documentation who were making major contributions in the United States. "I want to be a spokesperson for people that are new to this country," he has said. In recent years, he has been a leader in the House in the push to create a path to citizenship and a guest-worker program for illegal immigrants. In 2005, he was the lead Democratic sponsor of the House version of an overhaul in immigration policy, which passed the Senate in 2006 but was stopped by House Republicans. In the 110th Congress (2007–08), the bill was revived with a provision to allow illegal immigrants who had been employed in the U.S. before June 1, 2006 to apply for "conditional non-immigrant status."

His quick temper got the best of him during the immigration debate, when, after an appearance on an MSNBC broadcast, Gutierrez got into a shoving match with then Rep. Tom Tancredo of Colorado, a conservative Republican who advocated tough enforcement and deportation of illegal immigrants. Gutierrez said afterward, "It wasn't my best moment." To pursue his interest in immigration reform, he joined the Judiciary Committee in 2007. He angered some of his allies on the issue when he discussed with Rep. Jeff Flake, an Arizona conservative, a plan to increase the number of "guest workers" and tighten border security. In 2008, he criticized Democratic leaders who were encouraging enforcement-only legislation.

Though he often plays the rebel, Gutierrez has been capable of making accommodations with the establishment. He brought together Chicago's fractious Democratic politicians to maximize Latino influence. In 2005, Gutierrez said he would retire after seeking one final term in November 2006 and would explore a mayoral bid in February 2007. But after Democrats regained the House majority in 2006, Gutierrez decided against challenging Daley. He said he wanted to stay in Congress to complete his quest for a change in immigration policy.

In 2008, he was the subject of unflattering news coverage about real estate deals with local developers. The *Chicago Tribune* reported that starting in 2002, Gutierrez had made about $421,000 by investing in half a dozen real estate deals with campaign supporters and then exiting a short time later. Gutierrez told the newspaper that he had made a profit in five of those deals but lost a small amount of money on the sixth.

FIFTH DISTRICT

Mike Quigley (D)

Elected April 2009, 1st term; b. Oct. 17, 1958, Indianapolis, IN; home, Chicago; Roosevelt U., B.A. 1981; U. of Chicago, M.P.P. 1985; Loyola U., J.D. 1989; ; married (Barbara); 2 children.

Elected Office: Cook Cnty. commissioner, 1998–2009.

Professional Career: Cook Co. aldermanic aide, 1983–89; Adjct. prof., Roosevelt U., 2006–07; Adjct. prof. in political science, Loyola U. Chicago, 2002–09; Practicing atty., 1990–present.

State Offices:

Committees: *Judiciary* (15th of 24 D): Courts & Competition Policy; Crime, Terrorism & Homeland Security. *Oversight & Government Reform* (12th of 24 D): Government Management, Organization & Procurement; National Security & Foreign Affairs.

Group Ratings and Key Votes: Newly Elected

Election Results

2009 spec. general	Mike Quigley (D)	30,561	(69%)
	Rosanna Pulido (R)	10,662	(24%)
	Matt Reichel (Green)	2,911	(7%)
2009 spec. primary	Mike Quigley (D)	12,118	(22%)
	John Fritchey (D)	9,835	(18%)
	Sara Feigenholtz (D)	9,194	(17%)
	Victor Forys (D)	6,428	(12%)
	Pat O'Connor (D)	6,388	(12%)
	Charlie Wheelan (D)	3,681	(7%)
	Tom Geoghegan (D)	3,342	(6%)
2008 general	Rahm Emanuel (D)	170,728	(74%)
	Tom Hanson (R)	50,881	(22%)
	Alan Augustson (Green)	9,283	(4%)
2008 primary	Rahm Emanuel (D)	unopposed	

Population		Race/Ethnicity		Work	
Pop. 2007:	652,430	White:	60.8%	Private:	83.9%
Change since 2000:	Down 0.2%	Black:	3.0%	Government:	10.1%
Urban:	100.0%	Hispanic:	27.6%	Self-employed:	5.9%
Rural:	0.0%	Asian:	6.8%	Blue collar:	20.3%
Area size:	58 sq. mi.	Native Am.:	0.2%	White collar:	62.0%
		Hawaiian:	0.0%	Khaki collar:	0.0%
Age		Two+ races:	1.0%	Other:	17.7%
Median age:	35.5 yrs.	*Ancestry*		Median income:	$57,147
More than 65 yrs:	10.9%	Polish:	13.2%	Median home value:	$353,900
Less than 18 yrs:	20.6%	German:	10.9%	Poverty:	10.6%
Education		Irish:	10.5%	**Military Veterans**	
H.S. grad:	83.0%			% of Pop:	5.3%
College grad:	36.8%				
Grad degree:	13.8%				

Few places in America today have more ethnic and cultural variety than the North Side of Chicago. This has been the destination of one immigrant group after another and its neighborhoods harbor all manner of successful middle-class people. Wooden workingman's cottages from the late 19th century give way to sturdy brick houses from the early 1900s, and then to the prairie bungalows of the 1920s and the white-shuttered, orange-brick colonials of the 1950s. Chicago was America's top

2008 Presidential Vote
Obama (D) 181,458   (73%)
McCain (R)..............................63,733   (26%)

2004 Presidential Vote
Kerry (D)................................161,348   (67%)
Bush (R) 79,349   (33%)

Cook Partisan Voting Index: D + 19

immigrant destination for Poles, Lithuanians, Czechs, Slovaks, Ukrainians, and Romanians. Something about the heavy, dull clouds of the long winters, the short, hot summers, a climate suited to potatoes and cabbage and other hardy vegetables, may have reminded them of central and eastern Europe. By the late 1980s, upwardly mobile immigrants from Mexico and Guatemala, Korea and the Philippines were moving in. The 1990s witnessed new rounds of immigrants from Poland and Ukraine, and also from Pakistan, India, and Bosnia. Family ties, webs of acquaintances that reach back to ancestral villages, have made the North Side of Chicago a natural port of entry for Eastern bloc migrants, even as other newcomers arrive with relationships extending to Latin America and Southeast Asia.

The 5th Congressional District covers an oddly shaped swath across Chicago's North Side, running from the lakefront to the suburbs directly south of O'Hare Airport. The 5th includes Chicago's most glamorous lakefront apartments facing the Oak Street beach and the gentrified neighborhoods of Old Town, where Crate & Barrel was founded in 1962 and where old houses and factories are being converted into upscale condominiums, often over the objections of preservationists. Nearby Lincoln Park abounds with boutiques, clubs and restaurants and has the highest median household income of Chicago's 77 community areas. The district is home to baseball's famed Wrigley Field, which opened in 1914 and is a protected landmark that has defied the teardown trend in ballparks and endured the heartbreak of the Cubs. It takes in the Polish-American and Ukrainian-American neighborhoods, with their own museums around Milwaukee Avenue, and the old Italian neighborhoods running west on Grand Avenue. A couple of blocks from the Chicago River is the grand old St. Stanislaus Kostka Church—a traditional center of the Polish community since the 19th century that now conducts Masses in Spanish. With the increase of Hispanic population to 28% in 2007, a language other than English is spoken in 46% of the district's households. Across from Pulaski Park is the home of former Democratic Rep. Dan Rostenkowski, D-Ill., chairman of the House Ways and Means Committee from 1981 to 1994, for whom the district was designed in 1992. The district's politics are vintage Chicago. Longtime political consultant Don Rose says, "The 5th is the second-toughest machine-controlled Democratic congressional district in Chicago. It differs slightly from the conservative 3rd District because of a handful of independent-liberal lakefront precincts comprising 18 percent of the vote." This is a solidly Democratic district. In 2008, Barack Obama won here 73%-26%.

The new congressman from the 5th District is Mike Quigley, who won a special election in April 2009 to succeed Democratic Rep. Rahm Emanuel after Emanuel was named President Obama's White House chief of staff. Quigley grew up in the working-class suburb of Carol Stream in DuPage County. He graduated from Roosevelt University, got his law degree from Loyola University in Chicago, and practiced criminal law. He also taught political science part-time at Loyola. He started his career in politics as an aide to Ald. Bernard Hansen while studying for a master's degree in public policy from the University of Chicago. He got involved in a community battle to stop the addition of lights for night games at Wrigley Field, which is in the heart of an old gentrified neighborhood of young professionals. In 1998, after an unsuccessful run in 1991 to become aldermen of the 46th Ward on the Chicago City Council, Quigley was elected to the Cook County Board, where he became an independent voice and a frequent nemesis of board President John Stroger. He pushed reforms such as ending patronage jobs at the Cook County Forest Preserve District, promoted environmental action and sponsored a proposal to allow gay and lesbian couples to register as domestic partners. In 2005, Quigley decided to challenge Stroger for board president, but later dropped out and backed Forrest Claypool, saying the two would split the anti-incumbent vote if they both remained in the race. Claypool repaid the favor by endorsing Quigley for the House seat.

After Obama plucked Emanuel from the House, a long list of candidates jumped into the wide-open Democratic primary. State Rep. Sara Feigenholtz was endorsed by EMILY's List and had the early fundraising lead. Alderman Patrick O'Connor and state Rep. John Fritchey had local party machine support, but organized labor split its endorsements. The appointment of Roland Burris to the Senate by impeached Democratic Gov. Rod Blagojevich became a campaign issue, with candidates seeking to burnish their credentials as reformers and attacking their opponents for having been associated with the disgraced governor. Quigley and Feigenholtz said Burris should resign; Fritchey suffered from having defended Burris at a legislative hearing in January 2009. Quigley ran a late ad comparing Feigenholtz to President Richard Nixon, saying she had resorted to unfair campaign charges. That may have extinguished any lingering friendship between Quigley and Feigenholtz, who had dated briefly years earlier.

Despite their backgrounds as organization figures, the leading candidates all employed Obama's message of change. The influential Emanuel did not endorse anyone, but a yard sign for Feigenholtz appeared in front of his home, rumored to be put there by his wife. Quigley received key newspaper endorsements from the *Sun Times* and the *Chicago Tribune*, the latter praising him for an "outstanding record of independent, reform-minded performance in office." In a low-turnout event on March 3, Quigley won with 22% of the vote to 18% for Fritchey and 17% for Feigenholtz. He ran especially well in the "lakefront liberal" wards. Fritchey's support from organization bosses and Feigenholtz's backing by women's groups failed to deliver. Author Tom Geoghegan won plaudits from fellow writers, but only 6% of the vote.

Quigley breezed to victory in the April 7 general election against Republican Rosanna Pulido. He became heir to a district that has had a history of producing powerful if occasionally flawed national Democrats: the savvy Emanuel, who is known for his sharp tongue, the ethically challenged Blagojevich, and Rostenkowski, who did jail time for mail fraud after being accused of misusing his office accounts.

SIXTH DISTRICT

Peter Roskam (R)

Elected 2006, 2nd term; b. Sept. 13, 1961, Hinsdale; home, Wheaton; U. of IL, B.A. 1983, Chicago-Kent Col. of Law, J.D. 1989; Anglican; married (Elizabeth); 4 children.

Elected Office: IL House, 1992–98; IL Senate, 2000–06, Min. Whip, 2003–06.

Professional Career: Aide, U.S. Rep. Tom DeLay, 1985–86, U.S. Rep. Henry Hyde, 1986–87; High school teacher, 1983–85; Exec. Dir., Educational Assistance Ltd., 1987–1993; Practicing atty., 1994–2006.

DC Office: 507 CHOB, 20515, 202-225-4561; Fax: 202-225-1166; Web site: roskam.house.gov.

State Offices: Bloomingdale, 630-893-9670.

Committees: *Ways & Means* (15th of 15 R): Income Security & Family Support; Oversight; Select Revenue Measures.

Group Ratings

	ADA	ACLU	AFS	LCV	ITIC	NTU	COC	ACU	CFG	FRC
2008	10	18	14	23	50	78	94	96	87	100
2007	10	—	9	15	—	79	84	96	86	—

National Journal Ratings

	2007 LIB — 2007 CONS		2008 LIB — 2008 CONS	
Economic	24%	— 75%	17%	— 82%
Social	9%	— 85%	31%	— 62%
Foreign	0%	— 72%	35%	— 62%
Composite	17%	— 83%	30%	— 71%

Key Votes of the 110th Congress

1. Increase minimum wage	N	5. Share immigration data	Y	9. Withdraw troops 8/08	N
2. Expand SCHIP	N	6. Foreign aid abortion ban	Y	10. No operations in Iran	N
3. Raise CAFE standards	N	7. Ban gay bias in workplace	N	11. Free trade with Peru	Y
4. Bail out financial markets	N	8. Repeal D.C. gun law	Y	12. Overhaul FISA	Y

Election Results

2008 general	Peter Roskam (R)	147,906	(58%)	($2,708,859)
	Jill Morgenthaler (D)	109,007	(42%)	($827,457)
2008 primary	Peter Roskam (R)	unopposed		

Prior Winning Percentages: 2006 (51%)

Population		Race/Ethnicity		Work	
Pop. 2007:	665,774	White:	69.2%	Private:	87.2%
Change since 2000:	Up 1.9%	Black:	3.2%	Government:	8.7%
Urban:	100.0%	Hispanic:	16.6%	Self-employed:	3.9%
Rural:	0.0%	Asian:	9.7%	Blue collar:	20.6%
Area size:	215 sq. mi.	Native Am.:	0.2%	White collar:	66.8%
Age		Hawaiian:	0.1%	Khaki collar:	0.0%
Median age:	37.1 yrs.	Two+ races:	0.9%	Other:	12.5%
More than 65 yrs:	11.1%	*Ancestry*		Median income:	$69,273
Less than 18 yrs:	24.8%	German:	16.8%	Median home value:	$287,100
Education		Irish:	11.4%	Poverty:	5.8%
H.S. grad:	88.1%	Italian:	10.0%	**Military Veterans**	
College grad:	35.6%			% of Pop:	7.1%
Grad degree:	12.2%				

During World War II, the largest troop and cargo airplane, the Douglas C-54, was built at a military airstrip called Orchard Field, just northwest of Chicago. Today, Orchard Field is known as O'Hare International Airport, the nation's second-busiest. (O'Hare's three-letter code, ORD, borrows three letters from the word "orchard.") In the 1940s, Chicago politicians in search of a new airport site annexed Orchard Field, along with thousands of adjacent acres, and renamed it for a Navy flyer who lost his

2008 Presidential Vote		
Obama (D)	152,127	(56%)
McCain (R)	115,339	(43%)

2004 Presidential Vote		
Bush (R)	139,028	(53%)
Kerry (D)	121,344	(47%)

Cook Partisan Voting Index: Even

life in the war and hailed from Chicago, Lt. Edward O'Hare. Mayor Richard J. Daley, the father of the current mayor, opened O'Hare in 1955 and aggressively promoted its development, correctly concluding that a great airport in the 20th century could do for Chicago what railroad stations and rail yards did for the city in the 19th century. For years, O'Hare has vied with Atlanta's Hartsfield-Jackson as America's No. 1 or No. 2 airport, and it has done much to maintain Chicago as the most vibrant center of commerce in the Midwest. Today, with O'Hare operating close to capacity, Mayor Richard M. Daley's plans to reconfigure the runways and expand the airport are aimed at maintaining its pre-eminence. However, expansion is highly unpopular in the densely packed suburbs that surround O'Hare. Politically, these suburbs were for many years solidly Republican, convinced that civic virtues could best be realized by opposing the party of City Hall in Chicago, and that economic growth could best be assured by opposing the party that backed stifling government regulation. But in the 1990s, they became less Republican, as voters here recoiled from the national party's cultural conservatism.

The 6th Congressional District of Illinois includes O'Hare and much of the suburban area to its west. Most of the district is in DuPage County, the second-largest county in Illinois after Cook County. It includes the string of long-settled suburbs due west of the Loop: Elmhurst, Villa Park, Lombard, Glen Ellyn, and Wheaton. It takes in other suburbs along Interstate 290: Bensenville, Addison, Wood Dale, and Bloomingdale. Economically, this remains high-income territory; culturally, it is now cautiously moderate or even liberal. In 1988, George H.W. Bush carried DuPage by 124,000 votes, with 68% of the vote, but in 2004, his son carried it by only 39,000 votes, for a total of 54%—which tells you in a nutshell why the elder Bush carried Illinois in 1988 and the younger Bush twice wrote it off. In 2008, Illinois was a lost cause for Republicans opposed to favorite-son Democrat Barack Obama. John McCain lost DuPage by 45,000 votes.

The congressman from the 6th District is Peter Roskam, a Republican elected in 2006 to succeed the iconic Henry Hyde, who retired after 32 years. A native of DuPage County, Roskam was a varsity gymnast in high school, graduated from the University of Illinois, and got his law degree while directing a charitable organization that used corporate resources to fund college scholarships. During law school, he was part of a team that won a national mock trial competition. As a young man, he also once worked as an aide to Hyde. Roskam served six years in the state House, and six years in the Senate, where he was the Republican whip and floor leader. Between those legislative stints, he ran unsuccessfully in 1998 for the open congressional seat in the neighboring 13th District, losing 45%-40% against state House colleague Judy Biggert in the Republican primary. He attacked Biggert for support of abortion rights and was backed by national Republicans, but she raised far more money and had the endorsement of Gov. Jim Edgar and the incumbent representative, Harris Fawell. In 2006, Hyde, one of the most widely respected conservatives on Capitol Hill, stepped down. Roskam raised nearly $400,000 in two months, and managed to scare off potentially competitive Republican challengers. He ran unopposed for the GOP nomination, conserving his money for the general election.

In the general election campaign, his Democratic opponent was Tammy Duckworth, a former manager for Rotary International and an Iraq war veteran. The daughter of a retired Marine and an ethnically Chinese mother, she was born in Bangkok and spent much of her early life in Southeast Asia. She was famous as a Black Hawk helicopter pilot who served with the Illinois National Guard and lost both legs in Iraq after her helicopter was hit by a rocket-propelled grenade and crashed. As part of an effort to nominate military veterans for Congress, then-Rep. Rahm Emanuel, from the neighboring 5th District and chairman of the Democratic Congressional Campaign Committee, hand-picked Duckworth. Her high profile made this one of the nation's most closely watched House races, and one of the most expensive. First, she faced a competitive primary from technology consultant Christine Cegelis, who ran against Hyde in 2004 and held him to a 56%-44% win, his smallest margin since he was first elected. A political novice, Duckworth was slow to pick up campaign skills, but she was bolstered by Emanuel and other party leaders. She also benefited from a wave of favorable news coverage for her compelling personal story. Duckworth won the primary with 44% to 40% for Cegelis and 16% for a third candidate.

The two nominees sparred over tax cuts, earmarks, the Iraq war, and immigration policy. They also clashed over abortion rights, federal funding for embryonic-stem-cell research, and expansion of O'Hare, all of which Roskam opposed. Duckworth criticized Roskam as "a rubber stamp" for the Bush administration, and referred to the scandal-plagued House GOP Leader Tom DeLay of Texas as Roskam's "mentor." While Roskam was climbing a political ladder with DeLay, her campaign said, "Tammy Duckworth was climbing into helicopters and serving her country." Former President Clinton and actor Michael J. Fox made campaign appearances for her. Roskam disparaged Duckworth as the "candidate from the Chicago Democratic machine" because of her ties to the well-connected Emanuel. He also sought to portray her as a carpetbagger. In one of the few Republican successes in a competitive House contest that year, Roskam won with 51%-49%. Duckworth got 53% of the vote in Cook County, but Cook cast only 20% of the total vote. Roskam won 52%-48% in DuPage—sufficient, though not overwhelming.

In the House, Roskam votes near the center of the Republican Party. In May 2007, the House by 173-245 defeated his amendment to limit contributions to the affordable housing trust fund when the government is running a deficit. With Rep. John Shimkus, R-Ill., he unveiled in 2008 an energy-independence plan that was based on aggressive domestic production, conservation, and alternative fuels. That year, he also voted against the government bailout of the financial markets because, he said, it was not tough enough on Wall Street executives and "places too great a burden on taxpayers with no guarantee of success." As a constituent-outreach technique, he encouraged participation in his "There Oughta Be a Law" campaign soliciting proposals for new laws from residents of his district. In 2009, his solid freshman year and his friendship with party leaders got him a seat on the Ways and Means Committee.

Illinois Democratic Sen. Dick Durbin vowed that Democrats would give Roskam a strong challenge in 2008, but in July 2007 Duckworth, the party's top prospect, decided to stay in her job as head of the Illinois Veterans' Affairs Department. Instead, Democrats nominated another Iraq war veteran, retired Army Col. Jill Morgenthaler, who was the Army spokeswoman during the Abu Ghraib prison scandal. She campaigned on her support for President Bush's troop surge in Iraq, but said that democracy in Iraq must be "homegrown." She accused Roskam of having "extreme" views on abortion, health care, and the economy. Despite early Democratic hopes that Barack Obama's coattails would reach across Illinois, the national party gave little help to Morgenthaler. Roskam handily won a second term, 58%-42%, garnering 52% in the Cook County suburbs and 59% in DuPage. He and Democrat Debbie Halvorson, of the 11th District in Illinois, are the only members of Congress who served with Obama in the state Senate.

SEVENTH DISTRICT

Danny Davis (D)

Elected 1996, 7th term; b. Sept. 6, 1941, Parkdale, AR; home, Chicago; AR AM&N Col., B.A. 1961, Chicago St. U., M.S. 1968, Union Inst., Ph.D. 1977; Baptist; married (Vera); 2 children.

Elected Office: Chicago city alderman, 1979–90; Cook Cnty. commissioner, 1990–96.

Professional Career: Teacher, Chicago Public Schls., 1962–69; Health Care Planner, 1969–79.

DC Office: 2159 RHOB, 20515, 202-225-5006; Fax: 202-225-5641; Web site: www.house.gov/davis.

State Offices: Broadview, 708-345-6857; Chicago, 773-533-7520.

Committees: *Oversight & Government Reform* (16th of 24 D): Federal Workforce, Postal Service & the District of Columbia; Information Policy, Census & National Archives. *Ways & Means* (22nd of 26 D): Income Security & Family Support; Oversight.

Group Ratings

	ADA	ACLU	AFS	LCV	ITIC	NTU	COC	ACU	CFG	FRC
2008	80	100	100	92	83	8	56	0	0	5
2007	90	—	100	95	—	5	55	0	7	—

National Journal Ratings

	2007 LIB	—	2007 CONS		2008 LIB	—	2008 CONS
Economic	72%	—	27%		85%	—	0%
Social	92%	—	0%		82%	—	0%
Foreign	78%	—	20%		69%	—	30%
Composite	83%	—	18%		84%	—	16%

Key Votes of the 110th Congress

1. Increase minimum wage	Y	5. Share immigration data	N	9. Withdraw troops 8/08	Y
2. Expand SCHIP	Y	6. Foreign aid abortion ban	N	10. No operations in Iran	Y
3. Raise CAFE standards	Y	7. Ban gay bias in workplace	Y	11. Free trade with Peru	N
4. Bail out financial markets	Y	8. Repeal D.C. gun law	N	12. Overhaul FISA	N

Election Results

2008 general	Danny Davis (D)	235,343	(85%)	($413,001)
	Steve Miller (R)	41,474	(15%)	
2008 primary	Danny Davis (D)	129,865	(91%)	
	Robert Dallas (D)	12,629	(9%)	

Prior Winning Percentages: 2006 (87%); 2004 (86%); 2002 (83%); 2000 (86%); 1998 (93%); 1996 (83%)

Population		Race/Ethnicity		Work	
Pop. 2007:	614,247	White:	30.1%	Private:	80.7%
Change since 2000:	Down 6.0%	Black:	55.5%	Government:	14.1%
Urban:	100.0%	Hispanic:	8.1%	Self-employed:	5.1%
Rural:	0.0%	Asian:	5.0%	Blue collar:	13.8%
Area size:	59 sq. mi.	Native Am.:	0.1%	White collar:	71.6%
		Hawaiian:	0.0%	Khaki collar:	0.0%
Age		Two+ races:	0.9%	Other:	14.5%
Median age:	34.3 yrs.	*Ancestry*		Median income:	$48,486
More than 65 yrs:	10.6%	German:	7.1%	Median home value:	$297,900
Less than 18 yrs:	23.8%	Irish:	6.1%	Poverty:	22.2%
Education		Italian:	3.4%	**Military Veterans**	
H.S. grad:	81.8%			% of Pop:	6.3%
College grad:	36.9%				
Grad degree:	17.6%				

An airplane passenger on a cloudless day can get a clear view of the biggest man-made cityscape between the Atlantic and Pacific oceans: Chicago's Loop. Its high-rises and parks along Lake Michigan were pioneered a century ago, and the downtown district was named in 1897 for the quadrilateral shape the elevated train forms around the city's center. International School modernists built their most impressive collection of buildings here and along Lake Shore Drive in the years after World

2008 Presidential Vote

Obama (D)	260,925	(88%)
McCain (R)	34,481	(12%)

2004 Presidential Vote

Kerry (D)	227,018	(83%)
Bush (R)	45,071	(17%)

Cook Partisan Voting Index: D + 35

War II. In recent years, postmodernists have reinvented the skyscraper. The Loop now spreads beyond the elevated train, or the "El" as it's known locally. It reaches west beyond the financial exchanges to the 110-story Sears Tower—the third tallest building in the world—situated near the Chicago River. The Loop reaches north and stops at the Gold Coast, the wondrous shopping district along North Michigan Avenue. West of the Gold Coast is the River North neighborhood, which has become one of the city's most vibrant. This is the face Chicago likes to present to the world: giant structures rising where the prairies meet the inland sea, a vast concentration of brains and muscle, the nerve center of the nation's commodities markets.

Behind the lakefront are the muscle and sinew, gristle and fat of the city. There are parts that do not work so well: Houses and apartment buildings are abandoned, commercial space stands empty and vandalized, and public housing projects are crime racked. (Although Mayor Richard M. Daley has been systematically tearing down old housing projects, such as the Robert Taylor Homes, built by his famous mayor father in a failed experiment to concentrate the poor in a few locations.) The West Side of Chicago, the vast acres directly west of the Loop, for years was a grimy and dangerous slum, with some areas almost completely abandoned. The decay spread west to the Austin neighborhood, almost to the city border with upper-income and racially integrated Oak Park. Many factories that made Chicago the chocolate and candy center of the nation were shuttered, and production went mostly overseas. In the 1990s, there was some revival. The United Center, the erstwhile home court of Michael Jordan, sparked commercial development of the West Side, and lower crime rates raised land values. Former meatpacking buildings have been turned into art galleries. A massive new downtown dormitory houses students from nearby DePaul University, Roosevelt University and Columbia College.

The 7th Congressional District of Illinois contains the Loop and most of the North Michigan corridor and the Near North Side, where the infamous Cabrini-Green housing project has been replaced by new, mixed-market housing. It goes south, past landmark museums, Soldier Field and 19th-century mansions along Prairie Avenue to take in a few South Side neighborhoods chronicled in the groundbreaking 1945 book *Black Metropolis*. Its heart, demographically and spiritually, is the predominately African-American West Side, which is more depopulated and socially disorganized than the predominately black South Side. To the west, just outside city limits, are Oak Park, the boyhood home of writer Ernest Hemingway and the location of architect Frank Lloyd Wright's home and museum and many of his prairie-style houses. There is also well-heeled River Forest; more modest Maywood, which is a black-majority suburb; and Broadview and Hillside . Just over half of the residents of the district are African-American.

The congressman from the 7th District is Danny Davis, a Democrat first elected in 1996 after two unsuccessful tries in the 1980s. Davis grew up on a cotton farm in Arkansas, graduated from college in that state, then moved to Chicago and worked as a teacher, assistant principal and guidance counselor in Chicago public schools. For 10 years, he ran a community health project on the West Side. He was elected alderman in the 29th Ward in 1979, and supported Mayor Harold Washington, the city's first black mayor, in his notorious 1980s battles with white machine aldermen that were dubbed "Council Wars." In 1990, Davis was elected a Cook County commissioner and a year later, made a quixotic run for mayor against Richard M. Daley. In 1996, when Democratic Rep. Cardiss Collins retired after nearly 24 years in the House, Davis decided to run for the House again. His major opponents were 3rd Ward Alderman Dorothy Tillman, a Daley ally, and 37th Ward Alderman Ed Smith. Davis campaigned as a big-government liberal, calling for a $7.60 minimum wage, affirmative-action programs, and a nationalized health care plan. Davis won with 33%. He went on to win the general election with ease and has not faced a serious challenge since. But he lost his 29th Ward committeeman post to a Daley-backed challenger in 2000.

In the House, Davis has a liberal voting record, though he's moved closer to the center on economic issues in recent years. He has opposed income tax cuts, even when advocated by Democratic President Clinton. He opposed the sugar program as corporate welfare (Chicago remains the nation's leading candy manufacturer). On the Government Reform Committee, he was a champion of organized labor as he worked with a bipartisan coalition that in 2006 enacted major changes in the Postal Service. With his wife, Vera, who was then president of the West Side NAACP, Davis advocated a local program to increase the low share of black home ownership in his district by offering credit counseling and innovative forms of mortgage financing. He has created dozens of advisory task forces to get views from constituents. His devotion to issues affecting the poor won him respect even among Republicans during the dozen years of GOP control of Congress. With the view that everybody deserves a second chance, Davis has taken a deep interest in the problems of former convicts seeking to transition back to the mainstream. He and conservative Republican Rep. Mark Souder of Indiana proposed the Public Safety ex-Offender Self-Sufficiency Act, which used tax credits to encourage transitional housing and job training for former prisoners. This evolved into his Second Chance Act, which President Bush signed into law in April 2008.

Davis is eager for political advancement. In 2006, he sought to become Cook County Board president when incumbent John Stroger suffered a serious stroke. But Democratic committeemen overwhelmingly supported Stroger's son, Todd, for the nomination, and Davis was a distant second. After the 2008 election, he campaigned publicly to win the support of Democratic Gov. Rod Blagojevich to fill the Senate seat vacated by President-elect Barack Obama. "I'm eager to run, and eager to serve," he said, as he sought to rally support from ethnic groups in the city and from local officials across the state. Then Blagojevich was arrested and charged with trying to gain politically and personally from his power to make the appointment. The disgraced governor decided to go ahead and make the appointment anyway and called Davis his top choice. But Davis turned down what was bound to be viewed as a tainted appointment, saying the governor had "lost his moral authority." Blagojevich then appointed former Illinois Attorney General Roland Burris to the seat, but the appointment continued to be mired in controversy through the first part of 2009. As a significant consolation prize, the Democratic House leadership gave Davis a seat on the Ways and Means Committee.

EIGHTH DISTRICT

Melissa Bean (D)

Elected 2004, 3rd term; b. Jan. 22, 1962, Chicago; home, Barrington; Oakton Comm. Col., A.A. 1982, Roosevelt U., B.A. 2002; Serbian Orthodox; married (Alan); 2 children.

Professional Career: Technology and sales consultant, 1982–2004.

DC Office: 432 CHOB, 20515, 202-225-3711; Fax: 202-225-7830; Web site: www.house.gov/bean.

State Offices: Schaumburg, 847-517-2927.

Committees: *Financial Services* (22nd of 42 D): Capital Markets, Insurance & Government Sponsored Enterprises; Financial Institutions & Consumer Credit. *Small Business* (9th of 17 D): Contracting & Technology; Finance & Tax; Regulations & Healthcare.

Group Ratings

	ADA	ACLU	AFS	LCV	ITIC	NTU	COC	ACU	CFG	FRC
2008	65	82	71	85	100	25	83	20	22	5
2007	80	—	89	85	—	22	70	21	22	—

National Journal Ratings

	2007 LIB	—	2007 CONS		2008 LIB	—	2008 CONS
Economic	50%	—	49%		48%	—	50%
Social	54%	—	46%		51%	—	49%
Foreign	50%	—	50%		48%	—	51%
Composite	52%	—	49%		50%	—	51%

Key Votes of the 110th Congress

1. Increase minimum wage	Y	5. Share immigration data	N	9. Withdraw troops 8/08	Y
2. Expand SCHIP	Y	6. Foreign aid abortion ban	N	10. No operations in Iran	N
3. Raise CAFE standards	Y	7. Ban gay bias in workplace	Y	11. Free trade with Peru	Y
4. Bail out financial markets	Y	8. Repeal D.C. gun law	N	12. Overhaul FISA	Y

Election Results

2008 general	Melissa Bean (D)	179,444	(61%)	($2,986,001)
	Steve Greenberg (R)	116,081	(39%)	($990,574)
2008 primary	Melissa Bean (D)	64,255	(83%)	
	Bill Scheurer (D)	12,968	(17%)	

Prior Winning Percentages: 2006 (51%); 2004 (52%)

Population		Race/Ethnicity		Work	
Pop. 2007:	730,943	White:	72.2%	Private:	85.4%
Change since 2000:	Up 11.8%	Black:	3.8%	Government:	10.3%
Urban:	96.1%	Hispanic:	15.3%	Self-employed:	4.2%
Rural:	3.9%	Asian:	7.3%	Blue collar:	20.2%
Area size:	646 sq. mi.	Native Am.:	0.2%	White collar:	66.7%
Age		Hawaiian:	0.0%	Khaki collar:	0.2%
Median age:	35.5 yrs.	Two+ races:	1.0%	Other:	13.0%
More than 65 yrs:	8.9%	*Ancestry*		Median income:	$71,914
Less than 18 yrs:	26.9%	German:	18.9%	Median home value:	$248,100
Education		Irish:	11.6%	Poverty:	6.1%
H.S. grad:	89.6%	Polish:	9.4%	**Military Veterans**	
College grad:	35.7%			% of Pop:	7.8%
Grad degree:	12.1%				

Schaumburg may not be nationally known, but it is one of America's major corporate headquarters cities. Sixty years ago, this suburb northwest of Chicago was farmland. Today, Schaumburg—near the intersection of the Northwest Tollway and Interstate 290—is the site of the headquarters of Motorola and Zurich American Insurance. Nearby are the headquarters of Sears and Kemper Insurance, as well as the gargantuan Woodfield Mall and subdivisions as far as the eye can see. Schaumburg

2008 Presidential Vote		
Obama (D)	170,333	(56%)
McCain (R)	130,384	(43%)

2004 Presidential Vote		
Bush (R)	153,245	(56%)
Kerry (D)	121,710	(44%)

Cook Partisan Voting Index: R + 1

yearns for traditions. It has built a performing arts center, formed an orchestra for young people, and built from scratch a traditional downtown district. Lately, civic endeavors are taking a backseat to concerns about the recession, which hit here early. Motorola lost 3,000 jobs worldwide in 2008 alone.

The 8th Congressional District of Illinois is made up of Schaumburg and dozens of similar communities north and northwest of Chicago. A short drive from Schaumburg is Palatine and country-manor Barrington Hills. The district—whose population grew 12% from 2000 to 2007—includes the rapidly-growing western half of Lake County, with little lake communities being surrounded by new suburbs like Deer Park and Volo. It also includes the Lake Michigan town of Zion at the Wisconsin border. To the west, the 8th includes about half of fast-growing McHenry County, where Democrats have begun to show some life. The area lacks a regional identity, other than the "northwest suburbs." The local newspaper, the *Daily Herald* based in Arlington Heights, tried valiantly for a few years to give it a sense of place with a billboard campaign that dubbed it "Herald City." It didn't quite stick.

The tone of life is not elite, but people here are affluent. Culturally, it has more in common with the great rural Midwest than it does yeasty, lusty Chicago. Economically, its suspicion of government and trade restrictions has declined, as Motorola has become the victim of overseas competition, which has caused job upheaval in Schaumburg. Historically, this was one of the most Republican places in the nation. In the past decade, like other Chicago suburbs, it moved toward the Democrats. The Latino population has risen from 11% in 2000 to 15% in 2007, and Asian-Americans constitute 7%. If the 8th is still one of Illinois's most Republican districts, as measured by its 56% support of George W. Bush in both 2000 and 2004, it has become far less Republican than districts with similar demographics in Texas and Georgia. Like most of the Chicago metropolitan area, the district voted for Barack Obama in 2008. Obama won 56% here compared to John McCain's 43%.

The congresswoman from the 8th District is Melissa Bean, who on her second attempt at a House seat defeated Phil Crane, who had been the senior Republican in the House. Bean was born in Chicago and grew up in Park Ridge, Hillary Rodham Clinton's girlhood home. Bean's father owned a company that manufactured conveyor belts. She attended a local community college, then worked from home as a business consultant in technology sales, training executives at Motorola and other companies to develop marketing and sales campaigns. At age 40, she got a bachelor's degree in political science from Roosevelt University. She served on the local PTA and volunteered for Crane's Democratic challenger in 2000. Two years later, she ran for the seat herself. Although she got little assistance from national Democrats, she held Crane to 57% in 2002, the second-lowest performance of his long career.

Bean kept right on campaigning, with her sights set on 2004. Her energetic campaign offered a vivid contrast to Crane's sluggish and late-starting effort. Downplaying her party identification and keeping her distance from Democratic leaders, she handed voters jelly beans to help them remember her name, framed her candidacy as "a fresh start" and consistently talked about the need for a vigorous new voice. In this Republican district, she sharply attacked Crane for having lost touch back home while accruing little influence in Washington. Bean supported the war in Iraq, opposed the Bush tax cuts and favored abortion rights. Crane tried to depict her as an inexperienced newcomer who would be unable to deliver federal dollars for the district. But this is not a district that relies heavily on infusions of federal money. In October, the *Chicago Tribune*, historically Republican, endorsed Bean. Crane "has used his seat in Congress as a cozy sinecure," the paper griped. Crane complained, "I have been busting my hump for about five straight weeks" in the campaign. Bean won 52%-48%, making Crane one of only two Republican incumbents defeated in 2004. She won 56%-44% on her home turf of Cook County, 50.3%-49.7% in Lake County and trailed 49%-51% in McHenry County, running in each case well ahead of usual Democratic percentages in this historically Republican territory.

In the House, Bean became identified as a fiscal conservative and social moderate. In 2009, Bean became a vice-chairman of the centrist New Democrats. Perhaps Bean's most significant alliance has been her friendship with President Obama. They became friends campaigning together in 2004, and both were unlikely winners, she in the House and he in the Senate. They spoke "regularly and directly" during the 2008 presidential campaign. "He is open and receptive to new ideas, such as my interest in small business," Bean said after the election.

She has focused her work on the Financial Services Committee. She worked on the issues of identity theft and tax credits for adoptive families (Bean was adopted as a baby). She backed a bill to permit small businesses to join together and offer health coverage to employees. She won business support—and angered unions—as one of only 15 House Democrats to vote for the Central American Free Trade Agreement, which she said would benefit local companies. In 2007, she again drew fire from labor and progressive groups when she was the only Democrat to vote against the $607 billion spending bill for Labor and Health and Human Services programs, leading a public-employees-union lobbyist to comment, "We're profoundly disappointed, to put it mildly." A Bean spokesman said she was concerned that overall spending in the bill was too high. After initially supporting President Bush on the war in Iraq, she backed the February 2007 resolution opposing the president's plan for a "surge" of troops in Iraq. She collaborated with Republican Rep. Ed Royce of California in 2007 on a sweeping plan to overhaul regulation of insurance, and "remove barriers to innovation," Bean said. At home, she strongly opposed the takeover by Canadian National of a local rail line because of fears that increased Chicago-area freight service would make residential areas unsafe and harm the environment.

In two subsequent elections, Bean was a top Republican target. But she made skillful use of incumbency and solid constituency service, and moved quickly to build a campaign war chest. In 2006, she also benefited from a divisive six-candidate Republican primary. Former investment banker David McSweeney won the primary with 43% to 33% for Kathy Salvi, a personal-injury attorney with connections to local conservatives. Also in the general election was attorney Bill Scheurer, who ran as an independent with support from some national labor unions who felt betrayed by Bean. National Republicans spent more than $2 million here, some of it to encourage Scheurer, though he failed to get much traction. Bean won with 51% to 44% for McSweeney and 5% for Scheurer.

In 2008, Republicans again suffered from a fractious primary, Political neophyte Steve Greenberg, a wealthy businessman, was nominated with 57% of the vote. He put in nearly $90,000 of his own money for a total of $990,000, compared to Bean's more than $3 million. They disagreed on energy policy, a timetable for the troops to return from Iraq, federal coverage of health care, and abortion rights. With a turnout boost from Obama, Bean increased her margin to 61%-39%. Republicans will need a topflight challenger if they hope to oust her in 2010.

NINTH DISTRICT

Jan Schakowsky (D)

Elected 1998, 6th term; b. May 26, 1944, Chicago; home, Evanston; U. of IL, B.S. 1965; Jewish; married (Robert Creamer); 3 children.

Elected Office: IL House of Reps., 1990–98.

Professional Career: Founder, Natl. Consumers Unite, 1969–73; Prog. dir., IL Public Action, 1976–85; Exec. dir., IL State Cncl. of Sr. Citizens, 1985–90.

DC Office: 2367 RHOB, 20515, 202-225-2111; Fax: 202-226-6890; Web site: www.house.gov/schakowsky.

State Offices: Chicago, 773-506-7100; Evanston, 847-328-3409.

Committees: *Chief Deputy Whip. Energy & Commerce* (16th of 36 D): Commerce, Trade & Consumer Protections; Health; Oversight & Investigations. *Intelligence (Select):* (8th of 13 D): Oversight & Investigations (Chmn.), Intelligence Community Management.

Group Ratings

	ADA	ACLU	AFS	LCV	ITIC	NTU	COC	ACU	CFG	FRC
2008	100	100	100	100	86	7	61	0	0	0
2007	100	—	100	100	—	4	50	0	1	—

National Journal Ratings

	2007 LIB	—	2007 CONS		2008 LIB	—	2008 CONS
Economic	82%	—	0%		85%	—	0%
Social	92%	—	0%		67%	—	28%
Foreign	96%	—	0%		65%	—	32%
Composite	95%	—	5%		76%	—	24%

Key Votes of the 110th Congress

1. Increase minimum wage	Y	5. Share immigration data	N	9. Withdraw troops 8/08	Y
2. Expand SCHIP	Y	6. Foreign aid abortion ban	N	10. No operations in Iran	Y
3. Raise CAFE standards	Y	7. Ban gay bias in workplace	Y	11. Free trade with Peru	N
4. Bail out financial markets	Y	8. Repeal D.C. gun law	N	12. Overhaul FISA	N

Election Results

2008 general	Jan Schakowsky (D) 181,948	(75%)	($1,227,724)
	Michael Younan (R) 53,593	(22%)	($6,686)
	Morris Shanfield (Green) 8,140	(3%)	
2008 primary	Jan Schakowsky (D) 98,374	(88%)	
	John Nocita (D) 13,485	(12%)	

Prior Winning Percentages: 2006 (75%); 2004 (76%); 2002 (70%); 2000 (76%); 1998 (75%)

Population		Race/Ethnicity		Work	
Pop. 2007:	627,813	White:	62.9%	Private:	82.6%
Change since 2000:	Down 4.0%	Black:	9.7%	Government:	10.3%
Urban:	100.0%	Hispanic:	11.7%	Self-employed:	6.9%
Rural:	0.0%	Asian:	13.4%	Blue collar:	15.1%
Area size:	78 sq. mi.	Native Am.:	0.2%	White collar:	69.3%
Age		Hawaiian:	0.1%	Khaki collar:	0.0%
Median age:	39.3 yrs.	Two+ races:	1.5%	Other:	15.6%
More than 65 yrs:	14.7%	*Ancestry*		Median income:	$54,669
Less than 18 yrs:	19.9%	German:	11.6%	Median home value:	$345,000
Education		Irish:	9.3%	Poverty:	11.7%
H.S. grad:	88.0%	Polish:	8.7%	**Military Veterans**	
College grad:	43.1%			% of Pop:	6.1%
Grad degree:	18.3%				

"Make no little plans," architect Daniel Burnham once said, and he made no small plans for the Chicago lakefront. The glorious parks he designed are among America's urban jewels, and the row of high-rise apartment buildings—some austere works of masters of the International style, some in traditional styles evocative of some other place and time, some sleek Art Deco works of the 1920s and 1930s—is a splendid accompaniment. Beyond the lakefront is all the diversity of Chicago. In sturdy

2008 Presidential Vote
Obama (D) 189,497   (72%)
McCain (R) 69,081   (26%)

2004 Presidential Vote
Kerry (D) 175,288   (68%)
Bush (R) 81,138   (32%)

Cook Partisan Voting Index: D + 20

brick houses, with scarcely a shoehorn's space between them, or in stubby apartment buildings, are ethnic and racial groups of every sort, from Argentineans to Slavs, from Poles to Plains Indians. In the 1970s, the neighborhoods behind the lakefront seemed to be getting seedier and tipping downhill. But since the late 1980s, they have been gentrifying, as young couples and gays, professionals and entrepreneurs renovate old houses and open new businesses. Today, this part of Chicago has as much urban energy and lively diversity as any place in America.

The lakefront has long been the most heavily Jewish part of Chicago. The local Jewish community, prominent for more than a century, has never been as much a force as it is in New York, or connected to a glamorous industry as in Los Angeles. Yet these Jewish voters' liberal impulses have been strong: the 19th-century impulse to resist state authority and the imposition of cultural uniformity, and the 20th-century impulse to increase state responsibility for individuals' lives. Chicago's North Side Jews have been a solidly Democratic voting bloc, involved with—but always keeping at arm's length—the old Democratic machine. In city politics since the 1980s, Jewish voters and lakefront liberals of all backgrounds have been a key swing group.

The 9th Congressional District of Illinois covers most of Chicago's lakefront, from just north of Diversey Harbor past the thriving Asian and orthodox Jewish communities in West Rogers Park and on to Evanston, founded by Methodists to promote temperance (a cause that never prospered in Chicago). The home of Northwestern University, Evanston has moved gracefully from historic Yankee Republicanism to trendy, postgraduate Democratness. From Evanston and nearby Wilmette (which is shared with the 10th), the 9th presses inland through heavily Jewish Skokie to Morton Grove and Niles and includes most of Des Plaines. These bustling inner-ring suburbs have become the center of Chicagoland's job base. With its financial markets and the professionals that support them, the city once known as the hog butcher of the world has evolved into the hog belly trader of the world. The district extends west to once-rock-solid Republican territory—Park Ridge, with its characteristic Chicago brick houses in orderly rows, where Hillary Rodham Clinton grew up at 235 Wisner, and the cluster of office buildings and interchanges in Rosemont, next to O'Hare International Airport. This is an overwhelmingly Democratic district.

The congresswoman from the 9th District is Jan Schakowsky, a Democrat elected in 1998 and an outspoken progressive. She grew up in Rogers Park and worked for two years as a teacher. In 1969, she formed National Consumers Unite to fight for date-of-freshness labels on dairy products and other food. Later she joined Illinois Public Action, a consumer group. In 1985 she became executive director of the Illinois State Council of Senior Citizens, where she organized the pivotal 1989 protest of Democratic

Rep. Dan Rostenkowski's Medicare catastrophic health care law for seniors. Television news images of the powerful Rostenkowski fleeing an angry crowd of old people led Congress to repeal the benefit, which many said did not provide adequate coverage. In 1990, Schakowsky was elected to the state House from Evanston and Skokie, and served as Democratic floor leader. In 1998, Schakowsky was selected in the Democratic primary to replace Rep. Sidney Yates, a liberal Democrat who had represented the lakefront in Congress for 48 years. Her strategy was to run from the left— "I don't think I can be defined as too far left in a district like this" —and to build a volunteer organization. With ads in college papers, she hired young field organizers to set about identifying Schakowsky voters. She raised $1.4 million, with help from the women's fundraising group EMILY's List. Her opponent was state Sen. Howard Carroll, who had the support of most Democratic ward committeemen and attacked Schakowsky for her opposition to the death penalty. Schakowsky's 1,500 workers, 250 of them from labor unions, helped her to a 45%-34% win. She easily won the general election.

Schakowsky has one of the most liberal voting records in the House and regularly scores perfect ratings from liberal interest groups. She harshly criticized the 2003 enactment of prescription drug coverage for seniors, joining Democrats seeking to overhaul the Republican-drafted law, which liberals thought did not go far enough. To encourage food safety, she sponsored a bill to create a national database of school food suppliers. In 2006, she pushed a bill to require automakers to share technical information with repair shops but dropped her support after Republicans weakened the measure. When Democrats won a House majority that year, she pushed for aggressive oversight of the Bush administration. On the Energy and Commerce Committee, Schakowsky was a player in the enactment in 2008 of the child-product safety bill, which toughened regulations. An outspoken critic of the war in Iraq, she helped to win House passage in 2007 of a bill to hold military contractors in Iraq accountable for possible criminal violations.

A close ally of Speaker Nancy Pelosi, Schakowsky has worked with Democratic leaders on electoral strategy, gaining their support to expand her training program for political organizers. She was an early supporter of Pelosi for party whip, and Pelosi rewarded her with a chief deputy whip post. Her contacts with national liberal groups have helped her to become a major party fundraiser. When the McCain-Feingold law ended big soft-money contributions after the 2002 election, Schakowsky helped to assemble the House Democrats' program to expand contributions from small donors.

Schakowsky briefly considered a run for the Senate in 2004 but decided against it. In early 2006, she sought a higher leadership post as vice chairman of the Democratic Caucus, which would put her on a track to become chairman, the No. 3 leadership job. With support from Pelosi, Schakowsky was the early front-runner against New York's Joe Crowley and Connecticut's John Larson. But she unexpectedly was eliminated on the first ballot, finishing third behind Crowley and Larson. Schakowsky threw her support to Larson, who, like her, was an ally of Pelosi. Crowley was allied with Maryland's Steny Hoyer, Pelosi's archrival in leadership. With Schakowsky's former supporters, Larson prevailed. Some Democrats speculated that Schakowsky was hurt by the timing of the leadership contest; it occurred soon after her husband, Robert Creamer, the longtime head of Illinois Public Action Fund, pleaded guilty in August 2005 to bank fraud in a check-kiting scheme. He was sentenced to a five-month prison term. Schakowsky said that her husband had "made mistakes," but that she was unaware of his financial problems and was "proud of who Bob is.... He has been a constant crusader."

After Democrats won House control in November 2006, Schakowsky seconded the nomination of Pelosi for speaker, calling her "my treasured friend." She was an early backer of Barack Obama for president, giving cover to other prominent Democratic women who may have wanted to support him but felt beholden to support the first woman with a shot at the presidency, Hillary Rodham Clinton. Schakowsky was interested in pursuing the Senate seat left vacant by Obama, but after Illinois Gov. Rod Blagojevich was arrested on corruption charges in connection with an alleged scheme to sell the job to the highest bidder, she said that she would not accept an appointment from Blagojevich.

TENTH DISTRICT

Mark Kirk (R)

Elected 2000, 5th term; b. Sept. 15, 1959, Champaign; home, Highland Park; Universidad Nacional Autonoma de Mexico, 1977–78, Cornell U., B.A. 1981, London Sch. of Econ., M.Sc. 1982; Georgetown U., J.D. 1992; Congregationalist; divorced.

Military Career: U.S. Naval Reserve, 1989-present.

Professional Career: Parliamentary aide, British House of Commons, 1981–83; A.A., U.S. Rep. John E. Porter, 1984–89; Staffer, World Bank, 1990–91; Spec. asst., U.S. Dept. of State, 1991–93; Practicing atty., 1993–95; Counsel, U.S. House Cmte. on Intl. Relations, 1995–2000.

DC Office: 1030 LHOB, 20515, 202-225-4835; Fax: 202-225-0837; Web site: www.house.gov/kirk.

State Offices: Northbrook, 847-940-0202.

Committees: *Appropriations* (15th of 23 R): Financial Services & General Government; Homeland Security; State, Foreign Operations & Related Programs.

Group Ratings

	ADA	ACLU	AFS	LCV	ITIC	NTU	COC	ACU	CFG	FRC
2008	55	45	43	69	71	43	83	48	42	17
2007	40	—	27	90	—	36	84	40	33	—

National Journal Ratings

	2007 LIB	—	2007 CONS		2008 LIB	—	2008 CONS
Economic	45%	—	54%		42%	—	58%
Social	47%	—	53%		43%	—	56%
Foreign	44%	—	56%		41%	—	59%
Composite	46%	—	55%		42%	—	58%

Key Votes of the 110th Congress

1. Increase minimum wage	Y	5. Share immigration data	Y	9. Withdraw troops 8/08	N
2. Expand SCHIP	Y	6. Foreign aid abortion ban	N	10. No operations in Iran	N
3. Raise CAFE standards	Y	7. Ban gay bias in workplace	Y	11. Free trade with Peru	Y
4. Bail out financial markets	Y	8. Repeal D.C. gun law	N	12. Overhaul FISA	Y

Election Results

2008 general	Mark Kirk (R)	153,082	(53%)	($5,449,409)
	Daniel Seals (D)	138,176	(47%)	($3,566,123)
2008 primary	Mark Kirk (R)	unopposed		

Prior Winning Percentages: 2006 (53%); 2004 (64%); 2002 (69%); 2000 (51%)

Population		Race/Ethnicity		Work	
Pop. 2007:	656,807	White:	72.8%	Private:	82.0%
Change since 2000:	Up 0.5%	Black:	4.7%	Government:	11.6%
Urban:	99.6%	Hispanic:	14.2%	Self-employed:	6.2%
Rural:	0.4%	Asian:	7.0%	Blue collar:	14.3%
Area size:	252 sq. mi.	Native Am.:	0.1%	White collar:	72.4%
		Hawaiian:	0.1%	Khaki collar:	1.7%
Age		Two+ races:	1.0%	Other:	11.6%
Median age:	38.8 yrs.	*Ancestry*		Median income:	$81,486
More than 65 yrs:	13.0%	German:	14.6%	Median home value:	$408,800
Less than 18 yrs:	26.8%	Irish:	10.8%	Poverty:	5.1%
Education		Polish:	8.5%	**Military Veterans**	
H.S. grad:	90.3%			% of Pop:	8.2%
College grad:	51.0%				
Grad degree:	21.8%				

Since 1855, when the Chicago & Northwestern opened the railroad line from downtown Chicago north along the lakeshore, the North Shore suburbs along Lake Michigan have been home to Chicago's elite. The North Shore starts in Evanston, goes north through Wilmette, Winnetka, and Glencoe, then leaves Cook County and crosses into the eastern Lake County towns of Highland Park and Lake Forest. Each burg has a slightly different personality, each is long established and mightily prosperous, and each exudes a patina of age. These are communities of affluent, well-educated people living in an environment whose natural beauty—the vistas over Lake Michigan, the gentle rolling terrain, and the old trees—is carefully disciplined. Corporate headquarters fit comfortably here, including Baxter Healthcare, Abbott Laboratories, and Allstate Insurance. The North Shore suburbs were the setting for the 1980s films *Risky Business, Sixteen Candles,* and *Ferris Bueller's Day Off,* which depicted teen angst and lust for adventure among the pampered offspring of the rich. The one exception to the atmosphere of gracious high living is the area around the Great Lakes Naval Training Center, where income is lower to say the least.

The 10th Congressional District of Illinois is the North Shore district, starting on the lakefront in Wilmette and running north all the way to the blue-collar city of Waukegan and almost to the Wisconsin border. The district goes inland to Northbrook and Deerfield through what for many years were cornfields. Farther inland are suburbs like Arlington Heights, developed in the 1950s and 1960s on the Northwestern railroad line, and Wheeling, developed in the 1970s. To the north is Libertyville, near where

2008 Presidential Vote

Obama (D)	181,071	(61%)
McCain (R)	114,035	(38%)

2004 Presidential Vote

Kerry (D)	150,267	(53%)
Bush (R)	134,536	(47%)

Cook Partisan Voting Index: D+6

the Adlai Stevensons, the governor and two-time presidential candidate and his son the former senator, owned what is now one of the last farms only a few miles from Lake Michigan. After the family home on the property was donated to Lake County, it was restored as the Adlai Stevenson Center on Democracy in August 2008. With the big movement toward Democrats in the Chicago suburbs in the 1990s, this establishment Republican district voted narrowly for Al Gore in 2000 and by a slightly larger margin for John Kerry in 2004. Barack Obama ran strongly here in 2008, getting 61% of the vote to John McCain's 38%.

The congressman from the 10th District is Mark Kirk, a Republican first elected in 2000. Kirk was born in downstate Illinois but grew up mostly in tony Kenilworth, on the lake between Wilmette and Winnetka. The son of a telephone company executive, he graduated from Cornell University and the London School of Economics. He got a job in Republican Rep. John Porter's Washington office and rose to chief of staff in three years. Kirk left Capitol Hill in 1989 but stayed in Washington, doing stints first at the World Bank and then as a State Department aide working on the Central American peace process. Meanwhile, he worked toward a law degree from Georgetown University. After two years of international-law practice, he served five years as counsel to the House International Relations Committee. He is also a commander in the Naval Reserves, and has done tours of duty in Turkey, Serbia, Bosnia, Haiti, and Panama. In flights during the Gulf War, he was a frequent target of Iraqi guns. Kirk continues to work one weekend each month at the Pentagon's "war room," monitoring intelligence reports.

In 1999, when Porter announced his retirement, Kirk returned home to the 10th District, where he was one of 11 competitors in the Republican primary. This contest included six millionaires who spent nearly $4 million of their own money. Kirk did not spend nearly as much, but he had great advantages: the endorsement of the popular Porter, his positioning as the only candidate with moderate views on cultural issues, and his greater experience in government. He won the primary with 31%, ahead of Shawn Margaret Donnelley, the R.R. Donnelley & Sons printing company heiress, who got 15%, and Northbrook Mayor Mark Damisch, who got 14%. Democrats nominated state Rep. Lauren Beth Gash. Kirk and Gash campaigned as candidates in the Porter mold, promising to carry on his fiscally conservative, culturally moderate record. Gash tried to downplay Kirk's years in Washington, touting her own legislative experience while talking about the need for action on Social Security solvency and affordable prescription drugs. But Kirk won 51%-49%.

In the House, Kirk has compiled a centrist voting record that is a bit more liberal on social issues and conservative on foreign policy. His familiarity with the workings of the House and a helpful friendship with former GOP House Speaker Dennis Hastert of Illinois enabled him to get a seat on the Appropriations Committee. Kirk joined forces with other Republican moderates and deficit hawks in 2004 to try to curb federal spending; the House passed his amendment that requires the Congressional Budget Office to publish an annual report that compares projected annual spending for entitlement programs to the actual spending in the preceding year. He fought to eliminate funding for wasteful earmarks, the individual spending items that lawmakers often tuck into spending bills. Kirk also joined New York City Mayor Michael Bloomberg on a proposal to close a loophole that permits gun dealers to sell off their inventory without background checks of their customers. With other House GOP moderates in 2005, he successfully demanded a House vote on legislation to promote embryonic-stem-cell research as a condition for his support of that year's budget resolution.

Citing intelligence failures in Iraq, the typically well-prepared Kirk pushed for major changes in the structure of the intelligence community. In 2006, he demanded that the Pentagon do more about the opium crisis in Afghanistan and incidences of terrorism fueled by the sale of illegal narcotics. For three weeks in December 2008, he traveled with the Navy in Afghanistan as a special adviser for counternarcotics, making him the first House member since World War II to serve in a combat area. On his return, he called for more troops in Afghanistan to stabilize the region, and said that President Obama should spray the poppies there to curtail opium production.

On issues of parochial importance, Kirk teamed with Democratic Rep. Jesse Jackson Jr. to get the House Appropriations Committee to end subsidized loans for storage by sugar processing companies. Chicago-area candy producers have complained that high sugar prices forced them to cut thousands of jobs. The Kirk-Jackson effort failed. He also pushed for expansion of O'Hare International Airport and, after security breaches were discovered at O'Hare in 2007, he sponsored a bill requiring all airport employees in secure areas to be U.S. citizens. Kirk joined with then-Rep. Rahm Emanuel, D-Ill., in 2005 on a sweeping bill to clean up Lake Michigan.

Kirk has had two serious challenges to his re-election from Dan Seals, a marketing specialist who built well-financed grassroots campaigns. While largely maintaining his support for the war in Iraq, Kirk distanced himself from President Bush. In 2006, the Democratic Congressional Campaign Committee, then headed by Emanuel, did some last-minute spending for Seals, including a mailing in which Bush had his arm around Kirk. But it wasn't enough. Kirk won 53%-47%. He took 51% of the vote in Lake County and 55% in Cook, which cast 57% of the total vote.

Seals ran again in 2008. In a tough year for Republicans, especially Republicans from the home state of Democratic presidential nominee Barack Obama, Kirk kept his distance from the national GOP, and slammed John McCain's choice of Alaska Gov. Sarah Palin as his running mate by saying he would not have chosen her. Seals got early support from the DCCC, which ran ads depicting Kirk as a "rubber stamp" for Bush. Kirk cited his independence and campaigned more aggressively this time, calling Seals a carpet-bagger without a steady job. He raised $5.4 million to Seals's $3.5 million, and won convincingly, 53% to 47%. Seals won Lake County by 1,600 votes, but Kirk won the Cook suburbs with 55%.

Some Republicans wanted Kirk to run against Democratic Sen. Richard Durbin in 2008. He could well be a candidate for the Republican nomination for Obama's old Senate seat.

ELEVENTH DISTRICT

Debbie Halvorson (D)

Elected 2008, 1st term; b. March 1, 1958, Chicago Heights; home, Crete; Prairie State College, A.S. 1988; Governors St. U., B.A. 2001; M.A. 2003.; Lutheran; married (Jim Bush); 4 children.

Elected Office: Crete Township clerk, 1993–96; IL Senate, 1996–2008; Majority ldr., 2005–08.

Professional Career: Small businesss owner, cosmetics, 1979–1993.

DC Office: 1541 LHOB, 20515, 202-225-3635; Fax: 202-225-3521; Web site: halvorson.house.gov.

State Offices: Joliet, 815-726-4998.

Committees: *Agriculture* (16th of 28 D): Conservation, Credit, Energy & Research; General Farm Commodities & Risk Management. *Small Business* (17th of 17 D): Contracting & Technology; Finance & Tax. *Veterans' Affairs* (8th of 18 D): Disability Assistance & Memorial Affairs; Health.

Group Ratings and Key Votes: Newly Elected

Election Results

2008 general	Debbie Halvorson (D)	185,652	(58%)	($2,266,615)
	Marty Ozinga (R)	109,608	(34%)	($1,969,363)
	Jason Wallace (Green)	22,635	(7%)	($6,742)
2008 primary	Debbie Halvorson (D)	unopposed		

Population		Race/Ethnicity		Work	
Pop. 2007:	735,089	White:	79.9%	Private:	82.5%
Change since 2000:	Up 12.5%	Black:	8.0%	Government:	12.4%
Urban:	78.2%	Hispanic:	9.8%	Self-employed:	4.7%
Rural:	21.8%	Asian:	0.9%	Blue collar:	27.7%
Area size:	4,284 sq. mi.	Native Am.:	0.1%	White collar:	55.5%
		Hawaiian:	0.0%	Khaki collar:	0.0%
Age		Two+ races:	1.2%	Other:	16.8%
Median age:	34.3 yrs.	*Ancestry*		Median income:	$56,694
More than 65 yrs:	11.3%	German:	19.9%	Median home value:	$170,500
Less than 18 yrs:	25.7%	Irish:	13.0%	Poverty:	9.9%
Education		Italian:	7.2%		
H.S. grad:	87.6%			**Military Veterans**	
College grad:	21.0%			% of Pop:	9.4%
Grad degree:	7.1%				

The low-lying land west and south of Chicago, where sluggishly flowing rivers run circles around industrial sites, is a great divide over which French explorers portaged the easiest path from the Great Lakes to the Mississippi River valley. Today there is still a kind of borderland here, as the factories and shopping centers and subdivisions stop somewhere past the Cook County line and downstate prairies begin, cornfields bisected by highways and railroads radiating out from the Loop, and the rail

2008 Presidential Vote		
Obama (D)	175,808	(53%)
McCain (R)	148,600	(45%)

2004 Presidential Vote		
Bush (R)	162,779	(54%)
Kerry (D)	140,619	(46%)

Cook Partisan Voting Index: R + 1

yards of the nation's transportation hub. Politically, this is a borderland as well, between the traditionally Democratic Chicago area, with its hard-bitten machine politics, and heavily Republican downstate Illinois, with its tradition of governance by local civic leaders that stretches to the days of Abraham Lincoln.

The 11th Congressional District of Illinois covers much of this borderland. It includes most of Will County, the fastest-growing of the large suburban Chicago counties, and its county seat of Joliet. It is politically marginal territory, and Joliet grew by more than 35,000 people between 2000 and 2006, the largest jump in the state. Once a canal boat town, and later the producer of one-third of America's wallpaper, Joliet was home to the famed Joliet Correctional Center, the prison featured in the movie *The Blues Brothers*, until it closed in 2002. It is the location of a 75,000-seat NASCAR racetrack. It owes its current prosperity and growing tourist locales in part to riverboat gambling.

The number of Hispanic residents nearly doubled in Will County. Farther west, on bluffs above the Illinois River, are the factory towns of Ottawa, LaSalle, and Streator. South of Joliet is Kankakee, a county seat amid rich prairie earth on the Illinois Central main line and the home of convicted former GOP Gov. George Ryan. This is Republican territory. The 11th no longer includes the southernmost townships of Cook County, which were increasingly Democratic, but it has added two ungainly-looking appendages. One goes west to rural Bureau County; the other heads south at the intersection of interstates 80 and 39 and includes most of Bloomington in McLean County, one of the faster-growing downstate counties. The 2001 redistricting made this district more Republican than its 1990s incarnation, but recent votes show it trending Democratic. President Bush won here with 54% in 2004, but in 2008 Democrat Barack Obama took 53% to Republican John McCain's 45%.

The new congresswoman from the 11th District is Debbie Halvorson, a Democrat elected in 2008. Halvorson succeeds Republican Rep. Jerry Weller, who chose retirement amid political pressure over questionable Central American land deals. A former Mary Kay cosmetics saleswoman, Halvorson honed a business acumen that translated into political savvy in Springfield and on the campaign trail. Several years ago, she put a college education on hold while she raised two children as a single mother, juggling jobs selling the popular cosmetics brand and doing temp work for 10 years. She then went back to school, studying for her bachelor's and master's degrees while serving in the state Senate.

Halvorson was the Crete Township clerk when she was drafted in 1996 to attempt to unseat an 18-year Republican incumbent in the Illinois Senate, Aldo DeAngelis. Halvorson walked all 210 precincts campaigning for over a year, and won with 56% of the vote. DeAngelis's campaign manager later told Halvorson he knew she would win because "Aldo knew all the bank presidents, but Debbie knew all the tellers." In the Senate, Halvorson sponsored bills to make cheaper prescriptions available to senior citizens and to protect them from abuse in nursing homes. She also passed a bill toughening laws against hit-and run drivers. In 2005, Halvorson became the first woman in Illinois history to become Senate majority leader.

Halvorson was courted by national Democrats to run, and she was unopposed in the February 2008 primary. On the Republican side, New Lenox Mayor Tim Baldermann emerged as the top vote-getter in a three-way contest, but a few weeks later, he withdrew, saying he had underestimated the time and fundraising commitment. The GOP's substitute was concrete magnate Martin Ozinga. It was the local businessman's first foray into politics, but his name recognition and ability to self-fund made him an attractive candidate.

The general election campaign in the swing district quickly became one of the closest watched races in the country. Residents were bombarded by negative direct mail, robocalls, and television and radio advertising. Ozinga accused Halvorson of being a part of unpopular Gov. Rod Blagojevich's inner circle, though his attacks were muted by revelations that he had once made campaign contributions to Blagojevich. Ozinga also questioned Halvorson's motives in voting against an electricity rate freeze that would have affected a prominent Democratic donor. Halvorson tried to tie Ozinga to the unpopular Bush administration, highlighting Vice President Dick Cheney's planned visit to an Ozinga fundraiser. She also charged that his business deals had made him cozy with the Chicago political machine.

With Blagojevich coming under increased scrutiny in Illinois even before the election (he would later be impeached and removed from office in January 2009), it seemed as though some of Ozinga's salvos might be sticking. He earned an endorsement from the traditionally liberal *Chicago Sun-Times*, but Halvorson got the backing of the National Rifle Association. Polls showed Ozinga inching closer to Halvorson in the weeks before the election. But Election Day was a different story. Buoyed by a strong showing for Obama in the district, Halvorson cruised to election with 58% of the vote to Ozinga's 34%.

Once in Congress, Halvorson was appointed to the Agriculture, Small Business and Veterans' Affairs committees. But even with her wide margin of victory, Republicans were already making plans to recapture the seat: an early entrant for the GOP was Air Force pilot and Iraq War veteran Adam Kinzinger.

TWELFTH DISTRICT

Jerry Costello (D)

Elected Aug. 1988, 11th full term; b. Sept. 25, 1949, E. St. Louis; home, Belleville; Belleville Area Col., A.A. 1971, Maryville Col., B.A. 1973; Catholic; married (Georgia); 3 children.

Elected Office: Chmn., St. Clair Cnty. Bd. of Supervisors, 1980–88.

Professional Career: Dir., IL Court Svcs. & Probation, 1973–80; Chmn., Region's Cncl. of Govts., 1980–84.

DC Office: 2408 RHOB, 20515, 202-225-5661; Fax: 202-225-0285; Web site: www.house.gov/costello.

State Offices: Belleville, 618-233-8026; Carbondale, 618-529-3791; Chester, 618-826-3043; E. St. Louis, 618-397-8833; Granite City, 618-451-7065; West Frankfort, 618-937-6402.

Committees: *Science & Technology* (2nd of 26 D): Energy & Environment. *Transportation & Infrastructure* (4th of 44 D): Aviation (Chmn); Railroads, Pipelines & Hazardous Materials; Water Resources & Environment.

Group Ratings

	ADA	ACLU	AFS	LCV	ITIC	NTU	COC	ACU	CFG	FRC
2008	85	100	100	92	43	15	50	13	9	76
2007	95	—	100	75	—	7	47	16	1	—

National Journal Ratings

	2007 LIB — 2007 CONS		2008 LIB — 2008 CONS	
Economic	58%	— 41%	77%	— 22%
Social	56%	— 43%	52%	— 47%
Foreign	78%	— 20%	77%	— 22%
Composite	65%	— 35%	69%	— 31%

Key Votes of the 110th Congress

1. Increase minimum wage	Y	5. Share immigration data	N	9. Withdraw troops 8/08	Y
2. Expand SCHIP	Y	6. Foreign aid abortion ban	Y	10. No operations in Iran	Y
3. Raise CAFE standards	Y	7. Ban gay bias in workplace	Y	11. Free trade with Peru	N
4. Bail out financial markets	N	8. Repeal D.C. gun law	Y	12. Overhaul FISA	N

Election Results

2008 general	Jerry Costello (D)	212,891 (71%)	($830,944)
	Timmy Richardson (R)	74,382 (25%)	
	Rodger Jennings (Green)	10,907 (4%)	($8,229)
2008 primary	Jerry Costello (D)	unopposed	

Prior Winning Percentages: 2006 (100%); 2004 (69%); 2002 (69%); 2000 (100%); 1998 (60%); 1996 (72%); 1994 (66%); 1992 (71%); 1990 (66%); 1988 (53%); 1988 (51%)

Population		Race/Ethnicity		Work	
Pop. 2007:	653,304	White:	78.4%	Private:	75.8%
Change since 2000:	Down 0.1%	Black:	16.7%	Government:	19.0%
Urban:	76.7%	Hispanic:	2.2%	Self-employed:	5.1%
Rural:	23.3%	Asian:	1.0%	Blue collar:	23.6%
Area size:	4,556 sq. mi.	Native Am.:	0.2%	White collar:	55.2%
		Hawaiian:	0.0%	Khaki collar:	0.7%
Age		Two+ races:	1.3%	Other:	20.5%
Median age:	36.0 yrs.			Median income:	$41,241
More than 65 yrs:	13.9%	*Ancestry*		Median home value:	$90,500
Less than 18 yrs:	23.7%	German:	23.3%	Poverty:	15.6%
		Irish:	10.9%		
Education		English:	8.1%	**Military Veterans**	
H.S. grad:	84.9%			% of Pop:	13.5%
College grad:	20.0%				
Grad degree:	7.0%				

Their waters roiling together, the nation's two mightiest rivers, the Mississippi and Missouri, join just a few miles below Alton, Ill. Its 19th-century buildings recall its turbulent history, when it was the home of the antislavery agitator Elijah Lovejoy, who was murdered by a mob. More recently, it was the longtime home of conservative crusader and columnist Phyllis Schlafly. Nearby in Hartford, Lewis and Clark spent five months preparing their team and collecting supplies for their journey westward.

2008 Presidential Vote		
Obama (D)	.170,391	(56%)
McCain (R)	.131,443	(43%)
2004 Presidential Vote		
Kerry (D)	.152,055	(52%)
Bush (R)	.139,710	(48%)
Cook Partisan Voting Index:	D + 3	

Farther south along the Mississippi is East St. Louis, situated on the Illinois side of the river, with a view of the Gateway Arch in the city of St. Louis on the Missouri side. It is a terminus for dozens of rail lines and highways that funnel into bridges over the river. Once a rail and stockyard center second only to Chicago, East St. Louis is now one of America's poorest and most troubled cities, a half-abandoned slum with one of the nation's highest crime rates and a rapidly declining tax base. It is dependent on a riverboat casino and an adjacent waterfront hotel for local revenue, but casino taxes have increased and revenues have dipped, leaving the future of gambling in Illinois in question. After peaking at 82,000 in 1960, its population is now less than 29,000 and almost entirely African-American. East St. Louis is in St. Clair County, long heavily Democratic. Alton is in Madison County, which is politically more marginal.

South of East St. Louis and the industrial area around Belleville, the river counties are lightly inhabited. This was the site of the French Kaskaskia settlement that became Illinois's first capital in 1818, but repeated flooding turned it into an island and reduced its population to nine people and many more egrets. Farther south, the river abuts coal country and is not far from Carbondale, once a coal center but now, as the home of Southern Illinois University, bustling with students from downstate Illinois and Chicago. In 2006, Maytag shut its plant and eliminated 1,000 jobs in nearby Herrin. The land here is sometimes known as Little Egypt, the southern end of Illinois where the Ohio River meets the Mississippi: flat, fertile farmland, protected by giant constructed levees because it is susceptible to yearly floods. The marshy landscape has created the Sinkhole Plain, with more than 10,000 sinkholes. There is more than a touch of Dixie here: The unofficial capital of Little Egypt, Cairo (pronounced *KAY-roh*), is a declining town closer to Memphis than to Chicago. In his 1842 work *American Notes*, Charles Dickens described the town in these unflattering terms: "a hotbed of disease, an ugly sepulchre, a grave uncheered by any gleam of promise: a place without one single quality, in earth or air or water, to commend it: such is this dismal Cairo." A more enticing locale not far from Cairo is the Shawnee National Forest, which has preserved Native American sites that are 10,000 years old. The Cherokee Nation left here in the 1830s on its devastating forced march to Oklahoma, which became known as the Trail of Tears.

The 12th District of Illinois covers all of this Mississippi riverfront from Alton south to Cairo, with some inland territory as well. Most of its population is in the Metro East area in St. Clair and Madison counties. The largest employer in Southern Illinois is Scott Air Force Base near Belleville, home of the 932nd Airlift Wing, medical transport planes, and refueling tankers. George W. Bush lost this district twice. John McCain lost it to Barack Obama, 56%-43% in 2008.

The congressman from the 12th District is Jerry Costello, a Democrat first elected in 1988. He grew up in a St. Clair County political family—his father was the county sheriff. He graduated from high school in East St. Louis, then the family moved to Belleville. As a young man, Costello went to work for the county as a court bailiff, and eventually worked his way up to administrator of the county court system. He was elected to the St. Clair County Board of Supervisors and became chairman. He waited with some impatience for the retirement of Democratic Rep. Mel Price, who was first elected in 1944 and served for more than 40 years. Price died in office in April 1988. Experienced, well connected, supported by organized labor, Costello was the obvious successor. Yet he received only 51% of the votes in the special election and 53% for a full term.

Costello is a practical-minded, low-profile politician with a centrist voting record that is a bit more liberal on economics than on cultural issues. Seniority has moved him toward top posts on both the Science and Technology and the Transportation and Infrastructure committees, where he is chairman of the Aviation Subcommittee. In 2006, he pushed a bill to require contract talks between the Federal Aviation Administration and the air traffic controllers' union, but it fell 9 votes short of passage. He wants the federal government to make a much larger contribution to modernize the system. He has criticized airlines for not meeting their commitments for a "passenger bill of rights." In 2008, the Transportation Committee approved his proposal to ban cell phone use on planes. On the war in Iraq, Costello has been consistently opposed to Bush administration policies and voted against authorizing to use force against Iraq in 2002. (His son was a paratrooper during the Gulf War in 1991.)

In his district work, Costello is attempting to revive his district's largely dormant high-sulfur coal mines with incentives for clean-coal research and development and has been successful in including several provisions in recent energy bills. He also has worked to secure annual appropriations for the FutureGen clean-coal power plant just outside of his district, which is designed to burn coal without polluting the air. Costello also tries to get as much federal money as he can for infrastructure improvements for downtrodden East St. Louis. Despite setbacks, Costello finally won approval of a new Mississippi River bridge north of the current congested bridge on Interstate 70. In 2008, Costello sought Ethics Committee approval to continue seeking spending earmarks for Southwestern Illinois Community College after his wife, Georgia, was named president of the college.

Costello usually draws no serious challenges at election time. But in 1998, he faced Bill Price, an orthopedic surgeon and son of Mel Price, who switched parties and ran as a Republican. At the time, Costello had been weakened by disclosures at the trial of his former business partner, who ultimately was convicted of trying to obstruct a federal investigation. The trial brought out testimony that Costello was a silent partner in casino deals at a time when he was working on legislation to help an Indian tribe that owned the land for the proposed casinos. Despite an opponent with a well-known and respected name locally, Costello won by a solid 60%-40%. Since then, he has been easily re-elected every two years.

THIRTEENTH DISTRICT

Judy Biggert (R)

Elected 1998, 6th term; b. Aug. 15, 1937, Chicago; home, Hinsdale; Stanford U., B.A. 1959, Northwestern U., J.D. 1963; Episcopalian; married (Rody); 4 children.

Elected Office: Hinsdale Bd. of Ed., 1982–85; IL House of Reps., 1992–98.

Professional Career: Clerk, U.S. Ct. of Appeals, 1963–64; Practicing atty., 1975–98.

DC Office: 1034 LHOB, 20515, 202-225-3515; Fax: 202-225-9420; Web site: judybiggert.house.gov.

State Offices: Willowbrook, 630-655-2052.

Committees: *Education & Labor* (8th of 19 R): Early Childhood, Elementary & Secondary Education; Higher Education, Lifelong Learning & Competitiveness. *Financial Services* (9th of 29 R): Capital Markets, Insurance & Government Sponsored Enterprises; Housing & Community Opportunity; Oversight & Investigations (RMM). *Science & Technology* (8th of 17 R): Energy & Environment; Technology & Innovation.

Group Ratings

	ADA	ACLU	AFS	LCV	ITIC	NTU	COC	ACU	CFG	FRC
2008	35	27	14	38	71	63	94	84	65	35
2007	30	—	18	55	—	65	85	68	67	—

National Journal Ratings

	2007 LIB	—	2007 CONS	2008 LIB	—	2008 CONS
Economic	34%	—	66%	32%	—	68%
Social	43%	—	57%	31%	—	62%
Foreign	43%	—	56%	41%	—	59%
Composite	40%	—	60%	36%	—	64%

Key Votes of the 110th Congress

1. Increase minimum wage	Y	5. Share immigration data	Y	9. Withdraw troops 8/08	N
2. Expand SCHIP	N	6. Foreign aid abortion ban	Y	10. No operations in Iran	N
3. Raise CAFE standards	N	7. Ban gay bias in workplace	Y	11. Free trade with Peru	Y
4. Bail out financial markets	Y	8. Repeal D.C. gun law	Y	12. Overhaul FISA	Y

Election Results

2008 general	Judy Biggert (R)	180,888	(54%)	($1,585,536)
	Scott Harper (D)	147,430	(44%)	($1,070,201)
	Steve Alesch (Green)	9,402	(3%)	
2008 primary	Judy Biggert (R)	unopposed		

Prior Winning Percentages: 2006 (58%); 2004 (65%); 2002 (70%); 2000 (66%); 1998 (61%)

Population		Race/Ethnicity		Work	
Pop. 2007:	768,478	White:	74.9%	Private:	85.1%
Change since 2000:	Up 17.6%	Black:	6.3%	Government:	10.0%
Urban:	98.8%	Hispanic:	9.1%	Self-employed:	4.7%
Rural:	1.2%	Asian:	8.3%	Blue collar:	15.2%
Area size:	362 sq. mi.	Native Am.:	0.1%	White collar:	73.3%
		Hawaiian:	0.0%	Khaki collar:	0.0%
Age		Two+ races:	1.1%	Other:	11.5%
Median age:	35.6 yrs.	*Ancestry*		Median income:	$80,460
More than 65 yrs:	9.1%	German:	16.0%	Median home value:	$312,400
Less than 18 yrs:	27.5%	Irish:	13.4%	Poverty:	4.2%
Education		Polish:	10.6%	**Military Veterans**	
H.S. grad:	93.3%			% of Pop:	7.3%
College grad:	45.1%				
Grad degree:	17.4%				

Most residents of Chicagoland now live not in the city but in the suburbs, and increasingly not even in Cook County but in the collar counties all around Cook. DuPage County, straight west of Chicago, had 103,000 residents in 1940; in 2007, there were 929,000, with new subdivisions still springing up at the western edges. This is not a one-trick county of bedroom suburbs. Since 1970, DuPage has generated nearly half the new jobs in metropolitan Chicago. In Oak Brook are the headquarters of Ace

2008 Presidential Vote
Obama (D) 191,306 (54%)
McCain (R)..............................156,695 (45%)

2004 Presidential Vote
Bush (R) 175,705 (55%)
Kerry (D)................................142,397 (45%)

Cook Partisan Voting Index: R + 1

Hardware, Federal Signal, and most famously, McDonald's and its Hamburger University, an 80-acre campus where more than 80,000 trainees have received Bachelor of Hamburgerology degrees since it was founded in 1961. Nearby are graceful, old railroad-commuter towns like Hinsdale and Downers Grove, but also Naperville, once a country village, now an edge city, with a school district that is top-ranked globally in science and a top-rated public library. The Argonne National Laboratory, which conducts basic and applied research in disciplines that range from high-energy physics to biotechnology, has sparked numerous private research firms along the Sanitary and Ship Canal, the Des Plaines River, and the Illinois and Michigan Canal.

The 13th Congressional District of Illinois includes the southern part of DuPage County, including Oak Brook, Downers Grove, and Naperville; a small section of the southwest corner of Cook County; and a northern slice of Will County, including Bolingbrook, Romeoville, and Lockport. *Money* magazine rated Naperville No. 2 among the best places to live in the United States in 2006. Politically, this has been a heavily Republican area, suspicious of the motives and operations of Chicago Democrats, devoted to free enterprise and hostile to higher taxes. George W. Bush twice won the district with 55% of the vote. Barack Obama nearly reversed Bush's numbers, winning 54% to 45%.

The congresswoman from the 13th District is Judy Biggert, a Republican first elected in 1998. She grew up in affluent Kenilworth on the North Shore, graduated from New Trier Township High School, Stanford University and Northwestern Law School, and then clerked for a federal appeals judge. She raised four children in Hinsdale, practicing estate and real estate law out of her home. She served on the Hinsdale Township Board of Education and in 1992, was elected to the state House, where she was a member of the leadership. Biggert started running for the U.S. House in 1997, when incumbent Republican moderate Harris Fawell announced his retirement. He endorsed her as his successor. In the campaign, she portrayed herself as a "former car pool mom and assistant soccer coach." She supported abortion rights and opposed most gun-control measures. She had primary opposition from state Rep. Peter Roskam, who moved to the district to run (and later won the 6th District seat). Biggert put in $402,000 of her own money and got support from Planned Parenthood and the Human Rights Campaign. She won the primary 45% to 40% for Roskam and the general election 61%-39%.

In the House, Biggert has a moderate voting record, especially on cultural issues. In 2008, after a five-year campaign by Biggert, Congress passed her bill barring employers and insurers from denying a job or a health insurance policy on the basis of genetic tests. On the since renamed Education and the Workforce Committee, she was the prime sponsor of a bill to allow employees to take compensatory time rather than overtime, a measure she said would allow flexibility for working parents. The AFL-CIO lobbied heavily against it, and Republican leaders canceled a roll call after it was apparent they didn't have the votes to pass it. After Hurricane Katrina in 2005, she strongly opposed a proposed school-voucher program for evacuees. In 2007, Congress enacted her proposal to ensure that homeless youth have equivalent access to student aid. Also that year, she and other moderate Republicans tried unsuccessfully to bridge partisan differences on a Democratic initiative to expand the State Children's Health Insurance Program. (But in February 2009, she voted against enactment of a more comprehensive measure signed by President Obama.)

Biggert has been a strong supporter of the Argonne Lab. On the Science Committee, she has sponsored bills authorizing hundreds of millions of dollars for university nuclear science and engineering programs and for the Office of Science. In 2004, she sponsored a successful bill authorizing the Energy Department to spend $165 million to build a supercomputer. Her challenge in the 111th Congress (2009-10) was trying to persuade appropriators to sustain a high level of funding for research as the economy slipped into a recession. The funding is needed, she said, to avert a "brain drain" at the national labs. Another area of interest for Biggert is public education. She has sponsored bills to ensure that homeless children get schooling, to help children with eating disorders and to finance school construction.

In 2009, Biggert became the ranking Republican on the Financial Services Subcommittee on Oversight and Investigations. In the 110th Congress (2007-08), she had the senior minority slot on the subcommittee on Financial Institutions and Consumer Credit, where she worked on the mortgage crisis and bailout of the financial markets. The panel rejected her plan to allow the FHA to negotiate 40-year mortgages to assist troubled borrowers. At the local level, Biggert has worked to secure funding for electric fish barriers on the Chicago Sanitary and Ship Canal to keep the huge Asian carp from invading the Great Lakes.

Biggert has ambitions to get into the Republican leadership in the House. In November 2000, she lost a contest for secretary of the Republican Conference. At the request of former Republican Speaker Dennis Hastert, she agreed to serve on the House ethics committee, the panel that investigates ethics complaints against House members. It is generally thankless work, but a stint on the committee is often later rewarded by grateful party leaders. Biggert was on the four-member ethics panel that in 2006 investigated the case of former Florida Rep. Mark Foley, a Republican who had acknowledged improper contacts with former pages to House leaders, who then failed to take action. Biggert's panel detailed mistakes by Republican leaders and their top aides, but did not call for sanctions.

For years, she was not seriously challenged for re-election, even though in 1999, she abandoned her pledge to serve only three terms. But in 2008, she faced former health-care marketing executive Scott Harper, who criticized her as too friendly to corporate interests and out of touch with voters' economic anxieties. He was competitive financially, raising over $1 million, and criticized her for being "asleep at the wheel" for initially voting against the financial markets bailout. She later voted to support the legislation. She won 54%-44%, getting 54% in DuPage County and 60% in the Cook County suburbs, but only 50% in the outlying Will County suburbs.

FOURTEENTH DISTRICT

Bill Foster (D)

Elected Mar. 2008, 1st full term; b. Oct. 7, 1955, Madison, WI; home, Batavia; U. of WI-Madison, B.A., 1976, Harvard U., Ph.D., 1983.; No religious affiliation; married (Aesook); 2 children.

Professional Career: Co-founder, Electronic Theatre Controls, 1975-2007; Scientist, Fermi National Accelerator Laboratory, 1990-2006.

DC Office: 1339 LHOB, 20515, 202-225-2976; Fax: 202-225-0697; Web site: foster.house.gov.

State Offices: Batavia, 630-406-1114; Dixon, 815-288-0680; Geneseo, 309-944-3558.

Committees: *Financial Services* (30th of 42 D): Capital Markets, Insurance & Government Sponsored Enterprises; Financial Institutions & Consumer Credit. *Oversight & Government Reform* (22nd of 24 D): Domestic Policy; National Security & Foreign Affairs.

Group Ratings

	ADA	ACLU	AFS	LCV	ITIC	NTU	COC	ACU	CFG	FRC
2008	65	100	83	73	100	14	56	13	1	0
2007	—	—	—	—	—	—	—	—	—	—

National Journal Ratings

	2007 LIB	—	2007 CONS	2008 LIB	—	2008 CONS
Economic	*%	—	*%	52%	—	48%
Social	*%	—	*%	50%	—	50%
Foreign	*%	—	*%	64%	—	35%
Composite	*%	—	*%	56%	—	45%

Key Votes of the 110th Congress

1. Increase minimum wage	*	5. Share immigration data	*	9. Withdraw troops 8/08	*
2. Expand SCHIP	*	6. Foreign aid abortion ban	*	10. No operations in Iran	*
3. Raise CAFE standards	*	7. Ban gay bias in workplace	*	11. Free trade with Peru	*
4. Bail out financial markets	Y	8. Repeal D.C. gun law	Y	12. Overhaul FISA	N

Election Results

2008 general	Bill Foster (D) 185,404	(58%)	($5,047,815)
	Jim Oberweis (R) 135,653	(42%)	($5,084,489)
2008 primary	Bill Foster (D) 32,410	(42%)	
	John Laesch (D) 32,012	(42%)	
	Joe Serra (D) 6,033	(8%)	
	Jotham Stein (D)..5,865	(8%)	
2008 spec. general	Bill Foster (D) 52,205	(53%)	
	Jim Oberweis (R) 47,180	(47%)	
2008 spec. primary	Bill Foster (D) 32,982	(50%)	
	Kohn Laesch (D) 28,433	(43%)	
	Jotham Stein (D)..5,082	(8%)	

Population		Race/Ethnicity		Work	
Pop. 2007:	786,730	White:	68.7%	Private:	84.6%
Change since 2000:	Up 20.4%	Black:	4.8%	Government:	10.7%
Urban:	86.2%	Hispanic:	22.3%	Self-employed:	4.5%
Rural:	13.8%	Asian:	2.9%	Blue collar:	26.1%
Area size:	2,866 sq. mi.	Native Am.:	0.1%	White collar:	59.1%
Age		Hawaiian:	0.0%	Khaki collar:	0.0%
Median age:	32.3 yrs.	Two+ races:	1.1%	Other:	14.8%
More than 65 yrs:	8.7%	*Ancestry*		Median income:	$65,119
Less than 18 yrs:	27.9%	German:	20.3%	Median home value:	$227,300
Education		Irish:	10.8%	Poverty:	8.7%
H.S. grad:	85.1%	English:	5.9%	**Military Veterans**	
College grad:	29.7%			% of Pop:	7.9%
Grad degree:	9.7%				

Downstate Illinois, as it is known locally, is a misnomer. Although it certainly does refer to the territory south of Chicago, and therefore "down the state" from Chicago, it also means everything north and west of the nation's third-largest city. In the vernacular, downstate Illinois is everything that is not Chicago or its suburbs, just as upstate New York is everything that is not New York City. The 14th Congressional District is where downstate Illinois begins, at least where it begins in the westerly direction from the city. Where the densely packed suburban areas leave off, the district begins in western DuPage County. It is home to two great Illinois landmarks: Cantigny, the estate of Col. Robert McCormick, longtime publisher of the *Chicago Tribune*; and Fermilab, the world's fastest particle accelerator, which takes a staff of 2,000 people to operate. The 14th also contains the Fox River Valley and its industrial cities, Elgin and Aurora; Aurora's population grew 19% from 2000 to 2006 with a large influx of Hispanics. In contrast, there is urbane St. Charles, a small city bisected by the Fox River that is filled with antiques stores and restaurants and sponsors the well-attended annual Scarecrow Festival.

The district also includes Kendall County, rated the fastest-growing county in the nation in 2008. The county added some 42,000 people from 2000 to 2007, a 77% increase that edged out Flagler County, Fla., for fastest growth among U.S. counties with 10,000 people or more. Following a pattern established by cities and their close-in suburbs, Kendall exploded in population as people sought cheap land and more-affordable housing near job centers in suburban DuPage and Kane counties, which are a commute away. In effect, Kendall is a suburb of the suburbs. Since 2000, subdivisions and strip malls have sprouted out of its cornfields. Kendall's surge helps make this the fastest-growing congressional district in Illinois.

Farther west, the 14th passes through DeKalb County, long the world's leading manufacturer of barbed wire, and goes on to Lee County, to take in Ronald Reagan's boyhood home in Dixon. This was traditionally some of the most heavily Republican territory in the country. Northern Illinois was settled when Chicago was just a frontier village, by Yankees from Ohio, Indiana, upstate New York, and New England, and by Germans emigrating after the failed revolutions of 1848. They were the heart of the

2008 Presidential Vote

Obama (D) 181,329	(55%)
McCain (R)...........................145,345	(44%)

2004 Presidential Vote

Bush (R) 158,428	(55%)
Kerry (D) 125,269	(44%)

Cook Partisan Voting Index: R + 1

Republican Party from its founding in 1854, and the core of the Grand Army of the Republic a few years later. Their descendants remain mostly Republican today.

The congressman from the 14th District is Bill Foster, a Democrat who won a March 2008 special election to succeed Republican House Speaker Dennis Hastert. This contest was an early indicator of the good prospects for Democrats in that election year, when Illinois favorite-son Barack Obama was elected president and the party fattened its majorities in Congress. Foster began life as a Washington insider. His parents met in Washington, D.C., where each worked for a senator. His father became a law professor at the University of Wisconsin-Madison, and Foster grew up in Madison, graduated from the university, and went on to get his Ph.D. in physics from Harvard University. Foster was a physicist for 16 years at Fermilab, where he was involved in groundbreaking research in elementary particle physics; he also ran a theater-lighting business with his younger brother that made them both multimillionaires. He had not sought public office before volunteering in 2006 in the congressional campaign of Patrick Murphy, a Pennsylvania Democrat who ousted a Republican incumbent. "He was somebody I believed in, and he had a chance to win," said Foster, who, given his professional background, did more than stuff envelopes. Foster developed for Murphy a computerized get-out-the-vote system. At age 52, Foster then spent five months working on Murphy's Capitol Hill staff.

After Hastert resigned the seat in November 2007, Foster paid for a detailed poll that surprisingly revealed that the Republican-leaning district's voters could be wooed by a centrist Democrat who was "moderately pro-choice" on abortion rights and had a business and science background. "I went into the campaign knowing that it was long odds but that we had a chance to win," he says. Running in the Democratic primary against the more liberal Jonathan Laesch, who had lost to Hastert 60%-40% in 2006, Foster got a break when popular Illinois Sen. Richard Durbin endorsed him. "That was huge, and it divided the labor vote," Foster said. He also got backstage support from the Democratic Congressional Campaign Committee, whose chairman, Rep. Christopher Van Hollen of Maryland, quietly steered fundraising help to him. Foster won the primary 50%-43%.

Republicans nominated Jim Oberweis, a successful dairy owner who previously had lost numerous statewide campaigns but who had been endorsed by Hastert against state Sen. Chris Lauzen, an outspoken conservative. In a significant setback, Lauzen refused to endorse Oberweis following their divisive primary. Amid the clutter of negative charges and counter-charges, Foster seemed to get a boost from a 30-second ad by the Obama campaign, which endorsed Foster with Obama's presidential campaign theme of change. It said: "He'll focus on changing Washington to get results. I endorse Bill Foster for Congress because he represents the change we need." The outcome showed that Obama had coattails, according to House Democratic strategists. Foster won 53%-47%. In Kane County, which cast 61% of the vote, he led 54%-46%. Oberweis led in only three outlying rural counties. Each candidate spent more than $3 million, including about $2 million of his own money, with each national party kicking in more than $1 million. Foster and Oberweis faced each other again in November. But the outcome was viewed as a foregone conclusion and received little national attention. With another boost from Obama and with Republicans focused on other House races in Illinois, Foster this time won 58%-42%.

In the House, Foster got a seat on the Financial Services Committee, where he supported the bailout of the financial markets. He also helped to restore $62.5 million in funding for Fermilab. Republicans voiced hope of a competitive challenge in 2010.

FIFTEENTH DISTRICT

Tim Johnson (R)

Elected 2000, 5th term; b. July 23, 1946, Champaign; home, Urbana; U. of IL, B.A. 1969, U. of IL, J.D. 1972; Christian; divorced; 9 children.

Elected Office: Urbana City Council, 1971–76; IL House of Reps., 1976–2000.

Professional Career: Practicing atty., Johnson, Frank, Frederick & Walsh.

DC Office: 1207 LHOB, 20515, 202-225-2371; Fax: 202-226-0791; Web site: www.house.gov/timjohnson.

State Offices: Bloomington, 309-663-7049; Champaign, 217-403-4690; Charleston, 217-348-6759; Mt. Carmel, 618-262-8719.

Committees: *Agriculture* (4th of 18 R): General Farm Commodities & Risk Management; Horticulture & Organic Agriculture. *Transportation & Infrastructure* (11th of 30 R): Economic Development, Public Buildings & Emergency Management; Highways & Transit; Railroads, Pipelines & Hazardous Materials.

Group Ratings

	ADA	ACLU	AFS	LCV	ITIC	NTU	COC	ACU	CFG	FRC
2008	50	64	29	62	50	52	67	68	53	100
2007	35	—	36	75	—	39	84	60	43	—

National Journal Ratings

	2007 LIB	—	2007 CONS		2008 LIB	—	2008 CONS
Economic	44%	—	55%		41%	—	59%
Social	38%	—	62%		41%	—	59%
Foreign	45%	—	55%		43%	—	57%
Composite	43%	—	58%		42%	—	58%

Key Votes of the 110th Congress

1. Increase minimum wage	Y	5. Share immigration data	Y	9. Withdraw troops 8/08	N
2. Expand SCHIP	N	6. Foreign aid abortion ban	Y	10. No operations in Iran	N
3. Raise CAFE standards	Y	7. Ban gay bias in workplace	N	11. Free trade with Peru	Y
4. Bail out financial markets	N	8. Repeal D.C. gun law	Y	12. Overhaul FISA	N

Election Results

2008 general	Tim Johnson (R)..187,121	(64%)		($295,919)
	Steve Cox (D) 104,393	(36%)		
2008 primary	Tim Johnson (R).. unopposed			

Prior Winning Percentages: 2006 (58%); 2004 (61%); 2002 (65%); 2000 (53%)

Population		Race/Ethnicity		Work	
Pop. 2007:	666,704	White:	86.2%	Private:	74.3%
Change since 2000:	Up 2.0%	Black:	6.2%	Government:	18.8%
Urban:	64.2%	Hispanic:	2.9%	Self-employed:	6.7%
Rural:	35.8%	Asian:	3.2%	Blue collar:	25.4%
Area size:	10,122 sq. mi.	Native Am.:	0.1%	White collar:	57.7%
Age		Hawaiian:	0.0%	Khaki collar:	0.0%
Median age:	35.0 yrs.	Two+ races:	1.1%	Other:	16.9%
More than 65 yrs:	14.0%	*Ancestry*		Median income:	$44,193
Less than 18 yrs:	22.1%	German:	21.9%	Median home value:	$102,700
Education		Irish:	10.7%	Poverty:	14.8%
H.S. grad:	88.3%	USA:	10.6%	**Military Veterans**	
College grad:	26.1%			% of Pop:	10.4%
Grad degree:	10.1%				

South of Chicago, the Illinois Central Railroad heads to the city of New Orleans on a railbed elevated a few feet above the rich black soil of the Illinois prairie, topsoil reaching down not just inches but feet. This land dazzled its first settlers, who were accustomed to land that had to be cleared of trees and stumps before it could be plowed. This treeless prairie could be cultivated almost immediately, and with bounteous results. Today, the region is still farming country, made up not of small family

2008 Presidential Vote		
McCain (R)..............................152,222	(51%)
Obama (D) 143,965	(48%)

2004 Presidential Vote		
Bush (R)..................................174,928	(59%)
Kerry (D)..................................121,814	(41%)

Cook Partisan Voting Index: R + 6

farms, but of large and profitable commercial operations, typically of 1,000 acres or more. Cultivating this soil is a business, requiring judgments about crop selection, maximizing yields, proper pesticides, marketing, export prospects, and government programs. The chief crops are corn and soybeans. The prairie landscape of rural, eastern Illinois is marked by only a few towns, the largest of which are the sites of universities: the University of Illinois in Champaign-Urbana, Illinois State in Bloomington-Normal, Illinois Wesleyan, also in Bloomington. Politically, these prairie lands incline much more to the party of former House Speaker Joseph Cannon, a Republican from the manufacturing city of Danville east of Urbana, than to the party of Vice President Adlai Stevenson, a Democrat from Bloomington, who served under laissez-faire Democrat Grover Cleveland and was the grandfather of the Adlai Stevenson nominated by Democrats for president in 1952 and 1956.

The 15th Congressional District of Illinois occupies much of this prairie, beginning in Iroquois County and covering some 130 miles south to the old National Road and U.S. 40, traditionally the line between northern Republican and southern Democratic downstate Illinois. The biggest city here is Champaign-Urbana and the district includes parts of Normal and next-door Bloomington. The twin cities of Normal and Bloomington are split mostly along U.S. 51. Downtown Normal and Illinois State University are in the 11th District, while southern Normal and eastern Bloomington are in the 15th. The district also features a narrow corridor of land extending more than 100 miles along the Wabash River border with Indiana as far south as the Ohio River, with an extension to the town of Eldorado. The university towns are somewhat liberal, but the prairie counties have long been Republican, and on balance, this is a Republican-oriented district.

The congressman from the 15th District is Tim Johnson, a Republican first elected in 2000. Johnson was born in Champaign, grew up in Urbana, and graduated from the University of Illinois and its law school. He was elected to the Urbana City Council while still in law school and served four years before winning election to the state House in 1976. In the Legislature, Johnson worked his way up to deputy majority leader. He is a trial lawyer and managed a small farm operation until he sold it in 2005. Johnson ran for Congress after Republican Rep. Tom Ewing announced his retirement in 1999. Ewing and then GOP Speaker Dennis Hastert of Illinois had been close friends in Congress and previously in the state House, and Ewing backed his election as speaker. But Hastert was unhappy that Ewing delayed his retirement announcement until his 29-year-old son, Sam, could move back to the district from Texas to launch his candidacy to succeed his father. The speaker endorsed state Rep. Bill Brady, the scion of a prominent real estate family from Bloomington. Johnson had more political experience than either of the other Republican candidates and was a ferocious campaigner. The primary results broke along regional lines. Brady won his base of McLean County with 62% of the vote, while in Champaign, Johnson led Brady with 61%. Johnson carried seven of the 11 counties, winning 44% of the vote, to 36% for Brady and 17% for Ewing. Against Illinois State University instructor Mike Kelleher in the general election, the voting pattern was similar. Kelleher narrowly won his home of McLean County, while Johnson secured Champaign and 9 of the 11 counties, winning 53%-47% overall.

In the House, Johnson has compiled a moderate voting record, with maverick tendencies. He exercised notable independence from Hastert while Republicans were still in the majority, which helps to explain his modest committee assignments. But he found other routes to influence. He took issue with the Bush administration's environmental record and voted against opening the Alaska National Wildlife Refuge to oil drilling, winning him a re-election endorsement from the League of Conservation Voters. He also won over environmentalists for pressuring the Bureau of Land Management in 2005 to abandon plans for off-road vehicle use in Utah's Red Rock wilderness, an area Johnson termed "mankind's heritage." The same year, he was one of 14 House Republicans who voted against $50 billion in proposed domestic spending cuts.

Johnson also bucked the Republican administration on the war in Iraq. In February 2007, he was one of 17 House Republicans who voted for a resolution opposing President Bush's plan to try to bring an end to insurgent violence with "surge" of troop strength. However, Johnson later opposed Democratic proposals calling for a timetable to withdraw troops. In June 2008, he cited the impact on civil liberties when he was the only Republican to vote against renewal of the law to permit a secret court to approve intelligence surveillance, which the House passed 293-129. His maverick ways probably did not help his efforts to try to keep federal funding flowing to the giant FutureGen project, an experimental, clean-technology coal-fired power plant in Coles County in Johnson's district. In January 2008, the administration decided to curtail funding for the project. Johnson is hopeful that President Obama, with his ties to the state, will be more supportive; a few other Illinois heavyweights, such as Democratic Sen. Dick Durbin, are also behind FutureGen.

In May 2006, after the National Collegiate Athletic Associations reprimanded the University of Illinois for using a "demeaning" American Indian mascot it called Chief Illiniwek, Johnson filed a bill to limit the NCAA's ability to sanction colleges because of their athletic team's name, symbol, or mascot. At a field hearing in Champaign, Johnson told an NCAA official, "You do a good job of running basketball tournaments ... but you don't do a good job of social engineering." Yet the mascot made his last appearance in February 2007.

Johnson reneged on his term-limits pledge in October 2002. In subsequent bids for re-election, in 2004 and 2006, emergency-room physician David Gill challenged Johnson as the Democratic nominee, promoting universal health care as his prime issue. But Johnson prevailed by solid margins. In 2008, he breezed to a 64%-36% re-election.

SIXTEENTH DISTRICT

Don Manzullo (R)

Elected 1992, 9th term; b. March 24, 1944, Rockford; home, Egan; American U., B.A. 1967, Marquette U., J.D. 1970; Baptist; married (Freda); 3 children.

Professional Career: Practicing atty., 1970–92; author.

DC Office: 2228 RHOB, 20515, 202-225-5676; Fax: 202-225-5284; Web site: www.house.gov/manzullo.

State Offices: Crystal Lake, 815-356-9800; Rockford, 815-394-1231.

Committees: *Financial Services* (7th of 29 R): Capital Markets, Insurance & Government Sponsored Enterprises; International Monetary Policy & Trade. *Foreign Affairs* (6th of 19 R): Asia, the Pacific & the Global Environment (RMM); Terrorism, Nonproliferation & Trade.

Group Ratings

	ADA	ACLU	AFS	LCV	ITIC	NTU	COC	ACU	CFG	FRC
2008	20	27	0	8	29	68	83	92	78	100
2007	0	—	9	0	—	80	80	100	82	—

National Journal Ratings

	2007 LIB	—	2007 CONS		2008 LIB	—	2008 CONS
Economic	19%	—	80%		16%	—	83%
Social	31%	—	67%		20%	—	74%
Foreign	39%	—	60%		34%	—	66%
Composite	30%	—	70%		25%	—	76%

Key Votes of the 110th Congress

1. Increase minimum wage	N	5. Share immigration data	Y	9. Withdraw troops 8/08	N
2. Expand SCHIP	N	6. Foreign aid abortion ban	Y	10. No operations in Iran	N
3. Raise CAFE standards	N	7. Ban gay bias in workplace	N	11. Free trade with Peru	Y
4. Bail out financial markets	N	8. Repeal D.C. gun law	Y	12. Overhaul FISA	Y

Election Results

2008 general	Don Manzullo (R)	190,039	(61%)	($1,346,244)
	Robert Abboud (D)	112,648	(36%)	($501,317)
	Scott Summers (Green)	9,533	(3%)	($5,027)
2008 primary	Don Manzullo (R)	unopposed		

Prior Winning Percentages: 2006 (64%); 2004 (69%); 2002 (71%); 2000 (67%); 1998 (100%); 1996 (60%); 1994 (71%); 1992 (56%)

Population		Race/Ethnicity		Work	
Pop. 2007:	719,475	White:	81.9%	Private:	83.7%
Change since 2000:	Up 10.1%	Black:	5.6%	Government:	9.8%
Urban:	78.4%	Hispanic:	9.1%	Self-employed:	6.2%
Rural:	21.6%	Asian:	2.0%	Blue collar:	27.4%
Area size:	4,158 sq. mi.	Native Am.:	0.2%	White collar:	56.5%
Age		Hawaiian:	0.0%	Khaki collar:	0.0%
Median age:	36.6 yrs.	Two+ races:	1.0%	Other:	16.1%
More than 65 yrs:	12.4%	*Ancestry*		Median income:	$55,216
Less than 18 yrs:	25.9%	German:	23.9%	Median home value:	$152,900
Education		Irish:	11.0%	Poverty:	9.7%
H.S. grad:	86.9%	English:	6.5%	**Military Veterans**	
College grad:	23.0%			% of Pop:	10.1%
Grad degree:	7.4%				

The far northwest corner of Illinois is one of the heartlands of the Republican Party. In the town square of Freeport, some 15,000 people came to hear Abraham Lincoln and Stephen Douglas in one of their seven debates in 1858. Settled by New England Yankees, northern Illinois was one of the strongest Republican constituencies in 1860 and for years after. Not far away, on a little river once navigable by Mississippi River steamboats, is Galena, one of the earliest settlements in northern Illinois

2008 Presidential Vote		
Obama (D) 168,503	(53%)
McCain (R)............................145,795	(46%)
2004 Presidential Vote		
Bush (R)...............................168,303	(55%)
Kerry (D)..............................133,701	(44%)
Cook Partisan Voting Index: R + 2		

and the home of Ulysses S. Grant. Once larger than Chicago, Galena is now a tourist attraction. The second largest city in Illinois is Rockford, on the Rock River, settled by Swedes as well as Yankees and one of America's leading furniture manufacturers at one time. It is the nation's leading manufacturer of fasteners, and there is a big Chrysler plant a few miles east in Belvidere. But the city's manufacturing base steadily declined after World War II, and by the 1980s, Rockford had a serious unemployment problem. It has rebounded in recent years as it has moved aggressively toward becoming a center for professional services and high technology.

The 16th Congressional District of Illinois consists of much of the northwest part of the state. It includes the hilly, almost mountainous country around Galena and the Mississippi River, and the flatter plains in the farming counties to the east and south. The fastest-growing part of the district is in the east, in McHenry County and in Boone and Winnebago counties, three of the fastest-growing counties in Illinois in recent years. Politically, northern Illinois, perhaps in stubborn opposition to Democratic Chicago, remained steadfastly Republican for many years. It backed Herbert Hoover in 1932, Barry Goldwater in 1964, and George H. W. Bush in 1992 when the rest of Illinois was going the other way. But in recent years, the trend has reversed. In 2004, George W. Bush ran far behind his father's 1988 percentages in metro Chicago and in almost every one of the state's northern counties. In 2008, Barack Obama won 8 of the 9 counties in this district, winning 53% of the vote.

The congressman from the 16th District is Donald Manzullo, a Republican first elected in 1992. He grew up in Rockford, where his father ran a grocery store and Manzullo's Famous Italian Restaurant, from 1953 until it closed in 2004. While in college in Washington in the mid-1960s, Manzullo worked for Republican candidates and then practiced law in Illinois. For 20 years, he was a small-town lawyer in Oregon, Ill. He hosted a radio talk show for a while and wrote books on constitutional law. An ardent social conservative and passionate abortion-rights foe, Manzullo early in his career started the Northern Illinois Crisis Pregnancy Center. Later, he and his wife, a microbiologist, home-schooled their three children until the eighth grade, then sent them to a Christian high school. Manzullo ran for Congress in 1990 and lost the primary to a moderate Republican. Democrat John Cox won the seat, but was weakened when heavily Republican McHenry County was added during redistricting. Two years later, Manzullo ran again and, with support from conservative Christians, beat a moderate Republican in the primary, 56%-44%. In the general election, Cox campaigned for higher taxes; Manzullo for a 10% across-the-board income tax cut. Manzullo won with 56% of the vote. He has not been seriously challenged for reelection since.

Manzullo has a generally conservative voting record. He sponsored a law in 1998 requiring federally funded family-planning clinics to report evidence of child abuse and molestation. He has said that his proudest legislative achievement was helping to pass the 2001 law ordering the Veterans Administration to recognize Gulf War syndrome. Manzullo came to Congress as a market conservative and a strong supporter of free trade, and he supported the North American Free Trade Agreement and normalizing trade relations with China. He criticized the Bush administration's imposition of steel tariffs in 2002 and cited the impact on Rockford manufacturers. He worked to exclude products like tool-grade steel from the tariffs. But he has been dismayed by local job losses in manufacturing—some 13,000 in the Rockford area since 2000—which he attributes to Chinese competition, some of it in violation of international trade rules. He has worked to encourage a revival of manufacturing in America and has called for tax cuts for businesses that create jobs in the United States, an end to Chinese currency manipulation and enforcement of Buy American laws.

From 2001 to 2006, Manzullo was chairman of the Small Business Committee. He went to war with the Bush administration over funding cuts for the Small Business Administration and its guaranteed-loan program for small businesses. When the White House insisted on funding the program with higher fees on borrowers and lenders, Manzullo in 2004 got the House to add $79 million to the SBA budget. In 2005, when the SBA was criticized for not processing loans to Katrina victims rapidly enough, Manzullo defended the agency. In 2003 and 2004, he led a rebellion against the powerful chairman of the House Ways and Means Committee, Republican Bill Thomas of California. Forging a coalition of Democrats and lawmakers from heavy-manufacturing districts, Manzullo denied Thomas a majority on a corporate tax bill that Thomas favored until he agreed to more than $75 billion in tax incentives for manufacturers and small businesses. In 2006, Manzullo sponsored bills to allow small-business owners to deduct health care costs from their federal taxes.

Term limits forced Manzullo to give up the Small Business Committee gavel in 2007. He has since focused on his work on the Foreign Affairs Committee, where he is the top Republican on the Asia Subcommittee. That perch allows him to stay involved on U.S.-China trade issues. He also has a seat on the Financial Services Committee, where he has worked recently to try to accelerate tax breaks for domestic manufacturers. He was one of 32 House Republicans who voted for the bailout of the Big Three automakers in December 2008, after urging the companies to purchase U.S.-made supplies. In August 2008, Manzullo joined with other House conservatives in briefly occupying the House floor after Democratic Speaker Nancy Pelosi gaveled the House into recess without calling a vote on new domestic oil drilling and production. The group was protesting the absence of action on the issue as energy prices soared and also what they called strong-arm tactics by Pelosi.

On issues back home, Manzullo helped secure $12 million for Rockford's EIGERlab, a city-state-university center for the study of advanced manufacturing technologies like micromachining. It opened in 2004 in Rockford. With Democratic Sen. Dick Durbin of Illinois he secured over $40 million for construction of a new federal courthouse in Rockford.

SEVENTEENTH DISTRICT

Phil Hare (D)

Elected 2006, 2nd term; b. Feb. 21, 1949, Galesburg; home, Rock Island; Attended Black Hawk Community College, 1967–69; Catholic; married (Beckie); 2 children.

Military Career: Army Reserves, 1969–75.

Professional Career: Factory worker, Seaford Clothing Factory, 1969–82, Dist. dir., U.S. Rep. Lane Evans, 1982–2006.

DC Office: 428 CHOB, 20515, 202-225-5905; Fax: 202-225-5396; Web site: hare.house.gov.

State Offices: Carlinville, 217-854-2290; Decatur, 217-422-9150; Galesburg, 309-342-4411; Moline, 309-793-5760.

Committees: *Education & Labor* (20th of 29 D): Health, Employment, Labor & Pensions; Workforce Protections. *Transportation & Infrastructure* (36th of 44 D): Highways & Transit; Water Resources & Environment.

Group Ratings

	ADA	ACLU	AFS	LCV	ITIC	NTU	COC	ACU	CFG	FRC
2008	100	100	100	92	57	5	56	0	0	11
2007	100	—	100	85	—	4	55	0	1	—

National Journal Ratings

	2007 LIB	—	2007 CONS		2008 LIB	—	2008 CONS
Economic	69%	—	28%		69%	—	29%
Social	65%	—	34%		82%	—	0%
Foreign	65%	—	33%		78%	—	17%
Composite	67%	—	33%		81%	—	20%

Key Votes of the 110th Congress

1. Increase minimum wage	Y	5. Share immigration data	N	9. Withdraw troops 8/08	Y
2. Expand SCHIP	Y	6. Foreign aid abortion ban	N	10. No operations in Iran	Y
3. Raise CAFE standards	Y	7. Ban gay bias in workplace	Y	11. Free trade with Peru	N
4. Bail out financial markets	Y	8. Repeal D.C. gun law	N	12. Overhaul FISA	N

Election Results

2008 general	Phil Hare (D)	unopposed
2008 primary	Phil Hare (D)	unopposed

Prior Winning Percentages: 2006 (57%)

Population		Race/Ethnicity		Work	
Pop. 2007:	628,820	White:	85.5%	Private:	79.3%
Change since 2000:	Down 3.8%	Black:	7.7%	Government:	13.7%
Urban:	71.1%	Hispanic:	4.4%	Self-employed:	6.6%
Rural:	28.9%	Asian:	1.0%	Blue collar:	27.9%
Area size:	8,289 sq. mi.	Native Am.:	0.1%	White collar:	52.0%
		Hawaiian:	0.0%	Khaki collar:	0.1%
Age		Two+ races:	1.3%	Other:	20.0%
Median age:	38.5 yrs.			Median income:	$39,138
More than 65 yrs:	16.1%	*Ancestry*		Median home value:	$83,500
Less than 18 yrs:	22.3%	German:	22.1%	Poverty:	16.1%
		Irish:	11.2%		
Education		English:	8.5%	**Military Veterans**	
H.S. grad:	84.7%			% of Pop:	12.5%
College grad:	17.0%				
Grad degree:	5.7%				

Illinois's western prairies are some of America's richest agricultural land. They were first settled by Yankees coming overland from northern Indiana and Ohio and upstate New York. After 1848, Germans left their homeland in search of better opportunities and settled in a place that in many ways resembled the flat, orderly plains of northern Germany. These migrants farmed quarter-sections and built small towns, with banks and stores, community churches and libraries. As farming expanded,

2008 Presidential Vote		
Obama (D)	160,104	(57%)
McCain (R)	118,163	(42%)
2004 Presidential Vote		
Kerry (D)	148,562	(51%)
Bush (R)	139,251	(48%)
Cook Partisan Voting Index:	D + 3	

so did the need for agricultural equipment. Entrepreneurs and investors built farm-machinery factories, and the Quad Cities of the Mississippi—Davenport and Bettendorf in Iowa, and Rock Island and Moline in Illinois—became one of the nation's biggest agricultural-equipment manufacturing centers. The plants were unionized in the 1930s and 1940s, and in post-World War II America wages went up as the demand for more sophisticated machines increased on Midwest farms, many of them reliant on government subsidies. But eventually the cost of subsidies rose too high, and the market had its revenge. In the early 1980s, farm profits vanished, land values declined and orders for new machinery and equipment dried up. The result was a depression in western Illinois and neighboring Iowa, and a political swing toward the Democrats and away from the Republicans, who had been the ancestral party in most of this area. The Democratic tide has receded a bit, but this was still one of the few parts of rural America carried by Al Gore in 2000, John Kerry in 2004, and Barack Obama in 2008. Recent job losses and wildly oscillating farm prices have helped Democrats maintain majorities here. From 2000 to 2007, population in the region declined, with Rock Island down 3.2% and East Moline down 2.5%, and median household income fell 18% in Rock Island and 16% in East Moline.

The 17th Congressional District includes the Illinois portion of the Quad Cities plus several rural counties to the south. It takes in the entire Mississippi River border with Iowa almost to St. Louis. From there, the geography gets more imaginative. A thin strip of land along the Mississippi River and the lower Illinois River connects the district to an extension that includes rural Macoupin County and some parts east of there. Then another thin reed sprouts north from Macoupin to include central Springfield (but not the state Capitol building), and then reaches some 40 miles farther east to take in a portion of the city of Decatur. Decatur is home to politically influential Archer Daniels Midland, the world's largest agricultural processor and a key champion of ethanol. It would be fairly easy to drive directly from any part of the 17th District to another, but only if you crossed over into the 18th or 19th districts. There is, of course, a political explanation for this weird configuration. By removing the Republican counties east and north of the Quad Cities during redistricting, the 17th District was made more safely Democratic, and neighboring districts were reinforced for Republicans. Macoupin County is historically Democratic, and central Springfield and Decatur are solidly Democratic.

The congressman from the 17th District is Phil Hare, a Democrat elected in 2006. Hare was born in Galesburg, the son of a machinist. He attended Black Hawk Community College in Moline and was a union leader at the Seaford Clothing Factory in Rock Island, where he cut lining for men's suits for 13 years. The work could be hazardous, and during his time there, Hare says, he was one of only three employees with all 10 fingers intact. Hare went to work as an aide to Democratic Rep. Lane Evans and stayed 24 years, chiefly as his district director. Evans was the ranking minority member on the Veterans Affairs Committee and a leading prairie populist before suffering the debilitating effects of a long-running battle with Parkinson's disease. A week after winning the March 2006 Democratic primary, Evans announced that he would not run for a 13th term. Evans endorsed Hare as his successor, and Hare picked up the backing of labor unions and the Rock Island Democratic Party as well. But he had serious primary competition from State Sen. John Sullivan, state Rep. Mike Boland and Rock Island Mayor Mark Schweibert.

Hare campaigned on health care and expanding renewable fuels. He supported abortion rights but favored restrictions, such as requiring parental notification for minors, and he opposed a constitutional amendment to ban same-sex marriage. Under Illinois law, precinct committeemen from the 17th District were authorized to choose the party's replacement nominee for Evans in a weighted selection process. Hare says he spoke personally with nearly 350 of the roughly 400 eligible voters. He won 64% of the weighted vote to clinch the nomination. Boland criticized the "insider's game" and pressure from party and union leaders to support Hare. In the general election, Hare faced former Quad Cities television news anchor Andrea Zinga, but her campaign never really threatened. Hare struggled to raise money, and the national GOP took no interest in the race. Hare won 57% to 43% for Zinga.

In the House, Hare votes near the center of the Democratic Caucus. He has pursued his former boss's interest in veterans' issues, with proposals for automatic payment of at least a portion of a disabled veteran's claim at the time it is filed and for making veterans' programs mandatory rather than discretionary spending. Hare also managed to win approval for a new veterans' clinic in his district, an impressive feat for a freshman lawmaker. Following reports of bonuses to senior officials at the Veterans Administration, he cited the backlog of claims from soldiers plus security breaches at the department. In May 2007, Hare called for the resignation of Veterans Secretary Jim Nicholson.

On other issues, he was an outspoken critic of international trade agreements and publicly took issue with fellow Democrats who supported them. "I didn't come out here to be a backbencher," he said. When supporters said that the proposed free-trade deal with Colombia would help the Caterpillar plant in Hare's district, Hare said he believed the opposite would be true for workers at the plant. "Somebody's got to stand up for the American worker" and the adverse impact of past deals, he said. On the home front, he worked to secure as many earmarks as he could, despite controversy in recent years about the special provisions that lawmakers tuck into spending bills for their districts. "I don't consider it pork," he told the *Quad-City Times.* "My job is to get every penny I can back to this district." Hare had no Republican opponent in 2008.

EIGHTEENTH DISTRICT

Aaron Schock (R)

Elected 2008, 1st term; b. May 28, 1981, Morris, MN; home, Peoria; Bradley U., B.S. 2001; Baptist; single.

Elected Office: Peoria Bd. Of Education, 2001–05, V.P., 2003–04, Pres., 2004–05; IL House, 2005–08.

Professional Career: Founder, GarageTek, 2001–03; Dir. of devel. & construction, Petersen Co., 2007; Real estate investor/developer, 2001-present.

DC Office: 509 CHOB, 20515, 202-225-6201; Fax: 202-225-9249; Web site: schock.house.gov.

State Offices: Jacksonville, 217-245-1431; Peoria, 309-671-7027; Springfield, 217-670-1653.

Committees: *Oversight & Government Reform* (15th of 15 R): Domestic Policy; Government Management, Organization & Procurement. *Small Business* (10th of 12 R): Contracting & Technology (RMM); Rural Development, Entrepreneurship & Trade. *Transportation & Infrastructure* (29th of 30 R): Highways & Transit; Railroads, Pipelines & Hazardous Materials.

Group Ratings and Key Votes: Newly Elected

Election Results

2008 general	Aaron Schock (R)	182,589	(59%)	($2,602,218)
	Colleen Callahan (D)	117,642	(38%)	($607,734)
	Sheldon Schafer (Green)	9,857	(3%)	($9,074)
2008 primary	Aaron Schock (R)	55,610	(71%)	
	Jim McConoughey (R)	13,363	(17%)	
	John Morris (R)	9,160	(12%)	

Population		Race/Ethnicity		Work	
Pop. 2007:	656,128	White:	88.4%	Private:	79.5%
Change since 2000:	Up 0.4%	Black:	6.9%	Government:	14.2%
Urban:	68.0%	Hispanic:	2.2%	Self-employed:	6.1%
Rural:	32.0%	Asian:	1.1%	Blue collar:	23.5%
Area size:	8,302 sq. mi.	Native Am.:	0.1%	White collar:	58.7%
		Hawaiian:	0.0%	Khaki collar:	0.1%
Age		Two+ races:	1.3%	Other:	17.7%
Median age:	38.8 yrs.			Median income:	$49,079
More than 65 yrs:	15.2%	*Ancestry*		Median home value:	$107,400
Less than 18 yrs:	23.0%	German:	25.6%	Poverty:	10.6%
		Irish:	11.5%		
Education		USA:	9.3%	**Military Veterans**	
H.S. grad:	88.4%			% of Pop:	11.7%
College grad:	23.5%				
Grad degree:	7.8%				

Old vaudeville bookers, presented with a new act, used to ask, "Will it play in Peoria?" The implication was that if an act went over in this small city on the bluffs above the Illinois River, 154 miles from Chicago and 171 miles from St. Louis, it would go over just about anywhere. In the first half of the 20th century, Peoria did seem pretty typical of America. If its citizens were mostly of British or German descent, with a small percentage of African-Americans, that was the image of ordinary America that

2008 Presidential Vote		
McCain (R)	156,898	(50%)
Obama (D)	151,687	(48%)

2004 Presidential Vote		
Bush (R)	181,058	(58%)
Kerry (D)	130,669	(42%)

Cook Partisan Voting Index: R+6

prevailed through the 1960s, despite the great immigrations of 1880–1924 and the northward urban migrations of Southern rural blacks of 1940–1965. But Peoria's economy has changed, much as America's has changed. This is still a heavy manufacturing town, dominated by big plants that produce farm machinery and earth-moving equipment. Its biggest employer is Caterpillar, the world's leading producer of earth-moving and construction equipment, and one of America's major exporters. There are more than just memories here of the sharp divide between blue collar and white collar, union and management, Democrat and Republican—the basis of the class warfare politics that was the norm in heavy industrial metropolises of the Great Lakes region starting with the sit-down strikes of the late 1930s.

But the blue-collar workers now are not as numerous and the unions not as strong. The Peoria area went through terrible times in the 1980s, as big farm machinery plants laid off workers and even closed down. Then Caterpillar, struck by the United Auto Workers in 1992, hired replacement workers and continued to operate—not without some friction and inefficiency, but profitably—something unheard of a decade or more earlier. Not until 1998 did union members approve a settlement, pretty much on the company's terms. Memories of those hard times were revived by the recession in late 2008 and early 2009. Caterpillar was not immune from the national economic crisis, and the Peoria factory became one of the public faces of President Barack Obama's economic stimulus legislation. Obama claimed that Caterpillar promised to rehire some laid-off employees if the stimulus bill passed, but Caterpillar refuted those claims. Obama visited the Peoria plant on Feb. 12, 2009. Despite the passage of the bill, Caterpillar went ahead with its planned layoffs in mid-March, including more than 900 in Peoria.

The 18th Congressional District of Illinois, variously configured, has been the Peoria district since the 1940s. It includes all 11 counties that President Abraham Lincoln represented during his one term in Congress, 1847–49. It has been represented by two national Republican leaders: from 1933–49 by Everett McKinley Dirksen, who was elected senator in 1950 and was Senate Republican leader from 1959–69, and Robert Michel, a House member from 1957–95 and House Republican leader from 1981–95. The 18th's boundaries currently extend through rich farmland south along the Illinois River and east to include half of Springfield, including the state Capitol, and west within a few miles of Iowa. It is the home of Eureka College, which dedicated the Ronald Reagan Peace Garden in honor of its 1932 graduate and the end of the Cold War that he helped to achieve. George W. Bush won this district in 2004 with 58% of the vote, but in 2008 McCain eked out a win with 50% to Obama's 48%.

The new congressmen from the 18th District is Republican Aaron Schock, who at age 27 was the youngest member of the House when he took office in January 2009, and the first member to be born in the 1980s. Schock (*SHOK*) succeeded Republican Rep. Ray LaHood, who retired after the 110th Congress and then was chosen as Obama's Transportation secretary.

Ambitious even as a child—Schock started his own Individual Retirement Account at 14 and amassed $18,000 working in a gravel pit in high school—he graduated from Bradley University with a finance degree in just two years. While still in college, Schock decided to challenge the sitting Peoria school board president because the board had refused to let him graduate early from high school to comply with a rule that required four years of gym. The incumbent challenged Schock's petition signatures, and he was disqualified. Undeterred, Schock staged a write-in campaign and went door-to-door to campaign. On

Election Day, he won with 60% of the vote. After two years, he was elected vice president of the board, and the following year, at age 23, was unanimously elected school board president. Schock didn't stop at local politics. In 2004, he mounted a campaign against eight-year incumbent state Rep. Ricca Slone, a Democrat, in a district that trended 60% Democratic. He argued that her liberal votes stopped jobs from coming to the district. Despite being outspent by Slone, Schock relied on the same grassroots outreach that had made his school board campaigns successful, and again, he won.

In the Illinois General Assembly, Schock passed 11 bills in his first five months in office, including reforms in disability testing for students in elementary schools and a change in the way colleges report eligibility of transfer courses. Schock also worked on identity-theft, prescription drug affordability and road construction issues. He was also an outspoken opponent of Democratic Gov. Rod Blagojevich's economic policies. In January 2008, Schock proposed a bill to allow citizens who completed a safety course to carry concealed weapons.

When LaHood announced his retirement in July 2007 after seven terms, Schock quickly made plans to run for the open seat. He met with LaHood in mid-August to seek his support, and LaHood gave him the names of county chairmen to contact. Shortly afterward, LaHood learned his son was considering running for the seat, and so he called the chairmen to ask that they stay neutral, only to learn Schock had already received 11 endorsements. LaHood's son decided not to get into the contest. Still, LaHood withheld his initial support for Schock and later complained that Schock inappropriately used his name in his campaign literature.

During the campaign, Schock had some missteps. In November 2007, he called for China to impose sanctions on Iran in an effort to stop their nuclear program. If they refused, Schock suggested that the United States sell nuclear weapons to Taiwan to get China's attention. His two Republican challengers in the primary jumped on the statement. LaHood also said the remark showed immaturity. Schock later said that his statement was meant to underscore China's importance in dealing with Iran. And he won the February 2008 primary with 71% of the vote.

While President Bush's endorsement in 2008 sent some Republicans running in the other direction, Schock did not shy away from a fundraising visit by Bush over the summer, which netted his campaign more than $700,000. Former House Speaker Dennis Hastert, from the neighboring 14th District, also hosted a fundraiser for Schock and called him "the embodiment of the kind of candidates the Republican Party needs to win again."

His general election opponent, former television news reporter Colleen Callahan, was selected by the state Democratic Party to run after former Bradley University coach Dick Versace, who won the primary, withdrew. Schock greatly outpaced Callahan in fundraising, bringing in over $2.6 million compared to her $600,000. Callahan ran ads criticizing Schock after he was investigated for possibly backdating tax documents when serving as a notary public for his father. Two weeks before the election, the Peoria County state's attorney dropped the case. Schock won in November 59% to 38%, losing only Bureau County.

Schock arrived in Washington with near instant celebrity as the new "Generation Y" congressman, parlaying his youth into positive stories in the media and television appearances. Attractive and unmarried, the liberal blog *The Huffington Post* named him the "Hottest Freshman" of the 111th Congress. But one high profile admirer was rebuffed. Lobbying for Schock's vote on his economic stimulus bill, Obama invited the new congressman to ride with him on Air Force One during his February visit to the Caterpillar plant and then praised him in his public comments. Schock voted no anyway. He was also quick to capitalize on the controversy that erupted after soon-to-be-impeached Gov. Blagojevich named Democrat Roland Burris to Obama's Senate seat in spite of an investigation into whether the governor sought favors for the appointment. Schock's first bill would require special elections for Senate vacancies.

NINETEENTH DISTRICT

John Shimkus (R)

Elected 1996, 7th term; b. Feb. 21, 1958, East St. Louis; home, Collinsville; West Point Military Acad., B.S. 1980, Christ Col., Teaching Cert., 1990, S. IL U., M.B.A. 1997.; Lutheran; married (Karen); 3 children.

Military Career: Army 1980–85; Army Reserves, 1985–2008..

Elected Office: Collinsville Township trustee, 1989–93; Madison Cnty. treas., 1990–96.

Professional Career: High schl. teacher, 1986–90.

DC Office: 2452 RHOB, 20515, 202-225-5271; Fax: 202-225-5880; Web site: www.house.gov/shimkus.

State Offices: Centralia, 618-532-9676; Collinsville, 618-344-3065; Harrisburg, 618-252-8271; Olney, 618-392-7737; Springfield, 217-492-5090.

Committees: *Energy & Commerce* (7th of 23 R): Communications, Technology & the Internet; Energy & Environment; Health.

Group Ratings

	ADA	ACLU	AFS	LCV	ITIC	NTU	COC	ACU	CFG	FRC
2008	20	18	14	8	60	68	88	91	81	100
2007	15	—	27	10	—	70	85	84	75	—

National Journal Ratings

	2007 LIB	—	2007 CONS		2008 LIB	—	2008 CONS
Economic	29%	—	70%		23%	—	77%
Social	25%	—	74%		30%	—	70%
Foreign	0%	—	72%		22%	—	74%
Composite	23%	—	77%		26%	—	74%

Key Votes of the 110th Congress

1. Increase minimum wage	Y	5. Share immigration data	Y	9. Withdraw troops 8/08	N
2. Expand SCHIP	N	6. Foreign aid abortion ban	Y	10. No operations in Iran	N
3. Raise CAFE standards	N	7. Ban gay bias in workplace	N	11. Free trade with Peru	Y
4. Bail out financial markets	N	8. Repeal D.C. gun law	Y	12. Overhaul FISA	Y

Election Results

2008 general	John Shimkus (R)	203,434	(64%)	($1,209,093)
	Daniel Davis (D)	105,338	(33%)	($68,004)
	Troy Dennis (Green)	6,817	(2%)	
2008 primary	John Shimkus (R)	unopposed		

Prior Winning Percentages: 2006 (61%); 2004 (69%); 2002 (55%); 2000 (63%); 1998 (61%); 1996 (50%)

Population		Race/Ethnicity		Work	
Pop. 2007:	659,480	White:	93.2%	Private:	77.1%
Change since 2000:	Up 0.9%	Black:	3.3%	Government:	15.3%
Urban:	52.2%	Hispanic:	1.4%	Self-employed:	7.4%
Rural:	47.8%	Asian:	0.7%	Blue collar:	26.0%
Area size:	11,646 sq. mi.	Native Am.:	0.2%	White collar:	55.7%
		Hawaiian:	0.0%	Khaki collar:	0.1%
Age		Two+ races:	1.1%	Other:	18.2%
Median age:	38.9 yrs.	*Ancestry*		Median income:	$46,541
More than 65 yrs:	15.6%	German:	27.3%	Median home value:	$99,000
Less than 18 yrs:	22.7%	Irish:	11.2%	Poverty:	11.3%
Education		English:	9.3%	**Military Veterans**	
H.S. grad:	86.2%			% of Pop:	12.5%
College grad:	20.6%				
Grad degree:	7.2%				

Much of Southern Illinois is a land of prairies, of flat, treeless land sloping imperceptibly down to the Ohio and Mississippi rivers. It was settled almost entirely from the south by farmers coming overland from Kentucky, such as Abraham Lincoln's family. Just beyond the Ohio River, they found hilly terrain, some of which turned out to have coal deposits. As they traveled farther north, they must have been astonished, after miles of thick forest, to see the

2008 Presidential Vote

McCain (R)	176,342	(54%)
Obama (D)	142,316	(44%)

2004 Presidential Vote

Bush (R)	192,678	(61%)
Kerry (D)	123,172	(39%)

Cook Partisan Voting Index: R + 9

great American prairie stretch before them, a vast sea of empty land extending past the horizon. The prairie lands proved wondrously rich and were soon crisscrossed by rail lines taking their produce away and bringing in industrial products from St. Louis, Chicago and points east. About the same time, vast coal deposits were found in southern Illinois, and several mining towns sprouted. This was the home turf of John L. Lewis, the imperious leader of the United Mine Workers for half a century and, in the late 1930s and early 1940s, one of the most powerful and eloquent figures in American public life.

The 19th Congressional District of Illinois, the largest in the state, extends more than 200 miles up, down and across. It covers all or part of 30 counties in the rich heartland of southern Illinois—most of the land area south of Springfield, from the Ohio River to the Mississippi. Much of it is south of the old National Road, which became U.S. 40 and is paralleled by Interstate 70, the traditional boundary between the part of downstate Illinois settled by Southerners and the part settled by Yankees. The city of Effingham, which straddles that line, is where corn and soybean fields give way to hills and valleys with orchards and woodlands. The boundaries of the 19th are jagged, but there is a rational political explanation for them. The biggest voting blocs are in Madison, Clinton and Washington counties, part of the St. Louis metropolitan area, and the Sangamon County suburbs of Springfield, the state capital. The district includes the coal-mining area around Mount Vernon, sparsely settled areas along the Ohio River and some prairie counties along U.S. 40. Traditional Democrats have become harder to find here. George W. Bush won 61% of the vote in 2004, his best performance in the state. In 2008, John McCain won 26 of the 30 counties in the district.

The congressman from the 19th District is John Shimkus, a Republican first elected in 1996. Shimkus grew up in Collinsville, in Madison County. His father was an installer for Illinois Bell, and his mother a township trustee. He is of Lithuanian descent, as is his predecessor in the seat, Democratic Sen. Richard Durbin. Shimkus graduated from West Point, trained in the Army as a ranger and paratrooper, went to college in California, then came back to Collinsville to teach high school. Almost immediately, he began running for local office. In 1988, he ran for the Madison County Board and lost. The very next year, however, he was elected a Collinsville Township trustee. In 1990, at age 32, he beat a 12-year incumbent to become Madison County treasurer. He challenged then U.S. Rep. Durbin in 1992 and lost 57%-43%, a closer margin for Durbin than in his previous campaigns. In 1996, when Durbin ran for the Senate, Shimkus easily won the Republican primary, with 51% against seven other candidates. In the general election, he faced state Rep. Jay Hoffman. Both were anti-abortion rights, anti-gun control, and pro-balanced budget amendment. Hoffman raised more money and had the benefit of support and financial backing from the AFL-CIO, but Shimkus won, 50.3% to 49.7%. The following August, after taking classes part-time for six years, Shimkus received an MBA from Southern Illinois University.

In the House, Shimkus's voting record is at the center of House Republicans. In August 2008, he joined with other House Republicans in briefly occupying the House floor after Democratic Speaker Nancy Pelosi gaveled the House into recess without calling a vote on new domestic oil drilling and production. The group was protesting the absence of action on the issue as energy prices soared and also what they called strong-arm tactics by Pelosi. Shimkus has made several visits to Iraq and occasionally criticized the news media for not fully reporting the conditions there. In May 2007, he spurred liberal protests when he compared the current state of the war to a baseball game in which the St. Louis Cardinals left the field in the middle of a game with the Chicago Cubs. "You can't quit," Shimkus' spokesman said. Shimkus was a lieutenant colonel on active duty in the Army Reserves until he retired in 2008.

From his seat on the Energy and Commerce Committee early in his House tenure, Shimkus ushered to passage a locally important piece of legislation that qualified the soybean-diesel fuel blend B-20 for the alternative-fuels program. The bill passed despite objections from the Clinton administration. In 2008, Shimkus harshly criticized President Bush's decision to curtail funding the FutureGen project, an experimental, clean-technology coal-fired power plant that was to be built in the neighboring 15th District and could have provided an economic boost for his own district.

As a former high school teacher, Shimkus took what seemed to be a routine assignment as chairman of the House page board and imposed stricter review procedures for applicants. But five weeks before the 2006 election, revelations that Republican Rep. Mark Foley had sent inappropriate and sexually explicit e-mails to former male pages was a political bombshell for the party, including for Shimkus and GOP Speaker Dennis Hastert of Illinois. Both men had known of questionable contacts Foley had with pages and failed to launch an investigation. Shimkus said that in 2005 he had confronted Foley with reports of e-mail messages to young pages and alerted House officials. "I don't know of a single thing I would have done differently," he said. The Committee on Standards of Official Conduct found that Shimkus should have shared the information with other House members on the page board and should have demanded copies of all of Foley's e-mails. But the committee called for no sanctions against him. Later, Shimkus said he wished that he had done more to investigate the allegations about Foley, and he stepped down from the board.

In 2001, when the state's redistricting plan eliminated the seat held by Rep. David Phelps, a conservative Democrat, Phelps decided to run against Shimkus in the new 19th District. After a spirited contest, in which organized labor spent more than $1.5 million trying to dislodge Shimkus, he won 55% to 45% for Phelps. Since then, he has been re-elected easily. When he first ran for the seat, Shimkus said he would limit himself to six terms. But Shimkus reconsidered and in September 2005 called his earlier pledge "a mistake." He said, "Unless everyone plays by the same rules, term limits don't make sense."

★ INDIANA ★

Every year on Memorial Day, the nation's eyes turn to Indianapolis, the center of a state with the nation's most distinctive nickname—the Hoosier State—for a sports spectacle celebrating the taste for powerful machines that make the Midwest the nation's manufacturing center—the Indianapolis 500. This combination of sports and manufacturing is symbolic of Indiana's historic strengths and successes. Its industrial base and sports heritage sometimes seem as antique as the bricks that originally paved the Indianapolis Speedway, where all but one yard at the start-finish line has long since been asphalted. The Speedway is literally at the center of American manufacturing: Almost half of the country's manufacturing jobs are east of Indiana and the other half are west, almost half are north and half are south. Indiana has the nation's highest percentage of workers in manufacturing—20% in 2005—and the highest percentage of gross product attributable to manufacturing. It is the No. 2 steel producer in the country, with giant, heavily automated steel mills on the south shore of Lake Michigan and mini-mills scattered across the state. Indiana leads the nation in making elevators, refrigerators, engines, engine-electrical equipment, recreational vehicles, mobile homes, and truck and bus bodies. It gave the world canned pork and beans, tomato juice, the Coca-Cola bottle, and Alka-Seltzer. It has big General Motors and Chrysler plants and newer Toyota, Subaru, and Honda plants.

The downside of a manufacturing economy, apparent in the second half of 2008, is that it is prone to sharp contraction in a recession. Indiana managed to recover from the 2000–01 recession and was generating new jobs while neighboring states were losing them in 2006 and 2007. Growth was strong in metro Indianapolis, which with about one-quarter of the state's population accounted for 64% of its population growth from 2000 to 2007. Cummins and American Commercial Lines opened new factories in 2007, and Honda's plant in Greensburg opened in 2008. But manufacturing is increasingly capital-intensive. Indiana continues to churn out huge tonnages of steel to meet Chinese demands, but with only 19,000 workers. The recession of 2008 hit particularly hard in a state that ranks third nationally in auto-related manufacturing. Unemployment skyrocketed in November and December 2008, when the Detroit Three auto companies were threatened with bankruptcy. Indiana was projected to lose 147,000 jobs if the carmakers slid into Chapter 11. The jobless rate was especially high at year's end in Elkhart, which bills itself as the RV capital of the world. The bright spot for Indiana was that it has slowly been turning to other industries, especially life sciences. Biopharmaceutical development was under way at Indianapolis-based Eli Lilly; prosthetics, orthopedics, and biofuels were also growing—to the point that Indiana has been rated the nation's No. 3 or No. 4 life-sciences state in recent surveys.

Culturally, Indiana is like an earlier America. It retains some of the old norms that in the 1920s and 1930s attracted sociologists Robert and Helen Lynd, in their search for the typical American place, to "Middletown" (actually Muncie). Ethnically, Indiana seems like an earlier America too. Except for the steel area around Gary—really an extension of the Chicago metropolitan area—Indiana has relatively few descendants from the 1840–1924 wave of immigration and only a small flow of recent Hispanic or Asian immigrants. But it does have religious diversity, with 109 denominations, according to the Glenmary Center. Only six states have more. The major metropolitan area, Indianapolis, now has 1.6 million people but doesn't have the distinct singles and gay neighborhoods of larger cities. What it does have is one of the nation's largest foundations, the Lilly Endowment, which gives much of its money locally, and a willingness to create and innovate. In the 1980s, the Lilly Endowment urged Indianapolis to make itself a sports center. The city attracted the Colts professional football team to the Hoosier Dome, now the RCA Dome. In the late 1990s, Indianapolis's downtown filled with construction projects: the professional basketball Pacers' Conseco Fieldhouse, the new National Collegiate Athletic Association headquarters, a conservatory, and the Indiana State Museum. To cap it off, Indianapolis will host the 2012 Super Bowl.

The partisan patterns in Indiana state politics sometimes seem typical of an older America, too, with preferences anchored in the Civil War era and the union-organizing days of the 1930s. It was a crucial target state from the Civil War to the New Deal in the struggles between Republicans and Democrats. Party identification was handed down like religious affiliation—the Lynd research team noted that Presbyterians had little to do with Methodists, but that was nothing next to divisions between Republicans and Democrats. The people of Indiana, by and large, are descendants of its original settlers, Yankees from Ohio and New England, and "Butternuts," as they were called in the Civil War years, from Kentucky and the South. Most Yankees became Republicans and most Butternuts became Democrats, and that split has persisted over generations and been a factor in elections for state office from New Deal times until today. Those enduring traditions enabled Democrats to hold the governorship from 1988 to 2004 and to be competitive in state legislative elections. Democratic Sen. Evan Bayh has tended to run ahead in Butternut Indiana, whereas Republican Gov. Mitch Daniels fares well in Yankee Indiana. Two of the three U.S. House seats that Democrats captured in 2006 were in the Butternut south end of the state; the other was centered on industrial South Bend in the north.

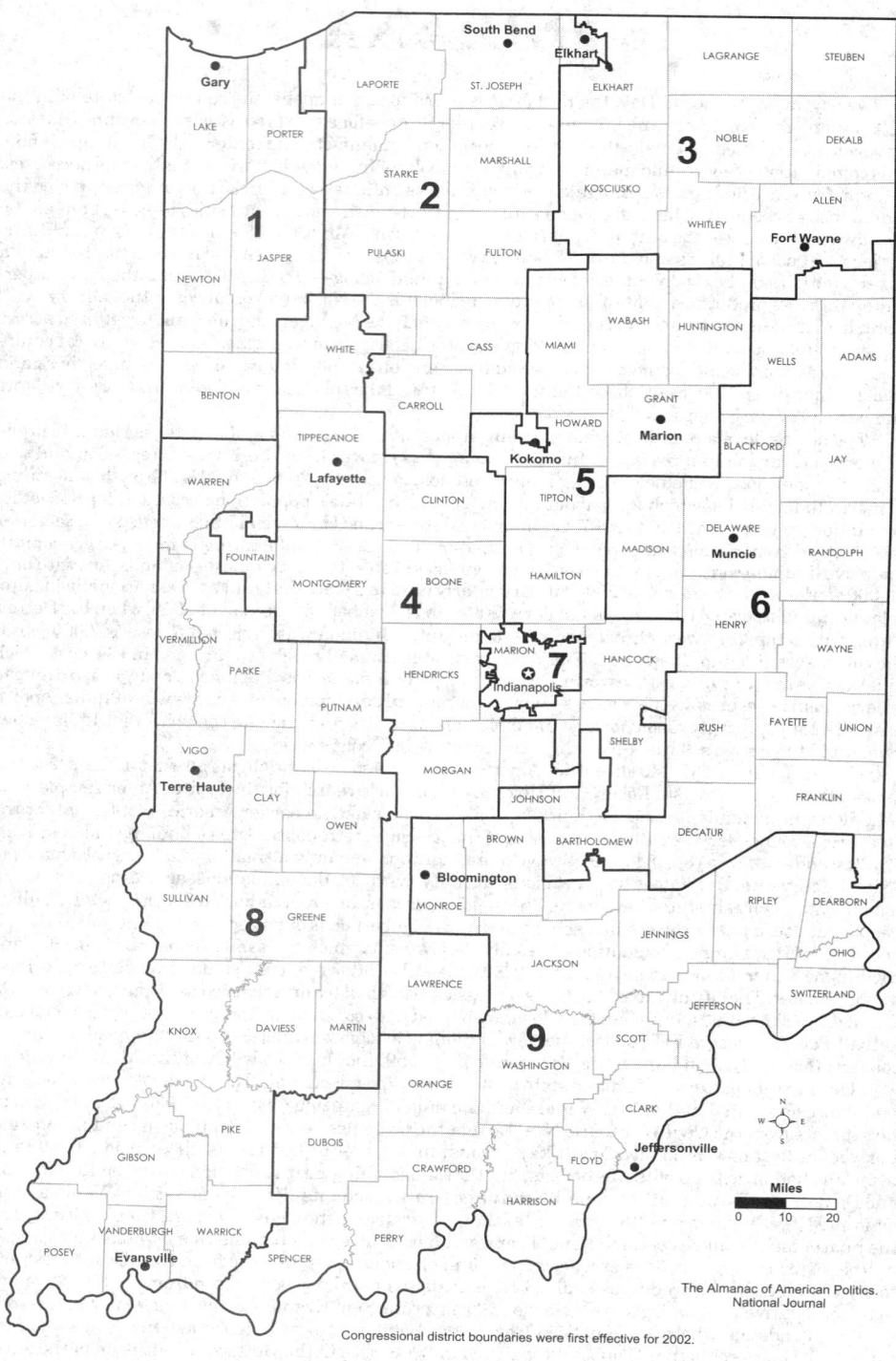

The Almanac of American Politics.
National Journal

Congressional district boundaries were first effective for 2002.

At the presidential level, Indiana's cultural conservatism and lack of a dovish tradition kept it in the Republican column for two generations. In 1964, it voted 56%-43% for Democrat Lyndon Johnson. But in the next 10 elections it was so resolutely Republican that it was never a target state for the Democrats, although the results were fairly close in 1976 and 1996. A main reason was that Indianapolis and the smaller factory towns were not as heavily Democratic as Detroit or Cleveland; indeed, they were usually Republican. In the 1920s the Lynds, liberal academics influenced by Marx's idea that political beliefs were determined by economic interests, were puzzled why the factory workers in "Middletown" didn't vote against the bosses. One reason may be that cultural identity and personal values tend to be permanent and so have usually been the critical determinants of political allegiance, especially in the United States, where economic status can often be changeable. Another factor may be that the economic interests of Indiana's highly skilled workers and its small and large factory owners may not be as adversarial as academics suppose.

In 2008, for the first time in nearly 45 years, Indiana voted Democratic for president. A state that went 60%-39% for George W. Bush in 2004 voted 50%-49% for Barack Obama four years later. This was the biggest swing in any of the 50 states, and is the product of many factors. The Obama campaign targeted Indiana from the beginning, vastly outspent the opposition, registered new young voters, and made inroads in the ailing industrial towns that had resisted Democratic nominees for many years. Metro Indianapolis, like metro Columbus, Ohio—which has a similar economic base and Republican past—moved sharply to the Democrats, particularly among affluent and better-educated voters. Obama did not run particularly well in the Butternut counties, but made up for it farther north in auto-dependent towns such as Fort Wayne, Anderson, and Muncie. Indiana began voting much more like Ohio and southern Michigan and less like the Great Plains states.

However, this did not hold true all the way down the ballot. Republican Gov. Mitch Daniels, who was George W. Bush's first-term budget director, was re-elected by a solid 58%-40% even as Obama was carrying the state, a considerably bigger victory than Daniels's initial 53%-45% win in 2004. The victory was all the more remarkable because two of the governor's policies were hugely controversial: the leasing for 75 years of the North Indiana Toll Road to an Australian-Spanish consortium and the adoption of daylight saving time. Indiana straddles the Eastern and Central time zones, with most counties in the Eastern time zone choosing not to observe daylight saving. Few issues impinge so drastically on personal lives, and several counties ended up outside their preferred time zone under Daniels's policy. Democrats put up an outcry, and in 2006 the party gained three seats in the state House, enough for a 51-49 majority, while the state Senate remained solidly Republican. For a time, Daniels posted low job-approval ratings and seemed vulnerable. But he emphasized his Indiana Economic Development Corp. which committed $700 million in incentives to bring a promised 75,000 jobs to the state, and a property-tax law that increased the sales tax by 1% but decreased the burden on local government.

Population		Household Income		Work	
Pop. 2007:	6,301,687	Under $15k:	13.1%	Private:	83.3%
State rank:	16th of 50	$15k to $50k:	39.8%	Government:	11.3%
Change since 2000:	Up 3.6%	$50k to $100k:	33.2%	Self-employed:	5.2%
Urban:	69.0%	$100k to $150k:	12.0%	Unemployment (3-yr. average):	4.5%
Rural:	31.0%	Over $150k:	2.0%	Poverty:	12.5%
Native of state:	68.5%	Median income:	$47,034	Blue collar:	29.1%
Not a citizen:	2.7%	**Home Value**		White collar:	54.7%
Area size:	36,418 sq. mi.	Under $100k:	38.4%	Khaki collar:	0.1%
Most populous cities		$100k to $300k:	54.7%	Other:	16.1%
1. Indianapolis	790,815	$300k to $500k:	5.1%	**Age**	
2. Fort Wayne	249,830	$500k to $1 mil:	1.6%	Median age:	36.3 yrs.
3. Evansville	113,627	Over $1 million:	0.3%	More than 65 yrs:	12.4%
4. South Bend	98,516	Median:	$119,400	Less than 18 yrs:	25.1%

Race/Ethnicity				Military Veterans		Registered Voters in 2008	
White:	83.7%	*Language*		% of Pop:	10.7%	No party registration	
Black:	8.6%	English:	92.6%	*Veterans by Period*		Voter turnout:	2,751,054
Hispanic:	4.7%	Spanish:	4.1%	WWII and before:	12.5%	Turnout as % of	
Asian:	1.3%	Asian:	0.9%	Korea:	11.9%	voting age:	57.4%
Native Am.:	0.2%	Other		Vietnam:	32.3%	**General Assembly**	
Hawaiian:	0.0%	European	2.1%	Gulf (pre-2001):	10.4%	Senate:	17 D 33 R
Two+ races:	1.3%	**Education**		Gulf (post-2001):	5.0%	House:	52 D 48 R
Ancestry		H.S. grad:	85.2%	Peace time:	27.8%		
German:	21.7%	College grad:	21.6%				
Irish:	10.5%	Grad degree:	7.9%				
USA:	8.4%						

Presidential politics   Indiana had seen little presidential campaigning since 1968, when Democrats Robert Kennedy and Eugene McCarthy battled in the May primary against Lyndon Johnson's stand-in, Gov. Roger Branigan. The closest the Democrats came to winning was President Clinton's loss by 5% to GOP presidential nominee Bob Dole in 1996, a year in which Clinton had more than enough electoral votes and did not seriously contest Indiana. The 2008 election was different.

Everyone had assumed that both parties' nominees would already be settled by the time of Indiana's May 6 primary. But Democrat Hillary Rodham Clinton was still battling Barack Obama and, after solid victories in Ohio and Pennsylvania, she hoped that a win in Indiana would balance an expected loss in North Carolina on the same day. Clinton had the active support of Democratic Sen. Evan Bayh, who had chosen not to run for president himself after some serious consideration in late 2006. And Indiana seemed demographically simi-

2008 Presidential Vote		
Obama (D)	1,374,039	(50%)
McCain (R)	1,345,648	(49%)
2008 Democratic Presidential Primary		
Clinton (D)	646,282	(51%)
Obama (D)	632,073	(49%)
2008 Republican Presidential Primary		
McCain (R)	320,318	(78%)
Huckabee (R)	41,173	(10%)
Paul (R)	31,612	(8%)
2004 Presidential Vote		
Bush (R)	1,479,438	(60%)
Kerry (D)	969,011	(39%)

lar to Ohio and Pennsylvania. But not quite. Indiana's population is a bit younger. Its African-American percentage is lower than Ohio's, and metro Indianapolis does not have the racially polarized urban politics that Cleveland and Cincinnati do (although Gary and Lake County do). Moreover, Indiana does not have party registration, as Pennsylvania does. Independents and Republicans could vote in the Democratic primary. And they did. Only 412,684 people voted in the Republican primary, less than in 2004, when there was only one candidate on the ballot, while nearly 1.3 million voted in the Democratic primary, *four times* as many as the 317,211 that voted in the 2004 Democratic contest. Obama won by huge margins among black and young voters. Clinton carried women, the elderly, and blue-collar voters by much smaller margins. Indianapolis and its suburbs voted heavily for Obama, who also carried the counties that included Gary, South Bend, Elkhart, and Fort Wayne, and the university towns of Lafayette and Bloomington. While Clinton emerged the winner, she was denied the satisfaction of announcing her victory on prime-time television because Lake County authorities held back their results, and network analysts, knowing there were many black voters there, refrained from calling her the winner. That was also the night that the late Tim Russert of NBC News declared, accurately, that Obama would ultimately be the Democratic nominee.

The Obama campaign's organizational work in the primary paid off in the general election. In a state that had seen no intensive presidential campaigning since the 1940s, the campaign opened 44 offices, hired 210 paid staff, attracted 80,000 volunteers, and had 50,000 people going door to door and making phone calls in the final week. The Obama team outspent Republican John McCain's campaign 5-to-1 in the state. Excitement was intense. Obama attracted a crowd of 30,000 in Indianapolis while McCain's vice presidential nominee, Sarah Palin, could muster a crowd of only 25,000 in suburban Noblesville in October. Obama carried only 15 of Indiana's 92 counties but racked up big enough margins to win 50% to McCain's 49% statewide.

The exit poll showed that 63% of young voters went for Obama, 61% of the elderly for McCain; 62% of white Protestants and 52% of white Catholics voted for McCain; 73% of whites with no religion and 90% of African-Americans voted for Obama. One precinct in Indianapolis gave 333 votes to Obama and none to McCain. Turnout was up 11% statewide and by about 25% in affluent Indianapolis suburbs (Hamilton, Hancock, and Hendricks counties) and in university towns (Tippecanoe and Monroe counties). Marion County, where Indianapolis is located and which had voted 51%-49% for John Kerry, voted 64%-35% for Obama. The Democrat did not run particularly well in the Butternut counties, but he made major gains in the industrial landscape between Indianapolis, Fort Wayne, and South Bend.

Congressional districting   Indiana lost one congressional district in the 2000 census, and that required significant changes in district lines that had stayed pretty much the same for 20 years. In charge were Democrats, who then had the governorship and a majority in the state House, though Republicans had a majority in the state Senate. Indiana law provides that if the House and Senate cannot agree, the decision goes to a five-member commission, with the tie-breaking member appointed by the governor.

111th Congress Lineup	
5 D	4 R
110th Congress Lineup	
5 D	4 R

In May 2001, the commission adopted a plan largely identical to that passed by the state House. Democrats hoped to retain the four seats they held and to improve their chances in at least one more. But as often happens with redistricting, the initial results were disappointing. In the marginal 2nd District, where Democrat Tim Roemer retired in 2002, Republican Chris Chocola picked up the seat. In 2004, Republican Mike Sodrel beat incumbent Democrat Baron Hill in the 9th District.

But the plan paid off for Democrats in 2006. The 2nd and 9th districts went 54% and 50% for Democrats Joe Donnelly and Baron Hill, respectively, with Hill reclaiming his former seat. Democrat Brad Ellsworth walloped six-term incumbent John Hostettler 61%-39% in the 8th District, which in the 1970s and 1980s was one of the nation's most frequently contested seats.

Indiana is not expected to lose a seat in the 2010 census. The re-election of GOP Gov. Mitch Daniels appears to give Republicans the upper hand in redistricting. The state Senate is solidly Republican and the state House is only narrowly Democratic. Even if Democrats hold on to the House in 2010, the House can probably be managed with finesse, as the Republican state Senate was in 2001, when Democrats were in charge of redistricting.

Governor

Mitch Daniels (R)

Elected 2004, term expires Jan. 2013, 2nd term; b. April 7, 1949, Monongahela, PA; home, Indianapolis; Princeton U., B.A. 1971, Georgetown U., J.D. 1979; Presbyterian; married (Cheri); 4 children.

Professional Career: Advisor, mayor of Indianapolis Richard Lugar, 1971–76; Chief of staff, U.S. Sen. Lugar, 1977–83; Exec. dir., NRSC, 1983–84; Senior adv., White House, 1985–87; CEO, Hudson Institute, 1987–90; Executive, Eli Lilly, 1990–2001; Dir., OMB, 2001–02.

Office: 200 W. Washington St., Room 206, Indianapolis, 46204, 317-232-1800; Fax: 317-232-3443; Web site: www.in.gov/gov.

Election Results

2008 general	Mitch Daniels (R)	1,563,885	(58%)
	Jill Thompson (D)	1,082,463	(40%)
	Andy Horning (Lib)	57,376	(2%)
2008 primary	Mitch Daniels (R)	unopposed	

Mitch Daniels has been the Republican governor of Indiana since 2005. He grew up in Indianapolis and graduated from Princeton University and Georgetown University's law school. He worked as a staffer for Republican Richard Lugar when Lugar was mayor of Indianapolis in the early 1970s, and was chief of staff for Lugar from 1977 to 1983 after Lugar moved to the Senate. He was political director in the Reagan White House until 1987, when he returned to Indianapolis to join the Hudson Institute think tank. In 1990, Daniels went to work for Eli Lilly and Company, the pharmaceutical giant based in Indianapolis. He had climbed the ranks to become president of Lilly's North American pharmaceutical operations, but resigned in 2001 to reenter government, liquidating at least $27 million in stock holdings. He turned down Gov. Robert Orr's offer to appoint him to the Senate in 1988 when Indiana Republican Dan Quayle was elected vice president. Instead, he became President Bush's director of the Office of Management and the Budget. In that role, he developed a reputation as a committed spending cutter and for having disdain for members of Congress, whose motto he said should be "'Don't just stand there, spend something.' This is the only way they feel relevant." Bush insiders referred to him as "the Blade," and veteran Democratic Sen. Robert Byrd of West Virginia called him "Little Caesar." Alaska's Sen. Ted Stevens, a fellow Republican, said the only way Daniels could fix his relationship with Congress was to "go home to Indiana."

He did go home, but not because Stevens told him to. In 2003, Daniels said he was tired of commuting between his family in Indianapolis and Washington. But he also saw an opportunity to run for governor of his home state. Democrats had held the office in mostly Republican Indiana since 1988—first Evan Bayh, elected in 1988 and 1992, then Frank O'Bannon, elected in 1996 and 2000. For most of that time, Bayh and O'Bannon cut taxes, cut welfare rolls and instituted education testing. But with the 2001 recession, state revenues plummeted, and O'Bannon took a different course. In 2002, the sales tax was raised. Out-year deficits loomed. Small scandals were exposed—DMV employees selling black market IDs, a state contracting official accepting favors, and child protective workers filing false reports. Lt. Gov. Joseph Kernan, a Vietnam veteran and POW for 11 months and a popular three-term mayor of South Bend, was widely assumed to be the strongest Democrat to succeed the term-limited O'Bannon. But in December 2002, Kernan shocked just about everyone by announcing that he would not run. "I just want to have a beer in my backyard on a Tuesday night," he said. "I've got a great job. I've enjoyed it, but I want to go back to South Bend."

Soon after he returned to Indiana, Daniels announced he was running for governor. All but one of the Republicans then running, including 2000 nominee and former U.S. Rep. David McIntosh, left the race and endorsed him. On a visit to the state, President Bush referred to "my man Mitch," at a time when that was still a politically advantageous thing to be. Vice President Dick Cheney and First Lady Laura Bush also put in appearances for him. Daniels campaigned around the state in plaid shirts and sweaters, traveling in an RV with supporters' signatures all over it. He went to every one of Indiana's 92 counties and eventually visited some of them repeatedly.

Then, in September 2003, O'Bannon suffered a major stroke and died within a few days. Kernan was sworn in as acting governor. He handled the tragic transition gracefully and reconsidered his decision not to run in 2004. In November, he announced his candidacy, and other Democrats ended their campaigns.

From there, it was a two-man race. While his former boss, President Bush, was on the defensive nationally for job losses in the manufacturing sector, Daniels was attacking Kernan and local Democrats for job losses in manufacturing in Indiana, saying it was time for a "new crew." He called for tax breaks for new business property investments, new hires and research and development. He said he would put more emphasis on winning federal grants, create a state agriculture department and provide tougher enforcement of child-support obligations. Daniels opposed importing U.S. drugs from Canada, saying he favored an online referral service to match patients with drug discount programs. He called for health savings accounts for state employees and credits for employees who stopped smoking and stayed fit. Kernan called for lower property taxes and for tax abatements for new business on a case-by-case basis. He endorsed full-day kindergarten. He criticized Daniels for his budget cuts as OMB director and for signing off on foreign contracts and job outsourcing. He blamed Indiana job losses on federal trade policy.

After enjoying modest leads in polls during most of the campaign, Daniels won 53% to 45%. He carried metro Indianapolis 57%-42%, but ran behind in northern Indiana and Kernan's home town of South Bend. Republicans increased their margin in the state Senate to 33-17 in 2004, and converted a 51-49 deficit in the state House to a 52-48 majority. It was the first time Republicans had won control of state government since 1986. Fiscal problems loomed. State government faced a $645 million deficit and owed $710 million in back payments to schools, universities, and local governments. Daniels achieved some notable but controversial successes in his first two years. With the help of business interests, he persuaded lawmakers to enact daylight-savings time to stop Indiana from being one of three states that does not go on daylight-savings time. And he persuaded the Department of Transportation to allow eight counties to switch to the Central time zone. He created a state economic-development corporation to replace the state Department of Commerce and a new inspector general post for ethics. He also got a small funding increase for schools, a voter-identification bill, and a crackdown on methamphetamine production. He signed a bill requiring state vehicles to run on agricultural-based fuels when possible. He reduced the state's property tax relief payments, and in turn sought to give local governments more control over how they raise revenue.

His most controversial plan was "Major Moves," a 10-year transportation plan that aimed to cover shortfalls in the state's transportation budget by privatizing transportation assets rather than raising gasoline taxes or state borrowing. The centerpiece was a 75-year deal to lease the Indiana Toll Road, a 157-mile-long span across northern Indiana that connects Ohio and Illinois, to an Australian-Spanish consortium in exchange for a $3.8 billion lump-sum payment. Daniels sold the plan as a way to raise cash to improve the state's road system and create jobs, while leaving toll collection and highway maintenance to the private sector. Democrats protested that the state would lose control of toll increases and decades of future revenue, while supporters of the plan argued that the highway was losing money because tolls had not been raised in 20 years. After the Republican Legislature approved the deal in 2006, Daniels proposed a spend $12 billion on the state's infrastructure over a decade, including the construction of an "Illiana Expressway" to ease traffic congestion between Illinois and Indiana and a privately funded toll beltway around metro Indianapolis.

The toll-road lease program and the switch to daylight-savings time proved unpopular. Daniels largely stayed off the campaign trail in 2006, and his political woes contributed to Republican losses in the state, including the ouster of three members of Congress. Democrats won a narrow 51-49 seat majority in the state House.

In 2007, the governor's plans to privatize the Hoosier Lottery were frustrated by House Speaker Patrick Bauer and a U.S. Justice Department ruling warning it would violate federal law. Daniels was able to privatize intake services at the Bureau of Motor Vehicles and at the Family and Social Services Administration. His Indiana Economic Development Corporation committed to $700 million in tax incentives to new businesses and took credit for deals that promised to generate more than 75,000 jobs. Tight fiscal policy resulted in an AA + credit rating for the state in 2006 and an AAA rating in 2008. In October 2007, Daniels proposed a 1% increase in the sales tax in return for a cap on property taxes of 1% of assessed value for homeowners, 2% for apartments and farms, and 3% for businesses. His tax proposal passed in March 2008, but he failed to get a limit on overall spending based on income growth.

Going into his 2008 re-election campaign, Daniels's job ratings were well under 50%, and Democrats sensed he was vulnerable. Most Democratic leaders supported South Bend architect Jim Schellinger, but Schellinger was upset, 51%-49%, in the May primary by former Rep. Jill Long Thompson. She attacked Daniels for privatizing the Indiana Toll Road and other government functions and on the switch to daylight-savings time. She advanced a Reinvest in Indiana program, with tax changes, business incentives and tax credits for health care and continuing education. Daniels called for a constitutional amendment making his property tax changes permanent and for a consolidation of local offices. He called for giving modest-income students tuition for two years at Ivy Tech Community College or an equivalent amount at another state school, to be funded by borrowing against future lottery proceeds. He outspent Long Thompson 3-to-1 and won 58% to 40%. He was especially strong in metro Indianapolis. He won 56% in Marion County, which Barack Obama won with 64%, and he carried affluent, fast-growing Hamilton County, 83%-15%. Democrats gained a seat in the state House and thus kept their majority there.

Daniels's victory, in a state carried by Obama and in a dismal year for Republicans, led some to urge him to consider a run for president. But Daniels seemed reluctant. One of his campaign ads showed him saying, "Here's some good news. This is the last time you'll have to watch me in an ad like this. See, governor is the only office I've run for or ever will." He stayed away from the Republican Governors Association meeting in Miami a few days after the November 2008 election and said again he would not run for president.

Senior Senator

Richard Lugar (R)

Elected 1976, term expires 2012, 6th term; b. April 4, 1932, Indianapolis; home, Indianapolis; Denison U., B.A. 1954, Rhodes Scholar, Oxford U., M.A. 1956; Methodist; married (Charlene); 4 children.

Military Career: Navy, 1957–60.

Elected Office: Indianapolis Bd. of Schl. Commissioners, 1964–67; Indianapolis mayor, 1968–75.

Professional Career: Mgr., family farm; V.P. & treas., Thomas L. Green & Co., 1960–67; Prof., U. of Indianapolis, 1976.

DC Office: 306 HSOB, 20510, 202-224-4814; Fax: 202-228-0360; Web site: lugar.senate.gov.

State Offices: Evansville, 812-465-6313; Ft. Wayne, 260-422-1505; Indianapolis, 317-226-5555; Valparaiso, 219-548-8035.

Committees: *Agriculture, Nutrition & Forestry* (2nd of 8 R). *Foreign Relations* (RMM of 7 R).

Group Ratings

	ADA	ACLU	AFS	LCV	ITIC	NTU	COC	ACU	CFG	FRC
2008	25	31	0	18	100	51	100	63	54	77
2007	45	—	14	53	—	53	91	60	57	—

National Journal Ratings

	2007 LIB — 2007 CONS		2008 LIB — 2008 CONS	
Economic	39%	— 60%	29%	— 70%
Social	46%	— 53%	41%	— 57%
Foreign	39%	— 60%	42%	— 56%
Composite	42%	— 58%	38%	— 62%

Key Votes of the 110th Congress

1. Raise CAFE standards	Y	5. Make English official language Y	9. Withdraw troops 3/08	N
2. Expand SCHIP	Y	6. Path to citizenship Y	10. Iran guard is terrorist group	N
3. Cap greenhouse gases	N	7. Fetus is unborn child Y	11. Increase missile defense $	Y
4. Bail out financial markets	Y	8. Prosecute hate crimes Y	12. Overhaul FISA	Y

Election Results

2006 general	Richard Lugar (R)	1,171,553	(87%)	($3,133,830)
	Steve Osborn (Lib)	168,820	(13%)	
2006 primary	Richard Lugar (R)	unopposed		

Prior Winning Percentages: 2000 (67%); 1994 (67%); 1988 (68%); 1982 (54%); 1976 (59%)

Richard Lugar became the most senior Republican in the Senate in the 111th Congress, with the retirement of Pete Domenici of New Mexico and the defeat of scandal-plagued Ted Stevens of Alaska. Lugar's career in public life stretches back to the late 1950s, when as a young Navy officer he prepared intelligence briefings for Chief of Naval Operations Arleigh Burke and also briefed President Eisenhower. He is the first Indiana senator ever elected to fourth, fifth, and sixth terms. Nationally, he is a powerful voice on foreign policy. Lugar grew up in Indianapolis, near his family's farm and food-machinery firm that dates back to 1893. He was an Eagle Scout, a straight-A student at Denison College, and a Rhodes scholar. After military service, Lugar returned to the family business; he was elected to the Indianapolis school board in 1964, and then elected mayor in 1967, at age 35. As mayor, he consolidated the city and Marion County into "Unigov," which brought in tax resources and suburban voters, keeping the city both solvent and Republican (until 1999, when a Democrat was elected mayor). In the late 1960s, Lugar bucked fashion and called for fewer rather than more federal programs, and he became known as President Nixon's favorite mayor. That was not a political asset in the Watergate scandal year of 1974, however, when Lugar challenged Democratic Sen. Birch Bayh. He lost 51%-46%. But in the more favorable climate of 1976 and against a weaker Democratic incumbent, Sen. Vance Hartke, Lugar won his Senate seat, 59%-40%.

Throughout his public life, Lugar's strength has been following his stubborn convictions and letting his considerable intellect guide him, regardless of political risk or reward. Over his long career, he has plenty of accomplishments but also some disappointments. His autonomous course has served him well in Indiana, but has produced mixed results in the Senate and in the national arena. Lugar has a mostly conservative voting record, with some exceptions. In 2007, he voted with Democrats more often than he ever had before. He voted to raise auto mileage standards, fund embryonic-stem-cell research, support the low-income heating program, raise the minimum wage, and expand the State Children's Health Insurance Program. In 1996, he ran for the Republican nomination for president on his own platform and without any concessions to the political shorthand or television sensibility of the day. Lugar based his campaign on "nuclear security and fiscal sanity" —deterring nuclear terrorism and backing a 17% national sales tax. But he got little media coverage, and after he finished seventh in the Iowa caucuses and fifth in the New Hampshire primary he left the race.

Lugar's great interest is foreign policy. He chaired the Foreign Relations Committee from 1985 to 1987 and from 2003 to 2007. With Democrats in control of the Senate, he is the ranking Republican on the panel. In 1985, he quickly took command over a committee sharply divided between conservative North Carolina Sen. Jesse Helms and liberal Democrats. Lugar was in the middle, backing aid to the Contra rebels in Nicaragua and favoring sanctions against the apartheid government of South Africa. Helms had allowed Lugar to ascend to Foreign Relations chairman that year, despite Helms's having more seniority, because the North Carolinian had made a campaign promise in the 1984 election to take the chairmanship of the Agriculture Committee. But after Republicans lost their Senate majority in 1986, Helms said he was no longer bound by his promise and invoked seniority. Lugar took the issue to the Republican Conference, but lost a vote there. So Helms was the ranking minority member and chairman for 16 years, while Lugar waited. Helms excluded Lugar from conference committees and seldom communicated with him. Lugar led the fight to ratify the chemical weapons treaty over Helms's opposition in April 1997, and won. He favored other arms control treaties, including START I in 1992 and START II in 1996, despite opposition from conservatives. Also in the 1990s, Lugar supported expansion of NATO and urged the U.S. to pay its dues to the United Nations. But in 1999, he joined other Republicans in voting against the Comprehensive Test Ban Treaty, arguing that the United States must keep testing to maintain its nuclear arsenal.

His greatest achievement was the Nunn-Lugar Cooperative Threat Reduction program to pay Russia, Ukraine, Belarus, and Kazakhstan to dismantle and destroy their nuclear weapons as well as some chemical and biological weapons. The goal of the 1991 legislation was to prevent weapons of mass destruction from falling into the hands of hostile powers or terrorists. Since then, Lugar has overseen the program to ensure its effectiveness and has gained considerable notice for this work—he and Nunn were nominated for the Nobel Peace Prize. As of 2005, the Nunn-Lugar program had resulted in the deactivation of 13,300 nuclear warheads, 1,473 intercontinental ballistic missiles, 831 ICBM silos, 442 ICBM mobile missile launchers, 233 bombers, 906 nuclear anti-ship missiles, and much more. All nuclear weapons have been removed from Ukraine, Belarus, and Kazakhstan. A facility to destroy nerve gas has been built at Shchuchye, Russia, and a pathogen storage facility in Tblisi, Georgia.

After September 11, 2001, Lugar called for a Nunn-Lugar approach to prevent chemical and biological weapons throughout the world from falling into the hands of terrorists. In 2004, Congress enacted legislation extending Nunn-Lugar to Albania. That year, Democratic presidential candidate Sen. John Kerry accused the Bush administration of slighting Nunn-Lugar, but Lugar credited the administration with getting $10 billion for the program from the other members of the Group of Eight, establishing the Global Threat Reduction Initiative to secure radioactive materials, ending weapons of mass destruction programs in Libya, and securing a U.N. resolution requiring states to criminalize nuclear proliferation. Lugar continues to monitor this work closely. In 2005, he and Democratic Sen. Barack Obama of Illinois made a trip to Russia, Ukraine, and Azerbaijan to monitor progress. He and Obama co-sponsored a measure extending the Nunn-Lugar program to target terrorists; President Bush signed the bill in January 2007.

Lugar kept a vigilant eye on Iraq throughout the 1990s. Starting in August 1990, he called for an end to Saddam Hussein's regime and said that U.S. ground troops might have to be sent to Iraq to kill Saddam. But he was not necessarily a team player for the Bush administration. In summer 2002, he and then-Foreign Relations Chairman Joe Biden, a Delaware Democrat, conducted hearings on the Iraq war, but the administration declined to send witnesses. In September 2002, Lugar and Biden drafted a use of force resolution to impose geographical limits on the authorization for war and require the administration either to obtain a U.N. resolution supporting the war or to certify to Congress that such efforts at the U.N. failed. Their work was bypassed when House Democratic Leader Dick Gephardt and Democratic Sens. Joe Lieberman of Connecticut and Evan Bayh of Indiana agreed with the administration on a different, less restrictive resolution. In late 2002, Lugar complained that the White House had not briefed him on postwar plans for Iraq. In early 2004, he said that the administration "failed to communicate" its plans to Congress and argued that the scheduled June 30 turnover of the government to the Iraqis was too soon; he also called for increasing the size of the Army by 80,000 soldiers. Later that year, he said that the administration's failure to spend more than $1 billion of $18 billion appropriated for Iraqi reconstruction resulted from a "lack of planning." Although Democrats have accused Republicans of failing to perform oversight while in the majority, Lugar in four years as chairman held 40 hearings on Iraq.

In January 2007, Lugar voted against a resolution before the Senate Foreign Relations Committee opposing the strategy to send a "surge" of troops into Iraq to restore order. And in June 2007 he dealt an unexpected blow to the Bush administration when he sharply criticized its Iraq policy and predicted that the surge strategy would fail. "In my judgment, the costs and risks of continuing down the current path outweigh the potential benefits that might be achieved," he said. "A course change should happen now, while there is still some possibility of constructing a sustainable bipartisan strategy in Iraq." With Republican Sen. John Warner of Virginia, he sponsored an amendment that would have required the administration to present an exit strategy by September 2007 and to begin withdrawing troops by December. But Majority Leader Harry Reid favored even stronger stands and pulled the amendment from the floor.

Lugar was chairman of the Agriculture Committee from 1995 to 2001. He liked to point out that he was the only working farmer on the committee—he owns 604 acres—and he played a key role in the 1996 passage of the Freedom to Farm Act, which purported to phase out over seven years the farm subsidies of which he had long been a critic. But low crop prices starting in 1998 resulted in disaster-relief payments that kept in place something very much like the old subsidy system. In 2001, Lugar opposed the House farm bill with its big increases for historically subsidized crops, and proposed his own bill, guaranteeing up to 80% of income of qualified farmers, but at far less cost. But with key Senate races coming up in states with historically subsidized farmers, the Senate passed a farm bill similar to the House's and President Bush signed it. Lugar took a similar course, with similar results, when the farm bill came up for renewal in December 2007. He sponsored an amendment to end almost all crop subsidies and to instead provide more crop insurance and conservation spending. It was defeated 58-37. Lugar voted against the final bill that passed in 2008.

Another Lugar issue is energy, particularly reducing dependence on oil. He has driven a Toyota Prius since 2005, and he grows carbon-sequestering walnut trees on his farm. In 2002, he voted for oil drilling in the Arctic National Wildlife Refuge, and, despite the importance of auto manufacturing in Indiana, he has voted to raise fuel-efficiency standards. He has supported ethanol production, but also sponsored a bill in 2007 to revoke the ethanol tax credit when oil prices rise above $45 a barrel. And he has often called for eliminating the 54% tariff on biofuels, which prevents the importation of cheap Brazilian sugar ethanol. With Iowa Democrat Tom Harkin, Lugar has worked to change the tax code to give pipeline companies incentives to transport ethanol. The two also co-sponsored a bill to require all cars to be flex-fuel and to make half of U.S. gas stations carry E-85 ethanol by 2016. In the 2007 energy bill, Lugar sought higher production of biofuels, stricter efficiency standards for appliances, and cash awards to inventors of replacements for 60-watt light bulbs and floodlights.

Lugar was one of the 23 Republicans who in May 2006 supported the Senate immigration bill, with its guest-worker program and path-to-legalization provisions. He also sponsored legislation to give conditional legal status to young illegal immigrants who graduate from U.S. high schools and either graduate from a two-year or four-year college or complete two years of military service.

In Indiana, Lugar has remained vastly popular. He was re-elected 68%-32% in 1988, 67%-31% in 1994, and 67%-32% in 2000. In 2006, former Democratic Rep. Timothy Roemer declined to run against him and he had no Democratic opponent. Democratic state Chairman Dan Parker said, "Let's be honest. Richard Lugar is beloved not only by Republicans, but by independents and Democrats." Lugar did not object when presidential candidate Barack Obama frequently mentioned their joint work on nuclear proliferation and used pictures of the Indianan in campaign ads. There was speculation in November 2008 that Lugar would get a position in the Obama administration, but he said he wanted to stay in the Senate. If he serves out this term, he will have served twice as long as any other Indiana senator.

Junior Senator

Evan Bayh (D)

Elected 1998, term expires 2010, 2nd term; b. Dec. 26, 1955, Shirkieville; home, Indianapolis; IN U., B.S. 1978, U. of VA, J.D. 1981.; Episcopalian; married (Susan); 2 children.

Elected Office: IN secy. of state, 1986–88; IN gov., 1988–96.

Professional Career: Practicing atty., 1981–86, 1997–98; Faculty., Indiana U., 1997–98.

DC Office: 131 RSOB, 20510, 202-224-5623; Fax: 202-228-1377; Web site: bayh.senate.gov.

State Offices: Evansville, 812-465-6500; Fort Wayne, 260-426-3151; Hammond, 219-852-2763; Indianapolis, 317-554-0750; Jeffersonville, 812-218-2317; South Bend, 574-236-8302.

Committees: *Aging (Special)* (4th of 13 D). *Armed Services* (9th of 15 D): Airland; Emerging Threats & Capabilities; Readiness & Management Support (Chmn). *Banking, Housing & Urban Affairs* (5th of 13 D): Financial Institutions; Securities, Insurance & Investment; Security & International Trade & Finance (Chmn). *Energy & Natural Resources* (10th of 13 D): Energy; National Parks; Water & Power. *Intelligence (Select)* (4th of 8 D). *Small Business & Entrepreneurship* (7th of 11 D).

Group Ratings

	ADA	ACLU	AFS	LCV	ITIC	NTU	COC	ACU	CFG	FRC
2008	70	57	78	82	100	15	63	29	11	22
2007	95	—	100	73	—	15	64	12	9	—

National Journal Ratings

	2007 LIB	—	2007 CONS		2008 LIB	—	2008 CONS
Economic	56%	—	42%		47%	—	52%
Social	66%	—	30%		48%	—	48%
Foreign	59%	—	36%		44%	—	55%
Composite	62%	—	38%		47%	—	53%

Key Votes of the 110th Congress

1. Raise CAFE standards	N	5. Make English official language N
2. Expand SCHIP	Y	6. Path to citizenship	Y
3. Cap greenhouse gases	Y	7. Fetus is unborn child	Y
4. Bail out financial markets	Y	8. Prosecute hate crimes	Y
		9. Withdraw troops 3/08	Y
		10. Iran guard is terrorist group	Y
		11. Increase missile defense $	Y
		12. Overhaul FISA	Y

Election Results

2004 general	Evan Bayh (D)	1,496,976	(62%)	($2,250,428)
	Marvin Scott (R)	903,913	(37%)	($2,242,526)
2004 primary	Evan Bayh (D)	unopposed		

Prior Winning Percentages: 1998 (64%); 1992 governor (62%); 1988 governor (53%)

Evan Bayh is a Democrat elected to the Senate in 1998. He is a former Indiana governor and the son of Birch Bayh, a U.S. senator from 1963 to 1981. (Father and son in fact have the same full name, Birch Evans Bayh, although they use different derivations.) Evan Bayh was just 6 years old when his father was elected to the Senate, and he grew up mostly in Washington, attending the prestigious St. Albans School and eventually earning a law degree from the University of Virginia. Bayh (BYE) returned to Indiana to practice law—and politics. His father, a popular figure in Indiana politics for decades, lost his 1980 re-election bid to Republican Rep. Dan Quayle. Six years later, his son picked up the family tradition of public service by winning election as Indiana secretary of state. In 1988, at age 32, Bayh ran for governor. Republicans had held the office and controlled most of the state government for 20 years. However, their smooth-running machine had grown sluggish. The Republican nominee promised change and innovation, but Bayh was a young, fresh face with a well-known political name. He won. As governor, he balanced the budget, cut taxes, and piled up a $1.6 billion budget surplus. He trimmed a deficit in state pension plans and reduced Medicaid spending. He claimed credit for the creation of 350,000 jobs that helped revive Indiana's manufacturing economy. He did less to reform education and other government services, but he was immensely popular when he left office.

A shot at his father's old Senate seat came along in 1998, when Republican Dan Coats decided not to seek re-election. At the time, Bayh was serving on the board of pharmaceutical giant Eli Lilly. The company, whose headquarters is in Indianapolis, is not only a major employer in the state but also a major political backer. Bayh's GOP opponent was Fort Wayne Mayor Paul Helmke, who had supported increasing the city's taxes and even expressed fondness for Bill and Hillary Rodham Clinton, whom he had known since law school. (He had narrowly won the Republican primary with 35% by besting two more conservative candidates.) In the campaign against Bayh, Helmke called his opponent "the empty suit." But Bayh's platform—a balanced budget, saving Social Security, raising education standards, and a "fairer, flatter" tax—pre-empted Helmke's pitch for the Hoosier State's political center. Bayh ran ads showing his wife, Susan, extolling his accomplishments, saying he "cracked down on deadbeat dads, sponsored Indiana's fatherhood initiative, . . . worked to make our schools safer and drug-free and to move people from welfare to work." Bayh won 64%-35%, carrying 88 of 92 counties.

If his father had a mostly liberal voting record, Evan Bayh has seemed more at home in the center of the Democratic Party in the Senate, even at times alienating liberal groups. He was one of the Democrats who early on indicated they would support the Iraq war resolution. He continued to support the Bush administration on Iraq through the fall of 2004. In 2005, he voted for a bankruptcy bill that was generally favorable to creditors. In September 2008, he supported an energy bill that permitted some offshore oil drilling. And he was the only Democrat to vote against the Democratic budget resolution in March 2008.

Indiana's economy is based heavily on manufacturing. In 2000, Bayh voted for normal trade relations with China, but more recently, he has been critical of China. In 2006, he called for tariffs on Chinese imports "until they get right the currency issue." In 2007, he pressed for countervailing duties on China and other countries that subsidize exports and keep their currencies artificially low. The following year, he said that the International Trade Commission should act against steel pipe imports from China. In 2005, he opposed the Central American Free Trade Agreement.

Bayh serves on the Armed Services and Select Intelligence committees. As an early backer of the Iraq war, he won votes in the Armed Services Committee for hundreds of millions of dollars for equipment for U.S. soldiers fighting overseas. Ultimately, he became disillusioned with the war effort, calling for Defense Secretary Donald Rumsfeld's resignation in December 2004. In 2005, he voted against the confirmation of Condoleezza Rice as secretary of State, saying that as an architect of the war she "did not deserve a promotion." But he also said: "To cut and run at this juncture would be a terrible mistake." In 2006, he voted against setting a date certain for the withdrawal of troops from Iraq. In May 2007, he and moderate Republican Sen. Olympia Snowe of Maine sponsored a bill for troop withdrawals starting in four months if the Iraqis did not meet certain political benchmarks. In July 2007, Bayh voted for a measure to withdraw troops in 120 days. He also co-sponsored a successful amendment in June 2008 to offload reconstruction costs from the United States to the Iraqi government.

During the debate over energy policy in the 110th Congress (2007–08), Bayh and Republican Sen. Richard Lugar of Indiana sponsored a bill to reduce U.S. oil consumption by 2.5 million barrels a day by 2016, with tax incentives for fuel-efficient vehicles and other incentives for ethanol and biodiesel. It passed as an amendment in June 2007. During debate on the immigration bill in 2007, Bayh sought to require the posting of job openings on a national website before employers could seek visas for foreign workers.

Bayh was serving on the Banking, Housing, and Urban Affairs Committee in September 2008 when the crisis in the financial markets hit. "There was a palpable sense that the nation's economy was hanging in the balance," he said. He voted for the $700 billion bailout of banks and financial institutions, calling the bill a "distasteful but necessary step to protect millions of innocent people from the malfeasance of a few." Indiana is a major auto-manufacturing state, and Bayh spoke out for the Big Three automakers bailout bill in December 2008. With Republican Gov. Mitch Daniels, he argued that any benefits from economic stimulus legislation should be distributed on the basis of a state's economic health. Bayh also said the legislation should include funding for next-generation vehicles.

His re-election in 2004 was never in doubt. He won a slightly lower percentage of votes than in 1998, but he prevailed 62%-37% and carried 86 of 92 counties. He received the highest number of popular votes ever for an Indiana senator, a noteworthy achievement considering that George W. Bush carried the state 60%-39% that year. Bayh has often been mentioned as a candidate for national office. (His father ran unsuccessfully for president in 1976, losing the nomination to Jimmy Carter.) In July 2000, he was on Al Gore's short list of vice presidential possibilities. But leaders of feminist organizations opposed him because of his vote to ban a procedure called "partial-birth" abortion. In June 2001, he announced that he wouldn't run for president in 2004 but held the door open for a vice presidential nomination. From 2001 to 2005, he chaired the moderate Democratic Leadership Council, which had helped foster Bill Clinton's national career. As the 2008 election approached, Bayh seemed open to taking the presidential plunge.

His voting record began to align more with that of his party. He joined filibusters to stop the constitutional amendment to ban same-sex marriage, the bill to limit medical malpractice lawsuits, and several judicial nominations. He joined almost all other Democrats in rejecting President Bush's 2005 proposal to add individual investment accounts to Social Security. He voted against the Supreme Court nominations of John Roberts and Samuel Alito. In 2005 and 2006, Bayh made frequent trips to the early presidential contest states of Iowa and New Hampshire, and by the fall of 2006, he had raised over $10 million. In early December 2006, he announced the creation of an exploratory committee, but two weeks later announced he was out of the running. "I concluded that due to circumstances beyond our control the odds were longer than I felt I could responsibly pursue," Bayh said. "This path, and these long odds, would have required me to be essentially absent from the Senate for the next year instead of working to help the people of my state and the nation." He may also have calculated that the Democratic victories of 2006 had made the party less receptive to a centrist nominee.

Bayh still seemed to harbor interest in the vice presidential nomination, however. In February 2007, he said, "I love being in the Senate and I'd like to think I make a difference here. But, you know, if you're president or vice president, I think you have an even greater opportunity to help our country, and that's what I'm all about. In September 2007, he endorsed Sen. Hillary Rodham Clinton, D-N.Y., for the party's nomination, and he traveled extensively to campaign for her. At that time, polls suggested that the Democrats had a chance to carry Indiana, which made Bayh attractive as a potential running mate. He campaigned hard for Clinton in the Indiana primary but failed to satisfy some of the Clinton people. They were displeased because her margin of victory there was small (she won 51%-49%) and because Bayh was unable to persuade Lake County officials to report the primary results early enough to get them on prime-time TV. Later, after Clinton lost the nomination fight, Bayh heartily supported Illinois Sen. Barack Obama. Ultimately, though, he was not Obama's choice for vice president.

FIRST DISTRICT

Peter Visclosky (D)

Elected 1984, 13th term; b. Aug. 13, 1949, Gary; home, Merrillville; IN U. Northwest, B.S. 1970, U. of Notre Dame, J.D. 1973, Georgetown U., LL.M. 1982; Catholic; married (Joanne Royce); 2 children.

Professional Career: Practicing atty., 1973–76, 1983–84; Aide, U.S. Rep. Adam Benjamin, 1976–82.

DC Office: 2256 RHOB, 20515, 202-225-2461; Fax: 202-225-2493; Web site: www.house.gov/visclosky.

State Offices: Merrillville, 219-795-1844.

Committees: *Appropriations* (6th of 37 D): Commerce, Justice, Science & Related Agencies; Defense; Energy & Water Development (Chmn).

Group Ratings

	ADA	ACLU	AFS	LCV	ITIC	NTU	COC	ACU	CFG	FRC
2008	80	100	100	85	43	16	53	8	8	11
2007	100	—	100	85	—	4	50	4	1	—

National Journal Ratings

	2007 LIB	—	2007 CONS	2008 LIB	—	2008 CONS
Economic	73%	—	27%	68%	—	32%
Social	69%	—	30%	82%	—	0%
Foreign	69%	—	29%	92%	—	0%
Composite	71%	—	29%	85%	—	15%

Key Votes of the 110th Congress

1. Increase minimum wage	Y	5. Share immigration data	N	9. Withdraw troops 8/08	Y
2. Expand SCHIP	Y	6. Foreign aid abortion ban	N	10. No operations in Iran	Y
3. Raise CAFE standards	Y	7. Ban gay bias in workplace	Y	11. Free trade with Peru	N
4. Bail out financial markets	Y	8. Repeal D.C. gun law	N	12. Overhaul FISA	*

Election Results

2008 general	Peter Visclosky (D)	199,954	(71%)	($1,664,250)
	Mark Leyva (R)	76,647	(27%)	($12,024)
2008 primary	Peter Visclosky (D)	unopposed		

Prior Winning Percentages: 2006 (70%); 2004 (68%); 2002 (67%); 2000 (72%); 1998 (73%); 1996 (69%); 1994 (56%); 1992 (69%); 1990 (66%); 1988 (77%); 1986 (73%); 1984 (71%)

Population		Race/Ethnicity		Work	
Pop. 2007:	692,645	White:	67.6%	Private:	84.8%
Change since 2000:	Up 2.5%	Black:	18.4%	Government:	11.1%
Urban:	87.0%	Hispanic:	11.6%	Self-employed:	3.9%
Rural:	13.0%	Asian:	1.0%	Blue collar:	29.2%
Area size:	2,443 sq. mi.	Native Am.:	0.2%	White collar:	53.7%
		Hawaiian:	0.0%	Khaki collar:	0.1%
Age		Two+ races:	1.0%	Other:	17.1%
Median age:	37.1 yrs.			Median income:	$50,112
More than 65 yrs:	12.6%	*Ancestry*		Median home value:	$133,500
Less than 18 yrs:	25.6%	German:	16.0%	Poverty:	13.9%
		Irish:	10.7%		
Education		Polish:	7.9%	**Military Veterans**	
H.S. grad:	86.2%			% of Pop:	10.8%
College grad:	19.3%				
Grad degree:	6.5%				

At the southernmost shore of Lake Michigan is a part of America made by steel. Here, in the northwest corner of Indiana, where the water highway of the Great Lakes comes closest to the rail highway of the transcontinental railroads, America's leading capitalists of a century ago identified an ideal site for manufacturing steel. On empty sand dunes, United States Steel, then the nation's largest corporation, founded Gary in 1906 and named it for the company's chairman, Chicago Judge Elbert Gary.

2008 Presidential Vote
Obama (D) 184,871   (62%)
McCain (R)............................111,895   (37%)

2004 Presidential Vote
Kerry (D)...............................148,698   (55%)
Bush (R) 118,417   (44%)

Cook Partisan Voting Index: D + 8

For nearly 70 years, the steel mills attracted a diverse workforce, more like Chicago than the rest of Indiana: Irish, Poles, Czechs, Ukrainians, and blacks from the South. Politics here has always been turbulent, from the long and unsuccessful steel strike of 1919 to the racially polarized politics of the 1960s and 1970s. The city has been the setting for other historical events: It is the birthplace of the late pop star Michael Jackson and lent its name to a famous tune in the Broadway musical *The Music Man*. But the tone of public life—the clash between union stewards and management foremen, between African-Americans and Eastern European ethnics, between the stalwarts of different factions vying for control of Gary's massive City Hall—was always abrasive, like the clash of steel on steel.

Steel brought sudden growth and sudden depression to northwest Indiana. The massive storefronts built on Gary's aptly named Broadway bear witness to the confidence and exuberance of the 1920s. Today they stand vacant—vandalized, whole blocks burned down—witness to steel layoffs, crime waves, and an acute sense of loss. The steel mills went cold during the Depression of the 1930s, but were again thronged with workers during World War II, and in the years afterward, their massiveness helped create the illusion that a robust economic life in the steel towns of Gary, Hammond, and East Chicago would last forever. But technological advances replaced increasingly expensive workers with increasingly efficient machines. And the efforts to seal off the U.S. steel market from the world inevitably failed. The oil crunch of 1979 was the catalyst for change, reducing the demand for large-sized autos, the biggest customer for steel. Steel employed 70,000 workers in northwest Indiana in 1979, 35,000 a few years later, and 18,500 in 2007. But with the average pay-and-benefits package exceeding $81,000 a year, the industry remains vital to the local economy. Obsolete mills were closed, old mills modernized, and new ones built that cut the number of man-hours needed by two-thirds. Just-in-time methods were introduced, and management and highly skilled workers cooperated to engineer higher-quality, less-expensive steel to meet market demands. In recent years, Indiana has been the No. 1 or No. 2 steel-producing state. In 2005, U.S. Steel announced a $260 million project to modernize its largest blast furnace in Gary. But the Environmental Protection Agency in 2007 blocked a permit for the facility, based on the amount of pollution that the mill would likely dump into the Grand Calumet River.

As the steel industry was shifting and changing, Gary was falling almost into ruins. Nobel Prize-winning economist Joseph Stiglitz in 2006 said the city was saddled with "the same problems facing less developed countries." In 1967, Gary elected a black mayor, Richard Hatcher, who was determined to use city government to cure poverty. But high crime rates gave Gary the distinction for many years as the "murder capital" of the country, with the most homicides per capita. White flight to the suburbs ensued, and the city's population steadily fell, from a peak of 178,000 in 1960 to 97,000 in 2007. In nearby majority-white Hammond, with many Hispanic immigrants, the population loss was not as dramatic. Local officials tried to promote the city's airport as a third Chicago-area airport, with only limited success. Since Hooters Air suspended operations in January 2006, the airport has had no regularly scheduled passenger service, although Chicago-based Boeing has parked its private-jet fleet at the airport. (In his presidential campaign, Barack Obama used the airport several times for his charter flights.) Like other economically desperate cities in the Midwest, such as East St. Louis, Gary has come to rely on gambling for tax income. It has two riverboat casinos.

Indiana's 1st Congressional District stretches from Gary and Hammond along the Lake Michigan shoreline, east almost to Michigan City. It includes Lake County, which was 25% African-American and 12% Hispanic in 2000, and Porter County to the east. In Porter is the city of Valparaiso, known locally as Valpo, notable for its annual Popcorn Festivals honoring longtime resident and developer of 300 popcorn hybrids Orville Redenbacher. The district includes three small Republican-leaning counties south of Gary, but nearly three-quarters of the population is in Lake County. This remains the most Democratic district in politically balanced Indiana, as it has been since the United Steelworkers' organizing drives of the late 1930s. In 2005, a nationwide research study ranked Gary as the second-most-liberal city in the nation, after Detroit.

The congressman from the 1st District is Peter Visclosky, a Democrat first elected in 1984. As the chairman of the Appropriations Subcommittee on Energy and Water Development, Visclosky was one of the powerful "cardinals" of the House. But he was forced to step aside, at least temporarily, in June 2009 after he was subpoenaed as part of a grand jury investigation into possible corruption in the appropriations process. The next-in-line in seniority, Democrat Ed Pastor of Arizona, took over the subcommittee for the duration of the investigation. In 2007, *The Indianapolis Star* reported that Visclosky had steered more than $12 million to out-of-state defense companies that contributed to his campaign. Much of that federal money had been secured through the efforts of a lobbying firm, PMA Group, that hired a former top Visclosky aide, Richard Kaelin, the newspaper reported. Visclosky said he expected to be cleared of wrongdoing. "I have always abided by the law and adhered to the rules and code of ethics of the House," he said in a June 2, 2009 statement.

Visclosky grew up in Lake County. His father was mayor of Gary in the early 1960s, and Visclosky went to college there and to law school at the University of Notre Dame. He practiced law and then worked for six years in Washington for 1st District Rep. Adam Benjamin, a Democrat. Benjamin died suddenly of a heart ailment in 1982, and Visclosky returned to Indiana. In 1984, he ran for the seat in the Democratic primary against Katie Hall, a black state senator who had been given the 1982 nomination—and thus the election, in this Democratic district—by Mayor Hatcher, who was also the district's party chairman. In the 1984 contest, she faced a determined Visclosky, who pulled out all the stops to connect with voters since he couldn't rely on the local Democratic establishment, which was backing Hall. He called himself the "Slovak Kid" to connect with the district's many European ethnic groups, and he held hot dog dinners to attract young people and others not usually seeped in local politics. Visclosky narrowly prevailed over Hall with 34% of the vote to her 33%.

Visclosky's voting record has trended in the direction of moderate, and he concentrates much of his effort on projects to help the local economy, especially the steel industry. He has a solid pro-union voting record. He is a leader of the Congressional Steel Caucus and has been vigilant in monitoring surges in steel imports. When George W. Bush was elected president in 2000 with critical help from steel-producing areas, Visclosky had greater leverage, and Bush did impose steel import quotas. But when the quotas were removed, Visclosky protested that Bush "stabbed the American steelworkers in the back." Visclosky, meanwhile, sought health benefits for unemployed and retired workers whose steel companies were unable to pay them, and he again called for close monitoring of imports. In 2005, he joined a bipartisan group of House members calling for repeal of permanent trade relations with China, which he termed "a one-way street." He criticized Bush for rejecting a recommendation to provide relief to American pipe-steel producers suffering from Chinese imports. In 2008, he sought to require that federally funded projects use only American-made steel, and he called for increased duties on subsidized steel, especially steel from China.

As the chairman of the appropriations subcommittee, Visclosky was adept at securing federal funding for projects in his district and doling them out to other lawmakers. One of his efforts was passing an exemption to the federal Johnson Act that made Lake Michigan waters eligible for gambling and thus allowing riverboat casinos for Gary. On broader national issues, Visclosky in 2007 rejected the Bush administration's request for $89 million for a new nuclear warhead, and he slashed from $405 million to $120 million the administration's proposed funding for reprocessing fuel rods in nuclear power plants, which was opposed by anti-nuclear-power environmentalists. He added more than $1 billion for the Energy Department's research and development of civilian energy technologies, including renewable fuels and energy efficiency.

At home, Visclosky appeared secure until he became a target in the corruption probe in early 2009.

SECOND DISTRICT

Joe Donnelly (D)

Elected 2006, 2nd term; b. Sept. 29, 1955, Massapequa, NY; home, Granger; U. of Notre Dame, B.A. 1977, J.D. 1981; Catholic; married (Jill); 2 children.

Elected Office: Mishawaka Marian High School Board, 1997–2001.

Professional Career: Practicing atty., 1981–96; Owner, Marking Solutions, 1996–2006.

DC Office: 1530 LHOB, 20515, 202-225-3915; Fax: 202-225-6798; Web site: donnelly.house.gov.

State Offices: La Porte, 219-326-6808 ext. 2414; Logansport, 574-753-2671; Michigan City, 219-873-1403 ext. 308; South Bend, 574-288-2780.

Committees: *Financial Services* (29th of 42 D): Capital Markets, Insurance & Government Sponsored Enterprises; Housing & Community Opportunity. *Veterans' Affairs* (12th of 18 D): Disability Assistance & Memorial Affairs; Health.

Group Ratings

	ADA	ACLU	AFS	LCV	ITIC	NTU	COC	ACU	CFG	FRC
2008	70	55	86	54	57	16	72	28	7	76
2007	85	—	82	85	—	15	60	44	1	—

National Journal Ratings

	2007 LIB —	2007 CONS	2008 LIB —	2008 CONS
Economic	48% —	51%	48% —	50%
Social	46% —	54%	46% —	52%
Foreign	46% —	53%	48% —	51%
Composite	47% —	53%	48% —	52%

Key Votes of the 110th Congress

1. Increase minimum wage	Y	5. Share immigration data	Y	9. Withdraw troops 8/08	Y
2. Expand SCHIP	Y	6. Foreign aid abortion ban	Y	10. No operations in Iran	N
3. Raise CAFE standards	Y	7. Ban gay bias in workplace	Y	11. Free trade with Peru	N
4. Bail out financial markets	Y	8. Repeal D.C. gun law	Y	12. Overhaul FISA	Y

Election Results

2008 general	Joe Donnelly (D)	187,416	(67%)	($1,599,268)
	Luke Puckett (R)	84,455	(30%)	($286,350)
	Mark Vogel (Lib)	7,475	(3%)	
2008 primary	Joe Donnelly (D)	unopposed		

Prior Winning Percentages: 2006 (54%)

Population		Race/Ethnicity		Work	
Pop. 2007:	676,813	White:	81.8%	Private:	84.5%
Change since 2000:	Up 0.2%	Black:	8.2%	Government:	10.3%
Urban:	72.8%	Hispanic:	7.0%	Self-employed:	5.0%
Rural:	27.2%	Asian:	1.0%	Blue collar:	33.0%
Area size:	3,719 sq. mi.	Native Am.:	0.3%	White collar:	50.2%
		Hawaiian:	0.0%	Khaki collar:	0.0%
Age		Two+ races:	1.6%	Other:	16.8%
Median age:	36.5 yrs.			Median income:	$44,237
More than 65 yrs:	13.2%	**Ancestry**		Median home value:	$108,400
Less than 18 yrs:	25.2%	German:	21.8%	Poverty:	12.8%
		Irish:	10.8%		
Education		Polish:	6.8%	**Military Veterans**	
H.S. grad:	82.8%			% of Pop:	11.0%
College grad:	18.5%				
Grad degree:	6.9%				

When the University of Notre Dame was founded in 1842, Catholics were still a rarity in most of America and certainly rare on the limestone-bottomed plains of northern Indiana. This was still farm country and South Bend no more than a crossroads on the St. Joseph River. But by the 1920s, both the school and the town had grown. Notre Dame, thanks to its football team, the Fighting Irish, was the most famous Catholic university in the land, and South Bend was a significant industrial city,

2008 Presidential Vote		
Obama (D) 153,363	(54%)
McCain (R) 126,796	(45%)
2004 Presidential Vote		
Bush (R) 146,000	(56%)
Kerry (D) 112,671	(43%)
Cook Partisan Voting Index: R+2		

home of Studebaker and Bendix and dozens of other factories. In the past 50 years, Notre Dame has grown in size and reputation, but South Bend, like many Rust Belt cities, diminished in size and reputation. In the 1960s, Studebaker went out of business. In the early 1980s, there were massive factory layoffs, and in the early 1990s, there were well-publicized layoffs in nearby Elkhart. But these high-visibility job losses were accompanied by the much less visible creation of jobs in small factories throughout the region. The work in those facilities required more skill than did the old assembly lines, and the products had to be more responsive to just-in-time prime contractors or computer-inventory retailers. In the late 1990s, many employers had trouble filling job openings, and the economic base was more secure than when it depended on the fate of two or three big companies. Notre Dame recently acquired the Midwestern Institute for Nanoelectronics Discovery, which in conjunction with other topflight colleges in the country, is doing research into the building blocks of the next generation of computers.

The 2nd Congressional District of Indiana is centered on South Bend, which for three decades has seen plenty of close congressional contests. This is an industrial and ethnic city, with one of the nation's largest percentage of Hungarian-Americans, plus a growing community of Mexican-Americans. It is strongly Democratic, as is LaPorte County around Michigan City. Also in the district is Kokomo, which has been trying to grow as an auto manufacturing center with plans for a new Chrysler plant. Those plans were jeopardized by the 2008 financial crisis in the domestic automobile market.

Elkhart County to the east is heavily Republican and conservative. There was a six-foot Ten Commandments monument in front of Elkhart City Hall until a 2005 lawsuit by the American Civil Liberties Union led to its removal. The 2nd District also includes several counties on the limestone plains to the south down past the Wabash River. This is an area rural in appearance but with much small manufacturing; politically, it has been part of the Republican heartland since the party was created in the 1850s. Indiana Democrats in 2002 drew the lines of the 2nd to maximize their chance to hold it by excluding much of heavily Republican Elkhart County, by including Democratic Michigan City, and by adding the industrial town of Kokomo at its southern edge. But it took four years to elect a Democrat, in 2006. In recent presidential contests, George W. Bush won the 2nd District with 53% in 2000 and 56% in 2004. Barack Obama won it with 54%.

The congressman from the 2nd District is Joe Donnelly, a Democrat first elected in 2006. Donnelly was born in Massapequa, New York, and grew up on Long Island's South Shore. He attended the University of Notre Dame, earning an undergraduate degree in government and a law degree in 1981. He practiced law in the area until 1996, when he opened Marking Solutions, a printing and rubber stamp company. Donnelly served on the state election board in 1988 and 1989, but his early bids for public office were disappointing to say the least. He ran unsuccessfully for the Democratic nomination for state attorney general in 1988, failed in a bid for the state Senate in 1990, and then lost his first attempt at a seat in Congress in 2004. However, he at least came in close in the latter contest, holding Republican Rep. Chris Chocola to 54% to his 45%. Donnelly compared himself to popular former Democratic Rep. Tim Roemer and said he would be more independent of his party than Chocola. But Donnelly raised less than half as much money as Jill Long Thompson, the 2002 Democratic nominee for the seat, and national Democrats made the race a low priority.

The year 2006 was much more difficult for Republicans like Chocola nationally, and he had some problems at home as well. Republican Gov. Mitch Daniels's move to daylight saving time and the privatization of the Indiana Toll Road, which runs through the district, proved unpopular. The liberal group MoveOn.org identified Chocola as an early target and ran negative television ads. This time, the Democratic Congressional Campaign Committee took a much greater interest in the race by installing a campaign manager for Donnelly and by elevating the race to its "Red to Blue" program. Republicans too recognized the seriousness of Chocola's predicament. President Bush's first 2006 campaign visit for a House candidate was for Chocola, who collected about $650,000 from the appearance. So Donnelly made Bush's handling of the Iraq war an issue in his campaign. Chocola again outspent Donnelly by more than 2-to-1, but it seemed it was finally Donnelly's year to win an election. He beat Chocola 54%-46%, carrying five of the district's 12 counties. Donnelly increased his margin in South Bend's St. Joseph County from 621 votes in 2004 to more than 12,700 in 2006.

In the House, Donnelly has a centrist voting record. An opponent of abortion rights and expanding federal funding for embryonic-stem-cell research, Donnelly urged Democratic leaders to advance a moderate agenda in Congress. He also joined the Blue Dogs, a group of conservative and centrist Democrats.

In the meantime, he went his own way on some issues, and was among 12 Democrats to vote against the Democratic budget in 2007.

He has focused on veterans' issues, working with Rep. Fred Upton, R-Mich., to expedite veterans' claims, and he took some credit for helping add $6.6 billion to veterans spending in 2007. On the Financial Services Committee, he backed the fall 2008 bailouts for the financial markets and big automobile companies. On the housing bill in 2007, he added a provision to raise loan limits for manufactured housing, which has a strong presence in Indiana.

Donnelly had an unexpectedly easy re-election campaign in 2008, after Republicans failed to recruit a strong challenger. Against Elkhart County businessman Luke Puckett, Donnelly won 67%-30% and took all 12 counties.

THIRD DISTRICT

Mark Souder (R)

Elected 1994, 8th term; b. July 18, 1950, Ft. Wayne; home, Ft. Wayne; IN U., B.S. 1972, Notre Dame U., M.B.A. 1974; Protestant; married (Diane); 3 children.

Professional Career: Furniture salesman, 1976–83; Staff dir., U.S. House Select Cmte. on Children, Youth & Families, 1984–89; Legis. dir., U.S. Sen. Dan Coats, 1989–91, Dep. chief of staff, 1991–93.

DC Office: 2231 RHOB, 20515, 202-225-4436; Fax: 202-225-3479; Web site: www.house.Gov/souder.

State Offices: Ft. Wayne, 260-424-3041; Goshen, 574-533-5802; Kendallville, 260-599-0557; Winona Lake, 574-269-1940.

Committees: *Education & Labor* (6th of 19 R): Early Childhood, Elementary & Secondary Education; Higher Education, Lifelong Learning & Competitiveness. *Homeland Security* (3rd of 13 R): Border, Maritime & Global Counterterrorism (RMM); Intelligence, Information Sharing & Terrorism Risk Assessment. *Oversight & Government Reform* (5th of 16 R): Domestic Policy; Federal Workforce, Postal Service & the District of Columbia.

Group Ratings

	ADA	ACLU	AFS	LCV	ITIC	NTU	COC	ACU	CFG	FRC
2008	20	11	0	31	67	51	94	72	57	94
2007	10	—	9	5	—	67	84	92	65	—

National Journal Ratings

	2007 LIB	—	2007 CONS	2008 LIB	—	2008 CONS
Economic	23%	—	77%	35%	—	65%
Social	17%	—	81%	9%	—	85%
Foreign	0%	—	72%	29%	—	69%
Composite	18%	—	82%	26%	—	74%

Key Votes of the 110th Congress

1. Increase minimum wage	N	5. Share immigration data	Y	9. Withdraw troops 8/08	N
2. Expand SCHIP	N	6. Foreign aid abortion ban	Y	10. No operations in Iran	N
3. Raise CAFE standards	N	7. Ban gay bias in workplace	N	11. Free trade with Peru	Y
4. Bail out financial markets	Y	8. Repeal D.C. gun law	Y	12. Overhaul FISA	Y

Election Results

2008 general	Mark Souder (R)	155,693	(55%)	($1,064,302)
	Michael Montagano (D)	112,309	(40%)	($854,573)
	William Larsen (Lib)	14,877	(5%)	
2008 primary	Mark Souder (R)	40,161	(77%)	
	Scott Wise (R)	11,946	(23%)	

Prior Winning Percentages: 2006 (54%); 2004 (69%); 2002 (63%); 2000 (62%); 1998 (63%); 1996 (58%); 1994 (55%)

Population		Race/Ethnicity		Work	
Pop. 2007:	708,467	White:	85.0%	Private:	85.6%
Change since 2000:	Up 4.9%	Black:	5.6%	Government:	8.6%
Urban:	65.1%	Hispanic:	5.9%	Self-employed:	5.5%
Rural:	34.9%	Asian:	1.2%	Blue collar:	33.5%
Area size:	3,292 sq. mi.	Native Am.:	0.2%	White collar:	52.2%
Age		Hawaiian:	0.0%	Khaki collar:	0.1%
Median age:	35.4 yrs.	Two+ races:	2.0%	Other:	14.2%
More than 65 yrs:	11.6%	*Ancestry*		Median income:	$49,132
Less than 18 yrs:	27.3%	German:	28.1%	Median home value:	$119,500
Education		Irish:	8.7%	Poverty:	10.3%
H.S. grad:	84.0%	USA:	7.7%	**Military Veterans**	
College grad:	20.6%			% of Pop:	9.8%
Grad degree:	6.8%				

The flat northeast corner of Indiana was first set-tled by people of New England Yankee stock, estab-lishing orderly communities with public schools and even colleges. They were joined by German im-migrants, who built tidy farms and their own civic institutions. In the northern part of the state, there are hills and lakes, and the strange swamp that is the central focus of Gene Stratton Porter's chil-dren's classic, *A Girl of the Limberlost*. The one large city here, Fort Wayne, was built on the flat terrain

2008 Presidential Vote
McCain (R)..............................162,147   (56%)
Obama (D) 123,558   (43%)

2004 Presidential Vote
Bush (R)..................................172,919   (68%)
Kerry (D)..................................79,674   (31%)

Cook Partisan Voting Index: R + 14

along the Maumee River that flows to Toledo, Ohio. It grew as a factory town, surging ahead and then falling back as large factories, often tied to the auto industry, opened and closed over the years. As much as anything else, this part of Indiana is a place where people make things. Northwest of Fort Wayne on U.S. Route 33, Elkhart County is a manufacturing hub where local companies make everything from pharmaceuticals to musical instruments—oboes, bassoons, and piccolos. The county is best known as the nation's manufacturing center for recreational vehicles, and doesn't much care what the greenies think of that. "I represent the biggest gas-guzzling district in the U.S.," its congressman, Republican Mark Souder, has said. But steep rises in gasoline prices, like those in recent years, can have a big impact in Elkhart, where several recent plant closings rippled through the economy to endanger suppliers and other dependent businesses. From August 2007 to August 2008, Elkhart had a larger increase in unem-ployment than any other metropolitan area in the nation, prompting *The New York Times* to call it "the white-hot center of the meltdown of the American economy." The story noted that the city council passed a law limiting residents to one garage sale per month. The mayor responded that the *Times* article was one-sided and "painted it much worse than it really is."

Neighboring Kosciusko (*Kosh-CHOO-shko*) County is renowned for medical supplies. In Warsaw, the orthopedics manufacturing capital of the world, residents have been making orthopedic devices for more than a century. But reflecting national trends, manufacturing jobs in the Fort Wayne area dropped by 22 per cent from 1998 to 2005. In 2007, Claypool opened a $150 million biodiesel complex, including a soybean processing plant, capable of producing 88 million gallons of fuel annually. This is a surprisingly diverse area. Its eclectic population mix includes a concentration of Amish, plus Central Americans, Bos-nians, Somalis, and the nation's largest population of Burmese refugees.

The 3rd Congressional District of Indiana consists of most of eight counties in the northeast part of the state. This part of Indiana has been heavily Republican since the Civil War, though it has sometimes veered Democratic in times of economic distress. The seat recently has sent its representatives on to high positions: Dan Quayle, elected here in 1976, was later a senator and vice president, and Dan Coats, who succeeded Quayle in the Senate seat, was ambassador to Germany for President Bush. GOP presidential candidates have won this district handily. In 2008, John McCain carried it with 56% of the vote.

The congressman from the 3rd District is Mark Souder (*SOW-dur*), a Republican first elected in 1994. Souder grew up in Grabill, 10 miles from Fort Wayne, where his Amish great-great-grandfather's family settled. In 1907, the family started Souders of Grabill, originally a harness shop and now a furniture store and manufacturer of store fixtures. As an undergraduate at Indiana University, where he was student body president, Souder wore a button that said, "I'm proud to be a square." He worked in the family busi-ness in Grabill, then went to work in 1984 for Coats as staff director of the House Select Committee on Children, Youth, and Families. He moved with Coats to the Senate in 1989, where Souder was his legisla-tive director. In 1993, he returned to Fort Wayne to run against Democratic Rep. Jill Long, who had won a special election to succeed Coats when he was appointed to the Senate. With a moderate record and a farm background, she was not an easy target. But Souder, after winning a six-candidate primary with 40%, raised more money. In a highly favorable year for Republicans, Souder won with 55% to 45% for Long.

Souder says that he is "most defined by the fact that I'm an evangelical Christian." He once told an interviewer with the Fort Wayne *Journal-Gazette* : It "isn't like it takes away all problems. It's just that you get a peace about the problems." In Washington, despite his solidly conservative views, he initially was a rebel in the House against his party leadership. As a leader of the Conservative Action Team, which was an influential faction in the 1990s, Souder challenged House appropriators for excessive spending, including their hitting-too-close-to-home members' office allowances. He often voted against Republican bills because they didn't go far enough to the right. He opposed the balanced-budget amendment of the mid-1990s because it did not require a supermajority to raise taxes. He takes a conservative's pro-gun-rights position, and in September 2008, the House passed his amendment to repeal the District of Columbia's new ban on handguns.

Souder has been active on issues to stem the domestic drug trade. As chairman of the Oversight and Government Reform subcommittee dealing with criminal justice and drug policy, Souder held hearings on growing addiction to methamphetamines, and he blamed weak enforcement in the 1990s for reviving drug abuse among the young. In 2006, President Bush signed his Combat Methamphetamine Epidemic Act, the most comprehensive government attack on meth trafficking to date; it included restrictions on consumer purchases, monitoring of sales at the wholesale level, and increased criminal enforcement. Souder also sponsored the reauthorization of the Office of Drug Control Policy Act. To clarify a controversial Clinton-era law he helped enact that denied those with past drug convictions access to federal student loans, Souder inserted the Drug-Free Student Loans amendment in the deficit-reduction law that specifies only students enrolled in college at the time of their drug conviction lose access to loans.

Although he had serious objections to Bush's military surge in Iraq in 2007, he objected that a proposal to condemn the plan was contrary to the national interest. Souder was also one of only 32 House Republicans who voted for the bailout of the Big Three automakers in December 2008. "My job is to defend my region," he said.

Over the years, Souder has faced a string of weak Democratic challengers. But after abandoning his original pledge to serve no more than 12 years, he faced credible opposition in 2006 from Tom Hayhurst, a retired pulmonary physician and Fort Wayne City Council member. Hayhurst called for affordable health care and opposed making abortion illegal. Souder purchased extensive advertising to tout his record. In a dismal year for Indiana Republicans, Souder was outspent by Hayhurst, but held on with a 54%-46% victory. He won all eight counties, though by fewer than 1,000 votes in Allen County, where he lost Fort Wayne. In 2008, he faced another competitive challenger: Mike Montagano, a 27-year-old attorney, a prolific fundraiser who attempted to nationalize the contest. Montagano said that Souder had failed to "make a difference" during 14 years in Congress; Souder cited his experience and deep roots in the district. Both candidates opposed abortion rights, backed gun ownership, and called for sealing the border before giving citizenship rights to illegal aliens. Souder won 55%-40%.

FOURTH DISTRICT

Steve Buyer (R)

Elected 1992, 9th term; b. Nov. 26, 1958, Rensselaer; home, Monticello; The Citadel, B.S. 1980, Valparaiso U., J.D. 1984; Methodist; married (Joni); 2 children.

Military Career: Army, 1984–87, 1990–91 (Persian Gulf); Army Reserves, 1980–84, 1987–present.

Professional Career: IN dep. atty. gen., 1987–88; Vice chmn., White Cnty. Repub. Party, 1988–90; Practicing atty., 1988–92.

DC Office: 2230 RHOB, 20515, 202-225-5037; Fax: 202-225-2267; Web site: stevebuyer.house.gov.

State Offices: Bedford, 812-277-9590; Monticello, 574-583-9819; Plainfield, 317-838-0404.

Committees: *Energy & Commerce* (10th of 23 R): Communications, Technology & the Internet; Health. *Veterans' Affairs* (RMM of 11 R).

Group Ratings

	ADA	ACLU	AFS	LCV	ITIC	NTU	COC	ACU	CFG	FRC
2008	25	18	33	15	33	64	81	84	64	82
2007	10	—	11	5	—	78	69	90	84	—

National Journal Ratings

	2007 LIB	—	2007 CONS		2008 LIB	—	2008 CONS
Economic	23%	—	77%		27%	—	73%
Social	19%	—	81%		27%	—	71%
Foreign	0%	—	72%		33%	—	66%
Composite	19%	—	81%		30%	—	71%

Key Votes of the 110th Congress

1. Increase minimum wage	*	5. Share immigration data	Y	9. Withdraw troops 8/08	N
2. Expand SCHIP	N	6. Foreign aid abortion ban	Y	10. No operations in Iran	N
3. Raise CAFE standards	N	7. Ban gay bias in workplace	*	11. Free trade with Peru	*
4. Bail out financial markets	N	8. Repeal D.C. gun law	Y	12. Overhaul FISA	Y

Election Results

2008 general	Steve Buyer (R)...192,526	(60%)	($969,469)
	Nels Ackerson (D)...129,038	(40%)	($870,680)
2008 primary	Steve Buyer (R)..45,538	(72%)
	Mike Campbell (R)..9,541	(15%)
	LaRon Keith (R)...8,545	(13%)

Prior Winning Percentages: 2006 (62%); 2004 (69%); 2002 (71%); 2000 (61%); 1998 (63%); 1996 (65%); 1994 (70%); 1992 (51%)

Population		Race/Ethnicity		Work	
Pop. 2007:	746,924	White:	90.3%	Private:	80.8%
Change since 2000:	Up 10.6%	Black:	2.6%	Government:	13.4%
Urban:	68.2%	Hispanic:	3.8%	Self-employed:	5.6%
Rural:	31.8%	Asian:	2.0%	Blue collar:	26.6%
Area size:	4,033 sq. mi.	Native Am.:	0.2%	White collar:	58.2%
Age		Hawaiian:	0.0%	Khaki collar:	0.1%
Median age:	34.7 yrs.	Two+ races:	0.9%	Other:	15.1%
More than 65 yrs:	11.2%	*Ancestry*		Median income:	$52,905
Less than 18 yrs:	24.9%	German:	20.6%	Median home value:	$134,400
Education		Irish:	10.8%	Poverty:	9.6%
H.S. grad:	88.1%	English:	9.8%	**Military Veterans**	
College grad:	25.4%			% of Pop:	10.3%
Grad degree:	9.5%				

The landscape of central Indiana is some of the most prosaic in the United States. It is mostly flat, with neat farms and towns of frame bungalows, looking mostly unchanged from many years ago. Across this landscape run some of the nation's chief transportation arteries. The earliest was the old National Road, from Baltimore to St. Louis, which was paralleled by U.S. 40 in the 1930s. The region was also crisscrossed by the great east-west rail lines carrying famed passenger trains like the old *Wabash Cannonball*. There is no *Cannonball* today. People bounce around the Midwest on commuter airlines from small city to hub, and U.S. 40 has been replaced by Interstate 70. The landscape still looks rural, and there are some large farms. But the economy is more industrial, with small factories in crossroads and courthouse towns. This is a part of America with little heritage from the early waves of immigration, relatively few blacks, and only modest numbers of Latino and Asian immigrants.

The 4th Congressional District of Indiana covers much of this territory, running from Indiana's northern plains to its southern hills. It includes all or part of 12 counties in western Indiana, including the far western edge of Indianapolis and Marion County. It extends south to Lawrence County, the source of the limestone used to rebuild the Pentagon after the September 11 attacks. The largest city is Lafayette, where the main employer is Purdue University. Growing and prosperous, the city has benefited from a 2006 partnership between Toyota and longtime local manufacturer Subaru to annually produce 100,000 Camry sedans while continuing to produce Subarus. Lafayette ranked sixth on *Forbes* magazine's 2009 list of "smartest small towns in America," and it tends to vote Republican. Even more Republican are the small counties and the suburban territory outside Indianapolis, such as fast-growing Hendricks County, which delivered 73% for George W. Bush in 2004 and 61% for John McCain in 2008.

The 4th District's congressman is Steve Buyer (*BOO-yer*), a Republican elected in 1992. Buyer grew up in White County, graduated from the Citadel, served in the Army, and then worked in Indianapolis. He

2008 Presidential Vote

McCain (R)............................185,843	(56%)
Obama (D) 142,930	(43%)

2004 Presidential Vote

Bush (R)................................196,010	(69%)
Kerry (D)................................85,179	(30%)

Cook Partisan Voting Index: R + 14

later started a family law practice in Monticello, where he joined all the civic organizations. As a captain in the Army Reserve, he was called to active duty in the fall of 1990, serving as legal adviser at a prisoner-of-war camp in the Persian Gulf. Buyer was enraged that most House Democrats, including then-Rep. Jim Jontz, voted against the war. After Buyer returned to Indiana, where he was White County Republican vice chairman, he began making speeches around the Hoosier heartland attacking Jontz on his Gulf War stand. Although a seasoned politician, Jontz lost to Buyer, 51%-49%.

In Washington in his early years, Buyer went to work on the Veterans' Affairs Committee, where he spent much time on the problems of returning soldiers suffering the effects of Gulf War syndrome. In 2003, still in the Army Reserves, Buyer was called to duty again, and he received a leave of absence from GOP Speaker Dennis Hastert. But the Army notified Buyer that his high-profile status as a congressman would jeopardize both him and fellow soldiers, and he was not deployed. In 2004, Buyer led an investigation that uncovered lapses in the hiring process for medical practitioners at Veterans Administration hospitals. When he chaired the Military Personnel Subcommittee on the House Armed Services Committee, he won enactment of an expansion of health care benefits for military retirees.

In early 2005, the House Republican leadership ousted Veterans' Affairs Chairman Chris Smith of New Jersey after he refused to go along with cuts in veterans' program spending. The leaders elevated Buyer to chairman, and in two years in that role, he worked to create a seamless transition between the Defense Department and the Veterans Administration, including the development of a system to share electronic medical records. To stop antiwar protesters from interfering with funerals of soldiers killed in Iraq, he filed a bill to restrict demonstrations at federal cemeteries. When Democrats took over the majority in 2007, Buyer clashed frequently with committee Chairman Bob Filner of California. In an interview with the *Filipino Express* in 2007, Buyer described himself as "schooled in honor and in trust and all the virtues and values that go with military bearing," in contrast to Filner, who he said was "a public activist, anti-institution and doesn't give a damn about the rules."

On the Energy and Commerce Committee, Buyer has focused on telecommunications and health care issues, including the creation of health savings accounts to pay for medical expenses. He defended the Indianapolis-based Eli Lilly Company, a major local employer, from industry critics—notably, fellow Republican Rep. Dan Burton, from an adjacent district—who wanted to permit states to create preferred lists for mental-health drugs for Medicaid patients. Buyer spoke out for increased domestic production of oil as well as alternative fuels.

In the redistricting in 2002, state Democrats sliced up Buyer's old 5th District so that its remains were grafted onto seven of Indiana's nine surviving districts. Buyer chose to run in the district with his hometown of Monticello (population 5,723), and that happened to be the most heavily Republican. It also happened to belong to the least senior member of the delegation—first-term Republican Brian Kerns. Still, this newly drawn 4th District was 97% new to Buyer. He emphasized that Kerns's home in Vigo County was 70 miles outside the new 4th District. Kerns said Buyer should run elsewhere. Buyer out-raised Kerns by more than 3-to-1, and the result wasn't close. Buyer bested Kerns 55%-30%, carrying every county. Buyer has won re-election easily since then.

FIFTH DISTRICT

Dan Burton (R)

Elected 1982, 14th term; b. June 21, 1938, Indianapolis; home, Indianapolis; IN U., 1958–59, Cincinnati Bible Seminary, 1959–60; Protestant; married (Samia); 4 children.

Military Career: Army, 1956–57, Army Reserves, 1957–62.

Elected Office: IN House of Reps., 1966–68, 1976–80; IN Senate, 1968–70, 1980–82.

Professional Career: Real estate broker; Founder, Dan Burton Insurance Agency, 1968.

DC Office: 2308 RHOB, 20515, 202-225-2276; Fax: 202-225-0016; Web site: www.house.gov/burton.

State Offices: Indianapolis, 317-848-0201; Marion, 765-662-6770.

Committees: *Foreign Affairs* (3rd of 19 R): Middle East & South Asia (RMM); Western Hemisphere. *Oversight & Government Reform* (2nd of 16 R): Domestic Policy; National Security & Government Reform.

Group Ratings

	ADA	ACLU	AFS	LCV	ITIC	NTU	COC	ACU	CFG	FRC
2008	10	18	0	0	43	82	89	100	94	100
2007	10	—	18	5	—	85	75	96	86	—

National Journal Ratings

	2007 LIB	—	2007 CONS		2008 LIB	—	2008 CONS
Economic	13%	—	87%		10%	—	89%
Social	27%	—	72%		16%	—	82%
Foreign	0%	—	72%		8%	—	89%
Composite	18%	—	82%		12%	—	88%

Key Votes of the 110th Congress

1. Increase minimum wage	N	5. Share immigration data	Y	9. Withdraw troops 8/08	N
2. Expand SCHIP	N	6. Foreign aid abortion ban	Y	10. No operations in Iran	N
3. Raise CAFE standards	N	7. Ban gay bias in workplace	N	11. Free trade with Peru	Y
4. Bail out financial markets	N	8. Repeal D.C. gun law	Y	12. Overhaul FISA	Y

Election Results

2008 general	Dan Burton (R)	234,705	(66%)	($1,810,296)
	Mary Etta Ruley (D)	123,357	(34%)	($18,624)
2008 primary	Dan Burton (R)	45,682	(52%)	
	John McGoff (R)	39,701	(45%)	

Prior Winning Percentages: 2006 (65%); 2004 (72%); 2002 (72%); 2000 (70%); 1998 (72%); 1996 (75%); 1994 (77%); 1992 (72%); 1990 (63%); 1988 (73%); 1986 (68%); 1984 (73%); 1982 (65%)

Population		Race/Ethnicity		Work	
Pop. 2007:	774,446	White:	90.4%	Private:	83.9%
Change since 2000:	Up 14.6%	Black:	3.7%	Government:	10.6%
Urban:	74.5%	Hispanic:	2.6%	Self-employed:	5.3%
Rural:	25.5%	Asian:	1.8%	Blue collar:	21.5%
Area size:	3,291 sq. mi.	Native Am.:	0.3%	White collar:	65.1%
Age		Hawaiian:	0.0%	Khaki collar:	0.1%
Median age:	36.4 yrs.	Two+ races:	1.1%	Other:	13.3%
More than 65 yrs:	11.5%	**Ancestry**		Median income:	$60,641
Less than 18 yrs:	26.3%	German:	22.8%	Median home value:	$148,800
Education		Irish:	11.6%	Poverty:	7.3%
H.S. grad:	90.8%	English:	10.1%	**Military Veterans**	
College grad:	34.6%			% of Pop:	10.3%
Grad degree:	12.0%				

Indiana's most rapid growth is taking place in the suburban ring counties around Indianapolis, especially in Hamilton County, directly north of the city. This is affluent suburbia, with subdivisions full of spacious houses, shopping centers, and office developments in what were not too long ago farm fields. Hamilton County's population increased from 82,000 in 1980 to 182,000 in 2000 and to 262,000 in 2007—a 43% jump in this decade, making it one of the fastest growing counties in the Midwest. It's

2008 Presidential Vote

McCain (R)	218,973	(59%)
Obama (D)	149,752	(40%)

2004 Presidential Vote

Bush (R)	233,215	(71%)
Kerry (D)	91,955	(28%)

Cook Partisan Voting Index: R + 17

now the fifth largest county in the state, soon to become the fourth, and it is certainly the most affluent. Indianapolis's wealthy used to be concentrated on the north side of the city; now they're more likely to be in the former farm communities of Carmel, Fishers, and Noblesville. These are not rich liberal suburbs. Hamilton County is the most Republican of the large counties in Indiana and one of the most Republican in the nation. It voted 74%-24% for George W. Bush in 2004 and 61%-38% for John McCain in 2008.

Almost half the people of the 5th Congressional District of Indiana live in Hamilton County. The district also includes suburban but less affluent (and less Republican) Hancock County, where the U.S. Lawn Mower Racing Association's championship is held every September. It takes in parts of Shelby and Johnson counties to the south. On its northern end, the district includes quite different parts of Indiana, with small industrial cities like Marion heavily dependent on the auto industry and suffering from auto-parts companies' bankruptcies and layoffs. The population is declining and new subdivisions are just about nonexistent. There is also Miami County, the birthplace of Cole Porter, and Wabash and Huntington counties, the birthplaces of two vice presidents: Democrat Thomas Marshall, Woodrow Wilson's vice president, was from North Manchester in Wabash County, and Republican Dan Quayle, the first George Bush's vice president, spent his high school years and later practiced law in Huntington. The latter town was in a Fort Wayne-based district when Quayle represented it in the House.

The congressman from the 5th District is Dan Burton, a Republican first elected to the House in 1982. He has been running for office since he was in his 20s. Burton had a horrific childhood. His father was abusive and left the family; his mother worked as a waitress and bought the kids' clothes at Goodwill. His father ultimately kidnapped his mother and went to jail, and the kids were sent to the county home. "I think part of my aggressive nature is because of my childhood," Burton told author Studs Terkel in an interview for *Hope Dies Last*. "The highest moment of hope in my childhood was when we finally got away from my father. When I was five, six years old, my mother used to stand between me and him when he'd start to beat me and take the blows. I was black and blue from my neck to my ankles." As a teenager, Burton earned money shining shoes and at age 18 enlisted in the Army. He never finished college but was successful as a real estate broker and insurance salesman. He also ran for public office, often losing but not giving up. He was finally elected to the Indiana House in 1966 and to the Indiana Senate in 1968. He lost races for Congress in 1970 and 1972, but won a seat in 1982 when the GOP-controlled Legislature created a heavily Republican suburban seat.

For years, Burton was regarded by many Democrats as a gadfly, excitedly pursuing lost causes. He once pushed for universal, mandatory AIDS testing. During the Clinton era, he long insisted that the suicide of White House counsel Vince Foster was a murder, and staged a reenactment in his backyard, using a gun and a pumpkin or watermelon–it was never clear which. For years, he has investigated the link between thimerosal, a mercury-based vaccine preservative, and autism, firm in his belief that his grandson's autism was caused by thimerosal. He has held hearings on vaccine safety and pressed for the removal of thimerosal. In 2004, he called the Institutes of Medicine "pawns for the pharmaceutical industry" when researchers reported finding no link between thimerosal and autism. His position puts him at odds with one of his district's major employers, Indianapolis-based Eli Lilly and Co., the company that developed thimerosal. Some 5,000 Lilly employees live in the district, and he has received no contributions from Lilly's political action committee since 2002.

But Burton is nothing if not fearless and often goes his own way in the face of pressure from GOP leaders to toe the line. He is an enthusiastic supporter of alternative medicine, and he favors importation of prescription drugs from Canada. He was one of only 25 Republican House members who voted against the creation of a prescription-drug benefit in Medicare in 2003, reasoning that the multi-billion-dollar benefit would cost the government too much. In 2007, Burton sided with Democrats to support giving the government power to negotiate lower drug prices with the pharmaceutical industry, a proposal staunchly opposed by most Republicans and by big companies like Eli Lilly. Some of his views on health care policy have evolved from his personal experience: Burton's wife died of cancer in 2002, and four years later, he married her doctor.

Burton has had some significant legislative successes, but his biggest achievement was the Helms-Burton Act of 1996. Drafted in response to the Cuban Air Force's downing of American planes, it stated that foreign companies could be sued in American courts if, as part of business deals with former Cuba Leader Fidel Castro's regime, they took over property expropriated from American owners. The low point of his congressional career was probably the tumultuous hearings he conducted into campaign-finance irregularities by the Clinton presidential campaign from 1997 to 2000. Burton was then chairman of the Government Reform Committee, and he promised bipartisan hearings. But they turned out to be quite partisan. Burton sealed that impression when he described Clinton to the *Indianapolis Star* in 1998: "This guy's a scumbag," he said. "That's why I'm after him."

Burton faced great resistance—some 90 witnesses took the Fifth Amendment or left the country—and perhaps even retaliation. In July 1997, the Federal Bureau of Investigation subpoenaed his finance records of his House campaigns. Burton worked doggedly to get internal White House documents dealing with campaign fundraising, and he was still seeking them in 2002, after the Bush administration came to power and claimed executive privilege. In another case, Burton tried to get internal Justice Department documents about an FBI scandal in which agents might have covered up evidence of crime by mobster informants in Boston from the 1960s to the 1980s and allowed an innocent man to go to jail for 30 years. Citing that case, he has called for taking former FBI Director J. Edgar Hoover's name off the FBI headquarters in Washington, D.C. His efforts to get those documents were opposed by the Bush administration, and he harshly criticized a 2001 Bush executive order that limited access to current and previous White House documents and records.

Because of Republican term limits on chairmen, Burton had to relinquish the Government Reform chairmanship in January 2003. He turned his focus to the Foreign Affairs Committee, where he had enough seniority to become chairman of the South Asia Subcommittee. Republican leaders judged Burton too compromised by his staunch support for Pakistan and denied him the gavel. Four years later, in 2007, Burton was in line to become chairman of the full committee, but leaders passed him over again and gave the job to the less senior Ileana Ros-Lehtinen, R-Fla. In 2009, he seemed to have redeemed himself with GOP leaders, who stood aside while Burton became the ranking Republican on the Middle East and South Asia Subcommittee. In 2007, Burton called for a closer U.S. friendship with Brazil, and opposed attempts to reduce U.S. aid to the country. He also warned against a "precipitous pullout" of troops from Iraq.

For all the negative press he has generated over his career in Congress, Burton won 14 terms mostly without difficulty—even after it was revealed in 1998 that he had fathered an illegitimate son some 15 years earlier. At the time of the revelations, Burton was being highly critical of Clinton's extramarital dalliances. The woman had not notified Burton at the time of the child's birth. When he found out, he took a blood test to confirm paternity and began to pay child support.

In 2008, he faced a serious primary challenger. John McGoff, a former Air Force flight surgeon in Iraq and Afghanistan and the Marion County Coroner, initially took advantage of negative publicity surrounding Burton's decision to skip 19 House votes to play in a Palm Springs golf tournament in 2007. McGoff ran as a reformer, promising to make public all of his meetings with special-interest groups. Burton apologized for his missed votes and blamed the news media for his problems. He spent $1.5 million to McGoff's $473,000 and won 52% to 45%. McGoff took the biggest counties, winning 55% in Hamilton and 59% in Marion; the two counties cast 55% of the total. But Burton won all of the outlying counties, some by 2-to-1 or better. He defeated a token opponent in the general election, 66%-34%. The result left Burton vulnerable to another primary challenge in 2010.

SIXTH DISTRICT

Mike Pence (R)

Elected 2000, 5th term; b. June 7, 1959, Columbus; home, Columbus; Hanover Col., B.A. 1981, IN U., J.D. 1986; Protestant; married (Karen); 3 children.

Professional Career: Practicing atty., 1986–91; Pres., IN Policy Review Fndt., 1991–93; Radio broadcaster, Network Indiana, 1992–99; Host, pub. affairs TV, UPN-23, 1995–99.

DC Office: 1431 LHOB, 20515, 202-225-3021; Fax: 202-225-3382; Web site: mikepence.house.gov.

State Offices: Anderson, 765-640-2919; Muncie, 765-747-5566; Richmond, 765-962-2883.

Committees: *Republican Conference Chairman. Foreign Affairs* (10th of 19 R).

Group Ratings

	ADA	ACLU	AFS	LCV	ITIC	NTU	COC	ACU	CFG	FRC
2008	5	18	0	0	57	88	81	100	100	94
2007	5	—	0	5	—	91	74	96	99	—

National Journal Ratings

	2007 LIB	—	2007 CONS		2008 LIB	—	2008 CONS
Economic	0%	—	97%		3%	—	97%
Social	28%	—	71%		0%	—	91%
Foreign	0%	—	72%		13%	—	84%
Composite	15%	—	85%		7%	—	93%

Key Votes of the 110th Congress

1. Increase minimum wage	N	5. Share immigration data	Y	9. Withdraw troops 8/08	N
2. Expand SCHIP	N	6. Foreign aid abortion ban	Y	10. No operations in Iran	N
3. Raise CAFE standards	N	7. Ban gay bias in workplace	N	11. Free trade with Peru	Y
4. Bail out financial markets	N	8. Repeal D.C. gun law	Y	12. Overhaul FISA	Y

Election Results

2008 general	Mike Pence (R)	180,608	(64%)	($1,575,412)
	Barry Welsh (D)	94,265	(33%)	($24,935)
	George Holland (Lib)	7,539	(3%)	
2008 primary	Mike Pence (R)	unopposed		

Prior Winning Percentages: 2006 (60%); 2004 (67%); 2002 (64%); 2000 (51%)

Population		Race/Ethnicity		Work	
Pop. 2007:	671,282	White:	92.2%	Private:	81.7%
Change since 2000:	Down 0.6%	Black:	4.1%	Government:	11.8%
Urban:	59.3%	Hispanic:	1.8%	Self-employed:	6.2%
Rural:	40.7%	Asian:	0.6%	Blue collar:	32.0%
Area size:	5,572 sq. mi.	Native Am.:	0.2%	White collar:	50.8%
		Hawaiian:	0.0%	Khaki collar:	0.1%
Age		Two+ races:	1.0%	Other:	17.1%
Median age:	38.3 yrs.			Median income:	$43,174
More than 65 yrs:	14.5%	*Ancestry*		Median home value:	$100,500
Less than 18 yrs:	23.6%	German:	22.3%	Poverty:	12.8%
		USA:	11.0%		
Education		Irish:	10.1%	**Military Veterans**	
H.S. grad:	84.2%			% of Pop:	11.4%
College grad:	16.4%				
Grad degree:	6.2%				

Muncie, Ind., became famous as the "Middletown" where sociologists Robert and Helen Lynd lived and did research for their report in 1924 and 1925. Another team of sociologists investigated Muncie and reported on it in 1976 and 1978. The Lynds were attracted to Muncie because it was typical of "every small city from Maine to California," as *Life* magazine put it. But it wasn't exactly. Muncie was a factory town in a country still almost 50% rural at that time, and it was almost entirely Protestant and

2008 Presidential Vote
McCain (R)............................151,601 (52%)
Obama (D) 133,461 (46%)

2004 Presidential Vote
Bush (R)................................177,214 (64%)
Kerry (D)................................97,781 (35%)

Cook Partisan Voting Index: R + 10

Northern in a country that was one-quarter Catholic and one-third Southern. Muncie was more typical in that it was culturally homogeneous but economically riven. In the 1920s, when General Motors opened a plant in Muncie, the city celebrated its common values and was loath to admit its economic disparities; Chevrolet took over the plant in 1935. In the 1930s, those differences were exposed when Muncie, like much of the industrial Midwest, was unionized, a process that sometimes led to violent clashes. Workers who were joining CIO unions and voting for Democrats fiercely opposed the business elite—local bankers, merchants, GM executives, and the Ball family's glass company. Partisan politics took on the sharp, bitter tone of a struggle for wealth between two rival classes whose claims seemed irreconcilable. Echoes of such class-warfare politics grow louder at times of economic distress, such as when Ball moved its headquarters to Colorado in 1998. When in 2006 Muncie was ranked ninth nationwide in poverty rates among cities its size or larger, local officials downplayed the situation as not unexpected in a small city with a large student population. In March 2006, GM closed its manual transmission plant, which had opened in 1935 and once employed 3,000 workers. But that loss was tempered by Honda's decision to build a car assembly plant on farmland in Greensburg, about 60 miles south of Muncie. After that facility opened in November 2008 with about 2,000 workers, Honda announced that the plant would produce the world's only passenger vehicles powered by compressed natural gas, the Civic GX.

This area's relative prosperity, based on high-skill manufacturing, has engendered something like a political consensus for tax cuts, tight budgets, and traditional cultural values, with strong support for candidates of either party who agree. Basketball is the civic religion here: Indiana has nine of the nation's 10 largest high school gyms. The Fieldhouse, in New Castle near the Indiana Basketball Hall of Fame, is No. 1 in size. Also noteworthy is Tom Raper Inc. in Richmond, the nation's largest RV dealer.

The 6th Congressional District of Indiana covers most of the east-central part of the state. It includes Muncie and Anderson in the north as well as Richmond, founded by a major branch of American Quakers and home to their Earlham College. In the north and south are suburban fringes of Fort Wayne and Cincinnati. The 6th is solidly Republican in presidential politics but has been a swing district in some state races. Barack Obama took Delaware County, which includes Muncie, 57%-42%, but John McCain won the district 52%-46%.

The congressman from the 6th District is Mike Pence, a Republican first elected in 2000. He grew up in Columbus, Ind., as a John F. Kennedy-admiring Catholic, but he graduated from Hanover College as a Republican evangelical Christian. He got his law degree from Indiana University, and then went into practice. Starting before he was 30, he ran as the Republican nominee for a U.S. House seat in 1988 and 1990 against longtime Democratic Rep. Philip Sharp, and then wrote "Confessions of a Negative Campaigner," an article in which he apologized for running negative ads. He was president of the conservative Indiana Policy Review Foundation, a think tank based in Fort Wayne, and then in 1994 began broadcasting "The Mike Pence Show," a conservative talk-radio program that was syndicated statewide. When the 6th District seat was vacated in 2000 by Republican Rep. David McIntosh, who left to challenge Democratic Gov. Frank O'Bannon, Pence decided to resume his quest for Congress. Pence prevailed in a six-candidate Republican primary, and then faced Democrat Robert Rock, an Anderson, Ind., lawyer and the son of former Lt. Gov. Robert Rock. Also in the contest was Bill Frazier, a former Republican state senator and four-time loser against Sharp who ran as an independent after the primary. All three candidates opposed abortion rights and gun control, and supported increased military spending. Frazier tried to tap into populist sentiment. Rock, a former marine, attacked Pence for not serving in the military, although Pence was only 13 when the draft was abolished and U.S. troops left Vietnam. Rock called for tax cuts for middle-income families, while Pence wanted across-the-board tax cuts and reform of Medicare financing. Pence got 51% of the vote to 39% for Rock and 9% for Frazier. He has since won re-election easily.

Pence quickly established himself as one of the House's more outspoken conservatives. He antagonized the business community by abandoning the bankruptcy bill in 2005 because he objected to a provision on abortion. As the only House member to become a plaintiff in the lawsuit challenging the constitutionality of the McCain-Feingold campaign finance law, Pence said that Arizona Republican McCain was "so deep in bed with the Democrats that his feet are coming out of the bottom of the sheets." He was one of 33 House Republicans to vote against President Bush's signature No Child Left Behind public schools bill in 2001, and one of just 25 to oppose the Republicans' Medicare prescription drug bill in 2003, calling it too costly. He claimed vindication when budget estimates showed rising costs in the program, though they ultimately leveled off. He did vote for the big-spending farm bill in 2002, conceding, "I don't have clean hands," and later voiced regret about his vote. With Republican Sen. Richard Lugar of Indiana, he sponsored a federal shield bill to protect journalists. The House passed the measure in October 2007. "As a conservative who believes in limited government, I believe the only check on government in real time is the freedom of the press," he told the House. He was the first House member to install a radio studio in his office.

In 2005, Pence became chairman of the Republican Study Committee, a group of the most conservative members of the House, and pushed to attract greater attention to the party's conservative message. "We win as conservatives when we communicate," Pence said. "If you can't communicate, you can't govern." Articulate, smart, and often charming, Pence gets frequent invitations to appear on cable television talk shows. He calls himself "Rush Limbaugh on decaf." Under his stewardship, the committee emphasized controlling federal spending. Pence's group worked with Majority Whip Roy Blunt and Budget Committee Chairman Jim Nussle to impose procedural roadblocks on appropriations bills that exceeded annual spending limits. Although some House insiders dismissed the outcome as a "fig leaf," Pence contended that the changes toughened budget discipline. He has shown skill and good timing in making political moves. When Majority Leader Tom DeLay in September 2005 said that it would be difficult to offset the costs of cleaning up the damage from Hurricane Katrina because Republicans had already cut most of the waste in government, Pence held a televised press conference to document $24 billion in possible spending cuts. GOP leaders were miffed at the stunt, but the conservative publication *Human Events* named Pence its "Man of the Year" in 2005.

In 2006, Pence's career took some unexpected twists. On immigration, he teamed with Republican Sen. Kay Bailey Hutchison of Texas on what they hoped would be a compromise bill to break the deadlock between the hard-line approach of House Republicans and the bipartisan proposal in the Senate. Their plan called for strengthening security along the border with Mexico and for sending illegal immigrants home, although it also permitted most of them to return and become eligible for citizenship. He won an audience with President Bush, but conservative activist Phyllis Schlafly called the proposal "a sick joke." The Pence-Hutchison plan went nowhere. Pence hoped that his activism with the RSC would help him land a meaty post in the GOP leadership. After Republicans suffered big losses in November 2006, Pence challenged Minority Leader John Boehner for the party's top job in the House. "We didn't just lose our majority," Pence said of the election outcome. "I believe we lost our way." But Boehner, who had spent less than a year as majority leader before the election, distanced himself from former Speaker Dennis Hastert and his team, and embraced conservative principles, including a leaner budget and entitlement reforms. Pence fared poorly in the showdown, winning just 27 votes to Boehner's 168.

In the minority, Pence served as the ranking Republican on the Middle East and South Asia Subcommittee of the Foreign Affairs Committee. During an April 2008 visit to Iraq, he drew flak back home after saying that the Baghdad market was like "a normal outdoor market in Indiana in the summertime." Pence conceded that his word choice was not ideal. On domestic issues, he was an outspoken critic of the government bailout of the financial markets. "Congress should act, but it must do the right thing, not just something," he said. "Economic freedom means the freedom to succeed and the freedom to fail." He worked on an alternative with loan guarantees, rather than outright grants. He was a leader of the spontaneous move by House Republicans to keep the chamber open in August after Democratic Speaker Nancy Pelosi called for a recess without first allowing a vote on a bill to step up oil exploration as a response to soaring gas prices. With enthusiastic support from Boehner, Pence in November 2008 was elected without opposition as chairman of the Republican Conference, the third-ranking minority leadership post. He took on assignments as a party spokesman and as the liaison to party conservatives. He is the first Hoosier in the House leadership since Democratic Whip John Brademas in the late 1970s.

Some conservative groups had hoped that Pence would be McCain's choice as running mate in 2008. Back home, some speculate that he might run for a Senate seat if one opens in the next few years.

SEVENTH DISTRICT

André Carson (D)

Elected March 2008, 1st full term; b. Oct. 16, 1974, Indianapolis; home, Indianapolis; Concordia U., B.A., 2003, IN Wesleyan U., M.S., 2005; Muslim; married (Mariama); 1 child.

Elected Office: Indianapolis/Marion City-Cnty. Cncl., 2007–08.

Professional Career: Investigator, IN State Excise Police, 1996–2005, Investigator, IN Dept. of Homeland Security, 2006–08.

DC Office: 425 CHOB, 20515, 202-225-4011; Fax: 202-225-5633; Web site: carson.house.gov.

State Offices: Indianapolis, 317-283-6516.

Committees: *Financial Services* (31st of 42 D): Capital Markets, Insurance & Government Sponsored Enterprises; International Monetary Policy & Trade.

Group Ratings

	ADA	ACLU	AFS	LCV	ITIC	NTU	COC	ACU	CFG	FRC
2008	75	—	100	91	—	12	53	4	0	100
2007	—	—	—	—	—	—	—	—	—	—

National Journal Ratings

	2007 LIB	—	2007 CONS		2008 LIB	—	2008 CONS
Economic	*%	—	*%		85%	—	0%
Social	*%	—	*%		82%	—	0%
Foreign	*%	—	*%		58%	—	41%
Composite	*%	—	*%		81%	—	19%

Key Votes of the 110th Congress

1. Increase minimum wage	*	5. Share immigration data	*	9. Withdraw troops 8/08	*
2. Expand SCHIP	*	6. Foreign aid abortion ban	*	10. No operations in Iran	*
3. Raise CAFE standards	*	7. Ban gay bias in workplace	*	11. Free trade with Peru	*
4. Bail out financial markets	Y	8. Repeal D.C. gun law	N	12. Overhaul FISA	N

Election Results

2008 general	André Carson (D)	172,650	(65%)	($1,600,844)
	Gabrielle Campo (R)	92,645	(35%)	($38,684)
2008 primary	André Carson (D)	66,659	(47%)	
	Woodrow Myers (D)	33,683	(24%)	
	David Orentlicher (D)	29,231	(20%)	
	Carolene Mays (D)	11,011	(8%)	
2008 spec. general	André Carson (D)	45,668	(54%)	
	Jon Elrod (R)	36,415	(43%)	
	Sean Shepard (Lib)	2,430	(3%)	

Population

Pop. 2007:	649,742
Change since 2000:	Down 3.8%
Urban:	99.7%
Rural:	0.3%
Area size:	265 sq. mi.

Age

Median age:	34.8 yrs.
More than 65 yrs:	10.8%
Less than 18 yrs:	26.6%

Education

H.S. grad:	81.0%
College grad:	22.3%
Grad degree:	8.1%

Race/Ethnicity

White:	58.1%
Black:	30.7%
Hispanic:	7.2%
Asian:	1.5%
Native Am.:	0.2%
Hawaiian:	0.1%
Two+ races:	2.1%
Ancestry	
German:	14.2%
Irish:	8.9%
English:	6.9%

Work

Private:	84.5%
Government:	11.1%
Self-employed:	4.2%
Blue collar:	24.7%
White collar:	57.3%
Khaki collar:	0.1%
Other:	17.9%
Median income:	$39,018
Median home value:	$106,700
Poverty:	18.7%

Military Veterans

% of Pop:	10.6%

Indianapolis, radiating outward from the soldiers and sailors statue in Monument Circle, is precisely at the center of Indiana and is the largest, and most dominant, city in the state. What residents once disparaged as Nap Town has become a thriving metropolis, including the downtown district. The city is the political and governmental capital, industrial and financial center, and the intellectual center of Indiana as well. It is symmetrically laid out: Just to the west of the circle is the state Capitol, to the north

2008 Presidential Vote		
Obama (D)	191,381	(71%)
McCain (R)	76,530	(28%)
2004 Presidential Vote		
Kerry (D)	130,779	(58%)
Bush (R)	93,347	(42%)
Cook Partisan Voting Index:	D + 14	

is the American Legion headquarters, to the east is the City-County building, and to the south is the Circle Center mall and the RCA Dome (formerly Hoosier Dome). Farther out are some classic and some new Indianapolis institutions: the Indiana University Medical Center; the Convention Center; the Eiteljorg Museum of American Indians and Western Art; Conseco Fieldhouse; and the NCAA's headquarters. Indianapolis has become the nation's amateur sports capital, especially for basketball, and it is a popular place for religious conventions. In 2006, a Brookings Institution study found that Indianapolis had the highest job growth of the 25 largest Rust Belt cities. It attracts many young Indianans looking for opportunity. With its strong service economy, Indianapolis continued to experience job growth even as the recession began, although the financial troubles of General Motors had an impact. In June 2009, the auto giant announced the closure of a local stamping plant that employed 760 people.

Politically, Indianapolis has long had robust competition in local and national races. Republicans held the mayor's office from 1967, when Richard Lugar won it, until 1999. Lugar expanded Indianapolis's city limits to include all of Marion County in a new entity called UniGov, which made it a solidly Republican constituency. But more recently, affluent young people have been moving to counties farther out, and Marion County has been trending Democratic. In 2004, the county voted for John Kerry by 51%-49%, even as seven surrounding suburban counties gave Bush 70% to 75% of the vote. Barack Obama took Marion County by a stunning 64%-35%. His 107,000-vote margin was nearly four times his lead in the entire state. But Republicans managed to pull off their own upset a year earlier, when management consultant Greg Ballard defeated two-term Indianapolis Mayor Bart Peterson, a Democrat.

Indiana's 7th Congressional District includes all of Indianapolis and most of Marion County. It also takes in Center Township, a Democratic stronghold with a large African-American population and a gentrified middle class. But it excludes the affluent, Republican northern edge of the county. The district extends west to include Speedway, where the Indianapolis 500 has been held on a 2.5-mile track since 1911, southward and east to modest neighborhoods, and it includes Amtrak's largest repair yard, which is in Beech Grove. The Mexican population nearly tripled in size during the 1990s and is the newest immigrant community. The 60% increase in Hispanic-owned businesses from 1997 to 2002 was twice the national average, and in 2007, the Hispanic share of the population was 7.2%. Within these boundaries, the 7th District leans Democratic, and it gave solid majorities to recent Democratic presidential nominees.

The congressman from the 7th District is André Carson, who won the seat in March 2008, succeeding his grandmother, Julia Carson, who represented the district for nearly 11 years until she died in office in late 2007. He is only the second Muslim to be elected to Congress; the other is Rep. Keith Ellison, a Minnesota Democrat.

As a child, André Carson was interested in the priesthood, and he studied religion. He also had an artistic side. He wrote poetry as a young man and performed as a rap artist. But his career took him into law enforcement. He got a bachelor's degree in criminal-justice management from Concordia University and a master's degree in business management from Indiana Wesleyan. Carson spent nine years as a plainclothes officer of the Indiana Excise Police, which enforces alcohol and tobacco laws. He recalled that his political interest began in 1984, at age 10, when he attended the Democratic convention in San Francisco. There, he heard civil-rights leader Jesse Jackson speak. Carson said that his thinking was transformed by reading *The Autobiography of Malcolm X,* and he attended Louis Farrakhan's Million Man March in 1995. In August 2007, at age 32, he won a seat on the Indianapolis City Council, his first elected office.

After Julia Carson died in December 2007 following multiple and lengthy illnesses, her grandson faced significant opposition for the Democratic nomination in the special election, which was held to fill the remainder of Carson's term. At the January 12 Democratic caucus, André Carson won 223 of the 439 votes; state Rep. David Orentlicher, a lawyer and doctor, got 123 votes; and Marion County Treasurer Michael Rodman came in third with 27 votes. Against Republican state Rep. Jon Elrod, a young lawyer, Carson received extensive assistance from the Democratic Congressional Campaign Committee. On issues, he called for U.S. troops in Iraq to come home "very soon," endorsed tax cuts for working families, and said that companies should have incentives to keep them from sending jobs overseas. Elrod emphasized aid to small businesses and tougher enforcement of immigration laws, and he called for an end to federal spending earmarks, the special provisions that lawmakers often tuck into appropriations bills. "I will be part of the solution and not part of the problem in Congress," he said. Carson won, 54%-43%.

Meanwhile, Carson had to continue campaigning for a May primary to determine the winner of a full term. That field included Orentlicher, former state health Commissioner Woodrow Myers, and state Rep. Carolene Mays. Running as the incumbent this time and with an endorsement from Barack Obama, Carson won the primary with 47% of the vote to 24% for Myers, 20% for Orentlicher, and 8% for Mays. In the contest for a full term, Elrod won the GOP nomination. But he soon withdrew and ran unsuccessfully to retain his seat in the state House. Carson faced minimal opposition.

In the House, Carson has established a liberal voting record, especially on economic and cultural issues. When he arrived, he got a seat on the Financial Services Committee and soon found himself embroiled in the debate over the $700 billion bailout of the financial markets in fall 2008. After initially opposing the bailout bill, he switched his position four days later to vote in favor after Obama encouraged him to support it.

EIGHTH DISTRICT

Brad Ellsworth (D)

Elected 2006, 2nd term; b. Sept. 11, 1958, Huntingburg; home, Evansville; U. of S. IN, B.S. 1981, IN St. U., M.A. 1993; Catholic; married (Beth); 1 child.

Elected Office: Vanderburgh Cnty. Sheriff, 1998–2006.

Professional Career: Chief deputy, Vanderburgh Cnty. Sheriff's Office, 1982–98.

DC Office: 513 CHOB, 20515, 202-225-4636; Fax: 202-225-3284; Web site: www.ellsworth.house.gov.

State Offices: Evansville, 812-465-6484; Terre Haute, 812-232-0523.

Committees: *Agriculture* (12th of 28 D): Conservation, Credit, Energy & Research; General Farm Commodities & Risk Management. *Armed Services* (19th of 36 D): Seapower & Expeditionary Forces; Terrorism, Unconventional Threats & Capabilities. *Small Business* (13th of 17 D): Contracting & Technology; Investigations & Oversight.

Group Ratings

	ADA	ACLU	AFS	LCV	ITIC	NTU	COC	ACU	CFG	FRC
2008	75	55	86	62	100	15	72	16	3	76
2007	75	—	73	75	—	15	70	36	18	—

National Journal Ratings

	2007 LIB	—	2007 CONS	2008 LIB	—	2008 CONS
Economic	51%	—	48%	48%	—	50%
Social	45%	—	54%	46%	—	52%
Foreign	47%	—	52%	47%	—	52%
Composite	48%	—	52%	48%	—	52%

Key Votes of the 110th Congress

1. Increase minimum wage	Y	5. Share immigration data	Y	9. Withdraw troops 8/08	Y
2. Expand SCHIP	Y	6. Foreign aid abortion ban	Y	10. No operations in Iran	Y
3. Raise CAFE standards	Y	7. Ban gay bias in workplace	Y	11. Free trade with Peru	Y
4. Bail out financial markets	Y	8. Repeal D.C. gun law	Y	12. Overhaul FISA	Y

Election Results

2008 general	Brad Ellsworth (D)..	188,693	(65%)	($1,366,664)
	Greg Goode (R)...	102,769	(35%)	($223,729)
2008 primary	Brad Ellsworth (D)..................................... unopposed			

Prior Winning Percentages: 2006 (61%)

Population

Pop. 2007:	678,829
Change since 2000:	Up 0.5%
Urban:	58.1%
Rural:	41.9%
Area size:	7,132 sq. mi.

Age

Median age:	38.0 yrs.
More than 65 yrs:	14.1%
Less than 18 yrs:	23.2%

Education

H.S. grad:	84.7%
College grad:	17.3%
Grad degree:	6.6%

Race/Ethnicity

White:	92.8%
Black:	3.9%
Hispanic:	1.2%
Asian:	0.8%
Native Am.:	0.2%
Hawaiian:	0.0%
Two+ races:	1.0%

Ancestry

German:	24.3%
USA:	13.3%
Irish:	10.9%

Work

Private:	82.0%
Government:	12.1%
Self-employed:	5.7%
Blue collar:	31.0%
White collar:	51.4%
Khaki collar:	0.1%
Other:	17.5%
Median income:	$42,483
Median home value:	$96,900
Poverty:	13.8%

Military Veterans

% of Pop:	12.0%

"Evansville," wrote John Bartlow Martin in 1947, "is the capital of a tri-state area comprising the neglected tag ends of Indiana, Kentucky, and Illinois." It was a factory town then, making car parts and refrigerators, drawing workers from Kentucky, Tennessee, and the picturesque but not very fertile hills of southern Indiana. Today, Evansville has become the headquarters for a number of midsize companies that offer many high-paying, skilled jobs. Car parts still get made here, though it is auto assembly

2008 Presidential Vote

McCain (R)	151,570	(51%)
Obama (D)	140,063	(47%)

2004 Presidential Vote

Bush (R)	170,390	(62%)
Kerry (D)	104,625	(38%)

Cook Partisan Voting Index: R+8

that helps anchor the local manufacturing economy. Toyota in 1998 opened a plant in nearby Princeton that builds SUVs and minivans, employing approximately 4,500 workers who take home as much as $28 an hour. It has seen hard times, such as the terrible flood of March 1997 and a November 2005 tornado that killed 24 people, but it also has Indiana's first riverboat casino and claims to have the nation's second-largest street festival, second only to New Orleans's Mardi Gras celebration. In 2008, construction began on the long-discussed Interstate 69 extension from Evansville to Indianapolis, which one local official said was "40 years too late."

Evansville is one of two major centers of the 8th Congressional District, which covers most of southwest and west-central Indiana. The other, in Vigo County, is Terre Haute, an old manufacturing town and the boyhood home of socialist Eugene Debs. It hosts a maximum-security penitentiary, which includes the only federal death chamber; Oklahoma City bomber Timothy McVeigh was executed there in 2001. In 2008, Pfizer closed a local plant that had employed about 800 workers producing the insulin drug Exubera. The district also takes in Vincennes, now a small town on the banks of the Wabash River but once a major metropolis. Downstream is New Harmony, established by Scottish philanthropist and visionary Robert Owen. His son was the first congressman from the area, elected in 1842 and 1844. Southern Indiana is ancestrally Democratic, just as northern Indiana is ancestrally Republican. These southern counties were hostile to the Union during the Civil War. In New Deal times, workers in Evansville again moved toward the Democrats.

The result has been a very close political balance, and this district has become known as the "Bloody 8th" for its tight congressional races. At one point in the 1970s, it sent four different members to the House in four successive elections. In 1984, the state certified the Republican as the winner by exactly 34 votes. The Democratic majority in the U.S. House overturned the result, however, in a fight that left many Republican members bitterly aggrieved. Since then, the district has been as fiercely contested as ever. The trend in presidential politics, however, is away from national Democrats. Bill Clinton twice carried the 8th by a 2% margin, George W. Bush won it with 56% in 2000, and again in 2004 with 62%. After campaigning there vigorously, Barack Obama won Vanderburgh and Vigo counties, but he narrowly lost the district, 51%-47%.

The congressman from the 8th District is Brad Ellsworth, a Democrat elected in 2006. He was born in Jasper, not far outside the current district, and his family moved to Evansville when he was 10 and his father took a job as crane operator at a nearby Alcoa plant. Brad graduated in 1981 from what was then called Indiana State University at Evansville, where he worked in the paint and hardware departments at Sears to pay his tuition, and then joined the Vanderburgh County Sheriff's Office as a deputy. Ellsworth steadily rose through the ranks while also earning a master's degree in criminology by taking weekend courses at Indiana State. He easily won his first election as county sheriff in 1998 and ran unopposed in 2002. During his eight years as sheriff, Ellsworth became a familiar name in Vanderburgh County, which is in the district's largest media market.

In 2006, Ellsworth took on Rep. John Hostettler, a conservative Republican iconoclast who had held the 8th District seat for six terms. Hostettler had never won with more than 53% of the vote, and his policy of never accepting political action committee donations made him a weak fundraiser and a perennial

Democratic target. He frequently bucked the GOP leadership in Congress, including voting against the 1995 balanced-budget amendment and the use of force in Iraq. Republican strategists each cycle worried about Hostettler's re-election but took comfort in his uncanny ability to eke out victories by mobilizing support among anti-abortion voters and Christian conservatives. After a string of disappointing challengers, Democrats thought they had found the ideal candidate for this culturally conservative district. Ellsworth touted gun-ownership rights and opposed abortion rights, same-sex marriage, and a hasty withdrawal of troops from Iraq. A quarter-century's experience as a police officer made him highly credible on crime and law enforcement issues. When a tornado devastated parts of southern Indiana in November 2005, Ellsworth was everywhere, helping people deal with the aftermath; while Hostettler was nearly invisible. Hostettler also found himself in the uncomfortable position of asking for federal disaster aid just two months after he had voted against Hurricane Katrina relief for the Gulf Coast.

Hostettler made few appearances and ran no ads until relatively late, leading to rumors that he had given up the race. In October, he ran a radio spot, in which an announcer impersonated Clint Eastwood's *Dirty Harry* movie character and warned that a vote for Ellsworth was a vote for Nancy Pelosi as House speaker. "Pelosi will then put in motion her radical plan to advance the homosexual agenda," the announcer warned. The attacks alienated many women who liked Pelosi, while baffling other potential voters who had no idea who she was. Meanwhile, Ellsworth was enjoying a surfeit of attention. Just weeks before the election, *The Washington Post* featured the "swaggering Indiana sheriff" in a front-page story about good-looking candidates running that year. Ellsworth also had a strong financial advantage, spending more than $1.7 million, three times as much as Hostettler's $580,000. On Election Day, Ellsworth crushed Hostettler 61%-39%, an unusually weak showing for a non-scandal-ridden incumbent. Ellsworth carried 14 of the district's 18 counties; he beat Hostettler by 11,500 votes in Vigo County and by nearly 15,000 votes in Vanderburgh County (63%-37%).

In the House, Ellsworth joined the conservative Blue Dog Democrats and established a centrist voting record. In 2008, he had a composite score of 47.8 in *National Journal*'s annual vote analysis. (A score of 50 is the exact ideological center of House, inclusive of both parties.) Ellsworth backed the Bush administration's troop surge in Iraq and split with his party on several issues, including his opposition to granting illegal immigrants a path to citizenship and to federal funding for embryonic-stem-cell research. "I vote like that because that's what I think the folks here want me to do," he told the *Evansville Courier & Press* in 2007. In 2008, he supported the massive bailout bill for the financial markets as necessary to assure loans to small businesses. He was also successful in getting the House to pass his bill barring companies with tax debts from receiving large government contracts or grants.

In his district-centered work, Ellsworth was among the most successful freshman Democrats in securing earmarks, special provisions tucked into spending bills. It was not an altogether positive distinction. Earmarks recently became highly controversial as federal spending ballooned and many of the projects were revealed to be unnecessary or wasteful. Ellsworth secured $5.6 million for AmeriQual, an Evansville company that produces packaged meals for the military. "Hoosiers play by the rules and pay their taxes, so it's only fair they receive some of the benefit of their tax dollars," Ellsworth said in defending his earmarks to the *Courier & Press*.

Republicans failed to recruit a top-flight challenger to Ellsworth when he sought re-election in 2008. He won 65%-35% against Greg Goode, a former Indiana State University public-affairs officer. Although he says he voted for Barack Obama in the Indiana primary, Ellsworth went to the Democratic convention as a delegate for Hillary Rodham Clinton because she carried his district.

NINTH DISTRICT

Baron Hill (D)

Elected 2006, 5th term; b. June 23, 1953, Seymour; home, Seymour; Furman U., B.A. 1975; Methodist; married (Betty); 3 children.

Elected Office: IN House of Reps., 1982–90; U.S. House of Reps., 1998–2004.

Professional Career: The Hill Agency (insurance), 1975–90; Exec. dir., IN Student Assistance Comm., 1990–94; Financial analyst, Merrill Lynch, 1994–98; Sr. advisor, mCapitol Management, 2005–06.

DC Office: 223 CHOB, 20515, 202-225-5315; Fax: 202-226-6866; Web site: baronhill.house.gov.

State Offices: Bloomington, 812-336-3000; Jeffersonville, 812-288-3999.

Committees: *Energy & Commerce* (26th of 36 D): Communications, Technology & the Internet; Energy & Environment. *Joint Economic Committee* (3rd of 6 D). *Science & Technology* (20th of 26 D): Space & Aeronautics.

Group Ratings

	ADA	ACLU	AFS	LCV	ITIC	NTU	COC	ACU	CFG	FRC
2008	75	91	71	85	57	22	61	20	16	17
2007	85	—	82	85	—	14	70	20	15	—

National Journal Ratings

	2007 LIB	—	2007 CONS	2008 LIB	—	2008 CONS
Economic	51%	—	48%	53%	—	47%
Social	49%	—	51%	50%	—	50%
Foreign	52%	—	47%	50%	—	48%
Composite	51%	—	49%	51%	—	49%

Key Votes of the 110th Congress

1. Increase minimum wage	Y	5. Share immigration data	Y	9. Withdraw troops 8/08	Y
2. Expand SCHIP	N	6. Foreign aid abortion ban	N	10. No operations in Iran	Y
3. Raise CAFE standards	Y	7. Ban gay bias in workplace	Y	11. Free trade with Peru	Y
4. Bail out financial markets	N	8. Repeal D.C. gun law	Y	12. Overhaul FISA	N

Election Results

2008 general	Baron Hill (D)	181,281	(58%)	($2,185,740)
	Michael Sodrel (R)	120,529	(38%)	($1,045,379)
	D. Eric Schansberg (Lib)	11,994	(4%)	($35,565)
2008 primary	Baron Hill (D)	99,332	(68%)	
	Gretchen Clearwater (D)	23,157	(16%)	
	John Bottorff (D)	18,963	(13%)	

Prior Winning Percentages: 2006 (50%); 2002 (51%); 2000 (54%); 1998 (51%)

Population		Race/Ethnicity		Work	
Pop. 2007:	702,539	White:	92.6%	Private:	82.0%
Change since 2000:	Up 4.0%	Black:	2.5%	Government:	12.3%
Urban:	52.3%	Hispanic:	2.0%	Self-employed:	5.5%
Rural:	47.7%	Asian:	1.3%	Blue collar:	32.1%
Area size:	6,670 sq. mi.	Native Am.:	0.2%	White collar:	51.1%
Age		Hawaiian:	0.0%	Khaki collar:	0.1%
Median age:	36.3 yrs.	Two+ races:	1.1%	Other:	16.7%
More than 65 yrs:	12.6%	*Ancestry*		Median income:	$43,940
Less than 18 yrs:	23.1%	German:	24.5%	Median home value:	$118,100
Education		Irish:	11.3%	Poverty:	14.2%
H.S. grad:	84.0%	USA:	11.0%	**Military Veterans**	
College grad:	18.4%			% of Pop:	10.5%
Grad degree:	7.7%				

The southeastern corner of Indiana swelled with new settlers in the early 19th century as Southerners, or "Butternuts," came across the Ohio River from Kentucky or over the mountains from Virginia. They built the first large Indiana settlements. Today, you can see their work in the marvelous old buildings of Madison, now a quiet hamlet but once one of the busiest ports on the river. Its landmark Broadway Fountain first appeared at the 1876 Centennial Exposition in Philadelphia. It arrived in Madison in 1886, thanks to the Independent Order of Oddfellows, which had purchased it after the exposition. Farther down the river is Corydon, which was the state capital from 1816 to 1825. Its early 19th-century buildings are well preserved. These small towns were bypassed first by the railroads, then by U.S. routes and interstate highways, and they are remote from today's major airports. The river remains an artery of commerce, although utilitarian barges have replaced all of the old steamers, except for riverboat casinos.

Butternut Indiana retained its affection for things Southern into the Civil War and beyond. In 1851, the state denied blacks the right to vote or serve in the militia. In 1862, the U.S. Senate expelled local politician Jesse Bright for "supporting the rebellion." The people who live in the hills along the Ohio River have typically voted Democratic, but the Clark County suburbs of Louisville have trended Republican. This part of Indiana is now filling up with migrants from Cincinnati, which was a Yankee and German abolitionist bastion in Bright's time but is an overwhelmingly Republican stronghold in ours.

2008 Presidential Vote

McCain (R)	160,248	(50%)
Obama (D)	154,629	(49%)

2004 Presidential Vote

Bush (R)	171,926	(59%)
Kerry (D)	117,647	(40%)

Cook Partisan Voting Index: R+6

The 9th Congressional District of Indiana comprises most of the state's Ohio River counties. It includes tiny Milan, home to the championship high school of *Hoosiers* movie fame, and Indiana University in Democratic-leaning Bloomington, the largest city in the district. To the east of Milan is Batesville, home of the Batesville Casket Co., which makes the coffins for U.S. military personnel who die in the line of duty. To the west of Batesville is French Lick, a former rural resort town, well known to basketball fans as the hometown of former Boston Celtics star Larry Bird. Most of the district is culturally conservative, but the area is highly competitive politically, both in local and national elections. George W. Bush won this district 59%-40% in 2004, but John McCain won it by the much narrower margin of 50%-48.5%. Barack Obama won Monroe County and Bloomington 66%-33%.

The congressman from the 9th District is Baron Hill, a Democrat first elected in 1998. He served three terms before losing the seat in 2004, only to regain it from Republican Mike Sodrel in 2006. Hill is the youngest of seven children. His parents worked in a shoe factory in Seymour. Seymour is the birthplace of John Mellencamp and the subject of his song *Small Town*. Hill, who was a basketball standout in high school and later at Furman University, was inducted into the Indiana Basketball Hall of Fame alongside Larry Bird in 2000. Hill returned home after college to join his family's insurance business and eventually served four terms in the state House. In 1990, he ran against U.S. Sen. Dan Coats and, despite a huge money disadvantage, held the Republican incumbent to a 54%-46% win. Then-Democratic Gov. Evan Bayh appointed Hill to head the state student assistance agency. In 1998, he won a competitive contest to replace Democratic Rep. Lee Hamilton, who had served in the House for 34 years and chaired the Foreign Affairs Committee.

Hill got off to a strong start. He joined the Blue Dog Coalition of moderate and conservative Democrats, the leadership made him a chief deputy whip, and he won a seat on the Agriculture Committee—an important posting for his district. In 2002, bus-company owner Sodrel spent more than $1 million of his own money to challenge Hill. But Hill won 51%-46%. Two years later, Sodrel returned for a rematch and this time defeated Hill by 1,425 votes in a campaign that centered on social issues such as gay marriage, abortion rights, and flag-burning. The National Republican Congressional Committee spent more than $1 million on ads against Hill, and top GOP leaders visited the district numerous times on Sodrel's behalf. On the coattails of President Bush, who carried the district with 59% that year, Sodrel won.

In 2006, a strong Democratic year, Sodrel's party affiliation worked against him. Bush, the Republican-controlled Congress, and Republican Gov. Mitch Daniels were far less popular than they were in 2004, and Democrats portrayed Sodrel as a drone for the Bush administration. Sodrel tried to counter by attacking Hill as a career politician who had become a Washington lobbyist. Hill insisted that he did consulting for local businesses and was not a lobbyist. Illegal immigration loomed large during the campaign, as did social issues such as same-sex marriage, but Hill left little daylight between his and Sodrel's positions on those matters. In early October, Hill put Sodrel on the defensive by linking him to the House GOP leaders who had failed to act quickly to punish Rep. Mark Foley, a Florida Republican who had sent sexually explicit e-mails to former congressional pages. Hill called himself "a family man with deep religious convictions," and he ran an ad opposing gay marriage. Hill won his third match with Sodrel, 50%-45%, with a margin of 9,985 votes. His big advantage was in Bloomington-based Monroe County, where he won 63%-32%, with a lead of nearly 8,000 votes.

Since 2007, Hill's voting record has put him almost precisely at the center of the House ideologically. He became policy co-chairman of the Blue Dog Democrats in 2009. In 2007, he won a seat on the influential Energy and Commerce Committee, where he wanted to target increased use of ethanol and biodiesel fuels and incentives for hybrid vehicles. But automaking is big business in Indiana, and Hill opposed sharply raising fuel economy standards for cars and trucks. Instead, he worked closely with the auto industry to limit the proposal. He and Rep. Lee Terry, R-Neb., sponsored a bill to set a 35-mile-per-gallon requirement for passenger cars by 2022. The industry and committee Chairman John Dingell, a Detroit-area Democrat, backed their bill. Congress ultimately enacted legislation setting that goal for all vehicles, but moved up the deadline to 2020.

Under pressure from party leaders, Hill voted in October 2007 to override President Bush's veto of expanding the State Children's Health Insurance Program; he initially voted against the bill because it raised cigarette taxes. In June 2008, Hill sponsored a bill to close loopholes in regulations for commodities, including gasoline. He voted against the bailout of the financial industry in the fall of 2008 because, he said, the legislation did not hold accountable the people responsible for the collapse of banks and other financial institutions. He later voted for the bailout of the Big Three automakers because of its impact on jobs in Indiana.

Hill and Sodrel faced each other once again in 2008, but the outcome was not nearly as close this time. Sodrel spent less than half of his 2006 total, and he had little national party help. He sought to hold Hill accountable for his 2006 campaign promises to spur the economy and reduce gas prices. Hill played up his independence in the House. He won 58%-38% and took 18 of the district's 20 counties.

★ IOWA ★

As Americans were surging westward in the 1840s, Iowa was filling up with Yankee farmers and German immigrants. Wagon trains headed to the Oregon Trail, and the thousands of Mormons mustered by Brigham Young traveled across Iowa's rolling hills to Council Bluffs on the Missouri River, and then to points further west. The state was young, and proud of its hundreds of schools and dozens of colleges, sending more than its share of young men back East to fight for the Union. After that war, Iowans built a solid civilization based on farming, farm-machine manufacturing, and meat processing that resisted the blandishments of William Jennings Bryan's populism and cheap money. Iowa became one of the most solidly Republican states in the nation.

But starting around 1900, Iowa's model society stopped attracting new transplants. "If you build it, they will come" was the theme from the movie *Field of Dreams*, set in Iowa. Yet during the 20th century, very few people came. The region's commercial and financial center remained the railroad hub of Chicago, Iowa's economy failed to diversify and develop the dense manufacturing base of the Great Lakes states, and its young people started to move east or west to make their fortunes. The state's population, which increased from 674,000 in 1860 to 2.2 million in 1900, did not reach 3 million until 2008. In 1900, Iowa had 11 congressional districts and California had seven. Now, Iowa has five and California 53. Iowa's solid Capitol, a memorial to its Civil War dead, its courthouses, and its sturdy but mostly old housing stock give testimony to Iowa's strengths but also suggest a lack of dynamism. Its great economic achievement has been the development of high-tech, ever more productive, but also less labor-intensive agriculture. Iowa is the nation's leading producer of pork, corn, and soybeans, yet it remains near the bottom in population growth.

Iowa had a particularly tough time in the 1980s. The number of Iowans whose principal occupation was farming dropped from 86,000 in 1982 to 56,000 in 1997, and the state's population dropped by 4.7% between 1980 and 1990, down to the 1960 level. However, the 1990s were a big improvement. Its high level of literacy and good work habits produced white-collar and high-tech growth in and around its pleasant small cities, especially Des Moines and Cedar Rapids. Even as many old factories closed, it grew by 5.4% in the 1990s. In this decade, the state grew by 1.6% from 2000 to 2007. Former Gov. Tom Vilsack hosted parties for Iowa natives in New York City and Chicago and urged them to come back home. Mexican immigrants moved to small towns with meatpacking plants as well as to Des Moines and the old industrial cities of Sioux City and Waterloo. Jobs and small-town life also attracted Bosnians and Liberians as well as Congolese, Sudanese and Somali refugees. Ethanol has boosted the Iowa economy since 1998, when Republican Sen. Charles Grassley got the ethanol tax credit extended to 2007; by the end of 2007, Iowa was producing almost one-third of the nation's ethanol, which the renewable fuel industry said generated as many as 96,000 jobs and helped raise corn prices, and therefore farmland prices. Soybean prices boomed as well. Some factory jobs have disappeared; in 2007, Whirlpool, which had bought Maytag the previous year, closed an Iowa plant. But the state has lost far fewer jobs in the recent recession than it did in the early 1980s. The housing bubble wasn't big here, financial institutions remained strong, and unemployment remained well below the national average.

For much of the 20th century, Iowa was a culturally and politically countercyclical state, headed in the opposite direction of the rest of the nation—determinedly, with confidence in its own chipper rectitude, unabashedly out of step. In the industrial New Deal era, it stayed mostly agricultural and Republican, even as Davenport and Des Moines radio announcer Ronald Reagan became an enthusiastic Roosevelt Democrat and headed to Hollywood. Iowa was dovish during the Vietnam War and afterward. In the 1980s, when Reagan, by then a conservative Republican, was president, Iowa's economy was hit hard and self-pity became the dominant note of Iowa's politics, as voters sought protection from the vagaries of the market. In the 1988 caucuses, Iowa Republicans voted against Reagan's vice president, George H.W. Bush, and Iowa Democrats voted for populist Dick Gephardt of Missouri. In the fall, it gave Democrat Michael Dukakis his second highest percentage of any state.

Since then, Iowa and the nation have converged politically. It voted twice for Bill Clinton and went for Al Gore by 4,144 votes in 2000 and for George W. Bush by 10,059 votes in 2004. It gave Barack Obama a decisive boost in its precinct caucuses and then voted 55%-44% for him in November. Its two U.S. senators are split, one Republican and one Democratic. After 30 years of Republican governors, Iowa elected Democrats three times, starting in 1998. Republicans won majorities in the Legislature in the 1990s, lost them in 2004 and failed to regain them in 2006. Collectively, these results indicate a sort of steady moderation, a desire to accept the verdict of the markets and to honor traditional values, with a little hedging on both counts. Iowa remains quirky in some respects. It is still probably one of the most dovish, isolationist-prone states, though very much aware of its role as an international exporter. Its delegation voted for the 1993 North American Free Trade Agreement and for normalizing trade relations with China in 1999 (Mexicans eat lots of corn and the Chinese buy a lot of pork). It is thrift-minded, seeing a balanced budget more as a badge of moral rectitude than as prudent economic policy. It pioneered legal riverboat

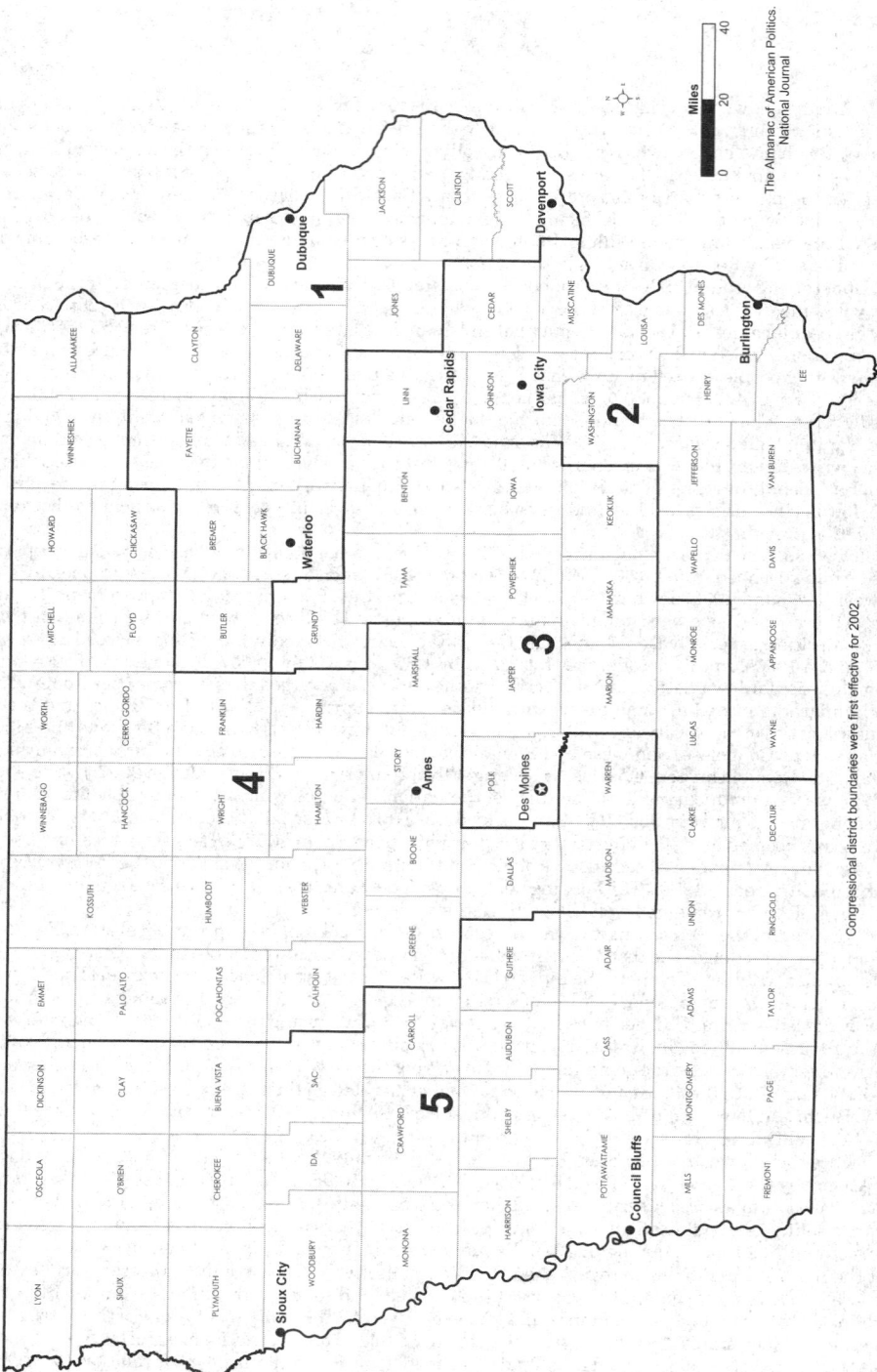

Congressional district boundaries were first effective for 2002.

Population		Household Income		Work	
Pop. 2007:	2,972,066	Under $15k:	12.8%	Private:	78.3%
State rank:	30th of 50	$15k to $50k:	40.8%	Government:	13.7%
Change since 2000:	Up 1.6%	$50k to $100k:	33.4%	Self-employed:	7.7%
Urban:	60.3%	$100k to $150k:	11.0%	Unemployment (3-yr. average):	3.4%
Rural:	39.7%	Over $150k:	2.0%	Poverty:	11.0%
Native of state:	72.5%	Median income:	$46,399	Blue collar:	25.7%
Not a citizen:	2.5%	**Home Value**		White collar:	57.6%
Area size:	56,272 sq. mi.	Under $100k:	43.0%	Khaki collar:	0.1%
Most populous cities		$100k to $300k:	50.8%	Other:	16.6%
1. Des Moines	197,039	$300k to $500k:	4.7%	**Age**	
2. Cedar Rapids	124,515	$500k to $1 mil:	1.3%	Median age:	37.9 yrs.
3. Davenport	97,090	Over $1 million:	0.2%	More than 65 yrs:	14.7%
4. Sioux City	82,385	Median:	$112,600	Less than 18 yrs:	23.9%

Race/Ethnicity				Military Veterans		Registered Voters in 2008	
White:	90.9%	Language		% of Pop:	11.1%	D:	736,244 (34.4%)
Black:	2.4%	English:	93.6%	Veterans by Period		R:	624,830 (29.2%)
Hispanic:	3.8%	Spanish:	3.5%	WWII and before:	14.7%	Other:	782,591 (36.5%)
Asian:	1.6%	Asian:	1.1%	Korea:	14.6%	Voter turnout:	1,537,123
Native Am.:	0.2%	Other		Vietnam:	32.8%	Turnout as % of	
Hawaiian:	0.0%	European	1.6%	Gulf (pre-2001):	9.0%	voting age:	67.1%
Two+ races:	1.0%	**Education**		Gulf (post-2001):	5.6%	**General Assembly**	
Ancestry		H.S. grad:	89.2%	Peace time:	23.4%	Senate:	32 D 18 R
German:	30.4%	College grad:	24.0%			House:	56 D 44 R
Irish:	11.8%	Grad degree:	7.5%				
English:	7.8%						

gambling in 1989, but also has a large anti-abortion rights movement. And it has its own traditional gatherings, which are often of political significance. One is the Iowa State Fair, held every August on the east side of Des Moines, complete with the traditional 600-pound butter cow. Another is RAGBRAI, the *Des Moines Register's* Annual Great Bike Ride Across Iowa, held in late summer every year since 1973. And then there are the Iowa precinct caucuses, held on a cold night in January in presidential years, the first occasion in which ordinary Americans decide who will be their next president.

Presidential Politics Every four years, tens of thousands of Iowans troop to caucuses in nearly 2,000 precincts to begin the formal process of electing a president. The precinct caucuses were scheduled early in the 1972 cycle by Democratic doves who wanted more leverage for their views, and that year, they started George McGovern on his way to the Democratic nomination. But the caucuses have had other, unanticipated consequences. In 1976, Jimmy Carter's strategist Hamilton Jordan determined that intensive campaigning could produce a surprise victory that could make a little-known candidate a national contender: Without Iowa and the next-up New Hampshire primary, Carter would not have become president.

2008 Presidential Vote
Obama (D) 828,940 (54%)
McCain (R).............................682,379 (44%)

2004 Presidential Vote
Bush (R) 751,957 (50%)
Kerry (D)................................741,898 (49%)

Then, for the next 20 years, the Iowa caucuses were less nomination determinative. In 1980, George H.W. Bush's intensive campaigning gave him a victory among Republicans, while Carter, still profiting from his 1976 contacts, trounced Sen. Edward Kennedy. But Bush lost the nomination to Ronald Reagan, and Carter lost in November. In 1984, Democratic favorite Walter Mondale won 49% of the "delegate strength" (Democrats don't compute the actual number of votes), but the momentum went to the 17% second-place finisher Gary Hart, though Mondale did win the nomination. In 1988, Iowa failed to pick the winners on either side. Dick Gephardt capitalized on Iowa's economic woes to win among Democrats, while George H.W. Bush finished in third place behind Kansas Sen. Bob Dole and televangelist Pat Robertson among Republicans—a sign of the rising strength of Christian conservatives in the Republican Party. But Gephardt and Dole lost in New Hampshire, and neither was nominated. In 1992, Iowa went dark. No Democrat challenged Iowa's Tom Harkin here, and Pat Buchanan began his campaign against Bush in New Hampshire. In 1996, Dole had the support of leading Republicans, led by Gov. Terry Branstad and Sen. Charles Grassley, and he had farm-state roots as well. Dole's very narrow victory was an omen of the weakness of his candidacy later.

In 2000, the Iowa caucuses became decisive again, for both parties, and remained so for Democrats in 2004 and 2008. The 2000 caucuses were moved to Monday, January 24, after New Hampshire surprised everyone by scheduling its primary for Tuesday, February 1. George W. Bush won the 25,000-strong

August 1999 Republican straw poll at Ames, Iowa, after which Dan Quayle, Lamar Alexander and Elizabeth Dole dropped out, and Pat Buchanan left the Republican Party altogether. Bush continued to build his organizational strength and won the caucus straw poll with 41% of the vote to Steve Forbes's 30%. Both got a share of religious conservatives, as did Alan Keyes, who was third with 14%. On the Democratic side, the race was between Al Gore and Bill Bradley. In his 1988 campaign, Gore had skipped what he called "madness" in "the small state of Iowa," but in June 1997, he was proclaiming, "I love Iowa." And in November 1998, he was on the phone congratulating Tom Vilsack before Vilsack himself realized he had been elected governor. Gore did not get Vilsack's support—he stayed neutral—but Gore did get vigorous support from Vilsack's wife, from Sen. Tom Harkin and, perhaps most important, from Iowa's labor unions. Gore won in "delegate strength" with 63% to Bradley's 35%. That gave Gore momentum in New Hampshire, which he won eight days later, though by only 50%-46%. With five weeks to the next Democratic contest, Bradley dropped out, and Gore was the nominee.

Iowa was dispositive in 2004 as well. President Bush had no opposition. This was the Democrats' show. The leader in Iowa polls from summer 2003 through the second week of January 2004 was Howard Dean. His opposition to the war in Iraq was popular among the state's overwhelmingly dovish caucusgoers. His thousands of out-of-state volunteers seemed to have built the best turnout organization. But as the year opened, Democrats suddenly confronted the possibility that they could actually defeat Bush, and the question for many became not who could most stridently criticize the president and his policies but who could defeat him. Dean's comment that the December 13 capture of Iraqi Leader Saddam Hussein "has not made America safer" raised doubts about his electability. Dean's irritated out-shouting of a 68-year-old Republican questioner in Oelwein January 11 was a breach of Iowa manners. His poll numbers immediately started plummeting. The question was who would rise. Gephardt, supported by labor unions and veterans of his campaign 16 years earlier, failed to gather new adherents. John Edwards, endorsed by the Des Moines Register, had only a few chipper out-of-staters organizing things. John Kerry, who mortgaged his Boston house for $6.4 million and put all of his effort into Iowa, had the best organization, the endorsement of Christie Vilsack—the governor was again technically neutral—and a strong message. Just days before the caucuses, he was joined by a Green Beret he had rescued in the waters of Vietnam. Kerry proclaimed that he could stand up to Bush on Iraq because he had volunteered and been decorated in the Vietnam War.

That was enough for victory on caucus night and later, the nomination. Howard Dean's 3,500 orange-stocking-capped Perfect Stormers were swarming in the streets of Des Moines. But Kerry got the votes. Under Iowa Democrats' procedures, the supporters of candidates who fail to meet a 15% threshold of the votes in any precinct can choose to caucus for another candidate. Entry polls at the caucuses showed Kerry well ahead, with Edwards, Dean, and Gephardt trailing. But Edwards had shrewdly targeted supporters of Dennis Kucinich, and their second-choice support for Edwards helped swell his numbers in the final standings, while Dean and Gephardt, failing to make the threshold in many precincts, saw their numbers dwindle below the entry poll. The final results, in "delegate strength": Kerry 38%, Edwards 32%, Dean 18%, and Gephardt 11%. Gephardt soon left the race. Dean was effectively finished even before he emitted his famous scream on caucus night. Edwards was left to finish second or third to Kerry until Kerry clinched the nomination six weeks and one day later. But it was Iowa Democrats—some 122,000 of them—who did the deciding.

In 2008, both parties had candidates competing in the Iowa caucuses, but the Democratic contest was much more vigorous. Outgoing Gov. Vilsack announced he was running in November 2006, but his entry still left other Democrats competitive in the polls, and in February 2007, he withdrew and endorsed Hillary Rodham Clinton. By the end of the year, Democratic candidates had more than 500 paid staffers in Iowa, while Republicans had fewer than 100. John Edwards had never really stopped visiting Iowa after the 2004 campaign, and by November 2007, he had made appearances in all 99 counties. Taking advantage of the propinquity of his home in Chicago, Barack Obama was in the state often. Joseph Biden and Christopher Dodd took time off from their duties as chairmen of the Senate Foreign Relations and Banking committees, respectively, to campaign frequently in the state. And in November, Dodd moved his family to Iowa and enrolled his daughter in a Des Moines kindergarten. Clinton visited less often, and in the spring, a staffer's memo recommending she skip Iowa leaked to the press. She led in initial polls, but her vote for the 2002 Iraq War resolution and her refusal to apologize for it (as Edwards did in 2005) hurt her with dovish Iowa Democrats. Her support of ethanol subsidies, a reversal of her previous opposition to them, did not seem to help much. But in the fall, she stepped up her Iowa campaign. The chief event of the Democratic race was the Jefferson-Jackson Day Dinner on November 10. All of the candidates had fans in the crowd, but the highlight was Obama's electrifying speech. The Obama campaign shrewdly distributed tapes of the almost entirely white crowd cheering their candidate to African-American Democrats in South Carolina and other states.

Republican candidates attracted less attention. Mitt Romney outspent all other Republicans combined and had many more staff in the state. He started running television ads in the spring and leapt to a lead in the polls. But Mike Huckabee, former governor of Arkansas, built a network made up largely of evangelical Christians, and on the stump, the former Baptist minister displayed an appealing sense of humor and knowledge of popular culture. At the Ames straw poll in August 2007, Romney finished first and Huckabee an impressive second. But turnout was only 14,300, about 10,000 less than in 1999. Fred Thompson trailed. Rudy Giuliani and John McCain, with unpopular positions on abortion and immigration respectively, did not show up.

About 239,000 people participated in the Democratic caucuses, more than double the record set in 2004. Obama won 38% of "state delegates," a clear lead. He had big leads in the counties with universities: Johnson (Iowa City), Story (Ames), Polk (Des Moines), Linn (Cedar Rapids), and Scott (Davenport). He won especially large margins among independents and among liberals, among unmarried voters and among affluent voters. Edwards, carrying mainly small, rural counties, finished second with 30% "delegate strength," just ahead of Clinton, with 29%. She carried western Iowa, the most conservative part of the state, but did not roll up big numbers in industrial counties, as Gore had in 2000. The 15% threshold essentially eliminated the rest of the field from the race: Bill Richardson, Biden, and Dodd. Obama's victory in a state where less than 3% of the population is black was decisive. Through December 2007, he had been splitting the black vote with Clinton in South Carolina and in other states. After Iowa, his support from black voters skyrocketed. Had Clinton won, she might have clinched the nomination on or before Super Tuesday. Her victory in the New Hampshire primary five days later was the beginning of a long, close race. Edwards fell to the wayside after his poor third in South Carolina, adjacent to his native North Carolina. But in retrospect, it's hard to see how Obama could have become president without winning the Iowa caucuses.

The result on the Republican side was far less decisive. Caucus turnout was 119,000, a little higher than the Republican record set in 1980 but only about half the level of the Democratic caucuses. Some 60% of caucus attendees told entrance poll-takers that they were evangelical or born-again Christians; 46% of them voted for Huckabee, who won with 35% of the total vote. Romney, for all his campaigning and spending, finished second, with 25%. Trailing were Thompson (13%), McCain (13%), Ron Paul (10%) and Giuliani (4%). Romney carried the eastern and western ends of the state. Paul carried Jefferson County, the home of Maharishi University. "Tonight we proved that American politics is still in the hands of ordinary folks like you," Huckabee proclaimed on caucus night. But in the primaries to come, he was not able to expand his appeal substantially beyond evangelical and born-again Christians, who made up a larger percentage of Iowa caucus-goers than of primary voters in almost any other state. Romney, defeated here and in New Hampshire, lost crucial primaries by narrow margins to McCain, who effectively clinched the nomination by Super Tuesday. He was the first Republican presidential nominee to have finished below third in Iowa.

In 2000 and 2004, Iowa was one of the closest states in presidential elections. It was one of only three that switched between the two elections, giving Gore a narrow margin in 2000 and Bush in 2004. These were battles between rival organizations. The Democrats, building on Harkin's campaigns in 1996 and 2002 and on the organizations built up for the precinct caucuses, prevailed in 2000. The Republicans, building a volunteer organization for Bush, prevailed in 2004. In 2008, it proved not to be such a close contest. Most polls throughout the year showed Obama well ahead of McCain, and the balance of enthusiasm, as demonstrated in caucus turnout, was on Obama's side. He returned to the state on May 20, so that the glow of his caucus victories would overshadow what was expected to be a tough evening of primary returns. (He lost Kentucky by a wide margin, and his victory in Oregon was not reported until most Americans had gone to bed.) In October, McCain and running mate Sarah Palin stumped half a dozen times in Iowa, though perhaps only because other potential target states looked farther out of reach. Obama carried Iowa 54%-44%, winning four of the five congressional districts. He was especially strong in eastern Iowa. He won 61%-36% among young voters and 49%-48% among the elderly. White evangelical Protestants voted 65%-33% for McCain, but Catholics, traditionally Democratic in Iowa, voted 59%-41% for Obama.

Iowa's first-in-the-nation status has been under attack, but was preserved against challenges at the 2004 Republican National Convention and by the rules adopted by the Democratic National Committee in August 2006. Provoked by the complaint by Michigan Sen. Carl Levin and others that Iowa and New Hampshire lack racial diversity (Iowa is less than 3% black and less than 4% Hispanic), Democrats staged a second early caucus in Nevada and, after the New Hampshire primary, a second early primary in South Carolina. At their 2008 national conventions, both parties reaffirmed New Hampshire's first-in-the-nation-primary status but were silent on the Iowa caucuses. Iowa politicians of both parties will surely try to maintain it. As David Yepsen, the dean of Iowa political reporters, wrote in September 2008, "Defending the caucuses is a never-ending battle and a never-ending responsibility of political leaders in both parties in Iowa." Alas, Yepsen later announced later his retirement from the *Des Moines Register*. His accurate and acute reporting, fair analysis, and sprightly writing helped keep the caucus process honest, and with him goes one of the arguments for letting Iowa vote first.

Congressional districting

Iowa's congressional district lines are drawn by the nonpartisan Legislative Services Bureau and then approved by the governor and Legislature—a process that is praised by many critics of partisan gerrymandering and bipartisan incumbent protection plans. But it is not entirely apolitical. The bureau is not supposed to take past voting patterns or a legislator's place of residence into account, and in good Iowa fashion, they don't. But the governor and legislators can and do. In May 2001, the Iowa Senate rejected the bureau's first plan after Republicans said the population disparities were too large. Its second plan placed Republican Reps. Jim Nussle and Jim Leach in the same district and separated Des Moines from suburban Dallas and Warren counties. Indeed, with the exception of the 5th District in western Iowa, all the districts combine very disparate parts of Iowa. Nevertheless, Vilsack and the Republican Legislature approved the plan. Two incumbents moved their residences, Leach into the 2nd District, most of which he had been representing, and Democrat Leonard Boswell into Des Moines in the new 3rd District, whose incumbent, Republican Greg Ganske, was running for the Senate.

The Iowa plan has produced more strenuous competition than has been seen in most states. In 2002, four of the five districts were contested seriously by both parties, and the 5th district had a spirited Republican primary. In 2004, only one district was seriously contested, and four of the five incumbents improved their percentages. In 2006, three districts were seriously contested.

Low population growth means that Iowa is likely to lose a seat in the reapportionment following the 2010 census, and there is no telling who will be the victim—or victims—of the Legislative Services Bureau and the governor and Legislature. The 2008 census estimates show the average district in a four-district plan would have 750,000 people—close to the 2008 population (767,000) of a district made up of Des Moines's Polk County and the eight surrounding counties. Its partisan tilt would reflect the statewide average, 54%-44% in the 2008 presidential election. If the bureau created such a district, it would presumably also create a heavily Republican western district and two Democratic-leaning eastern districts. If Democratic Gov. Chet Culver is re-elected in 2010 and Democrats retain their current large majorities in the state House and Senate, they would probably approve such a plan, which would probably put Republican incumbents Tom Latham and Steve King in the same district.

Governor

Chet Culver (D)

Elected 2006, term expires Jan. 2011, 1st term; b. Jan. 25, 1966, Washington, D.C.; home, Des Moines; VA Tech, B.A. 1988; Drake U., M.A.T. 1994; Presbyterian; married (Mari Thinnes); 2 children.

Elected Office: IA sec. of state, 1998–2006.

Professional Career: Consumer & environmental advocate, IA atty. gen.'s office, 1991–95; Teacher, Roosevelt High, 1995, Hoover High, 1996–1998.

Office: 1007 East Grand Avenue, Des Moines, 50319, 515-281-5211; Fax: 515-281-0217; Web site: www.governor.iowa.gov.

Election Results

2006 general	Chet Culver (D)	569,021	(54%)
	Jim Nussle (R)	467,425	(44%)
2006 primary	Chet Culver (D)	58,131	(39%)
	Michael Blouin (D)	50,728	(34%)
	Ed Fallon (D)	38,253	(26%)

Chet Culver, a Democrat, was elected governor of Iowa in 2006. He is the son of John Culver, a former U.S. House member (1965–75) and senator (1975–81). His Democratic father lost his Senate seat to Republican Charles Grassley in 1980, and Grassley has held it ever since. Chet Culver was born in Washington, during his father's first term in the House, went to high school in Maryland and college in Virginia. His family boasts not just politicians but also athletes. His father was a star football player at Harvard University, good enough to be drafted by the National Football League, and his mother was a champion diver and speed skater. His three sisters were college athletes, and he won a scholarship to play football for Virginia Tech University before a knee injury ended his career.

After college, Culver moved to Iowa, where his family name could open political doors. He was a field staffer for the state Democratic party, then chaired by Bonnie Campbell, who had been his father's state director. Culver went on to work for Campbell's husband, a statehouse lobbyist, before serving as Campbell's field director during her successful 1990 campaign for state attorney general. He spent several years working in the attorney general's office. Campbell ran for governor in 1994 but lost to Republican Terry Branstad. Culver dropped out of politics for a period, taking a job coaching football and teaching government and history at a Des Moines high school.

In 1998, at age 32, he was elected Iowa's secretary of state, the youngest in the nation at the time. A politician who wins statewide office at so young an age is typically marked as a future prospect for governor, and Culver did nothing in his two terms to take himself off that track. His critics, however, saw a partisan edge to his work. As the state's elections administrator, he frustrated GOP legislators who wanted changes to Iowa's voting system, and Republicans also criticized him in 2004 for mailing to every household a voter guide that included an absentee-ballot request. Traditionally, absentee ballots had worked to the advantage of Iowa Democrats. Culver responded that he was merely seeking to increase voter participation. He further angered Republicans when he failed to declare President George W. Bush the winner in Iowa until days after the 2004 election—making Iowa the last state to declare, even though few thought that the remaining uncounted ballots could change the outcome in the state.

In 2006, Democratic Gov. Tom Vilsack fulfilled a promise made in 1998 to serve only two terms. The only Democrat elected governor in Iowa since 1966, Vilsack was making plans to run for president in 2008. Culver entered the gubernatorial primary with two main opponents: former Rep. Michael Blouin and state Rep. Ed Fallon, who refused to take political action committee money or contributions from paid lobbyists. Blouin, who was the state's economic development director, had assembled support from most of the state's Democratic legislators and from organized labor. Fallon ran as a progressive and an outsider. He had supported Ralph Nader over Al Gore for president in 2000. Culver announced his candidacy in November 2005, months after Fallon and Blouin, and he highlighted economic development, education, and energy issues. He proposed a $100 million Iowa Power Fund to create energy-oriented businesses and attract new investment in alternative fuels and technologies. "In the past, Iowa has fed the world," he said. "Now it's time for Iowa to fuel the world."

Culver was the best fundraiser, and his solid support for abortion rights gave him an edge among party activists. He won 39% of the primary vote to Blouin's 34%. Fallon finished third with 26%. Culver carried 80 of 99 counties, but lost Dubuque County, the University of Iowa's Johnson County, and Cedar Rapids's Linn County to Blouin. Fallon's strength didn't extend far beyond his Des Moines home. He won Des Moines's Polk County and Iowa State University's Story County just to the north.

Awaiting Culver was U.S. Rep. Jim Nussle, who was unopposed in the Republican primary. An eight-term House veteran and the Budget Committee chairman, Nussle had more experience and polish, which the GOP highlighted. Culver's campaign responded to the perception that the Democrat was rough around the edges with a smart ad in which his wife, Mari, fondly refers to him as "a big lug." Culver tied Nussle to the unpopular Bush administration and the national Republican Party, while reminding Iowans about the explosion in the size of the federal budget deficit under Nussle's watch. Both Culver and Nussle urged more education spending. They were at odds on immigration policy, taxes, and economic development issues. The abortion-rights debate was especially divisive. Culver called Nussle's opposition to abortion rights and embryonic-stem-cell research an "extreme position." Nussle appeared to backtrack on abortion in the fall, though he later reiterated that he favored banning abortion except to save the life of the mother.

It was an awful year to run as a Republican in Iowa, and Culver won 54%-44%. He carried Des Moines's Polk County (56%-42%), Davenport's Scott County (56%-41%), and both Cedar Rapids's Linn County and Waterloo's Black Hawk County (59%-40%). In the University of Iowa's Johnson County, he won 68%-29%. As of early November, Democrats had cast 89,000 absentee ballots to 50,000 for Republicans, and these ballots accounted for more than a third of Culver's 99,000-vote margin. Democrats also picked up Nussle's open 1st District seat, defeated Republican Rep. Jim Leach in the 2nd District, and won majorities in the state House and Senate for the first time since 1992. Going into the election, the Senate was tied 25-25. Culver took office with a 30-20 Democratic advantage. Republicans had previously had a 50-49 edge (with one vacancy) in the House, but Democrats ended up with a 54-46 majority.

The 2007 legislative session marked the first time in 42 years that Democrats controlled the governor's office and both chambers of the Iowa state Legislature. It was a productive session for the new governor, who was able to pass several major initiatives. The Legislature approved $150 million to increase salaries for teachers and a boost in the hourly minimum wage from $5.15 to $7.25 in 2008, the first increase in 10 years. It also approved Culver's $100 million Iowa Power Fund. All told, state spending rose by roughly 10%, partially offset by an increase in the state's cigarette tax.

Culver also signed into law a bill allowing same-day voter registration. In 2007 conservative U.S. Rep. Steve King and immigration hard-liners sued the governor for violating the state's official English law by printing voter information in several languages. At the close of his first legislative session, Culver said, "I do feel good about the promises I made to voters."

By early 2009, however, Culver, like other governors nationwide, was facing budgetary pressures as the recession sent state revenues plummeting. In April, he proposed a $6.2 billion budget that called for $300 million in spending cuts, and said that many state programs would have slashed by up to 8%. The state's finances were also constrained by recovery efforts from severe tornados and flooding in 2008.

The governor had to tap $40 million in economic development funds to help businesses and homeowners waiting for federal disaster aid that was slow in arriving.

Culver's first term had some other low moments. He stopped payments to a consulting firm that had been hired to help cut costs when an auditor found that the firm cost the state more money than it saved. Chicago-based consulting firm A.T. Kearney was paid $4.8 million for finding a savings of $2.9 million in the fiscal year. In 2007, Culver came under fire from a citizens' advocacy group for refusing to reappoint three commissioners to an air- and water-quality oversight board. The commissioners were backed by several environmental groups. Among the replacements Culver named were two farmers, prompting the citizens' group to charge that he had caved in to "corporate agriculture pressure." Culver also lost important political support from labor unions in 2008 when he vetoed a bill that would have given Iowa's public employees broad rights to negotiate working conditions, including work shifts, leaves of absence, and early retirement. Several major unions stopped giving to his political fund.

Senior Senator

Charles Grassley (R)

Elected 1980, term expires 2010, 5th term; b. Sept. 17, 1933, New Hartford; home, New Hartford; U. of N. IA, B.A. 1955, M.A. 1956, U. of IA, 1957–58; Baptist; married (Barbara); 5 children.

Elected Office: IA House of Reps., 1958–74; U.S. House of Reps., 1974–80.

Professional Career: Farmer.

DC Office: 135 HSOB, 20510, 202-224-3744; Fax: 202-224-6020; Web site: grassley.senate.gov.

State Offices: Cedar Rapids, 319-363-6832; Council Bluffs, 712-322-7103; Davenport, 563-322-4331; Des Moines, 515-288-1145; Sioux City, 712-233-1860; Waterloo, 319-232-6657.

Committees: *Agriculture, Nutrition & Forestry* (7th of 8 R). *Budget* (2nd of 10 R). *Finance* (RMM of 10 R): Taxation, IRS Oversight & Long-Term Growth. *Joint Committee on Taxation. Judiciary* (3rd of 7 R): Administrative Oversight & the Courts; Antitrust, Competition Policy & Consumer Rights; Crime & Drugs; Immigration, Refugees & Border Security.

Group Ratings

	ADA	ACLU	AFS	LCV	ITIC	NTU	COC	ACU	CFG	FRC
2008	25	21	22	27	100	56	100	76	69	100
2007	30	—	14	33	—	52	64	84	51	—

National Journal Ratings

	2007 LIB — 2007 CONS		2008 LIB — 2008 CONS	
Economic	42%	— 57%	34%	— 65%
Social	17%	— 80%	0%	— 79%
Foreign	7%	— 92%	0%	— 84%
Composite	23%	— 77%	18%	— 82%

Key Votes of the 110th Congress

1. Raise CAFE standards	Y	5. Make English official language Y
2. Expand SCHIP	Y	6. Path to citizenship	N
3. Cap greenhouse gases	N	7. Fetus is unborn child	Y
4. Bail out financial markets Y		8. Prosecute hate crimes	N

9. Withdraw troops 3/08   N
10. Iran guard is terrorist group Y
11. Increase missile defense $ Y
12. Overhaul FISA   Y

Election Results

2004 general	Charles Grassley (R)	1,038,175	(70%)	($6,403,445)
	Arthur Small (D)	412,365	(28%)	($135,503)
2004 primary	Charles Grassley (R)	unopposed		

Prior Winning Percentages: 1998 (68%); 1992 (70%); 1986 (66%); 1980 (54%); 1978 House (75%); 1976 House (57%); 1974 House (51%)

Charles Grassley, the senior senator from Iowa, was first elected to the House in 1974 and to the Senate in 1980. He grew up on a farm in Butler County near Waterloo. His parents switched to the Republican Party when Franklin Roosevelt ran for a third term in 1940. Grassley received his bachelor's degree from the University of Northern Iowa, and while in graduate school, he ran for the state House in 1956, losing by only 70-some votes. Two years later, he ran again and was elected, at age 25. While he was in the state

Legislature, he worked as a sheet metal shearer and on an assembly line. He won an open U.S. House seat in 1974, the hugely successful post-Watergate year for the Democrats, and six years later, he won his Senate seat by beating incumbent Democratic Sen. John Culver, the father of Gov. Chet Culver. Sen. Culver was an uncompromising liberal who came under fire from religious conservatives in 1980. Grassley was a conservative who had built up strong loyalty in his north central Iowa House district, which gave him nearly half his statewide lead over Culver. In his other career, as a part-time farmer, Grassley inherited an 80-acre farm in 1960 and has added to it over the years. It's now a 710-acre concern that produces corn and soybeans. Grassley's son manages the farm, but the senator likes to go back to help out in the fields on weekends, sometimes conducting congressional business on the cellphone that he keeps tucked under his cap. He stays in touch with his state in other ways, too. He has held meetings in each of the state's 99 counties every year that he has served in the Senate.

Though he's a steady conservative on social issues—he opposes abortion rights and most gun control initiatives—Grassley is also a populist in the American agrarian tradition. He has distinguished himself in Congress as a defender of government whistle-blowers and other underdogs, and he has made oversight of bloated, indifferent or corrupt government agencies a focal point of his Senate career. To the chagrin of his party, Grassley also takes on well-heeled political contributors when they raise his ire, as many a pharmaceutical executive can attest. Throughout the George W. Bush era, Grassley repeatedly went after Food and Drug Administration officials who he thought were too cozy with the industries they were supposed to regulate. In 2006, he tried unsuccessfully to hold up the confirmation of FDA Commissioner Andrew von Eschenbach after accusing the agency of withholding key information about the antibiotic Ketek during a congressional investigation into whether the FDA based its approval of the drug on fraudulent clinical safety data. Back in the mid-1980s, Grassley's first major legislative achievement was passage of the Federal False Claims Act, which authorized lawsuits for fraud on behalf of the government; he says it has since brought the taxpayers more than $17 billion.

Over the years, Grassley has conducted intensive oversight of the FBI, the Homeland Security Department, the Centers for Medicare and Medicaid Services, and the FDA. One of his recent targets was Smithsonian Institution Chairman Lawrence Small, who was audited by Grassley's committee and found to have charged the government over $1 million for a mansion that was rarely used in an official capacity and for first-class travel around the globe for himself and his wife. Grassley lambasted Small for his "champagne lifestyle," and the once-powerful museums chief resigned. In 2007 and early 2008, Grassley went after televangelists, though they too are typically pro-Republican. To determine whether six preachers who espouse a "prosperity gospel" were abiding by the rules of their tax-exempt status, he demanded that they hand over information about their expenses, compensation, and amenities. Grassley has long advocated that Congress follow the same laws it imposes on citizens, and he was the chief Senate sponsor of the sweeping Congressional Accountability Act of 1995.

As a farmer, Grassley supported both the Republicans' 1996 Freedom to Farm law that attempted to phase out government subsidies and the subsequent disaster payments to farmers when they suffered financially under the law. He opposed the 2002 farm bill, drafted by Iowa Democratic Sen. Tom Harkin, on the grounds that it allowed a higher limit on subsidies than the $275,000 that Grassley had persuaded the Senate to vote for. "A number of folks have been saying this is a good bill, and I'd say those folks are part right. It's a good bill if you're a cotton and rice producer. The problem is, we don't grow those commodities in my state of Iowa." He has consistently argued that high payments to individual farmers put the whole program in political jeopardy. A July 2007 Government Accountability Office report that Grassley requested revealed that the Agriculture Department had given more than $1 billion to deceased farmers from 1999 to 2005. Grassley pushed an amendment to the 2008 budget to cap payments to farmers at $250,000. He also attacked the 2007 farm bill for lacking a ban on meatpackers' owning livestock, which he has long supported.

Grassley has served two stints as chairman of the powerful Senate Finance Committee, in the first half of 2001 and from 2003 to 2007. With Democrats in control of the Senate, Grassley is now the ranking Republican on the committee. Over the years, he has had close relations and weekly meetings with his Democratic counterpart, Max Baucus of Montana, often to the dismay of conservative Republicans who think Grassley is too accommodating of Baucus. But the working relationship between the two was crucial to many of the GOP initiatives during the George W. Bush era. Grassley and Baucus rounded up bipartisan support for the massive tax cuts early in Bush's first term. And Grassley was one of the leaders in passage of the prescription drug benefit under Medicare in 2003. Throughout the process he was careful to look after the interests of rural health care providers and to seek changes in the Medicare reimbursement formula that gave Iowa less reimbursement per beneficiary than any other state. After the bill passed, he defended it against continuing Democratic attacks and also monitored its implementation. In 2007, Grassley helped stop Democratic efforts to pass a measure that Republicans had expressly kept out of the earlier bill: to allow the government to negotiate drug prices with pharmaceutical companies. The industry balked at the greatly enhanced powers the bill would give the government in setting prices, and Grassley threatened to filibuster any such bill that came to the floor. Also in 2007, Grassley worked with Baucus to secure Senate support to expand the federal Children's Health Insurance Program, though

House Republicans then sustained a presidential veto. After pleading with Bush to sign the bill, Grassley accused the White House of "throwing cold water in my face."

Grassley argued in 2006 that major changes in Social Security could not happen even if Republicans had retained their majorities. "If you're going to change our entitlement programs or have a simplified tax system, it has to be an issue of national debate, and that can only happen in a presidential election." Instead, he worked for incremental changes. With his populist bent, he has for years pursued "fairness" in the tax code. He sought a charitable deduction for non-itemizers and tighter rules for foundations, with tougher penalties. He led the committee to tighten the rules on partial gifts of art, which allowed donors to retain possession while receiving tax deductions. "Call it what it is, a subsidy for millionaires to buy art. Where I come from, the word 'giving' doesn't mean 'keeping.'" He sent a letter to the Museum of Modern Art in New York City demanding to know the number of partial gifts and staff salaries. A headline in the *The New York Times* in 2006 called him "The Man Museums Love to Hate."

In 2007, Grassley joined Baucus in backing a bill to repeal the alternative minimum tax, which has been ensnaring an increasing number of middle-income taxpayers in addition to the wealthy itemizers it was designed to catch. But Grassley also said it would be unfair to raise other taxes to repeal the AMT. That year, he also questioned the tax exemption for college and university athletic activities, suggesting that donations to coaches' salaries amounted to a taxpayer subsidy. He scored a notable success in 2007 when several major universities with huge endowments agreed to spend a larger amount each year on student financial aid. "For the first time in years, we're hearing good news about tuition and affordability," he said.

Corn-based ethanol is an important product of Iowa's agribusiness, and Grassley has used his influence on the committee to win advantageous tax treatment of ethanol. He has also sought tax incentives for biodiesel, made with soybean oil or recycled cooking oil. The United States is a major exporter of agricultural products, and Grassley has been a supporter of free trade, with one major exception. He backed the North American Free Trade Agreement in 1993 and strongly supported normal trade relations with China and the Central American Free Trade Agreement in the 1990s. But he proposed an amendment to the Caribbean Basin Initiative to limit imports of duty-free ethanol. His goal was to avoid giving entry to Brazil's sugar-based ethanol, which would compete with Iowa's ethanol.

Grassley also serves on the Judiciary Committee, where for years he was the chief sponsor of the bankruptcy law overhaul bill that finally passed and was signed into law in 2005. He took special care to see that Chapter 12, which applies to farmers, would allow them to reorganize their debt without creditors' consent.

For more than two decades, Grassley has been the most popular politician in Iowa. "I commune with Iowans on a regular basis, and I think they know that. They appreciate it, and they don't feel like Washington has gone to my head. I suppose if I don't get smug and overconfident, I'll be re-elected," he said in 2004, shortly before he was returned to the Senate by a vote of 70%-28%. He regularly hosts dozens of foreign ambassadors at the Iowa State Fair to introduce them to agribusiness. In 1986, he became the first Iowa senator to win re-election in 20 years, with a record 66% of the vote. In 1992, he won 70%-27%, carrying all 99 counties. In 1998, against a Democrat who campaigned by taking trips down Iowa's rivers, he won 68%-30%, again carrying every single county. Grassley plans to run for re-election in 2010 and has now served Iowa in the Senate longer than anyone but William B. Allison, whose record he will beat if he stays until June 2016, three months before he turns 83. "With my seniority," Grassley says, "I am worth more to my employer, the people of Iowa, than I was before."

Junior Senator

Tom Harkin (D)

Elected 1984, term expires 2014, 5th term; b. Nov. 19, 1939, Cumming; home, Cumming; IA St. U., B.S. 1962, Catholic U., J.D. 1972; Catholic; married (Ruth); 2 children.

Military Career: Navy, 1962–67; Naval Reserves, 1969–72.

Elected Office: U.S. House of Reps., 1974–84.

Professional Career: Practicing atty., 1972–74; Staff aide, House Select Cmte. on U.S. Involvement in SE Asia, 1973–74.

DC Office: 731 HSOB, 20510, 202-224-3254; Fax: 202-224-9369; Web site: harkin.senate.gov.

State Offices: Cedar Rapids, 319-365-4504; Davenport, 563-322-1338; Des Moines, 515-284-4574; Dubuque, 563-582-2130; Sioux City, 712-252-1550.

Committees: *Agriculture, Nutrition & Forestry* (Chmn of 12 D). *Appropriations* (4th of 18 D): Agriculture, Rural Development, Food and Drug Administration & Related Agencies; Defense; Energy & Water Development; Labor, Health and Human Services, Education & Related Agencies (Chmn); State, Foreign Operations & Related Programs; Transportation, Housing and Urban Development & Related Agencies. *Health, Education, Labor & Pensions* (3rd of 14 D). *Small Business & Entrepreneurship* (4th of 11 D).

Group Ratings

	ADA	ACLU	AFS	LCV	ITIC	NTU	COC	ACU	CFG	FRC
2008	95	92	100	91	80	4	50	4	3	0
2007	95	—	100	87	—	5	36	8	0	—

National Journal Ratings

	2007 LIB — 2007 CONS		2008 LIB — 2008 CONS	
Economic	79%	13%	64%	35%
Social	76%	23%	80%	9%
Foreign	94%	2%	65%	6%
Composite	85%	15%	77%	24%

Key Votes of the 110th Congress

1. Raise CAFE standards	Y	5. Make English official language	N
2. Expand SCHIP	Y	6. Path to citizenship	N
3. Cap greenhouse gases	Y	7. Fetus is unborn child	N
4. Bail out financial markets	Y	8. Prosecute hate crimes	Y

9. Withdraw troops 3/08	Y
10. Iran guard is terrorist group	N
11. Increase missile defense $	N
12. Overhaul FISA	N

Election Results

2008 general	Tom Harkin (D)	941,665	(63%)	($5,022,490)
	Christopher Reed (R)	560,006	(37%)	($58,793)
2008 primary	Tom Harkin (D)	90,785	(99%)	

Prior Winning Percentages: 2002 (54%); 1996 (52%); 1990 (54%); 1984 (55%); 1982 House (59%); 1980 House (60%); 1978 House (59%); 1976 House (65%); 1974 House (51%)

Tom Harkin, a Democrat first elected to the House in 1974 and the Senate in 1984, is an accomplished veteran of Capitol Hill who brings the attitude of the aggrieved outsider to his work. Harkin grew up poor in a rural town where his father was a coal miner and his mother, a Slovenian immigrant, died when he was just 10. He worked his way through college and law school before spending five years in the Navy during the 1960s ferrying planes out of Vietnam for repair. In 1970, as an aide to Democratic Rep. Neal Smith of Iowa, Harkin returned to Vietnam and discovered the infamous "tiger cages." America's allies, the South Vietnamese, used these underground cells to hold and torture prisoners of war. (A young Harkin slipped past prison guards on a guided tour to confirm the existence of the secret cells.) Two years later, Harkin ran for a House seat and lost narrowly; he tried again in 1974 and won. In that campaign, he invented "work days," a technique widely imitated since: he spent a day working at each of a dozen local jobs to better understand people's experiences. He held the seat with solid percentages in four re-election contests. In 1984, he challenged Republican Sen. Roger Jepsen in the midst of a farm depression in Iowa. Harkin's support of subsidies for farmers contrasted Jepsen's advocacy of free-market solutions to economic woes. Jepsen was also vulnerable going into his first re-election. He voted in favor of selling Airborne Warning and Control System aircraft to Saudi Arabia after professing loyalty to Israel, which staunchly opposed the sale. He also came across as arrogant for claiming special privileges as a senator after being stopped for driving alone in high-occupancy vehicle lanes on the highway. Harkin won with 55% of the vote.

Harkin was chairman of the Agriculture Committee from June 2001 to January 2003, an advantageous assignment for a senator from a farm state. He regained the post in January 2007 when Democrats took control of the Senate. In both stints, Harkin controlled the gavel during reauthorization of the all-important farm bill. He steered to passage the 2002 farm measure, a considerable achievement because he fashioned a bill to restore subsidies phased out by the Republicans' 1996 Freedom to Farm Act. His top goals were to increase conservation programs, establish a formula for countercyclical aid, and fight concentration in agribusiness. In November 2001, Harkin introduced his bill, with no limit on farm subsidies. He also included a provision for more spending on conservation and food stamps aimed at securing votes from nonfarm states. The bill was defeated that December, but revived and passed in February 2002 with increased but limited subsidies for grain and cotton, and double the money for conservation. The total cost was an estimated $73.5 billion over 10 years. The bill went to a conference committee with the House. During those negotiations, Republicans led by Rep. Larry Combest, from cotton-farming West Texas, insisted on higher subsidy limits and the deletion of a ban on meatpackers owning livestock. Harkin brought the bill back and got the Senate to pass it.

While the Republicans controlled Congress, Harkin worked to make conservation payments an entitlement and promoted the use of ethanol and alcohol fuels. In 2004, Harkin held up a corporate tax bill to protest an appropriation for $2.8 billion in drought aid by deferring conservation spending and scaling back federal oversight of tobacco; he won a non-binding resolution to restore the conservation money. Farm exports are important to Iowa and Harkin, despite his warm feelings for labor unions, voted for the North American Free Trade Agreement in 1993 and for normalizing trade relations with China in 2000. Unions generally oppose free trade agreements as a threat to domestic jobs.

Democratic victories at the polls in 2006 made Harkin chairman again as the farm bill came up for reauthorization in 2007. His priorities were nutrition programs, increased conservation funds for environmentally friendly farming, and promotion of corn-based ethanol as fuel. In an unusual twist, key negotiations shifted to farm-state members of the Senate Finance Committee, led by Democrats Max Baucus of Montana and Kent Conrad of North Dakota and Republican Sen. Charles Grassley of Iowa. Harkin's critics said he was too protective of his pet programs. But eventually most of his programs were included in the bill: ethanol, more money for nutrition, modest caps on subsidies, and a renamed Conservation Stewardship Program. Two-thirds of the funds in the five-year, $300-billion bill were for food stamps and other nutrition programs. Harkin said his work on the complex legislation was "like giving birth to a porcupine."

Harkin also has had a substantial impact on health policy. Two of his sisters died from breast cancer and one brother died from thyroid cancer; another brother became deaf at age 9. Harkin was a key player in shaping the Americans with Disabilities Act of 1990, a major achievement and one that required a bipartisan coalition to overcome resistance to the cost and qualms about the real-world effect of the regulations. Later, in 2008, Harkin led the enactment of amendments to the law that mitigated the weakening effect of Supreme Court decisions. As chairman or senior Democrat on the appropriations subcommittee that funds health programs, Harkin worked with his Republican counterpart, Arlen Specter of Pennsylvania, to double the budget for the National Institutes of Health over five years. Harkin was also a chief Senate advocate of expanding federal funding for embryonic-stem-cell research, which uses excess embryos from the in vitro fertilization process. His bill passed 63-37 in July 2006 and 63-34 in April 2007, though not by sufficient margins to override vetoes by President Bush.

Throughout this decade, Harkin has been the Senate's leading advocate of better nutrition and fitness for children. "We need a new paradigm in American health care, a prevention paradigm," he said. Legislation he sponsored in 2004 required schools to set nutritional standards for food available during the school day and made Harkin Fresh Fruit and Vegetable grants to schools permanent. In 2005, he called for food companies to do less marketing to children and sponsored a bill to give the Federal Trade Commission authority to regulate advertising directed at children. He is a crusader against childhood obesity, pushing for nutritional standards for food sold in schools. A bill he sponsored in 2006 would have removed candy bars, french fries, ice cream bars, and non-diet soft drinks from schools. With GOP Sen. Lisa Murkowski of Alaska he sponsored a 2007 bill extending school nutrition standards to vending machines and giving the Agriculture Department authority to regulate schools' snack foods. Opposition came not only from food companies but from school districts eager to earn food revenues. Harkin also favors mandatory nutrition labels on menus in chain restaurants.

On foreign policy, Harkin's views have been shaped by the Vietnam War. He was a vocal opponent of aid to the Nicaraguan Contras in the 1980s and the Persian Gulf War resolution in 1991. But he favored the threat of force in Haiti in 1994, and voted to authorize the use of force in Iraq in 1998, when President Clinton sought it. Similarly, when President Bush requested congressional approval in October 2002, Harkin voted again for the use of force. But as the violence continued in Iraq, Harkin said in December 2003, it "may not be Vietnam, but, boy, it sure smells like it." In May 2004, he said abuses of prisoners at Abu Ghraib in Iraq reminded him of the tiger cages in Vietnam. He concluded, "It's time to fire the secretary of Defense." When Vice President Cheney in 2004 criticized presidential candidate John Kerry's Vietnam service, Harkin said, "When I hear this coming from Dick Cheney, who was a coward, who would not serve during the Vietnam War, it makes my blood boil. He'll be tough, but he'll be tough with someone else's kid's blood." In 2008, Harkin was one of only two senators who opposed the nomination of Gen. David Petraeus to take over the U.S. Central Command.

As an appropriator, Harkin is generous to Iowa and defends earmarks, the practice among lawmakers of designating specific projects for their districts and states. As he said in November 2006, "I happen to be a supporter of earmarks, unabashedly. But I don't call them earmarks. It is 'congressional directed spending.'" He cited the millions he directed toward breast cancer research. "Now, was that bad? If you left it to the Defense Department, they never would have done it." In 2007, Harkin's subcommittee on spending for the Labor, Health and Human Services, and Education departments approved a bill packed with more than 1,000 earmarks.

Harkin has been a major force in Iowa politics. His fervent stands on issues and his hard-edged campaigning give him a large base of loyal supporters as well as a large base of strong detractors. He has never won by a large margin, but in his career he has beaten no fewer than five members of Congress while rarely topping 55% of the vote. He ran for president in 1992. In angry phrases, with a Trumanesque zest, Harkin preached that incumbent George H.W. Bush and the Republicans helped only the rich and that government must get involved to help the poor and middle class. Organized labor withheld an early endorsement despite his 90%-plus AFL-CIO voting record—a great tactical victory for rival Bill Clinton, the Arkansas governor. Harkin's sweep of the Iowa caucuses on February 10 was mostly discounted by the media as a home-field advantage. He then finished with only 10% of the vote in the New Hampshire primary, and got just 7% in South Carolina on March 7 after campaigning there with civil-rights activist Jesse Jackson. Harkin quit the race. Four years later, he won re-election to the U.S. Senate.

In 2002, Harkin faced a serious challenge from Rep. Greg Ganske, a Des Moines plastic surgeon and Republican who had upset 36-year incumbent Neal Smith in 1994. Ganske argued that his work in the House regulating health maintenance organizations showed that he could find bipartisan solutions to problems. Harkin attacked Ganske for supporting Republican proposals to partially privatize the Social Security fund and touted passage of the farm bill. Polls showed the race fairly close in the summer. Harkin had far more money and, for the first time, the endorsement of the Iowa Farm Bureau Federation.

But he had to defend against an embarrassing incident involving his campaign staff. A former Harkin staffer changed his registration to Republican and contributed $50 to Ganske, then attended a Ganske fundraising meeting with a tape recorder in his pocket. After the meeting, he turned it over to a 21-year-old Harkin campaign staffer and a transcript was leaked to the media. Harkin's campaign manager at first denied involvement by the campaign, but he later resigned, and Harkin apologized. Many observers speculated that in squeaky-clean Iowa, the caper would cost Harkin votes. Perhaps it did, but not very many. Harkin won 54%-44%.

For the first time, he breezed to re-election in 2008. Despite early speculation, Iowa's two remaining Republican House members, Tom Latham and Steve King, declined to challenge Harkin. Instead, he ran against political neophyte Christopher Reed, a small-business owner who raised little money and had scant name recognition. In an October debate, Reed accused Harkin of "providing aid and comfort to the enemy" in Iraq, which Harkin called "beyond the pale." Following the television taping, Harkin told Reed, "You're a nice young man, and I thought you had a political future ahead of you. But that just ended your political career right there." Harkin won 63%-37%.

FIRST DISTRICT

Bruce Braley (D)

Elected 2006, 2nd term; b. Oct. 30, 1957, Grinnell; home, Waterloo; IA St. U., B.A. 1980, U. of IA, J.D. 1983; Presbyterian; married (Carolyn); 3 children.

Professional Career: Practicing atty., 1983–2006.

DC Office: 1019 LHOB, 20515, 202-225-2911; Fax: 202-225-6666; Web site: braley.house.gov.

State Offices: Davenport, 563-323-5988; Dubuque, 563-557-7789; Waterloo, 319-287-3233.

Committees: *Energy & Commerce* (35th of 36 D): Commerce, Trade & Consumer Protections; Health; Oversight & Investigations.

Group Ratings

	ADA	ACLU	AFS	LCV	ITIC	NTU	COC	ACU	CFG	FRC
2008	90	100	100	92	100	12	56	4	0	0
2007	90	—	91	85	—	5	63	0	0	—

National Journal Ratings

	2007 LIB — 2007 CONS		2008 LIB — 2008 CONS	
Economic	78%	— 18%	59%	— 41%
Social	63%	— 37%	82%	— 0%
Foreign	69%	— 31%	92%	— 0%
Composite	71%	— 29%	82%	— 18%

Key Votes of the 110th Congress

1. Increase minimum wage	Y	5. Share immigration data	Y	9. Withdraw troops 8/08	Y
2. Expand SCHIP	Y	6. Foreign aid abortion ban	N	10. No operations in Iran	Y
3. Raise CAFE standards	Y	7. Ban gay bias in workplace	*	11. Free trade with Peru	*
4. Bail out financial markets	Y	8. Repeal D.C. gun law	N	12. Overhaul FISA	N

Election Results

2008 general	Bruce Braley (D)	186,991	(65%)	($979,333)
	David Hartsuch (R)	102,439	(35%)	($54,604)
2008 primary	Bruce Braley (D)	10,596	(99%)	

Prior Winning Percentages: 2006 (55%)

Population		Race/Ethnicity		Work	
Pop. 2007:	585,134	White:	91.0%	Private:	80.7%
Change since 2000:	Unchanged	Black:	4.0%	Government:	12.2%
Urban:	66.3%	Hispanic:	2.5%	Self-employed:	6.8%
Rural:	33.7%	Asian:	1.1%	Blue collar:	28.0%
Area size:	7,291 sq. mi.	Native Am.:	0.2%	White collar:	54.8%
Age		Hawaiian:	0.1%	Khaki collar:	0.1%
Median age:	38.4 yrs.	Two+ races:	1.2%	Other:	17.0%
More than 65 yrs:	14.7%	*Ancestry*		Median income:	$44,672
Less than 18 yrs:	23.9%	German:	36.1%	Median home value:	$113,200
Education		Irish:	13.3%	Poverty:	11.8%
H.S. grad:	88.6%	English:	6.4%	**Military Veterans**	
College grad:	23.2%			% of Pop:	11.8%
Grad degree:	7.5%				

Northeast Iowa, along the Mississippi River and westward, has some of the loveliest landscape in America. Here the Mississippi flows past green bluffs, then broadens out in great quiet pools alongside picturesque towns. A century and a half ago, as settlers surged west of the Mississippi, Germans stopped at the river bluffs reminiscent of their native land and built neat farmhouses and substantial towns. Inland, on the rolling hills portrayed with surprisingly little exaggeration in the paintings of

2008 Presidential Vote		
Obama (D)	175,394	(58%)
McCain (R)	122,629	(41%)
2004 Presidential Vote		
Kerry (D)	157,380	(53%)
Bush (R)	138,073	(46%)
Cook Partisan Voting Index: D+5		

Iowa's Grant Wood, and in the more open territory to the west, New England Yankees and Midwesterners built their characteristic farmhouses, barns, town halls, church spires, and small colleges. Railroad companies, headquartered in Chicago, extended their networks of steel rails over the plains and rivers. Davenport, on the hills over the Mississippi, still has the look of the city where Ronald Reagan got his first radio job. German Catholics settled Dubuque, whose giant Victorian courthouse looks down on the river. Home to a giant John Deere facility that sells tractors worldwide, it is a self-styled green city that has other large factories but is also proud of its waterfront-generated tourism. However, major floods along the Mississippi in June 2008 extensively damaged many river towns. Farther west is Waterloo, which grew rapidly after 1900 when a John Deere tractor factory expanded and the eight-floor Rath factory became the largest meat-packing plant in the world. Rath closed in 1984 and Deere has laid off thousands, but Waterloo has rebounded somewhat with new industries from telemarketing to a high-tech Iowa Beef Processors factory, acquired by Tyson Foods in 2001.

The 1st Congressional District covers much of northeast Iowa, including the Mississippi riverfront, from the antiques town of McGregor south to Davenport, Iowa's part of the Quad Cities. From the river, it spans west 100 miles to Butler County. There is considerable political variation here. Davenport and next-door Bettendorf were historically Republican, but in 2000 and 2004, like much of eastern Iowa, they voted narrowly for Al Gore and John Kerry. In 2008, as Iowa began to look favorably on Barack Obama, these areas helped to lead the way. Dubuque, heavily German Catholic, was for years Iowa's most Democratic city, and still is unless abortion is the issue. But the rural counties along the river and farther west—more German Protestant, Scandinavian, and Yankee—were traditionally Republican. Waterloo and Cedar Falls, originally Republican, trended sharply Democratic in the 1980s. Overall, this district is pretty evenly balanced and has become a key battleground in presidential contests. At one point in 2004, President Bush and John Kerry were campaigning within blocks of each other in Davenport; thieves took advantage of the distraction and robbed three local banks. Bush lost the district by 7 percentage points each time, and Obama won it by 17 percentage points in 2008.

The congressman from the 1st District is Bruce Braley, a Democrat from Waterloo elected in 2006 to replace Republican Jim Nussle, who ran unsuccessfully for governor. Braley is a native of Brooklyn, Iowa. His mother was a teacher and his father was a farmer who died of injuries sustained in a fall down a grain elevator. The family struggled financially for years as a result. Braley graduated from Iowa State University and got his law degree from the University of Iowa. He was a trial lawyer and is a former president of the Iowa Trial Lawyers Association. His candidacy for Congress drew considerable financial support from the Association of Trial Lawyers of America and many of its members and officers, connections that made him the target of lawyer-bashing. National Republicans disparaged him as "a trial lawyer's trial lawyer." In the June primary, Braley overcame two competitive opponents: former state Rep. Rick Dickinson, an economic development official in Dubuque, and Bill Gluba, a real estate agent in Davenport. Although Braley was making his first run for office, he had a distinct fundraising advantage and the support of the Iowa AFL-CIO. He won 36% to 34% for Dickinson and 26% for Gluba. Meanwhile,

Republicans nominated Mike Whalen, a Harvard Law School graduate, wealthy entrepreneur, and owner of the Machine Shed restaurant chain.

From the start, Republicans knew it would be a tough contest. In his eight terms, outgoing Rep. Nussle never got more than 57% of the vote despite his prominence as the chairman of the House Budget Committee from 2001 to 2006. The candidates disagreed on many issues, including the Iraq war, tort reform, international trade deals, and abortion rights. Braley portrayed Whalen as an out-of-touch millionaire. He claimed that Whalen wanted to privatize Social Security, and he attacked Whalen's opposition to raising the hourly minimum wage. When Whalen insisted that all his employees were paid more than the federal minimum wage, Braley produced a Machine Shed waitress who claimed that, even with tips, she and her co-workers earned only the minimum wage. Whalen charged that Braley's litigious occupation contributed to higher health care costs and the medical liability crisis. Although the National Republican Congressional Committee spent heavily on direct mail and television ads against Braley, it wasn't enough to keep the seat in Republican hands. Braley won surprisingly easily, 55%-43%. He took each of the 12 counties, except for two rural counties. As expected, he ran strongly in Waterloo's Black Hawk County, with 59%; but he also took Whalen's Quad Cities base in Scott County, with 53%.

Braley initially got seats on the Transportation and Infrastructure Committee (to tend to local projects) and on the Oversight and Government Reform Committee (to utilize his trial-lawyer skills), and was among the more active members of his freshman class. He won House passage of a bill to require federal agencies to write in plain English, a longtime interest from his days practicing law. He took up the cause of veterans who had been neglected in government hospitals. The 2008 farm bill included his provision to fund advanced technology education centers to train technicians in renewable-energy resources. Braley's ambition led to talk of his joining the influential Energy and Commerce Committee, which he did in December 2008. That year, he also was re-elected easily. Some local Democrats have mentioned Braley as a possible contender if one of Iowa's two veteran senators retires.

SECOND DISTRICT

Dave Loebsack (D)

Elected 2006, 2nd term; b. Dec. 23, 1952, Sioux City; home, Mt. Vernon; IA St. U., B.S. 1974, M.A. 1976, U. of CA, Ph.D., 1985; Methodist; married (Teresa); 4 children.

Professional Career: Professor, Cornell Col., 1982–2006.

DC Office: 1221 LHOB, 20515, 202-225-6576; Fax: 202-226-0757; Web site: loebsack.house.gov.

State Offices: Cedar Rapids, 319-364-2288; Iowa City, 319-351-0789.

Committees: *Armed Services* (24th of 37 D): Military Personnel; Readiness. *Education & Labor* (17th of 30 D): Early Childhood, Elementary & Secondary Education; Health, Employment, Labor & Pensions.

Group Ratings

	ADA	ACLU	AFS	LCV	ITIC	NTU	COC	ACU	CFG	FRC
2008	90	100	100	92	57	6	56	0	0	0
2007	95	—	100	90	—	4	58	0	6	—

National Journal Ratings

	2007 LIB	—	2007 CONS	2008 LIB	—	2008 CONS
Economic	67%	—	31%	59%	—	41%
Social	89%	—	8%	82%	—	0%
Foreign	86%	—	11%	92%	—	0%
Composite	82%	—	18%	82%	—	18%

Key Votes of the 110th Congress

1. Increase minimum wage	Y	5. Share immigration data	N	9. Withdraw troops 8/08	Y
2. Expand SCHIP	Y	6. Foreign aid abortion ban	N	10. No operations in Iran	Y
3. Raise CAFE standards	Y	7. Ban gay bias in workplace	Y	11. Free trade with Peru	N
4. Bail out financial markets	Y	8. Repeal D.C. gun law	N	12. Overhaul FISA	N

Election Results

2008 general	Dave Loebsack (D)	175,218	(57%)	($805,024)
	Mariannette Miller-Meeks (R)	118,778	(39%)	($367,694)
	Wendy Barth (Green)	6,664	(2%)	
2008 primary	Dave Loebsack (D)	21,084	(99%)	

Prior Winning Percentages: 2006 (51%)

Population		Race/Ethnicity		Work	
Pop. 2007:	603,468	White:	90.3%	Private:	76.3%
Change since 2000:	Up 3.1%	Black:	2.6%	Government:	16.7%
Urban:	66.0%	Hispanic:	3.6%	Self-employed:	6.6%
Rural:	34.0%	Asian:	2.0%	Blue collar:	24.1%
Area size:	7,684 sq. mi.	Native Am.:	0.2%	White collar:	59.3%
Age		Hawaiian:	0.0%	Khaki collar:	0.1%
Median age:	36.6 yrs.	Two+ races:	1.2%	Other:	16.5%
More than 65 yrs:	13.1%	*Ancestry*		Median income:	$46,111
Less than 18 yrs:	23.5%	German:	28.7%	Median home value:	$117,200
Education		Irish:	12.3%	Poverty:	13.0%
H.S. grad:	89.8%	English:	8.6%	**Military Veterans**	
College grad:	27.9%			% of Pop:	10.4%
Grad degree:	9.8%				

Eastern Iowa is little known to outsiders. It is a land of rolling hills and deep river valleys, of undulant farm fields and big skies, of prosperous small towns and grain elevators and factories. Even political writers, who come to Iowa by the thousands for the quadrennial precinct caucuses, tend to hang out in Des Moines and do their reporting there or in the counties within an hour's drive of the city. The drive from Des Moines east to the second-largest city, Cedar Rapids, takes more than two hours. The biggest metropolis in these parts, Cedar Rapids has high-tech employers and contemporary office buildings. Unlike in most of Iowa, population boomed here in the past decade, and per capita income rose. Yet traditional industries are still a mainstay: go down by the river and you can't miss the smell of cooking oats coming from the Quaker Oats and General Mills factories. The town suffered a major setback in June 2008, when record floods caused $1.8 billion in damage, with the downtown area described as a war zone. Iowa City, just to the south, is a university town dotted with trendy bookstores and vegetarian eateries. The University of Iowa is known for its Writers' Workshop, which produced the nation's first creative writing degree program and some of its most gifted young authors. Iowa City elected a black mayor in 2006, though the African-American population is less than 4% of the total.

2008 Presidential Vote

Obama (D) 190,973   (60%)
McCain (R)............................122,395   (38%)

2004 Presidential Vote

Kerry (D)................................171,561   (55%)
Bush (R) 135,991   (44%)

Cook Partisan Voting Index: D + 7

Farther afield, Iowa's 2nd Congressional District offers up some offbeat claims to fame. Bentonsport, in Van Buren County near the Missouri border, was mostly bought up by the county's conservation board in the 1970s and restored; now it is an artists' and craftsmen's colony. Conesville, in Muscatine County near the Mississippi River, is the only city in Iowa with a Hispanic majority, a legacy of an abundance of farmwork in the area and, more recently, of the availability of jobs at the Iowa Beef Processors plant in nearby Columbus Junction. Anamosa, in Jones County just east of Cedar Rapids, is the site of the house depicted by Anamosa native Grant Wood in his famous *American Gothic* painting—the models for the two figures were his dentist and Wood's own sister, who died in 1990. Iowa's newest city, incorporated in 2001, is Vedic City, in Jefferson County, where followers of the Maharishi Mahesh Yogi built Maharishi University in 1973 and made the town a magnet for believers in transcendental meditation.

The 2nd is by most measures Iowa's most Democratic congressional district, thanks in large part to big Democratic majorities in Iowa City and Johnson County. Cedar Rapids and Linn County have also been inclined toward the Democrats in recent years.

The congressman from the 2nd District is Dave Loebsack (*LOBE-sak*), a Democrat elected in a stunning 2006 upset. He defeated 15-term Rep. Jim Leach, a Republican who often was out of step with his party but who held views that seemed well connected to this district. A native of Sioux City, Loebsack lived as a child in poverty with his mother, grandmother, and three siblings in a two-bedroom house, and worked as a high school janitor to pay for college. He got a master's degree at Iowa State University and went on to the University of California at Davis to earn a Ph.D. in political science. From 1982 until his election to Congress, he was a professor of international relations at Cornell College in Mount Vernon, a few miles from Cedar Rapids. He had been active in local politics for several years, including a stint as fundraising chairman for Linn County Democrats.

But his initial foray into electoral politics did not inspire confidence: He failed to get the appropriate number of signatures required to run for Leach's seat. Under Iowa law, if no candidate files for a party's nomination, the party can designate a candidate; so Democrats chose Loebsack. He insisted that his campaign was not an attack on Leach's three decades in Congress but rather on the GOP leadership in Congress; he called Leach, a moderate Republican, an "enabler" for his party leaders. The two had enjoyed a friendly relationship before the contest. A prominent member of the House Foreign Affairs Committee, Leach had lectured to Loebsack's classes on several occasions.

The war in Iraq was a pivotal issue from the start of this contest. In 2002, Leach was the only member of the Iowa delegation to oppose the war. Yet Loebsack sought to tie Leach to President Bush's defense secretary, Donald Rumsfeld, on the basis that Leach had been an aide to Rumsfeld for two years in the late 1960s, when Rumsfeld was a House member from Illinois, and he later served a stint under him at the Office of Economic Opportunity. Leach refused to disparage his former boss, calling him a friend and insisting that his ouster would not change the administration's policy in Iraq. The campaign remained civil, with Leach emphasizing the need to promote ethanol and Loebsack calling for national health insurance. But Leach may have underestimated the public's hostility toward the war in the district's population centers, especially in the university communities that welcomed Loebsack's anti-Iraq war message. Loebsack raised $522,000, which ordinarily would have not been nearly enough to win a competitive House race, and he had little support from the Democratic Congressional Campaign Committee. But Leach unwittingly helped Loebsack overcome those obstacles. Leach eschewed modern campaign practices, particularly negative campaigning, and was a notoriously reluctant fundraiser. When the Iowa Republican Party sent out negative mailers targeting Loebsack, Leach told them to stop and warned he would refuse to caucus with House Republicans if the negative tactics continued. He refused to accept contributions from political action committees or from sources outside the district, and raised only $491,000. Leach did earn the endorsement of the district's major newspapers, but it wasn't enough. Loebsack beat him, 51%-49%.

Of the district's 15 counties, Leach carried 10. Loebsack won by 367 votes in Linn County (Cedar Rapids), the largest county in the district. The election hinged on the second-largest county, Johnson (Iowa City), where Loebsack got 58%, a margin of 8,525 votes. He won in three other counties—Des Moines (Burlington), Lee (Fort Madison), and Wapello (Ottumwa)—by a total of nearly 5,000 votes. In a concession speech to teary supporters, Leach maintained his dignified approach to campaigning: "For three decades, I've had . . . the goal from the beginning of running positive campaigns. I want to express my deep respect for the Loebsack campaign." After the election, Leach joined the faculties at Princeton and Harvard universities. Loebsack went to Washington and got seats on the Armed Services and Education and Labor committees. One of his first official actions was to sponsor a measure to designate the federal building in Davenport, Iowa, as the James A. Leach Federal Building; it passed the House in May 2007. He spoke out against the war in Iraq and voiced frustration with the Democrats' failure to change Bush administration policy. However, after noting progress being made by U.S. forces during a 2007 visit to Anbar province, Loebsack abandoned his goal of removing all U.S. troops within one year. "The military has done a fantastic job, as always," he said.

Mostly, Loebsack tended the home fires in his first term, focusing on securing $28 million in earmarks, the often-criticized special provisions in appropriations bills added by individual lawmakers. In 2008, Loebsack won a comfortable re-election, 57%-39%, against political neophyte Mariannette Miller-Meeks, a Republican ophthalmologist and the first woman to be president of the Iowa Medical Society.

THIRD DISTRICT

Leonard Boswell (D)

Elected 1996, 7th term; b. Jan. 10, 1934, Harrison Cnty., MO; home, Davis City; Graceland Col., B.A. 1969; Community of Christ; married (Dody); 3 children.

Military Career: Army, 1956–76 (Vietnam).

Elected Office: IA Senate, 1984–96, Pres., 1992–96.

Professional Career: Farmer.

DC Office: 1427 LHOB, 20515, 202-225-3806; Fax: 202-225-5608; Web site: boswell.house.gov.

State Offices: Des Moines, 515-282-1909.

Committees: *Agriculture* (4th of 28 D): General Farm Commodities & Risk Management (Chmn); Livestock, Dairy & Poultry. *Transportation & Infrastructure* (12th of 44 D): Aviation; Highways & Transit; Railroads, Pipelines & Hazardous Materials.

Group Ratings

	ADA	ACLU	AFS	LCV	ITIC	NTU	COC	ACU	CFG	FRC
2008	95	82	100	85	100	6	61	4	0	5
2007	90	—	100	75	—	6	60	8	5	—

National Journal Ratings

	2007 LIB — 2007 CONS		2008 LIB — 2008 CONS	
Economic	58% —	41%	65% —	35%
Social	54% —	46%	52% —	48%
Foreign	73% —	26%	92% —	0%
Composite	62% —	38%	71% —	29%

Key Votes of the 110th Congress

1. Increase minimum wage	Y	5. Share immigration data	Y	9. Withdraw troops 8/08	Y
2. Expand SCHIP	Y	6. Foreign aid abortion ban	N	10. No operations in Iran	Y
3. Raise CAFE standards	Y	7. Ban gay bias in workplace	Y	11. Free trade with Peru	Y
4. Bail out financial markets	Y	8. Repeal D.C. gun law	Y	12. Overhaul FISA	Y

Election Results

2008 general	Leonard Boswell (D)	176,904	(56%)	($1,547,567)
	Kim Schmett (R)	132,136	(42%)	($155,895)
2008 primary	Leonard Boswell (D)	20,401	(61%)	
	Ed Fallon (D)	13,035	(39%)	

Prior Winning Percentages: 2006 (52%); 2004 (55%); 2002 (53%); 2000 (63%); 1998 (57%); 1996 (49%)

Population		Race/Ethnicity		Work	
Pop. 2007:	622,011	White:	88.2%	Private:	81.2%
Change since 2000:	Up 6.3%	Black:	3.4%	Government:	12.0%
Urban:	73.1%	Hispanic:	4.5%	Self-employed:	6.7%
Rural:	26.9%	Asian:	2.2%	Blue collar:	22.4%
Area size:	7,034 sq. mi.	Native Am.:	0.3%	White collar:	62.5%
Age		Hawaiian:	0.0%	Khaki collar:	0.1%
Median age:	37.0 yrs.	Two+ races:	1.2%	Other:	14.9%
More than 65 yrs:	12.9%	*Ancestry*		Median income:	$51,648
Less than 18 yrs:	25.4%	German:	25.0%	Median home value:	$131,300
Education		Irish:	11.8%	Poverty:	8.9%
H.S. grad:	90.0%	English:	8.4%	**Military Veterans**	
College grad:	27.2%			% of Pop:	10.5%
Grad degree:	7.9%				

Iowa, which today seems very much in the middle of the country, was once part of the West. It was not only the home of sober farmers and pious burghers, but also the eastern terminus of the first transcontinental railroad, a way station for people in a hurry to get across the Great Plains to the Rockies and the Pacific Northwest. Those who stayed behind used the wealth accumulated by methodical husbandry of their fertile farmlands to implant firmly the glories of Western civilization. One can feel that impulse today in Des Moines, looking across the river from downtown to the Victorian capitol, its gold dome above a Corinthian pediment. Terrace Hill, the beautifully restored governor's mansion, sits atop a hill overlooking the Raccoon River. Nearby Living History Farms, which recreates Indian villages, frontier towns, and turn-of-the-century farms, shows off the efforts of the early settlers.

2008 Presidential Vote

Obama (D)	173,932	(54%)
McCain (R)	143,771	(44%)

2004 Presidential Vote

Bush (R)	154,919	(50%)
Kerry (D)	154,652	(50%)

Cook Partisan Voting Index: D + 1

The 3rd Congressional District covers 12 counties in central Iowa, including Des Moines's Polk County, and it extends mostly to the east. It is the most urbanized district in Iowa and the only one that does not border another state or a major river on the east or west. Some 65% of its votes are cast in Polk County. However, it does not include rapidly growing Dallas or Warren counties in the Des Moines metropolitan area. The city itself remains classically Middle America, even as it gains a more lively downtown and spreads into the countryside while farm counties' population continues to decline. The area has become a sanctuary for people from outside of Iowa looking for a family-friendly urban lifestyle. More than 12,000 Bosnians have settled in Des Moines, where the climate reminds them of home. Insurance, agricultural supply, and printing and service businesses are expanding in office centers downtown and at freeway interchanges.

The remainder of the district is largely rural, with no city larger than 30,000. But these towns house some giant manufacturing plants. Pella (pop. 9,800) is home to the Pella window and door maker, which employs 3,000. Pella also was the site of the planned Earthpark—a combination rain forest, aquarium, and education center that was nixed by Congress after Republican Sen. John McCain of Arizona portrayed the $48 million federal grant as a wasteful use of public money. The famed Amana colonies, with seven quaint villages, were founded in 1855 by the Community of True Inspiration, German pietists who have retained many of their old customs. Newton (pop. 15,579) was the home of the Amana appliance business, acquired by Iowa-based Maytag in 2001, which in turn was purchased and then closed by Michigan-based Whirlpool in 2007. A year later, Newton became the site of 500 planned "green" jobs at a fiberglass wind turbine plant. Polk County has historically voted Democratic but has become more Republican as white-collar businesses overtake blue-collar ones. The district's other rural counties have mostly been Republican in the past. The result is a district split down the middle, about as evenly divided as any in the nation: It went 49%-48% for Al Gore in 2000 and 49.7%-49.6% for George W. Bush in 2004. In 2008, though, it favored Barack Obama 54%-44%.

The congressman from the 3rd Congressional District is Leonard Boswell, a Democrat first elected in 1996. Boswell grew up on farms in Ringgold and Decatur counties, near the Missouri border. He was drafted in 1956, at age 22, and was a private in the Army. He re-enlisted as an officer, graduated first in his class in both fixed-wing and helicopter flying school, served two years in Vietnam, and retired as a lieutenant colonel in 1976. He then taught at the Army command college at Fort Leavenworth, Kansas. Boswell settled down on his Decatur County farm and became head of the local farmers' co-op, which he managed to keep out of bankruptcy during the farm depression of the 1980s. In 1984, he was elected state senator from a six-county Republican district, served as chairman of the Appropriations Committee and, after 1992, Senate president. Boswell was also the Democratic nominee for lieutenant governor in 1994. In 1996, he ran for an open seat in the old 3rd District, which was largely rural and extended across the state's southern tier. Boswell flew his four-seater Piper Comanche 250 across the district, campaigning for a balanced federal budget, higher education spending, and fewer Medicare reductions, all to be financed with Pentagon cuts and elimination of waste in the Medicare medical program for the elderly. Poweshiek County attorney Mike Mahaffey ran as a moderate Republican. Boswell was endorsed by the Farm Bureau, which usually backs Republicans. He raised more money than Mahaffey and, like other Democrats, ran ads attacking GOP House Speaker Newt Gingrich of Georgia and cuts in Medicare. The result was a 49%-48% victory for Boswell.

Boswell got a seat on Agriculture, where he has supported normal trade relations with China, the world's biggest market for pork, a major Iowa commodity. A member of the Blue Dog Coalition, he has a voting record that has consistently placed him in the most conservative quadrant of House Democrats. On the Intelligence Committee, his extensive military background and his security clearance left him well positioned to investigate the nation's response to terrorism. He voted to authorize military action in Iraq, but later criticized the Bush administration for not spending enough money on counter-terrorism. In May 2006, when *The Washington Post* reported that he was absent from a closed committee meeting, he said that he was "appalled" that Republicans leaked the information. His attendance was a sensitive issue because Boswell had been absent from the House for three months in 2005, following removal of a noncancerous tumor from his abdomen and subsequent chemotherapy. Boswell lost 70 pounds but recovered. In November 2007, he won enactment of a bill for a suicide prevention program for veterans of the wars in Iraq and Afghanistan.

After Democrats won a House majority in 2006, Boswell initially took a seat on the influential Energy and Commerce Committee, but changed his mind when the 110th Congress convened in 2007 and kept his previous committee assignments. That positioned him to help write the new farm bill. As chairman of the Agriculture Subcommittee on Livestock, Dairy, and Poultry, he added provisions to the House bill that gave pricing benefits to food processors, and changed the dairy price support so that it was based on all dairy products, not just milk.

The nonpartisan June 2001 redistricting plan left Boswell with a dilemma and several tough subsequent re-elections. Only seven of the 27 counties and 24% of the population in his former district were moved to the new 3rd District. Decatur County, where he continued to operate his family farm, was one of eight counties moved to western Iowa's new, heavily Republican 5th District. His only other option was to move to the new 2nd District, which leans Democratic but where he would have faced a tough contest against incumbent Republican Rep. Jim Leach. Boswell decided to move to Des Moines and run in the newly redrawn 3rd. But Democratic state Sen. Matt McCoy had already said he would run in the Polk County-based district. Support for Boswell from national Democrats, including House Minority Leader Dick Gephardt of Missouri, eventually convinced McCoy to defer.

In the general election, Republican challenger Stan Thompson was less accommodating. A Des Moines lawyer who worked for George W. Bush in the 2000 Iowa caucuses, Thompson argued that Boswell was out of step with the new district's geography and philosophy. Thompson ran a credible campaign and won several endorsements, including a joint designation with Boswell from the Iowa Farm Bureau. Boswell won, 53%-45%. In a 2004 rematch, Thompson won endorsements from the farm bureau and from the *Des Moines Register*, which praised his energy and job-creating proposals, and said that Boswell had become "almost so low-key he is no longer heard." This time, Boswell won 55%-45%, and carried Polk County 57%-43%. Nonetheless, in 2006, he faced another tough challenge—from state Senate Co-President Jeff Lamberti, scion of a family-owned chain of convenience stores and gas stations. Lamberti got help from national Republicans and highlighted his differences with Boswell on taxes, spending, and border control. In a strongly Democratic year, Boswell won by only 52%-46%. His 13,269-

vote lead in Polk County accounted for more than his district-wide margin. Lamberti's showing was all the more impressive given the poor Republican performance elsewhere in Iowa.

In 2008, Boswell spent more than $1 million to defeat a primary challenge from Ed Fallon, a former state legislator, 61%-39%. Fallon, who suggested that Boswell might soon retire, was backed by the *Register*, which called Boswell "out of touch" in an editorial and criticized him for a relatively light record of accomplishments in Congress. In the general election, he attracted a politically savvy but little-known GOP challenger, lawyer Kim Schmett, and prevailed with 56% of the vote.

FOURTH DISTRICT

Tom Latham (R)

Elected 1994, 8th term; b. July 14, 1948, Hampton; home, Ames; Wartburg Col., 1966–67, IA St. U., 1967–70; Lutheran; married (Kathy); 3 children.

Professional Career: Farmer; Bank teller/bookkeeper, 1970–72; Independent Insurance agent, 1972–74; Hartford Insurance mktg. rep., 1974–76; Co–owner, Latham Seed Co., 1976–present.

DC Office: 2217 RHOB, 20515, 202-225-5476; Fax: 202-225-3301; Web site: latham.house.gov.

State Offices: Ames, 515-232-2885; Clear Lake, 641-357-5225; Fort Dodge, 515-573-2738.

Committees: *Appropriations* (9th of 23 R): Agriculture, Rural Development, FDA & Related Agencies; Transportation, HUD & Related Agencies (RMM).

Group Ratings

	ADA	ACLU	AFS	LCV	ITIC	NTU	COC	ACU	CFG	FRC
2008	30	18	29	23	57	60	89	88	69	100
2007	20	—	18	5	—	51	95	84	54	—

National Journal Ratings

	2007 LIB — 2007 CONS		2008 LIB — 2008 CONS	
Economic	32%	— 68%	29%	— 71%
Social	9%	— 85%	20%	— 74%
Foreign	32%	— 64%	39%	— 60%
Composite	26%	— 74%	31%	— 70%

Key Votes of the 110th Congress

1. Increase minimum wage	Y	5. Share immigration data	Y	9. Withdraw troops 8/08	N
2. Expand SCHIP	Y	6. Foreign aid abortion ban	Y	10. No operations in Iran	N
3. Raise CAFE standards	N	7. Ban gay bias in workplace	N	11. Free trade with Peru	Y
4. Bail out financial markets	N	8. Repeal D.C. gun law	Y	12. Overhaul FISA	Y

Election Results

2008 general	Tom Latham (R)...	185,458	(61%)	($1,627,654)
	Becky Greenwald (D)......................................	120,746	(39%)	($634,014)
2008 primary	Tom Latham (R)...	unopposed		

Prior Winning Percentages: 2006 (57%); 2004 (61%); 2002 (55%); 2000 (69%); 1998 (100%); 1996 (65%); 1994 (61%)

Population			Race/Ethnicity		Work	
Pop. 2007:	590,334		White:	93.2%	Private:	75.2%
Change since 2000:	Up 0.9%		Black:	0.9%	Government:	15.5%
Urban:	50.5%		Hispanic:	3.5%	Self-employed:	8.8%
Rural:	49.5%		Asian:	1.4%	Blue collar:	26.2%
Area size:	15,833 sq. mi.		Native Am.:	0.1%	White collar:	57.2%
Age			Hawaiian:	0.0%	Khaki collar:	0.1%
Median age:	38.1 yrs.		Two+ races:	0.7%	Other:	16.5%
More than 65 yrs:	15.9%		*Ancestry*		Median income:	$45,812
Less than 18 yrs:	22.6%		German:	31.1%	Median home value:	$105,500
Education			Irish:	10.6%	Poverty:	10.6%
H.S. grad:	90.3%		Norwegian:	9.0%	**Military Veterans**	
College grad:	23.4%				% of Pop:	11.2%
Grad degree:	7.1%					

Central Iowa is where the Great Plains begins—a land of farm fields marked off by straight roads and punctuated by occasional crossroads towns and grain elevators; the landscape rolls slightly upward to the west, topped by a sky that seems to fill the eyes. Pioneers coming here in the 1840s and 1850s found prairie grass with roots two feet thick, and girded trees with grubbing machines to cut off their roots belowground. Central Iowa has some of the world's most productive soil, and also some of its most creative agricultural scientists and farmers. A monument to one of them is the 12-foot statue of Norman Borlaug, a scientist who worked on increasing crop yield and ending hunger, in Borlaug's home-town of Cresco, in Howard County near the Minnesota border. This is long-settled land now, and Iowans' productivity means that there are fewer people living on farms than there were a century ago. But its towns and small cities remain centers of creativity. One is Ames, in Story County, home of Iowa State University and the host of the Iowa Republican straw poll, which has launched several GOP nomination contests. Ames is part of the growth zone around Des Moines, which is 30 miles to the south. Directly west of the city and its most affluent suburbs is fast-growing Dallas County. To the south is Madison County, famous for the wooden covered bridges that gave their name to a best-selling novel and movie; in 2002, five of the bridges caught fire and burned, so now there are just five left. To the north is Mason City, the boyhood home of *The Music Man* author Meredith Wilson. In Winnebago County is Winnebago Industries, which manufactures motor homes and recreation vehicles on computer-controlled assembly lines with robotic equipment; the main factory in Forest City employs 3,200, though increased gas prices and the recession have hit hard at sales. The first tractors were manufactured in Charles City, which calls itself "America's Hometown."

2008 Presidential Vote		
Obama (D)	166,104	(53%)
McCain (R)	142,396	(45%)
2004 Presidential Vote		
Bush (R)	155,587	(51%)
Kerry (D)	148,331	(48%)
Cook Partisan Voting Index:	Even	

The 4th Congressional District includes all these parts of central and northern Iowa, and covers 28 counties. It does not include Des Moines, but counties around Des Moines cast more than one-third of its votes. Like Iowa, the 4th District is closely divided politically: George W. Bush carried the district 49%-48% in 2000 and 51%-48% in 2004; Barack Obama won it in 2008, 53%-45%.

The congressman from the 4th District is Tom Latham, a Republican elected in 1994. Latham grew up on a farm in Franklin County, near Alexander (pop. 162), where his family has owned a seed company since 1947. For years, Latham was active in Republican politics, attending the national convention and serving as a farm adviser to GOP Rep. Fred Grandy. In 1994, Grandy challenged Republican Gov. Terry Branstad and lost a close primary, while Latham ran for the House. His Democratic opponent, Sheila McGuire, had been one of 47 health care professionals on an advisory panel for first lady Hillary Rodham Clinton's unpopular health care plan; Latham opposed it. He won 61%-39%.

In the House, Latham has a moderately conservative record and has usually been a quiet but diligent member who avoids the national spotlight. However, he has been a close ally and confidant of Minority Leader John Boehner of Ohio, whom Latham backed in a bitterly fought intraparty contest for majority leader in 2006. Latham has pursued local interests on the Appropriations Committee and its agriculture subcommittee, and helped to bring home money for causes ranging from disaster aid to farm research. He has been enthusiastic in securing federal funds for the National Animal Disease Center, a research center in Ames. He criticized the Senate Appropriations Committee, where Iowa Democrat Tom Harkin is a senior Democrat, for reducing funds needed to complete the center, which he described as essential to "agro-terrorism" prevention. In 2006, he enacted a bill to award a Congressional Gold Medal to Cresco scientist Borlaug.

In 2007, after a local Navy officer died in Iraq, Latham pushed to passage a law to permit grand-parents and other family members to get the military death benefit if they assume custody of a dead soldier's children. Earlier, he worked with Senate Republicans to give reserve and National Guard sol-diers the same health benefits as regular military personnel. He called for faster troop withdrawals from Iraq, but he opposed a deadline.

In 2002, redistricting made the district more competitive, and Latham faced the most vigorous cam-paign since he was elected. He had not been a robust fundraiser, and Democrats targeted the seat. Their nominee was John Norris, former chief of staff to Democratic Gov. Tom Vilsack and, in 2003 and 2004, presidential contender John Kerry's Iowa manager in the precinct caucuses. Norris attacked Latham for supporting Republican positions on taxes and health care, was an aggressive campaigner, and raised more than $1 million. But Latham won by a relatively comfortable 55%-43%, winning all 28 counties, though only by 9 votes in Ames's Story County, which cast the most votes.

In 2006, Latham's opponent was Selden Spencer, an Ames neurologist who spent two weeks in Afghanistan treating patients and training doctors shortly before the election. Spencer called for with-drawal of U.S. forces from Iraq. Latham commended Spencer for his medical contributions in the region, but said he disagreed with him on the war. Latham won, 57%-43%, carrying every county except Story County, which gave 52% to Spencer. Latham decided not to challenge Harkin in 2008. He again had a serious contest for re-election that year, against Democrat Becky Greenwald, a former marketing executive. He raised eyebrows by saying he did not want President Bush, by then unpopular with the public, to campaign for him. He won easily, 61%-39%.

FIFTH DISTRICT

Steve King (R)

Elected 2002, 4th term; b. May 28, 1949, Storm Lake; home, Kiron; NW MO St. U., 1967–70; Catholic; married (Marilyn); 3 children.

Elected Office: IA Senate, 1996–2002.

Professional Career: King Construction Co. owner, 1975–2002.

DC Office: 1131 LHOB, 20515, 202-225-4426; Fax: 202-225-3193; Web site: www.house.gov/steveking.

State Offices: Council Bluffs, 712-325-1404; Creston, 641-782-2495; Sioux City, 712-224-4692; Spencer, 712-580-7754; Storm Lake, 712-732-4197.

Committees: *Agriculture* (7th of 18 R): Conservation, Credit, Energy & Research; Department Operations, Oversight, Nutrition & Forestry; General Farm Commodities & Risk Management; Livestock, Dairy & Poultry. *Judiciary* (9th of 16 R): Commercial & Administrative Law; Constitution, Civil Rights & Civil Liberties; Immigration, Citizenship, Border Security & International Law (RMM). *Small Business* (4th of 12 R): Finance & Tax; Regulations & Healthcare; Rural Development, Entrepreneurship & Trade.

Group Ratings

	ADA	ACLU	AFS	LCV	ITIC	NTU	COC	ACU	CFG	FRC
2008	5	18	0	0	33	79	83	96	90	100
2007	0	—	0	0	—	85	75	100	98	—

National Journal Ratings

	2007 LIB	—	2007 CONS		2008 LIB	—	2008 CONS
Economic	8%	—	92%		5%	—	94%
Social	0%	—	91%		0%	—	91%
Foreign	0%	—	72%		0%	—	95%
Composite	9%	—	91%		4%	—	96%

Key Votes of the 110th Congress

1. Increase minimum wage	N	5. Share immigration data	Y	9. Withdraw troops 8/08	N
2. Expand SCHIP	N	6. Foreign aid abortion ban	Y	10. No operations in Iran	N
3. Raise CAFE standards	N	7. Ban gay bias in workplace	N	11. Free trade with Peru	Y
4. Bail out financial markets	N	8. Repeal D.C. gun law	Y	12. Overhaul FISA	Y

Election Results

2008 general	Steve King (R)	159,430	(60%)	($873,230)
	Rob Hubler (D)	99,601	(37%)	($290,089)
	Victor Vara (I)	7,406	(3%)	
2008 primary	Steve King (R)	22,663	(99%)	

Prior Winning Percentages: 2006 (59%); 2004 (63%); 2002 (62%)

Population		Race/Ethnicity		Work	
Pop. 2007:	571,119	White:	91.8%	Private:	78.1%
Change since 2000:	Down 2.4%	Black:	0.8%	Government:	12.0%
Urban:	49.4%	Hispanic:	5.1%	Self-employed:	9.5%
Rural:	50.6%	Asian:	1.0%	Blue collar:	28.1%
Area size:	18,429 sq. mi.	Native Am.:	0.4%	White collar:	53.5%
Age		Hawaiian:	0.0%	Khaki collar:	0.1%
Median age:	40.0 yrs.	Two+ races:	0.9%	Other:	18.4%
More than 65 yrs:	16.9%	*Ancestry*		Median income:	$44,006
Less than 18 yrs:	24.2%	German:	31.5%	Median home value:	$94,500
Education		Irish:	11.0%	Poverty:	10.8%
H.S. grad:	87.1%	English:	7.6%	**Military Veterans**	
College grad:	18.1%			% of Pop:	11.7%
Grad degree:	5.0%				

Sioux City, one of the oldest market towns on the Great Plains, is nestled in the loess bluffs above the Missouri River. Although still the largest city on the Plains west of Des Moines and north of Omaha, Sioux City has not grown much in the past half-century. Its original economic base has become obsolete: The waterfront, once raucous with boatmen and stockyard workers, is now quiet. Downtown stores have been replaced by shopping malls at the edge of town, where people spend a day doing a season's shopping and then drive for hours to get home. The stockyards, which employed thousands and slaughtered millions of hogs during their peak years in the 1920s, are shuttered. But there are still many hogs in western Iowa. Instead of meeting sellers in the markets of the Sioux City stockyard, packers now contract directly with large farms and build their modern slaughterhouses nearby. Tyson Foods has facilities in Buena Vista and Crawford counties. Meanwhile, wind farming has grown. Iowa is among the top states generating electricity from wind, over objections from some farmers to the noise and the hazard to birds.

2008 Presidential Vote		
McCain (R)	151,188	(54%)
Obama (D)	122,537	(44%)

2004 Presidential Vote		
Bush (R)	167,387	(60%)
Kerry (D)	109,974	(39%)

Cook Partisan Voting Index: R + 9

Sioux City is the largest city in the 5th Congressional District, which covers the western part of the state from Minnesota to Missouri and borders South Dakota and Nebraska to the west. This is the state's largest congressional district geographically, the one with the most 4-H members, and the nation's chief hog- and pig-producing district. In recent years, outside investors moved into the district's small towns for large-scale ethanol production. Council Bluffs is home to the mansion of General Grenville Dodge, who in 1859 lobbied Illinois lawyer Abraham Lincoln on the need for a transcontinental railroad. Lincoln got it through Congress in 1863, Dodge became its chief engineer, and Council Bluffs became its eastern terminus when it was completed in 1869. Surrounded by beef grazing territory, where federal intrusion has long been resented, Council Bluffs looks west across the Missouri River to Omaha, taking on the culturally more conservative tone of Nebraska and the conservative politics of the *Omaha World-Herald,* despite the presence of three Nevada-style casinos in the city. But Council Bluffs is also developing an economically hip side with Google's decision to open a data facility there. This is by far the most Republican district in Iowa, and George W. Bush twice carried it by wide margins. In 2008, McCain won it 54%-44%.

The congressman from the 5th District is Steve King, a Republican who won the seat in 2002. He was born in Storm Lake in western Iowa and attended Northwest Missouri State University, though he didn't graduate. In 1975, he founded the King Construction Company. After building up his business, he launched his political career in 1996, at age 47, with his election to the state Senate, where he quickly gained a reputation as an ultraconservative. He opposed abortion rights, racial quotas and preferences, and same-sex marriage. He sponsored Iowa's "God and Country" bill, which required Iowa schools to recognize that the United States "has derived its strength from biblical values," and he was a driving force behind the state's English-only law. On economic matters, King supported repeal of the state's inheritance tax, and backed a 15% state income-tax reduction and a national right-to-work law.

When the U.S. House seat came open in 2002, there were four main contenders in the Republican primary. King ran as a strong conservative and as the only rural candidate, and called for limiting federal control of local schools. King led in the June primary with 30% of the vote. Because no one candidate received the required 35% of the vote, the nomination was determined by a special party convention three weeks later. The 533 voting delegates needed three ballots to select a winner. King led on each ballot and defeated House Speaker Brent Siegrist of Council Bluffs, 272-253, in the final round, marking the first time in 38 years that Iowans used a convention to select a congressional nominee. The general election outcome was never in doubt. Democrat Paul Shomshor attempted to paint King as too conservative for the district, and won the endorsement of the *Omaha World-Herald,* but fell far short, 62%-38%. The conservative *National Review* magazine heralded King as the "Great Right Hope."

In the House, King has not been shy about sharing his strong views, and gets a fair amount of national press for controversial remarks. In 2005, the House passed his amendment to prohibit Medicare funds to reimburse for Viagra, a drug prescribed for male sexual dysfunction. He has been an outspoken proponent of tougher immigration laws. The House has twice passed his amendment to enforce a 1996 law that forbids localities from standing in the way if police officers want to report immigration information to the federal government. He advocates English as the official language of the United States. In April 2008, an Iowa district court judge ruled in favor of King's challenge to state officials who had placed bilingual voting forms on state websites. A Carroll *Daily Times Herald* columnist who assembled some of King's quotes into a book, *King Kong Krazy,* calls him "maniacally nationalistic."

In 2007, King became the ranking Republican on the immigration subcommittee of Judiciary, which put him in the middle of the high-profile debate. He criticized Democrats who voted for a fence along the Mexican border while they backed lawsuits to thwart its construction. When the subcommittee passed a bill to permit foreign fashion models into the country for a photo shoot, King called it the "Ugly American Bill" because he said it implied that attractive Americans could not be found for the work. After nine

Democrats voted against House passage of his resolution to recognize the importance of Christmas, he condemned their "assault on Christianity in America." He also has been vocal in urging Republican leaders to adopt a more aggressive strategy to regain the House majority. "There's got to be blood on the floor," he has said. On local issues, King has called for expansion of "value-added agriculture," including biotechnology and ethanol production, to strengthen the local economy. He successfully promoted an expanded tax credit for small ethanol and biodiesel producers as part of the 2005 energy law.

In his re-election bid in 2004, King carried all but one small county and won 63%-37% over Democrat Joyce Schulte. She ran again in 2006, accused him of "racist remarks" on immigration, and lost again, 59%-36%. King refused to debate her, saying that most voters already knew his views. After endorsing Republican Fred Thompson for president in 2008, he said in March that "radical Islamists and their supporters will be dancing in the streets" if Barack Obama won. John McCain's campaign condemned those remarks, but King declined to apologize.

★ KANSAS ★

With its relentlessly horizontal landscape, Kansas seems to invite the sort of weather systems that uprooted Dorothy's life in the children's classic *The Wonderful Wizard of Oz*. In 2007, a 205-mile-per-hour tornado—rated EF-5, the most dangerous category—destroyed the town of Greensburg, killing 10 people and prompting Gov. Kathleen Sebelius to complain that desperately needed National Guard equipment was tied up in Iraq. In this tragedy, there is an echo of Kansas's chief claim to literary fame; in the film, based on L. Frank Baum's 1900 novel, the Kansas from which Dorothy and Toto are swept by a tornado is shown in dreary black-and-white, in contrast to the brilliant Technicolor of Oz. Thomas Frank, author of the best-selling *What's the Matter With Kansas?*, seemed to get it right when he said, "Kansas may be the land of averageness, but it is a freaky, militant, outraged averageness." For the history of seemingly placid Kansas—it actually is flatter than a pancake, geographers announced in 2004 after comparing its topography to an IHOP product—has been punctuated by uprisings, intellectual and violent, by moments of anger and rage sweeping through the tall sheaves like a tornado wind. The history of Kansas began in a moment of violence, the Bleeding Kansas of the 1850s that led proximately to the terrible war that split the whole nation. The trigger was the Kansas-Nebraska Act of 1854, which left to local settlers the question of whether this new Kansas Territory would be a free or slave state. Pro-slavery "bushwhackers" rode over the line from Missouri, stealing elections and writing a pro-slavery constitution. But much larger numbers of free-soil "jayhawkers," from New England and the New England-Yankee-settled Great Lakes states, put down roots, and, despite the massacres of the mad John Brown, prevailed and established their own law and order. This was a civil war before the Civil War, and, as Wichita State historian Charles Miner points out, one conducted by literate people who produced mountains of documents that have not been fully mined by historians.

Kansas's effect on national politics was tumultuous. The Democratic Party was split on the slavery issue, the Republican Party was created, and the nation was plunged into Civil War. The ultimate effect on Kansas was calming: The antislavery majority bent the soil to the plow and built small towns with sturdy networks of schools, churches, and colleges. But the rebellious impulse did not totally die out. Kansans' livelihoods were always at risk: Hailstorms, grasshopper invasions, dry seasons or a drop in world farm prices could mean disaster for thousands of families. The high-rainfall 1880s attracted hundreds of thousands of new settlers to Kansas. The low-rainfall 1890s produced a bust and a populist rebellion. "What you farmers should do," said orator Mary Ellen Lease, "is to raise less corn and more hell." For a few years in the 1890s, and then in the farm rebellions of the 1930s, 1950s and 1970s, Kansans did, but afterwards, the state always returned to jayhawker Republicanism.

Kansas remains mostly Republican in the 21st century, but not in quite the same old way. Its most famous contemporary politician, former GOP Sen. Bob Dole, still returns occasionally to his small hometown of Russell, out on the plains. But Kansas' population is increasingly metropolitan. Some 52% of Kansans live in just five counties, which include Kansas City, Lawrence, Topeka, and Wichita. In 85 of the 100 other counties, the population declined between 2000 and 2007. A majority of Kansans live in or within easy reach of metropolitan Kansas City, which has a diverse economy that is by no means dependent on farming.

At the same time, some small towns on the plains are suffering, their city halls and post offices sometimes padlocked and their high schools closed because of low attendance. Some towns have bought land to be distributed free to homesteaders. The state promotes agritourism at buffalo ranches and the wild Tallgrass Prairie. But new office complexes and corporate headquarters are rising amidst the affluent suburbs of Johnson County, which has one of the highest job growth rates in the country. The smaller metropolitan area of Wichita, while less diversified, has an economy built on its role as the world's leading producer of small airplanes. Many World War II planes were built in Wichita, and today Cessna, Bombardier, Raytheon and other manufacturers make more than half the general-aviation aircraft in the world. Hispanics are flocking to work in meatpacking factories in towns like Dodge City, Garden City, and Liberal. With populations in 2000 that were more than 40% Hispanic, the towns experienced pro-immigration marches when Congress began debating major changes in immigration policy in 2005. Hispanics accounted for nearly half of Kansas's population growth in the 1990s and made up 9% of its population in 2005.

These demographic shifts have had political consequences. Some 40% of Kansas's votes in 2004 were cast in the mostly suburban counties from Kansas City west to Topeka and another 15% in Wichita's Sedgwick County. If rural Kansas once produced farm rebellions, these urban and suburban Kansans have produced their own kind of rebellion. Since the mid-1990s, Kansas has had in effect three-party politics—conservative Republicans versus moderate Republicans versus Democrats—and fought a kind of culture war over issues like abortion rights and the teaching of evolution in the schools. In 1994, the state elected as governor Republican Bill Graves, who was pro-abortion rights and pro-gun control. He was fiercely opposed by conservative Republicans in the Legislature and in his 1998 re-election primary.

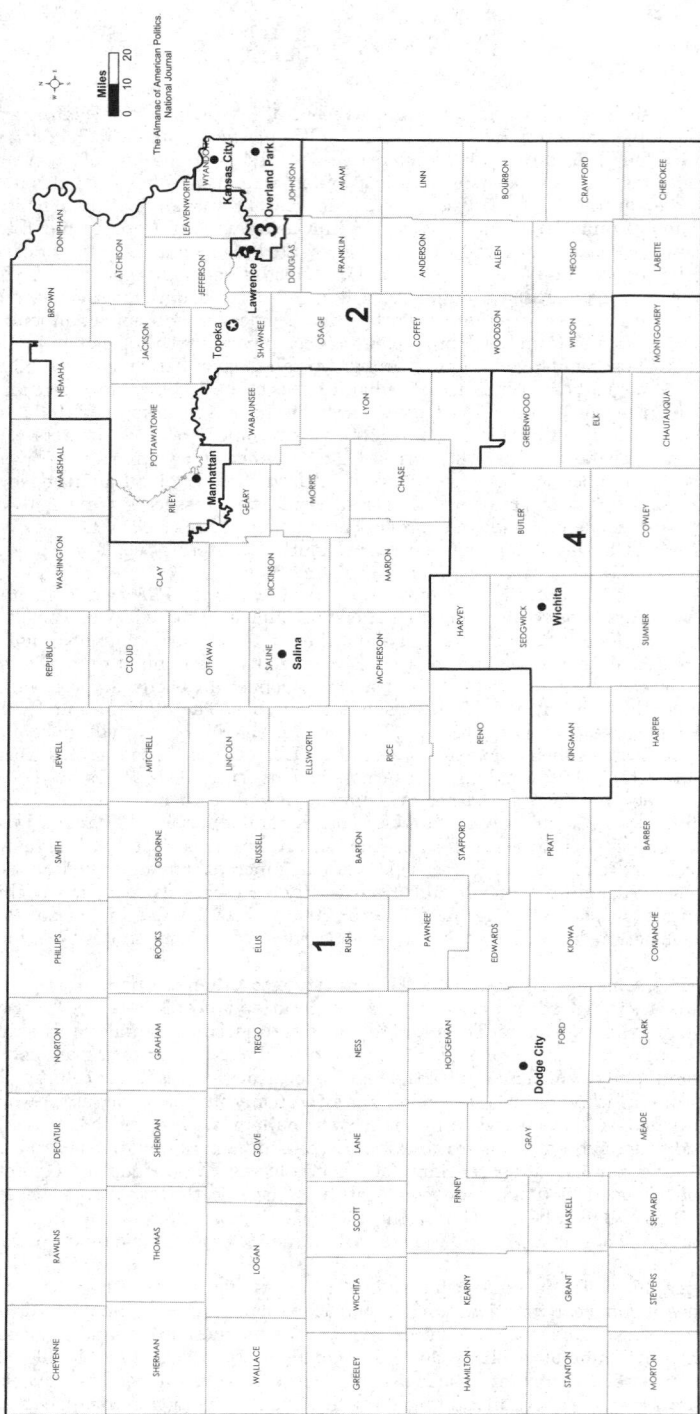

The Almanac of American Politics
National Journal

Congressional district boundaries were first effective for 2002.

He won easily, but traditionalists won a majority on the state Board of Education and in 1999 issued guidelines that treated evolution as a theory. There was a national uproar, and ever since, elections to this once obscure board have featured fierce fights, mostly in Republican primaries. The guidelines on evolution and science curricula have been revised four more times. In February 2007, the board repealed the guidelines questioning evolution on a 6-4 vote. In another snub of cultural conservatives, the Legislature voted in March 2007 to allow the Kansas Lottery to operate gambling casinos. Another hot issue is Sebelius's veto of plans to build coal-fired power plants in southwestern Kansas, out of concern for climate change. The Legislature didn't have the votes to override her veto.

The Republican split has created opportunities for the Democrats. The party captured the 3rd Congressional District seat in 1998 by beating a conservative who'd alienated suburban moderates, and it won the governorship in 2002 when Democrat Sebelius beat conservative Treasurer Tim Shallenburger. The battle raged on. Sebelius vetoed a bill for stricter regulation of abortion clinics, the Legislature considered a move to ban state-funded embryonic-stem-cell research and Republican Attorney General Phillip Kline sought abortion-clinic records from Dr. George Tiller. (Tiller was shot and killed by an anti-abortion extremist in 2009.) In 2006, Sebelius recruited former Republican state Chairman Mark Parkinson to be her running mate and won 58%-40%. Johnson County District Attorney Paul Morrison switched to the Democratic Party, ran against Kline and beat him 59%-41%. Also that year, conservatives lost their majority on the State Board of Education in the August GOP primaries. In January 2008, Morrison resigned after it was revealed that he had had a sexual affair with a subordinate. Kline, appointed Johnson County District Attorney, sought an indictment against Dr. Tiller for performing late-term abortions without a sign-off from a second doctor with no common financial interests. A grand jury declined to bring an indictment; Kline ran in the August 2008 primary for a full term as district attorney and was beaten.

Frank's book argued that Kansas voters have been hornswoggled into voting against their economic interests by big business operatives. That's not an entirely accurate picture. His hometown, which he cites as evidence of economic decline, is in booming Johnson County, and Kansas's unemployment rate has been well below the national average. And lots of other voters—liberals on the Upper East Side of New York, for example—vote against their short-term economic interests, because cultural issues are more important to them. The recent switches toward moderate Republicans and Democrats came not in the drought-stricken farm counties in southern and western Kansas, which are sustained by subsidized crop insurance and federal disaster payments, but in the economically vital metropolitan areas of Kansas, where the key swing voters were motivated, as Kansas's conservative Republican voters have been, by cultural issues.

In federal elections, Democrats had two of Kansas's four U.S. House seats in 2006, but lost one of them to a Republican in 2008. The state has remained Republican in presidential elections, and its two Republican senators were both first elected in 1996, when Dole resigned to run for president and moderate Sen. Nancy Landon Kassebaum retired. Kansas has not elected a Democratic senator since 1932—the

Population		**Household Income**		**Work**	
Pop. 2007:	2,757,827	Under $15k:	12.8%	Private:	75.4%
State rank:	33rd of 50	$15k to $50k:	40.3%	Government:	17.0%
Change since 2000:	Up 2.6%	$50k to $100k:	31.6%	Self-employed:	7.2%
Urban:	71.0%	$100k to $150k:	12.8%	Unemployment (3-yr. average):	3.7%
Rural:	29.0%	Over $150k:	2.5%	Poverty:	11.9%
Native of state:	59.0%	Median income:	$46,669	Blue collar:	23.8%
Not a citizen:	4.0%			White collar:	59.0%
Area size:	82,277 sq. mi.	**Home Value**		Khaki collar:	0.6%
		Under $100k:	43.7%	Other:	16.6%
Most populous cities		$100k to $300k:	48.8%		
1. Wichita	356,564	$300k to $500k:	5.6%	**Age**	
2. Overland Park	165,314	$500k to $1 mil:	1.5%	Median age:	36.1 yrs.
3. Kansas City	141,791	Over $1 million:	0.3%	More than 65 yrs:	13.0%
4. Topeka	121,184	Median:	$114,400	Less than 18 yrs:	25.2%

Race/Ethnicity					**Military Veterans**		**Registered Voters in 2008**	
White:	81.0%	*Language*			% of Pop:	11.5%	D:	484,710 (27.7%)
Black:	5.6%	English:	90.1%		*Veterans by Period*		R:	771,019 (44.1%)
Hispanic:	8.5%	Spanish:	6.3%		WWII and before:	13.6%	Other:	494,030 (28.2%)
Asian:	2.1%	Asian:	1.5%		Korea:	11.5%	Voter turnout:	1,235,872
Native Am.:	0.7%	Other			Vietnam:	32.0%	Turnout as % of	
Hawaiian:	0.0%	European	1.6%		Gulf (pre-2001):	11.8%	voting age:	58.8%
Two+ races:	1.9%	**Education**			Gulf (post-2001):	8.4%	**Legislature**	
Ancestry		H.S. grad:	88.5%		Peace time:	22.7%	Senate:	9 D 31 R
German:	24.5%	College grad:	28.3%				House:	48 D 77 R
Irish:	10.9%	Grad degree:	9.7%					
English:	9.1%							

only state that hasn't—and Republican incumbent Pat Roberts won re-election easily in the Democratic year of 2008. That could have changed in 2010, as the popular Sebelius, term-limited as governor, was widely expected to run for the seat being vacated by Republican Sam Brownback, who is running for governor. But in March 2009, Obama tapped Sebelius as his Secretary of Health and Human Services, likely dissuading her from a gubernatorial bid in 2010.

Presidential politics   Except for 1964, when it narrowly favored Lyndon Johnson over Barry Goldwater, Kansas has voted Republican for president throughout the past 60 years. In 2000 and 2004, George W. Bush carried 103 of its 105 counties, losing only those containing the old industrial city of Kansas City and the university town of Lawrence. Some polls showed the 2008 race could be closer, especially if Gov. Kathleen Sebelius were the Democratic vice presidential nominee. John McCain won by a solid but not overwhelming 57%-42% margin, carrying 102 of 105 counties. He lost the two that had gone for John Kerry, plus Crawford County in the southeast. In 1996, the state Legislature voted to cancel the April primary, and none has been held since.

2008 Presidential Vote		
McCain (R)	699,655	(57%)
Obama (D)	514,765	(42%)
2004 Presidential Vote		
Bush (R)	736,456	(62%)
Kerry (D)	434,993	(37%)

Congressional districting   In 2002, Republicans had full control of redistricting in Kansas for the first time since the 1960s, but did not use it to partisan advantage.

111th Congress Lineup
3 R   1 D
110th Congress Lineup
2 D   2 R

Why? As one legislator put it, "What's ground zero with reapportionment? I'd say it's Lawrence." In the previous plan, Lawrence, midway between Kansas City and Topeka and home of the University of Kansas, was in the 3rd District captured by Democrat Dennis Moore in 1998 and held in 2000. The 3rd District had to shed 61,000 people, and the obvious partisan move was to remove Lawrence, which Moore carried by wide margins, and place it in the heavily Republican 2nd District, where incumbent Republican Jim Ryun was thought to be unbeatable. But Lawrence civic leaders insisted that Lawrence be kept together in the 3rd District—they wanted the university to be in the same district as its hospital in Kansas City—and Republicans in the state House in March 2002 passed a plan splitting the city but keeping most of it, including the university, in the 3rd. The state Senate in April 2002 passed a different plan, promoted by national Republicans, which extended the western 1st District all the way to the southeast corner of the state. But the House's plan prevailed and was adopted in June. As it turned out, in 2006 Democrat Nancy Boyda won the portion of Douglas County included in the 2nd District, 61%-38%. Overall, she won by a much smaller margin in her 51%-47% upset win over Republican Jim Ryun. But in 2008, Douglas County was not enough to save Boyda, who lost 51%-46% to Republican state Treasurer Lynn Jenkins.

Governor

Mark Parkinson (D)

Assumed office April 2009, term expires Jan. 2011, 1st term; b. June 24, 1957, Wichita; home, Olathe; Wichita St. U., B.A. 1980; U. of KS, J.D. 1984; Methodist; married (Stacy); 3 children.

Elected Office: KS House of Reps., 1990–92; KS Senate, 1992–96; KS lt. gov., 2006–09

Professional Career: Practicing atty., 1984–96; Businessman, 1996–present

Office: State Capitol, 300 SW 10th Ave., Ste. 212S, Topeka, 66612, 785-296-3232; Fax: 785-368-8788; Web site: www.governor.ks.gov.

Election Results

2006 general	Kathleen Sebelius (D)	491,993	(58%)
	Jim Barnett (R)	343,586	(40%)
2006 primary	Kathleen Sebelius (D)	unopposed	

The new governor of Kansas is Mark Parkinson, a Democrat who was once a Republican. He switched parties in 2006 to run for lieutenant governor as Democratic Gov. Kathleen Sebelius' running mate, then assumed office as Sebelius' successor in April 2009 after she left to join the Obama Cabinet as secretary of Health and Human Services.

Parkinson was born in Wichita. His grandfather was a Scott City farmer who unsuccessfully ran for governor as a Democrat in the 1940s. His father worked in public relations and considered himself a moderate Republican. Parkinson attended Wichita public schools and went on to Wichita State University. He took a semester off during his junior year to run against Republican state Rep. Ben Foster. He lost to Foster in the GOP primary by 37 votes. Parkinson returned to Wichita State, graduated summa cum laude and went to law school at the University of Kansas, where he met his future wife, Stacy. He formed his own law firm in 1986 and practiced for 10 years. In 1990 he ran as a Republican for a seat in the Kansas House of Representatives. He was elected and two years later was elected to the state Senate. As a legislator, Parkinson helped write Kansas' death-penalty law. He earned a reputation as someone who was not afraid to stand out or to buck party leadership. He refused to support a GOP bill to ban flag burning and was a proponent of a controversial 1992 school-aid overhaul. Parkinson viewed himself as a moderate and grew frustrated with the long-standing rift between the moderate and conservative factions of the Republican Party. He decided not to seek re-election in 1996, opting instead to work with his wife to open a series of retirement homes and assisted-living facilities in Kansas.

Though he was no longer an elected official, Parkinson remained active in politics. He chaired the Kansas Republican Party from 1999 to 2003 and labeled Sebelius an "extreme liberal" during her 2002 gubernatorial campaign. He also said that "any Republican who supports Kathleen Sebelius for governor is either insincere or uninformed." Parkinson's longtime association with the Republican Party added to the shock value of his decision to accept Sebelius' invitation to join the re-election ticket in 2006. He switched his party registration one day before she announced that he would succeed Lt. Gov. John Moore, who planned to step down. Parkinson's presence on the ticket was a smart political play. It exploited the deep divisions between Kansas Republicans, made Sebelius a more attractive candidate to disaffected moderate Republicans, and laid the groundwork for a Democratic successor in 2010, when term limits would have prevented Sebelius from running again. But it brought harsh criticism from Republicans, who recalled that Moore too had been a Republican before running with Sebelius in 2002 and that Parkinson had disparagingly called the selection a gimmick. Sebelius and Parkinson went on to easily defeat Republican state Sen. Jim Barnett 58%-40%.

Sebelius' runaway victory in a state where registered Republicans outnumber Democrats, coupled with her 2007 chairmanship of the Democratic Governors Association, attracted national notice, leading to talk that she would make an attractive vice presidential candidate in 2008. "It's hard to imagine that her name's not going to appear on everybody's list," Democratic pollster Mark Mellman told the Associated Press. She endorsed Democratic Sen. Barack Obama of Illinois for president and campaigned for him in several states during his primary battle with New York Sen. Hillary Rodham Clinton. Obama considered her for running mate before choosing Delaware Sen. Joe Biden. He tapped her for the position of secretary of Health and Human Services after his first nominee, former South Dakota Sen. Tom Daschle, withdrew amid questions about his failure to pay incomes taxes. She was confirmed by the Senate on a 65-31 vote.

Parkinson was sworn in on April 28, 2009. He has stated that he has no intention of running for election to the job in 2010. "I admire those who are willing and able to make the sacrifices to serve the public for their entire careers, but I'm not one of them," he said. The two years he would spend in the governor's office looked to be challenging. The most pressing issue was a $328 million state budget deficit. In his first week in office, he signed an agreement to allow the Sunflower Electric Power Corp. to construct a coal-fired power plant near Holcomb. The deal differentiated Parkinson from Sebelius, who had blocked the company's previous efforts to gain approval for the project. His decision not to run in 2010 leaves the race wide open, with Republican Sen. Sam Brownback an early favorite.

Senior Senator

Sam Brownback (R)

Elected 1996, term expires 2010, 2nd full term; b. Sept. 12, 1956, Garnett; home, Topeka; KS St. U., B.S. 1978, U. of KS, J.D. 1982; Catholic; married (Mary); 5 children.

Elected Office: U.S. House of Reps., 1994–96.

Professional Career: Radio broadcaster, KKSU, 1978–79; Practicing atty., 1982–86, 1993; Prof., KS St. U. Law Schl., 1982–86; Ogden & Leonardville City Atty., 1983–86; KS secy. of agriculture, 1986–93; White House fellow, Office of USTR, 1990–91.

DC Office: 303 HSOB, 20510, 202-224-6521; Fax: 202-228-1265; Web site: brownback.senate.gov.

State Offices: Garden City, 620-275-1124; Overland Park, 913-492-6378; Pittsburg, 620-231-6040; Topeka, 785-233-2503; Wichita, 316-264-8066.

Committees: *Aging (Special)* (6th of 7 R). *Appropriations* (8th of 12 R): Agriculture, Rural Development, Food and Drug Administration & Related Agencies (RMM); Defense; Homeland Security; Military Construction, Veterans Affairs & Related Agencies; State, Foreign Operations & Related Programs; Transportation, Housing and Urban Development & Related Agencies. *Commerce, Science & Transportation* (9th of 11 R): Aviation Operations, Safety & Security; Communications, Technology & the Internet; Competitiveness, Innovation & Export Promotion; Surface Transportation & Merchant Marine Infrastructure, Safety & Security. *Energy & Natural Resources* (4th of 10 R): Energy; National Parks; Water & Power (RMM). *Joint Economic Committee.*

Group Ratings

	ADA	ACLU	AFS	LCV	ITIC	NTU	COC	ACU	CFG	FRC
2008	20	8	0	18	75	65	88	76	74	88
2007	5	—	0	7	—	77	86	95	82	—

National Journal Ratings

	2007 LIB	—	2007 CONS	2008 LIB	—	2008 CONS
Economic	0%	—	97%	17%	—	81%
Social	32%	—	67%	21%	—	73%
Foreign	36%	—	63%	29%	—	69%
Composite	24%	—	77%	24%	—	76%

Key Votes of the 110th Congress

1. Raise CAFE standards	*	5. Make English official language	Y	9. Withdraw troops 3/08	N
2. Expand SCHIP	N	6. Path to citizenship	N	10. Iran guard is terrorist group	Y
3. Cap greenhouse gases	N	7. Fetus is unborn child	Y	11. Increase missile defense $	Y
4. Bail out financial markets	N	8. Prosecute hate crimes	N	12. Overhaul FISA	Y

Election Results

2004 general	Sam Brownback (R)	780,863	(69%)	($2,476,585)
	Lee Jones (D)	310,337	(27%)	($102,931)
2004 primary	Sam Brownback (R)	286,839	(87%)	
	Arch Naramore (R)	42,880	(13%)	

Prior Winning Percentages: 1998 (65%); 1996 (54%); 1994 House (66%)

Sam Brownback grew up on a farm in Anderson County, some 50 miles south of Kansas City; he has family roots in Osawatomie, a center of evangelical abolitionism in Kansas in the 1850s. He was state president of Future Farmers of America while in high school and student body president at Kansas State University. As a young man, he had a daring side: He and a friend once herded cattle on motorcycles, and he wore his hair in a bushy style known in the 1970s as an "Afro." He worked briefly as a farm broadcaster before graduating from law school at the University of Kansas. He practiced law for four years in Manhattan, Kan., and then was appointed secretary of the state Board of Agriculture in 1986, serving until it was abolished in 1993. Brownback was a White House Fellow, working from 1990 to '91 for Special Trade Representative Carla Hills. In March 1994, when 2nd District Rep. Jim Slattery, a Democrat, ran for governor, Brownback announced his candidacy for the seat, condemning "a welfare system that discourages the work ethic and encourages the disintegration of families, and a government that can't say no to spending or yes to reform." He won the primary 48%-35% over Bob Bennie, who campaigned as a strong opponent of abortion rights. In the general election, Brownback defeated John Carlin, who was governor from 1978 to '86, by carrying every county in a 66%-34% win.

Brownback was among the "revolutionary" Republican freshmen in 1995 who tried to shake up Congress. He headed a group called the "New Federalists," which sought to abolish three Cabinet departments, and he denounced "influence peddling" in Washington. As the immigration issue heated up, he played a key role in separating the debate over illegal immigration from discussion of legal immigration, which led to passage of a tough measure against illegal immigrants but no major reductions in the number of legal immigrants. In 1995, he had a melanoma removed, and this brush with a fatal disease led him toward a deeper faith. "I did a lot of internal examination. My conclusion was that if this were to be terminal, at that point in time I would not be satisfied with how I had lived life," he told *The Weekly Standard* magazine . An evangelical Christian, Brownback later converted to Catholicism, with Sen. Rick Santorum of Pennsylvania as his sponsor; on Sundays in Topeka he attends both Catholic mass and a service at the Topeka Bible Church. Brownback believes that the nation has "re-engaged with its faith" in a spiritual revival. He chairs weekly meetings of the Values Action Team on Capitol Hill. At a prayer breakfast, he apologized to Sen. Hillary Rodham Clinton of New York for having despised her and her husband years earlier when President Clinton was in office. He also described washing the feet of a staffer at a farewell party to demonstrate respect and humility.

In May 1996, Republican Bob Dole of Kansas, in the midst of his presidential campaign, made the surprise announcement that he would resign from the Senate that June. Two days later, Brownback said he would seek the seat. But Republican Gov. Bill Graves chose a fellow moderate, Lt. Gov. Sheila Frahm, to fill the vacancy until the election, setting up a primary contest between Frahm and conservative Brownback. There were strong differences between the two: She favored abortion rights, and he opposed abortion. Brownback accused her of voting as a state legislator to raise taxes by $500 million; she criticized his "slash-and-burn" approach to federal spending. Brownback won the August primary, 55%-42%. In the fall race for the remaining two years of Dole's term, Brownback faced Democrat Jill Docking, a Wichita stockbroker and the wife of a former lieutenant governor whose father and grandfather both served as governor. Docking promised "Kansas common sense" and likened herself to Nancy Landon Kassebaum, a prominent moderate Republican who represented Kansas in the Senate for nearly 20 years. Brownback campaigned on the three R's: "Reduce, reform, and return. Reduce the size and scope of the federal government. Reform the Congress. Return to the basic values that built the country: Work and family and the recognition of a higher moral authority." He promised to serve only two terms. Both candidates spent liberally, and some fall polls showed the race to be close. But Brownback won by a convincing 54%-43%.

Brownback has had a mostly conservative voting record in the Senate and has taken on many issues because of his strong religious views. "I think every life is sacred and beautiful, whether it's the unborn or whether it's Ted Kennedy," he has said. "I really try to reach out and work with anybody and everybody I can." After September 11, Brownback and Kennedy, the liberal Massachusetts senator, co-sponsored a bill to strengthen the nation's borders. It provided for an automatic entry and exit system, the development of biometric identifiers and tracking of foreign students, and better coordination between immigration and anti-terrorism agencies. The bill became law in 2002. Brownback teamed up with Paul Wellstone, the late liberal senator from Minnesota, to gain passage of the Victims of Trafficking and Violence Protection Act of 2000. He led the fight for the Sudan Peace Act of 2002 and has worked to end slavery and the civil war there. With Kennedy, he co-sponsored the North Korea Refugee Act, saying in 2002, "If hell is the absence of God, I think you can see North Korea is the closest place to that on Earth." Using his seat on the Appropriations Committee, Brownback in 2006 called for $100 million to promote democracy in Iran and has pushed for action to combat AIDS and malaria in Africa.

Brownback has taken the initiative on many domestic issues. In 2005, after the Janet Jackson "wardrobe malfunction" at the Super Bowl, the Senate passed his bill raising the maximum fine on broadcasters for indecency from $32,500 to $325,000. With Rep. John Lewis, D-Ga., he worked to authorize the African-American museum on the National Mall, and with Sen. Byron Dorgan, D-N.D., he sponsored a resolution apologizing to American Indians for past government misdeeds. When the Senate approved the apology in 2008, Brownback said his hope was that it "helps heal the wounds that have divided America for too long." He has sponsored bills to require doctors to tell women seeking abortions that fetuses can feel pain and to bar doctors from prescribing controlled drugs for use in assisted suicides. On the Judiciary Committee, he supported most of President Bush's judicial appointees. In 2006, however, he held up the approval of District Court nominee Janet Neff of Michigan because she had attended a lesbian commitment ceremony; he was one of four senators to vote against her confirmation in 2007. To the dismay of many conservatives, Brownback was a leading co-sponsor of the immigration bill that passed in the Senate in 2006 and established a guest-worker program.

In 2003 and 2004, Brownback used his chairmanship of the Commerce Committee's Science Subcommittee to hold hearings on cloning and genetic testing. He is a staunch foe of federal funding for embryonic-stem-cell research, which uses excess embryos from in vitro fertilization procedures. Brownback says that the research destroys human life, and he compares it to Nazi experimentation on Jews. "While researchers in the private sector are free to destroy young human lives through embryonic-stem-cell research, the government should not be in the business of funding this ethically troubling research with taxpayer dollars," he says.

Brownback supported the Bush administration on the Iraq war until he made a trip there in early 2007. "I do not believe that sending more troops to Iraq is the answer," he said. "Iraq requires a political rather than a military solution." After meeting with Iraqi officials and U.S. military leaders, he called for Iraq to be divided into three relatively autonomous zones. The success of the military surge increased his frustration with the political stalemate in Iraq, and later in 2007 he continued to oppose additional troops.

Brownback was elected to a full six-year term in 1998 on a 65%-32% vote after well-known Democrats declined to run. In 2004, Democrats again had a hard time finding a candidate to run against him. Former House member and Agriculture Secretary Dan Glickman bowed out in September 2003, and Gov. Kathleen Sebelius also declined. The winner of the August 2004 primary withdrew from the race, and Brownback was re-elected 69%-27%, carrying 104 of Kansas's 105 counties.

After that election, conservatives encouraged Brownback to run for president. In June 2006, he said he was giving it serious consideration. "I could be the right person with the right message at the right moment. And I could be completely wrong, and I'll still be happy about it," he told *The Washington Post*. He made several trips to Iowa, where, he hoped, his background in agriculture and his strong religious convictions would resonate with Republican caucus-goers. After George Allen lost his Senate race in Virginia and former Sen. Bill Frist of Tennessee announced he would not run, Brownback seemed to be one of the few potential candidates whose stand on issues was in line with the cultural conservatives who have dominated the Republican selection process since 1980.

In January 2007, Brownback joined the race and offered himself as "a full-scale, Ronald Reagan conservative. . . . My positions are at the heart of where the Republican Party is." Two days later, he took part in the annual protest march at the Supreme Court on the anniversary of the *Roe v. Wade* decision legalizing abortion. His campaign blueprint was: "Move to Iowa. Consolidate the base. And tell your story." His platform included Social Security privatization and supported the development of alternative-fuel vehicles. But, lagging in the polls and in fundraising, he was unable to break out of the pack of Republican candidates. Brownback's moment of truth came at the Iowa straw poll in August 2007, when he finished third with 15% behind former Arkansas Gov. Mike Huckabee. *National Review* editor Rich Lowry wrote that Brownback's candidacy had reached the point of "extreme pointlessness." Brownback tried to refocus his campaign on bipartisanship and a broader political constituency. "I think it will really resonate with Iowa voters who are tired of the political bickering," he said. But Brownback withdrew on October 19, saying, "My yellow brick road just came short of the White House this time." Three weeks later, he endorsed Sen. John McCain of Arizona, and he worked to sell McCain to religious voters and other conservatives. He told *The Wichita Eagle,* "The most successful thing I did was get out of the race. That's what I got the most publicity for."

Brownback said that he will keep his pledge to serve only two full terms. In September 2008, he said he was "definitely considering the idea" of running for governor in 2010.

Junior Senator

Pat Roberts (R)

Elected 1996, term expires 2014, 3rd term; b. April 20, 1936, Topeka; home, Dodge City; KS St. U., B.A. 1958; United Methodist; married (Franki); 3 children.

Military Career: Marine Corps, 1958–62.

Elected Office: U.S. House of Reps., 1980–96.

Professional Career: Co–owner & editor, *The Westsider* (AZ newspaper) 1962–67; A.A., U.S. Sen. Frank Carlson, 1967–68; A.A., U.S. Rep. Keith Sebelius, 1968–80.

DC Office: 109 HSOB, 20510, 202-224-4774; Fax: 202-224-3514; Web site: roberts.senate.gov.

State Offices: Dodge City, 620-227-2244; Overland Park, 913-451-9343; Topeka, 785-295-2745; Wichita, 316-263-0416.

Committees: *Agriculture, Nutrition & Forestry* (5th of 8 R). *Ethics (Select)* (2nd of 3 R). *Finance* (7th of 10 R): International Trade, Customs & Global Competitiveness; Social Security, Pensions & Family Policy (RMM); Taxation, IRS Oversight & Long-Term Growth. *Health, Education, Labor & Pensions* (10th of 10 R). *Rules & Administration* (7th of 8 R).

Group Ratings

	ADA	ACLU	AFS	LCV	ITIC	NTU	COC	ACU	CFG	FRC
2008	20	14	11	18	80	60	88	72	77	100
2007	20	—	14	0	—	56	73	92	57	—

National Journal Ratings

	2007 LIB	—	2007 CONS	2008 LIB	—	2008 CONS
Economic	25%	—	74%	35%	—	64%
Social	14%	—	84%	21%	—	73%
Foreign	16%	—	79%	29%	—	69%
Composite	20%	—	80%	30%	—	70%

Key Votes of the 110th Congress

1. Raise CAFE standards	N	5. Make English official language	Y	9. Withdraw troops 3/08	N
2. Expand SCHIP	Y	6. Path to citizenship	N	10. Iran guard is terrorist group	Y
3. Cap greenhouse gases	N	7. Fetus is unborn child	Y	11. Increase missile defense $	Y
4. Bail out financial markets	N	8. Prosecute hate crimes	N	12. Overhaul FISA	Y

Election Results

2008 general	Pat Roberts (R)	727,121	(60%)	($6,297,288)
	Jim Slattery (D)	441,399	(36%)	($1,677,905)
	Randall Hodgkinson (Lib)	25,727	(2%)	
2008 primary	Pat Roberts (R)	unopposed		

Prior Winning Percentages: 2002 (83%); 1996 (62%); 1994 House (77%); 1992 House (68%); 1990 House (63%); 1988 House (100%); 1986 House (75%); 1984 House (76%); 1982 House (68%); 1980 House (62%)

Pat Roberts, the state's junior senator, is from a solid Kansas Republican background. His abolitionist great-grandfather "arrived in Kansas with a flat-bed press, a six-gun and a Bible" and founded Kansas' second-oldest newspaper, the *Oskaloosa Independent*. His father, Wes Roberts, was briefly Republican National Committee chairman during the Eisenhower years. Pat Roberts graduated from Kansas State University with a journalism degree. He served four years in the Marine Corps, then spent five years running a weekly newspaper in the suburbs of Phoenix. Starting in 1967, he worked for two years as an aide to Republican Sen. Frank Carlson and then 12 years as chief aide to 1st District GOP Rep. Keith Sebelius, the father-in-law of Health and Human Services Secretary Kathleen Sebelius, formerly the Democratic governor of Kansas. When Keith Sebelius retired in 1980, Roberts won the seat with 56% of the vote in a three-candidate Republican primary. For 14 years, he was in the minority party in the House. He concentrated on farm issues, learning their intricacies and minutiae, and traveling in a van to keep in touch with constituents in a district so large it took two weeks to visit every county seat. His voting record was moderate, and he looked after Kansas interests.

In 1995, after Republicans won majority control of Congress, Roberts became chairman of the House Agriculture Committee. He had long believed that the huge subsidies of the early 1980s would never return. Faced with Republican budget parameters, Roberts drafted the so-called Freedom to Farm bill designed to phase out subsidies over seven years. In September 1995, his bill failed in committee when Southern Republicans, eager to protect cotton, rice and peanut subsidies, voted against it. Two months later, Roberts persuaded Agriculture conferees to include most of his bill in the 1996 budget reconciliation bill, which President Bill Clinton vetoed. To attract more support, Roberts agreed to maintain cotton and rice marketing loans and managed to preserve the popular Conservation Reserve Program. But overall, his legislation was the biggest change in agriculture policy since the New Deal act of 1933. Roberts' revised bill passed the Agriculture Committee 29-17 in January 1996, the full House in February, and became law in April.

A Kansas Senate seat came open when in November 1995 Republican Nancy Landon Kassebaum announced her retirement. Although Roberts enjoyed considerable power as a committee chairman, the Republicans had imposed term limits on chairmen, and the Freedom to Farm law had diminished the Agriculture Committee's portfolio. In early 1996, Roberts announced his candidacy and went on to win the August primary with an overwhelming 78% of the vote in a four-way race. In the general election, he faced Democratic state Treasurer Sally Thompson and won easily, 62%-34%. Thus Roberts became the first House member to give up a committee chairmanship to run for the Senate since Lister Hill in 1938 (and Hill got appointed to his Senate seat).

In the Senate, Roberts got on Agriculture Committee and continued his focus on farm issues. The Freedom to Farm Act worked well in 1997, and farmers seemed pleased to be able to decide what crops to plant without getting government approval. But in 1998 crop prices plunged—in line with a long trend of falling prices for basic commodities—and some farmers demanded a return to the old system. Roberts resisted that, and bills were passed to accelerate $4.5 billion in payments and to give farmers an extra $4 billion in disaster assistance. In 2000, the pattern continued. Roberts argued that increased subsidies for crop insurance would mean less need for yearly assistance and that limiting production would not raise prices because the U.S. accounts for less than one-fifth of world production. The problem seemed intractable. The number of family farmers continued to fall in places like western Kansas, where farm communities were disappearing, yet prices were not sufficient to maintain many operations.

The Freedom to Farm Act came up for reauthorization in 2002, and this time, Democrats were in control of the Senate. Roberts was not chairman but the fifth-ranking member of the minority on the committee. He admitted that the Freedom to Farm Act "didn't work out as anybody would have hoped" and, with Mississippi Republican Thad Cochran, pushed for farm savings accounts. But in committee, that proposal was rejected in favor of Democratic Chairman Tom Harkin's approach: Revival of counter-cyclical subsidies when crop prices are low, plus a larger Conservation Reserve Program, which pays farmers not to farm their land in order to protect environmentally sensitive areas. Harkin prevailed on the Senate floor 58-40 in February 2002. Roberts wasn't even on the conference committee. "I've never seen such partisanship in a farm bill," he said. "This policy fails farmers." He argued that it would provide no aid when production was low and crop prices rose, which is exactly what happened when drought struck the Great Plains in the summer of 2002. Roberts has tried to encourage farm exports in many ways, opposing cargo preferences and urging expanded powers for the president to negotiate trade deals and replenishment of International Monetary Fund funds. He was a lead sponsor of the 2000 law to end the embargo on food to Cuba, and he and fellow Kansas Republican Sam Brownback sponsored the 1999 law allowing the president to lift the embargo on India and Pakistan. Roberts supported normalizing trade relations with China.

After Republicans lost their majority, Roberts let Georgia's Saxby Chambliss take the ranking minority position on Agriculture so that he could continue to be the top Republican on the Intelligence Committee. But he remained active in farm policy. As he once said, "When you're from Kansas, you're not appointed to [the Agriculture committee]. You're sentenced to it." Roberts has promoted food-aid programs that use U.S. surplus commodities, and in 2005, he opposed an administration plan to allow purchase of foreign commodities for the food-aid program. In 2006, he co-sponsored a bill to have federal food-labeling laws override state and local laws. The same year, he and Democrat Kent Conrad of North Dakota sponsored legislation to place trade sanctions on Japan unless it agreed to end its embargo on U.S. beef imports; Japan capitulated.

When the farm bill came up for reauthorization in 2007, Roberts pressed for maintaining protections against losses from weather and market fluctuations for producers of major commodities—wheat, corn and soybeans. "Somebody has to press the case for production agriculture. They are the people who are really responsible for our food supply," he told the *Topeka Capital-Journal*, not those in "Walden Pond agriculture," a reference to competing bids for government subsidies from fruit- and vegetable-growing states. Roberts moved successfully in committee to amend one farm program in a way that prevented corn growers from getting reductions in crop insurance at the expense of wheat growers in Kansas and other states.

In 1999, Roberts was named chairman of the new Emerging Threats and Capabilities Subcommittee of the Armed Services Committee. In hearings that attracted little attention, he probed the nation's vulnerability to terrorists and presciently asserted that targets would be "selected for their symbolic value, like the World Trade Center in the heart of Manhattan." He was particularly immersed in the issues of national security and intelligence gathering as the Intelligence chairman when Republicans controlled the Senate. But the panel grew increasingly partisan and therefore less productive. In 2003, Roberts resisted Democratic calls for an investigation of how Bush administration officials used intelligence on Iraq. The same year, a memo by Democratic staffers on the committee was leaked to the media; it cynically suggested a strategy of getting Roberts and the Republicans to go along with the release of pre-Iraq War intelligence, and then using whatever revelations came out to attack the Bush White House. After that, the committee's weekly meeting was suspended. Ranking Democrat Jay Rockefeller of West Virginia tried to mend relations, but he refused to apologize. Roberts wrote a guest column in the *Washington Post* that said: "The Democrats planned to undermine the integrity of the committee by conducting a partisan attack, which threatens to destroy the credibility of an institution that has served the U.S. Senate and the nation well for nearly 30 years."

But over time, both sides on the committee were arriving at the conclusion that pre-war intelligence was deeply flawed. It reported in 2004 that the Central Intelligence Agency had not seriously considered the possibility that Iraqi Leader Saddam Hussein had no weapons of mass destruction. Roberts proposed that the Intelligence panel take over from Armed Services oversight of Defense Department intelligence operations, but the proposal was predictably resisted. In July of 2004, the committee unanimously approved a report criticizing pre-war intelligence on Iraq. After the 9/11 Commission recommended changes in intelligence organizations, including a new national intelligence director, Roberts and committee Republicans came up with their own proposal: abolish the CIA and arrange its functions in three component organizations under a new national intelligence director. The CIA resisted, and the White House's response to the idea was frosty. But even the Democratic presidential nominee that year, John Kerry of Massachusetts, mentioned the proposal favorably. Soon thereafter, a bipartisan reorganization of intelligence operations was undertaken by the Senate Governmental Affairs Committee.

In early 2005, when Rockefeller called for an investigation of CIA treatment of terrorism suspects and renditions, Roberts refused, arguing that the committee covered that in normal oversight. "Let me assure you the Senate Intelligence Committee is well aware of what the CIA is doing overseas in the defense of our nation, and they are not torturing detainees." When Rockefeller filed an amendment to the emergency supplemental appropriations bill to require such an investigation, Roberts said that some members had an "almost a pathological obsession with calling into question the actions" of intelligence agencies.

The *New York Times* touched off another partisan squabble in the committee when it reported in December 2005 that the National Security Agency was secretly monitoring contacts between al Qaeda suspects abroad and people in the United States. Roberts noted that he and Rockefeller had been briefed on the program and that Rockefeller had said he approved it. Rockefeller nonetheless sought a committee investigation, while Roberts insisted that the program was not only within the president's constitutional powers but "legal, necessary and reasonable." In March 2006, the committee voted along party lines not to conduct an investigation into the domestic surveillance program but to establish a seven-member panel, approved by the Bush administration, charged with that responsibility. Roberts complained that some Democrats "believe the gravest threat we face is not Osama bin Laden and al Qaeda, but rather the president of the United States." Roberts rotated off the committee in January 2007. Long a supporter of the Bush administration on Iraq, he said in July of that year that his support was "not locked into concrete." He said, "We have to make some very tough decisions. We can't be engaged in a war which the American people do not support."

His rocky relationship with Rockefeller aside, Roberts can be a pragmatic about his dealings with Democrats to further his agenda. In spring of 2007, he worked with Edward Kennedy of Massachusetts and Tom Harkin of Iowa to limit consumer advertising on risky prescription drugs. He opposed Republican-inspired cuts in Medicare reimbursement rates for doctors, and told Treasury Secretary Henry Paulson in February 2008 that Medicare cuts were "just not gonna happen." The same year, he came out against moving Guantanamo detainees to Fort Leavenworth in Kansas, complaining that it would take hundreds of millions of dollars to outfit Leavenworth to equal the security standards at Guantanamo, and that the move could well put his constituents in harm's way. For years, Roberts has been promoting science and technology projects in Kansas, and in December 2008, he announced plans for a $450 million national biological defense facility at Kansas State University. He has demonstrated his clout in other ways. After visiting Greensburg, Kansas, just after the town was destroyed by a tornado in May 2007, he phoned President Bush and got him to say he would declare Kansas eligible for federal disaster aid. In 2005, Roberts secured $25 million for affordable housing for troops and civilians at Fort Riley. The base came out of the base-closing process with additional forces, including the 1st Infantry Division, which was to be moved from Germany to Kansas.

Around Washington, Roberts is known for his caustic but also dead-on sense of humor. He often makes the list of "funniest senators" in *Washingtonian's* biennial poll of congressional staffers. He once complained that he wasn't satisfied with the distinction. "I was lobbying for the 'hottie of the year,' but I can't even get to lukewarm," said the 70-something, utterly bald Roberts.

Roberts had no Democratic opponent in 2002 and was re-elected with 83% of the vote. In 2008, former Democratic Rep. Jim Slattery, who had been working as a Washington, D.C., lawyer and lobbyist since losing a race for governor in 1994, returned to the state to challenge Roberts. Slattery ran a vigorous campaign, with some ads that were memorable, if of questionable taste (one suggested a rich businessman urinating on a map of Kansas). But Roberts, who routinely visits all 105 Kansas counties, spent nearly $7 million and called Slattery a lobbyist, "Gucci loafers and all." He won 60%-36%, running ahead of GOP presidential nominee John McCain in the state. Slattery carried just three counties: Wyandotte (industrial Kansas City), Douglas (the University of Kansas) and Atchison (an old river town named after the Missouri Democrat who led pro-slavery forces in the Kansas Territory in the 1850s).

FIRST DISTRICT

Jerry Moran (R)

Elected 1996, 7th term; b. May 29, 1954, Great Bend; home, Hays; U. of KS, B.S. 1976, J.D. 1981; Methodist; married (Robba); 2 children.

Elected Office: KS Senate, 1988–96, Majority ldr., 1995–96.

Professional Career: Operations officer, Consolidated State Bank, 1975–77; Mgr., Farmers State Bank & Trust Co., 1977–78; Practicing atty., 1981–96; Instructor, Ft. Hays St. U., 1986.

DC Office: 2202 RHOB, 20515, 202-225-2715; Fax: 202-225-5124; Web site: jerrymoran.house.gov.

State Offices: Hays, 785-628-6401; Hutchinson, 620-665-6138; Salina, 785-309-0572.

Committees: *Agriculture* (3rd of 18 R): Conservation, Credit, Energy & Research; General Farm Commodities & Risk Management (RMM); Horticulture & Organic Agriculture. *Transportation & Infrastructure* (9th of 30 R): Aviation; Highways & Transit; Railroads, Pipelines & Hazardous Materials. *Veterans' Affairs* (3rd of 11 R): Economic Opportunity; Health.

Group Ratings

	ADA	ACLU	AFS	LCV	ITIC	NTU	COC	ACU	CFG	FRC
2008	15	36	17	15	57	72	89	92	76	100
2007	30	—	27	10	—	62	80	88	45	—

National Journal Ratings

	2007 LIB — 2007 CONS		2008 LIB — 2008 CONS	
Economic	33%	67%	25%	74%
Social	31%	67%	31%	62%
Foreign	39%	61%	35%	62%
Composite	35%	65%	32%	68%

Key Votes of the 110th Congress

1. Increase minimum wage	Y	5. Share immigration data	Y	9. Withdraw troops 8/08	N
2. Expand SCHIP	Y	6. Foreign aid abortion ban	Y	10. No operations in Iran	N
3. Raise CAFE standards	N	7. Ban gay bias in workplace	N	11. Free trade with Peru	Y
4. Bail out financial markets	N	8. Repeal D.C. gun law	Y	12. Overhaul FISA	Y

Election Results

2008 general	Jerry Moran (R)	214,549	(82%)	($2,769,946)
	James Bordonaro (D)	34,771	(13%)	($6,057)
	Kathleen Burton (Ref)	7,145	(3%)	
	Jack Warner (Lib)	5,562	(2%)	
2008 primary	Jerry Moran (R)	unopposed		

Prior Winning Percentages: 2006 (79%); 2004 (91%); 2002 (91%); 2000 (89%); 1998 (81%); 1996 (73%)

Population		Race/Ethnicity		Work	
Pop. 2007:	643,728	White:	82.3%	Private:	71.4%
Change since 2000:	Down 4.2%	Black:	1.9%	Government:	17.7%
Urban:	52.4%	Hispanic:	12.8%	Self-employed:	10.3%
Rural:	47.6%	Asian:	1.0%	Blue collar:	27.9%
Area size:	57,576 sq. mi.	Native Am.:	0.5%	White collar:	52.4%
Age		Hawaiian:	0.0%	Khaki collar:	0.4%
Median age:	39.0 yrs.	Two+ races:	1.4%	Other:	19.3%
More than 65 yrs:	16.4%	*Ancestry*		Median income:	$40,911
Less than 18 yrs:	24.2%	German:	30.1%	Median home value:	$79,500
Education		Irish:	9.0%	Poverty:	12.6%
H.S. grad:	84.5%	English:	8.3%	**Military Veterans**	
College grad:	19.6%			% of Pop:	11.6%
Grad degree:	6.0%				

"A prairie is not any old piece of flatland in the Midwest," writes Kansas-born reporter Dennis Farney. "No, a prairie is wine-colored grass, dancing in the wind. A prairie is a sun-splashed hillside, bright with wild flowers. A prairie is a fleeting cloud shadow, the song of the meadowlark. It is the wild land that has never felt the slash of the plow." The prairie Farney describes once covered almost all of Kansas. Now only a little virgin prairie can still be found, in the Flint Hills region west and south of

2008 Presidential Vote
McCain (R) 184,501   (69%)
Obama (D) 79,638   (30%)

2004 Presidential Vote
Bush (R) 199,554   (72%)
Kerry (D)................................73,309   (26%)

Cook Partisan Voting Index: R + 23

Topeka, where you can see 30 miles on a clear day and waist-deep sea of grass waves in the wind as it did when pioneers on the Santa Fe Trail passed through some 150 years ago. The 11,000-acre Tallgrass Prairie National Preserve was created in 1996 to protect this unique landscape, and it is the largest privately owned parcel of land in the National Park system. "The Flint Hills do not take your breath away," wrote western folklorist Jim Hoy. "They give you a chance to catch it." Much of the area was grazing land, first for buffalo, then for the cattle driven to Kansas railheads like Abilene and Dodge City in the 1870s and 1880s. This brief moment in history has been recaptured in the Boot Hill Museum of kitschy Dodge City, where Main Street is called Wyatt Earp Boulevard.

After the harsh winter of 1886–87 wiped out the cattle herds, farmers moved in with plows and barbed wire (commemorated in Lacrosse's Barbed Wire Museum), which enabled farmers to keep livestock out of their wheat fields. The farmers also brought Yankee civilization to this vacant landscape—schools and churches and some foreign traditions as well, like the Cathedral of the Plains built by German Catholics. Now this civilization is threatened. "My great-grandparents and grandparents were part of the stream of settlers who migrated to western Kansas after the Civil War to become wheat farmers," writes James Dickenson in his elegiac *Home on the Range.* "They broke the virgin sod, erected houses, barns, schools, churches and towns, and made the area one of the most agriculturally productive in the world. A little more than a century later, the population has ebbed away from this area and many of the farms, schools, churches and towns lie vacant, dilapidated and boarded up like old boomtowns." The average age of Kansas farmers has approached 60. But there are also signs of rejuvenation, including growing agri-tourism to supplement farm income. Some towns are attracting new residents by giving away land as homesteads. Big meatpacking plants in Dodge City, Garden City and Liberal (the "Golden Triangle of meatpacking") have attracted large numbers of Hispanic immigrants, many living in trailer parks. Nearly two-thirds of the schoolchildren in these counties are Hispanic, and Spanish-language radio is prominent. Wind farms have grown on prairie land, though some worry that they may disturb the prairie ecosystem.

The 1st Congressional District consists of most of this expanse of Kansas, almost everything west of the Flint Hills and Abilene, the boyhood home of President Dwight Eisenhower. It contains 66 full counties and parts of three others; only the Nebraska's 3rd District has more counties. The "Big First," which stretches 350 miles east from the Colorado border, is roughly the size of Illinois. Population increased from 76,000 people in 1870 to 570,000 in 1890, but it has not grown much since then. With its aging population, it has the most hospitals of any district in the nation. Kansas now has more "frontier counties," with between two and six people per square mile, than it did in 1890. It also has more farms and more acres in grain-sorghum production than any other state, and more cattle. And from 1995 to 2006, the district received the highest percentage of federal farm subsidies of any congressional district. Politically, the 1st District is solidly Republican. It voted for George W. Bush by nearly 3-to-1 in 2004, and it voted for John McCain by better than 2-to-1 in 2008. But it also voted narrowly for Democratic Gov. Kathleen Sebelius, whose late father-in-law, Republican Keith Sebelius, represented the district in the House for 12 years.

The congressman from the 1st District is Jerry Moran, a Republican first elected in 1996. Moran grew up in Plainville in Rooks County and got his start in politics as an intern for U.S. Rep. Keith Sebelius, which entitled him to a seat at the impeachment hearings of President Richard Nixon. Moran worked as a banker for four years before attending the University of Kansas Law School. He was elected to the state Senate in 1988 and became state Senate majority leader in 1995. When 1st District Rep. Pat Roberts, a Republican, ran for the Senate in 1996, Moran stepped into the race to succeed him. With the help of Republican leaders, he avoided serious primary competition and won with 76% of the vote in the primary, which was tantamount to election.

Moran's voting record is moderate, though he says he sees himself as a traditional Republican. He has sometimes gone his own way in pursuing district causes. To the dismay of Republican Speaker Dennis Hastert, he was one of the 25 House Republicans who opposed the GOP Medicare prescription-drug bill in 2003. "I have never been under such pressure to vote contrary to what I thought was right as I was with this vote," said Moran, who didn't think the legislation did enough to reduce drug prices. He has sought to give federal officials negotiating authority to lower prescription-drug costs, a popular Democratic notion, and he supported an expansion of the State Children's Health Insurance Program. He bucked the Republican leadership to lead bipartisan efforts to bar the Treasury Department from forcing Cuba, a major consumer of Kansas wheat, to pay in advance for shipments of food and medicine from the U.S. In 2007, Moran's amendment to ease restrictions on shipments of food and medicine to Cuba passed the House, though it was removed from the final legislation to avoid a White House veto.

Moran is the ranking member on the General Farm Commodities and Risk Management Subcommittee of the Agriculture Committee. He is a defender of the U.S. system of farm subsidies, which has brought billions of federal dollars to his district. During the debate over the 2008 farm bill, Moran argued that the legislation was diverting too much money away from farm subsidies for nutrition programs and other uses. He also said urban legislators had too much say in the process. "More and more of the farm bill is being written to satisfy the desires of urban constituencies—not by those of us who represent the nation's farmers and ranchers," he said. He voted against the final bill because it contained cuts to federal subsidies for farmers.

Each year, Moran logs about 50,000 miles visiting every county in the district; his constituents expect to be able to speak with their congressman without driving to the next county over. He was re-elected in 1998 with a record 81% of the vote and did not face another Democratic challenger until 2006, when he got 79% against first-time candidate John Doll, a former schoolteacher. In 2008, Moran got 82% of the vote. He resisted state party leaders' pressure to challenge popular Gov. Sebelius in 2006. In November 2008, Moran announced plans to run for the Senate seat being vacated by Republican Sam Brownback in 2010. He will face fellow Republican House member Todd Tiahrt in the race for the Republican nomination.

SECOND DISTRICT

Lynn Jenkins (R)

Elected 2008, 1st term; b. June 10, 1963, Holton; home, Topeka; KS St. U., A.S. 1985; Weber St. U., B.S., 1985; Methodist; divorced; 2 children.

Elected Office: KS House, 1999–2001; KS Senate, 2001–03; KS treasurer, 2003–08.

Professional Career: C.P.A., 1984–98.

DC Office: 130 CHOB, 20515, 202-225-6601; Fax: 202-225-7986; Web site: lynnjenkins.house.gov.

State Offices: Pittsburg, 620-231-5966; Topeka, 785-234-5966.

Committees: *Financial Services* (26th of 29 R): Capital Markets, Insurance & Government Sponsored Enterprises; Housing & Community Opportunity.

Group Ratings and Key Votes: Newly Elected

Election Results

2008 general	Lynn Jenkins (R)	155,532	(51%)	($1,666,239)
	Nancy Boyda (D)	142,013	(46%)	($1,760,726)
2008 primary	Lynn Jenkins (R)	34,278	(51%)	
	Jim Ryun (R)	32,966	(49%)	

Population		Race/Ethnicity		Work	
Pop. 2007:	691,527	White:	86.1%	Private:	69.5%
Change since 2000:	Up 2.9%	Black:	4.8%	Government:	23.3%
Urban:	59.8%	Hispanic:	4.3%	Self-employed:	7.0%
Rural:	40.2%	Asian:	1.3%	Blue collar:	24.5%
Area size:	14,318 sq. mi.	Native Am.:	1.1%	White collar:	56.7%
Age		Hawaiian:	0.0%	Khaki collar:	1.5%
Median age:	35.6 yrs.	Two+ races:	2.2%	Other:	17.3%
More than 65 yrs:	13.1%	*Ancestry*		Median income:	$43,575
Less than 18 yrs:	23.8%	German:	24.7%	Median home value:	$108,700
Education		Irish:	12.1%	Poverty:	13.3%
H.S. grad:	89.9%	English:	8.9%	**Military Veterans**	
College grad:	25.7%			% of Pop:	12.8%
Grad degree:	9.8%				

The green plains of eastern Kansas have seen more than their share of American history. In 1827, on bluffs above the Missouri River, settlers built Fort Leavenworth, famous in later years for its war college and military prison and now the oldest U.S. fort west of the Mississippi. In the 1850s, newly founded towns along the Kansas River and along the Missouri border were the centers of Bleeding Kansas, the name the state took after pro-slavery bush-whackers set up a state capital in tiny Lecompton

2008 Presidential Vote

McCain (R)	170,885	(55%)
Obama (D)	134,747	(43%)

2004 Presidential Vote

Bush (R)	176,764	(59%)
Kerry (D)	117,924	(39%)

Cook Partisan Voting Index: R + 9

and anti-slavery New Englanders established their stronghold down the river at Lawrence. Farther up the river is Manhattan, home of Kansas State University, and Fort Riley, once an outpost against Indians, then a major Army base. In 2005, the Pentagon designated Fort Riley the headquarters of the 1st Infantry Division—the "Big Red One." Topeka, the state capital, sits on a low bluff above the river; the city's system of legal segregation prompted the 1954 landmark case *Brown v. Board of Education.* Farther south, on the Missouri border, are the hills called "the Balkans," where coal miners of Eastern European origin lived in and near towns such as Pittsburg and Girard that were once a center of American socialism. Clarence Darrow and Upton Sinclair made pilgrimages to the area, and the local paper, *Appeal to Reason*, had a circulation of 750,000 across the nation. Population loss is not as great here as in western Kansas. The area around Lawrence has been growing as, in effect, the perimeter of metropolitan Kansas City. Coal-bed methane gas wells have provided an economic boost to southeast Kansas.

These disparate areas, Topeka and Manhattan, Fort Riley and Fort Leavenworth, the wheat-growing counties and the Balkans—most of eastern Kansas except the Kansas City metropolitan area—make up the 2nd Congressional District. The heritage of most of this area has been Republican ever since the jayhawks defeated the bushwhackers once the votes were counted honestly in the 1850s. Yet in recent decades, Democrats have been competitive in state races, especially in Topeka. For 20 of the years from 1970 to 1994, Democrats held the 2nd District seat. In the following dozen years, it voted for conservative Republicans, usually by comfortable margins.

The new congresswoman from the 2nd District is Republican Lynn Jenkins. She brought the seat back to the Republican Party by defeating Democratic Rep. Nancy Boyda in 2008. Two years earlier, Boyda had pulled off one of that year's biggest upsets by unseating Republican Jim Ryun, but she could not overcome the district's Republican tilt in a second election. Jenkins was born in Topeka and grew up in the rural town of Holton on a dairy farm, where her parents still live today. After graduating from college, she worked for close to 15 years as a certified public accountant. Her shift to public service began with her first successful run for the state House in 1998 and proceeded at a breakneck pace. She served one term in the House and one in the state Senate and in 2002, was elected Kansas Treasurer. In 2006, even as Kansas re-elected popular Democratic Gov. Kathleen Sebelius at the top of the ticket, they returned Jenkins as treasurer. Shortly into her new term, she set her sights on the 2nd District House seat.

Before she could take on the incumbent, Jenkins had to first get past the person Boyda defeated, former Rep. Ryun, who had held the seat for five terms and wanted it back. Ryun had barely left office in early 2007 when he announced plans to reclaim the seat. Jenkins's announcement also defied much of the state's Republican establishment, which looked at Ryun's loss as an anomaly that would be easily corrected through a rematch with Boyda in 2008. It also threatened to rupture the latent divide between the two wings of the state GOP. Ryun was one of the most conservative Republicans in the House during his career, while Jenkins had built a more moderate profile as a pro-business and pro-abortion rights Republican.

The primary proved spirited but largely avoided the self-immolating tendencies that had emerged in previous intraparty contests in the state. Ryun called on Jenkins to sign a "clean campaign pledge," and after she declined, he attacked her for voting to raise taxes as a member of the state Legislature. But Jenkins effectively turned Ryun's arguments against him. Calling him her "friend" all the way through the primary, she countered that Ryun had run up a large tab in Congress by adding earmarks for special projects to spending bills, and she promised to limit the number of earmarks she sought for the district. Although heavily outspent by Ryun, she eked out a win by just over 1,300 votes. Eager to dispel any notion of bitterness from the contest, Ryun heartily endorsed her.

Despite the strong GOP tilt of the district, Jenkins nonetheless faced an uphill battle in the general election. Swept into office on a Democratic wave, Boyda had carefully crafted a voting record mostly in line with her constituents' views. She sought to distance herself from her party in July 2008 by publicly renouncing the support of the Democratic Congressional Campaign Committee, although she had accepted $10,000 from the committee. But Jenkins still tied Boyda to liberal House Speaker Nancy Pelosi every chance she got and accused the incumbent of supporting tax increases by voting for Democratic budgets that phased out the Bush administration's tax cuts in the top income bracket.

The strategy ultimately paid off. By portraying Boyda as out-of-step with the district, Jenkins turned the come-from-behind winner in 2006 into one of the rare Democratic losers of 2008. She won 51%-46%. However, her personal life hit a sad note three days after her election victory, when her husband filed for divorce.

Although Jenkins railed against earmarks during the campaign, she soon succumbed to their political, constituent-pleasing appeal. The Club for Growth, a national anti-tax group, removed her from its "Sworn Off Earmarks" list in April 2009 after she submitted requests for 23 projects totaling $70 million to the Appropriations Committee. Like other self-described budget hawks who've had to contend with the contradiction of their active pursuit of earmarks, Jenkins responded that she would request money for legitimate projects in her district as long as earmarking remained the status quo in Congress.

THIRD DISTRICT

Dennis Moore (D)

Elected 1998, 6th term; b. Nov. 8, 1945, Anthony; home, Lenexa; U. of KS, B.A. 1967; Washburn U. Law Schl., J.D. 1970; Protestant; married (Stephene); 7 children.

Military Career: Army, 1970; Army Reserves, 1971–73.

Elected Office: Johnson Cnty. dist. atty., 1976–88; Johnson Cnty. Comm. Coll. Bd. of Trustees, 1993–98.

Professional Career: Asst. KS atty. gen., 1971–73; Practicing atty., 1973–76, 1989–98.

DC Office: 1727 LHOB, 20515, 202-225-2865; Fax: 202-225-2807; Web site: moore.house.gov.

State Offices: Kansas City, 913-621-0832; Lawrence, 785-842-9313; Overland Park, 913-383-2013.

Committees: *Financial Services* (11th of 42 D): Financial Institutions & Consumer Credit; Oversight & Investigations (Chmn). *Small Business* (2nd of 17 D): Finance & Tax.

Group Ratings

	ADA	ACLU	AFS	LCV	ITIC	NTU	COC	ACU	CFG	FRC
2008	80	91	100	85	100	6	71	4	0	5
2007	90	—	100	85	—	4	60	4	12	—

National Journal Ratings

	2007 LIB	—	2007 CONS	2008 LIB	—	2008 CONS
Economic	78%	—	18%	63%	—	36%
Social	60%	—	39%	62%	—	34%
Foreign	59%	—	41%	55%	—	43%
Composite	67%	—	34%	61%	—	39%

Key Votes of the 110th Congress

1. Increase minimum wage	Y	5. Share immigration data	N	9. Withdraw troops 8/08	Y
2. Expand SCHIP	Y	6. Foreign aid abortion ban	N	10. No operations in Iran	Y
3. Raise CAFE standards	Y	7. Ban gay bias in workplace	Y	11. Free trade with Peru	Y
4. Bail out financial markets	Y	8. Repeal D.C. gun law	Y	12. Overhaul FISA	Y

Election Results

2008 general	Dennis Moore (D)..202,541	(56%)	($1,868,504)
	Nick Jordan (R)..142,307	(40%)	($1,114,721)
	Joe Bellis (Lib) 10,073	(3%)	
2008 primary	Dennis Moore (D).......................................unopposed		

Prior Winning Percentages: 2006 (65%); 2004 (55%); 2002 (50%); 2000 (50%); 1998 (52%)

Population		Race/Ethnicity		Work	
Pop. 2007:	737,729	White:	77.0%	Private:	81.3%
Change since 2000:	Up 9.8%	Black:	8.6%	Government:	13.1%
Urban:	94.7%	Hispanic:	8.8%	Self-employed:	5.4%
Rural:	5.3%	Asian:	3.3%	Blue collar:	16.7%
Area size:	787 sq. mi.	Native Am.:	0.5%	White collar:	69.0%
		Hawaiian:	0.0%	Khaki collar:	0.1%
Age		Two+ races:	1.7%	Other:	14.2%
Median age:	34.6 yrs.			Median income:	$60,500
More than 65 yrs:	10.0%	*Ancestry*		Median home value:	$179,900
Less than 18 yrs:	25.9%	German:	21.2%	Poverty:	9.2%
		Irish:	12.0%		
Education		English:	9.5%	**Military Veterans**	
H.S. grad:	91.7%			% of Pop:	9.6%
College grad:	42.4%				
Grad degree:	14.5%				

Though its central core is in Missouri, in 2006 about 40% of metropolitan Kansas City's residents lived west of the state line in Kansas. Some are in Kansas City, Kan., or KCK as it is sometimes called, where the low-lying land near the Missouri River used to house one of the nation's largest stockyards. This is still a working-class town with lots of modest frame houses, new Latino neighborhoods, a large African-American community and a Catholic ethnic neighborhood. Kansas City's Wyandotte County has lost

2008 Presidential Vote		
Obama (D) 186,962	(51%)
McCain (R)............................177,564	(48%)

2004 Presidential Vote		
Bush (R) 186,476	(55%)
Kerry (D)...............................150,598	(44%)

Cook Partisan Voting Index: R + 3

35,000 people since the 1970s, and is 27% black and 22% Hispanic. South of Kansas City and Wyandotte is Johnson County, which is much more affluent and more than three times the size of Wyandotte. The newer neighborhoods are arrayed along the interstates, as subdivisions have replaced croplands. They have grown to the point that Overland Park, Olathe, Shawnee and Lenexa are among the largest cities in the state. These suburbs are not just residential. The Applebee's restaurant chain is headquartered in Lenexa, and Sprint Nextel is headquartered in Overland Park. Politically, Wyandotte County has an old Democratic-machine style of politics, though its influence has been tempered by the consolidation of city and county governments. Johnson County has long been heavily Republican, but with plenty of moderate and even liberal voters on cultural issues. It has also been a battleground for the fierce fights between the moderate and conservative wings of the Kansas Republican Party, which sometimes benefits the Democrats.

The 3rd Congressional District of Kansas consists of Johnson County, Wyandotte County and a section of Douglas County to the west, including the portion of Lawrence that is home to the University of Kansas campus. Douglas County was the only one of Kansas's 105 counties to oppose a 2005 constitutional amendment banning same-sex marriage. The majority of the district residents live in Johnson County, which is expected to become the largest county in metropolitan Kansas City by 2023. This is an affluent metropolitan district in a historically rural state.

The congressman from the 3rd District is Dennis Moore, a Democrat first elected in 1998. Moore grew up in Wichita, where his father, Warner Moore, ran for Congress in the 4th District and lost narrowly in 1958. Moore went to college and law school in Kansas, served in the Army, then practiced law in Johnson County. In 1976, at age 31, he was elected Johnson County district attorney and was twice re-elected. He went into private law practice, and was elected to the local community-college board in 1993. Five years later, when national Democrats were recruiting a candidate to run against conservative Republican incumbent Vince Snowbarger, Moore's electoral success made him a natural choice. The contest attracted outside interest, with the Sierra Club and the AFL-CIO spending heavily on television ads, mailings and phone banks to help Moore. He won 52%-48%, carrying Kansas City and Lawrence by wide margins. But his key wins came in the affluent, long-settled suburbs in northeast Johnson County.

In the House, Moore has styled himself as tightfisted on spending, pro-business, and eager to overhaul entitlement programs and long-term fiscal problems. He is a prominent voice in the Blue Dog Coalition, moderate and conservative Democrats who have sought to move the party toward the center. Moore was the group's policy co-chairman in the 110th Congress (2007–08). In December 2007, he unsuccessfully urged the House to adhere to pay-as-you-go rules by offsetting the cost of proposed legislation to scale back the alternative minimum tax to prevent it from raising tax bills for millions of middle-income Americans. However, he supported the $787 billion economic-stimulus legislation that passed the House in February 2009, even though its enormous price tag was not offset.

To the dismay of organized labor, he voted for normalizing trade relations with China and for giving the president broad powers to negotiate new free-trade agreements. In 2005, he was one of 15 Democrats who bucked party leaders to vote in favor of the Central American Free Trade Agreement. He led the effort in 2004 and 2005 to raise the death benefit for military personnel killed since September 11.

After Democrats won control of Congress in 2006, Moore was among the lawmakers who voiced hope for a bipartisan response to the nation's fiscal problems. He was one of 28 House members to sign the "Bipartisan Compact on Iraq Debate," which advocated the redeployment of troops from Iraq without setting a firm deadline for withdrawal.

Republicans would love to recapture this seat, but have been hampered by the moderate-conservative split in the Kansas party. But Moore has had to fight to hold on to the seat. In 2000, Republicans slugged it out in the primary, a contest between tax-cutting state Rep. Phill Kline and Overland Park Councilman Greg Musil. Kline won the primary 50%-37%, but in the general election campaign, Moore appealed to moderates by portraying himself as a fiscal conservative and a crime fighter. He won 50%-47%. In 2002, the GOP primary was between candidates on either side of the abortion-rights issue. Moderate United Airlines pilot Adam Taff, who supported abortion rights, won 52%-48%. Moore defeated him in the general election 50%-47%. In 2004, Taff ran again in the primary, only to be defeated by the conservative in the race, Overland Park Councilman Kris Kobach, a former top aide to conservative Attorney General John Ashcroft. In the general election, Kobach sought to rally the party base, but Moore had his biggest win yet: 55%-43%. In 2006, national Republicans took a pass on the district.

In 2008, Republicans coalesced behind state Sen. Nick Jordan. Unlike Moore's previous opponents, Jordan avoided a costly primary fight and was able to unite the party and focus exclusively on beating Moore. He ran ads that claimed Moore, as a member of the House Financial Services Committee, did not do enough to prevent the 2008 financial-markets crisis. But Moore cruised to victory in the strong Democratic year, winning 56%-40%.

After the 2004 election, a Johnson County Republican activist remarked, "Maybe we have to wait for Dennis Moore to retire." But Moore is probably not secure enough to avoid another tough challenge down the road.

FOURTH DISTRICT

Todd Tiahrt (R)

Elected 1994, 8th term; b. June 15, 1951, Vermillion, SD; home, Goddard; SD Sch. of Mines, 1969–71; Evangel Col., B.A. 1975; SW MO St. U., M.B.A. 1989; Assembly of God; married (Vicki); 3 children.

Elected Office: KS Senate, 1992–94.

Professional Career: Project engineer, Zenith Corp., 1978–81; Proposal mgr., Boeing Co., 1981–94.

DC Office: 2441 RHOB, 20515, 202-225-6216; Fax: 202-225-3489; Web site: tiahrt.house.gov.

State Offices: Wichita, 316-262-8992.

Committees: *Appropriations* (7th of 23 R): Defense; Labor, HHS, Education & Related Agencies (RMM).

Group Ratings

	ADA	ACLU	AFS	LCV	ITIC	NTU	COC	ACU	CFG	FRC
2008	15	20	17	15	86	71	94	91	74	100
2007	15	—	9	5	—	68	90	96	80	—

National Journal Ratings

	2007 LIB	—	2007 CONS		2008 LIB	—	2008 CONS
Economic	24%	—	75%		27%	—	72%
Social	20%	—	79%		38%	—	62%
Foreign	0%	—	72%		16%	—	83%
Composite	20%	—	80%		27%	—	73%

Key Votes of the 110th Congress

1. Increase minimum wage	N	5. Share immigration data	Y	9. Withdraw troops 8/08	N
2. Expand SCHIP	N	6. Foreign aid abortion ban	Y	10. No operations in Iran	N
3. Raise CAFE standards	N	7. Ban gay bias in workplace	N	11. Free trade with Peru	Y
4. Bail out financial markets	N	8. Repeal D.C. gun law	Y	12. Overhaul FISA	*

Election Results

2008 general	Todd Tiahrt (R)	177,617	(63%)	($964,059)
	Donald Betts (D)	90,706	(32%)	($210,358)
	Susan Ducey (Ref)	6,441	(2%)	
2008 primary	Todd Tiahrt (R)	.... unopposed		

Prior Winning Percentages: 2006 (64%); 2004 (66%); 2002 (61%); 2000 (54%); 1998 (58%); 1996 (50%); 1994 (53%)

Population		Race/Ethnicity		Work	
Pop. 2007:	684,843	White:	78.8%	Private:	78.8%
Change since 2000:	Up 1.9%	Black:	6.7%	Government:	14.3%
Urban:	78.8%	Hispanic:	8.3%	Self-employed:	6.6%
Rural:	21.2%	Asian:	2.7%	Blue collar:	27.1%
Area size:	9,596 sq. mi.	Native Am.:	0.8%	White collar:	56.4%
		Hawaiian:	0.0%	Khaki collar:	0.3%
Age		Two+ races:	2.5%	Other:	16.1%
Median age:	36.1 yrs.			Median income:	$45,157
More than 65 yrs:	12.7%	*Ancestry*		Median home value:	$99,400
Less than 18 yrs:	26.5%	German:	23.0%	Poverty:	12.6%
		Irish:	10.4%		
Education		English:	9.7%	**Military Veterans**	
H.S. grad:	87.6%			% of Pop:	11.9%
College grad:	24.2%				
Grad degree:	8.0%				

With about 360,000 people, Wichita may be smaller than 2 million-plus metro Kansas City, but it is a Great Plains metropolis of the magnitude of Omaha or Tulsa and still growing. It began as a farm market town and grew with local oil and gas discoveries in the 1920s. But its real impetus came during World War II and the years just afterward, when aircraft factories sprouted up on the Kansas plains, and Wichita suddenly became the nation's major producer of small planes. Today the big four—

2008 Presidential Vote		
McCain (R)	166,674	(58%)
Obama (D)	113,412	(40%)
2004 Presidential Vote		
Bush (R)	173,643	(64%)
Kerry (D)	93,129	(34%)
Cook Partisan Voting Index:	R+14	

Cessna, Raytheon, Boeing, Bombardier—are all located in Wichita. In the early 1990s, the general aviation industry was hurt by the recession and by lawsuits that held manufacturers liable for planes they had produced years earlier. Later in the decade, the demand for small planes was robust, and a federal limit on liability enlivened the industry. The September 11 attacks were a severe blow to the airline industry, with the loss of some 15,000 jobs in Wichita. But the Navy gave the area a boost in 2004 with a contract for 100 modified 737's to be used to hunt submarines. And more good news came with the opening of Cessna's huge hangar center to service business jets and increased production of new Cessna planes. Boeing, the area's largest employer, sold its commercial airplane operations in Kansas, but its military division remained strong. The aviation industry is just one facet of the local economy: Wichita also has become a regional health-care center in the Great Plains, as people from miles around come to the metropolis for treatment.

Kansas' 4th Congressional District is centered around Wichita, covering wheat-growing areas to the east and west, but with most of its people in Wichita and Sedgwick County. Politically, it has voted Republican in federal elections but has voted Democratic occasionally in state contests. The city elected its first African-American mayor, Democrat Carl Brewer, in April 2007.

The congressman from the 4th District is Todd Tiahrt (*TEE-art*), a Republican first elected in 1994. He grew up on his family's farm in South Dakota and got a scholarship to play football for the South Dakota School of Mines and Technology. When a knee injury ended his athletic career, Tiahrt transferred to Evangel College in Springfield, Mo., run by his church, the Assemblies of God. In 1976, Tiahrt and his wife moved to the Wichita area to be closer to her family, and Tiahrt went to work at Zenith as a project engineer and then at Boeing as a contract manager on the Air Force One, the Comanche helicopter and several other military craft. In 1990, he ran for the Kansas House and lost by just eight votes. In 1992, he was elected to the Kansas Senate, where he pushed to enact a concealed-weapons law.

In 1994, Tiahrt decided to run against Democratic U.S. Rep. Dan Glickman, who had been in the House for 18 years. Tiahrt ran ads playing on President Bill Clinton's unpopularity in the district, showing Glickman's face morphing into Clinton's. He also attacked Glickman for voting for gun-control laws. With his base among Wichita's numerous religious conservatives, who had come to dominate the local Republican Party, Tiahrt assembled a corps of 1,800 volunteers, many from his church contacts. Glickman outspent him more than 3-to-1, but he suffered serious losses in middle-income areas in Sedgwick County. Tiahrt won a solid 53%-47% victory.

In the House, Tiahrt has a strongly conservative voting record and has wielded influence on the Appropriations Committee, particularly on its Defense Subcommittee. Since 2003, he has inserted an amendment into the appropriation bills that restricts access to information on gun sales that is collected by the Bureau of Alcohol, Tobacco, Firearms and Explosives. New York City Mayor Michael Bloomberg, the leader of the Mayors Against Illegal Guns coalition, voiced opposition to the amendment in 2007 and ran ads in Tiahrt's district that accused him of putting police officers in harm's way. Liberal Democratic Rep. Patrick Kennedy of Rhode Island attempted to weaken the data restrictions with an amendment of his own, but Democrats from rural areas joined Republicans to defeat the effort. Tiahrt's amendment passed the House Appropriations Committee once again in July 2007.

Tiahrt chairs the House Economic Competitiveness Caucus, which seeks to eliminate federal regulations with the goal of making U.S. businesses more competitive in global trade. He has also campaigned over the years to eliminate various government programs he finds unnecessary, including the public-service program AmeriCorps.

Tiahrt has also been active on issues pertinent to his district. He has sponsored measures that help aircraft manufacturers and supported the Air Force's proposal to buy KC-767 aerial refueling tankers from Boeing. In 2008, he vehemently criticized the Air Force's decision to award a contract for a new fleet of refueling tankers to Northrop Grumman and the European Aeronautic Defence and Space Company. He had lobbied for Boeing to get the contract, which had the potential to add hundreds of jobs in the Wichita area. The Air Force nullified its initial decision and reopened the contract to bidding after the U.S. Government Accountability Office found errors in the awarding process.

After the devastating suicide of his teenage son, Luke, in 2004, Tiahrt created a foundation to help troubled teens.

Tiahrt has been stymied in his various attempts over the years to move up the ladder in the House, and in 2009, he announced that he would run for the Senate seat being vacated by Republican Sam Brownback in 2010. Fellow Republican Rep. Jerry Moran also had plans to run in the GOP primary. In early 2006, Tiahrt was among several Republicans who wanted to run for party whip when Rep. Roy Blunt of Missouri campaigned for Majority Leader. But Blunt lost and remained in the whip's job. Later that year, senior members of the Republican Study Committee backed Tiahrt as the group's new chairman, but he lost to insurgent Jeb Hensarling of Texas, whose backers said that Tiahrt was too close to Republican leaders.

Democrats targeted Tiahrt during his early years with well-financed opponents, but he appears to be safe for now. In 2000, Wichita attorney and former Glickman aide Carlos Nolla ran a tougher-than-expected challenge, But Tiahrt won, 54%-42%. In a rematch two years later, Nolla doubled his fundraising with support from national Hispanics, but still lost, 61%-37%. Since then, Tiahrt's opponents have been poorly funded and gotten little attention.

★ KENTUCKY ★

Kentucky, the first state west of the Appalachian chain to be admitted to the union, in many ways remains close to its beginnings. This is, literally, a Jeffersonian commonwealth: It is one of four commonwealths—the others are Massachusetts, Pennsylvania, and Virginia—and when the first settlers came here, in the years when Thomas Jefferson was writing his *Notes on Virginia*, this region was part of that state. Kentucky was admitted to the union in 1792, when Jefferson was secretary of state. Aroused by the Federalists' anti-sedition acts, Jefferson ghostwrote the Kentucky Resolutions, a defense of self-governance by the states, in 1798. Kentucky's largest county is named after Jefferson, and its largest city after the monarch to whom he was credentialed as ambassador to France, Louis XVI. To this day, Kentucky has a constitution informed by a Jeffersonian suspicion of concentrating power. Its one-term limit on governors was raised to two only in 1995. It limited its state Legislature to one 60-day session every two years until 2001, so much important business was done in special sessions. Every governor must swear that he or she has not participated in a duel (remember what Jefferson thought of Aaron Burr). Kentucky long favored the Democratic Party, which can trace its ancestry at least tenuously back to Jefferson. But here too there has been change recently. The state voted for George W. Bush twice, after twice voting, by diminishing margins, for Bill Clinton. In 2008, Kentucky remained immune to the charms of Barack Obama, who campaigned scarcely at all here and lost both the Democratic primary and the general election by wide margins. Both of Kentucky's senators and four of its six House members are Republicans, but Democrats still have a lead in party registration. They recaptured the governorship in 2007 and hold a nearly 2-1 ratio in the state House.

The agrarian Jefferson would approve of Kentucky's current demography, which is still quite rural, with well under half the population living in the big metropolitan areas of Louisville, Lexington, and the Northern Kentucky counties across the Ohio River from Cincinnati. And the tobacco planters, who once presided over what one historian called "the alcoholic republic," might not entirely disapprove of a Kentucky economy that remained for years heavily dependent on such century-old industries as whiskey (Bourbon County is where the beverage was invented in the 18th century), tobacco (Kentucky has long been the nation's number No.2 producer after North Carolina), and coal. But change is coming. Kentucky has ranked No. 1 in percentage of smokers, but the Lexington Urban County Council voted a ban on smoking in public places. Employment is down sharply in the coal and tobacco industries, although Kentucky still has big plants producing appliances, Toyotas, Ford trucks, and Lexmark printers. The state is also home to Humana health services and Ashland Oil. Still, this is an economy that did not partake in much of the bounteous growth of the past two decades.

Many of the buildings here are old: the small-town 19th-century courthouses, the cabins in the coal-mining Appalachians, the unpainted houses in the soggy lowlands beneath the levees by the Mississippi River. Kentucky is the home of some of the nation's oldest traditions, from bourbon to bluegrass music to religious revivals; the Disciples of Christ got their start in the enormous revival at Cane Ridge in 1801. Mother's Day was invented here in 1887, and a Louisville restaurant claims credit for inventing the cheeseburger. Some things have changed. Satellite dishes and four-lane highways have brought modern civilization into hollows and lowland farms that lacked indoor plumbing and electricity within living memory, and farmers have begun to diversify their crops. Eastern Kentucky farmers raise goats for meat production, and the state touts its vineyards and fruit orchards. But Kentuckians still have a strong attachment to place and family. Kentucky's population grew just 42% over the past 50 years, while the nation's almost doubled. Few outsiders have moved in, so most of today's residents are descendants of settlers who poured over the mountains in the 40 years after Daniel Boone made his way through the Cumberland Gap in 1775.

Kentucky has seen hearty, though lopsided, political competition, with most of the 120 counties stilly voting today as they did in the Civil War era. The eastern mountains were pro-Union and remain Republican, except for counties where coal miners were organized by the United Mine Workers in the 1930s. The Bluegrass region and the western end of the state were slaveholding territory and voted Democratic. However, both regions are prone to shift for specific candidates: Coal-mining country voted against Obama in November 2008. Louisville, with many German immigrants, was an anti-slavery town, and for years flirted with Republicans, but Jefferson County, which includes Louisville, was conspicuously more Democratic in 2004 and 2008 than the state as a whole. For years, all of this meant Democratic Party control, with the real battles in the primary elections. For nearly half a century, there was almost a two-party system within the dominant party, with factions going back to the 1938 primary, when Senate Majority Leader (and later Vice President) Alben Barkley was challenged by Gov. A.B. (Happy) Chandler, who was later a U.S. senator and commissioner of baseball. Barkley's faction was later led by Gov. Bert Combs (1959–63) and Gov. Wendell Ford (1971–74). Since then, partisan competition has been sharper. Democrat Paul Patton was only narrowly elected governor in 1995, although he easily won re-election in 1999. In 2003, after the term-limited Patton was tarred by scandal, Republican Ernie Fletcher beat

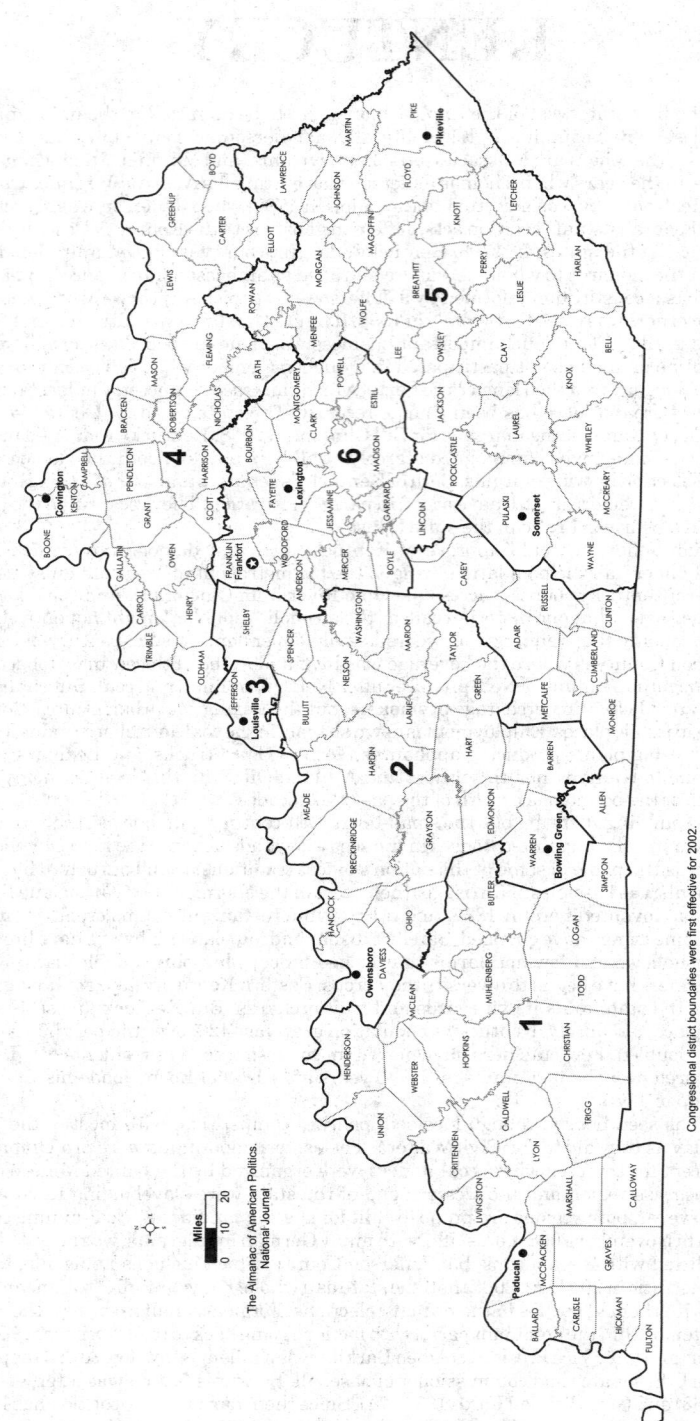

The Almanac of American Politics.
National Journal

Congressional district boundaries were first effective for 2002.

Population		Household Income		Work	
Pop. 2007:	4,205,648	Under $15k:	18.8%	Private:	77.5%
State rank:	26th of 50	$15k to $50k:	41.0%	Government:	15.7%
Change since 2000:	Up 4.1%	$50k to $100k:	28.4%	Self-employed:	6.5%
Urban:	55.0%	$100k to $150k:	10.1%	Unemployment (3-yr. average):	4.3%
Rural:	45.0%	Over $150k:	1.7%	Poverty:	17.1%
Native of state:	71.6%	Median income:	$40,138	Blue collar:	27.6%
Not a citizen:	1.7%	**Home Value**		White collar:	55.6%
Area size:	40,409 sq. mi.	Under $100k:	45.2%	Khaki collar:	0.4%
Most populous cities		$100k to $300k:	47.5%	Other:	16.4%
1. Louisville	560,454	$300k to $500k:	5.3%	**Age**	
2. Lexington	275,726	$500k to $1 mil:	1.6%	Median age:	37.3 yrs.
3. Bowling Green	53,463	Over $1 million:	0.4%	More than 65 yrs:	12.8%
4. Owensboro	53,408	Median:	$109,700	Less than 18 yrs:	23.9%

Race/Ethnicity		Language		Military Veterans		Registered Voters in 2008	
White:	88.1%	*Language*		% of Pop:	10.6%	D:	1,662,093 (57.2%)
Black:	7.5%	English:	95.8%	*Veterans by Period*		R:	1,053,871 (36.3%)
Hispanic:	2.1%	Spanish:	2.1%	WWII and before:	11.3%	Other:	190,845 (6.6%)
Asian:	0.9%	Asian:	0.6%	Korea:	11.1%	Voter turnout:	1,826,508
Native Am.:	0.2%	Other		Vietnam:	32.2%	Turnout as % of	
Hawaiian:	0.1%	European	1.2%	Gulf (pre-2001):	11.6%	voting age:	56.0%
Two+ races:	1.1%	**Education**		Gulf (post-2001):	7.4%	**Legislature**	
Ancestry		H.S. grad:	79.3%	Peace time:	26.3%	Senate:	15 D 22 R 1 I
USA:	17.0%	College grad:	19.7%			House:	65 D 35 R
German:	13.6%	Grad degree:	8.0%				
Irish:	11.5%						

Attorney General Ben Chandler, the grandson of Happy Chandler. Fletcher, himself touched by scandal, lost 59%-41% to Democrat Steve Beshear in 2007. Republicans won the offices of secretary of state and agriculture commissioner; Democrats won the offices of attorney general, treasurer, and auditor.

The change has been most pronounced in congressional elections. Much of this has been the work of Sen. Mitch McConnell, first elected in 1984 and now the Republican leader in the Senate. McConnell helped line up candidates who carried three formerly Democratic congressional districts in 1994 and 1996; he provided key support for Sen. Jim Bunning's 6,766-vote win in 1998 and his 22,652-vote win in 2004. In July and August 1999, party switches gave Republicans a 20-18 margin in the state Senate, where they had been outnumbered 30-8 in 1990. More recently, there has been a shift in the other direction. Chandler, after losing to Fletcher in 2003, won a House seat in a 2004 special election, and in 2006, Democrat John Yarmuth ousted Republican Anne Northup in the Jefferson County seat. McConnell himself was put on the defensive when health care executive Bruce Lunsford challenged him in 2008, but McConnell held on. Down the ballot, Republicans held their 4-2 edge in Kentucky's congressional delegation and their 22-15-1 margin in the state Senate, while Democrats failed to add to their 65-35 majority in the state House.

Presidential politics For many years, Kentucky was a competitive state when Democrats ran a Southerner or two on their ticket, as in such widely separated years as 1952, 1976, 1980, 1992, and 1996. In 2000, Al Gore initially targeted Kentucky, which is just north of his home state of Tennessee and which the Clinton-Gore ticket carried twice. But Kentucky was part of the rural trend away from Clinton Democrats and toward Republicans in the 1990s, and Gore had taken stands seen as hostile to the state's leading industries—tobacco, coal, and automobiles. Bush swept the state, 57%-41%. In 2004, Kentucky was never on anyone's list of battleground states, and Bush won 60%-40%. He lost Jefferson County 50%-49%, but carried 108 of the 119 other counties. John Kerry carried just Jefferson and 11 counties in the eastern mountains.

In the 2008 presidential election, Kentucky was a battleground state of sorts—not a target state but something in the nature of a killing field for the otherwise spectacularly successful Barack Obama.

2008 Presidential Vote
McCain (R) 1,048,462 (57%)
Obama (D) 751,985 (41%)

2008 Democratic Presidential Primary
Clinton (D) 459,511 (65%)
Obama (D) 209,954 (30%)

2008 Republican Presidential Primary
McCain (R) 142,918 (72%)
Huckabee (R) 16,388 (8%)
Paul (R) 13,427 (7%)

2004 Presidential Vote
Bush (R) 1,069,439 (60%)
Kerry (D) 712,733 (40%)

The state's May primary had not been critical in living memory, but the Democratic race was still undecided at that point, and Kentucky, voting on May 20, was coming on strong for Hillary Rodham Clinton.

As early as February 12, when the Virginia primary returns came in, it was apparent that Clinton was very strong or Obama was very weak—or both—in the great Appalachian chain settled by Scots-Irish who streamed southwest and over the mountains in the 18th and 19th centuries. These are fighting peoples, as Virginia Sen. Jim Webb has memorialized in his book *Born Fighting*, and they were the constituency least attracted to Obama in the primaries and most inclined to abandon him in the general election. Democratic registration in Kentucky spiked upward before the primary, but this did not benefit Obama as similar trends did in other states.

Clinton campaigned hard in the state, while Obama made only one appearance after August 2007, in the week before the primary. Clinton's ads portrayed her as a fighter for the people; Obama ran a few ads stressing his Christian faith—a response, perhaps, to polls that showed his long association with the controversial Rev. Jeremiah Wright hurting him with Kentucky voters. Clinton beat Obama 65%-30%. He carried Louisville's Jefferson County and Lexington's Fayette County, and lost the other 118 counties; in 19 counties he won less than 10% of the vote. Twenty percent of voters said that race was important in their vote, and 80% of those voters went for Clinton. But Obama, with his professorial demeanor and his promise to sit down without preconditions with the leaders of enemy states, was also out of sync with the martial traditions of the Scots-Irish Andrew Jackson and the Kentucky war hawk Henry Clay. Kentucky turned out to be Obama's third-weakest primary state, after Arkansas and West Virginia.

Obama did not target Kentucky in the general election; the state has a much smaller black population than either Virginia or North Carolina, which he targeted successfully, and fewer upscale whites than Indiana, which he also targeted successfully. An increase in Democratic registration did not help Obama. The exit poll showed that he won only 69% of the vote from self-identified Democrats, far lower than in almost any other state. Without much effort, John McCain carried Kentucky 57%-41%, the same as George W. Bush's victory in 2000. Of those who said they favored Clinton for the Democratic nomination, only 54% voted for Obama; 45% voted for McCain. Obama increased the Democratic percentage by 5% in Jefferson and Fayette counties and in Northern Kentucky, but he ran behind John Kerry's 2004 percentage in 63 of 120 counties. Those losses came in the Appalachian coal-mining counties in the east and south-central portions of the state, and in the far western area known historically as the Jackson Purchase. He carried only eight counties altogether—fewer in the Appalachian region than George McGovern carried in 1972—and made gains over previous Democratic showings in a few counties where it appears that the Obama campaign did some outreach to African-Americans. The exit poll showed that he carried young voters by only a 51%-48% margin and those with postgraduate degrees by just 52%-48%.

Congressional districting

111th Congress Lineup	
4 R	2 D
110th Congress Lineup	
4 R	2 D

Kentucky's 1991 redistricting plan, drawn by Democrats after the state lost one U.S. House seat in the 1990 census, was intended to protect Democratic incumbents but instead produced a delegation that was 5-1 Republican by 1996. Party control of the state Legislature in 2001 was split. House Democrats prepared a plan that would have made re-election more difficult for Republican Rep. Ed Whitfield, while state Senate Republicans backed a plan to add heavily Republican Oldham County to the 3rd District to strengthen Rep. Anne Northup. The impasse continued through January 2002, delaying the January 29 filing deadline for candidates. On February 1, the Legislature finally adopted a compromise plan that changed the lines very little, with one important exception: It removed increasingly Republican suburban Shelby County from the 4th District and added three and a half traditionally Democratic counties.

Kentucky is expected to keep all of its House seats in the reapportionment following the 2010 census. And if neither party has control of the process, the likely result is only a minor alteration of district boundaries.

Governor

Steve Beshear (D)

Elected 2007, term expires Jan. 2012, 1st term; b. Sept. 21, 1944, Dawson Springs; home, Lexington; U. of KY, B.A., 1966, U. of KY, J.D., 1968; Baptist; married (Jane); 2 children.

Military Career: U.S. Army Reserves, 1969–75.

Elected Office: KY Gen. Assembly, 1974–79, KY atty. gen., 1980–84, Lt. gov., 1984–88.

Professional Career: Attorney, 1968–71, 1989–2006.

Office: State Capitol, 700 Capitol Ave., Frankfort, 40601, 502-564-2611; Fax: 502-564-2517; Web site: gov.state.ky.us.

Election Results

2007 general	Steve Beshear (D)	619,552	(59%)
	Ernie Fletcher (R)	435,773	(41%)
2007 primary	Steve Beshear (D)	142,838	(41%)
	Bruce Lunsford (D)	74,578	(21%)
	Steve Henry (D)	60,893	(18%)
	Jody Richards (D)	45,433	(13%)
	Gatewood Galbraith (D)	20,704	(6%)

Kentucky's governor is Democrat Steve Beshear, elected in November 2007. The governor wields extraordinary authority in Kentucky, including broad appointment powers. Until the passage of a constitutional amendment in 2000, the Legislature met in regular session for only 60 days in even-numbered years. Beginning in 2001, it began meeting for 30 days in odd-numbered years as well. But the governor retains the power to shift around line items in the state budget and to call special sessions. Beshear defeated Republican Gov. Ernie Fletcher, whose administration was mired in a political hiring scandal.

The son and grandson of Baptist ministers, Beshear grew up in Dawson Springs, a small western Kentucky town with a population of less than 3,000. He has strong ties to the city—his father was also a funeral director and served as mayor. Valedictorian of his high school class, Beshear was able to attend the University of Kentucky thanks to a second mortgage on the family's home. He was elected student body president in his junior year and went on to earn a law degree from the school, graduating with honors. In a moot court national competition in New York City, Beshear impressed the judges with a skillful performance, and he was invited to interview with two international law firms. Offered a job by both, Beshear accepted a position with the Wall Street firm White & Case, and during that time, he joined an Army Reserve unit in the Bronx, serving as an intelligence analyst. But after three years in the Big Apple, Beshear was ready to return home to the Bluegrass State. He and his wife, Jane, whom he had met in college, settled in Lexington, where he took a job with a smaller firm. In 1973, he launched his first campaign for state representative to succeed a retiring member. Winning easily, Beshear went on to serve three terms in Frankfort, where he gained a reputation for supporting proposals to stimulate job growth and attract businesses to the state. But he was also in the minority among his peers for his support of abortion rights and his opposition to measures to stop school integration.

In 1979, Beshear made his first successful bid for statewide office, winning a race for attorney general at age 34. During his term, he took several stands that were unpopular in the conservative state. In 1982, he declared that a state law restricting abortion was unconstitutional. Then he announced that his interpretation of a U.S. Supreme Court decision meant that copies of the Ten Commandments had to be removed from Kentucky classrooms. His decision prompted thousands of calls to the governor's office and letters to newspapers. A billboard that said "Keep The 10 Commandments, Remove Steve Beshear" appeared in Lexington. In 1983, then-Lt. Gov. Martha Layne Collins captured the Democratic nomination for governor and selected Beshear as her running mate. The two defeated the Republican challenger, Jim Bunning (now a U.S. senator), by 10 points and more than 100,000 votes, making Collins the first and only female governor in the commonwealth's history. As the state's second-highest official, Beshear was responsible for overseeing the Kentucky Tomorrow Commission, which the Louisville *Courier-Journal* described as "an expansive, think-tank-style study of the state's direction" that brought together business, academic, and civic leaders.

In 1987, Beshear sought his party's nomination for governor. But the primary drew two other high-profile choices: KFC millionaire and former Gov. John Brown and wealthy bookstore businessman Wallace Wilkinson. Dwarfed by their ability to self-fund their campaigns, Beshear began attacking Brown, the better known of the two, for his high-stakes gambling. The strategy backfired, however, and the attacks ended up benefiting Wilkinson, who won the primary with 35% of the vote. Brown came in second with 25%, and Beshear finished a distant third with 18%. In 1996, Beshear challenged Republican Sen. Mitch McConnell, who was seeking a third term. McConnell had more than a 2-to-1 fundraising advantage and won handily, 55%-43%. Following his second loss, Beshear left public life and went back to private law practice in Lexington, working with business and community banking interests. While Democrats had once been the majority party in the state, by the mid-1990s, the congressional delegation and state offices were shifting toward Republicans, helped by the aggressive efforts of McConnell.

But in 2006, a different wave of change had begun, both across the Bluegrass State and across the nation. In the Democratic takeover of Congress, John Yarmuth had defeated GOP Rep. Anne Northup, a perennial Democratic target, in the state's 3rd District. In the 2nd District, GOP Rep. Ron Lewis also faced a credible Democratic challenger in conservative state Rep. Mike Weaver, though Lewis eventually won by a 10-point margin. In the race for the Governor's Mansion, always held in odd-numbered years, the time seemed ripe for Democrats to defeat Fletcher. His administration was tainted by a 15-month investigation into political patronage, and he faced possible indictment. A former Fletcher supporter and state Cabinet official turned over to investigators copies of e-mails and documents that included a list of civil service workers to be fired or transferred. The investigation also revealed the existence of a dozen officials called the "Disciples," who were tasked with replacing Democrats in state government. In May

2006, a grand jury indicted Fletcher on misdemeanor charges of criminal conspiracy, official misconduct, and political discrimination. But in August 2006, before the case went to trial, a judge ruled that Fletcher had immunity from prosecution for official acts and could not be tried unless he was out of office or impeached, which was unlikely even though Democrats controlled the Legislature. The case was settled, and Fletcher was cleared of the charges. But politically, he was still in deep trouble. His approval ratings had sunk below 30%, and a majority of voters supported his resignation. Republicans tried to use the scandal as evidence that Fletcher was unelectable, but he beat back primary challenges from Northup and his former finance chairman, Billy Harper, to win by 13 points.

In seeking the Democratic nomination to take on Fletcher, Beshear called for expanded gambling in the state, supporting a constitutional amendment that would bring casinos to Kentucky. Citing the huge sums Kentuckians were already spending at casinos across the border in Illinois, Indiana, and West Virginia, Beshear argued that legalized gambling could provide money for education reform and expanded health care. He won the May 2007 primary relatively easily, 41%-21%, beating hospital executive Bruce Lunsford and narrowly avoiding a runoff. In the five months leading up to the general election, Fletcher condemned Beshear's gambling proposal in an attempt to rally social conservatives to his side. He also emphasized Beshear's past support of abortion rights and his position on displaying the Ten Commandments in schools. But he was shadowed by the ethics controversy, and Beshear won, 59%-41%.

As governor, Beshear pressed to put his casino proposal before the voters, but the Legislature was slow to move. He also made waves among lawmakers for vetoing their $3.8 billion, two-year highway-improvement plan. Senate President David Williams, a Republican, said that the bill would fund needed road projects and bridges throughout the state and that Beshear's veto was unconstitutional because it was executed the day after the last legal day for issuing vetoes in the legislative session. Beshear argued that the Legislature's bill limited the Transportation Department's authority. In May 2008, Williams filed a lawsuit against Beshear, alleging that his veto was invalid and challenging the governor's alternative infrastructure plan. Beshear hired his former law firm, Stites & Harbison, to represent him.

Senior Senator

Mitch McConnell (R)

Elected 1984, term expires 2014, 5th term; b. Feb. 20, 1942, Sheffield, AL; home, Louisville; U. of Louisville, B.A. 1964, U. of KY, J.D. 1967; Baptist; married (Elaine Chao); 3 children.

Elected Office: Jefferson Cnty. judge exec., 1978–85.

Professional Career: Chief legis. asst., U.S. Sen. Marlow Cook, 1968–70; Dpty. asst. U.S. atty. gen., 1974–75.

DC Office: 361-A RSOB, 20510, 202-224-2541; Fax: 202-224-2499; Web site: mcconnell.senate.gov.

State Offices: Bowling Green, 270-781-1673; Ft. Wright, 859-578-0188; Lexington, 859-224-8286; London, 606-864-2026; Louisville, 502-582-6304; Paducah, 270-442-4554.

Committees: *Minority Leader. Agriculture, Nutrition & Forestry* (4th of 8 R). *Appropriations* (3rd of 12 R): Agriculture, Rural Development, Food and Drug Administration & Related Agencies; Commerce, Justice, Science & Related Agencies; Defense; Energy & Water Development; Military Construction, Veterans Affairs & Related Agencies; State, Foreign Operations & Related Programs. *Rules & Administration* (2nd of 8 R).

Group Ratings

	ADA	ACLU	AFS	LCV	ITIC	NTU	COC	ACU	CFG	FRC
2008	20	14	11	9	100	55	100	80	67	100
2007	10	—	0	7	—	77	82	92	84	—

National Journal Ratings

	2007 LIB	—	2007 CONS		2008 LIB	—	2008 CONS
Economic	3%	—	95%		14%	—	84%
Social	0%	—	91%		0%	—	79%
Foreign	30%	—	66%		16%	—	79%
Composite	14%	—	87%		15%	—	85%

Key Votes of the 110th Congress

1. Raise CAFE standards	N	5. Make English official language Y	9. Withdraw troops 3/08	N
2. Expand SCHIP	N	6. Path to citizenship N	10. Iran guard is terrorist group	Y
3. Cap greenhouse gases	N	7. Fetus is unborn child Y	11. Increase missile defense $	Y
4. Bail out financial markets	Y	8. Prosecute hate crimes N	12. Overhaul FISA	Y

Election Results

2008 general	Mitch McConnell (R)...953,816	(53%)	($21,306,296)
	Bruce Lunsford (D) 847,005	(47%)	($10,801,203)
2008 primary	Mitch McConnell (R)...168,127	(86%)	
	Daniel Essek (R) 27,170	(14%)	

Prior Winning Percentages: 2002 (65%); 1996 (55%); 1990 (52%); 1984 (50%)

Mitch McConnell is the Senate minority leader, making him the most powerful Republican in the Senate. First elected in 1984, he is known as a tough, thick-skinned leader who does not shrink from a fight. McConnell grew up in Alabama, where he overcame polio, and at age 13, moved to Louisville. He has been in politics for most of his adult life. Between college and law school at the University of Louisville, he was an intern for Republican Sen. John Sherman Cooper of Kentucky. Soon after graduating from law school, he became chief legislative assistant to Republican Sen. Marlow Cook of Kentucky. He served in the Ford administration Justice Department and then moved back to Louisville. In 1977, at age 35, McConnell won the office that had been Cook's political stepping-stone, Jefferson County judge-executive. In 1981, he was re-elected, and in 1984, he ran for the Senate against incumbent Democrat Walter ("Dee") Huddleston. McConnell ran a clever ad showing bloodhounds sniffing for Huddleston in vacation locales where Huddleston had collected fees for speeches while the Senate was in session. McConnell won by 5,169 votes out of 1.2 million cast. Part of a Washington power couple, he is married to former Bush administration Labor Secretary Elaine Chao.

McConnell began his Senate career with a seat on the Foreign Relations Committee. In 1992, he won a seat on the powerful Appropriations Committee and then moved up to become chairman of the Foreign Operations Subcommittee. In that role, he has worked since the early 1990s in opposing Burmese dictators who imprisoned Nobel Prize winner Aung San Suu Ki. With Democrat Dianne Feinstein of California, he sponsored bills imposing trade sanctions on the regime. McConnell has long been a strong supporter of Israel and an advocate for human rights in Cambodia, Egypt, and other nations. He frequently used his seat on Appropriations to channel aid to his home state, and he was particularly active on issues affecting the tobacco industry. In 2003, he forged an agreement for a buyout of tobacco quotas from farmers with the trade-off that the industry accept some Food and Drug Administration oversight of tobacco. In 2004, the Senate voted to add the buyout and FDA regulation to a must-pass corporate tax bill. But GOP conservatives in the House balked at FDA regulation, and in October 2004, the Senate backed the tobacco buyout without it, passing the corporate tax bill 69-17.

Another major area of interest for McConnell has been campaign finance law. He has been the Senate's leading opponent in recent years of efforts to curb political action committees and soft money, the large, unregulated contributions to political parties. He believes such restrictions are unconstitutional infringements of free speech. In October 1999, with more than 40 senators on his side, he killed a version of the McCain-Feingold campaign finance bill, the major reform bill of its day. In early 2001, Republican Sen. John McCain of Arizona brought the bill forward again, and despite McConnell's efforts, it passed. But it excluded many provisions from previous McCain-Feingold bills, including public subsidies for candidates and voluntary spending limits. McCain's bill was also amended with a provision to double the limit on individual contributions, which McConnell supported. When he was challenged about the potential inconsistency between his opposition to campaign finance regulation and his vote for amending the Constitution to allow the banning of flag-burning, another form of free expression, McConnell switched his position and became one of the few Republicans to consistently vote against measures to ban the burning of the American flag.

After the campaign finance law was enacted, McConnell filed a lawsuit challenging its constitutionality. In May 2003, a deeply divided three-judge federal court issued a 1,700-page opinion upholding some provisions of the law but not others. In December 2003, the U.S. Supreme Court upheld almost all of the legislation. "There won't be any less speech or money spent. Dramatically more will be spent, just in a different way," McConnell predicted, and warned that unregulated fundraising groups called 527s would raise and spend huge amounts of money, as indeed they did in the 2004 cycle. "You must have money in politics because it's the only way the candidates can get their message across," he said.

In 1990, McConnell began his quest to climb the leadership ladder. He ran for chairman of the National Republican Senatorial Committee, but lost to Texas Sen. Phil Gramm. He tried again in 1996 and won. But he was unable to get Republican senators to contribute as much to the campaigns of fellow Republicans as the Democrats gave to the campaigns of their fellow party members, and the GOP gained no seats in 1998. In the 2000 season, he had even tougher sledding. Republicans lost most of the close contests around the country, and the outcome was a 50-50 split that put Democrats in position to gain a majority a few months later, when Vermont's Jim Jeffords left the Republican Party in May 2001 to become an independent loosely affiliated with the Democrats.

In 2002, GOP Whip Don Nickles of Oklahoma stepped down from that position. McConnell campaigned for months among colleagues, and his only opponent, Larry Craig of Idaho, dropped out several days before the contest. Then in December, Republican Leader Trent Lott of Mississippi came under a storm of criticism when he spoke favorably of South Carolina Sen. Strom Thurmond's segregationist campaign for president in 1948 at an event honoring Thurmond on his 100th birthday. McConnell was Lott's strongest public defender, threatening retaliation against Democrats if they moved to censure Lott. But on December 20, as the controversy showed no sign of abating, he privately recommended to Lott that he "step down as soon as possible." Ordinarily, McConnell might have been in line for the leader's position as a result, but he did not challenge Tennessee's Bill Frist when Frist stepped up to fill the leadership void. Frist replaced Lott as Senate majority leader, and McConnell became whip and a key adviser to Frist, who was relatively unversed in Senate procedures. While others complained about heightened divisiveness in Congress, McConnell declined to join the lament. "I'm amazed at all the hand-wringing over the level of discourse and partisanship. It leads me to believe that nobody has read any history. The level of divisiveness now is really quite mild when it's compared with numerous periods in our history," McConnell said.

He showed considerable mastery of Senate rules and, anticipating Frist's plan to retire in 2006, ran for majority leader. It was a behind-the-scenes campaign, as described by his ally, Republican Robert Bennett of Utah. "Brick by brick, he built a firewall. So whenever somebody decided they wanted to run, all we had to do was sit down and say to them, 'This is what you're going to have to deal with.' One by one potential opponents said, 'Wait a minute, I don't want to run and lose,' " Bennett told the Associated Press. The election was a big disappointment for Republicans, who lost majority control of the Senate. As a result, McConnell became minority leader rather than majority leader, winning without opposition. Making a comeback in leadership, Lott narrowly beat Tennessee's Lamar Alexander for minority whip. "There will be nothing here [the Democrats] can do without some degree of cooperation from a very robust 49-vote minority," McConnell told the *New York Times* soon after the 2006 election. "The question is, Are you going to work together and try to do good things for the country or not?"

There was some bipartisan cooperation at first. Appropriations bills left over from the previous Congress were passed in early 2007, and agreement on a minimum-wage increase was reached after Democrats agreed to Republicans' demand for tax cuts for small businesses. But, predictably, harmony did not last long. In February, Senate Majority Leader Harry Reid introduced a resolution, supported by some Republicans, opposing President George W. Bush's strategy for a "troop surge" in Iraq. McConnell announced that he would block debate on Reid's resolution unless Republicans got votes on their resolutions opposing the cutoff of funds for the troops and setting 11 goals for the Iraqi government. On this, as on other issues throughout the next two years, McConnell was able to hold 41 or more Republicans together to get Reid to meet their demands. Republicans conducted a record number of filibusters during the 110th Congress (2007–08). McConnell observed that he lived by "an 80/20 rule." He spent 80% of his time trying to coax 20% of Republican senators to stick with the party.

On the issue of Iraq, he certainly succeeded. In June and July 2007, Democrats tried to put a timetable for withdrawing U.S. troops from Iraq in the defense bill. Even though Republicans admitted to doubts about the war, McConnell was able to hold a sufficient number of Republicans together to prevent passage of a timetable for troop withdrawals or a funding cutoff. Democrats were outraged, but it was an impressive legislative performance. By September, when signs of success in Bush's troop surge were starting to emerge, McConnell took the offensive and demanded that Democrats apologize after the liberal website MoveOn.org ran a newspaper ad attacking Gen. David Petraeus, the U.S. commander in Iraq, as "General Betray-Us." By December 2007, Democrats had abandoned their drive for withdrawal timetables and funding cutoffs.

On one issue, immigration, McConnell faced a deeply divided Republican Conference. He supported the attempts of Arizona Republican Jon Kyl to fashion a comprehensive bill that included a guest-worker program and a legalization process for illegal immigrants currently in the country. But most Republicans opposed the bill. It failed to survive a vote to end a filibuster against it, and an alternative was offered later in June. McConnell, recognizing its unpopularity in Kentucky (a state with a very small immigrant population), this time opposed it. On another issue, the Democrats' proposed expansion of the State Children's Health Insurance Program had the support of many Republicans. McConnell opposed it, but it passed and then was vetoed by Bush. McConnell warned the administration that if the president vetoed the farm bill, he would be overridden; the final version included a provision allowing racehorses to be depreciated in only three years—a matter of considerable interest in the Bluegrass country.

In December 2007 maneuverings on the budget, McConnell insisted Democrats hold down spending to the levels proposed by the Bush administration and to provide funding for the Iraq war without strings attached, and he prevailed. He forced the Democrats to back down on a tax increase they wanted to pay for an adjustment in the alternative minimum tax to prevent the tax from hitting middle-income tax payers. So-called "pay-as-you-go" rules embraced by both parties require that any spending increases or tax decreases be offset by tax and spending adjustments elsewhere in the budget. He opposed a bill by Virginia Republican John Warner and Connecticut independent Democrat Sen. Joe Lieberman to regulate reductions in carbon emissions on the grounds that it would impose "a stealth and giant tax on virtually every aspect of industrial consumer life."

Still, McConnell worked on a bipartisan basis on some issues. He cut an early deal with Reid that paved the way for Senate passage of the $700 billion financial industry bailout requested by the Bush administration in fall 2008. He also supported the loan package for the Detroit Three automakers. General Motors and Ford as well as Toyota have big plants in Kentucky. But bipartisanship did not survive the new Obama administration's introduction of a massive economic stimulus bill in Congress. The Senate approved the $787 billion bill 61-37 with only three moderate Republicans voting in favor of it. Speaking to the Conservative Political Action Conference in early 2009, McConnell veered sharply from the bipartisan script when he compared Obama's economic policies to those of socialist governments in Europe, citing in particular the stimulus bill and Obama's plan to expand government's role in health care. "Pushing back these efforts to basically Europeanize America will not be easy," McConnell said.

He also astutely found ways to maximize the minority's influence on committees. He appointed some of the party's most skillful senators to key panels: Michael Enzi of Wyoming, an expert in health care policy, and John Cornyn of Texas were given seats on the Finance Committee. Budget hawk George Voinovich of Ohio was assigned to the Appropriations Committee, and Lisa Murkowski of Alaska became the ranking Republican on Energy and Natural Resources. But he suffered a serious setback when Arlen Specter of Pennsylvania announced in late April 2009 that he would switch parties and join the Democrats, which gave the Democrats nearly a filibuster-proof majority of 59 (with the possibility of 60 if Democrat Al Franken was named the victor in the contested Minnesota Senate race, which he was in July 2009). However, McConnell got less of the blame for the defection than did staunch conservatives in the GOP caucus who have often picked fights with moderates such as Specter.

McConnell has never had an easy time of it in his re-election bids, and 2008 was no exception. Since 1984, he had won re-election three times, but always after spirited competition, from former Louisville Mayor Harvey Sloane in 1990; from now-Gov. Steve Beshear in 1996; and from Lois Combs Weinberg, daughter of former Gov. Bert Combs, in 2002. Sloane and Beshear held McConnell to 52% and 55% of the vote, respectively, although he did much better against Weinberg, winning 65%-35% and carrying 113 of 120 counties. He lost only a few Democratic strongholds in the eastern mountains. But in 2008, Democrats, still smarting from former Democratic Majority Leader Tom Daschle's defeat in 2004, were determined to put up a tough opponent against McConnell. They found Bruce Lunsford, a hospital and nursing home operator and multimillionaire who ran for governor in 2007 but lost the Democratic primary to Beshear. Lunsford spent some $10.8 million, more than $7 million of it his own money, and ran a string of negative ads against McConnell, including one showing dogs chasing the senator—a takeoff on McConnell's 1984 bloodhound ads—and another criticizing McConnell for supporting the financial industry bailout.

McConnell seemed unfazed by the political peril. He raised $20.9 million from 2003 to 2008 and ultimately spent $21.3 million. He started running ads immediately after the November 2007 state elections, comparing himself to Kentucky's long-serving Democratic Sen. Alben Barkley, who was Senate majority leader and later Harry Truman's vice president, and reminding voters of the money and projects his clout had made possible for the state. In the last two weeks of the campaign, he embarked on a 4,000-mile statewide bus tour with 62 stops in 55 counties. On November 1, just before the election, he announced that the Veterans Affairs Department had approved $75 million for a veterans hospital in Louisville.

McConnell won 53%-47%. In contrast, Republican presidential candidate McCain won 57% of the vote in Kentucky. McConnell lost the state's two largest urban counties, Jefferson and Fayette, where the Louisville and Lexington newspapers have long written unfavorable articles and editorials about him. He also lost some traditionally Democratic counties in the eastern mountains and in the western part of the state. He won 13% among African-Americans, more than McCain, and 44% among voters under 30. McConnell won 24% of Democrats and 58% of independents. Interestingly, given his yeoman's work to prevent Bush's troop surge from being undermined by a timetable for withdrawal, he won 57% among voters for whom Iraq was the most important issue.

His victory made McConnell the longest-serving senator in Kentucky history. Looking ahead after the election, he said, "It will be different with a different party in the White House. I'll be playing a different role. And how that will all play out lies in the future." When it appeared that Democrats might deprive Lieberman of his committee chairmanship, McConnell sounded him out about joining the Republicans.

McConnell has done much to build up Kentucky's long ailing Republican Party. In 1994, he helped Ed Whitfield pick up the 1st District House seat and helped Republican legislative candidates win in western Kentucky. He backed Anne Northup in her win in the Louisville-based 3rd District in 1996, and he helped rescue Sen. Jim Bunning's re-election campaign in 2004. He helped to persuade two Democratic state senators to switch parties in July and August 1999, which gave Republicans a 20-18 margin in the state Senate, and he has helped them hold that majority ever since. In 2003, McConnell backed the gubernatorial candidacy of Ernie Fletcher, who beat Democrat Ben Chandler 55%-45%. But that was McConnell's high-water mark. Chandler won Fletcher's House seat in a special election, and in 2006, Northup was defeated for re-election. Fletcher earned low job-approval ratings, and he lost his re-election bid to Democrat Beshear by a wide margin.

Junior Senator

Jim Bunning (R)

Elected 1998, term expires 2010, 2nd term; b. Oct. 23, 1931, Campbell Cnty.; home, Southgate; Xavier U., B.S. 1953; Catholic; married (Mary); 9 children.

Elected Office: Ft. Thomas City Cncl., 1977–79; KY Senate, 1979–83; U.S. House of Reps., 1986–98.

Professional Career: Pro baseball player, 1950–71; Investment broker & agent, 1960–86.

DC Office: 316 HSOB, 20510, 202-224-4343; Fax: 202-228-1373; Web site: bunning.senate.gov.

State Offices: Ft. Wright, 859-341-2602; Hazard, 606-435-2390; Hopkinsville, 270-885-1212; Lexington, 859-219-2239; Louisville, 502-582-5341; Owensboro, 270-689-9085.

Committees: *Banking, Housing & Urban Affairs* (3rd of 10 R): Financial Institutions; Securities, Insurance & Investment (RMM). *Budget* (5th of 10 R). *Energy & Natural Resources* (8th of 10 R): Energy; National Parks; Water & Power. *Finance* (5th of 10 R): Energy, Natural Resources & Infrastructure (RMM); Health Care; International Trade, Customs & Global Competitiveness.

Group Ratings

	ADA	ACLU	AFS	LCV	ITIC	NTU	COC	ACU	CFG	FRC
2008	5	23	0	18	80	79	75	88	93	100
2007	10	—	0	7	—	81	80	92	82	—

National Journal Ratings

	2007 LIB	—	2007 CONS	2008 LIB	—	2008 CONS
Economic	5%	—	94%	10%	—	89%
Social	21%	—	78%	0%	—	79%
Foreign	0%	—	93%	0%	—	84%
Composite	10%	—	90%	10%	—	90%

Key Votes of the 110th Congress

1. Raise CAFE standards	N	5. Make English official language Y	9. Withdraw troops 3/08	N
2. Expand SCHIP	N	6. Path to citizenship	N	10. Iran guard is terrorist group Y
3. Cap greenhouse gases	N	7. Fetus is unborn child	Y	11. Increase missile defense $	Y
4. Bail out financial markets	N	8. Prosecute hate crimes	N	12. Overhaul FISA	Y

Election Results

2004 general	Jim Bunning (R)	873,507	(51%)	($6,075,399)
	Daniel Mongiardo (D)	850,855	(49%)	($3,104,981)
2004 primary	Jim Bunning (R)	96,545	(84%)	
	Barry Metcalf (R)	18,395	(16%)	

Prior Winning Percentages: 1998 (50%); 1996 House (68%); 1994 House (74%); 1992 House (62%); 1990 House (69%); 1988 House (74%); 1986 House (55%)

The state's junior senator is Jim Bunning, a Republican elected in 1998 who has the distinction of being the first Baseball Hall of Fame player to serve in Congress. He plans to retire from the Senate when his current term is up in 2010.

Bunning grew up in Northern Kentucky, just across the Ohio River from Cincinnati. He started his sports career in baseball's minor leagues in 1950, but at his father's insistence, he finished college, getting a degree in economics from Xavier University. He made the majors in 1956, and the next year became the only pitcher to strike out Ted Williams three times in one game. Bunning threw a no-hitter for the Detroit Tigers in 1958 and pitched a perfect game for the Philadelphia Phillies in 1964, the first in the National League since 1880. Bunning also played for the Pittsburgh Pirates and the Los Angeles Dodgers. He retired in 1971 with a 224-184 record, a 3.24 ERA and 2,855 strikeouts; he was the second pitcher (Cy Young was the first) to achieve 1,000 strikeouts and 100 wins in both the American and the National Leagues. He was inducted into the Baseball Hall of Fame in 1996. Autograph signings account for more than half of the money his Jim Bunning Foundation raises each year, according to the *Wall Street Journal*. Jim Bunning and fellow pitcher Robin Roberts established the Major League Baseball Players Association in 1966, when the minimum player salary was $6,000. In recent years, he has criticized the sport's players for not accepting a salary cap, the big metro-area teams for not accepting revenue sharing and the team owners for not opening their books. Bunning has a large family; he and his wife have nine children (two sets of twins) and at last count 35 grandchildren. His son David Bunning, after 10 years as a federal prosecutor, was confirmed as a federal judge in 2002.

As a baseball player, Bunning was known for his skill and aggressiveness—he registered one of the highest totals in baseball history for hitting batters—and he's tried to apply those attributes to his second career in politics. He was elected to the Fort Thomas City Council in 1977 and to the state Senate in 1979, and he ran unsuccessfully for governor in 1983, though he posted a respectable 44% of the vote against Democratic Lt. Gov. Martha Layne Collins. When 4th District Rep. Gene Snyder retired in 1986, Bunning won the seat with 55% of the vote. In the House, Bunning spent six years on the ethics committee, leading the charge in 1992 against lawmakers who had multiple overdrafts at the House bank, which blossomed into a major scandal. He was one of the brash House conservatives of that decade who could scarcely conceal their contempt for President Clinton. In 1993, Bunning memorably called Clinton "the most corrupt, the most amoral, the most despicable person I've ever seen in the presidency."

When Democratic Sen. Wendell Ford announced in February 1997 that he would retire the following year, Bunning launched a campaign for the seat. The Democrats nominated U.S. Rep. Scotty Baesler, who represented the Lexington metro area in the 6th District and who was well known locally as a 1960s-era University of Kentucky basketball star. Baesler started out ahead of Bunning in the polls, but he was low on money. Bunning had no worries in that department; he had extensive help from Kentucky Sen. Mitch McConnell, who chaired the Republicans' Senate election efforts that year. Bunning invested some of his considerable money in devastating negative advertising against Baesler, including one television ad that depicted actors thanking Baesler, in Spanish and in Chinese, for voting for the North American Free Trade Agreement and for normal trade relations with China. This was the country's closest Senate race for months.

Bunning has compiled one of the most conservative voting records in the Senate. He has made headlines from his seat on the Banking Committee, which he has used to wage a campaign against the Federal Reserve. Bunning cast the Senate's lone dissenting vote against President Bush's nomination of Ben Bernanke as Federal Reserve chairman in 2006. He criticized Bernanke for not being more independent of outgoing Chairman Alan Greenspan and for stating he would continue the policy of raising interest rates to keep inflation in check. During the 2008 government rescue of mortgage lenders, he turned his sights on Treasury Secretary Henry Paulson, accusing him of "acting like the minister of finance in China" for bailing out Fannie Mae and Freddie Mac, and he called for Paulson's resignation. He was one of two Republican senators to oppose Robert Gates as successor to Defense Secretary Donald Rumsfeld, saying Gates lacked solutions for Iraq and Afghanistan. He also unsuccessfully opposed efforts to increase the Federal Deposit Insurance Corporation's coverage limits from $100,000 to $250,000.

Bunning is the first Kentucky senator in nearly 40 years to serve on the powerful Finance Committee. In 2007, he opposed expansion of the State Children's Health Insurance Program—which was to be financed by a tobacco tax hike—because "it taxes the poorest of our country that do most of the smoking." He is also immensely interested in any legislation dealing with baseball. Bunning has made steroid use in baseball a leading issue and has threatened to propose legislation against professional baseball's antitrust exemption if the league did not impose tougher penalties requiring abusers to sit out more games. Bunning maintains that athletes accused of steroid use should be stripped of their records and barred from entry into the Hall of Fame. He called former Sen. George Mitchell's 2007 report on steroid use "the saddest day in my life for baseball." His focus on baseball issues has prompted occasional portrayals of Bunning as a Senate lightweight. *Time* magazine in 2006 named Bunning the "Underperformer," saying that he "shows little interest in policy unless it involves baseball." In 2008, Bunning objected to the Senate extending a vote for the delayed Sens. Barack Obama of Illinois and Hillary Rodham Clinton of New York, which prompted long-serving Democratic Sen. Robert Byrd of West Virginia to scoff, "Who are you?" other than a "great baseball man."

But Bunning has also devoted himself to several Kentucky issues, including legislation promoting clean coal technologies. He has also criticized the Energy Department's cleanup of the USEC uranium enrichment plant in Paducah, ongoing since 1988. Particularly critical of the department's failure to compensate workers stricken with radiation-related diseases, he held several hearings on the issue and blocked the nomination of one of the agency's top officials to call attention to the problem. In 2004, Congress enacted his legislation to move the compensation process from DOE to the Labor Department and to have the government rather than private contractors compensate workers. The first claimants got their checks late in 2004.

When Bunning came up for re-election in 2004, it looked as though he would face a tough challenge from Democratic Gov. Paul Patton. But Patton declined to run after admitting to a sexual affair with a nursing-home operator who later sued him for sexual harassment. The Democratic nominee turned out to be state Sen. Daniel Mongiardo, a physician from the eastern mountains who had no statewide name recognition but who put up a surprisingly strong fight. Bunning raised and spent $6 million; the Democratic Senatorial Campaign Committee came to Mongiardo's aid in July, and he also gave his campaign $168,000 of his own money. He ran as a conservative Democrat, opposed to abortion rights and same-sex marriage. And he promised to reduce the cost of health care, while running ads attacking Bunning for accepting $75,000 from pharmaceutical company political action committees. Bunning ran ads calling his opponent a "Medicaid millionaire" and attacking him on national security and tax policy. Mongiardo got some help from Bunning's unusual campaign behavior. He refused to give the media covering him advance notice of his appearances, and he traveled with a security guard, citing "classified briefings that I have received in the U.S. Senate." In one campaign gaffe, Bunning said that Mongiardo looked like one of Iraqi leader Saddam Hussein's sons. Mongiardo accused Bunning of behavior "unbecoming of a Kentucky gentleman." And the senator later apologized for an "inappropriate comment."

Mongiardo closed the gap in the polls as the election neared, but Bunning squeaked to victory, 51%-49%, even as President Bush carried the state 60%-40%. Mongiardo ran well in his home area in the eastern mountains and in the ring of counties around Lexington. Bunning was rescued, as he had been in 1998, by his strong showing in his home area, the three counties of northern Kentucky, where he won 66.5% of the vote and which he carried by 48,000 votes, more than double his statewide margin of 22,000. Bunning, asked whether he had made mistakes, said, "Sure we made mistakes. Everybody makes mistakes. The only time I've ever been perfect was for about two hours and 10 minutes on June 21, 1964" (the date of his perfect game against the Phillies).

Bunning had planned to run for re-election in 2010 but then in July 2009 announced that he would not, blaming unnamed Republicans, presumably McConnell, for hindering his fundraising and forcing him to retire. McConnell and other senior Republicans were worried about Bunning's re-election prospects. Republicans Trey Grayson, the Kentucky secretary of state, and Rand Paul, the son of U.S. Rep. Ron Paul of Texas, were considering running against Bunning in the primary. Democrat Mongiardo announced he would seek a rematch. Bunning raised only $375,000 in the first quarter of 2009.

FIRST DISTRICT

Ed Whitfield (R)

Elected 1994, 8th term; b. May 25, 1943, Hopkinsville; home, Hopkinsville; U. of KY, B.S. 1965, J.D. 1969; Methodist; married (Connie); 1 child.

Military Career: Army Reserves, 1967–73.

Elected Office: KY House of Reps., 1974–75.

Professional Career: Practicing atty., 1969–79; Owner, Rhodes Oil Co., 1975–79; Cnsl., Seaboard System Railroad, 1979–83; V.P., CSX, 1983–91; Cnsl., Interstate Commerce Comm., 1991–93.

DC Office: 2411 RHOB, 20515, 202-225-3115; Fax: 202-225-3547; Web site: www.house.gov/whitfield.

State Offices: Henderson, 270-826-4180; Hopkinsville, 270-885-8079; Paducah, 270-442-6901; Tompkinsville, 270-487-9509.

Committees: *Energy & Commerce* (6th of 23 R): Commerce, Trade & Consumer Protections; Energy & Environment; Health.

Group Ratings

	ADA	ACLU	AFS	LCV	ITIC	NTU	COC	ACU	CFG	FRC
2008	35	18	17	38	57	61	72	78	70	94
2007	25	—	18	15	—	57	90	83	58	—

National Journal Ratings

	2007 LIB	—	2007 CONS	2008 LIB	—	2008 CONS
Economic	33%	—	67%	37%	—	63%
Social	21%	—	75%	20%	—	74%
Foreign	32%	—	64%	21%	—	78%
Composite	30%	—	70%	27%	—	73%

Key Votes of the 110th Congress

1. Increase minimum wage	Y	5. Share immigration data	Y	9. Withdraw troops 8/08	N
2. Expand SCHIP	N	6. Foreign aid abortion ban	*	10. No operations in Iran	N
3. Raise CAFE standards	N	7. Ban gay bias in workplace	N	11. Free trade with Peru	Y
4. Bail out financial markets	N	8. Repeal D.C. gun law	Y	12. Overhaul FISA	Y

Election Results

2008 general	Ed Whitfield (R)	178,107	(64%)	($1,052,635)
	Heather Ryan (D)	98,674	(36%)	($21,203)
2008 primary	Ed Whitfield (R)	unopposed		

Prior Winning Percentages: 2006 (60%); 2004 (67%); 2002 (65%); 2000 (58%); 1998 (55%); 1996 (54%); 1994 (51%)

Population		Race/Ethnicity		Work	
Pop. 2007:	686,014	White:	89.1%	Private:	73.3%
Change since 2000:	Up 1.8%	Black:	7.0%	Government:	17.6%
Urban:	36.5%	Hispanic:	2.1%	Self-employed:	8.7%
Rural:	63.5%	Asian:	0.5%	Blue collar:	33.2%
Area size:	12,058 sq. mi.	Native Am.:	0.2%	White collar:	47.9%
		Hawaiian:	0.0%	Khaki collar:	1.2%
Age		Two+ races:	1.0%	Other:	17.7%
Median age:	38.2 yrs.			Median income:	$35,773
More than 65 yrs:	14.8%	*Ancestry*		Median home value:	$79,800
Less than 18 yrs:	23.5%	USA:	16.4%	Poverty:	17.7%
		English:	10.6%		
Education		Irish:	10.2%	**Military Veterans**	
H.S. grad:	77.4%			% of Pop:	11.7%
College grad:	13.6%				
Grad degree:	5.5%				

The point where the Ohio River flows into the Mississippi—the intersection Huckleberry Finn and Jim missed in the fog—must have struck early settlers as a site for a great city. But no Pittsburgh or St. Louis grew up on this fertile black soil. Instead, the Kentucky land west of the dammed-up Tennessee and Cumberland rivers, bought from the Chickasaw Indians by Gen. Andrew Jackson and Gov. Isaac Shelby in 1818—the Jackson Purchase, it is still called—was settled by farmers. Most people here today are the descendants of these farmers, with memories of earlier generations living in family lore. Just to the east of the Tennessee and the Cumberland rivers is the Pennyrile (after pennyroyal, a common variety of local wild mint), a land of low hills and small farms, where you find the west Kentucky coalfields. There is Lyon County, founded by Matthew "Spitting" Lyon, who earned his epithet as a congressman from Vermont for spitting on a fellow member of Congress; he later represented western Kentucky from 1803 to 1811. The Land Between the Lakes, the boating and recreational haven created by the damming of the Tennessee and Cumberland Rivers just before the debouch into the Ohio, is the fastest-growing area in these parts, as the Jackson Purchase and the Pennyrile struggle economically. A uranium enrichment plant operated by the company USEC in Paducah has been under federal cleanup since 1988 and slated to be closed; in the meantime, the government has been slow to compensate workers stricken with radiation-related sickness.

2008 Presidential Vote
McCain (R)...........................176,807 (62%)
Obama (D) 104,626 (37%)

2004 Presidential Vote
Bush (R)...............................180,446 (63%)
Kerry (D)..............................102,346 (36%)

Cook Partisan Voting Index: R + 15

The 1st Congressional District of Kentucky is made up of the Jackson Purchase and much of the Pennyrile, plus a line of counties stretching some 200 miles east of the Mississippi in the mountains along the Tennessee border and then north toward the center of the state. There is a distinctive Southern atmosphere here—in the crops that are grown, in the historically low wages, and in the fact that the big city with the most influence locally is Nashville, not Louisville. Paducah has made some strides to reinvent itself with an artist-relocation program that has boosted development and made the small Ohio River town a U.S art destination. Turkey hunting also has become a big business here. The Army base at Fort Campbell, which is home to the 101st Airborne Division, has expanded with the activation of a Special Forces battalion.

The Jackson Purchase and the Pennyrile are ancestrally Democratic; Paducah produced one of the most enduring Democratic politicians of this century: Alben Barkley, whose career from 1912 to 1956 included 14 years in the House, 24 in the Senate and four as vice president. But the hills far from the Mississippi are Republican country, and this, combined with the Republican trend that reached north from Dixie to Paducah, has made the 1st District seriously contested territory in state elections—and one of the longtime Democratic rural areas that went solidly for George W. Bush in 2000 (58%) and 2004 (63%). In the close Senate election of 2004, Republican Jim Bunning won 48% in the Jackson Purchase. In 2008, John McCain won the district with 62% of the vote.

The congressman from the 1st District is Ed Whitfield, a Republican elected in 1994. Whitfield grew up in Hopkinsville and Madisonville, in a family with Pennyrile roots going back to before 1800. He served in the Army Reserves, practiced law in Hopkinsville and was elected to the Legislature in 1973 as a Democrat. After one term in Frankfort, Whitfield ran an oil distributorship in west Kentucky coalfields, then in 1979, moved to Washington to become an executive for the Seaboard and CSX railroads. He was legal counsel to the chairman of the Interstate Commerce Commission from 1991 to 1993, then returned to west Kentucky to run for Congress. The district long had been represented by quiet, long-serving, conservative Democrats. But the one-term incumbent, Tom Barlow, was a free-spirited supporter of the Clinton administration. Encouraged by Sen. Mitch McConnell, Whitfield ran as a Republican, turned aside criticism that he was carpetbagging and concentrated on attacking Barlow's vote for Clinton's first-term budget and tax increase. With help from the mountain counties and running strongly in the Pennyrile, Whitfield won 51%-49% in the big Republican sweep of 1994.

In the House, Whitfield has a moderate-to-conservative voting record and a seat on the Energy and Commerce Committee. One major concern has been aid to workers exposed to radiation at the uranium plant in Paducah. He overcame objections from the Bush administration to cleaning up the site, which is projected to cost more than $3 billion and last more than another decade. Whitfield is trying to work out a deal that keeps USEC's plant operating. He voted for normal trade relations with China after the Chinese agreed to lower tariffs on imported tobacco, and he supported the tobacco buyout bill, which handsomely benefited local farmers. Bush in 2005 signed into law a bill Whitfield authored to discourage "doctor shopping" by prescription-drugs addicts. It established an electronic data base that the states can use to monitor people who cross state lines to buy pharmaceuticals. A thoroughbred owner, Whitfield co-sponsored legislation in 2006 to ban the killing of horses for meat. The House overwhelmingly passed the bill, but it died in the Senate. He also has encouraged industry leaders to restrict performance-enhancing drugs given to racehorses.

When Republicans were in the majority, Whitfield was chairman of the Oversight and Investigations Subcommittee at Energy and Commerce. He held hearings on private data brokers who collect telephone records without customer permission, on the sexual exploitation of children on the Internet and on medical insurance for horse jockeys.

Whitfield has entrenched himself to the point that he is no longer much of a Democratic target. In 1996, when lawyer Dennis Null opposed him, Whitfield carried 18 of the district's 31 counties, including Paducah, which he lost in 1994. He won his first re-election 54%-46%. In 1998, former Rep. Tom Barlow ran again, and Whitfield won 55%-45%. Since then, he has won easily. He defeated Barlow a third time in 2006, increasing his winning margin to 60%-40%. And in 2008, he beat anti-war protester Heather Ryan 64%-36%. This longtime Democratic stronghold now seems to be a safe Republican seat.

SECOND DISTRICT

Brett Guthrie (R)

Elected 2008, 1st term; b. Feb. 18, 1964, Florence, AL; home, Bowling Green; U.S. Military Academy, B.S. 1987; Yale U., M.A. 1997.; Church of Christ; married (Beth); 3 children.

Military Career: Army, 1987–2001

Elected Office: KY Senate, 1998–2008.

Professional Career: V.P., Trace Die Cast, 2001–08.

DC Office: 510 CHOB, 20515, 202-225-3501; Fax: 202-226-2019; Web site: guthrie.house.gov.

State Offices: Bowling Green, 270-842-9896.

Committees: *Education & Labor* (14th of 19 R): Health, Employment, Labor & Pensions; Healthy Families & Communities; Higher Education, Lifelong Learning & Competitiveness (RMM). *Transportation & Infrastructure* (27th of 30 R): Aviation; Economic Development, Public Buildings & Emergency Management; Railroads, Pipelines & Hazardous Materials.

Group Ratings and Key Votes: Newly Elected

Election Results

2008 general	Brett Guthrie (R)	158,936	(53%)	($1,257,624)
	David Boswell (D)	143,379	(47%)	($900,518)
2008 primary	Brett Guthrie (R)	unopposed		

Population		Race/Ethnicity		Work	
Pop. 2007:	721,620	White:	89.8%	Private:	76.5%
Change since 2000:	Up 7.2%	Black:	5.9%	Government:	16.7%
Urban:	47.2%	Hispanic:	2.2%	Self-employed:	6.5%
Rural:	52.8%	Asian:	0.8%	Blue collar:	32.2%
Area size:	7,669 sq. mi.	Native Am.:	0.2%	White collar:	50.7%
		Hawaiian:	0.1%	Khaki collar:	1.1%
Age		Two+ races:	1.0%	Other:	16.0%
Median age:	36.4 yrs.	*Ancestry*		Median income:	$42,512
More than 65 yrs:	12.1%			Median home value:	$111,800
Less than 18 yrs:	24.7%	USA:	17.4%	Poverty:	15.1%
		German:	12.1%		
Education		Irish:	11.4%	**Military Veterans**	
H.S. grad:	80.6%			% of Pop:	12.0%
College grad:	16.2%				
Grad degree:	6.5%				

In the 1770s and 1780s, Americans began settling the limestone-soil country of central Kentucky, staking out towns like Bardstown and Elizabethtown and starting academies and colleges. They were well settled when Stephen Foster wrote "My Old Kentucky Home" just before the Civil War. The war tore deeply here. This part of Kentucky gave birth to Abraham Lincoln, and during the conflict, it lost thousands of soldiers, both Union and Confederate. The area is the home of several Kentucky landmarks—Fort Knox, the nation's gold depository; some of the nation's largest bourbon distilleries; and Mammoth Cave, the world's largest accessible cavern, near Bowling Green. Kentucky culture is more broadly disseminated than one might think. Executives at the five Japanese-owned plants in Bardstown feel at home there because Foster's songs, apparently well adapted to Japanese tones, are universally known in Japan. In 2004, a Japanese bluegrass band played at a bluegrass festival in Owensboro, the home of the International Bluegrass Music Museum.

2008 Presidential Vote		
McCain (R)	188,955	(61%)
Obama (D)	118,700	(38%)
2004 Presidential Vote		
Bush (R)	190,612	(65%)
Kerry (D)	100,580	(34%)
Cook Partisan Voting Index:	R + 15	

The 2nd Congressional District of Kentucky consists of much of the territory south and southwest of Louisville, starting with fast-growing Spencer County and proceeding south to Bowling Green and west along the Ohio River to Owensboro, a port with warehouses that receive aluminum alloys to make lightweight engine parts. The city has aggressively and successfully courted new economic development in recent years. It also hosts an annual international barbecue festival where mutton, a throwback to Welsh shepherds who settled in western Kentucky, remains a favorite.

Much of the district is rural and small-town country, where people have family roots that go back generations and a connection with the past not often found in metropolitan areas. Civil War loyalties are reflected in the election returns here. Kentucky was deeply split on secession, with some counties pro-South and others pro-Union. For many years, the balance of opinion here favored the Democrats. But in the 1990s, it moved toward the Republican Party, which better matched its conservative cultural leanings. In 2000 and 2004, this was George W. Bush's best district in Kentucky. In 2008, Republican nominee John McCain did well here, winning the district 61%-38% over Democrat Barack Obama.

The new congressman from the 2nd District is Brett Guthrie, a Republican elected in 2008 to succeed retiring GOP Rep. Ron Lewis. A graduate of West Point, Guthrie served 14 years in the U.S. Army, first in the Reserves, then as a field artillery officer with the 101st Airborne division at Fort Campbell. After his discharge, Guthrie joined the family business in Bowling Green, Ky., Trace Die Cast, Inc., a leading supplier of aluminum castings for the automobile industry with a workforce of more than 500. His father had started the business with his savings and just five employees in the 1980s. Guthrie eventually became vice president. In 1998, Guthrie was elected to the state Senate, where he focused on education issues and became chairman of the Transportation Committee, helping the state develop its highway budget. Republicans expected him to eventually join the leadership ranks, but Guthrie had his sights set on Congress.

After Lewis announced his retirement, his longtime chief of staff, Daniel London, jumped into the race to succeed him. Guthrie also got in and wound up running unopposed. Leading Republicans criticized Lewis and London, saying they'd set up a succession plan: Lewis had waited until just before the filing deadline to announce his retirement, leaving little time for candidates other than London to file. London apologized and withdrew from the race. Guthrie avoided a contested primary and marshaled his resources for the contested general election.

The Democratic nominee was state Sen. David Boswell, a 30-year veteran of Kentucky politics and a former Agriculture commissioner. He ran as a conservative Democrat, and the two contenders were virtually indistinguishable on the issues. Both opposed abortion rights and supported gun ownership, and both spoke out against the massive bailout for the financial industry passed by Congress that fall.

"These two candidates are very similar—their experiences in the Kentucky state Senate, committee assignments that they've worked on, their backgrounds," said Billy Ray Smith, a former Democratic agriculture commissioner. "They're very similar in a lot of their philosophies and political motivations."

National Democrats sensed they might be able to pick up a Republican House seat and made the contest one of their top priorities of 2008. Guthrie found himself neck and neck with Boswell in a district that had been held by a Republican for 15 years. He ran ads tying Boswell to liberal congressional Democrats and their opposition to offshore drilling, which Republicans argued would help lower gas prices. And he emphasized his military background to the district's sizable active and retired military population. The Democratic Congressional Campaign Committee ran an ad claiming that Trace Die Cast had sent jobs out of state to Mexico. Former President Bill Clinton stumped for Boswell in the district; First Lady Laura Bush put in an appearance for Guthrie. Guthrie proved more adept at fundraising, with a war chest of nearly $1.3 million; Boswell's barely topped $900,000.

Guthrie won 53%-47%. Once in the House, he was named to the Transportation and Infrastructure Committee and to the Education and Labor Committee. His colleagues predicted Guthrie would bring his bipartisan style to Congress. "He will work extremely hard on the one hand, but he's a little low-key on the other. He won't come in and try to run roughshod," state Sen. Charlie Borders told the *Louisville Courier-Journal*. "He'll try to find consensus and work with everyone sitting at the table."

THIRD DISTRICT

John Yarmuth (D)

Elected 2006, 2nd term; b. Nov. 4, 1947, Louisville; home, Louisville; Yale U., B.A. 1969, attended Georgetown, 1972–74, attended U. of Louisville, 1975; Jewish; married (Catherine); 1 child.

Professional Career: Stockbroker, 1969–71; Sr. aide, U.S. Sen. Marlow Cook, 1971–74; Publisher, Louisville Today magazine, 1976–82; Asst. vp of university relations, U. of Louisville, 1983–86; VP, Caretenders, 1986–90; Owner, columnist & executive editor, Louisville Eccentric Observer, 1990–2002; Co-host, Yarmuth & Ziegler, 2003; Commentator, Hot Button, 2004–05.

DC Office: 435 CHOB, 20515, 202-225-5401; Fax: 202-225-5776; Web site: yarmuth.house.gov.

State Offices: Louisville-A, 502-582-5129; Louisville-B, 502-935-6934.

Committees: *Budget* (14th of 24 D). *Ways & Means* (26th of 26 D): Select Revenue Measures; Social Security.

Group Ratings

	ADA	ACLU	AFS	LCV	ITIC	NTU	COC	ACU	CFG	FRC
2008	95	91	100	100	86	13	61	4	0	11
2007	100	—	100	100	—	6	53	0	1	—

National Journal Ratings

	2007 LIB	—	2007 CONS		2008 LIB	—	2008 CONS
Economic	58%	—	42%		69%	—	29%
Social	63%	—	36%		75%	—	18%
Foreign	86%	—	11%		78%	—	17%
Composite	70%	—	30%		76%	—	24%

Key Votes of the 110th Congress

1. Increase minimum wage	Y	5. Share immigration data	Y	9. Withdraw troops 8/08	Y
2. Expand SCHIP	Y	6. Foreign aid abortion ban	N	10. No operations in Iran	Y
3. Raise CAFE standards	Y	7. Ban gay bias in workplace	Y	11. Free trade with Peru	N
4. Bail out financial markets	Y	8. Repeal D.C. gun law	N	12. Overhaul FISA	Y

Election Results

2008 general	John Yarmuth (D)	203,843	(59%)	($2,138,457)
	Anne Northup (R)	139,527	(41%)	($1,708,081)
2008 primary	John Yarmuth (D)	unopposed		

Prior Winning Percentages: 2006 (51%)

Population		Race/Ethnicity		Work	
Pop. 2007:	685,701	White:	73.8%	Private:	83.5%
Change since 2000:	Up 1.7%	Black:	19.8%	Government:	11.4%
Urban:	98.3%	Hispanic:	2.8%	Self-employed:	5.0%
Rural:	1.7%	Asian:	1.7%	Blue collar:	21.5%
Area size:	379 sq. mi.	Native Am.:	0.2%	White collar:	63.1%
		Hawaiian:	0.1%	Khaki collar:	0.1%
Age		Two+ races:	1.4%	Other:	15.3%
Median age:	38.6 yrs.			Median income:	$43,831
More than 65 yrs:	13.5%	*Ancestry*		Median home value:	$141,500
Less than 18 yrs:	23.9%	German:	17.5%	Poverty:	14.3%
		Irish:	12.1%		
Education		English:	9.1%	**Military Veterans**	
H.S. grad:	85.7%			% of Pop:	11.0%
College grad:	27.7%				
Grad degree:	11.1%				

At the falls of the Ohio River, Americans more than 200 years ago founded one of their first inland metropolises, the river port and industrial city of Louisville. Established by George Rogers Clark in 1778, the city has always retained an air of the South. When Kentucky decided not to secede from the union in 1861, the decision was not unanimous, and the culture of tidewater Virginia is still evident in the Louisville lawn party. Mint juleps are served on the verandas of mansions, especially (but not

2008 Presidential Vote		
Obama (D)	193,260	(56%)
McCain (R)	150,552	(43%)
2004 Presidential Vote		
Kerry (D)	167,440	(51%)
Bush (R)	160,772	(49%)
Cook Partisan Voting Index:	D+2	

only) during Kentucky Derby week in May; horse racing is a preoccupation throughout the year. Although the Ohio River is crossed by many bridges and the accent across the river in Indiana may sound the same to outsiders, Louisville partakes of the Cavalier culture that second sons of big landowners from England brought to Virginia in the 17th century, and their heirs brought over the Appalachians to the valleys of Kentucky in the 18th century.

Louisville is Kentucky's largest city, surpassing Lexington in 2003 after Louisville voters decided to consolidate the city and surrounding Jefferson County. Louisville has not been growing as rapidly as many other Southern and Midwestern cities. Its economy is in many ways pre-postindustrial: It produces cigarettes and whiskey, large appliances and Ford automobiles. However, it is also the headquarters of Humana health services and of Yum! Brands, which owns KFC, Pizza Hut, Taco Bell and Long John Silver's. Its downtown hosts a new medical services center, the Muhammad Ali Center and the Owsley Brown Frazier Historical Arms Museum. The Louisville Bats's Slugger Field, which opened in 2000 on the riverfront, has attracted $100 million in development nearby. But the pace of growth in Louisville-Jefferson County is still slower than in the counties that ring it and in the counties across the river in Indiana. This regional growth has fueled plans to build two massive bridges over the Ohio River, at an estimated cost of $4 billion. Louisville has not yet attracted large numbers of immigrants, but has an interesting variety: Vietnamese, Bosnians, Cubans, Chinese, Indians, Koreans and Mexicans.

The 3rd Congressional District of Kentucky includes all but a dozen or so precincts of Louisville-Jefferson County. There is a large black population in the West End of Louisville and just south of the old city limits, and a lower-income white population along the strip highway that leads to Fort Knox. The suburbs to the east tend to be affluent. Small, elite neighborhoods—Mockingbird Valley, Glenview, Ten Broeck—are nestled in the hills above the Ohio River. Louisville has long been an odd duck in Kentucky politics. If its elite were Virginia Cavaliers, many of its burghers were Germans and Pennsylvanians who made this river town a Republican and anti-slavery island in a secessionist and pro-slavery sea. That tradition helps explain why Republican Mitch McConnell was able to get elected as Jefferson County judge-executive in 1977 and 1981, when the state was electing Democrats to most other offices. Since the 1990s, Louisville, like so many metro areas, has trended toward the Democrats, even as the rest of Kentucky trended Republican. The 3rd District voted by narrow margins for Al Gore in 2000 and John Kerry in 2004, while the state's other five districts all voted twice for George W. Bush. In 2008, the district voted for Barack Obama even as the rest of Kentucky went solidly for John McCain.

The congressman from the 3rd District is John Yarmuth, who won the district in 2006 by defeating five-term Republican Anne Northup. Yarmuth never held elected office before, but had spent four years as a Senate aide and more than two decades as a newspaper editor, publisher, and columnist. He comes from a wealthy family. His father, Stanley Yarmuth, founded National Industries, a conglomerate that started as a used car business; his maternal grandfather, Samuel Klein, ran the Bank of Louisville. John Yarmuth grew up in Louisville and went to Atherton High School, where he was elected student government president. After graduating from Yale University in 1969, he worked briefly as a stockbroker and then as an aide to Republican Sen. Marlow Cook. Yarmuth attended two years of law school but didn't finish his degree. In 1976, he founded *Louisville Today* magazine, and served as publisher until 1982. He ran unsuccessfully for Louisville alderman in 1975, and for county commissioner in 1981. He worked in public relations from 1983 to 1990 for the University of Louisville and for a health care company. Unhappy with the policies of President Reagan and the Republican Party, Yarmuth switched his party affiliation to Democrat in 1985. (He says he first registered as a Republican as a favor to his father, who was a fundraiser for President Nixon.) In 1990, Yarmuth founded the *Louisville Eccentric Observer*, a free newsweekly popularly known as LEO, and for the next 15 years, penned a column called "Hot Coals" that promoted his mostly liberal views. He sold the publication in 2003, but continued his column and also did political commentary on television.

In 2006, Northup was again vulnerable in this Democratic-leaning district, which she'd fought hard to keep by bringing in millions of dollars in federal funds from her perch on the House Appropriations Committee. The Democratic Congressional Campaign Committee touted attorney Andrew Horne, an Iraq War veteran and first-time candidate. But Yarmuth raised more money and proved a more formidable candidate than Horne, winning the four-way primary 54%-32%. He called for an immediate pullout of troops from Iraq and referred to Northup as a "rubber stamp" for President Bush. Northup campaigned on the Republican tax cuts and her work for the district. Yarmuth ran on his support for universal health coverage, a minimum-wage increase and revamping the Bush administration's No Child Left Behind education law.

The mother of six children, Northup suffered a wrenching personal tragedy during the campaign when her son died of an undiagnosed heart condition. She suspended her campaign for six weeks before returning to campaigning at the end of the summer. Then she unleashed a radio, television and Internet offensive that blasted Yarmuth for his liberal writings. She charged that Yarmuth supported doubling payroll taxes, removing the phrase "under God" from the Pledge of Allegiance and legalizing marijuana. Northup raised nearly $3.4 million to Yarmuth's $2.3 million, which included $700,000 of his own money. Northup, who carried the district while Bush lost it in 2000 and 2004, could not overcome a national tide against Republicans that year, an environment made worse locally by a patronage scandal surrounding Republican Gov. Ernie Fletcher. Yarmuth won 51%-48%.

In the House, Yarmuth is generally a moderate Democrat, though he is more liberal on foreign policy issues and more conservative on economic issues. When he was on the Education and Labor Committee in 2007 and 2008, he pressed for changes in the No Child Left Behind Act that would let states decide whether schools are meeting the law's requirements, which make federal funds contingent on students achieving proficiency on standardized tests. He also sponsored provisions in a higher-education bill to pay for more special education training for teachers and to forgive loans to teachers. He won House approval of his amendment to require Iraq to defray the costs of American troops stationed there. With his journalism background, Yarmuth co-sponsored a federal shield bill for news reporters and joined a "messaging" group that advises Speaker Nancy Pelosi and other Democratic leaders on media strategy. As he promised, he donated his congressional salary to Louisville-area community groups.

Northup came back for a rematch in 2008, after losing a primary challenge to Fletcher for governor. She criticized Yarmuth for supporting 2008's $700 billion bailout for the financial markets, and also attacked his "present" vote on a resolution honoring Christmas, asserting he'd lost touch with his constituents. (Yarmuth is Jewish.) Even though Northup raised more money than Yarmuth, he had a much easier time than in 2006, winning 59%-41%.

A scratch golfer who once played as many as 100 rounds of golf a year, Yarmuth says that the demands of Congress prompted him to scale back his plans to spend a month every year at a home he recently built near a golf course in Ireland.

FOURTH DISTRICT

Geoff Davis (R)

Elected 2004, 3rd term; b. Oct. 26, 1958, Montreal, Canada; home, Hebron; U.S.M.A., B.S. 1981; Christian; married (Pat); 6 children.

Military Career: Army, 1976–87.

Professional Career: Technology consultant, 1989–2004; Owner, Republic Consulting, 1992–2004.

DC Office: 1108 LHOB, 20515, 202-225-3465; Fax: 202-225-0003; Web site: www.geoffdavis.house.gov.

State Offices: Ashland, 606-324-9898; Fort Mitchell, 859-426-0080; LaGrange, 502-222-2233; Maysville, 606-564-6004; Williamstown, 859-824-3320.

Committees: *Ways & Means* (11th of 15 R): Select Revenue Measures; Trade.

Group Ratings

	ADA	ACLU	AFS	LCV	ITIC	NTU	COC	ACU	CFG	FRC
2008	15	18	14	8	43	70	89	96	82	94
2007	10	—	18	0	—	75	83	96	85	—

National Journal Ratings

	2007 LIB — 2007 CONS		2008 LIB — 2008 CONS	
Economic	23% —	77%	10% —	89%
Social	16% —	83%	9% —	85%
Foreign	0% —	72%	17% —	83%
Composite	18% —	82%	13% —	87%

Key Votes of the 110th Congress

1. Increase minimum wage	Y	5. Share immigration data	Y	9. Withdraw troops 8/08	N
2. Expand SCHIP	N	6. Foreign aid abortion ban	Y	10. No operations in Iran	N
3. Raise CAFE standards	N	7. Ban gay bias in workplace	N	11. Free trade with Peru	Y
4. Bail out financial markets	N	8. Repeal D.C. gun law	Y	12. Overhaul FISA	Y

Election Results

2008 general	Geoff Davis (R)	190,210	(63%)	($1,811,169)
	Michael Kelley (D)	111,549	(37%)	($19,531)
2008 primary	Geoff Davis (R)	30,189	(85%)	
	Warren Stone (R)	2,831	(8%)	
	G. E. Puckett (R)	2,427	(7%)	

Prior Winning Percentages: 2006 (52%); 2004 (54%)

Population		Race/Ethnicity		Work	
Pop. 2007:	712,819	White:	93.6%	Private:	81.2%
Change since 2000:	Up 5.8%	Black:	2.8%	Government:	12.5%
Urban:	59.7%	Hispanic:	1.5%	Self-employed:	6.1%
Rural:	40.3%	Asian:	0.7%	Blue collar:	25.4%
Area size:	5,770 sq. mi.	Native Am.:	0.1%	White collar:	58.8%
		Hawaiian:	0.0%	Khaki collar:	0.1%
Age		Two+ races:	1.1%	Other:	15.7%
Median age:	37.2 yrs.			Median income:	$47,727
More than 65 yrs:	11.8%	*Ancestry*		Median home value:	$126,500
Less than 18 yrs:	24.8%	German:	21.5%	Poverty:	13.3%
		Irish:	14.2%		
Education		USA:	13.1%	**Military Veterans**	
H.S. grad:	82.3%			% of Pop:	10.6%
College grad:	20.6%				
Grad degree:	7.6%				

Along the Ohio River are some very different parts of Kentucky. Ashland, near the West Virginia border, is industrial, the home of Ashland Oil; the river here is bound in by tight hills that hold smoke and soot close in the air. Farther down the river, the country is more bucolic. This is where Eliza fled across the ice floes in Harriet Beecher Stowe's *Uncle Tom's Cabin*. Farther west, between Louisville and Cincinnati, are counties that look like they're still in the 19th century. But metropolitan growth obtrudes. Oldham County, just upriver from Louisville, has some of Kentucky's oldest homes, and is by far the most affluent county in the state. The three Northern Kentucky counties across the river from Cincinnati—Campbell, Kenton and fast-growing Boone—are urban and suburban. Overlooking the suspension bridge built by John Roebling are new buildings on the Covington waterfront, and new subdivisions are rising on the hills in Boone County, above the river and near the Cincinnati-Northern Kentucky International Airport. In 2008, Fidelity Investments opened a campus in Covington with 4,600 employees. Newport, with its panoramic view of the Cincinnati skyline plus its entertainment and nightlife, has become a regional hot spot; local features include the aquarium and Labor Day fireworks on the river. It is also the hometown of one-time Republican presidential candidate Gary Bauer, the noted cultural conservative.

The 4th Congressional District of Kentucky is the most northernmost district in the state. It includes the counties along the Ohio and also lightly populated counties just inland. Economically, it runs the gamut from coal mining towns to rich suburbs. Politically, it has some of the most Democratic counties in America, like mountain-bound Elliott County, which voted 61%-36% for Barack Obama in 2008, his

2008 Presidential Vote

McCain (R)	189,008	(60%)
Obama (D)	118,773	(38%)

2004 Presidential Vote

Bush (R)	195,055	(63%)
Kerry (D)	111,049	(36%)

Cook Partisan Voting Index: R+14

strongest county in Kentucky, and 70%-30% for John Kerry in 2004. It also has some of the most Republican territory in Kentucky, like Oldham County, which voted 65%-34% for John McCain in 2008 and 69%-30% for George W. Bush in 2004. The three northern Kentucky counties across the river from Cincinnati cast nearly half the district's votes, and they too are heavily Republican.

The congressman from the 4th District is Geoff Davis, a Republican elected in 2004. He grew up in Pittsburgh and worked as a janitor in high school to help the family pay their bills. He was the victim of an abusive, alcoholic stepfather and left home right after high school to join the Army. His life turned around after he received an appointment to attend the prestigious U.S. Military Academy at West Point. He studied Arabic and Asian and European cultures, focusing his studies on national security and international affairs. In the service, Davis was an assault helicopter flight commander in the 82nd Airborne Division, and later ran U.S. Army aviation oversight on the Israel-Egypt border. After 11 years in the military, he moved to Fort Worth, Texas, then to Northern Kentucky, where in 1992 he started a consulting firm that advised companies on how to streamline manufacturing technology.

In 2002, he ran against U.S. Rep. Ken Lucas, a conservative Democrat first elected in 1998; Davis lost 51%-48% after receiving very little assistance from the national party. Lucas decided to honor his pledge to serve only three terms and announced his retirement in 2003. Davis became the frontrunner in this heavily Republican district in 2004, but he still faced a formidable challenge from Democrat Nick Clooney, a locally famous newspaper columnist and television commentator, and the father of actor George Clooney. Through his son, Clooney got checks from movie stars Paul Newman, Kevin Costner and Catherine Zeta-Jones. Davis charged that his opponent had more in common with the people of Southern California than with those in Northern Kentucky, and national Republicans called the Democrat "Looney Clooney."

Billing himself as a moderate, Clooney said he supported President Bush's tax cuts and opposed same-sex marriage and abortion rights. The Davis campaign unearthed columns Clooney had written over a period of 15 years, including one in which he criticized gun ownership. Davis touted his lifetime membership in the National Rifle Association. Despite Clooney's help from Hollywood, Davis had a big fundraising advantage; he spent $2.6 million to Clooney's $1.5 million. Clooney won rural and mining areas in the eastern end of the district, but Davis carried the three Cincinnati-area suburban counties and won the race, 54%-44%.

In the House, Davis established a solidly conservative voting record, especially on foreign policy. In 2006, Bush signed into law Davis's bill to protect military personnel from being sold overpriced insurance and investment products. He worked on other military issues, including increasing compensation for repeat deployments in combat zones. From his seat on the Financial Services Committee, which he held until 2009, he won passage in the House of a bill to require annual reports to Congress from federal regulators on the costs of financial reporting and another piece of legislation to make it easier for licensed insurance agents and brokers to do business across state lines. As a member of the committee, Davis pushed for a cap on interest rates on "payday" loans to members of the military. However, Davis received criticism on the issue after news stories reported a donation he had taken from a payday loan chain owner.

In 2006, national Democrats decided to challenge Davis by recruiting Lucas, a conservative who opposed abortion, same-sex marriage and gun control and who had held the district for three terms. Davis, usually a reliable vote for Bush administration policies, distanced himself from Bush by saying he strongly disagreed with the White House on immigration and on the partial privatization of Social Security. And Lucas had difficulty tapping into national anti-Republican sentiment or disenchantment with the Iraq war. He had voted for the Iraq invasion, which he later said he regretted. Davis won 52%-43%.

After the election, the House Oversight and Government Reform Committee investigated whether visits by two Cabinet members to Davis's district during 2006 were politically motivated. Davis said the visits were policy related and criticized the inquiry as partisan. In 2008, he easily won re-election against Oldham County physician Michael Kelley. But he was blasted after he referred to African American presidential candidate Barack Obama as a "boy" during a political dinner in April. Talking about Obama's lack of military experience, he said, "That boy's finger does not need to be on the button." Davis quickly made a public apology to Obama.

FIFTH DISTRICT

Harold Rogers (R)

Elected 1980, 15th term; b. Dec. 31, 1937, Barrier; home, Somerset; U. of KY, B.A. 1962, J.D. 1964; Baptist; married (Cynthia); 3 children.

Military Career: Army Natl. Guard, 1957–64.

Professional Career: Practicing atty., 1964–69; Pulaski–Rockcastle Commonwealth's Atty., 1969–80.

DC Office: 2406 RHOB, 20515, 202-225-4601; Fax: 202-225-0940; Web site: halrogers.house.gov.

State Offices: Hazard, 606-439-0794; Prestonburg, 606-886-0844; Somerset, 606-679-8346.

Committees: *Appropriations* (3rd of 23 R): Defense; Homeland Security (RMM).

Group Ratings

	ADA	ACLU	AFS	LCV	ITIC	NTU	COC	ACU	CFG	FRC
2008	20	18	14	8	86	60	94	84	75	100
2007	10	—	22	5	—	69	90	96	68	—

National Journal Ratings

	2007 LIB — 2007 CONS		2008 LIB — 2008 CONS	
Economic	25%	75%	23%	76%
Social	9%	85%	20%	74%
Foreign	0%	72%	22%	74%
Composite	17%	83%	24%	77%

Key Votes of the 110th Congress

1. Increase minimum wage	Y	5. Share immigration data	Y	9. Withdraw troops 8/08	N
2. Expand SCHIP	N	6. Foreign aid abortion ban	Y	10. No operations in Iran	N
3. Raise CAFE standards	N	7. Ban gay bias in workplace	N	11. Free trade with Peru	Y
4. Bail out financial markets	Y	8. Repeal D.C. gun law	Y	12. Overhaul FISA	Y

Election Results

2008 general	Harold Rogers (R)	177,024	(84%)	($796,760)
	Jim Holbert (I)	33,444	(16%)	
2008 primary	Harold Rogers (R)	unopposed		

Prior Winning Percentages: 2006 (74%); 2004 (100%); 2002 (78%); 2000 (74%); 1998 (78%); 1996 (100%); 1994 (79%); 1992 (55%); 1990 (100%); 1988 (100%); 1986 (100%); 1984 (76%); 1982 (65%); 1980 (67%)

Population		Race/Ethnicity		Work	
Pop. 2007:	675,258	White:	96.6%	Private:	74.0%
Change since 2000:	Up 0.2%	Black:	1.4%	Government:	18.7%
Urban:	21.3%	Hispanic:	0.6%	Self-employed:	7.0%
Rural:	78.7%	Asian:	0.4%	Blue collar:	32.5%
Area size:	10,759 sq. mi.	Native Am.:	0.2%	White collar:	49.7%
Age		Hawaiian:	0.1%	Khaki collar:	0.1%
Median age:	37.8 yrs.	Two+ races:	0.7%	Other:	17.7%
More than 65 yrs:	13.3%	*Ancestry*		Median income:	$27,324
Less than 18 yrs:	23.3%	USA:	32.8%	Median home value:	$64,100
Education		Irish:	9.3%	Poverty:	26.5%
H.S. grad:	66.9%	English:	8.9%	**Military Veterans**	
College grad:	11.9%			% of Pop:	8.5%
Grad degree:	5.7%				

Mountainous eastern Kentucky has been a unique place since Daniel Boone came through the Cumberland Gap in 1775. As Virginians poured through and created their version of a Tidewater civilization in the Bluegrass country, the people brought their assertive egalitarianism, loyalty to family and community, and passionate willingness to defend honor by feuds or violence. Most of the inhabitants of the mountains today are descendants of the Irish Protestant and Border Scot families who settled

2008 Presidential Vote		
McCain (R)	162,614	(67%)
Obama (D)	75,815	(31%)
2004 Presidential Vote		
Bush (R)	159,489	(61%)
Kerry (D)	102,142	(39%)
Cook Partisan Voting Index: R + 16		

there in the two or three generations after Boone. Handed down were living memories of the old ways of doing things from an era when there was little contact with the outside world. The first agent of change here was the Civil War; the second was the great United Mine Workers organizing drives in the coal mines in the 1930s. The Civil War made the mountains and the Cumberland Plateau a stronghold of the Republican Party. This was never slave territory—hardly any blacks have ever lived here—yet communities and families were riven by the rebellion of the South. Today, the counties around Somerset and Corbin in south central Kentucky cast some of the highest Republican percentages in the nation, election after election.

Early in the 20th century, vast seams of coal were discovered under the Kentucky mountains. Representatives of eastern capitalists (including the young Franklin D. Roosevelt) began prowling these hills, hiring town lawyers to buy up mineral rights from unsuspecting farmers, building industrial slum towns in hollows and creek beds beneath glowering, heavily forested mountains. Coal mining was harsh and deadly work. Mine accidents, black lung disease and simple exhaustion killed tens of thousands of miners, while low wages and company stores kept them poor. Then John L. Lewis's United Mine Workers came in, and open warfare followed, with neither mine operators nor union organizers reluctant to use violence and threats. The union mostly won in eastern Kentucky and in the short run raised wages and built hospitals for miners and their families. In the longer run, the impact of the UMW was a phasing out of many jobs in the mines in return for job security and health benefits, as use of oil expanded. Today, there are just over 400 mines in Kentucky, compared with 25 years ago, when there were 2,000. Politically, the UMW counties in the eastern part of the state became heavily Democratic.

In the mid-1960s, Lyndon B. Johnson came to eastern Kentucky and cited the poverty here in pushing for his Appalachian and anti-poverty bills. The high energy prices of the 1970s sparked strip mining, and eastern Kentucky's economy moved upward. High coal prices in 2004 stepped up the pace at existing mines, but the big mining companies that increasingly controlled production were wary of opening new mines. Mountaintop mining has become common, requiring huge machines and few workers. Most eastern coal counties have lost population since 1980, and counties off the interstate highways have a hard time attracting new businesses. But life here today is much closer to the ordinary American standard of living than it was in Johnson's era. Income levels are low, but so is the cost of living. Religion remains important here. The Pulaski County Fiscal Court in 2008 voted to appeal the ruling of a federal judge who had tried to stop the county's display of the Ten Commandments. And this part of Kentucky has produced stars in that quintessentially American medium, country music—Loretta Lynn, Ricky Skaggs, Dwight Yoakum, Crystal Gayle. The Hillbilly Days Festival draws 100,000 people every June to Pikeville.

The 5th Congressional District of Kentucky includes much of the Cumberland Plateau and most of the eastern mountains, a mixture of heavily Republican and heavily Democratic territories. There are huge political differences here between counties separated by just a mountain ridge or two, evidence of the depth of Civil War and United Mine Workers political loyalties, and only somewhat modulated by the recent trend toward Republicans in the coal country. The 5th District, created in the 1991 redistricting, combines most of two former districts, one Democratic and the other Republican. But overall this is a solidly Republican district—it voted 61% for Bush in 2004 and 67% for John McCain in 2008.

The congressman from the 5th District is Harold Rogers, a Republican first elected in 1980. Rogers grew up in Wayne County, went to the University of Kentucky, served in the National Guard, then practiced law in Somerset. He eventually bought the Citizens National Bank in Somerset. In 1969, at age 34, he was elected Pulaski-Rockcastle Commonwealth attorney. In 1979, he was the Republican nominee for lieutenant governor. The following year, when the 5th District congressman retired, Rogers was one of 11 Republicans in the primary. He got the nomination with 23% of the vote (Kentucky has no runoffs), and then easily won in November. His toughest race came in 1992, after redistricting. At first, his likely opponent was 7th District incumbent Rep. Chris Perkins, a Democrat and the son of longtime Rep. Carl Perkins. But then Perkins suddenly retired from Congress just before it was revealed that he had 514 overdrafts at the House bank when such overdrafts were developing into a major Washington scandal. Rogers ended up facing state Sen. John Doug Hays of Pike County. Rogers won with 55% of the vote. He won 71% in his old 5th District, which cast 52% of the new district's votes.

Rogers is now the third-ranking Republican of the powerful House Appropriations Committee. He is also the ranking GOP member of the Homeland Security Appropriations Subcommittee. His voting record is mostly, but not always, conservative. His district has long been hungry for federal aid, so Rogers finds it difficult to maintain a conservative record on spending issues. When Republicans were in control of Congress until 2006, he supported zeroing out domestic programs, except those important to his district—the Appalachian Regional Commission and the Legal Services Corporation. Over the years, he has worked to provide $162 million to protect the solvency of the funds for the United Mine Workers Combined Benefit Fund. After he became chairman of the Transportation Subcommittee in 2001, Kentucky became the fourth highest state in transportation funding per capita. The Daniel Boone Parkway, from London to Hazard, has been renamed the Hal Rogers Parkway. "The rate of return on highway spending far exceeds most other investments and is a proven engine," he wrote after the *Louisville Courier-Journal* criticized his appetite for highway spending.

Among the goodies for his district over the years have been: $100 million to rebuild the town of Martin above the floodplain, though the town's buildings are worth one-tenth that sum; $500,000 to pave a parking lot for Lee's Ford Marina Resort; and $15 million for a 760-seat theater and 23,000-square foot exhibition hall near Somerset. He was disappointed when the Homeland Security Department in 2007 rejected Pulaski County as the site for a $450 million bioterrorism research center. But he managed to secure $341 million for a massive concrete wall to close off leaks at Wolf Creek Dam at Lake Cumberland after the lowering of lake water levels caused a drop in tourism. The *Lexington Herald Leader* dubbed him "the Prince of Pork." Rogers says, "I'm two people. I'm a national legislator, and I'm a local congressman."

In his national role, Rogers has focused on spending for homeland security. Even before September 11, he lamented that most airport screeners were not U.S. citizens, and after Congress voted to federalize airport screeners, he kept a close watch on the new agency. After Hurricane Katrina in 2005, he berated the Federal Emergency Management Agency for failing to adapt its policy to reduce payments to contractors who failed to perform well and on time. In 2006, he took Homeland Security Secretary Michael Chertoff to task for a proposed budget that Rogers insisted was way short of meeting the country's needs. His subcommittee bill's that year was $1.8 billion above the administration's request; Rogers also demanded that the agency rearrange some of its priorities more to his liking. He has also been a supporter of the proposal for a fence along the border with Mexico.

The controversy in recent years over earmarks, the special provisions that lawmakers slip into spending bills for their districts and states, put an unaccustomed spotlight on Rogers and other powerful appropriators, who were used to going about their business quietly on Capitol Hill. He was criticized in a 2006 article in the *The New York Times* detailing the problems of the Transportation Worker Identification Credential program, which Rogers has fought to keep in Corbin, Ky., though arguably better technology for such cards was being developed elsewhere. When the *Lexington Herald Leader* criticized Rogers for keeping TWIC production in Corbin, Rogers fought back by writing in a column that Corbin was one of only three government facilities with sufficient security to produce the cards, and that it made no sense to have the work done by private firms. In 2005, Rogers generated more scrutiny when he inserted into a spending bill a provision requiring the Department of Homeland Security to hire a Virginia trade association that had sponsored several trips for the subcommittee chairman. The no-bid contract was later cancelled. Rogers has continued raising significant sums of political cash from firms that have won homeland security contracts. A *Washington Post* article in 2005 detailed these relationships, but did not allege any violations of House ethics rules or the law. Rogers's response was: "I've had a lot of fundraisers. Campaign contributions mean nothing on my watch." Citizens against Government Waste, a Washington-based watchdog group, regularly cites Rogers as a prime offender of pork barrel spending and has accused him of misusing his position to steer millions of dollars in earmarks to campaign contributors. Citizens for Responsibility and Ethics in Washington also has been harshly critical of him. Rogers says that he's created 15,000 jobs in his district and brought his constituents "peace of mind."

Since 1992, Rogers has been re-elected by overwhelming margins, carrying even the most Democratic counties. Many Republicans urged him to run for governor in 2003, but he said he felt he could do more for the state in Congress. After the 2004 election, he was one of three senior appropriators who sought the chairmanship of the Appropriations Committee. Rogers said he would impose a "sweeping attitudinal change of the entire committee," negotiate aggressively with the Senate and impose fundraising quotas on members. All this may have pleased the Republican Steering Committee, but the chairmanship went to the more senior Jerry Lewis of California. In 2008, Rogers won re-election without Democratic opposition.

SIXTH DISTRICT

Ben Chandler (D)

Elected Feb. 2004, 3rd full term; b. Sept. 12, 1959, Versailles; home, Versailles; U. of KY, B.A. 1983, J.D. 1986; Presbyterian; married (Jennifer); 3 children.

Elected Office: KY auditor, 1991–95; KY atty. gen. 1995–2004.

Professional Career: Practicing atty., 1986–95.

DC Office: 1504 LHOB, 20515, 202-225-4706; Fax: 202-225-2122; Web site: chandler.house.gov.

State Offices: Lexington, 859-219-1366.

Committees: *Appropriations* (33rd of 37 D): Interior, Environment & Related Agencies; State, Foreign Operations & Related Programs. *Science & Technology* (18th of 26 D): Energy & Environment.

Group Ratings

	ADA	ACLU	AFS	LCV	ITIC	NTU	COC	ACU	CFG	FRC
2008	85	64	100	100	71	15	61	12	12	17
2007	95	—	100	100	—	4	47	8	7	—

National Journal Ratings

	2007 LIB	—	2007 CONS		2008 LIB	—	2008 CONS
Economic	60%	—	40%		57%	—	41%
Social	55%	—	45%		54%	—	42%
Foreign	51%	—	49%		50%	—	48%
Composite	55%	—	45%		55%	—	45%

Key Votes of the 110th Congress

1. Increase minimum wage	Y	5. Share immigration data	N	9. Withdraw troops 8/08	Y
2. Expand SCHIP	Y	6. Foreign aid abortion ban	N	10. No operations in Iran	Y
3. Raise CAFE standards	Y	7. Ban gay bias in workplace	Y	11. Free trade with Peru	N
4. Bail out financial markets	N	8. Repeal D.C. gun law	Y	12. Overhaul FISA	Y

Election Results

2008 general	Ben Chandler (D)	203,764	(65%)	($481,994)
	Jon Larson (R)	111,378	(35%)	
2008 primary	Ben Chandler (D)	unopposed		

Prior Winning Percentages: 2006 (85%); 2004 (59%); 2004 (55%)

Population		Race/Ethnicity		Work	
Pop. 2007:	724,236	White:	85.8%	Private:	75.4%
Change since 2000:	Up 7.5%	Black:	8.2%	Government:	18.1%
Urban:	71.3%	Hispanic:	3.1%	Self-employed:	6.3%
Rural:	28.7%	Asian:	1.5%	Blue collar:	23.4%
Area size:	3,775 sq. mi.	Native Am.:	0.1%	White collar:	60.2%
		Hawaiian:	0.0%	Khaki collar:	0.1%
Age		Two+ races:	1.3%	Other:	16.3%
Median age:	35.6 yrs.			Median income:	$43,499
More than 65 yrs:	11.4%	*Ancestry*		Median home value:	$136,200
Less than 18 yrs:	22.9%	USA:	16.6%	Poverty:	15.9%
		German:	12.3%		
Education		Irish:	11.4%	**Military Veterans**	
H.S. grad:	82.9%			% of Pop:	9.9%
College grad:	27.9%				
Grad degree:	11.4%				

With its white picket fences, horse farms and small towns, the rolling plateau of Bluegrass in central Kentucky is the part of interior America longest settled by English speakers: Lexington was founded in 1775; the town of Hopewell was renamed Paris in 1789 out of gratitude for French help during the American Revolution and in a salute to the French Revolution (though the county name remained Bourbon even after Louis XVI was guillotined). Tobacco farming started here in the 1770s,

2008 Presidential Vote		
McCain (R)	180,526	(55%)
Obama (D)	140,811	(43%)
2004 Presidential Vote		
Bush (R)	182,787	(58%)
Kerry (D)	128,967	(41%)
Cook Partisan Voting Index:	R+9	

horse racing in 1787, and the first whiskey distillery, in Bourbon County, was built in 1790. Tobacco, whiskey and racehorses remained the staples of the Bluegrass economy for six generations, until 1956, when IBM built its typewriter plant in Lexington. IBM's arrival "really was the beginning of Lexington's industrial revolution," as University of Kentucky historian Carl Cone put it. But capitalism, as economist Joseph Schumpeter wrote, is a process of creative destruction. The personal computer eventually outclassed the typewriter, and the IBM plant was put on the block. The big employer here became Lexmark International, an independent IBM spinoff that makes inkjet and laser printers. Another mainstay is the Toyota plant built in the 1980s in Georgetown, a town with early-19th-century houses and lush countryside just one county north of Lexington. The plant can produce 500,000 cars annually, including the new Camry hybrid, and Toyota's $5.5 billion worth of investment has attracted auto-parts suppliers to the Georgetown area. Valvoline is among the companies that have done well locally. Lexington, which includes all of Fayette County, grew by a sprightly 24% between 1990 and 2007, and the 2000 census showed it to be the largest city in Kentucky, just ahead of Louisville. But Louisville voters decided to merge their city and Jefferson County, and in 2003, Louisville became the largest city-county again. Lexington is the host of the 2010 World Equestrian Games.

The 6th Congressional District of Kentucky includes Lexington and the surrounding counties—a natural unit, unlike some other Kentucky districts. Lexington casts 40% of the votes. It was the home base of the Whig Party's great leader Henry Clay, but in the first 140 years after his death, the Bluegrass country was mostly Democratic. In the 1990s, the area became more Republican, and George W. Bush carried the district in 2000 and 2004. John McCain won the district in 2008, 55% to 43%.

The congressman from the 6th District is Ben Chandler, a Democrat who won a special election in February 2004. He grew up in Versailles, in the horse country west of Lexington, the grandson of A.B. "Happy" Chandler, the former governor and senator who for five years was baseball commissioner. His father owned a local newspaper. Ben Chandler got his bachelor's degree and law degree from the University of Kentucky and practiced law for five years. In 1991, he was elected state auditor and in 1995 attorney general. In that job, he made a name for himself by prosecuting corrupt politicians. In 2003, Chandler ran for the Democratic nomination for governor and beat Speaker Jody Richards in the primary 50%-47%. But he lost the general election to 6th District Rep. Ernie Fletcher, 55%-45%. Chandler decided that if he could not defeat Fletcher, he would try to succeed him. He won the Democratic nomination for Fletcher's House seat without opposition and faced low-profile Republican state Sen. Alice Forgy Kerr in the general election. Both candidates supported the Iraq War and a constitutional amendment to ban same-sex marriage, and opposed amnesty for illegal aliens. National Democrats strongly backed Chandler, who carefully kept his distance from Democratic House Leader Nancy Pelosi, a liberal from California. Chandler scored an unexpectedly easy victory, 55%-43%, marking the first time since 1991 that Democrats captured a Republican seat in a special election. "It was a big, big deal," said Chandler. "I couldn't believe the enthusiasm I was greeted with on my arrival in Washington. My election was hailed at the time as a turning of the tide." In the next regularly scheduled election, in November 2004, Chandler defeated state Sen. Tom Buford, 59%-40%. His victories in 2004 kept alive Kentucky's record of electing at least one Democrat to Congress every year since Andrew Jackson founded the party in 1828, and since then, Chandler has become entrenched in what had been a safe Republican seat.

In the House, Chandler has a moderate voting record, though it is a bit more liberal on economic issues. In 2006, he proposed spending up to $32 billion over five years for grants and loans to fix the nation's schools, but the bill died without a hearing. From his seat on the Transportation and Infrastructure Aviation Subcommittee in 2006, Chandler hounded Federal Aviation Administration officials about the adequacy of air traffic control staffing at Lexington's Blue Grass Airport and nationally after the crash of Comair Flight 5191, which killed 49 people in August of that year. He criticized the National Transportation Safety Board for not holding hearings after the crash, and filed a bill to create an independent panel to review the FAA's safety-related programs.

After Democrats won the majority in 2006, he secured a plum seat on the House Appropriations Committee. Despite opposition from Republicans complaining about the loss of local authority for school districts, the House in June 2008 passed his bill to build more environmentally friendly public schools.

Some Kentucky political pundits thought Chandler would serve several years in Congress, then challenge Fletcher to a rematch in the 2007 gubernatorial race. But he decided he liked serving in the House.

"If you can maintain yourself here, if you can keep your nose clean, you will increase in your seniority and power," he told the *Lexington Herald Leader*. Chandler was his party's consensus favorite to run for governor in 2007, but after winning reelection with 85% in 2006 and after Democrats won control of the House, Chandler turned down another chance to seek the seat once held by his grandfather. He is frequently mentioned as a possible challenger to Republican Sen. Jim Bunning in 2010, but his endorsement of Democratic presidential candidate Barack Obama prior to the Kentucky primary as the candidate with "the best chance of bridging all of the divides that we face in this country" generated considerable local opposition.

★ LOUISIANA ★

L ouisiana often seems to be America's banana republic, with its charm and inefficiency, its communities interlaced by family ties and its public sector sometimes laced with corruption, with its own indigenous culture and its tradition of fine distinctions of class and caste. It is a state with an economy uncomfortably like that of an underdeveloped country, based on pumping minerals out of soggy ground and shipping grain produced in the vast hinterland drained by its great river, an economy increasingly dependent on businesses typical of picturesque Third World countries—tourism and gambling. Its politics, too, has its own peculiar election laws and a heritage of no-holds-barred conflict and demagoguery no other state can match: What other state has produced the likes of Huey Long or Edwin Edwards? Louisiana has a hereditary rich class and a large, low-wage working class. It has conservative cultural attitudes. Louisiana and Utah have the most-restrictive abortion laws in the United States, and Louisiana in 1997 became the first state to offer covenant marriages, in which spouses agree not to be covered by no-fault divorce laws. But Louisiana also has a lazy tolerance of rule-breaking, and feels more like the Caribbean or the Mediterranean than the North Atlantic or the Pacific Rim. This is not an entirely original observation. Five decades ago, journalist A.J. Liebling described Louisiana as an outpost of the Levant along the Gulf of Mexico. And more recently, architect Andres Duany noted, "New Orleans is not among the most haphazard, poorest, or misgoverned American cities, but rather the most organized, wealthiest, cleanest, and competently governed of the Caribbean cities."

It was, then, perhaps among the least equipped states to handle the aftermath of a Category 5 hurricane. On August 29, 2005, Hurricane Katrina raged in the Gulf waters off Louisiana and then slammed the coastline, resulting in flooding that devastated most of New Orleans and sent hundreds of thousands of evacuees to shelter on higher ground. One of the costliest natural disasters in the nation's history, Katrina destroyed large parts of Louisiana and, in the process, laid bare its political and economic frailties. New Orleans mostly withstood the initial winds and storm surge. But then the levees broke, submerging much of the city under water as water sought its level. The 17th Street Canal sprang a 200-foot gash through which came much of the water inundating 80% of New Orleans. Levees along the Industrial Canal, in the poverty-stricken 9th Ward, likewise failed to hold back water driven by a wave surge that reached 30 feet. The Mississippi River Gulf Outlet, built by the Army Corps of Engineers as a shipping channel (though precious few ships ever used it), funneled waters and winds into St. Bernard Parish east of the city and the lowlands of New Orleans, devastating all in its wake. More than half of the 270 miles of federally constructed levees and flood walls in Louisiana were breached or heavily damaged by winds and flood waters.

It had been known since New Orleans was founded by the French in 1718 that most of the land in and around it, beyond the two ridges piled high by the silt coming down the Mississippi River, was below sea level. It was known that New Orleans, the nation's fifth-largest city just before the Civil War, was at risk. It was no secret that the Mississippi River often flooded, as it did disastrously in 1927, or that hurricanes came roaring out of the Gulf, as one did that destroyed Galveston, Texas, in 1900. Yet in retrospect, it is clear that New Orleans was unprepared for the predictable disaster that caused more havoc in an American city than anything since the San Francisco earthquake of 1906.

Public officials responding to the disaster were responsible for moments of inspired decision-making but also of lamentable cluelessness. President George W. Bush was unwilling to cancel a West Coast speech and then told his Federal Emergency Management Agency Director Michael Brown, "You're doing a heckuva job, Brownie," a statement that was widely ridiculed. The Coast Guard moved in quickly and rescued perhaps 20,000 people, though no one knew it because the guardsmen didn't have room in their helicopters and boats for reporters and camera crews. On the other hand, as Harvard scholar and Clinton administration official Elaine Kamarck noted, the FEMA battle plan assumed that local first responders would not be incapacitated by the emergency, but that was not the case with Katrina (or with Hurricane Andrew in Miami in 1992). It was a mistake made by many administrations over many years. It could be argued that Democratic Gov. Kathleen Blanco was tardy in officially requesting federal assistance, but she also dispatched the boats of the Louisiana Fish and Wildlife Service to rescue thousands of people, again out of camera range. New Orleans Mayor Ray Nagin was pilloried for the school buses that were left under water when they could have been deployed to evacuate helpless people out of the city. But less dramatized was the fact that he had indeed sent city buses into neighborhoods as rescue vehicles. And the supposed murders and violence that were reported in the city's shelter in the Superdome never actually happened.

In actuality, the inundation of New Orleans was the result not of the inadequacies of the incumbent officeholders supposedly in charge but of the decisions made, and the derelictions committed, by federal, state, and local officials of both parties over many years before the disaster. The New Orleans levee boards were incompetent and corrupt. The Army Corps of Engineers never had a long-term strategy appropriate for a predictable disaster, and its congressional and executive overlords never insisted on one. The

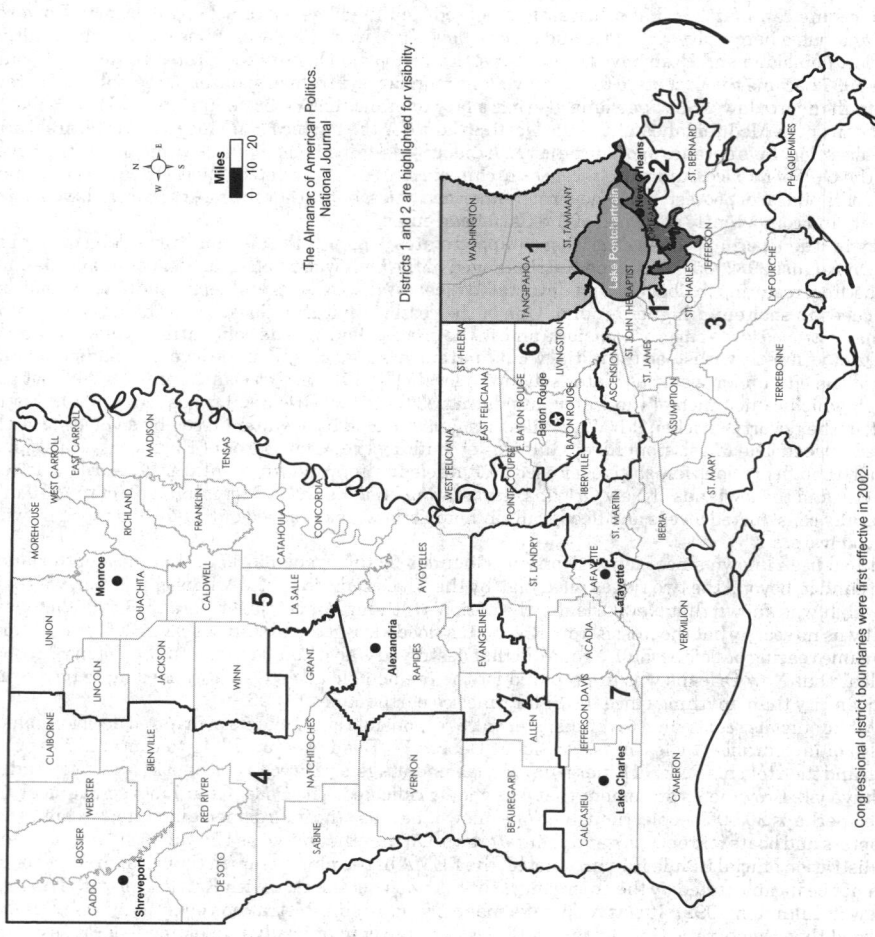

The Almanac of American Politics.
National Journal

Districts 1 and 2 are highlighted for visibility.

Congressional district boundaries were first effective in 2002.

destruction of so much of the city in the few days after August 29, 2005, was the result of decisions, over many years, of politicians operating out of full view, of congressional logrolling and administrative inertia, and of the particular civic and political culture of New Orleans and Louisiana, which, for all its charms, has been in many ways dysfunctional.

This is a product of history. The very things that made New Orleans distinctive—the look and feel of a French and Spanish outpost in the New World—were linked also to traditions of dirigiste centralized control and easygoing corruption. Louisiana is the only state whose law is based not on the common law of England but on the Napoleonic Code of France; the concept of civil liberties has shallower roots in Louisiana than in the other 49 states. It is also a state whose economy has always been based on the export of raw materials—sugar, rice, and cotton in the 19th century; oil and gas in the 20th century. Antebellum Louisiana's agricultural abundance generated the wealth that built grand plantation houses behind alleys of oaks running in from the Mississippi and made New Orleans the one significant city in the South by the time of the Civil War. Then came oil, discovered in 1901, at the dawn of the automobile age. The first offshore well, out of sight of land, came in 1947, at the start of the postwar boom. In 1921, Democratic Gov. John Parker and a young Public Service Commission chairman, Huey Long, got the idea of putting a severance tax on oil. In the 1970s, Democratic Gov. Edwin Edwards, a man similar in many ways to Long, changed it from a tax on amount of production to a tax on market value. Oil money came gushing into the Louisiana treasury and financed state government for six decades—and found its way into other pockets as well.

The most enduringly famous politician here, and by far the most talented, was Democrat Huey Long, who in less than a single term each as governor (1928–32) and U.S. senator (1932–35) left an imprint on the state's public life and imposed an organization on its politics that faded into history less than a generation ago. Long's genius was not that he promised to tax the rich to help the poor—hundreds of idealists and demagogues in America have done that—but that, to an amazing extent, he delivered. He dominated the Legislature so thoroughly that, as governor, he roamed the floors of both chambers at will, bringing to the podium bills he insisted lawmakers pass without changing a comma—and they did. He was ready to use bribery, intimidation, and physical violence. He built a new skyscraper Capitol, a new Louisiana State University, and more miles of roads than any other state but rich New York and huge Texas had. He also built a national following and, by 1935, was planning to run for president on a platform of "Share the wealth, every man a king." That year, Long was assassinated at age 42 in the hallway of the Capitol. The bullet holes can still be seen in the marble walls.

His impact was lasting. The Long threat may have moved President Franklin D. Roosevelt to embrace the liberal programs—the Wagner Labor Act, Social Security, steeply graduated taxes—of the second New Deal. For Louisiana, Long delivered a political structure that revolved around him even after he was dead—and a class of political leaders who, lacking his talents, treated the state as Long's incompetent doctors had treated his fatal wound, leaving Louisiana with neither a fully developed economy nor a fully competent public sector. For 50 years, until Huey's son, Democratic Sen. Russell Long, retired in 1986, Longs and Long protégés held high political office in Louisiana and elections were run along pro- and anti-Long lines. The Long experience strengthened Louisiana's already strong predispositions—tolerance of corruption, disinterest in abstract reform, and taste for colorful extremists regardless of their short-term means or long-term ends—in a way that helps explain the rise and fall of such unlikely politicians as the four-term Gov. Edwards and the onetime Ku Klux Klan leader and state legislator David Duke, both of whom by 2003 were spending time in jail. It also helps to explain the state's lack of economic dynamism. It has been a state with low incomes and workforce participation and low levels of education, with income disparities greater than almost anywhere else in the United States. New Orleans's rich, like many of their counterparts in Latin America, have been notoriously tight-knit, not venturesome, and determined to hold on to their wealth against the grasp of the impecunious and unlearned masses. This has made a huge difference over time. Metro New Orleans in 1940 had a population of 564,000; it was about the same size then as metro Houston (610,000) and metro Dallas (624,000). But in 2004, just before Katrina struck, metro Houston had 5.1 million people, metro Dallas 5.8 million, and New Orleans just 1.3 million.

The oil shocks of 1973 and 1979 did for Louisiana what they did for Saudi Arabia, Nigeria, and Venezuela: They made it suddenly hugely richer. Louisiana incomes reached national levels and 500,000 new jobs were generated between 1972 and 1981. But oil prices plummeted in the 1980s, Louisiana's rig count dropped by two-thirds, the state lost 150,000 jobs, and energy taxes fell from 41% of state revenues in 1982 to 9% in 1996. The state's economy has never regained much forward momentum. Gambling, legalized in 1991, produced less revenue than expected and nothing like the boom that some had promised. People have been leaving the state. From 1980 to 2005, Louisiana increased in population only 7%, far less than any other Southern state and less than any state nationally except two in the Great Plains and the industrial triangle of Ohio, Pennsylvania, and West Virginia. Then, as evacuees left New Orleans after Katrina, its population fell by some 250,000, according to Census estimates. It has slowly rebounded, as people have returned, but was still below 2005 levels in mid-2008. And despite the focus on those fleeing New Orleans's impoverished and predominately black 9th Ward, two-thirds of those who left the state were white, which is about the same proportion of whites in the state's population.

All this has accentuated long-term demographic trends. Within the state, people have been withdrawing from the lowland silt brought down over the centuries by the Mississippi River—from the city of New Orleans and low-lying St. Bernard Parish, from communities directly facing the Gulf, from the parishes fronting on the Mississippi north of Baton Rouge, and from much of rural northern Louisiana. One place where growth has been robust is along the Interstate 12-Interstate 10 corridor running west from the state line to Lafayette in the Cajun country. High-ground suburbs have burgeoned in St. Tammany and Tangipahoa parishes north of Lake Pontchartrain, in Livingston and Ascension parishes east and southeast of Baton Rouge, and in and around Lafayette Parish.

Louisiana has long had natural political divides. One is by religion. Catholic Cajun parishes (Louisiana has parishes rather than counties) cast about 30% of the state's vote; the New Orleans area casts 25% or so; and Protestant parishes from Baton Rouge on north cast about 45%. White Protestants for years have wanted nothing to do with national Democrats, while Cajuns sometimes will support them. Another divide is by race. Some 32% of Louisiana residents are black, the second-highest percentage after Mississippi. African-Americans are overwhelmingly Democratic, while whites are split in seriously contested state elections. A third divide is by income. Low- and high-income whites have voted very differently and are much less influenced than voters in most other states by candidates' cultural values, marital status, lifestyles, and the like. As a result, Louisiana politics since Huey P. Long's time has often been a struggle between reformist and conservative forces on one side and roguish populists on the other, a struggle waged in lavishly financed campaigns and with grandiloquent rhetoric. For a quarter-century, the lead role was played by Edwards as the roguish populist, with a number of rivals as reformist conservatives. Edwards was elected governor in 1971 and 1975, sat out 1979 because he was ineligible to run, and then in 1983 won a third term. While in office, he faced corruption charges and was acquitted by a jury in 1986. He lost a bid for re-election in 1987 but ran again in 1991. In Louisiana's (since altered) all-party system, he won 34% of the vote to 32% for Duke, the onetime Nazi sympathizer and Klansman who had won a special election to the Legislature as a Republican in 1989. Duke was repudiated by Republican National Chairman Lee Atwater and President George H.W. Bush as well as Louisiana Republicans. Bumper stickers read, "Vote for the crook—it's important," and Edwards won 61%-39%. He was convicted on corruption charges in May 2000 and went to prison.

In the years since, Louisiana politics has seen vigorous competition with volatile results. The state is one of only four to cast increasing percentages for Republican candidates for president in the past four elections, and its Legislature, long heavily Democratic, is now almost evenly divided. Its statewide races have also been close. Democratic Sen. Mary Landrieu has been elected to three terms starting in 1996 but never with more than 52% of the vote. Republican Sen. David Vitter was elected in 2004 with 51% under Louisiana's old system of multiparty primaries. Republican Bobby Jindal, defeated for governor by Democrat Kathleen Blanco in 2003, 52%-48%, came back in 2007 and, against split opposition, won the multiparty primary with 54% of the vote.

But the votes did not break the same way in all of these races. Republicans George W. Bush and John McCain carried Louisiana easily by running barely ahead in metro New Orleans, winning more robustly in metro Baton Rouge, and winning 60% or more in most of the rest of the state. The northern Protestant areas and the Cajun country areas cast large majorities for them. In 2008, the Democratic vote in metro New Orleans was down by 48,000 votes from 2004—evidence of black outmigration after Katrina. But the Republican vote there was also down, by 20,000, suggesting a net Katrina loss to Democrats of 1% to 2% of the total state vote, not nearly as much as some analysts had feared (or had hoped). Jindal in 2007 and Landrieu in 2008, although from different parties, ran best in metro New Orleans, with 58% and 59% of the vote there, respectively. They both carried metro Baton Rouge by narrower margins, and both barely ran ahead in the rest of the state. Vitter, from suburban New Orleans, ran about the same in all three regions, just barely clearing the 50% hurdle needed to avoid a runoff.

The impact of Katrina was most pronounced on the 2007 contest for governor. Jindal, the son of Indian immigrants, a Hindu-turned-Catholic, and a fast-talking policy wonk, had run four years earlier

Population		Household Income		Work	
Pop. 2007:	4,344,053	Under $15k:	19.7%	Private:	76.8%
State rank:	25th of 50	$15k to $50k:	39.5%	Government:	16.8%
Change since 2000:	Down 2.8%	$50k to $100k:	27.4%	Self-employed:	6.2%
Urban:	70.2%	$100k to $150k:	11.3%	Unemployment (3-yr. average):	4.9%
Rural:	29.8%	Over $150k:	2.2%	Poverty:	19.3%
Native of state:	79.5%	Median income:	$40,160	Blue collar:	25.6%
Not a citizen:	1.6%			White collar:	55.7%
Area size:	51,840 sq. mi.	**Home Value**		Khaki collar:	0.5%
		Under $100k:	44.0%	Other:	18.2%
Most populous cities		$100k to $300k:	47.6%		
1. New Orleans	301,016	$300k to $500k:	6.3%	**Age**	
2. Baton Rouge	224,555	$500k to $1 mil:	1.8%	Median age:	35.5 yrs.
3. Shreveport	200,528	Over $1 million:	0.4%	More than 65 yrs:	12.0%
4. Metairie	129,469	Median:	$113,500	Less than 18 yrs:	25.4%

Race/Ethnicity				Military Veterans		Registered Voters in 2008	
White:	62.1%	*Language*		% of Pop:	10.1%	D:	1,543,840 (52.5%)
Black:	31.8%	English:	91.6%	*Veterans by Period*		R:	743,367 (25.3%)
Hispanic:	3.0%	Spanish:	2.8%	WWII and before:	11.4%	Other:	653,778 (22.2%)
Asian:	1.4%	Asian:	1.0%	Korea:	11.0%	Voter turnout:	1,960,761
Native Am.:	0.5%	Other		Vietnam:	32.4%	Turnout as % of	
Hawaiian:	0.0%	European	4.4%	Gulf (pre-2001):	12.6%	voting age:	59.4%
Two+ races:	1.0%	**Education**		Gulf (post-2001):	9.0%	**Legislature**	
Ancestry		H.S. grad:	79.4%	Peace time:	23.6%	Senate:	22 D 15 R 2 V
French:	13.2%	College grad:	20.1%			House:	52 D 50 R 3 I
USA:	7.9%	Grad degree:	6.8%				
German:	7.5%						

and lost the runoff to Democrat Blanco. He had poor showings in the Cajun country and northern Louisiana, particularly after Democrats ran a television ad with his skin darkened. Two years later, Blanco's performance after Katrina left her politically wounded and she announced she would not run again. In the multiparty primary, Jindal won a solid 54% majority against split opposition. He persuaded the Legislature, with many new members and more Republicans, thanks to term limits, to pass major ethics legislation and tax legislation. As Louisianans continued to return after Katrina—and Louisiana's Road Home program financed many new homes—he called for stopping outmigration with grants for college graduates who buy homes and stay in the state for five years. With generally good reviews in his first months in office, Jindal was the subject of speculation about a future presidential run.

Presidential politics In recent years, Louisiana's presidential politics have been racially polarized, and the trend continued in 2008, when Republican nominee John McCain won 59%-40% over Democrat Barack Obama, the first African-American to be nominated by a major party. In 2004, whites voted 75%-24% for Republican President George W. Bush and African-Americans voted 90%-9% for Democrat John Kerry. Four years later, the difference was even starker. Whites voted 84%-14% for Republican John McCain, and blacks 94%-4% for Democrat Barack Obama. Even young whites voted 81% for McCain, as did 60% of white Democrats. Those who indicated that race was an important factor in their voting split almost evenly, which is to say, more in Obama's favor than the state's electorate as a whole. As a result, Louisiana was one of the few states that trended Republican in 2008, despite a significant increase in black registration and turnout. The exodus of African-Americans from New Orleans after the hurricane was one reason, but only a minor one. In terms of percentages, an exodus

2008 Presidential Vote		
McCain (R)	1,148,275	(59%)
Obama (D)	782,989	(40%)
2008 Democratic Presidential Primary		
Obama (D)	220,632	(57%)
Clinton (D)	136,925	(36%)
2008 Republican Presidential Primary		
Huckabee (R)	69,594	(43%)
McCain (R)	67,551	(42%)
Romney (R)	10,222	(6%)
Paul (R)	8,590	(5%)
2004 Presidential Vote		
Bush (R)	1,102,169	(57%)
Kerry (D)	820,299	(42%)

of whites from Republican St. Bernard Parish was even greater. And the metro New Orleans vote changed only marginally, from 50%-49% Republican in 2004 to 52%-46% Republican in 2008.

The biggest drops in Democratic percentage came in Cajun parishes—perhaps Kerry's Catholicism had some appeal there—and in the two heavily Cajun congressional districts, the 3rd and the 7th. The Democratic percentage rose in Baton Rouge and Shreveport and in rural parishes with large black populations. But the pattern was mixed, as might be expected in a state that was not targeted by either party in either election and in which the Obama campaign had far less occasion to organize than it did in target states such as Florida, North Carolina, and Virginia.

Louisiana has seldom played a significant role in presidential primaries and caucuses, with one odd exception. That was 1996, when Republican allies of candidate Phil Gramm set up a pre-Iowa and pre-New Hampshire caucus in Louisiana on February 6. The aim was to jump-start Gramm's campaign. Instead, the caucuses killed it. Only 20,000 Republicans showed up at 42 voting sites (compared with 100,000 at 2,000 sites later in Iowa), and conservative commentator Pat Buchanan won more votes than Gramm and took 13 of the 21 delegates. Gramm's campaign in Iowa faltered, and he left the race before the New Hampshire primary. The 2000 and 2004 primaries were held in March, after both parties' nominees had been chosen.

Louisiana did make at least a little bit of difference in 2008. Legislators chose to hold the primary in early February, but not on Super Tuesday, February 5, because that was Mardi Gras, and it was unthinkable to hold an election during Mardi Gras. Instead, the voting was set for the next Saturday, a day on which Louisiana has often held state elections. The decision left Louisiana at risk of irrelevance if both parties' nominations were settled on Super Tuesday, but they weren't. Obama came in and held a rally at Tulane University, and former President Bill Clinton spent Friday campaigning around the state for his wife, Democratic Sen. Hillary Rodham Clinton. In retrospect, the outcome should have been no surprise. As recently as 2000, the body of registered Democrats in Louisiana was 58% white and 40% African-American, but in 2008, after a big rush in registration, blacks made up nearly half of the state's registered Democrats. Democratic turnout in the primary was 384,000—roughly double what is was in 2004 and 2000 and almost identical to what is was in 1992, when Bill Clinton won 69% of the vote, but well below the 1988 record of 625,000. This time, the Clinton family didn't do as well. Obama won 57% of the vote (and about 80% of the African-American vote), and Clinton won 36%.

There was less enthusiasm on the Republican side because it was pretty clear after Super Tuesday that McCain would be nominated. Nonetheless, evangelical Christians and others set up telephone networks for Arkansas's Mike Huckabee. With a turnout of 161,000 voters, half the Democratic level but the highest Republican turnout in Louisiana ever, Huckabee won 43% of the vote to 42% for McCain. McCain carried metro New Orleans big and ran about even in the heavily Catholic Cajun country. Huckabee won large majorities in heavily Protestant northern Louisiana. But it didn't matter. A candidate must win 50% of the vote in Louisiana's Republican primary to win any delegates. A few days later, party insiders awarded 44 of the 47 delegates to McCain.

Congressional districting

Louisiana redrew its congressional districts three times in the 1990s. The first two plans created two black-majority districts, and in each case one of them was highly irregular in shape. They were declared unconstitutional in federal court in December 1993 and July 1994. The first plan was used in the 1992 elections, the second in 1994. In January 1996, a federal court came up with a plan, adopted by the Legislature, that cut through few parish boundaries and had much more regular lines. And it had only one black-majority district, centered in New Orleans. The plan was upheld by the Supreme Court in June 1996.

111th Congress Lineup	
6 R	1 D
110th Congress Lineup	
5 R	2 D

In August 2001, six of the seven House incumbents (one was running for the Senate) submitted a plan to the Legislature. Republican Gov. Mike Foster called a special session for redistricting in October, and the legislators made minor tweaks in the House incumbents' plan. It was opposed by the Black Legislative Caucus, which drew up a plan with a second black-majority district stretching from Lafayette and Baton Rouge along the Mississippi River to the Arkansas border. But the Legislature rejected that by solid margins. Foster signed the new plan in October, and the Justice Department approved it in April 2002. Generally, it has favored Republicans, but five of the seven districts have elected members of both parties in the elections from 2002 to 2008.

Louisiana's big population loss after Hurricane Katrina made it clear that the state would lose one House seat after the 2010 census. That might have happened anyway, given the state's sluggish pre-Katrina growth. Demographically, the 2nd District, centered in New Orleans, suffered the greatest population loss by far. But Voting Rights Act jurisprudence forbids the elimination of the state's one black-majority district and practically commands the 2011–2012 Legislature to create an African-American majority seat, perhaps by connecting part of New Orleans with part of Baton Rouge through a corridor running up the Mississippi River. That would leave a heavily Republican suburban New Orleans seat and four more districts in territory currently represented by four Republicans and one Democrat.

Governor

Bobby Jindal (R)

Elected 2007, term expires Jan. 2012, 1st term; b. June 10, 1971, Baton Rouge; home, Kenner; Brown U., B.A. 1991, Oxford U., M.Lit. 1994; Catholic; married (Supriya); 3 children.

Elected Office: U.S. House of Reps., 2004-2007.

Professional Career: Secy., LA Dept. of Health and Hospitals, 1996–98; Exec. dir., Natl. Bipartisan Comm. on the Future of Medicare, 1998–99; Pres., U. of LA System, 1999–2001; Asst. sec., U.S. Dept. of HHS, 2001–03.

Office: Office of the Governor, P.O. Box 94004, Baton Rouge, 70804, 225-342-0991; Fax: 225-342-7099; Web site: gov.state.la.us.

Election Results

2007 election			
Bobby Jindal (R)	699,275	(54%)
Walter Boasso (D)	226,476	(17%)
John Georges (R)	186,682	(14%)
Foster Campbell (D)	161,665	(12%)

Prior Winning Percentages: 2006 House (88%); 2004 House (78%)

The governor of Louisiana is Bobby Jindal, a Republican elected in October 2007. Jindal grew up in Baton Rouge, the son of immigrants from India who came to the United States so his mother could do graduate work at Louisiana State University. His given name was Piyush, but as a boy he insisted on being called Bobby, after his favorite character in the television series *The Brady Bunch*. As a teenager, he converted from Hinduism to Catholicism. He was an honors student at Baton Rouge High School, went on to graduate from Brown University with degrees in biology and public policy, then studied at Oxford as a Rhodes Scholar.

After college, Jindal worked briefly for McKinsey & Co. in Washington, D.C., then landed his first job in politics as an intern for 4th District Rep. Jim McCrery, a Republican. He quickly built an impressive resume. When McCrery assigned him to work on health-policy research, Jindal holed himself up in the Library of Congress for two weeks to master the complexities of the Medicare program. He eventually plopped on McCrery's desk a thick report spelling out possible solutions to the financial problems confounding the gigantic government-run medical program for the elderly. A few years later, Jindal, then age 24, set his sights on becoming the new head of Louisiana's Department of Health and Hospitals and asked McCrery to introduce him to the governor, Republican Mike Foster. "Bobby knocked their socks off," McCrery told the Baton Rouge newspaper, the *Advocate*. Foster gave Jindal the job of running a 13,000-employee agency that accounted for about 40% of the state budget. Jindal managed to erase a $400 million deficit within two years. He returned to Washington and, at age 27, became executive director of the National Bipartisan Commission on the Future of Medicare, co-chaired by Democratic Louisiana Sen. John Breaux and U.S. Rep. Bill Thomas, a Republican from California. Next he served as president of the 80,000-student Louisiana state university system. In 2001, he became assistant secretary for planning and evaluation at the U.S. Health and Human Services Department.

In 2003, Jindal ran for governor, his first race for elective office. He campaigned as a policy expert with ideas for restructuring state government, and he attracted national and even international attention; his candidacy was front-page news in India. In the October 2003 primary, he ran first, with 33% of the vote, ahead of three Democrats: Lt. Gov. Kathleen Blanco, with 18%; Attorney General Richard Ieyoub, with 16%; and former U.S. Rep. Buddy Leach, with 14%. Between the primary and the runoff, Blanco ran ads raising doubts about Jindal's success as the state health-department chief, to which Jindal failed to respond forcefully. In the November runoff, he lost to Blanco 52%-48%, but he carried the New Orleans, Baton Rouge, Shreveport and Monroe metro areas. Blanco carried her home area, the Cajun country, by a wide margin; Jindal carried only one of the northern parishes that most Republicans have won in other statewide races.

In 2004, Jindal considered running for the Senate when Breaux retired, but deferred to U.S. Rep. David Vitter, a Republican who won the seat. He then decided to run for Vitter's vacant House seat, ideally situated in a congressional district where Jindal's wife's family lived and where he had won 68% of the vote in his campaign for governor. Republican state Rep. Steve Scalise abandoned his campaign in August after trailing badly in fundraising and the polls, and Jindal was endorsed by state GOP leaders. He won 78% of the vote in November and was elected without a runoff. He was the first Indian-American elected to Congress since Democrat Dalip Saund won in the 29th District of California in 1956.

In the House, Jindal's voting record was moderate to conservative and his approach was earnest. With help from McCrery, he lobbied Republican leaders for an assignment to the Energy and Commerce Committee. But no freshman had been assigned there for years, and Jindal instead got seats on the Homeland Security and Natural Resources committees. He was elected president of the Republican freshman class and spoke out early for the GOP proposal to create private retirement accounts in the Social Security program. Following the devastation of Louisiana and other Gulf states by Hurricane Katrina in 2005, he worked on revamping the Federal Emergency Management Agency, the federal flood-insurance program and financial aid to state and local school boards. Perhaps his most significant achievement was enactment in December 2006 of a bill that opened more than 8 million acres in the Gulf of Mexico to offshore drilling, and mandated that a substantial portion of the revenues go to Louisiana and other Gulf states with Katrina damage.

Jindal never stopped thinking about running again for governor. He kept a campaign-style schedule during congressional recesses, traveling around the state to give speeches and hold fundraisers. Blanco had been widely criticized for her response to Katrina, and her job rating was low. In March 2007, when she announced she would not seek another term, Jindal was ready. Other prominent Louisiana politicians who might have given him a tough fight stayed out of the race for various reasons. Breaux considered running, but he had established residence in the Maryland suburbs outside Washington, and he decided not to run after Jindal supporters made it clear they would challenge his eligibility to run. Two other Democrats, Lt. Gov. Mitch Landrieu and former U.S. Rep. Chris John, also decided against running.

Three serious opponents did enter the race. Democratic State Sen. Walter Boasso spent personal money liberally and argued that he had worked to reduce patronage politics at levee boards. Businessman John Georges also spent millions and ran as a nonpartisan political unifier. Public Service Commissioner Foster Campbell, a Democrat, ran on a proposal to replace the state income tax with a levy on oil and gas producers. Jindal stressed his work in Congress on post-Katrina aid and promised to clean up the state's famously corrupt politics and rejuvenate Louisiana's economy. "We need a plan that won't just rebuild things the way they were, where we were 50th in health care and 50th in the best places to do business. We need to move to the top of those lists and others," he said. Jindal led in polls throughout the campaign and won 54% of the vote, more than the 50% required to avoid a runoff. The opposition was split: Boasso won 17% of the vote, Georges 14%, and Campbell 12%.

Taking office Jindal called a special session of the Legislature in February 2008 and won passage, with only minor changes, of an ethics bill requiring elected and appointed officials to disclose their personal finances and of another measure banning them from doing business with the state. Then he called a second special session in March to "eliminate unorthodox business taxes that are holding Louisiana's economy back." Almost without demur, the Legislature voted to accelerate $367 million in phaseouts of taxes on utilities, machinery purchases and corporate debt and to pass $20 million in tuition and home-schooling tax credits. In addition, he persuaded the Legislature to spend much of the $1.1 billion budget surplus on infrastructure—roads, bridges and ports—and on hurricane protection and coastal restoration. Also funded were repairs at public university buildings and the Pennington Biomedical Research Center. Another bill gradually reserved tax revenues from car and truck sales for transportation projects. "We should not be sitting on the sidelines of global economic competition while cities that were once small towns become giants of economic vitality," Jindal said.

In the regular session that followed, the Legislature did not always ratify Jindal's initiatives. The state House cut health and education funds in his budget and declined to pass his proposal for merit pay for teachers. He was dogged as well by his campaign's failure to report $100,000 in financial aid from the state Republican Party and by newspaper stories that one of the businesses benefiting from his Terrebonne Parish port expansion was a big contributor to his campaign. Jindal in turn vetoed $16 million of legislators' special projects. But his biggest misstep involved a raise in legislators' pay, stuck at $16,800 to $37,500 for many years. During his campaign, he had pledged to oppose a pay increase. On June 16, 2008, after the Legislature passed one, he said he would allow it to become law without his signature. There was widespread protest, and on June 27, papers were filed for a recall petition. He responded by vetoing the pay raise.

Jindal's early successes brought him into the national spotlight. He spent Memorial Day weekend at Republican presidential candidate John McCain's home in Sedona, Ariz., together with former Massachusetts Gov. Mitt Romney and Florida Gov. Charlie Crist. The next month, "Jindal for VP" bumper stickers" were circulating in Baton Rouge. But he was not a finalist for the job, and he canceled a speaking date at the Republican National Convention in September when Hurricane Gustav was headed toward New Orleans. Some 1.9 million people were evacuated from coastal parishes. Jindal gave frequent press conferences, rattling off wind speeds, shelter populations, damage descriptions, phone numbers and websites, seemingly in total command of the state response. Later in the month, he traveled to Washington to lobby Congress for relief. He rejected the idea of another Road Home program like the one following Katrina as too bureaucratic and slow moving.

Jindal's campaigning in 2008 and his trip to Iowa to deliver two speeches after the election stimulated talk of a presidential candidacy. "I am not running for the White House in 2012," he said. "I don't have any intent of running for any other office. I'd really like to go back to the private sector." He was chosen by Republican leaders to deliver the rebuttal to Democratic President Barack Obama's address to Congress in February 2009. In a speech he wrote himself, he talked about his immigrant heritage and attacked high government spending. But his delivery was uninspiring, and the critical postgame analysis was almost entirely negative. His response: "People ask, 'Well, did you have a debate coach or a speech coach?' Obviously, I didn't."

In 2009, Jindal, like most other governors, was no longer dealing with a state budget surplus but with a budget shortfall amid a deepening national recession. In March 2009, he presented a $26 billion budget that cut spending on health care and higher education and eliminated hundreds of state jobs. It included nearly $1 billion in federal economic stimulus funds, but he rejected stimulus unemployment benefits conditioned on a permanent increase in state spending levels. Jindal also called for redesigning the health-care system, with Medicaid being administered through private insurance companies. His plan required federal as well as legislative approval. Well before the 2011 state election, he had raised more than $3 million in campaign funds.

Senior Senator

Mary Landrieu (D)

Elected 1996, term expires 2014, 3rd term; b. Nov. 23, 1955, Arlington, VA; home, New Orleans; LA St. U., B.A. 1977; Catholic; married (Frank Snellings); 2 children.

Elected Office: LA House of Reps., 1980–88; LA treasurer, 1988–96.

DC Office: 328 HSOB, 20510, 202-224-5824; Fax: 202-224-9735; Web site: landrieu.senate.gov.

State Offices: Baton Rouge, 225-389-0395; Lake Charles, 337-436-6650; New Orleans, 504-589-2427; Shreveport, 318-676-3085.

Committees: *Appropriations* (12th of 18 D): Energy & Water Development; Financial Services & General Government; Homeland Security; Labor, Health and Human Services, Education & Related Agencies; Military Construction, Veterans Affairs & Related Agencies; State, Foreign Operations & Related Programs. *Energy & Natural Resources* (5th of 13 D): Energy; National Parks; Public Lands & Forests. *Homeland Security & Governmental Affairs* (6th of 10 D): Disaster Recovery (Chmn); Oversight of Government Management, the Federal Workforce & the District of Columbia; State, Local & Private Sector Preparedness & Integration. *Small Business & Entrepreneurship* (Chmn of 11 D).

Group Ratings

	ADA	ACLU	AFS	LCV	ITIC	NTU	COC	ACU	CFG	FRC
2008	65	57	100	55	80	26	75	32	33	44
2007	80	—	100	53	—	16	73	40	21	—

National Journal Ratings

	2007 LIB	—	2007 CONS		2008 LIB	—	2008 CONS
Economic	49%	—	49%		48%	—	51%
Social	54%	—	45%		45%	—	54%
Foreign	54%	—	44%		56%	—	40%
Composite	53%	—	47%		51%	—	49%

Key Votes of the 110th Congress

1. Raise CAFE standards	N	5. Make English official language	Y	9. Withdraw troops 3/08	Y
2. Expand SCHIP	Y	6. Path to citizenship	N	10. Iran guard is terrorist group	Y
3. Cap greenhouse gases	N	7. Fetus is unborn child	Y	11. Increase missile defense $	Y
4. Bail out financial markets	N	8. Prosecute hate crimes	Y	12. Overhaul FISA	Y

Election Results

2008 general	Mary Landrieu (D)	988,298	(52%)	($10,146,669)
	John Kennedy (R)	867,177	(46%)	($4,795,281)
2008 primary	Mary Landrieu (D)	unopposed		

Prior Winning Percentages: 2002 (52%); 1996 (50%)

Mary Landrieu, Louisiana's senior senator, is a Democrat who was first elected to the Senate in 1996. Landrieu (*LAN-drew*) has Louisiana politics in her blood. She grew up in New Orleans, the oldest of nine children of Moon Landrieu, the Democratic mayor of New Orleans from 1970 to 1978 and Housing and Urban Development secretary in the Carter administration. Her brother is Mitch Landrieu, Louisiana's lieutenant governor, who was defeated by incumbent Ray Nagin in the 2006 New Orleans mayor's race. She was educated at Ursuline Academy and Louisiana State University. In 1979, at age 23, she became the youngest woman ever elected to the Louisiana Legislature. In 1987, she was elected state Treasurer. A sharp critic of Democratic Gov. Edwin Edwards, she was re-elected in 1991. In 1995, she ran for governor and in the September primary finished third, 1% behind the second-place finisher, Democratic Rep. Cleo Fields. Democrats lost the governor's mansion that year to Republican Mike Foster.

Landrieu immediately started running for the Senate seat held by Democrat Bennett Johnston, who was retiring after 24 years in office. She had a well-known name and a moderate platform—she supported the proposed balanced-budget amendment and capital-gains tax cuts and promised to make education a top priority. Her competition was Attorney General Richard Ieyoub, also a Democrat, and Woody Jenkins, a 25-year state legislator and strong abortion opponent who had run twice unsuccessfully for the Senate as a Democrat and now was running as a Republican. Jenkins led the September primary with 26% to 22% for Landrieu and 20% for Ieyoub; former Ku Klux Klan member David Duke got 12%.

Going into the runoff, Jenkins looked like the favorite. But he had little money left, and Landrieu, who ultimately outspent him, ran ads attacking him as an extremist. The result was an exceedingly close election. The official results showed Landrieu ahead by 5,788 votes, 50.2% to 49.8% for Jenkins. He sued, claiming vote fraud, but withdrew the lawsuit and submitted his claim to the Senate. In October 1997, the Senate Rules Committee concluded that while "isolated instances" of voter fraud did occur, there was no evidence to prove a "widespread effort to illegally affect the outcome of this election" or that Landrieu was involved in the violation of election laws. Landrieu finally claimed the seat.

In the Senate, Landrieu's voting record places her among the more conservative Democrats. She voted for the Iraq war resolution in 2002. Her first bill was for a $5 million block grant for adoption services; her two children are adopted. She backs adoption tax credits and wants higher breaks for those who adopt special needs or foster children. She was the lead co-sponsor of the law providing for speedy citizenship for foreign-born children adopted by U.S. citizens. When it went into effect, it created the largest number of new U.S. citizens ever on a single day. Landrieu was the only Democrat who co-sponsored conservative Republican Sam Brownback's bills to prohibit human cloning for reproduction or research. In 2001, Landrieu secured a seat on the influential Appropriations Committee.

All the while she was running hard for re-election in 2002. She was an obvious Republican target, because of her small margin of victory in 1996 and because of President George W. Bush's popularity in Louisiana at the time. In 2001, 5th District Rep. John Cooksey, a Republican and a north Louisiana ophthalmologist, launched a challenge. But his candidacy was undone by one word: diaper. On September 18, 2001, a week after the September 11 attacks, Cooksey said in a radio interview in Louisiana, "If I see someone comes in that's got a diaper on his head and a fan belt wrapped around the diaper on his head, the guy needs to be pulled over." Cooksey spent $200,000 on radio ads defending his comments. But it was obvious that the Bush White House did not want to back a candidate who would be an embarrassment to the United States in the Middle East.

The National Republican Senatorial Committee encouraged other Republicans to run, banking on a strategy of getting multiple candidates in the field to hold Landrieu to under 50% of the vote, then beating her in the subsequent runoff. State Rep. Tony Perkins, a sponsor of a school-prayer bill, got into the contest, as did Elections Commissioner Suzanne Haik Terrell. In July, the NRSC started running what would eventually be $2 million worth of television ads against Landrieu. "There's just something about Mary and higher taxes," said one. "Landrieu voted in favor of higher taxes over 120 times." Playing defense, Landrieu ran ads saying she'd supported Bush 74% of the time and that only two Democrats, Georgia's Zell Miller and Louisiana's John Breaux, had voted more often with Bush.

At the end of August, the NRSC officially backed Terrell, and started spending money on her behalf, comparing Landrieu's voting record with New York Sen. Hillary Rodham Clinton's. Terrell, a New Orleans Catholic, was better positioned than Cooksey or Perkins, both northern Louisiana Protestants, to take votes away from Landrieu in the New Orleans area. However, GOP Gov. Foster endorsed Cooksey. In mid-October, Landrieu started running anti-Terrell ads, charging that taxes and spending went up in New Orleans when she was on the City Council. Perkins attacked Landrieu for living in a "Washington mansion." On November 5, Landrieu failed to clinch a victory. She won 46% of the vote, to 27% for Terrell, 14% for Cooksey and 10% for Perkins. The three Republicans together led Landrieu 51%-46%.

In the runoff, there was discontent on the Democratic side among black leaders about Landrieu's ads proclaiming her 74% support of Bush. In debates the two candidates tangled over abortion. In one case, on leaving the television studio, Landrieu said to Terrell, "This is your last campaign." Terrell, taken aback, said, "She threatened me." The candidates continued to argue about tax cuts, personnel rules for the Department of Homeland Security and privatizing government jobs. Then a Democratic opposition researcher made a propitious find—an article in the Mexican center-left newspaper *Reforma* reporting that the Bush administration had agreed with the Mexican government to double the amount of sugar that could be imported from Mexico, bad news for a major domestic sugar-producing state like Louisiana. The Office of Special Trade Representative and the State Department denied that any such agreement had been made. But Landrieu trumpeted the claim in ads and promised to do everything she could to stop any such agreement. It was a fine issue for Landrieu to use to document her claim that Terrell would be a "rubber stamp" for Bush, even though Terrell said she too opposed any deal. Landrieu met with trade and State Department officials in January 2003 and reported that she'd been assured there had not been a sugar deal with Mexico. The incident may have changed enough votes to give Landrieu her 52%-48% victory.

In her second term, Landrieu stepped into more national issues and into the limelight. As the ranking Democrat on the District of Columbia Appropriations Subcommittee, she insisted on restrictions on a program allowing D.C. parents to send their children to private schools on government vouchers. Voucher supporters ran an ad in the New Orleans newspaper saying, "My mom wants you to know that Sen. Mary Landrieu doesn't want me to go to the same school where her children go."

She supported oil drilling in the Arctic National Wildlife Refuge and, when it passed in March 2005, was one of three Democrats voting for it. (The others were the two senators from Hawaii.) In 2004, she won passage of an amendment eliminating the reduction in veterans' widows' pensions when they became eligible for Social Security. She isn't shy about putting holds on legislation or threatening to filibuster bills to force action on her issues. In 2004, she filibustered a corporate tax bill for three days in support of an amendment to give tax credits to employers who make up lost pay for reservists and National Guard troops called to active duty. She ultimately accepted a compromise limiting the tax credit to companies with 50 or fewer workers.

In the 2004 campaign she endorsed neither of the two well-known Democrats running for retiring Democratic Sen. John Breaux's seat, but campaigned extensively around the state against Republican David Vitter. "Don't send me a puppet to work with, send me a partner," she said over and over. On Election Night, she had an abrupt conversation with Vitter, who, against expectations, won the seat with 51% of the vote. She called Vitter to tell him the second-place finisher, Democrat Chris John, was not conceding, kicking off a rocky working relationship between Louisiana's two senators.

Hurricane Katrina forced them to grudgingly work together and put the outspoken Landrieu in the national spotlight as advocate for her state. "If my heart is a little heavy today, it's because I've seen more in the last two weeks than I've seen in my entire life," she said on her return from inspecting the damage to her home state and home city. Three of her siblings lost their homes to Katrina. In response to the post-hurricane comment by President Bush that nobody "anticipated the breach of the levees," she said tartly, "Everybody anticipated the breach of the levees, Mr. President." In early September, Landrieu said on national television that if anyone, including Bush, criticized the state and local government response to Katrina, "I might likely have to punch him. Literally."

Six weeks after the catastrophe, she objected that Louisiana was being treated less sympathetically than had other states during emergencies. Vitter disagreed with her protest. "She needs to learn a little statesmanship. She's been way too hotheaded," local political analyst Elliott Stonecipher told the Baton Rouge *Advocate*. But the criticism did not deter Landrieu. In April 2006, she said that she would block every presidential nomination until Bush agreed to $6 billion for repair of Louisiana levees. When the Senate approved that money and more a few weeks later, Landrieu backed off her general threat, but vowed to block nominees at the Energy and Interior departments until there was agreement on using royalties from offshore oil and gas production to pay for coastal restoration and additional hurricane protection. She played a major role when that bill finally was enacted in December 2006. "It is the cornerstone that has been laid down to protect and rebuild the Gulf Coast," she said.

In 2007, Landrieu complained of discrimination against Louisiana when the Federal Emergency Management Agency released $281 million for alternative housing in Mississippi. She promptly placed a hold on the nomination of the head of the Army Corps of Engineers, saying she would drop it only if she liked what he said after he visited the Gulf. She pushed Bush's Secretary of State Condoleezza Rice to implement policies to take advantage of foreign aid during disasters like Katrina. Then in February 2008, she added tenant vouchers to her rebuilding bill, although Vitter objected to rebuilding public-housing projects that no one might live in. She worked to include some $5.8 billion in recovery projects in the supplemental appropriation in July 2008, along with $73 million for housing not requested by Vitter or the Bush administration.

In the closely divided Senate in 2007 and 2008, Landrieu cast some key votes. She was one of two Democrats to vote in March 2008 to reduce the estate tax, and she voted for Vitter's amendment to cut community-policing funds for cities that refuse to help enforce immigration laws. She cast the deciding vote in December 2007 against eliminating a tax deduction for oil companies and directing the money to alternative fuels. She called it "one-sided policymaking" that left "Louisiana industry footing the bill." After hurricanes Gustav and Ike hit Louisiana, she sponsored a $1.2 billion farm disaster-relief bill, and threatened a filibuster until Senate Majority Leader Harry Reid, a Nevada Democrat, agreed to advance it. But in October 2008, the bill was stopped by an objection from Republican Sen. Tom Coburn of Oklahoma, who said the relief was duplicative.

Going into the 2008 election season, Republican strategists targeted Landrieu. Indeed, she was the only plausible target they could identify among incumbent Democratic senators. But they had difficulty finding a candidate. Rep. Richard Baker declined to run, as did Louisiana Secretary of State Jay Dardenne. Then in August 2007, state Treasurer John Kennedy, who had run third, with 15% of the vote, in the 2004 Senate race, switched from the Democratic to the Republican party and announced he would challenge Landrieu in November.

Landrieu had already been busy fundraising, which enabled her to maintain a significant advantage in cash on hand. Kennedy criticized her for voting against ending the moratorium on oil-shale development. She called him a "confused politician" and said he'd mismanaged the treasurer's office. Kennedy praised Coburn for blocking Landrieu's farm disaster-aid bill, although it was supported by Vitter and Republican state Agriculture Commissioner Mike Strain. The Landrieu campaign got endorsements from Republican local officials in St. Tammany and Jefferson parishes and from former Republican Gov. David Treen. Landrieu won 52%-46%. She won the votes of 96% of African-Americans, 33% of whites and 42% of white independents, while Democratic presidential nominee Barack Obama won only 14% of whites and 21% of white independents. Landrieu won Orleans Parish with 84%, more than the 80% she'd won in the 2002 runoff. Her work on recovery issues evidently more than offset the decline in the number of black voters there. She won 52% in metro Baton Rouge, 1% more than in 2002, and 52% in the rest of the state, the same as in 2002.

In January 2009, Landrieu became chairman of the Small Business Committee. And, continuing her heavy involvement in hurricane recovery, she threatened in March 2009 to stop federal housing spending in New Orleans unless Mayor Ray Nagin accounted for millions of dollars in unspent and expiring federal grants.

Junior Senator

David Vitter (R)

Elected 2004, term expires 2010, 1st term; b. May 3, 1961, New Orleans; home, Metairie; Harvard U., A.B. 1983, Rhodes Scholar, Oxford U., B.A. 1985, Tulane Law Schl., J.D. 1988; Catholic; married (Wendy); 4 children.

Elected Office: LA House of Reps., 1991–99; U.S. House of Reps., 1999–2004.

Professional Career: Practicing atty., 1988–99; Adjunct law prof., Tulane U. & Loyola U., 1995–98.

DC Office: 516 HSOB, 20510, 202-224-4623; Fax: 202-228-5061; Web site: vitter.senate.gov.

State Offices: Alexandria, 318-448-0169; Baton Rouge, 225-383-0331; Lafayette, 337-262-6898; Lake Charles, 337-436-0453; Metairie, 504-589-2753; Monroe, 318-325-8120; Shreveport, 318-861-0437.

Committees: *Armed Services* (10th of 11 R): Personnel; Seapower; Strategic Forces (RMM). *Banking, Housing & Urban Affairs* (8th of 10 R): Housing, Transportation & Community Development (RMM); Securities, Insurance & Investment. *Commerce, Science & Transportation* (8th of 11 R): Aviation Operations, Safety & Security; Communications, Technology & the Internet; Consumer Protection, Product Safety & Insurance; Oceans, Atmosphere & Coast Guard; Science & Space (RMM); Surface Transportation & Merchant Marine Infrastructure, Safety & Security. *Environment & Public Works* (3rd of 7 R). *Small Business & Entrepreneurship* (3rd of 7 R).

Group Ratings

	ADA	ACLU	AFS	LCV	ITIC	NTU	COC	ACU	CFG	FRC
2008	5	21	0	0	80	77	88	84	90	100
2007	10	—	0	0	—	76	73	96	83	—

National Journal Ratings

	2007 LIB	—	2007 CONS		2008 LIB	—	2008 CONS
Economic	20%	—	79%		11%	—	88%
Social	9%	—	87%		0%	—	79%
Foreign	14%	—	84%		0%	—	84%
Composite	16%	—	85%		10%	—	90%

Key Votes of the 110th Congress

1. Raise CAFE standards	N	5. Make English official language Y	9. Withdraw troops 3/08	N
2. Expand SCHIP	N	6. Path to citizenship	N	10. Iran guard is terrorist group Y
3. Cap greenhouse gases	N	7. Fetus is unborn child	Y	11. Increase missile defense $	Y
4. Bail out financial markets N	8. Prosecute hate crimes	N	12. Overhaul FISA	Y

Election Results

2004 primary				
	David Vitter (R)	943,014	(51%)	($7,206,714)
	Chris John (D)	542,150	(29%)	($4,868,165)
	John Kennedy (D)	275,821	(15%)	($1,919,874)

Prior Winning Percentages: 2002 House (81%); 2000 House (80%); 1999 House (51%)

Louisiana's junior senator is David Vitter, a Republican elected in 2004. He grew up in the New Orleans area, the son of a Chevron petroleum engineer. He graduated from Harvard University and Tulane University's law school and was a Rhodes Scholar. He was a business attorney and taught law at Tulane and Loyola. In 1991, Vitter was elected to the state House from the district that had been represented by former Ku Klux Klansman David Duke. There he passed a term-limits bill through a reluctant state Legislature and was noted for his ability to irritate other politicians. Many of them held grudges because of his crusade for term limits; others were put off by his crusades for ethics in government. Vitter led the effort to recall Democratic Gov. Edwin Edwards, who ultimately went to prison for racketeering. A popular sheriff sued Vitter three times after Vitter criticized his ethics.

Vitter ran for Congress and won in a May 1999 special election to replace Republican Bob Livingston, the Speaker-designate who announced in late 1998 that he would resign after confessing that he had had extramarital affairs. Many Republicans jumped into the race, and many Louisiana and national Republicans feared that Duke would run and embarrass the party by making it into the runoff. The establishment choice was David Treen, 70, who had served four terms in the House starting in 1972 and had been elected governor in 1979. Vitter argued, in effect, that Treen was too old, saying, "We need a younger congressman like me, so we can start building up the seniority we lost when Bob Livingston resigned." The top two vote-getters in the initial balloting were Treen, with 25%, and Vitter, with 22%. The two advanced to the runoff under the system then in use. Duke, unnervingly close to making the runoff, finished third with 19%. Low turnout was probably a factor in deciding the runoff, as Vitter rallied his troops and won 51%-49%.

Vitter had one of the most conservative voting records in the House and the most conservative in the delegation. He twice won re-election in his heavily Republican, suburban New Orleans district with at least 80% of the vote.

In December 2003, Democratic Sen. John Breaux announced that he would not seek a fourth term, and two days later, Vitter jumped into the contest. Wooden in manner, a self-described loner and highly conservative, Vitter was the stylistic opposite of Breaux, a gregarious dealmaker and respected centrist from Cajun country who had been a major force for reform of entitlements and health care. But the state party and national Republicans worked hard to clear the field for Vitter, viewing him as the strongest possible candidate, thanks to his suburban political base and his habit of traveling the state to announce projects secured from his perch on the Appropriations Committee. He was also familiar in Cajun country after his well-publicized opposition to an Indian casino in southwestern Louisiana.

On the Democratic side, three serious candidates joined the race: U.S. Rep. Chris John, a native of Crowley, the town that produced not only Breaux but Edwards; two-term state Treasurer John Kennedy; and state Rep. Arthur Morrell, an African-American from New Orleans. There was little doubt that Vitter would win the state's unique Election Day primary against a divided Democratic field; the real issue for Democrats was holding him below the 50%-plus-one threshold necessary to avoid a December runoff. Vitter ran as a strong supporter of President George W. Bush and called for making Bush's tax cuts permanent, new job creation and medical-malpractice restrictions. He opposed abortion rights, same-sex marriage and gun-ownership restrictions. He said he best represented "mainstream Louisiana values" and painted John as an out-of-touch Washington liberal who was close to John Kerry, the 2004 Democratic presidential nominee. John, the Democratic front-runner who had Breaux's endorsement, responded by referring to Vitter as a Republican Party puppet and strove to distance himself from Kerry's presidential campaign—a wise move in a state that Bush wound up carrying with 57% that November.

Sugar was an important issue. Louisiana is the prime cane-sugar-producing state, and producers worry about being undercut by cheap imports. Vitter broke with the Bush administration over the Central American Free Trade Agreement, opposing it because it did not exempt sugar imports from the deal. Vitter ran some of the best and most creative television ads of the election cycle, making light of his image as a stiff politician with humorous commercials featuring his daughter's home movies. Meanwhile, John failed to gain momentum and was caught in the crossfire between Vitter on the right and Kennedy and Morrell on the left. With Vitter leading in the polls going into November, the Democratic candidates began scrambling to keep him below the 50% threshold. The Democratic Senatorial Campaign Committee assisted by spending more than $1.5 million in ads criticizing Vitter's positions on prescription-drug reimportation and Social Security. It wasn't enough. Vitter won the race outright with 51%, becoming the first Republican in 121 years to represent Louisiana in the Senate. John was the leading Democratic vote-getter, with 29% to 15% for Kennedy and 3% for Morrell. Bush's strong performance helped Vitter, but he ran well on his own, winning Mississippi River parishes that Bush lost, carrying nearly all of Louisiana north of Baton Rouge, and posting large margins in the New Orleans suburbs. In populous St. Tammany Parish, which he had represented in Congress, Vitter won by more than 5-to-1. His 60,000-vote margin there was more than enough to erase John's 25,000-vote advantage in New Orleans.

In the Senate, Vitter has compiled a relatively conservative voting record with maverick touches. In January 2007, during the Senate's debate of the lobbying reform bill, he won passage of his amendments to increase criminal sanctions for willful violations. He sought to prohibit lobbying by spouses of senators. He also advocated for a lost cause in the Senate: a constitutional amendment to limit members of the House and Senate to 12 years of service. But Vitter continued to be a thorn in the side of lawmakers who prefer business as usual. In March 2009, he sponsored an amendment to require a vote on any annual congressional pay raise before it could take effect. Although the amendment was defeated, the move pressured Democratic Senate Majority Leader Harry Reid to put the pay raise to a stand-alone vote. It passed. After Democrat Barack Obama's election as president in 2008, Vitter was not inspired to try to make friends across the aisle. He cast one of the two votes against confirming New York Democrat Hillary Rodham Clinton as secretary of state, although her qualifications for the job were not an issue.

He continued to push for drug reimportation, which allows consumers to buy U.S.-made drugs from other countries, where they are often cheaper. In 2006, the Senate passed his amendment to stop customs agents from seizing small amounts of Food and Drug Administration-approved drugs that Americans had bought in Canada for their personal use.

In September 2007, his amendment to bar funding of organizations advocating international gun-control policies passed 81-10. But the following month, the Senate rejected 52-41 his amendment to deny family-planning funds to organizations that perform abortions. He frequently attacked the United

Nations, particularly when its Human Rights Council condemned the tearing down of New Orleans public-housing projects. In July 2008, the Senate passed his amendment giving inspectors general more access to documents on the Global Fund to Fight AIDS, Tuberculosis and Malaria. Vitter is particularly interested in law-and-order issues. In April 2008, he led a bipartisan group of senators supporting $50 million for the U.S. Marshals Service to track down child predators in April 2008. He also sponsored a bill to require all states to collect DNA samples from convicted felons.

At a Senate hearing two months before Hurricane Katrina, Vitter predicted that someday a huge storm would smash the city and leave it under water: "It's not a question of if. It's a question of when." After the catastrophe, he criticized the U.S. Army Corps of Engineers for failing to provide flood protection for the city. And he worked with Louisiana's Democratic senator, Mary Landrieu, in pressing for federal recovery funds, though the two famously don't get along personally. They presented a Louisiana commission's proposal for $250 billion in funding for repairs and reconstruction, which was widely regarded as unrealistic. On occasion, he attacked Landrieu for filibustering too much and told local reporters that he was well aware of the widespread view among Republicans in Congress that Louisiana would waste federal reconstruction funds. In September 2007, he criticized Reid for delaying the scheduling of a vote on a water-resources bill that authorized nearly $2 billion for Louisiana coastal-restoration projects and $886 million for a 72-mile system of levees and floodwalls for low-lying Terrebonne and Lafourche parishes. The next month, Vitter got 22 Republican senators to sign a letter urging Bush to abandon his threat to veto the bill. In February 2008, he got Landrieu to drop from her housing bill a requirement that all public-housing units be replaced and to add in its stead a provision for tenant vouchers that could be used for housing anywhere.

All in all, in the 110th Congress (2007–08), Vitter was productive for someone whose image and reputation had been dealt a major blow in July 2007, when it was revealed that between 1999 and 2001 his phone number had appeared on the call list of "D.C. Madam" Deborah Jeane Palfrey. A week later he appeared with his wife, Wendy, at his side and issued a public apology, saying he had committed "a very serious sin." In April 2008, Palfrey's defense attorney said he would ask the senator to testify, but in a stroke of luck for Vitter, the defense rested without calling witnesses. That same year, the Senate Ethics Committee debated whether to punish Vitter, but ruled that the conduct in question had occurred before he entered the Senate and took a pass. Vitter then tried to use his campaign funds to pay $160,000 in legal fees in the case, but the Federal Election Commission would not permit him to do so. In another round of negative publicity for Vitter, in March 2009, the Transportation Security Administration looked into an incident in which Vitter allegedly had opened a security gate to try to board a flight at Dulles Airport after the flight had been boarded and the doors locked; the attempt set off alarms. Vitter later claimed he had mistakenly gone through the wrong door at the gate. The TSA ruled that he had not posed a security threat.

Still, Louisianans continued to support Vitter; he maintained high job approval in 2008 and early 2009. He stayed in touch with constituents by attending more than 120 town-hall meetings across the state. There was talk that he would be opposed in the 2010 primary, but prominent possible challengers took a pass in early 2009. Vitter could face a Democratic challenge, however. The last time an incumbent Louisiana senator was defeated was in 1932.

FIRST DISTRICT

Steve Scalise (R)

Elected May 2008, 1st full term; b. Oct. 6, 1965, New Orleans; home, Jefferson; LA St. U., B.S., 1989; Catholic; married (Jennifer); 2 children.

Elected Office: LA Legislature, 1996–2007, LA Senate, 2008.

Professional Career: Systems engineer, Diamond Data Systems, eVenture Technologies.

DC Office: 429 CHOB, 20515, 202-225-3015; Fax: 202-226-0386; Web site: scalise.house.gov.

State Offices: Hammond, 985-340-2185; Mandeville, 985-893-9064; Metarie, 504-837-1259.

Committees: *Energy & Commerce* (23rd of 23 R): Commerce, Trade & Consumer Protections; Energy & Environment.

Group Ratings

	ADA	ACLU	AFS	LCV	ITIC	NTU	COC	ACU	CFG	FRC
2008	5	25	0	0	0	79	94	100	93	100
2007	—	—	—	—	—	—	—	—	—	—

National Journal Ratings

	2007 LIB — 2007 CONS		2008 LIB — 2008 CONS	
Economic	*% —	*%	0% —	98%
Social	*% —	*%	29% —	71%
Foreign	*% —	*%	8% —	92%
Composite	*% —	*%	13% —	87%

Key Votes of the 110th Congress

1. Increase minimum wage	*	5. Share immigration data	*	9. Withdraw troops 8/08	*
2. Expand SCHIP	*	6. Foreign aid abortion ban	*	10. No operations in Iran	*
3. Raise CAFE standards	*	7. Ban gay bias in workplace	*	11. Free trade with Peru	*
4. Bail out financial markets	N	8. Repeal D.C. gun law	Y	12. Overhaul FISA	Y

Election Results

2008 general	Steve Scalise (R) 189,168	(66%)	($1,628,134)
	Jim Harlan (D).......................................98,839	(34%)	($2,158,185)
2008 primary	Steve Scalise (R) .... unopposed		
2008 spec. general	Steve Scalise (R) 33,867	(75%)	
	Gilda Reed (D)......................................10,142	(23%)	
2008 spec. primary	Steve Scalise (R) 19,338	(58%)	
	Tim Burns (R) 13,958	(42%)	

Population		**Race/Ethnicity**		**Work**	
Pop. 2007:	649,497	White:	75.7%	Private:	79.5%
Change since 2000:	Up 1.7%	Black:	15.2%	Government:	13.6%
Urban:	79.6%	Hispanic:	5.8%	Self-employed:	6.5%
Rural:	20.4%	Asian:	1.8%	Blue collar:	20.6%
Area size:	2,840 sq. mi.	Native Am.:	0.2%	White collar:	64.3%
		Hawaiian:	0.0%	Khaki collar:	0.2%
Age		Two+ races:	1.1%	Other:	14.8%
Median age:	38.1 yrs.	*Ancestry*		Median income:	$49,015
More than 65 yrs:	13.3%	French:	15.5%	Median home value:	$172,900
Less than 18 yrs:	23.8%	German:	12.4%	Poverty:	13.4%
Education		Italian:	10.4%	**Military Veterans**	
H.S. grad:	84.9%			% of Pop:	10.7%
College grad:	28.5%				
Grad degree:	9.7%				

Founded in 1718 and the nation's fifth largest city at the outbreak of the Civil War, New Orleans is ancient for an American metropolis. It is still closely girded by the peculiar wilderness of the mushy Delta lands of the sluggish Mississippi River. For decades, you could climb a levee overlooking the Mississippi and see an expanse of water with untidy clumps of trees and disorganized-looking, seemingly abandoned docks—what Mark Twain had in his mind's eye while writing *Life on the Mississippi*

2008 Presidential Vote

McCain (R)..............................222,090	(73%)
Obama (D) 79,326	(26%)

2004 Presidential Vote

Bush (R)...................................215,538	(71%)
Kerry (D)..................................87,009	(28%)

Cook Partisan Voting Index: R + 24

in the 1870s. Drive just past the last block of a suburban subdivision and you were in unreclaimed swamp, vegetation thick with herons and alligators, flat as far as the eye could see. For years, the river funneled the products of half a continent down to a single port with an international heritage and flair. The New Orleans metropolitan area has lived off that geography and history, with an inward-looking elite preoccupied with who is in which Mardi Gras krewe and interested more in the genealogy of old families than in the geography of the Oil Patch. The old buildings of New Orleans are finely proportioned and its old neighborhoods charming, like those in France. Its early-20th-century improvements, like Olmstead's City Park, were grand. But its late-20th-century streetscapes and subdivisions were without ornament or charm, utilitarian works that were part of an attempt to master the below-sea-level environment.

After Hurricane Katrina struck with Category Four force on Aug. 29, 2005, many of those details changed dramatically. The city's population plummeted, housing stock was destroyed, some levees were breached and others were no longer reliable. The last act of nature to have wreaked so much damage on an American city was the San Francisco earthquake of 1906.

The 1st Congressional District of Louisiana encompasses some of the places hardest hit by Katrina, including much of the newer part of the New Orleans metropolitan area, spread over the soggy lands of the lower Mississippi and Lake Pontchartrain. About half of its people live south of the lake in affluent white neighborhoods, in the Uptown area and west of City Park, and in mostly white neighborhoods on the West Bank of the Mississippi. The district takes in the vast suburb of Metairie in Jefferson Parish and also part of suburbanizing St. Charles Parish. The boundaries have been drawn so that the next-door 2nd District has an African-American majority; the black percentage in the 1st (13%) is the lowest of any Louisiana district. The 1st extends across the 26-mile Lake Pontchartrain Causeway to include St. Tammany Parish, with its old towns lush with trees and clusters of new growth around giant intersections. This has been the growth area of metropolitan New Orleans. The population of the city fell 7% between 1990 and 2004, and Jefferson Parish's increased only 1%, while St. Tammany Parish's population increased 40%. Those figures fluctuated by as much as 50,000 people after Katrina, but previous trends seem likely to continue. Nearly 75% of the homes in St. Tammany were damaged to some degree, but much of the parish, with the notable exception of Slidell, was spared from the worst effects. As a result, the neighborhoods of St. Tammany recovered more quickly, and many evacuees found their way to its higher ground in the ensuing months . The local real estate market surged, and the population grew by about 23% in the first year after Katrina. The 1st District also includes, to the north and west, Washington and Tangipahoa parishes, still mostly rural. But Tangipahoa, which developed in the 19th century along the rail line linking New Orleans and Chicago, grew by 7% in the two years after Katrina.

This is the most upscale, affluent, highly educated district in Louisiana, and by far the most Republican, supportive of political reformers and against economic redistribution. George W. Bush got 71% of the vote here in 2004, by far his best performance in the state. John McCain bested Barack Obama 76%-22% in St. Tammany, and took the district 73%-26%.

The congressman from the 1st District is Steve Scalise, a Republican who won a special election in May 2008 to succeed GOP Rep. Bobby Jindal, who became governor. A native of New Orleans, Scalise grew up in Metairie. When his parents gave their son a battery-powered microphone, he played town crier on his neighborhood street, decorating his bicycle in red, white and blue and calling people to the polls—the start of his political career. He majored in computer science at Louisiana State University, where he was speaker of the student assembly. After college, he settled in Jefferson Parish as a systems engineer. In 1995, when he was 30, he was elected to the state House, where he served 12 years before winning a state Senate seat in October 2007. He pushed legislation to give incentives to the motion-picture industry to produce films in Louisiana. He helped to pass a bill that made Louisiana the first state to bar cities from suing gun manufacturers for the actions of criminals. Scalise had considered running for the open seat in this district in 1999 and 2004, but deferred first to David Vitter, now a U.S. senator, then to Jindal.

In the special election to replace Jindal, the key contest was the April 5 Republican runoff between Scalise and state Rep. Tim Burns of Mandeville in St. Tammany. Burns cited Scalise's opposition to a bill banning smoking in restaurants and tried to tie him to special interests. Scalise called for limits on "out-of-control spending" and said he had "the experience to hit the ground running from Day One." Scalise won 58%-42%, capturing 83% of the Jefferson Parish vote.

The May 3 contest against Democrat Gilda Reed, a college instructor and political neophyte, was never in doubt. Scalise won 75%-23%. But the following November, when Scalise had to defend the seat in regularly scheduled congressional election, he faced a bigger challenge. Democrat Jim Harlan, a venture capitalist, sank $1.8 million of his own money into the race and was not shy about negative advertising against Scalise. In one television ad, he tried to tie Scalise to a local scandal involving a federal investigation of the abuse of tax credits by the Louisiana Institute of Film Technology. Scalise had been a sponsor of the tax-credit program when he served in the state Legislature. Scalise cited his opponent's support of presidential candidate Barack Obama as evidence that Harlan was too liberal for the district. Scalise coasted to a 66%-34% win for a full two-year term, taking 71% in Jefferson Parish and 68% in St. Tammany, which together accounted for 71% of the total vote. In 2009, he joined the Energy and Commerce Committee, a useful assignment for this district. He called for more energy production, including offshore drilling.

SECOND DISTRICT

Joseph Cao (R)

Elected 2008, 1st term; b. March 19, 1967, Ho Chi Minh City, Vietnam; home, New Orleans; Baylor U., B.S. 1990; Fordham U., M.A. 1995; Loyola U., J.D. 2000; Catholic; married (Kate); 2 children.

Professional Career: Instructor, Loyola U.; Legal cnsl., Boat People SOS.; Mbr., Natl. Advisory Cncl. Of the U.S. Conf. of Catholic Bishops, 2002; New Orleans parish board of elections, 2007

DC Office: 2113 RHOB, 20515, 202-225-6636; Fax: 202-225-1988; Web site: josephcao.house.gov.

State Offices: New Orleans, 504-483-2325.

Committees: *Homeland Security* (12th of 13 R): Emergency Communications, Preparedness & Response; Management, Investigations & Oversight. *Transportation & Infrastructure* (28th of 30 R): Economic Development, Public Buildings & Emergency Management; Railroads, Pipelines & Hazardous Materials; Water Resources & Environment.

Group Ratings and Key Votes: Newly Elected

Election Results

2008 general	Anh "Joseph" Cao (R)...33,132	(50%)	($234,559)
	William Jefferson (D)...31,318	(47%)	($342,240)
	Malik Rahim (Green)...1,883	(3%)	($945)
2008 primary	Anh "Joseph" Cao (R)................................. unopposed		

Population		Race/Ethnicity		Work	
Pop. 2007:	463,384	White:	30.7%	Private:	77.1%
Change since 2000:	Down 27.4%	Black:	59.5%	Government:	15.8%
Urban:	99.4%	Hispanic:	4.9%	Self-employed:	6.9%
Rural:	0.6%	Asian:	3.3%	Blue collar:	24.2%
Area size:	444 sq. mi.	Native Am.:	0.3%	White collar:	54.5%
		Hawaiian:	0.0%	Khaki collar:	0.1%
Age		Two+ races:	1.1%	Other:	21.2%
Median age:	36.3 yrs.			Median income:	$36,159
More than 65 yrs:	11.0%	*Ancestry*		Median home value:	$136,200
Less than 18 yrs:	24.5%	French:	8.7%	Poverty:	22.9%
		German:	5.4%		
Education		Italian:	4.0%	**Military Veterans**	
H.S. grad:	77.3%			% of Pop:	8.6%
College grad:	20.7%				
Grad degree:	7.9%				

Founded by the French in 1718, ruled by the Spanish from 1763 until it was sold to the United States in 1803, New Orleans was a Creole city—part French, a bit Spanish, more than a touch Caribbean—when the American flag was raised over what is now Jackson Square. The statue of Andrew Jackson still seems an intrusion in a square set off by a French Market, the Cabildo, the Presbytere, the Pontalba apartments and Cathedral St. Louis.

2008 Presidential Vote		
Obama (D) 150,191	(75%)
McCain (R)..............................46,666	(23%)
2004 Presidential Vote		
Kerry (D)................................183,928	(75%)
Bush (R).................................58,855	(24%)
Cook Partisan Voting Index: D + 25		

New Orleans was the fifth largest American city from 1840 until the Civil War and the only sizable city in the South. Yet even as it was sending Southern cotton to the mills of Lancashire, it was an alien cultural force in both the nation and region. Urbanized, yet poor and in many ways primitive, New Orleans had yellow fever epidemics late in the 19th century, even as it was installing electric lights. It had a riot in which Italian immigrants were massacred, even as it was laying streetcar tracks and telephone lines. This was one of the most corrupt American cities during Reconstruction and the Gilded Age, when its votes were regularly bid for and bought. Like other Southern cities, it became rigidly segregated after 1890.

For a time during the 1970s oil boom, New Orleans seemed to be a fast-growing Sun Belt city. But in the 1980s, it was beset by economic woes. Its port lost business—oil to Houston and Latin American trade to Miami—though it still shipped large amounts of grain. In the 1990s, New Orleans took a turn for the better. Crime plummeted and no longer depressed tourism. Visitors wanted to see the gaudy bars of Bourbon Street, the graceful restored houses in the Garden District and the Mardi Gras parade. They wanted to dine in the storied restaurants, with a cuisine all New Orleans' own, spicy and rich and unaffected by trends in low-fat food. Incomes went up, and home ownership increased, among blacks as well as whites. Mayor Ray Nagin campaigned to tackle corruption, but was criticized by fellow African-Americans for not paying enough attention to community needs.

But the nation has since acquired other images of New Orleans. As Hurricane Katrina made landfall early on a Monday morning, Aug. 29, 2005, more than 20,000 people huddled at the downtown Superdome, the shelter of last resort. Although they were told to bring food, water and medicine, many did not. The scene inside was nightmarish, with no power or provisions, and conditions worsened when the storm ripped two holes in the roof. A few days later, city officials began to load people on buses for transport to cities that were better positioned to provide services. The breach of the city's levees led to a surge that churned through the low-income Ninth Ward, while the French Quarter, on higher ground, was largely untouched by the floodwaters. When the city started to dry out, Nagin begged people to return, though services were starkly limited.

During the months following the devastation, it became clear that the city was in for a very long recovery. Thousands of government trailers became semi-permanent homes. City residents who had fled the floodwaters only slowly trickled back, if at all. Only portions of the city got regular utility service. The recovery proceeded, but expectations repeatedly were downsized. In May 2007, the Kaiser Family Foundation issued a report saying, "Hurricane Katrina, and the failure of government at all levels to respond to it more effectively, was personally devastating for a large percentage of the Greater New Orleans population in ways that continue to reverberate today." Overall, a third of Greater New Orleans residents said their lives remain "very disrupted" or "somewhat disrupted," a sentiment shared by 59% of people living in Orleans Parish. In 2008, the last government trailer parks closed, and the restaurants in the French Quarter were back in business. But the numbers continued to tell the story of the city's struggle to rebound. Its population was down from 460,000 to about 320,000 in 2008, public-school enrollment was down 52% and transit riders were down 75%. As the city repopulated after Katrina, the population jumped nearly 14% from 2006 to 2007, but then it slowed dramatically in the next year, increasingly only 3% in 2008. "It's very clear we're going to have a much smaller, very different New Orleans," retired Brown University geographer Robert Kates told *USA Today*.

The 2nd Congressional District of Louisiana includes almost all of the city of New Orleans, everything except a few affluent white neighborhoods. It has nearly half of Jefferson Parish, African-American neighborhoods in Metairie and Kenner, and the West Bank towns of Harvey, Marrero, and Westwego. In the French Quarter—the *Vieux Carre* as it was originally called—are the 19th-century-row houses decked out in their island pastels and ornate wrought-iron railings. At street level are restaurants, art galleries and jazz and blues clubs, and the narrow sidewalks fill up nightly with diners, revelers, and patrons of the tiny voodoo establishments that are found only in New Orleans. South of the quarter is the downtown district, with its skyscrapers and the Superdome, and to the east is the old slum known as the Irish Channel, a reminder that New Orleans had more foreign immigrants than any other part of the South. Up St. Charles Avenue from the Vieux Carre is the Garden District, with the graceful intact homes of the rich early American settlers. The city's population was 60% African-American in 2007, and the district is solidly Democratic. John Kerry won 75% of the vote here in 2004 and Barack Obama got 75% in 2008.

The new congressman from the 2nd District is Joseph Cao, a Republican who won a December 2008 runoff. Cao (*GOW*) is the first Vietnamese-American elected to Congress. His victory in the overwhelmingly Democratic district was no doubt influenced by the legal problems of the ethically challenged incumbent, William Jefferson. Cao's life story offered voters an uplifting alternative to the sordid tale of Jefferson and his freezer full of illicit cash. Three days before Saigon fell to the North Vietnamese, in April 1975, Cao, then just 8, escaped in a U.S. military-transport plane with a brother and sister. His father had been a military officer and was sent to a Viet Cong "re-education camp;" he was reunited with the family years later. Cao settled with an uncle in Houston, where he graduated from high school and got a bachelor's degree in physics from Baylor University. He joined the Jesuit order, did missionary work in Mexico and Vietnam, and earned a master's degree in philosophy from Fordham University. Cao taught at Loyola University in New Orleans, got a law degree there, and began to represent immigrants in the local Vietnamese community. Following the devastation of Hurricane Katrina, he organized and gave legal advice to civic groups, helping one of them shut down a landfill that had been put in a Vietnamese neighborhood. In 2007, he ran for the state House and missed forcing the race into a runoff when he lost by just 250 votes.

Under ordinary circumstances, Cao, as a Republican, would have had no chance in this district. But he was running against nine-term Jefferson, whose career took a plunge after the Federal Bureau of Investigation raided his Capitol Hill home and found $90,000 in "cold cash" in his kitchen freezer, part of more than $400,000 that the investigators' affidavit called bribe money. House Speaker Nancy Pelosi stripped him of his seat on the powerful Ways and Means Committee, despite pleas from the Congressional Black Caucus to wait until Jefferson had his day in court. Even after Jefferson was indicted in June 2007 for bribery, he sought to retain his House seat. In a seven-candidate Democratic primary in October 2008, he led the first round with 25% of the vote. That forced a runoff with Helena Moreno, a former television news anchor who was making her first run for elected office. Jefferson refused to debate, and Moreno pledged to restore respect for Louisiana. Still, Jefferson won the primary runoff, 57%-43%.

Cao won the Republican nomination without opposition and raised $113,500 for his campaign. With turnout expected to be low for the Dec. 6 contest, he worked with local Republican activists to get out the vote among Republicans and the roughly 20,000 local Vietnamese. He campaigned on traditional conservative positions, opposing abortion rights and supporting government vouchers for private-school tuition and a reduction in the size of government. He promised to restore "ethics and honesty" to the office. Jefferson spent $342,240, and assured voters that despite losing his committee post, he maintained influence through his connections to other members of the Black Caucus. Cao won 50% to 47%. His margin of victory came from Jefferson Parish, which cast 32% of the vote and which Cao won 60% to 38%. Jefferson won in Orleans Parish, 51%-45%. The contest was held a month after Election Day, when Barack Obama took 79% of the vote in Orleans Parish.

Cao's victory was one of the few bright notes for Republicans in 2008. House Minority Leader John Boehner crowed in a post-election memo, "The Future Is Cao." The freshman got seats on the Homeland Security and the Transportation and Infrastructure committees. When Democrats said they would target him in 2010, Cao said that he had proved the political experts wrong in 2008 and "I'm sure we'll prove them wrong again." If he somehow manages to win a second term in this district, he might subsequently get a boost from redistricting.

THIRD DISTRICT

Charlie Melancon (D)

Elected 2004, 3rd term; b. Oct. 3, 1947, Napoleonville; home, Napoleonville; U. of SW LA, B.S. 1971; Catholic; married (Peachy); 2 children.

Elected Office: LA House, 1987–93.

Professional Career: Ex. dir., South Central Planning and Dev. Comm., 1973–79; Owner, Melancon Insurance Agency, 1980–93; Baskin-Robbins franchise owner; Pres. & gen. mgr., American Sugar Cane League, 1993–2004.

DC Office: 404 CHOB, 20515, 202-225-4031; Fax: 202-226-3944; Web site: melancon.house.gov.

State Offices: Chalmette, 504-271-1707; Gonzales, 225-621-8490; Houma, 985-876-3033; New Iberia, 337-367-8231.

Committees: *Budget* (13th of 24 D). *Energy & Commerce* (24th of 36 D): Communications, Technology & the Internet; Energy & Environment.

Group Ratings

	ADA	ACLU	AFS	LCV	ITIC	NTU	COC	ACU	CFG	FRC
2008	80	64	100	77	71	8	71	12	1	52
2007	85	—	91	55	—	11	75	36	9	—

National Journal Ratings

	2007 LIB	—	2007 CONS		2008 LIB	—	2008 CONS
Economic	47%	—	53%		47%	—	53%
Social	49%	—	50%		54%	—	42%
Foreign	47%	—	53%		54%	—	46%
Composite	48%	—	52%		52%	—	48%

Key Votes of the 110th Congress

1. Increase minimum wage	Y	5. Share immigration data	Y	9. Withdraw troops 8/08	Y
2. Expand SCHIP	Y	6. Foreign aid abortion ban	Y	10. No operations in Iran	N
3. Raise CAFE standards	N	7. Ban gay bias in workplace	N	11. Free trade with Peru	Y
4. Bail out financial markets	Y	8. Repeal D.C. gun law	Y	12. Overhaul FISA	Y

Election Results

2008 general	Charlie Melancon (D).................................	unopposed
2008 primary	Charlie Melancon (D).................................	unopposed

Prior Winning Percentages: 2006 (55%); 2004 (50%)

Population		Race/Ethnicity		Work	
Pop. 2007:	621,756	White:	66.9%	Private:	79.9%
Change since 2000:	Down 2.6%	Black:	27.1%	Government:	14.0%
Urban:	73.0%	Hispanic:	2.6%	Self-employed:	5.9%
Rural:	27.0%	Asian:	1.0%	Blue collar:	33.7%
Area size:	12,675 sq. mi.	Native Am.:	1.5%	White collar:	49.4%
Age		Hawaiian:	0.1%	Khaki collar:	0.2%
Median age:	35.3 yrs.	Two+ races:	0.8%	Other:	16.7%
More than 65 yrs:	11.1%	*Ancestry*		Median income:	$42,252
Less than 18 yrs:	26.5%	French:	20.5%	Median home value:	$103,500
Education		USA:	10.4%	Poverty:	17.7%
H.S. grad:	73.7%	German:	7.1%	**Military Veterans**	
College grad:	12.5%			% of Pop:	8.5%
Grad degree:	3.6%				

Below sea level, veined with bayous and creeks and crossed by only an occasional road or railroad, the wetlands of southern Louisiana are one of America's unique landscapes. Technically, most of this waterlogged land rests on islands in a broad river mouth, through which the waters of the Mississippi and its tributaries drain into the Gulf of Mexico. It is rich with animal life: herons and egrets, shrimp and crawfish, muskrats and alligators. Until August 2005, it supported more people than one might

2008 Presidential Vote

McCain (R)	167,046	(61%)
Obama (D)	101,427	(37%)

2004 Presidential Vote

Bush (R)	162,269	(58%)
Kerry (D)	115,011	(41%)

Cook Partisan Voting Index: R + 12

have thought, in surprisingly sturdy small towns with shopping malls on high ground and in bayou towns, where Cajun French remains the primary language. The steep-roofed Cajun houses were not the only structures. Here and there, jutting out of the swampy land, were huge elaborate metal sculptures—petrochemical plants and refineries, processing the oil and natural gas trapped under the wetlands and the shallow continental shelf of the Gulf. In the 1960s and 1970s, the oil industry, by providing well-paid jobs for young people, helped preserve Cajun culture and nurtured a Cajun pride that was seldom articulated a generation ago. Then oil payrolls plummeted and the wetlands were threatened by coastal erosion and battered by Hurricane Andrew in 1992. As erosion worsened, and the wetlands got less water because the Mississippi is not permitted to flood, shrimp fishermen found their catch declining and their profits threatened by competition from aquaculture-raised Asian and Latin American shrimp. But so long as the petrochemical plants, oil refineries, aluminum smelters, and sugar refineries provided decent jobs in these parts, most Cajuns remained in this land of good hunting and good food.

The good life changed on Aug. 29, 2005, when the eye of Hurricane Katrina made a direct hit on this district, inflicting more immediate damage than anywhere else along the Gulf Coast. Plaquemines and St. Bernard parishes were ravaged by high winds and floodwaters, and much of the population fled. By 2008, the population was starting to rebound, but in St. Bernard it remained far below pre-Katrina levels. One sign of the continuing difficulties was the absence of a local hospital. The parish's one hospital had been destroyed by the flood and had to be bulldozed; as of early 2009, it had not been replaced.

The 3rd Congressional District of Louisiana includes about half of Cajun country. It includes most of Louisiana's swamplands, covering Houma, where seven bayous converge. It takes in the parishes of St. Charles, St. John the Baptist, St. James, and Ascension on both sides of the Mississippi. Roughneck Morgan City services offshore oil rigs. Iberia Parish is the home of McIlhenny's Tabasco sauce. The district also has the remains of St. Bernard and Plaquemines parishes, downriver from New Orleans. Behind the Mississippi's western levee, hunkered side by side in Vacherie, are twin reminders of the region's grandeur and pain: the stately Oak Alley plantation, whose stunning vista stood in for the home of a fictional, aristocratic governor in the 1998 movie *Primary Colors,* and the slave cabins of Laura Plantation, believed to be the original home of the famous Br'er Rabbit stories. The ancestral politics in the district are Democratic, though a very conservative brand of Democratic. There has been an influx of Mexicans and other immigrants from Central America, many of whom work on the oil rigs or at the chemical plants. George W. Bush won 58% here in 2004, and John McCain took the district with 61% in 2008. In a measure of the continuing impact of Katrina, in working-class St. Bernard Parish, which votes Republican, the turnout in 2008 dropped 55% from the nearly 30,000 persons who voted in 2004. McCain got 71% of the smaller vote.

The congressman from the 3d District is Charlie Melancon (*meh-LAW-sawn*), a Democrat elected in 2004. He took a seat that had been held by a Republican and now is the only Democrat in the seven-member Louisiana delegation in the U.S. House of Representatives. He grew up in Napoleonville, on a dead-end street called Hog-Pen Alley. His father was mayor. After graduating with a bachelor's degree in agribusiness from the University of Southwestern Louisiana, Melancon worked on the 1971 campaign of Democrat Edwin Edwards for governor and then on his transition team. He returned to Napoleonville, where he worked on the South Central Planning and Development Commission. Later, he ran an insurance agency and owned several Baskin-Robbins ice cream franchises. He ran for the state House in 1975 and lost. He ran again in 1987 and was elected to the first of three terms. He co-sponsored the bill that resulted in creation of the state-backed Louisiana Workers Compensation Corporation. He resigned the Legislature in 1993 to become president of the American Sugar Cane League.

Melancon was one of three serious candidates in contention to succeed Republican Billy Tauzin, a popular, powerful lawmaker who chaired the Energy and Commerce Committee when the Republicans controlled the House. Tauzin left Congress in 2004 to head PhRMA, the giant pharmaceutical lobby. The early front-runner for the seat was his son, Billy Tauzin III, a lobbyist and regional manager for Bell South who inherited some financial advantages from Dad—the senior Tauzin gave $200,000 in political funds to the state Republican Party that could be used for his son's campaign. Also in the field was Craig Romero, an Iberia Parish cattle farmer and oil-field supply salesman who had served in the state Senate as a Republican since 1996. He criticized the younger Tauzin's lack of experience in politics and in south Louisiana.

In the nonpartisan November primary, some Democrats feared that Tauzin and Romero would be the two front-runners, leaving no Democrat in the runoff. But in the final weeks before the initial vote, Melancon benefited from a large investment in political advertising by the Democratic Congressional Campaign Committee. That spending proved to be a wise investment. In the November vote, Tauzin won 32% of the vote and led in eight parishes, mostly in the bayous. And Melancon edged out Romero, 24%-23%; each ran strongly in his political base. In the runoff campaign, Melancon and Tauzin split over tax cuts for the wealthy, school vouchers, tort reform and missile defense. Melancon voiced doubts about the war in Iraq, but said that he would not second-guess President Bush's decision. He said that he was pro-gun, anti-abortion and opposed to gay marriage, though he opposed amending the Constitution to ban same-sex marriage. He emphasized his experience and said that he would protect sugar interests from the Central America Free Trade Agreement. Tauzin fought to establish and identity apart from his father's and said that he was his own man, but he also benefited from large contributions by interest groups that had benefited from his father's work in Congress. Each national party spent close to $2 million in the runoff, mostly on negative ads. The final tally gave Melancon a victory by just 569 votes, 50.2%-49.8%. He carried six parishes in the northern and western parts of the district. Tauzin won all of the parishes along the Gulf, but it wasn't enough.

In the House, Melancon's voting record has been among the most conservative among Democrats. He joined the conservative Blue Dog Democrats and became their communications co-chairman in 2009. Following Hurricane Katrina, he was the only House member from Louisiana to join Sens. Mary Landrieu, a Democrat, and David Vitter, a Republican, in filing the proposed $250 billion relief package prepared by a home-state commission. Despite objections from Democratic Minority Leader Nancy Pelosi, he participated in a Republican-led select committee chaired by Rep. Tom Davis, R-Va., that investigated the federal response to the disaster. He worked with Republicans to craft details of the landmark legislation for Louisiana to share royalties from offshore drilling.

When the Democrats got majority control of the House in 2007, he criticized House Democratic leaders for "not moving fast enough" to address Katrina issues. He contended that people were still dying in his district because of Katrina, from the stress of life and from suicide. In response, Democrats created a working group on Gulf Coast recovery, led by Majority Whip James Clyburn of South Carolina. Melancon called for changes in immigration law to make it easier for seasonal businesses to hire temporary workers. On the Energy and Commerce Committee, where he is well positioned to work on oil and gas issues, he strongly opposed the move by Rep. Henry Waxman of California to oust John Dingell of Michigan as chairman, although Waxman ultimately succeeded. Melancon became a swing vote on climate-change issues, and with fellow Blue Dog Jim Matheson, D-Utah, he drafted principles for a "balanced approach" to guide legislation putting new emissions controls on U.S. factories. Melancon was one of seven House Democrats who voted against final passage of the energy bill in December 2007. Working on the 2008 farm bill, he helped pass the first increase in sugar loan rates in more than 20 years.

At home, Melancon appears to have secured the district. When he sought re-election the first time in 2006, Melancon had already proved himself to his constituents with his post-Katrina advocacy work. In a contest that became something of an afterthought, he won 55%-40% over Romero, who led only in Iberia Parish, his home base. Melancon was unopposed in 2008 and has been mentioned as a possible Senate candidate in 2010. The biggest challenge facing Melancon may be redistricting in 2012. With the state likely to lose a district, this Bayou district could be reshaped by population losses in the New Orleans-based 2nd District.

FOURTH DISTRICT

John Fleming (R)

Elected 2008, 1st term; b. July 5, 1951, Meridian, MS; home, Minden; U. of MS, B.S. 1973, M.D. 1976; Baptist; married (Cindy); 4 children.

Military Career: Navy, 1976–82

Elected Office: Webster Parish coroner, 1996–2000

Professional Career: Physician; Businessman

DC Office: 1023 LHOB, 20515, 202-225-2777; Fax: 202-225-8039; Web site: fleming.house.gov.

State Offices: Bossier City, 318-549-1712; Leesville, 337-238-0778; Shereveport, 318-798-2254.

Committees: *Armed Services* (22nd of 25 R): Air & Land Forces; Military Personnel; Readiness. *Natural Resources* (15th of 20 R): Energy & Mineral Resources; Insular Affairs, Oceans & Wildlife.

Group Ratings and Key Votes: Newly Elected

Election Results

2008 general	John Fleming (R)	44,501	(48%)	($1,828,695)
	Paul Carmouche (D)	44,151	(48%)	($1,844,290)
	Chester Kelley (I)	3,245	(4%)	($39,510)
2008 runoff	John Fleming (R)	43,012	(56%)	
	Chris Gorman (R)	34,405	(44%)	
2008 primary	John Fleming (R)	14,500	(35%)	
	Chris Gorman (R)	14,072	(34%)	
	Jeff Thompson (R)	12,693	(31%)	

Population		Race/Ethnicity		Work	
Pop. 2007:	644,663	White:	60.2%	Private:	71.3%
Change since 2000:	Up 1.0%	Black:	34.0%	Government:	22.5%
Urban:	59.3%	Hispanic:	2.8%	Self-employed:	6.1%
Rural:	40.7%	Asian:	1.0%	Blue collar:	26.7%
Area size:	11,151 sq. mi.	Native Am.:	0.7%	White collar:	51.1%
Age		Hawaiian:	0.0%	Khaki collar:	2.7%
Median age:	35.1 yrs.	Two+ races:	1.2%	Other:	19.5%
More than 65 yrs:	13.0%	*Ancestry*		Median income:	$36,751
Less than 18 yrs:	25.9%	USA:	10.4%	Median home value:	$87,000
Education		Irish:	8.8%	Poverty:	20.9%
H.S. grad:	80.9%	English:	7.0%	**Military Veterans**	
College grad:	18.3%			% of Pop:	13.0%
Grad degree:	6.3%				

Northwestern Louisiana, south of Arkansas and just east of Texas, is part of the Deep South. The overwhelming majority of people here are Protestants, not Catholics, and they are often tradition-minded, with names that are English or Scottish, not French. The tone is set not by wide-open New Orleans—which was not easily accessible by interstate until 1996, when the last chunk of I-49 was completed—but by the smaller Shreveport, which could be just another East Texas oil-patch town, al-

2008 Presidential Vote		
McCain (R)	162,198	(59%)
Obama (D)	108,273	(40%)

2004 Presidential Vote		
Bush (R)	156,298	(59%)
Kerry (D)	105,962	(40%)

Cook Partisan Voting Index: R + 11

beit one that has its own, comparatively sedate, Mardi Gras. The countryside is agricultural, though there are some vestiges of large riverfront plantations. Roots go back here a long way. Natchitoches is the oldest town in Louisiana, founded by Louis Antoine Juchereay de St. Denis in 1714. Shreveport was founded in the 1830s, when Capt. Henry Miller Shreve of the Army Corps of Engineers dispatched a young deputy named Robert E. Lee to break up a 100-mile blockade of logs in the Red River, moving the region's epicenter upriver to a new town, which was then named for the captain. Oil provided the basis for much of the economic growth of the 20th century, but natural gas has taken off in the 21st century, helping to sustain the region during the recession. Gas was discovered in 1870, and the nation's first gas pipeline was built from Caddo Field to Shreveport in 1908. However, it wasn't economical to drill until gas prices zoomed upward in 2000. The dark spot for the local economy is the General Motors assembly plant in Shreveport, which manufactures Hummers and which had big job cutbacks in 2008. There are defense installations nearby, notably Barksdale Air Force Base in Bossier City, one of the nation's largest airfields, where George W. Bush landed on Sept. 11, 2001, and spoke briefly to the nation. Politically, northern Louisiana voters, for more than 100 years, have been voting against cosmopolitan New Orleans and the Catholic Cajun south, sometimes for rip-roaring populists and more often recently for market-oriented Republicans.

The 4th Congressional District of Louisiana consists of the northwest corner of the state. More than half of the votes here are cast in Caddo and suburban Bossier parishes in the far corner around Shreveport, with the rest scattered around rural areas, like picturesque Natchitoches and strip-highway towns like Leesville near Fort Polk. This area seemed to be trending Republican in the 1980s, but in the middle 1990s, it went the other way. Both Bill Clinton and Sen. Mary Landrieu carried the district in 1996, a critical factor in Landrieu's narrow 5,788-vote statewide victory that year. In 2000, George W. Bush carried the area by a comfortable 55%, but it voted for Landrieu again in the close 2002 Senate race and for Democratic Gov. Kathleen Blanco in 2003 over Republican Bobby Jindal. In 2004, the district gave Bush 59% of the vote. John McCain won the district easily, with over 70% of the vote in Bossier; Barack Obama took Caddo 51%-48%.

The new Congressman from the 4th District is John Fleming, a Republican who narrowly won election in December 2008. He prevailed following three tough contests in two months. A physician, Fleming had little political experience, other than a four-year term in the 1990s as coroner of Webster Parish. He grew up in Meridian, Miss., the son of a utility substation operator who worked two or three jobs to make ends meet. His father died of a heart attack just before Fleming finished high school. His mother was disabled and so relied on Social Security to support Fleming and two younger siblings. After undergraduate and medical school at the University of Mississippi, he spent six years in the Navy, where he did his medical residency. He later opened a family medical practice in Minden, La., and as a sideline, operated 30 Subway restaurants in the state and had a stake in 130 UPS stores, from Mississippi to Texas. He also wrote a book called *Preventing Addiction: What Parents Must Know to Immunize Their Kids Against Drug and Alcohol Addiction.* In 2007, Fleming was on the social services advisory council of Republican Gov. Bobby Jindal's transition team.

The competition for the seat began when influential Rep. Jim McCrery, the ranking Republican on the Ways and Means Committee, announced his retirement in December 2007. (He later joined a Washington lobbying firm.) The early front-runners for the GOP nomination were trucking-company executive Chris Gorman and Bossier Chamber of Commerce President Jeff Thompson, who was supported by McCrery and the National Republican Congressional Committee. In the first round of voting, which was delayed a month because of Hurricane Gustav, Fleming led with 35%, to 34% for Gorman and 31% for Thompson. Next came a runoff campaign with Gorman. Both men held similar, conservative views, emphasizing the need to reduce federal spending and taxes, and both spent heavily. Fleming spent over $1 million, much of it his own money, while Gorman spent $1.8 million. Fleming captured the nomination 56%-44%.

Democrats lined up early behind Paul Carmouche, a 30-year Caddo Parish district attorney who styled himself as a centrist Blue Dog Democrat and ran an anti–abortion rights, anticrime campaign. Fleming emphasized his own conservative credentials, calling himself a Ronald Reagan Republican and emphasizing his opposition to abortion rights and support for gun ownership. He called for abolishing the Internal Revenue Service and replacing the current income-tax system with a national sales tax. And he said he favored tough measures against illegal immigrants, decrying an "invasion by illegal aliens." Fleming out-raised Carmouche $1.4 million to $1.2 million and got a big helping hand from the NRCC.

On Dec. 6, 2008, Fleming won by 350 votes. Carmouche led 57%-39% in Caddo Parish, which cast 43% of the vote. He also took four rural parishes outside Shreveport. Fleming ran strongly in the southern part of the district and in Bossier, which had the second largest vote and became the swing parish. He won there 61%-34%. In the House, Fleming got seats on the Armed Services and Natural Resources Committee and said that he expected a competitive re-election contest in 2010.

FIFTH DISTRICT

Rodney Alexander (R)

Elected 2002, 4th term; b. Dec. 5, 1946, Quitman; home, Quitman; attended LA Tech. U., 1965; Baptist; married (Nancy); 3 children.

Military Career: Air Force Reserves, 1965–71.

Elected Office: Jackson Parish Police Jury, 1972–87; President, 1980–87; LA House of Reps., 1988–2002.

Professional Career: Insurance agent, 1990–93; Contractor, 1993–present.

DC Office: 316 CHOB, 20515, 202-225-8490; Fax: 202-225-5639; Web site: www.house.gov/alexander.

State Offices: Alexandria, 318-445-0818; Monroe, 318-322-3500.

Committees: *Appropriations* (19th of 23 R): Agriculture, Rural Development, FDA & Related Agencies; Energy & Water Development; Labor, HHS, Education & Related Agencies.

Group Ratings

	ADA	ACLU	AFS	LCV	ITIC	NTU	COC	ACU	CFG	FRC
2008	25	18	14	0	57	62	94	84	72	100
2007	10	—	13	10	—	62	90	92	69	—

National Journal Ratings

	2007 LIB	—	2007 CONS	2008 LIB	—	2008 CONS
Economic	28%	—	72%	19%	—	81%
Social	25%	—	75%	31%	—	62%
Foreign	0%	—	72%	29%	—	69%
Composite	22%	—	78%	28%	—	72%

Key Votes of the 110th Congress

1. Increase minimum wage	Y	5. Share immigration data	Y	9. Withdraw troops 8/08	N
2. Expand SCHIP	N	6. Foreign aid abortion ban	Y	10. No operations in Iran	N
3. Raise CAFE standards	N	7. Ban gay bias in workplace	N	11. Free trade with Peru	Y
4. Bail out financial markets	Y	8. Repeal D.C. gun law	Y	12. Overhaul FISA	Y

Election Results

2008 general	Rodney Alexander (R)................................. unopposed		
2008 primary	Rodney Alexander (R)... 27,819	(90%)
	Andrew Clack (R)... 3,203	(10%)

Prior Winning Percentages: 2006 (68%); 2004 (59%); 2002 (50%)

Population		Race/Ethnicity		Work	
Pop. 2007:	634,428	White:	62.0%	Private:	74.5%
Change since 2000:	Down 0.6%	Black:	34.6%	Government:	19.1%
Urban:	52.9%	Hispanic:	1.6%	Self-employed:	6.2%
Rural:	47.1%	Asian:	0.5%	Blue collar:	25.3%
Area size:	14,225 sq. mi.	Native Am.:	0.4%	White collar:	53.8%
		Hawaiian:	0.0%	Khaki collar:	0.2%
Age		Two+ races:	0.8%	Other:	20.6%
Median age:	35.2 yrs.	*Ancestry*		Median income:	$33,231
More than 65 yrs:	13.4%	USA:	13.6%	Median home value:	$78,900
Less than 18 yrs:	25.2%	Irish:	8.6%	Poverty:	23.8%
Education		French:	8.2%	**Military Veterans**	
H.S. grad:	76.1%			% of Pop:	9.9%
College grad:	16.2%				
Grad degree:	5.3%				

Northeast Louisiana is perhaps the least known part of the state. Along the Mississippi River and the Red River and their dozens of tributaries, it was plantation country before the Civil War, and there are African-American majorities today in many parishes. Away from the rivers, in the hill country, small farmers scratched out a living on land connected to parish courthouses by dusty lanes. Such was Winn Parish, where Huey P. Long, the pivotal figure in modern Louisiana politics, was born in

2008 Presidential Vote

McCain (R)...........................177,344	(62%)
Obama (D) 106,026	(37%)

2004 Presidential Vote

Bush (R)................................168,484	(62%)
Kerry (D)...............................100,511	(37%)

Cook Partisan Voting Index: R + 14

1893 and from which he began his meteoric political career. Elected governor in 1928 and senator in 1930, he was a national figure threatening both parties when he was assassinated in 1935 in the new high-rise Capitol he built in Baton Rouge. Three-term Gov. Earl Long, Huey's younger brother, once joked that voters some day would elect "good government, and they won't like it."

The 5th Congressional District of Louisiana contains much of this country, from the river parishes to the hills of Winn Parish. The biggest urban areas here, with about 50,000 people each, are Monroe in the north and Alexandria in the south. Alexandria, in Rapides Parish, sits at the northernmost extension of Cajun, Catholic Louisiana and is majority black. Monroe in Ouachita Parish is heavily Protestant and home to one of the world's leading Bible collections, assembled by an heir to an early Coca-Cola bottler. Redistricting added some Cajun areas in Allen and Evangeline parishes and black precincts in Pointe Coupee and Iberville parishes, all Democratic areas. Overall, population has been declining in this area. Except for in the parishes along the river, Republicans have run strongly in this district. George W. Bush increased his vote here from 57% in 2000 to 62% in 2004, his second best showing in the state. John McCain won the district 62%-37%.

The congressman from the 5th District is Rodney Alexander, who was elected as a Democrat in 2002 and switched parties to become a Republican in 2004. He attended Louisiana Tech and won election to the Jackson Parish police jury in 1972 at the age of 25. In 1988, he was elected to the state House, where he chaired the Health and Welfare Committee. Although he was a Democrat then, he was pro–gun rights and anti–abortion rights, and he favored prayer in the public schools. When the 5th District seat opened, the primary turned out to be a regional contest. Alexander led with 29% of the vote, carrying three hill counties in his legislative district and five African-American parishes along the Mississippi. Republican Lee Fletcher, outgoing Representative John Cooksey's chief of staff for five years, was second with 25%, carrying Monroe's Ouachita Parish and three nearby parishes. Close behind, with 23%, was Republican Clyde Holloway, who had been elected congressman three times by narrow margins in 1986, 1988 and 1990 from the old 8th District. Alexander attacked Fletcher as a Washington insider and contrasted his "blue jeans" supporters with Fletcher's "blue blood" contributors. Alexander squeaked by with a 50.3%-49.7% victory, a margin of 974 votes. He carried two hill parishes, all of the Mississippi River parishes and all but one of the parishes in the southern end of the district.

In the House, Alexander was a Democratic maverick who voted for the Republican bill creating a prescription-drug benefit for Medicare in 2003. He voted to extend the tax cuts that Republicans enacted in 2001, and co-sponsored legislation to prohibit desecration of the flag and to bar gay marriages. Still, Democratic leaders worked to keep Alexander in the fold and helped him to raise money for his re-election. Alexander repaid these kindnesses by waiting until the last minute before the 2004 election filing deadline to switch parties, declaring himself a Republican. He claimed that had he remained a Democrat, the candidacy of Democrat Zelma Blakes, an African-American and a political neophyte, would draw votes away from him and leave him vulnerable to attacks from both the left and the right. His erstwhile Democratic friends were not sympathetic. "I've seen some cowardly things in my career, but this is the worst," said Louisiana Sen. Mary Landrieu. Louisiana Democrats filed suit to reopen the qualifying period, but the state appeals court rejected their case. Alexander promised to return campaign contributions from Democratic colleagues, but didn't until the donors complained about the delay.

National Republicans, who were not enthusiastic when Fletcher expressed interest in running again, quickly embraced Alexander. Democrats meanwhile coalesced around Blakes. But the election turned out to be an afterthought for both parties. It was overshadowed by other major happenings in Louisiana politics that year, including two hotly contested open-seat House races and a serious contest for the Senate seat of retiring Democrat John Breaux. Alexander won 59% of the vote, to 25% for Blakes and 16% for former state Rep. Jock Scott, a Republican. He carried all of the parishes except for two on the riverfront near Baton Rouge, where Blakes led.

Although Alexander and House Republican leaders insisted that they had made no deal before his switch, as soon as he arrived back in Washington as a Republican in January 2005 he got seats on the sought-after Appropriations Committee and its Agriculture Subcommittee, where he quickly secured funding for several road projects and a transportation and parking facility for the University of Louisiana at Monroe. He said that his views remained the same. But his voting record became markedly more conservative. In 2006, the scandal surrounding Florida Republican Mark Foley scandal unexpectedly swept in Alexander when it was revealed that he had sponsored a congressional page who was among those who received inappropriate, sexually explicit emails from Foley. Alexander and his chief of staff conveyed this information to Republican leaders and other officials, who failed to act. Alexander said that his office "did everything we thought we should have," and he voiced frustration that others did not respond. In its December report, the House Ethics Committee commended Alexander for his actions.

In the minority, Alexander has bucked Republican conservatives trying to end the use of earmarks, or pork barrel spending. He continued to secure money for the low-income areas of his district, including rural-development grants and pesticides to kill timber-threatening insects. "I don't want my voters to be neglected," he said. He also improved his relationship with Landrieu, a fellow appropriator. Democrats and liberal advocates sought unsuccessfully in 2007 to get his support to expand the State Children's Health Insurance Program. Also in recent years, Alexander has lobbied to end the trade embargo of Cuba, which could benefit Louisiana rice farmers.

House Democrats have failed to find a credible challenger to Alexander. In 2008, he ran for re-election unopposed. The increase in the district's African-American population to 35% could pose some redistricting jeopardy for Alexander, who is white, in the future, especially with Louisiana likely to lose a seat in 2010 redistricting.

SIXTH DISTRICT

Bill Cassidy (R)

Elected 2008, 1st term; b. Sept. 28, 1957, Chicago, IL; home, Baton Rouge; LA St. U., B.S. 1979; M.D., 1983.; Christian; married (Laura); 3 children.

Elected Office: LA Senate, 2006–08.

Professional Career: Internist and hepatologist, Cigna Med. Cntr, Los Angeles, CA, 1989–90; LA St. U., Asst. Prof. of Medicine, 1990–96; Assoc. prof. of medicine, 1996-present.

DC Office: 506 CHOB, 20515, 202-225-3901; Fax: 202-225-7313; Web site: cassidy.house.gov.

State Offices: Baton Rouge, 225-929-7711; Livingston, 225-686-4413.

Committees: *Agriculture* (17th of 18 R): Conservation, Credit, Energy & Research; Specialty Crops, Rural Development & Foreign Agriculture. *Education & Labor* (14th of 19 R): Early Childhood, Elementary & Secondary Education; Higher Education, Lifelong Learning & Competitiveness. *Natural Resources* (20th of 20 R): Insular Affairs, Oceans & Wildlife.

Group Ratings and Key Votes: Newly Elected

Election Results

2008 general	Bill Cassidy (R)	150,332	(48%)	($1,252,457)
	Donald Cazayoux (D)	125,886	(40%)	($2,766,865)
	Michael Jackson (I)..	36,198	(12%)	($212,215)
2008 primary	Bill Cassidy (R)	unopposed		
2008 spec. general	Don Cazayoux (D)	49,703	(49%)	
	Woody Jenkins (R)..	46,746	(46%)	
	Ashley Casey (I)	3,718	(4%)	
2008 spec. primary	Don Cazayoux (D)	19,806	(57%)	
	Michael Jackson (D)	15,068	(43%)	

Population		Race/Ethnicity		Work	
Pop. 2007:	679,262	White:	60.4%	Private:	75.6%
Change since 2000:	Up 6.4%	Black:	34.3%	Government:	18.7%
Urban:	75.5%	Hispanic:	2.3%	Self-employed:	5.5%
Rural:	24.5%	Asian:	1.7%	Blue collar:	22.6%
Area size:	3,210 sq. mi.	Native Am.:	0.2%	White collar:	59.7%
		Hawaiian:	0.0%	Khaki collar:	0.2%
Age		Two+ races:	1.1%	Other:	17.5%
Median age:	33.7 yrs.			Median income:	$45,373
More than 65 yrs:	10.2%	*Ancestry*		Median home value:	$133,000
Less than 18 yrs:	25.3%	French:	12.1%	Poverty:	17.1%
		Irish:	7.2%		
Education		German:	6.9%	**Military Veterans**	
H.S. grad:	84.5%			% of Pop:	9.4%
College grad:	25.6%				
Grad degree:	9.0%				

Baton Rouge is the central node of Louisiana, on the boundary between the French-speaking, Catholic Cajun country and the heavily Baptist region. Its skyscraper Capitol and Exxon refinery sit just beyond the levees that line the Mississippi River. Historically, it was part of the Florida parishes, the territory west of the Mississippi River and north of Lake Pontchartrain that was not included in the Louisiana Purchase in 1803. It still belonged to Spain, until the locals rebelled and declared their

2008 Presidential Vote

McCain (R)..............................	184,355	(57%)
Obama (D)	132,627	(41%)

2004 Presidential Vote

Bush (R)	172,080	(59%)
Kerry (D)................................	117,255	(40%)

Cook Partisan Voting Index: R + 10

own Republic of West Florida in 1810. Then it quickly became part of Louisiana and the United States, but the Florida parishes, like the states of Texas, California, Vermont, and Hawaii, can claim to have been separate republics (and a kingdom in the case of Hawaii) before their people became Americans. When the man who dominated Louisiana politics for decades, Huey P. Long, became governor at age 36 in the old (and still-standing) Gothic Capitol, Baton Rouge had only 30,000 people. He built the 34-story Art Deco Capitol next door to the Governor's Mansion, which he also built. Long also died in the capitol, the victim of an assassin in 1935. To the south, are the buildings of Louisiana State University, many of which he also built. Today, Baton Rouge is the center of a metropolitan area of 772,000 people that sits on the east bank of the Mississippi and reaches far inland to Livingston Parish. This is one of the faster-growing parts of Louisiana. Livingston and Ascension parishes outside Baton Rouge grew 27% and 29%, respectively, between 2000 and 2007, faster than any other parishes in the state. Baton Rouge grew more than that—no one knows how much more—in the weeks and months after Hurricane Katrina, when evacuees moved into motel rooms, spare rooms in people's houses, dorm rooms in LSU and Southern University, and the city's population may have momentarily doubled; certainly the traffic jams suggested it had. Many have moved on since then, and the growth has subsided. New Orleans was long the state's largest city, but Baton Rouge, with 225,000 people, now rivals the reduced, post-Katrina New Orleans in size.

The 6th Congressional District of Louisiana includes just about all of metropolitan Baton Rouge, plus three small, mostly rural parishes to the north. Overall, the district is 34% African-American, and historically it was Democratic. In the 1980s, the Baton Rouge area moved toward the Republicans, and in the 1990s, it was fairly closely balanced. In 2004, East Baton Rouge Parish voted 54% for George W. Bush, and Livingston Parish voted 77% for Bush; overall the 6th District voted 59% for Bush. In 2008, the shift was notable. Barack Obama won East Baton Rouge 50%-48%. The only other Democrat to have won the parish since 1964 was Bill Clinton, in 1996. But John McCain won Livingston Parish 85%-13%. McCain won the district 57%-41%.

The new Congressman from the 6th District is Republican Bill Cassidy. He was one of only five Republicans to defeat a House Democratic incumbent in the Democratic year of 2008. Republicans have held this Baton Rouge-based district for 30 years, except for the brief tenure of Democratic Rep. Don Cazayoux. He won a May 2008 special election to fill out the term of retiring GOP Rep. Richard Baker, who resigned to head a Washington trade group. Cazayoux held the seat until the regularly scheduled congressional election the following November, then lost it to Cassidy. The son of a life-insurance salesman, Cassidy grew up in Baton Rouge and went to college at Louisiana State University. He went on to graduate from LSU's medical school, and during his medical training, he met his wife, Laura, who is also a physician and formerly chief of surgery at Earl K. Long Hospital. Cassidy was an associate professor of medicine at LSU and taught at the same hospital. Cassidy went on to cofound the Greater Baton Rouge Community Clinic, which provides free dental and health care to the working uninsured. He developed a school-based hepatitis B vaccination program that has immunized more than 36,000 public, private, and parochial schoolchildren at no cost to parents or schools.

One of Cassidy's defining moments came when Hurricane Katrina hit in 2005. With the help of several other physicians, he created a makeshift field hospital in an abandoned Kmart store. In a PBS documentary, he recalled entering the store after the storm. "When we came in, there was grease all over the floor, dust, 90 percent of these lights were out. There was no electricity, no phone lines. No one had checked the plumbing, and we couldn't even open all the doors. Thirty-six to 48 hours after we began the process, we were ready to begin receiving patients." Cassidy won a December 2006 special election to the state Senate and was re-elected in 2007. He sponsored several bills to improve health standards in Louisiana, including one to overhaul the children's mental health system and another to expand Medicaid coverage to patients at new organ-transplant centers.

He passed on the opportunity to compete for Baker's seat in the special election. But after state Rep. Cazayoux defeated social conservative Woody Jenkins 49%-46%, with a big boost from the Democratic Congressional Campaign Committee, Cassidy vowed to take the district back for the Republicans. He described himself as a "pro-life, pro-gun-rights" social conservative in favor of free enterprise, limited government, and lower taxes. He made the economy the focus of his campaign, highlighting his record in the state Senate of voting against spending bills and cutting taxes for businesses and for parents with children in private schools. He also criticized Cazayoux for supporting Democratic presidential nominee Barack Obama's tax plan. Cazayoux ran an ad criticizing Cassidy for supporting the idea of private savings accounts in the Social Security program. State Rep. Michael Jackson, who is African-American, ran as an independent, due partly to his unhappiness over the national Democrats' early support for Cazayoux in the special election. Cassidy won comfortably, with 48% to 40% for Cazayoux and 12% for Jackson. In East Baton Rouge, which cast 62% of the total vote, Cassidy won 44%-42%. His margin of victory came in Livingston and Ascension parishes, which he won by more than 27,000 votes. Cazayoux ran strongly in the western part of the district, where he took three rural parishes. The shifting dynamics in this district could set up another competitive contest in 2010.

SEVENTH DISTRICT

Charles Boustany (R)

Elected 2004, 3rd term; b. Feb. 21, 1956, New Orleans; home, Lafayette; U. of SW LA, B.S. 1978, LA St. U., M.D. 1982; Episcopalian; married (Bridget); 2 children.

Professional Career: Practicing surgeon, 1982–2004.

DC Office: 1117 LHOB, 20515, 202-225-2031; Fax: 202-225-5724; Web site: boustany.house.gov.

State Offices: Lafayette, 337-235-6322; Lake Charles, 337-433-1747.

Committees: *Ways & Means* (13th of 15 R): Income Security & Family Support; Oversight (RMM).

Group Ratings

	ADA	ACLU	AFS	LCV	ITIC	NTU	COC	ACU	CFG	FRC
2008	20	18	17	8	57	55	94	83	54	100
2007	5	—	9	0	—	61	84	100	73	—

National Journal Ratings

	2007 LIB — 2007 CONS			2008 LIB — 2008 CONS	
Economic	21%	—	78%	28%	—	71%
Social	9%	—	85%	27%	—	71%
Foreign	0%	—	72%	22%	—	74%
Composite	16%	—	84%	27%	—	73%

Key Votes of the 110th Congress

1. Increase minimum wage	N	5. Share immigration data	Y	9. Withdraw troops 8/08	N
2. Expand SCHIP	N	6. Foreign aid abortion ban	Y	10. No operations in Iran	N
3. Raise CAFE standards	N	7. Ban gay bias in workplace	N	11. Free trade with Peru	Y
4. Bail out financial markets	Y	8. Repeal D.C. gun law	Y	12. Overhaul FISA	Y

Election Results

2008 general	Charles Boustany (R)	177,173	(62%)	($1,606,461)
	Donald Cravins (D)	98,280	(34%)	($623,426)
	Peter Vidrine (CP)	10,846	(4%)	
2008 primary	Charles Boustany (R)	unopposed		

Prior Winning Percentages: 2006 (71%); 2004 (55%)

Population		Race/Ethnicity		Work	
Pop. 2007:	651,063	White:	70.2%	Private:	79.3%
Change since 2000:	Up 2.0%	Black:	25.8%	Government:	13.9%
Urban:	68.9%	Hispanic:	1.8%	Self-employed:	6.4%
Rural:	31.1%	Asian:	0.9%	Blue collar:	26.8%
Area size:	7,294 sq. mi.	Native Am.:	0.2%	White collar:	54.9%
		Hawaiian:	0.0%	Khaki collar:	0.1%
Age		Two+ races:	1.0%	Other:	18.3%
Median age:	34.9 yrs.	*Ancestry*		Median income:	$37,340
More than 65 yrs:	12.1%	French:	20.4%	Median home value:	$96,300
Less than 18 yrs:	26.4%	German:	7.3%	Poverty:	20.2%
		Fr. Canadian:	6.8%		
Education				**Military Veterans**	
H.S. grad:	77.2%			% of Pop:	9.9%
College grad:	18.2%				
Grad degree:	5.6%				

More than 200 years ago, French-speaking settlers in Canada were forced to leave their land of Acadie, which the British had taken over and renamed Nova Scotia. They made their way to the wetlands of southern Louisiana. Here, without much notice, they built steep-roofed houses to slough off nonexistent snow and adapted French cuisine to the crawfish and muskrat they found in abundance in the pelican-tended swamps. They are the Cajuns, and the heart of their adopted homeland is around

2008 Presidential Vote		
McCain (R)	188,576	(63%)
Obama (D)	105,118	(35%)
2004 Presidential Vote		
Bush (R)	168,645	(60%)
Kerry (D)	110,623	(39%)
Cook Partisan Voting Index:	R + 14	

Lafayette, just west of the Atchafalaya Basin, where Mississippi waters pour through bayous and canals. A 30-mile section of Interstate 10 was built on elevated stilts. Cajun country thrived, thanks to the oil and gas plentiful here and just offshore in the Gulf of Mexico. Oil rigs are common, and every once in a while the swampy foliage parts to reveal a giant refinery or petrochemical plant. Cajun pride has experienced a resurgence. Cajun French is surviving decades of efforts to eliminate it, even by some older Cajun generations. Cajun music—and its black-influenced variant, zydeco—are popular here and nationally; spicy Cajun cooking attracts food lovers, who learn its secrets and then carry it off, in understated form, to other parts of the United States. About 45% of the people in Acadiana speak French as a second language. Lafayette, with its Acadian Village and plethora of oil exploration firms, features an annual *Festivals Acadiens* to celebrate music, food and crafts. Unlike New Orleans, its Mardi Gras reveries are still segregated affairs, with an all-white (and sometimes all-male) parade and an all-black parade. Cockfighting remains locally popular, despite efforts in the Legislature to prohibit it. Louisiana was the only state that still permitted cockfighting until it was finally banned in August 2008.

The oil-price crash of the middle 1980s hit Cajun country hard. Rising expectations, and the giddy sense that the oil industry promised lasting prosperity, suddenly collapsed, leaving borrowers overextended and ordinary homeowners unable to maintain the standard of living they expected. In 2005, Hurricane Rita, not Katrina, was the natural disaster with the most devastating local impact. With winds of 120 miles per hour and a storm surge of up to 15 feet, Rita left its own path of destruction 200 and 300 miles to the west of New Orleans. It virtually erased some coastal communities, especially in Cameron Parish. While the nation was spellbound by every development in New Orleans, local residents and officials complained that they were the victims of "Rita amnesia." Plans were hatched to move some villages along the coast more than 10 miles inland to higher ground. In September 2008, Hurricane Ike hit the area, although with much less devastation, thanks in part to new, stricter building codes.

The 7th Congressional District of Louisiana covers much of the Cajun country, from Lafayette and the Atchafalaya west along Interstate 10 to Lake Charles and the Texas border. Refineries and oil-field-support industries provide many jobs, as do rice and crawfish farming. Some 27% of the population claims either French or French-Canadian ancestry. Politically, Cajun country once gravitated to the Democrats, though it disapproved of the party's cultural liberalism, so at odds with the Cajun tradition of respecting the authority of the church while tolerating a certain amount of *laissez les bons temps rouler* spirit. The district voted for Bill Clinton in 1992 and 1996, as it had voted for Louisiana's foremost Cajun politician, Edwin Edwards, who was elected governor four times. But it gave George W. Bush solid majorities in 2000 and 2004, and gave John McCain 63% of the vote in 2008.

The congressman from the 7th District is Charles Boustany, who in 2004 became the first Republican elected from this area since 1884. Of Lebanese ancestry, Boustany (*Boo STON nee*) grew up in Lafayette, where his father was parish coroner. He graduated from the University of Southwestern Louisiana and from Louisiana State University's medical school. He worked as a cardio-thoracic surgeon and was active in civic and political affairs. In 2004, when Democrat Chris John ran for the Senate, Boustany was one of five candidates running to succeed him. The other Republican was David Thibodeaux of Lafayette, who had run unsuccessfully for the seat three times, most recently in 1996. But he raised little money, some party leaders viewed him as too conservative and Boustany quickly became the Republican favorite. The Democratic front-runners were two state senators: Don Cravins of the Breaux Bridge area, who was seeking to become the first African-American to hold this seat, and state Sen. Willie Mount of Lake Charles. Boustany raised plenty of money early and campaigned on his "prescription for prosperity" —expansion of health-savings accounts, high-speed Internet access for local small businesses and opposition to the Central American Free Trade Agreement. The National Republican Congressional Committee ran ads attacking Mount's support for higher taxes in the Legislature, presumably because it saw Cravins as a weaker candidate in a runoff. Boustany led the November primary with 39% of the vote, to 25.2% for Mount, 24.6% for Cravins, and 10% for Thibodeaux. In the December runoff, Cravins refused to endorse Mount, still angry over the state Democratic Party's "unity ballot" sent to black voters, which included Mount's name and not his. Cravins's neutrality hurt Mount in the Lafayette area. She pointed to her legislative experience, while Boustany emphasized his "values" agenda. Boustany won 55%-45%. Mount won 60% in Lake Charles's Calcasieu Parish, which cast 32% of the vote. But Boustany trumped that with 70% in Lafayette Parish, which cast 30% of the vote.

In the House, Boustany's voting record was relatively moderate for a Southern Republican. On the Education and the Workforce Committee, he was an active proponent of legislation to permit small businesses to join together in associations to pay less for health insurance. He also sought increased federal support for computerizing health records, which he said "remains trapped in the 20th century." His local priorities included more federal funding to restore Louisiana's eroding coastline and to complete Interstate 49 from Shreveport to Lafayette. After Hurricanes Katrina and Rita, he enacted initiatives to provide special rules for disaster-relief employment for individuals displaced by the storms and to assist the disabled. He pledged that southwest Louisiana would not be "a stepchild" to New Orleans in hurricane recovery. He pushed for expedited assistance payments from the Federal Emergency Management Agency and criticized the slow cleanup of debris in Cameron Parish. In March 2006, when Republican Speaker Dennis Hastert and Democratic Leader Nancy Pelosi led a delegation of House members to Katrina recovery sites, Boustany complained loudly that they overlooked his hard-hit district. In July of that year, Hastert returned to Boustany's district.

In 2008, Boustany, with Rep. Bart Stupak, D-Mich., sponsored a bill to increase visas for seasonal workers, notably for the crawfish industry. In recent years, he's also developed a close relationship with Minority Leader John Boehner, which helped him to fill the power vacuum following the departure of senior House Republicans from Louisiana. It also proved helpful to Boustany in early 2009, when he secured a seat on the powerful, tax-writing House Ways and Means Committee. On the panel, Boustany said he supports tax breaks as an incentive for people to use alternative fuels and more US oil drilling. In campaigning for the seat, Boustany distributed a packet to his colleagues grandly titled "The Next Conservative Leader for the Ways and Means Committee."

The Democratic Congressional Campaign Committee tried to recruit Chris John to run for his old seat in 2006, but he declined. With John out of the running, Boustany had an easy win against Democrat Mike Stagg, 71%-29%. In 2008, when state Sen. Don Cravins Jr., the son of Boustany's 2004 opponent, decided to challenge him, some Democrats were hopeful. But Cravins's pro–gun ownership, anti–abortion rights stance discouraged national party support. And internal party resentment lingered from the 2004 contest. Boustany won 62%-34%, carrying each parish except for Evangeline, which he narrowly lost.

★ MAINE ★

Maine possesses a distinctive personality—ornery, contrary-minded, almost bullheaded, rough-hewn. It is the state geographically closest to Europe, but it was not heavily settled until the mid-19th century, by people migrating from the south and the west. The typical pattern at the time was people moving *to* the west. In an urbanizing and rapidly changing country, Maine was famous for its pointed firs and steady habits, with a few dozen small factory towns and paper-mill towns but nothing like a major metropolis. Maine grew in a rush, and then mostly stopped. There were 600,000 people here in 1860, but the population dipped after the Civil War—many soldiers did not return—and did not top 1 million until the 1970s. Then the tremors of the New England high-technology booms of the 1980s and 1990s reverberated up Interstate 95 and reached Maine. The simple, back-to-nature Yankee style came into vogue. The antique dockside buildings on Portland's waterfront were restored and an old-style Public Market was constructed. The Maine Mall expanded and office parks sprang up nearby, a miniature edge city. Real estate prices rose by hundreds of percents, not just in vacation coves, but also in Portland and small towns that had never considered themselves picturesque. The L.L.Bean headquarters in Freeport, open 24 hours a day, 365 days a year, symbolized the boom. The two chaste initials and the Anglo-Saxon monosyl-lable suggested the dry understatement of Down East Yankees; the 24-hour-a-day schedule reflected the hard work needed to eke out a living from the cold waters of the North Atlantic to the pine-covered North Woods; and, the commercial success of the enterprise became a prime example of Maine's unexpected boom. Something like the Maine slogan: "The way life should be."

In the past two decades, Maine's economy has transformed. It has lost jobs in shoes, chicken process-ing, papermaking, leather processing, and timber, but gained them in tourism, call centers, high technol-ogy, and biotechnology. The Grand Banks have been overfished and fishing seasons shortened, but there's a new market among Northern Europeans for Maine shrimp. The lobster industry had been thriving, with prices at an all-time high, but it took a big cut when soaring fuel prices drove up costs, and a collapsing economy made lobster an extravagance to too many families, causing prices to fall. Scratching small Maine boiling potatoes out of the soil of Aroostook County has gotten harder. The nation's top potato producer 50 years ago, Maine fell to eighth place in the 1990s: small potatoes. Georgia-Pacific closed its paper mill in Old Town, near Bangor. But Loring Air Force Base, shuttered in 1994, has been redeveloped and is generating jobs in food manufacturing, aircraft disassembly and storage, telemarketing, and state government. Maine exports not just paper and lumber and seafood, but also computer and aircraft parts. Tourism continues to be the biggest business. Bath Iron Works, long the state's largest private employer, has a long-term contract to build 21 *Arleigh Burke* Class Naval destroyers. Maine politicians rallied when the Pentagon in 2005 recommended closing the Portsmouth Naval Shipyard, which repairs submarines. The base closing commission let the shipyard remain open but ordered the shutdown of Brunswick Naval Air Station, the state's second-largest employer. Maine, its economic development director still insists, has "the best work force on the planet," and Democratic Gov. John Baldacci's Pine Tree Zones have gener-ated 3,000 new jobs.

Now, in effect, there are two Maines—humming coastal Maine and declining interior Maine, one symbolized by the lobster and the other by the moose. Growth is greatest in York County and along the coast east of Portland to the Penobscot River. Population is stable in the North Woods and declining in the northern and eastern edges of the state. A slow-growth economy has some advantages: Maine didn't have much of a housing bubble in this decade and so has not had a housing bust like many other states Its unemployment rate has tracked the national average. Demographically, Maine is like Western Europe, with an aging population and the lowest birth rate in the United States. The country as a whole grew by 22% from 1990 to 2008, but Maine grew by just 7%, as young people continued to leave. An aging population has its advantages—Maine has the nation's lowest incarceration rate. But it also has disadvantages—health care costs are high, and the percentage of people with employer-provided health insurance is low. Maine has the highest high school graduation rate in the country, but its high schools and colleges have not been providing enough graduates to fill its job openings. There has been little immigration here and Maine is the whitest state in the nation. It is 1% black, 1% Hispanic, and 1% Asian. It treasures what diversity it has, however. French-Canadian immigrant children were once chided when they spoke French. Now the Legislature has a French-American day each year, when busi-ness is conducted in French and the Pledge of Allegiance recited in French.

In politics, Maine is contrary. Until 1958, it held state elections in September, a date originally chosen because it followed the state's early harvest. Starting in 1840, long before the advent of public opinion polls, the election results were taken as a gauge of national sentiment—hence the saying, "As Maine goes, so goes the nation." Actually, Maine didn't vote like the rest of the country most of the time. In September 1936, Maine voted 56% for a Republican for governor (Lewis Barrows) and in November, only Maine and Vermont voted for Republican Alf Landon over Democrat Franklin D. Roosevelt, prompting Roosevelt's campaign manager to observe, "As Maine goes, so goes Vermont." Maine's adherence to flinty Yankee

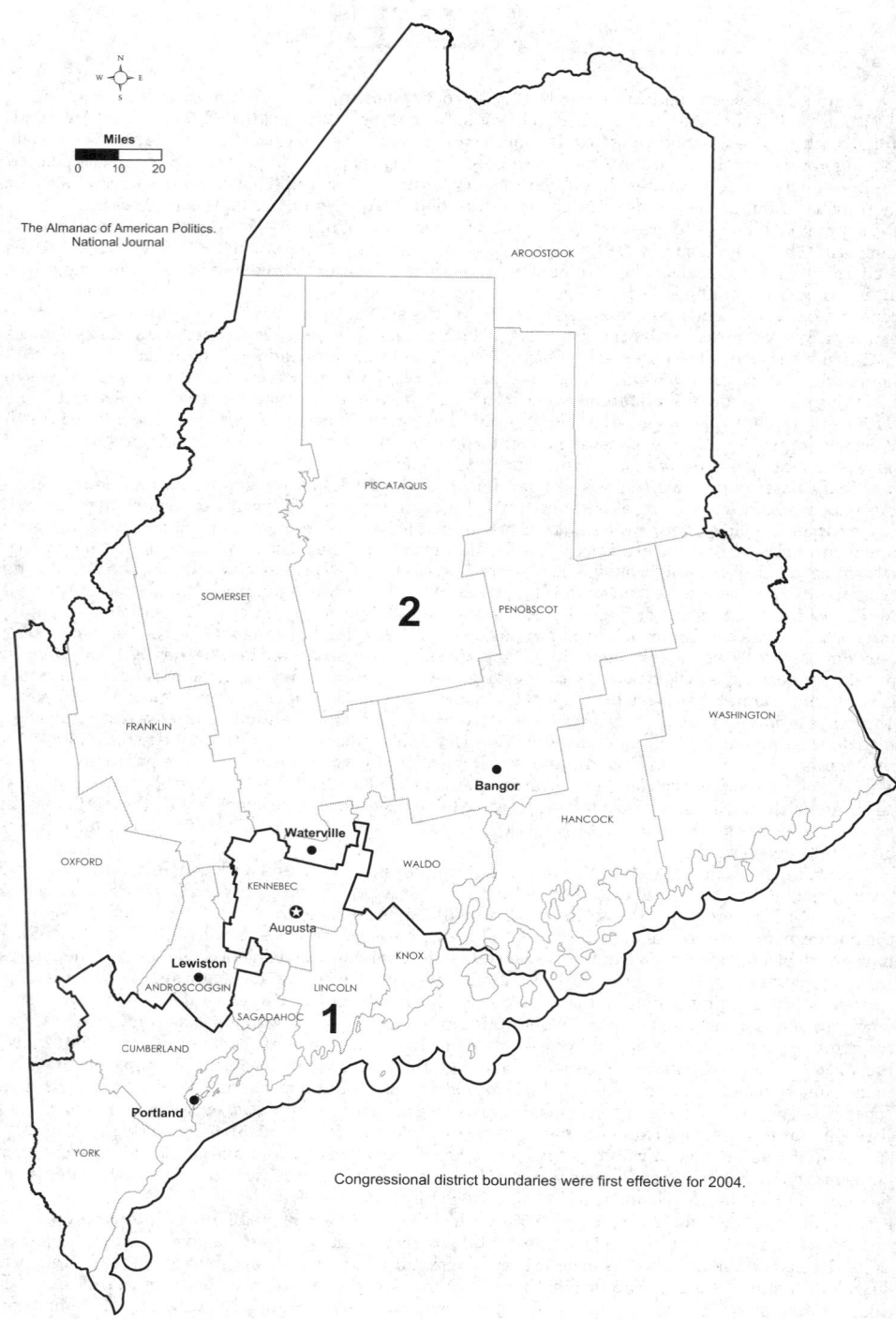

The Almanac of American Politics.
National Journal

AROOSTOOK

PISCATAQUIS

SOMERSET

2

PENOBSCOT

FRANKLIN

WASHINGTON

● Bangor

Waterville ●

OXFORD

KENNEBEC

WALDO

HANCOCK

✪
Augusta

Lewiston ●
ANDROSCOGGIN

KNOX

LINCOLN

1

SAGADAHOC

CUMBERLAND

Portland ●

YORK

Congressional district boundaries were first effective for 2004.

Republicanism and Prohibition was echoed almost nowhere else in the nation. Since then, it has voted for the loser in the close presidential elections of 1948, 1960, 1968, 1976, 2000, and 2004—a record equaled by no other state. Maine cast the nation's highest percentages for third-party presidential candidate Ross Perot, 30% in 1992 and 14% in 1996. In 1994 and 1998, it elected Angus King, an independent and former Democrat, as governor, as it had elected independent and former Republican James Longley in 1974. In the past eight gubernatorial elections, Maine voted twice for Republicans, four times for Democrats, and twice for independents.

If Maine's tradition-minded Yankees kept the state Republican long after the nation embraced the New Deal, the sons and daughters of its ethnic citizens—the Irish, French Canadian, Greek, and Arab immigrants have come to equal the numbers of WASPs (though these new Mainers in many ways share traditional Yankee traits and values)—made the Democrats competitive here in the 1980s even as they were losing ground in the rest of the nation. But there are exceptions. Maine has voted Democratic for president five times starting in 1992 and hasn't elected a Republican to the U.S. House since 1994. But it hasn't elected a Democratic U.S. senator since 1988, and only once since then has a Republican Senate candidate won less than 58% of the vote. Moderate GOP incumbents Olympia Snowe and Susan Collins wield considerable clout in the Senate. Maine has more partisan turnover in its Legislature than just about any other state. In its small legislative districts—the average population of a state House district is 8,724—Mainers vote for the person, not the party. In 2004, Republicans gained seats in the Legislature even as Democratic presidential nominee John Kerry carried the state, but in 2008, Democrats made significant gains. Vestiges of Maine's ethnic divides remain: Protestants voted for Republican George W. Bush in 2004 and John McCain in 2008, while Catholics cast bigger percentage margins for Democrats Kerry and Barack Obama. But young Mainers seem more volatile: Bush carried them in 2004; Obama won 71% of them in 2008. Yet when a group called Fed Up With Taxes put up a state ballot measure repealing fees on health insurers and repealing taxes on beer, wine, and soft drinks, it passed 65%-35%.

As the economy changed, Maine moved toward a consensus on how to balance economic growth and preserve the environment. But disagreement rages about the North Woods. The big paper companies, long the largest landowners in Maine, have been selling off millions of acres since 1998. As Conservation Commissioner Patrick McGowan put it, "For generations, the paper companies sort of managed everything for us up here. They gave sportsmen pretty much free rein, and in turn people up here helped out as stewards of the land. But with all of these new buyers, nobody quite knows what will happen now, and people are getting nervous." Local Mainers want to keep using the land for hunting, trapping, and snowmobiling. But a Concord, Mass., group called Restore the North Woods, with backing from Hollywood stars, wants to create a huge national park, bigger than Yellowstone and Yosemite combined. Environmentally minded people are buying up land with a view toward donating it for a national park. Roxanne Quimby, a beeswax lip-balm multimillionaire, bought 70,000 acres and has banned hunting and snowmobiling on her land. Mainers reacted angrily to advocates "from away," as they say; Baldacci called

Population		Household Income		Work	
Pop. 2007:	1,314,780	Under $15k:	14.7%	Private:	75.3%
State rank:	40th of 50	$15k to $50k:	40.0%	Government:	14.8%
Change since 2000:	Up 3.1%	$50k to $100k:	32.1%	Self-employed:	9.6%
Urban:	40.7%	$100k to $150k:	11.1%	Unemployment (3-yr. average):	3.8%
Rural:	59.3%	Over $150k:	2.1%	Poverty:	12.8%
Native of state:	64.4%	Median income:	$45,211	Blue collar:	23.4%
Not a citizen:	1.6%			White collar:	57.9%
Area size:	35,385 sq. mi.	**Home Value**		Khaki collar:	0.2%
		Under $100k:	25.2%	Other:	18.6%
Most populous cities		$100k to $300k:	56.3%		
1. Portland	62,986	$300k to $500k:	13.0%	**Age**	
2. Lewiston	37,807	$500k to $1 mil:	4.6%	Median age:	41.1 yrs.
3. Bangor	30,165	Over $1 million:	1.0%	More than 65 yrs:	14.7%
4. Biddeford	24,059	Median:	$167,700	Less than 18 yrs:	21.5%

Race/Ethnicity				Military Veterans		Registered Voters in 2008	
White:	94.8%	*Language*		% of Pop:	13.9%	D:	310,950 (33.0%)
Black:	1.0%	English:	92.4%	*Veterans by Period*		R:	258,147 (27.4%)
Hispanic:	1.1%	Spanish:	1.1%	WWII and before:	12.0%	Other:	373,728 (39.6%)
Asian:	0.9%	Asian:	0.6%	Korea:	12.2%	Voter turnout:	731,163
Native Am.:	0.5%	Other		Vietnam:	33.2%	Turnout as % of	
Hawaiian:	0.0%	European	5.5%	Gulf (pre-2001):	10.4%	voting age:	70.2%
Two+ races:	1.4%	**Education**		Gulf (post-2001):	6.0%	**Legislature**	
Ancestry		H.S. grad:	88.8%	Peace time:	26.0%	Senate:	20 D 15 R
English:	17.8%	College grad:	25.9%			House:	96 D 54 R 1 I
French:	13.2%	Grad degree:	8.9%				
Irish:	13.1%						

the national park proposal a "nonstarter," and has promoted alternatives. The Nature Conservancy in 2006 donated easements on 195,000 acres, with space for recreation and land available for sustainable timber harvests.

Presidential politics Maine has been a hard state to predict in recent presidential politics. It gave majorities to Republican George H.W. Bush in 1988 and Democrat Bill Clinton in 1996. In between, the 1992 race was very nearly a three-way tie, with Clinton in first place, Ross Perot in second, and Bush, who spent nearly every summer of his life in Maine, in third place. In 2000, Democrat Al Gore won 49%-44%, with 6% for Ralph Nader. But there has been a clear Democratic trend since then. Maine was on the campaigns' target lists in 2004, but Democrat John Kerry ended up carrying it 54%-45%. In 2008, GOP vice presidential nominee Sarah

2008 Presidential Vote		
Obama (D) 421,923	(58%)
McCain (R)............................295,273	(40%)
2004 Presidential Vote		
Kerry (D)................................396,842	(54%)
Bush (R)................................330,201	(45%)

Palin and husband Todd Palin campaigned in Hermon, Presque Isle, and Bangor after polls showed a close race between Republican Sen. John McCain and Democratic Sen. Barack Obama. Maine is one of two states (Nebraska is the other) that gives two electors to the statewide winner and one elector to the winner in each congressional district. The McCain campaign thought it might win the electoral vote of the northern 2nd District. But Obama's lead widened even while the Palins were on the stump, and McCain lost the 2nd District 55%-43%. McCain carried Piscataquis County, deep in the woods, with 51% of the vote—the only county he carried in New England. Statewide, Obama won 58%-40%, with his biggest percentages in metro Portland.

Maine held its first-ever presidential primary on March 5, 1996, in an attempt to attract the candidates' early attention. But the ploy didn't work, and the state abolished its presidential primary for 2004. In 2008, the parties held caucuses on different dates in early February. When Republicans voted on February 1, 2, and 3, some 5,000 people turned out. Republican Sens. Olympia Snowe and Susan Collins endorsed McCain early on, but that didn't make much difference. Former Massachusetts Gov. Mitt Romney won 52% of the Republican caucus vote, just days before his campaign was ended by the Super Tuesday results. McCain got 21% and U.S. Rep. Ron Paul of Texas got 18%. Democrats voted on February 10 when the race was still very much contested. Democratic Gov. John Baldacci endorsed Sen. Hillary Rodham Clinton and, in the week after Super Tuesday she campaigned in the mill town of Lewiston and at the University of Maine in Orono, while Obama campaigned in Bangor. Caucus turnout was only 3,500 people, and Obama won 59%-40%. Clinton carried Lewiston and three northern counties. Obama was strongest along the coast.

Congressional districting District lines in Maine are drawn by a 15-member, bipartisan Legislative Apportionment Committee. The Legislature may amend the plan and must approve it by a two-thirds vote. The governor has a veto, though presumably that's academic since there would be a two-thirds majority to override it. Under state law, the committee sent its last plan to the Legislature in spring 2003. This arguably violates the Constitution, since the 2002 elections were based on the congressional districts drawn from 1990, rather than 2000, census results. But no one has challenged the law, for the good reason that it makes no practical difference. There has been little change in the boundary between the two House districts since Maine lost its third seat after the 1960 census. In the 2003 session, however, the Legislature failed to adopt a map. On July 2, 2003, the state Supreme Court adopted a plan for the 2004 election, and it stayed in place.

111th Congress Lineup
2 D
110th Congress Lineup
2 D

Governor

John Baldacci (D)

Elected 2002, term expires Jan. 2011, 2nd term; b. Jan. 30, 1955, Bangor; home, Augusta; U. of ME, B.A. 1986; Catholic; married (Karen); 1 child.

Elected Office: Bangor City Cncl., 1978–81; ME Senate, 1982–94; U.S. House of Reps., 1994–2002.

Professional Career: Restaurateur.

Office: 1 State House Station, Augusta, 4333, 207-287-3531; Fax: 207-287-1034; Web site: maine.gov/governor.

Election Results

2006 general	John Baldacci (D)	209,927	(38%)
	Chandler Woodcock (R)	166,425	(30%)
	Barbara Merrill (I)	118,715	(22%)
	Patricia LaMarche (Green)	52,690	(10%)
2006 primary	John Baldacci (D)	40,314	(76%)
	Christopher Miller (D)	12,861	(24%)

Prior Winning Percentages: 2002 (47%)

Democrat John Baldacci was elected governor of Maine in 2002 and re-elected in 2006. Of Italian and Lebanese descent, Baldacci (*ball-DA-chee*) grew up in Bangor, where his family ran Momma Baldacci's, a restaurant started by his grandparents in 1933. (Former Maine Sen. William Cohen's father ran the bakery that supplied fresh rolls every day to Momma Baldacci's.) Like his seven siblings, Baldacci worked in the restaurant waiting tables. As an adult, he eventually bought a house right across the street from the one he grew up in. At age 23, he followed his father on the Bangor City Council in 1978. Four years later, he was elected to the state Senate, where he often dissented from Democrats and chaired the tax committee. When 2nd District Rep. Olympia Snowe ran for the Senate in 1994, Baldacci ran for her seat and campaigned by holding spaghetti dinners at $2 a head (children under 12 free). Maine's contrariness came out in the general election: Baldacci opposed Democratic President Bill Clinton's health care plan and pledged to oppose any new taxes; Republican nominee Richard Bennett was also not exactly in step with his party, being lukewarm on some of the planks in the congressional Republicans' Contract with America agenda that year. Baldacci won 46%-41%.

In the House, Baldacci had a mostly liberal voting record and was re-elected three times with more than 70% of the vote. Maine's congressional districts are good springboards to statewide office; each one is within both the Portland and Bangor television markets. Baldacci's three immediate predecessors in the 2nd District were all elected to the Senate. Baldacci's goal was the governorship, and he had pledged to serve only eight years in Congress. In 2002, independent Gov. Angus King was at the end of his second and last term, and Baldacci quickly became the front-runner. Yet there was plenty of competition. The leading Republican was former state Rep. Peter Cianchette. Independent candidate Jonathan Carter won the Green Party nomination (there was actually a primary) and also qualified for the state's public financing system, which gave him $902,000, while Baldacci's and Cianchette's campaigns each had roughly $1.5 million.

Baldacci campaigned against tax increases and on increasing state aid to public schools to hold down property taxes. He also promised to slow the growth of state spending and eliminate the property tax on business equipment. He said he would have a "balanced economic strategy" with different approaches for rural and urban areas and reiterated his promise to limit spending increases to the rate of inflation. Cianchette promised to cut the state tax burden by 20% and said he would veto any tax increase and "any budget that grows faster than your paychecks." He also called for a property-tax cap. Carter campaigned on a proposal to create a government-run health insurance system. On Election Day, Baldacci won a 47%-41% plurality over Cianchette; Carter got 9%. Baldacci won absolute majorities in the counties north and east of Bangor, and they accounted for 26,000 votes of his 29,000-vote plurality. Interestingly, these same counties were the strongest area that same day for Republican Sen. Susan Collins, who is from Aroostook County: hometown voting.

Baldacci immediately faced a budget shortfall estimated at $1.2 billion. In 2003, he and the Democratic Legislature managed to pass a balanced two-year budget without a tax increase. The governor also won enactment of his Pine Tree Opportunity Zones, to let economically ailing cities and towns offer business tax breaks, and of his Dirigo Health plan (*Dirigo*, the state motto, means "I lead"). Dirigo was designed to provide health insurance policies for low- and middle-income employees of small businesses and for people with no employers, with the state subsidizing individual premiums. It also authorized caps on fees for the state's 39 hospitals. In 2004, Baldacci sought bids from insurers, and only one, Anthem Blue Cross Blue Shield, already Maine's largest health insurer, responded. After a year in place, Anthem's DirigoChoice plan had enrolled just over 5,000 people and small businesses. Conservatives criticized the plan as not significantly cheaper than commercial alternatives, and Anthem greatly scaled back expectations of enrolling 31,000. In 2007, Baldacci proposed a host of changes to the program. Anthem dropped out and was replaced by Harvard Pilgrim Health Care. Baldacci called Dirigo, with 15,000 enrollees, only a "modest success."

In 2004, Maine voters passed a mandate for the state to pay 55% of education costs, up from 43%. But they rejected, by 63%, a proposal to limit property taxes to 1% of valuation. The Legislature increased state education spending by $340 million for the years 2006–10. And in December, Baldacci presented a package of tax measures that limited property taxes, capped spending increases at the rate of inflation, and proposed a constitutional amendment to allow towns and cities to freeze property taxes at current levels. But the following year was more troublesome financially. Baldacci had to ask the Legislature to borrow $450 million to balance the state budget; the request was approved. Republicans balked at the borrowing and began a drive to put the issue on the November ballot. Democrats responded by repealing the borrowing and making up the shortfall through spending cuts and targeted tax increases.

In January 2006, Baldacci signed a deal with Venezuela-owned CITGO Petroleum —in spite of Venezuelan President Hugo Chavez's fierce criticism of the United States—to supply $5.5 million in home heating oil to low-income Mainers. He also proposed an energy plan that would diversify the state's fuel use with tax breaks for biodiesel and incentives for wind and hydroelectric power. Also that year, he signed legislation to raise the minimum wage to $7 an hour, to eliminate property taxes on equipment for new businesses, and to crack down on people who drive with a suspended or revoked license. In 2007, Baldacci proposed a $6.4 billion budget and consolidation of 152 school administrative districts into 26. The Legislature approved most of his budget and agreed to reduce the number of districts to 80. It also passed a $1 cigarette tax increase. With additional spending cuts during the year, Baldacci again did not seek a general tax increase in 2008, and cut programs to cover a $95 million budget shortfall.

On other major issues in 2007, Baldacci vetoed a bill to allow the Passamaquoddy Tribe to build a racetrack casino along Maine's coast, signed a bill giving tax credits to Maine college graduates and employers who hire them as a way of keeping young talent in the state, and fought a National Marine Fisheries Service order requiring lobstermen to use sinking rope instead of floating rope. He also promoted a Green Seal program for labeling environmentally friendly cleaning supplies used in state buildings and sought legislation to reduce toxic chemicals in consumer products. In 2008, after the collapse of Minneapolis's I-35W bridge, Baldacci announced a $160 million four-year program to repair bridges. The next year, he and the Legislature tackled the vexing cultural issue of same-sex marriage. In the past, the governor had said he supported civil unions for homosexuals but opposed gay marriage. But in May 2009, after both houses of the Legislature by overwhelming margins passed a bill allowing same-sex marriages, Baldacci signed it into law.

Republicans considered Baldacci vulnerable in 2006. His proposed borrowing to cover budget gaps and the problems with Dirigo Health contributed to low popularity ratings. State Sen. Chandler Woodcock, a social conservative, won the three-way Republican primary in June by narrowly defeating a moderate Republican. Baldacci faced three other candidates in the general election, including independent state Rep. Barbara Merrill, a former Democrat. Woodcock campaigned on economic issues and supported a referendum on the November ballot that would have imposed a state spending cap. But Maine had not ousted an incumbent from Blaine House, the governor's mansion, in 40 years. Baldacci carried 12 of 16 counties and won 38% of the vote. Woodcock finished second with 30%, followed by Merrill with 22%. Voters also rejected 54%-46% the proposed spending cap. Baldacci vowed after the election to find a way to freeze increases in property valuations until a property is sold. Democrats gained seats in the House but lost them in the Senate in 2006. And in 2008, they gained seats in both houses.

Senior Senator

Olympia Snowe (R)

Elected 1994, term expires 2012, 3rd term; b. Feb. 21, 1947, Augusta; home, Auburn; U. of ME, B.A. 1969; Greek Orthodox; married (John McKernan).

Elected Office: ME House of Reps., 1973–76; ME Senate, 1976–78; U.S. House of Reps., 1978–94.

Professional Career: Dir., Superior Concrete Co., 1969–78; Auburn Bd. of Voter Registration, 1971–73.

DC Office: 154 RSOB, 20510, 202-224-5344; Fax: 202-224-1946; Web site: snowe.senate.gov.

State Offices: Auburn, 207-786-2451; Augusta, 207-622-8292; Bangor, 207-945-0432; Biddeford, 207-282-4144; Portland, 207-874-0883; Presque Isle, 207-764-5124.

Committees: *Commerce, Science & Transportation* (2nd of 11 R): Aviation Operations, Safety & Security; Communications, Technology & the Internet; Consumer Protection, Product Safety & Insurance; Oceans, Atmosphere, Fisheries & Coast Guard (RMM); Science & Space; Surface Transportation & Merchant Marine Infrastructure, Safety & Security. *Finance* (3rd of 10 R): Health Care; International Trade, Customs & Global Competitiveness; Taxation, IRS Oversight & Long-Term Growth. *Intelligence (Select)* (3rd of 7 R). *Small Business & Entrepreneurship* (RMM of 7 R).

Group Ratings

	ADA	ACLU	AFS	LCV	ITIC	NTU	COC	ACU	CFG	FRC
2008	80	57	67	91	100	12	71	12	12	22
2007	60	—	57	80	—	27	64	28	12	—

National Journal Ratings

	2007 LIB	—	2007 CONS	2008 LIB	—	2008 CONS
Economic	46%	—	52%	54%	—	45%
Social	49%	—	49%	47%	—	52%
Foreign	46%	—	53%	48%	—	47%
Composite	48%	—	52%	51%	—	49%

Key Votes of the 110th Congress

1. Raise CAFE standards	Y	5. Make English official language	Y	9. Withdraw troops 3/08	N
2. Expand SCHIP	Y	6. Path to citizenship	Y	10. Iran guard is terrorist group	Y
3. Cap greenhouse gases	Y	7. Fetus is unborn child	N	11. Increase missile defense $	N
4. Bail out financial markets	Y	8. Prosecute hate crimes	Y	12. Overhaul FISA	Y

Election Results

2006 general	Olympia Snowe (R)	402,598	(74%)	($2,773,431)
	Jean Hay Bright (D)	111,984	(21%)	($126,823)
	William Slavick (I)	29,220	(5%)	($5,580)
2006 primary	Olympia Snowe (R)	unopposed		

Prior Winning Percentages: 2000 (69%); 1994 (60%); 1992 House (49%); 1990 House (51%); 1988 House (66%); 1986 House (77%); 1984 House (76%); 1982 House (67%); 1980 House (79%); 1978 House (51%)

Olympia Snowe, Maine's senior senator, is a Republican who was first elected to the House in 1978 and to the Senate in 1994. After losing her mother to breast cancer when she was 8 years old and her father to heart disease at age 9, Snowe grew up with her aunt and uncle in Auburn. She worked her way through the University of Maine and took a job as a legislative staffer after college. Tragedy visited her again in 1973, when she lost her young husband, Peter Snowe, then a member of the Maine Legislature, in an auto accident. She was subsequently elected to his seat. In 1978, when Rep. William Cohen ran for the Senate, she made a bid for his U.S. House seat in the northern 2nd District and won. She maintained a moderate voting record, winning re-election by large margins throughout the 1980s but tighter ones in the 1990s. In 1989, she married Republican Gov. John McKernan. When Sen. George Mitchell announced his retirement in 1994, Snowe decided instantly to run for his seat. She went on the offense against her obvious Democratic opponent, 1st District Rep. Tom Andrews, attacking him for voting for the bill that closed Loring Air Force Base in northern Maine and for opposing the balanced budget amendment. She won 60%-36%.

In the Senate, Snowe has been one of the least conservative Republicans; she cast pivotal votes when the Senate was closely divided in 2001–02 and 2007–08. Her voting record puts her near the middle of the Senate. She has voted with Democrats on cultural issues and on some economic issues. She supports abortion rights. In 2001, she led a group that successfully pushed for legislation making the child care tax credit refundable. In the 2004 budget negotiations Snowe insisted on applying the "pay-as-you-go" rule to tax cuts as well as to spending increases, but the House would not go along and there was no budget resolution that year. In 2005, Snowe, along with fellow Maine Sen. Susan Collins joined the "Gang of 14" senators that diffused a showdown over President Bush's judicial nominees and preserved the Democrats' ability to filibuster, but only under "extraordinary circumstances."

Snowe supports legislation to allow the government to negotiate drug prices with pharmaceutical companies, which many Republicans oppose. She won a 63-28 vote in 2007 on a related issue that would allow drug reimportation from Canada and other industrialized countries. She has taken a lead role on many women's health issues, pushing for more money for women's health research, more screening for osteoporosis, and gender analysis in Food and Drug Administration clinical trials. With liberal Democrat Sen. Edward Kennedy of Massachusetts and conservative Republican Michael Enzi of Wyoming, she co-sponsored a bill to bar insurance companies from using genetic information to set premiums, which became law in 2008.

On the Finance Committee, Snowe exercised great influence over the Bush administration's economic agenda. During the 2005 debate over creating private savings accounts in Social Security, Snowe opposed using payroll taxes for private accounts. In May 2006, she was one of three Republicans to vote against passage of the eventual $70 billion tax-cut bill. In July 2006, Senate Republican leaders dropped plans to include repeal of the estate tax in a final draft of a pension bill after Snowe signaled that she would oppose it. She joined Democrats in voting against the Australia Free Trade Agreement, which she opposed because it would increase dairy imports. She also opposed the Colombia Free Trade Agreement, arguing that the Colombian government failed to prosecute killers of union leaders. Snowe also had a role in an early controversy over executive pay that ensnared the young Obama administration in early 2009. Snowe astutely predicted that high-dollar bonuses and "golden parachutes" to executives of financial companies being bailed out by American taxpayers would be unpopular with the public. She and Democrat Ron Wyden of Oregon won passage of a provision in that year's economic stimulus bill to prevent such bonus payments. But the stipulation was left out of the final bill at the insistence of the Obama administration, which said it was worried employees would sue to keep their bonuses, according to an account by Sen. Christopher Dodd, D-Conn. In late March 2009, there was an outpouring of public anger over bonuses paid to employees of troubled insurance giant AIG, which would have been prevented by the Snowe-Wyden legislation.

Snowe maintained her independence from the Bush administration on the Iraq war. In 2007, she co-sponsored a resolution criticizing the president's troop surge strategy. In April 2007, she voted against a Democratic proposal setting a timetable for withdrawal, but changed her mind in July 2007 and voted for it. She co-sponsored a bill setting benchmarks for the Iraqi government and mandating redeployment of American troops if the benchmarks were not met. "We need to have results, and the Iraqi political leadership needs to understand that," she said. Snowe also co-sponsored with Illinois Democrat Barack Obama a resolution to include soldiers with noncombat injuries in casualty reports.

In January 2003, Snowe became chairman of the Small Business Committee and promised to work for more affordable health insurance, regulatory relief, and access to foreign markets for small businesses. In 2007, after Democrats won control of the Senate, Massachusetts Sen. John Kerry became chairman and Snowe the ranking Republican on the committee. Together they sought a one-year delay for small businesses to comply with the Sarbanes-Oxley law's strict reporting requirements, and sought to change Small Business Administration procurement rules in economically distressed areas. Snowe sponsored a bill endorsed by both business leaders and labor unions to allow small businesses in different states to join together to buy health insurance.

Snowe's leadership role on the Oceans, Atmosphere, Fisheries, and Coast Guard Subcommittee of the Commerce, Science, and Transportation Committee gives her opportunities to shine for constituents. She helped pass the reauthorization of the Magnuson-Stevens fishery law in 2006. In October 2008, she declared that regulations had reduced fishing days by more than half and lamented that the government might "regulate our nation's first fishery out of existence." On other Commerce committee issues, Snowe and Democrat Maria Cantwell of Washington sponsored a measure to regulate foreign exchanges that trade in U.S. commodities; it passed as part of the 2008 farm bill. Snowe's provision to monitor electronic energy markets also got into the bill.

From her seat on the Finance Committee, Snowe has tinkered with legislation to include tax deferrals for military shipbuilding yards (Bath Iron Works would benefit), income averaging for fishermen, favorable accounting provisions for reforestation, and favorable treatment for energy plants that burn wood chips. She and Collins worked together in 2007 to get empowerment-zone designation for Aroostook County, to secure $617,500 to preserve landscape painter Winslow Homer's oceanfront studio in Scarborough, and to earmark $6 million for the Gulf of Maine Lobster Foundation in Kennebunk. In 2006, Snowe guided a bill through the Senate designating $1 billion for the Low Income Home Energy Assistance Program, an important federal program in the cold Northeast.

Snowe has enjoyed high job ratings in Maine. She was re-elected 69%-31% in 2000. Six years later, she easily turned back charges of being a "Bush enabler" to win re-election, 74%-21%, over Democrat Jean Hay Bright, an organic farmer, author, and environmental activist. She supported John McCain for president early on, in January 2007.

Junior Senator

Susan Collins (R)

Elected 1996, term expires 2014, 3rd term; b. Dec. 7, 1952, Caribou; home, Bangor; St. Lawrence U., B.A. 1975; Catholic; single.

Professional Career: Legis. aide, U.S. Sen. Bill Cohen, 1975–87, Staff dir., Oversight of Gov. Mgmt. Subcmte., 1981–87; Professional & Financial Regulation Comm., 1987–92; New England regional dir., U.S. Small Business Admin., 1992; ME dpty. treas., 1993; Exec. dir., Ctr. for Family Business, Husson Col., 1994–96.

DC Office: 413 DSOB, 20510, 202-224-2523; Fax: 202-224-2693; Web site: collins.senate.gov.

State Offices: Augusta, 207-622-8414; Bangor, 207-945-0417; Biddeford, 207-283-1101; Caribou, 207-493-7873; Lewiston, 207-784-6969; Portland, 207-780-3575.

Committees: *Aging (Special)* (3rd of 7 R). *Appropriations* (10th of 12 R): Agriculture, Rural Development, Food and Drug Administration & Related Agencies; Financial Services & General Government (RMM); Interior, Environment & Related Agencies; Military Construction, Veterans Affairs & Related Agencies; Transportation, Housing and Urban Development & Related Agencies. *Armed Services* (11th of 11 R): Emerging Threats & Capabilities; Personnel; Seapower. *Homeland Security & Governmental Affairs* (RMM of 6 R): Contracting Oversight (RMM); Investigations (Permanent).

Group Ratings

	ADA	ACLU	AFS	LCV	ITIC	NTU	COC	ACU	CFG	FRC
2008	75	50	78	100	100	26	75	20	30	22
2007	55	—	57	100	—	35	64	36	26	—

National Journal Ratings

	2007 LIB	—	2007 CONS		2008 LIB	—	2008 CONS
Economic	48%	—	51%		46%	—	53%
Social	47%	—	52%		48%	—	48%
Foreign	45%	—	54%		48%	—	47%
Composite	47%	—	53%		49%	—	51%

Key Votes of the 110th Congress

1. Raise CAFE standards	Y	5. Make English official language Y	9. Withdraw troops 3/08	N
2. Expand SCHIP	Y	6. Path to citizenship	N	10. Iran guard is terrorist group Y
3. Cap greenhouse gases	Y	7. Fetus is unborn child	N	11. Increase missile defense $	N
4. Bail out financial markets	Y	8. Prosecute hate crimes	Y	12. Overhaul FISA	Y

Election Results

2008 general	Susan Collins (R)	444,300	(61%)	($7,765,295)
	Tom Allen (D)	279,510	(39%)	($6,462,451)
2008 primary	Susan Collins (R)	unopposed		

Prior Winning Percentages: 2002 (58%); 1996 (49%)

Susan Collins, Maine's junior senator, is a Republican who was elected in 1996 in only her second run for elective office. She grew up in Caribou, in potato-growing Aroostook County, about as far northeast as you can get in the United States, closer to the capitals of New Brunswick and Quebec than to the capital of Maine. Her family is in the lumber business, and is also involved in politics. Her father was a state senator, her mother served as mayor, and her uncle was a state Supreme Court justice. She recalls that as a high school senior, she visited Washington as part of a Senate youth program, and home-state Republican Sen. Margaret Chase Smith talked with her for nearly two hours in her office. Right after college, she got a job as an intern with Republican Bill Cohen, then a Maine representative and a member of the Judiciary Committee who had voted to impeach President Nixon. Cohen hired Collins, and she remained on his staff for 12 years. She was staff director for the Senate Governmental Affairs Subcommittee on Oversight of Government Management, which Cohen chaired from 1981 to 1987. After Republicans lost their Senate majority, Collins returned to Maine to work for five years for GOP Gov. John McKernan as a financial regulation commissioner. In 1992, she was New England administrator of the Small Business Administration, and by 1994, she was running for governor. It was a disastrous campaign: She won the Republican nomination but was overshadowed by independent Angus King and ran third, with only 23% of the vote.

Two years later, Cohen announced his retirement from the Senate. Collins wanted to run, and indeed there was a precedent in Maine for a third-place gubernatorial finisher to be elected senator: Democrat George Mitchell was similarly humiliated in 1974, and then, after being appointed senator in 1980, won smashing victories in 1982 and 1988. In the Republican primary, Collins played up her resemblance to moderate Republican Sen. Olympia Snowe and Cohen on issues and called for a balanced-budget amendment, the presidential line-item veto, and term limits. She pledged to serve no more than two terms. Collins won with 56% of the vote. In the general election, she was opposed by former Gov. Joseph Brennan. Brennan attacked Collins on economic issues and gun control, but Collins raised much more money and won 49%-44%.

Collins has compiled a centrist voting record. She has joined Democrats on issues including tax cuts, campaign finance regulation, and a ban on "partial-birth" abortions. She was one of the Republicans who called for chopping the 2003 Bush tax cut in half; it ended up being trimmed but by considerably less than half. She also was one of the GOP members who insisted that the "pay-as-you-go" rule applies to tax cuts as well as spending increases in the budget in 2004. The following year, Collins joined the "Gang of 14" —seven Republicans and seven Democrats—who promised to vote against any effort by Republicans to halt the use of filibusters against judicial nominees as long as Democrats swore off future judicial filibusters in all but extraordinary cases. With then-Democratic Sen. Hillary Rodham Clinton of New York and Independent Sen. Joseph Lieberman of Connecticut, Collins sponsored a bill in 2007 to monitor mercury pollution. She also supported raising fuel-efficiency standards for cars to 35 miles per gallon in 2019 and requiring carbon dioxide emissions to be lowered to 1990 levels by 2020. Collins has been the lead Senate Republican sponsor of a bill to ban discrimination on the basis of sexual orientation. In 2009, Collins was given a coveted seat on the Appropriations Committee, the panel that controls federal spending.

Her first great cause in the Senate was campaign finance regulation: She was beaten by a millionaire in 1994 and faced two of them in the 1996 primary. Collins said that limits on self-financing candidates were a "cornerstone" of any reform for her, although such limits have been declared unconstitutional. In March 2001 she and Democrat Ron Wyden of Oregon sponsored an amendment requiring negative ads to include a picture of the candidate running them or otherwise be ineligible for the lowest discounted advertising rate.

In 2003, Collins became chairman of the Governmental Affairs Committee, the panel where she launched her career as a Senate staffer. Her highest-profile issue there was the reorganization of the intelligence community. Working closely with Lieberman, she fashioned a bill that established a director of national intelligence and a new counter-terrorism center. It was introduced in 2004 and adopted on a 96-2 vote after a two-week debate. With Lieberman's support, she beat back an amendment by Republican Ted Stevens of Alaska that would have kept secret the total amount of intelligence spending, and another amendment by Democrat Robert Byrd of West Virginia that would have limited the ability of the national intelligence director to shift funds and personnel. Collins worked with Democrat Patty Murray of Washington state on a 2006 bill requiring radiation screening of all cargo entering U.S. ports. Collins also moved legislation that would classify security threats at chemical facilities and require the operators to implement security measures or use safer chemicals.

Building on work from the previous Congress, Collins and Democrat Thomas Carper of Delaware moved a Postal Service reorganization bill through the Senate in 2006. The law pegged postal increases to inflation and shifted responsibility for the military retirement benefits of postal employees to the Treasury. On civil service issues, Collins generally supported Bush administration proposals to change federal work rules. Her March 2007 amendment to give Transportation Security Administration employees whistle-blower protection failed. She has also sponsored bills to strengthen the protection of whistle-blowers, increase competition in government procurement, and reduce the number of political appointees by one-third.

In late 2006, she won approval of a bill that allows minor league athletes and professional ice skaters to apply for P-1 immigration visas, making life easier for the many Canadian hockey players who skate for the Lewiston Maineiacs. On other local issues, Collins won protection for financially ailing fishermen under the Bankruptcy Act and sought a National Weather Service office for her hometown of Caribou. In 2007, she pushed a study to find ways to enhance the driver's license test, so that people crossing the Canadian border could use their licenses in lieu of passports.

In 2001, Collins got a seat on the Armed Services Committee, where she looks after the interests of Bath Iron Works, Maine's biggest private employer. In 2004, she secured a commitment that at least some work on the first new DD(X) destroyer will be done at Bath. Collins voted for the Iraq war resolution in 2002; in 2007, she opposed a Democratic attempt to set a timetable for withdrawing troops. But she sometimes sided with Democrats in imposing some restraints on the Bush administration. In 2008, with Democrats Ben Nelson of Nebraska and Evan Bayh of Indiana, Collins offered a successful amendment to make Iraq reconstruction funds a loan rather than an outright grant.

When Collins came up for re-election in 2002, national Democrats were optimistic about their chances. Their candidate, former state Senate Majority Leader Chellie Pingree, was energetic and politically creative, and was the chief sponsor of the state law allowing government negotiations with pharmaceutical companies as a way of lowering prescription drug costs. Eventually, both candidates spent more than $2 million. Not widely known in the state, Pingree ran a series of ads in 2001—positive spots on herself and tough attacks on Collins. The U.S. Senate debate over prescription drugs in July of that year helped Collins: She could say that her amendment to make prescription drugs less expensive had passed the Senate by a wide margin and that she had voted for a couple of different prescription drug benefit

1st District / **Maine**   683

programs. Pingree's ads insisted that Collins was "siding with the big drug companies." But Collins won by a solid 58%-42%.

In Collins's 2008 re-election bid, groups opposed to the Iraq war ran television ads targeting her, and Democratic Rep. Tom Allen announced he would challenge her with the war as a central issue in his campaign. Allen tried to tie Collins to Bush administration policies at a time when the president's popularity had sunk to historic lows. She fought back by highlighting her independence on such issues as oil drilling in the Arctic National Wildlife Refuge, which she opposed. Collins also ran ads touting her work getting emergency equipment for the Monmouth Fire Department and P-1 visas for the Lewiston Maineiacs. The war became a less salient issue as the success of the administration's troop "surge" strategy became evident. Collins maintained double-digit leads in the polls throughout the campaign. The two candidates appeared in 10 debates and spent more than $14 million. Collins won 61%-39%, and even achieved what she described as "my political dream" of carrying heavily Democratic Lewiston, as well as all 16 counties.

FIRST DISTRICT

Chellie Pingree (D)

Elected 2008, 1st term; b. April 4, 1955, Minneapolis, MN; home, Northaven; Col. of the Atlantic, B.A., 1979; Lutheran; divorced; 3 children.

Elected Office: ME Senate, 1992–2000, Majority ldr., 1996–2001.

Professional Career: Farmer, 1977–1980; Founder & pres., N. Island Designs Co., 1981–92; Pres. & CEO, Common Cause, 2003–07.

DC Office: 1037 LHOB, 20515, 202-225-6116; Fax: 202-225-5590; Web site: pingree.house.gov.

State Offices: Portland, 207-774-5019.

Committees: *Armed Services* (29th of 36 D): Oversight & Investigations; Seapower & Expeditionary Forces. *Rules* (8th of 9 D): Legislative & Budget Process.

Group Ratings and Key Votes: Newly Elected

Election Results

2008 general	Chellie Pingree (D)	205,629	(55%)	($2,213,642)
	Charles Summers (R)	168,930	(45%)	($644,690)
2008 primary	Chellie Pingree (D)	24,324	(44%)	
	Adam Cote (D)	15,706	(28%)	
	Michael Brennan (D)	6,040	(11%)	
	Ethan Strimling (D)	5,833	(11%)	

Population		Race/Ethnicity		Work	
Pop. 2007:	666,503	White:	95.1%	Private:	75.8%
Change since 2000:	Up 4.6%	Black:	1.2%	Government:	14.4%
Urban:	49.4%	Hispanic:	1.3%	Self-employed:	9.6%
Rural:	50.6%	Asian:	1.2%	Blue collar:	20.5%
Area size:	5,400 sq. mi.	Native Am.:	0.2%	White collar:	61.7%
		Hawaiian:	0.0%	Khaki collar:	0.2%
Age		Two+ races:	0.8%	Other:	17.6%
Median age:	41.2 yrs.			Median income:	$51,714
More than 65 yrs:	14.3%	*Ancestry*		Median home value:	$219,600
Less than 18 yrs:	21.9%	English:	18.0%	Poverty:	10.0%
		Irish:	14.1%		
Education		French:	12.2%	**Military Veterans**	
H.S. grad:	90.8%			% of Pop:	13.9%
College grad:	31.5%				
Grad degree:	10.8%				

The 1st District of Maine stretches from southern-most Kittery and nearby Kennebunkport to the craggy-shored ancestrally Republican counties to the east. The historic center is Portland, Maine's largest city, home to the yuppies and lawyers who have revived and renovated its downtown land-marks. Portland's antique charm, mostly booming economy and tolerant lifestyle have made it a haven for singles and gays. The 2000 census reported that

2008 Presidential Vote		
Obama (D) 232,145	(61%)
McCain (R).............................144,604	(38%)
2004 Presidential Vote		
Kerry (D)...............................211,703	(55%)
Bush (R) 165,824	(43%)
Cook Partisan Voting Index: D + 8		

Portland has the nation's third-largest concentration of women living together and the 10th-largest concentration of men living together. Maine legalized gay marriage in 2009. L.L.Bean is not far away in Freeport. Former farm towns have been transformed into suburbia, and old mill towns like Biddeford and Sanford have been redeveloped. The 2005 base-closing commission spared Portsmouth Naval Shipyard at Kittery, the nation's oldest continually operat-ing naval shipyard, and in 2009, Portsmouth announced the hiring of 400 more civilian workers. But the commission voted to close down the Brunswick Naval Air Station in 2011, costing the area $211 million in annual wages and military contracts. Redevelopment authorities faced decisions about what to do with the station's 3,200 acres of real estate, two runways, and 700 empty housing units.

Most voters in the 1st District live within a couple hours drive of the Maine Mall, which is just off the Maine Turnpike and Interstate 295 and is the state's heaviest concentration of retail and office space. But in a lifestyle more reminiscent of the Alaska wilderness, those who live on the district's remote islands depend on ferries and Cessna aircraft as their lifeline to the mainland. In the summer, the air traffic includes the families of *Fortune* 500 executives traveling to their estates. In the winter, lobstermen and local business owners board most flights. Lobsters are not just a tradition here but also an economic re-source. The industry experienced a boom for several years, but in 2008 the economic crisis sent sales plunging. Politically, the 1st District votes very much like the state as a whole: quirkily, often for indepen-dents, and splitting tickets with abandon. In 2008, every county voted not only for Democratic presidential nominee Barack Obama but also for Republican Sen. Susan Collins. Obama won 61%-38%. From 1968 to 1996, Maine elected three Democrats and three Republicans to the House, with each party holding the seat for 14 years.

The new congresswoman from the 1st District is Chellie Pingree, a Democrat elected in 2008. She succeeds Democratic Rep. Tom Allen, who unsuccessfully challenged Republican Sen. Susan Collins in 2008. Although Maine has a long history of electing women to office, Pingree is the first Democratic woman from Maine elected to Congress.

A veteran of the state Senate, Pingree is already an experienced legislator, but her path to elected office was hardly conventional. She grew up in Minnesota, the granddaughter of Scandinavian immi-grants who came to work as dairy farmers. Her parents moved to Minneapolis, where her father was an accountant and her mother a nurse. The city's anti-war activism during the Vietnam era had a profound influence on Pingree, and she left high school early for alternative education programs on the East Coast. At one program in Worcester, Mass., she met her future husband and followed him to Maine, where they settled on remote North Haven Island in Penobscot Bay. As disciples of the "back to the land" movement, they lived for years in a cabin without running water or electricity and made their living as organic farm-ers. Although the couple later divorced, Pingree thrived on the island, both politically and professionally. In 1981 she started her own business selling knitting kits. At its peak, the company, the North Island Design Company, distributed 100,000 mail-order catalogs. She started her political career in local offices on the island, including serving as tax assessor and sitting on the planning and school boards.

In 1991, she took her daughter to a local speech by then-Rep. Patricia Schroeder of Colorado, who briefly sought the Democratic presidential nomination in 1988. The speech inspired Pingree to take her friends seriously when they suggested that she run for an open seat in the state Senate. She went door to door in the traditionally Republican district in Knox County and won. Pingree rose to majority leader in 1996. As leader, she fought back a challenge from pharmaceutical companies and persuaded reluctant parties to agree to a law allowing the state to negotiate prescription drug prices, the first such law in the country.

Pingree left the state Senate in 2001, barred by term limits from seeking re-election. She ran unsuc-cessfully against Collins in 2002. Shortly after her loss, she received an offer to become president of Com-mon Cause, the Washington, D.C., government and campaign watchdog group. She took the reins of the nonprofit organization just as it had been thrust into the national spotlight by the push to overhaul the nation's campaign finance laws. That fight was not an easy one; she recalls an often strained relationship with Sen. John McCain of Arizona, a Republican who accused her of injecting partisanship into her work and is said to have pressured her to resign. As president, Pingree also directed Common Cause to lobby against media consolidation in the hands of a few powerful companies.

She left the job in early 2007 to run for the House seat that Allen gave up to campaign for the Senate. Although she had worked for years to limit the influence of money in politics, Pingree had no trouble raising far more of it that any of her five rivals for the Democratic nomination. She mostly eschewed money from political action committees but enjoyed the backing of EMILY's List, which funds women candidates who support abortion rights. Pingree won the primary with 44% of the vote.

　In the general election, she had a decisive fundraising advantage, bringing in $2.2 million compared with her Republican opponent, state Sen. Charles Summers, who raised about $645,000. Summers had run twice before for the 1st District seat, losing the 1994 primary to James Longley and the 2004 general election to Allen. Pingree consistently led in the polls in the Democratic-leaning district. On Election Day, she won 55%-45%.

　In Congress, Pingree was named to the Rules Committee, a prime assignment for a freshman, and to the Armed Services Committee. Drawing on her background at Common Cause, Pingree supported a bill creating a voluntary system for candidates to refuse political contributions from lobbyists and political action committees. Pingree's daughter, Hannah, is following in her mother's footsteps. She has served in the Maine House of Representatives since 2003, and in 2008 she was elected speaker of the state House.

SECOND DISTRICT

Michael Michaud (D)

Elected 2002, 4th term; b. Jan. 18, 1955, Millinocket; home, East Millinocket; Schenck H.S., 1973; Catholic; single.

Elected Office: ME House, 1980–94; ME Senate, 1994–2001, Pres., 2001.

Professional Career: Mill worker, Great Northern Paper, 1973–2002.

DC Office: 1724 LHOB, 20515, 202-225-6306; Fax: 202-225-2943; Web site: michaud.house.gov.

State Offices: Bangor, 207-942-6935; Lewiston, 207-782-3704; Presque Isle, 207-764-1036; Waterville, 207-873-5713.

Committees: *Small Business* (8th of 17 D): Finance & Tax; Rural Development, Entrepreneurship & Trade. *Transportation & Infrastructure* (18th of 44 D): Economic Development, Public Buildings & Emergency Management; Highways & Transit; Railroads, Pipelines & Hazardous Materials. *Veterans' Affairs* (4th of 18 D): Health (Chmn).

Group Ratings

	ADA	ACLU	AFS	LCV	ITIC	NTU	COC	ACU	CFG	FRC
2008	90	100	100	92	43	20	50	12	16	11
2007	85	—	91	100	—	7	55	0	1	—

National Journal Ratings

	2007 LIB	—	2007 CONS	2008 LIB	—	2008 CONS
Economic	77%	—	23%	62%	—	37%
Social	67%	—	33%	59%	—	38%
Foreign	62%	—	37%	92%	—	0%
Composite	69%	—	31%	73%	—	27%

Key Votes of the 110th Congress

1. Increase minimum wage	Y	5. Share immigration data	N	9. Withdraw troops 8/08	N
2. Expand SCHIP	Y	6. Foreign aid abortion ban	N	10. No operations in Iran	Y
3. Raise CAFE standards	Y	7. Ban gay bias in workplace	N	11. Free trade with Peru	N
4. Bail out financial markets	N	8. Repeal D.C. gun law	Y	12. Overhaul FISA	N

Election Results

2008 general	Michael Michaud (D)	226,274	(67%)	($569,114)
	John Frary (R)	109,268	(33%)	($311,470)
2008 primary	Michael Michaud (D)	unopposed		

Prior Winning Percentages: 2006 (71%); 2004 (58%); 2002 (52%)

Population		Race/Ethnicity		Work	
Pop. 2007:	648,277	White:	94.5%	Private:	74.9%
Change since 2000:	Up 1.7%	Black:	0.9%	Government:	15.3%
Urban:	31.0%	Hispanic:	1.0%	Self-employed:	9.5%
Rural:	69.0%	Asian:	0.7%	Blue collar:	26.6%
Area size:	29,985 sq. mi.	Native Am.:	0.8%	White collar:	53.6%
Age		Hawaiian:	0.0%	Khaki collar:	0.1%
Median age:	41.1 yrs.	Two+ races:	2.0%	Other:	19.7%
More than 65 yrs:	15.0%	*Ancestry*		Median income:	$39,544
Less than 18 yrs:	21.2%	English:	17.6%	Median home value:	$120,300
Education		French:	14.4%	Poverty:	15.6%
H.S. grad:	86.8%	Irish:	12.1%	**Military Veterans**	
College grad:	20.1%			% of Pop:	13.9%
Grad degree:	6.8%				

The 2nd District of Maine is heavily forested, rough-hewn, and enormous. It covers the northern three-quarters of the state, and is the largest congressional district east of the Mississippi River, larger than the states of New Hampshire, Vermont, and Massachusetts combined. The population is not evenly distributed. The district dips south to include the heavily Democratic mill town of Lewiston and also includes Eastport. At Belfast on Penobscot Bay, art galleries and boutiques have replaced fish-processing plants. There are several different Maines represented here: The bays of coastal Maine, with their small fishing towns; the potato fields of far northern Aroostook County (6,543 square miles in size); and the mill towns on the fast-running streams of western Maine. Some valleys have more moose than people. This was one of America's frontiers in the 1850s, when Bangor, on the Penobscot River, was the lumber capital of the world. Today, tiny Bangor is the second-largest city in the district after Lewiston.

2008 Presidential Vote
Obama (D) 189,778   (55%)
McCain (R)............................150,669   (43%)

2004 Presidential Vote
Kerry (D)...............................185,139   (52%)
Bush (R) 164,377   (46%)

Cook Partisan Voting Index: D + 3

This part of Maine has had its economic troubles, losing 22,000 jobs to neighboring Canada and other foreign markets after the 1993 passage of the North American Free Trade Agreement. Potato production is only half of what it was in 1980. A once-thriving sardine-canning business is virtually gone. Logging, long the largest industry in Maine, has suffered job cutbacks as big paper companies sell off acreage and shut down mills. A movement to set aside yet more acerage in a proposed North Maine Woods National Park, which would be larger than the Yellowstone and Yosemite parks combined, has sparked protests. Bumper stickers around the state read: "If you don't like cutting trees, try using plastic toilet paper." From 1998 to 2007, the Bangor area lost 3,700 manufacturing jobs. But there are also signs of life. Loring Air Force Base was closed in 1994, but new businesses, from aircraft repair to telemarketing, have replaced its civilian jobs and then some. And some long-standing industries are still humming. Washington County's sandy soil plains produce more than 90% of the nation's wild blueberry crop. The forest-products industry has explored new paper products and new ideas, such as turning sawdust into wood pellets for home heating. Politically, the district is iconoclastic and permanently enamored of neither major political party. This was Ross Perot's strongest congressional district in the United States in 1992 and 1996. Al Gore narrowly carried the 2nd in 2000 and John Kerry did only slightly better in 2004. Barack Obama won here, but by a closer margin than in Maine's other district, the 1st.

The congressman from the 2nd District is Mike Michaud *(mee-SHOO)*, a Democrat first elected in 2002. Michaud grew up in East Millinocket in the North Woods; he comes from a blue-collar family and is one of the few members of Congress who did not attend college. For 29 years, he was a mill worker and union member at Great Northern Paper. (The dominant employer in this economically depressed area, the company closed the plant a month after his election.) "I know what it's like to work the day shift, the midnight shift. I've been on strike. I know what it's like to worry about whether you will have a job or not," Michaud says. In 1980, he was elected to the state House and in 1994 to the state Senate, where he chaired the Appropriations Committee and became Senate president. Michaud has an eclectic mix of political views, which seem to be a throwback to earlier Democratic days. He is staunchly pro-labor, but opposes abortion rights. He opposes drilling for oil in the Arctic National Wildlife Refuge, but strongly supports gun ownership.

When Democrat John Baldacci left his 2nd District seat to run for governor in 2002, six Democrats lined up for the primary. Michaud's chief opponent was state Sen. Susan Longley of Lewiston, the daughter of former independent Gov. James Longley and sister of the 1st District's former Republican congressman, James Longley Jr. She emphasized her support for abortion rights. With strong support from organized labor, Michaud got 31% to Longley's 28%. It was a regional contest: Michaud carried the five most rural counties, and won 66% of the vote in Aroostook. Longley carried six counties chiefly in the southern part of the district, and won 59% in trendy coastal Waldo County. In the general election, Michaud faced

Kevin Raye, the veteran chief of staff to Republican Sen. Olympia Snowe. Michaud attempted to turn Raye's experience into a liability. His campaign slogan was, "I'm One of Us, Working for Us" —an attempt to contrast his blue-collar background and union membership with Raye's white-collar Washington experience. Hoping to appeal to feminists despite his opposition to abortion, Michaud set out a 10-point "women's equity agenda," including support for family planning, increased child care aid, breast cancer research, and equal pay for equal work. Raye had the support of abortion-rights groups. Michaud defeated Raye 52%-48%. He ran better than most Democrats in rural areas, winning 53% in the seven northern counties, where unions conducted a voter-turnout drive in the mill towns.

In the House, Michaud's voting record has been moderate for a Democrat. He has worked to create a caucus to unite workers and environmentalists on trade and other issues. Michaud co-founded the House Trade Working Group, whose members are highly skeptical of trade agreements. With Sen. Sherrod Brown, D-Ohio, he sponsored a bill in June 2008 calling for a review of all existing trade agreements and for halting new ones. In June 2004, he welcomed the reopening of the Great Northern mill under new ownership, but with significantly fewer employees.

On the Veterans' Affairs Committee, Michaud advocated more funding for the Togus Veteran Administration Medical Center and sponsored a bill to improve health care for rural veterans. As chairman of the panel's Health Subcommittee, he has taken an interest in the health needs of military personnel in Iraq. In May 2007, the House passed his bill to expand treatment of traumatic brain injuries.

After Democrats won the House majority in 2006, Michaud vied to become committee chairman, securing the support of retiring Illinois Rep. Lane Evans, the panel's top Democrat. Rep. Bob Filner had more seniority, but he worried some Democrats with occasional displays of bad temper, including an incident in which he shouted obscenities at VA employees after revelations that a stolen laptop had put the personal data of millions of veterans at risk. To boost his bid, Michaud had donated liberally to other House Democrats. He lost the election for chairman by a 24-20 vote in the Democratic Steering Committee; the result was close enough to force a vote in the full Democratic Caucus, which Filner won 112-69.

In 2004, Michaud faced Brian Hamel, a Republican with a record of job creation as the president of the Loring Development Authority. National Republicans took an early interest in the race. But Hamel, who had never held elected office, had trouble getting noticed in this sprawling district, especially with a presidential election and two controversial referenda on the ballot. Michaud was re-elected 58%-39%. With continued strong support from organized labor, he expanded his margin in 2006 and defeated Republican eye-care technician Laurence D'Amboise 71%-29%.

★ MARYLAND ★

Maryland, situated at the midpoint of the Atlantic coast, south of the Mason-Dixon Line but just north of the line between the Union and the Confederacy, is the crossroads state, with claims to both the North and South, and to both industrial and rural influences. This was the only one of the 13 colonies founded by Roman Catholics—the Calvert family—and its embrace of religious tolerance came less from high-minded ideals than from the Calverts' desire to protect their property from Protestant monarchs: a harbinger of Maryland's practical-mindedness. Similarly, although hot-blooded Baltimoreans wanted to secede from the Union in 1861 (the state song, "Maryland, My Maryland," is based on a poem condemning Abraham Lincoln's suppression of pro-Confederate rioters), cooler heads prevailed.

The Puritan impulse was never lively here. Prohibition was enforced only laxly in Baltimore, to the delight of its great journalist-cum-lexicographer H.L. Mencken, who called it Charm City. Slot machines were legal for years in the rural counties of the Western Shore and, after years of controversy and pleas from racetrack owners, were legalized statewide in 2008. An old state law guaranteeing blacks equal access to public accommodations specifically excluded the Eastern Shore. By not pursuing any one course rigorously, Maryland could be many things at once—Northern as well as Southern, moralistic as well as libertine, citified but also reliant on nature—mostly leaving people to their own devices. Perhaps as a result, much of Maryland's political history reads like a chronicle of rogues. Maryland's genial tolerance may have given it a little too savory a history, but this state cherishes its sense of uniqueness. The Chesapeake Bay is the nation's largest estuary, with water saltier than a river but fresher than the ocean and with unique watermen and shellfish. Pollution and years of overharvesting have drastically reduced its yield, however. The terrapin and Chesapeake oyster are rare today; oystermen harvested an average of 2.5 million bushels a year from the 1920s to the 1960s but an average of only 104,000 bushels in recent years. Rockfish and Chesapeake Bay blue crabs are much scarcer, too.

Maryland has some reason to be proud of the economy, or economies, it has built over the years. Half a century ago, half the state's population lived in the city of Baltimore and only one-fifth in the suburbs. Now the proportions are the other way around, and then some: 11% live in Baltimore, 76% in the suburbs. The Census Bureau classifies Washington-Baltimore as a single metropolitan area, the nation's fourth largest, with 8 million people. But Baltimore and Washington are not fraternal twins like Dallas and Fort Worth or Minneapolis and St. Paul. They are two quite separate cities, with different economic bases and different attitudes. Washington is a one-industry, white-collar capital city, while Baltimore started off as a port and an industrial city. Baltimore managed to stay diversified and successful as it spread out into the countryside from its new central core at the Inner Harbor and the solidly built edifices of its downtown streets. With its large suburban population, Maryland ranks second in median household income, after similarly suburban New Jersey. It is home to the Baltimore Orioles baseball team and their popular Oriole Park at Camden Yards (the first of the new-old ballparks of the 1990s) and to Johns Hopkins University with its Georgian buildings along the affluent corridor that runs directly north from downtown all the way to the developing edge city of Hunt Valley. But with its relatively high tax rates, increased under current Gov. Martin O'Malley, Maryland started to see net domestic out-migration in mid-decade, in contrast to the continuing domestic in-migration into neighboring Virginia and Delaware and into Lancaster, York, and suburban Philadelphia counties in Pennsylvania. And the long-term shrinking of the manufacturing workforce continues: Bethlehem Steel's Sparrows Point plant, which employed 30,000 in the 1950s, succumbed to bankruptcy, but it was bought by the Russian steelmaker Severstal in 2008 and now employs 6,000.

Baltimore remains the focus of Maryland's public life. Forty-seven percent of Marylanders still live in its metropolitan area, and its influence is far greater than Washington's on the Eastern Shore and in western Maryland. For years, most of Maryland's successful statewide politicians came from Baltimore. For more than two decades, its U.S. senators have lived there and commuted to Washington. Baltimore has a long Democratic tradition, and most of its voters are registered Democrats. Democrats currently hold more than two-thirds of the seats in both chambers of the Legislature, and they outnumber Republicans 7-1 in the state's U.S. House delegation. They have lost the governorship only once since 1966: in 2002, when Republican Bob Ehrlich, capitalizing on the unpopularity of incumbent Parris Glendenning, beat Democrat Kathleen Kennedy Townsend 52%-48%. But Democratic legislators battled Ehrlich ferociously, and despite a favorable job rating, he was defeated in 2006 by then-Baltimore Mayor O'Malley 53%-46%.

In national politics, Maryland for many years was a marginal state. It voted Republican for president in 1976 and as recently as 1988. But now it has become one of the most Democratic states in national politics, for two reasons. Almost 29 percent of Marylanders are African-American, the fourth-highest percentage among the states, after Mississippi, Louisiana, and Georgia (Maryland's black percentage passed South Carolina's in 2007). Many of Maryland's blacks, especially in Prince George's County, are college-educated and economically upscale, but they vote almost as heavily Democratic as do more-

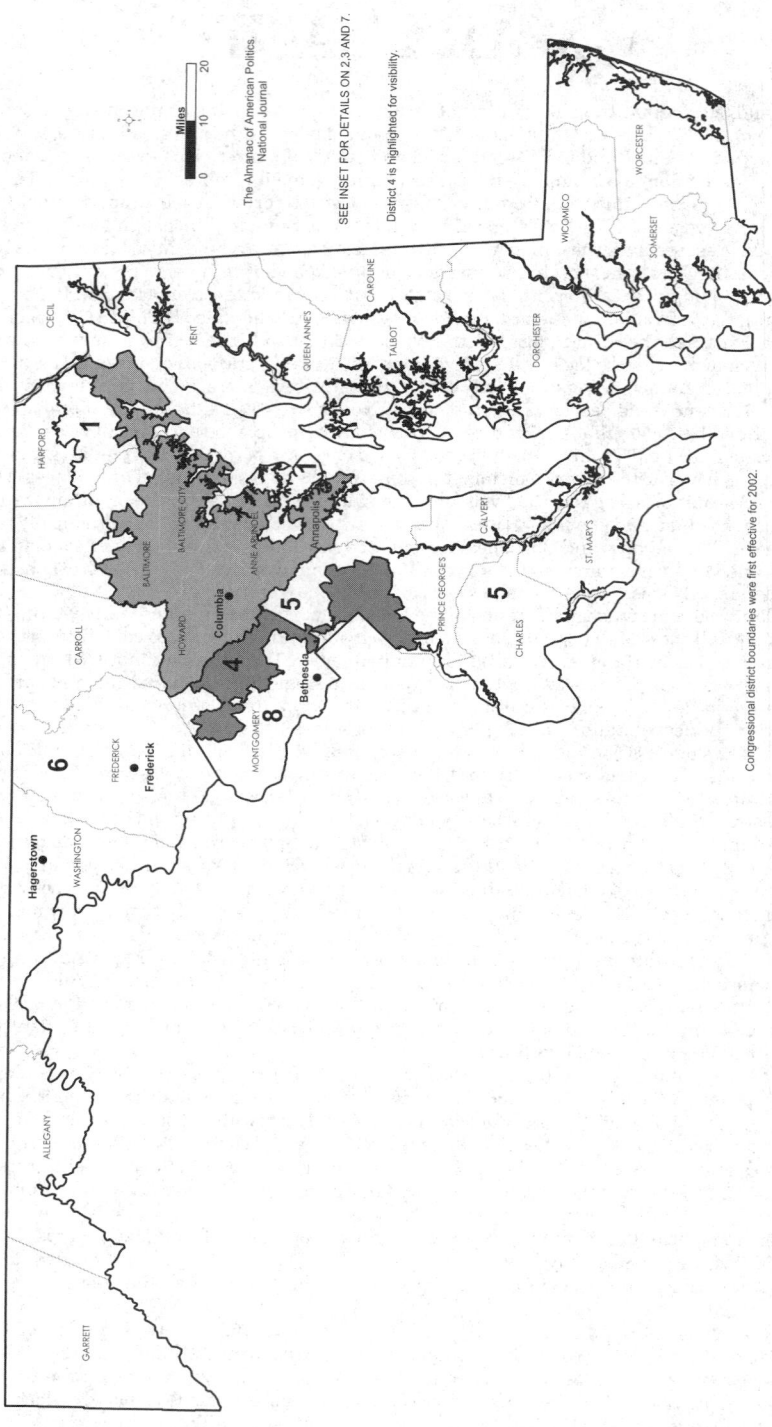

The Almanac of American Politics.
National Journal

SEE INSET FOR DETAILS ON 2, 3, AND 7.

District 4 is highlighted for visibility.

Congressional district boundaries were first effective for 2002.

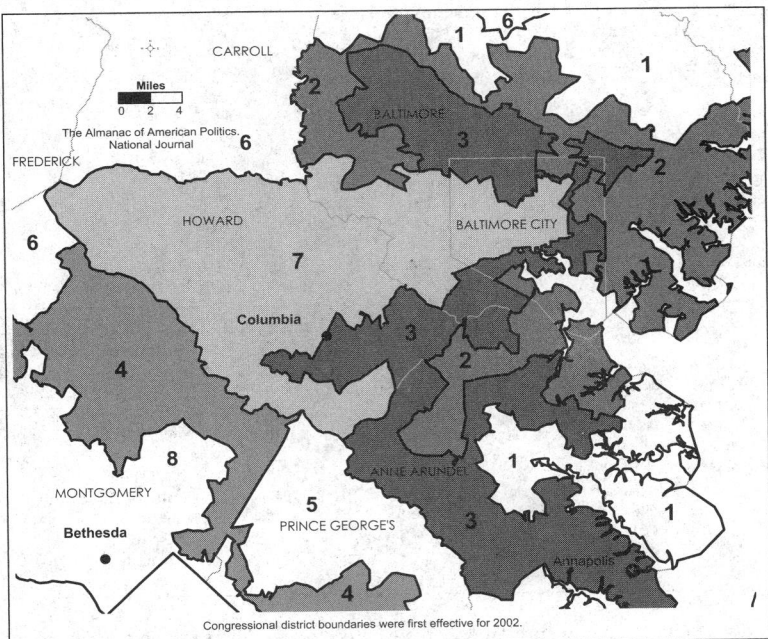

Congressional district boundaries were first effective for 2002.

downscale blacks. That was even the case in 2006, when the Republican candidate for an open U.S. Senate seat was Lt. Gov. Michael Steele, an African-American from Prince George's County. Steele made some inroads among black voters, but not enough. He got 25% of black voters statewide and 50% of white voters, in contrast to Ehrlich, who that year got 15% of blacks and 54% of whites in his failed re-election bid. Steele won 23% in Baltimore City and 24% in Prince George's, not much above George W. Bush's 17% in those jurisdictions. He lost the contest to Democratic Rep. Ben Cardin 54%-44%, and went on to become chairman of the Republican National Committee after the 2008 election. In the primary, Cardin had defeated former congressman and NAACP President Kweisi Mfume by a narrow 44%-41%.

The other reason for Maryland's Democratic strength is the increasing Democratic percentages in Montgomery and Prince George's counties, the two that are closest to Washington and that cast almost a third of the state's votes. In 1980, Montgomery and Prince George's weren't more Democratic than the rest of the state. Indeed, in the presidential race that year, they were slightly less so. But over a generation in which Republicans have backed smaller government and taken conservative cultural stands, Montgomery and Prince George's, like all of metro Washington, have become more Democratic than the rest of Maryland and the nation as a whole. In presidential elections from 1984 through 1996, Montgomery and Prince George's were about 10% more Democratic than the rest of Maryland. In the presidential elections of 2000 and 2004, with George W. Bush on the ballot, they were about 15% more Democratic than the rest of Maryland. In 2008, with Barack Obama on the ballot, and with his strong appeal to both black and high-income voters, Montgomery and Prince George's were 25% more Democratic than the rest of Maryland. To look at it another way, Maryland, excluding Montgomery and Prince George's counties, was in 1980 and is today not much more Democratic than the nation generally. This rest-of-Maryland gave Ronald Reagan and George H.W. Bush comfortable margins in 1984 and 1988; voted by about the national average for Bill Clinton in 1992 and 1996; gave small majorities to Al Gore in 2000 and George W. Bush in 2004; and voted 54%-44%—not much more than the national average—for Obama in 2008. In most of these contests this rest-of-Maryland would have been a GOP target state. But the heavy Democratic trend in the Washington suburbs has made Maryland solidly Democratic, and it has not been a Republican target state in 20 years.

Those trends seem likely to continue. Obama carried Maryland by a whopping 62%-36% (in only five other states did he win by a bigger margin). He won 94% of the votes from blacks and lost whites to John McCain by only 49%-47%. Turnout increased most in Charles County, which has had a large African-American migration from Prince George's, and in majority-black Prince George's and Baltimore City. The Democratic percentage was up most in Charles and Frederick counties, both with many new residents from closer-in Washington suburbs.

Population		Household Income		Work	
Pop. 2007:	5,597,843	Under $15k:	8.8%	Private:	72.2%
State rank:	19th of 50	$15k to $50k:	28.0%	Government:	22.4%
Change since 2000:	Up 5.7%	$50k to $100k:	33.1%	Self-employed:	5.3%
Urban:	84.9%	$100k to $150k:	23.9%	Unemployment (3-yr. average):	3.9%
Rural:	15.1%	Over $150k:	6.2%	Poverty:	8.2%
Native of state:	48.0%	Median income:	$66,873	Blue collar:	17.0%
Not a citizen:	6.7%			White collar:	67.1%
Area size:	12,407 sq. mi.	**Home Value**		Khaki collar:	0.4%
		Under $100k:	7.9%	Other:	15.5%
Most populous cities		$100k to $300k:	37.6%		
1. Baltimore	639,493	$300k to $500k:	32.4%	**Age**	
2. Columbia	91,398	$500k to $1 mil:	19.2%	Median age:	37.2 yrs.
3. Silver Spring	74,572	Over $1 million:	3.0%	More than 65 yrs:	11.6%
4. Ellicott City	64,257	Median:	$323,400	Less than 18 yrs:	24.4%

Race/Ethnicity				Military Veterans		Registered Voters in 2008	
White:	58.5%	*Language*		% of Pop:	11.2%	D:	1,946,823 (56.7%)
Black:	28.6%	English:	85.3%			R:	927,798 (27.0%)
Hispanic:	6.0%	Spanish:	5.8%	*Veterans by Period*		Other:	558,024 (16.3%)
Asian:	4.8%	Asian:	3.2%	WWII and before:	10.7%	Voter turnout:	2,631,596
Native Am.:	0.2%	Other		Korea:	10.1%	Turnout as % of	
Hawaiian:	0.0%	European	4.2%	Vietnam:	29.4%	voting age:	61.3%
Two+ races:	1.6%	**Education**		Gulf (pre-2001):	13.2%		
Ancestry		H.S. grad:	86.9%	Gulf (post-2001):	10.4%	**General Assembly**	
German:	13.7%	College grad:	34.7%	Peace time:	26.2%	Senate:	33 D 14 R
Irish:	10.3%	Grad degree:	15.4%			House of	
English:	7.7%					Delegates:	104 D 36 R 1 I

Maryland's strong Democratic preferences have helped its members of Congress wield major influence over important issues, though it is often quietly exercised. Paul Sarbanes retired in 2006 after 30 years in the Senate and served six years in the House before that; he was chief sponsor and shaper of the 2002 Sarbanes-Oxley Act, the wide-reaching crackdown on corporate accounting abuses. Barbara Mikulski was elected to the House in 1976 and the Senate in 1986; she is a senior member of the Appropriations Committee and up for re-election in 2010. Ben Cardin was elected to Sarbanes's seat in 2006 and had served for 20 years in the House before that. Maryland's most influential House member is Majority Leader Steny Hoyer, in Congress since 1981. Before becoming majority leader, Hoyer lost races for minority leader and House speaker to Nancy Pelosi, a Maryland native whose father, Thomas D'Alessandro, was a U.S. congressman and mayor of Baltimore. The two rivals once served together as interns in the office of Sen. Daniel Brewster. But Hoyer remains an influential and politically adept leader in the House and a major force in American politics.

Presidential politics　With its large black population, most prominently in Baltimore City and Prince George's County but also in other suburban counties, and with the increasing Democratic strength in the Washington suburbs of Montgomery County, Maryland has become one of the most Democratic states in presidential elections. It was Bill Clinton's third-best state in 1992 and fifth-best in 1996. It was Al Gore's fourth-best in 2000, John Kerry's fifth-best in 2004, and Barack Obama's sixth-best in 2008.

From 1992 to 2004, Maryland held its presidential primaries a week before Super Tuesday to try to get noticed, with limited success. The one significant result came in 1992, when Paul Tsongas beat Clinton 41%-33%, with all of his margin and more coming from suburban Baltimore and Montgomery County. In 2008, the primary was held on February 12, the same day that Virginia and the District of Columbia held their primaries. This was the single best day in the nomination contest for Obama. He won Virginia 64%-35%, D.C. 75%-24%,

2008 Presidential Vote		
Obama (D)	1,629,467	(62%)
McCain (R)	959,862	(36%)

2008 Democratic Presidential Primary		
Obama (D)	532,665	(61%)
Clinton (D)	314,211	(36%)

2008 Republican Presidential Primary		
McCain (R)	176,046	(55%)
Huckabee (R)	91,608	(29%)
Romney (R)	22,426	(7%)
Paul (R)	19,196	(6%)

2004 Presidential Vote		
Kerry (D)	1,334,493	(56%)
Bush (R)	1,024,703	(43%)

and Maryland 61%-36%. He garnered 79% in Prince George's County and 74% in Baltimore City and carried all of Maryland's major suburban counties as well. His lowest percentages there were 55% in Montgomery County and 56% in Baltimore County.

Congressional districting

111th Congress Lineup	
7 D	1 R
110th Congress Lineup	
6 D	2 R

Maryland was the scene of the Democrats' most successful partisan gerrymandering in the 2002 cycle. The convoluted shapes of the districts in the Baltimore area would have made Elbridge Gerry blush. The goal of the plan was to protect all four Democratic incumbents and to draw districts that would be impossible for 2nd District Republican Bob Ehrlich and 8th District Republican Connie Morella to win. The Bush 2000 percentage in the 2nd fell from 55% to 41%, and in the 8th from 36% to 31%. Ehrlich ran for governor and had his revenge, though as it turned out, for only four years. The 8th District attracted three Democratic challengers, each arguably a stronger candidate than any Morella had faced before, and she ended up losing narrowly to state Sen. Chris Van Hollen. The four Democratic incumbents had no problems. The two other districts, the 1st, based in the Eastern Shore, and the 6th, based in western Maryland, snake into the Baltimore suburbs to take in heavily Republican precincts and seemed to be safely Republican. But in 2008, after Republican state Sen. Andy Harris beat moderate Republican Wayne Gilchrest in the 1st District primary, Queen Anne's County state's attorney, Democrat Frank Kratovil, managed to win a narrow victory in the general election.

Governor

Martin O'Malley (D)

Elected 2006, term expires Jan. 2011, 1st term; b. Jan. 18, 1963, Washington, D.C.; home, Baltimore; Catholic U., B.A. 1985, U. of MD, J.D. 1988; Catholic; married (Katie); 4 children.

Elected Office: Baltimore City Cncl., 1992–99; Baltimore mayor, 1999–2006.

Professional Career: Field dir., pres. candidate Gary Hart, 1982–84; Sen. Barbara Mikulski, 1986–88; Baltimore asst. state's atty., 1988–90; Practicing atty., 1991–99.

Office: 100 State Circle, Annapolis, 21401, 410-974-3901; Fax: 410-974-3275; Web site: www.gov.state.md.us.

Election Results

2006 general	Martin O'Malley (D)	942,279	(53%)
	Robert Ehrlich (R)	825,464	(46%)
2006 primary	Martin O'Malley (D)	unopposed	

Martin O'Malley, a Democrat, was elected governor in 2006. He was born in Washington, D.C., grew up in the Maryland suburbs, and was truly a child of politics. His parents met at the Democratic National Committee headquarters. His father was a trial lawyer active in Montgomery County, Md., politics; his mother worked as a receptionist for Democratic Sen. Barbara Mikulski. Young O'Malley attended Gonzaga College High School in Washington, a private Jesuit academy in the shadow of the Capitol that also produced such illustrious graduates as political commentator Pat Buchanan and former Secretary of Education William Bennett. O'Malley went on to get a degree from Catholic University and the University of Maryland law school. He worked as a field organizer for Colorado Sen. Gary Hart's 1984 and 1988 presidential campaigns, and in between worked for Mikulski's 1986 run for Senate, where he met his future wife, Katie, the daughter of Joseph Curran, the longest-serving attorney general in Maryland history. After law school, O'Malley was a city prosecutor for two years, and then made his first bid for elected office, narrowly losing a state Senate race. In 1991, he ran for and won a seat on the Baltimore City Council. He spent eight years as a city councilman, during which time he became known for his energy, ambition, and penchant for headlines. In 1999, at the age of 36, he ran for mayor with a reform message and won the first of two terms as a white mayor in a majority-black city.

O'Malley was the kind of mayor who rides on snowplows and fire engines and seemed to be everywhere. He approached the job with a sense of urgency, calling for zero-tolerance policing and demanding accountability from city officials. Baltimore's high crime, drug use, and murder rates were a priority. He drew national acclaim for a reduction in crime, and he instituted a computerized system called CitiStat to track the performance of municipal government and to make agencies and department heads more efficient. During this time, O'Malley cultivated a national image, appearing on the cover of *Esquire* magazine in 2002 as the "best young mayor in America" and accepting a prime speaking role at the 2004 Democratic National Convention. In 2005, *Time* magazine called him one of the top five big-city mayors. He played a brief role as the mayor in the 2003 film *Ladder 49*, and sang with a Celtic rock band.

No doubt the youthful and telegenic O'Malley had ambitions beyond city hall, and in 2002 he considered running for governor but decided not to. In 2003, when he sought re-election to a second term, both his Democratic opponents in Baltimore and the state Republican Party groused that he was using the mayor's office as a stepping-stone to the governorship. In September 2005, O'Malley made the announcement that everyone in Maryland politics had been expecting: He would run against Robert Ehrlich, Maryland's first Republican governor since Spiro Agnew in the 1960s. Like O'Malley, Ehrlich had an unimpeachable résumé in Maryland politics. He was raised in the Baltimore suburbs, served in the state House of Delegates, and was a U.S. House member before his 52%-48% victory over Democratic Lt. Gov. Kathleen Kennedy Townsend in 2002. Ehrlich had decent approval ratings, but he had a stormy relationship with the *Baltimore Sun* and clashed with the Legislature on many issues. He entered the 2006 campaign as one of the most vulnerable governors in the nation. O'Malley did not have a clear path to the Democratic nomination at first; Montgomery County Executive Doug Duncan also entered the race. But in June 2006, Duncan, trailing O'Malley in both fundraising and in the polls, bowed out, citing a recent diagnosis of depression. This was a setback for Ehrlich, who stood to gain from a hard-fought, cash-draining Democratic primary that would have left little time for the victor to raise money and unite the party.

In a state where registered Democrats outnumber Republicans by 2-to-1 and where O'Malley led in the polls for virtually the entire campaign, Ehrlich nevertheless chose to run what he called a "non-campaign," a marked contrast to the aggressive, energetic O'Malley effort. He touted his record of tackling budget deficits and his initiatives to clean up the Chesapeake Bay, but otherwise insisted that the election was about governing, not promises. O'Malley offered a detailed agenda that called for, among other proposals, more funds for school construction, an affordable-housing trust fund, a $1 increase in the hourly minimum wage, and tax incentives for small businesses to join health insurance purchasing pools. The two candidates spent freely—together they spent more than $46 million—and did not pull punches. Ehrlich questioned O'Malley's record as mayor, pointing to Baltimore's high level of violent crime and troubled school system, while O'Malley referred to the governor as "$3 billion Bob," a reference to what his campaign said was the cumulative effect of the state property-tax increase and various other fees instituted during Ehrlich's tenure. O'Malley and state Democrats also sought to link Ehrlich to the unpopular Bush administration at every opportunity, referring to him as "the George Bush Mini-Me of Maryland."

O'Malley won 53%-46%. Ehrlich, the only incumbent Republican governor to lose in 2006, carried the Eastern Shore and Western Maryland, but O'Malley won by a landslide in Baltimore city (75%-23%) and in the populous Washington, D.C., suburban counties, Montgomery (62%-37%) and Prince George's (79%-21%).

His first legislative session was marked by a cordial relationship with Democratic legislative leaders who had harried Ehrlich at every turn. He signed a formal apology for Maryland's role in slavery, a freeze on in-state tuition at public universities, legislation to impose tighter automobile emission standards, and the nation's first statewide "living wage" law, requiring state contractors to pay employees more than the minimum wage. He also signed a law giving felons the right to vote as soon as they complete their prison terms. And Maryland became the first state to attempt to circumvent the Electoral College by agreeing to deliver its electoral votes to the winner of the national popular vote. It would not take effect until states that cumulatively hold 270 electoral votes, the number needed to win a presidential election, pass similar laws.

In October 2007, O'Malley called a special session of the Legislature, against the advice of legislative leaders, to try to resolve a $1.7 billion budget shortfall by raising taxes and increasing revenue by legalizing slot-machine gambling. A tax increase was needed, he said, to preserve "the very quality of life we all care about." O'Malley also said, "I did not put myself or my family through the meat grinder of public service to preside over decline." He sought to raise the state's income tax rate of 4.75% to 6.5% for high earners, as well as increasing taxes on corporate income, tobacco, and vehicle titles. Without the increases, he said, the state would have to lay off 10% of its workforce, close eight state parks, and freeze education spending. The Senate agreed to a top tax rate of 5.5%, rather than 6.5%, but the Legislature otherwise passed most of O'Malley's increases. It also authorized a November 2008 referendum on legalizing slot machines at racetracks. The issue had been heating up since neighboring Delaware legalized slots, and the Maryland horse-racing industry argued that slots were necessary to prevent their financial ruin. Ehrlich had supported slots, but was stymied by House of Delegates Speaker Michael Busch. O'Malley persuaded the Legislature to authorize the referendum, and despite the vocal opposition of state Comptroller Peter Franchot, it was approved 59%-41% in November 2008, carrying every county.

O'Malley proposed a $15.2 billion budget with $552 million in spending cuts and increased transportation spending, including for a new transit line between Montgomery and Prince George's counties' stations on the Washington-area Metro. On other issues, O'Malley and Virginia Gov. Tim Kaine, also a Democrat, jointly agreed to cut the blue crab catch 34%, an effort to rebuild Maryland's popular species of crab after the bay-wide population dropped 70% since 1993. O'Malley also called for spending $25 million to reduce runoff into Chesapeake Bay.

Like many other governors, O'Malley was actively engaged in the energy issue as gas prices soared. He signed a bill mandating a 15% reduction in electricity usage by 2015, and he supported the building of a new nuclear power plant at Calvert Cliffs. Amid the housing foreclosure crisis in 2008, the Legislature passed a bill extending the foreclosure timetable from 15 to 150 days and making mortgage fraud a crime. On a series of law-and-order measures, the Legislature agreed to expand the state's DNA database to include samples from persons arrested as well as those convicted of crimes. O'Malley, a death-penalty opponent, was unable to persuade the General Assembly to abolish the death penalty, but he delayed issuing new lethal injection guidelines in 2007 and 2008. Maryland's Supreme Court in 2006 ruled the state's lethal injection procedure was invalid. Lawmakers also rejected O'Malley's proposal for increased use of speed cameras on Maryland roads.

After the passage of his $1.4 billion tax increase, O'Malley's job-approval ratings declined but then rebounded somewhat in 2008. He endorsed Democrat Hillary Rodham Clinton for president, but she lost the Maryland primary to Barack Obama in February 2008. Meanwhile, former Gov. Ehrlich, who had launched a radio talk show, barraged the airwaves with criticism of O'Malley. He also began raising money, but polls in late 2008 showed him running far behind O'Malley.

Senior Senator

Barbara Mikulski (D)

Elected 1986, term expires 2010, 4th term; b. July 20, 1936, Baltimore; home, Baltimore; Mt. St. Agnes Col., B.A. 1958, U. of MD, M.S.W. 1965; Catholic; single.

Elected Office: Baltimore City Cncl., 1971–76; U.S. House of Reps., 1976–86.

Professional Career: Social worker, Baltimore Dept. of Social Svcs., 1965–70; Chmn., DNC Delegate Selection Comm., 1972; Adjunct prof., Loyola Col., 1972–76.

DC Office: 503 HSOB, 20510, 202-224-4654; Fax: 202-224-8858; Web site: mikulski.senate.gov.

State Offices: Annapolis, 410-263-1805; Baltimore, 410-962-4510; Greenbelt, 301-345-5517; Hagerstown, 301-797-2826; Salisbury, 410-546-7711.

Committees: *Appropriations* (5th of 18 D): Commerce, Justice, Science & Related Agencies (Chmn); Defense; Homeland Security; Interior, Environment & Related Agencies; State, Foreign Operations & Related Programs; Transportation, Housing and Urban Development & Related Agencies. *Health, Education, Labor & Pensions* (4th of 13 D). *Intelligence (Select)* (5th of 8 D).

Group Ratings

	ADA	ACLU	AFS	LCV	ITIC	NTU	COC	ACU	CFG	FRC
2008	90	50	100	91	100	2	63	0	0	0
2007	85	—	100	93	—	7	55	0	13	—

National Journal Ratings

	2007 LIB	—	2007 CONS	2008 LIB	—	2008 CONS
Economic	90%	—	6%	73%	—	25%
Social	72%	—	27%	64%	—	35%
Foreign	65%	—	32%	65%	—	6%
Composite	77%	—	23%	73%	—	27%

Key Votes of the 110th Congress

1. Raise CAFE standards	Y	5. Make English official language Y	9. Withdraw troops 3/08	Y
2. Expand SCHIP	Y	6. Path to citizenship Y	10. Iran guard is terrorist group Y
3. Cap greenhouse gases	Y	7. Fetus is unborn child N	11. Increase missile defense $ N
4. Bail out financial markets	Y	8. Prosecute hate crimes Y	12. Overhaul FISA Y

Election Results

2004 general	Barbara Mikulski (D)	1,504,691	(65%)	($5,997,093)
	E. J. Pipkin (R)	783,055	(34%)	($2,300,354)
2004 primary	Barbara Mikulski (D)	408,848	(90%)	
	Robert Kaufman (D)	32,127	(7%)	

Prior Winning Percentages: 1998 (71%); 1992 (71%); 1986 (61%); 1984 House (68%); 1982 House (74%); 1980 House (76%); 1978 House (100%); 1976 House (75%)

Barbara Mikulski, Maryland's senior senator, was first elected to the House in 1976 and to the Senate in 1986. She has deep roots in immigrant, urban America and a fascination for the new technology and jobs growing in edge cities and beyond. She doesn't look or sound like a traditional politician—just shy of 5 feet and stocky, she has a gruff and unpolished manner—but she is a savvy Senate insider. Her roots are in East Baltimore, where her Polish immigrant grandparents ran a bakery, and her father had a grocery store. She graduated from Mount St. Agnes College, earned a social work degree at the University of Maryland, and got a job as a social worker, helping at-risk children and educating seniors about Medicare. She entered politics by organizing a grassroots effort to stop a highway from going through the Highlandtown neighborhood where she grew up. She won, saving the now-thriving Inner Harbor, and went on to win a seat on the Baltimore City Council in 1971. She ran for the Senate in 1974, and got a respectable 43% against Republican incumbent Charles Mathias. When Democratic Rep. Paul Sarbanes ran for the other Senate seat in 1976, Mikulski made a bid for his 3rd District House seat and won. Ten years later, when Mathias retired, she gave up her safe seat for what seemed like a chancy Senate race. She won handily, with 50% in the primary to 31% for Democratic Rep. Michael Barnes, and 14% for Gov. Harry Hughes. In the general election, she beat Republican Linda Chavez, a Reagan-era civil-rights commission official, 61%-39%. She still lives in Baltimore and commutes to Washington. Her Baltimore office is in Fells Point, the city's original port area. She has a sideline writing mystery novels. She coauthored *Capitol Offense* and *Capitol Venture,* stories featuring the character Eleanor "Norie" Gorzack, a freshman senator from Pennsylvania.

Mikulski was the first woman elected to the Senate whose husband or father did not serve in high office. She is fond of calling herself "a social worker . . . with power." In her early years, the only other woman in the Senate was Republican Nancy Kassebaum of Kansas. Every two years since 1992, Mikulski has held workshops for new women senators to help them quickly learn the ropes in what is still a male-dominated realm. Mikulski is one of just 17 women in the Senate, and she takes seriously her role as dean of the women. "When I came . . . we were a bit of a novelty in the Senate," she said. "I think what we see now is that we're not viewed as a novelty. We're not viewed as celebrities. We're viewed as senators." Mikulski's policy agenda includes many initiatives aimed at women, such as establishing mammography clinic standards and homemaker IRAs.

In her first term, Mikulski won a seat on the Appropriations Committee, and within two years, she was chairman of a subcommittee handling housing, space, and veterans' programs. Now she chairs the revamped Commerce, Justice, and Science Subcommittee, which also includes NASA. Mikulski has been one of the Senate's chief advocates of the space program and an enthusiast for space exploration. She has paid close attention to funding for the Goddard Space Center, the Wallops Flight Facility, and Johns Hopkins's Applied Science Lab in Maryland. She is a champion of a future mission to Pluto, the only unexplored plant in the solar system, stating, "Pluto is a bargain at less than $500 million." She called the Hubble Space Telescope "the most successful NASA program since Apollo," and the best telescope "since Galileo invented the first one." And in 2004, she bitterly criticized NASA Administrator Sean O'Keefe for his decision to let the Hubble project die. The same year, she and Texas Republican Kay Bailey Hutchison moved to add $800 million to NASA's appropriation to repair the space shuttle fleet and service the Hubble Space Telescope. In 2006, she won a big victory when the new NASA Administrator, Michael Griffin, announced that the agency could repair and upgrade Hubble safely and within budget. The Hubble program provides about 1,000 jobs for Maryland. Her other work on the subcommittee has been directed at funding for Maryland highways, housing, homeland security at the Port of Baltimore, cleanup of the Chesapeake Bay, and research on oyster-bed reseeding in the bay. In 2008, her subcommittee bill would have increased President Bush's budget by $4.2 billion, but Congress did not complete work on the bill.

On domestic policy, Mikulski is a strong advocate of abortion rights and a solid liberal, although she sometimes votes for Republican initiatives, such as the bipartisan Welfare Reform Act of 1996. On the Health, Education, Labor, and Pensions Committee, she has taken a special interest in elder abuse and neglect, and long-term care. Her "Safety of Seniors Act," enacted in 2008, promoted education and research related to falls by senior citizens, a common cause of catastrophic injury. She has also been a leader in opposing Republican efforts to contract out government work to private firms. In 2005, she and Republican Sen. Mike DeWine of Ohio struck from a major pension bill a provision that would have required companies with poor credit to pay more into their pension funds, arguing that it would hurt small businesses. She has fought to extend a visa program to permit more seasonal foreign workers to assist Maryland's seafood processors. After voting for many years against higher fuel-efficiency standards—Maryland is home to auto assembly plants—Mikulski concluded in 2007, "It is time for a change." She supported the first major increase in fuel-efficiency standards in three decades.

Mikulski's toughest Senate election was her first, which she won against strong competition. Since then, she has not had a serious contest. In 2004, she faced Republican state Sen. E.J. Pipkin, a Dundalk native who made millions as a bond trader on Wall Street and returned to live on Maryland's Eastern Shore. He put $1 million of his own money into the race and argued that Mikulski's voting record was too far to the left ("Who knew?" his campaign spots asked), and that she had not done enough to preserve the health of the Chesapeake Bay. Mikulski managed to outspend him 2-1 in Maryland's most expensive Senate race, and won 65%-34%. Pipkin carried his state Senate district, two counties in western Maryland, and two exurban Baltimore counties. In 1995, Mikulski was mugged near her Fells Point townhouse, and subsequently moved to a more secure condominium building in Baltimore. In 2005, she was briefly hospitalized for an irregular heartbeat. Some Maryland Democrats have speculated that she might retire in 2010, at age 74, setting off a wide-open Democratic primary similar to 2006 when Sarbanes retired. But Mikulski has signaled she plans to seek a fifth Senate term. If she is re-elected in 2010, she would move into second place behind Sarbanes, who represented Maryland in the Senate for a record 30 years. In 2008, Mikulski was a national co-chair of Hillary Rodham Clinton's presidential campaign.

Junior Senator

Ben Cardin (D)

Elected 2006, term expires 2012, 1st term; b. Oct. 5, 1943, Baltimore; home, Baltimore; U. of Pittsburgh, B.A. 1964, U. of MD, LL.B., J.D. 1967; Jewish; married (Myrna); 2 children (1 deceased).

Elected Office: MD House of Delegates, 1966–86, Speaker, 1979–86; U.S. House of Reps., 1986–2006.

Professional Career: Practicing atty., 1967–86; Ways & Means Committee, MD, 1974–79; Chmn., MD Legal Services Corp., 1988–95.

DC Office: 509 HSOB, 20510, 202-224-4524; Fax: 202-224-1651; Web site: cardin.senate.gov.

State Offices: Baltimore, 410-962-4436; Bowie, 301-860-0414; Cumberland, 301-777-2957; Salisbury, 410-546-4250.

Committees: *Budget* (9th of 13 D). *Environment & Public Works* (5th of 12 D). *Foreign Relations* (6th of 11 D): African Affairs; International Development & Foreign Assistance, Economic Affairs & International Environmental Protection; Near Eastern & South & Central Asian Affairs; Western Hemisphere, Peace Corps & Global Narcotics Affairs. *Judiciary* (7th of 13 D): Administrative Oversight & the Courts; Constitution; Crime & Drugs; Human Rights & the Law; Terrorism & Homeland Security (Chmn). *Small Business & Entrepreneurship* (9th of 11 D).

Group Ratings

	ADA	ACLU	AFS	LCV	ITIC	NTU	COC	ACU	CFG	FRC
2008	100	93	100	100	100	4	63	8	3	0
2007	95	—	100	93	—	6	45	0	13	—

National Journal Ratings

	2007 LIB	— 2007 CONS	2008 LIB	— 2008 CONS
Economic	79%	— 13%	77%	— 13%
Social	81%	— 16%	91%	— 0%
Foreign	74%	— 24%	65%	— 6%
Composite	80%	— 20%	86%	— 14%

Key Votes of the 110th Congress

1. Raise CAFE standards	Y	5. Make English official language	Y	9. Withdraw troops 3/08	Y
2. Expand SCHIP	Y	6. Path to citizenship	Y	10. Iran guard is terrorist group	Y
3. Cap greenhouse gases	Y	7. Fetus is unborn child	N	11. Increase missile defense $	N
4. Bail out financial markets	Y	8. Prosecute hate crimes	Y	12. Overhaul FISA	N

Election Results

2006 general	Ben Cardin (D)	965,477	(54%)	($8,676,056)
	Michael Steele (R)	787,182	(44%)	($8,219,686)
2006 primary	Ben Cardin (D)	257,545	(44%)	
	Kweisi Mfume (D)	238,957	(41%)	
	Josh Rales (D)	30,737	(5%)	

Prior Winning Percentages: 2004 House (63%); 2002 House (66%); 2000 House (76%); 1998 House (78%); 1996 House (67%); 1994 House (71%); 1992 House (74%); 1990 House (70%); 1988 House (73%); 1986 House (79%)

The junior senator from Maryland is Ben Cardin, a Democrat elected in 2006 to succeed Sen. Paul Sarbanes, a Democrat and the longest-serving Maryland senator in history. Cardin is one of the many bright politicos who came from the Jewish neighborhoods of northwest Baltimore, the son and nephew of state legislators, a man who was elected to the state House at the age of 23—as soon as he was eligible to run. After serving four years as Ways and Means chairman in Annapolis, he became House speaker in 1979, at age 35. He had an interest in running for governor; but when Barbara Mikulski, now Maryland's senior senator, left her 3rd District House seat to run for the Senate in 1986, Cardin jumped into that race and was easily elected. In his second term in the House, Cardin got a seat on the Ways and Means Committee, where he was able to be a productive and creative legislator. He supported the 1993 North American Free Trade Agreement despite strong union opposition, backed a cap on medical-malpractice damages despite trial lawyers' opposition, and voted for normal trade relations with China after securing a rider designed to crack down on international dumping of subsidized steel in U.S. markets.

More than any other Democrat on the powerful tax-writing committee, he worked skillfully on bipartisan legislation at a time when few were sufficiently clever or independent enough to pursue such initiatives. *The Baltimore Sun* called him a "master of bipartisan lawmaking." Along with then-Rep. Rob Portman, R-Ohio, Cardin co-sponsored the 1998 Internal Revenue Service reform law. Again with Portman, he produced in 2000 bipartisan legislation to expand 401(k) savings and other retirement plans. In 2001, when Congress enacted the Bush tax cut, it included Cardin's provision to increase the limits for maximum IRA and 401(k) contributions. On Social Security, too, he has shown willingness to seek bipartisan reform with retirement accounts, but he was not receptive to President Bush's proposal for creating private savings accounts in the Social Security system. Cardin has also been a workhorse on health care and welfare, but with less bipartisan success. He criticized the prescription drug coverage for Medicare beneficiaries, which Congress approved in 2003, because it failed to provide sufficient benefits for senior citizens, and he proposed an alternative to authorize the government to negotiate lower drug prices, an idea the majority Republicans adamantly opposed.

Maryland Senate seats don't come open very often, so when one did, Cardin and 17 other Democrats filed to run. An experienced campaigner and fundraiser, Cardin began as the front-runner even though his earnest, somewhat bland demeanor raised questions about his viability as a statewide candidate. His toughest primary opponents were former Democratic Rep. Kweisi Mfume, who resigned his House seat in 1996 to chair the NAACP, and millionaire businessman Joshua Rales. Mfume and Cardin were friends—they were both elected to Congress in 1986—but Mfume and other black leaders warned that the state Democratic establishment's support for Cardin could breed resentment among African-American voters. The primary was expensive: Cardin, Rales, and Mfume together spent more than $12 million. Cardin outspent Mfume by nearly 4-to-1, but Mfume had a compelling life story and loads of charisma, especially compared with the low-key Cardin. Rales spent heavily from his own pocket but barely registered in the polls. Cardin won 44%-41%, carrying all but two counties and Baltimore City. The win was powered in part by Cardin's nearly 2-1 advantage over Mfume in suburban Washington's Montgomery County, the state's most populous county. Mfume ran best among black voters, winning Baltimore by more than 2-to-1, black-majority Prince George's County, and southern Maryland's Charles County, increasingly a destination for African-Americans moving in from Prince George's.

The Republican nominee was Lt. Gov. Michael Steele, the first African-American statewide officeholder in Maryland and a candidate exceptionally well-positioned to exploit Cardin's weaknesses. Steele combined his talent for retail politicking with quirky, unconventional ads designed to highlight his outsider status. Democrats, including Mfume, coalesced around Cardin and portrayed Steele as an inexperienced lightweight. Republicans criticized Cardin as a career pol who was closely tied to big-money special-interest groups. Without a legislative record, Steele made for an elusive target, so Cardin sought to link him to President Bush and criticized Steele for his support for the Iraq war. The issue of embryonic-stem-cell research, which uses donated eggs that have been fertilized in vitro, figured prominently in the election. Cardin ran stark ads featuring actor Michael Fox, who suffers from Parkinson's disease, saying, "George Bush and Michael Steele would put limits on the most-promising stem-cell research." Steele countered with an ad featuring his sister, a local doctor who revealed she had multiple sclerosis, saying Cardin was "using the victim of a terrible disease to frighten people, all for his own political gain." Cardin won 54%-44%, in what was a tough year for Maryland Republicans. Aside from Steele's defeat, Republican Gov. Bob Ehrlich lost his re-election bid. Steele won 18 of 23 counties, carrying the Eastern Shore and western Maryland, but Cardin carried all of the key suburban counties: 52%-47% in Baltimore County (which doesn't include the city); 54%-45% in Howard; 67%-32% in Montgomery. African-Americans voted overwhelmingly for Cardin. He won by landslide percentages in the city of Baltimore, 75%-23%, and in Steele's home base of suburban Prince George's County, 75%-24%. Two years later, in early 2009, Steele became the first African-American chairman of the Republican National Committee.

In his first year in the Senate, Cardin failed in his bid to win a seat on the influential Finance Committee, the Senate counterpart to the House Ways and Means panel. In spite of his impressive House career, he was still a freshman in the Senate. Majority Leader Harry Reid told Cardin: "Not gonna happen." Instead Cardin got seats on the Budget, Environment and Public Works, Foreign Relations, Judiciary, and Small Business committees.

In 2008, he unsuccessfully called for ending the use of a secret court—which gave President Bush broader surveillance powers in cases involving suspected terrorists—by sponsoring legislation that would allow the Foreign Intelligence Surveillance Act to "sunset" in four years instead of six. Many in Congress believed that the secret surveillance constituted a threat to civil liberties. Based on his recent campaign experience, Cardin sought to make it a crime for candidates to use misleading tactics against opponents. On an important local issue, he persuaded Washington, D.C., Mayor Adrian Fenty to explore alternative uses for land in Maryland's Anne Arundel County that had been chosen as the site for a juvenile detention facility for the District of Columbia. Cardin said that despite the partisanship in the Senate, he found it easier to continue the bipartisan approach that he had used in the House. His priorities included incentives for teachers at poorly performing schools, and Chesapeake Bay cleanup, a tried-and-true issue for Maryland lawmakers. During the final weeks of the 2008 presidential campaign, Cardin made numerous appearances for Barack Obama in Jewish neighborhoods in battleground states, where he had strong credibility as a Jewish U.S. senator with a solid record of support for Israel.

FIRST DISTRICT

Frank Kratovil (D)

Elected 2008, 1st term; b. May 29, 1968, Lanham; home, Stevensville; W. MD Col., B.A. 1990; U. of Baltimore, J.D. 1994.; Episcopalian; married (Kimberly); 4 children.

Elected Office: State's attorney, Queen Anne's County, 2002–08.

Professional Career: Practicing atty., 1994-present.

DC Office: 314 CHOB, 20515, 202-225-5311; Fax: 202-225-0254; Web site: kratovil.house.gov.

State Offices: Bel Air, 410-420-8822; Centreville, 443-262-9136; Salisbury, 410-334-3072.

Committees: *Agriculture* (21st of 28 D): Conservation, Credit, Energy & Research; Horticulture & Organic Agriculture; Livestock, Dairy & Poultry. *Armed Services* (32nd of 36 D): Air & Land Forces; Readiness. *Natural Resources* (28th of 29 D): Insular Affairs, Oceans & Wildlife.

Group Ratings and Key Votes: Newly Elected

Election Results

2008 general	Frank Kratovil (D)	177,065	(49%)	($1,994,553)
	Andy Harris (R)	174,213	(48%)	($3,024,144)
	Richard Davis (Lib)	8,873	(2%)	
2008 primary	Frank Kratovil (D)	28,566	(40%)	
	Christopher Robinson (D)	21,892	(31%)	
	Steve Harper (D)	11,904	(17%)	
	Joseph Werner (D)	8,753	(12%)	

Population		Race/Ethnicity		Work	
Pop. 2007:	713,133	White:	83.1%	Private:	75.2%
Change since 2000:	Up 7.7%	Black:	11.3%	Government:	18.0%
Urban:	64.2%	Hispanic:	2.3%	Self-employed:	6.6%
Rural:	35.8%	Asian:	1.8%	Blue collar:	20.2%
Area size:	3,702 sq. mi.	Native Am.:	0.2%	White collar:	64.1%
		Hawaiian:	0.1%	Khaki collar:	0.2%
Age		Two+ races:	1.1%	Other:	15.5%
Median age:	39.5 yrs.	*Ancestry*		Median income:	$65,395
More than 65 yrs:	14.1%	German:	17.6%	Median home value:	$298,800
Less than 18 yrs:	23.7%	Irish:	14.9%	Poverty:	7.4%
Education		English:	12.3%	**Military Veterans**	
H.S. grad:	87.9%			% of Pop:	12.6%
College grad:	30.5%				
Grad degree:	12.0%				

Chesapeake Bay is technically not a bay but an estuary. It was the central focus of the most thickly settled of the 13 colonies and today remains a central focus for much of modern Maryland. The first British here were amazed at the Chesapeake's oysters and terrapin turtles and crabs and rockfish. This was an estuary civilization in colonial days, with every little hamlet tied together by the highways of bays and creeks and inlets off the Chesapeake. The streets and docks of Chestertown, Oxford, St. Michaels and Cambridge still look something like they did when George Washington slept there.

2008 Presidential Vote

McCain (R)	216,896	(59%)
Obama (D)	148,029	(40%)

2004 Presidential Vote

Bush (R)	213,144	(62%)
Kerry (D)	124,163	(36%)

Cook Partisan Voting Index: R + 13

In post-colonial times, when most Americans were caught up in the romance of westward movement, these estuaries and peninsulas were mostly forgotten, located too far off the main lines of railroads and highways. In the 160 years between 1790 and 1950, the Eastern Shore counties of Maryland only doubled in population, perhaps the slowest growth rate on the Eastern Seaboard. Over the past half-century, much of the Chesapeake has changed beyond recognition, as the Eastern Shore has grown vigorously, with second-home buyers, retirees and commuters across the Chesapeake Bay Bridge. Now, this is a land of genteel estates fronting the water and of Frank Perdue's thriving chicken empire around Salisbury, of Easton's Waterfowl Festival and St. Michaels's Oysterfest, and of the swarms of motorboats and sailing ships making their way up and down the inlets or under the twin spans of the Bay Bridge. This growth has forced people along the Bay to confront issues that once would have been unimaginable here, such as high-rise condominiums obscuring the sunrise in an old fishing village like Crisfield.

But more threatening is pollution. Agricultural and suburban runoff have vastly depleted marine populations, and only a few watermen still make livings bringing crabs and oysters to shore. Since 1990, the blue-crab harvest has dropped by two-thirds. Various attempts at cleanup by governmental agencies over the years have been helpful but not entirely successful. In early 2009, the Chesapeake Bay Foundation filed a lawsuit seeking to force the Environmental Protection Agency to enforce limits on pollution entering the Bay.

The 1st Congressional District of Maryland includes all nine counties of the Eastern Shore. It extends across the Bay and grabs parts of Harford, Baltimore and Anne Arundel counties to strip Republican strongholds from the congressional districts that once contained them. The Baltimore and Harford county suburbs north of Baltimore are as solidly Republican as any part of Maryland. Although it is hard to avoid thinking of this district as the Eastern Shore district, nearly half the votes are cast on the west side of the Bay. This was one of only two districts in the state that twice voted for Republican George W. Bush—and comfortably. In 2008, it was one of two Maryland districts that voted for Republican presidential nominee John McCain, giving him 59%-40% over Democrat Barack Obama.

The new congressman from the 1st Congressional District is Frank Kratovil, a Democrat elected in 2008. After state Sen. Andy Harris ousted incumbent Rep. Wayne Gilchrest in the Republican primary, Kratovil upset Harris in a close November contest, becoming the first Democrat in 18 years to represent the Republican-leaning district.

Kratovil (*KRAT-o-vill*) was born in Lanham, Md. He received his bachelor's degree in political science from Western Maryland College, now McDaniel College, northwest of Baltimore, then went to law school in Baltimore. He worked in the city's public defender's office during school and after his graduation in 1994, then clerked for the Prince George's County Circuit Court. In 1997, he was appointed assistant state's attorney in Queen Anne's County. In 2002, he was elected state's attorney for the county, becoming one of the youngest state's attorneys in Maryland history. He was re-elected in 2006. During his tenure, he was also appointed by Republican Gov. Robert Ehrlich to the Maryland State Board of Victim Services.

After a brutal Republican primary in February 2008, nine-term incumbent Gilchrest was defeated by Harris. In that campaign, Harris had attacked Gilchrest, a Republican moderate, for voting with Democrats to support a timetable for withdrawing U.S. troops from Iraq. He painted Gilchrest as an economic liberal, a claim that was reinforced in advertising by the deep-pocketed Club for Growth, a national anti-tax group. Former Gov. Ehrlich also endorsed Harris over Gilchrest. Harris defeated Gilchrest 43%-33%. The presence of state Sen. E. J. Pipkin, one of three other Republicans in the contest, also worked against Gilchrest, as Pipkin carved out 20% of the vote. Gilchrest called his defeat "a clear sign the party is split between dogma and tolerance," and refused to call Harris to concede.

Kratovil bested three other candidates in the February Democratic primary, taking 40% of the vote. He entered the general election lagging in the polls and in fundraising, but got considerable help from the Democratic Party and unions. Kratovil portrayed himself as a Gilchrest moderate, campaigning on the need to clean up the Chesapeake Bay and expand access to health care. Gilchrest crossed party lines to use his considerable influence and name recognition in the district to help Kratovil, calling him "a man after my own heart." He campaigned actively for the Democratic nominee, even appearing in an ad for Kratovil.

Kratovil attacked Harris as a "just way out there" conservative, emphasizing his unwillingness to work with Democrats in the state Senate. The national Democratic Congressional Campaign Committee spent more than $2 million, mainly on ads attacking Harris for his ties to oil and banking interests and highlighting campaign contributions he'd received from insurance companies. The League of Conservation Voters and the Service Employees International Union also spent money on Kratovil's behalf. For his part, Harris worked to tie Kratovil to Democratic liberals such as House Speaker Nancy Pelosi and presidential nominee Barack Obama, calling Kratovil in one ad "clueless, liberal and very wrong." Harris also labeled him a "big spender."

On Election Night, Kratovil had a narrow lead of 916 votes, with absentee ballots yet to be counted. A week later, his lead had expanded to 2,852 votes, and Harris conceded. The final result was 49.1% for Kratovil to 48.3% for Harris. The Republican handily won the district's portions of Baltimore and Harford counties, which he had represented in the state Senate; he also carried Anne Arundel County. Kratovil carried the rest of the district's counties, with heavy support along the Eastern Shore.

In Washington, Kratovil pledged to be a moderate voice in the Gilchrest mold. On the first major issue before the 111th Congress in 2009, he was one of 11 Democrats to vote against President Obama's economic-stimulus bill. Kratovil later voted in favor of the revised bill that had passed the Senate, citing its spending cuts and increased focus on infrastructure development. He was one of four Democratic freshmen to join the conservative Blue Dog Democrats, and he received appointments to the Agriculture, Armed Services and Natural Resource committees. In what could shape up to be another close race, Harris announced in March 2009 that he would seek a rematch against Kratovil in 2010.

SECOND DISTRICT

Dutch Ruppersberger (D)

Elected 2002, 4th term; b. Jan. 31, 1946, Baltimore; home, Cockeysville; U. of MD, 1963–67, U of Baltimore, J.D. 1970; Methodist; married (Kay); 2 children.

Elected Office: Baltimore Cnty. Cncl. 1986–94; Baltimore Cnty. exec., 1994–2002.

Professional Career: Prosecutor, Baltimore Cnty. State's Atty. Office, 1970–75.

DC Office: 2453 RHOB, 20515, 202-225-3061; Fax: 202-225-3094; Web site: dutch.house.gov.

State Offices: Timonium, 410-628-2701.

Committees: *Appropriations* (32nd of 37 D): Commerce, Justice, Science & Related Agencies; Homeland Security; Legislative Branch. *Intelligence (Select)* (5th of 13 D): Oversight & Investigations; Technical & Tactical Intelligence; Terrorism, Human Intelligence, Analysis & Counterintelligence.

Group Ratings

	ADA	ACLU	AFS	LCV	ITIC	NTU	COC	ACU	CFG	FRC
2008	90	73	100	92	100	5	67	4	0	17
2007	90	—	100	80	—	4	63	8	12	—

National Journal Ratings

	2007 LIB	—	2007 CONS		2008 LIB	—	2008 CONS
Economic	64%	—	34%		78%	—	20%
Social	69%	—	31%		72%	—	26%
Foreign	55%	—	44%		48%	—	51%
Composite	63%	—	37%		67%	—	33%

Key Votes of the 110th Congress

1. Increase minimum wage	Y	5. Share immigration data	N	9. Withdraw troops 8/08	Y
2. Expand SCHIP	Y	6. Foreign aid abortion ban	N	10. No operations in Iran	Y
3. Raise CAFE standards	Y	7. Ban gay bias in workplace	Y	11. Free trade with Peru	Y
4. Bail out financial markets	Y	8. Repeal D.C. gun law	N	12. Overhaul FISA	Y

Election Results

2008 general	Dutch Ruppersberger (D)	198,578	(72%)	($636,162)
	Richard Matthews (R)	68,561	(25%)	($9,836)
	Lorenzo Gaztanaga (Lib)	8,786	(3%)	
2008 primary	Dutch Ruppersberger (D)	unopposed		

Prior Winning Percentages: 2006 (69%); 2004 (67%); 2002 (54%)

Population		Race/Ethnicity		Work	
Pop. 2007:	684,637	White:	60.2%	Private:	76.0%
Change since 2000:	Up 3.4%	Black:	31.4%	Government:	20.2%
Urban:	98.3%	Hispanic:	2.9%	Self-employed:	3.7%
Rural:	1.7%	Asian:	3.2%	Blue collar:	20.6%
Area size:	359 sq. mi.	Native Am.:	0.2%	White collar:	62.8%
Age		Hawaiian:	0.0%	Khaki collar:	0.9%
Median age:	36.3 yrs.	Two+ races:	2.0%	Other:	15.7%
More than 65 yrs:	12.1%	*Ancestry*		Median income:	$54,061
Less than 18 yrs:	24.3%	German:	16.8%	Median home value:	$213,900
Education		Irish:	11.2%	Poverty:	9.2%
H.S. grad:	84.1%	English:	6.6%	**Military Veterans**	
College grad:	23.6%			% of Pop:	12.9%
Grad degree:	8.8%				

The spokes of Baltimore's avenues spread out in all directions from the downtown district on the Inner Harbor, connecting the central city with the suburbs, where most residents of metropolitan Baltimore now live. The streets reach east to Dundalk and Essex, industrial suburbs where the tone of life was set for years by the giant Sparrows Point steel mill, long the biggest in the country. Northeastward, they extend to Havre de Grace and the oldest lighthouse in continuous use on the East Coast, as well as modest working-class suburbs in Harford County. The Aberdeen Proving Ground has generated both military and civilian job growth, but the locale is now better known for its Ripken Stadium, home of the Aberdeen Iron Birds, a Class A baseball team owned by hometown hero Cal Ripken, the Iron Man who set a baseball record by playing in 2,632 consecutive games for the Baltimore Orioles. In an arc northwest of downtown are middle-income towns from Randallstown to White Marsh. A couple of miles northwest of the county seat of Towson is Timonium, the site of the annual Maryland State Fair.

2008 Presidential Vote		
Obama (D)	176,198	(60%)
McCain (R)	111,909	(38%)
2004 Presidential Vote		
Kerry (D)	144,090	(54%)
Bush (R)	118,429	(45%)
Cook Partisan Voting Index:	D + 7	

The 2nd Congressional District of Maryland is an irregularly shaped hodgepodge that includes much of this territory. Most of the district is not far from the Chesapeake Bay, running south from Havre de Grace past the Aberdeen Proving Ground and the bustling Port of Baltimore, with its container facilities and large warehouses plus space for the more than 500,000 new cars and trucks that annually move through the port. To the south is the busy Baltimore/Washington International Airport, a major hub for low-cost airlines. Close by is Fort Meade, the large Army post that houses the National Security Agency and stands to gain more than 20,000 jobs from the realignment of military bases in recent years. (The post was a transit point for nearly 4 million soldiers in World War II.) The district angles inland to include some Baltimore County suburbs, residential neighborhoods in northeast Baltimore, and an industrial pocket in far southeast Baltimore. At that point, the district crosses the Harbor Tunnel to capture the row houses of Brooklyn and Curtis Bay, whose residents are mainly descendants of German and East European immigrants who moved there to work on the docks and in the factories along the Patapsco River and the harbor. The Democrats who drew the district lines connected Democratic suburban and city neighborhoods while including as little Republican territory as possible. About 60% of the district's population is in Baltimore County, with the remainder divided roughly equally among Anne Arundel and Harford counties and Baltimore city. The inclusion of Baltimore neighborhoods helped raise the percentage of African Americans in the district from 8% to 27%—which had grown to 31% by 2007.

The congressman from the 2nd District is Dutch Ruppersberger, a Democrat elected in 2002 in a district drawn specifically for him. Ruppersberger grew up in Baltimore, attended the University of Maryland, and graduated from the University of Baltimore Law School. Working as a Baltimore County assistant state's attorney, Ruppersberger had a near-fatal car accident in 1975 while investigating a drug-trafficking case. In 1986, he won a seat on the Baltimore County Council; in 1994, he was elected Baltimore County executive, a position once held by Republican Vice President Spiro Agnew.

Barred from seeking a third term in 2002, Ruppersberger seriously considered running for governor. But he was dissuaded by state party leaders who felt he was too politically vulnerable at the time. In 2000, he had backed a plan to give him the power of eminent domain to redevelop large pieces of the county, but in a resounding rebuke, voters rejected it 2-to-1 in a referendum. Compounding the situation for Ruppersberger was a damaging story in *The Baltimore Sun* saying that he had given county work to a firm to which he had financial ties. Kathleen Kennedy Townsend, the daughter of the late Robert F. Kennedy, became the gubernatorial candidate, while Ruppersberger got a favorable district for a House run when Democrats redrew the congressional map. However, he was still weakened politically and faced a primary fight. His little-known opponent, investment banker Osman (Oz) Bengur, spent more than $500,000 of his own money. But the state's Democratic establishment lined up behind Ruppersberger, and he won 50%-36%. The fall campaign was not much easier. The open seat attracted former Republican Rep. Helen Delich Bentley, who held the 2nd District seat for a decade until she ran, unsuccessfully, for governor in 1994. Bentley was 78 years old, but she offered an energetic campaign. With a strong record of constituent service and cross-party popularity, she had a chance to overcome the new district's Democratic leanings. Both candidates supported additional dredging of shipping channels in the Chesapeake Bay plus increased port security. Ruppersberger won, 54%-46%. His popular-vote margin was more than 13,000 in the small part of the district in Baltimore city, which he carried 79%-21%, and only 3,000 in the rest of the district.

In the House, Ruppersberger has had the least liberal voting record among Democrats from Maryland. With the help of Baltimore native and House Speaker Nancy Pelosi, he became the first freshman appointed to the Intelligence Committee, where he called for expanded oversight of the intelligence agencies and for shifting resources from the Iraq war to terrorist "safe havens" in Afghanistan. He initiated Operation Hero Miles to facilitate the use of frequent-flyer miles to assist U.S. troops in Iraq traveling home on civilian airlines during the Christmas season, and made the program permanent by including it in the Defense Department spending bill. Concerned about the potential sale of shipping operations at the Port of Baltimore to the United Arab Emirates, he helped to enact port-security legislation. In 2007, he got a seat on the Appropriations Committee, a useful assignment for his government-dependent district. In his first year, he worked on appropriating money for the protection of Chesapeake Bay. He also focused on expanding math and science schools near Fort Meade for the expected influx of specialized workers.

Ruppersberger has been re-elected easily. His earlier statewide ambitions have dimmed with the election of other Baltimore-area Democrats to vacant seats for governor and the Senate.

THIRD DISTRICT

John Sarbanes (D)

Elected 2006, 2nd term; b. May 22, 1962, Baltimore; home, Towson; Princeton, B.A. 1984, Harvard, J.D. 1988; Greek Orthodox; married (Dina); 3 children.

Professional Career: Clerk, Judge Fred Motz, 1988; Practicing atty., 1988-2006; Asst., MD Schls. Superintendent, 1998-2006.

DC Office: 426 CHOB, 20515, 202-225-4016; Fax: 202-225-9219; Web site: sarbanes.house.gov.

State Offices: Annapolis, 410-295-1679; Towson, 410-832-8890.

Committees: *Energy & Commerce* (30th of 36 D): Commerce, Trade & Consumer Protections; Health. *Natural Resources* (25th of 29 D): Energy & Mineral Resources; National Parks, Forests & Public Lands.

Group Ratings

	ADA	ACLU	AFS	LCV	ITIC	NTU	COC	ACU	CFG	FRC
2008	100	100	100	100	86	6	61	0	0	11
2007	100	—	100	85	—	4	50	0	6	—

National Journal Ratings

	2007 LIB	—	2007 CONS	2008 LIB	—	2008 CONS
Economic	73%	—	24%	81%	—	15%
Social	89%	—	8%	67%	—	28%
Foreign	90%	—	8%	70%	—	25%
Composite	85%	—	15%	75%	—	25%

Key Votes of the 110th Congress

1. Increase minimum wage	Y	5. Share immigration data	N	9. Withdraw troops 8/08	Y
2. Expand SCHIP	Y	6. Foreign aid abortion ban	N	10. No operations in Iran	Y
3. Raise CAFE standards	Y	7. Ban gay bias in workplace	Y	11. Free trade with Peru	N
4. Bail out financial markets	Y	8. Repeal D.C. gun law	N	12. Overhaul FISA	N

Election Results

2008 general	John Sarbanes (D)	203,711	(70%)	($799,506)
	Thomas Harris (R)	87,971	(30%)	
2008 primary	John Sarbanes (D)	86,598	(89%)	
	John Rea (D)	10,614	(11%)	

Prior Winning Percentages: 2006 (64%)

Population		Race/Ethnicity		Work	
Pop. 2007:	698,237	White:	70.8%	Private:	75.0%
Change since 2000:	Up 5.5%	Black:	17.9%	Government:	20.2%
Urban:	98.6%	Hispanic:	4.8%	Self-employed:	4.6%
Rural:	1.4%	Asian:	4.3%	Blue collar:	15.0%
Area size:	293 sq. mi.	Native Am.:	0.2%	White collar:	71.2%
		Hawaiian:	0.0%	Khaki collar:	0.4%
Age		Two+ races:	1.7%	Other:	13.4%
Median age:	36.5 yrs.			Median income:	$67,317
More than 65 yrs:	12.1%	*Ancestry*		Median home value:	$299,400
Less than 18 yrs:	22.9%	German:	14.9%	Poverty:	8.3%
		Irish:	12.3%		
Education		English:	8.0%	**Military Veterans**	
H.S. grad:	87.1%			% of Pop:	10.7%
College grad:	40.6%				
Grad degree:	18.5%				

Baltimore, one of America's major cities since the Revolution, has been transformed into one of America's star cities. Its Inner Harbor redevelopment, with a spectacular, multilevel aquarium on the water, and its ballpark at Camden Yards are national models. The local cuisine—crab cakes and steamed crabs spiced in a certain way—are known well beyond the watershed of the Chesapeake Bay. The city "prefers diners and taverns tucked into venerable row houses to newer, trendier spots,"

2008 Presidential Vote
Obama (D) 194,575   (59%)
McCain (R)............................128,342   (39%)

2004 Presidential Vote
Kerry (D)...............................163,088   (54%)
Bush (R) 136,672   (45%)

Cook Partisan Voting Index: D + 6

wrote *The New York Times*. The central city of Baltimore has had terrible urban problems—high crime, abandoned neighborhoods, poor schools—but the greater Baltimore area that has grown far beyond the city and county lines fares better and retains a distinctive character. This is a city built solidly on commerce, and one that has always maintained a relaxed air. To the south, Annapolis was laid out as a capital in 1694, with one circle planned for the Statehouse and one for the Church. The marble-halled Statehouse, built in 1772, is where the Continental Congress ratified the Treaty of Paris and is the oldest state capitol in continuous use. Annapolis is also the home of the U.S. Naval Academy, and the city's waterfront, though gentrified, is a waterman's port as well as a yachter's.

The 3rd Congressional District of Maryland consists of three oddly disjointed pieces of geography that extend from the locus of the Inner Harbor area. Its boundaries were designed by Democrats with politics in mind: The 3rd borders the majority-black 7th District on three sides and is itself bordered on three sides by the 2nd District, which redistricters made even more Democratic than the 3rd. One spoke extends northeast from black city neighborhoods into mostly white suburbs. Another extends north and west from the city to the Baltimore County seat of Towson and the heavily Jewish suburbs of Pikesville and Owings Mills, past the array of temples and synagogues on Park Heights Avenue in Baltimore city. The largest bloc of voters is in the crooked spoke that extends southwest, past the old row-house neighborhoods overlooking Fort McHenry and out past blue-collar Arbutus into Linthicum in Anne Arundel County and continuing to Annapolis. Just over one-third of the district population resides in Anne Arundel, including all of Annapolis; a quarter resides within Baltimore city, in such neighborhoods as Roland Park , and among the restaurants and bars of Little Italy and Fells Point. Another small slice of the 3rd consists of parts of Elkridge and Columbia in Howard County. Redistricting left the new 3rd District less Democratic than it had been; Bush's percentage of the vote increased from 34% in 2000 to 45% in 2004. But the district remains safely Democratic.

The congressman from the 3rd District is Democrat John Sarbanes, the son of the former longtime senator from Maryland. Sarbanes graduated from Princeton University and Harvard Law School, following the academic route taken by his dad, Democrat Paul Sarbanes, who retired in 2006 after more than 35 years in Congress. The younger Sarbanes returned to Baltimore to clerk for a federal District Court judge, and then joined the Venable law firm, where he chaired the health care practice and represented nonprofit hospitals and senior-living providers. He also spent seven years as special assistant to the Maryland superintendent of schools, serving as the liaison to the Baltimore schools.

Though his 2006 campaign was his first bid for public office, Sarbanes enjoyed a considerable advantage because of his name recognition. But the primary race was no cakewalk. Openings in the Maryland congressional delegation are rare, so when Democratic Rep. Ben Cardin announced he was giving up his seat to run for the Senate, eight candidates filed for the September primary. Contenders included veteran state Sen. Paula Hollinger and former Baltimore Health Commissioner Peter Beilenson, the son of former Democratic Rep. Anthony Beilenson of California. Sarbanes issued lengthy, detailed proposals on health care and education, which he called his top two legislative priorities. He supported repeal of the Bush tax cuts, calling them "fundamentally unfair and leading us down a road to financial disaster." Beilenson emphasized his experience managing a large government budget. Hollinger was endorsed by the teachers association, and had been an active state lawmaker as chairwoman of the Senate Education, Health, and Environmental Affairs Committee. Sarbanes, who had a small fundraising advantage, won the Democratic primary with 32% to 25% for runner-up Beilenson and 21% for Hollinger. Although his customarily low-profile father mostly stayed in the background, John Sarbanes acknowledged that he benefited from his name identification. He ran strongest in Anne Arundel County, which cast the most votes, trouncing Beilenson 40%-18%. Beilenson won more narrowly in Baltimore city, as did Hollinger in Baltimore County. Sarbanes finished second in each and also won the smaller vote in Howard County. Republican nominee John White, the founder and CEO of a marketing company, spent nearly a half-million dollars, most of it from his own pocket, but got little attention and lost the general election to Sarbanes, 64%-34%.

In the House, Sarbanes has had a solidly liberal voting record, though a bit to the center on economic issues. He became an advocate of cleaning up pollution in the Chesapeake Bay, and, with the thousands of federal workers in his district in mind, Sarbanes worked on a House-passed bill to allow qualified federal employees to telecommute at least 20 percent of their work hours. The House also passed his bill to rename a highway near Camden Yards "Cal Ripken Way," in honor of the all-star shortstop/third baseman who played his entire career for the Baltimore Orioles. Focusing on education from his seat on the Education and Labor Committee, Sarbanes won approval of amendments to bolster instruction in the schools on protecting the environment and to give local school officials more-specific guidelines on the objectives of the Bush-era No Child Left Behind education law. When Albert Wynn, D-Md., announced his resignation from the House in March 2008, Sarbanes was among several Democrats who sought to replace him on the Energy and Commerce Committee. He didn't get the seat, but set his marker for the future. Sarbanes was re-elected easily in 2008. In the 111th Congress, he finally attained his desired seat on the Energy and Commerce Committee, giving up posts on the Education and Labor Committee and the Oversight and Government Reform Committee.

FOURTH DISTRICT

Donna Edwards (D)

Elected June 2008, 1st full term; b. June 28, 1958, Yanceyville, NC; home, Fort Washington; Wake Forest U., B.A., 1980, Franklin Pierce Law Center, J.D., 1989; Baptist; separated; 1 child.

Professional Career: Lockheed Engineering, 1982–86; Lobbyist, Public Citizen and Congress Watch, 1992–94; Executive director, Center for a New Democracy, 1994–96; Co-founder and executive director, National Network to End Domestic Violence, 1996–99; Executive director, The Arca Foundation, 2000-present.

DC Office: 318 CHOB, 20515, 202-225-8699; Fax: 202-225-8714; Web site: donnaedwards.house.gov.

State Offices: Silver Spring, 301-562-7960; Suitland 301-516-7601.

Committees: *Science & Technology* (10th of 26 D): Energy & Environment; Space & Aeronautics (VChmn); Technology & Innovation. *Transportation & Infrastructure* (34th of 44 D): Economic Development; Public Buildings & Emergency Management; Highways & Transit; Water Resources & Environment.

Group Ratings: Newly Elected

Key Votes of the 110th Congress

1. Increase minimum wage	*	5. Share immigration data	*	9. Withdraw troops 8/08	*
2. Expand SCHIP	*	6. Foreign aid abortion ban	*	10. No operations in Iran	*
3. Raise CAFE standards	*	7. Ban gay bias in workplace	*	11. Free trade with Peru	*
4. Bail out financial markets	Y	8. Repeal D.C. gun law	N	12. Overhaul FISA	N

Election Results

2008 general	Donna Edwards (D)	258,704	(86%)	($1,443,942)
	Peter James (R)	38,739	(13%)	($23,514)
2008 spec. election	Donna Edwards (D)	16,481	(81%)	
	Peter James (R)	3,638	(18%)	
2008 primary	Donna Edwards (D)	78,008	(59%)	
	Albert Wynn (D)	48,885	(37%)	

Population		Race/Ethnicity		Work	
Pop. 2007:	678,636	White:	24.2%	Private:	68.0%
Change since 2000:	Up 2.5%	Black:	55.5%	Government:	27.1%
Urban:	97.9%	Hispanic:	11.5%	Self-employed:	4.8%
Rural:	2.1%	Asian:	6.6%	Blue collar:	15.4%
Area size:	318 sq. mi.	Native Am.:	0.2%	White collar:	66.9%
		Hawaiian:	0.1%	Khaki collar:	0.3%
Age		Two+ races:	1.6%	Other:	17.4%
Median age:	35.8 yrs.	*Ancestry*		Median income:	$70,530
More than 65 yrs:	8.6%	Subsaharan:	5.7%	Median home value:	$354,300
Less than 18 yrs:	26.4%	German:	5.3%	Poverty:	7.1%
		Irish:	4.7%		
Education				**Military Veterans**	
H.S. grad:	87.2%			% of Pop:	9.8%
College grad:	35.4%				
Grad degree:	15.4%				

In 1696, the proprietors of the colony of Maryland created a new county between the Potomac and Patuxent rivers and named it after the husband of the heir to the throne, Prince George of Denmark. During its 300 years, Prince George's County has not often won national fame—maybe briefly when investigators chased the plotters of Abraham Lincoln's murder here—but it might now. With a population that is nearly two-thirds African-American, Prince George's is the home of America's largest

2008 Presidential Vote		
Obama (D)	267,790	(85%)
McCain (R)	44,996	(14%)
2004 Presidential Vote		
Kerry (D)	217,549	(78%)
Bush (R)	58,170	(21%)
Cook Partisan Voting Index:	D + 31	

black middle class. It is also the wealthiest county with a majority black population. Historically, Prince George's was tobacco country, dotted by slave plantations and pretty much controlled by its white property owners. A hundred years after the Civil War, the population grew as middle-class blacks moved out of neighboring Washington, D.C., into modest suburbs at the county's edge and affluent subdivisions farther to the east. In the 1960s, this was one of the nation's fastest-growing suburban counties. Its African-American population increased from 14% in 1970, to 37% in 1980, to 65% in 2006, as the county's total population also grew. Prince George's is affluent by national standards, and 70 % of women here work outside the home, one of the highest percentages in the nation. With office and shopping mall development, it has lately been far more commercially vibrant than adjacent parts of the District of Columbia.

New economic development includes a 12-lane bridge across the Potomac River to replace the crumbling Wilson Bridge, and the nearby National Harbor hotel and convention center at Oxon Hill near the bridge, which is billed as the largest such non-casino facility on the East Coast. The county's median household income of more than $65,000 compares favorably with the national median of about $48,000 and is double the national median for black households. "The county ranks in the top 2 percent in the nation in income level, and in people who are employed in executive jobs," *Ebony* magazine reported. Yet amid this success, considerable problems remain: Prince George's accounts for half of Maryland's car thefts, and homicide rates tend to be high for a suburban county. The murder rate doubled from 2000 to 2004, though it has declined significantly since then.

The 4th Congressional District of Maryland includes most of Prince George's County inside the Capital Beltway that rings Washington. It also includes a large portion of Montgomery County that is mostly outside the Beltway, starting in Silver Spring, heading up Georgia Avenue and covering a sizable rural area all the way to Clarksburg at the Frederick County line. This Montgomery County area is heavily Democratic, as is Prince George's; Barack Obama won the latter by an extraordinary 89%-10% in 2008. Overall, this is the most Democratic district in Maryland. The biggest industry is government. It has the highest percentage of federal employees of any congressional district in the nation. Suitland, inside the Beltway in Prince George's, is the home of the Census Bureau.

The new congresswoman from the 4th District is Donna Edwards, who won a special election in June 2008 to succeed Albert Wynn. She is the first black woman to represent Maryland in Congress. Edwards was born in North Carolina, the second of six children. The family moved frequently as a result of her father's career in the Air Force. Edwards says she learned adaptability from her mother, and, as she told *The Washington Post*, "There's not a room I go in where I feel like a stranger." She was president of her high school class in New Mexico, and returned to her home state for college at Wake Forest University, where she was one of six African-American women in her class. She went to work for Lockheed at the Goddard Space Flight Center in Greenbelt, Md., and after the 1986 explosion of the space shuttle *Challenger,* she decided to attend law school. At Franklin Pierce University in New Hampshire, she focused on public-interest law. She settled in Fort Washington, Md., and clerked for a District of Columbia Superior Court judge. Later, she co-founded and was the first executive director of the National Network to End Domestic Violence. Edwards earned national recognition for her work on behalf of battered women. She was also executive director of the Center for a New Democracy, where she focused on campaign finance reform. In 2000, she became executive director of The Arca Foundation in Washington, which focuses on social equity and justice. After separating from her husband, she briefly was homeless and then lived with her young son in a room in her mother's home.

In 2006, Edwards challenged seven-term Wynn in the Democratic primary and surprised him with a well-funded and late-blossoming campaign. She ran to his left ideologically, benefited from strong local opposition to the Iraq war, which Wynn backed, and attacked the incumbent's close ties to business interests. Wynn accused Edwards of distorting his record. *The Washington Post* endorsed Edwards, writing, "Too often Wynn's votes have been at odds with good government and the interests of his constituents." Wynn won, but by a hair, 49.7%-46.4%. Wynn took his home Prince George's County, 57%-40%. In Montgomery, which cast 32% of the vote, Edwards led 60%-35%. Following that contest, Wynn increased his visibility in the district and co-sponsored a resolution to impeach Vice President Cheney. But Edwards almost immediately began preparing for a rematch in two years.

In 2008, she benefited in the primary from the support of MoveOn.org, the liberal grassroots group, and EMILY's List, the women's fundraising powerhouse. She did not take money from political action committees, and she criticized Wynn for his reliance on special-interest funds. Still, she was able to raise and spend $1 million to get her message to voters. The outcome this time was not close. Boosted by heavy turnout from the presidential primary, Edwards won the primary contest with Wynn, 59%-37%. She led 55%-41% in Prince George's, and 67%-27% in Montgomery County. Six weeks later, but before the general election, Wynn unexpectedly announced he was quitting Congress to join the Washington law firm of Dickstein Shapiro. That decision gave Edwards a chance to take the seat early and so have at least some seniority over other freshmen in the upcoming election. Wynn formally resigned on June 1, 2008. Democratic Gov. Martin O'Malley scheduled a special election for June 17; Edwards won 81%-18% over Republican Peter James, a technology developer, in a low-turnout event. She got some attention when she was among the House members who initially voted against the $700 billion bailout of the financial industry but then switched their votes to yes. Edwards said she voted for the revised version of the bill after a phone call from Obama urging her support.

FIFTH DISTRICT

Steny Hoyer (D)

Elected May 1981, 14th full term; b. June 14, 1939, New York, NY; home, Mechanicsville; U. of MD, B.S. 1963, Georgetown U., J.D. 1966; Baptist; widowed; 3 children.

Elected Office: MD Senate, 1966–78, Pres., 1975–78.

Professional Career: Practicing atty., 1966–80; MD Bd. of Higher Educ., 1978–81.

DC Office: 1705 LHOB, 20515, 202-225-4131; Fax: 202-225-4300; Web site: hoyer.house.gov.

State Offices: Greenbelt, 301-474-0119; Waldorf, 301-843-1577.

Committees: *Majority Leader.*

Group Ratings

	ADA	ACLU	AFS	LCV	ITIC	NTU	COC	ACU	CFG	FRC
2008	90	91	100	92	100	4	67	0	0	5
2007	90	—	100	90	—	3	55	4	11	—

National Journal Ratings

	2007 LIB	—	2007 CONS		2008 LIB	—	2008 CONS
Economic	82%	—	0%		81%	—	15%
Social	85%	—	13%		75%	—	18%
Foreign	60%	—	39%		59%	—	37%
Composite	79%	—	21%		74%	—	26%

Key Votes of the 110th Congress

1. Increase minimum wage	Y	5. Share immigration data	N	9. Withdraw troops 8/08	Y
2. Expand SCHIP	Y	6. Foreign aid abortion ban	N	10. No operations in Iran	Y
3. Raise CAFE standards	Y	7. Ban gay bias in workplace	Y	11. Free trade with Peru	Y
4. Bail out financial markets	Y	8. Repeal D.C. gun law	N	12. Overhaul FISA	Y

Election Results

2008 general	Steny Hoyer (D)	253,854	(74%)	($3,435,232)
	Collins Bailey (R)	82,631	(24%)	($27,681)
	Darlene Nicholas (Lib)	7,829	(2%)	
2008 primary	Steny Hoyer (D)	90,513	(83%)	
	James Cusick (D)	19,067	(17%)	

Prior Winning Percentages: 2006 (83%); 2004 (69%); 2002 (69%); 2000 (65%); 1998 (65%); 1996 (57%); 1994 (59%); 1992 (53%); 1990 (81%); 1988 (79%); 1986 (82%); 1984 (72%); 1982 (80%); 1981 (55%)

Population		Race/Ethnicity		Work	
Pop. 2007:	742,381	White:	52.9%	Private:	64.4%
Change since 2000:	Up 12.1%	Black:	34.7%	Government:	30.6%
Urban:	75.2%	Hispanic:	5.7%	Self-employed:	4.9%
Rural:	24.8%	Asian:	4.0%	Blue collar:	17.9%
Area size:	1,509 sq. mi.	Native Am.:	0.3%	White collar:	67.1%
Age		Hawaiian:	0.0%	Khaki collar:	0.8%
Median age:	35.9 yrs.	Two+ races:	2.1%	Other:	14.2%
More than 65 yrs:	9.3%	*Ancestry*		Median income:	$80,979
Less than 18 yrs:	25.3%	German:	11.0%	Median home value:	$358,300
Education		Irish:	9.6%	Poverty:	5.9%
H.S. grad:	89.8%	English:	8.1%	**Military Veterans**	
College grad:	32.0%			% of Pop:	13.7%
Grad degree:	13.1%				

Southern Maryland was established as a colony of the British Lords Baltimore, who were seeking a refuge for English Catholics in the New World. The Lords Baltimore, first George and then Cecil Calvert, founded St. Mary's in 1634, not long after the founding of Jamestown and Plymouth Rock. Maryland became one of the two great Chesapeake tobacco colonies, with plantation houses on every inlet off the broad Potomac and Patuxent rivers. For

2008 Presidential Vote
Obama (D) 233,930   (66%)
McCain (R).............................118,547   (33%)

2004 Presidential Vote
Kerry (D)...............................177,035   (57%)
Bush (R) 128,861   (42%)

Cook Partisan Voting Index: D + 11

years, the towns of southern Maryland grew slowly, and even today many of their residents are directly descended from the old families. The region was never Puritan country. Liquor flowed even during Prohibition, and for years, Maryland law specifically allowed slot machines. But tobacco farming is nearing an end, even if the area hasn't completely renounced its tobacco heritage. The highlight of the annual Charles County fair remains the crowning of Queen Nicotina, who must be a local high school senior. The area's economic base has owed much to government installations: the Civil War Point Lookout prisoner-of-war camp; the Navy's Patuxent River complex, where many astronauts began their training; and the Naval Air Warfare Center. Today, metro Washington and Baltimore are spreading into Southern Maryland, with rapid growth in Calvert County south of Annapolis—the fastest-growing county in Maryland from 2000 to 2007. Charles and St. Mary's counties are not far behind. Charles County has become the new home of many African-American families fleeing crime and troubled schools in Prince George's County. Today, most of Charles County's schoolchildren are black. Its median household income rose to more than $80,000 in 2008, thanks in part to many two-government-employee families. Also in 2008, minor league baseball arrived here when the Southern Maryland Blue Crabs took up residence in a new stadium in Waldorf.

The 5th Congressional District of Maryland comprises Calvert, Charles, and St. Mary's counties, plus most of Prince George's County outside of the Capital Beltway. Its lines were drawn to ensure a large African-American percentage in the adjacent 4th District, but blacks—both new suburbanites and descendants of old Southern Maryland families—made up 35% of the district's population in 2007. The district takes in College Park, home of the University of Maryland, and nearby Hyattsville, Greenbelt, Beltsville, Laurel, and Bowie. Historically, this is a Democratic area. Whites in the rural areas have trended Republican, but incoming blacks raised Charles County's voter turnout 19% between 2004 and 2008 and increased its Democratic percentage from 50% to 62%.

The congressman from the 5th District is Steny Hoyer, the Democratic majority leader and the second-most-powerful leader in the U.S. House, after Speaker Nancy Pelosi. He was first elected to the seat in 1981, and in June 2007, he became the longest-serving member of Congress from Maryland.

Hoyer is of Danish descent. His first name, he says, was his parents' adaptation of the Danish name Steen. He grew up in New York City, but moved from place to place with his mother and stepfather, who was in the Air Force. When Hoyer was in high school, his stepfather was transferred from Florida to Andrews Air Force Base in Maryland. Hoyer graduated from the University of Maryland, where in 1959 he listened to Democratic presidential candidate John F. Kennedy deliver a campaign speech that inspired him to switch his major from public relations to political science. While working on his law degree at Georgetown University in Washington, Hoyer interned one summer with Democratic Sen. Daniel Brewster. Another intern in Brewster's office that summer was young Nancy D'Alesandro, a Baltimore native who later married and became Nancy Pelosi. In 1966, just after graduating from law school, Hoyer was elected to the Maryland Senate, at age 27. He was Senate president from 1975–78, the youngest person to hold that post in Maryland history. In 1978, he ran for lieutenant governor on a losing ticket. In 1981, after incumbent Gladys Spellman was incapacitated by a heart attack, the 5th District seat was declared vacant. Hoyer won the special election, edging out Spellman's husband and several other Democrats in the primary and beating a well-financed Republican in the general. The district then was entirely in Prince George's County. That campaign launched Hoyer's long-standing friendship with then-Rep. Tony Coelho of California, who then chaired the Democratic Congressional Campaign Committee.

Hoyer has fine political instincts, works hard, and can speak in an old-fashioned, patriotic style that is genuinely moving. A fast riser in Maryland politics, he was also a fast riser in Congress. He excelled at constituency service and won a seat on the Appropriations Committee, where he worked with Republicans and became a champion for the Washington, D.C., metropolitan area. He once chaired the Treasury, Postal Service, and General Government Subcommittee, which oversaw several major components of the federal workforce and the White House budget. He has been an advocate of more spending for education programs and better pay and benefits for federal workers. He was the chief House sponsor of the Americans with Disabilities Act of 1990, which outlawed discrimination against the disabled. As ranking minority member on the House Administration Committee, he took the lead in crafting bipartisan election reform legislation and in enhancing security in the Capitol complex. When the political parties in the House became more polarized in the late 1990s, Hoyer initiated monthly lunches with Roy Blunt, R-Mo., who was then the chief deputy whip for the Republican majority. On September 11, 2001, it was Hoyer's idea to have lawmakers gather in front of the Capitol in a show of strength. The group spontaneously sang "God Bless America," an image captured vividly on television on a dark day in U.S. history.

His voting record is relatively moderate among Democrats, and less liberal than when he represented a near-black-majority district in the 1980s. He broke with the party by supporting the balanced budget amendment in 1995; he backed many of the free-trade initiatives of recent years that organized labor opposed, including the 1993 North American Free Trade Agreement. In October 2002, he voted to authorize military action in Iraq. Later he argued that the George W. Bush administration didn't send enough troops to Iraq and that the United Nations "has shirked its own responsibility." He is a former chairman of the Helsinki Commission and has been a champion of human rights around the world. On the district front, Hoyer has pushed for funding for Chesapeake Bay cleanup and for dredging the bay for Baltimore harbor. He has worked shrewdly to maintain and increase the number of jobs at the Goddard Space Flight Center in Greenbelt, at Patuxent River Naval Air Station, and at the Naval Surface Warfare Center at Indian Head. Another of his projects was getting the National Center for Weather and Climate Prediction based in College Park.

In 1989, Hoyer won his first leadership post as chairman of the Democratic Caucus. When he tried to move up to the job of majority whip in 1991, he lost, 160-109, to David Bonior of Michigan, who had the support of liberals and committee chairmen. Hoyer became chairman of the Democratic Steering Committee and has been the parliamentarian at four Democratic conventions. In 2001, Bonior, faced with unfavorable redistricting changes at home, decided to run for governor of Michigan. Both Hoyer and Pelosi sought to replace him as minority whip. Hoyer argued that he had greater experience in leadership positions and could do a better job of unifying the caucus. Pelosi had more publicly committed votes going into the October 2001 Democratic Caucus election, and she won 118-95. (Both did less well than predicted, as often happens in secret-ballot leadership contests.)

Although he was a two-time loser of leadership contests, Hoyer was undeterred when Missouri's Dick Gephardt stepped down as minority leader in 2002. With Pelosi running to succeed Gephardt as leader, Hoyer ran for minority whip. He collected commitments for months and was elected unanimously. In that position, it was his job to be partisan, and he often was. In 2004, after 11 Democrats voted for a parliamentary rule to consider the corporate tax bill, Hoyer sent a letter to all House Democrats admonishing them for supporting a procedure that prevented Democrats from offering amendments. This was standard. In the majority, both House Democrats and Republicans have taken a dim view of members of their party who buck their leadership on procedural issues. Since 1997, the two parties had had an ethics truce in which they promised not to file politically inspired ethics complaints against the other party's members and leaders. But in 2004, Hoyer called for consideration of complaints that powerful Republican Tom DeLay allegedly offered undue inducements to Republican Rep. Nick Smith of Michigan to vote for the Medicare prescription drug bill. At election time, Hoyer contributed to and campaigned tirelessly for Democratic House candidates.

The 2006 election rated as a stellar moment for Hoyer. It marked the culmination of four decades of political effort and left him well positioned to wield great influence in the House and within the party. In Maryland, he could take some credit for the successful Senate campaign of longtime friend Ben Cardin, for whom he was an early backer, to the dismay of former House colleague Kweisi Mfume and his backers. Nationally, Hoyer worked closely with Democratic Congressional Campaign Committee Chairman Rahm Emanuel to help Democrats running against Republican incumbents. In the two years preceding the election, he made at least 316 campaign stops in 80 districts in 33 states and raised more than $8 million for candidates and the DCCC. In September 2006, he predicted a gain of 30 House seats, which turned out to be right on the money. "We have close to 50 extraordinarily good candidates," he told National Journal's *CongressDaily*. Many of the freshmen subsequently credited the help Hoyer provided, especially those from swing districts where liberal Democratic leaders are not always welcome. Lost amid the euphoria were the occasional criticisms from liberal activists that Hoyer was an old-style pol and a Washington insider, with close ties to the lobbying community.

But right after the election, Hoyer waged a bitter 10-day contest for the coveted job of majority leader against Pennsylvania's John Murtha, who was the chosen candidate of Hoyer's old nemesis, Pelosi, who was about to rise to speaker. A defense hawk, Murtha had become an outspoken opponent of the Iraq war, while Hoyer supported the war effort, and Murtha contended that he could work better with Pelosi. Hoyer had little choice but to speak positively about his long-standing relationship with her—he calls her a "favorite daughter" of Maryland—and their success in largely unifying an often-unruly party. But he left no doubt about his dismay over her arm-twisting on Murtha's behalf. In spite of Pelosi's efforts for Murtha, Hoyer prevailed 149-86, a powerful endorsement for him. Democrats responded to his "ability, patience, know-how, and experience," said a Democratic lobbyist. Even more impressive, Hoyer won the support of many California Democrats who previously had been unified behind Pelosi and of numerous prospective committee chairmen who doubted Murtha's ability to do the job. "Nancy thought she could put these people away because of pressure," Coelho told *The New York Times.* "But these people that got elected understand relationships, and they're not going to flip away because of pressure. [Hoyer] has a tremendous capacity for friendship, and when you have that, people don't flake off on you."

As majority leader, Hoyer assumed responsibility for determining the floor schedule, helping guide Democratic initiatives to passage, and holding weekly press briefings. He describes his recipe for holding together what has historically been a fissiparous caucus this way: "First of all work very hard on communications, find out what people can do and can't do. Secondly, put together a consensus that, while it may not be the first choice of everybody, it is a choice they can live with." And for the most part the record justifies his boast that House Democrats, in their first two years in the majority, were "the most unified the Democratic Party has been in over half a century." Hoyer also kept in close touch with Blunt, until Blunt dropped out of the Republican leadership in January 2009; they maintained one of the best cross-party relationships on Capitol Hill.

Hoyer did find himself at odds with the majority of Democrats on some issues. He voted for military funding in Iraq and consistently against linking war funding to a timetable for withdrawing U.S. troops, earning him criticism from the liberal MoveOn.org. And, he worked on the negotiations on changes in the Foreign Intelligence Surveillance Act, which is a law enforcement tool in catching terrorists, and he backed the version of the legislation releasing telecommunications companies from legal liability for complying with government requests for warrantless surveillance of U.S. citizens' communications. Many Democrats did not want to let the companies off the hook.

On domestic issues, Hoyer was a strong supporter of the pay-go rule, which requires that spending increases and tax cuts be "paid for" by corresponding spending decreases or tax increases. He spoke out for maintaining the rule even as many Democrats favored dropping it to give middle-income taxpayers some relief from the alternative minimum tax. In early 2009, working with Pelosi, Hoyer steered to passage the $787 billion economic stimulus legislation, the first major initiative of the Obama administration. Only 11 House Democrats voted against it, and all of the Republicans opposed it. Weeks earlier, Hoyer strongly supported the bailout bill for the financial services industry although he expressed misgivings about the legislation. He also had a hand in the Democrats' successful efforts to increase the hourly minimum wage and in the adoption of most of the 9/11 commission's recommendations.

His toughest moment in the 110th Congress (2007–08) came in August 2007, when he urged Democratic Rep. Michael McNulty of New York, who was presiding over the House, to end a vote on limiting aid to illegal immigrants, when Democrats were ahead in the vote count. McNulty declared that the Democrats had prevailed, even though the voting machine lights showed otherwise. The incident was the subject of hearings in May 2008, during which McNulty and Hoyer admitted error. But Hoyer later maintained that the House rule against holding votes open beyond stated time limits was unenforceable.

Hoyer has been among the top 10 House members in securing earmarks for his district. He calls earmarks "congressional initiatives," but he hailed what he termed House Democrats' "substantial progress" in limiting them. More inclined to defer to committee chairs and hew to regular order than Pelosi is, he supported doing away with term limits for committee chairs, which the Republicans imposed when they were in the majority. Pelosi left term limits in place during the first two years of Democratic rule. (Term limits work to the advantage of the leadership because they make committee chairs less autonomous and therefore less powerful.) At Hoyer's urging, Pelosi agreed to repeal term limits in late 2008. "I am not for term limits for chairmen," Hoyer said. "It puts intellect on hold.

On local issues, he worked with Republican Rep. Tom Davis of Virginia and D.C. Democratic Delegate Eleanor Holmes Norton to pass a bill giving the District of Columbia a voting seat in the House. He sponsored bills allowing more government employees to work four-day weeks, granting eight weeks of paid parental leave, and raising the government contribution to federal employees' health care premiums from 72% to 80%. In the bitterly fought 2008 Democratic presidential primary, Hoyer stayed neutral even after the Maryland primary, which Illinois Sen. Barack Obama won. Obama carried Prince George's and Charles counties in Hoyer's district, but he ran only slightly ahead of New York Sen. Hillary Rodham Clinton in St. Mary's and Calvert counties.

The last time Hoyer had serious competition in a general election was in 1992, the first election after the district was reconfigured to extend beyond Prince George's County. He has won easily since then, and he has demonstrated an ability to win the loyalty of African-American voters in Democratic primaries.

SIXTH DISTRICT

Roscoe Bartlett (R)

Elected 1992, 9th term; b. June 3, 1926, Moreland, KY; home, Frederick; Columbia Union Col., B.A. 1947, U. of MD, M.S. 1949, Ph.D. 1952; Seventh Day Adventist; married (Ellen); 10 children.

Professional Career: Farmer; Prof., U. of MD, 1948–52; Asst. prof., Loma Linda Schl. of Medicine, 1952–54; Asst. prof., Howard U. Medical Schl., 1954–56; Research scientist, N.I.H., 1956–58; Research scientist, U.S. Naval Aerospace Medical Inst., 1958–62; Research scientist, Johns Hopkins U., 1962–67; Research mgr., IBM, 1967–74; Pres., Roscoe Bartlett & Assoc., 1974–86.

DC Office: 2412 RHOB, 20515, 202-225-2721; Fax: 202-225-2193; Web site: bartlett.house.gov.

State Offices: Cumberland, 301-724-3105; Frederick, 301-694-3030; Hagerstown, 301-797-6043; Westminster, 410-857-1115.

Committees: *Armed Services* (2nd of 25 R): Air & Land Forces (RMM); Seapower & Expeditionary Forces. *Science & Technology* (5th of 17 R): Energy & Environment. *Small Business* (2nd of 12 R): Contracting & Technology.

Group Ratings

	ADA	ACLU	AFS	LCV	ITIC	NTU	COC	ACU	CFG	FRC
2008	15	45	0	15	43	72	78	96	88	100
2007	15	—	0	45	—	76	80	88	87	—

National Journal Ratings

	2007 LIB — 2007 CONS		2008 LIB — 2008 CONS	
Economic	30%	— 69%	21%	— 78%
Social	31%	— 67%	31%	— 62%
Foreign	43%	— 56%	35%	— 62%
Composite	35%	— 65%	31%	— 69%

Key Votes of the 110th Congress

1. Increase minimum wage	N	5. Share immigration data	Y	9. Withdraw troops 8/08	N
2. Expand SCHIP	N	6. Foreign aid abortion ban	Y	10. No operations in Iran	Y
3. Raise CAFE standards	N	7. Ban gay bias in workplace	N	11. Free trade with Peru	Y
4. Bail out financial markets	N	8. Repeal D.C. gun law	Y	12. Overhaul FISA	Y

Election Results

2008 general	Roscoe Bartlett (R)	190,926	(58%)	($204,443)
	Jennifer Dougherty (D)	128,207	(39%)	($172,381)
	Gary Hoover (Lib)	11,060	(3%)	
2008 primary	Roscoe Bartlett (R)	51,635	(78%)	
	Joseph Krysztoforski (R)	5,686	(9%)	
	Tom Croft (R)	4,895	(7%)	
	John Kimble (R)	3,433	(5%)	

Prior Winning Percentages: 2006 (59%); 2004 (67%); 2002 (66%); 2000 (61%); 1998 (63%); 1996 (57%); 1994 (66%); 1992 (54%)

Population		Race/Ethnicity		Work	
Pop. 2007:	722,855	White:	87.6%	Private:	76.0%
Change since 2000:	Up 9.2%	Black:	5.9%	Government:	17.9%
Urban:	60.5%	Hispanic:	2.9%	Self-employed:	5.8%
Rural:	39.5%	Asian:	2.0%	Blue collar:	20.8%
Area size:	3,094 sq. mi.	Native Am.:	0.2%	White collar:	63.6%
		Hawaiian:	0.0%	Khaki collar:	0.2%
Age		Two+ races:	1.2%	Other:	15.5%
Median age:	38.2 yrs.			Median income:	$65,592
More than 65 yrs:	12.1%	*Ancestry*		Median home value:	$307,500
Less than 18 yrs:	24.5%	German:	23.7%	Poverty:	6.3%
		Irish:	13.0%		
Education		English:	9.4%	**Military Veterans**	
H.S. grad:	87.9%			% of Pop:	11.6%
College grad:	27.7%				
Grad degree:	10.7%				

One of America's first frontiers was Western Maryland, where the Appalachian ridges that cross the state diagonally from northeast to southwest cut through long sloping fields. The land was settled by Pennsylvania Dutch and Scots-Irish hill people, not Chesapeake Bay tobacco growers. Maryland is where the 19th century's great paths to the interior were staked out: The National Road; the nation's first railroad, the Baltimore & Ohio, which crossed the wide valleys of bounteous farms and climbed

2008 Presidential Vote		
McCain (R)............................200,652	(58%)
Obama (D) 139,421	(40%)
2004 Presidential Vote		
Bush (R)................................209,764	(65%)
Kerry (D)...............................110,821	(34%)
Cook Partisan Voting Index: R + 13		

over the Catoctin Mountains; and the Chesapeake and Ohio Canal, which began operating in 1828, primarily to haul coal from Western Maryland to the port of Georgetown in Washington. Towns grew up with narrow streets of row houses that today are overhung with telephone wires. They planted themselves among cornfields, pastureland, and ancient mountains. Across this placid land moved vast armies during the Civil War. In Frederick, city officials paid the Confederates $200,000 not to burn the town, and near Sharpsburg, blue- and gray-clad soldiers fought the Battle of Antietam, on the bloodiest day in American military history. A century later, on the steps of City Hall in Cumberland, near the coal-laced hills of Appalachia, President Johnson declared his War on Poverty. Poverty did fall here in the 1970s, but conditions worsened in the 1980s with the closure of several large factories. Hard-pressed as it is, Western Maryland is trying to preserve its natural wonders of small mountains and thick, deciduous forests. In 2008, opposition from residents halted a plan by a Pennsylvania company to sheer 400 mountaintop acres for a wind farm with 100 turbines. Cumberland has attempted to refashion itself as an arts community, with dozens of studios cropping up. To the east, Carroll County in metro Baltimore, and Frederick County in metro Washington, have grown rapidly in recent years and have become new hubs for outward expansion.

The 6th Congressional District includes all of Western Maryland, takes in a small part of northern Montgomery County, and runs eastward across the northern farmlands and hunt country of Baltimore and Harford counties all the way to the Susquehanna River. The political tradition in most of this area, unlike the rest of Maryland, is Republican. This was Union country during the Civil War and has been predominantly Republican ever since. The new rush of settlement—which has made this the fastest growing district in Maryland—is mostly made up of young families of modest incomes seeking respite from urban life, which is strengthening the area's already conservative leanings. Only seven of Maryland's 24 counties have more registered Republican voters than Democrats, and five of them are in this district.

The congressman from the 6th District is Roscoe Bartlett, a Republican first elected in 1992. In his early 80s, Bartlett is the second-oldest member of the House after Republican Ralph Hall of Texas. He is a curious character, a descendant of a signer of the Declaration of Independence and a Seventh Day Adventist with 10 children (he and his wife each have four children from previous marriages). He was born in Kentucky and grew up in poverty in Western Pennsylvania, where his father was a tenant farmer. After getting a bachelor's degree in theology and biology, he earned a Ph.D. in physiology at the University of Maryland, where he also taught and wrote more than 100 scientific articles. Over the years, he has also operated a 145-acre dairy farm, where he still milks goats. He was awarded 20 patents for inventing life-support equipment for pilots, astronauts, firefighters, and respiratory patients. In 1999, the Aeronautics and Astronautics Institute gave him an award for his career contributions to the advancement of medical knowledge and technologies. When Bartlett first ran for the House, he was a 65-year-old retired professor who seemed to have no chance of winning. Democrat Beverly Byron had represented the district for 14 years and had a conservative voting record. Bartlett lost to her in 1982, 74%-26%. But in 1992, Byron was upset in the primary by a liberal who favored national health insurance and abortion rights. Bartlett's conservative views and his attacks on his opponent's record in the state Legislature drove him to a 54%-46% victory.

Bartlett has proved a surprisingly durable, if quirky, politician. Profiled in *The Washington Post* as Maryland's "Mr. Right," he described a 2004 visit to Iraq, where he visited the "spider hole" where Iraqi Leader Saddam Hussein was captured after the U.S. invasion. "I was probably the only congressman who laid down there. It's very interesting dirt. It doesn't collapse. The water table is at 17 feet throughout most of Iraq." Bartlett is the only Republican in the state's congressional delegation, but his conservative views have not always followed Republican orthodoxy. "I'm not interested in politics," he says. "I am a conservative who wants to help restore the limited federal government envisioned and established in the Constitution by our nation's founders." He sometimes objects to his party's big spending, including President Bush's No Child Left Behind education law that mandated testing in public schools as a requisite for continued federal funding. But Bartlett voted for the 2003 bill creating a prescription drug benefit in the Medicare program. He also voted against renewal of the Bush administration's USA PATRIOT Act because he saw the anti-terrorism law as a threat to civil liberties. His fiscal conservatism was reflected in his opposition to expanded federal funds for a local Interstate highway. He was one of 33 House Republicans to oppose renewal of the Voting Rights Act. "He believes that when a disease is cured, you don't have to keep taking the same medicine," his spokeswoman said.

In the 110th Congress (2007–08), Bartlett was the only member of the Maryland delegation to oppose the $700 billion bailout of the financial markets, as well as the proposed expansion of the State Children's Health Insurance Program. He is also the only member of the delegation who opposes abortion rights. The first member of Congress to drive a hybrid car, Bartlett purchased a Toyota Prius in 2000. He has been a passionate advocate of alternative energy sources, and he powers his home with solar energy and a wood stove. When fellow Republicans voiced skepticism about former Vice President Gore's warnings about climate change, Bartlett chided them, saying, "It's possible to be a conservative without appearing to be an idiot."

On the Seapower and Expeditionary Forces Subcommittee of the Armed Services Committee, he has called on the Navy to build smaller, cheaper ships. He believes that the Navy needs more attack submarines and has urged a shift to nuclear power for surface ships because of concern about oil supply. And in 2006, Bush signed his bill to prohibit condominium associations and other residential group from barring members from displaying the American flag.

Bartlett has been re-elected by solid margins. In 2004, he faced an unusual primary challenge from Frederick County State's Attorney Scott Rolle, who criticized Bartlett for not supporting the Bush administration strongly enough. Bartlett responded by getting Vice President Cheney to make an appearance in his behalf before more than 700 people at a breakfast in Hagerstown just four days before the election. Bartlett won 70%-30% and carried Rolle's Frederick County base, 60%-40%. In 2008, against modestly funded Frederick Mayor Jennifer Dougherty, a Democrat, Bartlett won 58%-39%, his lowest percentage since he was first elected. But he won all eight counties, including 52%-44% in his opponent's home area. Maryland Democrats seem unlikely to take this final Republican outpost any time soon. In 2008, *Slate* magazine named him one of "America's silver lions," a list of the country's most influential people over the age of 80.

SEVENTH DISTRICT

Elijah Cummings (D)

Elected April 1996, 7th full term; b. Jan. 18, 1951, Baltimore; home, Baltimore; Howard U., B.S. 1973, U. of MD, J.D. 1976; Baptist; married (Maya Rockeymoore).

Elected Office: MD House of Delegates, 1982–96, Speaker pro tem, 1995–96.

Professional Career: Practicing atty., 1976–96.

DC Office: 2235 RHOB, 20515, 202-225-4741; Fax: 202-225-3178; Web site: www.house.gov/cummings.

State Offices: Baltimore, 410-685-9199; Catonsville, 410-719-8777; Ellicott City, 410-465-8259.

Committees: *Joint Economic Committee* (5th of 6 D). *Oversight & Government Reform* (4th of 24 D): Domestic Policy; Federal Workforce, Postal Service & the District of Columbia. *Transportation & Infrastructure* (11th of 44 D): Aviation; Coast Guard & Maritime Transportation (Chmn); Railroads, Pipelines & Hazardous Materials.

Group Ratings

	ADA	ACLU	AFS	LCV	ITIC	NTU	COC	ACU	CFG	FRC
2008	100	100	100	92	86	10	50	5	0	5
2007	100	—	100	95	—	4	50	0	7	—

National Journal Ratings

	2007 LIB	—	2007 CONS		2008 LIB	—	2008 CONS
Economic	73%	—	24%		85%	—	0%
Social	77%	—	17%		66%	—	33%
Foreign	78%	—	22%		92%	—	0%
Composite	78%	—	23%		85%	—	15%

Key Votes of the 110th Congress

1. Increase minimum wage	Y	5. Share immigration data	N	9. Withdraw troops 8/08	Y
2. Expand SCHIP	Y	6. Foreign aid abortion ban	N	10. No operations in Iran	Y
3. Raise CAFE standards	Y	7. Ban gay bias in workplace	Y	11. Free trade with Peru	N
4. Bail out financial markets	Y	8. Repeal D.C. gun law	N	12. Overhaul FISA	N

Election Results

2008 general	Elijah Cummings (D)	227,379	(80%)	($684,420)
	Michael Hargadon (R)	53,147	(19%)	($23,702)
2008 primary	Elijah Cummings (D)	98,027	(93%)	
	Charles Smith (D)	7,322	(7%)	

Prior Winning Percentages: 2006 (100%); 2004 (73%); 2002 (74%); 2000 (87%); 1998 (86%); 1996 (83%); 1996 (81%)

Population		Race/Ethnicity		Work	
Pop. 2007:	662,660	White:	33.3%	Private:	71.9%
Change since 2000:	Up 0.1%	Black:	57.9%	Government:	23.1%
Urban:	94.9%	Hispanic:	2.3%	Self-employed:	4.9%
Rural:	5.1%	Asian:	4.7%	Blue collar:	14.5%
Area size:	296 sq. mi.	Native Am.:	0.2%	White collar:	66.6%
Age		Hawaiian:	0.0%	Khaki collar:	0.1%
Median age:	37.0 yrs.	Two+ races:	1.3%	Other:	18.7%
More than 65 yrs:	11.7%	*Ancestry*		Median income:	$50,364
Less than 18 yrs:	24.6%	German:	8.6%	Median home value:	$237,600
Education		Irish:	6.9%	Poverty:	16.6%
H.S. grad:	81.2%	English:	5.1%	**Military Veterans**	
College grad:	31.4%			% of Pop:	10.0%
Grad degree:	14.7%				

At the junction of North and South, Baltimore is a product of both European immigration and the migration of African-Americans from the South. Its black community has a rich history. The *Afro-American* newspaper has been published here for more than 100 years, and there was once a black symphony orchestra. Eubie Blake, one of the founders of ragtime music, grew up here and now has a museum in his honor on Charles Street. Jazz great Billie Holliday was born here, as was Cab Calloway, the 1930s and 1940s big band leader, and Thurgood Marshall, the country's first African-American Supreme Court justice. Near downtown on the west side is the childhood home of slugger Babe Ruth and the home of writer H.L. Mencken. For years, this side of town had a biracial, bipartisan politics in which Democrats like Gov. Albert Ritchie and Republicans such as Gov. Theodore McKeldin competed zestfully for black and white votes. Baltimore has been a black majority city since the late 1970s, and most of its west-side neighborhoods are heavily African-American.

In the 1990s, Baltimore was hit by a terrible crime wave, with open drug markets on both the west and east sides. Democratic Mayor Martin O'Malley, elected in 1999, promised to build "a new Baltimore" with zero tolerance of crime; he went on to win the governorship in 2006. But many of the city's problems remained, with almost 20% of the city's residential areas classified as distressed.

Maryland's 7th Congressional District includes most of Baltimore's west side, plus the heavily African-American suburbs west of the city and extending to Catonsville along the old Baltimore National Pike. It also includes most of suburban Howard County. About 40% of the district's votes are cast in Baltimore City's precincts, largely north of Pratt Street, in places like Druid Heights; Harlem Park; Charles Village, which is home to Johns Hopkins University and poverty-stricken Sandtown-Winchester. Howard County is quite a different area. It grew 32% in the 1990s, and its largest community, Columbia, is a planned town that attracts a culturally liberal population. It tends to vote Democratic, and in 2004 cast 13% of the district's votes. There is a sharp socioeconomic contrast between these two parts of the district. Howard County is predominately white, has the third-highest median household income of all counties in the nation, and 4% of children under age 5 live in poverty. In Baltimore City, only 4% of households earn more than $100,000 and 40% of children are poor.

The congressman from the 7th District is Elijah Cummings, who won a 1996 special election after Kweisi Mfume resigned to become president of the NAACP. Cummings is the son of sharecroppers from South Carolina who moved north for a better life for their seven children. He grew up in Baltimore, graduated Phi Beta Kappa from Howard University, and then got a law degree from the University of Maryland. He practiced law for a time in Baltimore, and then in 1982, at age 31, he ran successfully for the Maryland House of Delegates, where he served 16 years and rose through the ranks to become speaker pro tem. When he ran for the U.S. House, his main competition was the Rev. Frank Reid III, stepbrother of Baltimore Mayor Kurt Schmoke, who raised $255,000. Cummings had support from local businesses and

2008 Presidential Vote

Obama (D)	234,123	(79%)
McCain (R)	60,134	(20%)

2004 Presidential Vote

Kerry (D)	192,081	(73%)
Bush (R)	69,545	(26%)

Cook Partisan Voting Index: D + 25

community-development organizations, and raised $450,000. He won with 37% of the vote to 24% for Reid. He has not been seriously challenged in a primary or general election since then.

Cummings lives in troubled west Baltimore, where he is a crusader against drug abuse and for stricter gun control. His voting record has been mostly liberal, but he has a pragmatic streak that allows him to work with Republicans in legislative coalitions. When the GOP controlled the House, he worked with Indiana conservative Republican Mark Souder to reauthorize the White House drug control office and to establish federal policy to combat rapidly multiplying methamphetamine labs. Once Democrats won the majority, he became chairman of the Coast Guard and Maritime Transportation Subcommittee at Transportation and Infrastructure, a useful niche for his port-dependent district and an opportunity for him to play a role in the debate on homeland security.

On the Oversight and Government Reform Committee, he worked closely with Democratic Chairman Henry Waxman of California on the investigation of performance-enhancing steroids in baseball, and emphasized the detrimental effect steroid use was having on young people who look up to successful athletes. "You're one of my heroes, but it's hard to believe you, sir," Cummings told former star pitcher Roger Clemens at a 2008 hearing. When Waxman in November 2008 was chosen to chair the Energy and Commerce Committee, some Democrats urged Cummings to challenge the more senior Rep. Edolphus Towns, D-N.Y., to replace Waxman as chairman of Oversight. But Cummings did not run, partly to avoid conflict within the seniority-sensitive Congressional Black Caucus, an influential group that Cummings once chaired. When Cummings led the CBC in 2003 and 2004, he spoke out on issues ranging from the presidential succession crisis in Haiti to the appointment of federal judges.

Cummings usually wins re-election by landslide margins, and in 2006 he was unopposed. He backed Mfume in the Democratic primary for the open Senate seat that year, and then played a constructive role in coalescing Democrats behind the eventual nominee, former Rep. Ben Cardin. In 2007, he bucked most of the Maryland Democratic establishment by announcing his early support of Barack Obama in the Democratic primary. In October 2008, he cited telephone calls from Obama in explaining why he reversed his initial opposition to the $700 billion bailout of the financial industry to a vote in favor of the bill. Cummings, who had been highly critical of the role of Wall Street managers in the financial collapse, expressed outrage when the media reported that officials of insurance giant AIG celebrated the bailout with a lavish golf and spa vacation at a California beach resort. He said, "They were getting their manicures, their facials, their pedicures and their massages while American people were footing the bill!"

EIGHTH DISTRICT

Chris Van Hollen (D)

Elected 2002, 4th term; b. Jan. 10, 1959, Karachi, Pakistan; home, Kensington; Swarthmore Col., B.A. 1982, Harvard U., M.P.P. 1985, Georgetown U., J.D. 1990; Protestant; married (Katherine); 3 children.

Elected Office: MD House of Delegates, 1990–94; MD Senate, 1994–2002.

DC Office: 1707 LHOB, 20515, 202-225-5341; Fax: 202-225-0375; Web site: vanhollen.house.gov.

State Offices: Hyattsville, 301-891-6982; Rockville, 301-424-3501.

Committees: *DCCC Chairman. Oversight & Government Reform* (17th of 24 D): National Security & Foreign Affairs. *Ways & Means* (18th of 26 D): Income Security & Family Support; Trade.

Group Ratings

	ADA	ACLU	AFS	LCV	ITIC	NTU	COC	ACU	CFG	FRC
2008	100	100	100	100	100	7	61	0	4	5
2007	90	—	100	95	—	5	55	0	12	—

National Journal Ratings

	2007 LIB	—	2007 CONS		2008 LIB	—	2008 CONS
Economic	82%	—	0%		78%	—	20%
Social	89%	—	8%		82%	—	0%
Foreign	81%	—	16%		85%	—	8%
Composite	88%	—	12%		86%	—	14%

Key Votes of the 110th Congress

1. Increase minimum wage	Y	5. Share immigration data	N	9. Withdraw troops 8/08	Y
2. Expand SCHIP	Y	6. Foreign aid abortion ban	N	10. No operations in Iran	Y
3. Raise CAFE standards	Y	7. Ban gay bias in workplace	Y	11. Free trade with Peru	Y
4. Bail out financial markets	Y	8. Repeal D.C. gun law	N	12. Overhaul FISA	N

Election Results

2008 general	Chris Van Hollen (D) 229,740	(75%)	($1,279,456)
	Steve Hudson (R) 66,351	(22%)	($59,213)
	Gordon Clark (Green) 6,828	(2%)	($36,305)
2008 primary	Chris Van Hollen (D) 104,108	(88%)	
	Deborah Vollmer (D)...11,052	(9%)	

Prior Winning Percentages:　2006 (77%); 2004 (75%); 2002 (52%)

Population		Race/Ethnicity		Work	
Pop. 2007:	695,304	White:	52.4%	Private:	71.8%
Change since 2000:	Up 5.0%	Black:	16.9%	Government:	21.4%
Urban:	98.8%	Hispanic:	16.1%	Self-employed:	6.7%
Rural:	1.2%	Asian:	12.2%	Blue collar:	11.4%
Area size:	307 sq. mi.	Native Am.:	0.2%	White collar:	74.2%
		Hawaiian:	0.0%	Khaki collar:	0.3%
Age		Two+ races:	1.8%	Other:	14.1%
Median age:	38.5 yrs.	*Ancestry*		Median income:	$85,238
More than 65 yrs:	12.9%	German:	8.5%	Median home value:	$502,800
Less than 18 yrs:	23.6%	Irish:	7.8%	Poverty:	5.8%
Education		English:	6.7%	**Military Veterans**	
H.S. grad:	89.3%			% of Pop:	8.0%
College grad:	55.9%				
Grad degree:	29.8%				

Colonial farmers once rolled barrels of tobacco to the port of Georgetown along an old road that is today the commercial spine of one of America's most affluent and best-educated areas. Wisconsin Avenue begins at the Potomac River in Washington, D.C., traverses the city, and then becomes Rockville Pike once it arrives in suburban Montgomery County, Md. For several decades, Montgomery County has ranked at or near the top among counties nationwide in income and education. Like all of Washing-

2008 Presidential Vote
Obama (D) ....234,927　(74%)
McCain (R)...............................78,223　(25%)

2004 Presidential Vote
Kerry (D)................................205,660　(69%)
Bush (R) ....90,108　(30%)

Cook Partisan Voting Index:　D + 21

ton's suburbs, the county is a creature of the federal government, which has huge facilities there—Bethesda Naval Hospital, the National Institutes of Health, the Food and Drug Administration, and the National Institute of Standards and Technology. Montgomery is also the center of America's biotech industry, the home of firms such as Celera and Human Genome Sciences which, in parallel with the Human Genome Project, have pioneered the study of the human genetic code. Some of the federal labs have high-security classification because of their research into biohazards and infectious diseases.

The downside is, Wisconsin/Rockville Pike and other main arteries in the county are overburdened by development and traffic-choked, though the problem is an embarrassment of riches. Retail shops and other sources of commerce along the Pike are decidedly upscale, with expensive condos among the office towers and well-reviewed restaurants thriving in the suburb of Bethesda. *New York Times* columnist David Brooks mocked Bethesdans as "urban exiles" who frequent "anti-chain chain stores . . . that cater to people who consider themselves too refined and individualistic to shop at the mall or the mass-market big-box stores." Historically, the typical Montgomery County voter was a high-ranking civil servant. "A candidate knocking on doors in the 8th District can reasonably expect to be questioned about a government regulation by the person who wrote it," once observed *The Washington Post.* But the picture is changing as growing private-sector employment outpaces government work, and new development reaches ever farther from D.C.'s borders to the far-flung cities of Gaithersburg and Germantown. Montgomery County is also becoming more racially and economically diverse. In 2006, the Census Bureau estimated that it was 17% African-American, 14% Hispanic, and 13% Asian. Many working-class neighborhoods have sprung up in Silver Spring and Wheaton just outside Washington.

The 8th Congressional District of Maryland includes most of the heavily populated parts of Montgomery County, which accounts for more than 90% of the district's population. In 2002, redistricting added a slice of strongly Democratic territory in neighboring Prince George's County. Perhaps the 8th's most unique precinct is Leisure World in Silver Spring, with its 6,000-plus senior citizens and an extraordinarily high voter-turnout rate. Democratic candidates practically camp out there during the primary season. This is the most Democratic white-majority district in the state. But still, the district has the largest share of Latinos in Maryland.

The congressman from the 8th District is Chris Van Hollen, first elected in 2002 in one of the nation's most competitive congressional races and now a major player in the House Democratic leadership. The son of a Foreign Service officer, Van Hollen was born in Pakistan, and grew up globally, living in several countries including the South Asian island of Sri Lanka, where his father was the U.S. ambassador. He graduated from Swarthmore College, and got a master's degree from Harvard University and a law degree from Georgetown University. In the 1980s, he worked for the Senate Foreign Relations Committee, where he co-authored a report on Iraq's use of chemical weapons. In 1990, he was elected to the Maryland House of Delegates and in 1994 to the state Senate. Wonky, self-assured, and telegenic, Van Hollen earned a prominent role in the Democratic House leadership after helping the party secure its majority in the chamber in 2006. He co-chaired the Democratic Congressional Campaign Committee's "Red to Blue" strategy, and *The Washington Post* dubbed him the party's "Mr. Fix-It."

Van Hollen's first race for Congress was his toughest by far. The 2002 contest attracted strong Democratic candidates who hoped to take advantage of redistricting changes that made the seat less friendly to longtime incumbent Connie Morella, a Republican moderate who had come to rely on crossover Democratic votes for her re-election victories. In the primary, Van Hollen had to compete against Del. Mark Shriver, a Kennedy cousin who had extensive labor support, and Ira Shapiro, a former Clinton administration trade official who touted his familiarity with federal policy issues. Bolstered by a crucial endorsement from *The Post*, Van Hollen defeated Shriver 43%-41%, with Shapiro getting 13%.

He then had only eight weeks to campaign against Morella, who was widely viewed as hard-working and congenial and who had a liberal voting record suited to the district's many Democrats. Morella had voted against the use of military force in Iraq and was often out of step with the conservative Republican leadership in the House. Van Hollen did not directly attack Morella but argued that she was an enabler of the Republican majority, that her vote to organize the House with Republicans kept in power conservatives who were out of sync with most district voters. Morella criticized Van Hollen's record in Annapolis, including his decision to quit a Senate subcommittee over proposed budget cuts. This time, *The Post* endorsed Morella, as did *The Baltimore Sun*. But it wasn't enough. In a race in which the two candidates together spent nearly $6 million, Van Hollen won 52%-47%. Democrats had redrawn the district for the express purpose of defeating Morella, and the gambit worked. Nearly half of Van Hollen's popular vote margin came from the piece of the district in Prince George's County, which is majority African-American. He won there, 78%-21%. If the contest had been held in the old district, Morella probably would have won.

In the House, Van Hollen has been an activist liberal on most issues. In his first term, he scored an unexpected victory when he got the chamber—including 26 Republicans, some of them conservatives—to approve his amendment to limit a Republican plan to outsource more federal jobs. Despite that vote, the Bush administration eventually prevailed. He also worked on lobbying legislation to eliminate conflicts of interests in earmarks, the special provisions tucked into spending bills by individual members. In 2005, he began to move up in the party leadership with his appointment to co-chair the DCCC with Illinois Democrat Rahm Emanuel and to manage candidate recruitment and execution of the "Red to Blue" campaign plan. Working closely with Emanuel, the lower-key Van Hollen traveled to many battleground districts for hands-on candidate mentoring.

In 2007, with Democrats now in control of Congress, Van Hollen was rewarded with a seat on the tax-writing Ways and Means Committee. He focused on revisions to the Alternative Minimum Tax to benefit the middle class, changes in federal law to make prescription drugs more affordable for lower-income groups, and legislation to curb speculation and market manipulation that contributed to high oil and gas prices. He also worked with Emanuel to require lobbyists to make additional disclosure of campaign contributions. On local issues, he sought more money for the regional Metro transit system and for initiatives to clean up the Chesapeake Bay.

House Speaker Nancy Pelosi showed her confidence in Van Hollen by appointing him to head the DCCC after Emanuel stepped down. In 2008, the Marylander worked closely with the new speaker on campaign strategy. In contrast to Emanuel's strained relations with Democratic National Committee Chairman Howard Dean, who like Emanuel is known for a fiery temperament, Van Hollen developed a harmonious relationship with Dean. Emphasizing that a "wave" election like 2006 almost always is followed by losses for the resurgent party, Van Hollen ran a smart operation that took advantage of opportunities. The party picked up important momentum with early victories in three Republican-held seats where incumbents had left midterm. Democrats won in springtime special elections in Illinois, Louisiana, and Mississippi in advance of the main show in the fall.

Democrats ultimately gained 21 seats in November, many of them in traditionally Republican areas, and Van Hollen and the DCCC got a good share of the credit. He protected the party's large freshman class, typically the most vulnerable incumbents. Only four first-term Democrats—all of them in Republican-leaning areas—were defeated out of a class of 33. Van Hollen ran a skillful in-house research operation and expanded the field program. He also performed well in the most important function for any DCCC chairman—raising money. The committee took in $176 million in the 2008 cycle, compared with $118 million for its GOP counterpart, the National Republican Congressional Committee. Early and aggressive challenges to veteran GOP incumbents influenced the disproportionately high number of House Republican retirements: 26 GOP incumbents did not seek re-election in 2008. Though his party stood to gain from the coattails of its eventual Democratic presidential nominee that year, Van Hollen took nothing for granted. He created pickup opportunities in red-state districts, including some in Alabama and Idaho, where candidates needed help with get-out-the-vote operations. "When I took over as chairman, I was determined to stay on the offensive and increase the majority," he said in May 2008. "We don't need to hunker down or circle the wagons."

At home, Van Hollen's earnest approach has made him nearly invulnerable to a re-election challenge, and his is now considered a safe Democratic seat. Following the retirement of Democratic Sen. Paul Sarbanes of Maryland in early 2005, Van Hollen gave serious thought to jumping into the multicandidate Democratic primary. But at the urging of Minority Whip Steny Hoyer of Maryland, and with the likely prospect of his advancement in the House, he decided against it. Although he was initially reluctant to take on another grueling two years as DCCC chairman, Pelosi persuaded him to stay on for the 2010 election cycle, giving him the additional title of assistant to the speaker. In 2009, the new position gave him more opportunity to coordinate policy with his close ally Emanuel, who had left the House to become President Obama's chief of staff, and to help manage the inevitable conflicts between the White House and Congress. If he chooses to remain in the House, Van Hollen is young enough—and the more senior House leaders are old enough—to allow him to move into the top ranks within the decade. But he no doubt will also keep his eye on a possible run for the Senate.

★ MASSACHUSETTS ★

It would be a city upon a hill, John Winthrop wrote of the Massachusetts Bay Colony that his fellow Puritans were building, an example to the entire world. And Massachusetts, in the nearly four centuries since, has always assumed that it has a lot to teach others. The Puritans' austere creed taught that only the elect would be saved and that they must extirpate the forces of Satan—Indians, Papists, tolerationists. For 150 years, New England was partial to learning, but it also was insular, hostile to outsiders, and economically stagnant. But after the American Revolution, the international war between royal Britain and revolutionary and Napoleonic France allowed New England's ship owners to cross enemy lines to become the world's leading merchants. They made vast profits and invested the money in textile mills, then railroads, then coal mines and steel mills, providing much of the capital that made industrial America.

Massachusetts remade the country in other ways. Intellectually, New England flowered in the 19th century, more than 200 years after Plymouth Rock. Writers from Boston, Cambridge, and Concord—Ralph Waldo Emerson, Henry Wadsworth Longfellow, Henry David Thoreau, John Greenleaf Whittier, Nathaniel Hawthorne—created an American literature and popularized an American philosophy. Hawthorne was as far away in time from the Salem witch trials as he is from us. Demographically, New England Yankees surged across the continent. Long blocked from upstate New York by mountains and the British-Iroquois alliance, they only reached Syracuse in the 1820s. By the 1850s, they were in Iowa, Kansas, and Oregon's Willamette Valley, and by the 1870s in Los Angeles. They helped found the Republican Party and did much to start—and win—the Civil War. They planted their economic system and their values, articulated in the *McGuffey Readers*, across the continent.

In the meantime, Massachusetts itself and Boston, the hub of the universe, were being remade. The Irish potato famine of the 1840s and an imploding economy sent Irish immigrants across the Atlantic, and many came to Boston, looking for work in the mills, docks, and factories of Massachusetts. Yankee Protestants had seen Catholics as their great political and cultural enemy since the 17th century, and they felt that their commonwealth was under siege. As Catholics became a majority, first in Boston and then statewide, Protestants feared that the Irish would use their political clout to ladle out government jobs and benefits to their own—and the Irish had a much better flair for politics than an instinct for commerce. But they encountered such bigotry and rejection by the Yankees that even as successful an Irish Catholic as Joseph Kennedy abandoned Boston for New York in 1927. Politics in Massachusetts for years was a kind of culture war between Yankee Republicans and Irish Democrats, an argument not so much over the distribution of income or the provision of services as over whose vision of Massachusetts should be honored, and whose version of history should be taught—an argument not unlike the battles being fought between cultural liberals and conservatives today.

Sometimes, the stakes were concrete—control of patronage, command of the Boston Police Department—but more often they were symbolic. Yankee Republicans tended to back activist government programs: public works and protective tariffs to help business; the Civil War and Reconstruction to help suitably distant oppressed people such as Southern blacks; uplifting (and productivity-enhancing) social movements such as temperance. The Irish found the 19th-century Democratic Party and its philosophy of laissez-faire more congenial. The Irish had come from a place where the government was the enemy, and they didn't want government spending money to help the rich or to stimulate commerce. They also didn't want government to restrict immigration, to advance blacks (potential competitors in the labor market), or to ban alcohol.

The Irish and Catholic percentages rose slowly over the years. Yankees had smaller families, moved west, intermarried with people of immigrant stock, and lost their Yankee identity. The Irish mostly stayed put, raised large families, and maintained their Catholic identity. Slowly but surely, Massachusetts moved from being one of the most Republican states to one of the most Democratic. Economically, early-20th-century Massachusetts progressed little. The descendants of the Yankees who had been so venturesome in the early 19th century became cautious investors in the early 20th. The predominance of the textile mills in their home state meant that for a century beginning in the 1820s, Massachusetts imported low-skill labor and exported high-skill people. As textile mills started moving south in the 1920s, Massachusetts started exporting low-skill people as well. From the waning of Yankee authority until the national rise of the Kennedys, Massachusetts seemed to run out of things to teach the rest of the nation. The state's Yankee Republicans were backward looking, out of power in Washington, on the defensive at home, and without a cause to champion. The Irish Democrats, not least the Kennedys, were hostile to Franklin Roosevelt's pro-British internationalism and were receptive to the anti-Communism of the very Irish Sen. Joe McCarthy.

Then came the Kennedys. Rose Kennedy was born in 1890 (and died in 1995), the daughter of John "Honey Fitz" Fitzgerald, who was elected to Congress at age 31 and was mayor of Boston in 1906–07 and 1910–14. Her husband, Joseph Kennedy, was chairman of the Securities and Exchange Commission in

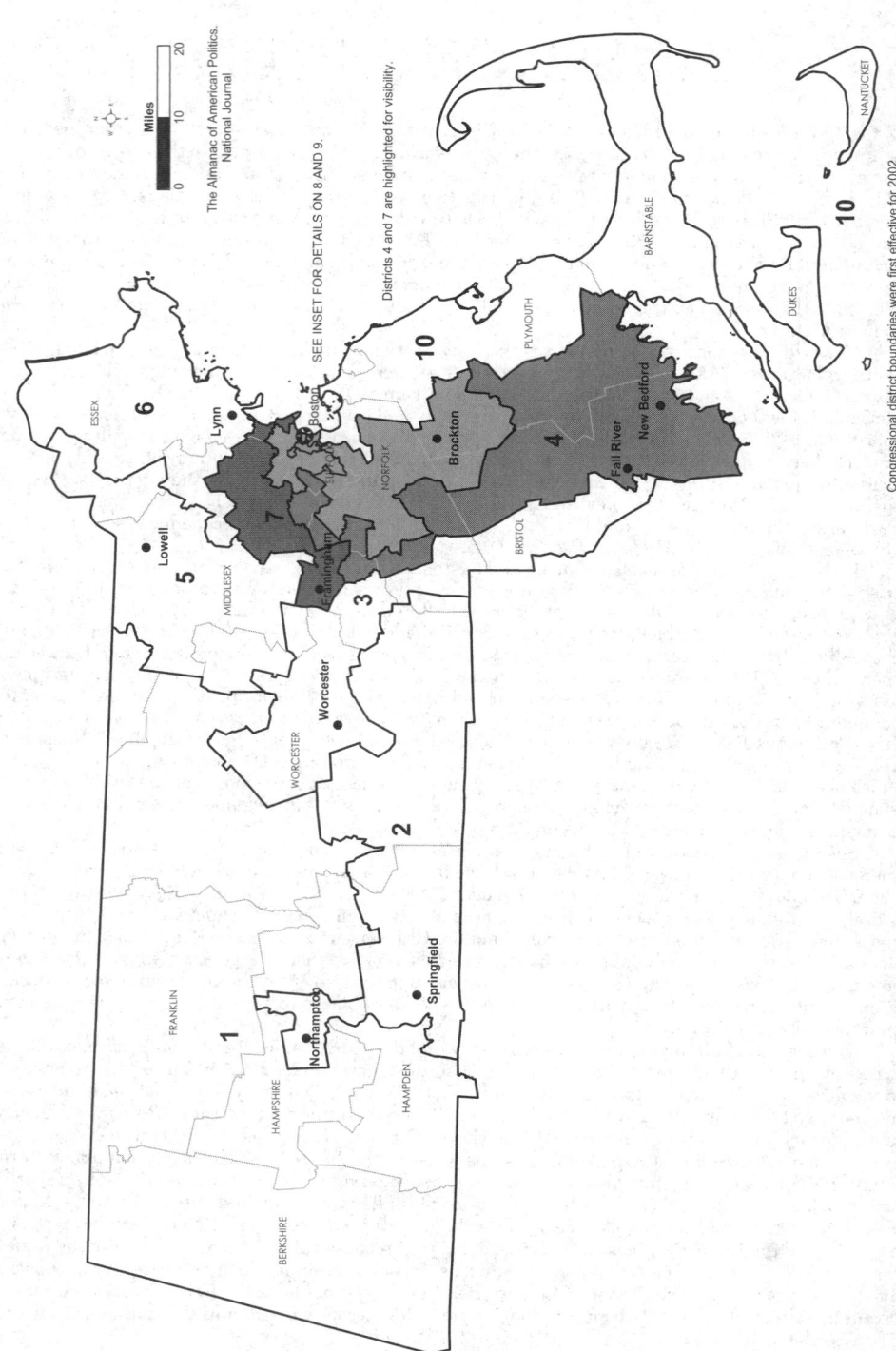

The Almanac of American Politics.
National Journal

SEE INSET FOR DETAILS ON 8 AND 9.

Districts 4 and 7 are highlighted for visibility.

Congressional district boundaries were first effective for 2002.

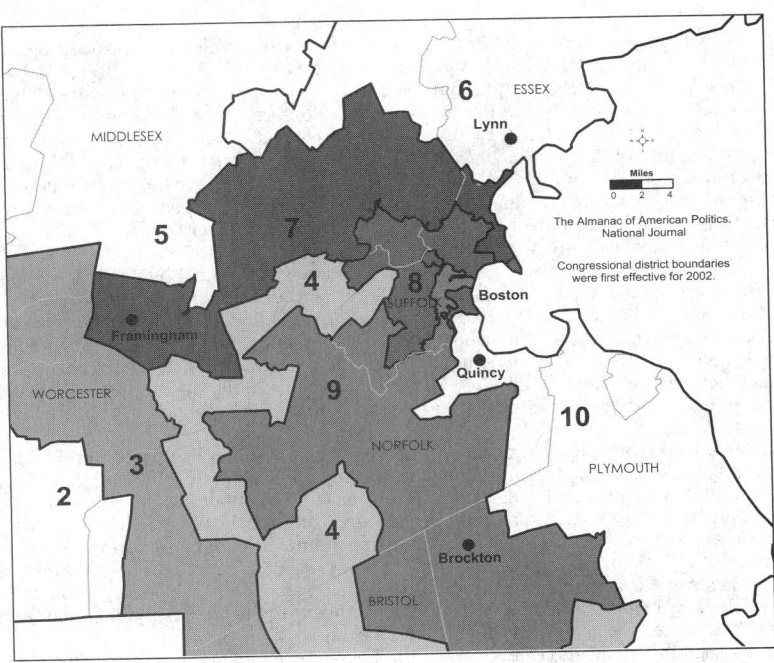

the 1930s and ambassador to the Court of St. James from 1937 to 1940. He was Catholic and uncommonly rich, and he was a shrewd and ruthless political operator. Their only residence in Massachusetts after 1927 was their summer home in Hyannis Port. In 1946, Joseph Kennedy moved his oldest surviving son, John, to Boston, and helped steer his election to the U.S. House that year, to the U.S. Senate in 1952, and to the presidency in 1960. With their elegant manners, charm, and great achievements, the Kennedys seemed like royalty to the Irish Catholics of Massachusetts. And Catholics across the country, 78% of whom voted for John Kennedy, greeted the Democrat's election in 1960 with great pride. Joseph and John Kennedy were, on many issues, conservative or skeptical. But JFK's administration was increasingly, even before his untimely death, identified as liberal. His example and that of his brother Edward Kennedy, who was elected to the U.S. Senate in 1962, moved Massachusetts Catholics to the left. At the same time, the leftward direction of the state's elite campuses in the 1960s influenced Massachusetts Protestants. The universities also provided the basis for a surging high-tech economy, to the point that Massachusetts started importing high-skill people even as it exported those with low skills.

In the 1970s and 1980s, Massachusetts, with one interval, had the most liberal governance and outlook on national politics of any state in the country. It was the only state to vote for Democratic presidential nominee George McGovern in 1972 and, although it voted twice for Republican Ronald Reagan, the son of an Irish Catholic, its Democratic percentage in presidential contests from 1968 to 1988 was 53%, just 0.4% behind Rhode Island and well ahead of every other state. During that span, it elected to the Senate Edward Kennedy, liberal Republican Edward Brooke, and Democrats Paul Tsongas and John Kerry. Liberal governors such as Republican Francis Sargent and Democrat Michael Dukakis vastly increased spending and endorsed policies that helped sink Dukakis' 1988 presidential campaign, notably the law that granted weekend furloughs to prisoners sentenced to life without parole. As historian David Hackett Fischer points out in *Albion's Seed*, the mind-set of the settlers remains strong even when the ethnicity of current residents is far different, and the spirit of the Puritans, the faith that they had much to teach the rest of the world, is strong in Massachusetts liberals: in the smug liberalism of Michael Dukakis, the hearty liberalism of Edward Kennedy, and the combative liberalism of John Kerry.

Then, in the early 1990s, Massachusetts had a momentary political revolution. The 1980s "Massachusetts miracle" had turned into a curse, as the state's economy sagged badly, as defense cutbacks sent unemployment rising, and as high-tech firms like Wang and Digital withered and Cambridge-based Lotus' software was eclipsed by Microsoft's. The Northeast real estate bubble burst, and Massachusetts banks foundered. The state government essentially went bankrupt. In 1990, as Dukakis retired as governor, voters embraced big tax cuts and elected Republican William Weld in his place.

Four different Republicans held the governorship for the next 16 years. Weld favored a government that taxed and spent lightly, that was friendly to gay rights, that exerted some effort to protect the environment, and that was tough on crime. Referenda limiting taxes and Weld's sharp spending cuts reduced the burden of government, and the state's private economy began recovering. Re-elected with 71% of the vote in 1994, Weld later left the state, but his basic approach prevailed, with variations, under his successors—Paul Cellucci, who took office in 1997 when Weld resigned; Jane Swift, who took office in 2001 when Cellucci resigned; and Mitt Romney, who was elected in 2002. But they were able to reduce the cost of government only so far. The biggest policy innovation was the health care plan passed by the Legislature and supported by Romney in 2006. It required all residents to buy health insurance, levied taxes on employers who do not provide it, and subsidized it for low-wage earners. Romney argued that universal coverage would reduce the need to provide free care to the uninsured.

The Massachusetts economy sagged noticeably after 2000. The state held its own in competition for high-tech and defense industries, but it showed little growth even as the nation's economy surged. Massachusetts experienced a net out-migration of nonimmigrants of some 298,000 people between 2000 and 2008; this migration slowed as the economy perked up in 2006 and 2007, only to be smacked down by the national recession in 2008. Most who left were young, many were professionals, and many were unable to afford Massachusetts' high housing costs. They have been only partly replaced by about 212,000 immigrants, about half of them Brazilians. Massachusetts has many descendants of Portuguese and Azorean immigrants, and the Brazilians have evidently been attracted to the most Lusophone part of the United States.

At the same time, the cultural liberalism that Weld championed has prevailed. Weld was one of America's first politicians to endorse gay rights, and he appointed Supreme Judicial Court Chief Justice Margaret Marshall, who pushed through the 4-3 decisions in November 2003 requiring the Legislature to give gays equal marriage rights. When the Legislature declined, the judge in May 2004 declared that same-sex couples have the right to marry. A short-lived stampede of same-sex couples to clerks' offices began: Some 2,500 same-sex marriages occurred the week after the court's decision but only 1,700 took place in the next six months. Romney opposed the decision, and state House Speaker Thomas Finneran, a Democrat, pushed the Legislature in 2004 to vote 105-92 to send to the voters a constitutional amendment banning same-sex marriage and endorsing civil unions.

But under the Massachusetts Constitution, the Legislature must vote for an amendment twice before it goes on the ballot. In the 2004 Democratic primaries and in the general election, opponents of same-sex marriage fared poorly, while Speaker Finneran was ousted by Salvatore DiMasi, a same-sex marriage backer from the gentrified North End of Boston. Signatures were gathered for a constitutional amendment banning same-sex marriage, but throughout 2006, DiMasi refused to let it come to a vote. After Romney sued to force the Legislature to act, the Supreme Judicial Court unanimously concluded that it was required to vote, but said it couldn't compel it to do so. Same-sex marriage advocates made gains in the 2006 elections, and opinion seemed to accept a change that was already occurring without notable disruption. In June, the state House voted 151-45 against the amendment, five votes shy of the 50 needed to place the measure on the ballot. Once again, there were lessons to be learned from the Massachusetts experience. Courts in Connecticut, New Hampshire, and Iowa, as well as the Maine and Vermont Legislatures, had legalized same-sex marriage by May 2009. The California Legislature and the New York Assembly also voted to do so. However, more than 40 states, stunned by the Massachusetts court's decision on same-sex marriage, have gone the other way and passed statutes or constitutional amendments barring same-sex marriage (as California did in 2008). Their actions make it harder for these states to follow Massachusetts' example if opinion shifts, as the attitudes of young voters in most of the nation suggests it will, in the Bay State's direction.

The continuing allegiance of Catholic voters (still a majority, according to the 2008 exit poll), the cultural liberalism of the Yankees and university elites, and the out-migration of Bay State natives who are not similarly minded has made Massachusetts one of the nation's most Democratic states. With Deval Patrick's 56%-35% victory in 2006 over Romney's lieutenant governor, Kerry Healey, Democrats now hold all six statewide offices, all 12 U.S. House and Senate seats, and 176 of the 200 seats in the state Legislature (whose official name is the Great and General Court). Republicans failed to contest six U.S. House seats and 154 state legislative seats in 2008. The state voted 62%-37% for John Kerry, the Democratic candidate for president in 2004, and 62%-36% for Democratic nominee Barack Obama in 2008. In recent elections, the most heavily Democratic parts of the state have not been the blue-collar wards of Boston (they're mostly either gentrified or heavily African-American or immigrant), but the university towns such as Cambridge, the Berkshires, and the college-rich Pioneer Valley in the west, and variously fashionable resort areas such as Martha's Vineyard, Nantucket, and Provincetown. The most heavily Republican (or less Democratic) areas are what political scientist Robert David Sullivan called the "Offramps"—towns near the Interstate 495 ring road and "cranberry country" in Plymouth County and Cape Cod; working-class Worcester County in the center of the state; and high-income Essex County in the northeast.

Population

Pop. 2007:	6,437,759
State rank:	15th of 50
Change since 2000:	Up 1.4%
Urban:	90.8%
Rural:	9.2%
Native of state:	64.1%
Not a citizen:	7.6%
Area size:	10,555 sq. mi.

Most populous cities

1. Boston	600,980
2. Worcester	165,965
3. Springfield	148,136
4. Lowell	100,659

Household Income

Under $15k:	12.3%
$15k to $50k:	28.6%
$50k to $100k:	31.6%
$100k to $150k:	21.7%
Over $150k:	5.8%
Median income:	$61,785

Home Value

Under $100k:	2.3%
$100k to $300k:	31.1%
$300k to $500k:	41.7%
$500k to $1 mil:	21.2%
Over $1 million:	3.7%
Median:	$366,200

Work

Private:	80.6%
Government:	12.7%
Self-employed:	6.6%
Unemployment (3-yr. average):	4.2%
Poverty:	10.1%
Blue collar:	17.4%
White collar:	66.3%
Khaki collar:	0.1%
Other:	16.2%

Age

Median age:	38.3 yrs.
More than 65 yrs:	13.3%
Less than 18 yrs:	22.5%

Race/Ethnicity

White:	79.4%
Black:	5.7%
Hispanic:	8.0%
Asian:	4.7%
Native Am.:	0.2%
Hawaiian:	0.0%
Two+ races:	1.2%

Ancestry

Irish:	17.8%
Italian:	10.8%
English:	9.1%

Language

English:	79.8%
Spanish:	6.9%
Asian:	3.4%
Other European	9.0%

Education

H.S. grad:	87.9%
College grad:	37.1%
Grad degree:	15.7%

Military Veterans

% of Pop:	9.0%

Veterans by Period

WWII and before:	17.9%
Korea:	14.4%
Vietnam:	30.3%
Gulf (pre-2001):	7.4%
Gulf (post-2001):	4.7%
Peace time:	25.3%

Registered Voters in 2008

D:	1,559,464 (37.0%)
R:	490,259 (11.6%)
Other:	2,170,765 (51.4%)
Voter turnout:	3,080,985
Turnout as % of voting age:	60.8%

General Court

Senate:	35 D 5 R
House:	143 D 16 R 1 I

Presidential politics

Over the last 11 presidential elections, Massachusetts has been the most Democratic state, giving Democratic nominees on average 56% of the vote. It was Bill Clinton's best state in 1996, Al Gore's second best state in 2000, John Kerry's best in 2004, and Barack Obama's sixth best in 2008 (after Hawaii and Vermont, and barely behind New York, Rhode Island, and Illinois). What is also striking about Massachusetts is how many serious presidential candidates it has produced over the last three decades: Edward Kennedy in 1980, Michael Dukakis in 1988, Paul Tsongas in 1992, Kerry in 2004, and Mitt Romney in 2008. Only California and Texas have produced more serious candidates over that period, but they are the No. 1 and No. 2 states in population, respectively, while Massachusetts is now No. 15, having recently fallen behind Washington and Arizona. Some credit must be given to New Hampshire, which holds the nation's first primary: The state is just north of Massachusetts and most of its residents receive Boston television stations. But even more credit must go to the hyperpolitical culture of Boston. Only Chicago seems as preoccupied by its local political figures, but for half a century, until 2008, that Midwestern city didn't share Boston's confidence that one of its own was capable of national leadership.

2008 Presidential Vote

Obama (D)	1,904,097	(62%)
McCain (R)	1,108,854	(36%)

2008 Democratic Presidential Primary

Clinton (D)	705,185	(56%)
Obama (D)	511,680	(41%)

2008 Republican Presidential Primary

Romney (R)	255,892	(51%)
McCain (R)	204,779	(41%)

2004 Presidential Vote

Kerry (D)	1,803,800	(62%)
Bush (R)	1,071,109	(37%)

Obama received 61.8% of the vote in Massachusetts—slightly trailing Kerry's 61.94%, which is understandable given the latter's home-state status. Obama did particularly well among young voters (78%) and women (68%; Massachusetts has a big gender gap). There's evidence in the exit poll of a split between the university elite and the private-sector affluent. Obama carried those earning more than $100,000 by only 50%-47%, while he won those with postgraduate degrees 69%-29%. Married voters with children voted 58% for Obama, but they made up only one-third of the electorate; the others voted 70% for Obama.

Massachusetts' presidential primary has long been held in early March and was once the scene of great commotion. It produced victories for native sons Dukakis, Tsongas, Kerry, and others. In 2000, it voted solidly for Democrat Gore and Republican John McCain, as many independents reregistered as Republicans. Candidates contesting New Hampshire always buy time on Boston television stations, which reach of much of the Granite State (most of the cost does not have to be charged against the low limit on spending in New Hampshire), and so their ads are widely seen in Massachusetts.

In 2008, Massachusetts voted on Super Tuesday, February 5, and it was one of the few states where polls showed close races in both parties. Obama was endorsed by Gov. Deval Patrick, Kerry, and U.S. Reps. Michael Capuano and Bill Delahunt. Sen. Edward Kennedy gave a rousing welcome to Obama at a rally the night before the primary in Boston's Faneuil Hall. But Hillary Rodham Clinton also had her Massachusetts supporters, including Boston Mayor Thomas Menino and U.S. Reps. Richard Neal, Jim McGovern, Barney Frank, and Stephen Lynch. And, as in New Hampshire, she had the support of downscale Democrats. While Obama carried the university towns, she carried the mill towns. She won majorities from Latino and Jewish voters, in a state where each of those groups outnumbers black voters, who overwhelmingly backed Obama. Clinton won 56%-41% in a turnout of 1.2 million voters.

Far fewer people, 500,000, voted in the Republican primary. Many Massachusetts Republicans are liberal on cultural issues, and Romney's turn to the right on those issues earlier in the election season may have produced a backlash. His two predecessors as governor, Paul Cellucci and Jane Swift, endorsed McCain of Arizona. Romney won, but by just 51%-41%. And because Massachusetts Republicans, unlike those in many other states, didn't have a winner-take-all rule, his delegate haul was minimal, while McCain on the same day was harvesting delegates in winner-take-all states such as New York, New Jersey, Missouri, and California.

Congressional districting

| 111th Congress Lineup |
| 10 D |
| 110th Congress Lineup |
| 10 D |

Massachusetts' convoluted congressional district lines deserve their own biographer, someone with a sure political instinct and a touch of whimsy. This is, after all, the state whose Gov. Elbridge Gerry gave his name to the term "gerrymander" in the early 19th century. The state lost two seats in the 1960 census, and one each in 1980 and 1990. It survived the 2000 census without losing another seat, but it will likely lose one in the 2010 count. And that will mean a Democratic loss.

The last time a Republican won a U.S. House seat here was in 1994; although the 5th District had a close special election in 2008, no Republican seems likely to win in 2010. (And if one did, he or she would probably lose out in the redistricting to follow, which would affect the 2012 election.) Demographics suggest that western Massachusetts, where population growth has been minimal or negative, will lose a seat, but the final decision will likely be a battle royal. The two most senior members of the delegation, Edward Markey and Frank, hold important committee positions that the state would not want to lose. The permutations and combinations—and the machinations of Beacon Hill politics—make predictions hazardous.

Governor

Deval Patrick (D)

Elected 2006, term expires Jan. 2011, 1st term; b. July 31, 1956, Chicago, IL; home, Milton; Harvard U., A.B. 1978, J.D. 1982; Presbyterian; married (Diane); 2 children.

Professional Career: Michael Clark Rockefeller Memorial Traveling Fellow, Sudan, 1978–79; Law clerk, 9th Circuit Court of Appeals, 1982–83; Practicing atty., 1983–94, 1997–99; Asst. U.S. Atty. Gen. for Civil Rights, 1994–97; Vice president and general counsel, Texaco, 1999–2001; Executive vice president and general counsel, Coca-Cola, 2001–04; ACC Capital Holdings, 2004–06.

Office: State House, Rm. 360, Boston, 2133, 617-725-4005; Fax: 617-727-9725; Web site: www.mass.gov/gov.

Election Results

2006 general	Deval Patrick (D)	1,234,984	(56%)
	Kerry Healey (R)	784,342	(35%)
	Christy Mihos (I)	154,628	(7%)
2006 primary	Deval Patrick (D)	452,229	(50%)
	Christopher Gabrieli (D)	248,301	(27%)
	Thomas Reilly (D)	211,031	(23%)

Deval Patrick, elected in 2006, is the state's first African-American governor and only the nation's second black governor. Virginia's Douglas Wilder was the first in 1989. Patrick grew up in a tough South Side Chicago neighborhood, and lived in an apartment where he shared a single room with his mother and sister; his father, a saxophone player, left the family when he was a child. He showed tremendous promise in elementary school, and a teacher recommended him to A Better Chance, an organization that sends gifted minority students to college preparatory schools. Patrick received a scholarship to the tony Milton Academy in Massachusetts. "(It) was like coming to a different planet," Patrick said later. He went on to graduate from Harvard College and then spent a year working in Africa on a United Nations youth training project in the Darfur region of Sudan. When he returned, he graduated from Harvard Law School and clerked for a federal appeals court judge in Los Angeles. In 1983, he joined the NAACP Legal Defense Fund in New York, and in 1986 he went into private law practice. During the Clinton administration, he was the assistant attorney general for civil rights. He returned to private practice in Boston in 1997, and later was general counsel for Texaco and Coca-Cola. Since Democrat Michael Dukakis left office in 1990, Massachusetts has had four Republican governors, the latest of which was Mitt Romney. Romney, running as an outsider in 2002, defeated Democratic state Treasurer Shannon O'Brien by 50%-45%. He faced large Democratic majorities in the statehouse, and after a single term, decided not to seek re-election but instead to run for president. The open governor's race attracted a formidable Democratic primary field that included Attorney General Thomas Reilly and venture capitalist Christopher Gabrieli. Patrick was a long shot in his first-ever run for elected office, but his grassroots campaign quickly built support among liberal activists who liked his outsider message and his criticism of the state's "backroom" political culture. He won the state party endorsement at its June 2006 convention, and after holding a steady lead in the polls throughout the summer, won the nomination decisively in the September 19 primary. Despite speculation that, as the most liberal of the three candidates, he would prove to be the weakest nominee, Patrick won 50% to Gabrieli's 27% and Reilly's 23%. The Republican nominee was Lt. Gov. Kerry Healey. Also running was Christy Mihos, a wealthy businessman and former director of the Massachusetts Turnpike Authority, who left the Republican Party to run as an independent. Mihos never gained traction, and Healey struggled to generate enthusiasm about her campaign. One reason was Romney, who was no asset in Healey's bid to succeed him. He had failed to build the state party in his four years, and his frequent out-of-state travel and the jibes he directed at Massachusetts while preparing to run for president left him with low job-approval ratings. Patrick consistently referred to the "Romney-Healey administration," and ran television ads featuring photos of Romney and Healey.

Healey called Patrick soft on crime and insisted he would raise taxes and increase state spending. Patrick pointed to his credentials as a Justice Department prosecutor and highlighted his executive-level experience at two Fortune 500 companies as evidence of his business-friendly background. Late in the campaign, Patrick was put on the defensive when Healey's campaign ran tough ads criticizing him for his advocacy on behalf of convicted rapist Benjamin LaGuer. Patrick declined to respond with an aggressive counterattack, insisting that his success so far was the result of avoiding such conventional political tactics. His instincts proved correct. The ensuing publicity surrounding the negative ads, which featured a woman walking alone in a parking garage, muted the charges that Patrick would weaken criminal justice laws. He won a sweeping 56%-35% victory, with 7% for Mihos. Patrick became the first Democrat in 20 years to win the Massachusetts governor's office. In office, he set about unraveling Romney's initiatives. He restored $384 million in budget cuts, rescinded an agreement with the federal government that empowered the state police to arrest illegal immigrants, ended a Romney plan to revamp the state's automobile insurance system and cut funding for abstinence-only sex education. But his honeymoon period ended quickly as a series of missteps tarnished his image. Lavish spending on his official state car, helicopter travel, a renovation of the governor's office that included $12,000 drapes and the hiring of a $72,000-a-year chief of staff for his wife led to weeks of bad press. Patrick acknowledged making a telephone call to Robert Rubin of Citigroup, which has significant business interests in the state, on behalf of the subprime mortgage lender Ameriquest, on whose board Patrick served from 2004 to 2006. The state Republican Party filed a complaint with the Massachusetts Ethics Commission, but the commission decided against reprimanding Patrick. Then he scaled back his public appearances after his wife, a prominent local lawyer, was revealed to be suffering from exhaustion and depression.

Patrick forged ahead, advancing big-ticket and bold new policies. He called for $1 billion in investment in biotechnology, which was passed by the Legislature in 2008. He called for major transportation projects, including a commuter rail service from Boston to New Bedford. His corporate tax reductions also passed. In January 2008, he proposed a $28 billion budget, with a $368 million increase for education, making possible longer school days and universal pre-kindergarten. He also called for tuition-free community colleges and in-state college tuition for children of illegal immigrants. He risked the wrath of teacher unions by proposing "readiness schools" modeled on charter schools and free from union, school district, and state regulations. He also proposed $213 million in programs for the elderly and disabled and for local policing. But revenues came in lower than expected, and in January 2009 Patrick engineered widespread cuts in planned spending. In March 2009, he proposed a 19-cent gas tax increase.

Ever since the state Supreme Judicial Court legalized same-sex marriage in a 4-3 decision in 2004, opponents had sought a vote on a constitutional amendment reversing the decision. To achieve that, they needed the votes of 50 of the state's 200 legislators in two successive legislatures, which they succeeded in getting in 2005. The issue came to a head in 2007. Patrick lobbied legislators heavily to vote against putting the issue on the ballot (although opinion had moved to the point that same-sex marriage might well have been approved), and in intense negotiations, switched 11 votes. The vote was 151-45 against a referendum, with same-sex marriage opponents coming up five votes short of the required 50. Patrick also pressed successfully for repeal of a 1913 law banning out-of-state couples from marrying in Massachusetts if their own state's laws prohibited the union.

Patrick had less luck with his casino gambling proposal. He proposed selling licenses for three resort casinos, with the Mashpee Wampanoag Tribe getting an option to seek federal approval of a fourth. He pointed out that gambling was an old tradition in Massachusetts: Historic Faneuil Hall in Boston had been financed by lotteries. Democratic Senate President Therese Murray strongly agreed, but Democratic Speaker Salvatore DiMasi was strongly opposed, and in March 2008, the House defeated the casino proposal 108-46. The vote came while Patrick was in New York negotiating a $1.35 million book contract.

In the hotly contested 2008 Democratic primary, Patrick endorsed Sen. Barack Obama of Illinois in October 2007 and spoke at a rally of 10,000 Obama supporters in Boston Common. Obama's chief strategist, David Axelrod, was a consultant on Patrick's 2006 campaign. Even so, Sen. Hillary Rodham Clinton of New York won the Massachusetts presidential primary. Patrick is expected to run for re-election in 2010.

Senior Senator

Edward Kennedy (D)

Elected 1962, term expires 2012, 8th full term; b. Feb. 22, 1932, Boston; home, Hyannis Port; Harvard U., B.A. 1956, The Hague Intl. Law Schl., 1958, U. of VA, LL.B. 1959; Catholic; married (Vicki); 5 children.

Military Career: Army, 1951–53.

Professional Career: Western states coord., John F. Kennedy Pres. Campaign, 1960; Asst. dist. atty., Suffolk Cnty., 1961–62.

DC Office: 317 RSOB, 20510, 202-224-4543; Fax: 202-224-2417; Web site: kennedy.senate.gov.

State Offices: Boston, 617-565-3170.

Committees: *Armed Services* (2nd of 15 D): Emerging Threats & Capabilities; Personnel; Seapower (Chmn). *Health, Education, Labor & Pensions* (Chmn of 13 D). *Joint Economic Committee.*

Group Ratings

	ADA	ACLU	AFS	LCV	ITIC	NTU	COC	ACU	CFG	FRC
2008	60	85	100	36	100	9	50	0	7	11
2007	85	—	100	93	—	8	64	0	14	—

National Journal Ratings

	2007 LIB	—	2007 CONS		2008 LIB	—	2008 CONS
Economic	66%	—	30%		*%	—	*%
Social	64%	—	35%		*%	—	*%
Foreign	94%	—	2%		*%	—	*%
Composite	76%	—	24%		*%	—	*%

Key Votes of the 110th Congress

1. Raise CAFE standards	Y	5. Make English official language	N	9. Withdraw troops 3/08	Y
2. Expand SCHIP	Y	6. Path to citizenship	Y	10. Iran guard is terrorist group	N
3. Cap greenhouse gases	*	7. Fetus is unborn child	Y	11. Increase missile defense $	*
4. Bail out financial markets	*	8. Prosecute hate crimes	Y	12. Overhaul FISA	*

Election Results

2006 general	Edward Kennedy (D)	 1,500,738	(69%)	($7,043,877)
	Ken Chase (R)	 661,532	(31%)	($853,730)
2006 primary	Edward Kennedy (D)	.... unopposed		

Prior Winning Percentages: 2000 (73%); 1994 (58%); 1988 (65%); 1982 (61%); 1976 (69%); 1970 (62%); 1964 (74%); 1962 (55%)

Democrat Edward Kennedy has served for more than 46 years in the Senate, longer than all but two other senators in American history and enduring through nine American presidencies. The only senators who served longer are the late Republican Strom Thurmond of South Carolina and incumbent Democrat Robert Byrd of West Virginia. A master of legislative deal-making and the keeper of the flame of liberalism, Kennedy is considered one of the giants of the Senate, with a place in history more earned than bestowed on him by the famous Kennedy name. News in May 2008 that he was suffering from a malignant brain tumor was received with great sadness on both sides of the political aisle.

He has been a presidential candidate and, while still in his 30s, was widely assumed to be the next president. To many, his reputation as an idealistic champion of the poor is unassailable, and the nation has watched him cope impressively time and again with family tragedy. To others, he is a symbol of personal immorality and unpunished criminal behavior, a man who has gotten away with things that would have ended the public career of almost anyone else. There is some basis for both views, but neither is an entirely fair picture of a politician who was re-elected without much fuss in 2006, and who has done much over the years to set national policy on any number of issues. Kennedy himself has acknowledged his failings. "I've made mistakes. Certainly there are things I'm not proud of," he once said.

For much of America, the luster of the Kennedys in their heyday is increasingly a distant memory. Most Americans—including the current president—have no actual recollection of the years John F. Kennedy was president. But Edward Kennedy has remained a major political force. There was little in the early life of this youngest of the Kennedy siblings to suggest he would be so important a public figure, much less for so long. He grew up in Bronxville, N.Y., a rich and heavily Catholic suburb. He was thrown out of Harvard University for cheating on a Spanish exam. He went off to do a stint in the Army, and then returned to earn degrees at Harvard and the University of Virginia Law School. He married a Bronxville woman, Joan Bennett, who never developed a taste for politics. Then one of his older brothers was elected president of the United States, and the 28-year-old Edward was a national celebrity. The imperious family patriarch, Joe Kennedy, insisted that he run for the Senate seat just vacated by his brother. A college roommate of President Kennedy's was appointed by Democratic Gov. Foster Furcolo to hold the seat until Kennedy reached the constitutional age of 30 in 1962. His family money and the enthusiasm among Massachusetts Catholics enabled him to beat strong candidates with good political names: Attorney General Edward McCormack, nephew of House Speaker John McCormack, in the Democratic primary; George Cabot Lodge, son and great-grandson of senators, in the general election. "He can do more for Massachusetts" was his slogan, as it had been John Kennedy's in his first Senate race 10 years before. Two years later, his brother, Robert Kennedy, was elected senator from New York, regarded generally as a carpetbagger although he had grown up from age 2 in the state. Robert Kennedy ran for president and was murdered just after winning the California primary in June 1968.

After the assassinations of his two brothers, Edward Kennedy was seen by many as their natural heir, and he could have been nominated for president in 1968, at 36, or in 1972, had he chosen to run. But his career would never completely recover from the accident at Chappaquiddick in July 1969, in which a young woman riding with Kennedy was killed after he lost control of the car and it plunged into a pond. Kennedy escaped, but passenger Mary Jo Kopechne died in the car. He did not call police until after her body was found, behavior he later blamed on being disoriented from the crash. Kennedy pleaded guilty to leaving the scene of an accident and was given a two-month suspended jail sentence. His poll ratings dropped, and Kennedy became a polarizing figure. In 1972, he delivered the first of many stirring convention speeches promoting his trademark liberalism. In 1979, he did run for president, and began the race against incumbent Democrat Jimmy Carter far ahead in the polls. But he was unable to articulate his reasons for running, and his candidacy stirred adverse reactions to him personally, as well as to his policies. It ended in a crushing defeat, relieved only by another stirring convention speech, after which he pointedly refused to raise Carter's hand on the podium in the traditional show of party unity. In retrospect, it is plain that Kennedy's presidential chances were ended by Chappaquiddick. But he has always been re-elected with solid margins in Massachusetts. His toughest competition was Mitt Romney, then a venture capitalist and later governor and presidential candidate, in the Republican year of 1994.

Kennedy has been a hardworking and practical politician who, after his brothers' deaths, took up liberal causes. He was elected Senate majority whip in 1967, but lost the post to Byrd in 1971. He worked hard for a quarter-century without friendly support from a Democratic administration, until the election of Bill Clinton. Among the laws that he played an important role in enacting were the National Teachers Corps; bilingual education; low-income heating assistance; the Women, Infants and Children (WIC) nutrition program; the Job Training Partnership Act; and the Americans With Disabilities Act. As chairman of the Judiciary Committee in 1979–80 (his chief aide was a young lawyer named Stephen Breyer, now on the U.S. Supreme Court), he supported abortion rights and feminist groups with energy and enthusiasm. He immediately pounced on Judge Robert Bork's nomination in 1987, but played a lesser role in the Clarence Thomas hearings, which came shortly after an incident in which his nephew William Kennedy Smith was arrested and charged with rape in Palm Beach, Fla. It marked another low point in Kennedy's personal life. Divorced from Joan Kennedy, he had spent several years on the party circuit, where his sometimes ribald behavior made news. The Smith trial revealed that the young man had been out on the town with Kennedy the night of the alleged rape.

The decade of the 1990s marked a turnaround for Kennedy. He stopped drinking heavily and dating beautiful, glamorous women. Instead he married one in 1992, Washington lawyer Victoria Reggie, an attractive, divorced mother of two. That year, Kennedy supported Clinton for president and Clinton paid repeated homage to the Kennedy family. Legislatively, Kennedy was productive, though not as much as he wished. As chairman of what is now the Health, Education, Labor, and Pensions Committee, Kennedy supported the higher spending sought by teachers' unions. He worked to pass direct student loans, AmeriCorps, Goals 2000, and the School-to-Work Opportunity Act. He again sponsored the Family and Medical Leave Act, which Republican President George H. W. Bush had vetoed. It was the first law Clinton signed when he succeeded Bush as president. After Republicans won a Senate majority in 1994, Kennedy shifted his focus from expanding government to protecting it from being downsized. In 1996, he went on the offensive. He pushed to passage the Kassebaum-Kennedy health care bill, an incremental measure to provide portability of health insurance and to limit exclusions for pre-existing conditions. He also had a hand in the Children's Health Insurance Program, passed as part of a grand compromise between Clinton and the Republican leadership in 1997.

When Republican George W. Bush took office, he may have been from the other political party, but he was no stranger to Kennedy, who went back a long time with the Bush family. Kennedy had served in the Senate with Bush's grandfather, Prescott Bush, whose last term ended in January 1963. And Kennedy got on well with his father, President George H. W. Bush in 1989–93. The new president started off his term in early 2001 by inviting Kennedy to the White House frequently, once to view *Thirteen Days*, a film about the Cuban missile crisis during John Kennedy's presidency. Kennedy also played a major role in producing Bush's first major bipartisan achievement, the No Child Left Behind education bill passed by the Senate in 2001 and signed in January 2002. This represented a change in course by Kennedy and by Rep. George Miller of California, the ranking Democrat on the House Education panel. They agreed to accept the accountability measures Bush sought, though they were opposed by the teachers' unions. The measures were designed especially to raise test scores among minority and disadvantaged pupils. When his bill came up for reauthorization in 2007, Kennedy again worked with the Bush administration. But this time, they did not reach agreement. The gulf between Democrats and Republicans on the level of funding necessary to pay for the law's mandates on school districts was too wide, and no bill was passed in 2008.

Kennedy broke with Bush in 2003 on the president's plan to create a prescription drug benefit in the Medicare program. Kennedy succeeded in getting a version to his liking through the Senate, but the House produced quite a different bill that largely prevailed in the conference committee. But he pursued other bipartisan causes—strengthening defenses against biological warfare with Tennessee Republican Bill Frist, Health Maintenance Organization regulation with Republican John McCain of Arizona, and hate crimes legislation with Republican Gordon Smith of Oregon. In 2005 and 2006, he worked closely with Gov. Romney, his 1994 opponent, on the universal health care program passed by the Massachusetts Legislature. Romney conceded that it would probably never have passed without Kennedy's involvement.

After the 2004 election, Kennedy was an increasingly sharp critic of the Bush administration, especially on the Iraq war, but continued to work on a bipartisan basis. He worked with conservative Republican Mike Enzi of Wyoming on an electronic health records bill in 2005. He and McCain developed a version of the immigration bill, with a guest worker program as well as border security provisions, which passed the Senate in May 2006 but ultimately was not enacted. He pushed through an amendment to stop universities from running school-as-lender programs, from which they pocketed the proceeds, and pressed Education Secretary Margaret Spellings to enforce it. On a local matter, he opposed the Cape Wind project to create a 130-turbine wind farm in the Horseshoe Shoal in Nantucket Sound. He pushed for a bill that would allow governors to veto such projects, knowing that Romney was prepared to do so.

But on other issues, Kennedy has continued to issue clarion calls for liberalism. On the Judiciary Committee, he opposed Bush's nominations of John Roberts and Samuel Alito to the Supreme Court. He pressed Attorney General Alberto Gonzales on interrogation policies for unlawful combatant detainees. He voted against the Iraq war resolution in 2002, while fellow Massachusetts Sen. John Kerry voted for it. Kennedy later called the case for the war "a fraud . . . cooked up in Texas." By early 2004, his spirit of cooperation with the Bush administration was depleted. In April of that year, he said, "Iraq is George Bush's Vietnam. This is the pattern and the record of the Bush administration [on] Iraq, jobs, Medicare, schools, issue after issue—mislead, deceive, make up the needed facts, smear the character of any critics. Again and again, we see this cynical, despicable strategy playing out." In January 2005, he presented a five-point plan for Iraqi self-government and a definite timetable for a phased withdrawal of U.S. troops.

After the 2006 elections, Kennedy became chairman of the Health, Education, Labor, and Pensions Committee for the third time. He focused on student loans, getting bills through the Senate in July 2007 to force lenders to take more risk, to streamline the financial aid process, and to raise the maximum Pell Grant from $4,500 to $5,100. He sponsored a bill to allow the Food and Drug Administration to approve generic versions of biologic drugs. And with Enzi, he shepherded to passage an FDA bill requiring more surveillance of drugs on the market. He also revived his bill for FDA regulation of tobacco. He introduced the Lilly Ledbetter Act to reverse a Supreme Court decision and extend the statute of limitations in job-discrimination cases. It was among the first pieces of legislation signed by newly elected President Barack Obama in January 2009. Kennedy also worked to pass a mental health parity act, which became law as part of the $700 billion bill to keep financial institutions afloat in October 2008.

In 2007, Kennedy once again took up the cudgel on immigration and introduced a comprehensive bill in May, with a guest-worker program, a path to legalization for illegal workers currently in the United States, and tougher enforcement provisions. With McCain on the campaign trail running for president, he worked with McCain's Arizona colleague Jon Kyl, a Republican. Kennedy joined Kyl in opposing amendments by liberals as "bill killers," but in June 2007 one such measure, which would sunset the guest-worker program, passed. Kennedy tried to salvage the legislation, but Democratic Majority Leader Harry Reid pulled it from the floor. Having failed to set a troop withdrawal deadline for Iraq, Kennedy took up the cause of Iraqis and Afghans adversely affected by the fighting. With Republican Richard

Lugar of Indiana, he sponsored a bill to vastly increase the number of special visas for Iraqi and Afghan translators and interpreters. His amendment to authorize 5,000 visas annually for Iraqis who worked for the U.S. government was included in the defense authorization in September 2007.

In May 2008, Kennedy was hospitalized in Boston and diagnosed with a cancerous brain tumor with a "grim" prognosis. He underwent surgery in June at the Duke Medical Center to remove as much of the tumor as possible. He was absent from the Senate for most of the rest of the year, but returned in July 2008 to cast a decisive vote for cancelling the scheduled 10.6% cut in Medicare reimbursements for doctors. He left the Senate Judiciary Committee in December 2008 after 46 years there.

Kennedy endorsed Illinois Sen. Barack Obama for president in 2008, and campaigned for him in many states during the primaries. Even after becoming ill, he traveled to Denver to the Democratic National Convention to give a brief speech for Obama. He also appeared at Obama's inauguration, but had a seizure at the lunch in the Capitol and had to be hospitalized overnight. Later, when Obama sent his health care bill to Congress, Kennedy was too ill to oversee the work of the HELP Committee. But he kept a hand in the legislation through his staff and through his stand-in as committee chairman, Democratic Sen. Christopher Dodd of Connecticut.

Kennedy was re-elected with 73% of the vote in 2000 and with 69% of the vote in 2006. He carried all but two towns in Hampden County, losing those by a combined 69 votes. He cast his 15,000th vote in the Senate in September 2007, one of only two senators to do so. Two months later, he signed a contract to write his memoirs and spent many hours in interviews for an oral history.

Junior Senator

John Kerry (D)

Elected 1984, term expires 2014, 5th term; b. Dec. 11, 1943, Aurora, CO; home, Boston; Yale U., A.B. 1966, Boston Col., LL.B. 1976; Catholic; married (Teresa Heinz); 5 children.

Military Career: Navy, 1966–70 (Vietnam), Naval Reserves, 1970–78.

Elected Office: MA lt. gov., 1982–84.

Professional Career: Organizer, Vietnam Veterans Against the War; Asst. Dist. Atty., Middlesex Cnty., 1976–81; Practicing atty., 1981–82.

DC Office: 218 RSOB, 20510, 202-224-2742; Fax: 202-224-8525; Web site: kerry.senate.gov.

State Offices: Boston, 617-565-8519; Fall River, 508-677-0522; Springfield, 413-785-4610.

Committees: *Commerce, Science & Transportation* (3rd of 14 D): Aviation Operations, Safety & Security; Communications, Technology & the Internet (Chmn); Competitiveness, Innovation & Export Promotion; Oceans, Atmosphere, Fisheries & Coast Guard; Science & Space; Surface Transportation & Merchant Marine Infrastructure, Safety & Security. *Finance* (5th of 13 D): Energy, Natural Resources & Infrastructure; Health Care; International Trade, Customs & Global Competitiveness. *Foreign Relations* (Chmn of 11 D). *Small Business & Entrepreneurship* (2nd of 11 D).

Group Ratings

	ADA	ACLU	AFS	LCV	ITIC	NTU	COC	ACU	CFG	FRC
2008	95	92	100	100	100	4	63	4	4	11
2007	90	—	100	93	—	8	50	4	6	—

National Journal Ratings

	2007 LIB — 2007 CONS		2008 LIB — 2008 CONS	
Economic	72%	— 23%	72%	— 27%
Social	75%	— 24%	80%	— 9%
Foreign	85%	— 8%	64%	— 35%
Composite	80%	— 21%	74%	— 26%

Key Votes of the 110th Congress

1. Raise CAFE standards	Y	5. Make English official language	N	9. Withdraw troops 3/08	Y
2. Expand SCHIP	Y	6. Path to citizenship	Y	10. Iran guard is terrorist group	N
3. Cap greenhouse gases	Y	7. Fetus is unborn child	Y	11. Increase missile defense $	N
4. Bail out financial markets	Y	8. Prosecute hate crimes	Y	12. Overhaul FISA	N

Election Results

2008 general	John Kerry (D)	1,971,974	(66%)	($12,279,425)
	Jeffrey Beatty (R)	926,044	(31%)	($2,070,528)
	Robert Underwood (Lib)	93,713	(3%)	
2008 primary	John Kerry (D)	342,446	(69%)	
	Edward O'Reilly (D)	154,395	(31%)	

Prior Winning Percentages: 2002 (80%); 1996 (52%); 1990 (57%); 1984 (55%)

John Kerry, Massachusetts' junior senator, the Democratic nominee for president in 2004, and the chairman of the Senate Foreign Relations Committee, has been a figure in national politics since 1971. The son of a Foreign Service officer, he grew up all over the world and attended boarding school in Switzerland. He graduated from Yale University in 1966 and, after exploring alternatives, enlisted in the Navy. He served on a swift boat in Vietnam—hazardous duty—and was awarded a Silver Star and three Purple Hearts. Once home, Kerry's disillusionment with America's role in the war led to a period of activism, and in the early 1970s, he became one of the leaders of Vietnam Veterans Against the War. He attracted much attention for his eloquence and for his cosmopolitan background, unusual for a Vietnam veteran. Testifying before the Senate Foreign Relations Committee in April 1971, he famously stated: "How do you ask a man to be the last to die for a mistake?" He condemned "war crimes committed in Southeast Asia," which, he said, were "not isolated incidents, but crimes committed on a day-to-day basis with the full awareness of officers at all levels of command." Kerry became familiar enough to be featured in *Doonesbury* and plunged quickly into politics. He moved to Lowell, Mass., and ran for a U.S. House seat in 1972, but lost to the Republican in a district carried by Democratic presidential nominee George McGovern that year. Chastened, he went to law school and became an assistant district attorney for Middlesex County. He was elected lieutenant governor on a ticket with Democrat Michael Dukakis in 1982, and ran for senator in 1984. In both races, he upset a favored rival for the Democratic nomination.

Kerry came to the Senate with a reputation as a strong liberal but has had a somewhat less liberal record than the state's senior senator, Edward Kennedy. For some years, Kerry seemed respectful of economic free markets and more inclined to support an expansive U.S. foreign and military policy. In his first 20 years in the Senate, Kerry was not a visibly active legislator (the website *factcheck.org* reported during the 2004 presidential campaign that only 11 of his bills became law), and was arguably more influential behind the scenes. One reason may have been the prominence of his senior colleague. Kennedy has been front and center in a number of legislative arenas, as well as in Massachusetts causes, and did not invite junior colleagues to play on his turf.

Kerry made his name more as an investigator, spending some time up blind alleys but also producing some important information. As the chairman of the Foreign Relations Subcommittee on the Western Hemisphere, Peace Corps, Narcotics, and Terrorism, he investigated the infamous Bank of Credit and Commerce International scandal. Kerry's other great investigation was as chairman of the Select Committee on POW/MIA Affairs, which probed whether Americans were left behind in Vietnam. Kerry and Republican Bob Smith of New Hampshire went to Vietnam to do their own investigation, and ultimately concluded that there was "no compelling evidence that any American remains alive in captivity in Southeast Asia." By May 1995, Kerry and fellow Vietnam veteran Sen. John McCain, R-Ariz., were convinced that Hanoi was fully cooperating and, aware they had standing on the issue, convinced President Bill Clinton to normalize relations with Vietnam. Kerry has remained close with McCain, except during the heat of presidential campaigns, and also with other Vietnam veterans in the Senate, namely Nebraska Democrat Bob Kerrey (1988–2000) and Nebraska Republican Chuck Hagel (1996–2008).

When Clinton was president, Kerry took some interesting positions on issues that put him at odds with Democratic interest groups. He supported the balanced-budget amendment and voted for the welfare overhaul of 1996. In 1998, he decried the "implosion" of public education and said it was caused not just by overcrowded classrooms but also by the "stifling bureaucracy" of school systems. His list of reforms, co-sponsored with Oregon Republican Gordon Smith, included proposals strongly opposed by the teachers' unions—important backers of the Democratic Party—such as ending teacher tenure, changing certification requirements to end the education-school monopoly, and allowing lateral entry into teaching. He favored normalizing trade relations with China and led the floor fight against the Thompson-Torricelli amendment, which would have required review of China's human rights practices. Kerry also spoke out strongly in favor of the bombing of Serbia in 1999.

After Republican George W. Bush became president, Kerry turned to sharp-edged opposition to administration policy. The Bush tax cut, he said, was "unfair, unaffordable, and unquestionably ineffective in growing our economy." On the environment, he was one of the most outspoken opponents of oil drilling in the Arctic National Wildlife Refuge and threatened to filibuster the bill. He criticized the administration for its rejection of the Kyoto Protocol on climate change, although he was one of 95 senators who voted in 1997 to reject Kyoto so long as it exempted developing nations like China and India, a main feature of the treaty then and now. On foreign policy, he criticized the administration for letting Afghan troops take the lead in Tora Bora in late 2001, and said that may have allowed Qaeda and Taliban leaders to escape. Despite considerable criticism of administration policy on Iraq, he voted for the Iraq war resolution in October 2002 but said shortly afterward, "I'm going to keep asking tough questions to hold the president accountable for his promise to insist on arms inspections first, act multilaterally, and only go to war as a last resort."

Like many senators, Kerry long harbored presidential ambitions. But in February 1999, with Clinton obviously smoothing the way for then-Vice President Al Gore, Kerry announced he would not run in 2000. There were no such obstacles in his way in 2004. He had an additional advantage: money. His wife, Teresa

Heinz Kerry, inherited $600 million when her first husband, Pennsylvania Republican Sen. John Heinz, died in a 1991 plane crash. Her net worth in 2004 was estimated at around $1 billion, making Kerry one of the richest members of Congress. (In 1996, when Kerry was fending off a challenge to his Senate seat by Republican William Weld, he borrowed $1.9 million against the couple's assets. Later, in 2003, when he was trailing Howard Dean in the polls in the presidential contest, Kerry borrowed $6.4 million against his share of their Beacon Hill townhouse.)

In early 2003, Kerry entered the presidential race as the favorite to win the nomination. But by July, he was trailing in the polls far behind Dean, whose outspoken opposition to the Iraq war attracted the left wing of the Democratic electorate and whose innovative use of the Internet generated an unprecedented number of small contributions. Kerry, who had voted for the war, began to criticize Bush's conduct of it, often in harsh terms. At year's end, he was still behind. Then, in mid-January 2004, Dean's poll numbers in Iowa and New Hampshire started dropping. Well organized in Iowa and well known in New Hampshire, Kerry was the Democrat best positioned to fill the vacuum. His record in Vietnam, he suggested, would protect him against criticisms that he was too soft on foreign and military policy. "Bring it on!" he said at the end of his speeches. He won a solid though not overwhelming victory in the Iowa caucuses and, eight days later, an impressive victory in New Hampshire, the one state where primary turnout zoomed upward. Kerry won all the primaries but three and clinched the Democratic nomination on March 2, exactly eight months before the general election.

As early as May, pollster John Zogby said the election was "Kerry's to lose." The Kerry campaign raised far more money than anyone expected, and was helped as well by outside organizations that spent more than $200 million to defeat Bush. Bush's job approval hovered under 50%, and he trailed Kerry in polls for much of the seven-month campaign. Kerry performed well in debates, being judged the winner in snap polls in all three. Yet he lost. One reason may have been encapsulated by his March 16 defense of his 2003 vote against the supplemental appropriation for Iraq: "I actually did vote for the $87 billion before I voted against it." The Bush campaign painted Kerry as a flip-flopper, and in fact he has had a propensity, common in politicians, to try to please those on all sides of an issue. More important, he was trying to rally a Democratic Party split between fiercely anti-war Bush haters and moderate Democrats who hoped for the best in Iraq but preferred a Democrat to Bush on most issues. Second, the credential which the Kerry campaign emphasized at the Democratic National Convention, his decorated service in Vietnam, was undermined by the ads and book sponsored by Swift Boat Veterans for Truth. Kerry had claimed—in the *Boston Herald* in 1979, on the Senate floor in 1986, and to the Associated Press in 1992—to have served on secret missions in Cambodia in the Christmas season of 1968. But those claims were withdrawn by his campaign in August, and no one, including the boat mates who supported him, came forward to corroborate his additional claim to have served in Cambodia in later months.

Finally, Kerry was vulnerable to attack as a Massachusetts liberal. The Bush campaign highlighted his rating by *National Journal* as the No. 1 liberal in the Senate in 2003—arguably unfairly, since he skipped many roll-call votes that year while campaigning for president. However, *National Journal* had ranked him as the 11th-most-liberal senator in the course of his career, well to the left of the midpoint. And the Massachusetts Supreme Judicial Court's legalization in May 2004 of same-sex marriage provided a vivid illustration of the difference between opinion in Massachusetts and majority opinion in the rest of the country. Democratic voter-turnout efforts were successful. Kerry won 59 million votes, 16% more than Gore and the second-highest total in American history. But Republican voter-turnout efforts were even more successful. Bush won 62 million votes, 23% more than he had four years earlier, and he won the popular vote 51%-48%.

His disappointment at losing was matched only by that of the many Massachusetts politicians who were longing to run for the Senate. The state has not had an open Senate seat since Kerry secured his 1984, and before that, since 1966.

Kerry in 2005 was the first senator to return to the Senate as a defeated presidential nominee since South Dakota Democrat George McGovern in 1973. He proceeded to stake out stands on important issues. He proposed a Kids First bill, to provide health insurance for every child. Kennedy, to whom he had usually deferred on health care issues, agreed to be the lead co-sponsor. He followed up with a proposal that would require all Americans to have health insurance by 2012. In a 2006 speech in Boston, he called for reducing oil consumption by 2.5 million barrels a day by 2015, and for sharp decreases in carbon dioxide emissions to address global warming. Kerry supported the Bush administration on one foreign-policy issue in 2006, the agreement on India's civilian nuclear program, provided it pushed India to agree to international standards for safeguarding civilian nuclear plants. But he increasingly opposed the administration's course in Iraq. In June 2006, as the Senate considered an amendment calling for redeployments from Iraq with no set date, Kerry and Democrat Russ Feingold of Wisconsin insisted on bringing up an amendment to withdraw all combat forces by July 2007. It was defeated 86-13.

Kerry's course during 2005 and 2006—his continued sharp criticisms of the administration, his new proposals on major issues, his heavy travel and fundraising schedule in support of Democratic candidates—suggested he was interested in running for president again in 2008. Criticized by some Democrats for having left $15 million in his presidential account long after the 2004 election was over, he contributed more than $1 million to Democratic candidates and the national Democratic campaign committees. Of his 2002 vote for the Iraq resolution, he wrote on the left-wing *Huffington Post* blog, "There's nothing—nothing—in my life in public service I regret more, nothing even close."

Then, on October 30, 2006, at Pasadena City College, he told a crowd of students, "Education: If you make the most of it, you study hard, you do your homework, and you make an effort to be smart, you can do well. If you don't, you get stuck in Iraq." The remark was interpreted as a disparaging comment about American military troops, and to some it was reminiscent of his 1971 Foreign Relations Committee testimony. In Seattle the next day, Kerry refused to apologize and blamed Bush adviser Karl Rove for instigating demands that he do so. When criticism continued, and Democratic candidates began to ask Kerry to skip scheduled campaign appearances, Kerry and his staffers said that the comment was "a botched joke," and that he had meant to say that "you get us stuck in Iraq" —an attack on Bush and his supposedly weak academic record, although in fact Bush's marks at Yale were slightly better than Kerry's. The explanation did not prevent the cancellation of all his appearances for Democratic candidates in the last week of the midterm congressional contests. Kerry had no public events in the seven weeks after the election, and on January 24, 2007, he announced he was not running for president in 2008.

No longer a presidential candidate, Kerry turned his focus to the Senate, especially to the foreign-policy issues that capture his attention. At the World Economic Forum in Davos, Switzerland, in January 2007, he proclaimed that under Bush the United States had become "a sort of international pariah." Later that year, he called for sending 5,000 more troops to Afghanistan. By then, many other Democrats had caught up with his thinking on Iraq and were demanding a timetable for the withdrawal of U.S. troops, similar to the position expressed in the Kerry-Feingold amendment of 2006.

As chairman of the Small Business Committee, Kerry has worked effectively with the senior Republican on the panel, Olympia Snowe of Maine. They got the Securities and Exchange Commission to delay for one year imposing the strict new Sarbanes-Oxley disclosure requirements on small businesses, and they added $100 million to the 2008 supplemental appropriations bill to help small businesses access credit. With then-Rep. Rahm Emanuel, D-Ill., an influential House leader, Kerry sought to prevent hedge-fund managers from deferring compensation to offshore tax havens.

On domestic issues, he has been arguably more involved than he was before he ran for president. In the last couple of years, Kerry staked out issues ranging from insurance coverage for mental illness to better access to sports programming for everyday people. With Kennedy, he pushed for mental health parity in the State Children's Health Insurance Program, which would require the health system to cover treatment for mental illness the same as for physical illnesses. He also sought to reverse the policy barring HIV-positive people from immigrating to the United States. With the publication of his book *This Moment on Earth*, he renewed his activism on global warming. He attended the United Nations climate-change talks, and in December 2007 again criticized the Bush administration for opposing the Kyoto Protocol. With Snowe, he sponsored a bill to reduce carbon emissions 65% below 1990 levels by 2050. Kerry also proposed legislation to set speed limits on ships in Massachusetts waters to protect whales. When Major League Baseball signed an exclusive programming agreement with DirecTV, Kerry complained to Federal Communications Commission Chairman Kevin Martin, and in 2007 the league agreed to keep the games on cable. Similarly, he demanded that the National Football League make the final regular season game of the New England Patriots available to all Massachusetts cable viewers. The NFL caved.

It has been a long time since a Democratic senator from Massachusetts has been defeated for re-election. It hasn't happened since 1946, when isolationist Democrat David Walsh was defeated by inter-nationalist Republican Henry Cabot Lodge Jr. Kerry's toughest re-election race came in 1996, when he was opposed by popular Republican Gov. Weld. Earlier, the two had worked together on some state problems and emphasized the similarity of their views, but the campaign inevitably produced disagreements and some gentlemanly acrimony. They held eight debates, spent liberally—Kerry, $12.6 million, Weld, $8 million—and attracted more national media attention than anyone else that year. But Democratic Massachusetts voted 52%-45% for its junior senator. In 2008, Kerry had primary opposition from Gloucester lawyer Edward O'Reilly, who got 31% of the vote. But he had no problems in the general election against Republican nominee Jeff Beatty, who criticized Kerry for voting for the Iraq war resolution. Kerry won, 66%-31%.

Kerry enjoyed good working relationships with both candidates in the hard-fought Democratic presidential primary in 2008, but he ultimately endorsed Illinois Sen. Barack Obama over New York Sen. Hillary Rodham Clinton. He campaigned heavily for Obama, gave him his 2004 e-mail list for fundraising, and delivered a stirring speech for him at the party's convention in Denver. After the election, it was made known that Kerry would be pleased to be nominated to be secretary of State, but the job went to Clinton. Kerry did not come out of the election season empty-handed, though. He got the chairmanship of the Foreign Relations Committee after Biden was sworn in as vice president in early 2009.

FIRST DISTRICT

John Olver (D)

Elected June 1991, 9th full term; b. Sept. 3, 1936, Honesdale, PA; home, Amherst; Rensselaer Polytechnic Inst., B.S. 1955, Tufts U., M.A. 1956, M.I.T., Ph.D. 1961; no religious affiliation; married (Rose); 1 child.

Elected Office: MA House of Reps., 1968–72; MA Senate, 1972–91.

Professional Career: Chemistry prof., U. of MA, Amherst, 1961–69.

DC Office: 1111 LHOB, 20515, 202-225-5335; Fax: 202-226-1224; Web site: www.house.gov/olver.

State Offices: Fitchburg, 978-342-8722; Holyoke, 413-532-7010; Pittsfield, 413-442-0946.

Committees: *Appropriations* (11th of 37 D): Energy & Water Development; Interior, Environment & Related Agencies; Transportation, HUD & Related Agencies (Chmn).

Group Ratings

	ADA	ACLU	AFS	LCV	ITIC	NTU	COC	ACU	CFG	FRC
2008	100	100	100	100	57	6	56	0	0	0
2007	90	—	100	100	—	5	50	0	1	—

National Journal Ratings

	2007 LIB	—	2007 CONS		2008 LIB	—	2008 CONS
Economic	82%	—	0%		85%	—	0%
Social	83%	—	17%		82%	—	0%
Foreign	96%	—	0%		92%	—	0%
Composite	91%	—	9%		93%	—	7%

Key Votes of the 110th Congress

1. Increase minimum wage	Y	5. Share immigration data	N	9. Withdraw troops 8/08	Y
2. Expand SCHIP	Y	6. Foreign aid abortion ban	N	10. No operations in Iran	Y
3. Raise CAFE standards	Y	7. Ban gay bias in workplace	*	11. Free trade with Peru	N
4. Bail out financial markets	Y	8. Repeal D.C. gun law	N	12. Overhaul FISA	N

Election Results

2008 general	John Olver (D)	215,696	(73%)	($857,631)
	Nathan Bech (R)	80,067	(27%)	($157,611)
2008 primary	John Olver (D)	33,513	(79%)	
	Robert Feuer (D)	8,765	(21%)	

Prior Winning Percentages: 2006 (76%); 2004 (100%); 2002 (68%); 2000 (68%); 1998 (72%); 1996 (53%); 1994 (100%); 1992 (52%); 1991 (50%)

Population		Race/Ethnicity		Work	
Pop. 2007:	639,172	White:	87.4%	Private:	75.7%
Change since 2000:	Up 0.7%	Black:	1.9%	Government:	16.4%
Urban:	69.3%	Hispanic:	7.2%	Self-employed:	7.7%
Rural:	30.7%	Asian:	2.0%	Blue collar:	22.7%
Area size:	3,192 sq. mi.	Native Am.:	0.2%	White collar:	59.8%
		Hawaiian:	0.0%	Khaki collar:	0.1%
Age		Two+ races:	1.1%	Other:	17.4%
Median age:	38.8 yrs.			Median income:	$51,992
More than 65 yrs:	13.6%	*Ancestry*		Median home value:	$225,100
Less than 18 yrs:	21.8%	Irish:	15.1%	Poverty:	12.2%
		French:	11.7%		
Education		English:	10.6%	**Military Veterans**	
H.S. grad:	88.1%			% of Pop:	11.1%
College grad:	28.8%				
Grad degree:	11.9%				

The stony hills and green mountains of western Massachusetts, where more trees dot the landscape today than when Henry David Thoreau was writing in the 1840s and where stone fencing once bounded one working farm from another, look a lot like they did 300 years ago. This was the frontier in the 17th century, where Puritan preachers founded towns in the wilderness, farmed the rocky soil, and preached against declension. This was also the site of the Indian uprising known as King Philip's War in 1676,

2008 Presidential Vote		
Obama (D) 196,565	(64%)
McCain (R).............................102,645	(33%)
2004 Presidential Vote		
Kerry (D)................................185,377	(63%)
Bush (R) 103,990	(35%)
Cook Partisan Voting Index: D + 14		

and the Indian raid, supported by the French in Quebec, at Deerfield in 1704. This was Yankee New England's western frontier for nearly 200 years. In the 19th century, the area was the home of writers and artists: Emily Dickinson lived quietly in Amherst, Edith Wharton grandly on her estate in Lenox. Herman Melville struck up a friendship with Nathaniel Hawthorne after purchasing a farm near Hawthorne's Pittsfield home, not far from where the Boston Symphony plays at the Tanglewood Festival each summer. Mill towns were here as well, jammed into valleys or along the wide Connecticut River. As the 20th century progressed, and trees grew on stony land once farmed, western Massachusetts came to look less settled. The exceptions were areas near giant factories like General Electric's now-closed electric transformer plant in Pittsfield and the Crane paper factory in Dalton, which since 1879 has been the only company to print money for the U.S. Treasury. Armed guards protect the facility's secret plating process, which is the benchmark for producing currency and preventing counterfeiting. The region's rolling hills and charming New England towns support a thriving tourist trade, featuring attractions such as Tanglewood and Jacob's Pillow, the only dance institution to be named a National Historic Landmark. There are year-round, weekend, and vacation homes throughout the Berkshires. Democratic Gov. Deval Patrick, who has a weekend home here, encouraged expansion of Internet access to many of these small towns. Truck farmers promote their sometimes-quirky products, including hard cider and pickles. But the area's iconic local fairs have fallen on hard times in recent years.

Western Massachusetts has changed politically. For many years, it was a heartland of the Republican Party—flinty, thrifty, and chilly, just like the area's most famous politician, Calvin Coolidge. But the area now contains some of the most liberal parts of the United States. Stockbridge attracted artist Norman Rockwell, and Alice's Restaurant in Great Barrington was immortalized by radical Arlo Guthrie in his antiwar song of the same name. The concentration of colleges and universities in the Pioneer Valley brought together a critical mass of liberal scholars and an even more leftist graduate student community; the University of Massachusetts in Amherst is the largest of these. Although the area's few remaining mills have shut down, the university continues to expand on former farmland. The results of the liberal trend showed up in election returns: Democratic presidential nominee Barack Obama carried Amherst 87%-10% over Republican John McCain in 2008. Western Massachusetts also voted heavily for Democrat Shannon O'Brien for governor in 2002, even as she lost the rest of Massachusetts to Republican Mitt Romney.

The 1st Congressional District is the state's largest congressional district geographically. It covers most of western Massachusetts—all of Berkshire and Franklin counties and their small towns; most of Hampshire County; Holyoke and West Springfield on the Connecticut River; and the more-working-class areas of northern Worcester County—and extends east to Pepperell in Middlesex County, about 40 miles from Boston. It borders four states and covers about 40% of the land area of Massachusetts. Over time, the solidly Democratic voting base has shifted from low-income mill workers in places like Holyoke and Pittsfield to liberal and radical academics in the college towns.

The congressman from the 1st District is John Olver, a Democrat who won a June 1991 special election after the death of longtime Republican Rep. Silvio Conte. Olver was educated at Tufts University and MIT, arriving at the University of Massachusetts as a chemistry professor in 1961, at age 25. His wife, Rose, is a professor of psychology and women's and gender studies at Amherst College. In 1968, he began a 22-year career in the Legislature. In the special election to replace Conte, his Pioneer Valley base helped him win 31% in the fragmented Democratic primary. In the general, he faced Steven Pierce, former state House Republican leader and Gov. William Weld's conservative opponent in the 1990 primary. With Massachusetts liberalism in disrepute after Gov. Michael Dukakis lost the 1988 presidential campaign, the contest was close. Weld made certain to schedule it after students' summer vacation began, when the area had emptied out of liberal voters. Olver nevertheless pulled off a close 50%-48% win, becoming the first Democrat to hold the seat since the Spanish-American War.

Olver has one of the most liberal voting records in the House. He has voted against international trade deals, and he favors conversion to a Canadian-style single-payer health care system. He chairs the Appropriations Subcommittee on Transportation, Housing and Urban Development, and Related Agencies, where he has sought to expand Amtrak train service and subsidies in the Northeast Corridor. In 2007, he increased funding for housing vouchers, public transit, and community development block grants. He was an early critic of President George W. Bush's Housing and Urban Development secretary, Alphonso Jackson, for "political favoritism" and called for Jackson's resignation 18 months before he finally quit in March 2008. Olver has also advocated increased federal support for bicycling, for recreation and transportation. His work to fund local projects drew criticism in the 110th Congress (2007–08) from congressional watchdog groups opposed to excessive earmarks, the special-projects funding that lawmakers insert into spending bills. Earmarks that he funded in 2007 included $6 million for the commuter train line from Fitchburg to Boston, $1 million for fiber-optics development along Interstate 91, and $265,000 for an arts center annex at the Amherst Cinema. Some Massachusetts Democrats have complained that as the state's only Appropriations member, he hasn't done much for the Boston area. He warned against expectations of an "easy pot of money."

Outside of his Appropriations work, Olver helped to organize the House bipartisan Climate Change Caucus and sponsored legislation to cap greenhouse gas emissions. In January 2008, the House passed his bill to add hiking trails in his district. On the housing mortgage bailout bills in 2008, he worked with Financial Services Committee Chairman Barney Frank of Massachusetts to increase aid for owners of foreclosed properties. Although he had earlier co-sponsored a resolution calling for an impeachment investigation of President Bush and Vice President Cheney—a popular idea in this district—he voted in 2007 against a resolution by Rep. Dennis Kucinich, a liberal Democrat from Ohio, to impeach Cheney, calling it a "totally destructive" move that would divide Democrats. Olver, who does not seem to be a politician by nature, dislikes fundraising. He prefers to rock climb, a solitary endeavor. In a state delegation filled with natural-born politicos, Olver is notably shy and ambivalent about the media limelight. An exception was his April 2006 arrest with four other House Democrats; all were handcuffed and briefly jailed for protesting the violence in Darfur at the Sudanese Embassy in Washington.

Olver has had only one close contest for re-election. In 1996, he beat Republican Jane Swift, then a state representative and later governor, 53%-47%. Obama's presidential campaign manager, David Plouffe, ran Olver's first re-election campaign. In 2008, Stockbridge lawyer Robert Feuer challenged Olver in the primary for his inaction on impeaching Bush; Olver won 79%-21%. With Massachusetts likely to lose a seat in 2010's reapportionment, Olver has acknowledged that his rambling district is an obvious target for Boston-area pols. The longer he holds the seat, the less likely a successor can stake a claim. In 2005, Olver was hospitalized with a brain infection, but he has recovered.

SECOND DISTRICT

Richard Neal (D)

Elected 1988, 11th term; b. Feb. 14, 1949, Springfield; home, Springfield; Amer. Intl. Col., B.A. 1972, U. of Hartford, M.A. 1976; Catholic; married (Maureen).

Elected Office: Springfield City Cncl., 1978–83; Springfield mayor, 1984–88.

Professional Career: Staff asst., Springfield Mayor William C. Sullivan, 1973–78; High schl. & col. teacher, 1978–83.

DC Office: 2208 RHOB, 20515, 202-225-5601; Fax: 202-225-8112; Web site: www.house.gov/neal.

State Offices: Milford, 508-634-8198; Springfield, 413-785-0325.

Committees: *Ways & Means* (6th of 26 D): Select Revenue Measures (Chmn); Trade.

Group Ratings

	ADA	ACLU	AFS	LCV	ITIC	NTU	COC	ACU	CFG	FRC
2008	100	100	100	100	100	4	61	0	0	5
2007	95	—	100	95	—	4	55	0	11	—

National Journal Ratings

	2007 LIB — 2007 CONS		2008 LIB — 2008 CONS	
Economic	82%	— 0%	85%	— 0%
Social	77%	— 17%	82%	— 0%
Foreign	90%	— 8%	85%	— 8%
Composite	87%	— 13%	91%	— 9%

Key Votes of the 110th Congress

1. Increase minimum wage	Y	5. Share immigration data	N	9. Withdraw troops 8/08	Y
2. Expand SCHIP	Y	6. Foreign aid abortion ban	N	10. No operations in Iran	Y
3. Raise CAFE standards	Y	7. Ban gay bias in workplace	Y	11. Free trade with Peru	Y
4. Bail out financial markets	Y	8. Repeal D.C. gun law	N	12. Overhaul FISA	N

Election Results

2008 general	Richard Neal (D) 234,369	(98%)	($766,166)
2008 primary	Richard Neal (D) .... unopposed		

Prior Winning Percentages: 2006 (100%); 2004 (100%); 2002 (100%); 2000 (100%); 1998 (100%); 1996 (72%); 1994 (59%); 1992 (53%); 1990 (100%); 1988 (80%)

Population		Race/Ethnicity		Work	
Pop. 2007:	652,404	White:	79.6%	Private:	79.5%
Change since 2000:	Up 2.8%	Black:	5.8%	Government:	13.9%
Urban:	84.8%	Hispanic:	11.3%	Self-employed:	6.4%
Rural:	15.2%	Asian:	1.8%	Blue collar:	21.6%
Area size:	952 sq. mi.	Native Am.:	0.1%	White collar:	60.6%
Age		Hawaiian:	0.0%	Khaki collar:	0.1%
Median age:	37.9 yrs.	Two+ races:	1.2%	Other:	17.7%
More than 65 yrs:	13.1%	*Ancestry*		Median income:	$54,420
Less than 18 yrs:	23.9%	Irish:	14.4%	Median home value:	$235,700
Education		French:	11.9%	Poverty:	11.8%
H.S. grad:	85.5%	Italian:	9.6%	**Military Veterans**	
College grad:	27.2%			% of Pop:	10.6%
Grad degree:	10.4%				

It's as American as apple pie, the place where basketball was invented, the city where the Webster's unabridged dictionaries (2nd and 3rd editions) were edited and published, and the site of the armory where unhappy soldiers mounted the Shays' Rebellion in 1786–87. This is Springfield, Mass., the third-largest city in the Bay State, but far from Boston. Historically overshadowed by Hartford as the center of the Connecticut River Valley, it is a medium-sized American city built by New England

2008 Presidential Vote		
Obama (D) 179,466	(59%)
McCain (R)...........................117,742	(39%)

2004 Presidential Vote		
Kerry (D)................................169,460	(59%)
Bush (R) 113,284	(40%)

Cook Partisan Voting Index: D + 9

Yankees. Immigrants from a dozen countries have worked their way up here. Blacks and Hispanics account for nearly half of its population. Like other New England city centers, Springfield's downtown has emptied and its tax base has shrunk. Business leaders have tried to revive it, in part with the expansion of the Basketball Hall of Fame. But the once-powerful city has suffered from corruption and serious crime, and in 2004, it was forced to submit to state control in a financial bailout. In 2007, the online *bizjournals* rated Springfield the worst metropolitan area in the country for small business, and in 2006, the Census Bureau said it was sixth in the nation in the number of children living in poverty. Recent efforts to revive downtown have included a new federal courthouse; a huge expansion of the Baystate Medical Center; and plans to redevelop Union Station, which has been empty since the early 1970s. Local companies, too, have had to adapt. In the 1990s, the gun manufacturer Smith & Wesson embraced the marketing restrictions sought by gun control advocates and then saw its sales sag, as gun control opponents—its natural market—shunned its products. Under new ownership, it abandoned that stance and sales rose again. Springfield is the home of *Talkers* magazine, known as "the bible of talk radio."

Springfield is the largest city in the 2nd Congressional District of Massachusetts, which stretches east from Springfield to a point 30 miles southwest of Boston. Its irregular boundaries travel north to South Hadley and Northampton ("Hamp" to locals; "NoHo" to the younger artsy crowd) and take in Mount Holyoke and Smith colleges. Since the downturn in the 1970s, trendy restaurants and avant-garde liberalism have revived these tourist destinations. To the east, the district stretches across stony hills and beyond Worcester to the antique center of Brimfield and the factory towns of the Blackstone Valley just north of Woonsocket, R.I. This was a Yankee Republican district for much of the 20th century, then a solidly Catholic Democratic district. Now it is more diverse culturally and even more solidly Democratic.

The congressman from the 2nd District is Richard Neal, a Democrat elected in 1988. Neal grew up in Springfield amid the acute racial tensions of the mid-1960s. His parents died when he was a teenager, and Neal and his younger sisters received monthly Social Security survivor benefits while being raised by their grandmother and aunt. He graduated from American International College and earned a master's degree in public administration from the University of Hartford. In Springfield, he worked for the mayor; and in 1978, while teaching high school and college history, he was elected to the City Council. As mayor from 1984 to 1988, Neal worked to rehabilitate the downtown area and revitalize neighborhoods. His congressional predecessor, 36-year-incumbent Edward Boland, a longtime pal of former Democratic House Speaker Thomas (Tip) O'Neill, essentially bequeathed him the House seat. Boland announced his retirement just before the filing deadline, and after Neal had traveled the district for a year. Unopposed in the Democratic primary, Neal won the general election with 80% of the vote.

Neal has a generally liberal voting record but has favored enough moderate initiatives to separate himself from more-liberal Massachusetts colleagues. Having depended on Social Security after the death of his parents, he reveres the legacy of Franklin D. Roosevelt. He voted for the 1996 welfare overhaul, a ban on partial-birth abortions, and a federal prohibition on same-sex marriages. He has reversed his earlier opposition to embryonic-stem-cell research. Neal serves on the influential House Ways and Means Committee. Major issues facing the committee over the years have included the North American Free Trade Agreement and normalization of trade relations with China, both of which Neal supported. He also sponsored legislation to drop the requirement that 401(k) plans offer at least one low-cost index fund. In October 2008, he helped to enact expanded tax credits for alternative forms of energy, but the Senate prevailed in blocking other tax hikes as offsets.

Neal is rising in seniority at Ways and Means, and he chairs the Select Revenue Measures Subcommittee, which handles many tax and tariff bills. He has tried to simplify the tax code and has crusaded for repeal of the alternative minimum tax, which was designed to ensure that the wealthy pay a fair share of taxes but which has been increasingly ensnaring middle-income taxpayers. In November 2007, he won House approval of a one-year fix of the alternative minimum tax that he "paid for" with offsets in other parts of the federal budget. The Senate, however, refused to support the bill. He took the lead for House Democrats on a popular proposal to clamp down on companies that incorporate in Bermuda and other offshore havens to avoid U.S. taxes. He gave the initiative additional bite when he directed its fire at companies that moved offshore after September 11, terming it the "Corporate Patriot Enforcement Act." He has held hearings to explore such topics as how the tax code penalizes veterans and their families, and a proposal to require businesses to enroll their employees in retirement savings accounts.

Like many other Irish Catholic politicians over the years, Neal has encouraged American attempts at reconciliation in Northern Ireland. He personally lobbied President Bill Clinton to grant a visa for Gerry Adams, president of Sinn Fein, to visit the United States, and he chairs the Friends of Ireland Committee. In 2005, he urged Adams to disband the Irish Republican Army "sooner rather than later," and he traveled to Ireland in April 2007 to reaffirm support for the peace process as the power-sharing agreement was signed. In spring 2008, outgoing Prime Minister Bertie Ahern praised Neal in a speech before a joint session of Congress. In other foreign-policy arenas, Neal in 2002 voted against the Iraq war resolution.

Neal has also focused on the economic problems of Springfield and in 2007 was instrumental in securing a $22 million grant for renovation of its Union Station. He confronted serious primary challenges in 1990 and 1992, but won re-election by satisfactory margins. Republicans have never mounted a credible opposition against him. He last faced a GOP challenger in 1996. He was an early supporter of Democrat Hillary Rodham Clinton for president in 2008 and actively campaigned for her. Neal teaches a course at the University of Massachusetts called The Politician and the Journalist.

THIRD DISTRICT

Jim McGovern (D)

Elected 1996, 7th term; b. Nov. 20, 1959, Worcester; home, Worcester; American U., B.A. 1981, M.P.A. 1984; Catholic; married (Lisa); 2 children.

Professional Career: Aide, U.S. Sen. George McGovern, 1977–80; Sr. aide, U.S. Rep. Joseph Moakley, 1982–96.

DC Office: 438 CHOB, 20515, 202-225-6101; Fax: 202-225-5759; Web site: mcgovern.house.gov.

State Offices: Attleboro, 508-431-8025; Fall River, 508-677-0140; Marlborough, 508-460-9292; Worcester, 508-831-7356.

Committees: *Budget* (9th of 24 D). *Rules* (2nd of 9 D): Rules & Organization of the House (Chmn).

Group Ratings

	ADA	ACLU	AFS	LCV	ITIC	NTU	COC	ACU	CFG	FRC
2008	100	100	100	100	86	6	50	0	4	5
2007	95	—	100	100	—	4	50	0	1	—

National Journal Ratings

	2007 LIB	—	2007 CONS	2008 LIB	—	2008 CONS
Economic	82%	—	0%	85%	—	0%
Social	92%	—	0%	82%	—	0%
Foreign	96%	—	0%	85%	—	8%
Composite	95%	—	5%	91%	—	9%

Key Votes of the 110th Congress

1. Increase minimum wage	Y	5. Share immigration data	N	9. Withdraw troops 8/08	Y
2. Expand SCHIP	Y	6. Foreign aid abortion ban	N	10. No operations in Iran	Y
3. Raise CAFE standards	Y	7. Ban gay bias in workplace	Y	11. Free trade with Peru	N
4. Bail out financial markets	Y	8. Repeal D.C. gun law	N	12. Overhaul FISA	N

Election Results

2008 general	Jim McGovern (D)...227,619	(98%)		($848,694)
2008 primary	Jim McGovern (D)... unopposed			

Prior Winning Percentages: 2006 (100%); 2004 (71%); 2002 (100%); 2000 (100%); 1998 (57%); 1996 (53%)

Population		Race/Ethnicity		Work	
Pop. 2007:	648,101	White:	83.5%	Private:	82.3%
Change since 2000:	Up 2.1%	Black:	3.1%	Government:	11.9%
Urban:	93.4%	Hispanic:	7.4%	Self-employed:	5.7%
Rural:	6.6%	Asian:	4.3%	Blue collar:	18.0%
Area size:	612 sq. mi.	Native Am.:	0.1%	White collar:	66.2%
		Hawaiian:	0.0%	Khaki collar:	0.0%
Age		Two+ races:	1.1%	Other:	15.7%
Median age:	37.8 yrs.	*Ancestry*		Median income:	$62,130
More than 65 yrs:	12.4%	Irish:	17.0%	Median home value:	$335,500
Less than 18 yrs:	24.4%	Italian:	10.0%	Poverty:	9.3%
Education		French:	9.1%	**Military Veterans**	
H.S. grad:	86.5%			% of Pop:	9.0%
College grad:	35.0%				
Grad degree:	13.2%				

Worcester is still pronounced with a particularly pungent Massachusetts accent making it sound as though it had no *r*'s. For more than 200 years, it has been one of the nation's centers of tinkering, contriving, and inventing, even though it is one of the few active industrial cities not located on a river, lake, or seacoast. In the mid-19th century, the city won renown as the valentine-making capital of the United States for its production of lavish valentines and other greeting cards. Fifty years ago, Worces-

2008 Presidential Vote

Obama (D)	175,951	(59%)
McCain (R)	117,862	(39%)

2004 Presidential Vote

Kerry (D)	167,402	(59%)
Bush (R)	112,957	(40%)

Cook Partisan Voting Index: D + 9

ter's biggest industries were wire-making, textiles, grinding wheels, and envelopes. It is where the birth control pill was invented and where Worcester native and Clark University professor Robert Goddard shot off experimental rockets before relieved locals saw him off to New Mexico.

In the 1970s and 1980s, electronics and computer firms sprouted along Interstate 495—the circumferential highway 20 miles east of Worcester—just as they had earlier around Route 128, closer to Boston. The high-tech boom brought prosperity, labor shortages, new residents, and higher housing prices to central Massachusetts. Then, in the early 1990s, the minicomputer industry slumped, bringing a recession. But Worcester's ingenious entrepreneurs and skilled labor force hustled, and local leaders set up a Biotechnology Research Institute to draw on the city's nine colleges and the University of Massachusetts Medical School to steer the city back on course. Holy Cross College offered free tuition to students of local families earning less than $50,000 annually. Just as the city's economy has changed, so has its face, with a 78% increase in Asians, 55% increase in blacks, and a 61% increase in Hispanics, mainly from Puerto Rico, in the 1990s. Overall, population declined 20% between 1950 and 1980 but increased 7% from 1980 to 2000 and an additional 5% since then, as the area attracted Hmong, Albanians, and Africans, many thousands of whom had fled the civil war in Liberia. The local cable television station airs Latino programming. That rebound contrasts with nearby Springfield and Hartford, and enabled Worcester to pass Providence as New England's second-largest city, behind Boston. Since 2000, Worcester County has led the state in growth.

The 3rd Congressional District of Massachusetts has Worcester as its largest city but not its geographic center. A little more than half of its residents live in Worcester and a cluster of adjacent towns. The other population cluster is 60 miles away, in and around the old textile mill town of Fall River, east of Rhode Island. The two are connected by a string of towns that reaches almost to Buzzards Bay. In national elections since 1992, this district has been solidly Democratic. In recent gubernatorial elections, however, the 3rd has been mixed. Worcester and Fall River (only a portion of which is in the district) voted by significant margins for Democrat Shannon O'Brien in 2002. But the Interstate 495 corridor and the towns northeast of Rhode Island gave even larger margins to Republican Mitt Romney. In 2006, Democrat Deval Patrick won by almost 3-1 ratios in Worcester and Fall River and lost only a handful of towns here.

The congressman from the 3rd District is Jim McGovern, a Democrat first elected in 1996. McGovern grew up in Worcester, where his parents owned a liquor store. He attended American University in Washington, and, while in graduate school, he worked in the office of then-Sen. George McGovern (no relation), a South Dakota Democrat. He ran McGovern's 1984 campaign in the Massachusetts presidential primary, where the senator finished third with 21% of the vote. He also nominated McGovern at the Democratic convention in San Francisco. He went to work as an aide to Boston-area Rep. Joe Moakley's office and became chief of staff just as Moakley ascended to chairman of the Rules Committee. McGovern got into the spotlight himself, leading a 1989 investigation of the murders of six Jesuits and two lay women in El Salvador, which led to a cutoff of U.S. aid to the country. In 1994, he ran for the House and lost in the Democratic primary, 38%-30%. In 1996, he ran again, this time with no primary opposition. In the general election, two-term Republican Rep. Peter Blute stressed his "independence" from the conservative Republican leadership in the House and attacked McGovern for liberal stands on abortion rights and Cuba. McGovern ran a humorous spot that asked, "If you wouldn't vote for Newt, why would you ever vote for Blute?" At age 36, McGovern won, 53%-45%.

With deft maneuvers reflecting his Capitol Hill experience, McGovern has positioned himself to become a power broker in the Democratic majority. In 2001, the dying Moakley personally asked Democratic Leader Dick Gephardt to help McGovern get a seat on Rules, which schedules most legislation for the House floor. As it turned out, the next seat went to Florida's Alcee Hastings, a member of the Congressional Black Caucus, but McGovern got a commitment for the next available Democratic seat, with seniority over Hastings. On Rules, he immediately showed familiarity with House procedures. As the No. 2 Democrat and in the majority for the first time, he said he gladly moved from "being a pain in the ass [in the minority] to more of an advocate for respect, inclusion, and fairness." With the roles reversed, he showed a sharp partisan edge as he embraced parliamentary maneuvers that led to cries of outrage from House Republicans. McGovern conceded, "We're not as open as I'd like," and said that Democratic leaders should be more willing to lose a few votes for the sake of inclusion. He also took a seat on the Budget Committee. With his considerable leverage, he became a party leader on strategizing Iraq war policy, though with little immediate success. In February 2007, he sponsored a bill to withdraw U.S. troops from Iraq in six months. The House defeated it in May on a surprisingly close 255-171 vote. In October 2007, he along with Democrats David Obey of Wisconsin and John Murtha of Pennsylvania proposed a war surtax, but Democratic leaders rejected it. In June 2008, McGovern called for the United Nations to replace U.S. forces in Iraq. The House Judiciary Committee in July 2008 approved his bill to prevent the summary deportation of foreign spouses of deceased U.S. citizens.

McGovern has a solid liberal voting record. He is a member of the Cuba Working Group, which has called for easing sanctions against the Castro regime. He has won bipartisan House votes to lift the travel ban to the island. He contends that the U.S. embargo has not achieved its goal of improving human rights and the economic situation in Cuba, and that only a change in policy, not continued sanctions, will improve living conditions and foment democratic reforms there. He also worked to release U.S. hostages held by the Colombian militant group FARC months before their July 2008 liberation in a government-led effort. Citing human rights violations, he has been a leading opponent of the U.S. free trade deal with Colombia. As the co-chair of the Human Rights Caucus, he called for a U.S. boycott of the 2008 Olympics in Beijing. McGovern chairs the Congressional Hunger Center, and in 2007 he participated in a one-week "food stamp challenge" in which he spent no more than $21 on food. He has pushed for more spending on international nutrition and for less support of biofuels, which he says have driven up food costs.

On issues affecting his district, McGovern led opposition to a proposed liquefied natural gas plant on the Taunton River. The Coast Guard ruled that the river was not safe for LNG tankers and blocked construction. In December 2007, he got $750,000 to redevelop the Blackstone Canal between Worcester and Providence. Although Republicans held this seat not long ago, they have given up on it. McGovern was unopposed in four of the past five congressional elections.

FOURTH DISTRICT

Barney Frank (D)

Elected 1980, 15th term; b. March 31, 1940, Bayonne, NJ; home, Newton; Harvard U., B.A. 1962, J.D. 1977; Jewish; single.

Elected Office: MA House of Reps., 1972–80.

Professional Career: Exec. asst., Boston Mayor Kevin White, 1967–71; A.A., U.S. Rep. Michael Harrington, 1971–72; Teaching fellow, Harvard JFK Schl. of Govt., 1978–80.

DC Office: 2252 RHOB, 20515, 202-225-5931; Fax: 202-225-0182; Web site: www.house.gov/frank.

State Offices: New Bedford, 508-999-6462; Newton, 617-332-3920; Taunton, 508-822-4796.

Committees: *Financial Services* (Chmn of 42 D).

Group Ratings

	ADA	ACLU	AFS	LCV	ITIC	NTU	COC	ACU	CFG	FRC
2008	100	100	100	100	100	6	61	0	4	0
2007	95	—	100	80	—	7	60	0	12	—

National Journal Ratings

	2007 LIB — 2007 CONS		2008 LIB — 2008 CONS	
Economic	82%	— 0%	85%	— 0%
Social	84%	— 15%	82%	— 0%
Foreign	93%	— 6%	85%	— 8%
Composite	90%	— 10%	91%	— 9%

Key Votes of the 110th Congress

1. Increase minimum wage	Y	5. Share immigration data	N	9. Withdraw troops 8/08	Y
2. Expand SCHIP	Y	6. Foreign aid abortion ban	N	10. No operations in Iran	Y
3. Raise CAFE standards	Y	7. Ban gay bias in workplace	Y	11. Free trade with Peru	Y
4. Bail out financial markets	Y	8. Repeal D.C. gun law	N	12. Overhaul FISA	N

Election Results

2008 general	Barney Frank (D)	203,032	(68%)	($2,953,741)
	Earl Sholley (R)	75,571	(25%)	($39,038)
	Susan Allen (I)	19,848	(7%)	
2008 primary	Barney Frank (D)	unopposed		

Prior Winning Percentages: 2006 (100%); 2004 (78%); 2002 (100%); 2000 (75%); 1998 (100%); 1996 (72%); 1994 (100%); 1992 (68%); 1990 (66%); 1988 (70%); 1986 (89%); 1984 (74%); 1982 (60%); 1980 (52%)

Population		Race/Ethnicity		Work	
Pop. 2007:	659,377	White:	85.8%	Private:	80.0%
Change since 2000:	Up 3.9%	Black:	3.1%	Government:	12.7%
Urban:	88.2%	Hispanic:	4.1%	Self-employed:	7.1%
Rural:	11.8%	Asian:	4.1%	Blue collar:	17.5%
Area size:	844 sq. mi.	Native Am.:	0.2%	White collar:	67.7%
		Hawaiian:	0.0%	Khaki collar:	0.1%
Age		Two+ races:	1.6%	Other:	14.7%
Median age:	38.5 yrs.			Median income:	$66,157
More than 65 yrs:	13.4%	*Ancestry*		Median home value:	$389,200
Less than 18 yrs:	23.1%	Irish:	14.4%	Poverty:	8.8%
		Portuguese:	13.9%		
Education		English:	9.7%	**Military Veterans**	
H.S. grad:	85.8%			% of Pop:	8.5%
College grad:	39.8%				
Grad degree:	19.3%				

The political transformation of Massachusetts is nowhere better illustrated than in the Boston suburbs of Brookline and Newton. These were Yankee enclaves a century ago, with avenues built to resemble the sweep of Haussmann's Grand Boulevards in Paris and villages of giant clapboard houses clustered within a few blocks of commuter rail stations. Brookline was where the Country Club (the very first one) was established in 1882, and where Joseph Kennedy, an Irish Catholic 20-something

2008 Presidential Vote

Obama (D)	198,079	(63%)
McCain (R)	107,758	(35%)

2004 Presidential Vote

Kerry (D)	194,914	(65%)
Bush (R)	99,878	(33%)

Cook Partisan Voting Index: D + 14

banker seeking respectability, moved his family in 1914. Brookline and Newton then were solidly Republican in politics, the base of such leading politicians as Christian Herter, the governor of Massachusetts and U.S. secretary of State in the 1950s. As late as 1960, Brookline, Newton, and adjacent wards of Boston were electing a Republican to Congress. Then came the transformation, personified by the election in 1962 of Michael Dukakis at age 29 to the Great and General Court (the Legislature). As Massachusetts' university-educated classes became more liberal, as Brookline's and Newton's Jewish populations grew, and as young, liberal-minded families refurbished the graceful old houses, these towns became Democratic bastions. Now there are an increasing number of Russian Jews and of Orthodox and Hasidic synagogues. Brookline and Newton are part of the liberal heart of Massachusetts. In recent presidential contests, they voted 73%-19% for Al Gore in 2000, 77%-22% for John Kerry in 2004, and 78%-21% for Barack Obama in 2008.

The 4th Congressional District of Massachusetts includes Brookline and Newton. Anchoring the hook-like northern tip of the district, they account for less than one-quarter of the district's votes. The shape results from successive redistrictings. New Bedford and Fall River are close to the ocean, and New

Bedford is proud of the Greek revival architecture of its great whaling days, when it was one of the richest cities in the country. It stages a daylong reading of *Moby Dick* every January 3, the day that Ishmael and his friend Queequeg sailed out under the command of Captain Ahab. Today, it is home to many Portuguese-Americans, many of them fishermen, who haul in groundfish and scallops. Fall River was famous for years as the home of Lizzie Borden, who was suspected of killing her father and mother with an ax in 1892. New Bedford and Fall River have long been working-class Democratic enclaves. Connecting the two sets of Democratic cities, in a corridor sometimes only a mile wide, is a series of towns—Wellesley, Dover, Sherborn, Millis, Norfolk, and Sharon. There is a little of bit of everything here: the high-income and WASPy denizens of Wellesley, the French-Canadian mill workers of Fall River, the sports-loving residents of Foxborough with its Patriots football stadium, the Orthodox Jews of Sharon, and the countrified atmosphere of Dover. This is a very Democratic district, although a handful of the suburban towns voted for Republican Lt. Gov. Kerry Healey for governor in 2006 over Democrat Deval Patrick. Democratic presidential nominee Obama carried the district 63%-35%.

The congressman from the 4th District is Barney Frank, an influential Democrat elected to the House in 1980. He is chairman of the Financial Services Committee, a savvy legislator known for his keen intelligence and sharp tongue. Frank grew up in Bayonne, N.J. His father ran a truck stop on the New Jersey Turnpike and loved to talk politics. All four of his children went on to careers in government service and politics. Barney distinguished himself as a student and was accepted at Harvard, where he got to know local politicians as well as political scientists. In 1967, he took a job as an aide to newly elected Boston Mayor Kevin White, and four years later, he arrived in Washington as an aide to Democratic Rep. Michael Harrington of Massachusetts. In 1972, Frank was elected to the Massachusetts House from Boston's Back Bay, which was transitioning from a staid Republican bastion to a liberal singles neighborhood. In 1980, when Democratic Rep. Robert Drinan retired after Pope John Paul II commanded Jesuits to leave elective office, Frank moved to Brookline and ran in the 4th District. With a strong base in Brookline and Newton, he won. After redistricting threw him in with Republican Rep. Margaret Heckler in 1982, he defeated her 60%-40%. He has been re-elected by wide margins since.

In the House, Frank quickly gained a reputation for his smarts and debating skills. He is perhaps one of the best debaters in modern American history, with a distinct, rapid-fire style that makes his less able opponents seem dull-witted by comparison. In a *Washingtonian* magazine poll of congressional staffers in 2006, he was voted the brainiest, funniest, and most eloquent member of the House. He is admired even by Republicans for his intellectual rigor and honesty. At the same time, he is a wily political operator. He does not profess to be a political theoretician, though few in the House exceed him as such. Frank once said, "My job is to be the mediator between people who have policy ideas and public policy. My strength is to be able to understand policy ideas and decide how best to implement them. I am about the political process. I know the rules of the House as much as anybody. I am a wonk about how to get things done, more than about what to do." In his early years in the House, he often worked behind the scenes on substantive issues. After Republicans won control of Congress in 1994, Frank started spending much more time on the floor, pouncing on the new majority's mistakes, criticizing its policies, and taking it to task when he felt its treatment of the minority was unfair.

Much of his focus in recent years has been on issues involving the House Financial Services Committee. He became the panel's ranking member in 2003 and its chairman in 2007, after Democrats became the House majority. The committee has not been as partisan as many in Congress, and Frank has frequently cooperated with Republicans. He worked with Rep. Spencer Bachus, R-Ala., now the ranking member, on debt relief for poor countries. Frank joined with the late Paul Gillmor, an Ohio Republican, to prevent Wal-Mart from getting into the banking business. He mastered the complex subjects covered by the committee: securities, corporate governance, accounting issues, and insurance. The regulatory matters that come before the committee are heavily lobbied, the negative effects of bad decisions can be long-lasting, and many issues do not break down along party lines.

Unlike previous Democrats who have chaired this committee—notably Wright Patman of Texas in the 1960s and 1970s—Frank believes in the efficiency and productivity of markets. "I think people may misunderstand what being a liberal means. I really do believe in the free market. You need inequality in the capitalist system, but we are at a point now where we are getting more inequality than is necessary for efficiency or socially helpful. The role of government should put some limits on that inequality, through raising the minimum wage, encouraging unions, providing public-sector programs that help people go to college," he says. Frank has argued that the U.S. economy is at an "inflection point" where it is easier to create wealth than jobs. During the 2006 election season, he spoke frequently about the need for a "grand bargain" between business and liberals. Such pro-growth policies as free-trade agreements and tax cuts, in his view, have tended to widen economic inequality. His grand bargain would have Republicans accept a hike in the minimum wage, a tax increase on high-income earners, and union certification based on the signatures of a majority of workers rather than a secret-ballot election. It would have Democrats accept free-trade agreements with labor and environmental measures that meet "minimal standards of civility," while accepting foreign direct investment in the United States without restriction. "I want to get the people who have been concerned about equity to support growth policies and the people who have been chafing that we aren't doing enough for growth to support policies that provide equity," Frank says. He can claim that he has been carrying out his side of the bargain: He has supported many free-trade agreements and has trenchantly criticized and voted against farm subsidies backed by most Democrats. He argues that "employer-paid health care is a mistake" that "depresses wages" — a point that former Republican President George W. Bush was fond of making.

An issue close to his heart is affordable housing. He has long been a supporter of the government-sponsored enterprises Fannie Mae and Freddie Mac, and has encouraged them to set higher affordable-housing goals. He sponsored legislation to require them to contribute a percentage of their after-tax income to an affordable-housing fund. He has also fought for more vouchers for public housing to replace the old Section 8 program. In 2007, Frank introduced a bill calling for strict limits on the GSEs' portfolios to deter abuses, along with his affordable-housing fund—his version of "getting the federal government back in the business of housing."

Frank has worked on a variety of other issues. He sponsored a predatory lending bill in 2005 that was modeled after a North Carolina law, highlighting data showing discrimination against African-Americans in setting mortgage rates. With then-Republican Committee Chairman Michael Oxley of Ohio, he sponsored a bill that year to allow national banks to engage in real estate brokerage and management. He opposed the Securities and Exchange Commission regulation requiring mutual funds to have independent directors. In 2006, during the furor over a proposal by Dubai Ports World, a United Arab Emirates company, to take over operations at six U.S. ports, Frank cautioned that it would be unwise to put too many limits on foreign direct investment in the United States.

In the majority, Frank initially focused on the credit crunch for housing, and then moved on to even more difficult challenges in the real estate and banking industries and in the overall economy. As the nation headed toward recession in September 2007, he won House approval of a bill designed to expand homeownership by easing loan rates to borrowers who were suffering from the meltdown in the subprime mortgage market. The next month, Frank won passage, with Republican support, of a bill to create an affordable-housing trust fund for low-income families, with the goal of producing 1.5 million housing units in the next decade. After the collapse of the investment bank Bear Stearns in March 2008, Frank moved a bill requiring investment banking houses to hold larger capital reserves similar to commercial banks. Major damage to the financial system "was done by inadequate regulation," he said. In July 2008, as federal mortgage giants Fannie Mae and Freddie Mac faced major capital losses, Frank moved to increase their credit lines and to give regulators broader oversight of the two housing banks. "This will begin to lay the groundwork for a turnaround in the housing market and hopefully in the broader economy as well," he said.

Like many Democrats, Frank has been dismayed at the widening gap between executives' and workers' compensation, but he opposes having the government set limits. A better fix, he says, is to require shareholder approval of public companies' executive compensation plans, with disclosure of performance targets for compensation and corporate jet use, plus recapture of bonuses that later financial results show weren't warranted. "I don't think the government should be telling people what to pay," he said. "I think the shareholders should." In April 2007, the House passed his bill permitting shareholders to cast a non-binding vote on executive pay, including "golden parachutes" for executives whose companies are being sold. Republicans called his proposal an unwarranted intrusion into the marketplace.

In September 2008, Frank survived a major legislative test after Treasury Secretary Henry Paulson Jr. and Federal Reserve Board Chairman Ben Bernanke told congressional leaders in a dramatic late-night session in House Speaker Nancy Pelosi's office that swift congressional action was needed to prevent several large financial firms from going under. The two recommended a plan for the government to purchase the bad assets of the financial institutions. Frank predicted quick agreement on the proposal, initially estimated to cost $700 billion. "It will be bipartisan, bicameral, bi-everything," he vowed. The subsequent discussions proved harrowing, with a toxic mix of presidential campaign politics, congressional pre-election jitters in both parties, a roller-coaster ride (mostly down) on Wall Street, and spreading fears of financial panic.

While Frank played a central role in crafting the bailout, he warned Republicans of the need for bipartisan support. "This is a Bush administration initiative," he said just hours before the September 29 vote. To Frank's embarrassment and dismay, 95 Democrats voted against the deal and it collapsed, 205-228, in a rank-and-file rebuke of leaders of both parties. The Dow Jones industrial average dropped 777 points that day, its worst single-day point loss ever. Frank and the other negotiators went back to work on the bill and agreed to add $150 billion in tax cuts that the Senate favored. Democratic presidential nominee Barack Obama telephoned recalcitrant House Democrats to urge their support. Four days later, the House passed the bailout legislation, with only 63 Democrats voting no. A veteran House Democrat later complained that one of the problems with the initial bill had been Frank trying to run "a one-man show."

As one of the House's most productive chairmen and a trusted confidant of Speaker Pelosi, Frank was constantly at her side in meetings with top officials of the Bush and Obama administrations. "They understand each other and have similar political backgrounds. Urban, ethnic, political," said a House insider who knows both members. "With that common background, they can communicate well, and they share the same values. Plus, humor helps." But even with his weighty responsibilities, Frank showed some independence. When House Rules Committee Chairwoman Louise Slaughter of New York rejected Frank's plea to permit Republicans to offer modest amendments to a flood insurance bill in 2007, he criticized her decision on the House floor.

For all his professional accomplishments, Frank's personal life once threatened to end his career. In 1987, in a seemingly casual answer to a reporter's question, Frank disclosed that he is gay. Then in 1989, *The Washington Times* newspaper reported that Frank had employed as a personal aide a male prostitute and convicted drug user, Steve Gobie, who was also living in Frank's apartment. He admitted paying Gobie but said he was careful never to use official or campaign funds. He also said he had ejected Gobie from his apartment. Frank voluntarily submitted to an investigation by the House Standards of Official Conduct (Ethics) Committee, which resulted in two minor charges. The committee recommended a reprimand but not censure. Frank made a contrite appearance before the House in July 1990, and the chamber voted 287-141 against censure. The vote for reprimand was 408-18. "I think members will agree that I have always had a reputation for honesty, not always tact or tolerance," Frank said in his remarks to the House.

Frank is now the leading House legislator on gay-rights issues. When the issue of gays in the military was raised in 1992, Frank, to the disappointment of many in the gay community, said he thought that allowing homosexuals to openly serve would not be accepted by most people in Congress or the Pentagon. But in the years since, Frank has criticized the military as the number of service members discharged for homosexuality increased. He has long sponsored a bill to allow benefits for same-sex partners of federal employees. Frank also hailed the Massachusetts Supreme Judicial Court's decision in 2003 that led to the legalization of same-sex marriage in that state. After 11 states passed bans on same-sex marriage, Frank said he thought that the gay movement made a mistake by engaging in mass weddings of same-sex couples. In 2009, he criticized as "deeply offensive and unfair" President-elect Obama's decision to invite evangelical pastor Rick Warren to deliver the invocation at his inauguration. Warren has compared homosexual sex to incest. "I think it was wrong to single [Warren] out for this mark of respect," Frank said.

In 2004, Frank was opposed for re-election by a former talk-radio host who claimed that changes Frank made to immigration law in the 1980s allowed the legal entry of the September 11 hijackers. Frank rebutted that by pointing out they could have been barred from entering under existing law. That year, Frank spent $350,000 on television ads, but less out of fear of losing his seat than out of a desire to gain more statewide name identification in case Democratic Sen. John Kerry was elected president. He may well have run for Kerry's Senate seat. Frank won re-election 78%-22%, carrying every city and town in his district, including four towns that voted for Bush for president.

FIFTH DISTRICT

Niki Tsongas (D)

Elected October 2007, 1st full term; b. April 26, 1946, Chico, CA; home, Lowell; Attended MI St. U., Smith Col., B.A. 1968, Boston U., J.D. 1988; Episcopalian; widowed; 3 children.

Professional Career: Social worker; Practicing attorney; Dean of external affairs, Middlesex Comm. Col., 1997–2007.

DC Office: 1607 LHOB, 20515, 202-225-3411; Fax: 202-226-0771; Web site: tsongas.house.gov.

State Offices: Acton, 978-263-1951; Lawrence, 978-681-6200; Lowell, 978-459-0101.

Committees: *Armed Services* (27th of 36 D): Air & Land Forces; Military Personnel. *Budget* (10th of 24 D). *Natural Resources* (27th of 29 D): Energy & Mineral Resources; National Parks, Forests & Public Lands.

Group Ratings

	ADA	ACLU	AFS	LCV	ITIC	NTU	COC	ACU	CFG	FRC
2008	100	100	100	100	75	5	56	0	0	50
2007	—	—	—	100	—	6	60	0	—	—

National Journal Ratings

	2007 LIB	—	2007 CONS	2008 LIB	—	2008 CONS
Economic	*%	—	*%	81%	—	15%
Social	*%	—	*%	82%	—	0%
Foreign	*%	—	*%	78%	—	17%
Composite	*%	—	*%	85%	—	15%

Key Votes of the 110th Congress

1. Increase minimum wage	*	5. Share immigration data	*	9. Withdraw troops 8/08	*
2. Expand SCHIP	*	6. Foreign aid abortion ban	*	10. No operations in Iran	*
3. Raise CAFE standards	Y	7. Ban gay bias in workplace	Y	11. Free trade with Peru	N
4. Bail out financial markets	Y	8. Repeal D.C. gun law	N	12. Overhaul FISA	N

Election Results

2008 general	Niki Tsongas (D)	225,947	(99%)	($3,287,403)
2008 primary	Niki Tsongas (D)	unopposed		
2007 spec. general	Niki Tsongas (D)	54,359	(51%)	
	Jim Ogonowski (R)	47,782	(45%)	
2007 spec. primary	Niki Tsongas (D)	19,821	(36%)	
	Eileen Donoghue (D)	17,385	(31%)	
	James Eldridge (D)	8,042	(14%)	
	Barry Finegold (D)	6,999	(13%)	
	James Miceli (D)	3,297	(6%)	

Population		Race/Ethnicity		Work	
Pop. 2007:	645,332	White:	75.7%	Private:	81.3%
Change since 2000:	Up 1.6%	Black:	2.2%	Government:	12.0%
Urban:	93.5%	Hispanic:	13.3%	Self-employed:	6.5%
Rural:	6.5%	Asian:	7.3%	Blue collar:	19.3%
Area size:	582 sq. mi.	Native Am.:	0.1%	White collar:	66.6%
Age		Hawaiian:	0.0%	Khaki collar:	0.1%
Median age:	37.8 yrs.	Two+ races:	0.9%	Other:	14.0%
More than 65 yrs:	11.3%	*Ancestry*		Median income:	$69,374
Less than 18 yrs:	26.1%	Irish:	17.7%	Median home value:	$374,100
Education		Italian:	10.6%	Poverty:	9.5%
H.S. grad:	86.5%	English:	9.1%	**Military Veterans**	
College grad:	37.1%			% of Pop:	8.6%
Grad degree:	16.0%				

The Merrimack River Valley at the northern edge of Massachusetts has had an erratic history: High-tech boom, bust, boom, bust, boom. When Massachusetts was a kind of maritime republic in the 19th century, with its farmers struggling to scratch out a living from the stony soil, a few clever Yankees used their profits from the sea trade to try to tame the rapidly flowing Merrimack and build cotton-spinning mills. Creating the cities of Lowell and Lawrence, they built model dormitories and recreation

2008 Presidential Vote

Obama (D)	176,547	(59%)
McCain (R)	117,877	(39%)

2004 Presidential Vote

Kerry (D)	158,455	(57%)
Bush (R)	114,874	(41%)

Cook Partisan Voting Index: D + 8

programs for their female workers. This was the center of America's textile industry for more than a century, long after the maritime industry faded. But in the 1920s, the price of labor rose and newly built mills in the Carolinas, much closer to the cotton supply, decimated the industry that Lawrence and Lowell built. Many residents, by then rather elderly, waited forlornly for an upturn in the local economy.

It came eventually, largely from an unexpected source. High-tech industry drove the growth, beginning in the 1960s around the Massachusetts Institute of Technology, and then moving out to the Route 128 ring road and eventually to Interstate 495, which passes through Lowell and Lawrence. Wang, headquartered in Lowell, grew spectacularly, and Democratic Sen. Paul Tsongas—the local kid who made it big before his early death to cancer—spearheaded a national historic restoration of the old mill area. This was the Massachusetts miracle of the 1980s. Then came the bust: Sales of Wang's word processors and minicomputers slumped as businesses purchased personal computers and linked them together in networks. But Lowell revived again. Its new immigrants provide vitality and entrepreneurial creativity. Cambodians own many small businesses and are nearly one-fifth of the local population, making Lowell second only to Long Beach, Calif. as a home for transplanted Cambodians in the United States. The first Spanish-language daily newspaper in New England began here in September 2008. The old Wang buildings are filled with health care, banking, telecommunications, and Internet companies, plus fledgling green-energy industries. Old mills have been converted to artists' lofts and upscale condos. The Tsongas Arena is home to a professional hockey team.

The 5th Congressional District of Massachusetts includes Lawrence and Lowell, which, along with a handful of nearby towns, account for about two-thirds of the district's population. The remainder of the district is the high-tech corridor south along I-495. The district also includes the tony suburbs near the Revolutionary War battleground of Concord, where the Minutemen stood their ground in 1775; the mountains along the New Hampshire state line; and the small towns west of Lowell. Fort Devens, which closed in 1996, is now a training site for members of the New England Army Reserve and National Guard. Except for Lowell and Lawrence, the district is ancestrally Yankee Republican. It is culturally liberal, with pockets of big wealth, and it trended Democratic in the early 1970s. Back then, the 5th District produced two Democratic candidates who would later run for president: Tsongas and John Kerry. In the 1980s and early 1990s, amid the high-tech boom, it went Republican in national and some statewide elections. In 1992, it gave Bill Clinton his lowest percentage in the state, while a big portion of the vote went to high-tech pioneer Ross Perot, the Texan who formed his own political party. But its cultural liberalism has moved it toward the Democrats, though not as far as some Massachusetts districts: Al Gore carried the 5th District 57%-36% in 2000, Kerry 57%-41% in 2004, and Barack Obama 59%-39% in 2008.

The congresswoman from the 5th District is Niki Tsongas, a Democrat who won the seat in a 2007 special election. She is the widow of Paul Tsongas and a political force in her own right. Growing up in an Air Force family, Niki Tsongas (*SONG-us*) never had a place to call home thanks to her father's frequent moves. While interning in Washington, D.C., during college, she was invited to a party where she met her future husband, who was an intern for 5th District Republican Rep. Brad Morse. On one of their early dates, he told her of his plans to get involved in electoral politics by running for the Lowell City Council. Inspired by his vision and vigor for local politics, Niki followed him to Lowell in 1968 to help with his successful campaign for city councilor. They were married soon after. Tsongas stumped for her husband several times during his various campaigns for office. "I couldn't have run for office if I hadn't spent time campaigning on my own," she recounted. Paul was first elected to the U.S. House in 1974 and to the U.S. Senate four years later. After retiring in 1984 with non-Hodgkin's lymphoma, he regained his health and launched a campaign for the 1992 Democratic presidential nomination. Although he won the New Hampshire primary, then-Arkansas Gov. Bill Clinton's surprise second-place finish in the Granite State gave him the momentum to overtake Tsongas, who withdrew in March 1992 after defeats in the Illinois and Michigan primaries. The Tsongases moved back to Lowell, and soon thereafter Paul's cancer returned. He succumbed to the disease in 1997.

While acting as a political adviser to her husband, Tsongas started the first all-woman law firm in Lowell, raised their three daughters, and eventually took a job at Middlesex Community College as the dean of external affairs. When Democratic Rep. Marty Meehan retired in July 2007 to become chancellor of the University of Massachusetts (Lowell), Tsongas said she wanted the chance to give back to the community that had welcomed her nearly 40 years earlier. Noting that Massachusetts had not had a female House member in more than 25 years, Tsongas was also motivated by what she saw as the need for change in Washington and her strong disagreement with the Bush administration on the Iraq war. Facing four other Democrats in a September primary, she was the early favorite and had endorsements from influential Democratic Rep. Barney Frank and Kitty Dukakis, the wife of former Democratic presidential nominee Michael Dukakis. Her most formidable challenge came from former Lowell Mayor Eileen Donoghue. Tsongas drew heavily on her ties to Lowell and emphasized her husband's years representing the district, but she erred during a debate in saying she spent 10 years in Washington representing the 5th District, a statement that actually described her husband's career. Tsongas's opponents seized on the comment to highlight her lack of elective experience and criticized her for moving away from Lowell to nearby Charlestown. Tsongas said she moved to be closer to her daughters, who were attending college in Boston. Donoghue also attacked Tsongas for accepting campaign money from outside the district while emphasizing her own local ties to the city. But Tsongas edged out Donoghue, 36% to 31%. Tsongas lost nearly 2-to-1 in Lowell but won most of the other towns.

In the general election, Tsongas faced a Republican with an intensely personal story and a recognizable name in the district. Retired Air Force Lt. Col. Jim Ogonowski's brother, John, was the pilot of the first plane to hit the World Trade Center on September 11. One of his ads featured John's widow, Margaret, extolling Jim's character and talking about how much he helped their family in the aftermath. Each candidate sought to wrap the Bush administration around the other. Ogonowski criticized Tsongas for supporting a path to citizenship for illegal immigrants, which Bush favored. Tsongas attacked Ogonowski for not supporting the expansion of the State Children's Health Insurance Program, then up for renewal in Congress. Both national parties spent heavily on the race, and EMILY's List backed Tsongas in the primary and general elections. Bill Clinton drew a crowd of several thousand during a campaign stop in her behalf. Sen. Edward Kennedy and House Speaker Nancy Pelosi also made appearances. Tsongas's victory was surprisingly close, 51%-45%. Ogonowski won 11 towns, mostly in the northern part of the district. Tsongas handily took Lowell and Lawrence, plus the area closer to Boston.

In the House, Tsongas traveled with a bipartisan delegation to Iraq and Afghanistan in January 2008, and sponsored a bill in February to begin withdrawing troops in 90 days while simultaneously creating an international agency to promote safety and economic stability in the region. On the Armed Services Committee, she pushed for reductions of U.S. forces in Iraq. During the Democratic presidential primaries, she criticized both Hillary Rodham Clinton and Barack Obama for failing to offer a strategy for the nation's cities. After her own tough contests a year earlier, she was re-elected without opposition. While setting up her office at the outset of her first term, Tsongas got a sentimental reminder of her late husband: Her House phone numbers had been his. "I think he'd be proud of me," she said.

SIXTH DISTRICT

John Tierney (D)

Elected 1996, 7th term; b. Sept. 18, 1951, Salem; home, Salem; Salem St. Col., B.A. 1973, Suffolk U., J.D. 1976; no religious affiliation; married (Patrice).

Professional Career: Practicing atty., 1976–96.

DC Office: 2238 RHOB, 20515, 202-225-8020; Fax: 202-225-5915; Web site: tierney.house.gov.

State Offices: Lynn, 781-595-7375; Peabody, 978-531-1669.

Committees: *Education & Labor* (9th of 29 D): Health, Employment, Labor & Pensions; Higher Education, Lifelong Learning & Competitiveness. *Oversight & Government Reform* (6th of 24 D): Domestic Policy; National Security & Foreign Affairs (Chmn).

Group Ratings

	ADA	ACLU	AFS	LCV	ITIC	NTU	COC	ACU	CFG	FRC
2008	95	100	100	100	57	13	59	4	4	0
2007	100	—	100	100	—	6	50	0	10	—

National Journal Ratings

	2007 LIB	—	2007 CONS		2008 LIB	—	2008 CONS
Economic	82%	—	0%		85%	—	0%
Social	75%	—	23%		82%	—	0%
Foreign	96%	—	0%		92%	—	0%
Composite	88%	—	12%		93%	—	7%

Key Votes of the 110th Congress

1. Increase minimum wage	Y	5. Share immigration data	N	9. Withdraw troops 8/08	Y
2. Expand SCHIP	Y	6. Foreign aid abortion ban	N	10. No operations in Iran	Y
3. Raise CAFE standards	Y	7. Ban gay bias in workplace	Y	11. Free trade with Peru	N
4. Bail out financial markets	Y	8. Repeal D.C. gun law	N	12. Overhaul FISA	N

Election Results

2008 general	John Tierney (D)	226,216	(70%)	($498,041)
	Richard Baker (R)	94,845	(30%)	($28,082)
2008 primary	John Tierney (D)	unopposed		

Prior Winning Percentages: 2006 (70%); 2004 (70%); 2002 (68%); 2000 (71%); 1998 (55%); 1996 (48%)

Population		Race/Ethnicity		Work	
Pop. 2007:	645,983	White:	87.5%	Private:	80.3%
Change since 2000:	Up 1.5%	Black:	2.3%	Government:	12.2%
Urban:	94.9%	Hispanic:	5.8%	Self-employed:	7.3%
Rural:	5.1%	Asian:	3.0%	Blue collar:	16.3%
Area size:	805 sq. mi.	Native Am.:	0.1%	White collar:	68.6%
Age		Hawaiian:	0.0%	Khaki collar:	0.1%
Median age:	40.8 yrs.	Two+ races:	0.9%	Other:	15.0%
More than 65 yrs:	14.5%	*Ancestry*		Median income:	$68,422
Less than 18 yrs:	23.3%	Irish:	20.1%	Median home value:	$422,600
Education		Italian:	14.3%	Poverty:	7.1%
H.S. grad:	91.0%	English:	11.1%	**Military Veterans**	
College grad:	39.4%			% of Pop:	10.3%
Grad degree:	15.7%				

The North Shore of Massachusetts Bay has often been at the leading edge of the nation's economy. In 1640, the Saugus Iron Works was built here—the beginning of American heavy industry. When Europe's great powers were convulsed in international war from 1792 to 1815, American ship owners suddenly became the richest in the world, and traders from Boston and Salem accumulated the capital needed to build textile mills and railroads and to finance much of the American Industrial Revolution.

2008 Presidential Vote

Obama (D)	192,995	(57%)
McCain (R)	136,116	(41%)

2004 Presidential Vote

Kerry (D)	185,264	(58%)
Bush (R)	130,924	(41%)

Cook Partisan Voting Index: D + 7

From the small port of Salem, ships left for China, bringing back porcelain and artifacts, which helped change American styles forever. Salem, first settled by Europeans in 1626, had the nation's first millionaire, Elias Hasket Derby. In 1900, it was the richest city per capita in the nation. Today, the North Shore is a quiet place. From Boston Harbor north to the mouth of the Merrimack River, it is a collection of ethnic factory towns from Lynn to Peabody (once one of the world's great leather producers with more than 100 tanneries) to the former shipbuilding Newburyport. There are a few high-income enclaves, such as Marblehead with its yachts, Beverly with its estates, and artsy Rockport. Salem's House of the Seven Gables is a popular tourist site. Built in 1668, it inspired the novel by Nathaniel Hawthorne and is the oldest surviving wooden mansion in New England. The Salem witch trials are probably the town's most famous legacy. More than two centuries later, they inspired Arthur Miller's play *The Crucible*, which used the trials as an allegory for the hearings of communist-baiter Sen. Joseph McCarthy. Moviegoers will recognize the fishing town of Gloucester as the homeport of the *Andrea Gail*, the 72-foot swordfishing boat whose tragic plight was dramatized in the novel and film *The Perfect Storm*. Although pleasure boating has surged, the ports were hit hard by overfishing of mackerel and herring in the 1970s and cod in the 1990s. A red tide scare closed clam-digging flats in July 2008. Some of the area's economic hopes are tied to a proposed marine research institute and a new cruise terminal that opened in 2007. Lynn is the district's largest city, and its General Electric jet engine plant has been the largest employer, although it has only a fraction of the jobs that it had at its peak of 13,000 in the late 1970s.

The 6th Congressional District includes the North Shore from Saugus and Lynn northward, plus towns and cities inland west to Burlington. Its high-income Yankee towns were historically liberal Republican, while Lynn, Salem, Peabody, and the Merrimack mill towns are still Irish working-class Democratic. The Hanscom Air Force Base in Bedford survived the base closing review in 2005, although hopes for additional high-tech aerospace research have been disappointed. The 6th has been a Democratic district since the 1960s, though only marginally in the 1980s and in the early 1990s. While this district is the site of the original gerrymander—named after Elbridge Gerry—the current 6th boundaries are hardly grotesque by contemporary standards.

The congressman from the 6th District is John Tierney, a Democrat elected in 1996. Tierney grew up in Salem in modest circumstances. He worked his way through Salem State College and Suffolk University Law School as a janitor on the night shift and as a clerk at a Boston law firm. For nearly 20 years, he practiced law in Salem. In 1994, he spied a political opening and ran for Congress. The incumbent, Peter Torkildsen, was a Republican elected in 1992 by beating veteran Democrat Nicholas Mavroules, who had been indicted on tax evasion and bribery charges. But in a year highly favorable to Republicans as 1994 was, Torkildsen managed to defeat Tierney by only 51%-47%. In 1996, Tierney ran again. His ads, along with the AFL-CIO's, assailed House Speaker Newt Gingrich, a Republican, and GOP cutbacks in Medicare. He called for health care insurance for children and criticized Torkildsen for not bringing enough defense dollars to the district. Torkildsen spent $1.1 million, while keeping his promise to accept no political action committee money. Tierney had $776,000 to spend, and he concentrated it on a blitz close to the election. The result was one of the closest races in the country. After several recounts, which stretched into December, Tierney won by 371 votes.

In the House, Tierney has been a solid ally of labor unions on the Education and Labor Committee and a consistently liberal vote. His work on that panel has included support for alternative paths to teaching, gang- and drug-free schools, and strengthened vocational education. In the 2008 higher education bill, Tierney won an amendment to penalize states that fail to meet budget benchmarks for college aid. He has been a leader among those Democrats trying to reduce prescription drug costs for senior citizens. Tierney has also raised questions with federal regulators about security procedures at the Seabrook nuclear plant in New Hampshire. In 2007, he joined the Intelligence Committee and also became chairman of the National Security and Foreign Affairs Subcommittee of the Oversight and Government Reform Committee, where he led the March 2007 hearings into poor conditions for patients at the Walter Reed Army Medical Center. "My question is, where have you been?" Tierney asked Army officials. In April 2008, he questioned the growing sales of military equipment on eBay and other websites. The House defeated his amendment in May 2008 to strip $966 million from missile defense programs. Tierney is well connected to House Speaker Nancy Pelosi. For several years, his top aide was her daughter Christine, who later became a political consultant in San Francisco.

Torkildsen challenged Tierney in a 1998 rubber match, but Tierney won 55%-42%. He has faced token opposition since then.

SEVENTH DISTRICT

Edward Markey (D)

Elected 1976, 17th full term; b. July 11, 1946, Malden; home, Malden; Boston Col., B.A. 1968, J.D. 1972; Catholic; married (Susan Blumenthal).

Military Career: Army Reserves, 1968–73.

Elected Office: MA House of Reps., 1973–76.

DC Office: 2108 RHOB, 20515, 202-225-2836; Fax: 202-226-0092; Web site: markey.house.gov.

State Offices: Framingham, 508-875-2900; Medford, 781-396-2900.

Committees: *Energy & Commerce* (3rd of 36 D): Communications, Technology & the Internet; Energy & Environment (Chmn); Oversight & Investigations. *Natural Resources* (15th of 29 D): Energy & Mineral Resources.

Group Ratings

	ADA	ACLU	AFS	LCV	ITIC	NTU	COC	ACU	CFG	FRC
2008	100	100	100	100	86	7	56	0	4	5
2007	100	—	100	95	—	5	58	4	9	—

National Journal Ratings

	2007 LIB	—	2007 CONS		2008 LIB	—	2008 CONS
Economic	69%	—	28%		81%	—	15%
Social	85%	—	15%		82%	—	0%
Foreign	96%	—	0%		92%	—	0%
Composite	85%	—	16%		90%	—	10%

Key Votes of the 110th Congress

1. Increase minimum wage	Y	5. Share immigration data	N	9. Withdraw troops 8/08	Y
2. Expand SCHIP	Y	6. Foreign aid abortion ban	N	10. No operations in Iran	Y
3. Raise CAFE standards	Y	7. Ban gay bias in workplace	Y	11. Free trade with Peru	N
4. Bail out financial markets	Y	8. Repeal D.C. gun law	N	12. Overhaul FISA	N

Election Results

2008 general	Edward Markey (D)	212,304	(76%)	($1,021,890)
	John Cunningham (R)	67,978	(24%)	($23,134)
2008 primary	Edward Markey (D)	unopposed		

Prior Winning Percentages: 2006 (100%); 2004 (74%); 2002 (100%); 2000 (100%); 1998 (71%); 1996 (70%); 1994 (64%); 1992 (62%); 1990 (100%); 1988 (100%); 1986 (100%); 1984 (71%); 1982 (78%); 1980 (100%); 1978 (85%); 1976 (77%).

Population		Race/Ethnicity		Work	
Pop. 2007:	641,263	White:	78.5%	Private:	82.8%
Change since 2000:	Up 1.1%	Black:	4.7%	Government:	11.0%
Urban:	99.5%	Hispanic:	6.7%	Self-employed:	6.0%
Rural:	0.5%	Asian:	7.6%	Blue collar:	14.2%
Area size:	188 sq. mi.	Native Am.:	0.1%	White collar:	70.6%
Age		Hawaiian:	0.0%	Khaki collar:	0.1%
Median age:	39.4 yrs.	Two+ races:	1.2%	Other:	15.1%
More than 65 yrs:	14.7%	*Ancestry*		Median income:	$67,458
Less than 18 yrs:	20.7%	Irish:	18.9%	Median home value:	$444,400
Education		Italian:	16.8%	Poverty:	7.2%
H.S. grad:	89.5%	English:	7.3%	**Military Veterans**	
College grad:	43.1%			% of Pop:	7.8%
Grad degree:	19.6%				

The Yankee Protestants and Irish Catholics who settled Massachusetts arrived by boat, the Yankees to a cold stony land with a few Indians, the Irish to a crowded city with Yankees who seemed no more welcoming. The Yankees whose ancestors once farmed the soil had, by the early 20th century, founded suburbs filled with solid brick and white frame houses. As the years went on, their local public schools emptied as young people with children moved out, and attendance at Protestant churches

2008 Presidential Vote		
Obama (D)	.193,130	(65%)
McCain (R)	.99,062	(33%)
2004 Presidential Vote		
Kerry (D)	.192,133	(66%)
Bush (R)	.96,374	(33%)
Cook Partisan Voting Index:	D + 15	

fell. The Irish, for decades heavily concentrated in the crowded wards of Boston, started moving out into the suburbs after World War II. There were other ethnic groups here and there (Jews, Italians, French-Canadians), but the major conflict—fought out in neighborhood playgrounds, in school committee meetings, and not least in political campaigns—was between Protestant Yankee Republicans and Catholic Irish Democrats.

The 7th Congressional District of Massachusetts is made up of Boston's northern and western suburbs, where vestiges of this conflict can still be seen. Geographically, it forms an arc around Boston, starting with the clapboard beach towns of Winthrop and Revere just beyond Logan Airport, going north as far as working-class Woburn (where Charles Goodyear developed the art of vulcanizing rubber), and west as far as modest-income Natick and Framingham. Brazilians were a significant immigrant group here after the war, when Boston-based mining companies began extracting mica from an area near the Brazilian city of Governador Valadares. The 7th also includes the university towns of Medford, home of Tufts University, and Waltham, home of Brandeis University. It includes the patriot town of Lexington, where minutemen fired the shots heard 'round the world in 1775, and high-income Lincoln and Weston. Many of these towns were Yankee Republican through the 1950s, but by the late 1960s, they were solidly Democratic. In state politics, the suburbanites of the 7th District have been less liberal: This district was close in the gubernatorial election of 1998 and again in 2002, when Republican Mitt Romney won 51%-49%. But Democrat Deval Patrick carried every town and city in the district in 2006. Like the rest of Massachusetts, recent presidential elections here have not been competitive.

The congressman in the 7th District is Democrat Edward Markey, first elected in 1976 at age 30, and now dean of the Massachusetts House delegation. He grew up in Malden, where his father was a milkman. He went to Malden Catholic High, Boston College, and Boston College law school, then immediately to the state House, at age 26. In 1976, he ran for the U.S. House and won a 12-candidate primary with 22% of the vote; he had never been to Washington before. Now he ranks 12th in House seniority and in February 2007 became the 12th current member to have served more than half his life in Congress.

In his first years in the House, Markey made his name as a fierce opponent of nuclear power plants and in the early 1980s as a crusader for the nuclear freeze. Speaker Thomas "Tip" O'Neill of Massachusetts put him in a position to be a serious legislator in the House from early on, and he has long since become one of the House's most legislatively productive and creative members. With O'Neill's help, he got a seat on the Commerce Committee. Impressed by the high-tech boom around Route 128, he joined the communications subcommittee early. Then, after only eight years in the House, he became chairman of the Energy Conservation and Power Subcommittee. After the 1986 election, with help from Chairman John Dingell of Michigan, who liked aggressive and loyal younger Democrats, Markey became chairman of the telecommunications subcommittee. This is one of the plum positions in the House, with lucrative possibilities for fundraising, and with subject matter that is intellectually more demanding (and, in lobbying terms, more fiercely contested) than almost anything else in Congress.

Markey has been an important shaper of public policy, often working with Republicans, often coming up with original initiatives, knowledgeable about the workings of the industries he oversees, and often inclined toward deregulation though he can just as often be found siding with consumers. In 1992, he shrewdly produced the cable television regulation bill on which both chambers of Congress overrode George H. W. Bush's veto—the only bill passed over his veto in his four-year term. Markey's influence was not greatly reduced when he became ranking minority member in 1995; bills in these areas are hard to pass without bipartisan consensus. He was a major player in the passage of the landmark Telecommunications Act of 1996. He has been an impetus as well behind the transition to digital television. He and Dingell pressed in 2005 to have the government pay for the converter boxes that would be required on old sets after digital television became universal in 2009. In 2007, he called on the Federal Communications Commission to regulate children's program advertising for unhealthy foods.

On the big telecom issues during the Bush administration, Markey favored allowing regional Bell and satellite companies to compete with cable companies locally (and cable companies compete with others nationally) in providing broadband and other Internet services, but only with a "build-out" requirement that new entrants serve all video customers in a geographic area. He has been a booster of so-called "net neutrality," which would prohibit Internet carriers from charging higher fees to big-volume users like Google and Yahoo. "If we don't protect the openness of the Internet for entrepreneurial activity, we're ruining a wonderful model for low-barrier entry, innovation, and job creation," Markey says. In other issues before the subcommittee, he called for a government investigation of the effect of electronic media on children and on hearing loss from portable music players.

In 2007, when Democrats took over the House, Markey was initially the chairman of the telecommunications subcommittee on the Energy and Commerce Committee. But in 2009, he gave up that gavel to become chairman of the Energy and Environment Subcommittee, giving him increased jurisdiction over the global warming issue. Speaker Nancy Pelosi had earlier designated him to take the lead on the issue by naming him chairman of the Select Committee on Energy Independence and Global Warming. (She deliberately put Markey in charge to get around Dingell, the more senior, Detroit-area congressman who did not agree with her on toughening car emission standards. Under pressure from Dingell, she announced it would not have authority to propose legislation, but she gave Markey free rein to hold hearings and travel widely—often with Pelosi—to make the case for a far-reaching bill to curb global warming.) In May 2008, Markey proposed an 85% cut in greenhouse-gas emissions by 2050, along with a cap-and-trade program that allows companies to "buy and sell" pollution emissions credits. With Democratic Reps. Henry Waxman of California and Jay Inslee of Washington, Markey separately issued a set of principles for guiding cap-and-trade legislation. Markey, working with Waxman and coal-state Democrats, crafted a sweeping climate change bill in 2009 that established a cap on greenhouse gas emissions with the goal of reducing them by 80% from 2005 levels by 2050. In June, the bill passed the House, 219-212.

For years, Markey pressed unsuccessfully for higher fuel-efficiency standards in cars and trucks and for windfall taxes on oil. He once proposed a bill to stop the favorable treatment of sports utility vehicles under the mileage standard—they're classified as light trucks, and indeed the SUV category seems to have emerged as a response to the fuel-economy regulations. In 2007, Markey, working closely with Pelosi, proposed an increase in fuel-efficiency standards to 35 miles per gallon by 2018. The domestic auto industry and unions criticized the plan as "extreme," and said that it would impose a far lower burden on foreign-based companies. Their allies backed a 2022 deadline and more flexible terms. Dingell's resistance to including the provision in that year's energy bill led to extended private negotiations with Markey, Pelosi, and others. The subsequent bill, which Bush signed, set the 35-miles-per-gallon standard for 2020, the first increase in the fuel-efficiency standards since 1975. Markey voiced regret that the Senate rejected a House-passed plan to require utilities to produce a larger share of electric power from renewable sources, but he promised to revive it.

Markey has opposed oil drilling in the Arctic National Wildlife Refuge and has a bill to declare it a permanently protected wilderness area. As gasoline prices surged in 2008, he unsuccessfully urged the Bush administration to release oil from the Strategic Petroleum Reserve. Another area of energy policy where Markey has had a heavy hand is nuclear power. He has long been a proponent of tougher regulation, and the subject often brings out in him his gift for memorable quotes. "We have a 'loose nuke' problem right here at home," he said in 2002, after 1,500 types of radioactive material had been lost in five years. That year, he called for a permanent end to the testing of nuclear weapons. He was one of the House's leading opponents of exempting India from the Nuclear Nonproliferation Act, and criticized the 2008 approval of the U.S.-India nuclear cooperation deal as a "historic mistake." In 2009, he said that he would seek a ban on radioactive materials used in "dirty bombs."

From his seat on the Homeland Security Committee, Markey worked effectively on air cargo security issues. He pointed out that while passenger luggage is X-rayed, commercial cargo went unscreened on passenger planes. In 2003, his amendment to require screening of all air cargo passed the House easily, but it was opposed by the Bush administration and went nowhere in the Senate. He claimed victory late in 2007 when Bush signed a bill that requires some inspection of all freight on commercial planes, though he promised to closely monitor implementation. Markey has also weighed in lustily on privacy issues. He co-sponsored a bill requiring that cell phone numbers be unpublished. The Internal Revenue Service, prompted by Markey, issued a Tax Guidance letter in 2005 requiring taxpayer consent before tax records are sent for preparation in other countries, where privacy protections are often weaker.

Markey has long coveted a Senate seat. In 1984, he wanted to run for the seat vacated by Democrat Paul Tsongas, but lost out to then-Lt. Gov. John Kerry. Nearly two decades later, Markey came to Kerry's aid during his presidential bid, which, if successful, could have opened a Senate seat for Markey. In 2003, when Kerry's campaign was faltering, Kerry named Markey political adviser Mary Beth Cahill as his campaign manager, and Markey, who had already endorsed Kerry, went to work to persuade colleagues in the House not to endorse anyone, especially Vermont Gov. Howard Dean, until the voters in Iowa and New Hampshire had a chance to speak. Markey predicted, correctly, that Dean would fade and Kerry would rally to victory, and he was mostly successful in keeping House members off the Dean team. In the meantime, gearing up for a possible run for Kerry's Senate seat, Markey spent $300,000 on ads in the Boston media market trumpeting his work against nuclear terrorism. So Markey more than commiserated with Kerry when he lost his campaign for president in 2004.

EIGHTH DISTRICT

Michael Capuano (D)

Elected 1998, 6th term; b. Jan. 9, 1952, Somerville; home, Somerville; Dartmouth Col., B.A. 1973, Boston Col., J.D. 1977; Catholic; married (Barbara); 2 children.

Elected Office: Somerville alderman Ward 5, 1977–79; Somerville alderman-at-large, 1985–89; Somerville mayor, 1989–98.

Professional Career: Chief legal cnsl., MA Legislature Taxation Cmte., 1978–84; Practicing atty., 1984–90.

DC Office: 1414 LHOB, 20515, 202-225-5111; Fax: 202-225-9322; Web site: www.house.gov/capuano.

State Offices: Cambridge, 617-621-6208.

Committees: *Financial Services* (12th of 42 D): Capital Markets, Insurance & Government Sponsored Enterprises; Housing & Community Opportunity. *House Administration* (3rd of 6 D): Capitol Security (Chmn). *Transportation & Infrastructure* (16th of 44 D): Aviation; Highways & Transit; Water Resources & Environment.

Group Ratings

	ADA	ACLU	AFS	LCV	ITIC	NTU	COC	ACU	CFG	FRC
2008	95	100	100	100	57	13	67	4	3	0
2007	95	—	100	95	—	6	50	0	10	—

National Journal Ratings

	2007 LIB	—	2007 CONS		2008 LIB	—	2008 CONS
Economic	73%	—	24%		81%	—	15%
Social	72%	—	28%		58%	—	42%
Foreign	90%	—	8%		85%	—	8%
Composite	79%	—	21%		77%	—	24%

Key Votes of the 110th Congress

1. Increase minimum wage	Y	5. Share immigration data	N	9. Withdraw troops 8/08	Y
2. Expand SCHIP	Y	6. Foreign aid abortion ban	N	10. No operations in Iran	Y
3. Raise CAFE standards	Y	7. Ban gay bias in workplace	Y	11. Free trade with Peru	N
4. Bail out financial markets	Y	8. Repeal D.C. gun law	N	12. Overhaul FISA	N

Election Results

2008 general	Michael Capuano (D)	185,530	(99%)	($554,013)
2008 primary	Michael Capuano (D)	unopposed		

Prior Winning Percentages: 2006 (91%); 2004 (100%); 2002 (100%); 2000 (100%); 1998 (82%)

Population		Race/Ethnicity		Work	
Pop. 2007:	615,720	White:	49.1%	Private:	85.1%
Change since 2000:	Down 3.0%	Black:	20.2%	Government:	9.8%
Urban:	100.0%	Hispanic:	17.5%	Self-employed:	5.0%
Rural:	0.0%	Asian:	9.1%	Blue collar:	12.0%
Area size:	92 sq. mi.	Native Am.:	0.2%	White collar:	68.4%
		Hawaiian:	0.0%	Khaki collar:	0.1%
Age		Two+ races:	1.6%	Other:	19.6%
Median age:	31.9 yrs.			Median income:	$47,845
More than 65 yrs:	9.7%	**Ancestry**		Median home value:	$456,200
Less than 18 yrs:	17.1%	Irish:	10.5%	Poverty:	21.8%
		Italian:	7.3%		
Education		English:	5.1%	**Military Veterans**	
H.S. grad:	83.1%			% of Pop:	3.9%
College grad:	44.3%				
Grad degree:	22.0%				

The "Hub of the Solar System" is what the elder Oliver Wendell Holmes called the Massachusetts State House in the 19th century, though over time, his statement has come to be remembered as referring to Boston as the "Hub of the Universe." Either way, this most political of cities has often been the focal point of essential moments in American history. On its streets, originally laid out as 17th-century cowpaths, Samuel Adams and Paul Revere plotted revolution, the abolitionist movement

2008 Presidential Vote
Obama (D) 205,113   (85%)
McCain (R)..............................33,104   (14%)

2004 Presidential Vote
Kerry (D)................................168,264   (79%)
Bush (R) 40,885   (19%)

Cook Partisan Voting Index: D + 32

helped ignite the Civil War, and various Kennedys opened their campaign headquarters. Today's Boston is different from the Boston of John F. Kennedy's time. Then it was a gray city with no new buildings and dust on every windowsill. The sky was dark with pollution, and the air was thick with ancient Yankee and Irish animosity. The old office buildings were full of Yankees seeking safe investments for their antique family fortunes. The Statehouse and City Hall were full of Irishmen, scampering after good patronage jobs and regaling one another with political battle stories. These days, that Boston is mostly gone. The new skyscrapers are full of well-educated venture capitalists, lawyers, and management consultants, many working for high-tech companies radiating from Cambridge out into the countryside. Of the 200 or so U.S. cities with populations greater than 160,000, only four (Boulder, Colo.; Madison, Wis.; San Jose, Calif.; and Stamford, Conn.) have a larger share of residents with college degrees than Boston. Most of the city's neighborhoods have changed. Minorities and young singles increasingly populate the central city, which has one of the nation's lowest percentages of school children. The city's population is down from 801,000 in 1950 to 600,000 in 2007, and more than 80% of the people in the metropolitan area live in the suburbs.

A generation ago, students from suburbs across the country who were exploring Boston from their dormitories and campuses felt as if they were pawing through the living remnants of 1920s America, a quaint town where the locals called traffic circles "rotaries" and milk shakes "frappes." But Massachusetts has evolved, and nowhere more than in Cambridge. As universities and high tech and biotech have become driving forces of economic growth, Cambridge has gone glitzy, with trendy restaurants and high-priced hotels, boutiques, and upscale condominiums. The Harvard University campus now has more land in Boston than in Cambridge. Greater Boston may well have a larger concentration of graduate students and post-graduate hangers-on than any other major U.S. city, and this graduate student community's world is centered on Cambridge, with outposts in lower-income Somerville and in the neighborhoods of tony Back Bay, funky Allston, and the more-family-oriented Brighton near Harvard Business School. Boston Harbor, which George H.W. Bush famously criticized for its pollution in 1988, has been cleaned up, and its port traffic is growing.

These communities are part of Massachusetts' 8th Congressional District, a region rich with historical sites, from the Paul Revere house in the North End to the frigate USS *Constitution* in the Charlestown docks. And with MIT and the software concentration in Cambridge's once-downscale Lechmere Square, the district is one of the high-tech capitals of America. The 8th includes all of Cambridge, Somerville, and economically revived Chelsea, and many Boston neighborhoods—newly upscale and diverse East Boston around Logan Airport, Brighton and the Back Bay, Fenway, Mattapan, Mission Hill, the South End. It shares Hyde Park, Roxbury, Dorchester, and Jamaica Plain with the neighboring 9th District. For the first time in its history, whites are a minority of Boston's population. Hispanics have replaced the many Irish and Italians who left in the 1970s because of court-ordered school busing. They have caused a population boom in Chelsea and in Dorchester, which annually celebrates one of the nation's largest Caribbean festivals. This is by far the most Democratic district in Democratic Massachusetts.

The congressman from the 8th District is Democrat Michael Capuano, the winner of a 10-candidate brawl in the 1998 primary who has been safe ever since. It has been said that over the past 70 years this district has been represented alternately by townies and Kennedys: James Michael Curley, the scampish five-term mayor of Boston and one-term governor; followed by John F. Kennedy in 1946. Then for many years, beginning in 1953, the seat belonged to Thomas (Tip) O'Neill, who rose to become speaker of the House. After his retirement in 1986, Joe Kennedy, son of Robert F. Kennedy, was elected to the seat. Then came Capuano, who was born and raised in Somerville. His paternal grandfather emigrated from Italy, and his father was the first Italian-American elected official in Somerville. His mother is the granddaughter of Irish immigrants. Capuano graduated from Dartmouth and Boston College Law School. He returned to Somerville to raise his family, practice law, and enter politics. By day, he worked for the Legislature's Joint Committee on Taxation and practiced law. In off-hours, he served as alderman of the 5th Ward, as his father had. He served as alderman-at-large from 1985 to 1989, then won election five times as Somerville mayor. For decades an Irish and Italian town, Somerville now attracts many graduate students and yuppies. Capuano seems to have been the right politician for this mix, with deep Somerville roots and a penchant for innovation and reform. He had a solid base of support to run for the 8th District seat when Joe Kennedy declined to seek re-election. In a 10-candidate field, Capuano led with 23%, with former Boston Mayor Ray Flynn (1983–93) the runner-up at 17%.

In the House, Capuano is well to the left on the political spectrum, although relatively centrist within the Massachusetts delegation. He supports same-sex marriage, opposed a ban on partial-birth abortion, and harshly criticized the Bush administration's handling of the war in Iraq. On the Financial Services Committee, he works closely with Chairman Barney Frank, another Massachusetts liberal Democrat.

Capuano is close to the Democratic leadership in the House. Speaker Nancy Pelosi trusts him to take on difficult assignments and quietly get the job done. Pelosi, who grew up in Baltimore as the daughter of a U.S. representative, shares with Capuano an urban, ethnic political background. After Democrats won majority control of the House in 2006 and Pelosi was elevated to the speakership, she tapped him to take charge of the myriad tasks in the transition. In some ways, it was a rocky exercise. With Pelosi, he backed Pennsylvania Democrat John Murtha's ill-fated challenge to Maryland's Steny Hoyer for the post of majority leader. Tasked with helping to revise party caucus rules and ethics guidelines, Capuano emphasized inclusion and reform, and stayed out of the spotlight. In March 2008, the House passed his reform package, which created an Office of Congressional Ethics, an independent board that for the first time allows non-lawmakers to review possible ethics violations by House members. Congressional watchdog groups have long favored setting up such a panel. Republicans opposed the plan for its failure to put teeth into the House Standards of Official Conduct (Ethics) Committee, and the reform had little practical impact during its first year.

He also chairs the House Administration Committee's Capitol Security Subcommittee, which puts him in charge of the Capitol Police force and other internal operations that affect the day-to-day lives of members of Congress. He was also assigned to head the Commission on Mailing Standards, which supervises franked mail, another sensitive insider task that requires the trust of House leaders. Republicans groused about possible free speech violations in a Capuano proposal to require House approval of members' postings on outside websites, but he responded that the criticism was "laughably inaccurate."

In the foreign policy arena, Capuano co-founded the Congressional Caucus on Sudan and traveled to the region in 2006 in support of United Nations peacekeeping forces.

Like any traditional Boston pol, he angles for federal goodies for his district. On the Transportation and Infrastructure Committee, he has worked to secure funding for the North Washington Street Bridge near North Station plus several rapid-transit extensions. After a fatal ceiling collapse in a tunnel that was part of Boston's "Big Dig" (a massive highway and tunnel project) in 2006, he sponsored a bill setting highway tunnel inspection standards, which passed the House. When Catholic bishops across the nation said in 2004 that they would deny communion to presidential candidate John Kerry of Massachusetts because of his support for abortion rights, Capuano was out front with a public reply to the bishops that Catholics should be able to vote their conscience. Capuano has expressed interest in running for the next available Senate seat in Massachusetts.

NINTH DISTRICT

Stephen Lynch (D)

Elected Oct. 2001, 4th full term; b. March 31, 1955, Boston; home, South Boston; Wentworth Inst., B.S. 1988, Boston Col. Schl. of Law, J.D. 1991, Harvard U. JFK Schl. of Gov., M.A. 1998; Catholic; married (Margaret); 2 children.

Elected Office: MA House of Reps., 1994–96; MA Senate, 1996–2001.

Professional Career: Structural ironworker, 1973–91; Practicing atty., 1991–2001.

DC Office: 221 CHOB, 20515, 202-225-8273; Fax: 202-225-3984; Web site: www.house.gov/lynch.

State Offices: Boston, 617-428-2000; Brockton, 508-586-5555.

Committees: *Financial Services* (17th of 42 D): Capital Markets, Insurance & Government Sponsored Enterprises; Housing & Community Opportunity; Oversight & Investigations. *Oversight & Government Reform* (9th of 24 D): Federal Workforce, Postal Service & the District of Columbia (Chmn); National Security & Government Reform.

Group Ratings

	ADA	ACLU	AFS	LCV	ITIC	NTU	COC	ACU	CFG	FRC
2008	95	91	100	100	86	15	53	8	8	5
2007	90	—	100	90	—	4	60	0	6	—

National Journal Ratings

	2007 LIB	—	2007 CONS	2008 LIB	—	2008 CONS
Economic	82%	—	0%	76%	—	23%
Social	57%	—	42%	67%	—	28%
Foreign	68%	—	31%	76%	—	24%
Composite	72%	—	28%	74%	—	26%

Key Votes of the 110th Congress

1. Increase minimum wage	Y	5. Share immigration data	Y	9. Withdraw troops 8/08	Y
2. Expand SCHIP	Y	6. Foreign aid abortion ban	N	10. No operations in Iran	Y
3. Raise CAFE standards	Y	7. Ban gay bias in workplace	Y	11. Free trade with Peru	Y
4. Bail out financial markets	N	8. Repeal D.C. gun law	N	12. Overhaul FISA	N

Election Results

2008 general	Stephen Lynch (D)..242,166	(99%)	($739,421)
2008 primary	Stephen Lynch (D)....................................... unopposed		

Prior Winning Percentages: 2006 (78%); 2004 (100%); 2002 (100%); 2001 (66%)

Population		Race/Ethnicity		Work	
Pop. 2007:	651,419	White:	75.1%	Private:	81.2%
Change since 2000:	Up 2.7%	Black:	11.9%	Government:	13.8%
Urban:	98.4%	Hispanic:	5.5%	Self-employed:	4.9%
Rural:	1.6%	Asian:	4.7%	Blue collar:	15.4%
Area size:	319 sq. mi.	Native Am.:	0.2%	White collar:	68.4%
		Hawaiian:	0.0%	Khaki collar:	0.1%
Age		Two+ races:	1.1%	Other:	16.1%
Median age:	38.5 yrs.			Median income:	$67,804
More than 65 yrs:	13.4%	*Ancestry*		Median home value:	$393,300
Less than 18 yrs:	23.3%	Irish:	24.5%	Poverty:	8.6%
		Italian:	11.5%		
Education		English:	7.5%	**Military Veterans**	
H.S. grad:	89.6%			% of Pop:	8.8%
College grad:	38.1%				
Grad degree:	15.7%				

The Irish remain the dominant political tribe in Boston, and in Massachusetts, though even in South Boston, long the center of Irish Boston, vestiges of the old neighborhoods are starting to gentrify. Southie's influence endures in the memory of two Irish Democrats who represented the area for all but two years from the Great Depression to the start of the 21st century. The first was John McCormack, an old-style backroom deal-maker who served as House speaker during the 1960s; the sec-

2008 Presidential Vote
Obama (D) 188,887	(60%)
McCain (R).............................120,394	(38%)

2004 Presidential Vote
Kerry (D)................................188,439	(63%)
Bush (R) 106,734	(36%)

Cook Partisan Voting Index: D + 11

ond was Joe Moakley, a close pal of Thomas (Tip) O'Neill's, who chaired the influential Rules Committee before Democrats lost the House majority in 1994.

The 9th Congressional District, historically anchored in Boston, has followed the move of the Irish to the suburbs. Today, fewer than one-third of its residents are in Boston, mostly in the still-Irish areas of South Boston, Hyde Park (shared with the 8th District), and West Roxbury. Completion of the transformational Big Dig highway construction project, with a new tunnel under Boston Harbor, has spurred economic development along the waterfront, including office buildings, hotels, condominiums, the John Joseph Moakley Courthouse, and a huge convention center. The development has reduced some of the parochialism in South Boston but has increased complaints of gentrification and of pricing the working class out of old neighborhoods.

Now that the ugly Central Artery, the north-south expressway that for five decades divided the city, has been moved underground, traffic flows far more efficiently (though progress came at a price: huge cost overruns drove the Big Dig bill to $15 billion, and the collapse of ceiling tile in a tunnel in July 2006 killed a woman). The 9th District also takes in much of Beacon Hill, including the gold-domed State House facing Boston Common. From there, the 9th heads west to the comfortable suburbs of Needham and Medfield, and southeast to Braintree, ancestral home of the presidential Adamses, and Brockton, the old shoe manufacturing town. Ethnically, this remains a heavily Irish congressional district, with Southie as home to an annual St. Patrick's Day parade preceded by a political breakfast and roast that is a must-attend for state politicians. Only the neighboring 10th District has more residents of Irish ancestry—further evidence of the Irish move out of Boston to the far suburbs.

The congressman from the 9th District is Democrat Stephen Lynch, who won a special election in October 2001 to succeed the late Joe Moakley. Lynch grew up in Boston's housing projects and took pride in making good by following the old ethnic precepts of hard work, family loyalty, and personal determination. After graduating from South Boston High School, he joined his father as a full-time ironworker while attending Wentworth Institute. Eventually, he became the youngest president in the history of the 2,000-member Local 7 of the Ironworkers union. After a fall on the job cut short his ironworking career, he graduated from Boston College Law School and opened a legal practice representing working people. In 1994, he was elected to the state House. Fourteen months later, he won a special election for a seat in the state Senate.

Lynch built a political base in South Boston and had strong union ties, advantages that led him to pursue the seat when Moakley announced in February 2001 that he would not seek re-election. The ailing Moakley, who was beloved by many House Democrats as a link between the party's old and new generations, died in May of that year. Lynch was one of several Democrats who had expressed interest in the race. The most prominent was Max Kennedy, son of Robert and Ethel Kennedy, but his campaign never gained traction. When Kennedy bowed out, Lynch became the front-runner. He stumbled after *The Boston Globe* revealed his student loan defaults years earlier, plus a tax lien that was resolved in 1998. He had also been arrested twice two decades earlier, for striking an anti-American student demonstrator and for smoking marijuana at a concert.

Three other state senators opposed Lynch, and the strongest among them was Cheryl Jacques, who is openly gay and had support from EMILY's List and other national feminist groups that criticized Lynch's anti-abortion views. But her switch in opposition to capital punishment stirred controversy. Moakley's two brothers, who wielded much influence, endorsed Lynch. Primary Election Day was September 11, 2001, but Republican Gov. Jane Swift decided not to postpone the vote despite the terrorist attacks. Lynch bested Jacques, 39% to 29%. In the anti-climactic general election five weeks later, he defeated another state senator, Jo Ann Sprague, 66%-33%.

In the House, Lynch falls roughly in the middle of the Democratic Caucus, and he has had the most conservative voting record in the Massachusetts delegation, especially on cultural issues. "That's like being called the slowest of the Kenyans in the marathon," he once quipped to the *Boston Herald*. Initially, he turned his attention to security, both at the nation's airports and in the war on terrorism. In 2006, he helped to secure $25 million for rail security in the Homeland Security spending bill, and he pushed for tighter port security. He was one of three Massachusetts House members to vote for the Iraq war resolution, and joined the first congressional delegation to Iraq after the overthrow of Saddam Hussein. Later, he criticized contractors' "disgraceful" abuse of war funding and questioned possible contract violations by the Blackwater International security firm. In 2006, he was one of 42 House Democrats to vote for a Republican resolution backing President Bush's policies in Iraq. And in December 2007, he was the only House member from Massachusetts to vote for a war spending bill. He showed unexpected support for gay-rights causes, developing a political alliance with Rep. Barney Frank, a liberal gay lawmaker from Massachusetts.

Lynch has been much engaged in the congressional investigations into steroid use in professional baseball. At hearings in 2005, he criticized Major League Baseball for a policy that "facilitates steroid abuse" and threatened additional congressional action. When former Red Sox star pitcher Roger Clemens testified in February 2008 that he had not used steroids, Lynch said he doubted that Clemens was telling the truth and called for prosecuting players who use steroids.

He has been re-elected without difficulty. In 2006, Lynch was challenged by Jack Robinson, who had run two statewide races. Robinson supported Bush's Social Security partial privatization plan and cuts in capital gains and income taxes, and called for dividing Iraq into three territories. Lynch had little reason for concern and won 78%-22%. Unopposed in 2008, he expressed interest in running for the Senate or for Boston mayor.

TENTH DISTRICT

Bill Delahunt (D)

Elected 1996, 7th term; b. July 18, 1941, Quincy; home, Quincy; Middlebury Col., B.A. 1963, Boston Col., J.D. 1967; Catholic; divorced; 2 children.

Military Career: Coast Guard, 1963; Coast Guard Reserves, 1963–71.

Elected Office: Quincy City Cncl., 1971; MA House of Reps., 1972–75.

Professional Career: Practicing atty., 1967–75; Asst. clerk, Norfolk Superior Court, 1969–71; Norfolk Cnty. dist. atty., 1975–96.

DC Office: 2454 RHOB, 20515, 202-225-3111; Fax: 202-225-5658; Web site: www.house.gov/delahunt.

State Offices: Hyannis, 508-771-0666; Quincy, 617-770-3700.

Committees: *Foreign Affairs* (8th of 28 D): Europe; International Organizations, Human Rights & Oversight (Chmn). *Judiciary* (10th of 24 D): Commercial & Administrative Law; Constitution, Civil Rights & Civil Liberties; Immigration, Citizenship, Border Security & International Law.

Group Ratings

	ADA	ACLU	AFS	LCV	ITIC	NTU	COC	ACU	CFG	FRC
2008	95	100	100	85	71	16	56	10	9	5
2007	95	—	100	90	—	3	50	0	7	—

National Journal Ratings

	2007 LIB	—	2007 CONS		2008 LIB	—	2008 CONS
Economic	82%	—	0%		85%	—	0%
Social	92%	—	0%		82%	—	0%
Foreign	93%	—	7%		85%	—	15%
Composite	93%	—	7%		90%	—	11%

Key Votes of the 110th Congress

1. Increase minimum wage	Y	5. Share immigration data	N	9. Withdraw troops 8/08	Y
2. Expand SCHIP	*	6. Foreign aid abortion ban	N	10. No operations in Iran	Y
3. Raise CAFE standards	Y	7. Ban gay bias in workplace	Y	11. Free trade with Peru	N
4. Bail out financial markets	N	8. Repeal D.C. gun law	N	12. Overhaul FISA	N

Election Results

2008 general	Bill Delahunt (D)	272,899	(99%)	($1,217,875)
2008 primary	Bill Delahunt (D)	unopposed		

Prior Winning Percentages: 2006 (64%); 2004 (66%); 2002 (69%); 2000 (74%); 1998 (70%); 1996 (54%)

Population		Race/Ethnicity		Work	
Pop. 2007:	638,988	White:	90.8%	Private:	77.2%
Change since 2000:	Up 0.5%	Black:	2.0%	Government:	13.1%
Urban:	92.2%	Hispanic:	1.4%	Self-employed:	9.6%
Rural:	7.8%	Asian:	3.6%	Blue collar:	17.6%
Area size:	2,969 sq. mi.	Native Am.:	0.4%	White collar:	65.4%
		Hawaiian:	0.0%	Khaki collar:	0.2%
Age		Two+ races:	1.1%	Other:	16.9%
Median age:	42.3 yrs.			Median income:	$66,291
More than 65 yrs:	17.0%	*Ancestry*		Median home value:	$410,300
Less than 18 yrs:	20.8%	Irish:	24.6%	Poverty:	5.8%
		English:	12.2%		
Education		Italian:	10.9%	**Military Veterans**	
H.S. grad:	93.0%			% of Pop:	11.9%
College grad:	37.8%				
Grad degree:	13.6%				

The South Shore of Massachusetts Bay, from Boston southward to Plymouth and then down Cape Cod (there is a lot of dispute about which way is up and down on the Cape), is Massachusetts's oldest settled territory. The Pilgrims landed here at Plymouth Rock in 1620. This stony land was farmed by John Adams's father, who was anything but the aristocrat some later members of the Adams family would have had you believe. Daniel Webster lived in the South Shore town of Marshfield, today a high-income suburb of Boston far out on the usually clogged Southeast Expressway. Joseph P. Kennedy used to summer with his young family on Nantasket Beach in Hull, before moving out of Massachusetts when the Yankees wouldn't let them into their beach club in Cohasset in the 1920s. But the Kennedys continue to summer at their Hyannis Port compound on the Cape. Provincetown, at the tip of the Cape, is still a fishing port, one of the major gay vacation areas in the country. The islands of Martha's Vineyard and Nantucket, rich whaling ports in the early 19th century, are favored summer resorts for the liberal rich of Boston, New York, and Washington. Half the nation's cranberry growers are clustered among the bogs along Cape Cod Bay. But the Cape is also filled with retirees who enjoy the beauty and quiet pace.

The 10th Congressional District of Massachusetts follows the South Shore from Quincy (QUIN zee), with its large Asian population, to the Cape. It juts inland almost, but not quite, to Brockton and includes Martha's Vineyard and Nantucket, where the glitterati have generated a "not in my backyard" fury over a proposed windmill farm in the nearby channel waters. With the loss of blue-collar jobs, business growth in the South Shore has been slower than elsewhere in the Boston area. The South Shore and the Cape were once exclusively Protestant and Yankee, but in the Massachusetts way, they have changed over the

2008 Presidential Vote

Obama (D)	197,365	(55%)
McCain (R)	156,294	(43%)

2004 Presidential Vote

Kerry (D)	194,092	(56%)
Bush (R)	151,209	(43%)

Cook Partisan Voting Index: D+5

years, with Irish and Italian surnames as common as Yankee ones (this is the nation's most heavily Irish congressional district), and the descendants of Portuguese-Azorean fishermen have fanned out into the countryside. Liberal politics, well established on the Vineyard and Nantucket, have spread inland as well. Although Republican Mitt Romney carried the area in 2002, the South Shore is generally Democratic territory.

The congressman from the 10th District is Bill Delahunt, a Democrat elected in 1996. Delahunt is a lifelong resident of Quincy, at the northern tip of the district. He graduated from Middlebury College and Boston College Law School and served in the Coast Guard. He practiced law and served on the Quincy Council. In 1972, he was elected to the state House. Democratic Gov. Michael Dukakis in 1975 appointed him district attorney of Norfolk County, a job that Delahunt held for two decades. He ran for the U.S. House in 1996, when 24-year incumbent Rep. Gerry Studds retired. He had serious primary competition from former state Rep. Philip Johnston and self-financed environmentalist Ian Bowles. The initial results showed 38% each for Delahunt and Johnston, with Johnston ahead by 266 votes. A recount declared Johnston still ahead by 175 votes.

But Delahunt filed suit, and on October 4, a judge ruled that more than 900 punch-card votes in Weymouth had not been properly tabulated. Foreshadowing another election challenge four years later, the judge ordered a recount of every ballot with an indentation, dimple or other mark. Only in this district and in 14 counties in Texas had dimpled chads ever been counted as votes in the United States until the Broward, Palm Beach and Miami-Dade County canvassing boards started counting them in November 2000. On October 10, Delahunt was declared the winner by 108 votes, even as Johnston was being hailed at a Quincy rally by Sens. Edward Kennedy of Massachusetts and Hillary Rodham Clinton of New York. Johnston called the result a "travesty," and Delahunt had less than a month to campaign for the general election against conservative state House Minority Leader Edward Teague. Both ran million-dollar campaigns. Eight years earlier, Republican George H. W. Bush carried this district over native son Dukakis. But reaction here to the new Republican majority in the House was hostile, and Delahunt won 54%-42%.

Delahunt has been an active legislator with a very liberal voting record and has kept a pledge to wear Cape Cod ties in the House and hand them out to colleagues of both parties. As the father of an adopted daughter who escaped Vietnam in the 1975 Operation Babylift, he has written laws to ease international adoptions. His positions on abortion offer a window on Massachusetts' move to the left. In 1974, as a state legislator he called the Supreme Court's *Roe v. Wade* decision legalizing abortion "a tragic decision," but he switched to a pro-abortion rights position before running for the House.

On the Judiciary Committee, Delahunt teamed with Illinois Republican Ray LaHood on the Innocence Protection Act, which includes federal funding to the states for DNA testing of people accused of crimes. The House passed it, 393-14, and it became law in 2004. His experience with contested elections made him an enthusiast for abolishing the Electoral College.

When the immigration issue heated up in recent years, Delahunt tried to increase the number of temporary visas, partly to boost the seasonal workforce on the Cape. He also chaired an investigation of Republican claims of improper handling by the House's presiding officer of an August 2007 vote on farm-bill benefits to illegal immigrants. Following a year-long inquiry, the panel unanimously found what Delahunt termed an "abundance of problems" with the vote and the voting system itself, but did not blame any particular member. As a member of the House Ethics Committee, Delahunt chaired the case of Rep. William Jefferson, D-La., who was accused by federal investigators of taking bribes.

Delahunt has generated controversy with his hands-on diplomatic efforts. He has met frequently with Venezuela president Hugo Chavez, partly with the goal of securing cheaper oil for low-income constituents. Critics accuse him of supporting a despot. Delahunt also joined several congressional delegations to visit Cuba to encourage democratic reforms. As the chairman of the International Organizations, Human Rights, and Oversight Subcommittee on the Foreign Affairs Committee, he sought to increase the independence of the State Department's inspector general following charges of obstruction of sensitive investigations. He also looked into claims that detainees at the federal prison at Guantanamo were held illegally and were tortured.

Delahunt has easily won his re-election bids, with no need to count dimpled chads. On Capitol Hill, he has taken some ribbing for his fraternity-house living quarters. To save on the expense of maintaining two homes, while in Washington Delahunt shares a small townhouse with Sens. Chuck Schumer of New York, Richard Durbin of Illinois, and their landlord, Rep. George Miller of California. Delahunt sleeps in the living room, as does Schumer, and the refrigerator is frequently empty.

★ MICHIGAN ★

When the French aristocrat Alexis de Tocqueville on his travels to America in 1831 wanted to visit the frontier, he went got on a boat and traveled across Lake Erie to what was then the Michigan Territory. Tocqueville was not the first Frenchman to travel there. Some two centuries before, French explorers and missionaries sailed the Great Lakes and slapped their version of Indian names on the landscape, which is why Michigan's *ch* is pronounced like *sh* and why Mackinac is pronounced with a silent final *c* (but Michiganders don't carry it to extremes: Detroit ends with a robust English *oit*). Michigan was not effectively occupied by the United States until 1796 and was bypassed in the initial westward rush into Ohio, Indiana and Illinois. Tocqueville was still able to travel through virgin woods occupied by Indian tribes, but only barely. In the 1830s, Michigan was settled in a rush by Yankee migrants from Upstate New York, who cut down trees and built farms and neat New England-style towns complete with schools and colleges. Politically, Michigan was full of Yankee reformers who hated slavery, manned the Underground Railroad, promoted temperance and in 1855 gave Michigan a constitution that banned (as it does to this day) capital punishment. Michigan was one of the birthplaces of the Republican Party, which held its first official meeting in Jackson in 1854 (The party held its first informal meeting in Ripon, Wis.) and swept the state in the elections later that year. Until 1929, Michigan was one of the most Republican states in the nation.

After the Civil War, Michigan developed an industrial economy. Its Lower Peninsula was mostly covered with trees, and lumber was the first boom industry on which Michigan overrelied. Forests were clear-cut or swept by blazes like the 1881 fire that burned out half the Thumb. In the late 1800s, huge copper deposits were discovered on the Keweenaw Peninsula, which juts from the Upper Peninsula into icy Lake Superior. Immigrants from Italy and Finland, Cornwall and Croatia came to work in the mines. Then came the auto industry. A combination of accident and shrewdness—the prickly genius of Henry Ford and the willingness of local bankers to finance auto start-ups—ensured that America's fastest-growing industry for the first 30 years of the 20th century was centered in Michigan. Detroit became a boomtown, the nation's fastest-growing major metropolitan area after Los Angeles. It zoomed from a population of 426,000 in 1900 to 2.2 million in 1930 (it was 4.2 million in 2000). The auto industry drew labor from Outstate Michigan, from southern Ontario and from the farms of Ohio and Indiana. It attracted Poles and Italians, Hungarians and Belgians, Greeks and Jews. During World War II and after, it brought whites from the Kentucky and Tennessee mountains and blacks from Alabama and Mississippi.

This influx of a polyglot proletariat eventually changed Michigan's politics. The catalyst was the Great Depression of the 1930s and company managers' desire to use machines efficiently, treating employees as extensions of machines and with great distrust. That culminated in the 1937 sit-down strikes organized by the new United Auto Workers (UAW). Management and labor fought, sometimes literally, for pieces of what both sides feared was a shrinking pie. The UAW won and organized most of the companies after Democratic Gov. Frank Murphy refused to send in troops to break the illegal strikes. In the years that followed, autoworkers became a heavily Democratic voting bloc.

Michigan politics became a kind of class warfare, conducted with a bitterness that split families and neighbors. The union mostly won, because demographics benefited the Democrats: Autoworkers and post-1900 immigrants produced more children than did Outstate Yankees or management. After Walter Reuther's election as UAW president in 1947, voters elected young, liberal G. Mennen Williams as governor in 1948. By 1954, the Democrats, closely tied to the UAW, seemed to have become the natural majority in the state. As growth continued, economic issues became less bitter. By the early 1960s, the class-warfare atmosphere had dissipated; in 1964, Henry Ford II joined Reuther in backing Democrat Lyndon Johnson for president. Republicans George Romney, the former American Motors president elected governor in 1962, and his successor, William Milliken, accepted the welfare-state policies endorsed by the UAW leadership and the Democrats. The state government was one of the nation's most generous, and not just to the poor and the unemployed. It supported one of the nation's most distinguished and extensive higher-education systems, built state parks and recreation areas, and pioneered efforts to end racial discrimination.

This system, which had seemed eternal, came crashing down with the collapse of the domestic auto industry after the oil shocks of the 1970s. Union-management relations had been static since 1941, and there had been no major technological changes in American autos since the automatic transmission in 1940. Michigan incomes had grown as Americans grew more affluent. The one-car household became the two-car household, and consumers enjoyed the tail fins and chrome of new car styling. But in 1979, this big-unit economy went bust. It became startlingly clear that the Big Three automakers and the UAW did not have a captive market, and that Americans did not have to buy a new full-sized American-made car every two or three years. Foreign competitors were producing better and cheaper cars that were more responsive to changes in gas prices and consumer preference. Big business and labor, so well adapted for growth in the quarter century after World War II, proved poorly adapted for the quarter century that

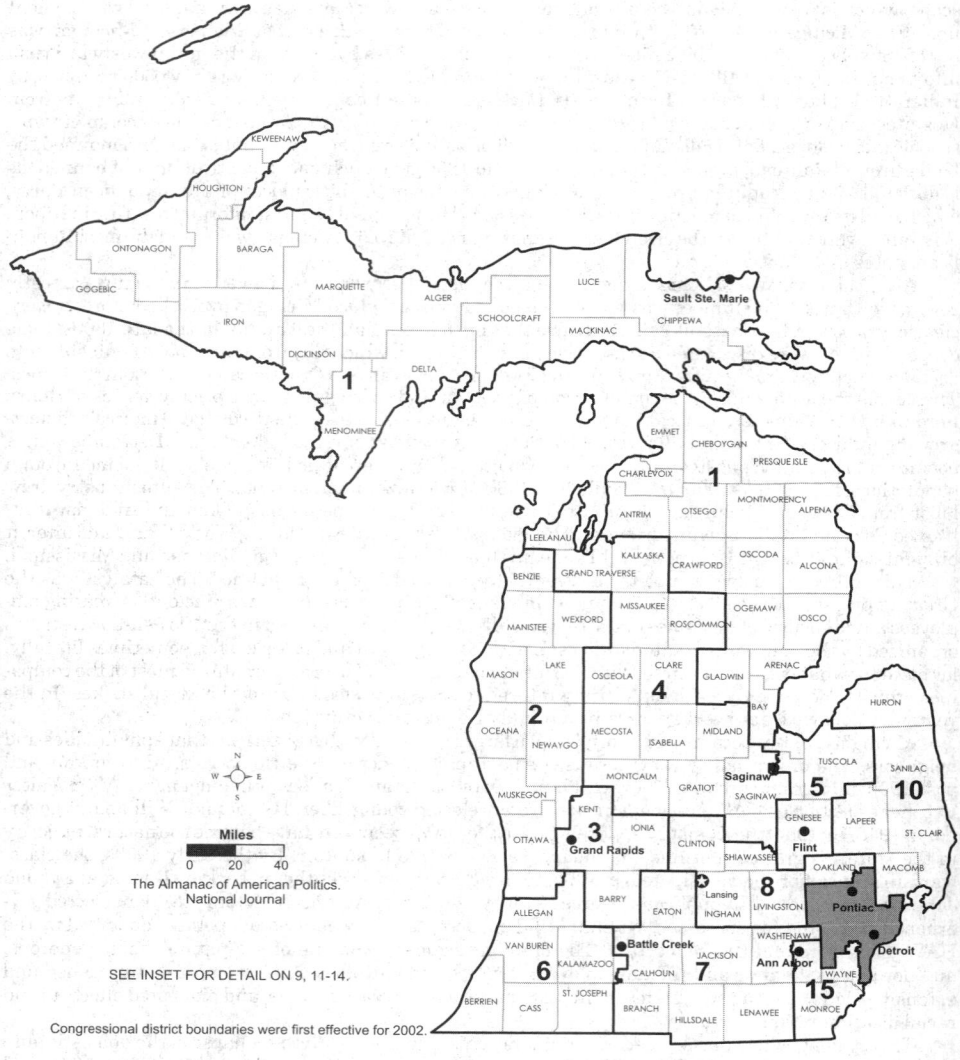

Miles

0   20   40

The Almanac of American Politics.
National Journal

SEE INSET FOR DETAIL ON 9, 11-14.

Congressional district boundaries were first effective for 2002.

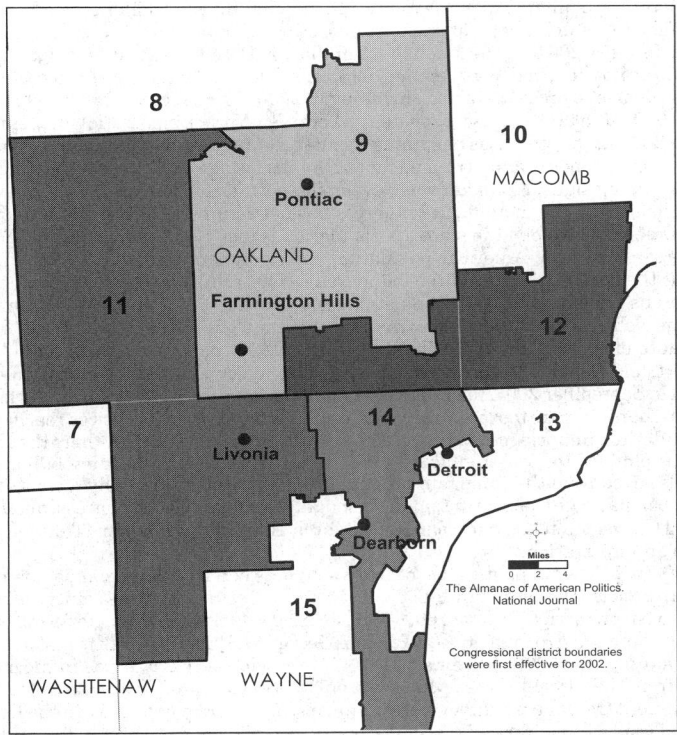

followed. Auto-industry employment in Michigan fell from 437,000 in October 1978 to 289,000 in October 1982. Chrysler nearly went bankrupt, Ford was in financial distress, and General Motors posted its first losses in years.

The collapse of its big-unit economy forced the state to experiment. The first to try was Gov. James Blanchard, a Democrat elected in 1982 with a record of supporting big units. His major achievement in eight years in Congress was managing the Chrysler bailout in the House. Blanchard worked to build a small-unit economy. He was proud of his efforts to stimulate high-skill, capital-intensive, flexible manufacturing, and he used $750 million of state pension funds as venture capital for manufacturers of items ranging from tape drives for microcomputers to fiberglass coffins. The second experiment came from John Engler, the Republican who beat Blanchard in 1990 and was resoundingly reelected in 1994 and 1998. Engler believed in less government activism and industrial policy. He cut taxes more than 30 times, and welfare rolls were cut by more than two-thirds. Engler pressed for public school choice and charter schools, and changed state pensions from defined benefits to defined contributions. Throughout the second half of the 1990s, the economy boomed. The auto industry, once an employer of thousands of low-skill workers, became more high-tech. The number of unionized autoworkers fell to 250,000 in 2000, but jobs required much higher skills and autoworkers' earnings averaged $60,000. With the auto companies requiring high standards and speedy turnaround from subcontractors, Michigan became the home of almost all the nation's auto-parts engineering centers and of much of the nation's large-scale manufacturing experts. Michigan's population rose 7% in the 1990s after staying even in the 1980s; median household incomes rose 5% after inflation. Large parts of the state—the western and northern suburbs of Detroit, greater Grand Rapids, the northwest corner of the Upper Peninsula—were unmistakably booming. The one glaring exception was the city of Detroit. Its population fell to 951,000 in 2000, almost exactly half the 1.8 million people it had in 1950. Starting with the riot of 1967, crime rates in Detroit were enormously high for 25 years, and much of the city simply vanished—houses were abandoned or burned down, commercial frontage had nearly 100% vacancy rates, the downtown was a beleaguered fortress surrounded by blasted-out square miles. But even Detroit began rebounding in the 1990s. Crime and welfare rolls were down, new stadiums and gambling casinos, even some new housing, were built downtown, and old theaters were refurbished.

But the recovery didn't last. Since 2000, efforts to diversify the economy and to encourage flexible manufacturing were not enough to compensate for the sharply deteriorating condition of the Big Three—or the Detroit Three, as they were called in November 2008, when their tin-eared CEOs flew in their corporate jets to Washington to seek a multi-billion-dollar taxpayer-financed bailout. The first signs came in 2000, when the state's unemployment rate rose above the national average; employment peaked at 4.9 million in January 2001 and declined to 4.1 million by December 2008. Michigan never recovered from the brief 2001 recession, and by December 2008, unemployment had risen to 10.5% of the labor force. The state's gross domestic product started shrinking in 2006. The net outmigration of people from 2000 to 2008 was 316,000—higher than any other state except New York. Democratic Gov. Jennifer Granholm came to office in 2003 as the state was beginning its most recent downward economic spiral. She encouraged "cool cities" developments and arranged for tax breaks for new facilities for the automakers. There were some encouraging signs. Michigan was developing new jobs in health care, professional services, finance and tourism. Still, the incremental progress has not stemmed the outflow of people. And immigrants by and large have avoided the state; its population is just 4% Hispanic and 2% Asian, and while it has the nation's largest Arab-American population, their numbers amount to less than 2% of the total.

Throughout the decade, the Big Three foundered—constrained by their contracts with the UAW, with their generous benefits and thousands of pages of work rules, and unable or unwilling to build the high-mileage vehicles that the public wanted and that government standards demanded. The bankruptcy of auto-electronics giant Delphi showed the UAW that its contracts could be torn up by a bankruptcy court, and General Motors was able to squeeze major concessions from the union in the contract negotiated in September 2007, including a stipulation that new hires could be paid lower wages and benefits. But the changes came too late. Big-car sales plummeted when gas prices reached $4 a gallon in May 2008, and after the financial crisis triggered by the failure of Lehman Brothers that September, the Big Three's sales plunged to catastrophic lows. GM and Chrysler were bleeding billions in cash every month. Ford was saved from the same fate because it had mortgaged virtually all of its assets in 2007. The $25-billion loan package that the automakers sought was defeated in Congress, and President Bush granted GM and Chrysler a temporary loan, until March 2009, of $13.4 billion. That left the problem to the new Obama administration.

Since the 1930s, Michigan politics has been divided between labor and management, and between the Detroit metro area and Outstate. In 1960, John F. Kennedy carried three-county metro Detroit 62%-38%, and Richard Nixon carried Outstate 60%-39%, for a 51%-49% Kennedy victory. In 2004, John Kerry carried the three-county metro area 56%-43%, while George W. Bush carried the rest of the state, which cast 61% of the vote, by only 52%-47%, for a 51%-48% Kerry victory. Kerry's lead in the metro area came almost entirely from the city of Detroit, which cast only 7% of the state's votes but voted 94% for Kerry. Kerry carried affluent Oakland County, where many upscale voters moved toward the Democrats in the 1990s on cultural issues. Bush carried Macomb County, historically more blue-collar and Democratic; it is pretty affluent now, and in the 1970s and 1980s, it trended away from Democrats on cultural issues. The Grand Rapids area, with its large Dutch-American population and many Christian conservatives, voted heavily Republican. The industrial Flint, Saginaw and Bay City areas, where unions remain relatively strong, voted heavily Democratic, as did the areas around Lansing, the state capital, and Ann Arbor, home of the University of Michigan. The Upper Peninsula, historically Democratic, voted for Bush.

Similar patterns are apparent in state elections. In 2006, against Republican Dick DeVos's expensive self-financed campaign, Democratic Gov. Granholm was re-elected 56%-42%. Also that year, Democratic Sen. Debbie Stabenow, a narrow winner in 2000, was re-elected 57%-41%. Democrats recaptured a majority in the state House, held by Republicans since 1994, and ran what turned out to be competitive races in four Republican congressional districts. Even so, there was one discordant result. The ballot measure banning racial quotas and preferences in state government and state universities, which was opposed and shunned by politicians of both parties, passed by a resounding 58%-42% margin, trailing only in the counties that include Detroit, the University of Michigan and Michigan State University.

The 2008 election results showed even more movement toward Democrats. At some points during the campaign, polls showed John McCain to be competitive in the state. The Democratic National Committee's decision invalidating Michigan's presidential primary meant that Barack Obama's campaign

Population		Household Income		Work	
Pop. 2007:	10,094,027	Under $15k:	13.6%	Private:	82.4%
State rank:	8th of 50	$15k to $50k:	37.6%	Government:	11.7%
Change since 2000:	Up 1.6%	$50k to $100k:	31.7%	Self-employed:	5.6%
Urban:	73.1%	$100k to $150k:	14.4%	Unemployment (3-yr. average):	6.1%
Rural:	26.9%	Over $150k:	2.7%	Poverty:	13.7%
Native of state:	75.7%	Median income:	$48,642	Blue collar:	24.6%
Not a citizen:	3.2%	**Home Value**		White collar:	57.8%
Area size:	96,716 sq. mi.	Under $100k:	25.0%	Khaki collar:	0.1%
Most populous cities		$100k to $300k:	61.2%	Other:	17.5%
1. Detroit	837,711	$300k to $500k:	10.2%		
2. Grand Rapids	193,671	$500k to $1 mil:	3.0%	**Age**	
3. Warren	132,464	Over $1 million:	0.6%	Median age:	37.3 yrs.
4. Sterling Heights	131,113	Median:	$152,200	More than 65 yrs:	12.6%
				Less than 18 yrs:	24.6%

Race/Ethnicity				Military Veterans		Registered Voters in 2008	
White:	77.6%	*Language*		% of Pop:	10.1%	No party registration	
Black:	14.0%	English:	91.0%	*Veterans by Period*		Voter turnout:	5,001,766
Hispanic:	3.9%	Spanish:	3.0%	WWII and before:	14.1%	Turnout as % of	
Asian:	2.3%	Asian:	1.4%	Korea:	12.9%	voting age:	65.7%
Native Am.:	0.5%	Other		Vietnam:	33.0%	**Legislature**	
Hawaiian:	0.0%	European	3.0%	Gulf (pre-2001):	9.0%	Senate:	17 D 21 R
Two+ races:	1.5%	**Education**		Gulf (post-2001):	4.4%	House:	67 D 43 R
Ancestry		H.S. grad:	87.0%	Peace time:	26.6%		
German:	17.2%	College grad:	24.5%				
Irish:	8.9%	Grad degree:	9.3%				
English:	8.1%						

got a late start organizing here. But after the national crisis in the financial markets in mid-September, the numbers shifted toward Obama, and the McCain campaign announced it was pulling out of the state. Obama carried Michigan 57%-41%, the best Democratic showing here since 1964. He carried Oakland County and Macomb County as well. He even carried, by a narrow margin, Grand Rapids's Kent County. The trend toward Democrats was especially strong in hitherto heavily Republican western Michigan. Sen. Carl Levin, Michigan's most popular Democrat, was re-elected to a sixth term by 63%-34%, his best margin ever; he carried 77 of 83 counties. Democrats increased their majority in the state House to 67-43 and captured two Republican seats in the U.S. House. Michigan, historically Republican and for some decades very marginal, now seems more Democratic than at any time in its history.

Presidential politics For a moment in history Michigan was a bellwether state. In three elections in a row—1984, 1988 and 1992—it voted within 1% of the national average for all major presidential candidates. It then voted 3% more Democratic in 1996, 2000 and 2004, close enough to make it a target state in the last two close contests. In 2008, it was 4% more Democratic. The shift in the 1990s occurred mainly in the most affluent areas, notably in Oakland County, which, like other suburban counties in the nation's largest metro areas, moved toward Democrats on cultural issues. The shift between 2004 and 2008 occurred mainly in western Michigan, where the economy was doing quite well in the 1990s but was suffering by 2008. Voters in union households voted 67%-31% for Obama and made up about one-third of the electorate, down from about half in the 1970s. Voters in nonunion households gave Obama a 52%-46% majority.

Michigan has had problems getting influence in the presidential selection process. One reason is that it does not have party registration, which is required by Democratic Party rules. So Michigan Democrats have to select their delegates through caucuses. Michigan Democrats, led by Sen. Carl Levin and Democratic National Committee woman Debbie Dingell, have worked to make Michigan one of the early primary states. They have argued, not unreasonably, that there is nothing sacred about Iowa and New Hampshire voting first. In 2003, they scheduled the Michigan Democratic Caucus for the same day as the New Hampshire primary, but the Democratic National Committee threatened not to recognize the results. They backed down after getting a pledge that a new commission would reexamine the delegate selection process after the 2004 election. It was duly appointed, and the DNC voted to allow two new early contests, a Nevada caucus and a South Carolina primary. It was certainly not the result Michigan Democrats had hoped for. In December 2006, Michigan Republican Chairman Saul Anuzis said that he and Democratic state Chairman Mark Brewer agreed that Michigan should hold simultaneous primaries. In September 2007, Granholm signed a bill setting a January 15 primary date, the earliest in state history.

But the DNC objected and asked presidential candidates to withdraw their names from the ballot. Barack Obama, John Edwards, Joe Biden and Bill Richardson did so in October. Hillary Rodham Clinton and Christopher Dodd did not (Dennis Kucinich did not file the right paperwork to withdraw and remained on the ballot). Two lower courts ruled against the primary law, but the state Supreme Court upheld it on November 21. On December 1, the DNC voted to strip Michigan of all of its delegates for holding its primary too early. The Republican National Committee, in contrast, stripped Michigan of only half its delegates, and its candidates did campaign in the state.

Only 600,000 people voted in the Democratic primary on January 15, compared with 869,000 in the Republican primary and 1.3 million in the Republican primary in 2000 (when exit polls showed that 17%

2008 Presidential Vote
Obama (D) 2,872,579 (57%)
McCain (R)...........................2,048,639 (41%)

2008 Democratic Presidential Primary
Clinton (D).............................328,309 (55%)
Uncommitted (D)...................238,168 (40%)

2008 Republican Presidential Primary
Romney (R)............................338,316 (39%)
McCain (R).............................257,985 (30%)
Huckabee (R) 139,764 (16%)
Paul (R)....................................54,475 (6%)

2004 Presidential Vote
Kerry (D)...............................2,479,183 (51%)
Bush (R)...............................2,313,746 (48%)

of those voters were self-identified Democrats, by far the largest such number that year). On the Democratic side, Clinton ran ahead of "uncommitted" by 55%-40%. She carried all but two of the 83 counties, and 13 of the 15 congressional districts. "Uncommitted" ran ahead in heavily black precincts and in the university towns; obviously these were mostly votes for Barack Obama, who had won the Iowa caucuses 12 days earlier.

On the Republican side, Mitt Romney beat John McCain 39%-30%, with 16% for Mike Huckabee. McCain had hoped to duplicate his Michigan victory in 2000, when he won among self-identified Democrats and independents and lost to George W. Bush among self-identified Republicans. But with at least a semblance of a contest on the Democratic side, there were fewer crossover voters this time. Romney grew up in Michigan, and his father, George Romney, was elected governor three times in the 1960s. He promised to restore the American auto industry, while McCain said that some jobs that had been lost would never be recovered. Romney ran strongest in metro Detroit and in affluent areas like the Traverse Bay area. McCain ran strongest in small-town western Michigan and in the Upper Peninsula.

The Michigan result was accepted by national Republicans, and no one was much troubled by the state's losing half its delegates. As it turned out, the Republicans' winner-take-all delegate allocation rules enabled McCain to essentially clinch the party's nomination by winning several close victories between January 15 and Super Tuesday, on February 5. In contrast, the Democrats' proportional-representation delegate-allocation rules, and the closeness of the race between Clinton and Obama, made Michigan (and Florida, which held its primary January 29), a continuing issue. Dingell and other Michigan Democratic leaders tried to schedule a rerun primary, but got no cooperation from the Republican-controlled state Senate. Michigan Democrats and the Clinton campaign sought some representation for Michigan, but the Obama campaign decried that as unfair. Pundits argued whether the Michigan and Florida numbers should be included wholly or partially when calculating which candidate had won the most popular votes. On May 31, the DNC met and voted to seat half the Michigan delegates, allocating 69 delegates to Clinton and 59 to Obama—a ratio more favorable to Obama than the election results.

Congressional districting

111th Congress Lineup	
8 D	7 R
110th Congress Lineup	
9 R	6 D

Michigan has now lost four seats in the last three censuses—one after the 1980 census, two after the 1990 census and one after the 2000 census. It has been losing population since 2005 and is likely to lose another seat after the 2010 census.

In 2001, for the first time since the 1930s, redistricting was controlled by Republicans, with GOP majorities in both houses of the Legislature and with Gov. John Engler determined to use the power to shift the Democrats' 9-7 edge to a 9-6 Republican edge. He succeeded. There was no pretense of bipartisanship: Bills were introduced in the House and Senate abruptly in June 2001 and passed on near party-line votes. The plan ended the 26-year congressional career of House Democratic Whip David Bonior and put two pairs of Democratic incumbents in the same districts. Jim Barcia of the 5th District decided to return to the state Senate, where he used to serve, while John Dingell, the dean of the House, beat liberal Democrat Lynn Rivers in the new 15th District. The 1st District, held by Democrat Bart Stupak, seems likely to go Republican if he is not running. A new Republican district was created in western Wayne and Oakland counties, and shaky Republican incumbents Mike Rogers and Joe Knollenberg were strengthened.

For a time, this was arguably the most successful partisan redistricting plan in the nation. But as is often the case, when the tide of opinion shifts, the partisan intentions of even the cleverest boundary drawers can be thwarted. In 2002, 2004 and 2006, Republicans won a 9-6 edge in the House delegation. But in 2008 they lost two seats—Joe Knollenberg's in suburban Oakland County, by a wide margin, and the seat of conservative freshman Tim Walberg, in south-central Michigan, by a narrow margin—and Democrats emerged with an 8-7 edge in the House delegation.

Who will control redistricting after the 2010 census? Currently, Republicans have a 21-17 majority in the state Senate and Democrats have a 67-43 majority in the state House. Democratic Gov. Granholm is term-limited. If the electoral patterns of 2008 continue into 2010, a Democrat is likely to be elected governor, and there would seem to be no chance that Republicans could overturn the Democrats' majority in the House. The focus then would be on the state Senate. In 2006, Republicans won nine seats and Democrats only one seat, with less than 55% of the vote, so Democrats would seem to have many targets from which to gain the three seats needed for control.

Governor

Jennifer Granholm (D)

Elected 2002, term expires Jan. 2011, 2nd term; b. Feb. 5, 1959, Vancouver, BC; home, Northville; U. of CA, B.A. 1984, Harvard U., J.D. 1987; Catholic; married (Daniel Mulhern); 3 children.

Elected Office: MI atty. gen., 1998–2002.

Professional Career: Prosecutor, U.S. Atty.'s Office, 1991–94; Corporation Cnsl., Wayne Cnty. exec., 1994–98.

Office: P.O. Box 30013, Lansing, 48909, 517-373-3400; Fax: 517-335-6863; Web site: www.michigan.gov/gov.

Election Results

2006 general	Jennifer Granholm (D)	2,142,513	(56%)
	Dick DeVos (R)	1,608,086	(42%)
2006 primary	Jennifer Granholm (D)	unopposed	

Prior Winning Percentages: 2002 (51%)

Democrat Jennifer Granholm was elected governor of Michigan in 2002 and 2006. She was born in British Columbia, Canada (and so is not eligible for the U.S. precidency), and moved to California at age 4, when her father, a bank-branch manager, was transferred there. In the 1960s, she lived in Anaheim, where she could watch the fireworks over Disneyland, and then in San Jose and San Carlos, a middle-class suburb on the peninsula south of San Francisco. She was a popular student in San Carlos High School and won the Miss San Carlos beauty and talent pageant. At age 18, she became a U.S. citizen. That year, she also moved to Los Angeles to try her luck as an actress, even though her parents wanted her to be the first in the family to graduate from college. She successfully completed the program at the American Academy of Dramatic Arts, but never got a major part in a film, though she once was a contestant on the television show *The Dating Game*. She made her living taking delivery complaints for the *Los Angeles Times* and as a tour guide at Universal Studios and at Marine World Africa USA, where she piloted tourist boats. She returned to San Carlos and in 1980 started her studies at the University of California at Berkeley. In 1984, she went off to Harvard Law School, where she demonstrated in favor of disinvestment in South Africa and edited the *Civil Rights-Civil Liberties Law Review*. While in Cambridge, she met her husband, Dan Mulhern, from Inkster, Mich., a suburb near Detroit's Metro Airport, and after she completed law school, they moved to Michigan.

Granholm clerked for federal appeals court Judge Damon Keith, then got a job in the U.S. attorney's office in Detroit. In 1994, she got what turned out to be her great political break when she was appointed corporation counsel to Wayne County Executive Ed McNamara, a man of impressive political skill (the new terminal at Detroit's Metro Airport is named after him). In 1998, Frank Kelley, Michigan's attorney general since January 1962, announced that he was retiring, and McNamara pushed Granholm to run for the office. She won the Democratic nomination at the state party convention in August 1998 and was elected in November—the only Democrat to win statewide, as Republican Gov. John Engler and Secretary of State Candice Miller were re-elected by wide margins. She might not have won if conservatives at the Republican state convention hadn't nominated a little-known candidate rather than Engler's choice, Scott Romney, son of former Gov. George Romney and brother of Massachusetts Gov. Mitt Romney, who ran for president in 2008.

Suddenly Granholm was the most visible Democrat in Michigan state government and an obvious candidate to succeed Engler in 2002, when he would be barred from running by term limits. She made an attractive candidate: She is articulate, poised, able to connect with an audience, and inclined to strike a note of consensus rather than confrontation. Granholm had serious competition in the Democratic primary from former Gov. Jim Blanchard and Rep. David Bonior. Much of the primary was a battle for endorsements. Bonior was endorsed by the state AFL-CIO and the United Auto Workers—endorsements that in the 1960s or 1970s would have clinched the nomination for him. But Granholm was endorsed in 2002 by the Teamsters and the Michigan Education Association—now at least as important in the state's Democratic politics. She also was backed by EMILY's List, the fundraising powerhouse for women candidates that brought in more than $400,000 for Granholm. Blanchard and Bonior decided to take state matching funds and accept a spending limit of $2 million. Granholm rejected the matching funds and raised and spent $5.7 million. Michigan does not have party registration, so voters can vote in either party's primary. In August 2002, 1.8 million voted, 58% of them in the Democratic primary, which was more seriously contested. Granholm won 48% of the vote, Bonior 28% and Blanchard 24%.

Granholm's general election opponent, Lt. Gov. Dick Posthumus, was not well-known to voters. A farmer from Grand Rapids's Kent County with solid conservative credentials, he tried to present himself as a blue-collar candidate. He called for tax cuts and for ending the single business tax. He split with Engler to oppose slant oil drilling under the Great Lakes and school vouchers, which had been beaten in a 2000 referendum. He attacked Granholm for favoring increases in property taxes and for opposing changes in welfare. But he concentrated much of his fire on her out-of-state origins. He portrayed himself as "raised in Michigan" and a product of Michigan public schools. "Let's just say I've got different values than come from Hollywood, Berkeley and Harvard," he said. But most voters did not seem to care that Granholm grew up somewhere else. She won by a closer than expected 51% to 47%. Only 220,000 Detroiters voted, but they cast more than 92% of their votes for Granholm and accounted for all of her popular-vote margin. Granholm carried Oakland County and suburban Wayne County, but lost Macomb County.

During Granholm's first term, most of the nation recovered from the 2001 recession, but not Michigan. Job losses continued, as the Big Three auto companies squeezed their subcontractors and still faced serious losses. In her first year, she faced a $3 billion shortfall in a $39 billion budget. Her first budget sliced aid to universities and cities, sold 2,500 state cars, rescinded $220 million in contracts and cut adult education by 70% and arts spending by 50%. More cuts followed in fall 2003, and in 2004 she persuaded the Legislature to raise the cigarette tax 75 cents, though not to replace the expiring estate tax with an inheritance tax. She cut or froze revenue-sharing grants to local governments by $523 million, got the Legislature to increase the casino tax from 18% to 24%, and put through $600 million in property tax relief for manufacturers moving to Michigan. In spite of her efforts, Michigan continued to lose jobs—the only state to do so in 2005, except for hurricane-ravaged Louisiana and Mississippi. Granholm accelerated spending on new roads and bridges. She welcomed new or expanded facilities by Hino Motors, Hyundai, Nissan, Suzuki, Aisin Seiki, and Toyota, but Michigan still failed to attract big new production plants from foreign automakers. She got the Legislature to raise the minimum wage, raise high school graduation requirements, and adopt her proposal for $4,000 Promise Grants to college students who maintain a 2.5 average their first two years.

Still, Granholm's job-approval ratings, which had been high her first two years, sagged in 2005 as Michigan's economy failed to grow. In June 2005, Republican Dick DeVos, son of the co-founder of Amway and president of the company (now called Alticor) until 2002, entered the race for governor. DeVos's ability to self-finance his campaign nudged others out of the race, and he began a heavy television advertising buy in February 2006. Altogether, he spent $42 million, $35 million of it his own money, while Granholm spent $14 million. He stressed his business experience and offered detailed programs on his website. "We have gone backward while the country has gone forward," he said. Granholm responded that the blame was misplaced and that "most people who work in the plants know that the shift of jobs to India or China is much more the result of federal policy and these trade agreements. . . . My tools can do only so much." Democrats attacked DeVos for his conservative stands on cultural issues, and he attacked Granholm for her veto of a ban on partial-birth abortions. Democrats charged that Amway had moved jobs from Michigan to China and attacked DeVos for sponsoring a school-voucher initiative that lost 69%-31% in 2000. In the August primary, in which voters can choose to vote for either party's candidate, DeVos won 52% of the votes to Granholm's 48%. Neither candidate had significant opposition within his/her own party.

Immediately after the primary, she began running ads and also had an online petition calling on President Bush to cap oil company profits. DeVos's businesslike demeanor contrasted with Granholm's ebullience in debates. By October 2006, she was leading in the polls and finally won by a solid 56%-42%. Turnout was 3.8 million, up 20% from the 3.1 million in 2002. The biggest increases were mostly in traditionally Republican areas, but it appears that many new Republican voters in 2004 were now voting Democratic. Granholm carried 55 of 83 counties, including many counties that have long voted Republican. Democrats also captured a majority of seats in the state House, but Republicans still held a 21-17 edge in the state Senate.

With Democrats in the majority at least in the House, Granholm in 2007 reached agreement with House and Senate leaders on a business tax to replace the 30-year-old system repealed in 2006. Granholm said the plan called for a tax cut for 70% of in-state businesses, and had provisions allowing new companies to pay lower taxes during their early start-up years. But a budget shortfall of up to $3 billion loomed. She refused to sign a budget extender while negotiations with the Legislature continued on her proposal to increase taxes to close the gap. And in October 2007, state government shut down for four hours, until the Legislature voted for the tax increases. Granholm went on the House floor to corral votes and persuaded two Republicans to vote for the bill. In the Senate, two Republicans defected and Lt. Gov. John Cherry cast the tie-breaking vote. The result was a $1.35 billion tax increase that raised the state income tax from 3.9% to 4.35%, extended the 6% sales tax to 23 new services and, as a sop to Republicans, revised teachers' health insurance. "This is a solution—not one of celebration, but one of resolve," Granholm said.

Granholm has pressed several initiatives to try to diversify the state's economy. She started a 21st Century Jobs Fund and a Venture Michigan Fund, which have put some $100 million into eight investment funds focusing on start-up companies. In 2008, she announced an Invest Michigan program that, with the help of a Business Leadership Council, would invest $300 million in state pension funds to attract small- and medium-sized businesses to Michigan. In 2008, Granholm reached an agreement with the

Legislature on the state budget earlier than in 2007, but could not get a deal on a requirement that specific percentages of electricity be produced from renewable sources. The Senate held out for a lower requirement than the House wanted. In June 2008, she vetoed a partial-birth abortion ban and a repeal of the motorcycle-helmet law. Also that month, the state Supreme Court ruled that the 2004 constitutional amendment banning same-sex marriage also barred public employers from offering health benefits to employees' same-sex domestic partners.

Democratic Sen. Carl Levin of Michigan and Democratic National Committeewoman Debbie Dingell have long pressed for an early presidential primary in Michigan, and with the agreement of both state parties, Granholm in September 2007 enthusiastically signed a bill setting the primary for Jan. 15, 2008. The Democratic National Committee said the move violated party rules, and most Democratic candidates withdrew their names. But Granholm's candidate, Hillary Rodham Clinton, kept hers on the ballot, and Granholm campaigned for her, even though the DNC voted in December to deprive Michigan of all of its delegates. "There's one candidate who said, 'I'm not going to abandon Michigan, and I'm going to keep my name on the ballot as a statement of how I support Michigan,' " Granholm said of Clinton. Efforts by Democrats to run a do-over primary failed, and the Clinton campaign continued to argue that the Michigan results (as well as those in Florida, which voted January 29) should count. Eventually, in May, the DNC voted to seat half the Michigan delegates, but soon afterward, Barack Obama clinched the nomination.

At the party's national convention in Denver, Granholm had a prime speaking spot, which she used to champion renewable energy sources. But she had a stickier problem at home—what to do about Detroit Mayor Kwame Kilpatrick. In 2008, the City Council asked her to remove him, under a provision of state law, for having the city enter into an $8.4 million settlement of a suit brought by three police officers. The settlement gave Kilpatrick custody of his text messages with his chief of staff, but the *Detroit Free Press* got hold of the messages, which indicated that the Democratic mayor had had a sexual relationship with his top aide. The Wayne County prosecutor brought criminal charges, and on Sept. 3, 2008, Granholm held a hearing in Detroit on the Kilpatrick matter. Soon afterward, he entered a guilty plea with the prosecutor, sparing Granholm the necessity of pursuing his forced removal from office.

Despite this negative publicity, Democrats did well in the fall election. Obama carried the state 57%-41%, just 1% better than Granholm's victory in 2006. Democrats also increased their majority in the state House to 67-43. Granholm is term-limited, and despite some speculation in the press, she did not receive an appointment in the new Obama administration.

Senior Senator

Carl Levin (D)

Elected 1978, term expires 2014, 6th term; b. June 28, 1934, Detroit; home, Detroit; Swarthmore Col., B.A. 1956, Harvard U., J.D. 1959; Jewish; married (Barbara); 3 children.

Elected Office: Detroit City Cncl., 1969–77, Pres., 1973–77.

Professional Career: Practicing atty., 1959–64, 1971–73, 1978–79; MI asst. atty. gen. & gen. cnsl., MI Civil Rights Comm., 1964–67; Detroit chief appellate defender, 1967–69.

DC Office: 269 RSOB, 20510, 202-224-6221; Fax: 202-224-1388; Web site: levin.senate.gov.

State Offices: Detroit, 313-226-6020; Escanaba, 906-789-0052; Grand Rapids, 616-456-2531; Lansing, 517-377-1508; Saginaw, 989-754-2494; Traverse City, 231-947-9569; Warren, 586-573-9145.

Committees: *Armed Services* (Chmn of 15 D). *Homeland Security & Governmental Affairs* (2nd of 10 D): Contracting Oversight; Federal Financial Management, Government Information, Federal Services & International Security; Investigations (Permanent) (Chmn); Oversight of Government Management, the Federal Workforce & the District of Columbia. *Small Business & Entrepreneurship* (3rd of 11 D).

Group Ratings

	ADA	ACLU	AFS	LCV	ITIC	NTU	COC	ACU	CFG	FRC
2008	100	86	100	100	100	3	63	0	3	0
2007	95	—	100	67	—	6	45	4	10	—

National Journal Ratings

	2007 LIB	—	2007 CONS		2008 LIB	—	2008 CONS
Economic	79%	—	13%		75%	—	24%
Social	79%	—	19%		80%	—	9%
Foreign	65%	—	32%		65%	—	6%
Composite	77%	—	24%		80%	—	20%

Election Results

2008 general	Carl Levin (D) 3,038,386	(63%)	($5,784,520)
	Jack Hoogendyk (R) 1,641,070	(34%)	($301,993)
2008 primary	Carl Levin (D) .... unopposed		

Prior Winning Percentages: 2002 (61%); 1996 (58%); 1990 (57%); 1984 (52%); 1978 (52%)

Democrat Carl Levin, first elected in 1978, is a member of one of Michigan's most respected political families and the longest-serving senator in state history. His older brother, Democrat Sander Levin, is Michigan's 12th District representative. Compared to his natty Senate colleagues, Levin is often rumpled and a bit tardy with a haircut, but also compared to many of the rest, he is articulate without political artifice, and he takes unpopular stands on issues. He grew up in Detroit, graduated from Swarthmore College and Harvard Law School, then went to work as counsel for the state Civil Rights Commission in the turbulent 1960s. After a stint as a public defender, Levin was elected to the Detroit City Council in 1969 with substantial support from both blacks and whites. In 1978, he ran for the U.S. Senate and was helped when Republican incumbent Robert Griffin indecisively got out of the race and then back in. Levin won 52%-48%. In 1984, he won his first re-election by a similar margin, and since then, he has returned four times by wide margins. Before Levin, Republican Arthur Vandenberg had held the record as a senator from Michigan, serving 23 years in office.

Levin is chairman of the Armed Services Committee. He has the skepticism of large-scale defense spending and military involvements common among Democrats in the 1970s and has built up an impressive expertise in military affairs. Levin was very dubious about the need for military action in Iraq in 2002 and argued fervently that any action should be multilateral. He argued in September 2002 that military action was not necessary because Iraqi leader Saddam Hussein could be deterred from using weapons of mass destruction if he had them and that in any case, the United States should not act without approval of the United Nations. He offered an alternative resolution calling on the Bush administration to get the UN to adopt a more vigorous weapons-inspection program, but not authorizing military action until it was approved by the UN. It was defeated 75-24. In 2004, Levin issued a report charging that Pentagon official Douglas Feith deliberately exaggerated ties between Hussein and the terrorist group Al Qaeda, and ignored corrections requested by the Central Intelligence Agency.

In June 2006, Levin and Rhode Island Democrat Jack Reed sponsored an amendment calling for a "phased redeployment" of U.S. troops in Iraq in six months, with no deadline for withdrawal; it also called for U.S. forces to transition to training Iraqi security forces. A more extreme alternative, Massachusetts Democratic Sen. John Kerry's amendment calling for withdrawal by July 2007, was defeated 86-13. But the Levin-Reed amendment also lost, 60-39. In late 2006, Levin described the situation in Iraq as "a low-grade civil war" and called for a bipartisan resolution supporting phased redeployment. "We have to force the Iraqis to take responsibility for their own nation, that we cannot save them from themselves," he said. "The president himself believes that what I'm saying is a useful thing for the Iraqis to hear." In December 2006, he called for implementation of the Iraq Study Group report, which he said could be "the beginning of a development of a new, realistic, bipartisan and hopefully successful approach." Despite his disagreements with administration policy, he voted to confirm the nomination of Defense Secretary Robert Gates, saying Gates was a "welcome break of honest, candid realism." In May 2007, Levin opposed a redeployment measure sponsored by Democrats Russ Feingold of Wisconsin and Harry Reid of Nevada that set a deadline for troops to be out of Iraq and cut funding thereafter. "I can't support a cutoff on funding and I cannot support a fixed date for removing all troops," he said. Even though it was clear that he could not get the 60 votes needed to force a vote—let alone the two-thirds majority needed to override a certain Bush veto—Levin continued to work with Reed on proposals to mandate the withdrawal of most U.S. troops within roughly 12 months. In 2008, the Senate continued to be deadlocked on troop redeployments from Iraq.

Levin has been a sharp-eyed overseer of the Pentagon, joining with Republican John McCain of Arizona in strongly questioning the Pentagon's leasing, rather than purchase, of KC-767 refueling tankers from Boeing. After e-mails obtained by McCain revealed improper negotiations between the Air Force and Boeing, Levin, McCain and Virginia Republican John Warner won approval in November 2003 of a proposal to lease only 20 of the aircraft and purchase 80 others, to keep the total cost down. In March 2004, Levin, McCain and Warner, disturbed by a Pentagon audit, imposed a hold on the entire project. Another of Levin's issues is the condition of the Army. During hearings in 2004, he said that the Army was stretched too thin, that there were not enough soldiers and protective gear in Iraq, that too many personnel were held in the service by stop-loss orders, and that the Army was not adequately replacing old equipment. Levin has been the Senate's most persistent critic of Republican-led efforts over the years to build a missile defense system for the United States. In 2001, he got the Armed Services Committee to move over $1 billion from missile defense to anti-terrorism programs. And in 2002, he got the committee to approve a defense-authorization bill that cut the Bush administration's missile-defense request by $812 million, though the Senate ultimately gave Bush the authority to restore the cuts. In 2004, Levin opposed $500 million in the defense budget for missile defense.

He has also weighed in on intelligence matters. He won passage of an amendment to the intelligence reorganization bill requiring the national intelligence director to be independent of the White House. He also objected to the National Security Agency surveillance of communications between Qaeda suspects abroad and people in the United States. In the intelligence realm, he has worked on laws for whistleblower protection, competition in government contracting and lobbying disclosure.

Levin generally has one of the most liberal records in the Senate, with some Michigan accents. He opposed the 1993 North American Free Trade Agreement, which the powerful labor unions in Michigan were fighting, and over the years, he has called for crackdowns on tax avoidance by foreign automakers and on Chinese and Japanese currency manipulation. He also has stood in the way of Democratic efforts to significantly raise fuel-efficiency standards for cars and trucks. In 2006, he called for the U.S. Department of Transportation rather than Congress to set fuel mileage standards and said the Bush administration's new light-truck standards were "reasonable." In 2007, he opposed the increase in fuel standards to 35 miles per gallon by 2020 that had passed the Senate Commerce Committee. Congress passed the tougher standards in December 2007, but Levin's resistance increased the leverage of then House Energy and Commerce Committee Chairman John Dingell, the Michigan Democrat, in gaining some concessions for the automobile industry.

In 2007, Levin held hearings on the "abusive practices and excesses" of the credit card industry. Some bank executives agreed to end some of the practices, but Levin continued to push for legislative restrictions. Also that year, with then–Sens. Barack Obama of Illinois and Norm Coleman, a Republican from Minnesota, he filed a bill to impose sanctions on corporations that operate offshore shelters to avoid taxes.

Michigan touches all but one of the Great Lakes, which have been threatened by invasive species. The zebra mussel has wiped out many native species, and Asian carp are making their way up the Illinois River and threatening to enter the lakes. In 2006, Levin worked with Ohio Republican Mike DeWine to reauthorize the Great Lakes Fish and Wildlife Restoration Act, and in October 2006, he celebrated the return, after eight decades, of whitefish to the Detroit River. Levin also sponsored a Great Lakes trust fund to pay for cleaning up the lakes, restoring wetlands and repelling invasive species. Also in 2006, he and fellow Michigan Democratic Sen. Debbie Stabenow negotiated an agreement with Ontario officials to stop by 2010 shipments of 415 truckloads a day of Canadian trash into Michigan.

When Levin ran for re-election in 2008, GOP state Chairman Saul Anuzis said the party would field a strong candidate. But Republican Reps. Candice Miller and Mike Rogers declined to run. Republicans nominated state Rep. Jack Hoogendyk, who waged a token challenge, and Levin breezed by, 63%-34%.

Junior Senator

Debbie Stabenow (D)

Elected 2000, term expires 2012, 2nd term; b. April 29, 1950, Gladwin; home, Lansing; MI St. U., B.A. 1972, M.S.W. 1975; United Methodist; married (Tom Athans); 2 children.

Elected Office: Ingham Cnty. comm., 1975–78, Chair, 1976–78; MI House of Reps., 1978–90; MI Senate, 1990–94; U.S. House of Reps 1996–2000.

Professional Career: Consultant & co–founder, MI Leadership Inst., 1995–96.

DC Office: 133 HSOB, 20510, 202-224-4822; Fax: 202-228-0325; Web site: stabenow.senate.gov.

State Offices: Detroit, 313-961-4330; East Lansing, 517-203-1760; Flint, 810-720-4172; Grand Rapids, 616-975-0052; Marquette, 906-228-8756; Traverse City, 231-929-1031.

Committees: *Democratic Steering & Outreach Committee Chairwoman. Agriculture, Nutrition & Forestry* (6th of 12 D). *Budget* (7th of 13 D). *Energy & Natural Resources* (11th of 13 D): Energy; National Parks; Water & Power (Chmn). *Finance* (9th of 13 D): Energy, Natural Resources & Infrastructure; Health Care; International Trade, Customs & Global Competitiveness; Taxation, IRS Oversight & Long-Term Growth.

Group Ratings

	ADA	ACLU	AFS	LCV	ITIC	NTU	COC	ACU	CFG	FRC
2008	100	86	100	100	40	15	50	4	13	0
2007	100	—	100	67	—	6	27	8	4	—

National Journal Ratings

	2007 LIB	—	2007 CONS	2008 LIB	—	2008 CONS
Economic	72%	—	23%	91%	—	0%
Social	85%	—	14%	74%	—	25%
Foreign	85%	—	8%	65%	—	6%
Composite	83%	—	17%	83%	—	17%

Key Votes of the 110th Congress

1. Raise CAFE standards	N	5. Make English official language N	9. Withdraw troops 3/08	Y
2. Expand SCHIP	Y	6. Path to citizenship	N	10. Iran guard is terrorist group	Y
3. Cap greenhouse gases	Y	7. Fetus is unborn child	N	11. Increase missile defense $	N
4. Bail out financial markets	N	8. Prosecute hate crimes	Y	12. Overhaul FISA	N

Election Results

2006 general	Debbie Stabenow (D)	2,151,278	(57%)	($11,220,506)
	Mike Bouchard (R)	1,559,597	(41%)	($6,050,148)
2006 primary	Debbie Stabenow (D)	unopposed		

Prior Winning Percentages: 2000 (49%); 1998 House (57%); 1996 House (54%)

Michigan's junior senator is Debbie Stabenow, a Democrat elected in 2000. Stabenow grew up in the small Outstate town of Clare, where her father was an Oldsmobile dealer and her mother was a nurse. She went to Michigan State University, where she got a master's degree in social work. She counseled kids in public schools and made extra money singing folk songs in coffeehouses. Young Stabenow also marched in antiwar rallies during the Vietnam War era and volunteered for antiwar presidential candidate George McGovern in 1972. Angered when the Ingham County Commission closed a nursing home, she ran for the commission two years later and, at age 24, beat an incumbent who referred to her as "that young broad." She was elected to the state House in 1978 at age 28 and was elected to the state Senate in 1990. Four years later, while running for governor, she was at the center of a storm in state politics. In response to Republican Gov. John Engler's call for changes in financing education, she proposed to zero out the property tax and start over, apparently calculating that he would reject such a drastic tax cut. Instead, he accepted her proposal and passed a plan reducing property taxes vastly and increasing the sales tax, which was approved by voters, 70%-30%, in March 1994. In the August primary, the state Democratic establishment opposed Stabenow: the Michigan Education Association, the UAW and AFL-CIO. She won 30% of the vote, behind former Rep. Howard Wolpe's 35%. She was chosen as Wolpe's running mate, but the ticket lost to Engler, 61%-38%.

Undaunted, Stabenow almost immediately began running for Congress. The 8th Congressional District seat, which included Lansing's Democratic Ingham County and heavily Republican Livingston County to the east, was held by freshman Republican Dick Chrysler. For the 1996 race, Stabenow raised more than $1 million in individual contributions, a tribute to her industriousness and the fundraising prowess of the feminist left; overall each spent $1.5 million. She won impressively, 54%-44%. In the House, Stabenow had a fairly liberal voting record. She opposed increasing the president's power to negotiate trade agreements and the partial-birth abortion ban. In March 1999, she announced she would run against first-term Republican Sen. Spencer Abraham in 2000. That day, Abraham took out full-page ads calling her a liberal.

This turned out to be one of the critical races among 2000 Senate contests. The first barrage of ads in the race came not from either candidate or their respective parties, but from the Federation for American Immigration Reform, which in early 2000 spent $700,000 attacking Abraham for his stands on immigration and charging that his stands cost Michigan workers jobs. In the summer, Abraham used his money advantage—he ultimately spent $13 million to Stabenow's nearly $8 million—to run ads spotlighting his own program for prescription drugs for senior citizens and attacked Stabenow as a free-spending liberal favoring increased bureaucracy and higher taxes, opposing welfare reform and supporting lenient sentences for criminals. Stabenow resisted pressure and hoarded her money for an October ad buy. This proved to be a good strategy. Stabenow was down by 17% in mid-October, but she answered charges that she was a liberal by citing her votes for a balanced budget and ending the marriage penalty. She kept herself in the good graces of labor by voting against normalizing trade relations with China. Stabenow said Abraham was beholden to corporations and special interests and attacked his stands on making prescription drugs affordable and regulation of health maintenance organizations. This race was heavy on ads by outside groups—the Sierra Club, Peace Action, and EMILY's List for Stabenow, and for Abraham, the Chamber of Commerce, Business Roundtable, Americans for Job Security, National Rifle Association, and Michigan Right to Life. It was the most expensive Senate race in Michigan history and the first since 1942 in which neither candidate won a majority of the vote. Stabenow won 49%-48%, carrying only 13 of the state's 83 counties.

To help her strengthen her grip on the seat, Senate Democrats made Stabenow head of a task force on prescription drugs, then among the hottest issues in the country. She organized bus trips of seniors to Canada and pressed for measures allowing the importation of U.S. drugs from Canada and permitting states to continue to negotiate prices with pharmaceutical companies on Medicaid drug purchases. In 2004, Stabenow won passage of an amendment for $2 billion in corporate tax cuts for manufacturers who create jobs in the United States.

Stabenow also focused on Michigan's environment issues. In 2003, Toronto began shipping all its trash to a landfill southwest of Detroit: 180 truckloads a day, or over 1 million tons a year. Stabenow argued that the practice violated a 1992 treaty and launched an online campaign to amass signatures to demand that the Environmental Protection Agency enforce the treaty, which required notification of each shipment and allowed the U.S. to decline. She presented 165,000 signatures to EPA Administrator Mike Leavitt, but he maintained that only hazardous-waste shipments violated the treaty. Stabenow argued that all waste was covered. The shipments continued, as did the fight. In August 2006, Stabenow and fellow Democratic Sen. Carl Levin of Michigan announced an agreement with Ontario's Environment Minister to end the shipment of municipal garbage by 2010. "This is real. It's concrete. It cannot be challenged in court," she said. Some skeptics were dubious that it was comprehensive or legally binding. By 2008, trash shipments from Canada and other states had been reduced, but by just 10%.

Late in her first term, Stabenow decided to try to get a toehold in leadership. In November 2004, when Sen. Barbara Mikulski, D-Md., stepped down as secretary of the Democratic caucus, Stabenow called Mikulski to ask for her support, and the two worked the phones. Stabenow got the job, the No. 3 position in the Senate Democratic leadership. It gave her a voice at leadership meetings, though her performance was limited. Other senior Senate Democrats quietly discussed replacing her after the 2006 election. Ultimately, the sides reached an agreement: Stabenow got a much-sought-after seat on the Finance Committee, and she became chair of the Democratic Steering and Outreach Committee, a liaison to grassroots groups across the nation. And Sen. Patty Murray, D-Wash., took over as conference secretary.

In the majority, Stabenow was a leading foe of President Bush's international trade agenda, insisting on protections for American workers who lose their jobs to foreign competition. In 2007 the Senate easily approved a bilateral trade deal with Peru despite her opposition. With Republican Jim Bunning of Kentucky, she sponsored a proposal to make it easier for U.S. manufacturers to show currency manipulation by other nations, a measure directed at China. With her seat on Finance, she also was a leading advocate of expanding the State Children's Health Insurance Program. With other rust-belt Democrats, she successfully fought Senate action on climate change legislation, which was opposed by heavy industries, and she opposed tougher fuel economy standards for the auto industry, which ultimately passed the Senate.

Facing re-election in 2006, Stabenow got early breaks when two Republican House members, Candice Miller and Mike Rogers, said that they would not run. Several second-tier candidates emerged, including wealthy Keith Butler, a former Detroit councilman, and Jerry Zandstra, a director at a Grand Rapids religious think tank. National Republicans encouraged Oakland County Sheriff Mike Bouchard, who initially demurred but announced his candidacy in October 2005. Bouchard won the August primary, 61%-39%. The general election campaign was overshadowed by the more competitive race for governor, and Bouchard struggled to gain attention and attract money. Republicans ran an ad mocking Stabenow for caving in to Canadian interests on trash shipments, and Bouchard called her ineffective. But incumbent Republican senators were struggling that year, and the GOP did not make this a high-priority contest. Stabenow won 57%-41%, taking 65 of the 83 counties.

Stabenow faced a personal challenge in 2008 when her husband, Tom Athans, a co-founder of the TalkUSA Radio network, acknowledged that he had solicited sex from a prostitute in Michigan, though he was not arrested.

FIRST DISTRICT

Bart Stupak (D)

Elected 1992, 9th term; b. Feb. 29, 1952, Milwaukee, WI; home, Menominee; NW MI Comm. Col., A.A. 1972, Saginaw Valley St. Col., B.S. 1977, Thomas Cooley Law Schl., J.D. 1981; Catholic; married (Laurie); 1 child (1 deceased).

Elected Office: MI House of Reps., 1988–90.

Professional Career: Escanaba Police Officer, 1972–73; MI St. Trooper, 1974–84; Practicing atty., 1981–92.

DC Office: 2268 RHOB, 20515, 202-225-4735; Fax: 202-225-4744; Web site: www.house.Gov/stupak.

State Offices: Alpena, 989-356-0690; Crystal Falls, 906-875-3751; Escanaba, 906-786-4504; Houghton, 906-482-1371; Marquette, 906-228-3700; Petoskey, 231-348-0657; West Branch, 989-345-2258.

Committees: *Energy & Commerce* (9th of 36 D): Commerce, Trade & Consumer Protections; Communications, Technology & the Internet; Oversight & Investigations (Chmn).

Group Ratings

	ADA	ACLU	AFS	LCV	ITIC	NTU	COC	ACU	CFG	FRC
2008	90	91	100	92	71	17	56	12	8	52
2007	95	—	100	70	—	5	55	12	1	—

National Journal Ratings

	2007 LIB	—	2007 CONS		2008 LIB	—	2008 CONS
Economic	53%	—	46%		71%	—	25%
Social	55%	—	44%		54%	—	42%
Foreign	65%	—	33%		78%	—	17%
Composite	58%	—	42%		70%	—	30%

Key Votes of the 110th Congress

1. Increase minimum wage	Y	5. Share immigration data	*	9. Withdraw troops 8/08	Y
2. Expand SCHIP	Y	6. Foreign aid abortion ban	Y	10. No operations in Iran	Y
3. Raise CAFE standards	Y	7. Ban gay bias in workplace	Y	11. Free trade with Peru	N
4. Bail out financial markets	N	8. Repeal D.C. gun law	Y	12. Overhaul FISA	Y

Election Results

2008 general	Bart Stupak (D)	213,216	(65%)	($1,281,683)
	Tom Casperson (R)	107,340	(33%)	($236,254)
2008 primary	Bart Stupak (D)	unopposed		

Prior Winning Percentages: 2006 (69%); 2004 (66%); 2002 (68%); 2000 (58%); 1998 (59%); 1996 (71%); 1994 (57%); 1992 (54%)

Population		Race/Ethnicity		Work	
Pop. 2007:	658,482	White:	93.0%	Private:	75.8%
Change since 2000:	Down 0.6%	Black:	1.4%	Government:	16.2%
Urban:	33.4%	Hispanic:	1.1%	Self-employed:	7.7%
Rural:	66.6%	Asian:	0.5%	Blue collar:	26.8%
Area size:	27,809 sq. mi.	Native Am.:	2.2%	White collar:	50.7%
Age		Hawaiian:	0.0%	Khaki collar:	0.1%
Median age:	42.2 yrs.	Two+ races:	1.7%	Other:	22.4%
More than 65 yrs:	18.0%	*Ancestry*		Median income:	$38,771
Less than 18 yrs:	20.5%	German:	19.6%	Median home value:	$111,100
Education		Irish:	8.9%	Poverty:	14.0%
H.S. grad:	86.5%	English:	8.9%	**Military Veterans**	
College grad:	18.0%			% of Pop:	14.4%
Grad degree:	6.1%				

Michigan's Upper Peninsula, commonly known as the UP, is a land apart. Surrounded on three sides by frigid Lakes Superior, Huron, and Michigan, the UP is no farther north than Montreal or Seattle, but there are places here that have some of the coldest climates in settled parts of North America. The area surrounding Keweenaw County, which juts into Lake Superior, often ranks high in the nation's heaviest snowfall. "In October, usually, the first snow falls steady on the northland," writes Dixie

2008 Presidential Vote

Obama (D)	166,185	(50%)
McCain (R)	160,142	(48%)

2004 Presidential Vote

Bush (R)	177,315	(53%)
Kerry (D)	151,450	(46%)

Cook Partisan Voting Index: R+3

Lee Franklin in *A Most Superior Land*, "whispering teasing promises of more to come" —for six or even eight months more. Far away from any major city, with ground too frozen and stony and a growing season too short for most crops, the Upper Peninsula was explored by French voyagers and missionaries more than 300 years ago but was never thickly settled until prospectors found rich veins of ore here. The mineral veins of the Keweenaw Peninsula produced 13.3 billion pounds of copper. The Marquette, Menominee, and Gogebic iron ranges have produced more than one billion tons of iron ore. Starting in the 1840s, immigrants flocked here to work the mines: Irish, Italians, Swedes, Norwegians, miners' sons from Wales and Cornwall, and most prominently Finns, who must have found this cold land with its lakes and hills much like home. Many were Roman Catholic, and they remain predominantly anti-abortion. Before 1900, the UP was a northern industrial belt, with a few bosses, some absentee overlords, and a workforce disposed to radical ideas and union movements. Timber was another major industry a century ago.

A major strike in 1913–14 and falling ore prices after World War I—events that would be long forgotten elsewhere—are recalled in the UP as accelerating the copper decline. The UP's population peaked at 332,000 in 1920. The accessible copper veins were mostly depleted by then, mining iron ore became less labor-intensive, and lumber and farming provided only a few thousand jobs. Other industries have grown since then: Marinette Marine, which builds Coast Guard cutters and military ships just across the state border in Wisconsin, is important to Menominee County. Enstrom Helicopter, founded in Menominee in the 1950s by a lumberman who wanted a helicopter suited for the rugged UP, sells models that are popular overseas and with law enforcement. But in the last half-century, there was great migration to Detroit for auto jobs, and to the West for mining. The UP's population has hovered around 300,000, rising to 315,000 in 2004. But "Yoopers" —who some say have their own dialect, "Yoopanese" —remain devoted to their land. "The U.P. is really a place of slow, steady economic decline. We actually find it kind of charming," says local writer Don Hunt.

The 1st Congressional District of Michigan includes the Upper Peninsula and 16 northern counties on the Lower Peninsula: geographically, almost half of all Michigan. Nearly half the people in the district live in the UP, in small towns spread across heavily forested distances. Often-snowbound Marquette, with 21,000 people, is the largest city in the district, followed by the "Soo," the more vibrant Sault Ste. Marie, with 14,000. The other half lives south of the breathtaking Mackinac Bridge, which connects the two peninsulas. This is a vast area, in sheer size the second-largest district east of the Mississippi, after Maine's 2nd District, and it has the most shoreline of any district. It is a 490-mile drive from Ironwood at the western end of the UP to the edge of Bay City on the southern tip of Saginaw Bay. The Lower Peninsula counties have two different personalities. On Lake Huron—the sunrise side—are smaller industrial towns and middle-class resorts. On Lake Michigan are affluent resort areas around Petoskey and Charlevoix, long summer places for people from Chicago (this is Ernest Hemingway's "up in Michigan"). Politically, the UP has long been Democratic, some parts more than others, but it can be contrarian. This is one part of Michigan that has not liked many national Democrats' environmental and gun control stands. The Lake Michigan shore of the Lower Peninsula is growing fast and heavily Republican; the sunrise side is growing more slowly and is politically marginal. The 1st District voted solidly for Bush in 2000 and 2004, narrowly for Republican gubernatorial candidate Dick Posthumus in 2002, and 50% for Barack Obama in 2008. But in 2006, Democratic Gov. Jennifer Granholm carried the 1st, winning every county in the UP and 61% farther south in Bay County.

The congressman from the 1st District is Bart Stupak, a Democrat and a "Yooper" from Menominee on the Wisconsin border, just a short jaunt from Green Bay. He was a police officer in Escanaba, then became a Michigan state trooper in 1974 and also earned a law degree. In 1984, he was injured in the line of duty and retired from the force. In 1988, he was elected to the Michigan House, and in 1990, he lost a race for the state Senate. Stupak got into the 1992 U.S. House race when incumbent Republican Bob Davis, who was caught up in the House bank scandal with 878 overdrafts, decided to drop out. In the general election, he beat Republican Philip Ruppe, who had represented the district from 1966 to 1978, 54%-44%.

Stupak's voting record has been centrist for House Democrats, and usually more conservative than most of them on cultural issues. He is strongly opposed to abortion rights, and spoke out against them at the 1996 Democratic National Convention. In 2003, the House passed a bill he co-sponsored to prohibit cloning, including for the production of embryos intended for research, but the bill stalled in the Senate. In 2006, he supported President Bush's veto of the bill to expand embryonic-stem-cell research, which uses excess embryos from in vitro fertilization. Stupak has paid fastidious attention to local issues. He claims to be the first elected official to oppose drilling for oil and natural gas under the Great Lakes, and he worked on the successful bill to permanently kill it in 2005. He has been a leading Democratic proponent of a measure to crack down on oil price-gouging. In 2007, he helped to organize a Congressional Water Caucus, which he hopes will devise a comprehensive water-use policy for the nation. The House defeated in June 2008 his proposal to approve land exchanges that would have permitted two Indian tribes in Michigan to open urban casinos away from their reservations in the UP.

On Mother's Day 2000, Stupak suffered a personal tragedy, which for a time raised questions about his political future. His 17-year-old son B.J., a high school football player and class president, killed himself on the morning after his prom. In coping with the tragedy, Stupak and his wife, Laurie, focused on their son's use of Accutane, a prescription drug for acne treatment that can have adverse psychological effects, including suicide attempts. Stupak held a hearing on the use of Accutane, and in December 2004, the Food and Drug Administration tightened restrictions on the drug, including creation of a mandatory registry for individuals who dispense or use it.

In 2007, Stupak took over as an aggressive chairman of the Oversight and Investigations Subcommittee at Energy and Commerce, which has long been a platform for then-committee chairman Rep. John Dingell, a Democratic home-state ally. He held hearings on several Democratic staples, including gas price-gouging, energy futures trading, and FDA regulation. Under pressure from Stupak, the FDA in 2008 reversed its plan to close seven field offices, including one in Michigan. "You have this [Bush] administration turning a blind eye to corporate America," Stupak said.

In 2000, Stupak faced a vigorous challenge from Chuck Yob, a Republican national committeeman, who criticized Stupak for taking more than 80% of his campaign money from special-interest groups. The NRA, an influential force in his district, endorsed Yob. Stupak argued that voters favored commonsense gun laws, and voters seemed to be in no mood for controversy in light of Stupak's family tragedy that year. He won 58%-40%, losing only one county. He hasn't had a competitive race since. Republicans hope to win the seat if Stupak does not run, but there is little chance as long as he does. In 2008, Republicans ran state Rep. Tom Casperson. But 2008 was a tough year for Republicans in Michigan, and Casperson never elevated the contest to make his run a serious threat. Stupak won 65%-33%. Stupak has been mentioned as a candidate for governor in 2010. But he likely would face a challenge in gaining support of Detroit-area Democrats in a primary.

SECOND DISTRICT

Pete Hoekstra (R)

Elected 1992, 9th term; b. Oct. 30, 1953, Groningen, Netherlands; home, Holland; Hope Col., B.A. 1975, U. of MI, M.B.A. 1977; Reformed Church of America; married (Diane); 3 children.

Professional Career: Furniture exec., Herman Miller Co., 1977–92.

DC Office: 2234 RHOB, 20515, 202-225-4401; Fax: 202-226-0779; Web site: hoekstra.house.gov.

State Offices: Cadillac, 231-775-0050; Holland, 616-395-0030; Muskegon, 231-722-8386.

Committees: *Education & Labor* (3rd of 19 R): Early Childhood, Elementary & Secondary Education; Workforce Protections. *Intelligence (Select)* (RMM of 9 R).

Group Ratings

	ADA	ACLU	AFS	LCV	ITIC	NTU	COC	ACU	CFG	FRC
2008	20	18	14	0	33	65	83	88	73	100
2007	5	—	9	5	—	79	68	92	80	—

National Journal Ratings

	2007 LIB — 2007 CONS		2008 LIB — 2008 CONS	
Economic	19%	— 80%	22%	— 77%
Social	9%	— 85%	19%	— 81%
Foreign	28%	— 71%	13%	— 84%
Composite	20%	— 80%	19%	— 81%

Key Votes of the 110th Congress

1. Increase minimum wage	N	5. Share immigration data	Y	9. Withdraw troops 8/08	N
2. Expand SCHIP	N	6. Foreign aid abortion ban	Y	10. No operations in Iran	N
3. Raise CAFE standards	N	7. Ban gay bias in workplace	N	11. Free trade with Peru	N
4. Bail out financial markets	Y	8. Repeal D.C. gun law	*	12. Overhaul FISA	Y

Election Results

2008 general	Pete Hoekstra (R)	214,100	(62%)	($828,852)
	Fred Johnson (D)	119,506	(35%)	($111,806)
2008 primary	Pete Hoekstra (R)	unopposed		

Prior Winning Percentages: 2006 (66%); 2004 (69%); 2002 (70%); 2000 (64%); 1998 (69%); 1996 (65%); 1994 (75%); 1992 (63%)

Population		Race/Ethnicity		Work	
Pop. 2007:	694,812	White:	86.4%	Private:	82.9%
Change since 2000:	Up 4.9%	Black:	4.3%	Government:	10.4%
Urban:	56.2%	Hispanic:	6.1%	Self-employed:	6.4%
Rural:	43.8%	Asian:	1.2%	Blue collar:	30.5%
Area size:	5,508 sq. mi.	Native Am.:	0.5%	White collar:	52.1%
		Hawaiian:	0.0%	Khaki collar:	0.1%
Age		Two+ races:	1.4%	Other:	17.3%
Median age:	36.1 yrs.			Median income:	$46,857
More than 65 yrs:	12.8%	*Ancestry*		Median home value:	$141,100
Less than 18 yrs:	25.5%	German:	18.2%	Poverty:	11.6%
		Dutch:	16.0%		
Education		Irish:	8.5%	**Military Veterans**	
H.S. grad:	87.5%			% of Pop:	10.9%
College grad:	21.0%				
Grad degree:	6.8%				

Lining the eastern shoreline of Lake Michigan, where the lake winds temper the frigid Michigan winters, are some of the nation's longest and highest sand dunes. In the late 19th century, this shoreline was America's lumber country. The river ports were choked with logs and full of lumbermen from Norway and Sweden, Ireland and Scotland, Quebec and New England. During the timber boom, the shoreline just to the south was the locus of the country's largest migration from the Netherlands and today still has the nation's largest concentration of Dutch-Americans. Wooden shoes are now seen only at the Tulip Festival in Holland, but conscientious Dutch work habits have produced many highly skilled workers, and this is a busy manufacturing area, with products ranging from baby food at Gerber in Fremont to self-dimming car mirrors at Gentex in Zeeland. It is also the center of the American office-furniture industry, with Herman Miller in Zeeland, Haworth in Holland and Steelcase in Grand Rapids. But the economic downtown of 2008 has had an impact, for sure. Pfizer recently shut down a factory in Holland. The territory away from the shore is fruit-growing country, with some of the nation's largest cherry orchards to the north and blueberry patches to the south.

2008 Presidential Vote		
McCain (R)	179,427	(51%)
Obama (D)	167,607	(48%)
2004 Presidential Vote		
Bush (R)	203,051	(60%)
Kerry (D)	131,552	(39%)
Cook Partisan Voting Index:	R + 7	

The 2nd Congressional District of Michigan occupies the Lake Michigan shoreline counties, plus a tier of inland counties, including a small part of Grand Rapids's Kent County. It stretches from the lumber country around Manistee south to Holland and the wealthy resort town of Saugatuck. For years, Dutch-American voters have been as strongly Republican as Cuban-Americans have been as an ethnically identifiable group, and the 2nd and 3rd Districts centered on Grand Rapids are the two most Republican districts in Michigan. Ottawa County voted 72% for George W. Bush in 2004, and 61% for John McCain in 2008.

The congressman from the 2nd District is Republican Pete Hoekstra, first elected to the House in 1992. He emigrated from the Netherlands with his family at age 3. He graduated from Hope College in Holland and spent a semester studying in Washington, D.C., during the Watergate scandal. He received an M.B.A. from the University of Michigan. Hoekstra (*HOOK-stra*) went to work at Herman Miller, where he helped develop the popular "Equa Chair" aimed at making office seating comfortable and ergonomic. He eventually became vice president for marketing. In 1992, he decided to run what seemed an improbable campaign for Congress against Rep. Guy Vander Jagt, 26-year incumbent and chairman of the National Republican Congressional Committee, the House GOP's political arm. Spending vacation time he'd saved up, Hoekstra took a bicycle tour of the district. With an earnestness that touched a chord, Hoekstra called for citizen politicians, refused political-action-committee money and supported abolishing such committees. He advocated 12-year term limits (though he subsequently broke his own term-limit pledge), promised to uphold family values and to oppose abortion rights. Hoekstra spent only $55,600 to Vander Jagt's $725,000. But on primary day, he carried the heavily Dutch Ottawa and Allegan counties 53%-31% and the district 46%-40%. He won the general election easily.

Hoekstra brought to Washington a mistrust of government and a desire to apply the participatory-management ideas he learned at Herman Miller. (He still works at a stand-up Herman Miller desk.) In the mid-1990s, he was a trusted ally of Speaker Newt Gingrich, who deployed newcomers like Hoekstra in pursuing his goals of reforming congressional ethical standards, making the House more efficient, and pushing an aggressive, conservative agenda through Congress after four decades of Democratic rule. Among Hoekstra's contributions were a ban on former members lobbying on the House floor and denying pensions to former members convicted of a felony.

To the dismay of the Republican leadership and the Bush administration, Hoekstra was not always a team player. He was given a highly visible role on what was then called the Education and the Workforce Committee, but he refused to toe the line on Bush's major education initiative, the 2001 No Child Left Behind. Hoekstra tried unsuccessfully to gut the law's call for mandatory testing. When it came up for renewal in 2007, he pushed an alternative that would let states come up with their own measures of schools' performance. "Does [Education Secretary] Margaret Spellings know more about educating kids in Michigan" than state officials? he asked. In his early years on the committee, Hoekstra was instructed by Gingrich to investigate labor unions, but he was largely ineffective. In attempting to investigate the Teamsters Union, Hoekstra asked the union for information, the union refused to give him any, and he had to cancel plans to hold public hearings.

For several years, Hoekstra was frustrated in his attempts to move up in the leadership, perhaps because of his less than perfect record of supporting leadership positions. In 1998, he ran for vice chairman of the House Republican Conference, but was eliminated on the second ballot. After the 2000 election, he expressed interest in succeeding Ohio Republican John Kasich as chairman of the Budget Committee, but the position went to Jim Nussle of Iowa. He sought the chairmanship of the Education and the Workforce Committee, but lost out to John Boehner of Ohio, who eventually became House minority leader.

Hoekstra seemed to find his niche on the Intelligence Committee, where he developed into an important voice on intelligence policy in the aftermath of the September 11 attacks. In 2002, he sponsored the bill to improve intelligence sharing between law enforcement and intelligence agencies that passed the House overwhelmingly. When Florida Republican Porter Goss left the chairmanship of the panel to become the director of the Central Intelligence Agency, GOP Speaker Dennis Hastert chose Hoekstra to replace Goss, though he was third in seniority. He established a good working relationship with the ranking Democrat, Jane Harman of California, and he could often get her to join him on issues, creating a strong bipartisan front. When President Bush issued executive orders increasing the authority of the CIA director, Hoekstra and Harman issued a joint statement saying that the orders had to be supported by legislation in Congress. Hoekstra supported intelligence reorganization along the lines recommended by the 9/11 Commission. And although the House passed a somewhat different bill, he hailed its passage in 2004.

Hoekstra pressed for publication of material captured in the 2003 invasion of Iraq, which he argued might shed light on the state of Iraqi leader Saddam Hussein's weapons of mass destruction programs. In 2005, Hoekstra and Senate Intelligence Committee Chairman Pat Roberts of Kansas called for declassifying 35,000 boxes of documents and for posting them on the Internet. In a 2006 letter to Bush, Hoekstra complained about not being informed of certain unspecified secret programs. He opposed the nomination of General Michael Hayden to be CIA chief on the grounds that there were too many military men in top intelligence positions already. He called Hayden "the wrong person at the wrong place at the wrong time."

After Democrats took the House majority in 2007 and Democratic Speaker Nancy Pelosi appointed Silvestre Reyes of Texas as the committee chairman, Hoekstra became ranking minority member and pledged to work with Reyes as Harman had with him. He said, "I think Silvestre and I are going to have the same kind of relationship." He bucked the Bush Administration on several sensitive topics in recent years, including the promotion of democracy in Iraq, the CIA's harsh interrogation practices, and plans by the intelligence agencies to study the impact of global warming on national security. And he harshly condemned the June 2008 decision to remove North Korea from the list of state sponsors of terror, saying that "the Bush administration has placed wishful thinking ahead of reality."

On issues affecting his district, Hoekstra has been a defender of the domestic furniture-making industry. In 2004, he successfully pushed through a bill to remove a federal requirement that the government buy its office furniture from Federal Prison Industries, which employs prisoners at bargain wages to produce office furniture and auto components. And Hoekstra joined with Illinois Democrat Rahm Emanuel to cosponsor the Great Lakes Financing Act, which aims to clean up the lakes and combat invasive species. He has opposed Indian gambling casinos and criticized the Justice Department for approving an Indian land trust in Allegan County.

Hoekstra speaks Dutch and is proud of his ethnic heritage. He cherishes his own naturalization papers and cites his own experience as a basis for supporting crackdowns on illegal immigration. "I describe it as one of the most valuable pieces of paper in the world. I really end up having a problem with giving one of the most valuable pieces of paper in the world to people who came here illegally," Hoekstra says.

In 1992, as term limits on state legislators passed in Michigan, Hoekstra pledged to serve only 12 years. By 2002, he said he had changed his mind and wrote an open letter to constituents saying he would run again. He has been re-elected without serious competition. He announced in March 2009 a bid for governor in 2010, when term limits prohibit Democrat Jennifer Granholm from running again.

THIRD DISTRICT

Vernon Ehlers (R)

Elected Dec. 1993, 8th full term; b. Feb. 6, 1934, Pipestone, MN; home, Grand Rapids; Calvin Col., 1952–55; U. of CA, A.B. 1956, Ph.D. 1960, U. of Heidelberg, Germany, 1961–62; Christian Reformed; married (Johanna); 4 children.

Elected Office: Kent Cnty. comm., 1974–82, Chmn., 1978–81; MI House of Reps., 1982–86; MI Senate, 1986–93, Pres. pro tem, 1990–93.

Professional Career: Prof., Calvin Col., 1966–82.

DC Office: 2182 RHOB, 20515, 202-225-3831; Fax: 202-225-5144; Web site: www.house.Gov/ehlers.

State Offices: Grand Rapids, 616-451-8383.

Committees: *Education & Labor* (7th of 19 R): Early Childhood, Elementary & Secondary Education; Higher Education, Lifelong Learning & Competitiveness. *Science & Technology* (6th of 17 R): Energy & Environment; Research & Science Education (RMM). *Transportation & Infrastructure* (6th of 30 R): Aviation; Coast Guard & Maritime Transportation; Water Resources & Environment.

Group Ratings

	ADA	ACLU	AFS	LCV	ITIC	NTU	COC	ACU	CFG	FRC
2008	40	30	14	69	71	51	100	61	60	88
2007	20	—	18	70	—	51	85	68	45	—

National Journal Ratings

	2007 LIB — 2007 CONS		2008 LIB — 2008 CONS	
Economic	40%	60%	39%	61%
Social	41%	58%	39%	60%
Foreign	43%	56%	42%	58%
Composite	42%	58%	40%	60%

Key Votes of the 110th Congress

1. Increase minimum wage	Y	5. Share immigration data	Y	9. Withdraw troops 8/08	N
2. Expand SCHIP	Y	6. Foreign aid abortion ban	Y	10. No operations in Iran	Y
3. Raise CAFE standards	N	7. Ban gay bias in workplace	N	11. Free trade with Peru	Y
4. Bail out financial markets	Y	8. Repeal D.C. gun law	*	12. Overhaul FISA	Y

Election Results

2008 general	Vernon Ehlers (R)	203,799	(61%)	($319,953)
	Henry Sanchez (D)	117,961	(35%)	($4,209)
	Erwin Haas (Lib)	11,758	(4%)	
2008 primary	Vernon Ehlers (R)	unopposed		

Prior Winning Percentages: 2006 (63%); 2004 (67%); 2002 (70%); 2000 (65%); 1998 (73%); 1996 (69%); 1994 (74%); 1993 (67%)

Population		Race/Ethnicity		Work	
Pop. 2007:	693,075	White:	80.2%	Private:	85.6%
Change since 2000:	Up 4.6%	Black:	8.2%	Government:	8.5%
Urban:	77.1%	Hispanic:	7.9%	Self-employed:	5.7%
Rural:	22.9%	Asian:	1.9%	Blue collar:	26.5%
Area size:	1,897 sq. mi.	Native Am.:	0.2%	White collar:	57.5%
		Hawaiian:	0.0%	Khaki collar:	0.1%
Age		Two+ races:	1.6%	Other:	16.0%
Median age:	34.7 yrs.			Median income:	$49,680
More than 65 yrs:	10.4%	*Ancestry*		Median home value:	$147,700
Less than 18 yrs:	26.8%	German:	17.4%	Poverty:	12.2%
		Dutch:	14.0%		
Education		English:	8.9%	**Military Veterans**	
H.S. grad:	87.1%			% of Pop:	9.1%
College grad:	26.9%				
Grad degree:	9.5%				

Grand Rapids is Michigan's second-largest city, the center of its most prosperous and confident metropolitan area. The city's roots are in trees: It grew as a center for processing and turning into furniture the hardwood forests of northern Michigan. By the early 20th century, Grand Rapids was the leading furniture manufacturer in the nation. The Depression knocked the bottom out of the residential furniture market, and many manufacturers moved to North Carolina, where labor was cheaper. So Grand

2008 Presidential Vote

McCain (R)	171,255	(49%)
Obama (D)	169,183	(49%)

2004 Presidential Vote

Bush (R)	197,493	(59%)
Kerry (D)	133,460	(40%)

Cook Partisan Voting Index: R+6

Rapids had to reinvent itself, and did. It went into office furniture, and today three of the nation's largest office furniture manufacturers—Steelcase, Haworth, and Herman Miller—are located here or nearby. It capitalized also on a knack for sales. Rich DeVos and Jay Van Andel started Amway, the direct-sales empire, which now has half of its sales abroad, and Frederik and Hendrik Meijer started Meijer's Thrifty Acres, combining supermarkets with discount stores in a way that even Wal-Mart has not been able to equal. Grand Rapids is also the center of a machine-tool empire; the home of Wolverine World Wide, maker of Hush Puppies shoes; and the headquarters of Bissell and its carpet sweepers. Fifty years ago Grand Rapids and its up-and-coming businesses were outshined by Detroit and the auto industry. Today, while Detroit's Big Three flirt with bankruptcy, Grand Rapids chugs along, although General Motor's financial troubles in 2009 led to the closure of a 900-employee stamping factory in the city.

One ingredient in Grand Rapids' success is its unique ethnic mix. It was founded by New England Yankees, but much of its character was set by the Dutch immigrants who began arriving in western Michigan in the 1870s, and are still coming today; 14% of people here claim Dutch ancestry (probably no other American city has such a high proportion of "V" pages in the phone book). The Dutch brought with them a piety witnessed in their Reform and Christian Reform churches, and a culture of hard work and precision craftsmanship. Their cultural conservatism and belief in market economics run deep. Dutch tradition and entrepreneurial success have been the ingredients of a civic activism that has given Grand Rapids a host of creative civic institutions—and an Alexander Calder stabile—that are the match of any city in the country. Grand Rapids' downtown has been thick with construction cranes. In 2007 the city opened the first certified "green" museum in the world, the new Grand Rapids Art Museum, with triple the space of the old, as well as a new hotel and medical buildings. Years ago Grand Rapids commissioned an Alexander Calder sculpture for the plaza outside its city hall, and now it has others by Calder, Andy Goldsworthy, and Maya Lin. Other draws for outsiders are the Gerald R. Ford Presidential Library and Museum and the outdoor Meijer Gardens.

Politically, Grand Rapids has been the center of Michigan Republicanism for much of the last century. It has also produced national Republican leaders. Arthur Vandenberg, originally a newspaper editor, was a U.S. senator from 1928 to 1951; once an isolationist, he provided key support for the bipartisan internationalist foreign policies of Franklin D. Roosevelt and Harry Truman. Another was Gerald Ford, who rose to House Republican leader in 1965, vice president in 1973, and then president after Richard Nixon resigned in 1974. The 3rd Congressional District of Michigan includes Grand Rapids and almost all of Kent County, plus Ionia and Barry counties to the east and south. Although it is one of the two most Republican districts in Michigan, it voted only narrowly for Republican nominee John McCain in 2008. He won the 3rd with 49.4% of the vote to Democratic nominee Barack Obama's 48.8%.

The congressman from the 3rd District is Republican Vernon Ehlers, the winner of a December 1993 special election. Ehlers grew up in small-town Minnesota, the son of a Christian Reform minister. He attended Calvin College in Grand Rapids, got a Ph.D. in physics at the University of California at Berkeley, and then returned to Calvin to teach for 17 years. In 1974, concerned about local waste management, he was elected Kent County commissioner. In 1982, he won a seat in the state House, and in 1986, the state Senate. After Republican Rep. Paul Henry died in July 1993, Ehlers ran to succeed him. He won the November primary with 33% of the vote, and a month later easily defeated the Democrat 67%-23%.

Ehlers brought to House Republicans, then entering their 40th year in the minority, a majority mindset. That brought him to the attention of Rep. Newt Gingrich, R-Ga., who as speaker named him to his transition team after the historic 1994 election gave control of the chamber to the GOP. He assigned Ehlers, the first research physicist in Congress, to lead efforts to revamp the House's computer system (there were 11 different e-mail systems). In 1995 Ehlers responded with a system making available vote tallies, public-hearing transcripts, and texts of amendments and bills, plus the Thomas Library of Congress website. He was responsible for convincing the House to migrate from onetime market leader Lotus Notes to the now ubiquitous Microsoft e-mail program.

His religious faith and scientific training have left Ehlers with a middle-of-the-House voting record. Ehlers often insists on research to determine public needs. In 2004 he passed an amendment to the transportation bill pegging future research at 1% of total spending. In 2007 he got the House to add $16 million to improve the training of math and science teachers, though President Bush vetoed the spending bill. When controversy arose over the composition of National Academy of Sciences advisory panels, he said, "A single, guiding principle should be applied—select the most qualified person for the job." But he added that on presidential appointments, "it is important that the scientists are in tune with the philosophy of the appointing president." A self-described nerd in high school, Ehlers is fond of telling high school groups: "They shouldn't look down on nerds because if they are not a nerd, they are going to end up working for one."

Ehlers chaired the Science subcommittee overseeing the Environmental Protection Agency and oceans programs until Republicans lost the majority in 2007. He sponsored several laws that won widespread backing, including one to study invasive species and another for a $9 million electric barrier in the Illinois River to prevent Asian carp from getting into the Great Lakes. He has continued to press with some success for more spending to solve Great Lakes problems. In 2008, he proposed a compact of eight Great Lakes states to prevent water diversions and the same year got committee approval for $775 million to restore contaminated areas of the lakes.

Ehlers was one of the Republicans who voted to repeal the section of the USA PATRIOT Act, the Bush administration's antiterrorism law, allowing agents access to library records. He also has been one of the House Republicans to oppose oil drilling in the Arctic National Wildlife Refuge and to force the Republican leadership to remove the issue from must-pass appropriation bills.

He is the former chairman of the House Administration Committee, which handles the managerial issues of running the House of Representatives as well as issues related to the conduct of elections. He led the debate on the bill to require photo IDs for voting, which passed in 2006. Ehlers has a penchant for compromise. As head of a three-member task force on California Republican Rep. Robert Dornan's challenge to his 984-vote defeat in 1996, Ehlers said there was evidence of vote fraud but not enough to vacate the seat.

Ehlers refuses to take more than 30% of his campaign money from outside the district and has been re-elected by wide margins.

FOURTH DISTRICT

Dave Camp (R)

Elected 1990, 10th term; b. July 9, 1953, Midland; home, Midland; Albion Col., B.A. 1975, U. of San Diego, J.D. 1978; Catholic; married (Nancy); 3 children.

Elected Office: MI House of Reps., 1988–90.

Professional Career: Practicing atty., 1978–90; MI special asst. atty. gen., 1980–84; A.A., U.S. Rep. Bill Schuette, 1984–87.

DC Office: 341 CHOB, 20515, 202-225-3561; Fax: 202-225-9679; Web site: camp.house.gov.

State Offices: Midland, 989-631-2552; Traverse City, 231-929-4711.

Committees: *Joint Committee on Taxation* (1st of 2 R). *Ways & Means* (RMM of 15 R).

Group Ratings

	ADA	ACLU	AFS	LCV	ITIC	NTU	COC	ACU	CFG	FRC
2008	20	18	14	0	57	56	94	83	60	100
2007	5	—	9	0	—	74	90	96	84	—

National Journal Ratings

	2007 LIB — 2007 CONS		2008 LIB — 2008 CONS	
Economic	21%	— 78%	24%	— 75%
Social	9%	— 85%	20%	— 74%
Foreign	30%	— 69%	22%	— 74%
Composite	21%	— 79%	24%	— 76%

Key Votes of the 110th Congress

1. Increase minimum wage	N	5. Share immigration data	Y	9. Withdraw troops 8/08	N
2. Expand SCHIP	N	6. Foreign aid abortion ban	Y	10. No operations in Iran	N
3. Raise CAFE standards	N	7. Ban gay bias in workplace	N	11. Free trade with Peru	Y
4. Bail out financial markets	Y	8. Repeal D.C. gun law	Y	12. Overhaul FISA	Y

Election Results

2008 general	Dave Camp (R)	204,259	(62%)	($2,568,143)
	Andrew Concannon (D)	117,665	(36%)	($121,971)
2008 primary	Dave Camp (R)	unopposed		

Prior Winning Percentages: 2006 (61%); 2004 (64%); 2002 (68%); 2000 (68%); 1998 (91%); 1996 (65%); 1994 (73%); 1992 (63%); 1990 (65%)

Population		Race/Ethnicity		Work	
Pop. 2007:	681,352	White:	91.4%	Private:	79.0%
Change since 2000:	Up 2.8%	Black:	2.4%	Government:	13.2%
Urban:	41.4%	Hispanic:	2.9%	Self-employed:	7.6%
Rural:	58.6%	Asian:	0.9%	Blue collar:	25.9%
Area size:	8,053 sq. mi.	Native Am.:	0.8%	White collar:	54.3%
		Hawaiian:	0.0%	Khaki collar:	0.1%
Age		Two+ races:	1.5%	Other:	19.8%
Median age:	38.0 yrs.			Median income:	$42,565
More than 65 yrs:	14.4%	*Ancestry*		Median home value:	$130,100
Less than 18 yrs:	22.6%	German:	23.4%	Poverty:	14.7%
		Irish:	10.2%		
Education		English:	10.1%	**Military Veterans**	
H.S. grad:	87.3%			% of Pop:	11.2%
College grad:	21.0%				
Grad degree:	7.8%				

Flat and treeless for miles, the central reaches of Michigan's Lower Peninsula are farm country, exposed to bitter winds and snowdrifts in winter and shining sun for precious weeks in summer. Like the steppes of Eastern Europe, these are farmlands that produce hearty crops: potatoes, navy beans, sugar beets. The little cities here are often small factory towns, with neat tree-lined streets that suddenly end and turn to bare fields. Each city has some

2008 Presidential Vote		
Obama (D)	170,251	(50%)
McCain (R)	163,855	(48%)
2004 Presidential Vote		
Bush (R)	181,314	(55%)
Kerry (D)	145,774	(44%)
Cook Partisan Voting Index:	R+3	

distinction. Midland in 1891 was a declining lumber town when Herbert Dow perfected an electrolytic process to extract chemicals from northern Michigan's extensive brine wells. That was the start of Dow Chemical, still headquartered in this now upscale town and today a large producer of pesticides and agricultural biotech products. Owosso in 1902 was the birthplace of Thomas E. Dewey, later New York governor and the Republican nominee for president in 1944 and 1948. It was also the home of novelist James Oliver Curwood and his Curwood Castle writing studio. Today it hosts the Curwood Festival, lovingly chronicled by Thomas Mallon in *Rockets and Rodeos*, and is the site of Mallon's novel *Dewey Defeats Truman*. As recently as the 1970s, Indian tribes in the area clashed with sportsmen over land and water use. An historic agreement in 2007 restored many Indian rights and allowed tribes to oversee their own hunters and anglers. Mount Pleasant, to the north, is the home of Central Michigan University.

The 4th Congressional District of Michigan, the state's second largest, includes much of this territory north of Lansing and Grand Rapids and west of Flint and Saginaw. It stretches north up the freeways, hemmed in between U.S. 131 to the west and Interstate 75 to the east. Thousands of people drive up the routes in the fall to hunt and in the winter to ski. The rolling country around Houghton Lake was once lumber country and is now a retirement and resort area, with trailers and condominiums between knotty-pine cottages clustered around icy green lakes. The 4th has more farms than any other district in Michigan. The district reaches economically vibrant Traverse City, which has the world's largest concentration of red tart cherry orchards and is burgeoning with vacation homes, resorts and more than two dozen wineries. Michigan leads the nation in production of tart cherries, blueberries and dry edible beans. In Greenville, hard-pressed economically after the closure of a large Electrolux plant, new solar-power manufacturing has enabled hundreds of jobs. Politically, the district remains mostly Republican territory, especially in the Midland and Traverse City areas, though some counties vote Democratic on occasion. George W. Bush won 54% here in 2000 and 55% in 2004. In 2008, Barack Obama won 50%-48%.

The congressman from the 4th District is Dave Camp, a Republican first elected in 1990. Camp grew up in Midland and returned there after school to practice law. In 1984, he managed the successful congressional campaign of his boyhood friend, Bill Schuette. In 1990, Schuette unsuccessfully ran against Democratic Sen. Carl Levin, and Camp ran for Congress after having served two years in the state House. His key victory was in the Republican primary, where he beat Al Cropsey, a former legislator who was allied with evangelical conservatives, 33%-30%.

Camp is influential on the Ways and Means Committee, where he is the ranking Republican and a potential bipartisan deal-maker on tax and health issues. He has a generally conservative voting record, especially on cultural issues. He worked with then-Illinois Democratic Rep. Rahm Emanuel in the House to expand tax credits for education costs, and advocated changes in the federal Hope scholarships to direct more benefits to low-income students. He has been a champion of free trade on the committee, while also trying to expand trade-adjustment assistance for workers. Camp was a guiding hand behind some of the major initiatives from the era of Republican control of the House, 1995 to 2006. Camp played a key role in passing the welfare overhaul in 1996, and he defended the party's signature 2003 Medicare prescription-drug bill against Democratic attacks. He championed the cause of making President Bush's 2001 tax cuts permanent, as well as the president's failed plan to create private savings accounts in the Social Security program. Active on the health care subcommittee, he called for tax changes to loosen the connection between jobs and health care. He also pushed legislation to assist patients with kidney disease, and he authored the Organ Donor Card Insert Act, under which an estimated 70 million taxpayers receive organ-donor information with their income-tax refunds.

When Louisiana Republican Rep. Jim McCrery announced that he would not seek re-election in 2008, Rep. Wally Herger of California had more seniority than Camp and was positioned to succeed McCrery in the ranking minority slot, the most powerful post for the minority party on a committee. Camp did the requisite party fundraising and networking on the K Street lobbying corridor to edge out the low-profile Herger. In the most important test—who could raise more money for Republicans in tough election battles—Camp was far and away Herger's superior, bringing in over $2 million for the party, while Herger raised about half that amount. Camp also had better ties to Republican leaders. In 1998, he ran Illinois Republican Dennis Hastert's successful campaign for House speaker. He also served on the leadership-driven Steering Committee, which makes committee assignments.

An important pet issue for Camp is adoption law. In 2000, he helped win enactment of the International Adoption Act, which designates the State Department to help adoptive parents in dealing with officials in other nations. And two years later, Congress passed his bill to create financial incentives for domestic adoptions. He also pushed for ratification by the Senate of a treaty on international adoption, which would remove additional obstacles. As a state legislator in Michigan, Camp had worked with parents and children in the foster-care system. On an issue of interest to his home state, Camp won enactment of a bill to protect the state's 120 lighthouses.

Camp has had minimal opposition in the 4th District. He keeps in close touch with the district by signing every constituent letter sent from his office, often with a personal note—roughly 30,000 each year.

FIFTH DISTRICT

Dale Kildee (D)

Elected 1976, 17th term; b. Sept. 16, 1929, Flint; home, Flint; Sacred Heart Seminary, B.A. 1952, U. of MI, M.A. 1961, Rotary Fellow, U. of Peshawar, Pakistan; Catholic; married (Gayle); 3 children.

Elected Office: MI House of Reps., 1964–74; MI Senate, 1974–75.

Professional Career: H.S. teacher, 1954–64.

DC Office: 2107 RHOB, 20515, 202-225-3611; Fax: 202-225-6393; Web site: www.house.gov/kildee.

State Offices: Bay City, 989-891-0990; Flint, 810-239-1437; Saginaw, 989-755-8904.

Committees: *Education & Labor* (2nd of 29 D): Early Childhood, Elementary & Secondary Education (Chmn); Health, Employment, Labor & Pensions. *Natural Resources* (2nd of 29 D): Insular Affairs, Oceans & Wildlife; National Parks, Forests & Public Lands.

Group Ratings

	ADA	ACLU	AFS	LCV	ITIC	NTU	COC	ACU	CFG	FRC
2008	100	91	100	92	57	5	61	0	0	23
2007	100	—	100	80	—	3	50	4	1	—

National Journal Ratings

	2007 LIB — 2007 CONS		2008 LIB — 2008 CONS	
Economic	73%	— 24%	81%	— 15%
Social	61%	— 39%	75%	— 18%
Foreign	65%	— 33%	65%	— 32%
Composite	67%	— 33%	76%	— 24%

Key Votes of the 110th Congress

1. Increase minimum wage	Y	5. Share immigration data	Y	9. Withdraw troops 8/08	Y
2. Expand SCHIP	Y	6. Foreign aid abortion ban	Y	10. No operations in Iran	Y
3. Raise CAFE standards	Y	7. Ban gay bias in workplace	Y	11. Free trade with Peru	N
4. Bail out financial markets	Y	8. Repeal D.C. gun law	N	12. Overhaul FISA	Y

Election Results

2008 general	Dale Kildee (D)	221,841	(70%)	($559,948)
	Matt Sawicki (R)	85,017	(27%)	
2008 primary	Dale Kildee (D)	unopposed		

Prior Winning Percentages: 2006 (73%); 2004 (67%); 2002 (92%); 2000 (61%); 1998 (56%); 1996 (59%); 1994 (51%); 1992 (54%); 1990 (68%); 1988 (76%); 1986 (80%); 1984 (93%); 1982 (75%); 1980 (93%); 1978 (77%); 1976 (70%)

Population		Race/Ethnicity		Work	
Pop. 2007:	649,971	White:	75.7%	Private:	83.2%
Change since 2000:	Down 1.9%	Black:	17.9%	Government:	11.3%
Urban:	79.4%	Hispanic:	3.6%	Self-employed:	5.4%
Rural:	20.6%	Asian:	0.8%	Blue collar:	26.9%
Area size:	1,780 sq. mi.	Native Am.:	0.4%	White collar:	52.7%
		Hawaiian:	0.0%	Khaki collar:	0.0%
Age		Two+ races:	1.6%	Other:	20.3%
Median age:	37.2 yrs.			Median income:	$42,040
More than 65 yrs:	12.9%	*Ancestry*		Median home value:	$118,200
Less than 18 yrs:	25.6%	German:	17.4%	Poverty:	17.3%
		Irish:	8.3%		
Education		English:	8.0%	**Military Veterans**	
H.S. grad:	86.4%			% of Pop:	10.5%
College grad:	17.4%				
Grad degree:	5.9%				

The flat plains south of Saginaw Bay, the inlet of Lake Huron that separates Michigan's Thumb (people really call it that) from the mitten of the Lower Peninsula, was once one of the nation's premier industrial areas. Some 130 years ago it was the nation's premier lumber country, with huge stands of virgin trees feeding 36 sawmills in Bay City and with logs piled high along both banks of the Saginaw River. When the trees were gone, farmers took over, and the land was sown with beans and sugar beets. A century ago, heavy industry followed. Flint, a small town on a minor branch of the Saginaw River, was the home base of W.C. Durant, the investor who merged several young auto firms to form General Motors. GM put its Chevrolet and Buick factories in Flint and its power-steering facility in Saginaw, chosen because it was already a center of precision machinery manufacturing. From 1910 through the 1960s, Flint grew lustily as it built Chevys and Buicks, attracting workers from the mountains of Kentucky and Tennessee and the Black Belt of Alabama. Country music, blues and soul, and Southern accents became common in an area originally settled by New England Yankees. There was turmoil, too. Flint was the scene in January 1937 of the great sit-down strike that forced GM to recognize the United Auto Workers as the bargaining agent for all its workers. The UAW-GM contracts produced the world's highest wages for industrial workers and lavish fringe benefits, including a generous health care plan.

2008 Presidential Vote		
Obama (D)	207,522	(64%)
McCain (R)	112,965	(35%)

2004 Presidential Vote		
Kerry (D)	187,671	(59%)
Bush (R)	129,457	(41%)

Cook Partisan Voting Index: D+11

Economic disaster struck with the energy crisis of the 1970s. Imports, especially from Japan, that were higher quality and lower priced than American cars, took an increasing share of the market. In 1979, GM employed more than 70,000 workers in its Flint plants, a huge share of the labor force in a metropolitan area of 430,000 people. Eventually, thousands left Flint as GM closed 13 of its 15 factories. By the late 2000s, the GM payroll had fallen below 12,000, and total local employment had dropped about 60%. Things got worse in 2008, when GM announced it was slashing its assembly-line production by 30%, including at its Flint facilities. In June 2009, the company filed for bankruptcy and shut yet another factory with 650 workers. The city's attempts to spruce up its downtown failed, and many storefronts have been boarded up. About one of five homes is unoccupied. One-third of Flint households are in poverty, and many skilled workers have fled what *Forbes* magazine calls one of "America's fastest-dying cites." Flint's economic woes forced the state to take control of the city government. Michael Moore, the liberal filmmaker, has used his hometown of Flint as the locale for much of his work about deteriorating life in America. Gritty Saginaw also suffered, with huge cutbacks by Delphi, its largest employer. But there are some modest positive developments. In the Saginaw area, small manufacturing operations requiring highly skilled workers have grown up in old factory buildings once considered worthless. This is part of southern Michigan's industrial belt with the expertise to sustain just-in-time manufacturing.

The 5th Congressional District of Michigan includes Flint and surrounding Genesee County, Saginaw and eastern Saginaw County, Bay City and eastern Bay County, and rural Tuscola County, which is part of the Thumb. Flint, evenly divided between the parties when the sit-down strikes divided the community in the 1930s, is now heavily Democratic, Saginaw and Bay City somewhat less so. Tuscola continues to vote Republican.

The congressman from the 5th District is Dale Kildee, a Democrat first elected in 1976. Kildee grew up in Flint, the son of an autoworker. He studied for the priesthood, then taught at a Catholic high school in Detroit and at Flint Central High School. Door-to-door campaigning got him elected to a state legislative seat in 1964, at age 35, and enabled him to beat a 26-year veteran of the state Senate in 1974. Two years later, he ran successfully for the U.S. House seat. Kildee has an intensity of conviction derived from the liberal tradition lively in the American Catholic Church, a tradition with little regard for market economics, a strong sense of obligation to the needy, and a cultural conservatism. He is almost always pro-union and requires his employees to drive to work in cars built by the UAW. He opposes abortion rights and is something of a stickler on ethics. On the Education and Labor Committee, he is a strong ally of teachers' unions, a backer of increased federal aid for education and an opponent of school choice.

Kildee was the first House member to argue that imported minivans should be subject not to the 2.5% tariff for cars but to the 25% tariff for trucks, which has been on the books since the early 1960s. The truck tariff has become a sticking point in U.S. negotiations with several countries, which led to Kildee's fierce opposition to a bilateral trade deal with Thailand. He also was a strong opponent of free-trade agreements with Mexico and Central America. On the Resources Committee, he is strong advocate for American Indians, influenced by his grandparents' friendships with Indians living on a reservation near their home in northern Michigan. His efforts to clean up the Great Lakes have produced commendations by environmentalists. Kildee has served more than two decades on the House board that oversees the page program. After Republican Rep. Mark Foley's improper contacts with former pages came to light, Kildee, who took over as chairman in 2007, implemented reforms.

As chairman of the Subcommittee on Early Childhood, Elementary and Secondary Education at Education and Labor, he has conducted extensive oversight of the Bush administration's No Child Left Behind education policy, while demanding adequate funding for its mandates on schools. He is a critic of government-paid vouchers for parents of private-school students. In 2007, he helped to enact an extension of the Head Start program, and successfully opposed a proposal that would have allowed faith-based organizations to hire teachers based on religion.

Kildee has been easily re-elected, except for a couple of tight races in the 1990s. In 2002, redistricting put him in the same heavily Democratic district as Bay City Democrat Jim Barcia, one of the more conservative Democrats in the House and, like Kildee, an opponent of abortion rights. Barcia opted to run for the state Senate rather than battle Kildee for the seat. As Kildee approached age 80, state Sen. John Gleason floated the idea of a primary challenge in 2008, but backed off just before the filing deadline.

SIXTH DISTRICT

Fred Upton (R)

Elected 1986, 12th term; b. April 23, 1953, St. Joseph; home, St. Joseph; U. of MI, B.A. 1975; Protestant; married (Amey); 2 children.

Professional Career: Project coord., U.S. Rep. David Stockman, 1975–80; Legis. affairs, O.M.B., 1981–83, Dir., 1984–85.

DC Office: 2183 RHOB, 20515, 202-225-3761; Fax: 202-225-4986; Web site: www.house.gov/upton.

State Offices: Kalamazoo, 269-385-0039; St. Joseph, 269-982-1986.

Committees: *Energy & Commerce* (3rd of 23 R): Communications, Technology & the Internet; Energy & Environment (RMM).

Group Ratings

	ADA	ACLU	AFS	LCV	ITIC	NTU	COC	ACU	CFG	FRC
2008	60	36	57	54	71	38	89	44	39	70
2007	40	—	18	35	—	54	100	56	41	—

National Journal Ratings

	2007 LIB	—	2007 CONS		2008 LIB	—	2008 CONS
Economic	41%	—	59%		41%	—	59%
Social	40%	—	59%		31%	—	62%
Foreign	42%	—	57%		44%	—	55%
Composite	41%	—	59%		40%	—	60%

Key Votes of the 110th Congress

1. Increase minimum wage	Y	5. Share immigration data	Y	9. Withdraw troops 8/08	N
2. Expand SCHIP	Y	6. Foreign aid abortion ban	Y	10. No operations in Iran	N
3. Raise CAFE standards	N	7. Ban gay bias in workplace	N	11. Free trade with Peru	Y
4. Bail out financial markets	Y	8. Repeal D.C. gun law	Y	12. Overhaul FISA	Y

Election Results

2008 general	Fred Upton (R)	188,157	(59%)	($1,527,587)
	Don Cooney (D)	123,257	(39%)	($84,883)
2008 primary	Fred Upton (R)	unopposed		

Prior Winning Percentages: 2006 (61%); 2004 (65%); 2002 (69%); 2000 (68%); 1998 (70%); 1996 (68%); 1994 (73%); 1992 (62%); 1990 (58%); 1988 (71%); 1986 (62%)

Population		Race/Ethnicity		Work	
Pop. 2007:	670,811	White:	83.5%	Private:	82.5%
Change since 2000:	Up 1.2%	Black:	8.4%	Government:	10.9%
Urban:	58.3%	Hispanic:	4.5%	Self-employed:	6.4%
Rural:	41.7%	Asian:	1.3%	Blue collar:	27.9%
Area size:	3,420 sq. mi.	Native Am.:	0.4%	White collar:	55.3%
		Hawaiian:	0.0%	Khaki collar:	0.1%
Age		Two+ races:	1.7%	Other:	16.7%
Median age:	36.9 yrs.			Median income:	$44,258
More than 65 yrs:	12.9%	*Ancestry*		Median home value:	$134,600
Less than 18 yrs:	24.5%	German:	20.6%	Poverty:	15.4%
		Irish:	9.7%		
Education		English:	8.9%	**Military Veterans**	
H.S. grad:	87.0%			% of Pop:	10.5%
College grad:	24.0%				
Grad degree:	9.2%				

The southwest corner of Michigan was settled by New England Yankees and Upstate New Yorkers in the 1830s and 1840s. They built small towns with schools and churches and colleges, supported temperance and opposed capital punishment. And in 1854, they started the Republican Party. There are towns in southwest Michigan that still recall proudly their past as termini of the Underground Railroad, and there are black families that claim ancestors who made their way north out of slavery

2008 Presidential Vote		
Obama (D)	177,497	(54%)
McCain (R)	145,045	(44%)

2004 Presidential Vote		
Bush (R)	164,595	(53%)
Kerry (D)	143,906	(46%)

Cook Partisan Voting Index: EVEN

to freedom. Later, big industries transformed some of the small towns into significant cities. Kalamazoo, started by Dutch-Americans who introduced celery to this country, became the home of Upjohn pharmaceuticals, which went through several corporate changes and is now part of Pfizer. Predominantly black and struggling Benton Harbor and predominantly white and prosperous St. Joseph, twin towns on Lake Michigan, were originally known for cherry and peach orchards, but now the dominant local fruit is the blueberry, and Benton Harbor is best known as the headquarters for Whirlpool. But many other local companies and other famous industrial names have moved out, along with their thousands of jobs. Like many other jurisdictions, the region is increasingly turning to casinos for an economic shot in the arm. The Pokagon Indian Tribe opened a large casino resort in Berrien County in 2007. Kalamazoo has had some success keeping its young people in school with a program that pays college tuition for high school students who graduate; it is the model for a statewide plan adopted by Democratic Gov. Jennifer Granholm in 2007. The southwest corner is where the influence of Michigan recedes: People here watch Chicago television and root for the Cubs or White Sox baseball teams rather than the Detroit Tigers.

The 6th Congressional District of Michigan occupies the southwest corner of the state, with Kalamazoo and Benton Harbor-St. Joseph its two major urban areas. It takes in three smaller counties and parts of two others. It was for many years arch-Republican territory, represented by a succession of conservative congressmen who deplored federal spending and welfare-state measures: New Deal opponent Clare Hoffman (1935–63), Nixon defender Edward Hutchinson (1963–77), and pork barrel critic and later Reagan Office of Management and Budget Director David Stockman (1977–81). In the 1990s, Kalamazoo trended toward the Democrats, and the 6th District cast small pluralities for Bill Clinton in the 1990s. George W. Bush carried the district twice but lost Kalamazoo County in 2000 and 2004, thanks in part to the influence of the Western Michigan University community and its 25,000 students. In 2008, Barack Obama won the district 54%-44%. Granholm won Kalamazoo County, 59%-39%, over western Michigan Republican Dick DeVos in 2006.

The congressman from the 6th District is Fred Upton, a Republican first elected in 1986. The grandson of one of the founders of Whirlpool, Upton grew up in St. Joseph, attended the University of Michigan and worked for David Stockman, first on Stockman's congressional staff, then from 1981 to 1985 at the White House in OMB. Upton returned home and ran in the 1986 Republican primary against Rep. Mark Siljander, a conservative and evangelical Christian, and won 55%-45%. Upton is less like the congressional David Stockman, a scourge when it came to federal spending, and more like the OMB Stockman, who rued the Reagan tax cuts.

Upton has a moderate voting record, and he freely exercised his independence when his party controlled the House from 1995 to 2006. He sought, with limited success, to use his leverage to reduce the size of tax cuts during the Bush presidency. He has backed increases in the minimum wage, increased funding for Amtrak, and Democratic measures to expand the State Children's Health Insurance Program. He also voted with Democrats to preserve the Endangered Species Act and to expand embryonic-stem-cell research, which uses discarded embryos from in vitro fertilization; both positions were at odds with those of his party. In February 2007, he broke with his party to oppose the Bush administration plan for a "surge" of troop strength in Iraq. "The Iraqis don't want us there. We're viewed as part of the problem, not the solution," he said. But he later backed Bush's veto of Democratic proposals to restrict spending on the war.

Upton is the third most senior Republican on the Energy and Commerce Committee, and is a strong candidate to become the top Republican on the panel in 2011, when the current ranking member, Republican Joe Barton of Texas, reaches his term limit. Next in line in seniority is Ralph Hall of Texas, but Hall will turn 88 in 2011, and would unlikely be the party's choice for such a critical committee post. Upton has been particularly involved in telecommunications issues on the committee and chaired the Telecommunications Subcommittee for six years when Republicans controlled the House. He supported a bill to allow regional telephone companies to provide broadband service more easily, and he pushed for higher fines against broadcasters for indecent programming, from $32,500 to $325,000. He also criticized the recording industry for inadequate parental advisory labels on music that contains sex, violence or strong language, but took the view that the First Amendment bars Congress from regulating the content. Bush signed his bill to create a "safe playground for kids" on the Internet, free of pornography and other inappropriate material. Overall, Upton has backed deregulation of the broadcast industry, including the lifting of cross-ownership media bans in the same market. In his committee work, Upton also has been a big booster of additional nuclear power facilities. As the one-time chairman of the Oversight and Investigations Subcommittee, Upton investigated the Salt Lake City Olympics scandal and defects in Firestone-Bridgestone tires.

Upton has been re-elected by wide margins. But in 2008, his defeat of outspoken liberal Kalamazoo City Councilor Don Cooney by 59% to 39% was his lowest percentage win since 1990, and was reflective of his gradually declining winning percentages in Berrien and Kalamazoo counties. In the 2006 election, he defeated Kim Clark, a modestly financed theater owner and former television producer, with 61%.

SEVENTH DISTRICT

Mark Schauer (D)

Elected 2008, 1st term; b. Oct. 2, 1961, Howell; home, Battle Creek; Albion Col., B.A. 1984; W. MI Univ., M.P.A., 1986; MI St. U., M.A. 1995; Methodist; married (Christine); 3 children.

Elected Office: Battle Creek city commissioner, 1994–96; MI House, 1997–2003; MI Senate, 2003–08, Majority ldr., 2007–08.

Professional Career: Urban planner, Calhoun Cnty., 1984–86; Exec. dir., Comm. Action Agency of S. Central MI, 1987–92; Prevention coordinator, Calhoun Cnty. Human Services Coordinating Cncl., 1992–97.

DC Office: 1408 LHOB, 20515, 202-225-6276; Fax: 202-225-6281; Web site: schauer.house.gov/.

State Offices: Jackson, 517-780-9075.

Committees: *Agriculture* (22nd of 28 D): Conservation, Credit, Energy & Research. *Transportation & Infrastructure* (38th of 44 D): Aviation; Highways & Transit; Railroads, Pipelines & Hazardous Materials.

Group Ratings and Key Votes: Newly Elected

Election Results

2008 general	Mark Schauer (D)	157,213	(49%)	($2,331,667)
	Tim Walberg (R)	149,781	(46%)	($2,128,559)
	Lynn Meadows (Green)	9,528	(3%)	
2008 primary	Mark Schauer (D)	17,270	(66%)	
	Sharon Renier (D)	9,034	(34%)	

Population		Race/Ethnicity		Work	
Pop. 2007:	685,170	White:	87.7%	Private:	79.2%
Change since 2000:	Up 3.4%	Black:	5.7%	Government:	13.7%
Urban:	54.0%	Hispanic:	3.5%	Self-employed:	6.8%
Rural:	46.0%	Asian:	1.2%	Blue collar:	28.0%
Area size:	4,365 sq. mi.	Native Am.:	0.3%	White collar:	55.3%
		Hawaiian:	0.0%	Khaki collar:	0.1%
Age		Two+ races:	1.5%	Other:	16.6%
Median age:	38.3 yrs.	*Ancestry*		Median income:	$48,872
More than 65 yrs:	13.0%	German:	21.2%	Median home value:	$144,300
Less than 18 yrs:	24.2%	English:	11.9%	Poverty:	12.2%
Education		Irish:	10.1%	**Military Veterans**	
H.S. grad:	88.4%			% of Pop:	11.4%
College grad:	21.7%				
Grad degree:	8.0%				

The small cities and towns spotting the farmland counties of south central Michigan have been incubators of innovation since they were settled by Yankees from New England 150 years ago. The state's public school system was established by two politicians from Marshall. A few miles away, in Battle Creek, sanitarium operator W.K. Kellogg invented cornflakes as a health food; he and his onetime patient, C.W. Post, both established factories in the late 19th century and created the American break-

2008 Presidential Vote
Obama (D) 171,566 (52%)
McCain (R).............................154,222 (47%)

2004 Presidential Vote
Bush (R)................................176,624 (54%)
Kerry (D)...............................145,979 (45%)

Cook Partisan Voting Index: R + 2

fast cereal industry. To the south is Hillsdale, where conservative Hillsdale College has been proudly admitting blacks and women since the 1850s and refusing all federal aid. Although the area today is politically marginal, it gave birth to the Republican Party. In 1854, the party was founded in the manufacturing and prison town of Jackson as a kind of reformist institution, growing out of the same activist impulse that produced support for women's rights and Prohibition and opposition to the death penalty. Southern Michigan mostly rejected New Deal tinkering and was hostile to the United Auto Workers union, but the people here were receptive to moral claims made by later 20th-century reformers challenging racial segregation, the Vietnam War, and the Watergate cover-up.

Recently, this region has suffered from debilitating economic woes, largely due to the decline of the automobile industry and heavy manufacturing. Unemployment and poverty rates here have nearly doubled since 2000, with unemployment reaching double digits by 2007, even before the lowest ebb of the national recession. Jackson County, with a population of 150,000, saw 1,400 home foreclosures in 2008 alone, and in May 2009 *Forbes* magazine ranked the cities of Jackson and Battle Creek as two of the four worst small cities for job seekers.

The 7th Congressional District takes in all of five counties in southern Michigan plus parts of two others. Although Battle Creek retains strong Republican enclaves and the area is still culturally conservative, Democrats have gained ground by focusing on economic issues. Democrat Bill Clinton carried the district by small pluralities in 1992 and 1996, and although Republican George W. Bush won it with 51% in 2000 and 54% in 2004, Democrat Barack Obama took 52% of the district's vote in 2008.

The new congressman from the 7th District is Democrat Mark Schauer, the latest beneficiary of the district's political volatility. (Voters have elected four different representatives in the past four elections.) Schauer was born and raised in the small town of Howell, Mich. His father was a high school science teacher and his mother was a nurse at a small medical practice. He grew up in the same town as his three living grandparents and calls himself the product of a close-knit family. Schauer cites as his most important influences his Methodist faith and his grandfather, a 45-year lineman for the Detroit Edison utility who taught him the value of work. The family's modest economic background would later push Schauer strongly into the Democratic fold when he launched his career in public service and community advocacy. He spent more than a decade organizing in south central Michigan, representing both local government and advocacy agencies. Schauer's work brought him into close contact with government at every level, and he came to view elected office as a promising opportunity. He served as a city commissioner in his hometown of Battle Creek for two years before launching his first successful run for the state House in 1996 in a Republican-leaning district. He served two terms in the state House and then won election to the Michigan Senate. There, he became the party floor leader, the second-ranking position in the Democratic conference. After winning a second Senate term in 2006, he was elevated to Democratic leader.

In August 2007, Schauer announced he would challenge 7th District Rep. Tim Walberg, a Republican who had limped into office in 2006 against poorly funded Democrat Sharon Renier. Walberg had won the Republican nomination by ousting moderate GOP Rep. Joe Schwarz with the help of the national anti-tax organization Club for Growth. Schauer labeled Walberg as too conservative for the district's voters. In the 2008 Democratic primary, Schauer easily bested Renier after securing the backing of most local Democrats and raising large sums of money.

With the local and national economies in free fall, Schauer focused his campaign on economic issues. The Democratic Congressional Campaign Committee attacked Walberg for supporting "unfair trade" and jobs outsourcing, and ran ads asking, "Is it that he doesn't get it? Or that he just doesn't care?" In supporting Walberg, the National Republican Congressional Committee declared that Schauer "failed our families" by voting for Democratic Gov. Jennifer Granholm's tax increases.

Schauer, a devout Methodist, was relatively insulated from criticism on cultural issues, although Walberg accused him of voting "to let adults send pornography to minors over the Internet." When a constituent complained to Walberg about the high level of negativity in the race, he responded by heatedly listing everything he saw as wrong with Schauer's positions, and asked, "How do you make a negative record like that sound positive?"

The Club for Growth again ran ads supporting Walberg, spending more than $500,000 attacking Schauer. But Schauer had strong union backing. The American Federation of State, County, and Municipal Employees spent $500,000 on his behalf, and he received $300,000 in campaign contributions from other labor groups. He was also endorsed by several prominent local Republicans, the most important being Schwarz, who criticized the Club for Growth's involvement in the race. Schauer narrowly won, beating Walberg 48.8%-46.5%, with Libertarian and Green Party candidates winning 4.7% of the vote between them. Schauer is the first Democrat to represent the district since it was created after the 1990 census. The candidates spent about $2 million apiece, and outside groups spent nearly as much as the candidates.

Schauer was appointed to the Agriculture Committee and the Transportation and Infrastructure Committee. He has said his main focus in Congress would be protecting jobs at home and encouraging investment in his district. He avidly supported the 2008 federal bailout of the domestic auto industry, a big employer in his district. With the fifth-lowest winning percentage of any House freshman, Schauer may be a Republican target in 2010.

EIGHTH DISTRICT

Mike Rogers (R)

Elected 2000, 5th term; b. June 2, 1963, Livingston Cnty.; home, Brighton; Adrian Col., B.A. 1985; Methodist; divorced; 2 children.

Military Career: Army, 1985–88.

Elected Office: MI Senate, 1995–2000, Maj. floor ldr., 1999–2000.

Professional Career: Co-founder, E.B.I. Builders, 1985; FBI spec. agent, 1988–94.

DC Office: 133 CHOB, 20515, 202-225-4872; Fax: 202-225-5820; Web site: mikerogers.house.gov.

State Offices: Lansing, 517-702-8000.

Committees: *Energy & Commerce* (16th of 23 R): Communications, Technology & the Internet; Health. *Intelligence (Select)* (4th of 9 R): Oversight & Investigations; Technical & Tactical Intelligence; Terrorism, Human Intelligence Analysis & Counterintelligence.

Group Ratings

	ADA	ACLU	AFS	LCV	ITIC	NTU	COC	ACU	CFG	FRC
2008	25	18	29	15	43	63	89	84	71	100
2007	5	—	18	5	—	70	90	100	83	—

National Journal Ratings

	2007 LIB	—	2007 CONS		2008 LIB	—	2008 CONS
Economic	29%	—	70%		31%	—	69%
Social	21%	—	75%		20%	—	74%
Foreign	0%	—	72%		22%	—	74%
Composite	22%	—	78%		26%	—	74%

Key Votes of the 110th Congress

1. Increase minimum wage	N	5. Share immigration data	Y	9. Withdraw troops 8/08	N
2. Expand SCHIP	N	6. Foreign aid abortion ban	Y	10. No operations in Iran	N
3. Raise CAFE standards	N	7. Ban gay bias in workplace	N	11. Free trade with Peru	Y
4. Bail out financial markets	N	8. Repeal D.C. gun law	Y	12. Overhaul FISA	Y

Election Results

2008 general	Mike Rogers (R)	204,408	(57%)	($1,565,888)
	Robert Alexander (D)	145,491	(40%)	($214,282)
2008 primary	Mike Rogers (R)	unopposed		

Prior Winning Percentages: 2006 (55%); 2004 (61%); 2002 (68%); 2000 (49%)

Population		Race/Ethnicity		Work	
Pop. 2007:	703,946	White:	87.0%	Private:	78.8%
Change since 2000:	Up 6.2%	Black:	4.9%	Government:	15.6%
Urban:	70.0%	Hispanic:	3.7%	Self-employed:	5.4%
Rural:	30.0%	Asian:	2.3%	Blue collar:	20.6%
Area size:	2,288 sq. mi.	Native Am.:	0.4%	White collar:	63.3%
Age		Hawaiian:	0.0%	Khaki collar:	0.1%
Median age:	35.9 yrs.	Two+ races:	1.5%	Other:	16.1%
More than 65 yrs:	9.7%	*Ancestry*		Median income:	$59,019
Less than 18 yrs:	24.4%	German:	19.0%	Median home value:	$193,800
Education		Irish:	10.5%	Poverty:	11.2%
H.S. grad:	91.7%	English:	10.3%	**Military Veterans**	
College grad:	31.6%			% of Pop:	9.0%
Grad degree:	11.8%				

Lansing is Michigan's state capital, chosen in 1847 because of its geographic position halfway between Lake Huron and Lake Michigan—and away from the border with Canada and the threat of invasion by British forces. The only drawback was fewer days with sunshine than anyplace else in the state. But it is a tidy and pleasant city with more than its share of amenities. It has a beautifully restored Capitol and a fine state history museum and is neighbor to Michigan State University in East Lansing, started

2008 Presidential Vote
Obama (D) 198,206   (53%)
McCain (R).............................172,344   (46%)

2004 Presidential Vote
Bush (R).................................191,287   (54%)
Kerry (D)................................161,282   (45%)

Cook Partisan Voting Index: R+2

in 1855 as America's first land-grant college. Its Oldsmobile plant stimulated growth in the first half of the 20th century, and state government did the same in the second half. GM closed its Olds line in 2004, but two new highly efficient GM assembly plants have been constructed in the Lansing area, and the Oldsmobile name remains alive at two local museums and at the baseball stadium where the Lansing Lugnuts play. Historically, the Lansing area voted Republican, up through the 1960s. But as public employee unions have grown in membership and strength, Lansing, like some other state capitals, has become heavily Democratic, as is university-influenced East Lansing.

Just east of Lansing's Ingham County is quite another part of Michigan, Livingston County (most of the counties in these parts were named for members of President Andrew Jackson's Cabinet: Livingston was secretary of State and Ingham secretary of the Treasury). Forty years ago, Livingston County was mostly rural, known mainly for its many lakes. But over the years, thousands of Detroit-area residents have driven out Interstate 96 to Brighton and Howell, and other Livingston townships and subdivisions, schools and shopping malls have sprouted up. Most of these people are conservatives, happy to leave the urban problems of Detroit behind, angry at high taxes, annoyed by government regulations, and hewing to traditional religious faiths. They have made Livingston Michigan's fastest-growing county—its population rose 59% from 1990 to 2007—and one of its most Republican. Meanwhile, Lansing's population has been slowly declining, and local leaders have begun to explore a merger with East Lansing. In 1970, Livingston had 58,000 people to Ingham's 261,000; in 2007, Livingston had 183,000 to Ingham's 279,000. So as Ingham has grown more Democratic, Livingston has been casting bigger Republican margins as a counterbalance to Ingham's Democratic margins. In the presidential election of 2004, 93,000 people voted in Livingston and gave George W. Bush a 25,000-vote margin. By comparison, 133,000 voted in Ingham and gave John Kerry a 22,000-vote-margin. In the 2008 election, Barack Obama won in Ingham by 48,000 votes, with 66% of the vote, and lost to John McCain in Livingston by 13,000 votes, getting 42% of the vote.

The 8th Congressional District of Michigan includes all of Ingham and Livingston Counties, Shiawassee County south of Owosso, plus Clinton County, directly north of Lansing. It also takes in the partisan battleground of northern Oakland County.

The congressman from the 8th District is Mike Rogers, a Republican first elected in 2000. (He is one of two Republican Mike Rogers in the House; the other one is from Alabama.) He grew up in Brighton, in Livingston County, and graduated from Adrian College in southeastern Michigan. He was commissioned by the ROTC as commander of an Army rapid-deployment unit. He graduated from the Federal Bureau of Investigation's academy and focused on public corruption cases as an FBI special agent in Chicago for six years. In 1994, he returned to Michigan, started a home-construction business and was elected to the state Senate, where in 1999 he became majority floor leader. In 2000, when Democrat Debbie Stabenow gave up the 8th District seat to run successfully for the Senate, Rogers and Democrat Dianne Byrum, a fellow state senator, both ran for the seat. Each candidate raised about $2 million, and it turned out to be the closest race in the country that year. It took six weeks to count the final tally, and Rogers won by 111 votes.

Rogers has described his political philosophy as a version of "compassionate conservatism," with a bit more conservatism on cultural issues than on the economy. With his military, law enforcement and legislative backgrounds, Rogers made an impression on colleagues with his sound advice in the aftermath of the September 11 attacks. He provided expertise on the high-technology tools used to track terrorists and on the use of wiretaps, and he urged that airport screeners have federal supervision.

He has been an activist member of the Energy and Commerce Committee. Citing the fact that only a few hundred gas stations nationwide have the requisite equipment, he won bipartisan House approval in 2006 of a bill to help independent businesses purchase equipment for ethanol gas pumps. The House also passed his bill to eliminate state food-safety warnings that are stronger than comparable federal warnings. He sponsored a bill to give Michigan more authority to limit its flow of trash from other states and Canada. "We love our Canadian neighbors. We love their trade. But you don't throw your trash in your neighbor's yard," he said when the House passed the bill in April 2007.

His energetic legislating has made Rogers popular among House Republicans, though Rep. Thaddeus McCotter in the adjacent 11th District was first to make it into the leadership, as chairman of the Republican Policy Committee. With his significant fundraising skills, Rogers has been tapped by Republican leaders for prime assignments in contested races. He positioned himself to run for House Republican whip in 2006, but Missouri's Roy Blunt did not relinquish the post. He showed his mettle in May 2007 when he stood up to a threat by the powerful Defense Appropriations Subcommittee Chairman John Murtha, a Pennsylvania Democrat and former Marine. On the floor, Rogers challenged a $23-million earmark for Murtha's congressional district, but failed. Rogers maintains that Murtha came over to him afterward and said, loudly: "I hope you don't have any earmarks in the defense appropriations bill, because they are gone, and you will not get any earmarks now and forever." Rogers replied (according to Rogers): "Is that supposed to make me afraid of you?" Republicans tried to officially reprimand Murtha, and although that effort was tabled, Murtha apologized. In 2008, Rogers also battled John Dingell, the most powerful member of the Michigan delegation, to stop a proposed casino in Port Huron near the Canadian border. Dingell favored settling a land claim by an Indian tribe that could allow it to operate a casino far from its reservation, but Rogers argued that the move would violate a 2004 statewide referendum to restrict expansions of casino gambling.

At home, Rogers has won re-election without major problems, but not by the huge margins that many incumbents enjoy. In 2006, he won 55%-43% against Royal Oak Deputy City Attorney Jim Marcinkowski, a former CIA agent. In the difficult climate for Republicans in 2008, Rogers was re-elected with 57% of the vote against East Lansing progressive activist Bob Alexander. Rogers lost Lansing's Ingham County by 11,500 votes, but he won Republican Livingston County by 37,757. Political insiders in Michigan have speculated that he might make a strong statewide candidate, though the recent climate has not been hospitable for Republicans.

NINTH DISTRICT

Gary Peters (D)

Elected 2008, 1st term; b. Dec. 1, 1958, Pontiac; home, Bloomfield Township; Alma Col., B.A. 1980; U. of Detroit, M.B.A. 1984; Wayne St. U., J.D. 1989; MI St. U., M.A. 2007; Episcopalian; married (Colleen); 3 children.

Military Career: Naval Reserve, 1993–2005.

Elected Office: Rochester Hills Cty. Cncl, 1991–93; MI Senate, 1995–2002.

Professional Career: Merril Lynch, asst. v.p., 1980–89; UBS/Paine Webber, v.p., 1989–2003; Michigan Lottery commissioner, 2003–07; Central MI U., professor 2007–08.

DC Office: 1130 LHOB, 20515, 202-225-5802; Fax: 202-226-2356; Web site: peters.house.gov.

State Offices: Troy, 248-273-4227.

Committees: *Financial Services* (41st of 42 D): Capital Markets, Insurance & Government Sponsored Enterprises; International Monetary Policy & Trade. *Science & Technology* (26th of 26 D): Technology & Innovation.

Group Ratings and Key Votes: Newly Elected

Election Results

2008 general	Gary Peters (D)	183,311	(52%)	($2,509,019)
	Joe Knollenberg (R)	150,035	(43%)	($4,135,864)
	Jack Kevorkian (I)	8,987	(3%)	($880)
2008 primary	Gary Peters (D)	unopposed		

Population		Race/Ethnicity		Work	
Pop. 2007:	667,143	White:	78.0%	Private:	85.7%
Change since 2000:	Up 0.7%	Black:	9.9%	Government:	8.5%
Urban:	99.3%	Hispanic:	3.5%	Self-employed:	5.5%
Rural:	0.7%	Asian:	7.0%	Blue collar:	13.0%
Area size:	323 sq. mi.	Native Am.:	0.2%	White collar:	74.9%
Age		Hawaiian:	0.0%	Khaki collar:	0.0%
Median age:	40.0 yrs.	Two+ races:	1.2%	Other:	12.1%
More than 65 yrs:	12.9%	*Ancestry*		Median income:	$71,158
Less than 18 yrs:	23.5%	German:	15.2%	Median home value:	$246,000
Education		Irish:	9.4%	Poverty:	7.2%
H.S. grad:	92.3%	English:	8.5%	**Military Veterans**	
College grad:	47.1%			% of Pop:	8.5%
Grad degree:	20.9%				

Oakland County, long considered just a suburban adjunct of Detroit, is now the center of a giant, spread-out, and mostly affluent urban area. It is only minutes on the Lodge or Chrysler Freeways from inner-city Detroit. North of Eight Mile Road, the terrain changes from Detroit's worn-out, abandoned neighborhoods to giant office buildings and expensive houses on large lots. There is one shopping mall after another, education levels are high, and crime rates are low. Even physically, the two

2008 Presidential Vote
Obama (D) 202,341   (56%)
McCain (R)..............................155,193   (43%)

2004 Presidential Vote
Bush (R) 180,073   (51%)
Kerry (D).................................174,078   (49%)
Cook Partisan Voting Index: D+2

areas are distinct: Detroit is on almost perfectly flat land, while much of Oakland County lies on a line of hills and lakes that marks the southernmost advance of an Ice Age glacier. Birmingham and Royal Oak, little suburbs set among farm fields half a century ago, are now upscale gentrified nodes amid a vast suburban expanse. Bloomfield Hills is metro Detroit's wealthiest community, and there are large corporate office centers in Auburn Hills. West Bloomfield is increasingly the focus of metro Detroit's Jewish community and has a large number of Asians, many from India and Pakistan; there are also Chaldeans, descended from Iraqi Catholics. Oakland County has become the population center of metro Detroit. In 1950, the city of Detroit had 1.8 million people, and Oakland County had 396,000. In 2007, Detroit had 917,000 people, and Oakland had 1.2 million.

But parts of the county are hurting economically in the wake of the dire financial troubles at the Detroit-based automakers. Interstate 75 in eastern and northern Oakland had developed as the nerve center of auto-company suppliers and manufacturers, and so took a big hit in 2008 and 2009 when General Motors and Chrysler closed several factories there. The old factory town of Pontiac has an African-American majority and major economic struggles in the wake of 1,500 layoffs at a GM plant and the company's decision to cancel the town's namesake brand. GM also suspended operations in Orion, furloughing another 3,400.

The 9th Congressional District of Michigan includes a little more than half the population of Oakland County. It does not include Southfield, Oak Park, Ferndale, Hazel Park or Madison Heights in the southeast—all heavily Democratic and part of the 12th District. It does include almost all of Royal Oak, all of Birmingham and Bloomfield Hills, Rochester Hills and Auburn Hills, Farmington Hills (you begin to see the prestige value of hills to people who grew up in the flatlands of Detroit) and West Bloomfield, Pontiac and Waterford Township. It is Michigan's most affluent congressional district, although the ongoing troubles at the domestic automakers could eventually have an impact on median income. The future of Chrysler's corporate headquarters in Auburn Hills and of the six-figure executives who work there was in doubt in 2009 after the Italian automaker Fiat bought the company.

The district trended toward the Democrats because of cultural issues in the 1990s. This has created problems for Republicans; there is a strong Right to Life movement in Michigan, and as anti-abortion rights activists have gained power at Republican conventions and won nominations, voters have moved toward Democrats. Republicans no longer win huge majorities in Birmingham and Bloomfield Township, and they run no better in fast-growing Troy and Rochester Hills. Royal Oak, Farmington Hills and West Bloomfield, once solidly Republican, now lean Democratic, though Waterford Township, with a more working-class population, leans Republican. Republican George W. Bush carried the 9th District by only 51%-49% in 2004, and Democrat Barack Obama won it 56%-43% in 2008.

The new congressman from the 9th District is Gary Peters, a Democrat elected in 2008. A fifth-generation Oakland County native, Peters grew up in Pontiac. While not known for his flair on the campaign trail, Peters has a broad array of interests. He had early success in his business career. He was vice president of investments for Paine Webber from 1989 to 2003, and before that he was an executive with Merrill Lynch for nine years. At age 34, Peters became a lieutenant commander in the Naval Reserves, training as a sharpshooter and ultimately spending a dozen years in the Reserves. In the early 1990s, he got involved in politics, landing a seat on the Rochester Hills City Council, where he helped unearth an overcharge to the city that saved taxpayers $400,000. In 1995, he was elected to the state Senate, where he pushed legislation to cut taxes for the middle class and to improve access to children's health insurance. He also led an effort to ban oil drilling in the Great Lakes. In 2002, Peters became the state's lottery commissioner. The *Detroit Free-* Press later praised him for increasing lottery sales.

In the 2008 election, he challenged eight-term Republican Rep. Joe Knollenberg. A fiscal conservative, Peters talked about middle-class tax cuts during the campaign, but didn't swear off raising taxes on the wealthy, a group that includes many of his district's constituents. Knollenberg criticized him for that stance. Peters attacked the incumbent for voting against legislation to expand the State Children's Health Insurance Program.

Knollenberg had faced some difficult races during the previous 16 years, but none that challenged him on nearly every front. He started out with a financial edge, but with the help of the national Democratic Party, Peters was able to bridge the gap. GOP presidential nominee John McCain pulled out of Michigan, making a tough political environment for Michigan Republicans even worse. Knollenberg also lost the endorsement of the powerful United Auto Workers, which backed Peters, despite Knollenberg's leadership in securing a $25 billion bailout for the industry. The incumbent tried to distance himself from the unpopular Bush administration and the GOP, even skipping the Republican National Convention in September.

A crowded field in the general election favored Knollenberg. The three other candidates, including the assisted-suicide advocate Dr. Jack Kevorkian, were expected to pull votes away from Peters. But the affluent district was mired in an economic downturn, which fueled anti-Republican sentiment. Peters defeated Knollenberg 52% to 43%; Kevorkian received 3% of the vote.

Peters sits on the Financial Services Committee and the Science and Technology Committee. In March 2009, he introduced legislation to place a surtax on bonuses paid to employees of companies that had received large sums of federal bailout money, but worded so as to encompass only insurance giant AIG. The proposed surtax, combined with existing federal and state taxes, would in effect tax the bonuses at a rate of 100%, returning the entire amount to the taxpayers.

TENTH DISTRICT

Candice Miller (R)

Elected 2002, 4th term; b. May 7, 1954, Detroit; home, Harrison Twnshp.; Macomb Cnty. Community Col., 1973–74, Northwood U.; Presbyterian; married (Donald); 1 child.

Elected Office: Trustee, Harrison Twnshp. Bd., 1979–80; Harrison Twnshp. supervisor, 1980–92; Macomb Cnty. treasurer, 1992–94; MI secy. of state, 1994–2002.

Professional Career: Secy.-Treas., D.B. Snider Inc. marina, 1972–79

DC Office: 228 CHOB, 20515, 202-225-2106; Fax: 202-226-1169; Web site: candicemiller.house.gov.

State Offices: Shelby Twnshp., 586-997-5010.

Committees: *Energy Independence & Global Warming* (5th of 6 R). *Homeland Security* (10th of 13 R): Border, Maritime & Global Counterterrorism; Transportation Security & Infrastructure Protection. *Transportation & Infrastructure* (23rd of 30 R): Highways & Transit; Railroads, Pipelines & Hazardous Materials; Water Resources & Environment.

Group Ratings

	ADA	ACLU	AFS	LCV	ITIC	NTU	COC	ACU	CFG	FRC
2008	50	27	57	31	43	46	78	63	44	88
2007	30	—	27	25	—	50	100	72	43	—

National Journal Ratings

	2007 LIB	—	2007 CONS		2008 LIB	—	2008 CONS
Economic	40%	—	60%		42%	—	58%
Social	29%	—	69%		31%	—	62%
Foreign	40%	—	60%		31%	—	67%
Composite	37%	—	63%		36%	—	64%

Key Votes of the 110th Congress

1. Increase minimum wage	Y	5. Share immigration data	Y	9. Withdraw troops 8/08	N
2. Expand SCHIP	Y	6. Foreign aid abortion ban	Y	10. No operations in Iran	N
3. Raise CAFE standards	N	7. Ban gay bias in workplace	Y	11. Free trade with Peru	Y
4. Bail out financial markets	N	8. Repeal D.C. gun law	Y	12. Overhaul FISA	Y

Election Results

2008 general	Candice Miller (R)..	230,471	(66%)	($756,978)
	Robert Denison (D)	108,354	(31%)	($7,440)
2008 primary	Candice Miller (R)..	unopposed		

Prior Winning Percentages: 2006 (66%); 2004 (69%); 2002 (63%)

Population		Race/Ethnicity		Work	
Pop. 2007:	722,996	White:	92.1%	Private:	83.8%
Change since 2000:	Up 9.1%	Black:	2.2%	Government:	10.5%
Urban:	66.0%	Hispanic:	2.5%	Self-employed:	5.4%
Rural:	34.0%	Asian:	1.8%	Blue collar:	27.7%
Area size:	3,663 sq. mi.	Native Am.:	0.3%	White collar:	56.6%
Age		Hawaiian:	0.0%	Khaki collar:	0.1%
Median age:	38.2 yrs.	Two+ races:	1.0%	Other:	15.6%
More than 65 yrs:	12.0%	*Ancestry*		Median income:	$58,260
Less than 18 yrs:	24.7%	German:	20.7%	Median home value:	$187,900
Education		Polish:	11.5%	Poverty:	8.3%
H.S. grad:	88.0%	Irish:	9.6%	**Military Veterans**	
College grad:	20.2%			% of Pop:	10.4%
Grad degree:	7.1%				

Macomb County, on the billiard-table-flat shore of Lake St. Clair just northeast of Detroit, has been one of the nation's most closely watched political battlegrounds, a place where it once seemed the electoral fate of Michigan and even the entire country might be determined. It owes much of that to its reputation as blue-collar suburbia, but that is no longer quite accurate: More people hold white-collar jobs than blue-collar jobs these days, and there is far less work in auto plants than in earlier generations.

2008 Presidential Vote

McCain (R).............................	179,768	(50%)
Obama (D)	173,920	(48%)

2004 Presidential Vote

Bush (R)	193,727	(57%)
Kerry (D)................................	147,288	(43%)

Cook Partisan Voting Index: R + 5

There are plenty of affluent subdivisions now, and boat ownership is close to the highest in the country. Macomb County is the product of the post-World War II boom. In 1940, it had 107,000 residents, many in the old sulphur-water spa town of Mount Clemens. Macomb passed the 400,000 mark in 1960 and the 600,000 mark in 1970. In 2007, it had 831,000 people, as farms continued to convert to subdivisions. Many people came here from the east side of Detroit. These new suburbanites were heavily Catholic, often blue collar, at least modestly affluent, and ancestrally Democratic. They accepted the New Deal as part of their natural heritage, but resented the efforts of Detroit politicians to tax them to pay for welfare programs, and they were fearful of the crime rates in Detroit's black neighborhoods.

In 1960, Macomb County was the most Democratic major suburban county in the United States, voting 63% for America's first Catholic president, John F. Kennedy. Over the next three decades, Macomb moved away from national Democrats—in 1962 because they would let Detroit tax suburbanites, in 1972 because they didn't vehemently oppose a metropolitan school busing plan. From 1976 to 1992, no Democratic presidential candidate got more than 40% of the vote here. In 1996, after great effort and with the advice of pollster Stan Greenberg, who has studied Macomb closely, Bill Clinton carried Macomb County 49%-39%. In 2000, Al Gore carried it 50%-48%, nearly the national average. But the Democratic tide receded a little. Central and northern Macomb County have been filling up with expensive subdivisions that have been growing rapidly—some by more than 40% in the 1990s—and that are not as culturally liberal as affluent parts of Oakland County. In 2004, President Bush carried Macomb 50%-49%. But as Republicans have suffered nationwide, so have they suffered in Macomb. In her successful re-election in 2006, Gov. Jennifer Granholm defeated Republican Dick DeVos in Macomb, 52%-46%. In 2008, Barack Obama defeated John McCain handily in Macomb, 53%-45%.

The 10th Congressional District of Michigan includes the northern two-thirds of Macomb County, with nearly half of its voters. It also includes Lapeer County, where once-rapid exurban growth has slowed. Also in the district are St. Clair County, with Port Huron and its Blue Water Bridge to Canada, and two rural counties in Michigan's "Thumb." Northern Macomb has become increasingly Republican, Lapeer and St. Clair have long been fairly Republican, and the Thumb has long been very Republican.

Overall this district has voted Republican in recent presidential elections—57% for Bush in 2004 , and 50% for John McCain in 2008.

The congresswoman from the 10th District is Candice Miller, a Republican elected in 2002. Miller grew up in Macomb County. In 1979, at age 25, she was elected Harrison Township trustee. A year later, she was elected as the youngest and first woman supervisor of the township. In 1986, she ran against Democratic Rep. David Bonior and lost 66%-34%. In 1992, she won an upset bid to become Macomb County treasurer. And two years later, she defeated 24-year incumbent Richard Austin to become the Michigan secretary of state. In 1998, she carried all of Michigan's counties and set a state record for total votes. Armed with huge name recognition as secretary of state but prevented from running for re-election by term limits, Miller was the favorite to succeed Bonior, who ran for governor in 2002. Democrats were enthusiastic about Macomb County Prosecutor Carl Marlinga, who had been in office for 20 years. But Marlinga could not keep pace with Miller's fundraising. He also called himself a "Hubert Humphrey Democrat" —not a big advantage in this district—while Miller called herself a "George W. Bush Republican" at a time such a claim still inspired voters. She opposed abortion rights, supported free-trade agreements, and favored making the Bush tax cuts permanent—all positions opposite Marlinga's. Both candidates supported gun-ownership rights. Citing her daughter's membership in the United Auto Workers, Miller reached out to unions and was endorsed by the Teamsters, but not the AFL-CIO. Miller won handily, 63%-36%, carrying Macomb County 61%-37%. She has been re-elected easily ever since.

In the House, Miller has had a moderate-to-conservative voting record; she tends to be more conservative on cultural issues. By 2007, her support for the Iraq war had softened, and she opposed the president's strategy for a "surge" of troop strength. But she opposed Democratic restrictions on war funding because of concerns it would demoralize U.S. troops. On the Armed Services Committee, she worked to protect the Selfridge Air National Guard Base, and sought additional Pentagon contracts for local firms, including the General Dynamics plant in Sterling Heights that manufactures the Army Stryker armored vehicle.

Miller takes seriously her district's proximity to the natural assets of the Great Lakes, and warned a congressional panel, "Do not look to the Great Lakes to solve the nation's water problems." She was "very disappointed" with Bush's veto in 2007 of the Water Resources Development Act, which included $20 million for the St. Clair River. Also in 2007, she condemned as "downright nuts" a proposed permit by Indiana that would allow British Petroleum to dump more pollutants in Lake Michigan with its expanded refinery. Mindful of the state's dependence on auto manufacturing, she also criticized advocates of tougher fuel-efficiency standards for seeking "to bankrupt Detroit." In April 2009, repeating assurances from Chrysler and the Obama administration, Miller declared in a floor speech that Chrysler's imminent bankruptcy would not result in plant closures in her district. The next day, it was revealed that Chrysler planned to close five plants, including one employing 1,400 in Sterling Heights in the district. Miller criticized the plan as "very troubling," citing Chrysler's decision to keep open a plant in Mexico with similar production abilities as the Sterling Heights facility.

Miller has sponsored a proposed constitutional amendment to exclude illegal aliens from the decennial congressional reapportionment process, calling it "absolutely outrageous" that noncitizens had "a profound impact on our political system."

The Ethics Committee admonished Miller after it reviewed the case of Majority Leader Tom DeLay of Texas and his efforts to influence the vote of Republican Rep. Nick Smith of Michigan during the close vote on the 2003 bill to create a prescription drug bill in Medicare. The committee concluded that Miller tried to intimidate Smith to vote for the bill. Miller told the *Detroit Free Press:* "If a black belt can be intimidated by an overweight, middle-age woman, that's too bad."

In 2008, Miller chaired recruitment for the National Republican Congressional Committee, but her efforts were unproductive in an election year that turned against Republicans.

ELEVENTH DISTRICT

Thaddeus McCotter (R)

Elected 2002, 4th term; b. Aug. 22, 1965, Detroit; home, Livonia; U. of Detroit, B.A. 1987, J.D. 1990; Catholic; married (Rita); 2 children.

Elected Office: Schoolcraft Community Col. Trustees Bd., 1989–92; Wayne Cnty. Commission, 1992–98; MI Senate, 1998–2002.

DC Office: 1632 LHOB, 20515, 202-225-8171; Fax: 202-225-2667; Web site: mccotter.house.gov.

State Offices: Livonia, 734-632-0314; Milford, 248-685-9495.

Committees: *Republican Policy Committee Chairman. Financial Services* (23rd of 29 R): Capital Markets, Insurance & Government Sponsored Enterprises; Housing & Community Opportunity.

Group Ratings

	ADA	ACLU	AFS	LCV	ITIC	NTU	COC	ACU	CFG	FRC
2008	40	10	43	15	43	56	82	72	64	88
2007	20	—	36	15	—	66	75	84	65	—

National Journal Ratings

	2007 LIB	—	2007 CONS	2008 LIB	—	2008 CONS
Economic	33%	—	67%	37%	—	62%
Social	29%	—	69%	15%	—	85%
Foreign	0%	—	72%	27%	—	72%
Composite	26%	—	74%	27%	—	73%

Key Votes of the 110th Congress

1. Increase minimum wage	Y	5. Share immigration data	Y	9. Withdraw troops 8/08	N
2. Expand SCHIP	N	6. Foreign aid abortion ban	Y	10. No operations in Iran	N
3. Raise CAFE standards	N	7. Ban gay bias in workplace	Y	11. Free trade with Peru	Y
4. Bail out financial markets	N	8. Repeal D.C. gun law	Y	12. Overhaul FISA	Y

Election Results

2008 general	Thaddeus McCotter (R)	177,461	(51%)	($1,058,502)
	Joseph Larkin (D)	156,625	(45%)	($28,957)
2008 primary	Thaddeus McCotter (R)	unopposed		

Prior Winning Percentages: 2006 (54%); 2004 (57%); 2002 (57%)

Population		Race/Ethnicity		Work	
Pop. 2007:	715,082	White:	83.4%	Private:	86.7%
Change since 2000:	Up 7.9%	Black:	6.7%	Government:	8.8%
Urban:	97.0%	Hispanic:	3.1%	Self-employed:	4.4%
Rural:	3.0%	Asian:	4.8%	Blue collar:	20.0%
Area size:	413 sq. mi.	Native Am.:	0.3%	White collar:	65.5%
		Hawaiian:	0.1%	Khaki collar:	0.0%
Age		Two+ races:	1.4%	Other:	14.5%
Median age:	38.9 yrs.			Median income:	$65,862
More than 65 yrs:	11.4%	*Ancestry*		Median home value:	$196,400
Less than 18 yrs:	24.7%	German:	15.9%	Poverty:	6.4%
		Irish:	10.5%		
Education		Polish:	9.9%	**Military Veterans**	
H.S. grad:	90.9%			% of Pop:	9.6%
College grad:	32.8%				
Grad degree:	12.5%				

The inexorable pattern of growth and its consequences is a vivid tale in the western suburbs of Wayne County, 15 miles from downtown Detroit. Just west of northwest Detroit is Livonia. Sixty years ago, the 36 square miles of Livonia had 17,000 people. By 1960, there were 66,000, and by 2000, 100,000. Similar growth was taking place just to the south in Westland, named after a shopping center. To the west, around the old towns of Plymouth and Northville, affluent subdivisions sprang up. To the

2008 Presidential Vote

Obama (D)	197,791	(54%)
McCain (R)	164,043	(45%)

2004 Presidential Vote

Bush (R)	183,835	(53%)
Kerry (D)	164,037	(47%)

Cook Partisan Voting Index: Even

southwest, Canton Township grew 34% with more modest subdivisions. To the northwest, Novi, in Oakland County, is one of the metro area's highest-income suburbs. Lyon Township has been another growth area. Livonia is aging now—its school-age population was 38,000 in the 1970s and 17,000 in 2002—with some vacant factories and closed malls. In June 2009, General Motors announced it would close an engine plant here and lay off 120 employees. But these suburbs all have been thriving in relation to troubled Detroit. Tying them together is Interstate 275, which runs along the western edge of Livonia and Westland and provides easy access to Metro Airport.

Livonia was originally the political base of longtime Wayne County Executive Ed McNamara (1986–2002), an old-style political boss who built the beautiful new midfield terminal at Metro, which is named after him. Livonia, originally settled by Detroiters, was long closely divided between the two major parties, but the recent affluent influx into western Wayne County has made those areas more Republican. Racial minorities have become a majority in Wayne County, due partly to the rapid growth of Hispanics and Asian-Americans, many of them doing high-tech work in what local officials trumpet as the Automation Alley, the long miles of open road between Detroit and Ann Arbor.

The 11th Congressional District of Michigan covers much of the territory in western Wayne and Oakland counties—Livonia and Redford Township just to the east, Westland and Canton Township,

Northville and Plymouth, Novi and several fast-growing townships to the north and west. The lines were carefully drawn to produce a district that voted 51% for George W. Bush in 2000 and with the clear intention of electing a Republican representative. But like nearby districts, Republican allegiance here has been slipping. Barack Obama won the district 54%-45% in 2008.

The congressman from the 11th District is Thaddeus McCotter, a Republican elected in 2002. He grew up in Livonia, where his mother was city clerk. He graduated from Detroit's Catholic Central High School, where he was a first-team all-Catholic football player, and from the University of Detroit and its law school. He was elected to the Wayne County Commission in 1992, at age 27, and became the driving force to change the county's charter to require a vote of two-thirds of the commission plus 60% of the voters in a referendum to pass a tax increase. In 1998, he was elected to the state Senate, where he became vice chairman of the Senate's reapportionment committee. He helped design the new 11th District, which included his entire Senate district, and so made himself the early front-runner for the 2002 election. He received encouragement from House Republican leaders and won the primary, 69%-31%. But McCotter did not win the seat without a contest. In the general election, he faced Democrat Kevin Kelley, the Redford Township supervisor. Kelley called himself a "centrist Democrat," and both candidates supported the Bush tax cuts and authorization of military force in Iraq, and both opposed creating individual investment accounts in Social Security. McCotter defined himself as a conservative who opposed abortion rights and gun control. Kelley supported abortion rights and restrictions on gun ownership. Kelley hoped to benefit from Democratic gubernatorial candidate Jennifer Granholm's local popularity. McCotter raised more money, much of it at a mid-October fundraiser with Bush. His 57%-40% victory was larger than expected.

In the House, McCotter established a moderate-to-conservative voting record, with streaks of independence. He is an avid rock-and-roll fan, with a quirky sense of humor, prone to quoting song lyrics. He has a large poster of Beatles legend John Lennon hanging on the wall in his congressional office. He enjoys playing the guitar, and with four other House members he formed the Second Amendments, a bipartisan rock and country band, which has performed for U.S. forces in Iraq and Afghanistan.

In 2006, he voted "present" on a Republican leadership resolution supporting the war in Iraq and rejecting a timetable for withdrawal. He called the resolution "strategically nebulous, morally obtuse, and woefully inadequate." In March 2007, he was one of 13 Republicans to vote for House passage of organized labor's bill to expedite union organization.

McCotter was an early supporter of John Boehner of Ohio for Majority Leader in 2006 and was welcomed into his inner circle. That may have helped him defeat California Republican Rep. Darrell Issa in a November 2006 contest for chairman of the Republican Policy Committee, a rung on the leadership ladder. He has used his leadership position to advocate the idea that Republicans should be less centralized and do a better job of engaging rank-and-file members. He took some innovative steps, such as opening Policy Committee membership to any House Republican who wanted to participate and starting a blog on its website. He skipped the Republican national convention in Minneapolis-St. Paul in September 2008 so that he could continue to lead the Republican protest on the floor—while the House was not in session—of the Democrats' inaction on energy policy.

In this competitive district, McCotter has been blessed by weak opposition. He has won re-election by unimpressive margins against underfinanced opponents. In 2006, he won 54%-43% against Tony Trupiano, an outspoken syndicated radio talk show host. While Democrats captured two adjacent districts in 2008, attorney Joseph Larkin ran a below-the-radar challenge to McCotter in 2008, and McCotter prevailed 51%-45%. A well-funded, top-tier Democratic opponent might give McCotter a tough race.

TWELFTH DISTRICT

Sander Levin (D)

Elected 1982, 14th term; b. Sept. 6, 1931, Detroit; home, Royal Oak; U. of Chicago, B.A. 1952, Columbia U., M.A. 1954, Harvard U., LL.B. 1957; Jewish; widowed; 4 children.

Elected Office: Oakland Bd. of Supervisors, 1961–64; MI Senate, 1964–70.

Professional Career: Practicing atty., 1957–64, 1970–76; Fellow, Harvard JFK Schl. of Govt., 1975; A.A., Agency for Intl. Devel., 1977–81.

DC Office: 1236 LHOB, 20515, 202-225-4961; Fax: 202-226-1033; Web site: www.house.gov/levin.

State Offices: Roseville, 586-498-7122.

Committees: *Joint Committee on Taxation* (3rd of 3 D). *Ways & Means* (3rd of 26 D): Income Security & Family Support; Trade (Chmn).

Group Ratings

	ADA	ACLU	AFS	LCV	ITIC	NTU	COC	ACU	CFG	FRC
2008	95	100	100	92	100	4	59	0	0	0
2007	90	—	100	90	—	5	56	0	12	—

National Journal Ratings

	2007 LIB	—	2007 CONS		2008 LIB	—	2008 CONS
Economic	67%	—	33%		85%	—	0%
Social	66%	—	33%		82%	—	0%
Foreign	69%	—	29%		70%	—	25%
Composite	68%	—	32%		85%	—	15%

Key Votes of the 110th Congress

1. Increase minimum wage	Y	5. Share immigration data	N	9. Withdraw troops 8/08	Y
2. Expand SCHIP	Y	6. Foreign aid abortion ban	N	10. No operations in Iran	Y
3. Raise CAFE standards	Y	7. Ban gay bias in workplace	Y	11. Free trade with Peru	Y
4. Bail out financial markets	Y	8. Repeal D.C. gun law	N	12. Overhaul FISA	N

Election Results

2008 general	Sander Levin (D)	225,094	(72%)	($660,710)
	Bert Copple (R)	74,565	(24%)	
2008 primary	Sander Levin (D)	unopposed		

Prior Winning Percentages: 2006 (70%); 2004 (69%); 2002 (68%); 2000 (64%); 1998 (56%); 1996 (57%); 1994 (52%); 1992 (53%); 1990 (70%); 1988 (70%); 1986 (76%); 1984 (100%); 1982 (67%)

Population		Race/Ethnicity		Work	
Pop. 2007:	631,704	White:	76.3%	Private:	85.8%
Change since 2000:	Down 4.7%	Black:	16.7%	Government:	9.7%
Urban:	100.0%	Hispanic:	1.7%	Self-employed:	4.4%
Rural:	0.0%	Asian:	3.1%	Blue collar:	24.3%
Area size:	160 sq. mi.	Native Am.:	0.3%	White collar:	59.0%
		Hawaiian:	0.0%	Khaki collar:	0.0%
Age		Two+ races:	1.8%	Other:	16.7%
Median age:	38.7 yrs.			Median income:	$48,410
More than 65 yrs:	15.1%	*Ancestry*		Median home value:	$152,000
Less than 18 yrs:	22.3%	German:	15.1%	Poverty:	10.7%
		Polish:	11.6%		
Education		Irish:	8.6%	**Military Veterans**	
H.S. grad:	85.6%			% of Pop:	9.9%
College grad:	21.8%				
Grad degree:	7.9%				

The flat expanse of land just north of Eight Mile Road, Detroit's northern city limit, was mostly vacant in the years just after World War II. A string of suburbs in Oakland County ran along Woodward Avenue from the Detroit city limits to the Shrine of the Little Flower Church in Royal Oak, where Father Charles Coughlin in the 1930s made his radio broadcasts opposing Franklin D. Roosevelt and denouncing bankers and Jews. In the 1950s and 1960s, Woodward was one of America's greatest cruising highways, where teenagers drove big Detroit cars up and down the eight lanes and where the lights were timed at 42 miles per hour. (Since 1994, the Woodward Dream Cruise of old cars has commemorated that era with a mega-celebration drawing more than 1 million.) To the east in Macomb County was some industrial development along Van Dyke Road, but this was mostly empty land, too. Then Polish-Americans began marching out Van Dyke from Hamtramck to Warren. Italian-Americans headed out Gratiot from Detroit's east side to Roseville and Clinton Township. Belgian-Americans from the Mack corridor moved out farther to St. Clair Shores. Today, these areas are well-settled suburbs, long since built up, a few neighborhoods edging toward seediness, many others continually renovated. Almost half of metro Detroit's population is now north of Eight Mile, in communities drawing on old traditions but crackling with economic creativity.

2008 Presidential Vote		
Obama (D)	212,850	(65%)
McCain (R)	108,752	(33%)

2004 Presidential Vote		
Kerry (D)	193,894	(61%)
Bush (R)	125,460	(39%)

Cook Partisan Voting Index: D + 12

The 12th Congressional District of Michigan is in this suburban territory, with two-thirds of its population in Macomb County. On the Oakland County side are the southern part of Royal Oak and other Woodward Avenue suburbs, which have been economically revitalized, attracting singles and gays as well as families. Oak Park, heavily Jewish in the 1950s, now also has sizable numbers of Arabs and blacks. Hazel Park and Madison Heights are mostly peopled with descendants of the Appalachian migrants of a few decades ago. Southfield, Michigan's largest office-space center (far ahead of Detroit), has a black middle-class majority. Ferndale, one of the original bedroom communities for autoworkers, has been revived with help from government bonds and is viewed as a model for rescuing aging suburbs. On the Macomb side are the county's more Democratic neighborhoods: Warren and the southern part of Sterling Heights, site of the General Motors Technical Center, a big Chrysler plant and the now-privatized M-1 tank plant. Farther east are blue-collar communities of Macomb: Eastpointe (formerly known as East Detroit, it voted to change its name to make it sound less like Detroit and more like tony Grosse Pointe), Roseville, St. Clair Shores, Clinton Township and Mount Clemens. Although still a small share at 7 percent, the black population has been growing rapidly in Macomb. This district is solidly Democratic.

The congressman from the 12th District is Sander Levin, a Democrat first elected in 1982, an influential lawmaker and a member of one of Michigan's most respected political families. He is the older brother by three years of Democratic Sen. Carl Levin. He grew up in Detroit and got degrees from the University of Chicago, Columbia University and Harvard Law School. He settled in the Woodward Avenue suburb of Berkley after school and was elected state senator in 1964. In 1970 and 1974, he ran for governor and lost narrowly each time to Republican William Milliken. During the Carter administration, he was a top appointee at the Agency for International Development. In 1982, a House seat suddenly opened up in redistricting. Levin won a spirited primary and held the seat without difficulty. The 1992 redistricting moved him east, into Macomb County, and placed him in the same district with Democrat Dennis Hertel, who decided to retire. Levin easily won the nomination and the election.

Levin is a hard worker and a details man, willing to spend endless hours with others working out solutions. Based on his work with local communities to create coalitions to combat drug and alcohol abuse, he co-authored the federal Drug Free Communities Act. On the Ways and Means Committee, he has played an important role on some significant issues. On welfare, Levin opposed the 1995 bills passed by Republicans but helped shape the bill enacted in August 1996 that overhauled the welfare program by introducing more work requirements. After the death of Robert Matsui of California in January 2005, Levin became the top Democrat on the Social Security Subcommittee. In that year's major debate, his outspoken opposition to personal retirement accounts in Social Security put Republicans on the defensive and helped to stymie serious action on the proposal. He said that Bush's initial warnings about the threats to the Social Security system were exaggerated, and he downplayed the need for Democrats to offer their own alternative. In opposing the use of force in Iraq, he consulted extensively with his brother, the chairman of the Senate Armed Services Committee. In their respective chambers, each Levin offered alternatives reflecting what the brothers view as a more internationalist approach, but each was defeated.

In the majority, Levin became chairman of the Trade Subcommittee, where he was a frequent obstacle to the Bush administration in the 110th Congress (2007–08). For years, Levin has been at the center of trade debates, seeking ways, as he often says, to shape globalization. He favored the free-trade agreement with Canada, which was designed in large part by auto manufacturers and the United Auto Workers. But he was wary of Japanese trade barriers and pushed unsuccessfully for stringent measures on Japanese minivans. He was a strong opponent of the North American Free Trade Agreement in 1993, but supported normal trade relations with China, playing an instrumental role in crafting details with the Clinton administration. He opposed giving the president expanded powers to negotiate trade agreements in both the Clinton and Bush years. He supported agreements that the Bush administration reached with Australia and Morocco, but he raised concerns over the impact on auto imports from a potential agreement with Thailand. In discussions on a bilateral trade deal with South Korea, a high priority of the Bush administration, he demanded "measurable benchmarks" for opening that market.

Reflecting Detroit's strong union heritage, Levin typically wants trade agreements to contain provisions on workers' rights, fair ways of settling workers' disagreements and environmental-protection provisions. In 2008, he cited labor-rights violations and other violence as he led opposition to House action on a free-trade deal with Colombia. Earlier, he got the Bush administration to make changes in labor and environmental protections in an agreement with Peru. And he pushed for steps to pressure China to reduce the value of its currency as a way to improve the U.S. trade imbalance with China. Democratic Speaker Nancy Pelosi, despite her professed support for expanded international trade, typically deferred to Levin on specific agreements. When Ways and Means Chairman Charles Rangel of New York was hurt by a spate of negative news stories about his ethics in 2008, some Democrats thought that if Rangel were forced to step down, Levin would be a more acceptable alternative to the more senior Pete Stark, D-Calif. After the 1992 redistricting, which removed much of metro Detroit's Jewish community from Levin's district and added unfamiliar territory in Macomb County, Levin had serious competition from Republican John Pappageorge, a retired Army colonel and M-1 tank executive. Levin outspent Pappageorge $1.18 million to $190,000 and won by just 53%-46%. In 1994, when Clinton was affirmatively unpopular, Levin again greatly outspent Pappageorge in a rematch and won 52%-47%. But in the more pro-incumbent environment of 1996, Levin improved his victory to 57%-41%. Since then, the local tide has shifted his way, and Levin has won easily. Just before the last election, Levin suffered a personal tragedy. His wife of over 50 years, Victoria Levin, an advocate for children's mental health issues, died of breast cancer. She had worked on many of her husband's campaigns and was his close political adviser.

THIRTEENTH DISTRICT

Carolyn Cheeks Kilpatrick (D)

Elected 1996, 7th term; b. June 25, 1945, Detroit; home, Detroit; Ferris St. U., 1965, W. MI U., B.S. 1972, U. of MI, M.S. 1977; African Methodist Episcopal; divorced; 2 children.

Elected Office: MI House of Reps., 1978–96.

Professional Career: Teacher, Detroit public schls., 1970–78.

DC Office: 2264 RHOB, 20515, 202-225-2261; Fax: 202-225-5730; Web site: www.house.gov/kilpatrick.

State Offices: Detroit, 313-965-9004; River Rouge. 313-297-6951.

Committees: *Appropriations* (20th of 37 D): Defense; Transportation, HUD & Related Agencies.

Group Ratings

	ADA	ACLU	AFS	LCV	ITIC	NTU	COC	ACU	CFG	FRC
2008	95	100	100	92	86	10	53	4	0	5
2007	95	—	100	80	—	4	63	0	0	—

National Journal Ratings

	2007 LIB	—	2007 CONS		2008 LIB	—	2008 CONS
Economic	73%	—	27%		85%	—	0%
Social	88%	—	12%		82%	—	0%
Foreign	84%	—	15%		76%	—	23%
Composite	82%	—	18%		87%	—	13%

Key Votes of the 110th Congress

1. Increase minimum wage	Y	5. Share immigration data	N	9. Withdraw troops 8/08	Y
2. Expand SCHIP	Y	6. Foreign aid abortion ban	N	10. No operations in Iran	Y
3. Raise CAFE standards	Y	7. Ban gay bias in workplace	Y	11. Free trade with Peru	N
4. Bail out financial markets	Y	8. Repeal D.C. gun law	N	12. Overhaul FISA	N

Election Results

2008 general	Carolyn Cheeks Kilpatrick (D)	167,481	(74%)	($1,066,838)
	Edward Gubics (R)	43,098	(19%)	
	George Corsetti (Green)	9,579	(4%)	
	Gregory Creswell (Lib)	5,764	(3%)	
2008 primary	Carolyn Cheeks Kilpatrick (D)	21,089	(39%)	
	Mary Waters (D)	19,303	(35%)	
	Martha Scott (D)	13,471	(25%)	

Prior Winning Percentages: 2006 (100%); 2004 (78%); 2002 (92%); 2000 (89%); 1998 (87%); 1996 (88%)

Population

Pop. 2007:	603,349
Change since 2000:	Down 8.9%
Urban:	100.0%
Rural:	0.0%
Area size:	108 sq. mi.

Age

Median age:	33.8 yrs.
More than 65 yrs:	10.7%
Less than 18 yrs:	29.1%

Education

H.S. grad:	75.1%
College grad:	14.9%
Grad degree:	5.9%

Race/Ethnicity

White:	28.2%
Black:	58.9%
Hispanic:	9.6%
Asian:	1.4%
Native Am.:	0.2%
Hawaiian:	0.0%
Two+ races:	1.3%

Ancestry

German:	6.0%
Irish:	4.7%
Polish:	4.4%

Work

Private:	83.6%
Government:	11.9%
Self-employed:	4.4%
Blue collar:	24.9%
White collar:	49.5%
Khaki collar:	0.0%
Other:	25.7%
Median income:	$31,721
Median home value:	$99,800
Poverty:	30.6%

Military Veterans

% of Pop:	8.2%

Few central cities in America were as vibrant in the 20th century as Detroit, or ever as diminished as Detroit is now. This was America's first automobile city, not just because it manufactured so many cars, but also because it was built to automobile scale. Detroit started the century as a second-ranked city, no bigger than Milwaukee, with less than half a million people and extending no farther than four or five miles out from the site where the French built Fort Pontchartrain on the Detroit River in 1701. As

2008 Presidential Vote		
Obama (D)	195,150	(84%)
McCain (R)	36,712	(16%)
2004 Presidential Vote		
Kerry (D)	188,555	(81%)
Bush (R)	45,019	(19%)
Cook Partisan Voting Index:	D+31	

the Motor City boomed, it grew outward along wide avenues and, starting in the 1950s, along freeways. The auto companies put their factories and headquarters near the edge of urban settlement. As early as 1954, the nation's first big suburban shopping center, with parking for 10,000 cars, was drawing retail trade from downtown. Metro Detroit expanded to 4 million people, each generation moving out the roadways rapidly in many directions, leaving behind the previous generation's neighborhoods and civic institutions.

Today, that trend has left large parts of Detroit literally empty. The central city had nearly 1.85 million people in 1950, dropped below 1 million in 2000, and stood at 917,000 in 2007. The reason is crime. For 30 years, Detroit had a murder rate drastically higher than its suburbs, and those who could afford to leave did so. Formerly iconic buildings in the downtown area have been torn down, and others are all but empty, while officials struggle to create new population centers and reestablish a business district. General Motors and Ford have been losing billions of dollars each year. (Chrysler went private and closed its finances to public inspection.) There have been some positive developments. GM bought for $72 million the 70-story Renaissance Center, built in the 1970s for $350 million, and the company moved several thousand employees there. Quicken agreed to move in from the suburbs. Beyond downtown, some of the city's jewels have been maintained: the Detroit Institute of Arts, the hospital center, the old Fox Theater. New baseball and football stadiums have opened just north of downtown, and in 2006, they hosted the World Series and the Super Bowl. Residential and commercial projects are planned on the long-neglected riverfront, with encouragement from a new shopping plaza and promenade at the Renaissance Center. But beyond these well-policed enclaves lie acres of vacant fields and half-empty blocks where there were once five-story apartments or brick houses. The big losses for the automakers in 2008 and the hemorrhaging of jobs showed no sign of abating.

Detroit's fate is all the more tragic because the city's liberal reformers once hoped to create model anti-poverty and anti-discrimination programs here. Democrat Coleman Young, Detroit's mayor from 1973 to 1993, spent his energy courting the Big Three automakers and bulldozed the viable Poletown neighborhood for a new Cadillac plant. Democrat Dennis Archer, who served the next eight years, took a different approach, and the city began to turn around, with lower crime, more jobs, new housing permits and the beginning of a thriving private sector. In 2001, Democrat Kwame Kilpatrick, a former state legislator, brought young blood when he was elected mayor at age 31, the self-styled "America's first hip-hop mayor." But despite the initial buzz, he was re-elected only narrowly. His tenure came to an ignominious end in September 2008, when he resigned after pleading guilty to obstruction of justice for lying under oath about an affair with his chief of staff. The controversy had paralyzed the city for months with a tawdry tale involving text messages on city phones. In its appraisal, the *Detroit Free Press* credited the mayor with presiding over the continued revival of parts of downtown, but complained that city services had continued to decline, along with the number of residents and businesses. "At his best, Kilpatrick called to mind an energetic, young Detroit. At his worst, he stood for a corrupt rust-belt city that seems to be running out of luck and time," the newspaper said.

The 13th Congressional District of Michigan includes more than half of Detroit, plus a few adjacent suburbs, from the affluent Grosse Pointe, with nearly 50,000 people looking out toward Lake St. Clair, to the down-river industrial towns of River Rouge, Ecorse, Lincoln Park and Wyandotte. It includes practically all of the east side of Detroit and the west side up to about five miles north of the Detroit River—the entire riverfront and downtown, the old General Motors and Fisher buildings, and most of Detroit's auto factories. At 108 square miles, this is the smallest district in the state, with the biggest problems. It has Michigan's highest rates of poverty and unemployment and the highest percentage of residents on public assistance. Politically, the 13th District is overwhelmingly Democratic, but voter turnout is low—225,922 in the House election in 2008, far below the 351,963 who turned out in the high-income 9th District. This is one of Michigan's two black-majority seats and one of the safest Democratic districts.

The congresswoman from the 13th District is Carolyn Cheeks Kilpatrick, a Democrat first elected in 1996 and the mother of the disgraced Detroit mayor. She was born and raised in Detroit, attended Ferris State University and graduated from Western Michigan University and the University of Michigan. She taught business education in Detroit public schools before being elected to the state House in 1978. She lost a race for the Detroit City Council, but won the 1996 Democratic primary for the congressional seat by a solid 51%-31% against her one-time political partner, incumbent Rep. Barbara-Rose Collins.

Kilpatrick, whose voting record once was among the most liberal in the House, has moderated slightly. She made a point of visiting the suburbs in her district, meeting local officials and assigning her staff to work with them—a contrast to Collins. She worked with others to successfully derail the proposed land swap that would have allowed two new Indian casinos to compete with those in Detroit. On the Appropriations Committee, she has taken credit for funding Detroit-area transportation projects and water and sewage facilities. She spurred the creation of the Detroit Area Regional Transportation Authority as a first step to increased national support for funding for the system. Her other focus on Appropriations has been increased foreign aid for countries in Africa, including additional hundreds of millions of dollars to combat the AIDS crisis overseas.

In January 2007, in the House majority for the first time, Kilpatrick took over as chair of the 43-member Congressional Black Caucus. She used that platform to speak out against the war in Iraq and to call for stepped-up recovery efforts after Hurricane Katrina, and for assurances that the 2010 census count would be complete. She clashed with Democratic House Speaker Nancy Pelosi in 2007 over the removal of Rep. William Jefferson, a Louisiana Democrat, from the Ways and Means Committee following his indictment on corruption charges.

In the midst of her son's legal problems, Kilpatrick faced a major campaign challenge that she barely survived. Her re-election became largely a referendum on her son the mayor, who at that time had not resigned. Her chief opponent in the primary, former Democratic state Rep. Mary Waters, harshly criticized Kilpatrick for "injecting herself" into the upheaval in city politics with her adamant defense of her son. In a broadcast debate, Kilpatrick replied derisively: "Girl, please. You can't even carry my bra." She benefited from campaign help from Pelosi, who appeared in suburban locales for her, and from Ways and Means Chairman Charles Rangel, a New York Democrat.

Kilpatrick won the August 2008 primary with 39% of the vote to 36% for Waters and 25% for state Sen. Martha Scott. She ran more strongly in the city, where she got nearly half the vote. In a two-way contest, Kilpatrick probably would have lost. Waters said that she might run again in 2010.

FOURTEENTH DISTRICT

John Conyers (D)

Elected 1964, 23rd term; b. May 16, 1929, Detroit; home, Detroit; Wayne St. U., B.A. 1957, LL.B. 1958; Baptist; married (Monica); 2 children.

Military Career: National Guard, 1948–50; Army, 1950–54 (Korea), Army Reserves, 1954–57.

Professional Career: Legis. asst., U.S. Rep. John Dingell, 1958–61; Practicing atty., 1959–61; Referee, MI Workmen's Comp. Dept., 1961–63.

DC Office: 2426 RHOB, 20515, 202-225-5126; Fax: 202-225-0072; Web site: www.house.gov/conyers.

State Offices: Detroit, 313-961-5670; Trenton, 734-675-4084.

Committees: *Judiciary* (Chmn of 24 D): Commercial & Administrative Law; Constitution, Civil Rights & Civil Liberties; Courts & Competition Policy.

Group Ratings

	ADA	ACLU	AFS	LCV	ITIC	NTU	COC	ACU	CFG	FRC
2008	100	100	100	85	71	17	50	9	12	5
2007	95	—	100	85	—	4	50	0	0	—

National Journal Ratings

	2007 LIB	—	2007 CONS	2008 LIB	—	2008 CONS
Economic	82%	—	0%	85%	—	0%
Social	92%	—	0%	82%	—	0%
Foreign	96%	—	0%	70%	—	25%
Composite	95%	—	5%	85%	—	15%

Key Votes of the 110th Congress

1. Increase minimum wage	Y	5. Share immigration data	N	9. Withdraw troops 8/08	Y
2. Expand SCHIP	Y	6. Foreign aid abortion ban	N	10. No operations in Iran	Y
3. Raise CAFE standards	Y	7. Ban gay bias in workplace	Y	11. Free trade with Peru	N
4. Bail out financial markets	N	8. Repeal D.C. gun law	N	12. Overhaul FISA	N

Election Results

2008 general	John Conyers (D) 227,841	(92%)	($1,196,772)
	Richard Secula (Lib) 10,732	(4%)	
	Clyde Shabazz (Green) 8,015	(3%)	
2008 primary	John Conyers (D) .... unopposed		

Prior Winning Percentages: 2006 (85%); 2004 (84%); 2002 (83%); 2000 (89%); 1998 (87%); 1996 (86%); 1994 (82%); 1992 (82%); 1990 (89%); 1988 (91%); 1986 (89%); 1984 (89%); 1982 (97%); 1980 (95%); 1978 (93%); 1976 (92%); 1974 (91%); 1972 (88%); 1970 (88%); 1968 (100%); 1966 (84%); 1964 (84%)

Population		Race/Ethnicity		Work	
Pop. 2007:	618,301	White:	34.1%	Private:	83.5%
Change since 2000:	Down 6.7%	Black:	61.1%	Government:	12.6%
Urban:	100.0%	Hispanic:	1.9%	Self-employed:	3.7%
Rural:	0.0%	Asian:	1.4%	Blue collar:	25.1%
Area size:	123 sq. mi.	Native Am.:	0.2%	White collar:	52.3%
		Hawaiian:	0.0%	Khaki collar:	0.0%
Age		Two+ races:	1.1%	Other:	22.6%
Median age:	35.6 yrs.	*Ancestry*		Median income:	$36,825
More than 65 yrs:	12.3%	Arab:	6.9%	Median home value:	$117,400
Less than 18 yrs:	27.6%	German:	5.5%	Poverty:	24.0%
Education		Polish:	4.6%	**Military Veterans**	
H.S. grad:	80.7%			% of Pop:	9.1%
College grad:	15.2%				
Grad degree:	5.5%				

Detroit's early auto factories—Packard, Hudson, Ford Highland Park, Dodge Main, Briggs, Ford Rouge, Cadillac, Kelsey-Hayes, Chrysler, Plymouth, DeSoto—were built between 1905 and 1925 about five miles from the city's center and at the edge of urban development. Almost instantly the flat farmlands all around were platted in grid streets and filled with wooden bungalows and brick prairie-style houses, often with a driveway at the side and a single elm in the front. Commercial strips

2008 Presidential Vote

Obama (D) 236,521	(87%)
McCain (R)...............................33,872	(12%)

2004 Presidential Vote

Kerry (D)................................219,075	(83%)
Bush (R) 46,240	(17%)

Cook Partisan Voting Index: D + 34

lined the mile-square and radial main streets, stretching straight as far as the eye could see. Detroit's neighborhoods filled up with factory workers and civil servants, professionals and maintenance men, corner-store owners and management personnel, Catholics and Protestants and Jews: a middle-class melting pot. With one exception—Detroit in those days had few blacks; they did not begin their big migration here from Alabama and the rest of the South until around 1940, when defense plants began hiring African-Americans in large numbers.

The history of black Detroit is one of conflict and uplift, inspiration and tragedy. The wartime mixture of Appalachian mountain whites and Deep South blacks in Detroit proved volatile, resulting in a violent race riot in June 1943. During the war years, blacks were pent up in a few severely overcrowded neighborhoods like the Black Bottom, most of it now covered by the Chrysler Freeway. After 1945, when African-Americans began moving outward, real estate agents played on racial fears, and in the 1950s, whole square miles of Detroit changed racial composition in a matter of months. In the 1960s, there was hope that the civil rights movement, encouraged by Walter Reuther's United Auto Workers union, and anti-poverty programs would improve blacks' fortunes, and in fact many black Detroiters found good jobs and made good incomes, bought their own homes and built community institutions. Then came the riot of July 1967, followed by extensive white flight and terrible increases in crime. Detroit's first black mayor, Democrat Coleman Young, elected in 1973, responded with policies that may have seemed appropriate in the 1960s but had disastrous results in the 1970s and 1980s: He pressured major employers like the Big Three auto companies to build facilities in Detroit, raised taxes to support a vast army of city employees, and attributed city problems to white racism. Violent crime became a part of everyday life, and arson became common.

Detroit took on a garrison atmosphere. Crime reduced the value of residential real estate to near zero, and the city's population dropped from 1.7 million in 1960 to 919,000 in 2007. In political dialogue, most black politicians called for an ever-increasing public sector. Yet the existing public sector, which took a larger share of residents' income than almost anywhere else in the country, served citizens poorly. Turnaround came agonizingly late in the 1990s, when Democratic Mayor Dennis Archer, elected in 1993, worked to fight crime and encourage private-sector growth. Incomes rose, and the median housing value doubled from $32,000 to $63,000. But the city has remained in decline by almost any measure, from the high rate of home foreclosures and to the low achievement of students in public schools.

The 14th Congressional District of Michigan consists of nearly half of Detroit, with the exception of the downtown area and some disparate suburbs. Its part of Detroit is north and west of where the old auto plants were built and is mostly residential—square mile after square mile of grid streets, some always working class, some middle-class, a few upscale, such as Palmer Woods, Sherwood Forest, Rosedale Park. In most of them, abandoned houses and empty lots are commonplace, and yet in many neighborhoods, residents struggle to maintain their houses and patrol their streets. Commercial frontage on Detroit's straight-line avenues is still patchy and often vacant. Politically, this is one of the most Democratic districts in the United States.

The suburbs of the 14th are diverse. Highland Park is like much of Detroit; Hamtramck still retains the flavor of its original Polish immigrants (on Fat Tuesday, this is where to find the best paczki), who made it America's fastest-growing city in 1910–20. It had 56,000 people in 1930 but only 21,000 in 2007. The 14th District now includes most of Dearborn, including the Ford headquarters, the Ford Rouge plant and Henry Ford's Greenfield Village. It is known today as the home of the nation's largest Arab-American community, with 30% of residents claiming Arab ancestry, among them Lebanese, Iraqis and Yemenis. From Dearborn, the district extends south, to take in the working-class suburbs of Melvindale, Allen Park, Southgate, Riverview, Trenton, and Gibraltar.

The congressman from the 14th District is John Conyers, the second most senior member of the House behind fellow Michigan Democrat, John Dingell, and the chairman of the House Judiciary Committee. He is the first African-American to chair the important congressional committee. First elected in 1964, he was a founder of the Congressional Black Caucus and has been among the most liberal members of the House. The son of a left-wing UAW operative, he grew up in Detroit. He played cornet at Northwestern and Cass Technical High Schools and watched jazz greats at Baker's Keyboard Lounge. In 1987, he passed a resolution declaring "the sense of Congress that jazz is [a] rare and valuable American national treasure." He served in the Army in Korea, practiced law and worked on the staff of a young John Dingell. Conyers was one of six blacks in the House when he was first elected in 1964, and the only one to take a militant approach to politics. He won his primary, in which 60,000 votes were cast, by 108 votes. Civil rights heroine Rosa Parks, who by then had moved to Detroit, worked in his 1964 campaign and then worked in his Detroit office until her retirement in 1988. Upon her death, he sponsored the resolution that she lie in state in the Capitol Rotunda, the first woman so honored. His response to the 1967 riots was to introduce the first bill for a guaranteed annual income. He sponsored the original Martin Luther King holiday bill just days after the civil rights leader was assassinated in 1968, and he persevered until it passed in 1983. Since 1989, he has sponsored bills to establish a commission to examine slavery and its lingering effects, and to consider whether reparations should be paid to descendants of slaves. He opposed the most controversial elements of the crime bills of the past three decades and the welfare changes of the 1990s.

In the early part of this decade, Conyers was the ranking minority member of Judiciary and worked hand-in-hand with the Republican chairman, James Sensenbrenner of Wisconsin, on anti-terrorism legislation in the tense weeks after the September 11 attacks. They agreed that the government could detain immigrants suspected of terrorism without bringing charges, but only for seven days, and they introduced the anti-terrorism bill together. In April 2002, Sensenbrenner got Conyers's support for splitting the Immigration and Naturalization Service into two agencies by agreeing to add counsel positions. Over time, Conyers displayed an ability to work with Sensenbrenner on a number of issues, despite the extreme ideological differences between the liberal Conyers and the conservative Sensenbrenner. In 2006, they passed through committee an amendment to prohibit telecommunications and cable companies from blocking or degrading Internet services. Conyers opposed the Iraq War resolution in 2002, and he co-sponsored New York Democrat Charles Rangel's bill to reinstitute the military draft and then, along with Rangel, voted against it on the floor. The exercise was their way of suggesting the war was going to consume more of America's troop strength than the Bush administration was willing to admit.

Conyers is the only member of the House ever to have served on two committees handling presidential impeachment, in 1974 and 1998. In May 1972, a month before the Watergate burglary, he called for impeaching Republican President Nixon because of his conduct of the Vietnam War. Later, as the hearings on Democrat Clinton's impeachment opened in 1998, Conyers, the ranking Democrat on Judiciary, performed ably. For all his criticisms of Clinton, Conyers rallied behind him and managed to craft an alternative investigation resolution that gave Clinton supporters a rallying point. In December 2005, he called on Congress to censure President Bush and Vice President Cheney for misleading Congress and the American people on the rationale for invading Iraq and called for creation of a special committee to investigate. Later, House Speaker Nancy Pelosi, in an effort to calm partisan tensions after the 2006 elections, said that impeachment would not be considered by the new Democratic majority.

Ascending to Judiciary Committee chairman in 2007, after Democrats won control of the House, Conyers examined the Bush presidency, including alleged abuse of presidential signing statements that went beyond the terms of the legislation. However, he drew criticism from liberal and anti-war activists who wanted to continue the pressure for impeachment proceedings, including Rep. Dennis Kucinich, the Ohio liberal who ran for president in 2008. But Conyers did not shrink from legal action against the White House in other matters. He pushed contempt charges against Bush White House Chief of Staff Joshua

Bolten and former Counsel Harriet Miers after they refused to give sworn testimony to his committee about the firings of U.S. attorneys across the country for alleged political reasons. During heated debate to extend the Foreign Intelligence Surveillance Act, which some feared was resulting in government eavesdropping on innocent Americans, Conyers sought measures to curb secret surveillance. He also sponsored a bill to end racial profiling. He successfully led opposition to a proposal for land transfers to allow two Indian tribes to open casinos in Michigan that would have competed with those in Detroit. Taking a hand in the huge government bailout of the financial sector in 2008, Conyers pushed to allow bankruptcy judges to lower mortgage rates or the principal for homeowners who go bankrupt.

Over the years, Conyers—described by the *Detroit News* as "part showman, part junkyard dog, part evangelist" —has been re-elected mostly without difficulty. He made two runs for mayor of Detroit, in 1989 and 1993. But he ran a desultory campaign the first time and almost no campaign the second, and came in far behind. During his long congressional tenure, he had two serious primary opponents in the 1994 House race, but finished well ahead of both, with 51% of the vote. He was an early supporter of Barack Obama for president.

In recent years, he has been the subject of negative news stories at home. In 2003, the *Detroit Free Press* reported that Conyers assigned his congressional staff to work on his political campaigns and also made them run personal errands and baby-sit his two children. In 2006, the House Ethics Committee concluded an investigation of the allegations by saying Conyers must take "a number of additional, significant steps to ensure that his office complies with all rules and standards regarding campaign and personal work by congressional staff." Then, in June 2009, his wife, Detroit City Council President Pro Tem Monica Conyers, pleaded guilty to taking bribes for helping a company called Synagro Technologies get a sludge-hauling contract with the city.

FIFTEENTH DISTRICT

John Dingell (D)

Elected Dec. 1955, 27th full term; b. July 8, 1926, Colorado Springs, CO; home, Dearborn; Georgetown U., B.S. 1949, J.D. 1952; Catholic; married (Deborah); 4 children.

Military Career: Army, 1944–46 (WWII).

Professional Career: Summer Park Ranger, 1947–52; Practicing atty., 1953–55; Wayne Cnty. asst. prosecuting atty., 1954–55.

DC Office: 2328 RHOB, 20515, 202-225-4071; Fax: 202-226-0371; Web site: www.house.Gov/dingell.

State Offices: Dearborn, 313-278-2936; Monroe, 734-243-1849; Ypsilanti, 734-481-1100.

Committees: *Energy & Commerce* (2nd of 36 D): Communications, Technology & the Internet; Energy & Environment; Health.

Group Ratings

	ADA	ACLU	AFS	LCV	ITIC	NTU	COC	ACU	CFG	FRC
2008	90	100	100	100	100	7	56	4	0	0
2007	95	—	100	90	—	5	65	0	6	—

National Journal Ratings

	2007 LIB	—	2007 CONS		2008 LIB	—	2008 CONS
Economic	73%	—	24%		71%	—	25%
Social	77%	—	17%		75%	—	18%
Foreign	65%	—	33%		92%	—	0%
Composite	74%	—	27%		83%	—	18%

Key Votes of the 110th Congress

1. Increase minimum wage	Y	5. Share immigration data	N	9. Withdraw troops 8/08	Y
2. Expand SCHIP	Y	6. Foreign aid abortion ban	N	10. No operations in Iran	Y
3. Raise CAFE standards	Y	7. Ban gay bias in workplace	Y	11. Free trade with Peru	Y
4. Bail out financial markets	Y	8. Repeal D.C. gun law	Y	12. Overhaul FISA	N

Election Results

2008 general	John Dingell (D)	231,784	(71%)	($2,522,180)
	John Lynch (R)	81,802	(25%)	($19,870)
	Aimee Smith (Green)	7,082	(2%)	
2008 primary	John Dingell (D)	unopposed		

Prior Winning Percentages: 2006 (88%); 2004 (71%); 2002 (72%); 2000 (71%); 1998 (67%); 1996 (62%); 1994 (59%); 1992 (65%); 1990 (67%); 1988 (97%); 1986 (78%); 1984 (64%); 1982 (74%); 1980 (70%); 1978 (77%); 1976 (76%); 1974 (78%); 1972 (68%); 1970 (79%); 1968 (74%); 1966 (63%); 1964 (73%); 1962 (83%); 1960 (79%); 1958 (79%); 1956 (74%); 1955 (76%)

Population		Race/Ethnicity		Work	
Pop. 2007:	697,833	White:	76.6%	Private:	80.3%
Change since 2000:	Up 5.3%	Black:	12.8%	Government:	15.2%
Urban:	87.7%	Hispanic:	3.5%	Self-employed:	4.4%
Rural:	12.3%	Asian:	4.7%	Blue collar:	22.8%
Area size:	981 sq. mi.	Native Am.:	0.3%	White collar:	60.4%
		Hawaiian:	0.0%	Khaki collar:	0.1%
Age		Two+ races:	1.9%	Other:	16.7%
Median age:	34.6 yrs.	*Ancestry*		Median income:	$53,630
More than 65 yrs:	10.3%	German:	17.1%	Median home value:	$171,400
Less than 18 yrs:	23.8%	Irish:	9.4%	Poverty:	12.8%
		English:	7.6%	**Military Veterans**	
Education				% of Pop:	9.1%
H.S. grad:	87.8%				
College grad:	29.8%				
Grad degree:	13.8%				

Compared with points further north in "the mitten," the southeast corner of Michigan is elevation challenged. Its flat marshlands along the shore of Lake Erie give way to flat farm lands, with rivers flowing lazily in summer and flashing with ice in winter. Here and there are power plants with giant smokestacks and factories. On the northern horizon is the sprawl of metro Detroit and of the great auto and steel and chemical plants along the Detroit River.

2008 Presidential Vote
Obama (D) 225,993   (66%)
McCain (R).............................111,041   (32%)

2004 Presidential Vote
Kerry (D)................................191,091   (62%)
Bush (R) 118,217   (38%)

Cook Partisan Voting Index: D + 13

The 15th Congressional District of Michigan includes much of the southeastern corner of the state and owes its shape to Republican redistricters, who in 2001 devised one of the most partisan plans of the decennial cycle. In Wayne County, the district takes in parts of Dearborn and most of Dearborn Heights. The most heavily Arab-American parts of Dearborn were put in the 14th District, and these are more middle-class, even affluent areas. All of Monroe County is in the district, as are Ypsilanti and Ann Arbor, home to the University of Michigan, in Washtenaw County.

There are several working-class Detroit suburbs: Taylor, Romulus (home of Detroit's Metro Airport), and Woodhaven, site of a big Ford plant. Flat Rock is home to a joint Ford-Mazda auto plant, one of the few Japanese plants in Michigan. Monroe County has a statue of Gen. George Armstrong Custer, who grew up there. Once agricultural, the county now is predominately industrial, and the southern part is in many ways an extension of Toledo, Ohio. (Michigan and Ohio almost went to war over the Toledo land in the 1830s; Ohio got Toledo and Michigan got the Upper Peninsula as recompense.) Ann Arbor is one of the nation's largest university towns, oriented to the university but also home to auto executives and young families who like a town with plenty of bookstores, coffeehouses and liberal neighbors. In 2004, the city voted 74% to legalize medical marijuana. In 2006, it landed the headquarters of Google's AdWords unit, which operates the company's "pay-per-click" advertising method, Google's main revenue source. The company planned to have a workforce of 1,000 in Ann Arbor by 2012. Ypsilanti, though it also has a university, Eastern Michigan, is less bookish and more industrial. With the decline of the auto industry, hard times have affected the entire district and infected other industries, including pharmaceuticals; in 2007 Pfizer announced the closing of a research plant in Ann Arbor. All of these areas tend to vote Democratic, though Monroe is sometimes marginal. But they are different kinds of Democrats. In Wayne County, union operatives have dominated Democratic party politics for 50 years. In Ann Arbor, the party is dominated by leftist peace activists, environmentalists and feminists. Democratic presidential candidates have won this area overwhelmingly.

The congressman from the 15th District is John Dingell, the dean of the House. He is the longest-serving sitting member of the House and hit a historic milestone in February 2009 by becoming the longest-serving U.S. representative ever. (In combined House and Senate years, Democratic Sen. Robert Byrd of West Virginia holds the record for total congressional service.) For many years, until recently, Dingell was also the fearsome chairman of the Energy and Commerce Committee. His father, John Dingell, Sr., was first elected to the House in 1932, from a district created as a result of the Detroit area's auto boom. The first Rep. Dingell was one of the most productive urban liberals of his day, a sponsor of the Social Security program and, starting in 1943, of national health insurance. His son has been around Capitol Hill almost as long. He was a House page from 1938-43, then served in the Army in World War II. He graduated from Georgetown University in Washington, D.C., and its law school, helping to pay his way by working as a Capitol elevator operator. He practiced law in Detroit and served as an assistant prosecutor in Wayne County. After his father died, in September 1955, Dingell was elected to succeed him the following December. He was 29 and represented a district entirely within Detroit with large Polish, African-American, and Jewish populations. He still uses his father's office furniture and every session continues to introduce as H.R. 15 (the number matches the district) the national health-insurance bill his father co-sponsored in 1943. He is fond of saying, "HMOs, foreign diplomats and the mentally insane are the only people in this country who are exempt from the consequences of their decisions." Dingell is the only member of the House who served in the 1950s. Indeed, only two others have been around since the 1960s—Democratic Reps. John Conyers of Michigan and David Obey of Wisconsin. It is a measure of his seniority that the second most senior member of the House, Conyers, once served on Dingell's staff. His personal life is also wrapped in his political career. He married, had children, but then divorced and was remarried in 1981 to a granddaughter of one of General Motors' Fisher brothers. Debbie Dingell is vice chairman of the General Motors Foundation and a Democratic national committeewoman. She headed the Michigan campaigns for Al Gore in 2000 and John Kerry in 2004, and helped each win 51% of the vote in this battleground state. In 2008, she was a central player in efforts to resolve the national party controversy over Michigan's unauthorized Democratic primary.

Dingell served as chairman of the powerful Energy and Commerce Committee from 1981 to 1995 and was also chairman of its Investigative and Oversight Subcommittee. He was one of the most powerful and effective committee chairmen ever. He grew his jurisdiction to the point that his committee handled up to 40% of all House bills; he had the largest budget and staff of any House committee. And as institutions will, the committee took on the character of its leader: bright, determined and domineering. Dingell, dubbed "the Truck," and his committee superintended the breakup of AT&T and the sale of Conrail by public offering. His 1992 cable reregulation bill was the only one on which Congress overrode President George H.W. Bush's veto. He was a key player in the legislation creating the Medicare program for the elderly in the 1960s. He had a hand in writing the Endangered Species Act, and after a decade of sparring over clean-air legislation, Dingell worked with Democrat Henry Waxman of California to produce the 1990 Clean Air Act.

On other issues, Dingell backed organized labor's agenda against the 1993 North American Free Trade Agreement and other agreements that followed. An avid outdoorsman and a hunter of deer, elk, caribou and moose, he long opposed gun control but voted for the 1994 crime bill and resigned from the National Rifle Association board. One of his proudest accomplishments is the creation in 2001 of the Detroit River International Wildlife Refuge, on both sides of the river, from Zug Island in River Rouge south to Lake Erie. Dingell worked to get donations of land or easements from private landowners, land preservation groups and the Army Corps of Engineers, and the refuge grew from 394 acres to over 5,000. In many ways, he is an old-fashioned Franklin D. Roosevelt Democrat, supporting big government and strenuous regulation, taking a conservative line on some cultural issues and backing an assertive foreign policy. He was the only Michigan Democrat to vote for the Gulf War resolution in January 1991, although he voted against the Iraq war resolution of 2002.

When the Republican majority took over in 1995, Dingell, as the senior House member, swore in Republican Newt Gingrich as speaker and then occasionally cooperated with Republicans to produce legislation. He developed a productive working relationship with Rep. Joe Barton of Texas, the Republican chairman of the committee beginning in 2004. Like many in the GOP, Dingell long opposed raising fuel-efficiency standards for cars and trucks. But when he was on the other side of an issue, which was often, Dingell was a formidable opponent. He not only refused to support the Republicans' 2003 Medicare prescription-drug bill, seeing it as too skimpy, but he went on the road to criticize it. President George W. Bush once called him the "biggest pain in the ass" in Congress. Dingell also sprang into action whenever Michigan's interests were threatened. In 2003, the city of Toronto started transporting its trash—180 truckloads a day—to a landfill in southwest Wayne County in his district. Dingell and Michigan's Democratic Sen. Debbie Stabenow insisted that Environmental Protection Agency enforce a 1992 treaty that they said required Canada to give notice of each shipment and allowed the U.S. to reject each one. EPA Administrator Mike Leavitt argued that only hazardous waste was covered by the treaty, but Dingell persisted and got a 12-4 subcommittee vote demanding enforcement.

After Democrats won the House majority in 2006, Dingell took over as Energy and Commerce chairman again. Asked about his priorities after 12 years of Republican policies, Dingell said, "We will kill the closest snake first." But while Dingell still had considerable power, it did not compare to his earlier stint as chairman. He no longer also chaired the investigative subcommittee that has been so effective in its heyday, taking on bungling federal bureaucracies and putting top government officials on the hot seat. Moreover, the Energy and Commerce jurisdiction was diminished during the era of Republican control, with securities, accounting and insurance legislation reassigned to the Financial Services Committee. In early 2007, Dingell and Financial Services Chairman Barney Frank, a Massachusetts Democrat, sparred briefly over jurisdiction over data-security legislation, then promised to cooperate. Despite a promise from Dingell that he would hold hearings on carbon emissions in spite of his close ties to the big automakers, newly installed House Speaker Nancy Pelosi went around him and created a select committee on global warming to consider legislation on carbon emissions—over Dingell's strenuous objections. "These [select] committees," he sniffed, "are as useful in relevance as feathers on a fish." He called the new panel, headed by fellow Democrat Edward Markey of Massachusetts, "the committee on world travel and junkets." In the 110th Congress (2007–08), energy legislation was Dingell's chief priority. After the Senate passed new fuel-efficiency standards for cars and trucks, Dingell moved to try to find a compromise that would be easier on Detroit. Negotiating chiefly with Pelosi, he argued for differences between cars and light trucks, and for additional time for the industry to comply. The result, he said, was "a strong bill that [auto companies] will hate but with which they can live." He firmly opposed state-mandated fuel standards or regulation by the EPA, but had to give in on those demands under pressure from Pelosi. Although liberal groups like MoveOn.org mocked him as a "Dingellsaurus," he was at the table for the final deal in December 2007. It produced a 35 mile-per-gallon average standard by 2020. Some environmentalists cheered him, while some of his friends in Detroit howled.

On other issues, Dingell worked with Pelosi to expand the State Children's Health Insurance Program. Although their plan drew bipartisan support, and a Senate-passed companion bill had two-thirds support to override a veto, it failed to attract sufficient backing from House Republicans to override a Bush veto. Dingell succeeded in enacting a bipartisan bill to strengthen product-safety regulation, however. And under pressure from Dingell and others, the Food and Drug Administration in 2007 abandoned plans to close seven labs across the nation, including one in Detroit that already had been downsized.

The 2008 election ended on an unexpectedly jarring note for Dingell. The morning after the Democrats' resounding victory at the polls, Waxman called to tell him he planned to challenge Dingell for the chairmanship of Energy and Commerce in the Congress opening in early 2009. The 82-year-old Dingell had suffered from health problems in recent years, undergoing two heart operations and the installation of an artificial hip, and he was recovering from knee surgery. Waxman said that in light of the election of a Democratic president, Barack Obama, "We have a narrow window to act" on big health and energy issues. Dingell was caught off guard and scrambled to put together a two-week campaign to defend his chairmanship as the party organized for the 111th Congress (2009–10). He was backed by the centrist Blue Dogs, who defended his record and raised alarms about the liberal Waxman. With Pelosi officially neutral—though her allies lobbied for Waxman—Dingell lost the chairmanship in a Democratic caucus vote, 137-122. "This was clearly a change year, and I congratulate my colleague Henry Waxman on his success today," Dingell said. "What will never change is my commitment to the working men and women of the 15th Congressional District of Michigan who have honored me with the opportunity to represent them here in Washington." Dingell and Waxman agreed that Dingell, as chairman emeritus of the full committee, would not have a subcommittee chairmanship but would "play an integral role in the negotiation" of national health care legislation on Capitol Hill and with the Obama administration. And despite his diminished status, Dingell was instrumental in crafting in December 2008 the federal bailout of $13.4 billion in short-term loans for the auto industry, which Bush approved after the Senate deadlocked.

Since his first election in December 1955, Dingell has had only two serious challenges, both in Democratic primaries after redistricting plans threw him into a district with another incumbent. In 1964, he ran in a district mostly new to him against John Lesinski of Dearborn, who was the only northern Democrat to vote against the Civil Rights Act of 1964. With strong support from the UAW, Dingell won 54%-46%. Then in July 2001, the Republican Legislature put him in the same district with Rep. Lynn Rivers, an Ann Arbor liberal first elected in 1994. Democratic leaders urged Rivers to run in the neighboring 11th District, but she declined. Rivers campaigned as someone who understood the problems of ordinary people, while Dingell campaigned as a veteran congressman who had gotten things done. Dingell posed the question to audiences: "Are you going to replace one of the most effective members of the House of Representatives with one of the least effective members?" Rivers emphasized their differences on abortion rights and gun control. Dingell parried by pointing to the women's issues he had worked on—breast and cervical cancer screening, minimum hospital stays after childbirth, and children's health insurance. This was Michigan's most expensive House primary ever. Dingell spent $2.5 million against Rivers, while she raised $1.5 million. Earning Dingell's everlasting enmity, Pelosi stepped in to support Rivers. In the August primary, Dingell won 59%-41%. He won 74%-26% in Wayne County, which cast 43% of the votes, even though part of it was in Rivers's old district, and 80%-20% in Monroe County, which cast 19% of the votes. Rivers won Washtenaw County 69%-31%. In the general election, Dingell won easily in this solidly Democratic district.

Given his health and the loss of his chairmanship, there was speculation in 2009 that Dingell would give up the seat and that his wife might seek to replace him. But Dingell insisted that he first wanted to help Obama enact legislation on which he—and his father—had worked for decades. "I creak a little more each year," he once said. "But I keep going. . . . I will burn out when I burn out. I don't know when the hell it will come. It probably will come in time. But I still give my people a full day's work. I still give them seven days a week. I still travel the district. I still work hard on legislation."

★ MINNESOTA ★

Located far up in America's frozen North, Minnesota is a distinctive commonwealth, a state that in commerce, culture, and politics has set one example after another for the rest of the nation. It is the node of the transcontinental railroads that linked the winter wheat fields of the northern prairies to Minneapolis, the greatest grain-milling center in the world, and to the great Pacific ports of Puget Sound. It is also the birthplace of Scotch tape, Betty Crocker, Target, and the Mall of America, and the home of dyspeptic chroniclers of small-town America from Sinclair Lewis to Garrison Keillor. Politically, Minnesota for much of the 20th century provided the nation with some of its most articulate and honorable leaders—Harold Stassen, Hubert Humphrey, Eugene McCarthy, Walter Mondale—and with traditions of probity, civic-mindedness, and innovation that are second to none.

Minnesota's distinctiveness derives from its history. The far northern states were ignored by most Yankee migrants, who headed straight west into Iowa, Nebraska, and Kansas. But others saw opportunity in Minnesota's icy lakes and ferocious winters. James J. Hill, the builder of the Great Northern Railroad, once said, "You can't interest me in any proposition in any place where it doesn't snow." He and other entrepreneurs operating out of Minneapolis and St. Paul—already twin cities by 1860—worked to attract Norwegian, Swedish, and German migrants who would find the terrain and climate congenial. By 1890, the Twin Cities—rivals that year in a census competition—were the nerve center of a sprawling and rich agricultural empire stretching west from Minnesota through the Dakotas into Montana and beyond. Minneapolis and St. Paul became the termini of its rail lines and the site of its grain-milling companies.

The Twin Cities also became the center of a three-party politics and an economic radicalism reminiscent of Scandinavia. (American regions do seem to mirror the geography of Europe, with the East Coast resembling the British Isles and France; the industrial Midwest reminiscent of Germany and Poland; the relatively poor and always hawkish South suggesting a Baptist Mediterranean; and the Upper Midwest of Minnesota, Wisconsin, and North Dakota standing in as North American versions of Scandinavia.) One can get lutefisk (smelly, lye-soaked cod) around Christmastime in Minneapolis restaurants. In politics these Upper Midwestern commonwealths pioneered this continent's welfare states and shaped national public policy far out of proportion to their numbers. Alarmed by the unprecedented concentration of economic power and wealth in the hands of a few identifiable millionaires who lived on St. Paul's Summit Avenue or on the hill above Minneapolis's Hennepin Avenue, the immigrants from Scandinavia drew on their native traditions of cooperative activity and bureaucratic socialism.

As in Wisconsin and North Dakota, a strong third political party developed here in the years after the Populist era. This Farmer-Labor Party elected senators in the 1920s and dominated state politics in the 1930s. Hurt by their ties to communists, the Farmer-Laborites were beaten by Gov. Harold Stassen's Republicans in 1938. But this was still a New Deal state, and by 1944 the bedraggled local Democrats were merged with the anti-communist faction of Farmer-Laborites to form the Democratic-Farmer-Labor Party. Hubert Humphrey, the mayor of Minneapolis in 1945 and the dazzling advocate of the civil-rights plank at the 1948 Democratic National Convention, played a key role. Humphrey's DFL—clean, idealistic, closely tied to labor, backed by many farmers—attracted dozens of talented politicians, including Eugene McCarthy, Orville Freeman, and Walter Mondale. Humphrey's convention speech helped put the Democrats on record for civil rights, and he was elected to the Senate at age 37.

In the years that followed, the DFL dominated Minnesota politics while a series of progressive businesses led the development of a strong, diversified economy. The DFL stood for a generous, compassionate government, for strong labor unions and high wages, for an expansionist fiscal policy to encourage consumer-led economic growth, for civil rights, and for an anti-communist, but not bombastic, foreign policy. Its base was among blue-collar workers in the Twin Cities, in Duluth and the Iron Range, and among farmers of Scandinavian origin. Minnesota's business leaders were politically conservative and professionally innovative. Over the years, with a pause during the Great Depression, Minnesota's economy mostly hummed along, growing robustly in prosperous years and not falling far behind in recessions, although the state's income growth started to lag the national average around 2004. Mergers eliminated the headquarters of Norwest Bank, Honeywell, and Northwest Airlines, and the Mall of America even lost its role as the nation's largest shopping mecca.

Minnesota has very low levels of crime, divorce, and aberrant behavior. Workforce participation is high, and women are an increasingly important power in the economy. Minnesota has more social connectedness than any other large state, author Robert Putnam noted in *Bowling Alone,* and this spirit of civic participation is echoed in everything from hockey (Minnesota has the nation's biggest high school hockey programs) to the party precinct caucuses and conventions. The 2008 DFL and Republican presidential precinct caucuses attracted 214,000 and 62,000 voters, respectively, more than in any other caucus state. Minnesota led the Midwest in population growth in the 1990s, although from 2000 to 2008, South Dakota edged ahead of Minnesota. The state has attracted an interesting array of immigrants:

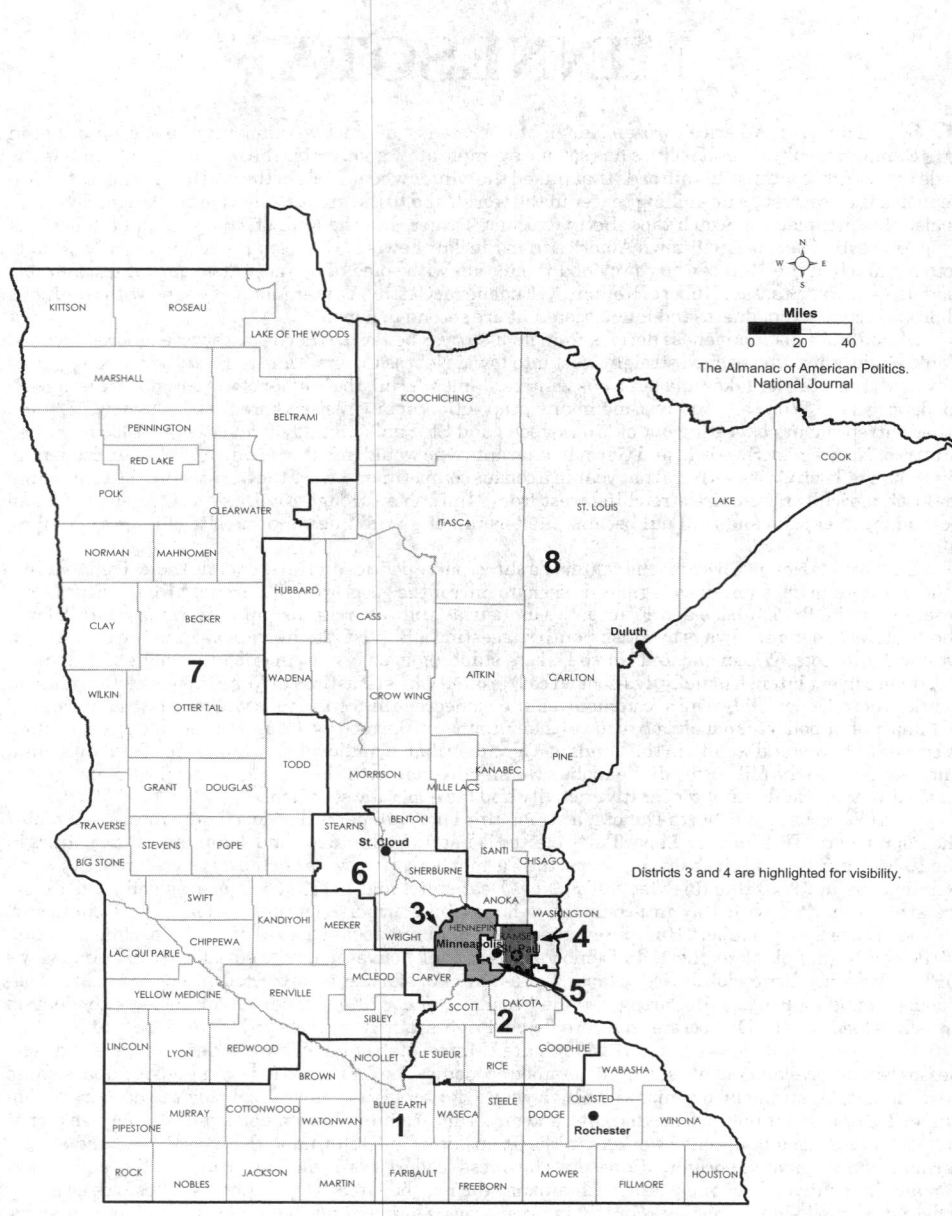

The Almanac of American Politics.
National Journal

Districts 3 and 4 are highlighted for visibility.

Congressional district boundaries were first effective for 2002.

Hmong and Vietnamese in the 1980s and 1990s, and Somalis since 2000. Once pretty much all white, its population is now 4% black, 4% Hispanic, and 3% Asian.

Over the years since the Humphrey breakthrough in 1948, Minnesota has been a mostly Democratic state, but the DFL has seldom had total dominance. The state has voted Democratic in every presidential election since 1976, and was presidential candidate George McGovern's second-best state in 1972. But in 1978, after DFL Gov. Wendell Anderson appointed himself to the Senate, voters reacted to his self-serving move by electing Republicans to the two U.S. Senate seats and the governorship. Liberal domination of DFL nominating conventions produced some weak statewide candidates, and, combined with conservative domination of the Republican nominating conventions, helped open the way for former professional wrestler and suburban mayor Jesse Ventura to be elected governor in 1998. Ventura's candidacy sparked a huge rise in turnout, especially in the Minneapolis-St. Paul media market beyond the Twin Cities core of Hennepin and Ramsey counties. This is family country and by far the fastest growing part of Minnesota; most counties outside the region lost population between 2000 and 2008.

In 2002, when Ventura did not run for re-election, the Twin Cities exurbs—the area just outside the Hennepin and Ramsey core—went heavily Republican, helping Tim Pawlenty win the governorship by a comfortable margin. In the Senate race, the tilt also boosted Norm Coleman, a DFLer-turned-Republican over Mondale; Democrats had named the former vice president to the ballot after Democratic Sen. Paul Wellstone died in an October plane crash. In 2004, the tide began to turn the other way. Minnesota was a target state in the presidential race, and heavy Democratic turnout in Hennepin and Ramsey counties enabled Democratic nominee John Kerry to win 51%-48%. In 2006, the DFL seized the tide. Pawlenty was re-elected by only 47%-46%, and the DFL's Amy Klobuchar won a Senate seat by a huge margin. Already in control of the Minnesota Senate, the DFL gained control of the House and picked up a U.S. House seat in the 1st Congressional District as well.

In 2008, Minnesota fell off the presidential candidates' target lists in late September, and turnout was up only 3% from 2004. The state has long had one of the nation's highest turnout rates and it seems that even the best organization can produce only marginal increases. Democratic presidential candidate Barack Obama won comfortably, but other DFL candidates lagged. DFL nominee Al Franken held Coleman to a 42%-42% tie, and, after eight months of ballot recounts and court challenges, was certified as the winner in July 2009. Dean Barkley, appointed to the Senate by Ventura to serve the last two months of Wellstone's term, got just 15% of the vote. The DFL fell short of winning the 3rd and 6th Congressional Districts and failed to win a veto-proof majority in the state House.

Population		Household Income		Work	
Pop. 2007:	5,155,344	Under $15k:	10.6%	Private:	80.9%
State rank:	21st of 50	$15k to $50k:	34.1%	Government:	12.1%
Change since 2000:	Up 4.8%	$50k to $100k:	34.8%	Self-employed:	6.8%
Urban:	69.2%	$100k to $150k:	17.0%	Unemployment (3-yr. average):	3.9%
Rural:	30.8%	Over $150k:	3.5%	Poverty:	9.6%
Native of state:	69.0%	Median income:	$55,616	Blue collar:	21.8%
Not a citizen:	3.8%			White collar:	62.1%
Area size:	86,939 sq. mi.	**Home Value**		Khaki collar:	0.1%
		Under $100k:	14.5%	Other:	16.1%
Most populous cities		$100k to $300k:	60.8%		
1. Minneapolis	362,513	$300k to $500k:	17.9%	**Age**	
2. St. Paul	271,203	$500k to $1 mil:	5.8%	Median age:	36.9 yrs.
3. Rochester	95,179	Over $1 million:	1.0%	More than 65 yrs:	12.2%
4. Duluth	84,532	Median:	$207,200	Less than 18 yrs:	24.5%

Race/Ethnicity				Military Veterans		Registered Voters in 2008	
White:	85.9%	*Language*		% of Pop:	10.6%	No party registration	
Black:	4.2%	English:	90.5%	*Veterans by Period*		Voter turnout:	2,910,369
Hispanic:	3.8%	Spanish:	3.5%	WWII and before:	13.4%	Turnout as % of	
Asian:	3.4%	Asian:	2.5%	Korea:	13.2%	voting age:	73.4%
Native Am.:	1.0%	Other		Vietnam:	34.3%	**Legislature**	
Hawaiian:	0.0%	European	2.1%	Gulf (pre-2001):	8.0%	Senate:	46 D 21 R
Two+ races:	1.4%	**Education**		Gulf (post-2001):	5.1%	House:	87 D 47 R
Ancestry		H.S. grad:	90.7%	Peace time:	25.9%		
German:	27.2%	College grad:	30.6%				
Norwegian:	12.0%	Grad degree:	9.7%				
Irish:	8.4%						

Presidential politics Minnesota is the state with the longest consecutive streak of voting Democratic for president. The last time Minnesota voted Republican was in 1972, and even then it gave Richard Nixon his lowest percentage margin over McGovern. But in 2000 and 2004, the state was seriously contested, and voters gave Al Gore and John Kerry only 48%-46% and 51%-48% victories, respectively, over Republican George W. Bush. One might attribute the increasing Democratic margin to the decision of 2000 Ralph Nader voters to back John Kerry, but that was only part of the reason. Total turnout

2008 Presidential Vote		
Obama (D) 1,573,354	(54%)
McCain (R).........................1,275,409	(44%)
2004 Presidential Vote		
Kerry (D)............................1,445,014	(51%)
Bush (R) 1,346,695	(48%)

was up 15% in a state that allows new voters to register on Election Day, and the Democratic-Farmer-Labor Party seems to have turned out more new voters. Bush's popular vote margin increased by 44,000 votes in the Twin Cities media-market counties outside the metropolitan core. But in the core counties of Hennepin and Ramsey, Kerry's popular vote margin was 71,000 votes more than Gore's. In 2008, turnout rose just 3%, but Democrat Barack Obama won 54%-44%, as Republican John McCain carried the Twin Cities exurbs by 51%-49%. Obama ran way ahead among young voters, and the Humphrey generation also went to Obama. White Protestants and Catholics gave small margins to McCain. Those with no religious affiliation voted 77% for Obama.

Minnesota has a tradition of selecting national convention delegates in caucuses. The DFL tried to attract more voters to its March 2000 caucuses by moving them from Tuesday night to Saturday and holding a presidential preference vote, with national convention delegates assigned proportionately. But by the time Minnesotans caucused, Gore had already clinched the nomination. Republican Gov. Tim Pawlenty tried but failed in 2003 to move the caucus date to February. In 2004, Minnesota was one of 10 states holding contests on March 2. Kerry carried 51% of the 55,000 votes cast in the presidential preference vote, North Carolina Sen. John Edwards took 27%, and Ohio Rep. Dennis Kucinich finished third with 17%. In 2008, the caucuses were held on February 5, Super Tuesday, and DFL turnout was a thumping 214,000. Obama beat Sen. Hillary Rodham Clinton 66%-32% in a contest in which more than half the votes were cast in Hennepin and Ramsey counties. Republican turnout was much lower, at 62,828. Despite Pawlenty's early endorsement of McCain, former Massachusetts Gov. Mitt Romney beat the Arizonan 41%-22%, with 20% for former Arkansas governor Mike Huckabee and 16% for Texas Rep. Ron Paul, who carried Red Lake County (Turnout: 30).

Minnesota competed to host the 2008 national political conventions, with politicians of both parties gamely pitching in. Minnesotans made it clear that they would go with whichever party chose them first. The Republicans, meeting on a Wednesday, picked St. Paul's Xcel Energy Center, a hockey arena that was a key project of Republican Sen. Norm Coleman when he was St. Paul's mayor. Coleman gave Minneapolis Mayor R. T. Rybak the news at noon. Rybak called Democratic National Chairman Howard Dean, who asked him to hold off for an hour. But Dean could not get Democrats to make a decision before their Friday meeting, at which they chose to convene in Denver. Rybak and St. Paul Mayor Chris Coleman, both staunch Democrats, and their townspeople gave the assembled Republicans a "Minnesota Nice" reception.

Congressional districting After the 2000 census, it never seemed likely that Minnesota's Republican House, DFL Senate, and Independence Party would agree on congressional redistricting, and they didn't—the new plan was drawn by a special panel of five judges appointed by Chief Justice Kathleen Blatz. The Republicans wanted to combine Minneapolis and St. Paul into one heavily Democratic district, in the hope of winning three of four suburban districts. Democrats designed a plan that would continue the long-standing pattern of predominantly rural districts anchored in each corner of the state, two districts dominated by Minneapolis and St. Paul, and two in the Twin Cities' suburbs. Gov. Jesse Ventura, of the Independence Party, submitted a plan with two urban, three suburban, and three rural districts, one of which stretched along the western side of the state from Iowa to Canada.

111th Congress Lineup	
5 D	3 R
110th Congress Lineup	
5 D	3 R

The special panel drew its own map, and, when Republicans, Democrats, and Ventura couldn't agree by the March 19, 2002, deadline, that plan went into effect. Minneapolis and St. Paul would each continue to dominate a district. The map created three suburban and three rural districts, one running along the southern end of the state from Wisconsin to South Dakota. Republican and Democratic leaders and Ventura all said they were pleased with the plan. The homes of two House incumbents, DFLer Bill Luther and Republican Mark Kennedy, ended up in the new 6th District. Luther, after pondering the decision for two months, decided to run in the new 2nd District, much of which he had represented, but he lost. The southernmost district, expected to be safely Republican, fell to the DFL in 2006.

Minnesota seems to be on the cusp of losing a House seat in the reapportionment following the 2010 census. Estimates by the political statistics firm Polidata, based on extrapolation of 2000–08 growth to 2010, show that Minnesota's eighth seat would be No. 438 in the formula used to apportion seats, and the House is limited to 435 seats. So if Minnesota's population growth shows a late spurt, it will probably hold the seat. If not, it won't. Loss of a seat would increase the pressure to move the central cities of Minneapolis and St. Paul into a single district; the 2008 estimates show that together the Twin Cities have a smaller population than a seven-district plan would require. But the DFL, with solid majorities in the Legislature, would surely reject any effort to combine them, and the election of a DFL governor in 2010 to succeed Pawlenty would surely prevent it.

The DFL would prefer to extend those two districts farther out into the suburbs and protect the 7th and 8th Districts represented by Collin Peterson, chairman of the House Agriculture Committee, and Jim Oberstar, chairman of the Transportation and Infrastructure Committee. The three primarily suburban 2nd, 3rd, and 6th Districts would then have to be combined into two, a move that would require a bit of legerdemain because they contain the fastest-growing areas in the state. Proposals to create an independent commission to redistrict, including one from a group led by Democrat Mondale, and former Republican Gov. Arne Carlson, are presumably not palatable to DFL politicians who, in early 2009, had reason to hope that their party would have total control of the redistricting process.

Governor

Tim Pawlenty (R)

Elected 2002, term expires Jan. 2011, 2nd term; b. Nov. 27, 1960, St. Paul; home, Eagan; U. of MN, B.A. 1983, J.D. 1986; Protestant; married (Mary); 2 children.

Elected Office: Eagan Planning Comm., 1988–89; Eagan City Cncl., 1990–92; MN House of Reps., 1992–2002, Maj. ldr., 1999–2002.

Professional Career: Practicing atty., 1986–92.

Office: 130 State Capitol, 75 Rev. Dr. Martin Luther King Jr. Blvd., St. Paul, 55155, 651-296-3391; Fax: 651-296-2089; Web site: www.governor.state.mn.us.

Election Results

2006 general	Tim Pawlenty (R)	1,028,568	(47%)
	Mike Hatch (DFL)	1,007,460	(46%)
	Peter Hutchinson (Ind)	141,735	(6%)
2006 primary	Tim Pawlenty (R)	147,622	(89%)
	Sue Jeffers (R)	18,490	(11%)

Prior Winning Percentages: 2002 (44%)

Republican Tim Pawlenty was elected governor of Minnesota in 2002 and re-elected in 2006. Pawlenty grew up in South St. Paul near the stockyards and a meatpacking plant. His early years were difficult. When he was 16, his mother died and his father lost his job at a trucking company. He worked his way through college and law school at the University of Minnesota, becoming the first college graduate in his family. At first he wanted to be a dentist, but he got involved in politics when interning for Republican Sen. David Durenberger of Minnesota. He practiced law until 1992, when he was elected to the state House from Eagan in suburban Dakota County. He distinguished himself in the Legislature, and planned a bid for governor in 1998. But he was persuaded to step aside for St. Paul Mayor Norm Coleman, who had switched parties and become a Republican. In 1999, Pawlenty was elected Minnesota House majority leader. In 2001, he set out to run against Democratic Sen. Paul Wellstone, but White House political strategist Karl Rove thought Coleman would be a stronger candidate. Vice President Dick Cheney called Pawlenty to say it would be better if he got out of the Senate race and ran for governor. For the second time, Pawlenty deferred to Coleman.

Running for governor in 2002 was a formidable task. The incumbent was Jesse Ventura, the former professional wrestler who, as the Reform Party candidate, was elected in 1998 over Coleman and Democrat Skip Humphrey and was enjoying high job-approval ratings. Pawlenty set his own agenda and put forward his own persona. He talked constantly of his South St. Paul roots and said he wanted Republicans to be "the party of Sam's Club, not the country club." He promised never to raise taxes and took conservative stands on abortion rights and other cultural issues. He had voted for a gay-rights measure as a freshman legislator, but now called his vote a mistake.

His opponent in the Republican primary was Brian Sullivan, a conservative and a self-financing businessman. A straw poll of those attending the March 2002 precinct caucuses showed Sullivan leading Pawlenty 51%-37%. But Pawlenty's organizational work put him even when the state convention assembled in June. Almost every state House Republican showed up wearing a Pawlenty blue shirt, and he ended up winning 58%-42%. The Democratic-Farmer-Labor nomination went to Roger Moe, the state Senate president since 1981, who had been waiting for the chance to run for governor. For the first time since 1978, no serious candidate challenged the candidate endorsed by either party's nominating convention.

The guiding assumption in both parties was that Ventura would run for another term. But on June 18, Ventura announced he wasn't running. Into that void stepped Tim Penny, a former Democratic congressman from a Republican-leaning district who had retired in 1994, saying he was disgusted with the partisanship of Washington. Several of Penny's former aides had been appointed to top jobs by Ventura. On June 26, Penny announced that he was switching to the Independence Party, the one most closely associated with Ventura, and running for governor. He chose a Republican state senator as his running mate, and Ventura supported him.

The three were by far more traditional politicians than Ventura, who had not cared about making friends in politics. Just about everyone in Minnesota politics agreed that Pawlenty, Moe, and Penny were decent, likeable people: a "Minnesota Nice" campaign. Of course there were differences on issues. Pawlenty pledged no tax increase. "The last thing I want to do is raise your taxes," Moe said. But also: "You pay a high income tax because you have high incomes in this state and we enjoy a higher quality of life." Penny said he "would keep taxes on the table as a last resort," and suggested there would have to be tax increases and spending cuts, and that he was the only candidate leveling with the voters. Pawlenty favored restrictions on abortion. Moe and Penny opposed them. Pawlenty and Penny favored a concealed-weapons law, and Moe did not.

For most of the campaign, polls showed the three in a three-way tie. Then in October, Pawlenty had a serious financing setback. All three candidates had accepted public financing of up to $400,000, which required them to limit spending to $2.2 million. The parties were allowed to spend money for their candidates, but not in cooperation with the campaigns. The Pawlenty campaign had sold some of its video—footage of the candidate talking about growing up in South St. Paul and making humorous comments—to the Republican Party. The state Campaign and Finance Disclosure Board ruled that the cost of the ads, about $1 million, had to be counted against Pawlenty's $2.2 million. After paying fines and the cost of the video, Pawlenty had only about $600,000 to spend in the closing days of the campaign. But he won with 44% of the vote to 36% for Moe and 16% for Penny.

This was a high point for Minnesota Republicans. Coleman was elected to the Senate over Walter Mondale, the former vice president's his first loss ever in Minnesota, and Republicans won narrow victories for secretary of state and auditor. The only statewide DFL winner was Attorney General Mike Hatch, who calmly and fairly handled the issue of replacing Wellstone on the ballot after his death in a plane crash. Republicans increased their majority in the state House to 82-52 and narrowed the DFL margin in the state Senate to 35-31-1.

Pawlenty took office with a budget shortfall estimated at $4.2 billion. He started off with good relations with legislative leaders of both parties, but much of that goodwill dissipated after an acrimonious budget battle. Pawlenty held to his no-new-taxes pledge and cut spending by more than $2 billion, explaining, "The days of a program for every problem and a state government that leads by blank check are over." There were small increases in health and human services, public education, and criminal-justice funding, but overall state spending fell slightly from 2003 to 2004 and increased by just 2.3% in 2005, the lowest increase in a consecutive two-year period in more than 40 years. "We're transitioning from a classic liberal state to a swing or transition or center-right state," Pawlenty told the Minneapolis *Star Tribune*. "That's not to say we are going to become North Carolina, nor should we be. We want the traditions of Minnesota, the heritage of Minnesota, the priorities of Minnesota updated for the times. There's more than one way to better health care, more than one way to better schools."

Among Pawlenty's other accomplishments in 2003 were a 24-hour waiting period for abortions, a concealed-weapons law, establishment of tax-exempt zones in distressed rural areas, and a bill requiring recitation of the Pledge of Allegiance in public schools. He proposed an ambitious mail-order program to buy cheaper prescription drugs from Canada through a state-sponsored website. In 2004, when the Legislature could not agree on a plan to close the state's $160 million budget deficit, Pawlenty balanced the budget largely by tapping a windfall of federal dollars that had been designated for the state's subsidized health insurance plan. Among his disappointments was the failure of his education initiatives, of a bill for stricter penalties for sexual predators, and of a $740 million bonding bill. A partisan impasse stalled a proposed same-sex marriage constitutional amendment.

Democrats in November 2004 reduced the Republican majority in the state House from 81-53 to a tenuous 68-66—the first time in 12 years the DFL gained seats in the House. In 2005, polarization increased. After Pawlenty and the Legislature could not agree on a budget, there was a partial shutdown of the state government in July, the first in Minnesota's history. Pawlenty got the Legislature to impose a 75-cent "health impact fee" on cigarettes—a retreat from his no-new-taxes pledge, many charged. Democrats also claimed that he was responsible for higher property taxes because of reductions in state aid. In 2006, he and the Legislature reached accord on bonding for a new University of Minnesota stadium and a ballpark for the Minnesota Twins. He vetoed only $1 million in spending and approved measures to conserve duck lands and reduce mercury levels in coal-fired plants.

Pawlenty entered campaign year 2006 with the most-polarized job ratings in SurveyUSA's 50-state polls: Republicans loved him, DFLers hated him. His DFL opponent was Attorney General Mike Hatch, who ran for governor in the primaries in 1990 and 1994 and was elected attorney general in 1998. Hatch charged that property taxes and college tuition had increased 50% on Pawlenty's watch, and that the governor had done little to improve access to health care, which he called "a right, not a privilege." Pawlenty said that Hatch's health care bill would encourage lawsuits against insurers and called for health savings accounts, price transparency, and patient incentives. "The future doesn't belong to the tax increasers or the education-without-accountability promoters and the folks who want to have government take over the health care system," he said. Polls showed the race between Pawlenty and Hatch close. In the last week Hatch was embarrassed when his running mate, Judi Dutcher, said she had never heard of E-85, the ethanol fuel sold at many Minnesota gas stations. On November 2, when a reporter asked Hatch to speak to Dutcher about that, Hatch said, "You're nothing but a Republican whore." This got widespread publicity throughout "Minnesota Nice" land. Hatch said he had called her a "Republican hack," but his explanation was not widely accepted. Pawlenty beat Hatch 47%-46%, with 6% going to former Minneapolis schools superintendent Peter Hutchinson, the Independence Party candidate. In the Twin Cities core counties of Hennepin and Ramsey, Hatch led 51%-39%. Pawlenty won 54%-39% in the outer counties in the Twin Cities media market. In the remainder of the state it was a standoff: Hatch led 48%-46% because of his big margins in the traditionally DFL Iron Range.

It was otherwise a good Election Day for the DFL. They unseated 1st District U.S. Rep. Gil Gutknecht and picked up many state legislative seats, giving them a 44-23 majority in the Senate and an 85-49 advantage in the House. DFL candidates were elected attorney general, secretary of state, and auditor. DFL Senate nominee Amy Klobuchar won 58%-38%.

After the election, Pawlenty struck a different note than he had in 2003, saying voters had sounded a warning to Republicans in the election: "'We're not much interested in your product, and we're choosing to go to your competitor.' We need to hear that message." Pawlenty still called for more accountability in education and, with a $2.2 billion budget surplus in sight, continued to stand against tax increases. But he promised little in the way of tax cuts. He called for health insurance for all children and an energy initiative including more E-85 pumps and more reliance on renewable sources. In February 2007, Pawlenty signed a bill requiring Minnesota to get 25% of its energy from renewable sources by 2025, to reduce carbon emissions 80% by 2050, and to reduce fossil fuel consumption 15% by 2015. He also supported higher auto gas-mileage standards. As the chairman of the National Governors Association in 2007–08, he steered the organization to agreement on a clean-energy initiative.

After the collapse of the Interstate 35W bridge in Minneapolis, the Legislature overrode Pawlenty's veto of a transportation bill that included a gas-tax increase and increases in local sales taxes. But most of his 34 vetoes in 2008 stood, including his refusal to sign bills on subprime mortgage relief and appropriations for light rail and an Asian Pacific Cultural Center. He prevented the Legislature from ending his JOBZ rural jobs program and announced a new Green JOBZ program, with tax exemptions for sustainable-energy projects. He got $24 million for his strategic entrepreneurial economic development program, and signed a bill to allow law enforcement officers to enforce federal immigration laws.

Things got progressively worse for Pawlenty in 2008. Republicans suffered further losses in state legislative contests, and the national recession had dramatically changed the budget outlook. In November, the DFL gained one seat in the Minnesota Senate, for a 46-21 advantage over Republicans, and gained two seats in the House, for an 87-47 edge. In December, the state was facing a $426 million shortfall in the current budget and a prospective $4.8 billion deficit in the 2010–11 budget. In January 2009, Pawlenty proposed a small increase for schools, maintenance of the State Children's Health Insurance Program, and large cuts in other spending. DFL legislative leaders favored a mix of spending cuts and tax increases. He called for freezing state-funded government pay for two years, cutting the corporate tax rate from 9.8% to 4.8% over six years, and replacing human service agencies in the 87 counties with 15 regional agencies.

In the GOP presidential contest in 2008, Pawlenty was the first governor to endorse Arizona Sen. John McCain, whom he called a "once-in-a-generation leader, one of the strongest, most courageous and fearless public servants I have ever met." He stuck with McCain when the campaign foundered in the summer of 2007, and stumped for him around the country in early 2008. Speculation of a possible vice presidency for Pawlenty was floated, as Pawlenty abandoned his mullet haircut in June and in July spoke sharply of "the audacity of hypocrisy" in Democrat Barack Obama's campaign. "Our question for Obama is, 'What have you done? And what have you run?' The answers are, 'Not much' and 'Nothing.'"

When McCain instead chose Alaska Gov. Sarah Palin as his running mate, Pawlenty gamely supported her and welcomed delegates to the Republican National Convention, which was held in St. Paul. He was given a six-minute speaking slot on the last night of the convention. After the election, he spoke to the Republican Governors Association in Miami Beach. He said, "The country is changing culturally, demographically, technologically, economically, and the like. And the Republican Party isn't changing in a way that reflects those major or macro changes across the country." Pawlenty announced in June 2009 he would not seek re-election, fueling speculation he is weighing a campaign for president in 2012.

Senior Senator

Amy Klobuchar (D)

Elected 2006, term expires 2012, 1st term; b. May 25, 1960, Plymouth; home, Minneapolis; Yale U., B.A. 1982, U. of Chicago, J.D. 1985; Protestant; married (John Bessler); 1 child.

Elected Office: Hennepin cnty. atty., 1998–2006.

Professional Career: Practicing atty., 1985–98.

DC Office: 302 HSOB, 20510, 202-224-3244; Fax: 202-228-2186; Web site: klobuchar.senate.gov.

State Offices: Minneapolis, 612-727-5220; Moorhead, 218-287-2219; Rochester, 507-288-5321; Virginia, 218-741-9690.

Committees: *Agriculture, Nutrition & Forestry* (10th of 12 D). *Commerce, Science & Transportation* (11th of 14 D): Aviation Operations, Safety & Security; Communications & Technology; Competitiveness, Innovation & Export Promotion (Chmn); Consumer Protection, Product Safety & Insurance. *Environment & Public Works* (7th of 12 D). *Joint Economic Committee. Judiciary* (9th of 12 D): Antitrust, Competition Policy & Consumer Rights; Crime & Drugs.

Group Ratings

	ADA	ACLU	AFS	LCV	ITIC	NTU	COC	ACU	CFG	FRC
2008	100	79	100	100	80	4	57	16	3	0
2007	100	—	100	87	—	5	45	4	7	—

National Journal Ratings

	2007 LIB — 2007 CONS		2008 LIB — 2008 CONS	
Economic	79%	— 13%	61%	— 36%
Social	66%	— 30%	75%	— 21%
Foreign	79%	— 17%	55%	— 44%
Composite	77%	— 23%	65%	— 35%

Key Votes of the 110th Congress

1. Raise CAFE standards	Y	5. Make English official language	Y	9. Withdraw troops 3/08		Y
2. Expand SCHIP	Y	6. Path to citizenship	Y	10. Iran guard is terrorist group		N
3. Cap greenhouse gases	Y	7. Fetus is unborn child	N	11. Increase missile defense $		N
4. Bail out financial markets	Y	8. Prosecute hate crimes	Y	12. Overhaul FISA		N

Election Results

2006 general	Amy Klobuchar (DFL)	1,278,849	(58%)	($9,095,671)
	Mark Kennedy (R)	835,653	(38%)	($10,347,739)
2006 primary	Amy Klobuchar (DFL)	294,671	(93%)	
	Darryl Stanton (DFL)	23,872	(7%)	

Amy Klobuchar, a Democrat elected in 2006, is Minnesota's senior senator and the fourth occupant of this Senate seat in as many elections. Klobuchar (*KLO-bu-shar*) was born in the Minneapolis suburb of Plymouth, the daughter of longtime Minneapolis *Star Tribune* columnist Jim Klobuchar. She attended Yale University, where she wrote a senior paper on the machinations behind the building of the Hubert H. Humphrey Metrodome, then graduated from the University of Chicago law school. After returning home, she worked primarily as a lawyer and as a lobbyist. In 1994, she ran for Hennepin County attorney but left the race when Mike Freeman, the officeholder at the time, lost a bid for the Democratic endorsement for governor and decided to run for re-election. In 1998, when Freeman ran for governor again, Klobuchar ran for the job and defeated the sister of 3rd District U.S. Rep. Jim Ramstad, a Republican, in the general election. Klobuchar served two terms as county attorney, was president of the Minnesota County Attorneys Association, and took credit for spearheading a crackdown on gun crimes and for securing nearly 300 homicide convictions.

Minneapolis's Hennepin County is home to almost a quarter of the state's population, so it provided an excellent springboard for Klobuchar to run for the Senate in 2006, after Democratic Sen. Mark Dayton announced he would not seek re-election. Dayton's standing had fallen in the polls in October 2004, when he announced that he was closing his Washington office because of security threats. Congress had recessed for the election, making the decision seem a bit alarmist. Also, Dayton, whose family fortune was made in department stores (Dayton Hudson, which became Target Corp.), had spent nearly $12 million on his campaign in 2000, and said he was not able to self-finance again. Quickly, Republican U.S. Rep. Mark Kennedy made it clear he was running. He was fresh from defeating a well-known and well-financed Democratic challenger in the 6th District, Patty Wetterling, a national child-safety advocate. While Republican Sen. Norm Coleman and other Minnesota Republicans quickly united behind Kennedy's candidacy, the Democratic field took time to shake out. Several prominent members of the Democratic-Farmer-Labor Party decided against the race, including former presidential candidate Walter Mondale, Justice Alan Page, Attorney General Mike Hatch, and radio talk-show host (and Minnesota native) Al Franken. Klobuchar was the first to formally announce her candidacy in April. But Wetterling was also interested in running, as was Minnesota Heart Institute Research Foundation President Ford Bell.

But Wetterling soon decided instead to run again for the 6th District seat, left open by Kennedy's Senate bid. Bell dropped out in July 2006, a month after Klobuchar received the party endorsement at the DFL state convention. With a clear path to the party nomination, Klobuchar was able to conserve her resources and focus her sights on Kennedy. Meanwhile, he struggled in his effort to distance himself from an unpopular Republican president, the war in Iraq, and the national GOP. In one television ad, Kennedy offered a list of issues on which he voted against the Bush administration and crossed party lines. He claimed he was an independent, bipartisan leader who would not "take up Senator Dayton's place on the fringe." He sought to portray Klobuchar as an ineffective liberal by linking her to the unpopular outgoing incumbent. And he also questioned the number of cases she actually prosecuted and highlighted the increasing rate of violent crime in Minneapolis.

This open Senate race at first figured to be one of the Republican Party's best opportunities to pick up a Democratic seat. But in her first bid for statewide office, Klobuchar built an early lead in the polls and never relinquished it. She referred to Kennedy as a "rubber stamp for President Bush" who supported Bush's policies more than 90% of the time. She talked about middle-class tax relief and called for an increase in the minimum wage. She emphasized her tough-on-crime credentials and ran on a more fiscally conservative platform than Dayton and the late Minnesota Democratic Sen. Paul Wellstone.

Klobuchar won 58%-38%, the biggest Minnesota Senate victory since 1978—only twice did Democratic Sen. Hubert H. Humphrey win a margin this big. She swept the Iron Range and won by 2-to-1 ratios in the Twin Cities core counties, carrying Hennepin County (64%-32%) and St. Paul's Ramsey County (66%-29%). She also showed strength in the eastern Twin Cities suburbs, winning Dakota County (56%-40%), Anoka County (55%-42%), and Washington County (55%-41%).

Bribery and corruption scandals had plagued Congress for the previous two years, and Klobuchar launched her Senate term by taking several high-profile steps to try to show she would be different. She announced that she would not accept gifts, meals, or trips from private groups or individuals, regardless of whether congressional rules allow them. She instituted "Minnesota Mornings," where every Thursday the Senate is in session she meets with visiting Minnesotans for coffee and *potica*, a traditional Slovenian holiday nut roll, a reminder to constituents of Klobuchar's ethnic heritage and Iron Range family roots.

Her lead issue was product safety. After news stories described the discovery of lead in children's toys made in China and Congress moved to tighten regulation, the Senate bill contained three of Klobuchar's provisions: a comprehensive ban on lead in children's products (including clothes), a requirement that toys contain batch numbers to make recalls easier, and a ban on the sale of recalled toys. Klobuchar also served on the conference committee that negotiated the final version, which raised the age for which products were regulated from 7 to 12. Congress passed the legislation in July 2008. She also co-sponsored a ban on industry-paid travel by staff of the Consumer Product Safety Commission. That bill passed the Senate in March 2008. In 2007, after a 6-year-old sustained serious injuries from a swimming pool drain in St. Louis Park, Minn., Klobuchar and Ramstad sponsored a bill banning swimming pool covers that fail to meet entrapment safety standards and requiring automatic drain shutoffs. It was signed into law in December 2007.

With a seat on the Agriculture Committee, Klobuchar also had a role in drafting the farm bill in 2007. She got into the final legislation provision creating incentives for farmers to switch from carbohydrate-based crops like corn to cellulosic crops like switchgrass to make ethanol. The provision no doubt made Minnesota switchgrass growers happy. She also sought to bar federal subsidies to farmers with incomes over $750,000 a year, but was unsuccessful. After gasoline prices spiked in May 2008, she backed a windfall profits tax on oil companies, and in September of that year, joined a bipartisan group pushing to permit states to allow offshore oil drilling along their coasts.

She also took up a cause affecting the multiple millions of cell phone consumers. With Democrat Jay Rockefeller of West Virginia, she co-sponsored a bill requiring cell phone companies to allow free termination of contracts for 30 days and prorated termination fees after that. "Sometimes I feel as if I work for these companies because I know all the dead spots on Interstate 35," she said. "If I know, the companies should know. And they should provide this information to consumers before they enter into a contract." Within six months, the major companies had announced they would prorate termination fees.

Klobuchar faces her first re-election test in 2012.

Junior Senator

Al Franken (D)

Elected 2008, term expires 2014, 1st term; b. May 21, 1951, New York City, NY; home, Minneapolis; Harvard U., B.A.1973; Jewish; married (Franni); 2 children.

Professional Career: Writer, network comedy show; Radio talk show host

DC Office: 320 HSOB, 20510, 202-224-5641; Fax: 202-224-0044; Web site: franken.senate.gov.

State Offices: None at press time.

Committees: *Aging (Special)* (13th of 13 D). *Health, Education, Labor & Pensions* (13th of 13 D). *Indian Affairs* (9th of 9 D). *Judiciary* (12th of 12 D).

Group Ratings and Key Votes: Newly Elected

Election Results

2008 general	Al Franken (DFL)	1,212,629	(42%)	($21,066,834)
	Norm Coleman (R)	1,212,317	(42%)	($19,011,108)
	Dean Barkley (Ind)	437,505	(15%)	($162,387)
2008 primary	Al Franken (D)	164,136	(65%)	
	Priscilla Faris (D)	74,655	(30%)	

Democrat Al Franken prevailed in his extremely close contest with Republican Sen. Norm Coleman, and was declared the winner of the November 2008 election after eight months of ballot recounts and court challenges. The Minnesota Supreme Court ruled 5-0 in the former comedian's favor on June 30, 2009, and Coleman immediately announced he would not appeal to the U.S. Supreme Court. The same day, Republican Gov. Tim Pawlenty signed the certificate of election declaring Franken the winner by 312 votes. Franken became the 60th Democrat in the Senate, giving the party a filibuster-proof majority.

Franken was born in New York City and moved at age 4 to Minnesota, where the family settled in the heavily Jewish suburb of St. Louis Park just west of Minneapolis. Franken's father was a printing salesman and his mother was a real estate agent. From a young age, Franken reconciled his competing political and comedic impulses by combining them. As a seventh grader, he ran for class president as "Honest Al" and hung posters in the hallways picturing him with a fake beard and a stovepipe hat. Franken graduated from Harvard University and took a writing job in New York for the then-new *Saturday Night Live* television show. For most of the next 20 years, Franken helped to define the program's sense of humor as it evolved from a fledgling variety show into a pop-culture mainstay. Franken also frequently appeared on the program, most memorably as Stuart Smalley, an obnoxious self-help guru.

Franken left *Saturday Night Live* in 1995 and began working as a political commentator. After the Republicans swept to victory in Congress in 1994, he authored four books, including *Rush Limbaugh Is a Big Fat Idiot.* In 2004, he joined the new liberal Air America Radio network with a daily, three-hour show opposite Limbaugh's influential conservative program. Franken spent the next three years excoriating conservatives of every stripe, from Bush administration officials to Fox News personality Bill O'Reilly. Franken began thinking about returning to Minnesota to run for the Senate after Democratic Sen. Paul Wellstone died in a plane crash in October 2002 while running for re-election against former St. Paul Mayor Coleman. Democrats chose former Vice President Walter Mondale to replace Wellstone on the ballot, and despite Mondale's prominence and long political history in the state, Coleman won by 2 percentage points.

In 2006, Franken moved his radio talk show from New York to Minneapolis, and in February 2007, he announced he would run for the Senate. Republicans immediately drew attention to Franken's ultra liberal on-air commentary. But his defenders noted that his program often featured in-depth interviews with policy experts. He appeared to have a clear shot at Coleman when trial lawyer Mike Ciresi dropped out of the Democratic-Farmer-Labor Party primary in March 2008. But damaging revelations on the eve of the DFL endorsement convention in June threatened his nomination. A sexually explicit satirical article that Franken wrote for *Playboy* magazine in 2000 about a virtual sex institute diminished enthusiasm for him among women's groups. He apologized for the article and secured the party's endorsement. But polling showed him looking increasingly weak against Coleman.

Franken slowly climbed back into contention, winning over skeptical Democrats and keeping pace with Coleman in fundraising. The dynamics of the race shifted considerably in July, when former Sen. Dean Barkley, who served the last two months of Wellstone's term in 2002, entered the race and secured the Independence Party line on the ballot. Throughout October, Barkley consistently drew about 20% in most polls. Franken attacked Coleman for reportedly receiving free suits and below-market rent in Washington from political benefactors. But Franken was embarrassed by disclosures that he owed

$70,000 in back taxes, and he paid a $25,000 fine to New York state for failing to carry workers' compensation insurance for his employees. This was an expensive contest; the candidates each spent more than $19 million. As the returns came in on election night, they showed the race to be exceedingly tight, with 42% for both Coleman and Franken and 15% for Barkley. In a state that Democratic presidential nominee Barack Obama carried 54%-44%, Franken ran 362,000 votes behind Obama. Coleman ran 64,000 votes behind Republican presidential nominee John McCain.

On November 18, the State Canvassing Board showed Coleman with a 206-vote lead. A recount began the next day. On January 5, 2009, the board certified a recount that had Franken 225 votes ahead. Coleman contended that 133 ballots were missing in the recount and contested the results. In Washington, Senate Majority Leader Harry Reid said he was ready to seat Franken, but Republicans protested that no one could be seated without a certificate of election; Senate Democrats had made the same argument when they questioned the validity of the certificate of election of Illinois Democrat Roland Burris earlier in the month. On January 26, a three-judge court began reviewing the ballots. On March 31, the court issued an order designating 400 absentee ballots for review; 351 of them were opened and counted. On April 13, the three judges issued an opinion that Franken had "received the highest number of votes legally cast" by a margin of 312. Coleman appealed to the state Supreme Court, and his attorneys suggested that he might appeal an adverse ruling to the U.S. Supreme Court on the grounds that different counties had used different standards in determining the validity of absentee ballots.

But after the state's high court ruled, Coleman called Franken to congratulate him and said he had decided against further court challenges. Coleman told the *St. Paul Pioneer Press:* "I just had a conversation with Al Franken congratulating him on his victory. I told him it's the best job he'll ever have, representing the people of Minnesota. The Supreme Court of Minnesota has spoken. I respect its decision and I will abide by its result."

Franken was sworn in on July 7, and took seats on the Judiciary Committee, the Health, Education, Labor and Pensions Committee, and also the Senate committees on Indian affairs and aging. The outcome of the Franken-Coleman battle topped a spectacular election season for the Democrats in 2008, which left them with control of the White House and both houses of Congress. With Franken's arrival in the Senate, Democrats secured the 60 votes they needed to stop Republicans from using the most powerful weapon at their disposal, the filibuster, to thwart the majority's proposals. Although Democrats went into the election in a strong position with voters, they were thought to have only a slim chance of achieving a 60-seat majority in the Senate.

FIRST DISTRICT

Tim Walz (D)

Elected 2006, 2nd term; b. April 6, 1964, West Point, NE; home, Mankato; Chadron St. Col., B.S. 1989, MN St. U., M.S. 2001; Lutheran; married (Gwen); 2 children.

Military Career: Army Natl. Guard, 1981–2005.

Professional Career: Teacher, Pine Ridge Indian Reservation, SD, 1984; Teacher, People's Republic of China, 1989–90; Founder, Educational Travel Adventures, 1991–2006; High school teacher, 1989–2006.

DC Office: 1722 LHOB, 20515, 202-225-2472; Fax: 202-225-3433; Web site: walz.house.gov.

State Offices: Mankato, 507-388-2149; Rochester, 507-206-0643.

Committees: *Agriculture* (13th of 28 D): Conservation, Credit, Energy & Research; General Farm Commodities & Risk Management. *Transportation & Infrastructure* (24th of 44 D): Economic Development, Public Buildings & Emergency Management; Highways & Transit; Railroads, Pipelines & Hazardous Materials. *Veterans' Affairs* (15th of 18 D): Oversight & Investigations.

Group Ratings

	ADA	ACLU	AFS	LCV	ITIC	NTU	COC	ACU	CFG	FRC
2008	85	91	100	77	71	20	50	20	20	11
2007	100	—	100	85	—	3	60	0	1	—

National Journal Ratings

	2007 LIB	—	2007 CONS		2008 LIB	—	2008 CONS
Economic	69%	—	28%		54%	—	45%
Social	58%	—	41%		59%	—	38%
Foreign	63%	—	35%		65%	—	32%
Composite	64%	—	36%		61%	—	40%

Key Votes of the 110th Congress

1. Increase minimum wage	Y	5. Share immigration data	N	9. Withdraw troops 8/08	Y
2. Expand SCHIP	Y	6. Foreign aid abortion ban	N	10. No operations in Iran	Y
3. Raise CAFE standards	Y	7. Ban gay bias in workplace	Y	11. Free trade with Peru	N
4. Bail out financial markets	N	8. Repeal D.C. gun law	Y	12. Overhaul FISA	N

Election Results

2008 general	Tim Walz (DFL)	207,753	(63%)	($2,707,385)
	Brian Davis (R)	109,453	(33%)	($1,094,278)
	Gregory Mikkelson (Ind)	14,904	(4%)	
2008 primary	Tim Walz (DFL)	unopposed		

Prior Winning Percentages: 2006 (53%)

Population		Race/Ethnicity		Work	
Pop. 2007:	627,854	White:	91.4%	Private:	80.0%
Change since 2000:	Up 2.1%	Black:	1.4%	Government:	11.0%
Urban:	56.5%	Hispanic:	3.8%	Self-employed:	8.7%
Rural:	43.5%	Asian:	2.1%	Blue collar:	25.4%
Area size:	13,521 sq. mi.	Native Am.:	0.3%	White collar:	57.0%
		Hawaiian:	0.0%	Khaki collar:	0.0%
Age		Two+ races:	0.9%	Other:	17.6%
Median age:	37.9 yrs.			Median income:	$49,034
More than 65 yrs:	15.1%	**Ancestry**		Median home value:	$138,400
Less than 18 yrs:	23.5%	German:	34.7%	Poverty:	10.0%
		Norwegian:	14.5%		
Education		Irish:	7.9%	**Military Veterans**	
H.S. grad:	88.9%			% of Pop:	10.8%
College grad:	24.4%				
Grad degree:	8.1%				

The Mississippi River flows majestically southeast from Minneapolis and St. Paul, cutting through rolling hills and, where it widens, forming calm lakes lapping at the bottomlands. It is one of the finest river landscapes of North America, exemplified by the river towns of Wabasha and Winona, with their 19th century stone storefronts and mountainlike rock outcroppings above the river. This far north, the westward tide of Yankee migrants thinned out. After the Civil War, most settlers fol-

2008 Presidential Vote		
Obama (D)	173,884	(51%)
McCain (R)	158,967	(47%)

2004 Presidential Vote		
Bush (R)	171,952	(51%)
Kerry (D)	159,776	(47%)

Cook Partisan Voting Index: R+1

lowing the railroads on the floodplains west of the river were Germans and Scandinavians, bringing their families to a terrain so much like the Rhineland and to the rolling uplands beyond, which resemble the northern European plain.

Southern Minnesota is a borderland between Yankee and German settlements. Along the Mississippi River, tourism spiked upward (from a nearly nonexistent base) after the old St. Paul and Milwaukee Railroad was converted to a hiker-biker nature trail in the 1990s. "Historic" Bluff Country now draws sufficient visitors to support not one but two upscale bed-and-breakfasts, former jails converted to new use with Minnesota practicality. A little to the west is Rochester, home to the Mayo Clinic, founded in 1863 when English-born physician William Mayo set up a practice to examine inductees into the Union Army. Rochester, with more than 31,000 employed at Mayo, is prosperous and the growth center of southern Minnesota. Austin, a county away, is headquarters of the Hormel meatpacking firm, which was the site of a bitter strike in the 1980s. The huge plant produces "miracle meat" Spam, Hormel chili, Dinty Moore stew and, say critics, too much ammonia-loaded waste. This is one place where class-conscious politics survives, with some tensions over the recent influx of Hispanic workers. The farther west you go, the more frequently you find communities with a German heritage, like New Ulm, where the "Hermann the German" monument guards the town and the Concord Singers—30 men decked out in lederhosen, red vests and white shirts—are known as one of the county's best male choruses. Farther south is dairy country, with a sprinkling of small industries. In tiny Ormsby, North County Seed breeds soybeans to match the wishes of its international customers.

The 1st Congressional District of Minnesota includes the state's two southern tiers of counties, running along Interstate 90 just north of the Iowa border. It stretches 280 miles from the South Dakota border at Sioux Falls to the Wisconsin border at LaCrosse. Historically, this was a political borderland, with Civil War Republicans in the east and Farmer-Laborites more common in the west. Rochester had long been a Republican stronghold, though like many communities with large numbers of professionals, it has been trending toward the Democrats. Austin, with its working-class tradition, has long been solidly Democratic-Farmer-Labor. To the west, the population-losing farm counties between Mankato and the South Dakota border continue to vote solidly Republican. The district swung to Democratic presidential nominee Barack Obama in 2008, 51%-47%.

The congressman from the 1st District is Tim Walz, a Democrat elected in one of the biggest upsets of 2006. Walz grew up in Nebraska and joined the Army National Guard when he was 17. When he retired from the military 24 years later, in 2005, he held the rank of command sergeant major. Walz earned his teaching degree in Nebraska, taught school in China for a year through a Harvard University program, and later established an educational travel company that helped high school students study in China. He and his wife moved to Minnesota in 1996 to take teaching jobs in Mankato. There he taught high school geography and coached the high school football team to two state championships.

Walz got into politics relatively late in life—he was 42 when he ran for Congress. In 2004, Bush made an appearance in the area as part of his re-election campaign. Walz took two students to the event, where campaign staffers demanded to know whether he supported the president and barred the students from entering after discovering one of them had a sticker for Bush's Democratic opponent, John Kerry, on his wallet. Walz suggested that it might be bad PR for the Bush campaign to arrest an Army veteran, and he and the students were allowed in. But the campaign kept a close eye on them. Walz said the experience sparked his interest in politics, first as a volunteer for the Kerry campaign and then as a congressional candidate in 2006. "I don't know if I'd necessarily call it an epiphany, but it was definitely one of those things that pushed me into that," Walz said.

Walz challenged six-term Republican Rep. Gil Gutknecht, an affable conservative who won re-election in 2004 with 60%, 9 points better than Bush. The district had sent Republicans to Washington for 100 of the previous 114 years, and Gutknecht was not considered especially vulnerable in 2006. Walz was not a polished campaigner. His speaking style was didactic compared to the ease with which Gutknecht, a former auctioneer, handled a crowd. But Walz decried declining middle-class wages, tax cuts for the wealthy and Congress's failure to hold Bush accountable on the Iraq War. He ran as a political outsider and painted Gutknecht as too closely tied to Bush.

By October, Republicans began to take the threat against Gutknecht seriously. Walz had raised $870,000 by then, keeping pace with Gutknecht, who had raised $1.2 million. Walz enjoyed independent support from VoteVets, a Democratic-oriented group of Iraq and Afghanistan war veterans, and labor support from AFSCME, the large public-employees union. National Democrats ran ads that criticized Gutknecht for votes against increasing military benefits while raising his own pay. Gutknecht sought to halt his slide by characterizing Walz as a liberal who was out of sync with this socially conservative district. Walz's support for abortion rights and his opposition to a constitutional amendment against same-sex marriage fell outside district norms, but his opposition to gun control was compatible with them. His military experience and football coaching gave an aura of authenticity to his campaign that made it harder to attack. On Election Day, Walz defeated Gutknecht 53%-47%. Walz carried Democratic areas around Mankato and Austin and won Rochester's Olmsted County by more than 1,800 votes (52%-48%). He became the highest-ranking enlisted soldier ever to serve in Congress.

Arriving in the House, Walz was chosen by his peers to split the freshman-class presidency with Rep. Paul Hodes, a New Hampshire Democrat. Walz established a mostly centrist voting record. He voted against President Bush's troop "surge" in Iraq, but he opposed Democratic proposals to set a deadline for withdrawal. He backed improved security to control illegal immigration, but voted against building a fence along the border with Mexico. With a seat on the Agriculture Committee, Walz secured increased access to credit and conservation opportunities for farmers in the 2008 farm bill. His district had been among the leading recipients of federal largesse through the farm program. On another local issue, Walz lobbied to have a high-speed train route from the Twin Cities to Chicago go through Rochester. The train had been proposed by Rep. Betty McCollum, D-Minn., who wanted it to follow a route down the Mississippi River.

Walz was initially a top target for Republicans in the 2008 election. But the party's preferred contenders decided not to run. National Republicans turned their focus to keeping their existing seats. Walz breezed to a 63%-33% victory, winning in all of his district's counties.

SECOND DISTRICT

John Kline (R)

Elected 2002, 4th term; b. Sept. 6, 1947, Allentown, PA; home, Lakeville; Rice U., B.A. 1969, Shippensburg U., M.P.A. 1988; Christian; married (Vicky); 2 children.

Military Career: Marine Corps, 1969–94 (Vietnam).

Professional Career: V.P., Cntr. of the American Experiment, 2001–02.

DC Office: 1210 LHOB, 20515, 202-225-2271; Fax: 202-225-2595; Web site: kline.house.gov.

State Offices: Burnsville, 952-808-1213.

Committees: *Armed Services* (12th of 25 R): Military Personnel; Terrorism, Unconventional Threats & Capabilities. *Education & Labor* (RMM of 19 R): Health, Employment, Labor & Pensions; Workforce Protections.

Group Ratings

	ADA	ACLU	AFS	LCV	ITIC	NTU	COC	ACU	CFG	FRC
2008	15	18	14	8	43	61	94	88	78	100
2007	0	—	9	0	—	84	80	100	96	—

National Journal Ratings

	2007 LIB — 2007 CONS		2008 LIB — 2008 CONS	
Economic	9% —	90%	10% —	89%
Social	0% —	91%	9% —	85%
Foreign	0% —	72%	8% —	89%
Composite	9% —	91%	11% —	89%

Key Votes of the 110th Congress

1. Increase minimum wage	N	5. Share immigration data	Y	9. Withdraw troops 8/08	N
2. Expand SCHIP	N	6. Foreign aid abortion ban	Y	10. No operations in Iran	N
3. Raise CAFE standards	N	7. Ban gay bias in workplace	N	11. Free trade with Peru	Y
4. Bail out financial markets	Y	8. Repeal D.C. gun law	Y	12. Overhaul FISA	Y

Election Results

2008 general	John Kline (R)	220,924	(57%)	($1,484,962)
	Steve Sarvi (DFL)	164,093	(43%)	($559,474)
2008 primary	John Kline (R)	unopposed		

Prior Winning Percentages: 2006 (56%); 2004 (56%); 2002 (53%)

Population		Race/Ethnicity		Work	
Pop. 2007:	707,057	White:	88.4%	Private:	83.6%
Change since 2000:	Up 15.0%	Black:	2.7%	Government:	11.0%
Urban:	80.1%	Hispanic:	3.6%	Self-employed:	5.2%
Rural:	19.9%	Asian:	3.5%	Blue collar:	20.4%
Area size:	3,154 sq. mi.	Native Am.:	0.4%	White collar:	65.7%
		Hawaiian:	0.0%	Khaki collar:	0.1%
Age		Two+ races:	1.2%	Other:	13.9%
Median age:	34.8 yrs.			Median income:	$72,571
More than 65 yrs:	8.2%	*Ancestry*		Median home value:	$245,900
Less than 18 yrs:	27.7%	German:	30.1%	Poverty:	4.8%
		Norwegian:	10.9%		
Education		Irish:	10.0%	**Military Veterans**	
H.S. grad:	93.4%			% of Pop:	9.7%
College grad:	35.0%				
Grad degree:	9.7%				

Drive south from the Twin Cities and one encounters big-box-store parking lots and new housing developments inhabited by youngish families working in managerial, business and technical careers. Many come from elsewhere, attracted by Minnesota's strong economy and pleasant living, and tolerant of its cold winters. They have turned places such as Eagan, Lakeville, Apple Valley, Mendota Heights and Burnsville in Dakota County into fast-growing "mall" suburbs. More upscale are the sub-

2008 Presidential Vote		
McCain (R)............................198,960	(50%)
Obama (D) 193,213	(48%)
2004 Presidential Vote		
Bush (R)................................203,538	(54%)
Kerry (D)..............................169,704	(45%)
Cook Partisan Voting Index: R+4		

urbs of Scott and Carver counties; Scott County grew by an impressive 44% from 2000 to 2008. In recent years, these suburban areas have begun to see an influx of lower-income residents, attracted by the same good schools and low crime rates that attracted the earlier population. Drive farther south on Interstate 35—a little farther every year—and suddenly one is surrounded by farm country. There are also modest-sized towns such as Northfield, the idyllic home of Carleton College and its late professor-turned-liberal senator, Paul Wellstone. Northfield is 40 miles from Minneapolis and St. Paul, and some people there commute to the Twin Cities core on I-35.

These 'burbs and hamlets make up the 2nd Congressional District of Minnesota. Dakota County, just south of St. Paul, casts nearly half the votes in the district and historically was marginally Democratic, while the other counties were fairly heavily Republican. But in 1998, this was Jesse Ventura country. In that three-way race, he carried all of the district's counties, with a sharply increased turnout. As the suburbs have continued growing, Ventura country has become more Republican. George W. Bush narrowly carried Dakota County in 2000 and 2004, and it produced big margins for Republican Sen. Norm Coleman and GOP Gov. Tim Pawlenty in 2002. But in 2006, Democrat Amy Klobuchar showed that Democrats can still compete in Dakota County, capturing 56% there. In 2008, Dakota was split: Democratic presidential nominee Barack Obama won the county 52%-46%, while Coleman was again successful, 46%-38%. The only remaining Democratic-Farmer-Labor strongholds here are Rice County, home of Northfield, and Washington County. Republican presidential candidate John McCain won the district overall, 49.8%-48.3%.

The congressman from the 2nd District is John Kline, a Republican first elected in 2002. Kline grew up in Corpus Christi, Texas, where his father owned a small hometown newspaper and his mother managed the Corpus Christi Symphony Orchestra for more than 40 years. After graduating from Rice University, he served for 25 years in the Marine Corps. During the Vietnam War, he commanded Marine aviation forces in Somalia, and his duties included responsibility for the Corps' $50 billion program-objective memorandum, a budget and planning analysis. Later, he was assigned to the White House and carried the so-called "football" —the package containing the nuclear launch codes—for presidents Jimmy Carter and Ronald Reagan; he surely has had more face time with presidents than most other members of Congress. When he retired in 1994, he settled in Lakeville, in Dakota County, where he managed his wife's family farm.

In 1998, Kline challenged Democratic Rep. Bill Luther in the old Minnesota 6th District, after Luther had had several expensive and fierce campaigns to keep the seat. Kline favored tax cuts, more military spending and the resignation of President Bill Clinton in that year's impeachment proceedings. He also opposed abortion rights. He spent only $283,000; Luther, who raised $1 million in the cycle, spent only $412,000. That might have been a mistake. Luther won by only 50%-46%. Kline hardly stopped running. More experienced and better financed in 2000, he made a rematch with Luther one of the nation's high-profile House contests. The result was closer across the board, but Luther survived 50%-48%, and Kline said he was unlikely to run again.

Then the unexpected happened. The redistricting plan ordered into effect by the state Supreme Court in March 2002 placed Kline's home in a new 2nd District that included the home of no incumbent. Republican leaders in Minnesota and Washington urged Kline to run again, and he agreed. But Luther's home was in the new 6th District, which was a dozen miles north of the new 2nd and considerably more Republican after the redistricting. He decided to take on Kline in the 2nd District. The acrimonious campaign resumed where it had left off in 2000. Luther called Kline an extremist who held "Texas values." Luther's campaign manager encouraged Sam Garst, a Sierra Club activist and Luther supporter, to enter the race as a candidate of a new "No New Taxes" party—a purposefully deceptive banner designed to siphon votes from the Republican column. At first, the Luther campaign denied all connection with Garst, but Luther had to admit he did not discourage the action, and the local media harshly criticized the scheme as "un-Minnesotan." It turned out to be no contest. Kline won by a comfortable 53%-42%.

In the House, Kline's voting record has put him among the chamber's most conservative members. He proposed legislation to replace Ulysses S. Grant with former President Ronald Reagan on the $50 bill. He later became a trusted deputy of Minority Leader John Boehner and was given responsibilities at the National Republican Congressional Committee, the campaign arm of House Republicans.

On the Armed Services Committee, Kline made frequent trips to Iraq and applauded the improved security after President Bush's troop "surge." On the Education and Labor Committee, Kline was a conferee on pension legislation signed into law in 2006. He worked to include relief for struggling airlines, including Minnesota-based Northwest Airlines, by giving them more time to make contributions to employee pensions. The House also passed a Kline bill that would require states to adopt policies that prevent schools from forcing parents to medicate children with behavioral problems.

Backed by Minnesota corn growers, Kline sponsored legislation requiring that gasoline contain 10% blended ethanol by 2010. But some local officials were unhappy in 2007 when Kline said he would no longer seek spending earmarks for his district in appropriations bills "until integrity is restored" to the process. By then, Congress' longtime practice of earmarking had fallen into disfavor with conservatives, who said it led to wasteful spending.

In 2006, Democrats appeared to have found a strong candidate in Colleen Rowley, a retired Federal Bureau of Investigation agent who was one of *Time*'s three "Persons of the Year" in 2002 for going public with the FBI's decision to ignore recommendations to investigate Zacarias Moussaoui, a figure in the September 11 attacks. But as a first-time candidate, Rowley struggled to find her footing, and the party lost interest in her campaign. She was forced to apologize to Kline for portraying him on her website as the incompetent Colonel Klink, a Nazi prison-camp commandant from the television series *Hogan's Heroes*. While other Republicans distanced themselves from Bush and the Iraq War, Kline was forthright about his support for the war, emphasizing his background as a former Marine and as the father of a young Army Blackhawk helicopter pilot (son John Daniel Kline) who did a tour of duty in Iraq. Kline won re-election 56%-40% over Rowley. In 2008, he again won re-election easily, with 57%-43% over Iraq War veteran Steve Sarvi.

THIRD DISTRICT

Erik Paulsen (R)

Elected 2008, 1st term; b. May 14, 1965, Bakersfield, CA; home, Eden Prairie; Olaf Col., B.A. 1987; Lutheran; married (Kelly); 4 children.

Elected Office: MN House, 1995–2008, Majority ldr., 2002–06.

Professional Career: Marketing analyst, Target Corp.

DC Office: 126 CHOB, 20515, 202-225-2871; Fax: 202-225-6351; Web site: paulsen.house.gov.

State Offices: Eden Prairie, 952-405-8501.

Committees: *Financial Services* (28th of 29 R): Financial Institutions & Consumer Credit; International Monetary Policy & Trade; Oversight & Investigations.

Group Ratings and Key Votes: Newly Elected

Election Results

2008 general	Erik Paulsen (R)	178,932	(48%)	($2,744,927)
	Ashwin Madia (DFL)	150,787	(41%)	($2,726,040)
	David Dillon (Ind)	38,970	(11%)	($161,181)
2008 primary	Erik Paulsen (R)	unopposed		

Population		Race/Ethnicity		Work	
Pop. 2007:	650,437	White:	82.6%	Private:	85.2%
Change since 2000:	Up 5.8%	Black:	6.3%	Government:	8.8%
Urban:	95.8%	Hispanic:	3.2%	Self-employed:	5.8%
Rural:	4.2%	Asian:	5.6%	Blue collar:	15.6%
Area size:	513 sq. mi.	Native Am.:	0.4%	White collar:	72.1%
Age		Hawaiian:	0.0%	Khaki collar:	0.0%
Median age:	38.9 yrs.	Two+ races:	1.6%	Other:	12.3%
More than 65 yrs:	11.1%	*Ancestry*		Median income:	$72,151
Less than 18 yrs:	26.1%	German:	23.4%	Median home value:	$273,300
Education		Norwegian:	11.1%	Poverty:	5.6%
H.S. grad:	94.4%	Irish:	8.7%	**Military Veterans**	
College grad:	42.5%			% of Pop:	10.1%
Grad degree:	13.3%				

Over the past half century, Minnesota's great twin metropolis has spread out from the neat streets inside the city limits of Minneapolis and St. Paul into the countryside all around. People have sorted themselves out geographically. In the lower lands along the Mississippi and Minnesota rivers, where rail lines fan out from the Twin Cities, are the blue-collar suburbs, with modest houses on grid streets and warehouses and factories near the tracks. In-

2008 Presidential Vote		
Obama (D)	200,240	(52%)
McCain (R)	175,728	(46%)
2004 Presidential Vote		
Bush (R)	190,339	(51%)
Kerry (D)	179,488	(48%)
Cook Partisan Voting Index:	EVEN	

land, around the lakes Minnesota is so proud of, in subdivisions with curved streets hugging the hills, are the Twin Cities' more affluent neighborhoods, quiet and unflashy in the Minnesota way, but comfortable whether blanketed with snow or with a nearby lake glinting in the summer sun. At the edge of Lake Minnetonka is Wayzata, the monied suburb that is the top ZIP code in Minnesota for political donations. In between are the freeway interchanges where some of the Twin Cities' great innovations can be seen—Southdale Shopping Center in Edina, the first enclosed mall and site of the first B. Dalton store, which begat the national book chains; huge indoor water parks; and the giant Mall of America, with its 4.2 million square feet, 520 stores, 86 eating options, 14 theaters, eight nightclubs and 11,000 year-round employees. Another nearly 6 million square feet, which include a 5,000-seat performing arts center and a rail connection to downtown Minneapolis, are in the works. The mall is the nation's No. 1 tourist attraction, attracting 40 million people annually.

The 3rd Congressional District of Minnesota takes in Hennepin County suburbs north, south and west of Minneapolis. On the north side of the district is working-class Brooklyn Park, long a Democratic-Farmer-Labor Party stronghold but more famous now for its former mayor, Jesse Ventura, the celebrity wrestler-turned-governor. On the south is middle-income Bloomington, home of the Mall of America. To the west are Edina, Plymouth, Wayzata and other towns around Lake Minnetonka, all traditionally Republican. It is the district's largest lake, and these are the most affluent communities in the Twin Cities area. The district is home to the headquarters of such diverse companies as Cargill and Radisson Hotels, and has large biotech facilities in Brooklyn Park and Maple Grove. This area trended Democratic in the 1990s, when Bill Clinton twice won pluralities here. The 3rd may be the home of Minnesota's traditional Republican establishment, but it voted just 51% for George W. Bush in 2004. In 2008, it flipped to the Democratic column, voting for Barack Obama 52%-46%.

The new congressman from the 3rd District is Erik Paulsen, a Republican elected in 2008 to succeed his retiring former boss, Republican Rep. Jim Ramstad. Raised in the Twin City suburbs, Paulsen was the oldest of four children. He attended nearby St. Olaf College, where he met his wife, Kelly, in a math class. After graduation, Paulsen followed a lifelong dream to work a summer in Yellowstone National Park, then returned to the Twin Cities to begin a career in marketing. He later took a job in Ramstad's Washington office, where he worked for a year and a half before returning to Minnesota as the director of Ramstad's district office. In 1995, he was elected to the Minnesota House of Representatives, rising to majority leader in 2003. He was a leading supporter of Republican Gov. Tim Pawlenty's no-new-taxes pledge. While in the Legislature, Paulsen also worked as a business analyst for the Minneapolis-based Target Corp.

Paulsen announced his candidacy for Ramstad's seat in January 2008. He faced no competition for the nomination and got an early fundraising lead. Democratic newcomer Ashwin Madia, an Iraq war veteran, was his opponent in the general election. Madia had upset better-known state Sen. Terri Bonoff to secure the Democratic-Farmer-Labor Party nomination, and he soon pulled even with Paulsen in the polls, making it a very competitive contest. At the Republican National Convention in September in Minneapolis-St. Paul, Paulsen was given a speaking role to help raise his profile. In his remarks, he emphasized fiscal discipline and called himself "one of a new generation of Republican reformers." On the stump, he emphasized his differences with Madia on taxes, contrasting his support for making the Bush-era tax cuts permanent with Madia's position allowing them to expire for people with annual incomes over $250,000.

The campaign was punctuated by negative ads. The Democratic Congressional Campaign Committee invested heavily in the race, with ads that attempted to link Paulsen to a Republican fundraiser at a Las Vegas strip club. Madia disavowed those attacks, but Paulsen complained that Madia could have had them pulled but didn't. Hitting back, Paulsen charged in his ads that Madia was lying about his own voting record and said Madia would vote for tax increases. The National Republican Congressional Committee ran an ad in the final days of the campaign that the Madia camp said deliberately depicted Madia's skin tone as darker than it is. Madia is of Indian descent. The NRCC denied it. Groups supporting Madia outspent Paulsen's backers nearly 4-to-1. The two candidates were neck and neck in fundraising, each raising $2.7 million. A third candidate, businessman David Dillon, ran as an independent. He raised little money but campaigned energetically.

Polls going into voting showed a tight race. Paulsen emerged the winner, with 48% to Madia's 41%. Dillon picked up a respectable 11%, drawing support in areas where Madia needed to perform well. Even as Obama won the district by 6 percentage points, Paulsen got strong support in Bloomington and Coon Rapids to ward off the national Democratic wave.

Paulsen was appointed to the House Financial Services Committee, where the first bill he sponsored was a measure to recoup some of the big executive bonuses paid by AIG after the failing insurance giant was bailed out by the government.

FOURTH DISTRICT

Betty McCollum (D)

Elected 2000, 5th term; b. July 12, 1954, Minneapolis; home, St. Paul; Inver Hills Comm. Col., A.A. 1980, Col. of St. Catherine, B.A. 1987; Catholic; divorced; 2 children.

Elected Office: N. St. Paul City Cncl., 1986–92; MN House of Reps., 1992–2000.

Professional Career: Teacher; Retail sales & management.

DC Office: 1714 LHOB, 20515, 202-225-6631; Fax: 202-225-1968; Web site: mccollum.house.gov.

State Offices: St. Paul, 651-224-9191.

Committees: *Appropriations* (29th of 37 D): Labor, HHS, Education & Related Agencies; Legislative Branch; State, Foreign Operations & Related Programs. *Budget* (12th of 24 D).

Group Ratings

	ADA	ACLU	AFS	LCV	ITIC	NTU	COC	ACU	CFG	FRC
2008	100	100	100	100	71	5	56	0	0	5
2007	90	—	100	95	—	3	58	0	12	—

National Journal Ratings

	2007 LIB	—	2007 CONS		2008 LIB	—	2008 CONS
Economic	82%	—	0%		85%	—	0%
Social	77%	—	17%		82%	—	0%
Foreign	86%	—	11%		92%	—	0%
Composite	86%	—	14%		93%	—	7%

Key Votes of the 110th Congress

1. Increase minimum wage	Y	5. Share immigration data	N	9. Withdraw troops 8/08	Y
2. Expand SCHIP	Y	6. Foreign aid abortion ban	N	10. No operations in Iran	Y
3. Raise CAFE standards	Y	7. Ban gay bias in workplace	Y	11. Free trade with Peru	Y
4. Bail out financial markets	Y	8. Repeal D.C. gun law	N	12. Overhaul FISA	N

Election Results

2008 general	Betty McCollum (DFL)	216,267	(68%)	($719,710)
	Ed Matthews (R)	98,936	(31%)	($79,648)
2008 primary	Betty McCollum (DFL)	unopposed		

Prior Winning Percentages: 2006 (70%); 2004 (57%); 2002 (62%); 2000 (48%)

Population		Race/Ethnicity		Work	
Pop. 2007:	600,252	White:	74.8%	Private:	81.4%
Change since 2000:	Down 2.4%	Black:	8.3%	Government:	13.5%
Urban:	99.9%	Hispanic:	6.3%	Self-employed:	5.0%
Rural:	0.1%	Asian:	7.9%	Blue collar:	17.2%
Area size:	220 sq. mi.	Native Am.:	0.5%	White collar:	67.2%
Age		Hawaiian:	0.0%	Khaki collar:	0.1%
Median age:	36.8 yrs.	Two+ races:	1.9%	Other:	15.5%
More than 65 yrs:	12.3%	*Ancestry*		Median income:	$53,233
Less than 18 yrs:	24.4%	German:	22.9%	Median home value:	$225,200
Education		Irish:	10.4%	Poverty:	12.8%
H.S. grad:	90.5%	Norwegian:	8.1%	**Military Veterans**	
College grad:	36.7%			% of Pop:	9.6%
Grad degree:	14.0%				

Above the Mississippi River bluffs stand the two great landmarks of St. Paul: the Minnesota Capitol and Archbishop Ireland's Cathedral. This is the older and smaller of the Twin Cities, settled mainly by Catholic Irish and German immigrants in the 1850s, while Minneapolis was attracting Protestant Swedes and Yankees. St. Paul became a major transportation hub, a railroad center and river port, while Minneapolis, farther upriver at the Falls of St. Anthony, became the nation's largest grain-milling center. Both industries stoked the ire of farmers in the Dakotas who had no choice but to deal

2008 Presidential Vote		
Obama (D)	217,984	(64%)
McCain (R)	113,600	(34%)
2004 Presidential Vote		
Kerry (D)	205,467	(62%)
Bush (R)	123,313	(37%)
Cook Partisan Voting Index:	D + 13	

with them to make a living. Beneath the Capitol and the cathedral, the city's skywalk-linked downtown is home to the Ordway Music Theater, the headquarters of Minnesota Public Radio and an active pop-music industry; the Winter Carnival is an annual highlight. Beyond the cathedral is Summit Avenue, on which capitalists like the Great Northern Railway's James J. Hill built grandiose Romanesque houses. With Monument Avenue in Richmond and Meridian Street in Indianapolis, it remains one of America's grand 19th century residential boulevards. The parallel Grand Avenue is home to a pleasant commercial strip with a walkable, urban feel; more modest neighborhoods elsewhere are notable for their grid streets lined with sturdy houses. In recent years, St. Paul has had a mixed bag of results in economic development. It scored a major coup by landing the 2008 Republican National Convention at its state-of-the-art Xcel Energy Center. But its fading industrial base took a blow when Ford Motor Co. announced that it would close its local plant by September 2009, at a cost of nearly 1,000 jobs. The facility made Ranger light trucks.

Minnesota's 4th Congressional District is made up of St. Paul, the Ramsey County suburbs to the north, and the southern suburbs of West St. Paul and South St. Paul. When a special panel of judges drew the new districts in 2002, they rejected a Republican proposal to combine Minneapolis and St. Paul into one district and made only modest changes in the boundaries. St. Paul was one of the most Democratic parts of Minnesota even before the Democratic-Farmer-Labor Party was formed in 1944, and it remained proudly DFL for a half-century. It voted to re-elect Mayor Norm Coleman in 1997 after he switched to the Republican party, but he failed to carry a single precinct in the city when he ran successfully for the Senate in 2002, and he lost Ramsey County 60% to 40% in his 2008 re-election bid. The area has become home to more than 24,000 Hmong immigrants, the largest concentration in any American city. The Hmong had been recruited by the Central Intelligence Agency and U.S. Special Forces during the Vietnam War and resettled here after Laos fell to the Communists in 1975. Another 5,000 refugees arrived from Thailand in 2004 and 2005. The 4th District seat has been held by the DFL since it elected Rep. Eugene McCarthy in 1948, and remains the second most Democratic district in the state.

The congresswoman from the 4th District is Betty McCollum, a Democrat first elected in 2000. The daughter of a military intelligence officer, she grew up in North St. Paul and graduated from the College of St. Catherine. For 11 years, she taught high school social studies and then was a retail sales manager for 14 years at Dayton's department store. She was also raising two children. After one of them was hurt on a slide in a city park, McCollum tried without success to get the city of North St. Paul to make immediate repairs. So in 1986, she ran for the North St. Paul City Council and was elected. She served until 1992, when she was elected to the state House of Representatives after defeating incumbents in both the primary and general.

In February 2000, Democratic Rep. Bruce Vento announced that he had malignant mesothelioma and would not seek re-election. He died on October 10, 2000. McCollum was endorsed by the Democratic-Farmer-Labor Party in the September primary. She faced three opponents, but with the DFL's endorsement, McCollum won easily, with 50% to 23% for state Sen. Steve Novak. Republicans nominated state Sen. Linda Runbeck, a vigorously anti-abortion candidate. McCollum backed prescription-drug coverage under Medicare and opposed tax cuts before Congress paid down the debt. Runbeck, who opposed gun control and took conservative positions on health care and education, attacked McCollum and her Democratic allies for running "hateful, vicious attack ads" that distorted her positions on guns. This was a three-way race, thanks to the candidacy of former Ramsey County prosecutor Tom Foley, a longtime DFLer who ran on the ticket of Gov. Jesse Ventura's Independence Party. Once again, McCollum won unexpectedly easily, 48%-31%, with 21% for Foley.

In the House, McCollum has a consistently liberal voting record. She is an ally of House Speaker Nancy Pelosi, whom she calls a mentor, and delivered the speech formally nominating Pelosi as party whip in October 2001. With Pelosi's help, McCollum has secured some plums, including a seat on the House Democratic Steering and Policy Committee and in 2006, the Appropriations Committee seat that had been held by former Rep. Martin Sabo, a Minnesota Democrat. In the 111th Congress (2009-10), McCollum was given a seat on the Budget Committee. Pelosi also named McCollum to a task force to consider how to enforce House ethics rules.

Earlier, McCollum worked on the Bush administration's No Child Left Behind education bill as a member of the Education and Labor panel and backed the House version of the bill; later, she joined the opposing camp because she said the administration had not put sufficient money into the program to make it work. She also sponsored legislation that would crack down on diploma mills that sell worthless degrees.

On the Foreign Affairs Committee, McCollum was a vocal critic of the war in Iraq, citing faulty intelligence as a reason for her strong opposition. In 2007, she was the chief House sponsor of the Global Child Survival Act, an attempt to decrease child-mortality rates.

An important local project for McCollum has been the Central Corridor, an 11-mile light-rail link between downtown St. Paul and Minneapolis. She had secured an initial $2 million for the project and was incensed when conservative Republicans targeted proposed additional funding as pork barrel spending. She and Republican Gov. Tim Pawlenty clashed over her insistence that he sign a statement supporting congressional funding for the project. When Pawlenty vetoed a companion state funding plan in April 2008, the project seemed dead; McCollum called the veto "reckless and irresponsible." Following the collapse of the Interstate 35W bridge over the Mississippi River in August 2007, she backed an increase in gasoline taxes for nationwide infrastructure rebuilding.

McCollum has been re-elected easily. In 2004, Peter Vento, son of the late congressman, ran as the Independent Party nominee. But he did not campaign much and got just 9% of the vote. McCollum is sometimes mentioned as a possible statewide candidate, but she has declined opportunities to run.

In 2008, she voiced unusually tough criticism of Democrat Al Franken in his campaign to unseat Republican Sen. Coleman. In May, she called some of the comedian's written work, which had appeared in *Playboy* and other publications, "pornographic writings that are indefensible." Then in August, McCollum, reverting to form as a party loyalist, endorsed Franken and said she would vote for him. In January, after the state canvassing board certified him as the winner in his close contest with Coleman, McCollum said Franken should be immediately seated.

FIFTH DISTRICT

Keith Ellison (D)

Elected 2006, 2nd term; b. Aug. 4, 1963, Detroit, MI; home, Minneapolis; Wayne St. U., B.A. 1985, U. of MN, J.D. 1990; Muslim; married (Kim); 4 children.

Elected Office: MN House of Reps., 2002–06.

Professional Career: Practicing atty., 1990–2002.

DC Office: 1122 LHOB, 20515, 202-225-4755; Fax: 202-225-4886; Web site: ellison.house.gov.

State Offices: Minneapolis, 612-522-1212.

Committees: *Financial Services* (25th of 42 D): Domestic Monetary Policy & Technology; Financial Institutions & Consumer Credit; Housing & Community Opportunity. *Foreign Affairs* (26th of 28 D): International Organizations, Human Rights & Oversight; Middle East & South Asia.

Group Ratings

	ADA	ACLU	AFS	LCV	ITIC	NTU	COC	ACU	CFG	FRC
2008	100	100	100	100	86	8	56	0	4	5
2007	100	—	100	100	—	6	50	0	6	—

National Journal Ratings

	2007 LIB — 2007 CONS			2008 LIB — 2008 CONS		
Economic	82%	—	0%	85%	—	0%
Social	89%	—	8%	82%	—	0%
Foreign	96%	—	0%	85%	—	8%
Composite	93%	—	7%	91%	—	9%

Key Votes of the 110th Congress

1. Increase minimum wage	Y	5. Share immigration data	N	9. Withdraw troops 8/08	Y
2. Expand SCHIP	Y	6. Foreign aid abortion ban	N	10. No operations in Iran	Y
3. Raise CAFE standards	Y	7. Ban gay bias in workplace	Y	11. Free trade with Peru	N
4. Bail out financial markets	Y	8. Repeal D.C. gun law	N	12. Overhaul FISA	N

Election Results

2008 general	Keith Ellison (DFL)	228,776	(71%)	($1,476,449)
	Barb White (R)	71,020	(22%)	($55,796)
	Bill McGaughey (Ind)	22,318	(7%)	
2008 primary	Keith Ellison (DFL)	33,988	(84%)	
	Gregg Iverson (DFL)	6,251	(16%)	

Prior Winning Percentages: 2006 (56%)

Population		Race/Ethnicity		Work	
Pop. 2007:	590,659	White:	69.0%	Private:	82.3%
Change since 2000:	Down 3.9%	Black:	13.6%	Government:	12.2%
Urban:	100.0%	Hispanic:	8.4%	Self-employed:	5.4%
Rural:	0.0%	Asian:	4.8%	Blue collar:	16.6%
Area size:	130 sq. mi.	Native Am.:	1.0%	White collar:	65.9%
		Hawaiian:	0.0%	Khaki collar:	0.0%
Age		Two+ races:	2.7%	Other:	17.5%
Median age:	35.5 yrs.			Median income:	$48,483
More than 65 yrs:	10.9%	*Ancestry*		Median home value:	$225,300
Less than 18 yrs:	21.0%	German:	18.6%	Poverty:	16.3%
		Norwegian:	9.3%		
Education		Irish:	8.4%	**Military Veterans**	
H.S. grad:	88.6%			% of Pop:	8.7%
College grad:	38.7%				
Grad degree:	13.4%				

From almost nowhere in Minneapolis today can you see the geographic feature that created the city: the Falls of St. Anthony, the head of navigation on the Mississippi River, where waters rush in rapids beneath low built-up downtown bridges. In olden days, every riverboat had to stop here, and the waterpower generated by the falls was the energy source first for the pioneers' grist mills and then for the giant grain mills that processed northern Great Plains wheat into food for the United States. By 1890, Minneapo-

2008 Presidential Vote

Obama (D)	254,796	(74%)
McCain (R)	81,757	(24%)

2004 Presidential Vote

Kerry (D)	237,418	(71%)
Bush (R)	92,797	(28%)

Cook Partisan Voting Index: D + 23

lis and St. Paul made up one of America's largest urban areas, living mainly off grain. Today, Minneapolis is a center of high-technology industry, banking and finance. It is the center of an economic region that extends almost 1,000 miles to the Rocky Mountains in Montana.

The city of Minneapolis, plus a few of its older, adjoining suburbs, make up the 5th Congressional District. In the southwest corner are the affluent neighborhoods around Lake Calhoun and Lake Harriet—long built-up and proudly maintained, amidst trees that turn beautifully golden in early autumn. Not far away are Minneapolis's skywalk-laced downtown skyscrapers, the museum quarter on the hill above Hennepin Avenue, and the Hubert H. Humphrey Metrodome, nicknamed the "Homerdome." Straddling the Mississippi River is the University of Minnesota, which has fostered the area's cutting-edge biotechnology research and medical innovations, and nearby Dinkytown, a student area where Robert Zimmerman discovered folk music and reinvented himself as Bob Dylan. Most of the 5th District is low on the income scale. Many of the working-class neighborhoods of small frame houses and ample parks are now kept up by new immigrants. The city is a haven for single young people. According to 2008 Census Bureau figures, it ranked second highest among cities for households of people living alone, and fourth lowest in elderly population.

For a place often thought of as monochromatically white and Scandinavian, the city is surprisingly diverse. To the northeast, behind the railroad and warehouse district along the Mississippi, are many Hmong from Laos. Hennepin County is home to the largest number of African immigrants in the state, following a decade in which African immigrants to Minnesota jumped sevenfold. The Jewish community here has increased as immigrants have come from the former Soviet Union. Ticket machines on the new Hiawatha Avenue light-rail line, from downtown to the airport and the Mall of America, do business in four languages—English, Spanish, Hmong and Somali. The 5th is the most heavily Democratic district in the state. Minneapolis's political liberalism is drawn from the Yankee tradition of clean government, the Scandinavian tradition of cooperative enterprise and the industrial-labor tradition of economic redistribution. Democratic presidential candidates Al Gore and John Kerry carried this district by more than 2-to-1 in 2000 and 2004 respectively. Barack Obama did better yet, with 74% to Republican John McCain's 24%.

The congressman from the 5th District is Keith Ellison, a Democrat elected in 2006. Ellison, previously a relatively unknown state legislator, garnered international attention when he became the first Muslim to serve in Congress and the first black representative from Minnesota. He was raised Catholic in Detroit, the son of a psychiatrist and the third of five boys. (Four became lawyers and the fifth a doctor.) Ellison studied economics at Wayne State University, and it was there that he converted to Sunni Islam. He moved to Minnesota in 1987 to study law at the University of Minnesota, worked in private practice, and ran a nonprofit criminal-defense firm while also hosting a public-affairs radio show. Ellison won the first of two terms in the state House in 2002.

The retirement of Democratic Rep. Martin Olav Sabo, who had held the seat since 1978, unleashed a torrent of pent-up political ambition. Nearly a dozen Democrats sought the party endorsement at the May 2006 Democratic-Farmer-Labor district convention. But the main contenders were Ellison, former DFL chairman and longtime Sabo aide Mike Erlandson, and former state Sen. Ember Reichgott Junge. Ellison, who strongly opposed the war in Iraq, attracted support from war opponents and key backers of the late Democratic Sen. Paul Wellstone. "I have the passion of a Wellstone and the practicality of a Sabo," he told convention activists. Ellison easily won the DFL endorsement, but Erlandson and Reichgott Junge did not heed the endorsement and competed for the Democratic nomination in a seven-way September 12 primary.

Ellison campaigned on his opposition to the war and on the need for environmental justice and government-funded universal health care. But he had to overcome a number of unhelpful personal revelations: unpaid parking tickets and moving violations that led to multiple suspensions of his driver's license; $25,000 he once owed in back taxes; and two fines from the state campaign-finance board for late filings. Most damaging were his ties to the controversial Nation of Islam leader Louis Farrakhan and Farrakhan's anti-Semitic pronouncements. Ellison said his association with the group was limited to 18 months during which he helped organize the 1995 Million Man March in Washington, D.C., although his writings about Farrakhan were traced back to his law-school days. Ellison reached out to local Jewish leaders, insisting that he'd been unaware of the group's anti-Semitic views. He relied on direct mail and grassroots campaigning and identifying potential new voters. Reichgott Junge courted suburban voters, while Erlandson, backed by Sabo, courted senior citizens. Despite the personal baggage, Ellison won the primary with 41%, followed by Erlandson with 31% and Reichgott Junge with 21%.

Heavily favored in the general election, Ellison faced two third-party candidates and Republican Alan Fine, who described Ellison as "an embarrassment to our district, our state, our country, and our world." But Ellison won with 56% of vote, while Fine and Independence Party candidate Tammy Lee each won 21%. Controversy followed Ellison after the election. A conservative commentator stirred up opposition to Ellison's plan to take the oath of office with the Quran, rather than the Bible. "If you are incapable of taking an oath on that book, don't serve in Congress," radio talk-show host Dennis Prager wrote on the Internet. In a politically adept move, Ellison borrowed a Quran from the Library of Congress that was once owned by Thomas Jefferson.

In the House, Ellison got a seat on the Judiciary Committee and again found himself the center of controversy in July 2007, when he compared September 11 to the burning of the Reichstag building in Nazi Germany, an event used by Adolph Hitler to suspend civil liberties. Several House Republicans wrote to Democratic House Speaker Nancy Pelosi asking her to reprimand Ellison, but he soon backed away from the comparison, saying, "It was probably inappropriate to use that example, because it's a unique historical event, without any clear parallels."

Ellison established a liberal voting record. On the Financial Services Committee, he challenged predatory-lending practices and foreclosures by credit-card and mortgage companies, which he said "have torn holes in the fabric of neighborhoods" in Minneapolis and across the nation. In November 2007, the House passed the Anti-Predatory Lending Act, which included provisions he helped craft.

He has championed the creation of a Department of Peace. In January 2009, he was one of 22 House members, all Democrats, who voted "present" on a resolution recognizing Israel's right to defend itself against attacks from Gaza. In December 2008, he became the first member of Congress to make the Hajj pilgrimage to the Muslim holy city of Mecca, later describing it as a "transformative" experience.

Ellison was an early supporter of Democrat Barack Obama for president, but said that he and other Muslims were frustrated by the candidate's refusal to appear at a mosque during the campaign. In 2008, Ellison was re-elected easily.

SIXTH DISTRICT

Michele Bachmann (R)

Elected 2006, 2nd term; b. April 6, 1956, Waterloo, IA; home, Stillwater; Winona State U., B.A. 1978, Oral Roberts U., J.D. 1986, Col. of William and Mary, LL.M. 1988; Lutheran; married (Marcus); 5 children.

Elected Office: MN Senate, 2000–06.

Professional Career: Practicing atty., 1995–2000.

DC Office: 107 CHOB, 20515, 202-225-2331; Fax: 202-225-6475; Web site: bachmann.house.gov.

State Offices: Waite Park, 320-253-5931; Woodbury, 651-731-5400.

Committees: *Financial Services* (21st of 29 R): Capital Markets, Insurance & Government Sponsored Enterprises; International Monetary Policy & Trade; Oversight & Investigations.

Group Ratings

	ADA	ACLU	AFS	LCV	ITIC	NTU	COC	ACU	CFG	FRC
2008	0	18	14	8	29	81	94	100	91	100
2007	0	—	9	0	—	86	75	100	98	—

National Journal Ratings

	2007 LIB	—	2007 CONS		2008 LIB	—	2008 CONS
Economic	6%	—	93%		6%	—	93%
Social	9%	—	85%		15%	—	85%
Foreign	0%	—	72%		8%	—	89%
Composite	11%	—	89%		10%	—	90%

Key Votes of the 110th Congress

1. Increase minimum wage	N	5. Share immigration data	Y	9. Withdraw troops 8/08	N
2. Expand SCHIP	N	6. Foreign aid abortion ban	Y	10. No operations in Iran	N
3. Raise CAFE standards	N	7. Ban gay bias in workplace	N	11. Free trade with Peru	Y
4. Bail out financial markets	N	8. Repeal D.C. gun law	*	12. Overhaul FISA	Y

Election Results

2008 general	Michele Bachmann (R)	187,817	(46%)	($3,565,248)
	El Tinklenberg (DFL)	175,786	(43%)	($2,515,420)
	Bob Anderson (Ind)	40,643	(10%)	
2008 primary	Michele Bachmann (R)	19,127	(86%)	
	Aubrey Immelman (R)	3,134	(14%)	

Prior Winning Percentages: 2006 (50%)

Population		Race/Ethnicity		Work	
Pop. 2007:	720,572	White:	92.3%	Private:	82.9%
Change since 2000:	Up 17.2%	Black:	1.6%	Government:	11.0%
Urban:	63.8%	Hispanic:	1.7%	Self-employed:	5.9%
Rural:	36.2%	Asian:	2.5%	Blue collar:	24.3%
Area size:	3,237 sq. mi.	Native Am.:	0.4%	White collar:	61.8%
		Hawaiian:	0.0%	Khaki collar:	0.1%
Age		Two+ races:	1.2%	Other:	13.8%
Median age:	34.4 yrs.			Median income:	$68,195
More than 65 yrs:	8.3%	*Ancestry*		Median home value:	$233,600
Less than 18 yrs:	26.7%	German:	31.3%	Poverty:	6.4%
		Norwegian:	10.5%		
Education		Irish:	8.4%	**Military Veterans**	
H.S. grad:	92.8%			% of Pop:	10.1%
College grad:	28.4%				
Grad degree:	8.3%				

The earliest settlers of the Twin Cities of Minneapolis and St. Paul came up the Mississippi River or up the rail lines that were soon built on the bottomlands beside it. They lived within walking distance of the mills and factories and rail yards. As the first streetcars and then automobiles allowed them to live farther from work, they spread out in St. Paul and Minneapolis and then all around the lake-strewn countryside. The flatlands are bleak here when the winter sun struggles to shine through

2008 Presidential Vote		
McCain (R)............................219,936	(53%)
Obama (D) 183,950	(45%)

2004 Presidential Vote		
Bush (R)................................216,574	(57%)
Kerry (D)..............................161,601	(42%)

Cook Partisan Voting Index: R + 7

gray clouds. The lakes are often surrounded by, and sometimes indistinguishable from, swamps. Stillwater, an old lumber-mill town built by pioneers on the hills above the St. Croix River, once nearly became Minnesota's capital, but later turned into an economic backwater, its Victorian structures ill tended. Even so, the creativity and productivity of Minnesotans have turned this superficially grim countryside into some of the nation's most pleasant suburbs. Taking maximum advantage of their lakes, they refurbished old towns and farmhouses and built comfortable homes in new subdivisions.

The 6th Congressional District of Minnesota is a suburban and exurban district north of St. Paul and Minneapolis. It dips as far south and east as Stillwater, with new riverfront housing developments along the St. Croix. It spreads north over Washington and Anoka counties, just north of the Twin Cities, with a mix of upscale and working-class suburbs. To the northwest, along the Mississippi River, are Wright, Sherburne and Benton counties, which have grown rapidly from a combined total of 141,000 people in 1990 to 247,000 in 2008. Young voters, usually from ancestrally Democratic-Farmer-Labor Party families, have become the key swing voters. Farther to the northwest, the district also includes the eastern half of St. Cloud-based Stearns County, a heavily German-Catholic area and a stronghold of anti-abortion rights sentiment. The 1990s saw an influx of Vietnamese, Chinese and Japanese into St. Cloud. And since 2000, several thousand Somalis have moved in and started up their own businesses. In 1998, the district, especially the fast-growing counties, was Jesse Ventura country; newcomers tended to vote Republican. George W. Bush carried the district 52%-42% in 2000 and 57%-42% in 2004, the latter his best showing in any Minnesota district. Likewise, Republican presidential candidate John McCain won here 53%-45% in 2008, his best in the state.

The congresswoman for the 6th District is Michele Bachmann, a Republican elected in 2006. Bachmann grew up in cities across the Midwest and attended Winona State University, where she met her husband while working on Democrat Jimmy Carter's 1976 presidential campaign. She became disillusioned with Carter and his party's position on abortion rights, and gravitated toward Ronald Reagan and the Republican Party. Bachmann and her husband, Marcus, both born-again Christians, moved to Tulsa, where she earned a degree at Coburn Law School at Oral Roberts University. After studying tax law at the College of William and Mary, Bachmann landed a job as a U.S. Treasury Department attorney in St. Paul, arguing criminal and civil tax cases. Her political career began in 1999, with a losing bid for the Stillwater school board. A year later, she won a seat in the state Senate by defeating a moderate Republican incumbent for the party's endorsement and then in the primary. In 2002, she defeated a ten-year Democratic incumbent when redistricting put them in the same state Senate district. In the Legislature, Bachmann sought to protect private-property rights, limit government spending and cut taxes. She was a prominent abortion-rights opponent and gained notoriety in 2004 for leading an unsuccessful fight for a state constitutional amendment to ban same-sex marriage.

When Republican incumbent Mark Kennedy gave up the 6th District seat to run for the U.S. Senate, Bachmann entered the Republican primary as the candidate to beat; she clinched the nomination at the party convention by defeating three other candidates. She had a following among social conservatives, but her stances also made her a polarizing figure. Clear ideological differences separated Bachmann and her Democratic opponent, Patty Wetterling, in the general election. Wetterling became a nationally recognized advocate for missing children after her 11-year-old son, Jacob, was abducted in 1989 and never found. Her support for abortion rights, her call for the withdrawal of U.S. troops from Iraq, and her opposition to a constitutional amendment outlawing same-sex marriage prompted Republicans to portray her as too liberal for this suburban and exurban seat. Neither candidate lacked money. Wetterling spent more than $3 million to Bachmann's $2.7 million. President Bush helped Bachmann raise money, and Wetterling enjoyed support from EMILY's List.

Bachmann downplayed her social positions and instead emphasized her opposition to taxes. Wetterling trailed in polls until October, when the congressional-page scandal suddenly thrust her into the national spotlight. With her background in child advocacy, Wetterling emerged as a top party spokeswoman on the scandal, in which Republican Rep. Mark Foley was discovered to have sent sexually explicit e-mails to young congressional pages. Democratic leaders tapped her to deliver the party's weekly radio address. But Bachmann was well-positioned to weather the political fallout. She is the mother of five children and, while in the Legislature, had sponsored legislation establishing a task force on Internet crimes against juveniles. She had also been a foster parent to 23 children. Polls showed that Wetterling had surged ahead after the scandal broke, but her lead was fleeting. In a political atmosphere that could not have been more hostile for Republicans, Bachmann won a decisive 50%-42% victory.

In the House, Bachmann has a strongly conservative voting record. She has received more than the usual share of attention for a junior House member because of her outspoken style. She has a good ear for issues that play well with conservatives, including her refusal to seek earmarks for her district, her opposition to the bailout of the financial markets in 2008, and her support for development of new energy resources when gas prices spiked. Some of the attention was less favorable. In early 2007, she said that Iran planned to split Iraq into two parts, one of them a "terrorist haven" that would launch attacks on the United States. When asked for evidence to support such a claim, Bachmann said her comments might have been "misconstrued."

In October 2008, she created a national sensation during the presidential contest when she went on MSNBC's *Hardball* political talk show and said that Democratic nominee Barack Obama "may have anti-American views." National Democrats sought to make Bachmann a poster child for intolerance. The publicity led to an immediate tightening of her re-election contest with Democratic challenger Elwyn Tinklenberg, a former state transportation commissioner. Nearly $2 million flowed into his campaign during the weeks that followed. In her defense, Bachmann said, "I have strong views," and she accused the show's host, Chris Matthews, of "full-fledged distortion" and the bloggers who'd picked up the story of being "motivated entirely by their hatred of me and my conservative beliefs."

Bachmann was aided by early fundraising that left her with a cash advantage, even against the Democratic onslaught. Independence Party candidate Bob Anderson may have saved Bachmann by drawing 10% of the vote, much of which probably would have gone to Tinklenberg. Bachmann prevailed 46%-43%, with a victory margin of 12,000 votes. She won 47%-43% in Anoka County and 51%-38% in Wright County. Tinklenberg took two counties at the opposite ends of the district, which had the second- and third-largest vote: He won 48%-44% in Washington and 48%-43% in Stearns. He also won in Benton County. After the election, Bachmann unsuccessfully sought a seat on the House Ways and Means Committee. She could face another competitive contest in 2010—in May 2009 Tinklenberg announced he would seek a rematch.

SEVENTH DISTRICT

Collin Peterson (D)

Elected 1990, 10th term; b. June 29, 1944, Fargo, ND; home, Detroit Lakes; Moorhead St. U., B.A. 1966; Lutheran; divorced; 3 children.

Military Career: Army Natl. Guard, 1963–69.

Elected Office: MN Senate, 1976–86.

Professional Career: Accountant, 1966–90.

DC Office: 2211 RHOB, 20515, 202-225-2165; Fax: 202-225-1593; Web site: collinpeterson.house.gov.

State Offices: Detroit Lakes, 218-847-5056; Marshall, 507-537-2299; Montevideo, 320-235-1061; Red Lake Falls, 218-253-4356; Redwood Falls, 507-637-2270; Willmar, 320-235-1061.

Committees: *Agriculture* (Chmn of 28 D).

Group Ratings

	ADA	ACLU	AFS	LCV	ITIC	NTU	COC	ACU	CFG	FRC
2008	80	64	86	85	43	21	50	20	19	82
2007	85	—	100	60	—	7	60	33	8	—

National Journal Ratings

	2007 LIB	—	2007 CONS	2008 LIB	—	2008 CONS
Economic	52%	—	47%	47%	—	53%
Social	50%	—	49%	54%	—	42%
Foreign	52%	—	47%	52%	—	46%
Composite	52%	—	48%	52%	—	48%

Key Votes of the 110th Congress

1. Increase minimum wage	Y	5. Share immigration data	Y	9. Withdraw troops 8/08	Y
2. Expand SCHIP	Y	6. Foreign aid abortion ban	Y	10. No operations in Iran	Y
3. Raise CAFE standards	Y	7. Ban gay bias in workplace	Y	11. Free trade with Peru	N
4. Bail out financial markets	N	8. Repeal D.C. gun law	Y	12. Overhaul FISA	Y

Election Results

2008 general	Collin Peterson (DFL)	227,187	(72%)	($1,036,463)
	Glen Menze (R)	87,062	(28%)	($13,401)
2008 primary	Collin Peterson (DFL)	unopposed		

Prior Winning Percentages: 2006 (70%); 2004 (66%); 2002 (65%); 2000 (69%); 1998 (72%); 1996 (68%); 1994 (51%); 1992 (51%); 1990 (54%)

Population		Race/Ethnicity		Work	
Pop. 2007:	615,090	White:	92.0%	Private:	74.2%
Change since 2000:	Up 0.0%	Black:	0.5%	Government:	14.7%
Urban:	34.0%	Hispanic:	3.2%	Self-employed:	10.7%
Rural:	66.0%	Asian:	0.7%	Blue collar:	28.2%
Area size:	33,745 sq. mi.	Native Am.:	2.5%	White collar:	52.8%
		Hawaiian:	0.1%	Khaki collar:	0.1%
Age		Two+ races:	1.0%	Other:	18.9%
Median age:	39.4 yrs.	*Ancestry*		Median income:	$44,014
More than 65 yrs:	16.9%	German:	31.4%	Median home value:	$123,500
Less than 18 yrs:	23.2%	Norwegian:	20.2%	Poverty:	11.7%
Education		Swedish:	7.2%	**Military Veterans**	
H.S. grad:	86.8%			% of Pop:	11.8%
College grad:	19.0%				
Grad degree:	5.2%				

Mark Twain's fabled Mississippi River begins modestly in Minnesota's Itasca State Park, 2,552 miles from the Gulf of Mexico. At that point, it can be crossed by foot on stepping-stones. The lake-strewn country in which the river begins has made its own contributions to American literature. More than a century ago, Sinclair Lewis grew up in the town of Sauk Centre, which provided grist for his critical but affectionate portrayals of small-town America in *Main Street* and *Babbitt*. In those years, this

2008 Presidential Vote
McCain (R).............................162,941   (50%)
Obama (D) 154,140   (47%)

2004 Presidential Vote
Bush (R)................................180,743   (55%)
Kerry (D)...............................140,332   (43%)

Cook Partisan Voting Index: R + 5

seemingly placid country was seething with rage, as WASP nationalists banned German from schools, renamed sauerkraut "liberty cabbage," and boycotted German-American businesses. This fed the bitter isolationism of the 1930s and 1940s, led by Charles Lindbergh, who grew up in Little Falls as the son of an isolationist congressman who voted against declaring war on Germany in 1917. This part of Minnesota is probably also the home of the fictional Lake Wobegon. Public radio host Garrison Keillor says he was inspired by small towns in Stearns County that were evenly divided between German Catholics and Norwegian Lutherans.

Farther south, where the plains rise above the river-cut gorges, is great farming country, settled more than 100 years ago by Yankees, Germans, and Scandinavians. Even today, farmers toil against the elements to make a profitable living, so productively that their lands are slowly but surely depopulating; 100,000 acres of farmland in the Minnesota River watershed has been taken out of production by the federal Conservation Reserve Program. This area is the nation's leading producer of sugar beets and a leading supplier of turkeys. It also produces wheat, soybeans, and oilseeds. On the shores of Plum Creek, near Walnut Grove, is where Laura Ingalls Wilder's family came on the way west to the *Little House on the Prairie* in South Dakota. After all of their struggles, Wilder's family left the farm for town as soon as they could. Their pain would be all too familiar to contemporary residents along the Red River of the North, which overflowed its banks in April 1997, inundating Grand Forks, N.D., and East Grand Forks, Minn., and dislocating 50,000 people—America's largest mass evacuation between the Civil War and Hurricane Katrina.

The 7th Congressional District of Minnesota covers almost all of the western part of the state. Its southeastern end is just 30 miles from Minneapolis, just beyond the zone of rapid exurban growth. Its population barely changed from 2000 to 2007, and many of its counties lost population. It takes in the wheat-farming plains adjoining North Dakota as well as the German Catholic areas, with their farm villages named for saints. Farmers have been increasingly turning to corn and soybeans, which have a greater variety of markets and uses. Many political traditions coexist here. Some of the wheat counties are heavily Democratic-Farmer-Labor Party, while heavily Norwegian Otter Tail County leans Republican. The 7th's political history reads like something out of Lake Wobegon Days. Back in 1958, DFL Rep. Coya Knutson was defeated for re-election when her husband, Andy, issued a plaintive statement urging her to come home from Washington and make his breakfast again. She was the only incumbent Democrat to lose in that heavily Democratic year. For the next three decades, this was one of America's prime marginal districts. In 2000, the unpopularity of Clinton administration environmental and gun control policies produced a 54%-40% victory for George W. Bush, his best showing in a Minnesota district. In 2004, Bush's won the district 55%-43%. In 2008, Republican nominee John McCain won this district by only 50%-47%, as ancestral DFL loyalties resurfaced.

The congressman from the 7th District is Collin Peterson, a Democrat who chairs the House Agriculture Committee. Peterson was born in Fargo, N.D., and grew up across the Red River of the North on a farm in Baker. He went to Moorhead State College, and then started a certified public accounting business in Detroit Lakes. All are within 50 miles of each other. In 1976, he was elected to the state Senate. In 1982, he lost a DFL caucus to run for the U.S. House, and then set out to prove that he's nothing if not persistent. Peterson tried three more times, losing to Republican Arlan Stangeland in 1984 and 1986 (by only 121 votes the second time), and losing the DFL primary in 1988. But in 1990, when the *St. Cloud Times* reported that Stangeland made 341 credit card calls to a woman who was not his wife, Peterson won with a robust 54%.

In office, he has been known as a free spirit, wearing cowboy boots and playing guitar in a band called the Second Amendments (the other four members are Republicans). He acted as his own campaign consultant and pilot on flights within the district. He has a small staff, with community economic development professionals rather than Washington policy wonks. He opposes abortion rights and gun control. He backs farm subsidies and labor unions, voted for the Iraq war resolution in 2002, for the Republicans' border-security bill, and for extending the Bush tax cuts. In October 2006, he called his vote on Iraq "a mistake." But he said withdrawal "would be more dangerous than anything we could do," and voted against war spending bills that carried with them timetables to withdraw from Iraq.

In the House, Peterson is a populist, with conservative leanings on social issues. His political fortune was bolstered by the Republican takeover of Congress in 1995, which made him a visibly different kind of Democrat. While voting for parts of the GOP's Contract With America agenda, he founded with California Democrat Gary Condit the Blue Dog Coalition, a group of conservative Democrats for "common sense legislation that embraces the ideas and values of mainstream America." He was one of 16 Democrats to vote for the Republicans' Medicare prescription drug bill in 2003. When Democratic Minority Whip Steny Hoyer of Maryland complained about his vote, Peterson said that the vote meant "life or death" for rural doctors and hospitals in his district. He opposed giving the president broad powers to negotiate free-trade agreements, and said that local farmers were furious about the Bush administration's trade deals. However, Peterson has supported lifting trade restrictions on Cuba, a move favored by farmers in Minnesota and elsewhere. Peterson is the opposite of many middle-of-the-House Republicans, who favor environmental restrictions. He takes the view of his constituents, who hunt and fish as a way of life and often see environmentalists' policies as hindrances.

When Democrat Charles Stenholm of Texas was defeated for re-election in 2004, Peterson was next in line to be the ranking minority member on the Agriculture Committee. But the Democratic leadership demanded that he pay $70,000 in back dues to the Democratic Congressional Campaign Committee, which helps Democrats in House elections. He agreed to be more of a team player and to raise money for other Democrats, although he said: "We have a lot of very liberal people in our caucus. They're misguided, in my opinion, in a lot of areas." But he supported Minority Leader Nancy Pelosi on the theory, he said, that only a liberal can tell liberals what to do. Pelosi accepted Peterson's invitation to attend Farm Fest in Redwood County in August 2006, where she wore cowboy boots and ate pork chops on a stick and got a warm reception. He supported her platform of raising the minimum wage, supporting increased ethanol production, and reinstituting pay-go rules requiring tax cuts be offset with spending decreases. After the Democrats won a House majority in 2006, there was no question about his becoming chairman. "She gets it," Peterson said of Pelosi. "She's going to govern from the center, and she will work with Republicans. There will be no getting even."

Peterson brought to the chairmanship several firm principles, which mostly reflected the views of his constituents. He had expressed reservations that the Republicans' 1996 Freedom to Farm Act would cause low prices and joined the bipartisan majority on the committee in restoring market controls when the farm program was renewed in 2002. In 2005 and 2006, Peterson worked unsuccessfully to advance supplemental disaster aid and to promote the party's ethanol agenda. He also called for extending the Conservation Reserve Program to keep millions of additional acres of farmland idle to produce switchgrass and plant waste that could be used to make ethanol. With a ready supply of raw material, Peterson predicted that cellulosic ethanol plants would prove to be profitable. He was skeptical about limiting farm subsidies to $200,000, a limit strongly opposed by Southern cotton and rice farmers. "Lots of people want to clamp down on payment limits, but if we do that, we are not going to pass a bill," he said.

In 2007 and 2008, Peterson worked with ranking Republican Bob Goodlatte of Virginia to achieve many of his goals on the farm bill enacted in May 2008. It was not easy. It took six short-term extensions of the bill and two votes to override Bush's veto of the legislation. He sought an income limit of $900,000 for subsidy payments, and the final deal set a ceiling of $750,000 for farmers receiving direct payments. It also barred payments to persons with more than $500,000 in nonfarm income. He finally got his permanent disaster fund so that farmers could get their aid more quickly following a drought or flood. He boosted the subsidy for cellulosic ethanol to $1 per gallon, while reducing the subsidy for corn ethanol from 51 cents to 45 cents per gallon.

With demands for new acreage, especially from the large fruit and vegetable states of Florida and California, the committee reduced the Conservation Reserve Program from 39 million acres to 32 million acres. Peterson, the former accountant, proved adept at figuring the costs of various commodity programs, and he established a solid working relationship with budget hawk Kent Conrad, a Democratic senator from North Dakota who was the chief Senate negotiator on the bill. Peterson accommodated lawmakers from urban areas by directing to the food stamp program an additional $10 billion over five years. "We have a bill that covers all of the interests in the country," Peterson said.

After Democrat Barack Obama was elected president in 2008, Peterson said that he wanted to focus on an overhaul of the Agriculture Department, which he said was "still in the 20th century as an organization." He also focused on improving food inspections by the Food and Drug Administration. But his maverick ways were not earning him friends in the new White House. Peterson was one of only seven House Democrats who voted against Obama's economic stimulus bill in February 2009.

A lasting contribution by Peterson was the change in the Democratic House rule prohibiting flying in private planes, which prevented Peterson from claiming reimbursement for flights in his Beechcraft Bonanza. He said he had to charter aircraft at nearly 10 times the cost of flying his own plane, and naturally he protested. "I threatened to put in a bill to make it illegal for any member to drive their own car until we got this fixed. And I told Nancy Pelosi that if she didn't get this fixed, I was going to quit and there was going to be a Republican in my place, that if I couldn't fly I wasn't going to do this anymore. She just kind of looked at me—she said it'll be fixed," Peterson recounted. In May 2007, the rule was changed to accommodate Peterson and other members who fly their own planes.

Peterson's politics have been a hit with 7th District voters and an irritant to local DFL activists. But he has not had a close contest since 1994. House Democrats did away with six-year term limits for chairmen, effective in 2009, which means Peterson could remain the chief farm policy maker in the House for many years.

EIGHTH DISTRICT

James Oberstar (D)

Elected 1974, 18th term; b. Sept. 10, 1934, Chisholm; home, Chisholm; St. Thomas Col., B.A. 1956, Col. of Europe, Bruges, Belgium, M.A. 1957; Catholic; married (Jean); 6 children.

Professional Career: Navy civilian language teacher, Haiti, 1959–63; A.A., U.S. Rep. John Blatnik, 1963–74; A.A., U.S. House Public Works Cmte., 1971–74.

DC Office: 2365 RHOB, 20515, 202-225-6211; Fax: 202-225-0699; Web site: www.house.gov/oberstar.

State Offices: Brainerd, 218-828-4400; Chisholm, 218-254-5761; Duluth, 218-727-7474; North Branch, 651-277-1234.

Committees: *Transportation & Infrastructure* (Chmn of 44 D).

Group Ratings

	ADA	ACLU	AFS	LCV	ITIC	NTU	COC	ACU	CFG	FRC
2008	80	100	100	92	67	6	56	4	0	41
2007	75	—	100	75	—	5	56	13	1	—

National Journal Ratings

	2007 LIB	—	2007 CONS		2008 LIB	—	2008 CONS
Economic	55%	—	45%		85%	—	0%
Social	68%	—	32%		72%	—	26%
Foreign	80%	—	20%		92%	—	0%
Composite	68%	—	32%		87%	—	13%

Key Votes of the 110th Congress

1. Increase minimum wage	Y	5. Share immigration data	N	9. Withdraw troops 8/08	Y
2. Expand SCHIP	Y	6. Foreign aid abortion ban	Y	10. No operations in Iran	Y
3. Raise CAFE standards	Y	7. Ban gay bias in workplace	*	11. Free trade with Peru	*
4. Bail out financial markets	Y	8. Repeal D.C. gun law	Y	12. Overhaul FISA	N

Election Results

2008 general	James Oberstar (DFL)	241,831	(68%)	($1,409,685)
	Michael Cummins (R)	114,871	(32%)	($15,751)
2008 primary	James Oberstar (DFL)	unopposed		

Prior Winning Percentages: 2006 (64%); 2004 (65%); 2002 (69%); 2000 (68%); 1998 (66%); 1996 (67%); 1994 (66%); 1992 (59%); 1990 (73%); 1988 (75%); 1986 (73%); 1984 (67%); 1982 (77%); 1980 (70%); 1978 (87%); 1976 (100%); 1974 (62%)

Population		Race/Ethnicity		Work	
Pop. 2007:	643,423	White:	94.0%	Private:	76.3%
Change since 2000:	Up 4.6%	Black:	0.8%	Government:	15.3%
Urban:	37.4%	Hispanic:	1.1%	Self-employed:	8.2%
Rural:	62.6%	Asian:	0.5%	Blue collar:	26.9%
Area size:	32,419 sq. mi.	Native Am.:	2.5%	White collar:	52.7%
Age		Hawaiian:	0.0%	Khaki collar:	0.1%
Median age:	39.8 yrs.	Two+ races:	1.1%	Other:	20.3%
More than 65 yrs:	15.8%	*Ancestry*		Median income:	$45,166
Less than 18 yrs:	22.1%	German:	23.6%	Median home value:	$160,300
Education		Norwegian:	11.6%	Poverty:	11.4%
H.S. grad:	89.6%	Swedish:	10.0%	**Military Veterans**	
College grad:	20.0%			% of Pop:	13.4%
Grad degree:	6.0%				

In the 1860s, prospectors in Minnesota's Arrowhead region, northwest of Lake Superior in the low hills of the Mesabi Range, happened upon one of the nation's largest veins of iron ore. They moved on, looking for gold. But in the 1880s, Duluth banker George Stone and Philadelphia financier Charlemagne Tower started mining the Iron Range and created the northern end of the lifeline of American heavy industry. Rail lines ran south from the Range to the port of Duluth, nestled on dramatic bluffs

2008 Presidential Vote
Obama (D) 195,147   (53%)
McCain (R)..............................163,520   (45%)

2004 Presidential Vote
Kerry (D)................................191,228   (53%)
Bush (R) 167,439   (46%)

Cook Partisan Voting Index: D + 3

over the always-cold and, for long months every winter, frozen waters of Lake Superior—one of the most beautiful settings for a city in North America, though also one of the most isolated. Duluth was a grain-shipping rival of Chicago and the premier iron ore port. Its city plan was drawn up by architect Daniel Burnham, who also planned Chicago, and its splendid turn-of-the-century buildings still celebrate the triumph of technology and civilization over wilderness and the elements. Millions of tons of ore have been dug out of the Range and loaded into railcars for the ride to Duluth, and into Great Lakes freighters for shipment to Chicago, Gary, Detroit, Cleveland, Pittsburgh, and Buffalo.

For most of the 20th century, in this land where the Arctic winds blow down over the Canadian Shield's thousands of inland lakes, about 100,000 people lived on the Iron Range and another 100,000 in Duluth, most of them descendants of America's 1880–1924 wave of immigration: Italians, Poles, Serbs and Croats, Jews, Swedes, and Finns. In this punishing environment, they worked to the point of exhaustion, built solid houses with staunch central heating, and wore layers of warm clothing to survive the brutal winter, which can be as extreme as 50 degrees below zero. Life was rough. The work was hard, the hours long, and the pay low. The churches, a separate one for each ethnic group, were the main community institutions. Living conditions improved vastly in the decades of great economic growth after World War II, but life remains rough-hewn today, and there is still economic distress. As iron mines and steel factories got more efficient, they needed fewer workers, and employment is well below its 1970s peak. As water fills abandoned open-pit mines, as factories close and mines are shut down, the Iron Range looks bleaker. In 2007, Duluth's population was down to 84,400, and the Iron Range's was about the same. Economic growth is sporadic. In the 1990s, Northwest Airlines built a large repair facility in Duluth and a reservations center in the Iron Range, and the call center survived the 2008 merger with Delta Airlines. The port of Duluth still ships large quantities of grain, and in the late 1990s a new taconite and steelmaking factory was built—the first big new plant in more than 20 years. People here have made the best of the frozen climate. Automakers test their new models' performance under extreme winter conditions at International Falls in Koochiching County. A new sports competition is the winter ultramarathon, a 135-mile endurance contest of walking, running, cycling, or skiing from International Falls to Tower.

The 8th Congressional District of Minnesota includes Duluth and the Iron Range, plus much of the north woods and lake country to the west and south. It extends all the way south to the boundaries of the Twin Cities metro area, to Isanti and Chisago counties, where young families are building new homes in pleasant old lakeside towns. This district has been a bulwark of Minnesota's Democratic-Farmer-Labor Party since the DFL was formed in 1944, and has been considered safely Democratic for years. But there are signs of change. The fast-growing counties in the south and west have trended toward Republicans, while Duluth and the Iron Range remain Democratic. However, issues like gun control and environmental regulation have sometimes moved those areas toward the Republicans. In 2004, Democratic presidential nominee John Kerry won here 53%-46% over President Bush. Four years later, Democrat Barack Obama had a similar 53%-45% win over Republican John McCain.

The congressman from the 8th District is James Oberstar, a Democrat first elected in 1974. He is the chairman of the House Transportation and Infrastructure Committee. Oberstar grew up in the Iron Range in the city of Chisholm. His father was an iron miner and union official who sent him off to St.

Thomas College with $2,500 saved in quarters at the Slovenian National Benefit Society. He studied French in college and in Belgium. For four years, he was a civilian employee of the U.S. Naval Mission to Haiti, teaching French and Creole to Marines, and French and English to Haitians. (Oberstar also speaks Serbo-Croatian, Italian, and Spanish, and has been known to break into polkas sung in Slovenian at Democratic retreats.) In 1963, at age 29, he landed a job as chief of staff to U.S. Rep. John Blatnik in the 8th District. When Blatnik retired in 1974, Oberstar won a primary over Tony Perpich, brother of Gov. Rudy Perpich, and went on to win easily in the general election. The *St. Paul Pioneer Press* has described him as "part scholar and part Iron Range street fighter, part pothole-filling ward healer and part workaholic."

Oberstar's views are in the liberal Catholic tradition. He believes in an economically active government and has little faith in economic markets. He was long dubious about American military involvement abroad. He voted against the Iraq war resolution in 2002 and has decried the results of U.S. intervention there since. He is an opponent of abortion rights and a backer of adoption, sponsoring bills to ensure family and medical leave and dependent deductions for families in the process of adopting. When he first proposed a $1,500 adoption tax deduction in the 1970s, he was not taken seriously by the tax-writing House Ways and Means Committee. Today, thanks in large part to his effort, there is a $5,000 tax credit. From this North Country district, Oberstar has been a supporter of local hunting and fishing activities and of the steel industry. When the issue of normalizing trade relations with China came before the House, he tried to get an amendment to treat steel slab imports as a direct threat to taconite miners. When the Bush administration wasn't interested, he voted against the bill.

Since October 1995, Oberstar has been the top Democrat on Transportation and Infrastructure—a position of real power. The committee has a long tradition of bipartisanship, and of sponsoring members' roads and public works projects. At 75 members, it is the largest in the House. For six years during the Republican majority, Oberstar worked with GOP Chairman Bud Shuster of Pennsylvania to make it more powerful than ever. Their great monument was the 1998 transportation bill, with $217 billion in spending, including $10 billion in projects earmarked by individual lawmakers. In April 2004, Oberstar and new Transportation Chairman Don Young, R-Alaska, persuaded the House to pass a $275 billion, six-year transportation bill; the Senate passed a $318 billion bill. The White House insisted on capping spending at $256 billion, and the deadlock resulted in no bill getting passed in 2003 and 2004. Oberstar and Young were unfazed. Finally, in July 2005, both chambers passed a $286 billion bill, with $24 billion for more than 6,000 earmarked projects, and Bush signed it.

Oberstar himself is a bicycling enthusiast, and logs 2,700 miles a year in Washington, D.C., in Duluth, on the Range, and in the Tour de Frog in St. Cloud. A special project of his is Safe Routes to School, grants for sidewalks, bike paths, and safe crossings to encourage kids to walk to school. Over five years, he pushed spending from an initial $20 million to $612 million in 2006. "I would say in time it will be the best thing I've ever done," Oberstar once said.

Oberstar was one of the architects of the airline bailout bill in 2001 and strongly pushed for federal rather than private employees in airport security. In 2006, the House adopted an Oberstar amendment to continue barring foreign companies from owning more than 25% of any U.S. airline stock. Also that year, he came out against plans backed by the Bush administration and many airlines to fund the Federal Aviation Administration entirely on user fees based on miles flown, with a quasi-governmental commission making spending decisions on air traffic control management and other matters. "There are some functions government must undertake in the public interest," Oberstar said. After the JetBlue airline left dozens of passenger-filled planes on the ground for 10 hours in February 2007, Oberstar called for hearings on flight delays.

Taking over as chairman of the Transportation committee in 2007 after Democrats won majority control, Oberstar spearheaded the passage of a $23 billion water resources bill, the first in six years. When Bush vetoed the measure, Congress overrode it easily. After the collapse in August 2007 of the Interstate 35W bridge in the Twin Cities, Oberstar quickly got passed a bill to fund reconstruction. The House also passed his legislation to tighten bridge safety standards and to require immediate inspection of all bridges deemed "structurally deficient."

Also that year, with approval from the Air Line Pilots Association, he won House approval of a bill to raise from age 60 to 65 the mandatory retirement age for airline pilots. In 2008, he vehemently opposed the merger of Minnesota-based Northwest Airlines with Delta as "the worst development in aviation history," not least because his constituents feared higher prices and a decline in service. While unsuccessfully urging the Justice Department to reject the deal as anti-competitive, he could do little to thwart approval by the Bush administration.

In 2009, with the transportation bill set to expire, Oberstar prepared for what was heralded as the most expensive public works bill in the nation's history—possibly $500 billion over six years. He was prepared to raise the gas tax, if necessary, to pay for expedited construction. But Oberstar was disappointed that Democratic leaders and appropriators signed off on less money for infrastructure than he had wanted in the anti-recession economic stimulus bill that passed the House in January 2009. Oberstar had called for $85 billion for highways, mass transit, rail, aviation, and clean-water programs, but the legislation provided for $66 billion. The stimulus bill was drafted chiefly by the Appropriations Committee, the longtime nemesis of the Transportation panel.

At home, Oberstar has worked to upgrade and widen to four lanes U.S. 53, which runs from Duluth through the Iron Range to the Canadian border. He succeeded in getting a dangerous interchange and railroad overpass rebuilt. On another issue, he favors more dredging of the Great Lakes, since lake levels have fallen in recent years.

Oberstar won tough primaries in 1980 and 1984, but he has been re-elected by wide margins. Longtime DFL voters may be moving away from Democrats higher up on the ticket, but they remain faithful to Oberstar. His one political setback came in 1984, when he ran for the Senate but did not get an endorsement by the liberal DFL convention. He is the longest-serving member of Congress from Minnesota.

★ MISSISSIPPI ★

Burdened with a tragic history, Mississippi has famously lagged behind the other states in just about every leading indicator. Yet there are signs the state is coming into its own in the post-civil-rights-movement era. This green land was settled in a rush in Jacksonian America, mostly by small farmers heading west from Georgia and south from Tennessee, and also by a few big planters who made and sometimes lost vast fortunes, built grand mansions, and sent their sons to fight in the Civil War. For a century afterward, as planters and engineers drained the Delta lands, Mississippi, with its racial segregation, subsistence farmers and sharecroppers, and low wages, lived apart from most of America. Faulkner's Mississippi never knew the Homestead Act, giant factories, the rushes of immigration, or the rise of the suburbs that characterized most of 20th-century America. Mississippi didn't develop great cities: Its two commercial metropolises—Memphis, Tenn., and New Orleans—lay just outside its borders. But if the state did not excel at commerce, it did produce great art. Mississippi gave us the blues and Elvis Presley. It gave the world writers William Faulkner and Eudora Welty, Walker Percy and Shelby Foote. The state with the lowest literacy rate has also produced the most Pulitzer Prize winners for literature. Their work was informed by a sense of the tragic that is missing or forgotten in most of America, where life is a triumphant sales pitch or a labor-saving invention. For years, no other state had such a painful contrast between image and reality, between an ideal sincerely strived for and the tawdry facts of everyday life. Magnolia trees on the lawns of antebellum mansions, golden-haired women in white dresses on the veranda, faithful black servants and retainers. This was once the ideal. And behind it stood loose-jointed frame houses and unpainted back-country stores, cabins without plumbing and poor white crossroads clustered with advertising signs hanging askew. As David Sansing wrote, "We at one time have the scent of magnolias and the smell of burning crosses."

Today, Mississippi still ranks 49th or 50th on many quality-of-life scales, but the gulf between the state and the rest of America has narrowed enormously. In 1940, Mississippi had an economy based on low-wage, subsistence or sharecropper agriculture and a system of racial segregation often enforced by violence. If history is, as Sir Henry Maine wrote, the story of the progress from status to contract, then old Mississippi was still at the beginning, for status—race—meant just about everything. In the years since, Mississippi has moved, not always willingly, from status to contract in its economy and in its race relations. Per capita income in Mississippi was 36% of the national average in 1940; in 1990 it was 67% and in 2008 it was 74%, still well below average but, given the lower cost of living here, a level recognizably American. Unlike New Orleans in neighboring Louisiana, the state quickly got up off the ground to start rebuilding after Hurricane Katrina struck in 2005. Mississippians of 50 years ago would be astonished by the physical comforts and mechanical marvels their grandchildren take for granted: Nearly every classroom in the state is air-conditioned and is being wired for the Internet.

The elder generation would be astonished as well by relations between whites and blacks, who make up 37% of the population, the highest of any state. As Mississippi native and columnist William Raspberry wrote in *The Washington Post*, "There is an easiness to relationships, a mutual respect and a willingness to move beyond race that, quite frankly, didn't exist during my years in the state. Mississippi is finally a good place to be." Forty years ago, blacks held no public offices in Mississippi. Now the state has more black elected officials than any other, with 27 black chairmen of state House committees. An African-American state senator from Tishomingo County in the far northeast part of the state was elected from a rural district that is 87% white. Voters have elected black mayors in Vicksburg, Jackson, Hattiesburg, Greenville, and Natchez. That's not to say the race issue has disappeared. It is still uncomfortably present in Mississippi elections. And as recently as 2001, 65% of voters chose to retain the Confederate battle cross—a symbol offensive to many African-Americans—in the state flag.. Yet Mississippi seems intent on moving forward rather than backward. Prosecutors have hunted down the Ku Klux Klan members who killed civil-rights activists in the 1960s. One was convicted in 2005 and another charged in 2007. Republican Gov. Haley Barbour signed bills authorizing a civil-rights curriculum in public schools and a civil-rights museum in Jackson. The Jackson airport is named for movement leader Medgar Evers. Ole Miss, which was integrated under force of arms in 1962, hosted Barack Obama, an African-American Democrat, and John McCain, a Republican who has Mississippi ancestors, for a presidential debate in September 2008.

Mississippi's economy once depended on cotton, but no longer. Manufacturing jobs have declined here, as elsewhere, in recent years, but northeast Mississippi around Tupelo remains the center of the nation's upholstered furniture industry and is the site of a $1.3 billion plant where workers will start assembling Priuses in 2010 (after the state offered Toyota $296 million in incentives). Growth has also been rapid around the $1.4 billion Nissan auto plant that opened in 2003 in Canton, just north of Jackson, attracted by $363 million in state aid and incentives. The factory, which builds 278,000 vehicles a year, provides 4,000 jobs and nearby suppliers employ thousands more. Highland Colony Parkway, heading north from Jackson in Madison County, and Lakeland Drive, heading east into Rankin County, anchor

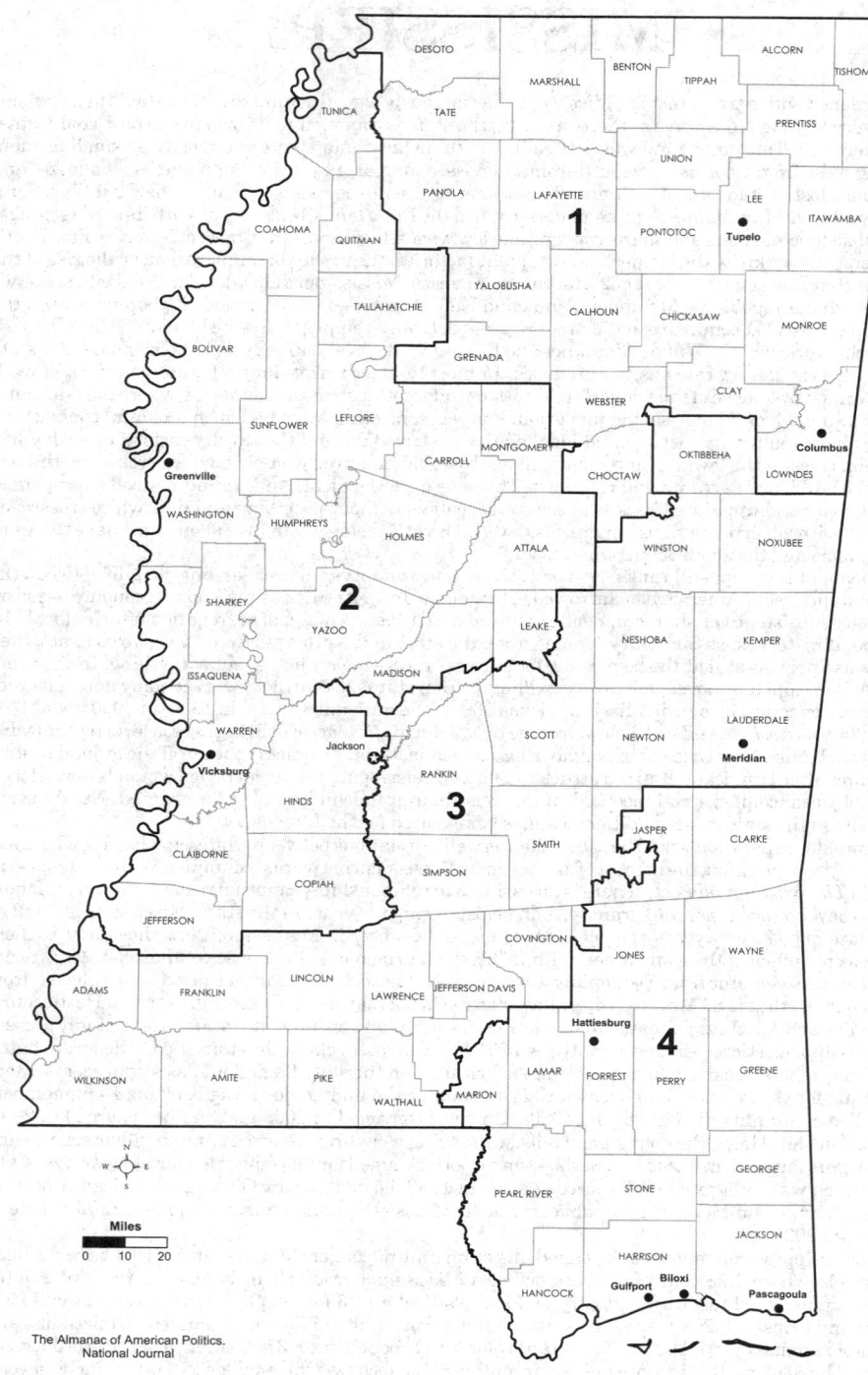

The Almanac of American Politics.
National Journal

Congressional district boundaries were first effective for 2002.

boom areas. Even more rapid growth has come in the DeSoto County suburbs of Memphis, just a few miles south of Elvis Presley's estate, Graceland. Population growth has been concentrated in these areas and also in inland counties as people after Hurricane Katrina drove them from the coast. Other sources of growth: Northrop Grumman's huge shipyard in former Senate Majority Leader Trent Lott's hometown of Pascagoula; the Richton salt dome, which is being developed for the Strategic Petroleum Reserve at a cost of $1 billion; General Electric's engine plant in Batesville; and a $175 million steel plant in Amory. Then there is gambling. Mississippi approved gambling in 1990, and in 1992, riverboat and dockside casinos started to open. Big gambling companies built some 29 casinos, nine in once-impoverished Tunica County, just south of Memphis, 12 on the Gulf Coast, and the rest scattered along the Mississippi River, all technically on boats and barges but tied to land. Mississippi is now No. 3 among states in gambling revenue, behind Nevada and New Jersey. The industry has produced thousands of service jobs at above-average wages, and some $500 million in state revenues a year.

To be sure, Katrina was a huge setback for Mississippi. The main force of the August 29, 2005, hurricane was directed at the state's Hancock County, not New Orleans; the Mississippi towns of Waveland, Bay St. Louis, and Pass Christian were totally wiped out. In a few hours, waves up to 55 feet high destroyed one-quarter of the structures in Biloxi and Gulfport. The homes of Democratic U.S. Rep. Gene Taylor in Bay St. Louis, and Lott in Pascagoula, the latter more than a century old, were swept away, as were many houses a quarter-mile from the Gulf. Floodwaters swept 10 miles inland. Some casinos were destroyed and others severely damaged. Federal emergency plans rest on the assumption that local officials and first responders will cope for the first three days, but Katrina left city halls without power and roads to hospitals blocked by fallen trees. In Mississippi, first responders went to work in spite of those obstacles, pulling 24-hour shifts. Barbour quickly took charge. Biloxi Mayor A.J. Holloway later described his city's response. "Our people have been good, too. You know, they shed some tears, work a little bit, cry again, and go back to work. We're not sitting on our behinds and waiting for someone to give us a hand."

Lawsuits brought against State Farm for denying hurricane-related claims were eventually settled in August 2008, when the insurer paid out $74 million. The Mississippi congressional delegation secured generous federal money to help with the recovery; it did not hurt that Republican Sen. Thad Cochran was chairman of the Senate Appropriations Committee. Barbour administered grants and low-interest loans to home and business owners who suffered uninsured losses, even as the Federal Emergency Management Agency shelled out $1.8 billion for National Flood Insurance Program claims. Barbour was criticized for his decision to spend $600 million in federal housing funds to restore and expand the port of Gulfport, which resulted in Chiquita entering into a long-term lease for its port facilities. A lawsuit was filed to halt the project in December 2008. With the closed casinos costing the state $500,000 a day in tax revenue, the state House and Senate changed the gambling law to allow casinos to be built on land within 800 feet of the shore. By 2007, the casinos were back in business, but the following year, gambling revenue fell 3% on the Gulf Coast and 8% on the riverboats. It turns out that gambling in Mississippi, as in Nevada, is not recession-proof. In March 2009 the governor signed a bill for a 30% sales tax rebate for casino developers who developed golf courses, hotels, convention facilities, and other non-gambling activities. Gambling was not the only part of Mississippi's economy hurt by the recession. Factories closed and in February 2009, unemployment reached 9%.

Politically, Mississippi is increasingly a Republican state, carried by Republicans in the last seven presidential elections. But Democrats have shown some signs of life. Republicans have held both U.S. Senate seats since the retirement of Democrat John Stennis in 1988. But after Barbour appointed U.S. Rep. Roger Wicker, a Republican, to fill Lott's seat, Democrat Travis Childers won the May 2008 special election to fill Wicker's 1st District House seat. That left Mississippi with a 3-1 Democratic House delegation, with Bennie Thompson safe in the black-majority 2nd District and conservative Democrat Gene Taylor holding on to the heavily Republican Gulf Coast district he first won in 1989. When Wicker ran for

Population		Household Income		Work	
Pop. 2007:	2,906,118	Under $15k:	21.6%	Private:	73.9%
State rank:	31st of 50	$15k to $50k:	42.5%	Government:	19.0%
Change since 2000:	Up 2.2%	$50k to $100k:	25.6%	Self-employed:	6.8%
Urban:	46.9%	$100k to $150k:	8.8%	Unemployment (3-yr. average):	5.6%
Rural:	53.1%	Over $150k:	1.6%	Poverty:	21.1%
Native of state:	72.1%	Median income:	$35,632	Blue collar:	29.1%
Not a citizen:	1.1%	**Home Value**		White collar:	52.7%
Area size:	48,430 sq. mi.	Under $100k:	56.7%	Khaki collar:	0.5%
Most populous cities		$100k to $300k:	37.8%	Other:	17.7%
1. Jackson	174,983	$300k to $500k:	4.1%	**Age**	
2. Gulfport	69,084	$500k to $1 mil:	1.1%	Median age:	35.1 yrs.
3. Hattiesburg	47,420	Over $1 million:	0.2%	More than 65 yrs:	12.4%
4. Southaven	42,469	Median:	$88,100	Less than 18 yrs:	26.3%

Race/Ethnicity				Military Veterans		Registered Voters in 2008	
White:	59.2%	*Language*		% of Pop:	10.2%	No party registration	
Black:	37.0%	English:	96.6%	*Veterans by Period*		Voter turnout:	1,289,865
Hispanic:	1.8%	Spanish:	1.9%	WWII and before:	10.9%	Turnout as % of	
Asian:	0.8%	Asian:	0.6%	Korea:	11.3%	voting age:	59.4%
Native Am.:	0.4%	Other		Vietnam:	30.5%	**Legislature**	
Hawaiian:	0.0%	European	0.6%	Gulf (pre-2001):	13.0%	Senate:	27 D 25 R
Two+ races:	0.8%	**Education**		Gulf (post-2001):	9.6%	House:	74 D 48 R
Ancestry		H.S. grad:	78.0%	Peace time:	24.6%		
USA:	12.1%	College grad:	18.6%				
Irish:	9.0%	Grad degree:	6.4%				
English:	7.5%						

the remainder of Lott's term in November 2008, he was held to 55%-45% by former Democratic governor Ronnie Musgrove.

At the state level, the pattern is mixed. In 2003, Musgrove lost his re-election bid to Barbour, who returned to Yazoo City from a Washington lobbying practice and a stint as Republican National Chairman. Barbour's surefooted response to Katrina, in contrast with that of Louisiana Gov. Kathleen Blanco, a Democrat, boosted his poll ratings. Going into the 2007 election, Barbour took credit for converting a $700 million deficit to a $70 million surplus and for boosting test scores in Mississippi public schools. He beat Democrat John Arthur Eaves by a solid 58%-42%. Republicans Phil Bryant and Delbert Hosemann were elected lieutenant governor and secretary of state, respectively, by similar margins. Over Barbour's years in office, Republicans narrowed the Democratic edge in the state Senate to 27-25, but Democrats maintained a solid 74-48 edge in the state House.

Presidential politics   Mississippi voted 56%-43% for Republican presidential nominee John McCain in 2008—a slight downtick from Republican George W. Bush's 58% in 2000 and 59% in 2004. It's difficult to avoid the conclusion that this is a racially polarized electorate. Whites voted 88%-11% for McCain over Democratic nominee Barack Obama, while African-Americans voted 98%-2% for Obama—both wider margins than four years before, when both presidential candidates were white. Blacks accounted for 33% of turnout, not much less than their share of adult population. White evangelical or born-again Protestants made up 46% of the electorate and voted 94%-6% for McCain. Young voters overall voted for Obama, but this was the result of a closer racial balance in the age group. Young whites voted 81% for McCain. It should be noted, however, that few Mississippi whites yearn for a return to racial segregation. They line up with Republicans on a raft of other issues—defense, crime, cultural attitudes, taxes—just as most African-Americans line up with Democrats on the same issues. And on some issues, blacks and whites in Mississippi are on the same page: On a proposed constitutional amendment banning same-sex marriage in November 2004, whites voted 89% in favor and blacks voted 77% in favor.

2008 Presidential Vote		
McCain (R)	724,597	(56%)
Obama (D)	554,662	(43%)
2008 Democratic Presidential Primary		
Obama (D)	265,502	(61%)
Clinton (D)	159,221	(37%)
2008 Republican Presidential Primary		
McCain (R)	113,074	(79%)
Huckabee (R)	17,943	(13%)
2004 Presidential Vote		
Bush (R)	684,981	(59%)
Kerry (D)	457,766	(40%)

Mississippi has held a presidential primary in the second week of March since 1988, too late to have made a difference in the 2000 and 2004 contests. That was the case again for Republicans in 2008. Former Arkansas Gov. Mike Huckabee withdrew from the contest the week before Mississippi voted. Some 145,000 people participated in the GOP primary—fewer than in 1988, 1992, and 1996—with 79% of voters supporting McCain. On the Democratic side, the race was still on. Turnout was 434,000, far more than the 76,000 voters in 2004, and topping the record of 359,000 in 1988. With voting along racial lines, Obama defeated Sen. Hillary Rodham Clinton 61%-37%, one of his highest percentage wins.

Congressional districting   Mississippi lost one of its five House districts in the 2000 census, marking the first time the state had just four representatives since the 1840s. In 2001, Democrats held the governorship and both houses of the Legislature, and one might have expected that they would draw a plan ousting one of the state's two Republican congressmen. But the state House, led by Democratic Speaker Tim Ford, and the state Senate, led by Republican Lt. Gov. Amy Tuck, could not agree on a plan.

111th Congress Lineup	
3 D	1 R
110th Congress Lineup	
2 D	2 R

Ford wanted to draw a map connecting northeast Mississippi home of Republican incumbent Roger Wicker, to DeSoto County, just south of Memphis, and including part of Rankin County, just east of Jackson and home of Republican incumbent Chip Pickering. Republicans called this the "tornado district" because it was shaped like a funnel cloud. The plan would have left Pickering with the choice of running against Wicker in a primary where he would be at a great geographic disadvantage or running in a new 3rd District against incumbent Democrat Ronnie Shows in a district that was 38% African-American. Tuck (who in December 2002 switched parties and became a Republican), state House Republicans, and northeast Mississippians in the Senate favored a plan that would combine most of the old 3rd and 4th Districts, represented by Pickering and Shows, that would be 34% black. Democratic Gov. Musgrove called a special session of the Legislature in November 2001, and on the first day, the Senate and House passed versions of Ford's and Tuck's plans. Negotiations for a compromise went nowhere, and the session was adjourned.

Action shifted to the courts. Democrats sued in state court, and Republicans sued in federal court. Hinds County Chancery Judge Patricia Wise adopted a plan put forward by Democrats with a 38% black 3rd District and it was forwarded it to the U.S. Justice Department for approval as required by the Voting Rights Act. But on January 15, 2002, a three-judge federal court ruling on the GOP lawsuit took the issue away from the Chancery Court, and put forward a map with a 30% black 3rd District, similar to the state Senate's plan. Democrats complained that the federal judges were improperly trying to impose a plan favoring Pickering, who is the son of federal Judge Charles Pickering. On February 25, the federal court ordered its own plan into effect, and U.S. Supreme Court Justice Antonin Scalia rejected an emergency appeal by furious Democrats, who argued that Scalia, a friend of the Pickering family, should have recused himself. But the districts in the federal court plan were about as compact as possible, given the state's geography, and it fulfilled the agreed-upon imperative of retaining a black-majority 2nd District. Democrats persisted in their appeal even though it was obvious its lines would be in effect for the November 2002 election. On March 31, the Supreme Court ruled against their claim.

Mississippi is expected to keep its four seats in the reapportionment following the 2010 census, and census population estimates suggest that the state's current districts could be redesigned to meet the equal population standard with just minor tweaking. Neither party appears likely to have complete control in 2011. Barbour will be serving his last year as governor, and Democrats likely will still have a majority in the state House.

Governor

Haley Barbour (R)

Elected 2003, term expires Jan. 2012, 2nd term; b. Oct. 22, 1947, Yazoo City; home, Yazoo City; Attended U. of MS; U. of MS, J.D. 1973; Presbyterian; married (Marsha); 2 children.

Professional Career: State dir., U.S. Census Bureau, 1969–70; RNC Committeeman, 1984–98; Dir., White House Office of Political Affairs, 1985–87; CEO & founder, Barbour, Griffith & Rogers, 1991-present; Chmn., RNC, 1993–97.

Office: State Capitol, P.O. Box 139, Jackson, 39205, 601-359-3150; Fax: 601-359-3741; Web site: www.governor.state.ms.us.

Election Results

2007 general	Haley Barbour (R)	430,807	(58%)
	John Eaves (D)	313,232	(42%)
2007 primary	Haley Barbour (R)	184,036	(93%)
	Frederick Jones (R)	13,611	(7%)

Prior Winning Percentages: 2003 (53%)

Republican Haley Barbour was elected governor of Mississippi in 2003 and re-elected in 2007. He is only the second Republican to win the office since Reconstruction. He grew up in Yazoo City in the Mississippi Delta. His father was a lawyer who died of a heart attack when Haley was 2 years old, leaving his 31-year-old mother to raise the three Barbour boys. A star athlete and class valedictorian, Barbour was voted Mr. Yazoo High School and won a scholarship to attend Ole Miss. But he left during his senior year to take a job on Republican Richard Nixon's 1968 presidential campaign. Barbour returned to Ole Miss and graduated from the university's law school in 1973. Three years later, he ran Republican Gerald Ford's presidential campaign in the Southeast, and he has been actively involved in GOP politics ever since. In 1980, Barbour worked on John Connally's White House bid. In 1982, he took on longtime Democratic Sen. John Stennis, then the chairman of the Armed Services Committee. Stennis had not faced a serious challenge since 1947, when he was elected to succeed Democratic Sen. Theodore G. Bilbo, and some expected that the octogenarian would not seek re-election in 1982. But he did, and Barbour approached the issue of Stennis's age gingerly. He ran with the slogan, "A senator for the '80s," knowing that it would remind voters that he was running against a senator who was in his 80s. The strategy didn't work. Stennis won 64%-36%, carrying 80 of 82 counties even though Barbour outspent him. At age 35, Barbour showed a sophisticated understanding of the nexus between money and politics. In what was then the most expensive race in state history, he raised and spent more than $1 million at a time when that amount could buy a great deal of attention in Mississippi.

It also got Barbour noticed in Washington, where he became Ronald Reagan's White House political director in 1985 and later an adviser to George H.W. Bush's presidential campaign. In 1991, he took advantage of his connections and hung out his shingle, founding Barbour Griffith & Rogers, now BGR Holdings, one of Washington's powerhouse lobbying firms. From 1993 to 1997, Barbour was chairman of the Republican National Committee, heading the party when it won a congressional majority for the first time in 40 years in 1994 and earning some of the credit. When he left the RNC and returned to his lobbying firm, he was positioned as one of Washington's most influential lobbyists, well connected to key members of the House and Senate and much sought-after by big corporate clients with interests before the Republican-controlled Congress.

In his years in Washington, Barbour maintained his ties back home. He served as a Republican national committeeman from 1984 until 1998, and regularly traveled to Yazoo City where his wife and sons lived. In 2002, he announced he would challenge Democratic Gov. Ronnie Musgrove, who, after winning just a 49.5% plurality in 1999, had been elected by the Mississippi House of Representatives. Much of Musgrove's term was taken up with controversy over the state flag, which had the Confederate battle cross in the upper-left-hand corner. The state Supreme Court ruled the flag illegal, but the new flag endorsed by Musgrove was rejected by voters in April 2001 by 65%-35%.

Barbour's main campaign issue was tort law and the civil justice system. Mississippi had become a trial lawyers' paradise, with seven product-liability judgments of $100 million or more in six years and medical-malpractice suits driving doctors out of an already underserved state. Musgrove got the Legislature to place limits on tort suits in 2002, but Barbour said they didn't go far enough. Musgrove fought back. "I've put Mississippi first. Haley Barbour has spent the last 20 years in Washington, D.C., putting special interests first," Musgrove said. He criticized Barbour for representing tobacco and pharmaceutical companies and lobbying for the North American Free Trade Agreement, which, Musgrove said, cost Mississippi 41,000 jobs. Barbour contended that Musgrove mismanaged the state economy and wasn't serious enough about fixing the civil justice system. Musgrove responded that Barbour was "running down Mississippi" and he claimed credit for attracting the Nissan plant to Madison County. Barbour reminded voters of Musgrove's endorsement of Democratic presidential candidate Al Gore in 2000 by airing a commercial with footage of Gore and Musgrove embracing. Musgrove was not helped by Senate Democrats' October 2003 filibuster of the nomination of Mississippi Judge Charles Pickering to the 5th Circuit Court of Appeals. Musgrove publicly backed Pickering's nomination, and sent senators a letter urging confirmation.

Barbour raised $10.6 million to Musgrove's $8.5 million, setting another record for the most expensive race in state history. Barbour won 53%-46%. He carried 51 of 82 counties and won big margins amid heavy turnout in key Republican counties such as fast-growing DeSoto County, just south of Memphis, and suburban Rankin County, just east of Jackson. That offset high African-American turnout, which Democrats had counted on because of the presence of two black statewide nominees in down-ballot races. Exit polls showed that blacks voted 94% for Musgrove and white voters went 77% for Barbour.

Barbour took office with Democratic majorities in the state House and Senate. But in 2004, he won approval of his bill to cap pain-and-suffering tort damages generally to $1 million and to $500,000 in medical-malpractice cases. The legislation also limited lawsuit forum-shopping and protected "innocent sellers" of faulty products. Barbour took credit for several economic development deals—a 500-job Textron Fastening Systems plant in Greenville and a 400-job FedEx Ground facility in Olive Branch. In 2005, he proposed cutting most agency budgets by 5%. The Legislature approved a tax increase on nursing home beds to help fund the state's ailing Medicaid program, and Barbour and the Legislature ultimately restored the program to solvency by borrowing $240 million from Mississippi's health care trust fund and instituting tighter restrictions on the number of prescriptions, emergency room visits, and home health care visits.

Hurricane Katrina slammed into the Gulf Coast on Barbour's watch, on August 29, 2005. He described its aftermath along the Mississippi coast as "nuclear destruction." The main force of the hurricane was directed at Hancock County, and the towns of Waveland, Bay St. Louis and Pass Christian were totally wiped out. Casinos were destroyed or severely damaged, costing the state $500,000 a day in revenue. The shrimping and shipbuilding industries were also disrupted by extensive damage to the state's 90-mile coastline. Barbour quickly took charge and drew national notice for his decisive leadership, particularly in contrast to the muddled reaction of Louisiana leaders to their hurricane-related problems.

The governor appointed a commission to coordinate the recovery, led by former Netscape chief Jim Barksdale. "We will rebuild bigger and better than ever," Barbour said. "It's going to take some time, and people have to be patient." The state's recovery was assisted by federal money secured by the powerful

Mississippi congressional delegation, and it did not hurt that Republican Thad Cochran was chairman of the Senate Appropriations Committee. Soon $5 billion was authorized for Mississippi, $3 billion of it for housing. Barbour administered grants and low-interest loans to home and business owners who suffered uninsured losses; the Federal Emergency Management Agency shelled out $2.4 billion for National Flood Insurance Program claims. The state House and Senate changed the gambling law to allow casinos to be built on land within 800 feet of the shore, and casino owners moved in rapidly to rebuild. By June 2006, the state had gained 30,000 jobs over 2005, wages were up, and developers were gentrifying what were once low-income Gulf Coast neighborhoods. Barbour's connections in Washington paid off, as D.C. lobbyists and friends sent supplies in the first days following the hurricane and later held fundraising events for the Mississippi Hurricane Recovery Fund that Barbour created not long after Katrina landed. Before the hurricane, Barbour's positive job rating in a SurveyUSA poll was 43%; after Katrina, his rating spiked to 58%. It remained above 50% for the rest of the year.

In July 2006, touting his job-creation efforts and fiscal restraint, Barbour announced the state's first budget surplus in years. He rebuffed efforts by Democrats to lower the grocery tax and raise the cigarette tax, saying that a lower grocery tax would have minimal impact on the poor because the state's 450,000 food stamp recipients were not subject to the tax. His credibility on economic development got a big boost when Toyota announced it had chosen a site near Tupelo as the site of a new 2,000-job assembly plant. In his 2007 State of the State address, Barbour told lawmakers, "There's no doubt in my mind that the future of Mississippi is brighter than it's ever been in our history.... As strange as it might seem, that awful catastrophe Katrina is part of the reason." He might as well have been discussing his own political future. His name was briefly floated as a possible presidential contender for 2008, but Barbour said he would not run because hurricane recovery demanded his full attention. He could be a possible candidate in 2012.

He ran for re-election as governor, however, starting the 2007 contest with $3.5 million. The Democratic nominee was John Arthur Eaves, a personal-injury lawyer from Madison County. During the campaign, Eaves called for cutting the grocery tax while Barbour promised an unspecified tax cut. Barbour also called for spending $125 million over five years to reduce school dropout rates and for higher pay for teachers with 25 years of service. Eaves emphasized prayers and faith, and, to Barbour's irritation, pressed for details of Barbour's blind trust. Barbour was helped by endorsements from some prominent Democrats, including former congressman and Agriculture Secretary Mike Espy and former Gov. Bill Waller. He won handily, 58%-42%.

After the election, Barbour immediately faced an unexpected issue when Republican Sen. Trent Lott announced in November 2007 that he would resign at the end of the year. Barbour said he would name an interim successor and he set the special election for the remaining four years of Lott's term for the day of the regularly scheduled general election in November 2008. He appointed U.S. Rep. Roger Wicker, a Republican, to fill the vacancy until then. But Democratic Attorney General Jim Hood argued that state law required an election within 100 days of Lott's resignation, and he sued to have the election held earlier. Democrats may have been betting they would have a better chance of winning the Senate seat in a low-turnout special election that would attract party activists rather than a more widely attended general election. A state court ruled in Hood's favor in January, but the Mississippi Supreme Court upheld Barbour 7-2 in February 2008.

Opening his second term, Barbour said in his inaugural speech, "Much of the state has the strongest economy and highest employment ever, but some areas are suffering, especially in the Delta and southwest Mississippi, where we must not only improve education and workforce skills, but also combat and reduce the scourge of illegitimacy." In 2008 he got full funding of the Mississippi Adequate Education Program for the first time in a non-election year. On other issues, Barbour supported a bill to require employers to use the eVerify system to determine the immigration status of employees. In July 2008, he was criticized for suspending the life sentence of a man convicted of murdering his wife; the convict had been working as a trusty in the Governor's Mansion. (Mississippi seems to be one of the last states to retain the curious practice of staffing the governor's residence with convicts.)

In 2008, gambling revenues were down, and overall revenues came in 9% under projections at the end of the year. Barbour demanded that legislators change the Medicaid law to eliminate a $90 million shortfall, and said he would make cuts in the program if they didn't. He trimmed the overall state budget by $42 million in November and in January promised more budget cuts, including in education programs. Barbour at first said he might not accept federal government's economic stimulus money, but as the budget problems worsened, he announced in March 2009 he would accept all but $50 million of the $2.3 billion for Mississippi. He also signed a bill for a 30% sales-tax rebate for casino developers who build golf courses, hotels, convention facilities, and other nongambling attractions worth at least $10 million.

After the national Republican Party's poor showing at the polls in 2008, Barbour said, "There are a lot of good questions Republicans need to ask themselves.... The fact of the matter is, we brought a lot of this on ourselves, a lot of it by not being faithful to what we told people that we believed in and not adhering to what people thought they had voted for." Asked whether he might run for president in 2012, Barbour declined to answer, saying that speculation about the election was premature and not helpful to the party's efforts to rebuild.

Senior Senator

Thad Cochran (R)

Elected 1978, term expires 2014, 6th term; b. Dec. 7, 1937, Pontotoc; home, Jackson; U. of MS, B.A. 1959, J.D. 1965, Rotary Fellow, Trinity Col., Ireland, 1963–64; Baptist; married (Rose); 2 children.

Military Career: Navy, 1959–61.

Elected Office: U.S. House of Reps., 1972–78.

Professional Career: Practicing atty., 1965–72.

DC Office: 113 DSOB, 20510, 202-224-5054; Fax: 202-224-9450; Web site: cochran.senate.gov.

State Offices: Gulfport, 228-867-9710; Jackson, 601-965-4459; Oxford, 662-236-1018.

Committees: *Agriculture, Nutrition & Forestry* (3rd of 8 R). *Appropriations* (RMM of 12 R): Agriculture, Rural Development, Food and Drug Administration & Related Agencies; Defense (RMM); Energy & Water Development; Homeland Security; Interior, Environment & Related Agencies; Labor, Health and Human Services, Education & Related Agencies (RMM). *Rules & Administration* (3rd of 8 R).

Group Ratings

	ADA	ACLU	AFS	LCV	ITIC	NTU	COC	ACU	CFG	FRC
2008	15	14	0	9	80	58	88	68	67	88
2007	15	—	0	0	—	64	82	83	64	—

National Journal Ratings

	2007 LIB — 2007 CONS		2008 LIB — 2008 CONS	
Economic	21%	— 78%	32%	— 67%
Social	24%	— 75%	36%	— 60%
Foreign	21%	— 73%	32%	— 67%
Composite	23%	— 77%	34%	— 66%

Key Votes of the 110th Congress

1. Raise CAFE standards	N	5. Make English official language	Y	9. Withdraw troops 3/08	N
2. Expand SCHIP	N	6. Path to citizenship	N	10. Iran guard is terrorist group	Y
3. Cap greenhouse gases	N	7. Fetus is unborn child	Y	11. Increase missile defense $	Y
4. Bail out financial markets	N	8. Prosecute hate crimes	N	12. Overhaul FISA	Y

Election Results

2008 general	Thad Cochran (R)	766,111	(61%)
	Erik Fleming (D)	480,915	(39%)
2008 primary	Thad Cochran (R)	unopposed	

Prior Winning Percentages: 2002 (85%); 1996 (71%); 1990 (100%); 1984 (61%); 1978 (45%); 1976 House (76%); 1974 House (70%); 1972 House (48%)

Republican Thad Cochran, Mississippi's senior senator, was elected to the House in 1972 and the Senate in 1978, where he sits at Jefferson Davis's old desk. He grew up in small towns in northern Mississippi and near Jackson, the son of a principal and a mathematics teacher. Cochran was extremely athletic in high school and lettered in football, basketball, and baseball. He was also valedictorian of his senior class. Cochran continued to excel academically at Ole Miss, where he was a cheerleader, which was not uncommon for men at that time and was in fact considered an honor. Cochran went on to get a law school degree from Ole Miss. He served in the Navy, spent a year abroad, and then practiced law in Jackson.

In 1968, he worked on the Nixon-Agnew presidential campaign in Mississippi, where Nixon ran third. Four years later, when Nixon was sweeping Mississippi, Cochran ran for Congress and was elected as a Republican from the Jackson-area district with a plurality against a white Democrat and a black independent. When segregationist Sen. James Eastland, a Democrat, retired, Cochran jumped into the race and once again won with a plurality over a white Democrat and a black independent. In the House and in the Senate, he has managed to amass a generally conservative record with little controversy or acrimony. His patrician demeanor, his refusal to engage in racial politics, and his Republican Party label—in a state where most whites have been voting Republican for president for three decades—have made him broadly acceptable to voters at home. His toughest race came in 1984, when he was opposed by popular former Democratic Gov. William Winter. Winter could make a case for himself but not against Cochran. Cochran outraised him $2.7 million to $738,000, and won 61%-39%.

Cochran is the ranking minority member on the Appropriations Committee, and was chairman from 2005 to 2007 when Republicans controlled the Senate. He has also been the ranking member since July 2008 on the Defense Appropriations Subcommittee, where he has been a key proponent of missile defense, and has worked to fund projects big and small for Mississippi. Timely amendments to appropriations bills that make major policy are a Cochran specialty.

In January 2005, Cochran succeeded Republican Ted Stevens of Alaska as chairman of the full committee, bringing a contrasting style of leadership to that of the grumpy, sometimes-abrasive Stevens. Even Stevens said of Cochran, "He's less confrontational, perhaps, more deliberate." Cochran promised to get appropriations bills passed on time, rather than rolling multiple bills into large "omnibus" measures, which had been done in the past when the appropriators could not complete their work on time. Cochran also said, "We're not going to have runaway spending on the Appropriations Committee when I'm chairman. I won't tolerate it." In spite of those assurances, earmarks and runaway discretionary spending were to remain major issues during his stewardship.

In June 2005, Cochran opened the appropriations season by allocating $843 billion to the subcommittees, switching $7 billion from defense to domestic spending. But then came Hurricane Katrina on August 29, which caused massive damage in Mississippi. Keeping tight controls on spending suddenly was not the chairman's prime concern. Cochran viewed the devastation by helicopter on August 31, and then persuaded the Senate to immediately vote for $10.5 billion in disaster relief. A week later, he persuaded it to vote for $52 billion more. In late October, President George W. Bush called for an additional $17 billion. Cochran, working closely with Republican Gov. Haley Barbour and others in the Mississippi and Louisiana delegations, pushed for $35 billion, with community development block grants available for homeowners and business owners with uninsured losses. This was a new policy, and one not included in the administration request. On December 21, Congress passed a $29 billion bill, with $11.5 billion for CDBG loans and grants. Mississippi received $5.1 billion of the CDBG funds, as Barbour said, "unprecedented amounts of money and unprecedented latitude in how we can spend that money." In the meantime, work on the regular appropriations bills bogged down, and Cochran and House Appropriations Chairman Jerry Lewis, R-Calif., resigned themselves to a continuing resolution for nine appropriations bills they couldn't get passed.

The following year, 2006, brought more vagaries in the appropriations process in the form of the Bush administration's request for large amounts of additional money for the war in Iraq. The president asked for a supplemental Iraq funding bill, a proposal sweetened with nearly $20 billion in additional funds for hurricane recovery. Cochran drafted a bill that included some controversial provisions: $700 million for building a CSX rail line inland, to replace the line on the Gulf Coast; $500 million for Northrop Grumman, which was in litigation with the insurers of its Pascagoula shipyard; and $1 billion for Katrina housing. The CSX line was labeled "the railroad to nowhere," an allusion to the infamous "bridge to nowhere" that Stevens once had slipped into a bill for Alaska. Cochran's fellow Republicans were among his biggest critics. Speaker Dennis Hastert and House Majority Leader John Boehner called his bill a "special-interest shopping cart," and conservative Republican Sen. Tom Coburn of Oklahoma tried to kill it. But Cochran prevailed on the Senate floor 50-47. Ultimately, Congress agreed to supplemental spending for Iraq and to $20 billion for Katrina recovery, although it rejected the railroad line.

As Cochran resumed trying to pass the regular appropriations bills on time, earmarked spending came increasingly under fire that year as more conservatives took issue with Congress's long-standing practice of approving special projects for individual lawmakers, projects that often were not requested by any government agency. Cochran and Lewis managed to get through both chambers just two of the 12 spending bills, those for defense and homeland-security appropriations. Budget hawks raised objections to earmarks in the remaining 10 bills, and GOP Majority Leader Bill Frist declined to bring them to the floor before the November 2006 election. Then Democrats won majorities in both houses. Congress passed a temporary measure to keep the government running, and work ceased on the remaining spending bills. Cochran lost his chairmanship, saying he was "terribly disappointed with the failure of this Congress to have passed the spending bills."

In 2007, the first year of the Democratic majorities in Congress, the appropriations bills became magnets for anti-war lawmakers. Cochran opposed Democrats' attempts to set timetables for troop withdrawals in the 2007 Iraq war supplemental spending bill, but his motion to eliminate a timetable was defeated 50-48. Cochran said, "I'm not going to belabor this point, but I think for us to continue to engage in who's going to win this political struggle about deadlines, forced redeployments ... it makes the world wonder whether our country is competent to deal with an emergency that threatens the very security of our country."

In May 2007, Cochran inserted into an appropriations bill $6 billion in hurricane relief aid to Mississippi and Louisiana and a provision calling for speedy approval of funding for Iraq. He also added to the bills "several items of interest to Mississippi," including $88 million for Army Corps of Engineers projects in the Yazoo Basin, $7.5 million for the Center for Marine Aquaculture at the University of Southern Mississippi, and $12 million for air traffic control facilities at the Gulfport airport. The watchdog group Citizens Against Government Waste put his final earmark tally that year at $892 million. And Cochran continued to wholeheartedly defend earmarks. "Analyses of how the executive branch spends discretionary federal dollars when left to its own devices show that rural states like Mississippi, states that often have a great deal of need, are largely ignored. This is why our founding fathers gave Congress the explicit power to direct spending, so that those who are elected by the people, not bureaucrats, decide how funds are spent," he said.

The other great area of interest for Cochran is farm legislation. On the Agriculture Committee, he played an important role in shaping the very different 1996, 2002, and 2008 farm bills. In 1996, he supported the Republican initiative to phase out most crop subsidies, although he insisted on maintaining the cotton marketing loan plan that he largely wrote in 1985. In 2002, he supported the strategy of reviving annual crop payments and of vastly increasing the Conservation Reserve Program. In 2005, Cochran defeated on the Senate floor, 53-46, Iowa Republican Charles Grassley's move to limit subsidies to farmers earning $250,000 or less. "You just can't change the rules from one year to the next and expect to have a dependable source of revenue to sustain an economy, a farm economy that is so important to the nation," he said. In 2006, he opposed Bush's proposed 5% cut in farm subsidies. And in 2008, he supported the farm bill that passed over Bush's veto. The president said the bill was too costly and did not go far enough to curb farm subsidies.

Also in 2008, Cochran got a new Mississippi partner in the Senate with the arrival of newly appointed Sen. Roger Wicker, a Republican. The two quickly teamed up to try to compel Congress to allow federal flood insurance policyholders to add wind coverage to protect themselves financially against future hurricanes. A former U.S. House member, Wicker was appointed by Barbour to replace GOP Sen. Trent Lott, who resigned from Congress. It was a welcome change for Cochran, who had competed with Lott over the years to advance in the leadership and usually wound up losing to him. In 1990, Cochran was elected to the chairmanship of the Senate Republican Conference, the No. 3 leadership position. Although he had less seniority than Cochran, Lott set his sights higher. Rather than wait his turn to move up, Lott challenged Wyoming's Alan Simpson for majority whip, the No. 2 position. Cochran pointedly endorsed Simpson, but Lott won anyway, with the support of junior Senate conservatives, and leapfrogged over Cochran to the higher-ranking post of whip. Then in 1996, the top job of Senate majority leader came open when Kansas Republican Bob Dole ran for president. Cochran and Lott both entered the race. Lott was able to sew up a majority of votes quickly. Cochran stayed in the contest and lost 44-8.

Some political observers wondered whether Cochran would run for re-election in 2008. In November 2007, he announced that he would. And Lott's decision to resign at the end of that year dissipated any possibility that Cochran would be seriously challenged. After all, it was much more appealing for high-profile Mississippi Democrats to take on Wicker, who was running for election to the remainder of Lott's term, than to take on the state's popular senior senator. Cochran even has friends and defenders among the state's Democrats. U.S. Rep. Gene Taylor, a Mississippi Democrat, said, "I would never encourage anyone to run against Thad Cochran." His challenger wound up being a former state representative with little money and no paid staff. Cochran spent $2.8 million and won 61%-39%, his closest margin since 1984.

In the presidential contest in 2008, Cochran backed former Massachusetts Gov. Mitt Romney, and his unflattering remarks about Romney's competitor in the primaries, Arizona Sen. John McCain, were widely quoted in the media. Cochran told the *Boston Globe*, "The thought of his being president sends a cold chill down my spine. He's erratic. He's hotheaded. He loses his temper, and he worries me." When McCain ultimately became the party's nominee, Cochran was conciliatory and called his earlier appraisal of McCain "ill advised." He added, "I didn't think he was going to win the nomination either."

After Democrat Barack Obama defeated McCain, Cochran said, "There are a lot of people coming in with a lot of enthusiasm. We need some people with a little gray hair to help be a calming influence. That is the role I will play."

In February 2007, Cochran became one of only 28 senators in U.S. history to cast 10,000 votes.

Junior Senator

Roger Wicker (R)

Appointed Dec. 2007, term expires 2012; 1st term; b. July 5, 1951, Pontotoc; home, Tupelo; U. of MS, B.A. 1973, J.D. 1975; Baptist; married (Gayle); 3 children.

Military Career: Air Force, 1976–80; Air Force Reserve, 1980–2004.

Elected Office: Tupelo city judge pro tem, 1986–87; MS Senate, 1987–94., U.S. House of Reps., 1995–2008.

Professional Career: Staff, U.S. House Rules Cmte., 1980–82; Practicing atty., 1982–94; Lee Cnty. public defender, 1984–87; Bd. of Visitors, U.S. Naval Academy, 2005.

DC Office: 555 DSOB, 20515, 202-224-6253; Fax: 202-228-0378; Web site: wicker.senate.gov.

State Offices: Gulfport, 228-604-2383; Hernando, 662-429-1002; Jackson, 601-965-4644; Pascagoula 228-762-5400; Tupelo, 662-844-5010.

Committees: *Armed Services* (8th of 11 R): Emerging Threats & Capabilities (RMM); Personnel; Seapower. *Commerce, Science & Transportation* (6th of 11 R): Aviation Operations, Safety & Security; Communications, Technology & the Internet; Consumer Protection, Product Safety & Insurance (RMM); Oceans, Atmosphere & Coast Guard; Surface Transportation & Merchant Marine Infrastructure, Safety & Security. *Foreign Relations* (7th of 7 R): East Asian & Pacific Affairs; European Affairs; International Development & Foreign Assistance, Economic Affairs & International Environmental Protection; International Operations & Organizations, Democracy & Global Women's Issues (RMM). *Small Business & Entrepreneurship* (7th of 7 R). *Veterans' Affairs* (3rd of 5 R).

Group Ratings (2007 House)

	ADA	ACLU	AFS	LCV	ITIC	NTU	COC	ACU	CFG	FRC
2008	10	14	0	9	50	62	88	80	75	100
2007	5	—	0	0	—	69	84	96	77	—

National Journal Ratings (2007 House)

	2007 LIB — 2007 CONS	2008 LIB — 2008 CONS
Economic	16% — 84%	26% — 72%
Social	0% — 91%	0% — 79%
Foreign	32% — 64%	24% — 71%
Composite	18% — 82%	21% — 79%

Key Votes of the 110th Congress (House)

1. Increase minimum wage	N	5. Share immigration data	Y	9. Withdraw troops 8/08	N
2. Expand SCHIP	N	6. Foreign aid abortion ban	Y	10. No operations in Iran	N
3. Raise CAFE standards	N	7. Ban gay bias in workplace	N	11. Free trade with Peru	Y
4. Bail out financial markets	*	8. Repeal D.C. gun law	*	12. Overhaul FISA	*

Election Results

2008 general	Roger Wicker (R)	683,409	(55%)	($6,160,116)
	Ronnie Musgrove (D)	560,064	(45%)	($5,371,030)

Prior Winning Percentages: 2006 House (66%); 2004 House (79%); 2002 House (71%); 2000 House (70%); 1998 House (67%); 1996 House (68%); 1994 House (63%)

Roger Wicker was appointed to the U.S. Senate in late 2007 by Republican Gov. Haley Barbour to fill the vacancy created by the resignation of Trent Lott, a powerful Mississippian who served at different times as both majority and minority leader of the Senate. Wicker, a Republican member of the U.S. House at the time of the appointment, went on to win election to the seat in November 2008.

Wicker grew up in Pontotoc, the same north Mississippi town where his senior colleague in the Senate, Republican Thad Cochran, spent part of his childhood. Wicker's father was a conservative Democrat, a state senator, and a circuit judge. He attended public schools and as a teenager became interested in Republican politics. From then on, his career was intertwined with the two more senior and well-established Mississippians, Lott and Cochran. He was a page in the House of Representatives and campaigned door to door for Cochran in his first race for Congress, in 1972. At Ole Miss, where both Lott and Cochran went to school, Wicker was associated student body president, and went on to get his law degree there. He then served for four years in the Air Force and remained in the Reserves until 2004. In 1980, he went to work for Lott on the House Rules Committee when Lott was still in the House. Wicker returned to Mississippi in 1982, set up a law practice, and was the county public defender in his wife's hometown of Tupelo. In 1987, at age 36, he was elected to the state Senate, the first Republican elected in north Mississippi since Reconstruction. In the Legislature, Wicker helped draft the state's strict abortion law and was also a leading advocate of government-sponsored vouchers for private-school tuition.

In 1994, longtime U.S. Rep. Jamie Whitten, a Democrat, momentously retired after becoming the longest-serving member of the House in history. His record of 53 years and 62 days was only recently broken by Michigan Democrat John Dingell in February 2009. The retirement of the powerful Whitten, the chairman of the Appropriations Committee, left large shoes to fill in Mississippi's 1st District. Pent-up demand produced a crowded primary field in both major parties. Six Republicans, including Wicker, and three Democrats lined up to run.

Carrying his home base around Tupelo, Wicker led the GOP primary 27%-19% over Grant Fox, a young former aide to Cochran. In the runoff, Wicker campaigned as a conservative, but Fox hammered him for voting to override Republican Gov. Kirk Fordice's veto of a sales tax increase. Wicker won, 53%-47%. Meanwhile, state Rep. Bill Wheeler, the Democratic nominee, had racked up support from African-Americans, labor unions, and teachers—an advantage in his party's primary but not necessarily in the general election in the conservative 1st District. The result wasn't even close. A district that had been held for five decades by a leading Democrat voted 63%-37% for the Republican, Wicker.

Wicker got off to a fast start in the House, elected president of the 73-member House freshman class, one of the largest in the 20th century and also one of the most historic. The incoming Republicans were by and large a feisty brand of conservatives who had nationalized the election of 1994, capitalized on public discontent with 40 years of Democratic control, and followed GOP firebrand Newt Gingrich to power. Wicker compiled a solidly conservative voting record. He got a seat on Appropriations—an unusual prize for a freshman. Appropriators tend to operate in an atmosphere of bipartisan cooperation, and while bitter fights between Republicans and Democrats flared on the floor of the House, Wicker worked quietly in subcommittees to get funding for the Natchez Trace Parkway, for Yalobusha River flood control, and for an interstate highway through DeSoto County. He delivered research dollars to Mississippi universities, and he worked with Lott, by then a senator, to attract defense technology firms to the state. Although north Mississippi was not badly hurt by Hurricane Katrina in August 2005, Wicker worked the House for Cochran as Cochran, the newly installed Senate Appropriations chairman, tried to direct federal aid to coastal Mississippi. Wicker's job was to convince his conservative Republican colleagues in the House that the state faced a genuine emergency.

In January 2007, Wicker finally reached the top GOP position on a subcommittee, but with a change in party control from the Republicans to the Democrats, he became the ranking minority member, not chairman, of the Military Construction, Veterans Affairs, and Related Agencies Subcommittee on Appropriations. He passed an amendment to place the words "In God We Trust" on the face of $1 presidential coins, and another to fund more legal representation for veterans claiming disability status. He sided with fellow appropriators and against conservatives in his party who tried to limit earmarked spending in recent years. For that, he earned the dubious distinction of No. 1 earmarker in the House by the watchdog group Citizens Against Government Waste. His achievement was securing $176 million in projects, most of it for his district. "I am a fiscal conservative, and I believe in keeping spending low," Wicker said in 2008, "but once the national budget is set, I think it is only fair to fight for our fair share for Mississippi."

In November 2007, Lott surprised just about everyone by announcing that he would retire from the Senate before the end of the year, after serving 19 years there and 16 in the House. (He is the only member of Congress to have served as his party's whip in both chambers.) Wicker was one of those vying for the seat. Others were 3rd district GOP Rep. Chip Pickering, who had already announced he wasn't running for re-election in 2008, and Netscape founder and Mississippi native James Barksdale. On December 31, 2007, Barbour appointed Wicker and set the election for the remaining years of Lott's term on November 4, 2008. Attorney General Jim Hood, a Democrat, argued that state law required a special election within 100 days of Lott's resignation and filed a lawsuit against Barbour. It seemed apparent that Democrats might fare better in a special election than with the wider electorate in November, and in fact Democrat Travis Childers did win Wicker's House seat—a district that had voted 62% for Republican President Bush in 2004—in the special election in May. Hood got a favorable verdict in a trial court on January 14, but on February 6, the state Supreme Court upheld Barbour 7-2.

Wicker took his seat in January, and got seats on the Armed Services, Veterans' Affairs, and Commerce committees. He continued to support Bush on the war in Iraq and to oppose timetables for a troop withdrawal. He supported Northrop Grumman and Airbus in their struggle against Boeing to get the Air Force's tanker contract. Airbus's big assembly plant was planned for Mobile, Ala., near the Gulf Coast of Mississippi. He worked closely with Cochran, who had often been at odds with Lott, in backing local projects and co-sponsoring bills. (Citizens Against Government Waste labeled Cochran and Wicker No. 1 and No. 3 Senate earmarkers respectively for 2008) Wicker also worked with Democrats to protect Mississippi's interests. With Democratic Rep. Gene Taylor, he pushed amendments allowing purchasers of federal flood insurance to add wind coverage to their policies, helpful to a hurricane-prone state. After Taylor got his bill passed in the House, Wicker tried to overcome resistance in the Senate from Banking Chairman Christopher Dodd of Connecticut, a state where many of the major insurers are headquartered. Wicker, Cochran, and the two Louisiana senators placed a hold on the flood insurance bill in March 2008. But they were eventually defeated, 74-19. Wicker also advanced a plan to allow those affected by the heavy hurricane season from 2004 to 2006 to take a onetime tax credit of up to $5,000 if their insurance premiums were increased by more than 100% over three years, and to take tax credits of up to $5,000 annually for hurricane mitigation home improvements. Wicker had been re-elected easily in the 1st District, but he spent his first year in the Senate facing a serious challenge in the upcoming November 2008 election. Mississippi Democrats had not seriously contested a Senate race in 20 years, but President Bush's low poll ratings, enthusiasm among African-American voters for Democratic presidential nominee Barack Obama, and Childers's Democratic victory in winning Wicker's old district gave both national and state Democrats reason to believe they might beat Wicker. He started the year little known outside his congressional district. The Democratic nominee was widely known: former Gov. Ronnie Musgrove, who was defeated for re-election by Barbour in 2003 and had good poll ratings. It was a battle between old friends: Wicker and Musgrove had both been elected to the state Senate for the first time in 1987 and roomed together in an apartment in Jackson.

Musgrove started out on the attack. He criticized Wicker for his support of earmarks and called him a "poster child" for a moratorium on pork-barrel spending; he liked to single out funding for the National Mule and Meatpackers Museum in California. Musgrove also criticized him for opposing increases in the minimum wage. Wicker said, "The people of Mississippi are tired of politicians like Mr. Musgrove and their negative attacks, and I don't think they're going to stand for his brand of politics." Musgrove even hinted at ethical misconduct, criticizing Wicker for securing a $6 million earmark, not sought by the Pentagon, for Aurora Flight Sciences to build unmanned aerial vehicles in north Mississippi, while company executives contributed $17,000 to his campaign and hired Wicker's former chief of staff to lobby for the project. Wicker said the effort was all about bringing high-paying jobs to Mississippi.

The tables turned on Musgrove when he was the subject of negative publicity after the indictment of three executives of a Georgia company that defaulted on a state government guaranteed loan of $54 million. They had contributed $59,000 to Musgrove's 2003 campaign. Wicker continued to make news on Katrina issues, notably his support of multi-peril insurance. He traveled extensively around the state, often with Cochran, who was up for re-election and was considered sure to win by a solid margin. Wicker outspent Musgrove, $6.2 million to $5.3 million. But the Democratic Senatorial Campaign Committee, flush with funds and aware that October polls showed the race to be within the margin of error, pumped in more than enough money to compensate for Wicker's advantage. Wicker won 55%-45%. Eighty-two percent of whites backed Wicker, 10% less than voted for Cochran, while 92% of blacks backed Musgrove.

Wicker comes up for re-election in 2012, a much less pressing date than he faced during 2008. In January 2009, he said he opposed further bills providing funding for endangered private firms. "I think Mississippians are properly skeptical about the bailout bills. And I have yet to see any positive effects come from those bills. I think my no vote is looking better and better," he said after Congress approved twin bailouts for the financial and domestic auto industries. In February 2009 he opposed the Democrats' economic stimulus bill, saying, "We need to slow this locomotive. The bill needs to be rebuilt from the bottom up."

FIRST DISTRICT

Travis Childers (D)

Elected May 2008, 1st full term; b. March 29, 1958, Booneville; home, Booneville; Northeast MS Jr. Col., A.A., 1978, U. of MS, B.A., 1980; Baptist; married (Tami); 2 children.

Elected Office: Prentiss Cnty. chancery clerk, 1991–2008.

Professional Career: Owner, Travis Childers Realty & Assoc., Owner, retirement and nursing homes.

DC Office: 1708 LHOB, 20515, 202-225-4306; Fax: 202-225-3549; Web site: childers.house.gov.

State Offices: Columbus, 662-327-0748; Hernando, 662-449-3090; Tupelo, 662-841-8808.

Committees: *Agriculture* (27th of 28 D): Department Operations, Oversight, Nutrition & Forestry; General Farm Commodities & Risk Management. *Financial Services* (33rd of 42 D): Capital Markets, Insurance & Government Sponsored Enterprises; Financial Institutions & Consumer Credit.

Group Ratings

	ADA	ACLU	AFS	LCV	ITIC	NTU	COC	ACU	CFG	FRC
2008	—	50	100	67	0	31	64	41	33	100
2007	—	—	—	—	—	—	—	—	—	—

National Journal Ratings

	2007 LIB	—	2007 CONS		2008 LIB	—	2008 CONS
Economic	*%	—	*%		*%	—	*%
Social	*%	—	*%		46%	—	54%
Foreign	*%	—	*%		42%	—	58%
Composite	*%	—	*%		*%	—	*%

Key Votes of the 110th Congress

1. Increase minimum wage	*	5. Share immigration data	*	9. Withdraw troops 8/08	*
2. Expand SCHIP	*	6. Foreign aid abortion ban	*	10. No operations in Iran	*
3. Raise CAFE standards	*	7. Ban gay bias in workplace	*	11. Free trade with Peru	*
4. Bail out financial markets	N	8. Repeal D.C. gun law	Y	12. Overhaul FISA	Y

Election Results

2008 general	Travis Childers (D)	185,959	(54%)	($1,822,307)
	Greg Davis (R)	149,818	(44%)	($1,437,823)
2008 runoff	Travis Childers (D)	20,797	(57%)	
	Steve Holland (D)	15,958	(43%)	
2008 primary	Travis Childers (D)	40,919	(41%)	
	Steve Holland (D)	30,274	(31%)	
	Marshall Coleman (D)	12,913	(13%)	
	Brian Neely (D)	10,624	(11%)	
2008 spec. runoff	Travis Childers (D)	58,037	(54%)	
	Greg Davis (R)	49,877	(46%)	
2008 spec. election	Travis Childers (D)	33,304	(49%)	
	Greg Davis (R)	31,117	(46%)	

Population		Race/Ethnicity		Work	
Pop. 2007:	757,113	White:	69.4%	Private:	78.3%
Change since 2000:	Up 6.5%	Black:	27.1%	Government:	14.8%
Urban:	38.5%	Hispanic:	2.0%	Self-employed:	6.7%
Rural:	61.5%	Asian:	0.5%	Blue collar:	34.8%
Area size:	11,647 sq. mi.	Native Am.:	0.1%	White collar:	49.5%
Age		Hawaiian:	0.0%	Khaki collar:	0.2%
Median age:	35.4 yrs.	Two+ races:	0.8%	Other:	15.4%
More than 65 yrs:	12.7%	*Ancestry*		Median income:	$36,993
Less than 18 yrs:	26.1%	USA:	12.1%	Median home value:	$89,300
Education		Irish:	11.2%	Poverty:	19.0%
H.S. grad:	76.3%	English:	9.3%	**Military Veterans**	
College grad:	15.9%			% of Pop:	9.6%
Grad degree:	5.3%				

The university town of Oxford—the "Jefferson" of William Faulkner's fictional Yoknapatawpha County—sits on a divide between the hill country of Mississippi and the flat farmlands of the Mississippi Delta. Named for Oxford, England, it is the home of the Center for the Study of Southern Culture and of the University of Mississippi, where violence broke out in 1962 when James Meredith became the school's first black student. Ole Miss, as it is known, now houses Meredith's papers in its

2008 Presidential Vote		
McCain (R)	213,479	(62%)
Obama (D)	129,940	(38%)

2004 Presidential Vote		
Bush (R)	187,979	(62%)
Kerry (D)	111,509	(37%)

Cook Partisan Voting Index: R + 14

library. In 1962, Republican Sen. Thad Cochran was a student at the Ole Miss law school, and former Senate Majority Leader Trent Lott of Mississippi was a senior. To the west is the Delta, with a large African-American majority, and also DeSoto County, just south of Memphis, Mississippi's fastest-growing county and one of its most affluent and most Republican. East of Oxford is the hill country, which stretches up to where the Tennessee River nicks the northeast corner of Tishomingo County. The Tennessee Valley Authority brought electricity here, the Tennessee-Tombigbee Waterway provided construction jobs for years, and a shipping canal was completed in 1985. The Tenn-Tom is the largest water resource project built in the United States. This was traditional farming country, but it is now more engaged in small manufacturing.

The Golden Triangle in the Starkville area has become a center for aerospace research, including work on unmanned air vehicle designs for improved surveillance and communications. The biggest town here is Tupelo, a stronghold of private enterprise and traditional values. It is home to an upholstered furniture industry that is the largest manufacturing sector in the state and has survived more prosperously than furniture centers elsewhere. Donald Wildmon's American Family Association, based in Tupelo, is a prominent Christian conservative organization. Elvis Presley was born in Tupelo in 1935, in a two-room house that is open to visitors, as is the Elvis Presley Museum with a modest collection of the rock 'n' roll idol's memorabilia. In February 2007, Toyota announced plans to build a plant near Tupelo. It would open in 2010 and eventually employ 2,000 workers producing 150,000 vehicles a year. Seven Toyota suppliers also planned support facilities nearby, with an estimated 2,000 additional jobs.

The 1st Congressional District of Mississippi includes Oxford, Tupelo, most of the hill country, and DeSoto County. This is the descendant of the district represented by Jamie Whitten, the longtime Democratic chairman of the Appropriations Committee and formerly the longest-serving House member. He served 53 years and 62 days, ending in January 1995, but Democratic Rep. John Dingell of Michigan surpassed his mark in February 2009. Historically this was conservative Democrat territory. In an April

2001 referendum, it voted overwhelmingly to keep the 1894 state flag with its Confederate battle cross—a symbol offensive to many African-Americans. The district voted solidly for Democratic Gov. Ronnie Musgrove in 1999, but in 2003 favored his Republican successor, Haley Barbour. In national politics it is solidly Republican, voting 59% for George W. Bush in 2000 and 62% in 2004. Similarly, the district voted 62% for Republican John McCain in 2008.

The new congressman from the 1st District is Travis Childers, a Democrat who won a May 2008 special election to fill the remainder of Republican Roger Wicker's congressional term. Wicker took an appointment to the Senate to finish retiring Republican Sen. Lott's unexpired term. Childers won a full term in November 2008.

A Mississippi native, Childers grew up in Prentiss County, where he still lives. His father died when Childers was 16 years old and still in high school. He worked nights and weekends at a local convenience store to help support his mother and sister. Childers earned an associate's degree at Northeast Mississippi Junior College before receiving a bachelor's degree in business administration from the University of Mississippi. While still at Ole Miss, he became a licensed real estate agent and joined a firm in his native Booneville. He later opened his own business, Travis Childers Realty & Associates. In 1991, he was elected Prentiss County chancery clerk, and he served in that position for five terms until 2008. He and his wife, Tami, also own a nursing home and skilled-care facility.

When Wicker was appointed to the Senate on December 31, 2007, Childers quickly took steps to run for his House seat. Describing himself as a "Mississippi Democrat" on social issues, Childers closely aligned with Republicans in opposition to gun control, abortion rights, and gay marriage. He highlighted his opposition to the Iraq war. Hoping to strike a chord with disaffected voters amid looming economic turmoil, Childers also highlighted his working class roots and his difficult early years. "True conservatism was going to work full-time when you're 16," Childers said on the stump. He won 41% of the vote in the special-election primary and, in a runoff in April, defeated state Rep. Steve Holland with 57% of the vote.

Southaven Mayor Greg Davis eventually won the Republican nod. As the special general election neared, the race drew national attention as a possible bellwether of Democratic strength in the 2008 congressional elections in November. But its value as a political indicator diminished with the presence of several third party candidates and exceptionally low voter turnout. Neither Childers nor Davis topped the 50% needed to avoid a runoff. Childers got 49.4%, which left him about 400 votes short of clinching the win outright. He ran strong in the more rural areas in the district, taking 58% in traditionally Republican Lee County and Tupelo. Davis received 46.3%, winning big in his native DeSoto County, a Memphis suburb and the largest county in the district.

In the runoff campaign, Republicans sought to link Childers to liberal national Democrats. In one ad, Davis said Childers had accepted Democratic presidential candidate Barack Obama's endorsement even "when Obama's pastor [the Rev. Jeremiah Wright] cursed America, blaming us for 9/11." Childers emphasized that Obama had not endorsed him, and his supporters accused Davis of attempting to play on racial prejudices.

The national parties each weighed in heavily. The Democratic Congressional Campaign Committee spent more than $1.5 million on the race. It sent out a controversial mailer in the final days of the campaign tying Davis to the Ku Klux Klan because he supported the erection of a statue of Confederate President Jefferson Davis in Southaven when he was mayor. The National Republican Congressional Committee spent $1.3 million. The conservative group Freedom's Watch also spent nearly $500,000 to benefit Davis, and Vice President Dick Cheney dropped in to campaign for him in the final hours of the campaign. In the end, Davis's negative ads backfired. Childers won with 54%, claiming a district that had been in Republican hands since 1995 and had voted for President Bush by 62% in 2004. Democrats heralded the win as a sign of things to come: "There is no district that is safe for Republican candidates," DCCC Chairman Chris Van Hollen told *The Washington Post*.

Once in Congress, Childers sought to burnish his conservative credentials, sponsoring a House amendment to legislation by District of Columbia Del. Eleanor Holmes Norton that sought to clarify D.C. gun rights in the wake of a U.S. Supreme Court decision striking down the District's ban on guns. His amendment would allow D.C. residents to own both handguns and rifles but continued the ban on sawed-off rifles, machine guns, and short-barreled rifles. Democrat Norton's bill was more restrictive on gun ownership. But Childers had the support of the powerful National Rifle Association and of other conservative Democrats in gun-friendly districts. His amendment passed by a wide margin in the House, though it later stalled in the Senate. Childers also voted against the $700 billion bailout of large financial firms in October 2008.

In November 2008, Davis sought a rematch, hoping that the presidential election on the same day would bring out many more voters who wanted to cast ballots for Republican nominee John McCain. Still, Republicans worried that Davis the suburban mayor did not have the same appeal as Childers, with his country boy persona. Childers also outpaced Davis in fundraising, $1.8 million to $1.5 million. Building on his May victory, he bested Davis by 11 points, 55% to 44%, even as McCain handily carried the district with 62% of the vote.

Childers is on the Financial Services Committee and the Agriculture Committee. Early in the 111th Congress, he fell more in line with other Democrats, particularly on economic issues. He supported the Democrats' proposed expansion of the State Children's Health Insurance Program and voted for President Obama's economic stimulus bill in February 2009.

SECOND DISTRICT

Bennie Thompson (D)

Elected April 1993, 8th full term; b. Jan. 28, 1948, Bolton; home, Bolton; Tougaloo Col., B.A. 1968, Jackson St. U., M.S. 1972; Methodist; married (London); 1 child.

Elected Office: Bolton Bd. of Aldermen, 1969–73; Bolton mayor, 1973–79; Hinds Cnty. Supervisor, 1980–93.

DC Office: 2432 RHOB, 20515, 202-225-5876; Fax: 202-225-5898; Web site: www.house.gov/thompson.

State Offices: Bolton, 601-866-9003; Greenville, 662-335-9003; Greenwood, 662-455-9003; Jackson, 601-946-9003; Marks, 662-326-9003; Mound Bayou, 662-741-9003.

Committees: *Homeland Security* (Chmn of 20 D).

Group Ratings

	ADA	ACLU	AFS	LCV	ITIC	NTU	COC	ACU	CFG	FRC
2008	90	91	100	92	71	15	50	8	8	5
2007	100	—	100	85	—	3	50	0	0	—

National Journal Ratings

	2007 LIB	—	2007 CONS		2008 LIB	—	2008 CONS
Economic	82%	—	0%		85%	—	0%
Social	71%	—	28%		75%	—	18%
Foreign	76%	—	23%		76%	—	23%
Composite	80%	—	20%		83%	—	18%

Key Votes of the 110th Congress

1. Increase minimum wage	Y	5. Share immigration data	N	9. Withdraw troops 8/08	Y
2. Expand SCHIP	Y	6. Foreign aid abortion ban	N	10. No operations in Iran	Y
3. Raise CAFE standards	Y	7. Ban gay bias in workplace	Y	11. Free trade with Peru	N
4. Bail out financial markets	N	8. Repeal D.C. gun law	N	12. Overhaul FISA	Y

Election Results

2008 general	Bennie Thompson (D)	201,606	(69%)	($1,081,785)
	Richard Cook (R)	90,364	(31%)	
2008 primary	Bennie Thompson (D)	111,077	(86%)	
	Dorothy Benford (D)	17,824	(14%)	

Prior Winning Percentages: 2006 (64%); 2004 (58%); 2002 (55%); 2000 (65%); 1998 (71%); 1996 (60%); 1994 (54%); 1993 (55%)

Population		Race/Ethnicity		Work	
Pop. 2007:	686,847	White:	32.0%	Private:	72.2%
Change since 2000:	Down 3.4%	Black:	65.4%	Government:	21.6%
Urban:	62.8%	Hispanic:	1.2%	Self-employed:	5.9%
Rural:	37.2%	Asian:	0.5%	Blue collar:	26.2%
Area size:	13,937 sq. mi.	Native Am.:	0.3%	White collar:	52.0%
		Hawaiian:	0.0%	Khaki collar:	0.2%
Age		Two+ races:	0.6%	Other:	21.6%
Median age:	33.4 yrs.			Median income:	$29,490
More than 65 yrs:	11.3%	*Ancestry*		Median home value:	$74,100
Less than 18 yrs:	27.9%	USA:	7.0%	Poverty:	28.7%
		Irish:	5.4%		
Education		English:	4.8%	**Military Veterans**	
H.S. grad:	74.4%			% of Pop:	7.9%
College grad:	18.1%				
Grad degree:	5.9%				

"The Mississippi Delta," wrote Delta native David Cohn, "begins in the lobby of the Peabody Hotel in Memphis and ends on Catfish Row in Vicksburg." For centuries, the flooding Mississippi and Yazoo rivers left their sediments here, producing a fertile, dark soil. Ironically, what may well be America's richest agricultural land has been home for more than a century to many of its poorest people. Criss-crossed by rivers and famously disease-ridden, the Delta wasn't much settled until after the Civil War.

2008 Presidential Vote		
Obama (D)	196,444	(66%)
McCain (R)	99,548	(33%)
2004 Presidential Vote		
Kerry (D)	153,786	(59%)
Bush (R)	104,749	(40%)
Cook Partisan Voting Index:	D + 12	

The tradition here is Reconstruction-era, profit-seeking operators who used late-19th-century technology to drain the land, line the river with levees, and build railroads on tracks above the rise of the river. Black sharecroppers and field hands worked here in conditions almost of bondage. From this episode of industrial farming came both great misery and great art: Clarksdale in Coahoma County was the real birthplace of blues music, the home of W.C. Handy and Muddy Waters, John Lee Hooker, Ike Turner, and Sam Cooke. Greenville on the Mississippi has produced writers of the caliber of Walker Percy and Shelby Foote. Yazoo City produced author Willie Morris and bluesman Skip James. Today, Vicksburg's antebellum mansions and battlefield monuments bring in 1.5 million tourists annually.

Twentieth-century technology changed life in the Delta. The mechanical cotton-picking machine, invented in 1944, came along just as Northern factories were seeking low-wage workers. The great exodus to Chicago and other cities in the North began, and the Delta's population has been declining ever since. Income levels remain very low, poverty is over 50% in some areas, and infant mortality is at Third World levels. City-style crime and drugs from Chicago have been brought back by Delta migrants returning home. Yet there are signs of hope. Soybeans have become a big-dollar crop here, poultry farms have become a major enterprise, and the Delta produces most of the nation's catfish. To control flooding and boost crop yield, farmers are pushing for the installation of pumps between the Mississippi and Yazoo rivers, but the Environmental Protection Agency has been reluctant to approve them.

Tunica County is by some measures the nation's poorest county, and the best it could do economically in recent years was to attract gambling businesses. It has nine casinos, and runways at the regional airport have been extended to accommodate jets bearing tourists and players in national poker tournaments. The casinos have increased local per capita income and decreased welfare rolls, but there is still a gulf between rich and poor. The Delta has been slow to develop a self-propelling market economy. At the edge of the Delta there are other economic stories. Just north of the fast-growing and affluent suburbs of Jackson, Nissan operates a 5,000-employee factory in Canton, historically a heavily African-American area. The plant produces the flexfuel Titan and Armada vehicles, and is expected to expand to build Nissan's new light commercial vehicle, the NV2500. One consequence was the tripling of land values, as thousands more jobs were created for suppliers, and property moved from agriculture to residential or commercial use.

The 2nd Congressional District of Mississippi includes the entire Delta, indeed the whole Mississippi riverfront from Tunica almost to Natchez. It includes most of heavily black and low-income Jackson and surrounding Hinds County except for the affluent Bellehaven neighborhood. This is Mississippi's one black-majority district, created in 1984. It includes a few counties in the east that are majority white and vote Republican, but the political tone of the district is set by the African-American neighborhoods in Jackson and the counties of the Delta. Before the Voting Rights Act of 1965, these were run politically by segregationists like Democratic Sen. James Eastland, a Delta cotton plantation owner and Senate Judiciary Committee chairman from 1955 to 1979. In 1986, the district elected its first black congressman since Reconstruction, Democrat Mike Espy, whose grandfather and father were among the biggest landowners in the state. In 2008, the 2nd was the only Mississippi district to vote for the nation's first African-American president, Democrat Barack Obama, who got 66% of the vote.

The congressman from the 2nd District is Democrat Bennie Thompson, who was elected in April 1993. He grew up in Bolton, in Hinds County outside Jackson, and graduated from Tougaloo College and Jackson State University. He was elected alderman in Bolton in 1969, at age 21, and elected mayor four years later. He was the first Mississippi politician to get a street named after the Rev. Martin Luther King Jr. A volunteer firefighter for much of his adult life, he got the first fire engine for Bolton, too. In 1980, he became a Hinds County supervisor. A lifelong grassroots activist and labor organizer, he successfully encouraged other African-Americans to run for office. After Espy resigned from Congress in 1993 to become President Bill Clinton's Agriculture secretary, Thompson ran for the seat in an all-party primary. He came out ahead of Henry Espy, Mike Espy's brother and mayor of Clarksdale, 28%-20%. Republican Hayes Dent, an aide to Gov. Kirk Fordice, led with 34%. Voting in the runoff was mostly along racial lines, and Thompson won 55%-45%, with his margin coming mostly from Hinds County.

Thompson has a solidly liberal voting record. He initially made no particular attempt to win white votes, making almost as few concessions across the racial divide as Eastland had. In time, he moderated his votes and reached out to whites, including some of the district's large farmers. After the Democrats won control of the House, Thompson became chairman of the Homeland Security Committee, where he has focused on the needs of first responders. Previously, he was the ranking minority member of the panel. When he first arrived on the committee in 2005, he caused some turmoil by firing some staffers, cutting the pay of others, and hiring more minority aides. But he also began a sometimes-productive working relationship with Republican Chairman Peter King of New York.

After Hurricane Katrina struck Louisiana and Mississippi in August 2005, revealing the weaknesses in the Federal Emergency Management Agency's ability to respond to a disaster of that magnitude, Thompson said, "It's like they brought a squirt gun to put out a forest fire." He found the federal assistance lines so tied up that he sent an aide with a cellphone to the Mississippi Emergency Management Agency. In 2006, House Republicans proposed to establish FEMA as an entirely independent agency, but Thompson and King instead called for keeping it within the Department of Homeland Security, but with the kind of autonomy the Coast Guard has there. Thompson worked with King on the first authorization bill for DHS, but his amendment to increase funding from $35 billion to $41 billion was defeated on a 16-13 party-line vote. Thompson negotiated with King on an agreement to restructure FEMA. As part of the deal, Thompson demanded an additional $3 billion for state and local governments to develop interoperable communications, and when King declined, he refused to support the bill. Ultimately, the authorization bill died in the Senate.

Thompson had a testy relationship with President Bush's Homeland Security chief, Michael Chertoff. He frequently criticized Chertoff, once accusing him of lapses in security at maritime cargo checkpoints and once of playing "political games" with chemical security legislation by opposing a bill allowing states to impose additional regulations at facilities. The department under Chertoff, Thompson complained, suffered from high turnover, low morale, and a lack of diversity.

Taking over as chairman in January 2007, Thompson shepherded through the House one of the new Democratic majority's "first 100 hours" bills, which was to adopt the recommendations of the 9/11 commission. It included a requirement to screen all passenger jet and ship cargo, and became law in August 2007. Thompson's priorities include encouraging awards of contracts to minority firms, making sure that contractors hire minorities, delivering research money to historically black colleges and universities, and ensuring that border security and Transportation Security Administration officers don't single out travelers because of race or ethnicity.

In the 111th Congress (2009–10), Thompson pushed to centralize oversight of the Homeland Security Department under his committee, ending the current practice of spreading jurisdiction among several committees. He persuaded the Democratic Caucus to adopt rules ensuring more bills would be referred to his committee. He also planned to conduct oversight of the planned closing of the detention facility at Guantanamo Bay.

Thompson's arguably confrontational politics have brought him opposition in the 2nd District. In 2002, he was re-elected by a less than impressive 55%-43% against Republican challenger Clinton LeSueur, a consultant to the Yazoo Community Action Agency. LeSueur ran again in 2004 and spent three times the money he had before, but Thompson increased his victory to 58%-41%. In 2006, state Rep. Chuck Espy, nephew of the former representative, challenged him in the primary, but Thompson prevailed 64%-35%. He also cruised to re-election in 2008, winning 69%-31%.

In 2009, Thompson came under fire from local Republicans after the *Jackson Clarion-Ledger* reported on trips to vacation destinations he took that were paid for by special-interest groups. The AFL-CIO labor union paid for him to travel to Las Vegas, the International Longshoreman's Association sent him to Fort Lauderdale, Fla., and the Carib News Organization, which publishes a newspaper on Caribbean issues, funded a trip to the island of St. Maarten in the Caribbean. Thompson defended the trips as necessary to learn firsthand about homeland-security issues, and said they were approved by the House Committee on Standards of Official Conduct.

THIRD DISTRICT

Gregg Harper (R)

Elected 2008, 1st term; b. June 1, 1956, Jackson; home, Pearl; MS Col., B.S. 1978; U. of MS, J.D. 1981.; Baptist; married (Sidney); 2 children.

Professional Career: Practicing atty.

DC Office: 307 CHOB, 20515, 202-225-5031; Fax: 202-225-5759; Web site: harper.house.gov.

State Offices: Brookhaven, 601-832-3400; Meridian, 601-693-6681; Pearl, 601-932-2410; Starkville, 662-324-0007.

Committees: *Budget* (14th of 15 R). *House Administration* (3rd of 3 R): Elections. *Judiciary* (16th of 16 R): Courts & Competition Policy; Immigration, Citizenship, Border Security & International Law.

Group Ratings and Key Votes: Newly Elected

Election Results

2008 general	Gregg Harper (R)	213,171	(63%)	($1,143,197)
	Joel Gill (D)	127,698	(37%)	($93,191)
2008 runoff	Gregg Harper (R)	29,351	(57%)	
	Charlie Ross (R)	22,178	(43%)	
2008 primary	Charlie Ross (R)	22,254	(33%)	
	Gregg Harper (R)	18,892	(28%)	
	David Landrum (R)	17,082	(26%)	
	John Rounsaville (R)	6,949	(10%)	

Population		Race/Ethnicity		Work	
Pop. 2007:	738,183	White:	62.1%	Private:	72.8%
Change since 2000:	Up 3.8%	Black:	34.2%	Government:	19.8%
Urban:	40.3%	Hispanic:	1.3%	Self-employed:	7.1%
Rural:	59.7%	Asian:	0.8%	Blue collar:	25.9%
Area size:	13,310 sq. mi.	Native Am.:	0.9%	White collar:	56.8%
		Hawaiian:	0.0%	Khaki collar:	0.5%
Age		Two+ races:	0.5%	Other:	16.8%
Median age:	35.8 yrs.	*Ancestry*		Median income:	$36,872
More than 65 yrs:	13.2%	USA:	16.4%	Median home value:	$88,600
Less than 18 yrs:	25.6%	Irish:	8.9%	Poverty:	19.1%
Education		English:	7.7%		
H.S. grad:	80.5%			**Military Veterans**	
College grad:	22.4%			% of Pop:	9.5%
Grad degree:	7.9%				

Mississippi, old and new. The old Mississippi is the Neshoba County fair, held every August since 1889 in the town of Philadelphia. What started as a farmer's picnic has become the traditional place where Mississippi politicians announce their candidacies, with the crowds watching to take their measure. The crowds are also there to watch the races on the state's only legal horse track. When Republican Ronald Reagan stumped here in 1980 and Democrat Michael Dukakis campaigned here in 1988,

2008 Presidential Vote
McCain (R) 213,025 (61%)
Obama (D) 134,878 (39%)

2004 Presidential Vote
Bush (R) 203,376 (65%)
Kerry (D) 106,455 (34%)

Cook Partisan Voting Index: R + 15

neither of them mentioned what Philadelphia and Neshoba County are best known for nationally. There is no memorial, except engraved stones at two African-American churches, to mark the events of the summer of 1964, when three civil-rights workers, two white and one black, were murdered for the crime of urging black American citizens to register to vote. In June 2005, a jury of nine whites and three blacks convicted Edgar Ray Killen, an 80-year-old preacher and sawmill operator, of manslaughter. He was sentenced to three life sentences. The new Mississippi is some 80 miles away, in Rankin and Madison counties east and north of Jackson, where subdivisions, shopping centers, and office complexes are sprouting up in the countryside, as well as the big Nissan plant operating in Canton since 2003, employing 5,000 workers. Even as other areas of the state were feeling the effects of the nationwide recession, Rankin County had the lowest unemployment rate in Mississippi.

The 3rd Congressional District of Mississippi includes the Jackson suburbs in Rankin County and south Madison County, plus the affluent neighborhoods of northeast Jackson in Hinds County. It stretches north to Starkville, home of Mississippi State University, and south almost to Laurel. In the southwest, it reaches over to include Natchez, where 600 antebellum mansions and other properties with live oaks sit atop bluffs overlooking the Mississippi River. The small town of Macon was the scene in 2007 of a first-ever Justice Department lawsuit against a black Democratic Party official for discriminating against the voting rights of minority whites. In the middle of the district are Neshoba County and Meridian, where Republican presidential candidate John McCain was once a Navy flight instructor at Naval Air Station Meridian. The airfield is named for his grandfather. The district's political tradition had been Democratic for many years, but its preference now is strongly Republican: Mississippi, old and new. In 2008, McCain had no problem winning the district, 61%-39%.

The new congressman from the 3rd District is Gregg Harper, a Republican elected in 2008 to succeed the retiring Chip Pickering, also a Republican. Harper was born in Jackson, where his father was a petroleum engineer and his mother was a homemaker. The family moved frequently because of his father's job, but always came back home to Mississippi. By the time he'd finished high school, Harper had attended 10 different schools. Harper became a Christian after attending a youth rally in high school, and later met his wife, Sidney, at a church function. They have a daughter, Maggie, and a son, Livingston, who suffers from a developmental disorder. Drawing on the challenges his family has faced, Harper promised to be an advocate for special-needs children in Congress.

Harper is new to elected office but he has long experience in politics. He has been the chairman of the Rankin County Republican Party and has worked on several local and state campaigns. As a young man, he campaigned for Pickering's father when he ran for the state Senate more than 30 years ago. Harper was a member of the state GOP executive committee and was a delegate to the 2000 and 2008 national Republican conventions. When the 2000 presidential election was in limbo and hinged on results in Florida, Harper volunteered as a legal observer for George W. Bush's recount efforts. Until his election, he was the prosecuting attorney for the cities of Brandon and Richland.

He jumped into the primary contest for the House seat as soon as Pickering announced his retirement. Harper's toughest Republican competitors were state Sen. Charlie Ross, considered the early favorite, and wealthy businessman David Landrum. On the Democratic side, popular former Rep. Ronnie Shows pondered a run but ultimately decided against it.

Ross shored up endorsements from local leaders and national groups such as the anti-tax Club for Growth, and both he and Landrum outspent Harper. But Harper rallied a hardworking core of young volunteers and family members, and focused on door-to-door campaigning. He also got one important endorsement, from former Senate Republican Leader Trent Lott of Mississippi, who appeared at a January fundraiser for him. In the March 2008 primary, Ross emerged as the top vote-getter with 33%, and Harper finished second with 28%. Because no candidate won more than 50%, the contest went to a runoff in April. In the runoff campaign, Ross emphasized his military background and 11 years in the state Legislature as a contrast to Harper's lack of legislative experience. Harper emphasized his conservative stances against abortion rights and same-sex marriage, in an appeal to the district's small-town voters. Harper's strategy worked, and the runoff results gave him 57% of the vote to Ross's 43%. Ross narrowly edged Harper in pivotal Meridian and Lauderdale County by 128 votes, but Harper won 63%-37% in Ross's native Rankin, the district's largest county.

In the November general election, Harper faced Democrat Joel Gill, a rancher and a Pickens alderman. Gill ran folksy ads that referred to him as "Joel the Cattleman." Still, a catchy ad was not enough in this Republican district, and Harper easily won with 63% of the vote.

In Washington, Harper promised to be a conservative vote in the model of Pickering, although he acknowledged it would be harder with Republicans in the minority. Harper was the only freshman elected to serve on the Republican Steering Committee, and was the only first-term lawmaker appointed to the House Administration Committee. Additionally, he got assignments on the Judiciary and Budget committees.

FOURTH DISTRICT

Gene Taylor (D)

Elected Oct. 1989, 10th full term; b. Sept. 17, 1953, New Orleans, LA; home, Bay St. Louis; Tulane U., B.A. 1974; Catholic; married (Margaret); 3 children.

Military Career: Coast Guard Reserve, 1971–84.

Elected Office: Bay St. Louis City Cncl., 1981–83; MS Senate, 1983–89.

Professional Career: Sales rep., Stone Container Corp., 1977–89.

DC Office: 2269 RHOB, 20515, 202-225-5772; Fax: 202-225-7074; Web site: www.house.gov/genetaylor.

State Offices: Bay St. Louis, 228-469-9235; Gulfport, 228-864-7670; Hattiesburg, 601-582-3246; Laurel, 601-425-3905; Ocean Springs, 228-872-7950.

Committees: *Armed Services* (4th of 36 D): Readiness; Seapower & Expeditionary Forces (Chmn). *Transportation & Infrastructure* (10th of 44 D): Coast Guard & Maritime Transportation; Highways & Transit; Water Resources & Environment.

Group Ratings

	ADA	ACLU	AFS	LCV	ITIC	NTU	COC	ACU	CFG	FRC
2008	75	64	86	77	43	20	56	24	10	94
2007	65	—	55	80	—	28	60	72	27	—

National Journal Ratings

	2007 LIB	—	2007 CONS		2008 LIB	—	2008 CONS
Economic	47%	—	53%		48%	—	50%
Social	45%	—	55%		54%	—	42%
Foreign	47%	—	53%		48%	—	52%
Composite	46%	—	54%		51%	—	49%

Key Votes of the 110th Congress

1. Increase minimum wage	Y	5. Share immigration data	Y	9. Withdraw troops 8/08	N
2. Expand SCHIP	N	6. Foreign aid abortion ban	Y	10. No operations in Iran	Y
3. Raise CAFE standards	Y	7. Ban gay bias in workplace	N	11. Free trade with Peru	N
4. Bail out financial markets	N	8. Repeal D.C. gun law	Y	12. Overhaul FISA	Y

Election Results

2008 general	Gene Taylor (D)...	216,542	(75%)	($513,266)
	John McCay (R)...	73,977	(25%)	($11,141)
2008 primary	Gene Taylor (D).. unopposed			

Prior Winning Percentages: 2006 (80%); 2004 (64%); 2002 (75%); 2000 (79%); 1998 (78%); 1996 (58%); 1994 (60%); 1992 (63%); 1990 (81%); 1989 (65%)

Population		Race/Ethnicity		Work	
Pop. 2007:	723,975	White:	71.4%	Private:	71.9%
Change since 2000:	Up 1.8%	Black:	23.1%	Government:	20.7%
Urban:	53.7%	Hispanic:	2.5%	Self-employed:	7.2%
Rural:	46.3%	Asian:	1.4%	Blue collar:	29.0%
Area size:	9,536 sq. mi.	Native Am.:	0.3%	White collar:	52.6%
		Hawaiian:	0.1%	Khaki collar:	0.9%
Age		Two+ races:	1.2%	Other:	17.5%
Median age:	35.7 yrs.	*Ancestry*		Median income:	$38,861
More than 65 yrs:	12.2%	USA:	12.3%	Median home value:	$101,200
Less than 18 yrs:	25.9%	Irish:	10.0%	Poverty:	18.2%
Education		English:	7.8%		
H.S. grad:	80.3%			**Military Veterans**	
College grad:	18.0%			% of Pop:	13.7%
Grad degree:	6.4%				

Coastal Mississippi along the Gulf of Mexico has gone through several transformations in its history. French explorers founded Biloxi in 1699, before New Orleans or St. Louis, and made it the capital of an empire extending to what is now Yellowstone National Park. Two hundred years later, rich people from New Orleans came to this section of the Gulf Coast in summer to get away from yellow fever and to rest on Victorian verandas. Six American presidents have vacationed here, and Pascagoula is

2008 Presidential Vote		
McCain (R)..............................	198,545	(67%)
Obama (D)	93,399	(32%)
2004 Presidential Vote		
Bush (R).................................	188,880	(68%)
Kerry (D).................................	86,010	(31%)
Cook Partisan Voting Index: R+20		

the birthplace of the original beach bum, singer Jimmy Buffett. More recently, the Gulf Coast grew more than any other major part of Mississippi. Along much of the shoreline, new 1,000-room hotels rose as part of the boom, and about 50,000 jobs were created. There is also a military flavor to the Gulf Coast. Biloxi's Keesler Air Force Base was once one of the four largest in the country. Pascagoula is home to more than 12,000 employees at Ingalls Shipyard, whose gray, hangarlike buildings and skeletons of ships under construction loom over the landscape. The Pentagon's 2005 base-closing actions hit hard here. Pascagoula Naval Station was closed, with its equipment and personnel shifted to Mayport, Fla. Keesler was scheduled to shrink by about 400 military jobs, but new plans suggest the base will actually expand by a few hundred. It is also bidding to host a new cyber-command center, which would bring thousands of high-technology jobs to the region,

The blow from the base closing, though severe, was trifling compared to the direct hit that the coastal communities took from Hurricane Katrina on August 29, 2005. From Waveland to Pascagoula, about 80 miles were obliterated: beachfront cottages, fishing villages, hotel casinos, oil-drilling platforms, and refineries all were either cruelly swamped or swept away. Status meant nothing. The homes of Confederate President Jefferson Davis in Biloxi and former Senate Majority Leader Trent Lott, R-Miss., in Pascagoula were destroyed. The eye of the monster storm passed over the area, and the devastation was, if anything, worse than that from the collapsed levees of New Orleans. In an instant, the storm ruined countless livelihoods, caused losses in the tens of billions of dollars, and laid waste to a way of life.

If there was a saving grace, many of these communities were left with a clean slate to restart development, with more control over the building of high-rises and strip malls that had started to overwhelm more-distinctive properties. With more organization and speed than in Louisiana, the state's officials planned for the future and quickly spent insurance proceeds and the money available from Washington. It helped to have Haley Barbour, a well-connected national Republican insider, as governor and Mississippi Sen. Thad Cochran as chairman of the Senate Appropriations Committee. Even while the cleanup continued, important decisions were made, especially in Biloxi. Condominium projects were more carefully managed; shrimp boaters got docks for their boats and places to sell their catch; casinos were permitted to be built on land, instead of the barges they were restricted to in the past. In Pascagoula, five new buildings were planned for the site of the naval station, and the state planned to use recovery funds to open a shipbuilding school.

This is the heart of the 4th Congressional District of Mississippi. Prior to Katrina, half of its people lived on the Gulf Coast. The rest were inland, in farm counties or around Hattiesburg and Laurel. This was mostly scrubland, not much good for plantations. With its low African-American percentage of the population, the district has been prime Republican territory. In close to its current form, it gave Republican President Richard Nixon his highest percentage in all 435 districts in 1972; it voted five times against fellow Southerners Jimmy Carter, Bill Clinton, and Al Gore, and it was represented for 16 years in the House by Lott, until he was elected to the Senate in 1988. In 2008, the district gave GOP presidential nominee John McCain his highest percentage in the Magnolia State, 67%, to Democratic nominee Barack Obama's 32%.

The congressman from the 4th District is Gene Taylor, a Democrat chosen in a 1989 special election. Taylor graduated from Tulane University, where he studied political science and history, and then served in the Coast Guard Reserves as skipper of a search-and-rescue boat for 13 years. He was elected to the Bay St. Louis City Council in 1981 and in 1983, at age 30, was elected to the state Senate. In 1988, when Lott ran for the Senate, Taylor ran for his House seat and won the Democratic primary, but lost the general election to Republican Larkin Smith 55%-45%. When Smith died in an August 1989 plane crash, Lott backed his own longtime aide, Tom Anderson, who had spent little time in the district and proved to be an abrasive candidate. Taylor, combining a barely reined-in aggressiveness with a down-home manner, won the special election 65%-35%.

In the House, Taylor has been among the most conservative Democrats, especially on cultural issues, and has bluntly criticized the leadership of both parties. Taylor is a peppery populist with a reasonably consistent view on issues. He is against abortion rights, gun control, foreign aid, and federal deficits. He is strongly pro-defense and boasts of bringing defense contracts to his district. As a senior Democrat on the Armed Services Committee, he has participated actively in expanding health benefits for military retirees. In 2007, he became chairman of the Seapower and Expeditionary Forces Subcommittee, a useful assignment for his coastal district. He is an advocate of requiring the Navy to use nuclear propulsion to fuel its large surface ships, both to decrease fuel costs and to enable the ships to spend more time at sea. He supported more competition for contracts on shipbuilding, and opposed an expansion of the DDG-1000 destroyer program, a ship built in his district, saying it could bankrupt the Navy's shipbuilding program.

Taylor has tended to oppose any U.S. military commitment that stops short of assured and total victory. He voted against the first Gulf War in 1991, lifting the arms embargo on Bosnia, and sending troops to Haiti. He won House passage of limits on forces in Colombia. Since then, he has become more willing to use military power. When faced with apparently ineffective American military involvement in Serbia in 1999, he said the United States should declare war. And in 2002, he voted for the use of force in the second Iraq conflict. Taylor is a protectionist, loudly opposing free-trade agreements for North America and Central America and opposing normalizing trade relations with China.

With his background in the Coast Guard and the geography of his district, Taylor is big on boats. He promotes Ingalls and other shipyards and succeeded in widening and deepening the Gulfport shipping channel. He protects the interests of the Merchant Marine fleet, champions the seafood industry, and wants to limit foreign-flag ships from competing with domestic shipping. With GOP Rep. Jo Ann Davis of Virginia, he organized the Shipbuilding Caucus to expand the Navy fleet. He vigorously opposed the 2005 base-closing round, and suffered a big defeat when Pascagoula Naval Station was shuttered. He has fought to give the National Guard membership in the Joint Chiefs of Staff.

Katrina preoccupied Taylor for many months, both personally and politically. He lost his home in Bay St. Louis and joined a lawsuit against State Farm for unpaid claims. He added links to his website to aid constituents seeking Social Security checks and missing persons. Despite opposition from Democratic Leader Nancy Pelosi to a Republican-led select committee investigation, Taylor participated. At a hearing a month after the storm, he grilled former Federal Emergency Management Agency Director Michael Brown about the inadequate response: "I was there, and I don't recall seeing you," he told Brown tartly. "You get an F-minus in my book." He filed a bill for retroactive federal compensation for homes and businesses without flood insurance. "After the storm, so many people who normally ask very little of their nation were now looking at losing everything, and they needed our help," he said in April 2006.

Two months later, the House passed his amendment requiring the Homeland Security Department to investigate whether insurance companies had wrongly denied claims after Katrina. Over criticism from the Bush White House in September 2007, the House also passed his amendment adding wind coverage to national flood insurance, but the bill stalled in the Senate and died at the end of the 110th Congress in late 2008. Taylor reintroduced the measure in early 2009 at the opening of the new Congress. He is the sponsor of a bill that goes even further for policyholders. As part of the National Flood Insurance Program, it would allow people in coastal areas to make claims for rebuilding costs no matter what the cause of damage from a natural disaster. The bill was supported by Gov. Barbour and the entire Mississippi congressional delegation, as well as the Democratic House leadership, but it never made it out of committee.

Taylor is hardly ever a reliable Democratic vote, especially on economic matters. In 2008, he voted against the $700 billion bailout for Wall Street, telling the *Biloxi Sun Herald* that he would not only vote no, "if there was a button that said 'hell no,' I'd push it." In February 2009, he was one of only seven Democrats who voted against President Obama's economic stimulus bill. Still, Taylor has rebuffed all importunings to switch parties. "I personally would feel like a prostitute. I still believe the average working person's best interest is best served by the Democratic Party," said Taylor, with his characteristically colorful choice of words. When it briefly looked like the House might have to decide the contested 2000 presidential election, he said then that he would vote for Republican Bush over Democratic nominee Al Gore to reflect the views of his constituents.

At home, he faced serious opposition only in 1996, when Republican Dennis Dollar challenged him for re-election. Taylor won with a solid 58%-40%, even as GOP presidential nominee Bob Dole was winning the district by a similar margin. If Taylor departs, Republicans would have a good chance to capture this seat. But he shows no signs of accommodating them. In 2008, he cruised to his 10th term with 75% of the vote.

★ MISSOURI ★

St. Louis, established by French frontiersmen and acquired by the United States as part of the Louisiana Purchase, was the place where Meriwether Lewis and William Clark set out on their expedition to the Pacific in May 1804. On high ground just below the point where the Missouri River swirls into the Mississippi, St. Louis was then the one well-established city in America's interior, with an aristocracy of French merchants, a brawling bourgeoisie of Yankee and Southern frontiersmen and fur traders, and a proletariat of black slaves. Several years later, in 1821, the city was part of the new state of Missouri, and for decades St. Louis and Missouri were the gateways to the frontier. West of St. Louis, Daniel Boone finally found elbow room; St. Joseph was the eastern terminus of the Pony Express; Westport, now part of Kansas City, was the starting point of the Santa Fe Trail. The Mississippi River steamboats celebrated by Mark Twain linked North and South before the Civil War; afterward, railroads reached across the continent, connecting the farmers on the prairies with their markets.

Missouri was not just the gateway to the frontier; it was also a focus of the furious battle over slavery. Missouri was the northernmost slave state in 1850. Missouri ruffians rode across the border and killed antislavery settlers in the Kansas Territory—acts that led proximately to the Civil War. The state had its own bloody civil war in the hilly counties along the Missouri River and in the southwest. Throughout the 19th century, both before and after the Civil War, Americans turned away from their oceans and headed inward to settle the great interior of the continent. They found Missouri at its heart, with farmland and mines, rivers and railroads and factories. In 1874, the Eads Bridge opened, one of the very few spans on the Mississippi, and St. Louis's Cupples Station was the largest rail hub in the world. At the turn of the 20th century, Missouri was the fifth-largest state and St. Louis was the fourth-largest city, site of the 1904 World's Fair and one of the few cities with two major league baseball teams, the Cardinals and the Browns. Missouri after the 1900 census had 16 congressional districts.

Today, Missouri does not loom as large in the national consciousness, yet it is in some ways still central. In the 20th century, Americans—like the Browns, who moved to Baltimore in the 1950s, and the football Cardinals, who moved to Phoenix in the 1980s—increasingly headed toward the coasts, to the big cities of the East and West, and eventually to Florida and Texas. Missouri has had below-average population growth since 1900, and today it is the 17th-largest state, with just nine congressional districts. But Missouri was the geographic center of the nation's population in the 2000 census: an imaginary, flat map of the United States population, if everyone weighed the same, would balance near Edgar Springs in Phelps County, Mo. Missouri started perking up demographically in the 1990s, growing 9%, its greatest decennial increase in a century. Growth was particularly strong in the outer suburbs of St. Louis and Kansas City, and in the Ozarks. Dozens of rural counties that had been losing population for most of the 20th century started regaining it. The state economy, long sluggish, was showing signs of solid growth. Some of St. Louis's major companies were acquired by outside firms—McDonnell-Douglas, TWA, Ralston Purina, May Department Stores, Monsanto, and Anheuser-Busch—yet St. Louis still produces lots of airplanes, chemicals, and beer. Meanwhile, unnoticed on the coasts, the Lake of the Ozarks region in central Missouri and southwest Missouri around the country music center of Branson have been attracting modest-income retirees looking for traditional lifestyles and inexpensive recreation.

Culturally, Missouri remains more conservative than most of the bigger states. Its relatively slow-growing metro areas have not overwhelmed the countryside, a land of farms and small towns thick with churches and modest-income shopping centers and laced with artificial lakes and boat launches. Only one town in rural Missouri, Springfield, has more than 150,000 residents, and in the state's 103 rural counties, life—and politics—seem not to have changed much over the past half-century. Missouri has some tough immigration laws, even though it has attracted relatively few immigrants. Local police agencies have seized many methamphetamine labs, but the state has one of the nation's few declining prison populations.

For more than a century, Missouri has been one of America's political bellwether states. It voted for every presidential winner but two from 1904 to 2008, narrowly backing Adlai Stevenson in 1956 and John McCain in 2008. From the 1960s to the 1990s, it mirrored national trends by moving its congressional politics from fairly solidly Democratic to leaning Republican. Starting with the excruciatingly close presidential vote in 2000, the results in Missouri have been very tight as well. In the state's 10 contests for president, senator, and governor between 2000 and 2008, only two were decided by wide margins: Republican Sen. Christopher (Kit) Bond's re-election in 2004 and Democratic Gov. Jay Nixon's election in 2008. In the eight other contests, Republicans got between 47% and 53% of the vote, Democrats between 46% and 50%.

The patterns in these 21st-century elections were very different from what prevailed for most of the 20th century. Then, Missouri's old Civil War political divisions still held: Democrats dominated in Little Dixie in the northeast, first settled by Virginians, and in the northwest, settled by Southerners. Republicans held sway in the Ozarks in the southwest, which was pro-Union, and the southeast was split, like next-door downstate Illinois. Now the real divide is between the state's two big metropolitan areas and

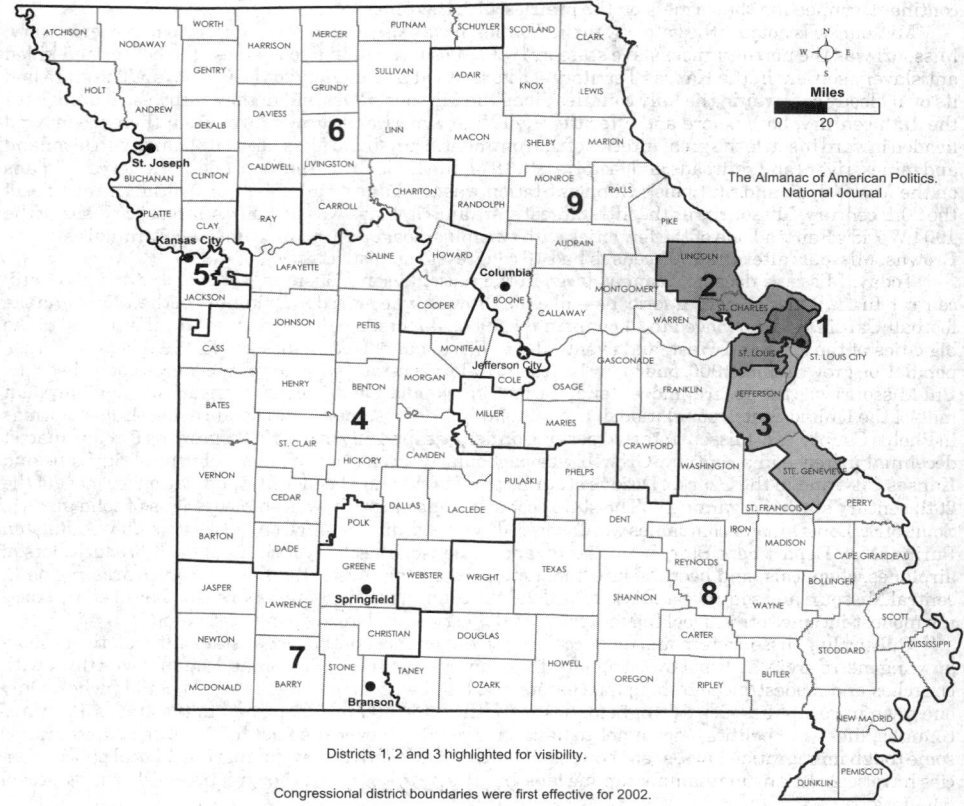

Districts 1, 2 and 3 highlighted for visibility.

Congressional district boundaries were first effective for 2002.

Population		Household Income		Work	
Pop. 2007:	5,834,644	Under $15k:	14.8%	Private:	79.4%
State rank:	18th of 50	$15k to $50k:	40.6%	Government:	13.5%
Change since 2000:	Up 4.3%	$50k to $100k:	30.8%	Self-employed:	6.8%
Urban:	68.2%	$100k to $150k:	11.7%	Unemployment (3-yr. average):	4.3%
Rural:	31.8%	Over $150k:	2.2%	Poverty:	13.4%
Native of state:	66.5%	Median income:	$44,545	Blue collar:	24.1%
Not a citizen:	2.0%			White collar:	58.8%
Area size:	69,704 sq. mi.	**Home Value**		Khaki collar:	0.3%
		Under $100k:	35.1%	Other:	16.9%
Most populous cities		$100k to $300k:	54.6%		
1. Kansas City	436,562	$300k to $500k:	7.4%	**Age**	
2. St. Louis	352,389	$500k to $1 mil:	2.4%	Median age:	37.3 yrs.
3. Springfield	153,727	Over $1 million:	0.6%	More than 65 yrs:	13.4%
4. Independence	116,214	Median:	$131,100	Less than 18 yrs:	24.4%

Race/Ethnicity		Language		Military Veterans		Registered Voters in 2008	
White:	82.4%	English:	94.4%	% of Pop:	11.9%	No party registration	
Black:	11.2%	Spanish:	2.6%	*Veterans by Period*		Voter turnout:	2,925,205
Hispanic:	2.9%	Asian:	1.0%	WWII and before:	12.5%	Turnout as % of	
Asian:	1.4%	Other		Korea:	12.8%	voting age:	65.1%
Native Am.:	0.4%	European	1.8%	Vietnam:	32.7%	**General Assembly**	
Hawaiian:	0.1%	**Education**		Gulf (pre-2001):	10.1%	Senate:	11 D 23 R
Two+ races:	1.5%	H.S. grad:	84.9%	Gulf (post-2001):	6.5%	House:	74 D 89 R
Ancestry		College grad:	24.0%	Peace time:	25.5%		
German:	21.6%	Grad degree:	8.6%				
Irish:	11.9%						
English:	8.5%						

the rural rest of Missouri. The St. Louis metro area voted 54%-45% for John Kerry in 2004; metro Kansas City, about half as big, voted 52%-47% for Kerry. But the rest of Missouri, casting 43% of the votes, went 63%-36% for George W. Bush. In 2008, Missourians moved toward the Democrats almost uniformly across the state, but not quite far enough to give Barack Obama Missouri's 11 electoral votes. Obama carried metro St. Louis 59%-41%, a big gain over 2004, and metro Kansas City 56%-43%, a similar gain. The rest of Missouri voted 59%-40% for McCain, and the Republican nominee carried 107 of 115 counties.

In downballot races, ancestrally Democratic rural counties have taken to electing Republicans to Congress and the state Legislature. Although Democrats seriously contested the open 9th Congressional District seat in 2008, they did not make much headway in state legislative races, gaining three seats in the House but losing three in the Senate. That left solid Republican majorities in both state chambers despite the election of Democrat Nixon as governor by an impressive 58%-40%. So, Missouri remains closely balanced politically, just as it is uniquely divided in another way: It is the only state whose name is pronounced two ways, depending on the region. In metro St. Louis, they say "Missouree;" in the rest of the state, it's "Missouruh."

Presidential politics   In 2008, Missouri departed from its pattern as a bellwether state by preferring McCain, who lost the presidential election to Obama. But in this race, and in both the Democratic

and Republican presidential primaries, Missouri was the site of some of the closest contests in the nation. On February 5, Obama won the Democratic primary over Hillary Rodham Clinton, 49.3%-47.9%. McCain won the Republican primary over Mike Huckabee, 33%-31.5%, with Mitt Romney capturing 29.3% of the vote. On November 4, McCain carried Missouri with 49.4% to 49.3% for Obama. Altogether, these three contests were decided by popular-vote margins totaling 24,046 votes out of 4.3 million cast.

All three elections showed similar patterns. Obama benefited in both the Democratic primary and general election by winning huge margins in St. Louis City; St. Louis County, whose population is now more than 20% black; and Jackson County, which includes most of the central city of Kansas

2008 Presidential Vote		
McCain (R)	1,445,814	(49%)
Obama (D)	1,441,911	(49%)

2008 Democratic Presidential Primary		
Obama (D)	406,917	(49%)
Clinton (D)	395,185	(48%)

2008 Republican Presidential Primary		
McCain (R)	194,053	(33%)
Huckabee (R)	185,642	(31%)
Romney (R)	172,329	(29%)

2004 Presidential Vote		
Bush (R)	1,455,713	(53%)
Kerry (D)	1,259,171	(46%)

City and some of its suburbs. In the primary, he also carried the counties including the state capital (Cole), the University of Missouri (Boone), and Northwest Missouri State University (Nodaway). In the general election, he carried rough-hewn Jefferson County south of St. Louis, Washington and Iron counties (old mining territory), Boone County, and Buchanan County (St. Joseph).

The pattern was a little more complicated in the three-way Republican primary. Romney, with his heavy television advertising and his appeal to high-income voters, carried most of the Kansas City media market plus Boone and Cole counties, St. Charles County (St. Louis exurbs), and Cape Girardeau County (Rush Limbaugh's hometown). McCain carried St. Louis City and St. Louis County, Jefferson and Franklin counties to the south and west, and a swath of counties in north-central Missouri. Huckabee, riding his strong appeal to evangelical conservatives, carried southwest Missouri by a wide margin and Little Dixie counties in the northeast.

Missouri joined the Super Tuesday primary for 1988, returned to multitiered caucuses to elect delegates in 1992 and 1996, then rejoined Super Tuesday in 2000. Expected victories for Missouri natives did not result: both Bill Bradley in 2000 and Dick Gephardt in 2004 were effectively out of the race before Missourians got to vote. In 2008, Obama's narrow victory over Clinton did not cost her much momentum, thanks to the Democrats' proportional representation delegate-allocation rules. But McCain's narrow victory, with less than one-third of the total votes, gave him all 58 of Missouri's GOP delegates thanks to the party's winner-take-all rules. That narrow victory played a key role in forcing Romney out of the race for the Republican nomination immediately; he was joined a few weeks later by Huckabee.

Congressional districting

111th Congress Lineup	
5 R	4 D

110th Congress Lineup	
5 R	4 D

Missouri did not lose any seats in the 2000 census, and control of redistricting was split between the parties: Democrats held the governorship and had a majority in the state House; Republicans had an 18-16 edge in the state Senate. The main problem was how to adjust for the declining population of St. Louis. Back in 1950, the city had 856,000 residents, enough for almost three congressional districts. By 2000, it had 348,000, not enough for half a district. But it is heavily Democratic, and in early 2001, 1st District Rep. William Lacy Clay was demanding more of the city, to keep the black percentage in his district above 50%. That was resisted by 3rd District Rep. Gephardt because the Democrat didn't want his district moved farther out into Republican suburbs. In April, Gephardt and Clay met at the St. Louis Labor Central headquarters and made a deal; the city would be divided roughly along Interstate 44.

In early May, Democrats passed a plan in the House that protected all incumbents and largely followed the Gephardt-Clay deal. In the Senate, Republicans prepared a proposal that would have given Gephardt a much more Republican district, but Democrats filibustered to keep it from the floor. On May 11, a deal was reached. Gephardt got the agreed-on portion of St. Louis and the close-in, increasingly Democratic suburbs of Maplewood, Richmond Heights, Clayton, and University City. Clay got the increasingly black northern suburbs of Florissant, Hazelwood, Bridgeton, and St. Ann plus affluent Creve Coeur and Ladue. Republican Todd Akin of the 2nd District lost all of those areas and got Sunset Hills, Sappington, and Concord from Gephardt's old district and new territory in suburban St. Charles and rural Lincoln counties. Akin was the only incumbent who didn't like the plan, but he said he wouldn't challenge it in court. It was a success for Republicans, considering that their sole leverage was a two-seat margin in the state Senate.

Since 2001, Missouri's population has been increasing more rapidly than that of most Midwestern states, but lags the national average. As a result, the state seems likely to lose a House seat in the reapportionment that will follow the 2010 census. Democratic Gov. Nixon will be in office during the redistricting cycle, but Democrats will have to pick up many seats in the state House and Senate in the 2010 elections to control the process. Demographically, the St. Louis area is even more at risk of losing a seat than it was in 2001. Population has been stagnant in St. Louis City and declining in St. Louis County, which together would be entitled to not quite two whole seats in an eight-district plan. Another district could be created from exurban counties around St. Louis. The district that is probably most vulnerable to elimination is the 9th, both because its central geographical position makes it easy to divide up among its neighbors and because its representative, Republican Blaine Luetkemeyer, elected by a narrow margin in 2008, has little seniority and is in the minority party in the House.

Governor

Jay Nixon (D)

Elected 2008, term expires Jan. 2013, 1st term; b. Feb. 13, 1956, DeSoto; home, Jefferson City; U. of MO, B.A., 1978; J.D., 1981.; Methodist; married (Georganne); 2 children.

Elected Office: MO Senate, 1986–1992; MO atty. gen., 1992–2008.

Professional Career: Practicing atty., 1981–1992.

Office: State Capitol Bldg., Rm. 216, Jefferson City, 65101, 573-751-3222; Fax: 573-751-1495; Web site: gov.mo.gov.

Election Results

2008 general	Jay Nixon (D)	1,680,611	(58%)
	Kenny Hulshof (R)	1,136,364	(39%)
2008 primary	Jay Nixon (D)	304,181	(85%)
	Daniel Carroll (D)	53,835	(15%)

Jay Nixon, the Democratic governor of Missouri, grew up in DeSoto, in Jefferson County, 47 miles southwest of St. Louis. His mother was president of the DeSoto school board and his father was mayor of DeSoto when *Look* magazine named it an "All-America City." Jay Nixon graduated from the University of Missouri and its law school and then practiced in Jefferson County. In 1986, when a state senator retired, he ran for the seat and won. In the state Senate, he spoke so often that he was warned he was angering senior colleagues. In 1988, at age 32, he ran against U.S. Sen. John Danforth, a Republican who had held statewide office in Missouri for 20 years. It was not an auspicious foray. His "Nixon '88" signs evoked memories of the disgraced former president, and his attacks on Danforth for running for a third term fell flat. He was trounced 68%-32%, carrying St. Louis city proper by an unimpressive margin and losing all 115 counties.

Nixon did not have to give up his state Senate seat, however, nor his ambition for statewide office. He made a name for himself by investigating a scandal at the State Agency for Surplus Property. In 1992, Nixon ran for attorney general, an office that Republicans had held for 24 straight years, and beat David Steelman. In four terms as attorney general, Nixon developed innovative programs such as No Call, which created a do-not-call list of more than 2.6 million names off-limits to telemarketers. He established the Agriculture and Environment Division to enforce Missouri's environmental laws. And in a landmark victory, Nixon argued before the U.S. Supreme Court to reinstate Missouri's campaign contribution limits. The decision was a catalyst for national campaign finance reform. He worked to end the protracted school desegregation cases in St. Louis and Kansas City, eventually reaching settlements.

In 1998, Nixon ran for the U.S. Senate again, against two-term incumbent Christopher (Kit) Bond. But Nixon was criticized by many black leaders for his stands in the school desegregation cases and got lukewarm support from Kansas City Mayor Emanuel Cleaver, a prominent African American who is now a House member. Bond, who had worked on housing and other issues with black leaders, clearly cut into the Democratic Party's normally near-unanimous African American vote and ended up winning 53%-44%.

As in his first U.S. Senate race, Nixon was in the middle of a four-year term and did not have to give up his state office. He was re-elected attorney general by wide margins in 2000 and 2004. In his second term as attorney general, he launched a political challenge to first-term Republican Gov. Matt Blunt. He criticized Blunt for cuts in Medicaid that removed 100,000 people from the rolls and for the sale of assets of the Missouri Higher Education Loan Authority. He also attacked Blunt's cuts in the First Steps program for children with autism and other problems; opposed the governor's limits on damages in lawsuits; and supported the request of a former official to retrieve Blunt's office e-mails, which were regularly deleted per administration policy. The request was rebuffed by the courts. Meanwhile, Nixon was ordered to reimburse the state $47,000 for the use of state vehicles to attend fundraisers.

Both candidates raised large sums—$6 million for Blunt and $3 million for Nixon by late 2007. But in July of that year, the state Supreme Court ruled that the law that had increased campaign fundraising limits was invalid; both Blunt and Nixon had to refund amounts over the limits, leaving them about equal in November 2007, with Blunt at $1.5 million and Nixon at $1.4 million. At this point, Blunt had low job-approval ratings, and the loss of his financial advantage made Nixon the favorite to win.

Then, in a move that surprised even his top staffers, Blunt announced in January 2008 that he would not run for a second term, saying he had accomplished most of what he had set out to do. Republicans scrambled for a nominee. Peter Kinder, the lieutenant governor, decided to run for re-election, and so the two leading GOP candidates were state Treasurer Sarah Steelman and 9th District Rep. Kenny Hulshof. It was a sharply negative campaign, with Steelman attacking Hulshof as a Washington insider. Hulshof was backed by Kinder and U.S. Sen. Bond, and these endorsements (Bond helped in the St. Louis area, Kinder in southeast Missouri) plus his popularity in his district enabled Hulshof to win 49%-45% despite Steelman's strength in the Springfield area, the most Republican part of the state.

The result set up a contest between two old friends, Nixon and Hulshof. Hulshof had worked in the attorney general's office as a roving prosecutor handling murder and other difficult cases. When he became attorney general, Nixon kept Hulshof on, despite his Republican affiliation, and the two men adopted a habit of lunchtime basketball games. Nixon even granted Hulshof a leave of absence in 1994 to run for Congress against the 18-year incumbent in the 9th District, Democrat Harold Volkmer. Hulshof lost the 1994 race, but he left the attorney general's office soon after to plot a rematch. In 1996, he challenged Volkmer again and won, eventually serving six terms. After Republicans lost control of the House in 2006, Hulshof began looking for other work. In 2008, the governorship came open.

Nixon entered the fall campaign with great advantages. He had good job-approval ratings and a big fundraising lead. Hulshof was short of money after the primary, and Steelman did not endorse him heartily. The national Democratic ticket—Nixon stayed carefully neutral until Barack Obama, the narrow primary winner in Missouri, clinched the nomination—seemed competitive in the state. He called for rescinding Blunt's Medicaid cuts, for expanding college scholarships for students from families with incomes under $80,000, and for regulation of payday loans. Nixon echoed Steelman's charge that Hulshof was a Washington insider and attacked him for voting for tax breaks for oil companies. To that, he contrasted his record of suing gas stations that raised prices beyond certain levels. He also attacked Hulshof for supporting school vouchers, in the form of tax credits for those who finance scholarships to private schools. Hulshof characterized Nixon as "old way Jay" and echoed Blunt's criticism of him for using no-bid contracts to hire lawyers and for seeking a contribution from the utility AmerenUE while investigating the collapse of its Taum Sauk reservoir. Hulshof called for using the state's "rainy day fund" to finance job-creating businesses, for tax incentives to build an oil refinery, and for bonuses for math and science teachers.

Nixon was the front-runner through most of the campaign season and won 58%-39%. He carried not only the cities but also 66 of the state's 115 counties, losing only in Hulshof's 9th Congressional District, in solidly Republican southwest Missouri, and in counties in the far southeast and northwest corners of the state. He came into office facing declining revenues but with a budget surplus. He also faced a Legislature with significant Republican majorities in both houses and a Republican lieutenant governor, his longtime critic Kinder, who had eked out a 50%-47% win.

Senior Senator

Christopher (Kit) Bond (R)

Elected 1986, term expires 2010, 4th term; b. March 6, 1939, St. Louis; home, Mexico; Princeton U., B.A. 1960, U. of VA, LL.B. 1963; Presbyterian; married (Linda Pell); 1 child.

Elected Office: MO auditor, 1970–72; MO gov., 1972–76, 1980–84.

Professional Career: Practicing atty., 1964–69, 1977–80; MO asst. atty. gen., 1969–70.

DC Office: 274 RSOB, 20510, 202-224-5721; Fax: 202-224-8149; Web site: bond.senate.gov.

State Offices: Cape Girardeau, 573-334-7044; Columbia, 573-442-8151; Jefferson City, 573-634-2488; Kansas City, 816-471-7141; Springfield, 417-864-8258; St. Louis, 314-725-4484.

Committees: *Appropriations* (2nd of 12 R): Agriculture, Rural Development, FDA & Related Agencies; Defense; Energy & Water Development; Financial Services & General Government; State, Foreign Operations & Related Programs; Transportation, Housing and Urban Development & Related Agencies (RMM). *Environment & Public Works* (6th of 7 R). *Intelligence (Select)* (VChmn of 7 R). *Small Business & Entrepreneurship* (2nd of 7 R).

Group Ratings

	ADA	ACLU	AFS	LCV	ITIC	NTU	COC	ACU	CFG	FRC
2008	20	14	0	18	100	51	100	75	59	100
2007	25	—	14	0	—	54	100	83	48	—

National Journal Ratings

	2007 LIB	—	2007 CONS	2008 LIB	—	2008 CONS
Economic	30%	—	68%	25%	—	74%
Social	17%	—	80%	0%	—	79%
Foreign	0%	—	93%	0%	—	84%
Composite	18%	—	82%	15%	—	85%

Key Votes of the 110th Congress

1. Raise CAFE standards	N	5. Make English official language Y	9. Withdraw troops 3/08	N
2. Expand SCHIP	Y	6. Path to citizenship N	10. Iran guard is terrorist group	Y
3. Cap greenhouse gases	N	7. Fetus is unborn child Y	11. Increase missile defense $	Y
4. Bail out financial markets	Y	8. Prosecute hate crimes N	12. Overhaul FISA	Y

Election Results

2004 general	Christopher (Kit) Bond (R)............................1,518,089	(56%)	($7,848,506)
	Nancy Farmer (D)..1,158,261	(43%)	($3,548,116)
2004 primary	Christopher (Kit) Bond (R)...............................541,998	(88%)	
	Mike Steger (R)..73,354	(12%)	

Prior Winning Percentages: 1998 (53%); 1992 (52%); 1986 (53%)

Christopher (Kit) Bond, Missouri's senior senator, was first elected to the Senate in 1986. The 69-year-old Republican stalwart of Missouri politics announced on January 8, 2009, that he would not seek another six-year term. "In 1973, I became Missouri's youngest governor," Bond said. "I do not aspire to become Missouri's oldest senator." His retirement was grim news for national Republicans, who, in addition to being fond of the genial Bond, were precariously close to falling below 40 seats in the Senate and handing the Democrats a filibuster-proof majority.

Bond grew up in the town of Mexico, Mo., where he still lives with his wife. His family was part-owner of the largest business in town, A.P. Green, which made heat-resistant bricks. He graduated from Princeton and the University of Virginia law school, and then clerked for one of the great pioneers of the civil-rights movement, Judge Elbert Tuttle of the 5th Circuit in Atlanta. Later, Bond returned to Missouri to practice law, and in 1968, at age 29, he ran for Congress but narrowly lost. He was elected state auditor in 1970 and then elected governor, at age 33, in 1972. He lost his 1976 re-election bid to Democrat Joseph Teasdale but won a comeback victory against Teasdale in 1980. After two years in private life, he ran for the Senate against Harriett Woods, who had come close to beating Bond's longtime ally, Republican Sen. John Danforth, in 1982. The campaign is best remembered for a negative ad that Woods ran depicting a farmer breaking into tears as he tells Woods about the foreclosure on his farm and names Bond as a board member of the insurance company that handled the foreclosure. The ad backfired, Woods fell in the polls, and Bond won, 53%-47%.

Bond has a moderate voting record in the Senate, and although he can be a strong partisan, he does much of his work behind the scenes in bipartisan alliances. In 2007, he became the ranking Republican on the Senate Select Intelligence Committee and proceeded to build a cooperative relationship with the committee's chairman, West Virginia Democrat Jay Rockefeller, whom he had known since they were fellow governors from 1980 through 1984. They agreed to merge the majority and minority staffs and to hold more hearings than in the past.

Bond supported the George W. Bush administration's surveillance of suspected terrorists abroad and worked to sustain its position in bills before the Senate. In August 2007, he and Minority Leader Mitch McConnell of Kentucky sponsored a bill to authorize such surveillance without a special court order, while Democrats pressed for requiring court approval of surveillance of U.S. citizens or individuals living in the United States. In October 2007, Bond and Rockefeller passed a bill in committee that required prior court approval of the terms of such surveillance and granted immunity from lawsuits to telecommunications companies that cooperated with government requests for surveillance. The House passed a different version of the immunity provision, and in early 2008, Bond and Rockefeller worked out a compromise with House leaders: A federal court would grant immunity if it determined that the telecom firms acted on assurances of legality and authorization by the president. This version, slightly altered, was passed into law in July 2008.

In other recent issues before the committee, Bond was a staunch defender of the nomination of Michael Hayden as Bush's director of the Central Intelligence Agency and pushed for more authority for the director of national intelligence. He also sponsored a bill with criminal penalties for government employees or contractors who leak classified information. In 2007, he lamented the intelligence agencies' inability to give senators "an unqualified financial statement."

Bond is a senior member of the Appropriations Committee and for years has been chairman of or ranking member on the panel's Transportation, Housing and Urban Development, and Related Agencies Subcommittee. There, he has worked in a generally bipartisan way with Democrats Barbara Mikulski of Maryland and Patty Murray of Washington state. In 2007, he and Murray opposed the Bush administration proposal to borrow $3.2 billion from mass transit funds to replenish the Highway Trust Fund. They favored using $8 billion of general funds instead, but the House declined to act. In 2008, Bond led the unsuccessful opposition to zeroing-out a pilot program allowing long-haul Mexican trucks to operate in the United States. Working in tandem with black community leaders in St. Louis and Kansas City over the years, Bond has taken a particular interest in housing issues that have come before the committee and has sponsored many amendments aiding inner-city organizations and encouraging small-business growth in troubled urban areas. In the 110th Congress (2007–08), he opposed administration cuts in housing subsidies, and he and Murray put $75 million more into their spending bill for shelters for homeless veterans.

Bond has also been active on the Defense Appropriations Subcommittee, working to continue operation of Boeing's F-15 production line at its plant next to the St. Louis airport. In 2004, he got $120 million for two more F-15s, which kept the production line open until 2008. In October 2007, he and then-Illinois Democratic Sen. Barack Obama called for a full accounting of troops who seek psychological help and questioned whether Veteran Affairs was inappropriately denying benefits to veterans by classifying their medical conditions as "pre-existing personality disorders."

He's done plenty of other work on Appropriations to help Missouri and is a stout defender of earmarks, the additional spending that lawmakers slip into appropriations bills for projects in their districts or states. In 2008, Bond obtained some $310 million in earmarks, or, as he prefers to call them, "strategic investments" for Missouri. The state is home to auto assembly plants, and Bond has frequently teamed with Michigan senators to help domestic automakers in their struggle to compete with the Japanese. In November 2008, he co-sponsored a bill to provide up to $25 billion in loans to rescue the Big Three automakers, which claimed to be on the verge of bankruptcy as a result of the nationwide credit crisis. The legislation had majority support in the Senate but failed because of a filibuster. Hoping to ward off a gathering political movement toward more-stringent fuel-efficiency standards in 2007, Bond and Democratic Sen. Carl Levin of Michigan sponsored an amendment to raise the standards to 36 miles per gallon for cars and 30 mpg for trucks by 2025. It was rejected in favor of greater and more-sustained increases in fuel efficiency.

Bond got his political start as a member of a group of young, reform-minded Republicans—his former Senate colleague Danforth was also a member—working against the Democratic political establishment in Missouri, and he can be a strong partisan on occasion. On Election Night 2000, he was furious when St. Louis Democrats persuaded a state judge to order the city's polls to remain open an extra three hours. An Appeals Court overturned the order within 45 minutes, but Bond maintained that the election had been stolen. Republican Jim Talent lost his bid for governor that year, and GOP Sen. John Ashcroft lost his re-election, both by narrow margins. In Washington, Bond became heavily involved in the election procedures bill in the wake of the 2000 presidential vote-count battle in Florida. The centerpiece of the bill was its national standards for voting equipment coupled with $3.5 million in federal aid for statewide voter registries.

Bond was re-elected 52%-45% in 1992, a year when Missouri Republicans lost every other major race. In 1998, running against Democrat Jay Nixon, then-state attorney general and now governor, he was re-elected 53%-44%. Democrats hoped to target Bond in 2004, but their best candidates did not run. State Treasurer Nancy Farmer stepped forward, but her fundraising fell short and Bond outspent her $8 million to $3.5 million. He lost metro St. Louis, 52%-47%, but he carried usually Democratic metro Kansas City, 51%-48%, and the rest of the state, 67%-33%, for a 56%-43% victory. The 13-point margin was his largest ever in a Senate or gubernatorial race.

Junior Senator

Claire McCaskill (D)

Elected 2006, term expires 2012, 1st term; b. July 24, 1953, Rolla; home, St. Louis; U. of MO, B.S. 1975, J.D. 1978; Catholic; married (Joseph Shepard); 7 children.

Elected Office: MO House of Reps., 1982–88; Jackson Cnty. legislature, 1990–92; Jackson Cnty. prosecutor, 1992–98; MO auditor, 1998–2006.

Professional Career: Law clerk, MO Court of Appeals, 1978; Asst. Jackson Cnty. prosecutor, 1978–82; Practicing atty., 1983–92.

DC Office: 717 HSOB, 20510, 202-224-6154; Fax: 202-228-6326; Web site: mccaskill.senate.gov.

State Offices: Cape Girardeau, 573-651-0964; Columbia, 573-442-7130; Kansas City, 816-421-1639; Springfield, 417-868-8745; St. Louis, 314-367-1364.

Committees: *Aging (Special)* (7th of 13 D). *Armed Services* (11th of 15 D): Airland; Personnel; Readiness & Management Support. *Commerce, Science & Transportation* (10th of 14 D): Aviation Operations, Safety & Security; Communications, Technology & the Internet; Competitiveness, Innovation & Export Promotion; Consumer Protection, Product Safety & Insurance. *Homeland Security & Governmental Affairs* (7th of 10 D): Contracting Oversight (Chmn); Disaster Recovery; Federal Financial Management, Government Information, Federal Services & International Security; Investigations (Permanent).

Group Ratings

	ADA	ACLU	AFS	LCV	ITIC	NTU	COC	ACU	CFG	FRC
2008	80	64	89	82	80	11	75	20	15	0
2007	90	—	100	73	—	17	9	8	13	—

National Journal Ratings

	2007 LIB	—	2007 CONS		2008 LIB	—	2008 CONS
Economic	51%	—	47%		49%	—	49%
Social	58%	—	41%		59%	—	40%
Foreign	59%	—	36%		45%	—	53%
Composite	57%	—	43%		52%	—	48%

Key Votes of the 110th Congress

1. Raise CAFE standards	N	5. Make English official language Y	9. Withdraw troops 3/08	Y
2. Expand SCHIP	Y	6. Path to citizenship	N	10. Iran guard is terrorist group N
3. Cap greenhouse gases	Y	7. Fetus is unborn child	N	11. Increase missile defense $	N
4. Bail out financial markets	Y	8. Prosecute hate crimes	Y	12. Overhaul FISA	Y

Election Results

2006 general	Claire McCaskill (D)	1,055,255	(50%)	($11,705,967)
	Jim Talent (R)	1,006,941	(47%)	($14,340,762)
2006 primary	Claire McCaskill (D)	282,767	(81%)	
	Bill Young (D)	67,173	(19%)	

Claire McCaskill, a Democrat, was elected Missouri's junior senator in 2006. She was born in Rolla, about halfway between St. Louis and Springfield, and grew up in the Missouri towns of Houston, Lebanon, and Columbia. She hails from a political family. Her father served for a time as state insurance commissioner, and her mother was the first female city council member in the university town of Columbia. McCaskill earned degrees from the University of Missouri and its law school, clerked for the state Court of Appeals in Kansas City, and worked as an assistant prosecutor. In 1982, at the age of 29, she was elected to the Missouri House, where she was the first sitting member to have a baby. Ten years later, she became Jackson County prosecutor. And in 1998, she decided to run statewide and was elected state auditor.

In 2004, halfway through her second term as auditor, McCaskill challenged incumbent Gov. Bob Holden in the Democratic primary. Holden's administration had started off on the wrong foot, holding a $1 million inaugural, the largest in state history. The inaugural committee wound up $417,000 in debt. Things didn't get much better as a tough economic climate necessitated deep spending cuts and Holden battled with the Legislature over education funding. Despite roots in the Ozarks, he was also hurt in outstate Missouri by his 2003 veto of a concealed-carry gun law. Democrats worried that they needed a stronger candidate to survive a Republican challenge in November. In stepped McCaskill, who defeated Holden 52%-45%. Holden graciously conceded, and the party and the state's major labor unions, which backed Holden, quickly united behind her against Republican Secretary of State Matt Blunt, the 33-year-old son of House Majority Whip Roy Blunt. This was not the first contest between the McCaskills and Blunts: Blunt's grandfather, Leroy Blunt, had been elected to the Missouri House in 1978 by defeating McCaskill's mother, Betty McCaskill.

In the general election campaign, Blunt promised to make state government more accountable and efficient. He supported concealed-carry legislation and the constitutional amendment banning same-sex marriage, and he opposed abortion rights. McCaskill supported abortion rights, though she opposed late-term abortions, with an exception for the life of the mother. She opposed the concealed-carry gun law and the constitutional amendment banning same-sex marriage. McCaskill sought to take advantage of Blunt's youth and relative inexperience in state government, noting that she would not need on-the-job training. She lost 51%-48%. McCaskill easily carried the Kansas City and St. Louis metropolitan areas but lost big in outstate Missouri, where Blunt won 90 of the 97 counties outside the two metro areas.

Despite the narrow loss, with three previous statewide races, McCaskill was a prize Senate recruit for the national party in 2006. She would be running for a seat that had changed partisan hands in both 2000 and 2002. In 2000, Republican John Ashcroft had lost 51%-48% to Mel Carnahan, the sitting governor whose name remained on the ballot after his death 22 days before the election. Carnahan's wife, Jean, was appointed to the vacancy. In the 2002 election for the remaining four years of the term, she lost 50%-49% to Republican Jim Talent. In most election years, Talent would have been well positioned for reelection. He had avoided ethics missteps, was attentive back home, and had quietly built a solid legislative record. But the war in Iraq and the unpopularity of the Bush administration were not helpful to a politician elected to the Senate with a thin 21,000-vote margin.

McCaskill announced her candidacy in August 2005 on the steps of the feed mill where her father once worked—a backdrop that telegraphed her focus on the rural counties that cost her the governor's election. She emphasized her country upbringing and promised to "never forget rural Missouri." She traveled in a 31-foot recreational vehicle through the rural region she once called "Ashcroftland" for its religious conservatism. She denounced tax breaks for oil companies, called for an increase in the minimum wage, and said she would push tax credits for first-time home purchases, child care, and college education. Throughout the campaign, McCaskill linked Talent to President George W. Bush. "He agrees with President Bush more than I agree with my husband," she liked to say. But the issue of embryonic-stem-cell research generated the most attention. A controversial proposed constitutional amendment forced both candidates to address whether they supported more government funding for the research, which uses surplus embryos from in vitro fertilization procedures. McCaskill supported it, and Talent was against it. Missouri Republicans were split: State business leaders backed the proposal in hopes of attracting biomedical research to the state, while religious conservatives opposed it, considering the destruction of embryos the destruction of human life.

In October, Talent flayed McCaskill over her family's personal finances and demanded that she release the tax returns of her husband, Joseph Shepard, a developer of low-income housing financed by government loans, who filed his taxes separately from her. Talent also suggested that they hadn't paid all of their taxes and accused McCaskill's husband of owning an offshore tax shelter. Through late October, polls showed the race to be a dead heat. On Election Day, McCaskill won 50%-47%, a difference of just 48,000 votes out of 2.1 million cast. It was the third consecutive election for the seat decided by fewer than 50,000 votes. Just as in the 2004 governor's race, McCaskill won big margins in the Kansas City and St. Louis metro areas, but unlike 2004, she held her own in outstate Missouri and carried 11 counties that she lost in 2004.

In her first year in the Senate, McCaskill emphasized her independence, voting against her party more often than most non-Southern Democrats. She was the first Democrat to back Arizona Republican Sen. John McCain's 2007 amendment blocking any bill containing spending earmarks, and she stepped forward to support South Carolina Republican Jim DeMint's one-year moratorium on earmarks. Her tough stance on earmarks put her at odds with her Missouri colleague Christopher "Kit" Bond, a Republican and longtime appropriator. But they also cooperated on Missouri issues like disaster aid for farmers and promotion of Boeing's C-17 military transport plane.

Unlike most Senate Democrats, McCaskill voted against measures to cut off military funding in Iraq and to set timetables to withdraw U.S. troops. She opposed the 2007 immigration bill that created a guest-worker program and a path to citizenship for illegal immigrants, and she declined to co-sponsor the Equal Rights Amendment. "The ERA, just because of the history of it, just in and of itself, is an incredibly divisive thing, and sometimes I'm not sure the divisiveness is worth it," McCaskill said. In June 2008, she declined to commit to Democratic Sen. Barbara Boxer's bill tightening restrictions on greenhouse gases. With Virginia Democrat Jim Webb, she sponsored a successful bill authorizing creation of a bipartisan commission to look into possible wartime profiteering, something like the committee Missouri Sen. Harry Truman chaired during World War II. Their bill passed as part of the defense bill in January 2008. In her first term, McCaskill established herself as a willing player in bipartisan legislation. With Republican Susan Collins of Maine, she sponsored a bill to make inspectors general more independent, giving them seven-year terms and their own legal counsel. It passed in April 2008.

In January 2008, after the New Hampshire primary and at the urging of her 18-year-old daughter, McCaskill endorsed Illinois Sen. Barack Obama for president. She spoke frequently on Obama's behalf during his primary campaign against New York Sen. Hillary Rodham Clinton. At one point, McCaskill accused former President Bill Clinton of trying "to manipulate the facts." Missouri was one of the few states where the margin in the presidential primary, and in the general election, was exquisitely close. Obama won the Missouri primary over Clinton 49.3%-47.9%, carrying just five counties and St. Louis City.

FIRST DISTRICT

William Lacy Clay (D)

Elected 2000, 5th term; b. July 27, 1956, St. Louis; home, St. Louis; U. of MD, B.S. 1983; Catholic; divorced; 2 children.

Elected Office: MO House of Reps., 1983–90; MO Senate, 1991–2000.

Professional Career: Asst. doorkeeper, U.S. House of Reps., 1976–83; Paralegal, 1982–2000; Real estate agent, 1986–2000.

DC Office: 2418 RHOB, 20515, 202-225-2406; Fax: 202-226-3717; Web site: lacyclay.house.gov.

State Offices: St. Louis, 314-367-1970; St. Louis County, 314-383-5240.

Committees: *Financial Services* (14th of 42 D): Domestic Monetary Policy & Technology; Financial Institutions & Consumer Credit; Housing & Community Opportunity. *Oversight & Government Reform* (7th of 24 D): Federal Workforce, Postal Service & the District of Columbia; Information Policy, Census & National Archives (Chmn).

Group Ratings

	ADA	ACLU	AFS	LCV	ITIC	NTU	COC	ACU	CFG	FRC
2008	100	100	100	92	86	15	47	8	8	0
2007	95	—	100	75	—	4	61	4	5	—

National Journal Ratings

	2007 LIB	—	2007 CONS	2008 LIB	—	2008 CONS
Economic	67%	—	33%	71%	—	25%
Social	92%	—	0%	82%	—	0%
Foreign	89%	—	10%	85%	—	8%
Composite	84%	—	16%	84%	—	16%

Key Votes of the 110th Congress

1. Increase minimum wage	Y	5. Share immigration data	N	9. Withdraw troops 8/08	Y
2. Expand SCHIP	Y	6. Foreign aid abortion ban	N	10. No operations in Iran	Y
3. Raise CAFE standards	Y	7. Ban gay bias in workplace	Y	11. Free trade with Peru	Y
4. Bail out financial markets	N	8. Repeal D.C. gun law	N	12. Overhaul FISA	N

Election Results

2008 general	William Lacy Clay (D)	242,570	(87%)	($622,529)
	Robb Cunningham (Lib)	36,700	(13%)	
2008 primary	William Lacy Clay (D)	unopposed		

Prior Winning Percentages: 2006 (73%); 2004 (75%); 2002 (70%); 2000 (75%)

Population		Race/Ethnicity		Work	
Pop. 2007:	596,414	White:	40.8%	Private:	82.7%
Change since 2000:	Down 4.1%	Black:	53.4%	Government:	13.1%
Urban:	99.2%	Hispanic:	1.9%	Self-employed:	4.0%
Rural:	0.8%	Asian:	2.0%	Blue collar:	19.1%
Area size:	227 sq. mi.	Native Am.:	0.2%	White collar:	59.7%
Age		Hawaiian:	0.0%	Khaki collar:	0.1%
Median age:	37.0 yrs.	Two+ races:	1.5%	Other:	21.1%
More than 65 yrs:	12.9%	*Ancestry*		Median income:	$40,572
Less than 18 yrs:	25.3%	German:	13.3%	Median home value:	$111,700
Education		Irish:	7.4%	Poverty:	18.9%
H.S. grad:	82.7%	English:	4.4%	**Military Veterans**	
College grad:	24.4%			% of Pop:	10.8%
Grad degree:	10.1%				

For a century or more, St. Louis seemed the center of America: the starting point for the Lewis and Clark expedition in 1804, the locus half a century later of the *Dred Scott* slavery case, and the site of the 1904 World's Fair, which introduced the hot dog and the ice cream cone and got 19 million people to *Meet Me in St. Louis*. Its 630-foot-high Gateway Arch is just below the point where the waters of the Missouri surge into the Mississippi, about halfway between New Orleans and Lake Superior, between the At-

2008 Presidential Vote		
Obama (D)	.246,448	(80%)
McCain (R)	.59,910	(20%)
2004 Presidential Vote		
Kerry (D)	.216,372	(75%)
Bush (R)	.71,367	(25%)
Cook Partisan Voting Index:	D + 27	

lantic and the Pacific. This first major American city west of the Mississippi River was the final resting place of Daniel Boone and for many years was Chicago's rival as the transportation hub of America. In 1904, St. Louis already had the Eads Bridge, one of America's first suspension bridges; the Wainwright Building, one of Louis Sullivan's first skyscrapers; and Union Station, the world's largest passenger train station when it opened in 1894. Some 600,000 people lived then in densely packed brick houses on street grids radiating outward from downtown. This was a heavily German city, with a Teutonic solidity and orderliness that distinguished it from the surrounding Southern-accented rural terrain. And from Mittel-europa came the founders of St. Louis's great businesses—the Anheuser-Busch brewery, May Company department stores, Joseph Pulitzer's *St. Louis Post-Dispatch* —and its first great politician, Carl Schurz, the senator and Interior secretary. There is almost a European aura to Forest Park, the site of the 1904 fair, and the dozen mansion-lined private streets nearby.

St. Louis is still one of the nation's 20 largest metro areas, but today it does not occupy as central a place in the national consciousness, and the central city itself has largely emptied out. The German order that made so many people comfortable living in close quarters and commuting by streetcar has yielded to an American desire for suburban spaces and the less restrictive automobile. St. Louis' population peaked at 856,000 in 1950; it was down to 353,500 in 2008, far less than the 1 million inhabitants of suburban St. Louis County. Downtown St. Louis has been spruced up admirably: the Gateway Arch was finished in 1965; Union Station has been redeveloped; Laclede's Landing and the former garment district are stocked with shops; and a new Busch Stadium opened with a panoramic view of the Arch and down-town. But most of St. Louis's old factories have closed, and many of its once tight neighborhoods are only a memory. A sign of the times: In October 2008, the International Bowling Museum and Hall of Fame near Busch Stadium closed and moved to an Arlington, Texas, entertainment district. A bigger local con-cern was the takeover of local icon Anheuser-Busch by Belgium-based InBev, even though the company said it would use St. Louis, with a reduced workforce, as its North American headquarters.

Missouri's congressional districts have followed the people out of St. Louis, where the Democratic organization has been weakened by the loss of patronage and by state approval of term limits. The 1st District has been historically based on the north side of the city, but now three-fourths of its residents live in suburban St. Louis County. The district includes St. Louis City north of Interstate 44, and the northern and some central portions of St. Louis County. It takes in all of the predominantly African-American suburbs north of the city, including Bellefontaine Neighbors, Ferguson, Spanish Lake, and Black Jack. It also includes working-class St. Ann and Bridgeton and, west of the city, parts of the affluent suburbs of University City, Ladue and Creve Coeur. The district is half African American, but blacks account for far more than half the votes in Democratic primaries. Barack Obama in November 2008 won the city 84%-16%. More telling was that he won St. Louis County, with more than triple the turnout, 60%-40%. In 2004, John Kerry won the county, 54%-45%.

The congressman from the 1st District is William Lacy Clay, a Democrat first elected in 2000 to the seat that his father Bill Clay had held for 32 years. Born in St. Louis, he moved to the Washington, D.C., area at age 12 after his father's election to the House in 1968. He attended public schools in suburban Silver Spring, Md., and then the University of Maryland, studying by night for seven years while he worked as a House staffer by day. He had started law classes at Howard University in 1983, when a special election for the state House drew him back to St. Louis. Party leaders appointed him the Demo-cratic nominee. Eight years later, he was again chosen by party leaders to run in a special election for a safely Democratic state Senate seat.

Then in 1999, his father decided to retire from Congress, after helping to enact many labor and educa-tion laws he had fought for. Clay wanted to take his father's place, but he had a serious primary contest. St. Louis Councilman Charlie Dooley raised nearly $400,000 and was an African American with a base of support in the mostly white suburbs of St. Louis County. Dooley campaigned that the office should not be "inherited," and he attacked what he called Clay's old-style tactics of political threats and bossism. The St. Louis Labor Council and Missouri AFL-CIO, long allied with Bill Clay, declined to endorse his son, but more than 30 locals endorsed him. Lacy Clay played up his father's name and revved up the still reliable machine. He won the primary 61%-28% over Dooley, winning St. Louis City 76%-12% and St. Louis County, where twice as many votes were cast, 49%-39%. In the general election, Clay won 75%-22%.

In the House, Clay has had a mostly liberal voting record, although it turned centrist on some economic issues in recent years. He has worked to protect voting rights for blacks and the reliability of electronic voting equipment. A member of the Oversight and Government Reform Committee, Clay chairs the Information Policy, Census and National Archives Subcommittee, with jurisdiction ranging from the Freedom of Information Act to the Census Bureau—a useful post for black Americans concerned about maximizing rights in the next redistricting after 2010. "The census is really about three things: money, information and political representation," Clay says. In 2007, he helped enact a rewrite of the freedom of information law to expedite requests and the handling of disputes; he also foiled an attempt by the Bush Administration to eliminate a Census Bureau program that provides information on the effect that federal programs have on the poor. On foreign policy, he called for the withdrawal of U.S. troops from Iraq in 2006 and famously described President Bush as an "incompetent chickenhawk." The following year, he cosponsored a bill to impeach Vice President Cheney. And Clay led opposition to the request of Rep. Stephen Cohen, a white Democrat from Tennessee, to join the Congressional Black Caucus. "It's an unwritten rule" that only African Americans can belong, Clay said.

Clay has not been seriously challenged for reelection. His biggest concern may be the declining population in his district, and its implications for the next round of redistricting. The 1st District was the only one in the state to lose population between 2000 and 2006.

SECOND DISTRICT

Todd Akin (R)

Elected 2000, 5th term; b. July 5, 1947, New York, NY; home, Town and Country; Worcester Polytech Inst. (MA), B.S. 1971, Covenant Theological Seminary (MO), M. Div. 1985; Presbyterian; married (Lulli); 5 children.

Military Career: Army Reserves 1972–80.

Elected Office: MO House of Reps., 1988–2000.

Professional Career: Marketing mgr., IBM, 1974–78; Mgmt. dir., Laclede Steel, 1977–80.

DC Office: 117 CHOB, 20515, 202-225-2561; Fax: 202-225-2563; Web site: akin.house.gov.

State Offices: St. Charles, 636-949-6826; St. Louis, 314-590-0029.

Committees: *Armed Services* (5th of 25 R): Air & Land Forces; Seapower & Expeditionary Forces (RMM). *Science & Technology* (9th of 17 R): Energy & Environment; Technology & Innovation. *Small Business* (3rd of 12 R): Contracting & Technology; Finance & Tax.

Group Ratings

	ADA	ACLU	AFS	LCV	ITIC	NTU	COC	ACU	CFG	FRC
2008	10	18	0	0	43	84	89	96	95	100
2007	0	—	0	5	—	86	80	100	91	—

National Journal Ratings

	2007 LIB — 2007 CONS		2008 LIB — 2008 CONS	
Economic	11%	— 88%	2%	— 97%
Social	0%	— 91%	0%	— 91%
Foreign	0%	— 72%	0%	— 95%
Composite	10%	— 90%	3%	— 97%

Key Votes of the 110th Congress

1. Increase minimum wage	N	5. Share immigration data	Y	9. Withdraw troops 8/08	N
2. Expand SCHIP	N	6. Foreign aid abortion ban	Y	10. No operations in Iran	N
3. Raise CAFE standards	N	7. Ban gay bias in workplace	N	11. Free trade with Peru	Y
4. Bail out financial markets	N	8. Repeal D.C. gun law	Y	12. Overhaul FISA	Y

Election Results

2008 general	Todd Akin (R)	232,276	(62%)	($838,986)
	William Haas (D)	132,068	(35%)	($52,218)
	Thomas Knapp (Lib)	8,628	(2%)	
2008 primary	Todd Akin (R)	unopposed		

Prior Winning Percentages: 2006 (61%); 2004 (65%); 2002 (67%); 2000 (55%)

Population		Race/Ethnicity		Work	
Pop. 2007:	683,694	White:	91.0%	Private:	86.3%
Change since 2000:	Up 10.0%	Black:	2.7%	Government:	8.3%
Urban:	91.7%	Hispanic:	2.1%	Self-employed:	5.3%
Rural:	8.4%	Asian:	2.8%	Blue collar:	16.1%
Area size:	1,288 sq. mi.	Native Am.:	0.2%	White collar:	71.2%
		Hawaiian:	0.1%	Khaki collar:	0.0%
Age		Two+ races:	1.1%	Other:	12.7%
Median age:	38.6 yrs.	*Ancestry*		Median income:	$71,094
More than 65 yrs:	12.1%	German:	29.5%	Median home value:	$211,700
Less than 18 yrs:	25.2%	Irish:	14.6%	Poverty:	4.5%
		English:	9.1%		
Education				**Military Veterans**	
H.S. grad:	92.1%			% of Pop:	11.3%
College grad:	40.6%				
Grad degree:	14.5%				

Just as the geographic center of the U.S. population has moved west from St. Louis to rural Phelps County, so has the center of metropolitan St. Louis moved farther west from the Gateway Arch on the Mississippi River. Now the midpoint is suburban St. Louis County, established in 1876 when the city, tired of paying for dusty back roads, separated itself from the sticks. That year, there were 350,000 people in the city and 31,000 in the county. In 2007, there were 347,000 in the city and just over 1 million

2008 Presidential Vote		
McCain (R)	215,450	(55%)
Obama (D)	172,169	(44%)

2004 Presidential Vote		
Bush (R)	215,123	(60%)
Kerry (D)	142,824	(40%)

Cook Partisan Voting Index: R + 9

in St. Louis County. By the 1960s, the center of office employment moved from downtown across the county line to Clayton. Now, the focus is fast moving out along the Daniel Boone Expressway (U.S. 40) to Chesterfield.

The 2nd Congressional District of Missouri consists of central and western St. Louis County, most of St. Charles County northwest across the Missouri River, and rural Lincoln County to the north. Along the expressway, in the center of St. Louis County, are long-settled suburbs: Kirkwood; most of high-income Town and Country and Ladue; fast-growing Chesterfield; and Sunset Hills to the south. They are all Republican areas, more so in newer family-oriented subdivisions than in the leafy precincts of the older enclaves. St. Charles County, where the supply of available land and affordable housing is tight, now casts more votes than the city of St. Louis and is the most Republican suburban county in Missouri. Fast-growing O'Fallon has been listed among the top 10 best places to live in the nation, according to a website of real estate professionals. Suburban Fallon is not doing quite as well. In 2009, Chrysler closed two local factories, idling 1,200 people. This conservative district voted 55% for John McCain in 2008, including 54%-45% in St. Charles County.

The congressman from the 2nd District is Todd Akin, a Republican first elected in 2000. He still lives in his boyhood home, a 60-year-old farmhouse in an upscale neighborhood in Town and Country. He graduated from Worcester Polytechnic Institute and earned a divinity degree at Covenant Seminary. After service as an Army combat engineer, he worked for IBM in the Boston area and then at Laclede Steel in Alton, Ill. The steel company was founded by his great-grandfather and his father once worked there, too. Akin was elected to the state House in 1988. An avid student and teacher of American history and the Constitution, Akin lectures at various public and private institutions. His religious beliefs are also a guiding force in his life, and Akin enjoys strumming gospel tunes on his guitar. While a state legislator, he sold standardized tests to parents who home-school their children; he and his wife home-schooled their six children. He also filed a lawsuit to stop the state's approval of riverboat gambling but was ultimately unsuccessful.

When U.S. Rep. Jim Talent, a Republican, launched his bid for governor in 1999, Akin ran for his House seat. He started off as the underdog to Gene McNary, a former Bush administration Immigration and Naturalization Service commissioner, well known locally from his 15 years as St. Louis County executive. Akin called himself "a conservative with a soft edge." He emphasized he had never voted to raise taxes and had strong support from religious conservatives. In a low-turnout, rainy-day primary, Akin rallied his committed voters to win the five-candidate contest by 56 votes over McNary. In the general election against Democratic state Sen. Ted House, Akin focused on their differences on taxes. House, whose television ads did not identify himself as a Democrat, depicted Akin as an extreme ideologue and an ineffective legislator. Akin carried St. Louis County 57%-40% and won overall, 55%-42%.

In the House, Akin has one of the most strongly conservative voting records. After a California federal appeals court ruled the reference to "one nation under God" in the Pledge of Allegiance was unconstitutional, Akin twice successfully ushered through a bill to strip lower courts of jurisdiction over challenges to the Pledge. But it went nowhere in the Senate. He sponsored the Parent's Right to Know Act, which bars funding to family planning projects that provide contraceptive drugs and devices to minors without parental consent. In 2003, Akin burned some bridges with Republican leaders when he voted against their bill creating a prescription drug benefit under Medicare, saying the new program would be a "budget buster" and attract more illegal immigrants to the country. He sponsored a bill in 2008 to encourage offshore energy exploration in the National Sea Grant Program.

On the Armed Services Committee, Akin has emphasized special operation forces, which he considers essential to the fight against terrorism. One of his sons was a Marine in Iraq. He is also a defender of Boeing, a major presence in his district. In May 2008, the House defeated his amendment to restore $193 million for the Army's Future Combat Systems program, a Boeing project. He may be motivated to try again given his increasing seniority on the committee.

Back home, Akin was easily re-elected. In 2006, Republican primary challenger Sherman Parker, a moderate African-American state representative, was arrested a week before the contest on charges of failing to register his car or to appear in court for a speeding ticket. Akin won 88%-12%. In the 2008 presidential contest, he did not endorse John McCain until midsummer, citing their differences on federal funding for embryonic-stem-cell research, campaign finance regulation and illegal immigration.

THIRD DISTRICT

Russ Carnahan (D)

Elected 2004, 3rd term; b. July 10, 1958, Columbia; home, St. Louis; U. of MO, B.S. 1979, J.D. 1983; Methodist; married (Debra); 2 children.

Elected Office: MO House of Reps., 2000–04.

Professional Career: Practicing atty., 1988–96; Consultant, BJC HealthCare, 1996–2004.

DC Office: 1710 LHOB, 20515, 202-225-2671; Fax: 202-225-7452; Web site: carnahan.house.gov.

State Offices: Crystal City, 636-937-8039; St. Louis, 314-962-1523.

Committees: *Foreign Affairs* (11th of 28 D): International Organizations, Human Rights & Oversight; Middle East & South Asia. *Science & Technology* (19th of 26 D): Research & Science Education. *Transportation & Infrastructure* (19th of 44 D): Aviation; Economic Development, Public Buildings & Emergency Management; Water Resources & Environment.

Group Ratings

	ADA	ACLU	AFS	LCV	ITIC	NTU	COC	ACU	CFG	FRC
2008	90	100	100	92	80	7	61	0	0	17
2007	100	—	100	90	—	5	55	4	1	—

National Journal Ratings

	2007 LIB	—	2007 CONS		2008 LIB	—	2008 CONS
Economic	64%	—	34%		71%	—	25%
Social	62%	—	37%		82%	—	0%
Foreign	69%	—	29%		59%	—	37%
Composite	66%	—	34%		75%	—	25%

Key Votes of the 110th Congress

1. Increase minimum wage	Y	5. Share immigration data	N	9. Withdraw troops 8/08	Y
2. Expand SCHIP	Y	6. Foreign aid abortion ban	N	10. No operations in Iran	Y
3. Raise CAFE standards	Y	7. Ban gay bias in workplace	Y	11. Free trade with Peru	N
4. Bail out financial markets	Y	8. Repeal D.C. gun law	N	12. Overhaul FISA	N

Election Results

2008 general	Russ Carnahan (D)	202,470	(66%)	($883,674)
	Chris Sander (R)	92,759	(30%)	($32,444)
2008 primary	Russ Carnahan (D)	unopposed		

Prior Winning Percentages: 2006 (66%); 2004 (53%)

Population		Race/Ethnicity		Work	
Pop. 2007:	642,628	White:	84.5%	Private:	84.8%
Change since 2000:	Up 3.4%	Black:	9.7%	Government:	9.9%
Urban:	86.7%	Hispanic:	2.2%	Self-employed:	5.2%
Rural:	13.3%	Asian:	2.1%	Blue collar:	22.3%
Area size:	1,266 sq. mi.	Native Am.:	0.2%	White collar:	61.1%
		Hawaiian:	0.0%	Khaki collar:	0.0%
Age		Two+ races:	1.1%	Other:	16.6%
Median age:	37.8 yrs.			Median income:	$48,990
More than 65 yrs:	12.5%	*Ancestry*		Median home value:	$151,900
Less than 18 yrs:	23.6%	German:	25.7%	Poverty:	11.3%
		Irish:	13.0%		
Education		English:	6.5%	**Military Veterans**	
H.S. grad:	84.6%			% of Pop:	10.8%
College grad:	26.5%				
Grad degree:	9.9%				

Middle America, it could be said, lies somewhere on the south side of metropolitan St. Louis. The geographical center of the country's population was here in 1980, just south of St. Louis in Jefferson County. While that point has moved further southwest, St. Louis is still the metro area nearest the demographic midpoint of the country. Geographically, this is a node where some of the nation's main arteries come together. The Missouri River flows into the Mississippi a few miles north of St. Louis's Gateway

2008 Presidential Vote
Obama (D) 189,727   (60%)
McCain (R)..............................124,536   (39%)

2004 Presidential Vote
Kerry (D)................................168,740   (57%)
Bush (R) 127,668   (43%)

Cook Partisan Voting Index: D + 7

Arch. The National Road and its successors, U.S. 40 and Interstate 70, cross the Mississippi just below the Arch. And the great tides of Southerners migrating west up the Mississippi and of Germans migrating overland met here to create one of the nation's largest and most bustling cities. The south side of St. Louis is famous for its pleasant parks and tight-knit, neat neighborhoods, including "Little Bosnia" in the Bevo Mill section. Its most famous symbols are the Anheuser-Busch brewery south of downtown and Grant's Farm, where Ulysses S. Grant lived in the 1850s and where Anheuser-Busch bred the Budweiser Clydesdales. But many more people now live in the suburbs. In St. Louis County and south St. Louis, the Catholic Church has closed more than 20 parishes and eight schools since 1970, and the number of registered parishioners has dropped by half, while suburban parishes have grown.

The 3rd Congressional District of Missouri consists of the south side of St. Louis, part of suburban St. Louis County and, to the south, Jefferson County and rural Ste. Genevieve County, the site of Missouri's oldest permanent settlement. Ste. Genevieve County also is the planned site of the nation's largest cement plant, scheduled to open in 2009. The district's St. Louis County portions are mostly suburbs close to the St. Louis City line—Clayton, Maplewood, Richmond Heights, Webster Groves, Affton, Lemay, and Oakville. This is the descendant of districts dominated by St. Louis voters, but today the city casts less than 25% of its votes; almost half are cast in St. Louis County. Ethnically, this has been a heavily German-American area since the mid-19th century. Politically, it has been Democratic since the New Deal of the 1930s. The district voted 57% for John Kerry in 2004 and 60% for Barack Obama in 2008. Obama carried each of its counties.

The congressman from the 3rd District is Russ Carnahan, a Democrat elected in 2004. He succeeded Richard Gephardt, a Democrat who rose to party leader in the House and who twice unsuccessfully sought the Democratic nomination for president. Carnahan is the son of the late Democratic Gov. Mel Carnahan and former Sen. Jean Carnahan, who was appointed to the Senate seat her husband had won shortly after he died in an airplane crash in October 2000. Russ Carnahan grew up in Rolla and graduated from the University of Missouri and its law school. He practiced law with his wife, Debra, until 1996, when he took a job as a lobbyist and consultant with BJC HealthCare, which operates several nursing homes and hospitals. In 1990, he ran unsuccessfully against Republican Rep. Bill Emerson in the old 10th Congressional District in southeast Missouri. In 2000, he was elected to the state House, and after the 2002 election, became chairman of the House Democratic Caucus. Two years later, he ran to succeed Gephardt, who was running for president.

Carnahan was among four current or former state legislators in the primary. Opponents ganged up on him, claiming he had a thin legislative record and was trading on his family name. His toughest opponent turned out to be Jeff Smith, a youthful political science instructor at Washington University in St. Louis. He was endorsed by the *St. Louis Post-Dispatch* and assembled a large corps of volunteers. Gephardt remained neutral, but many of his allies backed state Sen. Steve Stoll, who supported gun rights and opposed abortion. It turned out to be a very close race. Carnahan won with 23% of the vote; Smith finished second with 21%, and Stoll had 18%. Smith led in St. Louis City and County; Stoll led by a wide margin in Jefferson and Ste. Genevieve counties; Carnahan ran second or third in each—a sign that he had greater name recognition but lacked a committed core of supporters. In the general election, Carnahan faced Republican author Bill Federer, who spent heavily and ran on a platform of opposing abortion in all circumstances and most gun control laws, including a ban on assault weapons, which Carnahan supported. Carnahan called for increased funding for education and said that he would "retarget" Bush's tax cuts to the middle class. Carnahan won 53%-45%. Federer led 50%-48% in Jefferson County, but Carnahan carried St. Louis County, 52%-46%, and St. Louis City, 61%-36%.

In the House, Carnahan voted near the center of his party but a bit more conservatively on foreign policy. He helped to whip up support for a bill to provide federal funding for embryonic- stem-cell research, which uses excess embryos from in vitro fertilization. He worked with colleagues to enact the Combat Meth Act, with tough restrictions on production of methamphetamine, a major problem in Jefferson County. He also won passage in 2007 of a bill shifting federal land to St. Louis County to open access to a new casino in Lemay. Carnahan's wife has served on the national board of Planned Parenthood, and he has pushed for increased funding for contraceptives in developing nations.

Carnahan has had two easy re-elections. Smith, runner-up in the 2004 primary, thought about another run but instead sought and won a state Senate seat. In the 2008 presidential contest, Carnahan endorsed Barack Obama in May 2007 and encouraged him to campaign actively in Missouri.

FOURTH DISTRICT

Ike Skelton (D)

Elected 1976, 17th term; b. Dec. 20, 1931, Lexington; home, Lexington; Wentworth Military Acad. Jr. Col., 1949–51, U. of MO, A.B. 1953, LL.B. 1956; Disciples of Christ; widowed; 3 children.

Elected Office: MO Senate, 1970–76.

Professional Career: Lafayette Cnty. prosecuting atty., 1957–60; MO Special asst. atty. gen., 1961–63; Practicing atty., 1963–76.

DC Office: 2206 RHOB, 20515, 202-225-2876; Fax: 202-225-2695; Web site: www.house.gov/skelton.

State Offices: Blue Springs, 816-228-4242; Jefferson City, 573-635-3499; Lebanon, 417-532-7964; Sedalia, 660-826-2675.

Committees: *Armed Services* (Chmn of 36 D).

Group Ratings

	ADA	ACLU	AFS	LCV	ITIC	NTU	COC	ACU	CFG	FRC
2008	85	90	100	85	100	6	61	4	0	52
2007	85	—	100	70	—	6	72	25	12	—

National Journal Ratings

	2007 LIB	—	2007 CONS		2008 LIB	—	2008 CONS
Economic	59%	—	40%		57%	—	41%
Social	50%	—	50%		62%	—	34%
Foreign	53%	—	46%		65%	—	32%
Composite	54%	—	46%		63%	—	37%

Key Votes of the 110th Congress

1. Increase minimum wage	Y	5. Share immigration data	Y	9. Withdraw troops 8/08	Y
2. Expand SCHIP	Y	6. Foreign aid abortion ban	Y	10. No operations in Iran	Y
3. Raise CAFE standards	Y	7. Ban gay bias in workplace	N	11. Free trade with Peru	Y
4. Bail out financial markets	Y	8. Repeal D.C. gun law	Y	12. Overhaul FISA	Y

Election Results

2008 general	Ike Skelton (D)	200,009	(66%)	($1,203,525)
	Jeff Parnell (R)	103,446	(34%)	
2008 primary	Ike Skelton (D)	unopposed		

Prior Winning Percentages: 2006 (68%); 2004 (66%); 2002 (68%); 2000 (67%); 1998 (71%); 1996 (64%); 1994 (68%); 1992 (70%); 1990 (62%); 1988 (72%); 1986 (100%); 1984 (67%); 1982 (55%); 1980 (68%); 1978 (73%); 1976 (56%)

Population		Race/Ethnicity		Work	
Pop. 2007:	653,018	White:	91.4%	Private:	69.0%
Change since 2000:	Up 5.0%	Black:	3.0%	Government:	20.9%
Urban:	39.9%	Hispanic:	2.5%	Self-employed:	9.7%
Rural:	60.1%	Asian:	0.7%	Blue collar:	30.0%
Area size:	14,825 sq. mi.	Native Am.:	0.5%	White collar:	51.2%
Age		Hawaiian:	0.1%	Khaki collar:	1.9%
Median age:	37.7 yrs.	Two+ races:	1.6%	Other:	16.8%
More than 65 yrs:	14.5%	*Ancestry*		Median income:	$40,851
Less than 18 yrs:	24.3%	German:	23.8%	Median home value:	$111,600
Education		Irish:	11.7%	Poverty:	13.8%
H.S. grad:	83.3%	English:	9.6%	**Military Veterans**	
College grad:	16.6%			% of Pop:	14.2%
Grad degree:	5.6%				

Missouri was the first state settled west of the Mississippi, and the folks who settled it were a picture of pioneer diversity. Virginians and other Southerners made their way to counties north of the Missouri River, while Germans settled around the small capital, Jefferson City. A taste of that diversity can be found in the Capitol, with its mural by Thomas Hart Benton, great-grandnephew of one of Missouri's first senators, who championed hard money and westward expansion for 30 years and lost his seat

2008 Presidential Vote
McCain (R)............................187,394   (60%)
Obama (D) 117,978   (38%)

2004 Presidential Vote
Bush (R) 187,111   (64%)
Kerry (D)................................102,652   (35%)

Cook Partisan Voting Index: R + 14

for opposing the expansion of slavery. The painting depicts dance hall girls, black coal miners, and a mother diapering an infant.

The 4th Congressional District occupies central west Missouri. It includes part of Blue Springs and Oak Grove in Jackson County east of Kansas City, but the overall atmosphere here is rural and small-town. The rural counties around Kansas City were full of pro-slavery "bushwhackers" who rode across the Kansas line to thwart the anti-slavery Yankee "jayhawkers," and these areas today vote Democratic. The German area around Jefferson City was anti-slavery and remains among the most Republican parts of Missouri. The growing year-round resort areas around the man-made Lake of the Ozarks are mixed. The southern portion of the district, near Springfield, is predominantly Republican. There are two big military bases here: Fort Leonard Wood in Pulaski County, where Marines, sailors, and airmen train in joint exercises with Army troops; and Whiteman Air Force Base, near Knob Noster in Johnson County, from which the 21 original B-2 bombers flew to drop precision-targeted bombs in Afghanistan.

This is Harry Truman country. President Truman was born in Barton County, at the southern end of the district, and lived in Independence, a few miles from Blue Springs. He spent much of Election Night 1948, when just about everyone thought he would lose, in Excelsior Springs. In his long life, Truman spanned the gaps between country and city, South and North. His mother could remember her house being attacked by Yankee soldiers, and she remained pro-Confederate even when her son was in the White House. He got his political start in urban Independence and Kansas City and desegregated the military services.

The congressman from the 4th District is Ike Skelton, the chairman of the House Armed Services Committee, who can be called a Harry Truman Democrat. His father met the future president in 1928, when he was the Lafayette County prosecutor and Truman was a Jackson County judge, and they remained friends for life. His father supported Truman when he was nearly defeated in the 1940 Senate primary, and he took 17-year-old Ike to Washington for Truman's inauguration in 1949. Skelton is from a military family: His father served in the Navy, he and his brothers went to military academies, and his sons have served in the Army and Navy. A teenage bout with polio made him ineligible for military service, but Skelton was treated in Warm Springs, Ga., and recovered enough to run in 2-mile races on his high school track team. He grew up in Lexington and remembers walking down the street in 1944 watching C-47s droning overhead pulling gliders, training pilots for D-Day. Skelton graduated from the University of Missouri and its law school and returned to rural Lexington to practice law. He became county prosecutor in 1957, at age 25. In 1962, Truman urged him to run for Congress, but he continued practicing law with his father. He was elected to the Missouri Senate in 1970. Six years later, he ran for the U.S. House. In the Democratic primary, two candidates from Jackson County split 45% of the vote, allowing Skelton to emerge the winner with 40%. In the general, Skelton again pitched his campaign toward rural voters, and defeated Richard King, the mayor of Independence, with 56% of the vote.

In Congress, Skelton votes like an old-fashioned rural Missouri Democrat. His voting record puts him near the midpoint of the House. He has tended to support the same expansive, assertive foreign and defense policies that the preponderance of Democrats supported in the Truman days. He became chairman of the Armed Services Committee in 2007, after serving as ranking minority member from 1999 to 2006. Armed Services is among the House's least partisan committees. Most of its members are, like Skelton, strong defense supporters and the panel usually reports bills with bipartisan support. Skelton is greatly respected by Republicans as well as Democrats on the committee. His longtime mantra has been improving U.S. defense readiness. "Protecting our nation from direct attack is job one. Yet our allocation of forces does not match this imperative," he said at a 2008 hearing. He set military pay raises as a top priority and sought to increase the number of Navy ships. Naturally, Skelton also looks out for the interests of Fort Leonard Wood and Whiteman Air Force Base, which, as he points out, are major bases with unique functions and thus have been spared from the rounds of base closures in recent years.

Over the years, he has made significant contributions to military policy. He played a key role in passing the Goldwater-Nichols Act in 1986, which created the joint commands. He has worked to improve housing and facilities for service members and their families and has proposed offering 18-month enlistments plus four years of Reserve duty to attract more recruits. As part of his on-the-job training, Skelton drew up a list of 50 books on military history and analysis and read them all. Since he came to Congress, he has filled six blank books with quotes from military thinkers from Sun Tzu through the present day. Skelton was among the prominent hawks in Congress who took to task the first Bush administration and the Clinton administration for cutting the military too much, and he regularly pressed President George W. Bush to seek higher force levels. In 2005, Skleton told Defense Secretary Donald Rumsfeld: "A permanent addition to the force is needed. You're wearing 'em out, Secretary. That's the bottom line."

From the earliest stages, Skelton was deeply skeptical of the Bush administration's decision to go to war with Iraq. After a meeting in the White House in the fall of 2002, he wrote the president arguing that an occupation would be difficult. But he nonetheless voted for the war resolution when Bush sent the question to Congress in October. "I have no doubt that our military would decisively defeat Iraq's forces and remove Saddam," Skelton said at the time. "But like the proverbial dog chasing the car down the road, we must consider what we would do after we caught it." On the eve of military action, in March 2003, he wrote Bush another letter, saying that there was "great potential for a ragged ending to a war as we deal with the aftermath." The following year, he said that the war had caused greater strain on the military than he had seen in his entire career and that the Pentagon was pushing Reserve forces "nearly to the breaking point." After a trip to Iraq in 2006, Skelton enumerated his grievances with the occupation: a lack of planning, failure to deploy an adequate number of troops, failure to stop looting, disbanding the Iraqi army, kicking Baathists out of government jobs, lack of a strategy for dealing with militias, and the lack of an accounting of weapons given to Iraqi forces. "We are now, I think, strategically lost," Skelton concluded.

He was also skeptical of Bush's plan in 2007 for a "surge" in troop strength, a strategy that he said was "three-and-a-half years late and several hundred thousand troops short." Sun Tzu, he argued, "said never begin a war without its end in sight, and never have so many enemies that you cannot defeat all of them. We have violated both of these precepts in the Iraqi war." But Skelton always stopped short of calling for a cutoff of funds for the fighting. In May 2007, he sponsored a provision to the defense spending bill requiring all U.S. troops to pull out of Iraq by April 2008. The House passed it, but it died in the Senate. During debate on the 2009 defense appropriations bill, he backed away from a specific timetable in Iraq and sought to shift the focus to Afghanistan, which he worried was not a high enough priority for the administration. And in a sign that he'd lost faith in one of the key rationales for the war, Skelton banned references to "the war on terror" in the committee. "The Iraq war is separate and distinct from the war against terrorists, who have their genesis in Afghanistan and who attacked us on September 11, and the American people understand this," Skelton told *The Washington Times.*

On nonmilitary issues, Skelton tends to stick with the Democrats on taxes and economic policy, though he was one of only 20 Democrats who voted in 2001 and 2002 to give the president greater powers to negotiate free-trade agreements. His rural Missouri roots were at work in those decisions. "For me it was the right thing to do. I represent a rural area. We have a lot of farms, a lot of soybeans, wheat, and corn. And one-fourth of all that depends on foreign markets," Skelton said.

His toughest re-election was in 1982, when Missouri lost a congressional seat after the census and Skelton and a Republican incumbent, Wendell Bailey, were thrown into a newly drawn 4th District. Skelton won, 55%-45%, and he has not had a serious challenge since then. He is well-liked in a district that has trended Republican in recent elections. In 2004, when President Bush carried the district 64%-35%, Skelton was re-elected 66%-32%—more ticket-splitting than just about anywhere else in the country. It is widely assumed that when he retires, the 4th District will elect a Republican to replace him. However, Missouri seems likely to lose a House seat after the 2010 census, and the 4th District may be eliminated if Skelton chooses not to run in 2012, when he will be 80 years old.

FIFTH DISTRICT

Emanuel Cleaver (D)

Elected 2004, 3rd term; b. Oct. 26, 1944, Waxahachie, TX; home, Kansas City; Prairie View A&M U., B.S. 1968, St. Paul Schl. of Theology, M.Div. 1974; Methodist; married (Dianne); 4 children.

Elected Office: Kansas City Cncl., 1979–91; Mayor, 1991–99.

Professional Career: Pastor, 1970-present; Radio talk-show host, 2002–04.

DC Office: 1027 LHOB, 20515, 202-225-4535; Fax: 202-225-4403; Web site: www.house.gov/cleaver.

State Offices: Independence, 816-833-4545; Kansas City, 816-842-4545.

Committees: *Financial Services* (21st of 42 D): Domestic Monetary Policy & Technology; Financial Institutions & Consumer Credit; Housing & Community Opportunity. *Homeland Security* (15th of 20 D): Emergency Communications, Preparedness & Response; Transportation Security & Infrastructure Protection.

Group Ratings

	ADA	ACLU	AFS	LCV	ITIC	NTU	COC	ACU	CFG	FRC
2008	90	90	100	85	100	9	61	4	0	5
2007	95	—	100	85	—	4	55	0	5	—

National Journal Ratings

	2007 LIB	—	2007 CONS		2008 LIB	—	2008 CONS
Economic	82%	—	0%		85%	—	0%
Social	75%	—	23%		75%	—	18%
Foreign	78%	—	20%		92%	—	0%
Composite	82%	—	18%		89%	—	11%

Key Votes of the 110th Congress

1. Increase minimum wage	Y	5. Share immigration data	N	9. Withdraw troops 8/08	Y
2. Expand SCHIP	Y	6. Foreign aid abortion ban	N	10. No operations in Iran	Y
3. Raise CAFE standards	Y	7. Ban gay bias in workplace	Y	11. Free trade with Peru	Y
4. Bail out financial markets	Y	8. Repeal D.C. gun law	N	12. Overhaul FISA	Y

Election Results

2008 general	Emanuel Cleaver (D)	197,249	(64%)	($554,041)
	Jacob Turk (R)	109,166	(36%)	($56,599)
2008 primary	Emanuel Cleaver (D)	unopposed		

Prior Winning Percentages: 2006 (64%); 2004 (55%)

Population		Race/Ethnicity		Work	
Pop. 2007:	624,679	White:	64.7%	Private:	81.8%
Change since 2000:	Up 0.5%	Black:	23.9%	Government:	12.7%
Urban:	96.1%	Hispanic:	7.6%	Self-employed:	5.4%
Rural:	3.9%	Asian:	1.5%	Blue collar:	21.7%
Area size:	519 sq. mi.	Native Am.:	0.3%	White collar:	62.5%
Age		Hawaiian:	0.1%	Khaki collar:	0.1%
Median age:	36.7 yrs.	Two+ races:	1.8%	Other:	15.7%
More than 65 yrs:	12.6%	*Ancestry*		Median income:	$43,483
Less than 18 yrs:	25.3%	German:	15.2%	Median home value:	$124,900
Education		Irish:	10.2%	Poverty:	15.7%
H.S. grad:	86.3%	English:	8.5%	**Military Veterans**	
College grad:	25.9%			% of Pop:	11.3%
Grad degree:	9.1%				

Kansas City, named after a state it isn't in and a river it doesn't touch, is the center of one of America's large metro areas, the biggest on the central Great Plains. The first pioneers here started little towns on the bluffs above the Missouri River—Independence, Kansas City, Westport—that coalesced a few decades later. Here, traders on the Santa Fe Trail set out to cross the Sand Hills of Kansas to reach Mexican territory. Later, Jayhawkers and Bushwhackers fought for control of Bleeding Kansas during the Civil War. Kansas City was a rail center and, in the 1920s, had one of the largest stockyards in the country, a major commercial center with lean skyscrapers and the Country Club Plaza, the first shopping center in America. The city is famous also for its black community, its National Negro Leagues Baseball Museum, its historic jazz district that has been home to musicians like Scott Joplin, Charlie Parker and Count Basie, and for its much-praised barbecue. The area is also famous as the home of Harry Truman, who grew up on a farm now in the suburb of Grandview and who lived in his wife's family's house in Independence, the old county seat just to the east.

2008 Presidential Vote		
Obama (D)	201,337	(63%)
McCain (R)	114,030	(36%)
2004 Presidential Vote		
Kerry (D)	175,352	(60%)
Bush (R)	118,915	(40%)
Cook Partisan Voting Index:	D + 10	

The 5th Congressional District of Missouri includes most of Kansas City, the largest city in Missouri, plus Grandview and the bulk of Independence. The more suburban slices of Jackson County to the east have been filled with new subdivisions. It also includes fast-growing Belton and Raymore along U.S. 71 in Cass County just to the south. Most of the metro area's landmarks, including the Truman home, are here but much of the metropolitan area growth is across the state line in Kansas. One-quarter of the district's residents are black, the second highest percentage among Missouri districts. Politically, the seat has been solidly Democratic. John Kerry carried it 60%-40% in 2004, and Barack Obama won it 63%-36% in 2008.

The congressman from the 5th District is Emanuel Cleaver, a Democrat elected in 2004. He grew up in Waxahachie, Texas, in a three-room shack with no plumbing or electricity. He graduated from Prairie View A&M University, moved to Kansas City and earned a divinity degree, then became pastor of St. James United Methodist Church. He was elected to the City Council in 1979 and elected mayor in 1991. As mayor, Cleaver voiced support for the Clinton administration's changes in welfare policy, which he described as "corrective surgery." He backed expansion of downtown's Bartle Hall Convention Center and supported the renovation of the deteriorating Liberty Memorial, the country's largest World War I memorial. After leaving office, he hosted a radio talk show.

In December 2003, Democratic Rep. Karen McCarthy announced that she would not run for reelection, and Cleaver was widely expected to succeed her. Few expected just how tough Cleaver's road to Congress would be. In the primary, he faced former National Security Council aide Jamie Metzl, who raised substantial funds. Metzl hammered Cleaver on ethics issues, questioning the propriety of a loan that Cleaver took out to purchase a car wash business and his failure to pay $36,000 in back taxes on the business. Cleaver won the primary by 60%-40%. Metzl carried Cass County 59%-41% and ran 178 votes ahead in suburban Jackson County. But Cleaver led 68%-32% in Kansas City, where 57% of the votes were cast. In the general, Cleaver faced Republican businesswoman Jeanne Patterson, who said she would spend whatever it took to make the race competitive, including $3.2 million of her own money. Like Metzl, she made an issue of Cleaver's ethics, emphasizing bribery and fraud convictions of Cleaver's allies, though there was no evidence that he was involved in those crimes. Cleaver said that Patterson was politically inexperienced and was trying to buy the seat. He called himself a "hundred-aire" and criticized Patterson as a hypocrite for promising to create local jobs while her husband's company reportedly was outsourcing work to India. Cleaver won 55%-42%. In his Kansas City base, which cast 48% of the vote, he led 71%-27%. Patterson took Jackson County 54%-43%.

In the House, Cleaver's voting record is near the center of the Democrats. He led Congressional Black Caucus members seeking to play a role on environmental issues and got a seat on Speaker Nancy Pelosi's Select Committee on Energy Independence and Global Warming. She designated Cleaver to act as a liaison with mayors and faith communities on those issues. He proposed changing House rules to require members to lease energy-efficient vehicles in their districts. "The public would rather see a sermon than hear one," said Cleaver, whose own car runs on used cooking grease. In August 2007, the House approved, 218-196, a modified version requiring that leased congressional vehicles have low greenhouse gas emissions; the stipulation was also part of the major energy bill enacted that December. Cleaver has also sought protection for polar bears endangered by melting polar ice caps. On the Financial Services Committee, he testified for a bill to protect employees against discrimination because of sexual orientation, citing discrimination against his gay cousin.

Cleaver continued preaching regularly at his church in Kansas City but stepped down in 2008; his son replaced him. He has easily won re-election. He endorsed Hillary Rodham Clinton over Barack Obama for president in August 2007 and complained about pressure tactics directed at African-American superdelegates who backed her. He called the Democratic presidential primary process "about as stupid as human beings could put in place."

SIXTH DISTRICT

Sam Graves (R)

Elected 2000, 5th term; b. Nov. 7, 1963, Tarkio; home, Tarkio; U. of MO, B.S. 1986; Baptist; married (Lesley); 3 children.

Elected Office: MO House of Reps., 1992–94; MO Senate 1994–2000.

Professional Career: Farmer.

DC Office: 1415 LHOB, 20515, 202-225-7041; Fax: 202-225-8221; Web site: www.house.gov/graves.

State Offices: Liberty, 816-792-3976; St. Joseph, 816-233-9818.

Committees: *Agriculture* (5th of 18 R): Conservation, Credit, Energy & Research; General Farm Commodities & Risk Management. *Small Business* (RMM of 12 R). *Transportation & Infrastructure* (13th of 30 R): Aviation; Economic Development, Public Buildings & Emergency Management; Railroads, Pipelines & Hazardous Materials.

Group Ratings

	ADA	ACLU	AFS	LCV	ITIC	NTU	COC	ACU	CFG	FRC
2008	40	22	29	8	57	61	83	88	71	88
2007	15	—	9	5	—	64	95	82	55	—

National Journal Ratings

	2007 LIB	—	2007 CONS	2008 LIB	—	2008 CONS
Economic	31%	—	68%	34%	—	66%
Social	17%	—	81%	31%	—	62%
Foreign	0%	—	72%	19%	—	79%
Composite	21%	—	79%	30%	—	71%

Key Votes of the 110th Congress

1. Increase minimum wage	N	5. Share immigration data	Y	9. Withdraw troops 8/08	N
2. Expand SCHIP	N	6. Foreign aid abortion ban	Y	10. No operations in Iran	N
3. Raise CAFE standards	N	7. Ban gay bias in workplace	N	11. Free trade with Peru	Y
4. Bail out financial markets	N	8. Repeal D.C. gun law	Y	12. Overhaul FISA	Y

Election Results

2008 general	Sam Graves (R)	196,526	(59%)	($2,633,443)
	Kay Barnes (D)	121,894	(37%)	($2,801,656)
	Dave Browning (Lib)	12,279	(4%)	($4,519)
2008 primary	Sam Graves (R)	unopposed		

Prior Winning Percentages: 2006 (62%); 2004 (64%); 2002 (63%); 2000 (51%)

Population		Race/Ethnicity		Work	
Pop. 2007:	663,091	White:	90.2%	Private:	78.5%
Change since 2000:	Up 6.7%	Black:	3.2%	Government:	14.2%
Urban:	66.3%	Hispanic:	3.2%	Self-employed:	7.1%
Rural:	33.7%	Asian:	1.1%	Blue collar:	24.5%
Area size:	13,124 sq. mi.	Native Am.:	0.3%	White collar:	58.9%
		Hawaiian:	0.1%	Khaki collar:	0.1%
Age		Two+ races:	1.8%	Other:	16.4%
Median age:	37.5 yrs.			Median income:	$49,716
More than 65 yrs:	12.9%	*Ancestry*		Median home value:	$133,000
Less than 18 yrs:	24.5%	German:	22.2%	Poverty:	10.1%
		Irish:	13.1%		
Education		English:	9.8%	**Military Veterans**	
H.S. grad:	89.1%			% of Pop:	12.3%
College grad:	23.9%				
Grad degree:	7.5%				

The rolling fields along the Missouri River in north-west Missouri were settled in a rush in the late 19th century, and they lost people for most of the 20th century. Fewer hands were needed on farms than half a century ago, far fewer than a century ago. In 1940, this area had one of the largest meatpacking operations in the world, but the meatpacking business for years generated no new jobs here. Barge traffic on the Missouri has all but disappeared, a victim of low water levels that are the result of drought

2008 Presidential Vote		
McCain (R)	180,517	(54%)
Obama (D)	150,101	(45%)
2004 Presidential Vote		
Bush (R)	178,669	(57%)
Kerry (D)	132,007	(42%)
Cook Partisan Voting Index:	R + 7	

as well as recreational uses upstream and court rulings in favor of environmentalists. Just as Kansas City was the starting place for many wagon trains heading west, the river town of St. Joseph was the starting point for the Pony Express and its roughly 10-day transport of mail to Sacramento. Today, St. Joe is the biggest town north of Kansas City. With its meatpacking jobs as a draw, this has become the fastest-growing Hispanic community in the nation, with a 21% increase between July 2006 and July 2007; that has led to fear of law-enforcement raids among immigrants. The counties of northwest Missouri, aside from those in the Kansas City metro area, had 508,000 people in 1900, 452,000 in 1940 and 318,000 in 1990. But in the 1990s, the local economy began to perk up a little, and the number climbed to 330,000; some counties that had been losing population since 1900 started to gain. Biopharming—the use of genetically modified crops, such as rice, to grow medications—has become a growth industry in some of these rural communities. In 2008, Rock Port became the first area town to use only wind energy.

The 6th Congressional District of Missouri takes in all of the counties in northwest Missouri plus part of metro Kansas City—Clay and Platte counties and a small portion of Jackson County east of Independence, including Blue Springs. The Kansas City area casts about half the district's votes. The historic political tradition here was mostly Democratic, but it has been tempered by dislike for national Democrats' cultural liberalism. This was strong Perot country in 1992; Bill Clinton carried it with a plurality in 1992 and 1996. But the rural vote here, as across the nation, has moved toward Republicans. George W. Bush carried the district with 53% in 2000 and 57% in 2004. John McCain won all of the counties north of Kansas City, except for Buchanan, which he lost by 54 votes.

The congressman from the 6th District is Sam Graves, a Republican first elected in 2000. He is a lifelong resident of Tarkio in the northwest corner of the state. He graduated from the University of Missouri with a degree in agronomy, farmed with his father and brother, and joined the Farm Bureau. He ran for the state House in 1992 and beat a longtime Democratic incumbent. Two years later, he was elected to the state Senate. He attracted attention in 1998 with a five-hour filibuster against a school desegregation bill that he said put rural areas at a disadvantage, but the bill eventually passed.

Graves got his opportunity to run for the U.S. House when Democratic Rep. Pat Danner withdrew from her race for re-election just minutes before the filing deadline. Not by accident, the immediate favorite to succeed her was her son, state Sen. Steve Danner, also a Democrat. Graves entered the race within the short window provided by state law and drew support from national Republicans. Teresa Loar, a moderate Republican on the Kansas City Council, attacked Graves as the darling of extremist and sexist party leaders, but Graves beat her 68%-17%. In the general election, Danner billed himself as a conservative Democrat and switched from being pro-abortion rights to opposing abortion. In an editorial endorsing Graves, the *Kansas City Star* said that Danner's campaign switch on abortion showed that he "engaged in raw opportunism at the slightest opportunity." Graves won 51%-47%.

In the House, Graves showed some moderate instincts, especially on economic policy and has usually been a party loyalist. He has tended mostly to local issues. In 2005, the House passed his amendment to the transportation bill to preempt state laws governing liability for damages involving rental cars, a measure of interest to St. Louis-based Enterprise Rent-A-Car. In 2007, the House passed his amendment to the farm bill banning anyone found cheating federal farm programs from participating in the future. The House also approved his bill, which he sponsored with Rep. Jason Altmire, a Pennsylvania Democrat, to loosen restrictions on the eligibility of small businesses for investment capital.

Graves has had no trouble with re-election. Local Democrats and a few Republicans have complained that he uses hard-nosed political tactics. In 2006, the *Star* endorsed his opponent, Sara Jo Shettles, who chaired the Clay County Democrats, and criticized Graves as "reluctant to acknowledge serious problems facing the country." Graves won 62%-36%.

In 2008, national Democrats were excited when former Kansas City Mayor and St. Joseph native Kay Barnes announced she would challenge Graves. Republican Sen. Christopher "Kit" Bond publicly praised Barnes's record in office while she was being recruited to run against Graves. Bond and Graves have fought over local issues, including the removal of Graves's brother Todd Graves as local U.S. attorney in 2006, supposedly at Bond's urging, although he denied involvement. In the campaign, Democrats attacked Graves for his support of the Iraq war and opposition to expansion of the federal children's health insurance program. Barnes raised slightly more money than Graves and made appeals to the middle-class, attempting to mirror the success of Democrat Claire McCaskill's 2006 Senate campaign. Graves attacked Barnes for "San Francisco values" and supporting "a homosexual agenda" because her picture had appeared in a gay magazine. Graves did remarkably well against a tough candidate, winning 59%-37%. He won all counties, including 60%-37% in Barnes's base of Jackson.

SEVENTH DISTRICT

Roy Blunt (R)

Elected 1996, 7th term; b. Jan. 10, 1950, Niangua; home, Strafford; SW Baptist U., B.A. 1970, SW MO St. U., M.A. 1972; Baptist; married (Abigail Perlman); 4 children.

Elected Office: MO secy. of state, 1984–93.

Professional Career: H.S. teacher, 1970–73; Greene Cnty. clerk, 1973–85; Adjunct instructor, Drury Col., 1976–82; Pres., SW Baptist U., 1993–96.

DC Office: 2229 RHOB, 20515, 202-225-6536; Fax: 202-225-5604; Web site: blunt.house.gov.

State Offices: Joplin, 417-781-1041; Springfield, 417-889-1800.

Committees: *Energy & Commerce* (9th of 23 R): Communications, Technology & the Internet; Energy & Environment; Health. *Intelligence (Select)* (6th of 9 R): Intelligence Community Management; Oversight & Investigations.

Group Ratings

	ADA	ACLU	AFS	LCV	ITIC	NTU	COC	ACU	CFG	FRC
2008	15	18	0	0	57	66	83	88	76	100
2007	10	—	0	0	—	81	79	96	87	—

National Journal Ratings

	2007 LIB — 2007 CONS		2008 LIB — 2008 CONS	
Economic	11%	— 88%	3%	— 97%
Social	21%	— 75%	15%	— 85%
Foreign	0%	— 72%	5%	— 93%
Composite	16%	— 84%	8%	— 92%

Key Votes of the 110th Congress

1. Increase minimum wage	N	5. Share immigration data	Y
2. Expand SCHIP	N	6. Foreign aid abortion ban	Y
3. Raise CAFE standards	N	7. Ban gay bias in workplace	N
4. Bail out financial markets	Y	8. Repeal D.C. gun law	Y

9. Withdraw troops 8/08	N
10. No operations in Iran	N
11. Free trade with Peru	Y
12. Overhaul FISA	Y

Election Results

2008 general	Roy Blunt (R)	219,016	(68%)	($2,597,311)
	Richard Monroe (D)	91,010	(28%)	($55,453)
	Kevin Craig (Lib)	6,971	(2%)	
2008 primary	Roy Blunt (R)	unopposed		

Prior Winning Percentages: 2006 (67%); 2004 (70%); 2002 (75%); 2000 (74%); 1998 (73%); 1996 (65%)

Population		Race/Ethnicity		Work	
Pop. 2007:	681,744	White:	90.8%	Private:	81.0%
Change since 2000:	Up 9.7%	Black:	1.4%	Government:	10.6%
Urban:	59.1%	Hispanic:	3.7%	Self-employed:	8.1%
Rural:	40.9%	Asian:	0.9%	Blue collar:	26.0%
Area size:	5,555 sq. mi.	Native Am.:	0.7%	White collar:	56.3%
		Hawaiian:	0.1%	Khaki collar:	0.1%
Age		Two+ races:	2.4%	Other:	17.5%
Median age:	35.9 yrs.			Median income:	$39,479
More than 65 yrs:	13.9%	*Ancestry*		Median home value:	$111,300
Less than 18 yrs:	24.1%	German:	17.8%	Poverty:	14.4%
		USA:	11.9%		
Education		Irish:	11.3%	**Military Veterans**	
H.S. grad:	84.7%			% of Pop:	12.1%
College grad:	20.9%				
Grad degree:	6.9%				

One of the biggest tourist destinations in America today is Branson, Mo.—something almost no one would have predicted 30 years ago. Branson has only 7,010 residents, is served by two-lane roads, and is nowhere near a major airport, but it thrives thanks to the surging popularity of country and western music. The town has two dozen theaters with 56,000 seats—more than Broadway—and has become a hub for nonstop, low-cost, family-friendly entertainment. Nearby are fishing and boating and

2008 Presidential Vote

McCain (R)	208,231	(63%)
Obama (D)	116,660	(35%)

2004 Presidential Vote

Bush (R)	202,486	(67%)
Kerry (D)	97,557	(32%)

Cook Partisan Voting Index: R + 17

plenty of shopping. These diversions have made southwest Missouri the fastest-growing part of the state in the past 20 years, generating new businesses and attracting retirees as well as vacationers. A 1907 novel by Harold Bell Wright put Branson on the map early in the 20th century. *The Shepherd of the Hills* acquainted readers with the hardy people of the mountains, hills, and meadows of southwest Missouri, just north of Arkansas. When completion of the Ozark Beach Dam created Bull Shoals Lake in 1913, even more tourists came, lured by the native bass and stocked trout. In the 1960s, more man-made lakes were added, and entertainers—notably the four Mabe brothers, who as "The Baldknobbers" entertained audiences with comedy and country music, and Boxcar Willie from the Grand Ole Opry—started performing. Today, Branson is constantly undergoing new construction and hosts more than 7 million visitors a year, 80% of whom have been there before.

Springfield is the biggest city in southwest Missouri and the self-styled "buckle of the Bible Belt." It is home to more than 200 churches, including the headquarters of the Assemblies of God, one of the nation's largest and fastest-growing Protestant denominations. It is also the headquarters of such Middle American institutions as the Bass Pro Shops Outdoor World, perhaps the nation's largest fishing equipment store. Southwest Missouri is also dairy country and home to a growing poultry industry. Latinos have been moving into McDonald County to work in chicken-processing plants.

The 7th Congressional District of Missouri includes Branson and Springfield. Historically, this area has been Republican territory since 1861, when it opposed secession. Pro-Union Springfield changed hands several times as Missouri staged its own civil war. Its conservative response to the big-spending government of the 1960s and cultural liberalism of the 1970s reinforced its allegiance to the GOP, and now it is the most Republican part of Missouri. In the 2008 presidential election, Sen. John McCain, R-Ariz., won all of the counties here, many by 2-to-1.

The congressman from the 7th District is Roy Blunt, a Republican first elected in 1996 and formerly the House GOP whip. Blunt grew up on a dairy farm near Springfield, in a political family. His father was a state representative, who won election in 1978 by defeating Democratic Sen. Claire McCaskill's mother. In 1970, Blunt graduated from Southwest Baptist University, 25 miles north of Springfield; he later taught history and government at the high school and college levels. He got his start in politics in 1972, when he volunteered for Republican John Ashcroft's unsuccessful campaign for Congress. The story goes that he showed up at campaign headquarters in his pickup truck and Ashcroft asked, "Have you got gas in this truck?" When Blunt said that he did, he became Ashcroft's driver. In 1973, the 33-year-old governor, Christopher Bond, named the 23-year-old Blunt to be Greene County clerk. In 1980, GOP Sen. John Danforth asked him to run for lieutenant governor; he did and he lost. In 1984, at age 34, Blunt was elected Missouri secretary of state, the first Republican to win that office in half a century; he was re-elected with 60% of the vote in 1988. In 1992, he ran for governor and lost the Republican primary to William Webster, 44%-39%. Blunt then became president of Southwest Baptist University, his alma mater. In 1996, Republican Rep. Mel Hancock kept his pledge to serve only four terms and retired. Blunt ran in the subsequent primary, facing Gary Nodler, a businessman and onetime staffer to Republican Rep. Gene Taylor of Missouri, and won 56%-44%. In the general election, Blunt won 65%-32%, carrying every county. He has been re-elected easily ever since.

Blunt's voting record has been solidly conservative, with intermittent moves toward the center on social issues. He has on occasion pursued a bipartisan approach, usually on relatively minor legislation, as he did with his proposal to encourage Americans to increase their charitable giving. In 2006, he won passage of his Combat Meth Act, the first comprehensive approach to fighting the supply of methamphetamines. With then-Sen. Barack Obama, an Illinois Democrat, he sponsored a measure creating an Internet database of federal spending. Blunt's greater impact has been in his leadership roles in the House, which gave him a say in shaping a lot of the major legislation produced in the period that Republicans controlled Congress. For much of that time, Blunt had senior jobs in the whip operation, and from 2003 to 2008, he was the Republican whip. In 1999, Blunt was one of the 10 original members of then-Texas Gov. George W. Bush's presidential exploratory committee. Bush has called him "a leader who knows how to raise his sights and lower his voice."

Blunt's considerable political skills were apparent from his earliest days in the House. At the suggestion of then-Majority Whip Tom DeLay, R-Texas, he ran for and won the freshman spot on the Republican Steering Committee, a leadership-driven panel where he worked to get good committee assignments for freshmen. Then, in January 1999, DeLay plucked him from the ranks of 48 deputy whips and appointed him his chief deputy whip, the position that Dennis Hastert of Illinois held until his astonishing elevation to speaker. On a number of issues, Blunt's job was to make certain that bills the leadership hoped to pass were palatable to Republican conservatives, who often objected to compromises aimed at giving legislation broader appeal.

As chief deputy whip, Blunt spent a good deal of time meeting with lobbyists and organizing groups that were interested in various issues, including trade, taxes, and energy. He developed a reputation as a good listener with a soft touch, and he paid attention to party moderates. He mediated disputes between Republicans and went after votes on critical issues. In 2000, Blunt began keeping a list of members who would back him for a higher leadership position. He headed the Battleground 2002 operation, which contributed $5.6 million to Republican House candidates. When Majority Leader Dick Armey announced that he would retire in 2002, DeLay moved up to replace him, which left the post of whip available for Blunt. Ray LaHood of Illinois, a moderate Republican, announced that he, too, was running for whip. Within weeks, however, he bowed out after concluding that Blunt had locked up support not only from most conservatives but from many moderates as well. In November 2002, DeLay and Blunt were elected to their new positions without opposition.

For the most part, Blunt was successful as whip. He met his toughest challenge in passing the 2003 bill to create a prescription drug benefit as part of the Medicare program. He assembled a solid Republican bloc of support for the bill and brought along a few Democrats, as well. Still, in November, when GOP leaders took the final version to the floor, they were still short of the necessary 218 votes. The roll call started at 3 a.m. and lasted a record two hours and 53 minutes. Finally, two conservative Republicans who had opposed the legislation because of its cost were persuaded to switch their votes, and the bill passed, 220-215, just before dawn. Blunt and his vote-whipping operation could claim a significant victory. He ran into a couple of low points in this tenure as well. In 2002, the leadership was embarrassed by disclosures that Blunt had quietly inserted into a homeland security bill a provision benefiting Philip Morris, a tobacco giant with strong political ties to the whip. Still, Blunt's name often surfaced on lists of potential speakers of the House.

His star dimmed over time, in part because of his overweening ambition and in part because of events outside his control, mainly the political immolation of his old mentor, DeLay. On September 28, 2005, a Texas grand jury indicted DeLay and he was forced to step down as majority leader. Blunt persuaded Speaker Hastert to let him keep his post as whip while also assuming the majority leader's job temporarily. It was too heavy a burden, especially because the House was dealing with the devastating impact of Hurricane Katrina in the South. During the next three months, Republicans struggled to pass bills in the House. In January 2006, after DeLay announced that he would permanently give up his post as leader, Blunt positioned himself to take over and, after a week of lobbying his colleagues, claimed that he had the votes to win. His assertion proved to be a bluff. John Boehner of Ohio was aggressively campaigning against him, and the multiple DeLay controversies involving well-heeled lobbyists had indirectly hurt Blunt, who was viewed as being too cozy with Washington's vaunted K Street crowd. In a dramatic showdown, Boehner prevailed, 122-109, over Blunt, who suffered the double indignity of losing his bid and looking like a whip who couldn't count his votes.

Blunt remained in the leadership as whip and developed a smooth working relationship with Boehner. When House Republicans lost their majority in November 2006, he faced a new test. Republican Rep. John Shadegg of Arizona challenged him for the downsized post of minority whip. Blunt prevailed by an unexpectedly wide margin, winning 137-57. In the minority, he became more outspoken when criticizing the Democrats' management of the House and, with Boehner, fought the new majority on most issues. One exception was extension of the Foreign Intelligence Surveillance Act; for months, Blunt worked closely with Majority Leader Steny Hoyer, D-Md., on a compromise bill. In September 2008, Boehner gave him the thankless job of negotiating the $700 billion financial bailout bill, which proved to be wildly unpopular with his fellow Republicans.

In the 2008 elections, Republicans lost seats for a second consecutive time and the rank and file was itching for change. Boehner kept his job, but Eric Cantor of Virginia, Blunt's deputy, announced he would challenge Blunt for whip. Blunt quietly stepped down to avoid a likely defeat. "Ten years of asking people to do some things they don't want to do is a long time," he said in his valedictory. Hoyer praised Blunt's willingness "to achieving principled, bipartisan compromise."

Blunt's focus in the 111th Congress (2009–10) is his work on the Energy and Commerce Committee. In February 2009, Blunt announced he would be a candidate for Senate in 2010 when Republican Christopher (Kit) Bond retires.

EIGHTH DISTRICT

Jo Ann Emerson (R)

Elected Nov. 1996, 7th full term; b. Sept. 16, 1950, Washington, D.C.; home, Cape Girardeau; Ohio Wesleyan U., B.A. 1972; Presbyterian; married (Ron Gladney); 8 children.

Professional Career: Deputy communications dir., Natl. Repub. Cong. Cmte., 1984–91; Dir., State Relations & Grassroot Programs, Natl. Restaurant Assn., 1991–94; Sr. V.P., Pub. Affairs, American Insurance Assn., 1994–96.

DC Office: 2440 RHOB, 20515, 202-225-4404; Fax: 202-226-0326; Web site: www.house.gov/emerson.

State Offices: Cape Girardeau, 573-335-0101; Farmington, 573-756-9755; Rolla, 573-364-2455; West Plains, 417-255-1515.

Committees: *Appropriations* (11th of 23 R): Agriculture, Rural Development, FDA & Related Agencies; Financial Services & General Government (RMM).

Group Ratings

	ADA	ACLU	AFS	LCV	ITIC	NTU	COC	ACU	CFG	FRC
2008	65	27	57	15	71	37	83	56	34	88
2007	50	—	36	15	—	38	85	60	31	—

National Journal Ratings

	2007 LIB — 2007 CONS		2008 LIB — 2008 CONS	
Economic	41% —	59%	38% —	62%
Social	35% —	64%	38% —	61%
Foreign	43% —	57%	47% —	52%
Composite	40% —	60%	41% —	59%

Key Votes of the 110th Congress

1. Increase minimum wage	Y	5. Share immigration data	Y	9. Withdraw troops 8/08	N
2. Expand SCHIP	Y	6. Foreign aid abortion ban	Y	10. No operations in Iran	N
3. Raise CAFE standards	N	7. Ban gay bias in workplace	N	11. Free trade with Peru	Y
4. Bail out financial markets	Y	8. Repeal D.C. gun law	Y	12. Overhaul FISA	Y

Election Results

2008 general	Jo Ann Emerson (R)	198,798	(71%)	($1,285,597)
	Joe Allen (D)	72,790	(26%)	($62,069)
2008 primary	Jo Ann Emerson (R)	unopposed		

Prior Winning Percentages: 2006 (72%); 2004 (72%); 2002 (72%); 2000 (69%); 1998 (63%); 1996 (50%); 1996 special elec. (63%)

Population		Race/Ethnicity		Work	
Pop. 2007:	633,005	White:	91.6%	Private:	74.3%
Change since 2000:	Up 1.8%	Black:	4.8%	Government:	16.2%
Urban:	39.6%	Hispanic:	1.2%	Self-employed:	9.1%
Rural:	60.4%	Asian:	0.6%	Blue collar:	31.8%
Area size:	18,818 sq. mi.	Native Am.:	0.7%	White collar:	48.6%
		Hawaiian:	0.0%	Khaki collar:	0.1%
Age		Two+ races:	1.2%	Other:	19.6%
Median age:	38.4 yrs.			Median income:	$33,264
More than 65 yrs:	15.8%	*Ancestry*		Median home value:	$87,800
Less than 18 yrs:	23.6%	German:	17.5%	Poverty:	19.6%
		Irish:	12.6%		
Education		USA:	9.2%	**Military Veterans**	
H.S. grad:	75.9%			% of Pop:	12.8%
College grad:	13.4%				
Grad degree:	5.0%				

Mark Twain might not recognize life on the Mississippi below St. Louis today. The Ozark Mountains to the west flatten out, and the river is hidden behind levees, which ordinarily, except during the terrible flood of 1993, screen small towns and river roads from rows of barges tethered together, full of coal and corn and soybeans. The Mississippi today is an industrial waterway. But it was never really all that romantic. Twain's steamboats, as he was at

2008 Presidential Vote
McCain (R)..............................174,538   (62%)
Obama (D) 102,739   (36%)

2004 Presidential Vote
Bush (R)..................................173,378   (63%)
Kerry (D)..................................97,778   (36%)

Cook Partisan Voting Index: R + 15

pains to point out, were dangerous, noisy contraptions, forever blowing up or getting embedded in roots and branches in the river currents. This is one of the oldest settled parts of the United States. French settlers founded such Missouri towns as Cape Girardeau in the late 1700s. The big influx started a few years after the 1811 earthquake at New Madrid. The spongy Mississippi Valley land is seismically very active, and this was the site of one of the most devastating earthquakes in U.S. history.

The southeast quadrant of Missouri—the river valley and the hills to the west, with coal and lead mines, plus the Bootheel that hangs down in the far southeast—has not seemed to change much in half a century. For years, there has been a population outflow from the Bootheel, as machines replaced low-wage farmworkers and crops shifted from cotton to rice, corn, and soybeans. Dairy cattle, pigs, apples, and berries, plus some timber, are among the area's other products. But this is also home to Missouri's Lead Belt, a mining region rich in ore minerals such as lead, zinc, copper, silver, and cadmium. Reynolds and Iron counties produce about 80% of the nation's lead; the Environmental Protection Agency ordered a cleanup of massive piles of lead waste in recent years. An aluminum smelting plant in New Madrid provides more than 1,000 jobs. Still, the only big growth here has been around the retail and medical hub of Cape Girardeau and along Interstate 44. The poverty rate in the Bootheel is the highest in the state. At a point 20 miles south of Rolla, in Phelps County, is Edgar Springs, the home of 190 residents and the population center of the nation, according to the 2000 census. Ten years earlier, that designation was 35 miles to the northeast in Steelville.

The sprawling 8th Congressional District, the largest in Missouri, covers the state's southeast corner. Its political heritage is mixed. The Bootheel was as solidly Democratic as the Mississippi Valley around Memphis once was, and some mining counties show traces of Democratic sentiment. Cape Girardeau is heavily Republican and an incubator of Republican talent: It is the hometown of Rush Limbaugh and Lt. Gov. Peter Kinder. Once a safely Democratic district, it has been represented since 1980 by Republicans. This was one of the rural areas that trended Republican in the Clinton years. George W. Bush won 63% in 2004, and John McCain won 62% in 2008—including 66% in Cape Girardeau.

The congresswoman from the 8th District is Jo Ann Emerson, a Republican first elected in 1996 to replace her husband, Bill Emerson, who had died in office that June. Jo Ann Emerson grew up in Bethesda, Md., in a Republican family. Her father was executive director of the Republican National Committee, but her neighborhood was bipartisan. Next door lived Democrats Hale and Lindy Boggs, who served in Congress nearly 50 years. In 1975, she married Republican Bill Emerson, then a Washington lobbyist. In 1979, spotting the vulnerability of the Democratic incumbent in the Bootheel district, he went home to Missouri to run, and won with 55% of the vote. In 1995, he was diagnosed with cancer. After Bill's death, Jo Ann decided to put her considerable political résumé to work by running for his seat. She had worked for the American Insurance Association and the National Restaurant Association, and as a press aide for the National Republican Congressional Committee. Leading state and national Republicans quickly endorsed her. Missouri law bars reopening the filing deadline if an incumbent dies less than 11 weeks before the primary, so she ran as an independent. Democratic contender Emily Firebaugh, a timber company owner, attacked Emerson as a product of Washington, and spent $831,000, slightly more than Emerson. The Republican nominee, Richard Kline, was less trouble. In 1995, he had used pepper spray to try to place a Veterans Affairs Department doctor under citizen's arrest; his campaign never really got off the ground. Bill Emerson's record, Jo Ann Emerson's conservative views, and the poignancy of her situation all worked toward her victory. She won 50%; Firebaugh got 37%; and Kline, 11%.

In the House, Emerson has had a moderate-leaning voting record with sometimes conservative positions on cultural issues. On the Appropriations Committee and its Agriculture Subcommittee, her priority was rescuing falling farm commodity prices. She wrote the Trade Sanctions Reform Act of 2000, which partially lifted embargoes on five nations. And she worked with other members from farm districts to open agricultural trade with Cuba. She championed protection of U.S. food aid programs from international trade restrictions and crusaded for hunger relief, an issue that Bill Emerson popularized. She and Democratic Rep. Jim McGovern of Massachusetts lived for one week on a $21 food budget to dramatize the plight of some food stamp recipients and to gain additional funding for nutrition programs. Her bill to remove liability for federal agencies that donate excess food to shelters was enacted in 2008. By 2009, Emerson had accrued enough seniority to ascend to the ranking Republican slot on the Financial Services Subcommittee.

Emerson earned a footnote in history by casting the deciding vote in 2003 on the House version of the Republican bill creating a prescription drug benefit in the Medicare program. She initially opposed the bill, but changed her vote in exchange for a promise from Speaker Dennis Hastert for a subsequent floor vote on her priority bill, which would have allowed consumers to import American drugs from other countries where prices are lower. She got the vote as promised, but the second-ranking GOP leader, Majority Leader Tom DeLay, worked aggressively against it. Emerson won the floor vote, but the bill ultimately failed to pass Congress. Emerson took her revenge a few months later by voting against the final version of the prescription drug bill.

After Democrats took control of the House in 2007, Emerson voted for five of the six bills in the new majority's first "100-hour" agenda, including one she co-sponsored, to permit the government to negotiate prices with drug companies. She also voted for a Democratic bill to expand the Children's Health Insurance Program. On the major foreign-policy issue of the 110th Congress (2007–08), Emerson reluctantly supported President Bush's to send more troops into Iraq. But she voted "present" on a war-funding bill in April 2008 and said that she had many sleepless nights "thinking about this." Emerson, now remarried, has a personal connection to the war. Her stepdaughter served with the 1st Infantry Division in Iraq.

Her independence has not seemed to adversely affect her influence among House Republicans, perhaps because she has been up-front with party leaders about her views. And it has not affected her electoral prospects; she has won re-election without difficulty every two years. In 2008, she ended speculation about her future by declining to run for governor.

NINTH DISTRICT

Blaine Luetkemeyer (R)

Elected 2008, 1st term; b. May 7, 1952, Jefferson City; home, St. Elizabeth; Lincoln U., B.A. 1974; Catholic; married (Jackie); 3 children.

Elected Office: MO House, 1999–2005.

Professional Career: Loan officer, Bank of St. Elizabeth, 1978–2008; Pres., Luetkemeyer Insurance Agency, 1978–08; Dir., MO division of tourism, 2007–08.

DC Office: 1118 LHOB, 20515, 202-225-2956; Fax: 202-225-5712; Web site: luetkemeyer.house.gov.

State Offices: Columbia, 573-886-8929; Hannibal, 573-231-1012; Washington, 636-239-2276.

Committees: *Agriculture* (15th of 18 R): Conservation, Credit, Energy & Research; General Farm Commodities & Risk Management. *Small Business* (9th of 12 R): Finance & Tax; Rural Development, Entrepreneurship & Trade (RMM).

Group Ratings and Key Votes: Newly Elected

Election Results

2008 general	Blaine Luetkemeyer (R)	161,031	(50%)	($2,778,724)
	Judy Baker (D)	152,956	(47%)	($1,669,071)
	Tamara Millay (Lib)	8,108	(3%)	
2008 primary	Blaine Luetkemeyer (R)	21,543	(40%)	
	Bob Onder (R)	15,752	(29%)	
	Danielle Moore (R)	10,609	(20%)	
	Brock Olivo (R)	5,501	(10%)	

Population		Race/Ethnicity		Work	
Pop. 2007:	656,371	White:	91.7%	Private:	74.9%
Change since 2000:	Up 5.6%	Black:	3.9%	Government:	17.5%
Urban:	45.8%	Hispanic:	1.5%	Self-employed:	7.4%
Rural:	54.2%	Asian:	1.1%	Blue collar:	26.5%
Area size:	14,082 sq. mi.	Native Am.:	0.3%	White collar:	56.2%
		Hawaiian:	0.0%	Khaki collar:	0.1%
Age		Two+ races:	1.4%	Other:	17.2%
Median age:	36.0 yrs.			Median income:	$42,822
More than 65 yrs:	13.0%	*Ancestry*		Median home value:	$121,100
Less than 18 yrs:	23.9%	German:	26.1%	Poverty:	13.8%
		Irish:	12.3%		
Education		English:	9.3%	**Military Veterans**	
H.S. grad:	84.7%			% of Pop:	11.4%
College grad:	23.0%				
Grad degree:	9.0%				

Little Dixie, the swath of northeast Missouri along the Mississippi River, was settled by Southerners from Kentucky and Virginia. Its most famous native son is Mark Twain, born Samuel Langhorne Clemens in Hannibal, then as now a little town on bluffs overlooking the river. Hannibal was the thinly disguised St. Petersburg of Twain's classics, *The Adventures of Tom Sawyer* and *The Adventures of Huckleberry Finn*. Little Dixie was pro-Confederate during the Civil War, and Callaway County in

2008 Presidential Vote		
McCain (R)	181,181	(55%)
Obama (D)	144,729	(44%)
2004 Presidential Vote		
Bush (R)	180,362	(59%)
Kerry (D)	124,965	(41%)
Cook Partisan Voting Index: R+9		

fact declared its independence from the Union. For many years faithfully Democratic, Little Dixie has reared some notable politicians. One was Champ Clark, speaker of the U.S. House from 1911 to 1919 and a candidate for the Democratic presidential nomination in 1912. Another was Clarence Cannon, author of the definitive text on the House's parliamentary procedures and chairman of the House Appropriations Committee from 1941 to 1964, except for four years of Republican control.

The 9th Congressional District of Missouri is the descendant of the Little Dixie districts that elected Clark and Cannon, but slow population growth has expanded it far to the south and into the foothills of the Ozarks. It includes Columbia, home of the University of Missouri, and Fulton, home of Westminster College, where former Prime Minister Winston Churchill, accompanied by President Harry Truman, told the world in 1946: "From Stettin in the Baltic to Trieste in the Adriatic, an iron curtain has descended across the Continent." The district includes the western edge of the St. Louis metro area, western St. Charles County, and Franklin County south of the Missouri River. Its grain fields have become a center for ethanol production. Despite its Democratic heritage, the 9th votes mostly Republican now. George W. Bush carried the district with 59% in 2004, and John McCain carried it with 55% in 2008.

The new congressman from the 9th District is Blaine Luetkemeyer, a Republican with Missouri roots that stretch back five generations. He grew up in St. Elizabeth, where his father worked as an insurance agent and then owned a bank. Luetkemeyer *(LOOT-ka-myer)* was a star high school baseball player, but his tryouts with the Kansas City Royals and Pittsburgh Pirates were unsuccessful. He graduated from Lincoln University, a historically black college in Jefferson City, with a degree in political science. He and his wife settled on his great-grandfather's farm in St. Elizabeth. In addition to farming, Luetkemeyer became involved in his family's banking operations and founded the Luetkemeyer Insurance Agency.

In 1999, Luetkemeyer was elected to the Missouri House of Representatives, where he chaired the Financial Services Committee and developed a reputation as a thoughtful legislator. He campaigned for Missouri treasurer in 2004 but lost in the Republican primary. In 2007, Luetkemeyer was appointed director of the Missouri Division of Tourism. Two years later, the 9th District House seat came open when Republican Rep. Kenny Hulshof decided to run for governor to succeed retiring Republican Gov. Matt Blunt. Luetkemeyer entered a five-way GOP primary for Hulshof's seat. Missouri's Republican politicos viewed Luetkemeyer as the favorite. The conservative anti-tax group Club for Growth endorsed GOP state Rep. Bob Onder, although Luetkemeyer received a critical endorsement from the anti-abortion group Missouri Right to Life. The *St. Louis Post-Dispatch*, the dominant newspaper in the market, complained that no one among the candidates had a good grasp of issues. Still, Luetkemeyer trounced the competition, winning 40% of the vote.

In the general election, Luetkemeyer faced state Rep. Judy Baker, a health care consultant from Columbia. Republicans viewed Baker as an easy mark because they did not think her liberal message would play well in the district's conservative-leaning rural counties. Luetkemeyer ran as a social conservative opposed to abortion rights and same-sex marriage. He emphasized his farming background to the district's largely rural constituency. While Baker aligned herself with Democratic presidential nominee Barack Obama's message of change, Luetkemeyer was quick to point to Obama's campaign comments about small-town Americans. Describing people in small towns where jobs are disappearing, Obama said in April 2008 that they "get bitter, they cling to guns or religion or antipathy to people who aren't like them or anti-immigrant sentiment or anti-trade sentiment as a way to explain their frustrations."

Luetkemeyer also questioned Baker's health care credentials by pointing out that a private health care company she worked for in 2000 and 2001 lost more than $2 million from 1999 to 2001. Baker countered that she had helped to fix the company's problems even as auditors were discovering them. Democratic Sen. Claire McCaskill, who served as the state auditor during that period, also defended Baker's record.

Luetkemeyer opposed Baker's support for a Democratic proposal to expand federal funding for the State Children's Health Insurance Program, claiming it would be too costly. Baker criticized Luetkemeyer for sponsoring a bill that would have allowed Missouri insurance companies to offer health policies that did not cover mammograms, maternity benefits, or childhood immunizations. She neglected to note that Luetkemeyer eventually withdrew those controversial provisions from the bill. He also stressed his support for increased offshore drilling, a position that Baker tepidly supported. He was endorsed by the influential Missouri Farm Bureau. Luetkemeyer raised $2.8 million, two-thirds of it his own money; Baker raised $1.7 million. In the election, Baker managed to carry populous Boone County, but Luetkemeyer prevailed in the rural counties and those west of St. Louis in winning 50% to 47.5%.

★ MONTANA ★

In April 1805, Meriwether Lewis and William Clark and their pirogues wended up the Missouri River just past the Yellowstone into what now is Montana. It was wild, open country under a big sky—and most of it still is. To celebrate July 4, 1976, the late historian Stephen Ambrose took his family to Lemhi Pass at the other end of Montana, nearly 500 miles west, where Lewis was the first American to cross the Continental Divide. Ambrose noted that the terrain was little changed from when Lewis and Clark passed through. In recent years, many have come to Montana, to see for themselves this vast land—buying up ranchlands or condominiums, or campaigning politically, as Barack Obama did on July 4, 2008.

Yet American civilization has only lightly encroached on Montana. It is still a land of great empty vistas, with mountains in the west and vast expanses of plateaus and plains in the east—the 4th largest state in area and 44th in population. Almost nowhere in the state is the wilderness out of sight; it has the Lower 48's largest population of grizzly bears and buffalo. Montana sits atop the continental United States, spanning the Rockies so that on Interstate 15 one can cross the Continental Divide three times. Lewis and Clark found those mountains a fierce barrier, and Montana has not been much of a crossroads. The first Americans here were itinerant trappers seeking fur and miners seeking gold, silver and copper. They built ramshackle towns and in a few cases gained sudden wealth, which made them kings not of their barren homestead but of the metropolises back east. Then came the workers who built and serviced the Northern Pacific and Great Northern railroads, followed by wheat farmers and ranchers.

Statehood arrived in 1889, less than a century after Lewis and Clark. The mining economy gave Montana a radical, class-warfare political tradition. On one side was the Anaconda Mining Company, which until 1959 owned five of Montana's six daily newspapers, the Montana Power Company and many of its politicians. It had strong allies in the Stockmen's Association and the Farm Bureau. On the other side were progressives like Sen. Thomas Walsh, who exposed the Teapot Dome scandal, and Sen. Burton Wheeler, a New Dealer who broke with Franklin D. Roosevelt over court packing and isolationism. Allied with them were the labor unions (Montana has no right-to-work law and has been the most pro-union Rocky Mountain state), and pork barrel beneficiaries (for a while in the 1930s, Montana received more federal money per capita than almost any other state). The focus of all this was Butte, with its gold and copper mines on "The Richest Hill on Earth," with its gamblers, bootleggers, and millionaires, its company goons and union thugs, IWW organizers and its Socialist mayor. Today, Butte is far smaller. The mines are closed, the ore depleted, and the stone temples of commerce are grim; looming mine heads are being restored to a cleanliness they never enjoyed in the boom days.

Butte's population peaked in 1920, mines gradually closed all over the state, and agriculture—wheat growing and cattle grazing—became the mainstays of the economy. Class warfare died down. Other towns grew, though only Billings has topped 100,000. Others growth areas were the university town of Missoula, Great Falls just east of the Rockies, Kalispell near Flathead Lake, the university and resort town of Bozeman, and the state capital of Helena. The muscular tone of a land settled by ranch hands, miners and railroad workers, by men who do hard physical work and relax hard afterward, remains a link with Montanans going back to the mountain men, miners and cowboys who drove herds of Texas longhorns across the open range. And there is still the sense of space. Hunting and fishing opportunities abound; development in the small cities and resort areas has not been enough to drive the game away.

Over the past quarter-century, the Big Sky country attracted at first a trickle and then a flood of affluent Americans who purchased second homes here—high-visibility movie stars and billionaires like Ted Turner, but also just ordinary people buying small spreads near Big Sky or McLeod, near Bozeman, or around Flathead Lake or Big Timber or the Big Mountain ski resort in Whitefish. Many newcomers, from California and other urban states, are setting down roots here, as computers, modems and fax machines make it possible for small businessmen and entrepreneurs to work in Montana, far from their customers and clients but in an environment they love—and not far from the coffee houses and gambling parlors one finds along every highway. These new Montanas have added a spark of energy and inventiveness to a population that had consisted of those left behind when others moved elsewhere. Montana grew 13% in the 1990s and another 7% between 2000 and 2008, despite losses in the eastern plains. New Census Bureau estimates put total population at 967,440. The state's economy, fueled by construction and strong agricultural commodity and energy prices, continued to grow during the 2001 recession and after, and unemployment reached a historic low of 2.8% in 2007. Growth was especially vigorous around Bozeman and Big Sky, in Missoula and Ravalli County to the south, and around Kalispell and Lake Flathead to the north, while most of the eastern plains counties have lost population.

Sometimes newcomers are startled by the hardness of Montana life. The DeLorme Montana Road Atlas gives advice on what to do if you should encounter a bear. There are lively political arguments over the grizzly bears and gray wolves reintroduced to Montana in the 1990s. The American Prairie Foundation, funded by Manhattan and Silicon Valley millionaires, is buying up land in the northern plains to create a reserve where buffalo and prairie dogs can roam and to attract tourists and hunters. The Nature

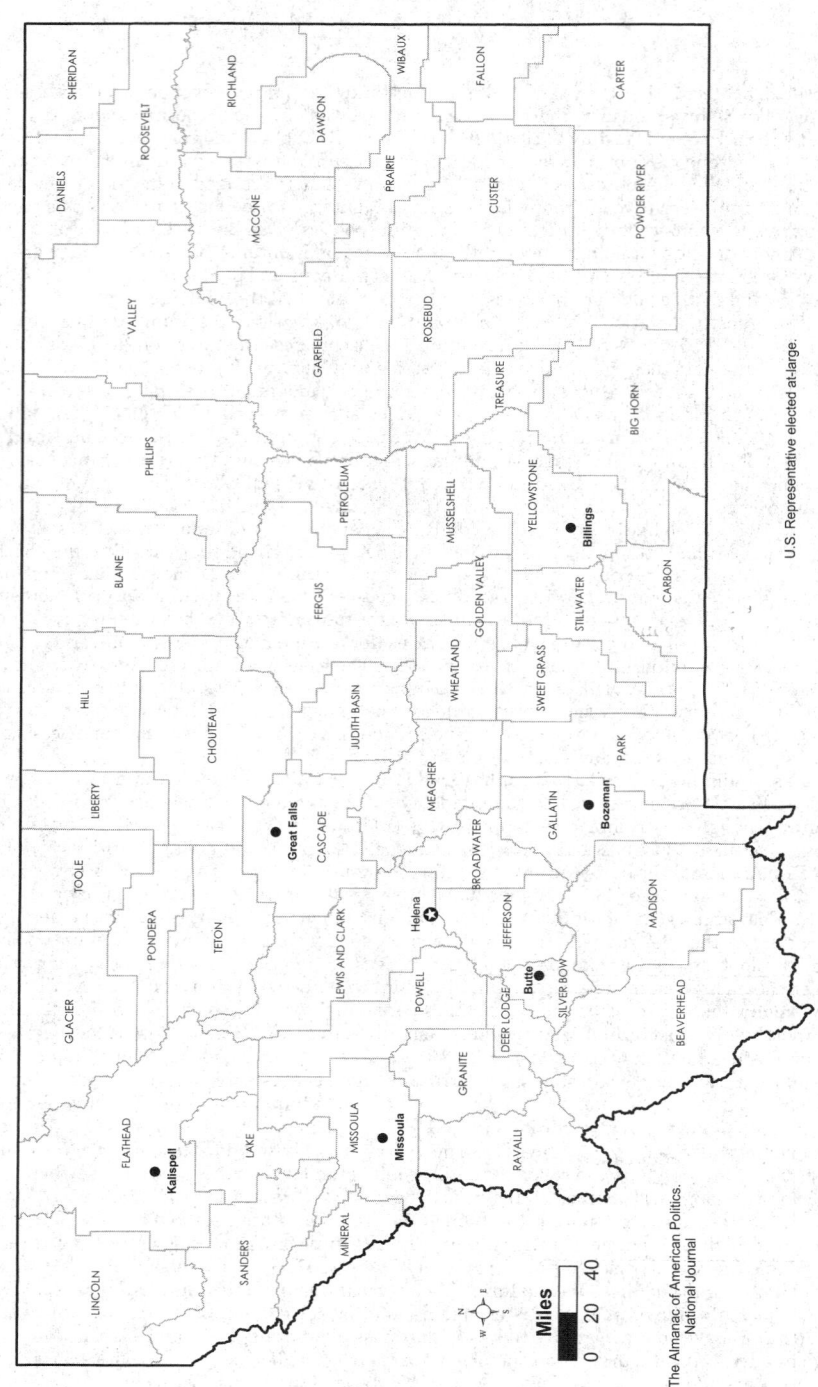

SHERIDAN

RICHLAND

WIBAUX

FALLON

CARTER

DANIELS

ROOSEVELT

DAWSON

MCCONE

PRAIRIE

CUSTER

POWDER RIVER

VALLEY

GARFIELD

ROSEBUD

TREASURE

PHILLIPS

PETROLEUM

MUSSELSHELL

YELLOWSTONE

● **Billings**

BIG HORN

BLAINE

FERGUS

GOLDEN VALLEY

STILLWATER

CABON

HILL

CHOUTEAU

JUDITH BASIN

WHEATLAND

SWEET GRASS

PARK

LIBERTY

MEAGHER

● **Bozeman**

TOOLE

● **Great Falls**

CASCADE

BROADWATER

GALLATIN

PONDERA

TETON

Helena ✪

JEFFERSON

MADISON

GLACIER

LEWIS AND CLARK

POWELL

DEER LODGE

● **Butte**

SILVER BOW

BEAVERHEAD

FLATHEAD

● **Kalispell**

LAKE

MISSOULA

● **Missoula**

GRANITE

RAVALLI

LINCOLN

SANDERS

MINERAL

N
W ● E
S

Miles

0   20   40

The Almanac of American Politics.
National Journal

U.S. Representative elected at-large.

Conservancy has been persuading ranchers in Phillips County to change their practices. The state conducted a lottery in 2006 for 50 licenses (Indian tribes were allotted 16 of them) to hunt buffalo north and west of Yellowstone National Park because ranchers fear that the buffalo will transmit brucellosis, which causes cows to abort, to their herds.

Montana has had two lively political traditions. One draws on its heritage of class-warfare politics, radical miners and angry labor unions, which made Montana for many years the most Democratic of the Rocky Mountain states. From 1952 to 1984, it elected only Democrats to the U.S. Senate, and since 2006, it has two Democratic senators again. The other, more recent tradition is in line with conservative activist Grover Norquist's "Leave-Us-Alone-Coalition" —a fierce opposition to higher taxes and federal government dictates. Montana has not elected a Democrat to the U.S. House since 1994, and Montana gave George W. Bush big majorities in 2000 and 2004. Barack Obama's campaigning and organization in 2008 held John McCain to a narrow plurality win. The Democratic tradition is strongest in the old mining towns like Butte and Anaconda, on Indian reservations (7% of Montanans are Indians), in old railroad towns like Great Falls and Havre, in university towns like Missoula and Bozeman, and in the state capital of Helena. The Republican tradition is strongest in the population-losing eastern plains counties and in fast-growing Flathead and Ravalli Counties in the west.

In recent years the Democratic tradition has mostly prevailed. Republican Dennis Rehberg, the state's lone U.S. representative, has continued to win House elections by wide margins, but Democrats have won by similarly impressive margins in other races. Rancher Brian Schweitzer, after running a strong race for senator in 2000, was elected governor by 50%-46% in 2004 and was rousingly re-elected, 65%-33%, in 2008. For several years, the Legislature has been closely divided between the two parties. In 2006, Democratic state Sen. Jon Tester edged out, 49%-48%, three-term U.S. Sen. Conrad Burns, who had received more contributions from Indian tribe clients of disgraced lobbyist Jack Abramoff than any other member of Congress. This was a key race in giving Democrats a majority in the Senate. And in 2008, Democratic Sen. Max Baucus, thought to be in trouble going into the 2002 cycle, was re-elected to his sixth term, 73%-27%, the biggest percentage victory in Montana since Democratic Sen. Mike Mansfield won 76%-24% in 1958, over a nuisance candidate. Baucus, as chairman of the Senate Finance Committee, wields more clout on Capitol Hill than any Montanan since Mansfield, who was the Senate majority leader, retiring in 1976.

Population		Household Income		Work	
Pop. 2007:	946,815	Under $15k:	15.1%	Private:	70.1%
State rank:	44th of 50	$15k to $50k:	43.1%	Government:	18.8%
Change since 2000:	Up 4.9%	$50k to $100k:	30.7%	Self-employed:	10.6%
Urban:	53.6%	$100k to $150k:	9.5%	Unemployment (3-yr. average):	3.4%
Rural:	46.4%	Over $150k:	1.6%	Poverty:	14.0%
Native of state:	54.2%	Median income:	$42,425	Blue collar:	22.6%
Not a citizen:	0.8%	**Home Value**		White collar:	57.3%
Area size:	147,042 sq. mi.	Under $100k:	29.7%	Khaki collar:	0.3%
Most populous cities		$100k to $300k:	52.8%	Other:	19.8%
1. Billings	97,053	$300k to $500k:	11.3%	**Age**	
2. Missoula	62,982	$500k to $1 mil:	4.7%	Median age:	39.3 yrs.
3. Great Falls	58,397	Over $1 million:	1.6%	More than 65 yrs:	13.8%
4. Bozeman	34,836	Median:	$152,300	Less than 18 yrs:	23.2%

Race/Ethnicity				Military Veterans		Registered Voters in 2008	
White:	88.3%	*Language*		% of Pop:	14.1%	No party registration	
Black:	0.6%	English:	95.5%	*Veterans by Period*		Voter turnout:	490,302
Hispanic:	2.5%	Spanish:	1.4%	WWII and before:	11.5%	Turnout as % of	
Asian:	0.7%	Asian:	0.4%	Korea:	11.8%	voting age:	65.6%
Native Am.:	5.9%	Other		Vietnam:	34.9%	**Legislature**	
Hawaiian:	0.1%	European	1.6%	Gulf (pre-2001):	10.0%	Senate:	23 D 27 R
Two+ races:	1.9%	**Education**		Gulf (post-2001):	8.1%	House:	50 D 50 R
Ancestry		H.S. grad:	90.1%	Peace time:	23.7%		
German:	22.0%	College grad:	26.7%				
Irish:	11.6%	Grad degree:	8.2%				
English:	9.4%			**Cook Partisan Voting Index:** R+7			

Presidential politics   Until very recently Montana, with its three electoral votes, didn't see much of presidential candidates. It holds its presidential primaries in June, at the end of the political primary season, and since 1992, it seemed too heavily Republican to be worth the time it takes to fly here for any Democrat on the national ticket. But 2008 was different. State Republicans, hoping to be relevant, opted for a February 5 caucus rather than a June primary. But only 1,630 party and local officials participated, giving a win to Mitt Romney, whose campaign was immediately ended by other Super Tuesday results.

2008 Presidential Vote		
McCain (R)	242,763	(50%)
Obama (D)	231,667	(47%)
2008 Democratic Presidential Primary		
Obama (D)	103,174	(57%)
Clinton (D)	74,889	(41%)
2004 Presidential Vote		
Bush (R)	266,063	(59%)
Kerry (D)	173,710	(39%)

Democrats, with more enthusiasm after the successive victories of Brian Schweitzer and Jon Tester, stuck with the June primary, by which time the nomination was still being contested. Obama's campaign early on spotted Montana, with its openness to new Democrats and its lack of racially polarized politics, as a state where he could have great appeal. Obama won 57%-41%, balancing Hillary Rodham Clinton's simultaneous win in South Dakota. He scored heavily on the Sioux reservation; in Missoula and Gallatin counties, with their university communities; in Flathead County, with its affluent new migrants; and in Lewis and Clark County, with its state government employees.

After Obama's July 4 visit to the state, polls showed him competitive with or ahead of John McCain, and he put together an impressive and enthusiastic organization. McCain's selection of Alaska Gov. Sarah Palin as his running mate revived his chances in the state, but after the crisis on Wall Street in mid-September, McCain's standing fell, while the Obama team ran television ads and organized new voters. It was not quite enough, but still impressive. Montana, which had voted 59%-39% for Bush in 2004, voted only 50%-47% for McCain. Obama received 32% more votes than John Kerry had in 2004; McCain got 9 fewer percentage points than Bush had four years earlier—a pattern common to states that were not battlegrounds in 2004 but were targeted by Obama in 2008. Obama had big wins on the Indian reservations in Silver Bow (Butte) and Missoula counties.

Congressional districting   Montana's population has not been growing rapidly enough in the 2000s to make it a contender for a second House seat in the reapportionment following the 2010 Census.

111th Congress Lineup
1 R
110th Congress Lineup
1 R

Governor

Brian Schweitzer (D)

Elected 2004, term expires Jan. 2013, 2nd term; b. Sept. 4, 1955, Havre; home, Georgetown Lake; CO St. U., B.S. 1978; MT St. U., M.S. 1980; Catholic; married (Nancy); 3 children.

Professional Career: Farm developer, 1980–86; Farmer, rancher, 1986-present; Committee member, Montana Farm Service Agency, 1993–99.

Office: P.O. Box 200801, State Capitol, Helena, 59620, 406-444-3111; Fax: 406-444-5529; Web site: governor.mt.gov.

Election Results

2008 general	Brian Schweitzer (D)	318,670	(66%)
	Roy Brown (R)	158,268	(33%)
2008 primary	Brian Schweitzer (D)	159,820	(91%)
	William Fischer (D)	9,865	(6%)

Prior Winning Percentages: 2004 (50%)

Brian Schweitzer, a Democrat who was elected governor of Montana in 2004, grew up on his family's ranch in the Judith Basin, east of Great Falls. His Irish grandparents had homesteaded in Hill County, near the Great Northern Railway line. He graduated from Colorado State with a degree in international agronomy and from Montana State with a degree in soil science. In the early 1980s, he went off to the Middle East on an agricultural adventure. He developed a 15,000-acre farm in the Sahara in Libya and helped oversee the development of a dairy farm in Saudi Arabia. In 1986, he returned to Montana and bought two farms. He raised cattle and exported bull semen and grew mint and dill. In 1993, when the Clinton administration took office, he was appointed to the three-member, part-time Farm Service Agency that helps distribute federal payments to farmers.

In 1999, with minimal political experience, he embarked on a race against two-term U.S. Sen. Conrad Burns. That fall, he organized a bus trip for senior citizens so they could go to Canada to buy prescription drugs at low prices. With armed guards, he strode into the Capitol in Helena and poured out $47,000 in cash—the amount, he said, of contributions to Burns from tobacco company political action committees. He attacked Burns for supporting a bill that would limit compensation to people with asbestos-related disease and shut down the giant asbestos tort cases. Burns, who had reneged on a 1988 promise to serve only two terms, outspent Schweitzer by 2-to-1 in the 2000 election but won by only 51% to 47%.

The Senate race made Schweitzer a formidable political figure and an obvious candidate for governor in 2004. The incumbent, Republican Judy Martz, elected in 2000 with only 51% of the vote, had had a rocky tenure. In August 2001, the state House majority leader was killed in a car crash; Martz's chief policy adviser, who was intoxicated, had been driving. She endured months of unfavorable publicity and in August 2003, threatened with a primary challenge, announced she would not run for a second term.

Schweitzer entered the race for governor as the clear front-runner in the Democratic primary. He campaigned against one-party rule—Montana had had Republican governors since 1988—and championed small businesses against out-of-state corporations. Montana had developed into a "salmon economy," he said: "All our young leave the state and then they come home to die." Republicans, he said, were to blame for high property taxes and for the state's low wage levels. He made common cause with both environmental advocates and hunters and fishermen by championing hunting and fishing rights on private lands and opposing the sale of public lands. He called for low-tuition technical colleges to provide training for young Montanans and for creation of pharmacy purchasing pools to buy prescription drugs in Canada. He named Republican state Sen. John Bohlinger as his lieutenant governor candidate and named him head of a Corps of Recovery to come up with $60 million of spending cuts without eliminating services. Schweitzer won the June 2004 Democratic primary 73%-27%. The winner of the Republican primary was Bob Brown, who had served 26 years in the Legislature and later was a lobbyist for USWEST (now Qwest), Columbia Falls Aluminum Co., and the state university system. Brown, like Schweitzer, declined to take the Americans for Tax Reform pledge not to raise taxes. Brown favored limited oil and gas exploration on the Rocky Mountain Front and the ballot proposition to repeal the state's ban on cyanide mining. Schweitzer took the opposite stand on both issues.

Schweitzer raised more money than Brown, some of it from out-of-state contributors to his 2000 Senate race. He billed himself as a "pickup-driving, God-fearing, gun-toting, red-meat-eating, take-responsibility-for-my-actions, invest-in-education kind of Democrat." Like Brown, he backed the referendum banning same-sex marriage, which passed with 67% of the vote. Schweitzer won by 50%-46%, even though George W. Bush carried the state by 59%-39%, and Democrats swept to a 27-23 majority in the state Senate and a 50-50 tie in the state House (thus giving them control because state law requires that in the case of a tie the speaker must come from the governor's party). Schweitzer carried not only the usual Democratic areas around Butte, the Indian reservations, and Missoula but also Billings, the state's largest city, and Helena, the capital.

Schweitzer announced an open-door policy in the governor's office, allowing reporters to come in any time they wanted (they got tired of this after a while) and brought his border collie, Jag, there every day. With a projected budget surplus, he and the Legislature froze the business equipment tax at 3% and eliminated it for 13,000 businesses that owned $20,000 worth of equipment or less. He signed a bill requiring country-of-origin meat labeling. He helped pass a law requiring public schools to teach American Indian history, and he made commencement speeches at high schools with one-student graduating classes.

He also unveiled a plan to spend some $31 million on building maintenance, energy programs, and the Indian Education for All program, which passed the two chambers. In addition, Schweitzer and the Legislature put $125 million into the teacher and state employee pension funds, which were figured to be $1.4 billion short because of investment losses and benefit increases. In 2007, again facing a surplus, Schweitzer got the Legislature to agree to a budget that raised spending 11% a year, with $400 rebates to homeowners. But that required a special session and came only after the House majority leader denounced Schweitzer in obscene terms. (The leader's colleagues subsequently ousted him from the post.) The Legislature also passed a law defying the federal Real ID Act, which requires states to verify a person's identity and citizenship before issuing a driver's license.

Schweitzer has emphasized energy issues. In 2005, he persuaded the Legislature to pass a bill requiring 10% of motor fuel to be a certain form of ethanol after state ethanol production reaches 55 million gallons a year, and another calling for 15% of electricity to be produced from renewable sources by 2015. Montana— "the Saudi Arabia of coal" —has the nation's largest coal reserves, in deep veins, and Schweitzer has promoted "clean coal" liquefaction, despite opposition from some environmental groups. In 2007, he got the Legislature to pass tax breaks for windmill farms, biofuels, and coal liquefaction plants, long-distance electric transmission lines, carbon dioxide sequestration, and liquid-fuel pipelines. When the Bush administration opened up national forestland to new logging roads, Schweitzer pressed local officials to request that none be built.

Schweitzer has had very high job ratings and shown shrewd political instincts. As he told *The Washington Post,* "In politics it doesn't matter what the facts are. It matters what the perceptions are. It is the way you frame it." In 2006, he campaigned for Senate candidate Jon Tester, a Democrat who beat incumbent Republican Burns. He also supported two ballot initiatives, an ethics measure that got 76% of the vote and a minimum-wage increase that got 73%. But Democrats, contrary to the national trend, lost seats in both chambers that year: The Senate went from 27-23 Democratic to 25-25, after which a Republican switched parties and made it 26-24. The House went from 50-50 to 49-50, with one Constitution Party member caucusing with Republicans, and a Republican became speaker. In political circles, there was talk of Schweitzer as a vice presidential nominee in 2008. "I am just a Montana farmer," he said in response. "I don't know if what I say or do is exportable. It is a long way from the Little League to playing for the Yankees." He delivered a spirited speech at the 2008 Democratic National Convention, but he appeared to go on after the allotted time, which meant that the next speaker, Sen. Hillary Rodham Clinton of New York, could not finish her speech before the end of prime time.

Schweitzer has his critics at home, and some circulated a *YouTube* video of a speech in which he bragged about increasing turnout on Indian reservations for Tester in 2006. But he has remained widely popular. In November 2008, he was re-elected by 66%-33% over GOP state Sen. Roy Brown. Republicans gained a 27-23 margin in the state Senate, but they lost ground in the state House, which was tied 50-50.

Senior Senator

Max Baucus (D)

Elected 1978, term expires 2014, 6th term; b. Dec. 11, 1941, Helena; home, Helena; Stanford U., B.A. 1964, LL.B. 1967; Protestant; divorced; 1 child.

Elected Office: MT House of Reps., 1973–74; U.S. House of Reps., 1974–78.

Professional Career: Staff atty., Civil Aeronautics Bd., 1967–69; Legal asst., Securities & Exchange Comm., 1969–71; Practicing atty., 1971–74.

DC Office: 511 HSOB, 20510, 202-224-2651; Fax: 202-224-9412; Web site: baucus.senate.gov.

State Offices: Billings, 406-657-6790; Bozeman, 406-586-6104; Butte, 406-782-8700; Great Falls, 406-761-1574; Helena, 406-449-5480; Kalispell, 406-756-1150; Missoula, 406-329-3123.

Committees: *Agriculture, Nutrition & Forestry* (4th of 12 D). *Environment & Public Works* (2nd of 12 D). *Finance* (Chmn of 13 D): Taxation, IRS Oversight & Long-Term Growth. *Joint Committee on Taxation.* (V. Chmn.)

Group Ratings

	ADA	ACLU	AFS	LCV	ITIC	NTU	COC	ACU	CFG	FRC
2008	80	86	89	100	100	11	75	8	20	11
2007	80	—	100	67	—	11	55	20	8	—

National Journal Ratings

	2007 LIB — 2007 CONS		2008 LIB — 2008 CONS	
Economic	53%	— 44%	57%	— 42%
Social	55%	— 43%	67%	— 31%
Foreign	59%	— 36%	65%	— 6%
Composite	57%	— 43%	68%	— 32%

Key Votes of the 110th Congress

1. Raise CAFE standards	Y	5. Make English official language Y	9. Withdraw troops 3/08	Y
2. Expand SCHIP	Y	6. Path to citizenship	N	10. Iran guard is terrorist group	Y
3. Cap greenhouse gases	Y	7. Fetus is unborn child	N	11. Increase missile defense $	N
4. Bail out financial markets	Y	8. Prosecute hate crimes	Y	12. Overhaul FISA	Y

Election Results

2008 general	Max Baucus (D) 348,289	(73%)	($8,164,703)
	Bob Kelleher (R)..129,369	(27%)	
2008 primary	Max Baucus (D).. unopposed		

Prior Winning Percentages: 2002 (63%); 1996 (50%); 1990 (68%); 1984 (57%); 1978 (56%); 1976 House (66%); 1974 House (55%)

Max Baucus, the state's senior senator, is from a well-known Montana ranching family. In 1897, his great-grandfather Henry Sieben started the huge Sieben Ranch, including the land in the book and film *A River Runs Through It*. Baucus grew up on the 125,000-acre (195 square miles) ranch near Helena and graduated from college and law school at Stanford University. He then worked four years at the now-abolished Civil Aeronautics Board and the Securities and Exchange Commission in Washington. Baucus returned to Montana in 1971, and he was executive director of the state constitutional convention in 1972. Two years later, at age 32, he won the western House seat (Montana had two seats until 1992) by walking 600 miles along highways through the district. He defeated three past or future holders: Democrats Pat Williams and Arnold Olsen in the primary and Republican Richard Shoup in the general. Baucus won his Senate seat in 1978 by easily beating an appointed senator in the primary and a conservative Republican in the general. In March 2005, he became the longest-serving senator in Montana history.

Since Sen. Daniel Patrick Moynihan of New York retired in 2000, Baucus has been the senior Democrat on the Senate Finance Committee. He was the chairman from June 2001 to January 2003 and got the post back when Democrats regained control of the Senate in January 2007. As chairman, Baucus is the most important Senate ally of President Obama on economic policy. This became apparent early in Obama's administration when he brought a massive economic stimulus bill to Congress as his first major initiative as president. Baucus is Obama's Senate point man on health care policy, another priority of the new administration.

Chairing the Finance Committee is a big job that comes with competing pressures. The panel has jurisdiction over tax, trade, and Medicare issues—all controversial in this decade—and the Senate Democratic leadership has sought a chairman loyal to party positions. But passing a bill in the Senate often requires 60 votes (to overcome potential filibusters), and they are easier to obtain when Baucus works out an agreement with his Republican counterpart, Charles Grassley of Iowa. This has been a tradition on Finance, adhered to by Moynihan and Republican William Roth of Delaware in the 1990s and Kansas Republican Bob Dole and Louisiana Democrat Russell Long in the 1980s. Also, as a Democratic senator from a generally Republican state—although one that has seemed less so since the victories of Gov. Brian Schweitzer in 2004 and Sen. Jon Tester in 2006 and the narrow loss by presidential candidate Obama in 2008—Baucus has political incentives to take a moderate course on some issues.

In 2001, Baucus, starting off in the minority, partnered with Grassley to unveil a $1.3 trillion tax cut package with specific provisions tailored to moderate Republicans and Democrats on the committee. The bill passed the committee 14-6 and the Senate 62-38 (with 12 Democrats, including Baucus, voting in favor). Key members of the coalition Baucus and Grassley assembled insisted that they would not accept major changes from the Senate bill, so something similar to the original came out of the House-Senate conference committee, and the first domestic priority of the Bush administration was passed into law. Around that same time, Sen. Jim Jeffords of Vermont was in the process of leaving the Republican Party to become an independent, handing effective control of the narrowly divided Senate to the Democrats. Tom Daschle of South Dakota, who became majority leader in June as a result of Jeffords's flip, was reportedly furious that Baucus refused to consult with the Democratic Caucus before the final drafting of the tax bill; he presumably wanted to hold out for a more Democratic tax cut. In October 2001, pressure from Daschle may have reined in Baucus when he introduced a $70 billion economic stimulus bill and Republicans urged him to negotiate a compromise with Grassley. Baucus instead called on President Bush to step in. A smaller Baucus plan passed the committee 11-10 in November (with Jeffords as the swing vote). Similarly, on welfare, Baucus was unable to come up with a united Democratic position, so the 1996 law was not reauthorized until 2006. In September 2002, Baucus summoned all Finance members and told them that Daschle would allow no prescription drug bill to come out of committee and, according to some reports that Baucus denied, said that Daschle would strip him of his chairmanship if he drafted one. Instead, Daschle brought his own bill to the floor.

After Republicans won the Senate majority in November 2002, Baucus began working closely again with Grassley on major legislation. The two came up with a corporate tax bill that passed the Senate 92-5 in 2004. Baucus also worked with Grassley in 2003 to draw up a bill creating a prescription drug benefit in the Medicare program, which won a majority in the Finance Committee and in the Senate. Baucus supported provisions, sought mostly by Republicans, for private health insurance to play a larger role in Medicare. However, he got Republicans to drop provisions that would allow greater prescription drug coverage in private plans than in Medicare.

On Social Security, Baucus joined Grassley and other moderates in 2004 to discuss changes in the system. But in spring 2005, Baucus stuck with Minority Leader Harry Reid and the party line by rejecting personal retirement accounts in the program. "Privatization has to be off the table because it exacerbates or makes more difficult [achieving] Social Security solvency," he said. He refused to discuss any proposal that included personal investment accounts and pressed other Democratic senators to do likewise. In 2005, he told AARP, an advocacy group for older Americans: "I'm the lead guy on this end, the person in charge of preventing privatization, and I love it. I've never had so much fun fighting for something that's right."

Trade issues are important to Baucus and his exporting state. Although he, like other Democrats, called for stronger labor and environmental standards in trade agreements, he has generally been more favorable to lowering trade barriers than most congressional Democrats. He was a leading advocate of normal trade relations with China, a potentially huge market for Montana wheat. He also supported an end to the trade embargo on Cuba. After Japan banned U.S. beef in December 2003, Baucus negotiated directly with the Japanese to reopen their market, which Japan later did. In 2007, Baucus called for renewing a measure that gives the president broad authority to negotiate free trade agreements, but said he would insist on stronger labor and environmental provisions.

As chairman again in 2007, with a narrowly divided Senate, Baucus continued to work closely with Grassley. "I care about results, and to get results, you have to work together and truly compromise," he says. With solid Democratic backing, they won Senate approval in October 2007 to expand the State Children's Health Insurance Program and also garnered a 68-31 vote to override Bush's veto. (But the House lacked the two-thirds support necessary for an override.) Baucus and Grassley also cooperated on a $60 billion fix of the alternative minimum tax in 2007 to reduce its impact on middle-income taxpayers, and on a similar one in 2008. The latter bill included long-term extensions of tax credits for renewable fuels. Another recent pursuit was a bill closing the "tax gap" of $370 billion between what is legally owed to the IRS annually and what is actually collected. They also sought legislation imposing a 25% tax on Internet pornography sites and creating a.xxx domain for pornography. In 2008, Baucus led committee members in cutting a final deal on that years' farm bill, with Baucus insisting on additional billions of dollars for disaster assistance, plus tax benefits for biofuels and conservation. For his state, Baucus added to the bill $500 million in tax credit bonds for the conservation of large tracts of land purchased by the government from Plum Creek Timber, Montana's largest land owner. Critics called it a tax giveaway to Plum Creek.

When Baucus was first elected in 1978, Montana had been represented exclusively by Democrats in the Senate since 1952. As the state trended Republican in the 1980s and 1990s, he was re-elected nonetheless, but was pressed in 1996 when challenged by Dennis Rehberg, then the Republican lieutenant governor and now the state's at-large House member. Baucus beat Rehberg by a slim margin, 50%-45%. Resentment over Clinton administration environment programs and George W. Bush's big victory here in 2000 suggested that he might have a serious challenge in 2002. One Republican who might have beaten him was Marc Racicot, who had high job ratings as governor from 1992 to 2000. But Racicot, having been the lowest-salaried governor in the nation, wanted to make money and refused to run despite pleas from President Bush. The Republican nomination was left to state Sen. Mike Taylor, a wealthy owner of a cosmetology school who eventually spent $1 million of his own money on the campaign.

But Baucus had much deeper pockets. As Finance chairman, his fundraising capacity was enormous, and in all, he spent over $6 million—almost four times as much as Taylor. In the fall, Montana Democrats ran an ad that slyly suggested Taylor was gay. It showed 1980s footage of Taylor massaging a man's face while applying facial cream and asserted that Taylor had failed to refund student-loan money when his cosmetology students dropped out. Taylor claimed that his wife made paperwork errors, and a Taylor aide said, "They're playing off the old stereotype of men who work in the hair-care profession." In any case, the race was probably already over. Taylor had only raised $658,000, he was still far behind Baucus in public polls, and national Republicans had decided it was not a priority race. Baucus won 63%-32%, carrying all but two small counties.

In 2008, after Racicot and Rehberg said they would not run, Baucus's re-election was all but a done deal. Running against Butte attorney and former Green Party nominee for governor, Bob Kelleher, who spent less than 1% of Baucus's total, Baucus hired more than 70 campaign staffers and took nothing for granted. He won 73%-27%, and this time took all 56 counties.

An avid runner, Baucus took a bad fall in a 50-mile race in Maryland in 2003 and two months later had surgery to relieve pressure on his brain. In June 2004 he had a pacemaker installed and the following month sustained minor injuries in a motorcycle crash in Montana. He suffered a tragic personal loss in July 2006 when his nephew, Cpl. Phillip Baucus, was killed in Iraq. The senator held the funeral at the Baucus family ranch in Montana.

Junior Senator

Jon Tester (D)

Elected 2006, term expires 2012, 1st term; b. Aug. 21, 1956, Havre; home, Big Sandy; U. of Great Falls, B.S. 1978; Christian; married (Sharla); 2 children.

Elected Office: Big Sandy Schl. Bd., 1982–92; MT Senate, 1998–2006; MT Senate pres., 2005–06.

Professional Career: Music teacher, Big Sandy Schl. Dist., 1978–80; Custom butcher, T-Bone Farms, 1978–98; Farmer, T-Bone Farms, 1978-present.

DC Office: 724 HSOB, 20510, 202-224-2644; Fax: 202-224-8594; Web site: tester.senate.gov.

State Offices: Billings, 406-252-0550; Bozeman, 406-586-4450; Butte, 406-723-3277; Glendive, 406-365-2391; Great Falls, 406-452-9585; Helena, 406-449-5401; Kalispell, 406-257-3360; Missoula, 406-728-3003.

Committees: *Appropriations* (17th of 18 D): Energy & Water Development; Financial Services & General Government; Homeland Security; Interior, Environment & Related Agencies; Legislative Branch. *Banking, Housing & Urban Affairs* (9th of 13 D): Economic Policy; Financial Institutions; Housing, Transportation & Community Development. *Homeland Security & Governmental Affairs* (8th of 10 D): Contracting Oversight; Investigations (Permanent); State, Local & Private Sector Preparedness & Integration. *Indian Affairs* (7th of 9 D). *Veterans' Affairs* (7th of 10 D).

Group Ratings

	ADA	ACLU	AFS	LCV	ITIC	NTU	COC	ACU	CFG	FRC
2008	85	93	89	100	60	23	63	16	30	0
2007	95	—	100	80	—	10	30	16	7	—

National Journal Ratings

	2007 LIB	—	2007 CONS		2008 LIB	—	2008 CONS
Economic	60%	—	38%		58%	—	40%
Social	57%	—	42%		71%	—	27%
Foreign	65%	—	32%		56%	—	40%
Composite	62%	—	38%		63%	—	37%

Key Votes of the 110th Congress

1. Raise CAFE standards	Y	5. Make English official language	Y
2. Expand SCHIP		6. Path to citizenship	N
3. Cap greenhouse gases	Y	7. Fetus is unborn child	N
4. Bail out financial markets	N	8. Prosecute hate crimes	Y

9. Withdraw troops 3/08	Y
10. Iran guard is terrorist group	N
11. Increase missile defense $	N
12. Overhaul FISA	N

Election Results

2006 general	Jon Tester (D)	199,845	(49%)	($5,588,292)
	Conrad Burns (R)	196,283	(48%)	($8,516,022)
2006 primary	Jon Tester (D)	65,757	(61%)	
	John Morrison (D)	38,394	(35%)	

Jon Tester, a Democrat, was elected Montana's junior senator in 2006. He grew up in a farming family, on the same prairie land his grandparents homesteaded almost a century ago near the small town of Big Sandy. His family ran a custom butcher shop behind their barn; at the age of 9 Tester lost three fingers from his left hand in a meat grinder. The accident, he says, changed him from a saxophone player to a trumpet player. He earned a music degree from the University of Great Falls and later taught music at a local elementary school before devoting himself to farming. He raised organic wheat, alfalfa, barley, buckwheat, lentils, millet, and peas. Tester also served on the local Soil Conservation Service Committee. He was elected in 1982 to the Big Sandy school board where he served for a decade. In 1998, when his neighbor, a Republican state senator, decided not to run for re-election, Tester ran for the seat and won.

Tester was chosen as minority leader in 2002. He became Senate president in 2005 after Democrats won a Senate majority. In that role, he helped pass a budget that cut taxes for small businesses and middle-class families while increasing funding for public education. When the 2005 legislative session adjourned, Tester announced he would challenge three-term Republican Sen. Conrad Burns. Tester was one of five Democrats seeking the party nomination; his only real opposition came from two-term state Auditor John Morrison. Morrison was a former president of the Montana Trial Lawyers Association, the son of a state Supreme Court justice who ran for governor, and the grandson of a former Nebraska governor. He outspent Tester nearly 2-to-1. But in a campaign that focused on Burns's ethics, Morrison was weakened by the disclosure that he had an extramarital affair in 1998 with the fiancée of a businessman who was later investigated by the auditor's office. This enabled Tester to rebut claims that Morrison was the more electable candidate, leading him to say he was the only Democrat who could go "belly-to-belly and toe-to-toe" with Burns. He ran as an unabashed populist, which made him a darling of liberal Internet activists, and he assembled a formidable grassroots operation with hundreds of volunteers. He won in a 61%-35% rout over Morrison.

Tester was taking on the only Republican senator Montana voters had ever re-elected. But by 2006, Burns, the 71-year-old conservative incumbent, had two serious problems. The first was his connection to disgraced and later convicted lobbyist Jack Abramoff. Beginning in 2005, national Democrats relentlessly hammered Burns for being the largest congressional recipient of campaign donations from Abramoff. He faced campaign accusations that he "sold his vote" and betrayed Montana's American Indian population by earmarking funds for Abramoff's Indian clients in other states. Burns urged U.S. Attorney General Alberto Gonzales to investigate the donations so that "these outrageous and wrongful allegations may be put to rest." The broader theme Tester used was that Burns was not the same down-to-earth Westerner Montanans had sent to Washington 18 years earlier.

Burns's second handicap was a gaffe-prone style, ill-suited for the *YouTube* era. His proclivity for making inappropriate and intemperate statements was one trait that had not changed in his two decades in Congress. In February 1999, he was forced to make a quick apology after referring to Arabs as "ragheads." In 2006, while discussing the war on terrorism, he spoke of enemies who "drive taxicabs in the daytime and kill at night." In July, he admonished a group of firefighters for doing a "piss-poor job" of battling a wildfire. A month later, he referred to his handyman as a "nice little Guatemalan man" and joked about the man's immigration status. "I can self-destruct in one sentence," he admitted. "Sometimes in one word." In the past, such blunders might have been overlooked as part of Burns's folksy appeal, but are harder to dismiss now that some of them are memorialized on video and on numerous websites. This was a bare-knuckled campaign. Burns spent $8.5 million, roughly twice as much as in 2000 and $3 million more than Tester. He was pummeled over his link to Abramoff while Republicans sought to portray Tester as too liberal for Montana. He was criticized for his opposition to a Bush-era anti-terrorism law called the USA PATRIOT Act and linked to "radical environmentalists" and liberal extremist bloggers. But Tester was not so easily caricatured. His signature $8 flattop haircut, highlighted in a television ad filmed at the Riverview Barbershop in Great Falls, his down-to-earth demeanor, his beefy farmer's build, and his agricultural background worked to temper the criticism. He also had the support of Democratic Gov. Brian Schweitzer, a Burns political enemy, who taped an ad saying, "Senator Burns and his crooked pals in Washington are lying about my friend Jon Tester."

The race was decided by just 3,562 votes. Burns carried 41 of 56 counties, including Yellowstone County, home to agriculture-industry-oriented Billings, the state's largest city. But Tester prevailed in several large counties including Cascade and Lewis and Clark, home to Great Falls and the state capital of Helena, respectively. He also won 64%-34% in Missoula County.

In Washington, Democrats hailed Tester's victory as a signal of a new political direction in the Mountain West. His distinctive look—he's tall, is barrel-chested, and wears cowboy boots—won him immediate notice in the Senate, as did his practice of prominently posting his daily schedule on the Internet, a Senate first. His physical stature stands in contrast to his modest attitude towards politics, "You have two ears and one mouth, act accordingly." Since arriving in Washington, Tester has stressed the importance of transparency and accountability in government, thus distancing himself from the questionable practices that hurt his predecessor. He strongly supported the Senate's 2007 ethics bill and in 2008 he voluntarily asked a retired Montana Supreme Court justice to conduct a comprehensive ethics audit of his office.

On matters relating to foreign policy and national security, Tester has taken a liberal stance. He sponsored a bill that increased the mileage reimbursement rate for veterans travelling to veterans' health care facilities from 11 cents per gallon to 28.5 cents per gallon. He cast votes against the Iraq war and the federal government's foreign eavesdropping programs. Tester also spoke out against the REAL ID law, which requires states to verify a person's citizenship before issuing a driver's license. He joined Democratic Sens. Jim Webb of Virginia and Claire McCaskill of Missouri in inserting an amendment to the National Defense Authorization Act that would have established a bipartisan commission to oversee private contractors in Iraq. President Bush signed the bill into law but attached a signing statement stipulating he felt justified in ignoring the amendment, a fact that did not sit well with Tester. "For the president to say, you know, 'I don't think this is a good idea and I can do that because I'm king,' is a big mistake," he said.

On domestic issues, Tester's positions are more moderate and generally reflect the interests of his home state. He voted against a GOP amendment that called for a one-year suspension of earmarks, spending projects requested by individual lawmakers, and a bill that would have granted immunity to illegal immigrants. He has joined other Montana politicians in promoting carbon-capture and sequestration technology as a feasible method of clean-energy production that could lead to the development of Montana's large coal reserves. "Montana is the Saudi Arabia of coal," Tester likes to say.

Representative-At-Large

Denny Rehberg (R)

Elected 2000, 5th term; b. Oct. 5, 1955, Billings; home, Billings; WA St. U., B.A. 1977; Episcopalian; married (Jan); 3 children.

Elected Office: MT House of Reps., 1984–90; MT lt. gov., 1991–96

Professional Career: Leg. asst., U.S. Rep. Ron Marlenee, 1979–82; Rancher, 1982-present.

DC Office: 2448 RHOB, 20515, 202-225-3211; Fax: 202-225-5687; Web site: www.house.gov/rehberg.

State Offices: Billings, 406-256-1019; Great Falls, 406-454-1066; Helena, 406-443-7878; Missoula, 406-543-9550.

Committees: *Appropriations* (17th of 23 R): Energy & Water Development; Labor, HHS, Education & Related Agencies; State, Foreign Operations & Related Programs.

Group Ratings

	ADA	ACLU	AFS	LCV	ITIC	NTU	COC	ACU	CFG	FRC
2008	40	18	43	8	57	60	89	84	70	100
2007	20	—	9	10	—	54	90	88	50	—

National Journal Ratings

	2007 LIB — 2007 CONS		2008 LIB — 2008 CONS	
Economic	26%	— 73%	29%	— 71%
Social	29%	— 69%	31%	— 62%
Foreign	0%	— 72%	34%	— 65%
Composite	24%	— 77%	33%	— 67%

Key Votes of the 110th Congress

1. Increase minimum wage	N	5. Share immigration data	Y	9. Withdraw troops 8/08	N
2. Expand SCHIP	Y	6. Foreign aid abortion ban	Y	10. No operations in Iran	N
3. Raise CAFE standards	N	7. Ban gay bias in workplace	N	11. Free trade with Peru	Y
4. Bail out financial markets	N	8. Repeal D.C. gun law	Y	12. Overhaul FISA	Y

Election Results

2008 general	Denny Rehberg (R)	308,470	(64%)	($897,187)
	John Driscoll (D)	155,930	(32%)	
	Mike Fellows (Lib)	16,500	(3%)	
2008 primary	Denny Rehberg (R)	unopposed		

Prior Winning Percentages: 2006 (59%); 2004 (64%); 2002 (65%); 2000 (51%)

Denny Rehberg, a Republican first elected in 2000, is a fifth-generation Montanan and a rancher from Billings who raises cattle and cashmere goats on the same ranch that his great-grandfather homesteaded at the turn of the 20th century. A helicopter owner and pilot, he frequently flies to appointments around the state. Rehberg has been involved in politics most of his life: His father was a state legislator who ran against Democratic Rep. John Melcher in 1970.

After college, Rehberg (*REE-berg*) worked in real estate before moving to Washington so his wife could attend law school. While there, he worked for Republican Rep. Ron Marlenee of Montana. He returned to his home state in 1982 to rebuild and run the family ranch, a third of which—including the house in which Rehberg grew up—had been sold to help pay the inheritance tax levied after his great-grandmother passed away. At 29, Rehberg was elected to the state House. He managed Republican Conrad Burns's first campaign for the U.S. Senate in 1988, and then served as Burns's state director for two years. He was appointed lieutenant governor by Republican Gov. Stan Stephens and was elected to that post on the ticket headed by Marc Racicot in 1992. Four years later, Rehberg ran against Democratic Sen. Max Baucus. Rehberg backed term limits, promised to forgo pay increases, and attacked Baucus for backing the 1993 tax increase and the assault-weapons ban. Baucus called Rehberg a "special interest" candidate who would cut taxes for the rich. Rehberg was outspent $4.3 million to $1.4 million, but he made it a serious contest, holding Baucus to 50% of the vote to his 45%.

Rehberg returned to ranching. In 2000, he annexed part of his ranch into the Billings city limits, divided the land into salable lots, and founded Rehberg Ranch Estates. Today, his wife, Jan, manages the company, which contributes significantly to the couple's wealth. In 2006, the Center for Responsive

Politics, a watchdog group, listed Rehberg as the 24th richest member of Congress, with an estimated worth of $6 million to $55 million.

The opportunity to again run for Congress came in September 1999, when Republican Rep. Rick Hill, re-elected with only 53% of the vote the previous year and facing vigorous opposition from Democratic Superintendent of Public Instruction Nancy Keenan, announced he would not run again because of complications from eye surgery. Rehberg was unopposed for the GOP nomination, and then faced Keenan in the general election, which turned into a classic contest between a conservative Republican and a liberal Democrat. Rehberg and Keenan agreed on several issues: They both favored gun rights, repeal of the so-called marriage-tax penalty, and letting patients sue health maintenance organizations. The race turned on their disagreements—on abortion rights, inheritance taxes, and a prescription drug benefit. (Rehberg favored giving the drug benefit to the needy; Keenan favored it for all.) The tone got testy as outside groups—the AFL-CIO, the NEA, the U.S. Chamber of Commerce, and the National Federation of Independent Business spent more than $100,000 each. Rehberg ran ads with strong endorsements from Gov. Racicot and often depicting his family, especially his 2-year-old daughter, an implicit contrast with Keenan, a former copper smelter worker and special education teacher who had never married. Rehberg won 51%-46%, almost precisely the same ratio as in the races for governor and senator that year. He was surely helped by George W. Bush's 58%-33% victory over Al Gore in the presidential contest.

As a freshman, Rehberg concentrated on Montana issues. He worked with Sen. Burns in 2002 to put $752 million in drought relief for farmers into the farm bill. He successfully sought repeal of Clinton-era restrictions on snowmobiling in Yellowstone National Park, although it continues to be regulated. In his second term, Rehberg took up the cause of preserving mandatory country-of-origin labeling of meat, a regional issue that pitted Texas cattlemen, who import much of their livestock from Mexico, against their northern counterparts. Rehberg framed country-of-origin labeling as a way to assure consumers that meat products sold under the USDA label came from animals that were born, raised, and processed in the United States. In 2008, Rehberg backed a provision in that year's farm bill requiring country-of-origin labeling, which became law after the House and Senate overrode President Bush's veto by comfortable margins.

Rehberg has strongly supported Bush on the Iraq war but has disagreed on other issues. He joined Democrats on the House Appropriations Committee in criticizing the level of funding in Bush's fiscal 2009 budget for "No Child Left Behind" education mandates. He specifically attacked the amount of money allocated for Impact Aid, a program important to Montana's seven American Indian reservations. He supported the FutureGen clean-coal project, partly because Montana has the largest coal reserves in the United States. FutureGen was a partnership between government and private industry aimed at building a coal-fueled, near-zero-emissions power plant. It was later canceled by the Energy Department. During the debate over immigration, Rehberg opposed guest worker and legalization provisions. And he has harshly criticized the Endangered Species Act for leading farmers and ranchers to "shoot, shovel, and shut up" —killing endangered animals living on their property rather than report the animals' presence and risk having their land confiscated by the government.

Rehberg was re-elected with 65% of the vote in 2002 and 64% in 2004. In 2005, he secured a seat on the Appropriations Committee, a sign that he might be settling in for a long career in the House. Then, in 2006, he was opposed by Billings-area state Rep. Monica Lindeen, whose family started Montana's largest Internet service provider. Rehberg was more vulnerable than usual that year. He had received about $17,000 in contributions from Indian tribes represented by disgraced lobbyist Jack Abramoff, plus $2,000 from Abramoff himself. He returned the tribes' money and donated Abramoff's $2,000 to domestic violence centers on Montana reservations. Lindeen raised $518,000, with notable contributions from Baucus and former Baucus staffers. Rehberg raised $1.2 million. He prevailed 59%-39%, his worst re-election showing since he won the seat.

In July 2007, Rehberg announced he would seek re-election to the House, declining a repeat run against Baucus for the Senate, although polls suggested that he would be competitive. He won a fifth House term easily in 2008.

★ NEBRASKA ★

When the first travelers on the Oregon Trail in the 1840s crossed the Missouri River, they found themselves in "the sea of Nebraska"—not actually a single river, but a braid of streams that weaves a silver chain around sandbars and islands, flooding the level floor of the great plain; a mile wide, as the saying goes, and six inches deep. The wagons on the Oregon Trail passed through, and Nebraska was largely settled in a single rush in the 1880s, when its population increased from 452,000 to 1 million. It increased less than that, to 1.6 million in the next 100 years. In the 1880s, Omaha became a major railroad center, Lincoln the state capital, and farming and food products the main businesses. And for about a century, Nebraska remained pretty much the same. This is not what its founders intended. They hoped that Nebraska would develop a diversified farming, industrial, and commercial economy like that found in Illinois, Missouri, or Ohio. But climate is hard to predict. Rains were plentiful in the 1880s, but the 1890s were years of drought, and Nebraska abruptly stopped growing. Many rural counties and even Omaha lost population, and Nebraska exported people for 100 years: 48% of Nebraskans in 1890 were children; in 2000, only 26% were. For a long time the creative energies in the American economy seemed to have skipped over the Great Plains and moved far to the west.

The sudden boom of the 1880s and the bust of the 1890s produced the most colorful—and atypical—politics of Nebraska's history: the populist movement and William Jennings Bryan, the "silver-tongued orator of the Platte." Bryan was only 36 when he delivered his Cross of Gold speech at the 1896 Democratic National Convention and was swept to the Democratic nomination. He was so radical that Democratic President Grover Cleveland wouldn't support him, but he still won 47% of the popular vote in the first of his three attempts at the presidency. Since Bryan's time, Nebraska's most notable politician has been George Norris, who led the House rebellion against Speaker Joseph Cannon in 1911 and in the 1930s championed the state's unicameral, nonpartisan Legislature (in which every bill gets a public hearing where anyone can speak). In Washington, Norris sponsored the Norris-LaGuardia Anti-Injunction Act, the first federal pro-union legislation, and the Tennessee Valley Authority. But most Nebraskans were repelled by the New Deal, which seemed to threaten their way of life. Although it often elects Democratic governors and senators, Nebraska over the past half-century has been the second-most Republican state in presidential elections.

Since 1990, Nebraska has been growing robustly for the first time in decades. Its population grew 12%, to 1.8 million between 1990 and 2007, less than the national average but more than Nebraska has grown since the 1910s. The age tilt has changed, too. Nebraska's percentages of old people and children are now within 1% of the national average. The growth has not been even. In 68 of its 93 counties, population has declined since 2000. In tiny county seats, stores are closing, and across the Plains, farmhouses are shuttered and small school buildings are half-empty. The acreage of irrigated land has been rising, but ground water irrigation may have peaked during the drought years of 2000–07. Even so, farm incomes have been high, helped by increasing demand for corn because of federal ethanol subsidies, and Nebraska has been exporting more than $2 billion to foreign countries, much of it in food products.

For years, Nebraska's aging population was not producing enough young people to fill its jobs, but for the first time in a century there has been migration into the state. A hundred years ago, Czechs, Germans, and Danes came to work the factories in Omaha and farms on the Plains—Willa Cather tells the story beautifully in her novels. Now, Hispanics have been coming from Texas and Mexico to work in meat-packing factories; they account for half of the state's population increase. And their share of the population rose from 2% in 1990 to 7% in 2007. The population also no longer tilts toward the elderly: The biggest increases in age groups between 2000 and 2007 came in the under 5 and 18-24 categories (primarily Hispanics), as well as in the 45-64 group, (the Baby Boomers). Hispanic percentages are highest in the counties around Lexington (30%), South Sioux City (29%), Scottsbluff (19%), and Grand Island (18%). Meanwhile, farm counties keep losing population. Drought in 2002 caused ranchers to cull their herds, and another dry spell in 2006 caused $342 million in agricultural losses. Demographically, Nebraska increasingly looks like a Rocky Mountain state, with population concentrated in two cities and several smaller factory towns, with relatively few people spread out over farmlands. Every Saturday during the fall when the 'Huskers (Nebraskans don't say Cornhuskers) play in Lincoln, one out of every 25 Nebraskans is there.

Nebraska may be heavily Republican, but it is also a small enough community that attractive Democrats can win high office. The pattern has been this: A Republican governor raises taxes, a Democrat defeats him or her, and that Democrat then goes on to serve in the U.S. Senate. This is the template for the careers of James Exon, elected governor in 1970 and senator from 1978 to 1996; Bob Kerrey, elected governor in 1982 and senator from 1988 to 2000; and Ben Nelson, elected governor in 1990 and senator in 2000. But Republicans have grown stronger. Republican Chuck Hagel beat Nelson when he first ran for the Senate in 1996. Former Gov. Mike Johanns, a Republican elected in 1998, opposed tax increases, some of which were passed over his veto, and was re-elected easily in 2002. After a stint as Agriculture

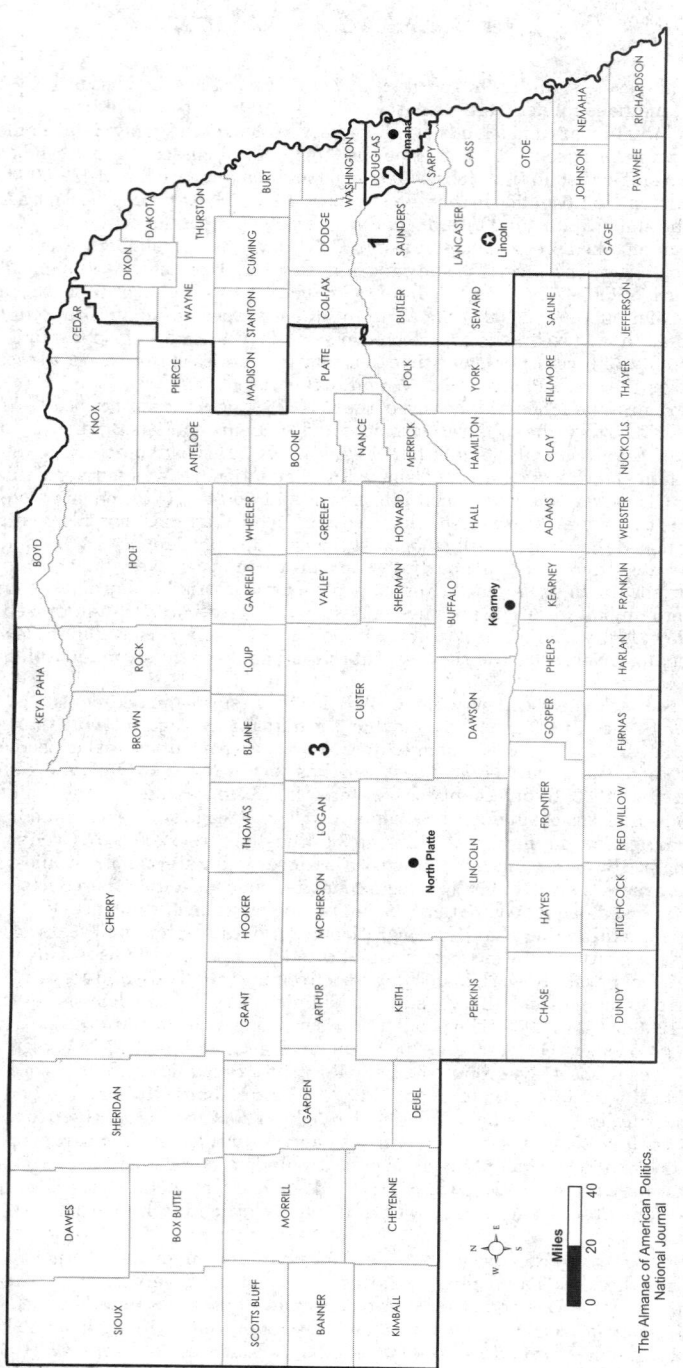

Congressional district boundaries were first effective for 2002.

The Almanac of American Politics.
National Journal

Population

Pop. 2007:	1,764,131
State rank:	38th of 50
Change since 2000:	Up 3.1%
Urban:	69.3%
Rural:	30.7%
Native of state:	65.8%
Not a citizen:	3.8%
Area size:	77,354 sq. mi.

Most populous cities

1. Omaha	379,851
2. Lincoln	247,246
3. Grand Island	43,793
4. Bellevue	43,643

Household Income

Under $15k:	13.0%
$15k to $50k:	40.0%
$50k to $100k:	33.2%
$100k to $150k:	11.8%
Over $150k:	2.0%
Median income:	$46,954

Home Value

Under $100k:	39.0%
$100k to $300k:	54.5%
$300k to $500k:	4.8%
$500k to $1 mil:	1.4%
Over $1 million:	0.2%
Median:	$118,200

Work

Private:	76.8%
Government:	14.8%
Self-employed:	8.1%
Unemployment (3-yr. average):	3.4%
Poverty:	11.3%
Blue collar:	23.0%
White collar:	59.4%
Khaki collar:	0.3%
Other:	17.3%

Age

Median age:	36.0 yrs.
More than 65 yrs:	13.3%
Less than 18 yrs:	25.3%

Race/Ethnicity

White:	84.8%
Black:	4.0%
Hispanic:	7.3%
Asian:	1.6%
Native Am.:	0.7%
Hawaiian:	0.1%
Two+ races:	1.5%

Ancestry

German:	31.4%
Irish:	11.0%
English:	7.2%

Language

English:	91.0%
Spanish:	5.9%
Asian:	1.1%
Other European	1.5%

Education

H.S. grad:	89.4%
College grad:	27.2%
Grad degree:	8.5%

Military Veterans

% of Pop:	11.5%

Veterans by Period

WWII and before:	13.2%
Korea:	13.7%
Vietnam:	30.4%
Gulf (pre-2001):	11.7%
Gulf (post-2001):	8.0%
Peace time:	23.0%

Registered Voters in 2008

D:	393,468 (34.0%)
R:	558,308 (48.2%)
Other:	205,569 (17.8%)
Voter turnout:	801,281
Turnout as % of voting age:	60.0%

Unicameral

Senate:	49 I

secretary, Johanns returned home to be elected to the Senate by 58%-40% in 2008. His successor, Dave Heineman, compiled a popular enough record that in the 2006 primary he beat 3rd District Rep. (and former 'Huskers football coach) Tom Osborne by 50%-44% and won the general election 73%-24%. That gave the Republicans the governorship for 12 years, their longest such stretch since the 1950s.

The last time a Democrat won one of Nebraska's three congressional seats was in 1992, and Republicans hold all five down-ballot statewide offices. In 2004, George W. Bush carried the state 66%-33%, winning 92 of the state's 93 counties (the exception, Thurston County, is an Indian reservation). He ran under 60% in only five counties, two of them the counties containing Omaha and Lincoln. But Nebraska's Democrats are a game bunch, and they came close to snatching the 2nd District House seat in 2008 from the incumbent, Republican Lee Terry, as a result of a burst of enthusiasm for Democratic presidential nominee Barack Obama. The senator from Illinois competed successfully in the 2nd District for one of three electoral votes that Nebraska law awards on the basis of congressional districts. Two years earlier, Democrats nearly captured the 3rd District seat, thanks to an attractive young candidate, Scott Kleeb. Omaha Democrats can also count in their ranks one of the country's two richest men, investor Warren Buffett, whose father was a Republican member of Congress in the 1940s and early 1950s when Warren was starting his business career as a newspaper carrier.

Presidential politics   Over the past 50 years, Nebraska has voted more Republican in presidential elections than all but one other state—65% to Utah's 66.5%. It was the last state Democratic President Bill Clinton visited in 1996, and the 2004 exit poll showed that no significant demographic group came close to going Democratic. But 2008 was different. Nebraska Democrats decided to stir up interest by choosing their delegates in a February 9 caucus rather than in the traditional May primary, which hasn't had much significance since Robert Kennedy and Eugene McCarthy contested it in 1968 and Frank Church won a surprise victory in 1976. As in other caucus states, Barack Obama's presidential campaign was enthusiastic and well organized, while Hillary Rodham Clinton's was well nigh invisible. Obama carried the caucus vote 68%-32%, running up big margins in Lincoln and Omaha and receiving scattered support in the west (some counties out in the sparsely populated SandHills cast one vote). The difference that Obama's organization made in the caucus setting can be gauged by the fact that his margin over Clinton in the admittedly inconsequential May primary was only 49%-47%.

2008 Presidential Vote
McCain (R) 452,979 (57%)
Obama (D) 333,319 (42%)

2008 Democratic Presidential Primary
Obama (D) 46,670 (49%)
Clinton (D) 43,979 (47%)

2008 Republican Presidential Primary
McCain (R) 118,876 (87%)
Paul (R) 17,772 (13%)

2004 Presidential Vote
Bush (R) 512,814 (66%)
Kerry (D) 254,328 (33%)

The strength of the Obama organization was evident in the general election as well. Targeting the 2nd District, which includes all of Omaha's Douglas County and most of its Sarpy County suburbs, Obama opened three offices and enlisted some 1,500 volunteers. Taking alarm, the campaign of GOP rival John McCain sent in Sarah Palin, his popular vice presidential pick. In the end, Obama carried the 2nd District by just 3,370 votes out of 277,809 cast, allowing him to capture one electoral vote. Given his large Electoral College margin, the vote ultimately didn't matter. But if, in one scenario that seemed realistic earlier in the campaign, McCain had carried all the states that George W. Bush won in 2004 except Iowa, New Mexico, and Nevada, the 2nd District's single electoral vote would have made the difference between a 270-268 win for Obama and a 269-269 tie. A tie would have sent the election to the House of Representatives, where, to be sure, Democrats ended up with majorities of most state delegations.

Congressional districting

| 111th Congress Lineup |
| 3 R |
| 110th Congress Lineup |
| 3 R |

Nebraska has had three congressional districts since the 1960 census. Redistricting in 2002 meant only marginal changes in the boundaries. Democrats were angered when traditionally Democratic Saline County was moved from the 1st to the 3rd District. No Democrat has been elected from a Nebraska district since 1992, but Democrats have put up a fight in at least one of the districts in each of the past three House elections.

Governor

Dave Heineman (R)

Assumed office Jan. 2005, term expires Jan. 2011, 1st full term; b. May 12, 1948, Falls City; home, Fremont; U.S. Military Acad., B.S. 1970; Eastern Orthodox; married (Sally Ganem); 1 child.

Military Career: Army Ranger, 1970–75.

Elected Office: Fremont City Cncl., 1990–94; NE treasurer, 1994–2001; Lt. gov., 2003–05.

Professional Career: Ex. dir., NE Republican party, 1979–81; Chief of staff, U.S. Rep. Hal Daub, 1983–88.

Office: P.O. Box 94848, Lincoln, 68509, 402-471-2244; Fax: 402-471-6031; Web site: www.governor.nebraska.gov.

Election Results

2006 general	Dave Heineman (R)	435,507	(73%)
	David Hahn (D)	145,115	(24%)
2006 primary	Dave Heineman (R)	138,216	(50%)
	Tom Osborne (R)	121,973	(44%)
	Dave Nabity (R)	14,786	(5%)

Republican Dave Heineman became governor of Nebraska in January 2005, when Mike Johanns resigned the post to become President Bush's secretary of Agriculture. Heineman, the state's lieutenant governor, moved up to the top job and then ran successfully in 2006 for a full four-year term.

Heineman was born in Falls City (pop. 4,375) in the state's southeastern corner, 100 miles equidistant from Omaha and Lincoln. He grew up in a handful of small towns across the state, the son of an itinerant J.C. Penney store manager, before graduating from Wahoo High School. He went east to attend the U.S. Military Academy at West Point and expected to see action in Vietnam, but the war ended first. He served five years in the Army, graduating from Airborne and Ranger schools and rising to the rank of captain. When his tour ended in 1975, Heineman returned to Nebraska and immediately dove into politics as an envelope-stuffing volunteer for the Republican party in Omaha. He met Hal Daub, the future Omaha mayor and U.S. representative who became his political mentor. Daub also introduced the 28-year-old to his future wife, Sally Ganem, a Fremont school principal. In 1979, Heineman was named the party's executive director, a job he held for two years; for the rest of the decade, he worked as campaign manager and aide to Daub, as a political consultant, and as the local office manager for then-Rep. Doug Bereuter. Even in those early stages of his career, Heineman harbored an ambition to become governor.

In 1990, he won his first elective office, a seat on the Fremont City Council. He was elected state treasurer in 1994 and re-elected in 1998. Heineman modernized the state's money-management system and its methods of returning unclaimed property to residents. In 2002, he ran for lieutenant governor on a ticket with Johanns; they won 69%-28%. As lieutenant governor, Heineman was the state's official lobbyist in Washington, its homeland security director, and chairman of Nebraska's Information Technology Commission; at the commission, he helped to create a telecommunications backbone for state government, state medical facilities, and the University of Nebraska. When Bereuter announced he would not seek re-election in 2004, Heineman declined to run for the open 1st District House seat, saying he was focused on running for governor in 2006, when term limits would prevent Johanns from running again. "I would rather pursue my dream of becoming governor, even if that opportunity never materializes, than to pursue another office that I am not committed to."

The dream came true sooner than expected with Johanns's surprise Cabinet appointment in 2005. Heineman was able to step up to the job immediately and to run for the post the following year as the incumbent, a powerful advantage. In March, Attorney General Jon Bruning announced he would not run for the governorship and would instead seek a second term as attorney general. On April 11, Heineman signaled his intention to run, and popular GOP Sen. Chuck Hagel endorsed Heineman's candidacy the same day. From there, Heineman was expected to waltz to election—until Rep. Tom Osborne, one of Nebraska's most popular politicians and former University of Nebraska football coach, entered the race that spring. After Osborne announced he would give up his seat in Congress to run for governor, national party officials tried to persuade Heineman to change course and to challenge Democratic Sen. Ben Nelson. But Heineman told *The Lincoln Journal Star* in May that his interest in serving in the Senate, on a scale of zero to 100, was "minus-1,000 and dropping."

Heineman moved quickly to cement his hold on the governor's office before the election. That summer, he led a 10-member trade delegation to encourage Cuba to purchase Nebraska-grown products. Despite criticism from several anti-Castro Republican House members from Florida, Heineman met for four hours with Cuban President Fidel Castro and came back with an agreement to sell 5,000 metric tons of dry beans, with the future prospect of exporting 25,000 metric tons of corn, 25,000 metric tons of wheat, and 15,000 metric tons of soybeans and soy meal. In August, Heineman signed an agreement with Cuban officials for a total of $30 million in agricultural products.

He also challenged the Legislature on a number of controversial issues. Nebraska's unicameral Legislature, the Senate, (often called the Unicam), has 49 members, who are not grouped by political party as in most other legislatures. In 2006, Heineman vetoed a pay raise for the state's top elected officials, a bill to improve retirement benefits for state workers, and a third measure to allow children of illegal immigrants to qualify for in-state tuition rates at state colleges and universities. The Legislature overrode all three vetoes.

The eager new governor also waded into a highly contentious boundary dispute involving the Omaha public schools. In 2006, the Legislature was grappling with a bitter feud touched off by the Omaha school district's attempt to take over 25 schools in suburban Millard and Ralston. The Millard and Ralston school superintendents resisted and were joined in opposition by two other suburban districts. In an attempt to resolve the matter, the Legislature passed a bill dividing the Omaha area into three racially identifiable districts—one largely Latino, one largely black, and one largely white. Heineman signed the bill and then defended it against a barrage of outside criticism that it was state-sanctioned resegregation. "This bill is far from perfect, and I'll be honest, there are parts that make me less than comfortable, and parts that would make me pause as a parent," he said. "It is clear to me that the motivation behind [this] proposal is neither segregation nor separation, but instead the goal of improving student achievement and the responsiveness of schools."

Meanwhile, the May primary showdown was looming. Heineman trailed badly in some 2005 polls but by April 2006 he had drawn even with Osborne. Omaha businessman David Nabity, who played up his private-sector experience, was a distant third. Heineman's hard-charging approach contrasted with the more sedate campaign style of the 69-year-old Osborne, who had never been seriously challenged in his brief political career. Heineman got key endorsements from the state Farm Bureau, Nebraska Right to Life, and the National Rifle Association. The state employees and teachers' unions also backed him. Heineman gained traction by criticizing Osborne's support for the in-state college tuition law for illegal immigrants' children; Osborne said he didn't believe that children should be penalized for their parents' actions. For his part, Osborne accused Heineman of embarrassing Nebraska nationally by signing the school boundary bill.

Without a top-tier Democratic candidate in the race, the Republican primary drew heightened interest. As many as 10,000 Nebraskans switched parties so that they could vote in the primary. Famed investor and Omaha resident Warren Buffett, a Democrat, said he would change his party affiliation to vote for Osborne. Osborne said that if he won the governorship, Buffett would oversee a top-to-bottom review of state government operations. But Heineman won 50%-44%, with Nabity finishing third with 5%. Osborne carried the state's two most populous counties, Omaha's Douglas County (47%-44%) and Lincoln's Lancaster County (53%-43%), but not by enough to erase Heineman's margins elsewhere. Heineman's early position in the Omaha schools dispute, in which he sided with suburban schools targeted for takeover by the city, boosted him with suburban voters. He carried the central and eastern parts of the state and also won 54 of the 69 counties in Osborne's western Nebraska-based congressional district.

The general election against Democrat David Hahn, an attorney and Internet entrepreneur from Lincoln, was largely an afterthought. Hahn scoffed at talk of tax cuts and supported abortion rights. Even before the Republican nomination was settled, Hahn was forced to deny that he was a "sacrificial lamb." In a year that featured competitive Senate and House races, the long-shot governor's race was a low Democratic priority. Hahn trailed badly in the polls and Heineman won 73%-24%, the largest margin in a Nebraska governor's race since Dwight Griswold won re-election in 1944 with 76% of the vote.

With that boost of voter confidence, Heineman tackled some new initiatives and took pains to close the book on the sensitive schools issue. He signed a new bill passed by the Legislature that scrapped the old plan and replaced it with one that left school boundaries intact but compelled more affluent districts to share tax revenues with poorer districts. Heineman also sent to the Legislature a get-tough immigration bill to repeal the law making children of illegal immigrants eligible for in-state tuition rates. The measure, which also called for checking the immigration status of anyone applying for government benefits or licenses, stayed bottled up in committee. In mid-2008, with an unexpected rise in state tax revenues of $100 million, Heineman vowed to make tax relief a major push, but the subsequent souring of the national economy late in the year put a crimp in those plans.

In 2008, Heineman won plaudits from conservatives for successfully pressuring the University of Nebraska to rescind a speaking invitation to 1960s radical William Ayers, a co-founder of the violent Weather Underground, who now is a college professor. Republicans criticized Democratic nominee Barack Obama for maintaining political ties to Ayers. But Heineman did himself no public relations favors with his heavy-handed treatment of the *Daily Nebraskan* in the spring of 2008 after it ran a story he didn't like. The governor banned the college newspaper's reporters from his press conferences after they reported, accurately, that a man convicted of second-degree murder was giving tours at the Governor's Mansion as part of a rehabilitation program. Heineman rescinded the ban the same day.

If he seeks and wins a second term in 2010, Heineman could leave office as the longest-serving governor in state history. No Nebraska governor has served more than eight years.

Senior Senator

Ben Nelson (D)

Elected 2000, term expires 2012, 2nd term; b. May 17, 1941, McCook; home, Omaha; U. of NE, B.A. 1963, M.A. 1965, LL.B. 1970; Methodist; married (Diane); 4 children.

Elected Office: NE Gov., 1991–98.

Professional Career: Gen. cnsl., Central Natl. Group Insurance, 1972–74, Pres. & CEO, 1977–81; NE insurance dir., 1975–76; Exec. V.P., Natl. Assn. of Insurance Commissioners, 1982–85; Practicing atty., 1985–90.

DC Office: 720 HSOB, 20510, 202-224-6551; Fax: 202-228-0012; Web site: bennelson.senate.gov.

State Offices: Kearney, 308-293-5818; Lincoln, 402-441-4600; Omaha, 402-391-3411; Scottsbluff, 308-631-7614; South Sioux City, 402-209-3595.

Committees: *Agriculture, Nutrition & Forestry* (7th of 12 D). *Appropriations* (15th of 18 D): Agriculture, Rural Development, Food and Drug Administration & Related Agencies; Commerce, Justice, Science & Related Agencies; Financial Services & General Government; Interior, Environment & Related Agencies; Legislative Branch (Chmn); Military Construction, Veterans Affairs & Related Agencies. *Armed Services* (8th of 15 D): Emerging Threats & Capabilities; Personnel (Chmn); Strategic Forces. *Rules & Administration* (7th of 11 D).

Group Ratings

	ADA	ACLU	AFS	LCV	ITIC	NTU	COC	ACU	CFG	FRC
2008	75	50	89	91	100	9	71	16	11	88
2007	75	—	86	67	—	17	64	32	15	—

National Journal Ratings

	2007 LIB	—	2007 CONS		2008 LIB	—	2008 CONS
Economic	46%	—	52%		52%	—	47%
Social	44%	—	55%		46%	—	53%
Foreign	48%	—	51%		48%	—	47%
Composite	47%	—	53%		50%	—	50%

Key Votes of the 110th Congress

1. Raise CAFE standards	Y	5. Make English official language Y	9. Withdraw troops 3/08	Y
2. Expand SCHIP	Y	6. Path to citizenship	N	10. Iran guard is terrorist group Y
3. Cap greenhouse gases	Y	7. Fetus is unborn child	Y	11. Increase missile defense $	N
4. Bail out financial markets	Y	8. Prosecute hate crimes	Y	12. Overhaul FISA	Y

Election Results

2006 general	Ben Nelson (D)	378,388	(64%)	($6,992,058)
	Pete Ricketts (R)	213,928	(36%)	($13,417,690)
2006 primary	Ben Nelson (D)	unopposed		

Prior Winning Percentages: 2000 (51%); 1994 governor (73%); 1990 governor (50%)

Ben Nelson, a former two-term governor of Nebraska, is a Democrat who was elected to the Senate in 2000. He grew up in McCook, a small town that has produced some of the state's political giants, including legendary Sen. George Norris, who led the revolt against Speaker Joe Cannon in 1910, and Ralph Brooks, Nelson's high school principal who became governor in the 1950s. McCook is also the birthplace of Willa Cather, whose novels powerfully depict frontier life on the Great Plains. Nelson graduated from the University of Nebraska, practiced law, served as state insurance director, and headed a major insurance company. He is a man of varied avocations. He has collected several hundred clocks, for instance, and is an avid hunter of turkeys and bears. Disdaining the customary senatorial pretensions, the bushy-headed Nelson has a self-deprecating sense of humor and tolerates his staff's pet names for him, which include "Hair Force One."

In 1990, Nelson ran for governor, taking on Bill Hoppner, former staff aide to Democratic Sen. Bob Kerrey, in the primary; he won by all of 42 votes. In the general election, he narrowly beat Gov. Kay Orr, 50%-49%. Orr had lost popularity after raising taxes, and her campaign bungled its television advertising, handing challenger Nelson several advantages. As governor, Nelson built prisons, trimmed workmen's compensation payments, and reorganized the human services department. He cut property taxes and reduced income and sales taxes. His record won him high job ratings and re-election by a 73%-26% vote in the strongly Republican year of 1994. When Nelson ran for the Senate in 1996, he led in polls most of the way, but then fell behind in October and lost to Republican Chuck Hagel, 56%-42%.

Early in 2000, Nebraska's other Senate seat came open when Sen. Bob Kerrey, one of the Democratic Party's national stars, shocked just about everyone when he said that he would not seek re-election. Nelson, then practicing law in Omaha, was the strongest possible Democratic nominee, and he entered the race in February. Attorney General Don Stenberg won the Republican primary, with 50% of the vote against five opponents. Nelson and Stenberg both opposed abortion rights and backed tax cuts. But they had significant differences in style and a long history of clashes. Stenberg ran as part of the "Bush-Hagel-Stenberg Team." Nelson led from the start in the polls, and he raised and spent more money. The popular Kerrey also actively campaigned for his fellow Democrat. Nelson's lead in the polls narrowed in October, but this time, he won, 51%-49%.

Second only to Zell Miller of Georgia, Nelson turned out to be the Senate Democrat most likely to support Bush. He helped to broker the administration's tax cuts of 2001 and 2003. In 2002, Nelson was one of the senators who put together a compromise to permit President Bush to cancel collective bargaining rights for homeland security workers, although the measure also allowed future presidents to overturn the decision. Nelson generally supported Bush on the Iraq war, joining Republicans in March 2007 to oppose a plan to start troop withdrawals a year later. With moderate GOP Sen. Susan Collins of Maine, he also authored benchmarks for Iraqi progress. Nelson joined Republicans again to turn back a proposal to restrict funds for Vice President Cheney's office, and shunned his party on global warming by criticizing legislation for setting what he called unrealistic deadlines for new technologies.

His Democratic colleagues tolerated these apostasies. As one said, "He needs to do what he needs to do to keep his seat" in one of the most Republican states in the nation. Nelson has stuck with his party in a few tough fights. He voted against the GOP's Federal Marriage Amendment, for example, arguing that same-sex marriage was a state issue. He also was an early and enthusiastic supporter of Illinois Sen. Barack Obama for president after being impressed by the record audience that Obama drew at a 2006 Nebraska campaign event for Nelson. He often is found in the middle of battles between the extremes of both parties. He was part of the "Gang of 14" senators who in 2005 sought a middle ground on judgeships, thus scuttling possible filibusters against Bush's judicial nominees while preserving the Senate's ability to filibuster future nominations.

During his first Senate term, Republicans tried to persuade Nelson to switch parties. According to the *Omaha World-Herald,* White House strategist Karl Rove in 2004 offered Nelson the job of Agriculture secretary; Nelson considered it for five days before declining. If he had accepted, then-Republican Gov. Johanns would have appointed his successor, allowing the GOP to pick up a Senate seat.

Nelson has focused much of his legislative work on home-state concerns. When the Great Plains were hit by a drought in 2002, he argued that affected areas should get disaster relief, just as states hit by hurricanes and floods do. He has been fighting for such parity ever since. The compensation, he maintains, would be for crops or livestock lost, rather than property destroyed. Twice Nelson got the Senate to pass drought relief, but the House rejected it both times. In 2003, he called for help for farmers hurt by "Drought David," following the custom of naming hurricanes. The following year, when a bill for hurricane aid came up, Nelson and Hagel attached nearly $3 billion for farmers affected by drought. The House accepted the bill but reduced farm conservation spending as an offset.

During debate of the 2008 farm bill, Nelson criticized a reduction in drought assistance and was vocally unhappy that fellow Nebraskan Mike Johanns quit as Agriculture secretary before passage of the bill. (Johanns returned home to run for Hagel's Senate seat.) With Nebraska's farmers in mind, Nelson in 2007 joined a bipartisan farm-state group that secured an increase in ethanol production to 15 billion gallons by 2015.

With a seat on the Appropriations Committee, Nelson is able to direct federal dollars to Nebraska. His Senate website boasts of his earmarks for the state in defiance of critics who say that the often narrowly targeted special provisions in spending bills are wasteful. In 2008, Nelson touted his work on nearly $9 million for communications at the Air National Guard base in Lincoln, $9 million for Antelope Valley development, and $9.7 million for the University of Nebraska.

Most observers assumed that Johanns would run against Nelson in 2006. But in 2005, Bush appointed Johanns Agriculture secretary. Soon afterward, Republican Reps. Lee Terry and Tom Osborne said that they would not run for the Senate, leaving the Republican nomination wide open. National party officials hoped to persuade Gov. Dave Heineman to run, but Heineman said he had no interest in the Senate. Former Attorney General Don Stenberg, the Republican nominee in 2000, announced he would seek a rematch but he created little enthusiasm; Republicans instead rallied behind Pete Ricketts, an executive with TD Ameritrade and a self-financing multimillionaire.

Running on a platform of tax cuts and smaller government, Ricketts sought to appeal to traditional red-state values. He won the primary with 48% to 36% for Stenberg and 16% for former state Republican Chairman David Kramer. In the general election against Nelson, Ricketts supported a guest-worker program for immigrants, allowing Nelson to position himself to the right of the Republican by making demands to seal the border. Ricketts supported private savings accounts as a first step in "modernizing" Social Security; Nelson opposed such accounts. Ricketts opposed spending earmarks in the federal budget, but Nelson backed them as vital for sparsely populated states. Ricketts spent more than $13 million, most of it from his own deep pockets. The combined $20 million-plus spending by the two candidates was roughly three times the previous record for a statewide contest in Nebraska. But the result wasn't close. Nelson won 64%-36%, dominating in Omaha's Douglas County, 65%-35%, and in Lincoln's Lancaster County, 70%-30%. Ricketts won just 13 of 93 counties, all of them sparsely populated and west of the city of North Platte.

Junior Senator

Mike Johanns (R)

Elected 2008, term expires 2014, 1st term; b. June 18, 1950, Osage, IA; home, Omaha; St. Mary's Col. (MN), B.A. 1971; Creighton U., J.D. 1974.; Catholic; married (Stephanie); 2 children.

Elected Office: Lancaster Cnty. Bd. of Commissioners, 1983–87; Lincoln City Cncl., 1989–1991; Lincoln mayor, 1991–98; NE gov., 1998–05.

Professional Career: Atty., Cronin and Hannon, 1975–76; Atty., Nelson, Johanns, Morris, Holdeman and Titus, 1976–1991; Clerk, Hon. Hale McCown, NE Supreme Court; U.S. secy. of agriculture, 2005–07.

DC Office: 404 RSOB, 20510, 202-224-4224; Fax: 202-228-0436; Web site: johanns.senate.gov.

State Offices: Kearney, 308-236-7602; Lincoln, 402-476-1400; Omaha, 402-758-8981; Scottsbluff, 308-632-6032.

Committees: *Agriculture, Nutrition & Forestry* (6th of 8 R). *Banking, Housing & Urban Affairs* (9th of 10 R): Housing, Transportation & Community Development; Securities, Insurance & Investment; Security & International Trade & Finance. *Commerce, Science & Transportation* (11th of 11 R): Aviation Operations, Safety & Security; Communications & Technology; Competitiveness, Innovation & Export Promotion; Science & Space; Surface Transportation & Merchant Marine Infrastructure, Safety & Security. *Indian Affairs* (6th of 6 R). *Veterans' Affairs* (4th of 5 R).

Group Ratings and Key Votes: Newly Elected

Election Results

2008 general	Mike Johanns (R)	455,854	(58%)	($3,781,316)
	Scott Kleeb (D)	317,456	(40%)	($1,911,771)
2008 primary	Mike Johanns (R)	112,191	(78%)	
	Pat Flynn (R)	31,560	(22%)	

Prior Winning Percentages: 2002 governor (69%); 1998 governor (54%)

The junior senator from Nebraska is Republican Mike Johanns, a former governor and secretary of Agriculture in the Bush administration. He was born in Iowa and is of Luxembourgian descent. Johanns grew up on a dairy farm in Osage, Iowa, and started doing chores at age 4. He attended college in Minnesota, earned a law degree at Creighton University in Omaha, and, after clerking for a judge there for a year, settled into a career in Nebraska rather than returning to his native state. He practiced law in O'Neill and got involved in local politics in 1982, when he was elected to the Lancaster County Board of Commissioners. He also served on the Lincoln City Council and was elected mayor of Lincoln in 1991. Johanns was a Democrat until 1988.

Though re-elected mayor of Lincoln in 1995, Johanns began laying the groundwork for a gubernatorial run in 1998 by traveling to each of the state's 93 counties. He faced vigorous competition in the Republican primary: State Auditor John Breslow had a large campaign treasury, and 2nd District House Rep. Jon Christensen had strong support from religious conservatives. A week before the May primary, Christensen distributed fliers accusing Johanns of allowing obscene and racist broadcasts to air on Lincoln's public access cable channel. Johanns maintained that he had, in fact, tried to stop the broadcasts, and the state's nationally respected senator, Republican Chuck Hagel, called the flier "absolute trash." This was a high-spending contest. Breslow spent $3.8 million, Christensen $1.8 million, and Johanns $1.7 million. Johanns prevailed with 40% of the vote to 30% for Breslow and 28% for Christensen. In the general election, Johanns faced Democrat Bill Hoppner, longtime aide to former Sens. James Exon and Bob Kerrey. The campaign was conducted civilly but with major differences on issues. Johanns's solid conservatism was more in step with the Republican leanings of the state and he won, 54% to 46%.

As governor, Johanns's low-key nature belied his strong policy convictions. During his first term, he vetoed 26 bills in five days, the state's strongest use of the veto pen in a decade. He vetoed a moratorium on the death penalty and a bill raising elected officials' salaries and his own salary from the nation's lowest, $65,000 annually. He got passed a $10 million bill for tax credits and entrepreneurship grants to firms that opened businesses in rural areas. In 2001, Nebraska's revenues started coming in below estimates, but Johanns pushed ahead with plans to cut spending by $171 million. "I'm not here to sign tax increases," he said. "Government tends to operate better when it's under pressure." In 2002, state revenues decreased further, but Johanns vetoed temporary increases in the sales, income, and cigarette taxes, though the Legislature overrode his vetoes. Johanns cut school aid and terminated the Rural Development Commission. He also proposed cuts in Medicaid and a freeze on higher-education spending. He called raising taxes to solve the budget crisis "the last alternative." Johanns was easily re-elected in 2002 without a serious challenge. During his second term, he joined President Bush's Cabinet as Agriculture secretary.

In that role, Johanns more than doubled the number of acres in conservation programs nationwide and focused on opening foreign markets to domestic farm products. By far his biggest undertaking was representing the administration on Capitol Hill as Congress wrote a new bill governing farm and agricultural programs. The administration wanted to reduce farm spending by $88 billion over five years and eliminate government payments to farmers who made more than $200,000 a year, a proposal aimed at complying with international demands to reduce farm subsidies in the United States. Although Johanns and the president were in agreement on the bill, both houses of Congress opposed it. Top Democrats on the Agriculture committees widely criticized Johanns for leaving the post to run for the Senate in the middle of the negotiations to pass a farm bill, which was set to expire at the end of 2007.

His election to the Senate in 2008 was two years later than some Republicans envisioned. The GOP had heavily courted Johanns to challenge Sen. Ben Nelson, a Democrat who was up for re-election in 2006. Several months later, Johanns apparently saw the opportunity he was waiting for. Hagel announced his retirement in September 2007, leaving an open Senate seat, an easier mark than one inconveniently occupied by an incumbent. Johanns quit his administration job and returned home to campaign.

When jockeying for the Senate began, other prominent Republicans, including Nebraska Attorney General Jon Bruning and Omaha Mayor Hal Daub, were contenders, with Bruning able to raise an impressive $780,000 a year out from the election. But the two men stepped aside as it became increasingly clear that Johanns would win. For the general election, national Democrats aggressively tried to recruit former Gov. Bob Kerrey, but he opted to remain in his job as president of the New School in New York City. The Democrats turned to rancher and college instructor Scott Kleeb, who in 2006 came within 10 percentage points of winning the open House seat in Nebraska's heavily Republican 3rd District.

Johanns and Kleeb differed on a variety of issues. Johanns advocated increased offshore drilling and exploration in the Arctic National Wildlife Refuge, while Kleeb said he favored more "green" solutions to energy shortages, such as the development of wind energy, ethanol, and biofuels. They also clashed on the seriousness of global warming. Kleeb called the issue a "moral test" for policy leaders, and Johanns took the more typically conservative position that potential fixes should take the costs to industry into account and that reducing carbon emissions to the levels touted by his opponent was unrealistic.

Nelson criticized Johanns for leaving the administration before work on the farm bill was complete. And Kleeb tried mightily to tie Johanns to Bush, by then extremely unpopular in public opinion polls. Johanns responded by saying that he hadn't been in Washington long enough to be defined by the administration he served. "I was in D.C. less time than Barack Obama has been," Johanns was fond of saying on the campaign trail, contrasting himself to the first-term U.S. senator from Illinois then running for the Democratic presidential nomination. It turns out that Johanns's affiliation with Bush hardly resonated in this red state. He won the election with 58%, 1-percentage point higher than John McCain earned in the state. Kleeb got 40% of the vote. The Democrat prevailed in just seven of 93 counties, including in Lancaster County, which is home to Lincoln, the state capital. However, Johanns beat him in most rural counties and in Omaha in Douglas County. Johanns has never lost an election, including six general elections and six primaries.

FIRST DISTRICT

Jeff Fortenberry (R)

Elected 2004, 3rd term; b. Dec. 27, 1960, Baton Rouge, LA; home, Lincoln; LA St. U., 1982, Franciscan U. of Steubenville, M.A. 1985, Georgetown U., M.P.P. 1986; Catholic; married (Celeste); 5 children.

Elected Office: Lincoln City Cncl., 1997–2001.

Professional Career: Staffer, U.S. House Comm. on Ag., 1986; Research assoc., Gulf South Research Inst., 1987–89; Asst. dir., Baton Rouge Downtown Dev. District, 1989–92; Sales rep., Sandhills Publishing, 1995–2004.

DC Office: 1535 LHOB, 20515, 202-225-4806; Fax: 202-225-5686; Web site: www.house.gov/fortenberry.

State Offices: Fremont, 402-727-0888; Lincoln, 402-438-1598; Norfolk, 402-379-2064.

Committees: *Agriculture* (10th of 18 R): Department Operations, Oversight, Nutrition & Forestry (RMM). *Foreign Affairs* (15th of 19 R): Africa & Global Health; Middle East & South Asia; Western Hemisphere. *Oversight & Government Reform* (13th of 15 R): Domestic Policy; National Security & Foreign Affairs.

Group Ratings

	ADA	ACLU	AFS	LCV	ITIC	NTU	COC	ACU	CFG	FRC
2008	40	18	29	46	86	57	72	84	70	100
2007	15	—	9	45	—	50	90	88	56	—

National Journal Ratings

	2007 LIB	—	2007 CONS		2008 LIB	—	2008 CONS
Economic	36%	—	64%		35%	—	65%
Social	21%	—	75%		38%	—	61%
Foreign	0%	—	72%		43%	—	57%
Composite	24%	—	76%		39%	—	61%

Key Votes of the 110th Congress

1. Increase minimum wage	N	5. Share immigration data	Y	9. Withdraw troops 8/08	N
2. Expand SCHIP	N	6. Foreign aid abortion ban	Y	10. No operations in Iran	N
3. Raise CAFE standards	N	7. Ban gay bias in workplace	N	11. Free trade with Peru	Y
4. Bail out financial markets	N	8. Repeal D.C. gun law	Y	12. Overhaul FISA	Y

Election Results

2008 general	Jeff Fortenberry (R)	184,923	(70%)	($341,030)
	Max Yashirin (D)	77,897	(30%)	($24,232)
2008 primary	Jeff Fortenberry (R)	unopposed		

Prior Winning Percentages: 2006 (58%); 2004 (54%)

Population		Race/Ethnicity		Work	
Pop. 2007:	599,787	White:	88.6%	Private:	75.2%
Change since 2000:	Up 5.2%	Black:	1.7%	Government:	17.4%
Urban:	65.1%	Hispanic:	5.5%	Self-employed:	7.1%
Rural:	34.9%	Asian:	1.8%	Blue collar:	24.3%
Area size:	12,034 sq. mi.	Native Am.:	1.1%	White collar:	58.5%
Age		Hawaiian:	0.1%	Khaki collar:	0.2%
Median age:	35.3 yrs.	Two+ races:	1.2%	Other:	17.0%
More than 65 yrs:	12.9%	*Ancestry*		Median income:	$48,710
Less than 18 yrs:	24.4%	German:	35.3%	Median home value:	$124,500
Education		Irish:	10.1%	Poverty:	10.7%
H.S. grad:	90.0%	English:	6.9%	**Military Veterans**	
College grad:	27.3%			% of Pop:	10.6%
Grad degree:	8.4%				

The eastern half of Nebraska, between the Missouri River and the 98th parallel, was laid out in relentless Midwestern mile-square grids and became some of America's prime farmland during the 1880s. The Plains here have completed most of their gentle decline from the Rockies to sea level, and the land has contours just regular enough, and weather just favorable enough, to make farming economically viable. The area was settled by Yankee-descended farmers from the Midwest and immigrants

2008 Presidential Vote
McCain (R)............................148,179   (54%)
Obama (D) 121,411   (44%)

2004 Presidential Vote
Bush (R)................................169,888   (63%)
Kerry (D)................................96,314   (36%)

Cook Partisan Voting Index: R + 11

from Germany and other countries. Traces of the immigrant heritage can still be found. Many people from Luxembourg, for example, settled along the Platte River in Butler County, where St. Mary's Presentation Parish still has a statue of Our Lady of Luxembourg. Not far away are villages with names that recall other immigrant groups—Prague (Czechs), Malmo (Swedes), Aloys (Germans). Today, a new wave of immigrants is coming to eastern Nebraska, including Latinos from Mexico and the southwest United States, to work in the meatpacking factories in the area. Wakefield, in Dixon County, had the highest percentage increase in Hispanic population in the country in the 1990s at 8,700%, though the number is less impressive considering the Hispanic population grew from 4 to 348. But there are larger numbers in other towns, and the district's demographic face is changing.

The 1st Congressional District of Nebraska comprises 22 full counties and parts of two others in an easternmost slice of the state. It surrounds but does not take in Omaha and most of its suburbs, which are in the 2nd District. It's anchored by Lincoln, the state capital and home of the beloved University of Nebraska Huskers football team. Lincoln has been growing rapidly. It is affluent, with above-national-average incomes and unemployment among the lowest in the United States. Underway east of downtown Lincoln is the $238 million Antelope Valley urban renewal project, which is expected to spur further economic development. In the smaller towns, there are significant numbers of farm equipment and meatpacking factories. Population growth has been robust around Schuyler, Norfolk, and Dakota City. Politically, Lincoln is fond of moderate Democrats but is still on balance Republican in national contests. The district voted 63% for George W. Bush in 2004 and 54% for John McCain in 2008.

The congressman from the 1st District is Jeff Fortenberry, a Republican elected in 2004. Fortenberry grew up in Baton Rouge, La., where his father was a life insurance salesman and his mother worked as a 4-H Club extension agent. Fortenberry got the political bug early as a page to a Democratic state senator, but switched to the Republican Party after he graduated from Louisiana State University. He earned one master's degree in theology from Franciscan University of Steubenville, Ohio, and then another one in public policy from Georgetown University in Washington, D.C. (For a time, he studied for the priesthood but changed his mind.) In 1995, the congressman moved to Nebraska to take a public relations position with Sandhills Publishing, a publisher of trade magazines for the trucking, aircraft, and computer industries. He later got into the sales end of the business. Fortenberry's first foray into local politics came in 1997, when he won a seat on the Lincoln City Council. He served for four years, focusing on neighborhood concerns and on increasing the police force.

When U.S. Rep. Doug Bereuter, who was first elected in 1978, announced he would not run again in 2004, three candidates mounted competitive campaigns for the Republican nomination: Fortenberry; Curt Bromm, the speaker of the state's unicameral Legislature; and Greg Ruehle, a former executive vice president of the Nebraska Cattlemen Association. Bromm, a moderate who was endorsed by Bereuter, began as the front-runner. But he quickly lost momentum after a barrage of negative television ads financed by the Club for Growth, a national anti-tax group that supported Ruehle. Fortenberry, a social conservative, drew criticism from his opponents as a single-issue candidate, but his superior grassroots operation and fundraising carried him to victory. He won just seven of the 24 counties, but in Lincoln's Lancaster County, which cast 43% of the votes, he got 52% to 29% for Bromm and 13% for Ruehle. The vote in the rest of the district was closer: 29% for Fortenberry, 36% for Bromm and 27% for Ruehle. Overall, Fortenberry won with 39% of the vote, to 33% for Bromm and 21% for Ruehle.

In November, Fortenberry faced state Sen. Matt Connealy, a farmer from Decatur who sought to exploit Republican divisions—Bromm refused to endorse Fortenberry after the primary—and who characterized Fortenberry as a stranger to Nebraska farm issues, a potent charge in a state where one in four jobs is connected to agriculture. "If you want a guy in a slick suit with slick answers, I'm probably not your guy," Connealy said. Fortenberry responded by promising to improve trade policies for farmers and to support ethanol development. His main message, however, focused on socially-conservative themes: opposition to abortion, support of capital punishment, and a ban on same-sex marriage. Connealy gained traction briefly by hammering his opponent's attendance record as a city councilman but lost ground when Fortenberry responded with an ad explaining that the absences were connected to his infant daughter's open-heart surgery. Fortenberry won 54%-43%, losing only two American Indian reservation counties. In Lancaster County, which cast 46% of the votes, he won by only 49%-47%.

In the House, Fortenberry is a backbencher but has gained a reputation as a brainy policy expert. More conservative than Bereuter, Fortenberry voted against expanded embryonic-stem-cell research, saying that using discarded human embryos from in vitro fertilization "poses profound ethical dilemmas." But he has been a centrist on some economic issues. Teaming with Democratic U.S. Rep. Stephanie Herseth Sandlin of South Dakota, he supported renewable energy sources and pushed for an overhaul of subsidy payments in the 2008 farm bill. In November 2007, he was the only one of the three House Republicans from Nebraska to vote to override President Bush's veto of the appropriations bill for labor, education, and health and human services. He also was part of a swing group of Republicans who unsuccessfully sought middle ground that year with Democrats on a children's health insurance bill. On the International Relations Committee, he supported Bush on the war in Iraq, won House approval of an increase in visas for Iraqi translators, and worked on the deal to promote nuclear cooperation with India.

In Fortenberry's first re-election campaign, former Democratic Lt. Gov. Maxine Moul cited the need for benchmarks in Iraq. Although her fundraising was competitive, Moul's campaign attack ads did not catch fire in the district, which has not elected a Democrat since 1964. Fortenberry won 58%-42%, including 53% of the vote in Lancaster County. Moul won only in Burt County, where she was born and raised. In 2008, Fortenberry had an even easier ride to reelection with 70% of the vote against Iraq War veteran Max Yashirin. Fortenberry was an early supporter of John McCain in the presidential contest.

SECOND DISTRICT

Lee Terry (R)

Elected 1998, 6th term; b. Jan. 29, 1962, Omaha; home, Omaha; U. of NE at Lincoln, B.A. 1984; Creighton U., J.D. 1987; Protestant; married (Robyn); 3 children.

Elected Office: Omaha City Cncl., 1991–98, Pres., 1995–96.

Professional Career: Practicing atty., 1988–98.

DC Office: 2331 RHOB, 20515, 202-225-4155; Fax: 202-226-5452; Web site: leeterry.house.gov.

State Offices: Omaha, 402-397-9944.

Committees: *Energy & Commerce* (15th of 23 R): Commerce, Trade & Consumer Protections; Communications, Technology & the Internet.

Group Ratings

	ADA	ACLU	AFS	LCV	ITIC	NTU	COC	ACU	CFG	FRC
2008	15	18	14	15	71	69	100	92	80	100
2007	10	—	9	15	—	74	90	88	84	—

National Journal Ratings

	2007 LIB — 2007 CONS		2008 LIB — 2008 CONS	
Economic	28%	— 71%	22%	— 77%
Social	15%	— 85%	31%	— 62%
Foreign	0%	— 72%	31%	— 67%
Composite	19%	— 81%	30%	— 70%

Key Votes of the 110th Congress

1. Increase minimum wage	N	5. Share immigration data	Y	9. Withdraw troops 8/08	N
2. Expand SCHIP	N	6. Foreign aid abortion ban	Y	10. No operations in Iran	N
3. Raise CAFE standards	N	7. Ban gay bias in workplace	N	11. Free trade with Peru	Y
4. Bail out financial markets	Y	8. Repeal D.C. gun law	Y	12. Overhaul FISA	Y

Election Results

2008 general	Lee Terry (R)	142,473	(52%)	($1,838,836)
	Jim Esch (D)	131,901	(48%)	($843,515)
2008 primary	Lee Terry (R)	23,146	(84%)	
	Steven Laird (R)	4,288	(16%)	

Prior Winning Percentages: 2006 (55%); 2004 (61%); 2002 (63%); 2000 (66%); 1998 (66%)

Population		Race/Ethnicity		Work	
Pop. 2007:	609,182	White:	76.8%	Private:	82.1%
Change since 2000:	Up 6.8%	Black:	9.6%	Government:	12.9%
Urban:	97.8%	Hispanic:	8.6%	Self-employed:	4.9%
Rural:	2.2%	Asian:	2.2%	Blue collar:	18.0%
Area size:	421 sq. mi.	Native Am.:	0.2%	White collar:	65.7%
		Hawaiian:	0.2%	Khaki collar:	0.7%
Age		Two+ races:	2.3%	Other:	15.6%
Median age:	33.5 yrs.			Median income:	$52,229
More than 65 yrs:	10.1%	*Ancestry*		Median home value:	$140,400
Less than 18 yrs:	27.2%	German:	24.6%	Poverty:	11.3%
		Irish:	12.8%		
Education		English:	7.1%	**Military Veterans**	
H.S. grad:	90.5%			% of Pop:	12.2%
College grad:	35.2%				
Grad degree:	11.5%				

Omaha is the commercial heart of Nebraska and the largest city on the Great Plains north of Kansas City and west of Minneapolis. It got its start from the government, when President Lincoln picked it as the eastern terminus of the Union Pacific railroad, from which emerged the stockyards and livestock exchange that made it a thriving town. Over the years, Omaha filled up with cattle hands and European immigrants, especially Germans and Czechs. It developed fine civic institutions, from the

2008 Presidential Vote
Obama (D) 138,809   (50%)
McCain (R).............................135,439   (49%)

2004 Presidential Vote
Bush (R) 153,041   (60%)
Kerry (D)................................97,858   (38%)

Cook Partisan Voting Index: R + 6

Joslyn Art Museum to Boys Town, an orphanage founded by the Rev. Edward Flanagan (Father Flanagan) in 1917 and the subject of a 1938 movie. Today, the facility is a gender-neutral home for troubled youth called Boys and Girls Town. Though a major city by the 1880s, Omaha has remained small enough to be manageable. One doesn't feel distant, physically or psychologically, from the other side of town, and residents usually know people from a broader range of backgrounds than they might in a large, homogeneous, big-city neighborhood. The older, less affluent part of Omaha is near Iowa and the Missouri River. Downtown and the riverfront have experienced a construction boom; the Tower at First National Center is the tallest structure between Minneapolis and Denver. To the west, the city has been quietly flourishing with the rise of upscale neighborhoods and new shopping malls. Omaha has also entered into the Wall Street vernacular as the place where investor Warren Buffett lives and works.

Omaha's economy has been changing. It remains dependent on the overseas trade of meat and is home to many processors of food products, including ConAgra Foods, Omaha Steaks, and Nebraska Beef. However, it has also become the nation's telecommunications hub, handling 20 million '800' and '900' calls a day and employing more than 30,000 people in more than three dozen telemarketing centers. The city is also ethnically diverse: About 30% of students in the Omaha public schools are black and about 20% are Hispanic.

The 2nd Congressional District of Nebraska includes most of metropolitan Omaha: Douglas County, which includes Omaha and its western suburbs, and the eastern part of fast-growing Sarpy County, which houses Bellevue and the Offutt Air Force Base, headquarters of the U.S. Strategic Air Command. STRATCOM opened a foreign language training center here in 2005 and in 2008, local leaders pushed for a new cyber-command headquarters. Politically, Omaha has long had competitive politics, with Democrats strong on the south side around the stockyards and the northeast and Republicans strong on the west side. But as Omaha and Nebraska have boomed, they have become more Republican, and increasingly it is the Republican primary that decides elections here. But in 2008, Democratic nominee Barack Obama banked on the district being competitive, and opened three offices and enlisted some 1,500 volunteers. His efforts paid off. He won the district 50%-49%.

The congressman from the 2nd District is Lee Terry, a Republican first elected in 1998. Terry grew up in Omaha and became interested in politics at age 14 when his father, television anchor Lee Terry Sr., a conservative Republican, ran and lost a race for the House in 1976 against Democrat John Cavanaugh. Terry Sr. remained a prominent local commentator on politics, and his son went off to college and law school, practiced law, and at 29, was elected to the Omaha City Council from an affluent west-side district. When Republican U.S. Rep. Jon Christensen ran for governor, Terry announced his bid for the House seat. His chief opponents were Brad Kuiper, owner of a pest control business, and Steve Kupka, former chief of staff to Omaha Mayor Hal Daub and an official in President Reagan's Office of Management and Budget. The contrast among the three was less on issues—all were for lower taxes and against abortion —than on style and approach. Kuiper, with less money than the other two, targeted religious conservatives and emphasized cultural issues. Kupka assembled Washington endorsements and, spending the most money, went on the attack. He criticized Terry for not opposing a 1991 garbage fee and said Terry had increased the city's budget. Terry won 40% to 30% for Kupka and 26% for Kuiper. The general election was anticlimactic. Despite the fact that Democrats had won open seats here in 1976 and 1988, Terry won 66%-34% against Democrat Michael Scott. In April 1999, shortly after taking office, he reneged on his pledge to serve only three terms.

In Washington, Terry has a moderate-to-conservative voting record and occasionally is a consensus-seeker. On the Energy and Commerce Committee, he worked with Democratic Rep. Rick Boucher of Virginia to provide federal funds for high-speed Internet service to low-income and rural areas. In 2007, he successfully joined Democrat U.S. Rep Baron Hill of Indiana on a bill to increase average fuel efficiency standards to 35 miles per gallon for cars, although he opposed raising the standard to that level for light trucks, widely used by Nebraska farmers. Terry is generally low key, so it surprised his colleagues in August 2007 when he told Rep. Jesse Jackson Jr. of Illinois to "shut up" after Jackson said that Republicans could not be trusted during a House floor debate. Terry stormed across the aisle and reportedly cursed at Jackson, who then suggested they "go outside." But the two men did not come to blows.

Terry has survived some well-funded, re-election opponents. In 2004, state Sen. Nancy Thompson ran an aggressive campaign against him while other Democrats mocked his "decency" values when he held a Washington fundraiser at a Madonna concert. A Terry spokesman called her a legitimate entertainer. Despite polls indicating a tight contest, Terry won 61%-36%. Two years later, political newcomer Jim Esch, who worked for the Omaha Chamber of Commerce, held him to a 55%-45% win. Terry got only 53% in Douglas County, which cast 82% of the vote. He attributed the closer outcome to discontent over the war in Iraq, which was "deeper than I perceived it to be, honestly."

In 2008, Esch decided to run again, encouraged by Barack Obama's grassroots efforts in the 2nd District, where the presidential candidate and U.S. senator from Illinois was vying for one of three electoral votes that Nebraska awards on the basis of congressional districts. Douglas County Democrats registered a slew of new voters and outnumbered Republicans in total voters for the first time since 1994. Esch linked his candidacy to Obama's and attacked Terry's congressional record, questioning why he had not been elected to a leadership position during a decade in Washington. Terry hit back by criticizing Esch for accepting $100,000 in agriculture subsidies.

Terry was cognizant of Obama's appeal in urban areas. His campaign mailed post cards to independent women urging them to split their ballot by voting Obama-Terry, and the campaign ran a television ad in which a young woman says, "I'll admit, I'm voting for Obama and Lee Terry." He also did not underestimate Esch or the projected strength of Obama's coattails. Terry outraised Esch more than 2-to-1 and went door-to-door asking for support, and both national parties got involved. Sen. Hillary Rodham Clinton of New York and Republican vice presidential nominee Sarah Palin of Alaska made campaign stops in the district. Two weeks before the election, the National Republican Campaign Committee poured $400,000 into the race and the Democratic Congressional Campaign Committee spent $745,801.

Terry won with 52% of the vote. He narrowly prevailed in Douglas County, which Obama carried by 51%, but he won by big margins in Republican-leaning Sarpy County.

THIRD DISTRICT

Adrian Smith (R)

Elected 2006, 2nd term; b. Dec. 19, 1970, Scottsbluff; home, Gering; Attended Liberty U., 1989–90, U. of NE, B.S. 1993; Evangelical Free; single.

Elected Office: Gering City Council, 1994–98, NE Unicameral, 1998–2006.

Professional Career: Realtor, Buyer Realty, 1997–2006; Owner, My Other Garage, 2003–06.

DC Office: 503 CHOB, 20515, 202-225-6435; Fax: 202-225-0207; Web site: adriansmith.house.gov.

State Offices: Grand Island, 308-384-3900; Scottsbluff, 308-633-6333.

Committees: *Agriculture* (12th of 18 R): Conservation, Credit, Energy & Research; Livestock, Dairy & Poultry. *Natural Resources* (12th of 20 R): Water & Power. *Science & Technology* (15th of 17 R): Technology & Innovation (RMM).

Group Ratings

	ADA	ACLU	AFS	LCV	ITIC	NTU	COC	ACU	CFG	FRC
2008	15	18	0	8	57	75	89	96	91	100
2007	10	—	0	5	—	79	95	96	85	—

National Journal Ratings

	2007 LIB	—	2007 CONS	2008 LIB	—	2008 CONS
Economic	14%	—	85%	6%	—	93%
Social	9%	—	85%	9%	—	85%
Foreign	0%	—	72%	5%	—	93%
Composite	14%	—	87%	8%	—	92%

Key Votes of the 110th Congress

1. Increase minimum wage	N	5. Share immigration data	Y	9. Withdraw troops 8/08	N
2. Expand SCHIP	N	6. Foreign aid abortion ban	Y	10. No operations in Iran	N
3. Raise CAFE standards	N	7. Ban gay bias in workplace	N	11. Free trade with Peru	Y
4. Bail out financial markets	N	8. Repeal D.C. gun law	Y	12. Overhaul FISA	Y

Election Results

2008 general	Adrian Smith (R)	183,117	(77%)	($623,810)
	Jay Stoddard (D)	55,087	(23%)	
2008 primary	Adrian Smith (R)	55,225	(87%)	
	Jeremiah Ellison (R)	7,947	(13%)	

Prior Winning Percentages: 2006 (55%)

Population		**Race/Ethnicity**		**Work**	
Pop. 2007:	555,162	White:	89.5%	Private:	72.9%
Change since 2000:	Down 2.7%	Black:	0.4%	Government:	14.0%
Urban:	46.1%	Hispanic:	7.8%	Self-employed:	12.6%
Rural:	53.9%	Asian:	0.6%	Blue collar:	27.0%
Area size:	64,899 sq. mi.	Native Am.:	0.7%	White collar:	53.6%
		Hawaiian:	0.0%	Khaki collar:	0.1%
Age		Two+ races:	0.9%	Other:	19.4%
Median age:	40.2 yrs.			Median income:	$40,569
More than 65 yrs:	17.2%	*Ancestry*		Median home value:	$84,600
Less than 18 yrs:	24.1%	German:	35.0%	Poverty:	11.8%
		Irish:	10.1%		
Education		English:	7.8%	**Military Veterans**	
H.S. grad:	87.6%			% of Pop:	11.8%
College grad:	19.0%				
Grad degree:	5.7%				

West of Grand Island, Nebraska is wheat and livestock country. For miles on end you can see nothing but rolling brown fields, sectioned off here and there by barbed wire fences, and in the distance, a grain elevator towering over a tiny town and its miniature railroad depot. The winds, rain and tornadoes that come suddenly out of the sky remind you that the original settlers likened this part of the country to an ocean and thought themselves in their wooden wagons almost as helpless as passengers at sea in a

2008 Presidential Vote		
McCain (R)	169,361	(68%)
Obama (D)	73,099	(30%)
2004 Presidential Vote		
Bush (R)	189,885	(75%)
Kerry (D)	60,156	(24%)
Cook Partisan Voting Index:	R + 24	

rowboat. Settlers passed through here on the Oregon Trail in the 1840s, then set down roots in the 1880s. But the rain they hoped for fell too unreliably, and wheatlands gave way to pasture and open range. It is a beautiful but hard land, exacting much from its people, as the novels of western Nebraska's Willa Cather make poignantly clear. Chimney Rock—a clay and sandstone spire that marked a good camping spot and offered reliable spring water for travelers and their animals—was the landmark that travelers on the Oregon Trail most frequently mentioned in their journals. This symbol of westward expansion now graces the Nebraska issue of the U.S. quarter. Dozens of small counties today have fewer people than they did in 1900. Severe droughts in recent years have seemed a kind of end point, as the grasslands turned dry and brown, reservoirs and aquifers began to run dry and ranchers sold off their thinning and sickening herds. But some economic life survives. In North Platte, Bailey Yard is the world's largest railroad classification yard, covering 2,850 acres and handling 10,000 rail cars every 24 hours. The Union Pacific line from North Platte east to Gibbon is the busiest freight rail corridor in the world. Farther west on Interstate 80 is the town of Sidney, home of Cabela's, the world's largest mail order and Internet business for hunting, fishing and camping gear.

The 3rd Congressional District of Nebraska has one-third of the state's people, 85% of its acreage and exists in two time zones. At nearly 65,000 square miles, it is one of the largest congressional districts—bigger than the state of New York and with more counties. Except along the interstate and around Scottsbluff, the 3rd has been losing population for decades as beef production continues to drop, and several of the western ranching counties are among the poorest in the nation. The Census Bureau reported a loss of 23,000 residents in Nebraska's rural population in the first eight years of this decade. Valley County is one of many fighting for economic survival, creating a "business coach" to assist local firms in selling on the Internet. Still, the 3rd is a major agricultural producer, with the highest total in U.S. farm subsidies, more farms than all but one other congressional district, and more cattle and calves than any other place in the nation. Geographically and politically, the 3rd District is where the Midwest becomes the West. For years people here welcomed farm subsidies even as they angrily opposed federal interference. Politically, it is heavily Republican and sometimes ornery: In 1992 Ross Perot got more votes here than Bill Clinton. The district voted 75% for George W. Bush in 2004 and 68% for John McCain in 2008.

The congressman from the 3rd District is Adrian Smith, the youngest of the 13 freshmen Republicans elected to the House in 2006. He hails from a politically active family—his father is a former county Republican chairman, and his mother is the state GOP secretary. But the most significant political influence in Smith's life was President Reagan. When he was in fourth grade, Smith recalls, adults around him were weighing Reagan's attributes against that of Democrat Jimmy Carter's, and it sunk into the boy's head that Reagan favored a strong defense. "It just made sense to me that we needed a strong military," said Smith, whose congressional office is filled with portraits of the former president. In college, Smith served as an intern in the Nebraska governor's office and as a page in the state's unicameral Legislature. At 23, shortly after graduating from the University of Nebraska, he won election to the Gering City Council in his hometown. Four years later, he knocked off a Democratic incumbent to win the first of two terms in the Legislature. There, Smith devoted his efforts to opposing abortion rights, protecting Nebraskans' right to bear arms, fighting tax increases, and blocking efforts to expand casino gambling. He also worked as a real estate agent and storage-business owner. In May 2005, two weeks after U.S. Rep. Tom Osborne, a Republican, announced his ultimately unsuccessful primary bid for governor, Smith joined the race for Osborne's seat in Congress.

The crowded Republican primary field included Grand Island Mayor Jay Vavricek and John Hanson, Osborne's former district director. Smith championed tax incentives to attract new residents and encourage investment in the district, which is threatened with elimination in the next census because of population declines. He also promised to expand markets globally for Nebraska farmers. Still, his opponents charged that he betrayed rural Nebraska by accepting more than $300,000 in contributions from members of the Club for Growth, a national anti-tax group that opposes farm subsidies. Smith supports caps on subsidies, which many of his farming constituents do not. In response to his opponents' criticism, he pointed to his support from the Nebraska Farm Bureau. Smith ultimately carried 39 of the 69 counties to win the nomination with 39%. Hanson finished second with 29% and was strongest in the Republican River valley south of North Platte, while Vavricek's 27% came mainly from the Grand Island area.

For the 2006 general election, the Democratic Party fielded an unusually strong nominee: Yale-educated, cattle rancher Scott Kleeb. He accused Smith of "distorting the truth" about the Club for Growth's opposition to farm subsidies. Smith responded that the group backed him because of his record on taxes. Smith sought to link Kleeb to Democrats who supported a timetable for the withdrawal of troops from Iraq, and he portrayed Kleeb as a political carpetbagger who grew up overseas on military bases and attended schools in Colorado and Connecticut before settling in Nebraska on a family-owned ranch. Kleeb's retort was, "You don't run as a Democrat in the 3rd District because you thought it would be easy." Kleeb called for changes in farm policy to emphasize niche markets and made the contest much closer than anybody expected. Each candidate raised more than $1 million. After late-October polling showed a virtual toss-up, the Democratic Congressional Campaign Committee ran an ad attacking Smith for accepting campaign money from "Washington special interests." President Bush made one of his final campaign stops of the season here to try to help Smith. He won 55%-45%, though Kleeb won a dozen counties in the eastern portion of the district.

In Washington, Smith landed a seat on the Agriculture Committee and focused his early efforts on the rewrite of farm policy, working to expand rural development programs, increase research of algae biomass and other biofuels, and seek international markets for Nebraska crops. He stood by President Bush as support for the war in Iraq waned, even turning down the Democrats' offer of billions of dollars in drought relief if he joined them in pushing timetables for withdrawing troops. Smith describes himself as an economic conservative in Reagan's mold: "I believe in a market-based approach. Government is not the solution to everything. That's why I'm not in a rush to introduce a whole lot of bills. I'll introduce bills that I think are a good idea and work for their passage."

In the 2008 primary, Smith easily defeated Jeremiah Ellison, an activist supporter of libertarian Ron Paul of Texas. Kleeb turned down a rematch against Smith and instead ran for the U.S. Senate.

★ NEVADA ★

Las Vegas is unlike any other place on Earth. As your plane descends for a landing, you see a pyramid rising from the desert; just across the street from the Sphinx-like lion are New York City-style skyscrapers. Nearby are a fair-sized Eiffel Tower, the gondolas of Venice, and a flaming pirate ship. These surrealistic monuments, and miles of spreading subdivisions, are set in one of North America's most forbidding landscapes, a bowl-shaped desert valley rimmed by barren peaks. "Geologically, Nevada is a gigantic, post-oceanic ditch between the Rockies and the Sierras, filled with rough, secondary mountain ranges that stack and twine across the naked landscape like ranks of FEMA house trailers in a storage lot," writes Las Vegas art critic Dave Hickey. The first settlers came to mine silver and gold, starting with the Comstock Lode in 1859, which produced $500 million worth of silver in the next 20 years. Abraham Lincoln's Republicans made Nevada a state in 1864 even though it did not meet the population requirement, because the GOP thought it might need three more electoral votes. But for years Nevada was not a viable state; by the early 20th century, its population had shrunk, and in the early 1930s there were only 91,000 Nevadans. The state government was about to go bankrupt, so Nevada decided to roll the dice: It reduced its residency requirement for divorce to six weeks and legalized gambling. Catering to what most Americans considered sin—casinos, pawnshops, divorce mills, quick-wedding chapels, even legal brothels—turned out to be good business. Nevada has been America's fastest-growing state for two decades. Its population doubled, from 1.2 million to 2.5 million, from 1990 to 2007.

Las Vegas, a mere dot on the map when gambling was legalized, is the center of a metropolitan area of 1.8 million people. Reno, known as "the biggest little city in the world," now has, together with Lake Tahoe and the capital of Carson City, 506,000 people. Gaming—the Nevada word for gambling—generates most of this growth: Las Vegas had 150,000 hotel rooms in 2007, with 40,000 more scheduled to be built by 2010, requiring 100,000 new workers. Las Vegas' tourists spend more than $33 billion a year and Reno's about $4 billion, and not just in casinos and hotels but also in increasingly upscale restaurants and shopping malls. They come from all over the United States and from foreign countries, especially Japan. Though at least one form of gambling is now available in 48 states, Las Vegas has made itself a destination; it has more than twice as much convention exhibit space as the No. 2 city, Chicago. This is definitely a service economy: Of the more than 1 million people employed, nearly 90% provide services rather than goods. The 6.75% gambling receipts tax has generated enough revenue to make it unnecessary for Nevada to impose income, corporate, or inheritance taxes. The cost of living is low, housing is relatively inexpensive, and a newcomer doesn't stand out in the crowd. Some 5,000 people were moving in every month before the global financial crisis hit in 2008.

From mining to gambling, Nevada has been a second-chance state, a place for outcasts to succeed and misfits to rebound. Like Alaska, it is one of the few states with more men than women. At 14%, Nevada has the highest percentage of divorced residents in the nation. Only 23% of Nevadans were born in the state, the lowest of any state; in Stateline, on Lake Tahoe, just 5% were born in Nevada. The state has been an avenue of success for ethnic groups who faced roadblocks elsewhere. The four owners of the Comstock Lode—MacKay, Fair, Flood, and O'Brien—were Irishmen. The first big hotel on the Las Vegas strip, the Flamingo, was built in 1946 by Jewish gangster Bugsy Siegel, who was later gunned down in his Beverly Hills home. Most of the big casinos were owned by mobsters until industrialist Howard Hughes—a different kind of outcast—bought them up in the late 1960s. Since 1990, Latinos have moved here in large numbers, attracted by the strong job market. Nevada's minority population in 2007 was 24% Hispanic, 7% black, and 6% Asian. Some 4% of Nevadans told the 2000 census takers that they were of multiple races, the fourth highest percentage of any state. Nevadans tend to be nonreligious and not highly educated: About 34% belonged to a church in 2000, a proportion lower than any other state except Oregon and Washington. Only 17% of adults in Las Vegas and Clark County had college degrees, one of the lowest percentages for any big metropolitan area.

By 2007, Nevada was feeling the heat from the recession. That year, taxable revenue declined nearly 10% and the unemployment rate rose above the national average. In 2008, things got worse. Gambling collections were down 23% in May, hotel occupancy was falling, thousands of construction workers were laid off, the Tropicana was headed into bankruptcy, and Starbucks closed 10% of its Las Vegas outlets. Casino stocks took a nosedive in late 2008, and much of the fortunes of casino magnates Kirk Kerkorian and Sheldon Adelson vanished. Real estate values, which were rising rapidly as late as 2005, crashed, and subdivisions built farther and farther out in the desert seemed empty. Nevada ranked No. 1 among the states in foreclosures, with rates running close to 100 per 1,000 households. Speculators with adjustable-rate mortgage loans and Hispanic construction workers with subprime mortgages suddenly found themselves far under water in the desert. Las Vegas, with all of its glitter and growth, found itself at the epicenter of the financial crisis that struck America in the fall of 2008.

All of this poses the greatest challenge that Las Vegas and Nevada have faced in years. As gambling has spread across the nation, Las Vegas has changed its focus, from Frank Sinatra and the Rat Pack, to

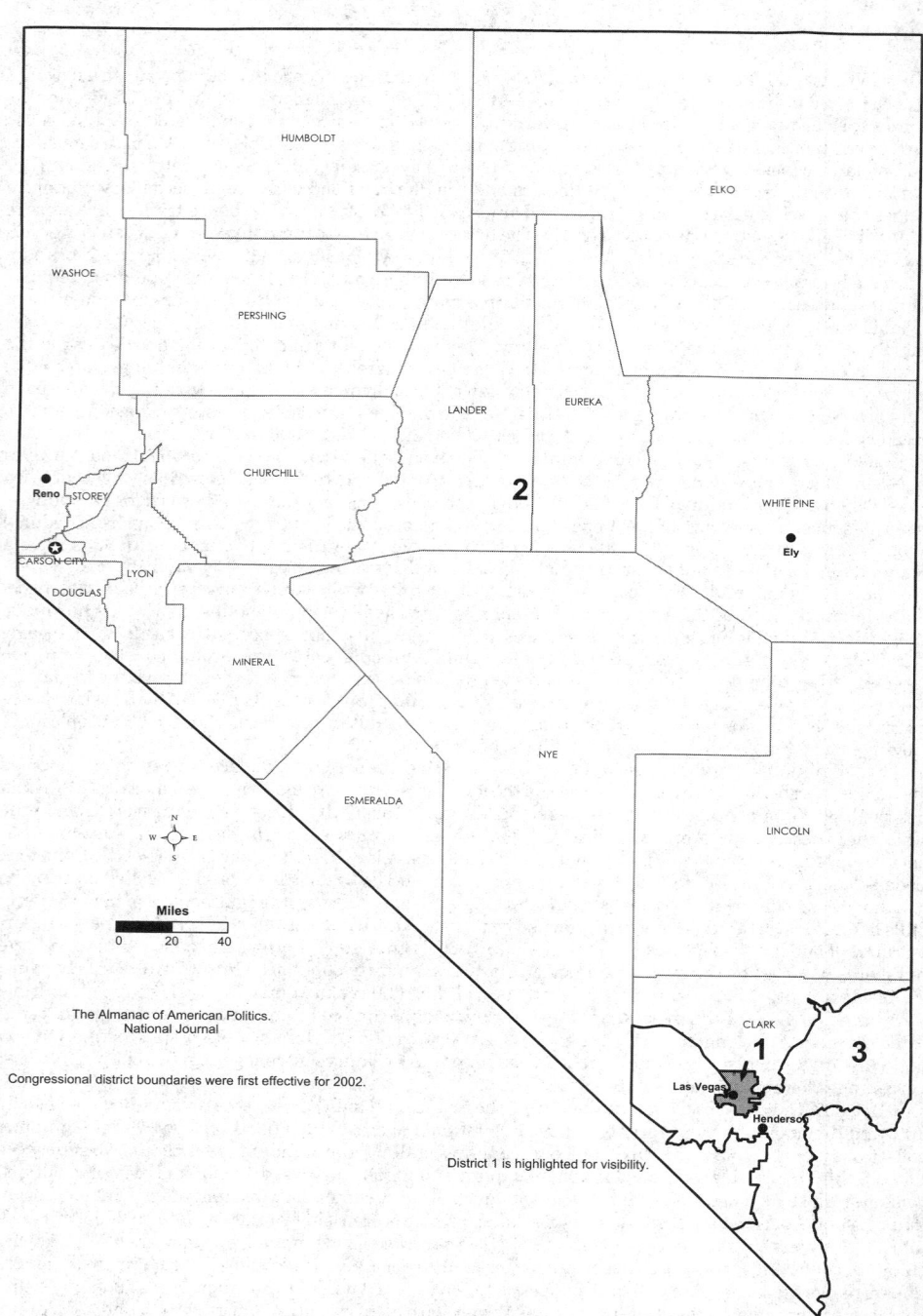

HUMBOLDT

ELKO

WASHOE

PERSHING

LANDER

EUREKA

2

WHITE PINE

CHURCHILL

Reno STOREY

CARSON CITY

Ely

LYON

DOUGLAS

MINERAL

NYE

ESMERALDA

N
W — E
S

LINCOLN

Miles

0   20   40

Congressional district boundaries were first effective for 2002.

CLARK

1   **3**

Las Vegas

Henderson

District 1 is highlighted for visibility.

Population		Household Income		Work	
Pop. 2007:	2,488,917	Under $15k:	9.9%	Private:	82.8%
State rank:	35th of 50	$15k to $50k:	36.2%	Government:	12.1%
Change since 2000:	Up 24.6%	$50k to $100k:	34.8%	Self-employed:	4.9%
Urban:	83.7%	$100k to $150k:	15.8%	Unemployment (3-yr. average):	3.8%
Rural:	16.3%	Over $150k:	3.3%	Poverty:	10.8%
Native of state:	22.7%	Median income:	$53,753	Blue collar:	23.1%
Not a citizen:	11.6%	**Home Value**		White collar:	51.9%
Area size:	110,561 sq. mi.	Under $100k:	8.4%	Khaki collar:	0.3%
Most populous cities		$100k to $300k:	41.1%	Other:	24.8%
1. Las Vegas	558,892	$300k to $500k:	34.3%	**Age**	
2. Henderson	236,506	$500k to $1 mil:	13.8%	Median age:	35.6 yrs.
3. Reno	211,183	Over $1 million:	2.4%	More than 65 yrs:	11.1%
4. Paradise	203,890	Median:	$302,600	Less than 18 yrs:	25.8%

Race/Ethnicity				Military Veterans		Registered Voters in 2008	
White:	58.9%	*Language*		% of Pop:	12.8%	D:	625,134 (43.2%)
Black:	7.1%	English:	73.3%	*Veterans by Period*		R:	513,629 (35.5%)
Hispanic:	24.3%	Spanish:	19.1%	WWII and before:	9.1%	Other:	307,775 (21.3%)
Asian:	5.8%	Asian:	4.4%	Korea:	11.0%	Voter turnout:	967,848
Native Am.:	1.0%	Other		Vietnam:	34.3%	Turnout as % of	
Hawaiian:	0.4%	European	2.5%	Gulf (pre-2001):	12.5%	voting age:	50.1%
Two+ races:	2.2%	**Education**		Gulf (post-2001):	6.7%	**Legislature**	
Ancestry		H.S. grad:	83.4%	Peace time:	26.3%	Senate:	12 D 9 R
German:	11.7%	College grad:	20.9%			Assembly:	28 D 14 R
Irish:	8.8%	Grad degree:	7.0%				
English:	8.4%						

family-friendly destination, to "what happens in Vegas stays in Vegas." It has promoted lavish shopping malls and hosted giant conventions (although neither of the major political parties has shown an interest). The city has even experimented with museums: The Guggenheim Heritage Museum in the Venetian closed in 2008, but the Neon Museum was scheduled to open in La Concha Motel in 2009 and the Museum of Organized Crime and Law Enforcement (locals call it the mob museum) in the old federal courthouse was to debut in 2010.

There are other businesses in Nevada besides gambling and other places besides Las Vegas (although 71% of Nevadans live in Clark County). The state's low taxes have made it a regional distribution and credit card operations center, and it has attracted warehouses and factories from California. There is still some mining, mostly in gold, which has been booming since the Clinton administration's mining regulations were scrapped and the price of gold rose. Nevada also mines the less glamorous diatomaceous earth, used for swimming pool filters and cat litter. And a lot of older Californians cash out their expensive homes and retire to low-tax Nevada. A Wild West atmosphere endures in the "cow counties" beyond Las Vegas and Reno. Half of the 37,000 wild horses that roam the American West can be found in Nevada.

Presidential politics   Politically, Nevada was closely divided in the four presidential elections from 1992 to 2004, but in 2008 it went strongly Democratic, which is its historic preference. For years, this sparsely populated desert sent politically shrewd Democrats to Washington and kept them there to protect the interests of a state heavily dependent on the federal government. The most powerful were Key Pittman, chairman of the Senate Foreign Relations Committee, who backed Franklin Delano Roosevelt's foreign policy only after Roosevelt agreed to buy absurdly large amounts of Nevada's silver; and Sen. Pat McCarran, author of the repres-

2008 Presidential Vote
Obama (D) 533,736   (55%)
McCain (R) 412,827   (43%)

2004 Presidential Vote
Bush (R) 418,690   (50%)
Kerry (D) 397,190   (48%)

sive McCarran Act, who shamelessly pushed aid for Reno and Las Vegas (the airport there is named for him) and became suddenly solicitous of civil liberties when mobsters and casino owners were called to testify before the Kefauver committee investigating racketeering. In the 1980s, Nevada swung heavily Republican. In the 1990s, it twice voted narrowly for Democrat Bill Clinton, partly because he promised to stop the proposed nuclear-waste repository in Yucca Mountain, some 90 miles from Las Vegas. In 2000 and 2004, it was a target state again, narrowly carried both times by George W. Bush, who arguably would have done better here had he taken the same pledge to oppose the repository; instead, he was agnostic. In 2006, Nevada again seemed closely divided, electing Republican Jim Gibbons as governor and re-electing Republican Sen. John Ensign.

But it changed in 2008 for three reasons. One was presidential politics. The Democratic National Committee, under heavy pressure from Senate Democratic Leader Harry Reid, named Nevada as one of its four states allowed to hold early contests, along with Iowa, New Hampshire, and South Carolina. Reid argued that largely white Iowa and New Hampshire were not typical of an increasingly diverse nation and that Nevada—with its mix of Hispanics, blacks, and Asians—was. (In South Carolina, the fourth early state, most of the Democratic primary voters are black.) Labor leaders pointed out that Nevada, unlike the three other states, has a large number of union members: The Nevada casinos are the only growth industry in the nation where most employees are union members. Other Democrats argued, presciently as it turned out, that Nevada was one of several Western states trending Democratic. So the Democrats held a caucus on January 19, just 16 days after the Iowa caucuses. Hillary Rodham Clinton and Barack Obama both organized in the state; Clinton came out the winner, in the metrics Democrats use, 51%-45%, her only caucus victory all year.

Democrats did not quit organizing after the caucus, which is the second reason for their surge. In October 2006, Nevada had 494,000 registered Democrats and 482,000 registered Republicans. But in this fastest-growing state, there were plenty of new residents to be signed up, and Democrats got them. The Democratic registration advantage rose to 523,000 to 479,000 by January 2008, and by October 2008, it was a whopping 624,000 to 513,000.

Boosting your lead in registered voters from 12,000 to 111,000 is a great organizational achievement, but the effort was greatly aided by the third reason for Nevada's Democratic trend: the state's sudden and thudding economic slowdown. Nevada's new Hispanic voters, many dependent on the construction and casino industries, found themselves laid off and their subprime mortgages under water. Those who had gambled on Nevada's economy continuing to boom found they had made very bad bets, with the effects more visible here than in many other states before September's financial crisis. The Obama campaign was instrumental in getting more than half of the state's voters to cast their ballots early. And they tended to vote a straight party ticket: Republican Rep. Jon Porter was defeated in the Las Vegas suburbs, while Democrats captured the state Senate for the first time in 18 years and widened their majority in the state House to 28-14. The fact that Republican Gov. Jim Gibbons was unpopular and under investigation (he was exonerated after the election) didn't help his party.

Obama won 76% of the Hispanic vote (15% of the electorate), 94% of the black vote, and lost the white vote by only 51%-47%. Voters under 30 cast 67% of their ballots for Obama, and voters 30 to 44 were almost equally supportive, 60%. Voters in union households, nearly a quarter of the electorate, backed him 62%. Obama carried Las Vegas's Clark County by a solid 59%-40% and also won Reno's Washoe County 55%-43%, a real feat because it has voted Republican for years. John McCain carried the cow counties 58%-38%, but that did not even make it close statewide.

The election left the state's congressional delegation with a Democratic majority. Their seats are all a bit unsteady, if only because Nevada has so many new voters. Democrat Reid and Republican Ensign have noted that nearly half of the voters in their Senate re-election contests weren't Nevada residents when they won six years before. Reid and Ensign have had a kind of nonaggression pact ever since Reid beat Ensign, then a congressman, by only 428 votes in 1998. Reid's partisan stances as Senate majority leader may have caused his job rating to fall in 2007, but his clout may enable him to win as easily in 2010 as he did in 2004.

Some observers say that Nevada has a third party that always wins—the gambling party— that is closely allied with the Culinary Union, which has seen its membership increase to 60,000. Las Vegas gambling interests have backed every recent governor, from Democrat Bob Miller, who first won in 1990, to Republicans Kenny Guinn and Gibbons, who won in 1998 and 2006, respectively. Reid has been close to the gambling industry over a political career that goes back to the 1960s. His colleague Ensign's stepfather was chairman of the company that owns the Mandalay Bay Resort and Casino until 2005.

One issue that has long preoccupied Nevada is the proposed Yucca Mountain nuclear-waste repository. The federal government took responsibility for the country's nuclear waste in 1982, and the Yucca Mountain site was chosen by Congress in 1987, when the Nevada delegation was unusually weak: Reid was in his first year in the Senate and Republican Chic Hecht seemed to be facing sure defeat in 1988. The plan is to bury the waste deep within the mountain, 1,300 feet above the water table, in reinforced steel containers in a 1,400-acre maze with 100 miles of storage tunnels. Many Nevadans argue that rainwater will flush the radioactive material out of the repository and into the water table. More recently, Yucca Mountain opponents have charged that the site is geologically flawed and within an earthquake zone, and that transportation of nuclear waste across the country would be hazardous, especially after September 11. President Clinton promised to veto a temporary site, but veto-proof majorities in the House approved such a site in Nevada. Sens. Richard Bryan and Reid lobbied furiously to get enough votes to prevent a veto override in the Senate and succeeded in 1995, 1997, and 2000. In 2000, candidate George W. Bush pledged not to place a temporary storage site in the state. But he refrained from promising to veto a permanent repository, saying that his decision would be based on "sound science and not politics." In February 2002, President Bush, on the recommendation of Energy Secretary Spencer Abraham, designated Yucca Mountain as the permanent site. The law provided for a veto by the governor, which could be overridden by majorities in both chambers of Congress. In April 2002, with great ceremony, Gov. Guinn issued his veto. In May 2002, the House cast a large majority for Yucca Mountain. In the Senate, Reid and Ensign lobbied hard for votes, but in July 2002 the designation was affirmed 60-39. Many Nevadans cheered when the U.S. Court of Appeals for the D.C. Circuit ruled in July 2004 that the Environmental Protection Agency's health and safety standards were insufficient. But the court also upheld the selection of the site and said that the standards could be changed. The permanent site is not slated to open until 2012, and additional regulatory proceedings and lawsuits could alter the schedule. The Nevada delegation in Congress has vowed not to work for concessions on the repository's construction but to fight it every step of the way. With the Democratic victory in November 2006, Reid became majority leader and promised that any legislation advancing Yucca Mountain would never get to the Senate floor.

Congressional districting

111th Congress Lineup	
2 D	1 R
110th Congress Lineup	
2 R	1 D

Nevada gained a second congressional district in the 1980 census and a third district in the 2000 census. It is expected to gain a fourth district in the 2010 census. Redistricting was easy in the 1980s and 1990s. The 1st District was the inner part of Clark County, politically marginal and won by both parties in the 1990s; the 2nd District was the rest of the state, heavily Republican.

It was a little more difficult in 2001, with a third district and control of redistricting split between a Republican governor and state Senate and a Democratic Assembly. Clark County, with 69% of the population, was entitled to two of the seats and a small part of the third. For a time, Republicans argued that two or all three of the districts should combine part of Clark County with part of the rest of the state, but that idea was dropped in the June 2001 special legislative session. Eventually, agreement was reached on a plan: The city of Las Vegas proper would make up the 1st District; a 2nd District would comprise all of the remaining counties plus much of outer Clark County; and a Y-shaped 3rd District would have much of the Las Vegas suburbs. The 1st District was safe for Democrat Shelley Berkley, the 2nd was safe for Republican Jim Gibbons, and the 3rd was drawn to be evenly split in party registration; it cast narrow pluralities for Al Gore in 2000 and Bush in 2004 but went solidly for Obama in 2008. Republican Jon Porter won it in 2002, 2004, and 2006, and Democrat Dina Titus won it in 2008.

Democrats currently have a small majority in the state Senate and a 2-1 ratio in the state House; Republican Gibbons is governor. Party control of redistricting depends on whether this balance is maintained. It seems unlikely that Democrats will lose their House majority, so they will have at least some say, and they could control the proceedings if Gibbons is defeated in 2010 and Republicans do not gain seats in the state Senate.

Governor

Jim Gibbons (R)

Elected 2006, term expires Jan. 2011, 1st term; b. Dec. 16, 1944, Sparks; home, Reno; U. of NV, B.S. 1967, M.S. 1973; Southwestern U., J.D. 1979; Mormon; separated; 3 children.

Military Career: Air Force, 1967–71 (Vietnam), NV Air Natl. Guard, 1975–96 (Persian Gulf).

Elected Office: NV Assembly, 1988–94; U.S. House of Reps., 1996–2006.

Professional Career: Pilot, Western Airlines, 1979–87, Delta Airlines, 1987–96.

Office: 101 N. Carson St., Carson City, 89701, 775-684-5670; Fax: 775-684-5683; Web site: gov.state.nv.us.

Election Results

2006 general	Jim Gibbons (R)	279,003	(48%)
	Dina Titus (D)	255,684	(44%)
	None of these candidates	20,699	(4%)
2006 primary	Jim Gibbons (R)	67,717	(48%)
	Bob Beers (R)	40,876	(29%)
	Lorraine Hunt (R)	25,161	(18%)

Prior Winning Percentages: 2004 House (67%); 2002 House (74%); 2000 House (65%); 1998 House (81%); 1996 House (59%)

Republican Jim Gibbons was elected governor of Nevada in 2006, the first from northern Nevada since Republican Robert List won election in 1978 and the first Nevada-born governor since Republican Paul Laxalt in 1966. Gibbons grew up in Sparks, next door to Reno, and like Bush strategist Karl Rove, was a graduate of Sparks High School. He graduated from the University of Nevada and served in the Air Force during the Vietnam War. He went to law school and practiced law, but was also a mining geologist, a hydrologist, a pilot for Delta and Western airlines and vice commander of the Nevada Air National Guard. In 1988, he was elected to the Nevada Assembly and, two years later, was called up to active duty in the Gulf War. While he was flying unarmed air reconnaissance missions of enemy targets in Kuwait, his wife, Dawn Gibbons, took his place in the Legislature. After his celebrated return, he proposed a ballot initiative to require a two-thirds supermajority to raise any state tax; it passed with more than 70% of the votes in 1994. However, the law was suspended in 2003 when the state Supreme Court required the Legislature to pass Republican Gov. Kenny Guinn's tax increase by a majority vote. In 1994, Gibbons ran for governor. He beat Secretary of State Cheryl Lau 52%-32% in the primary, but lost the general election to Democratic incumbent Bob Miller, 53%-41%. In 1996, after Republican Rep. Barbara Vucanovich retired, Gibbons ran for the 2nd District House seat and won, 59%-35%.

He served five terms, representing the sprawling and heavily Republican district, which covers most of the state's land area and a small part of Las Vegas's Clark County. He opposed federal intrusion on local rights, the nuclear waste repository at Yucca Mountain and the proposed temporary storage at the Nevada Test Site. He showed an independent streak that placed him toward the center of the House on cultural issues. In August 2005, he announced he would run for governor to replace term-limited Guinn in 2006. He appeared to be the front-runner, but Dawn Gibbons sparked controversy by running to replace her husband in the House, raising objections that she would not be able to fulfill her duties as Nevada's first lady. She lost the Republican primary.

In the contest for governor, Gibbons had to first prevail in the Republican primary, up against state Sen. Bob Beers, Lt. Gov. Lorraine Hunt and adult-movie star Melody Damayo. Beers ran a hard-hitting campaign with an anti-tax focus. Hunt spent nearly $800,000 of her own money. Damayo, using her stage name Mimi Miyagi, posted a racy campaign website. Gibbons campaigned as a fiscal conservative promising to make education a priority and won with 48% of the vote. Beers finished second with 29%, followed by Hunt, who had 18%. Damayo won 1%.

The Democratic nominee was state Senate Minority Leader Dina Titus, a political science professor who represented the Las Vegas Strip and who had defeated Henderson Mayor Jim Gibson, 54%-36%, in the primary. In Titus and Gibbons, the governor's race featured approximate versions of the two Nevadas: Gibbons a native of northern Nevada, Titus a Southern-born migrant to Las Vegas. Titus sought to portray Gibbons as an "inconsequential" Washington backbencher and ran on a theme of the five "E's" : economic development, education, energy, environment and ethics. She criticized Gibbons's support for the Bush administration's No Child Left Behind education law and said full-day kindergarten would be one of her first priorities in office. Gibbons advocated merit pay for teachers and called Titus a tax-and-spend liberal, dubbing her "Dina Taxes." He ran ads on Reno television saying, "Dina Titus called Washoe County a sponge and called us rascals who want handouts. Jim Gibbons calls Washoe County home and calls us neighbors and friends."

In the final weeks of the campaign, Gibbons suffered through a stretch of publicity so negative it is a wonder he won. In mid-October, a casino cocktail waitress filed a complaint alleging that he had propositioned and threatened to sexually assault her in a parking garage after an evening of drinking at a restaurant. Gibbons denied her account, contending that he merely caught her when she tripped. He called for the release of tapes from video cameras at the garage, but the videotapes failed to show either of them in the garage. In early December, the Las Vegas police recommended that no charges be filed. He also confronted disclosures that he had employed an illegal immigrant as a nanny in the late 1980s. The Gibbons campaign accused Titus of instigating the release of embarrassing information. Then, less than one week before Election Day, *The Wall Street Journal* reported that in 2005 Gibbons took a weeklong Caribbean cruise that was paid for by entrepreneur Warren Trepp, a contributor whom the congressman had helped to win federal software contracts.

As a result of the negative bombardment, Gibbons's lead in the polls dwindled. But he still managed to win, 48%-44%, outspending Titus $5.7 million to $3.6 million. He lost Las Vegas's Clark County, where he trailed by 23,000 votes, but won everywhere else. He received enough votes in the capital of Carson City, in Reno's Washoe County, and in fast-growing Douglas County to overcome Titus's advantage in southern Nevada. She failed to break 41% anywhere outside of Clark County. Titus, who was later reelected as Senate minority leader, did not take defeat well. "I wouldn't be surprised if he got indicted while in office," she told *The Las Vegas Sun.*

Gibbons had a rocky start as governor. Citing unspecified homeland-security concerns, he was sworn in 12 seconds after midnight on January 1, a move widely viewed as an attempt to prevent outgoing Gov. Guinn from making an appointment to the Gaming Control Board. Early in 2007, *The Wall Street Journal* reported that a federal corruption inquiry into his relations with Trepp had been opened. Gibbons publicly speculated that the newspaper had been paid by Democrats to write the damaging stories. In March, *The Journal* reported that Dawn Gibbons had been paid $35,000 in consulting fees by a Sparks company that her husband was helping win contracts. In April, she filed for divorce and Gibbons sought a court order to remove her from the governor's mansion. In June, it was reported that Gibbons had sent 867 text messages to another woman over his state-owned cellphone. Then it was reported that Gibbons and a state tax official had pressured the Elko County assessor to change the designation of a vacant parcel of land he owned from residential to agricultural, reducing his property taxes from about $5,000 to $15.

Gibbons's job ratings fell, and so did the economy of what has been the nation's fastest-growing state. It turned out that developers had overbuilt, and Nevada clocked the nation's highest home-foreclosure rate. Gibbons, who had vowed not to raise taxes, asked legislators in November 2007 to find ways to cut $285 million in state spending. He was criticized for holding secret budget sessions in an effort to find more cuts. The chancellor of the state university system refused to submit lists of possible budget cuts, and Gibbons was booed at commencement ceremonies at the University of Nevada at Las Vegas. The estimated revenue shortfall had ballooned to $800 million by March 2008. Gibbons ordered a 4.5% across-the-board cut in spending, and postponed the expansion of all-day kindergarten.

Gibbons also did himself no favors with Nevadans in July 2007, when he concurred with the state engineer's decision to let the U.S. Department of Energy continue to use Nevada water for 30 more days to collect samples of data needed for licensing the enormously unpopular nuclear-waste repository at Yucca Mountain. By mid-2008, Gibbons had become nearly radioactive himself, at least politically, and the John McCain presidential campaign made sure he was not present at its campaign events around the state. In early 2009, his re-election prospects were dimming.

Senior Senator

Harry Reid (D)

Elected 1986, term expires 2010, 4th term; b. Dec. 2, 1939, Searchlight; home, Searchlight; S. UT St. Col., A.S. 1959, UT St. U., B.S. 1961, George Washington U., J.D. 1964, U. of NV, 1969–70; Mormon; married (Landra); 5 children.

Elected Office: NV Assembly, 1968–70; NV lt. gov., 1970–74; U.S. House of Reps., 1982–86.

Professional Career: Practicing atty., 1969–82; Henderson City atty., 1964–66; Chmn., NV Gaming Comm., 1977–81.

DC Office: 522 HSOB, 20510, 202-224-3542; Fax: 202-224-7327; Web site: reid.senate.gov.

State Offices: Carson City, 775-882-7343; Las Vegas, 702-388-5020; Reno, 775-686-5750.

Committees: *Majority Leader.*

Group Ratings

	ADA	ACLU	AFS	LCV	ITIC	NTU	COC	ACU	CFG	FRC
2008	70	79	67	100	80	15	75	16	11	11
2007	85	—	86	87	—	7	45	0	11	—

National Journal Ratings

	2007 LIB	—	2007 CONS	2008 LIB	—	2008 CONS
Economic	72%	—	23%	77%	—	13%
Social	94%	—	0%	70%	—	29%
Foreign	94%	—	2%	65%	—	6%
Composite	89%	—	11%	77%	—	23%

Key Votes of the 110th Congress

1. Raise CAFE standards	Y	5. Make English official language	N	9. Withdraw troops 3/08	Y
2. Expand SCHIP	Y	6. Path to citizenship	Y	10. Iran guard is terrorist group	Y
3. Cap greenhouse gases	Y	7. Fetus is unborn child	N	11. Increase missile defense $	N
4. Bail out financial markets	Y	8. Prosecute hate crimes	Y	12. Overhaul FISA	N

Election Results

2004 general	Harry Reid (D)	494,805	(61%)	($7,040,588)
	Richard Ziser (R)	284,640	(35%)	($647,500)
2004 primary	Harry Reid (D)	unopposed		

Prior Winning Percentages: 1998 (48%); 1992 (51%); 1986 (50%); 1984 House (56%); 1982 House (58%)

Democrat Harry Reid is the Senate majority leader. He was first elected to the Senate in 1986, and before that, he served in the U.S. House. Reid grew up in Searchlight, Nev., in the scorching desert south of

Las Vegas. It was a hard life. His father, a hard-rock miner, was an alcoholic who killed himself at age 58. His mother did laundry for a nearby bordello to keep the family afloat. Reid grew up in a small house without indoor plumbing, and hitchhiked 40 miles to high school in Henderson, where his civics teacher and boxing coach, Mike O'Callaghan, became his political mentor. As a young man, Reid was a middle-weight boxer of some local renown, but he aspired to better himself through education. Henderson businessmen helped him pay for college, and he graduated from Southern Utah State, where he and his wife became Mormons. To put himself through law school at George Washington University in Washington, D.C., he worked nights as a Capitol Police officer. He likes to say, "I would rather dance than fight, but I know how to fight." He returned to Henderson to practice law. At age 28, Reid was elected to the Nevada Assembly. In 1970, his mentor O'Callaghan was elected governor and Reid, running separately, was elected lieutenant governor. In 1974, Reid came within 624 votes of beating Republican Paul Laxalt in the race for senator, and two years later, he ran for mayor of Las Vegas and lost that election too. O'Callaghan named him to head the Nevada Gaming Commission from 1977 to 1981, a sensitive post overseeing the state's top industry at a time when it was controlled by organized crime. Reid later recounted that his life was threatened and his car wired with a bomb. In 1982, when Nevada got two U.S. House seats for the first time and Rep. at-large Jim Santini ran for the Senate, Reid ran in the Las Vegas-based 1st District and won. As Reid was completing his second term in the House, Laxalt retired and Reid tried for the Senate seat again. His opponent turned out to be Santini, who had switched parties at the last minute and ran as a Republican. Reid won 50%-45%.

Over the years, Reid has had a more moderate voting record than many Senate Democrats. He voted for banning "partial-birth" abortions and against resolutions endorsing *Roe v. Wade,* the Supreme Court ruling legalizing abortion. He co-sponsored the constitutional amendment to outlaw flag-burning. Reid was one of the few Senate Democrats to vote for the Persian Gulf War resolution in 1991, and he voted for the Iraq war resolution in 2002. He has consistently opposed environmental groups on mining issues and blocked attempts to impose higher fees on hard-rock miners. He has opposed most gun control measures. Reid has steered counter-terrorism money to Nevada and has worked to transform the old Nevada nuclear test site, with its hundreds of underground tunnels, into a $250 million center for training first responders to confront acts of terrorism. He has been a strong supporter of the gambling industry. When President Bill Clinton proposed a 4% gambling tax, Reid vowed, "I will become the most negative, the most irresponsible, the most obnoxious person of anyone in the Senate." He effectively blocked a bill, backed by Republican Sen. John McCain of Arizona and others, to prohibit betting on college and amateur sports, which is legal only in Nevada.

For two decades, the key federal issue for Nevada has been the proposed nuclear waste repository at Yucca Mountain. In the late 1980s, the federal government named the site as the top candidate for a permanent repository for waste from nuclear reactors that had been piling up at temporary sites in 39 states. Reid has opposed the repository at Yucca Mountain with every parliamentary and political tool at his command as senators from states with temporary sites have pressed hard for it. Clinton carried Nevada by narrow margins in 1992 and 1996 largely because he promised to veto the establishment of even a temporary site at Yucca Mountain. So Reid's task was to assemble sufficient votes to prevent an override of Clinton's veto, which he did consistently through 2000. In 2002, President George W. Bush, based on the recommendation of Energy Secretary Spencer Abraham, designated Yucca Mountain as the permanent site. The law provided for a veto by the governor, which could be overridden by majorities in both chambers of Congress. In April 2002, Republican Gov. Kenny Guinn issued his veto. In May 2002, the House cast a large majority for Yucca Mountain. Reid lobbied furiously for Democratic votes, while John Ensign, his 1998 opponent and now his Republican colleague, lobbied desperately for Republican votes. Reid argued that the site was geologically flawed and that transporting nuclear waste to it would be hazardous, especially after the September 11 terrorist attacks. Altogether, he got 34 Democrats and independent James Jeffords to vote his way. With the Bush administration lobbying in the other direction, Ensign could get only two other Republicans. The site was approved 60-39.

But for Reid, the fight was not over. Lawsuits were filed against the plan, and Reid, as the chairman of the Appropriations subcommittee with jurisdiction over the Energy Department, blocked funding for the repository year after year. In November 2004, Reid, now the minority leader, negotiated with the Bush administration over judicial appointments and agreed to approve 175 Bush nominees in return for the appointment of his aide, Gregory Jaczko, to the Nuclear Regulatory Commission, which had to approve the site before it could go forward. In 2006, when he was chosen majority leader, Reid said he would use his power to control the Senate schedule to block the Yucca Mountain measure.

Reid's rise to leader was set in motion when he won the post of minority whip in 1998. For the next six years, he was a constant presence on the floor, advancing his party's causes and maintaining civil relations with GOP leaders. He played a key role in persuading Vermont's Sen. Jeffords to leave the Republican Party in May 2001 and become an independent who caucused with the Democrats; that move effectively put the Democrats in the majority. When Republicans held all-night sessions in November 2003 to protest Democratic filibusters of nominees for Appellate Court judgeships, Reid retaliated by speaking for nine hours, reading from his book about his upbringing in Searchlight. In 2004, he campaigned for fellow Democrats and contributed generously to their political treasuries. When Democratic

Leader Tom Daschle of South Dakota lost his seat in a stunning upset, Reid had already lined up the votes he needed to be elected minority leader. (Republicans were back in control of the majority.) Sen. Christopher Dodd of Connecticut was interested in the post but declined to run. Reid was not the Senate's best orator and not much of a policy visionary, but his colleagues knew him as a crafty parliamentarian who would be a scrappy and effective defender of their interests. "I know my limitations," said Reid, who became minority leader in 2005. "I haven't gotten where I am by my good looks, my athletic ability, my great brain, (or) my oratorical skills."

Reid worked deftly behind the scenes, giving up his committee seats to accommodate other Democrats and pledging to rely on committee chairmen on policy. He blocked nongermane amendments from bills. He staunchly opposed Bush's proposal for private individual retirement accounts in Social Security, and the president's efforts to get Democratic support went nowhere. "President Bush should forget about privatizing Social Security. It will not happen," Reid said. "They are trying to destroy Social Security by giving this money to the fat cats on Wall Street, and I think it's wrong." The Republican National Committee blasted him in an e-mail as "chief Democratic obstructionist," and pointed out that his son and a son-in-law were lobbyists, though both had let their lobbyist registrations drop. When Bush renominated several filibustered judicial appointees, Reid promised to filibuster them again and threatened to bring the business of the Senate to a halt if Republicans tried to change the rules by majority vote. But in May 2005, he acquiesced in the agreement of the bipartisan "Gang of 14" to allow some of the nominees to come to a vote. He voted to confirm John Roberts as chief justice but joined most Democrats in opposing the Supreme Court nomination of Samuel Alito. Reid sometimes undercut himself as a leader by resorting to indecorous comments or insults. He once called Bush a "loser" and a "liar," Federal Reserve Board Chairman Alan Greenspan "a political hack," and Supreme Court Justice Clarence Thomas "an embarrassment."

Reid has been vulnerable on the ethics front, although he has maintained that none of the issues raised against him over the years have had merit. After a 2003 *Los Angeles Times* story pointed out that his son and a son-in-law were lobbying in Washington for Nevada companies, Reid banned relatives from lobbying his office. He was a leading recipient of contributions from the Indian tribe clients of disgraced lobbyist Jack Abramoff, and Republican Rep. Jon Porter of Nevada called on him to return the money. Reid refused and pointed out that he had always opposed expansion of Indian gambling, as anyone protecting Las Vegas' interests would. From 2003 to 2005, Reid accepted free seats at Las Vegas boxing matches from the Nevada Athletic Commission. In December 2006, the Senate Ethics Committee said that he had violated no rule because the money came from a state government agency. In October 2006, it was reported that Reid had not disclosed a transaction on a land deal that netted him more than $1 million in 2004. Reid said that he had purchased the land in 1998 at market price, then sold it to a friend's corporation in 2001 in return for a stake in that corporation. He got his share of the proceeds in 2004, he said, when the property was sold to a shopping center developer. Reid reported the 1998 and 2004 transactions and said he would revise his disclosure form to report the 2001 transaction as well.

In 2006, Democrats won the six seats they needed to regain the Senate majority and Reid ascended to majority leader. After the election, Reid deftly juggled committee and leadership posts, giving Michigan's Debbie Stabenow a seat on the Finance Committee and giving Stabenow's leadership job as conference secretary to Washington's Patty Murray, who was considered better suited to the role. He reappointed New York's Charles Schumer as head of the Democratic Senatorial Campaign Committee, and as a reward for Schumer's work on successful Democratic campaigns in 2006, Reid also named him to the new leadership post of vice chairman of the Democratic Conference. In another move to increase resistance to Bush administration proposals, liberals Ben Cardin of Maryland and Sheldon Whitehouse of Rhode Island got seats on the Judiciary Committee. Connecticut's Joe Lieberman, whose vote would be crucial to keeping the majority, was given the chairmanship of the Homeland Security and Governmental Affairs committee even though he had been re-elected as an independent.

On other issues, Reid was often stymied by the Senate Republicans' constant resort to filibusters. His efforts to place limitations on Bush's handling of the Iraq war mostly fell short of the 60 votes required to shut off debate. And there seemed to be no preventing conservative Oklahoman Tom Coburn from blocking even seemingly acceptable bills from the Senate floor. The contrast to the more lockstep House under Speaker Nancy Pelosi of California was a source of some embarrassment to Senate Democrats. Reid also rushed to judgment with an announcement in 2008 that Illinois Democrat Roland Burris, appointed by Gov. Rod Blagojevich to an open Senate seat amid a "pay-to-play" scandal in the Blagojevich administration, would not be seated when he arrived at the Senate. Reid capitulated after leading Democrats said that Burris should be seated while Illinois authorities investigated the circumstances of his appointment. Reid misread the sentiments of his caucus in another highly publicized case, as well. In April 2009, he smoothed the way for Republican Arlen Specter of Pennsylvania to switch parties, bringing the Democrats within one vote of a filibuster-proof 60-vote majority. As part of the deal with Reid, Specter said, he would keep his seniority, putting him in line for a subcommittee or full committee chairmanship. But in an embarrassing rebuke to Reid, rank-and-file Senate Democrats refused to go along and stripped Specter of his seniority on committees.

Despite these setbacks, the electoral success of Senate candidates in 2006 and 2008 engendered enormous goodwill for Reid. With a Democratic majority in Congress, and the election of a Democratic president in 2008, he slipped into the role most comfortable for him, that of behind-the-scenes deal-maker. Reid won bipartisan support for tough new ethics and lobbying rules and expansion of the student loan program. In early 2009, he guided the new administration's $787 billion economic stimulus bill to passage. (The bill happened to include funding for a high-speed bullet train between Las Vegas and Anaheim, Calif., that Reid has championed.) When the $700 billion bailout for the financial industry was in trouble in the House, Reid made several changes to the Senate bill to attract additional votes, including a tweak to the tax code to protect middle-income taxpayers from the alternative minimum tax. "Inaction is not an option," Reid said at the time. "This is, I repeat, a crisis. We've got to get this done." That and other modifications were popular with lawmakers in both parties in the House, and the bill ultimately passed. The Senate also approved an expansion of the State Children's Health Insurance Program. Another happy outcome of the 2008 election for Reid was the new administration's willingness to consider alternative locations to Yucca Mountain for a permanent nuclear waste repository.

Reid faced one serious challenge to his Senate seat, in 1998 when Republican Rep. John Ensign ran a well-financed campaign against him. Both Reid and Ensign, whose stepfather was head of the Mandalay Resort Group, one of the big Las Vegas casino operations, raised large amounts of money from the gambling industry. Reid spent $4.9 million and Ensign $3.5 million. After a nasty campaign, Reid prevailed by just 459 votes. Ensign called for a recount, and finally conceded on December 9, with Reid ahead by 428 votes. Two years later, Ensign was elected to Nevada's other Senate seat. Despite the bitterness of the 1998 campaign, Reid and Ensign have worked together on many home-state projects.

In his 2004 re-election bid, Reid had a different sort of political problem. Nevada had so many newcomers, many of them Republicans, that few were familiar with his work in almost 40 years of public life. About 5,000 people were moving to the Las Vegas area every month—which meant that nearly 300,000 Nevadans in 2004 were not in the state during Reid's 1998 campaign. Some 436,000 Nevadans voted in 1998, when Reid faced Ensign; 830,000 would vote in November 2004, so about half of the voters (some 1998 voters died or dropped out) had never seen Reid's name on a November ballot. For Reid, the solution was to preclude serious opposition from GOP Rep. Jim Gibbons or one of Nevada's several Republican statewide officeholders by showing strong support from Las Vegas big hitters, who are unusually bipartisan and have been the motivating force in Nevada state politics. They supported the election of Democratic Gov. Bob Miller in 1990 but also that of Republican Gov. Guinn in 1998. Reid got early support from Guinn, former Reagan appointee Sig Rogich and gambling executives Terry Lanni and Mike Ensign. The Republican nominee, Richard Ziser, an evangelical Christian who led the drive to ban same-sex marriages on the 2000 and 2002 ballots, got little financial support in Nevada or from national Republicans. Reid won 61%-35%, carrying Las Vegas' Clark County 65%-31% and Reno's Washoe County 58%-38%.

As the parties looked ahead to the 2010 election, many Republicans expressed hope of toppling Reid in the same way that Daschle was defeated in 2004 at the pinnacle of his power. Reid and his supporters dismiss any parallel, pointing out that, in contrast to Daschle's situation in South Dakota, Reid has rebuilt and invigorated the Democratic Party in Nevada. Reid makes regular visits back home, and there was little evidence that Nevada Republicans would produce the sort of threat to Reid that Republican John Thune posed to Daschle. Still, with Reid having to reintroduce himself to new Nevadans every six years, he could become a target in 2010.

Junior Senator

John Ensign (R)

Elected 2000, term expires 2012, 2nd term; b. March 25, 1958, Roseville, CA; home, Las Vegas; Attended UNLV; OR St. U., B.S. 1981; CO St. U., D.V.M. 1985; Christian; married (Darlene); 3 children.

Elected Office: U.S. House of Reps. 1994–98.

Professional Career: Veterinarian, 1987–93; Gen. mgr., Gold Strike Hotel, 1991–93.

DC Office: 119 RSOB, 20510, 202-224-6244; Fax: 202-228-2193; Web site: ensign.senate.gov.

State Offices: Carson City, 775-885-9111; Las Vegas, 702-388-6605; Reno, 775-686-5770.

Committees: *Budget* (7th of 10 R). *Commerce, Science & Transportation* (3rd of 11 R): Aviation Operations, Safety & Security; Communications, Technology & the Internet (RMM); Competitiveness, Innovation & Export Promotion; Science & Space; Surface Transportation & Merchant Marine Infrastructure, Safety & Security. *Finance* (8th of 10 R): Health Care; Social Security, Pensions & Family Policy; Taxation, IRS Oversight & Long-Term Growth. *Homeland Security & Governmental Affairs* (5th of 6 R): Federal Financial Management, Government Information, Federal Services & International Security; Investigations (Permanent); State, Local & Private Sector Preparedness & Integration (RMM). *Rules & Administration* (7th of 8 R).

Group Ratings

	ADA	ACLU	AFS	LCV	ITIC	NTU	COC	ACU	CFG	FRC
2008	0	14	0	18	100	74	88	92	58	100
2007	0	—	0	33	—	86	56	91	90	—

National Journal Ratings

	2007 LIB — 2007 CONS		2008 LIB — 2008 CONS	
Economic	11%	— 88%	0%	— 96%
Social	9%	— 87%	0%	— 79%
Foreign	21%	— 73%	0%	— 84%
Composite	16%	— 85%	7%	— 93%

Key Votes of the 110th Congress

1. Raise CAFE standards	Y	5. Make English official language	Y	9. Withdraw troops 3/08	N
2. Expand SCHIP	N	6. Path to citizenship	N	10. Iran guard is terrorist group	Y
3. Cap greenhouse gases	N	7. Fetus is unborn child	Y	11. Increase missile defense $	Y
4. Bail out financial markets	Y	8. Prosecute hate crimes	N	12. Overhaul FISA	Y

Election Results

2006 general	John Ensign (R)	322,501	(55%)	($4,456,881)
	Jack Carter (D)	238,796	(41%)	($2,264,708)
2006 primary	John Ensign (R)	127,023	(90%)	
	None of these candidates	6,754	(5%)	
	Edward Hamilton (R)	6,649	(5%)	

Prior Winning Percentages: 2000 (55%); 1996 House (50%); 1994 House (48%)

Republican John Ensign was elected to the Senate in 2000, in his second try for the office. Ensign grew up in northern Nevada and moved to Las Vegas at age 6. For a time his mother had a low-level job at a Reno casino, supporting three children with no help from her ex-husband. Then she married Mike Ensign, who became a top executive at Circus Circus and was chairman of the Mandalay Resort Group until 2005. John Ensign graduated from Oregon State in 1981 and from veterinary school at Colorado State in 1985. While in college, he became a born-again Christian. He built a successful veterinary practice in Las Vegas, with the first 24-hour clinic, and also got involved in civic affairs. At his wife's suggestion, he became active in Promise Keepers, an evangelical ministry for men. Disturbed at cultural trends in national life, they decided he would run for the House in 1994, against 1st District Democratic Rep. James Bilbray. This was the more Democratic of Nevada's then two House seats, and Bilbray was an eight-year incumbent. But 1994 was also a Republican year, and with the help of his stepfather's connections in the gambling industry, he was able to raise substantial funds. On election night, Bilbray claimed victory, but when the totals came in, Ensign had won by 1,436 votes. In the House, Ensign compiled a generally conservative voting record and got a seat on the influential Ways and Means Committee. In the summer of 1996, he and GOP colleague Dave Camp of Michigan persuaded Speaker Newt Gingrich to separate the welfare and Medicaid issues and present President Clinton with a welfare bill, which the president signed. Ensign can reasonably claim to be one of the fathers of the 1996 Welfare Reform Act. He was re-elected in 1996, 50%-44%.

Ensign decided to run against Democratic Sen. Harry Reid in 1998. This was a hard-fought, high-spending race, targeted by both national parties and engaged with intensity by the candidates. Reid spent $5 million and Ensign $3.5 million. Reid attacked Ensign harshly as an "extremist" who would gut Social Security and environmental regulation. "You send Ensign to the Senate, you send nuclear waste to Nevada," he said. The Election Night tally showed Reid ahead by 459 votes. Ensign called for a recount, and it turned out that the Washoe County ballots had been misprinted, preventing some from being read by machines. The hand count there took weeks, and Ensign finally conceded on December 9, with Reid ahead by 428 votes.

Just two months later, in February 1999, Democratic Sen. Richard Bryan announced that he would not run for re-election in 2000. Ensign announced his candidacy the next day. Democrats tried to enlist their strongest candidate, Bob Miller, who had just completed eight years as governor, but he preferred to remain in the private sector in Las Vegas. Then Attorney General Frankie Sue Del Papa launched her candidacy. An April poll showed Ensign with a narrow 45%-40% lead, but he was much further ahead in money: $1.1 million to $250,000. In September, Del Papa abruptly withdrew from the race, citing difficulties in fundraising; her bad relations with Las Vegas unions did not help. Democratic efforts to recruit Brian Greenspun, owner of the *Las Vegas Sun*, failed. That left the Democratic banner in the hands of Ed Bernstein, a wealthy personal injury lawyer. Bernstein put in $1.1 million of his own money and emphasized the high cost of prescription drugs and abortion rights. The candidates engaged in six debates. Naturally both candidates promised to fight nuclear waste storage in Nevada, and Ensign was careful to return a contribution from a Yucca Mountain contractor. Ensign won, 55%-40%, carrying Las Vegas and Clark County 51%-45%, Reno and Washoe County 58%-35%, and the cow counties 68%-27%.

Ensign and Reid, bitter rivals in 1998, quickly became cooperative colleagues. In December 2000, they announced that their first priority was blocking the move by Arizona Sen. John McCain and Kansas Sen. Sam Brownback to prohibit betting on college and amateur sports—they argued that sports books are well regulated by Nevada authorities. Ensign sponsored a bill to outlaw the slaughter of horses in the U.S. for human consumption in other countries, and in 2005, after Hurricane Katrina hit the Gulf Coast, he traveled to Louisiana to review federal efforts at rescuing pets displaced by the storm. In 2004, Ensign persuaded Republican Budget Chairman Don Nickles to delete from the 2004 budget resolution a proposal requiring casinos to withhold winnings from gamblers behind on child support payments.

In 2006, Ensign won Senate passage, by a 65-34 vote, of a bill making it a federal crime to help minors cross state lines to avoid parental-notification laws on abortion. Democrats said the vote was engineered to motivate social conservatives for the midterm elections, but Ensign said the bill represented "reasonable restrictions" on abortion that a majority could accept. Democrat Richard Durbin of Illinois blocked the Senate from negotiating a final bill with the House. On foreign policy issues, Ensign has opposed limits on enemy-interrogation methods that fall short of torture, including sleep deprivation and "waterboarding," in which the detainee has water poured over his or her face to simulate drowning. He moved through Congress an amendment that permits the president to authorize the military to use tear gas against an enemy, as domestic police departments can do to control a riot. Opponents argued the Chemical Weapons Convention prohibits the use of riot-control agents in war.

A prime federal issue for Nevada is the proposed nuclear-waste repository in Yucca Mountain, 90 miles northwest of Las Vegas. Creation of a temporary storage site in Yucca Mountain was prevented during the Clinton era by President Clinton's promise to veto it—probably the reason he carried Republican-leaning Nevada twice by narrow margins. In 2002, President Bush designated Yucca Mountain as the permanent site. The law provided for a veto by the governor, which could be overridden by majorities in both houses of Congress. In April 2002, Gov. Kenny Guinn issued his veto. In May 2002, the House cast a large majority for creating the site at Yucca Mountain. In the Senate, Reid lobbied furiously for votes among Democrats, most of whom had stood with him before on the issue, while Ensign lobbied desperately for Republican votes, a difficult task in light of the Bush administration's desire to go forward with Yucca Mountain. Reid got 35 Democrats and independent James Jeffords of Vermont to vote his way. Ensign could get only two other Republicans, so the site was approved 60-39. But the fight was not over. Lawsuits had been filed against the plan, and the Energy Department had to get approval from the Nuclear Regulatory Commission, which threatened to consume many years. Meanwhile, Ensign has worked with Reid to block funding of a Yucca Mountain repository.

Ensign's re-election in 2006 was not seriously contested, but Democratic nominee Jack Carter, the eldest son of former President Carter, attracted a level of national interest not usually afforded a long-shot candidate. An investment consultant who moved into the state in 2002, Carter benefited from his father's famous name and campaign appearances, as well as a national donor base, but that was about all. Jimmy Carter had lost Nevada in both 1976 and 1980, the latter election by 36 points. At the urging of Reid, Las Vegas Mayor Oscar Goodman considered challenging Ensign but declined. When Ensign launched his campaign in March, he commended Bush for fighting the war on terrorism. He called for adding 10,000 new Border Patrol agents and cutting taxes and government spending. Ensign criticized Carter as a carpetbagger and ran warm-and-fuzzy television ads of himself as a veterinarian, stethoscope in hand, holding a small dog. Carter was forced off the campaign trail for two weeks in September by a severe bout of colitis. Back on his feet, he assailed Ensign for supporting a failed strategy in Iraq and the Bush agenda. He largely ignored such critical state issues as Yucca Mountain and water resources, and his admitted youthful use of marijuana, an admission that got him discharged from the Navy 36 years earlier. During an October debate, Ensign noted his good working relationship with Reid, by then the powerful minority leader of the Senate, asserting that it had brought the state billions of dollars in federal help. Ensign won re-election, 55%-41%.

On the Finance Committee in the 110th Congress (2007–08), Ensign opposed Democratic plans to raise taxes on U.S. corporations operating overseas. He also got into a showdown with the solar industry, which has a growing presence in Nevada, when he opposed plans to raise other business taxes to pay for tax breaks for solar energy. His stance put Ensign in an awkward position with Reid, an enthusiastic backer of the solar industry and its legislative agenda.

Ensign's desire for a bipartisanship working relationship with Reid was also sorely tested in the 110th Congress (2007–08), when Ensign became chairman of the National Republican Senatorial Committee, the party's political arm charged with electing Republicans to the Senate. Reid by then was majority leader, the most powerful position in the Senate, and that role gave him a strong hand in trying to expand the Democrats' majority. Republicans began the 2008 election cycle with the challenge of defending 21 Senate seats, while Democrats had just 12 senators up for re-election. Ensign's challenge became more onerous when five Republican senators announced their retirement. Of those seats, the one in Virginia quickly became a likely Democratic pickup, and Democrats established themselves as front-runners in Colorado and New Mexico. Ensign and the Republicans also were seriously tested by vigorous Democratic challenges to incumbents in New Hampshire, Minnesota, Oregon, and Alaska. "There are no easy races this year," Ensign said in May 2008. "There are just none." He also was outgunned by Democrats in fundraising, a critical measure of success for a NRSC chairman. Ensign raised $93 million in the two-year election cycle, compared with $156 million collected by Sen. Charles Schumer of New York, the chairman of the corresponding Democratic political committee. At one point, Ensign predicted it would be a "terrific night" if Republicans lost only three seats in November. But in the end, in a terrible political climate for Republicans, the party ended up losing eight seats and ceding enormous power to the Democrats, who ultimately expanded their Senate majority to 60-40.

After his leadership at the NRSC, Ensign was chosen by his peers to lead the Republican Policy Committee, giving him an important role in developing party positions. He also made a visit to Iowa to test the water for a possible presidential run in 2012. But in June 2009, his star dimmed considerably when he publicly admitted to having an extramarital affair with the wife of his top Senate aide. The day after his admission, Ensign resigned his leadership post but said he remained committed to remaining in the Senate. In July 2009, Ensign admitted that his parents had paid the woman $96,000, but said the money was a gift and not intended to buy her silence.

FIRST DISTRICT

Shelley Berkley (D)

Elected 1998, 6th term; b. Jan. 20, 1951, South Fallsburg, NY; home, Las Vegas; UNLV, B.A. 1972; U. of San Diego, J.D. 1976; Jewish; married (Larry Lehrner); 4 children.

Elected Office: NV Assembly, 1982–84; Regent, U. Commun. Col. System of NV, 1990–98.

Professional Career: Cnsl., SW Gas Corp., 1977–82; VP, Sands Hotel, 1989–98; Chair, NV Hotel & Motel Assn., 1994.

DC Office: 405 CHOB, 20515, 202-225-5965; Fax: 202-225-3119; Web site: berkley.house.gov.

State Offices: Las Vegas, 702-220-9823.

Committees: *Foreign Affairs* (20th of 28 D): Europe; Middle East & South Asia. *Ways & Means* (16th of 26 D): Health; Income Security & Family Support.

Group Ratings

	ADA	ACLU	AFS	LCV	ITIC	NTU	COC	ACU	CFG	FRC
2008	85	82	100	92	86	12	67	4	4	5
2007	85	—	100	75	—	6	58	8	6	—

National Journal Ratings

	2007 LIB — 2007 CONS		2008 LIB — 2008 CONS	
Economic	62%	— 37%	63%	— 37%
Social	72%	— 28%	59%	— 41%
Foreign	51%	— 49%	55%	— 43%
Composite	62%	— 38%	59%	— 41%

Key Votes of the 110th Congress

1. Increase minimum wage	Y	5. Share immigration data	N	9. Withdraw troops 8/08	Y
2. Expand SCHIP	Y	6. Foreign aid abortion ban	N	10. No operations in Iran	N
3. Raise CAFE standards	Y	7. Ban gay bias in workplace	Y	11. Free trade with Peru	N
4. Bail out financial markets	Y	8. Repeal D.C. gun law	N	12. Overhaul FISA	Y

Election Results

2008 general	Shelley Berkley (D)	154,860	(68%)	($1,985,063)
	Kenneth Wegner (R)	64,837	(28%)	($15,794)
	Caren Alexander (AMI)	4,697	(2%)	
2008 primary	Shelley Berkley (D)	19,444	(90%)	
	John Budetich (D)	2,222	(10%)	

Prior Winning Percentages: 2006 (65%); 2004 (66%); 2002 (54%); 2000 (52%); 1998 (49%)

Population		Race/Ethnicity		Work	
Pop. 2007:	791,733	White:	44.4%	Private:	86.3%
Change since 2000:	Up 18.9%	Black:	12.5%	Government:	9.7%
Urban:	99.9%	Hispanic:	34.2%	Self-employed:	3.9%
Rural:	0.1%	Asian:	5.3%	Blue collar:	25.8%
Area size:	177 sq. mi.	Native Am.:	0.6%	White collar:	46.0%
		Hawaiian:	0.4%	Khaki collar:	0.4%
Age		Two+ races:	2.3%	Other:	27.9%
Median age:	33.5 yrs.			Median income:	$48,569
More than 65 yrs:	9.2%	*Ancestry*		Median home value:	$275,100
Less than 18 yrs:	28.0%	German:	9.3%	Poverty:	13.4%
		Irish:	7.1%		
Education		English:	5.4%	**Military Veterans**	
H.S. grad:	77.4%			% of Pop:	11.3%
College grad:	17.0%				
Grad degree:	5.9%				

Las Vegas, that garish and improbable city, had a fittingly colorful beginning. It began as a Paiute Indian settlement that in the late 1700s served as a watering stop for Spanish priests making the 1,200-mile trek between New Mexico and California. By the 1800s, the Old Spanish Trail, as it came to be known, was used by horse and mule smugglers, by white explorers like John Fremont and by Mormon emigrants heading west. Las Vegas was still a small crossroads when Nevada, its mining industry a

2008 Presidential Vote
Obama (D) 158,367   (64%)
McCain (R)............................85,193   (34%)

2004 Presidential Vote
Kerry (D)................................121,453   (57%)
Bush (R) 89,800   (41%)

Cook Partisan Voting Index: D + 10

shambles, legalized gambling in the 1930s. The *WPA Guide* to Nevada, published in 1940, when the city had 10,000 people, describes a prim Las Vegas: "Relatively little emphasis is placed on the gambling clubs and divorce facilities—though they are attractions to many visitors—and much effort is being made to build up cultural attractions. No cheap and easily parodied slogans have been adopted to publicize the city, no attempt has been made to introduce pseudo-romantic architectural themes, or to give an artificial glamour or gaiety."

All that changed big-time after World War II, when gangster Bugsy Siegel built the Flamingo hotel and casino on what became the Strip south of the city limits. Pseudo-romantic architectural themes became the order of the day (flamingos are found in the waters of Florida, not in the deserts of Nevada), and one casino followed another. Organized crime provided much of the money and muscle for Las Vegas, and investment capital came from Teamsters pension funds. In the late 1960s, eccentric billionaire Howard Hughes moved into the Desert Inn, bought most of the casinos and hired Mormons to run them. After Hughes abruptly left town, most of his hotels eventually were torn down, and other operators built casinos like Caesars Palace and Circus Circus, the Mirage and Excalibur, the lavish Bellagio and Venetian. In the 1970s, the casinos were the haven of flashy high rollers, of Frank Sinatra and girl shows. In the 1990s, diversification became the buzz. Las Vegas began to produce more family-oriented entertainment, shopping, and even high art, with the Bellagio's museum-quality art collection on view. Las Vegas also built the biggest convention center in the country. But recent promotions have sounded a naughtier theme: "What happens in Vegas stays in Vegas." The scent of the underworld has not entirely disappeared. The flashy Oscar Goldman, a former mob lawyer, was elected mayor and actively promoted the city. Today, it remains one of the great leisure destinations in the world. Since the 1960s, Las Vegas has grown faster than any other metropolitan area in the nation. At least 5,000 people move here each month, though roughly half that number depart. Because of the city's dependence on leisure-time spending, the economic crisis hit hard here in 2008, with gambling down, joblessness up and many new homes unsold. The resorts began to aggressively market to foreigners.

The 1st Congressional District of Nevada consists of the inner core of Las Vegas that visitors are most likely to see. They cross into it as soon as they drive their rental cars out of the lot at McCarran International Airport. On the three-mile Strip you can find 14 of the nation's 15 largest hotels, each with thousands of rooms. North of Sahara Avenue, Las Vegas Boulevard enters the city of Las Vegas, the older and less glamorous part of town. The district continues north for another dozen miles through the housing developments and scrubland that follow the U.S. 95 and Interstate 15 diagonals, to include the sizable Hispanic and black communities of North Las Vegas. The 1st District is also home to the University of Nevada-Las Vegas and includes the Clark County Government Center, a circular sandstone complex whose beautiful Indian-inspired architecture is a testament to the power of the gambling dollar. The district has a high percentage of union members and poverty levels below the national average. More than 80,000 Jewish Americans live in the area, supporting 18 synagogues and a kosher supermarket. Overall, this is a safely Democratic district.

The congresswoman from the 1st District is Shelley Berkley, a Democrat elected in 1998. Berkley was born on the Lower East Side of New York and moved to Las Vegas as a child. "I am not a politician who happens to be Jewish. I am a Jew who happens to be in politics," she likes to say. Her parents emigrated from Eastern Europe after World War II. Her mother, an artist, was held in Auschwitz and painted watercolors of Gypsies and other prisoners for Nazi doctor Josef Mengele. Her work saved her from extermination, and she later sought the return of her portraits, which were displayed at the Auschwitz museum in Poland. Berkley's father worked at the Sands and rose to maitre d'. In college, Berkley waited tables and was a keno runner. She was the student body president at the University of Nevada, then went to law school. She chaired the Nevada Hotel and Motel Association, was government and legal-affairs vice president at the Sands and the in-house counsel at Southwest Gas. She was elected to one term in the state House.

After 1st District Rep. John Ensign, a Republican, decided to run against Democratic Sen. Harry Reid in the 1998 election, Berkley made a bid for the House seat. Brassy and effusive, she lacked a serious Republican opponent for several weeks and seemed headed for an easy election. But 15 minutes before the filing deadline, Judge Donald Chairez resigned his post to run for the seat. Then came a bombshell that threatened to unravel her campaign. The *Las Vegas Review-Journal* reported the existence of taped 1997 telephone conversations and of a memo in which Berkley seemed to advise Sands owner Sheldon Adelson to make campaign contributions to local judges and to grant concessions to Clark County commissioners as a way of improving chances for approval of his Venetian hotel. Berkley publicly apologized. The Clark County district attorney found no cause for prosecution. But Chairez made his slogan "Fairness, not favors." With strong support from the gambling industry, Berkley outspent Chairez $1.2 million to $554,000 and won only narrowly, 49%-46%.

In the House, Berkley's voting record has been moderate, especially on foreign issues. She keeps a close watch on the interests of the gambling industry. She led opposition in the House to a proposal by the National Collegiate Athletic Association to bar Nevada casinos from accepting bets on college sports. When Democrats took majority control in the 110th Congress (2007–08), she won a seat on the powerful House Ways and Means Committee, where she has fought proposals to tax Internet gambling, saying those decisions should be left to the states.

With other Nevada officials, she fought the plan to store nuclear waste at Yucca Mountain, but managed to win only 80 House votes on an amendment in June 2007 to stop funding for the site. In 2006, Berkley authored a bill that would repeal subsidies and tax breaks for the nuclear power and oil and gas industries, in favor of incentives for renewable energy.

She has shown a strong interest in Middle East affairs and is an advocate for Israel. She forcefully backed President Bush's use of force in Iraq in 2002 and 2003, but later said that she was misled by phony intelligence and called for Defense Secretary Donald Rumsfeld's resignation. In April 2007, she criticized Democratic Speaker Nancy Pelosi for leading a House delegation to Syria. A strong gay-rights supporter, Berkley favors repeal of the Pentagon's "don't ask, don't tell" policy.

Berkley initially faced tough re-election contests. In 2000, Republican state Sen. Jon Porter revived the 1998 Sands hotel controversy, but Berkley won 52%-44%. Porter then ran and won in the state's newly created 3rd District in 2002. That year, Berkley faced Las Vegas City Council member Lynette Boggs-McDonald, a former Miss Oregon and former Democrat who hoped to become the first Republican black woman elected to the House. But redistricting had removed many suburban precincts favorable to the GOP, and Berkley won with 54%. Since then, she has faced only weak opposition.

SECOND DISTRICT

Dean Heller (R)

Elected 2006, 2nd term; b. May 10, 1959, Castro Valley, CA; home, Carson City; U. of S. CA, B.A. 1985; Mormon; married (Lynne); 4 children.

Elected Office: NV Assembly, 1990–94, NV sec. of state, 1994–2006.

Professional Career: Stockbroker, 1983–88; Chief deputy state treas., 1988–90; Public funds rep., Bank of America, 1990–95.

DC Office: 125 CHOB, 20515, 202-225-6155; Fax: 202-225-5679; Web site: heller.house.gov.

State Offices: Elko, 775-777-7920; Las Vegas, 702-255-1651; Reno, 775-686-5760.

Committees: *Ways & Means* (14th of 15 R): Income Security & Family Support; Select Revenue Measures.

Group Ratings

	ADA	ACLU	AFS	LCV	ITIC	NTU	COC	ACU	CFG	FRC
2008	25	18	29	23	71	67	89	80	71	88
2007	15	—	9	15	—	78	80	96	92	—

National Journal Ratings

	2007 LIB	—	2007 CONS	2008 LIB	—	2008 CONS
Economic	27%	—	72%	32%	—	68%
Social	21%	—	75%	42%	—	57%
Foreign	0%	—	72%	8%	—	89%
Composite	22%	—	79%	28%	—	72%

Key Votes of the 110th Congress

1. Increase minimum wage	N	5. Share immigration data	Y	9. Withdraw troops 8/08	N
2. Expand SCHIP	N	6. Foreign aid abortion ban	Y	10. No operations in Iran	N
3. Raise CAFE standards	N	7. Ban gay bias in workplace	N	11. Free trade with Peru	Y
4. Bail out financial markets	N	8. Repeal D.C. gun law	Y	12. Overhaul FISA	Y

Election Results

2008 general	Dean Heller (R)	170,771	(52%)	($1,605,810)
	Jill Derby (D)	136,548	(41%)	($1,131,582)
	John Everhart (AMI)	11,179	(3%)	
2008 primary	Dean Heller (R)	43,112	(86%)	
	James Smack (R)	7,009	(14%)	

Prior Winning Percentages: 2006 (50%)

Population		Race/Ethnicity		Work	
Pop. 2007:	786,047	White:	70.6%	Private:	77.9%
Change since 2000:	Up 18.0%	Black:	2.5%	Government:	15.8%
Urban:	78.5%	Hispanic:	19.1%	Self-employed:	6.1%
Rural:	21.5%	Asian:	3.4%	Blue collar:	26.6%
Area size:	105,635 sq. mi.	Native Am.:	2.0%	White collar:	52.7%
Age		Hawaiian:	0.3%	Khaki collar:	0.3%
Median age:	37.0 yrs.	Two+ races:	2.0%	Other:	20.4%
More than 65 yrs:	12.6%	*Ancestry*		Median income:	$52,324
Less than 18 yrs:	24.9%	German:	13.6%	Median home value:	$286,200
Education		English:	11.5%	Poverty:	11.1%
H.S. grad:	85.0%	Irish:	10.0%	**Military Veterans**	
College grad:	21.8%			% of Pop:	14.1%
Grad degree:	7.4%				

Outside of metro Las Vegas, huge, empty, and mountainous Nevada has only one sizable population center, a cluster of small cities and towns near the border with California: the casino cities of Reno and Sparks, the small capital of Carson City, the restored Comstock Lode boomtown of Virginia City and the resort areas that surround (and endanger) the deep, impossibly blue waters of Lake Tahoe. Reno is so remote from Las Vegas that the only practical way to get there is by air. It takes more than

2008 Presidential Vote
McCain (R)	167,920	(49%)
Obama (D)	167,831	(49%)

2004 Presidential Vote
Bush (R)	172,422	(57%)
Kerry (D)	123,490	(41%)

Cook Partisan Voting Index: R+5

nine hours to drive, eight of which are on two-lane highways that pass through just a handful of towns, none bigger than 7,000 people. Ghost towns that once bustled with miners dot the parched, sand-swept deserts of Nevada. In some places, these lands remain distinctly rutted from the wagon trains that crossed them more than 100 years ago. Today, Nevada's small towns survive on mining, ranching and, in some cases, servicing the human sins of greed and lust: It is generally in the small counties that you find Nevada's legal brothels. Immigrant Basque shepherds once tended their flocks in remote portions of northern Nevada and made carvings on aspen trees to pass the time. Today, Basque festivals, social clubs, and restaurants can be found in Winnemucca, Ely and Elko, while Reno is home to the national sheepherder's monument and the nation's only Basque Studies Department, at the University of Nevada-Reno.

The military has vast holdings in the Nevada interior: the Fallon Naval Air Station, home to the Navy Fighter Weapons "Top Gun" School, and the 3.1 million-acre Nellis Air Force Gunnery Range. Also found there is the U.S. Energy Department's Nevada Test Site, where more than 800 underground tests of nuclear weapons were held, as well as 100 aboveground tests, before 1962. These explosions have left the Rhode Island-sized facility pockmarked with unstable "subsidence craters" as far as the eye can see.

Many places in Nevada are dependent on other federal government programs: the Newlands Irrigation Project near Fallon was among the first of its kind, and Nevada's gold-mining operations, booming since 2000, do not have to pay royalties to the federal government thanks to the Mining Act of 1872. Economic diversification is limited to budding solar- and wind-energy enterprises, bio-agriculture and high-precision technologies. Some 87% of the land in Nevada is owned by the federal government—a constant source of tension with local officials, ranchers, loggers and miners, whose pursuits, frequently solitary and often ornery, shaped Nevada's culture from its earliest days. On the desolate frontier, speculation runs wild: Art Bell used to broadcast his popular radio show about the paranormal, aliens and other unexplained phenomena from tiny Pahrump, while the government's top-secret aviation experiments at places like Area 51 on the Nellis Gunnery Range have stoked UFO lore to the point that adjoining Route 375 was rededicated as the Extraterrestrial Highway in 1996. Anti-establishment views also flourish here in more mainstream ways. Nevada residents have long opposed a nuclear-waste repository 1,000 feet beneath Yucca Mountain, 90 miles northwest of Las Vegas. Congress finally approved the project in 2002, with a scheduled opening of 2012, but stubborn opponents continue their battle.

The 2nd Congressional District of Nevada takes in all of this and the vast majority of Nevada's land area. Excluding single-member states, this is the largest congressional district in the nation. After the 2000 census results came in, two districts were created entirely within Clark County, which had 69% of the state's population; the 2nd consisted of all the other counties, plus small slices of Clark County. About one-half of the district's population is in Washoe County, which contains Reno and Sparks. Half a century ago, Reno was Nevada's largest city. "The Biggest Little City in the World," reads the neon sign across downtown Virginia Street. It has grown steadily, but vastly less than Las Vegas, which now overshadows it. Reno is the state's third-largest city behind Henderson. Its casinos were hit hard by competition from Indian casinos in California, and the growth trend gravitates toward Lake Tahoe, just to the west. People here are from all over: the Tahoe communities of Stateline, Zephyr Cove, and Incline Village are among the U.S. cities with the smallest percentage of residents born in the state. A new city, Coyote Springs, is being built about 60 miles north of Las Vegas, with plans for 159,000 homes and its own groundwater resources. Historically, Reno has been Republican and Las Vegas Democratic. In the 1990s, when the federal government was widely viewed as unfriendly to mining, grazing and timber interests, the cow counties, as the counties outside Reno and Las Vegas are called, became even more Republican. All that has made the 2nd District heavily Republican.

The congressman from the 2nd District is Dean Heller, a Republican elected in 2006. Heller was a political fixture in Carson City long before he ran for the House seat, left vacant when five-term Republican Jim Gibbons ran for governor. Heller got his first taste of politics during childhood when his newspaper route included deliveries at the state Capitol. He graduated from the University of Southern California in 1985 with a degree in business administration, then worked as a stockbroker and traded on the Pacific Stock Exchange. In 1990, he won the first of two terms in the Nevada House, and in 1994, he was elected to the first of three terms as Nevada secretary of state. During his 12-year tenure, Heller streamlined the corporation registration process, and revenues increased tenfold. He has supported increased public access to government records and greater transparency in the state campaign finance system. Nevada was seen as a national model in 2004, when it became the first state to create a paper trail for its electronic voting machines.

Heller faced competition for the Republican nomination from Assemblywoman Sharron Angle and former Assemblywoman Dawn Gibbons, the outgoing congressman's wife. Heller and Gibbons began with the strongest name recognition, but Gibbons' candidacy was underfunded and never took off. Angle, a Christian conservative, emerged as a serious primary rival after she picked up the endorsement and financial support of the deep-pocketed Club for Growth, a national anti-tax group. Angle ran as the race's true conservative, while Heller campaigned on his record in state office and called for cuts in taxes and government spending. Heller won 36% of the vote, giving him a 421-vote victory over Angle, who got 35%. Gibbons finished third with 25%. Rather than request a recount, Angle filed a lawsuit seeking a new election because some polling locations in Washoe County had opened late. A judge denied her request, and she conceded two weeks after the primary.

Heller entered the general election campaign with a depleted campaign treasury to face Democrat Jill Derby, an 18-year veteran of the Nevada Board of Regents. He ran the race as a referendum on President Bush and his policies, emphasizing his support for the Iraq war, for making Bush's tax cuts permanent and for creating private Social Security accounts for younger workers. While many Republican candidates elsewhere considered Bush a liability in 2006, the president stumped twice for Heller in the final weeks of the campaign. Bush's stops helped Heller rebuild his campaign reserves and motivate the traditionally Republican-leaning rural vote. Derby emphasized her rural roots, criticized Heller for his stance on the war and framed the election as a chance for voters to reject Republican control in Washington. In October, the Democratic Congressional Campaign Committee mounted a late attack on Heller, insinuating that federal drug investigators in 2005 had seized Heller's race car (he is a stock car racing enthusiast) in connection with a drug case involving Heller's friend Eddie Floyd, a former Reno talk-show host who was a convicted sex offender. Heller said he did not own the car, but had been helping Floyd's son build it.

The controversy wasn't enough to overcome the district's wide Republican voter-registration advantage. Heller defeated Derby 50%-45%.

In the House, Heller broke with conservatives on issues such as federal funding for embryonic-stem-cell research and the September 11 commission recommendations, and he got a seat on the Financial Services Committee. He supported nuclear energy on the condition that the radioactive waste would be stored where it is produced, not at Yucca Mountain. Heller also got into an unusual family squabble when he criticized the limited impact of the Republican takeover of the House led by Republican Newt Gingrich in 1994. "They came to Washington, and Washington changed them," he said, adding that he thought it was time for Republicans to clean house. This district has not elected a Democrat since it was created after the 1980 census. That didn't stop Derby and the Democrats from trying again in 2008. But Heller took a comfortable lead in early polls and won the rematch, 52% to 41%.

THIRD DISTRICT

Dina Titus (D)

Elected 2008, 1st term; b. May 23, 1950, Thomasville, GA; home, Las Vegas; Col. of William & Mary, B.A. 1970; U. of GA, M.A. 1973; FL St. U., Ph.D., 1976; Greek Orthodox; married (Tom Wright).

Elected Office: NV Senate, 1989–2008, Minority ldr., 1993–2008

Professional Career: N. TX St. U., Asst. prof., 1975–76; UNLV, Chmn., Dept. of Public Admin., 1979–1980, Asst. prof., 1977–1982, Assoc. prof., 1982–1990, Prof., 1990-present.

DC Office: 319 CHOB, 20515, 202-225-3252; Fax: 202-225-2185; Web site: titus.house.gov.

State Offices: Las Vegas, 702-387-4941.

Committees: *Education & Labor* (29th of 29 D): Early Childhood, Elementary & Secondary Education; Higher Education, Lifelong Learning & Competitiveness. *Homeland Security* (20th of 20 D): Emergency Communications, Preparedness & Response; Transportation Security & Infrastructure Protection. *Transportation & Infrastructure* (43rd of 44 D): Railroads, Pipelines & Hazardous Materials; Water Resources & Environment.

Group Ratings and Key Votes: Newly Elected

Election Results

2008 general	Dina Titus (D)	165,912	(47%)	($1,777,641)
	Jon Porter (R)	147,940	(42%)	($3,182,799)
	Jeffrey Reeves (I)	14,922	(4%)	
	Joseph Silvestri (Lib)	10,164	(3%)	
2008 primary	Dina Titus (D)	22,232	(85%)	
	Barry Michaels (D)	2,312	(9%)	

Population		Race/Ethnicity		Work	
Pop. 2007:	911,137	White:	61.4%	Private:	84.0%
Change since 2000:	Up 36.8%	Black:	6.4%	Government:	11.0%
Urban:	96.3%	Hispanic:	20.2%	Self-employed:	4.8%
Rural:	3.7%	Asian:	8.4%	Blue collar:	18.0%
Area size:	4,749 sq. mi.	Native Am.:	0.5%	White collar:	56.2%
		Hawaiian:	0.5%	Khaki collar:	0.2%
Age		Two+ races:	2.4%	Other:	25.7%
Median age:	36.5 yrs.	*Ancestry*		Median income:	$59,957
More than 65 yrs:	11.5%	German:	11.9%	Median home value:	$335,500
Less than 18 yrs:	24.6%	Irish:	9.2%	Poverty:	8.1%
Education		English:	8.0%		
H.S. grad:	86.9%			**Military Veterans**	
College grad:	23.3%			% of Pop:	13.0%
Grad degree:	7.6%				

Las Vegas, "The Meadows" in Spanish, began as a stop along the Old Spanish Trail trading route between Santa Fe and California in the 1830s. Water from artesian wells had created vast grasslands in the area and let traders replenish their supplies. In the early 20th century, Las Vegas was one of the termini of the Las Vegas & Tonopah Railroad, a link to Nevada's silver mines. Even at the end of the 1930s, when gambling was legalized in Nevada, it was still a town of less than 10,000. Then came decades of

2008 Presidential Vote		
Obama (D)	207,439	(55%)
McCain (R)	159,624	(43%)
2004 Presidential Vote		
Bush (R)	156,335	(50%)
Kerry (D)	152,150	(49%)
Cook Partisan Voting Index:	D + 2	

amazing growth, as Las Vegas became America's destination for gambling and topflight entertainment. From 2000 to 2008, the Las Vegas metro area grew by 36%, to 1.9 million, making it the seventh-fastest-growing metropolitan area in America. But given the fast pace of building in the Las Vegas metro area, it was particularly hard hit by the crisis in the credit markets, and the red-hot real estate market bottomed out. Clark County had one of the highest rates of pre-foreclosure filings in the nation in 2007, and the number of foreclosures increased in 2008. This is still frontier country, one of the few places in the nation with more men than women. Las Vegas has spread across the desert in every direction from the few blocks around Fremont Street that it occupied in the 1930s, and today it is an exuberant, undisciplined and chaotic city.

The 3rd Congressional District is a Y-shaped segment of Nevada's Clark County made up of most of the suburbs of Las Vegas. It includes the south end of the Las Vegas Strip and McCarran International Airport, and spreads west, northeast and south. It includes active retiree communities, blue-collar towns such as Blue Diamond that still have a rural flavor, and a variety of planned (and often gated) areas like Summerlin, where young families have come for job opportunities and retired baby boomers have purchased vacation homes. Southeast of Las Vegas, the district takes in two additional population hubs: Henderson, ranked third in the nation in per capita online commercial activity by the auction site eBay, and Boulder City, originally built for federal workers at Hoover Dam. (Under an old agreement with the federal government, Boulder City is the only place in Nevada where gambling is prohibited.) The 3rd also includes the Nevada halves of Lake Mead and Lake Mohave on the Arizona border, and the state's southernmost tip, where Searchlight, the hometown of Senate Majority Leader Harry Reid, is found. The district was created after the 2000 census to have an equal number of registered Democrats and registered Republicans. Clark County historically was the most Democratic part of Nevada, but newcomers in the 1990s tilted Republican. The district gave small pluralities to Al Gore in 2000 and George W. Bush in 2004. Democrats gained a 40,000-person advantage in registered voters before the 2008 election, and Democratic nominee Barack Obama carried the district with 55% of the vote.

The new congresswoman from the 3rd District is Dina Titus, a Democrat elected in 2008. Titus' life-long interest in politics can be traced to her upbringing in Tifton, Ga. Her grandfather owned a restaurant across from the courthouse, where community officials would gather to discuss politics. Her father ran for the City Council, and her Republican uncle served in the Georgia Legislature. Titus recalls attending a campaign rally for Hubert Humphrey, the Minnesota Democrat who ran unsuccessfully for president in 1968. She followed her interest in politics to William and Mary University, where she majored in political science. She then got a Ph.D. in government from Florida State University. In 1977, she began teaching at the University of Nevada-Las Vegas, where she has authored two books on atomic testing at the Nevada Test Site.

After a decade of teaching, Titus was ready for some practical experience. In 1988, she was elected to the Nevada Senate, and in 1993, she was elevated to minority leader. As a state legislator, Titus fought development that threatened the rural areas of the Las Vegas Valley. In 2003, she authored a bill to halt development around Red Rock Canyon. It passed both houses of the Legislature unanimously. She also advocated for the rights of disabled persons.

In 2006, Titus ran for governor. In the Democratic primary, she defeated Henderson Mayor Jim Gibson 54%-36%. In the general election, she faced GOP Rep. Jim Gibbons. The two candidates were a stark contrast: Gibbons was a native-born northern Nevadan who embodied the "cow counties" north of Las Vegas, whereas Titus was more representative of the Las Vegas metro area. Titus attacked Gibbons as an "inconsequential" Washington backbencher and offered a campaign platform of "five E's: economic development, education, energy, environment and ethics." Gibbons called Titus a tax-and-spend liberal—he referred to her as "Dina Taxes" —and ran ads on Reno television reminding voters of disparaging remarks she had made about northern Nevada years before. Gibbons heavily outspent Titus and won, despite suffering a rash of very negative publicity in the weeks prior to the election, including allegations from a casino cocktail waitress that he had propositioned and then threatened her. No charges were filed in the case. After the long and bruising campaign, Titus returned to the state Senate with the hope that the Democratic caucus could retake the majority in the next election, and she could cap her career by becoming majority leader.

By 2008, the Democratic Congressional Campaign Committee was ready to target Republican Jon Porter's seat. Porter had been elected to three consecutive terms but by increasingly smaller margins.

Democratic Clark County prosecutor Robert Daskas contemplated taking on Porter, but opted out. The DCCC then recruited Titus, though she had said in 2007 she wasn't interested in running for the seat. After one legislative session, which gave her time to recuperate from her grueling gubernatorial campaign, she changed her mind.

Some Nevada politicos initially wrote Titus off, but the district's politics were volatile and ripe for change. Between the 2006 and 2008 elections, the district was feeling the effects of the high housing foreclosure rates, and by July 2008, Democrats held a distinct advantage in registered voters. Titus campaigned as a moderate and touted a renewable-energy plan to create jobs in Nevada. She claimed that in Congress, Porter had favored the financial interests of oil companies over those of ordinary citizens, and she tried to tie him to the unpopular Bush administration. Porter and the conservative group Freedom's Watch took a page from Gibbons' campaign and ran ads painting Titus as a politician who had a history of supporting higher taxes. Another Porter ad claimed Titus was guilty of double-dipping because she had simultaneously received a salary as a University of Nevada professor and as a state legislator. Titus, who had taken unpaid leaves of absence during legislative sessions, responded, "I hope Nevadans are as disgusted as my mother is by [Porter's] lies and distortions."

Porter outspent Titus $3 million to $1.8 million, but his financial advantage could not overcome the district's increasingly Democratic tilt. Titus won 47% to 42%. Over half of the registered voters in Clark County cast early ballots, and over half of those ballots were cast by registered Democrats. In an ironic twist, Democrats won control of the Nevada state Senate, but the woman who had once aspired to be majority leader was headed to Washington. She got seats on committees that oversee education and labor, homeland security and transportation and infrastructure.

★ NEW HAMPSHIRE ★

To be precise, New Hampshire has just 43 one-hundredths of 1% of the nation's population. Yet every four years, it is the epicenter of the political universe, the place where the contest for the American presidency is temporarily based, where every vote is avidly sought and where members of the national political press vie for access to candidates and for tables at the latest cycle's most fashionable bars and restaurants. New Hampshire has had impact far beyond its miniature size: It gave a huge boost to Republican Dwight Eisenhower's candidacy in 1952, it prompted the retirement of Democrat Lyndon Johnson in 1968, it launched Democrat Jimmy Carter in 1976, then Republican Ronald Reagan in 1980 and then Republican George H.W. Bush in 1988. The lever with which this small state has sometimes moved the political world is its first-in-the-nation presidential primary, given that status by Democratic rules writers in the 1970s and exploited by Republicans in the 1980s. Its disproportionate weight in presidential elections is even more impressive considering that its public policies are atypical of the nation and its political terrain is unusual if not eccentric. This is one of the few states that over the past half-century have had more registered Republicans than Democrats, and it was for many years the state with the most antipathy to taxes. Yet in the last dozen years, New Hampshire's ability to pick winners and losers has waned. The last three presidents have finished second in the New Hampshire primary. It gave conservative commentator Patrick Buchanan a surprising 37% of the vote in 1992 and a 27% victory in 1996, but he never did as well elsewhere and wound up leaving the Republican Party in 1999. It gave Republican John McCain a thumping victory over George W. Bush in 2000, but that proved to be a harbinger for the Northeast and not the rest of the country. It gave Democrat Hillary Rodham Clinton a surprise victory in 2008. New Hampshire played a key role in nominating Democrats Al Gore in 2000 and John Kerry in 2004, but both lost the general election. However, the big increase in turnout in the 2004 Democratic primary proved prescient, as New Hampshire has moved sharply toward the Democrats. Gov. John Lynch, a Democrat elected narrowly in 2004, was re-elected by wide margins in 2006 and 2008. In 2008, Democratic presidential nominee Barack Obama won a solid 54%-45% victory in a state that had voted 58%, 69% and 62% for Republican presidents in the 1980s, and Jeanne Shaheen became the first Democrat elected U.S. senator from New Hampshire since 1974.

New Hampshire has always been distinct. In a country that prides itself on its feistiness and freedom from outside direction, it has always been even feistier and more lightly fettered by authority. Before the Revolutionary War, New Hampshire was almost an outlaw colony, its great fortunes made by poachers in the king's forests and by smugglers avoiding taxes. It was the first colony with an independent government and was fighting the British before the Minutemen stood at Lexington and Concord. In this environment, 19th century entrepreneurs built textile mills along fast-flowing rivers. The Amoskeag Mills in Manchester, lining the Merrimack River for a mile, were once the largest cotton mills in the world, employing 17,000 people and producing enough cloth every two months to put a band around the world. Around the mills grew a city of red brick dormitories and three-family frame houses filled with immigrants from Canada, Ireland, Poland and Greece, set down amid villages of dirt roads and flinty Yankee farmers and mechanics. New Hampshire held to its traditions of local government and little external control, and for years its refusal to join most other states in enacting an income or sales tax, or to provide statewide guidance of schools and social services, seemed to doom it to continued backwardness.

Instead, low taxes proved to be New Hampshire's fortune. From the 1960s to the 1990s, New Hampshire had the fastest growth in the Northeast, attracting businesses from Massachusetts and other high-tax states. It became a location of choice for entrepreneurs and high-tech innovators, attracting an increasing number of people skeptical of government programs. From 1965 to 2000, Massachusetts grew from 5.5 million to 6.3 million, up 15%, while New Hampshire grew from 676,000 to 1.2 million, up 83%. The bedraggled New Hampshire of 50 years ago, of poor Yankee farmers and French Canadian mill hands, has largely disappeared, and in its place is one of the nation's most prosperous economic communities. The low taxes that spurred New Hampshire's growth would probably have been raised in the late 1960s or early 1970s, as they were in so many states at the time but for the far from gentle advocacy of Manchester's *Union Leader* newspaper and its owner, William Loeb. *The Union Leader* insisted that governors and legislators "take the pledge" to vote for no sales or income tax and, from 1970 to 1998, almost all did. The two who didn't were defeated. The result was that education and welfare remained local responsibilities. At the same time, New Hampshire boasted the highest SAT scores in the country and had the brainpower to participate fully in New England's high-tech boom. The old Amoskeag Mills were converted to offices, and once-grimy Manchester is now a high-tech center. Fidelity Investment, BAE Systems, Liberty Mutual and Timberland are big employers, and New Hampshire has one of the nation's highest growth rates in information-technology jobs.

This "Nouvelle Hampshire," as *Washington Post* writer Henry Allen dubbed it, has none of the architectural purity of Amoskeag. Its shopping centers and new subdivisions have a slapdash, half-built look, as if there were no time for details in the hurry to build. But it is also a state that claims to have the highest

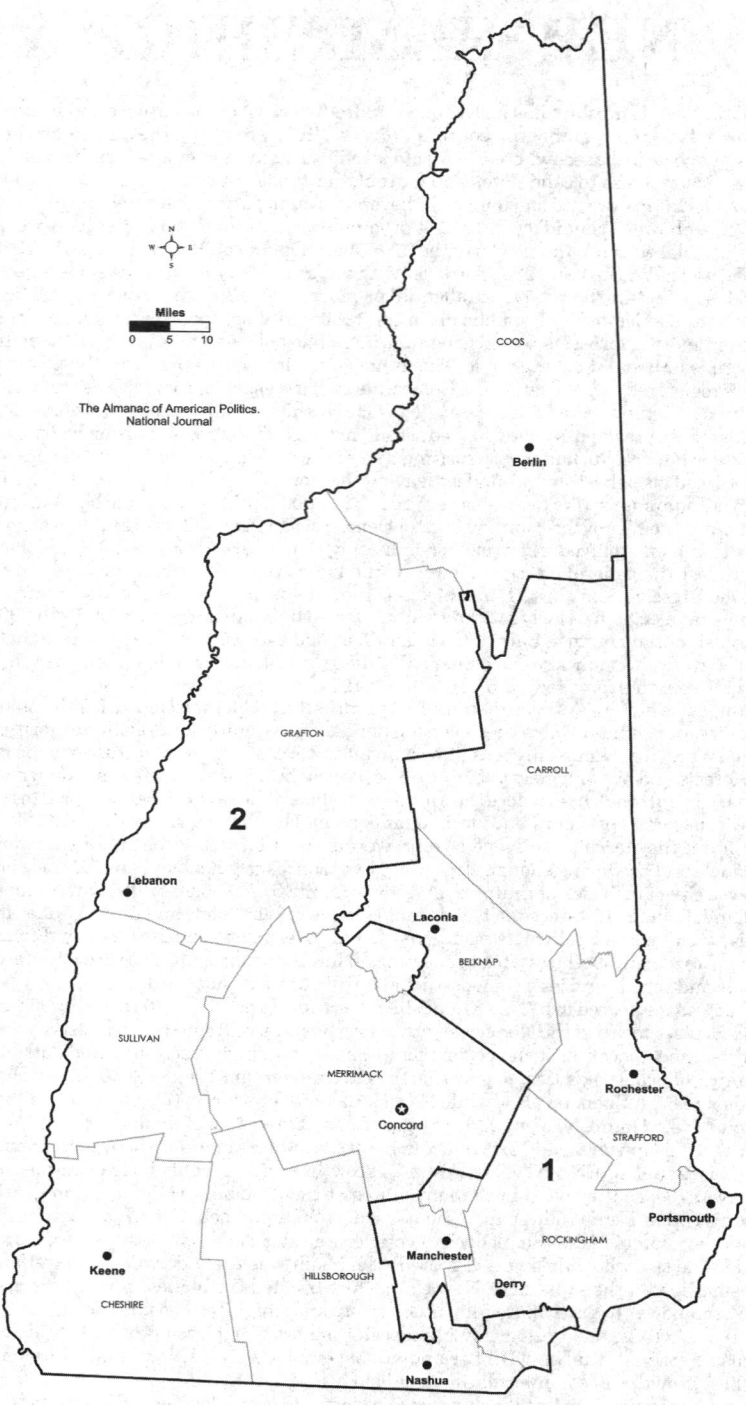

N
W E
S

Miles
0   5   10

COOS

Berlin

GRAFTON

2

CARROLL

Lebanon

Laconia

BELKNAP

SULLIVAN

Rochester

MERRIMACK

STRAFFORD

Concord

1

Portsmouth

Keene

Manchester

ROCKINGHAM

Derry

HILLSBOROUGH

CHESHIRE

Nashua

Congressional district boundaries were first effective for 2002.

proportion of high-tech jobs and the highest percentage of citizens with Internet access. It also is a big center for financial services, with giant mutual-fund campuses. New Hampshire has not been without its problems. The booming state priced itself out of the growth market. Its giddily high real estate prices in the late 1980s kept out the new workers its businesses needed to continue expanding. The recession of the early 1990s was harsher here than anywhere else. Thousands of jobs disappeared; real estate prices crashed so that ordinary people lost not only short-term income but also long-term wealth. By the mid-1990s, growth had returned, and during the national recession of 2001–02, New Hampshire's unemployment stayed low, real estate prices were rising and incomes ranked seventh in the nation. However, the state also has virtually no racial minorities; its population is 1% black, 2.4% Hispanic and 2% Asian. There has been less migration to the state in recent years, perhaps because Massachusetts and other states have lowered their taxes. The biggest in-migration since 2000 has been around Concord and the Lake Country, not along the Massachusetts border.

This helps to explain the state's political gyrations over the last dozen years. In 1992, in-migration had stopped, and New Hampshire was reacting angrily to recession and rapidly declining house prices. In that year's presidential contest, it held Republican George H.W. Bush to an unimpressive 53%-37% win over Buchanan, then voted for Democrat Bill Clinton over Bush in November. This turned out not to be a fluke. Like most states dominated by big metropolitan areas (most of New Hampshire gets Boston television), New Hampshire moved toward the Democrats in the 1990s, reassured by economic growth and comfortable with the Democrats' liberal stands on cultural issues. In 1996, New Hampshire voted 49%-39% for Clinton and elected Democrat Shaheen as governor, and Republican Sen. Bob Smith came so close to losing that he was proclaimed the loser by the networks on Election Night.

Then New Hampshire's tax regime came under attack. The state Supreme Court in December 1997 ruled the state's school-financing system unconstitutional because it left some districts with less taxable resources than others (at that time, the state provided only 10% of funding, far less than in the 49 other states) and gave the state an April 1999 deadline to come up with a new system. The result was a statewide property tax—not anybody's first choice, but it was what the Democratic governor and Senate and the Republican House could agree on. There were also increases in business, cigarette and property-sales taxes and a new tax on rental cars. By 2008, the state was providing nearly 39% of school funding. In 2002, Republican Clark Benson was elected governor over a Democrat who favored the new taxes. Two years later, Democrat Lynch took the anti-tax pledge and won the gubernatorial contest 51%-49%. Lynch kept his pledge even after the state Supreme Court once again rejected the Legislature's school-funding plan in September 2006. That November, Democrats won a smashing, across-the-board victory, and despite losing some seats in the state House in 2008, they continue to hold majorities in the state House and Senate and on the five-member Executive Council. Lynch continues to oppose a broad-based tax, and the Legislature has moved on to other matters, including voting to legalize same-sex marriage in 2009.

Population		Household Income		Work	
Pop. 2007:	1,310,254	Under $15k:	9.1%	Private:	78.5%
State rank:	41st of 50	$15k to $50k:	31.0%	Government:	13.2%
Change since 2000:	Up 6.0%	$50k to $100k:	36.2%	Self-employed:	8.1%
Urban:	57.5%	$100k to $150k:	20.0%	Unemployment (3-yr. average):	3.3%
Rural:	42.5%	Over $150k:	3.8%	Poverty:	7.7%
Native of state:	42.0%	Median income:	$61,459	Blue collar:	22.0%
Not a citizen:	2.9%	**Home Value**		White collar:	62.6%
Area size:	9,350 sq. mi.	Under $100k:	8.8%	Khaki collar:	0.1%
Most populous cities		$100k to $300k:	53.4%	Other:	15.2%
1. Manchester	109,777	$300k to $500k:	29.3%	**Age**	
2. Nashua	86,969	$500k to $1 mil:	7.2%	Median age:	39.3 yrs.
3. Concord	42,019	Over $1 million:	1.1%	More than 65 yrs:	12.4%
4. Rochester	30,039	Median:	$250,700	Less than 18 yrs:	23.1%

Race/Ethnicity				Military Veterans		Registered Voters in 2008	
White:	93.4%	*Language*		% of Pop:	12.7%	D:	282,421 (29.5%)
Black:	1.0%	English:	91.6%	*Veterans by Period*		R:	280,507 (29.3%)
Hispanic:	2.4%	Spanish:	2.1%	WWII and before:	11.9%	Other:	395,600 (41.3%)
Asian:	1.9%	Asian:	1.1%	Korea:	11.7%	Voter turnout:	710,970
Native Am.:	0.3%	*Other*		Vietnam:	33.6%	Turnout as % of	
Hawaiian:	0.0%	European	4.7%	Gulf (pre-2001):	9.9%	voting age:	69.5%
Two+ races:	0.9%	**Education**		Gulf (post-2001):	5.4%	**General Court**	
Ancestry		H.S. grad:	89.9%	Peace time:	27.5%	Senate:	14 D 10 R
Irish:	15.9%	College grad:	31.8%			House:	225 D 175 R
English:	14.0%	Grad degree:	11.3%				
French:	12.0%						

Presidential politics   Since 1920, New Hampshire has held the first-in-the-nation primary, and since 1952, when candidates' names were first put on the ballot, it has had extraordinary influence on the presidential selection process—a fact that will surely strike 23rd century historians as bizarre. To be sure, there are arguments for having early contests in small states that provide a venue for "retail politics," in which candidates meet voters in person, listen to them, exchange ideas and allow citizens to gauge their character. Unlike Iowa, New Hampshire is small enough physically that candidates can efficiently meet voters. Everything except the lightly populated North Country is within an hour's drive of Manchester, and for all the state's abstract dislike of government, New Hampshire does an excellent job of keeping its roads clear of snow. New Hampshire's retail politics offers little-known candidates the ability to propel themselves into the national spotlight, though over the last 25 years none of those candidates has gone on to win his party's nomination. The last to do so were Democrats George McGovern and Jimmy Carter in the 1970s.

2008 Presidential Vote		
Obama (D)	384,826	(54%)
McCain (R)	316,534	(45%)
2008 Democratic Presidential Primary		
Clinton (D)	112,404	(39%)
Obama (D)	104,815	(36%)
Edwards (D)	48,699	(17%)
Richardson (D)	13,269	(5%)
2008 Republican Presidential Primary		
McCain (R)	88,713	(37%)
Romney (R)	75,675	(32%)
Huckabee (R)	26,916	(11%)
Giuliani (R)	20,344	(8%)
Paul (R)	18,346	(8%)
2004 Presidential Vote		
Kerry (D)	340,511	(50%)
Bush (R)	331,237	(49%)

In any case, New Hampshire retains its first-in-the-nation status not on the merits but because it has insisted on having its way. In the 1970s, Democrats tried to confine primaries to a "window" period in which New Hampshire would have competition. But New Hampshire, with its outlaw tradition, insisted it would hold its primary before the window if necessary, confident that candidates and reporters would pay it heed even if its tiny delegation was not seated at the national convention as punishment. Republicans made no such rules, but in 1996, let Iowa Gov. Terry Branstad and New Hampshire Gov. Steve Merrill, both Republicans, threaten voter retaliation against candidates who took part in caucuses or primaries held before those in their states or even during the week after their states' events. Democratic Gov. Jeanne Shaheen continued the tradition in December 1998, demanding that candidates take a pledge not to participate in earlier contests. In 2000, the Democrats imposed a five-week window of no contests after New Hampshire, which made Democrat Al Gore's 50%-46% victory here decisive. Bill Bradley's candidacy effectively died of inattention before he could reach Super Tuesday. Fortunately for Republican George W. Bush, the laissez-faire Republicans did not restrict other states as much as the Democrats, and he could recover from his loss in New Hampshire 19 days later in South Carolina. John McCain's smashing 49%-30% victory in the GOP primary knocked the wind out of the Bush campaign for only about a week.

In 2003, the Michigan Democratic Party, led by U.S. Sen. Carl Levin, attempted to challenge New Hampshire's first-in-the-nation status by moving the 2004 Michigan Democratic caucuses to the same January date as New Hampshire's primary. After a noisy debate, Michigan backed down. But Levin got the national party to promise to convene another commission in 2005 to study the nomination process.

New Hampshire is still one of the few states with more registered Republicans than Democrats, but it effectively chose, or ratified, Iowa caucus-goers' choice of Democratic nominee in both 2000 and 2004. Once upon a time, New Hampshire's registered Democrats were mill workers in Manchester and other factory towns, ethnics who rejected the Yankee Republican consensus of the state. Those days are long gone. Democratic turnout is not concentrated in the two largest cities, Manchester and Nashua, which often vote Republican, but in the state capital of Concord and clusters of towns around universities—the area around Durham (the University of New Hampshire) and Dover in southeast New Hampshire, the area around Keene (Keene State College) in the southwest and the area around Hanover (Dartmouth College). The typical Democratic primary voter here now is more likely to be an assistant professor. In 2000, the upscale character of the electorate was already clear. Gore, with strong support from labor unions, had won a wide victory in Iowa. But in New Hampshire, he was fortunate to squeeze out a 50%-46% victory against Bradley, who ran to his right on some economic issues and to his left on cultural issues.

In the 2004 cycle, New Hampshire was the first venue in which Democrat Howard Dean raced to a lead, far ahead of New Hampshire's Massachusetts neighbor John Kerry. Some voters in the western part of the state were perhaps familiar with Dean's somewhat moderate record as governor of Vermont. But his real appeal—what kept volunteers buzzing at their computers in his crowded Manchester headquarters and his poll numbers above 50% in a multicandidate field—came from his vitriolic denunciations of President Bush, especially on the war in Iraq. About half of Dean's support evaporated after his third-place showing in Iowa and his infamous election night rant. But he had already set the tone of the campaign and stirred the enthusiasm of New Hampshire Democrats. Turnout was up 42%. Kerry argued, as he had in Iowa, that he was the Democrat best able to defeat Bush. New Hampshire gave him 38% of its votes, to 26% for Dean, 12.4% for Wesley Clark, who had skipped Iowa, 12% for John Edwards, who had done much better in Iowa, and 9% for Joe Lieberman, who had also skipped Iowa. In retrospect, New Hampshire nailed the nomination for Kerry: Lieberman soon dropped out, as did Dean. Clark was never able to make himself Kerry's chief rival, and although Edwards did, he never overtook Kerry.

In the 2008 election season, Michigan scheduled its primary on January 15 in an attempt to outflank New Hampshire, but in August 2007, the Democratic National Committee commanded the Democratic candidates not to campaign there. In November, after the Michigan Supreme Court upheld the state's January date, New Hampshire Secretary of State William Gardner announced that his state's primary would be held on January 8, five days after the Iowa caucuses, restoring New Hampshire's first-in-the-nation place.

Campaigning proceeded through most of 2007, and for the first time, with both nominations contested, turnout was higher in the Democratic primary than in the Republican primary. Democrat Hillary Rodham Clinton, who had led in polls most of the year, began to trail Barack Obama after Obama's win in the Iowa caucuses. But shortly before the primary, at a coffeehouse in Portsmouth, Clinton was asked how she was withstanding the rigors of campaigning, and in response, she seemed to tear up as she talked about how she felt so strongly the country needed to change. This was the one primary in 2008 in which the result differed from the late polls. Clinton edged Obama 39%-36%; John Edwards got just 17%, Bill Richardson 5%. Turnout was 289,000 people, up 30% from 2004 and nearly double that of 2000. Clinton carried Manchester, the southeast and the North Country. She won among women and downscale voters, much as Gore had in 2000. Obama carried Concord and towns in the west, and won among upscale and well-educated voters, much as Bradley had eight years earlier. Clinton's victory ended the possibility that Obama might wrap up the nomination early.

Turnout on the Republican side was 239,000, almost identical to that in 2000. And the winner was again McCain, who had prevailed in 2000. He edged Mitt Romney 37%-32%; 11% went for Mike Huckabee and 8% for Rudy Giuliani, who had essentially abandoned serious efforts in the state in November. McCain carried western and northern New Hampshire. Romney carried the southeastern corner of the state, where he was well known from his four years as governor of Massachusetts. That left Romney, who had been considered by many the front-runner and the best-financed Republican, without a victory in either Iowa or New Hampshire. It injected life into the McCain candidacy, which had nearly collapsed just six months before.

Up through 1992, political reporters left New Hampshire the day after the primary and never returned for the general election in the fall. It was assumed that the state would go Republican. But Clinton carried New Hampshire twice, and in 2000, the general election contest was close again. Gore unaccountably visited the state just once, yet Bush still carried it by only 48%-47%, with a popular-vote margin of 7,211. In 2004, New Hampshire was a target state for both campaigns, and the enthusiasm evoked by the Dean campaign and transferred to Kerry in New Hampshire seemed to carry over into the fall. This was the only Bush 2000 state that went for Kerry. Again the vote was close, 50%-49%, with a popular-vote margin of 9,274—without which it would not have mattered whether Bush carried Ohio.

In 2008, New Hampshire was again a target state, but the Democratic tide was rising at a considerable clip. One clue: McCain had won more votes in the 2000 primary than in the 2008 primary. Another indication was that the Obama campaign had 100 organizers in the state, far more than the Republicans. Obama won by a solid 54%-45%. He got 61% of the votes from women and voters under 30. Interestingly, McCain ran even among Catholics and ahead among Protestants, but those who characterized their religion as "other" or "none," who accounted for 23% of the electorate, voted 76% for Obama.

Congressional districting

111th Congress Lineup
2 D
110th Congress Lineup
2 D

With only slight changes, New Hampshire's two congressional districts basically have had the same boundaries since 1881, neatly separating the Merrimack River mill towns of Manchester and Nashua, the state's largest cities. That was done originally to split the Catholic Democratic vote, but now both cities are high-tech towns. For years, that split helped Republicans hold both districts; now it helps Democrats.

Governor

John Lynch (D)

Elected 2004, term expires Jan. 2011, 3rd term; b. Nov. 25, 1952, Waltham, MA; home, Hopkinton; U of NH, B.A. 1974, Harvard U., M.B.A. 1979, Georgetown U., J.D. 1984; Catholic; married (Susan); 3 children.

Professional Career: Ex. Dir., NH Dem. party, 1975–77; Dir. of Admissions, Harvard Bus. Schl., 1982–86; Partner, consulting firm, 1987–94; Pres. and CEO, Knoll Inc., 1994–2001; Pres., Lynch Group, 2001–04.

Office: State House, 25 Capitol St., Concord, 03301, 603-271-2121; Fax: 603-271-2130; Web site: www.state.nh.us/governor.

Election Results

2008 general	John Lynch (D)	479,042	(70%)
	Joe Kenney (R)	188,555	(28%)
	Susan Newell (Lib)	14,987	(2%)
2008 primary	John Lynch (D)	44,549	(91%)
	Katy Forry (D)	4,444	(9%)

Prior Winning Percentages: 2006 (74%); 2004 (51%)

John Lynch, a Democrat, was elected governor of New Hampshire in 2004 in his first run for public office. Lynch grew up in Waltham, Mass., the fifth of six children. His father ran a local Boys' Club and his mother was a schoolteacher. He graduated from the University of New Hampshire in 1974, got an M.B.A. from Harvard Business School in 1979, and earned a law degree from Georgetown University in 1984. He took an interest in politics in college, interned for Democratic Sen. Tom McIntyre in 1975 and not long after became executive director of the New Hampshire Democratic State Committee. He left state politics to attend business school. In 1994, he became president and chief executive of Knoll Inc., a Pennsylvania-based office-furniture maker. He maintained his New Hampshire political network, however, and commuted from Knoll's headquarters in East Greenville, Pa., to his home in Hopkinton. He also was the president of the University of New Hampshire alumni association. In the mid-1980s and 1990s, Lynch worked for the Merrimack County Democratic Party, contributing to various campaigns and working to establish a New Hampshire chapter of the centrist Democratic Leadership Council. In 2001, he left Knoll and later opened his own management consulting firm in Manchester. In 2000, Democratic Gov. Jeanne Shaheen appointed Lynch to the University System of New Hampshire's Board of Trustees; he served as chairman from 2001 to 2004, when he resigned to run for governor.

Lynch challenged incumbent Republican Gov. Craig Benson, a wealthy political outsider who won his first term in 2002 in the state's most expensive gubernatorial race. A high-tech entrepreneur, Benson was one of three Republican former CEOs elected to New England governorships that year. (Massachusetts' Mitt Romney and Rhode Island's Donald Carcieri were the others.) Benson was the only one with the advantage of a Republican-controlled Legislature. He had a rough transition to the public sector, however; his brusque and heavy-handed style alienated legislators from both parties. Nonetheless, the governor fared well in public opinion polls in his first year. Voters gave him high approval ratings for his hard-charging style and his call for a constitutional amendment to limit tax increases. But Benson's popularity began to fade after frequent missteps and controversies. Several of his appointees were forced to step down for ethical lapses. Benson and his state safety commissioner were accused of interfering with an investigation of sexual-harassment allegations against Attorney General Peter Heed. Benson was ultimately cleared, but the safety commissioner was disciplined. In the Democratic primary, Lynch easily defeated former legislator Paul McEachern, who was making his fourth try for the office. The general election was dominated by two issues: taxes and ethics. In his campaign kickoff speech, Lynch said he would "restore integrity, trust, and a bipartisan spirit" to state government. He highlighted his opposition to a sales or income tax but did back an increase in the cigarette tax. He said he would provide targeted aid to schools while phasing out the state property tax adopted in 1999. Benson hewed to a hard anti-tax position and insisted that Lynch's plan to repeal the state property tax would lead to a "back-door income tax." Lynch insisted that existing revenues would enable him to pay for his spending priorities. He focused on what he called Benson's "culture of corruption," and pointed out that Benson had been cited twice for having illegal landscaping in front of his beachfront home. The candidates, both multimillionaires, largely self-financed their campaigns. Benson, after spending more than $9 million from his deep pockets in 2002, put up $3.3 million of his own money, out of a total of $4 million raised. Lynch raised $3 million, $2 million of it his own money. That was enough to keep him competitive through Election Day. He won 51%-49%.

The election results closely tracked presidential returns that year: Democrat John Kerry ran just 600 votes ahead of Lynch, carrying the state 50%-49% over Republican President George W. Bush. Lynch and Kerry won the same six counties, both carrying western New Hampshire and Concord's Merrimack County and both losing in Manchester's Hillsborough County and Rockingham County. Benson became the first freshman governor in 78 years to be denied a second term. Ever the outsider, he failed to give a concession speech or to speak to campaign supporters on election night. In Lynch's first act in office, he issued an executive order requiring everyone who worked in the governor's office to file a financial disclosure form that detailed their sources of income, loans of $5,000 or more, the location of real estate holdings other than homes, and businesses that they or their spouses were involved in if the investment was 1% or more of the outstanding stock or securities issued by the business.

His mild-mannered and cautious style offered a marked contrast to Benson and enabled him to work productively with the Republican-controlled Legislature. Lynch stressed the importance of bipartisanship. "I was not elected to represent a party," he said. In October, the governor drew praise for his leadership when severe flooding devastated parts of southwestern New Hampshire. He flew back from a European trade mission to oversee recovery efforts and surprised homeowners and local officials by handing them laminated cards that included phone numbers of key state and National Guard officials, as well as his own personal cell phone number. Lynch failed to achieve everything he wanted in his first year—he was unable to repeal the statewide property tax, for example—but his work with the state's congressional delegation to help keep the Portsmouth Naval Shipyard open and his response to the flood led to high approval ratings. He was able to establish an ethics commission for the executive branch; he signed a tough law cracking down on child sexual predators; and he pushed through "Michelle's Law," which required health insurers to continue covering severely ill college students whom doctors certified were unable to maintain their status as full-time students. The law was named for a cancer-stricken student who had to continue attending classes to keep her insurance benefits.

Vermont and New Hampshire are the last two states with two-year gubernatorial terms and, Benson the exception, voters in both states are inclined to grant their chief executives a second term. With 70% job-approval ratings, Lynch in 2006 was far ahead of his Republican challenger, state Rep. Jim Coburn. In September 2006, the state Supreme Court ruled that New Hampshire's system of funding education was unconstitutional because its heavy reliance on local property taxes resulted in inequities in per pupil spending. The court set a June 2007 deadline before it would impose its own financing system. Coburn supported a constitutional amendment to remove control of the education financing system from the courts. Lynch argued that the state could fund the public schools without a sales or income tax and said he would consider a narrowly written constitutional amendment designed to give the state more flexibility. Coburn argued that Lynch's position left open the possibility of broad-based taxes. But Lynch won 74%-26%, the largest victory ever for a gubernatorial candidate in New Hampshire. Democrats also gained 89 seats in the state House to give them a 239-161 majority, along with their 14-10 majority in the state Senate. For the first time since the Civil War era, New Hampshire had a Democratic Legislature and governor.

In 2007, the Legislature enacted one of Lynch's priorities, raising the legal school dropout age from 16 to 18, and lawmakers also increased the minimum wage and hiked the cigarette tax. The Legislature repealed the state's parental-notification abortion law, and Lynch also signed a measure that made New Hampshire the fourth state to allow civil unions. But the state House rejected 253-108 Lynch's fix for the school financing problem. He proposed a constitutional amendment requiring the state to pay for 50% of school funding, up from 7%, as a way to lessen the schools' reliance on local property taxes, which varied widely by locality. Even so, Lynch was able to avoid signing an income or sales tax, and in June 2008, the budget included $80 million in bonds for school construction. The November 2008 election was anticlimactic: Lynch beat state GOP Sen. Joseph Kenney 70%-28%, although Republicans gained seats in the state House and reduced Democrats' majority to 225-175.

Lynch faced new challenges in his third term. When the recession hit New Hampshire hard, the governor was forced to lay off hundreds of state workers and to close the Laconia prison, eight district courts, and several state liquor stores. Also in early 2009, the Legislature considered passing a mandatory seat belt law, which would end New Hampshire's distinction as the only state without one. The Senate put off action, however. In April 2009, both chambers passed a law legalizing same-sex marriage. He said in a statement that he saw no need for the law since the state had adopted civil unions two years earlier. When the bill arrived on his desk, Lynch said he would sign it provided the Legislature added a clause allowing religious organizations to refuse to conduct same-sex weddings if they contradict their beliefs. In June 2009, the Legislature approved his condition and Lynch signed the bill. He said he had come to agree with "compelling arguments that a separate system is not an equal system."

Lynch said in 2009 that he would not run for Republican Sen. Judd Gregg's U.S. Senate seat when it comes up in 2010, and that he had not decided whether to seek another term as governor. No New Hampshire governor has been elected four times since the state extended the term of office to two years in 1880. No one has served longer than six years since Federalist John Gilman won 11 one-year terms from 1794 to 1804.

Senior Senator

Judd Gregg (R)

Elected 1992, term expires 2010, 3rd term; b. Feb. 14, 1947, Nashua; home, Rye; Columbia U., A.B. 1969, Boston U., J.D. 1972, LL.M. 1975; Protestant; married (Kathleen); 3 children.

Elected Office: NH Exec. Cncl., 1978–80; U.S. House of Reps., 1980–88; NH gov., 1988–92.

Professional Career: Practicing atty., 1976–80.

DC Office: 201 RSOB, 20510, 202-224-3324; Fax: 202-224-4952; Web site: gregg.senate.gov.

State Offices: Berlin, 603-752-2604; Concord, 603-225-7115; Manchester, 603-622-7979; Portsmouth, 603-431-2171.

Committees: *Appropriations* (5th of 12 R): Commerce, Justice, Science & Related Agencies; Defense; Homeland Security; Interior, Environment & Related Agencies; Labor, Health and Human Services, Education & Related Agencies; State, Foreign Operations & Related Programs (RMM). *Budget* (RMM of 10 R). *Health, Education, Labor & Pensions* (2nd of 10 R).

Group Ratings

	ADA	ACLU	AFS	LCV	ITIC	NTU	COC	ACU	CFG	FRC
2008	15	17	11	9	80	64	86	83	70	77
2007	10	—	0	60	—	78	82	72	79	—

National Journal Ratings

	2007 LIB	—	2007 CONS		2008 LIB	—	2008 CONS
Economic	26%	—	72%		12%	—	87%
Social	31%	—	68%		21%	—	73%
Foreign	30%	—	66%		24%	—	71%
Composite	30%	—	70%		21%	—	79%

Key Votes of the 110th Congress

1. Raise CAFE standards	Y	5. Make English official language	Y	9. Withdraw troops 3/08	N
2. Expand SCHIP	N	6. Path to citizenship	Y	10. Iran guard is terrorist group	Y
3. Cap greenhouse gases	*	7. Fetus is unborn child	Y	11. Increase missile defense $	N
4. Bail out financial markets	Y	8. Prosecute hate crimes	Y	12. Overhaul FISA	Y

Election Results

2004 general	Judd Gregg (R)	435,846	(66%)	($1,897,466)
	Doris Haddock (D)	221,544	(34%)	($177,199)
2004 primary	Judd Gregg (R)	60,597	(92%)	

Prior Winning Percentages: 1998 (68%); 1992 (48%); 1986 House (74%); 1984 House (76%); 1982 House (71%); 1980 House (64%)

Judd Gregg, a Republican, was elected a senator from New Hampshire in 1992. He grew up in Nashua and was involved in politics early on. In 1952, when he was 5 years old, his father, Hugh Gregg, was elected governor and remained a power in presidential primary politics for many years. In 1988, Hugh Gregg provided crucial backing for Republican presidential candidate George H.W. Bush. He died in September 2003. Judd Gregg was a student at Columbia University during the student riots of 1968, but stayed true to New Hampshire Republicanism and didn't partake. He graduated from Boston University law school and returned to Nashua to practice law. In 1978, at age 31, he was elected to the Executive Council, which dates to the colonial era and approves state appointments and expenditures. In 1980, he was elected to the U.S. House, where he was an eager soldier in the Reagan revolution. In 1988, he ran for governor and won handily. He was easily re-elected in 1990. During those years, New Hampshire's housing prices and economy crashed, but Gregg resisted all efforts to impose an income tax or sales tax.

In 1992, when Republican Warren Rudman retired, Gregg ran for the Senate and in his taciturn way seemed sure he would win. But with the New Hampshire economy souring, indeed in worse shape than it was in early 2009, the race turned close. In the September primary, he beat a construction-company owner by only 50%-38%. In the general election, he faced retired businessman John Rauh, a Democrat who backed the line-item veto and balanced-budget amendment and attacked Gregg for opposing abortion rights. Gregg won by an unimpressive 48%-45%.

In the Senate, Gregg accrued sufficient seniority to become chairman of the Health, Education, Labor and Pensions Committee for five months in 2001 and again from 2003 to 2005. (He was ranking

Republican when the Senate was under Democratic control in 2001 and 2002.) He was the lead Senate supporter of the Bush administration's No Child Left Behind education initiative and worked with Democratic Sen. Edward Kennedy of Massachusetts on the details. His amendment to allow vouchers for private-school tuition was rejected in June 2001 on a 58-41 vote. In November 2001, he and Kennedy and Republican Reps. John Boehner of Ohio and George Miller of California reached a final compromise. It left in place the Bush proposal for annual testing in math and reading from grades three to eight. It allowed economically disadvantaged students to use federal funds for private tutoring and summer school. The bill passed and was signed in January 2002.

In September 2005, Gregg proposed cash grants that parents of New Orleans area schoolchildren could use in public or private schools. As a result, a larger percentage of children in the New Orleans school district are in charter schools than in any other district in the country. Gregg worked on consensus health legislation with Democrats and other Republicans—a law requiring the Food and Drug Administration to test the effects of drugs on children and a bill limiting pharmaceutical companies to one 30-month stay of an application to sell a generic drug. He got the Senate to approve FDA regulation of tobacco, together with a buyout of tobacco quotas in the 2004 corporate tax bill, although the FDA regulation was ultimately dropped from the final legislation. Gregg voted against the overall bill on the grounds that it cost too much. He co-sponsored the Biodefense Act of 2005, which promoted the development of vaccines, and a bill setting down strict criteria for plaintiffs seeking punitive damages from health care providers or medical product manufacturers. In 2003, Gregg and his New Hampshire colleague Republican Sen. John Sununu voted against the energy bill because it banned the state of New Hampshire's lawsuit against the manufacturers of MTBE, a gasoline additive that was found to be polluting groundwater supplies. They effectively blocked the energy bill from passing that year.

In 2004, Gregg gave up the chairmanship of the HELP Committee to become chairman of the Budget Committee. He promised "very strong enforcement measures" of budget rules and sought to "put the brakes on the growth of entitlements." In April 2005, he pushed through a budget resolution but failed to get the tight limits on Medicaid spending he had wanted. In 2003, he worked to hold the cost of the Republicans' Medicare prescription drug bill to $400 billion over 10 years, which was the projection when it was passed. Often frustrated with the resolve of Congress to set limits in the budget, Gregg once said, "Are we going to pass budgets that mean something, or are we going to pass budgets for show?" In 2007 and 2008, back in the minority as ranking Republican on the committee, Gregg worked with Democratic Chairman Kent Conrad on trying to establish a bipartisan commission to modify entitlements.

Gregg passed up a chance to get on the Finance Committee and remained on Appropriations, where he has been more tightfisted than many of his colleagues. He has procured federal money to buy land to preserve Lake Tarleton, expand the Hubbard Brook Experimental Forest, and maintain the Great Bay Estuarine Research Reserve, the Mount Washington Observatory Weather Discovery Center, and the St. Anselm's College civic-education program. He has gotten funding for the purchase of easement rights on the extensive lands owned by paper companies in New Hampshire and elsewhere in northern New England—a major conservation project. However, he was criticized for investing in land around the Pease Tradeport, a commercial-industrial development with an airport that he helped fund to replace a closed Air Force base. In 2007, he became the ranking member on the Appropriations subcommittee on State, Foreign Operations, and Related Programs.

After Democrats won a majority in the Senate in 2006, Gregg became active on the floor in trying to stop Democratic initiatives. In December 2006, he raised objections to the $39 billion end-of-session spending bill, opposing especially its assumption of coal companies' insurance liability, at a cost of $4 billion. In January 2007, he introduced an amendment to the Senate ethics bill giving the president line-item rescission power over earmarks in spending bills. He withdrew it when Democratic Sen. Robert Byrd of West Virginia threatened a filibuster. Democratic Majority Leader Harry Reid called Gregg "the designated 'see-if-we-can-mess-up-the-legislation' guy this year." Gregg responded, "I don't think I came here to be a potted plant." In March 2007, when Democrats allowed Republicans a floor vote on an alternative proposal to their resolution calling for a troop withdrawal from Iraq, Republicans chose Gregg's resolution calling for fully funding the troops. It passed 82-16. In September 2008, Gregg was a chief Republican negotiator on the $700 billion bailout of the financial industry. He supported the bipartisan bill, explaining later, "What we were facing was the meltdown of the entire financial system of the United States."

Gregg has maintained a network of supporters in New Hampshire, but the organization his father ran that was so effective for George H. W. Bush in 1988 has not been duplicated, and Gregg was unable to deliver a primary victory for the last three candidates he endorsed—Bob Dole in 1996, George W. Bush in 2000 and Mitt Romney in 2008. Gregg's standing in New Hampshire seems strong. In 1998, he was opposed by an underfinanced Democrat who called him a "draft dodger" and a "wimp." Gregg won 68%-28%. In 2004, in the general election, he had a challenge from state Sen. Burt Cohen, but Cohen eventually dropped out. New Hampshire Democrats, eager for a nominee, found Doris "Granny D" Haddock, a 94-year-old longtime leftish activist who in 2000 walked 3,225 miles across America to support campaign finance regulation. Granite Staters may have admired her pluck, but not very many voted for her. Gregg won 66%-34% and became the first New Hampshire senator elected to a third term since Norris Cotton in 1968.

In February 2009, Gregg was Democratic President Barack Obama's surprise pick for Commerce secretary. (Gregg persuaded Democratic Gov. John Lynch to appoint a Republican to replace him in the Senate, one who would not seek a full term in 2010. Lynch named J. Bonnie Newman, a former Gregg aide and Lynch supporter.) But his philosophy and Obama's proved too different. Gregg favored an economic-stimulus package, but opposed the Senate Democrats' version on the grounds that it unduly increased the national debt. Another issue was equally sensitive. The Commerce Department supervises the Census Bureau, and Gregg had opposed using sampling procedures in the 2000 census. Sampling tends to increase the count in urban areas, to the disadvantage of Republicans. On February 5, apparently to mollify African-American and Hispanic Democrats who objected to Gregg's appointment based on the census issue, White House Chief of Staff Rahm Emanuel gave assurances that the director of the Census Bureau would report directly to the White House. On February 12, Gregg withdrew his name from consideration. "I'm a fiscal conservative, as everybody knows, a fairly strong one," he said. "And it just became clear to me that it would be very difficult, day in and day out, to serve in this Cabinet or any Cabinet."

Gregg quickly reverted to form and harshly criticized the Democratic budget in March and April 2009, predicting that it would lead to "bankruptcy for the United States" and might lead to levels of debt seen in a "banana republic." He especially took issue with a provision that in effect would allow a health care bill to pass with a simple majority, rather than the filibuster-proof 60 votes typically necessary in the Senate. Gregg likened it to "running over the minority, putting them in cement and throwing them in the Chicago River."

Gregg said in early 2009 that he would not run for re-election in 2010. Obama carried New Hampshire handily in 2008, and Democrats were hopeful that they could win the seat. Democratic U.S. Rep. Paul Hodes announced his candidacy. When Gregg retires from the Senate, he will at least be able to do it in comfort. In 2005, he won more than $853,000 in the Powerball lottery in New Hampshire.

Junior Senator

Jeanne Shaheen (D)

Elected 2008, term expires 2014, 1st term; b. Jan. 28, 1947, St. Charles, MO; home, Madbury; Shippensburg Coll., B.A. 1969, U. of MS, M.A. 1973; Protestant; married (William); 3 children.

Elected Office: NH Senate, 1990–96; NH gov., 1997–2003.

Professional Career: Teacher, 1969–71; A.A., U. of NH, 1973–74, Parents' Assoc. Program Coord., 1982–86; Mgr., seasonal retail business, 1973–76; Campaign mgr., Carter/Mondale NH pres. campaign, 1979–80; Hart NH pres. campaign, 1983–84; McEachern NH gov. campaign, 1986–88.

DC Office: 520 HSOB, 20510, 202-224-2841; Fax: ; Web site: shaheen.senate.gov.

State Offices: Claremont, 603-542-4872; Dover, 603-750-3004; Manchester, 603-647-7500; Nashua, 603-883-0196.

Committees: *Energy & Natural Resources* (13th of 13 D): Energy; Public Lands & Forests; Water & Power. *Foreign Relations* (9th of 11 D): African Affairs; European Affairs (Chmn); International Development & Foreign Assistance, Economic Affairs & International Environmental Protection; International Operations & Organizations, Democracy & Global Women's Issues. *Small Business & Entrepreneurship* (10th of 11 D).

Group Ratings and Key Votes: Newly Elected

Election Results

2008 general	Jeanne Shaheen (D)	358,438	(52%)	($8,225,580)
	John Sununu (R)	314,403	(45%)	($8,010,010)
	Ken Blevens (Lib)	21,516	(3%)	
2008 primary	Jeanne Shaheen (D)	42,968	(88%)	
	Henry Stebbins (D)	5,281	(11%)	

Prior Winning Percentages: 2000 governor (49%); 1998 governor (66%); 1996 governor (57%)

Jeanne Shaheen, a Democrat, was elected to the Senate in 2008. She is the first woman in U.S. history to be elected both a governor and a senator. Shaheen grew up in St. Charles County, Mo., north of St. Louis, and graduated from Shippensburg College in Pennsylvania. She got a master's degree at the University of Mississippi. She moved to New Hampshire in 1973, where she worked as a teacher and ran a silver and leather business with her husband, attorney William Shaheen. She worked as a staffer on Democrat Jimmy Carter's successful presidential primary campaigns in New Hampshire in 1976 and

1980, and worked on other Democratic campaigns as well. She managed Democrat Gary Hart's 1984 campaign in the New Hampshire primary, in which he beat Walter Mondale 37%-28%. She also worked for the unsuccessful gubernatorial campaigns of Paul McEachern in 1986 and 1988, when he lost to John Sununu and Judd Gregg, respectively.

In 1990, Shaheen was elected to the state Senate, where she supported expanded health care coverage and needle-exchange programs, but also term limits on federal and state legislators. In 1996, she ran for governor. She had no serious primary opposition, while the Republicans had a close race between U.S. Rep. Bill Zeliff and Board of Education Chairman Ovide Lamontagne, a strong conservative who won the nomination. Shaheen took a pledge not to support an income or sales tax and won the general election 57%-39%, carrying every county. As governor, Shaheen won more funding from the Legislature for kindergarten programs and signed a bill creating a needle-exchange pilot program. She vetoed bills that would have abolished the estate tax and the death penalty. A December 1997 state Supreme Court ruling that outlawed New Hampshire's system of local school financing provided a continual challenge. Shaheen proposed increasing state revenues through slot machine gambling and a hike in the tobacco tax, but the court invalidated her plan in 1998. That same year, when her two-year term was up, Shaheen was re-elected by 66%-31%. But she then abandoned her pledge to oppose an income or sales tax and was re-elected in 2000 by only 49%-44%. During that term, the controversy over school funding continued, and the Republican-controlled Legislature refused to pass either an income or sales tax.

In 2002, Shaheen ran for the Senate. As in her 1996 race, Republicans had a seriously contested primary in which U.S. Rep. John Sununu, son of the former governor and George H.W. Bush White House chief of staff, defeated the very conservative incumbent Robert Smith 53%-45%. Shaheen supported President George W. Bush's tax cuts and the authorization of military force in Iraq passed by Congress in October 2002. But her abandonment of the tax pledge came back to haunt her in the gubernatorial race that year, when the Democratic nominee for governor, Mark Fernald, took a strong stand backing the imposition of a state income tax. Polls showed the Senate race as one of the closest in the country, and Sununu won 51%-46%.

In the 2004 election season, Shaheen was the national chairwoman of Democrat John Kerry's presidential campaign and helped orchestrate his sudden rise in the polls and his victory in the New Hampshire primary, as competitor Howard Dean's support collapsed. After that election, in April 2005, Shaheen became director of the Kennedy School of Government's Institute of Politics at Harvard. She said she had no interest in running for office again. But after the Democratic sweep of November 2006, many local Democrats pressed her to run against Sununu in 2008. Other candidates were already in the race, including Katrina Swett, wife of former U.S. Rep. Dick Swett and daughter of the late California Rep. Tom Lantos. She raised $1.2 million for the race. A July 2007 poll showed Shaheen far ahead of Sununu in a theoretical matchup, with Swett and other Democrats running behind him. In September, Shaheen quit her job at Harvard and announced that she was running. She said that if she had known in 2002 what she knew in 2007, she would have opposed the Iraq war resolution. Swett and others dropped out of the race.

Much of New Hampshire's attention over the next few months was devoted to the presidential race. In December 2007, Shaheen's husband William, co-chairman of Hillary Clinton's national and New Hampshire campaigns, told reporters that Republicans would attack Democratic competitor Barack Obama for admitting in his autobiography that he "got into drinking" and "experimented with drugs." The next day, Clinton apologized, and Shaheen's husband resigned his position in her campaign.

The campaign was a rematch between two candidates in a very different political atmosphere. In 2002, Shaheen had emphasized areas where she agreed with Bush and congressional Republicans; in 2008, she emphasized her disagreements with them. She attacked Sununu for votes against changing the tax treatment of oil companies and was supported by environmental groups. She decried the state of the economy and attacked Sununu for supporting the Bush administration's economic policies. Shaheen led in polls throughout the campaign, but Sununu rebounded after gas prices reached $4 a gallon, and he criticized Shaheen's opposition to offshore oil drilling. He also attacked her for doubling state spending in her six years as governor. But he may have lost ground in October 2008, when he voted for the $700 billion government bailout for the financial industry, which Shaheen, like many challenger candidates in both parties, opposed.

It was one of the most closely contested Senate races in the country, and both candidates raised and spent more than $8 million. The outcome was a reversal of 2002. Shaheen won 52%-45%, a spread just slightly greater than Sununu's six years earlier. It was the first Democratic Senate victory in New Hampshire since 1974.

FIRST DISTRICT

Carol Shea-Porter (D)

Elected 2006, 2nd term; b. Dec. 2, 1952, New York, NY; home, Rochester; U. of NH, B.A. 1975, M.P.A. 1979; Catholic; married (Gene); 2 children.

Professional Career: Social worker; Comm. col. instructor; Lecturer.

DC Office: 1330 LHOB, 20515, 202-225-5456; Fax: 202-225-5822; Web site: shea-porter.house.gov.

State Offices: Dover, 603-743-4813; Manchester, 603-641-9536.

Committees: *Armed Services* (22nd of 36 D): Military Personnel; Readiness. *Education & Labor* (23rd of 29 D): Healthy Families & Communities; Workforce Protections. *Natural Resources* (26th of 29 D): Insular Affairs, Oceans & Wildlife; National Parks, Forests & Public Lands.

Group Ratings

	ADA	ACLU	AFS	LCV	ITIC	NTU	COC	ACU	CFG	FRC
2008	90	100	100	100	43	18	50	12	12	11
2007	95	—	100	90	—	5	50	0	1	—

National Journal Ratings

	2007 LIB — 2007 CONS		2008 LIB — 2008 CONS	
Economic	78% —	18%	71% —	25%
Social	73% —	27%	52% —	47%
Foreign	81% —	16%	78% —	17%
Composite	79% —	22%	69% —	31%

Key Votes of the 110th Congress

1. Increase minimum wage	Y	5. Share immigration data	N	9. Withdraw troops 8/08	Y
2. Expand SCHIP	Y	6. Foreign aid abortion ban	N	10. No operations in Iran	Y
3. Raise CAFE standards	Y	7. Ban gay bias in workplace	Y	11. Free trade with Peru	N
4. Bail out financial markets	N	8. Repeal D.C. gun law	Y	12. Overhaul FISA	N

Election Results

2008 general	Carol Shea-Porter (D)	176,435	(52%)	($1,576,897)
	Jeb Bradley (R)	156,338	(46%)	($1,447,187)
	Robert Kingsbury (Lib)	8,100	(2%)	
2008 primary	Carol Shea-Porter (D)	20,839	(98%)	

Prior Winning Percentages: 2006 (51%)

Population		Race/Ethnicity		Work	
Pop. 2007:	656,912	White:	93.4%	Private:	79.0%
Change since 2000:	Up 6.4%	Black:	1.2%	Government:	12.9%
Urban:	66.6%	Hispanic:	2.5%	Self-employed:	7.9%
Rural:	33.4%	Asian:	1.7%	Blue collar:	21.9%
Area size:	2,688 sq. mi.	Native Am.:	0.2%	White collar:	62.4%
Age		Hawaiian:	0.0%	Khaki collar:	0.1%
Median age:	38.9 yrs.	Two+ races:	0.9%	Other:	15.6%
More than 65 yrs:	11.8%	*Ancestry*		Median income:	$63,171
Less than 18 yrs:	23.3%	Irish:	16.5%	Median home value:	$265,500
Education		English:	13.3%	Poverty:	8.1%
H.S. grad:	90.3%	French:	12.2%	**Military Veterans**	
College grad:	31.5%			% of Pop:	12.6%
Grad degree:	11.0%				

The greatest growth in New Hampshire over the past two decades has been in the southeast and south-central parts of the state—the Seacoast and the Manchester area. Manchester was once famous for the Amoskeag Mills, the world's largest textile mill complex. In the first half of the 20th century, it was the quintessential mill town, with a few mansions for mill owners and managers and closely packed neighborhoods of frame houses for mill workers, many of them immigrants—from Quebec,

2008 Presidential Vote		
Obama (D) 186,370	(53%)
McCain (R).............................164,403	(47%)
2004 Presidential Vote		
Bush (R) 171,013	(51%)
Kerry (D)................................163,191	(48%)
Cook Partisan Voting Index: Even		

Ireland, and Greece (Manchester has America's largest percentage of Greek-Americans). By the beginning of the 21st century, it was something quite different: a high-tech city, with big shopping malls at freeway interchanges, a spiffy new airport and downtown arena, spruced-up neighborhoods, and growth extending to the wooded suburbs all around. The Seacoast, within easy commuting distance of Massachusetts, is a collection of towns of ancient pedigree and high-tech growth. The biggest city on the coast is Portsmouth, the colonial capital of New Hampshire, with its busy naval shipyard and old seaport with well-preserved houses and a solid local economy that includes many galleries and bars.

Pease Air Force Base, shuttered in 1991, has been successfully redeveloped as the Pease International Tradeport, with office buildings and an airplane runway, resulting in the addition of more than 160 businesses and nearly 10,000 jobs in the Seacoast, as the region along the state's 18-mile coast is known. Not far to the southwest are Stratham, where Swiss chocolate maker Lindt completed in 2007 a multimillion-dollar expansion, and Exeter, home of Phillips Exeter Academy, the elite boarding school. A quarter of New Hampshire residents claim French or French-Canadian ties; racial minorities are sparse here.

The 1st Congressional District of New Hampshire includes the Manchester area and the Seacoast from Manchester and next-door Bedford, its most affluent suburb, east to Portsmouth. It also extends north to Laconia and gentrifying Lake Winnipesaukee, studded with summer resorts and new mansions, and Ossipee in Carroll County. Politically, this is the slightly more Republican of New Hampshire's two congressional districts. It was the destination of many people fleeing high taxes in Massachusetts. Manchester, the largest city in the state, still has more registered Democrats than Republicans—a relic of its mill town days—but usually votes Republican in general elections. Portsmouth, with its trendy coffee shops, is Democratic, as are Durham, home of the University of New Hampshire, and nearby Dover, once a mill town. Most of the smaller towns in the Seacoast and to the north have been solidly Republican, though that is changing. George W. Bush narrowly carried the district twice, but Democratic presidential nominee Barack Obama won it 53%-47% in 2008, despite Republican nominee John McCain's past popularity here.

The congresswoman from the 1st District is Carol Shea-Porter, a Democrat elected in one of the biggest upsets of 2006. She was born in New York City and grew up in a large extended family in New Hampshire. After her high school guidance counselor recommended she go to secretary school, Shea-Porter figured she could do better and enrolled in the University of New Hampshire. She worked her way through college and graduate school, ultimately getting a master's degree in public administration. She moved to Colorado with her husband, an officer stationed at an Army medical center. There she witnessed soldiers returning from the Vietnam War in need of medical and psychological care, an experience that would contribute to her anti-war candidacy decades later. She and her family moved to New Orleans, and then to the Washington, D.C., area, before returning to New Hampshire. Shea-Porter worked as a social worker, directed programs for senior citizens, and lectured at a community college. She worked on retired Gen. Wesley Clark's 2004 presidential primary campaign and served as the chairman of the Rochester Democrats, cultivating a network of liberal activists. She started following Republican U.S. Rep. Jeb Bradley from event to event, asking pointed questions about the issues. She got the media's attention with a stunt in February 2005. Shea-Porter was escorted from a town hall meeting with President Bush after she removed her sweater to reveal a T-shirt that read, "Turn your back on Bush." On relief trips to New Orleans, she concluded that the federal government had failed to help its citizens recover from Hurricane Katrina and decided to run for Congress.

Taking on Bradley, Shea-Porter campaigned as staunchly against the war in Iraq, advocated the creation of a federal institute dedicated to reducing dependence on foreign oil, and called for a nationalized health care system. National Democrats questioned her viability in a general election, and the Democratic Congressional Campaign Committee backed state House Minority Leader Jim Craig in the four-way primary. Craig proved to be a disappointing candidate. He ran well in his Manchester base but lost nearly everywhere else in the district. Shea-Porter had assembled a deeply committed grassroots network that turned out many voters. She won 54%-34%, a surprise to political observers: "Oh my God, I think I'm going to faint," she told supporters on primary night.

Shea-Porter entered the general election a decided underdog. She was outspent by more than 3-to-1. Bradley defended Bush on the Iraq war and argued that withdrawing troops would destabilize the Middle East. Polls showed Bradley leading narrowly but hampered by Bush's unpopularity. The largest union at the Portsmouth Naval Shipyard, which Bradley helped protect during the 2005 base-closing round, endorsed Shea-Porter. Three weeks before the election, national Republican strategists recognized Shea-Porter's late surge and dispatched help to Bradley. National Democrats remained skeptical and instead pumped $1 million into the neighboring 2nd District to help candidate Paul Hodes, who won. Shea-Porter won 51%-49%. The victory surprised Democratic National Committee Chairman Howard Dean, the former governor of neighboring Vermont, who could not remember Shea-Porter's name in a morning-after press conference.

In the House, Shea-Porter established a centrist voting record. In June 2008, she joined most Democrats in voting against Iraq war funding. On the Education and Labor Committee, she has sought major changes in the Bush administration's 2001 No Child Left Behind education law, which she compared to a "beautiful-looking car [that] doesn't start."

Shea-Porter has focused on legislation affecting families. Her main bill would protect family savings in the case of a costly medical crisis by sheltering $250,000 in home value from debt collectors. She has also sponsored legislation to reverse restrictions placed on the 1993 Family and Medical Leave Act during Bush's two terms. Among other changes, it would end limitations on the use of accrued paid leave if a worker invokes the act to take time off and prohibit the denial of attendance bonuses when a worker takes an FMLA-sanctioned leave of absence.

Shea-Porter was a prime campaign target for Republicans in 2008. Bradley wanted a rematch against her, but first faced a primary race with John Stephen, the former New Hampshire health commissioner. Stephen criticized Bradley for having supported wasteful spending during his two terms in Congress, but Bradley won 51%-46%. In the general election contest, he faced a better-financed Shea-Porter, who was finally getting help from the national party. She sought to link Bradley to Bush, while he criticized the policies of the liberal-dominated Democratic majority in Congress. Shea-Porter won 52%-46%.

Following the election, she briefly considered a run for the open New Hampshire Senate seat in 2010 but decided against it. She would have had a primary contest with the other New Hampshire House member, Hodes, who had announced his candidacy for the Senate. However, she can expect competition to keep her seat in 2010. Manchester Mayor Frank Guinta, a Republican, has said he would run against her.

SECOND DISTRICT

Paul Hodes (D)

Elected 2006, 2nd term; b. March 21, 1951, New York, NY; home, Concord; Dartmouth Col., A.B. 1972, Boston Col., J.D. 1978; Jewish; married (Peggo Horstmann Hodes); 3 children.

Professional Career: NH asst. atty. gen., 1979–82; NH special prosecutor, 1982–83; Practicing atty., 1983–2006; Musician and founder, Peggosus, 1985-present.

DC Office: 1317 LHOB, 20515, 202-225-5206; Fax: 202-225-2946; Web site: hodes.house.gov.

State Offices: Berlin, 603-752-4680; Concord, 603-223-9814; Keene, 603-358-1023; Littleton, 603-444-8967; Nashua, 603-579-6913.

Committees: *Financial Services* (24th of 42 D): Capital Markets, Insurance & Government Sponsored Enterprises; Financial Institutions & Consumer Credit. *Oversight & Government Reform* (19th of 24 D): Government Management, Organization & Procurement; National Security & Foreign Affairs.

Group Ratings

	ADA	ACLU	AFS	LCV	ITIC	NTU	COC	ACU	CFG	FRC
2008	90	100	100	100	43	18	56	12	12	0
2007	100	—	100	100	—	5	50	0	6	—

National Journal Ratings

	2007 LIB	—	2007 CONS	2008 LIB	—	2008 CONS
Economic	78%	—	18%	62%	—	37%
Social	65%	—	34%	59%	—	38%
Foreign	81%	—	16%	70%	—	25%
Composite	76%	—	24%	65%	—	35%

Key Votes of the 110th Congress

1. Increase minimum wage	Y	5. Share immigration data	N	9. Withdraw troops 8/08	Y
2. Expand SCHIP	Y	6. Foreign aid abortion ban	N	10. No operations in Iran	Y
3. Raise CAFE standards	Y	7. Ban gay bias in workplace	Y	11. Free trade with Peru	N
4. Bail out financial markets	N	8. Repeal D.C. gun law	Y	12. Overhaul FISA	N

Election Results

2008 general	Paul Hodes (D)	188,332	(56%)	($2,021,750)
	Jennifer Horn (R)	138,222	(41%)	($552,317)
	Chester Lapointe (Lib)	7,121	(2%)	
2008 primary	Paul Hodes (D)	22,638	(99%)	

Prior Winning Percentages: 2006 (53%)

Population		Race/Ethnicity		Work	
Pop. 2007:	653,342	White:	93.4%	Private:	78.0%
Change since 2000:	Up 5.7%	Black:	0.8%	Government:	13.5%
Urban:	51.7%	Hispanic:	2.3%	Self-employed:	8.3%
Rural:	48.3%	Asian:	2.1%	Blue collar:	22.2%
Area size:	6,662 sq. mi.	Native Am.:	0.3%	White collar:	62.8%
Age		Hawaiian:	0.0%	Khaki collar:	0.1%
Median age:	39.8 yrs.	Two+ races:	0.9%	Other:	14.9%
More than 65 yrs:	13.0%	*Ancestry*		Median income:	$59,829
Less than 18 yrs:	22.8%	Irish:	15.3%	Median home value:	$239,600
		English:	14.8%	Poverty:	7.3%
Education		French:	11.8%	**Military Veterans**	
H.S. grad:	89.4%			% of Pop:	12.9%
College grad:	32.1%				
Grad degree:	11.7%				

Political reporters covering New Hampshire's first-in-the-nation primary usually stay in Manchester, the state's largest city and within an hour's drive of the rest of the state except for the North Country. Yet there are other noteworthy cities and towns in New Hampshire. Concord, north of Manchester, is the state capital. On one side of Main Street is the handsome, small, granite Capitol, and on the other you can usually find the headquarters of the two political parties and many candidates: an entire

2008 Presidential Vote

Obama (D)	198,456	(56%)
McCain (R)	152,131	(43%)

2004 Presidential Vote

Kerry (D)	177,320	(52%)
Bush (R)	160,224	(47%)

Cook Partisan Voting Index: D+3

state's politics within 100 yards. Nashua, south of Manchester and on the Massachusetts line, is the state's second-largest city, a high-technology and financial services center that has been booming for two decades. To the east is prosperous and growing Salem, first chartered in 1750 and the largest of the border suburbs. To the west of Nashua, past the pleasant country around Mount Monadnock, is Keene, the hub of southwest New Hampshire. To the north are the towns along the Connecticut River; some are mill towns, and some are vacation home enclaves. New Hampshire's prosperity has spread to most of these, just across the river from Vermont. Hanover, home of Dartmouth College, is a tiny, picturesque town set in the mountains. And every political reporter's itinerary has to include a trip, usually by plane, to the little lumber mill city of Berlin in the middle of the North Country (although the paper mills have cut many jobs), and perhaps also to Dixville Notch in the White Mountains, where the town's roughly two dozen voters cast their ballots at a minute past midnight and provide the first reported returns in every presidential election. (Hint for doing election analysis: If Dixville Notch doesn't go heavily Republican, the Republicans are in trouble.)

The 2nd Congressional District of New Hampshire includes Concord, Nashua, Salem, Keene, the Connecticut River counties, Hanover, Berlin, and Dixville Notch. It also includes Mount Washington, with its spectacularly violent weather and winds that have measured up to 231 miles per hour. Not surprisingly, entrepreneurs have been exploring the possibility of wind-power parks in the North Country. The district also takes in the Bretton Woods resort, where the world monetary system was established at a conference in 1944. Politically, this region is mixed, but much of it has been trending Democratic. Nashua is more Democratic than Manchester, Salem more Republican. The area between Mount Monadnock and Keene and the territory running north along the Connecticut River to Hanover and Dartmouth has become very Democratic, much like Vermont across the river. Overall, this is the more Democratic of New Hampshire's two congressional districts. Republican George W. Bush twice lost this district with 47% of the vote. In 2008, GOP nominee John McCain lost by a more decisive 56%-43%.

The congressman from the 2nd District is Paul Hodes, a Democrat elected in 2006. He grew up in New York City, the grandson of Russian and Hungarian Jewish immigrants. His younger brother died of

Hodgkin's disease in his childhood. While studying at Dartmouth, his father's alma mater, Hodes became disillusioned by the Vietnam War. After college, Hodes worked as an actor, playwright, musician (he began playing guitar at 15), and documentary filmmaker. Then he decided to accept his grandmother's advice to have a fallback plan and got a law degree from Boston College. Hodes was hired by then-New Hampshire Attorney General David Souter as a state prosecutor, and then went into private practice in Concord, eventually becoming a partner in the firm of Shaheen and Gordon. (William Shaheen, the lead partner, is the husband of Democratic Sen. Jeanne Shaheen.) Still, Hodes refused to give up on entertaining. He and his wife, Peggo, founded Peggosus, a children's rock group whose repertoire includes the songs "If My School Was a Zoo" and "Cheerios in My Kazoo." President Bill Clinton invited the duo to perform at the White House in 1996.

Hodes first ran for Congress in 2004, when he challenged Republican Rep. Charles Bass and lost, 58%-38%. But Hodes tried again in 2006, when the political environment was far more hostile to Republicans. This time he had more support from the national party and raised much more money, outspending Bass $1.6 million to $1.2 million. Bass claimed he was an "independent voice for New Hampshire" in an attempt to distance himself from the unpopular Republican congressional leadership and the Bush administration. His claim was not entirely unfounded. Earlier that year, Bass helped launch the petition for new House Republican leadership elections that prompted scandal-plagued Majority Leader Tom DeLay to give up plans to try to retake his post. Bass also cast maverick votes against drilling in the Arctic National Wildlife Refuge and against the same-sex marriage ban. Hodes nevertheless continually tied Bass to President Bush and the Iraq war, calling for a "new course for this country." The liberal MoveOn.org also ran a television ad suggesting Bass had voted for wasteful Iraq reconstruction funds, including payments to Halliburton, Vice President Dick Cheney's former firm. As the incumbent's lead in the polls started to fade in October, both national parties took an interest in the race and began pouring money in. Hodes won 53%-46%.

In the House, Hodes established a voting record toward the center of the Democratic Caucus. He was elected president of the Democratic freshman class, and got a seat on the Financial Services Committee. He sponsored a bill to create the Northern Border Regional Development Commission to invest federal money in economic development and job creation in the Northeast. In 2008, he was successful in passing "Michelle's Law," which is designed to ensure that college students who take a medically necessary leave of absence do not lose their health insurance coverage. His legislation, based on a New Hampshire statute, was named after Michelle Morse, a cancer patient in Manchester who was diagnosed in 2003 and was forced to stay in school to keep her medical coverage.

In 2008, Republicans nominated Jennifer Horn, a radio talk-show host who competed in a five-candidate primary as a conservative and a political outsider. In the general election campaign, Horn called for tax cuts and opening more areas to oil drilling, and expressed support for the war in Iraq. She criticized Hodes for his support of liberal Democratic House Speaker Nancy Pelosi. Hodes emphasized his constituent service, and won 56%-41%. He ran most strongly in the Connecticut River counties, and trailed only in the Salem area.

After Republican Sen. Judd Gregg said in February 2009 that he would not seek re-election, Hodes announced his candidacy for the Senate. Bass and Horn were among the potential Republican candidates for the House seat.

★ NEW JERSEY ★

"**A** valley of humility between two mountains of conceit": That was how Benjamin Franklin described New Jersey, which even in colonial days was overshadowed by New York City and Philadelphia. New Jersey was named by King James II, then Duke of York, for the Channel Island on which he was sheltered during the English Civil War. New Jersey was plagued in its early years by rival claims from its neighbors and, still defensive in the 1980s, went to the U.S. Supreme Court to argue that it and not New York owns the Statue of Liberty and Ellis Island. New Jersey eventually got most of the islands' acreage, but New York got the immigrant museum and Great Hall, which are built on fill land. New Jersey, though, has much to say for itself. It is "a sort of laboratory in which the best blood is prepared for other communities to thrive on," Woodrow Wilson said when he was governor, just a tad defensively.

From its modest beginnings, New Jersey grew in the 20th century to become one of America's powerhouse states. Its economy transitioned from a reliance on vegetable farming—hence the name the Garden State—to cutting-edge technology. Thomas Edison churned out inventions in his laboratory at Menlo Park and gave birth to General Electric and Bell Labs. On open fields near large labor pools, U.S. automakers built assembly plants in the years after World War II, and the container port on the New Jersey side of New York harbor overshadowed the crumbling, racketeer-plagued docks of Manhattan and Brooklyn. The pharmaceutical industry came to be concentrated here, housing the headquarters of Merck; Johnson & Johnson; Bristol-Myers Squibb; Novartis; and Schering-Plough. Connected to Wall Street by Hudson tubes and ferries, New Jersey became the home of finance professionals and their back offices as well. This economy has given the state a high-income, well-educated workforce and a prosperous middle class, with a relatively high concentration of scientists and engineers. New Jersey has long had the highest or second-highest median household income of any state, although it trails others in per capita income and wealth. This state is the home not only of high-income Ph.D.s but also of *The Sopranos*.

Physically, New Jersey has been transformed. The oil tank farms and swamplands of the Meadowlands have become sports palaces and office complexes. The Singer factory in Elizabeth, the Western Electric factory in Kearny, the Ford Motor plant in Mahwah, and the Shulton plant in Clifton are all gone, replaced by shopping centers and hotels and other development. The General Motors plant in Linden, the state's last auto plant, closed in 2005. The intersection of Interstates 78 and 287 has become a major shopping and office-edge city. U.S. 1 north from Princeton to North Brunswick has become one of the nation's high-tech centers. Casting off its suburban image, New Jersey has developed an identity of its own. It is the home of big-league football, basketball, and hockey franchises and of the world's longest expanses of boardwalk, on the Jersey Shore from Cape May to Sandy Hook. New Jersey is also the East Coast's premier gambling getaway. Atlantic City, an hour from Philadelphia and two hours from Manhattan, had gambling revenues in 2006 of $5.5 billion, a close second behind the Las Vegas Strip's $6.7 billion.

Within New Jersey's close boundaries is great diversity: geographically, from beaches to mountains; demographically, from old Quaker stock to new Hispanic arrivals; economically, from inner-city slums to hunt-country mansions. Although New York writers are inclined to look on New Jersey as a land of 1940s diners and 1970s shopping malls, the state much more closely resembles the rest of America than does Manhattan, although drivers will find some peculiarities: horizontal traffic lights, jughandle intersections (to make a left turn, you exit to the right and then cross over after the light has changed), and a ban on self-service gas stations. The Jersey City row houses one encounters on emerging from the Holland Tunnel give way within a few miles to the skyscrapers of Newark and its new performing arts center. Farther out are comfortably packed middle-income suburbs and the horse country around Far Hills, the university town of Princeton, old industrial cities such as Paterson and Trenton, and dozens of suburban towns and small factory cities where people work and raise families over generations. Among them are commuter towns such as Middletown, whose commuter trails lead to Lower Manhattan. (Middletown lost dozens of residents on September 11.)

Regardless of which state holds legal title to Ellis Island, New Jersey has long been a magnet for immigrants. In its post-World War II years of rapid growth, the state was a quilt pattern of WASPs, Irish, Italians, Jews, and Hungarians (the nation's largest concentration of the latter was in Middlesex County). Small-town-like suburbs centered on Dutch Reform or Episcopal churches became heavily Catholic or Jewish. Immigrant growth is concentrated in North and Central Jersey, within range of New York City. South Jersey (as in adjacent Philadelphia) has few immigrant communities. Overall in 2007, the state's population was 13% African-American, 16% Hispanic, and 7% Asian. One-third of New Jersey schoolchildren had immigrant parents. Hudson County, the land along the ridge opposite Manhattan, was the home of hundreds of thousands of Irish, Italian, Polish and Jewish immigrants in the early 20th century, and is now more than 40% Hispanic, a grouping that includes Cubans, Puerto Ricans, Dominicans and Mexicans. Immigrants are also plentiful in the small middle-American towns of Bergen County: Filipinos in Bergenfield, Guatemalans in Fairview, Koreans in Leonia, Indians in Lodi, and Chinese in Palisades Park. The old cities of Elizabeth and Paterson are half Hispanic and nearly one-quarter of the residents

Districts 6, 8, 9, 10, and 13 are highlighted for visibility.

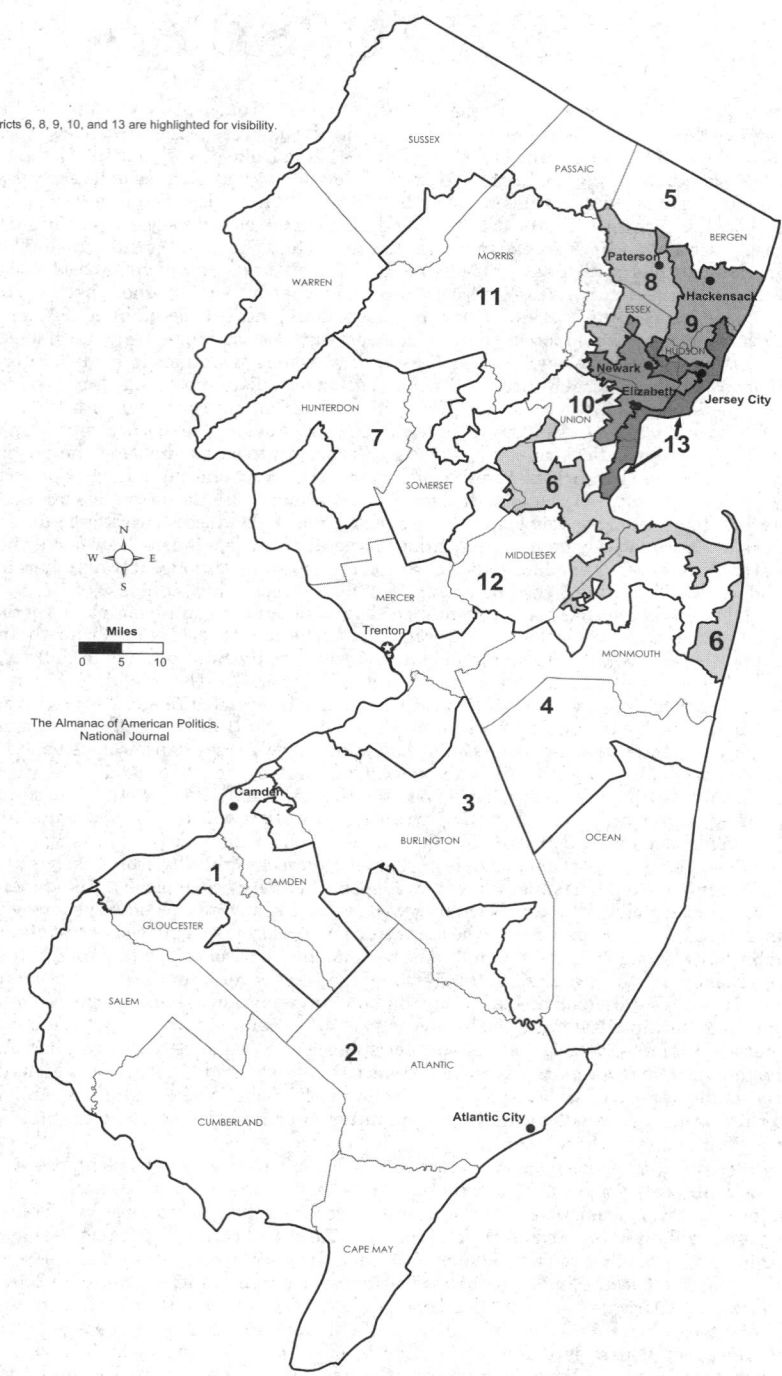

The Almanac of American Politics.
National Journal

Congressional district boundaries were first effective for 2002.

of the area from Woodbridge to New Brunswick in Middlesex County are Asian. Newark still has a black majority, but it includes many of the Brazilians in the Ironbound district.

For all its strengths, New Jersey has faced difficulties in the new century. Population growth has slowed to a crawl, with only very small patches of suburban boom and of growth in gated, adult-only communities. Immigrant inflow from 2000 to 2008 was 4.8% of the 2000 population, but there was an even higher nonimmigrant outflow. Only Ocean County, with its retirement communities, and Gloucester County, on the New Jersey Turnpike outside of Philadelphia, attracted significant numbers of nonimmigrant new residents. New Jersey's emblematic private sector firms have found themselves in trouble. Lucent, the successor to Bell Labs, was burned in the high tech bust and was acquired in 2006 by the French firm Alcatel, which soon cut thousands of jobs. The pharmaceutical firms, battered by class-action lawsuits, the threat of drug reimportation, and the difficulty of developing and getting approval for new blockbuster drugs, have seen their business model founder. Merck, Bristol-Myers Squibb, Schering-Plough, Pfizer, and Ortho Biotech have cut their New Jersey payrolls. The state had 20% of U.S. pharmaceutical jobs in 1990 but only 13% by 2008. Two New Jersey industries that once seemed launched on eternal growth trajectories found themselves in trouble in 2008. Gambling revenues fell steeply in Atlantic City, and casino owners were actively fighting a state proposal to ban smoking, which they said would drive away more customers. Banks and financial service firms in distress cut back sharply both on Wall Street and New Jersey back-office jobs. Unemployment rose from 4.2% in February 2007 to 8.3% in March 2009. Experts predicted that the state would end up with a zero increase in private-sector jobs in the decade. New Jersey did reap some gain from a 20% tax credit for moviemakers, but the results, at least in *The Wrestler*, were less than flattering to the state's image.

State government has played a role in building New Jersey's identity, but it also has placed heavy burdens on its private sector. In the 1970s, Democratic Gov. Brendan Byrne started the Meadowlands sports complex and legalized casino gambling in Atlantic City. He also pushed through an income tax in a state that, until that point, had far lower taxes than New York. Gov. Tom Kean in the 1980s reformed education and promoted the state shamelessly ("New Jersey and you: perfect together"). The revolt against Democratic Gov. Jim Florio's tax increase in 1990 was led by the first all-New Jersey talk radio station and took on national significance with his defeat by Republican Christine Todd Whitman in 1993—a harbinger, as it turned out, of the big Republican congressional victories in 1994. In the 1990s, crime and welfare rolls dropped, but auto insurance and property taxes remained the highest in the nation. Health insurance premiums skyrocketed 71% from 2000 to '07, thanks to state mandates requiring all policies to cover all manner of treatments. Property taxes kept rising, and the Legislature increased the sales tax in 2006. When he came to power that year, Gov. Jon Corzine pledged to support all-day kindergarten and community health clinics; he also backed the rehabilitation of Port Newark and low-interest loans for first-time homebuyers. Corzine's proposal to lease the Turnpike and raise tolls for the first time in years would have eliminated one of New Jersey's few bargains. The state Legislature voted to spend $270 million on embryonic-stem-cell research, not normally a state government function, and to require sharp decreases in carbon emissions, and hence higher electricity rates, in the near future.

New Jersey leaned Republican for many years. But it has become a Democratic bastion because of a growing immigrant population and the presence of many affluent suburbanites who reject conservative stands on cultural issues. No Republican has won 50% of the state vote for president or for governor since presidential candidate George H.W. Bush in 1988 and gubernatorial candidate Thomas Kean in 1985. No Republican has been elected to the U.S. Senate since Clifford Case in 1972. Starting in 2000, New Jersey has voted between 53% and 57% Democratic and between 42% and 46% Republican for president, senator, and governor. On a map showing election results by city and township, Democrats carry the spine of the state, on either side of the Metroliner route and through the South Jersey suburbs of Philadelphia. Republicans carry the outliers, most of the Jersey Shore on the east, and the affluent suburban and exurban areas on the northwest. The Democrats' margins have been augmented by the steady absorption of immigrants and the outflow of modest-income Americans from the formerly middle-class suburbs within close range of the Metroliner spine. In early 2009, with polls showing Corzine running behind potential Republican challengers in the November 2010 election, the Democratic string seemed threatened. But in a state where 12% of the voters are African-American, 9% Latino, and 4% Asian, Republicans need to get about 60% of the votes from whites to win.

A number of factors have helped Democrats. Corzine, who amassed a $300 million fortune when Goldman Sachs went public in the 1990s, spent more than $100 million on his races for senator in 2000 and for governor in 2005, and he has generously subsidized other Democratic campaigns in between. New Jersey is the second-most expensive political state in the nation because candidates have to buy ads in the New York and Philadelphia media markets. Second, New Jersey's high-earning, relatively well-educated voters tend not to vote in often crucial primaries—some 47% are not registered in either party—and those who do vote tend to defer to the choices of county and city political machines, which are of varying degrees of competence and cronyism. For candidates in both parties, it is a great advantage to have the designation of the local county party on the primary ballot. A 1993 campaign finance law also increased the power of parties and its leaders—it allows county parties to accept contributions 18 times as large as what candidates can receive; party chairmen, as a result, increasingly raise money and dole it out to favored candidates. These chairmen in turn sometimes control local government and possess the power to dole out contracts—the Jersey term is "pay to play." Corzine has given hundreds of thousands of dollars to county Democratic machines, which has enabled him to wield the power once held by the party bosses of yore.

A third factor has been the readiness of Democrats to pitch losers aside, and the willingness of the legal and political establishments to go along. In September 2002, Democratic Sen. Robert Torricelli, plagued by scandal, dropped out of his race for re-election. In a bipartisan decision, the state Supreme Court upheld the right of Democrats to substitute on the ballot former Sen. Frank Lautenberg (whose relations with Torricelli were famously acerbic). In August 2004, Democratic Gov. Jim McGreevey, already in trouble because of his ties to later-convicted fundraiser Charles Kushner, announced that he would resign on November 15; this was prompted by the revelation that he had appointed a gay lover as his homeland-security adviser. McGreevey's delayed announcement prevented a special election, which a Republican might have won. Democratic Senate President Richard Codey stepped in as acting governor, and he considered running for a full term in November. But Corzine, with his capacity to spend unlimited amounts of money, was able to muscle Codey aside and seize the gubernatorial nomination, which proved to be tantamount to election.

The outlook for New Jersey in election year 2009 seems bound to be determined by the voters' choice between two competing visions. One view is that state government has ambitiously and courageously set out to solve major societal problems, using the resources of a bounteously prosperous society, and should remain poised to resume doing so when the inevitable economic recovery occurs. Another view is that state government has been draining the life out of a productive private sector to the point that people and production are migrating elsewhere. Those two views will be tested in 2009 and the years ahead.

Population		Household Income		Work	
Pop. 2007:	8,669,815	Under $15k:	9.8%	Private:	80.4%
State rank:	11th of 50	$15k to $50k:	27.9%	Government:	14.3%
Change since 2000:	Up 3.0%	$50k to $100k:	31.5%	Self-employed:	5.1%
Urban:	93.6%	$100k to $150k:	23.6%	Unemployment (3-yr. average):	4.1%
Rural:	6.4%	Over $150k:	7.2%	Poverty:	8.7%
Native of state:	52.5%	Median income:	$66,509	Blue collar:	18.5%
Not a citizen:	10.0%	**Home Value**		White collar:	65.8%
Area size:	8,721 sq. mi.	Under $100k:	4.6%	Khaki collar:	0.1%
Most populous cities		$100k to $300k:	33.0%	Other:	15.6%
1. Newark	265,375	$300k to $500k:	37.2%	**Age**	
2. Jersey City	234,914	$500k to $1 mil:	21.9%	Median age:	38.2 yrs.
3. Paterson	142,443	Over $1 million:	3.4%	More than 65 yrs:	13.0%
4. Elizabeth	126,538	Median:	$358,400	Less than 18 yrs:	24.0%

Race/Ethnicity				Military Veterans		Registered Voters in 2008	
White:	62.5%	*Language*		% of Pop:	8.0%	D:	1,782,556 (33.3%)
Black:	13.2%	English:	72.5%	*Veterans by Period*		R:	1,055,403 (19.7%)
Hispanic:	15.6%	Spanish:	13.7%	WWII and before:	17.8%	Other:	2,513,710 (47.0%)
Asian:	7.2%	Asian:	4.2%	Korea:	14.8%	Voter turnout:	3,868,237
Native Am.:	0.1%	Other		Vietnam:	30.0%	Turnout as % of	
Hawaiian:	0.0%	European	8.2%	Gulf (pre-2001):	6.5%	voting age:	58.3%
Two+ races:	1.0%	**Education**		Gulf (post-2001):	5.1%	**Legislature**	
Ancestry		H.S. grad:	86.3%	Peace time:	25.9%	Senate:	23 D 17 R
Italian:	14.2%	College grad:	33.7%			General Assembly:	48 D 32 R
Irish:	12.7%	Grad degree:	12.4%				
German:	10.0%						

Presidential politics   For most of the 20th century, New Jersey was a close state in close presidential elections, giving small margins to winners in 1960 and 1968 and to losers in 1948 and 1976, but no more. In the 1980s, the vast suburban expanses of New Jersey leaned toward the Republicans. Since 1995, they have leaned to the Democrats. This is a state with relatively few voters on the Religious Right and with a high number of secular residents and Jews. It also has a rising number of immigrant voters.

In 2004, President Bush's campaign strategists kept an eye on New Jersey's polls to see whether for some reason—the impact of September 11, for example—the state might be worth contesting. A few public polls showed the race close or tied, but others placed Democratic candidate John Kerry well ahead, and Kerry carried the state 53%-46%. In 2008, no one targeted New Jersey. Polls showed the race tightening in the spring and again in early

2008 Presidential Vote		
Obama (D)	2,215,422	(57%)
McCain (R)	1,613,207	(42%)
2008 Democratic Presidential Primary		
Clinton (D)	613,500	(54%)
Obama (D)	501,372	(44%)
2008 Republican Presidential Primary		
McCain (R)	313,459	(55%)
Romney (R)	160,388	(28%)
Huckabee (R)	46,284	(8%)
2004 Presidential Vote		
Kerry (D)	1,911,430	(53%)
Bush (R)	1,670,003	(46%)

September, but Republicans could not afford to put money into New York television (there was some question whether they could afford Philadelphia) and Democrats saw no need to. Barack Obama carried the state 57%-42%, the best Democratic showing since 1964, although it barely bested Democratic nominee Al Gore's 56%-40% in 2000. Young voters went 67% for Obama, and senior citizens went 53% for Republican John McCain. Whites voted 50%-49% for McCain, African-Americans 92%-8% for Obama. Catholics voted 55% for McCain, close to the 58% Bush received from them in 2004. (With his support coming from the elderly, white Catholics, and white Protestants, McCain was carrying the New Jersey of the 1950s but not the New Jersey of the 2000s.) Despite his stand on immigration, McCain won only 21% of Latinos. A comparison of Obama's and Gore's percentages showed big Democratic gains in North Jersey, with large black and immigrant populations, and Democratic losses in all the Jersey Shore counties, including the largest in fast-growing Ocean County.

For years, New Jersey held its presidential primary in early June, but it was usually overshadowed by the California primary on the same day. In 1996, California voted in March, and New Jerseyans did not get to the polls until long after the nominations were sewn up. The pattern continued in the next two presidential contests. In April 2007, the primary date was changed to February 5, Super Tuesday. But New Jersey again got lost in the shuffle. Polls showed Democrat Hillary Rodham Clinton and Republican John McCain with solid leads here and in New York, which also voted on Super Tuesday. So the campaigns had little need to buy New York television. Democratic turnout was 1.1 million, nearly double the previous record. Clinton beat Obama in the Democratic primary 54%-44%. She carried Jewish and Latino voters, while Obama carried blacks and did well in high-income suburbs, except those with large Jewish populations. Turnout on the Republican side was only 566,000, more than ever before but only half the number of Democrats who voted. McCain defeated Mitt Romney by a surprisingly large 55%-28%. Romney was unable to duplicate here the appeal he demonstrated in high-income suburbs in several other states. McCain received more than 50% of the vote in all but two counties.

Congressional districting   New Jersey has a Congressional Redistricting Commission, made up of 12 members appointed by the party leaders in the Legislature. The members pick an arbiter, and in both 1991 and 2001, they chose professor Alan Rosenthal of the Eagleton Institute at Rutgers University. The 13th member breaks a tie, produces a compromise plan of his own, and sees whether a majority will accept it. If not, he forwards the two plans to the state Supreme Court. In 1991, Rosenthal picked the Republican plan, with grotesquely shaped districts. But given New Jersey's Democratic trend, it had yielded by 2000 the Republicans only six of the state's 13 congressional seats.

111th Congress Lineup	
8 D	5 R
110th Congress Lineup	
7 D	6 R

In 2001, the 13 incumbents agreed on a bipartisan congressional delegation plan and submitted it to the commission. Rosenthal liked the incumbent-protection plan, and in October the commission adopted it with slight changes. The result is a map with very erose district lines and oddly shaped districts, drawn explicitly to protect incumbents and blessed by an esteemed political scientist. The partisan tilt is plain from the presidential election returns. Within these lines, Bush carried only three of these districts in 2000, when he won 40% of the vote in New Jersey. But in 2004, he carried all six of the districts represented by Republicans. In 2008, McCain carried three of them, while Democrats picked up the open seat in the 3rd District.

New Jersey will likely lose a seat after the 2010 census, as it did after the censuses of 1970 and 1980. The state has grown slowly and was passed in population by Georgia in 2002 and by North Carolina in 2005. Any new plan will surely maintain the majority-black 10th District and the heavily Hispanic 13th District (although the latter will presumably have to be renumbered), and the lines are unlikely to be disturbed much in South Jersey, which has grown faster than the rest of the state. Yet the latter's growth means squeezing out a North Jersey seat. Several of these districts have convoluted shapes and could easily be divided among their neighbors. Democrats would presumably prefer to divide up the 7th District, which was retained by Republican Leonard Lance in an open-seat contest in 2008. Republicans might prefer to divide up the 8th District, centered on Paterson; its Democratic towns could be added to the 9th, 10th, and 13th districts, which will have to be expanded geographically because of low population growth.

Governor

Jon Corzine (D)

Elected 2005, term expires Jan. 2010, 1st term; b. Jan. 1, 1947, Taylorville, IL; home, Hoboken; U. of IL (Urbana-Champaign), B.A. 1969; U. of Chicago, M.B.A. 1973; Christian; divorced; 3 children.

Military Career: Marine Corps Reserve, 1969–75.

Elected Office: U.S. Senate, 2000–05.

Professional Career: Officer, Continental IL Natl. Bank, 1970–73; Asst. V.P., BancOhio, 1973–75; Goldman Sachs, Bond Trader 1975–80, Partner 1980–99, Chmn. & CEO 1994–99.

Office: P.O. Box 001, Trenton, 08625, 609-292-6000; Fax: 609-292-3454; Web site: www.state.nj.us/governor.

Election Results

2005 general	Jon Corzine (D)	1,224,493	(53%)
	Douglas Forrester (R)	985,235	(43%)
2005 primary	Jon Corzine (D)	207,670	(88%)
	James Kelly (D)	19,512	(8%)

Prior Winning Percentages: 2000 Senate (50%)

Democrat Jon Corzine was elected governor in 2005, and had been a U.S. senator from New Jersey since 2001. Corzine grew up on the family farm in Christian County in rural Illinois. In addition to farming, his father was an insurance salesman and his mother a teacher. Corzine got his undergraduate degree at the University of Illinois, which was three counties over from home, and went on to get a business degree from the University of Chicago. He served six years in the Marine Corps Reserve. His first job after college was as a financial analyst for Continental Bank in Chicago. In 1975, he joined the Goldman Sachs investment banking house in New York. His entry-level position included fetching coffee for his boss, but in a few years, Corzine was a successful bond trader and a protégé of Robert Rubin, who became Treasury secretary in the Clinton administration. In 1980, Corzine was made a general partner at Goldman Sachs, and 14 years later he was co-chairman and chief executive officer. In May 1999, when Goldman Sachs went public, the $3.6 billion initial public offering netted Corzine more than $300 million. He retired from the firm after a management shake-up that year. By that time, he had moved to New Jersey. Aside from contributing to Democratic (and some Republican) candidates, he had not been engaged politically except to co-chair a 1997 presidential commission on increasing investment in technology, infrastructure, and schools.

In February 1999, Democratic Sen. Frank Lautenberg announced he would not seek re-election in 2000 (Lautenberg later returned to win election to Bob Torricelli's seat in 2002). Former Democratic Gov. Jim Florio, still remembered for increasing state taxes by $2.8 billion in 1990, got into the contest, as did former Republican Gov. Christine Todd Whitman, who, unlike Florio, was still popular in the state. (She defeated Florio in 1993.) Many Democratic leaders feared that Whitman would win, and, searching for an alternative to Florio, they found Corzine. Having just retired from investment banking, Corzine had time and money on his hands, about $300 million in fact. Without any real experience in electoral politics, Corzine traveled around the state to meet leaders of the county Democratic organizations, who are vital in the primary. He also began to contribute large sums to community groups and political organizations that could be helpful in a statewide campaign. Between 1999 and 2007, his foundation gave $48 million to charities, including African-American churches, arts groups, and Jewish organizations. His wealth and willingness to spend it cleared the field. Whitman withdrew in September 1999, although Florio was not dissuaded and stayed in the race. He attacked Corzine's inexperience and the fact that he hadn't voted in every election. In March, three months before the primary, Corzine went up with television ads in the New York and Philadelphia markets. He spent a whopping $35 million on the primary race, and won 58%-42%.

Meanwhile, the low-turnout Republican primary was won by 7th District Rep. Bob Franks, a member of the same church as Corzine. With a big disadvantage in finances, Franks went on the attack, criticizing Corzine's lack of experience in government and accusing him of trying to buy the Senate seat. He called on Corzine to disclose his income-tax returns, which Corzine refused to do. (However, in mid-September, he released records showing that in 1996–99 he made $145 million, paid $43 million in taxes, and contributed $25 million to charity.) Franks also benefited from endorsements by *The New York Times* and *Philadelphia Inquirer*, and Corzine's beginner's mistakes. Corzine told the Sierra Club he had voted for an open space referendum in 1998, when in fact he had not voted that year. Still stuck below 50% in the polls, Corzine started running negative ads against Franks, and dominated the airwaves in the weeks before the election. He spent $7.4 million on turnout efforts, including busing in residents of Philadelphia homeless shelters and halfway houses to work on his campaign. In total, he spent $63 million, a record that still stands. He won 50%-47%, with big margins in the central cities. But he ran behind Democratic presidential nominee Al Gore's 56%-40% showing in New Jersey that year.

In his first year in the Senate, the September 11 attacks occurred, hitting New Jersey especially hard. Ten people from Corzine's hometown of Summit died. His major initiative that year was a chemical-security bill to require businesses to conduct vulnerability assessments and consider safer security technology. He was also a co-sponsor of the Terrorism Risk Insurance Act, which became law in November 2002. With a seat on the Banking Committee, where he had considerable expertise, he worked on the 2002 Sarbanes-Oxley Act, which dramatically tightened accounting regulations after a series of accounting scandals. He also fought successfully that year to delay for a year the Education Department's plan to reduce deductions for state taxes when parents and students calculate their eligibility for Pell college grants. The change would hurt most in high-income, high-tax states like New Jersey. Corzine worked to raise the maximum jail penalty, from six months to 10 years, for willful worker-safety violations that result in an employee's death.

Corzine became an active partisan in New Jersey and national politics. He supported the election of Democratic Gov. Jim McGreevey in 2001, and showed skill at handling difficult political situations in the imbroglio over whether his scandal-plagued Senate colleague, Democrat Bob Torricelli, should drop out of the 2002 Senate race. He had backed Torricelli but helped to negotiate his departure and also Lautenberg's Senate comeback to replace Torricelli. In 2003, he liberally supported county Democratic organizations, which helped Democrats win majorities in both houses of the Legislature. In late 2002, Senate Democratic Leader Tom Daschle named Corzine as chairman of the Democratic Senatorial Campaign Committee. His major responsibility was fundraising for the party's candidates for Senate, and he was good at it, out-raising the Republicans' Senate committee in the 2004 election season. He sought out candidates capable of self-financing their races and discouraged primary competition in four of the five Southern states where Democrats were retiring. Through the summer, he said, not unreasonably, that Democrats had a chance to gain seats. But in the end, the close races went the other way, and Democrats lost all five Southern seats, and in the biggest blow, Daschle lost his re-election bid.

In 2004, Gov. McGreevey was in trouble. His job rating was low, there was talk of replacing him with another candidate, and hanging over state government was a cloud of corruption. U.S. Attorney Christopher Christie obtained indictments of two prominent McGreevey fundraisers, one of whom was accused of trying to thwart a federal investigation by luring a grand jury witness into a tryst with a prostitute. At the Democratic National Convention in July 2004, Corzine, not McGreevey, was head of the New Jersey delegation. Then, on August 12, McGreevey announced that he had had an extramarital affair with a man whom he had appointed as his homeland security adviser and would resign effective November 15. Some state Democrats urged him to resign sooner so that state Senate President Richard Codey could become acting governor and get a head start on running for the post in his own right. McGreevey refused, and Codey was stymied from moving up. But he began to lay the groundwork for a campaign.

Meanwhile, after the Democratic losses at the polls, Corzine was facing the prospect of at least another two years in the minority. While he said he was happy in the Senate, he also said he missed being in an executive position. And the New Jersey governor wields broad executive powers. The state has the strongest governor in the nation, the only statewide elected official who appoints all others, including the attorney general and the 21 county district attorneys. Corzine decided to run, and quickly lined up endorsements from dozens of Democrats, including U.S. representatives Bob Menendez and Frank Pallone, both of whom were interested in being appointed to Corzine's Senate seat if he won. He also got the backing of New Jersey Speaker Albio Sires and many others whom he had supported generously over the years. Corzine said his wealth ensured that he would be "unbought and unbossed" as governor. In addition to Codey, 1st District Rep. Rob Andrews, who narrowly lost the 1997 gubernatorial primary to McGreevey, was also interested in the Democratic nomination for governor, and with his base in South Jersey, he looked like a formidable contender. But it became clear that Corzine had much more support than the other two. In the Republican primary, Doug Forrester, a health benefits administrator who had lost the 2002 Senate race to Lautenberg after spending $8 million of his own money, was able to defeat his competition, former Jersey City Mayor Bret Schundler. Organization Republicans disliked Schundler for his maverick ways and conservative views on abortion. Forrester spent $10 million of his own money to defeat Schundler, 36%-31%.

New Jersey's property taxes, the highest in the country, were the main issue in the contest between Corzine and Forrester, and both presented property-tax relief plans. Forrester called for a 30% cut over three years and said he would pay for it by spending cuts and layoffs of state employees. Corzine called for graduated rebates over four years averaging 10%, with higher rates for those with lower incomes and for senior citizens. Corzine charged that Forrester's plan would end senior-citizen rebates, and Forrester charged that Corzine's spending programs would be unsustainable. The arguments over policy became overshadowed by personal attacks. Forrester charged that Corzine sought a government subsidy as part of a group seeking to buy the New Jersey Nets. Corzine said Forrester's firm benefited from government contracts made by officials to whom he gave campaign contributions. Both charges were based on flimsy evidence. Forrester trumpeted the revelation that Corzine had loaned $470,000 to girlfriend Carla Katz, who was the head of the largest state public employee union, and that he had forgiven the loan around the time he announced for governor. In the final week of the campaign, Forrester ran an ad that quoted Corzine's former wife of 33 years telling *The New York Times*: "When I saw the campaign ad where Andrea Forrester said, 'Doug never let his family down and he won't let New Jersey down,' all I could think was that Jon did let his family down and he'll probably let New Jersey down too." But despite the flood of negative ads, Corzine won 53%-43%, racking up big margins in the central cities. Forrester carried only three counties on the shore and five counties from affluent Morris and Somerset west to the state line. Interestingly, Corzine's old hometown of Summit split evenly, 3,328 to 3,328.

When he took office, Corzine pledged to take only $1 a year in salary and soon started wearing what became his trademark navy blue sweater-vest. One of his first orders of business was to appoint his successor, and he chose Democrat Robert Menendez, the 13th District House member and a member of the House leadership. In January, Corzine faced a projected $4 billion budget deficit. His $31 billion budget imposed on hospitals a $620 monthly per bed fee, froze state aid to poor school districts, and increased the sales tax from 6% to 7%. New Jersey Speaker Joe Roberts, a Democrat, balked and forced an impasse in July 2006. The state government shut down and so did Atlantic City's casinos, which require state monitoring to stay open. Corzine threatened to spend his own money on ads targeting Roberts, and the Assembly backed down and the sales tax was increased, with a promise that half of the proceeds would go to property-tax relief.

In January 2007, Corzine asked the Legislature to cap property-tax increases at 4% a year; they had been capped at 7% a year. When lawmakers missed their deadline to act, he threatened to call for a constitutional convention in the fall. He also demanded that the bill include a ban on double officeholding; New Jersey had allowed its legislators to hold local office while serving in the Legislature. The ban passed in June, with exemptions for current legislators. And the Legislature came up with a bill that met his specifications, with graduated property-tax rebates up to 20% and a 4% cap on increases. In June 2007, he signed a $33.5 billion budget with property-tax relief and, for the first time in six years, no tax increases. Corzine was less successful at "asset monetization," his plan to lease the often-jammed New Jersey Turnpike and increase tolls.

In April 2007, Corzine was seriously injured in an auto accident. A state trooper driving him on the Garden State Parkway from Atlantic City to a meeting in New Brunswick was traveling over 90 miles per hour when a truck veered into its path. The governor's sport-utility vehicle crashed into a guardrail, with Corzine in the front seat and not wearing a seat belt. He suffered a broken breastbone, collarbone, and leg and many broken ribs; he was on a ventilator for several days and returned weeks later to the governor's mansion, Drumthwacket. When he recovered, Corzine, who had championed mandatory seat belt laws, publicly apologized for not wearing his seat belt, paid a $46 fine, and filmed a 30-second public service announcement in which he said, "I'm New Jersey Governor Jon Corzine, and I should be dead."

Late in 2007, Corzine called for "transformational change" in state finances, and argued again for leasing the turnpike to realize $38 billion in higher tolls. He paid $4 million to a Manhattan law firm to analyze the legality of such an arrangement in which a state leasing corporation would be tax-exempt. In early 2008, he rolled out a $33.5 billion budget, with no spending increase but with the turnpike leasing plan. It also included $168 million in cuts in state aid to 323 municipalities, which was an attempt to force them to consolidate services. His budget plan drew hostile receptions in a series of town hall meetings, and in February, he admitted he didn't have the votes in the Legislature for the turnpike leasing plan. (It didn't help that Lautenberg weighed in against it.) In the meantime, Corzine pushed for nearly $4 billion in borrowing for school construction to meet the terms of a state Supreme Court decision. In June, after some back-and-forth with the Legislature, Corzine signed a $32.9 billion budget. Property taxes increased only 3.7% in 2008, the lowest rate in 10 years and below Corzine's 4% cap.

Although he lost on the turnpike leasing plan, Corzine nonetheless chalked up several successes in the legislative session. In July, with former vice president turned environmental activist Al Gore at this side at the Meadowlands, he signed a bill requiring a 20% reduction in carbon emissions by 2020, and an 80% reduction by 2050. His proposal for universal health insurance coverage passed and was put into place in July 2008. It mandates coverage of all children in three years. His proposal for 12 weeks of paid family leave, which he backed fervently after his own convalescence, was pared down to six weeks and passed in May 2008. And the death penalty, not administered in New Jersey since

1963, was abolished. However, voters rejected Corzine's ballot proposal to borrow $450 million for embryonic-stem-cell research.

Also in 2008, Corzine played a role in presidential politics. He heartily supported New York Sen. Hillary Rodham Clinton for president and had the satisfaction of helping her win the New Jersey primary on February 5. In March, he and Pennsylvania Gov. Ed Rendell, also a Clinton supporter, pledged to raise $15 million to fund rerun primaries in Michigan and Florida, which Clinton had won but which were not recognized by the national Democratic Party because of a dispute with those states over the timing of their primaries. However, rerun primaries were not held. When Illinois Sen. Barack Obama clinched the Democratic nomination in June, Corzine fully supported him.

At home, Corzine faced continued controversy over his relationship with union leader Carla Katz. Steve Lonegan, the mayor of Bogota and an unsuccessful candidate for the Republican gubernatorial nomination in 2005, brought an ethics complaint against him for forgiving a $475,000 mortgage when their relationship ended in 2004. Corzine had also given her large undisclosed sums that enabled her to send her children to private school and to purchase a $1 million apartment in the same Hoboken building where Corzine had his residence. The complaint ultimately was dismissed, but that wasn't the end of the publicity. Republican state Chairman Tom Wilson brought a lawsuit seeking disclosure of e-mails between Corzine and Katz and her brother-in-law, Rocco Riccio. The suit alleged that Corzine had given Riccio $15,000 and promised to get him a private-sector job. In May 2008, a judge ordered disclosure of the e-mails, and Corzine appealed. In November, Corzine admitted he had paid $350,000 to Riccio after Riccio threatened to sue for breach of the promise to get him a job. In January 2009, a state appeals court reversed the decision ordering release of the e-mails, and the state Supreme Court declined to review the decision, ending the case.

By early 2009, the recession had brought its bad tidings to New Jersey, and Corzine started the year facing a $2.1 billion budget shortfall. He proposed an 18-month freeze on state pay increases and ordered cuts in aid to community health centers and school districts. In March 2009, he proposed a $29.8 billion state budget—well below previous levels—with reductions in property-tax rebates, a one-year suspension of property-tax deductions, and cuts in aid to small municipalities. "Tough choices to do the right thing," he said. He pledged $12 million in aid for homeowners threatened with foreclosure and small businesses short of credit as a result of the crisis in the financial markets.

With Virginia, New Jersey is one of two states that elects its governor in the year after the presidential election, putting Corzine up for re-election in 2009. He began in parlous political shape. Polls in March 2009 showed him with negative job ratings and trailing Republican Christopher Christie, who as U.S. attorney secured convictions of dozens of New Jersey politicians of both parties. Christie launched his campaign in February with a series of appearances across the state. Also running in the June GOP primary was his old nemesis in the ethics controversy, Lonegan, the Bogota mayor. Christie called for overhauling the pension system and requiring supermajorities for tax increases. And Lonegan called for replacing the state income tax with a flat tax and reducing the state budget to $27 billion. Christie easily won the June primary, besting Lonegan 55%-42%.

Corzine said in December 2008: "I really would like to be re-elected. But it's more important that I use the time that I have to do the best I can to try to address the challenges that the people of the state have." It was unclear whether he could finance his own campaign as lavishly as in 2000 and 2005. His income declined from about $55 million in 2006 to $4 million in 2007, and presumably his blind trust suffered significant losses in the market crash.

Senior Senator

Frank Lautenberg (D)

Elected 2002, term expires 2014, 5th term; b. Jan. 23, 1924, Paterson; home, Cliffside Park; Columbia U., B.S. 1949; Jewish; married (Bonnie); 4 children.

Military Career: Army Signal Corps, 1942–46 (WWII).

Elected Office: U.S. Senate, 1982–2000.

Professional Career: Co-founder, Automatic Data Processing, 1952–82; NY & NJ Port Authority Comm., 1978–82.

DC Office: 324 HSOB, 20510, 202-224-3224; Fax: 202-228-4054; Web site: lautenberg.senate.gov.

State Offices: Camden, 856-338-8922; Newark, 973-639-8700.

Committees: *Appropriations* (14th of 18 D): Commerce, Justice, Science & Related Agencies; Energy & Water Development; Financial Services & General Government; Homeland Security; State, Foreign Operations & Related Programs; Transportation, Housing and Urban Development & Related Agencies. *Commerce, Science & Transportation* (8th of 14 D): Aviation Operations, Safety & Security; Communications, Technology & the Internet; Oceans, Atmosphere, Fisheries & Coast Guard; Surface Transportation & Merchant Marine (Chmn). *Environment & Public Works* (4th of 12 D).

Group Ratings

	ADA	ACLU	AFS	LCV	ITIC	NTU	COC	ACU	CFG	FRC
2008	100	93	100	91	100	2	63	4	0	0
2007	90	—	100	93	—	9	55	0	18	—

National Journal Ratings

	2007 LIB	—	2007 CONS	2008 LIB	—	2008 CONS
Economic	94%	—	0%	89%	—	9%
Social	94%	—	0%	91%	—	0%
Foreign	79%	—	17%	65%	—	6%
Composite	92%	—	8%	88%	—	12%

Key Votes of the 110th Congress

1. Raise CAFE standards	Y	5. Make English official language	N	9. Withdraw troops 3/08	Y
2. Expand SCHIP	Y	6. Path to citizenship	Y	10. Iran guard is terrorist group	Y
3. Cap greenhouse gases	Y	7. Fetus is unborn child	N	11. Increase missile defense $	N
4. Bail out financial markets	Y	8. Prosecute hate crimes	Y	12. Overhaul FISA	N

Election Results

2008 general	Frank Lautenberg (D)	1,951,218	(56%)	($8,135,752)
	Dick Zimmer (R)	1,461,025	(42%)	($1,498,731)
2008 primary	Frank Lautenberg (D)	203,012	(59%)	
	Robert Andrews (D)	121,777	(35%)	
	Donald Cresitello (D)	19,743	(6%)	

Prior Winning Percentages: 2002 (54%); 1994 (50%); 1988 (54%); 1982 (51%)

Democrat Frank Lautenberg is New Jersey's senior senator. He was first elected in 1982, retired from the Senate in 2000, and then returned to run again in October 2002 after Democratic Sen. Robert Torricelli withdrew from his re-election race. Lautenberg grew up in Paterson, the son of Russian and Polish immigrants. His father, a silk worker who also once ran a tavern, died of cancer while Lautenberg was still in high school, and he worked nights and weekends to help with the family finances. He served in the Army Signal Corps in World War II and says he could not have gone to college without the GI Bill. He graduated from Columbia University and in 1952 started a company called Automatic Data Processing, which organized information using punch-card machines—the forerunner to computers. In time, ADP was processing the payroll for nearly 10% of the private-sector jobs in the United States. When the company went public in 1961, Lautenberg's stock was valued at $50,000; now his net worth exceeds $40 million, according to his financial disclosure forms, and ADP is still in business as one of the world's largest providers of outsourced business services. (Lautenberg's charitable foundation, however, lost most of its $14 million by investing with Bernard Madoff, the former NASDAQ chief who pleaded guilty in 2009 to a massive fraud scheme.) Lautenberg was a contributor to Democratic campaigns and landed on President Richard Nixon's "enemies list" after he gave $90,000 to Democratic presidential candidate George McGovern in 1972.

In 1982, Democratic Sen. Harrison Williams resigned as the Senate was considering his expulsion after his conviction in the Abscam bribery scandal, and his appointed successor, Republican Nicholas Brady, made it clear he was not running for a full term. Lautenberg ran, spending $5 million of his own money and touting his experience in technology. He defeated several more-seasoned politicians in the primary. In the general election, he faced Republican U.S. Rep. Millicent Fenwick, an eccentric 72-year-old who was satirized in the *Doonesbury* comic strip. Lautenberg, who's now in his mid-80s, made an issue of Fenwick's age by referring to her as a "national monument" and questioning her "fitness" and "ability to do the job." He won 51%-48%.

Lautenberg says he believes that government helped him and others work their way up, and in his first three terms in the Senate he established a solidly liberal voting record. He bucked his party only occasionally. One of his successes then was his battle against smoking in public places. A former smoker himself, Lautenberg got Congress to ban smoking in federal buildings and on airplanes on all domestic flights. In recent years, he has called for stricter labeling of the ingredients in cigarettes. He has also been a strong backer of stricter gun laws and is the author of the 1996 law barring people convicted of domestic abuse from possessing firearms. The statute was upheld 7-2 by the Supreme Court in February 2009. In 1997, Lautenberg was one of the few Democrats to enthusiastically support the balanced-budget deal that President Bill Clinton forged with the Republican majority in Congress. His support was key to Clinton's success in getting the measure through the Senate. With money to burn on his campaigns—New Jersey is the second-most-expensive state in politics because candidates must run ads in both the New York and Philadelphia television markets—Lautenberg won re-election relatively easily over retired Gen. Pete Dawkins in 1988 and state Assembly Speaker Chuck Haytaian in 1994. In 1998, he seemed primed to run again, and no well-known Republican appeared eager to challenge him. But in February 1999 he announced that he would retire in 2000.

Before long, however, national Democrats were facing a big problem with New Jersey's other Senate seat. The U.S. Attorney's Office in Manhattan was investigating charges that businessman David Chang had given lavish gifts and cash to Torricelli and that Torricelli had worked to advance Chang's business interests in South Korea. Torricelli did give such assistance, but he denied receiving gifts and said he had reimbursed Chang. In January 2002, U.S. Attorney Mary Jo White announced that Torricelli would not be prosecuted, but she sent her evidence to the Senate Ethics Committee. On July 30, the committee "severely admonished" Torricelli for violating the Senate rule against receiving gifts over $50, but the panel did not make the evidence public. His Republican opponent, businessman Doug Forrester, made much of Torricelli's problems and, as details leaked out, Torricelli plummeted in the polls; a September *Star-Ledger* newspaper survey gave Forrester a 47%-34% lead—a devastating result. The following Sunday, Gov. Jim McGreevey, Sen. Jon Corzine (who had succeeded Lautenberg), and other New Jersey Democratic leaders met in Trenton, and in a conference call with Senate Majority Leader Tom Daschle, they discussed the need for Torricelli to withdraw from the race. On Monday, he did.

New Jersey Democrats were now in need of a well-known candidate to replace Torricelli. U.S. Rep. Robert Menendez was seeking a leadership position in the House and was not interested. Rep. Robert Andrews was vetoed by McGreevey, who had narrowly defeated him in the 1997 gubernatorial primary. Other prominent Democrats, including former Sen. Bill Bradley, took a pass. By then realizing that he missed being a senator, Lautenberg let it be known he was available. It seems unlikely that Torricelli would have withdrawn if he had known that Lautenberg would get the nomination: The two had an acrimonious relationship when they served together. But there was nothing he could do to stop him. Lautenberg was well known and was capable of self-financing a race. McGreevey and the other Democrats quickly agreed on him.

New Jersey law does not contain a provision for substituting a new candidate so late in the campaign unless a candidate has died. Ballots with Torricelli's name had already been printed. But the New Jersey Supreme Court is made up of judicial activists from both parties with a propensity to accommodate party insiders. In October 2002, it quickly approved state Democrats' request to substitute Lautenberg for Torricelli and ordered the state Democratic Party to pay the $800,000 needed to print new ballots. The Lautenberg campaign moved into Torricelli's headquarters and Lautenberg was again a candidate for the Senate, and without having to spend months fundraising. The easiest source of funds proved unavailable: In a final expression of his feelings toward Lautenberg, Torricelli would not send over a dime from his $5 million campaign treasury.

The Republican in the race, Forrester, had to switch gears. He could no longer introduce himself as "the guy running against Bob Torricelli." He did run a cute ad on cable television showing a kid slamming his hand on his desk and saying, "I can't do this. I quit! If I fail this test, can I have Frank Lautenberg take it for me?" Forrester attacked Lautenberg as soft on defense and terrorism, citing his 1991 vote against the Persian Gulf War resolution, and he questioned whether Lautenberg at 78—six years older than Millicent Fenwick was when Lautenberg questioned her ability to do the job—was too old. Lautenberg hit Forrester on the issues and made a special point of noting his positions against state-paid abortions and gun control. Forrester spent $10 million altogether, including $7.5 million of his own money, but got little help from national Republicans, who did not target the race. Lautenberg spent $1.5 million of his own money, and was helped by $1.2 million from national and New Jersey Democrats. He won 54%-44%, a better showing than he'd had in 1994, when the state was significantly less Democratic.

Back in the Senate, Lautenberg was disappointed when the Democratic Caucus did not give him full credit for his seniority. But he quickly directed his ire toward the Bush administration. He moved aggressively to stop privatization of the air traffic control system, holding up the Federal Aviation Administration's reauthorization in summer 2003 until the FAA swore off privatization. Lautenberg voted against the Republican-drafted Medicare prescription drug bill that year, even though it was supported by many New Jersey pharmaceutical companies. During 2004, Lautenberg kept up a drumbeat of criticism of the Pentagon for awarding sole-source contracts to Halliburton, Vice President Dick Cheney's former employer. And he sponsored an amendment, aimed at Halliburton, to keep foreign subsidies of U.S. corporations from doing business with nations on the terrorist watch list. He also opposed the administration on the Iraq war. He sponsored an amendment to allow the media to photograph the coffins of fallen service personnel being returned to their families through Dover Air Force Base in Delaware, and as a protest against the war, Lautenberg used a foyer outside his Senate office to display photos of U.S. troops killed in Iraq and Afghanistan. When Bush made a campaign stop in New Jersey in October 2004, Lautenberg said, "President Bush, time and time again, has made decisions that made New Jersey more vulnerable to terrorism. He's here because of November 2, not 9/11." He seemed distinctly more outspoken in his second stint, and his New Jersey colleague in the Senate at the time, Democrat Jon Corzine, observed, "He's less risk-averse. I think Frank couldn't care less." Lautenberg said, "I do feel unconstrained."

From his seat on the Commerce Committee, Lautenberg has looked after his state's transportation needs with an emphasis on guarding against terrorist threats. He advocated that the Port Authority of New York and New Jersey break its lease with Dubai Ports World if the foreign-owned company was allowed to assume operations of the Newark port. He has pressed for better security at airports, seaports, and railroads. Lautenberg won a seat on the powerful Appropriations Committee in 2007 after giving up his seat on the Homeland Security and Governmental Affairs Committee. (He had been frustrated in his effort to chair the committee by invoking his years of previous experience and leapfrogging Joe Lieberman, a Connecticut independent who frequently voted with the Democrats and needed to be kept satisfied.) From Appropriations, he was able to secure funding for his pet transportation and security projects. In 2007, he inserted provisions in appropriations bills barring federal pre-emption of tougher state chemical safety laws, such as New Jersey's. He sponsored a bill on vessel safety, requiring double hulls on fuel tankers. "The last thing America needs is another Exxon Valdez," Lautenberg said. He and Menendez, now a senator, sponsored a bill, based on the 9/11 commission's recommendations, to require radiation scanning of all shipping cargo containers by 2012. Also in 2007, Lautenberg secured $14.7 million to begin engineering work on a new rail tunnel from northern New Jersey to Manhattan. And he co-sponsored a five-year reauthorization of Amtrak that provided $14.4 billion in funding over five years, while also requiring better efficiency and more state aid.

On other issues, Lautenberg teamed with Republican John Warner of Virginia on a bill to establish an Office of High Performance Green Buildings to help make federal buildings more energy efficient. With Republican Richard Lugar of Indiana, he sponsored an amendment to the farm bill to end crop subsidy programs and substitute more spending on conservation, energy, nutrition, and rural development. This was a major challenge to the Agriculture Committee's version of the farm bill, and it was defeated 58-37 in December 2007.

In 2008, in contrast to eight years before, Lautenberg showed no hesitancy in seeking another term. "There is a lot that remains to be done," he told the Bergen *Record*. "The people respect what I do. They know I'm straightforward in my efforts for my state. And I want to continue doing it." He started fundraising early. And when all three Republican candidates for the seat in February 2008 opposed Democratic Gov. Corzine's plan to lease the New Jersey Turnpike and raise tolls, Lautenberg came out against it too, despite his close relationship with Corzine. In April, Andrews announced he was running in the June Democratic primary. There was an obvious contrast in their ages—Lautenberg was 84, Andrews was 50—and in their political bases. Andrews is from Camden County in South Jersey, and in his previous statewide primary, for governor in 1997, he had won big margins in the Philadelphia media market. Lautenberg had already won the backing of all of the county party organizations, usually decisive in New Jersey's light-voting primaries, but Andrews accumulated some endorsements, including prominent state legislators from Union and Middlesex counties, as well as Speaker Joseph Roberts from Camden County.

Lautenberg campaigned aggressively. "Age has nothing to do with it," he argued. "It's about effectiveness, and I've been effective in office." He ran an ad attacking Andrews for his support for the Iraq war resolution in October 2002, with pictures of President Bush and Vice President Cheney. (At the time, Lautenberg issued statements generally supporting military action but, being out of office, did not vote on the resolution.) Andrews countered that he would be a more vigorous senator. His supporters noted that Lautenberg's wife was registered to vote on Park Avenue in New York City. Lautenberg spent $5.7 million, lending his campaign $1.65 million, while Andrews spent $3 million. The voting ran along regional lines. Andrews won 71% of the votes in South Jersey and Lautenberg won 75% in North Jersey. Unfortunately for Andrews, three-quarters of the votes were cast in North Jersey, and Lautenberg won 59%-35%. But Andrews managed a soft landing by figuring out a way to save his place in the House. He had his wife put her name on the ballot in the election for his House seat, so when he lost the Senate race, all he had to do was substitute as the Democratic nominee, which he did.

In the general election, Lautenberg faced Republican Dick Zimmer, a former House member who had lost to Torricelli 53%-43% in 1996. Zimmer criticized Lautenberg for sponsoring spending earmarks and for supporting the $700 billion bailout of the financial industry. Lautenberg said that the measure "isn't perfect, but it is real action when we need it," and he defended the earmarks as worthwhile for New Jersey and the country. To keep campaign funds flowing, Lautenberg petitioned the Federal Election Commission in August to overturn the requirement that candidates' loans to their campaigns of more than $250,000 be repaid within 20 days of the election, arguing that it was "constitutionally suspect." Zimmer spent only $945,000 and national Republicans, on the defensive in many other states, did not target the race. Lautenberg won 56%-42% and became the first New Jersey senator in history to be elected to a fifth term. Asked during the campaign whether he would serve the full term, he said, "Yeah. Why not?"

Junior Senator

Robert Menendez (D)

Appointed Jan. 2006, term expires 2012, 1st full term; b. Jan. 1, 1954, New York, NY; home, Union City; St. Peter's Col., B.A. 1976, Rutgers Law Schl., J.D. 1979; Catholic; married (Jane Jacobsen-Menendez); 2 children.

Elected Office: Union City Bd. of Ed., 1974–82; Union City mayor, 1986–92; NJ Assembly, 1987–91; NJ Senate, 1991–92; U.S. House of Reps., 1992–2006.

Professional Career: Practicing atty., 1980–92.

DC Office: 528 HSOB, 20510, 202-224-4744; Fax: 202-228-2197; Web site: menendez.senate.gov.

State Offices: Newark, 973-645-3030; Barrington 856-757-5353.

Committees: *DSCC Chairman. Banking, Housing & Urban Affairs* (6th of 13 D): Financial Institutions; Housing, Transportation & Community Development (Chmn); Securities, Insurance & Investment. *Budget* (8th of 13 D). *Energy & Natural Resources* (7th of 13 D): Energy; National Parks; Public Lands & Forests. *Finance* (12th of 13 D): Health Care; International Trade, Customs & Global Competitiveness; Taxation, IRS Oversight & Long-Term Growth. *Foreign Relations* (5th of 11 D): European Affairs; International Development & Foreign Assistance, Economic Affairs & International Environmental Protection (Chmn); International Operations & Organizations, Human Rights, Democracy & Global Women's Issues; Western Hemisphere, Peace Corps & Global Narcotics Affairs.

Group Ratings

	ADA	ACLU	AFS	LCV	ITIC	NTU	COC	ACU	CFG	FRC
2008	100	93	100	91	100	2	63	4	0	0
2007	95	—	100	93	—	7	55	0	13	—

National Journal Ratings

	2007 LIB	—	2007 CONS		2008 LIB	—	2008 CONS
Economic	94%	—	0%		89%	—	9%
Social	92%	—	6%		75%	—	21%
Foreign	85%	—	8%		65%	—	6%
Composite	93%	—	7%		82%	—	18%

Key Votes of the 110th Congress

1. Raise CAFE standards	Y	5. Make English official language N	9. Withdraw troops 3/08	Y
2. Expand SCHIP	Y	6. Path to citizenship	Y	10. Iran guard is terrorist group	Y
3. Cap greenhouse gases	Y	7. Fetus is unborn child	N	11. Increase missile defense $	N
4. Bail out financial markets	Y	8. Prosecute hate crimes	Y	12. Overhaul FISA	N

Election Results

2006 general	Robert Menendez (D)	1,200,843	(53%)	($13,328,665)
	Thomas Kean Jr. (R)	997,775	(44%)	($7,762,373)
2006 primary	Robert Menendez (D)	159,604	(84%)	
	James Kelly (D)	30,340	(16%)	

Prior Winning Percentages: 2004 House (76%); 2002 House (78%); 2000 House (79%); 1998 House (80%); 1996 House (79%); 1994 House (71%); 1992 House (64%)

Robert Menendez, New Jersey's junior senator, was appointed by Democratic Gov. Jon Corzine in January 2006, and won election to a full term 10 months later. His ascension to the Senate was no lucky break, but rather the culmination of a career marked by an ability to adapt to and thrive in bruising political arenas. He is of Cuban descent and grew up in Union City, America's most densely populated city (in 2000 it had 60,000 people in 1.3 square miles), and got into politics early. He was elected to the school board in 1974, at age 20. He worked for Union City Mayor William Musto in the 1970s, but quit and testified against Musto in a corruption trial, wearing a bulletproof vest for protection because of death threats. Menendez was elected mayor in 1986, and elected to the Assembly in 1987 and Senate in 1991; he served both as mayor and legislator, which had been a common practice in New Jersey, until his 1992 election to Congress. Menendez was the first New Jersey Latino in the state Legislature and in Congress. When new district lines were created and incumbent Frank Guarini retired, Menendez won the 1992 primary 68%-32% and the general election 64%-31%. As head of the Democratic Party organization in Hudson County, which has the highest number of registered Democrats of any county in the state, he was for many years a major player in state politics.

In the House, Menendez was a strong supporter of anti-Castro legislation, including the 1992 Cuban Democracy Act and the 1996 Helms-Burton Act. He sponsored a bill in 2004 to put illegal immigrants on the path to permanent worker status and citizenship. Noting the increasing importance of the financial services industry in Hudson County, his home base, he broke with many Democrats to support the 2005 bankruptcy bill and financial services deregulation.

By the late 1990s, Menendez was on the track to a leadership position in the House and to a possible Senate candidacy in New Jersey. In November 1998, he was elected vice chairman of the Democratic Caucus. In February 1999, when Democratic Sen. Frank Lautenberg announced his retirement, Menendez was widely expected to run for the seat, but support was not forthcoming from New Jersey Sen. Bob Torricelli, the Democratic Senatorial Campaign Committee chairman, who preferred Jon Corzine, a wealthy former investment banker who could self-finance his campaign. Minority Leader Dick Gephardt urged Menendez to stay in the House, arguing that as a leader of a Democratic majority—and Democrats came within a few seats of winning a majority in November 2000—he would have more influence than as a junior minority-party senator. In November 1999, Menendez endorsed Corzine for the Senate and began running for Democratic Caucus chairman, the third-ranking minority leadership post. He raised more than $4 million for House Democrats in the 2000 and 2002 elections, and traveled around the country campaigning. His Hispanic background was an asset, and not just within the 20-member Hispanic Caucus. "There are 50 to 60 members who are not Hispanic but have significant Hispanic communities in their districts," he said.

The decisive leadership election came in 2001, when David Bonior, running for governor of Michigan, resigned his position as minority whip. In a decision with major reverberations today, the caucus picked California's Nancy Pelosi over Maryland's Steny Hoyer to succeed Bonior as whip. Menendez announced he would run for caucus chairman in November 2002, against Rosa DeLauro of Connecticut. Pelosi endorsed DeLauro, and Hoyer endorsed Menendez. Then, on the last day of September 2002, another opportunity came to run for the Senate. Torricelli dropped out of his race for re-election amid an ethics scandal, and Democratic Gov. Jim McGreevey and state Democratic leaders sought another candidate. With more than $2 million in his campaign treasury, Menendez probably could have had the nomination for the asking. But he decided not to run, saying he was already too committed to getting a Democratic majority in the House and becoming caucus chairman. Instead, Lautenberg became the nominee and was elected to the Senate in November. But Democrats once again failed to win a majority in the House in 2002. Menendez walked into the caucus meeting after the election with a list of 107 members who had agreed to openly support him. On the secret ballot he won 104-103.

As caucus chairman, Menendez continued to show his fundraising prowess. By June 2003, he had $2.8 million in his campaign fund, more than any other House member, and over the 2003–04 election season he raised $3.6 million. On August 12, McGreevey announced that he had had an affair with a man he'd hired as his homeland-security chief and would resign on November 15. Menendez, along with Camden County Democratic Chairman George Norcross and Middlesex County Chairman John Lynch, urged McGreevey to resign before September 3, which would trigger a November special election in which Corzine could run and which he would probably win, at which point he could appoint Menendez senator. But McGreevey refused, and Senate President Richard Codey, a political adversary of Norcross's and Lynch's, became acting governor for 14 months until January 2006.

In December 2004, after Corzine announced he would run for governor and before acting Gov. Codey took himself out of the race, Menendez made it known that if Corzine were elected, he would run for the Senate even if Corzine named someone else to the seat. As the presumed front-runner to succeed Corzine, Menendez had amassed more than $4 million for a statewide campaign, far more than two potential Democratic rivals—U.S. Reps. Robert Andrews and Frank Pallone. By May 2005, Menendez began spending time on the Senate side of the Capitol at news conferences and developing relationships with senators. Menendez, Pallone, and Andrews all actively campaigned for Corzine's gubernatorial bid, while at the same time positioning themselves for a Senate campaign.

After Corzine won the election in November 2005, he waited a month before revealing his chosen successor. Codey was the favorite of DSCC Chairman Charles Schumer because of his popularity and name recognition, but Codey took his name out of consideration before Thanksgiving. Democrats worried about Menendez's Hudson County political baggage, and had questions about Menendez's relationship with former aide Kay LiCausi and his efforts to steer lobbying and consulting work her way. In December, Corzine announced he would appoint Menendez as his replacement, and did so in January after he was sworn in as governor. Menendez joined Sens. Mel Martinez of Florida and Ken Salazar of Colorado as the chamber's Hispanic members. In his first actions, Menendez won $2.6 million in additional funding for the New Jersey National Guard and won passage of a measure that would fund $60 million for a United Nations mission in the Darfur region in Sudan.

Much of his attention was devoted to the Senate election. Andrews and Pallone each decided they probably couldn't compete with Menendez and declined to challenge him in the primary, leaving Menendez free to focus on his Republican opponent, state Sen. Tom Kean Jr., son and namesake of popular former Republican Gov. Thomas Kean. Menendez campaigned against the Iraq war, while Kean said he would have voted for the Iraq war resolution and opposed a timetable for withdrawing U.S. troops. But

Kean also called for the resignation of Defense Secretary Donald Rumsfeld and criticized President Bush's handling of the conflict, which Menendez called a "clumsy" attempt to find political cover for the unpopular war. Kean reminded voters of Menendez's influence in Hudson County. In September 2006, U.S. Attorney Christopher Christie subpoenaed records from a lease arrangement between Menendez and an anti-poverty group for which he had sought federal funding and that paid him some $300,000 in rent on a building he owned in Union City. Republicans spread rumors that Menendez might drop out as Torricelli had in 2002. Menendez responded with an attack ad linking Kean to contributors with ethics problems. Then it was revealed that the Kean campaign's opposition researchers had contacted former Hudson County Executive Robert Janiszewski, who was serving time in federal prison on corruption charges. Menendez struck back with a television ad accusing Kean of a smear campaign: "Federal prisoner 25038-050. He's Tom Kean Jr.'s newest adviser." Polls late in the season showed Menendez with only a slight lead, and for a moment it seemed Republicans had one of the few opportunities to contest a Democrat-held seat in 2006. But Menendez held on to win 53%-44%.

In the Senate, Menendez took part in bipartisan discussions aimed at coming up with a comprehensive immigration bill, but walked out in May 2007, arguing that Democratic Sen. Edward Kennedy of Massachusetts had made too many concessions to Republicans and that the bill would "tear at the fabric of family reunification." The proposed $19,000 fees required for legalization for a family of four, he said, were "punitive" and "impractical." Menendez said, "Under this bill, my father and mother would never have made it here. The parents of Colin Powell would probably not have made it, or Jonas Salk or Bob Hope or plenty of others I consider great Americans." He sponsored his own unsuccessful amendment to make green card holders eligible for legalization from May 2005 to January 2007. He continued to speak out on immigration after the bill died in June 2007. He defended tax rebates to illegal immigrants under the 2008 economic stimulus bill. "This new dimension about whether that person is undocumented or not—if in fact they paid taxes, then it seems to me that they are also going to continue to stimulate the economy," Menendez said. After the House extended for five years the eVerify system, used by employers to check the immigration status of new hires, Menendez tried to block it in the Senate by backing an amendment to make hundreds of thousands of unused family visas dating back to 1992 available for use.

He weighed in on other issues. With Lautenberg, he sponsored a bill based on recommendations of the 9/11 commission and requiring 100% radiation scanning of shipping cargo containers by 2012. When the *Asbury Park Press* spotlighted huge increases in the cost of closing Fort Monmouth by 2011, he and Lautenberg sponsored a bill to require a review of base-closing costs if they went over 25% of original estimates. Menendez also sponsored a bill on beef safety after a recall of beef purchased in volume for New Jersey schools. In January 2009, he succeeded in adding a one-year fix to the alternative minimum tax patch to the economic stimulus bill, which would protect middle-income taxpayers from having to pay a tax originally aimed at wealthy taxpayers who sheltered most of their earnings. In March 2009, he placed a hold on two of Obama's nominees to administration jobs to protest a provision easing travel restrictions to Cuba that was included in a $410 billion catchall appropriations bill. "It's a horrid process to start going down the road on. It means a handful of members can change the foreign policy of the United States," Mendendez said of mixing Cuba policy with appropriations legislation. His refusal to vote for the spending bill prevented it from getting the needed 60 votes until he was offered assurances by the administration that the Cuba rider would have little impact.

The investigation of Menendez's ties with LiCausi produced no indictments. Menendez was criticized for blocking a promotion for a prosecutor investigating Puerto Rican Gov. Anibal Acevedo-Vila, a friend of Menendez who, as the nonvoting delegate from Puerto Rico in the House, had cast a decisive vote for Menendez in the caucus chairman race in 2002. The prosecutor was in line to become the U.S. attorney in Puerto Rico, and at the time was investigating Acevedo-Vila's fundraising practices. Menendez had also raised $250,000 in campaign funds in Puerto Rico for his congressional campaigns. The prosecutor got the appointment in the end, and Acevedo-Vila was indicted for violating campaign finance and tax laws in March 2008, and was defeated for re-election in November 2008.

In the 2008 election season, Menendez was the deputy director of the DSCC and worked with Chairman Schumer to raise money for the 2008 campaigns. In November 2008, he succeeded Schumer as DSCC chairman, the fourth-ranking leadership position in the Senate Democratic majority. The campaign committee has been headed by senators from New Jersey or New York in five of the last six cycles—Torricelli in 2000, Corzine in 2004, Schumer in 2006 and 2008, and Menendez in 2010. In February 2009, Menendez said, "I think a cursory look at the map shows that the fear should be on the other side," and indicated that he would target Republican-held seats in Florida, Kansas, Kentucky, Louisiana, Missouri, New Hampshire, North Carolina, Ohio, and Pennsylvania.

He endorsed New York Sen. Hillary Rodham Clinton for president in June 2007, and she carried Hudson County 62%-36%. When Illinois Sen. Barack Obama won the nomination, he offered Menendez a pre-prime-time speech slot at the party's national convention in Denver, but he declined.

FIRST DISTRICT

Robert Andrews (D)

Elected Nov. 1990, 10th full term; b. Aug. 4, 1957, Camden; home, Haddon Heights; Bucknell U., B.A. 1979, Cornell U., J.D. 1982; Episcopalian; married (Camille); 2 children.

Elected Office: Camden Cnty. Bd. of Chosen Freeholders, 1987–90.

Professional Career: Practicing atty., 1982–90; Adjunct prof., Rutgers Law Schl., 1985–86, 1989–90.

DC Office: 2265 RHOB, 20515, 202-225-6501; Fax: 202-225-6583; Web site: www.house.gov/andrews.

State Offices: Haddon Heights, 856-546-5100; Woodbury, 856-848-3900.

Committees: *Armed Services* (12th of 36 D): Strategic Forces; Terrorism, Unconventional Threats & Capabilities. *Budget* (15th of 24 D). *Education & Labor* (4th of 29 D): Health, Employment, Labor & Pensions (Chmn); Higher Education, Lifelong Learning & Competitiveness.

Group Ratings

	ADA	ACLU	AFS	LCV	ITIC	NTU	COC	ACU	CFG	FRC
2008	85	100	100	85	86	6	63	0	0	5
2007	100	—	100	100	—	4	50	0	7	—

National Journal Ratings

	2007 LIB	—	2007 CONS		2008 LIB	—	2008 CONS
Economic	82%	—	0%		77%	—	23%
Social	75%	—	25%		82%	—	0%
Foreign	62%	—	37%		*%	—	*%
Composite	76%	—	24%		*%	—	*%

Key Votes of the 110th Congress

1. Increase minimum wage	Y	5. Share immigration data	*	9. Withdraw troops 8/08	Y
2. Expand SCHIP	Y	6. Foreign aid abortion ban	N	10. No operations in Iran	Y
3. Raise CAFE standards	Y	7. Ban gay bias in workplace	Y	11. Free trade with Peru	N
4. Bail out financial markets	Y	8. Repeal D.C. gun law	N	12. Overhaul FISA	N

Election Results

2008 general	Robert Andrews (D)	206,453	(72%)	($3,502,678)
	Dale Glading (R)	74,001	(26%)	($26,034)
2008 primary	Camille Andrews (D)	32,108	(83%)	
	John Caramanna (D)	4,342	(11%)	
	Mahdi Ibn-Ziyad (D)	2,222	(6%)	

Prior Winning Percentages: 2006 (100%); 2004 (75%); 2002 (93%); 2000 (76%); 1998 (73%); 1996 (76%); 1994 (72%); 1992 (67%); 1990 (54%); 1990 (55%)

Population		Race/Ethnicity		Work	
Pop. 2007:	664,156	White:	68.0%	Private:	81.0%
Change since 2000:	Up 2.6%	Black:	17.2%	Government:	14.6%
Urban:	98.6%	Hispanic:	9.8%	Self-employed:	4.2%
Rural:	1.4%	Asian:	3.4%	Blue collar:	20.1%
Area size:	352 sq. mi.	Native Am.:	0.1%	White collar:	63.7%
		Hawaiian:	0.0%	Khaki collar:	0.1%
Age		Two+ races:	1.3%	Other:	16.0%
Median age:	36.6 yrs.			Median income:	$58,674
More than 65 yrs:	11.8%	*Ancestry*		Median home value:	$201,000
Less than 18 yrs:	24.6%	Irish:	17.6%	Poverty:	10.6%
		Italian:	15.5%		
Education		German:	13.7%	**Military Veterans**	
H.S. grad:	84.4%			% of Pop:	9.5%
College grad:	23.8%				
Grad degree:	7.3%				

The closely built streets of the little city of Camden, across the Delaware River from Philadelphia, have seen a fair amount of history. This was where the poet Walt Whitman lived when he wrote some of the versions of his *Leaves of Grass*. It was an immigrant-jammed industrial city then, with tinkerers and inventors. In 1894, a Camden machinist named Eldridge Johnson produced the Victor Talking Machine, the birth of the recorded music industry and a company that became RCA Victor in 1929. A few

2008 Presidential Vote		
Obama (D)	198,194	(65%)
McCain (R)	103,994	(34%)
2004 Presidential Vote		
Kerry (D)	170,786	(61%)
Bush (R)	111,073	(39%)
Cook Partisan Voting Index:	D + 12	

years later, the new Campbell Soup Company began producing condensed soups. Camden remained for years afterward a major industrial locus on the New Jersey side of the Delaware River, not the broadest and certainly not the most picturesque of Atlantic estuaries, but probably the East Coast's premier industrial waterway, with a concentration of steel factories, chemical plants, and oil tank farms equal to any in the country. The flatlands all around, mostly ignored in the 19th century, had easy access to cheap water transport and plenty of skilled labor from the Philadelphia area. For a quarter-century starting in the 1940s, this was one of the country's fastest-growing industrial areas.

In the 1980s and 1990s, Camden emptied out. Many of its factories had closed, and fewer than 10,000 manufacturing jobs remained. Its neighborhoods were beset by crime, its mostly minority residents were heavily dependent on public assistance, and its mayor was convicted for doing favors for Philadelphia's organized crime leaders. Camden, ranked among the poorest cities in America, continues to struggle today. The median family income in 2006 was $24,612, compared with $65,026 for New Jersey as a whole. The state underwrites much of the budget of the nearly bankrupt city, and national crime data place Camden in the top five most crime-ridden cities. The bright spots are a newly-developed riverfront park, the New Jersey Aquarium, and the Sony Music/Pace amphitheater. There are plans for a new Campbell's world headquarters. The port of Camden has rebounded, spurred by Del Monte's large fruit-processing plant, plus large imports of foreign steel and exports of scrap metal.

The 1st Congressional District is, more or less, greater Camden, the Delaware riverfront from Riverton south to a point across from the Delaware state line, and the suburbs running southeast to the flat vegetable fields of South Jersey. The district is traversed by Black Horse Pike and White Horse Pike. Both routes date back two centuries; today, they connect Philadelphia to its middle-class South Jersey suburbs. Many of these boroughs and townships developed over the past half-century as a result of flight from Camden. The district includes a growing number of Hispanics, who now make up more than 40% of Camden's population. Politically, this area has a Democratic heritage.

The 1st District is represented by Robert Andrews, a Democrat first elected in 1990. He grew up in Bellmawr, the son of a shipyard worker. At age 14, he got a job with the Suburban Newspaper Group, dreaming of covering basketball games and becoming a sportswriter. But his editor had other ideas; assigned to cover city halls, police departments, and zoning boards, Andrews developed an interest in the machinations of government and politics. He excelled in college, became the first in his family to get a degree, and went on to law school. While still in his 20s, he was elected to the Camden County Board of Chosen Freeholders, with the help of then-Democratic U.S. Rep. Jim Florio. When Florio left Congress to become governor in January 1990, he postponed the special election for a successor until November and supported Andrews for the post. Andrews had other help. His Republican opponent switched positions on abortion rights and lied about his college attendance. Andrews won 54%-43%.

Andrews has a mostly moderate record, particularly on foreign policy. After Democrats lost control of the House in 1995, he kept a hand in shaping legislation by working with Republicans. He typically introduces more than 100 bills in a two-year term, the most of any House member.

As the ranking Democrat on the Employer-Employee Relations Subcommittee of the Education and the Workforce Committee, he worked with John Boehner, R-Ohio, chairman of the full committee, to expand the panel's focus on pensions and retirement issues. When Democrats regained the majority in 2007, Andrews became chairman of the Health, Employment, Labor, and Pensions Subcommittee. With Chairman George Miller, D-Calif., he spearheaded House approval of the controversial labor-backed Employee Free Choice Act, which would make it easier for unions to organize in a workplace by gathering the signatures of more than half of the employees in a bargaining unit. Under current law, an employer can demand that an election be held after the signatures are gathered. Andrews also has ambitious plans to expand health coverage for the uninsured, perhaps paid for by higher taxes on the top 1% of taxpayers. In a first for Congress, Andrews in 2008 chaired hearing on transgender rights in the workplace.

Andrews was a longtime ardent proponent of the use of force in Iraq. Even when conditions in Iraq worsened after the overthrow of Iraqi Leader Saddam Hussein, Andrews remained convinced that the situation was "better than leaving Saddam Hussein in power." But in 2006, he called for Iraqi soldiers to take a stronger role in maintaining civil order in the country. And in 2007, he opposed Bush's troop "surge" in Iraq. Andrews said he concluded that it was a mistake to try to referee a civil war.

Andrews has been re-elected by overwhelming margins and has continued to live with his family in Haddon Heights, commuting by train to Washington and occasionally sleeping overnight in his office. He has been frustrated in his efforts to attain higher office. He ran for governor in 1997, but was defeated in the primary by then-state Sen. James McGreevy. When McGreevy announced his resignation as governor in 2004, Andrews was interested in running again but stood little chance after Democratic Sen. Jon Corzine announced his candidacy. In the end, Andrews declined to run and endorsed Corzine, with the hope of winning appointment as Corzine's successor in the Senate, but that didn't happen.

In the 2008 election season, he surprised and angered many local Democrats when he challenged Democratic Sen. Frank Lautenberg in the primary. An Andrews ad called for change in "stale, tired, old politics," an allusion to the 84-year-old Lautenberg's age. Another ad did not even bother with the pretense of subtlety. "Lautenberg will be 91 at the end of his term—91," it said. Andrews portrayed the contest as a "David versus Goliath" challenge to the Democratic establishment. Lautenberg shot back, calling Andrews "an enabler" for the Bush administration, especially on the war in Iraq. Lautenberg started with a big lead in the polls, and he benefited from a fundraising advantage. He won the Democratic primary 59%-35%.

Andrews had said that if he lost the contest for Senate, he would not run again for the House. But political insiders questioned whether he in fact maneuvered to keep the seat warm in case things didn't work out for him in the Senate race: Andrews' wife, Camille, ran for the Democratic nomination for his House seat in the primary and secured it. Then, on September 4, 2008, after Andrews had lost the Senate primary, he announced he wanted to run for his former House seat after all. Camille Andrews immediately bowed out, allowing the local Democratic committee to designate her husband as the new nominee. Although Andrews called the turnabout a simple change of heart, the upshot was, he was able to circumvent a prohibition on candidates running simultaneously for the Senate and the House. Republican challenger Dale Glading, a minister, accused Andrews for lying to his constituents. Still, he was handily elected, 72%-26%.

SECOND DISTRICT

Frank LoBiondo (R)

Elected 1994, 8th term; b. May 12, 1946, Bridgeton; home, Ventnor; St. Joseph's U., B.A. 1968; Catholic; married (Tina); 2 children.

Elected Office: Cumberland Cnty. Bd. of Chosen Freeholders, 1985–88; NJ Assembly, 1987–94.

Professional Career: Operations mgr., LoBiondo Bros. Motor Express Inc., 1968–94.

DC Office: 2427 RHOB, 20515, 202-225-6572; Fax: 202-225-3318; Web site: www.house.gov/lobiondo.

State Offices: Mays Landing, 609-625-5008.

Committees: *Armed Services* (9th of 25 R): Air & Land Forces; Readiness; Terrorism, Unconventional Threats & Capabilities. *Transportation & Infrastructure* (7th of 30 R): Aviation; Coast Guard & Maritime Transportation (RMM); Water Resources & Environment.

Group Ratings

	ADA	ACLU	AFS	LCV	ITIC	NTU	COC	ACU	CFG	FRC
2008	60	27	57	85	43	48	72	52	43	76
2007	50	—	55	90	—	24	63	44	16	—

National Journal Ratings

	2007 LIB — 2007 CONS		2008 LIB — 2008 CONS	
Economic	51%	— 48%	46%	— 54%
Social	40%	— 60%	42%	— 58%
Foreign	29%	— 70%	31%	— 67%
Composite	40%	— 60%	40%	— 60%

Key Votes of the 110th Congress

1. Increase minimum wage	Y	5. Share immigration data	Y	9. Withdraw troops 8/08	N
2. Expand SCHIP	Y	6. Foreign aid abortion ban	Y	10. No operations in Iran	N
3. Raise CAFE standards	Y	7. Ban gay bias in workplace	Y	11. Free trade with Peru	N
4. Bail out financial markets	N	8. Repeal D.C. gun law	Y	12. Overhaul FISA	Y

Election Results

2008 general	Frank LoBiondo (R)	167,701	(59%)	($1,520,178)
	David Kurkowski (D)	110,990	(39%)	($192,143)
2008 primary	Frank LoBiondo (R)	16,026	(89%)	
	Donna Ward (R)	2,025	(11%)	

Prior Winning Percentages: 2006 (62%); 2004 (65%); 2002 (69%); 2000 (66%); 1998 (66%); 1996 (60%); 1994 (65%)

Population		Race/Ethnicity		Work	
Pop. 2007:	681,555	White:	69.1%	Private:	77.1%
Change since 2000:	Up 5.3%	Black:	13.8%	Government:	17.9%
Urban:	79.0%	Hispanic:	12.2%	Self-employed:	4.8%
Rural:	21.0%	Asian:	3.0%	Blue collar:	21.2%
Area size:	2,683 sq. mi.	Native Am.:	0.3%	White collar:	54.0%
		Hawaiian:	0.0%	Khaki collar:	0.1%
Age		Two+ races:	1.2%	Other:	24.6%
Median age:	38.4 yrs.	*Ancestry*		Median income:	$54,829
More than 65 yrs:	13.8%	Irish:	15.4%	Median home value:	$226,800
Less than 18 yrs:	23.9%	Italian:	14.4%	Poverty:	11.1%
Education		German:	13.8%	**Military Veterans**	
H.S. grad:	82.8%			% of Pop:	10.6%
College grad:	21.2%				
Grad degree:	6.4%				

The builders of the Camden & Atlantic Railroad in 1852 may not have known it, but when they extended their line to the little inlet town of Absecon, they were starting America's biggest beach resort, Atlantic City. Like all resorts, it was a product of developments elsewhere—of industrialization and spreading affluence, of railroad technology and the conquest of diseases that used to make summer a time of foreboding. In the years after the Civil War, Atlantic City and then the Jersey Shore from

2008 Presidential Vote		
Obama (D)	165,982	(54%)
McCain (R)	137,440	(45%)

2004 Presidential Vote		
Bush (R)	141,123	(50%)
Kerry (D)	138,797	(49%)

Cook Partisan Voting Index: D + 1

Brigantine to Cape May became America's first seaside resort, and Atlantic City developed its characteristic features: the boardwalk in 1870, the amusement pier in 1882, the rolling chair in 1884, salt water taffy in the 1890s, and the Miss America pageant in 1921. By 1940, when 16 million Americans visited every summer, Atlantic City was a common man's resort of old traditions. It declined in the years after World War II, and by the early 1970s, Atlantic City was grim, featuring a bedraggled convention hall (site of the 1964 Democratic National Convention), empty hotels, and bleak streets of Philadelphia-style row houses.

Then in 1977, New Jersey voters legalized casino gambling in Atlantic City, and gleaming new hotels sprang up, big-name entertainers came in, and the resort became more glamorous than it had been in 90 years. But it's not that way for all of its residents: Casino and hotel jobs tend to be low-wage, and decrepit neighborhoods began just feet from the casinos' massive parking lots. Atlantic City's gambling business had been thriving. For years, its dozen casinos had net annual revenues of more than $5 billion, nearly as much as Las Vegas's casinos. The recession hit hard here. For the first time, revenues fell in both 2007 and 2008. The hotels laid off 3,000 people in 2008. The casinos also suffered from the competition of slots parlors in New York and Pennsylvania. A smoking ban on the gambling floors was suspended in November 2008 for at least a year in hopes of drawing customers back. Still, Atlantic City in prosperous times has one of the nation's largest tourism economies and is developing into what Las Vegas has become, not just a collection of gaudy casinos but also a gaggle of theme parks, with entertainment for the family as well as adults.

Beach resorts populate the Jersey Shore south of Atlantic City. There is the old Methodist town of Ocean City, where Gay Talese grew up the son of Italian immigrants, a story he told movingly in *Unto the Sons*. He likely would not recognize today's Ocean City, which is jammed with high-rise condominiums and bars and attracts rowdy spring-break college crowds. There is Wildwood, with its refurbished 1950s motels and the doo-wop revival, and Cape May, with its lovingly preserved Victorian houses and a "ghosts of Cape May" trolley tour. West of the Shore are swamps and flatlands, the Pine Barrens and vegetable fields that gave New Jersey its "Garden State" nickname. Growth has been slow in these small towns and gas station intersections. Some towns are clustered around low-wage apparel factories or petrochemical plants on the Delaware estuary. The Northeast high-tech and service economy has not reached this far south in Jersey yet.

The 2nd Congressional District covers this part of South Jersey. Politically, it has strong Democratic leanings in the chemical industry towns along the Delaware River and in Vineland and a strong Republican presence in Cape May. Atlantic City often votes Democratic, but it has an antique Republican machine that goes back generations. Al Gore carried this district by 54%-43% in 2000. In 2004, it swung back to the Republicans and George W. Bush, 50%-49%, but in 2008, Democratic nominee Barack Obama won 54% to 45%. Republican John McCain won only in Cape May County.

The congressman from the 2nd District is Frank LoBiondo, a Republican first elected in 1994. He grew up in Vineland, on the vegetable farm his grandparents established after leaving Sicily. LoBiondo's father started transporting his produce to market himself in a used truck, and as Atlantic City boomed in the early 20th century, he found that he could making a good living transporting the produce of other farmers as well. He created LoBiondo Brothers Motor Express, where the son worked when he was young. In 1987, Frank LoBiondo was elected to the New Jersey Assembly; there, he stoutly opposed new taxes and gun control laws. LoBiondo ran against veteran U.S. Rep. William Hughes, a Democrat, in 1992 and lost 56%-41%. After Hughes decided to retire in 1994, LoBiondo ran again. In the primary, he competed with state Sen. William Gormley, whom LoBiondo portrayed as favoring tax increases and gun control laws. A National Rifle Association ad called Gormley "a liberal in Republican clothing." LoBiondo won 54%-35%, and then easily won the general election, 65%-35%.

In the House, LoBiondo has compiled a moderate voting record, especially on economic and labor issues, although he retains his conservative stance on gun control. On the Transportation and Infrastructure Committee, he is the ranking Republican on the Coast Guard and Maritime Transportation Subcommittee, a useful assignment for New Jersey. LoBiondo opposes oil drilling within 125 miles of the Jersey coast, and he worked against the Bush administration proposal to reduce the federal contribution to beach replenishment. He helped to enact the Delaware River Protection Act, increasing the liability for single-hull oil tankers that pollute.

In the 110th Congress (2007–08), he crossed party lines to work with Democrats on legislation to increase the minimum wage and, despite the opposition of GOP leaders, voted in June 2008 for extended unemployment benefits. In 2008, he voted against the massive bailout of the financial markets because he said that taxpayers were not sufficiently protected. On the Armed Services Committee, LoBiondo said he thought "all the time" about breaking with President George W. Bush on the Iraq war, but he opposed efforts to set a timetable for a troop withdrawal. He backed a ban on earmarks, advocating disclosure of the sponsors of such spending, but said he would continue to pursue them actively for his district.

LoBiondo maintains a low profile on Capitol Hill and seems content to climb the seniority ladder at the Transportation and Infrastructure Committee. When he was first elected, LoBiondo promised to serve no more than 12 years but has since broken that pledge. Still, he routinely wins re-election with 60% of the vote or more. In 2008 he was re-elected 59%-39%, the first time that he had fallen short of 60% but still impressive in a competitive district in a Democratic year.

THIRD DISTRICT

John Adler (D)

Elected 2008, 1st term; b. Aug. 23, 1959, Philadelphia, PA; home, Cherry Hill; Harvard U., B.A. 1981; J.D., 1989.; Jewish; married (Shelley); 4 children.

Elected Office: Cherry Hill Township Cncl., 1988–89; NJ Senate, 1992–2008.

Professional Career: Atty., Adler and Gold, 1992–98; Cozen and O'Connor, 1998–99; John H. Adler, Atty. at Law LLC, 2000; Earp Cohn P.C., 2000-present.

DC Office: 1223 LHOB, 20515, 202-225-4765; Fax: 202-225-0778; Web site: adler.house.gov.

State Offices: Marlton, 856-985-2777; Toms River, 732-608-7235.

Committees: *Financial Services* (35th of 42 D): Capital Markets, Insurance & Government Sponsored Enterprises; Domestic Monetary Policy & Technology; Oversight & Investigations. *Veterans' Affairs* (16th of 18 D): Economic Opportunity; Oversight & Investigations.

Group Ratings and Key Votes: Newly Elected

Election Results

2008 general	John Adler (D)	166,390	(52%)	($2,863,993)
	Chris Myers (R)	153,122	(48%)	($1,259,800)
2008 primary	John Adler (D)	unopposed		

Population		Race/Ethnicity		Work	
Pop. 2007:	682,907	White:	80.5%	Private:	76.2%
Change since 2000:	Up 5.5%	Black:	8.9%	Government:	18.0%
Urban:	96.2%	Hispanic:	5.2%	Self-employed:	5.5%
Rural:	3.8%	Asian:	3.6%	Blue collar:	17.8%
Area size:	1,180 sq. mi.	Native Am.:	0.1%	White collar:	66.9%
		Hawaiian:	0.0%	Khaki collar:	0.4%
Age		Two+ races:	1.4%	Other:	14.9%
Median age:	40.7 yrs.			Median income:	$68,338
More than 65 yrs:	16.8%	*Ancestry*		Median home value:	$283,100
Less than 18 yrs:	22.7%	Irish:	16.9%	Poverty:	5.3%
		Italian:	16.8%		
Education		German:	14.3%	**Military Veterans**	
H.S. grad:	89.9%			% of Pop:	12.6%
College grad:	31.6%				
Grad degree:	10.9%				

The Pine Barrens of New Jersey is one of the last vacant spots on the eastern seaboard—not quite terra incognita, but still not thickly populated. Encroached upon by the Philadelphia suburbs of South Jersey on the west and burgeoning retirement developments of the Jersey Shore on the east, the 1 million acres of heavy forest and white sand, with their unusual plant life, are crossed mostly by narrow two-lane roads. There are only a few small towns here, plus Fort Dix and McGuire Air Force

2008 Presidential Vote
Obama (D) 180,999   (52%)
McCain (R).............................162,335   (47%)

2004 Presidential Vote
Bush (R) 167,254   (51%)
Kerry (D)...............................159,041   (49%)

Cook Partisan Voting Index: R + 1

Base. For years, the Pine Barrens was seen as a barrier to development. Only recently have environment-minded Jerseyites come to see the relatively unspoiled area as a natural treasure.

The 3rd Congressional District of New Jersey spans the Pine Barrens and thousands of acres of farmland. It includes large parts of Burlington and Ocean Counties and Cherry Hill in Camden County. Most of its residents live in the South Jersey suburbs of Philadelphia; in spread-out Cherry Hill, with its 1960s-vintage shopping centers; in the older towns along the Delaware River or in the newer developments inland toward McGuire. This is comfortable, but not affluent, suburban territory. Lockheed Martin in Moorestown is a big employer, with its naval electronics and surveillance-system plant. It is the birthplace of the Aegis radar. Politically, it is competitive territory, with big Democratic margins in Willingboro and Cherry Hill.

East of the Pine Barrens is Ocean County, including the barrier islands from Normandy Beach south to Little Egg Harbor, with older communities on the beachfront and larger clusters of new subdivisions and condominiums inland. Ocean County has been the fastest-growing part of New Jersey, a kind of Frost Belt Florida, with many retirees from New York and North Jersey eager to leave urban crime and high taxes. While Ocean County is Republican, the district as a whole is closely divided. It voted 54%-43% for Democrat Al Gore in 2000, but 51%-49% for President George W. Bush in 2004. In 2008, the pendulum swung back to the Democrats, with nominee Barack Obama winning 52% to Republican John McCain's 47%.

The new congressman from the third district is Democrat John Adler, who prevailed in a close and nasty campaign in 2008 to replace retiring Republican Rep. Jim Saxton.

Adler was born in Philadelphia but grew up on the New Jersey side of the Delaware River in Haddonfield, where his family owned a dry cleaner. His father suffered from heart trouble and died when Adler was a teenager. Social Security benefits were crucial in keeping Adler and his widowed mother financially afloat after his father's death and in allowing Adler to attend Harvard University, where he earned his undergraduate and law degrees. After law school, Adler returned to New Jersey and settled in the Camden suburb of Cherry Hill with his wife, Shelley. In 1987, he won a seat on the Cherry Hill Township Council, where he wrote the township's ethics ordinance. He ran unsuccessfully against Saxton for the House in 1990.

In 1991, he beat an incumbent Republican to win a seat in the state Senate, and went on to become chairman of the Judiciary Committee. He sponsored a statewide public-smoking ban that became law in January 2006 and a law to reduce auto emissions. He adroitly secured grant money for Cherry Hill over the course of his tenure, at one point spurring an ethics complaint because his wife sat on the township council. But he also showed some independence from the Democratic establishment and Gov. Jon Corzine, particularly during his House campaign. Adler opposed Corzine's plan to boost tolls on New Jersey roads and in December 2007, asked the state attorney general to investigate whether Corzine had paid his ex-girlfriend's brother to step down from a state job.

In September 2007, Adler announced that he would run for a second time against Saxton, who was in his 12th term. His chances got markedly better when Saxton, who had been diagnosed with prostate cancer, announced that he would retire at the end of his term. Adler shot to the top of the Democratic

Congressional Campaign Committee's list of challengers in the November 2008 election. While Republicans fought out an acrimonious primary, Adler faced no opposition for the Democratic nomination and used his time out of the spotlight to raise money. By the time Lockheed Martin executive Chris Myers emerged from the Republican primary in June, Adler had raised nearly $1.5 million. Myers had only $426,000 and had spent most of it on the primary.

Adler embraced a strategy of tying Myers to the unpopular Republican president and congressional Republicans. Myers responded in kind, labeling Adler a "Trenton insider" and seeking to tie him to what he called a culture of cronyism and scandal in the state capital. But as the campaign wore on, the disparity in campaign funds hurt Myers. The National Republican Congressional Committee spent only $16,500 against Adler, while the DCCC pumped more than $42,000 into the district against Myers. Adler won the backing of the Sierra Club and other environmental groups, an influential lobby in the district that is home to the largely undeveloped Pine Barrens. Saxton, one of the most environmentally friendly Republicans in the House, had consistently enjoyed the Sierra Club's endorsement.

Adler won, but not by a landslide: 52%-48%. The candidates split their home turf on Election Day, Myers carrying the Republican stronghold of Ocean County with 56% of the vote and Adler winning Democratic Camden County with 65% of the vote. In Burlington County, which cast nearly half of the district's votes, Adler won with 56 percent.

In the House, Adler got a seat on the House Financial Services Committee and said that oversight of the $700 billion government bailout of the financial industry would be his top priority. He also was assigned to the Veterans Affairs Committee. The first bill he introduced would allocate money from the 2009 economic-stimulus bill to senior citizens and veterans who would not otherwise get a rebate.

FOURTH DISTRICT

Chris Smith (R)

Elected 1980, 15th term; b. March 4, 1953, Rahway; home, Hamilton; Trenton St. Col., B.S. 1975; Catholic; married (Marie); 4 children.

Professional Career: Sales exec., family–owned sporting goods business, 1975–80; Exec. dir., NJ Right to Life, 1976–78.

DC Office: 2373 RHOB, 20515, 202-225-3765; Fax: 202-225-7768; Web site: chrissmith.house.gov.

State Offices: Hamilton, 609-585-7878; Whiting, 732-350-2300.

Committees: *Foreign Affairs* (2nd of 19 R): Africa & Global Health (RMM); Western Hemisphere.

Group Ratings

	ADA	ACLU	AFS	LCV	ITIC	NTU	COC	ACU	CFG	FRC
2008	65	45	71	77	71	39	67	28	27	100
2007	55	—	45	85	—	26	70	44	22	—

National Journal Ratings

	2007 LIB	—	2007 CONS		2008 LIB	—	2008 CONS
Economic	48%	—	51%		50%	—	50%
Social	42%	—	58%		45%	—	54%
Foreign	43%	—	57%		46%	—	53%
Composite	45%	—	56%		47%	—	53%

Key Votes of the 110th Congress

1. Increase minimum wage	Y	5. Share immigration data	Y	9. Withdraw troops 8/08	N
2. Expand SCHIP	Y	6. Foreign aid abortion ban	Y	10. No operations in Iran	N
3. Raise CAFE standards	Y	7. Ban gay bias in workplace	N	11. Free trade with Peru	N
4. Bail out financial markets	N	8. Repeal D.C. gun law	N	12. Overhaul FISA	Y

Election Results

2008 general	Chris Smith (R)...	202,972	(66%)	($1,076,919)
	Joshua Zeitz (D)...	100,036	(33%)	($481,166)
2008 primary	Chris Smith (R)... unopposed			

Prior Winning Percentages: 2006 (66%); 2004 (67%); 2002 (66%); 2000 (63%); 1998 (62%); 1996 (64%); 1994 (68%); 1992 (62%); 1990 (63%); 1988 (66%); 1986 (61%); 1984 (61%); 1982 (53%); 1980 (57%)

Population		Race/Ethnicity		Work	
Pop. 2007:	712,724	White:	77.0%	Private:	78.2%
Change since 2000:	Up 10.1%	Black:	8.8%	Government:	16.2%
Urban:	93.2%	Hispanic:	9.8%	Self-employed:	5.4%
Rural:	6.8%	Asian:	3.3%	Blue collar:	18.3%
Area size:	762 sq. mi.	Native Am.:	0.2%	White collar:	65.9%
		Hawaiian:	0.0%	Khaki collar:	0.1%
Age		Two+ races:	0.7%	Other:	15.7%
Median age:	38.2 yrs.	*Ancestry*		Median income:	$65,510
More than 65 yrs:	15.5%	Italian:	16.1%	Median home value:	$326,200
Less than 18 yrs:	24.8%	Irish:	15.9%	Poverty:	7.6%
Education		German:	12.0%	**Military Veterans**	
H.S. grad:	87.9%			% of Pop:	10.0%
College grad:	29.1%				
Grad degree:	9.9%				

An invisible and not-well-defined line divides North Jersey and South Jersey. North of the line people watch New York television stations, eat hero sandwiches, and root for the Yankees. South of the line they watch Philadelphia television, eat hoagies, and root for the Phillies. The state capital of Trenton lies south of the line, which passes east somewhere around Six Flags Great Adventure and Wild Safari in the Pine Barrens and heads southeast past Lakewood and Bricktown to the little village of Mantoloking on the Jersey shore. But on both sides of the line a stronger New Jersey identity has developed over the last two decades. The big cities—New York and Philadelphia—are not all that close, particularly when traffic is heavy, which is often. And the economy of central New Jersey has its own special character, with big pharmaceutical companies and Fort Dix and McGuire Air Force Base. New Jersey politics is also centered in Trenton. The city has been a manufacturing mecca since the 19th century, with the Lenox and Boehm china factories and the old Roebling ironworks, which produced parts for many of our great bridges (hence the sign on a span across the Delaware River that boasts, "Trenton Makes, the World Takes"). But much of this area is also spanking new, with growing subdivisions just west of the shore and office buildings stretching north from Princeton. Even Trenton has had some growth. Preservationists are eyeing its antique buildings and, long the only state capital without a hotel, it now has the Marriott Lafayette Yard Conference Hotel.

2008 Presidential Vote

McCain (R)	172,987	(52%)
Obama (D)	154,256	(47%)

2004 Presidential Vote

Bush (R)	172,369	(56%)
Kerry (D)	134,220	(44%)

Cook Partisan Voting Index: R+6

The 4th Congressional District of New Jersey covers much of the central part of the state. It stretches from the eastern part of Trenton to Mantoloking, Point Pleasant, Sea Girt, and Spring Lake on the shore. The district includes the old colonial town of Burlington on the Delaware River and the new spacious subdivisions of Colts Neck just west of the shore, as well as what was Lakehurst Naval Air Station, where the German zeppelin *Hindenburg* exploded while docking in 1937. Population movement has been eastward, away from the old neighborhoods of Trenton and its close-in suburbs and toward the new subdivisions of coastal and exurban Ocean County, which grew 10% from 2000 to 2007. Some towns have curtailed sprawl with laws to preserve farmland and open space. Politically, it is a mixed bag. The Trenton area has long been solidly Democratic, but the Pine Barrens and Jersey shore have leaned Republican. After George W. Bush won this district 56%-44% in 2004, Barack Obama won it back for the Democrats in 2008, 52%-47%.

The congressman from the 4th District is Chris Smith, a Republican first elected in 1980. Smith grew up in the Trenton area, worked in his family's sporting goods business, and, after graduating from college, became executive director of the New Jersey Right to Life Committee in 1976. Four years later, he ran for the House in a Trenton-centered 4th District and defeated 26-year Rep. Frank Thompson, a Democrat convicted in the Abscam bribery scandal. Now tied as the sixth-most-senior House Republican, Smith is a youthful-looking lawmaker who brings passion to his pursuit of conservative causes, sometimes as a maverick within his party. He won passage of 30 bills from 1991 to 2008, the fifth-largest number for any member of Congress during that period.

He is best known for his fight against legalized abortion. Smith has worked to stop abortions in military hospitals, and he persuaded the Bush administration to reinstate Reagan-era restrictions that denied federal funds to family planning organizations that promote abortions abroad. (In 2009, new Democratic President Barack Obama rescinded the restrictions during his first week in office.) Smith was a prime mover of legislation to ban "partial-birth" abortions. He has fought not only Democrats but also the House Republican leadership on the abortion issue. In the 2002 bankruptcy bill, he took exception to a provision that prevented the dropping of court-imposed fines levied against abortion protesters in the event of bankruptcy. Smith rounded up a group of like-minded Republicans who threatened to vote no on the bankruptcy bill unless the provision was removed. The abortion section was ultimately stripped out, and the bill passed the House. As retribution for his protest against the bankruptcy legislation, GOP House leaders stalled Smith's bill to provide loans to small businesses in developing countries.

Smith has long crusaded for his Unborn Child Pain Awareness Act, which would require doctors to inform pregnant women that some experts say that a fetus can feel pain after 20 weeks of gestation. When Republicans were in the majority, the bill never advanced out of committee, and it is even more unlikely to get to the floor with Democrats in control of the House. Smith also has a bill to revoke the Food and Drug Administration's approval of the abortifacient RU-486, which Smith calls "baby pesticide." Smith has opposed federal funding for embryonic-stem-cell research, which uses excess embryos from in vitro fertilization, but he has been a champion of other stem-cell research. In 2005, Congress enacted his Stem Cell Therapeutic and Research Act, which provides $265 million for research and therapy using umbilical cord stem cells and cells from bone-marrow transplants.

Smith has brought his strong moral views to his work against human-rights abuses abroad. He has sharply criticized China for its forced sterilizations and abortions, and its persecution of Christians and other religious minorities. As a result, he opposed normalizing trade relations with Beijing. Smith has condemned Russia for barring entry of foreign Catholic priests, and he criticized the Saudis for treating foreign servants as slaves. In 2000, Congress enacted his legislation to combat sex trafficking around the world, including requiring yearly reports on each nation's record. In 2005, he won passage of $361 million for prosecution of domestic trafficking and to compensate victims of trafficking. At one point, Smith learned of Ukrainian girls being held against their will in brothels in Montenegro; he personally called the Montenegran prime minister, who ordered a raid on the operation.

After Democrats took over Congress in 2007, Smith became the ranking member of the renamed Africa and Global Health Subcommittee of the Foreign Affairs Committee. On the eve of the Olympics in July 2008, Smith tried to meet human-rights lawyers in Beijing, but they were placed under house arrest. He fought to require greater disclosure of censorship by Internet companies in their dealings with China and other repressive governments, and he unsuccessfully urged President Bush not to attend the Olympic opening ceremonies. "I'm not against the Olympics. I love sports, but not there," he said. In August 2008, he traveled to Tbilisi in the Georgia Republic and helped to rescue two young New Jersey girls who were at risk during the Russian invasion there. In 2005, Smith won passage of a bill doubling U.S. contributions to international peacekeeping efforts, to support of democracy in Haiti, and to permanently fund Radio Free Asia.

Smith's tendency to buck his party for the sake of his beliefs was best illustrated by events in 2005, when Republicans still controlled the House. As chairman of the Veterans' Affairs Committee, Smith angered budget conservatives by pushing generous government benefits for veterans, including increasing disability payments by $2.5 billion and GI Bill spending by 46%; $1 billion in aid to homeless veterans; and an additional $100 million in health care benefits for surviving spouses of veterans. In 2004, in a major breach of party protocol, he voted against the Republican-drafted budget and for the Democratic spending plan because it contained more money for veterans. In early January 2005, the GOP leadership had had enough. The Republican Steering Committee booted Smith from his committee chairmanship and gave it to Steve Buyer of Indiana. Veterans groups expressed outrage, to no avail. But Smith's warnings that veterans programs were being underfunded proved true that June, when Veterans Affairs Secretary Jim Nicholson announced that the department had underestimated the number of returning Iraq war veterans by a factor of four and that it needed an additional $2.6 billion.

Smith's devotion to principle and his reputation for tending to constituent problems have made him popular in the politically marginal 4th District. Since 1984, he has received at least 61% of the vote in easily winning re-election. In 2008, Democratic challenger Joshua Zeitz, a first-time candidate, accused him of being a resident of Virginia because Smith owns a home in the Old Dominion and his daughter paid in-state tuition there. Smith rents a town house in Hamilton Township, N.J. He was re-elected 66%-33%.

FIFTH DISTRICT

Scott Garrett (R)

Elected 2002, 4th term; b. July 9, 1959, Englewood; home, Wantage; Montclair St. U., B.A. 1981, Rutgers U., J.D. 1984; Protestant; married (Mary Ellen); 2 children.

Elected Office: NJ Assembly, 1990–2002.

Professional Career: Practicing atty., 1984–2002.

DC Office: 137 CHOB, 20515, 202-225-4465; Fax: 202-225-9048; Web site: garrett.house.gov.

State Offices: Glen Rock, 201-444-5454; Newton, 973-300-2000.

Committees: *Budget* (2nd of 15 R). *Financial Services* (13th of 29 R): Capital Markets, Insurance & Government Sponsored Enterprises (RMM); Financial Institutions & Consumer Credit.

Group Ratings

	ADA	ACLU	AFS	LCV	ITIC	NTU	COC	ACU	CFG	FRC
2008	5	9	0	8	43	85	78	100	98	100
2007	0	—	0	20		88	70	100	98	—

National Journal Ratings

	2007 LIB	—	2007 CONS		2008 LIB	—	2008 CONS
Economic	9%	—	90%		9%	—	90%
Social	20%	—	79%		0%	—	91%
Foreign	0%	—	72%		34%	—	65%
Composite	15%	—	85%		16%	—	84%

Key Votes of the 110th Congress

1. Increase minimum wage	N	5. Share immigration data	Y	9. Withdraw troops 8/08	N
2. Expand SCHIP	N	6. Foreign aid abortion ban	Y	10. No operations in Iran	N
3. Raise CAFE standards	N	7. Ban gay bias in workplace	N	11. Free trade with Peru	Y
4. Bail out financial markets	N	8. Repeal D.C. gun law	Y	12. Overhaul FISA	Y

Election Results

2008 general	Scott Garrett (R)	172,653	(56%)	($1,726,631)
	Dennis Shulman (D)	131,033	(42%)	($1,194,535)
2008 primary	Scott Garrett (R)	unopposed		

Prior Winning Percentages: 2006 (55%); 2004 (58%); 2002 (59%)

Population		Race/Ethnicity		Work	
Pop. 2007:	666,834	White:	81.5%	Private:	79.8%
Change since 2000:	Up 3.0%	Black:	1.9%	Government:	13.4%
Urban:	82.7%	Hispanic:	6.2%	Self-employed:	6.6%
Rural:	17.3%	Asian:	9.0%	Blue collar:	14.8%
Area size:	1,130 sq. mi.	Native Am.:	0.1%	White collar:	73.2%
		Hawaiian:	0.0%	Khaki collar:	0.0%
Age		Two+ races:	1.0%	Other:	11.9%
Median age:	40.9 yrs.			Median income:	$87,505
More than 65 yrs:	13.3%	*Ancestry*		Median home value:	$456,500
Less than 18 yrs:	25.2%	Italian:	17.4%	Poverty:	3.8%
		Irish:	15.6%		
Education		German:	13.4%	**Military Veterans**	
H.S. grad:	92.5%			% of Pop:	8.6%
College grad:	42.2%				
Grad degree:	15.6%				

The northern edge of New Jersey was settled three centuries ago by the Dutch, for whom this plateau of land behind the Hudson River Palisades seemed a natural part of Nieuw Amsterdam. The Dutch influence is seen in old, steep-roofed farmhouses and in many of the place names—Bergen County, Cresskill, Closter. And some "Dutchness" remains in local communities. But overall, northernmost New Jersey has the well-settled look of so many northeastern suburbs, with touches of both affluence and small-town hominess, criss-crossed at its edges with limited-access highways and shopping centers. In the late 1950s, Paramus was transformed from celery farms to the site of two of the nation's first large shopping malls—and constant traffic jams. Not far away are Saddle River and Franklin Lakes, with million-dollar houses on multi-acre lots, and Park Ridge, with office buildings and condominiums. This area may look like WASP suburbia on the surface, but in fact it is home to successful people of all ethnic groups, many of them descended from those who first saw the Statue of Liberty from steerage and passed through the inspection queues at Ellis Island. A curiosity: Asian women in Bergen County have the nation's longest life expectancy, 91 years.

The 5th Congressional District of New Jersey comprises most of northern Bergen County, plus a swath of North Jersey stretching west to the hill-enclosed upper reaches of the Delaware River, crossing one ridge of mountains after another, and then running south to Interstate 78. About 60% of its population is in Bergen County. To the west, little subdivisions set amid the lakes of western Passaic County are filling up with young families. Farther west are once rural, now more or less suburban Sussex and Warren counties. In 2008, the recession took a toll on many of these suburban enclaves as foreclosures and a large inventory of unsold homes sent property values plummeting. Politically, this area has long been solidly Republican, although as with the rest of New Jersey, it has moved toward the Democrats since the 1990s.

2008 Presidential Vote

McCain (R)	179,801	(54%)
Obama (D)	152,544	(46%)

2004 Presidential Vote

Bush (R)	184,530	(57%)
Kerry (D)	137,019	(43%)

Cook Partisan Voting Index: R+7

In 2004, Republican George W. Bush won the district 57%-43%, his second-best showing in the state. In 2008, Democratic nominee Barack Obama lost it 54%-46%.

The congressman from the 5th District is Scott Garrett, a Republican elected in 2002. Garrett grew up on a farm in Wantage, where his parents grew tomatoes and Christmas trees. The family's main income came from his father's job as a salesman for Uniroyal. A conservative from the start, Garrett questioned his high school administration's spending practices and kept a picture of David Stockman, the father of Reaganomics, at his desk. He graduated from Montclair State College and Rutgers law school, and became a trial lawyer in Sussex County. He's a born-again Christian who meets most Saturday mornings for three hours with a small group that calls itself Joshua Men.

In 1989, he was elected to the New Jersey General Assembly, where he quickly became one of the most conservative members. In 1998 and 2000, he challenged veteran U.S. Rep. Marge Roukema, a moderate Republican, in the primary. He attacked Roukema for supporting abortion rights and gun-control laws. She pointed to her conservative votes on economic issues and was backed by the conservative House Republican leadership. Each time, Garrett carried the western part of the district but Roukema ran strongly in her Bergen County base, winning by 53%-47% in 1998 and 52%-48% in 2000.

In 2001, Roukema announced that she would not seek another term. Garrett ran again in 2002. His challenge in the primary was to sell his views in Bergen County, where Sussex County is viewed as a distant province somewhere near Idaho. Two well-known Republicans from Bergen entered the race: state Sen. Gerald Cardinale and Assemblyman David Russo. They argued that nominating Garrett would put the seat at risk. But Garrett won the primary with 41% to 26% for Russo and 25% for Cardinale. Garrett won 81% of the vote in Sussex and 68% in Warren. But he won just 25% in Bergen County, raising Democratic hopes. The Democratic nominee was Anne Sumers, a former Republican who switched parties in early 2002 and stressed her agreement with Roukema on most issues. With help from the national Democrats, Sumers attacked Garrett as an "extremist," pointing to his support for limited federal aid to education. Garrett pounced on Sumers's failure to vote in local school board elections and her musings on a liberal website, where she characterized American patriotism as "jingoistic." At the urging of the House Republicans' campaign committee, Garrett soft-pedaled some of his more conservative views. Sumers outspent Garrett, $1.6 million to $1.3 million, including nearly $400,000 of her own money. But national Republicans spent heavily on issue ads on Garrett's behalf. This turned out to be less of a contest than many people expected. Garrett won 59%-38%. In Bergen County, which cast 64% of the total vote, he led 55%-43%.

In the House, Garrett is the most conservative member of the New Jersey delegation and a budget hawk. His vote against the Republicans' Medicare prescription drug bill in 2003 angered GOP leaders and limited Garrett's influence in the House. When the state delegation sent a letter to President Bush opposing oil exploration off the New Jersey coast, Garrett was the only member who did not sign it. In 2008, he was among 17 House members who opposed extension of the Americans with Disabilities Act, and among 10 who voted against fighting AIDS in Africa. In 2006, the House passed his amendment to require disclosure of earmarks in tax bills as well as in spending measures.

Garrett got a furious reaction in July 2007 when he challenged as "overspending" $34 million for Alaska natives in the education appropriations bill. Angry that he had not received a warning, Republican Don Young of Alaska told the House, "I suggest New Jersey ought to elect some new representatives." Garrett lost the amendment, 74-352. As the Republican Conference became more conservative, Garrett became more of a presence. Even though many of his constituents work on Wall Street, he opposed the bailout of the financial markets in 2008. "I am wary of using taxpayer dollars to prop up failing businesses," he said.

In 2009, he leapfrogged other members and became the ranking Republican on the Subcommittee on Capital Markets, Insurance, and Government-Sponsored Enterprises at the Financial Services Committee, which has authority over the Fannie Mae and Freddie Mac housing finance authorities. Garrett has clashed repeatedly with full committee Chairman Barney Frank, a Democrat from Massachusetts.

Garrett has faced serious re-election challenges. In 2006, Paul Aronsohn, who was communications director for Democratic Gov. Jim McGreevey, called Garrett "too extreme, too disconnected to the people he represents." He raised nearly $600,000 and cut Garrett's margin in Bergen to 51%-48%. But with more than 60% of the vote in Sussex and Warren, Garrett won 55%-44%.

His 2008 challenger was unconventional, and the contest attracted national attention. The Democratic nominee was Dennis Shulman, a blind rabbi and psychologist who was a first-time political candidate. He got help from the Democratic Congressional Campaign Committee, labor unions, and robo-calls featuring former President Bill Clinton. Shulman criticized Garrett as too conservative, a recipient of money from special interests, and a participant in a "corrupt" tax break for farmland on which his brother grows Christmas trees. Garrett countered that Shulman was the "extremist," and he emphasized his independence from President Bush. Garrett spent $1.7 million to Shulman's $1.1 million. Garrett won 56%-42%, carrying all four counties, including 53% of the vote in Bergen.

SIXTH DISTRICT

Frank Pallone (D)

Elected 1988, 11th full term; b. Oct. 30, 1951, Long Branch; home, Long Branch; Middlebury Col., B.A. 1973, Fletcher Schl. of Law & Diplomacy, M.A. 1974, Rutgers U., J.D. 1978; Catholic; married (Sarah); 3 children.

Elected Office: Long Branch City Cncl., 1982–88; NJ Senate, 1983–88.

Professional Career: Asst. prof., Rutgers U., 1979–80; Practicing atty., 1981–83; Instructor, Monmouth Col., 1984–86.

DC Office: 237 CHOB, 20515, 202-225-4671; Fax: 202-225-9665; Web site: www.house.gov/pallone.

State Offices: Long Branch, 732-571-1140; Monmouth, 732-571-1140; New Brunswick, 732-249-8892.

Committees: *Energy & Commerce* (5th of 36 D): Commerce, Trade & Consumer Protections; Energy & Environment; Health (Chmn). *Natural Resources* (5th of 29 D): Insular Affairs, Oceans & Wildlife.

Group Ratings

	ADA	ACLU	AFS	LCV	ITIC	NTU	COC	ACU	CFG	FRC
2008	100	100	100	100	80	7	67	0	6	0
2007	100	—	100	100	—	4	45	0	6	—

National Journal Ratings

	2007 LIB — 2007 CONS		2008 LIB — 2008 CONS	
Economic	82% —	0%	69% —	29%
Social	92% —	0%	66% —	34%
Foreign	78% —	20%	85% —	8%
Composite	89% —	11%	75% —	25%

Key Votes of the 110th Congress

1. Increase minimum wage	Y	5. Share immigration data	N	9. Withdraw troops 8/08	Y
2. Expand SCHIP	Y	6. Foreign aid abortion ban	N	10. No operations in Iran	Y
3. Raise CAFE standards	Y	7. Ban gay bias in workplace	Y	11. Free trade with Peru	N
4. Bail out financial markets	Y	8. Repeal D.C. gun law	N	12. Overhaul FISA	N

Election Results

2008 general	Frank Pallone (D)	164,077	(67%)	($1,542,502)
	Robert McLeod (R)	77,469	(32%)	($12,364)
2008 primary	Frank Pallone (D)	unopposed		

Prior Winning Percentages: 2006 (69%); 2004 (67%); 2002 (66%); 2000 (68%); 1998 (57%); 1996 (61%); 1994 (60%); 1992 (52%); 1990 (49%); 1988 (52%); 1988 special (52%)

Population		Race/Ethnicity		Work	
Pop. 2007:	656,854	White:	57.6%	Private:	81.3%
Change since 2000:	Up 1.5%	Black:	15.6%	Government:	14.2%
Urban:	99.7%	Hispanic:	14.7%	Self-employed:	4.3%
Rural:	0.3%	Asian:	10.5%	Blue collar:	19.4%
Area size:	388 sq. mi.	Native Am.:	0.1%	White collar:	64.7%
		Hawaiian:	0.0%	Khaki collar:	0.0%
Age		Two+ races:	1.1%	Other:	15.9%
Median age:	36.3 yrs.	*Ancestry*		Median income:	$66,215
More than 65 yrs:	11.6%	Italian:	13.8%	Median home value:	$360,000
Less than 18 yrs:	22.7%	Irish:	12.5%	Poverty:	9.0%
Education		German:	8.0%		
H.S. grad:	86.9%			**Military Veterans**	
College grad:	33.7%			% of Pop:	7.8%
Grad degree:	12.9%				

For generations, great transportation arteries have brought people out of the huge central cities of New York and Philadelphia and into the flatlands and hills of New Jersey—to vacation, to raise families, to work toward affluence, and to build communities. The railroads of the late 19th century created the towns of the Jersey shore. After 1874, when the first train from New York City reached Long Branch, the shore became the summer home of seven presidents from Grant to Wilson (Garfield, convalescing after

2008 Presidential Vote		
Obama (D)	165,261	(60%)
McCain (R)	104,932	(38%)
2004 Presidential Vote		
Kerry (D)	144,105	(57%)
Bush (R)	109,729	(43%)
Cook Partisan Voting Index:	D+8	

he was shot, died there in 1881) and of New York racehorse owners and socialites. But over time, the ambiance became honky-tonk, and the fishing pier and much of the boardwalk went up in flames in 1987. Only recently have developers sought to revive it. The great freight rail lines in the New York-Philadelphia corridor sparked electrical and chemical industries here. They built on the inventions of Thomas Edison, many of them produced in his Menlo Park laboratory just off the rail lines, where a 131-foot tower stands as a memorial to the inventor. The same corridor was the site of America's first cloverleaf intersection, at the junction of U.S. 1 and U.S. 9, and of the intersection of two of America's great post-World War II highways, the New Jersey Turnpike and the Garden State Parkway. The turnpike, now 12 lanes wide in stretches, roars past oil tank farms and petrochemical plants, major rail lines, Newark International Airport, and the oily waters of Raritan Bay. The parkway links leafy affluent suburbs with the Jersey shore.

The 6th Congressional District inelegantly ties together these great transportation nodes, and the upward mobility and economic progress that have taken place around them. The district is shaped something like an overturned capital F, with a long string of towns running from Piscataway to Sandy Hook, and two appendages running south: one along the Middlesex-Monmouth county line, the other along the Atlantic Ocean. Middlesex and Monmouth counties account for 90% of the district's population. It includes the central core of Middlesex County: New Brunswick, Highland Park, Metuchen, Sayreville, and parts of Edison Township and surrounding communities—a heavy industry area that, since the time of Edison, has also housed some of America's great research and development facilities, plus Rutgers, the state university of New Jersey. In recent years, Edison Township has seen an influx of immigrants from India, many of them engineers and doctors.

The 6th also includes Monmouth County territory overlooking Lower New York Bay, with spacious estates on highlands above little port towns from Sandy Hook, home to the nation's oldest operating lighthouse (1764), south to the mile-long boardwalk of Belmar. Between them are Asbury Park, founded as a Christian resort, immortalized by a Bruce Springsteen album, and now plagued by a high poverty rate; and Ocean Grove, founded in 1869 as a square-mile Methodist resort, still dry for teetotalers who throng to its 10,000-seat Great Hall, built in 1894. Ocean Grove also has the nation's greatest concentration of Victorian homes. The shore has remained a summer vacation area that attracts millions, but it also hosts year-round communities, with their own upward-striving families. These are comfortable Democratic working-class bastions, wedged between heavily minority urban districts and upscale suburbia. In 2008, Barack Obama won this district 60%-38%.

The congressman from the 6th District is Frank Pallone, a Democrat elected in 1988. Pallone is the son of a disabled Long Branch policeman. He has been an environmentalist since 1969, when as a Middlebury College freshman in Vermont he worked for that state's first-in-the-nation bottle deposit law. After getting a master's degree in international relations from Tufts University and a law degree from Rutgers, he was elected to the Long Branch City Council in 1982, at age 31, and to the New Jersey Senate a year later. After the death of U.S. Rep. Jim Howard, a Democrat who chaired the Public Works and Transportation Committee, Pallone ran for the House. The district leaned Republican, but residents were angry about untreated sludge, plastic containers, and medical waste washing up on the beach. Pallone's bumper sticker, which didn't mention party affiliation, said, "Stop Ocean Dumping." That, combined with his conservative stands on taxes and crime, helped him to win 52% in both the special and general elections.

Pallone, moderate to liberal, started as a political maverick but became more loyal to the party when Democrats were the minority. His environmental focus turned to the ever-lively border war with New York, and he opposed offshore dumping near Sandy Hook of highly contaminated material dredged from New York Harbor. In 2006, he won passage of a bill to reduce and prevent debris in the marine environment. In 2008, he was the lead sponsor of a bipartisan bill to rebuild American fisheries, in part by requiring a review of factors that lead to over-fishing.

As chairman of the influential Energy and Commerce Subcommittee on Health, he has criticized shortfalls in children's health funding. In 2009, he helped steer to passage the Democrats' expansion of the State Children's Health Insurance Program, which he called "a down payment to ensuring that all Americans have access to affordable health care." When the Obama administration's economic stimulus bill came up for debate, he backed an increase in the federal matching rate for Medicaid as a step to reduce the program's financial burden on states. Pallone was also critical of President Bush's plan to allow insured workers to switch to lower-cost health coverage and of the Republicans' Medicare prescription drug program. With fellow Energy and Commerce members John Dingell and Bart Stupak, both Michigan Democrats, he promised action in 2009 on their bill to strengthen the authority of the Food and Drug Administration.

In a bow to the many people of Armenian descent in the district, Pallone helped push congressional approval of normalizing trade relations for Armenia. He sponsored the resolution that labeled the 1915 killing of Armenians by Ottoman Turks as genocide. But he agreed in October 2007 to defer a vote under pressure from the Turkish government and the Bush administration.

Since 1994, Pallone has been re-elected with at least 60% of the vote, with one exception. In 1998, he faced a tough challenge from 28-year-old Republican Mike Ferguson, an ally of former GOP Gov. Thomas Kean. An insurance group unhappy with Pallone's support for President Bill Clinton's plan to regulate health maintenance organizations spent nearly $2 million on Ferguson's campaign. But Pallone won 57%-40%.

His ambitions for statewide office have been frustrated. When Democratic Sen. Frank Lautenberg announced his retirement in 1999, Pallone formed an exploratory committee but did not run. He again thought about running when Democratic Sen. Robert Torricelli quit the 2002 Senate race. When Democratic Sen. Jon Corzine ran for governor in 2005, Pallone endorsed him and said that he would like to fill Corzine's Senate seat. But after winning the gubernatorial race, Corzine appointed U.S. Rep. Robert Menendez to his Senate seat.

SEVENTH DISTRICT

Leonard Lance (R)

Elected 2008, 1st term; b. June 25, 1952, Easton, PA; home, Clinton Township; Lehigh U., B.A., 1974; Vanderbilt U., J.D. 1977; Princeton U., M.P.A. 1982; Catholic; married (Heidi Rohrbach); 1 child.

Elected Office: NJ Assembly, 1991–2001; NJ Senate, 2002–08, minority leader 2002-08.

Professional Career: Law clerk, Warren Cnty Court, 1977–78; Asst. cnsl., Gov. Thomas H. Kean, 1983–1990.

DC Office: 114 CHOB, 20515, 202-225-5361; Fax: 202-225-9460; Web site: lance.house.gov.

State Offices: Flemington, 908-789-2869; Westfield, 908-518-7733.

Committees: *Financial Services* (29th of 29 R): Domestic Monetary Policy & Technology; Financial Institutions & Consumer Credit.

Group Ratings and Key Votes: Newly Elected

Election Results

2008 general	Leonard Lance (R)	148,461	(50%)	($1,419,698)
	Linda Stender (D)	124,818	(42%)	($2,621,407)
	Michael Hsing (I)	16,419	(6%)	($213,817)
2008 primary	Leonard Lance (R)	10,094	(39%)	
	Kate Whitman (R)	5,052	(20%)	
	P. Hatfield (R)	3,902	(15%)	
	Martin Marks (R)	3,211	(13%)	
	Tom Roughneen (R)	1,845	(7%)	

Population		Race/Ethnicity		Work	
Pop. 2007:	671,277	White:	73.2%	Private:	81.7%
Change since 2000:	Up 3.7%	Black:	5.1%	Government:	12.4%
Urban:	90.4%	Hispanic:	10.1%	Self-employed:	5.7%
Rural:	9.6%	Asian:	10.2%	Blue collar:	14.8%
Area size:	603 sq. mi.	Native Am.:	0.1%	White collar:	74.1%
Age		Hawaiian:	0.0%	Khaki collar:	0.0%
Median age:	40.1 yrs.	Two+ races:	1.0%	Other:	11.1%
More than 65 yrs:	12.6%	*Ancestry*		Median income:	$90,502
Less than 18 yrs:	24.6%	Italian:	15.6%	Median home value:	$442,200
Education		Irish:	13.1%	Poverty:	3.5%
H.S. grad:	91.0%	German:	11.1%	**Military Veterans**	
College grad:	45.0%			% of Pop:	7.5%
Grad degree:	18.1%				

The transportation arteries beneath the First Watchung Mountain played a large role in New Jersey's development. The rail lines of the late 19th century opened up commuter suburbs. In the 1940s, the four lanes of U.S. 22 made those communities readily accessible by car. And finally, Interstate 78, completed in the mid-1980s, put Newark only an hour's distance from the Pennsylvania line. The interstate stimulated the development of an edge city called Bridgewater Commons halfway between

2008 Presidential Vote		
Obama (D)	161,497	(50%)
McCain (R)	159,529	(49%)
2004 Presidential Vote		
Bush (R)	164,176	(53%)
Kerry (D)	144,767	(47%)
Cook Partisan Voting Index:	R + 3	

Philadelphia and Manhattan. An enormous shopping mall and office developments, which included the headquarters of AT&T, rose up in the horse country around Far Hills and Bernardsville, where the likes of Malcolm Forbes and Charles Engelhard owned huge estates. (New Jersey claims more horses per square mile than any other state.) These towns are in Somerset County, with a median household income in 2007 of $97,658, the fourth highest among U.S. counties.

The 7th Congressional District of New Jersey, with its contorted boundaries, covers these several generations of suburban development. It ranges across the breadth of the state, from the edge of Pennsylvania's Lehigh Valley in the west almost to Staten Island in the east. It is an agglomeration of places, not a district with a distinct character. The 7th includes parts of four counties, and parts of Edison, Woodbridge, Bridgewater, Linden and Union. Edison has become a cultural melting pot in recent years, with a majority nonwhite population; it is 36% Asian, 9% African-American and 7% Hispanic. The district's easternmost points are in Union County, just shy of Newark International Airport. It includes Summit, Scotch Plains and North and South Plainfield, but not heavily Democratic Plainfield. It follows I-78 and the Watchung Mountains to western Somerset County. It takes in fast-growing Hunterdon County, where the county seat of Flemington was the site of the "trial of the century" for the kidnapping and murder of the 20-month-old son of aviator Charles Lindbergh. There is, of course, a political imperative behind the weird shape of the district. It was designed as part of a bipartisan incumbent-protection plan, and it put heavily Democratic areas into the adjacent 12th, 6th and 10th Districts, while moving Republican areas formerly in those districts to the 7th. Republican President George W. Bush won comfortably here by 53%-47% in 2004, but in 2008, Democrat Barack Obama won, though by a much narrower margin, 1,968 votes. Obama got 49.7% to Republican John McCain's 49.1%.

The new congressman from the 7th District is Leonard Lance, a Republican elected in 2008 to succeed retiring GOP Rep. Mike Ferguson. Lance's English-German ancestors have lived in Hunterdon County for 300 years, and he and his twin brother, James, grew up there in the small town of Glen Gardner. Politics is in Lance's blood. His father, Wesley Lance, was a state senator and eventually rose to Senate president. The younger Lance went to Lehigh University in neighboring Pennsylvania, then headed south to Vanderbilt University to go to law school. He returned to New Jersey to pursue a master's degree from Princeton University. One of his early jobs was as Republican Gov. Thomas Kean's assistant counsel for county and municipal matters. In 1990, he was elected to the New Jersey Legislature, where he made a name for himself as a budget hawk and independent thinker. He is fond of saying, "I am New Jersey's leading opponent of borrowing without voter approval," and his record bears that out. In 2004, when he was the state Senate minority leader, Lance successfully sued Democratic Gov. Jim McGreevy over a plan to borrow from public coffers to close a budget gap. When he was in the state Assembly, he opposed a spending plan by GOP Gov. Christine Todd Whitman, a move that cost him the Budget Committee chairmanship. He was known by fellow legislators as a workhorse with a pragmatic streak. In many respects, he is a prototypical Northeastern Republican: fiscally conservative but socially moderate. He supports abortion rights and calls himself an "Eisenhower Republican." He tends to favor bipartisanship over ideology.

In 2006, Ferguson narrowly won re-election to his fourth term, beating Democratic Assemblywoman Linda Stender by just under 3,000 votes. Facing a 2008 rematch against Stender, Ferguson announced his retirement in November 2007, leaving the GOP field wide open. Well-known in the district, Lance announced his candidacy in January 2008, joining six other candidates. Lance was the establishment Republicans' pick and considered the frontrunner, but he faced tough competition from Whitman's daughter, Kate Whitman, who outraised him and questioned his fiscal bona fides. He was forced to spend nearly all of his funds early on, yet he won the primary by a surprisingly large margin, besting Whitman 39%-20%.

Drained by the primary, Lance started the general election campaign seriously outmatched by Stender in fundraising. By midsummer, he had collected $485,000 compared with her $1.6 million. Stender criticized Lance for opposing her legislation to make it mandatory for pharmacies to fill prescriptions for birth-control pills, including emergency contraception. Lance said he voted against the bill because he believed that mom-and-pop pharmacies should have the right to decide whether to fill such prescriptions. Both political parties pulled out all the stops for this seat. President Bush stumped for Lance and helped him raise money, but that seemed to give Stender more ammunition to assert that Lance was a clone of the unpopular outgoing president. Democratic House Speaker Nancy Pelosi and

New York Sen. Hillary Rodham Clinton both came to the district to campaign for Stender. But Lance got a boost from the Newark *Star-Ledger* newspaper, which gave him a glowing endorsement and called him "that rarest of birds, an old-fashioned, thrifty, genuinely moderate Republican. He is a thoughtful, principled lawmaker with a knack for bipartisanship."

Stender outspent Lance nearly 2-to-1— $2.6 million to $1.4 million. But Lance did better than expected, winning by 50%-42%. Once in the House, he was appointed to the Financial Services Committee.

EIGHTH DISTRICT

Bill Pascrell (D)

Elected 1996, 7th term; b. Jan. 25, 1937, Paterson; home, Paterson; Fordham U., B.A. 1959, M.A. 1961; Catholic; married (Elsie); 3 children.

Military Career: Army, 1961; Army Reserves, 1962–67.

Elected Office: Pres., Paterson Bd. of Ed., 1979–82; NJ Assembly, 1987–97, Minority ldr. pro tem; Paterson mayor, 1990–97.

Professional Career: High Schl. teacher, 1960–74; Dir., Paterson Dept. of Public Works, 1974–77; Dir., Paterson Dept. of Policy, 1977–87.

DC Office: 2464 RHOB, 20515, 202-225-5751; Fax: 202-225-5782; Web site: www.pascrell.house.gov.

State Offices: Bloomfield, 973-680-1361; Passaic, 973-472-4510; Paterson, 973-523-5152.

Committees: *Homeland Security* (14th of 20 D): Border, Maritime & Global Counterterrorism; Emergency Communications, Preparedness & Response; Management, Investigations & Oversight. *Ways & Means* (15th of 26 D): Health; Oversight.

Group Ratings

	ADA	ACLU	AFS	LCV	ITIC	NTU	COC	ACU	CFG	FRC
2008	95	100	100	92	71	12	56	4	4	5
2007	95	—	100	100	—	6	55	0	12	—

National Journal Ratings

	2007 LIB	—	2007 CONS		2008 LIB	—	2008 CONS
Economic	82%	—	0%		78%	—	20%
Social	85%	—	13%		66%	—	33%
Foreign	73%	—	26%		92%	—	0%
Composite	84%	—	17%		81%	—	20%

Key Votes of the 110th Congress

1. Increase minimum wage	Y	5. Share immigration data	N	9. Withdraw troops 8/08	Y
2. Expand SCHIP	Y	6. Foreign aid abortion ban	N	10. No operations in Iran	Y
3. Raise CAFE standards	Y	7. Ban gay bias in workplace	Y	11. Free trade with Peru	Y
4. Bail out financial markets	Y	8. Repeal D.C. gun law	N	12. Overhaul FISA	N

Election Results

2008 general	Bill Pascrell (D)	159,279	(71%)	($1,137,316)
	Roland Straten (R)	63,107	(28%)	($82,227)
2008 primary	Bill Pascrell (D)	unopposed		

Prior Winning Percentages: 2006 (71%); 2004 (69%); 2002 (67%); 2000 (67%); 1998 (62%); 1996 (51%)

Population		Race/Ethnicity		Work	
Pop. 2007:	648,791	White:	49.2%	Private:	81.9%
Change since 2000:	Up 0.2%	Black:	13.1%	Government:	13.1%
Urban:	100.0%	Hispanic:	30.2%	Self-employed:	4.8%
Rural:	0.0%	Asian:	6.0%	Blue collar:	21.0%
Area size:	110 sq. mi.	Native Am.:	0.1%	White collar:	63.1%
		Hawaiian:	0.0%	Khaki collar:	0.0%
Age		Two+ races:	0.8%	Other:	15.9%
Median age:	37.3 yrs.			Median income:	$59,610
More than 65 yrs:	12.8%	*Ancestry*		Median home value:	$410,800
Less than 18 yrs:	25.1%	Italian:	15.0%	Poverty:	12.2%
		Irish:	7.8%		
Education		German:	5.5%	**Military Veterans**	
H.S. grad:	82.1%			% of Pop:	5.8%
College grad:	31.0%				
Grad degree:	11.6%				

Paterson is one of the few American cities that have turned out pretty much as planned. It was the brainchild of Alexander Hamilton, who in the 1790s journeyed 20 miles from Manhattan to the Great Falls of the Passaic River in New Jersey. Watching the water surge down 72 feet—the highest falls along the East Coast—he predicted an industrial city would rise on the site. Hamilton formed the Society for Establishing Useful Manufactures, which opened a calico factory in 1794, and got Pierre

2008 Presidential Vote		
Obama (D)	163,359	(63%)
McCain (R)	91,690	(36%)
2004 Presidential Vote		
Kerry (D)	142,081	(59%)
Bush (R)	99,239	(41%)
Cook Partisan Voting Index:		D + 10

L'Enfant, the designer of Washington, D.C., to design Paterson (named after then-Gov. William Paterson). In 1836, Samuel Colt began manufacturing revolvers here. One of the first American locomotives, the Sandusky, was built in Paterson in 1837. A walkout of cotton workers in 1828 was America's first factory strike. Paterson ultimately became America's "Silk City," employing 25,000 silk-mill workers before the great strike of 1913 led by the radical Industrial Workers of the World. Paterson kept producing locomotives and, after the silk mills started closing down following another unsuccessful strike in 1924, became a cloth-dyeing center. Throughout, it attracted immigrants from England, Ireland, and, after 1890, Italy and Poland. The city continues to attract them today, even if its economy produces more service jobs and fewer manufacturing jobs. In 2000, Paterson's population was 50% Hispanic, up from 30% in 1990. The city has gained a lively artists' community in its postindustrial setting, and downtown's "Little Palestine" reflects the city's sizable Arab community—Turks, Palestinians, Lebanese, Syrians, and Jordanians. There is also a politically active Islamic Center in Paterson.

The 8th Congressional District includes Paterson (its largest city) and much suburban and industrial territory west and south of Paterson and north of Newark. More than half the population lives in Passaic County; the rest are in Essex County. The district includes the mixed factory and middle-class towns south of Paterson on the Passaic River—Clifton, Nutley, Belleville, Bloomfield, and Passaic, which is majority Hispanic. On higher ground is affluent Montclair, with large populations of well-off African-Americans and Manhattan-oriented Boomers, the most Democratic part of the district outside of Paterson. Over the Watchung Mountain are affluent West Orange and South Orange, both heavily Democratic, and the small Republican towns of Cedar Grove and Verona. In the 1980s, the district leaned Republican; in the 1990s, it became heavily Democratic and remains so.

The 8th District representative is Bill Pascrell, a Democrat elected in 1996. He grew up in Paterson, the grandson of Italian immigrants. His father worked for the railroad, and Pascrell was the first one in his family to graduate from college. He worked his way through Fordham University, served in the Army, and then taught high school for 14 years. From there Pascrell went into politics, first as director of Paterson's public works department, and then as school board president. In 1987, he was elected to the New Jersey Assembly. In 1990, Pascrell was elected mayor of Paterson but continued to serve in the Assembly—a common practice in New Jersey until the Legislature voted in 2007 to stop the practice. In 1996, Pascrell challenged first-term U.S. Rep. Bill Martini, a Republican, whom Pascrell portrayed as the tool of an "extremist" House leadership. His ads showed Martini's face on a puppet being manipulated by Republican House Speaker Newt Gingrich. Despite Martini's support from the Sierra Club and labor unions, Pascrell rode the coattails of President Clinton, who got 58% of the vote in the district. Pascrell won 51%-48%. Since then, he has received at least 62% of the vote against weak challengers.

In the House, Pascrell has compiled a liberal record on economics and a more moderate one on cultural and foreign issues. He has voted for some restrictions on abortion, including a ban on "partial-birth" abortions and a parental-notification requirement when a woman under 18 crosses state lines for an abortion. In 2002, he voted to authorize the use of force in Iraq, and, on the Homeland Security Committee, he has been a voice for strengthening homeland defense, calling for improved communications among first responders. "How is it we can talk to people on the moon, but we can't talk one block away?" Pascrell asked. In 2008, he urged then President-elect Barack Obama to conduct a security review of "America's most dangerous 2 miles"—the refineries, chemical plants, and rail yards between Newark Liberty International Airport and Port Elizabeth.

Pascrell landed a seat on the powerful House Ways and Means Committee in 2007 after years of lobbying for a spot. He worked with labor and consumer groups to promote "fair trade," and to expand the Trade Adjustment Assistance program for workers who have lost their jobs. Two other pet projects of Pascrell's were successful: A bill to designate Paterson's Great Falls as a 120-acre national park, which was enacted in March 2009, and a bill to increase federal research funding for brain injuries, which passed the House in 2008. When later that year a Montclair High School football player died from a brain injury, Pascrell introduced a bill requiring states to pay for neurological testing of student athletes.

Pascrell has harbored ambitions for statewide office. He expressed interest in running for governor in 2001. But his support of former Gov. Jim Florio in the 2000 Senate Democratic primary against Jon Corzine left him on the losing side of the state's Democratic establishment. In 2005, he supported Corzine for governor in the hopes of succeeding him in the Senate, but the appointment went to U.S. Rep. Robert Menendez. Having gained a Ways and Means seat, Pascrell is less likely to move elsewhere.

NINTH DISTRICT

Steven Rothman (D)

Elected 1996, 7th term; b. Oct. 14, 1952, Englewood; home, Fair Lawn; Syracuse U., B.A. 1974, Washington U., J.D. 1977; Jewish; married (Jennifer); 5 children.

Elected Office: Englewood mayor, 1983–89; Bergen Cnty. Surrogate Court judge, 1993–96.

Professional Career: Practicing atty., 1978–93.

DC Office: 2303 RHOB, 20515, 202-225-5061; Fax: 202-225-5851; Web site: rothman.house.gov.

State Offices: Hackensack, 201-646-0808; Jersey City, 201-798-1366.

Committees: *Appropriations* (23rd of 37 D): Defense; Homeland Security; State, Foreign Operations & Related Programs. *Science & Technology* (15th of 26 D): Investigations & Oversight; Space & Aeronautics.

Group Ratings

	ADA	ACLU	AFS	LCV	ITIC	NTU	COC	ACU	CFG	FRC
2008	100	100	100	92	50	17	56	8	10	5
2007	95	—	100	90	—	4	44	0	7	—

National Journal Ratings

	2007 LIB	—	2007 CONS		2008 LIB	—	2008 CONS
Economic	82%	—	0%		65%	—	34%
Social	77%	—	17%		67%	—	28%
Foreign	67%	—	32%		78%	—	17%
Composite	80%	—	21%		72%	—	28%

Key Votes of the 110th Congress

1. Increase minimum wage	Y	5. Share immigration data	N	9. Withdraw troops 8/08	Y
2. Expand SCHIP	Y	6. Foreign aid abortion ban	N	10. No operations in Iran	N
3. Raise CAFE standards	Y	7. Ban gay bias in workplace	Y	11. Free trade with Peru	*
4. Bail out financial markets	N	8. Repeal D.C. gun law	N	12. Overhaul FISA	N

Election Results

2008 general	Steven Rothman (D)	151,182	(68%)	($1,288,656)
	Vincent Micco (R)	69,503	(31%)	($34,363)
2008 primary	Steven Rothman (D)	unopposed		

Prior Winning Percentages: 2006 (71%); 2004 (68%); 2002 (70%); 2000 (68%); 1998 (65%); 1996 (56%)

Population		Race/Ethnicity		Work	
Pop. 2007:	649,640	White:	55.3%	Private:	82.3%
Change since 2000:	Up 0.4%	Black:	7.1%	Government:	12.0%
Urban:	100.0%	Hispanic:	23.5%	Self-employed:	5.4%
Rural:	0.0%	Asian:	12.6%	Blue collar:	18.4%
Area size:	100 sq. mi.	Native Am.:	0.1%	White collar:	67.2%
		Hawaiian:	0.0%	Khaki collar:	0.1%
Age		Two+ races:	1.0%	Other:	14.3%
Median age:	39.7 yrs.			Median income:	$62,406
More than 65 yrs:	14.5%	*Ancestry*		Median home value:	$418,800
Less than 18 yrs:	20.4%	Italian:	14.1%	Poverty:	8.6%
		Irish:	8.4%		
Education		German:	6.3%	**Military Veterans**	
H.S. grad:	85.8%			% of Pop:	6.2%
College grad:	34.9%				
Grad degree:	12.5%				

The George Washington Bridge, one of several wondrous suspension bridges completed in America in the 1930s, strides the Hudson River, its west tower almost up against the green cliffs of New Jersey's Palisades. It is one of the glories of modern engineering, enabling people and goods to be transported through the irregular terrain of metropolitan New York—tidal rivers and cliffs and broad expanses of swamp. For a century, the dramatic beauty of the Palisades contrasted with the sprawl

2008 Presidential Vote		
Obama (D)	158,911	(61%)
McCain (R)	99,129	(38%)
2004 Presidential Vote		
Kerry (D)	144,723	(59%)
Bush (R)	101,229	(41%)
Cook Partisan Voting Index:	D + 9	

of the Hackensack River Valley and the Jersey Meadowlands not far to the west, which conveyed the image of New Jersey for many—a landscape of gas station signs, oil tank farms, truck terminals, and 12 lanes of New Jersey Turnpike. The Meadowlands, once 8,400 acres of wetlands and home to thousands of species of animals and plants, was developed in the 1970s. The state built in East Rutherford the Meadowlands Sports Complex—Giants Stadium, where the Giants and Jets play; the Meadowlands Racetrack; the Brendan Byrne Arena, later Continental Airlines Arena. Private development followed—hotels, warehouses, light industry, shopping centers—in what became a small city. Now, a generation later, the state is building a new $1.6 billion stadium at the Meadowlands for the National Football League's Giants and Jets. The nearby $2 billion Xanadu retail and entertainment center was scheduled to open in late 2009.

The 9th Congressional District of New Jersey includes much of the Palisades and the Meadowlands. The scenery here is familiar to fans of the cable television series *The Sopranos* : Jersey City, Kearny, North Arlington, Lodi, which is home to the fictitious Bada Bing strip club. The 9th takes in the high-rise towers of Fort Lee, Cliffside Park, and fast-growing Edgewater, where dwellers in luxury apartment houses brag about their views of New York City. It goes west and north to the leafy suburbs of Englewood and Teaneck, and southwest to the high land overlooking the Meadowlands and the Passaic River. Old towns like Rutherford have enclaves of Polish-, German-, and Italian-Americans. Blue-collar Palisades Park has Korean-Americans. Teaneck and Englewood are home to middle-class blacks and young, Orthodox Jewish families.

Fairview, Bergenfield, and Hackensack, an old industrial town and the Bergen County seat, are home to growing numbers of Hispanics. The county has about 80% of the district's voters. This was a growth area in the 1950s and 1960s, as New Yorkers moved out of the city. It lost population in the 1970s and 1980s, as young people moved farther out and left empty nesters behind. Now the population in some towns is rising because of new immigrants. From 2000 to 2007, the Hispanic population in Bergen County grew more than 40% to 130,000. In 2008, Democratic presidential candidate Barack Obama won 54% of the vote in Bergen, and won the district 61%-38%.

The congressman from the 9th District is Steve Rothman, a Democrat first elected in 1996. Rothman grew up in Englewood and Tenafly, the grandson of Jewish immigrants from Russia, Poland, and Austria. His father was a tool and die maker but later found industrial real estate to be more profitable. Rothman went to school at Syracuse University and Washington University law school in St. Louis, and then practiced law. From 1983 to 1989, he was mayor of Englewood. In 1993, he became a judge in the Bergen County Surrogate's Court. When Democrat Bob Torricelli ran for the Senate in 1996, Rothman resigned his judgeship to run for Torricelli's House seat. With the party endorsement, Rothman faced Republican Kathleen Donovan, a former Bergen County clerk, state assemblywoman, and chairwoman of the New York-New Jersey Port Authority. She was endorsed by the New Jersey Education Association. But this part of New Jersey swung sharply to the Democrats after Republicans won control of Congress in 1994. The 9th District voted overwhelmingly for Bill Clinton for president that year, and voted 56%-42% for Rothman.

In the House, Rothman often has been more liberal on economic issues than on foreign-policy and defense issues. He voted for the Iraq war resolution in 2002, although in 2007 he backed a deadline for withdrawal of U.S. forces. The House in June 2007 passed, 411-2, his resolution condemning Iranian President Mahmoud Ahmadinejad for calling for the destruction of Israel.

On local issues, his most innovative work has been to limit further development of the Meadowlands and to get protections for environmentally sensitive areas. He secured $5.2 million to help create an 8,400-acre state park in the one-third of the Meadowlands that had not been developed. "From an industrial waste dump to a nature preserve," is how Rothman describes the project. He fought proposals to expand the Teterboro Airport in the Meadowlands, and in 2003 the House approved his provision to ban noisy 737s at Teterboro. In 2006, he brokered a noise-control agreement for the airport, including a weight limit for jets and overnight curfews on flights.

Rothman's district work naturally includes pitching for transportation dollars, including for projects to relieve ever-congested Route 17. On the Appropriations Committee, he has secured money for commuter rail projects in Bergen County, to expand public transportation into and out of Manhattan, and to clean up pollution in the Passaic River. Rothman also authored a bill, passed by Congress, that creates federal grants for better security in public schools, including for metal detectors, security cameras, and security training. He has obtained $50 million for the program in recent years. He often takes an interest in issues related to veterans benefits, and has been pushing to restore Bush-era cuts that eliminated health care benefits to veterans who fail to qualify as low income.

Rothman has won re-election by wide margins, and has ambitions to run for the Senate.

TENTH DISTRICT

Donald Payne (D)

Elected 1988, 11th term; b. July 16, 1934, Newark; home, Newark; Seton Hall, B.A. 1957; Baptist; widowed; 3 children.

Elected Office: Essex Cnty. Bd. of Chosen Freeholders, 1972–78, Dir. 1977–78; Newark Municipal Cncl., 1982–89.

Professional Career: Elem. & high schl. teacher, 1957–64; Exec., Prudential Insurance Co., 1964–72; Pres., YMCAs of the U.S., 1970; V.P., Urban Data Systems Inc., 1975–88.

DC Office: 2310 RHOB, 20515, 202-225-3436; Fax: 202-225-4160; Web site: www.house.gov/payne.

State Offices: Elizabeth, 908-629-0222; Jersey City, 201-369-0395; Newark, 973-645-3213.

Committees: *Education & Labor* (3rd of 29 D): Early Childhood, Elementary & Secondary Education; Workforce Protections. *Foreign Affairs* (4th of 28 D): Africa & Global Health (Chmn); International Organizations, Human Rights & Oversight; Western Hemisphere.

Group Ratings

	ADA	ACLU	AFS	LCV	ITIC	NTU	COC	ACU	CFG	FRC
2008	95	100	100	100	43	17	47	8	11	5
2007	100	—	100	75	—	5	42	0	1	—

National Journal Ratings

	2007 LIB	—	2007 CONS		2008 LIB	—	2008 CONS
Economic	82%	—	0%		68%	—	32%
Social	85%	—	15%		67%	—	28%
Foreign	90%	—	10%		85%	—	8%
Composite	89%	—	11%		75%	—	25%

Key Votes of the 110th Congress

1. Increase minimum wage	Y	5. Share immigration data	N	9. Withdraw troops 8/08	Y
2. Expand SCHIP	Y	6. Foreign aid abortion ban	N	10. No operations in Iran	Y
3. Raise CAFE standards	Y	7. Ban gay bias in workplace	Y	11. Free trade with Peru	N
4. Bail out financial markets	N	8. Repeal D.C. gun law	N	12. Overhaul FISA	N

Election Results

2008 general	Donald Payne (D)	169,945	(99%)	($502,611)
2008 primary	Donald Payne (D)	unopposed		

Prior Winning Percentages: 2006 (100%); 2004 (97%); 2002 (84%); 2000 (88%); 1998 (84%); 1996 (84%); 1994 (76%); 1992 (78%); 1990 (81%); 1988 (77%)

Population		Race/Ethnicity		Work	
Pop. 2007:	637,152	White:	18.2%	Private:	78.4%
Change since 2000:	Down 1.6%	Black:	56.7%	Government:	17.1%
Urban:	100.0%	Hispanic:	19.1%	Self-employed:	4.4%
Rural:	0.0%	Asian:	4.3%	Blue collar:	22.4%
Area size:	69 sq. mi.	Native Am.:	0.2%	White collar:	54.5%
		Hawaiian:	0.0%	Khaki collar:	0.1%
Age		Two+ races:	0.8%	Other:	23.1%
Median age:	34.6 yrs.			Median income:	$44,493
More than 65 yrs:	10.6%	*Ancestry*		Median home value:	$318,000
Less than 18 yrs:	26.4%	West Indian:	8.8%	Poverty:	17.5%
		Subsaharan:	3.9%		
Education		Italian:	3.5%	**Military Veterans**	
H.S. grad:	79.0%			% of Pop:	5.3%
College grad:	21.1%				
Grad degree:	6.7%				

Newark was once the heart of New Jersey. All of the main transportation arteries led there, and its corporate headquarters buildings were the tallest in the state. In 1930, 442,000 people lived in Newark, 1 of every 9 in New Jersey. Newark fell on hard times in the latter half of the 20th century. The city was plagued by terrible schools and high crime. Whole sections of the city were dominated by criminals and deserted by most law-abiding residents. By the year 2000, there were just 273,000 people left

2008 Presidential Vote		
Obama (D)	208,070	(87%)
McCain (R)	30,395	(13%)
2004 Presidential Vote		
Kerry (D)	167,707	(82%)
Bush (R)	36,660	(18%)
Cook Partisan Voting Index:	D+33	

in Newark, representing 1 in every 30. In recent years, Newark has been attempting a turnaround. Population was up to 280,000 in 2007; new office buildings have joined the Prudential and Public Service Electric & Gas headquarters, and the New Jersey Performing Arts Center has been a big hit for city-dwellers seeking a less expensive experience than Manhattan. There are new restaurants and trendy bars, and a new downtown arena houses the hockey team the Devils. An assortment of condominium projects are on the drawing board. Crime rates have declined, the state has taken over the schools, and life is returning to deserted streets. The young and charismatic mayor, Democrat Cory Booker, brought energy to the city and has declared war on street gangs.

There has been industrial development around Newark Airport. The glass and aluminum facility has been greatly expanded for international carriers and is prospering as a hub for Continental, the most thriving of the legacy airlines. Port Newark-Elizabeth Marine Terminal is the largest container port on the East Coast and ranks nationally behind only Los Angeles and Long Beach. Old warehouses there have been cleared for more-modern facilities. The question is whether the city's finances will stabilize and Newark can become once again the vital center of New Jersey. Mayor Booker's friendship with President Obama certainly won't hurt.

The 10th Congressional District of New Jersey is centered in Essex County and is made up of most of Newark—the Central, South, and West wards—plus Irvington, most of the Oranges, and part of Montclair to the west. It also takes in much of Elizabeth, Rahway, and Linden to the south. Its boundary lines wiggle around to include African-Americans in Jersey City, Montclair, and Elizabeth, while leaving Hispanics in the next-door 13th District. Overall the district is 57% black and is by far the most Democratic district in New Jersey. Obama won Essex County 76%-24%, and the district 87%-13%.

The congressman from the 10th District is Donald Payne, a Democrat first elected in 1988 and the first African-American to represent a New Jersey district in Congress. He grew up in a working-class section of Newark. His mother died when he was just 7, and Payne stayed with his grandmother while his father worked long shifts on the docks. A community organization dedicated to children and teens in tough neighborhoods helped him win a college scholarship, and Payne became a high school history teacher and football coach. He was later the community liaison for Newark-based Prudential. In the 1970s, Payne was elected to the Essex Board of Chosen Freeholders. In 1980 and 1986, he ran against Democratic U.S. Rep. Peter Rodino, who was chairman of the House Judiciary Committee when it voted to impeach President Richard Nixon. Payne lost, even as an African-American in a district with a black majority. But when Rodino retired in 1988, Payne, at age 54, won 73% of the vote in the Democratic primary and easily won the general election. He has not faced a serious re-election challenge since.

Payne has a strongly liberal voting record. He served as chairman of the Congressional Black Caucus in 1995 and 1996, just as Republicans were taking control of Congress. He successfully lobbied the new majority to keep the Africa Subcommittee on the Foreign Relations Committee. Active in issues related to Africa, Payne sponsored a resolution to cut off new investment in Sudan because of its practice of slavery. In July 2004, the House passed his resolution condemning the war in Sudan as "genocide." In 2006, Payne helped to negotiate a bipartisan deal in the House to expand presidential authority to promote peace and accountability in Darfur, and he joined a delegation led by House Speaker Nancy Pelosi to Darfur and elsewhere in Africa.

Payne agitates for increased foreign aid for United Nations peacekeeping operations, and likes to point out that the more than 700 million people of Africa receive less aid from the United States than do the 6 million of Israel. In 2003, President George W. Bush named Payne as one of two congressional delegates to the United Nations. Payne also came to the defense of UN Secretary-General Kofi Annan in December 2004, when Republicans called for his resignation amid allegations concerning corruption in the Iraq oil-for-food program

He was one of 22 House members who voted "present" on the March 2003 resolution authorizing the use of force in Iraq, calling the war "ill-conceived" and one that "could have been avoided through diplomacy." In the majority, Payne chairs the expanded Foreign Affairs Subcommittee on Africa and Global Health. In October 2007, the House passed his Ethiopian Democracy and Accountability Act, which condemned Ethiopia's human-rights record and raised the option of sanctions against the country. He also joined with Republican Rep. John Boozman of Arkansas to get more U.S. assistance to African countries fighting malaria.

ELEVENTH DISTRICT

Rodney Frelinghuysen (R)

Elected 1994, 8th term; b. April 29, 1946, New York City; home, Harding; Hobart Col., B.A. 1969; Episcopalian; married (Virginia); 2 children.

Military Career: Army, 1969–71 (Vietnam).

Elected Office: Morris Cnty. Bd. of Freeholders, 1974–83; NJ Assembly, 1983–94.

Professional Career: Aide, Morris Cnty. Bd. of Freeholders, 1972–74.

DC Office: 2442 RHOB, 20515, 202-225-5034; Fax: 202-225-3186; Web site: frelinghuysen.house.gov.

State Offices: Morristown, 973-984-0711.

Committees: *Appropriations* (6th of 23 R): Defense; Energy & Water Development (RMM).

Group Ratings

	ADA	ACLU	AFS	LCV	ITIC	NTU	COC	ACU	CFG	FRC
2008	15	27	14	62	71	59	100	80	55	29
2007	30	—	18	70	—	53	80	56	55	—

National Journal Ratings

	2007 LIB	—	2007 CONS		2008 LIB	—	2008 CONS
Economic	39%	—	60%		33%	—	66%
Social	45%	—	55%		38%	—	61%
Foreign	42%	—	57%		22%	—	74%
Composite	42%	—	58%		32%	—	68%

Key Votes of the 110th Congress

1. Increase minimum wage	Y	5. Share immigration data	Y	9. Withdraw troops 8/08	N
2. Expand SCHIP	N	6. Foreign aid abortion ban	N	10. No operations in Iran	N
3. Raise CAFE standards	N	7. Ban gay bias in workplace	Y	11. Free trade with Peru	Y
4. Bail out financial markets	Y	8. Repeal D.C. gun law	Y	12. Overhaul FISA	Y

Election Results

2008 general	Rodney Frelinghuysen (R)	189,696	(62%)	($1,206,615)
	Tom Wyka (D)	113,510	(37%)	($93,651)
2008 primary	Rodney Frelinghuysen (R)	24,304	(87%)	
	Kate Erber (R)	3,731	(13%)	

Prior Winning Percentages: 2006 (62%); 2004 (68%); 2002 (72%); 2000 (68%); 1998 (68%); 1996 (66%); 1994 (71%)

Population

Pop. 2007:	672,527
Change since 2000:	Up 3.9%
Urban:	93.5%
Rural:	6.5%
Area size:	628 sq. mi.

Age

Median age:	40.1 yrs.
More than 65 yrs:	12.6%
Less than 18 yrs:	24.6%

Education

H.S. grad:	92.9%
College grad:	48.6%
Grad degree:	19.6%

Race/Ethnicity

White:	78.5%
Black:	2.9%
Hispanic:	9.1%
Asian:	8.4%
Native Am.:	0.1%
Hawaiian:	0.0%
Two+ races:	0.8%

Ancestry

Italian:	17.8%
Irish:	14.8%
German:	11.9%

Work

Private:	82.6%
Government:	11.5%
Self-employed:	5.8%
Blue collar:	13.5%
White collar:	74.6%
Khaki collar:	0.1%
Other:	11.9%
Median income:	$94,562
Median home value:	$488,500
Poverty:	3.5%

Military Veterans

% of Pop:	8.4%

Morris County in New Jersey, west of the Watchung Mountains, was one of the first parts of the United States west of the seaboard to be settled. It has long been a place of comparative wealth, the home of skilled craftsmen during the Revolutionary War and plenty of water mills and iron forges by the 19th century. But only in the late 20th century did it come into its own, as one of the most affluent parts of the United States. And it is not just a collection of country estates, but a well-rounded community

2008 Presidential Vote		
McCain (R)	182,731	(54%)
Obama (D)	154,076	(45%)
2004 Presidential Vote		
Bush (R)	186,993	(58%)
Kerry (D)	135,578	(42%)
Cook Partisan Voting Index:	R + 7	

with all the appurtenances of urbanity except high crime and poverty rates. The very rich have lived here for some time, connected to Manhattan by commuter rail lines. But starting in the 1970s, new residents rushed out the newly completed interstates. Prompted by court-required zoning changes, old farms and woods have been cleared to make way for new subdivisions. This is not just a bedroom community. New Jersey's economic energy, entrepreneurial creativity, and research expertise is found in new office complexes and corporate headquarters. Large forested areas of state parkland remain, including the Wildcat Ridge Wildlife Management Area. The preservation of the state's Highlands region, a 1,000-square-mile forest- and lake-filled stretch from Ringwood southwest to Warren County, has been a priority.

The 11th Congressional District of New Jersey includes all of Morris County plus small slices of Sussex, Passaic, Essex, and Somerset counties. It ranks second in the nation in median household income. It is family territory, with relatively few singles, not a strongly cultural-conservative area, but not aggressively liberal either. It is predominantly white. There is a small community of Hispanics, many of whom arrived as day laborers and some of whom have settled comfortably. One of its biggest immigrant populations is of Indians, whose household incomes are double the national average. Politically, it is the most Republican district in New Jersey, and one of the most Republican in the Northeast. President George W. Bush won 58% of the district's vote in 2004, and Republican presidential nominee John McCain won 54% of the vote in 2008.

The congressman from the 11th District is Rodney Frelinghuysen (*FREE - ling-high-zen*), a Republican first elected in 1994. He is the scion of one of New Jersey's most durable political families. The Frelinghuysens emigrated from Germany near the Dutch border in 1720 and settled in what is now the 11th District. Four Frelinghuysens served as senators from New Jersey, starting in 1793 and as recently as 1923. Theodore Frelinghuysen was the candidate for vice president in 1844 (spawning the memorable chant, "Hurrah! Hurrah! The country's risin',' for Henry Clay and Frelinghuysen"). Frederick Frelinghuysen was President Chester Arthur's secretary of state. Peter Frelinghuysen, Rodney's father, was elected to the House in 1952 and served until his retirement in 1974. History tends to repeat itself, and Frelinghuysens have been involved in every presidential impeachment. Rodney Frelinghuysen's great-great-grandfather Frederick voted to convict Andrew Johnson in 1868, and his father, Peter, after the revelations of July 1974, would have voted to impeach Richard Nixon if the president had not resigned. The current-generation Frelinghuysen voted to impeach Bill Clinton in December 1998.

As a child, Rodney Frelinghuysen lived in the large brick house on Georgetown's N Street now owned by former *Washington Post* editor Ben Bradlee and his wife, Sally Quinn. He attended St. Albans preparatory school with the future Democratic vice president, Al Gore. After college, he served in the Army in Vietnam, where he built roads in the Mekong Delta. In 1972, he was an aide to Morris County Freeholder Dean Gallo, who was later elected to Congress from the 11th District. Frelinghuysen was a freeholder himself from 1974 to 1983, and was elected to the state Assembly in 1983. Frelinghuysen ran for Congress in 1990 in what is now the 12th District but lost the primary to Dick Zimmer. In August 1994, Gallo retired because of illness; he died two days before the election. Frelinghuysen was chosen to be the Republican nominee at a September party convention and was elected with 71% of the vote.

Frelinghuysen has taken moderate and even liberal stands on some issues, but is more conservative on defense and foreign policy. He supported President Bush on the war in Iraq, and after a visit to the country in July 2008, said he found "real progress" being made.

He showed his insider skills by winning a seat on the Appropriations Committee while still a freshman, a rarity. New Jersey had no senator on the Senate Appropriations Committee between 2000 and 2006, so Frelinghuysen in the House became the go-to guy for the entire delegation on projects benefiting New Jersey. He concentrated on big projects: construction of the Hudson-Bergen light rail, dredging of channels in the Port of New York and New Jersey, millions to slow erosion on the Jersey Shore. In 2008, he got $20 million in earmarks for the Picatinny Arsenal in Morris County. Frelinghuysen was a subcommittee chairman for a short time, on the panel overseeing appropriations for the District of Columbia. But he lost his gavel in 2005 when Republicans eliminated the subcommittee. He continued to gain seniority, and in 2009 he became the ranking Republican of the Energy and Water Development Subcommittee.

In response to the stock market decline in 2008, Frelinghuysen proposed suspension of the requirement that 70-year-olds withdraw funds from their individual retirement accounts or 401(k) retirement savings plans. He initially opposed the government bailout of the financial markets but then voted in favor of it, he said, because Americans needed protection from "economic shockwaves from problems they did not create."

Frelinghuysen was the sponsor of the "Know Your Caller" law, which bars telemarketers from interfering with Caller ID systems of customers seeking to avoid such solicitations. Another of his pet projects is environmental cleanup in his district, which he says has more Superfund sites than any other. He tours the sites annually with environmental and local officials to get updates on cleanup progress. In 2004, he won enactment of legislation to protect the New Jersey Highlands.

Frelinghuysen has not been seriously challenged for re-election. In 2006, he was among the House Republicans targeted by the liberal MoveOn.org for supporting the war in Iraq. Against first-time candidate Tom Wyka, who hammered him on Iraq, he was re-elected with his smallest margin since he took office, but a still-comfortable 62%-37%. In a 2008 rematch, Frelinghuysen won with the identical result.

TWELFTH DISTRICT

Rush Holt (D)

Elected 1998, 6th term; b. Oct. 15, 1948, Weston, WV; home, Hopewell Township; Carleton Col., B.S. 1970, N.Y.U., PhD. 1981; Protestant; married (Margaret Lancefield); 3 children.

Professional Career: Prof., Swarthmore Col., 1981–89; Asst. Dir., Princeton Plasma Physics Lab., 1989–98.

DC Office: 1214 LHOB, 20515, 202-225-5801; Fax: 202-225-6025; Web site: www.holt.house.gov.

State Offices: West Windsor, 609-750-9365.

Committees: *Education & Labor* (12th of 29 D): Early Childhood, Elementary & Secondary Education; Health, Employment, Labor & Pensions. *Intelligence (Select)* (4th of 13 D): Intelligence Community Management; Technical & Tactical Intelligence. *Natural Resources* (7th of 29 D): Energy & Mineral Resources; National Parks, Forests & Public Lands.

Group Ratings

	ADA	ACLU	AFS	LCV	ITIC	NTU	COC	ACU	CFG	FRC
2008	100	100	100	100	57	8	61	0	6	5
2007	90	—	100	100	—	5	50	0	1	—

National Journal Ratings

	2007 LIB — 2007 CONS		2008 LIB — 2008 CONS	
Economic	82%	0%	69%	29%
Social	77%	17%	67%	28%
Foreign	96%	0%	92%	0%
Composite	90%	10%	79%	22%

Key Votes of the 110th Congress

1. Increase minimum wage	Y	5. Share immigration data	N	9. Withdraw troops 8/08	Y
2. Expand SCHIP	Y	6. Foreign aid abortion ban	N	10. No operations in Iran	Y
3. Raise CAFE standards	Y	7. Ban gay bias in workplace	N	11. Free trade with Peru	N
4. Bail out financial markets	Y	8. Repeal D.C. gun law	N	12. Overhaul FISA	N

Election Results

2008 general	Rush Holt (D)	193,732	(63%)	($1,268,760)
	Alan Bateman (R)	108,400	(35%)	($32,959)
2008 primary	Rush Holt (D)	unopposed		

Prior Winning Percentages: 2006 (66%); 2004 (59%); 2002 (61%); 2000 (49%); 1998 (50%)

Population		Race/Ethnicity		Work	
Pop. 2007:	682,342	White:	68.2%	Private:	79.2%
Change since 2000:	Up 5.4%	Black:	10.9%	Government:	15.1%
Urban:	93.2%	Hispanic:	6.5%	Self-employed:	5.5%
Rural:	6.8%	Asian:	12.8%	Blue collar:	12.3%
Area size:	642 sq. mi.	Native Am.:	0.1%	White collar:	76.4%
		Hawaiian:	0.0%	Khaki collar:	0.1%
Age		Two+ races:	1.3%	Other:	11.2%
Median age:	39.3 yrs.	*Ancestry*		Median income:	$86,316
More than 65 yrs:	13.0%	Italian:	13.8%	Median home value:	$407,800
Less than 18 yrs:	24.2%	Irish:	12.3%	Poverty:	5.6%
Education		German:	9.5%	**Military Veterans**	
H.S. grad:	91.6%			% of Pop:	7.4%
College grad:	47.1%				
Grad degree:	20.7%				

It was once the main East Coast arterial highway, carrying the nation's highest volume of truck traffic. Today it is crowded with cars taking high-salaried workers and clerical help to one of the East Coast's thickest concentrations of office buildings in one of the bigger edge cities spawned in the 1980s. U.S. 1, which once just connected the industrial cities of Trenton and New Brunswick on its way from Philadelphia to New York, is better thought of now as connecting the university towns around

2008 Presidential Vote		
Obama (D)	194,988	(58%)
McCain (R)	136,374	(41%)
2004 Presidential Vote		
Kerry (D)	165,776	(54%)
Bush (R)	138,454	(46%)
Cook Partisan Voting Index:	D + 5	

Princeton and Rutgers, and as a locus of telecommunications and pharmaceutical research. This had been empty bucolic country, to be enjoyed by F. Scott Fitzgerald's undergraduates from their Gothic Princeton towers. Now it is filled with post-modern office campuses, hotels, and restaurants.

The 12th Congressional District of New Jersey meanders across the breadth of central New Jersey, from the Delaware River to the Atlantic Ocean. It extends several dozen miles on either side of U.S. 1 as it slices through Mercer and Middlesex counties. It is home to both an Englishtown and a Frenchtown. To the west, it takes in some of the rolling country of Hunterdon County. On the other side of U.S. 1, the 12th includes Princeton University and some modest-income suburbs—Franklin in Somerset County, East Brunswick in Middlesex County—and some fast-growing Monmouth County areas, such as Rumson, part of Middletown, and Holmdel. Monmouth, Marlboro, and Manalapan, all in the district, have been rated among the best small towns on the East Coast. Monmouth is undergoing a transition as the Army prepares to close the 1,100-acre Fort Monmouth in 2011. The 90-year-old research facility with 5,000 employees is in a busy commercial area, and will be redeveloped. The 12th had been represented for most of the 1990s by a Republican, but redistricting earlier this decade made it more Democratic.

The congressman from the 12th District is Rush Holt, a Democrat first elected in 1998. He has an impressive political pedigree. His father, Rush D. Holt, was a favorite of United Mine Workers leader John Lewis, and was elected as the "boy senator" from West Virginia in 1934 when he was just 29. He had to wait until he turned age 30 in June 1935 to actually take the seat. But he clashed often with President Franklin D. Roosevelt and lost the Democratic primary to Harley Kilgore in 1940. Sen. Holt died when the young Rush was just 6 years old. He grew up in Washington, D.C., where his mother, Helen Holt, who had been West Virginia secretary of state, was an official in the Federal Housing Agency. He went off to Carleton College in Minnesota and to New York University, where he earned advanced degrees in physics and researched alternative energy, eventually becoming assistant director of the Princeton Plasma Physics Laboratory. He later was an arms control specialist for the State Department. There can be no doubt he's brainy: Holt is a five-time *Jeopardy!* champion.

He got into politics in 1996, when Republican U.S. Rep. Dick Zimmer ran for the Senate against Democratic Rep. Bob Torricelli. (Zimmer lost.) Holt ran for Zimmer's seat and finished third in the Democratic primary. Conservative Republican Mike Pappas won the general election, but by only 50%-47%. Two years later, Holt came back for a rematch. It was 1998, the year of the impeachment of President Bill Clinton. New Jersey was pro-Clinton, anti-impeachment territory, and Pappas made the mistake of taking the House floor to recite: "Twinkle, Twinkle Kenneth Starr, now we see how brave you are. We could not see which way to go, if you did not lead us so." His ditty was replayed on network newscasts and incorporated into a Holt ad. It proved a liability, and Holt won 50%-47%.

In Congress, Holt has compiled a solidly liberal voting record. As the second research physicist in the House, he worked with the first research physicist in the House, Republican Rep. Vern Ehlers of Michigan, to promote science education and to give science equal standing with reading and math. (In 2008, Democratic Rep. Bill Foster of Illinois became the third physicist in the House.)

Holt is perhaps the House's most prominent crusader on election reform, an interest sparked in part by a belief that his father's close defeat in a bid for West Virginia governor resulted from ballot fraud.

"One of my earliest memories is the talk in the family about votes being stolen and ballot boxes being found on the riverbanks," he has said. He sponsored the Voter Confidence and Increased Accessibility Act, which calls for an improved paper trail for electronic voting machines. But local election officials have objected to the cost, and Democratic leaders pulled his plan from the House schedule in 2007. He introduced a scaled-down version in 2008 that authorizes funding for states to buy the machines that produce paper trails.

On the House Intelligence Committee, Holt was an outspoken critic of the Bush administration's reluctance to disclose more information to Congress. In 2007, he became chairman of the new Select Intelligence Oversight Panel, a hybrid group of members from the Appropriations and Select Intelligence committees. Although details of the panel's work mostly remain behind closed doors, Holt has pressed for more vigorous review of intelligence-gathering. In 2008, he continued his call for a deadline for the withdrawal of U.S. troops from Iraq.

Another of his interests is gun legislation, and he has sponsored an assortment of gun control measures, including one to require licensing and registration of all handguns (it attracted no co-sponsors). Locally, he has secured funding for open space and helped to get added protection for the lower Delaware River.

In his first bid for re-election in 2000, Holt faced a challenge from Zimmer, who won the Republican primary against Pappas, 62%-38%. The Democratic Congressional Campaign Committee ran $2 million in negative ads against him, and Zimmer acknowledged that the political terrain had changed. "There's a cultural divide between the Northeast and what's become the Republican base," he said. "The world looks different from suburban New Jersey than it does from Texas." Still, Zimmer was competitive against Holt. In one of the closest races in the nation that year, Holt won by a bit more than 1,000 votes.

In 2001, the new congressional district boundaries drawn in redistricting reduced the number of Republicans in the 12th. Holt has made this a safe Democratic seat.

THIRTEENTH DISTRICT

Albio Sires (D)

Elected Nov. 2006, 2nd full term; b. Jan. 26, 1951, Bejucal, Cuba; home, West New York; St. Peter's Col., B.A. 1974, Middlebury Col., M.A. 1985; Catholic; married (Adrienne); 1 child.

Elected Office: West New York mayor, 1995–2006; NJ Assembly, 1999–2006; NJ Assembly speaker, 2002–06.

Professional Career: High schl. Spanish and ESL teacher, 1975–85; Special asst., NJ Dept. of Community Affairs, 1985; Part-owner, A.M. Title Agency, 1986–2006.

DC Office: 1024 LHOB, 20515, 202-225-7919; Fax: 202-226-0792; Web site: www.house.gov/sires.

State Offices: Bayonne, 201-823-2900; Carteret, 732-969-9160; Jersey City, 201-222-2828; Perth Amboy, 732-442-0601; West New York, 201-558-0800.

Committees: *Foreign Affairs* (12th of 28 D): Europe; Western Hemisphere. *Transportation & Infrastructure* (33rd of 44 D): Highways & Transit; Railroads, Pipelines & Hazardous Materials.

Group Ratings

	ADA	ACLU	AFS	LCV	ITIC	NTU	COC	ACU	CFG	FRC
2008	90	91	100	85	71	5	71	0	0	5
2007	95	—	100	95	—	5	55	0	12	—

National Journal Ratings

	2007 LIB	—	2007 CONS	2008 LIB	—	2008 CONS
Economic	82%	—	0%	77%	—	22%
Social	77%	—	17%	72%	—	26%
Foreign	69%	—	29%	83%	—	15%
Composite	80%	—	20%	78%	—	22%

Key Votes of the 110th Congress

1. Increase minimum wage	Y	5. Share immigration data	N	9. Withdraw troops 8/08	Y
2. Expand SCHIP	Y	6. Foreign aid abortion ban	N	10. No operations in Iran	Y
3. Raise CAFE standards	Y	7. Ban gay bias in workplace	Y	11. Free trade with Peru	Y
4. Bail out financial markets	Y	8. Repeal D.C. gun law	N	12. Overhaul FISA	Y

Election Results

2008 general	Albio Sires (D)	120,382	(75%)	($802,335)
	Joseph Turula (R)	34,735	(22%)	
	Julio Fernandez (I)	3,661	(2%)	
2008 primary	Albio Sires (D)	unopposed		

Prior Winning Percentages: 2006 (78%); 2006 special (97%)

Population		Race/Ethnicity		Work	
Pop. 2007:	643,056	White:	30.1%	Private:	85.5%
Change since 2000:	Down 0.6%	Black:	11.5%	Government:	10.3%
Urban:	100.0%	Hispanic:	48.9%	Self-employed:	4.1%
Rural:	0.0%	Asian:	7.3%	Blue collar:	27.5%
Area size:	74 sq. mi.	Native Am.:	0.1%	White collar:	53.9%
		Hawaiian:	0.0%	Khaki collar:	0.0%
Age		Two+ races:	0.7%	Other:	18.6%
Median age:	34.6 yrs.			Median income:	$47,209
More than 65 yrs:	10.0%	*Ancestry*		Median home value:	$371,600
Less than 18 yrs:	22.7%	Italian:	6.8%	Poverty:	15.7%
		Irish:	5.5%		
Education		Polish:	3.4%	**Military Veterans**	
H.S. grad:	72.6%			% of Pop:	3.7%
College grad:	26.0%				
Grad degree:	8.5%				

Standing in New York Harbor since 1886, the Statue of Liberty has been the symbol of America's receptiveness to immigrants. Actually, the statue is on the New Jersey side of the harbor, and so is, as the U.S. Supreme Court ruled in 1998, most of Ellis Island, where immigrants once were processed. So it's natural that the towns atop the granite and gneiss ridge of Hudson County, overlooking the harbor, became immigrant territory. Many chil-

2008 Presidential Vote

Obama (D)	154,219	(75%)
McCain (R)	50,525	(25%)

2004 Presidential Vote

Kerry (D)	127,168	(69%)
Bush (R)	57,278	(31%)

Cook Partisan Voting Index: D+21

dren and grandchildren of Irish and Italian immigrants stayed in Hudson County, living in the same neighborhoods, working on the same docks or factories, and voting the dictates of the same political machine. Hudson County was the setting of one of America's classic political machines, undisciplined by any metropolitan elite. From 1917 to 1949, the boss of Hudson County was Frank ("I am the law") Hague. His machine chose governors and U.S. senators, prosecutors and judges, and had influence in the White House of Franklin D. Roosevelt. Hague collected high taxes from industries clustered here, who then passed them on to consumers everywhere, and in return, he gave them an orderly city, free of most crime and vice, and a workforce insulated against racketeers and militant unions. Hague's successor, John V. Kenny, was boss from 1949 to 1971—continuous power for 54 years.

But Hudson County began changing. New immigrants were coming in—refugees from Castro's Cuba and other Latinos and Asians arrived after the 1965 immigration act. Union City became predominantly Cuban; Jersey City neighborhoods became heavily Latino. Starting in the 1980s, huge new condominium and office developments went up in Jersey City, with back-office buildings for big banks and securities firms and, later, Internet content businesses. Upscale young singles looking for lower rents moved into Hoboken's five-story Victorians that sparkle with light off the Hudson; they were just a quick commute through the PATH tubes to Wall Street or Greenwich Village. In Hoboken, the home of Frank Sinatra and the Oreo cookie, shopping and apartment complexes have taken up the waterfront sites where Maxwell House Coffee and Lipton Tea once had factories (and where the movie classic *On the Waterfront* was filmed). Bayonne has become a cruise-ship port. Ferries from Weehawken assisted in the miraculous rescue of the US Airways flight that made an emergency landing in the Hudson River in January 2009. Meanwhile, new immigrants continue to arrive. As middle-class Cubans move to Bergen County suburbs and the Jersey mainstream, Union City is less Cuban and more Colombian, Ecuadoran, Peruvian, Dominican, and Filipino. Hudson County, which seemed to be dying a generation ago, is now pulsing with new life.

The 13th Congressional District of New Jersey includes most of Hudson County, plus most of the immigrant entry ports along the water, from West New York and Weehawken, where Alexander Hamilton was killed in a duel with Vice President Aaron Burr in 1804, south past Jersey City and Bayonne, where you can still find bocce courts. It extends past the Port of New York and New Jersey to the waterfront areas of Elizabeth, Linden, Carteret (with a large Sikh community), Woodbridge, and Perth Amboy. The district's population is 49% Hispanic and also includes the Ironbound district of Newark, with its Portuguese and Brazilian immigrants; working-class Harrison, an aging factory town where European immigrants have been replaced by Hispanic immigrants; and part of industrial Kearny. The 13th is heavily Democratic.

The congressman from the 13th District is Democrat Albio Sires (*SEAR-eez*), who replaced Robert Menendez, also a Democrat, after he was appointed to the Senate in January 2006. Sires, who was born in Cuba, remembers the book burning following the Communist revolution there. His family fled Fidel Castro's regime in 1962 when he was 10. He attended St. Peter's College on a four-year basketball scholarship, and then earned a master's degree from Middlebury College. He became a high school Spanish teacher. On his fourth try, he was elected mayor of West New York as a Republican in 1995, and held that post until 2006. He focused on the creation of more-affordable housing in the small but densely populated town and won praise for merging the fire department with three neighboring departments. He switched parties in 1999 and, with the support of party leaders, defeated a veteran Democratic incumbent in the primary to win a state House seat (dual officeholding was then a common practice in New Jersey). With strong support from newly elected Democratic Gov. Jim McGreevey in 2002, he became speaker of the Assembly.

After newly elected Democratic Gov. Jon Corzine appointed Menendez to replace him in the U.S. Senate, Sires immediately became the front-runner for the House seat. In the primary, Sires faced a fierce challenge from Joe Vas of Perth Amboy, who likewise was a state House member and a mayor. Vas assailed Sires as a puppet of the Hudson County Democratic machine. He also questioned whether Sires was a true Democrat. Sires had started his political career as a Democrat, run for Congress in 1986 as a Republican, and was elected to local office as an independent before rejoining the Democratic Party. Sires responded by depicting Vas as soft on crime and won the support of most leading Democrats, except for his longtime rival Menendez, who remained neutral. Vas accused Sires of ties to organized crime; Sires linked Vas to drug dealers. But the shrill tenor of the campaign made little difference. Although Vas carried his home base of Middlesex County 76%-24%, Sires crushed him 80%-20% in Hudson County, which cast 74% of the total vote. Overall, Sires won 72%-28%. In the general election, Republicans nominated John Guarini, who raised little money and posed no threat. Sires won 78%-19%. He succeeded Menendez as the only Cuban-American House member from a state other than Florida.

In the House, Sires established a liberal voting record. He allied himself in 2007 with South Florida members who wanted to keep U.S. sanctions on Cuba in place and supported President George W. Bush's pro-democracy programs in Cuba. Sires lobbied most of the House freshman class with his personal story about Cuba. On the Financial Services Committee, he got approval in 2007 of his bill to increase penalties, up to $1 million in some cases, for identity theft. In February 2008, the House debated his bill to give more management flexibility to small public housing agencies like New Jersey's, but postponed final action after Republicans tried to tack on a provision prohibiting the enforcement of the District of Columbia's gun laws.

Sires also showed an interest in getting involved in the House Democratic leadership. He was appointed one of the vice chairs of the Democratic Congressional Campaign Committee, and was put in charge of member participation and outreach. He was re-elected easily in 2008.

★ NEW MEXICO ★

New Mexico has some of the oldest settlements in America and some of its newest technologies, often in surrealistic proximity to one another. The oldest permanently inhabited city in the United States is not Plymouth or Jamestown or St. Augustine; it is probably Acoma, which apparently thrived in what is now New Mexico long before the Spanish conquistadors arrived in 1540 and has been continuously inhabited for the nearly 470 years since. While the settlers of Jamestown and Plymouth were building flimsy wood houses, the Indians in New Mexico were living in extensive dwellings hundreds of years old, made with the adobe that is still the characteristic building material here. They used small pebbles as mulch to retain scarce moisture on the rocky desert land. Nearly five centuries later, much of what makes New Mexico distinctive derives from the people found here by the first European explorers—something true of no other state but Hawaii. The cultures in other states are mostly an outgrowth of what early European settlers brought to the land. The native people have mostly disappeared, either killed off by disease or maltreatment, or driven onto reservations. Not so in New Mexico, the northernmost salient of the great Indian-Spanish civilizations of the Cordillera, which extend along the mountain chain through Mexico and Central and South America to the southern end of Chile. The Spanish settled in Santa Fe in 1609, and though their hold on the town was often tenuous, their imprint remains. There are still 19 Indian pueblos in New Mexico today, plus the reservations of the Navajo and the Jicarilla and the Mescalero Apache. A very substantial minority of today's New Mexicans are descendants of those Indians, or the Spanish, or both. New Mexico's population was 44% Hispanic in 2007, the highest percentage of any state, and 9% American Indian. Almost one-third of the people in this state speak Spanish in everyday life, but relatively few are recent immigrants from Latin America. Only 9% of New Mexicans are foreign-born, less than the national average.

Modern New Mexico is also a civilization built on technology. It was to a remote mesa called Los Alamos that Gen. Leslie Groves brought his Manhattan Project scientists during World War II to build a secret town and develop a secret weapon that would, in two explosions, end World War II and change the course of history. Los Alamos is still a government laboratory, and an occasional source of controversy as it was in 1999, when revelations surfaced that Chinese spies had obtained hundreds of computer files from the lab. (The facility is now slated for substantial layoffs by the Obama administration.) New Mexico has other high-tech sites as well: the White Sands Missile Range near Alamogordo, where the first atomic bomb was detonated in July 1945; and the Sandia National Laboratories near Albuquerque, run by Lockheed Martin for the government, a non-nuclear weapons research facility with one of the fastest computers in the world, used to simulate nuclear explosions. Near Carlsbad is the federal Waste Isolation Pilot Plant (WIPP), where the U.S. Energy Department deposits transuranic radioactive waste. And at the western edge of White Sands in Sierra County is the Virgin Galactic spaceport, a project by billionaire Richard Branson to send people on tours of space beginning in late 2010. With the state and federal governments financing the runways, and 275 investors paying $35 million total for rights to early rides, Branson plans to launch his SpaceShipTwo crafts from the bellies of airplanes at 55,000 feet and fly them at 2,500 miles per hour on an arc up to 68 miles into space, where passengers can float in glassed-in cabins for six minutes and then glide back down to Earth. Democratic Gov. Bill Richardson, a big booster and prospective early passenger, proclaimed, "This sends a message that will be heard around the world, that New Mexico is a state that embraces entrepreneurs, adventurers, and pioneers."

New and old New Mexico intermingle in varying proportions in this land of majestically vast vistas. The Hispanic and Indian cultures predominate north and west of Albuquerque, with picturesque old towns and active pueblos, backward Indian reservations and lavish casino resorts. "Little Texas," in the south and east, has small cities, plenty of oil wells, vast cattle ranches, and desolate military bases; the region resembles, economically and culturally, the adjacent West Texas high plains. Here, as everywhere in New Mexico, government is a prime employer, accounting for 23% of jobs, one of the highest figures in the country, and often the moving force in the local economy. While New Mexico had neither the housing boom nor the housing bust of next-door neighbor Arizona, its economy in early 2009 was sagging despite its relatively recession-proof reliance on government jobs.

In the middle of the state is Albuquerque, which, with the arrival of air conditioning, grew from a small desert town of 35,000 in 1940 into a Sun Belt metropolis of 841,000 today. The city's economy is heavily based on technology, especially nuclear power, but its people have relatively low income and education levels. New Mexico ranks high among states in the percentage of residents living in poverty—the downscale Sun Belt. It also has high rates of drunk driving (and a state law requiring ignition interlocks for DWI offenders), accidental deaths, teenage pregnancies, and drug overdoses. But over the years, its amazing scenery and unique culture have attracted writers such as D.H. Lawrence and painters such as Georgia O'Keefe. Santa Fe today is a magnet for young people with a taste for alternative lifestyles and with the trust funds to comfortably finance them. Other migrants are attracted by the 10 or so destination golf courses built by Indian tribes next to their reservation casinos.

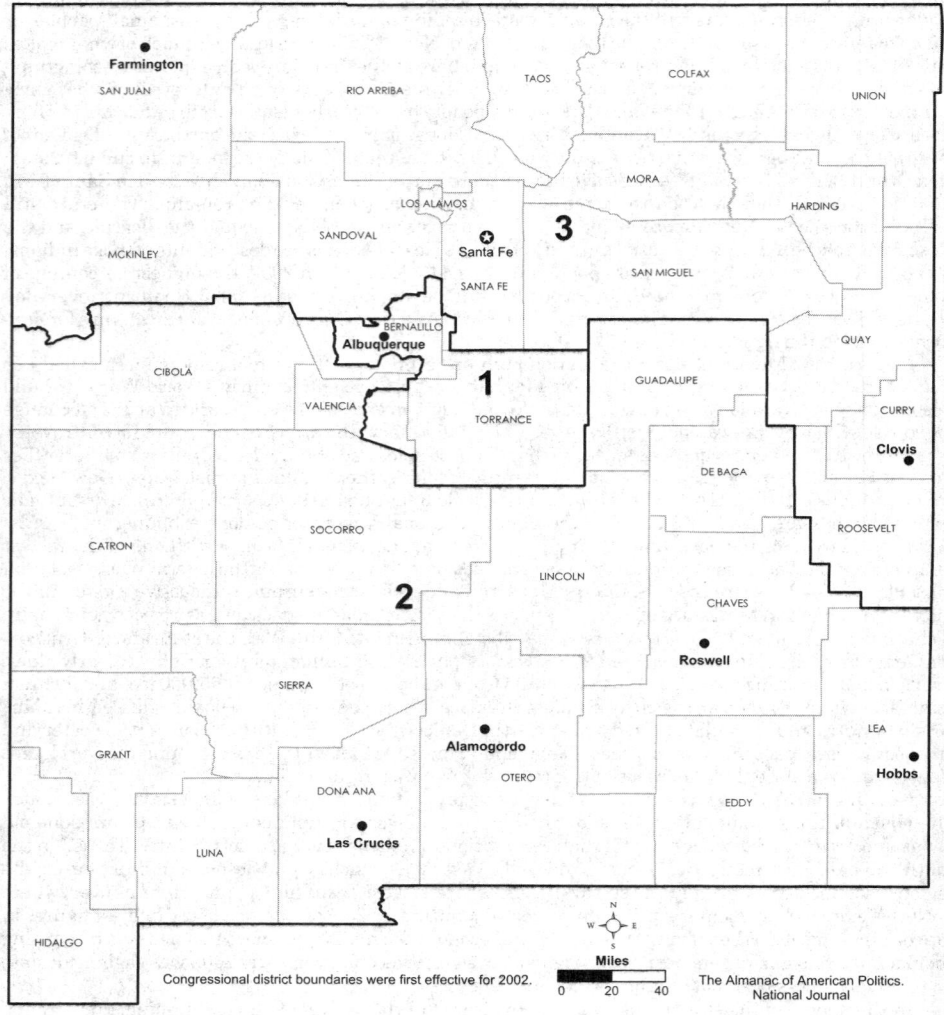

For many years, New Mexico politics was a somnolent business. Local bosses—first Republican, later Democratic—controlled the large Hispanic vote. Elections in many counties featured irregularities that would have made a Chicago ward committeeman blush. New Mexico had for years another feature of boss-controlled politics: the balanced ticket, one Spanish and one Anglo U.S. senator, with the offices of governor and lieutenant governor split as well. But for all its distinctiveness, in national politics New Mexico was a bellwether, voting for every winning presidential candidate from 1912, when it became a state, until 1976, when it backed losing Republican Gerald Ford. In the 1988 and 1996 elections, the state was just 1% off the national mark. In 2000, it voted narrowly for Democrat Al Gore. Four years later, it voted just a bit less narrowly for Republican George W. Bush. In 2008, New Mexico moved sharply toward the Democrats, after Sen. Barack Obama opened offices around the state and boosted voter turnout sharply in Democratic areas. The strong Democratic base in the north, from Hispanics and from liberal newcomers in Santa Fe and Taos, grew even stronger. Albuquerque and its surging suburb of Rio Rancho, long politically marginal, went solidly Democratic, as did Las Cruces, just north of El Paso, Texas. Turnout sagged in Little Texas, which remained Republican but was heavily outvoted by the rest of the state. Obama carried New Mexico; the seat of 36-year veteran GOP Sen. Pete Domenici, who retired, was won by Democrat Tom Udall. All three of New Mexico's House members ran for the Senate in 2008, and all three open seats went Democratic. With Sen. Jeff Bingaman in his fifth term, New Mexico has an all-Democratic congressional delegation for the first time since 1968.

The dominant figure in New Mexico state politics in this decade has been Gov. Bill Richardson, who came to Santa Fe to run the state Democratic party in 1978, was elected to Congress in 1982, and later had prominent roles in the Clinton administration as the secretary of Energy and ambassador to the United Nations. Richardson returned to the state in 2001 and was easily elected governor in 2002; he dominated the Democratic state Legislature and built a record popular with voters of both parties. He has signed bans on smoking and cockfighting, and he abolished the death penalty—New Mexico is changing. But Richardson has suffered a series of disappointments. He failed to break into the top ranks of presidential contenders in 2008, and after Obama was elected, Richardson's nomination for secretary of Commerce was derailed. He is barred from seeking a third term as governor in 2010.

Population			Household Income		Work	
Pop. 2007:	1,942,847		Under $15k:	17.2%	Private:	69.5%
State rank:	36th of 50		$15k to $50k:	41.5%	Government:	22.5%
Change since 2000:	Up 6.8%		$50k to $100k:	28.1%	Self-employed:	7.7%
Urban:	76.3%		$100k to $150k:	11.1%	Unemployment (3-yr. average):	4.1%
Rural:	23.7%		Over $150k:	2.1%	Poverty:	18.4%
Native of state:	51.6%		Median income:	$41,042	Blue collar:	21.9%
Not a citizen:	6.5%		**Home Value**		White collar:	58.3%
Area size:	121,589 sq. mi.		Under $100k:	33.9%	Khaki collar:	0.4%
Most populous cities			$100k to $300k:	50.9%	Other:	19.4%
1. Albuquerque	505,578		$300k to $500k:	10.3%	**Age**	
2. Las Cruces	91,294		$500k to $1 mil:	3.9%	Median age:	35.6 yrs.
3. Rio Rancho	69,080		Over $1 million:	0.9%	More than 65 yrs:	12.5%
4. Santa Fe	65,163		Median:	$140,100	Less than 18 yrs:	25.6%

Race/Ethnicity				Military Veterans		Registered Voters in 2008	
White:	42.4%	*Language*		% of Pop:	12.3%	D:	594,229 (50.1%)
Black:	2.0%	English:	64.0%	*Veterans by Period*		R:	375,619 (31.7%)
Hispanic:	44.1%	Spanish:	28.4%	WWII and before:	10.9%	Other:	215,591 (18.2%)
Asian:	1.3%	Asian:	0.8%	Korea:	11.7%	Voter turnout:	830,158
Native Am.:	8.7%	Other		Vietnam:	31.6%	Turnout as % of	
Hawaiian:	0.1%	European	1.1%	Gulf (pre-2001):	12.8%	voting age:	56.0%
Two+ races:	1.2%	**Education**		Gulf (post-2001):	9.0%	**Legislature**	
Ancestry		H.S. grad:	81.7%	Peace time:	23.9%	Senate:	27 D 15 R
German:	9.3%	College grad:	24.9%			House:	45 D 25 R
English:	7.1%	Grad degree:	10.6%				
Irish:	6.7%						

Presidential politics   New Mexico has been a battleground state in the last three presidential elections, but the results were very different the third time. In 2000, after some ragged vote counting, the state gave a 365-vote margin to Democrat Al Gore. In 2004, it reported a 5,988-vote margin for Republican George W. Bush. Voter rolls and turnout swelled that year, thanks to Gov. Bill Richardson's well-publicized efforts to register new Democrats and to the Bush campaign's less-noticed organizational efforts. Overall turnout rose 26% from 2000 to 2004 even though the state's population increased just 5% in that period. High Democratic turnout in Santa Fe and Albuquerque was balanced by high Republican turnout in Little Texas. In addition, Bush won 44% of the Hispanic vote, up from 32% in 2000.

2008 Presidential Vote		
Obama (D)	472,422	(57%)
McCain (R)	346,832	(42%)

2008 Democratic Presidential Primary		
Clinton (D)	73,105	(49%)
Obama (D)	71,396	(48%)

2008 Republican Presidential Primary		
McCain (R)	95,378	(86%)
Paul (R)	15,561	(14%)

2004 Presidential Vote		
Bush (R)	376,930	(50%)
Kerry (D)	370,942	(49%)

The 2008 contest was another story, with Democrat Barack Obama beating Republican John McCain 57%-42%. As in other states that were targeted in both 2004 and 2008, turnout inched up just marginally, 10%. The Obama campaign opened 39 offices across the state and vastly out-organized the Republicans. But the turnout numbers show that Obama's team shrewdly concentrated its efforts where there were new Democrats. In most counties, turnout rose only 1% to 9% and in twelve counties it actually dropped. But it rose 7% or more in metro Albuquerque, Santa Fe, and Taos, in heavily Hispanic Rio Arriba County, and in the two heavily Indian counties to the west, in and around Las Cruces. Obama won 74% of first-time voters, 71% of young voters, and 83% of young Latino voters. McCain won whites 56%-42%, almost identical to Bush's 56%-43% support from those voters in 2004. But McCain won only 30% of the Latino vote, far below Bush's level and more in line with historic norms.

New Mexico traditionally held its presidential primary in June, long after every major party nomination since 1984 was settled. For 2008, with Richardson as a candidate, New Mexico scheduled its Democratic primary for February 5, Super Tuesday. By that time, Richardson had withdrawn, but the race between Obama and Sen. Hillary Rodham Clinton was so close it took nine days to count all the votes, including 17,000 provisional ballots. Clinton won 49%-48%, carrying heavily Hispanic counties and Little Texas. Obama carried metro Albuquerque, Santa Fe, Taos, and two other rural counties. The Republicans did not stage their primary until June, when no one was paying attention. McCain beat Rep. Ron Paul of Texas 86%-14%.

Congressional districting   The boundaries of New Mexico's three congressional districts have been substantially the same since 1982. Control of the redistricting process in 2001 was split between the Democratic Legislature and Republican Gov. Gary Johnson. In June 2001, the Legislature passed a plan that would make the 1st District, held by Republican Heather Wilson, more Democratic; Johnson vetoed it. In September 2001, the Legislature passed a plan that would make the 2nd District, held by Republican Joe Skeen, more Democratic; Johnson vetoed it. Republicans took the issue to court. In January 2002, state District Judge Frank Allen, a Democrat, imposed his own plan. He said he was reluctant to make major changes, and his map shifted only 22,000 people into different districts. Democrats were disappointed; Republicans were pleased.

111th Congress Lineup	
3 D	
110th Congress Lineup	
2 R	1 D

In February 2003 state Senate President Richard Romero, who unsuccessfully challenged Wilson in 2002 and 2004, pressed the Legislature to redraw the lines once again. But national Democrats urged caution and Richardson seemed uninterested, perhaps because a new plan might have jeopardized his good relations with Republican Sen. Pete Domenici, who would have opposed a plan that hurt Wilson. In December 2006, after Wilson was very narrowly re-elected, Democratic state Sen. Jerry Ortiz y Pino called for a redistricting map that would make the 1st District more Democratic; Richardson said he was willing to listen to the proposal but it never went anywhere. Now that Democrats hold all of New Mexico's House seats and have large majorities in both chambers of the state Legislature, redistricting after the 2010 census likely will be an all-Democratic exercise, unless a Republican is elected governor or one of the House members loses re-election in 2010. With Democrats in charge, only minor changes in the boundaries are expected.

Governor

Bill Richardson (D)

Elected 2002, term expires Jan. 2011, 2nd term; b. Nov. 15, 1947, Pasadena, CA; home, Santa Fe; Tufts U., B.A. 1970, Fletcher Schl. of Law and Diplomacy, M.A. 1971; Catholic; married (Barbara).

Elected Office: U.S. House of Reps., 1982–97.

Professional Career: Congressional rel., U.S. Dept. of State, 1973–75; Staff, Senate Foreign Relations Subcmte., 1975–78; Exec. Dir., NM Dem. Party, 1978; Pres., Richardson Trade Group, 1978–82; U.S. Ambassador to U.N., 1997–98; Secy., U.S. Dept. of Energy, 1998–2000.

Office: Office of the Governor, 490 Old Santa Fe Trail, Room 400, Santa Fe, 87501, 505-476-2200; Fax: 505-576-2226; Web site: www.gover nor.state.nm.us.

Election Results

2006 general	Bill Richardson (D)	384,806	(69%)
	John Dendahl (R)	174,364	(31%)
2006 primary	Bill Richardson (D)	unopposed	

Prior Winning Percentages: 2002 (55%); 1994 House (64%); 1992 House (67%); 1990 House (74%); 1988 House (73%); 1986 House (71%); 1984 House (61%); 1982 House (64%)

Democrat Bill Richardson was elected governor of New Mexico in 2002. Richardson is a unique politician—a Hispanic with an Anglo name, a newcomer when he was first elected in New Mexico (where many families go back 300 years), and an adept politician who has also been an international negotiator. He was born in California and grew up in the Coyoacan neighborhood of Mexico City. His father was a banker from Boston who became head of Citibank in Mexico City, and his mother was a native of Mexico. The family lived securely behind high walls but young Bill liked to sneak out to play baseball with the neighborhood kids. Richardson was sent East for prep school at Middlesex in Concord, Mass., and then on to his father's alma mater, Tufts University in Medford, Mass., where he stood out as a baseball player. For many years, he claimed that he was drafted by the Kansas City Athletics and Los Angeles Dodgers. But after the *Albuquerque Journal* investigated the story, he conceded that it was not true. In any case, an elbow injury in his junior year ended his pitching career, and after raising his grades, he went on to the distinguished Fletcher School of Law and Diplomacy at Tufts and earned a master's degree. This was the era of campus unrest over the Vietnam War, but Richardson did not take part in protests, and he received a medical draft deferment. After graduation, he went to Washington, where his first job was working for the Wednesday Group, a faction of moderate Republicans. He worked for the State Department's congressional relations office, served on the Senate Foreign Relations Committee's staff on human rights, and did a stint on Democratic Sen. Hubert Humphrey's staff.

In 1975, Richardson visited New Mexico for the first time. He met with state Democratic leaders and told them he was interested in moving to the state and running for Congress. Most were nonplussed, although in 1978, the outgoing governor's state party chairman hired him to be his executive director. But the winner of the 1978 Democratic primary for governor, Bruce King, got Richardson fired within a month. Richardson managed to get a job with the Bernalillo County Democratic Party in Albuquerque, and then hung out his shingle as a consultant after the election. In February 1980, he filed to run against Republican Rep. Manuel Luján. This was a Republican year, and Luján had deep roots in Albuquerque and had been in office since 1968. But Richardson held him to a 51%-49% victory. New Mexico got a third congressional district after the 1980 census, and the Legislature drew a new, heavily Hispanic 3rd District in northern New Mexico. Richardson, based in Santa Fe, had won much of this territory in the 1980 race, and he ran for the new seat. He had substantial competition in the Democratic primary, from Lt. Gov. Roberto Mondragon and Tom Udall, who is now a senator. Richardson was accused of exaggerating the importance of some of his Washington jobs, but he won 36% of the vote to Mondragon's 31%. He won the general election 64%-35%. At age 35, after just four years in New Mexico, he had a safe seat in the House.

In the House, Richardson landed a spot on the powerful Energy and Commerce Committee in his first term. He established a moderate voting record, favoring abortion rights, opposing gun control, favoring the death penalty, and voting to criminalize flag burning. He voted against the Persian Gulf War resolution, but called his stance a mistake in his 2005 autobiography. He lobbied hard for ratification of the North American Free Trade Agreement in 1993. In the 1990s, he spent more time on foreign policy issues. In 1994, he traveled to Haiti and met with Gen. Raoul Cedras; in a five-hour conversation, he unsuccessfully sought to get Cedras to cede power. The same year, he was traveling to North Korea when two U.S. helicopter pilots were shot down; Pyongyang claimed that they had violated the country's airspace. He was able to negotiate the release of the surviving pilot. In 1995, he met with Iraqi leader Saddam Hussein to seek the release of two Americans who had crossed into Iraq. In 1996, he met with

Cuban dictator Fidel Castro and obtained the release of three dissidents. He took to calling himself the Undersecretary of Thugs and described his negotiating technique. "I listen a lot. I try not to impose my views. It's important to listen, but it's important to be forceful, too."

In recognition of his talents on the foreign stage, President Bill Clinton nominated Richardson as U.N. ambassador. It was an opportunity to be a major player in foreign policy. He negotiated agreements between the Taliban regime in Afghanistan and opposition forces, and secured the release of Red Cross workers held hostage in Sudan. The only embarrassing thing about his service was the fact, later disclosed, that at the request of a White House staffer and without asking why, he offered a job to Monica Lewinsky; she rejected it as insufficiently grand. When Energy Secretary Federico Pena resigned in 1998, Clinton was eager to replace him with a Hispanic and gave the post to Richardson. This was not really a promotion. The department is made up of several unrelated agencies, and some of them had deep troubles at the time. One of those was Los Alamos National Laboratory, from which, it seemed, secret documents about the assembly of nuclear weapons had made their way to China. Richardson was much criticized in Congress for security failures at the national laboratories, and his connection to the Wen Ho Lee security case was a political liability. He was mentioned as a possible vice presidential candidate in 2000—the Democrats would have loved to run a Hispanic—but his name soon fell off the list.

After Democrat Al Gore's defeat, Richardson returned to Santa Fe to run for governor. He had considered running before, especially in 1994, but ultimately didn't. The governor elected that year, Republican Gary Johnson, had been re-elected in 1998 and was ineligible to run again. Richardson announced his candidacy in January 2002 and pledged to shake 600 hands a day. On September 16, he broke Theodore Roosevelt's record of 8,513, set on New Year's Day 1908, by shaking 13,392 hands at the New Mexico State Fair and at a tailgate party at the University of New Mexico. His campaign flew in a representative of Guinness World Records to document the feat. He faced opposition from two Democrats, but at the state Democratic convention in March, Richardson won 1,288 of 1,705 votes, and the others failed to even qualify for the ballot. With his energy and his national contacts, Richardson raised and spent large sums, eventually $6.8 million, more than twice as much as both parties' candidates spent in 1998.

The Republican nominee was state Rep. John Sanchez, a roofing contractor from Albuquerque's North Valley, who by 206 votes in 2000 defeated the man who was New Mexico House speaker for 30 years. Sanchez called for merit pay for teachers and government vouchers for private-school tuition. He ran a series of ads recounting his rise from poverty, using the theme "Dream Big." But Richardson had much more money and took many more-specific stands on issues. He called for cutting the state income tax—New Mexico's 8.2% top rate was much higher than those of surrounding states—and eliminating the gross-receipts tax. Amid news of drought and water conservation measures, he called for a statewide water policy and sketched one out in considerable detail. He opposed vouchers but supported charter schools and tax credits for parochial schools. Like Sanchez, he favored the death penalty and a concealed-weapons law. Sanchez criticized Richardson for serving on the board of a company that misstated its earnings. Richardson ran ads criticizing Sanchez for absenteeism in the Legislature and a spot poking fun at his earlier stint as a flight attendant. It said, "While Bill Richardson was cutting taxes for New Mexico, John Sanchez was serving orange juice at 30,000 feet." There was little suspense about the result. Richardson won 55%-39%. Inevitably, he was asked whether he had ambitions for national office. He said, "I love this state, and I think the governor can make an enormous difference in people's lives, more so than any job I have held. I see this as a sort of culmination of my career. I am not interested in going back to Washington."

In office, he did not act like a governor whose horizon ended at the state line. He frequently traveled out of state—to Davos, Switzerland, for the World Economic Forum; to Chicago, to talk businesses into relocating to New Mexico; to Hollywood, to promote the state as a good location for shooting movies; to Mexico City, where he grew up, to meet with President Vicente Fox. In Sante Fe, he met with a North Korean delegation for three days of discussions about nuclear weapons; it became known as "green chile diplomacy." Other foreign dignitaries who visited were Spain's prime minister, Jose Maria Aznar; Saudi Arabia's ambassador, Prince Bandar bin Sultan; and Prince Andrew of Great Britain. In January 2007 he was involved in negotiations between the Sudanese government and rebel factions that led to a 60-day cease-fire in Darfur. He was a familiar face in the national media and in Times Square, too, where his picture appeared on a giant billboard advertising the virtues of New Mexico and its tax policy. In September 2003, he hosted the first party-sanctioned presidential debate in Albuquerque.

Richardson's first year in office was among the most productive and successful of all the governors elected in his class of 2002. "We will move so fast! You're not going to see us," he said in his address to the opening of the 2003 Legislature. He immediately started lobbying lawmakers of both parties for his tax cut. Later that year, Richardson signed a bill reducing the top income-tax rate from 8.2% in steps to 4.9% and cutting the capital-gains tax in half over five years. He signed a bill to crack down on drunken drivers, an especially vexing problem in New Mexico, and signed an executive order that extended employee benefits to the domestic partners of gay and lesbian state workers. In September, voters approved two constitutional amendments strongly backed by Richardson, one to create a Cabinet-level education secretary appointed by the governor and the other to permit the state to increase the annual payout from the state's Land Grant Permanent Fund for public schools. Less successful was a fall special session where

Richardson called for more-fundamental changes in tax laws. A bill he backed to further tax cuts and increase some state and local taxes and fees failed to pass. Among the proposed increases was a hike in alcohol taxes, already among the highest in the nation. Critics said it would hurt the tourism and hospitality industry.

The next year, Richardson got the food-tax cut he wanted after threatening to call the Legislature back into session, although the gross-receipts tax on other goods and services increased and Republicans complained about his "bullying tactics." The Legislature also passed tougher drunken-driving penalties and a stronger truancy law. Also in 2004, Richardson played a highly visible role in state and national Democratic politics, including chairing the Democratic National Convention in Boston. At home, he used his $2 million campaign fund, Moving America Forward, to register new voters and to influence state and local elections. He was the driving force in 2003 behind a bill allowing parties to hold caucuses in lieu of presidential primaries, and state Democrats held their presidential nominating caucus in February 2004. New Mexico traditionally held its presidential primary in June, usually long after the party nomination had been settled. As chairman of the Western Governors' Association, he pushed members to agree to work toward establishing a single date for the Western states' presidential primaries and caucuses in 2008 to give the region more clout in the nominating process and to focus attention on such issues as water rights, energy, the environment, and immigration.

In 2005 and 2006, Richardson got the Legislature to require that DUI offenders install ignition interlocks in their vehicles to prevent drunken driving; to give National Guard members $250,000 life insurance policies; and to cut the income tax. Richardson called for a huge increase in pre-kindergarten education funding, and got lawmakers to approve $12.5 million. He also won passage of a 5% pay increase for teachers and a 16% hike for state police. The governor urged that schools have more physical education and less junk food, and more security cameras and Global Positioning System devices for school buses. The Legislature approved a solar energy tax credit but failed to pass other Richardson energy proposals. In March 2006, the state entered the Chicago Climate Exchange's cap-and-trade system for reducing carbon dioxide emissions and took other steps to cut pollution. But Richardson was unable to stop the Navajo Nation from building a coal-fired plant on its reservation. He has been a big booster of billionaire Richard Branson's Virgin Galactic space tourism business, and got $30 million from the Legislature to help pay for the runways near the White Sands Missile Range. Branson's plan is for space vehicles to be released by aircraft at 55,000 feet; they would fly at 3,000 miles per hour outside the atmosphere and then glide back down to Earth. Flights are slated to begin in late 2010, and Richardson has signed on to be a passenger.

Richardson was up for re-election in 2006, but the result was never in doubt. His opponent was former Republican state Chairman John Dendahl, an ally of former Gov. Gary Johnson, who got some attention when he said that teachers shortchange the basics because they are too interested in "the three S's—sexuality, self-esteem, and socialism." Richardson raised $14 million and won 69%-31%, the highest percentage for a governor in New Mexico history. He lost only one county, by only 6 votes. He also raised $13 million for the Democratic Governors Association, which he headed. In 2007, Richardson got the Legislature to approve a minimum wage increase and, with an eye on his national image, he persuaded it to outlaw cockfighting, which every other state except Louisiana had done.

By early 2007, however, his sights were trained beyond New Mexico. In January, he announced on his website, in English and Spanish, that he was running for president. "I wouldn't run as a Hispanic candidate. I would run as an American, proud to be Hispanic," he said. "Most importantly, I can bring this country together. I'm a negotiator. I've brought countries together, closer, on peace treaties. I've rescued American hostages and servicemen. What we have right now is an opportunity to deal with major issues that really are dividing this country. I have the experience, I've been in Iraq. I've negotiated with Saddam Hussein. I was secretary of Energy. I increased energy efficiency in our country. I've been a governor. I created 86,000 jobs in four years. I've cut taxes. I've brought economic growth to our state. I've made our schools better. I've got the strongest record on the environment and dealing with clean energy and fighting global warming." He said he was not interested in the vice presidency, only the nation's top job. "I got a better job as governor of New Mexico. If I don't get the nomination, I'll come back" to Santa Fe.

Richardson spent much of 2007 on the campaign trail, though he did squeeze in a trip to North Korea in April 2007 to retrieve the remains of U.S. troops killed there during the Korean War. (He also announced that the Communist regime shut down its main nuclear reactor one day after the United States lifted restrictions on a bank in Macao through which regime leaders obtained luxury goods.) In Iowa and New Hampshire, he shook hands and recruited supporters. He participated in 24 debates among the Democratic candidates. Some charged that he was going easy on fellow candidate Hillary Rodham Clinton in hopes of ultimately being chosen as her running mate.

Iowa and New Hampshire turned out to be a three-candidate race, with Richardson running fourth. He won only 2.11% of state delegate equivalents in the Iowa caucuses on January 3 and 4.6% of the vote in the New Hampshire primary on January 8. Two days later, he withdrew from the presidential contest and returned to "the job I love as governor of New Mexico." He went through a "period of decompression," grew a beard, and attended boxing matches in New Mexico. He was courted by both the Obama and Clinton camps, and was widely expected to support Clinton because of his work in her husband's administration. But on March 21 in Oregon, he endorsed Barack Obama as "a once-in-a-lifetime candidate." The Clintons were bitterly disappointed. Longtime adviser James Carville compared Richardson to Judas, and the former president broke off relations. Yet, despite his well-timed endorsement when Obama was getting tepid support from Hispanic voters, Richardson did not later receive serious consideration as Obama's running mate.

He returned to work in the Capitol, pushing the Legislature to pass a universal health care bill. But lawmakers rejected his mandatory insurance requirement and his proposed tax on employers who do not provide insurance. And he got only pared-down versions of his tax rebate and children's health care program. Richardson resumed his freelance diplomacy, flying to Venezuela in April to seek leader Hugo Chavez's help in rescuing U.S. hostages from FARC guerrillas in Colombia. They were later freed in a Colombian government raid.

After the election, on December 3, 2008, Obama nominated Richardson to be his Commerce secretary, arguably not as important a post as those he held in the Clinton administration. But on January 4, Richardson withdrew his acceptance, he said, because of a pending "pay-to-play" investigation of allegations that his aides pressured state agencies to hire financial firms that had contributed to Richardson's campaigns. Facing a $454 million budget shortfall, Richardson declared 2009 to be "the year of fiscal restraint" and trimmed his budget requests. Despite his former support of the death penalty, he signed a bill abolishing it in March 2009.

Richardson is not eligible to run for a third term, and he passed on running in 2008 for New Mexico's first open U.S. Senate seat since 1972. He seems now to have no obvious path ahead in electoral politics.

Senior Senator

Jeff Bingaman (D)

Elected 1982, term expires 2012, 5th term; b. Oct. 3, 1943, El Paso, TX; home, Santa Fe; Harvard U., B.A. 1965, Stanford U., LL.B. 1968; United Methodist; married (Anne); 1 child.

Military Career: Army Reserves, 1968–74.

Elected Office: NM atty. gen., 1978–82.

Professional Career: NM asst. atty. gen., 1969; Practicing atty., 1970–78.

DC Office: 703 HSOB, 20510, 202-224-5521; Fax: 202-224-2852; Web site: bingaman.senate.gov.

State Offices: Albuquerque, 505-346-6601; Farmington, 505-325-5030; Las Cruces, 575-523-6561; Roswell, 575-622-7113; Santa Fe, 505-988-6647.

Committees: *Energy & Natural Resources* (Chmn of 13 D). *Finance* (4th of 13 D): Energy, Natural Resources & Infrastructure (Chmn); Health Care; International Trade, Customs & Global Competitiveness. *Health, Education, Labor & Pensions* (5th of 13 D). *Joint Economic Committee* (3rd of 6 D).

Group Ratings

	ADA	ACLU	AFS	LCV	ITIC	NTU	COC	ACU	CFG	FRC
2008	100	93	100	100	100	4	50	0	3	0
2007	90	—	100	93	—	5	45	4	13	—

National Journal Ratings

	2007 LIB	—	2007 CONS		2008 LIB	—	2008 CONS
Economic	77%	—	21%		77%	—	13%
Social	70%	—	28%		80%	—	9%
Foreign	68%	—	30%		94%	—	0%
Composite	73%	—	27%		88%	—	12%

Key Votes of the 110th Congress

1. Raise CAFE standards	Y	5. Make English official language	N	9. Withdraw troops 3/08	Y
2. Expand SCHIP	Y	6. Path to citizenship	N	10. Iran guard is terrorist group	N
3. Cap greenhouse gases	Y	7. Fetus is unborn child	N	11. Increase missile defense $	N
4. Bail out financial markets	Y	8. Prosecute hate crimes	Y	12. Overhaul FISA	N

Election Results

2006 general	Jeff Bingaman (D)	394,365	(71%)	($2,628,276)
	Allen McCulloch (R)	163,826	(29%)	($555,511)
2006 primary	Jeff Bingaman (D)	unopposed		

Prior Winning Percentages: 2000 (62%); 1994 (54%); 1988 (63%); 1982 (54%)

Jeff Bingaman, a Democrat first elected in 1982, is New Mexico's senior senator. He was born in Texas but reared in Silver City, a mining town in New Mexico. His father was a professor at Western New Mexico University in Silver City, and his mother was a schoolteacher. His uncle was campaign manager for longtime Democratic Sen. Clinton Anderson (1949–73). Bingaman graduated from Harvard University and Stanford Law School, then returned to New Mexico. A year out of law school, he was counsel to the state constitutional convention. Later he went into law practice in Santa Fe with former Democratic Gov. Jack Campbell. Bingaman's wife, Anne, started a highly successful law practice of her own that helped finance his first campaigns. She later was assistant attorney general for antitrust in President Bill Clinton's first term. In a small state, bright young people like Jeff Bingaman can rise fast. He ran for attorney general in 1978 and won. In 1982, he ran against Republican Sen. Harrison Schmitt, the former astronaut, also from Silver City, and won with 54%, partly because it was a recession year, but also because Schmitt ran misleading and negative ads.

For years, Bingaman followed a course in the Senate much like that of New Mexico Democrat Clinton Anderson, who used his influence behind the scenes to great effect but shunned national publicity. Since 1999, Bingaman has been the top-ranking Democrat on the Energy and Natural Resources Committee; he was chairman from 2001 to 2003 and again in January 2007, when Democrats assumed control of the Senate.

Bingaman is a longtime proponent of federal support for renewable-energy sources. He also is a major advocate of imposing restrictions on greenhouse gases to reduce global warming. In the 110th Congress (2007–08), he led the Senate to passage of a major energy bill that had been in the works for nearly a year. The centerpiece was a boost in vehicle fuel efficiency standards from 25 miles per gallon to 35 miles per gallon by 2020. Bingaman also pushed the Senate to agree to a substantial change in policy that would have forced utilities to generate at least 15% of their electricity from renewable sources such as wind and solar energy by 2020. But Republicans balked, and Bingaman's amendment fell four votes short of passage. Still, Bingaman called the final legislation "the most important energy efficiency legislation that has ever passed in this country." It was the first increase in fuel-economy standards for cars and trucks since 1975. Bingaman planned to try again in 2009 to pass his renewable-sources mandate, introducing the bill early in the new Congress.

Another big priority for Bingaman is so-called "cap and trade" legislation aimed at reducing greenhouse gases linked to global climate change. The bill places a cap on emissions levels and then lets industries buy and sell emission "allowances." Companies that do a better job of cutting emissions can profit by selling their allowances to "dirtier" companies. In 2007, Bingaman and then-Republican and now-Democratic Sen. Arlen Specter of Pennsylvania sponsored a greenhouse-gas-emissions bill. Opponents argued that it would drive up the cost of energy at a time of high gas prices, and Bingaman and other backers were unable to get the 60 votes they needed to stop a filibuster. A years-long effort by the Alaska delegation and Republicans to open the Arctic National Wildlife Refuge in Alaska to oil exploration is unlikely to get very far as long as Bingaman chairs the committee. In 2002, a majority on the committee made clear that they favored advancing an ANWR drilling measure for a vote. Bingaman refused to support the bill, though he did allow it to be brought to the floor in 2002 without committee consideration, a highly unusual tactic for such complex legislation. The Senate failed to pass it.

From 2003 to 2009, Bingaman's New Mexico colleague Pete Domenici was the senior Republican on the committee, the first time in history that the two top members on a Senate committee were from the same state. While they disagreed on some issues, they worked together on many others. In 2005, Bingaman and Domenici made a point of emphasizing areas of agreement during work on the energy bill, and House Republicans agreed to drop a controversial provision to protect oil companies from liability for adding the pollutant MTBE to gasoline. There was also bipartisan agreement on incentives for building more electricity lines to avert major blackouts and for the start-up of advanced-design nuclear power plants. The bill passed, and Bingaman praised Domenici's cooperation. Both also were united in efforts to limit cuts in the budget for New Mexico's Los Alamos and Sandia national laboratories. The partnership ended when Domenici retired from the Senate in 2008.

In May 2008, Bingaman opposed Senate Majority Leader Harry Reid's proposal for a windfall-profits tax on oil companies. When Republicans sought more offshore oil drilling, Bingaman claimed it wouldn't lower gas prices and supported suspending deposits in the Strategic Petroleum Reserve until oil prices fell below $75 a barrel. The February 2009 economic stimulus bill included Bingaman's provisions for tax credits of 30% on the cost of building renewable energy manufacturing facilities and 20% on renewable-energy research and development.

In the debate about illegal immigration in 2007, Bingaman sponsored an amendment, supported by labor unions, to reduce the number of permitted guest workers from 400,000 to 200,000 and to eliminate a clause that allowed increases in guest workers in response to economic need. It passed, 74-24. When Arizona Republican Jon Kyl, trying to negotiate a final immigration bill, said that Bingaman's provision could be a deal-breaker, Bingaman said, "I'd say the deal's broken then." In late June, as crucial votes loomed, Bingaman said he was undecided, then voted against the bill, arguing that it "unnecessarily complicated the guest worker program that would have depressed American wages and encouraged immigrants to overstay their visas, while making dramatic changes—but not necessarily for the better—to the process individuals would use to legally immigrate to our country." The immigration bill ultimately failed because of disputes over several key provisions.

On local issues, he and Domenici directed $10 million to the descendants of Hispanic homesteaders who had been paid only a few dollars an acre in the 1940s for land that became part of the Los Alamos National Laboratory. The two also shepherded through the Senate in 2006 the Valle Vidal Protection Act, which covered 102,000 acres of Forest Service lands in the Raton Basin of northeast New Mexico. Bingaman was the lead sponsor of the public-lands-management bill passed by the Senate in early 2009. It would set aside more than 2 million acres in nine states as protected wilderness and 100 miles of wild and scenic rivers. It included a 5,300-acre national monument to protect Paleozoic fossilized tracks in the Robledo Mountains north of Las Cruces.

Bingaman has been re-elected four times. He faced his most serious challenge in the Republican year of 1994, when Republican Colin McMillan, a rancher and former assistant Defense secretary, spent over $1 million of his own money on his campaign. He attacked Bingaman's vote for Clinton's 1993 tax increase and for what McMillan said was a vote to increase grazing fees. Bingaman ads boasted of his work on defense conversion, national education standards and education technology. Bingaman won 54%-46%. Given New Mexico's sharp swing to the Democrats in 2008, his prospects for re-election in 2012 look better than ever.

Junior Senator

Tom Udall (D)

Elected 2008, term expires 2014, 1st term; b. May 18, 1948, Tucson, AZ; home, Santa Fe; Prescott Col., B.A. 1970; Cambridge U., B.L. 1975; U. of NM, J.D. 1977; Mormon; married (Jill Cooper); 1 child.

Elected Office: NM atty. gen., 1990–98; U.S. House of Reps., 1999–08.

Professional Career: Law clerk, 10th Circuit Court of Appeals, 1977; Asst. U.S. atty, 1978–81; Practicing atty., 1981–83, 1985–90; Chief cnsl., NM Health & Environment Dept., 1983–84.

DC Office: 110 HSOB, 20510, 202-224-6621; Fax: 202-228-3261; Web site: tomudall.senate.gov.

State Offices: Albuquerque, 505-346-6791; Las Cruces, 575-526-5475; Santa Fe, 505-988-6511.

Committees: *Commerce, Science & Transportation* (12th of 14 D): Communications, Technology & the Internet; Competitiveness, Innovation & Export Promotion; Consumer Protection, Product Safety & Insurance; Science & Space; Surface Transportation & Merchant Marine Infrastructure, Safety & Security. *Environment & Public Works* (9th of 12 D). *Indian Affairs* (8th of 9 D). *Rules & Administration* (10th of 11 D).

Group Ratings (House)

	ADA	ACLU	AFS	LCV	ITIC	NTU	COC	ACU	CFG	FRC
2008	90	100	100	92	71	17	47	12	8	11
2007	100	—	100	100	—	5	47	0	7	—

National Journal Ratings (House)

	2007 LIB	—	2007 CONS		2008 LIB	—	2008 CONS
Economic	78%	—	18%		61%	—	39%
Social	77%	—	23%		59%	—	38%
Foreign	81%	—	16%		78%	—	17%
Composite	80%	—	20%		67%	—	33%

Key Votes of the 110th Congress (House)

1. Increase minimum wage	Y	5. Share immigration data	N	9. Withdraw troops 8/08	Y
2. Expand SCHIP	Y	6. Foreign aid abortion ban	N	10. No operations in Iran	Y
3. Raise CAFE standards	Y	7. Ban gay bias in workplace	Y	11. Free trade with Peru	N
4. Bail out financial markets	N	8. Repeal D.C. gun law	Y	12. Overhaul FISA	N

Election Results

2008 general	Tom Udall (D)	505,128	(61%)	($7,841,887)
	Steve Pearce (R)	318,522	(39%)	($4,626,706)
2008 primary	Tom Udall (D)	unopposed		

Prior Winning Percentages: 2006 House (75%); 2004 House (69%); 2002 House (100%); 2000 House (67%); 1998 House (53%)

Democrat Tom Udall was elected to the House in 1998 and to the Senate in 2008. He belongs to a political clan that is well known in the West and nationally. He is the son of Steward Udall, the Arizona congressman (1955–61) and U.S. Interior secretary (1961–69), and the nephew Morris "Mo" Udall, an Arizona congressman (1961–91). He is also the first cousin of Sen. Mark Udall of Colorado and a distant cousin of former Oregon Sen. Gordon Smith, the only Republican in the bunch—sometimes called the "Kennedys of the West." Tom Udall grew up in Tucson and in McLean, Va., went to Prescott College in Arizona, got a degree at Cambridge University in England and graduated from the University of New Mexico Law School. He worked as a law clerk for a federal judge, then as a lawyer in the New Mexico state government before going into private law practice. Politics was obviously on his mind. He ran for Congress in 1982, when the 3rd District was newly created, and finished last among four candidates, with 13% of the vote. The winner was Democrat Bill Richardson, now governor. In 1988, Udall ran in the open, Albuquerque-based 1st district, won the Democratic nomination but lost the general to Republican Steven Schiff, 51%-47%. In 1990, he was elected state attorney general of New Mexico.

In 1997, when Richardson resigned the 3rd District seat, Republican Bill Redmond, an independent Christian minister from Los Alamos, won it in an upset, assisted by a Green Party candidate nominee who won 17%. In 1998, Udall decided he had a shot at the seat, given the district's heavy ratio of Democrats to Republicans. He worked to consolidate the Democratic and leftist vote. Drawing on lawyers, the arts community and friends of the Udall family, he raised daunting sums. The Sierra Club and the League of Conservation Voters criticized Redmond and ran waves of ads against him. As for the third-party threat, Udall said, "I intend to make peace with the Greens." He won with 53% of the vote. Redmond got the same 43% he had won 18 months before, while Green Party nominee Carole Miller saw her 17% evaporate to 4%. Udall won re-election without serious challenges four times.

Udall had a seat on the House Resources Committee, on which his father served and which his uncle chaired. He helped to enact a bill to explore establishment of a national historical park at Los Alamos. With Republican Roscoe Bartlett of Maryland, he formed a bipartisan coalition to seek alternatives to high-priced and finite petroleum resources. Locally, he called for a ban on oil drilling in the Valle Vidal area of the Carson National Forest, which was passed in 2006. He opposed Republican attempts to permit salvage logging in national forests as well.

With a largely liberal voting record, he voted against the Bush administration's USA PATRIOT Act, which gave law enforcement greatly expanded powers to catch terrorists. He proposed revisions in the act to limit police authority to obtain search warrants and to restore civil liberty protections for libraries and bookstores. He also called for an independent agency to monitor civil liberties abuses in the war on terrorism. Udall also opposed the 2002 Iraq war resolution and called "misguided" a bill to restrict illegal immigrants from obtaining driver's licenses. With the rest of the New Mexico delegation, he protested the Pentagon's recommendation to close Cannon Air Force Base in Clovis, which would have meant the loss of roughly 20% of the local workforce. Instead, the Pentagon decided to move its Special Operations Wing to Cannon.

In January 2007, after Democrats took control of the House, Udall secured a seat on the powerful Appropriations Committee. His bill to allow Indian tribal governments to apply for grants to investigate and shut down methamphetamine labs was passed unanimously by the House in February 2007. He tried to amend the energy and water appropriations bill to restore $192 million of the $300 million being cut for national laboratories, including Los Alamos National Laboratory in New Mexico, but his amendment was defeated 312-121. Despite losing that battle, Udall voted for the final bill, unlike New Mexico Republicans Heather Wilson and Steve Pearce, who voted against it. He was criticized at home for voting for the appropriations bill, and defended his position as a signal to the labs that their missions needed to change from a focus on nuclear weapons to alternative-energy research and other areas. But when the House voted in June 2008 to shut down the plutonium-manufacturing program at Los Alamos, Udall voted against.

On the 2007 energy bill, he sponsored an amendment requiring 15% of electricity to be generated from renewable sources other than nuclear power by 2020. The Democratic leadership supported this amendment, and the bill passed 220-190 in August. Democratic House Speaker Nancy Pelosi insisted that Udall's proposal remain in the legislation when it went to a House-Senate conference committee, but the Senate refused to accept it, and it was dropped from the legislation that was signed into law.

In October 2007, Republican Sen. Pete Domenici announced he would not run for re-election in 2008. Wilson and Pearce, the state's two Republican congressmen, immediately jumped into the race; several Democrats, including moderate Albuquerque Mayor Martin Chavez, considered it as well. This was the first open Senate seat in New Mexico since 1972, and only the second open seat since 1948. Udall at first said he wasn't interested. But Gov. Richardson and Democratic Senatorial Campaign Committee Chairman Charles Schumer of New York urged him to run. On November 10, a little less than a year out from the election, Udall announced his candidacy, which quickly cleared the Democratic field.

Meanwhile, Wilson and Pearce battled for the Republican nomination. Pearce attacked Wilson for supporting the Democrats' expansion of the State Children's Health Insurance Program, which he called "socialized medicine," and for voting to raise taxes. Wilson hit Pearce for votes against additional guards on the U.S. border with Mexico and against keeping Cannon Air Force Base open. Domenici, long thought to favor Wilson, stayed neutral. But when the national anti-tax organization Club for Growth ran ads against her, Domenici denounced "out-of-state" people interfering in the contest and endorsed her a few days before the June primary. But Pearce still won, 51%-49%. Wilson won 66% in Albuquerque's Bernalillo County, but had lower percentages in suburban counties and northern New Mexico. Pearce won large majorities in southern New Mexico and in the southeastern "Little Texas" region.

The primary drained Pearce's war chest, and Udall was able to significantly outspend him, $7.8 million to $4.6 million. Pearce went on the attack, painting Udall as captive to the liberal wing of the Democratic Party and its "hippie" traditions. A former oil-industry executive, Pearce also hammered Udall for his opposition to new oil exploration in environmentally sensitive areas. Udall responded that he was for a "do-it-all" approach to energy. It was apparent long before November that this wasn't much of a contest. Udall won 61%-39%. Pearce carried only Little Texas in the southeast and the San Juan Basin in the far northwest corner.

In the Senate, Udall joined his cousin Mark Udall, who had just won election to a Colorado Senate seat. The two were awarded more seniority credit than other freshmen because of their House service. In one of his first moves, Udall proposed designating 17,000 acres in San Miguel County as wilderness. It was added to Democratic Sen. Jeff Bingaman's lands bill and passed in January 2009. A Udall amendment providing tax credits for employers hiring military veterans discharged after 2001 was included in the February 2009 economic-stimulus bill.

FIRST DISTRICT

Martin Heinrich (D)

Elected 2008, 1st term; b. Oct. 17, 1971, Fallon, NV; home, Albuquerque; U. of MO, B.S.E. 1995; Lutheran; married (Julie); 2 children.

Elected Office: Albuquerque City Cncl., 2004–07, Pres., 2006–07.

Professional Career: New Mexico National Resources Trustee

DC Office: 1505 LHOB, 20515, 202-225-6316; Fax: 202-225-4975; Web site: heinrich.house.gov.

State Offices: Albuquerque, 505-346-6781.

Committees: *Armed Services* (31st of 36 D): Readiness; Strategic Forces. *Natural Resources* (13th of 29 D): Energy & Mineral Resources; National Parks, Forests & Public Lands.

Group Ratings and Key Votes: Newly Elected

Election Results

2008 general	Martin Heinrich (D)	166,271	(56%)	($2,481,040)
	Darren White (R)	132,485	(44%)	($1,778,319)
2008 primary	Martin Heinrich (D)	22,341	(44%)	
	Rebecca Vigil-Giron (D)	12,660	(25%)	
	Michelle Grisham (D)	12,074	(24%)	
	Robert Pidcock (D)	4,273	(8%)	

Population		Race/Ethnicity		Work	
Pop. 2007:	668,643	White:	44.7%	Private:	73.8%
Change since 2000:	Up 10.3%	Black:	2.7%	Government:	19.4%
Urban:	91.3%	Hispanic:	45.1%	Self-employed:	6.6%
Rural:	8.7%	Asian:	2.0%	Blue collar:	19.8%
Area size:	4,720 sq. mi.	Native Am.:	3.6%	White collar:	62.3%
Age		Hawaiian:	0.1%	Khaki collar:	0.5%
Median age:	35.6 yrs.	Two+ races:	1.3%	Other:	17.4%
More than 65 yrs:	11.7%	*Ancestry*		Median income:	$44,461
Less than 18 yrs:	24.8%	German:	10.5%	Median home value:	$164,700
Education		Irish:	7.4%	Poverty:	15.2%
H.S. grad:	84.9%	English:	7.1%	**Military Veterans**	
College grad:	30.2%			% of Pop:	12.6%
Grad degree:	13.5%				

New Mexico's past and future come together in its single metropolis, Albuquerque. The city's Spanish and Indian past is memorialized in its name (for a 17th-century Spanish nobleman) and in its age (founded in 1706) and in its quaint Old Town. But Albuquerque's future is decidedly high-tech. For decades, the Sandia National Laboratories, Kirtland Air Force Base and the University of New Mexico have attracted scientists and engineers to Albuquerque and promoted private-sector technology

2008 Presidential Vote

Obama (D)	180,790	(60%)
McCain (R)	118,972	(39%)

2004 Presidential Vote

Kerry (D)	139,820	(51%)
Bush (R)	130,946	(48%)

Cook Partisan Voting Index: D + 5

growth. When rocket scientist Robert Goddard moved here in 1930 and nuclear scientist J. Robert Oppenheimer reconnoitered the site in 1940, Albuquerque was still a town of 35,000 at the junction of the Rio Grande River and old U.S. 66, which paralleled the Santa Fe Railroad. "A dirty, red sod-hut tortilla desert highway city," novelist Tom Wolfe wrote. Now, metro Albuquerque, spreading out from Bernalillo County into Sandoval and Valencia counties, has more people (846,000 in 2008) than all of New Mexico did when the scientists first arrived. Bill Gates founded a little company called Microsoft here in 1975, although the software maker moved its 16 employees to Seattle in 1979. Intel now employs about 3,300 local residents in an advanced chip-making facility. The city's prosperous neighborhoods have climbed the gently rising heights to the east; poorer residents have spread north and south along the Rio Grande. In the Old Town Plaza, some of the adobe buildings date to the 18th century. Hemmed in by the Sandia Mountains and by federal installations, growth is moving west and north, especially to the new town of Rio Rancho, home of the Intel plant and facilities for Sprint PCS and Victoria's Secret. Despite its cold winters, Albuquerque is part of the Sun Belt. While Albuquerque has seen some growth in tourism— every October, it hosts the International Balloon Fiesta, which features many resident balloonists— it is heavily dependent on federal jobs.

The 1st Congressional District of New Mexico includes Albuquerque and some of its suburbs. It is 45% Hispanic and takes in most of Bernalillo County and sparsely populated Torrance County in the desert. But the 1st does not include most of the big-growth suburbs of Corrales and Rio Rancho to the north in Sandoval County or Isleta and Las Lunas to the south in Valencia County. This has been one of the nation's most competitive districts: It voted 51%-48% for John Kerry in 2004—Kerry visited Albuquerque six times during his campaign—but 60%-39% for Barack Obama in 2008. The district had elected a Republican to Congress since its creation in 1969, but the trend ended in 2008.

The new congressman from the 1st District is Democrat Martin Heinrich (*HYN-rihk*). He defeated Republican Bernalillo County Sheriff Darren White after incumbent Rep. Heather Wilson gave up the seat to run for the Senate. Heinrich was born in Fallon, Nev., earned a bachelor's degree in engineering from the University of Missouri and moved to New Mexico in 1995. He founded a political consulting business and served as executive director of the Cottonwood Gulch Foundation, which runs adventure programs in the Southwest. In 2003, he was elected to the Albuquerque City Council. His signature issue was increasing New Mexico's minimum wage, and Heinrich worked with the city's business leaders and community activists to produce compromise legislation mandating a gradual increase. It passed in 2006. He also lobbied for federal protection of the Ojito Wilderness, and Democratic Gov. Bill Richardson appointed him the state's national resources trustee in 2006.

Encouraged by Richardson, Heinrich announced that he would challenge Wilson in 2008. National Democrats backed Heinrich's candidacy from the start, and he defeated three other hopefuls in the June 3 primary, including former New Mexico Secretary of State Rebecca Vigil-Giron. In October 2007, Wilson announced her intention to relinquish the seat to run for the Senate. Republicans fielded a strong replacement candidate in Darren White, who has had a long career in New Mexico politics, including two terms as sheriff of Bernalillo County, and early polls showed he had better name recognition than Heinrich.

But Heinrich made steady gains. He tied White to the unpopular incumbent president by reminding voters that White had served as President George W. Bush's Bernalillo County re-election chairman in 2004. White in turn questioned Heinrich's business practices, saying he had been paid by nonprofit groups for advocacy work without first registering as a lobbyist. Heinrich had worked as a political consultant for the Coalition for New Mexico Wilderness from 2002 to 2005 and lobbied on its behalf. During the campaign, he maintained that the law had not required him to register as a federal or state lobbyist. The campaign took an especially negative turn in the final weeks. Heinrich's campaign ran an ad featuring a group of New Mexico state police officers' wives who in 1996 accused White of policies they claimed compromised their husbands' safety. White's campaign hit back with an ad in which the mother of a slain Bernalillo County sheriff's deputy referred to Heinrich as "despicable."

Late polls showed a close race. But Heinrich defeated White 56% to 44%, carrying three of the district's five counties. He crushed White by 33,786 votes in populous Bernalillo County, which Wilson had lost by a mere 1,250 votes in 2006. Heinrich's surprisingly large victory can be attributed in part to money. White was not nearly as good a fundraiser as Wilson, who spent nearly $5 million to defend the seat in 2006. Heinrich outraised White $2.5 million to $1.8 million, and the Democratic Congressional Campaign Committee poured $2 million into the race. The cash-strapped National Republican Congressional Committee ignored it. Heinrich was also helped by the Democratic wave that swept through New Mexico in 2008. Democratic presidential nominee Barack Obama defeated Republican nominee John McCain 57% to 42%, in a state where the two previous presidential elections had been decided by a percentage point or less. In other contests, Democrat Tom Udall snatched a Senate seat from the Republicans, that of the retiring Sen. Pete Domenici, and New Mexico's two other House seats were secured by non-incumbent Democrats.

Before arriving in Washington, Heinrich had already generated some inside-the-industry buzz. A poll conducted by the website Politics1.com named the handsome Heinrich the "Hottest Man in Politics," ahead of such well-known political heartthrobs as Sen. John Thune of South Dakota. Once in the House, Heinrich got seats on the Armed Services Committee and the Natural Resources Committee, where he is focusing on legislation to make the country energy independent.

SECOND DISTRICT

Harry Teague (D)

Elected 2008, 1st term; b. June 29, 1949, Gracemont, OK; home, Hobbs; Attended Hobbs H.S.; Baptist; married (Nancy); 2 children.

Elected Office: Lea Cnty. Bd. of Commissioners, 1998–2006, chmn. 2003–06.

Professional Career: Pres., Teaco Energy Services

DC Office: 1007 LHOB, 20515, 202-225-2365; Fax: 202-225-9599; Web site: teague.house.gov.

State Offices: Hobbs, 575-393-0510; Las Cruces, 575-522-3908; Los Lunas, 505-865-7802; Roswell, 575-622-4178; Socorro, 575-835-8919.

Committees: *Transportation & Infrastructure* (44th of 44 D): Railroads, Pipelines & Hazardous Materials; Water Resources & Environment. *Veterans' Affairs* (10th of 18 D): Economic Opportunity; Health.

Group Ratings and Key Votes: Newly Elected

Election Results

2008 general	Harry Teague (D)	129,572	(56%)	($3,408,821)
	Edward Tinsley (R)	101,980	(44%)	($2,389,508)
2008 primary	Harry Teague (D)	20,281	(52%)	
	Bill McCamley (D)	18,597	(48%)	

Population		Race/Ethnicity		Work	
Pop. 2007:	629,931	White:	41.4%	Private:	66.8%
Change since 2000:	Up 3.9%	Black:	1.8%	Government:	24.6%
Urban:	71.0%	Hispanic:	49.4%	Self-employed:	7.9%
Rural:	29.0%	Asian:	0.7%	Blue collar:	24.3%
Area size:	69,598 sq. mi.	Native Am.:	5.3%	White collar:	53.1%
Age		Hawaiian:	0.0%	Khaki collar:	0.4%
Median age:	35.1 yrs.	Two+ races:	1.2%	Other:	22.2%
More than 65 yrs:	13.8%	*Ancestry*		Median income:	$35,366
Less than 18 yrs:	26.1%	German:	8.8%	Median home value:	$93,700
Education		English:	6.4%	Poverty:	22.2%
H.S. grad:	77.0%	Irish:	6.3%	**Military Veterans**	
College grad:	18.3%			% of Pop:	12.8%
Grad degree:	7.0%				

Southeastern New Mexico is a disparate landscape: endless sagebrush-strewn acreage and then, suddenly, 9,000-foot mountain peaks rising along the Continental Divide. The eastern part of this region—places like Clovis and Portales, Lovington and Hobbs—speaks with a Texas twang rather than a northern New Mexico lilt. In Little Texas, as southeastern New Mexico is known, oil has long been the economic mainstay. Cattle ranching is common, and cotton is grown on irrigated land. One

2008 Presidential Vote

McCain (R)	118,063	(50%)
Obama (D)	114,928	(49%)

2004 Presidential Vote

Bush (R)	127,391	(58%)
Kerry (D)	91,073	(41%)

Cook Partisan Voting Index: R + 6

of the larger towns is Roswell, site of a supposed flying-saucer landing in 1947 and now home of the International UFO Museum and Research Center. Farther west is White Sands National Monument, with its immaculate gypsum dunes and specially evolved animals with white coloration that allows them to elude predators in the harsh environment. Close by is Alamogordo, where the first atomic bomb was exploded at 5:29:45 a.m. Mountain War Time on July 16, 1945. Virgin Galactic, a company started by billionaire Richard Branson, has leased land near White Sands to build the nation's first commercial spaceport. It plans to send passengers to the edge of space starting in 2010.

As in many places on America's high plains, population here is thinning and old economic pillars are crumbling. Once reliant on potash mining, Carlsbad aggressively sought the Waste Isolation Pilot Plant, a nuclear-waste repository. East of Carlsbad, a uranium-enrichment plant is under construction in Eunice, the first such facility licensed by the Nuclear Regulatory Commission. In central and western New Mexico, the scrubland shades into desert, and people cram into small cities, protected from summer's burning heat and winter's deathly cold. The Hatch Valley, in the desert adjoining Interstate 25, is home to perhaps the world's finest chili peppers—the traditional cornerstone of the Southwest's spicy cuisine. Places like Silver City and Bayard were built on mining and occasional discord. The story of a strike by Mexican-American workers at a zinc mine here in 1950 and 1951 was told in the film *Salt of the Earth*. Now home to miners, artists, ranchers and outdoor enthusiasts alike, Silver City lacks the polish of Santa Fe or Taos, but locals like to say it offers "the real New Mexico experience."

Las Cruces, New Mexico's second-largest city, has grown at rates well above the statewide average, thanks to migrants from Mexico coming up the Rio Grande. Nearby are the Robledo Mountains, hailed by the Smithsonian Institution as the world's greatest repository of pre-dinosaur era fossil tracks. For decades, Anglo and Mexican ranchers across the border spoke "the common language of cattle." Communities frequently shared public services with their cross-border neighbors and left the gates open at night for stragglers stuck too late on the wrong side of the border. But rapid development due to 1993 North American Free Trade Agreement, a surge in illegal immigration and a sharp uptick in drug trafficking have brought enormous strains. Still, the New Mexico portion of the U.S.-Mexico border remains far sleepier than elsewhere, and the border posts that dot New Mexico's largely empty 150-mile frontier apprehend considerably fewer illegal immigrants than those in Arizona. The national training center for border-patrol agents has been consolidated in Artesia.

The 2nd Congressional District of New Mexico covers this southern part of the state, going as far north as the suburb of Las Lunas and the Isleta Pueblo south of Albuquerque and the Acoma Pueblo to the west. Demographically and politically, it is diverse. It includes most of New Mexico's Little Texas—majority Anglo and solidly conservative, though with a Democratic heritage. It includes the politically marginal Las Cruces and the Democratic mining counties in the southwest corner of the state. And it includes the Indian country around the pueblos, which is strongly Democratic. The district is 49% Hispanic and 5% Indian. More Hispanics are ineligible to vote here than in the 1st and 3rd districts.

The new congressman from the 2nd District is Democrat Harry Teague. Teague defeated Republican nominee Edward Tinsley to become the first Democrat to represent the district since 1980. Republican Rep. Steve Pearce had given up the seat to run for the Senate.

Teague was born in Gracemont, Okla., and moved to eastern New Mexico at 9 years old. When he was a senior at Hobbs High School, his father became ill, and Teague dropped out of school to work in the oil fields along the New Mexico-Texas border. His starting rate was $1.50 an hour, which he used to help support the family. Today, Teague is president of his own company, the Hobbs-based Teaco Energy Services, Inc., which services oil wells in New Mexico and Texas and employs more than 250 workers. Teague served for eight years on the Lea County Board of Commissioners. Though the commission was controlled by Republicans, he was voted chairman for more than three years. As a commissioner, Teague pushed for bringing the National Enrichment Facility, which processes fuel for nuclear power plants, to Lea County.

In the contest for the House seat, Teague and Tinsley, owner of the K-Bob's Steakhouse chain and a rancher, both supported more domestic drilling as well as the development of alternative energy. Teague tried to link Tinsley to Republican President Bush as much as possible, emphasizing his opponent's support for making the Bush tax cuts permanent, and he criticized Tinsley for opposing an increase in the federal minimum wage. During debates, Teague slammed Tinsley for once being tardy in paying his payroll taxes, noting that Tinsley had had to pay the Internal Revenue Service $65,000 for late filings and late payments. Tinsley brought up a sexual-harassment suit against a vice president of Teague's company.

Teague got the endorsement of Democratic Gov. Bill Richardson, an early contender for the presidential nomination in 2008. He also had solid union support, winning endorsements from the American Federation of Teachers and the United Steelworkers of America. Tinsley was endorsed by the *Las Cruces Sun-News*, the dominant newspaper in the district. He also got the backing of retiring Republican Sen. Pete Domenici, the U.S. Chamber of Commerce and former Las Cruces Mayor Bill Mattiace. Teague raised $3.4 million, half of it his own money, while Tinsley raised $2.4 million. Teague won, 56%-44%, performing better than statewide Democratic candidates in the district's conservative southeastern counties and winning comfortably in more liberal areas such as Dona Ana County.

Once in the House, Teague got seats on the Transportation and Infrastructure Committee and the Veterans' Affairs Committee.

THIRD DISTRICT

Ben Ray Luján (D)

Elected 2008, 1st term; b. June 7, 1972, Santa Fe; home, Nambé; NM Highlands U., B.B.A., 2007.; Catholic; single.

State Offices: Farmington, 505-324-1005; Gallup, 505-863-0582; Las Vegas, 505-454-3038; Rio Rancho, 505-994-0499; Tucumcari, 575-461-3029.

Committees: *Homeland Security* (13th of 20 D): Emerging Threats, Cybersecurity & Science and Technology; Transportation Security & Infrastructure Protection. *Science & Technology* (12th of 26 D): Energy & Environment; Technology & Innovation (VChmn).

Group Ratings and Key Votes: Newly Elected

Election Results

2008 general	Ben Ray Luján (D)	161,292	(57%)	($1,520,908)
	Daniel East (R)	86,618	(30%)	($190,884)
	Carol Miller (I)	36,348	(13%)	($42,154)
2008 primary	Ben Ray Luján (D)	26,775	(42%)	
	Donald Wiviott (D)	16,497	(26%)	
	Benny Shendo (D)	10,148	(16%)	
	Harry Montoya (D)	7,234	(11%)	

Population		Race/Ethnicity		Work	
Pop. 2007:	644,273	White:	40.9%	Private:	67.0%
Change since 2000:	Up 6.3%	Black:	1.5%	Government:	24.0%
Urban:	62.8%	Hispanic:	37.9%	Self-employed:	8.7%
Rural:	37.2%	Asian:	1.0%	Blue collar:	22.0%
Area size:	47,271 sq. mi.	Native Am.:	17.2%	White collar:	58.3%
Age		Hawaiian:	0.0%	Khaki collar:	0.4%
Median age:	36.0 yrs.	Two+ races:	1.2%	Other:	19.3%
More than 65 yrs:	12.0%	*Ancestry*		Median income:	$43,324
Less than 18 yrs:	26.0%	German:	8.6%	Median home value:	$156,600
Education		English:	7.7%	Poverty:	18.0%
H.S. grad:	82.8%	Irish:	6.2%	**Military Veterans**	
College grad:	25.6%			% of Pop:	11.5%
Grad degree:	10.9%				

"The dancing ground of the sun," is what the Pueblo Indians called the land of northern New Mexico, where the long vistas, dotted with low-lying scrub, are painted in pastel hues in the cold light and clear air. For 100 years, artists have been coming here, attracted by the scenery and by a unique civilization that is part Indian, part Anglo, part Spanish, and a little Mexican (northern New Mexico was under Mexican control only from 1821–46). The region's long-surviving traditions, however, mask the instabilities of this blended civilization. The Indians were here first and built adobe pueblos, including some of the world's earliest apartment buildings. The Spanish conquistadors and priests brought the Catholic religion, the baroque architectural accents and the Spanish language. Successive waves of American settlement have changed New Mexico in multiple ways. The Indian crafts that thrive today nearly died out in the 1880s. The Palace of the Governors, built in Santa Fe in 1610, was shorn of a Victorian balustrade and returned to its original appearance in 1913. Along the back roads in Rio Arriba or Taos counties, one can find a religion that mixes Catholicism with adaptations of Indian festivals, buildings not that much different from the old pueblos and a standard of living reminiscent of the Indian past, although sometimes punctuated by high rates of drug abuse. It's quite a contrast with the chichi ski lodges in the Taos Valley, the high-security research facilities of Los Alamos and the affluent, bohemian lifestyles of modern-day Santa Fe, where zoning laws decree that the color of all buildings must be adobe brown.

The 3rd Congressional District of New Mexico contains most of the state's historic Spanish-speaking and Indian parts. In 2007, Rio Rancho, with 76,000 residents, became the district's most populous city,

2008 Presidential Vote

Obama (D)	176,704	(61%)
McCain (R)	109,797	(38%)

2004 Presidential Vote

Kerry (D)	139,336	(54%)
Bush (R)	118,350	(45%)

Cook Partisan Voting Index: D + 7

but trendy Santa Fe, where painter Georgia O'Keeffe was a major cultural force and local spas have encouraged the tourism boom, remains its most dominant. The 3rd runs from the High Plains along the Texas border, past the haunting Sangre de Cristo Mountains, through the vast ridges and isolated buttes in the center, to the windy and dusty desertlike plains. Its Hispanic population is 38%, the lowest of the state's three districts. Another 17% of the district population is Indian, the most of the state's three districts. Concentrated in and around the Navajo Reservation in the west, the district's Indians live in abject poverty.

The politics of northern New Mexico are unique. For years, debate was conducted and votes bartered in Spanish, not by separatists, but by Republicans and Democrats, often cynically, sometimes corruptly. Loyalties ran to families and communities more than to principles or parties. In the backcountry, you can still find more than just vestiges of the old communities and old politics—though no one is going to let you in on them, even if you speak good Spanish. Republican territory includes the Little Texas counties, the Albuquerque suburb of Rio Rancho, the mining and ranching country around Farmington, and the nuclear scientists of Los Alamos, but on the whole, this is a Democratic district. Both Hispanics and Indians are solidly Democratic, and in Santa Fe and Taos, the affluent and hippie migrants have produced a strong leftist tilt. Politically, this is a sharply divided district. Santa Fe, Taos and San Miguel counties voted more than 70% for John Kerry in 2004 and more than 75% for Barack Obama in 2008. President George W. Bush in 2004 won 65% to 77% in the counties on the Texas border and 66% in Farmington's San Juan County. Republican nominee John McCain's 2008 winning percentages in those counties ranged from 59% to 70%. Overall, the district voted 54%-45% for Kerry in 2004 and 61%-38% for Barack Obama in 2008.

The new congressman from the 3rd District is Democrat Ben Ray Luján, who was elected in 2008 to the seat vacated when Democrat Tom Udall ran for the Senate. A seventh-generation New Mexican, Luján (*LOO-han*) is the son of state House Speaker Ben Luján. Luján was born in Santa Fe and grew up on his family's farm, where he and his three siblings helped raise cattle, sheep and chickens. Luján's father was a union ironworker who was elected to the New Mexico House of Representatives in 1975. Luján's mother worked as a secretary for the Pojoaque Valley School District. After graduating from Pojoaque High School, Luján worked as a card dealer in a casino while attending classes at New Mexico Highlands University. In 2002, he became a deputy state treasurer, and a year later, he went to the New Mexico Department of Cultural Affairs as its chief financial officer and director of administrative services.

Luján's first experience with electoral politics was 2004, when he was elected to the New Mexico Public Regulation Commission, which regulates utilities, telecommunications, insurance and transportation in the state. Despite his somewhat sparse credentials, his fellow commissioners elected him chairman. The most pressing issue was the failure of Qwest Communications to invest a promised $788 million in its New Mexico communications network. Under Luján's leadership, the PRC ordered Qwest to invest in infrastructure or refund the money to customers. Qwest refused, and Democratic Gov. Bill Richardson advocated for a settlement. But Luján and the PRC steadfastly rejected Qwest's settlement offer, opting instead to take the company to the New Mexico Supreme Court. In 2006, the court sided with the commission, and Qwest ultimately agreed to spend $270 million in the state over three years.

When Udall gave up his House seat to run for the Senate, there was speculation that Luján's connections to the state's Democratic establishment might help him seal the party's nomination without competition from other interested candidates. A year earlier, the New Mexico Legislature passed a law stipulating that candidates had to receive 20% of the delegate vote at their respective party's pre-primary nominating convention in order to get their names on the primary ballot. The district's Democratic delegation consisted largely of elected officials, which worked in Luján's favor. New Mexico developer Donald Wiviott filed a lawsuit seeking to overturn the law. The state Legislature then changed the law to allow candidates who fell short of 20% to get on the ballot by gathering additional signatures from registered voters. At the Democratic nominating convention, Luján got 40% of the vote and Wiviott 30%; both were on the primary ballot. Also on the ballot was Benny Shendo, former head of the New Mexico Indian Affairs Department.

The primary race quickly turned negative. Wiviott ran ads claiming Luján's father had helped him secure his job as deputy state treasurer and criticizing Luján's attendance record on a governor-appointed Telehealth Commission. He also called for Luján to release his college transcripts. Luján responded with ads claiming that Wiviott's Texas trailer-parts company had been charged by the Federal Trade Commission with price-fixing and called for Wiviott to release his tax returns. But Shendo caused the race's biggest controversy when he implied that Luján was gay at a candidate forum. In a later email, he said Luján's parents had hired a woman to pretend that she was Luján's girlfriend. Shendo, who had been gaining traction among the district's liberal voters, drew criticism from local gay-rights groups.

Luján picked up endorsements from Richardson, local labor unions and the Sierra Club environmental group. Wiviott was endorsed by Joe Wilson, husband of ex-CIA officer Valerie Plame Wilson, a former covert agent whose outing by officials in the Bush administration caused a major controversy in

2003–07; the couple had recently moved to Santa Fe. Wiviott invested almost $1.6 million of his own money in the campaign. Luján spent less than $800,000. Luján won with 42% of the vote to Wiviott's 25%. Shendo got 16%.

In the general election, Luján faced Republican Daniel East, a building contractor, and independent Carol Miller. The district's strong Democratic leanings and Luján's aggressive fundraising made the race a foregone conclusion. He won with 57% of the vote. East received 30%, Miller 13%.

Luján sits on the Committee on Homeland Security and the Science and Technology Committee.

★ NEW YORK ★

New York City is America's largest city, its financial capital, its center of arts and letters and media, and its largest immigrant destination. Since September 11, 2001, it also has been a symbol of the country's war on the constant yet unseen threat of terrorism. New York's achievements were not inevitable. They happened because New Yorkers—and not least those who came from elsewhere and opted to become New Yorkers—worked to make them happen. They did it in a city that has a certain enduring character that goes back to its birth as the 17th-century Dutch colony of Nieuw Amsterdam. Simon Schama's *The Embarrassment of Riches* paints a picture of the Old World Amsterdam that speaks to the character of the New World settlers. They came to America from "the richest city in the world; full of people who work hard all day and stay up late at night, smoke too much tobacco and drink too much coffee and gin, but are dazzlingly smart and shrewd; people who know their way around every corner of the globe and can make fine aesthetic discriminations, but are attached to their uncomfortable, crowded, bad-smelling city. They were merchants and manipulators with no aristocratic pedigree, welcoming any religious or ethnic group who can achieve and accumulate and show good taste, cherishing education and culture but indifferent to credentials." Probably fewer than 2% of today's New Yorkers are descended from the Dutch of Nieuw Amsterdam, but the character of the place endures in daily life and in its great institutions, and helps explain its miraculous growth. Combine Amsterdam and America, Dutch character with British-born political freedoms and American military strength, and you have the opportunity to build a city-state that can lead the world—and be the natural target of terrorists who hate that civilization.

New York was not always the nation's leader. In 1776, it was only the seventh-most populous colony. Only in the 19th century did the descendants of Dutch patroons, Huguenot refugees, British West Indies traders and Yankee farmers become the nation's most successful merchants and capitalists, forging the first routes to the great American interior through the valleys of the Hudson and the Mohawk and building grand brownstone mansions on broad midtown Manhattan avenues. That early diversity provides one clue to New York's success. If New York has been cynical, ready to cooperate with Loyalists and Revolutionaries, depending on who was ahead, it has also been tolerant, ready to accept anyone smart or rich enough to be counted a success. It has been propelled upward at each stage—forging ahead of London as a financial and manufacturing center by World War I and staying ahead of surging Chicago—by incorporating every immigrant wave and consistently rewarding intelligence and hard work, with no concern about preserving hierarchies.

New York's success has been a product not only of market economics, but also of government—and politics. The English saw New York as a pivotal point in North America, a connecter of its northern and southern colonies and an avenue to the interior. That is why the Lord High Admiral, 30-year-old James, Duke of York, ordered his fleet to take Nieuw Amsterdam in 1664; the city and state are named for the man who was later King James II. The Iroquois, the most deeply rooted and militarily strong Native Americans, were kept in place for 100 years by an alliance with British troops, then were driven out of their homelands in upstate New York after the Revolution. The Erie Canal, which connected western New York State with the Hudson River, was the project of Federalist Gov. DeWitt Clinton's state government. New York led the nation in political innovation. Martin Van Buren's Albany Regency was the first state political machine, an ally of New York City's Tammany Hall. Van Buren invented or institutionalized the Democratic Party, the national convention and the inaugural parade. His adversaries, Thurlow Weed and William Seward, formed the Whig Party and ultimately became Republicans. Noting that Van Buren's Democrats were winning large margins from Irish Catholics and other immigrants, the Republicans too made bids for the newcomers' votes. Both parties served the function of mediating between the divergent interests of the New York City masses and upstate New York's farmers and burghers, a conflict still evident in New York between city and country, immigrant and native, Catholic and Protestant, the Big Apple and the apple-knockers.

Both parties also worked to protect New Yorkers against the untrammeled workings of free economic and political markets. Old-line Democrats embarked on an unprecedented, labor-intensive campaign to build infrastructure, the bridges and tunnels that made Greater New York possible. The tradition carried on from the time of Mayor Abram Hewitt, elected in 1886 over the single-taxer Henry George and the young Theodore Roosevelt, up through the time of Gov. Al Smith in the 1920s and his protégé Robert Moses, who built bridges, tunnels, highways, beaches and two World's Fairs. Progressive Republicans, from Theodore Roosevelt through Elihu Root and Henry Stimson, worked to create civil-service laws and bureaucratized purchasing and spending to protect taxpayers from corrupt party machines. The Democratic Tammany machine led by Charles F. Murphy and the talented young men he advanced, Smith and Robert Wagner, responded to the shocking 1911 Triangle Shirtwaist fire—when hundreds of women jumped 11 floors to their death because fire escapes were blocked—by passing labor and safety laws. The results included minimum wages, maximum work hours, working-condition regulations, encourage-

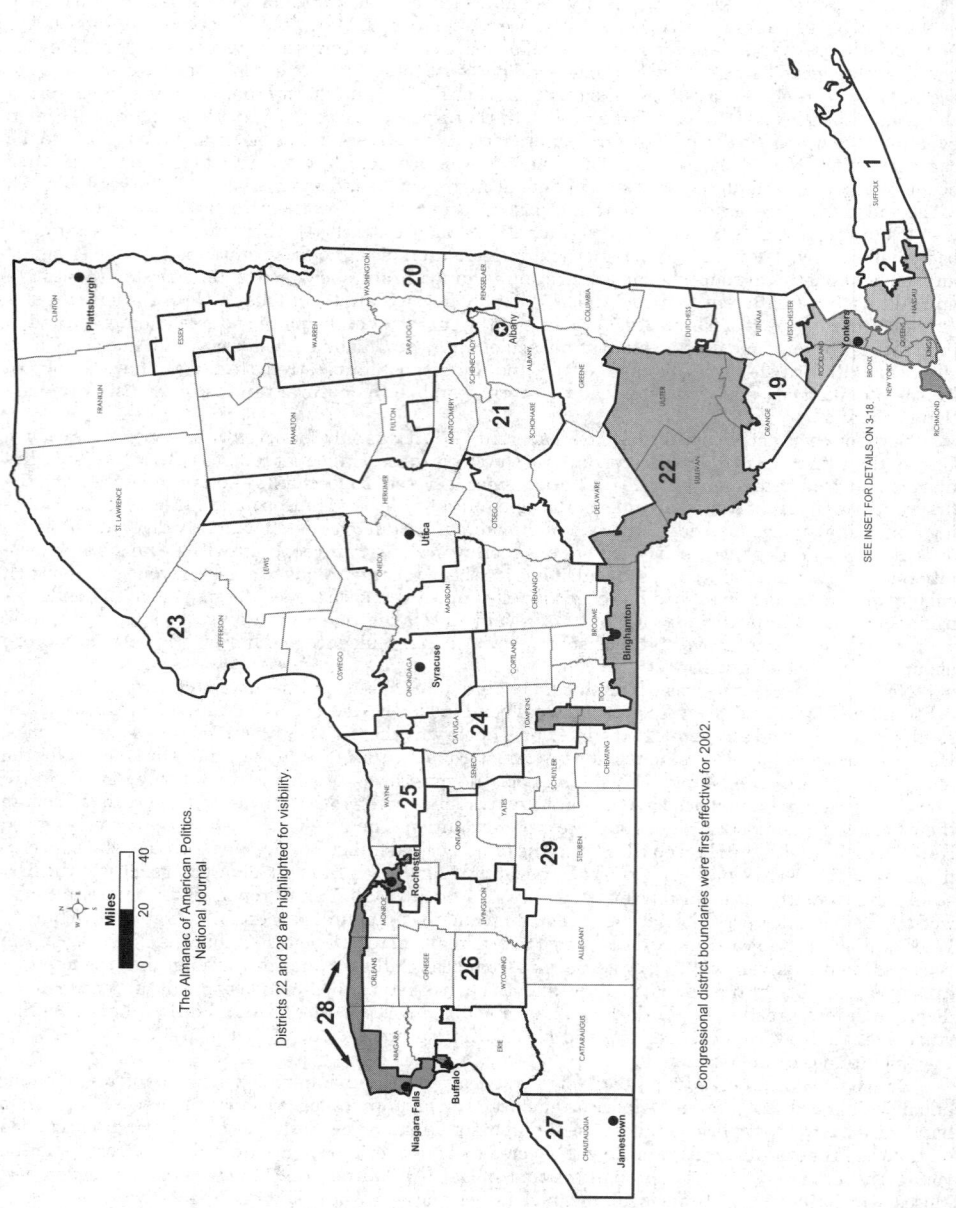

The Almanac of American Politics.
National Journal

Districts 22 and 28 are highlighted for visibility.

Congressional district boundaries were first effective for 2002.

SEE INSET FOR DETAILS ON 3-18.

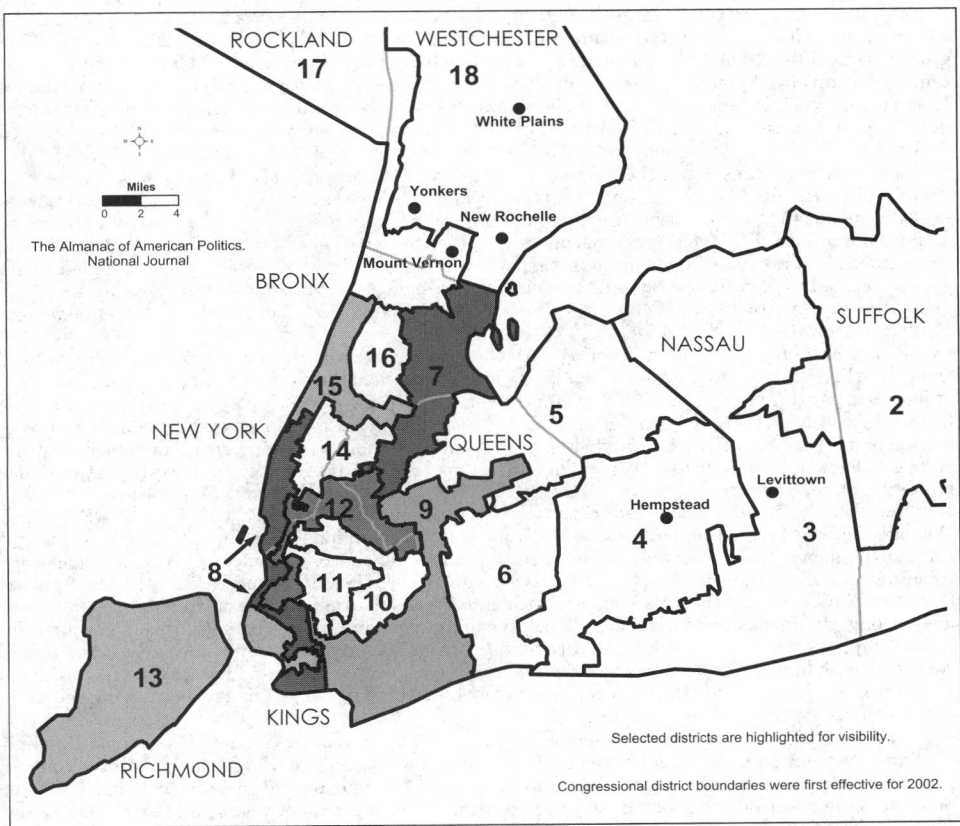

The Almanac of American Politics.
National Journal

Selected districts are highlighted for visibility.

Congressional district boundaries were first effective for 2002.

ment of unions, and state-owned electric utilities—the prototype of the New Deal, 20 years later, and the first American welfare state. In later years, New York pioneered public-housing and fair-housing laws, industry-wide unions (in the garment trades), rent control and dairy-price controls to help both New York City tenants and upstate farmers.

Statewide elections were exceedingly close, with Democrats carrying the New York City Catholic vote and Republicans winning upstate Protestants. Swing votes were cast by the 2 million Jewish immigrants, who supported a generous welfare state but mistrusted the Tammany machine and valued civil rights. The politician who combined these appeals most cannily was Fiorello LaGuardia, a nominal Republican but almost a socialist, an Episcopalian who was half Jewish as well as Italian, and the man who, as mayor of New York City from 1933 to 1945, built much of the public housing and many of the civic monuments that still stand. Incensed that New York had no airport, he built what is now LaGuardia within a year. Both parties produced politicians whose positions appealed to these swing voters, politicians who became nationally prominent and often presidential candidates at a time when the national media was much more concentrated in Manhattan than in Washington, D.C.: Democrats Smith, Wagner, Franklin D. Roosevelt and Averell Harriman; Republicans Thomas Dewey, Wendell Willkie, Nelson Rockefeller and Dwight Eisenhower, who was a New Yorker by virtue of the fact he was president of Columbia University when he was elected president in 1952.

The polity that these men built was productive, generous, tolerant and closely regulated. The country was becoming accustomed to working in big units—being employed by big corporations, represented by big unions, regulated by big government—and in this, New York was a natural leader. The financial dominance of Wall Street and the big banks was protected by federal regulation. The high-technology thrust of America in the mid-20th century was directed by big companies headquartered in New York's suburbs or upstate: General Electric and IBM, Eastman Kodak and Xerox. New York took for granted the productivity of its thousands of entrepreneurs and the high skills of its largely immigrant-born, public- and Catholic-school-educated workforce. It was blasé about its own miraculous infrastructure—the bridges and subways, electronic cables and electric wires connecting it better than anyplace else with every corner of the world.

But in the last quarter of the 20th century, New York's public strengths became weaknesses. The state that was clearly the national leader of a big-unit America lost the leadership of a country where growth had shifted to small economic units, where flexibility and adaptability had become more important than centralized planning. The institutions, practices and infrastructure that had helped produce New York's successes became ossified. Welfare-state benefits became too expensive, measures meant to protect against corruption stifled innovation, and both failed to achieve their objectives: Ghettos throbbed with the pains of disorganization, and payoffs and rackets remained part of the everyday cost of doing business in New York as in no other place in the country. The noble aim of creating a public sector that would guarantee cheap rents and top-notch public schools, colleges and public hospitals, instead guaranteed that none of these were readily available. Rent control kept housing scarce, school bureaucracies and teacher unions stifled good teaching, public hospitals rationed care. The attempt to create a fail-safe government had produced a government that was sure to fail. The government that intended to aid growth seemed to be cutting it off—not completely, but enough to explain why New York State, which grew 32% in population from 1940 to 1965, grew only 1% from 1965 to 1990; during that same period, California grew 67% and Texas 64%.

People and businesses started voting with their feet, especially during the terms of Mayor John Lindsay, a liberal Republican who caved to municipal unions' demands and borrowed against next year's revenues to pay this year's bills. That brought the city to the brink of bankruptcy in 1975, two years after he left office. In the 1970s, the population of New York, city and state, dropped by 1 million, an unprecedented hemorrhage of talent and productivity. Retrenchment followed, and private financiers and the state government took control of city government, cut spending and negotiated cutbacks in jobs and salaries with public-employees' unions. In the 1980s, Wall Street boomed, and Manhattan once again brimmed with confidence. Taxes were cut further under Democratic Mayor Edward Koch (1978–90) and Democratic Gov. Mario Cuomo (1983–95), public-employees' unions were for a time reined in, and rational management was installed. But institutional problems remained. New York's Legislature remained unusually tightly controlled by the two chambers' leaders, the Democratic Assembly Speaker, from New York City, and the Republican state Senate President, from upstate or the suburbs, and these leaders engaged in classic political logrolling, lavishing taxpayers' dollars on each other's pet projects. Public-employees' unions reestablished their stranglehold. The mild recession of the early 1990s struck New York with force. Big upstate companies—Xerox, Kodak, IBM—suffered serious reverses, and a private sector that had grown little if at all outside Wall Street could no longer finance the growing demands of the oversized welfare state.

By the end of the 1990s, New York seemed to have adapted and changed. Republican Mayor Rudolph Giuliani, first elected in 1993, cut crime and welfare rolls in half and cut hard deals with the unions. Republican Gov. George Pataki, first elected in 1994, imposed huge tax and spending cuts in 1995. Wall Street and the financial-services industry boomed in the late 1990s, to the point that the jobs lost in the 1990–94 recession were replaced. Then came September 11, 2001.

It was a beautiful fall morning, the sunshine lighting a blue sky above the skyscrapers of Manhattan, commuters hurrying through the streets and subways to work. At 8:46 a.m., the first plane hit the North Tower of the World Trade Center, and everything changed. When the second plane hit the South Tower 16 minutes later, it was clear that America was under attack, at war, even as office workers fled the burning buildings and New York firefighters streamed in. The terrorists had chosen to attack a facility in the seat of government in Washington—the Pentagon (and a second target, but they were stopped by the heroes of United Flight 93)—and the seat of commerce in New York, to inflict the maximum possible damage. The people of New York, like those at the Pentagon and on United 93, responded with courage, determination and devotion to duty. Firefighters, police officers and rescue workers risked death to help others. Strangers helped strangers. People who had no experience with disaster figured out how to cope and help others. Millions volunteered to give blood, sent money, and provided food and supplies. The *Wall Street Journal*, headquartered across the street from the World Trade Center, scrambled to put out a newspaper that was distributed at the regular time across the nation the next day. In less than a week, the New York Stock Exchange reopened.

Giuliani and Pataki performed well in the national spotlight. But New York faced an economic downturn and a turn in the course of government. Despite heroic efforts at recovery, Manhattan and New York lost 200,000 jobs in 2001 and 2002. Downtown real estate values tumbled as financial-services firms decentralized and sought office space elsewhere. Giuliani was term-limited, and all the leading contestants were well to his left. Media billionaire Michael Bloomberg, long a Democrat, became a Republican and spent $70 million of his own money on the campaign; he beat Public Advocate Mark Green 45.1%-44.5%. Pataki, running for re-election in 2002, made a $1.8 billion deal with the hospital workers' union and ensured that he would be re-elected without serious opposition. Faced with a fiscal crunch in 2002, Bloomberg increased property taxes 18% and raised other taxes as well. In his third term as governor, Pataki tried to hold down spending, but big tax increases, supported by Assembly Democrats and Senate Republicans, were passed over his veto. Nevertheless, the financial industry boomed as never before, generating revenues well beyond expectations. But the boom turned out to be fueled by mortgage-backed securities and other toxic assets, and in September 2008, the financial industry collapsed, with repercussions nationally and internationally, and with grave consequences for New York City and New York State.

New York City's growth in the first decade of the 21st century was fueled almost entirely by immigration. The city's population grew 3% from 2000 to 2007, to 8.2 million, and the four close-in suburban counties grew by a similar percentage as well. But this small change masked much greater movements. In those seven years, there was an immigrant inflow of 8% of the 2000 population and a domestic outflow of 14%. For the most part, the people moving out were the elderly, who headed to Florida, and middle-income workers and young blue-collar workers, who headed to lower-cost and lower-tax states like Virginia, Georgia and the Carolinas. Moving in were immigrants, who streamed into outer-borough neighborhoods and created new businesses, churches and neighborhood institutions—Caribbean blacks in Flatbush; Chinese in Flushing, Borough Park and on Staten Island; Colombians and Mexicans in Corona; Pakistanis and Bangladeshis in Jackson Heights; Greeks in Astoria; Russians in Brighton Beach; and Dominicans in Washington Heights and much of the Bronx. The Bronx is now majority Hispanic. New York City has about the same number of Puerto Ricans as it did in 1970, 800,000, but the number of other Hispanics has risen from 467,000 to 1.5 million.

Today's immigrants are arriving in a different sort of city. New York has long since lost most of its manufacturing jobs, and many corporate headquarters have moved elsewhere. The financial-services industry paid enormous salaries and bonuses to those at the very top and generated service-sector jobs for those who tend to the needs of the rich. But even those jobs were cut back drastically starting in 2008. As historian Fred Siegel points out, the outer boroughs are increasingly dependent on public-sector jobs, with one-third of jobs in Brooklyn and half in the Bronx directly dependent on the city or state governments. New York's Medicaid program, designed by Republican Gov. Nelson Rockefeller in 1966 to be far more generous than any other state's, provides a lot of jobs, including many for immigrants: Hospitals are major employers in the outer boroughs and did not cut back during the recession. The bad news is, the trend tends to squeeze the life out of the private sector. Subprime mortgages encouraged immigrants to buy houses in the outer boroughs at what turned out to be unsustainable prices.

The suburbs have similar problems, exacerbated by much higher property taxes than those in the city. The immigrant inflow in the four close in suburban counties of Nassau, Rockland, Suffolk and Westchester is smaller, 3% from 2000 to 2008, with a domestic outflow of 6%. Places like Levittown, buzzing with young families moving in from Brooklyn in the 1950s, are aging and losing population. The high property taxes are in effect tuition to good suburban school districts, but become a heavy burden when the kids go off to college. Immigrant communities are coalescing in low-income suburbs whose first residents have departed. But with their high taxes and utility rates, the suburbs are not attractive to new businesses—the hedge-fund sector bloomed across the line to Greenwich, Conn.—and population is growing more sluggishly than in the city.

Upstate New York has even greater problems. Burdened with a state tax system constructed to support New York City's welfare state, it has been at a substantial disadvantage compared with nearby Northeastern states, not to mention the Sun Belt, when it comes to attracting jobs. Medicaid mandates have forced upstate counties to raise property taxes as much as 70%. Large, formerly paternalistic companies have been shedding jobs. In the 1990s, IBM cut back heavily in the Hudson Valley. Kodak, hard hit by competition from digital cameras, employed 60,000 people in the Rochester area in 1981 but had cut its workforce by half by 2007. Xerox jobs in the area fell from 16,000 to 8,000. General Electric, which employed 40,000 in Schenectady in the 1950s, cut the payroll there to 3,000 in 2006. Buffalo, once one of the nation's great steel producers, has become a center for the debt-collection industry. The 7 million population of upstate New York increased by only 6,000 people between 2000 and 2008, and 32 of 50 counties lost population. (Only two, Orange and Saratoga, gained more than 5%.)

In the first half of the 20th century, New York politics was a battle between the Democratic city, then with more than half the state's population, and the Republican upstate. Jewish voters, concentrated in the city and moored to neither party, provided critical swing votes. In the post-World War II period, the suburbs grew and tended to produce small Republican majorities. Today the picture is different. New York voters turned to state and city Republicans amid the economically straitened and crime-ridden early 1990s—Giuliani as mayor, Pataki as governor. But they left no political heirs unless you count Bloomberg, a Democrat who changed his party registration so that he could run for mayor without the inconvenience of going through a left-wing gauntlet in a Democratic primary. (Bloomberg changed again in 2007, to unaffiliated, then persuaded the City Council to abolish term limits so he could run for re-election in 2009.)

In national politics, New York is one of the most Democratic states. In 2008, Democratic presidential nominee Barack Obama carried New York City 79%-20%. But even if the city had not cast a single vote, he would have won comfortably. He carried the four suburban counties, 55%-44%, and he carried upstate New York, which had voted against upstate native Franklin Roosevelt in four presidential races. Large numbers of Jewish and black voters have turned Westchester from a Republican to a Democratic county. On Long Island, Nassau and Suffolk County threw out Republican machine politicians and installed Democrats. The upstate counties containing Buffalo, Rochester, Syracuse, Albany and Binghamton produced Democratic margins to counterbalance Republican margins in smaller counties. Democratic Sen.

Charles Schumer, who defeated Republican incumbent Alfonse D'Amato in a close race in 1998, was re-elected in 2004 by 71%-24%. That was the pattern again in 2006. Democrat Eliot Spitzer, who narrowly defeated a Republican incumbent attorney general in 1998, used the office to bring charges of wrongdoing against corporate executives and Wall Street figures, and in the process restructured securities-market regulation. Even before Pataki announced that he would not seek a fourth term, it was apparent that Spitzer would be the next governor, and he won 70%-29%. Democratic Sen. Hillary Rodham Clinton, the 55%-43% winner in a vigorously contested Senate race in 2000, did not draw a serious opponent and was re-elected 67%-31%. Democrats hold a 109-41 margin in the Assembly. The state Senate got a Democratic majority in 2008, although that was thrown into limbo in June 2009, when two Democrats announced they were defecting from their party and joining Republicans on organizational issues affecting party control of the chamber. A few weeks later, the two returned to the fold, and majority control was back in Democratic hands.

For all of the recent Democratic triumphs, New York politics seems to be in flux. The huge victories of Spitzer and Clinton in 2006 suggested they could hold two of New York's highest offices indefinitely. But Spitzer resigned in March 2008 after he was caught patronizing prostitutes, and Clinton, having narrowly lost the Democratic nomination for president in 2008, resigned in early 2009 to become Obama's secretary of State. Incoming Democratic Gov. David Paterson wrestled with budget problems and dithered over whether to appoint presidential daughter Caroline Kennedy to fill Clinton's vacancy in the Senate. His job ratings fell, and in polls in spring 2009, he trailed behind Attorney General Andrew Cuomo in the Democratic primary and Giuliani in the general election. His appointee to the Senate, U.S. Rep. Kirsten Gillibrand of upstate New York, had no statewide name recognition and was threatened with opposition in the Democratic primary. Cruising above all this was Schumer. His position in New York is impregnable, and in his two terms as chairman of the Democratic Senatorial Campaign Committee, Democrats gained 14 seats in the U.S. Senate. In the Democratic Senate leadership, Schumer is a steadying force behind Majority Leader Harry Reid of Nevada and Majority Whip Dick Durbin of Illinois, soothing tempers behind the scenes even as he, a notorious media hound, races to the microphones and cameras to comment on the latest developments. He seems to have a long and consequential career ahead of him in American politics.

Population			Household Income		Work	
Pop. 2007:	19,280,753		Under $15k:	14.4%	Private:	76.9%
State rank:	3rd of 50		$15k to $50k:	33.0%	Government:	16.6%
Change since 2000:	Up 1.6%		$50k to $100k:	29.8%	Self-employed:	6.4%
Urban:	87.3%		$100k to $150k:	17.5%	Unemployment (3-yr. average):	4.3%
Rural:	12.7%		Over $150k:	5.3%	Poverty:	14.0%
Native of state:	64.4%		Median income:	$52,944	Blue collar:	18.1%
Not a citizen:	10.5%		**Home Value**		White collar:	62.8%
Area size:	54,556 sq. mi.		Under $100k:	20.6%	Khaki collar:	0.2%
Most populous cities			$100k to $300k:	29.9%	Other:	18.9%
1. New York	8,246,310		$300k to $500k:	23.6%	**Age**	
2. Buffalo	263,030		$500k to $1 mil:	21.1%	Median age:	37.4 yrs.
3. Rochester	199,697		Over $1 million:	4.8%	More than 65 yrs:	13.1%
4. Yonkers	195,817		Median:	$293,400	Less than 18 yrs:	23.2%

Race/Ethnicity				Military Veterans		Registered Voters in 2008	
White:	60.3%	*Language*		% of Pop:	7.3%	D:	5,831,445 (48.5%)
Black:	14.8%	English:	71.4%			R:	3,054,520 (25.4%)
Hispanic:	16.2%	Spanish:	14.1%	*Veterans by Period*		Other:	3,145,347 (26.1%)
Asian:	6.7%	Asian:	4.2%	WWII and before:	17.2%	Voter turnout:	7,640,640
Native Am.:	0.3%	Other		Korea:	14.2%	Turnout as % of	
Hawaiian:	0.0%	European	8.3%	Vietnam:	29.8%	voting age:	50.7%
Two+ races:	1.1%	**Education**		Gulf (pre-2001):	7.2%	**Legislature**	
Ancestry		H.S. grad:	83.9%	Gulf (post-2001):	5.5%	Senate:	32 D 30 R
Italian:	11.8%	College grad:	31.2%	Peace time:	26.1%	Assembly:	109 D 41 R
Irish:	10.8%	Grad degree:	13.3%				
German:	9.6%						

Presidential politics   In the first half of the 20th century, New York was the most pivotal—indeed, arguably the dominant—state in presidential politics. It had the most electoral votes—45 from 1912–28, 47 from 1932–48, and 45 from 1952–60—and of all the large states, it was usually the most evenly divided between the two parties. New York, with 33 electoral votes in 2000, 31 in 2004 and 2008, and most likely 30 in 2012, has come to be the most heavily Democratic large state; in 2008, only Hawaii and Vermont cast higher percentages for presidential nominee Barack Obama. How did this come to pass? One reason is that Jewish voters, who did not identify strongly with either major party in the first half of the 20th century, became strong Democrats in the second. Increases in the percentages of black and Hispanic voters raised the Democratic percentage. White Catholic voters took conservative positions on cultural issues like crime and foreign policy in the 1970s and 1980s, one reason that Sen. James Buckley was elected on the Conservative Party line in 1970, that Republican Ronald Reagan won New

2008 Presidential Vote		
Obama (D-WF)	4,804,701	(63%)
McCain (R-Ind-C)	2,752,728	(36%)
2008 Democratic Presidential Primary		
Clinton (D)	1,068,496	(57%)
Obama (D)	751,019	(40%)
2008 Republican Presidential Primary		
McCain (R)	333,001	(50%)
Romney (R)	178,043	(27%)
Huckabee (R)	68,477	(10%)
Paul (R)	40,113	(6%)
2004 Presidential Vote		
Kerry (D-WF)	4,314,280	(58%)
Bush (R-C)	2,962,567	(40%)

York's electoral votes narrowly in 1980 and 1984, and that Republican George H. W. Bush was beaten by only 52%-48% in 1988. But today, these voters, or their descendants, are more likely to take liberal stands on cultural issues salient in the 1990s, such as gun control and abortion rights. In the past four elections, Democratic presidential nominees have won 60%, 60%, 58% and 63% of New York's votes.

The low point for Democrats was 2004, when George W. Bush's percentages rose sharply among Catholics, Latinos and Jews in response to his leadership after September 11. Obama ran weakly among all three groups in New York's presidential primary in February 2008. But in November, he won 59% of Catholics. Obama carried 36 of 62 counties and 25 of 29 congressional districts, and did not run below 46% of the vote in any of them.

New York Democrats have had presidential primaries since 1980; Republicans voted not for candidates but for slates of delegates through 2000. For 2008, New York scheduled regular primaries for both parties on February 5, Super Tuesday. It was one of more than a dozen states voting that day and got little attention from candidates (except for Park Avenue fundraisers) because New York's own, Clinton and Giuliani, were well ahead in polls. When Giuliani dropped out after the Florida primary on January 29, he endorsed Arizona Sen. John McCain, who went on to win New York's GOP primary on Super Tuesday.

Turnout in the Democratic primary was high, 1.9 million voters, beating the record of 1.5 million set in 1988, when Mayor Edward Koch's endorsement of Democrat Al Gore stirred angry talk from civil rights leader Jesse Jackson but did not prevent the victory of Democrat Michael Dukakis. In 2008, Clinton beat Barack Obama 57%-40%, carrying 26 of the 29 congressional districts—all but three heavily black districts in Brooklyn and Queens—and 61 of 62 counties, the exception being Tompkins County, home of Cornell University. Blacks tended to vote for Obama, but not unanimously. Jews, Latinos and white ethnics gave about two-thirds of their votes to Clinton. A little under half of all Democratic primary votes were cast in New York City, 18% in the four suburban counties and 30% upstate.

Republican turnout was only 670,000 voters, far fewer than the 2 million who voted for delegate slates in 2000. McCain beat Mitt Romney 50%-27%, carrying every county and congressional district and, with the Republicans' winner-take-all rule, winning all the delegates. Only 12% of Republican primary votes were cast in New York City; 25% came from the suburbs and 63% from upstate counties.

New York law allows third parties to cross-endorse major-party candidates, and once upon a time, third parties played a serious role in the state's politics. The Liberal Party and its predecessor, the American Labor Party, were founded to give Jewish garment workers a line on which to vote for Franklin D. Roosevelt for president but against local Tammany Hall candidates; the Liberal line was a help to Giuliani in the 1993 and 1997 mayoral elections. But in 2002, the Liberals lost their ballot position when their candidate for governor, Andrew Cuomo, received far fewer than the 50,000 votes required. The Conservative Party was formed in the 1960s to oppose Rockefeller Republicans and provided a line on the ballot for William F. Buckley Jr.'s quixotic run for mayor in 1965 and for his brother James Buckley's successful race for the U.S. Senate in 1970. It endorsed Republicans Alfonse D'Amato for the Senate and George Pataki for governor, but has had only spotty influence on local races since. The newest third party is the Working Families Party, formed in 1998 by labor unions and usually endorsing selected Democrats. The most successful recent third-party-line effort was Mayor Michael Bloomberg's creation of an Independent line to support his re-election as mayor in 2009.

Congressional districting

111th Congress Lineup	
26 D	3 R
110th Congress Lineup	
23 D	6 R

When John Kennedy was elected president in 1960, New York elected 43 members of Congress, California 30 and Texas 22. Now, New York elects 29 members of Congress, California 53 and Texas 32. Starting in 2012, according to projections, New York will elect 28 House members, California 53 and Texas 36. Reapportionment has been carnage time for New York. The state lost five districts in the 1980 census, another three in 1990 and two more in 2000. In 2002, as in 1992, New York produced a convoluted redistricting plan. New York has more than 200 state legislators, but legislative decisions are made by three powerful figures: the governor, Assembly speaker and Senate president. In 2002, they were Republican Pataki, Republican state Senate President Joseph Bruno and Democratic Assembly Speaker Sheldon Silver. Party discipline was so strong that Bruno and Silver could always deliver majorities, and Pataki had a veto. Although New York lost two seats that year, the census figures showed that most of the state's growth had come in New York City.

Frederick Lacey, a former federal judge, was appointed as a special master with orders to draft a plan that could be adopted if the Legislature failed to act. He presented a plan placing two pairs of upstate members—Republican Sherwood Boehlert and Democrat Maurice Hinchey, and Republican Jack Quinn and Democrat John LaFalce—in the same districts. A three-judge court adopted the plan, but gave the Legislature more time to act and said it would gladly accept the Legislature's plan if it offered one. The pressure was on. Silver wanted to protect Hinchey and other Democrats. Bruno got a call from Republican Vice President Dick Cheney urging him to deal, since the Lacey plan seemed to put some Republican seats at risk. The three political decision-makers decided to target Rochester Democrat Louise Slaughter and Republican Benjamin Gilman. Slaughter said she would run in the primary against Democrat LaFalce, and Gilman threatened to switch parties and run against Republican Sue Kelly. Still, the new plan was passed and signed June 5. Slaughter went to the court and asked it to adopt the Lacey plan, but the court accepted the Legislature's plan, and the Justice Department gave it clearance under the Voting Rights Act. LaFalce announced that he would not run against Slaughter. And Gilman, who was 79 and was serving his 30th year in the House, announced that he would retire. All the incumbents running were easily re-elected in 2002, except for 1st District Republican Felix Grucci, who lost for reasons that had nothing to do with redistricting.

New York is expected to lose just one seat in the 2010 census, but the political lineup will be different from that in 2002. Democratic Gov. David Paterson had exceedingly low poll ratings in early 2009, and the strongest candidate to succeed him seemed to be another Democrat, Attorney General Andrew Cuomo. Speaker Silver commands better than a 2-to-1 Democratic majority in the Assembly. But in early 2009, the state Senate was in flux. Democrats won a majority in 2008, but two crucial Democrats refused to support the party leader for Senate president. Of the House members who were in jeopardy in 2002, only Hinchey and Slaughter remain in Congress. Today Slaughter is the chairman of the House Rules Committee and likely will be untouchable. And the U.S. House delegation consists of 26 Democrats and only three Republicans. Provided they can agree, Democrats will probably be in control. They are unlikely to squeeze out incumbent Republicans Peter King in Long Island for fear of endangering adjacent Democrats. Another Republican, Christopher Lee, is a freshman from western New York, which lost population between 2000 and 2008. But targeting him might put another adjacent Democrat at risk, unless Slaughter, who turns 83 in 2012, chooses to retire. In that case, her heavily Democratic territory could be parceled out to strengthen Democrats in several districts.

Governor

David Paterson (D)

Assumed office March 2008, term expires 2010, 1st term; b. May 20, 1954, Harlem; home, Brooklyn; Columbia U., B.A., 1977, Hofstra U., J.D., 1982; Catholic; married (Michelle); 2 children.

Elected Office: NY St. Sen., 1985–2007, NY lt. gov, 2007–08.

Office: State Capitol, Albany, 12224, 518-474-8390; Fax: 518-474-1513; Web site: www.ny.gov/governor.

Election Results

2006 general	Eliot Spitzer (D-Ind-WF)	3,086,709	(70%)
	John Faso (R-C)	1,274,335	(29%)
2006 primary	Eliot Spitzer (D)	624,684	(82%)
	Tom Suozzi (D)	138,263	(18%)

Democrat David Paterson is the governor of New York and the first African-American to hold the office. Elected lieutenant governor in 2006, he unexpectedly ascended to the governorship on March 14, 2008, after Eliot Spitzer resigned in a prostitution scandal. Paterson was born in Brooklyn and grew up in Harlem in a powerful political family. His father, Basil Paterson, thrived in Harlem's Democratic machine as a longtime state senator and later as New York's secretary of state and the deputy mayor of New York City. The elder Paterson was for years one of Harlem's major political leaders, part of the "Gang of Four," which included U.S. Rep. Charles Rangel, Manhattan Borough President Percy Sutton and Mayor David Dinkins. The younger Paterson faced an unexpected challenge in childhood. As an infant, he contracted an ear infection that spread to his optic nerve and left him legally blind. His parents enrolled him in school on Long Island, where he could receive special education, and from there he went to Columbia and Hofstra University Law School.

Paterson followed his father into New York politics. In 1985, he worked on Dinkins's successful campaign for Manhattan borough president. The same year, he ran for the state Senate seat once held by his father and won. In the Legislature, he compiled a liberal voting record and earned a reputation as an approachable, good-humored dealmaker. In 1993, he ran for public advocate (the position formerly known as City Council president) and lost the Democratic primary to Mark Green. In 1995, he was elected deputy party leader in the Senate, where Democrats were in the minority. After the 2002 election, Paterson challenged and beat Minority Leader Martin Connor. The Senate for many years had been run more or less singlehandedly by the Republican Senate president. Paterson didn't challenge that arrangement, instead working amicably with GOP Senate President Joseph Bruno. He imposed new ethical guidelines on Democratic members, admonishing them not to direct state money toward sources with which they shared family or other ties. However, his success in getting financial help for North General Hospital, for which his wife worked as a registered lobbyist, seemed to run afoul of his own guidelines. He also worked to elect more Democrats, with considerable success: They gained one seat in 2004 and two seats in 2006, leaving them just two shy of a majority, which they achieved in 2008.

In 2006, the city's African-American leaders urged Attorney General Eliot Spitzer, who easily won the Democratic governor nomination, to choose a black running mate and recommended Leecia Eve, daughter of longtime Buffalo Assemblyman Arthur Eve. But the independent-minded Spitzer preferred Paterson. Loath to give up a chance at real power as Senate president if Democrats gained just two seats in 2008, Paterson initially resisted but ultimately agreed. The prospect also loomed of his being appointed to replace Democrat Hillary Rodham Clinton in the Senate should she be elected president. Then in March 2008, it was reported that Spitzer had patronized a prostitute at the Mayflower Hotel in Washington, D.C., and as a result had been caught in a Federal Bureau of Investigation probe of a prostitution ring. After three days of drama, Spitzer announced that he would resign. He delayed the effective date to give Paterson time to prepare. New Yorkers were suddenly introduced to a governor they knew little about. In his initial press conference, Paterson, determined to get scandal stories behind him, told them perhaps more than they wanted to know about his and his wife's extramarital affairs and his past drug use. He had warm words for Speaker Sheldon Silver and Senate President Bruno, who would be intimately involved in negotiating the state budget and other major issues.

In Paterson's early days as governor, the contrast with Spitzer's pugnacious style was vivid. The state faced a $4.6 billion shortfall, and an agreement with the legislative leaders was reached in time to meet deadlines. He startled some by calling for the state to recognize same-sex marriages entered into in other states, and he signed bills providing binding arbitration for Suffolk County police. In July 2008, with a looming shortfall of $5 billion, he called the Legislature back into session, and the two sides agreed to cut $1 billion over 18 months, although Silver and Senate President Dean Skelos (who had replaced Bruno after his indictment) opposed cuts in school funding. All the while, Paterson continued to be active politically. His support of Clinton in her presidential-primary fight with black Democrat Barack Obama of Illinois provoked some criticism by African-American politicians. Paterson's fundraising for Democratic state Senate candidates paid off when Democrats gained two seats and a Senate majority in November 2008 for the first time since 1965. But he suffered a setback when his close aide, Charles O'Byrne, resigned in October 2008 after it was revealed that he had failed to pay federal and state income taxes for five years.

New York's unusual system of party discipline and leadership control of both houses of the Legislature has yielded upward pressure on state spending, which, in the financial crisis of 2008, led to enormous fiscal challenges. The Democratic Assembly tended to favor high spending for New York City and its employees and Medicaid programs that have been a burden on upstate New York. The Republican state Senate tended to favor high spending on suburban school aid (to hold down high property taxes) and on state employees, many of whom are located in upstate communities. Democrats briefly gained control of the Senate after the 2008 elections, complicating the status quo, but then in June 2009, two disgruntled Democrats kicked off a power struggle when they announced they were defecting from their party and joining Republicans on organizational issues affecting party control of the chamber. That put Republicans back in command, at least for a few weeks, and Paterson was viewed in some quarters as out-of-the-loop and powerless to influence the outcome. The renegades ultimately returned to the fold and Democrats were back in control.

In November 2008, Paterson sought $5.2 billion in spending cuts over 16 months, mostly in health care and education. The state's total budget was $121 billion. In his State of the State speech to the Legislature in January 2009, Paterson warned of yet more belt-tightening to come, as protesters outside, including members of state employees' unions, blasted his budget cuts. "Hey hey, ho ho, Paterson's budget has got to go," they shouted. Inside the Capitol, Paterson said soberly: "The state of the state is perilous. Our economy is damaged. . . Our confidence is shaken." On other issues, he announced two initiatives, one to battle childhood obesity, which he called an "epidemic," and another on energy conservation. He called for a ban on trans fats in restaurants and for posting calorie counts in fast-food outlets. And he announced a plan for the state to meet 45% of its energy needs through renewable sources or conservation within 15 years.

Also in Paterson's early months as governor, he had the opportunity, and the burden, of appointing a U.S. senator who might serve for a long time. (Since direct election of senators came into being, no Democratic senator from New York has been defeated for re-election.) Paterson evidently considered appointing Attorney General Andrew Cuomo to the seat, which came open after President-elect Obama announced that he would nominate Clinton as secretary of State. That move would have eliminated Cuomo as a possible primary opponent in 2010, when Paterson had to stand for election. But then on December 3, Caroline Kennedy, the daughter of the iconic former president, indicated she was interested in the seat, and Paterson gave many indications that he would appoint her. But Kennedy performed weakly in upstate visits and in an interview with the *New York Times*. Republican U.S. Rep. Peter King of Long Island let it be known that he would oppose her in 2010, and other Democrats began threatening to run in the primary. By the end of December, Paterson complained that Kennedy's promoters had made it appear that he had made a choice and were trying to box him in. Then on January 21, Kennedy announced that she was withdrawing her name "for personal reasons." The next day, Paterson announced that he was appointing U.S. Rep. Kirsten Gillibrand of the 20th District to the Senate seat.

In 2008, Paterson started raising money for a 2010 campaign, yet by March 2009, his job ratings were the lowest in state history. Suburbanites were angry about cuts in school funding, New York City residents were angry about cuts in city aid, and leaders of public employee unions were angry about proposed layoffs and revisions in fringe benefits. The muddy process for appointing a senator did not help. Polls showed Cuomo beating Paterson by wide margins in a theoretical Democratic primary and Republican Rudy Giuliani, the former New York City mayor, leading Paterson in a general election, though running behind Cuomo.

Senior Senator

Charles Schumer (D)

Elected 1998, term expires 2010, 2nd term; b. Nov. 23, 1950, Brooklyn; home, Brooklyn; Harvard U., B.A. 1971, J.D. 1974; Jewish; married (Iris Weinshall); 2 children.

Elected Office: NY Assembly, 1974–80; U.S. House of Reps., 1980–1998.

DC Office: 313 HSOB, 20510, 202-224-6542; Fax: 202-228-3027; Web site: schumer.senate.gov.

State Offices: Albany, 518-431-4070; Binghamton, 607-772-6792; Buffalo, 716-846-4111; Hudson Valley, 914-734-1532; Long Island, 631-753-0978; New York City, 212-486-4430; Rochester, 585-263-5866; Syracuse, 315-423-5471.

Committees: *Democratic Conference Vice Chairman. Banking, Housing & Urban Affairs* (4th of 13 D): Financial Institutions; Housing, Transportation & Community Development; Securities, Insurance & Investment. *Finance* (8th of 13 D): Health Care; Social Security, Pensions & Family Policy; Taxation, IRS Oversight & Long-Term Growth. *Joint Economic Committee* (1st of 6 D). *Judiciary* (5th of 12 D): Administrative Oversight & the Courts; Antitrust, Competition Policy & Consumer Rights; Crime & Drugs; Immigration, Refugees & Border Security (Chmn); Terrorism & Homeland Security. *Rules & Administration* (Chmn of 11 D).

Group Ratings

	ADA	ACLU	AFS	LCV	ITIC	NTU	COC	ACU	CFG	FRC
2008	100	86	100	91	100	2	63	4	0	0
2007	90	—	100	93	—	7	55	0	6	—

National Journal Ratings

	2007 LIB — 2007 CONS		2008 LIB — 2008 CONS	
Economic	89%	— 10%	77%	— 13%
Social	78%	— 21%	91%	— 0%
Foreign	79%	— 17%	65%	— 6%
Composite	83%	— 17%	86%	— 14%

Key Votes of the 110th Congress

1. Raise CAFE standards	Y	5. Make English official language	N
2. Expand SCHIP	Y	6. Path to citizenship	Y
3. Cap greenhouse gases	Y	7. Fetus is unborn child	N
4. Bail out financial markets	Y	8. Prosecute hate crimes	Y

9. Withdraw troops 3/08	Y
10. Iran guard is terrorist group	Y
11. Increase missile defense $	N
12. Overhaul FISA	N

Election Results

2004 general	Charles Schumer (D-Ind-WF) 4,769,824	(71%)	($15,467,530)
	Howard Mills (R)...1,625,069	(24%)	($628,578)
2004 primary	Charles Schumer (D) .... unopposed		

Prior Winning Percentages: 1998 (55%); 1996 House (75%); 1994 House (73%); 1992 House (89%); 1990 House (80%); 1988 House (78%); 1986 House (93%); 1984 House (72%); 1982 House (79%); 1980 House (77%)

Democrat Charles Schumer is New York's senior senator, first elected in 1998. He grew up in Flatbush, Brooklyn, where his father had a small exterminating business. Schumer graduated first in his class at James Madison High School, the alma mater of Supreme Court Justice Ruth Bader Ginsburg. It's safe to say that Schumer was interested in politics from the start. He graduated from Harvard College and Law School and, with his law degree fresh in hand in June 1974, he immediately began running for an open New York Assembly seat. He won, at age 23, becoming the state's youngest Assembly member since Theodore Roosevelt. In 1980, just before turning 30, he was elected to the U.S. House from an open Brooklyn seat. Through energy, imagination, hard work, and a certain amount of chutzpah, he became a skilled legislator and a politician noted—and sometimes resented—for attracting publicity. (Former presidential candidate and Sen. Bob Dole of Kansas was one of the first to say that the most dangerous place to be in Washington was between Schumer and a television camera.)

Schumer got a seat on the Banking Committee, a panel that most talented members lobby to leave. But like another talented member of the class of 1980, Democrat Barney Frank of Massachusetts, he stayed on, aware of its importance to New York's financial industry. Schumer did some of his most noteworthy work on the Judiciary Committee, where he eventually chaired the Crime Subcommittee. Schumer sponsored the 1994 crime bill that banned assault weapons and shepherded President Bill Clinton's proposal to add 100,000 police officers across the country. The legislation also created "three strikes" mandatory life terms for repeat violent criminals. Schumer was the House sponsor of the Brady bill, which created waiting periods for handgun purchases and was passed over the strong opposition of the National Rifle Association. Schumer also contributed key provisions to the immigration acts in 1986 and 1990.

The idea of running for statewide office was surely never far from his mind. In 1997, Schumer considered seeking the governorship, but by April of that year, Gov. George Pataki's strong job ratings persuaded Schumer to use his $5 million campaign treasury to run instead against Republican Sen. Alfonse D'Amato. It was by no means obvious that Schumer would win. D'Amato was known for his assiduous constituent service and for his ability to dominate the tabloid wars that are a mainstay of metropolitan New York political campaigns. D'Amato was chairman of the Senate Banking Committee and excelled at raising money. Schumer started off largely unknown outside his district, and he faced serious primary opposition from Geraldine Ferraro, the 1984 vice presidential nominee, and Mark Green, the New York City public advocate and D'Amato's 1986 opponent. By summer, Schumer was leading in polls and was much better financed than his rivals; in September, he won the primary with 51% of the vote.

In the general election campaign, Schumer immediately launched an attack on D'Amato, saying that the incumbent had told "too many lies for too long," which echoed D'Amato's earlier criticisms of his opponents as "too liberal for too long." Schumer maintained that he was tougher on crime than D'Amato, and he emphasized his support of abortion rights and gun regulation. D'Amato concentrated heavily on Schumer's missed votes while running for Senate, but the implication that the high-voltage Schumer was lazy was implausible. Still, by mid-October, most of Schumer's poll leads were less than the statistical margin of error. Then, in a closed meeting before a Jewish group, D'Amato called Schumer a "putzhead," Yiddish slang for "jerk." When the remark became public, he denied it, before backtracking unconvincingly after his own supporter, former Democratic Mayor Edward Koch, confirmed it. D'Amato lost momentum, and by early November, was sagging in the polls. Schumer had announced in October that he would vote against impeaching Clinton, although he said he believed that the president lied under oath about a sexual relationship with White House intern Monica Lewinsky. Schumer was the beneficiary of two visits from Clinton and no less than four from Hillary Rodham Clinton (the rousing receptions she got may have encouraged her to run for the Senate in New York two years later). Although outspent, Schumer won 55%-44%.

In the Senate, Schumer established a solidly liberal voting record. And he honed his skills for hogging the limelight. Schumer makes a practice of visiting all 62 counties each year, and he regularly spends Mondays on upstate swings that get him on Buffalo, Rochester, Syracuse, and Albany television. He holds regular Sunday press conferences, to take advantage of the slow news digest that day, a tactic that often gets him coverage on television news programs and in the Monday editions of newspapers.

Schumer gladly returned to work on financial services issues with a seat on the Banking Committee. He supported the 1999 Gramm-Bliley-Leach bill eliminating the barriers between banks and investment banks, and in 2001 he joined Republican Sen. Phil Gramm of Texas in successfully halving the fees paid by Wall Street firms to the Securities and Exchange Commission. In 2002, Schumer played a key role in scuttling a Republican bankruptcy bill by persuading the Senate to pass an amendment that made fines and penalties for attacking abortion clinics not dischargeable in bankruptcy cases; abortion-rights opponents were increasingly declaring bankruptcy to avoid paying such fines. Abortion opponents in the House refused to vote for the bill as long as it contained Schumer's amendment. The bill died but was revived in 2005. This time, Schumer's abortion amendment was voted down, 53-46, in the Senate, and the bill was ultimately enacted. He long opposed moves to toughen regulation of the government-sponsored mortgage institutions, Fannie Mae and Freddie Mac, citing the rising rate of homeownership and the possibility of increased interest rates. In 2007, Schumer called for increasing the limit on their investment in mortgage-backed securities by 10%, or $145 billion, but that move was defeated. Schumer also opposed taxing the carried interest income of hedge-fund operators. He has proposed establishing an Office of Identity Theft in the Federal Trade Commission to set minimum security standards. Despite his opposition to many Bush administration policies, he strongly supported some Bush nominees—former Republican Rep. Christopher Cox for appointment to the SEC in July 2005 and Goldman Sachs chief executive officer Henry Paulson Jr. as Treasury secretary in June 2006.

On the Judiciary Committee, Schumer argued that senators should reject Bush appointees on "purely ideological grounds." Starting with the nomination of Miguel Estrada to the U.S. Court of Appeals, he led the opposition to Bush judicial nominees whom he and liberal lobbying groups judged to be out of the mainstream. Schumer, along with other Democrats, used the filibuster to block the appointment of federal judges who enjoyed majority support, forcing the nominee to earn 60 votes to be confirmed. He took strong exception to Senate Republicans who advocated changing the rules to allow nominations to be considered by majority vote. In 2005, Schumer tried to pin down Supreme Court nominee John Roberts in committee hearings and was one of 22 senators who later voted against him and noted later, "Roberts was quite stealthy, but he was so brilliant he could pull it off." When Bush nominated Samuel Alito in 2005, Schumer said he was "sad that the president felt he had to pick a nominee likely to divide America" and wondered "whether [Alito] would use that seat to reverse much of what Rosa Parks and so many others fought so hard and for so long to put in place." In 2007, Schumer pounced on the Bush administration's firings of seven U.S. attorneys around the country, demanding the resignation of Attorney General Alberto Gonzales. However, also that year, he voted for Michael Mukasey as attorney general, although the nominee declined to say whether he considered waterboarding terrorism suspects a form of torture.

Schumer played a major role in shepherding recovery money through Congress after the September 11 attacks. On that fateful day in 2001, Schumer's daughter was in school a few blocks from the World Trade Center, although she was unharmed. He immediately requested $20 billion in aid for New York, which Bush readily approved. The Bush administration then turned to Schumer to rally support for its centerpiece anti-domestic terrorism law, the USA PATRIOT Act. More generally, Schumer has secured federal grants for all manner of projects for New York, ranging from an ambulance for the volunteer fire department in St. Lawrence County to funding for tritium cleanup at the Brookhaven National Laboratory. Schumer gets along well with New York City Mayor Michael Bloomberg, the nominal Republican. Schumer's wife, Iris Weinshall, was Bloomberg's transportation commissioner and in 2004, Bloomberg endorsed Schumer for re-election.

Schumer has been a prodigious fundraiser since his early days in the House. In 2004, his money skills enabled him to raise nearly $12 million and ward off a serious challenge to his re-election. Constant traveling in upstate New York also made him as well known there as in New York City. The 2004 Republican nominee, Assembly member Howard Mills, was little known and poorly financed, and Schumer won easily, 71%-24%, exceeding the 67%-31% record set by Democrat Daniel Patrick Moynihan in 1988. Schumer won 66% of the vote in the suburbs, 63% in upstate, and 86% in the city. No Democratic incumbent has been defeated in New York since the direct election of senators began (although seven incumbent Republicans have lost).

Some speculated that Schumer would run for governor in 2006, but that issue was settled when he agreed to accept Democratic Leader Harry Reid's appointment as chairman of the Democratic Senatorial Campaign Committee and got a seat on the powerful Finance Committee to boot. The task ahead looked difficult. The lineup of Senate seats up in 2006 left Republicans with more target seats than Democrats. But Schumer did a brilliant job of persuading Democratic incumbents from states that Bush carried in 2004—Jeff Bingaman of New Mexico, Kent Conrad of North Dakota, Ben Nelson of Nebraska, and Bill Nelson of Florida—not to retire. Then he worked on getting strong challengers to Republican incumbents. In Pennsylvania, he aggressively recruited state Treasurer Bob Casey Jr., son of the late governor who is known for his strong opposition to abortion rights. Schumer calculated that Casey would make inroads in the culturally conservative base of incumbent Republican Rick Santorum and would be acceptable to abortion-rights voters in suburban Philadelphia. Abortion-rights groups that had worked closely with Schumer on the Judiciary Committee protested to no avail. Casey ran and won by a wide margin. Schumer made a pitch over dinner in London to Claire McCaskill to compete in Missouri, where she had shown some strength in her losing 2004 gubernatorial race. She ran and won narrowly. He tried to recruit U.S. Rep. Jim Langevin to enter in Rhode Island, and although he declined, Democrat Sheldon Whitehouse beat incumbent Lincoln Chafee, a moderate Republican, anyway. In Montana, Schumer spent money on ads against incumbent Republican Conrad Burns, reminding voters that he had received more contributions from the clients of disgraced lobbyist Jack Abramoff than any other member of Congress. Campaign committee chairmen rarely make endorsements in seriously contested primaries, but Schumer did so in Virginia, where he backed Jim Webb, a decorated Vietnam veteran who served as President Reagan's Navy secretary, over liberal lobbyist Harris Miller. Webb won a narrow victory in the primary and went on to defeat incumbent Republican George Allen, who had been heavily favored to win the general election.

Schumer also deftly exploited issues. The award of a contract to United Arab Emirates' Dubai Ports World to manage major U.S. ports aroused little interest at first; Schumer, however, held a press conference in New York in February 2006, after which such Republicans as Sen. Tom Coburn of Oklahoma and House Homeland Security Chairman Peter King of New York expressed reservations about the deal, and the deal was eventually halted. During the campaign, Schumer wrote a book, *Positively American: Winning Back the Middle-Class Majority One Family at a Time*, in which he urged Democrats to offer 50% solutions—increase math and reading scores by 50%, cut property taxes by 50%, reduce illegal immigration by 50%, and so forth. But he didn't press his candidates to adopt these issues. He did advise them to campaign against the perceived incompetence of the Bush administration.

Schumer's success in helping to win a Democratic majority in 2006 impelled Reid to ask him to lead the DSCC again in the 2008 election season. As an inducement, Reid created a leadership position for Schumer as vice chairman of the Democratic Caucus, although the new post did not come with a staff and detailed portfolio. Schumer effectively became the confidential adviser of the hotheaded and sometimes contradictory Reid of Nevada and of the mellifluous but sometimes malapropism-prone Majority Whip Dick Durbin of Illinois. And, once again, he played a key role in producing winning candidates at election time. When Republican Pete Domenici announced his retirement in New Mexico and second-tier Democratic candidates emerged, Schumer persuaded U.S. Rep. Tom Udall to run, and he won. Late in the election season, he and Reid persuaded Anchorage Mayor Mark Begich to take on 40-year veteran Sen. Ted Stevens after Stevens was indicted in July and convicted in October of failure to disclose receiving gifts. Stevens's conviction was overturned in April 2009, but that was after Begich had won his seat, 48%-47%, in November. In North Carolina, Schumer and former Gov. Jim Hunt pressed state Sen. Kay Hagan to take on incumbent Elizabeth Dole and helped Hagan wage an aggressive, upstart campaign that resulted in an impressive victory. Schumer's incapacity for embarrassment also served him well. With Wall Street as a constituency, he was among the first senators to support the $700 billion bailout for financial services firms in September 2008. The DSCC then financed ads criticizing Republicans who supported it.

All told, Democrats picked up six seats in 2006 and seven in November 2008 while losing none. A 45-seat minority became, pending the dispute in the exceedingly close 2008 Minnesota contest, a 58- or 59-seat majority. (Ultimately, Democrats won the Minnesota seat and picked up a seat in Pennsylvania when incumbent Sen. Arlen Specter switched parties in 2009, giving them a filibuster-proof 60.) In at least five of those races, Schumer arguably made the difference, urging reluctant candidates to run or tipping the balance in favor of the stronger candidate in a primary. A less proactive, less politically savvy chairman might have produced a Senate with about 53 Democrats, rather than one with close to 60—a huge difference in the political balance. Seldom has one senator made such a difference in the partisan composition of the body. And seldom if ever has the No. 3 person in a party's leadership done as much to determine his party's policy stands or political positioning in the Senate. As Texas Republican John Cornyn said ruefully but with admiration, "In my opinion his influence is supreme. He's everywhere."

Schumer's position in New York politics is also paramount. When Hillary Rodham Clinton was elected senator in 2000, many thought that she would overshadow Schumer. The earthier Schumer seemed to get along better with Bush, while the more disciplined Clinton seemed to get along better with some Republican senators. And then there are the lifestyle differences. While Clinton held fundraisers in her $2.8 million house in Georgetown, Schumer shares a spare Capitol Hill townhouse with Durbin and Democratic U.S. Reps. Bill Delahunt of Massachusetts and George Miller of California. But Schumer supported Clinton's 2008 presidential campaign, and her appointment as secretary of State in the Obama administration made him indisputably New York's lead senator. Schumer provided helpful mentoring to Clinton's replacement, Democratic U.S. Rep. Kirsten Gillibrand, who was appointed to the Senate seat by Gov. David Paterson. Schumer told reporters that Gillibrand's conservative stands on gun control and other issues were representative of an upstate constituency and would be modified as she sought support from a more liberal statewide electorate in the 2010 election.

Schumer likely has earned several footnotes in history, but one of them is that he is one of three Americans to have cast two votes on the impeachment of the same president. The other two are Mike Crapo of Idaho and Jim Bunning of Kentucky. All three are former members of the House who were elected to the Senate in 1998. Schumer voted against impeaching Clinton in the House in December 1998 and against conviction in the Senate in February 1999.

Junior Senator

Kirsten Gillibrand (D)

Appointed Jan. 2009, term expires 2010, 1st term; b. Dec. 9, 1966, Albany; home, Hudson; Dartmouth Col., A.B. 1988, U.C.L.A., J.D. 1991; Catholic; married (Jonathan); 2 children.

Elected Office: U.S. House of Reps., 2006- 09

Professional Career: Practicing atty, 1991–2006; Special counsel, HUD, 2000.

DC Office: 478 RSOB, 20510, 202-224-4451; Fax: 202-228-0282; Web site: gillibrand.senate.gov.

State Offices: Albany, 518-431-0120; Buffalo, 716-854-9725; Hudson Valley, 845-875-4585; Long Island, 631-249-2825; New York City, 212-688-6262; North Country, 315-376-6118; Rochester, 585-263-6250; Syracuse, 315-448-0470; Westchester, 914-725-9294.

Committees: *Aging (Special)* (10th of 13 D). *Agriculture, Nutrition & Forestry* (12th of 12 D). *Environment & Public Works* (11th of 12 D). *Foreign Relations* (11th of 11 D): East Asian & Pacific Affairs; International Development & Foreign Assistance, Economic Affairs & International Environmental Protection; International Operations & Organizations, Democracy & Global Women's Issues; Western Hemisphere, Peace Corps & Global Narcotics Affairs.

Group Ratings (House)

	ADA	ACLU	AFS	LCV	ITIC	NTU	COC	ACU	CFG	FRC
2008	70	90	100	69	86	21	69	23	9	5
2007	95	—	100	95	—	7	60	8	12	—

National Journal Ratings (House)

	2007 LIB — 2007 CONS		2008 LIB — 2008 CONS	
Economic	64% —	34%	55% —	45%
Social	54% —	46%	46% —	52%
Foreign	57% —	43%	*% —	*%
Composite	59% —	41%	*% —	*%

Key Votes of the 110th Congress (House)

1. Increase minimum wage	Y	5. Share immigration data	Y	9. Withdraw troops 8/08	Y
2. Expand SCHIP	Y	6. Foreign aid abortion ban	N	10. No operations in Iran	Y
3. Raise CAFE standards	Y	7. Ban gay bias in workplace	Y	11. Free trade with Peru	Y
4. Bail out financial markets	N	8. Repeal D.C. gun law	Y	12. Overhaul FISA	Y

Election Results

2006 general	Hillary Rodham Clinton (D-Ind-WF)	3,008,428	(67%)	($34,358,255)
	John Spencer (R-C)	1,392,189	(31%)	($5,660,688)
2006 primary	Hillary Rodham Clinton (D)	640,955	(84%)	
	Jonathan Tasini (D)	124,999	(16%)	

Democrat Kirsten Gillibrand is New York's junior senator. She had been in the House for just one term when Democratic Gov. David Paterson in 2009 appointed her to the Senate seat vacated by Secretary of State Hillary Rodham Clinton. Gillibrand (*JILL-uh-brand*) hails from a politically sophisticated family. Her father, Douglas Rutnik, is an attorney and lobbyist who had close ties to Zenia Mucha, a top aide to former Republican Gov. George Pataki. Her grandmother, Polly Noonan, was a prominent Democratic activist in Albany and longtime companion of Albany Mayor Erastus Corning (1942–83). Her grandmother used to bring Gillibrand along with her on the campaign trail. Gillibrand attended the all-girls Emma Willard School in Troy and graduated from Dartmouth College, where she majored in Asian studies. She traveled widely, worked as a summer intern for Republican Sen. Alfonse D'Amato, graduated from law school at the University of California (Los Angeles), and did a United Nations internship in Vienna, Austria. After law school, Gillibrand clerked for a Reagan-appointed federal Appeals Court judge and served briefly as special counsel for Housing and Urban Development Secretary Andrew Cuomo. She then joined a major New York law firm, Boies, Schiller & Flexner. Gillibrand raised money for Clinton's first Senate campaign in 2000.

In 2005, she launched a quixotic campaign against four-term U.S. Rep. John Sweeney, a rising Republican star with a seat on the Appropriations Committee, who had never faced a serious re-election challenge. With hard work but also a lot of luck, Gillibrand won the seat. Although Sweeney was a strong incumbent, he developed some serious vulnerabilities during the campaign. He missed several weeks of House votes after he was hospitalized in February 2006 for the treatment of vasculitis, an inflammation of the blood vessels. He got negative press about a fundraising event in Utah that included a ski vacation and dinner at the home of a pharmaceutical lobbyist. In April 2006, there were more negative news stories, including accounts of Sweeney's visit to a college fraternity party. He denied college newspaper reports that he had been intoxicated. The state Democratic Party issued a press release asking, "What is a 50-year-old congressman doing at a frat party at 1 a.m.?"

Still, as late as August, polls showed Sweeney with a solid lead. He called Gillibrand a carpetbagger who lived not in the Hudson Valley-based congressional district but in a Manhattan high-rise. He also accused her campaign of making anonymous and intimidating phone calls to his wife. He emphasized his independence from the unpopular Bush administration and contrasted his working-class background with Gillibrand's prep-school pedigree. Gillibrand did plenty of negative campaigning of her own. She demanded that Sweeney release police reports from two arrests in 1977 and 1978 and from a 2001 automobile accident; he called on her to release her income-tax returns. In October, it was revealed that Sweeney had traveled to the Northern Mariana Islands with Tony Rudy, an associate of disgraced lobbyist Jack Abramoff, who pleaded guilty to conspiracy charges in a scandal that involved several congressional junkets to the islands. Then, one week before the election, the Albany *Times Union* reported that Sweeney's wife had called local police in December 2005 to complain that the congressman was "knocking her around." Sweeney's campaign at first insisted that the police report on the incident was "false and concocted by our opposition," but he eventually conceded that state police were called to his home.

Sweeney had spent $3.4 million to Gillibrand's $2.6 million. But in a year when Clinton and Democratic Gov. Eliot Spitzer were heading to landslide statewide victories and Republicans were dragged down by Bush, Gillibrand won 53%-47%.

When she arrived in the House, Gillibrand began posting a "Sunlight Report" of her daily schedule, including meetings with lobbyists. She held "office hours" in grocery stores throughout the district. She got the committee seats she wanted—on Agriculture and Armed Services. On the issue of Iraq, she voted for a nonbinding resolution calling for withdrawing troops but also for a bill providing funding for the war without a timetable for troop withdrawal. She cast conservative votes on gun-related issues, compiling a 100% score from the National Rifle Association. Gillibrand said she grew up in a family of hunters and "always believed in protecting hunters' rights. . . . It's a core value for our region and our state." She opposed driver's licenses for illegal immigrants and voted for a controversial bill granting immunity to telecommunications companies that had cooperated with government requests for warrantless surveillance of U.S. citizens' communications.

Defending the seat for the first time in 2008, Gillibrand did prodigious fundraising and collected $4.6 million. Her opponent was state Republican Chairman Sandy Treadwell, who spent nearly $6 million of his own money on his campaign. But Gillibrand's moderate-to-conservative stands on issues paid off. She won 62%-38%.

After the election, she pushed for a seat on the prestigious Ways and Means Committee, ahead of the more senior Rep. Brian Higgins of New York. Her unmasked ambition raised eyebrows even in the ambition-saturated Congress, and House Speaker Nancy Pelosi turned her down for Ways and Means.

When Clinton was named President-elect Barack Obama's choice for secretary of State, Gillibrand was not the first person to spring to mind as a likely successor to Clinton. Gov. Paterson, who had ascended to the state's top job after Spitzer resigned amid a prostitution scandal, considered appointing New York Attorney General Cuomo, which would have removed Cuomo as a possible primary opponent to Paterson in 2010. But then, on December 3, 2008, Caroline Kennedy, the daughter of the late president, indicated she was interested in the seat. Paterson gave her selection serious thought. But Kennedy performed weakly in series of upstate public appearances and in an interview with *The New York Times*. Other Democrats began to hint at running against her in the primary. On January 21, 2009, Kennedy withdrew "for personal reasons."

Two days later, Paterson announced that he was appointing Gillibrand, a surprise pick considering that several more-prominent state political figures and more-senior House members were interested. But arguing in Gillibrand's favor was her moderate politics on some issues, which may play well statewide when she and Paterson stand for election in 2010. She has more-traditional liberal stances on other issues, like her support for abortion rights and gay marriage, which will appeal to loyal Democrats. The announcement was made in Albany, with former Sen. D'Amato and several current Democratic members of the U.S. House in attendance. Conspicuously absent were several politicians who had wanted the job: Cuomo and House Democrats Higgins, Steve Israel, Carolyn Maloney, and Jerrold Nadler.

On January 27, Gillibrand was sworn in as the youngest U.S. senator. "I realize that for many New Yorkers this is the first you've heard my name and you don't know much about me," said the 42-year-old. "Over these next two years, you will get to know me. But much more importantly, I will get to know you." She held early meetings with Paterson, Clinton, and Charles Schumer, New York's senior senator and a member of the Democratic leadership. Soon afterward, Gillibrand began modifying some of her positions that are out of step with the party's liberal mainstream, particularly on gun control. "There're a lot of concerns in many of our city communities about gun violence, about keeping our children safe, and keeping guns out of the hands of criminals," she said. And Schumer noted that Gillibrand's old district is "more like Montana than New York City." Gillibrand promised to work with Democratic Rep. Carolyn McCarthy, a staunch gun control proponent, on gun legislation. But, with the vast majority of the state's Democratic primary votes cast in New York City, an upstate Democrat such as Gillibrand, with a history of moderate votes, may well attract a serious primary opponent. On the Republican side, Rep. Peter King in early 2009 was contemplating running. Also early in 2009, *The New York Times* published an unflattering front-page article that said Gillibrand, as a lawyer for Philip Morris in 1996, helped defend the tobacco company against allegations that it lied about the existence of internal research on the health effects of smoking.

Gillibrand holds a seat occupied by distinguished predecessors going back half a century—Clinton, Daniel Patrick Moynihan, James Buckley, Robert Kennedy, Kenneth Keating, and Irving Ives. Moynihan and Kennedy were Democrats, Keating and Ives were Republicans, and Buckley belonged to the Conservative Party.

FIRST DISTRICT

Tim Bishop (D)

Elected 2002, 4th term; b. June 1, 1950, Southampton; home, Southampton; Holy Cross Col., A.B. 1972; Long Island U., M.P.A. 1981; Catholic; married (Kathy); 2 children.

Professional Career: Admin., Southampton College, 1973–2002.

DC Office: 306 CHOB, 20515, 202-225-3826; Fax: 202-225-3143; Web site: www.house.gov/timbishop/.

State Offices: Coram, 631-696-6500; Southampton, 631-259-8450.

Committees: *Budget* (21st of 24 D). *Education & Labor* (15th of 29 D): Higher Education, Lifelong Learning & Competitiveness; Workforce Protections. *Transportation & Infrastructure* (17th of 44 D): Coast Guard & Maritime Transportation; Highways & Transit; Water Resources & Environment.

Group Ratings

	ADA	ACLU	AFS	LCV	ITIC	NTU	COC	ACU	CFG	FRC
2008	85	91	100	100	100	7	71	0	4	11
2007	95	—	100	100	—	6	55	0	6	—

National Journal Ratings

	2007 LIB	—	2007 CONS	2008 LIB	—	2008 CONS
Economic	78%	—	18%	71%	—	25%
Social	77%	—	17%	74%	—	25%
Foreign	86%	—	11%	83%	—	15%
Composite	83%	—	18%	77%	—	23%

Key Votes of the 110th Congress

1. Increase minimum wage	Y	5. Share immigration data	N	9. Withdraw troops 8/08	Y
2. Expand SCHIP	Y	6. Foreign aid abortion ban	N	10. No operations in Iran	Y
3. Raise CAFE standards	Y	7. Ban gay bias in workplace	Y	11. Free trade with Peru	Y
4. Bail out financial markets	Y	8. Repeal D.C. gun law	*	12. Overhaul FISA	Y

Election Results

2008 general	Tim Bishop (D-Ind-WF)	162,083	(58%)	($1,478,623)
	Lee Zeldin (R-C)	115,545	(42%)	($864,720)
2008 primary	Tim Bishop (D-Ind-WF)	unopposed		

Prior Winning Percentages: 2006 (62%); 2004 (56%); 2002 (50%)

Population		Race/Ethnicity		Work	
Pop. 2007:	676,805	White:	81.9%	Private:	74.4%
Change since 2000:	Up 3.4%	Black:	4.0%	Government:	19.7%
Urban:	94.0%	Hispanic:	9.4%	Self-employed:	5.7%
Rural:	6.0%	Asian:	3.3%	Blue collar:	18.5%
Area size:	1,944 sq. mi.	Native Am.:	0.1%	White collar:	65.2%
Age		Hawaiian:	0.0%	Khaki collar:	0.1%
Median age:	38.8 yrs.	Two+ races:	1.1%	Other:	16.3%
More than 65 yrs:	12.9%	*Ancestry*		Median income:	$79,231
Less than 18 yrs:	24.3%	Italian:	22.5%	Median home value:	$424,800
Education		Irish:	18.8%	Poverty:	6.0%
H.S. grad:	90.1%	German:	13.7%	**Military Veterans**	
College grad:	31.9%			% of Pop:	9.3%
Grad degree:	14.7%				

Long Island—"the Island" to most New Yorkers—is the largest and most populous island in the mainland United States. It stretches 103 miles, from the two-century-old Montauk Point lighthouse on a crumbling bluff at its eastern extremity to Fort Hamilton at the foot of the Verrazano-Narrows Bridge. Ranging from 12 to 20 miles wide, Long Island is ringed by gentle hills and cliffs above Long Island Sound and sand-spit beaches that front the Atlantic Ocean. Including the populations of

2008 Presidential Vote
Obama (D) 165,805   (52%)
McCain (R).............................153,419   (48%)

2004 Presidential Vote
Bush (R) 154,249   (49%)
Kerry (D)................................152,165   (49%)

Cook Partisan Voting Index: Even

Brooklyn and Queens, some 7.5 million people live on Long Island, more than in all but 12 states. Brooklyn, at the island's western end, is urban and thickly settled, while the Hamptons in the east are carefully manicured countryside, preserved as a playground for the New York elite. Demographically, the Hamptons are only a small part of Long Island. More important economically are the suburbs created in the post-World War II migration out of the city.

Developers looking for cheaper land for aircraft factories, shopping centers, subdivisions, and office parks found them first in Nassau County, just east of Queens, and then farther out in Suffolk County. Suffolk attracted young families of Irish and Italian descent looking for more space and less crime. More recently the county has been attracting Latinos, who are now 13% of the population and include Salvadorans and Puerto Ricans in lower-income areas. Over the past 30 years, the island's economy soured as defense plants were decimated by the end of the Cold War, cost overruns on nuclear plants led to electricity rate increases, and young people fled older suburbs for jobs elsewhere. The Bush administration's defense buildup resulted in a temporary increase in defense jobs at Northrop Grumman, and the Long Island Power Authority wants to build wind farms and run underwater cables from Connecticut to bring more energy across Long Island Sound. High taxes and expensive housing remain endemic problems.

The 1st Congressional District of New York consists of the eastern end of Long Island and covers eastern Suffolk County. It runs as far west as Smithtown on the North Shore and Patchogue on the South Shore. It includes Shelter Island, located between the north and south forks of Long Island's "fishtail," and Plum Island, which houses the nation's only animal infection research site, operated by the Homeland Security Department but scheduled to be closed in 2015 and replaced by a lab in Kansas. A few farmers remain on Long Island, where they grow sweet corn and pumpkins. The 1st District includes two areas frequented in the summer by urban sophisticates: the Hamptons, with their extravagant prices, and most of Fire Island National Seashore, the only federal wilderness area in New York state and a magnet for gay vacationers for decades. The district also includes Brookhaven National Laboratory, a physics research lab, and the defense plants in the center of the Island. Suffolk County was long one of the most conservative parts of New York, though not very conservative by today's national standards. Republican voter registration remains robust, despite the district's trending Democratic in recent presidential elections. The district voted solidly for Democrat Al Gore in 2000 but swung narrowly to Republican George W. Bush in 2004—a September 11 effect. It backed Democratic nominee Barack Obama in 2008.

The representative from the 1st District is Tim Bishop, a Democrat elected in 2002. He grew up in Southampton, the son of a telephone lineman, and graduated from Holy Cross College and Long Island University. He spent his entire professional career at Southampton College, where he began in 1973 as an admissions counselor and by 1986 had become provost. He chaired the town of Southampton's Board of Ethics and was on the board of the Eastern Long Island Coastal Conservation Alliance. Few paid much attention when Bishop announced he would oppose Rep. Felix Grucci, the first-term Republican who had won the seat in 2000. That year, Mike Forbes, a Republican elected in 1994 as part of the GOP revolution, lost the low-turnout Democratic primary by 35 votes to Regina Seltzer after he switched from the Republican Party and became a Democrat. The turn of events allowed Grucci to easily win the general election, 56%-41%.

Grucci seemed headed for re-election in 2002 when, in late September, he ran an ad accusing Bishop of falsifying rape statistics at Southampton College and "turning his back on rape victims." This turned out to be untrue. The basis for the allegations was several college newspaper articles riddled with inaccuracies. Grucci's campaign refused to repudiate the ad, on the ground that no correction had ever appeared in print. National Democrats saw an opportunity to pick up a seat, and soon the airwaves were saturated with ads attacking Grucci both for the rape commercial and for his voting record on the environment. In one spot, the Grucci family's famed fireworks enterprise was linked to the chemical contamination of local drinking water. Republican operatives privately fumed that Grucci had failed to tell them about the college rape ad and that he had blundered in failing to offer a positive message. Bishop won 50%-49%.

In the House, Bishop compiled a voting record near the center of House Democrats. He opposed the war in Iraq and supported abortion rights and a rollback of the Bush tax cuts. With his extensive background in academia, he played a leading role on the Education and Labor Committee in the 2008 higher education bill that enacted spending increases for colleges and universities. And he has championed more federal funding to help schools adapt to the demands of the 2001 No Child Left Behind law. Bishop lobbied for $100 million for Long Island schools in the economic stimulus bill enacted in February 2009. With California Democrat Hilda Solis, he won passage of an amendment in 2005 to bar the Environmental Protection Agency from testing pesticides on humans. One of his key issues is adjusting the alternative minimum tax to stop it from ensnaring middle-class taxpayers; the tax was created to ensure that the wealthy pay at least some taxes.

On local issues, Bishop successfully fought proposed cutbacks at Brookhaven and sought funds for a third track on the Long Island Railroad. Like other members of Congress representing vacation spots, he has sought to increase seasonal worker visas. Mindful of the high turnover rate in the district in recent years, Bishop has paid close attention to constituent services.

Republicans think of Bishop as a prime target, but they have not been able to seriously threaten him in recent elections. In 2004, their nominee was Bill Manger, who served four years as a village trustee in Southampton. He emphasized his independence from national Republicans and attacked Bishop for opposing tax cuts. But Bishop won handily, 56%-44%. Since then, he has won twice, barely breaking a sweat against political novices who were too conservative for the area. Voting trends in the state and on the Island are going Bishop's way.

SECOND DISTRICT

Steve Israel (D)

Elected 2000, 5th term; b. May 30, 1958, Brooklyn; home, Dix Hills; George Wash. U., B.A. 1983; Jewish; married (Marlene Budd); 2 children.

Elected Office: Huntington Town Council., 1993–2000, Maj. ldr., 1997–2000.

Professional Career: Legis. asst., U.S. Rep. Richard Ottinger, 1980–83; Fundraising dir., Touro Law Ctr., 1985–88; Pres., Steve Israel Assoc., Inc., 1992–98; Pres. & CEO, Inst. on Holocaust and Law, 1998–2000.

DC Office: 2457 RHOB, 20515, 202-225-3335; Fax: 202-225-4669; Web site: www.house.gov/israel.

State Offices: Long Island, 631-951-2210.

Committees: *Appropriations* (30th of 37 D): Energy, Water Development & Related Agencies; Military Construction, Veterans Affairs & Related Agencies; State, Foreign Operations & Related Programs.

Group Ratings

	ADA	ACLU	AFS	LCV	ITIC	NTU	COC	ACU	CFG	FRC
2008	95	100	100	100	100	7	61	0	0	11
2007	85	—	100	100	—	6	58	0	13	—

National Journal Ratings

	2007 LIB	—	2007 CONS		2008 LIB	—	2008 CONS
Economic	63%	—	36%		71%	—	25%
Social	74%	—	26%		67%	—	28%
Foreign	81%	—	19%		69%	—	30%
Composite	73%	—	27%		71%	—	29%

Key Votes of the 110th Congress

1. Increase minimum wage	Y	5. Share immigration data	N	9. Withdraw troops 8/08	Y
2. Expand SCHIP	Y	6. Foreign aid abortion ban	N	10. No operations in Iran	*
3. Raise CAFE standards	Y	7. Ban gay bias in workplace	Y	11. Free trade with Peru	Y
4. Bail out financial markets	Y	8. Repeal D.C. gun law	N	12. Overhaul FISA	N

Election Results

2008 general	Steve Israel (D-Ind-WF)	161,279	(67%)	($1,436,880)
	Frank Stalzer (R-C)	79,641	(33%)	($15,500)
2008 primary	Steve Israel (D-Ind-WF)	unopposed		

Prior Winning Percentages: 2006 (70%); 2004 (67%); 2002 (58%); 2000 (48%)

Population		Race/Ethnicity		Work	
Pop. 2007:	670,944	White:	67.5%	Private:	78.9%
Change since 2000:	Up 2.5%	Black:	10.5%	Government:	15.6%
Urban:	99.7%	Hispanic:	16.7%	Self-employed:	5.4%
Rural:	0.3%	Asian:	4.1%	Blue collar:	18.4%
Area size:	330 sq. mi.	Native Am.:	0.2%	White collar:	66.2%
Age		Hawaiian:	0.0%	Khaki collar:	0.0%
Median age:	38.2 yrs.	Two+ races:	0.9%	Other:	15.5%
More than 65 yrs:	12.3%	*Ancestry*		Median income:	$85,847
Less than 18 yrs:	25.9%	Italian:	20.0%	Median home value:	$460,400
Education		Irish:	14.3%	Poverty:	5.0%
H.S. grad:	88.3%	German:	10.6%	**Military Veterans**	
College grad:	33.5%			% of Pop:	8.1%
Grad degree:	14.8%				

Shortly after World War II, hundreds of thousands of New York City residents, many of them young veterans and their families, moved to detached suburban houses built on the former potato fields of central Long Island. Those in the first wave of postwar migration settled in Nassau County, and they included a cross-section of all but the poorest New Yorkers. About half were Catholic, a quarter Protestant, and a quarter Jewish. As Long Island developed its own employment base, another wave

2008 Presidential Vote

Obama (D)	164,106	(56%)
McCain (R)	125,978	(43%)

2004 Presidential Vote

Kerry (D)	148,625	(53%)
Bush (R)	127,626	(45%)

Cook Partisan Voting Index: D+4

moved farther east into Suffolk County. This group was more Catholic, less Jewish, and more blue-collar. Ancestrally Democratic, these voters were culturally conservative, and in the 1970s and 1980s, they tended to vote Republican. Since then, voters in Suffolk County have joined the rest of the New York metro area in shunning the Republican Party as it has increasingly drifted to the right.

The 2nd Congressional District of New York includes most of western Suffolk County, part of the town of Islip and a small portion of Nassau County—Plainview, Woodbury, and part of Jericho. For the most part, the 2nd is the humbler part of Long Island: farther east than most of the fashionable commuter suburbs, well south of the picturesque North Shore, not as far east as the ritzy Hamptons, and, aside from a handful of ferry-only resort towns on Fire Island, located inland from the southern shore. With some of the lowest-priced housing on the Island, this area has been attracting minorities and immigrants. Brentwood, settled in 1851 as part of a free-love social experiment that lasted 13 years, is now more than half Hispanic. Once a destination for Puerto Ricans, it also has attracted large numbers of Salvadorans, Guatemalans, and Mexicans. Illegal immigration has been a divisive issue in Suffolk. In 2006, officials barred day laborers from loitering on public roads while looking for work. Historically Republican, the 2nd District has not voted for a Republican presidential nominee since 1992. In 2008, Democrat Barack Obama won it with 56% of the vote.

The congressman from the 2nd District is Steve Israel, a Democrat first elected in 2000. He grew up in Wantagh and graduated from George Washington University in 1983. While in college, he worked full-time on Capitol Hill, first doing constituent work for Democratic Rep. Robert Matsui of California, and then as a legislative assistant for Rep. Richard Ottinger of New York, also a Democrat. After college, Israel returned to Long Island, where he was Suffolk director for the American Jewish Congress, fundraising director for Touro Law School, and assistant for intergovernmental relations to Suffolk County Executive Patrick Halpin for three years. Then he started his own public-relations and marketing firm and was president of the Institute on the Holocaust and the Law. In 1993, Israel was the only Democrat elected to the Huntington Town Council, where he built a reputation as a bipartisan leader who helped revive the town's finances. After Republican U.S. Rep. Rick Lazio announced he was running for the Senate, Israel ran for Lazio's seat and squeaked out a 45%-41% victory in the Democratic primary. In the general election, he faced Republican Joan Johnson, who had a compelling life story as a 66-year-old who grew up under segregation, moved to New York to become a schoolteacher, and later was elected town clerk of Islip. She would have been the first black Republican woman elected to Congress. She also had the Suffolk County GOP's supposed organizational muscle behind her. But despite help from Lazio, Johnson was a disappointing candidate. She pulled a television ad attacking Israel for voting to raise taxes after Israel protested that he had opposed tax increases. Israel won by a surprisingly easy 48%-35%.

In the House, Israel's voting record is moderate and a tad more liberal on cultural issues. In an early sign of his dexterity with House politics, he was elected as the freshman representative to the Democratic Steering Committee, which makes the all-important committee assignments. Israel joined the fiscally conservative Blue Dog Coalition and was one of 28 House Democrats who voted for President George W. Bush's tax cuts in 1981. Israel supported the use of force in Iraq but later said that the case for war was based on a "false pretense." After irritating Democratic leaders by voting for the Republicans' prescription drug bill in 2002 because of a provision that increased annual Medicare payments on Long Island, Israel redeemed himself with his party when he voted against the GOP's Medicare prescription drug bill in 2003.

Israel believes that national Democrats can learn something from the successes of centrist Democrats on Long Island. They prevailed locally, he said, by taking positions that protected national security, balanced government budgets, and championed civil and human rights. The party icon, Israel added, should be former Sen. Scoop Jackson of Washington, a defense hawk in the 1960s and 1970s, whose views are hardly in today's Democratic mainstream. In internal party politics, he favored Maryland's Steny Hoyer over California's Nancy Pelosi for minority whip as Pelosi was beginning her climb up the leadership. Pelosi won that contest, and went on to become House speaker. Although both are liberal, Hoyer is more conservative on defense issues than Pelosi.

In 2007, Israel snagged a seat on the powerful House Appropriations Committee, useful for delivering federal dollars back home, and a sign that he had mended fences with Pelosi. On the committee, he promoted international human rights and pushed for additional funds for renewable energy. With Rep. Jay Inslee, D-Wash., in January 2009 he formed the Sustainable Energy and Environment Coalition to promote climate-change legislation and more funding for green technology projects. He also has a "next generation" energy plan designed to reduce the nation's dependence on foreign energy sources. Israel joined the select intelligence oversight panel on Appropriations, where he voiced concern about the anti-Israel views of Charles Freeman, who was nominated to chair President Barack Obama's National Intelligence Council. Under pressure, Freeman withdrew.

When Lazio decided not to run again for this seat in March 2002, local Republicans grumbled about his delay in deciding, and quietly threw in the towel. Israel won 58%-40% and since then, he has become increasingly secure in the seat. After Sen. Hillary Rodham Clinton resigned to become secretary of State in 2009, Israel was among the names discussed as a possible successor. But he did not line up as well in polling as others considered by Gov. David Paterson, including U.S. Rep. Kirsten Gillibrand, who got the appointment. Disappointed, Israel talked openly about challenging Gillibrand in the 2010 Democratic primary for the Senate seat. In the House, he won additional assignments, including as head of candidate recruiting for the Democratic Congressional Campaign Committee in 2009.

THIRD DISTRICT

Peter King (R)

Elected 1992, 9th term; b. April 5, 1944, Manhattan; home, Seaford; St. Francis Col., B.A. 1965, U. of Notre Dame, J.D. 1968; Catholic; married (Rosemary); 2 children.

Military Career: Army Natl. Guard, 1968–73.

Elected Office: Hempstead Town Cncl., 1977–81; Nassau Cnty. comptroller, 1981–92.

Professional Career: Practicing atty., 1968–72, 1978–81; Dep. atty., Nassau Cnty., 1972–74; Exec. asst., Nassau Cnty. exec., 1974–76, Gen. cnsl., comptroller, 1977.

DC Office: 339 CHOB, 20515, 202-225-7896; Fax: 202-226-2279; Web site: peteking.house.gov.

State Offices: Massapequa Park, 516-541-4225; Suffolk County, 631-541-4225.

Committees: *Financial Services* (3rd of 29 R): Capital Markets, Insurance & Government Sponsored Enterprises; Financial Institutions & Consumer Credit. *Homeland Security* (RMM of 13 R). *Intelligence (Select)* (9th of 9 R)

Group Ratings

	ADA	ACLU	AFS	LCV	ITIC	NTU	COC	ACU	CFG	FRC
2008	45	18	43	23	100	43	94	50	36	88
2007	30	—	27	30	—	45	90	68	50	—

National Journal Ratings

	2007 LIB — 2007 CONS		2008 LIB — 2008 CONS	
Economic	42%	— 58%	36%	— 64%
Social	27%	— 72%	43%	— 56%
Foreign	0%	— 72%	39%	— 60%
Composite	28%	— 72%	40%	— 60%

Key Votes of the 110th Congress

1. Increase minimum wage	Y	5. Share immigration data	Y	9. Withdraw troops 8/08	N
2. Expand SCHIP	Y	6. Foreign aid abortion ban	Y	10. No operations in Iran	N
3. Raise CAFE standards	N	7. Ban gay bias in workplace	N	11. Free trade with Peru	Y
4. Bail out financial markets	Y	8. Repeal D.C. gun law	N	12. Overhaul FISA	Y

Election Results

2008 general	Peter King (R-Ind-C)	172,774	(64%)	($875,084)
	Graham Long (D-WF)	97,525	(36%)	($42,361)
2008 primary	Peter King (R)	6,847	(88%)	
	Robert Previdi (R)	897	(12%)	

Prior Winning Percentages: 2006 (56%); 2004 (63%); 2002 (72%); 2000 (60%); 1998 (64%); 1996 (55%); 1994 (59%); 1992 (50%)

Population		Race/Ethnicity		Work	
Pop. 2007:	640,423	White:	83.4%	Private:	77.1%
Change since 2000:	Down 2.1%	Black:	2.7%	Government:	17.5%
Urban:	99.6%	Hispanic:	8.2%	Self-employed:	5.2%
Rural:	0.4%	Asian:	4.6%	Blue collar:	15.6%
Area size:	393 sq. mi.	Native Am.:	0.2%	White collar:	70.2%
		Hawaiian:	0.1%	Khaki collar:	0.0%
Age		Two+ races:	0.7%	Other:	14.2%
Median age:	41.6 yrs.	*Ancestry*		Median income:	$87,066
More than 65 yrs:	14.7%	Italian:	24.4%	Median home value:	$473,900
Less than 18 yrs:	22.9%	Irish:	18.1%	Poverty:	4.6%
Education		German:	12.3%	**Military Veterans**	
H.S. grad:	91.4%			% of Pop:	8.9%
College grad:	35.5%				
Grad degree:	14.8%				

September 1947 was a pivotal moment in American history: 300 families moved into 750-square-foot houses that sold for $6,990, with no money down for veterans. The location was Levittown—America's first mass-produced suburb, where delivery trucks dropped off piles of prefabricated materials 60 feet apart, to be picked up by roving teams of specialized workers with power tools. By the time the final house was sold for $9,500 in November 1951, Levittown, a former potato field, had become synony-

2008 Presidential Vote

McCain (R)	164,682	(52%)
Obama (D)	149,995	(47%)

2004 Presidential Vote

Bush (R)	162,181	(52%)
Kerry (D)	147,317	(47%)

Cook Partisan Voting Index: R + 4

mous with instant suburbanization. Southern State Parkway, the road that drew New York City's working- and middle-class families out to Long Island, was originally constructed in the 1920s by the legendary city-builder Robert Moses as a way of linking New Yorkers, at least those affluent enough to own a car, with the newly constructed Jones Beach State Park. Three decades later, Moses widened the parkway to accommodate the growing ranks of long-distance commuters who populated Long Island's bedroom communities and worked in New York City. More than a half-century later, aging Nassau County is all but built out and is sometimes referred to as the nation's "first mature suburb." Its population, 450,000 in 1940, zoomed to 1.4 million in 1970. In recent years, it has stabilized at 1.3 million.

As the prototype suburb, Nassau County created what may have been the nation's premier county Republican machine. Among other pols, it produced three-term Sen. Alfonse D'Amato, a former Hempstead supervisor. The GOP-run county government, which was one of the highest-salaried, highest-spending in America, thrived until the late 1990s, when fiscal laxity dropped the county's credit rating to near junk-bond status despite tax rates that were among the highest in the country. Voters rebelled in 1999, by giving Democrats their first-ever majority in the county legislature, and in 2001, by electing

Democrat Thomas Suozzi as county executive. He shook up the local government and agreed to abide by the bipartisan legislative majority.

The 3rd Congressional District of New York includes roughly half of Nassau County. It covers much of the southern shoreline of Long Island, taking in the old railroad resort of Long Beach, plus Baldwin, Merrick, and Massapequa in Nassau County; and Amityville, Lindenhurst, most of Babylon, Bay Shore, and Islip in Suffolk County. Nearly one-fourth of the district's population lives in Suffolk County. The district runs north all the way to Long Island Sound, where old estates—including Sagamore Hill, the home Theodore Roosevelt built on Cold Spring Harbor in 1885—alternate with more-modest homes and newer subdivisions. Most of the people in the district live in towns strung along either side of Sunrise Highway or just off the Southern and Northern State parkways: Levittown, Syosset, Hicksville (home to Billy Joel), and Bethpage (home to a major Northrop Grumman facility). For a district so close to New York City, its minority population remains low. Although few of Greater New York's wealthiest live in the 3rd District, the overall level of affluence is high. Democratic presidential nominee Al Gore carried the district 52%-44% in 2000, but it broke for Republican George W. Bush in 2004, 52%-47%. In 2008, Republican nominee John McCain beat Democratic nominee Barack Obama by an identical 52%-47%.

The congressman from the 3rd District is Peter King, a Republican elected in 1992. King grew up in Sunnyside, Queens. His parents were Irish immigrants and Democrats, his father a New York City police detective. He went to St. Francis College and law school at the University of Notre Dame, and he clerked one summer at former Republican President Richard Nixon's law firm with a Long Islander named Rudolph Giuliani. After law school, he followed the trek to the suburbs and became part of the Nassau County Republican machine. He worked as a lawyer and staffer in county government beginning in 1972, and in 1981, he became county comptroller. When 22-year Republican Rep. Norman Lent retired in 1992, King ran for the seat and won the Republican primary. In the general election, King ran as a political insider, fiscal conservative, and abortion-rights opponent. He won by just 50%-46%. He has not faced a close re-election since.

King's voting record ranks him near the ideological center of the House. He is more conservative on foreign-policy issues than on economic or social ones, but with distinctive interests. He opposes abortion rights, racial quotas and preferences, bilingual education, and gun regulation. He supports English-only laws and opposes aid to illegal immigrants. He has been an ardent supporter of the Irish Republican Army. Within days of his election in 1992, he flew to Belfast to meet with leaders of Sinn Fein, the IRA's political arm, and he had a role in 1998 peace negotiations carrying messages between the IRA and the Irish government. His activism on the issue led to an unusually close bipartisan relationship with President Bill Clinton, who helped broker the agreement. But in 2005, after Sinn Fein's suspected involvement in a bank robbery and a highly publicized murder, King called for the IRA to disband. He often seemed more comfortable with Democrats and labor leaders—the sort of people he dealt with in Nassau County—than with Southern or Western Republicans. Over the years, King has been a provocative presence on radio and television chat shows. He also gained attention with two novels about politics and diplomacy in Northern Ireland. In one of them, *Deliver Us From Evil*, a thinly disguised Long Island congressman is the protagonist.

After the September 11 attacks, in which 160 of his constituents died, King became more of a Republican Party regular and focused on legislation to prevent a repeat of the attacks. After Republican Rep. Christopher Cox of California resigned to become chairman of the Securities and Exchange Commission in 2005, GOP leaders tapped King to succeed him as chairman of the Homeland Security Committee. A major part of his job, he said, was to "articulate the Republican view on homeland security." In 2006, he was the first House Republican to attack the Bush administration's plan to give control of six major U.S. ports to a company in Dubai in the United Arab Emirates, and he subsequently helped to enact tighter controls on port security. During the debate over illegal immigration in 2007 and 2008, King criticized Democrats, including Speaker Nancy Pelosi, who called for an end to federal raids of work sites known to employ illegal aliens. "We need more enforcement, not less," he said. In 2009, he bucked his friends in organized labor by opposing their "card-check" bill to facilitate union organizing by requiring employers to recognize a union if it persuades a majority of workers to sign union authorization cards. Secret-ballot elections would be held only if they were requested by the unions, which would have little incentive to do so. King originally supported the controversial bill but cited "the most severe economic crisis in 75 years" to explain his switch.

As one of the few remaining moderate Republicans in Congress, King has decried the party's losses of local offices in Nassau County and said that the GOP had "no overwhelming vision or course." Freshman Nassau County legislator David Mejias, a Democrat, ran against King in 2006 with an endorsement from the AFL-CIO. He sought to link King to President Bush and "special interests." But in an otherwise dismal year for New York Republicans, King won 56%-44%, providing evidence of his hold on his district. He had another easy win in 2008.

FOURTH DISTRICT

Carolyn McCarthy (D)

Elected 1996, 7th term; b. Jan. 5, 1944, Brooklyn; home, Mineola; Glen Cove Nursing Schl., L.P.N. 1964; Catholic; widowed; 1 child.

Professional Career: Nurse, 1964–93; Gun control activist, 1993–96.

DC Office: 2346 RHOB, 20515, 202-225-5516; Fax: 202-225-5758; Web site: carolynmccarthy.house.gov.

State Offices: Garden City, 516-739-3008.

Committees: *Education & Labor* (8th of 29 D): Health, Employment, Labor & Pensions; Healthy Families & Communities (Chmn). *Financial Services* (15th of 42 D): Capital Markets, Insurance & Government Sponsored Enterprises; Financial Institutions & Consumer Credit.

Group Ratings

	ADA	ACLU	AFS	LCV	ITIC	NTU	COC	ACU	CFG	FRC
2008	95	91	100	100	100	7	65	0	0	11
2007	90	—	100	100	—	6	58	0	7	—

National Journal Ratings

	2007 LIB	—	2007 CONS		2008 LIB	—	2008 CONS
Economic	67%	—	31%		64%	—	35%
Social	77%	—	23%		75%	—	18%
Foreign	78%	—	22%		70%	—	25%
Composite	74%	—	26%		72%	—	28%

Key Votes of the 110th Congress

1. Increase minimum wage	Y	5. Share immigration data	N	9. Withdraw troops 8/08	Y
2. Expand SCHIP	Y	6. Foreign aid abortion ban	N	10. No operations in Iran	Y
3. Raise CAFE standards	Y	7. Ban gay bias in workplace	Y	11. Free trade with Peru	Y
4. Bail out financial markets	Y	8. Repeal D.C. gun law	N	12. Overhaul FISA	Y

Election Results

2008 general	Carolyn McCarthy (D-Ind-WF)	164,028	(64%)	($1,520,492)
	Jack Martins (R-C)	92,242	(36%)	($496,029)
2008 primary	Carolyn McCarthy (D-Ind-WF)	unopposed		

Prior Winning Percentages: 2006 (65%); 2004 (63%); 2002 (56%); 2000 (61%); 1998 (53%); 1996 (57%)

Population		Race/Ethnicity		Work	
Pop. 2007:	647,082	White:	56.1%	Private:	77.7%
Change since 2000:	Down 1.1%	Black:	18.9%	Government:	17.0%
Urban:	100.0%	Hispanic:	17.1%	Self-employed:	5.0%
Rural:	0.0%	Asian:	6.1%	Blue collar:	16.7%
Area size:	103 sq. mi.	Native Am.:	0.1%	White collar:	66.8%
		Hawaiian:	0.0%	Khaki collar:	0.1%
Age		Two+ races:	1.1%	Other:	16.5%
Median age:	39.0 yrs.	*Ancestry*		Median income:	$80,700
More than 65 yrs:	13.9%	Italian:	16.6%	Median home value:	$465,800
Less than 18 yrs:	24.0%	Irish:	11.9%	Poverty:	5.8%
Education		German:	7.6%		
H.S. grad:	86.6%			**Military Veterans**	
College grad:	35.5%			% of Pop:	6.8%
Grad degree:	14.7%				

By the mid-20th century, Nassau County had changed from being almost entirely rural to being almost entirely suburban. One of its first suburbs was Garden City, with its wide avenues and single-family homes. It was founded in 1869 by New York City retailer A.T. Stewart at a time when urban planners were urging that new communities retain the commercial vitality and social interaction of the city within a setting that preserved the healthful openness of the countryside. After World War II,

2008 Presidential Vote
Obama (D) 171,346   (58%)
McCain (R)............................122,166   (41%)

2004 Presidential Vote
Kerry (D)...............................153,546   (55%)
Bush (R) 124,617   (44%)

Cook Partisan Voting Index: D + 6

freeways replaced highways, and shopping centers sprang up at intersections. But many of the middle- and upper-income residents there continue to depend on the Long Island Railroad to speed them to jobs in New York City. Garden City has maintained high real estate prices and is surrounded by some of Nassau County's key institutions: the county seat of Mineola; Hofstra University in Hempstead; and Roosevelt Field, where Charles Lindbergh took off for Paris (it's now a shopping center). In November 2008, officials announced plans to turn the former Northrup-Grumman complex in Bethpage into a high-technology industrial site.

The 4th Congressional District of New York comprises Garden City and the towns around it. The district takes in several suburbs just north of the Jericho Turnpike—New Hyde Park, Mineola, Westbury—as well as a large swath of southern Nassau County east of the Queens County line. This territory includes Hempstead, Uniondale, Rockville Center, and ethnically diverse Valley Stream, as well as the "Five Towns"—the railway suburbs of Lawrence, Inwood, Cedarhurst, Hewlett, and Woodmere—many of which have more elementary and high school students in private schools (mostly yeshivas) than in public schools. Nassau County has traditionally been Republican, and both Garden City and heavily Catholic East Meadow remain that way. But the Five Towns are heavily Democratic, and more than a third of the district's residents are African-Americans or Hispanics who generally vote Democratic. Elmont, near the Queens line and once heavily white, now has a large Caribbean and Latin American population. The traditional Republican heritage in the 4th District is becoming a dim memory. The county legislature is now led by a Democratic majority, something that would have seemed unimaginable just a few decades ago. Democratic presidential nominee Barack Obama won easily here in 2008.

The congresswoman from the 4th District is Carolyn McCarthy, a Democrat elected in 1996. She was born in Brooklyn, trained as a nurse, and then married and raised a family on Long Island. Originally, she was a Republican, but her life and politics changed dramatically in 1993. That year, her husband, Dennis, a stockbroker, was killed and her adult son, Kevin, was seriously injured in the "Long Island Railroad Massacre." A gunman opened fire on passengers riding a commuter train as it crossed the Nassau County line. McCarthy spoke movingly at the killer's trial, and her strength in tragedy won many admirers. She began campaigning for gun control laws and, in 1995, lobbied her congressman, Republican Daniel Frisa, to vote against repeal of the assault weapons ban. After Frisa voted for repeal, McCarthy inquired about running against him in the GOP primary. When Nassau County Republicans discouraged her, Democrats who had been eyeing the seat for some time recruited her. Initially, McCarthy knew little about politics. When told that Minority Leader Dick Gephardt wanted to meet her, she reportedly asked, "Who's Dick Gephardt?" But she learned quickly. As the Democratic nominee, she called for stricter gun laws and attacked Frisa as too close to Republican House Speaker Newt Gingrich, a Georgia conservative. Frisa abruptly stopped campaigning the week before the election, did not show up at his election night party, and never made a concession statement. McCarthy won 57%-41%.

In the House, McCarthy has a voting record that is one of the least liberal among New York Democrats, especially on economic issues and on some foreign-policy issues. She backed the use of force in Iraq in 2002, and she voted for a Republican resolution supporting the war in 2006.

On guns, however, she has remained committed to liberal positions. She has called for childproof locks on handguns, fines for parents of children who get possession of handguns, and mandatory jail terms for crimes committed with guns. The House approved her bill to help states gain more access to the federal background check system for gun buyers. The 2002 sniper spree in the Washington, D.C., area gave her the opportunity to gain approval in the House of her bill—the Our Lady of Peace Act—to strengthen laws prohibiting the mentally ill from buying guns and requiring states to file records with the national background check system. In 2004, she led an unsuccessful effort to force a House vote on extending the assault weapons ban. Then-GOP Majority Leader Tom DeLay said there were not enough votes to extend the ban and refused to schedule a vote; McCarthy criticized President George W. Bush for "winking" at the National Rifle Association on the issue, but she also blamed Democrats for their lack of support. She has also called for a ban on .50-caliber sniper rifles.

With only limited success on gun issues, McCarthy has broadened her portfolio, using her experience as a mother and nurse to become active in education and health care. In 2002, Bush signed her bill giving incentives to hospitals to hire more nurses to remedy acute shortages. She chairs the Education and Labor Subcommittee on Healthy Families and Communities, which deals with issues ranging from child nutrition and gang violence to low-income energy assistance. In March 2009, she sponsored a bill to boost federal support for early child care. Also in 2009, she was the House sponsor of the successful Serve America Act, a bill sponsored by Democratic Sen. Edward Kennedy of Massachusetts that represented a significant expansion of national service opportunities. It triples the number of federally supported volunteers to 250,000 and establishes new service corps for clean energy, education, health care, and veterans' services.

McCarthy had a tougher than usual re-election in 2002, when she was challenged by ophthalmologist Marilyn O'Grady, a Republican who took a hard line on terrorism and immigration and opposed abortion rights. She also ran ads criticizing McCarthy for taking a 1998 contribution from actress and singer Barbra Streisand. Although O'Grady received little party support, she held McCarthy to a 56%-43% victory. Since then, McCarthy has been re-elected easily. She strongly criticized the appointment of Democratic Rep. Kirsten Gillibrand to fill the Senate seat vacated by Secretary of State Hillary Rodham Clinton of New York. She cited Gillibrand's "awful" record on gun control. She has some influential ties to the Obama White House. Her former chief of staff, Jim Messina, is Obama's deputy chief of staff.

FIFTH DISTRICT

Gary Ackerman (D)

Elected Mar. 1983, 13th full term; b. Nov. 19, 1942, Brooklyn; home, Jamaica Estates; Queens Col., B.A. 1965; Jewish; married (Rita); 3 children.

Elected Office: NY Senate, 1978–83.

Professional Career: Jr. high schl. teacher, 1966–70; Editor & publisher, *Queens Tribune*, 1970–78; Pres., advertising agcy., 1972–78.

DC Office: 2243 RHOB, 20515, 202-225-2601; Fax: 202-225-1589; Web site: www.house.gov/ackerman.

State Offices: Bayside, 718-423-2154.

Committees: *Financial Services* (8th of 42 D): Capital Markets, Insurance & Government Sponsored Enterprises; Financial Institutions & Consumer Credit. *Foreign Affairs* (2nd of 28 D): Asia, the Pacific & the Global Environment; Middle East & South Asia (Chmn).

Group Ratings

	ADA	ACLU	AFS	LCV	ITIC	NTU	COC	ACU	CFG	FRC
2008	100	91	100	100	100	5	67	0	0	5
2007	90	—	100	85	—	5	55	0	11	—

National Journal Ratings

	2007 LIB	—	2007 CONS		2008 LIB	—	2008 CONS
Economic	76%	—	23%		85%	—	0%
Social	87%	—	12%		59%	—	38%
Foreign	74%	—	25%		85%	—	8%
Composite	80%	—	21%		81%	—	20%

Key Votes of the 110th Congress

1. Increase minimum wage	Y	5. Share immigration data	*	9. Withdraw troops 8/08	Y
2. Expand SCHIP	Y	6. Foreign aid abortion ban	N	10. No operations in Iran	N
3. Raise CAFE standards	Y	7. Ban gay bias in workplace	Y	11. Free trade with Peru	Y
4. Bail out financial markets	Y	8. Repeal D.C. gun law	Y	12. Overhaul FISA	Y

Election Results

2008 general	Gary Ackerman (D-Ind-WF)	112,724	(71%)	($988,775)
	Elizabeth Berney (R)	43,039	(27%)	($24,367)
2008 primary	Gary Ackerman (D-Ind-WF)	unopposed		

Prior Winning Percentages: 2006 (100%); 2004 (71%); 2002 (92%); 2000 (68%); 1998 (65%); 1996 (64%); 1994 (55%); 1992 (52%); 1990 (100%); 1988 (100%); 1986 (77%); 1984 (69%); 1983 (49%)

Population		Race/Ethnicity		Work	
Pop. 2007:	649,534	White:	41.1%	Private:	81.0%
Change since 2000:	Down 0.7%	Black:	4.2%	Government:	11.3%
Urban:	100.0%	Hispanic:	24.3%	Self-employed:	7.4%
Rural:	0.0%	Asian:	28.9%	Blue collar:	17.3%
Area size:	85 sq. mi.	Native Am.:	0.1%	White collar:	62.9%
		Hawaiian:	0.0%	Khaki collar:	0.0%
Age		Two+ races:	0.8%	Other:	19.8%
Median age:	40.5 yrs.			Median income:	$59,705
More than 65 yrs:	15.7%	*Ancestry*		Median home value:	$602,400
Less than 18 yrs:	19.9%	Italian:	9.9%	Poverty:	10.2%
		Irish:	5.5%		
Education		Russian:	3.7%	**Military Veterans**	
H.S. grad:	81.3%			% of Pop:	4.7%
College grad:	36.1%				
Grad degree:	15.0%				

Queens is to most Americans the mystery borough, little explored even by many Manhattanites, although it contains both LaGuardia and John F. Kennedy airports. Some of it is almost suburban: Bayside, Douglaston, and Little Neck are upper-middle-income neighborhoods far beyond the subway lines, with detached houses with driveways and views across the water. Other Queens neighborhoods are more modest, with houses crowded together and plain-Jane apartment buildings lining

2008 Presidential Vote
Obama (D) 128,158   (63%)
McCain (R)..............................73,125   (36%)

2004 Presidential Vote
Kerry (D)................................128,252   (63%)
Bush (R) 74,635   (36%)

Cook Partisan Voting Index: D + 12

the avenues. In the past two decades, Queens has become the No. 1 immigrant destination in New York City. Corona was once predominantly Italian and African-American (Louis Armstrong, Duke Ellington, and Malcolm X lived here). Today, there is a large Latin American community, with many Dominican immigrants and also many Asians—a modern-day melting pot. Flushing, long a modest-income Jewish and white ethnic neighborhood, is now the biggest Asian neighborhood in the city. West of 138th Street, Queens is dominated by Taiwanese and ethnic Chinese from Malaysia, Vietnam, and Thailand; shops have a more urban "Chinatown" feel and feature an amazing variety of delicacies. (New York City has three Chinatowns—one each in Manhattan, Brooklyn, and the largest in Queens.) East of 138th Street is predominantly Korean, with development following a more suburban pattern. As Chinese businesses moved into Flushing's Main Street commercial strip, Korean storeowners moved east to Union Street, a major north-south artery, and to Northern Boulevard. In most of the years since 2004, the area has been represented in the state Assembly by either Chinese businessman Jimmy Meng from Flushing or his daughter, Grace Meng. The city's most ambitious Asian politician may be City Council member John Liu of Flushing, who ran for city comptroller in 2009. Just east of Flushing and its large new condominium development is Flushing Meadow, the huge drainage basin and former dumping ground that hosted two World's Fairs (1939 and 1964) and now is home to the U.S. Open tennis tournament, a new Mets baseball park, and endless pickup soccer games played among Queens' many immigrant groups.

Just a few miles but a world away is the North Shore of Long Island. For a century it has had an upper-crust ambiance—peninsulas jutting out into Long Island Sound, vast green lawns, and the great capitalist mansions that inspired East Egg and West Egg in *The Great Gatsby*. In the 19th century, millionaires commuted from Manhattan to their estates on steam yachts. During Prohibition, the richest people in business and entertainment spent their leisure time playing croquet while their servants unloaded bootleggers' shipments at private docks. By the middle of the 20th century, the city had encroached, and the Great Neck and Sands Point peninsulas became affluent, predominantly Jewish suburbs with stately Tudor homes. Lately, many wealthy Asians have moved here.

The 5th Congressional District of New York takes in this territory in Queens and suburban Nassau County. The district includes most of Queens east of Flushing Meadow and north of Union Turnpike—Flushing, Bayside, Douglaston, Little Neck (but not the airports). And it includes the northwest corner of Nassau County—Great Neck, super-rich Sands Point, Lake Success, Port Washington, and Kings Point, home of the U.S. Merchant Marine Academy. The district's population is 29% Asian and 24% Hispanic. Sixty percent of the people speak a language other than English at home. Both the Queens and Nassau County portions of the district have long voted heavily Democratic.

The congressman from the 5th District is Gary Ackerman, a Democrat first elected in 1983. Ackerman grew up in Flushing. His father was a cab driver and, true to the character of the district, his mother was a Polish immigrant. As a young man, Ackerman cultivated a variety of interests and careers. He graduated from Queens College, and taught social studies in junior high school. After he and his wife had their first child, Ackerman successfully sued the New York City school district for the right of fathers, as well as mothers, to take time off for a new child. For a time, Ackerman ran an advertising agency, and then started the weekly *Queens Tribune* in 1970, which he sold in 1978. That year, he was elected to the

New York Senate. He won his seat in the U.S. House in a special election from a district that was then centered in the heavily Jewish apartment complexes in central Queens. Ackerman is a colorful character. In Washington, he lives on a houseboat on the Potomac River called the *Unsinkable II,* successor to the *Unsinkable I,* which sank. He hosts an annual "Taste of New York" fundraiser, featuring pastrami sandwiches and stuffed cabbage, with waiters imported from the city. Acerbic but humorous, he is a pungent speaker, with a humor that makes even opponents smile. He always wears a white carnation in his lapel, a habit he started as a teacher to remind his students that "every day is special."

Ackerman has a penchant for taking on worthy but neglected causes. His once solidly liberal voting record has moderated on foreign-policy issues. Despite opposition from many constituents, including his wife, Ackerman voted in 2002 to authorize war in Iraq; in 2005 he said he regretted it. He is the chairman of the Middle East and South Asia Subcommittee on the Foreign Affairs Committee, a panel of great interest to his constituents. He has met frequently with leaders in the region. Between 2006 and 2008, he helped win congressional approval of the nuclear energy deal with India, under which India gained U.S. expertise and nuclear fuel to meet its rapidly rising energy needs in exchange for opening its nuclear facilities to international inspections. A longtime supporter of India—Queens is home to a large Indian-American community— he also urged President George W. Bush not to sell sophisticated weapons and F-16s to Pakistan, although he has been willing to offer counter-narcotics, anti-terrorism, and peacekeeping aid to Pakistan along with intelligence information.

In 2007 and 2008, Ackerman won overwhelming House passage of five nonbinding resolutions on foreign policy, most of them dealing with the Middle East. They included measures calling for the release of Israeli soldiers held by the Muslim groups Hamas and Hezbollah and condemning Syria for taking control of the internal affairs of Lebanon. In the same period, he pushed a bill to freeze the personal assets of corporate executives whose companies invest in oil in Iran. "You can't invest with Al Capone without underwriting gangsterism," said Ackerman, deploying one of his trademark analogies. "And you can't invest in Iran without underwriting terrorism." Peace activists from the group Code Pink protested what they deemed his "provocative" anti-Iran rhetoric by blockading his houseboat with rafts. Ackerman came on deck and discussed the issue with the activists.

On domestic issues, Ackerman in 1995 helped to pass the "Baby AIDS" bill requiring HIV testing of newborns and disclosure of the results to the mother. The bill also bars insurers from terminating coverage because of HIV/AIDS test results. As one of five New York Democrats on the Financial Services Committee, Ackerman worked in 2007 to extend the terrorism insurance program. He occasionally stands out as a lonely liberal, such as when he was one of only three House members to vote against a resolution criticizing a federal Appeals Court that ruled unconstitutional the phrase "under God" in the Pledge of Allegiance.

Ackerman was an outspoken opponent of the short-lived publicity boomlet in 2008 to appoint Caroline Kennedy, the daughter of the late president, to the Senate seat vacated by Hillary Rodham Clinton when she became secretary of State. "I don't know what Caroline Kennedy's qualifications are, except that she has name recognition, but so does J-Lo," he told a local radio station, referring to pop singer Jennifer Lopez. He twice has survived redistricting, and he takes pride in tending to constituent projects ranging from environmental issues to saving the Merchant Marine Academy. Ackerman regularly wins re-election by large margins. His chief political threat might be a candidacy from one of the fast-growing immigrant communities in his district. And redistricting in advance of the 2012 election could prove a problem. Population growth in his Nassau County base is stagnant while growing minority communities in Queens seek to wield more clout.

SIXTH DISTRICT

Gregory Meeks (D)

Elected Feb. 1998, 6th full term; b. Sept. 25, 1953, Harlem; home, Far Rockaway; Adelphi U., B.A., 1975, Howard U., J.D., 1978; Baptist; married (Simone-Marie); 3 children.

Elected Office: NY Assembly, 1992–98.

Professional Career: Asst. dist. atty., Queens Co., NY, 1978–84; NY St. Comm. of Investigations, 1984–85; Judge, NY St. Workers Compensation Bd., 1985–92.

DC Office: 2342 RHOB, 20515, 202-225-3461; Fax: 202-226-4169; Web site: www.house.gov/meeks.

State Offices: Far Rockaway, 718-327-9791; Jamaica, 718-725-6000.

Committees: *Financial Services* (10th of 42 D): Domestic Monetary Policy & Technology; Financial Institutions & Consumer Credit; International Monetary Policy & Trade (Chmn). *Foreign Affairs* (9th of 28 D): Africa & Global Health; Asia, the Pacific & the Global Environment; Western Hemisphere.

Group Ratings

	ADA	ACLU	AFS	LCV	ITIC	NTU	COC	ACU	CFG	FRC
2008	90	90	100	100	100	6	65	0	1	11
2007	95	—	100	90	—	6	58	0	12	—

National Journal Ratings

	2007 LIB	—	2007 CONS	2008 LIB	—	2008 CONS
Economic	82%	—	0%	85%	—	0%
Social	77%	—	17%	75%	—	25%
Foreign	78%	—	20%	69%	—	31%
Composite	83%	—	17%	79%	—	21%

Key Votes of the 110th Congress

1. Increase minimum wage	Y	5. Share immigration data	N	9. Withdraw troops 8/08	Y
2. Expand SCHIP	Y	6. Foreign aid abortion ban	N	10. No operations in Iran	Y
3. Raise CAFE standards	Y	7. Ban gay bias in workplace	Y	11. Free trade with Peru	Y
4. Bail out financial markets	Y	8. Repeal D.C. gun law	N	12. Overhaul FISA	Y

Election Results

2008 general	Gregory Meeks (D).....................................unopposed	($1,756,925)
2008 primary	Gregory Meeks (D).....................................unopposed	

Prior Winning Percentages: 2006 (100%); 2004 (100%); 2002 (97%); 2000 (100%); 1998 (100%); 1998 (57%)

Population		Race/Ethnicity		Work	
Pop. 2007:	671,275	White:	11.5%	Private:	76.5%
Change since 2000:	Up 2.6%	Black:	51.6%	Government:	18.0%
Urban:	100.0%	Hispanic:	17.2%	Self-employed:	5.4%
Rural:	0.0%	Asian:	13.1%	Blue collar:	20.3%
Area size:	46 sq. mi.	Native Am.:	0.6%	White collar:	55.4%
Age		Hawaiian:	0.0%	Khaki collar:	0.1%
Median age:	36.0 yrs.	Two+ races:	1.5%	Other:	24.3%
More than 65 yrs:	11.4%	*Ancestry*		Median income:	$54,501
Less than 18 yrs:	25.3%	West Indian:	18.4%	Median home value:	$425,900
Education		Italian:	2.7%	Poverty:	11.4%
H.S. grad:	78.6%	USA:	2.7%	**Military Veterans**	
College grad:	21.6%			% of Pop:	4.2%
Grad degree:	6.9%				

The eastern edge of Queens has been an important transportation hub for New York for almost 250 years. In the 1750s, the British laid out what is now Jamaica Avenue to help them defend Long Island. In the 1830s—nearly a century before most present-day commuters would have guessed—the Long Island Rail Road was built. Today, this corner of Queens is sliced by the Belt Parkway and the Van Wyck Expressway—two integral parts of Robert Moses's midcentury highway network. And it

2008 Presidential Vote
Obama (D) 185,890   (89%)
McCain (R)..............................22,302   (11%)

2004 Presidential Vote
Kerry (D)...............................154,468   (84%)
Bush (R) 27,352   (15%)

Cook Partisan Voting Index: D+36

is home to John F. Kennedy International Airport, a major hub for air travelers entering the United States. The neighborhood of Jamaica is so well situated with transportation links that officials have worked mightily to improve its commercial vitality. The old elevated subway line on Jamaica Avenue has been buried underground, so that shoppers have a less claustrophobic experience. Now, billions of dollars are being spent for a Long Island Rail Road line from Queens to Grand Central Terminal in Manhattan. Property seizures have prompted citizen protests, but the massive project has spurred downtown revitalization in Jamaica.

This part of Queens is home to New York City's largest concentration of middle-class black homeowners, with a median income higher than white households in Queens. A half-century ago, there was a small black community in South Jamaica, and since then many African-American families have bought houses and raised their families in neighborhoods that fan east from Jamaica. They fought to maintain the relatively spacious streets, relishing the plenitude of natural light, safe schools, and good neighborhood stores. There is block upon block of low-rise, frame and brick houses, built mostly from the 1920s to the 1950s, in the neighborhoods of Springfield Gardens and Laurelton (the home of financial-scam mastermind Bernard Madoff), St. Albans and Rosedale, Cambria Heights and Queens Village. These middle-class areas never experienced the kind of riots that damaged Harlem and parts of Brooklyn.

The 6th Congressional District of New York contains all of these southeast Queens neighborhoods, plus others less affluent and orderly in southern Queens. It is bounded on the north, more or less, by Jackie Robinson Parkway; on the east by the Nassau County line; and on the west by Cross Bay Boulevard. To the south, it includes part of the Rockaway Peninsula across Jamaica Bay from the rest of Queens. Richmond Hill and Ozone Park, previously white ethnic neighborhoods, now have sizable numbers of Latinos and Asians. South Ozone Park is home to many immigrants from Guyana, Jamaica, Haiti, the Dominican Republic, and Trinidad and Tobago. Despite being just a few blocks from the beach, the Rockaway portions of the district are a relatively undeveloped backwater, leveled by urban renewal in the late 1960s but never completely rebuilt. The 6th District is 52% African-American, 17% Hispanic, and 13% Asian. The common denominator is the amount of time that residents spend on the road: The district is among the nation's worst for commuters, at 41.7 minutes of mean travel time to work. Politically, the district is overwhelmingly Democratic.

The congressman from the 6th District is Gregory Meeks, a Democrat elected in 1998. Meeks grew up in public housing projects in Harlem. He was inspired by his mother, who went back to school when her four children were older and encouraged community service volunteerism. Meeks's childhood hero was Supreme Court Justice Thurgood Marshall. After graduating from college and law school, Meeks moved to Far Rockaway. He became an assistant district attorney in 1978 and a workers' compensation judge in 1985. After losing a City Council race in 1991, he was elected to the New York state Assembly in 1992. He became an ally of Democratic Rep. Floyd Flake, a minister whose Allen A.M.E. Church congregation grew from 1,400 members in 1976 to 12,000 in 2000. When Flake retired, Meeks won a majority of Democratic committee members at a January 1998 endorsement meeting and thus became the party's nominee. Democratic state Sen. Alton Waldon and Assemblywoman Barbara Clark ran as independents. With the support of Flake, influential Rep. Charles Rangel of New York, and civil-rights leaders Al Sharpton and Jesse Jackson, Meeks won with 57% of the vote, to Waldon's 21%, and Clark's 13%.

Meeks has a mostly liberal voting record on social issues, but his stance on economic issues is more pro-business than most other New York City Democrats. In 2009, he became chairman of the House Financial Services Committee's International Monetary Policy and Trade Subcommittee. That role gives him oversight of the World Bank and International Monetary Fund. He has said he plans to focus on reducing poverty and on global economic growth and stability. As a committee member, he sponsored a bill to enable more accounting firms to conduct audits of large companies.

In 2000, Meeks was a pivotal vote in the proposal to normalize trade relations with China. Both sides lobbied him furiously, including Rangel and President Bill Clinton, and he went on a White House-sponsored trip to China to meet with senior officials to discuss the country's economic growth. After Republican House Speaker Dennis Hastert agreed to extend tax breaks and public investment to distressed urban and rural areas, Meeks voted for the measure. Later, in 2005, Meeks also voted for the Central American Free Trade Agreement, citing increased traffic for JFK Airport.

Meeks has shown a desire to advance within the party. When several House Democratic leadership positions opened up in late 2002, he campaigned for vice chairman of the Democratic Caucus but was bested by Rep. James Clyburn of South Carolina. In 2004, Meeks spent considerable time on the campaign trail with Democratic presidential nominee John Kerry and advised Kerry on relationships with minority groups across the nation. After the election, Meeks sought a leadership post at the Democratic National Committee, but he lost out to Rep. Mike Honda of California. In 2008, Meeks endorsed Sen. Hillary Rodham Clinton of New York in her pitched primary battle with Sen. Barack Obama of Illinois for the presidential nomination.

Meeks has sought to bring business deals to Queens by meeting with leaders of other nations, and his many overseas trips have attracted attention. His personal life has caused some political problems. A Federal Election Commission audit in 2006 reprimanded him for using more than $6,000 in 2004 campaign funds for a personal trainer. When his wife, Simone, expressed interest in running for the New York City Council in 2007, Meeks refused to endorse her and she deferred to the candidacy of her husband's aide. In 2008, Meeks became chairman of the Congressional Black Caucus's political action committee. He reportedly was considered for appointment to the Senate after Clinton resigned her seat to become President Obama's secretary of State.

SEVENTH DISTRICT

Joseph Crowley (D)

Elected 1998, 6th term; b. March 16, 1962, Elmhurst, NY; home, Elmhurst; C.U.N.Y. Queens College, B.A. 1985; Catholic; married (Kasey); 3 children.

Elected Office: NY Assembly, 1986–98.

DC Office: 2404 RHOB, 20515, 202-225-3965; Fax: 202-225-1909; Web site: www.crowley.house.gov.

State Offices: Bronx, 718-931-1400; Bronx, 718-320-2314; Jackson Heights, 718-779-1400.

Committees: *Chief Deputy Whip. Foreign Affairs* (21st of 28 D): Middle East & South Asia; Western Hemisphere. *Ways & Means* (17th of 26 D): Select Revenue Measures; Social Security.

Group Ratings

	ADA	ACLU	AFS	LCV	ITIC	NTU	COC	ACU	CFG	FRC
2008	100	91	100	92	100	6	67	0	1	11
2007	95	—	100	95	—	6	60	0	12	—

National Journal Ratings

	2007 LIB	—	2007 CONS	2008 LIB	—	2008 CONS
Economic	82%	—	0%	66%	—	34%
Social	89%	—	8%	75%	—	18%
Foreign	81%	—	16%	70%	—	25%
Composite	88%	—	12%	72%	—	28%

Key Votes of the 110th Congress

1. Increase minimum wage	Y	5. Share immigration data	N	9. Withdraw troops 8/08	Y
2. Expand SCHIP	Y	6. Foreign aid abortion ban	N	10. No operations in Iran	Y
3. Raise CAFE standards	Y	7. Ban gay bias in workplace	Y	11. Free trade with Peru	Y
4. Bail out financial markets	Y	8. Repeal D.C. gun law	N	12. Overhaul FISA	Y

Election Results

2008 general	Joseph Crowley (D-WF)	118,459	(85%)	($1,729,732)
	William Britt (R-C)	21,477	(15%)	
2008 primary	Joseph Crowley (D-WF)	unopposed		

Prior Winning Percentages: 2006 (84%); 2004 (81%); 2002 (73%); 2000 (72%); 1998 (69%)

Population		Race/Ethnicity		Work	
Pop. 2007:	677,842	White:	25.2%	Private:	77.6%
Change since 2000:	Up 3.6%	Black:	16.0%	Government:	16.8%
Urban:	100.0%	Hispanic:	41.5%	Self-employed:	5.4%
Rural:	0.0%	Asian:	15.2%	Blue collar:	20.9%
Area size:	42 sq. mi.	Native Am.:	0.2%	White collar:	54.4%
Age		Hawaiian:	0.1%	Khaki collar:	0.0%
Median age:	36.8 yrs.	Two+ races:	0.8%	Other:	24.6%
More than 65 yrs:	13.5%	*Ancestry*		Median income:	$44,960
Less than 18 yrs:	22.4%	Italian:	9.5%	Median home value:	$398,600
Education		Irish:	4.5%	Poverty:	15.9%
H.S. grad:	76.3%	West Indian:	4.0%	**Military Veterans**	
College grad:	21.9%			% of Pop:	4.7%
Grad degree:	7.8%				

Over the past two decades, hundreds of thousands of immigrants moved into many of New York City's modest neighborhoods—neighborhoods that had been emptying out as the children of the immigrants who came to New York between 1890 and 1924 died or moved to the suburbs. These are places that affluent New Yorkers and traveling journalists seldom see as they whiz by on freeways to destinations in Manhattan. Rather, these are the neighborhoods that pop star Jennifer Lopez sings about.

2008 Presidential Vote		
Obama (D)	148,242	(79%)
McCain (R)	38,170	(20%)
2004 Presidential Vote		
Kerry (D)	129,909	(74%)
Bush (R)	44,607	(25%)
Cook Partisan Voting Index:	D + 26	

Most of the housing was built in the decades after 1910, when the subways first started connecting these neighborhoods with job sites in Manhattan. In the East Bronx, off the Bruckner Expressway and near the cluster of highways north of the Bronx-Whitestone Bridge, are such places as Bruckner, Morris Park, Schuylerville, and Throgs Neck. (Work began in 2008 on a $200 million reconstruction and widening of the Bronx-Whitestone Bridge, which opened in 1939.) The Hunts Point meat and produce markets are where some of the city's toniest restaurants handpick their daily provisions and where plans are under way for a $100 million modernization.

Increasingly, the neighborhoods are filling with Latinos, many from Puerto Rico, but many also from the Dominican Republic and other Caribbean and Latin American countries. Lopez hails from Castle Hill; her *On the 6* album is a reference to the Number 6 subway train that whisked her to Manhattan auditions. Home for many immigrants is one of two massive apartment projects: the Parkchester, built just before World War II by Metropolitan Life Insurance in the center of the Bronx, and the sprawling Co-op City, consisting of 35 buildings that house more than 50,000 residents in 15,000 apartments that were built by a consortium of labor unions in the late 1960s on marshy land near Eastchester Bay. Out past the bay is City Island, a Cape Cod-like resort area with boat makers and plenty of seafood restaurants.

Across the bridges in Queens are Jackson Heights, home to Little India and a sizable Latino community; Elmhurst, a place so diverse that one local hospital counted more than 100 different languages and dialects; and Woodside, a long-settled enclave with residents from 49 nations who speak 34 languages. One can find Pakistanis and Peruvians, Koreans and Dominicans, Indians and Filipinos, Mexicans and Bangladeshis.

These Bronx and Queens neighborhoods are all in the 7th Congressional District of New York. The district is a polyglot: In 2007, it was 16% black, 42% Hispanic, and 15% Asian. Sixty percent speak a language other than English at home, and 40% are foreign-born. Since 2000, the share of workers and high school graduates has increased and the poverty level has dropped slightly. But a major difference in satisfaction levels separates the residents of the Bronx and Queens. A January 2009 report by the Citizens Committee for New York found that the happiest New Yorkers, 51%, are from Queens, and the least happy, 24%, are from the Bronx. Politically, the 7th District votes heavily Democratic.

The congressman from the 7th District is Joseph Crowley, a Democrat elected in 1998. He grew up in Woodside, where his family was involved in politics. His Uncle Walter Crowley was elected to the New York City Council in 1984. When he died in 1985, Joseph Crowley wanted to succeed him, though he was only 23. But Tom Manton, the boss of the efficient Queens County Democratic Party, chose his chief of staff instead. The following year, Assemblyman Ralph Goldstein from Elmhurst died. Fresh from Queens College, Crowley ran and won, with support from Manton. Crowley was interested in Irish affairs and sponsored the law that requires public school students to be taught about the Irish potato famine. He played guitar and sang tenor with the Budget Blues Boys, a group of assemblymen who performed on cold Albany nights. When political boss Manton decided it was time for Crowley to go to Congress, he went.

In 1998, Manton was the 7th District incumbent. He filed for re-election by the July 16 deadline. Then at 11 a.m. on July 21, he convened a meeting of Queens Democratic committeemen, announced that he was retiring, and got them to vote in Crowley as the Democratic nominee. Other potential candidates were not notified beforehand and were naturally miffed but resigned to reality. Manton argued that Crowley, at 36, was in a position to accumulate seniority and power in Washington. Crowley was delighted. "What you're hearing is not so much about the process, but sour grapes. What happened here is simply that I was offered an ice cream cone, and I took it." His Republican opponent had no money and no chance. Crowley won in November, 69%-26%.

Once elected, Crowley voted as a centrist Democrat and demonstrated leadership ambition. He was the freshman Democrats' class president that year. Over time, he changed his position from opposing abortion rights to favoring them, a stance in line with the party position. He now has a seat on the powerful, tax-writing House Ways and Means Committee, where he is an ally of Chairman Charles Rangel of New York. His local priorities include aid for city hospitals and adjusting the alternative minimum tax to reduce the number of middle-income taxpayers who are forced to pay it.

An active participant in leadership activities, Crowley has had setbacks in seeking a top post. In 2005, he sought the chairmanship of the Democratic Congressional Campaign Committee, highlighting his fundraising connections to New York's financial community. But as an ally of Minority Whip Steny Hoyer of Maryland, he was on the wrong side of Democratic Leader Nancy Pelosi, who has competed with Hoyer to move up the leadership ladder. The DCCC appointment went to Rep. Rahm Emanuel of Illinois, who led Democrats to victory in the next election in 2006. Crowley was named to lead the DCCC's Business Council, a key fundraising post. After that election, Crowley sought to move up to vice chairman of the Democratic Caucus. On the first ballot, he received the most votes, 79. John Larson of Connecticut, a Pelosi ally, got the next highest number, 66, and Jan Schakowsky of Illinois, another Pelosi ally, was eliminated when she came in third. But on the second ballot, the Schakowsky-Pelosi voters moved to Larson rather than to Crowley, and Larson prevailed, 116-87. Crowley remained a team player and did some bridge-building with Pelosi and her allies. When the caucus vice chairmanship opened again after the 2008 election, he expressed interest but deferred when Pelosi backed Rep. Xavier Becerra of California.

The September 11 attacks hit Crowley especially hard as a member of Congress. His district lost many local firefighters, including his first cousin, who was a battalion chief. He won passage of an amendment to issue the Public Safety Officers Medal of Valor to the 414 first responders who died on September 11. He fought to change funding formulas for homeland security, which he said shortchanged New York. In June 2007, the House passed his amendment to restore $50 million for homeland-security funding in high-threat urban areas. On another issue with local interest, Crowley was an active proponent of the U.S.-India agreement on nuclear energy, which Congress approved in October 2008. It allows India to gain U.S. expertise and nuclear fuel to meet its rapidly rising energy needs in exchange for opening its nuclear facilities to international inspections. There is a sizable community of Indian-Americans in Queens, many of whom are foreign-born. During the George W. Bush administration, Crowley worked with Republicans on behalf of business interests to gain approval of bilateral free-trade agreements, earning praise from GOP Whip Roy Blunt for helping to secure Democratic votes.

Crowley has not faced serious opposition at election time. After the 2000 census, redistricting radically changed his constituency. In the old district, Queens cast 74% of the votes. Now the Bronx casts 62% (Crowley remains a Mets fan, though). He has been a leader in the delegation's efforts to help Democrats win more House seats from New York by assisting the successful campaigns of Tim Bishop in Suffolk County in 2002, Brian Higgins for an open Buffalo-area seat in 2004, and Michael Arcuri in his bid for the seat of retiring Republican Rep. Sherwood Boehlert in 2006. After Manton died in July 2006, Crowley became Queens Democratic chairman.

EIGHTH DISTRICT

Jerrold Nadler (D)

Elected 1992, 9th full term; b. June 13, 1947, Brooklyn; home, Manhattan; Columbia U., B.A. 1970, Fordham U., J.D. 1978; Jewish; married (Joyce Miller); 1 child.

Elected Office: NY Assembly, 1976–92.

Professional Career: Legis. asst., NY Assembly, 1972; Law clerk, 1976.

DC Office: 2334 RHOB, 20515, 202-225-5635; Fax: 202-225-6923; Web site: www.house.gov/nadler.

State Offices: Brooklyn, 718-373-3198; Manhattan, 212-367-7350.

Committees: *Judiciary* (4th of 24 D): Constitution, Civil Rights & Civil Liberties (Chmn); Crime, Terrorism & Homeland Security. *Transportation & Infrastructure* (6th of 44 D): Highways & Transit; Railroads, Pipelines & Hazardous Materials.

Group Ratings

	ADA	ACLU	AFS	LCV	ITIC	NTU	COC	ACU	CFG	FRC
2008	95	100	100	100	86	4	53	0	0	11
2007	95	—	100	95	—	4	47	0	6	—

National Journal Ratings

	2007 LIB	—	2007 CONS		2008 LIB	—	2008 CONS
Economic	78%	—	18%		85%	—	0%
Social	77%	—	17%		82%	—	0%
Foreign	96%	—	0%		68%	—	31%
Composite	86%	—	14%		84%	—	16%

Key Votes of the 110th Congress

1. Increase minimum wage	Y	5. Share immigration data	N	9. Withdraw troops 8/08	Y
2. Expand SCHIP	Y	6. Foreign aid abortion ban	N	10. No operations in Iran	*
3. Raise CAFE standards	Y	7. Ban gay bias in workplace	N	11. Free trade with Peru	N
4. Bail out financial markets	Y	8. Repeal D.C. gun law	N	12. Overhaul FISA	N

Election Results

2008 general	Jerrold Nadler (D-WF)	160,730	(80%)	($1,044,454)
	Grace Lin (R-C)	39,047	(20%)	
2008 primary	Jerrold Nadler (D-WF)	unopposed		

Prior Winning Percentages: 2006 (85%); 2004 (81%); 2002 (76%); 2000 (81%); 1998 (86%); 1996 (82%); 1994 (82%); 1992 (81%); 1992 (100%)

Population		Race/Ethnicity		Work	
Pop. 2007:	710,291	White:	69.6%	Private:	82.5%
Change since 2000:	Up 8.5%	Black:	4.6%	Government:	7.8%
Urban:	100.0%	Hispanic:	10.8%	Self-employed:	9.5%
Rural:	0.0%	Asian:	13.5%	Blue collar:	9.2%
Area size:	28 sq. mi.	Native Am.:	0.2%	White collar:	79.2%
		Hawaiian:	0.0%	Khaki collar:	0.0%
Age		Two+ races:	1.0%	Other:	11.6%
Median age:	37.6 yrs.	*Ancestry*		Median income:	$63,544
More than 65 yrs:	13.7%	Italian:	8.2%	Median home value:	$712,900
Less than 18 yrs:	18.3%	Russian:	7.2%	Poverty:	17.2%
Education		Irish:	6.1%	**Military Veterans**	
H.S. grad:	86.9%			% of Pop:	3.4%
College grad:	54.9%				
Grad degree:	25.5%				

Over the course of the 20th century, New York City spread so far beyond its original boundaries in lower Manhattan that, for a while, it became easy to forget how pivotal the southern end of the island had been in making the city what it is today. That all changed in an instant, on the morning of September 11, 2001, when Al Qaeda terrorists flew two hijacked jets into the twin towers of the World Trade Center, killing approximately 2,800 people and laying waste to 13 city blocks. The target

2008 Presidential Vote		
Obama (D)	184,682	(74%)
McCain (R)	63,769	(26%)
2004 Presidential Vote		
Kerry (D)	180,080	(72%)
Bush (R)	66,948	(27%)
Cook Partisan Voting Index:	D + 22	

had been chosen deliberately. The terrorists struck the tallest buildings in America's biggest city, toppling a complex whose name embodied the reach of American capitalism. Lower Manhattan has long been home to Wall Street and the Financial District, but over the years it has represented America's striving spirit in other ways as well. The Brooklyn Bridge, begun in 1867 just a few blocks east of the Twin Towers site and completed in 1883, was half again as long as any bridge then standing and seven times higher than any buildings in the adjoining boroughs. The Holland Tunnel, built in 1927, was the first underwater vehicular tunnel built anywhere in the world. Just offshore are Ellis Island, where members of the great immigration wave first set foot on American soil, and the Statue of Liberty, the symbol of freedom they saw as they sailed in.

The 8th Congressional District of New York includes all of these places. From the Battery, at the very southern tip of Manhattan Island, the 8th spreads north and south. As it moves up the west side of Manhattan, it takes in the Financial District and many of the neighborhoods synonymous with New York: Battery Park City, the attractive modern apartments and parks built on 32 acres of infill in an area that city planners now describe as a "harbor district"; sophisticated TriBeCa, with its artists' lofts; SoHo, the international shoppers' paradise; Greenwich Village; and Chelsea, with its many art galleries. Clinton is the new, economically diverse incarnation of the old slum known as Hell's Kitchen. There is also the economically revived Theater District and the cleaned-up Times Square, where neon signs have been replaced by digital screens. The Upper West Side is home to the Lincoln Center and the American Museum of Natural History. Also in the district is the huge Port Authority bus terminal. South from the Battery, the 8th District crosses into Brooklyn, running along the waterfront before taking in the inland neighborhood of Borough Park and the waterside enclaves of Sea Gate, Brighton Beach and Coney Island, once known as the world's largest playground and now the site of several thousand proposed apartments. In the Financial District, young families and wealthy professionals have filled new condos and hotel rooms despite the economic woes of the city's financial institutions, which have not seemed to have trickled down locally. Endless infighting has frustrated redevelopment at Ground Zero. Although the 8th

District has some of the world's biggest concentrations of wealth, it also has a 17% rate of poverty. There are more Asians, 14%, than Hispanics, 11%, and the district is only 5% African-American.

Both parts of the 8th District have a strong Jewish heritage. The city's Dutch founders hailed from a European country that was then most tolerant of Jews. German Jews came to New York in large numbers in the 19th century, and a few of them founded merchant banking, retail and clothing empires. Around 1890, Ashkenazi Jews from Eastern Europe began arriving from Poland, Lithuania, Belarus, Ukraine, Hungary and Romania. In the years after World War I, as many as 400,000 Jews a year debarked at Ellis Island until a 1924 law virtually shut down immigration. (Had a nativist Congress not done that, perhaps 2 million of the 6 million who perished in the Holocaust would instead have become Americans.) Ashkenazi Jews initially lived on the Lower East Side but moved out to Brooklyn and the Bronx almost as soon as the subways were built. Their children moved up faster than those of any new group in memory, despite the incredible odds against them given the widespread prejudice in the professions and in educational institutions. These immigrants invented new businesses, from the rag trade to showbiz—second-caste people from third-rate countries almost immediately becoming America's elite. Today, New York has the largest Jewish population behind Tel Aviv.

The venerable apartment buildings along Central Park West, West End Avenue and Riverside Drive, and the brownstones on the cross streets, house some of the country's most dedicated liberals (and radicals). These professional people—lovingly satirized on *Seinfeld,* the long-running sitcom that resonated far beyond Manhattan—include a mix of wealthy and less-affluent intellectuals. In the 1950s, West Siders took up the reform banner and eviscerated the old Tammany Hall Democratic machine. In the 1960s, they protested the Vietnam War. Another big voting area is Greenwich Village, which in the 1910s was America's original Bohemia but now has a mix of expensive apartments and cheaper dwellings. Politically, the Village has long had a taste for the radical, though some of its ideas are now mainstream, such as the historic preservation and urbanist policies developed in the Village's successful fight against a proposed lower Manhattan expressway. The effort was led by Jane Jacobs, author of *The Death and Life of Great American Cities.*

The Brooklyn part of the district is probably more Jewish than the Manhattan part. Brighton Beach ("Little Odessa") and Coney Island house the largest concentration of recent Russian Jewish immigrants in New York. Here one can see Cyrillic as well as Roman letters on store signs. Borough Park has one of the nation's largest Orthodox communities, with Yiddish-language ATMs and Russian bathhouses. The political attitudes in these neighborhoods are quite different from those of most American Jews, who are liberal on both cultural and economic issues. The Russians, many of whom live close to poverty, are anti-socialist. The Hasidic Jews of Borough Park are conservative and hostile to racial preferences, and they favor tough police treatment of crime. Still, voters in these areas tend to register as Democrats and vote Democratic in most elections. In 2008, the district voted 74%-26% for Democratic presidential nominee Barack Obama over Republican nominee John McCain, although McCain prevailed 55%-44% in the Brooklyn part of the district, which cast 29% of the total vote.

The congressman from the 8th District is Jerrold Nadler, a West Side liberal Democrat elected in 1992. He was born in Brooklyn and moved around with his family as a child. His parents bought a chicken farm in New Jersey, but the business failed, and they moved back to the city. His father ran a gas station on Long Island and owned an auto parts store. Interested in politics from a young age, Nadler campaigned for Democrat Eugene McCarthy for president while at Columbia University, where he roomed with Dick Morris, who would later become a top adviser to President Bill Clinton. The two were at Columbia during the 1968 campus riots. After getting his law degree from Fordham University, Nadler ran for the New York Assembly in 1976, at age 29. In the primary, he beat Ruth Messinger, the Democratic nominee for mayor in 1997, by 73 votes. In 1992, he was suddenly presented with the opportunity to run for Congress. Ted Weiss, long an Upper West Side icon, died the day before the September primary, which he won posthumously. The nomination was decided by a convention of almost 1,000 county Democratic committee members. Nadler won 62% of the votes to secure the nomination and thus the election. He has not been seriously challenged since.

Nadler's voting record has been among the most liberal in the House, with a strong civil libertarian bent. In 2007, he became chairman of the Constitution, Civil Rights and Civil Liberties Subcommittee of the House Judiciary Committee, where he has been a counterweight to lawmakers of both parties seeking expanded police powers to crack down on terrorism. It is not because Nadler, as the representative of the site of the September 11 attacks, is unsympathetic to their cause. But he has worked to narrow the definition of "enemy combatants" and to remove restrictions on detainees to protect their habeas corpus rights. In 2008, he sponsored a bill requiring the Federal Bureau of Investigation to surmount higher legal hurdles before being allowed to use "national security letters," which are government demands for information not subject to judicial review. He vigorously opposed the USA PATRIOT Act, which was the Bush administration's centerpiece anti-terrorism law. On foreign policy, he has been a staunch supporter of Israel, but he opposed the Iraq war resolution in 2002.

In early 2009, Nadler held hearings to document what he viewed as the "criminal" abuses of the Bush administration and demanded that former Bush aide Karl Rove testify about the "politicization of the Justice Department" after the firing of several U.S. attorneys around the country allegedly for political reasons. As the ranking Democrat on the subcommittee when Republicans were in control, Nadler opposed proposed constitutional amendments to overturn court rulings and legislation to curb abortion rights. He also led the fight in the House against the proposed Federal Marriage Amendment, which would ban same-sex marriage. With Democratic Sen. Patrick Leahy of Vermont, he sponsored a 2007 bill to permit gay and lesbian Americans to sponsor their foreign-born partners for legal residency.

In the aftermath of the September 11 attacks, Nadler found that his work life became both sad and frenetic. When the second airplane struck the tower, he rushed to catch a 10 a.m. train from Washington to Manhattan. After delays en route, he finally arrived at 6 p.m. and saw a scene he later described as "surrealistic." He worked with city, state and federal officials as well as local business leaders to identify immediate needs and then to secure $20 billion for rebuilding. He spearheaded numerous actions on behalf of affected families and small businesses.

On other local issues, he successfully fought developer Donald Trump's attempts to alter the West Side Highway to accommodate his luxury housing project on old rail yards between 59th and 72nd Streets. In a book, Trump termed Nadler "one of the most egregious hacks in contemporary politics." As a senior member of the Transportation and Infrastructure Committee, Nadler has fought to get more rail competition east of the Hudson and to save Amtrak. His biggest project has been a rail-freight tunnel under the Hudson. Lack of a rail-freight line means that New York gets only a tiny share of its freight by rail; a new line could mean cheaper freight and therefore lower consumer prices. The cost would be billion of dollars. Nadler's proposal was ridiculed for years, but he persisted and got $12 million for a two-year design and environmental study of a tunnel. And in 2007, the Port Authority of New York and New Jersey agreed to spend more than $100 million in federal funds on an environmental-impact study. Mayor Michael Bloomberg has sided with neighborhood groups in Queens that object to the plan because it would increase noise.

NINTH DISTRICT

Anthony Weiner (D)

Elected 1998, 6th term; b. Sept. 4, 1964, Brooklyn; home, Queens; S.U.N.Y. Plattsburgh, B.A. 1985; Jewish; single.

Elected Office: NY City Cncl., 1991–98.

Professional Career: Aide, U.S. Rep. Charles Schumer, 1985–91.

DC Office: 2104 RHOB, 20515, 202-225-6616; Fax: 202-226-7253; Web site: weiner.house.gov.

State Offices: Brooklyn, 718-743-0441; Kew Gardens, 718-520-9001; Rockaway, 718-318-9255.

Committees: *Energy & Commerce* (21st of 36 D): Commerce, Trade & Consumer Protections; Communications, Technology & the Internet; Health. *Judiciary* (20th of 24 D): Crime, Terrorism & Homeland Security; Immigration, Citizenship, Border Security & International Law.

Group Ratings

	ADA	ACLU	AFS	LCV	ITIC	NTU	COC	ACU	CFG	FRC
2008	100	100	100	92	100	5	59	0	1	17
2007	90	—	100	90	—	6	60	0	12	—

National Journal Ratings

	2007 LIB	—	2007 CONS		2008 LIB	—	2008 CONS
Economic	78%	—	18%		76%	—	24%
Social	69%	—	31%		67%	—	28%
Foreign	93%	—	7%		77%	—	22%
Composite	81%	—	19%		74%	—	26%

Key Votes of the 110th Congress

1. Increase minimum wage	Y	5. Share immigration data	N	9. Withdraw troops 8/08	Y
2. Expand SCHIP	Y	6. Foreign aid abortion ban	*	10. No operations in Iran	Y
3. Raise CAFE standards	Y	7. Ban gay bias in workplace	N	11. Free trade with Peru	Y
4. Bail out financial markets	Y	8. Repeal D.C. gun law	N	12. Overhaul FISA	N

Election Results

2008 general	Anthony Weiner (D-WF)	112,205	(93%)	($524,607)
	Alfred Donohue (C)	8,378	(7%)	
2008 primary	Anthony Weiner (D-WF)	unopposed		

Prior Winning Percentages: 2006 (100%); 2004 (71%); 2002 (66%); 2000 (68%); 1998 (66%)

Population		Race/Ethnicity		Work	
Pop. 2007:	667,255	White:	62.1%	Private:	76.7%
Change since 2000:	Up 2.0%	Black:	4.2%	Government:	16.8%
Urban:	100.0%	Hispanic:	14.7%	Self-employed:	6.3%
Rural:	0.0%	Asian:	17.6%	Blue collar:	17.3%
Area size:	103 sq. mi.	Native Am.:	0.2%	White collar:	66.2%
		Hawaiian:	0.0%	Khaki collar:	0.0%
Age		Two+ races:	0.8%	Other:	16.5%
Median age:	40.4 yrs.			Median income:	$54,130
More than 65 yrs:	16.1%	*Ancestry*		Median home value:	$498,400
Less than 18 yrs:	21.4%	Italian:	11.5%	Poverty:	11.2%
		Irish:	7.2%		
Education		Russian:	6.9%	**Military Veterans**	
H.S. grad:	86.2%			% of Pop:	5.2%
College grad:	36.7%				
Grad degree:	13.8%				

Forty years ago, most of the neighborhoods in New York's outer boroughs were almost all-white. A few were WASPy and high-income—Forest Hills in Queens, with its famous tennis stadium and large Tudor houses on winding lanes within view of massive high-rises, was a notable example. But most of them were filled by descendants of the great mass of immigrants who came over from eastern and southern Europe between 1890 and 1924 and from northern Europe earlier—Irish and Italians, Jews

2008 Presidential Vote		
Obama (D)	111,237	(55%)
McCain (R)	88,307	(44%)
2004 Presidential Vote		
Kerry (D)	111,850	(56%)
Bush (R)	87,449	(44%)
Cook Partisan Voting Index:	D+5	

and Hungarians, Poles and Czechs and Greeks. The great pitched battles of city politics in the 1960s were between John Lindsay, a liberal Manhattan Republican, and his mostly outer-borough opponents. Lindsay won big margins in Manhattan from Harlem blacks, Upper East Side Republicans, and Upper West Side and Greenwich Village liberal Democrats, but he lost the other four boroughs both times he ran and was elected each time only by a plurality. Lindsay's attitudes and policies resulted in high taxes and crime-addled neighborhoods, and fueled an exodus of middle-class New Yorkers. The city lost 1 million people in the 1970s. Some of this neighborhood change would have happened anyway. Neighborhoods settled by immigrants in the 1920s were full of old people, and increasing numbers of African-Americans were bound to move out of the old ghettoes. Unnoticed, increasing numbers of immigrants started coming to the United States after the 1965 changes in immigration law, and eventually large numbers settled in New York.

Some white upper-middle- and lower-middle-class neighborhoods remain in the outer boroughs, though they are ethnically more diverse than those of 40 years ago. Many of these neighborhoods are gathered within the convoluted boundaries of the 9th Congressional District, which includes parts of Queens and Brooklyn. The 9th begins in Queens near Fresh Meadows, just inside Nassau County. It runs west through Pomonok and the old rail suburbs of Kew Gardens and Forest Hills, with houses built to resemble English cottages. It continues west to Rego Park ("Regostan"), which has many 1950s high-rise apartments and is where Wal-Mart abandoned plans for a store because of community opposition; Middle Village; Glendale, an old German neighborhood that is now more Eastern European; and part of Maspeth. From there, the 9th heads south, taking in Woodhaven, Lindenwood and Howard Beach. It crosses over open parkland to include the shoreline areas of Bergen Beach, Mill Basin, Mill Island, Marine Park and Sheepshead Bay. It takes in Broad Channel, the only inhabited island in Jamaica Bay's Gateway National Recreation Area, where many descendants of the original fishing families still live. In recent years, the U.S. Army Corps of Engineers helped revive dozens of acres of marshland and removed toxic wastes from the bay. On the Rockaway Peninsula, the district encompasses the neighborhoods of Seaside, Rockaway Park, Belle Harbor, Roxbury and the tight-knit enclave of Breezy Point, a clannish, white-ethnic, middle-class enclave where the bungalows and brick homes often change hands by word of mouth. While some of Rockaway has been largely abandoned, parts in the Arverne area have thousands of new housing units.

The population of the 9th District is only 4% black and 15% Hispanic, and some of its neighborhoods, like the Italian Howard Beach on Jamaica Bay, have remained remarkably parochial and seemingly unaffected by change. But the district's 18% Asian population has added diversity. The district also has a large and diverse Jewish population, with both liberal voters and politically conservative Orthodox voters. This is unquestionably a Democratic district, but conservative by New York City standards: It voted 67%-30% for Democrat Al Gore for president in 2000, but in 2004, after President George W. Bush's response to September 11, it gave Democrat John Kerry only 56%. It was the greatest swing of any congressional district in the nation that year. In 2008, Democrat Barack Obama won with 55%-44% over Republican John McCain. Obama lost the Brooklyn portion of the district, 57%-42%.

The congressman from the 9th District is Anthony Weiner, a Democrat elected in 1998. He grew up in Park Slope section of Brooklyn, the son of a lawyer and a teacher. Weiner (*WEE-ner*) went to college upstate at the State University of New York-Plattsburgh, where he became interested in politics. He majored in political science and ran for student government with the slogan "Vote for Weiner—he'll be frank." After graduation, he went to work as an aide to Democratic Rep. Charles Schumer. In 1991, Weiner was elected to the New York City Council; he was only 27, which made him the body's youngest member ever. In 1997, as Schumer prepared to run for the Senate, Weiner began running for the House. In the Democratic primary, he faced two members of the Assembly and another councilman. This was mainly a battle of organizations and endorsements, and in the final weeks, Schumer endorsed Weiner. The primary was so close that the results weren't certified for two weeks. In a turnout of 45,000 voters, Weiner won with 28.1%, to 27.5% for the runner-up. He won the general election easily.

In the House, Weiner usually votes with liberals but styles himself a moderate on issues dealing with business and crime. Like his mentor, Schumer, he has a lust for the media limelight and is always eager to appear on cable talk shows. On issues, he is particularly interested in pro-consumer legislation and, given the many senior citizens in his district, in policy affecting the elderly. On foreign policy, he is a staunch defender of Israel and has been active in recent years in opposing U.S. foreign aid and arms sales to Saudi Arabia, citing Saudi support of terrorists.

In 2007, he got a seat on the influential Energy and Commerce Committee. In 2007, he sponsored a bill creating an online registry of sex offenders' e-mail addresses. And in 2008, the House passed his bill to reduce illegal cigarette sales and ensure the collection of tobacco taxes after contraband sales were suspected of helping to finance international terrorism groups. He sought to protect local pharmacies from the invasion of chain drug stores by permitting them to negotiate collectively with insurance and drug companies, and he sponsored legislation to bar pharmaceutical firms from owning a controlling interest in a pharmacy benefit management company.

In 2005, Weiner sought the Democratic nomination for New York City mayor and tried to build an outer-borough base that focused on the needs of working people. He called for a new football stadium in Queens and for a 10% cut in income taxes for people earning less than $150,000 that would be financed by a tax increase on millionaires. In the September primary, Weiner finished second, with 29% to Bronx borough President Fernando Ferrer's 40%. Weiner generated political goodwill by choosing not to seek a runoff. Republican Michael Bloomberg then trounced Ferrer to win a second term. In 2007, Weiner was planning to run again for mayor in 2009, but scrapped the idea after Bloomberg got the City Council to extend the eight-year limit on elected city officials, giving Bloomberg the chance to run for a third term.

TENTH DISTRICT

Edolphus Towns (D)

Elected 1982, 14th term; b. July 21, 1934, Chadbourn, NC; home, Brooklyn; NC A&T, B.S. 1956, Adelphi U., M.S.W. 1973; Baptist; married (Gwendolyn); 2 children.

Military Career: Army, 1956–58.

Professional Career: Baptist minister; Social worker; Prof., Medgar Evers Col.; NY public schl. teacher; Dpty. hospital admin., 1965–71; Brooklyn Dpty. Borough Pres., 1976–82.

DC Office: 2232 RHOB, 20515, 202-225-5936; Fax: 202-225-1018; Web site: www.house.gov/towns.

State Offices: Brooklyn, 718-855-8018; Brooklyn, 718-272-1175; Brooklyn, 718-774-5682; Brooklyn, 718-434-7931.

Committees: *Oversight & Government Reform* (Chmn of 24 D).

Group Ratings

	ADA	ACLU	AFS	LCV	ITIC	NTU	COC	ACU	CFG	FRC
2008	100	100	100	92	100	6	56	0	0	5
2007	90	—	100	90	—	5	65	0	12	—

National Journal Ratings

	2007 LIB	—	2007 CONS		2008 LIB	—	2008 CONS
Economic	82%	—	0%		85%	—	0%
Social	75%	—	23%		82%	—	0%
Foreign	85%	—	14%		70%	—	25%
Composite	84%	—	16%		85%	—	15%

Key Votes of the 110th Congress

1. Increase minimum wage	Y	5. Share immigration data	N	9. Withdraw troops 8/08	Y
2. Expand SCHIP	Y	6. Foreign aid abortion ban	N	10. No operations in Iran	Y
3. Raise CAFE standards	Y	7. Ban gay bias in workplace	N	11. Free trade with Peru	Y
4. Bail out financial markets	Y	8. Repeal D.C. gun law	N	12. Overhaul FISA	N

Election Results

2008 general	Edolphus Towns (D)..155,090	(94%)	($1,568,247)
	Salvatore Grupico (R-C) 9,565	(6%)	
2008 primary	Edolphus Towns (D).................................... unopposed		

Prior Winning Percentages: 2006 (92%); 2004 (91%); 2002 (98%); 2000 (90%); 1998 (92%); 1996 (91%); 1994 (89%); 1992 (96%); 1990 (93%); 1988 (89%); 1986 (89%); 1984 (85%); 1982 (84%)

Population		Race/Ethnicity		Work	
Pop. 2007:	681,074	White:	17.8%	Private:	71.5%
Change since 2000:	Up 4.1%	Black:	60.5%	Government:	23.8%
Urban:	100.0%	Hispanic:	16.7%	Self-employed:	4.6%
Rural:	0.0%	Asian:	3.2%	Blue collar:	16.0%
Area size:	18 sq. mi.	Native Am.:	0.1%	White collar:	58.9%
Age		Hawaiian:	0.0%	Khaki collar:	0.1%
Median age:	32.3 yrs.	Two+ races:	1.0%	Other:	25.1%
More than 65 yrs:	10.2%	*Ancestry*		Median income:	$37,464
Less than 18 yrs:	28.7%	West Indian:	18.2%	Median home value:	$467,600
Education		USA:	3.5%	Poverty:	26.1%
H.S. grad:	76.7%	Subsaharan:	3.3%	**Military Veterans**	
College grad:	22.6%			% of Pop:	3.4%
Grad degree:	8.2%				

African-Americans began settling in Brooklyn's Bedford-Stuyvesant neighborhood in the 1930s, with the opening of the subway line that was celebrated in Duke Ellington and Billy Strayhorn's "Take the A Train." After World War II, the pace accelerated, as crime and crowding in Harlem—as well as a large influx of African-Americans from the South—drove black New Yorkers to the aging but solid brownstones of "Bed-Stuy." When job growth slowed, Bed-Stuy faced more than its share of

2008 Presidential Vote
Obama (D) 205,929 (91%)
McCain (R)..............................19,677 (9%)

2004 Presidential Vote
Kerry (D)................................166,840 (86%)
Bush (R) 25,359 (13%)

Cook Partisan Voting Index: D + 38

poverty and crime. But after a 1966 visit by New York's two senators, Democrat Robert F. Kennedy and Republican Jacob Javits, Bed-Stuy won a Model Cities designation, which brought federal development funds and the establishment of the Bedford-Stuyvesant Restoration Corporation, the first such community-development organization in the United States. Even as the black community expanded across Brooklyn, Bed-Stuy became almost as powerful a symbol of black New York as Harlem. As a New York University film student in 1983, Brooklyn native Spike Lee made *Joe's Bed-Stuy Barbershop: We Cut Heads*, about a tonsorial parlor fronting for the numbers racket. Five years later, he shot *Do the Right Thing* on Stuyvesant Avenue between Lexington Avenue and Quincy Street, a film that succinctly captured the racial tensions then brewing in the old neighborhood. From a different perspective, pop singer Billy Joel, who is white, sang in the 1980s, "I've been stranded in the combat zone. I walked through Bed-Stuy alone." The neighborhood also gave birth to rappers Jay-Z and Notorious B.I.G., both of whom had a major impact on the hip-hop scene of the 1990s. By the new century, Bed-Stuy was in better shape than many other areas of Brooklyn. The neighborhood's stately, Hopperesque architecture largely avoided the wrecking ball, and community vigilance kept the streets maintained. The revitalized residential area has developed a Caribbean flavor that, combined with modest prices for handsome brownstones and new shops and galleries, has led to a noticeable wave of gentrification.

The 10th Congressional District of New York takes the shape of a sideways "V" as it zigzags across Brooklyn. It takes in several neighborhoods near, but not on, the East River, including part of affluent Brooklyn Heights; downtown Brooklyn, with Borough Hall and the $670 million courthouse complex; Fort Greene, a rising arts area; and part of Williamsburg (shared with the 12th District), inhabited by large Hasidic families and a recent influx of European investors buying up new condos. From there, it runs southeasterly through Bed-Stuy, Clinton Hill and East New York until it hits the Queens border, where it turns to the southwest to take in three communities along Jamaica Bay: Spring Creek, the huge middle-income apartment complex of Starrett City, and Canarsie, the site of Jonathan Rieder's classic sociological study of Jewish and Italian flight from increasingly black neighborhoods. In the 1990s, Canarsie again experienced significant demographic change, as the neighborhood's black population grew from

10% to 60%, mainly due to an influx of Caribbean immigrants who prize the backyards and single-family homes. The 10th also includes Remsen Village, Flatlands and part of East Flatbush. In East New York, gutted blocks have been torn down and in many cases rebuilt, even though crime has hardly disappeared. The district is 61% African-American—the highest of any New York district—and it is 17% Hispanic. Politically, it is one of the most Democratic districts in the nation. Voter turnout in the 2008 presidential primary, with the first black major-party presidential nominee, was up 17% over 2004, and Democrat Barack Obama won this district with 91% of the vote.

The congressman from the 10th District is Edolphus Towns, first elected in 1982. He is a Democrat from East New York who is as experienced in government as in politics. He was born in North Carolina, the son of a tobacco sharecropper. He graduated from the historically black North Carolina A&T State University, served two years in the Army and then moved to Brooklyn. He got a job teaching in the public schools and at Medgar Evers College. He became a social worker and hospital administrator, and was active in community affairs. In 1976, he became Brooklyn's deputy borough president, a position he held for six years.

In recent years, Towns's voting record has lost some of its liberal edge, especially on economic issues, where he occasionally sides with business. He now chairs a major House committee, the Oversight and Government Reform Committee, having overcome initial qualms among Democratic leaders. In November 2008, when Rep. Henry Waxman of California gave up the chairmanship of the Oversight and Reform panel to take over at Energy and Commerce, Towns was the next most senior Democrat. But some senior Democrats worried that the low-key Towns would not be aggressive enough in the role, and they considered Elijah Cummings of Maryland as an alternative. But as Towns made his case in one-on-one conversations and rallied support, opposition quickly dissipated, especially after Towns agreed to relinquish his seat on Energy and Commerce. Towns pledged vigorous oversight of the executive branch, although there naturally would be less of it with a Democratic president than there had been in the previous Congress (2007–08), when Republican George W. Bush was in the White House. Taking over as chairman, Towns sought to tamp down the panel's rancorous internal dealings. Some Democrats worried that he was giving Republicans too much leeway, but Towns cited President Barack Obama's call for bipartisanship.

In the past, Towns has demonstrated an ability to work effectively across party lines. Working with Republican Mike Rogers of Michigan, he got the House to pass a bill imposing uniform safety rules on food. In 2005, he infuriated Minority Leader Nancy Pelosi by breaking ranks to vote for the Central American Free Trade Agreement on a very close roll-call vote. The agreement passed 217-215. She demanded an explanation and threatened to deprive Towns, and a few other maverick Democrats, of their committee seats. When Democrats took over the House in 2007, Towns did not get a subcommittee chairmanship on Energy and Commerce, perhaps as a result of Pelosi's unhappiness over his CAFTA vote.

Still, he managed to get a few things done once Democrats were in the majority. He won enactment of a bill to permit state and local governments to purchase equipment for homeland security and law enforcement at the discount prices available to federal agencies. And he won passage of a provision in the higher-education bill to aid minority colleges. Earlier in his House career, Towns had sponsored the Student Athlete Right-to-Know Act, which required colleges to report the graduation rates of student athletes.

Towns has faced serious primary challenges in recent elections. In 1997, he endorsed Republican Rudolph Giuliani for re-election as mayor of New York City. Voters in Bedford-Stuyvesant were not wild about Giuliani, and in 1998, Kings County Democratic Chairman Clarence Norman recruited Barry Ford, a Harvard-educated Wall Street lawyer, to run against Towns in the primary. Towns's critics concentrated on his opposition to anti-tobacco legislation, which he'd argued would hurt farmers. The Campaign for Tobacco-Free Kids put up billboards reading, "Representative Towns: Big Tobacco or Kids?" Towns beat Ford 52%-36%. Emboldened by his decent showing against a longtime incumbent, Ford barely stopped campaigning over the next two years. Towns defended his support of Giuliani by pointing to the mayor's support for commercial development, and he refused campaign contributions from tobacco companies. This time Towns beat Ford 57%-43%.

In 2006, his opponents in the primary were Councilman Charles Barron, who said that Towns had been "missing in action for years," and Assemblyman Roger Green. But the challengers had their own problems. Barron's call for reparations for descendants of slaves was controversial, and Green had pleaded guilty in 2004 to petty larceny for phony travel expenses while in office. Towns stayed above the fray and raised a lot of money. He won the primary with 47%, to 37% for Barron and 15% for Green— less-than-impressive results for a 12-term incumbent. Towns fared better in 2008 against Kevin Powell, a television reality show celebrity. Powell criticized Towns for his lack of influence in Congress and for endorsing Sen. Hillary Rodham Clinton in the Democratic presidential primary while many of his constituents supported Obama. But Towns stepped up his own campaigning and defended his support for his home-state senator, and he won 68%-32%.

There has been speculation that the incumbent would like to pass the district to his son, Assemblyman Darryl Towns, when he retires. But his rise to a chairmanship at age 74 might delay that prospect.

ELEVENTH DISTRICT

Yvette Clarke (D)

Elected 2006, 2nd term; b. Nov. 21, 1964, Brooklyn; home, Brooklyn; Attended Oberlin Col.; Protestant; single.

Elected Office: NY City Cncl., 2001–06.

Professional Career: Childcare specialist, Erasmus Neighborhood Fed., 1987–89; Leg. aide, state Sen. Velmanette Montgomery, 1989–91; Exec. asst., NY Workers' Compensation Bd., 1992–93; Youth program dir., Hospital League/Local S.E.I.U. 1199 Training and Upgrading Fund, 1993–97; Bus. devel. dir., Bronx Overall Devel. Corp., 1997–2001.

DC Office: 1029 LHOB, 20515, 202-225-6231; Fax: 202-226-0112; Web site: clarke.house.gov.

State Offices: Brooklyn, 718-287-1142.

Committees: *Education & Labor* (21st of 29 D): Health, Employment, Labor & Pensions; Healthy Families & Communities. *Homeland Security* (10th of 20 D): Emerging Threats, Cybersecurity & Science and Technology (Chmn); Intelligence, Information Sharing & Terrorism Risk Assessment. *Small Business* (12th of 17 D): Contracting & Technology; Rural Development, Entrepreneurship & Trade.

Group Ratings

	ADA	ACLU	AFS	LCV	ITIC	NTU	COC	ACU	CFG	FRC
2008	100	100	100	92	67	8	56	0	1	11
2007	75	—	100	80	—	5	64	0	13	—

National Journal Ratings

	2007 LIB	—	2007 CONS		2008 LIB	—	2008 CONS
Economic	82%	—	0%		76%	—	23%
Social	83%	—	17%		82%	—	0%
Foreign	92%	—	8%		85%	—	8%
Composite	89%	—	11%		85%	—	15%

Key Votes of the 110th Congress

1. Increase minimum wage	Y	5. Share immigration data	N	9. Withdraw troops 8/08	Y
2. Expand SCHIP	Y	6. Foreign aid abortion ban	N	10. No operations in Iran	Y
3. Raise CAFE standards	Y	7. Ban gay bias in workplace	N	11. Free trade with Peru	Y
4. Bail out financial markets	Y	8. Repeal D.C. gun law	N	12. Overhaul FISA	N

Election Results

2008 general	Yvette Clarke (D-WF)	168,562	(93%)	($545,983)
	Hugh Carr (R)	11,644	(6%)	
2008 primary	Yvette Clarke (D-WF)	unopposed		

Prior Winning Percentages: 2006 (90%)

Population		Race/Ethnicity		Work	
Pop. 2007:	658,512	White:	25.5%	Private:	75.3%
Change since 2000:	Up 0.6%	Black:	56.0%	Government:	17.9%
Urban:	100.0%	Hispanic:	12.2%	Self-employed:	6.7%
Rural:	0.0%	Asian:	4.3%	Blue collar:	14.3%
Area size:	12 sq. mi.	Native Am.:	0.3%	White collar:	60.9%
Age		Hawaiian:	0.0%	Khaki collar:	0.0%
Median age:	33.8 yrs.	Two+ races:	1.1%	Other:	24.8%
More than 65 yrs:	9.8%	*Ancestry*		Median income:	$44,177
Less than 18 yrs:	25.5%	West Indian:	23.1%	Median home value:	$541,000
Education		Subsaharan:	6.2%	Poverty:	19.7%
H.S. grad:	82.4%	USA:	5.1%	**Military Veterans**	
College grad:	31.8%			% of Pop:	3.1%
Grad degree:	12.5%				

Brooklyn. Just saying the word in a comedian's monologue used to elicit laughter. It evoked an accent of twisted English, a raucous, in-your-face style, a sense of humor with an edge, and the chip-on-the-shoulder assertiveness of those sure they will always be in second place. Brooklyn would never be more important than Manhattan; the Dodgers would always lose the World Series to the Yankees or the pennant to the Giants, and when they finally did win, in 1955, they moved to Los Angeles two years later. As its name testifies, Brooklyn was a separate community (named after the Dutch town Breukelen) from the 17th century on, and in the 19th century, it was one of the largest cities in the country, with its own celebrities—Henry Ward Beecher, Walt Whitman, John Roebling. By 1898, when the five boroughs were welded into Greater New York, 1 million people lived in Brooklyn, but the Brooklyn of the comedians really came into being as the subways were built in the early 20th century. In 1913, a transit agreement was struck to link the city's then-independent lines and triple the track to 619 miles. The agreement helped Brooklyn expand well beyond its established neighborhoods near the Brooklyn Bridge and into then-rural southwestern Brooklyn.

2008 Presidential Vote		
Obama (D)	206,656	(91%)
McCain (R)	20,709	(9%)

2004 Presidential Vote		
Kerry (D)	172,654	(86%)
Bush (R)	26,172	(13%)

Cook Partisan Voting Index: D+38

Suddenly, Manhattan factory workers no longer had to live in the crowded Lower East Side tenements that social reformer Jacob Riis had exposed in the 1890s. They moved in droves into neighborhoods of three- to five-story apartments and four-family houses. Brooklyn grew from 1.1 million in 1900 to 1.6 million in 1910 to 2 million in 1920 and to 2.6 million in 1930. The old Brooklynites were mostly Protestant—Dutch, Yankee and German, plus some Catholic Irish. The new Brooklynites were heavily Italian and Jewish, and they populated the sports and entertainment businesses for a long generation, making their hometown nationally famous. In 1940, Brooklyn had 2.7 million people: One of every 49 Americans lived in Brooklyn. The heart of the old Brooklyn was Ebbets Field, where the Dodgers played. Around the time Jackie Robinson suited up for the Brooklyn Dodgers in 1947 as the first black player in Major League Baseball, Brooklyn was experiencing an influx of blacks into Brownsville and Crown Heights near Ebbets Field. Just as rapid was the flight of ethnic whites, driven away by "blockbusting," in which hard-nosed real estate brokers stoked white fears, then bought their homes cheaply and re-sold high. After "Dem Bums" left for Los Angeles in 1958 and Ebbets Field was knocked down for an apartment complex, Brooklyn's black neighborhoods continued to grow.

By 2007, Brooklyn had 2.5 million people and was no longer a staple of national comedy. Some of its old neighborhoods have been ravaged by crime, but there is also great vitality among upwardly mobile Hispanic, Asian, Caribbean and Russian immigrants, among the hard-working, middle-class blacks, and among new generations of Italians and Jews. A change in zoning laws in 2004 resulted in a burst of new residential and office-space construction that reinvigorated Brooklyn's commercial district.

The 11th Congressional District of New York begins at the edge of downtown Brooklyn and includes some of the borough's jewels: the Grand Army Plaza, the Parisian-style Eastern Parkway (the world's first six-lane parkway) and Prospect Park, home to the Brooklyn Library, the Brooklyn Museum and the Brooklyn Botanic Garden, with its Japanese landscaping and placid duck ponds. Park Slope, on Prospect Park's west side, has become increasingly affluent, filling up with young professionals who appreciate the easy commute to downtown Manhattan. On the east side of Prospect Park is Crown Heights, with its mix of modest apartment buildings and nicely restored row houses. However, it was the scene of violent clashes between blacks and Hasidic Jews in 1991 (the Lubavitch Hasidim, who make up the largest Hasidic sect in the world, are headquartered in Crown Heights). Prospect Park South, also adjoining the park, is an affluent neighborhood with artsy yuppies whose stately mansions contrast sharply with the vibrant Caribbean street life just around the corner on Flatbush's Church Avenue and with struggling, depopulated Brownsville to the east. Most of these neighborhoods have great ethnic diversity. One minute you are in "La Saline," a center of the Haitian community in the East Flatbush-Crown Heights area, nicknamed for the slum district of Port-au-Prince, and the next, you are in "Little Pakistan" in Midwood, home to the largest concentration of Pakistanis in America. The district's population is 56% black, roughly half Caribbean in origin, and 12% Hispanic. Politically, the district is overwhelmingly Democratic, but the borough's party organization has been weakened by allegations of corruption.

The congresswoman from the 11th District is Yvette Clarke, a Democrat elected in 2006. She was born in Brooklyn to immigrant parents from Jamaica. As a young girl, she tagged along to political meetings and events with her mother, Una Clarke, who in 1991 became the first Jamaican elected to the New York City Council. Yvette Clarke attended Oberlin College in Ohio, but fell short of graduating by six credit hours. She returned to New York, helped train child-care workers, worked as a state legislative aide and served as business-development director for the Bronx Overall Economic Development Corp. In 2001, when term limits forced her mother off the City Council, Clarke defeated four other candidates to succeed her in the predominately Caribbean area of Flatbush and East Flatbush.

Since its creation in 1968 until 2006, the 11th District had been represented by just two people, both Democrats—trailblazer Shirley Chisholm, the first black woman elected to Congress and a 1972 presidential candidate, and Major Owens, who succeeded her in 1982. Owens had announced in 2004 that he would serve just one more term and hoped that his son Chris, a health-industry administrator, would succeed him. But Clarke was also part of a political family that had designs on the seat. Her mother had run against Owens, an African-American, in the 2000 Democratic primary, a bitter contest that exposed divisions between the local Caribbean-American community and the African-American community. Una Clark accused Owens of being ineffective and anti-immigrant. Owens accused Clarke of betraying their friendship, and he won 54%-46%. Four years later, Yvette Clarke and fellow City Councilwoman Tracy Boyland challenged Owens in the Democratic primary, both aware that his son would likely run for the seat two years later. Owens won the low-turnout primary with an unimpressive 45%, to 29% for Clarke and 22% for Boyland. When Clarke faced re-election to the council in 2005, Owens retaliated by backing, unsuccessfully, her primary-election opponent.

Clarke decided to run again in 2006, but first had to navigate a competitive primary field. New York City Councilman David Yassky, who is white, jumped in, only to be called a "colonizer" by Owens for running in a majority-black district that had been created in 1968 in response to a Voting Rights Act lawsuit. The black community feared that the well-financed Yassky, who had moved three blocks into the district to run for the seat, would be the beneficiary if the black vote was splintered among the three prominent black candidates: Clarke, Chris Owens and state Sen. Carl Andrews. By the end of August, Yassky had raised over $1.3 million, more than the other three candidates combined.

But Yassky had an awkward campaign style that made it difficult for him to connect with voters. Clarke's status as the only woman in the contest and her support among Caribbean-Americans were helpful. On the leading local issue, Clarke supported a plan to build a Nets arena and other development in Brooklyn, while Owens vigorously opposed it. Clarke stumbled when she was forced to backtrack from her claim that she had graduated from Oberlin. But she picked up the endorsement of the Service Employees International Union's powerful Local 1199, which worked to turn out votes. In the September 12 primary, the only election that mattered in this heavily Democratic district, Clarke defeated Yassky 31%-27%, while Andrews finished third with 23% and Owens last with 19%.

In the House, Clarke has had a solidly liberal voting record. In her activist freshman class, she operated largely in the background and waited nine months to file her first bill, which sought to reduce the backlog of immigration applications. In June 2008, the House passed her bill to create an appeals process for individuals wrongly denied rights in homeland- security investigations.

Clarke occasionally goes her own way. In November 2007, she voted against passing a bill to ban workplace discrimination against gays and lesbians because it did not also protect transgender workers. She was one of nine Democrats who voted in December 2007 against a resolution recognizing the importance of Christmas. Because of a conflict with Democratic adviser Howard Wolfson that had lingered after the 2006 campaign, she was the final member of the New York delegation to endorse Sen. Hillary Rodham Clinton in the 2008 presidential campaign.

Clarke ran unopposed in the 2008 Democratic primary and was re-elected with 93% of the vote in November. But past conflicts and political changes in Brooklyn could affect redistricting and pose problems for her.

TWELFTH DISTRICT

Nydia Velázquez (D)

Elected 1992, 9th term; b. March 28, 1953, Yabucoa, PR; home, Brooklyn; U. of PR, B.A. 1974, N.Y.U., M.A. 1976; Catholic; married (Paul Bader).

Elected Office: NY City Cncl., 1984–86.

Professional Career: Instructor, U. of PR, 1976–81; Adjunct prof., Hunter Col., 1981–83; Special asst., U.S. Rep. Edolphus Towns, 1983; Migration dir., PR Dept. of Labor & Human Resources, 1986–89; Secy., PR Dept. of Community Affairs in the U.S., 1989–92.

DC Office: 2466 RHOB, 20515, 202-225-2361; Fax: 202-226-0327; Web site: www.house.gov/velazquez.

State Offices: Brooklyn, 718-599-3658; Brooklyn, 718-222-5819; Manhattan, 212-673-3997.

Committees: *Financial Services* (6th of 42 D): Capital Markets, Insurance & Government Sponsored Enterprises; Housing & Community Opportunity. *Small Business* (Chmn of 17 D).

Group Ratings

	ADA	ACLU	AFS	LCV	ITIC	NTU	COC	ACU	CFG	FRC
2008	100	100	100	92	86	7	50	0	0	5
2007	95	—	100	85	—	4	60	0	6	—

National Journal Ratings

	2007 LIB	—	2007 CONS		2008 LIB	—	2008 CONS
Economic	82%	—	0%		85%	—	0%
Social	77%	—	17%		82%	—	0%
Foreign	96%	—	0%		92%	—	0%
Composite	90%	—	10%		93%	—	7%

Key Votes of the 110th Congress

1. Increase minimum wage	Y	5. Share immigration data	N	9. Withdraw troops 8/08	Y
2. Expand SCHIP	Y	6. Foreign aid abortion ban	N	10. No operations in Iran	Y
3. Raise CAFE standards	Y	7. Ban gay bias in workplace	N	11. Free trade with Peru	N
4. Bail out financial markets	Y	8. Repeal D.C. gun law	N	12. Overhaul FISA	N

Election Results

2008 general	Nydia Velázquez (D-WF)....................................123,046	(90%)	($816,108)
	Allan Romaguera (R-C) 13,747	(10%)	
2008 primary	Nydia Velázquez (D-WF)............................ unopposed		

Prior Winning Percentages: 2006 (90%); 2004 (86%); 2002 (96%); 2000 (87%); 1998 (84%); 1996 (85%); 1994 (92%); 1992 (77%)

Population		**Race/Ethnicity**		**Work**	
Pop. 2007:	671,803	White:	25.6%	Private:	81.3%
Change since 2000:	Up 2.7%	Black:	8.5%	Government:	11.5%
Urban:	100.0%	Hispanic:	46.8%	Self-employed:	7.1%
Rural:	0.0%	Asian:	17.3%	Blue collar:	23.8%
Area size:	20 sq. mi.	Native Am.:	0.2%	White collar:	51.4%
		Hawaiian:	0.0%	Khaki collar:	0.0%
Age		Two+ races:	0.7%	Other:	24.8%
Median age:	34.6 yrs.			Median income:	$37,435
More than 65 yrs:	10.5%	*Ancestry*		Median home value:	$548,000
Less than 18 yrs:	22.9%	Italian:	4.7%	Poverty:	25.0%
		Polish:	4.6%		
Education		Irish:	3.7%	**Military Veterans**	
H.S. grad:	66.9%			% of Pop:	2.8%
College grad:	23.3%				
Grad degree:	7.9%				

In 1957, amid a vast wave of Puerto Rican migration to New York, Leonard Bernstein wrote his musical *West Side Story*, with Romeo as an Italian-American and Juliet as a Manhattan Puerto Rican. Before World War II, there were 60,000 Puerto Ricans in New York City. Three decades later, with cheap airfares and no need to go through passport control, there were 800,000. But as the city's industrial base grew stagnant, the number of Puerto Ricans in New York declined, and young New

2008 Presidential Vote		
Obama (D) 154,394	(86%)
McCain (R)...............................23,504	(13%)

2004 Presidential Vote		
Kerry (D)................................130,019	(80%)
Bush (R) 29,942	(19%)

Cook Partisan Voting Index: D + 33

Yorkers of Puerto Rican descent increasingly moved to Puerto Rico. By the late 1990s, New York City was experiencing a large influx of Latinos from places not under the U.S. flag, and today most Hispanics in the city come not from Puerto Rico but from the Dominican Republic, Colombia, Mexico, Panama and Peru.

The 12th Congressional District of New York was designed to stitch together many of these diverse people. More than two-thirds of the district's population is in Brooklyn, with the remainder split between Queens and Manhattan. In Brooklyn, the district hugs the waterfront and dips inland to include areas with many Hispanics. But this is New York, so it takes in many other ethnicities as well. Overall, the district in 2007 was 47% Hispanic and 17% Asian (mostly Chinese). Sixty-seven percent spoke a language other than English at home. The 12th includes the upscale Brooklyn Heights waterfront, with its stunning but after September 11, haunting views of Lower Manhattan, and nearby Carroll Gardens with young professionals intermingled with Italian immigrants. To the south is Sunset Park, once the home of Irish, Polish and Norwegian immigrants, now filled with Chinese, Puerto Ricans, Colombians and Ecuadorans. North of Brooklyn Heights is DUMBO (Down Under the Manhattan Bridge Overpass), with artists in old industrial lofts, and just above that, Vinegar Hill. Williamsburg has many Orthodox Jews and recent Latino arrivals as well as some hip young people.

Inland is Bushwick, with low-income Latinos. Just a few streets away, across the Brooklyn-Queens border, is Ridgewood, once mostly Irish, then Polish, now filled with new arrivals from Poland, Romania, Albania, Serbia and Bosnia. Nearby is industrial Maspeth. In Manhattan, the 12th District includes parts of the Lower East Side, Chinatown and Little Italy, although today there are virtually no Italians (only

Italian restaurants), but still many Chinese, including the largest Chinese Roman Catholic church in the nation. The Bowery, which a century ago was the city's entertainment center, is the birthplace of punk rock and is slowly gentrifying. Politically, the 12th District is heavily Democratic.

The congresswoman from the 12th District is Nydia Velázquez, a Democrat elected in 1992. She grew up in Puerto Rico, one of nine children of sugarcane-field workers. Although her father never finished elementary school, he was a political leader in her hometown of Yabucoa and inspired her to pursue politics as a career. She studied political science at the University of Puerto Rico and taught there in the 1970s. After graduate school in New York City, she went to work for Rep. Edolphus Towns of New York. In 1983, she became the first Hispanic woman to be elected to the New York City Council. When the 12th District was created in 1992, Velázquez was a major contender in the Democratic primary but had to overcome Rep. Stephen Solarz, who had decided to run in the new district rather than in the Manhattan-dominated 8th or in the 9th District, where incumbent Democrat Charles Schumer had a heavy advantage. Velázquez got the endorsements of Mayor David Dinkins and civil rights leader Jesse Jackson, and in a light turnout election, beat Solarz 34% to 28%. After the primary, confidential hospital records that were leaked to a New York tabloid indicated that in September 1991, Velázquez had attempted suicide, was hospitalized and underwent counseling. Evidently, it was of little concern to voters. She won in November with 77% of the vote.

In the House, Velázquez has a solidly liberal voting record, with occasional pro-business votes on economic issues. She is the chairman of the Small Business Committee, where she has sought to give small businesses more time to comply with the tougher accounting standards of the 2002 Sarbanes-Oxley law. In 2008, she tried to win enactment of a bill that would have expanded subsidies for small-business innovation by diverting $650 million from other federal research funds, but she backed off after the Bush administration strongly objected. In March 2009, she praised the Obama administration for requiring the nation's largest banks to report monthly on how much lending they do to small businesses.

Earlier, when the Republicans controlled the House and Velázquez was the ranking Democrat on the panel, she joined with Chairman Don Manzullo of Illinois to reinstate a Small Business Administration loan program that had guaranteed lenders a 75% return if a borrower defaulted on loans of up to $750,000. The Bush administration insisted on abolishing the SBA subsidy and funding the program with higher fees to borrowers and lenders. In 2004 Manzullo and Velázquez won approval to add $79 million to the SBA budget to support the loan program, although some fees were also increased. Velázquez also initiated an annual scorecard to show whether the federal government had met its goal of granting 23% of contracts to small businesses. In 2005, the SBA Office of Advocacy found that the agency had miscoded a significant number of loans to small divisions of large firms and had counted them as small-business loans. Velázquez accused the Bush administration of "cooking the books." In 2006, her scorecard showed that the government had miscoded $12 billion in contracts and that only 22% of contracts went to small businesses. She also charged that the SBA repeatedly fell short of its goal of granting 5% of loans to women.

She has been equally vigilant in overseeing SBA problems in approving loans to small businesses affected by Hurricane Katrina in 2004. After a government report pointing to chaotic service, failure to plan for increased staff and office space, and a loan approval process that lagged behind demand, she said, "At this point, SBA has given us no reason to believe it can adequately respond to another Katrina, and that is simply not acceptable." She called on Administrator Hector Barreto to resign, and in 2006, he did resign.

Velázquez has been a leading voice on issues related to Puerto Rico and the ongoing debate over whether to change the commonwealth's status. She favors an inclusive process that would allow the people of Puerto Rico to determine the status of the island. Velázquez has authored legislation authorizing a constitutional convention which would produce a recommendation that would then be subject to a referendum. Those results would then be submitted to Congress. In 2007, she opposed a bill sponsored by New York Democratic Rep. José Serrano, which she said bypassed a consensus process. She strongly advocated clemency for several members of the FALN terrorist group who had sought Puerto Rican independence; they'd been responsible for the deaths of six people and had been imprisoned for 19 years, after being convicted on seditious-conspiracy and weapons charges. When President Bill Clinton granted clemency in 1999, on condition that they renounce violence, Velázquez said that clemency should be unconditional. The House condemned the clemency move, 311-41. Velázquez also champions the cause of immigrants. She favors no time limits on welfare and benefits for legal immigrants, and in 2006, she participated in a Brooklyn march protesting immigration-restriction proposals. "*Si se puede,*" she cried, adding, "We should not be in the business of criminalizing undocumented immigrants."

In 2009, Velázquez became chairman of the Hispanic Caucus, an influential group of Hispanic House members. She had run for the post two years earlier and been beaten by California Democrat Joe Baca. Her friendship with House Speaker Nancy Pelosi has contributed to her rising influence. A longtime combatant in New York City's political wars, Velázquez she has won re-election easily every two years. In the contested 2008 Democratic presidential primary, she was an enthusiastic backer of Hillary Rodham Clinton for president in 2008, and she voiced doubts about how well Barack Obama was "connecting" to Hispanics.

THIRTEENTH DISTRICT

Michael McMahon (D)

Elected 2008, 1st term; b. Sept. 12, 1957, Staten Island; home, Staten Island; NYU., B.A. 1980, NY Law School J.D. 1985; U. of Heidelberg, A.S. 1982; Catholic; married (Judith); 2 children.

Elected Office: NY City Cncl., 2001–08

Professional Career: Counsel, NY St. Assemblymen Eric Vitaliano & Elizabeth Connelly, 1987–2000; Partner, O'Leary, McMahon & Spero, 1993–2008

DC Office: 323 CHOB, 20515, 202-225-3371; Fax: 202-226-1272; Web site: mcmahon.house.gov.

State Offices: Brooklyn, 718-630-5277; Staten Island, 718-351-1062.

Committees: *Foreign Affairs* (14th of 28 D): Europe, the Middle East & South Asia; Terrorism, Nonproliferation & Trade. *Transportation & Infrastructure* (41st of 44 D): Aviation; Coast Guard & Maritime Transportation; Railroads, Pipelines & Hazardous Materials.

Group Ratings and Key Votes: Newly Elected

Election Results

2008 general	Michael McMahon (D-WF)	114,219	(61%)	($1,272,811)
	Robert Straniere (R)	62,441	(33%)	($162,474)
	Timothy Cochrane (C)	5,799	(3%)	
	Carmine Morano (Ind)	4,947	(3%)	($51,424)
2008 primary	Michael McMahon (D)	11,792	(74%)	
	Stephen Harrison (D)	3,885	(26%)	

Population		Race/Ethnicity		Work	
Pop. 2007:	699,459	White:	66.5%	Private:	76.0%
Change since 2000:	Up 6.9%	Black:	6.7%	Government:	19.6%
Urban:	100.0%	Hispanic:	14.1%	Self-employed:	4.3%
Rural:	0.0%	Asian:	11.7%	Blue collar:	18.3%
Area size:	113 sq. mi.	Native Am.:	0.1%	White collar:	63.7%
		Hawaiian:	0.0%	Khaki collar:	0.1%
Age		Two+ races:	0.6%	Other:	17.9%
Median age:	38.2 yrs.			Median income:	$61,433
More than 65 yrs:	13.6%	*Ancestry*		Median home value:	$486,100
Less than 18 yrs:	22.8%	Italian:	27.8%	Poverty:	11.1%
		Irish:	10.9%		
Education		German:	4.2%	**Military Veterans**	
H.S. grad:	84.7%			% of Pop:	6.5%
College grad:	27.3%				
Grad degree:	10.9%				

Staten Island is part of New York City, yet is a land apart, closer geographically and culturally to New Jersey than to the city's other boroughs. The sixth-largest island in the continental U.S., its inclusion in Greater New York as part of the great 1898 consolidation was something of an afterthought. It was connected to the rest of the city only by ferry or through Bayonne, N.J., until the Verrazano Narrows Bridge—one of Robert Moses's last and most impressive infrastructure achievements—opened

2008 Presidential Vote		
McCain (R)	112,491	(51%)
Obama (D)	108,439	(49%)

2004 Presidential Vote		
Bush (R)	118,370	(55%)
Kerry (D)	96,474	(45%)

Cook Partisan Voting Index: R + 4

to traffic in 1965. Hilly Staten Island (or Richmond County) is the state's southernmost county, one-tenth as densely populated as Manhattan, and that's after it grew 22% between 1990 and 2004, the fastest growth rate of any county in New York state. Its rate of home ownership, 70%, is nearly double that of the rest of New York City and nearly meets the national average. Ethnically, the 13th District has the highest percentage of residents of Italian ancestry in the nation. The signs on coffee shops read *Caffe* and on delicatessens, *Salumeria*. The Staten Island Ferry docks at St. George, the home of the Staten Island Yankees' new ballpark. The north and south shores that spread out from there are notable for their pleasant Victorian homes, while the island's west shore is industrial marshland, with plans for the eventual development of a 2,200-acre park—more than twice as large as Central Park—on top of the now-closed Fresh Kills dump. Staten Island's interior consists of blocks of suburbia alternating with scrubland that's rapidly being turned into suburbia. Population growth, plus a shortage of mass transit, has brought significant traffic congestion to the island, which is more dependent on cars than the other boroughs.

Culturally, Staten Islanders are more conservative than people from the boroughs, particularly the Manhattanites who live a 20-minute ferry ride away. Taking a cue from Fresh Kills, their motto is "Don't dump on us." Not many people here read the *New York Times*; the local paper is the *Staten Island Advance*. Fed up with the city's high income taxes and social programs, Staten Island residents voted in 1993 for secession, but the Legislature never acted to carry out their wish. In that same election, Staten Islanders provided the margin of victory for Republican Mayor Rudolph Giuliani, whose agenda of cutting crime and welfare rolls soothed the secessionist fervor. The Giuliani years produced an economic boom, with a new ferry terminal, additional shops and hundreds of new houses near cleaned-up beaches. The biggest victory was the closing of Fresh Kills in 2001, though it opened again temporarily for the cleanup of the World Trade Center site. The September 11 attacks killed nearly 250 residents of Staten Island. They made up nearly 10% of the dead and nearly a fourth of all the firefighters who died.

The 13th Congressional District of New York is made up of Staten Island plus Brooklyn neighborhoods with similar demographics. These include heavily Catholic and Italian Bay Ridge, Dyker Heights and Bensonhurst, middle-class enclaves with large single-family brownstones that are nowhere near a subway stop and thus impervious to the gentrification spreading across Brooklyn. The entertainment industry has found some memorable characters in these neighborhoods: The Three Stooges (Moe, Curly and Shemp) grew up in Bensonhurst, which also was the home to the fictional Ralph Kramden of *The Honeymooners*. John Travolta danced to fame in the film *Saturday Night Fever* on the streets of Bensonhurst and Bay Ridge. The district also includes Gravesend, with its large population of Sephardic Jews, and Fort Hamilton, the only active-duty military base in New York City and one of the oldest military posts still in operation in the United States.

The 13th is seeing a rising number of immigrants. There are growing numbers of Muslims in Bay Ridge and an influx of newcomers from West Africa, Mexico, South America, Southeast Asia, and Russia in white ethnic neighborhoods near St. George. But Staten Island remains New York's whitest borough and has the fewest immigrants. It is only 7% black and 14% Hispanic. Voters here solidly backed Republican George Pataki for governor and gave then-Republican Mayor Michael Bloomberg his slim winning margin in 2001. The district voted 52%-44% for Democrat Al Gore in 2000, but snapped back to Republican George W. Bush four years later, 55%-45%. In 2008, it voted for McCain 51%-49%.

The new congressman from the 13th District of New York is Michael McMahon, a Democrat who won the seat in 2008 after Republican Rep. Vito Fossella tumbled into the national spotlight for all the wrong reasons. A drunk-driving arrest in Virginia led to revelations about an extramarital affair and a child born out of wedlock. Three weeks after his arrest, Fossella, a one-time rising GOP star, announced that he would retire.

A lifelong Staten Islander and self-described moderate, McMahon grew up in Stapleton, the middle child of seven children. His father was as an insurance underwriter, and his mother, a German immigrant, worked as a hotel bookkeeper. While bartending and waiting tables, he earned a degree in political science and history from New York University. He spent two years at the University of Heidelberg in Germany studying to teach German, then returned home to get his law degree at New York Law School. McMahon practiced law as a counsel to two state Assembly members from Staten Island and as a partner at the law firm of O'Leary, McMahon and Spero. While working for the Assembly, McMahon helped write legislation in the early 1990s that would have let Staten Island secede from New York City. He has said that since then, better borough planning and a more attentive mayoral administration under Bloomberg have put the secession question to rest. In 2001, McMahon ran for the New York City Council on the island's North Shore. He won the Democratic primary by a narrow 170-vote margin but easily won the seat that November. As a councilman, he worked to keep the Fresh Kills dump closed, to increase service for the Staten Island Ferry and to require nurses in all city schools. The national Democratic Congressional Campaign Committee long viewed McMahon as a promising candidate in the district, but McMahon had resisted their entreaties.

In 2008, after a year of the Fossella scandal—an unending political drama all but gift-wrapped for headline writers at the *New York Post*—Republicans lost their dominance in Staten Island. After the incumbent announced that he would not seek re-election, McMahon jumped into the primary race, where he faced Brooklyn lawyer Stephen Harrison, the Democratic candidate against Fossella in 2006. The borough's Democratic and Working Families parties immediately endorsed McMahon, and the DCCC quickly followed suit. Harrison refused to drop his campaign, charging that McMahon was not a true Democrat. But the longtime councilman compiled a long roster of support that included local labor unions, Democrats from the city's House delegation and both U.S. senators from New York. He cruised to victory by a 3-to-1 margin in the September primary.

The open seat should have portended a competitive race, but a situation that had started out badly for the GOP only got worse. The party's choice to replace Fossella, retired Wall Street executive Frank Powers, died of a heart attack in June. To replace him, Republicans turned to Robert Straniere, a controversial former assemblyman rejected by much of the GOP establishment because of his questionable business dealings and past battles with other local Republicans. Straniere criticized McMahon for supporting a property-tax increase on the City Council in 2002; McMahon countered that the hike was needed to salvage the city's finances after the terrorist attacks. With his own party divided over his candidacy, Straniere never had much of a chance against the well-funded McMahon, who outspent Straniere 9-to-1 and picked up endorsements from Bloomberg and Conservative Party Borough President James Molinaro. He won easily, beating Straniere 61% to 33%. He won by wide margins everywhere but in the Republican strongholds on the South Shore, where he ran nearly even with Straniere. He became the first Democrat in 28 years to represent Staten Island.

McMahon was given seats on the Foreign Affairs and Transportation and Infrastructure committees. He had sought a spot on the Transportation panel in order to try to secure federal money to expand ferry service and to construct rail lines on the north and west shores. In his first few months in the House, McMahon was a party-line voter in the House and supported President Obama's $787 billion economic-stimulus bill. His first bill mandated confidential mental-health screenings for military personnel returning from Iraq and Afghanistan.

FOURTEENTH DISTRICT

Carolyn Maloney (D)

Elected 1992, 9th term; b. Feb. 19, 1946, Greensboro, NC; home, Manhattan; Greensboro Col, A.B. 1968; Presbyterian; married (Clifton); 2 children.

Elected Office: NY City Cncl., 1982–92.

Professional Career: NYC Bd. of Ed., 1970–77; Legis. aide, NY Assembly & NY Senate, 1977–82.

DC Office: 2232 RHOB, 20515, 202-225-7944; Fax: 202-225-4709; Web site: maloney.house.gov.

State Offices: Astoria, 718-932-1804; Manhattan, 212-860-0606.

Committees: *Financial Services* (4th of 42 D): Capital Markets, Insurance & Government Sponsored Enterprises; Domestic Monetary Policy & Technology; Financial Institutions & Consumer Credit. *Joint Economic Committee* (Chmn of 6 D). *Oversight & Government Reform* (3rd of 24 D): Information Policy, Census & National Archives; National Security & Foreign Affairs.

Group Ratings

	ADA	ACLU	AFS	LCV	ITIC	NTU	COC	ACU	CFG	FRC
2008	95	100	100	92	100	6	65	0	1	0
2007	90	—	100	100	—	6	58	0	6	—

National Journal Ratings

	2007 LIB — 2007 CONS		2008 LIB — 2008 CONS	
Economic	76%	— 23%	65%	— 34%
Social	75%	— 23%	82%	— 0%
Foreign	86%	— 11%	70%	— 25%
Composite	80%	— 20%	76%	— 24%

Key Votes of the 110th Congress

1. Increase minimum wage	Y	5. Share immigration data	N	9. Withdraw troops 8/08	Y
2. Expand SCHIP	Y	6. Foreign aid abortion ban	N	10. No operations in Iran	Y
3. Raise CAFE standards	Y	7. Ban gay bias in workplace	Y	11. Free trade with Peru	Y
4. Bail out financial markets	Y	8. Repeal D.C. gun law	N	12. Overhaul FISA	N

Election Results

2008 general	Carolyn Maloney (D-WF)	183,190	(80%)	($1,257,989)
	Robert Heim (R)	43,365	(19%)	
2008 primary	Carolyn Maloney (D-WF)	unopposed		

Prior Winning Percentages: 2006 (84%); 2004 (81%); 2002 (75%); 2000 (74%); 1998 (77%); 1996 (72%); 1994 (64%); 1992 (50%)

Population		Race/Ethnicity		Work	
Pop. 2007:	645,763	White:	67.3%	Private:	83.0%
Change since 2000:	Down 1.3%	Black:	4.1%	Government:	8.1%
Urban:	100.0%	Hispanic:	14.1%	Self-employed:	8.8%
Rural:	0.0%	Asian:	12.3%	Blue collar:	6.8%
Area size:	15 sq. mi.	Native Am.:	0.1%	White collar:	82.9%
		Hawaiian:	0.1%	Khaki collar:	0.0%
Age		Two+ races:	1.2%	Other:	10.2%
Median age:	38.2 yrs.			Median income:	$74,669
More than 65 yrs:	13.7%	*Ancestry*		Median home value:	$712,200
Less than 18 yrs:	14.5%	Italian:	8.1%	Poverty:	10.5%
		Irish:	8.0%		
Education		USA:	6.6%	**Military Veterans**	
H.S. grad:	90.2%			% of Pop:	4.2%
College grad:	62.8%				
Grad degree:	28.1%				

The Upper East Side of Manhattan, the home of people with more accumulated wealth than anywhere else in the world, began as much of New York City did, as farmland. Its eastern border was established at Fifth Avenue when work began on Central Park in 1857, but most of the area was still farmland when the park was completed in 1873. During the 1880s, the avenues—Fifth, Madison, Park, Lexington, Third, Second, First—were paved, and rich New Yorkers as well as many who had made their

2008 Presidential Vote
Obama (D) 212,802   (78%)
McCain (R)..............................56,946   (21%)

2004 Presidential Vote
Kerry (D)...............................201,782   (74%)
Bush (R) 66,494   (24%)

Cook Partisan Voting Index: D + 26

money elsewhere, including Pittsburgh steel baron Andrew Carnegie and Montana mining magnate William Clark, built mansions on Fifth Avenue. Third Avenue, with its elevated train line, was lined with walk-ups for working- class commuters, while the side streets off Fifth Avenue were filled with massive brownstones shielded from the industrial haze along the East River. The Upper East Side began taking on its present character in 1913, when Grand Central Terminal was opened and the New York Central rail line was buried under Park Avenue. What had been a filthy railroad cut became a broad boulevard lined with grand apartment buildings. The federal income tax, passed the same year, had the unintended consequence of encouraging New York's rich to dispense with grand mansions and live, quietly and out of sight, in apartment buildings where doormen protected their privacy. The Upper East Side remains a world apart from ordinary folks. Even as the recession hit in 2008, it set records for the number of $5 million-plus residential sales, and the locals complained about how tough it was to exist on a mere $500,000 annual income—which President Obama set as the top salary for executives in banks receiving federal bailout money.

The emergence of the modern Upper East Side represented yet another iteration of the pattern noticed by the mid-19th-century New York diarists Philip Hone and George Templeton Strong: On such a compact island, it took only a generation or so before buildings were torn down and rebuilt. Even today, New York is being transformed by gleaming postmodern skyscrapers and high-priced storefronts, though its most enduring landmarks were products of the first half of the 20th century: the Flatiron Building, built in 1901; the Woolworth Building and Grand Central, in 1913; the Chrysler Building, in the 1920s; and the Empire State Building and Rockefeller Center, in the 1930s. The United Nations headquarters, the world's first glass-fronted skyscraper, went up after World War II. This area also holds the more humble distinction of being the site of the first public-housing project in America: The First Houses were built in lower Manhattan in 1935 by Mayor Fiorello LaGuardia.

The 14th Congressional District of New York includes within its irregular borders the Upper East Side and nearly all of these famous buildings. It begins at East 96th Street, the historic dividing line between Manhattan's wealthiest and poorest neighborhoods, and runs all the way down to East 9th Street in the East Village. It includes all of Central Park, much of the midtown corporate district, Murray Hill in the 30s and Gramercy Park to the south. It takes in parts of the East Village, with its pricey lofts and busy nightlife, and the Lower East Side. Midtown Manhattan's skyscrapers and the Garment District are also here, as is Roosevelt Island, a 147-acre expanse in the East River that was transformed in the 1970s from a hospital-and-prison complex into an ethnically diverse residential neighborhood (and stripped of its old name, Welfare Island). The 14th also encompasses part of Queens across the East River; blue-collar Long Island City; Steinway, part of historically Irish Sunnyside; and vibrant Greek Astoria, now with many Asians, Latinos and Arabs. The district's cultural landmarks are among the world's finest: the Metropolitan Museum of Art, the Guggenheim, the Whitney and the Frick, but also a rising arts cluster in Long Island City with the contemporary-art gallery P.S. 1 and the American Museum of the Moving Image.

The district has always been dominated by its affluent and highly educated voters, leaders in securities, publishing, advertising, entertainment, broadcasting and communications. Historically, they mistrusted the city's usually Democratic immigrant masses, the politics of Theodore Roosevelt, the old *New York Herald Tribune* and Henry Luce's *Time* magazine. But the attitude of the Manhattan elite was transformed from liberal Republican to leftish Democratic in a way personified by the Silk Stocking district's most famous politician, John Lindsay. He was elected to Congress in 1958 as a liberal Republican, an advocate of civil liberties and full of mistrust of machine Democrats and unions. In 1965, he was elected mayor of New York and eventually ran up huge debts that led the city to the brink of bankruptcy in 1975. Neighborhoods deteriorated, and the city lost 1 million people in the 1970s. He was succeeded as congressman and ultimately as mayor by Democrat Edward Koch, who managed to clean up the mess he left in the city's finances, but then alienated the liberal elite by favoring capital punishment, opposing racial quotas and questioning the efficacy of poverty programs. Since then, Republican Mayor Rudolph Giuliani and his successor, Michael Bloomberg, who lives in a town house on East 79th Street, have been cultural liberals on abortion rights, gay rights and gun control. To the national Republican Party of former House Speaker Newt Gingrich in the 1990s and President George W. Bush, who brought the Republican Convention of 2004 to a less-than-enthralled Manhattan, the Upper East Side was unremittingly hostile. When the rest of the country narrowly favored Bush over Democrats Al Gore and John Kerry, the Upper East Side voted for the Democrats by wide margins. The Upper East Side's 10021 zip code was the nation's top zip code for Democratic campaign contributions in 2004 and 2008. The district voted for Democrat Barack Obama over Republican John McCain 78% to 21% in 2008.

The congresswoman from the 14th District is Carolyn Maloney, a Democrat elected in 1992. Born and educated in North Carolina, she visited New York in 1970 at the age of 22, loved it and "just stayed." She taught adult-education classes in East Harlem and, from 1977 to 1982, was an influential legislative staffer in Albany. She was elected to the New York City Council in 1982. Redistricting in 1992 made the Silk Stocking district more Democratic, and Maloney ran against incumbent Bill Green, an independent Republican who shared Manhattan's cultural liberalism. But he was poorly positioned to appeal to voters in the outer-borough neighborhoods that had been added to the district, who preferred Republicans to be conservative on cultural issues but liberal on economics. Maloney lost the Manhattan part of the district 50%-44% but carried Queens heavily, winning 50%-48% overall.

Maloney has a mostly liberal voting record. Long an active and effective legislator, she won new prominence in early 2009 when she became chairman of the Joint Economic Committee, a House and Senate panel that tackles pressing economic issues. She is also a senior member of the Financial Services Committee, where she has been a prominent voice on banking issues. Her priorities include limits on predatory loans and protections from inaccurate credit reports. She worked hard to win House passage in September 2008 of her bill to promote more transparent practices by credit card companies and to restrict abusive lending practices. She called the bill "a much-needed correction to a market that is out of balance." With a boost from President Obama, the bill was enacted in May 2009. Even though many bankers are her constituents, she had tough rhetoric for bankers who took millions of dollars in bonuses after their firms received federal bailout money in 2008. In earlier years, she worked to keep banks from controlling other businesses, sought more oversight of the Federal Reserve, and added privacy provisions to financial modernization bills. She helped to craft reforms tightening rules for foreign investment. With an eye to her corporate constituents, she voted for normal trade relations with China.

A leader of the Women's Caucus, she demanded that the Food and Drug Administration permit over-the-counter sales of morning-after birth-control pills, and she opposed separating men and women in basic training in the military. She introduced a bill to create an office within the Internal Revenue Service to prosecute sex traffickers who violate tax laws. In 2007, with Sen. Edward Kennedy, D-Mass., she introduced the Women's Equality Amendment, a latter-day version of the Equal Rights Amendment, which fell three states short of constitutional ratification in the 1970s. In June 2008, the House passed her bill to give eight weeks of paid leave to federal employees for the birth or adoption of a child. Also in 2008, she authored a book, *Rumors of Our Progress Have Been Greatly Exaggerated: Why Women's Lives Aren't Getting Any Easier — And How We Can Make Real Progress for Ourselves and Our Daughters.*

With part of her district in Lower Manhattan and close to Ground Zero, Maloney was heavily involved in the government response to the September 11 attacks. She was among the most outspoken House Democrats urging President George W. Bush to quickly send New York the $20 billion that Congress approved for cleanup and recovery, and she urged him to appoint a coordinator to work with the city. But her proposal to give a $1,000 tax credit to visitors to the city went nowhere.

Maloney has a firm lock on the district. In the Republican year of 1994, City Councilman Charles Millard of Manhattan spent almost $1 million running against her, but Maloney won 64%-35%. Aside from the perils of redistricting, she has not had to worry about re-election since then. She was bitterly disappointed when New York Gov. David Paterson appointed the less-seasoned Democratic Rep. Kirsten Gillibrand to the Senate seat vacated by Hillary Rodham Clinton when she became secretary of State in 2009. Maloney publicly questioned Gillibrand's conservative stance on issues such as gun control and curbing illegal immigration, and she began raising money for a primary challenge in 2010. As the first woman in Congress to get a black belt in martial arts, she should not be underestimated.

FIFTEENTH DISTRICT

Charles Rangel (D)

Elected 1970, 20th term; b. June 11, 1930, New York City; home, Harlem; N.Y.U., B.S. 1957, St. John's U., LL.B. 1960; Catholic; married (Alma); 2 children.

Military Career: Army, 1948–52 (Korea).

Elected Office: NY Assembly, 1966–70.

Professional Career: Asst. U.S. atty., S. Dist. of NY, 1959–64; Legal cnsl., NYC Housing & Redevel. Bd., Neighborhood Conservation Bureau, 1963–68; Gen. cnsl., Natl. Advisory Comm. on Selective Svc., 1966.

DC Office: 2354 RHOB, 20515, 202-225-4365; Fax: 202-225-0816; Web site: rangel.house.gov.

State Offices: Manhattan, 212-663-3900.

Committees: *Joint Committee on Taxation* (Chmn of 3 D). *Ways & Means* (Chmn of 26 D).

Group Ratings

	ADA	ACLU	AFS	LCV	ITIC	NTU	COC	ACU	CFG	FRC
2008	85	100	100	92	100	5	61	0	0	0
2007	95	—	100	90	—	4	60	0	12	—

National Journal Ratings

	2007 LIB	—	2007 CONS		2008 LIB	—	2008 CONS
Economic	82%	—	0%		85%	—	0%
Social	77%	—	17%		82%	—	0%
Foreign	69%	—	29%		83%	—	15%
Composite	80%	—	20%		89%	—	11%

Key Votes of the 110th Congress

1. Increase minimum wage	Y	5. Share immigration data	N	9. Withdraw troops 8/08	Y
2. Expand SCHIP	Y	6. Foreign aid abortion ban	N	10. No operations in Iran	Y
3. Raise CAFE standards	Y	7. Ban gay bias in workplace	Y	11. Free trade with Peru	Y
4. Bail out financial markets	Y	8. Repeal D.C. gun law	N	12. Overhaul FISA	N

Election Results

2008 general	Charles Rangel (D-WF) 177,060	(89%)	($4,209,400)
	Edward Daniels (R) 15,668	(8%)	
2008 primary	Charles Rangel (D-WF) .... unopposed		

Prior Winning Percentages: 2006 (94%); 2004 (91%); 2002 (88%); 2000 (92%); 1998 (93%); 1996 (91%); 1994 (97%); 1992 (95%); 1990 (97%); 1988 (97%); 1986 (96%); 1984 (97%); 1982 (97%); 1980 (96%); 1978 (96%); 1976 (97%); 1974 (97%); 1972 (96%); 1970 (87%)

Population		Race/Ethnicity		Work	
Pop. 2007:	675,536	White:	20.5%	Private:	78.3%
Change since 2000:	Up 3.2%	Black:	27.9%	Government:	14.0%
Urban:	100.0%	Hispanic:	45.6%	Self-employed:	7.7%
Rural:	0.0%	Asian:	3.5%	Blue collar:	13.2%
Area size:	16 sq. mi.	Native Am.:	0.1%	White collar:	62.1%
		Hawaiian:	0.0%	Khaki collar:	0.1%
Age		Two+ races:	1.6%	Other:	24.6%
Median age:	35.3 yrs.	*Ancestry*		Median income:	$34,768
More than 65 yrs:	11.6%	Irish:	3.0%	Median home value:	$614,400
Less than 18 yrs:	22.0%	West Indian:	2.8%	Poverty:	27.2%
		German:	2.8%		
Education				**Military Veterans**	
H.S. grad:	72.2%			% of Pop:	3.4%
College grad:	33.1%				
Grad degree:	15.3%				

Harlem, for many years America's most famous black ghetto, is rebounding from decades of grim times. Harlem's development came relatively late in New York City's history. When Alexander Hamilton and Roger Morris built mansions in northern Manhattan, they were far out in the countryside. Early critics of Central Park questioned the necessity of setting aside open land when picnickers could always go to Harlem. By the late 19th century, Harlem had become a commuter neighborhood for

2008 Presidential Vote		
Obama (D)	226,049	(93%)
McCain (R)	14,954	(6%)
2004 Presidential Vote		
Kerry (D)	194,186	(90%)
Bush (R)	20,049	(9%)
Cook Partisan Voting Index:	D + 41	

Germans and then Jews and Italians. After the turn of the century, real estate speculators began constructing blocks of impressive brownstones, hoping to capitalize on the impending arrival of the subway. But overbuilding led to high vacancy rates, and some landlords, in desperation, agreed to rent to African-Americans, as long as they were willing to pay a premium. After generations of being shunted from one neighborhood to the next as the city developed, black residents were willing, and the neighborhood soon turned into the locus of New York City's African-American community. Harlem expanded from its nucleus around Lenox Avenue and 125th Street, while the Italian neighborhood to the east later known as Spanish Harlem grew outward from 116th Street and Pleasant Avenue. Many great black Americans—W. E. B. DuBois, Thurgood Marshall, Ralph Ellison, Joe Louis—lived in northwest Harlem's Sugar Hill.

For a long moment in history, Harlem was a center of writers and professionals and entertainers. The rosters of the Apollo Theater on 125th Street in the 1920s and 1930s were filled with the names of great artists still remembered today. Back then, the *WPA Guide* described Harlem as "the spiritual capital of Black America." But starting with the riot in the summer of 1964, Harlem endured decades of deterioration. Hundreds of brownstones were abandoned or pulled down. As successful black families moved out—to Springfield Gardens in Queens or Williamsbridge in the Bronx or to the Westchester or New Jersey suburbs—Harlem's population shifted increasingly toward welfare dependency and criminal gangs, and it declined by a third between 1970 and 1990.

Starting in the 1990s, Harlem began to recover. The federal government gave $300 million in investment capital, and the huge drop in crime under Republican Mayor Rudolph Giuliani made Harlem real estate valuable again. Brownstones were renovated, vacant city buildings were sold off, neighborhood schools were upgraded, and arts spaces were opened. Harlem was made a federal enterprise zone, with favorable federal and state tax treatment, and the Metropolitan Economic Revitalization Fund pumped money into new developments, as did Calvin Butts's Abyssinian Baptist Church. Younger African-Americans are returning, while visitors from overseas, especially Japan and Europe, flock to the area for historical tours, prompting a boomlet in niche hotels and guest houses. The façade of the Apollo Theater has been restored, a new Harlem pier has been constructed, and supermarkets and chain stores have opened. In 2001, former President Bill Clinton opened his post presidential office at 55 W. 125th Street in Harlem. There has been a double-digit percentage increase in median household income in Harlem since 2000. The upward trend abated somewhat in 2008 as Wall Street's problems reduced investment and charitable donations.

Politically, Harlem has been heavily Democratic ever since the 1930s, when black voters switched from the Republican Party of Abraham Lincoln to the Democratic Party of Franklin Roosevelt. Harlem got its own congressional district in 1944 and elected Adam Clayton Powell Jr., minister at the Abyssinian Baptist Church and a brilliant orator who became the most famous black politician of his time. He was the chairman of the Education and Labor Committee when it passed the Great Society programs in 1965, but was excluded from Congress in 1967 (illegally, the Supreme Court later ruled) for refusing to honor a New York decree in a libel case.

Today, the 15th Congressional District of New York includes not just Harlem but all of northern Manhattan, down to 89th Street on the west side and 96th Street on the east side. On the west side, the district's southern reaches include portions of the white, liberal Upper West Side as well as the Morningside Heights precincts around Columbia University. On the east side, at 96th Street, the railroad comes out of the tunnel that runs under Park Avenue to Grand Central Station, and the Upper East Side gives way to Harlem. Spanish Harlem, just to the north, was once Italian (it was Fiorello LaGuardia's political base) and later heavily Puerto Rican. Today, "El Barrio" has fewer Puerto Ricans and more Mexicans and Dominicans along with some gentrifying whites. Still farther north, the district includes Washington Heights and Inwood, both heavily Latino and the center of Dominican life in New York as Dominicans replace Puerto Ricans as New York's most numerous Latino group. Overall, the district in 2007 was 28% black and 46% Hispanic, figures that testify to decades of black flight from Harlem and the continuing inflow of immigrants from the Western Hemisphere. In 2004, this was the most heavily Democratic congressional district in the nation, voting 90% for John Kerry for president. Democrat Barack Obama won it in 2008 with 93%, his second best in the nation, after New York's adjacent 16th District.

The congressman from the 15th District is Democrat Charles Rangel, first elected to the House in 1970 and now chairman of the House Ways and Means Committee. Rangel grew up in Harlem and served in the Army in Korea, where he rescued 40 men from behind the lines in Kunu-ri and was awarded the Bronze Star. He graduated from New York University and St. John's University law school, served as legal counsel in several government agencies and was elected to the New York Assembly in 1966. He was part of a group of young black politicians—among them Basil Paterson, Carl McCall and Percy Sutton—who for many years dominated Harlem and greatly influenced New York politics. In 1970, Rangel challenged Powell in the Democratic primary and narrowly won. Remarkably, these two iconic and often controversial figures have been the district's only representatives for two-thirds of a century. Like most Harlem politicians, Rangel has long argued that government aid and racial preferences are needed to solve Harlem's problems.

Aside from some early successes on trade and increasing the minimum wage, Rangel's first two years as chairman in the 110th Congress (2007–08) proved relatively unproductive and often contentious, as his proposals came under veto threat from the Republican White House. Despite pressure from liberal Democrats, Rangel made little effort to alter the Bush-era tax cuts, which were scheduled to expire in 2010. He won House passage of a bill extending an adjustment in the alternative minimum tax to protect middle-income taxpayers, who increasingly have been forced to pay a tax that originally targeted only wealthy taxpayers. The Senate passed a similar bill. Rangel worked with other Democrats to expand the State Children's Health Insurance Program, but failed in October 2007 to get a sufficient number of Republican votes to override Bush's promised veto. He collaborated with other House committees on changes in tax law for the energy bill of 2007. And in 2008, he backed the federal bank bailout of financial institutions, though Ways and Means played a relatively minor role.

In 2009, Rangel said he was eager to "have a head start" in legislative planning for the new administration. "Time is not our friend," he warned in July 2008, describing the multiple challenges on tax policy, health care and entitlements legislation. With Obama as president, Rangel moved quickly to enact the long-discussed children's health-insurance expansion, and he helped craft $348 billion in tax cuts over five years in the administration's $787 billion economic-stimulus bill. He also joined other senior House Democrats in extended discussions on health reform. Somewhat less expected was his assertive role on climate-change legislation. Environmental legislation traditionally has been under the control of the Energy and Commerce Committee, but Rangel held numerous hearings on a proposed carbon tax.

Rangel's chairmanship has been marred by numerous ethics controversies uncovered by the *New York Times*. It reported that Rangel maintained four rent-controlled apartments in Harlem, despite state and city regulations stating that such apartments were supposed to be primary residences, that he failed to report rental income from a real estate investment in the Dominican Republic, and that he used his congressional stationery to raise funds for the Charles B. Rangel Center for Public Service at the City College of New York. Perhaps most damaging, The *Times* reported that Maurice Greenberg, one of the biggest shareholders in financially troubled American International Group, gave the Rangel school $5 million from a foundation he controlled in 2007, and that Rangel in early 2008, supported a provision in a tax bill that saved AIG several million dollars a year. Rangel steadfastly denied wrongdoing, and in September 2008 he requested a review by the House Committee on Standards of Official Conduct. Republicans demanded that he be removed as chairman while the inquiry was ongoing, but House Speaker Nancy Pelosi declined to do so.

Rangel combines political shrewdness with a lot of personal charm and a penchant for extravagant rhetoric. When a bipartisan majority voted to end racial preferences in broadcasting in 1995, Rangel lashed out in a letter to then Ways and Means Chairman Bill Archer, a Texas Republican, saying, "Just like under Hitler, people say they don't mean to blame any particular individuals and groups, but in the U.S. those groups always turn out to be minorities and immigrants." Archer refused to speak to Rangel, the ranking member of the committee, except in public committee meetings. During the 1990s, Rangel defended President Bill Clinton against impeachment with great vigor, but he did not always get along with Clinton. And he resented it when the administration negotiated directly with Republicans, leaving congressional Democrats out of the loop.

Republican Bill Thomas of California succeeded Archer as chairman. Notoriously acerbic and uncollegial, Thomas made few if any moves toward bipartisanship. In 2003, a Ways and Means meeting on pension legislation ended in chaos when Democrats led by Rangel walked out in protest, charging they hadn't had time to review a substitute bill the committee was considering. Thomas called the Capitol Police to remove the Democrats from the library where they had gathered, and in their absence, Republicans approved the bill by voice vote. Rangel later offered a resolution to nullify the meeting and chastised Thomas but dropped the effort after Thomas went to the House floor and made a tearful apology. Yet the committee was never able to work in a bipartisan way. Rangel also protested when Thomas excluded him from the House-Senate conference committee on the 2003 Medicare prescription-drug bill. The only Democrats Thomas allowed to participate were Senate Finance Committee members Max Baucus of Montana and John Breaux of Louisiana, who favored Thomas' bill.

Rangel has opposed some of the international free-trade agreements of recent years, but has proven open to compromise on others. After becoming chairman in 2007, Rangel moved to have the full committee, not the Ways and Means Trade Subcommittee, handle trade agreements. The subcommittee is chaired by liberal Democrat Sander Levin of Michigan, who has taken a harder line on labor and environmental provisions. In 2000, Rangel worked hard for a bill to cut tariffs on apparel and other imports from sub-Saharan Africa, despite opposition from labor unions, textile interests and other members of the Congressional Black Caucus. During 2004, Rangel did not take a position on the Central American-Dominican Republic Free Trade Agreement, though many Democrats opposed the agreement. There are many Dominican and Central American immigrants in New York.

One of Rangel's priorities is a permanent change in the alternative minimum tax to prevent it from ensnaring middle-class taxpayers. Rangel has suggested making up the lost revenue by restricting foreign tax shelters or by narrowing the gap between taxes owed and taxes paid. But he has made it plain many times over the years that he would adamantly oppose eliminating the deduction for state and local taxes—a deduction worth a great deal to New Yorkers, whose state and local taxes are relatively high. Rangel opposed President George W. Bush's proposal for individual investment accounts in Social Security in 2005, saying, "There's no guarantee the market's going to work for you." He helped write the Federal Empowerment Zone law, the Low Income Housing tax credit and the Targeted Jobs tax credit. He was a key sponsor of the 1993 increases in the Earned Income Tax Credit. All those would help turn around places like Harlem.

On foreign policy, Rangel has long advocated eliminating sanctions on trade with Cuba. He favors allowing Haitian and Dominican immigrants into the United States on the same basis as refugees from Cuba. Rangel voted against the Iraq war resolution in 2002 and the following year called for the resignation of Donald Rumsfeld. Late in 2002, he called for a revival of the military draft, contending that "a disproportionate number of the poor and members of minority groups make up the enlisted ranks of the military, while the most privileged Americans are underrepresented or absent." He introduced a bill in 2003 to require some form of national service, military or civilian, from Americans ages 18 to 26, and found 13 cosponsors. When House Republican leaders brought it to a vote in October 2004, he called it a "political maneuver to kill rumors of the president's intention to reinstate the draft after the November election" and voted against it, saying it had had no committee hearings. It was voted down 402-2.

Earlier in his House career, Rangel's main emphasis had been trying to curb the illegal drug trade. Starting in 1983, he chaired the Select Committee on Narcotics Abuse and Control and seldom missed a chance to relate other social problems to the prevalence of drug abuse; he was chairman until 1993, when the committee was abolished along with other House select committees.

In the 2008 election, he was an early and vocal supporter of home-state Sen. Hillary Rodham Clinton in her pitched battle with Obama for the Democratic nomination. "This ain't no time for a beginner," he told the *New York Times* in January 2008, referring to Obama's relative inexperience in the Senate. Despite pressure from many Democrats, including many of his constituents, he stuck with Clinton until the end; he reportedly advised her on, and encouraged, her June 2008 decision to withdraw from the race. He was denied a speaking appearance at the Democratic National Convention in Denver that summer.

Rangel has long been a major player in New York's city and state politics. He strongly backed his old friend, Democrat Carl McCall, for governor in 2002, and in December 2001, he said he would vote for Republican George Pataki if the nomination went to McCall's rival, Democrat Andrew Cuomo. But in 2006, he gave Cuomo a hearty endorsement for attorney general. That same year, he was frosty toward Democratic Gov. Eliot Spitzer after Spitzer chose a running mate who was not Rangel's first choice: "When Eliot Spitzer, the world's smartest man, is telling me that he has picked his candidate and knows that his candidate can win, who am I to question the world's smartest man?" Rangel said.

Rangel has been easily re-elected every two years. In 1994, he faced primary opposition from the son of his predecessor, the Puerto Rico-raised Councilman Adam Clayton Powell IV. Rangel spent $1.4 million and won 61%-33. In 2007, he published a memoir, *And I Haven't Had a Bad Day Since: From the Streets of Harlem to the Halls of Congress.*

SIXTEENTH DISTRICT

José Serrano (D)

Elected Mar. 1990, 10th full term; b. Oct. 24, 1943, Mayaguez, PR; home, Bronx; Lehman Col.; Catholic; divorced; 5 children.

Military Career: Army Medical Corps, 1964–66.

Elected Office: Dist. 7 Schl. Bd., 1969–74; NY Assembly, 1974–90.

Professional Career: Banker, 1961–69.

DC Office: 2227 RHOB, 20515, 202-225-4361; Fax: 202-225-6001; Web site: serrano.house.gov.

State Offices: Bronx, 718-620-0084.

Committees: *Appropriations* (8th of 37 D): Commerce, Justice, Science & Related Agencies; Financial Services & General Government (Chmn); Homeland Security.

Group Ratings

	ADA	ACLU	AFS	LCV	ITIC	NTU	COC	ACU	CFG	FRC
2008	100	100	100	100	71	17	39	8	8	5
2007	95	—	100	85	—	5	55	0	7	—

National Journal Ratings

	2007 LIB — 2007 CONS		2008 LIB — 2008 CONS	
Economic	73% —	24%	85% —	0%
Social	74% —	25%	67% —	28%
Foreign	85% —	15%	85% —	8%
Composite	78% —	22%	84% —	17%

Key Votes of the 110th Congress

1. Increase minimum wage	Y	5. Share immigration data	N	9. Withdraw troops 8/08	Y
2. Expand SCHIP	Y	6. Foreign aid abortion ban	N	10. No operations in Iran	Y
3. Raise CAFE standards	Y	7. Ban gay bias in workplace	Y	11. Free trade with Peru	N
4. Bail out financial markets	N	8. Repeal D.C. gun law	N	12. Overhaul FISA	N

Election Results

2008 general	José Serrano (D-WF)	127,179	(97%)	($386,734)
	Ali Mohamed (R)	4,488	(3%)	
2008 primary	José Serrano (D-WF)	unopposed		

Prior Winning Percentages: 2006 (95%); 2004 (95%); 2002 (92%); 2000 (96%); 1998 (95%); 1996 (96%); 1994 (96%); 1992 (91%); 1990 (93%); 1990 (92%)

Population		Race/Ethnicity		Work	
Pop. 2007:	666,055	White:	2.3%	Private:	79.0%
Change since 2000:	Up 1.8%	Black:	28.5%	Government:	14.0%
Urban:	100.0%	Hispanic:	65.3%	Self-employed:	6.9%
Rural:	0.0%	Asian:	1.8%	Blue collar:	22.6%
Area size:	13 sq. mi.	Native Am.:	0.2%	White collar:	40.8%
Age		Hawaiian:	0.1%	Khaki collar:	0.0%
Median age:	28.8 yrs.	Two+ races:	0.6%	Other:	36.5%
More than 65 yrs:	7.2%	*Ancestry*		Median income:	$21,764
Less than 18 yrs:	32.6%	Subsaharan:	5.1%	Median home value:	$321,200
Education		West Indian:	4.4%	Poverty:	40.0%
H.S. grad:	57.9%	Italian:	0.9%	**Military Veterans**	
College grad:	9.8%			% of Pop:	2.5%
Grad degree:	2.9%				

It may not quite be "the beautiful Bronx," as borough historian Lloyd Utlan calls it, but The Bronx seems to have rebounded from rock bottom. The beautiful days were in the 1930s and 1940s, when Presidents Roosevelt and Truman rode down 138th Street, and when Babe Ruth, Lou Gehrig and Joe DiMaggio knocked home runs out of Yankee Stadium. Art deco apartment buildings were built along the Grand Concourse, and shoppers thronged Tremont Avenue stores. Bronx County Democratic

2008 Presidential Vote		
Obama (D)	158,671	(95%)
McCain (R)	8,437	(5%)

2004 Presidential Vote		
Kerry (D)	130,109	(89%)
Bush (R)	14,766	(10%)

Cook Partisan Voting Index: D+41

Chairman Ed Flynn chaired the Democratic National Committee in the early 1940s. In the 1880s, the Bronx (then known as the Northside and only recently annexed from Westchester County) had been linked to the level eastern half of Manhattan by elevated steam locomotives. The borough really took off in 1906 with the arrival of the first subway, which allowed the children of immigrants to move from grim Lower East Side tenements to spacious walk-up apartments flooded with light. The Bronx population grew from 200,000 in 1900 to 430,000 in 1910 to 1.2 million in 1930. Its population peaked at nearly 1.5 million in 1950. After a quarter-century of deterioration, the population had shrunk to 1.2 million by 1990. Now, it's up again, to nearly 1.4 million, as new immigrants revive neighborhoods that had been given up for dead.

The fall began in the mid-1960s, when several factors led to the destruction of neighborhoods. Rent control, insisted upon by tenants, guaranteed that many owners of low-rent property wouldn't maintain it. Once empty, buildings were torched for the insurance money, sometimes as many as four blocks of buildings a week. At the same time, a drop in low-income, low-skill jobs in Manhattan and the Bronx, abetted by high union wages, led to a rise in welfare dependency and crime, and empty building shells became the perfect venue for drug dealing. The 13-year, $250 million effort to build the Cross-Bronx

Expressway—a brainchild of Robert Moses that crossed 113 streets and avenues, hundreds of utility mains and ten mass-transit lines—only made things worse. As workers plowed through acres of tough bedrock, the project shredded entire neighborhoods, forcing 40,000 people to move from their homes. In the upheaval, longtime residents fled in droves, and the rapid turnover strained civic institutions. A vicious cycle emerged: Crime drove away jobs, which drove away fathers, which produced more crime. When Tom Wolfe imagined the "wrong turn" that sank a high-flying Wall Street career in *Bonfire of the Vanities*, he set it in the South Bronx. The movie version filmed the scene under the Bruckner Expressway.

Presidents and presidential candidates came in—Democrat Jimmy Carter in 1977, Republican Ronald Reagan in 1980—promising help. The borough's saviors were churches and creative community groups that built single-family, pastel bungalows and small-scale apartment projects for the elderly, for single-parent families and for the homeless. The South Bronx turned a corner. A building spree created the Bronx's first new wave of housing starts since the 1950s, and the first new cluster of private residences since the 1930s. As immigrants from the Dominican Republic, Jamaica, Ecuador, and Central America settled in, the population began to increase. A few corners of the South Bronx, such as Mott Haven, have even seen yuppies and artists colonizing old industrial spaces where gang wars prevailed not long ago. Charlotte Street, which Carter and Reagan visited as the worst of the slums, is now Charlotte Gardens, with owner-occupied houses. After decades of decay, some businesses—warehouses, distribution centers, small industrial parks—have begun to move back in, leaving declining and more expensive space nearby. The new Yankee Stadium, at $1.5 billion the most expensive sports facility ever built in the United States, opened in April 2009 and focused attention on the area's economic renewal. But this remains a low-income area, with many people on public assistance, and check-cashing outlets are still easier to find than banks.

The 16th Congressional District of New York includes most of the South Bronx. It is bounded by the Harlem River on the west, the East River on the south, the Bronx River and Bronx Park (home of the Bronx Zoo) on the east, and it goes just past Fordham Road on the north. It also includes Belmont, the industrial flatlands of Bruckner Boulevard and Hunts Point (though not the meat and produce markets). The district is 29% black, and it has the highest share of Hispanics—65%—of any New York district. This has long been New York's largest concentration of Puerto Ricans, but about 60% of Hispanics here are now from other parts of Latin America. Measured by median income and percentage of families below poverty status, it ranks as the one of the most impoverished congressional districts in the nation. This was the most heavily Democratic district in the nation in 2000 (92% for Al Gore) and the second most heavily Democratic in 2004 (89% for John Kerry). In 2008, voter turnout increased 15% with the enthusiasm for Democrat Barack Obama's candidacy, and he won nearly 95% of the vote, his best showing of any congressional district.

The congressman from the 16th District is Democrat José Serrano, who won the seat in a 1990 special election. A native of Mayaguez, Puerto Rico, he grew up in the Mill Brook project in Mott Haven. After serving in the Army, he worked at a bank and as a school administrator. Serrano moved up while other Bronx politicians fell by the wayside because of corruption. He was elected to the New York Assembly in 1974 and chaired its Education Committee. In 1985, he ran for Bronx borough president, bucking the Democratic organization, and nearly won. Then in January 1990, U.S. Rep. Robert García of the South Bronx was convicted of accepting money from the minority contractor Wedtech. His conviction was later reversed, but his resignation paved the way for Serrano's election to the House.

Serrano has one of the most liberal voting records in the House. As one of the Appropriations subcommittee chairmen, he is a member of the powerful "college of cardinals," which wields great influence over spending decisions. He also brings as many federal dollars home to his economically strapped district as he can. Serrano chairs the Subcommittee on Financial Services and General Government, which oversees many federal regulators

Serrano is a critic of outsourcing government services, and in 2007, he moved to end the Internal Revenue Service's use of private debt-collection companies for delinquent taxes. He was the only House member from New York City who voted in 2008 against the federal bailout for banks and other financial-services companies. He said he couldn't justify giving money to the wealthy people who'd created the problem. In 2008, his subcommittee's appropriations bill included a policy rider that relaxed travel restrictions on Cuba; it also lifted restrictions that barred the District of Columbia government from using local funds for needle-exchange programs for drug users.

A big local priority for Serrano has been cleaning up the Bronx River, and he delivered about $30 million for the effort. (When the river progressed to the point where it could support wildlife, a beaver appeared and was dubbed "José" in honor of Serrano's work in behalf of the waterway.) In 2007, he helped broker a $2 million deal to purchase for the city the heavily wooded, seven-acre South Brother Island in the East River.

Although he has an important subcommittee post, Serrano's attempts to join the Democratic leadership have been stymied. In 1997, Democratic Minority Leader Dick Gephardt passed over him and picked the less-senior Robert Menendez of New Jersey, who was a better fundraiser, to be chief deputy whip. In 1998, Serrano ran for Democratic Caucus vice chairman as "the candidate who refuses to raise money to buy your vote for leadership." He again lost out to Menendez, who went on to become a senator.

In opposition to Cuban Hispanics in Congress, Serrano has been Fidel Castro's greatest champion in the House. He has sought repeal of economic sanctions against Cuba. When questions arose about Castro's future after major surgery in July 2006, Serrano issued a press release telling President George W. Bush, "Hands Off Cuba." When Castro's brother, Raúl Castro, took control, Serrano said that it was "long past time to end the charade and begin dialogue and engagement with Cuba." Another of his issues is statehood for Puerto Rico, which he calls an American "colony." He backs a long-stalled referendum to determine the status of the island. In 2000, Serrano was arrested at the White House while protesting the Navy's bombing range at Vieques, Puerto Rico. He also took credit for working with Venezuelan President Hugo Chávez and Citizen Energy Corp. to strike a deal to bring cheaper oil to the South Bronx. He has criticized the reluctance of House Democratic leaders to pass immigration reform.

In New York politics, Serrano backed former Bronx Borough President Fernando Ferrer for mayor in 2001 and 2005. He backed civil-rights activist Al Sharpton for president in 2004. His son José, a former city councilman, ousted a Republican incumbent in 2004 to win a state Senate seat. Serrano the elder remains secure in his district.

SEVENTEENTH DISTRICT

Eliot Engel (D)

Elected 1988, 11th term; b. Feb. 18, 1947, Bronx; home, Bronx; Hunter-Lehman Col., B.A. 1969, C.U.N.Y., Lehman Col., M.A. 1973, NY Law Schl., J.D. 1987; Jewish; married (Patricia); 3 children.

Elected Office: NY Assembly, 1977–88.

Professional Career: Teacher, guidance counselor, NYC public schl., 1969–77.

DC Office: 2161 RHOB, 20515, 202-225-2464; Fax: 202-225-5513; Web site: www.house.gov/engel.

State Offices: Bronx, 718-796-9700; Mt. Vernon, 914-699-4100; West Nyack, 845-735-1000.

Committees: *Energy & Commerce* (10th of 36 D): Energy & Environment; Health. *Foreign Affairs* (7th of 28 D): Asia, the Pacific & the Global Environment; Middle East & South Asia; Western Hemisphere (Chmn).

Group Ratings

	ADA	ACLU	AFS	LCV	ITIC	NTU	COC	ACU	CFG	FRC
2008	95	86	100	92	100	5	65	0	0	5
2007	80	—	100	85	—	5	53	0	12	—

National Journal Ratings

	2007 LIB	—	2007 CONS		2008 LIB	—	2008 CONS
Economic	82%	—	0%		85%	—	0%
Social	87%	—	13%		59%	—	38%
Foreign	72%	—	28%		59%	—	41%
Composite	83%	—	17%		71%	—	29%

Key Votes of the 110th Congress

1. Increase minimum wage	Y	5. Share immigration data	N	9. Withdraw troops 8/08	Y
2. Expand SCHIP	Y	6. Foreign aid abortion ban	N	10. No operations in Iran	*
3. Raise CAFE standards	Y	7. Ban gay bias in workplace	Y	11. Free trade with Peru	Y
4. Bail out financial markets	Y	8. Repeal D.C. gun law	N	12. Overhaul FISA	Y

Election Results

2008 general	Eliot Engel (D-Ind-WF)	161,594	(80%)	($776,808)
	Robert Goodman (R-C)	40,707	(20%)	
2008 primary	Eliot Engel (D-Ind-WF)	unopposed		

Prior Winning Percentages: 2006 (76%); 2004 (76%); 2002 (63%); 2000 (90%); 1998 (88%); 1996 (85%); 1994 (78%); 1992 (80%); 1990 (61%); 1988 (56%)

Population		Race/Ethnicity		Work	
Pop. 2007:	675,475	White:	38.2%	Private:	78.2%
Change since 2000:	Up 3.2%	Black:	31.2%	Government:	16.7%
Urban:	99.9%	Hispanic:	23.7%	Self-employed:	4.9%
Rural:	0.1%	Asian:	4.6%	Blue collar:	16.5%
Area size:	146 sq. mi.	Native Am.:	0.3%	White collar:	62.1%
		Hawaiian:	0.0%	Khaki collar:	0.1%
Age		Two+ races:	1.1%	Other:	21.4%
Median age:	35.5 yrs.	*Ancestry*		Median income:	$52,821
More than 65 yrs:	12.8%	West Indian:	11.9%	Median home value:	$433,700
Less than 18 yrs:	26.1%	Irish:	8.4%	Poverty:	14.5%
Education		Italian:	7.5%	**Military Veterans**	
H.S. grad:	82.2%			% of Pop:	5.7%
College grad:	30.7%				
Grad degree:	13.5%				

The Bronx, settled mostly in the early 20th century, was originally a collection of middle-class neighborhoods clustered around subway stops, places where the children of immigrants left behind Manhattan's gloomy tenements and walk-ups and basked in the sunlight, wide avenues and hilly vistas. Different ethnic groups collected here: Irish in Kingsbridge, in the valley between Riverdale and the Grand Concourse; well-to-do WASPs and Jews in Riverdale, on the palisades above the Hudson River; middle-class

2008 Presidential Vote
Obama (D) 172,479   (72%)
McCain (R)..............................66,027   (28%)

2004 Presidential Vote
Kerry (D)................................149,727   (67%)
Bush (R) 73,896   (33%)

Cook Partisan Voting Index: D + 18

blacks in Williamsbridge, in the north-central part of the borough. When neighboring areas in the South Bronx began to deteriorate, many of their residents fled to the southern cities of Westchester County, on the Bronx border. Others drove over the Tappan Zee Bridge to the pleasant suburbs of Rockland County, just north of Bergen County, N.J. In 2008, serious discussions began over the possible replacement—not repair—of the 52-year-old Tappan Zee; the cost likely would exceed $6 billion.

The 17th Congressional District of New York includes the bulk of these Bronx neighborhoods, plus Baychester, Eastchester and Spuyten Duyvil. It has the century-old Van Cortlandt Park, at 1,146 acres New York City's third-largest park. It also includes leafy Woodlawn, still a magnet for Irish immigrants and more like neighboring Westchester County than the Bronx. The district skips around Marble Hill, an African-American and Latino enclave on the Bronx mainland that was kept as part of Manhattan after engineers diverted the Harlem River around it in 1895, hoping to improve water flow for shipping. The 17th extends deep into the suburbs, taking in black-majority Mount Vernon, financially troubled Yonkers and a narrow strip of land running north from Yonkers along the Hudson River. Across the Tappan Zee, the district encompasses the southern half of Rockland County, including Nyack, Orangetown, Suffern, Ramapo and part of Clarkstown. In 2007, the minority population of the district was 31% African-American and 24% Hispanic. The Bronx casts 38% of the vote, Rockland casts 37% and Westchester 25%. In 2008, Democratic presidential nominee Barack Obama carried the district, 72% to 28%

The congressman from the 17th District is Eliot Engel, a Democrat elected in 1988. He is the son of a welder and grew up in the Bronx. As a boy, he was a political junkie who memorized the names of all 100 senators. He graduated from Hunter-Lehman College, got a master's in guidance and counseling from the City University of New York, then taught in the New York City public schools. He was also a guidance counselor. After 14 years, he went back to school for a law degree from New York Law School. In 1977, at age 30, he was elected to the New York Assembly in a special election to replace a convicted incumbent. He won election to the House in 1988, replacing Democratic Rep. Mario Biaggi, who'd been convicted of bribery.

Engel's once strongly liberal voting record has become more moderate in recent years, especially on foreign policy. On the Foreign Affairs Committee, he made his name as the backer of downtrodden ethnic groups. He has been a prime sponsor of the resolution to recognize Jerusalem as the capital of Israel. He called for investigation of the internment of Italian nationals and other harsh restrictions in this nation during World War II, and he has co-chaired the Congressional ad hoc Committee on Irish Affairs to foster the peace process in that country. Engel is not a 1970s-style dove: He supported the Gulf War resolution in 1990, the bombing of Serbia to get a settlement in Bosnia, and the use of force in Iraq in 2002, though he criticized President George W. Bush's handling of that conflict following the ouster of Iraqi Leader Saddam Hussein. As chairman of the Western Hemisphere Subcommittee, he has criticized socialist Venezuelan President Hugo Chavez for his attitude toward the United States, accusing him of "provocation."

On the Energy and Commerce Committee, Engel has pushed for energy conservation and steps to address climate change. With Republican Jack Kingston of Georgia, he worked across the aisle to promote alternative and renewable sources of energy. In 2008, he helped enact a bill renaming the research library in the Ellis Island immigration museum to honor longtime comedian Bob Hope.

Engel has a personal tradition of staking out an aisle seat many hours before the start of the annual State of the Union address so that he can shake the president's hand or occasionally give a hug. In February 2009, CNN anchor Anderson Cooper called Engel "pathetic" for waiting 12 and a half hours for Obama's address to Congress. Engel replied that Cooper was "pathetic" for failing to share his enthusiasm. At home, Engel relentlessly stays on top of constituent service.

Given his minority-majority district, Engel can never feel quite secure in his seat. In the 2000 primary, Assemblyman Larry Seabrook argued that the district needed "real leadership" and attacked Engel for living in suburban Maryland. Engel won 50%-41%. After redistricting made his district more suburban in 2002, Engel had vigorous competition from Rockland County Executive Scott Vanderhoef, a Republican who criticized Engel for voting against tax cuts and defense spending. Vanderhoef carried Rockland County by 53%-45%. But Engel won big in Westchester and the Bronx, for a 63%-34% overall victory. In 2004, New York City firefighter Kevin McAdams challenged Engel in the primary, denouncing his support of the Iraq War, but Engel won easily, 59%-20%. In the 2006 Democratic primary, progressive Jessica Flagg criticized his support of "Bush war policies," but he got 83% of the vote. In 2008, he had no primary foe and only token Republican opposition. But redistricting after the 2010 census could pose a new set of challenges, depending on how much of the Bronx remains in his district.

EIGHTEENTH DISTRICT

Nita Lowey (D)

Elected 1988, 11th term; b. July 5, 1937, Bronx; home, Harrison; Mt. Holyoke Col., B.A. 1959; Jewish; married (Stephen); 3 children.

Professional Career: Asst. for Econ. Devel. & Neighborhood Preservation, NY Secy. of State; Dep. dir., Division of Econ. Opportunity, 1975–85; NY asst. secy. of st., 1985–87.

DC Office: 2329 RHOB, 20515, 202-225-6506; Fax: 202-225-0546; Web site: lowey.house.gov.

State Offices: Rockland, 845-639-3485; White Plains, 914-428-1707.

Committees: *Appropriations* (7th of 37 D): Homeland Security; Labor, HHS, Education & Related Agencies; State, Foreign Operations & Related Programs (Chmn).

Group Ratings

	ADA	ACLU	AFS	LCV	ITIC	NTU	COC	ACU	CFG	FRC
2008	100	91	100	100	100	6	67	0	0	0
2007	95	—	100	95	—	5	56	0	12	—

National Journal Ratings

	2007 LIB	—	2007 CONS		2008 LIB	—	2008 CONS
Economic	82%	—	0%		78%	—	20%
Social	89%	—	8%		72%	—	26%
Foreign	86%	—	11%		70%	—	25%
Composite	90%	—	10%		75%	—	25%

Key Votes of the 110th Congress

1. Increase minimum wage	Y	5. Share immigration data	N	9. Withdraw troops 8/08	Y
2. Expand SCHIP	Y	6. Foreign aid abortion ban	N	10. No operations in Iran	Y
3. Raise CAFE standards	Y	7. Ban gay bias in workplace	Y	11. Free trade with Peru	Y
4. Bail out financial markets	Y	8. Repeal D.C. gun law	N	12. Overhaul FISA	Y

Election Results

2008 general	Nita Lowey (D-WF)......................................174,791	(68%)	($1,489,302)
	Jim Russell (R-C)...80,498	(32%)	($19,906)
2008 primary	Nita Lowey (D-WF)...................................... unopposed		

Prior Winning Percentages: 2006 (71%); 2004 (70%); 2002 (92%); 2000 (67%); 1998 (83%); 1996 (64%); 1994 (57%); 1992 (56%); 1990 (63%); 1988 (50%)

Population		Race/Ethnicity		Work	
Pop. 2007:	671,156	White:	64.0%	Private:	77.8%
Change since 2000:	Up 2.6%	Black:	9.7%	Government:	13.9%
Urban:	99.3%	Hispanic:	18.3%	Self-employed:	8.2%
Rural:	0.7%	Asian:	6.4%	Blue collar:	13.0%
Area size:	270 sq. mi.	Native Am.:	0.1%	White collar:	71.0%
		Hawaiian:	0.0%	Khaki collar:	0.0%
Age		Two+ races:	1.0%	Other:	16.0%
Median age:	39.4 yrs.	*Ancestry*		Median income:	$85,163
More than 65 yrs:	14.2%	Italian:	17.5%	Median home value:	$602,700
Less than 18 yrs:	24.6%	Irish:	10.9%	Poverty:	6.4%
Education		German:	6.3%	**Military Veterans**	
H.S. grad:	88.1%			% of Pop:	6.7%
College grad:	48.1%				
Grad degree:	24.2%				

The great granite ridges that form the spine of Manhattan and the Bronx move north into lower Westchester County, the thin peninsula of land between Long Island Sound and the Hudson River. This was active territory from early on. Washington Irving, the first fully professional writer in America, sent his headless horseman on a chase for schoolmaster Ichabod Crane through Sleepy Hollow, a fictionalized version of Tarrytown, on the east bank of the Hudson. Revolutionary War battles were fought

2008 Presidential Vote
Obama (D) 184,182 (62%)
McCain (R)............................112,214 (38%)

2004 Presidential Vote
Kerry (D)................................164,342 (58%)
Bush (R) 119,981 (42%)

Cook Partisan Voting Index: D + 9

here, and figures like John Peter Zenger, Alexander Hamilton and John Jay lived here. Blessed with some of America's loveliest scenery and easily accessible from Manhattan by train since the mid-19th century, this became some of America's first suburban terrain, with grand estates built by great millionaires—Jay Gould's Gothic revival Lyndhurst and John D. Rockefeller's spectacular Kykuit, with villages for retainers clustered around the railroad stations. Today, Westchester still looks suburban, perhaps more than ever now that it has the patina of age. It has little commuter-railroad stations across from faux Tudor drugstores, soda fountains and cobblestone post offices. But it also has shopping malls and galleries and plenty of corporate headquarters, from IBM and Texaco to PepsiCo and Reader's Digest (as well as corporate watchdogs: *Consumer Reports* magazine is based in Yonkers). Intensive development slows north of White Plains, for Westchester is crossed by the first of several mountain ridges just to the north—the closest the Appalachians come to the ocean. The county does have its share of homeless people and impoverished ghettos. And to the north, in Ossining, on the Hudson River, looms the famed Sing Sing maximum-security prison.

The 18th Congressional District of New York contains the heart of suburban Westchester County and also crosses the Hudson River into Rockland County to Haverstraw. It includes a host of affluent suburbs, many within easy reach of Grand Central via the Metro North rail lines—Bronxville, Tuckahoe, Eastchester, New Rochelle, Scarsdale, White Plains, Larchmont, Mamaroneck, Rye, Harrison, Armonk and Chappaqua, where former President Bill Clinton and Secretary of State Hillary Rodham Clinton have a home. Historically, Westchester was a Republican county, with a successful Republican machine and an electorate of affluent professionals who naturally preferred the political party that opposed the big city political bosses and labor union leaders. But today, Westchester is mostly Democratic, after a heavy influx of Jews who broke down many legal restrictions and other barriers to residence after World War II. These Jewish voters, long Democratic, became even more so thanks to the visibility of Christian conservatives in the Republican Party. Another reason is that on the cultural issues of greatest import, gun control and abortion rights, affluent suburbanites in America's biggest metropolitan area have been strongly on the liberal side. Westchester County is more diverse than one might imagine and the 18th District reflects this: It is 10% black, 18% Hispanic and 6% Asian. Former Republican Gov. George Pataki, who began his political career as mayor of Peekskill in northern Westchester, carried the county by handsome margins in 1998 and 2002. But the county gave strong support to Democrats Al Gore and John Kerry in the presidential elections of 2000 and 2004, and unlike the Long Island suburbs, it voted for Hillary Rodham Clinton for Senate in 2000. In 2008, Democratic presidential nominee Barack Obama won Westchester, 63%-36%.

The congresswoman from the 18th District is Nita Lowey, a Democrat elected in 1988. She was born in the Bronx, and after graduating from Mount Holyoke College with a degree in marketing, she moved to Queens, where she became a homemaker raising three children. She first got involved in politics when her neighbor, Mario Cuomo, got Lowey to help out in his campaign for lieutenant governor. He lost that race but was appointed New York secretary of state and hired Lowey as his assistant in 1975. Cuomo later became New York governor. In the 1988 Democratic primary for the House seat, Lowey faced Hamilton Fish III, who was politically well connected but as a former publisher of the *Nation* was considerably to the left of Lowey. She won 44%-36%. In the general election, she challenged two-term Republican Rep. Joseph DioGuardi, who was dogged by charges of illicit contributions. She won 50%-47%. Each spent over $1 million, with Lowey spending $657,000 of her own money.

In the House, Lowey's voting record is liberal, though she is more moderate on foreign policy. She has been a strong advocate of aid to Israel and voted for the 2002 Iraq war resolution.

She's a member of the powerful Appropriations Committee and chairs its State and Foreign Operations subcommittee, which makes her one of the subcommittee chairmen known as the "cardinals" for their influence on spending decisions. In 2007, she opposed President George W. Bush's call to increase troop strength in Iraq, but she backed his request for more money for military operations in Afghanistan. In that year's appropriations bill, she set aside $5 billion for programs to combat HIV/AIDS around the world and increased by $300 million Bush's $1.5 billion budget for global health and child survival. She strongly criticized the president's opposition to allowing international health organizations to receive donated contraceptives to prevent disease and unintended pregnancies and to reduce abortions. In 2009, she secured $424 million for climate-change and clean-energy programs, and $538 million for educational and cultural exchanges to "strengthen America's image abroad." On Homeland Security, she worked to implement recommendations of the 9/11 Commission and pursued a grant program for interoperable communications for local governments.

In the 1990s, Lowey was a Clinton loyalist when it was tough to be so, voting for the 1993 budget and tax package in this high-income district and splitting with most New York Democrats and organized labor to support both the North American Free Trade Agreement and normalizing trade relations with China. When Clinton proposed to change the health-care financing system, she organized 72 House members to demand that it cover abortions. Much of Lowey's legislative work has been on the Appropriations Committee. On domestic issues, she has actively supported the National Endowment for the Arts; she has also been a big supporter of biomedical research and helped increase spending on cancer research at the National Institutes of Health. Pursuing her interest in feminist issues, she has backed funds for international family planning. In 2008, she won passage of a bill to authorize research centers to study environmental factors linked to breast cancer.

Since Lowey first won, the boundaries of her district have been radically altered twice by redistricting, but she has been re-elected by wide margins. She thought about a Senate bid in 2000, but deferred to First Lady Hillary Rodham Clinton, and in 2008, she was an enthusiastic supporter of Clinton's presidential campaign. Her party loyalty and avid fundraising led Minority Leader Dick Gephardt to appoint her to chair the Democratic Congressional Campaign Committee for the 2002 election. Lowey optimistically said that Democrats would be able to capture a House majority, but it didn't happen on her watch. Ultimately, Democrats defeated only three Republican incumbents and lost five of their own. The GOP's six-seat gain was an acute disappointment to Lowey, who quietly bowed out of the chairmanship. In 2008, she was mentioned as a possible successor to Clinton in the Senate after Clinton became Secretary of State, but the plum went to Democratic U.S. Rep. Kirsten Gillibrand of New York.

NINETEENTH DISTRICT

John Hall (D)

Elected 2006, 2nd term; b. July 23, 1948, Baltimore, MD; home, Dover Plains; Attended U. of Notre Dame, Loyola Col. (MD); Protestant; married (Pamela); 1 child.

Elected Office: Ulster Cnty. Legislature, 1989–91; Saugerties Bd. of Educ., 1996–99.

Professional Career: Singer/songwriter.

DC Office: 1217 LHOB, 20515, 202-225-5441; Fax: 202-225-3289; Web site: johnhall.house.gov.

State Offices: Carmel, 845-225-3641x371; Goshen, 845-291-4100.

Committees: *Transportation & Infrastructure* (29th of 44 D): Aviation; Highways & Transit; Water Resources & Environment. *Veterans' Affairs* (7th of 18 D): Disability Assistance & Memorial Affairs (Chmn); Oversight & Investigations.

Group Ratings

	ADA	ACLU	AFS	LCV	ITIC	NTU	COC	ACU	CFG	FRC
2008	95	100	100	100	86	8	56	0	0	5
2007	100	—	100	95	—	4	50	0	6	—

National Journal Ratings

	2007 LIB	—	2007 CONS		2008 LIB	—	2008 CONS
Economic	64%	—	34%		71%	—	25%
Social	58%	—	41%		67%	—	28%
Foreign	76%	—	23%		77%	—	23%
Composite	67%	—	33%		73%	—	27%

Key Votes of the 110th Congress

1. Increase minimum wage	Y	5. Share immigration data	N	9. Withdraw troops 8/08	Y
2. Expand SCHIP	Y	6. Foreign aid abortion ban	N	10. No operations in Iran	Y
3. Raise CAFE standards	Y	7. Ban gay bias in workplace	Y	11. Free trade with Peru	N
4. Bail out financial markets	Y	8. Repeal D.C. gun law	N	12. Overhaul FISA	N

Election Results

2008 general	John Hall (D-Ind-WF)......................................164,859	(59%)	($2,136,773)
	Kieran Lalor (R-C)...116,120	(41%)	($612,220)
2008 primary	John Hall (D-Ind-WF)................................ unopposed		

Prior Winning Percentages: 2006 (51%)

Population		Race/Ethnicity		Work	
Pop. 2007:	698,637	White:	78.7%	Private:	74.3%
Change since 2000:	Up 6.8%	Black:	5.8%	Government:	19.8%
Urban:	78.7%	Hispanic:	10.7%	Self-employed:	5.8%
Rural:	21.3%	Asian:	3.1%	Blue collar:	16.7%
Area size:	1,470 sq. mi.	Native Am.:	0.2%	White collar:	66.1%
		Hawaiian:	0.0%	Khaki collar:	1.7%
Age		Two+ races:	1.4%	Other:	15.6%
Median age:	38.2 yrs.			Median income:	$79,800
More than 65 yrs:	11.5%	*Ancestry*		Median home value:	$388,200
Less than 18 yrs:	25.1%	Italian:	18.7%	Poverty:	7.1%
		Irish:	17.3%		
Education		German:	11.2%	**Military Veterans**	
H.S. grad:	89.7%			% of Pop:	9.7%
College grad:	35.1%				
Grad degree:	15.4%				

The great interior of America can be said to begin where the Hudson River squeezes through the series of Appalachian ridges at the Hudson Highlands. This choke point became a barrier to British military power during the Revolutionary War, when American forces put a chain across the river to keep the British from sailing north. Benedict Arnold betrayed his country over control of this part of the Hudson, and the new nation built its Military Academy high on the cliffs at West Point. The Hud-

2008 Presidential Vote

Obama (D) 160,645	(51%)
McCain (R)..............................153,424	(48%)

2004 Presidential Vote

Bush (R).................................162,960	(54%)
Kerry (D).................................137,432	(45%)

Cook Partisan Voting Index: R+3

son was the impetus for the builders of the Erie Canal and the water-level New York Central Railroad, two great projects that made New York City the port of the American interior as well as the port for the builders of the nearby Croton Aqueduct, which provided the water without which New York could not grow. (It also carried the first cockroaches to the city.) Some distant day the great aqueduct may crumble, but the cockroaches will remain.

The 19th Congressional District of New York covers much of the lower Hudson Valley, sprawling across parts of five counties. West of the Hudson, the district takes in much of Orange County, New York's fastest-growing county from 2000 to 2007. There, old farming villages like Warwick adjoin mountains, farms and new, middle-income subdivisions on the nation's biggest deposit of muck soil outside the Everglades. Orange County is also home to the Stewart Airport, which many have viewed as a possible alternate airport for New York City. The Port Authority of New York and New Jersey took control the facility in 2007, but its service has remained scant. The county includes Kiryas Joel, a politically controversial Satmar Hasidic settlement where two-thirds of residents live below the poverty line. (Its 20,000 residents function almost as a single voting unit, without much regard to partisan affiliation, a fact that has not escaped the notice of the state's top politicians, who regularly court local leaders.)

While the district excludes two of Orange County's biggest population centers, Middletown and Newburgh, it takes in portions of northern Rockland County, including Stony Point. The district crosses the Hudson near West Point. East of the river, the district begins in northern Westchester County, including Croton-on-Hudson, Yorktown, Mount Kisco, and Peekskill, where Republican George Pataki was mayor before becoming governor. Farther north, the 19th takes in all of Putnam County and part of Dutchess County, including the suburbs, but not the center city, of Poughkeepsie and Wappingers Falls. Putnam has become popular with first-time home buyers who make the 80-minute commute to Grand Central Station. The region also has proved attractive to middle- and higher-income public and corporate employees seeking reasonably priced housing in safe areas, a trend that has led to robust growth at a time when other areas of New York state are losing population. Immigrants from Ecuador who have settled here find the farmland and mountains similar to those back home. Politically, this area moved toward the Democrats in the 1990s, voted for Republican George W. Bush for president in 2004, but switched again to vote for Democrat Barack Obama in 2008.

The congressman from the 19th District is John Hall, a Democrat elected in 2006. The singer-songwriter is the second professional rock musician to serve in Congress. (The late Sonny Bono, who represented a California district, was the first.) Hall was raised in upstate New York and began playing the piano at age 4. His father was a Westinghouse engineer, his mother a college professor. He entered Notre Dame University at age 16 and studied physics for just a year, later attending Loyola College in Baltimore. Hall dropped out of school to pursue a music career, performing in the West Village and writing music for Broadway musicals. In the 1960s and 1970s, he recorded with such top artists as Janis Joplin, Bonnie Raitt, and Jackson Browne. In 1972, he helped found the soft-rock band Orleans, which performed the smash hits "Still the One" and "Dance With Me."

Even then Hall was a budding policy wonk and activist, occasionally holding forth on the dangers of plutonium production. He also became an activist for anti-nuclear and environmental causes. He founded the anti-nuclear group Musicians United for Safe Energy and in 1979 organized a series of "No Nukes" concerts. Hall won his first elected office in the early 1990s, when he served two years in the Ulster County legislature and then four years on the Saugerties School Board. In October 2004, he attracted fleeting national attention for noisily protesting the Bush campaign's use of "Still the One" at campaign events. The Bush campaign did not have Hall's permission and stopped using the song. Hall decided to challenge moderate Republican Rep. Sue Kelly of New York, he said, "because my wife told me to stop yelling at the TV." He was egged on by Democratic Rep. Maurice Hinchey, who represents an adjoining district, and by Democratic Rep. Debbie Wasserman Schultz of Florida, who overheard Hall complaining backstage about the Iraq War during a concert in her state.

In the 2006 Democratic primary, party strategists preferred lawyer Judy Aydelott, a former Republican, because of her fundraising skills and apparent crossover appeal. Hall was viewed as too liberal for the district, but he had considerable grassroots strength, and his star power and music-industry contacts won him attention and enough money to remain competitive. He defeated Aydelott 49%-27% in the four-way primary.

Hall worked to tie Kelly to the unpopular Republican president. Kelly portrayed herself as an "independent voice" and attacked Hall as a tax-raising liberal who would vote to impeach Bush, advocate for socialized medicine and summarily withdraw U.S. troops from Iraq. During the general election, a mailer surfaced showing the reprinted cover of the Orleans' 1976 "Waking and Dreaming" album, in which Hall appeared bearded and bare-chested, a contrast to the pinstripes and wing tips he was sporting 30 years later as a congressional candidate. The caption read: "John Hall, wrong for America." Against the advice of his advisers, Hall sang an impromptu duet of "Dance With Me" with television comedy host Stephen Colbert, a scene that played repeatedly on the Internet. Republicans have an 18,000-voter enrollment advantage in the district, and Kelly appeared well-positioned for another term. But late in the campaign, she became tarred by the scandal involving Florida Republican Rep. Mark Foley and the sexually explicit emails he had sent to former congressional pages. A former member of the board overseeing the page program, Kelly faced questions about whether she had been aware of Foley's behavior, and a television crew filmed her running away from questions about the Foley scandal. Hall won the general election 51%-49%, by less than 5,000 votes, with the winning margin coming from Westchester County.

In his first term in the House, Hall established a relatively centrist voting record and kept a low profile for a former rock star. As a freshman, he chaired the Veterans' Affairs Subcommittee on Disability Assistance and Memorial Affairs, where in 2007 he won passage of a bill to increase the compensation rates for veterans with service-connected disabilities. In 2008, the House also passed his bill to modernize the disability-claims process. On a topic of personal interest, he supported the effort by Rep. Howard Berman, D-Calif., to require radio stations to pay an added fee for performance rights.

As the 2008 election approached, Hall was an early target of Republicans, who talked up Andrew Saul, a wealthy businessman and philanthropist, as a challenger. But Saul withdrew in November 2007 for unspecified personal reasons, after having raised $1.5 million, nearly half of it his own money. After failing to recruit another strong candidate, Republicans nominated Kieran Lalor, an Iraq War vet and political novice. The contest never became competitive, and Hall won 59%-41%. He easily carried all five counties in the district, outperforming Democratic presidential nominee Obama, who won only Dutchess and Westchester.

TWENTIETH DISTRICT

Scott Murphy (D)

Elected 2009, 1st term; b. Jan. 19, 1970, Columbia, MO; home, Glens Falls; Harvard U., A.B. 1992; Methodist; married (Jennifer Hogan); 3 children.

Professional Career: Aide, Roger Wilson for lt. gov., 1992; Aide, Gov. Mel Carnahan, 1992; Owner, Small World Software, 1993–98; COO, iXL New York, 1998–2001; Depty. chief of staff, Gov. Roger Wilson, 2000–01; Managing dir., Advantage Capital Partners, 2001–08

DC Office: 120 CHOB, 20515, 202-225-5614; Fax: 202-225-1168; Web site: scottmurphy.house.gov.

State Offices: Glens Falls, 518-743-0964; Hudson, 518-828-3109; Saratoga Springs, 518-581-8247.

Committees: *Agriculture* (25th of 28 D). *Armed Services* (35th of 36 D): Strategic Forces; Terrorism, Unconventional Threats & Capabilities.

Group Ratings and Key Votes: Newly Elected

Election Results

2008 spec. election	Scott Murphy (D-Ind-WF)	80,833	(50%)	
	Jim Tedisco (R-C)	80,107	(50%)	
2008 general	Kirsten Gillibrand (D-WF)	193,651	(62%)	($4,489,391)
	Sandy Treadwell (R-Ind-C)	118,031	(38%)	($7,038,552)
2008 primary	Kirsten Gillibrand (D-WF)	unopposed		

Population		Race/Ethnicity		Work	
Pop. 2007:	677,533	White:	92.1%	Private:	72.6%
Change since 2000:	Up 3.5%	Black:	2.5%	Government:	18.9%
Urban:	44.9%	Hispanic:	2.7%	Self-employed:	8.2%
Rural:	55.1%	Asian:	1.4%	Blue collar:	21.7%
Area size:	7,200 sq. mi.	Native Am.:	0.1%	White collar:	60.3%
		Hawaiian:	0.0%	Khaki collar:	0.2%
Age		Two+ races:	1.0%	Other:	17.8%
Median age:	40.0 yrs.	*Ancestry*		Median income:	$54,941
More than 65 yrs:	14.1%	Irish:	16.4%	Median home value:	$186,600
Less than 18 yrs:	21.8%	German:	13.6%	Poverty:	8.5%
Education		Italian:	11.1%		
H.S. grad:	88.5%			**Military Veterans**	
College grad:	27.9%			% of Pop:	12.0%
Grad degree:	12.0%				

The Hudson River, an avenue of commerce in colonial days and an inspiration to artists in the new federal republic, is still one of America's great sights, though it is no longer central, as it was, to the nation's consciousness and politics. The classic mansions overlooking the river, like Clermont, whose builder Robert Livingston financed Robert Fulton's first steamboat, and Montgomery Place, built by Janet Livingston Montgomery, widow of the general who attacked Quebec in 1775, are

2008 Presidential Vote		
Obama (D)	167,827	(51%)
McCain (R)	157,879	(48%)

2004 Presidential Vote		
Bush (R)	170,307	(54%)
Kerry (D)	145,289	(46%)

Cook Partisan Voting Index: R+2

reminders of the cool serenity of the 18th-century mind and the daring nature of its spirit. Robert Livingston, whose descendants include former first lady Eleanor Roosevelt, former New Jersey Gov. Thomas Kean, and former U.S. Rep. Bob Livingston of Louisiana, administered the first oath of office to George Washington in 1789 and helped negotiate the Louisiana Purchase in 1803. On a visit to his land in the 1790s, James Madison and Aaron Burr welded the Virginia-New York alliance that set the course of American political history. The Hudson was also a center of American culture during the Romantic era. From Frederick Church's Moorish mansion, Olana, one can see the still-unspoiled river landscape that inspired his art and that of others of the Hudson River School of painters. James Fenimore Cooper lived farther up the river, near the placid shores of Lake George, and his classic work *The Last of the Mohicans* abounds with descriptions of the area. Later, the photographer Alfred Stieglitz and his wife, painter Georgia O'Keeffe, drew inspiration from the same waters, woods, and hills.

The Hudson gave birth to America's passionate party politics. Nearby is Kinderhook, home of Martin Van Buren, the innkeeper's son who in alliance with Andrew Jackson invented the torchlight parade, the national party convention, and some argue the Democratic Party itself. Later in the 19th century, the Hudson was lined with the palaces of the nation's first great millionaires and the comfortable country homes of New York's gentry. One of the latter, Springwood in Hyde Park, was the birthplace and home of Franklin D. Roosevelt. He greatly expanded government at home and was the victorious commander-in-chief of American military forces throughout the world, but was most comfortable looking out over his sloping lawn down to the river, where he used to go iceboating during the winter.

The sprawling 20th Congressional District of New York circles the Albany metro area and includes much of the Hudson Valley—the grand river south of Albany and the smaller river, freshly fed by the Adirondacks, to the north. It includes four full counties (Warren, Washington, Columbia, and Greene), most of Saratoga County, and parts of five others (Dutchess, Essex, Rensselaer, Delaware, and Otsego). The northern extreme of the 20th extends right up to Lake Placid in the Adirondacks, site of the 1980 Winter Olympics. The southern extreme in Dutchess County is close enough for commuters from New York City to travel back and forth regularly. Just to the north is Columbia County, where city dwellers go to introduce their children to "the country." The district extends west just short of Cooperstown, home of the National Baseball Hall of Fame, but it includes Oneonta, home of the less-well-known National Soccer Hall of Fame. It also includes Saratoga Springs with its grand racetrack and the nearby battlefield where the British were decisively stopped in 1777. This area had been Republican territory since the Civil War. Indeed, Roosevelt never carried his home territory except when he ran for the state Senate in 1910. The 20th was one of only six New York districts to vote for Republican George W. Bush in 2000 and one of nine to vote for him in 2004. In recent years, the district has trended Democratic, like much of upstate New York. While registered Republicans still outnumber registered Democrats, the district voted for both Sen. Hillary Rodham Clinton and Gov. Eliot Spitzer in 2006. Also that year, it elected Democrat Kirsten Gillibrand, now a senator, over longtime Republican Rep. John Sweeney. In 2008, the district voted narrowly for Barack Obama, 51%-48%.

The new congressman from the 20th District is Scott Murphy, a Democrat elected in 2009 after Gillibrand was appointed to the Senate seat vacated by Secretary of State Hillary Rodham Clinton. Murphy is the son of a postal worker and a teacher and grew up in Columbia, Mo. After graduating magna cum laude from Harvard University in 1992, Murphy planned on working on Democrat Bill Clinton's presidential campaign, but returned home because his mother was ill. He instead worked on Democrat Roger Wilson's successful campaign for Missouri lieutenant governor, and then worked as an aide to Missouri Gov. Mel Carnahan. After that taste of politics, Murphy moved to New York City to work as a venture capitalist, with a focus on high-technology and Internet-related companies. He invested money in *baazee.com*, an Indian auction website that eBay later bought for $50 million. He also co-founded Small World Software, which developed the first online fantasy sports leagues. In 2000, after Gov. Carnahan's death in a plane crash, Wilson became governor for a few months and asked Murphy to be his deputy chief of staff. Murphy commuted back and forth from New York for a few months and then returned to his work as a venture capitalist.

Murphy's opportunity to jump back into politics came when New York Gov. David Paterson appointed Gillibrand to the Senate in late January 2009, triggering a special election. Both national parties immediately took a strong interest in the race. Republicans saw an opportunity for a much-needed win in a GOP-friendly district, while Democrats very much wanted to hold the seat. Michael Steele, the chairman of the Republican National Committee, and Rep. Pete Sessions of Texas, chairman of the National Republican Campaign Committee, both made the race a top priority. As Steele wrote to GOP insiders on March 19, "Some have advised me to downplay this race in case we lose. NONSENSE. We have to do all we can to win it."

Republicans quickly settled on New York Assembly Minority Leader James Tedisco as their candidate. Democrats first tried to recruit former New York Rangers goalie Mike Richter. Once he declined, they chose Murphy out of a weak field of three other Democrats, partially because of his ability to self-fund. Murphy started the race with very little name recognition and trailed. A poll conducted two days after he was nominated had him behind Tedisco by 21 points and showed only 17% of voters had an opinion of him. The Republican Party accused him of failing to pay taxes on some of the businesses he owned and charged that he was "part of the problem" on Wall Street, an issue with real resonance after the government's massive bailout of financial services firms in 2008. National Democrats countered with charges that Tedisco had used a state-owned sport-utility vehicle and spent $21,000 of taxpayer money for his personal use.

The election turned on the state of the economy. Murphy called himself "Mr. Jobs" and argued that his business acumen would create jobs in the district. The NRCC in turn accused him of outsourcing jobs at *baazee.com*. Tedisco might have erred by refusing to take a stand on the $787 billion economic stimulus bill, arguing that since he wasn't currently in Congress, the question was "hypothetical." He eventually opposed the plan. Polls indicated that the NRCC's negative campaigning was hurting Tedisco's campaign, and he complained that he "didn't have a handle about the information about [himself] going out." He called for an end to the negative advertising. The NRCC ignored him and continued to run attack ads.

Pundits predicted a close race, and it did not disappoint. On Election Night on March 31, Tedisco led Murphy by a few dozen votes. As absentee ballots were counted and the tallies grew, Murphy built a small lead. Tedisco conceded on April 24, and Murphy's final margin of victory was a mere 726 votes. The two candidates raised and spent more than $3.7 million, a large amount considering the entire race and vote tallying lasted fewer than three months. Murphy outraised Tedisco $2 million to $1.7 million. Total spending on the race topped $6 million.

Murphy credited his victory to his family, and for once this might not have been a political platitude: He dines weekly with more than 50 members of his wife's extended family, and many were very active in the campaign. If each of them recruited 15 voters, Murphy's entire margin of victory could be accounted for. Murphy said after the election that his primary goal was to help fix the economy, sticking with the issue he had focused on during the campaign. He was named to the Agriculture and Armed Services committees, taking prime slots previously held by Gillibrand. He will likely be a target in 2010.

TWENTY-FIRST DISTRICT

Paul Tonko (D)

Elected 2008, 1st term; b. June 18, 1949, Amsterdam; home, Amsterdam; Clarkson U., B.S. 1981; Catholic; single.

Elected Office: Montgomery Cnty Bd. of Supervisors, 1974–83, Chmn. 1981; NY Assembly, 1983–2007

Professional Career: NY Dept. of Transportation, 1972–74; NY Dept. of Public Service, 1974–83; Pres. & CEO, NY St. Energy Research & Development Authority, 2007–08

DC Office: 128 CHOB, 20515, 202-225-5076; Fax: 202-225-5077; Web site: tonko.house.gov.

State Offices: Albany, 518-465-0700; Amsterdam, 518-843-3400; Schenectady, 518-374-4547.

Committees: *Education & Labor* (26th of 29 D): Healthy Families & Communities; Higher Education, Lifelong Learning & Competitiveness. *Science & Technology* (13th of 26 D): Energy & Environment; Research & Science Education; Technology & Innovation.

Group Ratings and Key Votes: Newly Elected

Election Results

2008 general	Paul Tonko (D-WF)	171,286	(62%)	($753,520)
	James Buhrmaster (R-C)	96,599	(35%)	($504,378)
	Phillip Steck (Ind)	7,965	(3%)	($552,513)
2008 primary	Paul Tonko (D)	15,932	(40%)	
	Tracey Brooks (D)	12,166	(30%)	
	Phillip Steck (D)	7,498	(19%)	
	Darius Shahinfar (D)	4,002	(10%)	

Population		Race/Ethnicity		Work	
Pop. 2007:	663,629	White:	82.1%	Private:	70.3%
Change since 2000:	Up 1.4%	Black:	8.2%	Government:	24.5%
Urban:	84.3%	Hispanic:	4.1%	Self-employed:	5.1%
Rural:	15.7%	Asian:	3.1%	Blue collar:	17.7%
Area size:	1,962 sq. mi.	Native Am.:	0.2%	White collar:	65.5%
		Hawaiian:	0.0%	Khaki collar:	0.1%
Age		Two+ races:	1.7%	Other:	16.6%
Median age:	38.4 yrs.			Median income:	$50,032
More than 65 yrs:	14.4%	*Ancestry*		Median home value:	$151,200
Less than 18 yrs:	21.6%	Irish:	16.4%	Poverty:	12.8%
		Italian:	13.3%		
Education		German:	13.1%	**Military Veterans**	
H.S. grad:	88.4%			% of Pop:	10.4%
College grad:	29.5%				
Grad degree:	13.5%				

As readers of its novelist laureate William Kennedy know, Albany is within living memory an antique city. Its solid row houses show its 19th-century prosperity. Its once-teeming lumberyards and railroad car shops, restaurants and hotels, have the patina of age and the accumulated grime of decades of coal smoke burned during six-month-long winters. Its history dates to 1624, when the Dutch built Fort Orange on the banks of the Hudson so seagoing ships could dock at the edge of the great gloomy for-

2008 Presidential Vote		
Obama (D)	179,322	(58%)
McCain (R)	123,378	(40%)
2004 Presidential Vote		
Kerry (D)	169,693	(55%)
Bush (R)	133,016	(43%)
Cook Partisan Voting Index: D + 6		

ests near the confluence of the Hudson and the Mohawk—the natural crossroads of upstate New York even before the building of the Erie Canal and the New York Central Railroad. This was one of America's early industrial centers. A few miles upriver, Troy was a steel town rivaling Pittsburgh in the 1840s, and later the leading producer of detachable collars. Cohoes, at the junction of the Hudson and the Mohawk, became a leading textile producer. Schenectady, a few miles up the Mohawk, was the site of Charles Steinmetz's fabled General Electric laboratories (with help from Thomas Edison) and long remained a GE town. Albany was one of America's biggest lumber towns in addition to serving as New York's state capital.

Albany is home to the state capitol of New York, but for a long time, it also had one of the nation's most famed Democratic political machines, dating to 1921, when Daniel O'Connell and his brothers and local aristocrat Edwin Corning took control of City Hall. They never really relinquished it. O'Connell died in 1977 at age 91, still boss after 56 years, and his early partner's son, Erastus Corning II, was mayor from 1942 until his death in 1983. The machine was sustained by legions of city and county employees, by a certain creativity when it came to counting votes, and by the raffish atmosphere that was found in the speakeasies of so many cities during Prohibition and lingered in Albany for decades after. Read Kennedy's novels and you are there. Curiously, the machine made possible the transformation of Albany into the shinier metropolis it is today. Mayor Corning and Republican Gov. Nelson Rockefeller collaborated on a smorgasbord of civic improvement projects: the Empire State Plaza with 11,000 employees in 10 government buildings on 98 acres; the distinctive, ovoid performing arts center known as the Egg; and a renovated Union Station.

The 21st Congressional District of New York includes most of the Albany metro area: all of Albany County; Schenectady County, including Schenectady; Montgomery County, including Amsterdam, a carpet-making town until the mills moved south in 1955, rural Schoharie County, and parts of Rensselaer, including the gentrified Troy, with its bustling antique shops. It also takes in Fulton and Saratoga counties. Times have been tough here: Albany lost 5% of its population during the 1990s, Schenectady lost 6%, and Troy lost 9%. While the outer counties lean Republican, the Democratic machine vote in Albany makes this a comfortably Democratic district. Even Democrat Carl McCall, who lost every other county in the state outside New York City, beat incumbent Republican Gov. George Pataki in Albany County in 2002. Gov. Eliot Spitzer and Sen. Hillary Rodham Clinton each took more than 70% of the vote there in 2006. Democratic presidential nominee Barack Obama won 64% of Albany County's vote in 2008.

The congressman from the 21st District is Paul Tonko, a Democrat elected in 2008. The grandson of Polish immigrants, Tonko was born in the old mill town of Amsterdam, N.Y., where he still lives. His working-class background gave him an appreciation for the "underdog" that remains the underpinning of his political beliefs. Attracted from a young age to public service, he built his career in state government, first at the New York Department of Transportation and then as an engineer at the Department of Public Service, the state's utilities regulator. In 1974, at age 26, he became the youngest person ever elected to the Montgomery County Board of Supervisors. He was elected board chairman in 1981. Tonko won a seat in the New York Assembly in a 1983 special election, and served for nearly a quarter-century. He won passage of a law requiring health insurers to cover most mental illnesses and another requiring social services workers to report all cases of suspected child abuse to the state. But he exercised his greatest influence over state energy policy, serving as chairman of the Assembly's energy committee from 1992 to 2007, when he resigned to accept an appointment as head of the state's Energy Research and Development Authority.

His tenure there was short-lived. When Democratic Rep. Michael McNulty announced in October 2007 that he would not seek an 11th term in the 2008 election, Tonko began exploring a campaign to succeed him, and entered the race the following May. By then, the primary had already taken shape around two front-runners, Phil Steck, an Albany County legislator, and Tracey Brooks, a former regional director for New York Democratic Sen. Hillary Rodham Clinton. Both enjoyed a head start raising money. Brooks won the backing of the powerful women's fundraising group EMILY's List and other national women's campaign groups, along with high-profile endorsements from U.S. Rep. Carolyn Maloney of Manhattan and former Democratic vice presidential nominee Geraldine Ferraro. But most of the local Democratic establishment lined up behind Tonko (McNulty remained neutral). Tonko won two important union endorsements, from the American Federation of State, County and Municipal Employees and the local Service Employees International Union, as well as the backing of the state's Working Families

Party. With few differences between the candidates on major issues, the local support likely made the difference. Outraised and outspent by both Brooks and Steck, Tonko sailed to victory over both. He finished narrowly behind Brooks in her home base of Albany County, but won with huge margins on his own turf in Montgomery and Schenectady counties.

In the general election Tonko faced Republican Jim Buhrmaster, a Schenectady County legislator who hoped that his appeal to independents might help him overcome the huge registration advantage for Democrats in the district. But it was too tall an order for a seat Democrats have held since the 1950s. Tonko won with 62% of the vote. Buhrmaster received 35%, and Steck, who ran as an independent, received 3%.

Tonko got seats on the Science and Technology Committee and the Education and Labor Committee. He says he wants to focus on the issue he knows best, energy policy.

TWENTY-SECOND DISTRICT

Maurice Hinchey (D)

Elected 1992, 9th term; b. Oct. 27, 1938, New York, NY; home, Saugerties; S.U.N.Y. New Paltz, B.S. 1968, M.A. 1969; Catholic; married (Allison Lee); 3 children.

Military Career: Navy, 1956–59.

Elected Office: NY Assembly, 1974–92.

Professional Career: Cement plant worker, 1959–64; NY St. Thruway toll collector, 1959–68; Analyst, NY St. Dept. of Educ., 1971–74.

DC Office: 2431 RHOB, 20515, 202-225-6335; Fax: 202-226-0774; Web site: www.house.gov/hinchey.

State Offices: Binghamton, 607-773-2768; Ithaca, 607-273-1388; Kingston, 845-331-4466; Middletown, 845-344-3211; Monticello, 845-791-7116.

Committees: *Appropriations* (16th of 37 D): Agriculture, Rural Development, FDA & Related Agencies; Defense; Interior, Environment & Related Agencies. *Joint Economic Committee* (2nd of 6 D). *Natural Resources* (17th of 29 D): Energy & Mineral Resources; National Parks, Forests & Public Lands.

Group Ratings

	ADA	ACLU	AFS	LCV	ITIC	NTU	COC	ACU	CFG	FRC
2008	95	100	100	100	43	15	50	12	8	5
2007	100	—	100	95	—	4	45	0	6	—

National Journal Ratings

	2007 LIB	—	2007 CONS	2008 LIB	—	2008 CONS
Economic	82%	—	0%	85%	—	0%
Social	88%	—	11%	52%	—	47%
Foreign	96%	—	0%	92%	—	0%
Composite	93%	—	8%	80%	—	20%

Key Votes of the 110th Congress

1. Increase minimum wage	Y	5. Share immigration data	N	9. Withdraw troops 8/08	Y
2. Expand SCHIP	Y	6. Foreign aid abortion ban	N	10. No operations in Iran	Y
3. Raise CAFE standards	Y	7. Ban gay bias in workplace	Y	11. Free trade with Peru	N
4. Bail out financial markets	N	8. Repeal D.C. gun law	Y	12. Overhaul FISA	N

Election Results

2008 general	Maurice Hinchey (D-Ind-WF)	168,558	(66%)	($735,253)
	George Phillips (R-C)	85,126	(34%)	($150,490)
2008 primary	Maurice Hinchey (D-Ind-WF)	unopposed		

Prior Winning Percentages: 2006 (100%); 2004 (67%); 2002 (64%); 2000 (62%); 1998 (62%); 1996 (55%); 1994 (49%); 1992 (50%)

Population		Race/Ethnicity		Work	
Pop. 2007:	668,526	White:	75.9%	Private:	74.3%
Change since 2000:	Up 2.2%	Black:	8.3%	Government:	18.9%
Urban:	67.8%	Hispanic:	10.5%	Self-employed:	6.6%
Rural:	32.2%	Asian:	3.2%	Blue collar:	20.5%
Area size:	3,334 sq. mi.	Native Am.:	0.1%	White collar:	59.7%
Age		Hawaiian:	0.0%	Khaki collar:	0.0%
Median age:	36.4 yrs.	Two+ races:	1.8%	Other:	19.7%
More than 65 yrs:	13.1%	*Ancestry*		Median income:	$47,751
Less than 18 yrs:	21.7%	Irish:	14.4%	Median home value:	$181,800
Education		German:	13.0%	Poverty:	14.8%
H.S. grad:	85.9%	Italian:	11.5%	**Military Veterans**	
College grad:	27.0%			% of Pop:	9.8%
Grad degree:	12.2%				

In colonial days, the Catskills looming over the mid-Hudson River Valley were a mysterious place where Rip Van Winkle was said to have fallen asleep for 20 years after drinking with nine pipe-playing dwarfs and where Indians lurked in the days of James Fenimore Cooper. Eventually, the area became part of a great pathway west, along the Erie Lackawanna and Delaware & Hudson Railroad lines, with engines steaming over giant viaducts and along narrow river valleys through the

2008 Presidential Vote
Obama (D) 170,379   (59%)
McCain (R).............................112,669   (39%)

2004 Presidential Vote
Kerry (D)................................151,890   (54%)
Bush (R) 127,253   (45%)

Cook Partisan Voting Index: D+6

hills and mountains. Later in the 19th century, huge kosher hotels were built in Sullivan County in the Catskills, the Jewish resort area popularly known as the Borscht Belt. These thrived when Jews were excluded from other resorts, but fell on hard times in the late 20th century, as discrimination against Jews waned. Some survive to cater to Russian-Jewish immigrants and a kosher clientele. Today, the Catskills are no longer on great transportation lines. There is little passenger train service, and the area is bypassed by major airlines. In recent years, there have been attempts, none successful, to open an Indian casino in the Catskills.

The sprawling 22nd Congressional District of New York includes all of Sullivan and Ulster counties and most of the Catskills area. It covers part of the Hudson Valley and parts of the counties along the New York-Pennsylvania border. Its two population centers are on its east and west ends. On the east are Newburgh, Poughkeepsie, and Kingston, old towns in the Hudson Valley. Poughkeepsie is the home of Vassar College, and Kingston, in Ulster County, was the political base of George Clinton, the former longtime governor and two-term vice president. This area has been growing relatively rapidly, with new residents from metro New York. In the west, connected to the rest of the district by a narrow corridor of southern-tier townships, are Binghamton and Ithaca, where Cornell University sits high above the Cayuga River and is by far the largest employer in Tompkins County. Ithaca has attracted a number superlative designations in recent years, including "lesbian-friendliest," "best fly-fishing," one of the "greatest places to retire," and "largest share of commuters who walk or bicycle to work." The district also includes Bethel, site of the 1969 Woodstock music festival, one of the watershed events of the hippie counterculture era. Most of this territory voted Republican for many years, though Sullivan County, with the only large rural Jewish population in the United States, has long been Democratic. Today most of the area is Democratic, especially the university towns of Ithaca, Poughkeepsie, and New Paltz in Ulster County, and the actual Woodstock (not where the festival was held), a favorite country house location for New Yorkers. Democratic presidential nominee Barack Obama won the district in 2008 with 59% of the vote.

The congressman from the 22nd is Maurice Hinchey, a Democrat elected in 1992. The son of a cement plant worker, Hinchey grew up in Greenwich Village in humble circumstances. After high school, he enlisted in the Navy at age 18 and served on a destroyer in the Pacific. When he got home, he worked in the cement factory for five years. But Hinchey wanted to go to college, and since his parents couldn't afford to send him, he worked his way through as a New York State Thruway toll collector. After getting his degree, he was an analyst for the state education department. Then, in the Democratic year of 1974, Hinchey was elected as the first Democrat from Ulster County to the New York Assembly since 1912, and served for nine terms. When he ran for Congress, Hinchey called for national health insurance, a repeal of Reagan-Bush tax cuts for upper-income taxpayers and corporations, and "reindustrializing America." His Republican opponent, Bob Moppert, a Binghamton moving company owner, campaigned on reducing government spending and trimming the size of the federal bureaucracy. Hinchey won 50%-47%.

Hinchey has one of the most liberal voting records for a nonurban member in the House. He is frequently the leader of lost causes. In 2008, he co-sponsored a bill calling for the impeachment of President George W. Bush. When Republicans controlled the White House, he once sparked a House debate with a proposal to prohibit the private donation of food and beverages for official events at the vice president's residence; it was defeated, with 54 Democrats voting no. In 2004, he was one of 16 House members voting against a resolution of sympathy for the victims of the September 11 attacks. He objected to the Republicans' inclusion of "political" language with the "destruction of two terrorist regimes" in Afghanistan and Iraq, and called the measure "back-slapping, self-congratulatory." Following an incident at a Rosendale street fair in July 2008, a local official of the National Rifle Association filed harassment charges against Hinchey for allegedly hitting him on the head following a heated exchange. An Ulster County judge dismissed the charges in November 2008.

Hinchey has been a vocal opponent of the war in Iraq, and condemned the "deplorable" humanitarian conditions that the United States had created there. With other Democrats, Hinchey organized the Future of American Media Caucus to "address critical media policy issues," where he has advocated a return of the Federal Communications Commission's Fairness Doctrine requiring equal time for differing political viewpoints. He says that the television networks give disproportionate airtime to conservatives on their Sunday morning talk shows.

On the Appropriations Committee, his focus has been ensuring the independence of the Food and Drug Administration from the pharmaceutical industry, and demanding that owners of oil and gas leases pay "fair market prices." When Republicans in 2008 sought repeal of oil-drilling restrictions, Hinchey countered by seeking increased penalties for gas-price gouging and pressing for more use of renewable fuels. He joined the Defense Subcommittee in 2009, where his focus is seeking money for local defense contractors. Earlier, he directed several appropriations grants to the revitalization of downtown Poughkeepsie.

Hinchey was the subject of unfavorable press coverage in recent years when New York newspapers reported extensively on his more than 20 privately funded foreign trips to exotic places, ranking him among the top members of Congress who received travel gifts. The *New York Post* dubbed him a "junket junkie." He has since cut back on his foreign travel.

Early in his House tenure Hinchey was a Republican target, but since the mid-1990s he has won re-election easily. His district became more secure after the 2002 redistricting with the help of Assembly Speaker Sheldon Silver, a friend of Hinchey's from their time in the Legislature.

TWENTY-THIRD DISTRICT

John McHugh (R)

Elected 1992, 9th term; b. Sept. 29, 1948, Watertown; home, Pierrepont Manor; Utica Col., B.A. 1970, S.U.N.Y. Albany, M.P.A. 1977; Catholic; divorced.

Elected Office: NY Senate, 1984–92.

Professional Career: Confidential asst., Watertown City Mgr., 1971–76; Research & liaison chief, NY Sen. Douglas Barclay, 1976–84.

DC Office: 2366 RHOB, 20515, 202-225-4611; Fax: 202-226-0621; Web site: www.mchugh.house.gov.

State Offices: Canastota, 315-697-2063; Mayfield, 518-661-6486; Plattsburgh, 518-563-1406; Watertown, 315-782-3150.

Committees: *Oversight & Government Reform* (3rd of 15 R): Federal Workforce, Postal Service & the District of Columbia.

Group Ratings

	ADA	ACLU	AFS	LCV	ITIC	NTU	COC	ACU	CFG	FRC
2008	60	18	57	38	57	30	83	40	25	82
2007	45	—	40	45	—	30	78	60	15	—

National Journal Ratings

	2007 LIB	—	2007 CONS	2008 LIB	—	2008 CONS
Economic	44%	—	56%	44%	—	56%
Social	29%	—	69%	31%	—	62%
Foreign	28%	—	71%	29%	—	69%
Composite	34%	—	66%	36%	—	64%

Key Votes of the 110th Congress

1. Increase minimum wage	Y	5. Share immigration data	Y	9. Withdraw troops 8/08	N
2. Expand SCHIP	Y	6. Foreign aid abortion ban	Y	10. No operations in Iran	N
3. Raise CAFE standards	N	7. Ban gay bias in workplace	Y	11. Free trade with Peru	N
4. Bail out financial markets	Y	8. Repeal D.C. gun law	Y	12. Overhaul FISA	Y

Election Results

2008 general	John McHugh (R-Ind-C)	143,029	(65%)	($645,795)
	Michael Oot (D-WF)	75,871	(35%)	($107,714)
2008 primary	John McHugh (R-Ind-C)	unopposed		

Prior Winning Percentages: 2006 (63%); 2004 (71%); 2002 (100%); 2000 (74%); 1998 (79%); 1996 (71%); 1994 (79%); 1992 (61%)

Population		Race/Ethnicity		Work	
Pop. 2007:	655,696	White:	92.4%	Private:	68.4%
Change since 2000:	Up 0.2%	Black:	2.5%	Government:	23.7%
Urban:	34.7%	Hispanic:	2.3%	Self-employed:	7.6%
Rural:	65.3%	Asian:	0.8%	Blue collar:	25.1%
Area size:	14,739 sq. mi.	Native Am.:	0.9%	White collar:	51.5%
Age		Hawaiian:	0.1%	Khaki collar:	1.6%
Median age:	36.7 yrs.	Two+ races:	0.9%	Other:	21.8%
More than 65 yrs:	12.9%	*Ancestry*		Median income:	$42,473
Less than 18 yrs:	22.1%	Irish:	13.9%	Median home value:	$88,100
Education		German:	12.3%	Poverty:	14.9%
H.S. grad:	85.4%	English:	11.9%	**Military Veterans**	
College grad:	18.3%			% of Pop:	12.2%
Grad degree:	7.7%				

Some early-19th-century visionaries believed that the North Country of upstate New York—a battleground in both the Revolutionary War and the War of 1812—was the land of the future. Financier Gouverneur Morris, French slave trader James Leray, and Dutch silver speculator David Parish bought up thousands of acres between the Adirondacks and the St. Lawrence River and tried to unload them on farmers unaware of the shortness of the growing season and the unnavigability of the

2008 Presidential Vote

Obama (D)	133,367	(52%)
McCain (R)	119,944	(47%)

2004 Presidential Vote

Bush (R)	134,174	(51%)
Kerry (D)	123,216	(47%)

Cook Partisan Voting Index: R + 1

river. These developers left behind grand mansions, but their hopes for huge profits were frustrated when the Erie Canal turned the stream of settlement westward, and Canadians built their new capital of Ottawa far north of the river. (Queen Victoria picked the site, and put it as far from the U.S. border as possible.) But northern New York was not without its business successes: It was in Watertown in 1878 that 26-year-old Frank Woolworth put a sign over a table of odds and ends that read "Any Article 5 Cents," starting America's first retail chain and inventing the concept of discount stores.

More recently, the North Country has looked to government for help. The St. Lawrence Seaway proved too small for most oceangoing freighters and remains frozen three months of the year. The locks are slow, and icebreakers would wreck the shoreline. The state government has built prisons in Ogdensburg and Cape Vincent and Malone. North Country and Vermont members of Congress tried to get Lake Champlain declared one of the Great Lakes, to qualify for funding for various programs. The gambit failed as Michigan members howled in protest. A General Motors power-train factory in Massena closed in May 2009, wiping out 500 jobs. The biggest initiative has been the enlargement of Fort Drum, near Watertown and adjacent to Lake Bonaparte, where despite the Army's preference for warm-weather training sites, a 10,000-person light infantry division, the 10th Mountain Division, has been stationed since 1985. (The 10th Mountain has performed valiantly in difficult environs in Afghanistan and Iraq.) Private developers have built big malls in Watertown and Massena, attracting Canadians, as even New York has lower taxes than Ontario. While the dollar was cheap, Canadian tourism and shopping here were strong, notably at the Adirondack State Park.

The 23rd Congressional District of New York covers most of the North Country, starting at Lake Champlain, running westward along the St. Lawrence Seaway and over the Adirondacks Forest Preserve to Lake Ontario. It includes Madison County to the south. The district has only a few population centers, including Plattsburgh on Lake Champlain and Watertown and Oswego on Lake Ontario. Oswego, which occasionally docks oceangoing bulk vessels, bills itself as the first U.S. port of call on the Great Lakes from the Seaway. Geographically it is the largest district in New York state, and one of the largest in the East. Politically, it is ancestrally Republican but more inclined toward moderates than conservatives and increasingly divided in its loyalties to the two parties. It gave Republican George W. Bush a small plurality in 2000 and a small majority in 2004. And it gave Democratic presidential nominee Barack Obama 52% of the vote over Republican John McCain's 47% in 2008.

Since 1993, the 23rd District had been represented by Republican John McHugh. However, in early June 2009, McHugh accepted President Barack Obama's offer to become secretary of the Army. McHugh had been the ranking Republican on the House Armed Services Committee, and is well versed in defense issues. "I grew up in the shadow of Fort Drum," McHugh said. "The Army's always had a special place in my heart."

At press time for the *Almanac* in July 2009, McHugh was expected to be easily confirmed by the Senate. The appointment was one in a series of high-profile positions offered to moderate Republicans early in the Obama administration, a sign that the president's political team was intent on capturing those seats for the Democrats. With McHugh's anticipated departure, there were just two remaining Republicans in the New York congressional delegation, down from 10 as recently as 2004. Although the region has long been Republican, Democrats have been making inroads. Republicans have a registration advantage of about 46,500 voters in the 23rd, but Obama carried it by five percentage points. McHugh's appointment quickly touched off a hotly contested special election campaign to choose a successor. Several prominent state politicians from both parties were weighing the race. Democrats were feeling especially confident, having recently prevailed in a special election in an adjacent upstate New York district. Democrat Scott Murphy defeated Republican James Tedisco, the New York Assembly minority leader, on March 31, 2009 by a margin of just 726 votes. Murphy succeeded U.S. Rep. Kirsten Gillibrand, a Democrat, who was appointed to the Senate after Obama named New York Democrat Hillary Rodham Clinton his secretary of State.

McHugh has been in government almost his entire career. His first public job was as assistant city manager of Watertown, N.Y., his hometown. After five years, he went to work for state Sen. Douglas Barclay, a prominent Republican, and stayed for nearly a decade. In 1984, he was elected to succeed his boss in the state Legislature. When U.S. Republican Rep. David Martin announced his retirement in 1992, McHugh easily won the Republican primary and the general election, 61%-24%. He was re-elected every two years against modest opposition. In the House, McHugh had a moderate voting record, especially on economic issues, and was frequently at odds with GOP conservatives. But he was a steadfast supporter of the Bush administration on the war in Iraq.

During Republican control of Congress, McHugh was chairman of the Military Personnel Subcommittee on Armed Services, where he had jurisdiction over a broad range of issues dealing with military benefits and quality of life. He won passage of a permanent increase of nearly 40,000 Army and Marine troops. His early years on the committee were focused on protecting military installations in his district during several rounds of base closings. He successfully lobbied to preserve Fort Drum, the largest employer in northern New York, in the 2005 base-closing round. The base got an expansion of another 6,000 troops, and in 2006 he stuck in the defense bill another $200 million for housing at Fort Drum. McHugh became ranking member of the full committee in early 2009.

TWENTY-FOURTH DISTRICT

Michael Arcuri (D)

Elected 2006, 2nd term; b. June 11, 1959, Utica; home, Utica; S.U.N.Y. Albany, B.A. 1981; NY Law Schl., J.D. 1984; Catholic; married (Sabrina); 3 children.

Elected Office:　Oneida Cnty. D.A., 1993–2006.

Professional Career:　Practicing atty., 1984–93.

DC Office:　127 CHOB, 20515, 202-225-3665; Fax: 202-225-1891; Web site: arcuri.house.gov.

State Offices:　Auburn, 315-252-2777; Cortland, 607-756-2470; Utica, 315-793-8146.

Committees:　*Rules* (6th of 9 D): Rules & Organization of the House. *Transportation & Infrastructure* (26th of 44 D): Economic Development, Public Buildings & Emergency Management; Highways & Transit; Railroads, Pipelines & Hazardous Materials.

Group Ratings

	ADA	ACLU	AFS	LCV	ITIC	NTU	COC	ACU	CFG	FRC
2008	90	73	100	92	86	8	67	4	0	0
2007	100	—	100	90	—	4	55	0	0	—

National Journal Ratings

	2007 LIB	—	2007 CONS		2008 LIB	—	2008 CONS
Economic	78%	—	18%		64%	—	35%
Social	63%	—	36%		54%	—	42%
Foreign	63%	—	35%		52%	—	46%
Composite	69%	—	31%		58%	—	42%

Key Votes of the 110th Congress

1. Increase minimum wage	Y	5. Share immigration data	N	9. Withdraw troops 8/08	Y
2. Expand SCHIP	Y	6. Foreign aid abortion ban	N	10. No operations in Iran	Y
3. Raise CAFE standards	Y	7. Ban gay bias in workplace	Y	11. Free trade with Peru	N
4. Bail out financial markets	Y	8. Repeal D.C. gun law	Y	12. Overhaul FISA	Y

Election Results

2008 general	Michael Arcuri (D-WF)	130,799	(52%)	($1,616,138)
	Richard Hanna (R-Ind-C)	120,880	(48%)	($1,090,713)
2008 primary	Michael Arcuri (D-WF)	unopposed		

Prior Winning Percentages: 2006 (54%)

Population		Race/Ethnicity		Work	
Pop. 2007:	649,431	White:	90.9%	Private:	73.9%
Change since 2000:	Down 0.8%	Black:	3.5%	Government:	18.0%
Urban:	50.5%	Hispanic:	2.7%	Self-employed:	7.8%
Rural:	49.5%	Asian:	1.3%	Blue collar:	22.9%
Area size:	6,356 sq. mi.	Native Am.:	0.2%	White collar:	57.5%
		Hawaiian:	0.0%	Khaki collar:	0.1%
Age		Two+ races:	1.3%	Other:	19.5%
Median age:	39.0 yrs.	*Ancestry*		Median income:	$44,298
More than 65 yrs:	14.8%	German:	14.5%	Median home value:	$92,800
Less than 18 yrs:	21.4%	Irish:	14.3%	Poverty:	13.0%
		English:	11.5%		
Education				**Military Veterans**	
H.S. grad:	85.5%			% of Pop:	11.3%
College grad:	22.3%				
Grad degree:	9.2%				

One of the first American frontiers was the Mohawk River Valley of upstate New York. But from the establishment of Fort Orange in 1624 in what now is Albany until the Revolutionary War, white settlers did not dare move west along the Mohawk. The British used their Iroquois allies as a buffer against the French and in return kept New England Yankees from moving westward. Only after the French were driven from the colonies in 1759 did the pressures for westward settlement prevail. Once the Revolu-

2008 Presidential Vote
Obama (D)	139,832	(50%)
McCain (R)	133,277	(48%)

2004 Presidential Vote
Bush (R)	147,509	(53%)
Kerry (D)	130,568	(47%)

Cook Partisan Voting Index: R+2

tionary War started, Iroquois dominion ended. Those events are the background of *Drums Along the Mohawk* and of James Fenimore Cooper's *Leatherstocking Tales*. But there is little in these rolling hills today to evoke the bloody violence of the conflict or the later digging of the Erie Canal and the building of the New York Central Railroad. The canal was a staggering engineering feat. In 1811, it cost more to ship goods 30 miles inland from New York City than it cost to send them to England. But after eight years of work by 9,000 men, the canal opened in 1825, ahead of schedule and on budget, effectively tying together the nation and cementing the importance of New York City to America's future. Then the New York Central built its water-line route, and the Mohawk Valley became one of the nation's early industrial centers. The little Oneida County hamlets of Utica and Rome, where the canal builders had to dig through the route's highest ground, became sizable factory towns. Even the utopian Oneida Community, with its believers in plural marriage and communal ownership, operated a stainless steel factory. First settled by New England Yankees, these towns attracted a new wave of immigration from the Atlantic coast in the early 20th century, including many Italian- and Polish-Americans.

The 24th Congressional District of New York sprawls through parts of 11 counties in central New York, few of them heavily populated. The biggest towns are Utica and Rome in Oneida County and Auburn in Cayuga County, which sits amid the Finger Lakes. Nearby Seneca Falls was the birthplace of the women's movement in 1848, when Boston transplant Elizabeth Cady Stanton and Lucretia Mott produced a Declaration of Sentiments that initiated the push for women's suffrage. Abolition and temperance were also popular here. Today, this is a part of upstate New York that feels itself bypassed by more recent economic growth. Young people increasingly see their futures in larger cities like Albany or Syracuse, rather than in Utica. Oneida County's population fell 7% between 1990 and 2007 as the county lost many industrial jobs. Seven of the district's counties have experienced population declines since 2000. The booming business here is the Oneida Indians' Turning Stone Resort Casino, the largest employer in the area. At the south end of Otsego Lake is Cooperstown, home of the Baseball Hall of Fame. In March 2009, the state announced plans to improve rail service in upstate New York as a way of potentially sparking more economic activity. The 24th District is historically Republican, but trended to Democrats in the 1990s. Republican George W. Bush carried it only narrowly in 2000 and by 53%-47% in 2004. In 2008, the district voted for Democrat Barack Obama 50%-48%.

The congressman from the 24th District is Michael Arcuri, a Democrat elected in 2006. He grew up in Utica and went to college at the State University of New York at Albany, where he distinguished himself as a Division III football star. Arcuri (*ar-CURE-ee*) got his law degree at New York Law School in Manhattan and returned home to open a law practice. In 1993, he was elected Oneida County district attorney, the first Democrat elected to the position in 40 years. During his tenure, he boasted of a conviction rate above 90% and sometimes pursued unpopular prosecutions, including the convictions of a veteran local politician and an assistant fire chief. He ran for the House after 12-term Rep. Sherwood Boehlert, a leading Republican centrist, announced his retirement in 2006. Democrats united behind Arcuri while Republicans chose state Sen. Ray Meier. Although Republicans had nearly 40,000 more registered voters than Democrats, the district's nearly 72,000 unaffiliated voters and Democratic voting trends made this a highly competitive race.

Arcuri and Meier hewed to the ideological center, but Arcuri most closely reflected Boehlert's viewpoints. "I've been calling myself, much to my opponent's chagrin, a Boehlert Democrat," Arcuri said during the campaign. Meier opposed abortion rights, while Arcuri supported them as Boehlert had. Meier had Boehlert's endorsement, and said that although he was more conservative than Boehlert, he would stand up to his party and seek bipartisan compromises in Congress. Arcuri had no legislative record to defend, making it difficult for Republicans to argue that he was too liberal for the district. Both veterans of Oneida County politics, Arcuri and Meier remained relatively civil for much of the campaign, even as the national parties spent millions attacking the candidates. The Democratic Congressional Campaign Committee sponsored one direct-mail piece, titled "Spending like a Drunken Sailor," that showed Meier holding a champagne bottle. The National Republican Congressional Committee ran a racy ad featuring the silhouette of a dancing woman that accused Arcuri of charging the county for calls to a phone sex line. The allegation was later discredited. Both national parties spent about $2 million apiece on the contest. In a strongly Democratic year in New York, Arcuri won decisively, 54%-45%, helped by landslide victories for Democratic Gov. Eliot Spitzer and Sen. Hillary Rodham Clinton.

In the House, Arcuri's voting record was among the most conservative among New York Democrats. He won a seat on the influential Rules Committee, a prominent posting for a freshman on the leadership-driven committee that sets the ground rules for legislation on the floor. He voted with his party on most issues, but backed tougher border security during the debate over illegal immigration in the 110th Congress (2007–08). He joined the fiscally conservative Blue Dog Coalition. In February 2009, Arcuri and a group of Blue Dogs met with Obama to try to convince him to consider deep spending cuts and other belt-tightening measures. On local issues, Arcuri was involved in efforts to stop a proposed New York Regional Interconnect high-voltage power line from going through his district. The line is designed to deliver excess energy from upstate markets to power-starved New York City. He also tried to prevent the Interior Department from approving a request by the Oneida Indians to place 17,370 acres of nonreservation land into a federal Indian trust. Local governments in the area object to the plan.

The district remains winnable territory for the right Republican candidate. In 2008, Arcuri failed to respond to attack ads from GOP challenger Richard Hanna and did not take the threat from the self-funding multimillionaire as seriously as he should have, as he later acknowledged. Hanna, the owner of a construction company, spent $1.1 million against Arcuri, campaigned as a moderate, and criticized Arcuri for some of his votes with House Democrats. The two candidates agreed on their support for abortion rights and opposition to gun control. Arcuri was re-elected narrowly, 52%-48%, two weeks after the election when the results of absentee ballots came in. He carried all but Herkimer, Broome, and Tioga counties. In April 2009, the National Republican Congressional Committee ran ads in the district criticizing Arcuri's support for the Democratic budget, a sign he will be a target again in 2010.

Upstate New York will likely lose at least one seat in redistricting after the 2010 census, and Arcuri could find his district squeezed by more-urban-based Democrats.

TWENTY-FIFTH DISTRICT

Dan Maffei (D)

Elected 2008, 1st term; b. July 4, 1968, Syracuse; home, DeWitt; Brown U., B.A. 1990; Columbia U., M.S. 1991; Harvard U., M.P.P. 1995; Catholic; married (Abby).

Professional Career: TV reporter, 1991–93; Press secy., U.S. Sen. Bill Bradley, 1996; Press secy., U.S. Sen. Daniel Patrick Moynihan, 1997–98; Aide, House Ways & Means Committee, 1999–2005; Campaign coordinator, Matt Driscoll for mayor of Syracuse, 2005; Sr. VP, Pinnacle Capital Management, LLC 2006–08

DC Office: 1630 LHOB, 20515, 202-225-3701; Fax: 202-225-4042; Web site: maffei.house.gov.

State Offices: Rochester, 585-336-7291; Syracuse, 315-423-5657.

Committees: *Financial Services* (42nd of 42 D): Housing & Community Opportunity; International Monetary Policy & Trade. *Judiciary* (24th of 24 D): Commercial & Administrative Law.

Group Ratings and Key Votes: Newly Elected

Election Results

2008 general	Dan Maffei (D-WF)	157,375	(55%)	($2,410,865)
	Dale Sweetland (R-C)	120,217	(42%)	($403,189)
	Howie Hawkins (Green)	9,483	(3%)	($6,132)
2008 primary	Dan Maffei (D-WF)	unopposed		

Population		Race/Ethnicity		Work	
Pop. 2007:	656,045	White:	85.4%	Private:	78.7%
Change since 2000:	Up 0.3%	Black:	7.3%	Government:	15.9%
Urban:	79.0%	Hispanic:	2.8%	Self-employed:	5.2%
Rural:	21.0%	Asian:	2.1%	Blue collar:	19.8%
Area size:	2,561 sq. mi.	Native Am.:	0.5%	White collar:	64.3%
		Hawaiian:	0.0%	Khaki collar:	0.1%
Age		Two+ races:	1.7%	Other:	15.8%
Median age:	38.9 yrs.	*Ancestry*		Median income:	$50,501
More than 65 yrs:	13.9%	German:	15.9%	Median home value:	$116,300
Less than 18 yrs:	23.8%	Irish:	15.2%	Poverty:	11.8%
Education		Italian:	13.3%		
H.S. grad:	88.5%			**Military Veterans**	
College grad:	30.0%			% of Pop:	10.4%
Grad degree:	12.5%				

Syracuse is a Middle American city in the middle of upstate New York, halfway between Albany and Buffalo on the Erie Canal and the old New York Central Railroad, which were for years the nation's major east-west transportation routes. Built on a swamp that was a salt spring, Syracuse is the home of many practical-minded inventions—the dental chair, Stickley mission furniture, the drive-in bank teller, the serrated knife, and the foot measuring devices used in shoe stores. It is the site of the New

2008 Presidential Vote		
Obama (D)	177,800	(56%)
McCain (R)	135,941	(43%)
2004 Presidential Vote		
Kerry (D)	158,063	(50%)
Bush (R)	150,098	(48%)
Cook Partisan Voting Index:	D+3	

York State Fair, which attracts 1 million visitors annually, and of Syracuse University, which plays basketball inside the Carrier Dome, the largest domed stadium on a college campus. The agricultural hinterland is rich with specialty crops like wine grapes, and its industrial jobs are mostly high-skill. But Onondaga County has been losing population since 1990, with a big loss in the 20-35 age group. Manufacturing jobs are being lost, but there are job gains in business services, education, and health care. Because local housing prices increased only modestly during the real estate boom, the area suffered little from the sharp decline in housing prices in 2008 and 2009.

The 25th Congressional District of New York includes all of Syracuse and Onondaga County. West of Syracuse, it includes territory just south of Lake Ontario, northern Cayuga County, and Wayne County, where in the village of Palmyra, Joseph Smith had his vision of the angel Moroni and saw the golden tablets that led him to found the Mormon Church. The district's western end is in the suburbs of Rochester in Monroe County, which is split up between four districts. Historically, Syracuse and Rochester have been heavily Republican, partly out of antipathy to New York City. But in the 1990s, economically ailing upstate New York trended sharply toward national Democrats even as it voted for Republican Gov.

George Pataki. In 2007, Democrats had the majority of voter registrations in Onondaga for the first time. This district voted 50% for Democratic presidential nominee John Kerry in 2004 and 56% for Democratic nominee Barack Obama in 2008.

The congressman from the 25th District is Dan Maffei, a Democrat elected in 2008. He was born in Syracuse, the son of social workers, and grew up a self-described "nerd" who wrote computer code after school to make extra money. Maffei (*Mu-FAY*) earned three Ivy League degrees, from Brown University, the Columbia School of Journalism, and the Kennedy School of Government at Harvard. He briefly worked as a reporter for a local television station, and in 1996 Maffei went to Washington to pursue a career on Capitol Hill, working as press secretary to Sens. Bill Bradley, D-N.J., and Daniel Patrick Moynihan, D-N.Y., for a year each. He then spent six years as a press aide to the Democratic minority on the House Ways and Means Committee, where he forged a relationship with ranking Democratic Rep. Charles Rangel of New York. Maffei picked up valuable political experience as a coordinator for Democrat Matt Driscoll's successful 2005 campaign for Syracuse mayor. In 2006, few observers gave Maffei much of a chance when he launched a campaign against nine-term Republican Rep. James Walsh. But his anti-war focus, coupled with the favorable national climate for Democrats, provided the ingredients for a near-upset. Maffei fell short by fewer than 3,500 votes.

With encouragement from Democratic Sen. Hillary Rodham Clinton of New York and flush with cash from the Democratic Congressional Campaign Committee, Maffei was set for a rematch with Walsh in 2008. Then, in January 2008, Walsh unexpectedly announced he would not run for re-election, leaving open one of the few remaining districts in Republican hands that backed Democrat Kerry for president in 2004. Maffei avoided primary competition but weathered criticism over the generous campaign contributions he accepted from Rangel while the Ways and Means chairman was under investigation for charges of tax fraud. He had received some $75,000 from Rangel's political action committee and from a birthday gala for Rangel at Tavern-on-the-Green in Manhattan. Maffei defended the contributions as proper and legal, and declined to return them. Republicans also criticized him for campaigning with national party figures like party Chairman Howard Dean, but the outcry failed to resonate in this liberal-leaning district. Outraised almost 6-to-1, GOP nominee Dale Sweetland, a farmer and former Onondaga County legislator, proved unable to replicate Walsh's success. Maffei defeated him 55%-42%. In his election night speech, he cited one of Moynihan's aphorisms: "America is a land of the second chance." His victory over Sweetland nudged congressional Republicans further along the road to extinction in New York. In the past three election cycles, Democrats have picked up seven House seats in the state. After four years of practically uninterrupted campaigning for the seat, Maffei ended not only with a seat in Congress, but a partner to share it with—he married his fiancée, Abby Davidson, in July 2008.

In the House, he emphasized his moderate stripes and nonideological pragmatism. He joined the New Democrat Coalition, a group of moderate Democrats. He got seats on the Financial Services and Judiciary committees. During his first month in office, Maffei fought to include billions of dollars for school construction in the Democrats' economic stimulus bill. He also sought to direct funds to his district for "green jobs" and high-tech development. In a sign that the GOP has not given up on the seat, the National Republican Congressional Committee aired a series of radio commercials in Syracuse accusing Maffei of placing pork-barrel spending over job creation. With an eye on re-election in 2010, Maffei got an early start on fundraising with $440,000 in the first quarter of 2009, ranking him the third-most-prodigious fundraiser among freshmen Democrats. (He says he keeps a photograph of hard-charging Rahm Emanuel, the White House chief of staff and former Illinois lawmaker, in his office closet as a reminder of the need to raise money.)

Maffei says his district leans more Democratic than those of three other upstate Democrats, which should help him in the case of a likely Republican challenge in 2010. Another political goal for him is to keep Onondaga County whole during redistricting in 2012, in contrast to Rochester-based Monroe County, which was split into four districts in 2002.

TWENTY-SIXTH DISTRICT

Chris Lee (R)

Elected 2008, 1st term; b. April 1, 1964, Kenmore; home, Clarence; U. of Rochester, B.A. 1987; Chapman U., M.B.A. 1997; Protestant; married (Michele); 1 child.

Professional Career: Microtek Lab, Sales operations mgr., 1990–92, Dir. of sales, 1993–94; Enidine, Inc., Sales, 1995–97, Dir. of international sales & marketing, 2000–02, Gen. mgr., 2003–07; Pres., Automation Group, 2003–07

DC Office: 1711 LHOB, 20515, 202-225-5265; Fax: 202-225-5910; Web site: chrislee.house.gov.

State Offices: Greece, 585-663-5570; Williamsville, 716-634-2324.

Committees: *Financial Services* (27th of 29 R): Financial Institutions & Consumer Credit; Housing & Community Opportunity; Oversight & Investigations.

Group Ratings and Key Votes: Newly Elected

Election Results

2008 general	Chris Lee (R-Ind-C)	148,607	(55%)	($2,220,960)
	Alice Kryzan (D)	109,615	(41%)	($1,206,640)
	Jonathan Powers (WF)	12,104	(4%)	($1,183,545)
2008 primary	Chris Lee (R)	unopposed		

Population		Race/Ethnicity		Work	
Pop. 2007:	666,224	White:	90.7%	Private:	77.7%
Change since 2000:	Up 1.8%	Black:	3.6%	Government:	16.3%
Urban:	71.2%	Hispanic:	2.3%	Self-employed:	5.8%
Rural:	28.8%	Asian:	2.0%	Blue collar:	21.5%
Area size:	2,749 sq. mi.	Native Am.:	0.3%	White collar:	62.1%
		Hawaiian:	0.0%	Khaki collar:	0.1%
Age		Two+ races:	1.0%	Other:	16.3%
Median age:	39.4 yrs.	*Ancestry*		Median income:	$53,102
More than 65 yrs:	14.1%	German:	22.0%	Median home value:	$119,400
Less than 18 yrs:	22.3%	Irish:	13.6%	Poverty:	9.6%
Education		Italian:	13.5%	**Military Veterans**	
H.S. grad:	89.5%			% of Pop:	10.5%
College grad:	27.7%				
Grad degree:	12.0%				

The destination of the Erie Canal, the great state engineering project that made New York the Empire State, is Lake Erie. The final 100 miles of the canal passed through the rolling countryside of western New York when it was scarcely settled, except by American Indians. In some ways, the region has a Midwest flavor. People speak not in the pungent accents of New York City but in flat Midwestern tones. The economy, based originally on farming, was dominated by heavy industry by the

2008 Presidential Vote

McCain (R)	166,862	(52%)
Obama (D)	148,577	(46%)

2004 Presidential Vote

Bush (R)	176,235	(55%)
Kerry (D)	137,543	(43%)

Cook Partisan Voting Index: R+6

late 19th century. The land was settled mostly by New England Yankees, with cultural folkways quite different from those of New York City. Later, they were joined by Irish, Italian, and Polish immigrants who came to work in the factories of Buffalo and Rochester. For most of its history, western New York had an economy more prosperous than that of the rest of the country, as you can still see in the solid houses and schools, stores, and factories built to weather the upstate winters. But in the past three decades, economic growth has lagged behind the rest of the nation. Many of Buffalo's factories have closed, and the large Delphi plant in Lockport—where the locks of the Erie Canal are near Main Street—had major cutbacks following the company's bankruptcy in 2005. Rochester's premier industries, Eastman Kodak and Xerox, have fallen on hard times and laid off thousands of workers.

The 26th Congressional District of New York covers much of western New York. About half its people are in the suburbs of Buffalo in Erie and Niagara counties. It extends from the city limits of Buffalo to the city limits of Rochester and includes Rochester's northwestern suburbs. In between is rural and small-town territory. One of them is Attica, scene of a terrible prison uprising in 1970. Politically, this is ancestrally Republican country, based on upstaters' general distrust of Democratic New York City. But as economic growth has lagged, upstate New York has trended toward the Democratic Party. The 26th District still leans Republican, however. It was one of six New York districts that voted for Republican George W. Bush in both 2000 and 2004, and it was one of four New York districts that voted for GOP presidential nominee John McCain in 2008.

The new congressman from the 26th District is Chris Lee, a Republican who was one of the rare success stories for the GOP in 2008. He withstood a strong Democratic wind blowing through the state to win the House seat formerly held by Republican Rep. Tom Reynolds. Born in Buffalo, he grew up in the western New York town of Tonawanda, where his father ran a small machine shop. He stayed close to home to earn his undergraduate degree at the University of Rochester, and then moved across the country to work in California's burgeoning information-technology industry. While working on the West Coast, Lee went back to school to earn his MBA at Chapman University. In 1995, he returned home to take a job at his family's business, which by then had grown into a multinational conglomerate of manufacturing companies called International Motion Control. He worked for eight years as a manager at the company's flagship enterprise in Orchard Park. In 2003, he became a division president at IMC, overseeing offices on three continents.

He likely would have stayed there had it not been for Reynolds's announcement in March 2008 that he would step down at the end of his term. Eager to avoid a contentious primary, the district's Republican leaders chose to interview potential candidates privately and throw their support behind a consensus nominee. Lee had no prior political experience but knew one of the county chairmen, and was included among the seven candidates interviewed. He impressed them with his long-standing ties to the district, his business experience, and his ability to fund his own campaign with up to $1 million of his own money. Once Lee had the backing of the party establishment, the other candidates bowed out.

Initially expected to be one of the most competitive of the year, the race took a surprising turn when the Democrats' top prospects failed to survive the primary. Jack Davis, a local billionaire who nearly defeated Reynolds in 2006, and Jon Powers, an Iraq war veteran backed by the Democratic Congressional Campaign Committee, both lost to attorney Alice Kryzan. Although Kryzan's upset victory made the race a lower priority for the DCCC, the group continued to pour money into her campaign. But her fundraising was no match for Lee's, especially after he pumped more than $1 million of his personal fortune into the campaign. Lee outraised Kryzan $2.2 million to $1.2 million. Campaigning as a business-oriented fiscal conservative and criticizing both parties' records in Washington, Lee distanced himself from national Republicans in a year when the GOP brand was especially damaged in New York. Democratic presidential nominee Barack Obama threatened to provide Democrats some powerful coattails, but the traditional Republican lean of the district played to Lee's advantage.

The race took on a negative tone during its final stretch. The DCCC financed a television commercial that claimed Lee had profited from selling a family-owned company to a firm that had been fined for selling secrets to China. Lee admitted to the sale but pointed out that the purchasing firm's legal problems occurred six years earlier. But Lee won a solid victory, 55%-41%, over Kryzan.

Although he heads to Washington as a member of the minority party in the House—and an even more extreme minority as a New York Republican—Lee says he is undaunted by the challenge. He hopes to draw on his local business experience to create job opportunities in the region. His appointment to the Financial Services Committee gives him a platform to pursue his agenda. Early in 2009, Lee supported a bill that would have stopped members of Congress from receiving a scheduled pay raise. He also set up a special website to track government spending that he deems wasteful.

TWENTY-SEVENTH DISTRICT

Brian Higgins (D)

Elected 2004, 3rd term; b. Oct. 6, 1959, Buffalo; home, Buffalo; S.U.N.Y. Buffalo, B.A. 1984, M.A. 1985, Harvard U. M.P.A. 1996; Catholic; married (Mary Jane); 2 children.

Elected Office: Buffalo City Cncl., 1987–93; NY Assembly, 1998–2004.

Professional Career: Chief of staff, Erie Cnty. Leg., 1994–98; Lecturer, Buffalo State College, 2000–03.

DC Office: 431 CHOB, 20515, 202-225-3306; Fax: 202-226-0347; Web site: house.gov/higgins.

State Offices: Buffalo, 716-852-3501; Jamestown, 716-484-0729.

Committees: *Ways & Means* (25th of 26 D): Oversight; Select Revenue Measures.

Group Ratings

	ADA	ACLU	AFS	LCV	ITIC	NTU	COC	ACU	CFG	FRC
2008	80	82	100	85	57	7	65	4	0	0
2007	95	—	100	95	—	5	50	0	2	—

National Journal Ratings

	2007 LIB	—	2007 CONS		2008 LIB	—	2008 CONS
Economic	72%	—	27%		68%	—	31%
Social	61%	—	38%		62%	—	34%
Foreign	69%	—	29%		70%	—	25%
Composite	68%	—	32%		68%	—	32%

Key Votes of the 110th Congress

1. Increase minimum wage	Y	5. Share immigration data	N	9. Withdraw troops 8/08	Y
2. Expand SCHIP	Y	6. Foreign aid abortion ban	N	10. No operations in Iran	Y
3. Raise CAFE standards	Y	7. Ban gay bias in workplace	Y	11. Free trade with Peru	N
4. Bail out financial markets	Y	8. Repeal D.C. gun law	Y	12. Overhaul FISA	Y

Election Results

2008 general	Brian Higgins (D-WF)...	185,713	(74%)	($850,357)
	Daniel Humiston (R-Ind)...................................	56,354	(23%)	($190,451)
	Harold Schroeder (C)...	7,478	(3%)	($3,635)
2008 primary	Brian Higgins (D-WF)................................. unopposed			

Prior Winning Percentages: 2006 (79%); 2004 (51%)

Population		Race/Ethnicity		Work	
Pop. 2007:	630,157	White:	87.2%	Private:	78.1%
Change since 2000:	Down 3.7%	Black:	5.3%	Government:	16.9%
Urban:	81.5%	Hispanic:	5.1%	Self-employed:	4.9%
Rural:	18.5%	Asian:	0.7%	Blue collar:	22.9%
Area size:	2,444 sq. mi.	Native Am.:	0.6%	White collar:	57.8%
		Hawaiian:	0.0%	Khaki collar:	0.1%
Age		Two+ races:	1.0%	Other:	19.2%
Median age:	40.3 yrs.	*Ancestry*		Median income:	$42,872
More than 65 yrs:	15.8%	German:	20.6%	Median home value:	$96,400
Less than 18 yrs:	21.7%	Polish:	15.4%	Poverty:	13.6%
		Irish:	13.7%	**Military Veterans**	
Education				% of Pop:	11.5%
H.S. grad:	85.9%				
College grad:	22.3%				
Grad degree:	9.3%				

With its massive 1920s skyscraper City Hall overlooking the Niagara River and Lake Erie, Buffalo declares itself to be a city of substance. But it has gone through some rough times in recent decades. The butt of jokes about the snow that piles up at the eastern end of Lake Erie and that supposedly keeps it immobilized half the year, Buffalo also can claim credit for building a heavy industrial base in the late 19th and early 20th centuries, as America's No. 1 grain milling center and as a major steel producer.

2008 Presidential Vote

Obama (D)	156,635	(54%)
McCain (R)............................	127,249	(44%)

2004 Presidential Vote

Kerry (D)................................	158,433	(53%)
Bush (R)	132,416	(45%)

Cook Partisan Voting Index: D + 4

Today, the area still benefits from cheap hydroelectric power, but the Lackawanna steel mills are shuttered, and grain milling waned after the St. Lawrence Seaway opened in the 1950s. Buffalo has been eclipsed economically by the bigger Great Lakes industrial cities of Cleveland, Detroit, and Chicago, and its architecturally bold downtown skyscrapers are overshadowed by the high-rise horizon of Toronto, not many miles away. Buffalo was the nation's 15th-largest city in 1950 when it had a population of 580,000. By 2007, it was 69th-largest, with a population reduced by half to 273,000. Surrounding Erie County, once well over 1 million, had 910,000 people in 2008. Right across Buffalo's Peace Bridge is the richest part of Canada, the golden horseshoe from Niagara Falls through Hamilton to Toronto. But Buffalo's hopes of becoming Toronto's back office have faded, and New York taxes are still high enough to leave Buffalo at a serious competitive disadvantage. Local boosters have criticized state capital powerbrokers for lavishing excessive attention on New York City as the state's economic engine. And, to add insult to injury, the Buffalo Bills franchise in the National Football League has moved some of its home games to Toronto. Still, Buffalo retains some considerable assets: a high-skill labor force and inexpensive real estate, including a gentrified and handsome waterfront on a now-cleaner Lake Erie, and some impressive cultural institutions.

The 27th Congressional District of New York consists of the eastern and southern two-thirds of Buffalo, plus most of the Erie County suburbs east and south of the city, from working-class Cheektowaga and Lackawanna to higher-income Hamburg and Orchard Park. The 27th also includes Chautauqua County, which is sufficiently rural to harbor some black bears and also is the famed birthplace of a movement to promote high-minded discourse. It was there that a training camp for Methodist Sunday school teachers was founded in 1874, attracting some 25,000 people to educational talks and inspirational lectures from the likes of Ralph Waldo Emerson and William Jennings Bryan. The rounds of summer lectures continue today. Although some Buffalo suburbs are Republican, this district is solidly Democratic. But as Buffalo struggles, it has become politically volatile. In 1992, Buffalo gave third-party presidential candidate Ross Perot 28% of the vote, his best showing in a central city anywhere. In 1994, Democrat Mario Cuomo lost Erie County to Republican George Pataki in the governor's race. In recent contests for president and statewide offices, Buffalo and Erie County have been solidly Democratic.

The congressman from the 27th District is Brian Higgins, a Democrat elected in 2004. Higgins grew up in Buffalo, the son of a skilled tradesman who was prominent in local politics, serving on the Buffalo City Council and later as commissioner of the New York State Workers Compensation Board. His mother was a schoolteacher. Higgins graduated from Buffalo State College and later got a master's degree from Harvard. A political junkie, he launched his career in government with staff jobs in the Erie County sheriff's office, the state Assembly, and the county Legislature. In 1993, after six years on the Buffalo City Council, he ran for county comptroller and lost. In 1998, he was elected to the Assembly and served three terms. In a district crowded with unionized workers, Higgins often reminded voters that his father and uncle were bricklayers and he stressed his Irish immigrant heritage.

A House seat unexpectedly opened up in 2004 when Republican Rep. Jack Quinn announced he was retiring after 12 years in Congress. Nancy Naples, a former Merrill Lynch executive in Manhattan and a popular local figure with strong name recognition, quickly wrapped up the Republican nomination, while five Democrats battled for their party's nomination. Higgins was the favorite of local and national Democratic leaders, organized labor, and the *Buffalo News*, which called him "an unusually productive member of a largely dysfunctional legislative body" in Albany. He won the primary with 44% of the vote. In the contentious general election, Higgins reminded voters that Naples supported many of President George W. Bush's policies, including his handling of national security. He criticized Republicans for shifting the tax burden from the rich to the middle class, and promised that he would make health care more available and that he would protect Social Security benefits. Naples criticized Higgins for supporting tax increases in Albany. Higgins won 51%-49%. Naples took 57% of the vote in Chautauqua County, which cast 20% of the district's votes. Higgins won 53% in Erie County. It took 16 days of recounts and a court challenge before Naples conceded the nearly 3,800-vote victory.

In the House, Higgins established a centrist voting record, and after spending his first years securing his hold on the seat with an array of mostly successful efforts for his district, he was rewarded with a seat on the powerful House Ways and Means Committee in 2009.

Higgins got $42 million for local projects in the 2005 highway bill and he helped to eliminate toll barriers on Interstate 90 in Buffalo. He helped to broker an agreement with the New York Power Authority for local financial aid, including waterfront improvements, in exchange for its long-term right to operate the Niagara Power Project. The issue strained his relationship with Democratic Rep. Louise Slaughter in the adjoining district, who disagreed with his strategy. In 2008, he won a change in policy from the Federal Emergency Management Agency that resulted in 2,700 homeowners in Buffalo's floodplain being released from having to pay flood insurance premiums. He also demanded changes by the Social Security Administration to eliminate a nearly two-year wait for local appeals of disability claims.

On national issues, Higgins's support for the USA PATRIOT Act, which gave law enforcement enhanced powers in terrorism investigations, and his opposition to a deadline for the withdrawal of troops from Iraq led to complaints from some liberals. But those positions may have been a net plus for him in the district. Republicans wanted to try to defeat Higgins in 2006 but couldn't come up with a credible challenger. Higgins initially got the endorsement of local conservative leaders, but the state Conservative Party chairman overruled it. Still, he won 79%-21% against Assistant District Attorney Michael McHale. He appears safe, at least until redistricting, when he likely will join Buffalo leaders in seeking to unify the entire city into a single district. However, western New York as a whole could lose a district in the 2010 census, which would add a high degree of volatility to redistricting in that region.

TWENTY-EIGHTH DISTRICT

Louise Slaughter (D)

Elected 1986, 12th term; b. Aug. 14, 1929, Harlan Cnty., KY; home, Fairport; U. of KY, B.S. 1951, M.S. 1953; Episcopalian; married (Robert); 3 children.

Elected Office: Monroe Cnty. Legislature, 1976–79; NY Assembly, 1982–86.

Professional Career: Regional coord., Lt. Gov. Mario Cuomo, 1976–79.

DC Office: 2469 RHOB, 20515, 202-225-3615; Fax: 202-225-7822; Web site: www.louise.house.gov.

State Offices: Buffalo, 716-853-5813; Niagara Falls, 716-282-1274; Rochester, 585-232-4850.

Committees: *Rules* (Chmn of 9 D): Legislative & Budget Process; Rules & Organization of the House.

Group Ratings

	ADA	ACLU	AFS	LCV	ITIC	NTU	COC	ACU	CFG	FRC
2008	95	100	100	92	83	5	47	0	0	5
2007	100	—	100	95	—	3	47	0	0	—

National Journal Ratings

	2007 LIB	—	2007 CONS		2008 LIB	—	2008 CONS
Economic	82%	—	0%		85%	—	0%
Social	92%	—	0%		82%	—	0%
Foreign	90%	—	10%		92%	—	0%
Composite	92%	—	8%		93%	—	7%

Key Votes of the 110th Congress

1. Increase minimum wage	Y	5. Share immigration data	N	9. Withdraw troops 8/08	Y
2. Expand SCHIP	Y	6. Foreign aid abortion ban	N	10. No operations in Iran	Y
3. Raise CAFE standards	Y	7. Ban gay bias in workplace	Y	11. Free trade with Peru	N
4. Bail out financial markets	Y	8. Repeal D.C. gun law	N	12. Overhaul FISA	N

Election Results

2008 general	Louise Slaughter (D-Ind-WF)............................172,655	(78%)	($756,579)
	David Crimmen (R-C)..48,690	(22%)	
2008 primary	Louise Slaughter (D-Ind-WF)...................... unopposed		

Prior Winning Percentages: 2006 (73%); 2004 (73%); 2002 (62%); 2000 (66%); 1998 (65%); 1996 (57%); 1994 (57%); 1992 (55%); 1990 (59%); 1988 (57%); 1986 (51%)

Population		Race/Ethnicity		Work	
Pop. 2007:	602,298	White:	60.5%	Private:	80.8%
Change since 2000:	Down 8.0%	Black:	29.4%	Government:	14.6%
Urban:	93.5%	Hispanic:	5.9%	Self-employed:	4.5%
Rural:	6.5%	Asian:	2.0%	Blue collar:	20.1%
Area size:	2,282 sq. mi.	Native Am.:	0.5%	White collar:	59.7%
Age		Hawaiian:	0.0%	Khaki collar:	0.0%
Median age:	36.4 yrs.	Two+ races:	1.4%	Other:	20.2%
More than 65 yrs:	13.7%	*Ancestry*		Median income:	$36,201
Less than 18 yrs:	23.5%	German:	14.9%	Median home value:	$86,000
Education		Italian:	11.7%	Poverty:	21.2%
H.S. grad:	83.4%	Irish:	10.2%	**Military Veterans**	
College grad:	23.4%			% of Pop:	9.8%
Grad degree:	10.1%				

Rochester, with a metro area of just over 1 million, is one of the major cities of upstate New York. Located where the Erie Canal crosses the Genesee River, Rochester became a major industrial city—the Flour City—in the 1830s, as it milled the wheat produced by western New York farmers. Then, it was one of the early high-tech cities, after a bank clerk named George Eastman began making photographic dry plates and marketed the first still camera and film for Thomas Edison's motion picture

2008 Presidential Vote		
Obama (D) 184,209	(69%)
McCain (R) 81,517	(30%)
2004 Presidential Vote		
Kerry (D)..................................162,319	(63%)
Bush (R) 92,627	(36%)
Cook Partisan Voting Index: D + 15		

camera. Later, Bausch & Lomb developed its lens business in Rochester, and the optics and imaging industry continues to be a significant regional employer. Its great industries—Bausch & Lomb, Eastman Kodak, and Xerox, which started here as Haloid—have thrived on technical innovation, precision workmanship, high reliability, and customer service, giving Rochester an affluent and well-educated population as well as fine civic institutions, including the George Eastman House, one of the world's leading repositories of photographic and motion picture history. Rochester was also the home base of women's suffrage leader Susan B. Anthony and abolitionist Frederick Douglass. This was the city that in 1918 invented the Community Chest and at one time had the nation's highest United Way contributions. Unhappily, Rochester's big employers have fallen on hard times, and young professionals have been leaving the area. Kodak, hard hit by competition from digital cameras, employed 60,000 people in the Rochester area in 1981; by 2008 that was down to 9,200. Xerox jobs in the area were down to half of what they once were, from 16,000 to 7,400. The city's population—332,000 in 1950—dropped below 207,000 in 2007. That decline has been accompanied by an increase in crime and poverty in areas only a few blocks from historic homes.

Not far west of Rochester is a very different part of upstate New York, the Niagara Frontier—the local name for the Buffalo-Niagara Falls area. The Niagara Frontier was once an armed frontier, between the United States and British-held Upper Canada, where American troops crossed the raging Niagara River during the War of 1812 to fight the Battle of Lundys Lane. Later in the 19th century, Niagara Falls became a prime vacation spot, a must-see sight for European tourists and American honeymooners. Few tourists today notice the huge water intakes farther up the river or the hydroelectric power lines strung out on giant pylons fanning out in every direction, providing cheap public power for the chemical and steel factories that made the Niagara Frontier one of the heavy-industry capitals of America. But the city of Niagara Falls has suffered hard times. Tourists tend to stay on the Canadian side, which has better views of the Falls and loose enforcement of sex and gambling laws that make it, as some say, the "Las Vegas of the North." Niagara Falls has lost much of its manufacturing since the 1960s and has suffered double-digit unemployment and population losses. The downtown, leveled by urban renewal, remains troubled.

The 28th Congressional District of New York, created by redistricting in 2002, includes Rochester, Niagara Falls, and part of Buffalo, all connected by a thin strip of land along Lake Ontario and the Niagara River. A bit more than 46% of the district is in Monroe County, and a bit less than 37% is in Erie County. Most of Rochester's suburbs are in three other districts, but the 28th includes Grand Island, Tonawanda, and the northeast quadrant of Buffalo, where it takes in much of the city's downtown and its fine cultural institutions. This is mainly a central city district. Twenty-nine percent of residents are African-American, the highest percentage in any upstate district. Politically, this is a solidly Democratic district.

The congresswoman from the 28th District is Louise Slaughter, a Democrat elected in 1986 and the chairman of the powerful Rules Committee, which sets the ground rules for debate that can make or break a piece of legislation on the House floor. A coal miner's daughter and a descendant of Daniel Boone (and a cousin of Armed Services Committee Chairman Ike Skelton, D-Mo.), she grew up in Kentucky and still speaks with the accent and distinctive phraseology of the mountains. She wound up in New York in the 1950s when she moved there with her husband. Her involvement in community issues led to a career in government. Slaughter became a staffer for Mario Cuomo when he was lieutenant governor in the 1970s, and she won a seat on the Monroe County legislature in 1976. She was elected to the New York Assembly in 1982. Four years later, she beat one-term conservative Republican Rep. Fred Eckert, 51%-49%, after charging that he did nothing to free *Associated Press* reporter Terry Anderson, a Rochester native held hostage in Lebanon. She secured what had been a marginal seat by tending carefully to local problems and by winning the support of area businessmen and the local *Democrat & Chronicle* newspaper.

Slaughter, the first woman to chair the Rules Committee, has a solidly liberal voting record. She backs feminist causes and is active on health issues. In 2008, she capped a years-long campaign by winning enactment of her bill to bar discrimination in employment or health insurance based on the use of genetic information. "Americans can finally take advantage of the tremendous potential of genetic research without the fear that their own genetic information will be used against them," she said. A microbiologist by training, and consistent with the Rochester-area research mindset, Slaughter opposed proposals to ban human cloning and was an outspoken proponent of federal support for embryonic-stem-cell research, which uses excess embryos from in vitro fertilization. In 1991 she was one of the seven women House members who marched on the Senate to protest its treatment of Anita Hill, the law professor who accused Supreme Court nominee Clarence Thomas of sexual harassment.

As a loyal lieutenant of Democratic House Speaker Nancy Pelosi, Slaughter became an outspoken critic of Republican policies and the management of the House during 12 years of Republican control. She was among the most outspoken critics of the Republican "culture of corruption," a prime talking point in Pelosi's campaign message in 2006. She accused Republicans of "strong-arm tactics" and a "win-at-all-costs mentality" to move legislation. In January 2007, she helped to bring the first legislation to the House floor for the new majority: an overhaul of House rules, largely dictated by Pelosi and her lieutenants. Slaughter hailed the result as "a Congress people can be proud of again." But Republicans quickly cried foul when Democrats next moved to the floor six bills from their campaign agenda, without committee action and with no opportunity for amendments. Her dismissal of procedural objections led to regular flare-ups with ranking Republican David Dreier of California and other Republicans. But there also has been occasional Democratic criticism of the committee's strong-arm tactics. Financial Services Committee Chairman Barney Frank, D-Mass., in September 2007 voiced "regret" that the Rules Committee had barred Republican amendments to a flood insurance bill. But Pelosi—whom Slaughter termed "the best politician that I have ever seen"—seemed satisfied with her assistance in helping to manage the House.

Slaughter's ascension to the chairmanship of Rules capped several years of struggle to move up in the Democratic leadership. In 1994, she lost to Barbara Kennelly of Connecticut in the race for vice chairman of the Democratic Caucus, and in 1996 she was defeated by John Spratt of South Carolina for the ranking Democrat post on the Budget Committee. She became the ranking Democrat on the Rules Committee in 2005.

In 2002, redistricting was a perils-of-Pauline nightmare for Slaughter. Sluggish population growth meant that upstate New York had to lose one congressional district, and after much political maneuvering, Slaughter was placed in the same district with Democratic Rep. John LaFalce, the party's ranking member on the Banking Committee. Luckily for Slaughter, LaFalce decided to retire. In the general election that year, she campaigned on much new territory, but most of it was Democratic. She won 73% of the vote in Monroe County and 60% in Erie County, for a 62%-38% victory against an inexperienced Republican challenger.

TWENTY-NINTH DISTRICT

Eric Massa (D)

Elected 2008, 1st term; b. Sept. 16, 1959, Charleston, SC; home, Corning; U.S. Naval Academy, 1981; Catholic; married (Beverly).

Military Career: Navy, 1977–2001 (Beirut, Desert Storm)

Professional Career: Special asst. to NATO Supreme Allied Commander Gen. Wesley Clark (Bosnia)

DC Office: 1208 LHOB, 20515, 202-225-3161; Fax: 202-226-6599; Web site: massa.house.gov.

State Offices: Corning, 607-654-7566; Olean, 716-372-2090; Pittsford, 585-218-0040.

Committees: *Agriculture* (18th of 28 D): Conservation, Credit, Energy & Research; Horticulture & Organic Agriculture. *Armed Services* (33rd of 36 D): Air & Land Forces; Seapower & Expeditionary Forces. *Homeland Security* (19th of 20 D): Border, Maritime & Global Counterterrorism; Transportation Security & Infrastructure Protection.

Group Ratings and Key Votes: Newly Elected

Election Results

2008 general	Eric Massa (D-WF)	140,529	(51%)	($2,159,314)
	John Kuhl (R-Ind-C)	135,199	(49%)	($1,501,652)
2008 primary	Eric Massa (D-WF)	unopposed		

Population		Race/Ethnicity		Work	
Pop. 2007:	656,293	White:	91.7%	Private:	77.6%
Change since 2000:	Up 0.3%	Black:	2.6%	Government:	15.0%
Urban:	58.4%	Hispanic:	1.8%	Self-employed:	7.1%
Rural:	41.6%	Asian:	2.2%	Blue collar:	21.6%
Area size:	5,761 sq. mi.	Native Am.:	0.5%	White collar:	61.2%
		Hawaiian:	0.0%	Khaki collar:	0.1%
Age		Two+ races:	1.1%	Other:	17.1%
Median age:	39.2 yrs.	*Ancestry*		Median income:	$48,215
More than 65 yrs:	14.8%	German:	18.5%	Median home value:	$105,100
Less than 18 yrs:	22.6%	Irish:	14.7%	Poverty:	10.9%
Education		English:	12.2%	**Military Veterans**	
H.S. grad:	89.0%			% of Pop:	11.6%
College grad:	28.9%				
Grad degree:	13.3%				

The southern tier of New York is one of the nation's forgotten stretches of territory, yet it has an interesting and distinctive history. Elmira was the hometown of Mark Twain's beloved wife, Olivia, and is where Twain is buried. Corning is the headquarters of Corning Glass Works, a company successful over the years not only in manufacturing but also in its artistic distinction, which is showcased at a well-visited glass museum. This area has an Indian presence, with small reservations as well as the Seneca-Iroquois National Museum in Salamanca, plus miles and miles of dairy farms. Sheltered by hills, the lands at the edge of upstate New York's deep lakes constitute the nation's largest grape-growing area outside California and are the headquarters of prime New York wineries. But the region is isolated, and ill-served by air travel or interstate highways. Cattaraugus County, slightly inland from Lake Erie, is actually 110 miles closer to Washington, D.C., than it is to New York City, though getting to either

2008 Presidential Vote		
McCain (R)	153,487	(51%)
Obama (D)	146,758	(48%)
2004 Presidential Vote		
Bush (R)	171,317	(56%)
Kerry (D)	127,481	(42%)
Cook Partisan Voting Index:	R+5	

destination requires considerable patience. The cruelest cut was the Internet bust. Corning's prospects grew dramatically when fiber optics and other high-tech components were being installed at a feverish pace, but the reduction in orders following the bust forced the company to lay off more than 1,000 of its local workers in a town of only 11,000 people. In 2007, *Forbes* reported that the company was making a comeback as demand increased for its fiber products, which are key components of the liquid crystal display (LCD) glass used in flat-screen televisions and computers.

The 29th Congressional District of New York includes much of the state's southern tier, from Elmira to Cattaraugus County. To the north, it includes the westernmost of the Finger Lakes and the southern suburbs of Rochester. Politically, this has been Republican country since the party's founding. The towns and the countryside are no longer homogeneously Protestant, and the trend in upstate New York has been toward national Democrats, but the 29th remains comfortably Republican for now. This was Republican presidential candidate George W. Bush's best congressional district in New York in both 2000 and 2004. And it was one of four New York congressional districts that voted for Republican nominee John McCain in 2008, albeit narrowly. He got 50.5% of the vote.

The new congressman from the 29th District is Democrat Eric Massa, who returned this seat to Democrats by ousting two-term Republican Rep. Randy Kuhl in 2008. Born on a naval base in Charleston, S.C., Massa is the son of a nurse and career Navy aviator. A decade ago, he moved to Corning to work for Corning Inc. as a telecommunications specialist. Massa describes himself as "a rural FDR Democrat," an appealing image to a politically moderate constituency primarily concerned with pocketbook, rather than social, issues. The gregarious Massa is no political neophyte, despite never having held public office. He spent more than two decades in the Navy and did a stint as a GOP aide to the House Armed Services Committee. He later switched parties. Massa opposed the invasion of Iraq in 2003, becoming disenchanted with what he called "the party of Karl Rove," a reference to President Bush's top political adviser, and signed on to retired Gen. Wesley Clark's 2004 Democratic presidential campaign. Massa had worked as a special assistant for Clark from 1998 to 2001, when Clark was NATO's supreme allied commander.

Massa in fact credits Clark with saving his life. Clark ordered Massa to see a doctor after Massa's wife, Beverly, surreptitiously called him with concerns over her husband's health. Massa was diagnosed with non-Hodgkin's lymphoma. Massa said that his experience with cancer is what got him into politics. "My passion in life became understanding the health insurance system," he said.

Massa first battled Kuhl for the seat in 2006, narrowly losing by 6,033 votes. In their rematch, Massa benefited from high name recognition and a sizable war chest. By the end of September, he'd raised $1.7 million, compared to Kuhl's $1.2 million. His impressive fundraising and near-win two years earlier attracted the attention and resources of the Democratic Congressional Campaign Committee. Massa also capitalized on an electorate eager for change. "The feel on the ground is fundamentally different this time than in 2006," he said during his 2008 bid. "Instead of upriver, I feel like I am with the current."

Kuhl was also well known in the district, having spent 24 years in the New York state Legislature. But Massa ran a more organized campaign this time around and benefited from the Democratic wave that swept through the state. He defeated Kuhl 51%-49%.

Early in 2009, Massa decided to begin accepting campaign contributions from corporate political action committees to help build a war chest for his re-election bid in 2010 even though he criticized Kuhl for such contributions in the 2008 race. The decision prompted the National Republican Congressional Committee to label Massa a newly converted Washington insider.

★ NORTH CAROLINA ★

In the first decade of the 21st century, North Carolina emerged as one of America's leading-edge states, with a booming demography and vibrant culture that are in many ways typical of the way the nation was going—or wanted to go. North Carolina had the third-largest-percentage population increase in 2008, trailing only Utah and Arizona (and tying Texas and Colorado), and also experienced the biggest percentage increase in turnout in the 2008 presidential election. Four decades ago, few people picked North Carolina as a state that would chart a path to the future. It had no great central city, no Atlanta primed to become another Los Angeles or Chicago, but rather a series of small metropolitan areas spaced out over thickly settled countryside. It did not have what seemed to be cutting-edge industries. The biggest employer was textiles, typically an underdeveloped nation's first industry, and the next two were stolid furniture and soon-to-be-disfavored tobacco. Geographically, it seemed to be off the nation's main lines of commerce, and meteorologically, it was too steamy to be businesslike in the summer and too cold to be a resort in the winter. Yet North Carolina has emerged as one of America's leading growth states. Its population nearly doubled from 1970 to 2008, from 5.1 million to 9.2 million, making it the 10th-largest state. Its economy has diversified and grown steadily, while businesses that dominated the state's political dialogue 40 years ago have faded in importance. Textile jobs peaked in 1973. The government's 2004 tobacco buyout, ending tobacco allotments, left in its wake only about 1,800 tobacco farmers and 11,500 tobacco workers. (State Agriculture Commissioner Steve Troxler even quit growing tobacco.) Some former tobacco farmers have shifted to blueberries and pumpkins. High Point still hosts annual furniture-industry shows, but the furniture factories have been pressed by competition from China.

In place of farming and furniture, research and technology have taken root. One key has been the success of Research Triangle Park, which was established between Raleigh, Durham, and Chapel Hill—and their universities—in 1959. Its first breakthrough was the opening of a big IBM facility in 1965. Today, it's one of the world's leading biotech, pharmaceutical, medical device, and telecommunications centers. New investment in the state hit a record high in 2006. The Triangle's core counties had 537,000 people in 1970 and 1.5 million in 2008. Its success has been echoed farther west in the Piedmont Research Triad between Winston-Salem, Greensboro, and High Point. And North Carolina has become one of the nation's leading banking centers. Charlotte is the headquarters of Bank of America (formerly NationsBank and NCNB), which came out of the 2008 financial crisis a winner after purchasing Merrill Lynch. Not far away on Tryon Street is the headquarters of Wachovia, whose roots were in Winston-Salem. Wachovia merged with Charlotte's First Union in 2001 and was acquired by Wells Fargo in 2008. Metro Charlotte and Raleigh-Durham have accounted for more than half of the state's population growth for a generation, and they are now major metropolitan areas, with national sports franchises and huge hub airports. North Carolina has one of the nation's least unionized workforces, something the state's Democratic leaders have done little to change, and it has long been rated one of the best places to relocate a business. "Our biggest advantage over who we compete with—San Diego, San Francisco, Massachusetts, and the Maryland-Virginia area," said former Gov. Mike Easley, "is that we can do everything they can do, if not more, but we can do it 20 to 25 percent cheaper when you look at labor and capital investment." The unemployment rate was low enough that thousands of Latinos moved into North Carolina seeking jobs in construction and in meat and chicken factories. The state's Hispanic population rose from 77,000 in 1990 to 638,000 in 2007. Yet for all its metropolitan growth, life in North Carolina has not lost its rural tone. The state is the nation's No. 2 hog producer, with big feedlots and sewage lagoons. One is never out of sight of others, but there is also plenty of green space and reminders of rural roots, from barbecue stands to country Baptist churches to stock car tracks.

The forces behind the change are diverse and sometimes even hostile. North Carolina historically had a small and erudite elite, which looked for guidance from the University of North Carolina at Chapel Hill and the liberal editors of the state's newspapers, most prominently the Raleigh *News & Observer* and *The Charlotte Observer*. Quite different attitudes are nurtured by tradition-minded churches in a state where churchgoing is deeply ingrained, reinforced for years by Sunday blue laws and strengthened periodically by religious revivals. When North Carolina was an economically backward state, infant mortality was common, indoor plumbing was not, and religion was a fountain of hope and a source of discipline, as it is still for many in this now-bustling, air-conditioned, Internet-connected commonwealth.

North Carolina has grown with the aid of both its progressive and tradition-minded citizens, and in spite of—sometimes because of—the polarized politics that have developed between the two. North Carolina's professionals tend to share progressive values; its businesspeople and conservative Protestants tend to share tradition-minded values. Both groups have contributed to the state's economic dynamism and cultural energy. Liberal progressivism has provided an impetus toward building good schools and universities, as well as highways and amenities like the nation's first state-funded symphony and state high schools for science, mathematics, and the arts. Religious conservatism has provided a commu-

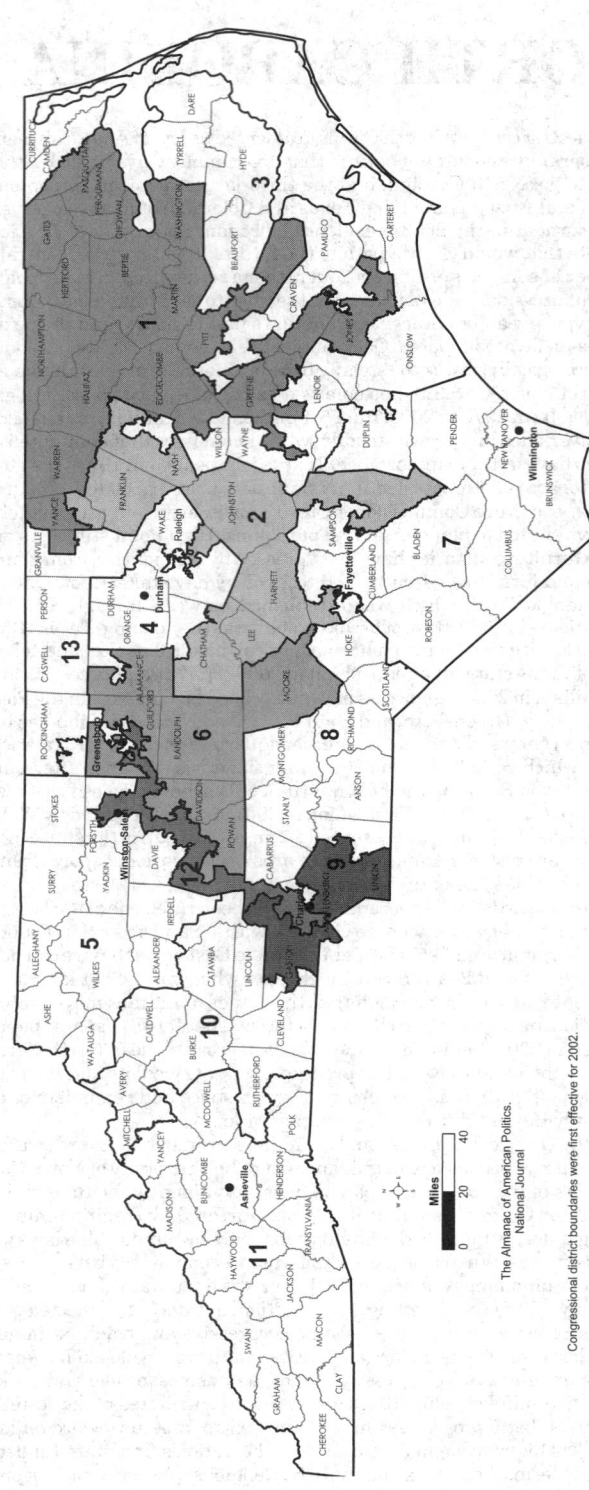

The Almanac of American Politics.
National Journal

Congressional district boundaries were first effective for 2002.

Districts 1, 2, 6, 9 and 12 are highlighted for visibility.

nitarian spirit and charitable impulses, and a moral undertone that anchors those who might go astray. Each side also has its excesses: the historic racism that undergirded segregation, and the impulses that led black leaders and university professors to cheer on a rogue prosecutor when he brought a baseless case against three Duke lacrosse players.

From these two strands of North Carolina tradition there developed a polarized, increasingly party-line politics, waged partly on economic issues but even more on cultural attitudes. This politics was built on historic partisan patterns. Coastal North Carolina settlers tended to be British Anglicans who became Methodists, slaveholders who supported the Confederacy and voted Democratic. Piedmont settlers by contrast tended to be Scots-Irish Presbyterians, with a scattering of German sects; they were Union men in 1861 and Republicans ever after. The most effective paladins of both traditions for the last quarter-century, Republican Sen. Jesse Helms and Democratic Gov. Jim Hunt, were each elected to statewide office five times over 25 years, and in 1984 waged what was then the most expensive Senate race in U.S. history. Once bitter rivals, they later reconciled. Hunt left office in 2000 but has remained active in state affairs. Helms did not seek re-election in 2002 and died in 2008 at age 86.

Over the last four decades, Republicans tended to win federal elections in North Carolina, and Democrats tended to do well in state elections. In five elections, Helms never got more than 55% of the vote. But Republicans carried the state for president in every election from 1968 to 2004, except 1976. George W. Bush won 56%-43% in 2000 and, despite the presence of North Carolinian John Edwards on the Democratic ticket, 56%-44% in 2004. At the same time, Democrats have continued to dominate state politics as they have not in other fast-growing Southern states, such as South Carolina, Georgia, Florida, and Virginia. Hunt was succeeded as governor by Republican Jim Martin in 1984, but in 1992 and 1996, Hunt won his third and fourth terms by solid margins. Democrat Michael Easley, a moderate from eastern North Carolina, was elected governor by solid margins in 2000 and 2004. Lt. Gov. Bev Perdue kept the governorship in Democratic hands by beating Charlotte Mayor Pat McCrory in 2008. (There seems to be a Charlotte jinx in North Carolina: Two of McCrory's predecessors as mayor, Republican Richard Vinroot and Democrat Harvey Gantt, also lost statewide races.) Most of the other statewide races were decided by similar margins. In general, these Democrats have followed Hunt's lead in policies that are characterized as pro-business but also pro-environment, and in supporting increased spending on education but also insisting on testing and accountability.

The 2008 campaign may have been a turning point in North Carolina politics.

Population		Household Income		Work	
Pop. 2007:	8,869,861	Under $15k:	15.6%	Private:	77.3%
State rank:	10th of 50	$15k to $50k:	40.3%	Government:	16.1%
Change since 2000:	Up 10.2%	$50k to $100k:	29.7%	Self-employed:	6.4%
Urban:	59.3%	$100k to $150k:	11.8%	Unemployment (3-yr. average):	4.5%
Rural:	40.7%	Over $150k:	2.6%	Poverty:	14.8%
Native of state:	59.8%	Median income:	$43,867	Blue collar:	25.8%
Not a citizen:	4.9%			White collar:	56.8%
Area size:	53,819 sq. mi.	**Home Value**		Khaki collar:	1.1%
		Under $100k:	32.4%	Other:	16.3%
Most populous cities		$100k to $300k:	53.9%		
1. Charlotte	649,578	$300k to $500k:	9.2%	**Age**	
2. Raleigh	341,891	$500k to $1 mil:	3.7%	Median age:	36.6 yrs.
3. Greensboro	237,423	Over $1 million:	0.8%	More than 65 yrs:	12.1%
4. Winston-Salem	213,889	Median:	$136,800	Less than 18 yrs:	24.4%

Race/Ethnicity				Military Veterans		Registered Voters in 2008	
White:	67.8%	*Language*		% of Pop:	11.1%	D:	2,849,979 (45.7%)
Black:	21.1%	English:	90.6%	*Veterans by Period*		R:	1,994,494 (32.0%)
Hispanic:	6.7%	Spanish:	6.3%	WWII and before:	10.3%	Other:	1,388,857 (22.3%)
Asian:	1.8%	Asian:	1.2%	Korea:	10.3%	Voter turnout:	4,310,789
Native Am.:	1.1%	Other		Vietnam:	31.9%	Turnout as % of	
Hawaiian:	0.0%	European	1.6%	Gulf (pre-2001):	13.7%	voting age:	61.8%
Two+ races:	1.3%	**Education**		Gulf (post-2001):	8.8%	**General Assembly**	
Ancestry		H.S. grad:	82.2%	Peace time:	25.0%	Senate:	30 D 20 R
USA:	10.4%	College grad:	25.0%			House:	68 D 52 R
German:	10.2%	Grad degree:	8.3%				
English:	9.5%						

Presidential politics For a quarter-century after 1980, North Carolina was not a competitive state in presidential elections. Democrats hoped to change that in 2004 when John Kerry named then-Sen. John Edwards of North Carolina as his running mate. But Edwards had won just one election in the state, with 51% of the vote in 1998, and his appeal proved limited. The Kerry-Edwards campaign took its ads off the air in North Carolina in August. Edwards himself returned to the state only to vote in October.

2008 Presidential Vote		
Obama (D)	2,142,651	(50%)
McCain (R)	2,128,474	(49%)
2008 Democratic Presidential Primary		
Obama (D)	887,391	(56%)
Clinton (D)	657,669	(42%)
2008 Republican Presidential Primary		
McCain (R)	383,085	(74%)
Huckabee (R)	63,018	(12%)
Paul (R)	37,260	(7%)
2004 Presidential Vote		
Bush (R)	1,961,166	(56%)
Kerry (D)	1,525,849	(44%)

The 2008 campaign was quite another matter. North Carolina's presidential primary, held on the same day in May as its state primary, had played a serious role in presidential politics only once before, in 1976, when after five straight losses, Ronald Reagan started denouncing the Panama Canal Treaty and won his first victory over Gerald Ford. That kept the Reagan campaign viable until the Republican convention. If it had gone the other way, Reagan might not have been a plausible candidate in 1980.

Barack Obama's campaign, quick to spot opportunities, staked out North Carolina as a target, first in the primary and then in the general election. Like Virginia, it had a large African-American population (21%), much of which had never been politically organized. Its universities and its 2007 state law authorizing same-day-registration early voting meant that a large student vote could be mobilized. The relatively recent arrival of highly educated outsiders provided another opening.

The results justified the Obama campaign's calculations. New registrations in the first three months of 2008 were nearly triple the number in the same months of 2004. Hillary Rodham Clinton, fresh from March and April victories in Ohio, Texas, and Pennsylvania, was still in the race and was endorsed by Gov. Michael Easley. But on May 6, Obama won by a solid 56%-42%, carrying not only four districts with high black percentages but also two others with affluent white populations in the Research Triangle and Charlotte areas. Clinton carried rural whites in the east and west of the state. Obama's big margin in North Carolina, and Clinton's small margin of victory the same day in Indiana, prompted the late Tim Russert of NBC News to declare that the nomination race was decided, for Obama, that night.

In the fall, John McCain was reluctant to spend resources in North Carolina, where he thought he stood a good shot of winning. The campaign strategy was to target states where McCain could expand his base of support, not simply hold his own. Organizing for the primary gave the Democrats a head start on the general, and they made good use of it. Early voting was heavy, and overall turnout was up 23%, the largest gain of any state. Some 36% of early voters, many of them registering the same day, were African-American. McCain got 9% more votes than George W. Bush had four years before. But Obama got 40% more votes than Kerry and Edwards did, with especially large increases in heavily black eastern counties and in the Research Triangle and metro Charlotte areas. Obama carried the state 49.7%-49.4%. African-American voters went for Obama 95%-5%. But he also got 35% of the votes of whites, up from 27% for Kerry-Edwards. Obama won young voters 74%-26%, and ran behind among voters 30 and over. He carried first-time voters, who were 13% of the total, by 68%-32%.

But at the same time, the vote for state office and national office seemed to be converging. Democrat Bev Perdue was only barely elected governor, and Democrats lost a seat in the state Senate. Democratic state Sen. Kay Hagan was able to oust Republican U.S. Sen. Elizabeth Dole by a wider margin, but the results suggest that North Carolina may be moving toward a more even partisan balance in both federal and state elections. The 2008 exit poll showed that North Carolina's African-Americans voted heavily for Obama, while white evangelical Protestants voted 74%-25% for McCain. Since blacks formed 23% (down from 26% four years earlier) of those who voted and white evangelical Protestants 44%, they basically canceled each other out—as did the third of voters who did not fit into either category. One question for the future is whether those who came out primarily to vote for Obama will be motivated to vote in the future. Some 140,000 North Carolinians voted for president only and skipped the down-ballot races, more than double the 63,000 people who did so in 2004.

Congressional districting North Carolina won a 12th House seat in the 1990 census and a 13th seat in the 2000 census. It beat out Utah for the latter by just 856 people, because its apportionment population includes some 18,000 U.S. troops and diplomats who claim North Carolina as their home. In the 1990s, North Carolina was the epicenter of race-based redistricting litigation, home to a legal controversy that went to the U.S. Supreme Court four times. Democratic legislators created their plans for 2002 with this litigation in mind. The state House and Senate passed the same plan in November 2001;

111th Congress Lineup	
8 D	5 R
110th Congress Lineup	
7 D	6 R

in North Carolina the governor does not have a veto on redistricting bills. The plan created a new 13th District seat in the northern Piedmont, which leaned Democratic in state elections although it was even in the 2000 presidential race. The district ended up electing Democrat Brad Miller, not coincidentally the chairman of the Senate redistricting committee. The plan significantly weakened 8th District Republican Rep. Robin Hayes, who faced serious challenges in the next four elections and was defeated in 2008. It created six heavily Republican districts and three solidly Democratic districts, with the four other districts tailored to the needs of local Democrats. Republicans filed suit, prevailed in the state courts, but ultimately lost the case when the U.S. Supreme Court refused to intervene.

North Carolina is not expected to gain a 14th seat in the 2010 census. With a Democratic governor in place and large Democratic majorities in the Legislature, it seems likely that the current Democratic redistricting plan will be adjusted only slightly, to meet the equal population standard, for 2012.

Governor

Bev Perdue (D)

Elected 2008, term expires 2012, 1st term; b. Jan. 14, 1947, Grundy, VA; home, New Bern; U. of KY, B.A. 1969; U. of FL., M.Ed. 1974, Ph.D. 1976; Episcopalian; married (Bob Eaves); 2 children.

Elected Office: NC House of Reps., 1986–1990; NC Senate 1990–2000; Lt. gov., 2000–08.

Professional Career: Public schl. teacher; Consultant.

Office: Office of the Governor, 20301 Mail Service Center, Raleigh, 27699, 919-733-4240; Fax: 919-733-2120; Web site: www.governor.state.nc.us.

Election Results

2008 general	Bev Perdue (D)	2,146,189	(50%)
	Pat McCrory (R)	2,001,168	(47%)
	Michael Munger (Lib)	121,584	(3%)
2008 primary	Bev Perdue (D)	840,342	(56%)
	Richard Moore (D)	594,028	(40%)

Bev Perdue, a Democrat, was elected governor of North Carolina in 2008. Perdue grew up in the coal-mining town of Grundy in southwest Virginia, near the borders of West Virginia and Kentucky. Her father, Alfred Moore, was a coal miner, and her mother was a homemaker. Neither parent earned a high school diploma, but they were nonetheless an upwardly mobile family. Her father later became a mine owner and utility executive. Beverly Moore became the first college graduate in the family when she got her degree from the University of Kentucky. She taught kindergarten for several years and then went back to school to get advanced degrees in her field of education from the University of Florida. She also took courses in gerontology and volunteered with a local program for senior citizens. In 1975, she and her first husband moved to New Bern, an old colonial town at the confluence of the Neuse and Trent rivers in east North Carolina, where she worked as a geriatric health care consultant at a local hospital.

In 1986, frustration with state government policies affecting senior citizens prompted her to run for the state House. She ran as a Democrat—Republicans seldom won east North Carolina races in those years—and was elected. In 1989, she joined other Democrats and Republicans in favor of ousting House Speaker Liston Ramsey, and then backed out on the morning of the vote. Out of favor in the House, she ran for the state Senate in 1990 and won. In 1995, she sought to become co-chair of the Appropriations Committee, with power over the state budget. Senate President Marc Basnight went to her office to give her the bad news that he was passing her over for the job. But as he listened to her describe her ideas and plans for the committee, he changed his mind and offered her the post. (A decade later Basnight named Kay Hagan to the same post, and she went on to be elected U.S. senator in 2008.) Perdue worked successfully to raise teachers' salaries, which was her top goal, and to pass a children's health insurance program.

In 2000, Perdue ran for lieutenant governor, an office elected separately from governor in North Carolina and one with few explicit duties. She won 64% of the vote in a four-candidate Democratic primary and won in November, 52%-46%, becoming the first female lieutenant governor in state history. She was re-elected 55%-43% in 2004. In the role, she took on assignments from Democratic Gov. Michael Easley, who made her chairman of the Health and Wellness Trust Fund Commission, where she worked to create a prescription drug benefit for seniors and to reduce smoking among young people. She also organized local communities to lobby to maintain North Carolina's military bases.

As many in North Carolina political circles expected, Perdue decided to run for governor in 2008, when incumbent Easley was term-limited. She faced spirited competition in the Democratic primary from state Treasurer Richard Moore. She attacked Moore for investing in what she said were risky hedge funds, for increasing fees to money managers, and for raising $1.5 million in campaign funds from Wall Street and other financial interests. Moore ran an ad criticizing her 1987 vote against a bill authorizing state police to conduct investigations of secret organizations like the Ku Klux Klan—an ad that former Gov. Hunt, who had appointed Moore head of state law enforcement, said went over the line. Perdue raised some $10 million and spent most of it on the May primary. She won 56%-40%. Republicans nominated Pat McCrory, the mayor of Charlotte since 1995.

McCrory raised issues like crime, particularly gang violence, and illegal immigration. He had developed a long-range transit plan and the Lynx light rail system in Charlotte and called for a 50-year transportation plan for the state. He attacked Perdue for her "100%" opposition to offshore oil drilling in August, which many North Carolina voters supported. She backed off and said she would appoint a panel to study the issue. "I'm proud that I'm able to stand up and say, 'Hey, the world's changed and perhaps I need to change,'" she said. Perdue supported increasing the number of college scholarships for North Carolina students. McCrory emphasized vocational training, saying that four-year college programs did not interest all high school graduates. Endorsed by teachers' unions grateful for her efforts in the Legislature that increased teacher salaries, Perdue criticized McCrory's support for government vouchers for private-school tuition. McCrory called her part of the status quo and tried to link her with Democrats Jim Black, the former state House speaker, and Frank Ballance, a former North Carolina U.S. representative, who were both convicted on corruption charges. He also tried to connect her to a member of the Transportation Board who resigned after pressing Roanoke Rapids officials for contributions to Perdue's campaign. She criticized McCrory for opposing embryonic-stem-cell research, which uses cells harvested from surplus embryos at fertility clinics.

It was a closely fought election. Perdue won 50%-47%. She clearly benefited from the voter-registration and turnout efforts of Barack Obama's presidential campaign, which targeted North Carolina. McCrory carried the Charlotte area, though narrowly losing Mecklenburg County. Perdue carried the Research Triangle and Triad areas solidly and ran far ahead on her home turf in east North Carolina. Even in a state that has had a boom economy, Perdue was facing fiscal problems when she took office in 2009. The year before, Easley had ordered agencies to cut up to 5% of their budgets.

Senior Senator

Richard Burr (R)

Elected 2004, term expires 2010, 1st term; b. Nov. 30, 1955, Charlottesville, VA; home, Winston-Salem; Wake Forest U., B.A. 1978; Methodist; married (Brooke); 2 children.

Elected Office: U.S. House of Reps., 1994–2004.

Professional Career: Natl. sales mgr., Carswell Distributing, 1978–94.

DC Office: 217 RSOB, 20510, 202-224-3154; Fax: 202-228-2981; Web site: burr.senate.gov.

State Offices: Asheville, 828-350-2437; Gastonia, 704-833-0854; Rocky Mount, 252-977-9522; Wilmington, 910-251-1058; Winston-Salem, 336-631-5125.

Committees: *Armed Services* (9th of 11 R): Airland; Emerging Threats & Capabilities; Readiness & Management Support (RMM). *Energy & Natural Resources* (2nd of 10 R): Energy; National Parks (RMM). *Health, Education, Labor & Pensions* (4th of 10 R). *Intelligence (Select)* (5th of 7 R). *Veterans' Affairs* (RMM of 5 R).

Group Ratings

	ADA	ACLU	AFS	LCV	ITIC	NTU	COC	ACU	CFG	FRC
2008	5	14	0	18	100	64	100	79	80	88
2007	0	—	0	7	—	85	73	92	97	—

National Journal Ratings

	2007 LIB	—	2007 CONS		2008 LIB	—	2008 CONS
Economic	0%	—	97%		6%	—	93%
Social	17%	—	80%		0%	—	79%
Foreign	0%	—	93%		16%	—	79%
Composite	8%	—	92%		12%	—	88%

Key Votes of the 110th Congress

1. Raise CAFE standards	N	5. Make English official language	Y	9. Withdraw troops 3/08	N
2. Expand SCHIP	N	6. Path to citizenship	N	10. Iran guard is terrorist group	Y
3. Cap greenhouse gases	N	7. Fetus is unborn child	Y	11. Increase missile defense $	Y
4. Bail out financial markets	Y	8. Prosecute hate crimes	N	12. Overhaul FISA	Y

Election Results

2004 general	Richard Burr (R)	1,791,450	(52%)	($12,853,110)
	Erskine Bowles (D)	1,632,527	(47%)	($13,359,764)
2004 primary	Richard Burr (R)	302,319	(88%)	
	John Hendrix (R)	25,971	(8%)	
	Albert Wiley (R)	15,585	(5%)	

Prior Winning Percentages: 2002 House (70%); 2000 House (93%); 1998 House (68%); 1996 House (62%); 1994 House (57%)

Richard Burr, North Carolina's senior senator, was first elected to the House in 1994 and to the Senate in 2004. A distant relative to Vice President Aaron Burr, he grew up a minister's son in Winston-Salem, was a star football player at Reynolds High School and Wake Forest University, then worked in sales for a wholesaling firm. In 1992, Burr ran against Rep. Steve Neal, a Democrat first elected in 1974. Although outspent 3-to-1 by Neal, he lost by a relatively narrow 53%-46%. Neal retired in 1994 and Burr ran again, this time winning a solid 57% of the vote. He did not have a serious challenger in the next four House elections.

In the House, Burr had a mostly conservative voting record. On the Energy and Commerce Committee, his early cause became streamlining the Food and Drug Administration's drug and medical-device approval process, which he argued kept lifesaving products from the market. For over two years, he worked with the agency, doctors, patients, consumer groups, and the pharmaceutical industry to come up with a consensus. With broad bipartisan support, his FDA Modernization Act became law in 1997. He helped to set up the National Institute for Biomedical Imaging and Bioengineering at the National Institutes of Health. After September 11, he sponsored laws to improve defenses against bioterrorism and to compensate people injured by smallpox vaccination. He strongly opposed FDA regulation of tobacco and, with others from North Carolina, later called for an optional buyout of tobacco quotas. He sought a crackdown on illegal textile imports but backed President Bush's call for trade promotion authority after securing promises that the local textile industry would have a seat at the table. He called it a difficult vote but said it could help make U.S. textiles more competitive internationally.

By 1999, Burr made no secret of his interest in running for the Senate. He had promised to serve only five terms in the House, and was looking ahead to 2002, when GOP Sen. Jesse Helms would turn 80, and to 2004, when Democratic Sen. John Edwards' seat would come up. In 2002, he deferred to Elizabeth Dole on the Helms seat when it became apparent that the Bush White House was pushing her. By 2003, Edwards was running for president, giving Burr the shot he was looking for. He had $2 million in his campaign account and this time was encouraged by White House political strategist Karl Rove.

Burr's Democratic opponent was Erskine Bowles, the former White House chief of staff under President Clinton who had lost the 2002 race to Dole. Despite his many years in Washington, Bowles had deep roots in North Carolina. His father, Hargrove "Skipper" Bowles, was the Democratic nominee for governor in 1972, and his wife, Crandall Close, was the chief executive officer of Springs Industries, a large textile firm started by her family. As Clinton's top aide, Bowles negotiated the 1997 legislation that helped produce a balanced federal budget for the first time in years. He had earned the respect of Republican leaders even as they seethed with mistrust of Clinton. With greater name identification than Burr, Bowles led by about 10% in most polls until September. He started running ads six months before the election and had the resources to continue. Burr didn't run ads until September, hoping to match whatever Bowles could spend in the final weeks. In the end they spent about the same, Burr $12.8 million and Bowles $13.4 million, making their contest the third-most-expensive Senate campaign in 2004.

Bowles ran on a 10-point economic program and, pointing to recent losses of furniture and textile jobs, said he was "the only candidate with a real jobs plan." He called for expanding health insurance for children and providing tax credits for health insurance for small businesses. He touted his ability to work with both parties while depicting Burr as the king of the special interests, especially the pharmaceutical and tobacco companies. A major issue in the campaign was the tobacco buyout. The proposal was before Congress, and the entire North Carolina delegation favored ending the tobacco quota system in place since 1938; tobacco quotas had been cut back in recent years and seemed likely to be again. At issue was whether the buyout should be coupled with FDA regulation of tobacco. The Senate passed a corporate tax bill with both the buyout and FDA regulation. In the House, Burr voted for the buyout without the FDA regulation caveat. He argued that the toxicity of cigarettes should be regulated by the Centers for Disease Control and Prevention, and that packages and labeling should fall under the Federal Trade Commission. Bowles charged that Burr's position was influenced by R.J. Reynolds, based in Winston-

Salem, which opposed FDA regulation. In the fall, Bowles interrupted his campaign to lobby for the buy-out, and later claimed that he had persuaded Senate Democrats not to filibuster the legislation.

Burr was appointed by House Republican leaders to the conference committee on the bill. When the House held out for the buyout without FDA regulation, the Senate yielded and the bill was enacted. Republicans made much of Burr's role. Senate Majority Leader Bill Frist of Tennessee came to North Carolina and proclaimed, "It took monumental leadership, and without Richard Burr providing that monumental leadership, this bill would not have occurred." This may have been the turning point of the campaign. Burr had pulled even with Bowles in polls by late September. His ads linked Bowles to Clinton and to his policies on tax increases, welfare for immigrants, trade with China, and trade policy generally. One ad dubiously called Bowles Clinton's "chief negotiator" on the North American Free Trade Agreement. Both candidates skittered back from previous free-trade positions. And a Burr ad said Bowles "doesn't have the courage to stand up for traditional marriage."

That year, President Bush carried North Carolina 56%-44%. Burr beat Bowles 52%-47%. Burr ran 4% behind Bush in the state's three big metropolitan areas, which cast just over half the votes. He ran 5% behind Bush in the rest of the state. Bowles won big majorities in rural black-majority counties and in the counties with Durham and Chapel Hill. Burr carried almost every rural county in the Piedmont and the mountains.

In the Senate, Burr leaned conservative on cultural issues and toward the center on foreign policy. Starting off in the majority, he sought to review the work of NIH after it had received a doubling of funds over five years. Unlike Bush, he supported using frozen embryos in fertility clinics in stem-cell research. He won enactment of a bill to create the Biomedical Advanced Research and Development Authority to develop vaccines and other countermeasures to biological terrorism or a pandemic. Opponents criticized the bill for its secret operations and for protecting companies that make ineffective or harmful medicines. Burr responded that the agency would become the "venture capitalist" for private-sector initiatives, and would have complete access to their data. Biotech firms applauded the bipartisan deal.

After pledging to vote against the Central American Free Trade Agreement in the campaign, Burr voted for the agreement in 2005, saying "new side agreements" that would boost the state's economy persuaded him to support it. In 2006, he voted against the Senate immigration overhaul bill because he said it would lead to "blanket amnesty" for illegal immigrants. During negotiations on the compromise bill in 2007, Burr supported the "touchback" amendment that would have forced illegal immigrants to return to their home countries before applying for visas. When the amendment was voted down, he voted against allowing the compromise bill to advance.

In 2007, Burr became the ranking minority member on the Veterans' Affairs Committee. In February 2008, he sponsored a bill to give transition payments for soldiers moving from active duty to veteran status. In March 2008, he proposed an amendment transferring funds for Filipino World War II veterans not living in the United States or suffering from service-connected disabilities in order to free $220 million for benefits for Afghanistan and Iraq war veterans. It was killed by Chairman Daniel Akaka, D-Hawaii, who opposed transfers from Filipino veterans. In July 2008, he tried to prevent the Veterans Administration from listing veterans as "mentally defective" in its background check database without a judicial determination. And in August 2008, he got the Senate to pass a bill setting the cost-of-living adjustments for veterans with service-connected disabilities to the same rate as Social Security. Burr co-sponsored with Republican Sens. Lindsey Graham of South Carolina and John McCain of Arizona a revision of the GI Bill of Rights that would allow veterans to transfer half their benefits to spouses or children after six years and all of them after 12 years. The Senate passed a bill by Democratic Sen. Jim Webb of Virginia that went even further, allowing veterans with three years' service to get tuition at the most expensive of their state's public colleges. Burr argued that Webb's version would discourage re-enlistments.

Burr's other recent legislative projects have included advocating a form of equalized tax treatment of employer-provided and non-employer-provided health insurance, with a tax credit of up to $5,400 per family. He sponsored a bill to bar NIH from recalling from their haven in Keithville, La., chimpanzees retired earlier from medical research. In April 2007, he fought the Navy's proposal to build a landing field near the Pocosin Lakes National Wildlife Refuge in eastern North Carolina. In January 2008, as Congress considered a bipartisan economic stimulus bill, Burr called for a sales tax holiday from April 3 to 13.

In 2007, Burr lost a bid to move up the ladder to Republican Conference chairman to Lamar Alexander of Tennessee on a 31-16 vote among Senate Republicans. However, he was selected co-chairman of the 2008 Republican National Convention's Platform Committee, and his legislative acumen paid off when, in January 2009, he was named chief deputy whip in the Republican leadership.

In 2008, Obama's victory in North Carolina—and even more, Dole's defeat for re-election to the Senate—increased speculation that Burr would encounter serious opposition when he comes up for re-election in 2010. He has reportedly spent more time in the state than did Dole, who chaired the Senate Republicans' campaign committee in 2005–06, a job demanding much time and travel. Several Democrats would be plausible opponents; the strongest, based on previous electoral performance, probably would be Attorney General Roy Cooper. In addition, there seems to be a jinx on this seat. Since Democrat Sam Ervin retired in 1974, none of its holders has won a second term.

Junior Senator

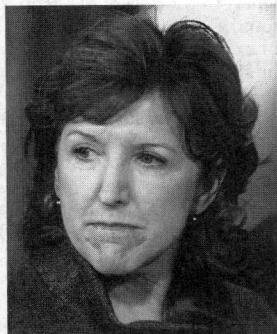

Kay Hagan (D)

Elected 2008, term expires 2014, 1st term; b. May 26, 1953, Shelby; home, Greensboro; FL St. U., B.A. 1975; Wake Forest U., J.D. 1978; Presbyterian; married (Chip); 3 children.

Elected Office: NC Senate, 1999–2008

Professional Career: Lawyer; Banker

DC Office: 521 DSOB, 20510, 202-224-6342; Fax: 202-228-2563; Web site: hagan.senate.gov.

State Offices: Greensboro, 336-333-5311; Raleigh, 919-856-4630.

Committees: *Armed Services* (13th of 15 D): Airland; Personnel; Seapower. *Health, Education, Labor & Pensions* (11th of 13 D). *Small Business & Entrepreneurship* (11th of 11 D).

Group Ratings and Key Votes: Newly Elected

Election Results

2008 general	Kay Hagan (D)	2,249,311	(53%)	($8,953,274)
	Elizabeth Dole (R)	1,887,510	(44%)	($17,468,134)
	Christopher Cole (Lib)	133,430	(3%)	
2008 primary	Kay Hagan (D)	801,920	(60%)	
	Jim Neal (D)	239,623	(18%)	
	Marcus Williams (D)	170,970	(13%)	

Kay Hagan, a Democrat, upset Republican incumbent Elizabeth Dole to be elected to the U.S. Senate in 2008. Hagan was born in Shelby in Cleveland County, which in the 20th century produced an unusually high proportion of prominent state Democratic politicians. When she was a child, her parents moved to Lakeland, Fla. Her father, Joe Ruthven, worked in the tire business, was a real estate broker, and was elected mayor of Lakeland. There were other political influences in her life. Her uncle was Lawton Chiles, who was a state senator from Lakeland in the 1960s, was elected to the U.S. Senate in 1970, 1976, and 1982, and went on to become Florida governor in 1990. Hagen helped out in Chiles's campaigns, and also interned in his Senate office in the 1970s.

Hagan graduated from Florida State and then went to law school at Wake Forest University, in Winston-Salem, where she met her husband, Chip Hagan. After graduation they moved to his hometown, Greensboro, where she worked as an attorney in the trust department at NationsBank (now Bank of America). After her third child was born, she was a stay-at-home mom and got involved in civic affairs—the Greensboro Coliseum, Greensboro Day School—and Democratic politics. In 1992 and 1996, she was Greensboro chairman for Democratic Gov. Jim Hunt's campaigns. In 1998, Hunt persuaded her to run for the state Senate, convincing her that she could still balance her kids' soccer practices and Scout meetings.

With campaign help from Chiles, Hagan defeated an incumbent Republican. Once in Raleigh, Hagan befriended Democratic Senate President Marc Basnight, who became her mentor, giving her important committee posts. Hagan was able to secure money for several projects in her district, including funding for the International Civil Rights Museum, the International Furnishings Market, and Center City Park. As a senator, she cast votes in favor of a state lottery, a two-year moratorium on executions, and financial incentives for corporations to create new jobs. She opposed a constitutional amendment to ban same-sex marriage, citing a state law already in place against it. She also proved an able fundraiser, bringing in more than $325,000 for each of her re-election races in 2002 and 2004.

In 2007, when it looked like GOP Sen. Elizabeth Dole would be re-elected without serious opposition, state and national party leaders looked around for a candidate. Former Clinton-era White House chief of staff Erskine Bowles, who lost the 2002 and 2004 Senate races, declined to run again. Democratic Gov. Michael Easley, though barred from running for a third term, declined also, as did Rep. Brad Miller and Attorney General Roy Cooper. In early October 2007, Hagan announced she would not be a candidate. But Hunt and Democratic Senatorial Campaign Committee Chairman Charles Schumer of New York pressed her hard to run, and later in the month she announced her candidacy. In a five-way May primary, Hagan's chief rival was Chapel Hill investment adviser Jim Neal, who criticized Hagan as too moderate. She was the only candidate to run ads in the May primary and won with 60% of the vote.

At that point, Dole was the clear favorite. She had raised nearly $10 million, far more than Hagan. But Dole had also spent much of 2005 and 2006 traveling around the country on behalf of GOP candidates as the chairman of the National Republican Senatorial Committee. Dole had spent little time in North Carolina until the May 2008 primary. Hagan seized on this, accusing Dole of being a Washington insider and promising to give her a pair of ruby-red slippers to send her to her husband's home state of Kansas.

(Dole is married to former Republican senator and presidential candidate Bob Dole of Kansas.) Hagan ran ads accusing Dole of blindly supporting the Bush administration and being "in the pocket of big oil" because of political contributors who worked for energy companies. National Democrats also subtly raised the issue of Dole's age with a television ad featuring two elderly men in rocking chairs debating whether Dole was 92, the percentage of her votes in support of Bush administration stands, or 93, her effectiveness ranking in the Senate, according to the website *Congress.org*. At the time, Dole was 72. She attacked Hagan for supporting higher taxes on a state Senate budget committee and said she was a creature of national Democrats. Dole dubbed her "Fibber Kay." She emphasized her work in the Senate on North Carolina issues, such as the 2004 tobacco buyout, preserving military bases, and protecting the state's Medicaid funding.

By October, Hagan was consistently leading Dole in polls. With one week to go, Dole ran an ad attacking Hagan for attending a fundraiser in the Massachusetts home of one of the leaders of the Godless America Political Action Committee, a group opposed to having Christmas as a national holiday. The announcer said, "Godless Americans and Kay Hagan. She hid from cameras. Took godless money. What did Hagan promise in return?" Hagan, citing her Sunday school teaching and status as a Presbyterian elder, said Dole should be "ashamed" of the ad, which she said was "bearing false witness against fellow Christians." Hagan threatened to sue for libel and slander. Some 3,600 people sent in contributions to Hagan.

Some North Carolina analysts said the "godless" ad backfired on Dole, and the polling evidence suggests it didn't help her. Hagan won 53%-44%, running 3 percentage points ahead of Barack Obama while Dole ran 5 points behind John McCain. Hagan won 71% of voters under 30, while losing narrowly among voters over the age of 44. Dole carried white evangelical Christians 67%-31%, running 7 percentage points behind McCain among that group. Hagan clearly benefited from the huge increase in the number of young and African-American voters prompted both by the Obama campaign organization and spontaneous enthusiasm for Obama. But she probably would have prevailed in any case, as she ran ahead of most statewide Democratic candidates.

FIRST DISTRICT

G.K. Butterfield (D)

Elected July 2004, 3rd full term; b. April 27, 1947, Wilson; home, Wilson; NC Central U., B.A. 1971, J.D. 1974; Baptist; divorced; 2 children.

Military Career: Army, 1968–70.

Elected Office: NC Superior Ct., 1988–2001, 2002–04; NC Supreme Ct., 2001–02.

Professional Career: Practicing atty., 1974–88.

DC Office: 413 CHOB, 20515, 202-225-3101; Fax: 202-225-3354; Web site: www.house.gov/butterfield.

State Offices: Weldon, 252-538-4123; Wilson, 252-237-9816.

Committees: *Chief Deputy Whip. Energy & Commerce* (23rd of 36 D): Commerce, Trade & Consumer Protections; Communications, Technology & the Internet; Energy & Environment. *Standards of Official Conduct* (3rd of 5D)

Group Ratings

	ADA	ACLU	AFS	LCV	ITIC	NTU	COC	ACU	CFG	FRC
2008	100	91	100	92	86	18	56	12	16	0
2007	95	—	100	70	—	3	58	0	5	—

National Journal Ratings

	2007 LIB — 2007 CONS		2008 LIB — 2008 CONS	
Economic	63%	37%	76%	24%
Social	74%	25%	75%	18%
Foreign	63%	35%	78%	17%
Composite	67%	33%	78%	22%

Key Votes of the 110th Congress

1. Increase minimum wage	Y	5. Share immigration data	N	9. Withdraw troops 8/08	Y
2. Expand SCHIP	Y	6. Foreign aid abortion ban	N	10. No operations in Iran	Y
3. Raise CAFE standards	Y	7. Ban gay bias in workplace	Y	11. Free trade with Peru	Y
4. Bail out financial markets	N	8. Repeal D.C. gun law	N	12. Overhaul FISA	Y

Election Results

2008 general	G.K. Butterfield (D) 192,765	(70%)	($703,692)
	Dean Stephens (R) 81,506	(30%)	
2008 primary	G.K. Butterfield (D) .... unopposed		

Prior Winning Percentages: 2006 (100%); 2004 (64%); 2004 (71%)

Population		Race/Ethnicity		Work	
Pop. 2007:	607,849	White:	43.2%	Private:	73.0%
Change since 2000:	Down 1.8%	Black:	50.4%	Government:	21.2%
Urban:	47.7%	Hispanic:	3.9%	Self-employed:	5.7%
Rural:	52.3%	Asian:	0.5%	Blue collar:	31.0%
Area size:	7,664 sq. mi.	Native Am.:	0.8%	White collar:	45.8%
		Hawaiian:	0.0%	Khaki collar:	1.2%
Age		Two+ races:	1.1%	Other:	22.1%
Median age:	37.7 yrs.	*Ancestry*		Median income:	$30,753
More than 65 yrs:	14.2%	USA:	9.8%	Median home value:	$86,800
Less than 18 yrs:	24.6%	English:	7.2%	Poverty:	24.3%
Education		Irish:	4.9%	**Military Veterans**	
H.S. grad:	74.9%			% of Pop:	10.9%
College grad:	12.7%				
Grad degree:	4.1%				

In colonial days, eastern North Carolina was a smaller version of the Chesapeake Bay colonies of Virginia and Maryland, a fertile land laced by dozens of rivers and inlets, with tobacco plantations and farms with docks on waterways that were accessible to the ocean and so to London. North Carolina was settled later than the Chesapeake colonies, and was poorer, with smaller landholdings. But vestiges of its 18th-century past can still be seen in New Bern with its Tryon Palace, the governor's house

2008 Presidential Vote

Obama (D) 179,431	(63%)
McCain (R)............................103,679	(37%)

2004 Presidential Vote

Kerry (D)................................128,129	(57%)
Bush (R) 94,738	(42%)

Cook Partisan Voting Index: D + 9

when this was the capital, and in the tiny, well-preserved town of Edenton on Albemarle Sound, where 51 women in 1774 protested the taxing of tea and cloth. It is considered the first women's political protest on these shores.

Today, east Carolina survives with remnants of Tobacco Road, and is still largely inhabited by the descendants of the original white settlers and black slaves of 250 years ago. They live in small towns and cities and in some of the most thickly settled rural land in the United States. Tobacco was a labor-intensive crop that for many years produced yields of $4,000 an acre; a family lucky enough to have a tobacco quota could make a living off 40 acres. In 2004, Congress enacted a $10 billion buyout of quota holders, and many old east Carolina tobacco fields are now planted with cucumbers, sweet potatoes, blueberries, and especially cotton. Tobacco's political influence has diminished as well. Hog farming in this area makes North Carolina the second-largest producer behind Iowa. But there have been socioeconomic troubles in this region in recent years. Several rural counties have had high HIV infection rates. Seven counties in northeast North Carolina lost population from 2000 to 2006. Perdue closed a chicken-processing plant, and even fast-food giant Hardee's, founded here in Rocky Mount, decamped to St. Louis. In Beaufort County, more than one-third of African-Americans live in poverty.

The 1st Congressional District of North Carolina is among the poorest in the nation. It covers much of the old tobacco country of east Carolina, touches Albemarle and Pamlico sounds in the east, and juts inland to reach African-American neighborhoods in Greenville and Goldsboro. It includes Halifax County, the state's No. 1 deer-hunting county. Together, the 1st and the 3rd districts blanket the eastern quarter of the state, with intricately drawn boundaries whose fingers reach deep into each other's territory, like clasped hands. There is a political reason for this. The 1st is 50% percent black, the highest percentage of any district in the state, and solidly though not overwhelmingly Democratic. The 3rd is only 16% African-American and, with retirees and new residents in fast-growing coastal counties, votes heavily Republican. The 1st is also notable for its curious gender ratio: In 2006, there were 55,000 more female voters here than male voters—a greater disparity than in any other congressional district in the state.

The congressman from the 1st District is G.K. (George Kenneth) Butterfield, a Democrat who won a special election in July 2004. Butterfield grew up in Wilson County, where his father was a dentist and the first black elected official in Wilson in the 20th century. His mother was a schoolteacher for 48 years. He got his bachelor's degree and a law degree from North Carolina Central University. A civil rights lawyer who represented poor people, Butterfield took on many voting rights cases. As a Superior Court judge for 12 years, he handled thousands of civil and criminal cases in 46 counties until February 2001, when Democratic Gov. Michael Easley appointed him to the state Supreme Court. After Butterfield lost election in 2002 to a full term, Easley appointed him as a special Superior Court judge. In the July 2004 special election to replace the retiring Democratic Rep. Frank Balance, who later pleaded guilty to federal fraud charges in the operation of his antidrug foundation, party caucuses selected the nominees, and the six-week contest in this safe Democratic district received little local or national attention. Butterfield said that his priorities would be strengthening the rural economy and halting U.S. job losses. He won 71%-27% and has not been seriously challenged since.

In the House, he has a liberal voting record. One of his issues was urging the Federal Communications Commission to move slowly to all-digital cable television. "In poor rural places like eastern North Carolina, this could leave a lot of people in the dark when it comes to watching television," he said. He lobbied to include in an exhibit in the new Capitol Visitor Center a portrayal of the slave labor that was employed in building the Capitol and a description of the careers of the 22 African-Americans who served in Congress during and following Reconstruction. He also pushed for renewal of the Voting Rights Act, noting that his father lost his seat on the local city council in 1957 because of a discriminatory voting law change.

A longtime friend of Democratic Rep. James Clyburn of South Carolina, Butterfield managed his successful campaign for majority whip in 2006, and the two were virtually inseparable for 12 days before the November election—in South Carolina and at campaign events across the nation. Butterfield said, "I was his conscience and insisted that he make his calls. He called about 200 members, with the help of four or five cell phones and an occasional staffer. Now he is grateful to me." In 2009, Butterfield became secretary of the Congressional Black Caucus, an influential faction in the House.

With his connections to the leadership, Butterfield got a seat in 2007 on the influential Energy and Commerce Committee, where he has worked to prohibit states from passing on their Medicaid costs to counties. In his district, many counties spend more of their property-tax revenues on Medicaid than on the public schools. He advocated incentives to develop energy from hog and chicken waste. With vestiges of tobacco farming in his district, Butterfield fought to limit the size of an increase in the cigarette tax when House Democrats identified the tax as a source to expand the State Children's Health Insurance Program. In May 2007, Butterfield worked with Rep. David Price, D-N.C., for House passage of a ban on a Navy airstrip planned in Washington and Beaufort counties. Like many older African-Americans, Butterfield was deeply moved by Barack Obama's election as president. "I did not think it would happen in my lifetime," he said.

SECOND DISTRICT

Bob Etheridge (D)

Elected 1996, 7th term; b. Aug. 7, 1941, Turkey; home, Lillington; Campbell U., B.S. 1965; Presbyterian; married (Faye); 3 children.

Military Career: Army, 1965–67.

Elected Office: Harnett Cnty. Comm., 1973–76, Chmn., 1975–76; NC House of Reps., 1978–88; NC Superintendent of Public Instruction, 1989–96.

Professional Career: Farmer, 1965–present; V.P. sales, Sorensen Industries, 1968–87; Owner, Layton Hardware, 1973–90; Co–owner, WLLN Radio, 1979–91.

DC Office: 1533 LHOB, 20515, 202-225-4531; Fax: 202-225-5662; Web site: www.house.gov/etheridge.

State Offices: Lillington, 910-814-0335; Raleigh, 919-829-9122.

Committees: *Budget* (11th of 24 D). *Ways & Means* (23rd of 26 D): Oversight; Trade.

Group Ratings

	ADA	ACLU	AFS	LCV	ITIC	NTU	COC	ACU	CFG	FRC
2008	85	82	100	92	71	6	67	0	0	29
2007	90	—	91	85	—	9	65	8	9	—

National Journal Ratings

	2007 LIB	—	2007 CONS		2008 LIB	—	2008 CONS
Economic	56%	—	43%		71%	—	29%
Social	57%	—	42%		75%	—	18%
Foreign	61%	—	39%		59%	—	37%
Composite	58%	—	42%		70%	—	30%

Key Votes of the 110th Congress

1. Increase minimum wage	Y	5. Share immigration data	N	9. Withdraw troops 8/08	Y
2. Expand SCHIP	N	6. Foreign aid abortion ban	N	10. No operations in Iran	Y
3. Raise CAFE standards	Y	7. Ban gay bias in workplace	Y	11. Free trade with Peru	Y
4. Bail out financial markets	Y	8. Repeal D.C. gun law	N	12. Overhaul FISA	Y

Election Results

2008 general	Bob Etheridge (D)	199,730	(67%)	($984,575)
	Dan Mansell (R)	93,323	(31%)	($21,861)
2008 primary	Bob Etheridge (D)	unopposed		

Prior Winning Percentages: 2006 (67%); 2004 (62%); 2002 (65%); 2000 (58%); 1998 (57%); 1996 (53%)

Population		Race/Ethnicity		Work	
Pop. 2007:	687,531	White:	58.1%	Private:	71.9%
Change since 2000:	Up 11.0%	Black:	28.7%	Government:	22.1%
Urban:	49.5%	Hispanic:	10.0%	Self-employed:	5.8%
Rural:	50.5%	Asian:	1.0%	Blue collar:	28.5%
Area size:	3,979 sq. mi.	Native Am.:	0.4%	White collar:	50.4%
		Hawaiian:	0.1%	Khaki collar:	4.5%
Age		Two+ races:	1.5%	Other:	16.6%
Median age:	33.7 yrs.			Median income:	$41,521
More than 65 yrs:	9.9%	*Ancestry*		Median home value:	$114,800
Less than 18 yrs:	25.6%	USA:	10.1%	Poverty:	16.6%
		English:	8.3%		
Education		German:	7.6%	**Military Veterans**	
H.S. grad:	79.4%			% of Pop:	11.8%
College grad:	17.3%				
Grad degree:	5.1%				

The coastal plain of North Carolina was long bypassed by history. It was settled after Virginia and South Carolina, and only filled in with English settlers as Scots-Irish families were streaming down the valley of Virginia to the western Piedmont. This had long been tobacco country, a high-yield crop that for many years could support a family on 40 acres. Tobacco, an important colonial crop, became even more so after James B. Duke created Bull Durham tobacco and Lucky Strike cigarettes. But this was long a backward area. Its small farms and little cities were populated mainly by tenant farmers and mill hands, people raising families in thin-walled frame houses, often with no electricity or running water.

2008 Presidential Vote

Obama (D)	158,878	(53%)
McCain (R)	141,448	(47%)

2004 Presidential Vote

Bush (R)	128,220	(54%)
Kerry (D)	107,912	(46%)

Cook Partisan Voting Index: R+2

In many ways, life here has improved, in large part because this region adjoins one of the nation's fastest-growing metropolitan areas, Raleigh-Durham. The population of Wake County, which includes Raleigh, grew 33% from 2000 to 2007. Similar growth is taking place in surrounding Franklin (21%), Johnston (29%), Harnett (19%), and Chatham (25%) counties. The dynamic local economy has generated tens of thousands of jobs, with subdivisions and retirement communities sprouting up. While counties to the east have seen denim mills close and tobacco farms reduced by half since Congress in 2004 ended price supports, other parts of the region have boomed. Raleigh combines North Carolina State University and glitzy new cultural institutions with country-cured hams and collard greens at such culinary destinations as Big Ed's City Market Restaurant. In Chatham County, a co-op in 2006 opened the state's first biodiesel production plant.

The 2nd Congressional District of North Carolina consists of an irregular loop south of Raleigh, taking in parts of nine counties, including Wake County, which is split among three congressional districts. It covers all of Johnston County, the state's top tobacco-producing county, and parts of hog-producing Sampson County and Cumberland County, including portions of the Army's Fort Bragg and Pope Air Force Base. The Hispanic population has grown to 10% as Latinos flock to jobs in meat- and chicken-processing factories, but many are not registered to vote. This is by and large the blue-collar, country music part of the booming Raleigh-Durham metro area, a place where most voters have a Democratic heritage but many have gotten into the habit of voting Republican for major offices. In 2000, the district voted for Republican George W. Bush for president and for Democrat Michael Easley for governor. Despite the presence of native-son John Edwards on the Democratic ticket as the vice presidential nominee in 2004, the 2nd voted for Bush again. But in Barack Obama's narrow victory in North Carolina in 2008, he beat John McCain in this district, 52.5%-47%.

The congressman from the 2nd District is Bob Etheridge, a Democrat first elected in 1996. His biography seems tailored to the district: He was born in the hamlet of Turkey in Sampson County, grew up in Johnston County, went to Campbell University in Harnett County, where he was a basketball star, and owned a hardware store in Lillington, the county seat. He is a tobacco farmer who served four years on the Harnett County Commission in the 1970s. He was elected to the North Carolina House in 1978 and served 10 years, eventually chairing the Appropriations Committee. In 1988 and 1992, he was elected state superintendent of public instruction. In the mid-1990s, Democratic Gov. Jim Hunt called for abolishing the superintendent's post and transferred 300 employees to the state Board of Education. Etheridge decided to run for the U.S. House against freshman David Funderburk, a Republican and longtime ally of conservative firebrand Jesse Helms in the Senate. When Funderburk tried to tie Etheridge to the Food and Drug Administration's announcement that tobacco could be regulated as a drug, Etheridge responded by citing his own tobacco credentials: "I own tobacco allotments and have for years. I'd like to know how many days Mr. Funderburk spent priming tobacco, setting tobacco, and how many days he spent under the hot sun in the tobacco fields." Etheridge won 53%-46%.

In the House, Etheridge has compiled a moderate voting record that is generally more liberal on economic issues. He belongs to the centrist New Democrats. The only tobacco farmer in Congress, Etheridge vigorously opposed all attempts to regulate the crop and worked for years on the tobacco buyout bill, which finally was enacted in 2004 and reportedly paid him and his wife $31,000. Utilizing his previous experience as an educator, he won a provision in the Higher Education Reauthorization Act to teach values in public schools. He also pushed legislation to allow states to obtain interest-free loans to build schools. He supported the flag-burning amendment, a ban on "partial-birth" abortions, and later, in 2002, supported the use of force in Iraq. He also split with his party when he voted for trade promotion authority for Bush, which made it easier for the president to negotiate free-trade deals. North Carolina high-tech and farm interests supported the measure. The state has suffered setbacks from expanded trade, he said, but added, "We've been a net winner."

After his district was devastated by Hurricane Floyd in 1999, Etheridge won enactment of his bill to assist weather forecasters to improve hurricane warnings for inland areas. In another assist for his district, he passed a measure to name the post office in Smithfield for actress Ava Gardner, who "did live the American dream, but never forgot her beginnings in Johnston County."

After Democrats won majority control of the House in 2006, Etheridge became chairman of the Agriculture Subcommittee on General Farm Commodities and Risk Management. From that perch, he helped to shape the 2008 farm bill, including reduced subsidies for big farmers. With Rep. Jerry Moran, R-Kan., he won passage of a bill to permit small farmers to qualify for farm programs, overturning a controversial federal agency ruling. In 2007, he traveled to Cuba and sought to end the U.S. trade embargo on that country, a move supported by many American farmers. During the recent spike in energy prices, Etheridge in 2008 pushed a bill designed to reduce market manipulation and excessive speculation, but it fell 13 votes short of passage. He is also a major enthusiast for production of renewable fuels. In 2009, he stepped down as chairman to join the powerful, tax-writing Ways and Means Committee, where he was positioned to be a deal-cutter for moderate Democrats, a measure of the growing size and influence of the Democrats in the North Carolina congressional delegation. He is the only House member from the state on Ways and Means, where he landed a spot on the Trade Subcommittee to pursue his interest in that area.

The Democratically controlled state Legislature's redistricting plan after the 2000 census added part of Raleigh, making this district more Democratic. Since then, Etheridge has won easily. In 2008, he caused a minor stir when, in an appearance at a local elementary school, he referred to Republican nominee John McCain as "an old white man." Etheridge later apologized. In recent years, he twice thought about running for an open Senate seat, but was pre-empted by wealthy former Clinton chief of staff Erskine Bowles, who was able to self-finance some of his campaign. Etheridge seems safe, but an open-seat contest in this district could be competitive.

THIRD DISTRICT

Walter Jones (R)

Elected 1994, 8th term; b. Feb. 10, 1943, Farmville; home, Farmville; NC St. U., 1962–65, Atlantic Christian Col., B.A. 1967; Catholic; married (Joe Anne); 1 child.

Military Career: NC Natl. Guard, 1967–71.

Elected Office: NC House of Reps., 1982–92.

Professional Career: Mgr., Walter B. Jones Office Supply Co., 1967–73; Salesman, Dunn Assoc., 1973–82; Pres., Benefit Reserves Inc., 1989–94; Pres., Judson Co., 1990–94.

DC Office: 2333 RHOB, 20515, 202-225-3415; Fax: 202-225-3286; Web site: jones.house.gov.

State Offices: Greenville, 252-931-1003.

Committees: *Armed Services* (4th of 25 R): Military Personnel; Oversight & Investigations. *Financial Services* (8th of 29 R): Financial Institutions & Consumer Credit; Housing & Community Opportunity.

Group Ratings

	ADA	ACLU	AFS	LCV	ITIC	NTU	COC	ACU	CFG	FRC
2008	50	33	57	15	43	54	59	58	45	100
2007	50	—	45	40	—	50	79	71	43	—

National Journal Ratings

	2007 LIB — 2007 CONS		2008 LIB — 2008 CONS	
Economic	40%	— 59%	39%	— 60%
Social	37%	— 62%	20%	— 80%
Foreign	48%	— 52%	45%	— 54%
Composite	42%	— 58%	35%	— 65%

Key Votes of the 110th Congress

1. Increase minimum wage	Y	5. Share immigration data	Y	9. Withdraw troops 8/08	Y
2. Expand SCHIP	N	6. Foreign aid abortion ban	Y	10. No operations in Iran	Y
3. Raise CAFE standards	N	7. Ban gay bias in workplace	N	11. Free trade with Peru	N
4. Bail out financial markets	N	8. Repeal D.C. gun law	Y	12. Overhaul FISA	*

Election Results

2008 general	Walter Jones (R)	201,686	(66%)	($915,298)
	Craig Weber (D)	104,364	(34%)	($21,761)
2008 primary	Walter Jones (R)	23,699	(59%)	
	Joe McLaughlin (R)	16,491	(41%)	

Prior Winning Percentages: 2006 (69%); 2004 (71%); 2002 (91%); 2000 (61%); 1998 (62%); 1996 (63%); 1994 (53%)

Population		Race/Ethnicity		Work	
Pop. 2007:	675,222	White:	75.3%	Private:	62.2%
Change since 2000:	Up 9.1%	Black:	16.2%	Government:	30.2%
Urban:	53.2%	Hispanic:	5.0%	Self-employed:	7.4%
Rural:	46.8%	Asian:	1.2%	Blue collar:	23.8%
Area size:	10,048 sq. mi.	Native Am.:	0.4%	White collar:	53.9%
		Hawaiian:	0.0%	Khaki collar:	5.8%
Age		Two+ races:	1.8%	Other:	16.4%
Median age:	35.2 yrs.	*Ancestry*		Median income:	$44,659
More than 65 yrs:	12.2%	English:	11.3%	Median home value:	$132,800
Less than 18 yrs:	24.4%	USA:	10.4%	Poverty:	13.3%
Education		Irish:	10.3%		
H.S. grad:	85.2%			**Military Veterans**	
College grad:	21.9%			% of Pop:	14.8%
Grad degree:	7.3%				

Nearly 500 years ago, Giovanni da Verrazano sailed past the Gulf Stream and landed on a sand-spit island he thought was the outer edge of China. It was the Outer Banks of North Carolina. These are probably America's most unstable barrier islands, constantly changing shape and cut by new inlets as they are battered by ocean currents and storm winds. In 2003, 30-foot waves from Hurricane Isabel pounded the beaches. The islands were settled early by Europeans. Sir Walter Raleigh's Roanoke

2008 Presidential Vote		
McCain (R)	193,564	(62%)
Obama (D)	117,365	(38%)

2004 Presidential Vote		
Bush (R)	169,674	(68%)
Kerry (D)	79,936	(32%)

Cook Partisan Voting Index: R+16

colony was founded here in 1587, then vanished shortly thereafter. Edward Teach, better known as Blackbeard, and other pirates lurked in Pamlico and Albemarle sounds behind the islets. History is still very much alive on the Outer Banks. An antique form of English is spoken on Ocracoke Island, reachable only by ferry. A pack of wild horses—believed to be the last remaining descendants of late-16th-century Spanish mustangs—roams free in a 12,000-acre sanctuary on Corolla's beaches. The 208-foot lighthouse on Cape Hatteras, America's tallest, looks out on some of the most treacherous currents in the Atlantic. The sands along Kitty Hawk, with their constant winds, brought the Wright brothers to the Outer Banks to undertake mankind's first heavier-than-air flight in December 1903. The Outer Banks are prime vacation and retirement country, with affluent beachfront communities around Kitty Hawk, Nags Head, and Duck and, much farther south, on the "Crystal Coast" around Beaufort (*BOWfort*, not *BEWfort* as in South Carolina) and Morehead City.

Inland, amid swamps, is the Marine Corps' Camp Lejeune, home base for one-fifth of the Corps, many of whose members have served in Iraq. Past and present military families at the base were shaken by admissions by the government in June 2007 that as many as 1 million people consumed tainted water at Camp Lejeune from 1957 to 1987. The base's drinking wells were contaminated with industrial solvents like TCE and PCE in concentrations as much as 40 times higher than today's safety standards. Many victims have filed health claims against the government. On the other side of the Croatan National Forest is Cherry Point, the world's largest Marine Corps air station. The flatlands of east Carolina have long been tobacco- and peanut-growing country, and are now also hog-raising land.

The 3rd Congressional District of North Carolina covers the Outer Banks and much of the coastal plain of North Carolina, though the northeastern tier moves more in the orbit of Virginia's Hampton Roads than North Carolina's Research Triangle. The 3rd exists in balance with the 1st, with which it shares most of eastern North Carolina. Fingers of the 3rd District reach deeply inland to include mostly white portions of Goldsboro and Greenville, where tobacco farms are fading and a pharmaceutical company is the largest industrial employer. The 3rd is predominantly white and Republican, compared with the 1st, which is half African-American and heavily Democratic. Party registration here is misleading, an artifact of the past. There are 27,000 more registered Democrats than Republicans, but the district voted for George W. Bush by 68%-32% in 2004. John McCain comfortably won the district with 62% even as he lost the state.

The congressman from the 3rd District is Walter Jones, a Republican first elected in 1994. He grew up in eastern North Carolina, attended North Carolina State and Atlantic Christian College, and served in the National Guard. His father, Walter Jones Sr., was a Democratic representative from the old 1st District. The senior Jones served for a quarter-century and chaired the Merchant Marine and Fisheries Committee. The younger Jones was elected in 1982 to the state House, where he voted to oust the Democratic speaker and often broke with Democratic leaders. In 1992, he ran as a Democrat in the new black-majority 1st District after his father decided to retire. He led the primary with 38% but lost the runoff to Democrat Eva Clayton, an African-American who got 55% to Jones' 45%. In April 1993, Jones switched to the Republican Party and soon announced he was running in the 3rd District. This pitted him against four-term Rep. Martin Lancaster, a Democrat who had worked hard on local projects. But Lancaster voted for the Clinton budget and tax bills plus his crime legislation, and failed to persuade the Clintons to drop the cigarette tax from their health care legislation. Jones ran an ad showing Lancaster jogging with Clinton. It said, "How'd Martin Lancaster get so out of touch? Well, look who he's running around with in Washington." Jones won 53%-47%.

In the House, Jones got a seat on the Armed Services Committee and also on the Resources Committee, which had absorbed his father's Merchant Marine panel. His voting record began consistently conservative and hawkish, but over the years moderated as he took issue with President Bush's policies, especially on national security. Jones has favored more defense spending. He had a remarkable conversion on the issue of the war in Iraq. Jones voted to authorize the use of force in Iraq in 2002, as did all but six House Republicans. He even led the 2003 effort, widely spoofed by late-night comics, to rename the House cafeteria's french fries as "freedom fries" after France declined to support the invasion. But not long afterward, he was profoundly affected by a local Marine's funeral, setting the stage for an unlikely conversion from conservative war supporter to Bush administration antagonist.

In 2005, he joined with some of the most liberal members of the House to co-sponsor a resolution calling for the Bush administration to publish a timetable for withdrawing troops from Iraq. Then Jones began writing letters to the families of every soldier killed in Iraq. He told *Mother Jones*, the liberal opinion magazine whose cover he graced in January 2006, that he had written more than 2,000 by that time, penning them every Saturday while sitting alone in his Greenville office. He called the letters his "mea culpa to my Lord" for voting for the war. In February 2007, he was one of 17 House Republicans to vote for the Democrats' resolution disapproving of Bush's plan for a "surge" of troops in Iraq to try to bring order to the country, torn by civil and sectarian strife. He voted for a war-funding bill that set an August 2008 deadline for withdrawal from Iraq, but Jones drew the line at a Democratic proposal to attach conditions to future war funding, saying that attempts to "starve" the war to bring it to a close were wrong.

Jones was one of only two House Republicans to vote against expanding the scope of the Bush administration's secret surveillance program, and he also supported the closing of the prison at Guantanamo Bay. With Rep. Bill Delahunt, D-Mass., Jones explored changes in the War Powers Resolution to strengthen the role of Congress, insisting that problems with the law went beyond Iraq. In January 2007, he sponsored a resolution seeking to ensure that the president get specific authorization from Congress before initiating the use of military force against Iran. His independence from the president and his party cost him the top Republican post on the Readiness Subcommittee on Armed Services in 2007. After his punishment at the hands of GOP leaders, Democrats approached Jones about switching parties, but he declined, saying his opposition to abortion rights would make him ill at ease in the party.

Jones has attracted attention at home as well. In North Carolina, he has generated controversy by intervening in conflicts outside his district. He called for the state school superintendent to remove from an elementary school in Wilmington a book about two gay princes who get married; he opposed full recognition to the Lumbee Indians for fear that they would build a big casino on Interstate 95; and he called for a federal review of the Durham County district attorney's prosecution of three Duke University lacrosse players on sexual assault charges. Jones, who posted the Ten Commandments in his Capitol Hill office, supported politically active churches with his proposal to permit them to endorse candidates without losing their tax-exempt status. The bill generated lots of traffic on the Internet, but the House defeated it 178-239 in 2002.

With other Republicans during the immigration debate, he pushed for 700 miles of double-layered fencing along the border with Mexico. He opposed normalizing trade relations with China, which, he said, "steals technology and sells it to our enemies, steals our nuclear secrets, and tries to influence our election process." And he joined Democrats in opposing the Central America Free Trade Agreement. On Resources, Jones fought oil drilling on the North Carolina coast and a Bush administration proposal to shift to local governments a greater share of the cost for beach restoration.

His outspoken criticism of Iraq war policy brought him a serious primary challenge in 2008 from Onslow County Commissioner Joe McLaughlin, a financial planner and former Army Ranger officer. McLaughlin called Jones "a poster boy for the Left" and said he was "standing shoulder to shoulder with Nancy Pelosi." But Jones seemed to benefit from Iraq fatigue among the public, even among military families. McLaughlin was significantly outspent, and the deep-pocketed Club for Growth, a national anti-tax group, declined to invest in his race. Jones won 59%-41%, with McLaughlin carrying only Carteret, Pimlico, and Craven counties. In November, he defeated poorly funded television meteorologist Craig Weber 66%-34% in a rematch from 2006. Jones was the only House Republican to endorse Texas Rep. Ron Paul's presidential campaign.

FOURTH DISTRICT

David Price (D)

Elected 1996, 11th term; b. Aug. 17, 1940, Erwin, TN; home, Chapel Hill; U. of NC, B.A. 1961, Yale U., B.D. 1964, Ph.D. 1969; Baptist; married (Lisa); 2 children.

Elected Office: U.S. House of Reps., 1986–94.

Professional Career: Legis. aide, U.S. Sen. Bartlett, 1963–67; Prof., Yale U., 1969–73, Duke U., 1973–present; Exec. dir., NC Dem. Party, 1979–80, Chmn., 1983–84; Staff dir., DNC Comm. on Pres. Nominations, 1981–82.

DC Office: 2162 RHOB, 20515, 202-225-1784; Fax: 202-225-2014; Web site: price.house.gov.

State Offices: Chapel Hill, 919-967-7924; Durham, 919-688-3004; Raleigh, 919-859-5999.

Committees: *Appropriations* (13th of 37 D): Homeland Security (Chmn); Interior, Environment & Related Agencies; Transportation, HUD & Related Agencies.

Group Ratings

	ADA	ACLU	AFS	LCV	ITIC	NTU	COC	ACU	CFG	FRC
2008	100	100	100	92	71	6	61	0	0	0
2007	95	—	100	95	—	3	55	0	11	—

National Journal Ratings

	2007 LIB	—	2007 CONS	2008 LIB	—	2008 CONS
Economic	82%	—	0%	81%	—	15%
Social	85%	—	13%	82%	—	0%
Foreign	94%	—	4%	85%	—	8%
Composite	91%	—	9%	88%	—	13%

Key Votes of the 110th Congress

1. Increase minimum wage	Y	5. Share immigration data	N	9. Withdraw troops 8/08	Y
2. Expand SCHIP	Y	6. Foreign aid abortion ban	N	10. No operations in Iran	Y
3. Raise CAFE standards	Y	7. Ban gay bias in workplace	Y	11. Free trade with Peru	Y
4. Bail out financial markets	Y	8. Repeal D.C. gun law	N	12. Overhaul FISA	N

Election Results

2008 general	David Price (D)	265,751	(63%)	($940,570)
	B.J. Lawson (R)	153,947	(37%)	($573,572)
2008 primary	David Price (D)	unopposed		

Prior Winning Percentages: 2006 (65%); 2004 (64%); 2002 (61%); 2000 (62%); 1998 (57%); 1996 (54%); 1992 (65%); 1990 (58%); 1988 (58%); 1986 (56%)

Population		Race/Ethnicity		Work	
Pop. 2007:	744,395	White:	65.9%	Private:	76.6%
Change since 2000:	Up 20.2%	Black:	19.0%	Government:	17.6%
Urban:	83.2%	Hispanic:	7.5%	Self-employed:	5.6%
Rural:	16.8%	Asian:	5.5%	Blue collar:	12.4%
Area size:	1,298 sq. mi.	Native Am.:	0.2%	White collar:	75.2%
Age		Hawaiian:	0.0%	Khaki collar:	0.1%
Median age:	35.0 yrs.	Two+ races:	1.6%	Other:	12.4%
More than 65 yrs:	8.4%	*Ancestry*		Median income:	$61,416
Less than 18 yrs:	25.1%	English:	11.5%	Median home value:	$213,900
Education		German:	11.2%	Poverty:	9.6%
H.S. grad:	90.6%	Irish:	8.8%	**Military Veterans**	
College grad:	50.9%			% of Pop:	8.7%
Grad degree:	20.9%				

Back in the 1950s, few people would have predicted that the countryside around Raleigh and Durham would become one of America's high-tech boom areas. But Democratic Gov. Luther Hodges did, and he started the 6,900-acre Research Triangle Park as a research-and-development industrial park between the musty state capital of Raleigh, the Lucky Strike-manufacturing city of Durham, and the small university town of Chapel Hill. With the drawing power of three universities—North

2008 Presidential Vote		
Obama (D)	267,368	(62%)
McCain (R)	162,591	(37%)

2004 Presidential Vote		
Kerry (D)	193,126	(55%)
Bush (R)	154,743	(44%)

Cook Partisan Voting Index: D+8

Carolina State in Raleigh, Duke in Durham, and the University of North Carolina in Chapel Hill—Research Triangle Park slowly began attracting top-tier R&D organizations, which in turn spawned a dynamic entrepreneurial sector. Today, the big-name employers there include IBM, GlaxoSmithKline, Cisco, Nortel, and RTI International. There are smaller businesses too. A little more than half of Triangle employers had 10 or fewer employees. A sleepy metro area that once trailed the nation in income is now a vibrant, affluent metropolis and the prime engine of North Carolina's growth. The Raleigh-Durham airport, which had four gates in the 1970s, has expanded steadily and will have 60 gates by 2010. Local planners are working on a light-rail system for the area.

Three decades of solid economic growth have made the Triangle affluent and one of the nation's hottest job markets. But it still prides itself on its homier touches, from slow-cooked pit barbecue to a minor-league baseball stadium in Durham that features a smoke-snorting replica of a bull, a prop made famous by the movie set in the region, *Bull Durham*. College basketball makes the headlines here, and UNC, NC State, and Duke have fielded more March Madness contenders than any similarly sized area. This combination of upscale and down-home has proved to be a popular draw. From 1990 to 2007, the Raleigh-Durham metro area grew by 75%, from 855,000 to 1.5 million. The area's one setback in recent years was the notorious Duke lacrosse rape case, in which Durham prosecutor Mike Nifong charged three Duke players with rape based on evidence so thin the charges were dropped. Nifong resigned in 2007 and was stripped of his law license. Three players later settled a civil suit against the city.

The 4th Congressional District of North Carolina covers much of the fast-growing Research Triangle area. It includes Durham County and Chapel Hill's Orange County, part of Chatham County to the south and a little less than half of Wake County. Politics here revolves around cultural issues. The Democratic base here is made up of two parts: the black community, with 19% of the district's population, and whites and blacks with postgraduate degrees. *Black Enterprise* magazine ranks the region as the third-best in the nation (behind Washington, D.C., and Atlanta) for African-Americans to live and work. This part of the Triangle has one of the highest concentrations of Ph.D.s in the nation, and their livelihoods—in academia, in the sciences, in the social services—tend to depend on government. Durham and Orange counties are heavily Democratic, usually that party's strongest area in North Carolina, except for a few rural counties with large African-American percentages. The burgeoning suburbs of Wake County are pretty heavily Republican, like so many fast-growing areas at the edge of metropolitan development across the nation, and provide some counterweight. On balance, though, this is a district that votes for Democrats, not only local moderates but also liberals like Barack Obama, who got 62% in the district in 2008.

The congressman from the 4th District is David Price, a Democrat first elected in 1986. He lost the seat in 1994 and regained it in 1996. Price grew up in east Tennessee, the son of a school principal and an English teacher. He is an interesting blend of political scientist, practical politician, and lay Baptist preacher, and he has quietly become one of the most influential House members. He came to Chapel Hill to go to college, worked as a young aide on Capitol Hill, earned a degree in divinity and a doctorate in political science at Yale University and taught there for four years. In 1973, he took a job as a political science professor at Duke. He was executive director of the North Carolina Democratic Party in the 1980 election season and chairman in 1983–84, which were both, in effect, appointments of Gov. Jim Hunt. Price helped develop North Carolina's robust straight-ticket politics. He worked for Hunt when he headed a commission on revising the Democratic Party's nominating rules. In 1986, he ran for the House and beat Republican Rep. Bill Cobey, who had won in the 1984 sweep. In 1994, Price lost 50.4%-49.6% to Fred Heineman, a former New York City police officer and Raleigh police chief in the 1970s. In 1996, Heineman was outspent by Price, who regained the seat 54%-44%. Price has written four books, including *The Congressional Experience*, about his observations on Congress.

In the House, Price's voting record typically places him near the center of House Democrats. During his first years, Price helped pass laws increasing the percentage of a home's value the government can insure, aiding technical education at community colleges, and setting up an Advanced Technological Education program at the National Science Foundation. His Education Affordability Act, "my personal centerpiece," on which he had been working for a dozen years, was folded into the 1997 Balanced Budget Act and became law. It made interest on student loans tax deductible and allowed penalty-free withdrawals from individual retirement accounts for education expenses.

Price has combined strong opposition to Bush administration policies in Iraq and elsewhere with his work on homeland security issues on the Appropriations Committee. He voted against the Iraq war resolution in 2002 and later called the Bush administration "out of touch and out of control." In 2005, he and North Carolina Rep. Brad Miller, also a Democrat, sponsored a resolution to require withdrawal of troops from Iraq as soon as possible. In January 2007, they sponsored a bill to curtail the administration's ability to pursue the military effort after December 2007. In 2006, Price called the Iraq war "a major failure" and "indicative of the diversion" away from the goal of hunting down Osama bin Laden and other Al Qaeda leaders.

Price was one of the founders of the House Democracy Assistance Commission, which has worked with leaders of emerging democracies, and as part of that effort he was in Lebanon on July 4, 2006, just before the Hamas attack on Israel. He voted for the resolution supporting Israel's response to the attack. In January 2007, Price became chairman of the Appropriations Homeland Security Subcommittee, on which he had served quietly under Rep. Harold Rogers, R-Ky., during the years of GOP control of the House. Price pledged to take a bipartisan approach, as he said Rogers had. But he consistently sought higher levels of spending for homeland security measures, like support for first responders, than requested by the Bush administration. The 2007 homeland security spending bill increased by about 33% Bush's funding request for the Federal Emergency Management Agency. Also that year, the House passed Price's bill establishing a code of conduct for private security contractors in Iraq and Afghanistan. A target of the bill was North Carolina-based Blackwater, whose activities in Iraq, including the shooting of 17 people in a Baghdad square, have been controversial. The Bush White House cited his provision prohibiting such defense contractors from interrogating detainees as the chief factor for its veto of the 2008 intelligence bill. In the 2008 appropriations debate, Price sought more aid for first responders and demanded higher priority for the deportation of criminal illegal immigrants held in U.S. jails.

In the appropriations process, Price has nurtured local projects, including $272 million for a new Environmental Protection Agency complex in Research Triangle Park. Price has also been active in campaign finance law. He sponsored the "stand by your ad" requirement for candidates to appear in the full frame of television ads reading their disclaimers on the air, so they would more likely be held responsible for negative ads. His proposal became part of the campaign reform law in 2002. He wants a similar requirement for Internet ads. In 2007, he sponsored a bill to double the amount of public financing presidential candidates could receive if an opponent outside the public financing system spends more than 120% of the public financing limit. It would be financed by increasing the check-off on tax returns to $10.

Since his return to the House in 1996, Price has been re-elected by wide margins. In 2008, he won 63%-37% over a well-funded technology-company executive, B.J. Lawson. In Wake County, the fastest-growing part of the district, responsible for 47% of the total vote, he won just 52%. He ran much better in the areas dominated by universities: 77% in Durham County, 72% in Orange County, and 62% in Chatham County.

FIFTH DISTRICT

Virginia Foxx (R)

Elected 2004, 3rd term; b. June 29, 1943, Bronx, NY; home, Banner Elk; U. of NC, A.B. 1968, M.A.C.T. 1972, U. of NC-Greensboro, Ed.D. 1985; Catholic; married (Thomas); 1 child.

Elected Office: Watauga Bd. of Ed., 1976–88; NC Senate, 1994–2004.

Professional Career: Owner, Grandfather Mountain Nursery, 1976-present; Asst. Dean of General College, Appalachian St. U., 1976–1984; Pres. Mayland CC, 1987–1994.

DC Office: 1230 LHOB, 20515, 202-225-2071; Fax: 202-225-2995; Web site: foxx.house.gov.

State Offices: Boone, 828-265-0240; Clemmons, 336-778-0211.

Committees: *Rules* (4th of 4 R): Rules & Organization of the House.

Group Ratings

	ADA	ACLU	AFS	LCV	ITIC	NTU	COC	ACU	CFG	FRC
2008	5	18	0	0	29	89	78	100	100	100
2007	0	—	0	10	—	89	70	100	89	—

National Journal Ratings

	2007 LIB — 2007 CONS		2008 LIB — 2008 CONS	
Economic	4% —	95%	3% —	95%
Social	0% —	91%	0% —	91%
Foreign	0% —	72%	0% —	95%
Composite	8% —	92%	4% —	96%

Key Votes of the 110th Congress

1. Increase minimum wage	N	5. Share immigration data	Y
2. Expand SCHIP	N	6. Foreign aid abortion ban	Y
3. Raise CAFE standards	N	7. Ban gay bias in workplace	N
4. Bail out financial markets	N	8. Repeal D.C. gun law	Y

9. Withdraw troops 8/08	N
10. No operations in Iran	N
11. Free trade with Peru	Y
12. Overhaul FISA	Y

Election Results

2008 general	Virginia Foxx (R)	190,820	(58%)	($852,649)
	Roy Carter (D)	136,103	(42%)	($238,153)
2008 primary	Virginia Foxx (R)	unopposed		

Prior Winning Percentages: 2006 (57%); 2004 (59%)

Population		Race/Ethnicity		Work	
Pop. 2007:	657,309	White:	84.7%	Private:	80.4%
Change since 2000:	Up 6.2%	Black:	7.4%	Government:	11.7%
Urban:	42.9%	Hispanic:	5.6%	Self-employed:	7.5%
Rural:	57.1%	Asian:	1.0%	Blue collar:	29.4%
Area size:	4,424 sq. mi.	Native Am.:	0.3%	White collar:	54.8%
		Hawaiian:	0.0%	Khaki collar:	0.1%
Age		Two+ races:	0.8%	Other:	15.7%
Median age:	39.5 yrs.			Median income:	$43,892
More than 65 yrs:	14.3%	*Ancestry*		Median home value:	$131,700
Less than 18 yrs:	22.5%	USA:	17.0%	Poverty:	12.9%
		German:	12.4%		
Education		English:	10.6%	**Military Veterans**	
H.S. grad:	79.7%			% of Pop:	10.2%
College grad:	21.5%				
Grad degree:	6.9%				

From the Atlantic Ocean, the terrain of North Carolina rises slowly through the Piedmont, a transitional land of modest hills that lies between the coastal plain and the Blue Ridge mountains. The Blue Ridge, named for the mysterious blue haze that blankets it, provides the headwaters of the New River, which cuts majestic crevasses—alternately lush and mined-out—as it flows north to West Virginia. The lower Piedmont lands of North Carolina were first settled by independent-minded Scots-Irish farmers and by followers of British and German sects like the Moravians. This was hardscrabble farm country before the Civil War, with few slaves. By the late 19th century, it was becoming industrialized, with textile mills alongside streams, furniture factories not far from hardwood forests, and R.J. Reynolds' cigarette factories in Winston-Salem. The Piedmont economy was hailed as the basis of a progressive New South, although textile mills paid low wages and tobacco employed fewer workers.

Today, the region's pharmaceutical companies, banking institutions, and high-skill Piedmont factories have contributed to the state's overall affluence. Lowe's, the $31 billion home-improvement giant, is based in Wilkesboro, population 3,200. The merger of banking giants Wachovia and First Union proved bittersweet for Winston-Salem, Wachovia's home base since 1879. First Union let the new company keep Wachovia's name but shifted its headquarters to Charlotte. In 2005, Dell opened a plant in Winston-Salem that produced 2 million computers and 1,100 jobs in its first year. However, Dell's future in the region was clouded by its attempt in 2008 to sell its factories nationwide. New wineries are gaining recognition in the Yadkin Valley. Yet large swaths of the region remain rural, from chicken-raising Wilkes County to Appalachian State University in Boone (named for Daniel), a center for resurgent pride in the culture of Appalachia, a region so often the target of either pity or condescension. In September 2007, the university's football team pulled off one of the biggest upsets in college football history when it defeated the University of Michigan in a game at Ann Arbor.

All of these places lie within the boundaries of the 5th Congressional District. The 5th begins in the heart of the Piedmont: the suburbs of Winston-Salem (though not the city, which is in the 12th District). From there, it drops south just short of the outer fringes of metropolitan Charlotte. It heads west and north to the Tennessee line, taking in mountain communities like Boone. The core of its population base is the Winston-Salem suburbs in Forsyth County, plus small industrial cities in Stokes and Surry counties, including Mount Airy, the model for Mayberry in *The Andy Griffith Show*. The district is solidly Republican.

The congresswoman from the 5th District is Virginia Foxx, a Republican first elected in 2004 after emerging from a fiercely contested Republican primary. She graduated from the University of North Carolina and had a diverse professional and political background before winning election to Congress at age 61. She owned a nursery and landscape company, and taught sociology and was assistant dean of the General College at Appalachian State University. Later, she was president of Mayland Community College. She served 12 years on the Board of Education of Watauga County, on the western edge of the district (nearly as close to Knoxville, Tenn., as to Winston-Salem). In 1994, Foxx was elected to the state Senate. In the Legislature she sponsored a constitutional amendment to ban same-sex marriage and a bill to deny Social Security benefits to illegal aliens. She actively supported gun rights and home schooling, and she opposed abortion rights.

In 2004, Foxx was one of five serious candidates in the Republican primary for the U.S. House seat. Collectively, they spent more than $6 million. Ed Broyhill, the son of former Republican Sen. James Broyhill, started off as the early front-runner. Broyhill was endorsed by his father's onetime colleague Sen. Jesse Helms. Also in the race was Winston-Salem Councilman Vernon Robinson, a retired Air Force officer who campaigned as a staunch conservative, "the black Jesse Helms," as he put it. Robinson finished first in the primary, with 24% of the vote. Foxx unexpectedly finished second, with 22%, just 511 votes ahead of Broyhill.

The four-week campaign for the runoff was heatedly contested. Robinson said that Foxx was "fighting the cultural war on the wrong side," and he aired several controversial ads targeting his tougher position on illegal immigrants. Foxx warned voters that Robinson's aggressive style would make him a weak general election candidate who could lose, although that seemed unlikely in a district that twice voted 66% for George W. Bush. Foxx won 55%-45%, with between 73% and 82% in her home area in the three mountain counties. Robinson carried Forsyth County, which cast 40% of the vote, but by only 38 votes. In the general election, Foxx won 59%-41%.

In the House, Foxx has a solidly conservative voting record and an outspoken style. She reinforced her reputation as a tightfisted spender when she was one of 11 members voting against House passage of the $52 billion relief package following Hurricane Katrina. "The real issue for me was accountability," Foxx said. She was more generous for local projects, taking credit for $500,000 for a teapot museum in Sparta, which President Bush later criticized as wasteful spending. After such earmarked spending became controversial, Foxx said in December 2007 that she no longer would seek earmarks, but she also

2008 Presidential Vote
McCain (R)............................200,520   (61%)
Obama (D) 126,178   (38%)

2004 Presidential Vote
Bush (R)................................191,034   (66%)
Kerry (D)................................95,811   (33%)

Cook Partisan Voting Index: R+15

criticized Democrats for "hypocrisy" when they attacked the lack of "transparency" in her requested projects. Foxx opposed federal support for embryonic-stem cell research, which uses frozen embryos from in vitro fertilization. "Killing human life does not have to be accomplished to create efficacious treatment," she said. In November 2008, Foxx sponsored legislation to prevent unspent portions of the $700 billion in bailout funds for the financial industry from being distributed, complaining there had been no meaningful oversight of the way the first $290 billion were used by private companies.

Foxx has been re-elected by unimpressive margins against low-profile opponents.

SIXTH DISTRICT

Howard Coble (R)

Elected 1984, 13th term; b. March 18, 1931, Greensboro; home, Greensboro; Appalachian St. U., 1949–50, Guilford Col., B.A. 1958, U. of NC, J.D. 1962; Presbyterian; single.

Military Career: Coast Guard, 1952–56, 1977–78, Coast Guard Reserves, 1960–81.

Elected Office: NC House of Reps., 1968–70, 1978–84.

Professional Career: Claims rep., State Farm Ins., 1961–67; Asst. Guilford Cnty. atty., 1967–69; Asst. U.S. atty., NC Middle Dist., 1969–73; Secy., NC Dept. of Revenue, 1973–77; Practicing atty., 1979–83.

DC Office: 2468 RHOB, 20515, 202-225-3065; Fax: 202-225-8611; Web site: coble.house.gov.

State Offices: Asheboro, 336-626-3060; Graham, 336-229-0159; Granite Quarry, 704-209-0428; Greensboro, 336-333-5005; High Point, 336-886-5106.

Committees: *Judiciary* (3rd of 16 R): Commercial & Administrative Law; Courts & Competition Policy (RMM). *Transportation & Infrastructure* (4th of 30 R): Aviation; Coast Guard & Maritime Transportation; Highways & Transit.

Group Ratings

	ADA	ACLU	AFS	LCV	ITIC	NTU	COC	ACU	CFG	FRC
2008	20	20	14	15	100	65	89	88	73	88
2007	10	—	0	5	—	81	88	83	81	—

National Journal Ratings

	2007 LIB	—	2007 CONS	2008 LIB	—	2008 CONS
Economic	21%	—	79%	13%	—	86%
Social	26%	—	74%	0%	—	91%
Foreign	36%	—	63%	44%	—	56%
Composite	28%	—	72%	21%	—	79%

Key Votes of the 110th Congress

1. Increase minimum wage	N	5. Share immigration data	Y	9. Withdraw troops 8/08	N
2. Expand SCHIP	N	6. Foreign aid abortion ban	Y	10. No operations in Iran	N
3. Raise CAFE standards	N	7. Ban gay bias in workplace	N	11. Free trade with Peru	Y
4. Bail out financial markets	Y	8. Repeal D.C. gun law	Y	12. Overhaul FISA	Y

Election Results

2008 general	Howard Coble (R)	221,018	(67%)	($688,818)
	Teresa Sue Bratton (D)	108,873	(33%)	($105,750)
2008 primary	Howard Coble (R)	unopposed		

Prior Winning Percentages: 2006 (71%); 2004 (73%); 2002 (90%); 2000 (91%); 1998 (89%); 1996 (73%); 1994 (100%); 1992 (71%); 1990 (67%); 1988 (62%); 1986 (50%); 1984 (51%)

Population		Race/Ethnicity		Work	
Pop. 2007:	681,171	White:	81.6%	Private:	80.6%
Change since 2000:	Up 10.0%	Black:	9.7%	Government:	12.6%
Urban:	51.6%	Hispanic:	5.7%	Self-employed:	6.6%
Rural:	48.4%	Asian:	1.4%	Blue collar:	28.9%
Area size:	2,989 sq. mi.	Native Am.:	0.4%	White collar:	56.5%
		Hawaiian:	0.0%	Khaki collar:	0.2%
Age		Two+ races:	1.0%	Other:	14.5%
Median age:	39.3 yrs.			Median income:	$48,288
More than 65 yrs:	14.0%	*Ancestry*		Median home value:	$139,800
Less than 18 yrs:	23.6%	German:	12.8%	Poverty:	11.7%
		USA:	12.7%		
Education		English:	12.0%	**Military Veterans**	
H.S. grad:	82.4%			% of Pop:	11.4%
College grad:	24.0%				
Grad degree:	7.1%				

For more than half a century, furniture store managers and owners from all over the country twice a year have converged on the huge Furniture Mart in High Point, the center of the U.S. furniture business. The giant trade show put on by manufacturers now attracts about 70,000 visitors. High Point sits amid rolling farmland originally settled by Quakers. It was the site of the Battle of Guilford Courthouse in the Revolutionary War. The furniture business grew here early in the 20th century

2008 Presidential Vote
McCain (R)............................212,548   (63%)
Obama (D) 120,805   (36%)

2004 Presidential Vote
Bush (R) 200,942   (69%)
Kerry (D)................................87,295   (30%)

Cook Partisan Voting Index: R + 18

because of the hardwoods in the mountains not far west and the abundance of low-wage labor in the flatlands not far east. For many years, the furniture business has proven more resilient than textiles and tobacco, but lately it has faced serious competition from China, and many furniture jobs have been lost, including more than 6,000 jobs in this area since 2000. Some local businesses have been reaching out to China, with increased textile and fabric exports. The Triad area—Greensboro, High Point, and Winston-Salem—has been forced to scramble for new engines of economic growth to keep pace with booming Raleigh-Durham and Charlotte. FedEx planned to open in 2009 a new hub at Piedmont Triad International Airport, between Winston-Salem and Greensboro, with some 1,500 workers. That has led other firms to plan distribution centers to utilize the new facility as part of what one business expert termed an "aerotropolis." At the same time, the region's Hispanic population is growing. The town of Robbins in Moore County—the childhood home of John Edwards, former Democratic vice presidential candidate and North Carolina senator—was 48% Hispanic by 2007, as Latinos moved in for jobs in chicken processing and furniture making.

The 6th Congressional District of North Carolina is centered on greater Greensboro and High Point, which collectively cast about one-third of its votes. The Furniture Mart itself is not physically located within the 6th, but the district takes in other parts of High Point, which calls itself "North Carolina's International City," plus Quaker-settled Randolph County. Moore County and its numerous golf courses are in the district, as are parts of furniture-manufacturing Davidson County, most of textile-making Alamance County, much of populous Guilford County (though not central Greensboro), and the eastern half of Rowan County. Many of these areas are historically Republican, and others have moved in that direction in the past generation. This district has the highest share of registered Republicans in North Carolina.

The congressman from the 6th District is Howard Coble, a Republican first elected in 1984. He grew up in Guilford County and went to Guilford College. After wrecking his father's car, he fled to the Coast Guard, where he started off collecting garbage and served for five years. He was an insurance claims representative, went to law school, and became an assistant U.S. attorney and the state revenue commissioner. He served in the state House for eight years. Coble was elected to Congress in what was then a swing district. It was the third time the 6th District had changed parties in three elections. Coble won re-election in 1986 by just 79 votes, in a contest that Democrats complained was decided by the Guilford County election board's refusal to hold a recount. But his personal popularity and redistricting have made this a safe seat.

Coble is a friendly man who asks visitors if they mind if he smokes his cheap cigars. He likes bluegrass music and eats pork brains and eggs for breakfast. His voting record is mostly conservative, with interesting twists. He is tightfisted, and since his first term, he has tried to pass legislation to abolish pensions or health coverage for congressional retirees, which he calls "a taxpayer rip-off." He hasn't found many co-sponsors, but he has refused to back down on his pledge to boycott the program himself. Like many of his constituents, he is leery of free trade. He initially opposed the North American Free Trade Agreement but voted for it in 1993. But he has opposed subsequent trade initiatives, including normalizing trade relations with China and the 2005 Central America Free Trade Agreement.

"I see my role more as one of keeping bad legislation off the books," Coble once said. But as a subcommittee chairman he was legislatively productive. As chairman of the Courts and Intellectual Property Subcommittee of the Judiciary Committee, Coble argued that industries that depend on copyrights produce more GDP than does manufacturing, and he has supported greater protection for intellectual property. When the Bush administration sought budget cuts from the Patent and Trademark Office, Coble told the appropriators to "keep their grubby paws out of the PTO's coffers." In 2002, he shepherded the enactment of additional changes in the patent law, including the development of an electronic system for the filing and processing of patent and trademark applications. In 2004, the Judiciary Committee approved his bill to protect commercial databases from piracy. Despite his own limitations in operating a computer, the nearly 80-year-old Coble is a major cheerleader for the digital revolution and says he has come to appreciate the Internet.

In 2003, when Republicans controlled the House, Coble was chairman of the Crime, Terrorism, and Homeland Security Subcommittee of Judiciary. The House passed his bill to modernize the Bureau of Alcohol, Tobacco, Firearms, and Explosives with new investigative powers against rogue dealers of firearms. He was in line to become the senior Republican on the Judiciary Committee in 2007, after Democrats won control, but GOP leaders gave the post to Lamar Smith of Texas, a more prolific party fundraiser. Coble, instead, got the top Republican post on the Subcommittee on Courts, the Internet, and Intellectual Property.

Coble voted in 2002 to authorize the use of force in Iraq, but by 2005 he began to distance himself from the party position and raised questions about President Bush's war policy. In February 2007, he was one of 17 House Republicans to vote for the resolution opposing Bush's plans for a "surge" of troop strength to try to restore order in Iraq. But he opposed Democratic measures imposing a timetable to withdraw U.S. troops. In January 2008, he was one of 35 House members who voted against tax rebates that were designed to stimulate the economy, saying the rebates were like "applying a Band-Aid to a problem that requires major surgery." After first opposing the $700 billion bailout of the financial markets later that year, he cited warnings from local business leaders of a looming liquidity crisis and voted for the bill.

In July 2008, Coble broke James Broyhill's record for the longest tenure in the U.S. House of a Republican from North Carolina. Broyhill served 23 years, from 1963 to 1986. When Coble faces a Democratic opponent, which isn't very often, he typically exceeds 70% of the vote. Democrats view this seat as possibly competitive once Coble departs, but that seems a stretch. More likely, the district's future could hinge on redistricting.

SEVENTH DISTRICT

Mike McIntyre (D)

Elected 1996, 7th term; b. Aug. 6, 1956, Lumberton; home, Lumberton; U. of NC, B.A. 1978, J.D. 1981; Presbyterian; married (Dee); 2 children.

Professional Career: Practicing atty., 1981–96.

DC Office: 2437 RHOB, 20515, 202-225-2731; Fax: 202-225-5773; Web site: www.house.gov/mcintyre.

State Offices: Bolivia, 910-253-0158; Fayetteville, 910-323-0260; Lumberton, 910-735-0610; Wilmington, 910-815-4959.

Committees: *Agriculture* (3rd of 28 D): Conservation, Credit, Energy & Research; Specialty Crops, Rural Development & Foreign Agriculture (Chmn). *Armed Services* (10th of 36 D): Air & Land Forces; Terrorism, Unconventional Threats & Capabilities.

Group Ratings

	ADA	ACLU	AFS	LCV	ITIC	NTU	COC	ACU	CFG	FRC
2008	85	55	100	77	43	29	61	32	21	100
2007	85	—	91	75	—	10	65	44	10	—

National Journal Ratings

	2007 LIB	—	2007 CONS	2008 LIB	—	2008 CONS
Economic	51%	—	48%	57%	—	41%
Social	46%	—	53%	46%	—	52%
Foreign	50%	—	49%	52%	—	46%
Composite	50%	—	51%	53%	—	47%

Key Votes of the 110th Congress

1. Increase minimum wage	Y	5. Share immigration data	Y	9. Withdraw troops 8/08	Y
2. Expand SCHIP	N	6. Foreign aid abortion ban	Y	10. No operations in Iran	Y
3. Raise CAFE standards	Y	7. Ban gay bias in workplace	N	11. Free trade with Peru	N
4. Bail out financial markets	N	8. Repeal D.C. gun law	Y	12. Overhaul FISA	Y

Election Results

2008 general	Mike McIntyre (D)	215,383	(69%)	($1,160,679)
	Will Breazeale (R)	97,472	(31%)	($89,219)
2008 primary	Mike McIntyre (D)	unopposed		

Prior Winning Percentages: 2006 (73%); 2004 (73%); 2002 (71%); 2000 (70%); 1998 (91%); 1996 (53%)

Population		Race/Ethnicity		Work	
Pop. 2007:	689,448	White:	63.6%	Private:	76.4%
Change since 2000:	Up 11.3%	Black:	20.8%	Government:	15.7%
Urban:	45.1%	Hispanic:	5.7%	Self-employed:	7.7%
Rural:	54.9%	Asian:	0.6%	Blue collar:	28.5%
Area size:	6,510 sq. mi.	Native Am.:	7.8%	White collar:	51.7%
		Hawaiian:	0.1%	Khaki collar:	0.6%
Age		Two+ races:	1.4%	Other:	19.2%
Median age:	37.3 yrs.			Median income:	$38,616
More than 65 yrs:	13.2%	*Ancestry*		Median home value:	$118,700
Less than 18 yrs:	24.1%	USA:	10.9%	Poverty:	19.1%
		English:	8.9%		
Education		Irish:	8.3%	**Military Veterans**	
H.S. grad:	79.5%			% of Pop:	12.0%
College grad:	20.3%				
Grad degree:	6.3%				

Southernmost North Carolina was long a somnolent part of America. Its one port, Wilmington, was far overshadowed by Charleston, S.C., and Norfolk, Va. Its miles of beaches seemed too hot in the summer and too cold in the winter to attract many tourists. Its inland farmlands were mainly planted in tobacco. Tobacco was America's first export crop, and one that can be cultivated profitably in only a few places in the world. Under the quota system estab-

2008 Presidential Vote

McCain (R)	165,960	(52%)
Obama (D)	151,172	(47%)

2004 Presidential Vote

Bush (R)	141,459	(56%)
Kerry (D)	110,589	(44%)

Cook Partisan Voting Index: R + 5

lished in 1938, tobacco farmers could make a living off small plots; it probably produced more voters per federally assisted acre than any other crop. But in recent decades, as smoking declined and tobacco companies were hit by lawsuits, tobacco fell out of favor with the public. In 2004, Congress passed a $10 billion buyout and in the process abolished the quota system. So tobacco farmers are diversifying; some have switched to blueberries, pumpkins, and other crops.

The coastal counties of southern North Carolina and some inland counties, nevertheless, have been growing fast. One reason is the military. Wilmington is home to the World War II battleship USS *North Carolina*, and a little farther south, the Army runs the 16,000-acre Military Ocean Terminal at Sunny Point, the largest ammunition port in the United States, and the Army's main deep-water port on the East Coast. The state is planning a new deep-water port in Brunswick County near Southport. Condominiums have sprouted along the beaches north and south of Wilmington, and tourism has boomed. This area also has some of the busiest American movie- and television-production facilities outside Los Angeles, and the state Legislature in 2006 approved new incentives to further boost the business. In Sampson and Duplin counties, the growth industry is hog farming, which has been criticized by environmentalists for its enormous output of hog waste. One Smithfield Foods facility, which is believed to be the largest slaughterhouse in the world, handles 8.5 million animals a year. The company is among those researching the potential for turning the abundance of methane gas produced by the hog waste on the farms into a usable source of energy.

The 7th Congressional District of North Carolina covers much of this territory. The district consists of three main areas: the Wilmington region, with affluent condo dwellers along the beach and retiree subdivisions reclaimed from timbered-out pinelands further inland; the outskirts of Fayetteville, heavily dependent on Fort Bragg and Pope Air Force Base; and economically disadvantaged Robeson County, the home of the Lumbee Indians, whose origins have been lost to antiquity but who were recognized as a tribe by the state in 1885. For many years, this was a solidly Democratic district. Robeson County—with 20% of the district's population, where whites, blacks, and Lumbees each constitute about a third of the population—remains heavily Democratic in both national and state elections. But the Wilmington area and the hog-farming counties are now Republican. The Fayetteville area and the old tobacco counties are politically marginal. The result is a district Republican in national contests but still Democratic in some state races. George W. Bush twice won the district, and Republican John McCain also won here in 2008, 52%-47%.

The congressman from the 7th District is Mike McIntyre, a Democrat first elected in 1996. McIntyre grew up in Lumberton, in Robeson County, graduated from college and law school at Chapel Hill, and practiced law in Lumberton, where his family has been prominent for 200 years. When he was an intern in the office of Democratic Rep. Charlie Rose, where he watched the Watergate hearings and President Nixon's resignation speech, he told his father that he would like to run for Rose's seat someday. McIntyre finally got that chance in 1995, when Rose decided to retire. McIntyre's chief opposition in the primary was Rose Marie Lowry-Townsend, a Lumbee and a liberal who had support from the National Education Association, labor unions, and national women's groups. Lowry-Townsend led McIntyre 30%-23% in the primary. In the runoff campaign, McIntyre called for smaller government, cited his close ties to the district and his involvement in community activities, and got a boost from local African-American leaders, who supported him. He won 52%-48%. In the general election, McIntyre's platform was almost as conservative as that of his Republican opponent, New Hanover County Commissioner Bill Caster, who ridiculed McIntyre's emphasis on his community ties. "While it's all well and good to coach Little League, that doesn't mean you're ready to go to Congress," Caster said. McIntyre won 53%-46%.

McIntyre joined the conservative "Blue Dog" Democrats and got seats on Armed Services and Agriculture. His voting record—conservative among Democrats, especially on cultural issues—is centrist in the House as a whole. He voted for some restrictions on abortion and a constitutional ban on same-sex marriage. But he supported racial quotas and preferences, and opposed government vouchers for private-school tuition. He opposed normal trade relations with China, and he sought to impose a higher tariff on new imports of Caribbean Basin footwear. Converse's plant west of Lumberton was once the country's largest shoe factory. He proposed additional subsistence payments and job-training assistance for workers who have lost their jobs because of the 1993 North American Free Trade Agreement. He estimated the loss at nearly 10,000 jobs in Robeson and Columbus counties.

As many of the troops based in the district headed to the Persian Gulf, McIntyre voted to authorize the use of force in Iraq in 2002, but he later criticized the Bush administration for its post-victory planning and its slowness in turning control over to the Iraqis. In March 2007, he voted for the bill to set a timetable to withdraw U.S. forces from Iraq.

McIntyre has sought to break the deadlock in the century-old battle for federal recognition of the Lumbees. In June 2007, he won House passage of his Lumbee Recognition bill, which included a ban on gambling and gave the state jurisdiction over criminal offenses and civil actions. But it died in the Senate. He did successfully guide to passage a bill to increase grants to state agencies for veterans-outreach programs. As chairman of the Agriculture subcommittee on specialty crops and rural development, McIntyre crafted a compromise on the peanuts title of the 2008 farm bill that reduced the acres eligible for federal payments and increased the loan rate for direct payments.

In this swing district, McIntyre has not faced a serious challenge. In the traditional Southern Democrat style, he has quietly built seniority and influence.

EIGHTH DISTRICT

Larry Kissell (D)

Elected 2008, 1st term; b. Jan. 31, 1951, Biscoe; home, Biscoe; Wake Forest U., B.A. 1973; Baptist; married (Tina); 2 children.

Professional Career: Union Carbide, production mgmt., 1973–74; Russell Hosiery, 1974–2001; Social studies teacher, East Montgomery HS, 2001–08

DC Office: 512 CHOB, 20515, 202-225-3715; Fax: 202-225-4036; Web site: kissell.house.gov.

State Offices: Concord, 704-786-1612; Fayetteville, 910-920-2070; Rockingham, 910-997-2070.

Committees: *Agriculture* (23rd of 28 D): Conservation, Credit, Energy & Research; General Farm Commodities & Risk Management; Rural Development, Specialty Crops, Biotechnology & Foreign Agriculture. *Armed Services* (30th of 36 D): Air & Land Forces; Readiness.

Group Ratings and Key Votes: Newly Elected

Election Results

2008 general	Larry Kissell (D)	157,185	(55%)	($1,509,753)
	Robin Hayes (R)	126,634	(45%)	($3,808,201)
2008 primary	Larry Kissell (D)	unopposed		

Population		Race/Ethnicity		Work	
Pop. 2007:	664,902	White:	57.7%	Private:	75.4%
Change since 2000:	Up 7.4%	Black:	28.0%	Government:	18.6%
Urban:	69.4%	Hispanic:	8.8%	Self-employed:	5.8%
Rural:	30.6%	Asian:	1.9%	Blue collar:	27.8%
Area size:	3,318 sq. mi.	Native Am.:	1.5%	White collar:	52.5%
		Hawaiian:	0.1%	Khaki collar:	2.0%
Age		Two+ races:	1.7%	Other:	17.7%
Median age:	34.3 yrs.			Median income:	$41,273
More than 65 yrs:	10.5%	*Ancestry*		Median home value:	$116,100
Less than 18 yrs:	26.4%	USA:	10.0%	Poverty:	16.9%
		German:	9.9%		
Education		English:	7.3%	**Military Veterans**	
H.S. grad:	81.8%			% of Pop:	12.3%
College grad:	19.4%				
Grad degree:	5.8%				

In the Carolina Piedmont, from Atlanta to Durham along Interstate 85, lies the thickest concentration of America's once-mighty textile industry. Within North Carolina, I-85 brushes past Concord and Kannapolis, the latter named for its founding company, Cannon Mills. While eastern Carolina was settled by Englishmen, the Piedmont was settled mainly by Scots and diverse groups like Quakers and Moravian sects, coming down the Blue Ridge from Pennsylvania through Virginia. These migratory patterns were reflected in Civil War divisions and continue in current voting habits. The coastal counties all the way up through the Sand Hills were Confederate and are now Democratic. The textile mill towns along the interstate were anti-secession and are now Republican.

2008 Presidential Vote
Obama (D) 151,707   (52%)
McCain (R).............................135,607   (47%)

2004 Presidential Vote
Bush (R) 126,041   (54%)
Kerry (D)................................105,248   (45%)

Cook Partisan Voting Index: R+2

Parts of both of these areas are in the 8th Congressional District. The most populous county in the district is Cabarrus County, which includes the southern end of the textile corridor around Kannapolis and Concord. In recent years, Cabarrus, fed by migration from Charlotte, has moved beyond its textile and small-town roots and become an exurban county, growing by 25% from 2000 to 2007; it was the 29th-fastest-growing county in the nation in 2007. Cabarrus casts one-fourth of the district's votes. The bankruptcy of Pillowtex (formerly Cannon Mills) in 2003 eliminated some 4,000 jobs in Cabarrus and Rowan counties. As if the region didn't have trouble enough, South Carolina sued in 2007 to try to stop North Carolina from diverting water from the Catawba River basin to Concord and Kannapolis. South Carolina views the river as a recreational resource, while the North Carolina areas rely on it to fill depleted reservoirs and for industrial uses.

The 8th District extends east to include part of Fayetteville's Cumberland County, which casts 20% of the vote, but stops short of the military neighborhoods outside Fort Bragg. Democratic redistricters included as much of the Democratic Sand Hills as they could, and removed most of Union County, a fast-growing and heavily Republican area just east of Charlotte. They added central-city precincts in Charlotte with a mix of African-Americans and white liberals. This split-personality district has usually been carried by Republican presidential candidates and by North Carolina Democrats in close statewide contests. Both parties have long targeted it as a marginal district. Barack Obama increased the local turnout by nearly 20% compared with 2004, and won here with 52%.

The new congressman from the 8th District is Larry Kissell, a Democrat who was elected in 2008 on his second try for the seat. A strong Democratic tailwind helped the social studies teacher across the finish line in his rematch with Rep. Robin Hayes, a five-term Republican. Kissell is a native of Biscoe, at the edge of the Uwharrie National Forest. His mother was a mathematics teacher, and his father was the town's postmaster for many years. After graduating from Wake Forest University, Kissell returned home to work in the local textile mills. He started at Union Carbide, and then joined Russell Hosiery in the town of Star, where he stayed for 27 years. At the time, many of the plants were closing as jobs were shipped overseas, so he switched careers to become a teacher. He says he was inspired by his mother, and also by a recognition that the exodus of factory jobs in the region put a premium on children getting an education. Kissell is a conservative Democrat who espouses smaller government and lower taxes, but says he believes that social issues like abortion rights are matters of individual choice. During the campaign, he said he supported increasing the hourly minimum wage.

He first ran against Hayes in 2006, and although he lost, he held the incumbent to less than 54% of the vote. Democratic Congressional Campaign Committee Chairman Rahm Emanuel, then a representative from Illinois, conceded that the race was a missed opportunity for the national party. Two years later, the DCCC had the contest in its sights. Kissell ran an effective grassroots campaign, using a "common man" message in a year when most "common men" were feeling anxious about the economy. His small-town upbringing and background as a former mill worker had appeal for many district voters who had not forgiven Hayes, a wealthy hosiery-mill owner, for casting a decisive vote in favor of the 2005 Central American Free Trade Agreement after vowing to vote against it because of the potential impact on textile workers. Kissell dubbed the vote Hayes' "CAFTA betrayal," and focused his speeches on job creation in the economically struggling region.

Kissell was outspent $3.8 million to $1.5 million, but he was helped by $2.4 million in DCCC spending and by Barack Obama's aggressive voter registration efforts in North Carolina. Hayes added to his own woes with a controversial remark a few days before the election at a rally for John McCain, saying that "liberals hate real Americans that work and achieve and believe in God." He later said his remarks were a mistake.

In their second contest, it wasn't close. Kissell won 55%-45%, capturing eight of the 10 counties. He took the urban-area counties of Mecklenberg, 75%-25%, and Cumberland, 59%-41%. Hayes won the two large suburban counties: 57%-43% in Cabarrus and 62%-38% in Stanly. Although Republicans promised to compete for the seat and make this a test of Democratic control of Washington in 2010, Kissell's 30,000-vote advantage will be formidable.

In the House, Kissell landed a seat on the Armed Services Committee and also on the Agriculture Committee.

Kissell's first act was to co-sign legislation turning back the pay increase Congress was slated to get this year.

NINTH DISTRICT

Sue Myrick (R)

Elected 1994, 8th term; b. Aug. 1, 1941, Tiffin, OH; home, Charlotte; Heidelberg Col., 1959–60; Methodist; married (Ed); 5 children.

Elected Office: Charlotte City Cncl., 1983–85; Charlotte mayor, 1987–91.

Professional Career: Pres. & CEO, Myrick Advertising, 1985–94; Pres. & CEO, Myrick Enterprises, 1992–94.

DC Office: 230 CHOB, 20515, 202-225-1976; Fax: 202-225-3389; Web site: myrick.house.gov.

State Offices: Charlotte, 704-362-1060; Gastonia, 704-861-1976.

Committees: *Energy & Commerce* (17th of 23 R): Commerce, Trade & Consumer Protections; Health. *Intelligence (Select)* (5th of 9 R): Intelligence Community Management (RMM); Terrorism, Human Intelligence, Analysis & Counterintelligence.

Group Ratings

	ADA	ACLU	AFS	LCV	ITIC	NTU	COC	ACU	CFG	FRC
2008	10	18	14	0	57	72	94	91	76	100
2007	10	—	0	10	—	88	74	96	90	—

National Journal Ratings

	2007 LIB — 2007 CONS		2008 LIB — 2008 CONS	
Economic	13%	— 86%	14%	— 85%
Social	15%	— 84%	9%	— 85%
Foreign	0%	— 72%	17%	— 83%
Composite	14%	— 86%	15%	— 86%

Key Votes of the 110th Congress

1. Increase minimum wage	N	5. Share immigration data	Y	9. Withdraw troops 8/08	N
2. Expand SCHIP	N	6. Foreign aid abortion ban	Y	10. No operations in Iran	N
3. Raise CAFE standards	N	7. Ban gay bias in workplace	N	11. Free trade with Peru	Y
4. Bail out financial markets	Y	8. Repeal D.C. gun law	Y	12. Overhaul FISA	Y

Election Results

2008 general	Sue Myrick (R)	241,053	(62%)	($1,164,506)
	Harry Taylor (D)	138,719	(36%)	($252,020)
2008 primary	Sue Myrick (R)	51,402	(92%)	
	Jack Stratton (R)	4,370	(8%)	

Prior Winning Percentages: 2006 (67%); 2004 (70%); 2002 (72%); 2000 (69%); 1998 (69%); 1996 (63%); 1994 (65%)

Population		Race/Ethnicity		Work	
Pop. 2007:	777,420	White:	76.5%	Private:	85.7%
Change since 2000:	Up 25.6%	Black:	13.1%	Government:	8.4%
Urban:	84.2%	Hispanic:	6.3%	Self-employed:	5.8%
Rural:	15.8%	Asian:	2.5%	Blue collar:	18.5%
Area size:	1,018 sq. mi.	Native Am.:	0.3%	White collar:	69.7%
		Hawaiian:	0.1%	Khaki collar:	0.0%
Age		Two+ races:	1.0%	Other:	11.8%
Median age:	36.6 yrs.	*Ancestry*		Median income:	$61,071
More than 65 yrs:	9.5%	German:	12.5%	Median home value:	$182,500
Less than 18 yrs:	26.4%	Irish:	10.1%	Poverty:	7.5%
		English:	9.9%		
Education				**Military Veterans**	
H.S. grad:	89.0%			% of Pop:	10.3%
College grad:	39.0%				
Grad degree:	11.7%				

"An agreeable village but in a damn rebellious country," recorded Gen. Cornwallis when, before the unpleasantness at Yorktown, he visited Charlotte, North Carolina. Settled by Scots-Irish and German colonists who came down from Pennsylvania along the Blue Ridge Mountains, Charlotte is a rapidly growing metropolitan area of some 1.7 million people. Before the California gold rush, Charlotte was the gold-mining capital of the country; in 1837, the U.S. Mint established a branch here. And the city

2008 Presidential Vote
McCain (R)............................215,045   (55%)
Obama (D) 174,265   (44%)

2004 Presidential Vote
Bush (R)................................193,419   (63%)
Kerry (D)................................110,769   (36%)

Cook Partisan Voting Index: R + 11

has continued its preoccupation with the financial sector. It is headquarters to one of the nation's biggest banks: Bank of America, formed from the 1998 merger of Charlotte-based NationsBank and San Francisco's Bank of America. But it was not immune to the tumult in the financial markets in late 2008. The Charlotte-based Wachovia, which was the area's second-largest employer, was taken over in early 2009 by San Francisco-based Wells Fargo, a move that likely saved Wachovia from failure. Still, for a city its size, Charlotte has a respectable share of *Fortune* 500 companies. Nine are headquartered in the Charlotte area, including Lowe's, Family Dollar Store, Duke Energy, Sonic Automotive, and B.F. Goodrich. It is also the center of the nation's biggest textile manufacturing region. Charlotte's metro area is projected to equal Atlanta's by 2030. The city was rated America's best place to live by the *RelocateAmerica.com* website in 2008. The downside of its rapid growth is that the city has the worst sprawl of 15 fast-growing metro areas. In November 2007, a 9.6-mile light-rail system began operations and exceeded ridership expectations, with plans for expansion.

The past two decades have brought cultural development to Charlotte worthy of its increasing business stature. It now boasts a $50 million performing arts center across from the 60-story Bank of America tower, and is home to the Carolina Panthers professional football team and the Charlotte Bobcats basketball franchise owned by Black Entertainment Television founder Robert Johnson. The rebelliousness Cornwallis noted can be seen in this region's passion for the stock-car circuit. One of the nation's biggest auto-racing tracks is here, and just up the road is Mooresville, home of the late Dale Earnhardt and the family's racing business. In 2010, the NASCAR Hall of Fame is scheduled to open in Charlotte. The city has built a boosterish pride in its capacity for accommodation. It is proud that it responded amicably to a busing order approved in a landmark Supreme Court case in 1971; that it twice elected an African-American Democrat as mayor, Harvey Gantt, and then replaced him with conservative Republican Sue Myrick, who now represents the city's district in Congress. (Charlotte can't seem to produce a political star, however. Five mayors have run statewide since 1984, and all have lost—most recently, Pat McCrory in the 2008 race for governor. In the 1990s, Gantt lost two challenges to the late Sen. Jesse Helms, a conservative Republican.)

The 9th Congressional District of North Carolina includes about half of Mecklenburg County. It extends west to include most of Gaston County, long a textile center, and south to take in upscale bedroom communities in Union County, the seventh-fastest-growing county in the nation. Mecklenburg County as a whole is politically competitive, with Barack Obama winning it 62%-38%, but the 9th District overall is Republican. President Bush won here with 63% in 2004, but John McCain dropped to 55% in 2008.

The congresswoman from the 9th District is Sue Myrick, a Republican first elected in 1994. She was born on a peach farm in Ohio and graduated from college there. She owned an advertising agency and Amway distributorship in Charlotte, where she also raised her family. In 1983, she was elected to the Charlotte City Council. She ran for mayor and lost in 1985, then beat Harvey Gantt in 1987. In her tenure, Myrick made infrastructure improvements in the city and prevented increases in property taxes. She ran for the U.S. Senate in 1992, but was beaten by Republican Lauch Faircloth in the primary 48%-30%. In 1994, after Rep. Alex McMillan retired, she ran for his House seat. In the first round of the primary, against state House Minority Leader David Balmer, Myrick led 34%-28%. Before the runoff three weeks later, it was revealed that he had falsely claimed on his résumé to have graduated in the top 20% of his law school class and to have played varsity soccer. Myrick won 68%-32%, then easily won the general election. A leader of the brash 1994 Republican freshman class, Myrick served on House Speaker Newt Gingrich's transition team and was the freshman liaison to the leadership. Then in 1997, she joined a group of junior members who had grown disillusioned with Gingrich and wanted to force him to step down as speaker. The plan failed, and with Gingrich still in power, Myrick's influence waned. That year, she lost by 110-65 the leadership post of Republican Conference secretary to Deborah Pryce of Ohio, whom Gingrich backed.

A reliable conservative, Myrick has taken a lead role on many Republican initiatives. Representing a prosperous and growing district, she once turned down $15 million for Charlotte's freeways because she felt the transportation bill would bust the budget: "I said when I ran for this job, 'If you want somebody to bring home the bacon, don't send me,' " she said. In 2003, she was chairman of the Republican Study Committee, a group of activist conservatives who have urged spending restraint and tax cuts. A vocal opponent of illegal immigration, she won House approval in 2005 of a measure to deport illegal immigrants convicted of drunken driving, and more recently advocated slashing federal aid to colleges that knowingly admit illegal immigrants.

Myrick had surgery and follow-up treatment for breast cancer in 1999, and was later declared cancer-free. But the disease changed her focus. After that, she sponsored the law to provide Medicaid coverage for mammograms and pap smears for low-income women. She also co-sponsored with New York Democrat Nita Lowey a bill to require the National Institutes of Health to explore the connection between environmental pollutants and cancer. On the Energy and Commerce Committee, she has focused on health care, including mental health. On energy issues on the committee, Myrick in 2008 sponsored a bill to give the states authority to permit oil drilling in the ocean within 100 miles of their coasts. Also outspoken on antiterrorism issues, Myrick in April 2008 demanded the revocation of former President Carter's passport after he met with Hamas, which the U.S. government considers a terrorist group.

Myrick has considered but declined to run for the Senate in recent years, and she also turned down a chance to run for governor in 2008. She has won re-election easily.

TENTH DISTRICT

Patrick McHenry (R)

Elected 2004, 3rd term; b. Oct. 22, 1975, Charlotte; home, Cherryville; Attended NC St. U., Belmont Abbey Col., B.A. 1999; Catholic; single.

Elected Office: NC House of Reps., 2002–04.

Professional Career: Real estate broker, 2000–02.

DC Office: 224 CHOB, 20515, 202-225-2576; Fax: 202-225-0316; Web site: mchenry.house.gov.

State Offices: Hickory, 828-327-6100; Shelby, 704-481-0578; Spruce Pine, 828-765-2729.

Committees: *Budget* (6th of 15 R). *Financial Services* (18th of 29 R): Financial Institutions & Consumer Credit; Oversight & Investigations. *Oversight & Government Reform* (10th of 15 R): Information Policy, Census & National Archives (RMM); National Security & Foreign Affairs.

Group Ratings

	ADA	ACLU	AFS	LCV	ITIC	NTU	COC	ACU	CFG	FRC
2008	10	18	14	0	29	83	78	100	94	100
2007	0	—	0	0	—	87	75	100	89	—

National Journal Ratings

	2007 LIB	—	2007 CONS	2008 LIB	—	2008 CONS
Economic	12%	—	87%	12%	—	87%
Social	0%	—	91%	0%	—	91%
Foreign	0%	—	72%	8%	—	89%
Composite	10%	—	90%	9%	—	91%

Key Votes of the 110th Congress

1. Increase minimum wage	N	5. Share immigration data	Y	9. Withdraw troops 8/08	N
2. Expand SCHIP	N	6. Foreign aid abortion ban	Y	10. No operations in Iran	N
3. Raise CAFE standards	N	7. Ban gay bias in workplace	N	11. Free trade with Peru	Y
4. Bail out financial markets	N	8. Repeal D.C. gun law	Y	12. Overhaul FISA	Y

Election Results

2008 general	Patrick McHenry (R)..	171,774	(58%)	($1,587,880)
	Daniel Johnson (D)	126,699	(42%)	($684,167)
2008 primary	Patrick McHenry (R)..	34,457	(67%)	
	Lance Sigmon (R)...	16,892	(33%)	

Prior Winning Percentages: 2006 (62%); 2004 (64%)

Population		Race/Ethnicity		Work	
Pop. 2007:	659,941	White:	83.2%	Private:	80.9%
Change since 2000:	Up 6.6%	Black:	8.9%	Government:	13.0%
Urban:	49.9%	Hispanic:	5.0%	Self-employed:	5.9%
Rural:	50.1%	Asian:	1.5%	Blue collar:	33.9%
Area size:	3,362 sq. mi.	Native Am.:	0.2%	White collar:	50.5%
		Hawaiian:	0.0%	Khaki collar:	0.0%
Age		Two+ races:	1.0%	Other:	15.6%
Median age:	38.9 yrs.			Median income:	$40,855
More than 65 yrs:	13.9%	*Ancestry*		Median home value:	$115,900
Less than 18 yrs:	23.5%	German:	14.5%	Poverty:	13.9%
Education		USA:	13.8%		
H.S. grad:	77.7%	Irish:	9.5%	**Military Veterans**	
College grad:	17.1%			% of Pop:	10.9%
Grad degree:	5.1%				

Steeped in the hues that gave them the name Blue Ridge, the heavily wooded mountains of North Carolina seem placid and ancient. Geologically, they are some of the oldest ranges in the world. Economically, the region is blue-collar and oriented toward manufacturing, though there is some cotton farming, too. During the 1990s, residents here benefited from investment in fiber-optic factories, which, along with the general economic boom, helped reduce the local unemployment rate to near-record

2008 Presidential Vote

McCain (R)............................	192,076	(63%)
Obama (D)	108,546	(36%)

2004 Presidential Vote

Bush (R)................................	169,484	(67%)
Kerry (D)...............................	82,965	(33%)

Cook Partisan Voting Index: R + 17

lows. But the Internet bust hurt the fiber-optic business. Textiles and furniture were also troubled, and the local unemployment rate rose. At the same time, this corner of North Carolina is adapting—as are so many other rural areas in the U.S.—to growing diversity. County seats like Morganton in Burke County are now home not just to Hispanics but to newcomers from Laos; the influx of recent arrivals has prompted some anti-immigrant backlash in this previously insular region, including the occasional rejection of school bond proposals on the grounds that they could help immigrants disproportionately. The Catawba Valley is home to the Hosiery Technology Center and produces about one-third of the nation's hosiery. It remains a furniture center, but it has suffered major job losses due to international competition and is at risk of more competitive threats from Central America and China. The one bright spot in the local economy was Google. The Internet search engine company in 2007 broke ground in Lenoir on a $600 million data center after the city and county offered it millions of dollars in tax rebates to locate a so-called server farm there.

The 10th Congressional District of North Carolina stretches across the state from Tennessee, where the mountains are high enough to support a modest ski industry, to the South Carolina border. It is composed mostly of small towns, and is still predominantly white. It ranks first among 435 congressional districts in the percentage of manufacturing and blue-collar jobs. The largest population center in the 10th is Hickory in Catawba County, which accounts for just over 20% of the district's population. This remains a very Republican area—home to a rough-hewn, hill variety of Republicanism that is unsympathetic to government regulators, from factory inspectors to revenuers on the lookout for illegal stills. Despite job losses and worries about international competition that increasingly have made this a service economy, it remains one of North Carolina's most Republican districts. George W. Bush got 67% here in 2004, and John McCain 63% in 2008.

The congressman from the 10th District is Patrick McHenry, a Republican elected at age 29 in 2004. He grew up in Cherryville, and graduated from Belmont Abbey College, where he was president of the state College Republicans. After school, he was a real estate broker. As a young staunch conservative, he cut his political teeth on his hatred of the Clintons. He once dressed up in an Abraham Lincoln costume at a North Carolina appearance by President Clinton after Clinton was accused by Republicans of rewarding big contributors with overnight stays in the Lincoln bedroom in the White House. In 2000, he ran a website, *notHillary.com*, opposing Hillary Rodham Clinton's Senate candidacy in New York. McHenry worked on several Republican campaigns in North Carolina, including Rep. Robin Hayes' unsuccessful run for governor in 1996. At the start of the Bush administration, he was appointed to a job in the Labor Department. And in 2002, he was elected to the state House.

He was in the state Legislature for less than two years when GOP Rep. Cass Ballenger retired, leaving an open seat in Congress. In the Republican primary, his chief competition was Catawba County Sheriff David Huffman, and both men made conservative "Christian values" their main issue. Huffman finished first with 35% but was forced into a runoff with McHenry, who got 26%. In the four weeks to the runoff, the campaign took a negative turn. Huffman questioned McHenry's record as a businessman and accused him of having all-night parties at his house, which also served as a residence for his campaign staff. McHenry's neighbors insisted Huffman's claim was untrue. McHenry accused Huffman of campaign finance irregularities. McHenry ran an energetic, door-to-door grassroots campaign, billing himself as a "pro-life, pro-gun, anti-gay-marriage" Christian conservative. He won the runoff by just 85 votes, after a recount. Huffman carried Catawba County 59%-41%. But McHenry rolled up huge majorities in the counties south of Interstate 40 and close to his Gaston County home. He easily won the general election against Democrat Anne Fischer, who called herself a part-time stress release facilitator.

In the House, McHenry was an atypical newcomer. Rather than keeping a low profile and doing constituent work to sew up his seat as most freshmen do, he became a noisy partisan and party pit bull. He courted the limelight, making repeat appearances on talk shows for his ability to serve up red meat and good quotes. He cited as his role model the late Sen. Jesse Helms, the legendary North Carolina conservative who employed race-baiting in his campaigns as recently as the mid-90s. On the House floor, he took on Democrats, no matter how powerful or how senior, picking verbal fights with liberal Democratic Rep. Barney Frank of Massachusetts, known for his debating prowess. In 2007, McHenry accused Speaker Nancy Pelosi of California of abusing her office by using military jets to fly home to San Francisco during congressional recesses (although former Republican Speaker Dennis Hastert of Illinois did the same thing).

Although he rarely breaks with his party, McHenry in 2005 voted against President Bush on the Central American Free Trade Agreement because of its potential impact on jobs in this district. He also opposed the president on giving illegal immigrants a path to citizenship, which McHenry called "amnesty with makeup." On the Financial Services Committee, he won enactment of his bill allowing financial institutions involved in multiple transactions to combine them into one contract, something helpful to the banking industry in nearby Charlotte. On other issues, he won passage of his amendment to limit foreign aid to nations that refuse to extradite suspects accused of killing U.S. law enforcement officers. In the 111th Congress (2009–10), he is the ranking Republican on the Oversight and Government Reform Subcommittee on Information Policy, Census, and National Archives, where he was poised to go toe-to-toe with the Obama administration over the 2010 census. McHenry objects to Obama's plan to have the Census Bureau report directly to the White House as it oversees the politically sensitive task of tallying the population numbers that will directly affect the next congressional reapportionment.

But it's his shoot-from-the-hip remarks that get McHenry the most attention. At a private meeting in January 2008, he asked aloud why Republicans "shouldn't be physically ill at the prospects of a President McCain." The Pentagon took McHenry to task the same year after he apparently violated military security rules by posting on his website video footage of a Green Zone rocket attack that he witnessed in Baghdad. He subsequently removed the video. After McHenry repeatedly took to the floor to criticize special spending provisions called earmarks added to bills by other lawmakers, the House in 2007 took the rare step of voting down an individual earmark—$129,000 that McHenry had slipped into a bill to expand a Christmas crafts store in Mitchell County. The vote was a resounding 249-174.

In 2006, McHenry was re-elected easily. In 2008, former Air Force attorney Lance Sigmon challenged him in the primary, saying his Iraq video put American lives at risk. McHenry won 67%-33%. But in November, his 58%-42% victory over well-funded former prosecutor Daniel Johnson, a Democrat who lost both legs during training in the Navy, was his closest House election.

ELEVENTH DISTRICT

Heath Shuler (D)

Elected 2006, 2nd term; b. Dec. 31, 1971, Bryson City; home, Waynesville; U of TN, B.A. 2001; Baptist; married (Nikol); 2 children.

Professional Career: Pro football player, 1994–98; Owner, Heath Shuler Real Estate, 1998–2003; Property development investor.

DC Office: 422 CHOB, 20515, 202-225-6401; Fax: 202-226-6422; Web site: shuler.house.gov.

State Offices: Asheville, 828-252-1651; Murphy, 828-835-4981; Sylva, 828-586-1962.

Committees: *Small Business* (3rd of 17 D): Investigations & Oversight; Rural Development, Entrepreneurship & Trade (Chmn). *Transportation & Infrastructure* (25th of 44 D): Economic Development, Public Buildings & Emergency Management; Highways & Transit.

Group Ratings

	ADA	ACLU	AFS	LCV	ITIC	NTU	COC	ACU	CFG	FRC
2008	75	45	86	69	43	26	56	24	22	100
2007	80	—	82	75	—	15	55	44	2	—

National Journal Ratings

	2007 LIB	—	2007 CONS	2008 LIB	—	2008 CONS
Economic	55%	—	45%	50%	—	50%
Social	44%	—	56%	48%	—	52%
Foreign	50%	—	50%	55%	—	43%
Composite	50%	—	50%	51%	—	49%

Key Votes of the 110th Congress

1. Increase minimum wage	Y	5. Share immigration data	Y	9. Withdraw troops 8/08	Y
2. Expand SCHIP	Y	6. Foreign aid abortion ban	Y	10. No operations in Iran	N
3. Raise CAFE standards	Y	7. Ban gay bias in workplace	N	11. Free trade with Peru	N
4. Bail out financial markets	N	8. Repeal D.C. gun law	Y	12. Overhaul FISA	Y

Election Results

2008 general	Heath Shuler (D)	211,112	(62%)	($769,941)
	Carl Mumpower (R)	122,087	(36%)	($134,199)
	Keith Smith (Lib)	7,517	(2%)	
2008 primary	Heath Shuler (D)	unopposed		

Prior Winning Percentages: 2006 (54%)

Population
Pop. 2007:	662,289
Change since 2000:	Up 7.0%
Urban:	43.9%
Rural:	56.1%
Area size:	6,088 sq. mi.

Age
Median age:	41.7 yrs.
More than 65 yrs:	18.0%
Less than 18 yrs:	20.9%

Education
H.S. grad:	83.1%
College grad:	23.8%
Grad degree:	8.7%

Race/Ethnicity
White:	87.7%
Black:	4.8%
Hispanic:	4.1%
Asian:	0.7%
Native Am.:	1.5%
Hawaiian:	0.0%
Two+ races:	1.1%

Ancestry
USA:	12.9%
German:	11.9%
English:	11.2%

Work
Private:	75.7%
Government:	14.6%
Self-employed:	9.5%
Blue collar:	27.2%
White collar:	53.1%
Khaki collar:	0.0%
Other:	19.6%
Median income:	$39,488
Median home value:	$152,400
Poverty:	14.5%

Military Veterans
% of Pop:	12.7%

Western North Carolina, the protrusion of the Tar Heel State deep into the eastern United States' highest and oldest mountains, is a land of long and ornery traditions. First settled not long after the Revolutionary War, it still has Indian communities and hollows where people are descended from the first white settlers. Its biggest city, Asheville, memorialized in Thomas Wolfe's novels, was a retreat for lung patients. Asheville was also the home of the brilliant eccentric George Vanderbilt, who built the 255-room Biltmore mansion amid a vast forest where he pioneered scientific forestry. A dozen miles east is Black Mountain College, frequented by such innovators as Buckminster Fuller and minimalist composer John Cage. Asheville's historic structures, from Gothic Revival to Art Deco, remain well preserved and are a magnet for gay couples and tourists, who in turn support a handful of coffeehouses, microbreweries, and artsy cinemas. The city's minor league baseball team is called the Tourists. Not far to the west is the Eastern Band of Cherokee's casino, which has given the tribe a yearly budget of $130 million and considerable political influence. Over a ridge is the Great Smoky Mountains National Park, the nation's most heavily visited. Its forested, fog-wisped mountains are 20 degrees cooler in the summer than the lowland towns an hour or so away. The Fraser fir trees grown on farms in the mountains are America's favorite Christmas tree.

The 11th District of North Carolina includes the western end of the state, including Asheville's Buncombe County, which accounts for one-third of the votes. The orneriness of the mountain country has been manifest in its politics. This part of the state was reluctant to secede in the Civil War. There were few slaves and many small farmers loyal to the Union, and those who took up the Confederate cause did so out of loyalty to Gov. Zebulon Vance, an Asheville native and reluctant secessionist. In modern times,

2008 Presidential Vote
McCain (R)	178,875	(52%)
Obama (D)	159,839	(47%)

2004 Presidential Vote
Bush (R)	169,872	(57%)
Kerry (D)	126,979	(43%)

Cook Partisan Voting Index: R+6

the 11th has been one of the nation's most closely contested districts, throwing out incumbents in five of six elections between 1980 and 1990. Coinciding with an influx of retirees in the mountains south of Asheville, it has tilted Republican in the past few presidential elections, including 2008, when John McCain won it by 52%-46.5%. However, Barack Obama won Buncombe County, where liberal-leaning Asheville is located, 56%-42%.

The congressman from the 11th District is Heath Shuler, a Democrat elected in 2006. The son of a mailman, Shuler grew up on Toot Hollow Road in tiny Bryson City, closer to the Tennessee line than to Asheville. He led Swain County High School to three state football championships and starred as quarterback at the University of Tennessee, where he was the 1993 runner-up for the Heisman Trophy. The Washington Redskins picked Shuler, then a college junior, third in the 1994 draft and first among quarterbacks. He played three disappointing seasons before being traded to the New Orleans Saints, where he injured his left foot when a 334-pound defensive tackle fell on him. He attempted a comeback, but was reinjured while playing for the Oakland Raiders. Despite the disappointments in his pro football career, Shuler remained a hero in Swain County and western North Carolina. He founded a successful real estate business in Knoxville, Tenn., with his brother and returned to North Carolina with his family in 2003. Shuler still cuts the figure of a professional athlete, wears his NFL alumni ring, and as in his playing days, does not smoke or drink alcohol or soda. Republicans in 2002 tried to get Shuler to run for public office, but he declined. Democrats aggressively recruited him in 2006 to run for Congress. Then-Rep. Rahm Emanuel, D-Ill., who led the Democratic Congressional Campaign Committee, allayed Shuler's fears about missing time with his children by calling Shuler on his cell phone each time he dropped his own children off at school or attended their events.

Shuler challenged eight-term incumbent Charles Taylor, a Republican who had faced competitive races the past three elections. Taylor was weakened by his business dealings after two associates at a bank Taylor controlled pleaded guilty to bank-fraud charges. He was vulnerable on other fronts. Though he later blamed a glitch in the House electronic voting machine, Taylor did not show a recorded vote for the 2005 Central American Free Trade Agreement, which passed only narrowly. This was no small matter in the district, where trade pacts are blamed for the loss of textile jobs. Taylor sought to tie Shuler to national Democrats. "Rookie Heath Shuler is following the playbook of San Francisco liberal Nancy Pelosi," claimed one radio ad. Shuler was not an easy target. He had no legislative record to mine for controversial votes, and his politics were in line with the socially conservative district. He campaigned on "mountain values," opposing abortion rights, gay marriage, and gun control. Taylor, who was an Appropriations subcommittee "cardinal," campaigned on his ability to bring home federal money. Then, in October, with polls showing Taylor trailing, *The Wall Street Journal* ran a story about spending earmarks sought by Taylor that had the effect of benefiting many of his own business interests. The incumbent poured $2.5 million of his own money into his race, and spent $4.4 million overall, compared with Shuler's $1.8 million. But Shuler won 54%-46%, an impressive showing for a novice candidate against an incumbent.

In the House, Shuler joined the "Blue Dog" coalition of conservative Democrats, where he was outspoken for "pay-as-you-go" budgeting. He voted for the Democrats' initial "100-hour" legislative agenda, except for lifting the ban on federal funding for embryonic-stem cell research. He dove into the immigration debate with a bill that emphasized toughening controls at the borders and requiring employers to use an Internet-based verification system to weed out illegal workers. Republicans supported Shuler's bill, but it was extremely unpopular in his own party. The Hispanic Caucus condemned it, and Democratic leaders ignored his pleas to bring it to a vote. He had more success with small-business legislation. Although he was just a freshman, Shuler got the chairmanship of the Small Business Subcommittee on Rural and Urban Entrepreneurship, where he was able to pass a bill increasing the number of federal contracts awarded to small businesses. Congress also enacted his bill to increase investment in small producers of biofuels and other new, clean energy sources. But Shuler also attracted some negative publicity in his first term when *The Knoxville News-Sentinel* published a story in August 2008 saying that the Tennessee Valley Authority had approved lake access for a development group whose investors included Shuler, who also sits on the committee that oversees the TVA.

Expectations that he would face strong Republican opposition in 2008 evaporated. Taylor waited a long time before eventually deciding not to seek a rematch, and other potentially strong candidates took a pass as well. The Republican nominee, Asheville City Councilor Carl Mumpower, was poorly funded, got little national party support, and temporarily suspended his campaign. Shuler won easily, 62%-36%, taking all 15 counties.

TWELFTH DISTRICT

Melvin Watt (D)

Elected 1992, 9th term; b. Aug. 26, 1945, Mecklenburg; home, Charlotte; U. of NC, B.S. 1967, Yale U., J.D. 1970; Presbyterian; married (Eulada); 2 children.

Elected Office: NC Senate, 1984–86.

Professional Career: Practicing atty., 1971–92; Co–owner, East Town Manor nursing home, 1989–2008; Campaign mgr., Harvey Gantt Senate Campaign, 1990.

DC Office: 2304 RHOB, 20515, 202-225-1510; Fax: 202-225-1512; Web site: watt.house.gov.

State Offices: Charlotte, 704-344-9950; Greensboro, 336-275-9950.

Committees: *Financial Services* (7th of 42 D): Domestic Monetary Policy & Technology (Chmn); Financial Institutions & Consumer Credit; International Monetary Policy & Trade. *Judiciary* (6th of 24 D): Commercial & Administrative Law; Constitution, Civil Rights & Civil Liberties; Courts & Competition Policy.

Group Ratings

	ADA	ACLU	AFS	LCV	ITIC	NTU	COC	ACU	CFG	FRC
2008	100	100	100	92	100	5	61	0	0	5
2007	90	—	100	95	—	4	55	0	12	—

National Journal Ratings

	2007 LIB	—	2007 CONS		2008 LIB	—	2008 CONS
Economic	82%	—	0%		85%	—	0%
Social	92%	—	0%		67%	—	28%
Foreign	93%	—	7%		85%	—	8%
Composite	93%	—	7%		84%	—	17%

Key Votes of the 110th Congress

1. Increase minimum wage	Y	5. Share immigration data	N	9. Withdraw troops 8/08	*
2. Expand SCHIP	Y	6. Foreign aid abortion ban	N	10. No operations in Iran	Y
3. Raise CAFE standards	Y	7. Ban gay bias in workplace	Y	11. Free trade with Peru	Y
4. Bail out financial markets	Y	8. Repeal D.C. gun law	N	12. Overhaul FISA	N

Election Results

2008 general	Melvin Watt (D)	215,908	(72%)	($646,075)
	Ty Cobb (R)	85,814	(28%)	($25,584)
2008 primary	Melvin Watt (D)	unopposed		

Prior Winning Percentages: 2006 (67%); 2004 (67%); 2002 (65%); 2000 (65%); 1998 (56%); 1996 (71%); 1994 (66%); 1992 (70%)

Population		Race/Ethnicity		Work	
Pop. 2007:	662,095	White:	41.3%	Private:	83.9%
Change since 2000:	Up 6.9%	Black:	43.5%	Government:	11.5%
Urban:	88.5%	Hispanic:	10.6%	Self-employed:	4.5%
Rural:	11.5%	Asian:	2.7%	Blue collar:	28.1%
Area size:	827 sq. mi.	Native Am.:	0.4%	White collar:	53.0%
		Hawaiian:	0.0%	Khaki collar:	0.1%
Age		Two+ races:	1.3%	Other:	18.9%
Median age:	34.2 yrs.			Median income:	$37,833
More than 65 yrs:	10.6%	*Ancestry*		Median home value:	$121,300
Less than 18 yrs:	26.0%	German:	8.1%	Poverty:	20.2%
		USA:	6.4%		
Education		English:	5.5%	**Military Veterans**	
H.S. grad:	79.0%			% of Pop:	9.6%
College grad:	21.7%				
Grad degree:	6.6%				

"This is perhaps the Negro's temporary farewell to Congress," said George White, a Tarboro, N.C., lawyer and Republican, in his last days in the House of Representatives in 1901. Segregation was being imposed by law, and blacks informally but effectively were being driven from the voting rolls in the rural South. It was 28 years until another black candidate was elected to Congress (from Chicago), and 72 years until another African-American won in the South (in Atlanta). When White said his farewell,

2008 Presidential Vote
Obama (D) 220,586   (71%)
McCain (R)..............................88,958   (29%)

2004 Presidential Vote
Kerry (D)...............................149,940   (63%)
Bush (R) 88,955   (37%)

Cook Partisan Voting Index: D + 16

most North Carolina blacks lived on farms or in tiny towns. Through the 20th century, few moved to the textile towns, where most mills hired only whites, but some African-Americans did move to North Carolina's larger cities. In the years after the Voting Rights Act of 1965, they were numerous enough to elect members to the state Legislature. And some black candidates were successful with white-majority constituencies, notably Charlotte Mayor Harvey Gantt. But North Carolina blacks were not concentrated in high enough numbers either in the rural areas or in the cities to become the majority of any congressional district, at least not one drawn compactly. No African-American from North Carolina followed White to Congress until the Democratic Legislature, after the 1990 census, drew two irregularly shaped black-majority districts. That resulted in the election in 1992 of Eva Clayton in the mostly rural and small-town 1st District, and the election of Melvin Watt in the 12th District.

This 12th Congressional District of North Carolina was the most litigated district in the country during the 1990s, and was the focus of no fewer than four cases that went to the U.S. Supreme Court. It originally was made up of a series of scattered black precincts connected in some places by nothing wider than the lanes of Interstate 85, and it stretched 160 miles from Gastonia all the way to Durham. In the current version, drawn in 2001, the 12th remains a 100-mile-long, snake-like agglomeration that roughly parallels I-85 and includes African-American voters in Charlotte, Winston-Salem, Greensboro, Lexington, Salisbury, and High Point, the international furniture center. A near-majority, 44%, of its residents are black. The Charlotte-area precincts account for a bit more than one-third of the district population, the Greensboro area is slightly more than 20%, and the Winston-Salem portion accounts for a little under 20%. In recent years, Hispanics have increased to 11%. This is North Carolina's most urban district and includes the major banking center in downtown Charlotte. Politically, it is reliably though not overwhelmingly Democratic.

The congressman from the 12th District is Melvin Watt, a Democrat first elected in 1992. Watt grew up in a place called Dixie outside Charlotte, in a tin-roofed house with no electricity or running water. His dream was to attend the University of North Carolina, and he was one of the first black students to go there. He had a superb academic record and went on to Yale Law School. He set up a civil rights law practice in Charlotte. He served one term in the state Senate, then decided not to seek office again until his sons completed high school. He managed Harvey Gantt's campaigns for City Council and mayor in the 1980s and for the U.S. Senate in 1990. In 1992, Watt decided to run for the 12th District seat. The contest turned out to be the kind of friends-and-neighbors Democratic primary common in the South. Watt won 47% in a four-way race. His base in Charlotte was bigger than those of his rivals, and he made inroads in other counties as well. He won the general election easily.

In the House, Watt has compiled a voting record among the most liberal of Southern Democrats, and he's not afraid to go his own way. He voted against crime bills because of death-penalty provisions, against the popular notion of increased prison sentences for crimes against children because he said they would interfere with the U.S. Sentencing Commission's autonomy, and against the constitutional amendment to prohibit flag desecration. He vehemently opposed the 1996 Welfare Reform Act, which President Clinton forged with the Republican Congress. And he cast the only vote in the House against Megan's Law requiring registration of convicted sex offenders because, he said, individuals ought to be able to get on with their lives once they have paid their debt to society.

In the 109th Congress (2005–06), Watt was chairman of the Congressional Black Caucus. He showed his independence by voting against a formal challenge by several Black Caucus members to the November 2004 presidential vote count in Ohio. He led the CBC members to try to open up a legislative dialogue with Bush, who then included what appeared to be a couple of the CBC's proposals in his State of the Union address. But other than on the broadly backed 25-year extension of the Voting Rights Act, the two sides reached little common ground. His chairmanship was marked by frequent clashes with House Speaker Nancy Pelosi, notably his vigorous objection to her decision to remove Rep. William Jefferson from the Ways and Means Committee after the Louisiana Democrat was caught up in a federal bribery investigation. Watt criticized the "political expediency" of taking on a Black Caucus member when Pelosi did not take comparable action against ethically tainted white Democrats. Watt also was a sounding board for Illinois Sen. Barack Obama in his early stages of considering whether to run for the Democratic nomination for president. Watt initially doubted that the nation would elect a black president, and he backed former North Carolina Sen. John Edwards. He later endorsed Obama prior to the North Carolina primary.

As chairman of the Oversight and Investigations Subcommittee on Financial Services, he faced a challenge balancing consumer concerns with those of his banker constituents, who have been major contributors to his campaigns. The committee approved his bill to require bank regulators to file annual reports on their efforts to promote minority-owned banks. With Rep. Luis Gutierrez, D-Ill., he sponsored a bill to prohibit insurance companies from using credit scores to set rates for auto policies if the Federal Trade Commission found that racial discrimination resulted. In 2007, he worked behind the scenes with committee Chairman Barney Frank, D-Mass., on legislation to overhaul the housing finance market, including requiring lenders to establish that borrowers have a reasonable chance to repay loans. But moderate Democrats opposed Watt's plan to give $40 million in legal aid to borrowers facing foreclosure. Watt also co-sponsored a bill to protect consumers from predatory mortgages.

Watt was a vocal critic of the Bush administration's policies in Iraq, once accusing the president of lying about the justification to go to war. In July 2007, Watt apologized for the remark, which was made on the House floor, after Republicans threatened to have him reprimanded for violation of House rules requiring respectful debate. The following year, Watt teamed with Republican Rep. Howard Coble of North Carolina to sponsor a timetable for the withdrawal of U.S. troops from Iraq.

Watt, whose great-great-grandmother was a Cherokee, threatened to deny housing assistance to the Cherokee Nation after the tribe voted in March 2007 to rescind the tribal citizenship of African-American slaves.

Despite the many twists and turns in the 12th District since he was first elected, Watt has shown the ability to endear himself to voters regardless of their race. His toughest re-election contest came in 1998, when the black share of the district's population had shrunk to 36% and Republicans put up a candidate who attacked him as an "extreme liberal." Watt won 56%-42%, with support from the district's many white liberals. He has not been seriously challenged since. Watt hates fundraising, but he has not needed to do much of it in recent elections.

THIRTEENTH DISTRICT

Brad Miller (D)

Elected 2002, 4th term; b. May 19, 1953, Fayetteville; home, Raleigh; U. of NC, B.A. 1975, London Schl. of Economics, M.S.C. 1978, Columbia U., J.D. 1979; Episcopalian; separated.

Elected Office: NC House of Reps., 1992–94; NC Senate, 1996–2002.

Professional Career: Clerk, Judge J. Dickson Phillips Jr., U.S. Fourth Circuit Ct. of Appeals, Durham, 1979–80; Practicing atty., 1980–2002.

DC Office: 1127 LHOB, 20515, 202-225-3032; Fax: 202-225-0181; Web site: bradmiller.house.gov.

State Offices: Greensboro, 336-574-2909; Raleigh, 919-836-1313.

Committees: *Financial Services* (18th of 42 D): Capital Markets, Insurance & Government Sponsored Enterprises; Financial Institutions & Consumer Credit. *Foreign Affairs* (23rd of 28 D): Africa & Global Health; Europe. *Science & Technology* (7th of 26 D): Investigations & Oversight (Chmn).

Group Ratings

	ADA	ACLU	AFS	LCV	ITIC	NTU	COC	ACU	CFG	FRC
2008	100	100	100	92	86	6	61	0	0	11
2007	100	—	100	90	—	4	47	0	6	—

National Journal Ratings

	2007 LIB	—	2007 CONS	2008 LIB	—	2008 CONS
Economic	82%	—	0%	81%	—	15%
Social	70%	—	29%	82%	—	0%
Foreign	73%	—	26%	70%	—	25%
Composite	78%	—	22%	82%	—	18%

Key Votes of the 110th Congress

1. Increase minimum wage	Y	5. Share immigration data	N	9. Withdraw troops 8/08	Y
2. Expand SCHIP	Y	6. Foreign aid abortion ban	N	10. No operations in Iran	Y
3. Raise CAFE standards	Y	7. Ban gay bias in workplace	Y	11. Free trade with Peru	N
4. Bail out financial markets	Y	8. Repeal D.C. gun law	N	12. Overhaul FISA	N

Election Results

2008 general	Brad Miller (D)..221,379	(66%)	($925,429)
	Hugh Webster (R) 114,383	(34%)	($34,655)
2008 primary	Brad Miller (D)...113,254	(88%)	
	Derald Hafner (D)...14,744	(12%)	

Prior Winning Percentages: 2006 (64%); 2004 (59%); 2002 (55%)

Population		Race/Ethnicity		Work	
Pop. 2007:	700,289	White:	59.6%	Private:	79.2%
Change since 2000:	Up 13.1%	Black:	27.5%	Government:	14.9%
Urban:	73.7%	Hispanic:	8.8%	Self-employed:	5.7%
Rural:	26.3%	Asian:	2.1%	Blue collar:	23.8%
Area size:	2,294 sq. mi.	Native Am.:	0.4%	White collar:	60.3%
Age		Hawaiian:	0.0%	Khaki collar:	0.1%
Median age:	35.3 yrs.	Two+ races:	1.2%	Other:	15.8%
More than 65 yrs:	10.5%	*Ancestry*		Median income:	$45,023
Less than 18 yrs:	23.9%	English:	9.3%	Median home value:	$145,000
Education		USA:	9.0%	Poverty:	14.9%
H.S. grad:	83.5%	German:	8.0%	**Military Veterans**	
College grad:	29.7%			% of Pop:	9.4%
Grad degree:	9.4%				

Metropolitan growth has come to the long-humble countryside of North Carolina. A generation ago, Raleigh, Durham, Burlington, and Greensboro were a string of small cities connected by Interstate 85 across the central Piedmont, moderately prosperous, with textile, tobacco, and furniture factories, but not very big. Just a few miles from the center of town, farm fields started, dotted by country towns with barbecue restaurants and churches. The counties to the north were almost purely rural,

2008 Presidential Vote

Obama (D) 206,520	(60%)
McCain (R)..............................137,599	(40%)

2004 Presidential Vote

Kerry (D)................................147,144	(52%)
Bush (R) 132,581	(47%)

Cook Partisan Voting Index: D+5

with a few factory towns. Today, many of the old tobacco fields are used for growing other crops. The booming metropolitan areas of North Carolina have spread far beyond the old city and county lines into the adjacent counties. Wake County, which includes Raleigh, grew 33% between 2000 and 2007. Rural roads are clogged in the morning with commuters headed for jobs in new office parks, and income levels have risen far above what they once were.

Much of this territory makes up the 13th Congressional District of North Carolina, created after the 2000 census. Half of its residents live in Wake County, including the center of Raleigh and its expanding skyline. A tangent goes off to North Carolina State University and much of the northern part of the county, except for the affluent new subdivisions that are mostly in the 4th District. In 2007, *Forbes* magazine rated Raleigh the nation's best city in which to find a job. Another 16% of district residents live in Guilford County, with African-American neighborhoods and the University of North Carolina's Greensboro campus. The rest of the district includes all or most of four counties up to the Virginia border—Granville, Person, Caswell, and Rockingham—with fairly large black percentages. The district lines were drawn by the Democratic Legislature to produce a new Democratic district, one of the few created in the South in recent decades that does not have a majority or near-majority of blacks. The district is 28% African-American. But the rural counties have a historical Democratic heritage, and university neighborhoods are heavily Democratic. The district has been closely divided in presidential races, but Barack Obama won it with 59.5% in 2008. George W. Bush won the district narrowly in 2000 and John Kerry won it by a slight margin in 2004.

The congressman from the 13th District is Brad Miller, a Democrat first elected in 2002. Born and raised in Fayetteville by his widowed mother, a school cafeteria bookkeeper, he graduated from the University of North Carolina. He went on to get a master's degree at the London School of Economics and a law degree from Columbia University. After clerking for a federal appeals court judge, Miller practiced law in Raleigh. In 1992, he was elected to the state House. But he was swept away in the 1994 Republican landslide. He was elected in 1996 to the state Senate where, like many members of the House, he had a hand in drawing his own congressional district as chairman of the Senate's redistricting committee.

Miller drew a district very much in his own political interest, but he couldn't be sure he could get the seat. Utah brought a lawsuit against the Census Bureau, arguing that because the census counted service members overseas with legal residence North Carolina, it should count Mormon missionaries domiciled in Utah but serving overseas. Such a count would have increased Utah's population enough that it, rather than North Carolina, would have gotten the 435th congressional district that year. Utah lost in federal court, and the Supreme Court affirmed the decision.

Four experienced Democrats, including Miller, launched an 11-week sprint to the September primary, which seemed likely to determine the winner in November. Miller raised the most money and got early endorsements from teachers' and other labor unions, plus the League of Conservation Voters. In the primary, he led with 40%, enough to avoid a runoff, to 24% for former Rep. Robin Britt. In the general election, Miller faced Carolyn Grant, a commercial real estate broker and former head of the Raleigh Chamber of Commerce. Grant called Miller a tax-and-spend Democrat, and also criticized him for voting to cut prescription drug assistance for the elderly. Miller said that North Carolina had the second-best record of any state in cutting taxes while he was in the Legislature. Grant got little help from national Republicans, and Miller won 55%-42%.

In the House, Miller has a relatively liberal record, especially on economics. He joined the Financial Services Committee, a useful post for home-state banking interests. In November 2006, the Raleigh *News & Observer* wrote that Miller "remains somewhat uncomfortable with the rituals of Congress" and often sits alone on the House floor reading memos while colleagues chat up each other in the aisles. "He doesn't make a lot of noise, but he's doing the work," Democratic Rep. Bob Etheridge told the newspaper. He also displays flashes of wry humor. Following a congressional delegation visit to Antarctica in 2006, Miller said of his trip to the magnetic South Pole: "I thought, 'Every other politician who thinks the world is revolving around them is wrong. It actually revolves around me.'"

With Rep. Melvin Watt, D-N.C., he was able to get passed in November 2007 a bill to prohibit predatory lending practices. He spearheaded a proposal approved by the House Judiciary Committee in 2007 to permit bankruptcy judges to lighten mortgage terms to help borrowers avoid foreclosure, although the bill did not come up for a vote. When Democrats became the majority party in 2007, Miller ascended to chairman of the Science and Technology Subcommittee on Investigations and Oversight, where he explored allegations of politicizing of scientific research in the Bush administration. He clashed with NASA over its inspector general's job performance and the agency's refusal to release a study about the safety of commercial aviation. Then-Gov. Sarah Palin of Alaska, the 2008 GOP vice presidential nominee, criticized Miller for suggesting that polar bears should be classified as an endangered species.

Back home, he appears safe. In 2006, his Republican challenger was Vernon Robinson, an outspoken and conservative African-American, who criticized Miller as soft on illegal immigration and gay rights. "If Miller had his way, America would be nothing but one big fiesta for illegal aliens and homosexuals," said Robinson, who was well funded but received little national party assistance. Miller won 64%-36%. In 2008, he seriously considered challenging Republican Sen. Elizabeth Dole, and perhaps wishes now that he had. Dole lost the election to a less-seasoned candidate than Miller, Democratic state Sen. Kay Hagan, in one of the biggest upsets of the year. Miller went on to be re-elected easily.

★ NORTH DAKOTA ★

A little more than two centuries ago, in late 1804, the Lewis and Clark expedition paddled up the Missouri River and reached what is now North Dakota. The explorers bivouacked for the winter across the river from what is now the state capital of Bismarck. Lewis and Clark, North Dakota proudly proclaims, spent more nights in North Dakota, 146, than in any other state. And on the Lewis and Clark Trail you can still see much of the pristine land that the expeditioners saw—a vast unfenced land where the Indians built a civilization based on the buffalo and, a Spanish import, the horse. The history of North Dakota is short: Theodore Roosevelt did not arrive until nearly 80 years after Lewis and Clark, and bicentennial tourists came just a little more than 120 years after Roosevelt. There are still a few North Dakotans alive today who knew the men and women who settled this land and saw the state enter the Union in 1889. As children, these old-timers walked in the ruts left by the early settlers' wagon trains. They saw the Indians, recently defeated and herded into reservations by the white settlers' government covetous of their land. This was some of the best wheat-growing acreage in the world, empty by then of buffalo, connected to markets by rail, ready to become a cog in the industrial world.

In a sudden rush of settlement during the 20 years before World War I, North Dakota filled up to pretty much its present population. There were 632,000 people in 1920 and in counts since then, the number has fluctuated between 617,000 and 680,000. The 2000 census count was 642,000, making it the state with the lowest growth rate since 1950. Wheat—mostly spring wheat but also durum (used to make pasta)—is the biggest crop here but not the only one. North Dakota ranks first in production of sunflowers, barley, dry edible beans, oats, and dry peas; it ranks high in sugar beets and rye. There is also plenty of cattle ranching and livestock grazing on the arid plains in the western half of the state.

Its dependence on agriculture shaped North Dakota's politics. Farmers, as much as they like to extol their way of life, are seldom content with the workings of the market. When prices are high, it is often because of low production; when they are low, farmers seek protection. The boosterish optimism of the first settlers was soon followed by cries, reverberating with varying intensity, for government protection against market forces. Since commodity prices tend to fall during periods of economic growth, there has been a countercyclical force at work in North Dakota politics, a tendency to vote against the national trends, and a radical strain going back to the 1910s and still lively in recent decades. That strain also owes much to the immigrant origins of so many of North Dakota's early settlers: Norwegians in the eastern part of the state; Canadians along the northern border; and colonies of Poles, Czechs, Icelanders, and Germans throughout the state. German is still spoken on the streets of some towns, and the state is proud of its Nordic Initiative which welcomed Princess Martha Louise of Norway to Grand Forks in April 2006.

These immigrants produced orderly small towns and grain cooperatives. They also provided support for the Non-Partisan League, which operated as an independent force from its founding in 1915 to its alliance with the Democratic Party in 1956. The league appealed to marginal farmers, cut off in many cases from the wider American culture by language barriers and seemingly at the mercy of the grain millers of Minneapolis, the railroads of St. Paul, the banks of New York, and the commodity traders of Chicago. The NPL's program was socialist—government ownership of railroads and grain elevators—and its members, like most North Dakota ethnics, opposed going to war with Germany. The NPL often determined the outcome of the usually decisive Republican primary but sometimes swung its support to the otherwise heavily outnumbered Democrats, instituting reforms and creating a state-owned bank and grain elevator. In the 1950s, the NPL more or less melded into the Democratic Party, a merger symbolized by the election of the late Democratic Sen. Quentin Burdick, whose father, Usher Burdick, served 20 years in the House as an NPL-endorsed Republican. North Dakota's leading Democrats of recent decades, Sens. Kent Conrad and Byron Dorgan, have championed a politics clearly of NPL lineage: boosterish of government farm programs, wary if not hostile to American military involvement abroad, and cheerful championing of the little guy from North Dakota against out-of-state corporations.

This is a place where everyone knows everyone else. For years there has been no voter registration because people obviously spot anyone who is not eligible. People live longer here too. The 2000 census reported that North Dakota had the highest proportion of any state of residents age 85 and older, and tiny McIntosh County had the highest proportion of any county. Communal closeness has produced an innate conservatism in North Dakota. Divorce is as uncommon here as anywhere in the United States, the two-parent family is still very much the norm, and abortions are available in just one clinic in the state. Politics is personal, too, in a state where every politician is known to many voters. North Dakota is one of five states with an all-Democratic congressional delegation (Hawaii, Massachusetts, New Mexico, and Rhode Island are the others; the five don't have much else in common). The two senators and single at-large congressman are all allies who have worked together for decades.

Yet there are signs of change. The land, it seems, is emptying out. Increasing agricultural productivity has meant fewer farmers living directly off the land, and more people living in towns and working in other sectors. People from out of state are buying up farmland for vacation hunting; North Dakota sits

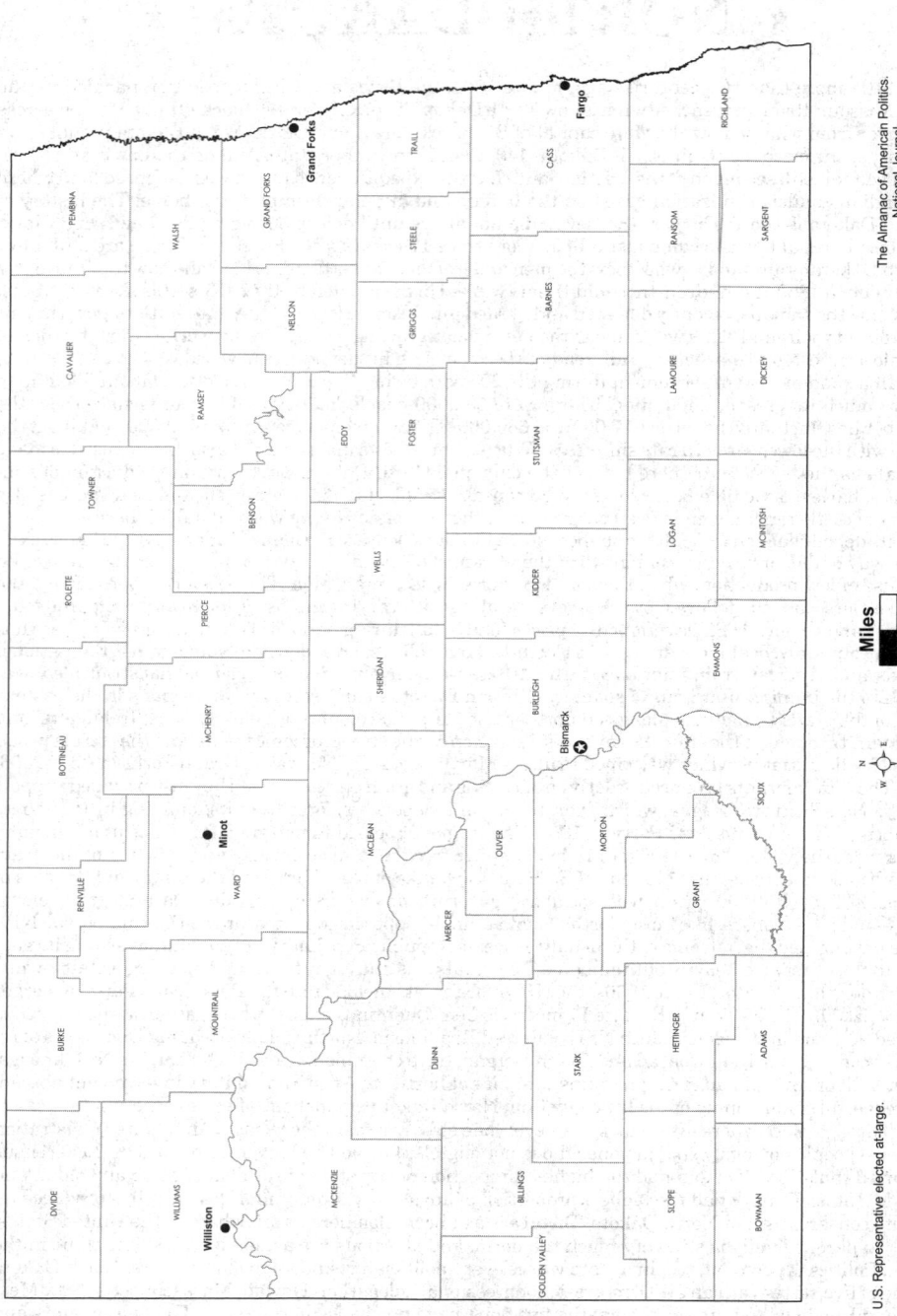

The Almanac of American Politics.
National Journal

U.S. Representative elected at-large.

below the North American Migration Flyway, which makes for good fowl hunting. Bison have been reintroduced, and the idea circulated two decades ago that North Dakota would become a "buffalo commons" may be coming true.

At the same time, North Dakota's small cities have grown. Back in 1955, North Dakota-born sociologist Carl Kraenzel predicted in *The Great Plains in Transition* that "sutland" communities, places on transportation lines, would grow and "yonland" communities, places away from transportation lines, would wane. And so it has happened. North Dakota's four biggest counties, home to Fargo, Grand Forks, Bismarck, and Minot, grew from 134,000 people in 1930 to 338,000 in 2007, while the state's other 49 counties dropped from 546,000 people to 301,000 in the same period. In 2008, these four counties cast 54% of the state's votes. In effect, North Dakota is developing the demographics of the Rocky Mountain states, with population concentrated in a few cities and towns.

Microsoft bought Great Plains Software in 2000 for $1.1 billion, and the company's Fargo campus is the headquarters of its business systems division, handling all of Microsoft's U.S. and Canada payroll operations. It is the state's third-largest employer. Alien Technology's Fargo plant produces the tiny radio frequency tags used by Wal-Mart and the military. Grand Forks, devastated by flood in 1997, generously provided its "lessons learned" to its sister city, Biloxi, Miss., in 2005 when flood struck there. Grand Forks is the home of the University of North Dakota, with a Center of Excellence in Life Sciences and Advanced Technology starting up. In 2007, the school settled a lawsuit with the NCAA allowing it to keep the nickname Fighting Sioux for its sports teams if the two local Sioux tribes agreed within three years.

North Dakota is making some progress on a problem it has wrestled with for years: how to retain its young people. The government spends more per capita on state colleges than any other state, and a smaller proportion of graduates seem to be heading off to Minneapolis, Denver, Chicago, and Los Angeles. Fargo, Bismarck, Grand Forks, and Minot still have the coldest winters of any American cities, but they are also spouting hip restaurants and Starbucks, industrial parks, and office buildings. The Census Bureau estimates that North Dakota's population started rising after years of decline in 2003. The state's unemployment rate lately has been one of the lowest in the nation; its wages and incomes have been rising more than the national average and its farm incomes are among the highest ever. Before the recession of 2008, state government faced the pleasant problem of dealing with budget surpluses.

The state also abounds in something the nation needs: energy. Counting coal, oil, wind, and ethanol, North Dakota is the No. 6 energy-producing state in the nation. The coal country west of Bismarck supports six electric power plants. And with the world's largest lignite reserves, North Dakota has the potential to build a large coal-gasification industry if oil prices remain high enough. The Bakken Formation's oil shale is estimated by the U.S. Geological Survey to contain the largest potential oil reserves in the lower 48 states. Only 1% has been commercially recoverable in recent years, but even so, North Dakota surpassed Kansas as the eighth-largest oil-producing state in 2006. Oil production rose from 29.3 million barrels in 2003 to 39.9 million barrels in 2007. North Dakota supports six ethanol and three biodiesel plants and can easily grow vast quantities of switchgrass to make cellulosic ethanol. The state has enough wind power potential to export plenty of energy, provided that electric transmission lines can be financed and built. Republican Gov. John Hoeven's Empower North Dakota plan sets benchmarks for increasing energy production from oil, natural gas, biofuels, wind, and lignite coal, with a goal of doubling energy production from all sources by 2025.

These developments could alter the state's political traditions. If the typical elderly North Dakotan is a hardworking retired farmer, with fond memories of NPL agitation and a belief in government programs, the typical young North Dakotan has a family and a college education and is more trusting of markets and the private sector. Republican President George W. Bush won the state 63%-35% in 2004. GOP presidential nominee John McCain's weaker 53%-45% win in 2008 was largely a result of younger voters' attraction to Democratic nominee Barack Obama. McCain won about the same percentage among voters over 60 as Bush had, but his percentage among those under 45 was 54%, 15% lower than Bush's. By contrast, Hoeven swept to a third term with a landslide victory, attracting 79% of the vote from people

Population		Household Income		Work	
Pop. 2007:	637,709	Under $15k:	15.1%	Private:	71.8%
State rank:	48th of 50	$15k to $50k:	41.7%	Government:	18.5%
Change since 2000:	Down 0.7%	$50k to $100k:	31.7%	Self-employed:	9.3%
Urban:	56.3%	$100k to $150k:	9.8%	Unemployment (3-yr. average):	2.4%
Rural:	43.7%	Over $150k:	1.7%	Poverty:	11.9%
Native of state:	70.5%	Median income:	$43,442	Blue collar:	23.1%
Not a citizen:	1.4%	**Home Value**		White collar:	57.6%
Area size:	70,700 sq. mi.	Under $100k:	51.5%	Khaki collar:	0.7%
Most populous cities		$100k to $300k:	44.6%	Other:	18.6%
1. Fargo	94,603	$300k to $500k:	3.0%	**Age**	
2. Bismarck	58,820	$500k to $1 mil:	0.8%	Median age:	37.0 yrs.
3. Grand Forks	50,743	Over $1 million:	0.2%	More than 65 yrs:	14.5%
4. Minot	36,682	Median:	$97,400	Less than 18 yrs:	22.5%

Race/Ethnicity				Military Veterans		Registered Voters in 2008	
White:	90.2%	*Language*		% of Pop:	11.6%	No party registration	
Black:	0.9%	English:	94.3%	*Veterans by Period*		Voter turnout:	316,621
Hispanic:	1.6%	Spanish:	1.5%	WWII and before:	11.8%	Turnout as % of	
Asian:	0.8%	Asian:	0.5%	Korea:	12.1%	voting age:	63.5%
Native Am.:	5.0%	Other		Vietnam:	31.3%		
Hawaiian:	0.1%	European	3.1%	Gulf (pre-2001):	9.3%	Legislative Assembly	
Two+ races:	1.3%	**Education**		Gulf (post-2001):	12.5%	Senate:	21 D 26 R
Ancestry		H.S. grad:	88.1%	Peace time:	23.0%	House:	36 D 58 R
German:	33.4%	College grad:	25.6%				
Norwegian:	21.7%	Grad degree:	6.6%				
Irish:	5.7%			**Cook Partisan Voting Index:** R+10			

under 45. Still, the heirs of the NPL tradition continue to do well. The state's two Democratic senators have been re-elected by wide margins—Byron Dorgan won with 68% in 2004, Kent Conrad got 69% in 2006, and Democratic Rep. Earl Pomeroy won with 62% in 2008. These were consensus elections: In their most recent elections, Dorgan and Conrad carried all 53 counties, Hoeven carried 52, and Pomeroy 45. Republicans hold most of the down-ballot statewide offices and have majorities in both houses of the Legislature. North Dakota prizes frugality in government and values Senate Budget Committee Chairman Conrad's denunciations of federal budget deficits. But the state was happy to receive some $7.4 billion in farm subsidies from 1995 to 2006, and has fought mightily against Air Force base cutbacks in Grand Forks.

Presidential politics   North Dakota, for the first time since 1964, was a competitive state in the 2008 presidential election. In 2000 and 2004, it cast 61% and 63% of its votes, respectively, for George W. Bush, but by 2008 this historically dovish state was plainly unhappy with the incumbent. And though it has virtually no black residents (and most of them live on military bases), the state was plainly intrigued by Democratic nominee Barack Obama. With North Dakota scheduled to hold caucuses on Super Tuesday, February 5, the Obama campaign moved in early, bought television time, and, more important, set up offices with paid staff and volunteers in Fargo, Grand Forks, Bismarck, and Minot. Conrad, Dorgan, and Pomeroy endorsed Obama.

2008 Presidential Vote		
McCain (R)............................168,601	(53%)
Obama (D) 141,278	(45%)
2004 Presidential Vote		
Bush (R)................................196,651	(63%)
Kerry (D)...............................111,052	(35%)

The effort paid off on caucus day. Altogether, 19,012 North Dakotans participated in the Democratic caucuses and only 9,785 in the Republican caucuses. Obama outpolled Hillary Rodham Clinton 61% to 37% and got more votes than all of the Republicans put together. Mitt Romney was the winner on the Republican side, with 36% of the vote; ahead of McCain, 23%; Ron Paul, 21%; and Mike Huckabee, 20%. A SurveyUSA poll in late February showed Obama ahead of McCain in the state, and the few polls taken from then until the national conventions showed the candidates within the margin of error. McCain's selection of Alaska Gov. Sarah Palin seemed to have had great appeal in this often-snowbound state, at least judging from two post-convention polls showing the Republican ticket far ahead. But after the financial crisis hit the housing, banking, and insurance markets in mid-September, North Dakota became closely contested again. McCain won 53%-45%, doing a little better than late polls suggested but far below George W. Bush's percentages. Obama carried Fargo, Grand Forks and the Indian reservations, but McCain carried Bismarck and Minot by wider margins, and most rural counties as well.

Governor

John Hoeven (R)

Elected 2000, term expires Dec. 2012, 3rd term; b. March 13, 1957, Bismarck; home, Bismarck; Dartmouth, B.A. 1979; Northwestern U., Kellogg Grad. Schl., M.B.A. 1981; Catholic; married (Mikey); 2 children.

Professional Career: Exec. V.P., First Western Bank, 1986–93; Pres. & CEO, Bank of ND, 1993–2000.

Office: State Capitol, 600 E. Boulevard, Bismarck, 58505, 701-328-2200; Fax: 701-328-2205; Web site: www.governor.nd.gov.

Election Results

2008 general	John Hoeven (R)	235,009	(74%)
	Tim Mathern (D)	74,279	(24%)
	DuWayne Hendrickson (I)	6,404	(2%)
2008 primary	John Hoeven (R)	unopposed	

Prior Winning Percentages: 2004 (71%); 2000 (55%)

North Dakota's John Hoeven is the longest serving governor in the United States. The Republican was first elected in November 2000 and was sworn into office on Dec. 15, 2000—six days before the second-longest serving governor, Republican Rick Perry of Texas, who took office from then President-elect George W. Bush. Hoeven (*HO-ven*) was born in Bismarck and grew up in Minot. He graduated from Dartmouth College and received an M.B.A. from Northwestern University. In 1981, he entered the family business, First Western Bank in Minot, and became executive vice president. In 1993, he was chosen to be head of the state-owned Bank of North Dakota—a creation of the democratic-socialist Non-Partisan League by a board that included his predecessor as governor, Republican Ed Schafer, and his 2000 Democratic opponent, Attorney General Heidi Heitkamp. Under Hoeven's stewardship, the bank's worth rose from $990 million to $1.6 billion, and its loan portfolio increased from $200 million to $1 billion. In 1996, Hoeven considered running as a Democrat against Schafer, but after Schafer announced his retirement in October 1999, Hoeven decided to remain a Republican.

His 2000 contest with Heitkamp was relatively civil. The two candidates knew each other well; Bismarck is a small town, where officeholders can scarcely avoid each other, and North Dakotans generally are a civil people. Hoeven cited his work in attracting jobs by founding Minot's Magic Fund, a city sales tax used for business development, and by organizing to keep Minot Air Force Base off Congress' base-closure list. He called for economic development with an emphasis on the technology industry and on improving education; he pledged more money for teacher training and salaries. Heitkamp, who grew up in the town of Mantador (population 77), was elected tax commissioner in 1984 and 1988 and attorney general in 1992 and 1996. She said she would try to keep young people in the state through a recruitment and mentoring program, by reinstating a living wage for employees of companies receiving financial assistance and by giving tax incentives to companies that guarantee high-wage jobs.

As the fall campaign heated up, Heitkamp announced in September that she had breast cancer. She underwent a mastectomy the same month, and Hoeven suspended his ads for two days. Quickly, she returned to the campaign trail. For several weeks, she led in polls, but the momentum went back to Hoeven, and he won 55%-45%. Voters over the age of 60 backed the Democrat, voters under 60, the Republican, which is a familiar North Dakota pattern. North Dakota's skyscraper Capitol, towering over neatly kept Bismarck and the rolling plains beyond, now contained more Republicans in high office than at any time since the NPL allied with the Democrats around 1960.

As governor, Hoeven has used North Dakota's burgeoning revenues to fund programs to stimulate economic development. In his first years, he combined several state agencies into a Department of Commerce. In 2002, he presented a budget that drew $50 million from two trust funds and borrowed $20 million to complete the state telecommunications network and to fund teacher salary increases. He promoted the use of ethanol fuel and required it in state vehicles. He brought a lawsuit to roll back the Burlington Northern Santa Fe Railroad's rate increases and eliminated the sales tax on used farm machinery and parts.

In 2002, Hoeven announced an ambitious research and development program, borrowing $50 million to generate $150 million for university projects that would help commercialize new technology. From 2005 to 2007, more than $40 million in state funds, combined with double that in private funds, were invested in the Center of Excellence in Life Sciences and Advanced Technology and other new research centers devoted to developing technology and making greater use of North Dakota's natural resources. These included research facilities for hydrogen technology, crop oils and petroleum, aerospace science, electronics, and biopharmaceuticals.

Much of this was aimed at exploiting North Dakota's considerable energy resources, including oil, coal, ethanol and other biofuels, wind and hydrogen. In 2002, Hoeven announced his Empower North Dakota energy plan, which aims to build three new biodiesel plants by 2015, to have wind supply 10% of electricity by 2015 (up from 5%), to require that ethanol account for 75% of gasoline consumption by 2015 and to build at least one coal-to-liquid energy plant by 2012. Other projects include commercializing hydrogen by using wind power to separate water into hydrogen and oxygen.

Water is a controversial issue in river-crossed North Dakota. For years, there was concern about the rising water level in land-locked Devils Lake, which was submerging farmland and houses after heavy rains and threatening local roads. The three North Dakotans in Congress tried to get the federal government to act. But when progress was slow on that front, Hoeven stepped in, and construction began in 2003 on a channel to divert the water through the Sheyenne River, which drains into the northward-flowing Red River of the North. The move generated loud protests from Minnesota and Manitoba officials, worried about water quality and invasive species. The two sides battled in court, but a 14-mile channel was opened in 2005 and drainage began. Hoeven and North Dakota ultimately agreed to install filters to prevent invasive species and pollutants from moving downstream.

Hoeven has had one of the highest job-approval ratings of any American governor. In 2004, he was re-elected, 71%-27%, over former state Sen. Joseph Satrom, who opposed the constitutional amendment banning same-sex marriage that was approved by 73% of the voters. Hoeven's percentage of victory was the largest for a North Dakota governor since Republican C. Norman Brunsdale was re-elected in 1952. In 2005 and 2007, Hoeven submitted budgets with big increases in education spending targeted at teachers' salaries and with reductions in local property taxes. His budgets have also included the largest tax-relief measure in state history, the biggest increase in higher-education funding in state history, a renewable-energy package, and a landmark K-12 education bill that featured a more equitable school-aid formula and funding for statewide all-day kindergarten. He negotiated with Manitoba Premier Gary Doer to develop "enhanced" state and provincial driver's licenses to avoid the need for passports for locals crossing the U.S.-Canada border. He responded in spirited fashion to a 2008 *National Geographic* article on "The Emptied Prairie" by saying North Dakota has "a growing economy, well-educated citizens, low crime, great infrastructure, and one of the cleanest environments in America."

Taking note of Hoeven's high approval ratings, national Republicans have hoped that he would run against one of North Dakota's two Democratic senators. He was pressed to run in 2006 against Kent Conrad by top Bush political adviser Karl Rove. Conrad took Hoeven's potential candidacy seriously: He raised $2.7 million by June 2005, more than he had ever spent over the course of an entire election cycle, and began running ads in September 2005. Later that month, Hoeven announced he would not run. In 2007, he announced he would run for a third four-year term, and in November 2008, he defeated state Sen. Tim Mathern, 74%-24%, as Republicans dominated all the down-ballot offices. He is now set to equal Democrat William Guy's record of serving 12 years as governor. Guy won two-year terms in 1960 and 1962 and four-year terms in 1964 and 1968. Before the 2008 election, Hoeven brushed aside speculation that he would run against Sen. Byron Dorgan or Rep. Earl Pomeroy in 2010, but did not pledge to serve out his third term. "I'm focused on what we are doing now, working to serve the people of North Dakota," he told the *Bismarck Tribune*. "I'm not ruling anything out or in."

Senior Senator

Kent Conrad (D)

Elected 1986, term expires 2012, 4th full term; b. March 12, 1948, Bismarck; home, Bismarck; Stanford U., B.A. 1971, George Washington U., M.B.A. 1975; Unitarian; married (Lucy Calautti); 1 child.

Elected Office: ND tax commissioner, 1981–86.

Professional Career: Asst., ND tax commissioner, 1974–80; Dir., mgmt. planning & personnel, ND Tax Dept., 1980.

DC Office: 530 HSOB, 20510, 202-224-2043; Fax: 202-224-7776; Web site: conrad.senate.gov.

State Offices: Bismarck, 701-258-4648; Fargo, 701-232-8030; Grand Forks, 701-775-9601; Minot, 701-852-0703.

Committees: *Agriculture, Nutrition & Forestry* (3rd of 12 D). *Budget* (Chmn of 13 D). *Finance* (3rd of 13 D): Energy, Natural Resources & Infrastructure; Social Security, Pensions & Family Policy; Taxation, IRS Oversight & Long-Term Growth (Chmn). *Indian Affairs* (3rd of 9 D). *Joint Committee on Taxation* (3rd of 3 D).

Group Ratings

	ADA	ACLU	AFS	LCV	ITIC	NTU	COC	ACU	CFG	FRC
2008	90	64	100	91	80	5	57	0	3	33
2007	80	—	86	73	—	6	45	12	8	—

National Journal Ratings

	2007 LIB	—	2007 CONS		2008 LIB	—	2008 CONS
Economic	53%	—	44%		67%	—	32%
Social	55%	—	43%		65%	—	33%
Foreign	59%	—	36%		60%	—	39%
Composite	57%	—	43%		65%	—	35%

Key Votes of the 110th Congress

1. Raise CAFE standards	Y	5. Make English official language	Y	9. Withdraw troops 3/08	Y
2. Expand SCHIP	Y	6. Path to citizenship	Y	10. Iran guard is terrorist group	Y
3. Cap greenhouse gases	*	7. Fetus is unborn child	N	11. Increase missile defense $	N
4. Bail out financial markets	Y	8. Prosecute hate crimes	Y	12. Overhaul FISA	Y

Election Results

2006 general	Kent Conrad (D)..	150,146	(69%)	($3,532,732)
	Dwight Grotberg (R)	64,417	(30%)	($259,081)
2006 primary	Kent Conrad (D)...	unopposed		

Prior Winning Percentages: 2000 (62%); 1994 (58%); 1992 (63%); 1986 (50%)

Kent Conrad, North Dakota's senior senator, was first elected to the Senate in 1986. He grew up in North Dakota, and knew personal tragedy early. Conrad was raised by his grandparents after both his parents were killed in an automobile accident when he was just five. One of his grandfathers owned a biweekly newspaper in Bismarck and had been the North Dakota chairman for Robert LaFollette's Progressive campaign for president in 1924. His other grandfather was the physician for longtime Republican Gov. and Sen. William Langer. It was a family full of connections in the small world of North Dakota politics. Conrad's first political effort was to lead, in 1968, a campaign to grant voting rights to 19-year-olds. After graduating from Stanford University, he went to work for Democrat Byron Dorgan's unsuccessful 1974 House campaign. Conrad ran for tax commissioner in 1980 and won. When Dorgan declined to run against Republican Sen. Mark Andrews in 1986, Conrad ran and won, 50%-49%. In 1986, he earnestly promised not to run again unless "the federal deficit, the trade deficit and real interest rates will be brought under control." By 1992, the latter two arguably were, and he could claim to have worked to trim the budget deficit. Early 1992 polls showed Conrad well ahead, but in April 1992, shortly after his wife was mugged and dragged down a street near their Capitol Hill home in Washington, D.C., Conrad announced he was retiring because he had not kept his pledge. Dorgan ran successfully for his seat.

Then, in September 1992, the elderly Sen. Quentin Burdick, a Republican and no ally of Dorgan and Conrad, died. State law said a special election had to be held after November but before January. Experiencing a change of heart about leaving the Senate, Conrad ran for Burdick's seat while serving out the last month in his own. He was nominated unanimously at the Democratic state convention. His Republican opponent was Jack Dalrymple, the lieutenant governor. Conrad had far more money and won easily, 63%-34%. For a few hours in December 1992, Conrad technically held both of North Dakota's Senate seats: He was sworn in December 14 to fill Burdick's term, and a few hours later, Dorgan was sworn in to fill his. In 1994, Conrad's new Senate seat came up again. Republican Ben Clayburgh, the 70-year-old former head of the state medical association, accused him of voting most of the time with President Clinton. Conrad responded with an ad saying he voted with Republican leader Bob Dole of Kansas more than half the time. In a Republican year, Conrad won by a reduced 58%-42%.

Conrad is an active deal-maker and the chairman of the Budget Committee. His votes have placed him close to the center of the Senate, especially on economic and cultural issues. Throughout his career, he has called for balanced budgets and decried deficits. From the 1930s to the 1970s, Republicans were the great critics of deficits, calling, usually ineffectually, for lower spending. Since the 1980s, Democrats have increasingly taken that stand, Conrad foremost among them, often calling for changes in tax laws to increase uncollected taxes owed, to clamp down on tax shelters and havens and, if necessary, to increase tax rates. When he argues his case on the Senate floor, he often comes equipped with his trademark charts, chock full of numbers and graphs, and familiar to any regular viewer of C-SPAN. In 2001, he lambasted the Bush administration for its tax cut proposals, arguing that lower than expected revenue would lead to deficits. But he did not seek to undo the tax cut. In March 2002, Conrad presented a $2 trillion budget with a $90 billion deficit, which he said would pay more of the national debt than Bush's budget. His plan passed in committee, but in the 51-49 Senate there were not enough senators willing to constrain appropriators, and Conrad's budget never came to a vote. For the first time since the Budget committees in both chambers were established in 1974, no budget resolution passed Congress.

When Republicans held the majority in 2003, Conrad became the ranking minority member on Budget. That year, the Republicans dropped the "pay-go" rule, in place since 1990 and supported by Conrad, that required spending increases and tax cuts to be "paid for" by corresponding spending decreases or tax increases. The change made possible passage of the 2003 Bush tax cuts on dividends and capital gains, and later the extension of various Bush tax cuts. Conrad continued to press, unsuccessfully, for restoration of the pay-go rule. Conrad also tried to focus attention on the surplus in Social Security revenues over benefits, which was reducing the nominal federal budget deficit. But that financial comfort was in jeopardy of disappearing in roughly a decade, when Social Security benefits would begin to exceed revenues. Conrad also complained about Bush's escalating requests for money to pay for the Iraq war without a long-range plan for covering the costs. He told *The Washington Post,* "The president, this is his policy. He's got an obligation to tell us how to pay for it."

When Democrats assumed the majority in 2007, Conrad unveiled a budget resolution that put the budget into balance by 2012, ended the supplemental appropriations strategies used heavily by the Bush administration, and provided for a two-year fix of the Alternative Minimum Tax, which had been designed to ensure that the wealthy paid taxes but in effect had for several years been snaring middle-income taxpayers. His budget called for cutting in half interest rates on student loans, more spending on homeland security, extending the child tax credit and the 10% tax bracket, and eliminating the marriage penalty. Republicans charged that it all amounted to a tax increase, but Democrats envisioned that the Bush tax cuts, set to expire in 2010, would be either allowed to expire or offset at that time. Conrad and House Budget Committee Chairman John Spratt, a South Carolina Democrat, pushed similar packages through the two chambers in April 2007, and they reached a final agreement in May. The next year, when Bush proposed his final budget, Conrad called it "debt on departure" for the lame-duck president. The Senate and House resolved minor differences between the two chambers and adopted a budget, but they postponed major issues until after the 2008 election.

Conrad also has a seat on the influential Finance Committee, where he voted against the Bush tax cuts and against repeal of the estate tax. But he has been willing to work with Republicans on other issues. He was one of 11 Democratic senators to vote for the 2003 GOP bill creating a prescription drug benefit in the Medicare program—not a perfect bill, in his view, but a step forward. He sponsored bills that in his view would improve it, including one to allow federal negotiation of prices with pharmaceutical companies, a step adamantly opposed by Republicans. In 2005, some advisers in the Bush White House, noting Conrad's continual warnings about the fiscal difficulties facing Social Security as baby boomers reach retirement age, hoped that he would join in discussions on a long-term Social Security fix. Conrad did sponsor a bill with Republican Gordon Smith of Oregon giving employees automatic enrollment in 401(k) accounts unless they opted out and extending tax credits for voluntary savings accounts. But he, like other prominent Democrats, steered clear of any public discussions or negotiations, and House Republicans, leery of the issue, were happy to see it disappear from the agenda later in the year when Hurricane Katrina struck. In 2007, Conrad supported expansion of the State Children's Health Insurance Program, which Bush vetoed. In September 2008, he was among the small number of lawmakers who crafted the $700 billion bailout package for wobbling financial markets.

Conrad is a big booster of government aid for farmers. On the Agriculture Committee, he helped write a generous 2002 farm bill that abandoned the principles of the 1996 Freedom to Farm Act, which had tried to end farm subsidies. As he said then, "No one did better than North Dakota under the current bill." The state received the equivalent of $2,368 per person in payments, more than any other state. During work on the 2008 farm bill, Conrad used his multiple committee posts to significantly influence the details, including passage of a permanent $3.8 billion disaster fund for farmers and a new sugar-subsidy program. When it came time for the final deal-cutting, he worked with Southern senators on commodity programs and largely preempted Agriculture Committee Chairman Tom Harkin of Iowa, who opposed permanent disaster aid.

North Dakota's farm interests, particularly its sugar beet farmers and processors, have been increasingly affected by trade agreements. Conrad's objections helped ensure that sugar was not included in the Australia Free Trade Agreement, but his effort to give House and Senate committees veto power over waivers of limits on Australian beef imports was characterized as unconstitutional and failed. In 2004, when the Bush administration included limited sugar imports from the Dominican Republic in the Caribbean Free Trade Agreement, Conrad spoke out strongly against them. "This is about whether we have sugar in our future," he said. "This is whether we have 30,000 jobs in the valley. This is about whether we have a strong and vibrant economy in the Red River Valley of North Dakota and Minnesota."

On another issue vital to his home state, Conrad assumed an active role in energy legislation in the 110th Congress (2007–08). He was a major supporter of increased use of ethanol and biodiesel, plus coal liquefaction and tax credits for wind energy. North Dakota produces corn used to make ethanol, has major coal deposits suitable for liquefaction and has more wind-energy potential than any other state. In 2008, Conrad organized with Republican Sen. Saxby Chambliss of Georgia, the bipartisan "Gang of Ten" that sought middle ground on the issue of oil and gas development in the outer continental shelf.

When Conrad came up for re-election in 2006, the Bush White House encouraged popular Republican Gov. John Hoeven to run against him. Conrad ran ads touting his Senate accomplishments, and Hoeven decided not to run. Conrad instead faced a far less serious GOP threat that year in Barnes County farmer Dwight Grotberg. Conrad spent $3.5 million and won 69%-30%, carrying every county. In June 2008, he was embarrassed by disclosures that Countrywide loan officers gave him special treatment on a home mortgage, which he claimed was done unknowingly on his part. He agreed to donate $10,500 to charity and promised to disclose all the details of the transaction.

Conrad is bound to be regarded warmly at the White House during the new Obama administration. Early in the 2008 campaign, he was the second senator to endorse Obama and made appearances on his behalf in early Democratic contests in Iowa and New Hampshire.

Junior Senator

Byron Dorgan (D)

Elected 1992, term expires 2010, 3rd term; b. May 14, 1942, Dickinson; home, Bismarck; U. of ND, B.S. 1965, U. of Denver, M.B.A. 1966; Lutheran; married (Kimberly); 4 children.

Elected Office: ND Tax Commissioner, 1969–80; U.S. House of Reps., 1980–92.

Professional Career: Martin–Marietta Exec. Develop. Prog., 1966–68; ND dpty. tax commissioner, 1968–69.

DC Office: 322 HSOB, 20510, 202-224-2551; Fax: 202-224-1193; Web site: dorgan.senate.gov.

State Offices: Bismarck, 701-250-4618; Fargo, 701-239-5389; Grand Forks, 701-746-8972; Minot, 701-852-0703.

Committees: *Democratic Policy Committee Chairman. Appropriations* (8th of 18 D): Agriculture, Rural Development, Food and Drug Administration & Related Agencies; Commerce, Justice, Science & Related Agencies; Defense; Energy & Water Development (Chmn); Interior, Environment & Related Agencies; Transportation, Housing and Urban Development & Related Agencies. *Commerce, Science & Transportation* (4th of 14 D): Aviation Operations, Safety & Security (Chmn); Communications, Technology & the Internet; Competitiveness, Innovation & Export Promotion; Consumer Protection, Product Safety & Insurance; Surface Transportation & Merchant Marine Infrastructure, Safety & Security. *Energy & Natural Resources* (2nd of 13 D): Energy; National Parks; Water & Power. *Indian Affairs* (Chmn of 9 D).

Group Ratings

	ADA	ACLU	AFS	LCV	ITIC	NTU	COC	ACU	CFG	FRC
2008	90	100	100	91	60	20	50	8	23	22
2007	85	—	86	87	—	5	27	12	3	—

National Journal Ratings

	2007 LIB	—	2007 CONS	2008 LIB	—	2008 CONS
Economic	60%	—	38%	53%	—	46%
Social	51%	—	48%	71%	—	27%
Foreign	64%	—	35%	65%	—	6%
Composite	59%	—	41%	68%	—	32%

Key Votes of the 110th Congress

1. Raise CAFE standards	Y	5. Make English official language Y	9. Withdraw troops 3/08	Y
2. Expand SCHIP	Y	6. Path to citizenship	N	10. Iran guard is terrorist group	Y
3. Cap greenhouse gases	N	7. Fetus is unborn child	N	11. Increase missile defense $	N
4. Bail out financial markets	N	8. Prosecute hate crimes	Y	12. Overhaul FISA	N

Election Results

2004 general	Byron Dorgan (D)	211,843	(68%)	($2,676,756)
	Mike Liffrig (R)	98,553	(32%)	($381,125)
2004 primary	Byron Dorgan (D)	unopposed		

Prior Winning Percentages: 1998 (63%); 1992 (59%); 1990 House (65%); 1988 House (71%); 1986 House (76%); 1984 House (79%); 1982 House (72%); 1980 House (57%)

Byron Dorgan, North Dakota's junior senator, was first elected to the House in 1980 and to the Senate in 1992. Dorgan grew up in Regent, N.D. (population 268), where his family had a farm-equipment and petroleum business and raised cattle and horses. He was one of nine students in his high school graduating class. After college and business school, he worked for a Denver aerospace firm. Then in 1969, at age 26, he was appointed state tax commissioner, becoming the youngest constitutional officer in the state's history. His politics are very much out of North Dakota's democratic-socialist Non-Partisan League tradition: He has a strong mistrust of economic markets, a deep belief that government should intervene to protect the family farmer and small businessman, and a capacity to frame issues in a popular and un-threatening way. His first big issue as tax commissioner was taxing out-of-state corporations, which struck a chord in a state always hostile to big out-of-state money. Dorgan brought zest and cornball good humor to his work, and had a bright future in state politics. He ran for the House in 1974, and lost to Republican Mark Andrews. In 1980, when Andrews ran for the Senate, Dorgan was elected to the House. The cautious Dorgan declined to challenge Andrews for the Senate in 1986, a race that his successor as tax commissioner, Kent Conrad, won. And he declined to take on 80-year-old Sen. Quentin Burdick, a fellow Democrat, in 1988. But four years later, when Conrad unexpectedly announced he would not seek re-election, Dorgan finally ran for the Senate. (Conrad had a change of heart and came back to the Senate in a special election after Burdick died in office.) Dorgan and his Republican opponent both backed normal trade relations with China, a major buyer of North Dakota wheat, but remained wary of free trade otherwise. Dorgan won by a solid 59%-39%.

In the Senate, Dorgan's voting record has been similar to Conrad's—generally moderate to liberal, and more centrist on cultural issues. This is one case where senators of the same party from the same state have worked harmoniously together. They call themselves, along with Earl Pomeroy, the state's at-large representative, "Team North Dakota." Dorgan strongly backed South Dakotan Tom Daschle for Senate Democratic leader in 1994 and became an assistant floor leader. In 1998, he considered running for whip against Harry Reid of Nevada, but withdrew and became co-chairman of the Democratic Policy Committee. In 2004, when Daschle was defeated for re-election and it became apparent that Reid had the votes to succeed him as minority leader, Dorgan started running for party whip, but quickly dropped out when it was clear Richard Durbin of Illinois had the votes. "It seemed to me that a number of our members felt that, for our two top spots, at least one should be from a blue state," he said. Unhappy with the Republican-controlled Senate's lack of oversight of the Bush administration, he used the policy committee to hold quasi-hearings on topics ranging from post-Hurricane Katrina relief to contracting abuses in Iraq. When Democrats returned to the majority in 2007, Dorgan made his Policy Committee chairmanship more visible in setting the party's agenda in the Senate. Dorgan took on oil speculators and media moguls trying to concentrate their holdings, investigating the merger of two satellite-radio companies. He was also a strong advocate of loosened restrictions on importation of prescription drugs from abroad.

Dorgan continues to be a champion of family farms, even as their numbers decline. He has been a leading proponent of crop insurance and disaster relief packages. On both the 2002 and 2008 farm bills, he and Republican Charles Grassley of Iowa led the move to cap farm subsidies at $250,000. He argued that too much would go to a few rich farmers and said he feared that such payments would instigate opposition to the farm bill. (Anyway, not many North Dakota or Iowa farmers qualify for huge payments.) Their effort failed under both Republican and Democratic control.

A theme throughout Dorgan's voting record is a distrust of unfettered economic markets. During the 1990s, he often criticized Federal Reserve Chairman Alan Greenspan for backing high interest rates, and he was one of four senators to vote against his reconfirmation as Fed chairman in 2000. He advocates a more vigorous antitrust policy, with temporary bans on agribusiness and airline mergers. He opposes individual investment accounts for Social Security and has sought to expand access to broadband Internet service in rural communities. In July 2006, he promoted his new book, *Take This Job and Ship It: How Corporate Greed and Brain-Dead Politics Are Selling Out America*. Dorgan believes that free-trade deals have led to sweatshop production, and in 2007 he strongly opposed renewing a grant of broad negotiating authority for the president in free-trade deals with other countries. In the 110th Congress (2007–08), he led opposition to expanding guest-worker programs during the immigration debate. But his objections to trade stopped at his state's border. To promote North Dakota grain sales, Dorgan has been a prime mover in scaling back the embargo on Cuba. He has called the embargo "one of the greatest follies of American foreign policy." He attacked the Bush administration proposal to require Cuban purchasers to make payments before goods were shipped. His amendment to permit travel to Cuba for agricultural purposes was dropped from the final farm spending bill in 2007 because of fears that Bush would veto it.

Dorgan has backed wind-energy projects, in which North Dakota is a leader. During debate on the 2007 energy bill, he teamed with Republican Larry Craig of Idaho on a measure to increase fuel-efficiency standards for cars and trucks by 4% a year from 2012 to 2030. He has worked for several years to create a Red River Valley Research Corridor, to link North Dakota colleges and businesses with federal research contracts.

Dorgan is the chairman of the Indian Affairs committee. In the last Congress (2007–08), he was able to get passed the first overhaul of Indian health programs since 1992. "We spend twice as much on health services for federal prisoners as we do on health services for American Indians," he asserted. He also wants to expand economic development and youth centers, and to encourage the settlement of long-running litigation over Interior Department mismanagement of Indian trust funds. While in the minority, Dorgan teamed with Arizona Republican John McCain to investigate abuses by GOP lobbyist Jack Abramoff and the bilking of Indian tribes. When news reports documented large campaign contributions to Dorgan from some of those tribes, the senator heatedly replied that he had long backed the Indian projects and others "will try to spin a web of deception to smear and discredit those of us who are investigating the wrongdoing."

Dorgan has been easily re-elected. In 1998, he beat state Sen. Donna Nalewaja 63%-35%, carrying every county but one, where the vote was tied. For 2004, national Republicans tried to recruit former Gov. Ed Schafer, but he declined. The Republican nominee, rancher Mike Liffrig, attacked Dorgan for supporting human cloning (in response, Dorgan altered a bill he'd sponsored). One opposition ad portrayed gay couples at the altar, with two men in black ties about to kiss. The voiceover said, "You can kiss our North Dakota values goodbye or you can kiss Senator Dorgan goodbye." But with far more money and more than three decades of winning statewide races, Dorgan won easily, 68%-32%. This time he carried every county. He seems safe for an easy re-election in 2010, unless Republican Gov. Mike Hoeven challenges him.

Representative-At-Large

Earl Pomeroy (D)

Elected 1992, 9th term; b. Sept. 2, 1952, Valley City; home, Bismarck; U. of ND, B.A. 1974, J.D., 1979; Presbyterian; married (Mary Berglund); 2 children.

Elected Office: ND House of Reps., 1980–84; ND insurance commissioner, 1984–92.

Professional Career: Practicing atty., 1979–84; Natl. Assn. of Insurance Commissioners., V.P. 1989, Pres. 1990.

DC Office: 1501 LHOB, 20515, 202-225-2611; Fax: 202-226-0893; Web site: www.house.Gov/pomeroy.

State Offices: Bismarck, 701-224-0355; Fargo, 701-235-9760.

Committees: *Agriculture* (26th of 28 D): Conservation, Credit, Energy & Research; General Farm Commodities & Risk Management. *Ways & Means* (10th of 26 D): Health; Social Security; Trade.

Group Ratings

	ADA	ACLU	AFS	LCV	ITIC	NTU	COC	ACU	CFG	FRC
2008	85	73	100	85	100	6	61	4	0	17
2007	85	—	100	85	—	4	60	4	12	—

National Journal Ratings

	2007 LIB	—	2007 CONS		2008 LIB	—	2008 CONS
Economic	69%	—	28%		57%	—	41%
Social	55%	—	45%		62%	—	34%
Foreign	58%	—	41%		63%	—	36%
Composite	61%	—	39%		62%	—	38%

Key Votes of the 110th Congress

1. Increase minimum wage	Y	5. Share immigration data	Y
2. Expand SCHIP	Y	6. Foreign aid abortion ban	N
3. Raise CAFE standards	Y	7. Ban gay bias in workplace	Y
4. Bail out financial markets	Y	8. Repeal D.C. gun law	Y

9. Withdraw troops 8/08	Y
10. No operations in Iran	Y
11. Free trade with Peru	Y
12. Overhaul FISA	Y

Election Results

2008 general	Earl Pomeroy (D)	194,577	(62%)	($1,795,718)
	Duane Sand (R)	119,388	(38%)	($1,944,099)
2008 primary	Earl Pomeroy (D)	unopposed		

Prior Winning Percentages: 2006 (66%); 2004 (60%); 2002 (52%); 2000 (53%); 1998 (56%); 1996 (55%); 1994 (52%); 1992 (57%)

Earl Pomeroy, North Dakota's lone House member, is a Democrat first elected in 1992. Pomeroy grew up in Valley City and after college served as Byron Dorgan's driver during Dorgan's unsuccessful bid for a House seat in 1974. After law school, Pomeroy practiced law in Valley City. In 1980, when Dorgan and Kent Conrad won statewide elections, Pomeroy, at age 28, won a seat in the Legislature. In 1984 and 1988, he was elected insurance commissioner. In 1992, he was planning to retire from politics and join the Peace Corps in Russia. But then, the at-large House seat came open; Dorgan was running for Conrad's seat in the Senate after Conrad decided not to seek re-election. (Conrad came back to the Senate in a special election after Democratic Sen. Quentin Burdick died in office.) Pomeroy put his overseas plans on hold and decided to run for Dorgan's House seat. Articulate, cheerful and sincere, a critic of insurance companies yet unabrasive, he was nominated unanimously by the state Democratic convention. He won the general election, 57%-39%, almost exactly Dorgan's margin in the Senate election that year. The three North Dakotans—Pomeroy, Dorgan and Conrad—are good friends and often band together to defend the state's interests.

Pomeroy has compiled a moderate to liberal voting record, working with Republicans as well as Democrats on issues. In the Republican-controlled Congress, he strongly supported the adoption tax credit and brought his two-year-old daughter, adopted from Korea, onto the floor for the vote. He also strongly supported normal trade relations with China and has pushed for more exports of North Dakota wheat to China. In 2001, he got a coveted seat on the House Ways and Means Committee, where he is considered an expert on pension and insurance policy. During debate over repeal of the estate tax, Pomeroy supported raising the $1 million exemption to $3 million. In 2003, Pomeroy supported the GOP bill to create a prescription drug bill in the Medicare program; the bill increased the Medicare reimbursement rate for rural and small city hospitals, which was worth $48 million to Bismarck hospitals alone and $183 million statewide. In 2005 and 2006, he co-chaired the House Democrats' Social Security Task Force. And in 2007, he worked to revive the wind energy production tax credit, enacted in 1992 but allowed to expire in 1999, 2001 and again in 2003. The extended credit, popular in windy North Dakota, was part of the $700 billion financial industry bailout enacted in October 2008.

In 2003, Democratic leaders allowed Pomeroy to regain a seat on the Agriculture Committee while staying on Ways and Means, something not permitted for most other members but viewed as important in keeping Pomeroy safe politically. He is often an ally on the committee of Chairman Collin Peterson, a Democrat from adjoining farm-state Minnesota. As the only House member on both Agriculture and Ways and Means, Pomeroy played a key role in the 2008 farm bill in expanding tax credits, including for cellulosic ethanol production. In 1996, when Republicans controlled the House, Pomeroy opposed the GOP's Freedom to Farm Act, which phased out farm subsidies, and was a booster of the subsequent annual disaster-relief bills that continued to provide hefty government support for farmers. He backed the 2002 farm act that reversed much of Freedom to Farm. In that bill, Pomeroy pressed successfully for country-of-origin meat labeling.

Many of the biggest agricultural issues are related to trade, over which Ways and Means has jurisdiction. When Special Trade Representative Robert Zoellick negotiated an allowance of sugar imports from the Dominican Republic as part of the Central American Free Trade Agreement in 2004, Pomeroy protested vigorously and said that the only way to settle sugar issues was through World Trade Organization negotiations, not regional trade agreements. North Dakota has a thriving sugar-beet industry. He voted against the Australian Free Trade Agreement in 2004, and he led the fight in 2005 against ratification of the Central American-Dominican Republic Free Trade Agreement, opposed by the Red River Valley Sugarbeet Growers Association but backed by the North Dakota Wheat Commission. When Agriculture Secretary Mike Johanns sought to allay concerns by saying that the sugar provisions amounted to only two additional small packets of foreign sugar per U.S. consumer, Pomeroy replied, "Those two little packets of sugar cost us $180 million in lost income to farmers."

During devastating floods in Grand Forks in April 1997, Pomeroy helped man dikes and slept in a nearby Air Force shelter. He later got nearly $500 million in flood relief and has continued to work for a $300 million system of levees and flood walls. Another vital local project for him is federal funding for an emergency outlet for Devils Lake, which has no natural outlet. Water has risen to record levels and flooded more than 100,000 acres. In 2003, the state started work on a channel to connect the lake with the Sheyenne River and through it, the Red River of the North; the first waters started flowing out in 2005.

Pomeroy had a serious challenge in 2002 from Tax Commissioner Rick Clayburgh, who argued that North Dakota would do better with a Republican congressman. He attacked Pomeroy for leaving the Agriculture Committee just before work on that year's farm bill began. Republicans also hit Pomeroy for voting against estate tax repeal and for backing the partial "privatization" of Social Security. But Pomeroy won 52%-48%, carrying Fargo, Minot and Grand Forks, Clayburgh's hometown; Clayburgh carried Bismarck.

In 2004, Pomeroy was opposed by Duane Sand, a 15-year Navy officer who in 2000 lost a challenge to Conrad, 62%-38%. Sand was reinforced by a late October appearance by then Republican Speaker Dennis Hastert, who said, "When we're talking about water policy, when we talk about farm policy, there's really nobody there to represent North Dakota." Pomeroy's campaign shot back that he had delivered on Medicare reimbursement, disaster relief legislation and agricultural policy. The result was Pomeroy's widest victory yet, 60%-40%, even as Bush carried the state 63%-35%. In 2006, Pomeroy had little serious opposition from political newcomer Matt Mechtel, a Cass County farmer. In a 2008 rematch against Sand, Pomeroy won 62%-38%. He got a dollop of national media attention in August 2007 when, addressing the issue of impeaching Bush, he said: "The people I represent don't want to impeach this clown." He got the local media's attention in 2009, when Pomeroy announced he was going to marry Grand Forks teacher Mary Berglund on July 2. He has two adopted children from his first marriage, which ended in divorce in 2002.

★ OHIO ★

Connecting the East with the great interior, bordering the South yet also on the Great Lakes, Ohio was the first entirely American state. The original 13 states started as British colonies, and the next three, Vermont, Kentucky and Tennessee, were spun off from them. But Ohio sprang Athena-like from the head of Congress, as the first state formed from the Northwest Territory. The Northwest Ordinance of 1787 established 6-mile-square townships, which imposed geometric order on diverse American landscapes west to the Pacific. It set aside one square mile per township for public schools, and the land was soon peppered with schoolhouses and small colleges, the foundation stones of a literate republic. The ordinance prohibited slavery, opening the way for free labor to clear fields, raise crops, and build mills and factories. In less than half a century, the former wilderness was one of the most productive parts of the young country. In the years after the Civil War, Ohio became one of the great industrial states, the original headquarters of John D. Rockefeller's Standard Oil, the site of major steel mills along the narrow and languidly flowing Cuyahoga and Mahoning rivers, and the location of the biggest soap companies, machine tool makers and tire manufacturers. Dayton was the home of the Wright brothers, who developed the airplane; of James Patterson, the inventor and manufacturer of the cash register; and of Charles Kettering, the inventor of the automobile starter. Akron was the home of Harvey Firestone, B. F. Goodrich and F. A. Seiberling—the great tire manufacturers. Cincinnati was the headquarters of the founders of Procter & Gamble. The state was settled by New Englanders in the northeast (in the Western Reserve) and by Virginians in the south, creating a split between the Southern-accented counties south of the National Road and U.S. 40 and the Northern-accented cities and towns to the north. It was also divided between Butternut and Copperhead territory that didn't want to fight the Civil War and Yankee territory that fiercely prosecuted the war and Reconstruction afterward.

This split heritage made Ohio politically a closely divided state—and a nationally pivotal one. A little more than a century ago, Ohio produced the candidate and campaign manager who won the presidency in 1896 and 1900: former Gov. William McKinley and iron and coal industrialist Mark Hanna. They inaugurated a 34-year period of Republican national majorities. McKinley's Republicans were for high tariffs and hard money and had a friendly regard for workers and even some unions, but they had no patience with large unions. They preached a nationalist Americanism tempered by wariness about making major commitments abroad. Republicans were the majority in this increasingly industrial Ohio, losing rural Butternut counties but carrying the big industrial cities of the north.

Then came the Depression of the 1930s, and Ohio became the scene of something like class warfare, with sit-down strikes and victories for the CIO industrial unions in autos, steel and tires. CIO cities (Cleveland, Akron, Youngstown, and Toledo) moved sharply toward the Democrats, while places with fewer union members (Cincinnati, Columbus, the dozens of small factory towns dotting the flat limestone plains of northern Ohio) stayed Republican. The political fighting was fierce, and the stakes were high. CIO leaders hoped to organize the entire workforce and build a Scandinavian-style welfare state. Republican leaders like Ohio's Sen. Robert Taft feared union control of business would imperil freedoms and throttle the economy. In the 1930s and 1940s, the unions made great gains, but Taft held them off, reducing union power with the Taft-Hartley Act of 1947 and his own re-election to the Senate in 1950.

In the years since, Ohio has oscillated as it's been courted by national campaigns. It has not voted for the loser in a presidential election since 1960. Democrat Bill Clinton carried the state twice, but by the narrowest of his margins in any large state—40%-38% in 1992, 47%-41% in 1996. And Al Gore lost here 50%-46% in 2000. Ohio Republicans won smashing victories in 1994 and 1998 and held their own in 1996 and 2000. The leading figure was George Voinovich, elected governor in 1990 by 56%-44%, re-elected in 1994 by 72%-25%, by far the biggest margin since 1826, when neither the Republican nor the Democratic party existed. From 1976 to 1994, Ohio was represented by two Democrats in the Senate, but when they retired, they were replaced by Republicans: Mike DeWine and Voinovich, both of whom had run unsuccessfully for the Senate before. In 1998, Republican Bob Taft, bearer of a great Ohio name, was elected governor over Democrat Lee Fisher by 50%-45%. Until that election, Ohio's governorship had been passed back and forth between the two parties, with neither holding it for more than eight years since Republican George K. Nash won in 1899. Republicans also held every other statewide office, had seemingly impervious margins in both houses of the Legislature, and made up the majority of the U.S. House delegation. Despite the state's lagging economy, President George W. Bush carried Ohio 51%-49% in 2004, as turnout surged as much as 20% in a state with very little population growth.

Then in 2006 came a great turn toward the Democrats. Unused to having one party in control for more than a decade, Ohio recoiled against the Republicans. It did not help that the supposedly fiscally conservative party had raised taxes several times or that individual Republicans were tarred with scandal. Ohio's state and local tax burden, rated 45th highest in the nation in 1977 by the Tax Foundation, was rated seventh in 2008, and Republicans had held the governorship for 24 of those 31 years. Gov. Taft pleaded no contest in 2005 to criminal violations for failing to report some $6,000 in gifts. The state Bureau

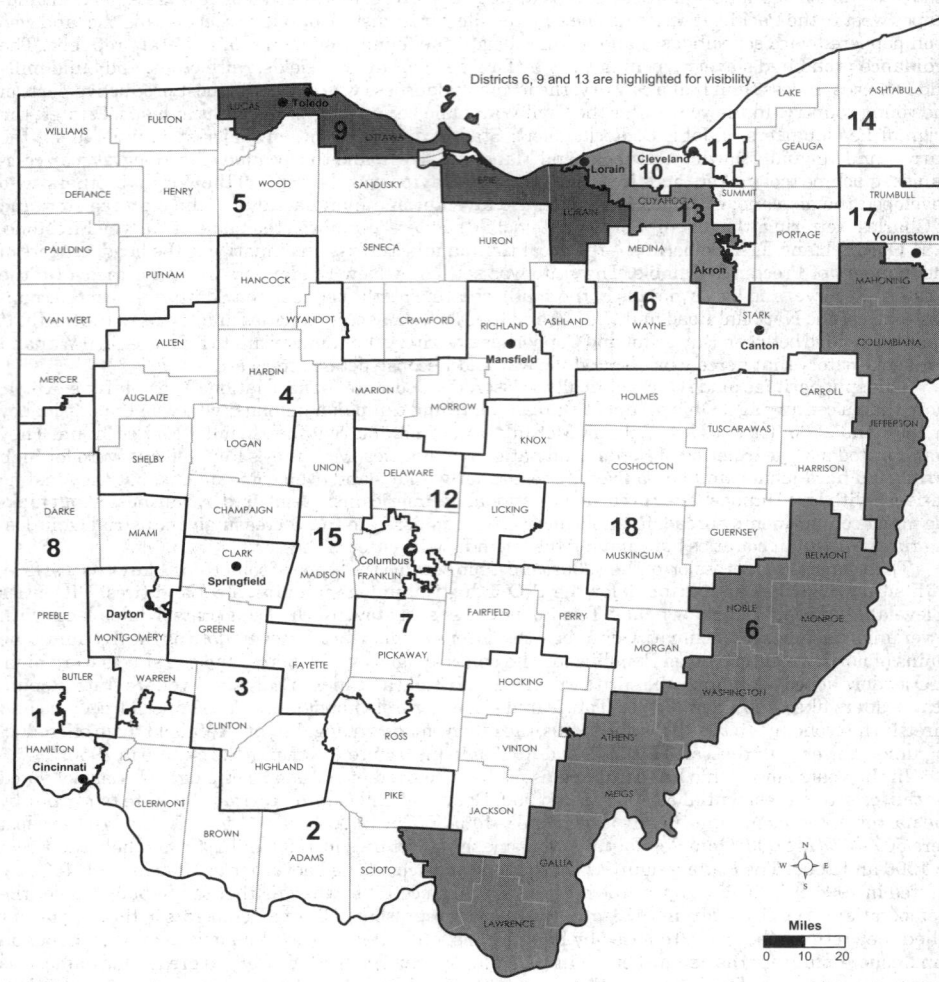

Districts 6, 9 and 13 are highlighted for visibility.

Congressional district boundaries were first effective for 2002.

The Almanac of American Politics.
National Journal

of Workmen's Compensation, controlled by Republicans, was under investigation for placing $50 million in investments in a rare-coin business run by a major GOP contributor, with $13 million of state assets missing. Democratic U.S. Rep. Ted Strickland, a former minister and prison psychologist, was elected governor by 61%-37% over Secretary of State Ken Blackwell, a Taft critic from the right. Strickland carried 72 of 88 counties; the only major metro area Blackwell carried was his home base of Cincinnati. Democrats won the offices of attorney general, secretary of state and treasurer. Democratic Rep. Sherrod Brown beat two-term GOP Sen. Mike DeWine by a solid 56%-44%. Democrats did not quite sweep the board. Republicans won the race for auditor and two seats on the state Supreme Court, and they held on to majorities in the Legislature.

The Democratic trend continued in 2008. Ohio was once again a target state in the presidential contest, with Republicans hoping that Democratic nominee Barack Obama would be a weak candidate in a state where he had lost the Democratic primary to Hillary Rodham Clinton, carrying only five of 18 congressional districts. Ohio was the scene of many candidate visits. Republican nominee John McCain introduced Alaska Gov. Sarah Palin as his vice presidential nominee in Dayton, and there were intensive organizational efforts on the part of both campaigns. This was the third campaign in a row in which Ohio was a major—arguably, the major—target state, and a certain fatigue may have set in. Turnout was up only marginally from 2004, the lowest increase in the nation. Obama carried the state 52%-47%. Democrats made further gains, winning two open U.S. House seats and seven seats in the state House, giving them majorities of 10-8 in the House delegation and 53-46 in the state House.

The Republican trend of the 1990s and the Democratic trend of 2006–08 occurred in a state that is still more industrial than post-industrial, a state changed by the immigration of the early 20th century but little touched by the immigration of the late 20th century, a state where cultural liberalism has a far smaller constituency than it does on either coast or even in nearby Illinois and Michigan. It used to be said that Ohio was a typical state, a great test market, close to the national average in income levels, urban-rural balance, and ethnic mix, as well as presidential percentages. But economically and culturally, it is different, a template perhaps for Indiana and Missouri but not for Oregon and Arizona. There are few immigrants here, and the population is only 2% Hispanic. In manufacturing jobs, Ohio trails only California and Texas—which have three and two times as many people, respectively—yet it has 500,000 fewer than it did in the peak year, 1969. From 2000 to 2007, it had a lower rate of population growth than any other state except West Virginia, North Dakota, Rhode Island and Louisiana. Ohio economy's never seemed to recover from the 2001–02 recession. The state has one of the lowest rates of business start-ups in the nation, according to the Kauffman Foundation, and its income levels have languished as first the steel companies, then the auto subcontractors and finally the Detroit Three laid off thousands of workers. Honda decided in 2006 not to build a fourth plant in Ohio but to go to Indiana instead. The state's encouragement of bioscience and high-tech businesses has not generated nearly as many offsetting jobs. Columbus, the one metro area with significant post-industrial growth, nonetheless seemed threatened by the 2008 crisis in the financial-services markets.

For over half a century, there have been two politically distinct parts of Ohio. Northeast Ohio—centered on Cleveland and extending westward to Toledo and south and east to the factory towns of Akron and Canton, Youngstown and Warren and the gritty industrial cities south along the Ohio River—has been the state's Democratic heartland, with the highest percentages of union members and a large black population in Cleveland. In 2008, this area remained Democratic, but there was no significant trend toward Obama except in northwest Ohio around Toledo, an area hurt by the troubles of the auto subcontractors and Detroit auto companies. Indeed, in Youngstown, Warren and the Ohio River counties, Obama's percentages ran behind those of Democratic nominee John Kerry four years earlier, an example, at least in part, of his weakness among voters of Scots-Irish Appalachian origin that was so evident in the Democratic primaries. The other part of Ohio—south and west of the industrial belt and including Columbus, Cincinnati and Dayton—was never as heavily unionized and in national elections has tended to vote Republican, much like most of Indiana. In 2008, in contrast to Indiana, which gave Obama a narrow

Population		**Household Income**		**Work**	
Pop. 2007:	11,463,403	Under $15k:	14.5%	Private:	81.5%
State rank:	7th of 50	$15k to $50k:	39.0%	Government:	12.7%
Change since 2000:	Up 1.0%	$50k to $100k:	31.4%	Self-employed:	5.7%
Urban:	75.7%	$100k to $150k:	12.8%	Unemployment (3-yr. average):	4.8%
Rural:	24.3%	Over $150k:	2.3%	Poverty:	13.2%
Native of state:	75.0%	Median income:	$46,296	Blue collar:	25.1%
Not a citizen:	1.9%			White collar:	58.1%
Area size:	44,825 sq. mi.	**Home Value**		Khaki collar:	0.1%
		Under $100k:	30.5%	Other:	16.7%
Most populous cities		$100k to $300k:	60.6%		
1. Columbus	724,095	$300k to $500k:	6.7%	**Age**	
2. Cleveland	405,014	$500k to $1 mil:	1.9%	Median age:	37.6 yrs.
3. Cincinnati	302,471	Over $1 million:	0.3%	More than 65 yrs:	13.4%
4. Toledo	289,103	Median:	$134,400	Less than 18 yrs:	24.2%

Race/Ethnicity				Military Veterans		Registered Voters in 2008	
White:	82.8%	*Language*		% of Pop:	11.2%	No party registration	
Black:	11.7%	English:	93.9%	*Veterans by Period*		Voter turnout:	5,708,350
Hispanic:	2.4%	Spanish:	2.1%	WWII and before:	13.9%	Turnout as % of	
Asian:	1.5%	Asian:	0.9%	Korea:	12.4%	voting age:	65.2%
Native Am.:	0.2%	Other		Vietnam:	32.1%	**General Assembly**	
Hawaiian:	0.0%	European	2.5%	Gulf (pre-2001):	9.8%	Senate:	12 D 21 R
Two+ races:	1.3%	**Education**		Gulf (post-2001):	5.1%	House:	53 D 46 R
Ancestry		H.S. grad:	86.3%	Peace time:	26.7%		
German:	22.1%	College grad:	23.3%				
Irish:	11.2%	Grad degree:	8.5%				
English:	7.8%						

victory, this area continued to vote Republican, although by lesser margins. Obama carried the counties containing the central cities of Columbus, Cincinnati and Dayton, but ran behind in the latter two metro areas and won only a small lead in metro Columbus.

Presidential politics   From its beginnings, Ohio has been a crucial state in presidential politics, and it has never been more so, with its 20 electoral votes, than in the elections of 2000, 2004 and 2008.

Of the large northern states, it has generally been the most Republican, except in 1976, when Jimmy Carter ran well in the Southern-accented counties below U.S. 40 and carried the state by 11,000 votes. (Gerald Ford carried Michigan and Illinois.) No Republican has ever been elected president without carrying Ohio. No Democrat, in today's electoral-vote arithmetic, can be sure of winning without it.

Even so, the dynamics of the presidential race in Ohio have been quite different in the past three elections. In 2000, Republican George W. Bush, despite holding narrow leads in polls, made Ohio a priority state from start to finish, while the campaign of Democrat Al Gore, looking to opportunities elsewhere, pulled out much of its advertising in mid-October—perhaps its greatest strategic mis-

2008 Presidential Vote		
Obama (D)	2,940,044	(52%)
McCain (R)	2,677,820	(47%)
2008 Democratic Presidential Primary		
Clinton (D)	1,259,620	(53%)
Obama (D)	1,055,769	(45%)
2008 Republican Presidential Primary		
McCain (R)	656,687	(60%)
Huckabee (R)	335,356	(31%)
2004 Presidential Vote		
Bush (R)	2,859,764	(51%)
Kerry (D)	2,741,165	(49%)

take. Bush carried Ohio by only 50%-46%. In 2004, both campaigns recognized that Ohio was a major target state. Job losses, especially in manufacturing, seemed to make the atmosphere especially favorable to Democrats. They and anti-Bush 527 organizations ran a classic industrial-era registration and turnout drive aimed particularly at African-American neighborhoods in central cities and at university communities. By all measures, it was spectacularly successful. The Democratic popular-vote margin increased by 60,000 votes in Cleveland's Cuyahoga County, and Democratic margins increased as well in the counties containing Columbus, Cincinnati, Akron, Toledo, Lorain, Youngstown and Warren and in a five-county cluster centered on the university town of Athens. But the Bush campaign ran a post-industrial registration and turnout organization in all 88 counties, with some 65,000 volunteers networking with evangelical and Catholic churches, farmers, doctors and community organizations. That gave Bush a lead of 136,000 votes over Kerry in the initial count. When 155,000 provisional ballots were counted, the Bush margin was reduced to 119,000.

In 2008, Ohio was once again a central focus of both campaigns, although Democrat Barack Obama's lead in polls in states like Virginia and Colorado that Bush had won in 2004 made it seem less crucial. Yet the intense organizational efforts of both campaigns were only barely enough to match the turnout that the organizational efforts of 2004 had produced. Barack Obama carried the state 52%-47%, winning 198,879 more votes than John Kerry had. Republican John McCain got 181,944 fewer votes than Bush, suggesting a decline in Republican turnout and an increase in Democratic turnout compared to 2004. Obama carried union-household voters by about the same margin as Kerry had, but he also narrowly won voters in nonunion households. Republican John McCain won small margins from both Catholics and Protestants, but not enough to overcome the big Obama margins among those registering no religion. Young voters went 61% for Obama, providing about two-thirds of his popular-vote margin. Those with graduate-school degrees preferred Obama 54%-44%, a margin much lower than he won among those voters in coastal states.

In 1996, Ohio switched its presidential primary from May to March and voted on the same day as Illinois, Michigan and Wisconsin. But even then, just four weeks after New Hampshire, the race was already over. For the 2000 election, the state Legislature voted to move the date to March 7, and Ohio was seriously contested. Bush and Gore won overwhelming victories as they clinched their parties' nominations. In 2004, Ohio held its primary on March 2, with seven other states; John Kerry won easily here and elsewhere and clinched the Democratic nomination exactly nine months before the general election.

In 2008, the Republican contest was effectively over on March 4, when Ohio voted. Mike Huckabee remained an active candidate, but McCain beat him 60%-31%, carrying all 88 counties. In contrast, there was a spirited contest on the Democratic side. Fresh from a series of stunning victories in February, Obama hoped to end Hillary Rodham Clinton's candidacy by beating her in Ohio and Texas. But Clinton, casting herself as a fighter for working families, rallied and won an impressive 53%-45% victory here, which, with a narrower win in Texas, kept her in the race for three more months. Obama carried only five counties, including the central cities of Cleveland, Columbus, Cincinnati and Dayton, and he carried only five of 18 congressional districts. He was particularly weak in white working-class areas—the west side of Cleveland and its close-in suburbs, the Mahoning Valley steel country around Youngstown and Warren, and the Democratic-leaning small industrial counties along the Ohio River. Clinton got as much as 80% of the vote in some counties, evidence of Obama's weakness in Appalachia. That weakness showed up, in muted form, in the general election, when Obama ran behind John Kerry's percentages in many of the same areas—not enough to prevent him from carrying Ohio, but enough to prevent him from making the major gains from previous Democratic showings that he did in states like Virginia, North Carolina and Indiana.

Congressional districting

Ohio lost one House seat in the 2000 census and now has a House delegation of 18 members, its smallest since the 1820s. In 2001, Republicans had majorities in the Legislature and held the governorship, and so had control of the process. It was clear that the Republicans could eliminate the seat of 13th District Democratic Rep. Sherrod Brown and imperil the chances of 6th District Democratic Rep. Ted Strickland. But Strickland threatened to run in the 18th District against Republican Rep. Bob Ney, and Brown made it clear that if his seat was eliminated, he would run for governor. Republican Gov. Taft did not want to face a well-financed and politically adept challenger and asked Republican legislators not to target Brown.

111th Congress Lineup
10 D   8 R

110th Congress Lineup
11 R   7 D

The Legislature did not act in 2001, and in 2002 the Republicans effectively lost control, since under Ohio law a statute passed that close to the February 21 filing deadline could take immediate effect only if it had a two-thirds vote in both houses. This meant the Republicans had to get the votes of at least one Democrat in the Senate and seven in the House. Given the circumstances, the Republicans constructed a pretty ingenious plan. All 11 Republican incumbents got districts very similar to their current ones, as did the two Cleveland Democrats. Every other Democrat got a significantly different district. The incumbent put into the most parlous position was the 17th District's Jim Traficant, a Democrat. But he was facing trial on bribery charges and had been voting with Republicans on many issues; Democrats obviously preferred to sacrifice him. The 3rd District was made significantly more Republican, but incumbent Democrat Tony Hall had long run far ahead of party lines, so as long as he continued to run, the seat seemed safely Democratic. The 14th District's Tom Sawyer was given much of Traficant's old territory. Strickland was given a district that was much more Democratic than his previous one, and Brown was left alone. So the Democrats made a deal. They would provide the votes to allow the plan to go into effect immediately and avoid having to reschedule the congressional primary for August or September at a cost to taxpayers of $7 million. The plan passed on January 22.

The 3rd district seat turned Republican after Democratic incumbent Hall left the House in 2002. Strickland and Brown were re-elected twice and then were elected governor and senator in 2006. Also that year, Republicans lost scandal-plagued Bob Ney's seat. In 2008, Democrats won seats in the 1st, 15th and 16th districts. So a House delegation that had been 12-6 Republican immediately after redistricting had become 10-8 Democratic six years later.

Ohio is expected to lose two seats in the reapportionment following the 2010 census. In early 2009, the odds appeared to favor another bipartisan plan. Democratic Gov. Strickland had a high job rating, and Democrats held a majority in the state House, but they would have to capture a net five seats in the state Senate in 2010 to overcome the Republicans' 21-12 advantage there. A bipartisan plan would presumably cost each party a seat, and there would likely be an incentive to strengthen incumbents of both parties.

Governor

Ted Strickland (D)

Elected 2006, term expires Jan. 2011, 1st term; b. Aug. 4, 1941, Lucasville; home, Bexley; Asbury Col., B.A. 1963, M.Div. 1967, U. of KY, Ph.D. 1980; Methodist; married (Frances).

Elected Office: U.S. House of Reps., 1992–94, 1996–2006.

Professional Career: Assoc. minister, Trinity Methodist Church, 1967–68; Administrator, KY Methodist Home, 1968–70, 1975–76; Consulting psychologist, Southern OH Correctional Facility, 1985–92, 1995–96; Prof., Shawnee St. U., 1988–92, 1995–96.

Office: Governor's Office, Riffe Center, 30th Floor, 77 S. High Street, Columbus, 43215-6108, 614-466-3555; Fax: 614-466-9354; Web site: governor.ohio.gov.

Election Results

2006 general	Ted Strickland (D)	2,435,384	(61%)
	Kenneth Blackwell (R)	1,474,285	(37%)
2006 primary	Ted Strickland (D)	634,114	(79%)
	Bryan Flannery (D)	166,253	(21%)

Democrat Ted Strickland was elected governor of Ohio in 2006. He was born and raised in Lucasville in Appalachian Ohio, the son of a steelworker with a sixth-grade education and the eighth of nine children. His family lived a hardscrabble existence, briefly living in a chicken coop after their home burned down. College did not seem within the realm of possibilities but a high school teacher took him on a trip to visit Asbury College and Theological Seminary in Kentucky and he ended up graduating from there with degree in history in 1963. He went on to get a master's degree in divinity in 1967. Strickland became a Methodist minister and served in various roles at the Methodist Home for Children in Versailles, Ky. In 1980, he got a Ph.D. in counseling psychology from the University of Kentucky and went to work as a prison psychologist. He was also a psychology professor at Shawnee State University in Portsmouth, Ohio.

There was little in his early political career to suggest he might one day end up as governor. Strickland ran for the U.S. House unsuccessfully in 1976, 1978 and 1980, and then ran again in 1992 when redistricting placed two Republican incumbents in the same district. One lost in the primary 50.2%-49.8% and Strickland defeated the other 51%-49%. In his first term in the House, Strickland voted for President Bill Clinton's budget and tax package, but against the 1994 crime bill because of its gun control provisions. He also voted against the North American Free Trade Agreement. As the 1994 election neared, Strickland suggested there might be a need for tax increases to pay for health care programs. Republican challenger Frank Cremeans seized on the statement and beat Strickland 51%-49%. In a 1996 rematch, Strickland attacked Cremeans for Medicare "cuts" and scaling down the earned income tax credit, which he called a tax increase on the poor. Strickland won 51%-49%. In Congress, Strickland's voting record was generally moderate but a bit more liberal on foreign policy.

In May 2005, he decided to run for governor after Columbus Mayor Michael Coleman, the leading Democratic candidate, seemed to falter. The governor at the time, Republican Bob Taft, was ineligible for a third term and had extremely low job approval ratings. In any case, Ohio Democrats argued that Republicans had been in office too long, having held the governorship and majorities in the legislature for 16 years, the longest period since Thomas Jefferson's Democratic Republicans in 1803–22. It did not help that the supposedly fiscally conservative party had raised taxes several times, and that was not mitigated by cuts in the income tax made by Taft and the Legislature in 2005. As often happens when a party is in power for many years, there was scandal. In August 2005, Taft pleaded no contest to criminal violations of state ethics laws for failing to report some $6,000 of gifts, including free golf outings, meals, and hockey tickets. It the first time an Ohio governor had been convicted of a crime. At the same time, the state Bureau of Workmen's Compensation, controlled by Republicans, was under investigation for placing $50 million in investments in a rare coin business run by major Republican contributor, Tom Noe. In May 2005, the *Toledo Blade* reported that as much as $13 million of state assets were missing. A year later, Noe pleaded guilty to violating federal campaign finance laws.

Strickland won a 79%-21% victory over former state Rep. Bryan Flannery in the May primary, and faced Secretary of State Kenneth Blackwell, a strong fiscal and cultural conservative, in the general election. Like Strickland, Blackwell had a compelling life story: The son of a meatpacker, he lived in a Cincinnati housing project until he was 6, attended Xavier University on a football scholarship and later became Cincinnati mayor, a U.S. Department of Housing and Urban Development undersecretary and Ohio treasurer. Blackwell was sharply critical of Taft and Republican legislative leaders. Strickland campaigned on a platform called "Turnaround Ohio," a plan to strengthen the state's economy, improve education, retrain workers for the global economy and increase access to health care. Blackwell called for repeal of the sales tax increase and a constitutional amendment limiting the growth of state spending. Both candidates opposed gun control and legalizing same-sex marriage, though Strickland supported legal benefits for gay partners. Religious faith played an unusually prominent role; both candidates incorporated biblical verses into their speeches and Strickland ran ads on Christian radio saying that "biblical principles" would guide his actions as governor. He won 61%-37%, carrying 72 of 88 counties and accruing more votes than Republican Gov. George Voinovich had in 1994. However, Republicans held on to majorities in the Legislature, losing just one seat in the state Senate and seven in the House.

On his first day in office, Strickland angered Republicans by vetoing a law limiting non-economic damages in civil lawsuits to $5,000; Taft had intended to allow it to become law without his signature. But Strickland also embarked on a bipartisan course. He moved his office from a high-rise to the old State House and installed a round conference table, where he held weekly meetings with the Republican House speaker and Senate president—the atmosphere was frosty at first, but warmed up. He worked to come up with policies that would have their support, and in 2007 he told *The Washington Post*, "If you act with respect toward the people who disagree with you, they'll give you a break and won't cut you off." One result was the passage in June 2007, with just one dissenting vote, of a $52 billion, two-year budget. It included a freeze on tuition increases at state colleges and universities after a decade of 9% average increases, $100 million of additional college aid, an expansion of Medicaid eligibility and an increase of the state share of education funding from 48% to 54%. Republicans opposed Strickland's line-item veto of a tuition voucher program for special needs students and $500,000 for abstinence-only sex education. Strickland firmly opposed any tax increase. In December 2007 he told the *Toledo Blade*, "I feel the economy is fragile, and a tax increase would not be helpful to the economy." He reduced state spending pretty much across the board in September 2008 when revenues came in under estimates.

Energy was another issue Strickland took on. Electric rate stabilization plans were scheduled to expire in 2008, with the likely result being much higher electricity rates. He endorsed a plan to require that 25% of energy generated in Ohio in 2025 be from "advanced" sources—wind, fuel cells, clean coal—and his bill allowed consumers to choose between market rates and those set by the Public Utilities Commission of Ohio. His plan passed the Senate unanimously and the bill was signed into law in May 2008.

In early 2008, Strickland proposed that the state borrow $1.7 billion and invest the proceeds in various projects to create 80,000 jobs, including $250 million in renewable energy, $200 million in biomedical industries, $150 million in bridges, ports and roads, $100 million in bioproducts for renewable sources for plastics (Akron is a major polymer producer), $400 million for local infrastructure and $200 million to redevelop city centers.

In January 2009, Strickland called for sweeping reforms to the education system, with plans to reduce classroom sizes, require day-long kindergarten and add 20 days to the school year. The House passed a plan similar to Strickland's, but the Senate balked, stripping the changes from their budget. This set up a contentious fight between the houses as they sat down to negotiate a compromise budget that June.

For all his bipartisanship, Strickland has proved to be an effective party leader. When Democratic Attorney General Marc Dann was revealed to have had an affair with a female subordinate, Strickland joined other Democrats calling for him to resign, which Dann did in May 2008. Strickland also took an active role in presidential politics. He endorsed New York Sen. Hillary Rodham Clinton for president. Her 53%-45% victory in the March 4 Ohio primary, which brought her especially large margins in Strickland's old congressional district, kept her in the race with Illinois Sen. Barack Obama for another three months. After Clinton withdrew in June, Strickland endorsed Obama and campaigned with him in the fall. As the highly popular governor of a state that had been crucial to the outcome in 2004, he was widely mentioned as a possible vice presidential nominee. But he announced in June 2008 that he would not accept the vice presidential nomination. The November election turned out well for Strickland. Obama carried Ohio and Democrats gained seven seats in the House to capture a 53-46 majority. But the GOP retained control of the Senate, 21-12.

Into 2009, Strickland generally enjoyed solid job approval ratings although, like governors around the country, he faced hard economic times ahead. Also, Democrats need to capture five seats in the state Senate in 2010 to get control of congressional redistricting after the every-decade census, a tall order.

Senior Senator

George Voinovich (R)

Elected 1998, term expires 2010, 2nd term; b. July 15, 1936, Cleveland; home, Cleveland; Ohio U., B.A. 1958, Ohio St. U., J.D. 1961; Catholic; married (Janet); 4 children.

Elected Office: OH House of Reps., 1966–71; Cuyahoga Cnty. auditor, 1971–76; Cuyahoga Cnty. commissioner, 1977–78; OH lt. gov., 1979; Cleveland mayor, 1979–89; OH Gov., 1990–98.

Professional Career: OH asst. atty. gen., 1963–64.

DC Office: 524 HSOB, 20510, 202-224-3353; Fax: 202-228-1382; Web site: voinovich.senate.gov.

State Offices: Cincinnati, 513-684-3265; Cleveland, 216-522-7095; Columbus, 614-469-6697; Nelsonville, 740-441-6410; Toledo, 419-259-3895.

Committees: *Appropriations* (11th of 12 R): Commerce, Justice, Science & Related Agencies; Energy & Water Development; Homeland Security (RMM); Transportation, Housing and Urban Development & Related Agencies. *Environment & Public Works* (2nd of 7 R). *Homeland Security & Governmental Affairs* (4th of 6 R): Federal Financial Management, Government Information, Federal Services & International Security; Oversight of Government Management, the Federal Workforce & the District of Columbia (RMM); State, Local & Private Sector Preparedness & Integration.

Group Ratings

	ADA	ACLU	AFS	LCV	ITIC	NTU	COC	ACU	CFG	FRC
2008	25	29	22	18	100	44	88	52	43	88
2007	25	—	0	20	—	58	82	48	46	—

National Journal Ratings

	2007 LIB	—	2007 CONS		2008 LIB	—	2008 CONS
Economic	41%	—	58%		40%	—	59%
Social	42%	—	57%		41%	—	57%
Foreign	41%	—	58%		33%	—	66%
Composite	42%	—	58%		39%	—	61%

Key Votes of the 110th Congress

1. Raise CAFE standards	N	5. Make English official language Y	9. Withdraw troops 3/08	N
2. Expand SCHIP	N	6. Path to citizenship	N	10. Iran guard is terrorist group	Y
3. Cap greenhouse gases	N	7. Fetus is unborn child	Y	11. Increase missile defense $	Y
4. Bail out financial markets	Y	8. Prosecute hate crimes	Y	12. Overhaul FISA	Y

Election Results

2004 general	George Voinovich (R) 3,464,356	(64%)	($8,956,380)
	Eric Fingerhut (D) 1,961,171	(36%)	($1,166,538)
2004 primary	George Voinovich (R) 640,082	(77%)	
	John Mitchel (R) 195,476	(23%)	

Prior Winning Percentages: 1998 (56%); 1994 governor (72%); 1990 governor (56%)

George Voinovich, Ohio's senior senator, is a Republican who will have spent 44 years in elected office by the time he retires in 2010. Facing the prospect of a tough re-election fight that year, he announced in January 2009 that he would leave the Senate at the end of his current term.

Voinovich is of Serbian and Slovenian descent and grew up in the heavily ethnic, working-class neighborhood of Collinwood in Cleveland, where he still lives. He graduated from Ohio University and from the Ohio State University law school, then practiced law in Cleveland. He was elected to the state House in 1966 at the age of 30, elected Cuyahoga County auditor in 1971 and county commissioner in 1977. In 1978, he was chosen by Republican Gov. James Rhodes to be lieutenant governor. In 1979, after Cleveland went into bankruptcy under Democratic Mayor Dennis Kucinich (now a House member), Voinovich ran for mayor. It was a strenuous campaign—he was running as a Republican in a heavily Democratic city—and one touched by tragedy: His nine-year-old daughter was killed in an auto accident during the campaign. But he won, and in 10 years in office, he fixed the budget and helped spark the city's renaissance. In 1990, he ran for governor and beat Attorney General Anthony Celebrezze Jr. 56%-44%, and in 1994, he was re-elected by a resounding 72%-25%. Although he increased taxes in 1992, Voinovich got the state government's fiscal house in order.

When Democratic Sen. John Glenn announced plans to retire in 1998, Voinovich, not eligible to run for re-election as governor, was the favorite. His Democratic opponent was Cuyahoga County Commissioner Mary Boyle, who campaigned on education, blaming Voinovich for allowing Ohio schools to decline. Voinovich mostly ignored her attacks and outspent her almost 3-to-1, running ads that highlighted his record as governor. In November, his margin over Boyle was a decisive but not overwhelming 56%-44%.

After 32 years in public office, Voinovich came to the Senate as a big-government Republican, willing to increase tax rates and dubious about cutting them. In his previous positions, he had been required to balance budgets, and he was put off by budget deficits. In April 2000, he was one of only two Republicans to vote against the Republican budget. The same year, he voted against repeal of the estate tax and marriage-penalty relief. He did support President George W. Bush's tax cuts in 2001, when it looked as if the government's budget surplus would be permanent. But later that year, he worked to scale back the tax cuts in the House Republicans' economic-stimulus bill. In 2003, he came out against the $700 billion Bush tax cut, and that April, he and Maine Republican Olympia Snowe insisted they would back no tax cut higher than $350 billion. That led GOP Finance Chairman Charles Grassley and Republican Majority Leader Bill Frist to say they were willing to compromise on the figure, enraging the House Republican leadership. In 2004, Voinovich declined to back the "pay-go" amendment, which required all tax cuts and spending increases to be offset elsewhere in the budget, but in March 2005, he agreed to back an unsuccessful pay-go measure.

In September 2005, Voinovich said that the Bush Social Security changes were "not going to happen now" and continued to argue against extending earlier tax cuts. In May 2006, he was one of three Republicans to vote against the tax bill extending the capital-gains and dividend tax cuts and providing a one-year fix of the alternative minimum tax to stop it from ensnaring middle-income taxpayers (it is aimed at wealthy taxpayers). Also that year, he joined most Democrats in voting against the Republican leadership's trifecta bill, which included estate-tax reductions, a minimum-wage increase and extensions of other tax cuts. "Instead of making the tax cuts permanent, we should be leveling with the American people about the fiscally shaky ground we are on," he said. "I have to say this, and I know it is controversial, but if you look at the extraordinary costs that we have had with the war and homeland security and Katrina, the logical thing that one would think about is to ask for a temporary tax increase to pay for them."

In 2007, Voinovich proposed repealing the tax code by 2010 to force major changes in it. He was one of two Senate Republicans to vote against permanent repeal of the estate tax that year, and in March 2008, he said that a federal tax increase might be necessary to meet future challenges. However, he was one of the few Senate Republicans to vote against a proposal for greater disclosure of spending earmarks and joined 77 other senators to override Bush's veto of a $23 billion water-resources bill. In October 2008, as the economy faltered, Voinovich agreed to vote for the bipartisan $700 billion bailout of the financial-services industry, calling it necessary but "like being punched in the gut." He was one of four Republican senators President Barack Obama and Democratic Senate Majority Leader Harry Reid targeted as possible votes for Obama's $787 billion economic-stimulus bill in January 2009. Voinovich initially indicated that he was leaning toward voting for the bill, but after days of deliberations with centrist Republicans and Democrats, he said there "was too much in the Democratic counterproposal that was not stimulative" and voted against the bill.

In May 2009, Voinovich introduced legislation with independent Sen. Joe Lieberman of Connecticut to create a commission to explore ways to revamp the nation's tax code and to reform entitlement programs, including Social Security and Medicare. He also has led the unpopular fight to raise the gas tax, arguing that in order to fix highways, "It's going to take a gas tax [increase]. I think the sooner we face up to it, the better off we're going to be."

Before the collapse of Fannie Mae and Freddie Mac in 2008, Voinovich had called for tighter regulation of the twin mortgage giants. In 2007, he and Michigan Democrat Debbie Stabenow sponsored a successful amendment for mortgage-cancellation relief, which reduced taxes when mortgages were reduced by agreement. A booster of the domestic auto industry, he co-sponsored a successful amendment to let auto companies use accumulated research and development credits to make new investments. With other senators in November 2008, Voinovich fashioned an auto-company relief bill to let them use for general purposes the $25 billion in loan funds approved for use in clean-car development. "We must ensure that the American auto industry remains whole. During these uncertain and fragile economic times, in my opinion, bankruptcy is not an option," he said. Reid and Democratic House Speaker Nancy Pelosi swatted the idea down immediately, but eventually the Senate considered a similar but smaller version of bill, though it failed to garner the 60 votes necessary to avoid a filibuster.

Voinovich has also been deeply involved in energy issues. In 2003, he managed Bush's Clear Skies Initiative, which created a cap-and-trade system to allow companies to swap permits to emit sulfur dioxide, nitrogen oxide and mercury. But he rejected calls for carbon dioxide controls, which he said would disproportionately hurt the economy in Ohio, which has a coal-mining sector in its southern tier and is heavily reliant on coal as an energy source. The bill bogged down amid disagreements between members of both parties on the Environment and Public Works Committee. In 2005, Voinovich floated a compromise, with a voluntary carbon-dioxide-emissions program, but it was rejected in committee. In 2008, he opposed a similar bill sponsored by Lieberman and Sen. John McCain of Arizona, a Republican, saying it would "have a dramatic impact on the standard of living on the people of Ohio." He called for a greater reliance on nuclear power and development of clean-coal technology.

Voinovich has sometimes surprised colleagues with his stands on foreign issues. He is the only Serbian-American in the Senate and as a college freshman wrote a paper on how the United States sold out Yugoslavia at the February 1945 Yalta conference. In 1991, his Serbian relatives were forced out of their homes in the newly independent Croatia. In March and April 1999, he strongly opposed the bombing of Serbia, but he called Slobodan Milosevic a "war criminal" and tried to persuade the State Department to support forces that wanted to depose him. In February 2008, he criticized the Bush administration's recognition of Kosovo's unilateral declaration of independence. On Iraq, Voinovich joined Indiana Republican Richard Lugar in June 2007 in calling for the withdrawal of troops, though without a timetable. In June of the following year, he urged Bush not to negotiate an agreement with Iraq that committed the next administration to defend it against internal and foreign aggressors.

In 2004, a good year for Republicans, Voinovich came up for re-election. There was talk that he would be opposed by Democrat Jerry Springer, the successful talk-show host, who had served competently as councilman and mayor in Cincinnati in the 1970s and 1980s. But in August 2003, Springer decided against a race. The Democratic nominee was state Sen. Eric Fingerhut, a former U.S. House member who hiked across Ohio as part of his campaign. But he had only $1 million to Voinovich's $9 million. The incumbent won 64%-36%, carrying all 88 counties and almost beating Glenn's record percentage in a Senate race, set in 1974. But Ohio has trended Democratic over the years, in part because of a scandal involving Republican state officials and GOP fundraiser Tom Noe, who persuaded the Ohio Bureau of Workmen's Compensation to make what turned out to be disastrous investments in rare coins. Newspapers revealed that the bureau made its first investment with Noe when Voinovich was governor. Noe was later convicted on campaign-finance and fraud charges. Voinovich said he had been mistaken in believing that Noe and bureau officials were honest.

In his final two years in the Senate, Voinovich will serve on the powerful Appropriations Committee, an appointment he secured in early 2009. His retirement announcement caused an electoral scrum, as numerous candidates in both parties indicated interest in the race. Republicans are worried about holding the seat in the increasingly Democratic state.

Junior Senator

Sherrod Brown (D)

Elected 2006, term expires 2012, 1st term; b. Nov. 9, 1952, Mansfield; home, Avon; Yale U., B.A. 1974, OH St. U., M.A. 1979, M.A. 1981; Lutheran; married (Connie Schultz); 4 children.

Elected Office: OH House of Reps., 1974–82; OH secy. of state, 1982–90, U.S. House of Reps., 1993–2006.

Professional Career: Prof., OH St. U. at Mansfield, 1979, 1981, 1991.

DC Office: 713 HSOB, 20510, 202-224-2315; Fax: 202-228-6321; Web site: brown.senate.gov.

State Offices: Cincinnati, 513-684-1021; Cleveland, 216-522-7272; Columbus, 614-469-2083; Lorain, 440-242-4100.

Committees: *Agriculture, Nutrition & Forestry* (8th of 12 D). *Banking, Housing & Urban Affairs* (8th of 13 D): Economic Policy (Chmn); Housing, Transportation & Community Development; Securities, Insurance & Investment. *Ethics (Select)* (3rd of 3 D). *Health, Education, Labor & Pensions* (9th of 13 D). *Veterans' Affairs* (5th of 10 D).

Group Ratings

	ADA	ACLU	AFS	LCV	ITIC	NTU	COC	ACU	CFG	FRC
2008	95	93	100	91	80	8	63	8	13	0
2007	95	—	100	87	—	6	36	0	0	—

National Journal Ratings

	2007 LIB — 2007 CONS		2008 LIB — 2008 CONS	
Economic	71%	— 28%	61%	— 36%
Social	79%	— 19%	80%	— 9%
Foreign	77%	— 22%	65%	— 6%
Composite	76%	— 24%	76%	— 24%

Key Votes of the 110th Congress

1. Raise CAFE standards	Y	5. Make English official language	N	9. Withdraw troops 3/08	Y
2. Expand SCHIP	Y	6. Path to citizenship	N	10. Iran guard is terrorist group	N
3. Cap greenhouse gases	N	7. Fetus is unborn child	N	11. Increase missile defense $	N
4. Bail out financial markets	Y	8. Prosecute hate crimes	Y	12. Overhaul FISA	N

Election Results

2006 general	Sherrod Brown (D)...2,257,369	(56%)	($10,752,665)
	Mike DeWine (R)..1,761,037	(44%)	($14,161,402)
2006 primary	Sherrod Brown (D)..583,776	(78%)	
	Merrill Keiser (D)..163,628	(22%)	

Prior Winning Percentages: 2004 House (67%); 2002 House (69%); 2000 House (65%); 1998 House (62%); 1996 House (60%); 1994 House (49%); 1992 House (53%)

Sherrod Brown, Ohio's junior senator, is a Democrat first elected to the House in 1992 and to the Senate in 2006. He grew up in Mansfield, the son of a doctor, graduated from Yale in 1974, and won a seat in the state House later that year. Another House member, mistaking him for an intern, gave him a dollar to get her a cup of coffee. He later got master's degrees in education and public administration from the Ohio State University. Brown has spent more than half his life in public office. In 1982, when he was 29, he was elected Ohio secretary of state and worked to increase voter registration and turnout. In 1990, after serving two terms, he lost that office to Republican Bob Taft, who was later elected governor. In 1992, Brown ran for the open 13th District House seat. With solid labor support, he campaigned loud and hard against the North American Free Trade Agreement and championed universal health care. He won 53%-35%.

For many years Brown has worn a self-designed lapel pin of a canary in a cage, to commemorate underground miners who were at risk back in the days before labor unions and government safety inspections. He had a consistently liberal voting record in the House. On trade, he was one of the most voluble pro-labor and "fair-trade" members from the Great Lakes area, attacking the string of free-trade agreements and policies that followed NAFTA in 1993. He sponsored bus trips to Canada for consumers to buy prescription drugs, and he helped to pass the Children's Health Act, which created a new Pediatric Research Institute. In 2003, he helped to secure an increase in Medicaid funding. He urged a ban on the use of antibiotics in farm animals, including penicillin and tetracycline. He called for enforcement of laws against importing goods made with slave labor in China and helped to increase funding for international programs to fight tuberculosis. He authored *Congress From the Inside*, a book that examines why House Democrats lost the majority in 1994. He has also authored a book titled *Myths of Free Trade*. In 2007, his wife, *Cleveland Plain Dealer* columnist Connie Schultz, wrote *And His Lovely Wife: A Memoir From the Woman Beside the Man* about Brown's 2006 campaign for Senate.

Brown long had had his eye on statewide office. In 2005, he at first said he would not challenge two-term Republican Sen. Mike DeWine, which left Iraq War veteran Paul Hackett as the Democratic front-runner. Hackett, who had won some fame after nearly pulling off a major upset in an August 2005 House special election, was an attractive candidate, but there were questions about whether he could raise enough money, and his shoot-from-the-hip style aroused concerns about how he would play statewide. Brown reconsidered and entered the race in October 2005. "The culture of corruption plaguing state and federal government has led our state down the wrong path, and it is time for a change," he said in a statement announcing his Senate candidacy. Hackett reacted angrily—he accused Brown of reneging on a promise of support—and in February 2006 withdrew from the race. With Hackett out of the picture, Brown breezed to the Democratic nomination.

DeWine, meanwhile, won a lackluster 72% in the GOP primary against two little-known opponents, a reflection of conservative dissatisfaction with his votes on gun control and his role in the bipartisan compromise to end Senate filibusters on federal judicial nominees. DeWine also had the misfortune of running for re-election in an unusually hostile political environment for Ohio Republicans. There was an undertow from various scandals associated with the Republican-controlled state government, though DeWine was not implicated, plus the drag from the unpopular Bush administration. Brown charged that DeWine was a "rubber stamp" for President George W. Bush and tied him to Bush's Iraq War policy. He campaigned as a populist progressive, calling for an increase in the minimum wage, denouncing free-trade agreements and criticizing the 2003 Medicare prescription-drug law as a windfall for the pharmaceutical industry. While Brown sought to nationalize the race, DeWine pursued a more localized approach. He focused on his accomplishments and his ability to work across party lines, hoping to heighten the contrast between himself and the more sharply partisan Brown, whose legislative effectiveness had been limited under Republican rule.

Brown won 56%-44%, dominating nearly all of Ohio's population centers: Cleveland's Cuyahoga County (71%-29%), Toledo's Lucas County (66%-33%), Akron's Summit County (64%-36%), Columbus's Franklin County (59%-41%), and Dayton's Montgomery County (53%-47%). DeWine carried Cincinnati's Hamilton County, but by just 2,000 votes; in his 2000 re-election bid, he had won Hamilton by 94,000 votes. DeWine carried much of the state west of Interstate 75, where the tone is more Midwestern. Brown carried everything east of Interstate 77, where the coal and steel counties look to Pennsylvania and West Virginia and where his high-profile opposition to free trade resonated.

In the Senate, Brown opposed Bush's troop-surge policy in Iraq. "The president calls it a surge, but it's an escalation of the war. It's reprehensible and it's wrong," he told the *Cleveland Jewish News* in February 2007. In October of that year, he won passage of an amendment requiring the government to deliver dead soldiers' remains to the airport chosen by his or her family.

Brown surprised environmental groups in April 2007 when he said, "We should look at nuclear power," adding, "It has to absolutely be safe." In June 2008, he disappointed them again when he was one of four Democratic senators to vote against allowing a vote on a bill to cut greenhouse-gas emissions to 70% below 2005 levels by 2050. At the same time, he sponsored a bill to increase the notification for mass layoffs or plant closings from 60 to 90 days. In 2007, he and several other big-state Democrats co-sponsored a bill providing $300 million for housing-foreclosure relief. With Missouri Republican Christopher "Kit" Bond, he sought increased funding for research into children's diseases and for children's hospitals.

Early in 2009, Brown fought to include in the Democrats' economic-stimulus bill requirements that stimulus money be used on American-made goods. The provision was included in the bill that passed the House and Senate, but it was watered down to allow goods to be purchased from some of America's largest trading partners. Trade continued to be a signature issue for Brown. "While they call those of us who support labor and environmental standards protectionists, they call it free trade when they protect drug companies and Hollywood films," he said. "Now, I support intellectual-property protections. But if we can protect Hollywood films, we can protect the environment. If we can protect the drug companies, we can protect workers." He co-sponsored a bipartisan bill allowing competitors to bring lawsuits against companies that profit from sweatshop goods, and he sought to reinstate the law, repealed in 2006, that allocated penalties in dumping complaints to the complaining companies. Brown also called for the Government Accountability Office to review how past trade agreements had affected the U.S. economy, and he sponsored a bill to rescind normal trade relations with China.

On the Agriculture Committee, he and Illinois Democrat Dick Durbin advanced an amendment that would offer farms the option of a program protecting their overall revenue rather than protecting crop prices. It was included in the Senate farm bill in 2007. But Brown failed to get $2 billion moved from crop insurance to conservation and nutrition programs.

FIRST DISTRICT

Steve Driehaus (D)

Elected 2008, 1st term; b. June 24, 1966, Cincinnati; home, Cincinnati; Miami U., B.A. 1988; Indiana U., M.P.A., 1995; Catholic; married (Lucienne); 3 children.

Elected Office: OH House, 2000–08, Minority whip, 2005–08.

Professional Career: Community organizer.

DC Office: 408 CHOB, 20515, 202-225-2216; Fax: 202-225-3012; Web site: driehaus.house.gov.

State Offices: Cincinnati, 513-684-2723.

Committees: *Financial Services* (37th of 42 D): Housing & Community Opportunity; International Monetary Policy & Trade; Oversight & Investigations. *Oversight & Government Reform* (24th of 24 D): Information Policy, Census & National Archives; National Security & Foreign Affairs.

Group Ratings and Key Votes: Newly Elected

Election Results

2008 general	Steve Driehaus (D)	155,455	(52%)	($1,447,544)
	Steve Chabot (R)	140,683	(47%)	($2,410,292)
2008 primary	Steve Driehaus (D)	unopposed		

Population		Race/Ethnicity		Work	
Pop. 2007:	627,620	White:	66.6%	Private:	82.8%
Change since 2000:	Down 0.5%	Black:	28.2%	Government:	11.8%
Urban:	94.8%	Hispanic:	1.8%	Self-employed:	5.3%
Rural:	5.2%	Asian:	1.2%	Blue collar:	22.2%
Area size:	420 sq. mi.	Native Am.:	0.1%	White collar:	59.9%
Age		Hawaiian:	0.0%	Khaki collar:	0.0%
Median age:	37.0 yrs.	Two+ races:	1.8%	Other:	17.8%
More than 65 yrs:	12.9%	*Ancestry*		Median income:	$42,498
Less than 18 yrs:	25.2%	German:	26.5%	Median home value:	$132,100
Education		Irish:	10.9%	Poverty:	16.0%
H.S. grad:	84.5%	English:	5.9%	**Military Veterans**	
College grad:	23.5%			% of Pop:	10.2%
Grad degree:	8.4%				

From its seven hills, Cincinnati looks down on the curves of the Ohio River. It was Ohio's first major metropolis and a heavily German beehive of riverboats and sausage factories, known in the 1850s as Porkopolis. In the 19th century, Cincinnati was the nation's fourth-largest city and at the outbreak of the Civil War, it was a chief destination for slaves on the Underground Railroad. The city has long given off an air of the recent past. Mark Twain once said he'd like to be there for the apocalypse because everything in Cincinnati is 10 years behind. Growing slowly over many decades, Cincinnati's long-settled good looks and urbanity are somehow consistent with its natural terrain: the bottomlands along the river, the hills and rolling terrain above. In the middle of Cincinnati is Mill Creek, lined with factories. On the hills to the west, above the restored Union Terminal housing several museums, are the modest streetcar suburbs of the 19th century and the early years of the 20th. On Mount Adams and toward the northeast are a string of affluent neighborhoods, with stately mansions like the William Howard Taft house, and the comfortable Tudors and colonials of the 20th century bourgeoisie—Reform Jewish as well as WASP and German. Families have lived for generations in the same neighborhoods, though typically not in ethnic enclaves.

2008 Presidential Vote		
Obama (D)	165,843	(55%)
McCain (R)	134,715	(44%)
2004 Presidential Vote		
Bush (R)	152,441	(51%)
Kerry (D)	149,180	(49%)
Cook Partisan Voting Index: D+1		

Cincinnati was the site of great innovations: the first iron suspension bridge, built in 1867, which connects Cincinnati to northern Kentucky and was designed by John Roebling, who later built the Brooklyn Bridge; the first baseball team, the Red Stockings, who began playing in 1869; and the country's leading Reform Jewish seminary, Hebrew Union College, opened in 1875. It spawned not flashy but solid industries, including America's biggest concentration of machine tool makers, the industry now a fraction of its once-robust size, and the Procter & Gamble soap business, with its twin-towered headquarters at the edge of downtown. Its Ivorydale manufacturing facility has made soap since the 1880s. Downtown Cincinnati's spruced-up Fountain Square shows off well-maintained skyscrapers of the past plus a revival of museums, arts institutions and retail shops. Its first-class restaurants still attract a dressy clientele. Old ethnic neighborhoods on the west side, crowded with brick row houses on steep hills, keep their thick local accents and special local foods, from German sauerbrauten to Cincinnati chili. Baseball's career-hitting (and, alas, sports-betting) leader Pete Rose grew up here, and many Catholic schools remain. Yet the city has faced tough times. Crime is a problem and there has been flight to the suburbs. With fewer recent immigrants than comparable northern cities, Cincinnati's population declined in the 1990s, although it made modest gains since 2000.

The 1st Congressional District of Ohio includes almost all of Cincinnati, except for parts of its affluent eastern edge, plus most of the middle-class suburbs that cling to the woody hills west of Interstate 71 and south of I-275. It covers the southwest quarter of Butler County plus the western parts of Hamilton County all the way to the Indiana border, including North Bend, the home of President William Henry Harrison. City elections here were for years competitive between old-line Republicans and a combination of Democrats and Charterites (the latter started by Charles Taft, liberal brother of GOP Sen. Robert Taft Sr. and great-uncle of recent Republican Gov. Bob Taft). As its population has declined, Cincinnati has become noticeably more Democratic, but the suburbs, which now cast more votes than the city, remain heavily Republican. This makes the 1st a closely divided district. Republican George W. Bush carried the district with just 51% of the vote in 2000 and 2004 presidential elections and Democratic nominee Barack Obama won it with 55% in 2008.

The new congressman from the 1st District is Steve Driehaus, a Democrat who defeated seven-term Republican Rep. Steve Chabot in a contest that became a symbol of how far giddy Democrats could go in plundering GOP seats in 2008.

The fifth of eight children, Driehaus (*DREE house*) ran for the seat his father sought unsuccessfully 40 years earlier. His father was the late Don "Dreamy" Driehaus, a salesman and longtime fixture in Cincinnati politics. The younger Driehaus attributes his zeal for public service to his father. He graduated from Miami University in Ohio and got a master's degree in public administration from the University of Indiana. After spending a year abroad in Europe during college, Driehaus worked in Senegal as a Peace Corps volunteer. As a result of his time there, Driehaus speaks Wolof, Senegal's dominant language, which actually comes in handy for him: The Cincinnati area experienced an influx of Senegalese immigrants during the past decade. Now in his early 40s, Driehaus spent most of his career as a state legislator. He also was an aide to former Democratic Rep. Charles Luken, and worked as a community organizer at Cincinnati's Xavier University. He was elected in 2000 to the state House of Representatives and in 2005 was chosen as minority whip.

The race for the 1st District seat was expensive. Both Republican and Democratic congressional campaign committees poured money into the contest, with the Democrats doling out over $1 million for television ads and the Republicans spending about $400,000. Chabot surpassed Driehaus in the money chase, spending $900,000 more. The two traded barbs over taxes and the bailout legislation for the financial services industry. Citing the many local home foreclosures, Driehaus criticized Chabot for voting against the financial rescue plan but stopped short of saying he would have supported the bill. Republicans ran an ad attacking Driehaus for missing a vote in the Ohio Legislature on a bill providing help to families facing foreclosure to attend a fundraiser in Washington. A battle-tested pol, Chabot had managed to fend off several vigorous challengers over his 14 years in the House. Obama's success in turning out new voters in the district and its changing demographics, including a 28% African-American population in the district, favored Driehaus. He won 52%-47% overall, a margin of more than 14,000 votes.

An anti-abortion-rights, fiscally conservative Catholic, Driehaus calls himself a "raging moderate" interested in housing and tax reform. "I tend to be very open-minded on a whole host of issues," he said, adding that he worked closely with Republican leaders in Columbus. "I know what it's like to be on the minority side." In the House, Driehaus got seats on the Financial Services Committee and the Oversight and Government Reform Committee. In March 2009, the House passed Driehaus' first bill. It directs the U.S. archivist to establish a universal system for classifying federal documents to eliminate pseudo-classifications, such as "for official use only," which certain federal agencies used to prevent private citizens from accessing information.

SECOND DISTRICT

Jean Schmidt (R)

Elected Aug. 2005, 2nd full term; b. Nov. 29, 1951, Cincinnati; home, Miami Township; U. of Cincinnati, B.A. 1974; Catholic; married (Peter); 1 child.

Elected Office: Miami Township Bd. of Trustees, 1989–2000; OH House of Reps., 2000–04.

Professional Career: Branch mgr., Midwest Savings Assoc., 1971–78; Fitness instructor, Elaine Powers, 1984–86; Teacher, 1986–90; President, Right to Life of Greater Cincinnati, 2004–05.

DC Office: 418 CHOB, 20515, 202-225-3164; Fax: 202-225-1992; Web site: www.house.gov/schmidt.

State Offices: Cincinnati, 513-791-0381; Portsmouth, 740-354-1440.

Committees: *Agriculture* (11th of 18 R): Conservation, Credit, Energy & Research; Department Operations, Oversight, Nutrition & Forestry; Horticulture & Organic Agriculture (RMM). *Transportation & Infrastructure* (22nd of 30 R): Aviation; Highways & Transit; Railroads, Pipelines & Hazardous Materials.

Group Ratings

	ADA	ACLU	AFS	LCV	ITIC	NTU	COC	ACU	CFG	FRC
2008	15	18	14	8	71	64	94	87	68	100
2007	15	—	18	10	—	75	89	92	80	—

National Journal Ratings

	2007 LIB	—	2007 CONS	2008 LIB	—	2008 CONS
Economic	29%	—	71%	28%	—	72%
Social	9%	—	85%	9%	—	85%
Foreign	0%	—	72%	29%	—	69%
Composite	18%	—	82%	23%	—	77%

Key Votes of the 110th Congress

1. Increase minimum wage	Y	5. Share immigration data	Y	9. Withdraw troops 8/08	N
2. Expand SCHIP	N	6. Foreign aid abortion ban	Y	10. No operations in Iran	N
3. Raise CAFE standards	N	7. Ban gay bias in workplace	N	11. Free trade with Peru	Y
4. Bail out financial markets	Y	8. Repeal D.C. gun law	Y	12. Overhaul FISA	Y

Election Results

2008 general	Jean Schmidt (R)	148,671	(45%)	($1,276,573)
	Victoria Wulsin (D)	124,213	(37%)	($1,972,691)
	David Krikorian (I)	58,710	(18%)	($191,083)
2008 primary	Jean Schmidt (R)	41,987	(58%)	
	Tom Brinkman (R)	28,897	(40%)	

Prior Winning Percentages: 2006 (50%); 2005 (52%)

Population		Race/Ethnicity		Work	
Pop. 2007:	669,775	White:	90.5%	Private:	82.7%
Change since 2000:	Up 6.2%	Black:	4.9%	Government:	10.9%
Urban:	73.0%	Hispanic:	1.1%	Self-employed:	6.2%
Rural:	27.0%	Asian:	2.0%	Blue collar:	21.3%
Area size:	2,630 sq. mi.	Native Am.:	0.2%	White collar:	64.1%
		Hawaiian:	0.1%	Khaki collar:	0.0%
Age		Two+ races:	1.2%	Other:	14.5%
Median age:	37.4 yrs.	*Ancestry*		Median income:	$53,952
More than 65 yrs:	12.5%	German:	24.4%	Median home value:	$160,100
Less than 18 yrs:	24.9%	Irish:	13.1%	Poverty:	10.3%
Education		English:	9.4%	**Military Veterans**	
H.S. grad:	86.4%			% of Pop:	10.4%
College grad:	31.5%				
Grad degree:	11.5%				

For a long time, one of the most Republican urban areas in the nation has been the Cincinnati suburbs. Back in the 1850s, when Harriet Beecher Stowe wrote *Uncle Tom's Cabin* here, Cincinnati was an island of German, pro-Union, Republican sentiment in a Southern, Democratic, pro-slavery region. Later, Cincinnati attracted fewer southern and eastern European immigrants than Great Lakes industrial cities like Cleveland, Detroit and Chicago. The city's ethnic character and political

2008 Presidential Vote		
McCain (R)	201,215	(59%)
Obama (D)	137,804	(40%)
2004 Presidential Vote		
Bush (R)	211,489	(64%)
Kerry (D)	119,139	(36%)
Cook Partisan Voting Index:	R + 13	

preference, like its physical appearance, remained pretty well fixed until very recently. Even many descendents of the Appalachians here are Republicans, from Civil War Republican counties in the hills. Democratic constituencies here never got very large. Economically, it was never a strong union town, and culturally, its conservatism was revealed in a strong anti-pornography movement that made this the site of obscenity charges filed against *Hustler* publisher Larry Flynt. The local Republican record remains intact: It was the only million-plus metro area that George H.W. Bush and Bob Dole carried by more than 50% in 1992 and 1996, and George W. Bush twice won the district handily. In 2008, Republican presidential nominee John McCain beat Democrat Barack Obama in the metro area.

For 140 years after 1852, Cincinnati and surrounding Hamilton County were divided by a north-south line into two congressional districts. But today, both Cincinnati-based districts include territory in other counties. Ohio's 2nd Congressional District includes the eastern edge of Cincinnati and the boutiques of Hyde Park Square, a more transient area than the west side neighborhoods; the mostly affluent suburban subdivisions of eastern Hamilton County; and the fast-growing suburbs of Clermont County and southern Warren County. In once-rural Clermont, Miami Township has become a bedroom community and a center of commercial development along the Interstate 275 Loop. The district also ranges farther east on the Ohio River, all the way to the old industrial city of Portsmouth and the hills of rural Pike County. These are distinctly different places— "the richest to the poorest, and everything in between," as one area mayor put it. The metropolitan parts of the district, with roughly 80% of the people, are mostly affluent and Republican. The counties farther east are less well off, with most of the old factories gone and with pockets of high unemployment and poverty. They are close to marginal in most elections, and Pike County has a Democratic tradition. Portsmouth, on the district's eastern fringe, has a depressed economy and an Appalachian frame of mind. Overall, this is a very Republican district with a tiny minority population. McCain won the district with 59% to Obama's 40%.

The congresswoman from the 2nd District is Jean Schmidt, who won an August 2005 special election. A lifelong resident of Clermont County, she grew up on her family's farm. Her father, a well-known local banker, owned a motor-car racing team and she spent time on the racing circuit. "I'd rather smell ethanol than Chanel No. 5," Schmidt once told the *Cincinnati Enquirer*. An avid runner, she has competed in marathons and continues to run in long-distance races. In 2008 and 2009, she finished first among women members of Congress in an annual charity race for lawmakers, executive branch officials and the media. Schmidt majored in political science at the University of Cincinnati and entered public life as an anti-abortion rights activist. She served 10 years as a Miami Township trustee and two terms in the state House. In 2004, she lost a state Senate primary by 22 votes. After Republican Rep. Rob Portman resigned his House seat to become the United States Trade Representative, Schmidt ran in the special election to replace him.

An early favorite in the contest was Republican Pat DeWine, the son of then-U.S. Sen. Mike DeWine. He had the highest name identification and the most lavish financing, with the help of his father and the Cincinnati business establishment. But his election the previous November as Hamilton County commissioner led many to believe that he was too eager to move up the political ladder. He had also recently divorced his wife, the mother of their three small children, after having an affair with a business lobbyist. The other leading contenders were former U.S. Rep. Bob McEwen, a Washington-based lobbyist after he was defeated in 1992, and GOP state Rep. Tom Brinkman. The contest demonstrated the perils of negative campaigning. As DeWine's support dropped, he ran negative ads against McEwen. The national anti-tax group Club for Growth ran ads against Schmidt for backing Republican Gov. Bob Taft's tax hikes. Conservatives ended up dividing their votes among McEwen, Brinkman and Schmidt. Benefiting from her strong base in Clermont County, Schmidt was the surprise winner with 31%, to 26% for McEwen and 20% for Brinkman. DeWine was a distant fourth with 12%.

Democrats nominated attorney and Iraq war veteran Paul Hackett for what was expected to be a mere formality given the GOP tilt of the district. Instead, it became a harbinger of the 2006 midterm elections nationally. Hackett raised hundreds of thousands of dollars on the Internet from liberal activists. He called President George W. Bush a "chicken hawk" for his failure to serve in the Vietnam War, and strongly attacked Bush's decision to invade Iraq. Schmidt squeaked to victory with 51.6% to Hackett's 48.4%. Her entire margin of victory came from her Clermont base, which cast 26% of the vote and where she led by nearly 5,000 votes. She won just 51% in Republican Hamilton County, which cast 43% of the vote, and 58% in Warren County. The next day, Democratic Congressional Campaign Committee Chairman Rahm Emanuel, then an Illinois House member, gloated that the outcome was a "wake-up call" for Republicans.

As a junior member of the House, Schmidt gained much attention, not all of it positive. In November 2005, she blundered politically by suggesting that Democratic Rep. John Murtha of Pennsylvania, a decorated Marine, was a coward. She said that a local Marine had advised her to stay the course in Iraq and added: "He also asked me to send Congressman Murtha a message, that cowards cut and run. Marines never do." Across the aisle, Democrats exploded in shouts and boos. Schmidt, who had apparently been oblivious to Murtha's military background, quickly retracted her comments and apologized. She was dubbed "Mean Jean" in the blogosphere and *The Cincinnati Enquirer* editorialized that she was "way out of line." Local Democrats drove a "billboard on wheels" across the district that said: "Shame on you, Jean Schmidt. Stop attacking veterans." Then, the *Enquirer* reported two plagiarism incidents in which columns Schmidt wrote contained passages identical to those in columns written by former Rep. Deborah Pryce, R-Ohio, and by an Ohio highway patrol official. In 2008, Schmidt repeated as fact Vice President Dick Cheney's false claim that the Chinese government was drilling for oil off the coast of Florida.

Her first-term performance assured she would be challenged in 2006. McEwen ran again in the primary, citing his 12 years of congressional experience and calling for the start to troop withdraws in Iraq. Schmidt claimed that McEwen was a resident of Virginia and had voted illegally in Ohio. She won the primary by an unimpressive 48%-43%. Without her 4,000-vote lead in Clermont County, she would have lost. Democrats nominated Victoria Wulsin, a local physician who had finished a distant second to Hackett a year earlier and was not expected to pose a serious challenge. But Murtha stepped in to campaign for her and Wulsin ran the "cowards" speech in a television ad. Schmidt got more unwelcome attention when she said that it might be a good idea to send nuclear waste from around the world to a storage facility in Pike County. (Later, in May 2007, she introduced a bill to prohibit storage of waste there.) Schmidt won, after the three weeks it took to count absentee and provisional ballots, by 50.5%-49.4%. She carried Clermont by 7,900 votes and Warren by 5,700 votes, but lost Hamilton County by nearly 5,800 votes.

She faced tough sledding in 2008 as well. Brinkman, and the state representative she beat in the 2005 special election, jumped in late to challenge her in the primary, prompting former Hamilton County commissioner Phil Heimlich to unexpectedly drop out six weeks before the vote. Schmidt won 58%-40%, and led in all of the counties. Wulsin, running again, had another campaign visit from Murtha, who said that Schmidt "shouldn't be in Congress." Four weeks before the election, Schmidt was treated for broken ribs and vertebrae after being struck by a hit-and-run driver while she was out running. Unlike in 2006, Wulsin this time out-spent Schmidt, with financial help from the Democratic Congressional Campaign Committee. But Schmidt won, this time increasing her margin of victory over Wulsin but still not winning resoundingly. She got 45% of the vote to 37% for Wulsin and 18% for independent candidate David Kirkorian, a businessman. Schmidt got only 48% in her home base of Clermont, lost Hamilton by one point, and got less than 40% in Pike and Scioto counties. Her strongest showing was 53% in Warren County, which may have resulted from party-line Republican voting.

THIRD DISTRICT

Mike Turner (R)

Elected 2002, 4th term; b. Jan. 11, 1960, Dayton; home, Dayton; OH N. U., B.A. 1982, Case Western Reserve U., J.D. 1985, U. of Dayton, M.B.A. 1992; Protestant; married (Lori); 2 children.

Elected Office: Dayton mayor, 1993–2001.

Professional Career: Practicing atty.

DC Office: 1740 LHOB, 20515, 202-225-6465; Fax: 202-225-6754; Web site: www.house.gov/miketurner.

State Offices: Dayton, 937-225-2843; Wilmington, 937-383-8931.

Committees: *Armed Services* (11th of 25 R): Air & Land Forces; Readiness; Strategic Forces (RMM). *Oversight & Government Reform* (7th of 15 R): Domestic Policy; National Security & Foreign Affairs.

Group Ratings

	ADA	*ACLU*	*AFS*	*LCV*	*ITIC*	*NTU*	*COC*	*ACU*	*CFG*	*FRC*
2008	55	20	67	23	43	48	81	63	51	100
2007	25	—	18	10	—	48	100	80	37	—

National Journal Ratings

	2007 LIB	—	*2007 CONS*		*2008 LIB*	—	*2008 CONS*
Economic	38%	—	61%		39%	—	61%
Social	21%	—	75%		20%	—	74%
Foreign	32%	—	64%		29%	—	69%
Composite	32%	—	68%		31%	—	69%

Key Votes of the 110th Congress

1. Increase minimum wage	Y	5. Share immigration data	Y	9. Withdraw troops 8/08	N
2. Expand SCHIP	Y	6. Foreign aid abortion ban	Y	10. No operations in Iran	N
3. Raise CAFE standards	N	7. Ban gay bias in workplace	N	11. Free trade with Peru	Y
4. Bail out financial markets	N	8. Repeal D.C. gun law	Y	12. Overhaul FISA	Y

Election Results

2008 general	Mike Turner (R)	200,204	(63%)	($1,058,000)
	Jane Mitakides (D)	115,976	(37%)	($462,075)
2008 primary	Mike Turner (R)	unopposed		

Prior Winning Percentages: 2006 (59%); 2004 (62%); 2002 (59%)

Population		Race/Ethnicity		Work	
Pop. 2007:	642,565	White:	78.9%	Private:	81.3%
Change since 2000:	Up 1.9%	Black:	16.5%	Government:	13.2%
Urban:	84.7%	Hispanic:	1.5%	Self-employed:	5.3%
Rural:	15.3%	Asian:	1.4%	Blue collar:	23.6%
Area size:	1,610 sq. mi.	Native Am.:	0.1%	White collar:	59.5%
		Hawaiian:	0.0%	Khaki collar:	0.2%
Age		Two+ races:	1.3%	Other:	16.6%
Median age:	38.0 yrs.			Median income:	$46,521
More than 65 yrs:	13.9%	*Ancestry*		Median home value:	$131,500
Less than 18 yrs:	24.4%	German:	20.8%	Poverty:	13.1%
		Irish:	10.8%		
Education		USA:	9.6%	**Military Veterans**	
H.S. grad:	86.4%			% of Pop:	12.4%
College grad:	25.0%				
Grad degree:	9.4%				

The underestimated Dayton can hold its own against bigger cities known for fostering creative American genius in commerce. It has strong traditions of tinkering and innovation, practical organization and mechanical dreaming, as well as small-town neighborliness. Just south of the old National Road that spans the Midwest was the home of James Ritty, who in 1879 invented the cash register—that indispensable instrument of mass retail trade—and of John Henry Patterson, who

2008 Presidential Vote

McCain (R)	170,431	(52%)
Obama (D)	156,611	(47%)

2004 Presidential Vote

Bush (R)	178,323	(54%)
Kerry (D)	148,978	(45%)

Cook Partisan Voting Index: R+5

bought it from Ritty for $6,500 in 1884 and established the National Cash Register company. Dayton was the home of a former employee of Patterson's, Tom Watson Sr., who feuded with Patterson and went off in a huff to found IBM. In Dayton in the 1890s, Wilbur and Orville Wright, tinkering in their bicycle shop and observing the horseless carriages driven through Dayton's streets, experimented with kites and gliders and constructed the first wind tunnel in the world and the first heavier-than-air flying machine, which they took to windy Kitty Hawk, N.C., for a test flight in December 1903. A few years later, Dayton's Charles Kettering invented the automatic starter for cars and became one of the leaders of the budding automobile industry. More recently, in 1995, Dayton was a most unlikely but effective player on the international stage. It was the site the international peace negotiations that led to the agreement among countries to stop the bloody fighting in the former Yugoslavia. The 21-day summit took place at nearby Wright-Patterson Air Force Base. "From the time we landed at the airport," wrote U.S. negotiator Richard Holbrooke, "until the time we left, we felt that we were in a community that was literally praying for us. People were lighting candles in their windows, there were signs all over the airport and on the byways. That would never have happened in New York or in Washington. And it made a tremendous impression on people."

In the 1970s and 1980s, Dayton's economy sputtered. General Motors, then the area's largest employer, was in trouble and NCR was taken over in a merger. Manufacturing jobs continue to exit, especially with the bankruptcy of GM parts supplier Delphi Corp, but the local economy eventually turned around. Wright-Patterson base became the biggest employer, and is the Air Force's largest site for analyzing intelligence about foreign aerospace and weapons technology. Today there are more scientists, engineers, computer specialists and technicians here than GM workers. The area's small manufacturers and suppliers have produced more patents per capita than any other city in the nation. Dayton entered another period of economic gloom in 2008 and 2009 as the national economy soured. It has been bleeding manufacturing jobs for two years, and in November 2008, DHL closed an air cargo hub at the Wilmington Air Park in Clinton County, costing the region 10,000 jobs. Then, in a major psychological as well as economic blow for the city, NCR announced in June 2009 that it was leaving after 125 years, taking away Dayton's last Fortune 500 company and the 1,300 jobs it provided.

The 3rd Congressional District of Ohio includes most of Dayton and all but the northeast corner of Montgomery County. It takes in the northern half of fast-growing suburban Warren County, and the mostly rural and small town Clinton and Highland counties. Republican George W. Bush won 54% of the vote in the 2004 presidential election, and GOP nominee John McCain got 52% in 2008.

The congressman from the 3rd District is Mike Turner, a Republican elected in 2002. Turner grew up in Dayton, where his father worked 42 years for GM. He graduated from Ohio Northern University, Case Western law school and the University of Dayton business school and became a corporate lawyer. In 1993, at age 33, he narrowly defeated a scandal-tainted Democratic incumbent to win the first of two terms as mayor of Dayton. He narrowly lost a bid for re-election in 2001. Ohio and national Republican leaders recruited him to challenge 3rd District Democratic Rep. Tony Hall, who had served 12 terms but was vulnerable after post-2000 census redistricting made his turf considerably more Republican. In early 2002, Turner announced he was running for Congress, the same day the Ohio Legislature passed their redistricting plan. A week later, President Bush nominated Hall as ambassador to the United Nations' Food and Agriculture Organization in Rome.

In the Republican primary, Turner had fierce opposition from newspaper publisher Roy Brown, grandson and son of former U.S. Reps. Clarence Brown and Clarence Brown Jr., who had represented the neighboring 7th District from 1938 to 1982. Brown spent $1.3 million of his own money in the primary, largely on ads attacking Turner's record on taxes and crime and lambasting him for being insufficiently conservative. Brown owned more than 50 newspapers, 10 in the 3rd District. Turner contended that Brown's campaign guided his newspapers' coverage of the race. Then, a few days before the primary, the Ohio Election Commission ruled that Brown violated state law with false statements in a televised ad. Voters evidently took the same view. Turner beat Brown 80%-14%. The general election was comparatively sedate. The Democratic nominee was Rick Carne, Hall's chief of staff. He had little support from the national party but he raised nearly $600,000, with help from a local appearance by Dayton native Martin Sheen, who played President Bartlet on popular *The West Wing* television series. Turner won 59%-41%.

In the House, Turner got a seat on Armed Services and worked successfully to keep the Wright-Patterson base off the base-closing list and to expand its jobs, including a new center for research on fixed-wing aircraft—solid first steps for a new member of Congress. In October 2007, he worked to pass a bipartisan bill in the House to require the Bush administration to prepare contingency plans to withdraw troops from Iraq. And Turner collaborated with Rep. Jane Harman, D-Calif., to review the military's handling of sexual assault charges. Also in 2007, he was successful in getting the Office of the Architect of the Capitol to return the word "God" to the official certificates with flags that are sent to constituents.

Turner formed a caucus of former mayors serving in Congress to focus on urban issues. In 2006, he worked on House-passed legislation to accelerate clean-up of polluted brownfields by making it easier for communities to apply for federal grants for revitalization efforts. He also promoted the kind of public-private partnerships that he used for economic development in Dayton. In March 2009, Turner was one of seven House Republicans to support a bill that would give bankruptcy judges the power to restructure the terms of home mortgages. House Minority Leader John Boehner, R-Ohio, called the bill "just the worst idea in the world."

Turner seems entrenched in what had been a safe Democratic district. In 2006, three months after veterinarian Stephanie Studebaker won the Democratic nomination to challenge him, both she and her husband were arrested at their home and charged with domestic violence. She withdrew as a candidate. In September, federal prosecutor Richard Chema won a special primary to replace her, but Turner won easily. In 2008, Democratic challenger and investment manager Jane Mitakides ran, criticizing Turner for supporting Bush's policies. And in August before the election, Ohio Democrats made an issue of the fact that he had not disclosed a five-year business relationship between his wife, Lori Turner, and home builder Tom Peebles, who had contributed to Turner's campaign. Turner asked for a ruling from the House Committee on Standards of Official Conduct and the panel concluded he did not have to disclose the relationship between Peebles and his wife. Turner won 63%-37%.

FOURTH DISTRICT

Jim Jordan (R)

Elected 2006, 2nd term; b. Feb. 17, 1964, Troy; home, Urbana; U. of WI, B.A. 1986, OH St. U., M.Ed. 1991, Capital U., J.D. 2002; Christian; married (Polly); 4 children.

Elected Office: OH House of Reps., 1994–2000; OH Senate, 2000–06.

Professional Career: Asst. wrestling coach, OH St. U., 1987–95; Wrestling camp coach, clinician, 1987–2006.

DC Office: 515 CHOB, 20515, 202-225-2676; Fax: 202-226-0577; Web site: jordan.house.gov.

State Offices: Findlay, 419-423-3210; Lima, 419-999-6455; Mansfield, 419-522-5757.

Committees: *Budget* (9th of 15 R). *Judiciary* (12th of 16 R): Commercial & Administrative Law; Constitution, Civil Rights & Civil Liberties. *Oversight & Government Reform* (11th of 15 R): Domestic Policy (RMM); National Security & Foreign Affairs.

Group Ratings

	ADA	ACLU	AFS	LCV	ITIC	NTU	COC	ACU	CFG	FRC
2008	0	18	0	0	29	89	83	100	100	100
2007	0	—	0	5	—	91	70	100	96	—

National Journal Ratings

	2007 LIB	—	2007 CONS		2008 LIB	—	2008 CONS
Economic	5%	—	94%		0%	—	98%
Social	15%	—	84%		0%	—	91%
Foreign	0%	—	72%		22%	—	74%
Composite	12%	—	88%		10%	—	90%

Key Votes of the 110th Congress

1. Increase minimum wage	N	5. Share immigration data	Y	9. Withdraw troops 8/08	N
2. Expand SCHIP	N	6. Foreign aid abortion ban	Y	10. No operations in Iran	N
3. Raise CAFE standards	N	7. Ban gay bias in workplace	N	11. Free trade with Peru	Y
4. Bail out financial markets	N	8. Repeal D.C. gun law	Y	12. Overhaul FISA	Y

Election Results

2008 general	Jim Jordan (R)	186,154	(65%)	($436,919)
	Mike Carroll (D)	99,499	(35%)	($27,697)
2008 primary	Jim Jordan (R)	unopposed		

Prior Winning Percentages: 2006 (60%)

Population		Race/Ethnicity		Work	
Pop. 2007:	630,187	White:	91.0%	Private:	82.6%
Change since 2000:	Down 0.1%	Black:	4.9%	Government:	11.0%
Urban:	58.6%	Hispanic:	1.4%	Self-employed:	6.1%
Rural:	41.4%	Asian:	0.8%	Blue collar:	34.5%
Area size:	4,642 sq. mi.	Native Am.:	0.2%	White collar:	48.9%
		Hawaiian:	0.0%	Khaki collar:	0.1%
Age		Two+ races:	1.4%	Other:	16.6%
Median age:	37.7 yrs.			Median income:	$45,022
More than 65 yrs:	13.9%	*Ancestry*		Median home value:	$112,800
Less than 18 yrs:	24.3%	German:	29.0%	Poverty:	12.0%
		Irish:	10.5%		
Education		USA:	9.0%	**Military Veterans**	
H.S. grad:	85.6%			% of Pop:	11.6%
College grad:	15.1%				
Grad degree:	5.2%				

Central Ohio looks mostly like farmland to the traveler. Yet this is manufacturing country, indeed one of America's premier manufacturing areas, where the economy is based on factories in small towns and on rural highways. These places seem far from anywhere important, yet are on one of the great east-west routes—the old rail lines and newer highways—that cross the country. They seem old-fashioned and rooted in an older technological time, with some exceptions. Wapakoneta is the home-

2008 Presidential Vote
McCain (R)..............................180,255   (60%)
Obama (D) 114,956   (38%)

2004 Presidential Vote
Bush (R)................................193,875   (65%)
Kerry (D)................................102,332   (34%)

Cook Partisan Voting Index: R + 15

town of Neil Armstrong, the first man on the moon, and has the Neil Armstrong Air and Space Museum. A county away is Bellefontaine, site of the first concrete street in America. Politically, this crossroads on the flat limestone plains of northern Ohio is one of the Republican heartlands of the United States. It has been quietly prosperous most of the years since World War II, though it has been hurt by the continuing erosion of the automobile, steel and coal industries and troubled by recent manufacturing job losses, in-cluding the planned closing of a General Motors facility in Mansfield that employs 700 people. In 2008, Siemens announced that it was closing its plant in Bellefontaine. But considering its old-line economic base, central Ohio seemed to be surviving the recession better than other parts of the state. Lima had reason to be optimistic when Procter & Gamble made plans to build a massive new warehouse to distrib-ute liquid Tide detergent, which is produced in a factory a mile away. And ethanol production is a growth industry in the area.

Much of central Ohio makes up the 4th Congressional District. It includes Lima, where Standard Oil drilled what was once the largest oil field in the nation; Marion, where young socialist-to-be Norman Thomas delivered newspapers edited by president-to-be Warren Harding; and Mansfield, home of John Sherman, one of Ohio's great 19th century Republican statesmen, and his brother General William Te-cumseh Sherman, who marched his troops through Georgia for the Union. This has been a Republican stronghold since the Civil War. Republican George W. Bush twice carried the district with 62% and 65% of the vote respectively in 2000 and 2004. The district was one of the reasons he carried Ohio, and the presidency, a second time. Republican presidential nominee John McCain carried the district with 60% in 2008.

The congressman from the 4th District is Jim Jordan, a Republican elected in 2006. Jordan grew up in Champaign County and graduated from Graham High School in 1982, after earning four state wres-tling championships and a 150-1 record. At the University of Wisconsin, Jordan won two NCAA wrestling championships in the 134-pound weight class and was inducted into the Badger Hall of Fame. After grad-uating in 1986 with an economics degree, Jordan worked as an assistant wrestling coach at Ohio State University, where he earned a master's degree in education before completing a law degree at Capital University. He won a state House seat in 1994, won re-election twice, and then won a tough primary in 2000 for the state Senate. During his time in the Legislature, Jordan compiled a solidly conservative voting record. He sponsored legislation creating Ohio's "Choose Life" license plates, backed a ban on same-sex marriage, and supported government vouchers for private school tuition. When Jordan announced he was running to succeed Republican Rep. Michael Oxley, *The Columbus Dispatch* called Jordan "one of the best-known conservative Republicans in the Ohio legislature."

Oxley, who chaired the House Financial Services Committee, retired after 12 terms. Jordan entered the six-way Republican primary with the most name recognition and had support from the Ohio Right to Life, the National Rifle Association and the national anti-tax group Club for Growth. Findlay real estate developer Frank Guglielmi spent $1.6 million of his own money and saturated the television airwaves with ads. Jordan raised plenty of money but did not break the $1 million mark until a month after the May primary. While money mattered, so did geography. Jordan won with 51%, carrying eight of 11 counties. Guglielmi carried only his home county and one other to finish second with 30%. Kevin Nestor, president of the Mansfield-Richland Area Chamber of Commerce, came in third with 11%. Despite the tough political environment for Republicans in 2006, Democrats never mounted a competitive campaign for the seat. Jordan beat Lima attorney and Vietnam veteran Rick Siferd 60%-40%.

In the House, Jordan established a solidly conservative voting record. In 2007, he set his mark early as one of 50 Republicans to vote against all of the Democrats' "Six for '06" agenda. Also that year, he filed nine amendments to limit spending in the appropriations bills; none of them passed. On the Budget Committee, he advocated a commission to reduce government waste. In May 2009, Jordan, who likes to say he came to Washington to protect families, sponsored a bill that would define marriage in the District of Columbia as the union between a man and woman.

He was re-elected easily in 2008.

FIFTH DISTRICT

Bob Latta (R)

Elected 2007, 1st full term; b. April 18, 1956, Bluffton; home, Bowling Green; Bowling Green St. U., B.A., 1978, U. of Toledo Col. of Law, J.D., 1981.; Catholic; married (Marcie); 2 children.

Elected Office: Wood Cnty. commissioner, 1991–96, Ohio Senate, 1997–2001, Ohio Gen. Assembly, 2001–07.

Professional Career: Attorney, 1981–1991.

DC Office: 1531 LHOB, 20515, 202-225-6405; Fax: 202-225-1985; Web site: latta.house.gov.

State Offices: Bowling Green, 419-354-8700; Defiance, 419-782-1996; Norwalk, 419-668-0206.

Committees: *Agriculture* (13th of 18 R): Conservation, Credit, Energy & Research; General Farm Commodities & Risk Management. *Budget* (15th of 15 R). *Transportation & Infrastructure* (26th of 30 R): Highways & Transit; Railroads, Pipelines & Hazardous Materials; Water Resources & Environment.

Group Ratings

	ADA	ACLU	AFS	LCV	ITIC	NTU	COC	ACU	CFG	FRC
2008	15	25	0	0	0	73	89	96	90	100
2007	—	—	—	—	—	—	—	100	—	—

National Journal Ratings

	2007 LIB — 2007 CONS		2008 LIB — 2008 CONS	
Economic	*% —	*%	10% —	89%
Social	*% —	*%	9% —	85%
Foreign	*% —	*%	19% —	79%
Composite	*% —	*%	14% —	86%

Key Votes of the 110th Congress

1. Increase minimum wage	*	5. Share immigration data	*	9. Withdraw troops 8/08	*
2. Expand SCHIP	*	6. Foreign aid abortion ban	*	10. No operations in Iran	*
3. Raise CAFE standards	*	7. Ban gay bias in workplace	*	11. Free trade with Peru	*
4. Bail out financial markets	N	8. Repeal D.C. gun law	Y	12. Overhaul FISA	Y

Election Results

2008 general	Bob Latta (R)	188,905	(64%)	($2,051,669)
	George Mays (D)	105,840	(36%)	
2008 primary	Bob Latta (R)	54,093	(75%)	
	Scott Radcliffe (R)	12,347	(17%)	
	Michael Reynolds (R)	5,873	(8%)	
2007 spec. general	Bob Latta (R)	56,114	(57%)	
	Robin Weirauch (D)	42,229	(43%)	
2007 spec. primary	Bob Latta (R)	32,392	(44%)	
	Steve Buehrer (R)	29,850	(40%)	
	Mark Hollenbaugh (R)	4,955	(7%)	
	Fred Pieper (R)	4,252	(6%)	

Population		Race/Ethnicity		Work	
Pop. 2007:	629,765	White:	92.6%	Private:	82.9%
Change since 2000:	Down 0.2%	Black:	1.2%	Government:	11.4%
Urban:	48.9%	Hispanic:	4.4%	Self-employed:	5.5%
Rural:	51.1%	Asian:	0.6%	Blue collar:	36.8%
Area size:	6,158 sq. mi.	Native Am.:	0.1%	White collar:	46.8%
		Hawaiian:	0.0%	Khaki collar:	0.1%
Age		Two+ races:	1.0%	Other:	16.3%
Median age:	37.6 yrs.	*Ancestry*		Median income:	$47,214
More than 65 yrs:	13.7%	German:	35.3%	Median home value:	$117,400
Less than 18 yrs:	24.0%	Irish:	9.5%	Poverty:	10.0%
Education		English:	7.4%	**Military Veterans**	
H.S. grad:	87.1%			% of Pop:	11.1%
College grad:	16.0%				
Grad degree:	5.9%				

Undergirded by limestone, as flat and fertile as any place in America, northwest Ohio was economically productive from the time it was settled. Parts of it were known as the "Firelands," reserved for Connecticut Yankees whose farms were burned in the Revolution, and neat and substantial small towns were built by German Protestants in the mid-19th century. Northwest Ohio is the beginning of the great corn and hog belt that stretches through Indiana and Illinois into Iowa, and has long been a Re-

2008 Presidential Vote
McCain (R)...........................165,762 (53%)
Obama (D) 141,321 (45%)

2004 Presidential Vote
Bush (R)................................188,935 (61%)
Kerry (D)...............................119,308 (39%)

Cook Partisan Voting Index: R + 9

publican heartland. Fremont, settled by abstemious Yankees, was the home of President Rutherford B. Hayes, whose wife, Lucy, served only lemonade in the White House. Nearby Sandusky was settled by Germans who built big wineries and breweries.

This is also prime industrial country. Its limestone, rail connections and location near the Great Lakes have spurred the growth of a factory economy that financially is far more important than agriculture. After the first settlement, northwest Ohio grew steadily for many decades, surging ahead in the 1950s and 1960s as its small factories supplied the big auto plants in Detroit and in cities in Ohio. Growth lagged noticeably in the 1980s, when the domestic auto industry collapsed, but rebounded somewhat as small firms sold not only to the Big Three but to foreign customers. That gave this area the highest percentage of blue-collar workers in the state. Honda has dozens of suppliers in the area, though many parts companies continue to cut back with the continuing financial troubles of the domestic auto industry.

The 5th Congressional District of Ohio sweeps across northwest Ohio, from northern Ashland County, almost within the ambit of metro Cleveland, across the limestone plains through Sandusky County and Fremont, past the university town of Bowling Green and the Toledo suburb of Perrysburg, to the towns of Defiance and Napoleon and on to the northwest corner where Ohio borders Michigan and Indiana. Its factories include the aromatic Heinz ketchup plant in Fremont—the world's largest, with the equivalent of 4 million 14-ounce bottles produced every day—and the largest Whirlpool washing machine plant in Clyde, both in Sandusky County. Bowling Green is the site of the state's first wind turbines and gets about 20% of its electricity from renewable sources. Locals now call it "Blowing Green." Historically, this has been a solidly Republican district since the Civil War. President George W. Bush won it 61%-39% in 2004, and Republican nominee John McCain won it 53% to 45% in 2008.

The congressman from the 5th District is Bob Latta, a Republican who won a special election for the seat in 2007. Latta is the son of Delbert Latta, who held the seat for 30 years, from 1959 to 1989). Bob Latta was born in Ohio but split his early years between his native Bluffton, Ohio and Washington. Growing up helping in his father's campaigns, Latta says he learned the business of catering to constituents. Young Latta was frequently interrupted during his homework to answer their phone calls and remembers his father following up with federal agencies to try to get results from the vast government bureaucracy. Latta also spent time driving around the district with his dad, going to meetings and events. During college at Bowling Green State University, Latta volunteered in his father's office, where he met his wife, Marcia, who worked for his father.

He graduated from law school at the University of Toledo, and his father had one bit of career advice for him: Don't get into politics. Bob Latta did his best to follow that guidance, and practiced law for several years. But when his father announced his retirement from Congress in 1988, the 31-year-old couldn't pass on the opportunity to try to follow in his footsteps. However, he first had to get by Paul Gillmor, a Republican state senator who had been waiting for a congressional seat to open up during Del Latta's long tenure. In the primary contest with Gillmor, Bob Latta argued that, like his father, he would start out young and eventually gain enough seniority to preside over powerful committees. After a spirited race, Gillmor beat Latta by just 27 votes out of 57,361 cast. With the close loss behind him, Latta focused on local politics, first getting elected to the Wood County Commission, and then to the Ohio Legislature, where he served in both the Senate and the state General Assembly. One of his major efforts was to repeal the Ohio estate tax, which he succeeded in doing for 78% of Ohioans, although the tax was not eliminated entirely. An avid hunter, Latta also championed conservation issues, including lengthening hunting seasons and expanding wildlife reserves.

On Sept. 5, 2007, Gillmor died at his Washington home, apparently from a fall down stairs. Latta got into the contest for a successor, but had to overcome a brutal Republican primary fight and a Democratic challenger heavily financed by the national party. As the primary field took shape, Gillmor's wife, Karen, briefly considered running for her late husband's seat, but ultimately declined. Latta's major primary opponent was state Sen. Steve Buehrer, who was backed by the national anti-tax group Club for Growth, which spent $290,000 in Beuhrer's behalf. Club for Growth ran several ads attacking Latta as an advocate of higher taxes to increase public school funding. Latta attacked Buehrer for accepting donations from a former fundraiser for President George W. Bush in Ohio, Tom Noe, a convicted money launderer. But it came to light that Latta had also taken money from Noe. In the end, Latta defeated Buehrer by only 2,542 votes out of 74,191 cast.

His Democratic opponent, Robin Weirauch, a former public administrator who had twice run against Gillmor, had backing from national labor unions and the fundraising group EMILY's list. She also got the endorsements of U.S. Sen. Sherrod Brown and Gov. Ted Strickland, both prominent Ohio Democrats. She attacked Latta on economic issues and on his support for the Iraq war. Still, despite Weirauch's best efforts to capitalize on the anti-incumbent, anti-Washington sentiment in the country that year, she came up short in the solidly Republican district. Latta won 57%-43%.

In the House, Latta joined the Republicans' House Energy Action Team and made energy independence his central issue. He supports new oil refineries, new nuclear power plants and tax incentives for commercial ventures using clean coal, hydrogen, wind, solar and biofuels. His bill calling for increased domestic production and offshore drilling as well as expanded reliance on renewable and alternative sources became one of the GOP's main alternatives to Democratic proposals. Latta dubbed it the "all of the above" strategy to solving the country's energy shortage. He opposes the proposed "cap and trade" system that would set pollution limits on companies but let them swap credits when they need to increase their output of carbon emissions. He says such a law would hurt American industry during tough financial times.

In early 2009, Latta became an assistant whip, part of a leadership group that helps whip up support for the House Republicans' agenda.

SIXTH DISTRICT

Charlie Wilson (D)

Elected 2006, 2nd term; b. Jan. 18, 1943, Martins Ferry; home, St. Clairsville; Cincinnati Col. of Mortuary Science, 1967, OH U., B.A. 1980; Catholic; divorced; 4 children.

Elected Office: OH House of Reps., 1996–2004; OH Senate, 2004–06.

Professional Career: Welder, painter, assembly-line worker, 1963–64; Owner, Wilson Funeral and Furniture Co., 1966–2006; Owner, Wilson Realty Co., 1978–2006.

DC Office: 226 CHOB, 20515, 202-225-5705; Fax: 202-225-5907; Web site: charliewilson.house.gov.

State Offices: Bridgeport, 740-633-5705; Canfield, 330-533-7250; Ironton, 740-533-9423; Marietta, 740-376-0868; Wellsville, 330-532-3740.

Committees: *Financial Services* (27th of 42 D): Capital Markets, Insurance & Government Sponsored Enterprises; Financial Institutions & Consumer Credit. *Science & Technology* (22nd of 26 D): Investigations & Oversight; Space & Aeronautics.

Group Ratings

	ADA	ACLU	AFS	LCV	ITIC	NTU	COC	ACU	CFG	FRC
2008	80	82	100	77	50	6	67	4	0	52
2007	85	—	100	60	—	6	63	21	1	—

National Journal Ratings

	2007 LIB — 2007 CONS		2008 LIB — 2008 CONS	
Economic	57%	— 43%	53%	— 47%
Social	53%	— 47%	54%	— 42%
Foreign	55%	— 44%	59%	— 37%
Composite	55%	— 45%	57%	— 43%

Key Votes of the 110th Congress

1. Increase minimum wage	Y	5. Share immigration data	N	9. Withdraw troops 8/08	Y
2. Expand SCHIP	Y	6. Foreign aid abortion ban	Y	10. No operations in Iran	Y
3. Raise CAFE standards	Y	7. Ban gay bias in workplace	Y	11. Free trade with Peru	N
4. Bail out financial markets	Y	8. Repeal D.C. gun law	Y	12. Overhaul FISA	Y

Election Results

2008 general	Charlie Wilson (D)	176,330	(62%)	($598,718)
	Richard Stobbs (R)	92,968	(33%)	
	Dennis Spisak (Green)	13,812	(5%)	
2008 primary	Charlie Wilson (D)	unopposed		

Prior Winning Percentages: 2006 (62%)

Population		Race/Ethnicity		Work	
Pop. 2007:	620,806	White:	94.6%	Private:	79.2%
Change since 2000:	Down 1.6%	Black:	2.6%	Government:	14.2%
Urban:	50.0%	Hispanic:	0.9%	Self-employed:	6.3%
Rural:	50.0%	Asian:	0.7%	Blue collar:	28.6%
Area size:	5,236 sq. mi.	Native Am.:	0.2%	White collar:	52.5%
		Hawaiian:	0.0%	Khaki collar:	0.0%
Age		Two+ races:	1.1%	Other:	18.9%
Median age:	39.7 yrs.			Median income:	$37,550
More than 65 yrs:	15.6%	*Ancestry*		Median home value:	$96,400
Less than 18 yrs:	21.4%	German:	19.4%	Poverty:	17.1%
		Irish:	12.5%		
Education		English:	9.0%	**Military Veterans**	
H.S. grad:	85.3%			% of Pop:	11.8%
College grad:	15.9%				
Grad degree:	5.8%				

In the years after the American Revolution, the Ohio River was one of the great highways west. From Pittsburgh, where the Allegheny and Monongahela Rivers meet to form the Ohio, the river led south and west toward the Mississippi and the great port of New Orleans. Shipping goods downriver by raft was cheaper than sending them over the Appalachian Mountains, and so the Ohio became a great highway of commerce. For hundreds of miles, the Ohio twisted this way and that through

2008 Presidential Vote

McCain (R)	150,850	(50%)
Obama (D)	142,846	(48%)

2004 Presidential Vote

Bush (R)	153,983	(51%)
Kerry (D)	149,080	(49%)

Cook Partisan Voting Index: R+2

rounded-off mountains and rolling hills, land that marked the boundary between post-Revolutionary Virginia and the Northwest Territory, between slaveholding territory and free soil as determined by the Confederation Congress of 1787. Across this boundary, settlers made their way in those years—Yankees in 1788 to Marietta, Ohio's first town, and, in larger numbers, Virginians. By the late 19th century, the Ohio was an industrial river. Coal was nearby, barge transportation was available and railroads were built in the narrow valleys between the hills. Steel mills went up on the riverfront. This produced prosperity for a while, but it also produced pollution—Steubenville on the Ohio River once had the nation's dirtiest air—and after the old-line steel industry fell on hard times, the Ohio River was lined with some of the least prosperous parts of America. Even with mandates from the Clean Air Act, the pollution in much of this area from coal-fired power plants remains. Construction was scheduled to start in 2009 on a $2.9 billion clean coal power plant in Meigs County to employ ammonium scrubbers.

The 6th Congressional District of Ohio is made up of a string of counties running 325 miles along the Ohio River, plus part of the Mahoning Valley, named after a narrow tributary of the Ohio. In the north, it includes the Youngstown suburbs of Boardman, Canfield and part of Poland in Mahoning County, and East Liverpool and Steubenville on the river. It curves along the lightly populated stretch of the river south from Marietta, past the old industrial town of Ironton and extends to the city limits of Portsmouth, not quite in the Cincinnati metropolitan area. Much of this area is part of poverty-ridden Appalachia. Athens County, with a poverty rate of 32% in 2007, is the state's poorest county. The steel and coal areas in the north became Democratic during the 1930s and the southern counties started trending Republican in the 1960s. This mix makes for a Democratic-leaning district but the cultural conservatism of this region, much like that of West Virginia and eastern Kentucky across the river, put it narrowly in George W. Bush's column, by 49% in 2000 and 51% in 2004. In 2008, the close trend continued with John McCain narrowly winning 50%-48%.

The congressman from the 6th District is Charlie Wilson, a Democrat elected in 2006, and just the fifth person to reach Congress by running a write-in campaign. Wilson was born in Martins Ferry, across the Ohio River from Wheeling, W.V. He worked as a UAW welder, painter and assembly line worker before earning his mortician's license from Cincinnati College of Mortuary Science in 1967. He started the Wilson Funeral and Furniture Company in 1966 and the Wilson Realty Company in 1978 and, as a 37-year-old businessman, got his bachelor's degree from Ohio University. In 1996, Wilson won the first of four terms in the Ohio House, where he served as Democratic whip and assistant leader. In 2004, he was term-limited in the House and won a seat in the state Senate. Wilson worked in the Legislature to improve health care, spur job creation and promote economic development in the Ohio Valley. When Democratic incumbent Ted Strickland announced he would run for governor, Democrats touted Wilson as their top candidate to run for the seat.

Despite a decade in the Legislature, Wilson made a classic rookie mistake that nearly sunk his campaign. He failed to file the nominal 50 valid signatures to register his candidacy. His son, acting as campaign manager, submitted 96 signatures, but only 46 came from within the district and were valid. The bungled filing was an enormous embarrassment and national Democrats began to wonder about Wilson's ability to capture the seat, especially against a strong Republican candidate, Chuck Blasdel, the speaker pro tempore of the Ohio State House. Wilson could either run as an independent or mount a write-in campaign for the Democratic nomination, both uphill endeavors. He chose the latter.

The Democratic Congressional Campaign Committee agreed to help, but insisted on installing a professional manager. The DCCC flooded the district with radio and television ads while the Ohio AFL-CIO mobilized the district's union members by making 120,000 phone calls and putting 300 volunteers in the field. Wilson says he knocked on 40,000 doors and wrote 4,000 personal letters. The field work paid off. Wilson won the primary with an astounding 66%, with 43,687 write-in votes. In the meantime, Blasdel won the GOP primary with a lackluster 47%, and by the fall the district had fallen off the Republicans' list of targeted Democratic seats. Wilson defeated Blasdel 62%-38% in the general election and won all 12 counties in the district.

In the House, Wilson established a centrist voting record and joined the Blue Dog Coalition of moderate and conservative Democrats. He got behind the effort to impose "pay as you go" budgeting on lawmakers, which requires any tax cuts or spending increases be offset elsewhere in the budget. He got a seat on the Financial Services Committee, and during the housing market crisis, he worked with Ohio Republicans on a plan to direct a larger share of funds to buy foreclosed homes to harder-hit states. In January 2007, Wilson was one of only 16 House Democrats to vote against additional federal funding for embryonic-stem-cell research, which uses excess cells from in vitro fertilization. On the war in Iraq, he was a strong supporter of "benchmarks" for progress, but opposed deadlines for withdrawing U.S. troops.

Wilson has had to withstand some good-natured ribbing from colleagues that he is not the *real* Rep. Charlie Wilson, the swashbuckling Texan of the same name who dated gorgeous women, fought the mujahudeen in Afghanistan and was featured in a 2007 film starring Tom Hanks. That Charlie Wilson is now retired from Congress. The new Charlie Wilson got re-elected with an impressive 62%-33% in 2008.

SEVENTH DISTRICT

Steve Austria (R)

Elected 2008, 1st term; b. Oct. 12, 1958, Cincinnati; home, Beavercreek; Marquette U., B.A. 1981; Catholic; married (Eileen); 3 children.

Elected Office: OH House, 1998–2000; OH Senate, 2000–08, Majority whip, 2004–08.

Professional Career: Financial advisor.

DC Office: 1641 LHOB, 20515, 202-225-4324; Fax: 202-225-1984; Web site: austria.house.gov.

State Offices: Lancaster, 740-654-5149; Springfield, 937-325-0474.

Committees: *Budget* (13th of 15 R). *Homeland Security* (13th of 13 R): Emerging Threats, Cybersecurity & Science and Technology; Transportation Security & Infrastructure Protection.

Group Ratings and Key Votes: Newly Elected

Election Results

2008 general	Steve Austria (R)	174,915	(58%)	($1,196,189)
	Sharen Swartz Neuhardt (D)	125,547	(42%)	($855,332)
2008 primary	Steve Austria (R)	42,499	(55%)	
	Ron Hood (R)	25,984	(34%)	
	Dan Harkins (R)	4,817	(6%)	
	John Mitchel (R)	4,030	(5%)	

Population		Race/Ethnicity		Work	
Pop. 2007:	656,335	White:	86.1%	Private:	77.7%
Change since 2000:	Up 4.1%	Black:	8.8%	Government:	16.4%
Urban:	71.3%	Hispanic:	1.7%	Self-employed:	5.6%
Rural:	28.7%	Asian:	1.2%	Blue collar:	24.3%
Area size:	2,866 sq. mi.	Native Am.:	0.2%	White collar:	58.9%
		Hawaiian:	0.0%	Khaki collar:	0.4%
Age		Two+ races:	1.8%	Other:	16.4%
Median age:	36.7 yrs.			Median income:	$49,425
More than 65 yrs:	12.3%	*Ancestry*		Median home value:	$134,600
Less than 18 yrs:	24.1%	German:	21.3%	Poverty:	11.6%
		Irish:	11.7%		
Education		USA:	10.0%	**Military Veterans**	
H.S. grad:	86.7%			% of Pop:	12.9%
College grad:	20.5%				
Grad degree:	7.8%				

The hills and plains of central Ohio are dotted with towns and small cities that have been manufacturing centers almost since they were settled in the early 19th century, when the dominant technologies were the waterwheel and the open forge. In the decades after, new technologies—the automobile and the airplane—arrived, and the local manufacturing economy, sometimes in uncomfortable fits and starts, adjusted and advanced. This has been the story of Springfield, often studied as a typical

2008 Presidential Vote
McCain (R)..............................172,647   (54%)
Obama (D) 143,778   (45%)

2004 Presidential Vote
Bush (R) 176,365   (57%)
Kerry (D).................................132,124   (43%)

Cook Partisan Voting Index: R + 7

American city. In the early 1980s, International Harvester, the city's largest employer, went bankrupt, downsized dramatically and was renamed Navistar. In 1996, the company cut 3,000 jobs from its Springfield plant, and by 2002, the workforce had been pared down to 2,800. Navistar was on the rebound in 2008 after securing a deal to assemble General Motors medium-duty trucks, but that prospect went up in smoke in 2009 when GM went bankrupt. But amid these highly publicized and visible examples of capitalism's creative destruction, there have been less-noticed examples of its creativity. Small manufacturing businesses have grown up in empty factory spaces, and service employment has grown.

The 7th Congressional District of Ohio is made up of a portion of south-central Ohio. It includes Springfield and Clark County and, just to the south, the growing Greene County suburbs of Dayton around Wright Patterson Air Force Base. Although Wright Patterson gained a few hundred jobs in the base-closing review of 2005, Springfield's Air National Guard station lost its F-16 training unit. Other population centers are in Fairfield County, southeast of Columbus, and a slice of Franklin County, including part of the east side of Columbus. Fairfield is home to the 5,200-seat World Harvest Church, where politically active Pastor Rod Parsley is one of the nation's leading evangelicals and a prominent opponent of abortion rights and gay marriage. Early in the 2008 presidential campaign, Republican candidate John McCain referred to Parsley as "a spiritual guide," but he denounced the pastor's endorsement of his candidacy after Parsley made derogatory comments about the religion of Islam.

Farther east in Perry County, coal mining has revived as the price of oil skyrocketed. The district has always been Republican territory. It backed the policies of Ohio Republican President William McKinley (tariff protection, railroad regulation, antitrust suits against monopolies, discouragement of labor unions) and of Republican Gov. James Rhodes (low taxes, promotion of new businesses and jobs). It is culturally conservative as well. In 2008, Republican presidential nominee John McCain won the district, 54% to 45%.

The new congressman from the 7th district is Steve Austria, a protégé of Republican Rep. Dave Hobson, the longtime incumbent whose retirement paved the way for Austria's ascension to the U.S. House. His father, Dr. Clement Austria, was born in the Philippines but moved to Cincinnati to attend medical school. Austria was born in Cincinnati and grew up in Xenia, Ohio, with eight younger siblings. He graduated from Marquette University with a bachelor's degree in political science, then returned home and founded his own financial-planning business. He worked for the local GOP, and his wife, Eileen, worked for Hobson when Hobson was a state senator. She was Hobson's U.S. House district director from 1990 to 2007.

In 1998, Austria launched his political career by challenging incumbent state Rep. Marilyn Reid, a fellow Republican embroiled in an ethics scandal. Austria upset Reid in the GOP primary and easily defeated the Democratic candidate in the general election. Two years later, he was elected to the state Senate, where he served two terms as majority whip. In the Legislature, Austria focused on law and order issues. He sponsored a bill that stiffened penalties for soliciting sex from minors over the Internet. He also sponsored a bill that toughened penalties for child rapists. In 2003, he won praise for helping to broker a deal on a bill that allowed Ohioans to carry concealed handguns.

When Hobson announced his retirement in October 2007, Austria got into the contest for the seat as the front-runner. Democrats hoped that Clark County Sheriff Gene Kelly would enter the race, but he opted against it saying, "I don't know of a Democrat out there that can take on Steve Austria." Still, Austria had primary competition. Former state Rep. Ron Hood and Clark County Republican Party Chairman Dan Harkins also vied for the Republican nomination. Austria was not helped by the *Dayton Daily News*, which editorialized: "What he's most likely to do is settle into a long, long career of keeping people back home happy, while remaining on the congressional back benches." Nevertheless, Austria won, with 55% to Hood's 34% and Harkins's 6%. In the general election, Austria faced attorney Sharen Neuhardt. Democrats claimed Neuhardt could run a competitive race, but the Democratic Congressional Campaign Committee did not put her on their top-rated Red to Blue list until early September. The powerhouse fundraising group EMILY's List also endorsed her. But Austria still outraised her $1.2 million to $900,000.

A couple months before the election, Austria's campaign had a setback when political blogger Jeff Coryell revealed that sections of a column Austria wrote for the *Xenia Gazette* closely resembled text from a U.S. Department of Labor website. Neuhardt accused Austria of plagiarism, but the attention the incident got paled in comparison to the flak Neuhardt took a few weeks later, when the *Dayton Daily News* revealed that for six years she had housed a Rwandan refugee who was not legally in the United States for part of that period. The National Republican Congressional Committee criticized Neuhardt for harboring an illegal immigrant. The Rwandan man also had been arrested for disorderly conduct and cited for driving without a license. In the campaign's final stretch, Neuhardt blamed the Republican Party for the job losses in the district, but the message failed to resonate. Austria defeated her 58% to 42%, carrying every county in the district except Franklin.

In the House, Austria got seats on the Budget Committee and the Homeland Security Committee. During a February 2009 interview with the *Columbus Dispatch*'s editorial board, Austria compared President Barack Obama's economic-stimulus bill to former President Franklin Roosevelt's economic policies and claimed government spending under Roosevelt caused the Great Depression. A week later, liberal MSNBC news commentator Keith Olbermann ridiculed Austria's take on American history.

EIGHTH DISTRICT

John Boehner (R)

Elected 1990, 10th term; b. Nov. 17, 1949, Cincinnati; home, West Chester; Xavier U., B.S. 1977; Catholic; married (Debbie); 2 children.

Military Career: Navy, 1969.

Elected Office: Union Township Bd. of Trustees, 1981–85, Pres., 1984; OH House of Reps., 1984–90.

Professional Career: Pres., Nucite Sales Inc., 1976–90.

DC Office: 1011 LHOB, 20515, 202-225-6205; Fax: 202-225-0704; Web site: www.johnboehner.house.gov.

State Offices: Troy, 937-339-1524; West Chester, 513-779-5400.

Committees: *Minority Leader.*

Group Ratings

	ADA	ACLU	AFS	LCV	ITIC	NTU	COC	ACU	CFG	FRC
2008	0	18	0	0	43	76	94	92	89	100
2007	5	—	0	0	—	87	79	100	92	—

National Journal Ratings

	2007 LIB	—	2007 CONS	2008 LIB	—	2008 CONS
Economic	0%	—	97%	0%	—	98%
Social	0%	—	91%	9%	—	85%
Foreign	0%	—	72%	5%	—	93%
Composite	7%	—	93%	6%	—	94%

Key Votes of the 110th Congress

1. Increase minimum wage	N	5. Share immigration data	Y	9. Withdraw troops 8/08	N
2. Expand SCHIP	N	6. Foreign aid abortion ban	Y	10. No operations in Iran	N
3. Raise CAFE standards	N	7. Ban gay bias in workplace	N	11. Free trade with Peru	Y
4. Bail out financial markets	Y	8. Repeal D.C. gun law	Y	12. Overhaul FISA	Y

Election Results

2008 general	John Boehner (R)	202,063	(68%)	($5,342,022)
	Nicholas Von Stein (D)	95,510	(32%)	($15,425)
2008 primary	John Boehner (R)	unopposed		

Population		Race/Ethnicity		Work	
Pop. 2007:	645,065	White:	89.6%	Private:	82.8%
Change since 2000:	Up 2.3%	Black:	5.1%	Government:	11.3%
Urban:	78.1%	Hispanic:	1.9%	Self-employed:	5.8%
Rural:	21.9%	Asian:	1.6%	Blue collar:	28.2%
Area size:	2,031 sq. mi.	Native Am.:	0.2%	White collar:	55.4%
		Hawaiian:	0.0%	Khaki collar:	0.1%
Age		Two+ races:	1.4%	Other:	16.3%
Median age:	36.2 yrs.			Median income:	$48,305
More than 65 yrs:	12.4%	*Ancestry*		Median home value:	$134,000
Less than 18 yrs:	24.9%	German:	24.9%	Poverty:	12.0%
		USA:	12.5%		
Education		Irish:	10.6%	**Military Veterans**	
H.S. grad:	85.2%			% of Pop:	11.3%
College grad:	20.0%				
Grad degree:	7.0%				

Since the early 20th century, the far west end of Ohio—where U.S. 40, the old National Road, heads straight as an arrow in its last miles across Ohio and into Indiana—has been some of the nation's prime industrial country. The Great and Little Miami rivers drain south into the Ohio, and U.S. 40 jogs southward twice to go over the Miami and Stillwater river dams, built after the great flood of 1913, which killed 361 people in Dayton and caused $1 billion in damage. After the recession of the early

2008 Presidential Vote
McCain (R).............................191,639   (61%)
Obama (D) 119,834   (38%)

2004 Presidential Vote
Bush (R) 199,265   (64%)
Kerry (D) 109,374   (35%)

Cook Partisan Voting Index: R + 14

1980s, Ohioans around Dayton and Cincinnati, in large factory towns like Middletown and Hamilton and smaller factory towns like Troy and Piqua, adapted to new conditions and began to produce exports for Europe, Latin America and Asia as well as for the American market. At the same time, people leaving the central cities of Dayton and Cincinnati moved into new subdivisions amid shopping malls and office parks in Butler County. Hamilton, the Butler County seat founded in 1791, lost jobs when International Paper shut down a plant, but many more were created. Again this decade, the region was hit inordinately hard by a recession because of its reliance on manufacturing. In 2007, AK Steel moved its corporate headquarters and 300 employees from Middletown, the area's second-largest city, to nearby West Chester Township. And in 2008, *Forbes* magazine called Middletown one of America's fastest-dying cities, citing rising poverty and the relatively low percentage of college graduates. In February 2009, the unemployment level in Butler County reached a 25-year high, and Middletown and Hamilton also reported double-digit jobless rates. West Chester Township has been one of the few bright spots in recent years. Its population has steadily increased since 2000, and its business-friendly climate has attracted new economic activity, including a new Amylin Pharmaceuticals facility and a new GE Aviation facility.

The 8th Congressional District of Ohio covers much of this territory. It includes all of Butler County, except four lightly populated townships, two counties to the north on the Indiana line and part of a third. It also includes Miami County north of Dayton and the northeastern corner of Montgomery County, including part of Dayton, all of Huber Heights and part of Wright-Patterson Air Force Base. Politically, this is very Republican territory; the district twice gave George W. Bush more than 60% of the vote. It voted 61% for GOP presidential nominee John McCain in 2008.

The congressman from the 8th District is John Boehner, a Republican elected in 1990 and the House Minority Leader. Boehner (pronounced *BAY-ner*) grew up in Cincinnati, the second-oldest of 12 children in a home with two bedrooms. His father ran Andy's Café, a neighborhood restaurant and bar. Playing at a much heavier weight than he is now, he was a linebacker for Cincinnati's Archbishop Moeller High School on a team coached by Gerry Faust, before Faust went to Notre Dame. Boehner worked his way through college as a janitor and graduated from Xavier University, the first college graduate in his family. He moved to Butler County, where he went to work for a small business that sold plastics for packaging and eventually took it over and developed it into a highly successful enterprise. He served on the Union Township Board of Trustees and in 1984, at age 34, was elected to the Ohio House. In 1990, he ran against Republican incumbent Rep. Donald (Buz) Lukens, who inexplicably sought re-election after he was convicted of having sex with a 16-year-old girl. Also in the GOP primary was Tom Kindness, a former House member who ran unsuccessfully for the Senate in 1986 and then became a lobbyist in Washington. Boehner won the primary with 49%, to 32% for Kindness and 17% for Lukens. The win was tantamount to victory in the heavily Republican district, and Boehner has since been re-elected without difficulty.

In the House, Boehner has a consistently conservative voting record, though he is also pragmatic and more apt to look for compromise on legislation than his more hard-edged ideological colleagues. In his early years, he was a rabble-rousing reformer. He joined the Gang of Seven, young freshman Republicans who insisted on naming all 355 members who'd had overdrafts at the House bank, a scandal that revealed that members had routinely abused their tax-subsidized banking privileges. He went on to assail Democrats as well as Republicans who supported a congressional pay raise. Boehner's Gang of Seven infuriated House veterans but struck a chord with the public, and the junior lawmakers earned recognition beyond their years of service. In the process, Boehner became a top ally of Minority Whip Newt Gingrich of Georgia, who was raising money for Republican candidates with the goal of toppling the entrenched Democratic majority in the House. Boehner also managed Gingrich's campaign for Republican leader, though he later would sour on Gingrich and participate in efforts to curb his power.

Boehner was one of the architects of the 10-point Contract With America, the policy manifesto that Republicans ran on in their successful 1994 drive to win a majority in the House for the first time in 40 years. After the election, he ran for chairman of the Republican Conference, and with the backing of Gingrich, the new speaker of the House, he beat California's Duncan Hunter 122-102. That made Boehner the fourth-most-powerful member of the new Republican leadership, with the responsibility of preparing the party's message and enforcing discipline.

The Gingrich years were a turbulent time for Boehner. An ethics investigation of Gingrich instigated by the Democrats placed Boehner in the middle of a legal altercation after a Florida couple taped one of Boehner's cell-phone conversations with Republican leaders while he was driving through the state. The tape eventually reached Jim McDermott of Washington, the senior Democrat on the Committee on Standards of Official Conduct, who made the contents available to the *New York Times*. In 1998, Boehner sued McDermott in federal court for invasion of privacy. Despite attempts to settle the case, the two could not agree on terms, and the case wound its way through the court system over the course of several years, finally reaching the U.S. Supreme Court. In 2008, the high court denied further review, and a federal district court judge ordered McDermott to pay Boehner more than $1 million in legal fees.

By 1997, many rank-and-file House Republicans had lost confidence in the leadership team, especially the brilliant but erratic Gingrich. Boehner and other high-level members of the leadership team held secret discussions about whether to try to force Gingrich out as speaker. When their plotting was made public, the plan backfired, and the plotters took most of the heat for appearing to be disloyal and self-serving. GOP Whip Tom DeLay of Texas admitted his role and was forgiven. Dick Armey of Texas retained his majority leadership post even though he had misled members by saying he had nothing to do with the plotting. Boehner did not survive. After the 1998 elections, during which Republicans lost five seats, Gingrich lost power and Boehner also lost the conference chairmanship to J.C. Watts of Oklahoma, who argued that the GOP needed a more diversified leadership. Watts was backed by DeLay.

Boehner's ejection from the leadership was humiliating. But he quickly set about rebuilding his reputation as a leader. He plunged into his role as a subcommittee chairman on what was then called the Education and the Workforce Committee. In six months, the subcommittee passed eight bills restructuring employer-run health-insurance plans. Pleased by Boehner's initiative and dismayed that other committees had not been as effective, Speaker Hastert adopted many of the subcommittee's bills as the Republican health-care agenda. After the 2000 election, Boehner secured the chairmanship of the full committee.

When President George W. Bush assumed office in 2001, he made an overhaul of education policy a top priority, putting Boehner in the driver's seat of the new administration's chief domestic initiative. Early on, the chairman established a working relationship with the chief Democrat on the panel, George Miller of California. Miller had been teaching school dropouts and believed that current programs weren't helping disadvantaged children keep up with their peers, and Boehner shared his concern. While other committees dissolved into partisan stalemate, Boehner and Miller worked together on the House version of Bush's No Child Left Behind Act, which included the president's mandates for annual testing and increased accountability. It passed the committee and was later overwhelmingly approved by the House, 384-45. Boehner and Miller then worked with their Senate counterparts, Republican Judd Gregg of New Hampshire and Democrat Edward Kennedy of Massachusetts, on a compromise final draft that would be acceptable to both chambers. The House passed the final bill 381-41, with most of the no votes coming from Republicans, and it passed the Senate, 87-10. As a sign of Boehner's enduring partnership with Kennedy, the two sponsored an annual dinner in Washington, D.C., that raised more than $1 million for underfunded Roman Catholic schools in the city and featured motivational speakers, including First Lady Laura Bush, and good-natured ribbing between the two hosts.

In 2003 and 2004, Boehner worked successfully on the reauthorization of the special-education act, again making it a bipartisan undertaking. The final bill contained a provision sought by teachers' unions that disabilities be taken into account when students are disciplined. It also provided stronger certification requirements and withholding of state funds if local districts fail to comply with the act. Waivers on paperwork requirements were authorized for 15 states, and Boehner agreed to annual increases in funding for special-education programs. The committee also tackled the complex issue of pensions.

In January 2005, as bankrupt airlines began ceding their pension obligations to the federal Pension Benefit Guaranty Corporation, Boehner said, "We have a huge pension underfunding problem." Once again with bipartisan support, he pushed for a comprehensive solution to pension problems around the country and then played a leading role in months of painstaking House-Senate negotiations. The legislation, passed in summer 2006, represented a major change in pension law. It closed loopholes that had permitted many companies to underfund their plans by an estimated $450 billion, set deadlines for them to make payments, and created automatic enrollment in 401(k) plans for many workers.

In the fall of 2005, the House Republican leadership was again in turmoil. DeLay, by then the majority leader, was forced to step down after being indicted for alleged campaign fundraising irregularities. Speaker Hastert tapped Majority Whip Roy Blunt of Missouri to serve as acting leader. Boehner had been quietly planning for a return to the leadership. In January 2006, he announced that he would run against Blunt for majority leader, although Blunt, in his capacity as acting leader, had styled himself the heir apparent. Boehner believed that restiveness among House Republicans would support an alternative to Hastert's hand-chosen candidate, and he offered a 37-page campaign manifesto that called for "one big, bold goal" each year and more reliance on the committees to generate legislation. When leadership elections were held, Boehner was in a three-way race with Blunt and conservative Rep. John Shadegg of Arizona. Shadegg was forced out on the first ballot, getting only 40 votes to 110 for Blunt and 79 for Boehner. On the second ballot, Boehner got most of the Shadegg's supporters as well as a few defectors from Blunt. He won 122-109.

In contrast to the reserved Hastert, Boehner was sociable and adept at the glad-handing side of politics. He regularly held court just off the House floor with reporters and fellow members, puffing on ever-present Barclay cigarettes and sporting the year-round tan he maintains through his devotion to golf. (His Ohio home backs onto the tenth green of a golf course, though chronic back problems, which often cause him acute pain, have reduced his time on the green.) In his early days as majority leader, Boehner focused on lobbying reform and a crackdown on spending earmarks, which had exploded under Republican control and diminished the party's message of fiscal responsibility. In October 2006, he visited the districts of many endangered House Republicans and made numerous national-media appearances, largely in a bid to turn out the Republican vote. The efforts were for naught. Fed up with scandal and the party's unpopular president, voters delivered a strong rebuke to Republicans, who lost control of Congress. Hastert announced that he was stepping down from the leadership, leaving it to Boehner to vie for minority leader against only a relatively weak challenger, conservative Mike Pence of Indiana. Boehner won, 168-27. "To earn our majority back, House Republicans must rededicate ourselves to the spirit of reform, and we must regain our confidence and courage to tackle the big issues the American people care about," Boehner said following his selection.

Adapting to life in the minority, Boehner has occasionally cooperated with Democratic leaders, notably on the February 2008 economic-stimulus bill and the handling of Iraq War funding. He also helped deliver votes for the $700 billion rescue of the financial-services industry, despite dubbing it a "crap sandwich." But mostly he has been outspoken in leading the opposition to their policies. He led the charge, unsuccessfully, to oust House Ways and Means Committee Charles Rangel of New York after questions were raised about Rangel's ethics and financial dealings. On immigration reform, he dropped his earlier advocacy of a middle ground and joined Republican hard-liners who emphasized border security and opposed a path to citizenship for illegal aliens. He remained an ardent supporter of the war in Iraq.

A low moment for Boehner came in the spring of 2008 with the loss of three longtime Republican-held seats in special elections. Having privately told his members to get off their "dead asses," Boehner had little alternative other than to buck up his party with assurances that November was "not going to be as bad as people think." He turned the focus to the soaring price of oil to spotlight policy differences between the two parties. Then in November, Republicans lost 21 more House seats—including three in Ohio, an abysmal showing and a setback for Boehner, whose only words of encouragement were that it could have been worse, given the party's low public approval and Bush's unpopularity. With Bush gone, Boehner entered the Obama presidency with his best opportunity to try to guide House Republicans back to victory in November 2010.

Boehner's first major political strategy of the 111th Congress (2009–10) was persuading the Republican conference to unanimously vote against Obama's $787 billion economic-stimulus bill. He derided it as wasteful government spending, and while he couldn't block its passage, he created a clear distinction between Democratic and Republican approaches to the recession. He characterized the House Republicans as an "entrepreneurial insurgency" that would oppose Democratic policies through all means at their disposal. In May 2009, he harshly criticized Speaker Nancy Pelosi after she claimed that in 2002 the Central Intelligence Agency failed to inform her about the use of a form of coercion called water boarding on suspected terrorists. Pelosi's unfavorable ratings with voters increased during that time.

NINTH DISTRICT

Marcy Kaptur (D)

Elected 1982, 14th term; b. June 17, 1946, Toledo; home, Toledo; U. of WI, B.A. 1968, U. of MI, M.A. 1974, M.I.T., 1981–82; Catholic; single.

Professional Career: Urban planner, Lucas Cnty. Planning Comm., 1969–75; Urban planning consultant, 1975–77; White House Asst. Dir. for Urban Affairs, 1977–80; Dpty. secy., Natl. Consumer Coop. Bank, 1980–81; Author.

DC Office: 2186 RHOB, 20515, 202-225-4146; Fax: 202-225-7711; Web site: kaptur.house.gov.

State Offices: Toledo, 419-259-7500.

Committees: *Appropriations* (5th of 37 D): Agriculture, Rural Development, FDA & Related Agencies; Defense; Transportation, HUD & Related Agencies. *Budget* (3rd of 24 D). *Oversight & Government Reform* (13th of 24 D).

Group Ratings

	ADA	ACLU	AFS	LCV	ITIC	NTU	COC	ACU	CFG	FRC
2008	100	100	100	92	43	17	47	13	14	35
2007	95	—	100	80	—	3	47	8	0	—

National Journal Ratings

	2007 LIB — 2007 CONS		2008 LIB — 2008 CONS	
Economic	57%	— 42%	68%	— 31%
Social	70%	— 29%	82%	— 0%
Foreign	81%	— 16%	64%	— 35%
Composite	70%	— 30%	75%	— 25%

Key Votes of the 110th Congress

1. Increase minimum wage	Y	5. Share immigration data	N	9. Withdraw troops 8/08	Y
2. Expand SCHIP	Y	6. Foreign aid abortion ban	Y	10. No operations in Iran	Y
3. Raise CAFE standards	Y	7. Ban gay bias in workplace	Y	11. Free trade with Peru	N
4. Bail out financial markets	N	8. Repeal D.C. gun law	N	12. Overhaul FISA	N

Election Results

2008 general	Marcy Kaptur (D)	222,054	(74%)	($501,404)
	Bradley Leavitt (R)	76,512	(26%)	
2008 primary	Marcy Kaptur (D)	unopposed		

Prior Winning Percentages: 2006 (74%); 2004 (68%); 2002 (74%); 2000 (75%); 1998 (81%); 1996 (77%); 1994 (75%); 1992 (74%); 1990 (78%); 1988 (81%); 1986 (78%); 1984 (55%); 1982 (58%)

Population		Race/Ethnicity		Work	
Pop. 2007:	624,100	White:	78.4%	Private:	81.9%
Change since 2000:	Down 1.1%	Black:	14.0%	Government:	13.0%
Urban:	86.0%	Hispanic:	4.5%	Self-employed:	4.9%
Rural:	14.0%	Asian:	1.2%	Blue collar:	26.3%
Area size:	1,244 sq. mi.	Native Am.:	0.1%	White collar:	55.9%
		Hawaiian:	0.0%	Khaki collar:	0.1%
Age		Two+ races:	1.7%	Other:	17.7%
Median age:	37.6 yrs.			Median income:	$45,597
More than 65 yrs:	13.5%	*Ancestry*		Median home value:	$131,100
Less than 18 yrs:	24.2%	German:	24.1%	Poverty:	15.0%
		Irish:	10.4%		
Education		Polish:	7.1%	**Military Veterans**	
H.S. grad:	86.6%			% of Pop:	11.2%
College grad:	21.5%				
Grad degree:	7.7%				

Toledo was one of America's boomtowns in the 1920s, "a decade of fabulous figures," as historian Harlan Hatcher wrote. The Willys-Overland plant employed 25,000 workers and turned out an automobile every 30 seconds. The Libbey-Owens-Ford merger made Toledo, with local supplies of natural gas and sand, the nation's largest glass manufacturer. The city built docks for coal and iron-ore shipments and later erected an airport that could handle transcontinental flights. Toledo had long been

2008 Presidential Vote		
Obama (D)	195,240	(62%)
McCain (R)	113,800	(36%)
2004 Presidential Vote		
Kerry (D)	181,889	(58%)
Bush (R)	129,825	(42%)
Cook Partisan Voting Index: D + 10		

well situated, where the Maumee River empties into Lake Erie, where two dozen rail lines connected it with the East Coast, Chicago, and the coal fields of Kentucky and West Virginia. It was well positioned to be a center of the brash auto industry and became a national leader when it first produced the Jeep in the 1940s. During World War II, it also produced aircraft parts, rockets and other military equipment. But by the early 1980s, the domestic auto industry was faltering, as foreign competitors brought to the market better, lower-maintenance cars that were more economical to drive. Toledo and other auto-dependent cities went through tough times.

But revival was on the way. Toledo's small manufacturers in search of markets showed energy and ingenuity. Sport utility vehicles were invented here, and the city produced one of America's hottest vehicles, the Jeep Cherokee. The old Jeep plant was set to close, but the city offered Chrysler $300 million in incentives to stay, and a new plant was built along Interstate 75. For years, the Jeep Liberty and Jeep Wrangler factories here were barely able to meet demand. Then, with competition and higher gasoline prices, the good times ended. In 2007, Jeep eliminated its third shift and 750 workers, and the following year, Chrysler dropped the second shift at the same plant. The continuing loss of auto and other manufacturing jobs took a toll. In 2008, the Milken Institute ranked Toledo 194th among 200 cities in job growth; most of the other bottom cities were in Ohio and Michigan.

The 9th Congressional District of Ohio is centered on Toledo, spreading east through the flatlands of Ottawa and Erie counties on the Lake Erie shore and inland to southern Lorain County southwest of Cleveland. It includes Oberlin, home of Oberlin College, founded in 1833 and the first American college to admit women and blacks. Port Clinton, on Lake Erie, bills itself as the "Walleye Capital of the World" and drops a plastic walleye in place of a glittering ball on New Year's Eve. Sandusky is home to the giant Cedar Point amusement park , with some of the country's fastest roller coasters. Not far away is Milan, birthplace of the great inventor and capitalist Thomas Edison. Politically, Toledo has been heavily Democratic since CIO unions organized the plants in the late 1930s. The collapse of the auto industry so unnerved the district it voted for Republican Ronald Reagan in 1980 and elected a Republican congressman, but it switched back to the Democrats in 1982 and has stayed with them in almost every election since. In 2008, the district voted 62% to 36% for Democratic candidate Barack Obama.

The congresswoman from the 9th District is Marcy Kaptur, a Democrat first elected in 1982. She is now the most-senior woman among Democrats in the House, a distinction not lost on her in her occasional clashes with Democratic House Speaker Nancy Pelosi. Kaptur grew up in a blue-collar neighborhood in Toledo, the daughter of Polish-American parents who worked at local auto plants. The family also operated a small grocery store, but her father sold it to get a job with health benefits. "It broke his heart," she said. She has spent almost her entire career in public service. She and her brother, Steve, live in the house where they grew up. She graduated from the University of Wisconsin, the first in her family to attend college, got a master's degree from the University of Michigan, then spent eight years as an urban planner in Toledo. She worked on urban revitalization in the Carter White House, returning home in 1980 with thoughts of running for elected office. That year, Republican Ed Weber defeated 26-year Democratic incumbent Thomas Ashley. In 1982, when no other Democrat would run against Weber, she did and won 58%-39% despite being outspent 3-to-1.

Kaptur is a plainspoken, old-fashioned Democrat and dedicated opponent of free trade. She has long been convinced that Toledo and places like it have lost jobs and industry because of unfair trade practices and low-wage competition from countries like Mexico and China. She pressured the Japanese to buy more American auto parts, but has been leery of Japanese investment in the United States. Kaptur was probably Congress's most dedicated opponent of the 1993 North American Free Trade Agreement. She criticized Democratic President Bill Clinton for doing nothing for sagging U.S. industries and for ignoring Democrats opposed to NAFTA. She became something of a national figure in 1995, when she appeared before Texas businessman Ross Perot's United We Stand party and made a rousing speech on trade that had delegates cheering. Perot, running as a third-party candidate for president in 1996, offered her the vice presidential nomination a year later, but she turned it down. She was a vocal opponent of normal trade relations with China and of expanded free-trade negotiating powers for President George W. Bush, and she predicted that the 2005 Central American Free Trade Agreement would destroy jobs in Ohio. She backed a resolution calling for the United States to withdraw from the World Trade Organization, citing "the $600 billion trade deficit and the fact that these trade agreements are hollowing out our country."

Reflecting on those early trade wars years later, Kaptur criticized Pelosi's support of NAFTA. "That's where the real knife was put in the flesh," she said. When Pelosi announced in May 2007 an agreement with Treasury Secretary Hank Paulson on principles for international trade policy, an uninvited Kaptur glared from the back of the room. "It was quite disappointing to see that our leadership talked to the White House and Republican leadership before they talked to the Democratic Caucus," Kaptur complained. In 2002, she ran a quixotic, one-day campaign for minority leader against Pelosi but, predictably, got nowhere against the powerful California Democrat. In 2008, Kaptur challenged Pelosi ally Xavier Becerra of California for the leadership post of Democratic Caucus vice chairman and lost badly, 175-67.

Kaptur has a liberal voting record but departs from party orthodoxy on abortion—she opposes funding for abortion and embryonic-stem-cell research, which uses excess cells from in vitro fertilizations. She is a strong advocate of alternative energy sources such as ethanol and biofuels for Ohio. Strongly opposed to the war in Iraq, Kaptur and Texas Republican Kay Granger in 2005 became the first women to serve on the Defense Appropriations Subcommittee. Kaptur gave up the senior Democratic slot on the Agriculture Subcommittee to make the move.

She keeps close tabs on her district. A constituent gave her the idea to sponsor the legislation that authorized the World War II Memorial on the Washington Mall. On the Appropriations Committee, she has focused on improvements to bridges, roads, and rail and port facilities in her district. Kaptur is unabashed about working to secure spending earmarks in the appropriations bills for her district, a practice that has come under harsh criticism in recent years. In 2007, she earmarked $77 million for projects back home and ranked 25th among the top earmark recipients in the House, according to the group Taxpayers for Common Sense. She once challenged Republicans on the committee to limit farm payments, but when they threatened her favorite spending projects, she backed off. "I may be blockheaded sometimes, but I'm not stupid," Kaptur said.

She is proud of her role as a successful woman in what is still a male-dominated realm and has pushed for more portraits and statues of women in the Capitol. She also wrote a book on women in Congress. She is exceedingly popular in Toledo and is rarely seriously challenged at election time. In 2004, her Republican opponent, Lucas County Auditor Larry Kaczala, criticized Kaptur for comparing terrorist Osama bin Laden to American revolutionaries. But Kaptur won 68%-32%.

TENTH DISTRICT

Dennis Kucinich (D)

Elected 1996, 7th term; b. Oct. 8, 1946, Cleveland; home, Cleveland; Cleveland St. U., 1967–70, Case Western Reserve U., B.A., M.A., 1973; Catholic; married (Elizabeth Harper); 1 child.

Elected Office: Cleveland City Cncl., 1969–75, 1983–85; Cleveland mayor, 1977–79; OH Senate, 1994–96.

Professional Career: Clerk, municipal courts, 1976–77; Radio talk show host, 1979, 1989; Lecturer, 1980–83; Consultant, 1986–94; TV Reporter, Channel 8, 1989–92.

DC Office: 2445 RHOB, 20515, 202-225-5871; Fax: 202-225-5745; Web site: kucinich.house.gov.

State Offices: Lakewood, 216-228-8850; Parma, 440-845-2707.

Committees: *Education & Labor* (10th of 29 D): Early Childhood, Elementary & Secondary Education; Health, Employment, Labor & Pensions. *Oversight & Government Reform* (5th of 24 D): Domestic Policy (Chmn); Federal Workforce, Postal Service & the District of Columbia; National Security & Foreign Affairs.

Group Ratings

	ADA	ACLU	AFS	LCV	ITIC	NTU	COC	ACU	CFG	FRC
2008	95	100	86	92	17	25	39	8	11	11
2007	70	—	82	80	—	15	35	4	6	—

National Journal Ratings

	2007 LIB	—	2007 CONS	2008 LIB	—	2008 CONS
Economic	48%	—	52%	64%	—	35%
Social	92%	—	0%	52%	—	48%
Foreign	55%	—	45%	55%	—	43%
Composite	66%	—	34%	58%	—	43%

Key Votes of the 110th Congress

1. Increase minimum wage	Y	5. Share immigration data	N	9. Withdraw troops 8/08	N
2. Expand SCHIP	N	6. Foreign aid abortion ban	N	10. No operations in Iran	Y
3. Raise CAFE standards	Y	7. Ban gay bias in workplace	Y	11. Free trade with Peru	N
4. Bail out financial markets	N	8. Repeal D.C. gun law	N	12. Overhaul FISA	N

Election Results

2008 general	Dennis Kucinich (D)	157,268	(57%)	($2,430,560)
	Jim Trakas (R)	107,918	(39%)	($381,135)
	Paul Conroy (Lib)	10,623	(4%)	
2008 primary	Dennis Kucinich (D)	72,646	(50%)	
	Joe Cimperman (D)	50,760	(35%)	
	Barbara Ferris (D)	9,362	(6%)	
	Thomas O'Grady (D)	7,264	(5%)	

Prior Winning Percentages: 2006 (66%); 2004 (60%); 2002 (74%); 2000 (75%); 1998 (67%); 1996 (49%)

Population		Race/Ethnicity		Work	
Pop. 2007:	604,029	White:	83.7%	Private:	83.0%
Change since 2000:	Down 4.2%	Black:	6.7%	Government:	12.6%
Urban:	99.4%	Hispanic:	6.3%	Self-employed:	4.3%
Rural:	0.6%	Asian:	2.0%	Blue collar:	21.6%
Area size:	196 sq. mi.	Native Am.:	0.2%	White collar:	60.7%
		Hawaiian:	0.0%	Khaki collar:	0.1%
Age		Two+ races:	1.0%	Other:	17.6%
Median age:	40.3 yrs.	*Ancestry*		Median income:	$45,562
More than 65 yrs:	15.4%	German:	17.7%	Median home value:	$137,600
Less than 18 yrs:	23.1%	Irish:	13.6%	Poverty:	12.7%
Education		Polish:	8.9%	**Military Veterans**	
H.S. grad:	85.9%			% of Pop:	10.8%
College grad:	25.0%				
Grad degree:	8.7%				

Cleveland, one of America's great cities at the beginning of the 20th century, faced major hardships in the latter half of the century. It grew up as a center of heavy industry. This was the original base of John D. Rockefeller's Standard Oil. The city's deep, twisting Cuyahoga River was the site of several of the nation's largest steel mills. Great industrial fortunes built civic institutions like the museums in Wade Park, Case Western University and the Cleveland Symphony, and they financed the campaigns of

2008 Presidential Vote		
Obama (D)	174,598	(59%)
McCain (R)	115,025	(39%)

2004 Presidential Vote		
Kerry (D)	175,149	(58%)
Bush (R)	125,102	(41%)

Cook Partisan Voting Index: D + 8

northeast Ohio Republican Presidents James Garfield and William McKinley. On the old Public Square, designed like a New England town green by the Yankees who settled this Western Reserve (the northeast corner of Ohio) in the early 19th century, the two eccentric Van Sweringen brothers, trolley magnates of the early 20th century, built the Terminal Tower, for many years the highest skyscraper in interior America. As an ethnic city with more than 40 nationalities—Hungarians, Czechs, Serbs, Croatians, Poles, Italians, Germans—and many distinct ethnic neighborhoods, it produced a robust two-party politics. In the 1930s, after CIO unions organized steel factories and auto-assembly plants, Cleveland became solidly Democratic, though with some affluent Republican suburbs.

Disgruntled by local taxes, Rockefeller and his corporate operations moved to New York, and Cleveland never led the nation as it had hoped. America's fourth largest city in 1910, it was overtaken in size first by Detroit and eventually by the likes of Houston and Dallas. Today, it's the center of the nation's 26th-largest metropolitan area, having fallen below Cincinnati in 2007. That year, more people left Cleveland and Cuyahoga County than any other major city or county. The central city declined from 914,000 in 1950 to 405,000 in 2007, with a Census Bureau projection that it may soon fall below 400,000. As the children who grew up in the tightly packed neighborhoods have made more money and moved to the close-in suburbs and then outer suburban counties, fewer new immigrants have taken their place; a modest sign of hope has been the growth of the Asian community. The 1970s were a hard decade for Cleveland, which became an object of ridicule nationally. Its heavy industries were fast declining, corporate headquarters were departing, Lake Erie and the Cuyahoga River were badly polluted (the river caught fire in June 1969), and the city faced bankruptcy under the youthful Democratic Mayor Dennis Kucinich. The city government was rescued by Republican George Voinovich, elected mayor in 1979. Downtown Cleveland slowly revived, with the theater district center at Playhouse Square, the Jacobs Field baseball stadium, Gund Arena, and the Rock and Roll Hall of Fame. People now swim in a restored Lake Erie.

Restaurants and pleasure-boat docks line the Cuyahoga. In Brook Park, NASA's Glenn Research Center is developing the service module for the next generation of the space shuttle.

The 10th Congressional District of Ohio includes most of the west side of Cleveland and the western and southern suburbs in Cuyahoga County. Excluded is one salient of mostly black Cleveland precincts, which are attached to the 11th District across the river. Suburbs in the 10th include Lakewood, still comfortable middle-class territory, plus Rocky River and Bay Village. Inland is Parma, a creation of the 1950s, when second- and third-generation ethnics moved out to subdivision houses set amid what was once America's densest concentration of bowling alleys. The political tradition is primarily Democratic. In 2008, Democratic presidential nominee Barack Obama won the district with 59% of the vote to 39% for Republican John McCain.

The congressman from the 10th District is Dennis Kucinich, elected in 1996 and an iconoclastic candidate for president in 2004 and 2008. The son of a truck driver who was frequently out of work, Kucinich (*Koo SIN ich*) grew up as the oldest of seven children. The family moved 21 times to various parts of Cleveland and during particularly rough patches slept in the family's car. As the oldest, Kucinich went to work at 12 as a shoe-shine boy. He was driven and continued working to put himself through college. In 1969, at age 23, he was elected to the Cleveland City Council. He saw himself as the champion of the working man and had a confrontational relationship with Cleveland's business establishment. He was elected mayor in 1977, then the youngest-ever mayor of a major American city. But the city was in dire financial straits, and Kucinich was unwilling or unable to balance the budget and meet obligations. When bankers demanded that he sell city-owned properties, he refused, and they called in their loans. The public verdict was negative. In 1979, after surviving a recall petition by just 236 votes out of 120,000 cast, Kucinich was defeated. He argued that his primary goal had been to preserve the city-owned Muny Light electric system, and that in succeeding, he had saved residents millions of dollars on their electric bills. "This was a case of the bank blackmailing the city, pure and simple," he once said. He taught at Cleveland State and Case Western Reserve universities, hosted a radio talk show and was a television reporter. In 1994, he staged a political comeback and was elected to the state Senate. Two years later, he ran for the U.S. House against Republican Rep. Martin Hoke. He campaigned against the North American Free Trade Agreement and as a friend of labor. Many of his former critics rallied around him. The Cleveland City Council named a public power plant for him, and President Bill Clinton campaigned for him in Parma. Kucinich won, but by only 49%-46%.

Kucinich's voting record is liberal. He has been a vocal foe of international trade agreements and bars his staff from parking foreign cars in congressional lots. Even in a Democratic-controlled House, he remains largely out of the mainstream. A vegan since before he was elected to Congress, Kucinich has attacked companies that produce genetically modified foods. Active in the Progressive Caucus, his agenda includes a national health-care system, universal pre-kindergarten, the abolition of all nuclear weapons, and repeal of the USA PATRIOT Act. He continues to emphasize his local roots, with a tab on his website dedicated to polka, bowling and kielbasa, or Polish sausage.

In early 2003, Kucinich decided to run for president, based on his opposition to American military action in Iraq and elsewhere. He voted to authorize the use of force in Afghanistan after the September 11 attacks, but after the defeat of the Taliban government, he focused on nonviolent responses and called for the creation of a Department of Peace. He joined five other House Democrats in a lawsuit to prevent President George W. Bush from invading Iraq without an explicit declaration of war. In seeking the Democratic nomination in the 2004 presidential contest, he called himself an "FDR Democrat" who wanted to "return the Democratic Party to its roots," with strong ties to organized labor. "Miracles occur," he claimed when he announced his candidacy. He spoke to enthusiastic audiences of peace activists. Long an opponent of abortion, he had voted present on two anti–abortion rights bills in 2002. After he launched his presidential campaign, he changed his position completely. "I want to state clearly that no one will be appointed to the U.S. Supreme Court if they don't commit to supporting *Roe v. Wade* and a woman's right to choose," he said.

Even though he did not come close to winning a single state, trailing far behind Vermont's Howard Dean in winning the support of party leftists, Kucinich remained buoyant and enjoyed the attention. Long after Massachusetts Sen. John Kerry had clinched the nomination, Kucinich continued his campaign. At the Democratic convention in Boston, the 67 Kucinich delegates were a rump group for "peace and justice" and for moving the party further to the left.

Running again in 2008, he more than ever marched to his own drummer, and his candidacy was not taken seriously by other Democrats or the news media. He challenged corporate America, emphasized world peace, and promised to protect the little guy. "Why should people vote for a Democrat if you can't tell the difference?" he said. But he picked up no delegates in the Iowa caucuses and got just 1% of the vote in the New Hampshire primary. Citing his exclusion from national debates, he ended his campaign in late January 2008 to shift his attention to a competitive primary for his House seat.

Back in the House, Kucinich gained a wide-ranging platform as chairman of Oversight and Government Reform's Domestic Policy Subcommittee. In 2007 and 2008, with full committee Chairman Henry Waxman of California, he held hearings on high mortgage-foreclosure rates in the Cleveland area, the use of taxpayer money for athletic stadiums, and the dealings of U.S. oil companies in Iraq after the fall of Saddam Hussein. His chief initiative was a series of resolutions and votes with the goal of impeaching Bush and Vice President Cheney for lying to Congress about the justification for invading Iraq. "The war was totally unnecessary, unprovoked and unjustified," Kucinich told a House Judiciary Committee hearing in July 2008, after the House voted 238-180 to send the resolution to committee. Democratic leaders saw the move as an unwelcome distraction. As Bush's term was coming to an end, Kucinich called for a "national truth and reconciliation commission," but neither party expressed interest.

He has faced some trouble at home in recent elections. In 2006 the *Cleveland Plain Dealer* endorsed his primary opponent Barbara Anne Ferris, a former Peace Corps worker, in part because of Kucinich's failure to address local problems. But he won 76%-24%. In 2008, Cleveland City Councilman Joe Cimperman spent more than $600,000 to challenge him in the primary and criticized Kucinich for having little influence in Congress. The *Plain Dealer* endorsed Cimperman and said that Kucinich had indeed ignored his district for "an absolutely hopeless quest for the White House." But Kucinich won 50%-35%. In the general election, he defeated Republican Jim Trakas, a former state representative from Independence, who criticized him for "misplaced priorities" and for playing "political games" with impeachment. Kucinich won 57%-39%.

ELEVENTH DISTRICT

Marcia Fudge (D)

Elected 2008, 1st full term; b. Oct. 29, 1952, Cleveland; home, Warrensville Heights; OH St. U., B.S. 1975; Cleveland St. U., J.D. 1983; Christian; single.

Elected Office: Warrensville Heights mayor, 2000–08.

Professional Career: Practicing atty.; Aide to U.S. Rep. Stephanie Tubbs Jones, 1991-2000.

DC Office: 513 CHOB, 20515, 202-225-7032; Fax: 202-225-1339; Web site: fudge.house.gov.

State Offices: Warrensville Heights, 216-522-4900.

Committees: *Education & Labor* (24th of 29 D): Health, Employment, Labor & Pensions; Higher Education, Lifelong Learning & Competitiveness. *Science & Technology* (11th of 26 D): Research & Science Education; Space & Aeronautics.

Group Ratings and Key Votes: Newly Elected

Election Results

2008 spec. general	Marcia Fudge (D)	8,597	(100%)	
2008 general	Marcia Fudge (D)	212,667	(85%)	($94,049)
	Thomas Pekarek (R)	36,708	(15%)	
2008 spec. primary	Marcia Fudge (D)	10,753	(74%)	
	Jeffrey Johnson (D)	2,028	(14%)	
2008 primary	Stephanie Tubbs Jones (D)	unopposed		

Population		Race/Ethnicity		Work	
Pop. 2007:	563,144	White:	35.7%	Private:	79.5%
Change since 2000:	Down 10.7%	Black:	58.4%	Government:	14.9%
Urban:	100.0%	Hispanic:	2.3%	Self-employed:	5.5%
Rural:	0.0%	Asian:	2.0%	Blue collar:	18.1%
Area size:	135 sq. mi.	Native Am.:	0.1%	White collar:	61.2%
		Hawaiian:	0.0%	Khaki collar:	0.1%
Age		Two+ races:	1.3%	Other:	20.7%
Median age:	38.0 yrs.			Median income:	$34,564
More than 65 yrs:	15.3%	*Ancestry*		Median home value:	$118,600
Less than 18 yrs:	24.7%	German:	7.1%	Poverty:	22.0%
		Irish:	5.6%		
Education		Italian:	5.2%	**Military Veterans**	
H.S. grad:	82.3%			% of Pop:	10.0%
College grad:	25.1%				
Grad degree:	11.6%				

Like most great American cities, Cleveland grew in great bursts of migration, during periods when the economy expanded and attracted low-wage workers from around the country and the world. Cleveland's greatest surge of growth started in the 1890s and lasted through the 1920s, as tens of thousands of immigrants from central and southern Europe arrived, looking for jobs in the steel, automobile and other factories. Bohemians came to the tightly

2008 Presidential Vote		
Obama (D)	245,341	(85%)
McCain (R)	41,601	(14%)
2004 Presidential Vote		
Kerry (D)	237,469	(81%)
Bush (R)	52,372	(18%)
Cook Partisan Voting Index:	D+32	

packed neighborhoods along Broadway, Hungarians settled in the northeast, and Jews moved in north of University Circle along East 105th Street. Italians ran produce markets along Mayfield Road. As the nation's heavy industries geared up for World War II and enjoyed years of prosperous growth afterward, a second surge of immigrants came, this time blacks from the South. Starting from Cleveland's old ghetto, south of Carnegie Avenue downtown to East 105th, the rapidly increasing number of African-Americans covered most of the east side by the middle 1960s, when only a few Bohemian and Italian enclaves remained east of the Cuyahoga River. Migration stopped around 1965, but African-Americans continued to move beyond the city limits to the east-side suburbs. These bursts of migration led to political changes. A string of ethnic mayors—Frank Lausche, Anthony Celebrezze, Ralph Locher—was followed by the election in 1967 of Carl Stokes, the nation's first black big-city mayor. Cleveland had racially polarized politics for much of the 1970s. Even so, the west side stayed mostly white, and Cleveland did not have a black majority until the 2000 census, when its declining population was 51% black. The Census Bureau reported in 2008 that Cleveland was second to Detroit as the poorest of the nation's big cities, with 45% of all children living in poverty.

The 11th Congressional District of Ohio includes most of the east side of Cleveland, plus the suburbs just to the east, which together have about as many people as the city now does. Some of these communities—East Cleveland, Warrensville Heights—are mostly black. Some, notably Shaker Heights, have stable black percentages in carefully maintained neighborhoods where racial integration has succeeded. Near the campus of Case Western Reserve University on the east side, Severance Hall is one of the nation's grand symphony-orchestra homes. Downtown, Cleveland State University has a large campus. The average age of its roughly 16,000 students is 25 years old. The city's No. 1 employer is health services, and the Cleveland Clinic, with 1,800 doctors, is internationally renowned, especially for cardiac care. Other suburbs are the destination of African-Americans seeking low-crime neighborhoods and middle-class schools. Still others have attracted Cleveland's relatively few new immigrants, most of them from Eastern Europe—Russians in Mayfield Heights and Serbs in South Euclid. Overall, 58% of the people in the 11th District are African-American. Politically, this is by far the most Democratic district in Ohio.

The new congresswoman from the 11th District is Marcia Fudge, who succeeded her former mentor and friend Rep. Stephanie Tubbs Jones, after the five-term Tubbs Jones died on Aug. 20, 2008, from a cerebral aneurysm. Fudge, like many African-Americans of her generation, was greatly influenced by the civil rights movement and got active politically when she was young.

She grew up in Cleveland, but her family moved to the suburb of Shaker Heights when she was 12. During high school, Fudge volunteered with "Young Folks for Stokes," a coalition of young people helping to elect Carl Stokes mayor. She helped with get-out-the-vote efforts and with distributing campaign literature. After graduating from the Ohio State University with a degree in business administration, she received her law degree from Cleveland State University. She practiced mainly criminal defense law in the Cleveland area, along with some probate and corporate work, until she went to work for Tubbs Jones. Fudge and Tubbs Jones first met as members of the national Delta Sigma Theta Sorority alumnae association. Fudge later served as national president of the group of predominately African-American women. When Tubbs Jones became the Cuyahoga County prosecutor in 1991, Fudge served as her administrative assistant. When her boss was elected to Congress in 1998, Fudge came with her to Washington as chief of staff.

After a few years, Fudge felt the pull of elected office herself. When the Warrensville Heights mayor resigned after pleading guilty to improper solicitation, she decided to run. She faced four other candidates in the Democratic primary, including the interim mayor, and came just two votes short of the required 50% to avoid a runoff. On the next ballot, she won, becoming the first African-American woman to be elected mayor of the city. In nine years as mayor, Fudge focused on economic development and claimed credit for creating 3,000 new jobs and bringing in $500 million for development and infrastructure. "I believe people started to feel really good about where they lived, and I think that when people feel good about where they live, that pride transitions into so many things," Fudge said. She also built relationships with other community leaders and business executives.

Tubbs Jones' sudden death just a few days before the Democratic National Convention in Denver saddened local and national Democrats, and her funeral in Cleveland drew a huge crowd, including Speaker Nancy Pelosi, who had recently named Tubbs Jones to chair the House Committee on Standards of Official Conduct. In deciding to seek the nomination, Fudge said she was motivated by a desire to carry on her political mentor's legacy. "People didn't really understand what an impact she had on this district, and on the nation, until she was gone," Fudge said.

Since Tubbs Jones already had won the Democratic primary before her death, members of the district's Democratic Executive Committee named her replacement on the ballot. Fudge called each member of the committee to explain why she would be the best choice to carry on Tubbs Jones' legacy. The strategy paid off. There were four candidates, and the committee nominated Fudge with 175 votes. Former state Sen. C. J. Prentiss was a distant second, with 64 votes. In the ten-way special primary on October 14 to fill the remainder of Tubbs Jones' term, Fudge cruised to victory with 74%. She won the general election 85%-15% and had no Republican challenger for the Nov. 18 special general election, allowing her to be sworn in before other freshmen members that year.

In the House, Fudge got seats on the Education and Labor Committee and on the Science and Technology Committee, where she is vice chairman of the Subcommittee on Research and Science Education. She also joined the Congressional Black Caucus. In April 2009, she traveled with other caucus members to Cuba to meet with Cuban President Raúl Castro to try to improve U.S.-Cuba relations.

TWELFTH DISTRICT

Pat Tiberi (R)

Elected 2000, 5th term; b. Oct. 21, 1962, Columbus; home, Columbus; OH St. U., B.A. 1985; Catholic; married (Denice); 4 children.

Elected Office: OH House of Reps., 1992–2000, Maj. ldr., 1999–2000.

Professional Career: Staff asst., U.S. Rep. John Kasich, 1984–92; Realtor, ReMax Achievers, 1995–2000.

DC Office: 113 CHOB, 20515, 202-225-5355; Fax: 202-226-4523; Web site: tiberi.house.gov.

State Offices: Columbus, 614-523-2555.

Committees: *Ways & Means* (9th of 15 R): Income Security & Family Support; Select Revenue Measures (RMM); Social Security.

Group Ratings

	ADA	ACLU	AFS	LCV	ITIC	NTU	COC	ACU	CFG	FRC
2008	35	18	43	38	71	62	94	72	60	94
2007	20	—	9	15	—	69	85	88	65	—

National Journal Ratings

	2007 LIB	—	2007 CONS		2008 LIB	—	2008 CONS
Economic	32%	—	68%		36%	—	64%
Social	29%	—	69%		31%	—	62%
Foreign	0%	—	72%		13%	—	84%
Composite	25%	—	75%		28%	—	72%

Key Votes of the 110th Congress

1. Increase minimum wage	N	5. Share immigration data	Y	9. Withdraw troops 8/08	N
2. Expand SCHIP	Y	6. Foreign aid abortion ban	Y	10. No operations in Iran	N
3. Raise CAFE standards	N	7. Ban gay bias in workplace	Y	11. Free trade with Peru	Y
4. Bail out financial markets	Y	8. Repeal D.C. gun law	Y	12. Overhaul FISA	Y

Election Results

2008 general	Pat Tiberi (R)	197,447	(55%)	($1,714,042)
	David Robinson (D)	152,234	(42%)	($180,974)
	Steven Linnabary (Lib)	10,707	(3%)	
2008 primary	Pat Tiberi (R)	63,450	(90%)	
	David Ryon (R)	6,681	(10%)	

Prior Winning Percentages: 2006 (57%); 2004 (62%); 2002 (64%); 2000 (53%)

Population		Race/Ethnicity		Work	
Pop. 2007:	699,651	White:	71.3%	Private:	79.5%
Change since 2000:	Up 10.9%	Black:	21.1%	Government:	14.3%
Urban:	88.1%	Hispanic:	2.3%	Self-employed:	6.0%
Rural:	11.9%	Asian:	3.3%	Blue collar:	15.3%
Area size:	1,031 sq. mi.	Native Am.:	0.1%	White collar:	70.1%
		Hawaiian:	0.1%	Khaki collar:	0.1%
Age		Two+ races:	1.6%	Other:	14.6%
Median age:	34.8 yrs.			Median income:	$55,146
More than 65 yrs:	9.8%	*Ancestry*		Median home value:	$179,300
Less than 18 yrs:	26.8%	German:	20.1%	Poverty:	11.9%
		Irish:	10.7%		
Education		English:	8.7%	**Military Veterans**	
H.S. grad:	90.6%			% of Pop:	9.6%
College grad:	37.3%				
Grad degree:	12.9%				

Columbus is on the verge of becoming a major metropolis. With city limits stretching toward farmland at each point of the compass, the central city of Columbus had 724,000 people in 2007, far more than Cleveland, with 405,000, or Cincinnati, with 332,000. Columbus's Franklin County passed the one million mark in the 1990s and was at 1.1 million in 2007. Columbus is centrally located, not only in the center of Ohio, but also just a one-day truck drive from more than half of the nation's population.

2008 Presidential Vote
Obama (D) 209,237   (54%)
McCain (R) 171,448   (45%)

2004 Presidential Vote
Bush (R) 178,080   (51%)
Kerry (D) 171,881   (49%)

Cook Partisan Voting Index: D + 1

It was the only one of the 15 largest cities in Ohio to gain population in the 1990s and has the advantages of being the state capital, the home of the Ohio State University, and a major white-collar employment town. It is the home of Nationwide Insurance, Wendy's International, and Red Roof Inns. The Limited is based at the Easton Town Center, a huge mall built in the 1990s. Columbus likes to brag that its airfreight operations at Port Columbus, the airport, make it the largest in the country dedicated to cargo. The city's economic base and civic infrastructure have attracted the kind of upscale, enterprising people who have produced much of America's growth in recent years. Its rapidly growing foreign-born population—Latinos, Asians, Ethiopians, Russian Jews, and Somalis—exceeds that of Cleveland or Detroit. But the city also has suffered from traditional big-city problems as well, which has spurred a migration of students from public to private schools. The politics of Columbus traditionally were Republican. It had few of the Eastern European immigrants and CIO unions that made Cleveland so Democratic. But in 1999, Columbus elected African-American Democrat Michael Coleman as mayor, and in 2000, Franklin County was carried, though just barely, by Democratic presidential candidate Al Gore. In 2004, thanks to out-migration of whites and a vigorous registration and turnout drive by Democrats, John Kerry carried the county 54%-45%. In 2008, Barack Obama carried it 60%-39%.

The 12th Congressional District of Ohio is one of two districts dominated by Columbus and Franklin County. It includes 39% of the city, including most of the east side, plus the affluent suburb of Bexley, site of the Governor's Mansion, and the northeastern suburbs in Franklin County. It also includes Delaware County, directly north of Columbus, which is Ohio's fastest-growing county; it grew 50% from 2000 to 2008 and was the 21st-fastest-growing county in the nation. The district takes in most of Licking County east of Columbus, including the small industrial town of Newark and the lovely college town of Granville. With big margins in Delaware and Licking Counties, George W. Bush won here 51%-49% in 2004. But Obama's Ohio victory switched this district to 54%-45% in his favor.

The congressman from the 12th District is Pat Tiberi, a Republican elected in 2000. The son of Italian immigrants, Tiberi (*TEE berry*) grew up in Columbus and graduated from the Ohio State University. He worked as a real estate agent and then as an assistant to Republican U.S. Rep. John Kasich for eight years. Kasich helped Tiberi win a seat in the state House, where he became majority leader and supported business-friendly legislation and tort-law changes. In 1999, Kasich, then chairman of the Budget Committee, announced his retirement from the House. Tiberi won support to replace his mentor from most of the Republican establishment and from the U.S. Chamber of Commerce. He faced a noisy but not very effective primary challenge from state Sen. Gene Watts, who sought to rally the conservative base. Tiberi won 73%-21%. The resounding victory gave him a big boost heading into the general election against Maryellen O'Shaughnessy, a Democratic City Council member in Columbus. She had a compelling personal story as the single mother of a 10-year-old son. Tiberi played up his Columbus roots and his membership in the Ohio State marching band and held O'Shaughnessy responsible for negative Democratic Party ads that labeled him a defender of insurance companies on the issue of affordable prescription drugs. This was one of the most-watched House races in the nation. With campaign help from Kasich, Tiberi won 53%-44%.

In the House, Tiberi's record has been conservative on economic and cultural issues but occasionally centrist on defense and foreign policy. He has called for scrapping the income-tax code and for creating a national commission to craft a new tax system, and he supports lifting the trade embargo on Cuba. On the Financial Services Committee, he has focused on housing and home-ownership issues, including a bill to require an increase in zero-down-payment mortgages for first-time home buyers. In July 2006, he joined a group of Republican mavericks who urged a vote to increase the minimum wage.

When U.S. Rep. Rob Portman of Ohio resigned from the House in 2005, Tiberi was the Ohio delegation's choice to fill his seat on the Ways and Means Committee. After a bruising intraparty fight, the seat went to Devin Nunes of California. Then in January 2007, Tiberi finally won a Ways and Means seat, with a boost from Republican Leader John Boehner of Ohio. Tiberi had been campaign manager for Boehner in his successful bid for majority leader in early 2006, and he later helped Boehner fix organizational problems at the National Republican Congressional Committee. He typically toes the party line against Democratic proposals on Ways and Means, but he supported their bills to expand the State Children's Health Insurance Program.

Despite the district's narrow partisan balance, Tiberi has easily won re-election. In 2006, he faced an unusual challenge from 79-year-old Bob Shamansky, a lawyer and real-estate investor who held the seat for two years before Kasich defeated him in 1982. Shamansky criticized the Iraq War and the congressional failure to allow the government to negotiate with pharmaceutical companies in the Medicare prescription-drug program. He also loaned his campaign $1.4 million. Tiberi distanced himself from President George W. Bush on Iraq, and he won 57%-43%. In 2008, he was challenged by businessman and climate-control advocate David Robinson, a political novice who ran on the need for change in Congress. The result was similar to that in 2006. Tiberi lost 51%-46% in Franklin County, which cast 61% of the vote, but won 55%-42% overall, with 69%-28% in Delaware and 67%-31% in Licking. The election of Democrat Mary Jo Kilroy in the neighboring 15th District could give Tiberi protection in redistricting if Democrats are shifted to her district to bolster her job security.

THIRTEENTH DISTRICT

Betty Sutton (D)

Elected 2006, 2nd term; b. July 31, 1963, Barberton; home, Copley Township; Kent St. U., B.A. 1985, U. of Akron, J.D. 1990; Methodist; married (Doug Corwon); 2 children.

Elected Office: Barberton City Cncl., 1989–91; Summit Cnty. Cncl., 1991–92; OH House of Reps., 1992–2000.

Professional Career: Practicing atty., 2001–06.

DC Office: 1721 LHOB, 20515, 202-225-3401; Fax: 202-225-2266; Web site: sutton.house.gov.

State Offices: Akron, 330-865-8450; Lorain, 440-245-5350.

Committees: *Energy & Commerce* (34th of 36 D): Commerce, Trade & Consumer Protections; Health; Oversight & Investigations.

Group Ratings

	ADA	ACLU	AFS	LCV	ITIC	NTU	COC	ACU	CFG	FRC
2008	100	100	100	92	86	11	61	4	0	0
2007	100	—	100	85	—	4	55	0	0	—

National Journal Ratings

	2007 LIB	—	2007 CONS		2008 LIB	—	2008 CONS
Economic	64%	—	36%		81%	—	15%
Social	89%	—	8%		82%	—	0%
Foreign	81%	—	19%		85%	—	8%
Composite	79%	—	22%		88%	—	13%

Key Votes of the 110th Congress

1. Increase minimum wage	Y	5. Share immigration data	N	9. Withdraw troops 8/08	Y
2. Expand SCHIP	Y	6. Foreign aid abortion ban	N	10. No operations in Iran	Y
3. Raise CAFE standards	Y	7. Ban gay bias in workplace	Y	11. Free trade with Peru	N
4. Bail out financial markets	Y	8. Repeal D.C. gun law	N	12. Overhaul FISA	N

Election Results

2008 general	Betty Sutton (D)	192,593	(65%)	($719,608)
	David Potter (R)	105,050	(35%)	($28,165)
2008 primary	Betty Sutton (D)	unopposed		

Prior Winning Percentages: 2006 (61%)

Population		Race/Ethnicity		Work	
Pop. 2007:	649,318	White:	81.0%	Private:	83.9%
Change since 2000:	Up 2.9%	Black:	12.0%	Government:	11.4%
Urban:	92.7%	Hispanic:	3.7%	Self-employed:	4.6%
Rural:	7.3%	Asian:	1.6%	Blue collar:	22.5%
Area size:	537 sq. mi.	Native Am.:	0.2%	White collar:	61.5%
		Hawaiian:	0.0%	Khaki collar:	0.0%
Age		Two+ races:	1.3%	Other:	15.9%
Median age:	38.9 yrs.	*Ancestry*		Median income:	$50,681
More than 65 yrs:	13.4%	German:	18.8%	Median home value:	$150,700
Less than 18 yrs:	24.6%	Irish:	11.7%	Poverty:	11.8%
Education		English:	7.1%	**Military Veterans**	
H.S. grad:	88.3%			% of Pop:	11.4%
College grad:	26.3%				
Grad degree:	9.5%				

Fifty years ago, most of the people of metro Cleveland were clustered in the city itself, in tightly packed blocks of houses above the Cuyahoga River valley and its giant steel mills. Around the city, were some comfortable suburbs, and beyond them, miles of farm fields before you encountered the nearby industrial cities—Akron, the "Rubber Capital" with its Firestone, B. F. Goodrich and Goodyear tire factories, and Lorain, a sort of mini-Cleveland on Lake Erie with steel mills lining the narrow

2008 Presidential Vote
Obama (D) 185,742   (57%)
McCain (R).............................137,374   (42%)

2004 Presidential Vote
Kerry (D).................................177,472   (56%)
Bush (R) 140,908   (44%)
Cook Partisan Voting Index: D + 5

Black River. Since then, the population of Cleveland has fallen by half, and the metropolitan area has spread out over the northern Ohio countryside. The suburbs now spread from Cleveland to Akron without interval. The shoreline from Cleveland to Lorain has been filled in. Medina County, between Lorain and Akron, has also been transformed from farmland to suburbia. Only the Cuyahoga River valley between Cleveland and Akron has been off-limits to development, protected by the creation of the Cuyahoga Valley National Park. The economy has changed as well. In 1950, Cleveland depended on heavy manufacturing, especially steel, and Akron was reliant on tires. Today, most of the steel mills are shuttered or torn down, most of the old tire factories have been converted to other uses, and in 2005, Ford closed its assembly plant in Lorain. But Akron has memorialized the past in the National Inventors Hall of Fame and has developed itself as the "Polymer Center of America," with 80% of the nation's polymer research and a first-class polymer engineering program at the University of Akron. In 2007, the city began an innovative project to turn sewage sludge into electricity. Downtown Akron has been revived by entertainment areas, the University of Akron, and some upscale housing. Still, the city's population dropped by 7,300 from 2000 to 2006.

The 13th Congressional District of Ohio is made up of much of this metro Cleveland area, though none of the city itself. It includes the west side of Akron and its western suburbs. The lines separating it from the 14th and 17th Districts in Akron's Summit County are absurdly convoluted. It encompasses the northern and eastern parts of Lorain County, including Lorain and Elyria just to the south; the southern tier of suburban townships in Cleveland's Cuyahoga County—Strongsville, North Royalton, Broadview Heights; and the northern tier of suburban townships in Medina County, including Brunswick. Fifty years ago, this area would have been Republican, with Democratic precincts in Akron and Lorain. Today, as Clevelanders have spread far and wide, it is Democratic, though not overwhelmingly so. Republican presidential candidate George W. Bush twice got 44% of the vote here. In 2008, Democrat. Barack Obama won the district with 57%.

The congresswoman from the 13th District is Democrat Betty Sutton, elected in 2006. Sutton grew up in Barberton as the youngest of six children. Her mother was a library clerk and her father a boilermaker. She graduated from Kent State University and then earned a law degree from the University of Akron. In 1989, while still in law school, Sutton won an at-large seat on the Barberton City Council and in 1991, was elected to the Summit County Council. In 1992, at age 29, she became the youngest woman to win a seat in the state House, where she worked on employment issues like health care, pensions and retirement benefits. In 1993, after speaking publicly about an abusive first marriage, she worked to pass legislation to protect women from domestic violence. She fought passage of a Republican bill to cut workers compensation benefits and then led a referendum to repeal the law. She served in the Legislature until term limits forced her out in 2000 and afterward worked as a labor lawyer.

When Democratic Rep. Sherrod Brown announced that he would run for the Senate, Sutton quickly emerged as a leading contender to succeed him. She faced significant opposition in the primary from former eight-term U.S. Rep. Tom Sawyer and from shopping-center heiress Capri Cafaro. Sawyer had good name recognition but struggled to raise money and was dogged by his 1993 vote for the North American Free Trade Agreement, which was blamed for sending many of the district's manufacturing jobs overseas. Cafaro, who had run unsuccessfully in 2004 against Republican U.S. Rep. Steven LaTourette, poured more than $2 million of her own money into the primary. Sutton ran aggressively as an anticorruption crusader. She criticized Sawyer for taking privately financed trips and Cafaro for her ties to a federal investigation of former Democratic U.S. Rep. James Traficant of Ohio, who had been convicted of 10 counts of bribery in 2002. Cafaro had been an executive of a company run by her father, who had pleaded guilty in 2001 to bribing Traficant.

Sutton enjoyed strong backing from organized labor, but an endorsement from EMILY's List proved just as decisive. The group's Ohio affiliate built grassroots support and sent out direct mail against Sawyer. Sutton won the eight-way primary with 31%, ahead of Cafaro with 25% and Sawyer with 22%. In the general election, her Republican opponent was Lorain Mayor Craig Foltin, an accountant who campaigned for sound fiscal management. National Republicans were interested in his candidacy because he had won two races in a Democratic city and had raised an impressive $250,000 for his last mayoral campaign. Democrats attempted to tie Foltin to Republican scandals in Ohio, and Sutton said there was "rampant corruption" in Lorain. She raised twice as much as Foltin, including more than $300,000 from EMILY's List donors. The poor political environment for Republicans and the district's large union presence proved too much for Foltin to overcome. Sutton won 61%-39%.

As a freshman, Sutton impressed Democratic leaders and won a seat on the exclusive, leadership-run Rules Committee. In June 2008, the House passed her bill mandating nationwide access to automated external defibrillators, a proposal suggested by an Akron cardiologist. She joined other Ohio Democrats as an outspoken foe of President Bush's free-trade agenda, and she was a leader in pushing for organized labor's "card check" bill, which would bypass the traditional union election process and allow workers to be certified as a bargaining unit if a majority signed cards indicating their support for a union.

In 2008, Sutton was re-elected easily. In early 2009, Democratic leaders gave her a seat on the influential Energy and Commerce Committee. In March, she introduced in committee a "cash for clunkers" bill that would give vouchers of $3,500 to $4,500 to people trading in old cars for more gas-efficient vehicles. The bill quickly passed the committee and gained momentum in late April, when Sutton agreed to drop provisions requiring that cars purchased with help from the legislation be made in North America.

FOURTEENTH DISTRICT

Steven LaTourette (R)

Elected 1994, 8th term; b. July 22, 1954, Cleveland; home, Madison; U. of MI, B.A. 1976, Cleveland St. U., J.D. 1979; Methodist; married (Jennifer Laptook); 5 children.

Elected Office: Lake Cnty. district atty., 1988–94.

Professional Career: Lake Cnty. asst. public defender, 1980–83; Practicing atty., 1983–88.

DC Office: 2371 RHOB, 20515, 202-225-5731; Fax: 202-225-3307; Web site: www.house.gov/latourette.

State Offices: Painesville, 440-352-3939; Twinsburg, 330-425-9291.

Committees: *Appropriations* (22nd of 23 R): Interior, Environment & Related Agencies; Legislative Branch; Transportation, HUD & Related Agencies.

Group Ratings

	ADA	ACLU	AFS	LCV	ITIC	NTU	COC	ACU	CFG	FRC
2008	60	18	57	38	43	40	76	52	33	64
2007	55	—	45	40	—	35	65	52	18	—

National Journal Ratings

	2007 LIB	—	2007 CONS		2008 LIB	—	2008 CONS
Economic	43%	—	57%		44%	—	56%
Social	41%	—	58%		31%	—	62%
Foreign	41%	—	59%		35%	—	62%
Composite	42%	—	58%		38%	—	62%

Key Votes of the 110th Congress

1. Increase minimum wage	Y	5. Share immigration data	Y	9. Withdraw troops 8/08	N
2. Expand SCHIP	Y	6. Foreign aid abortion ban	Y	10. No operations in Iran	N
3. Raise CAFE standards	N	7. Ban gay bias in workplace	Y	11. Free trade with Peru	N
4. Bail out financial markets	N	8. Repeal D.C. gun law	Y	12. Overhaul FISA	Y

Election Results

2008 general	Steven LaTourette (R)	188,488	(58%)	($1,425,133)
	Bill O'Neill (D)	125,214	(39%)	($553,388)
	David Macko (Lib)	9,511	(3%)	
2008 primary	Steven LaTourette (R)	unopposed		

Prior Winning Percentages: 2006 (58%); 2004 (63%); 2002 (72%); 2000 (69%); 1998 (66%); 1996 (55%); 1994 (48%)

Population		Race/Ethnicity		Work	
Pop. 2007:	653,462	White:	92.2%	Private:	83.1%
Change since 2000:	Up 3.6%	Black:	3.3%	Government:	10.5%
Urban:	74.1%	Hispanic:	1.8%	Self-employed:	6.1%
Rural:	25.9%	Asian:	1.6%	Blue collar:	22.8%
Area size:	1,820 sq. mi.	Native Am.:	0.2%	White collar:	63.0%
Age		Hawaiian:	0.0%	Khaki collar:	0.0%
Median age:	40.4 yrs.	Two+ races:	0.9%	Other:	14.2%
More than 65 yrs:	14.2%	*Ancestry*		Median income:	$57,084
Less than 18 yrs:	24.2%	German:	19.0%	Median home value:	$176,000
Education		Irish:	11.9%	Poverty:	7.7%
H.S. grad:	89.6%	Italian:	10.6%	**Military Veterans**	
College grad:	30.1%			% of Pop:	11.5%
Grad degree:	10.9%				

The imprint of the westward track of New England Yankee migration is still apparent today on the shores of Lake Erie in northern Ohio. The Yankees, cooped up in New England for 200 years, shot west across the country through upstate New York, across Ohio and Michigan to Chicago, and on to Kansas and southern California in just two or three generations, providing inspiration, manpower and technical might for the Union victory in the Civil War and leaving their imprint along the way. One

2008 Presidential Vote

McCain (R)	169,495	(49%)
Obama (D)	168,753	(49%)

2004 Presidential Vote

Bush (R)	178,510	(53%)
Kerry (D)	159,929	(47%)

Cook Partisan Voting Index: R+3

place they stopped was the Western Reserve, the northeast corner of Ohio, created for the excess population of Connecticut. Its towns, colleges and cultural institutions were established by Yankees. This area produced some of the nation's strongest opposition to slavery and strongest support of the Union armies and the Republican Party; Lake Erie ports were prime transit points for the Underground Railroad to Canada. Its thrifty, hardworking, well-educated citizens built communities with fine schools and, with their accumulated savings, invested in what became some of the nation's leading industries. A century ago, that brought great masses of immigrants to Cleveland and the other cities of northeast Ohio. Now, like Connecticut and Massachusetts, it may be moving toward a post-industrial economy. Factory employment has dropped. Chrysler is scheduled to close its Twinsburg factory and lay off 1,250 people in late 2010. But total jobs are holding steady. Small, adaptive business units with highly skilled workers are the growth sectors.

The 14th Congressional District of Ohio takes in parts or all of seven counties of northeast Ohio and the old Western Reserve. It includes Lake County, northeast of Cleveland, and Geauga County, with prosperous suburbs amid Western Reserve villages that still yield 25% of the state's maple syrup even though the loss of farmland has cut production. Ashtabula, home to 17 covered bridges and several wineries, is in the district, as is the northern part of Trumbull County, which is industrial. The district includes the affluent suburbs at the eastern edge of Cleveland's Cuyahoga County, the comfortable suburbs in northern Summit County and some of Portage County to the east. In the 19th century, the Western Reserve was heavily Republican. The congressman from the area from 1863 to 1880 was James Garfield, a Civil War general who was elected president in 1880 and assassinated the following year. In the 1930s, the area became politically competitive, as Cleveland became heavily Democratic, and it has remained so in most years since. But the district was designed to gather together Republican territory in the Western Reserve, and it voted twice in presidential elections for Republican George W. Bush. In 2008, Republican nominee John McCain won the district, 49.4%-49.2%.

The congressman from the 14th District is Steven LaTourette, a Republican elected in 1994. He grew up in the Cleveland area and went to law school at Cleveland State University. In the 1980s, he worked as a public defender and in 1988, became Lake County district attorney. Well-known and well-liked, he won a three-candidate Republican primary with 54% of the vote to compete for the House seat. In the general election, he challenged freshman Rep. Eric Fingerhut. LaTourette attacked Fingerhut for backing President Bill Clinton's budget and tax increases and for being soft on crime. He won 48%-43%. In

January 2009, LaTourette won a seat on the coveted Appropriations Committee, though to get the spot, he had to give up his seats on the House Financial Services Committee and House Transportation and Infrastructure Committee.

In the House, LaTourette has the most moderate voting record of Ohio's Republican members. He was an ardent advocate of a minimum-wage hike and broke with House Republicans to oppose normalizing trade relations with China, though he did deliver crucial, last-minute support for the Central American Free Trade Agreement. He later said that he regretted that vote. In a major break with his party in January 2007, he voted for most of the bills in the new Democratic majority's agenda, except for the energy proposal.

As a senior member of the Transportation panel, LaTourette's high-priority projects have included improvements of Ohio Routes 82 and 8, plus enactment of legislation to add Ashtabula, Mahoning and Trumbull counties to the Appalachian Regional Commission. In May 2009, he was promised by the Obama administration and Chrysler company officials that, despite the company's imminent bankruptcy filing, the plant in his district would remain open and its 1,250 employees would keep their jobs. Days later, after the bankruptcy proceedings became official, the company announced that the plant would close. LaTourette accused the administration and Chrysler of lying, and a Chrysler lobbyist called him to apologize for the "misunderstanding."

As a member of the Committee on Standards of Official Conduct in 2004, LaTourette took seriously the responsibility of committee members to render bipartisan decisions and joined in unanimous committee votes to admonish GOP Majority Leader Tom DeLay on three ethics charges. When GOP Speaker Dennis Hastert, without explanation, removed him from the committee in 2005, LaTourette was privately unhappy with his punishment but did not say so publicly. In 2007, he voiced disapproval of attacks on Democratic Rep. William Jefferson of Louisiana, who was a suspect in a federal bribery investigation. The partisan skirmishing over Jefferson, he said, amounted to "the dumbing-down of the House," with both parties to blame.

In contrast to many members of the Class of 1994, LaTourette quickly secured his formerly Democratic seat without a competitive challenger. In 2004, the challenger was Democrat Capri Cafaro, a 26-year-old shopping-center heiress who spent nearly $2 million of her own money. Cafaro struggled with the issues, and LaTourette won 63%-37%. During the campaign, however, he acknowledged an affair with his former chief aide, who had become a lobbyist and whom he soon married. His former wife endorsed Cafaro and complained, "Washington corrupts people." In 2008, retired Appeals Court Judge William O'Neill spent $550,000 on a campaign and had some name recognition in the district, but LaTourette won 58%-39%.

FIFTEENTH DISTRICT

Mary Jo Kilroy (D)

Elected 2008, 1st term; b. April 30, 1949, Euclid; home, Columbus; Cleveland St. U., B.A. 1977; OH St. U., J.D. 1980; Catholic; married (Robert); 2 children.

Elected Office: Columbus Schl. Bd., 1991–2000; Franklin Cnty. Commission, 2000–08, pres. 2005-07.

Professional Career: Practicing atty, Handelman & Kilroy.

DC Office: 1237 LHOB, 20515, 202-225-2015; Fax: 202-225-3529; Web site: kilroy.house.gov.

State Offices: Columbus, 614-294-2196.

Committees: *Financial Services* (36th of 42 D): Capital Markets, Insurance & Government Sponsored Enterprises; Housing & Community Opportunity; Oversight & Investigations. *Homeland Security* (18th of 20 D): Emerging Threats, Cybersecurity & Science and Technology; Management, Investigations & Oversight.

Group Ratings and Key Votes: Newly Elected

Election Results

2008 general	Mary Jo Kilroy (D)	139,584	(46%)	($2,611,122)
	Steve Stivers (R)	137,272	(45%)	($2,244,221)
	Mark Noble (Lib)	14,061	(5%)	
	Don Eckhart (I)	12,915	(4%)	
2008 primary	Mary Jo Kilroy (D)	unopposed		

Population		Race/Ethnicity		Work	
Pop. 2007:	659,682	White:	82.0%	Private:	78.6%
Change since 2000:	Up 4.6%	Black:	8.6%	Government:	16.0%
Urban:	91.3%	Hispanic:	3.7%	Self-employed:	5.1%
Rural:	8.8%	Asian:	3.8%	Blue collar:	18.3%
Area size:	1,182 sq. mi.	Native Am.:	0.2%	White collar:	66.6%
		Hawaiian:	0.0%	Khaki collar:	0.1%
Age		Two+ races:	1.6%	Other:	15.0%
Median age:	33.9 yrs.			Median income:	$49,549
More than 65 yrs:	9.7%	*Ancestry*		Median home value:	$158,100
Less than 18 yrs:	24.1%	German:	22.0%	Poverty:	15.4%
		Irish:	12.3%		
Education		English:	8.5%	**Military Veterans**	
H.S. grad:	87.4%			% of Pop:	8.9%
College grad:	34.1%				
Grad degree:	12.5%				

Smack in the center of Ohio, Columbus was founded in 1812 as the state capital. Its flat-domed Capitol at Broad and High, with the statue of President William McKinley out front, is surrounded by high-rises; the city has grown in all directions into the countryside and is on the verge of becoming a large metropolis. It is the headquarters of state government and the Ohio State University, which, with more than 52,000 students, has the highest enrollment of any campus in the nation. It is the head-

2008 Presidential Vote
Obama (D) 173,526   (54%)
McCain (R).............................143,468   (45%)

2004 Presidential Vote
Bush (R) 154,105   (50%)
Kerry (D)................................151,869   (50%)

Cook Partisan Voting Index: D + 1

quarters of the Batelle Memorial Institute, the think tank that helped invent compact discs, office copy machines and the Universal Product Code; a major industry here is data retrieval. After annexing many suburbs and doubling its geography since 1967, Columbus is now Ohio's largest central city by far, with 724,000 people in 2007. Franklin County has nearly 1.1 million. Given the suburban growth, more people in the seven-county metro area now live outside than inside the Interstate 270 outer belt, which was completed in the 1980s. Former farm towns are booming. Columbus has built civic landmarks—the Center of Science and Industry on the riverfront, the Jerome Schottenstein Center for sports and concerts at OSU, a hockey stadium for the Columbus Blue Jackets and the nation's first stadium built for a professional soccer team, the Columbus Crew, the Major League Soccer champions in 2008. There is residential building downtown in thriving entertainment districts. With the nation's highest proportion of residents age 25 to 34, Columbus has been attracting young professionals and immigrants and continues to be a prime test market for commercial products. BET.com ranked Columbus second, behind Charlotte, N.C., as the nation's best city for African-American families.

The 15th Congressional District of Ohio includes all of Columbus except the east side, plus southern and western Franklin County and once-rural Madison and Union counties to the west. Honda has invested $6 billion in Union County—its projects included a motorcycle plant in 1979 and an auto plant in 1982—though in 2009 it decided to stop production of motorcycles because of declining sales. The 15th includes white working-class areas on the south side of the city and in nearby Grove City. Politically, these Democratic areas long were balanced by the heavily Republican suburb of Upper Arlington, across the Olentangy River from Ohio State, and by Republican subdivisions sprouting up in the exurbs. But since 2004, Columbus has been the target of highly successful registration and turnout drives by Democrats. The 15th District voted only narrowly for Republican President George W. Bush in 2004 and four years later, gave Democratic nominee Barack Obama a 54%-45% win.

The new congresswoman from the 15th Congressional District is Mary Jo Kilroy, the first Democrat since 1982 to represent a Columbus-area House district. In 2008, she won the seat of retiring Republican Rep. Deborah Pryce, who had prevailed in a contest against Kilroy two years earlier by only 1,055 votes. The daughter of a pipe fitter, Kilroy was born in Euclid in the Cleveland area. She worked her way through college, taking jobs at hospitals and restaurants. After receiving her law degree from the Ohio State University, she went into private practice with her husband, and in 1991, she was elected to the Columbus School Board. Her next stop, in 2000, was the Franklin County Commission, where she rose to become commission president in 2005 and was instrumental in creating the Franklin County Affordable Housing Trust Corporation, aimed at increasing the number of minority homeowners.

In 2006, the national Democratic Congressional Campaign Committee recruited Kilroy to take on Pryce, a popular former member of the Republican leadership in the House. When news stories broke that year about Florida Republican Rep. Mark Foley's lewd email messages to male congressional pages, Kilroy publicized Pryce's personal friendship with Foley in attack ads that aired on Christian and conservative radio stations. Pryce's slim victory remained in limbo until a recount in December, after which Kilroy immediately began preparing for a rematch. But Pryce decided to retire, and Kilroy had to shift to a new opponent. The GOP nominee was state Sen. Steve Stivers, who like Pryce, was a moderate Republican and backed abortion rights. He had impressive political and military credentials as well: five years in the Ohio Senate and service in the Ohio Army National Guard, including a stint in Iraq. Kilroy seized on Stivers's résumé prior to being elected to the Legislature, when he was a lobbyist for Bank One. Lobbyists were unpopular with voters in 2008 because several prominent members of Congress had been tainted by their association with self-interested lobbyists. And as the election neared, the economy was slipping into recession, in part as a result of widespread bad lending practices by banks and mortgage companies. The DCCC, which invested heavily in the race, also attacked Stivers for his association with the financial industry. Stivers cited his work on behalf of Medicaid recipients with disabilities, criticized Kilroy for raising taxes locally, and said that she would impose government-run health care. He also got support from local veterans groups. Each candidate spent more than $2 million.

Stivers led in the initial results. But after rulings by the Secretary of State and court challenges of provisional ballots, Kilroy was certified the winner by 2,312 votes—a 45.9% victory over Stivers's 45.2%. He won easily in the suburban counties, with 58% in Madison County and 62% in Union County, but they cast only 13% of the total. Kilroy won Franklin County by almost 15,000 votes. She was helped by two third-party candidates: college instructor Don Eckhart, an anti-abortion conservative who siphoned off 4.3% of the vote among Christian conservatives, and Libertarian Mark Noble, who got 4.6%. Stivers's loss was a blow to the prestige of GOP House Minority Leader John Boehner, the powerful Ohioan who had personally recruited him to run for the seat. Republicans promised to make Kilroy a top target in 2010.

SIXTEENTH DISTRICT

John Boccieri (D)

Elected 2008, 1st term; b. Oct. 5, 1969, Youngstown; home, Alliance; St. Bonaventure U., B.S. 1992; Webster U., M.A., M.P.A. 1996; Catholic; married (Stacey Kennedy-Boccieri); 4 children.

Military Career: Air Force Reserve, 1994-present (Iraq, Afghanistan).

Elected Office: Ohio House of Reps., 2000-06; Ohio Senate, 2006-08.

Professional Career: Pro baseball player, 1992; Leg. aide, state Rep. Rich Cordray, 1992-94

DC Office: 1516 LHOB, 20515, 202-225-3876; Fax: 202-225-3059; Web site: boccieri.house.gov.

State Offices: Canton, 330-489-4414.

Committees: *Agriculture* (24th of 28 D): Conservation, Credit, Energy & Research. *Transportation & Infrastructure* (37th of 44 D): Aviation; Highways & Transit.

Group Ratings and Key Votes: Newly Elected

Election Results

2008 general	John Boccieri (D)	169,044	(55%)	($1,722,377)
	Kirk Schuring (R)	136,293	(45%)	($1,208,527)
2008 primary	John Boccieri (D)	71,038	(64%)	
	Mary Cirelli (D)	40,429	(36%)	

Population		Race/Ethnicity		Work	
Pop. 2007:	644,439	White:	91.8%	Private:	83.3%
Change since 2000:	Up 2.2%	Black:	4.7%	Government:	10.5%
Urban:	73.6%	Hispanic:	1.1%	Self-employed:	6.1%
Rural:	26.4%	Asian:	0.8%	Blue collar:	26.9%
Area size:	1,741 sq. mi.	Native Am.:	0.2%	White collar:	56.0%
Age		Hawaiian:	0.0%	Khaki collar:	0.0%
Median age:	39.0 yrs.	Two+ races:	1.3%	Other:	17.0%
More than 65 yrs:	14.4%	*Ancestry*		Median income:	$47,788
Less than 18 yrs:	24.0%	German:	25.6%	Median home value:	$137,900
Education		Irish:	11.2%	Poverty:	10.5%
H.S. grad:	87.4%	English:	7.8%	**Military Veterans**	
College grad:	21.3%			% of Pop:	11.9%
Grad degree:	7.1%				

A little more than a century ago, Canton, Ohio, was at the center of American politics. It was already an industrial city, though unlike Youngstown and Cleveland, it didn't have huge steel factories. Its high-skill workers were fashioning new kinds of plows and reapers, making watches and, beginning in 1899, roller bearings. Canton did not attract masses of immigrants. Its factories did not run on harsh stopwatch discipline, and the class-warfare politics of other northern Ohio industrial cities did

2008 Presidential Vote		
McCain (R)	160,914	(50%)
Obama (D)	152,509	(48%)
2004 Presidential Vote		
Bush (R)	171,561	(54%)
Kerry (D)	146,066	(46%)
Cook Partisan Voting Index:	R + 4	

not take root here. Its most famous citizen was Republican President William McKinley, who rose to the rank of major at 22 in the Civil War, was elected congressman and governor, and chaired the House Ways and Means Committee. As the Republican nominee for president in 1896, McKinley campaigned from his front porch in Canton, meeting with delegations brought in by train from around the country. This spectacle, displaying both technological virtuosity and personal modesty, sounded a reverberating note in American politics, as did the McKinley platform—the "full dinner pail," the gold standard, the enforcement of law and order in labor relations. More than a century later, Canton is a community still based on manufacturing, but one troubled by manufacturing job losses, including those stemming from the crash of the domestic auto industry in 2009. Less widely reported are new jobs in smaller factories, like an Alliance casting plant reopened to make rail-car parts with 420 jobs. However, Canton has suffered a net loss of jobs in recent years. It has become best known as the home of the Professional Football Hall of Fame, with its football-shaped roof.

The 16th Congressional District of Ohio includes all of Canton and Stark County, plus Wayne County to the west and most of Ashland and Medina counties. Wayne County is home to the College of Wooster and the headquarters of Smuckers, which has acquired new brands from other food companies—Jif peanut butter, Hungry Jack pancakes, and Folgers Coffee. In the southern part of the county is the largest Amish settlement in the world, where people drive horse-drawn tractors, eschew automobiles and electricity, and quit school after the eighth grade. Tourism has been a growth industry in Amish country, with restaurants, bed-and-breakfasts and gift shops. Ashland is a smaller, non-metropolitan county. Johnny Appleseed once lived on what is now the campus of Ashland University. Medina County, north of Wayne, is part of the Cleveland metropolitan area. Politically, this area is generally Republican, though not always by wide margins. Stark County was the only Ohio county that Republican George W. Bush carried in 2000 but lost in 2004, both times by narrow margins. In 2008, Democratic presidential nominee Barack Obama won the county 52%-46%, but it wasn't enough for him to win the entire district, which voted 50%-48% for Republican John McCain.

The new congressman from the 16th Congressional District is John Boccieri, a Democrat elected in 2008. The son of schoolteachers, Boccieri grew up in Youngstown and went to college on a baseball scholarship, graduating from New York's St. Bonaventure University in 1992 with a degree in economics. He tried out for several Major League baseball teams and played a season as an outfielder and catcher in the independent professional Frontier League. He made the transition to politics by taking a job as a legislative aide to Democratic state Rep. Rich Cordray, who later became Ohio treasurer. In 2000, Boccieri was elected to the Ohio House, where he rose to assistant minority whip, the fourth-ranking Democratic position in the House. (A member of the Air Force Reserve, he had to give up the post in 2003 when he was called to Iraq to fly cargo planes.) In 2006, he won a seat in the state Senate, where he carved out a niche working on veterans issues. He sponsored a bill that sought job protection for service members returning from active duty. His cosponsor was Republican state Sen. Kurt Schuring, who would become his opponent for the House seat.

Boccieri decided to run for the U.S. House after 18-term Rep. Ralph Regula announced his retirement at age 84. Schuring was Regula's handpicked successor and won the GOP primary 47%-42% against Ashland County Commissioner Matt Miller. Money and the issue of residency played major roles in the general election campaign. Boccieri raised nearly $1.8 million to Schuring's $1.2 million. The Democratic Congressional Campaign Committee invested heavily in the race, spending more than $300,000 just days before the election. The National Republican Congressional Committee, strapped for cash, all but gave up on the seat in the weeks leading up to the election. Schuring complained that the Democrats were "trying to buy the seat" and criticized Boccieri for having only recently moved to Alliance from outside the district and for changing his voter registration. But Boccieri won this formerly Republican territory by a surprisingly large 55%-45% split. In Stark County, which cast 59% of the vote, he led 57%-43%. He lost 51%-49% in Ashland, the smallest county in the district.

In the House, Boccieri was named to the Transportation and Infrastructure Committee and to the Agriculture Committee for the 111th Congress (2009–2010).

SEVENTEENTH DISTRICT

Tim Ryan (D)

Elected 2002, 4th term; b. July 16, 1973, Niles; home, Niles; Bowling Green St. U., B.A. 1995, Franklin Pierce Law Ctr., J.D. 2000; Catholic; divorced.

Elected Office: OH Senate, 2000–02.

Professional Career: Aide, U.S. Rep. Jim Traficant, 1995–97.

DC Office: 1421 LHOB, 20515, 202-225-5261; Fax: 202-225-3719; Web site: timryan.house.gov.

State Offices: Akron, 330-630-7311; Warren, 330-373-0074; Youngstown, 330-740-0193.

Committees: *Appropriations* (31st of 37 D): Energy & Water Development; Labor, HHS, Education & Related Agencies; Legislative Branch.

Group Ratings

	ADA	ACLU	AFS	LCV	ITIC	NTU	COC	ACU	CFG	FRC
2008	90	100	100	77	57	4	61	4	0	11
2007	95	—	100	80	—	4	55	0	1	—

National Journal Ratings

	2007 LIB	—	2007 CONS		2008 LIB	—	2008 CONS
Economic	73%	—	24%		69%	—	29%
Social	60%	—	40%		75%	—	18%
Foreign	76%	—	23%		59%	—	37%
Composite	70%	—	30%		70%	—	30%

Key Votes of the 110th Congress

1. Increase minimum wage	Y	5. Share immigration data	N	9. Withdraw troops 8/08	Y
2. Expand SCHIP	Y	6. Foreign aid abortion ban	N	10. No operations in Iran	Y
3. Raise CAFE standards	Y	7. Ban gay bias in workplace	Y	11. Free trade with Peru	N
4. Bail out financial markets	Y	8. Repeal D.C. gun law	Y	12. Overhaul FISA	N

Election Results

2008 general	Tim Ryan (D)	218,896	(78%)	($1,151,775)
	Duane Grassell (R)	61,216	(22%)	($850)
2008 primary	Tim Ryan (D)	unopposed		

Prior Winning Percentages: 2006 (80%); 2004 (77%); 2002 (51%)

Population		Race/Ethnicity		Work	
Pop. 2007:	603,933	White:	83.6%	Private:	82.7%
Change since 2000:	Down 4.2%	Black:	11.8%	Government:	11.9%
Urban:	84.3%	Hispanic:	2.0%	Self-employed:	5.2%
Rural:	15.7%	Asian:	1.0%	Blue collar:	28.6%
Area size:	1,033 sq. mi.	Native Am.:	0.1%	White collar:	52.5%
		Hawaiian:	0.0%	Khaki collar:	0.0%
Age		Two+ races:	1.3%	Other:	18.8%
Median age:	38.6 yrs.			Median income:	$40,434
More than 65 yrs:	14.7%	*Ancestry*		Median home value:	$106,200
Less than 18 yrs:	22.1%	German:	18.0%	Poverty:	15.4%
		Irish:	11.6%		
Education		Italian:	9.7%	**Military Veterans**	
H.S. grad:	86.1%			% of Pop:	12.2%
College grad:	17.4%				
Grad degree:	5.9%				

For nearly a century, the Mahoning Valley, between the Lake Erie docks that unload iron ore from Great Lakes freighters and the coalfields of western Pennsylvania and West Virginia, was one of the steel capitals of the United States. The first coal mine opened in 1826, canals followed, and in 1892 the first steel mill was built in Youngstown. The valley soon filled up with mills, converters, and furnaces. Now the steel mills stand empty, smokeless and silent—except those that have been dynamited

2008 Presidential Vote
Obama (D) 183,083 (62%)
McCain (R).............................106,337 (36%)

2004 Presidential Vote
Kerry (D)...............................188,531 (63%)
Bush (R) 111,663 (37%)

Cook Partisan Voting Index: D + 12

or torn down. Big-steel management allowed foreign producers to gain a technological edge in the 1950s and 1960s, and worldwide overcapacity in steel grew as almost every developing country decided it needed its own steel mills. Meanwhile, an agreement between the United Steelworkers and management after a 119-day strike in 1959 boosted wages and fringe benefits to levels that helped price domestic steel out of the market. Import restrictions kept the furnaces hot for a while, but the oil shock of the 1970s produced sharply higher energy prices and a collapse in the U.S. auto and steel markets. Every plant in the Mahoning Valley closed, with a loss of 40,000 jobs. In the early 1980s, Youngstown had one of the nation's highest unemployment rates. From 1990 to 2004, the population of Youngstown's Mahoning County declined by 6% and next-door Trumbull County's by 3%. Steel has since revived, but not here. The high-wage living standard has vanished. Several aluminum plants opened in nearby Warren, but young people looking for opportunities routinely leave. In 2007, Youngstown's population was 74,000, less than half its size in the 1950s. That same year the Census Bureau reported that Youngstown had the lowest median household income in the nation among cities with 65,000 to 250,000 people. Organized crime infiltrated local government, and a federal investigation in the late 1990s led to more than 70 convictions; among those sentenced were a prosecutor, a sheriff and a congressman. Today, Youngstown is struggling to rebound, though it has managed to attract a few high-tech firms, including the fast-growing Turning Technologies software company.

The 17th Congressional District of Ohio encompasses most of the Mahoning Valley industrial area—Youngstown (though not its southern Mahoning County suburbs), Warren, and most of Trumbull County. It includes nearly all of Portage County to the west and part of eastern Summit County and Akron. It contains two loci of 1970s protest—Kent State University, where four war-protesting students were killed by National Guardsmen, and Lordstown, site of the General Motors plant where workers purposely built shoddy cars to protest the tedium of the assembly line. This is a Democratic district. It voted 63% for John Kerry in 2004, his second-best district in Ohio. In 2008, Democratic nominee Barack Obama did not fare quite as well among the district's mostly white working-class voters, but his 62%-36% victory was comfortable enough.

The congressman from the 17th District is Tim Ryan, a Democrat elected in 2002 at age 29. Ryan grew up in Niles, was a star quarterback before a knee injury ended his career, and graduated from Bowling Green State University. His first job was with 17th District Rep. James Traficant, a Democrat later convicted of racketeering and bribery. In 2000, after graduating from Franklin Pierce Law Center, Ryan was elected to the state Senate. His opening to run for Congress came when Traficant was forced to resign in disgrace after his conviction in 2002. For years, Traficant had been a colorful if coarse figure in the House, whose ranting orations ("Beam me up, Scottie" was his expression of incredulity at hearing an opposing viewpoint) and retro haircut ("I do my hair with a weed whacker") were a regular source of fascination for C-SPAN viewers.

Most 17th District insiders thought Akron-based Rep. Tom Sawyer, a Democrat who had been thrown into the district by reapportionment based on the 2000 census, had the inside track to succeed Traficant. And by standard measures, Sawyer should have won easily: He outspent Ryan nearly 6-to-1. But his record on issues gave Ryan an opening. Sawyer had voted for the 1993 North American Free Trade Agreement, and he was one of the few Rust Belt Democrats to vote for normalizing trade relations with China. Ryan hammered on these votes in the Mahoning Valley, where it is gospel that free trade drove the region's high-paying jobs abroad. Ryan also got the endorsement of the National Rifle Association in a district with many hunters. He beat Sawyer 41%-27%. The Republican nominee was state Rep. Ann Womer Benjamin. Ryan slammed her and the Ohio Republican Legislature for votes that had led to higher tuition at state universities. Republicans fired back with ads highlighting several disorderly conduct charges lodged against Ryan while he was in college. The district's Democratic leanings and Ryan's labor support proved decisive. He won 51% of the vote to 34% for Womer Benjamin and 15% for Traficant, who ran as an independent even though he'd been carted off to jail.

Ryan has leaned to the left on economic and foreign policy, while his splits with Democrats on abortion rights and gun control have placed him closer to the center on social issues. With abortion-rights advocate Rosa DeLauro, D-Conn., he sponsored the "Reducing the Need for Abortion and Supporting Parents Act," with federal dollars to fight teen pregnancy, while increasing aid for women who become pregnant; Democratic activists depicted this as a move toward party consensus on a difficult issue. Worried about the loss of local call-center jobs, Ryan was one of just seven House members who voted against the national do-not-call list. For several years, he sponsored the Chinese Currency Act, which sought to counter China's alleged manipulation and undervaluation of its currency.

With the encouragement of then Minority Leader Nancy Pelosi, Ryan and other young Democratic newcomers to the House created the "30-Something Working Group" as a partisan device to reach young C-SPAN viewers with their late-night House speeches. After challenging the Republicans' advocacy of the partial privatization of Social Security in 2005, Ryan said the group noticed that poll numbers were changing among young people. However, Ryan sided with Republicans on some issues, such as repeal of the estate tax and the construction of a security fence along the border with Mexico.

He was a vocal backer of the powerful Pennsylvania Democrat John Murtha in his unsuccessful bid against Maryland's Steny Hoyer for majority leader in 2006, which endeared him to Murtha-Backer Pelosi and earned Ryan a coveted seat on the House Appropriations Committee. He immediately went to work securing earmarked projects for his hard-pressed district, including more than $26 million in 2007 alone.

Ryan has not faced serious re-election problems. He considered a run for the Senate in 2006 but decided against it. Democratic Gov. Ted Strickland discussed a shared ticket with Ryan in 2010, but Ryan decided to remain in the House, largely because of his new assignment on Appropriations.

EIGHTEENTH DISTRICT

Zack Space (D)

Elected 2006, 2nd term; b. Jan. 27, 1961, Dover; home, Dover; Kenyon Col., B.A. 1983, OH St. U., J.D. 1986; Greek Orthodox; married (Mary); 2 children.

Elected Office: Dover law director, 2000–06.

Professional Career: Public defender, 1986–87; Practicing atty., 1986–2006; Hotel developer, 1995–2004.

DC Office: 315 CHOB, 20515, 202-225-6265; Fax: 202-225-3394; Web site: space.house.gov.

State Offices: Chillicothe, 740-779-1636; Dover, 330-364-4300; Zanesville, 740-452-6338.

Committees: *Energy & Commerce* (32nd of 36 D): Commerce, Trade & Consumer Protections; Communications, Technology & the Internet; Health. *Veterans' Affairs* (14th of 18 D): Oversight.

Group Ratings

	ADA	ACLU	AFS	LCV	ITIC	NTU	COC	ACU	CFG	FRC
2008	80	64	100	85	86	5	61	12	0	11
2007	95	—	91	60	—	8	58	20	6	—

National Journal Ratings

	2007 LIB	—	2007 CONS		2008 LIB	—	2008 CONS
Economic	54%	—	46%		61%	—	38%
Social	50%	—	50%		51%	—	49%
Foreign	49%	—	50%		49%	—	50%
Composite	51%	—	49%		54%	—	46%

Key Votes of the 110th Congress

1. Increase minimum wage	Y	5. Share immigration data	Y	9. Withdraw troops 8/08	Y
2. Expand SCHIP	Y	6. Foreign aid abortion ban	N	10. No operations in Iran	N
3. Raise CAFE standards	Y	7. Ban gay bias in workplace	Y	11. Free trade with Peru	N
4. Bail out financial markets	Y	8. Repeal D.C. gun law	Y	12. Overhaul FISA	Y

Election Results

2008 general	Zack Space (D)	164,187	(60%)	($2,041,891)
	Fred Dailey (R)	110,031	(40%)	($391,524)
2008 primary	Zack Space (D)	87,503	(85%)	
	Mark Pitrone (D)	15,980	(15%)	

Prior Winning Percentages: 2006 (62%)

Population		Race/Ethnicity		Work	
Pop. 2007:	639,527	White:	95.5%	Private:	78.4%
Change since 2000:	Up 1.4%	Black:	1.9%	Government:	13.3%
Urban:	43.3%	Hispanic:	0.8%	Self-employed:	7.8%
Rural:	56.7%	Asian:	0.3%	Blue collar:	32.9%
Area size:	6,876 sq. mi.	Native Am.:	0.2%	White collar:	48.7%
		Hawaiian:	0.0%	Khaki collar:	0.1%
Age		Two+ races:	1.3%	Other:	18.3%
Median age:	37.6 yrs.	*Ancestry*		Median income:	$39,662
More than 65 yrs:	14.3%	German:	22.3%	Median home value:	$105,400
Less than 18 yrs:	24.4%	Irish:	11.1%	Poverty:	14.5%
Education		USA:	9.5%	**Military Veterans**	
H.S. grad:	80.9%			% of Pop:	11.7%
College grad:	12.5%				
Grad degree:	4.6%				

The hills of eastern Ohio are one of those obscure parts of America, seen by most Americans, if at all, from airplanes or speeding cars on the interstates on their way to someplace else. They were settled early on in U.S. history, in the 1790s, mostly by Virginians, and for the most part remained sparsely populated. This was hard land to clear and hard land to farm, better suited for dairy cattle than the plains that lay beyond. In some places near the Ohio River, there was industrial development early on.

2008 Presidential Vote
McCain (R)............................150,461   (53%)
Obama (D) 128,058   (45%)

2004 Presidential Vote
Bush (R) 163,121   (57%)
Kerry (D)................................121,495   (43%)

Cook Partisan Voting Index: R + 7

The local clay was used to make pottery, the coal that lies near the surface was dug up, a green-vitriol works was built, and a nail factory went into operation, all before 1814. In time, the area became dotted with small factory towns and coal mines. Farther south there was little industrial development, and today that landscape has a timeless feel. This region was little affected by the flow of immigrants from Europe in 1880–1924, southern blacks in 1940–1965 or Latino and Asian immigrants since 1970. Some counties have seen sharp job losses, as coal mines and factories have shut down. Others, despite objections from some local farmers, have benefited from the construction of a gasoline pipeline from the Ohio River to Columbus and beyond to Colorado. As the price of oil and natural gas rose, the coal industry began to rebound, reopening some mines and returning some jobs. The most distinctive people here are the Amish, who drive their horses and buggies over covered bridges in Holmes, Tuscarawas and Wayne counties. They make up the largest concentration of Amish in the world. They run shops now as well as farms, get energy from solar power, and no longer eschew all farm machinery.

The 18th Congressional District of Ohio covers much of this hill country, from Holmes and Tuscarawas counties in the north to Ross and Jackson counties in the south. Geographically, it is the largest district in the state, spanning five media markets, including two in West Virginia. It includes such cities as New Rumley, the birthplace of Gen. George Custer; Zanesville, the birthplace of writer Zane Grey and architect Cass Gilbert; and Chillicothe, the first capital of Ohio, on the Scioto River. Politically, much of this area is ancestrally Democratic, but Republican presidential candidate George W. Bush won 55% of the vote here in 2000 and 57% in 2004. Republican nominee John McCain beat Barack Obama here 53%-45% in 2008.

The congressman from the 18th District is Democrat Zack Space, elected in 2006. He was born in Dover and named after his grandfather Zacharias, a Greek immigrant who won U.S citizenship for his World War I service. Space attended Kenyon College, where he distinguished himself as a Division III All-American football player. He earned a law degree from the Ohio State University and started Space & Space Company, a law practice with his father, Socrates Space. While practicing consumer-rights law for two decades, Space also served as a public defender and as the business manager of a local hotel company. He was appointed Dover law director in 2000 and was twice elected to the position.

In 2006, Space was one of a handful of Democrats seeking to oust six-term Republican Rep. Bob Ney, chairman of the House Administration Committee. In early 2006, when reports about his relationship with corrupt lobbyist Jack Abramoff began to surface, Ney gave up his chairmanship, saying that he had become a distraction for the party. The Democratic Congressional Campaign Committee initially favored Chillicothe Mayor Joe Sulzer in the primary, but he proved unable to expand his base outside the southern part of the sprawling district. Space campaigned against corruption and signed an ethics pledge saying he would not accept gifts from lobbyists. He also talked about economic issues such as lost manufacturing jobs and health care. He won the May primary with 39%; Ohio Board of Education member Jennifer Stewart got 26% and Sulzer got 24%.

In August, Ney bowed to House Republican leadership pressure and withdrew his candidacy for re-election. In October, he pled guilty to corruption charges, but he did not resign the seat until November 3, 2006, four days before the election, ensuring that the specter of scandal lingered over the campaign.

Republican leaders anointed state Sen. Joy Padgett, who was also Ney's preferred successor. She easily won a five-way September 14 special-election primary, but her late start gave Space an advantage. She attacked Space for taking contributions from MoveOn.org and other liberal groups, and the National Republican Congressional Committee poured in over $2 million to defend the seat. Despite being tagged as a liberal, Space took positions on tax cuts, gun-ownership rights, trade and illegal immigration that were not all that different from Padgett's. Democrats emphasized Padgett's ties to unpopular Republican Gov. Bob Taft, who had appointed her director of the Office of Appalachia. They also noted that her family's office-supply business had gone bankrupt in 2005 and that Padgett and her husband had filed for personal bankruptcy protection as recently as 2006. Space spent over $1.6 million to Padgett's $850,000 and won 62%-38%.

In the House, Space joined the Blue Dog Coalition of moderate and conservative Democrats and fit comfortably in the center of the House. His "Renew Ohio 18" program focused on local issues, including extension of commodity programs in the farm bill, expansion of Internet broadband services to underserved areas, and alternative energy sources. He made an emotional plea for embryonic-stem-cell research, citing his son's "thousands of injections and blood tests" in his battle with juvenile diabetes. Party leaders recruited him to take a prominent role on their ethics-reform legislation, but in 2007, he alienated some Democrats when he drew parallels to Ney in calling for Democratic Rep. William Jefferson of Louisiana to resign after Jefferson became the target of a federal bribery investigation. On foreign policy, Space initially supported then opposed Democratic proposals establishing deadlines for troop withdrawals from Iraq.

In early 2009, Space got a seat on the influential Energy and Commerce Committee, where he hoped to play a moderating role between the two parties on health and energy issues. That May, he repaid the Democrats who had put him on the committee by supporting legislation that sought to cap carbon emissions, a move that surprised local Democrats in his coal-heavy district .

Space was a target for Republicans in 2008. Cattle farmer and longtime state Department of Agriculture Director Fred Dailey won the GOP primary after more-experienced party regulars declined to run. Republicans criticized Space for supporting the Democratic budget and other parts of Speaker Nancy Pelosi's agenda. Space avoided his party's national convention in Denver in August 2008, saying he had "too much work to do" in his district, but noted that he fully supported the presumed nominee, Barack Obama. Dailey complained about his lack of national party resources and was heavily outspent by Space. The incumbent won 60%-40%, carrying traditionally Republican Holmes and Knox counties in the Amish country.

★ OKLAHOMA ★

Oklahoma's Capitol dome, left unconstructed when the Capitol was opened in 1917, was finally finished in 2002. Similarly, Oklahoma's history has been a story of stops and sudden starts. It was settled in a rush, first by the Five Civilized Tribes driven west by Andrew Jackson's troops over the Trail of Tears in the 1830s. Then came white settlers one morning in April 1889, when, in the great land rush memorialized by novelist Edna Ferber and half a dozen Hollywood movies, thousands of homesteaders drove their wagons across the territorial line at the sound of a gunshot, the most adventurous or unscrupulous of them literally jumping the gun—the Sooners. In 1905, a convention of the Civilized Nations, as they became known, sought to have eastern Oklahoma admitted as a separate state of Sequoyah. The federal government turned a deaf ear to the Indians, and ended the tribal government. It combined the Indian and Oklahoma territories as a single state, which was admitted to the union in 1907.

The heritage of these hurried settlements is evident today. Oklahoma has the second-largest Indian population in the country, after California—273,000 in the 2000 census—though there is just one reservation and the status of many other tribal entities is often disputed. Some Indian tribes here have unsuccessfully sought a return of native lands and face high unemployment rates. But there has been much intermarriage over the years, and many Oklahomans—and not a few of its politicians—proudly claim Indian blood. There is an ongoing struggle to keep the Cherokee, Choctaw, Chickasaw and Seminole languages from dying out—you can see street signs in the Cherokee alphabet in Tahlequah. The counties with a large Indian heritage in the eastern part of the state have been growing, while the Great Plains farm and oil counties west of Oklahoma City and Tulsa have lost population. Indians own 6% of businesses in Oklahoma, and make up about 7% of the population. In 2009, the Cherokee Nation purchased an aerospace company.

The Rodgers and Hammerstein musical recalled an Oklahoma on the brink of statehood in 1907, at which point the territory rapidly filled up with farmers, rising from 1.5 million people in 1907 to 2.4 million in 1930. Oil helped. The first well was drilled here in 1897 and by 1920, Tulsa was an oil boom town. Then in the 1930s came a decade of bust—or dust—as soil loosened by erosion was whipped into giant swirling clouds: The Dust Bowl. "On a single day, I heard, 50 million tons of soil were blown away," American journalist John Gunther reported later. "People sat in Oklahoma City, with the sky invisible for three days in a row, holding dust masks over their faces and wet towels to protect their mouths at night, while the farms blew by." Okies headed in droves west on U.S. 66 to the green land of California, and Oklahoma's population steadily declined, falling to 2.2 million in 1950. It did not to reach its 1930 level again until 1970. The state's population is 7% American Indian, 7% African-American, and 7% Hispanic.

Oil brought another boom. As the oil shocks of 1973 and 1979 sent oil prices up, Oklahoma's population rose from 2.5 million in 1970 to 3 million in 1980 and 3.3 million in 1983. Then, with the collapse of oil prices and of Oklahoma's farm economy as well, it was bust again. A giddy rise was followed by a giddier fall. The rig count went from 882 in 1982 to 232 in 1983 and was just 186 in 2007. The 1990 census reported just 3.1 million Oklahomans. But in the 1990s, Oklahoma began building a more diversified economy, with high-tech employers as well as oil and gas firms. Population rose 10% in the decade, to 3.5 million in 2000, and another 5% to 3.6 million in 2008. High oil prices made it worthwhile to squeeze more from marginal wells, and Oklahoma's natural gas—it's the third state in production—has commanded high prices given strong demand. At the same time, Oklahoma has been one of the leading states in developing wind power, with utilities offering customers electricity produced from wind although at slightly higher than ordinary rates. Oklahoma continues to have above-average rates of divorce, teenage pregnancy and crime, and a low rate of college graduates. But unemployment has been low, and the housing bust and the subsequent 2007–09 recession caused less distress here than in many faster-growing states.

Historically, Oklahoma was a Democratic state, with big Democratic margins in eastern counties and in southeast's Little Dixie. But northwestern Oklahoma, settled by Kansans, has always been Republican, and starting in the 1950s, Tulsa and Oklahoma City leaned Republican too. Vestiges of its Democratic heritage remain. There are more registered Democrats than Republicans (though the 2008 exit poll showed conservatives outnumbering liberals 39%-16%). Oklahoma has not voted Democratic for president since 1964 and has not come close lately. Republican President George W. Bush carried all 77 counties in 2004, as did GOP nominee John McCain in 2008. Oklahoma has elected only one Democratic senator, David Boren, since 1966, and the only Democrat in its congressional delegation is his son Dan Boren. Lots of Oklahomans identify as conservative Democrats, and helped elect Democrat Brad Henry as governor in 2002 and to re-elect him by 67%-33% in 2006. But Republicans captured a 57-44 majority in the state House in 2004 and expanded it to 61-40 in 2008. For the first time in history, they won a majority, 26-22, in the state Senate in 2008.

In some respects Oklahoma politics has been a struggle between Oklahoma City and Tulsa Republicans and rural Democrats. Tulsa-based Republican Frank Keating, governor from 1994 and 2002, managed to get voters to pass a right-to-work law, long opposed by Democrats in the Legislature, by 54%-46%

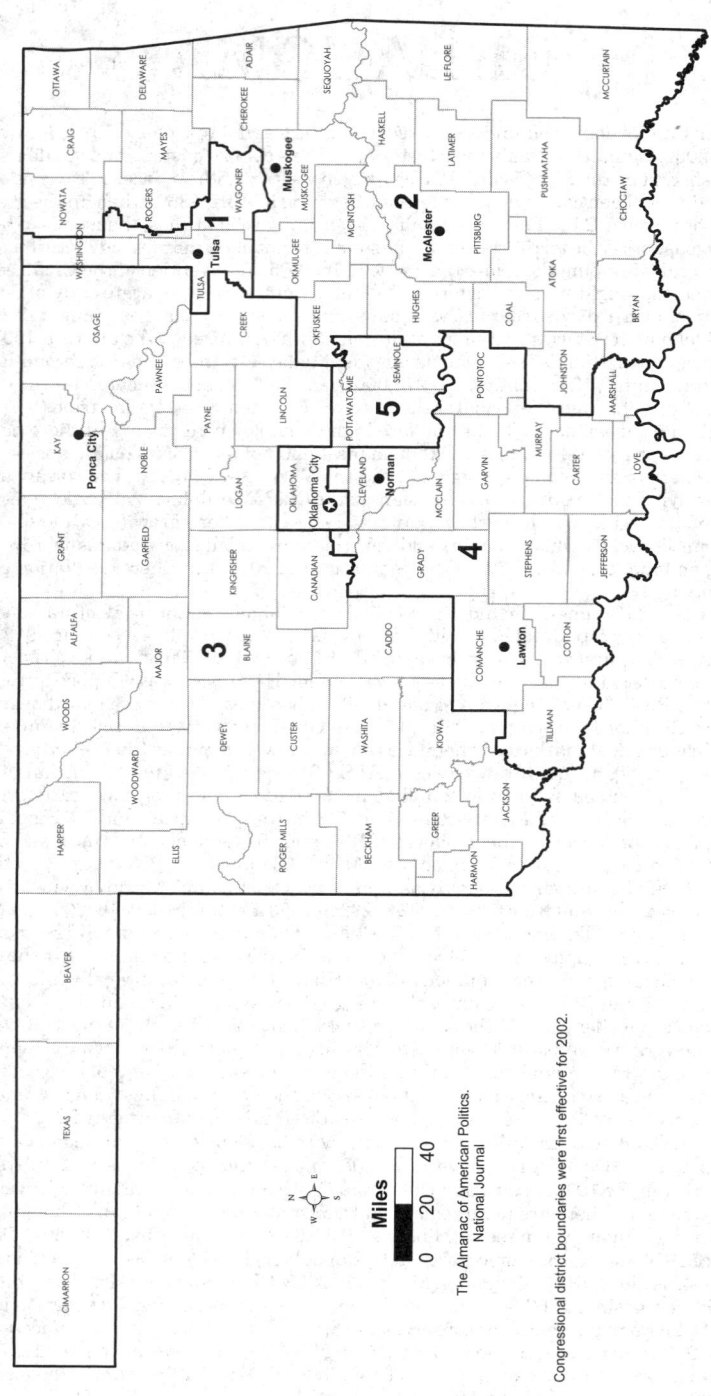

The Almanac of American Politics.
National Journal

Congressional district boundaries were first effective for 2002.

Population		**Household Income**		**Work**	
Pop. 2007:	3,576,929	Under $15k:	17.1%	Private:	74.3%
State rank:	28th of 50	$15k to $50k:	42.9%	Government:	17.6%
Change since 2000:	Up 3.7%	$50k to $100k:	28.4%	Self-employed:	7.7%
Urban:	65.1%	$100k to $150k:	9.8%	Unemployment (3-yr. average):	3.8%
Rural:	34.9%	Over $150k:	2.0%	Poverty:	16.6%
Native of state:	61.7%	Median income:	$40,371	Blue collar:	25.1%
Not a citizen:	3.4%	**Home Value**		White collar:	56.6%
Area size:	69,898 sq. mi.	Under $100k:	53.3%	Khaki collar:	0.7%
Most populous cities		$100k to $300k:	41.6%	Other:	17.6%
1. Oklahoma City	540,321	$300k to $500k:	3.6%	**Age**	
2. Tulsa	384,040	$500k to $1 mil:	1.2%	Median age:	36.0 yrs.
3. Norman	103,057	Over $1 million:	0.3%	More than 65 yrs:	13.2%
4. Lawton	90,346	Median:	$95,200	Less than 18 yrs:	24.9%

Race/Ethnicity				**Military Veterans**		**Registered Voters in 2008**	
White:	72.1%	*Language*		% of Pop:	12.5%	D:	1,079,373 (49.4%)
Black:	7.4%	English:	91.8%	*Veterans by Period*		R:	859,872 (39.4%)
Hispanic:	6.9%	Spanish:	5.3%	WWII and before:	11.3%	Other:	244,847 (11.2%)
Asian:	1.6%	Asian:	1.2%	Korea:	11.3%	Voter turnout:	1,462,661
Native Am.:	6.6%	Other		Vietnam:	33.2%	Turnout as % of	
Hawaiian:	0.1%	European	1.0%	Gulf (pre-2001):	12.1%	voting age:	53.5%
Two+ races:	5.2%	**Education**		Gulf (post-2001):	9.1%	**Legislature**	
Ancestry		H.S. grad:	84.2%	Peace time:	23.0%	Senate:	22 D 26 R
German:	12.9%	College grad:	22.2%			House:	40 D 61 R
Irish:	10.6%	Grad degree:	7.3%				
USA:	9.1%						

in a September 2001 referendum. But small town-based Democrat Henry profited from a referendum on quite a different subject, a ban on cockfighting, in his 2002 gubernatorial run. Oklahoma was one of only three states that allowed this "sport," and urban voters helped the ban pass 56%-44%. But opposition to the ban brought out rural voters in droves, and they helped ban-opponent Henry defeat Republican Rep. Steve Largent 43.3%-42.6%. Henry is barred from running for a third term in 2010, and it's not clear whether another cross-cutting issue will help determine who succeeds him. One possibility is immigration. In 2007, state Republican Rep. Randy Terrill led the drive that resulted in the Legislature passing one of the nation's toughest laws on illegal immigrants. Law enforcement personnel are required to check the citizenship status of everyone arrested, applicants for driver's licenses must establish their legal status, and public and private employers are required to use the federal eVerify system to establish legal status. The law has been challenged in federal court.

Presidential politics   Oklahoma has been a solidly Republican state in presidential elections since the 1950s. There are no large blocs of voters here who back national Democrats, and most Oklahomans find national Republicans acceptable. It has been a long time since Oklahoma has been on anyone's list of target states, and seems unlikely to be in the near future. While Tulsa and Oklahoma City were the Republicans' strongholds from the 1950s to the 1990s, now many rural counties are even more so. President George W. Bush in 2004 and Republican nominee John McCain in 2008 carried all 77 counties in the state. This was McCain's best state. He won with 65.6% of the vote, about the same as Bush in 2004. Indeed the two elections were almost carbon copies. McCain got 373 more votes than Bush and 2008 Democratic nominee Barack Obama got 1,470 fewer votes than 2004 Democratic nominee John Kerry. But this was not Obama's worst state. He had lower percentages in Wyoming and Utah, where there were third-party candidates, while Oklahoma alone of all the 50 states had none. There

2008 Presidential Vote
McCain (R)............................960,165   (66%)
Obama (D) 502,496   (34%)

2008 Democratic Presidential Primary
Clinton (D) 228,480   (55%)
Obama (D) 130,130   (31%)
Edwards (D)...........................42,725   (10%)

2008 Republican Presidential Primary
McCain (R)............................122,772   (37%)
Huckabee (R) 111,899   (33%)
Romney (R) 83,030   (25%)

2004 Presidential Vote
Bush (R)................................959,792   (66%)
Kerry (D)...............................503,966   (34%)

was no significant gender gap in Oklahoma and not much of an age gap: Young voters went 60% for McCain. And there are lots of conservative Democrats: 41% of white Democrats voted for McCain.

Oklahoma has had a presidential primary since it joined the Super Tuesday contests in 1988. That year, it voted 37%-35% for Texas neighbor George H. W. Bush over Kansas neighbor Bob Dole in the Republican primary, and it gave Al Gore a solid win in the Democratic primary. In the next three cycles, it was not seriously contested, and for 2004, the Legislature scheduled the primary for February, a week after New Hampshire. As one of two primaries in a southern-accented state that day (the other was South Carolina), Oklahoma was targeted by John Edwards and Wesley Clark, both desperate for a win after John Kerry's triumphs in Iowa and New Hampshire. Clark won here—his first and only electoral victory—but with just 29.9%, to 29.5% for Edwards and 27% for Kerry. Kerry carried the counties including Oklahoma City, Tulsa and Norman (home of the University of Oklahoma), and not much else; Clark got big pluralities in the counties around Fort Sill and Altus Air Force Base, and not much else. Edwards carried most suburban and rural counties, but seldom by big pluralities.

In 2008, Oklahoma was joined by many other states on Super Tuesday on February 5, and did not attract too much attention. In the Democratic primary, Hillary Rodham Clinton was the early favorite here, and beat Obama 55%-31%. John Edwards got 10% although he had already dropped out of the race. Obama carried Oklahoma County (Oklahoma City), and Clinton carried the other 76 counties, with very big margins in eastern Oklahoma counties near her longtime home in Arkansas. Edwards finished second in three rural counties. Turnout was 417,000, a record, but not significantly higher than in 1988 or 1992. The Republican race was much closer. Fresh off victories in New Hampshire and Florida, McCain won with 37% of the vote, to 33% for Mike Huckabee and 25% for Mitt Romney. Oklahoma's party registration law—and the fact that so many rural conservatives are still registered as Democrats—probably cost Huckabee a victory. He carried the eastern portion of the state, with a high of 58.5% in Adair County, on the border of his home state of Arkansas. McCain ran strongest in the western part of the state, with his best showing, 50%, in rural Ellis County. Turnout was 335,000, a record, and 27% above the previous high in 1996, a sign that the Republican Party continues to gain strength in the state.

Congressional districting

111th Congress Lineup	
4 R	1 D
110th Congress Lineup	
4 R	1 D

Oklahoma lost one of its six House seats in the 2000 census, and for months there was a deadlock over redistricting between Republican Gov. Frank Keating and the Democratic Legislature. Keating wanted to keep a Tulsa-centered district, especially before the December 2001 special election in which his wife, Cathy Keating, ran for the Tulsa-centered 1st District seat vacated by Republican Rep. Steve Largent. But she lost the Republican nomination. In 2002, the solution appeared after 3rd District Rep. Wes Watkins announced his retirement. Watkins was a Republican (and a former Democrat) and the 3rd District was centered in Little Dixie; the seat was safe for Watkins, but Democrats carry the area in state elections and would have a good chance to win an open seat contest. The issue went to court, and in May 2002, a county judge ordered the adoption of a plan that eliminated Watkins's district and gave the other incumbents safe seats. It also had the virtue of creating an Oklahoma City-centered district rather than splitting the city between several districts as it had been since 1981. Democrats, happy that Democratic incumbent Rep. Brad Carson got a safe seat, let the matter drop. Carson ran for the Senate in 2004 and lost to Tom Coburn, but Democrat Dan Boren has easily held the seat since.

Demographic projections indicate that Oklahoma will not gain or lose a seat after the 2010 census. Republicans, having won majorities in the state House in 2004 and in the state Senate in 2008, would likely draw the lines, no matter who is elected governor. But that probably makes little difference, because it is hard to imagine lines that will endanger Boren in the 2nd District or that will weaken the GOP's hold on any of the other four seats.

Governor

Brad Henry (D)

Elected 2002, term expires Jan. 2011, 2nd term; b. July 7, 1963, Shawnee; home, Shawnee; U. of OK, B.S. 1985, J.D. 1988; Baptist; married (Kim); 3 children.

Elected Office: OK Senate, 1992–2002.

Professional Career: Practicing atty., 1989–2002; Atty., City of Shawnee, 1990–2002.

Office: State Capitol Bldg., 2300 N. Lincoln Blvd., Rm. 212, Oklahoma City, 73105, 405-521-2342; Fax: 405-521-3353; Web site: governor.state.ok.us.

Election Results

2006 general	Brad Henry (D)	616,135	(67%)
	Ernest Istook (R)	310,327	(33%)
2006 primary	Brad Henry (D)	226,957	(86%)
	Andrew Marr (D)	37,510	(14%)

Prior Winning Percentages: 2002 (43%)

Brad Henry, a Democrat, was elected governor of Oklahoma in an upset in 2002, defeating Republican Steve Largent, a homegrown gridiron star and member of Congress. Henry grew up in Shawnee, one county east of Oklahoma City. As a boy, he built a tree house with multiple floors and once borrowed $10,500 from a bank to buy 15 crossbred cow-calf pairs for a Future Farmers of America project. He graduated from the University of Oklahoma and its law school and returned home to practice law. In 1992, at 29, he was elected to the state Senate. There, he achieved little statewide notice. So, at the beginning of the 2002 race for governor, Henry was not on anyone's political radar. The candidate considered most likely to win was Republican U.S. Rep. Largent, a football standout at the University of Tulsa who later played professionally for the Seattle Seahawks. He resigned his House seat in February 2002 to campaign for governor. The favorite for the Democratic nomination was Oklahoma City restaurateur Vince Orza, a former Republican who came close to winning the 1990 GOP gubernatorial runoff. Henry was not even sure whether to run, and did not announce until the breathtakingly late date of June 24.

But he had a good campaign plan. Henry had one big issue—a state lottery to finance education; one big vehicle—an RV in which he traveled around the state; and one big supporter—former University of Oklahoma and Dallas Cowboys football coach Barry Switzer. Voters may not be much interested in meeting politicians, but Oklahoma voters are very interested in meeting football coaches. Henry's folksy, aw-shucks manner appealed to rural voters; for them it was a gratifying contrast to the other major figures in gubernatorial politics: Gov. Frank Keating, Largent, and Orza, who are from Oklahoma's two major cities. In the Democratic primary on August 27, two months and three days after Henry announced, Orza led with 44% of the vote, short of the 50% needed to avoid a runoff; Henry finished second with 29%, carrying only five counties. In the runoff campaign, Orza called for ending reliance on the state income tax, which presumably meant a higher sales tax. Henry backed the lottery as a solution to bolstering state revenues, and also touted a tax exemption on seniors' retirement income. Henry had the support of the primary's third-place finisher, state Sen. Kelly Haney, a full-blooded Seminole-Creek, and he took care to meet with tribal chiefs, who were conducting a big voter registration drive. Henry won the September runoff, 52%-48%.

In the general election campaign, there were clear contrasts with Largent. The Republican opposed the lottery and called for moving from the income tax to consumption taxes over 10 years; he also supported eliminating the sales tax on food. Henry backed across-the-board teacher salary increases and opposed merit pay—the teachers union positions—while Largent took the other side on both issues. Another important local issue set the candidates apart: a proposed ban on cockfighting. Largent endorsed the ban, a popular stand in urban Oklahoma. Henry came out against it, putting him on the side of Little Dixie in southeastern Oklahoma, where cockfighting is part of the local culture.

Also a factor in the race was the independent candidacy of businessman Gary Richardson, who spent $2 million of his own money on his campaign. Richardson called for eliminating a whole raft of taxes and replacing them with a levy on the gross revenues of all business operations. Polls showed Richardson with double-digit support, but his issue positions were less important than his ads attacking Largent. Congress was in session on September 11, 2001, but Largent was bow hunting in Idaho and couldn't be reached by his staff, so he was unaware of the monumental events occurring. Richardson's ads showed one of the World Trade Center towers collapsing, raised the issue of Largent's whereabouts that day, and then showed Largent angrily responding to a reporter's question about the situation. While all of this was working against Largent, Henry ran ads featuring his young family and showcasing his folksy style. October polls showed the race tightening. In November, Henry won by fewer than 7,000 votes out of more than 1 million cast, 43.3%-42.6%, with 14% for Richardson. Largent led 46%-40% in the Oklahoma City area and 45%-39% in the Tulsa area—far less than the usual Republican leads in those cities—while Henry carried the rest of Oklahoma, which cast 44% of the total vote, 48%-39%. This, in many ways, was a victory for rural Oklahoma over urban Oklahoma.

The new governor rolled out his program: A cigarette-tax increase to pay for health care, a statewide lottery to raise teachers' salaries to levels competitive with surrounding states, expansion of tribal casinos, plus a permanent cut in the top income-tax rate from 7% to 6.65% and zero capital-gains tax on the sale of Oklahoma property. In May 2004, Henry achieved major victories on his platform. Most legislators may have been unwilling to vote for his proposals outright, but they voted to put them on the November ballot. All passed, most of them by handsome margins.

But Henry also suffered a major setback in 2004. Republicans captured the state House, only the second time since statehood that Democrats failed to win control of that chamber. His job was suddenly more difficult. His plan to reduce the cost of prescription drugs failed, and his tort reform proposal died in the Democratic-controlled Senate when all 22 Republicans and a handful of Democrats opposed it.

However, Henry did win a permanent reduction in the top income-tax rate. In 2006, high oil and gas prices gave the state a $1 billion surplus, but the warring House and Senate were unable to agree on the budget and were forced to hold a special session. A budget accord, reached in June, reduced personal income-tax rates from 6.25% to 5.25% over four years, eliminated the estate tax, granted pay raises to state workers and teachers, and gave an additional $130 million to higher education.

Going into the 2006 election campaign, Henry was in remarkably good shape for a Democratic governor elected with just 43.3% of the vote in a Republican state. His approval ratings were high, and he could point to a record that seemed in line with Oklahoma values. Henry had opposed a federal constitutional amendment banning same-sex marriages, but he firmly backed Oklahoma's state ban and signed a bill barring adoption by same-sex couples. He also signed a bill authorizing the death penalty for repeat offenders in sex crimes involving children, and approved several abortion-related measures, including one that required parental consent before a minor could have an abortion.

Republican Ernest Istook, a U.S. House member, was the Republican nominee after winning 55% of the vote against three competitors. A conservative who considered running for the Senate in 2004, Istook had hit a wall in Congress. As chairman of the Transportation Appropriations Subcommittee, and thus a member of the so-called College of Cardinals, he had angered his Republican colleagues in 2004 when, without notice, he cut funds from transportation projects sought by 21 House Republicans who had signed a letter calling for increased Amtrak funding, which Istook opposed. The same year, Republicans were embarrassed by the disclosure of an Istook provision allowing the Appropriations chairman and designated staff to inspect individual tax returns. The following year, Republican leaders stripped Istook of his cardinalship when the number of subcommittees was reduced from 13 to 10.

Istook hammered Henry over illegal immigration, criticizing him for not doing enough to stop the influx and for signing a bill that made Oklahoma high school graduates eligible for in-state college tuition as long as they were working toward legal immigrant status. Istook insisted he would repeal the law, and he ran a radio ad that included a Western-style jingle with the lyrics, "If you sneak across the border, there's some help that you can get in a place called Oklahoma. . . . If you re-elect Brad Henry, he'll never take a stand. Illegal immigration will continue in your land."

Henry defended himself with ads emphasizing that he had instructed the state highway patrol to apprehend illegal immigrants. He maintained that illegal immigration was a federal issue that Congress had failed to address. The two candidates clashed over education, with Istook calling for merit pay for teachers and Henry asserting that teachers' salaries were rising on his watch. Henry outspent Istook and won in a landslide, 67%-33%, making him just the third governor in state history to capture back-to-back terms. He won all but the three Panhandle counties. His rousing victory immediately sparked speculation that Henry would run for the Senate in 2008 against Republican incumbent James Inhofe. But in late 2006, a spokesman for the governor said, "He does not plan to run for the Senate in two years or four years."

In his second term, Henry seemed to get the hang of divided government. He racked up a string of successes in the Legislature, and was given a fair measure of credit for attracting a professional basketball team to the state. In 2008 the Sonics took up his offer of lucrative tax credits, renamed themselves the Thunder and moved from Seattle to Oklahoma City. Henry applied the veto pen smartly. When the Legislature failed to produce a budget to his liking in 2007, he withheld his signature from a tax bill sought by Republican lawmakers until they agreed to some of his budget priorities. Henry won a $1,000-a-year pay increase for teachers and $5 million for programs for children, and he expanded Medicaid eligibility for 42,000 uninsured youngsters. He also secured $10 million for a new biofuels research center as part of his quest to reduce the state's reliance on oil and natural gas as economic mainstays. However, he failed to get the Legislature to agree to an increase in the minimum wage, long on Henry's wish list. And perhaps as a result of the criticism he suffered at Istook's hands in his re-election campaign, Henry signed a Republican bill setting stiff penalties for employers who knowingly hire illegal immigrants.

Senior Senator

James Inhofe (R)

Elected 1994, term expires 2014, 3rd full term; b. Nov. 17, 1934, Des Moines, IA; home, Tulsa; U. of Tulsa, B.A. 1973; Presbyterian; married (Kay); 4 children.

Military Career: Army, 1957–58.

Elected Office: OK House of Reps., 1966–69; OK Senate, 1969–77, Repub. ldr., 1975–77; Tulsa mayor, 1978–84; U.S. House of Reps., 1986–94.

Professional Career: Businessman, land developer, 1962–86.

DC Office: 453 RSOB, 20510, 202-224-4721; Fax: 202-228-0380; Web site: inhofe.senate.gov.

State Offices: Enid, 580-234-5105; McAlester, 918-426-0933; Oklahoma City, 405-608-4381; Tulsa, 918-748-5111.

Committees: *Armed Services* (2nd of 11 R): Airland; Readiness & Management Support; Strategic Forces. *Environment & Public Works* (RMM of 7 R). *Foreign Relations* (8th of 8 R).

Group Ratings

	ADA	ACLU	AFS	LCV	ITIC	NTU	COC	ACU	CFG	FRC
2008	5	21	0	9	40	80	63	96	94	100
2007	10	—	0	0		83	80	100	91	—

National Journal Ratings

	2007 LIB	—	2007 CONS	2008 LIB	—	2008 CONS
Economic	6%	—	93%	9%	—	90%
Social	0%	—	91%	0%	—	79%
Foreign	28%	—	70%	0%	—	84%
Composite	13%	—	87%	9%	—	91%

Key Votes of the 110th Congress

1. Raise CAFE standards	N	5. Make English official language	Y	9. Withdraw troops 3/08	N
2. Expand SCHIP	N	6. Path to citizenship	N	10. Iran guard is terrorist group	Y
3. Cap greenhouse gases	N	7. Fetus is unborn child	Y	11. Increase missile defense $	Y
4. Bail out financial markets	N	8. Prosecute hate crimes	N	12. Overhaul FISA	Y

Election Results

2008 general	James Inhofe (R)	763,375	(57%)	($5,477,730)
	Andrew Rice (D)	527,736	(39%)	($2,868,819)
	Stephen Wallace (I)	55,708	(4%)	
2008 primary	James Inhofe (R)	116,371	(84%)	
	Evelyn Rogers (R)	10,770	(8%)	
	Ted Ryals (R)	7,306	(5%)	

Prior Winning Percentages: 2002 (57%); 1996 (57%); 1994 (55%); 1992 House (53%); 1990 House (56%); 1988 House (53%); 1986 House (55%)

James Inhofe, Oklahoma's senior senator, was first elected to the Senate in 1994. He grew up in Tulsa, served in the Army, and worked in real estate and insurance. Inhofe (*IN hoff*), was elected to the Oklahoma House in 1966, at age 31, and to the Oklahoma Senate in 1969. He ran for governor in 1974 and lost to David Boren, 64%-36%. In 1976, Inhofe ran for the U.S. House against Jim Jones and lost. From 1979 to 1984, he was mayor of Tulsa. He won the heavily Republican 1st District House seat in 1986, when Jones ran unsuccessfully for the Senate, but held it with uninspiring margins. He was hurt by negative publicity from a family business lawsuit and charges of campaign finance irregularities, often leveled by the liberal-leaning *Tulsa World*. Inhofe's greatest achievement in the House was reforming the arcane discharge petition rule. For years, House rules kept secret the names of signers of petitions to force bills stuck in committees to the floor for action; anonymity allowed lawmakers to claim they had worked to bring legislation to the floor when they in fact had done the opposite. That was changed in 1993, and one of the first bills to benefit from the new rules was an aviation liability reform bill, co-sponsored by flying buff Inhofe and limiting the liability of small airplane manufacturers in lawsuits resulting from crashes.

Inhofe jumped into the 1994 Senate race after Boren, a conservative Democrat who carried every precinct in 1990, announced he was retiring to become president of the University of Oklahoma with two years left in his Senate term. The Democratic nominee was moderate Dave McCurdy, a congressman from southwest Oklahoma since 1980 who was favored to win. But in Oklahoma in 1994, the burden of President Clinton's unpopularity among conservatives was too much for McCurdy. He was closely associated with Clinton's policies, having voted for the 1993 budget and tax package and for the 1994 crime bill with its ban on assault weapons. Inhofe won by a solid 55%-40%. In the Senate, Inhofe was president of the conservative-leaning freshman class of 11 senators. In 1996, he was elected to a full six-year term over James Boren, David Boren's cousin, by 57%-40%.

Inhofe has a solidly conservative voting record and is blunt and even acerbic at times. "I'm not afraid of controversy. I'm not afraid to say what's on my mind and what's on a lot of people's minds," he says. He speaks his mind in pungent terms, with his barbs often targeted at his opponents in the green movement. He once accused Clinton environmental protection Administrator Carol Browner of "Gestapo tactics." And in recent years, as the most senior Republican on the Environment and Public Works Committee, he has been a leader of conservatives who deny the existence of a global warming problem caused by humans. In 2003, Inhofe said that the idea that man-made emissions have caused global warming was "the greatest hoax ever perpetrated on the American people."

Inhofe was chairman of the committee from 2003 to 2007. He favored oil drilling in the Arctic National Wildlife Refuge and more oil and gas drilling exploration in the United States generally. He also has low regard for the Endangered Species Act. "America has adopted an attitude that places more value on the life of a critter than on a human being. We want to protect the Arkansas River shiner, a bait fish in Oklahoma, yet we will allow unborn babies to have their brains sucked out in a partial-birth abortion," he once said. He supported President Bush's Clear Skies initiative, but complained that the administration failed to speak out more strongly for it, and the committee deadlocked 9-9 on the bill in 2005. Later that year, after gasoline prices had soared because of Hurricane Katrina, he called for incentives to build refineries at shut-down military bases; the refinery bill also died in his committee, 9-9.

Much of Inhofe's tenure as chairman was devoted to an issue on which he was opposed by the Bush administration and fiscal conservatives—the reauthorization of the transportation act, generally known as the highway bill, one of the main institutional responsibilities of the committee. By early 2004, Inhofe had hammered out agreement in the Senate on a $318 billion transportation bill. House Transportation Committee Chairman Don Young, R-Alaska, was seeking a $375 billion bill, while the Bush administration wanted to cap spending at $256 billion. Inhofe argued that money was needed to maintain the highway system and would be funded entirely by user fees, primarily the gas tax. With bipartisan support, he got the Senate to pass the $318 billion bill, which would have increased Oklahoma spending by 42%, by 76-21. But the White House renewed its veto threat. Meanwhile, Young got the House, cowed by the veto threat, to pass a $275 billion bill. Inhofe was the chairman of the House-Senate conference committee, and his goal was to get a bill passed in 2004. But he could not work out a settlement given the great disparity in funding levels with the House. The political differences were also significant. A goal of Inhofe's bill was to guarantee that every state got 95% of its gas tax money back, but when the total spending was decreased, that meant other states would lose projects. So the issue was deferred to 2005. By that point, Republican leaders were eager to cut a final deal with Bush. Even Inhofe backed a scaled-down version of a transportation bill. In a conference committee with the House, he agreed to a $286 billion bill, though Oklahoma fared well, needless to say.

After Democrats won control of the Senate, Inhofe in January 2007 withstood a backroom challenge from Sen. John Warner of Virginia to become the ranking minority member of the Environment and Public Works Committee. Prospects for his cooperation with incoming Democratic Chairman Barbara Boxer of California were nil. As she talked about the need for action on global warming, Inhofe had this terse response: "Hysteria sells." He spoke out strongly against her bill to impose a mandatory cap on greenhouse gas emissions and challenged activists from former Vice President Al Gore to singer Sheryl Crow to lower their "carbon footprints" to the level of average Americans. When Boxer's proposal died in the Senate in June 2008, he said that it showed "momentum is going our way."

Inhofe is now the second-ranking Republican on the Armed Services Committee, after Sen. John McCain of Arizona. Inhofe has been a strong supporter of missile defense and was one of the leaders of the successful fight to deny Clinton's effort to ratify the Comprehensive Test Ban Treaty. He supported the Bush administration on the Iraq War and argued that the public's skepticism about the war could be attributed to the administration's failure to make a stronger case that there were connections between Iraqi Leader Saddam Hussein and al Qaeda before September 11. In 2006, he called the U.S. military results in Iraq "nothing short of a miracle."

Inhofe has also been a leader in the movement to make English the official language. During the 2006 debate on overhauling immigration policy, Inhofe got the Senate to pass his amendment to make English the national language. "This is not just about preserving our culture and heritage, but also about bettering the odds for our nation's newest potential citizens," he said. When immigration reform returned to the Senate in 2007, Inhofe again was able to get his language amendment passed.

In 2002, Inhofe was re-elected despite a challenge from former Democratic Gov. David Walters, who had years earlier pleaded guilty to a misdemeanor count of violating campaign finance laws. The result was almost identical to those in 1994 and 1996. Inhofe won statewide 57%-36%, with solid margins in metro Oklahoma City (62%-31%) and metro Tulsa (60%-34%) and slightly smaller margins (52%-41%) in the rest of the state. When Democratic Gov. Brad Henry ruled out running against him in 2008, Inhofe looked to be a solid bet for re-election. Democrats eventually settled on state Sen. Andrew Rice as their nominee and tried to portray Inhofe as outside the political mainstream. Early in the campaign, Democrats held out hope that the contest would be competitive. But Rice failed to raise sufficient funds to make it a serious contest. Inhofe won 57%-39%, taking all but four counties in the Muskogee area.

Inhofe has for years regularly flown airplanes and is one of the few certified commercial pilots in Congress. He flew around the world following the historic route of Wiley Post, the first pilot to fly solo around the globe. But he encountered problems in October 2006 when the small plane he was flying spun out of control and suffered significant damage on landing in Tulsa, though he and an aide escaped injury. His penchant for daredevil stunts in the air is well-known around the Capitol, and few of his aides will take him up on his offers of airplane rides.

Junior Senator

Tom Coburn (R)

Elected 2004, term expires 2010, 1st term; b. March 14, 1948, Casper, WY; home, Muskogee; OK St. U., B.S. 1970, OK U., M.D. 1983; Southern Baptist; married (Carolyn); 3 children.

Elected Office: U.S. House of Reps., 1994–2000.

Professional Career: Mgr., Coburn Optical Industries, 1970–78; Practicing physician, 1983–present.

DC Office: 172 RSOB, 20510, 202-224-5754; Fax: 202-224-6008; Web site: coburn.senate.gov.

State Offices: Oklahoma City, 405-231-4941; Tulsa, 918-581-7651.

Committees: *Health, Education, Labor & Pensions* (9th of 10 R). *Homeland Security & Governmental Affairs* (2nd of 6 R): Contracting Oversight; Federal Financial Management, Government Information, Federal Services & International Security; Investigations (Permanent) (RMM). *Indian Affairs* (4th of 6 R). *Intelligence (Select)* (6th of 7 R). *Judiciary* (7th of 7 R): Constitution (RMM); Crime & Drugs; Human Rights & the Law (RMM); Terrorism & Homeland Security.

Group Ratings

	ADA	ACLU	AFS	LCV	ITIC	NTU	COC	ACU	CFG	FRC
2008	0	21	0	9	60	81	75	96	95	100
2007	5	—	0	7	—	89	50	100	97	—

National Journal Ratings

	2007 LIB	—	2007 CONS		2008 LIB	—	2008 CONS
Economic	13%	—	86%		5%	—	94%
Social	20%	—	79%		0%	—	79%
Foreign	9%	—	87%		0%	—	84%
Composite	15%	—	85%		8%	—	92%

Key Votes of the 110th Congress

1. Raise CAFE standards	*	5. Make English official language	Y	9. Withdraw troops 3/08	N
2. Expand SCHIP	N	6. Path to citizenship	N	10. Iran guard is terrorist group	Y
3. Cap greenhouse gases	N	7. Fetus is unborn child	Y	11. Increase missile defense $	Y
4. Bail out financial markets	Y	8. Prosecute hate crimes	N	12. Overhaul FISA	Y

Election Results

2004 general	Tom Coburn (R)	763,433	(53%)	($5,078,647)
	Brad Carson (D)	596,750	(41%)	($6,172,076)
	Sheila Bilyeu (I)	86,663	(6%)	
2004 primary	Tom Coburn (R)	145,974	(61%)	
	Kirk Humphreys (R)	59,877	(25%)	
	Bob Anthony (R)	29,596	(12%)	

Prior Winning Percentages: 1998 House (58%); 1996 House (55%); 1994 House (52%)

Tom Coburn, a Republican who previously served six years in the House, was elected Oklahoma's junior senator in 2004. Coburn grew up in Muskogee, where his father started Coburn Optical Services, which became the town's biggest employer. Coburn graduated from Oklahoma State, and while there, married his childhood sweetheart, who was Miss Oklahoma 1967. His father moved his company to Virginia, and Coburn followed to join the business. These were years of campus and youth rebellions, but not for Coburn. "I was focused on business, kind of driven. I was sort of aloof to the counterculture. I never even heard of marijuana," he says. Coburn took over the lens division of the company and increased sales from $100,000 to $40 million. In 1975, the company was sold to Revlon. After being stricken with melanoma, Coburn decided to go to the University of Oklahoma Medical School. He graduated at age 35, moved to Muskogee, Okla., and opened Maternal and Family Practice Associates. In addition to running his practice, he went on medical missions around the world. In 1994, he read in his local newspaper that Democratic U.S. Rep. Mike Synar from Oklahoma's 2nd District was talking about a greater role for the government in running the health care system, and decided to run against him. As it turned out, Synar lost to a 71-year-old retired middle school teacher in the Democratic primary, and Coburn went on to prevail in the general election, 52%-48%.

Coburn was an outspoken member of "revolutionary" class of Republicans who came to power with House Speaker Newt Gingrich in 1995 determined to make big changes in Washington. He regularly angered appropriators by opposing their bills and offering multiple amendments. A strong opponent of abortion rights, Coburn sponsored bills requiring AIDS counseling for pregnant women and labels on condoms disclosing that they don't prevent infections that lead to cervical cancer. He became known around the Capitol for conducting somewhat graphic slide shows for lawmakers and staff about the effects of sexually transmitted diseases. Eventually, Coburn and a small band of similarly radicalized Republicans got fed up with Gingrich, whom they faulted for poor judgment and for being too accommodating to the Clinton administration. The group tried to oust Gingrich in July 1997, and although the attempt failed, it spelled the beginning of the end for Gingrich, who did not seek re-election as Speaker in 1998. In 2000, Coburn kept his campaign promise to serve only three terms, and did not run for re-election. He went home to his medical practice in Muskogee. He also wrote a book, *Breach of Trust: How Washington Turns Outsiders into Insiders*, in which he called members of Congress "Pharisees" and attacked Republican leaders by name.

In 2003, when Republican Sen. Don Nickles announced that he would not seek a fifth term, several politicians lined up to succeed him—Oklahoma City Mayor Kirk Humphreys and state Corporation Commissioner Bob Anthony, both Republicans, and Rep. Brad Carson, a Democrat who had been elected to Coburn's old House seat in 2000. Coburn was urged by many to run, but declined because of health concerns; he had been treated for colon cancer that year. But Coburn changed his mind, saying he had "an impression in my spiritual life that I was supposed to do this." He observed: "Politically, it's stupid to get into a race six to nine months after everyone's already into it. But it's kind of been one of those things that's marked my life. I learned to be obedient to that still inner voice." (In 2007, Coburn had surgery for the removal of a benign pituitary tumor.)

Leading Republicans already had gotten behind Humphreys, including endorsements from Sens. Nickles and James Inhofe, and Reps. John Sullivan and Tom Cole. Polls showed a close race, with Coburn slightly ahead of Humphreys. Humphreys attacked Coburn for attending a Las Vegas fundraiser, prompting Coburn to return contributions from gambling figures, and also ran an ad attacking Coburn for voting against intelligence and airport spending bills. The anti-tax group Club for Growth, supporting Coburn, replied with ads claiming the bills were loaded with pork barrel spending. Coburn's cultural and fiscal conservatism, his opposition to Washington insiders and his adherence to his House term-limit pledge had earned him fans across the state, and he won the primary with 61% to 25% for Humphreys and 12% for Anthony. Coburn carried 76 of 77 counties.

The winner of the Democratic nomination, with 79% of the primary vote, was Carson, who was part Cherokee and a Southern Baptist and had a sterling resume. He was an honors graduate at Baylor University, a Rhodes Scholar, graduated from law school at Oklahoma, was a White House Fellow, then practiced with a big firm in Oklahoma City before settling in eastern Oklahoma. After replacing Coburn in the 2nd Congressional District, he had one of the most moderate voting records of any House Democrat; he favored gun rights, the death penalty and the war in Iraq. Happy to have a politically adept candidate with a chance in a heavily Republican state, national Democrats eagerly supported him, and Carson raised more money than Coburn.

Coburn described himself as a part-time lawmaker, determined to uphold principle and willing to take on his own party's leadership. Carson described himself as a practical-minded lawmaker, committed to "fight[ing] for Oklahoma" and eager for bipartisanship. Carson was aided by Coburn's penchant for impolitic statements, saying Coburn "already made us a laughingstock all across not only the country but the whole globe." State Democratic Chairman Jay Parmley called Coburn "just flat crazy" and an "extremist." Coburn sought to link Carson to high profile liberals in his party, saying: "Brad Carson is a vote for Ted Kennedy and Hillary Clinton to run the Senate." The race was close going into September, when the most incendiary issue was raised. News broke of a lawsuit, long since settled, by a woman who claimed Coburn in 1990 sterilized her without her consent when operating on her ectopic pregnancy, and then filed a false Medicaid claim. Coburn said the woman gave oral consent and that he'd never sought reimbursement for the sterilization. A Carson ad said Coburn "sterilized an underage girl without her consent," then committed Medicaid fraud "to get paid for the illegal procedure." Coburn charged that Democrats had connived with reporters to raise the issue.

In spite of some negative fallout from the revelations, Coburn won by a solid 53%-41%. Carson carried all but two of the counties in his congressional district and won in some other rural, historically Democratic counties. But Coburn won in the major cities, 56%-37% in the Oklahoma City area and 55%-41% in the Tulsa area. Interestingly, exit polls showed that more voters considered Carson more extreme than Coburn.

In the Senate, Coburn resumed the belligerent politics honed during his House days. He was delighted to discover that Senate rules give any one individual the ability to obstruct proceedings far more than is the case in the House. Coburn said, "I'll be sleeping every night" with the 1,500-page *Riddick's Senate Procedure*. He was a quick study, turning his attention to the nation's "unsustainable course financially," and the need for accountability and transparency in federal spending. He vowed he would not seek earmarks, the special provisions that lawmakers insert into appropriations bills for their home districts and states. And he became a self-appointed taxpayers' watchdog on the Senate floor, often criticizing the earmarks of fellow senators. More than once, he was the only senator opposing passage of an appropriations bill. When he tried to delete $453 million that had been added for two bridges in Alaska, Republican Sen. Ted Stevens of Alaska exploded in anger: "If the Senate decides to discriminate against our state. . . . I will resign from this body," he said. Coburn lost that vote, 82-15, but he felt that he had made his point.

On dollars and cents issues, Coburn can be just as tough on members of his own party as he is on Democrats. He complained that the Bush administration's handling of budget requests for the war in Iraq through "emergency" supplemental spending bills was a phony way to do business. He teamed with Illinois liberal Sen. Barack Obama in 2006 to win enactment of a proposal to create a central database for citizens to track federal grants and contracts. "This bill is a small but significant step toward changing the culture in Washington," he said. Obama talked up their collaboration during his presidential campaign in 2008.

Coburn has established a solidly conservative voting record. Pursuing his interest in health care, he sponsored a bill to fund research of embryonic stem cells so long as the research would not harm a human embryo. He also unveiled a sweeping market-based health care reform package designed to provoke debate, including a malpractice court that would be similar to the workers' compensation system. Coburn challenged the Senate rule that bars senators from earning money practicing medicine. When the Rules and Administration Committee directed him to stop practicing medicine because it was a conflict of interest with his Senate duties, Coburn adamantly objected and insisted that it "will make me a better senator" who understands real world problems. In 2005, on a procedural vote to permit him to see patients without making a profit, Coburn got 51 votes, but that was short of the 60 required to prevail. The result was "a moral victory," he said, and he vowed to continue the fight. He prefers to be called Dr. Coburn.

But many Democrats call him Dr. No. After Democrats took the majority in January 2007, Coburn was aggressive in challenging Senate operations and repeatedly delayed routine measures, infuriating Democratic Majority Leader Harry Reid. When Reid bundled them together in an attempt to pass them, Democrats sarcastically described it as the "Coburn Omnibus Bill." Republicans complained Coburn was being unfairly targeted.

One of Coburn major efforts in recent years is an "A to Z" rewriting of the federal budget, and he joined other Senate Republicans on a "fiscal watch team." He said in 2007, "My intention is not to create ill will. My intention is to follow my oath. . . . How are we affording the government that we have? The answer to that is, we're borrowing from the next two generations. I'd much rather have the ill will of my peers here than place a much larger burden on the next generation."

Democrats believe that they could give Coburn a stiff re-election contest in 2010, especially if popular Gov. Brad Henry runs.

FIRST DISTRICT

John Sullivan (R)

Elected Jan. 2002, 4th full term; b. Jan. 1, 1965, Tulsa; home, Tulsa; Northeastern St. U., B.B.A., 1992; Catholic; married (Judy); 4 children.

Elected Office: OK House of Reps., 1994–2001.

Professional Career: Trucking salesman, 1988–92; Gas and Fleet sales rep., 1991–98; Realtor, 1997–2002.

DC Office: 434 CHOB, 20515, 202-225-2211; Fax: 202-225-9187; Web site: sullivan.house.gov.

State Offices: Bartlesville, 918-336-6500; Tulsa, 918-749-0014.

Committees: *Energy & Commerce* (18th of 23 R): Commerce, Trade & Consumer Protections; Energy & Environment; Oversight & Investigations.

Group Ratings

	ADA	ACLU	AFS	LCV	ITIC	NTU	COC	ACU	CFG	FRC
2008	20	18	14	8	50	68	100	92	73	76
2007	5	—	9	5	—	83	71	100	95	—

National Journal Ratings

	2007 LIB	—	2007 CONS		2008 LIB	—	2008 CONS
Economic	14%	—	85%		22%	—	78%
Social	20%	—	79%		20%	—	74%
Foreign	0%	—	72%		0%	—	95%
Composite	16%	—	84%		16%	—	84%

Key Votes of the 110th Congress

1. Increase minimum wage	N	5. Share immigration data	Y	9. Withdraw troops 8/08	N
2. Expand SCHIP	N	6. Foreign aid abortion ban	*	10. No operations in Iran	N
3. Raise CAFE standards	N	7. Ban gay bias in workplace	N	11. Free trade with Peru	Y
4. Bail out financial markets	Y	8. Repeal D.C. gun law	Y	12. Overhaul FISA	Y

Election Results

2008 general	John Sullivan (R)	193,404	(66%)	($1,171,990)
	Georgianna Oliver (D)	98,890	(34%)	($566,307)
2008 primary	John Sullivan (R)	33,563	(92%)	
	Fran Mo-Ghaddam (R)	3,025	(8%)	

Prior Winning Percentages: 2006 (64%); 2004 (60%); 2002 (56%); 2002 (54%)

Population		Race/Ethnicity		Work	
Pop. 2007:	717,540	White:	71.3%	Private:	82.9%
Change since 2000:	Up 4.0%	Black:	9.3%	Government:	9.9%
Urban:	89.6%	Hispanic:	7.8%	Self-employed:	6.9%
Rural:	10.4%	Asian:	1.7%	Blue collar:	22.6%
Area size:	1,790 sq. mi.	Native Am.:	4.9%	White collar:	61.4%
		Hawaiian:	0.1%	Khaki collar:	0.0%
Age		Two+ races:	4.8%	Other:	15.9%
Median age:	36.1 yrs.			Median income:	$44,610
More than 65 yrs:	12.2%	*Ancestry*		Median home value:	$115,900
Less than 18 yrs:	25.9%	German:	13.2%	Poverty:	14.5%
		Irish:	10.2%		
Education		English:	8.9%	**Military Veterans**	
H.S. grad:	87.4%			% of Pop:	11.5%
College grad:	27.6%				
Grad degree:	8.2%				

The gushers of the 1905 Glenn Pool discovery made Tulsa one of America's oil boomtowns, settled not just by people from the immediate hinterland but also by Midwesterners and New Englanders of Yankee stock. In the 1920s, as its art deco skyscrapers rose on the heights above the Arkansas River, it was still a raw town, but one intent on becoming more cultural. It was optimistic and ready to seek economic change, yet culturally and politically conservative, with a Yankee elite and an American Indian heritage recalled today in one of the nation's best collections of Western art at the Gilcrease Museum—left by oil millionaire Thomas Gilcrease, who was one-eighth Creek Indian. In the decades since, Tulsa has boomed and occasionally busted. The city also is the headquarters of Oral Roberts University and its 60-story City of Faith Hospital. It has remained cosmopolitan but conservative. A travel writer for *The Washington Post* once termed Tulsa "a fine replica of European grandeur." People here do not resent the oil companies or the new rich; they identify with them. In 2003, voters approved the Vision 2025 economic development referendum, a $900 million investment funded by a one-cent sales tax increase, as part of Tulsa's efforts to diversify from being solely one of America's leading petroleum centers. After Citgo Petroleum announced that it was moving its corporate headquarters from Tulsa to Houston, local officials persuaded American Airlines to move its maintenance and engineering center and over 7,000 jobs to Tulsa from Kansas City; that move spurred other aerospace-related development in the city. In 2008, the Salary.com website ranked Tulsa 12th-best among 69 cities for building personal wealth. Plano, Texas came in first, and New York City was last.

The 1st Congressional District of Oklahoma includes Tulsa, Wagoner, and Washington counties, and slices of Rogers and Creek counties—just about all of the Tulsa metropolitan area. The political tradition here is heavily Republican, strengthened in recent decades by opposition to national Democrats' cultural liberalism. Even during the collapse of oil prices in the 1980s, Tulsa maintained its contagious enthusiasm for new business enterprises and innovations. But some business groups worried that the state's strict 2007 law to force out illegal immigrants would cause a loss of workers and hurt Tulsa's economic base.

The congressman from the 1st District is John Sullivan, a Republican who won a January 2002 special election to succeed Steve Largent, who resigned to run for governor. Sullivan grew up in Tulsa and graduated from Northeastern Oklahoma State University. In Tulsa, he worked in the transportation, oil and gas, and real estate industries. In 1994, at age 29, he was elected to the state House, where he served as Republican whip. In the December 2001 primary for the 1st District seat, the best-known candidate was Cathy Keating, wife of Republican Gov. Frank Keating, who enthusiastically backed her campaign.

2008 Presidential Vote

McCain (R)	205,482	(64%)
Obama (D)	114,174	(36%)

2004 Presidential Vote

Bush (R)	206,744	(65%)
Kerry (D)	109,486	(35%)

Cook Partisan Voting Index: R + 16

She had a big fundraising advantage, but she stumbled in the course of the five-week campaign. Sullivan accused her of being too moderate for the conservative district, and she had no legislative record to dispute his claims. Sullivan, meanwhile, built a strong grassroots network among conservative activists. He led the first round of balloting, 46%-30%. Under state law, Sullivan's failure to win 50% entitled Keating to a runoff. But his unexpectedly large lead, plus the unlikelihood that four weeks of additional campaigning over Christmas and New Years would capture voter attention, convinced Keating to drop her candidacy. In January, Sullivan faced the Democratic nominee, Doug Dodd, a Tulsa lawyer and former school board member. Dodd ran a spirited campaign and raised money from organized labor. Even though this is a district that George W. Bush carried with more than 60% of the vote in 2000 and 2004, Sullivan won by only 54%-44%, and national Democrats may have regretted ignoring the race.

Sullivan won a seat on the Energy and Commerce Committee, where oil and gas issues are often front and center. With help from GOP Sen. James Inhofe of Oklahoma, who managed the 2005 highway bill, Sullivan fought for Tulsa's share of highway and transit funds. He sponsored a measure for a monument commemorating the 1921 Tulsa race riot, during which more than 300 people died, but he opposed a proposal to suspend the statute of limitations on families seeking legal damages from the riot. He pushed for tougher controls on illegal immigration, contending that truckloads of illegals have been dumped into Tulsa neighborhoods, and he criticized President Bush for not taking a tougher stand against amnesty for illegal immigrants living in the United States. Although Sullivan is a conservative, he declined to join a conservative-led campaign to ban earmarks, the special projects that lawmakers insert into spending bills for their districts and states. "I don't want to cut myself off from helping my district," he told a local reporter.

Sullivan has slowly tightened his hold on the seat in two campaign rematches against Dodd. In the first one, Sullivan raised his margin of victory to 56%-42%. In 2004, he faced a primary challenge from Bill Wortman, who attacked Sullivan's veracity on several issues and was backed by two disgruntled ex-consultants who complained that Sullivan had failed to pay for their services. Sullivan won 70%-25%. In the fall campaign against Dodd, his challenger focused on the high cost of the "mess" in Iraq and the loss of U.S. jobs to outsourcing, but Sullivan ran as an insider and cited the accomplishments of the Bush administration and the Republican congressional majorities. He won 60%-38%. In 2006, he defeated Bartlesville lawyer Alan Gentges 64% to 31%.

In 2008, Democrat Georgianna Oliver, a Tulsa technology company executive who funded her own campaign, challenged Sullivan's record, charging that he was not attuned to local needs and that he flip-flopped on the bailout bill for financial institutions. Sullivan dismissed Oliver, saying, "I wouldn't know her if she came up to me." With national Democrats busy elsewhere, Oliver had little help from the party, and Sullivan won easily. He gained attention with some quotable comments, such this quip about New York Sen. Hillary Rodham Clinton's presidential bid: "The Clintons are like cockroaches. They could survive a nuclear holocaust." And he had this explanation for filing a workers' compensation claim for injuries—including a blind left eye—he sustained when an aide drove into a barrier while speeding him to a vote at the Capitol. "I am looking at all of my options. I have four children. I may not be in this job forever. What happens then?"

SECOND DISTRICT

Dan Boren (D)

Elected 2004, 3rd term; b. Aug. 2, 1973, Shawnee; home, Muskogee; TX Christian U., B.S. 1997, U. of OK, M.B.A. 2000; Methodist; married (Andrea); 1 child.

Elected Office: OK House of Reps., 2002–04.

Professional Career: Aide, OK Corp. Comm., 1997–98; Loan processor, Banc First Corp., 1999–2000; Staffer, U.S. Rep. Wes Watkins 2000–01.

DC Office: 216 CHOB, 20515, 202-225-2701; Fax: 202-225-3038; Web site: www.house.gov/boren.

State Offices: Claremore, 918-341-9336; Durant, 580-931-0333; McAlester, 918-423-5951; Muskogee, 918-687-2533.

Committees: *Armed Services* (36th of 36 D): Air & Land Forces; Readiness. *Intelligence (Select)* (13th of 13 D): Oversight and Investigations; Terrorism, Human Intelligence, Analysis & Counterintelligence. *Natural Resources* (11th of 29 D): Energy & Mineral Resources; National Parks, Forests & Public Lands.

Group Ratings

	ADA	ACLU	AFS	LCV	ITIC	NTU	COC	ACU	CFG	FRC
2008	65	45	71	69	100	16	78	24	14	70
2007	50	—	44	15	—	24	94	57	19	—

National Journal Ratings

	2007 LIB — 2007 CONS		2008 LIB — 2008 CONS	
Economic	43% —	57%	46% —	54%
Social	43% —	56%	48% —	52%
Foreign	45% —	54%	47% —	52%
Composite	44% —	56%	47% —	53%

Key Votes of the 110th Congress

1. Increase minimum wage	Y	5. Share immigration data	Y	9. Withdraw troops 8/08	N
2. Expand SCHIP	N	6. Foreign aid abortion ban	Y	10. No operations in Iran	N
3. Raise CAFE standards	N	7. Ban gay bias in workplace	*	11. Free trade with Peru	*
4. Bail out financial markets	Y	8. Repeal D.C. gun law	Y	12. Overhaul FISA	Y

Election Results

2008 general	Dan Boren (D)	173,757	(70%)	($960,350)
	Raymond Wickson (R)	72,815	(30%)	
2008 primary	Dan Boren (D)	66,041	(85%)	
	Kevin Coleman (D)	11,438	(15%)	

Prior Winning Percentages: 2006 (73%); 2004 (66%)

Population		Race/Ethnicity		Work	
Pop. 2007:	706,849	White:	69.6%	Private:	72.3%
Change since 2000:	Up 2.4%	Black:	3.8%	Government:	18.6%
Urban:	35.6%	Hispanic:	3.2%	Self-employed:	8.8%
Rural:	64.4%	Asian:	0.4%	Blue collar:	31.3%
Area size:	21,225 sq. mi.	Native Am.:	14.5%	White collar:	49.3%
		Hawaiian:	0.1%	Khaki collar:	0.1%
Age		Two+ races:	8.4%	Other:	19.3%
Median age:	37.9 yrs.			Median income:	$34,328
More than 65 yrs:	15.3%	*Ancestry*		Median home value:	$78,000
Less than 18 yrs:	23.9%	Irish:	11.4%	Poverty:	19.8%
		German:	10.3%		
Education		USA:	8.6%	**Military Veterans**	
H.S. grad:	79.7%			% of Pop:	12.8%
College grad:	14.6%				
Grad degree:	4.9%				

The land that is now northeast Oklahoma used to be Indian territory, the place where in the 1830s the Five Civilized Tribes were driven from Georgia and Alabama over the Trail of Tears. Almost 15% of people here report their race as American Indian, and in some counties, one-third or more say they are part Indian. The Native American identity is highest in the hilly counties just west of the Ozarks of Arkansas, where county names—Cherokee, Osage, Sequoyah—recall the Civilized Tribes.

2008 Presidential Vote

McCain (R)	174,230	(66%)
Obama (D)	91,760	(34%)

2004 Presidential Vote

Bush (R)	166,826	(59%)
Kerry (D)	114,113	(41%)

Cook Partisan Voting Index: R + 14

The street signs in scenic Tahlequah, the Cherokee capital since 1839, are written in both English and Cherokee. The Creek Nation chose its tribal site in Okmulgee in the belief that tornadoes would not strike the area; history has proven the choice correct so far. In the northeast corner of the state, Ottawa County has been home to more Indian tribes than any other county in the nation. This pleasant land of gentle hills and man-made lakes recently has grown at a healthy pace, with the advent of Indian-owned casinos and population spread from Tulsa.

South of Indian country is Oklahoma's Little Dixie, settled between 1889 and 1907 by white Southerners, most of them poor. Some of the county names—LeFlore, Pontotoc—are borrowed straight from Mississippi. Interstate highways and turnpikes connect people to jobs in more-vibrant metropolitan areas, while dam-made lakes have spurred resort and retirement communities. Still, traditional cultural attitudes and folkways remain strong. When Oklahoma voted in 2002 to outlaw cockfighting, voters in many Little Dixie towns turned out in large numbers to oppose the ban.

The 2nd Congressional District includes most of the eastern third of Oklahoma, except for metropolitan Tulsa. It includes Muskogee, which inspired Merle Haggard's song "Okie From Muskogee"; Claremore, Will Rogers's hometown; and McAlester, former House Speaker Carl Albert's home. McAlester, originally a rail center for the coal mining industry, is the site of a massive Army ammunition plant that manufactures non-nuclear bombs (during the war in Iraq, it was forced to add a night shift). The abandoned Tar Creek lead and zinc mines left a destructive legacy, and the region became a huge Superfund site in the 1980s. This area was ancestrally Democratic, but in the 1980s, it trended Republican on cultural issues. In the past decade, voters moved back toward the Democrats. Brad Henry carried every county here in his two races for governor. Al Gore was competitive with a 52%-47% loss to George W. Bush, but John Kerry lost 59%-41%. In 2008, John McCain defeated Barack Obama 66%-34%.

The congressman from the 2nd District is Dan Boren, who was elected in 2004 and hails from one of Oklahoma's prominent political families. His grandfather, Lyle Boren, represented southeastern Oklahoma in Congress from 1937 to 1947. His father, David Boren, a Democrat, was elected governor in 1974 and senator in 1978. David Boren was chairman of the Senate Intelligence Committee before he resigned from Congress in 1994 to become president of the University of Oklahoma. Dan Boren grew up in Shawnee and in Longview, Texas, where he lived with his mother and stepfather. He graduated from Texas Christian University and the University of Oklahoma Business School. He worked as a college fundraiser, as a staffer on the state Corporation Commission, and as a district aide to Republican Rep. Wes Watkins, who represented Little Dixie until he retired in 2002. Based in rural Okfuskee County, Boren ran for the state House in 2002 at age 29, raised $200,000, and unseated a Republican who had switched from the Democratic Party. He became chairman of the Democratic Caucus.

When Boren was still in his first term, the Democratic incumbent in the 2nd Congressional District, Brad Carson, announced he was running for the Senate, and Boren decided to make a play for Carson's seat. The Democratic primary narrowed to a contest between Boren and former district prosecutor Kalyn Free. Boren had the backing of local business and was the more conservative candidate. While he supported abortion rights, he favored restrictions, such as parental consent for minors. Unlike many other Democrats, Boren opposed repeal of the Bush-era tax cuts, and he said he would have voted to authorize the use of force in Iraq. His positions aroused significant opposition from left-leaning interest groups. Several labor unions, environmental groups, and MoveOn.org endorsed Free. EMILY's List poured more than $500,000 into her campaign, but it wasn't enough. Boren won the Democratic primary 58%-36%. In the general election, he won 66%-34% against Republican horse breeder Wayland Smalley.

His voting record places Boren among the most conservative Democrats in the House. He was the only Democrat to oppose limits on prosecutors seeking to review library records in terrorism investigations, and he supported repeal of the federal estate and gift taxes. On the Armed Services Committee, Boren sponsored a bill to ban the use of names and images of military members in anti-war commercial enterprises. Although he sometimes disagreed with the tactics in Iraq, he mostly supported the Bush administration's policies there and in Afghanistan.

Boren won re-election easily in 2006 and 2008. Over the past 30 years, this district has sent young and inexperienced candidates to Washington: Democrat Mike Synar at age 28 in 1978; Republican Tom Coburn, after a career in obstetrics, in 1994; and Democrat Carson at age 33 in 2000. Boren, at age 31 and with only two years in the Legislature, was part of that tradition. He appears to have a safe seat, but he may some day run for governor, as his father did, or for senator, as his two 2nd District predecessors did. Despite considerable support from other Democrats, he dismissed a possible challenge to Republican Sen. James Inhofe in 2008. And he said in November 2008 that he will not run statewide in 2010. He declined to endorse Democratic Nominee Barack Obama for president because, he said, Obama was too liberal.

THIRD DISTRICT

Frank Lucas (R)

Elected May 1994, 8th full term; b. Jan. 6, 1960, Cheyenne; home, Cheyenne; OK St. U., B.S. 1982; Baptist; married (Lynda); 3 children.

Elected Office: OK House of Reps., 1988–94.

Professional Career: Farmer & rancher.

DC Office: 2311 RHOB, 20515, 202-225-5565; Fax: 202-225-8698; Web site: www.house.gov/lucas.

State Offices: Stillwater, 405-624-6407; Woodward, 580-256-5752; Yukon, 405-373-1958.

Committees: *Agriculture* (RMM of 18 R). *Financial Services* (5th of 29 R): Capital Markets, Insurance & Government Sponsored Enterprises; Domestic Monetary Policy & Technology. *Science & Technology* (7th of 17 R): Space & Aeronautics.

Group Ratings

	ADA	ACLU	AFS	LCV	ITIC	NTU	COC	ACU	CFG	FRC
2008	15	18	17	0	43	65	89	96	84	100
2007	10	—	0	0	—	71	85	100	81	—

National Journal Ratings

	2007 LIB	—	2007 CONS	2008 LIB	—	2008 CONS
Economic	20%	—	80%	20%	—	80%
Social	21%	—	75%	27%	—	71%
Foreign	0%	—	72%	13%	—	84%
Composite	19%	—	81%	21%	—	79%

Key Votes of the 110th Congress

1. Increase minimum wage	N	5. Share immigration data	Y	9. Withdraw troops 8/08	N
2. Expand SCHIP	N	6. Foreign aid abortion ban	Y	10. No operations in Iran	N
3. Raise CAFE standards	*	7. Ban gay bias in workplace	N	11. Free trade with Peru	Y
4. Bail out financial markets	N	8. Repeal D.C. gun law	Y	12. Overhaul FISA	Y

Election Results

2008 general	Frank Lucas (R)	184,306	(70%)	($644,446)
	Frankie Robbins (D)	62,297	(24%)	($28,612)
	Forrest Michael (I)	17,756	(7%)	($73,167)
2008 primary	Frank Lucas (R)	unopposed		

Prior Winning Percentages: 2006 (67%); 2004 (82%); 2002 (76%); 2000 (59%); 1998 (65%); 1996 (64%); 1994 (70%); 1994 (54%)

Population		Race/Ethnicity		Work	
Pop. 2007:	699,329	White:	79.2%	Private:	70.6%
Change since 2000:	Up 1.3%	Black:	3.8%	Government:	19.6%
Urban:	50.7%	Hispanic:	6.5%	Self-employed:	9.2%
Rural:	49.3%	Asian:	1.1%	Blue collar:	27.5%
Area size:	34,384 sq. mi.	Native Am.:	5.3%	White collar:	53.4%
Age		Hawaiian:	0.1%	Khaki collar:	0.4%
Median age:	36.9 yrs.	Two+ races:	4.0%	Other:	18.8%
More than 65 yrs:	14.1%	*Ancestry*		Median income:	$40,014
Less than 18 yrs:	23.7%	German:	16.4%	Median home value:	$83,000
Education		Irish:	11.1%	Poverty:	16.7%
H.S. grad:	84.0%	USA:	8.9%	**Military Veterans**	
College grad:	19.7%			% of Pop:	12.0%
Grad degree:	6.4%				

Settled just a century ago, western Oklahoma is a fertile land forever at the mercy of the elements. The western plains are scorching hot under the summer sun and blown frozen by bitter winter winds. Visitors to the Tallgrass Prairie Preserve, maintained by the Nature Conservancy near Pawhuska, can experience what settlers found when they arrived here: a swaying ocean of 10-foot-high grasses filled with insects emitting a dull, incessant roar. One can still get a sense of what the old towns looked like. In

2008 Presidential Vote

McCain (R)	210,074	(73%)
Obama (D)	78,426	(27%)

2004 Presidential Vote

Bush (R)	209,598	(72%)
Kerry (D)	82,670	(28%)

Cook Partisan Voting Index: R + 24

1910, three years after statehood, Oklahoma moved its capital south 25 miles, from Guthrie to Oklahoma City, leaving behind what has become one of the nation's largest historic preservation districts. Many rural counties here are not much more populated than they were 100 years ago, when the land was virgin sod. Far fewer people live here than did before the Dust Bowl days in the 1930s, and fewer than during the Anadarko Basin oil and natural-gas boom of the 1970s. Today, local entrepreneurs see the possibility of economic revival in another abundant natural resource: the wind. The region is one of the windiest parts of America and is being billed locally as the "Saudi Arabia of wind." It is also home to the world's largest plot of switchgrass, and there are hopes that the grass too can be turned into a profitable source of alternative energy at the new cellulosic ethanol production plant near Guymon.

The 3rd Congressional District includes Oklahoma's western plains and nearly half of the state's land, from the Panhandle to the northern fringes of Oklahoma City. The 3rd extends to north central Oklahoma, including Ponca City, the university town of Stillwater, and Osage County, site of the state's lone Indian reservation. A few of the southern counties, settled by farmers crossing the Red River from Texas, are ancestrally Democratic. But farmers coming south from Kansas settled most of these plains, and they always have been heavily Republican. In Kingfisher County, George W. Bush won by more than 3-to-1 in 2004, and John McCain trounced Barack Obama there 84%-16% in 2008. Farther west in the Panhandle is Beaver County, which claims to be the cow-chip-throwing capital of the world, and Texas and Cimarron counties; they are the only three counties that Democratic Gov. Brad Henry failed to carry in his landslide re-election in 2006. Few blacks live in this part of Oklahoma, but an increasing number of Hispanics are moving here to work on hog farms and in meatpacking plants.

The congressman from the 3rd District is Frank Lucas, a Republican chosen in a 1994 special election that prefigured the GOP's historic takeover of the House later that year. Lucas' family roots in western Oklahoma extend more than 100 years; he owns a farm and cattle ranch in Roger Mills County and was elected to the Oklahoma House in 1988, at age 28. He got his chance to run for Congress when Glenn English, a 19-year conservative Democrat, resigned to head the National Rural Electric Cooperative Association. Lucas had serious competition in both the primary and the general election. In the initial voting in the primary, he trailed state Sen. Brooks Douglass, who campaigned from his Oklahoma City base, 36%-34%. In the runoff, Lucas ridiculed "some Johnny-come-lately dressed up like a drugstore cowboy" and carried all of the rural areas to win 56%-44%. In the general, he faced Dan Webber, the 27-year-old press secretary to former U.S. Sen. David Boren. Lucas ran an ad depicting the U.S. Capitol and saying, "This is where Dan Webber has worked his entire adult life." The ad also displayed a picture of Oklahoma farmland and said, "This is where Frank Lucas has worked his entire adult life." Lucas won 54%-46%. Since then, he has been re-elected by wide margins.

Lucas' voting record is mostly conservative, but less so on cultural issues. His main focus is the pragmatic work of the Agriculture Committee, where he became the ranking Republican in the 111th Congress (2009–10), taking over from the term-limited Rep. Bob Goodlatte, a Republican from Virginia. Lucas says he wants to stay in Congress long enough to become chairman of the committee, where he has had a large role in writing the last two farm bills. As the chairman of an Agriculture subcommittee during the drafting of the 2002 bill, he helped to unravel the 1996 Freedom to Farm Act and its attack on government subsidies, although he had once embraced the law and its conservative philosophical underpinnings. Lucas helped write provisions to control erosion, aid farmers hit by drought, and protect air and water quality. He successfully fought a plan to reduce the number of Farm Service Agency field offices. In the minority party during the work on the 2008 farm bill, Lucas strongly opposed an overhaul of farm programs as "a threat to the nutrition of the whole, entire world," and he mostly succeeded in preserving subsidies for his district, which ranked 15th in the amount of subsidies it receives.

Also with an eye on his district, Lucas helped to write the final provisions in the 2005 energy bill governing rural grants and biodiesel tax credits. He remains a proponent of government support for alternative fuels, particularly switchgrass. As the representative at the time of the site of the Oklahoma City bombing, he introduced the resolution condemning it and the bill to authorize the bombing monument and make it part of the national park system.

Back home, Lucas's main challenge is the physical size of the district. From his home in Cheyenne, it extends 80 miles south, 240 miles west to the Panhandle, and 270 miles east to Tulsa's outskirts—more than 34,000 square miles in total. But the real trouble for the easygoing Lucas seems to be on his ranch, which he operates. He broke his nose years ago when a cow slammed a gate on him, and he lost a tooth while trying to attach an identification tag to a 250-pound heifer.

FOURTH DISTRICT

Tom Cole (R)

Elected 2002, 4th term; b. April 28, 1949, Shreveport, LA; home, Moore; Grinnell Col., B.A. 1971, Yale U., M.A. 1974, U. of OK, Ph.D. 1984; Methodist; married (Ellen); 1 child.

Elected Office: OK Senate, 1988–91.

Professional Career: OK GOP Chmn., 1985–89; Exec. dir. NRCC, 1991–95; OK secy. of state, 1995–99; Pol. consultant, 2000–2002.

DC Office: 2458 RHOB, 20515, 202-225-6165; Fax: 202-225-3512; Web site: cole.house.gov.

State Offices: Ada, 580-436-5375; Lawton, 580-357-2131; Norman, 405-329-6500.

Committees: *Appropriations* (23rd of 23 R): Interior, Environment & Related Agencies; Labor, HHS, Education & Related Agencies; Legislative Branch.

Group Ratings

	ADA	ACLU	AFS	LCV	ITIC	NTU	COC	ACU	CFG	FRC
2008	10	18	14	8	50	57	94	88	67	94
2007	10	—	9	0	—	73	84	100	86	—

National Journal Ratings

	2007 LIB	—	2007 CONS		2008 LIB	—	2008 CONS
Economic	18%	—	81%		13%	—	86%
Social	9%	—	85%		30%	—	70%
Foreign	0%	—	72%		19%	—	79%
Composite	15%	—	85%		21%	—	79%

Key Votes of the 110th Congress

1. Increase minimum wage	N	5. Share immigration data	Y	9. Withdraw troops 8/08	N
2. Expand SCHIP	N	6. Foreign aid abortion ban	Y	10. No operations in Iran	N
3. Raise CAFE standards	*	7. Ban gay bias in workplace	N	11. Free trade with Peru	Y
4. Bail out financial markets	Y	8. Repeal D.C. gun law	Y	12. Overhaul FISA	Y

Election Results

2008 general	Tom Cole (R) 180,080	(66%)	($1,116,842)
	Blake Cummings (D) 79,674	(29%)	($12,369)
	David Joyce (I) 13,027	(5%)	
2008 primary	Tom Cole (R) .... unopposed		

Prior Winning Percentages: 2006 (65%); 2004 (78%); 2002 (54%)

Population		Race/Ethnicity		Work	
Pop. 2007:	728,895	White:	76.0%	Private:	69.0%
Change since 2000:	Up 5.6%	Black:	6.7%	Government:	24.0%
Urban:	63.3%	Hispanic:	5.7%	Self-employed:	6.8%
Rural:	36.7%	Asian:	2.0%	Blue collar:	23.7%
Area size:	10,409 sq. mi.	Native Am.:	5.0%	White collar:	56.9%
		Hawaiian:	0.1%	Khaki collar:	2.5%
Age		Two+ races:	4.4%	Other:	16.9%
Median age:	34.9 yrs.			Median income:	$43,569
More than 65 yrs:	12.2%	*Ancestry*		Median home value:	$99,200
Less than 18 yrs:	24.9%	USA:	13.1%	Poverty:	14.1%
		German:	12.6%		
Education		Irish:	10.8%	**Military Veterans**	
H.S. grad:	86.1%			% of Pop:	14.1%
College grad:	22.0%				
Grad degree:	7.6%				

In the years after 1900, the brown hills west of Oklahoma City and north of the Red River suddenly filled up with farmers riding north from Texas, past the quenched green lands of the east toward the bare pasture lands of the west. The first settlers here arrived just as the buffalo were dying out, from an estimated 60 million animals to no more than 1,000. So in 1901, Republican President William McKinley established the nation's first wildlife preserve in the Wichita Mountains, 25 miles northwest

2008 Presidential Vote

McCain (R)............................200,353	(67%)
Obama (D) 101,115	(33%)

2004 Presidential Vote

Bush (R)................................194,977	(67%)
Kerry (D)................................96,100	(33%)

Cook Partisan Voting Index: R + 18

of Lawton. Fifteen bison were donated by the New York Zoological Society and arrived at the preserve via rail in 1907—a major factor in the survival of the species. Today this habitat supports grazing for Rocky Mountain elk, white-tailed deer and Texas longhorn cattle. Government has played a role in the survival of the people, too. Population in southwest Oklahoma clusters around major government institutions: the state capital in Oklahoma City; the University of Oklahoma in Norman, which was the world's first school of petroleum geology; Tinker Air Force Base in southern Oklahoma City; the Army Field Artillery School at Fort Sill in Lawton. Sill also is the new home of the Army Air Defense Artillery School, which was relocated from Fort Bliss, Texas.

The 4th Congressional District of Oklahoma begins a few miles from the capitol in Oklahoma City, smack dab in the middle of the state, and proceeds south and west to cover half of Oklahoma's Red River Valley. Demographically, this district is becoming more suburban, but the cultural tone remains countrified. That is true even in the Oklahoma City suburbs, where in new subdivisions people still prefer chicken-fried steak to stir-fried chicken and watermelons from Rush Springs. Ancestrally, this is Democratic country, but Norman, Lawton and the Oklahoma City fringe have voted solidly Republican since the 1990s.

The congressman from the 4th District is Tom Cole, a Republican first elected in 2002 after a long career working for other politicians. With the retirement of Republican Sen. Ben Nighthorse Campbell of Colorado in 2004, Cole became the only American Indian in Congress and a leading defender of Indian interests in Washington. He grew up in Moore, south of Oklahoma City and north of Norman. He is a fifth-generation Oklahoman, and his mother was a state representative and senator. He's also a member of the Chickasaw Nation tribe; more than half of the nation's Chickasaw Indians live in the district. Cole's father served in the Air Force and later worked at Tinker Air Force Base. Cole graduated from Grinnell College, got a master's degree at Yale University and a Ph.D. in British history at the University of Oklahoma, studying for a year at the University of London. From 1985 to 1989, he was the Oklahoma Republican Party chairman. In 1988, he was elected to the state Senate. He moved to Washington in 1991 to become executive director of the National Republican Congressional Committee, then returned to Oklahoma and was appointed secretary of state, becoming the first Republican to hold that office. He went back to Washington to serve as the chief of staff for the Republican National Committee during the 2000 presidential campaign. During much of that period, he was also the president of a polling and political consulting firm in Oklahoma City.

In 2002, Rep. J.C. Watts, a member of the House leadership as chairman of the Republican Conference, announced that he would not seek re-election. Cole moved quickly to run. Despite his party connections and an endorsement from Watts, he faced formidable opposition from attorney Marc Nuttle. The two shared positions on most issues and extensive party connections. Nuttle had been Cole's predecessor at the NRCC, and had worked on Republican Pat Robertson's 1988 presidential campaign. Nuttle and Cole also had worked together to pass an Oklahoma right-to-work law in a 2001 referendum. In the showdown between the strategists, Cole won 60%-33%. He had tough competition in the general election, from former state Senate Majority Leader Darryl Roberts, who appealed to the "yellow dog" Democratic tradition that is particularly strong in the Red River counties. Cole countered by linking Roberts to all of the past Democratic presidential nominees he had supported, and described him as "pro-tax," "pro-abortion" and "pro-lawsuit." Roberts had only limited national party support compared to Cole and Cole won 54%-46%.

In the House, Cole has a mostly conservative voting record. He began his House career on the Armed Services Committee, a seat of obvious importance to the district, before leaving the panel in 2005 to serve on the Rules Committee, which launched him on a career in leadership. He has been actively involved in issues related to American Indians and has urged tribal leaders to educate Americans about the importance of Indian sovereignty. In the wake of an influence-peddling scandal involving Republican lobbyist Jack Abramoff, who represented several tribes, Cole strongly opposed proposed limits on the right of tribes to contribute to political campaigns. In 2008, he accused the chairman of the House Financial Services Committee of "legislative blackmail" for delaying an Indian housing bill unless a provision was added to punish the Cherokee nation for a long-running tribal conflict. As a member of the House ethics committee in 2005, Cole excused himself from a high-profile investigation of Majority Leader Tom DeLay to avoid an appearance of impropriety; he had previously contributed to DeLay's legal defense fund.

Following the dismal 2006 election for Republicans, Cole was elected by his peers to be chairman of the NRCC, the fifth-ranking GOP leadership job and one that put him in charge of national Republican efforts to regain the party's majority in the House in 2008. Cole defeated Texan Pete Sessions, 102 to 81, to take over the committee, where he'd cut his teeth as a political strategist years before. He vowed to expand the playing field of competitive seats and proclaimed that 2008 "will be a year to hunt with a shotgun, not a rifle." His initial targets were the 30 freshman Democrats who defeated or replaced retiring House Republicans in 2006, handing control of the chamber to the Democrats. "It's hard to imagine a cycle that will be worse" than 2006, Cole said. But conditions got much worse, and his two-year chairmanship became a nightmare. "The hits keep on coming," he lamented in May 2008, after Republicans in the prior two months unexpectedly lost three special elections for seats that had been held by prominent Republicans, that of former Speaker Dennis Hastert in Illinois, Richard Baker in Louisiana, and Roger Wicker in Mississippi.

Cole faced myriad problems: The party had had a rough transition to the minority after a dozen years in control, the committee was $19 million in debt, and there were an inordinate number of GOP retirements. Plus, the committee had a huge fundraising disparity with the Democratic Congressional Campaign Committee. Cole and the Republicans raised $116 million in the 2007–2008 election cycle, compared to $171 million for the Democrats. On top of all that the committee had internal problems, notably the discovery that its longtime treasurer had embezzled hundreds of thousands of dollars. Retiring Rep. Tom Davis of Virginia, a former NRCC chairman himself, circulated a memo warning that the party's campaign apparatus was badly broken and its message "stale" and "obsolete." But the biggest obstacle was largely out of Cole's control: Bush's abysmally low public-approval ratings, which made re-election an uphill climb for most Republicans, despite their efforts to distance themselves from the president.

Before long, the relationship between Cole and Minority Leader John Boehner deteriorated, with public sniping and second-guessing over who was to blame for the party's failure to gain traction in House contests. Boehner believed that Cole's top staffers at the NRCC were not sufficiently aggressive at fundraising and candidate recruitment. He created an advisory group to look over Cole's shoulder at the committee. Even in the absence of a spiraling political decline, the two men might not have gotten along. Sessions, the man Cole defeated for the job, was a Boehner ally. And Cole had publicly backed Republican

Rep. Roy Blunt of Missouri over Boehner in the bitterly contested race for majority leader in 2006, an event that left long-lasting enmity among Republican colleagues.

The results of 2008 were disappointing for Cole, to say the least. Republicans lost rather than gained seats in the House, winding up at a 257-178 disadvantage. Nevertheless, after the election, Cole decided to seek re-election to another two years as NRCC chairman. He noted that the losses could have been considerably worse and that the party was well-positioned for gains in 2010. "House Republicans performed far better than expectations, holding losses down in what was the worst political environment many of us have ever experienced," he wrote in a post-election memo to his colleagues. Once again, Sessions was seeking the post, with the active support of Boehner. Sensing he could well lose the showdown this time when the decision went to a vote by all House Republicans, Cole withdrew. In a gesture of conciliation, Boehner gave him a seat on the powerful Appropriations Committee in 2009.

FIFTH DISTRICT

Mary Fallin (R)

Elected 2006, 2nd term; b. Dec. 9, 1954, Warrensburg, MO; home, Oklahoma City; Attended OK Baptist U., OK St. U., B.S. 1977, attended U. of Central OK; Christian; divorced; 2 children.

Elected Office: OK House of Reps., 1990–94; Lt. Gov., 1994–2006.

Professional Career: OK Dept. of Tourism and Rec., OK Securities Comm., OK Office of Personnel Mgt., 1977–82; Hotel mkting. and mgt., 1983–90.

DC Office: 1432 LHOB, 20515, 202-225-2132; Fax: 202-226-1463; Web site: fallin.house.gov.

State Offices: Oklahoma City, 405-234-9900; Shawnee, 405-273-1733.

Committees: *Armed Services* (20th of 25 R): Air & Land Forces; Military Personnel; Readiness. *Small Business* (7th of 12 R): Contracting & Technology; Investigations & Oversight (RMM). *Transportation & Infrastructure* (24th of 30 R): Aviation; Economic Development, Public Buildings & Emergency Management; Highways & Transit.

Group Ratings

	ADA	ACLU	AFS	LCV	ITIC	NTU	COC	ACU	CFG	FRC
2008	15	18	14	8	57	60	94	92	72	100
2007	5	—	0	0	—	75	85	100	88	—

National Journal Ratings

	2007 LIB	—	2007 CONS		2008 LIB	—	2008 CONS
Economic	14%	—	85%		19%	—	80%
Social	9%	—	85%		31%	—	62%
Foreign	0%	—	72%		13%	—	84%
Composite	14%	—	87%		23%	—	77%

Key Votes of the 110th Congress

1. Increase minimum wage	N	5. Share immigration data	Y	9. Withdraw troops 8/08	N
2. Expand SCHIP	N	6. Foreign aid abortion ban	Y	10. No operations in Iran	N
3. Raise CAFE standards	N	7. Ban gay bias in workplace	N	11. Free trade with Peru	Y
4. Bail out financial markets	Y	8. Repeal D.C. gun law	Y	12. Overhaul FISA	Y

Election Results

2008 general	Mary Fallin (R)	171,925	(66%)	($1,081,684)
	Steven Perry (D)	88,996	(34%)	
2008 primary	Mary Fallin (R)	unopposed		

Prior Winning Percentages: 2006 (60%)

Population		Race/Ethnicity		Work	
Pop. 2007:	724,316	White:	64.5%	Private:	76.3%
Change since 2000:	Up 5.0%	Black:	13.0%	Government:	16.2%
Urban:	87.5%	Hispanic:	11.3%	Self-employed:	7.2%
Rural:	12.5%	Asian:	2.9%	Blue collar:	21.8%
Area size:	2,089 sq. mi.	Native Am.:	3.6%	White collar:	60.5%
		Hawaiian:	0.1%	Khaki collar:	0.4%
Age		Two+ races:	4.5%	Other:	17.4%
Median age:	34.9 yrs.			Median income:	$39,322
More than 65 yrs:	12.5%	*Ancestry*		Median home value:	$103,600
Less than 18 yrs:	26.0%	German:	11.8%	Poverty:	17.8%
		Irish:	9.5%		
Education		English:	7.9%	**Military Veterans**	
H.S. grad:	83.7%			% of Pop:	11.9%
College grad:	27.2%				
Grad degree:	9.1%				

Oklahoma City, like many state capitals, was not the spontaneous creation of commerce but the deliberate creation of government, sited in the geographic center of the state on what turned out to be oil land. Rigs were pumping crude on the grounds of the Capitol until 1989, and a derrick still stands sentinel outside the governor's window. The land here is browner and more eroded by creeks than the rolling Oklahoma farmland farther east. From its center, Oklahoma City has grown far out into the countryside, and, as has happened in so many southwestern cities, its limits expanded so that the city now extends into four counties and three congressional districts, and covers 621 square miles. The capital captured worldwide attention in April 1995 when a bomb destroyed the Alfred P. Murrah Federal Building, killing 168 people and injuring more than 500. The profound grief here was channeled into the construction of the Oklahoma City National Memorial on the site of the blast, movingly dedicated exactly five years later in April 2000. In 2006, fueled by the oil boom and sales tax revenues, the city moved to rebuild its downtown with condominiums, a baseball stadium, and a canal through the Bricktown area. The revival was set back by the closing of a General Motors assembly plant the same year. But overall, the area's soaring farm commodities prices have helped to keep the economy strong while much of the nation moved toward recession. Local pride spiked in October 2008 when the Seattle SuperSonics of the National Basketball Association relocated to the city and became the Oklahoma City Thunder, the state's first major sports franchise.

The 5th Congressional District includes Oklahoma City and all but a small section of Oklahoma County where Midwest City and Tinker Air Force Base are located. It also takes in Pottawatomie and Seminole counties to the east. These two counties partake of the ancestral Democratic leanings of most of Oklahoma. But Oklahoma City is solidly Republican in state and national politics, and Oklahoma County casts about 90% of the district's votes.

The congresswoman from the 5th District is Republican Mary Fallin, first elected in 2006. She was born in Missouri but raised in Tecumseh; her mother and father were Democrats and each served as mayor of the town. After graduating from Oklahoma State University, Fallin managed hotel properties and was a commercial real estate broker. In 1990, she was elected to the state House, where she championed victims' rights and health care reform. She became lieutenant governor four years later, making her the first Republican and the first woman to hold the office in Oklahoma. During her three terms as lieutenant governor, she expanded her reach well beyond the office's traditional ribbon-cutting responsibilities. With a focus on economic development, she compiled a pro-business record and played a key role in bringing the right-to-work issue to a successful statewide vote. But in 2005, she failed to get the Democratic-controlled Senate to overhaul the state worker compensation system. Her star had dimmed a bit in 1998 when, in the course of a bitter divorce, she was accused of having a sexual relationship with a state trooper assigned to her security detail; both of them denied the charge. Democrats used the scandal to attack Republican Gov. Frank Keating for refusing to criticize Fallin, even though he had earlier been a vocal critic of President Clinton's sexual relationship with White House intern Monica Lewinsky.

In June 2005, Fallin announced that she would seek a fourth term as lieutenant governor. But she changed her mind when GOP Rep. Ernest Istook decided to relinquish his House seat and run for governor. She joined a wide-open primary race for Istook's seat as one of six Republican candidates. Her chief opponents were state Corporation Commissioner Denise Bode and Oklahoma City Mayor Mick Cornett. Bode's Republican credentials were suspect because she was a former aide to U.S. Sen. David Boren, a Democrat. Cornett had the backing of Christian conservatives, who were pleased that the mayor had removed gay-themed books from the children's section of public libraries. In the initial July balloting, Fallin led with 35% and Cornett's base in Oklahoma City propelled him to a second-place finish with 24%.

2008 Presidential Vote
McCain (R) 170,027 (59%)
Obama (D) 117,019 (41%)

2004 Presidential Vote
Bush (R) 181,644 (64%)
Kerry (D) 101,595 (36%)

Cook Partisan Voting Index: R + 13

Bode came in third with 19%. Fallin and Cornett competed in an August runoff. The two candidates had few differences on the issues, but Fallin had a big fundraising advantage. She defeated Cornett, 63%-37%, even though Oklahoma County cast 93% of the vote. In this solidly Republican district, the general election was an afterthought. Against Oklahoma City physician David Hunter, Fallin won 60%-37% to become the first woman sent to Washington by Oklahoma since 1922.

In the House, Fallin quickly established her bona fides as an ardent conservative, and she sought leadership roles as a freshman. In June 2007, she saw her first bill passed in the House: a revamping of federal grants for women's business centers. She joined a group of 38 Republicans who staked out negotiating positions in opposition to the Democrats' proposal to expand the State Children's Health Insurance Program. In July 2008, she was part of a House Republican delegation that traveled to Alaska to try to bolster the case for oil drilling in the Arctic National Wildlife Refuge. Fallin became politically active on the executive committee of the National Republican Congressional Committee, which fellow Oklahoman Tom Cole chaired. In the 2008 presidential contest, she was an enthusiastic backer of Alaska Gov. Sarah Palin as the GOP vice presidential nominee, calling her "an excellent model for other women." Fallin took a vocal role in defending Palin against attacks by Democrats. At home, Fallin was re-elected easily in 2008 and is a contender for governor in 2010.

★ OREGON ★

L ong an American outpost on the Pacific Rim, Oregon prides itself on being an experimental common-wealth and a laboratory of reform, a maker of national trends. It is far removed from where most Americans live but has made its mark on the rest of the nation nonetheless. Oregon has led the way with bike trails and Nike sneakers, light-rail trams and Pendleton shirts. In public policy, it was first to sanction assisted suicide and to adopt mail-in ballot elections. Oregon is an affluent, high-tech civilization where one can still see much the same land that Lewis and Clark saw in 1805 when they came down the Columbia River gorge, past the Willamette River, to the vast Pacific Ocean.

Oregon was settled by Americans when John Jacob Astor set up his fur trading post at Astoria in 1811. New England Yankees in the 1840s rode the Oregon Trail and floated down the Columbia to the well-watered Willamette Valley. In this remote land, nearly 2,000 miles from the Mississippi River frontier and 700 miles from the small Mexican settlements in California, they built an orderly, productive society—a kind of western New England. It grew steadily, with a few booms—in the early 1900s as timber harvesting surged, during the world war years, and then again in the 1970s, when home building skyrocketed and Oregon's natural environment began to be widely appreciated.

Oregon leaders since Republican Gov. Tom McCall in the 1970s have warned against population growth, but the state has grown significantly over the past two decades. In the 1990s, newcomers filled Portland's postmodern skyscrapers, the high-tech offices in Silicon Forest to the west, and the smaller cities and towns of the green Willamette Valley. More recently, the fastest growth has been east of the Cascades, around Bend, as land-use restrictions limited growth in the Portland area. Nearly 40 percent of Oregon's population increase since 2000 has been accounted for by Hispanics, who now make up 10% of the state's population, far more than blacks (2%), American Indians (1%), and Asians (3.5%). Despite brisk population growth, Oregon has also had setbacks. Lumber production was sharply curtailed in the 1990s (though Oregon is still No. 1 in Christmas trees), and the high-tech bust of 2000–03 hit the state hard. Unemployment was the highest of any state, peaking at 8.1% in February 2002. State government revenues, heavily dependent on the income tax (Oregon has no sales tax), fell sharply, and voters twice, in 2003 and 2004, rejected income-tax increases sought by Democratic Govs. John Kitzhaber and Ted Kulongoski.

Its Yankee settlers brought town meeting-style government to Oregon. This was the first state to give people direct decision-making via the initiative and referendum; it pioneered recall of elected officials and the election of U.S. senators by popular vote; and it was the first state to institute Labor Day. Over the years, Oregon has had more ballot propositions than any other state. The November 2000 ballot had no fewer than 26 initiatives, more than any state since North Dakota in 1932, and the voters' guide ran 376 pages. A comparatively small 12 measures were on the November 2008 ballot, with a voters' guide of a modest 156 pages.

In recent decades, Oregon, founded by New England churchmen, has become America's most non-churchgoing state, with the lowest rate of church membership—in the 2008 exit poll, 31% of voters said their religion was "other" or "none" —and large numbers of believers in astrology and New Age spiritualism. Oregon's public institutions, like those in New England, have been friendly to the innovations of the cultural Left. Over the last two generations, the state produced the first bottle-deposit law, decriminalized medical marijuana, legalized most abortions before the U.S. Supreme Court's *Roe v. Wade* decision, and backed limits on land development and use of property. It is one of two states that ban self-service gas; the other is New Jersey. The 2007 Legislature, controlled by Democrats, imposed limits on smoking, banned discrimination on the basis of sexual orientation, and instituted mandatory recycling of discarded electronics materials.

Oregon legalized assisted suicide, in referenda in 1994 and 1997, to the point that doctors can prescribe but not administer lethal drugs. U.S. Attorney General John Ashcroft angered many Oregonians by announcing in 2001 that the federal government would prosecute doctors prescribing lethal drugs. A federal judge quickly blocked that decision, and the Supreme Court ruled 6-3 in January 2006 that the federal government had overstepped its powers. Another innovation was Kitzhaber's Oregon Health Plan that went into effect in 1994. State Medicaid officials drew up lists of some 700 medical treatments and ranked them by effectiveness and importance to basic health. Then, based on cost estimates, the state decided how many treatments it could afford to pay.

The state also has been more receptive than most to gay couples. The Multnomah County Commission chairwoman ordered clerks to issue marriage licenses to same-sex couples in 2004. Then, across Oregon, petitions were quickly circulated to put the issue on the ballot. A record 244,000 signatures were filed in July, far more than the 108,000 required, and Oregon was clearly the most culturally liberal state voting on the issue that year. Despite $2.9 million spent against the ballot measure, it passed 57%-43%. Later, in 2007, the Legislature endorsed civil unions.

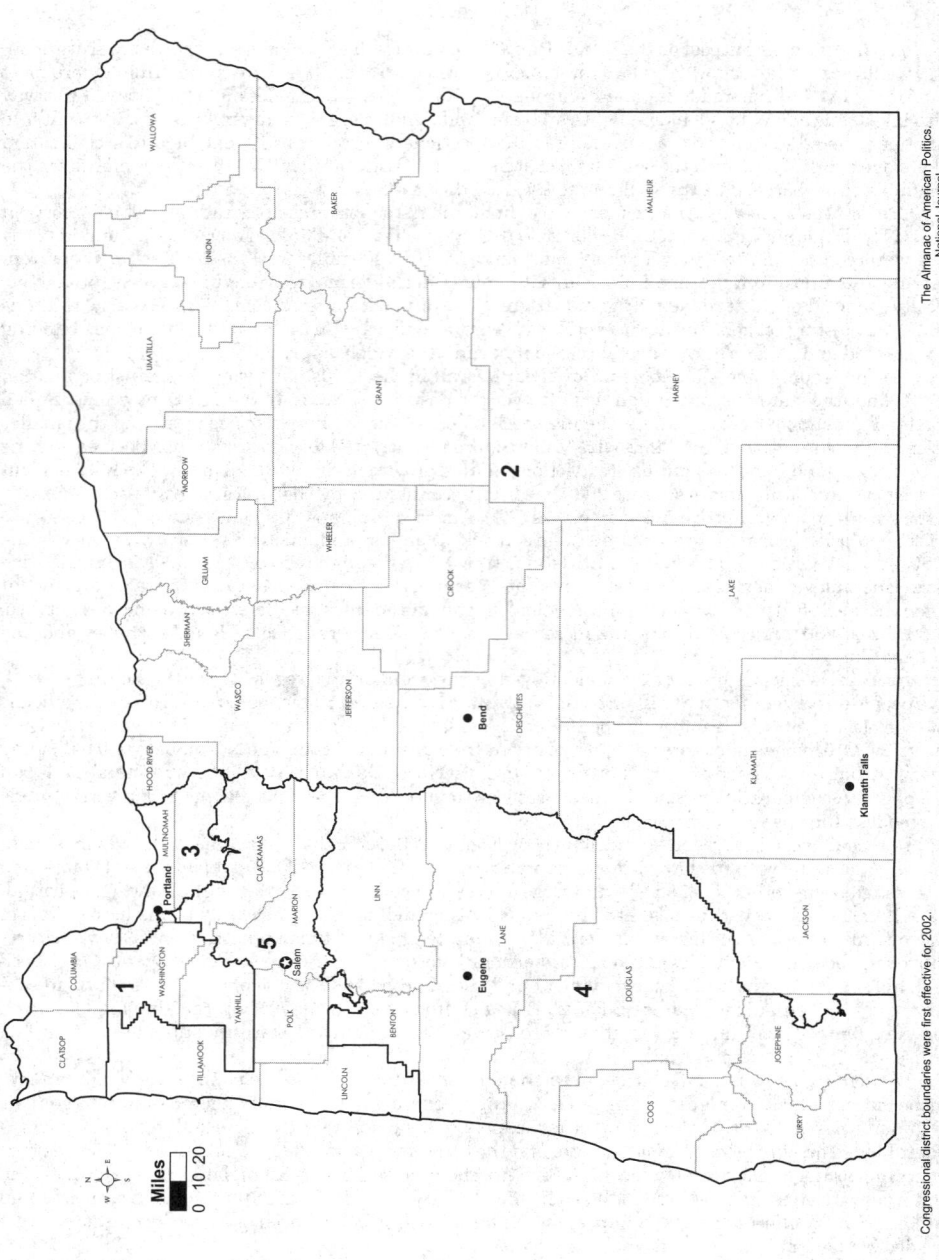

The Almanac of American Politics.
National Journal

Oregon pioneered state land-use regulation and restriction. In 1973, it passed a law that in many ways limited development, and in the 1990s, the Portland metro area sharply restricted growth and what many considered sprawl. These measures were popular in Portland and the university towns and to a lesser extent in the suburbs. But environmental restrictions have raised hackles in nonmetropolitan Oregon. Logging in the Pacific Northwest was largely wiped out because of restrictions imposed to protect the threatened spotted owl. This provoked sharp protests and a migration to the Republican Party in timber country. In 2001, the Interior Department cut off water to 1,000 farmers in the Klamath Basin to protect the endangered sucker fish. This became a major issue locally, and helps explain why parched eastern Oregon has become as heavily Republican as Portland is Democratic. In 2004, the discontent seemed to spread statewide. State land-use laws prevented landowners from building houses on land without farming it, even if the land was unsuitable for farming. An aggrieved landowner sparked a petition drive for a ballot measure requiring state and local governments to excuse property owners from rules enacted after they bought land or to compensate them for complying. It passed 61%-39%, carrying even Portland's Multnomah County.

If there is a common thread in Oregon's ballot issues, it seems to be a regard for personal autonomy and a readiness to discard traditional ways of doing things. Another seems to be a desire for limits on the ability of officeholders to spend public money. Voting on most of these measures has followed similar patterns, with Portland and the university towns of Eugene and Corvallis taking liberal positions, and counties east of the Cascades and outside the metro area taking more conservative stands. These cultural and regional differences have been reflected increasingly in Oregon's partisan politics. In the 1980s and 1990s, the gulf between liberal Portland and conservative eastern and southern Oregon widened, and since 2000, it has been a chasm. In 2004, John Kerry carried Multnomah County 72%-27%, and George W. Bush carried the counties east of the Cascades 63%-36%. In 2008, Barack Obama won Multnomah with 76.6% to John McCain's 20.6%, while McCain bested him 56%-41% in the east. Starting in 1986, Oregon has elected only Democratic governors, though only once by a wide margin. Kulongoski was re-elected in 2006, but by a not overwhelming 51%-43%. For a dozen years, Oregon's two Senate seats were held by a Republican and a Democrat who had run against each other in a special election in early 1996. Democrat Ron Wyden won that contest narrowly, and Republican Gordon Smith won the other seat in the November election that year. For some years, they held town meetings together across the state, and each was re-elected comfortably. But in 2008, Smith found himself running in an unfriendly environment for Republicans, and was beaten 49%-46% by Democratic House Speaker Jeff Merkley.

In 1998, Oregonians voted by referendum to hold all elections by mail, so there are no polls open on Election Day. Voters have until that night to get their ballots to the election clerk. Proponents of mail-in ballots argue that they increase the percentage of people who vote, which has always been high in Oregon anyway, and they give voters time to read over and think about the numerous ballot initiatives. Opponents say they increase the possibility of fraud. Because Oregon has no statewide registry, unscrupulous voters could cast votes in multiple counties.

Population		Household Income		Work	
Pop. 2007:	3,689,498	Under $15k:	13.5%	Private:	77.5%
State rank:	27th of 50	$15k to $50k:	38.9%	Government:	13.5%
Change since 2000:	Up 7.8%	$50k to $100k:	31.9%	Self-employed:	8.7%
Urban:	79.2%	$100k to $150k:	13.0%	Unemployment (3-yr. average):	4.5%
Rural:	20.8%	Over $150k:	2.6%	Poverty:	13.5%
Native of state:	45.3%	Median income:	$47,385	Blue collar:	22.5%
Not a citizen:	6.4%	**Home Value**		White collar:	59.0%
Area size:	98,381 sq. mi.	Under $100k:	11.0%	Khaki collar:	0.1%
Most populous cities		$100k to $300k:	54.6%	Other:	18.5%
1. Portland	541,550	$300k to $500k:	23.5%	**Age**	
2. Eugene	150,430	$500k to $1 mil:	9.4%	Median age:	37.6 yrs.
3. Salem	148,233	Over $1 million:	1.6%	More than 65 yrs:	12.9%
4. Gresham	101,537	Median:	$232,000	Less than 18 yrs:	23.2%

Race/Ethnicity				Military Veterans		Registered Voters in 2008	
White:	80.8%	*Language*		% of Pop:	12.5%	D:	929,741 (43.2%)
Black:	1.7%	English:	85.9%	*Veterans by Period*		R:	695,677 (32.3%)
Hispanic:	10.2%	Spanish:	8.5%	WWII and before:	13.5%	Other:	528,496 (24.5%)
Asian:	3.5%	Asian:	2.6%	Korea:	11.1%	Voter turnout:	1,827,864
Native Am.:	1.0%	Other		Vietnam:	35.0%	Turnout as % of	
Hawaiian:	0.2%	European	2.6%	Gulf (pre-2001):	9.9%	voting age:	62.5%
Two+ races:	2.5%	**Education**		Gulf (post-2001):	5.0%	**Legislature**	
Ancestry		H.S. grad:	87.5%	Peace time:	25.6%	Senate:	18 D 12 R
German:	16.8%	College grad:	27.6%			House:	36 D 24 R
English:	10.6%	Grad degree:	10.0%				
Irish:	9.8%						

Presidential politics   Oregon was once the most Republican state in the West, voting for Thomas Dewey over Harry Truman for president in 1948; it voted for Republicans who lost the presidency in 1948, 1960, and 1976. By the late 1980s, it had become one of the most Democratic states, voting for Democrats who lost the race for president in 1988, 2000, and 2004. For a time, the unpopularity of Clinton-era logging policies in much of Oregon threatened to make the state competitive, and Al Gore carried it by only 47%-46.5% in 2000, with 5% for Green Party candidate Ralph Nader. Nader was not on the ballot in 2004, and John Kerry won here by 51%-47%. During most of the 2008 election cycle, Oregon seemed solidly Democratic, though poll results from the first half of September suggested it might be competitive. But after the financial crash of mid-September, Oregon was not seriously contested, and Obama carried the state by a solid 57%-40%.

2008 Presidential Vote		
Obama (D)	1,037,291	(57%)
McCain (R)	738,475	(40%)
2008 Democratic Presidential Primary		
Obama (D)	375,385	(59%)
Clinton (D)	259,825	(41%)
2008 Republican Presidential Primary		
McCain (R)	285,881	(81%)
Paul (R)	51,100	(14%)
2004 Presidential Vote		
Kerry (D)	943,163	(51%)
Bush (R)	866,831	(47%)

Oregon once had an important presidential primary, scheduled in late May. In 1948, Oregon ended Republican Harold Stassen's presidential prospects, when he lost 52%-48% to Dewey. In 1968, Oregon gave Democrat Robert Kennedy his only defeat when it voted 44%-38% for his primary rival, Eugene McCarthy. Oregon in those days was part of a West Coast campaign swing, just before the California primary, at a time when candidates were not used to routinely crisscrossing the country. Like National Football League teams in the 1950s, they scheduled West Coast contests together to minimize travel time. For 1992 and 1996, Oregon scheduled its primary for Super Tuesday in March, but it was overshadowed by bigger contests in the South. In 2000 and 2004, the primary was held again in May. That, of course, was well after the parties' nominees were determined. But in 2004, Ohio Democrat Dennis Kucinich spent four weeks campaigning in Oregon, hoping to rally a constituency with his New Age, Department of Peace ideas. He nonetheless lost to Kerry, 79%-16%. In 2008, the primary was again held in May, when the race between Democrats Obama and New York Sen. Hillary Rodham Clinton was still raging. Obama carried Oregon, 59%-41%.

Congressional districting   Oregon's current congressional map is the product of a partisan battle between a Republican legislature and a Democratic governor. The Republican redistricters wanted to move solidly Democratic western Multnomah County from the arguably marginal 1st District to the hugely Democratic 3rd District. But in June 2001 Democratic Gov. John Kitzhaber vetoed the GOP plan, and in the inevitable lawsuit, a Multnomah County judge chose the Democratic alternative, saying it was less disruptive and better preserved communities of interest.

111th Congress Lineup	
4 D	1 R
110th Congress Lineup	
4 D	1 R

Oregon seems likely to gain an additional House seat in the reapportionment following the 2010 census. Democrats currently hold the governorship and both houses of the state Legislature by comfortable margins, and if they continue to do so, they will presumably try to add to the party's 4-1 edge in the state's U.S. House delegation. That may prove difficult, however, since the fastest-growing areas of the state tend to vote Republican. Democrats may decide to settle for strengthening their current four districts and take their chances in a marginal sixth seat.

Governor

Ted Kulongoski (D)

Elected 2002, term expires Jan. 2011, 2nd term; b. Nov. 5, 1940, Missouri; home, Portland; U. of MO, B.A. 1967, J.D. 1970; Catholic; married (Mary); 3 children.

Military Career: Marine Corps, 1959–63.

Elected Office: OR House of Reps., 1974–78; OR Senate, 1978–82; OR Atty. Gen., 1992–96; OR Sup. Ct., 1996–2001.

Professional Career: Practicing atty., 1971–87; OR insurance commissioner, 1987–92.

Office: 160 State Capitol, 900 Court St., Salem, 97301, 503-378-3111; Fax: 503-378-6827; Web site: www.governor.state.or.us.

Election Results

2006 general	Ted Kulongoski (D)	699,786	(51%)
	Ron Saxton (R)	589,748	(43%)
	Mary Starrett (CNP)	50,229	(4%)
2006 primary	Ted Kulongoski (D)	170,944	(54%)
	Jim Hill (D)	92,439	(29%)
	Pete Sorenson (D)	51,346	(16%)

Prior Winning Percentages: 2002 (49%)

Ted Kulongoski was elected governor of Oregon in 2002. He was born in rural Missouri, and, after his father died, was raised by nuns in a Catholic boys' home from ages 4 to 14. After high school, Kulongoski (*koo-lun-GAW-ski*) joined the Marine Corps, and later saved enough money working in a steel mill and as a truck driver to attend the University of Missouri; he graduated from college and law school there at ages 26 and 29. He moved to Eugene, Ore., and practiced labor law, representing mostly unions. He also worked as a state legislative staffer, helping to write a law giving public employee unions collective bargaining rights. Kulongoski was elected to the Oregon House in 1974 and the Oregon Senate in 1978. In the Legislature, he was regarded as a champion of labor unions. In 1980, he ran against Republican Sen. Bob Packwood and held him to 52% in a Republican year. In 1982, he ran against GOP Gov. Victor Atiyeh and lost by a humiliating 61%-36%. Kulongoski moved to Portland and practiced law. In 1987, his political career was revived by Gov. Neil Goldschmidt, who appointed him insurance commissioner. He went on to help broker changes in workmen's compensation laws, which earned him resentment from his old friends in the unions. In 1992, after a tough Democratic primary, he was elected attorney general, and then in 1996, he won election to the Oregon Supreme Court. In 2001, he resigned to campaign for governor.

Of the six major candidates, three Democrats and three Republicans, Kulongoski was the best-known, having been elected to jobs in the legislative, executive, and judicial branches of state government. He argued that he had the experience to solve Oregon's major problems—unemployment, a budget shortfall, and shoring up the state employees' pension fund. Outgoing Gov. John Kitzhaber and the preceding two Democratic governors, Barbara Roberts and Goldschmidt, quickly endorsed him. Against former state Treasurer Jim Hill and former Multnomah County Commission Chairman Bev Stein, Kulongoski depicted himself as the more moderate choice. With late contributions from public employees unions, he outspent the others and won the May 2002 primary with 49% of the vote, to 26% for Hill and 22% for Stein.

The winner of the Republican primary was Kevin Mannix, a Democratic state representative from 1988 to 1996 and a Democratic candidate for attorney general in 1996. He switched parties in 1997 and was elected to the state Senate as a Republican the following year. Mannix was a prolific drafter of legislation—135 of his bills became law in 10 years. He also sponsored several ballot initiatives, and his three tough-on-crime measures won in 1996. He ran as a "populist Republican," pledging to oppose new taxes and abortion rights.

Kulongoski called Mannix "divisive" and criticized him for invoking the abortion issue in the primary, but the campaign focused more on fiscal issues. The overriding concern at the time was a budget shortfall estimated at $720 million out of a $16 billion budget. Oregon has no sales tax and relies heavily on the income tax. In addition, Measure 5, passed in 1990, limits property-tax increases, so the state provides 80% of school funding. In 2002, the Legislature made significant cuts in planned spending and authorized a special referendum to raise the top income-tax rate from 9% to 9.8%. Kulongoski supported the proposal, reluctantly he said; Mannix opposed it, and said he could make enough cuts to make it unnecessary. (The measure ultimately failed.) Kulongoski called on localities to pay a greater share for education, promising to develop a consensus for a permanent, stable funding base, with even a sales tax in the mix—long verboten in Oregon politics. He called for all children to be covered by the Oregon Health Plan even if it meant removing some adults from the program. Mannix campaigned with gusto, handled debates well, and accurately banked on the tax issue to unite Republicans, which brought him large contributions in the final weeks of campaigning.

By all measures—party label, experience, and familiarity to voters—Kulongoski seemed to be an easy winner. But on election night, Mannix was ahead in the count, and Kulongoski pulled off a victory only narrowly, 49%-46%. He carried just eight of 36 counties—Multnomah, the counties containing the state's two big universities, three on the Pacific coast, and two on the Columbia River on either side of Portland.

Kulongoski had a stormy first term, marked by a recession that hit Oregon harder than most states. After voters rejected the tax-increase referendum, he was forced to cut spending drastically, and some public schools had to shorten their school year. Then in August 2003, he persuaded the divided Legislature—Republicans had a majority in the House; the Senate was 15-15—to vote for a tax increase. Anti-tax-increase groups quickly got out petitions to put the issue to the voters in February 2004. Kulongoski quietly supported the tax hike, but it was rejected 59%-41%. Kulongoski let $545 million in scheduled spending cuts go into effect, with the Oregon public health plan particularly hard hit. On a brighter note, Kulongoski succeeded in getting the Legislature to pass a 10-year bill to borrow $2.5 billion to repair bridges. By December 2004, the state found that half the bridges were in good shape and the money could be used on road projects.

Also in his first term, Kulongoski's longtime political friendship with Neil Goldschmidt turned into a grave liability for him. Elected mayor of Portland in 1972 at age 32, then going on to serve as Jimmy Carter's Transportation secretary, Goldschmidt was once Oregon's political wunderkind. He had supported Kulongoski in all of his campaigns for public office, and had rescued Kulongoski's career with the appointment as insurance commissioner after the failed gubernatorial bid. In turn, when he became governor, Kulongoski appointed Goldschmidt to head the state Board of Higher Education and PGE, the Portland utility. Then, on April 26, 2004, Goldschmidt abruptly resigned, and the reason surfaced a few days later. On May 6, after the *Willamette Week* put the story on its website, Goldschmidt admitted to the Portland *Oregonian* that he had had an affair with a 14-year-old girl in 1975 and 1976, when he was Portland mayor. The offense was a felony, though the statute of limitations had passed. Kulongoski said he "had no knowledge" of the charge, but a Goldschmidt aide insisted he had told Kulongoski about it in the 1990s. Kulongoski said Goldschmidt had "betrayed" him.

Going into his 2006 reelection campaign, Kulongoski looked to be one of the nation's most vulnerable governors. His job-approval ratings were below 50%. Within his own party, there was considerable dissatisfaction with his performance, particularly among labor groups, which resented his efforts to reduce pension benefits of public employees and to freeze state salaries. Republicans slammed him for supporting two statewide income-tax increases that were defeated by Oregon voters. Kulongoski had made some progress on creating jobs, and he had earned goodwill by attending the funeral of almost every Oregon soldier who died in the Iraq war. But candidates on the left and the right were lining up against him.

Kulongoski got a break in January 2006 when his Democratic predecessor, John Kitzhaber, announced he would not challenge him in the May primary. The state economy was also in better shape than when Kulongoski took office. But he still had serious opposition on the left from former state Treasurer Jim Hill, who finished second in the 2002 primary for governor, and Lane County Commissioner Pete Sorenson, both of whom criticized him not doing enough on education and health care. Hill went so far as to call Kulongoski a "bad Democrat." Kulongoski won the low turnout affair with 54%, carrying all but two small counties and winning by 2-1 in Portland's Multnomah County and in suburban Portland's Washington and Clackamas counties. Hill finished second with 29%, followed by Sorenson with 16%.

The nominee from the bruising Republican primary was Ron Saxton, who had lost to Mannix in the 2002 primary but returned to defeat him in 2006. A former Portland School Board member, Saxton had run as a moderate in 2002, but this time he made a play for conservative votes, advocating tough immigration policies and courting abortion-rights opponents on issues such as a late-term abortion ban and parental notification. He did not have a clear shot at Kulongoski in the general election. State Sen. Ben Westlund, a Republican who re-registered as an independent, announced in February that he was running too.

Kulongoski talked about stabilizing school funding, providing more health insurance coverage for children, and increasing the state's use of renewable energy. He generated controversy by suggesting that the state suspend its practice of sending rebate checks to taxpayers when there were excess state revenues and instead spend the money on schools and health care; he later backed away from that idea but did not rule out various tax increases. Saxton said "our views of government could not be more different" and insisted that the state had enough money for essential services. He called for tax cuts and more efficiency in state government. On the environment, there were also clear differences. Kulongoski touted his clean-car initiative, similar to California's aggressive move to reduce car emissions; Saxton wanted to overturn it.

In August, Westlund dropped out of the race, saying he could not win and did not want to be a spoiler candidate—a sign that Kulongoski had made considerable progress toward uniting Democrats behind his candidacy. In October, he endorsed Kulongoski and campaigned with him across the state. Kulongoski ended up winning 51%-43%. He carried just 12 of 36 counties and lost everything east of the Cascades, but won 68%-25% in Portland's Multnomah County, enough to power him to victory. Kulongoski won by 110,000 votes statewide; his 112,000-vote margin in Multnomah County made all the difference. It was an unimpressive victory in what was a Democratic year nationally, but it hardly mattered. Republicans remained shut out of the governor's office, having last won it in 1982. Democrats captured the state House, giving them control of the governorship and the Legislature for the first time in 16 years.

In 2007, Kulongoski approved a nearly 18% increase in K-12 education spending, funding for 100 more state troopers, and domestic partnerships for same-sex couples. The session was widely described as the state's "greenest" in decades, with an expansion of Oregon's bottle bill to require deposits on bottled water containers and a plan to require utilities to generate a quarter of their electricity from renewable sources by 2025. But the overall picture was mixed: The governor failed to deliver on his pledge to overhaul the state's archaic tax structure, the Legislature rejected his Brand Oregon marketing plan, and voters were largely disenchanted with state government.

Senior Senator

Ron Wyden (D)

Elected Jan. 1996, term expires 2010, 2nd full term; b. May 3, 1949, Wichita, KS; home, Portland; Stanford U., B.A. 1971, U. of OR, J.D. 1974; Jewish; married (Nancy Bass); 4 children.

Elected Office: U.S. House of Reps., 1980–96.

Professional Career: Co–dir. & co–founder, OR Gray Panthers, 1974–80; Dir., OR Legal Svcs. for the Elderly, 1977–79; Prof. of Gerontology, U. of OR, 1976, Portland St. U., 1979, U. of Portland, 1980.

DC Office: 223 DSOB, 20510, 202-224-5244; Fax: 202-228-2717; Web site: wyden.senate.gov.

State Offices: Bend, 541-330-9142; Eugene, 541-431-0229; La Grande, 541-962-7691; Medford, 541-858-5122; Portland, 503-326-7525; Salem, 503-589-4555.

Committees: *Aging (Special)* (2nd of 13 D). *Budget* (3rd of 13 D). *Energy & Natural Resources* (3rd of 13 D): Energy; Public Lands & Forests (Chmn). *Finance* (7th of 13 D): Health Care; International Trade, Customs & Global Competitiveness (Chmn); Taxation, IRS Oversight & Long-Term Growth. *Intelligence (Select)* (3rd of 8 D).

Group Ratings

	ADA	ACLU	AFS	LCV	ITIC	NTU	COC	ACU	CFG	FRC
2008	95	93	89	100	80	18	50	8	14	0
2007	95	—	100	87	—	8	55	4	13	—

National Journal Ratings

	2007 LIB — 2007 CONS		2008 LIB — 2008 CONS	
Economic	59% —	40%	73% —	25%
Social	81% —	16%	75% —	21%
Foreign	85% —	8%	65% —	6%
Composite	77% —	23%	77% —	23%

Key Votes of the 110th Congress

1. Raise CAFE standards	Y	5. Make English official language	Y	9. Withdraw troops 3/08	Y
2. Expand SCHIP	Y	6. Path to citizenship	Y	10. Iran guard is terrorist group	N
3. Cap greenhouse gases	Y	7. Fetus is unborn child	N	11. Increase missile defense $	N
4. Bail out financial markets	N	8. Prosecute hate crimes	Y	12. Overhaul FISA	N

Election Results

2004 general	Ron Wyden (D)	1,128,728	(63%)	($2,817,706)
	Al King (R)	565,254	(32%)	($32,930)
2004 primary	Ron Wyden (D)	unopposed		

Prior Winning Percentages: 1998 (61%); 1996 (48%); 1994 House (73%); 1992 House (77%); 1990 House (81%); 1988 House (99%); 1986 House (86%); 1984 House (72%); 1982 House (78%); 1980 House (72%)

Ron Wyden, Oregon's senior senator, was first elected to the House in 1980 and to the Senate in January 1996. He grew up in California, graduated from Stanford University, and came to Oregon to attend the University of Oregon Law School. After graduating in 1974, he founded the Oregon chapter of the Gray Panthers, an advocacy group for the elderly. His first foray into electoral politics was sponsoring a success-ful referendum reducing the price of dentures. In 1980, at age 31, he boldly launched a primary challenge to Democratic Rep. Robert Duncan in the 3rd Congressional District, which covers most of Portland, and won 60%-40%. He went on to easily capture the seat in the heavily Democratic district. Wyden's way to the Senate was opened by the Senate Ethics Committee's decision in September 1995 to expel Sen. Bob Packwood, R-Ore., for ethical misdeeds related to the sexual abuse of former aides and lobbyists. Wyden, who had long been eyeing the seat, decided to run in the special election to replace Packwood—the first election Oregon conducted by mail-in ballot. With his home base in Portland, where the local television broadcasts reach most of the state, Wyden had greater name identification than his competitors. But he had spirited opposition in the Democratic primary from Eugene-based Rep. Peter DeFazio, who carried his own district overwhelmingly, holding Wyden to a 50%-44% win. The Republican nomination went to state Senate President Gordon Smith, a frozen-vegetable tycoon from eastern Oregon who spent $2 mil-lion of his own money. Most polls had the race in a dead heat, and negative ads flooded the airwaves. Wyden picked up strength the week before the Jan. 30 mail deadline, and won 48%-47%.

Ten months later, Smith won the state's other Senate seat, marking the first time two senators were elected who had run against each other in the same year. With the departure of Packwood and Republican Sen. Mark Hatfield, Oregon had lost 56 years of Senate seniority and had gained two senators who everyone expected would be bitter enemies. Instead, they became friends and collaborators, holding dozens of joint town meetings across Oregon and having lunch every Thursday with their chiefs of staff. The bipartisan working alliance between the two ended in 2008 when Smith lost his re-election bid to Democrat Jeff Merkley.

In his years in Washington, Wyden has displayed a genius for coming up with sensible-sounding ideas no one else had thought of and a knack for making the counterintuitive political alliances that prove helpful in passing bills. He says, "Look at my record. My record is based on the proposition that if you want to get anything done, it's got to be bipartisan. But sometimes you have to stand alone." An illustration was Wyden's work with Republican Sen. Olympia Snowe, of Maine, in early 2009. Wyden and Snowe astutely predicted that high-dollar bonuses and "golden parachutes" for executives of financial companies being bailed out by American taxpayers would be unpopular with the public. They won passage of a provision in that year's economic stimulus bill to prevent such bonus payments. But the stipulation was left out of the final bill at the insistence of the Obama administration, which said it was worried that employees would sue to keep their bonuses, according to an account by Sen. Christopher Dodd, D-Conn. In late March 2009, there was an outpouring of public anger over bonuses paid to employees of troubled insurance giant AIG, which ensnared the fledgling Obama administration and which would have been prevented by the Wyden-Snowe legislation.

Wyden's portfolio of interests is wide, ranging from Senate procedure to new technology. In 1997, he and Republican Sen. Charles Grassley of Iowa shook things up in the tradition-bound Senate by calling for disclosure of the names of senators who place "holds" on legislation, which allow individual senators to tie up legislation for months or years. One of Wyden's bills was the victim of such a hold. Wyden and Grassley were rebuffed in their efforts for years, but made slow progress. In March 2006, the Senate voted 84-13 for a Wyden-Grassley amendment requiring senators to announce their opposition in the *Congressional Record* within three days of objecting to legislation or a nominee. The provision was included in the Senate version of the lobbying reform bill that passed in January 2007.

Another Wyden cause has been the Internet. He and former California Rep. Christopher Cox, a Republican, sponsored the three-year ban on Internet taxation that passed in 1998. Three years later, they sought to extend the ban permanently, but also set up a procedure to allow states to tax Internet sales if they adopt uniform sales tax rules and provide a means to file and remit sales taxes electronically; the ban was extended until 2005. In 2004, the Senate passed a four-year extension that grandfathered in pre-1998 taxes and permitted states to apply telephone taxes to voice-over-Internet protocol (VOIP) services. The bill was signed in December 2004. Wyden has also worked on Internet privacy issues and on anti-spam legislation, which passed in 2003. As spam purveyors evolved, he moved to restrict spam messages over text-messaging systems and cell phones. In 2006, he backed network neutrality legislation, which would bar Internet service providers from giving preference to websites that pay fees.

Health care has long captured Wyden's interest too. He was one of 11 Senate Democrats to vote for the Republican-authored Medicare prescription drug law in 2003 in the face of criticism from many fellow Democrats and former allies. "It was clearly the toughest call I've ever had to make. It wasn't a bill I would have written. But I thought it was the right thing to do to get started," he said. He won amendments creating a national commission on health care and to extend a managed care option for rural Oregon. Later, with Snowe, he sponsored a bill to allow the federal government to negotiate drug prices with pharmaceutical companies.

In 2006, Wyden and Smith sponsored a bill for pilot projects for health care plans designed to increase reliance on private insurance over employer-based insurance, and to shield individuals from high out-of-pocket costs. In December 2006, Wyden announced a bill for a private health insurance system, including a federal-state system of premium collection and subsidies. Individuals would be required to buy private health insurance, with subsidies for low earners making as much as 400% of the poverty level. Medicaid, the federal health care program for the poor, would be abolished. And the proposal would essentially eliminate the current system of employer-based coverage. In the first two years after enactment, employers would transfer money that they had been spending on health benefits to wages. By 2008, the proposal was cosponsored by seven Democrats and seven Republicans, including chief cosponsor Robert Bennett, a conservative Utah Republican. And Wyden's bill got a boost from a Congressional Budget Office analysis that concluded the plan would be revenue-neutral in its first year of operation and subsequently would create budget surpluses.

Wyden has also been a staunch defender of the state's assisted-suicide law, the only one like it in the nation. He has fought various legislative attempts to nullify the law over the years, and also vocally opposed Attorney General John Ashcroft's decision in 2001 to prosecute doctors who prescribe lethal drugs for terminally ill patients. That decision was challenged in court, and in January 2006, the high court ruled 6-3 against the federal government.

For years, Wyden has been trying to put together a bipartisan approach to taxes and has called for the first major restructuring of the tax code since 1986. In December 2005, Rep. Rahm Emanuel, D-Ill., joined him on a bill they called the Fair Flat Tax, which would create three individual rates and a 35% corporate income-tax rate while eliminating most current deductions and credits. Capital gains would be taxed at the individual rate rather than at 15%, and the popular home mortgage deduction would be retained. The following year, he and Sen. Larry Craig, R-Idaho, pushed a similar measure. "It's very clear that the tax system is a monstrosity and abomination," Wyden said.

As chairman of an Energy and Natural Resources subcommittee in 2001 and 2002, Wyden was thrust into national controversies. After the huge forest fires in the summer of 2002, he worked with Sen. Dianne Feinstein, D-Calif., on a compromise national forest thinning plan, which resulted in passage of the Healthy Forests Restoration Act in 2003. Some environmental groups were unhappy, but the legislation was popular in rural Oregon. In November 2006, noting the recession in the hardwood industry, Wyden called for an investigation of China's timber subsidies, fraudulent labeling, and illegal logging of hardwood.

In the foreign-policy realm, Wyden voted against the Iraq war resolution and in July 2003 criticized the Bush administration for using "any snippet of information to justify the decision they had made." He serves on the Intelligence Committee and in December 2004 was criticized for revealing allegedly classified information when he publicly referred to a "major acquisition program." A day later, *The Washington Post* said the program was a $9.5 billion spy satellite system. Wyden said his words were authorized by committee Chairman Pat Roberts, R-Kan.

Wyden takes pains not to neglect Oregon's interests. He supported permanent repeal of the estate tax, pointing out the problems it caused for family businesses that own large stands of timber. In 2003, he worked to block the reauthorization of welfare programs because the bill didn't extend the 1996 waiver for Oregon's welfare-to-work program, which counts mental health treatment and drug treatment toward working hours. Using a hold, in June 2006 he got into a fisheries bill a provision for federal disaster relief for Klamath River salmon fishermen after the federal government reduced catch limits and fishing days.

His devotion to state issues, and to keeping his visibility up at home—he continues to hold open meetings in all 36 counties every year, even heavily Republican counties—has paid off at election time. In November 1998, Wyden was elected to a full term, 61%-34%. For his 2004 campaign, he raised $5 million but spent only $2.8 million, donating $500,000 to other Democratic Senate campaigns. His Republican opponent was Klamath County rancher Al King, a former county Republican chairman. While web-surfing at a friend's house the day before the filing deadline, King noticed that no well-known people had filed to run against Wyden and so mouse-clicked his name in, together with the filing fee. King won the six-candidate primary with 35% of the vote. But Wyden easily prevailed in the general, 63%-32%, carrying 33 of 36 counties; the three counties he lost have 26% of Oregon's land area but cast only 1% of its votes. In the 2008 Democratic presidential primary, Wyden was neutral, but his chief of staff was Oregon co-chairman for New York Sen. Hillary Rodham Clinton.

With his seat on the Finance Committee and with Congress moving to address some of the issues Wyden has focused on in recent years, he is positioned to be a major policy player in the 111th Congress (2009–10).

Junior Senator

Jeff Merkley (D)

Elected 2008, term expires 2014, 1st term; b. Oct. 24, 1956, Myrtle Creek; home, Portland; Stanford U., B.A. 1979; Princeton U., M.P.P. 1982; Lutheran; married (Mary Sorteberg); 2 children.

Elected Office: OR House, 1999–2008, House Speaker, 2006–08.

Professional Career: Pres. fellow, Office of the Secy. of Defense, 1982–85; Natl. security analyst, CBO, 1985–1989; Exec. dir., Portland Habitat for Humanity, 1991–94; Dir. of housing development, Human Solutions, 1995–96; Pres., World Affairs Cncl. of OR, 1996–2003.

DC Office: 107 RSOB, 20510, 202-224-3753; Fax: 202-228-3997; Web site: merkley.senate.gov.

State Offices: Bend, 541-318-1298; Eugene, 541-465-6750; Medford, 541-608-9102; Pendleton, 541-278-1129; Portland, 503-326-3386; Salem, 503-362-8102.

Committees: *Banking, Housing & Urban Affairs* (12th of 13 D): Economic Policy; Financial Institutions; Housing, Transportation & Community Development. *Budget* (13th of 13 D). *Environment & Public Works* (10th of 12 D). *Health, Education, Labor & Pensions* (12th of 13 D).

Group Ratings and Key Votes: Newly Elected

Election Results

2008 general	Jeff Merkley (D)	864,392	(49%)	($6,501,315)
	Gordon Smith (R)	805,159	(46%)	($11,372,481)
	Dave Brownlow (CNP)	92,565	(5%)	
2008 primary	Jeff Merkley (D)	246,482	(45%)	
	Steve Novick (D)	230,889	(42%)	
	Candy Neville (D)	38,367	(7%)	

The junior senator from Oregon is first-term Democrat Jeff Merkley. He was born in Myrtle Creek, Ore., to parents who worked at a local sawmill. A declining local economy forced them into career adjustments during Merkley's formative years. The sawmill closed when he was 2 years old, obliging his father to work as a logger and homebuilder in the neighboring town of Roseburg. When those jobs disappeared, the family moved to Portland where his father took a job as a mechanic. During these times, the Merkley family lived frugally. "My parents lived with an ethic of making sure they saved and spent very little money on frills," he says. In high school, Merkley broadened his perspective on economic struggles by spending a summer in Ghana as part of the American Field Service Exchange Program. The family he stayed with had two prized possessions: a bicycle and an iron. The first in his own family to attend college, Merkley pursued international affairs and travel as an undergraduate at Stanford University. He spent a trimester in Florence, Italy, and a summer hitchhiking around Israel. After graduating with a bachelor's degree in international relations, he took an internship with the Carnegie Endowment of International Peace. In the summer of 1980, Merkley and a fellow intern traveled through war-torn Central America by bus. He earned a master's degree in public policy from Princeton University, landed a presidential fellowship at the Pentagon in 1982, and then worked as an analyst in the Congressional Budget Office.

Merkley moved back to Portland in the early 1990s and took a job as director of the city's Habitat for Humanity chapter, where he concentrated on affordable housing and skills training for at-risk youth and low-income families. In 1998, he was elected to the state House, campaigning on his desire to improve Oregon's school system. He achieved his first legislative victory in 1999 with a bill establishing Individual Development Accounts to help low-income families save money for buying homes, attending school, or starting businesses. As a state legislator, Merkley supported fee increases on deeds and other home purchase filings to increase funding for low-income housing. In 2003, the Democratic House minority leader stepped down, and Merkley, who had gained a reputation as an unassuming policy wonk, was surprisingly elected to succeed her. Fellow House members cited Merkley's consensus-building ability. But House Republicans had concentrated their power and restricted the Democratic caucus's influence, and the ensuing partisanship prevented cooperation on major legislation. Merkley demonstrated a competitive edge by aggressively campaigning on behalf of Democratic House candidates in 2006. One controversial television ad accused Republican House Speaker Karen Minnis of covering up suspected sexual misconduct by her brother-in-law. State Republicans condemned the ad as too personal, but Merkley stood by it. Democrats won control of the Oregon House for the first time in 16 years, and Merkley was unanimously elected speaker.

During his tenure as speaker, the Legislature passed several reforms, including an expanded indoor smoking ban and greater rights for same-sex couples. He also pushed through an ethics bill aimed at curbing gifts and other perks from lobbyists to lawmakers. In 2007, Merkley fought Oregon's payday loan industry by sponsoring a bill that imposed an interest-rate cap of 36% annually on consumer loans less than $50,000. He also negotiated the establishment of a state rainy-day fund to protect schools and other state services from recessions; an increase in the state's corporate minimum tax paid for the fund. *The Oregonian* called the session "one of the most successful legislative sessions of recent years."

Merkley got the attention of Democratic Senatorial Campaign Committee Chairman Chuck Schumer of New York, who recruited him to challenge incumbent GOP Sen. Gordon Smith in the 2008 election. National Democrats thought Merkley would appeal to the same voters who had elected the moderate and pragmatic Smith to two Senate terms. Despite the endorsements and financial backing of his national party, Merkley faced stiff primary competition from liberal activist and political consultant Steve Novick, who had opposed Merkley's elevation to House minority leader in 2003. Merkley initially ignored Novick and focused his campaign on Smith. But Novick, who stands just 4 feet, 9 inches tall, built support among the state's most liberal voters. He ran ads saying he would "stand up for the little guy," and labeled Merkley as pro-war for a vote he cast in favor of a 2003 resolution that praised both President Bush and American troops for courage in the war against Iraq. Without sharp disagreements on policy, the two candidates reverted to criticizing each other through negative ads and spirited debates. Merkley narrowly defeated Novick, 45%-42%. Novick won liberal Multnomah County around Portland by 12 percentage points, but Merkley's large victories in rural areas gave him the nomination.

The general election was one of the most expensive and closely watched contests of 2008. In Smith, Merkley faced a moderate Republican who had demonstrated an independent policy streak and willingness to work across the aisle. Smith had broken with his party by voting for higher automobile mileage standards and against oil drilling in the Arctic National Wildlife Refuge. In August 2006, *The Oregonian* wrote, "As a Republican senator from a politically divided state, Smith's Senate terms are six-year balancing acts in which he must please both conservatives in this party and enough liberal Oregonians to get re-elected. In an increasingly polarized political world, Smith straddles a rare middle ground."

To combat Smith's centrist appeal, Merkley allied himself with Barack Obama and his presidential campaign's theme of change. The message resonated in a state where Bush's approval ratings were below the national average. In late October, Merkley aired a television ad that featured Obama urging voters to bring about "real change" by casting their ballots for Merkley. Former Vice President Gore—noticeably absent from the campaign trail for most of the election cycle—also stumped for Merkley. Smith touted his reputation for working across the aisle, particularly with fellow Oregon Sen. Ron Wyden, a Democrat. He attempted to distance himself from Bush, running ads that featured Wyden and Democratic icon Sen. Edward Kennedy of Massachusetts. Cognizant of Oregonians' anti-GOP sentiments, Smith featured Obama in three of his own ads, including one touting that the two senators had worked together to increase mileage standards.

On issues, Merkley criticized Smith for supporting the $700 billion government bailout of financial institutions. The two-term senator also faced renewed questions about the legal status of seasonal immigrant workers at his family business, Smith Frozen Foods. Ironically, as House speaker, Merkley had helped kill the bill that would have required Oregon employers to verify the legal status of foreign workers; Smith has voted for such legislation in Congress. Merkley also called on Smith to return campaign contributions from Republican Sen. Ted Stevens of Alaska, who was convicted in a corruption scandal. (The conviction was later thrown out.) Smith ran an ad that claimed Merkley had voted to increase taxes 44 times in the state House. An independent review showed that Merkley had voted eight times to directly raise taxes. In one of the campaign season's oddest attack ads, the National Republican Senatorial Committee aired an unflattering clip of Merkley gobbling a hot dog and fielding questions about Russia's invasion of Georgia with his mouth full. In addition to capturing an inelegant moment for Merkley, the ad also caught him uninformed on the issue. Smith later condemned the ad.

Another hurdle for Smith was the candidacy of Constitution Party candidate Dave Brownlow, a libertarian who threatened to attract conservative voters estranged by Smith's moderate platform. Late polls showed Brownlow taking 3% to 5%, despite running an almost no-budget campaign. On November 4, Merkley defeated Smith 49%-46% with Brownlow getting a significant 5%. Smith out-raised Merkley $13 million to $7 million, but the DSCC and other outside groups poured $11 million into the race. In a post-election tribute to the defeated incumbent, *The Oregonian* editorialized, "The across-party working relationship he developed with Democrat Ron Wyden—even if it frayed in this political season—became a model for bipartisan cooperation worth emulating in other circumstances, nationally and locally."

FIRST DISTRICT

David Wu (D)

Elected 1998, 6th term; b. April 8, 1955, Hsinchu, Taiwan; home, Portland; Stanford U., B.S. 1977; Harvard Med. Schl., 1978; Yale Law Schl., J.D. 1982; Presbyterian; married (Michelle); 2 children.

Professional Career: Law clerk, 9th Circuit Court of Appeals, 1982–83; Campaign staff, Gary Hart for president, 1984; Practicing atty., 1984–98.

DC Office: 2338 RHOB, 20515, 202-225-0855; Fax: 202-225-9497; Web site: www.house.gov/wu.

State Offices: Portland, 503-326-2901.

Committees: *Education & Labor* (11th of 29 D): Health, Employment, Labor & Pensions; Higher Education, Lifelong Learning & Competitiveness. *Science & Technology* (5th of 26 D): Space & Aeronautics; Technology & Innovation (Chmn).

Group Ratings

	ADA	ACLU	AFS	LCV	ITIC	NTU	COC	ACU	CFG	FRC
2008	90	100	100	92	86	13	50	4	0	0
2007	100	—	100	100	—	5	50	0	6	—

National Journal Ratings

	2007 LIB	—	2007 CONS		2008 LIB	—	2008 CONS
Economic	82%	—	0%		68%	—	32%
Social	67%	—	32%		67%	—	28%
Foreign	73%	—	26%		92%	—	0%
Composite	77%	—	23%		78%	—	22%

Key Votes of the 110th Congress

1. Increase minimum wage	Y	5. Share immigration data	N	9. Withdraw troops 8/08	Y
2. Expand SCHIP	Y	6. Foreign aid abortion ban	N	10. No operations in Iran	Y
3. Raise CAFE standards	Y	7. Ban gay bias in workplace	Y	11. Free trade with Peru	N
4. Bail out financial markets	Y	8. Repeal D.C. gun law	N	12. Overhaul FISA	N

Election Results

2008 general	David Wu (D)	237,567	(72%)	($1,214,535)
	Joel Haugen (I)	58,279	(18%)	($7,563)
	Scott Semrau (CNP)	14,172	(4%)	
	H. Joe Tabor (Lib)	10,992	(3%)	
	Chris Henry (Green)	7,128	(2%)	
2008 primary	David Wu (D)	91,466	(78%)	
	Will Hobbs (D)	19,659	(17%)	
	Mark Welyczko (D)	5,982	(5%)	

Prior Winning Percentages: 2006 (63%); 2004 (58%); 2002 (63%); 2000 (58%); 1998 (50%)

Population		Race/Ethnicity		Work	
Pop. 2007:	767,732	White:	77.1%	Private:	82.2%
Change since 2000:	Up 12.2%	Black:	1.3%	Government:	9.9%
Urban:	86.7%	Hispanic:	12.0%	Self-employed:	7.5%
Rural:	13.3%	Asian:	6.1%	Blue collar:	18.7%
Area size:	3,236 sq. mi.	Native Am.:	0.5%	White collar:	64.7%
		Hawaiian:	0.3%	Khaki collar:	0.1%
Age		Two+ races:	2.5%	Other:	16.5%
Median age:	36.0 yrs.	*Ancestry*		Median income:	$55,615
More than 65 yrs:	10.1%	German:	16.8%	Median home value:	$273,500
Less than 18 yrs:	24.5%	English:	10.5%	Poverty:	10.8%
Education		Irish:	9.5%	**Military Veterans**	
H.S. grad:	89.7%			% of Pop:	11.1%
College grad:	35.9%				
Grad degree:	13.1%				

Post-modern skyscrapers rising above the riverfront and below a range of hills: This is downtown Portland. The city—which would have been named Boston if a coin toss had gone the other way—started here, along the Willamette River just before it flows into the Columbia. Downtown Portland was built on the narrow strip of land west of the river and below the hills, not on the flat expanse that stretches east toward the snow-capped peak of Mount Hood. It was once a dowdy place, proper in a

2008 Presidential Vote
Obama (D) 228,817 (61%)
McCain (R) 135,975 (36%)

2004 Presidential Vote
Kerry (D) 200,489 (55%)
Bush (R) 161,738 (44%)

Cook Partisan Voting Index: D+8

New England kind of way, with a few formal buildings above the warehouses and factories. But in the last 30 years, there has been an explosion of affluence and creativity here, symbolized by handsome high-rises—the pyramid-crested brick KOIN Tower, the wedge-shaped Justice Center—restored Victorian storefronts, a downtown transit trolley, and a light-rail line known as MAX (for Metropolitan Area Express). There is a free wireless network in Pioneer Courthouse Square, and just across the river is the Oregon Museum of Science and Industry. The well-to-do neighborhoods in the hills overlooking downtown are full of old lumber barons' mansions with splendid views.

Just over the hills are the valleys and interstices between green mountains of suburban Washington County. This was once farm country, with 39,000 people in 1940; now it has 522,000 and is an integral part of metro Portland. It continues to be fast-growing; the population rose 68% between 1990 and 2007. And it enjoys a high-tech, healthy-lifestyle affluence. Its towns are cushioned by protected forests and anchored by major employers that include Tektronix, Intel, IBM, Columbia Sportswear, and Adidas. Beaverton has the world headquarters of Nike, housed in 16 buildings spread over 178 acres. Like Silicon Valley, the Silicon Forest has an environment that appeals to a highly skilled workforce: Nestled at the foot of mountains, it is woodsy and even rustic, but it's outfitted with all the comforts of modern life. As they say locally, wood chips have been replaced by computer chips.

The 1st Congressional District of Oregon includes downtown Portland and its western hills, and all of suburban Washington County. The 1st also proceeds nearly 100 miles northwest from Portland along the Columbia River to the rain-swept port of Astoria on the Pacific Coast, where Lewis and Clark spent the winter of 1805–06 at what is now the Fort Clatsop National Memorial. To the southwest is Yamhill County, a prime location for turkey farms during the 1960s but lately the site of metro expansion. Beaverton has become known for its wineries, and coastal Newport is popular for its oysters. Like Oregon, the

1st District is historically New England Republican, electing only GOP members of Congress from 1892 to 1972. Like New England, it then trended sharply left on cultural issues, even as its high-tech economy brought new affluence. Starting in 1974, it has elected only Democrats. In 2004, John Kerry won the district 55%-44%, and in 2008, Barack Obama won it with 61%.

The congressman from the 1st District is David Wu, a Democrat elected in 1998 and the first Chinese-American to serve in the House. He was born in Taiwan in 1955 and came to the United States with his family to join his father, who was studying at Rensselaer Polytechnic Institute, in 1961. He grew up mostly in Orange County, Calif., graduated from Stanford, started medical school at Harvard, and then switched to law school at Yale. He clerked for a federal judge in Portland and settled there. He worked on Jimmy Carter's presidential campaign in 1980 and Gary Hart's in 1984. He started his own law firm in 1988 and served on the Portland Planning Commission. When the House seat became available, the Democratic front-runner was Linda Peters, who was well known as the Washington County Board chairwoman and had the financial backing of EMILY's List. Wu left his law practice and spent $100,000 of his own money. He attacked Peters in ads for taking a personal loan from a developer and accused her of misspending tax dollars while traveling on county business. He won the primary 52%-43%. The Republican nominee, 29-year-old Molly Bordonaro, the daughter of a prominent real estate businessman in Portland, came out of the primary with more money than Wu and a more united party behind her. She and Wu were running even in the polls. With help from national Democrats and labor unions, Wu caught up on fundraising. He used his life story to extol America's system of education and to call for more spending on Head Start (his wife was a Head Start teacher) early education and aid to college students. He won 50%-47%.

In the House, Wu joined the New Democrat Coalition and developed a centrist voting record. With one notable exception, he has been a reliable Democratic vote on education, health care, abortion, and gun control. As chairman of the House Science panel's Subcommittee on Technology and Innovation, Wu has pushed for environmentally friendly transportation construction and has championed a bill to promote technology innovation. He angered local tech firms by voting against normal trade relations with China because of "the sacrifices of countless families like mine." In November 2003, he had a rare moment in the national spotlight as one of only 16 House Democrats to vote for the Republican leadership's Medicare prescription drug bill. During the extended, three-hour roll call, he sat stoically and silently among acutely displeased Democrats on the floor, looking as though he wanted to be anywhere else in the world. He said he has decided that the bill was good for his constituents but had promised his leaders that he would not cast his yea vote until a majority of House members had cast theirs. His was the final, and by then largely irrelevant, vote in support of the bill, which passed 220-215. Afterward, Wu conceded that he would have to mend fences with Democrats on Capitol Hill and at home. Redemption was slow to arrive. When the party took control of the House in 2007, other Oregon Democrats gained influence in the new majority while Wu remained a backbencher, criticized by some back home as increasingly marginalized. On the air, conservative radio host Rush Limbaugh poked fun of Wu's use of metaphors from the television program *Star Trek* to criticize President Bush's policy in Iraq.

In the 2004 election, Wu faced spirited competition from Goli Ameri, an Iranian-born communications consultant who was new to politics but showed a good grasp of local economic issues and raised lots of money. Ameri supported Bush on the war in Iraq and tax cuts, but she differed with the administration on embryonic stem cell research, which she supported, and oil drilling in the Arctic National Wildlife Refuge, which she opposed.

In mid-October, the Portland *Oregonian* published a lengthy article setting out in great detail allegations that Wu had sexually harassed and physically attacked a former girlfriend when they were both Stanford undergraduates. The newspaper reported that he was not arrested and that no criminal charges were filed, but that the university disciplined him and he privately apologized. After the story was published, Wu issued a statement taking responsibility and admitting to "inexcusable behavior." Some Wu supporters questioned the newspaper's decision to run the story so close to the election and just a few days after it had endorsed Ameri. In a debate three days later, Ameri raised the matter. "I cannot in good conscience stand here and pretend that violating the most fundamental human right, a woman's safety, is merely a wrongdoing." Wu replied that Ameri's attack was "unfortunate." She ran campaign ads featuring the incident, but the news story and the extensive coverage that followed appeared to cause little political harm to Wu. He won 58%-38%, carrying Washington County 55%-41%.

By 2006, the incident from his past had disappeared locally. Wu was re-elected 63%-34%, and his victory over state House majority whip and self-styled maverick Derrick Kitts was never in serious doubt. Kitts raised little money and Wu avoided debates. In 2008, Wu endorsed presidential contender Barack Obama a month before the Oregon primary, and Wu was easily re-elected over businessman Joel Haugen, an independent.

SECOND DISTRICT

Greg Walden (R)

Elected 1998, 6th term; b. Jan. 10, 1957, The Dalles; home, Hood River; U. of OR, B.S. 1981; Episcopalian; married (Mylene); 1 child.

Elected Office: OR House of Reps., 1988–94, Majority ldr., 1991–93; OR Senate, 1994–96.

Professional Career: Press secy., U.S. Rep. Denny Smith, 1981–84, Chief of staff, 1984–86; Owner, Columbia Gorge Broadcasters Inc., 1986–2008.

DC Office: 2352 RHOB, 20515, 202-225-6730; Fax: 202-225-5774; Web site: walden.house.gov.

State Offices: Bend, 541-389-4408; La Grande, 541-624-2400; Medford, 541-776-4646.

Committees: *Energy & Commerce* (14th of 23 R): Communications, Technology & the Internet; Energy & Environment; Oversight & Investigations (RMM).

Group Ratings

	ADA	ACLU	AFS	LCV	ITIC	NTU	COC	ACU	CFG	FRC
2008	30	30	14	8	100	53	89	75	55	52
2007	30	—	18	20	—	57	90	68	56	—

National Journal Ratings

	2007 LIB	—	2007 CONS		2008 LIB	—	2008 CONS
Economic	34%	—	65%		30%	—	70%
Social	41%	—	59%		30%	—	70%
Foreign	32%	—	64%		35%	—	65%
Composite	37%	—	64%		32%	—	68%

Key Votes of the 110th Congress

1. Increase minimum wage	Y	5. Share immigration data	Y	9. Withdraw troops 8/08	N
2. Expand SCHIP	N	6. Foreign aid abortion ban	N	10. No operations in Iran	N
3. Raise CAFE standards	Y	7. Ban gay bias in workplace	Y	11. Free trade with Peru	Y
4. Bail out financial markets	Y	8. Repeal D.C. gun law	Y	12. Overhaul FISA	Y

Election Results

2008 general	Greg Walden (R)	236,560	(70%)	($1,646,853)
	Noah Lemas (D)	87,649	(26%)	
	Tristin Mock (Green)	9,668	(3%)	
2008 primary	Greg Walden (R)	83,087	(99%)	

Prior Winning Percentages: 2006 (67%); 2004 (72%); 2002 (72%); 2000 (74%); 1998 (61%)

Population		**Race/Ethnicity**		**Work**	
Pop. 2007:	744,054	White:	84.3%	Private:	74.3%
Change since 2000:	Up 8.7%	Black:	0.4%	Government:	14.5%
Urban:	64.2%	Hispanic:	10.1%	Self-employed:	10.9%
Rural:	35.8%	Asian:	1.0%	Blue collar:	26.1%
Area size:	70,227 sq. mi.	Native Am.:	1.7%	White collar:	53.2%
Age		Hawaiian:	0.1%	Khaki collar:	0.1%
Median age:	39.5 yrs.	Two+ races:	2.2%	Other:	20.6%
More than 65 yrs:	15.5%	*Ancestry*		Median income:	$43,704
Less than 18 yrs:	23.2%	German:	16.5%	Median home value:	$216,300
Education		English:	10.8%	Poverty:	13.5%
H.S. grad:	86.2%	Irish:	10.2%	**Military Veterans**	
College grad:	21.1%			% of Pop:	14.4%
Grad degree:	7.2%				

The Cascade Mountains that wall off eastern Oregon from the rest of the state are a magnificent chain of once (and quite possibly still) active volcanic mountains that drain almost every drop of moisture out of the air blowing in from the Pacific Ocean. They separate green, wet, western Oregon from brown, parched, eastern Oregon. The eastern part has 70% of the state's land, but only 477,000 of its 3.7 million people, most of whom still make their living off the land: beef and dairy cattle, timber and

2008 Presidential Vote		
McCain (R)............................193,002	(54%)
Obama (D) 154,848	(43%)
2004 Presidential Vote		
Bush (R)...............................218,288	(61%)
Kerry (D)..............................135,560	(38%)
Cook Partisan Voting Index: R + 10		

lumber, fish from the Columbia River, and wheat and sugar beets from the irrigated plains. The effect of the Cascades can be felt in the one place they are breached—by the Columbia River Gorge. There, surrounded by brown hills on both sides, funneled winds pound in steadily from the west, making the confluence of the Columbia and Hood rivers the best windsurfing site in the United States. The world's largest wind farm opened here in 2002, featuring 400 windmills capable of generating electricity for 60,000 homes.

The 2nd Congressional District of Oregon covers all of the state east of the Cascades and the southernmost valley between the Cascades and the Coast Range. Much of this land is forested and unpopulated: Harney County, with a land area larger than that of nine states, has just 7,000 residents. Population centers are miles apart. Pendleton is a genuine rodeo town amid the northeastern wheat fields. In the town of The Dalles, where the Columbia River Gorge begins, housing prices spiked after Internet giant Google purchased 30 acres of riverfront land for a 100-employee data center to be powered by cheap hydroelectricity. In the town of Bend, in the fastest-growing part of eastern Oregon, sawmills have closed but the wilderness and high desert plateau attract lots of outdoor activity, tourism and telecommuters. In the mid-2000s, "trophy ranches" were catching on and driving up land prices in Wallowa County as wealthy exurbanites bought up huge parcels for vacation retreats and retirement dream homes. Crook County has also seen an invasion of real estate developers.

Until it voted for George H.W. Bush for president over Bill Clinton in 1992, Crook County was a bellwether, the only county in the country to have voted for the winning presidential candidate in every election in the 20th century. Like the district as a whole, it has become more Republican, voting 68% for George W. Bush in 2004 and 61.5% for John McCain in 2008. In the district's southwestern corner, lying west of the Cascades, is the 1,932-foot-deep Crater Lake, the deepest in the nation, created when the top blew off a huge volcano. The local economy is dominated by lumber and pear orchards around Klamath Falls, Ashland, Medford and Grants Pass.

Politically, the 2nd District has grown very suspicious of the federal government and very Republican. The cultural liberalism of Portland isn't welcome here. This is part of the leave-us-alone Rocky Mountain Basin, not the hipster West Coast. The federal government owns three-quarters of the district's land, with much of it fenced off from local use by various government decrees. Court decisions protecting the spotted owl eviscerated the logging industry here, and the cutoff of water in 2001 from the Klamath Basin to protect the endangered suckerfish threatened to destroy the livelihoods of 1,400 local farmers. The flow of water was restored, but logging remains endangered, with a lasting impact locally. In 2007, rural Jackson County was forced to shut down all of its 15 libraries after Congress ended "safety net" payments to communities hard hit by efforts to protect endangered species. The county has just one large sawmill left, compared with 91 in its heyday.

The representative from the 2nd District is Greg Walden, a Republican elected in 1998. He grew up on an 80-acre cherry orchard near The Dalles in the Columbia Gorge; his father ran radio stations that had been in the family since the 1930s and also served in the state House. Walden followed his father into both pursuits. As a young man, he was a disc jockey and talk show host. Then, he got involved in politics as the press secretary and chief of staff for Republican Rep. Denny Smith from 1981 to 1987. Walden returned to Hood River to run the family's five-station broadcast business, Columbia Gorge Broadcasters. In 1988, he was elected to the state House, eventually becoming majority leader. He is conservative on economics but more moderate on cultural issues; he supports abortion rights and embryonic stem cell research, but opposes federal funding of abortions.

When the 2nd District seat opened in 1998 with the retirement of GOP Rep. Bob Smith, Walden ran and faced substantial primary opposition from Perry Atkinson, a Christian broadcaster who was backed financially by Gary L. Bauer's Campaign for Working Americans and Americans for Limited Terms. Walden stayed competitive by raising $500,000 and prevailed over Atkinson with 55% of the vote. In the anticlimactic general election against a conservative Democrat, Walden won 61%-35%.

In the House, Walden has been an active legislator with a focus on a national issue with strong local implications—forest management. He played a central role in 2003 in assembling bipartisan support for the Healthy Forests Restoration Act, which was a legislative response to wildfires raging across the West from unlogged dry timber. He also successfully sought to reopen the flow of water to farmers in the Klamath Basin. Later, he pushed for legislation to expedite logging after natural disasters. In July 2006, the House passed his bill to expand the Mount Hood wilderness area, but the Senate did not act. Walden has worked to curb regulations under the Endangered Species Act by encouraging a greater role for outside scientists to review government proposals. In recent years, he also has tried to restore timber payments to rural counties, joining forces with home-state Sen. Ron Wyden, a Democrat.

In 2007, Walden was a leader of a coalition to stop efforts to restore the Fairness Doctrine in broadcasting, which forced broadcasters to offer views opposing those of their on-air commentators. The rule was abandoned in 1987, and liberals have pushed to revive it to counter the influence of popular conservative talk show hosts such as Rush Limbaugh. Recalling his own days in broadcasting, Walden told *The Oregonian* newspaper that it was difficult to figure out who qualified to offer opposing viewpoints when his father read editorials on the air, so the family stopped airing editorials altogether. Political chatter over the broadcast network tends to be conservative, he said, but that should not matter. "Is it more conservative than liberal? Yeah," Walden told the newspaper. "Are there a lot more country-western stations than polka stations? Yeah. Listeners make these determinations. The marketplace decides." Also in 2007, Walden was appointed by Minority Leader John Boehner to the Select Committee on Energy Independence and Global Warming.

Walden has been re-elected easily. He has twice declined to run for governor, but may have another opportunity to run in this swing state in 2010. "Greg Walden will be governor of Oregon one day," former Sen. Gordon Smith told *The Oregonian*.

THIRD DISTRICT

Earl Blumenauer (D)

Elected May 1996, 7th full term; b. Aug. 16, 1948, Portland; home, Portland; Lewis & Clark Col., B.A. 1970, J.D. 1976; no religious affiliation; married (Margaret); 4 children.

Elected Office: OR House of Reps., 1972–78; Multnomah Cnty. Comm., 1978–86; Portland City Cncl., 1986–96.

Professional Career: Asst. to pres., Portland St. U., 1970–77.

DC Office: 2267 RHOB, 20515, 202-225-4811; Fax: 202-225-8941; Web site: www.house.gov/blumenauer.

State Offices: Portland, 503-231-2300.

Committees: *Budget* (6th of 24 D). *Ways & Means* (13th of 26 D): Health; Select Revenue Measures.

Group Ratings

	ADA	ACLU	AFS	LCV	ITIC	NTU	COC	ACU	CFG	FRC
2008	95	100	100	100	86	24	53	12	15	0
2007	85	—	100	100	—	11	50	0	16	—

National Journal Ratings

	2007 LIB	—	2007 CONS		2008 LIB	—	2008 CONS
Economic	72%	—	28%		78%	—	20%
Social	85%	—	13%		82%	—	0%
Foreign	93%	—	7%		92%	—	0%
Composite	84%	—	16%		89%	—	11%

Key Votes of the 110th Congress

1. Increase minimum wage	Y	5. Share immigration data	N	9. Withdraw troops 8/08	Y
2. Expand SCHIP	Y	6. Foreign aid abortion ban	N	10. No operations in Iran	Y
3. Raise CAFE standards	Y	7. Ban gay bias in workplace	Y	11. Free trade with Peru	Y
4. Bail out financial markets	N	8. Repeal D.C. gun law	N	12. Overhaul FISA	N

Election Results

2008 general	Earl Blumenauer (D)	254,235	(75%)	($1,132,494)
	Delia Lopez (R)	71,063	(21%)	
	Michael Meo (Green)	15,063	(4%)	
2008 primary	Earl Blumenauer (D)	121,176	(87%)	
	John Sweeney (D)	9,389	(7%)	
	Joseph Walsh (D)	8,783	(6%)	

Prior Winning Percentages: 2006 (73%); 2004 (71%); 2002 (67%); 2000 (67%); 1998 (84%); 1996 (67%); 1996 (68%)

Population		Race/Ethnicity		Work	
Pop. 2007:	723,163	White:	74.4%	Private:	79.6%
Change since 2000:	Up 5.7%	Black:	5.1%	Government:	11.9%
Urban:	93.1%	Hispanic:	10.5%	Self-employed:	8.3%
Rural:	6.9%	Asian:	5.9%	Blue collar:	21.8%
Area size:	1,054 sq. mi.	Native Am.:	0.5%	White collar:	60.2%
		Hawaiian:	0.4%	Khaki collar:	0.0%
Age		Two+ races:	3.1%	Other:	17.9%
Median age:	36.7 yrs.			Median income:	$47,621
More than 65 yrs:	10.4%	*Ancestry*		Median home value:	$242,900
Less than 18 yrs:	23.8%	German:	15.6%	Poverty:	15.3%
		Irish:	9.3%		
Education		English:	8.8%	**Military Veterans**	
H.S. grad:	86.9%			% of Pop:	10.4%
College grad:	28.7%				
Grad degree:	10.1%				

Portland, the Rose City set between Mount Hood to the east and the Tualatin Mountains to the west, spans the Willamette River and keeps its industrial back to the Columbia. Still one of America's least-known major cities, it's also one of its most distinctive. For most of its history Portland was a prosaic city, a blue-collar town that piled Oregon lumber and Oregon pears into freight cars or unloaded machines from back East or automobiles from Japan on its docks. But in the past three decades, Portland

2008 Presidential Vote
Obama (D) 260,156   (71%)
McCain (R)............................93,934   (26%)

2004 Presidential Vote
Kerry (D)..............................242,075   (67%)
Bush (R) 118,442   (33%)

Cook Partisan Voting Index: D + 19

has been transformed. Out on the Pacific Rim, it increasingly makes its living on foreign trade with Asia. It has become a home to high-tech industries, particularly in the Silicon Forest suburbs. Government has also produced change. Oregon's land-use act, passed in 1973, required local governments to set geographic limits on growth. Metro, the regional government established in 1979 just as growth was accelerating, is a counterweight against the endless population spread outward into former farmland. With gentrification in the city, old neighborhoods have been revived with new names: "NoPo" refers to north Portland. With its first light-rail service, Portland encouraged the development of high-density commercial space and housing around transit stops. Bicycle paths wind throughout the metropolitan area, and downtown, west of the Willamette River, boasts postmodern structures amid classic masonry buildings. Portland in fact is the nation's most bicycle-friendly large city, with the highest percentage of bike commuters. Local leaders now are seeking to make Portland the nation's leader for biodiesel and other renewable fuels.

In the process, the central city of Portland, like San Francisco and Seattle, has attracted political and cultural liberals. And, like those two cities, Portland has its share of traffic congestion and high home prices. Earlier in the decade, *Money* magazine rated it among the most livable cities, but its standing has since declined. For a time, the metropolitan region had one of the country's highest unemployment rates, due partly to the dot-com bust and perhaps exacerbated by excessive controls on growth. *Money* dropped Portland from its top-100 list in 2006. Still, growth has continued despite the national economic downturn in 2008.

The 3rd Congressional District of Oregon includes the large part of Portland and Multnomah County east of the Willamette River and some of suburban Clackamas County to the south. It extends over plains and hills to the exquisite scenery of Mount Hood high in the Cascades and Bonneville Dam in the Columbia River Gorge. Politically, it remains dominated by cultural liberalism, which sets Portland apart from its suburbs and the rest of Oregon. In 2004, Multnomah County voted 72%-27% for John Kerry over George W. Bush, and in 2008, Barack Obama beat John McCain in Multnomah, 77%-21%.

The congressman from the 3rd District is Earl Blumenauer, who won a special election in May 1996 to replace Ron Wyden, elected to the Senate that year. Blumenauer grew up in Portland, graduated from Lewis and Clark College and its Northwestern Law School. He was inspired by the civil-rights and anti-war movements of the 1960s, while in his teens. In 1969 in college, he headed a statewide campaign to lower Oregon's voting age. He has held public office almost all of his adult life. In 1972, at age 23, he was elected to the Oregon House; in 1978, he was elected to the Multnomah County Board of Commissioners. In 1986, he was elected to the Portland City Council. He championed many of the policies that have made Portland distinctive—regional light-rail transit, curbside recycling, and aggressive land-use planning. He encouraged bicycle riding and "regional rail summits," which bring neighborhood residents into the planning for higher densities at transit nodes. Blumenauer has had some setbacks, notably when he lost the 1992 mayoral race. But he was the obvious successor to Wyden and won the special election 68%-25%. His campaign slogan was, "Vote Earl, Vote Often." He has been easily re-elected since.

In the House, Blumenauer has a liberal voting record and a distinctive agenda. To promote biking as an alternative to driving, he rides his bicycle everywhere he travels around Washington from his Capitol Hill apartment. He formed a Bicycle Caucus that boasts over 100 members and fought for showers for bike commuters at the Capitol. Blumenauer was astonished to find that the House subsidized parking for employees, but not mass transit; now, employees can get subsidized transit fares. He is interested in what seem like quixotic projects now but may seem less so in time: an interstate highway system for bicycle paths and less dependence on driving as a tool to improve public health. "The rise of bicycles is a metaphor for change in this country," Blumenauer says. Blumenauer proudly terms Portland a model for the future of the American city. And the sometimes-nerdy policy wonk has taken his gospel of livability and civic values elsewhere, through his Livable Cities Task Force and his political action committee. The Internet-savvy Blumenauer sets his BlackBerry to notify him when he is mentioned in a blog posting, and he responds on a regular basis.

On economic issues, he has actively promoted trade across the Pacific, a key element of Portland's economy. He supported normal trade relations with China, but he joined most House Democrats in opposing the Central American Free Trade Agreement. With Republican Rep. Jeff Flake of Arizona, he has railed against wasteful government spending. When Democrats assumed the majority in 2007, Blumenauer bolstered his influence with a seat on the tax-writing House Ways and Means Committee and became a more active lawmaker. He gave the panel a new focus on the environment and urban planning, including his call for tax subsidies for bicycle commuting and for closing a loophole that allowed businesses to write off the cost of sport utility vehicles. He worked on increased labor and environmental standards in a free-trade agreement with Peru. But he continued his independent ways as one of 14 House Democrats who voted in May 2008 to sustain President Bush's veto of the farm bill they decried as bloated. "We're giving money to the richest [farmers] who are going to squeeze small and medium-sized farmers out," he told the *Oregonian*. And Blumenauer resigned from the U.S.-Vietnam Caucus, a group he once led, following the conviction of pro-democracy Vietnamese activists.

He seriously considered running for mayor of Portland in 2004 and surprised some local Democrats when he decided against it. Blumenauer was also mentioned widely as a possible challenger to GOP Sen. Gordon Smith in 2008 but declined to run. However, he kept the door open to a run for governor in 2010.

FOURTH DISTRICT

Peter DeFazio (D)

Elected 1986, 12th term; b. May 27, 1947, Needham, MA; home, Springfield; Tufts U., B.A. 1969, U. of OR, M.S. 1977; Catholic; married (Myrnie).

Military Career: Air Force, 1967–71.

Elected Office: Lane Cnty. Bd. of Commissioners, 1982–86.

Professional Career: Dist. dir., U.S. Rep. James Weaver, 1977–82.

DC Office: 2134 RHOB, 20515, 202-225-6416; Fax: 202-225-0032; Web site: www.defazio.house.gov.

State Offices: Coos Bay, 541-269-2609; Eugene, 541-465-6732; Roseburg, 541-440-3523.

Committees: *Homeland Security* (4th of 20 D): Management, Investigations & Oversight; Transportation Security & Infrastructure Protection. *Natural Resources* (16th of 29 D): National Parks, Forests & Public Lands; Water & Power. *Transportation & Infrastructure* (3rd of 44 D): Aviation; Highways & Transit (Chmn); Railroads, Pipelines & Hazardous Materials.

Group Ratings

	ADA	ACLU	AFS	LCV	ITIC	NTU	COC	ACU	CFG	FRC
2008	90	100	100	100	29	22	50	20	18	5
2007	90	—	100	95	—	6	37	4	3	—

National Journal Ratings

	2007 LIB	—	2007 CONS		2008 LIB	—	2008 CONS
Economic	61%	—	38%		55%	—	44%
Social	58%	—	41%		59%	—	38%
Foreign	81%	—	16%		78%	—	17%
Composite	68%	—	33%		66%	—	35%

Key Votes of the 110th Congress

1. Increase minimum wage	Y	5. Share immigration data	Y	9. Withdraw troops 8/08	Y
2. Expand SCHIP	Y	6. Foreign aid abortion ban	N	10. No operations in Iran	Y
3. Raise CAFE standards	Y	7. Ban gay bias in workplace	Y	11. Free trade with Peru	N
4. Bail out financial markets	N	8. Repeal D.C. gun law	Y	12. Overhaul FISA	N

Election Results

2008 general	Peter DeFazio (D) 275,143	(82%)	($471,179)
	Jaynee Germond (CNP) 43,133	(13%)	
	Mike Beilstein (Green) 13,162	(4%)	
2008 primary	Peter DeFazio (D) 119,366	(99%)	

Prior Winning Percentages: 2006 (62%); 2004 (61%); 2002 (64%); 2000 (68%); 1998 (70%); 1996 (66%); 1994 (67%); 1992 (71%); 1990 (86%); 1988 (72%); 1986 (54%)

Population		Race/Ethnicity		Work	
Pop. 2007:	714,140	White:	87.9%	Private:	74.8%
Change since 2000:	Up 4.4%	Black:	0.7%	Government:	15.4%
Urban:	69.2%	Hispanic:	5.4%	Self-employed:	9.4%
Rural:	30.8%	Asian:	2.1%	Blue collar:	24.8%
Area size:	18,034 sq. mi.	Native Am.:	1.3%	White collar:	55.9%
		Hawaiian:	0.1%	Khaki collar:	0.1%
Age		Two+ races:	2.3%	Other:	19.2%
Median age:	40.1 yrs.			Median income:	$41,081
More than 65 yrs:	15.9%	*Ancestry*		Median home value:	$195,400
Less than 18 yrs:	20.8%	German:	16.5%	Poverty:	15.4%
		English:	11.3%		
Education		Irish:	10.6%	**Military Veterans**	
H.S. grad:	87.6%			% of Pop:	14.4%
College grad:	23.3%				
Grad degree:	9.0%				

Eugene is nestled in the southernmost bit of lowland in Oregon's Willamette Valley, and is surrounded by mountains on three sides. It is a farming center, a lumber metropolis and, most notably, a university town. Settlers arrived here in 1846, farming in the valley and cutting timber in the hills. In 1876, the University of Oregon was established, a symbol of the state's strong Yankee cultural ethic. Eugene and next-door Springfield, once a lumber town and now a center for the manufacture of computer chips, have grown into comfortable midsized towns. Eugene has bicycle paths along the riverbanks and its main streets, and likes to bill itself as the "Running Capital of the Universe" —Phil Knight and his former University of Oregon track coach, Bill Bowerman, started Nike here, the first soles formed on a waffle iron. Now the second-largest city in Oregon, behind Portland, and often described as one of the most livable in the nation, Eugene has small-town ambience and urban sensibilities (local laws permit nude beaches, but only with individuals of the same sex), and its liberal voters have been vital to Democrats statewide.

2008 Presidential Vote		
Obama (D) 201,143	(54%)
McCain (R) 161,079	(43%)

2004 Presidential Vote		
Kerry (D) 188,479	(49%)
Bush (R) 187,292	(49%)

Cook Partisan Voting Index: D+2

Beyond Eugene and Springfield are southwest Oregon's green-clad mountains, and for years the region cut more timber than anywhere else in the country. But demand for wood is volatile, dependent on the vagaries of interest rates. East Asia increasingly wants unprocessed logs rather than milled lumber, which means fewer jobs for Oregon. The 1980s were tough on this region. Recession reduced demand for housing, and the cutting of old-growth forests was banned to protect the endangered spotted owl. But even as the lumber industry languished, a robust local economy and active job retraining resulted in local job gains in the 1990s. Recent economic development has been diverse, with gains in health care, tourism, and retiree migration from California. But Timber Country, including forest-product businesses, continues to struggle. With the 2006 closing of Weyerhaeuser's plywood plant, Lane County's wood-products-sector employment dropped by two-thirds from its 1977 peak of 14,000 jobs. The decline of commercial fishing also hit coastal towns of southwest Oregon hard.

The 4th Congressional District of Oregon includes Eugene, Springfield, and surrounding Lane County; it goes south on Interstate 5 to include Roseburg in Douglas County, once one of the premier logging counties in the United States. It extends north to Albany and includes most of Corvallis, except for Oregon State University. It includes the entire southern half of Oregon's stunning Pacific coastline down to the California border. Eugene is heavily Democratic. Roseburg, the vacation town of Albany, and their surrounding counties vote heavily Republican. The travails of the logging industry moved the area to the right: The 4th District (with only slightly different boundaries) voted 54%-44% against George H. W. Bush in 1988, but 49%-44% for George W. Bush in 2000. In 2004, the 4th voted narrowly for John Kerry, one of just two districts in the nation to flip from Bush to Kerry. It voted 54%-43% for Barack Obama in 2008.

The congressman from the 4th District is Peter DeFazio (*da-FAH-zee-oh*), a Democrat first elected in 1986. He grew up in Massachusetts, came to Oregon for graduate school, was a bike mechanic, and went to work for 4th District Rep. Jim Weaver, a Democrat. In 1982, DeFazio moved to Springfield and won a seat on the county commission. When Weaver retired in 1986, DeFazio won his House seat in a tight race. He beat Bill Bradbury 34%-33% in the primary and won the general election 54%-46%. DeFazio has compiled a record that seems to satisfy both Eugene and the rest of the district: He's liberal on most issues, and moderate on social issues. An original founder of the loose-knit Progressive Caucus, he has not been shy to express his anger that millions of working Americans suffered during the boom years before 2008. He opposed the Clinton-era North American Free Trade Agreement and later was a leader in the fight to defeat normal trade relations with China.

DeFazio often takes idiosyncratic views. During the period of GOP control of Congress, he offered a specific proposal to fix Social Security, unlike most Democrats. He called for removing the payroll deduction limitation that benefits the top wage earners. He took the lead in the House effort to permit airline pilots to carry guns in the cockpit, and although the Bush administration opposed it, DeFazio won by an astonishing 250-175. The Senate later followed suit. After catastrophic wildfires in the summer of 2002, DeFazio teamed with Oregon Republican Rep. Greg Walden to seek a middle ground to speed the thinning of brush in the forests; DeFazio's environmental allies denounced him as a turncoat, but his proposal was enacted.

When Democrats won control of the House in 2006, DeFazio took the influential post of chairman of Transportation and Infrastructure's Highways and Transit Subcommittee. He called for taxing oil companies, rather than imposing a gas tax on consumers, after high gas prices prompted people to drive less, with a resulting falloff in revenues in the highway trust fund. He also criticized loopholes in the highway-safety law that were blamed for inadequate oversight of drug and alcohol use by truck drivers.

DeFazio has routinely won re-election by more than 60% in a marginal district. Against former FBI agent Jim Feldkamp, who favored more local control of forests and spent a total of $1 million in back-to-back challenges in 2004 and 2006, DeFazio got 61% and 62%, respectively. The vote was close in the southern counties of Curry, Douglas, and Josephine, but DeFazio exceeded two-thirds of the vote in Lane County. After GOP Sen. Bob Packwood resigned in 1995, DeFazio ran to succeed him. In the primary, he had far less money than Democratic Rep. Ron Wyden. His opposition to gun control and NAFTA provided clear contrasts to Wyden, but Wyden won 50%-44% and went on to prevail in the general election. In the 2002 election, DeFazio considered running again for the Senate, this time against Republican Gordon Smith. But he said he would run only with the "strongest possible support" from Democratic leaders. They in turn declined to help unless he showed he could raise a significant amount of money and get traction in the early polls. DeFazio opted to remain in the House. Should he ever decide not to seek re-election, this might well be a seriously contested seat.

FIFTH DISTRICT

Kurt Schrader (D)

Elected 2008, 1st term; b. Oct. 19, 1951, Bridgeport, CT; home, Candy; Cornell U., B.A. 1973; U. of IL, D.V.M. 1977; Christian; married (Martha); 4 children.

Elected Office: OR House, 1997–2003; OR Senate, 2003–08.

Professional Career: Former aide, AK Gov. office; Veterinarian, 1978–2008.

DC Office: 1419 LHOB, 20515, 202-225-5711; Fax: 202-225-5699; Web site: schrader.house.gov.

State Offices: Oregon City, 503-557-1324; Salem, 503-588-9100.

Committees: *Agriculture* (15th of 28 D): Department Operations, Oversight, Nutrition & Forestry; General Farm Commodities & Risk Management; Horticulture & Organic Agriculture. *Budget* (24th of 24 D). *Small Business* (5th of 17 D): Contracting & Technology; Finance & Tax (Chmn).

Group Ratings and Key Votes: Newly Elected

Election Results

2008 general	Kurt Schrader (D)	181,577	(54%)	($1,389,050)
	Mike Erickson (R)	128,297	(38%)	($2,594,663)
	Sean Bates (I)	6,830	(2%)	
2008 primary	Kurt Schrader (D)	51,980	(54%)	
	Nancy Moran (D)	18,597	(19%)	
	Steve Marks (D)	17,643	(18%)	
	Andrew Foster (D)	6,104	(6%)	

Population		Race/Ethnicity		Work	
Pop. 2007:	740,409	White:	80.5%	Private:	75.9%
Change since 2000:	Up 8.2%	Black:	0.9%	Government:	16.2%
Urban:	80.4%	Hispanic:	12.7%	Self-employed:	7.6%
Rural:	19.6%	Asian:	2.5%	Blue collar:	21.6%
Area size:	5,829 sq. mi.	Native Am.:	0.9%	White collar:	59.7%
		Hawaiian:	0.2%	Khaki collar:	0.1%
Age		Two+ races:	2.2%	Other:	18.7%
Median age:	37.2 yrs.			Median income:	$51,130
More than 65 yrs:	13.0%	*Ancestry*		Median home value:	$232,500
Less than 18 yrs:	23.7%	German:	18.7%	Poverty:	12.9%
		English:	11.5%		
Education		Irish:	9.6%	**Military Veterans**	
H.S. grad:	87.3%			% of Pop:	12.0%
College grad:	29.0%				
Grad degree:	10.7%				

The Willamette Valley was the great Promised Land at the end of the Oregon Trail, shielded from the cold storms of the Pacific by mountains but squeezing most of the moisture out of the clouds in the form of rain, fog, and persistent mist. New England Yankees planted small towns they called Salem and Oregon City, founded schools and colleges, built tall-spired churches and eventually Salem's distinctive Art Deco state Capitol. This was one of the few valleys in the West that settlers found

2008 Presidential Vote		
Obama (D)	192,327	(54%)
McCain (R)	154,485	(43%)
2004 Presidential Vote		
Bush (R)	181,070	(50%)
Kerry (D)	176,558	(49%)
Cook Partisan Voting Index: D + 1		

readily suitable for agriculture. The Willamette Valley's soil is fertile, the plain created by the waters of the Willamette sweeping down from the mountains is broad, but industrial runoff has made the river among the most polluted in the nation. Metro Portland has also intruded on the land, with young people leapfrogging most of the parcels protected from development and into Clackamas and Marion counties to the south. Salem and Eugene are battling for the distinction of Oregon's second-largest city. In 2003, rapidly-growing Salem passed Eugene in population, but Eugene regained second-largest-city status in 2007, according to the Center for Population Research at Portland State University.

The 5th Congressional District of Oregon includes much of the northern Willamette Valley. Near Portland is the old pioneer town of Oregon City, which was the end point of the Oregon Trail. The district spreads south to the state capital of Salem, also home of Willamette University, the oldest university west of the Mississippi River. It includes part of Corvallis, home of Oregon State University and its renowned agricultural science department. Then it hops over the Coast Range to take in Lincoln and Tillamook counties, which are fishing and logging and cheese-making communities. The district also includes all of rural Polk County. Although the area remains one of the nation's chief producers of processed vegetables, its crops of beans and berries have dropped significantly, while nurseries have become a new growth industry. The Willamette Valley is also home to a burgeoning wine industry that produces prize-winning Pinot Noir. In 2007, wine grapes became one of Oregon's top 10 money-producing crops. Historically, the valley was Republican, like the original home of many of its settlers, New England. But like New England, it has been trending Democratic, and now is marginal territory. The Corvallis area is heavily Democratic, the Salem area more likely to be Republican while Clackamas County is competitive. George W. Bush won this district by fewer than 5,000 votes in both the 2000 and 2004 presidential elections. In 2008, Barack Obama defeated John McCain 54%-43%.

The congressman from the 5th District is first-term Democrat Kurt Schrader. Schrader was born in Bridgeport, Conn., the oldest of three children of a chemical engineer and his wife. He studied government at Cornell University in Ithaca, N.Y., where he met his wife, Martha, also a Cornell student. Schrader went on to pursue his passion for veterinary medicine at the University of Illinois. After college, the couple wanted to move West, and settled in Oregon. Schrader currently runs two veterinary clinics in Canby, Ore., and his wife is a Clackamas County commissioner. They live on a 60-acre gentleman's farm listed on the National Register of Historic Places.

Schrader launched himself into public service as a member of the Canby planning commission for 15 years, assisting in development of the city's land use plan. In 1997, he won a seat in the state House, and six years later was elected to the state Senate. There, he was co-chairman of the Joint Ways and Means Committee, with jurisdiction over taxation. His major focus was improving public education, and Schrader pushed legislation to tax new construction to pay for schools. He developed a reputation as a conservative Democrat by opposing his party on some key issues, such as increasing the minimum wage.

The 5th District seat opened when six-term Democratic Rep. Darlene Hooley announced her retirement in February 2008. Schrader was the first Democrat to file for the race. He lent his campaign $130,000 during the primary and won over 50% of the vote against three opponents. In the general election, he faced shipping entrepreneur and 2006 GOP nominee Mike Erickson. Erickson had challenged Hooley two years earlier, and held her to 54% of the vote. In that contest, he spent $1.8 million, most of it his own money. In the 2008 Republican primary, Erickson lent his campaign $1.6 million and ran a series of ads attacking the legislative record of his chief rival, former state Rep. Kevin Mannix. But Mannix hit back and in the process contributed what would become the race's defining story, when he publicized allegations that Erickson had impregnated a woman in 2000 and then paid for an ensuing abortion. Erickson admitted to the relationship but denied paying for an abortion. He defeated Mannix by just over 1,000 votes.

The general election was initially considered wide open. This was George W. Bush territory in 2000 and 2004, and Hooley had faced competitive contests in previous years. But the district had experienced a surge in new Democratic voters in the latter half of 2008, giving Democrats their first voter-registration advantage in the district in 12 years.

As the race progressed, Schrader emerged as the favorite. Erickson was unable to shake the allegations pertaining to his earlier romantic relationship—it was the subject of a June article in *The Oregonian* —and he limited his public appearances during the campaign. Erickson attempted to slow Schrader's momentum by running ads claiming his opponent would vote for "the largest tax increase in American history." He also attacked Schrader for failing to pay his property taxes on time, as the local news media reported in 2005. But Schrader received major endorsements from the Oregon Farm Bureau, and *The Oregonian* and the *Statesman Journal* newspapers. He also got financial help from the Democratic Congressional Campaign Committee. Erickson outspent Schrader by over $1 million, but Schrader prevailed 54% to 38%. He carried every county in the district and won 74 percent of the vote in the liberal stronghold of Multnomah County.

As a member of Congress, Schrader earned a spot on the House Agriculture Committee, a good fit for his agriculture-heavy district.

★ PENNSYLVANIA ★

Pennsylvania started off as the center of America. Philadelphia was the 13 colonies' largest city when it hosted the Continental Congress in 1776 and the Constitutional Convention in 1787. It was one of the newer colonies, founded 52 years after Massachusetts and 75 years after Virginia. Under the benevolent rule of the Penn family and with its Quaker traditions, Pennsylvania soon became the major settlement in the Middle Colonies. Its tolerance attracted Englishmen of many religious sects and thousands of Germans as well. Bordermen from Scotland, Yorkshire and Northern Ireland crossed the corduroy-like ridges of the Appalachians and settled the mountainous interior where Gen. Edward Braddock had been beaten by the French and Indians not long before. Pennsylvania, in the geometric lines founding father William Penn had obtained from King Charles II, connected two major river systems—the golden triangle where the Allegheny and Monongahela rivers joined to form the Ohio, and the wide Delaware estuary, with its thriving commerce and rich hinterland. Philadelphia was, after London and Dublin, the largest Georgian city in the late 18th century, seemingly destined to be the London of America, the metropolis of government and commerce and culture. Pittsburgh was the frontier metropolis, the gateway to the great interior of North America and the fulcrum point of American expansion.

But Philadelphia—and Pennsylvania—failed to hold the central position the founding founders had expected. As part of a political deal, the young nation's capital was located on a site along the Potomac River rather than on the Delaware. And the railroad built from the Hudson to Lake Erie channeled trade away from Philadelphia to New York. Philadelphia lost its chance to be the nation's financial capital when Andrew Jackson in righteous rage vetoed the rechartering of the Second Bank of the United States. Philadelphia's Quaker tradition, tolerant of diversity, was overshadowed in intellectual life by New England's Puritan tradition, morally stern, angrily intolerant, ready to use the state to impose cultural values from abolition to prohibition. Instead, Pennsylvania became America's energy and heavy industry capital. The reason was coal. Northeast Pennsylvania was the nation's primary source of anthracite, the hard coal used for home heating, and western Pennsylvania was laced with bituminous coal, the soft coal used in steel production. Connected with Philadelphia by the Pennsylvania Railroad, Pittsburgh was the center of the nation's steel industry by 1890.

Immigrants poured in from Europe and from the surrounding hills to work in western Pennsylvania's mines and factories. Pittsburgh became synonymous with industrial prosperity. In 1900, Pennsylvania was the nation's second-largest state and growing rapidly. But the boom ended conclusively with the Great Depression of the 1930s, and in parts of Pennsylvania it has never returned. After World War II, both home heating and industry switched away from coal. Even when coal prices boomed in the 1970s, strip mining created relatively few new jobs. Similarly, Pennsylvania steel began its decline three decades ago, when management decided not to keep up with new technology and agreed to big wage and benefit increases with the mistaken confidence they could pass the costs along. Big steel got import quotas as long ago as 1969—Pennsylvania has been a protectionist state since the first Bessemer converter furnaces were lit—but they didn't create jobs. By the time quotas lapsed in the 1990s, the industry had modernized, but mostly in huge new Indiana mills and in small mini-mills scattered far from the factories that once lined the Monongahela. Only the embers remain, or, the fires: The Red Ash colliery fire, ignited in 1915, burns on beneath the hills above Wilkes-Barre, as do 35 other fires in abandoned coal mines.

The result has been the slowest population growth of any major state: There were 9.6 million Pennsylvanians in 1930, and 12.4 million in 2008. Pennsylvania cast 36 electoral votes for Franklin Roosevelt in 1940 and 21 for Barack Obama in 2008. It had 30 House members, as many as California, in 1960, but now has 19 to California's 53. People growing up here are as likely to leave as they are to stay, and few outsiders move in. Pennsylvania looks and sounds today like it did in the 1940s, with the significant difference that Pennsylvania in 1940 had lots of young people, while the Pennsylvania of today has the second largest elderly population, after Florida, of any state. In recent years, eastern Pennsylvania has enjoyed a boomlet of refugees from high-tax, adjacent states. From 1990 to 2008, the population of the 19 counties east of the first major Appalachian ridge grew 11% with newcomers pouring in from New York and New Jersey. Marylanders have settled in Lancaster and York counties west of Philadelphia. It has been mainly white-collar growth. In the same period, the population of the 48 counties west of the ridge declined 3%.

Although Pennsylvania started off as the country's center of government, government has not been central to Pennsylvania for most of its history. During the Civil War, Pennsylvania was the site of the northernmost advance of the Confederate Army, at Carlisle, just north of Gettysburg. For generations afterward, it was the most Republican of the large states, because of Abraham Lincoln and the Union, and because of the steel industry and the high tariff. Its malodorous Republican machines built parties that were not representative of one ethnic segment but had a place for just about everyone. In 1932, Pennsylvania was the only big state that stuck with Republican Herbert Hoover and voted against Democrat Franklin Roosevelt. But then, the political landscape changed. The New Deal, John L. Lewis's United

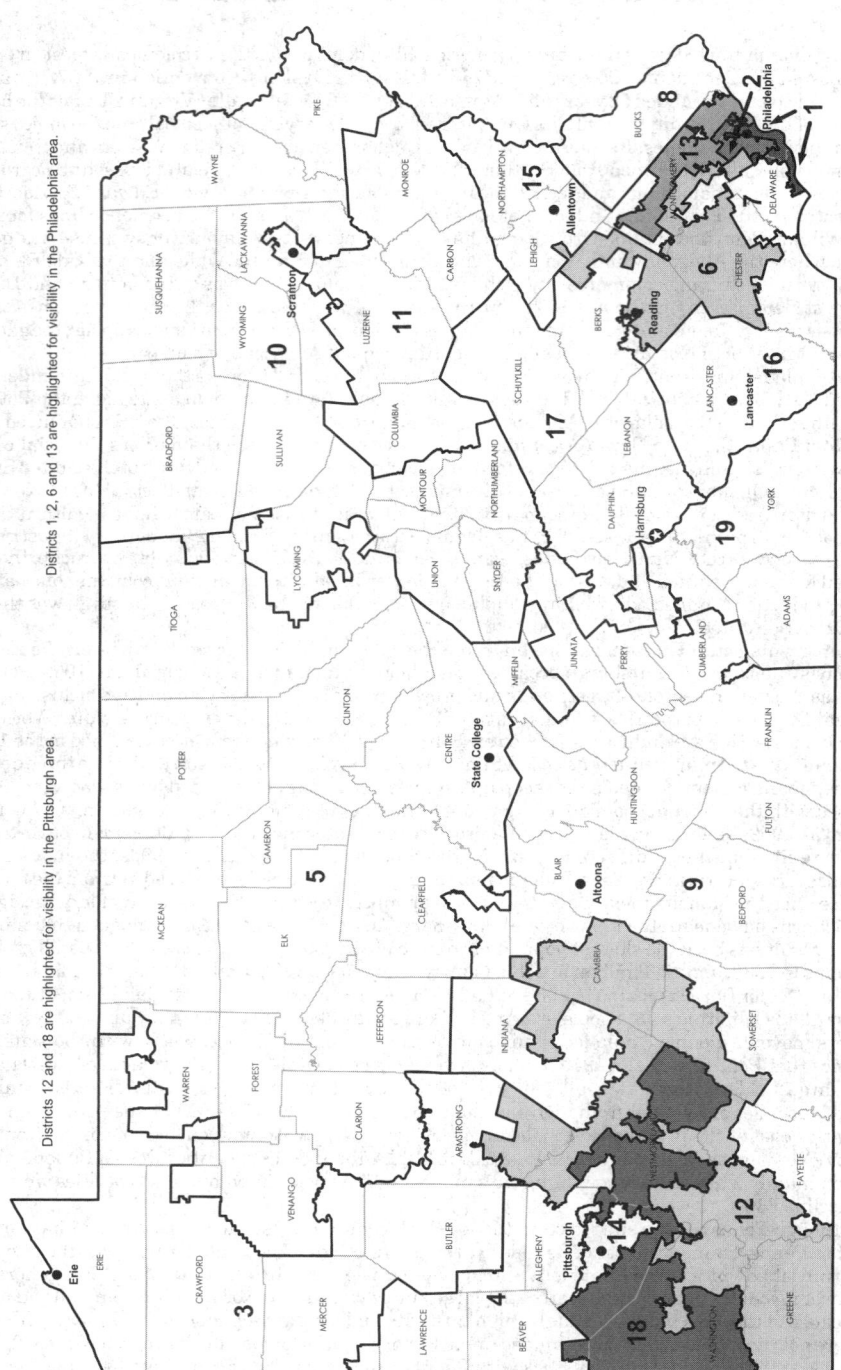

Districts 1, 2, 6 and 13 are highlighted for visibility in the Philadelphia area.

Districts 12 and 18 are highlighted for visibility in the Pittsburgh area.

The Almanac of American Politics.
National Journal

Congressional district boundaries were first effective for 2004.

Mine Workers and the CIO industrial union movement, and a series of bloody strikes made industrial Pennsylvania almost as Democratic in the 1930s and 1940s as it had been Republican from the 1860s to the 1920s. Even then, parts of Pennsylvania not heavy with big steel factories and coal mines—the northern tier of counties along the New York border, the central part of the state around Altoona, and the Pennsylvania Dutch country around Lancaster—remained the strongest Republican voting bloc in the East. Philadelphia became a heavily Democratic city, but in the suburban counties, the old Republican machines stayed in control. The result was a pivotal marginal state in presidential elections from the 1950s to the 1990s.

In the 1980s, prosperous eastern Pennsylvania trended Republican and ailing western Pennsylvania trended Democratic. In the 1990s, culturally liberal eastern Pennsylvania trended Democratic and culturally conservative western Pennsylvania trended Republican. The east is larger—metro Philadelphia cast 34% of the state's votes in 2004 and metro Pittsburgh 24%—and the state has mostly gone its way. Pennsylvania voted Republican for president three times in the 1980s and Democratic for president in the five elections from 1992 to 2008. Metro Philadelphia, which voted 50%-49% for Democrat Michael Dukakis in 1988, voted 66%-33% for Democrat Barack Obama in 2008. Metro Pittsburgh, which voted 59%-40% for Dukakis, gave Obama only 51%-48%. Similarly, the eastern 19 counties, which voted 54% for George H.W. Bush in 1988, voted 54% against his son in 2004 and 59% for Obama in 2008. The western 48 counties, which voted 52% against Bush Sr. in 1988 and then voted 52% for Bush Jr. in 2004 gave Republican presidential nominee John McCain a 50%-49% victory in 2008. Western Pennsylvania's slight move to the Republicans was thus more than counterbalanced by eastern Pennsylvania's move to the Democrats. Eastern Pennsylvania's share of the statewide vote increased from 53% in 1988 to 58% in 2008.

The persistence of these countervailing trends has given Pennsylvania a balance on cultural issues that is different from any other state's. In 1986, the state elected a Democratic governor, Robert Casey, who was a strong opponent of abortion rights. In 1994, it elected a pro-abortion rights Republican, Tom Ridge. Then, Democrat Ed Rendell won the 2002 election largely because of his huge margins in his home area of metropolitan Philadelphia. From 1994 to 2006, Pennsylvania had two Republican senators, moderate Arlen Specter and conservative Rick Santorum, whose opposite stands on issues can be illuminated by recognizing that the first is from Philadelphia and the second from Pittsburgh.

In 2006, after Santorum had taken his anti-abortion rights position to un-Pennsylvania-like extremes, national Democrats put up an anti-abortion candidate, Bob Casey Jr., to challenge Santorum. Casey beat him 59%-41%. Democrats also transformed a 12-7 Republican edge in the state's congressional delegation—the result of a partisan districting plan—into a 12-7 Democratic advantage in 2008. When GOP Sen. Arlen Specter switched parties in 2009, after being threatened in the 2010 primary by a diehard conservative, Pennsylvania had two Democratic senators for the first time (except for two years in the 1940s) since 1856.

Population		Household Income		Work	
Pop. 2007:	12,400,959	Under $15k:	13.9%	Private:	81.9%
State rank:	6th of 50	$15k to $50k:	37.9%	Government:	11.8%
Change since 2000:	Up 1.0%	$50k to $100k:	31.2%	Self-employed:	6.1%
Urban:	76.6%	$100k to $150k:	13.9%	Unemployment (3-yr. average):	4.0%
Rural:	23.4%	Over $150k:	3.0%	Poverty:	11.9%
Native of state:	75.5%	Median income:	$47,913	Blue collar:	23.0%
Not a citizen:	2.6%			White collar:	60.5%
Area size:	46,055 sq. mi.	**Home Value**		Khaki collar:	0.1%
		Under $100k:	32.5%	Other:	16.5%
Most populous cities		$100k to $300k:	50.7%		
1. Philadelphia	1,454,382	$300k to $500k:	12.1%	**Age**	
2. Pittsburgh	296,324	$500k to $1 mil:	4.1%	Median age:	39.5 yrs.
3. Allentown	108,900	Over $1 million:	0.7%	More than 65 yrs:	15.2%
4. Erie	100,393	Median:	$144,100	Less than 18 yrs:	22.6%

Race/Ethnicity				Military Veterans		Registered Voters in 2008	
White:	82.0%	*Language*		% of Pop:	11.2%	D:	4,480,691 (51.2%)
Black:	10.1%	English:	90.7%	*Veterans by Period*		R:	3,243,391 (37.0%)
Hispanic:	4.3%	Spanish:	3.7%	WWII and before:	16.7%	Other:	1,033,949 (11.8%)
Asian:	2.3%	Asian:	1.5%	Korea:	13.6%	Voter turnout:	6,013,272
Native Am.:	0.1%	Other		Vietnam:	30.9%	Turnout as % of	
Hawaiian:	0.0%	European	3.5%	Gulf (pre-2001):	8.0%	voting age:	62.1%
Two+ races:	1.0%	**Education**		Gulf (post-2001):	4.7%	**General Assembly**	
Ancestry		H.S. grad:	86.3%	Peace time:	26.0%	Senate:	20 D 30 R
German:	21.4%	College grad:	25.6%			House:	104 D 99 R
Irish:	13.4%	Grad degree:	9.7%				
Italian:	9.6%						

Presidential politics   From 1976 to 2004, Pennsylvania was a seriously contested state in every presidential general election, while its presidential primary had little impact on outcomes. In 2008 that pattern came close to being reversed. Falling six weeks after contests in Ohio and Texas, Pennsylvania's April primary was an epic battleground in the close contest between Democrats Barack Obama of Illinois and Hillary Rodham Clinton of New York. In the general election, both parties started off targeting Pennsylvania, and all candidates campaigned extensively in the state. But the final result—a 54%-44% Obama victory—made it clear that Pennsylvania was not really in contention.

Pennsylvania was not supposed to be a Democratic primary battleground in 2008. Typically, by the time the state voted in April, someone had clinched the nomination in the caucuses and primaries held in the nine weeks between January 3 and March 4. But this time, the March 4 results left the Democrats nearly deadlocked. Obama had a

2008 Presidential Vote		
Obama (D) 3,276,363	(54%)
McCain (R)........................2,655,885	(44%)

2008 Democratic Presidential Primary		
Clinton (D)........................1,275,039	(55%)
Obama (D) 1,061,441	(45%)

2008 Republican Presidential Primary		
McCain (R)............................595,175	(73%)
Paul (R)................................129,323	(16%)
Huckabee (R) 92,430	(11%)

2004 Presidential Vote		
Kerry (D)...........................2,938,095	(51%)
Bush (R) 2,793,847	(48%)

narrow lead in delegates, but Clinton had just won in Ohio and Texas, two of the seven largest states, and Pennsylvania looked, demographically and politically, a lot like Ohio. By contrast, Obama seemed to be headed into hostile territory. Videotapes of divisive, black-versus-white speeches by his pastor, the Reverend Jeremiah Wright of Chicago, were played over and over on cable television, and Obama felt he needed to respond. He delivered a thoughtful, frank and stirring speech on race relations in the United States in Philadelphia.

But he also squandered goodwill in other quarters with his off-the-cuff comments that people in small towns were "bitter" about their economic straits, and "they cling to guns and religion." News of his remarks, made at a fundraiser in San Francisco, did not play well in blue-collar Pennsylvania. Moreover, it was plain from earlier results in Ohio, Virginia, Tennessee and Georgia that he was particularly weak in Jacksonian America, in the Appalachian chain that stretches from Alabama and Georgia in the south to southwestern Pennsylvania, a weakness that some ascribed to racism. But that explanation overlooked the fact that southwest Virginia counties who rejected Obama by overwhelming margins had voted for Douglas Wilder, an African-American, for governor in 1989. Obama had the support of Democratic Sen. Bob Casey, Jr., who hoped to help Obama carry his base in the anthracite coal country around Scranton. But Clinton had the support of Democratic Gov. Ed Rendell, who had strong appeal in metro Philadelphia, especially in the suburban counties that Obama hoped to carry.

The battle turned out to be a milestone of the primary season, complete with bowling and cheese steaks and 2.3 million registered Democrats who voted. More than 130,000 of them switched their party registration to do so. This was far above the 1.3 million-1.5 million turnouts in Democratic primaries from 1972 to 1992, and triple the 700,000-odd turnouts in 2000 and 2004, when Pennsylvania Democrats voted after the contest was long over.

Clinton won a convincing 55%-45% victory. As in earlier contests in other states, she ran strongest among older and downscale voters, and she won among Jewish and Latino voters, enabling her to carry suburban Montgomery and Bucks counties. Obama carried only seven counties—Philadelphia, Delaware and Dauphin, with large black populations; Chester and Lancaster, relatively affluent areas; and Centre and Union, dominated by Penn State University and Bucknell College. Nonetheless, Obama's huge majority in Philadelphia enabled him to carry the 19 counties of eastern Pennsylvania by 52%-48%. Clinton won 69% to 79% in five counties just southwest of Pittsburgh and beat Obama 63%-37% in the 48 counties of western Pennsylvania.

As November approached, Obama's apparent weakness among key electoral groups, plus the fact that Democratic presidential candidates Al Gore and John Kerry had carried Pennsylvania with just 51% of the vote in 2000 and 2004, put Pennsylvania on everyone's list of target states. After the Democratic National Convention in August, Obama and running mate Joe Biden of Delaware headed straight for Beaver County, just northwest of Pittsburgh, to campaign in the old steel country that Obama had lost 69%-30% in the primary. Later in the campaign, Biden campaigned in Scranton, Pa., where he had been born and lived for the first years of his life. Republican opponent John McCain sent in vice presidential candidate Sarah Palin, the governor of Alaska, for multiple visits. Polls showed a tight race for most of September. Then, Obama established a substantial lead the first week of October. But McCain strategists, having conceded Michigan, continued to contest Pennsylvania, on the accurate assumption that without it, their candidate had no chance of an electoral-vote majority.

Obama won Pennsylvania 54%-44%. He carried the 19 counties of eastern Pennsylvania 59%-40%, running far ahead of Democrats John Kerry in 2004 and Al Gore in 2000. He lost the 48 counties of western Pennsylvania by only 50%-49%, a marginal improvement on Kerry's results and virtually the same as Gore's. Turnout was up only 4% from 2004, far less than the turnout increase of 17% from 2000 to 2004, similar to the pattern in Ohio and Florida, which were also furiously contested in all three elections. (Even the most assiduous turnout drives eventually produce diminishing returns.) Turnout rose more than average in areas where Obama ran well, a sign of his organizing prowess. It was up in Philadelphia, in fast-growing counties in eastern Pennsylvania and in the university counties of Centre and Union. Overall, turnout rose 7% in the 19 counties of eastern Pennsylvania and only 1% in the 48 counties of western Pennsylvania. Obama's biggest percentage gains over Kerry in 2004 came not so much in metro Philadelphia but in fast-growing counties along the state's eastern and southeastern borders. Newcomers leaving high-tax states may have been, if less liberal than voters in the states they left, more liberal than most voters in Pennsylvania.

There was little evidence of an increase in voter turnout among Republicans. The national exit poll showed that party identification switched from 41%-39% Democratic in 2004 to 44%-37% Democratic in 2008, presumably mostly because of changes in eastern Pennsylvania. Young voters preferred Obama 65%-35% and Baby Boomers (age 45-64) preferred him 55%-43%. The rest of the electorate was evenly split. The anthracite area around Scranton delivered handsome majorities to the Obama-Biden ticket, despite its primary votes, as did Jewish and Latino voters. Southwestern Pennsylvania tended to vote against the Democratic ticket. White Catholics voted 54% for McCain and white Protestants 61% for him, but blacks voted 95% for Obama, and voters registering no religion—11% of the total—voted 84% for Obama. Voters with incomes over $150,000, a group heavily concentrated in the Philadelphia suburbs, voted 58% for Obama.

Congressional districting

111th Congress Lineup
12 D   7 R
110th Congress Lineup
11 D   8 R

Pennsylvania is projected to lose one of its 19 House seats after the 2010 census. Because western Pennsylvania has been losing population, it is likely to forfeit a seat. But the current grotesque district boundaries—Pennsylvania has been rated the second most gerrymandered state—plus the possibility that incumbents of both parties could lose in 2010, make any prediction hazardous.

In 2001 and 2002, Republicans held the governorship and majorities in both houses of the Legislature, and so were in firm control of redistricting. They were determined to redraw the lines in such a way that an 11-10 advantage in the congressional delegation would be a 13-6 advantage. Demographics suggested eliminating one district each from Philadelphia and the Pittsburgh area. In late 2001, state Senate Republicans unveiled their plan, which put three pairs of Democratic incumbents in the same districts: Tim Holden and Paul Kanjorski, John Murtha and Frank Mascara, and Joe Hoeffel and Robert Borski. It created new Republican-leaning districts with no incumbents in metro Philadelphia and Pittsburgh, and it seemed likely to raise the Republican edge to 13-6.

But state House Majority Leader John Perzel, a Republican from Philadelphia, had a different idea. Perzel is from Northeast Philadelphia, and wanted to preserve three Philadelphia seats, which meant putting more Philadelphia Democrats than suburban Democrats in the new district pairing Philadelphian Bob Borski and suburbanite Joe Hoeffel. Perzel's House plan protected Murtha, the second-ranking Democrat on the House Appropriations Committee, and did not create a new Republican-leaning suburban Pittsburgh district. In the days that followed, Perzel got phone calls from National Republican Congressional Campaign Chairman Tom Davis of Virginia and White House political strategist Karl Rove. Democrats in Georgia had just passed a redistricting plan that seemed likely to cost Republicans seats the two had counted on, and they asked Perzel to accept the Senate plan. In January 2002, an agreement was reached. The new plan made adjustments in western Pennsylvania to please Murtha. Instead of pairing Democrats Holden and Kanjorski, it put Holden and Republican George Gekas in the same district. Overall, it eliminated four Democratic seats and created two Republican-leaning seats.

Lawsuits were filed in both federal and state courts. Democrats argued that the plan was unconstitutional as an obvious partisan gerrymander. But the U.S. Supreme Court, in redistricting cases in the 1990s, had said that while it was unconstitutional to draw contorted boundaries for racial reasons, it was permissible to do so for partisan reasons.

The plan achieved most of its partisan aims, but only for a while. Republicans took the new suburban districts, and Murtha won re-election handily. Borski decided to retire from the House. But Democrat Holden beat Republican Gekas in the new Republican-leaning 17th District. The result was a 12-7 Republican delegation, and indicated that Republicans' hold on several districts was shaky. That was born out by the results of the 2006 elections. Democrats gained four seats in the House delegation and emerged with an 11-8 edge. They captured an additional seat in 2008 and now have a 12-7 edge.

Governor

Ed Rendell (D)

Elected 2002, term expires Jan. 2011, 2nd term; b. Jan. 5, 1944, New York, NY; home, Harrisburg; U. of PA, B.A. 1965, Villanova U., J.D. 1968; Jewish; married (Marjorie); 1 child.

Military Career: Army Reserve, 1968–74.

Elected Office: Dist. atty., City of Philadelphia, 1977–85; Philadelphia mayor, 1991–99.

Office: 225 Capitol Bldg., Harrisburg, 17120, 717-787-2500; Fax: 717-772-8284; Web site: www.governor.state.pa.us.

Election Results

2006 general	Ed Rendell (D)	2,470,517	(60%)
	Lynn Swann (R)	1,622,135	(40%)
2006 primary	Ed Rendell (D)	unopposed	

Prior Winning Percentages: 2002 (53%)

Ed Rendell, a Democrat, was elected governor of Pennsylvania in 2002, the first Philadelphian elected to that position since 1914. He won re-election in 2006. Rendell (*Ren DEL*) grew up in Manhattan, in an apartment overlooking the Hudson on Riverside Drive. His father was a middleman in the women's clothing business and an ardent New Dealer; his mother's family owned a big women's clothing manufacturer that clashed often with unions. After his father died when he was 14, Rendell went through a difficult phase and was thrown out of Riverdale Country School for a year. He graduated from the University of Pennsylvania and from the Villanova University School of Law, and never left Philadelphia. He got a job prosecuting homicides in the office of Philadelphia District Attorney Arlen Specter, then a Republican. In 1977, Rendell was elected district attorney at age 33, and served two terms. The office is high-profile not just in Philadelphia, but also in the entire Philadelphia media market, where some 40% of Pennsylvania voters live. Former occupants are now Pennsylvania's governor and the senior U.S. senator (Specter). In 1985, Rendell started running for governor. Since 1955, the two major parties have alternated in the governor's office every eight years. Republican Gov. Richard Thornburgh was ineligible to run in 1986, and it seemed it was the Democrats' turn. In the Democratic primary, Rendell faced former Auditor General Robert Casey, who had lost in gubernatorial primaries in 1966, 1970 and 1978. This time Casey won, 51%-40%. Rendell carried the Philadelphia market, but in the rest of the state, he seemed perhaps too young, too brash, and too Philadelphia.

In 1987, Rendell ran unsuccessfully in the Democratic primary against Philadelphia's first black mayor, Wilson Goode. At 43, Rendell seemed to be through politically. But in 1991, with Goode ineligible to run again and the city's finances in dreadful shape, Rendell ran again, campaigning with his usual high energy. He won the Democratic primary 49%-27%. In the general election, he faced former Mayor Frank Rizzo. But Rizzo died of a heart attack in July 1991, and Rendell won easily in November, 64%-30%. Especially in his first term, Rendell clashed with public employee unions and whittled away at their generous contracts. Brash, cheerful, rumpled and sports-crazy, he became a popular public figure in the Philadelphia area. In his second term in 1998, he did a stint as a commentator on a Philadelphia Eagles football post-game show on cable television. In 2000, out of office as mayor, Rendell was named Democratic National Chairman. He campaigned for presidential nominee Al Gore, who had called him "America's mayor."

Rendell set out to run again for governor in 2002, when two-term Republican Gov. Tom Ridge would be ineligible to run. In 2001, Ridge was named President George W. Bush's homeland security adviser and was succeeded by Lt. Gov. Mark Schweiker. In the Democratic primary, Rendell faced Auditor General Bob Casey Jr., whose father had defeated him 16 years earlier. Early polls showed a close race, and many thought that Rendell, as in 1986, would be seen as too pro-Philadelphia for the rest of the state. Casey, like his father, opposed abortion rights and gun control. Rendell had the opposite view on both. On economic issues, Rendell had an economic development initiative for parts of the state that missed the 1990s boom. Casey concentrated on extending government benefits, creating low-cost health insurance for unemployed workers and raising the minimum wage by a $1 an hour. There was also a stylistic contrast. Rendell traveled the state in a bus caravan, campaigning with his usual brio, while Casey was tightly scripted, polite and earnest.

Pennsylvania allows unlimited contributions to state campaigns, and this was a big money race. The two candidates spent more than $25 million on the primary. Rendell raised huge amounts from his Philadelphia and national contacts. Casey raised over $5 million from unions, including public employee unions still bitterly opposed to Rendell. Casey ran largely negative ads, calling Rendell's Philadelphia story a half-truth and blaming him for the conditions of the city's public schools, which had been taken over by the state. Some of the Casey ads were scorching; a Philadelphia police officer was shown saying about Rendell, "He lies. Cops deal with liars all the time, and we have no respect for anybody who lies." The Democratic state committee endorsed Casey, and he counted on local endorsements from influential state Sen. Vince Fumo and union leaders to dent Rendell's margin in Philadelphia. Rendell spent $740,000 on Election Day activities, including $450,000 cash to be handed out in the city's 66 wards. But his popularity in the suburbs was even more decisive. Rendell won 79% of the vote in Philadelphia and even more in the suburbs. Altogether he carried the eight counties in the Philadelphia media market 79%-21%. Overall, Rendell won 57%-43%, though he carried only two of the 59 counties outside the Philadelphia market, Lancaster and the county containing Penn State University.

After the primary, Rendell led conservative Attorney General Mike Fisher in the polls, but not by much. Ridge and Schweiker had high job ratings. Pennsylvania elects judges in off-years, the auditor and treasurer in presidential years, and so there is a statewide partisan race every year, and Republicans had been winning almost all of them since 1990. Republicans held majorities in both houses of the Legislature. Fisher had more experience in state government. He had been elected to the state House in 1974 and the state Senate in 1980 and as attorney general in 1996 and 2000. His opposition to abortion rights was by no means a political liability in Pennsylvania. Nor was his platform—cutting the corporate income tax, expanding the state's prescription drug program with revenue from gambling, and requiring school districts to give voters a choice between the property tax and an earned income tax. After the primary, Rendell was almost out of money.

Fisher raised $14 million for the campaign, but Rendell did much better, with $42 million for the entire campaign, more than any other candidate in 2002 except the incumbent governors of California, Texas and New York. In the end, Rendell won on his popularity in the Philadelphia media market, where he won 68%-30%. Outside of Pennsylvania's two big media markets, Fisher led 58%-39%. But Rendell also did extremely well in the suburbs, where Republicans have a huge registration advantage and where they usually win in statewide races. Turnout was higher in the Philadelphia media market, which cast 41% of the state's votes.

Once in office, Rendell set about paring the state budget. He had problems with the Republican-controlled General Assembly, a far more partisan and far less malleable body than the overwhelmingly Democratic City Council he had been used to. He proposed a 33% increase in the state income tax to help pay for early childhood education, but legislators scaled it down to 10%. His ambitious plan for slot machines to pay for property tax relief failed. The state got stuck in a bitter, nine-month budget stalemate after Rendell vetoed the $4 billion education appropriation.

But in his second year in office, Rendell won a victory on the most important piece of his agenda—slot machines. The fractious issue of legalizing gambling to pay for property tax relief created divisions within both parties. Rendell traveled the state in support of his legalized gambling plan and promised Republicans that he would not campaign against them if they supported his tax package, which included the slots proposal. He said an expansion of gambling would staunch the flow of dollars to adjacent states like Delaware, New Jersey and West Virginia, all of which permit slots and other forms of wagering. The plan passed in July. The final deal authorized as many as 61,000 slot machines at 14 locations, more slots than any state other than Nevada. The 14 licenses for horse racing tracks, resorts and casinos were expected to bring in $1 billion per year in revenues to help the state reduce property taxes by an average of 20% statewide.

Also in 2004, the Legislature passed several items on his environmental agenda, including a bill requiring that 18% of the state's electricity come from renewable sources within 15 years and one that provided funding for rebuilding sewer and water systems. In November, Rendell won a Pittsburgh bailout package that gave the city new taxing authority. But he failed to secure a permanent funding solution for troubled transit systems in Philadelphia and Pittsburgh, caught between urban mass transit needs and those of rural areas seeking dollars for aging highways and bridges. His relations with the Legislature remained stormy. When asked to assess his own performance after two years, Rendell described his achievements as "winning ugly." Ever the sports fan, he postponed the annual budget address in 2005 "in consideration of potential scheduling difficulties for those traveling out of state during the days immediately preceding Feb. 8." Translation: The Eagles were in the Super Bowl and he was planning to attend.

In May 2005, Rendell suffered a blow that threatened to kill his signature achievement. A companion bill to the legalized gambling legislation allowed school districts to opt into the property tax relief system; they would then receive a share of the gambling revenues in exchange for lowering property tax rates. The vast majority of the state's 501 school districts, it turned out, voted against participating in the distribution scheme, in part because opting in would make it more difficult for them to increase property taxes in the future. That made it difficult for Rendell to enact property tax relief.

There was more bad news for him starting in July, when legislators voted to increase their pay from $69,700 to about $81,000, a figure on the low end since many were also entitled to extra pay for being committee chairmen, vice chairmen or members of the leadership. And they took their raise right away, despite a state constitutional clause that bars legislators from taking salary raises in the same term that they are passed in. Rendell signed the bill, which also increased pay for judges and executive branch officials, but said he would not accept his own raise. Legislative pay raises are never popular with the voting public, but this one, with increases ranging from 15% to 34% and passed without debate at 2:30 a.m. as lawmakers prepared to leave for the summer, created a firestorm. In November 2005, at the first opportunity to register their anger, voters ousted one state Supreme Court justice and nearly ousted another. This jarring result, the first time a justice had lost a retention race, spurred the Legislature to action. Eight days after the election, Rendell signed a bill repealing the raises.

Between the ill will surrounding the pay raise and his failure to enact statewide property tax relief, the cornerstone of his agenda, Rendell entered 2006 in a less than ideal position. His poll ratings were decent, but in May, it became clear that the pay raise fiasco remained fresh in voters' minds as 17 legislators lost in primaries. But in June, Rendell got the silver bullet he had been seeking. He signed into law a $1 billion property tax cut, the largest in state history, with senior citizens slated to receive tax relief immediately, even before gambling revenues began to flow—an important consideration in a state with the second-largest elderly population after Florida.

Republicans nominated former professional football player Lynn Swann, a Hall of Famer who starred on the Pittsburgh Steelers Super Bowl champion teams of the 1970s and settled in the Pittsburgh suburbs. Swann dismissed Rendell's property tax plan as a "Band-aid solution" and promised "real property tax relief" pegged to passage of a constitutional amendment that would replace the current assessment-based system with one based on the purchase price of the home or other real property. Rendell, one of the most prolific fundraisers in American politics, had a large cash advantage. He began 2006 with $12 million in the bank, and had $10 million more cash-on-hand than Swann through mid-September, enabling him to blanket the state in ads touting his accomplishments. He built a double-digit lead in the polls and ended up with a runaway 60%-40% victory, powered by huge margins in the Philadelphia media market. As expected, he won big in the city (89%-11%), but he also racked up remarkable margins in the vote-rich Philadelphia suburbs that once provided the foundation for Republican state-wide victories.

Rendell declared that this, his 14th election, would be his last, and waved away speculation that he was interested in running for president. He again sparred with the Legislature over the budget and ordered a shutdown of state services and an employee furlough in July 2007. It lasted one day, until agreement was reached on a $27 billion budget and the $945 million in transportation spending Rendell wanted. His efforts to lease the Pennsylvania Turnpike for 75 years for $13 billion were met with more resistance. In February 2009, he proposed giving $400 rebates to low earners but abandoned the plan the following month. His proposals to extend health insurance to 800,000 households in 2007, scaled back to 250,000 in 2008, failed to pass.

Rendell played an outsized role in national politics in 2008, despite his stated lack of interest in the vice presidency. He said, "If I'm asked a question, I answer it and I tell the truth. That probably isn't a good idea for someone who is No. 2 on the ticket." Former President Bill Clinton had appointed his wife, Marjorie Rendell, to a federal appeals judgeship in 1997, and his feelings for the Clintons remained warm. He endorsed New York Sen. Hillary Rodham Clinton in 2008 and became a major spokesman in her primary battle with Illinois Sen. Barack Obama. But he did not excel in the role, for the same reason he was a poor choice as a presidential running mate. When Clinton failed to clinch the nomination by Super Tuesday on February 5, Rendell said, "It sure didn't look like they had a game plan after Super Tuesday." He stirred more controversy when he said of Pennsylvania in February: "You've got some conservative whites here, and I think there are some whites who are probably not ready to vote for an African-American candidate."

After Clinton's victories on March 4 in Ohio and Texas, there was no major contest until the Pennsylvania primary April 22, and Rendell took command of the Clinton campaign in the state, hiring top staff members, dictating schedules, organizing events and determining where the candidate and Bill Clinton would appear. He spoke warmly of Clinton as "the best prepared Democratic presidential contender," even while responding to questions with a frankness that would make most politicians wince. Rendell rejoiced when Clinton carried Pennsylvania 55%-45%. Obama won Philadelphia by a wide margin, but Clinton ran ahead of him in the suburban counties, a contrast to her usual weakness in affluent suburbs and perhaps a testament to Rendell's popularity there.

When Obama became the nominee, Rendell switched gears and heartily campaigned for him while taking potshots at Republican opponent John McCain. "Everything Senator McCain has done has been to widen the gap between the richest and most powerful corporations and small businesses," he said. Even as McCain continued to target Pennsylvania, Rendell insisted Obama would carry the state, which he did by 54%-44%. After the campaign, Rendell backed the new president's economic stimulus bill as head of the National Governors Association. In April 2009, Rendell played a key role in persuading Sen. Specter to switch back to the Democratic Party, which he had left after being elected district attorney in 1965. Along with Obama and Vice President Joe Biden, he promised to support Specter in the 2010 election.

Like other governors around the country, Rendell was preoccupied in 2008 and 2009 with the state's own recession-induced troubles. In October 2008, he ordered state agencies to cut spending by 4% to help address an expected $1.6 billion budget shortfall. In January 2009, Rendell told the unions there would be no pay increases and possible furloughs. He asked the Legislature to approve video poker, with proceeds going to tuition relief.

Senior Senator

Arlen Specter (D)

Elected 1980, term expires 2010, 5th term; b. Feb. 12, 1930, Wichita, KS; home, Philadelphia; U. of PA, B.A. 1951, Yale U., LL.B. 1956; Jewish; married (Joan); 2 children.

Military Career: Air Force, 1951–53.

Elected Office: Philadelphia dist. atty., 1965–73.

Professional Career: Practicing atty., 1955–56, 1974–80; Asst. cnsl., Warren Comm., 1964; PA asst. atty. gen., 1964–65.

DC Office: 711 HSOB, 20510, 202-224-4254; Fax: 202-228-1229; Web site: specter.senate.gov.

State Offices: Allentown, 610-434-1444; Erie, 814-453-3010; Harrisburg, 717-782-3951; Philadelphia, 215-597-7200; Pittsburgh, 412-644-3400; Scranton, 570-346-2006; Wilkes-Barre, 570-826-6265.

Committees: *Aging (Special)* (12th of 13 D). *Appropriations* (18th of 18 D): Agriculture, Rural Development, Food and Drug Administration & Related Agencies; Defense; Homeland Security; Labor, Health and Human Services, Education & Related Agencies; State, Foreign Operations & Related Programs; Transportation, Housing and Urban Development & Related Agencies. *Environment & Public Works* (12th of 12 D). *Judiciary* (11th of 12 D): Antitrust, Competition Policy & Consumer Rights; Constitution; Crime & Drugs (Chmn); Human Rights & the Law. *Veterans' Affairs* (10th of 10 D).

Group Ratings

	ADA	ACLU	AFS	LCV	ITIC	NTU	COC	ACU	CFG	FRC
2008	45	43	56	27	100	34	86	42	39	22
2007	60	—	71	60	—	34	82	40	39	—

National Journal Ratings

	2007 LIB	—	2007 CONS		2008 LIB	—	2008 CONS
Economic	45%	—	54%		42%	—	57%
Social	48%	—	51%		52%	—	47%
Foreign	42%	—	57%		39%	—	60%
Composite	46%	—	55%		45%	—	55%

Key Votes of the 110th Congress

1. Raise CAFE standards	Y	5. Make English official language	Y	9. Withdraw troops 3/08	N
2. Expand SCHIP	Y	6. Path to citizenship	Y	10. Iran guard is terrorist group	Y
3. Cap greenhouse gases	*	7. Fetus is unborn child	N	11. Increase missile defense $	Y
4. Bail out financial markets	Y	8. Prosecute hate crimes	Y	12. Overhaul FISA	Y

Election Results

2004 general	Arlen Specter (R)	2,925,080	(53%)	($20,307,099)
	Joe Hoeffel (D)	2,334,126	(42%)	($4,540,209)
	James Clymer (CNP)	220,056	(4%)	($212,896)
2004 primary	Arlen Specter (R)	530,839	(51%)	
	Pat Toomey (R)	513,693	(49%)	

Prior Winning Percentages: 1998 (61%); 1992 (49%); 1986 (56%); 1980 (50%)

Arlen Specter is Pennsylvania's senior senator. He was elected as a Republican in 1980, but in April 2009, he shook up national politics by announcing his switch to the Democratic Party. The move helped give Democrats a filibuster-proof majority of 60 seats in the Senate in 2009.

Specter grew up in Russell, Kan., also the hometown of former Republican presidential candidate and Senator Bob Dole. His father was a Jewish immigrant from the Ukraine who worked as a tailor and a peddler, owned a junkyard, and sent four children through college. Specter came to Philadelphia at age 17 to attend the University of Pennsylvania. After college, he served in the Air Force, graduated from Yale Law School and practiced law in Philadelphia. In 1964, he was a top staffer for the Warren Commission investigating the Kennedy assassination and helped develop the single-bullet theory that a lone gunman was responsible. (At one point, he held assassin Lee Harvey Oswald's weapon and aimed it out the Texas Schoolbook Depository window toward Dealey Plaza.) Specter then returned to his law practice and, dismayed by what he considered corruption, ran as a Republican for district attorney in Democratic Philadelphia in 1965 and 1969. As district attorney, he hired as his assistant a young lawyer from New York named Ed Rendell, who is now the Pennsylvania governor. In 1973, he lost his re-election bid. He tried to restart his political career but was beaten in Republican primaries for senator in 1976 and governor in 1978. In 1980, Specter ran for the Senate again. He narrowly (36%-33%) edged out a former state Republican chairman in the primary and beat a low-spending Democrat 50%-48% in the general election. In 1986, he won re-election by 56%-43%. In 1992, he was only barely re-elected by 49%-46% after he became a target of feminists for his questioning of law professor Anita Hill during the confirmation hearings of Clarence Thomas, which focused on Hill's allegations of sexual harassment against Thomas. Specter ran for president in 1995 but withdrew before the first caucus or primary.

Throughout this career of narrow victories, Specter's assets have been brains and hard work. He is respected by colleagues and constituents, though with his tendency toward arrogance, he is not always well-liked. He has sided with conservatives on some divisive issues, and with liberals on others, building up no permanent credit with either. He is aggressive and prosecutorial, well-prepared and persuasive once he takes a stand. These traits are both his strengths and weaknesses. They explain why he was vulnerable in 1992, and why he won. His voting record for years has been almost precisely at the midpoint of the Senate, and he has played key roles on countless issues. He is pro-abortion rights, he pushes tough penalties for crime, and he supports capital punishment. On a closely divided and rancorous Judiciary Committee, he played a key role on several Supreme Court nominations. More than anyone else, he defeated ultra conservative nominee Robert Bork in 1987 and, more than anyone except for then Republican Sen. John Danforth of Missouri, he secured Thomas' confirmation in 1991. On many issues, Specter has been one of the few Republicans voting with Senate Democrats—on the Republican tax cut in August 1999, on the minimum wage in November 1999, on the federal tobacco lawsuit in July 2000, and on overtime regulations in 2003 and 2005.

Specter has often backed trial lawyers on legal issues, opposing a $250,000 limit on pain and suffering damages in medical malpractice cases, arguing that there should be no limit for egregious cases of severe bodily impairment, disfigurement or death. (His son, Shanin Specter, is a Philadelphia malpractice lawyer.) In April 2005, he proposed a $140 billion trust fund, to be financed by asbestos manufacturers and insurers, to compensate people who have asbestos-caused disease. It was opposed by powerful Democrats like Illinois Sen. Richard Durbin, who wanted trial lawyers to be able to press pending cases, and also by Republicans who had other reservations. The Judiciary Committee approved the bill, but in January 2006 it lost on the Senate floor by one vote.

Specter was in a position of considerable influence after he became chairman of the Judiciary Committee in 2005, although conservative Republicans had tried to deny him the posting. After he warned President George W. Bush not to nominate judges who would overturn *Roe v. Wade*, the decision that legalized abortion, abortion opponents protested his appointment as chairman and then-Majority Leader Bill Frist pointedly refrained from endorsing him. But the Bush White House weighed in on his behalf as did all the Judiciary Committee Republicans. And he had to eat his earlier words on *Roe v. Wade*: "I have not and would not use a litmus test to deny confirmation to pro-life nominees," Specter said.

As chairman, he was pressed by many Republicans to block Democratic filibusters of judicial nominees, the so-called "nuclear option" that would have disrupted longstanding prerogatives of senators to filibuster. Instead, he urged Frist to seek accommodation with Democrats, which ultimately resulted in formation of a bipartisan "Gang of 14" senators that reached a compromise on the issue. Specter presided over the confirmation of John Roberts to replace retiring Supreme Court Justice Sandra Day O'Connor. He backed the White House's refusal to turn over memos Roberts wrote while in the solicitor general's office, a stand endorsed by former solicitor generals of both parties. He sharply admonished liberal Democrats Edward Kennedy of Massachusetts and Joe Biden of Delaware, both former chairmen of the committee, to let Roberts complete his answers without interruption. After the hearings, he announced his support of Roberts and the committee approved him 13-5. In October, after Harriet Miers' nomination was withdrawn, he said she was the victim of a "one-sided debate" and could not survive "the heavy decibel level against her." When Samuel Alito was nominated in 2005, committee opinion was split on party lines, but Alito was confirmed by the Senate, 58-42.

In 2005, Specter worked for reauthorization of the USA PATRIOT Act, the Bush administration's main anti-terrorism law, which the Senate passed with more restrictions than the House measure. Several Senate Republicans had qualms about the measure and blocked agreement on the conference report in December, but the bill passed in March 2006. When *The New York Times* reported that month that the National Security Agency was conducting surveillance of communications between al Qaeda terrorism suspects abroad and persons in the United States, Specter said that the action violated the Foreign Intelligence Surveillance Act of 1978. He introduced a bill requiring that surveillance of U.S. citizens in the country must be conducted according to FISA, streamlining the approval process in the FISA court and requiring individual warrants for surveillance targets. But other committee Republicans failed to back

Specter and the bill did not come to the floor. In the controversy over suspected enemy combatants held in Guantanamo, Specter called for an independent commission to investigate incarceration policies. He visited Guantanamo in 2005, but the Defense Department blocked him from holding a hearing there. And in July 2007, he called for habeas corpus rights for unlawful combatants taken prisoner. He got 56 votes for the measure in September 2007, but fell short of the 60 needed to cut off a filibuster by opponents.

In 2006, Specter introduced his own immigration bills, a guest worker bill with no limit on numbers and stays up to six years, and a legalization bill providing for gold cards for eligible illegal aliens that could be renewed every two years indefinitely. Ultimately, the Senate passed a compromise worked out by Kennedy and Arizona Republican John McCain. But the House leadership refused to go to conference on the bill, and it died. In September, the House and Senate passed a bill authorizing a 700-mile fence along the Mexico border. In July 2007, after another attempt to pass a more comprehensive immigration bill failed, Specter called again for his version, which would provide legalization but not a path to citizenship for illegal immigrants living in the United States. The following year, he introduced a bill for quicker deportations of illegal immigrants convicted of violent crimes.

In March 2007, Specter also weighed the alleged political firings of eight U.S. attorneys around the country, pressing Attorney General Alberto Gonzales for an explanation of the firings. He concluded that the Justice Department would be better off if Gonzales resigned, but he did not expressly call for Bush's attorney general to step down. In October 2007, Specter co-sponsored a media shield bill to protect reporters from being forced to reveal confidential sources unless a judge rules otherwise. It passed the Judiciary Committee 15-2, and a similar bill passed the House, but Bush threatened a veto and it was stopped in its tracks.

Specter has brought his legalistic approach to foreign policy. In 1999, he sponsored an amendment to the annual defense bill invoking the War Powers Act to prevent the deployment of ground troops in the former Yugoslavia. It failed 52-48. During debate on the 2002 resolution authorizing military action in Iraq, Specter expressed doubts about whether Congress can delegate such authority to the president, but he voted for the resolution. In January 2007, he called for the president to agree to "sharing" the decision-making power in Iraq. "I would suggest respectfully to the president that he is not the sole decider," Specter said. He called for U.S. troops to be withdrawn from urban centers in Iraq and help train Iraqi troops. He was not swayed by Bush's plan for a "surge" of troop strength in Iraq. "The current plan is not working, and 21,500 additional troops—it's a snowball in July. It's not going to work," he said. In September 2007, he called for sending a United Nations peacekeeping force into Iraq. He also backed engagement with Syria. Specter defended Democratic House Speaker Nancy Pelosi after her April 2007 trip to Damascus, and in December 2007 traveled there with Democratic Rep. Patrick Kennedy of Rhode Island and offered to assist in negotiations between Syria and Israel.

Specter, who has had serious health problems in recent years, has played a major role in encouraging medical research. He cited his own experiences with a brain tumor and with stage IV-B Hodgkin's lymphoma, for which he underwent chemotherapy for several months first in 2005 and then again in 2008, all without missing a Senate session. He wrote a book on the subject called, *Never Give In: Battling Cancer—and Politicians—in the Senate*. He and Iowa Democrat Tom Harkin, as their parties' leaders on the health and human services appropriations subcommittee, shepherded the process of doubling the National Institutes of Health budget over five years from 1999 to 2004. He has supported federal funding of embryonic-stem-cell research, which uses excess embryos from in vitro fertilization and is opposed by many conservatives. In September 2008, Specter criticized fellow Republicans for not reflecting nominee John McCain's support for such research in the party platform.

In politically marginal Pennsylvania, without a firm base in either party, Specter has never had an entirely safe seat. Yet he has been, since November 2005, the longest-serving senator in Pennsylvania history. (The old record was held by Republican Boies Penrose, who served from 1897 to 1921.) He has had opposition in each Republican primary. The most serious challenger was conservative U.S. Rep. Pat Toomey, an opponent of abortion and advocate of tax cuts, who set out to run against him in 2004. Bush threw his weight behind Specter and sent White House Chief of Staff Andrew Card to a fundraiser for Specter in Toomey's congressional district. But conservatives were arrayed against him. *National Review* called Specter "the worst Republican senator." Former Judge Robert Bork and former Attorney General Edwin Meese supported Toomey and the anti-tax group Club for Growth raised $1 million for him and spent another $1 million on ads. But Specter had much more. He spent $15 million up through the April 2004 primary, and campaigned on his seniority and his seat on the Appropriations Committee. His campaign slogan was: "Courage. Clout. Convictions." "I would say it's an election to see if there's going to be any place in the Republican Party for a big tent," he said. Toomey's message was that the party was letting an opportunity to govern "with a common sense conservative agenda" slip away by re-electing a liberal. But the message was undercut by frequent appearances for Specter by Bush, Vice President Dick Cheney and conservative Sen. Rick Santorum of Pennsylvania. Specter had not backed Santorum in his 1994 primary, but had provided him critical help in the general election that year.

After 24 years in the Senate, Specter won the primary by only 51%-49%. He carried metro Philadelphia 57%-43%, but Toomey carried metro Pittsburgh 58%-42%. Toomey won 2-to-1 in his 15th District in the Lehigh Valley and carried Lancaster and York counties in the Pennsylvania Dutch territory and several industrial counties in the ring around Pittsburgh. Perhaps decisive were Specter's large majorities in most of the state's small counties. "I have a very strong bond with the people of Pennsylvania. It comes from having visited every one of the counties," he said.

In the general election, against U.S. Rep. Joe Hoeffel, a suburban Philadelphia Democrat, Specter trumpeted his differences with the Bush administration on issues like overtime pay for workers, private school tuition vouchers and embryonic-stem-cell research. Hoeffel protested that Specter was "meek, a supporter of the Bush program, which has alarmed a lot of moderates, with the budget deficits growing and the deceptions in Iraq and all the rest." Specter had the money advantage. He spent $20.3 million to Hoeffel's $4.5 million, and outspent Hoeffel by $1.2 million to $450,000 in the final weeks of the campaign. National Democrats were reluctant to pour money into an iffy race in a large and expensive state. In September, Specter was endorsed by the Philadelphia Black Clergy and the state AFL-CIO. In debates Specter relished taking the center position between Hoeffel, who had a very liberal voting record, and Constitution Party nominee James Clymer, who attacked him from the right and ended up winning 4% of the vote. Specter won 53%-42%, trailing 53%-47% in metro Philadelphia and leading 51%-49% in metro Pittsburgh. Specter won 25% among blacks, 48% in union households, and 23% among liberals. But his overall percentage of 53% was not much above Bush's 48%.

Republicans' Senate losses in 2008 made Specter's frequent departures from party orthodoxy more visible and potentially decisive. On the new Obama administration's nominations, Specter characteristically took a mixed approach. He supported Eric Holder for attorney general after his explanation of his role in several pardons at the end of the Clinton administration, but he opposed Timothy Geithner for Treasury secretary after it was revealed that Geithner had failed to pay self-employment taxes. In February 2009, as the Democrats' economic stimulus bill was being debated in the Senate but was still short of the needed 60 votes, Specter entered negotiations with Majority Leader Harry Reid, White House Chief of Staff Rahm Emanuel and fellow Republican Sen. Susan Collins of Maine. They cut some $145 billion from the plan, and Specter, Collins and fellow Maine Sen. Olympia Snowe, a moderate Republican, voted for the final $787 billion version, the only three Republicans in the Senate to do so. Specter said, "I believe that my duty is to follow my conscience and vote what I think is in the best interest of the country. And the political risks will have to abide."

But the risks didn't abide. Toomey, who had been heading the Club for Growth, announced he would challenge Specter again in 2010, when he is up for re-election. Reid, Vice President Joe Biden and other prominent Democrats began discussions with Specter urging him to switch parties. But he demurred. On March 15, 2009, the head of the Pennsylvania AFL-CIO said he would pull out all the stops to try to re-elect Specter if Specter supported the unions' card check bill, which would allow a union to form when a majority of workers sign a public declaration. But Specter declined, saying he could not support a bill that eliminated the secret ballot in union elections.

Reid said that Specter's position pretty much precluded a party switch. But then polls were published showing Specter getting only about 30% of the vote in a hypothetical primary matchup with Toomey. Specter began to explore alternatives. On March 18, he declined to rule out an independent candidacy. But Pennsylvania does not allow a candidate defeated in a primary to file as an independent, as Joseph Lieberman did in Connecticut in 2006. (Lieberman went on to win as an independent.) In any event, Specter could not count on pulling supporters away from a strong challenger, as Lieberman did when he faced only a nuisance Republican challenger. Specter sounded out Republican state senators on changing Pennsylvania laws to allow independents to vote in party primaries, but they were not receptive.

With other options exhausted, Specter in April announced he was switching parties, as he had done shortly before he was elected district attorney in Philadelphia in 1965 (from Democrat to Republican). He acknowledged he could not win a Republican primary, and he said he did not want his 30-year record in the Senate judged by Republican primary voters. Obama, Biden and Gov. Rendell all said they would campaign for Specter in 2010, and Reid said that he would get credit for seniority as a Democrat. But the leaders promised more than they could deliver. The Senate Democratic Caucus refused to honor Specter's seniority. That decision dashed Specter's hope of becoming chairman of the appropriations subcommittee overseeing labor and health and human services programs, and he even found himself sitting in the junior-most chair on the platform of the Judiciary Committee, which just a few years earlier he had so forcefully chaired.

One of the arguments Specter had long made—that his seniority enabled him to be a force on national issues and a benefactor for Pennsylvania—was undercut as well, and potential 2010 challengers started lining up to take him on.

Junior Senator

Robert Casey, Jr. (D)

Elected 2006, term expires 2012, 1st term; b. April 13, 1960, Scranton; home, Scranton; Col. of the Holy Cross, B.A. 1982, Catholic U., J.D. 1988; Catholic; married (Terese); 4 children.

Elected Office: PA aud. gen., 1996–2004; PA st. treas., 2004–06.

Professional Career: Practicing atty., 1988–96.

DC Office: 383 RSOB, 20510, 202-224-6324; Fax: 202-228-0604; Web site: casey.senate.gov.

State Offices: Bellefonte, 814-357-0314; Erie, 814-874-5080; Harrisburg, 717-231-7540; Lehigh Valley, 610-782-9470; Philadelphia, 215-405-9660; Pittsburgh, 412-803-7370; Scranton, 570-941-0930.

Committees: *Aging (Special)* (6th of 13 D). *Agriculture, Nutrition & Forestry* (9th of 12 D). *Foreign Relations* (7th of 11 D): East Asian & Pacific Affairs; European Affairs; International Development & Foreign Assistance, Economic Affairs & International Environmental Protection; Near Eastern & South & Central Asian Affairs (Chmn). *Health, Education, Labor & Pensions* (10th of 13 D). *Joint Economic Committee* (5th of 6 D).

Group Ratings

	ADA	ACLU	AFS	LCV	ITIC	NTU	COC	ACU	CFG	FRC
2008	90	71	100	100	80	3	63	8	3	55
2007	100	—	100	100	—	7	36	8	0	—

National Journal Ratings

	2007 LIB	—	2007 CONS		2008 LIB	—	2008 CONS
Economic	90%	—	6%		91%	—	0%
Social	63%	—	36%		62%	—	36%
Foreign	57%	—	41%		65%	—	6%
Composite	71%	—	29%		79%	—	21%

Key Votes of the 110th Congress

1. Raise CAFE standards	Y	5. Make English official language	N	9. Withdraw troops 3/08	Y
2. Expand SCHIP	Y	6. Path to citizenship	Y	10. Iran guard is terrorist group	Y
3. Cap greenhouse gases	Y	7. Fetus is unborn child	Y	11. Increase missile defense $	N
4. Bail out financial markets	Y	8. Prosecute hate crimes	Y	12. Overhaul FISA	Y

Election Results

2006 general	Robert Casey, Jr. (D)	2,392,984	(59%)	($17,592,210)
	Rick Santorum (R)	1,684,778	(41%)	($25,832,567)
2006 primary	Robert Casey, Jr. (D)	629,271	(85%)	
	Chuck Pennacchio (D)	66,364	(9%)	
	Alan Sandals (D)	48,113	(6%)	

Robert Casey, Jr., a Democrat elected in 2006, is the junior senator from Pennsylvania. He was born in the former coal town of Scranton, the oldest son in a large Irish-Catholic political family. Casey's father, Robert Casey, lost in three Democratic primaries before winning the first of his two terms as governor in 1986. He was a feisty, tradition-minded practitioner of New Deal-style politics, known best nationally as a steadfast opponent of abortion rights. In 1992, he was prevented from speaking at the Democratic National Convention, a decision certainly related to his stance on abortion but also brought on by his skepticism about Bill Clinton as the right candidate. Robert Casey, Jr.'s brother, Pat Casey, twice ran unsuccessfully for the House with another Casey brother serving as his campaign manager.

Like his father, Robert Jr. graduated from the College of the Holy Cross in Massachusetts. He taught in an inner city Philadelphia school for the Jesuit Volunteer Corps and got his law degree from Catholic University in Washington, D.C. He practiced law in Scranton, and then won election as state auditor general in 1996. He was re-elected in 2000. In 2002, running as a cultural conservative with strong labor support, he lost a bitter and expensive primary for governor to former Philadelphia Mayor Ed Rendell. Casey's tightly-scripted campaign and negative ads tarnished his image, but he showed some resilience by returning two years later to win the state treasurer's office with 3.4 million votes, more than any other candidate in Pennsylvania history.

In 2005, national Democrats were looking for a strong challenger against Republican Sen. Rick Santorum, a high-profile social conservative with a red-state following and a blue-state electorate. First in the House and then in the Senate, Santorum showed a knack for winning elections against tough odds.

But the state's political landscape had shifted considerably since his first election to the Senate in 1994. Pennsylvania had voted Democratic in the last four presidential elections, and in 2002, Democrat Rendell captured the governorship and easily carried the populous and once-Republican Philadelphia suburbs.

Democratic Senatorial Campaign Committee Chairman Charles Schumer of New York considered Casey the only prospective heavyweight challenger to Santorum and quickly moved to clear the field to avoid a cash-draining primary. There was one problem: Casey, like his father, opposes abortion rights, which made him anathema to many cultural liberals in the Philadelphia area. But Schumer believed that Casey could make inroads into Santorum's culturally conservative and "pro-life" base, and, as the Democratic alternative to Santorum, also could be acceptable to "pro-choice" voters in suburban Philadelphia. The national party's heavy-handed involvement rankled many Democrats. For a time, former NARAL Pro-Choice America President Kate Michelman contemplated running as an independent. Resistance to Casey's candidacy faded in the run-up to the election as Casey maintained a steady and sizable lead over Santorum in the polls.

Santorum began the campaign in a difficult position. Though he was mentioned as a potential presidential candidate, his standing at home was tenuous. As early as April 2005, he trailed Casey by double digits in the polls. That summer, he released a book titled, *It Takes a Family: Conservatism and the Common Good*. The year before he stood for re-election was perhaps not the best timing for a frank discourse on some of the most divisive cultural issues of the day. Despite his stature as a member of the Senate Republican leadership, his avid support for the increasingly unpopular Bush administration was unhelpful in 2006. Casey hammered him for voting "98 percent of the time" with Bush and characterized Santorum as having close ties to the oil, pharmaceutical and insurance industries. Democrats sought mileage from the issue of Santorum's residence—an issue Santorum had used against his opponent in his first House campaign in 1990—and questioned whether his Virginia home disqualified him from casting a vote in Penn Hills, the Pittsburgh suburb where Santorum owned a home and was registered to vote. Democrats also criticized him for using Penn Hills school district taxpayer dollars to educate his children in a Pennsylvania-based online charter school though they spent much of their time in Virginia.

Santorum did not run like an incumbent nor Casey like a challenger. Santorum, who trailed in the polls from beginning to end, campaigned aggressively across the state while Casey limited his public appearances in the early stages of the campaign. Santorum in November 2005 called for 10 debates— a typical challenger's move—while Casey was vague about debates. The two candidates clashed over the war in Iraq, Social Security and immigration. Casey's socially conservative positions—he also opposes gun control and same-sex marriage—helped cut into Santorum's advantage outside the state's metropolitan areas.

Together the two candidates raised $43 million. Santorum outspent Casey by more than $8 million, but it wasn't enough. Casey won 59%-41%, to become the first Pennsylvania Democrat elected to a full Senate term since Joe Clark in 1962, and the first senator elected from Northeastern Pennsylvania. Casey won by huge margins in Pittsburgh's Allegheny County, 65%-35%, and in Philadelphia, 84%-16%, while holding his own in the Republican "T" that stretches from Pennsylvania Dutch country around Lancaster to the northern tier of sparsely-populated counties along the New York border. Casey also swept the populous Philadelphia suburbs, winning 62% in Delaware and Montgomery counties, 59% in Bucks County and 55% in Chester County.

In the Senate, Casey voted against expanding federal funding for embryonic-stem-cell research, which uses cells from the in vitro fertilization process. But his votes for funding family planning organizations that don't reject abortion as an option gave him a 65% rating from NARAL-Pro-Choice America. In 2007 and 2009, he sponsored bills to provide financial aid and counseling to pregnant women. He spent more energy on promoting funding for the State Children's Health Insurance Program, similar to a program his father instituted in Pennsylvania in 1992. He said he was guided "by an enduring belief that every child in America—every child—is born with a bright light burning inside them. I feel a real abiding obligation to do everything I can as a public official to keep that bright light burning." Also in 2007, he co-sponsored a bill to provide $35 billion over five years for pre-kindergarten programs, and worked with New York Democratic Sen. Hillary Rodham Clinton to promote it.

From his seat on the Foreign Relations Committee, Casey in 2007 called for timetables on U.S. involvement in Iraq, but later acknowledged that Bush's strategy for a "surge" of U.S. troops to restore civil order in Iraq showed signs of being effective. He said in December 2007, "I think if you look at individual metrics in isolation on the so-called surge you could make an argument in a positive way." In July 2007, while chairing a committee hearing on nuclear weapons, he said, "The administration has shown a blatant disregard for the diplomacy and multilateral cooperation so essential to a strong nonproliferation regime."

Casey is skeptical about the free trade policies of the last two decades, and in May 2007 he called for Congress to have the power to terminate future trade agreements that fail to meet benchmarks for creating U.S. jobs, improving U.S. wages or opening markets to U.S. products. On other issues of strong local interest, Casey opposed the building of high-voltage transmission lines from the Appalachian chain to the East Coast as "federal government arrogance" and in October 2007 threatened to block the reconfirmation of the Federal Energy Regulatory Commission chairman. The Department of Energy had classified 52 of Pennsylvania's 67 counties as a "national interest electric transmission corridor." In December 2008, he strongly supported government aid to the Detroit auto companies. "The cost of doing nothing is beyond catastrophic," he said. "We can't continue to live in a country where there's less and less of an opportunity, year in and year out, to make things."

In the 2008 presidential campaign, Casey endorsed fellow Democratic Sen. Barack Obama of Illinois. "I believe in this guy like I've never believed in a candidate in my life, except my father," he said. He campaigned hard for Obama in the coal country around his native Scranton and in the southwest part of the state. But Obama lost the Pennsylvania primary to Clinton 55%-45%. He lost Scranton's Lackawanna County 73%-26% and ran behind by similar margins in other coal and industrial areas. Casey spoke about the economy at the Democratic National Convention in Denver and continued to campaign for Obama in the fall. In winning Pennsylvania, Obama carried Lackawanna County 63%-37%, though he failed to win the coal country in southwestern Pennsylvania.

FIRST DISTRICT

Robert Brady (D)

Elected May 1998, 6th full term; b. April 7, 1945, Philadelphia; home, Philadelphia; St. Thomas More H.S.; Catholic; married (Debra).

Elected Office: 34th Ward Dem. exec. cmte. mbr., 1967–present, Ward ldr., 1980.

Professional Career: Carpenter; Real estate salesman; Philadelphia dpty. mayor for labor, 1984–87; Chmn., Philadelphia Dem. Party, 1986; Legis. rep., Metro. Regional Cncl. of Carpenters & Joiners, 1987–98; Lecturer, U. of PA, 1997-present.

DC Office: 206 CHOB, 20515, 202-225-4731; Fax: 202-225-0088; Web site: www.brady.house.gov.

State Offices: Chester, 610-874-7094; Philadelphia, 215-389-4627; Philadelphia, 215-426-4616; Philadelphia, 267-519-2252

Committees: *Armed Services* (11th of 36 D): Air & Land Forces. *House Administration* (Chmn of 6 D): Capitol Security.

Group Ratings

	ADA	ACLU	AFS	LCV	ITIC	NTU	COC	ACU	CFG	FRC
2008	100	100	100	92	86	5	56	0	0	0
2007	85	—	100	85	—	4	44	0	6	—

National Journal Ratings

	2007 LIB — 2007 CONS		2008 LIB — 2008 CONS	
Economic	82%	0%	85%	0%
Social	83%	16%	82%	0%
Foreign	77%	22%	92%	0%
Composite	84%	16%	93%	7%

Key Votes of the 110th Congress

1. Increase minimum wage	Y	5. Share immigration data	N	9. Withdraw troops 8/08	Y
2. Expand SCHIP	Y	6. Foreign aid abortion ban	N	10. No operations in Iran	Y
3. Raise CAFE standards	Y	7. Ban gay bias in workplace	Y	11. Free trade with Peru	N
4. Bail out financial markets	Y	8. Repeal D.C. gun law	N	12. Overhaul FISA	N

Election Results

2008 general	Robert Brady (D)	242,799	(91%)	($1,013,835)
	Mike Muhammad (R)	24,714	(9%)	
2008 primary	Robert Brady (D)	unopposed		

Prior Winning Percentages: 2006 (100%); 2004 (86%); 2002 (86%); 2000 (88%); 1998 (81%); 1998 (74%)

Population		Race/Ethnicity		Work	
Pop. 2007:	631,369	White:	27.6%	Private:	81.2%
Change since 2000:	Down 2.3%	Black:	47.8%	Government:	14.7%
Urban:	100.0%	Hispanic:	17.2%	Self-employed:	3.8%
Rural:	0.0%	Asian:	5.3%	Blue collar:	20.1%
Area size:	68 sq. mi.	Native Am.:	0.2%	White collar:	55.1%
		Hawaiian:	0.1%	Khaki collar:	0.1%
Age		Two+ races:	1.0%	Other:	24.6%
Median age:	33.3 yrs.	*Ancestry*		Median income:	$31,393
More than 65 yrs:	10.8%	Irish:	8.5%	Median home value:	$91,000
Less than 18 yrs:	28.1%	Italian:	7.1%	Poverty:	30.1%
Education		German:	4.6%	**Military Veterans**	
H.S. grad:	73.9%			% of Pop:	7.2%
College grad:	16.3%				
Grad degree:	6.5%				

Everywhere in Center City Philadelphia, American history is close at hand. The statue of William Penn, who founded the city in 1682, stands 37 feet high atop the ornate, Empire-style City Hall built in the 1880s at Market and Broad. To the east is Independence Hall, where Americans in the 1780s drew up the nation's Constitution, and not far away are the restored townhouses of Society Hill. Philadelphia is built on a certain order. Other American colonies were settled by practical men, out to make

2008 Presidential Vote
Obama (D) 256,940 (88%)
McCain (R).............................34,276 (12%)

2004 Presidential Vote
Kerry (D)................................227,327 (84%)
Bush (R)..................................41,509 (15%)

Cook Partisan Voting Index: D + 35

money or replicate a farm settlement back home. But Penn was a Quaker, a member of one of the 17th century sects that prized reason, and he imposed order on his new environment: no cow-path street patterns here, like those in Boston or Charleston, but a grid of numbered and named streets, with precisely spaced open squares. Penn's city of brotherly love grew to be a commercial and industrial metropolis that spread out over the countryside until Philadelphia was the young nation's largest city. Today, the old colonial-era structures are interspersed with architect I.M. Pei's modernist Society Hill Towers, and with the masonry-faced skyscrapers of the 1920 and glass-and-steel versions of recent decades.

For all the grandeur of its City Hall, Philadelphia has seldom had a city government to be proud of. "Corrupt beyond redemption" is how journalist Lincoln Steffens described the city more than a century ago. Corruption and incompetence have reigned here off and on since then. While the city's private economy grew robustly in the 1980s, the city government lurched toward bankruptcy under Democratic Mayor Wilson Goode. Then in 1991, Democrat Ed Rendell was elected mayor, and did well enough to become in 2002 the first former Philadelphia mayor to be elected governor since 1906. Unfortunately, Rendell's push for reform stalled in the mid-1990s. Philadelphia still has an inordinately expensive city government. And it has neighborhoods ravaged by crime that have emptied out over the years. But there are signs of hope. Philadelphia has some of the nation's most vibrant and socially active churches. Center City remains attractive to young professionals, a growing number with families, and the population there increased 11% from 2000 to 2007. The metropolitan area is fifth largest in the country.

The 1st Congressional District of Pennsylvania contains much of Philadelphia east of Broad Street and all of 18th century Philadelphia: Independence Hall, the U.S. Mint, and Elfreth's Alley, the oldest continually occupied residential block in the country. It also takes in Chinatown, Society Hill, Overbrook, the Northern Liberties village, and Penn's Landing, and Philadelphia's four-square-block convention center, the largest in the Northeast. North of Center City, the district includes much of heavily black North Philadelphia, a couple of wards of Northeast Philadelphia (connected to the rest by irregular boundaries), and Kensington and its closely packed 19th century homes, where descendants of Irish and Italian immigrants lived for years in tiny frame houses that are increasingly occupied by Hispanic immigrants. The 1st includes once-heavily Italian South Philadelphia, where families and their small stores and restaurants have been pressed tightly into narrow streets. The *Rocky* movies were filmed there and the Philadelphia cheese steak originated there. Nearby, the district takes in the city's stadium and arena complex. The 1st continues along the Delaware River shore southwest into Delaware County to impoverished Chester. And it takes in three wards in heavily black West Philadelphia and a few small adjacent suburbs. The population of the minority-majority district in 2007 was 48% African-American and 17% Hispanic (mainly Puerto Rican), the highest of any Pennsylvania district. Despite growth in Center City, the district's population overall fell 2% since 2000, and Philadelphia itself has lost 30% since 1950. This is a heavily Democratic district that gave the party's 2008 nominee, Barack Obama, 88% of the vote.

The congressman from the 1st District is Robert Brady, a Democrat elected in 1998. He is the personification of Philadelphia's old-fashioned urban politics, one of the last white ethnic party bosses left in big-city America. He grew up in Overbrook Park in West Philadelphia, with an Irish father who was a policeman and an Italian mother. After high school, he went to work as a carpenter, quickly rose through the ranks of the carpenters' union, and remains a dues-paying member. He entered politics in 1967, at age 22, when the local ward leader wouldn't replace a burnt-out streetlight. Brady was elected to the 34th Ward Democratic Executive Committee, and in 1980 he was elected ward leader. In 1986, he became chairman of the Philadelphia Democratic Party. He depicts himself as a roll-up-your-sleeves guy who represents working class voters, and says he's proud to be the boss of what he calls the nation's largest big-city machine—or, as he calls it, an "organization." Brady is known for making "arrangements" with others— "They're always arrangements, never deals," he insists—and he has been chairman for more than two decades.

In November 1997, Democratic Rep. Thomas Foglietta, a veteran of South Philly politics, became ambassador to Italy, and Brady ran for the seat. The district's ward leaders determined the Democratic nomination for the special election and they favored Brady. With the endorsement of many black leaders and a strong Election Day organization, he won the special election with 74% of the vote.

After his election to the House, Brady's focus remained back home. "Ninety-five percent of my day is not Congress," he once said. He mediated a local teachers' strike in 2000, and he sought common ground between the mayor and City Council on a deal for two new stadiums. His ties to City Hall and to local unions gave him credibility with both sides. Brady worked to resolve local intra-party conflicts. According to the *Philadelphia Daily News,* he chewed out feuding City Council Democrats at one memorable private meeting. "You are a [f____] embarrassment. You're embarrassing me, embarrassing yourselves. You're like a bunch of 10-year-old children. If you're not careful, you're not going to be here next year," he said, banging the table. "I've got 30 ward leaders who don't want to support you and 30 more who want to run against you."

Brady has a liberal voting record and keeps a low-profile in Washington. For "the most powerful man in Philadelphia," *Philadelphia* magazine once wrote, "Washington gas-bagging is not his thing." His initiatives reflect his local orientation. He says he decided that he was in favor of abortion rights after asking his mother. His loyalty to unions led him to buck environmentalists and most Democrats to vote for drilling in the Arctic National Wildlife Refuge. In 2007, House Speaker Nancy Pelosi may have found the perfect job for him. Brady became chairman of the House Administration Committee, the so-called "Mayor of Capitol Hill" who oversees operations of the House and doles out favors like choice office space. As part of the opening of a new visitors' center at the Capitol, he approved memorials to honor African-Americans who had been slave laborers during the original construction of the building.

Prior to becoming chairman, he ran for Philadelphia mayor in the May 2007 primary. He joined the field late and had significant opposition, including from three veteran local black officials who had operated largely outside Brady's organization—U.S. Rep. Chaka Fattah, state Rep. Dwight Evans and former City Councilman Michael Nutter. Brady's platform was standard fare, including a call for more open government, safer streets, improved schools and lower taxes—though the details were not always certain. Democratic ward leaders endorsed him, in overwhelming numbers but with varying enthusiasm.

And his campaign ran into an unusual stumbling block: a lawsuit seeking to remove Brady from the ballot because he did not include his union pension on a candidate disclosure form. Brady revealed in court that his pension benefits were accruing as though he was working a full work week, a curiosity, given the fact that he was serving in Congress. The *Philadelphia Inquirer* reported that his "stumbling performance on the witness stand" raised "a harsh question: Is Bob Brady smart enough to be mayor?" He paid nearly $20,000 in fines for violating the city's campaign-finance laws. He finished a distant third in the primary, with 15% of the vote. Ever the party loyalist, Brady immediately dismissed the results as a "family squabble" and moved quickly to endorse primary winner Nutter. But in Philadelphia's Byzantine politics, Brady's weak performance—he lost even his home ward in Overbrook—raised questions about his political vulnerability. There was talk of a 2008 primary challenge from an African-American candidate, but it never materialized. Brady had no opposition in the 2008 primary and won the general election with 91%.

SECOND DISTRICT

Chaka Fattah (D)

Elected 1994, 8th term; b. Nov. 21, 1956, Philadelphia; home, Philadelphia; Community Col. of Philadelphia, U. of PA, M.A. 1986, Harvard U. Kennedy Schl. of Gov., 1984; Baptist; married (Renee Chenault Fattah); 4 children.

Elected Office: PA House of Reps., 1982–88; PA Senate, 1988–94.

Professional Career: Asst. dir., House of Umoja, 1977–79; City of Philadelphia, Spec. asst. to dir. of Housing & Community Dev., 1980, Spec. asst. to managing director, 1981.

DC Office: 2301 RHOB, 20515, 202-225-4001; Fax: 202-225-5392; Web site: www.house.gov/fattah.

State Offices: Philadelphia, 215-848-9386; Philadelphia, 215-387-6404.

Committees: *Appropriations* (22nd of 37 D): Commerce, Justice, Science & Related Agencies; Energy & Water Development & Related Agencies; Financial Services & General Government.

Group Ratings

	ADA	ACLU	AFS	LCV	ITIC	NTU	COC	ACU	CFG	FRC
2008	95	100	100	92	100	6	53	0	0	5
2007	75	—	100	90	—	5	55	0	12	—

National Journal Ratings

	2007 LIB	—	2007 CONS		2008 LIB	—	2008 CONS
Economic	82%	—	0%		85%	—	0%
Social	75%	—	25%		67%	—	28%
Foreign	80%	—	19%		92%	—	0%
Composite	82%	—	18%		86%	—	14%

Key Votes of the 110th Congress

1. Increase minimum wage	Y	5. Share immigration data	N	9. Withdraw troops 8/08	Y
2. Expand SCHIP	Y	6. Foreign aid abortion ban	N	10. No operations in Iran	Y
3. Raise CAFE standards	Y	7. Ban gay bias in workplace	Y	11. Free trade with Peru	Y
4. Bail out financial markets	Y	8. Repeal D.C. gun law	N	12. Overhaul FISA	N

Election Results

2008 general	Chaka Fattah (D)	276,870	(89%)	($699,411)
	Adam Lang (R)	34,466	(11%)	($4,729)
2008 primary	Chaka Fattah (D)	unopposed		

Prior Winning Percentages: 2006 (89%); 2004 (88%); 2002 (88%); 2000 (98%); 1998 (87%); 1996 (88%); 1994 (86%)

Population		Race/Ethnicity		Work	
Pop. 2007:	580,773	White:	30.2%	Private:	79.0%
Change since 2000:	Down 10.1%	Black:	59.3%	Government:	16.3%
Urban:	100.0%	Hispanic:	3.4%	Self-employed:	4.5%
Rural:	0.0%	Asian:	5.2%	Blue collar:	13.6%
Area size:	60 sq. mi.	Native Am.:	0.2%	White collar:	66.8%
Age		Hawaiian:	0.0%	Khaki collar:	0.0%
Median age:	35.7 yrs.	Two+ races:	1.4%	Other:	19.6%
More than 65 yrs:	13.8%	*Ancestry*		Median income:	$34,450
Less than 18 yrs:	22.6%	Irish:	8.0%	Median home value:	$114,400
Education		Italian:	5.9%	Poverty:	24.4%
H.S. grad:	81.1%	German:	5.4%	**Military Veterans**	
College grad:	28.2%			% of Pop:	7.9%
Grad degree:	13.2%				

Looking out over the Schuylkill River north of Center City Philadelphia, you can still see the landscape painted 100 years ago by Philadelphia artist Thomas Eakins: the tightly-packed but formidable rowhouses, the old fieldstone houses of Germantown, the gray-blue water flowing past boat houses below the small Greek temples of the Water Works and the larger temple of the Philadelphia Museum of Art. On both sides of this romantic scene are some of Philadelphia's long-established black

2008 Presidential Vote

Obama (D)	298,834	(90%)
McCain (R)	31,584	(10%)

2004 Presidential Vote

Kerry (D)	266,174	(87%)
Bush (R)	37,811	(12%)

Cook Partisan Voting Index: D + 38

neighborhoods: West Philadelphia, across the Schuylkill on either side of Market Street; North Philadelphia, on either side of Broad Street; historic Germantown to the northwest, off the narrow diagonal of Germantown Avenue. Pennsylvania never had slavery, thanks to William Penn and his Quaker legacy, and Philadelphia has been home to a large black community since before the Civil War. That heritage is reflected in places like the John Coltrane House on North 33rd Street, designated a national historic landmark in celebration of the jazz innovator's early years here. Suburban Cheltenham Township includes old, comfortable communities like Cheltenham, Melrose Park, Elkins Park and Glenside. Some neighborhoods continue to suffer from poverty and blight, and the city has 600,000 fewer people today than it did in 1950. In 2006, it fell behind Phoenix to become the sixth-largest city (although as a metropolitan area, it ranks 5th). From 2000 to 2007, it had the biggest population loss of the nation's 10 largest cities.

The 2nd Congressional District of Pennsylvania takes in much of the city of Philadelphia west of Broad Street, plus Cheltenham Township in suburban Montgomery County. It doesn't include the key colonial landmarks—they're in the neighboring 1st—but it does include most of the skyscrapers of Center City and well-heeled Rittenhouse Square, the Philadelphia Zoo (America's first), the University of Pennsylvania and Drexel University. It also includes lush Fairmount Park, the largest landscaped urban park in the world, which climaxes at the grand Philadelphia Museum of Art, where a *Rocky* -like run up the steps became *de rigueur* for tourists. The district takes in West Oak Lane, Strawberry Mansion and, further west, the distinguished old neighborhoods of Mount Airy, Chestnut Hill and East Falls. The 2nd also covers Roxborough and the old mill area of Manayunk, now an artsy enclave. With a 59% African-American population, it is Pennsylvania's only black-majority district. From 2000 to 2007, the district suffered a 10% population loss, which could force an expansion in redistricting after the 2010 census. The district is heavily Democratic, and was Republican nominee John McCain's fifth-worst performing district in the nation in 2008. He got just 10% of the vote. The bottom four were all in New York.

The congressman from the 2nd District is Chaka Fattah (*SHOCK-ah Fu-TAH*), a Democrat first elected in 1994. He was born Arthur Davenport, one of six children of a poor single mother in Philadelphia. She changed his name after she married community activist David Fattah; his first name was taken from a Zulu warrior. His parents were both politically active, producing a magazine for African-Americans and opening their home as a neighborhood gathering spot for teens at risk of joining street gangs. Fattah dropped out of high school, but later got an equivalent diploma and went on to earn a master's degree in government administration at the University of Pennsylvania. In 1982, at age 25, was elected to the Pennsylvania General Assembly, its youngest member ever. Six years later, he was elected to the state Senate. In 1991, Democratic Rep. William Gray, the powerful House majority whip, resigned to become head of the United Negro College Fund. In the special election to succeed him, local Democratic ward leaders nominated Councilman Lucien Blackwell, a former longshoreman and labor union stalwart. Fattah ran under the Consumer Party label while state Welfare Secretary John White ran as an independent. Blackwell won with 39% to 28% for Fattah and 27% for White. In 1994, Fattah ran again, this time taking on the Democratic establishment in the primary. Blackwell relied mostly on ward politicians. Fattah was endorsed by the Black Clergy of Philadelphia and Vicinity. This time Fattah won, 58%-42%. He has had no serious primary or general election challenge since. Fattah's wife, Renee Chenault-Fattah, is a local television news anchor in Philadelphia.

Fattah has a liberal voting record. Unlike Rep. Robert Brady, the city's other congressman, Fattah's focus is more nationally oriented. "A policy wonk with savvy," the *Philadelphia Inquirer* called him. He has advocated eliminating the federal tax code and replacing all individual and corporate taxes with a system that would tax all individual transactions, an idea that generated some interest among Republicans. But most Democrats are leery of anything that looks like a consumption tax.

Much of Fattah's focus has been on education. He worked on the "Gear Up" program to prepare low-income students for college, although in 2007, the *Philadelphia Daily News* reported that the program had limited effectiveness for local kids, and the city's schools phased it out. In late 2008, he had another setback in his education initiatives when he abruptly shut down a federally funded scholarship program he founded called CORE Philly after it became the target of an FBI investigation. In the past, Fattah also has secured money to curb witness intimidation in Philadelphia, and to combat the use of unsafe blood supplies that transmit HIV/AIDS in Africa.

In December 2007, House Speaker Nancy Pelosi named Fattah chairman of the Congressional Urban Caucus, with the goal of legislation to address urban challenges.

Fattah ran and lost a campaign for Philadelphia mayor in 2007. "I want to transform this city from a city of Brotherly Love to the city of Real Opportunity," he said. The move prompted grumbling among local Democrats planning to run for mayor that he was giving up his clout as an appropriator, and even some threats that Fattah would face a primary challenge for his House seat. Also in the crowded primary race was Brady, of the neighboring 1st District, former City Councilman Michael Nutter, and wealthy businessman Thomas Knox. Fattah began the race as the early frontrunner, but his campaign struggled to raise money and drew criticism over his refusal to release his income tax returns. Nutter was the eventual winner with 37% of the vote, followed by Knox with 25%. Fattah finished fourth with 15%, less than 200 votes behind Brady, who also had 15%. In 2008, Fattah won re-election easily.

THIRD DISTRICT

Kathy Dahlkemper (D)

Elected Nov. 2008, 1st term; b. Dec. 10, 1957, Erie; home, Erie; Edinboro U., 1982; Catholic; married (Dan); 5 children.

Professional Career: Dahlkemper Landscape Architects, HR mgr. & dir. of Special Projects, 1997–2008; Director, Lake Erie Arboretum, 2000–08; Dietician

DC Office: 516 CHOB, 20515, 202-225-5406; Fax: 202-225-3103; Web site: dahlkemper.house.gov.

State Offices: Erie, 814-456-2038.

Committees: *Agriculture* (17th of 28 D): Conservation, Credit, Energy & Research; Department Operations, Oversight, Nutrition & Forestry. *Science & Technology* (23rd of 26 D): Investigations & Oversight. *Small Business* (4th of 17 D): Regulations & Healthcare (Chmn); Rural Development, Entrepreneurship & Trade.

Group Ratings and Key Votes: Newly Elected

Election Results

2008 general	Kathy Dahlkemper (D)	146,846	(51%)	($1,301,838)
	Phil English (R)	139,757	(49%)	($2,633,349)
2008 primary	Kathy Dahlkemper (D)	43,858	(45%)	
	Kyle Foust (D)	24,672	(25%)	
	Tom Myers (D)	18,584	(19%)	
	Mike Waltner (D)	10,532	(11%)	

Population		Race/Ethnicity		Work	
Pop. 2007:	640,211	White:	93.0%	Private:	82.0%
Change since 2000:	Down 0.9%	Black:	3.6%	Government:	10.9%
Urban:	58.4%	Hispanic:	1.6%	Self-employed:	6.9%
Rural:	41.6%	Asian:	0.6%	Blue collar:	28.0%
Area size:	4,777 sq. mi.	Native Am.:	0.1%	White collar:	53.4%
Age		Hawaiian:	0.0%	Khaki collar:	0.1%
Median age:	39.7 yrs.	Two+ races:	1.1%	Other:	18.5%
More than 65 yrs:	15.4%	*Ancestry*		Median income:	$41,909
Less than 18 yrs:	22.4%	German:	25.9%	Median home value:	$102,400
Education		Irish:	12.8%	Poverty:	13.2%
H.S. grad:	87.4%	Italian:	8.4%	**Military Veterans**	
College grad:	19.9%			% of Pop:	12.4%
Grad degree:	6.7%				

The best natural harbor on Lake Erie is in Erie, Pennsylvania, protected by the Presque Isle ("almost an island") peninsula—a cowlick-shaped, seven-mile-long sand spit blanketed by mature forest, with a lighthouse dating to 1872. Erie is in Pennsylvania's far northwest corner, only about 100 miles from Cleveland but 428 miles from Center City Philadelphia. There is farmland here, and even some woods, but the land between the Great Lakes and the basin of the Ohio River has been prime

2008 Presidential Vote

McCain (R)	143,433	(49%)
Obama (D)	143,416	(49%)

2004 Presidential Vote

Bush (R)	152,473	(53%)
Kerry (D)	133,764	(47%)

Cook Partisan Voting Index: R + 3

heavy industry territory for more than a century. The jeep, which Gen. George Marshall called America's greatest contribution to World War II, was invented in Butler County. In the 1990s, under Republican Gov. Tom Ridge, an Erie native, the state invested $100 million in Erie's waterfront to develop a cruise ship terminal, hotel and convention center, a ballpark for the single-A Erie SeaWolves baseball team, and restorations to the Warner Theatre. The effort spruced up a dying downtown, but it didn't buffer Erie from a subsequent economic downturn. International Paper, American Meter, Gunite/EMI and American Sterilizer laid off employees and closed plants. Local colleges document a brain drain as high as 70%

from the region. General Electric, the area's largest employer for much of the 20th century, also had major cutbacks, though it still had 5,500 employees in 2008.

The 3rd Congressional District of Pennsylvania occupies this northwest corner of the state—all of Erie County, most of Mercer, Crawford and Butler counties and about half of Warren, Venango, and Armstrong counties. Erie County has 44% of the district's population, and had almost no population gains from 2000 to 2007. Growth has been modest in Butler County, on the northern edge of the Pittsburgh metropolitan area, while other parts of the district have lost population. Politically, the mix of industrial and rural voters makes for closely balanced territory. Erie and Mercer counties vote Democratic in most national elections, but they have also voted for Republicans with working class appeal, like Ridge, who is from a Catholic working-class family in Erie. The other counties are culturally conservative and solidly Republican. In 2008, GOP presidential nominee John McCain won the district by a mere 17 votes out of more than 291,000 cast. McCain won all of the outlying counties, but Democrat Barack Obama carried Erie, 59%-39%.

The new congresswoman from the 3rd District is Kathy Dahlkemper, a Democrat who unexpectedly overcame a significant fundraising disadvantage to bring down Republican Rep. Phil English in 2008. Her father was a member of the Erie County Council and chaired the county Democratic party. She graduated from Edinboro University and is a dietician by training. After working in Houston for four years as a clinical dietician, she returned to her hometown of Erie in 1986 to open her own consulting shop. Like a lot of women, Dahlkemper has balanced work and family for most of her life. After she and her first husband divorced, she raised her son from that marriage on her own for a time. She has four children with her second husband, Dan Dahlkemper. Her daughter, Linden, serves in the U.S. Coast Guard, and several extended family members are in the military. In 1997, she and her husband took over a landscaping business. She was a political newcomer when she decided to challenge English, a seven-term incumbent. Dahlkemper said bringing jobs back to blue-collar Western Pennsylvania and enticing young people to raise their families there were her top priorities.

In the April primary, she won 45% of the vote against three other Erie-based opponents. In the general election campaign, English outraised Dahlkemper by more than $1.3 million, although the national Democratic Party helped narrow the gap. The result said more about voters' desire for change than about the ideologically similar candidates, and English ultimately fell victim to the electorate's disillusionment with the Bush administration. Like English, Dahlkemper is an anti-abortion rights Catholic, supports gun ownership, and, as part of her "whole life" view, opposes the death penalty. She repeatedly sought to tie English to President George W. Bush, and criticized him for voting in February 2008 against a Democratic bill to increase taxes on big oil companies. English ran an ad criticizing Dahlkemper for refusing to release her tax returns, and the National Republican Congressional Committee aired a spot calling her ideas on conserving energy, which included walking and biking, as "wacky."

But aside from the usual back-and-forth between competitive candidates, the race never turned nasty. English suffered from the loss of some of his traditional labor support. The American Federation of State, County and Municipal Employees, which had endorsed him early in his career, ran $500,000 in television advertising targeting English's support for Bush's economic policies. A few weeks before the election, when polls showed her with an eight-point advantage over English, Dahlkemper said of her first political campaign, "I've had to learn a lot." She added that the time she had to spend raising money "is really daunting, and I know it keeps a lot of good people from running for office." Dahlkemper won by more than 7,000 votes, 51% to 49%.

In the House, Dahlkemper got seats on the Agriculture, Science and Technology, and Small Business committees. And she said she intended to be a centrist, citing as a model the voting pattern of Democratic Rep. Jason Altmire in the adjacent 4th District.

FOURTH DISTRICT

Jason Altmire (D)

Elected 2006, 2nd term; b. March 7, 1968, Kittaning; home, McCandless Twnshp.; FL. St. U., B.S. 1990, George Washington U., M.H.A. 1998; Catholic; married (Kelly); 2 children.

Professional Career: Aide, U.S. Rep. Pete Peterson, 1991–96; Asst. VP, Fed. of American Hospitals, 1996–98; VP of Govt. Relations, U. of Pittsburgh Med. Ctr., 1998–2005.

DC Office: 332 CHOB, 20515, 202-225-2565; Fax: 202-226-2274; Web site: altmire.house.gov.

State Offices: Aliquippa, 724-378-0928; Natrona Heights, 724-226-1304.

Committees: *Education & Labor* (19th of 29 D): Early Childhood, Elementary & Secondary Education; Higher Education, Lifelong Learning & Competitiveness. *Small Business* (11th of 17 D): Investigations & Oversight (Chmn); Regulations & Healthcare. *Transportation & Infrastructure* (23rd of 44 D): Aviation; Highways & Transit; Railroads, Pipelines & Hazardous Materials.

Group Ratings

	ADA	ACLU	AFS	LCV	ITIC	NTU	COC	ACU	CFG	FRC
2008	80	64	100	77	43	21	61	24	8	35
2007	95	—	91	80	—	12	55	28	8	—

National Journal Ratings

	2007 LIB	—	2007 CONS		2008 LIB	—	2008 CONS
Economic	56%	—	43%		54%	—	45%
Social	49%	—	51%		48%	—	50%
Foreign	48%	—	51%		46%	—	53%
Composite	51%	—	49%		50%	—	50%

Key Votes of the 110th Congress

1. Increase minimum wage	Y	5. Share immigration data	Y	9. Withdraw troops 8/08	Y
2. Expand SCHIP	Y	6. Foreign aid abortion ban	Y	10. No operations in Iran	N
3. Raise CAFE standards	Y	7. Ban gay bias in workplace	Y	11. Free trade with Peru	N
4. Bail out financial markets	N	8. Repeal D.C. gun law	Y	12. Overhaul FISA	Y

Election Results

2008 general	Jason Altmire (D)	186,536	(56%)	($2,986,360)
	Melissa Hart (R)	147,411	(44%)	($1,362,528)
2008 primary	Jason Altmire (D)	unopposed		

Prior Winning Percentages: 2006 (52%)

Population		Race/Ethnicity		Work	
Pop. 2007:	645,777	White:	93.0%	Private:	83.6%
Change since 2000:	Down 0.1%	Black:	3.6%	Government:	9.8%
Urban:	78.5%	Hispanic:	1.0%	Self-employed:	6.5%
Rural:	21.5%	Asian:	1.3%	Blue collar:	18.9%
Area size:	1,318 sq. mi.	Native Am.:	0.1%	White collar:	65.9%
Age		Hawaiian:	0.0%	Khaki collar:	0.0%
Median age:	42.6 yrs.	Two+ races:	1.0%	Other:	15.1%
More than 65 yrs:	17.0%	*Ancestry*		Median income:	$53,635
Less than 18 yrs:	22.6%	German:	23.7%	Median home value:	$132,600
Education		Irish:	14.2%	Poverty:	7.5%
H.S. grad:	90.9%	Italian:	13.4%	**Military Veterans**	
College grad:	31.5%			% of Pop:	12.1%
Grad degree:	11.8%				

For a century, one of America's great industrial zones was near the intersection of the Beaver and Ohio rivers in western Pennsylvania. This was steel country, with mills rising black and brooding from the bottomlands and filling the narrow river valleys with smoke. Immigrant families lived in small frame houses on hillsides, looking down on riverscapes lined with piles of iron ore, limestone, and coal and littered with cranes, stocks and furnaces. This was not an environmentalist's idea of perfection, but it was a land of opportunity for thousands whose lives were worse before moving to steel country. One grandchild of a Hungarian immigrant steelworker in Beaver Falls grew up to be Joe Namath, one of the many great quarterbacks produced by southwestern Pennsylvania (fellow Hall of Famers Jim Kelly, Joe Montana and Dan Marino are a few of the others). During the heady years, high union wages and early retirement plans made working in the mills a path to the middle class. But the industry crashed after the oil shock of 1979. Many mills closed and jobs vanished. Today, thousands of workers who long ago exhausted their unemployment benefits have given up and left the Beaver and Ohio valleys.

The 4th Congressional District of Pennsylvania includes much of steel country and, equally important, a large swath of suburban Pittsburgh. The 4th begins around Farrell in Mercer County, located as close to Erie as to Pittsburgh, then travels south along Route 60 through steel-mill country in Lawrence and Beaver counties. Aliquippa, a typically distressed former steel-mill city, is where composer Henry

2008 Presidential Vote

McCain (R)	185,052	(55%)
Obama (D)	149,661	(44%)

2004 Presidential Vote

Bush (R)	179,855	(54%)
Kerry (D)	149,070	(45%)

Cook Partisan Voting Index: R+6

Mancini and football icon Mike Ditka grew up but then left for brighter futures elsewhere. The district then turns to the east, taking in a fast-growing tier of suburban southern Butler County and the longer-established Allegheny County suburbs north of Pittsburgh. It includes old-money Fox Chapel and Sewickley, which is now attracting the region's high-tech wealth, and affluent McCandless and middle-class Ross in the North Hills. It also takes in a tiny portion of Westmoreland County. The steel mill areas tend to be Democratic, with unions still capable of flexing some muscle. The suburbs of Butler County are tax-averse and strongly Republican, with solid growth in Cranberry and Seven Fields. The older suburbs in Allegheny County, with some of the highest senior citizen populations in the country, are politically marginal; they are more Democratic than Butler, but much more Republican than the city of Pittsburgh. Overall, the district's heritage is Democratic but it has been trending slightly toward the Republicans. George W. Bush carried this district with 54% of the vote in 2004. Although 2008 Democratic presidential nominee Barack Obama launched his post-convention campaign in Beaver County, Republican John McCain won it with 55% of the vote.

The congressman from the 4th District is Jason Altmire, a Democrat elected in 2006. Altmire grew up outside of Pittsburgh, the only child of a single mother who was a school teacher. He was a star high school athlete until he suffered a knee injury. He attended Florida State University, worked to rehabilitate his knee and made the football team as a walk-on player. He suffered another injury as the team trained to play in the Sugar Bowl. Altmire volunteered for the successful campaign of Florida Democrat Pete Peterson for the U.S. House, and then worked as Peterson's legislative aide for six years, developing expertise in health care issues. Altmire earned a master's degree in health administration at George Washington University while working on Capitol Hill, and at age 25, was appointed to President Bill Clinton's health care task force. Following a short stint with the Federation of American Hospitals, he returned home to western Pennsylvania in 1998 for a job with the University of Pittsburgh Medical Center, eventually becoming vice president for government relations. Sixteen months before the general election in 2006, Altmire quit his $130,000-a-year job and jumped into the race against Republican Rep. Melissa Hart, who had held the seat since 2000. A conservative, Hart was seen as one of the Republican Party's rising stars and had faced only light opposition in her re-election campaigns.

In the Democratic primary, Altmire defeated businesswoman Georgia Berner, who supported abortion rights while Altmire stressed his opposition to both abortion rights and gun control. He was outspent, but he enjoyed support from key labor groups. He won 55%-45% with strong support from his Allegheny County base, which he carried by nearly 10,000 votes. In the general election campaign, Altmire positioned himself as more socially conservative than the national Democratic Party, but also turned to two liberal lightning rods to help fill his coffers. In July, he went door-to-door with Democratic National Committee Chairman Howard Dean, and in October, comedian (and later senator) Al Franken appeared at an Altmire fundraiser. An ad financed by the Democratic Congressional Campaign Committee tied the incumbent to the sinking popularity of Bush and conservative Sen. Rick Santorum of Pennsylvania. An Altmire ad criticized Hart for voting to "raid" the Social Security trust fund and to cut veterans' benefits and student loans. Hart outspent Altmire by more than $1 million, but she was fighting an anti-Republican current in a traditionally Democratic district. Altmire won 52%-48%, narrowly losing Allegheny County but winning by large margins in traditionally Democratic Beaver County.

In the House, Altmire went his own way from Democratic Party leaders. His voting record left him almost precisely at the center of the House in each of his first two years. He joined the centrist New Democrats and the Blue Dog Coalition of conservative Democrats. When anti-war groups in 2007 criticized his votes to support military funding for the Iraq war, Altmire responded, "I am never going to vote to cut funding for our troops when they are on the field of battle."

With his legislative experience, he scored some accomplishments. His proposal for increased screening for traumatic brain injuries for U.S. soldiers returning from Iraq was included in the defense spending bill that became law in January 2008. With help from Majority Leader Steny Hoyer of Maryland, Altmire won passage of a bill to prevent the military from curtailing bonuses to soldiers who ended their service because of serious injury. But he made life difficult for Hoyer in 2009 by insisting on repeal of the District of Columbia's strict gun control laws as a condition for his support for D.C. gaining a voting member in the House.

On the Small Business Committee, Altmire tended to his district's technology interests in 2007 by pushing a bill through the House to permit small businesses to qualify for research grants even if they have benefited from venture capital.

Hart sought a rematch in 2008. She blasted his votes for higher taxes and said that he failed to take action on high gas prices. Altmire said Hart was "wrong then and now." Altmire raised twice as much money as Hart and easily held the seat, 56%-44%. But he cannot take the seat for granted, as he could be a Republican target again.

FIFTH DISTRICT

Glenn Thompson (R)

Elected 2008, 1st term; b. July 27, 1959, Bellefonte; home, Howard Township; PA St. U., B.S. 1981; Temple U., M.Ed. 1998; Church of Christ; married (Penny); 3 children.

Elected Office: Bald Eagle Area Schl Bd., 1990–96

Professional Career: Therapist, Williamsport Hospital, 1982–1995; Adjct. faculty, Cambria Cnty. Comm. Col, 1997–1999; Mgr., Susquehanna Health Rehabilitation Services, 1995–2008; Centre Cnty. GOP Chmn., 2002–08; Firefighter & EMT

DC Office: 124 CHOB, 20515, 202-225-5121; Fax: 202-225-5796; Web site: thompson.house.gov.

State Offices: Bellefonte, 814-353-0215; Titusville, 814-827-3985.

Committees: *Agriculture* (16th of 18 R): Conservation, Credit, Energy & Research; Rural Development, Biotechnology, Specialty Crops & Foreign Agriculture. *Education & Labor* (19th of 19 R): Healthy Families & Communities; Higher Education, Lifelong Learning & Competitiveness. *Small Business* (11th of 12 R): Contracting & Technology; Regulations & Healthcare; Rural Development, Entrepreneurship & Trade.

Group Ratings and Key Votes: Newly Elected

Election Results

2008 general	Glenn Thompson (R)	155,513	(57%)	($442,425)
	Mark McCracken (D)	112,509	(41%)	($98,895)
	James Fryman (Lib)	6,155	(2%)	
2008 primary	Glenn Thompson (R)	13,988	(19%)	
	Derek Walker (R)	13,153	(18%)	
	Matt Shaner (R)	12,860	(18%)	
	Jeffrey Stroehmann (R)	9,921	(14%)	
	Keith Richardson (R)	7,094	(10%)	
	Lou Radkowski (R)	5,083	(7%)	
	John Stroup (R)	4,550	(6%)	
	Chris Exarchos (R)	4,376	(6%)	

Population		Race/Ethnicity		Work	
Pop. 2007:	637,283	White:	94.9%	Private:	76.4%
Change since 2000:	Down 1.4%	Black:	1.6%	Government:	16.0%
Urban:	46.0%	Hispanic:	1.1%	Self-employed:	7.4%
Rural:	54.0%	Asian:	1.5%	Blue collar:	29.8%
Area size:	11,108 sq. mi.	Native Am.:	0.2%	White collar:	51.3%
Age		Hawaiian:	0.0%	Khaki collar:	0.1%
Median age:	38.7 yrs.	Two+ races:	0.7%	Other:	18.8%
More than 65 yrs:	15.9%	*Ancestry*		Median income:	$38,566
Less than 18 yrs:	19.8%	German:	26.1%	Median home value:	$90,300
Education		Irish:	10.9%	Poverty:	14.5%
H.S. grad:	86.2%	English:	7.8%	**Military Veterans**	
College grad:	19.3%			% of Pop:	12.2%
Grad degree:	7.6%				

North central Pennsylvania, isolated from the rest of the country by mountains and off the main east-west rail and highway lines until the 1970s, is one of those empty spaces that make even the northeastern states seem lightly populated compared to the densely packed terrain of Western Europe or East Asia. Forest County has the highest percentage of second homes or cottages of any county in the nation. Pressed tightly by narrow valleys and fast-flowing rivers, roads here are often forced to

2008 Presidential Vote

McCain (R)	153,015	(55%)
Obama (D)	123,485	(44%)

2004 Presidential Vote

Bush (R)	165,343	(61%)
Kerry (D)	105,295	(39%)

Cook Partisan Voting Index: R+9

switch back as they wind their way precariously over the mountains. Tioga County is home to Pine Creek Gorge, known as "Pennsylvania's Grand Canyon." This part of the state is a prime area for hunting—225 black bears were shot in Clinton County in 2006—fishing and snowmobiling. There are wide open spaces like the Allegheny National Forest, which sprawls across four counties and is a popular recreational area. Neatly-preserved Ridgway, just outside the Allegheny National Forest, holds the largest chainsaw carving event in the world. Elk County and the Elk State Forest feature a free-roaming herd of elk, of course, but also are home to a new trout hatchery.

Titusville is where Col. Edwin Drake sank the first successful oil well in 1859, and Oil City was the headquarters of Quaker State Oil from 1931 until it left for Texas in 1995. The last oil and natural gas wells were capped here in 1964. DuBois in Clearfield County is home to glass production and a powdered metal industry. In Bradford, Zippo manufactures lighters. Punxsutawney in Jefferson County is home of the legendary groundhog Phil, who predicts the arrival of spring every year based on whether he sees his shadow on Gobbler's Knob on Feb. 2. The 1993 movie *Groundhog Day* sparked a tourism boomlet in this town of 6,000, even though the movie was filmed in Woodstock, Ill. To the southeast is the Nittany Valley, home of State College and Pennsylvania State University. Penn State has long been known for its powerful football teams coached by iconic Joe Paterno ("JoePa," locally), and the university's cutting-edge facilities have spawned a high-skills job market. Interstate 80 makes this part of Pennsylvania accessible to big markets, and there has been some modest population growth since 1990.

The 5th Congressional District of Pennsylvania is the state's most rural and its largest in land area, taking in an enormous swath of north central Pennsylvania. It's one of the largest districts east of the Mississippi River. Politically, this area became Republican in the 1850s when the party was founded, and it has remained heavily Republican since. In 2004, President George W. Bush won 61% of the vote here, and in 2008, GOP nominee John McCain did not do as well, but still won with 55%.

The new congressman from the 5th District is Republican Glenn Thompson, who cruised to victory in 2008 to retain the GOP seat of Rep. John Peterson. A lifelong resident of Centre County, Thompson was born in Bellefonte, Penn., where he grew up with a sister and two brothers, one of whom was adopted. Staying close to home for college, he attended Penn State in nearby State College. After graduating, he launched his career in health care at Williamsport Hospital, which later consolidated with two other area hospitals to form the community health network Susquehanna Health, where he worked as a rehabilitation services manager when he launched his campaign for the House. Now a resident of Howard Township, Thompson served as a member of the board of the Bald Eagle Area School District from 1990 to 1996. He ran twice for state representative, both times unsuccessfully, but was elected to three terms as chairman of the Centre County Republican Party. In 2004, he was a member of Pennsylvania's delegation to the Republican National Committee.

Peterson announced in early January 2008 that he would not seek re-election. In the nine-candidate primary, Thompson's hopes at first appeared dim against the robust spending by rivals. Two of his opponents, businessmen Matt Shaner and Derek Walker, financed their own campaigns, and took to the airwaves hoping to reach voters across the geographically expansive district. Thompson instead hit the pavement, crisscrossing the district in a low-key campaign that emphasized his Republican positions and focused on rural issues. He opposed tolling on local Interstate 80 and called for expanding rural Medicare initiatives. He also spoke of the Iraq war in personal terms; his son, Logan, was injured by a landmine in late 2007 while serving there.

Two developments late in the campaign likely provided Thompson with the boost he needed to break out of the pack. Less than two weeks before the primary, Peterson threw his support behind Thompson as the candidate who would follow in his legacy and who best understood rural issues. The following week, the Clearfield County district attorney filed charges against Walker for allegedly breaking into his ex-girlfriend's apartment. Together, Peterson's endorsement and Walker's personal problems allowed Thompson to eke out a small victory. Vastly outspent, he won 19% of the vote to beat Walker by just over 800 votes.

The general election was a breeze by comparison. Thompson's opponent, Clearfield County Commissioner Mark McCracken, did not raise much money and received little help from the Democratic Party. Thompson won 57% to 41%, carrying 16 of the district's 17 counties. The aftermath was unusually civil: Thompson invited McCracken to attend President Barack Obama's first primetime joint address to Congress as his guest.

In the House, Thompson broke with the majority of House Republicans in January 2009 by voting to expand the State Children's Health Insurance Program. Rural causes remain a priority for him. He has seats on the Agriculture Committee, and also the Education and Labor and Small Business committees.

SIXTH DISTRICT

Jim Gerlach (R)

Elected 2002, 4th term; b. Feb. 25, 1955, Ellwood City; home, Chester Springs; Dickinson Col., B.A. 1977, J.D. 1980; Presbyterian; married (Karen); 6 children.

Elected Office: PA House of Reps., 1990–94; PA Senate, 1994–2002.

Professional Career: Practicing atty., 1980–2002.

DC Office: 308 CHOB, 20515, 202-225-4315; Fax: 202-225-8440; Web site: www.house.gov/gerlach/.

State Offices: Exton, 610-594-1415; Trappe, 610-409-2780; Wyomissing, 610-376-7630.

Committees: *Financial Services* (15th of 29 R): Capital Markets, Insurance & Government Sponsored Enterprises; Domestic Monetary Policy & Technology; Financial Institutions & Consumer Credit. *Transportation & Infrastructure* (17th of 30 R): Aviation; Highways & Transit; Railroads, Pipelines & Hazardous Materials.

Group Ratings

	ADA	ACLU	AFS	LCV	ITIC	NTU	COC	ACU	CFG	FRC
2008	60	36	71	54	71	41	81	48	37	64
2007	40	—	27	70	—	35	90	52	32	—

National Journal Ratings

	2007 LIB	—	2007 CONS		2008 LIB	—	2008 CONS
Economic	45%	—	55%		42%	—	58%
Social	38%	—	60%		44%	—	56%
Foreign	32%	—	64%		40%	—	60%
Composite	39%	—	61%		42%	—	58%

Key Votes of the 110th Congress

1. Increase minimum wage	Y	5. Share immigration data	Y	9. Withdraw troops 8/08	N
2. Expand SCHIP	Y	6. Foreign aid abortion ban	Y	10. No operations in Iran	N
3. Raise CAFE standards	Y	7. Ban gay bias in workplace	Y	11. Free trade with Peru	Y
4. Bail out financial markets	Y	8. Repeal D.C. gun law	Y	12. Overhaul FISA	Y

Election Results

2008 general	Jim Gerlach (R)	179,423	(52%)	($2,310,342)
	Bob Roggio (D)	164,952	(48%)	($663,236)
2008 primary	Jim Gerlach (R)	unopposed		

Prior Winning Percentages: 2006 (51%); 2004 (51%); 2002 (51%)

Population		Race/Ethnicity		Work	
Pop. 2007:	699,747	White:	82.5%	Private:	84.9%
Change since 2000:	Up 8.3%	Black:	7.5%	Government:	8.9%
Urban:	85.8%	Hispanic:	5.7%	Self-employed:	6.0%
Rural:	14.2%	Asian:	2.8%	Blue collar:	17.9%
Area size:	819 sq. mi.	Native Am.:	0.1%	White collar:	68.3%
Age		Hawaiian:	0.0%	Khaki collar:	0.1%
Median age:	38.5 yrs.	Two+ races:	1.2%	Other:	13.7%
More than 65 yrs:	13.0%	*Ancestry*		Median income:	$67,521
Less than 18 yrs:	23.9%	German:	19.9%	Median home value:	$236,200
Education		Irish:	14.5%	Poverty:	7.7%
H.S. grad:	89.6%	Italian:	10.5%	**Military Veterans**	
College grad:	38.3%			% of Pop:	10.4%
Grad degree:	15.2%				

The gentle hills of southeastern Pennsylvania, settled in the 18th century by Quaker townsmen, Welsh farmers, German peasants, and members of pietistic sects who became known as the Pennsylvania Dutch, were America's first polyglot interior. Before and after independence, a diverse lot looking for tolerance in the area above Philadelphia and the Delaware River found a land that yielded riches, first in crops, then in ironworking and other industry. Valley Forge is where Gen. George Washington and his men spent the terrible winter and spring of 1777–78, while the British luxuriated in Philadelphia 25 miles away. In Revolutionary times, the area was countryside, a long day's ride from the markets and docks of Philadelphia. Then, rail lines were built from Philadelphia: The Main Line of the Pennsylvania Railroad headed west to industrial Pittsburgh and the Midwest, and the Reading Railroad headed northwest to Reading and the anthracite coalfields beyond. Factories were built in some of the towns here, and many farms continued to thrive, but by the late 19th century some of this land had become commuter territory.

2008 Presidential Vote		
Obama (D)	206,593	(58%)
McCain (R)	147,207	(41%)
2004 Presidential Vote		
Kerry (D)	167,431	(51%)
Bush (R)	156,634	(48%)
Cook Partisan Voting Index:	D+4	

The most lavish Philadelphia suburbs were built on the Main Line, where in mansions shaded by huge trees, Philadelphia's captains of commerce could get respite from the rowhouses and narrow streets of the city. By the late 20th century, highways and giant shopping centers had sprung up. This was affluent suburbia for the masses, or a large part of them. Prosperity even came to some of the factory towns. Reading, the decaying industrial town described in John Updike's *Rabbit* novels, in the 1970s was the site of the first factory outlet store, when a company called Vanity Fair began selling seconds and overruns of stockings and lingerie at wholesale prices.

The 6th Congressional District of Pennsylvania includes parts of this countryside in Chester County, which has about 40% of the population, and Berks and Montgomery counties, with 30% each. Chester County has the highest median income levels in Pennsylvania and is its fastest growing major county, though mushroom farming remains abundant. The boundaries of the 6th District are irregular. Geographically, the main body of the district is northern Chester County, including Coatesville, Downingtown and Phoenixville, and southern Berks County. The district also includes a salient that runs northward in eastern Berks County, with its rapidly growing exurbs. Another, much more heavily populated salient reaches into Montgomery County from Pottstown to Lower Merion Township, which is home to some of Philadelphia's wealthiest people. The district includes Valley Forge, with its American Revolution Center, part but not all of Reading, and most of the Main Line suburbs: Ardmore, Bryn Mawr, and part of Paoli. Until the 1990s, the area had been heavily Republican, and the district was drawn for a Republican. But the suburbs of Philadelphia, like those in other large metropolitan areas, have trended to the Democrats since 2000. Democratic presidential nominee John Kerry carried it 51%-48% in 2004. Barack Obama won it 58%-41% in 2008. He led comfortably in each of the three counties, illustrative of his strong showing in the Philadelphia suburbs.

The congressman from the 6th District is Jim Gerlach, a Republican elected in 2002. He grew up in Ellwood City, Penn., midway between Pittsburgh and Youngstown, Ohio. He graduated from Dickinson College and its law school, just west of Harrisburg. He continued moving east, settled in Chester County and practiced law. He was elected to the state House in 1990 and to the state Senate in 1994. When Republicans in 2002 created a new district in suburban Philadelphia, Gerlach was the obvious intended beneficiary. He had spirited competition from Democrat Dan Wofford, a former adviser to Democratic Gov. Robert Casey. Wofford had not previously run for office, but his name was well known; his father, Harris Wofford, was elected to the Senate in a 1991 special election. Gerlach ran on his legislative accomplishments, including votes to expand Pennsylvania's prescription drug program for low-income seniors. Wofford attacked Gerlach as a career politician. They disagreed on abortion and Medicare. Polls showed the race close, and national Republicans spent more than $1.5 million on ads for Gerlach. The outcome was not clear until the early morning hours. Gerlach won 51%-49%.

In the House, Gerlach's voting record is mostly moderate though more conservative on foreign policy. He was a strong supporter of Bush-era tax cuts and eliminating the marriage penalty in the tax code, but he opposed the Bush administration's proposal to create personal retirement accounts in Social Security.

In October 2005, his late vote helped Republican leaders to win narrow passage of a bill to facilitate construction of new oil refineries. When anti-war activists targeted his support for Bush's troop surge in Iraq in 2007, Gerlach said that the Democrats' withdrawal timetable sent the wrong message to enemies. In 2009, he termed President Barack Obama's $787 billion economic stimulus bill "massive, wasteful government spending," and he called for Pennsylvania to create a bipartisan oversight board to monitor the state's share of the money. But Gerlach bucked his party in 2007 by supporting a Democratic plan to expand the State Children's Health Insurance Program. In April 2005, the House passed his bill to improve access to services for non-members, as well as members, of federal credit unions.

Gerlach has been a prime Democratic target in recent elections. In 2004, he faced Democratic attorney Lois Murphy, who managed Rendell's 2002 campaign in Montgomery County. A former staffer for

NARAL ProChoice America, she received strong support from the women's fundraising group EMILY's List and criticized Gerlach for a lack of leadership in Congress. The well-financed Murphy made it an unexpectedly close contest, but Gerlach won, again by 51%-49%. Two years later, Murphy ran again with strong encouragement from EMILY's List and the Democratic Congressional Campaign Committee. She was better-known and the issues were similar, but the campaign rhetoric was harsher. Gerlach may have benefited from more aggressive attacks by his campaign on alleged inconsistencies in Murphy's agenda. And he accused her of supporting a tax increase on the wealthy. For the third consecutive election, Gerlach won by 51%-49%. In 2008, Gerlach had a more than 3-to-1 fundraising advantage over Democrat Robert Roggio, a retired corporate executive. But he still managed only a 52%-48% win. Republicans could be hard-pressed to hold this district now that Gerlach has announced plans to run for governor in 2010.

SEVENTH DISTRICT

Joe Sestak (D)

Elected 2006, 2nd term; b. Dec. 12, 1951, Secane; home, Edgemont; U.S. Naval Academy, B.S. 1974, Harvard U., M.P.A. 1980, Ph.D. 1984; Catholic; married (Susan); 1 child.

Military Career: Navy, 1974–2005 (Kuwait, Afghanistan, Iraq).

Professional Career: Dir. for Defense Policy, National Security Council, 1994–97; Anti-terrorism unit dir., 2001–02; Commander, George Washington Aircraft Carrier Battle Group, 2002–03.

DC Office: 1022 LHOB, 20515, 202-225-2011; Fax: 202-226-0280; Web site: sestak.house.gov.

State Offices: Media, 610-892-8623.

Committees: *Armed Services* (25th of 36 D): Air & Land Forces; Oversight & Investigations; Seapower & Expeditionary Forces. *Education & Labor* (16th of 29 D): Early Childhood, Elementary & Secondary Education; Health, Employment, Labor & Pensions. *Small Business* (14th of 17 D): Contracting & Technology; Finance & Tax; Regulations & Healthcare.

Group Ratings

	ADA	ACLU	AFS	LCV	ITIC	NTU	COC	ACU	CFG	FRC
2008	90	91	100	92	100	7	61	0	4	5
2007	95	—	100	100	—	7	60	0	6	—

National Journal Ratings

	2007 LIB — 2007 CONS		2008 LIB — 2008 CONS	
Economic	64%	— 34%	68%	— 31%
Social	62%	— 37%	75%	— 18%
Foreign	60%	— 39%	58%	— 42%
Composite	63%	— 37%	68%	— 32%

Key Votes of the 110th Congress

1. Increase minimum wage	Y	5. Share immigration data	Y	9.Withdraw troops 8/08	Y
2. Expand SCHIP	Y	6. Foreign aid abortion ban	N	10. No operations in Iran	Y
3. Raise CAFE standards	Y	7. Ban gay bias in workplace	Y	11. Free trade with Peru	Y
4. Bail out financial markets	Y	8. Repeal D.C. gun law	N	12. Overhaul FISA	Y

Election Results

2008 general	Joe Sestak (D)	209,955	(60%)	($1,162,719)
	Craig Williams (R)	142,362	(40%)	($598,846)
2008 primary	Joe Sestak (D)	unopposed		

Prior Winning Percentages: 2006 (56%)

Population		Race/Ethnicity		Work	
Pop. 2007:	668,358	White:	83.3%	Private:	84.6%
Change since 2000:	Up 3.4%	Black:	8.7%	Government:	10.0%
Urban:	98.6%	Hispanic:	2.0%	Self-employed:	5.2%
Rural:	1.4%	Asian:	4.8%	Blue collar:	14.4%
Area size:	294 sq. mi.	Native Am.:	0.1%	White collar:	72.7%
		Hawaiian:	0.0%	Khaki collar:	0.1%
Age		Two+ races:	0.9%	Other:	12.8%
Median age:	39.6 yrs.			Median income:	$67,299
More than 65 yrs:	14.4%	*Ancestry*		Median home value:	$253,000
Less than 18 yrs:	23.5%	Irish:	22.5%	Poverty:	6.3%
		Italian:	15.3%		
Education		German:	13.9%	**Military Veterans**	
H.S. grad:	91.1%			% of Pop:	10.1%
College grad:	39.5%				
Grad degree:	16.2%				

The close-in suburbs of the great Eastern cities were home to some of the longest-lasting political machines in America. They were Republican; they were ethnic as well as WASP; they had a tolerance for patronage and corruption that was sharply at odds with their supposed embodiment of middle-class morality. And they were as much a part of the urban landscape as trolley lines. One such machine was the War Board of Pennsylvania's Delaware County, a ruthlessly effective Republican organiza-

2008 Presidential Vote
Obama (D) 203,407   (56%)
McCain (R)............................157,367   (43%)

2004 Presidential Vote
Kerry (D)...............................184,392   (53%)
Bush (R) 163,095   (47%)

Cook Partisan Voting Index: D + 3

tion that continues to influence local politics even in its current and greatly diminished form. Republicans retain a decided advantage in party registration in Delaware County, though they lost their board majority in 2008. And Democratic presidential candidates have been winning in the county by increasing margins since the 1990s, including a 56%-43% victory for Barack Obama in 2008. The reasons are partly demographic—in recent decades many Democrats have moved out to the suburbs from Philadelphia—and partly ideological. Republicans of the Newt Gingrich stripe are unfamiliar here, and Sun Belt Republicanism is not popular.

The 7th Congressional District of Pennsylvania includes almost all of Delaware County, except for a few towns with large African-American populations that are appended to Philadelphia's 1st District. The 7th extends north to include a few Montgomery County suburbs, such as modest Conshohocken, an old Schuylkill River factory town that is now the U.S. headquarters for Swedish home furnishings retailer Ikea. It also includes affluent Upper Merion Township and King of Prussia, an edge city where the Schuylkill Expressway intersects the Pennsylvania Turnpike. The 7th takes in southeastern Chester County, including the commercial hub of West Chester and a few further-out suburbs such as Malvern and part of Paoli. About 70% of the population is in Delaware County, with the remainder split between Montgomery and Chester counties. The 7th includes the elite small colleges of Haverford and Swarthmore, and the refined farm country of Chadds Ford, home to generations of Wyeth artists. Its housing is aging but well maintained. Its population is above average in income and people here have deep roots in greater Philadelphia, although they may rarely venture into Center City.

The congressman from the 7th District is Joe Sestak, a Democrat elected in 2006. Sestak is a retired admiral who spent 31 years in the Navy, and he is the highest ranking former military officer ever elected to Congress. (Navy Admiral Thomas Hart was appointed to the Senate from Connecticut.) He grew up in a large family in Delaware County, and followed his father, a World War II captain, into the Navy. He graduated second in his class from the U.S. Naval Academy, and rose through the ranks to become a three-star admiral. He has a doctoral degree from Harvard University. During his career, Sestak held various operational commands. He was a defense adviser for the National Security Council during the Clinton administration. He commanded the George Washington aircraft carrier battle group during combat operations in Afghanistan. After the September 11 terrorist attacks, Sestak was the director of "Deep Blue," an anti-terrorism think tank within the Navy. In July 2005, his young daughter was diagnosed with a malignant brain tumor, and he and his family's life revolved around a Washington hospital for four months. He said his experience with families lacking quality health insurance caused him to rethink his life priorities. After officially retiring from the Navy, and after his daughter was declared free of cancer, Sestak in early 2006 launched his campaign for Congress against 10-term incumbent Republican Curt Weldon, who had not been seriously challenged since he won the seat in 1986.

A political novice, Sestak needed time to polish his retail campaigning skills. But he established his credibility by raising $1.1 million by June 2006. Weldon, on the other hand, struggled to shake off the cobwebs. In April, Weldon drew criticism for suggesting that Sestak should have sent his daughter to a Pennsylvania hospital rather than to one in Washington, D.C. The comment was part of Weldon's strategy to portray Sestak, who had spent roughly three decades away from the suburban Philadelphia district, as an outsider. The Democratic Congressional Campaign Committee played up news reports that Weldon planned a Memorial Day expedition to Iraq to look for alleged weapons of mass destruction, contributing to the view that Weldon had indulged his interest in national security ahead of his district's economic needs. Weldon responded by adopting a more energetic fundraising pace, relying heavily on contributions from the defense industry.

Sestak voiced support for a U.S. withdrawal of troops from Iraq, which Weldon opposed. Weldon questioned Sestak's temperament, citing an August 2005 *Navy Times* report that he was relieved of his duties as deputy chief of naval operations a month earlier because of a "poor command climate." But Weldon's offensive was abruptly rendered moot when the Federal Bureau of Investigation raided the homes of Weldon's daughter and a close associate as part of a probe into whether Weldon improperly used his influence to win contracts for his daughter's lobbying firm. Weldon denied wrongdoing and questioned the curious timing of the raid, which the FBI said was necessary to preserve evidence from destruction. In a tough political environment against an aggressive, well-funded challenger, Weldon sank quickly. The national Republican Party scaled back its ad buys and financial support for his campaign. Sestak won by 56%-44%.

In the House, Sestak has steered close to the ideological center and spent much time cementing his roots at home. On the Armed Services Committee, he began 2007 by introducing a bill to withdraw all U.S. troops from Iraq by the end of the year, but he later voted to continue funding without deadlines. "Do you play chicken with our troops? Absolutely not," he told the Harrisburg *Patriot-News.* "There has to be a strategy, [not just] get out tomorrow." By August 2007, he said that withdrawal could take two years. "As we say in the military, amateurs do tactics, experts do logistics." Those views put him at odds with U.S. Rep. John Murtha, the powerful chairman of Defense Appropriations Subcommittee from Pennsylvania who was the chief proponent of withdrawal deadlines.

On the Education and Labor Committee, Sestak won passage of his proposal to increase flexibility for veterans repaying student loans. On local issues, he opposed the Federal Aviation Administration's flight-path changes that increased noise over parts of the Delaware County.

Republicans failed to recruit a top-flight challenger to Sestak in 2008, and he won easily against former federal prosecutor and Gulf War veteran Craig Williams.

EIGHTH DISTRICT

Patrick Murphy (D)

Elected 2006, 2nd term; b. Oct. 19, 1973, Philadelphia; home, Bristol; Attended Bucks Cnty. Comm. Col., King's Col., B.S. 1996, Widener U., J.D. 1999; Catholic; married (Jennifer); 1 child.

Military Career: Army, 1996–2004 (Bosnia, Iraq); Army Reserves, 2004-present.

Professional Career: Asst. professor and staff atty., U.S. Military Academy, West Point, 1999–2004; Practicing atty., 2004–06; Adjct. prof., Mt. S. Mary's Col.; Lecturer, Widener U.

DC Office: 1609 LHOB, 20515, 202-225-4276; Fax: 202-225-9511; Web site: www.patrickmurphy.house.gov.

State Offices: Bristol, 215-826-1963; Doylestown, 215-348-1194.

Committees: *Armed Services* (20th of 36 D): Military Personnel; Terrorism, Unconventional Threats & Capabilities. *Intelligence (Select)* (10th of 13 D); Intelligence Community Management; Oversight & Investigations; Tactical & Technical Intelligence.

Group Ratings

	ADA	ACLU	AFS	LCV	ITIC	NTU	COC	ACU	CFG	FRC
2008	85	82	86	92	57	12	67	12	4	5
2007	95	—	91	90	—	13	55	4	2	—

National Journal Ratings

	2007 LIB	—	2007 CONS		2008 LIB	—	2008 CONS
Economic	56%	—	43%		62%	—	37%
Social	52%	—	47%		48%	—	50%
Foreign	60%	—	39%		59%	—	37%
Composite	57%	—	44%		58%	—	43%

Key Votes of the 110th Congress

1. Increase minimum wage	Y	5. Share immigration data	Y	9.Withdraw troops 8/08	Y
2. Expand SCHIP	Y	6. Foreign aid abortion ban	N	10. No operations in Iran	Y
3. Raise CAFE standards	Y	7. Ban gay bias in workplace	Y	11. Free trade with Peru	N
4. Bail out financial markets	Y	8. Repeal D.C. gun law	Y	12. Overhaul FISA	Y

Election Results

2008 general	Patrick Murphy (D)	197,869	(57%)	($3,917,416)
	Tom Manion (R)	145,103	(42%)	($1,138,048)
2008 primary	Patrick Murphy (D) .... unopposed			

Prior Winning Percentages: 2006 (50%)

Population		Race/Ethnicity		Work	
Pop. 2007:	665,860	White:	88.9%	Private:	82.9%
Change since 2000:	Up 3.2%	Black:	3.7%	Government:	10.9%
Urban:	90.8%	Hispanic:	3.2%	Self-employed:	6.0%
Rural:	9.2%	Asian:	3.2%	Blue collar:	19.0%
Area size:	634 sq. mi.	Native Am.:	0.1%	White collar:	68.4%
		Hawaiian:	0.0%	Khaki collar:	0.1%
Age		Two+ races:	0.8%	Other:	12.5%
Median age:	40.3 yrs.			Median income:	$70,522
More than 65 yrs:	13.6%	*Ancestry*		Median home value:	$305,500
Less than 18 yrs:	23.5%	German:	19.8%	Poverty:	5.2%
		Irish:	19.5%		
Education		Italian:	11.8%	**Military Veterans**	
H.S. grad:	90.5%			% of Pop:	9.9%
College grad:	33.5%				
Grad degree:	12.9%				

Bucks County was one of founding father William Penn's three original settlements and the launching point for George Washington's crossing of the frigid Delaware River to surprise English and Hessian forces on Christmas Day 1776. But it has had a split personality from the start. Upper Bucks County was at once a bucolic paradise of rolling hills and creeks running into the Delaware River and, after Penn's secretary, James Logan, built the Durham Furnace iron works in 1727, it became

2008 Presidential Vote
Obama (D)	192,570	(54%)
McCain (R)	160,695	(45%)

2004 Presidential Vote
Kerry (D)	177,008	(51%)
Bush (R)	165,239	(48%)

Cook Partisan Voting Index: D + 2

one of the nation's major industrial sites. In the 1920s, Bucks County's well-settled farmland, old field-stone houses and covered bridges captured the imagination of writers and artists, attracting the New York theatrical crowd—Oscar Hammerstein, Moss Hart, Dorothy Parker, S. J. Perelman. New Hope remains a popular weekend spot with hip boutiques and restaurants. After World War II, its location between Philadelphia and Trenton, N.J., brought industrial Lower Bucks County to the forefront. The ocean-navigable Delaware River and several rail lines resulted in huge new developments: U.S. Steel's Fairless Works, one of the few big postwar steel plants, and the Levitt organization's second Levittown, in what had been a swamp between U.S. 13 and U.S. 1. Most of the steel mill closed in 1991, and today, Bucks County's largest employers are in the health care field.

Bucks County's politics were heavily Republican, but more recently, it has been marginally Democratic. This was the home of Republican Sen. Joseph Grundy, longtime head of the Pennsylvania Manufacturers Association, who opposed the 1930 Smoot-Hawley tariff as insufficiently protectionist. Development in Bucks came after the New Deal, unlike other suburban Philadelphia counties where most blue-collar immigration occurred years earlier. Lower Bucks around the Fairless Works and Levittown, with its tightly-packed homes filled with blue collar workers, became Democratic. Upper Bucks, faster-growing and attracting trendy New Yorkers, has favored Democratic policies such as green space programs to keep developers away.

The 8th Congressional District of Pennsylvania includes all of Bucks County, a tiny finger of Montgomery County and parts of two wards in Northeast Philadelphia. Bucks has a small minority population and the third highest income of any county in the state. The 8th was marginal in elections during the 1980s. Since then, it has moved with other Philadelphia suburban areas toward the Democrats and has voted for Democratic presidential candidates since 1992. It also joined the rest of southeastern Pennsylvania in voting decisively for Democrat Ed Rendell for governor in 2002 and 2006. Democratic presidential nominee Barack Obama won the district 54%-45% in 2008.

The congressman from the 8th District is Patrick Murphy, a Democrat elected in 2006 and the first Iraq war veteran elected to Congress. Murphy grew up in Northeast Philadelphia, the son of a Philadelphia policeman and a legal secretary. He attended Bucks County Community College, enrolled as a cadet in the Army ROTC program at King's College, and after graduation, earned a commission in the Army as a second lieutenant. He obtained his law degree at Widener University, got a job as a staff attorney at West Point, and later taught there as a professor. Murphy trained as paratrooper with the 82nd Airborne Division and served four months in Bosnia in 2002 and seven months in Iraq beginning in mid-2003. In Iraq, he worked as a JAG Corps attorney, handling court-martial cases and claims made against U.S. troops by Iraqis, and rebuilding the Iraqi justice system. After returning from Iraq, he practiced law at a Philadelphia firm, and volunteered as a veterans' liaison in Pennsylvania for Democratic presidential nominee John Kerry in 2004.

He was a first-time candidate when he decided to challenge Republican Rep. Mike Fitzpatrick in 2006. He first had a competitive primary with recent Democratic convert Andrew Warren, who was better known to voters after four terms as a Republican Bucks County commissioner. Warren called for rapid troop withdrawal from Iraq, while Murphy offered a three-phase troop redeployment that would bring U.S. troops home by the end of 2007. Murphy won, 65%-35%.

First-term incumbent Fitzpatrick had been hurried onto the ballot in 2004 after longtime GOP Rep. Jim Greenwood announced he was leaving Congress, and so had only a weak hold on the seat. His conservative positions on abortion rights and stem cell research differed from Murphy's. And Murphy's military credentials gave him credibility on Iraq and forced Fitzpatrick to stray from the party line; in one mailer the incumbent declared, "Mike Fitzpatrick to President Bush: 'America needs a better, smarter plan in Iraq.'" Murphy too was critical of President George W. Bush's handling of the war, but struck a different tone than other Democratic war opponents. "I'm not antiwar. I'm not pro-war. I'm pro-troops," Murphy told the *Philadelphia Inquirer*.

Fitzpatrick tried to distance himself from the by-then unpopular administration by noting he had voted against the Republican budget and a constitutional ban on same-sex marriage, and that he had earned endorsements from environmental groups. He also charged that Murphy had moved into the district to further his political ambitions. In one debate, he stumped Murphy by asking him how many school districts there are in Bucks County. The National Republican Congressional Committee pumped $3.5 million in independent ads into the district, compared to the Democratic Congressional Campaign Committee's $1.7 million. Fitzpatrick outspent Murphy $3.2 million to $2.4 million. But Murphy won 50.3%-49.7%. Fitzpatrick actually carried Bucks County, which includes almost all the district, by just over 1,000 votes. But Murphy carried smaller areas of Northeast Philadelphia and Montgomery County by large enough margins to win the district by just over 1,500 votes. Shortly before taking office, Murphy generated some controversy by signing a book deal with a $100,000 advance, which Republicans called a possible violation for the outside-income rule. The book, *Taking the Hill*, was published in February 2008.

In the House, Murphy established a centrist voting record, especially on social issues. He quickly became a favorite of Speaker Nancy Pelosi, who made him a party spokesman on the issue of a troop withdrawal from Iraq. With seats on the Armed Services and Intelligence committees, he was a leading voice against Bush's troop "surge" plan to send more combat troops to Iraq to restore order. And he was a leading proponent of the Democrats' initial plan to require redeployment of all combat troops by March 2008. Murphy contended that once the Iraqis knew that American forces were departing, they would take more responsibility.

On other issues, Murphy won House approval of his amendment to the higher education bill to require universities to estimate their long-range charges for tuition and other costs.

In 2008, Murphy had an easy ride to re-election against pharmaceutical executive Tom Manion, a former Marine whose son was killed in Iraq. After spending nearly $4 million to Manion's $1.1 million, Murphy won 57%-42%.

NINTH DISTRICT

Bill Shuster (R)

Elected May 2001, 4th full term; b. Jan. 10, 1961, McKeesport; home, Hollidaysburg; Dickinson Col., B.A. 1983; American U., M.B.A. 1987; Lutheran; married (Rebecca); 2 children.

Professional Career: Mgr., Goodyear Tire & Rubber Co., 1983–87; District mgr., Bandag Inc., 1987–90; Owner & gen. mgr., Shuster Chrysler, 1990–2001.

DC Office: 204 CHOB, 20515, 202-225-2431; Fax: 202-225-2486; Web site: www.house.gov/shuster.

State Offices: Chambersburg, 717-264-8308; Hollidaysburg, 814-696-6318; Indiana, 724-463-0516; Somerset, 814-443-3918.

Committees: *Armed Services* (15th of 25 R): Readiness; Terrorism, Unconventional Threats & Capabilities. *Natural Resources* (10th of 20 R): National Parks, Forests & Public Lands. *Transportation & Infrastructure* (14th of 30 R): Highways & Transit; Railroads, Pipelines & Hazardous Materials (RMM); Water Resources & Environment.

Group Ratings

	ADA	ACLU	AFS	LCV	ITIC	NTU	COC	ACU	CFG	FRC
2008	20	18	14	15	100	62	94	92	69	88
2007	10	—	9	5	—	74	89	96	78	—

National Journal Ratings

	2007 LIB — 2007 CONS		2008 LIB — 2008 CONS	
Economic	19% —	81%	19% —	80%
Social	17% —	81%	20% —	74%
Foreign	0% —	72%	0% —	95%
Composite	17% —	83%	15% —	85%

Key Votes of the 110th Congress

1. Increase minimum wage	N	5. Share immigration data	Y	9. Withdraw troops 8/08	N
2. Expand SCHIP	N	6. Foreign aid abortion ban	Y	10. No operations in Iran	N
3. Raise CAFE standards	N	7. Ban gay bias in workplace	N	11. Free trade with Peru	Y
4. Bail out financial markets	Y	8. Repeal D.C. gun law	Y	12. Overhaul FISA	Y

Election Results

2008 general	Bill Shuster (R)	174,951	(64%)	($979,174)
	Tony Barr (D)	98,735	(36%)	($47,417)
2008 primary	Bill Shuster (R)	unopposed		

Prior Winning Percentages: 2006 (60%); 2004 (69%); 2002 (71%); 2001 (52%)

Population		Race/Ethnicity		Work	
Pop. 2007:	651,289	White:	95.4%	Private:	78.3%
Change since 2000:	Up 0.7%	Black:	1.7%	Government:	13.4%
Urban:	40.5%	Hispanic:	1.3%	Self-employed:	8.0%
Rural:	59.5%	Asian:	0.5%	Blue collar:	32.0%
Area size:	7,199 sq. mi.	Native Am.:	0.1%	White collar:	50.4%
		Hawaiian:	0.0%	Khaki collar:	0.1%
Age		Two+ races:	0.8%	Other:	17.4%
Median age:	40.6 yrs.	*Ancestry*		Median income:	$42,162
More than 65 yrs:	16.5%	German:	30.7%	Median home value:	$109,300
Less than 18 yrs:	21.8%	Irish:	11.6%	Poverty:	11.6%
Education		USA:	6.5%	**Military Veterans**	
H.S. grad:	83.7%			% of Pop:	12.7%
College grad:	15.3%				
Grad degree:	5.4%				

The old towns of south central Pennsylvania look much as they did 60 years ago: farmhouses and red barns set amidst rolling hills in the shadow of mountain ridges, seemingly isolated from the pulsing rhythms of 21st century America. But this tranquility was shattered on September 11, 2001, when United Airlines Flight 93 crashed into an empty former coalfield near Shanksville in Somerset County, killing all 40 passengers and crew on board. To Americans, the crash site became a symbol of both

2008 Presidential Vote

McCain (R)	176,023	(63%)
Obama (D)	98,430	(35%)

2004 Presidential Vote

Bush (R)	183,717	(67%)
Kerry (D)	89,208	(33%)

Cook Partisan Voting Index:　R + 17

sadness and pride at the passengers' effort to wrest back control of the plane, initiated by the now-famous cry of "Let's roll!" The bravery of the passengers prevented the plane from reaching the hijackers' target, probably the Capitol or perhaps the White House. The National Park Service is racing to complete a permanent memorial to Flight 93 by the tenth anniversary of the attacks. In 2002, Somerset County was struck by another bolt of lightning when nine miners at the Quecreek coal mine were trapped by rising waters 240 feet underground. As a breathless nation looked on, rescuers strained to dig rescue shafts, and this time, the outcome was happy. After 77 hours in confinement, the miners were lifted one by one to safety.

The Appalachian Mountains run like a series of vertebrae up and down central Pennsylvania, long posing a formidable barrier. Up close, the mountains look tantalizingly low; you imagine that you could hike over them in an hour or so. But they are much more daunting. During the 18th century, the mountains provided Quaker Pennsylvania with a rampart against Indian attacks, and allowed the Common-wealth to become the richest and most populous of the colonies. But the colonials led by Gen. Edward Braddock to defeat near Pittsburgh in 1754 found the mountains hard-going, despite guidance from George Washington. Nineteenth century pioneers in Conestoga wagons found it not much easier, for there are few gaps in the ridges. Later, the mountains proved to be a barrier to commerce, and people flocked to the easier routes through New York: the Erie Canal and the New York Central Railroad. It took the aggressive capitalists who built the Pennsylvania Railroad to get trains over these ridges. Conquering the mountains near Altoona required the work of several hundred Irish laborers, equipped with hand tools, gunpowder and pack animals. They built Horseshoe Curve between 1851 and 1854, one of the finest examples of railroad engineering anywhere. The local AA baseball team is called the Altoona Curve. Though Pennsylvania's rail links remained important—the Nazis considered them key sabotage targets during World War II—the war-bound nation in 1940 opened the road of the future here: the Pennsylvania Turnpike, the first highway in America that was able to move vehicles dependably at high speeds over long distances. "The Pennsylvania Turnpike is a triumph of engineering," wrote Tom Lewis in *Divided Highways*, a study of the Interstate highway system. "The road tunnels under the Allegheny Mountains and cuts about five hours off the journey between the cities.

Pennsylvania's 9th Congressional District takes in a wide swath of south and central Pennsylvania, including six full counties and parts of eight others. Most of the 9th is not coal country and was thus spared the boom-bust cycles of northeastern Pennsylvania and West Virginia. But this is a slow-growth, low-income area today. The largest city is Altoona, which withered from 82,000 people in 1930 to 46,000 in 2007 as the once-prosperous Pennsylvania Railroad succumbed to competition from truck traffic. One bright spot economically is the resort in Bedford Springs, which was reopened in 2007 after being shut for 21 years with a $120 million refurbishing. A century earlier, it was a magnet for captains of business and government. Politically, this part of Pennsylvania has been solidly Republican since 1860, when Mercersburg native James Buchanan left the White House, and has not come close to electing a Democrat to Congress for decades. George W. Bush won 64% of the vote here in 2000 and 67% in 2004. John McCain won the district with 63% in 2008, his best performance in the Northeast.

The congressman from the 9th District is Bill Shuster, a Republican who won a May 2001 special election to succeed his father, Bud Shuster, for six years the powerful chairman of the Transportation and Infrastructure Committee. Bill Shuster grew up in the Pittsburgh area, where his father started a successful business. After graduating from Dickinson College and American University's business school, he moved to Blair County, where he took over the family's car dealership, Shuster Chrysler in East Freedom, near Altoona. He sold the business in 2002.

Bud Shuster announced his resignation in January 2001, shortly after being re-elected to a 14th term. He was disgruntled that he failed to get an exemption from the House Republicans' term limit on chairmanships. The contest for the House seat was for all practical purposes decided at a district-wide Republican convention. Facing nine other contenders, Shuster, with back-room help from his father, ran an insider campaign that took advantage of the family's years of service. Although there was some local grumbling about a Shuster dynasty, opponents failed to coalesce behind a single candidate. Shuster won 69 of the 133 votes, two more than the required majority. National Democrats ignored the race in the heavily Republican district, which seemed to them hopeless. But Democrat H. Scott Conklin campaigned vigorously as an opponent of abortion rights and gun control. Shuster won by a closer than expected 52%-44%. National Republicans attributed the narrow margin to residual intra-party ill will over Shuster's nomination.

In the House, Bill Shuster has a solidly conservative voting record. Naturally, he ended up on the Transportation and Infrastructure Committee. Following Hurricane Katrina in 2005, he questioned whether parts of New Orleans below sea level should be rebuilt. Since 2007, Shuster has been the senior Republican on the Railroads, Pipelines, and Hazardous Materials Subcommittee, where he has backed additional funding for Amtrak rail service and for freight-rail capacity. He has advocated more energy production, including drilling in the Arctic National Wildlife Refuge, producing liquid fuel from coal and the building of more nuclear power plants.

In his father's tradition, Shuster has been an avid practitioner of earmarked spending for his district, a practice that in recent years has been attacked by budget conservatives as wasteful. In 2008, he claimed $22 million in earmarks, including $8.3 million for water and sewer grants and $250,000 for a covered bridge near Greencastle. Democrats lampooned him in March 2009 for taking credit for $9 million to his district from President Barack Obama's economic stimulus bill, even though he had voted against the legislation. He was less amenable to funding for Berkeley, Calif., seeking unsuccessfully to cut $2 million for the city from an appropriations bill in 2008. After Berkeley told Marine recruiters they were unwelcome to set up shop in the city, Shuster called Berkeley "ground zero for radicals and leftist zealots."

Shuster had an unusually strong challenge in the 2004 primary from Michael DelGrosso, a management consultant whose family owns a Blair County tomato sauce company. He said that the district needed a new economic approach. DelGrosso carried Blair County and three nearby counties in the northern part of the district, but Shuster ran strongly elsewhere and squeezed by with a 51%-49% win. He has not been seriously challenged in recent elections.

TENTH DISTRICT

Christopher Carney (D)

Elected 2006, 2nd term; b. March 2, 1959, Cedar Rapids, IA; home, Dimock; Cornell College, B.S. 1981, U. of WY, M.A. 1983, U. of NE, Ph.D. 1993; Catholic; married (Jennifer); 5 children.

Military Career: Naval Reserve, 1995-present.

Professional Career: Prof., PA St. U.-Worthington Scranton, 1992–2006.

DC Office: 416 CHOB, 20515, 202-225-3731; Fax: 202-225-9594; Web site: carney.house.gov.

State Offices: Clarks Summit, 570-585-9988; Shamokin, 570-644-1682; Williamsport, 570-327-1902.

Committees: *Homeland Security* (9th of 20 D): Intelligence, Information Sharing & Terrorism Risk Assessment; Management, Investigations & Oversight (Chmn). *Transportation & Infrastructure* (28th of 44 D): Economic Development, Public Buildings & Emergency Management; Highways & Transit; Railroads, Pipelines & Hazardous Materials.

Group Ratings

	ADA	ACLU	AFS	LCV	ITIC	NTU	COC	ACU	CFG	FRC
2008	85	55	100	85	43	18	59	20	8	23
2007	85	—	91	80	—	9	53	28	1	—

National Journal Ratings

	2007 LIB	—	2007 CONS	2008 LIB	—	2008 CONS
Economic	52%	—	47%	57%	—	41%
Social	47%	—	53%	46%	—	52%
Foreign	49%	—	50%	46%	—	54%
Composite	50%	—	50%	50%	—	50%

Key Votes of the 110th Congress

1. Increase minimum wage	Y	5. Share immigration data	N	9.Withdraw troops 8/08	Y
2. Expand SCHIP	Y	6. Foreign aid abortion ban	N	10. No operations in Iran	N
3. Raise CAFE standards	Y	7. Ban gay bias in workplace	Y	11. Free trade with Peru	N
4. Bail out financial markets	N	8. Repeal D.C. gun law	Y	12. Overhaul FISA	Y

Election Results

2008 general	Christopher Carney (D)	160,837	(56%)	($2,333,358)
	Chris Hackett (R)	124,681	(44%)	($3,226,168)
2008 primary	Christopher Carney (D)	unopposed		

Prior Winning Percentages: 2006 (53%)

Population		Race/Ethnicity		Work	
Pop. 2007:	648,097	White:	93.9%	Private:	77.8%
Change since 2000:	Up 0.2%	Black:	2.5%	Government:	13.4%
Urban:	44.6%	Hispanic:	2.0%	Self-employed:	8.5%
Rural:	55.4%	Asian:	0.7%	Blue collar:	29.1%
Area size:	6,663 sq. mi.	Native Am.:	0.1%	White collar:	53.8%
		Hawaiian:	0.0%	Khaki collar:	0.1%
Age		Two+ races:	0.7%	Other:	17.0%
Median age:	41.4 yrs.			Median income:	$42,546
More than 65 yrs:	16.6%	*Ancestry*		Median home value:	$124,600
Less than 18 yrs:	21.6%	German:	22.5%	Poverty:	11.6%
		Irish:	13.4%		
Education		Italian:	9.0%	**Military Veterans**	
H.S. grad:	86.2%			% of Pop:	12.6%
College grad:	19.7%				
Grad degree:	7.2%				

The northeast corner of Pennsylvania is a land of crevassed valleys and rugged mountains, criss-crossed by giant viaducts built for the railroads linking the East Coast with the Great Lakes and the mines to the big cities that heated their houses with the region's anthracite coal. Except for a row of anthracite coal cities from Scranton to Wilkes-Barre, this part of Pennsylvania still has a wild look to it. The superstructure of railroads and Interstate

2008 Presidential Vote		
McCain (R)............................155,438	(54%)
Obama (D) 131,168	(45%)
2004 Presidential Vote		
Bush (R)................................170,880	(60%)
Kerry (D)...............................112,923	(40%)
Cook Partisan Voting Index: R+8		

80 pass through an area that seems otherwise little touched by recent prosperity. The region has numerous long-established small towns, with solidly built courthouses and banks and elderly citizens. It's a part of the Northeast that seems worlds away from the region's huge central cities and growing suburbs. The biggest towns here are Lewisburg, home of Bucknell University and a major federal penitentiary, and Williamsport, home of the Little League World Series. Only at the eastern edge is there significant growth. Pike County on the Delaware River is the state's fastest-growing county. It increased in population by 29% since 2000, mostly as a result of people fleeing high taxes in New Jersey and New York. The local Pocono Mountains are a destination for weekenders and, for a few days each November, for bear hunters. In the winter months, hunters in increasing numbers turn to tracking coyote in the fresh snow.

The 10th Congressional District of Pennsylvania includes all of northeast Pennsylvania except for Scranton, Wilkes-Barre and fast-growing Monroe County, which are in the 11th District. The area's most consequential congressman was probably David Wilmot, who in the 1840s introduced the Wilmot Proviso barring slavery from the New Mexico and California Territories acquired in the Mexican War; this raised the issue of slavery in the territories which led proximately to the Civil War. Wilmot was a founder of the Republican Party. Most people in this part of Pennsylvania have been Republicans ever since. John McCain won the district with 54% in 2008, a sizable dip from George W. Bush's 60% win in 2004.

The congressman from the 10th District is Christopher Carney, a Democrat elected in 2006. Carney was born in Cedar Rapids, Iowa, and studied at Cornell College, the University of Wyoming and the University of Nebraska. In 1992, Carney moved his family to Pennsylvania to take a job as an associate professor at Penn State University's Scranton campus. After the September 11 terrorist attacks, Carney, a Navy reservist, was called up to go to Afghanistan, but instead ended up at the Pentagon analyzing CIA intelligence for Undersecretary of Defense Douglas Feith in search of connections between al-Qaeda terrorists and the government of Iraq. His conclusion, which he has defended, was that there were "high-level" contacts between the two, but he said the Bush administration took the evidence too far when Defense Secretary Donald Rumsfeld declared the connection was "bulletproof."

Carney told the Wilkes-Barre *Times Leader* he decided to run for Congress after he saw Republican Rep. Don Sherwood at a gas station, preparing to go to Washington to vote on the end-of-life case of Terri Schiavo, a comatose Florida woman whose feeding tube was ordered removed by the courts. Congressional Republicans stepped in to try to reverse that decision. "This was the Republicans trying to capitalize on this family's misery and it made me mad. I'm Irish and I had a couple hundred more miles to go before I was home, and actually somewhere right around Wilkes-Barre I decided, 'Dammit, I'm going to do this.'"

Sherwood represented a reliably Republican district, but the seat was put into play after the *Times Leader* reported in April 2005 that police had been called to Sherwood's Capitol Hill apartment in September 2004 by a 29-year-old woman who accused him of punching and choking her. Sherwood said he was giving her a back rub. Sherwood's accuser later said she had a five-year affair with the married congressman and filed a lawsuit against him seeking $5.5 million in damages. It was settled in November 2005, reportedly for $500,000. Sherwood faced an unusually competitive challenge in the May 2006 Republican primary from an underfunded candidate who ran on family values and held the incumbent to just 56%-44%.

In an attempt to steer the campaign back to safer territory in this conservative district, Sherwood portrayed Carney as a supporter of tax increases and accused Carney of deceiving voters on his position in favor of abortion rights. A cancer survivor, Carney also supported federal funding for embryonic stem cell research, which many conservatives consider a form of abortion. Carney criticized Bush's execution of the war and advocated the redeployment of a U.S. battalion for each equivalent Iraqi security force trained as a replacement. Because of Carney's opposition to the war, activists were willing to overlook his role in helping to make the White House case for intervention in Iraq.

Carney avoided direct mention of Sherwood's affair for most of the campaign until late September, when he aired a television ad that featured a one-time Sherwood supporter holding a photo of his 26-year-old stepdaughter and saying, "How can I tell her I support Don Sherwood and feel good about myself?" Sherwood issued a direct apology to the district for the affair and denied that any abuse occurred. "Should you forgive me, you can count on me to continue fighting for you and your family," Sherwood said in his own TV ad. National Republican leaders including President Bush and House GOP Leader John Boehner of Ohio visited the district in an attempt to save Sherwood. But Carney won 53%-47%.

In the House, Carney has a voting record almost precisely in the center of the 435 members. He disappointed liberal activists with his support for Bush's domestic surveillance legislation and his opposition to Democratic proposals for Iraq. Although he voted for a resolution opposing the "surge" in Iraq, he was one of only nine Democrats in April 2007 who voted against a provision setting a timetable for withdrawal in Iraq. "I do not want partisan bickering over timetables to delay funding for our troops," he said. In 2008, Carney was promoted to commander in the Navy Reserve and serves one weekend each month at the Pentagon.

As a freshman, he became chairman of the Homeland Security Committee's Management, Investigation and Oversight Subcommittee. His proposal for increased transparency in Transportation Security Administration contracting was included in the omnibus appropriations bill enacted in December 2007. Attempting to secure his hold on the seat, Carney led all freshman Democrats in 2007 in the amount of earmarked spending he got for his district in the appropriations bills, some $18 million.

Republicans naturally targeted this district in 2008, but a contentious primary weakened their nominee, Luzerne County businessman Chris Hackett. Although Carney was outspent $3.2 million to $2.3 million, with Hackett spending $1.2 million of his own money, he successfully attacked Hackett's support for a national sales tax. Carney won 56%-44%.

ELEVENTH DISTRICT

Paul Kanjorski (D)

Elected 1984, 13th term; b. April 2, 1937, Nanticoke; home, Nanticoke; Temple U., 1957–61, Dickinson Law Schl., 1962–65; Catholic; married (Nancy); 1 child.

Military Career: Army Reserves, 1960–61.

Professional Career: Practicing atty., 1966–85; Nanticoke City solicitor, 1969–81; Admin. law judge, 1971–80.

DC Office: 2188 RHOB, 20515, 202-225-6511; Fax: 202-225-0764; Web site: kanjorski.house.gov.

State Offices: Mount Pocono, 570-895-4176; Scranton, 570-496-1011; Wilkes-Barre, 570-825-2200.

Committees: *Financial Services* (2nd of 42 D): Capital Markets, Insurance & Government Sponsored Enterprises (Chmn); Financial Institutions & Consumer Credit; Housing & Community Opportunity. *Oversight & Government Reform* (2nd of 24 D): Government Management, Organization & Procurement; Information Policy, Census & National Archives.

Group Ratings

	ADA	ACLU	AFS	LCV	ITIC	NTU	COC	ACU	CFG	FRC
2008	80	91	86	92	57	7	67	12	0	17
2007	90	—	100	70	—	5	45	17	6	—

National Journal Ratings

	2007 LIB — 2007 CONS		2008 LIB — 2008 CONS	
Economic	50%	— 50%	57%	— 41%
Social	59%	— 41%	54%	— 42%
Foreign	63%	— 37%	59%	— 37%
Composite	57%	— 43%	58%	— 42%

Key Votes of the 110th Congress

1. Increase minimum wage	Y	5. Share immigration data	N	9.Withdraw troops 8/08	*
2. Expand SCHIP	Y	6. Foreign aid abortion ban	Y	10. No operations in Iran	Y
3. Raise CAFE standards	Y	7. Ban gay bias in workplace	Y	11. Free trade with Peru	N
4. Bail out financial markets	Y	8. Repeal D.C. gun law	Y	12. Overhaul FISA	Y

Election Results

2008 general	Paul Kanjorski (D)	146,379	(52%)	($3,153,006)
	Lou Barletta (R)	137,151	(48%)	($1,315,969)
2008 primary	Paul Kanjorski (D)	unopposed		

Prior Winning Percentages: 2006 (72%); 2004 (94%); 2002 (56%); 2000 (66%); 1998 (67%); 1996 (68%); 1994 (67%); 1992 (67%); 1990 (100%); 1988 (100%); 1986 (71%); 1984 (59%)

Population		Race/Ethnicity		Work	
Pop. 2007:	671,427	White:	88.6%	Private:	81.1%
Change since 2000:	Up 3.9%	Black:	4.2%	Government:	12.9%
Urban:	72.6%	Hispanic:	5.1%	Self-employed:	5.7%
Rural:	27.4%	Asian:	1.2%	Blue collar:	26.8%
Area size:	2,249 sq. mi.	Native Am.:	0.1%	White collar:	54.9%
Age		Hawaiian:	0.0%	Khaki collar:	0.1%
Median age:	40.1 yrs.	Two+ races:	0.7%	Other:	18.2%
More than 65 yrs:	16.4%	*Ancestry*		Median income:	$42,079
Less than 18 yrs:	21.2%	German:	16.8%	Median home value:	$122,200
Education		Irish:	14.5%	Poverty:	12.7%
H.S. grad:	85.9%	Italian:	13.2%	**Military Veterans**	
College grad:	18.6%			% of Pop:	12.2%
Grad degree:	6.5%				

"Coal is the theme song of this city in the hills," the *WPA Guide* said of Scranton in 1940, but even as those words were written, the anthracite kingdom around Scranton and Wilkes-Barre was crumbling. In the 19th century, anthracite had become America's main home heating fuel and the valley along the East Branch of the Susquehanna River was the No. 1 source of anthracite. Thousands of immigrants flocked to the valley, settling in a chain of little cities north and south of Wilkes-Barre, which is named

2008 Presidential Vote		
Obama (D)	164,646	(57%)
McCain (R)	121,916	(42%)
2004 Presidential Vote		
Kerry (D)	143,205	(53%)
Bush (R)	127,866	(47%)
Cook Partisan Voting Index:	D+4	

for two backers of the American Revolution, and Scranton, which is named for its founding family. They took jobs with long hours, modest pay, poor working conditions and high death rates—facts of life that made the violently pro-union Molly Maguires popular here and that spawned periodic clashes between workers and the Pinkerton security forces hired by the industrial moguls. While the supply of coal was endless—the area produced 40% of the world's hard coal—demand proved fleeting. Anthracite production peaked in 1917, with long strikes in 1922 and 1925 quickening the conversion to oil and gas. Demand for anthracite began to fall in the 1920s and plummeted in the 1940s. The counties containing Wilkes-Barre and Scranton, Luzerne and Lackawanna, had 755,000 people in 1930 and 521,000 in 2008. As the area's 50 collieries shut down, the once-ubiquitous coal dust vanished. The local ethnic mix—Irish, Polish, Ukrainian and Welsh—grew less distinctive. Former boomtowns full of young families became time-worn communities of senior citizens with modest household incomes.

The 11th Congressional District of Pennsylvania is the anthracite district. It includes almost all of Luzerne County, plus Scranton and surrounding towns in Lackawanna County. It also includes Columbia County west of Luzerne, Carbon County to the south, and Monroe County to the east. Monroe is a different sort of place. It contains most of the Pocono Mountain resorts and the often-congested Interstate 80 bridge to New Jersey; New Yorkers and New Jerseyites looking for lower taxes and pleasant scenery have moved here in large numbers and the county's population rose 72% from 1990 to 2008. More typical of the district are small towns like Centralia, site of a massive underground fire that has burned unchecked since 1962 and might burn for another 100 years, inspiring a 2007 book, *The Day the Earth Caved In*. The town of Jim Thorpe was created in 1953 from the unification of neighboring Mauch Chunk and East Mauch Chunk. The cities changed their name after offering to provide a gravesite for the great football, baseball and Olympic track star when Thorpe's widow was shopping his remains to whichever town agreed to build him a suitable memorial. Downtown is lively today, with tourists and thousands of cyclists who flock to the town's numerous downtown trails. Hazleton gained national notoriety in 2006 after passing a tough ordinance aimed at cracking down on illegal immigrants, including fines on landlords and employers. In 2007, a federal judge ruled that law unconstitutional.

Since the 1930s, miners have been a large Democratic voting bloc, and this is a solidly Democratic district. But the district's Democrats tend to be cultural conservatives who are pro-gun and anti-abortion rights. In 2008, Democratic presidential candidate Barack Obama had trouble connecting to this district after his off-the-cuff comment at a San Francisco fundraiser that working-class people there were "bitter," they cling to guns or religion or antipathy to people who aren't like them." When Democratic vice presidential nominee Joe Biden made his first post-convention visit here in 2008, it had special significance: Scranton was his birthplace and first hometown. Obama won the district, 57%-42%.

The congressman from the 11th District is Paul Kanjorski, a Democrat first elected in 1984. Kanjorski grew up in Nanticoke, near Wilkes-Barre. As a 16-year-old page in the House of Representatives in 1954, he was on the floor when Puerto Rican terrorists started shooting from the gallery and wounded five congressmen. Sprayed by dust from the gunfire, Kanjorski helped to bring stretchers into the chamber. He attended, but did not graduate from, college and law school, then passed the bar exam and returned home to practice law. He was a workmen's compensation administrative law judge for nine years and Nanticoke city solicitor for 12. He ran for Congress and won the Democratic primary by pointing out that the incumbent was in Central America while flooded Wilkes-Barre area residents were boiling water to drink.

In the House, Kanjorski is a tough partisan whose voting record was once liberal but has moved toward the center, especially on cultural issues. He opposes abortion rights but has voted for international family planning aid. He voted to authorize the use of force in Iraq, but later voiced regret for his vote and criticized the Bush administration for diverting funds from fighting Al Qaeda to Iraq. In April 2007, he bucked his party as one of six House Democrats who voted against giving the District of Columbia full voting representation in the House of Representatives.

On the Financial Services Committee, Kanjorski is the No. 2 Democrat and chairman of the Subcommittee on Capitol Markets, Insurance and Government Sponsored Enterprises. He helped to write the post-Enron scandal bill to crack down on corporate fraud, and he pushed a "subprime lending" bill to protect consumers from predatory practices. In 2007, he took the lead on renewing the terrorism risk-insurance program, including a requirement that insurance carriers offer coverage of a nuclear, biological, chemical or radiological attack. He also has proposed steps toward federal regulation of the insurance industry, starting with a Treasury Department office to collect information about the industry. Major insurance companies staunchly oppose the measure.

Most important to Kanjorski is helping his economically ailing district. With help from powerful home-state ally Rep. John Murtha, he has directed millions of federal dollars to local projects; *The New York Times* has called him "a master of earmarking." But his eagerness to deliver money back home has gotten him some unwelcome notice. The Scranton *Times-Tribune* reported in 2007 that since the late 1990s, Kanjorski has earmarked nearly $10 million in federal funding to Cornerstone Technologies, a troubled high-tech research and development company controlled by his relatives. The company was supposed to turn coal into minute particles for use in carbon fibers, but the end product was disappointing and Cornerstone filed for bankruptcy in 2006, with more than $1 million in debt. "It was just like the Three Stooges meet anthracite," a Penn State professor who worked with the firm told the *Times-Tribune*. Former employees charged that Kanjorski "often took an active role in its operations," according to the newspaper account. In 2008, the U.S. Transportation Department had blocked $5.6 million that Kanjorski had earmarked for a parking garage in Nanticoke.

Republicans have targeted Kanjorski, and succeeded in tightening his margin. In 2008, his opponent was Hazleton Mayor Louis Barletta, who had challenged him in 2002 and lost. Given his role on the Financial Services Committee, Kanjorski was a prime target for grass-roots opposition against the $700 billion bailout of the financial services industry that committee Democrats shepherded through the House in 2008. Polls in September showed Kanjorski was deadlocked or trailing Barletta, who criticized him for weak oversight of the financial industry, including the many companies whose executives had made campaign contributions to Kanjorski. "I'm elected to Congress to do the right thing, not to get reelected," he told *The Citizens' Voice* in Wilkes-Barre.

Barletta ran ads criticizing Kanjorski's support of the bailout, and he talked up the need for federal action to control illegal immigration. Kanjorski outspent Barletta $3.2 million to $1.3 million, and he received campaign help from Biden and former President Bill Clinton. He won by only 52%-48%. Barletta won three of the five counties, including the district's largest, Luzerne. Kanjorski prevailed with 60% in gritty Lackawanna and 56% in fast-growing Monroe. Kanjorski has had some health problems in recent years, including triple bypass surgery in 2007.

TWELFTH DISTRICT

John Murtha (D)

Elected Feb. 1974, 18th full term; b. June 17, 1932, New Martinsville, WV; home, Johnstown; U. of Pittsburgh, B.A. 1962, Indiana U. of PA, 1963–64; Catholic; married (Joyce); 3 children.

Military Career: Marine Corps, 1952–55, 1966–67 (Vietnam); Marine Corps Reserves, 1955–66, 1967–90.

Elected Office: PA House of Reps., 1969–74.

Professional Career: Owner, Johnstown Minute Car Wash.

DC Office: 2423 RHOB, 20515, 202-225-2065; Fax: 202-225-5709; Web site: murtha.house.gov.

State Offices: Johnstown, 814-535-2642.

Committees: *Appropriations* (2nd of 37 D): Defense (Chmn).

Group Ratings

	ADA	ACLU	AFS	LCV	ITIC	NTU	COC	ACU	CFG	FRC
2008	85	91	100	92	100	7	65	4	0	23
2007	95	—	100	75	—	4	50	8	5	—

National Journal Ratings

	2007 LIB — 2007 CONS		2008 LIB — 2008 CONS	
Economic	56% —	44%	64% —	35%
Social	66% —	33%	62% —	34%
Foreign	61% —	39%	59% —	37%
Composite	61% —	39%	63% —	37%

Key Votes of the 110th Congress

1. Increase minimum wage	Y	5. Share immigration data	N	9.Withdraw troops 8/08	Y
2. Expand SCHIP	Y	6. Foreign aid abortion ban	Y	10. No operations in Iran	N
3. Raise CAFE standards	Y	7. Ban gay bias in workplace	Y	11. Free trade with Peru	Y
4. Bail out financial markets	Y	8. Repeal D.C. gun law	Y	12. Overhaul FISA	Y

Election Results

2008 general	John Murtha (D)	155,268	(58%)	($3,656,397)
	William Russell (R)	113,120	(42%)	($3,492,873)
2008 primary	John Murtha (D)	unopposed		

Prior Winning Percentages: 2006 (61%); 2004 (100%); 2002 (73%); 2000 (71%); 1998 (68%); 1996 (70%); 1994 (69%); 1992 (100%); 1990 (62%); 1988 (100%); 1986 (67%); 1984 (69%); 1982 (61%); 1980 (59%); 1978 (69%); 1976 (68%); 1974 (58%); 1974 (50%)

Population		Race/Ethnicity		Work	
Pop. 2007:	627,426	White:	94.1%	Private:	81.6%
Change since 2000:	Down 2.9%	Black:	3.7%	Government:	12.6%
Urban:	62.5%	Hispanic:	0.7%	Self-employed:	5.6%
Rural:	37.5%	Asian:	0.6%	Blue collar:	28.0%
Area size:	2,781 sq. mi.	Native Am.:	0.1%	White collar:	52.9%
		Hawaiian:	0.0%	Khaki collar:	0.1%
Age		Two+ races:	0.8%	Other:	19.1%
Median age:	41.8 yrs.	*Ancestry*		Median income:	$37,053
More than 65 yrs:	18.0%	German:	21.4%	Median home value:	$86,900
Less than 18 yrs:	20.0%	Irish:	12.2%	Poverty:	14.8%
Education		Italian:	11.5%		
H.S. grad:	85.4%			**Military Veterans**	
College grad:	16.4%			% of Pop:	12.7%
Grad degree:	5.7%				

The mountains and valleys within a 100-mile radius of Pittsburgh comprise one of America's most beautiful—and economically troubled—regions. This has been tough, hard-working country ever since Scots-Irish farmers settled here in the 1790s. Their first big product was whiskey—this was the site of the Whiskey Rebellion of 1794—but historically the most important product was bituminous coal. Discovered in the 19th century, it was the basic energy source for the production of iron and steel.

2008 Presidential Vote		
McCain (R)	133,543	(49%)
Obama (D)	132,670	(49%)

2004 Presidential Vote		
Kerry (D)	141,046	(51%)
Bush (R)	133,088	(49%)

Cook Partisan Voting Index: R + 1

The offspring of the original settlers were joined by immigrants from Italy, Poland and Czechoslovakia, living in little frame houses packed into the towns on interstices between hills and rivers, within walking distance of steel factories, foundries and coal mine shafts. It is an industrial landscape and yet there are spots of natural beauty, like the swirling waters of the Youghiogheny River, now much enjoyed by rafters. Its best known community is Johnstown, where on May 31, 1889, floodwater from the ruptured South Fork Dam, gaining speed during an 18-mile trip down steep-walled valleys, poured into the little industrial city with a force equal to Niagara Falls. During 10 awful minutes, buildings crumpled like paper, and tumbling hearths and gaslights ignited the wreckage, creating a flaming pile of debris over a 30-acre expanse; 2,209 people died. It was the worst single-day civilian loss of life in American history until September 11, 2001, when airliners crashed into the World Trade Center and the Pentagon, and another airliner came down in a field just 50 miles southwest of Johnstown near Shanksville.

The 1889 flood had class overtones. The dam was owned by western Pennsylvania's richest families, and had been negligently maintained, facts that are thoughtfully documented by the Johnstown Flood Museum in the old Carnegie Library. The museum provides an offset to the economic woes of Johnstown, whose population fell from 67,000 in 1920 to 22,000 in 2006, a decline similar to that of many communities in this region. Life was never easy here. After some prosperous years in the 1960s and 1970s, the "Cradle of the American Steel Industry" was hit hard by the recession that followed the 1979 oil shock. Young people have been leaving the area for years, downtown has been deserted and this district now has the highest elderly percentage in the state. Yet there are some signs of revival. The Johnstown area gained jobs mid-decade, thanks in part to defense firms locating here, and Texas investors, noting the area's low incomes, are putting in money too. But this small revival is so far not drawing newcomers. Johnstown ranks No. 1 among the 318 metropolitan areas in the percentage of residents born in the state, 90%.

The 12th Congressional District of Pennsylvania, with highly irregular boundaries, contains much of this coal and steel country. It includes all of Greene County and parts of Fayette, Somerset, Cambria, Indiana, Armstrong, Washington and Westmoreland counties. The boundaries were drawn by Republican legislators who wanted to create a new Republican-leaning 18th District in the southern suburbs of Pittsburgh while also accommodating Democratic Rep. John Murtha, the second ranking Democrat on the Appropriations Committee who has brought millions of federal dollars to the region. The district unites Murtha's home base of Johnstown and Democratic territory in the southwestern corner of the state.

Politically, this was one of the most Republican parts of America from the Civil War up to the 1930s. Republican policies, including high tariffs and hostility to labor unions, were seen as protecting jobs and increasing growth in the steel economy centered on Pittsburgh. With the coming of the New Deal, and success of the United Mine Workers and the United Steelworkers, the area began voting mostly Democratic. Since 1945, on the Monday before primary and general elections, Democratic pols from across southwestern Pennsylvania have attended the "rally in the valley" held at the Slovak Home in the mill town of Monessen. But this area has not followed the national Democratic Party on all issues. Voters here have strongly favored trade restrictions on steel imports and have opposed the free trade agreements of recent years. Voters here also tend to take conservative stands on cultural issues and foreign policy. This carefully carved district voted 55%-44% for Democrat Al Gore for president in 2000. But after Republican President George W. Bush imposed import quotas on steel and boosted clean coal technology, the district voted only 51%-49% for Democrat John Kerry. In 2008, it voted by 49.4%-49.0% for Republican John McCain, making it the only district in the country that voted for Kerry in 2004 and McCain in 2008.

The congressman from the 12th District is John Murtha, a Democrat first elected in a February 1974 special election that signaled the political weakness of President Richard Nixon. He was the first Vietnam veteran elected to Congress. Murtha grew up in the Johnstown area, attended Washington and Jefferson College, then in 1952 enlisted in the Marine Corps. He became a drill instructor at Parris Island and was selected for officer candidate school in Quantico, Va. He graduated from the University of Pittsburgh and re-enlisted in the Marines in 1966, at age 34, and then served in Vietnam. For his distinguished service, he was awarded the Bronze Star, two Purple Hearts and the Vietnamese Cross for Gallantry.

Murtha is a member of the Appropriations Committee and chairman of the Defense Appropriations Subcommittee, making him one of the most powerful "cardinals," as the appropriations subcommittee chairmen are known. He is the Democrats' go-to guy on the defense budget. His voting record over many years—hawkish on foreign policy, interventionist on economics and usually tradition-minded on cultural issues—is perfectly suited to steel and coal country. He opposes abortion rights and gun control. Murtha is also one of those old-time politicians who operates best in secret, holding court in the back corner of the House chamber, "the Murtha corner" as it's known, where he trades gossip and votes with colleagues who crowd around him. For most of his career, he spoke for attribution to few national or local reporters, hardly ever appeared on television, and rarely spoke on the House floor unless it was about the annual defense spending bill, which often passes with little debate. He wields power not only on his committee work but also on many back-room issues dear to his colleagues, including congressional pay raises and committee assignments.

When Republicans controlled the House, Murtha was caught sometimes between Democratic demands for lower defense spending and Republican desires to spend even more on defense, but in the bipartisan culture of the Appropriations Committee, he exerted major influence even while in the minority. Appropriations Chairman David Obey, D-Wis., has called him a man "who likes to get things done with virtually no spoken words." Murtha voted for the Gulf War resolution in 1991, but opposed intervention in Bosnia and deployment in Somalia, arguing that United Nations officials lacked the know-how to command U.S. troops. Inside the Democratic Caucus, he wielded considerable clout, and became an ally of Nancy Pelosi in her quest for ever higher positions in leadership. In 2001, after David Bonior of Michigan resigned as Minority Whip, Murtha managed Pelosi's campaign for that post against the more senior Steny Hoyer of Maryland, and Pelosi won 118-95, a victory that put Pelosi on the road to the speakership. It was a role similar to that played by coal-country Democrat Wayne Hays for San Francisco's Phil Burton in his quest for the majority leadership in 1976, providing assurance to conservative and traditional Democrats that a West Coast liberal would be acceptable. Murtha's admiration for Pelosi is unbounded. In January 2007, he said, "The speaker has the best political mind I've ever seen."

Murtha voted for the Iraq war resolution in October 2002, contrary to Pelosi and most House Democrats. But he had reservations about the war early on. He complained loudly that troops in Iraq were poorly equipped, with both personal gear and machines, and he questioned the civilian decision-making. In May 2004, he said, "We cannot prevail in this war as it is going today. We either have to mobilize or we have to get out." In October 2004, he was one of two House members who voted to reinstate the military draft, advanced on the theory that Congress would be less willing to support wars if their constituents were subject to conscription. In early November 2005, he called the Central Intelligence Agency's secret prisons "absolutely outrageous." Then on November 17, to much publicity, he called for withdrawal from Iraq. "It is time for a change in direction," he said, decrying "a flawed policy wrapped in illusion." This was treated in the press as the sudden conversion of a military hawk, but Murtha's previous statements about the stress on the troops suggested that his thinking was moving in that direction for some time. When Vice President Dick Cheney criticized his statement, Murtha dismissed comments from "people with five deferments." When Ohio Republican Rep. Jean Schmidt, probably to her everlasting regret, suggested Murtha was a "coward" for wanting to withdraw from Iraq, she set off a firestorm in defense of Murtha and was forced to apologize. Murtha's position made him a hero to many House Democrats, but not to all. Hoyer, by then minority whip, said that a premature withdrawal from Iraq would be a "disaster." House Republicans insisted on a vote on a resolution stating that "deployment of United States forces be terminated immediately" and it failed 403-3.

After Democrats won a majority in the House in 2006, Murtha challenged Hoyer for majority leader with Pelosi's blessing. It was a closely watched contest, one that pitted Pelosi and her handpicked candidate, Murtha, against her old nemesis in the race for power in the House, Steny Hoyer. Most of the conservative Blue Dog Democrats backed Hoyer, as did senior incoming committee chairmen like John Dingell of Michigan, Henry Waxman of California and Barney Frank of Massachusetts. Democrats had won in 2006 in part by campaigning against a Republican "climate of corruption," and some Democrats thought Murtha's record was inconsistent with that theme. Videotape was unearthed of Murtha's interchange with a purported sheik, actually an undercover FBI agent, in the Abscam scandal in 1980. It showed the "sheik" offering Murtha $50,000, and Murtha responding that he wasn't interested "at this point," but "I want to get [expletive] jobs in the area, you know, a few bank deposits. . . . Later on, after we've dealt a while . . . we might want to do more business." Back then, the Committee on Standards of Official Conduct voted not to bring charges against Murtha, after which its special counsel resigned in protest; Murtha was a cooperating witness against two other members. After the old video was unearthed, Murtha explained himself to MSNBC's Chris Matthews, "Listen, I wanted to negotiate with them about investment in the district. That's what I was interested in. It's the only thing I was interested in." In October 2006, *The New York Times* ran an article on how Murtha "often delivers Democratic votes to Republican leaders in a tacit exchange for (spending) earmarks for himself and his allies." The story said Murtha sided with Republicans on close votes 169 times since 1994, more than all but three other Democrats. Despite confident statements that he would win, Murtha lost to Hoyer on the secret ballot 149-86.

Despite this loss, Murtha continued to be a leading spokesman for House Democrats as Defense Appropriations chairman. In January 2007, he said that the military faced a $100 billion shortfall in equipment because of Iraq. "We have no ability to deploy and sustain a deployment in Iran or Korea, and the enemy knows this," he said. During consideration of a bill for supplemental spending for the war, Murtha wanted to attach conditions that troops must have at least one year between deployments, that no deployment last more than a year and that the stop-loss program end. He got a harsh reaction from many quarters, including fellow Democrats. Antiwar Republican Rep. Walter Jones of North Carolina called it an attempt to "starve" the war. And Senate Armed Services Chairman Carl Levin, a Michigan Democrat, said that it "sends the wrong message to our troops."

Later that year, Murtha again proposed attaching conditions to a war spending bill. He wanted to add to the defense appropriations bill amendments mandating troop reductions within 60 days, full training for soldiers before deployment and the closure of the prison camp at Guantanamo Bay, Cuba. But there was waning support in Congress for conditions once Bush's strategy for a surge in troop strength in Iraq began showing results late in 2007. In November, Murtha said, "I think the surge is working." Early in 2008, he voiced no objection when the Democratic leadership sent a war supplemental bill to the floor directly, bypassing his subcommittee. However, he did manage to insert into the defense appropriations bill that year $500-per-month in compensation to service members retained on duty by stop-loss orders since 2001.

Murtha is an energetic earmarker of special projects for his district, despite the controversy surrounding the practice in recent years that it results in grossly wasteful spending of tax dollars. Johnstown has a Murtha highway, a Murtha airport and Murtha health centers. In 1988, Murtha persuaded the University of Pittsburgh to set up a nonprofit organization called Concurrent Technologies, which would use Navy money to establish a Center for Excellence in Metalworking Technology in Johnstown. Between 1999 and 2006, military and other federal agencies spent nearly $1 billion on contracts and grants to Concurrent. Meanwhile, Concurrent executives donated $114,000 to Murtha's 2000, 2002 and 2004 re-election campaigns. Concurrent also paid about $500,000 a year to a lobbying firm, the PMA Group, founded by Paul Magliocchetti, a Murtha aide in the 1980s. Executives of PMA and its clients contributed some $2.4 million to Murtha from 1989 to 2008 as well as about $1 million each to his Defense Appropriations Subcommittee colleagues Peter Visclosky of Indiana and Jim Moran of Virginia. In 2007 and 2008, Murtha, Visclosky and Moran sponsored $137 million in earmarks to PMA clients, and PMA became one of Washington's 10 largest lobbying firms. At the least, the revelations furthered the perception of insider wheeling and dealing on Murtha's part.

In May 2007, Murtha tried to get a $23 million earmark for the National Drug Intelligence Center in Johnstown, which the Office of Management and Budget had recommended not funding. After Michigan Republican Rep. Mike Rogers objected, Murtha approached him on the House floor and said, according to Rogers, "I hope you don't have any earmarks in the defense appropriation bill, because they are gone and you will not get any earmarks now and forever." Rogers accused him of violating a new House rule by the Democrats that barred members from considering the inclusion of earmarks on the basis of a member's vote on other matters, and he sought to have Murtha officially reprimanded. The matter came to the floor on May 22 and the Democratic leadership moved to table Rogers' resolution. All but two Democrats voted to table. But on May 23, Murtha sent a written apology to Rogers.

More serious publicity for Murtha came after a Federal Bureau of Investigation raid on PMA's offices in Virginia and Pennsylvania in November 2008. Murtha said he was not approached by the FBI and defended his work by holding up a copy of the Constitution. "What it says is the Congress of the United States appropriates the money. Got that?" he said. In the spring of 2009, Republicans demanded roll call votes on resolutions demanding the ethics committee investigate Murtha. They were voted down largely on party lines, but with increasing numbers of Democrats defecting.

Before 2008, Murtha seldom got involved in presidential politics. Five weeks before the Pennsylvania primary, he endorsed New York Sen. Hillary Rodham Clinton in her primary battle with Illinois Sen. Barack Obama. Yet his involvement was not exactly helpful. He made a few controversial remarks, such as: "Obama's got a problem with the race issue in western Pennsylvania," and "There's no question western Pennsylvania is a racist area." In any case, Clinton carried the state and carried the 12th district with more than 70% of the vote. Murtha endorsed and campaigned for Obama after he clinched the nomination.

Murtha gets re-elected every two years without a fuss. In 2006, after the release of the Abscam tapes and Murtha's outspoken opposition to the war, Washington County Commissioner Diana Irey, a Republican, opposed him. Murtha won 61%-39%, a convincing margin but one considerably smaller than in 2002. In 2008, William Russell, a veteran of the Gulf and Iraq wars, moved from Northern Virginia to Pennsylvania to run against Murtha. As a Reserve member, he was deployed during the campaign, which prevented him from actively campaigning until he resigned from the military in August 2008. He called Murtha the "king of pork," and criticized his vote in the fall for the $700 billion rescue of the financial services industry. Former President Bill Clinton came to the district to campaign for Murtha. He won 58%-42%, leading in all but one county.

In early 2009, as President Obama was preparing to step up U.S. involvement in Afghanistan, Murtha said, "I'm very nervous about getting too far in Afghanistan." But he supported Obama's commitment to close Guantanamo and said that the government could hold detainees in maximum security prisons in the United States. In January 2010, he would be the longest-serving House member from Pennsylvania ever.

THIRTEENTH DISTRICT

Allyson Schwartz (D)

Elected 2004, 3rd term; b. Oct. 3, 1948, Queens, NY; home, Jenkintown; Simmons Col., B.A. 1970, Bryn Mawr Col., M.S.W. 1972; Jewish; married (David); 2 children.

Elected Office: PA Senate, 1990–2004.

Professional Career: Exec. dir., Elizabeth Blackwell Center, 1975–88; Dep. comm., Philadelphia Human Svcs. Dept., 1988–90.

DC Office: 330 CHOB, 20515, 202-225-6111; Fax: 202-226-0611; Web site: schwartz.house.gov.

State Offices: Jenkintown, 215-517-6572; Philadelphia, 215-335-3355.

Committees: *Budget* (2nd of 24 D). *Ways & Means* (20th of 26 D): Select Revenue Measures; Social Security.

Group Ratings

	ADA	ACLU	AFS	LCV	ITIC	NTU	COC	ACU	CFG	FRC
2008	90	100	100	100	71	7	56	0	4	11
2007	90	—	100	95	—	7	55	4	12	—

National Journal Ratings

	2007 LIB	—	2007 CONS		2008 LIB	—	2008 CONS
Economic	67%	—	31%		71%	—	25%
Social	66%	—	33%		82%	—	0%
Foreign	61%	—	39%		63%	—	36%
Composite	65%	—	35%		76%	—	24%

Key Votes of the 110th Congress

1. Increase minimum wage	Y	5. Share immigration data	N	9.Withdraw troops 8/08	Y
2. Expand SCHIP	Y	6. Foreign aid abortion ban	N	10. No operations in Iran	N
3. Raise CAFE standards	Y	7. Ban gay bias in workplace	Y	11. Free trade with Peru	Y
4. Bail out financial markets	Y	8. Repeal D.C. gun law	N	12. Overhaul FISA	N

Election Results

2008 general	Allyson Schwartz (D)	196,868	(63%)	($1,745,577)
	Marina Kats (R)	108,271	(35%)	($500,141)
	John McDermott (CNP)	8,374	(3%)	
2008 primary	Allyson Schwartz (D)	unopposed		

Prior Winning Percentages: 2006 (66%); 2004 (56%)

Population		Race/Ethnicity		Work	
Pop. 2007:	658,434	White:	79.6%	Private:	82.5%
Change since 2000:	Up 1.7%	Black:	8.3%	Government:	11.8%
Urban:	98.5%	Hispanic:	4.8%	Self-employed:	5.5%
Rural:	1.5%	Asian:	5.8%	Blue collar:	18.3%
Area size:	258 sq. mi.	Native Am.:	0.1%	White collar:	67.4%
		Hawaiian:	0.0%	Khaki collar:	0.1%
Age		Two+ races:	1.1%	Other:	14.2%
Median age:	40.4 yrs.	*Ancestry*		Median income:	$58,319
More than 65 yrs:	15.8%	Irish:	20.3%	Median home value:	$228,200
Less than 18 yrs:	23.8%	German:	16.2%	Poverty:	8.6%
		Italian:	10.9%		
Education				**Military Veterans**	
H.S. grad:	88.3%			% of Pop:	10.1%
College grad:	32.9%				
Grad degree:	13.0%				

Montgomery County is the proximate hinterland of Philadelphia: rolling hills cut on one side by the Schuylkill River and at intervals by the Pennsylvania and Reading Railroad lines radiating outward from Center City. Older suburbs, both rich and modest, grew up around rail stations, with comfortable houses within walking distance for commuters. Further out are 18th and 19th century villages, once surrounded by farm fields, now encroached by subdivisions where people depend

2008 Presidential Vote

Obama (D)	192,968	(59%)
McCain (R)	133,740	(41%)

2004 Presidential Vote

Kerry (D)	182,552	(56%)
Bush (R)	140,900	(43%)

Cook Partisan Voting Index: D+7

on cars, not rail lines, to get to work. Montgomery County has its shopping malls and office parks, but not many freeways. Most of the traffic here is along roads on the area's diagonal grid or along the old pikes laid out when Pennsylvania was a colony. It is the most populous and second most affluent county, behind Chester, in suburban Philadelphia, with solid job growth prospects.

Quite a different place, though adjacent to southern Montgomery County, is Northeast Philadelphia. This is relatively new urban territory, with more than half its houses built after 1950. When the alley-wide streets of North and South Philadelphia and the river wards were already teeming with people, and the Main Line suburbs were well-settled, the workers of Philadelphia's docks, factories and offices were just starting to fill up vacant land here. They settled in neighborhoods like Bustleton, Somerton and Torresdale. Many of Philadelphia's Hispanics live in the industrial river wards along the Delaware River, but the other wards of Northeast Philadelphia are still mostly white and ethnic. Outside investors and Hasidic Jews from New York looking for more space and opportunity have bid up residential prices and have revived a vibrant Jewish community.

The 13th Congressional District of Pennsylvania includes much of southeastern and central Montgomery County and most of Northeast Philadelphia. From 2000 to 2007, the district's population increased 2%. Historically, Montgomery was quintessentially Republican, with a style of politics set for years by Ivy-educated Republican men. But the county, like other affluent suburbs in the Boston-Washington corridor, swung toward the Democratic Party in national politics in the 1990s, with abortion rights and other cultural issues usually trumping economic interests. Montgomery voted by large margins for Republicans Ronald Reagan and George H.W. Bush in the 1980s, but has voted strongly for Democratic presidential candidates since then. Northeast Philadelphia has a different political heritage. Its feisty Republican organization has won some elections and shown facility in making deals to get its share of patronage. Republican John McCain's presidential campaign made a big advertising and organizational drive in this area in 2008, but Democrat Barack Obama won 60% of the vote in Northeast Philly and 57% in Montgomery County, for an overall 59%-41% win in the district.

The congresswoman from the 13th District is Allyson Schwartz, a Democrat elected in 2004. Her mother fled Vienna as a teenager in 1938, after the Germans annexed Austria, and traveled alone to the United States, where she was taken in by a Jewish foster home in Philadelphia. Her father was a dentist in Flushing, Queens, where she grew up. A graduate of Simmons College with a master's degree in social work from Bryn Mawr College, Schwartz started a women's health center in 1975 and worked on health care issues as first deputy commissioner for the Philadelphia Department of Human Services. Her husband is a cardiologist. In 1990, Schwartz was elected to the state Senate. In 2000, she ran for the U. S. Senate and finished second in the Democratic primary, with 27% of the vote, behind U.S. Rep. Ron Klink, who had 41%.

The 13th District seat opened when Democratic Rep. Joe Hoeffel ran, unsuccessfully, against then-Republican Sen. Arlen Specter in 2004. Schwartz faced two rounds of serious competition. In the primary, her opponent was Joe Torsella, an aide to then-Philadelphia Mayor Ed Rendell. She was backed by EMILY's List, which spent $170,000 on her behalf and also phoned voters and sent out mailings. Torsella did well in the city portion of the district, but Schwartz carried Montgomery County with 62%, for an overall win of 52%-48%.

In the general election, her opponent was Republican Melissa Brown, an ophthalmologist who supported abortion rights. "The two opponents proved that women can sling mud as capably as any men," *The Philadelphia Inquirer* wrote. Schwartz called herself a "new Democrat," not a liberal, but Brown labeled her a radical. Schwartz called Brown "sleazy" because of her links to a bankrupt health maintenance organization and a lawsuit that the state insurance department filed against her. Both candidates emphasized health care. Schwartz emphasized her sponsorship of the State Children's Health Insurance Program, which provided health insurance for 133,000 children from low-income families. Brown, a physician with an M.B.A, called for changes in tort law, arguing that it would keep doctors' liability insurance down and lower the cost of health care. Schwartz won 56%-41%, getting 60% of the vote in Northeast Philadelphia and 53% in Montgomery County.

In the House, Schwartz has voted with moderate Democrats, and she is vice-chairman of the New Democrat Coalition. She has focused on health care, joining with then-Rep. Rahm Emanuel of Illinois to support a plan to automatically enroll all children eligible for the federal SCHIP program, including those with pre-existing conditions. In early 2007, Schwartz got a seat on the powerful Ways and Means Committee, which has broad jurisdiction over health issues and where she made universal insurance coverage a priority. She sought more funds for preventive health care programs and improved health-information systems. In January 2008, she joined with two other Democrats, Reps. Jason Altmire of Pennsylvania and Lois Capps of California, in advocating a set of principles to modernize the U.S. medical system with innovation, insurance reform and improved care. In other issues on the committee, Schwartz played a central role in the House's November 2007 passage of the bilateral trade agreement with Peru. As a condition of her support, she secured assurances of environmental and labor protections in that country.

She has been re-elected easily.

FOURTEENTH DISTRICT

Mike Doyle (D)

Elected 1994, 8th term; b. Aug. 5, 1953, Pittsburgh; home, Forest Hills; PA St. U., B.S. 1975; Catholic; married (Susan); 4 children.

Elected Office: Swissvale Borough Cncl., 1977–81.

Professional Career: Insurance agent, 1975–77; Exec. dir., Turtle Creek Valley Citizens Union, 1977–79; Chief of Staff, PA Sen. Frank Pecora, 1978–94; Co–Founder/owner, Eastgate Insurance Agency, 1983–present.

DC Office: 401 CHOB, 20515, 202-225-2135; Fax: 202-225-3084; Web site: www.house.gov/doyle.

State Offices: Pittsburgh, 412-261-5091.

Committees: *Energy & Commerce* (14th of 36 D): Communications, Technology & the Internet; Energy & Environment; Oversight & Investigations.

Group Ratings

	ADA	ACLU	AFS	LCV	ITIC	NTU	COC	ACU	CFG	FRC
2008	95	100	100	92	86	5	56	0	0	5
2007	95	—	100	80	—	3	53	4	0	—

National Journal Ratings

	2007 LIB	—	2007 CONS		2008 LIB	—	2008 CONS
Economic	72%	—	28%		85%	—	0%
Social	68%	—	31%		82%	—	0%
Foreign	85%	—	15%		83%	—	17%
Composite	75%	—	25%		89%	—	11%

Key Votes of the 110th Congress

1. Increase minimum wage	Y	5. Share immigration data	N	9.Withdraw troops 8/08	Y
2. Expand SCHIP	Y	6. Foreign aid abortion ban	N	10. No operations in Iran	Y
3. Raise CAFE standards	Y	7. Ban gay bias in workplace	Y	11. Free trade with Peru	N
4. Bail out financial markets	Y	8. Repeal D.C. gun law	N	12. Overhaul FISA	N

Election Results

2008 general	Mike Doyle (D)	242,326	(91%)	($838,611)
	Titus North (Green)	23,214	(9%)	
2008 primary	Mike Doyle (D)	unopposed		

Prior Winning Percentages: 2006 (90%); 2004 (100%); 2002 (100%); 2000 (69%); 1998 (68%); 1996 (56%); 1994 (55%)

Population		Race/Ethnicity		Work	
Pop. 2007:	584,252	White:	70.2%	Private:	84.0%
Change since 2000:	Down 9.6%	Black:	23.5%	Government:	11.4%
Urban:	99.8%	Hispanic:	1.7%	Self-employed:	4.5%
Rural:	0.2%	Asian:	2.3%	Blue collar:	16.3%
Area size:	170 sq. mi.	Native Am.:	0.1%	White collar:	63.2%
		Hawaiian:	0.0%	Khaki collar:	0.1%
Age		Two+ races:	2.0%	Other:	20.4%
Median age:	39.6 yrs.	*Ancestry*		Median income:	$33,738
More than 65 yrs:	16.5%	German:	16.8%	Median home value:	$76,900
Less than 18 yrs:	20.0%	Irish:	12.9%	Poverty:	19.3%
Education		Italian:	10.8%		
H.S. grad:	87.6%			**Military Veterans**	
College grad:	26.0%			% of Pop:	11.2%
Grad degree:	11.2%				

The Golden Triangle is the inevitable focus of Pittsburgh, the tip of land where the Allegheny and Monongahela rivers come together to form the Ohio. It has been a strategic site for more than 200 years. During the French and Indian War, British Gen. Edward Braddock's army was heading to Fort Duquesne, with George Washington helping lead the way, when it was ambushed and famously defeated in 1754. A few years later, the first American city west of the Appalachian chain was carved out

2008 Presidential Vote

Obama (D)	209,749	(70%)
McCain (R)	86,703	(29%)

2004 Presidential Vote

Kerry (D)	205,636	(69%)
Bush (R)	88,316	(30%)

Cook Partisan Voting Index: D + 19

of the wilderness and named after the English statesman William Pitt. Pittsburgh grew rapidly in the days when most of the nation's commerce moved over water. When railroads became ascendant, Pittsburgh still did nicely, since rail lines tend to run along the riverside rather than scaling mountains. Then came Andrew Carnegie, a Scottish immigrant working as a telegrapher for the Pennsylvania Railroad who foresaw that steel would replace iron for railroad bridges. He built a steel factory in Pittsburgh, which was then not much more than a rail junction but one blessed with ready deposits of coal and access to iron ore from the Great Lakes. With associates like Henry Clay Frick and Henry Phipps, Carnegie built his capacity to the point that when he sold out in 1901, the resulting U.S. Steel Corporation held a near-monopoly.

The Pittsburgh that Carnegie and his steel men built was one of giant mills in the bottomlands along the rivers and massive buildings downtown, such as H.H. Richardson's classic stone City-County Building. There were once 12 cable cars going up the Duquesne Incline and other routes connecting mills with the neighborhoods above. Back then, the smog—a word used here long before it was a problem in Los Angeles—was so bad that street lights had to stay on all day downtown. A famous 1947 photograph shows a midnight-like darkness at nine in the morning. But then, an alliance of local elected officials and corporate titans, including the leaders of such local Fortune 500 companies as USX, Heinz, Alcoa, and PPG, pushed through a series of forceful and visionary projects designed to improve the city's quality of life. Early on, this model produced tremendous successes. In the 1950s, Mayor David Lawrence and financier Richard King Mellon led efforts to cut air pollution, control river flooding, and construct an advanced network of highways and tunnels. They also turned a derelict industrial zone at the three-rivers confluence into Point State Park, a triangular gem that remains popular with office workers. But as the steel industry and other blue-collar industries contracted over the years, so did Pittsburgh. In 1940, it was the nation's 10th largest city, with 672,000 people. In 2007, it was the 59th largest, with 296,000 people, which represents a population decline of 38,000 since 2000.

Pittsburgh is a city of neighborhoods, built on or beneath vertiginous hills, with more bridges, it is often said, than any other city in the world except Venice. Neighborhoods that are situated right next to each other on the map are in fact quite separate and distinct. There is the uptown neighborhood around Carnegie-Mellon University and the University of Pittsburgh, with its neo-Gothic "cathedral of learning." These institutions have helped to spur robust high-technology and medical sectors that have replaced some of the lost manufacturing jobs. The city also has become a banking center. Local universities and hospitals now have far more workers than the downsized U.S. Steel Corporation, which, with the economic downturn in 2008, suspended plans for a new $1 billion coke plant in Clairton. Among and atop the hills are neighborhoods as different as the predominantly black Hill District, where the famed Pittsburgh Crawfords of baseball's Negro Leagues once played and playwright August Wilson set most of his chronicles. There are WASPy Shady Side and Jewish Squirrel Hill, with fine mansions and fashionable shops. Along the Monongahela River are small industrial neighborhoods and towns, like Clairton, where the classic movie *The Deer Hunter* was set and filmed. Although the city boasts that it has fared better than Cleveland or Detroit, its poverty rate far exceeds the national average and its population is aging.

The 14th Congressional District of Pennsylvania includes all of Pittsburgh and the mostly working class suburbs to the east, south and west. There is some suburbia here, but much of the district is in the Monongahela (or Mon) Valley, where the old steel mills stand or once stood, and the hills above. More affluent suburbs to the north and south are in the 4th and 18th Districts. This is a heavily Democratic district.

The congressman from the 14th District is Mike Doyle, a Democrat first elected in 1994. Of Irish and Italian descent, Doyle grew up in the Mon Valley town of Swissvale and worked in steel mills during summers off from Penn State. He became an insurance agent and was elected to the Swissvale Borough Council in 1977, at age 24. In 1978, he became chief of staff to state Sen. Frank Pecora, a Republican. Pecora switched parties in 1992 and briefly gave Democrats control of the state Senate. In 1994, Doyle, who had just switched himself to the Democratic Party, ran for the House seat vacated by Republican Rep. Rick Santorum, who ran successfully for the Senate. Doyle was one of seven Democrats and four Republican candidates. With endorsements from labor unions and community leaders, he won the primary. In the general election, he faced John McCarty, an aide to the late Republican Sen. John Heinz. McCarty was pro-abortion rights and Doyle opposed abortion rights. Doyle also campaigned for sweeping health care changes. In a Republican year, he won 55%-45%.

In the House, Doyle has a mixed voting record, often on the right on cultural issues and on the left on economics. Doyle rarely seeks attention, nor has he caused much of a ruckus. He has worked to reduce foreign imports, and he pushed a bill to create a national historic site at the former U.S. Steel facilities along the Mon River as part of the local Rivers of Steel program. On the Energy and Commerce Committee, his focus has been on high-tech initiatives, including increased availability of broadband services in underserved areas. He has been a leading advocate of the "Do Not Call" restrictions on telephone marketers, and won passage in 2008 a bill to make the national list permanent. During the debate over so-called cap and trade legislation, which would cap harmful carbon emissions but allow companies to trade on the right to pollute, he vigorously advocated the interests of steel and other Rust Belt industries, even as he sought to work out a compromise with environmentalists.

Doyle can often be found on the House floor in the "Pennsylvania Corner," seated next to his close ally, the powerful appropriator, Democrat John Murtha of Pennsylvania. Like Murtha, he is an avid earmarker of spending projects for his district, a practice that has become increasingly controversial with budget conservatives, who say it's a prime example of wasteful Washington spending. One of Doyle's favorite beneficiaries is the Doyle Center for Manufacturing Technology in South Oakland, which was started in 2003 by a $1.5 federal million grant he helped secure.

FIFTEENTH DISTRICT

Charlie Dent (R)

Elected 2004, 3rd term; b. May 24, 1960, Allentown; home, Allentown; PA St. U., B.A. 1982, Lehigh U., M.P.A. 1993; Presbyterian; married (Pamela); 3 children.

Elected Office: PA House of Reps., 1990–98; PA Senate, 1998–2004.

Professional Career: Development officer, Lehigh U., 1986–90.

DC Office: 1009 LHOB, 20515, 202-225-6411; Fax: 202-226-0778; Web site: www.dent.house.gov.

State Offices: Bethlehem, 610-861-9734; East Greenville, 215-541-4106.

Committees: *Homeland Security* (7th of 13 R): Intelligence, Information Sharing & Terrorism Risk Assessment; Transportation Security & Infrastructure Protection (RMM). *Standards of Official Conduct* (4th of 5 R). *Transportation & Infrastructure* (19th of 30 R): Aviation; Highways & Transit; Railroads, Pipelines & Hazardous Materials.

Group Ratings

	ADA	ACLU	AFS	LCV	ITIC	NTU	COC	ACU	CFG	FRC
2008	55	36	71	46	71	48	83	56	41	35
2007	45	—	18	55	—	41	100	52	33	—

National Journal Ratings

	2007 LIB	—	2007 CONS		2008 LIB	—	2008 CONS
Economic	43%	—	56%		41%	—	59%
Social	43%	—	57%		41%	—	58%
Foreign	42%	—	57%		38%	—	62%
Composite	43%	—	57%		40%	—	60%

Key Votes of the 110th Congress

1. Increase minimum wage	Y	5. Share immigration data	Y	9. Withdraw troops 8/08	N
2. Expand SCHIP	Y	6. Foreign aid abortion ban	N	10. No operations in Iran	N
3. Raise CAFE standards	N	7. Ban gay bias in workplace	Y	11. Free trade with Peru	Y
4. Bail out financial markets	Y	8. Repeal D.C. gun law	Y	12. Overhaul FISA	Y

Election Results

2008 general	Charlie Dent (R)	181,433	(59%)	($1,775,398)
	Sam Bennett (D)	128,333	(41%)	($950,043)
2008 primary	Charlie Dent (R)	unopposed		

Prior Winning Percentages: 2006 (54%); 2004 (59%)

Population		Race/Ethnicity		Work	
Pop. 2007:	696,392	White:	82.1%	Private:	84.6%
Change since 2000:	Up 7.8%	Black:	3.8%	Government:	9.5%
Urban:	87.2%	Hispanic:	10.5%	Self-employed:	5.8%
Rural:	12.8%	Asian:	2.2%	Blue collar:	23.2%
Area size:	851 sq. mi.	Native Am.:	0.1%	White collar:	61.6%
Age		Hawaiian:	0.0%	Khaki collar:	0.0%
Median age:	39.1 yrs.	Two+ races:	1.1%	Other:	15.2%
More than 65 yrs:	14.7%	*Ancestry*		Median income:	$55,333
Less than 18 yrs:	23.2%	German:	22.8%	Median home value:	$198,300
Education		Irish:	10.7%	Poverty:	8.7%
H.S. grad:	86.0%	Italian:	9.3%	**Military Veterans**	
College grad:	26.0%			% of Pop:	11.2%
Grad degree:	9.8%				

Allentown has long been derided by songwriters, from "42nd Street" back in 1933, in which it was scorned as the polar opposite of Broadway, to Billy Joel's "Allentown" in 1982, with its grim picture of closed factories and joblessness. Though both contain nuggets of truth, neither is an entirely fair portrait of Pennsylvania's Lehigh Valley today. Allentown and next-door Bethlehem did suffer when big employers—Mack Truck in Allentown and Bethlehem Steel in Bethlehem—closed down massive

2008 Presidential Vote		
Obama (D)	179,589	(56%)
McCain (R)	139,396	(43%)
2004 Presidential Vote		
Kerry (D)	150,939	(50%)
Bush (R)	150,213	(50%)
Cook Partisan Voting Index:	D+2	

plants in the 1980s. But the Lehigh Valley around Allentown and Bethlehem in recent years had solid growth and low unemployment, thanks to a mix of regional health care networks, telephone call-centers for insurance companies and banks, and long-surviving industries, such as Air Products and Chemicals, energy utility PPL and the remnants of Mack Truck's local operations. Its numerous small startups don't earn the visibility of the big closedowns, but the fact is more new jobs have been created than those that were lost. In the Lehigh Valley, two-thirds of the employers have 10 or fewer workers.

If the Lehigh Valley is off the main lines of traffic, it does have several features that make it attractive to people from the big city, which helps to explain why its population increased 7% from 2000 to 2007, in contrast to the stagnant growth in the Philadelphia area. Commuters seeking less expensive housing and lower taxes are connected by Interstate 78 to New York and by the Turnpike Extension to Philadelphia. It has a cluster of colleges—Lehigh, Muhlenberg, Moravian—and a strong regional newspaper—the Allentown *Morning Call*. It has both Dorney Park, one of the nation's oldest amusement parks, and the delightful and child-friendly Crayola Crayon factory in Easton. Easton's old industrial buildings, just across the Delaware River from New Jersey, have become something of a magnet for artists seeking inexpensive loft and warehouse space.

The 15th Congressional District of Pennsylvania consists of the Lehigh Valley plus a small adjoining slice of northern Montgomery County, which has 11% of the district's population. Some 11% of the population here is Hispanic, an increase from 8% in 2000 and higher than in any other Pennsylvania metropolitan area and a sure sign that the area is generating new jobs. In Allentown, the Hispanic share is 35%. Politically, this has long been a classic swing area, located at the intersection of heavily Democratic industrial precincts and the Republican farmlands of the Pennsylvania Dutch Country. The valley backed Republican Ronald Reagan twice, Republican George H.W. Bush in 1988 and Democrat Bill Clinton twice. It voted for Democrats Al Gore and John Kerry in 2000 and 2004, respectively, by miniscule margins. In the past six governors' races, it voted for the winner each time: twice for Democrat Robert Casey, twice for Republican Tom Ridge and twice for Democrat Ed Rendell. Again reflecting the national vote, the district gave Democratic presidential nominee Barack Obama a 56%-43% win in 2008.

The congressman from the 15th District is Charlie Dent, a Republican elected in 2004. Dent grew up in Allentown, graduated from Penn State University and got a graduate degree at Lehigh, where he later worked as a development officer. In 1990, he was elected to the state House and in 1998 to the state Senate. When Republican Rep. Pat Toomey announced that he would run against Sen. Arlen Specter in the 2004 Republican primary, Dent was the front-runner to succeed him. Dent's lifelong residence in the Lehigh Valley was in sharp contrast to the background of the Democratic nominee, businessman Joe Driscoll. Driscoll grew up in Massachusetts, where he went sailing with the Kennedys and made enough money to spend $2 million on this race. But he lived for years in posh Lower Merion Township in Montgomery County, just outside Philadelphia. He bought a townhouse in Upper Macungie Township to run for the seat, though his wife and children continued living outside the district.

Dent framed the campaign as a contest between a native son and a carpetbagging outsider who thought of the Lehigh Valley as "a speed bump on his way to Congress." Driscoll sought to deflect the residency issue with aggressive criticism of the Bush administration, asserting that a vote for Dent was an endorsement of Bush's by then unpopular policies. Dent's moderate record, which included support for abortion rights, made it difficult to tie him to Bush, and he insisted he would be an independent voice in Washington. Dent won 59%-39%. A few weeks after the election, Driscoll's real estate agent said that he put his townhouse here up for sale and moved back to Lower Merion Township.

In the House, Dent has a mostly centrist voting record. With a seat on the Transportation and Infrastructure Committee, he worked to deliver local spending projects, in contrast to Toomey, who considered congressional earmarks a waste of taxpayer money. Dent supported more federal funding for embryonic-stem-cell research, which uses surplus embryos from in vitro fertilization. He opposed Bush's plan for partial "privatization" of Social Security, and he was a last-minute supporter of the Central American Free Trade Agreement. Dent initially voiced skepticism about Bush's troop "surge" in Iraq, but he voted against the House Democrats' resolution to oppose the surge.

On the Homeland Security Committee, Dent pushed a bill to use the Civil Air Patrol to prevent illegal crossings at the border. And he has introduced a bill to deport illegal immigrants convicted of crimes in the United States. In October 2007, he was one of 44 Republicans who voted to override Bush's veto of the Democrats' expansion of the State Children's Health Insurance Program. In February 2009, President Barack Obama invited Dent and his family to the White House to watch the Super Bowl, with the hope of getting his vote on his economic stimulus bill. But Dent said the bill cost too much and voted no. In 2009, Dent was appointed to the House Committee on Standards of Official Conduct.

Democrats tried, but failed, to find a credible opponent to Dent in 2006. Northampton County Councilman Charles Dertinger got on the ballot as a write-in candidate, and made lots of noise criticizing Dent for Bush's policies and "the culture of corruption." Dent won by a surprisingly narrow 54%-43%. In 2008, Democrats nominated Siobhan "Sam" Bennett, who ran an Allentown charity. She spent $950,000, but lost to Dent 59%-41%.

SIXTEENTH DISTRICT

Joe Pitts (R)

Elected 1996, 7th term; b. Oct. 10, 1939, Lexington, KY; home, Kennett Square; Asbury Col., B.A. 1961, West Chester U., M.Ed. 1972; Protestant; married (Virginia); 3 children.

Military Career: Air Force, 1963–69 (Vietnam).

Elected Office: PA House of Reps., 1972–96

Professional Career: High schl. teacher, 1969–72; Owner, Landscape & Nursery Co., 1974–90.

DC Office: 420 CHOB, 20515, 202-225-2411; Fax: 202-225-2013; Web site: www.house.gov/pitts.

State Offices: Lancaster, 717-393-0667; Unionville, 610-444-4581.

Committees: *Energy & Commerce* (12th of 23 R): Commerce, Trade & Consumer Protection; Energy & Environment; Health.

Group Ratings

	ADA	ACLU	AFS	LCV	ITIC	NTU	COC	ACU	CFG	FRC
2008	5	18	0	8	43	84	88	100	100	100
2007	0	—	0	10	—	87	75	100	92	—

National Journal Ratings

	2007 LIB	—	2007 CONS		2008 LIB	—	2008 CONS
Economic	9%	—	90%		6%	—	94%
Social	9%	—	85%		15%	—	84%
Foreign	0%	—	72%		8%	—	89%
Composite	12%	—	88%		10%	—	90%

Key Votes of the 110th Congress

1. Increase minimum wage	N	5. Share immigration data	Y	9. Withdraw troops 8/08	N
2. Expand SCHIP	N	6. Foreign aid abortion ban	Y	10. No operations in Iran	N
3. Raise CAFE standards	N	7. Ban gay bias in workplace	N	11. Free trade with Peru	Y
4. Bail out financial markets	N	8. Repeal D.C. gun law	*	12. Overhaul FISA	Y

Election Results

2008 general	Joe Pitts (R)	170,329	(56%)	($621,729)
	Bruce Slater (D)	120,193	(39%)	($92,274)
	John Murphy (I)	11,768	(4%)	($5,484)
2008 primary	Joe Pitts (R)	unopposed		

Prior Winning Percentages: 2006 (57%); 2004 (64%); 2002 (88%); 2000 (67%); 1998 (71%); 1996 (59%)

Population		Race/Ethnicity		Work	
Pop. 2007:	685,223	White:	82.7%	Private:	83.9%
Change since 2000:	Up 6.0%	Black:	4.2%	Government:	8.2%
Urban:	76.0%	Hispanic:	10.3%	Self-employed:	7.5%
Rural:	24.0%	Asian:	1.6%	Blue collar:	27.1%
Area size:	1,326 sq. mi.	Native Am.:	0.1%	White collar:	57.1%
Age		Hawaiian:	0.0%	Khaki collar:	0.0%
Median age:	36.5 yrs.	Two+ races:	0.9%	Other:	15.8%
More than 65 yrs:	13.5%	**Ancestry**		Median income:	$53,851
Less than 18 yrs:	25.9%	German:	27.7%	Median home value:	$182,400
Education		Irish:	9.9%	Poverty:	10.7%
H.S. grad:	81.0%	English:	6.9%	**Military Veterans**	
College grad:	26.1%			% of Pop:	9.4%
Grad degree:	8.9%				

The Pennsylvania Dutch Country, settled by Germans in the 18th century when it was Pennsylvania's frontier, remains a distinctive part of America. These Germans were Amish and Mennonite, pietistic sects seeking religious liberty and determined to farm rich lands in the same intensive way they had in Germany. Today, many of their descendants—the Eisenhower family is the most famous example—have blended into mainstream America.

2008 Presidential Vote
McCain (R)............................161,844   (51%)
Obama (D) 150,341   (48%)

2004 Presidential Vote
Bush (R) 182,856   (61%)
Kerry (D)...............................113,193   (38%)

Cook Partisan Voting Index: R + 8

But in the Dutch area around Lancaster, many "Plain People" still live in the old way, though today they are willing to use some modern devices, such as battery-powered electricity. Though larger communities exist in Ohio and Indiana, tourists can still see families of Plain People clad in black, clattering over the back roads in horse-drawn carriages, with scrupulously tended farms set amid rolling hills and barns decorated with hex signs. The scene was captured memorably in the 1983 film *Witness*. Beneath the surface, Amish communities are facing the strains of modernity. In recent years, Amish teens have attracted public attention for using drugs and alcohol while participating in the "rumschpringes," a period when adolescents are freed from their community's rigid rules and mores, before being given the choice of returning to the fold as an adult.

Modern-style crime also interrupts their peaceful lifestyle from time to time. In October 2006, five girls were killed and five others seriously wounded by a gunman at their one-room schoolhouse in Nickel Mines. The local Amish community quickly demolished the building and erected a new one six months later. The community remains robust, and tourism, much of it linked to interest in the Amish, brings in more than 5 million people annually. Agriculture is the other pillar of the local economy. Farmers here produce some of the highest per-acre yields on earth. Within an easy drive from Philadelphia, Baltimore and Washington, the area has also become home to outlet malls, a fitting development given that the first Woolworth's five-and-dime store opened in Lancaster in 1879. Lancaster County and Chester County grew by double-digit rates in the 1990s—partly from religious families, partly from newcomers moving in—making this the heart of one of Pennsylvania's fastest-growing regions, though the pace has slowed in recent years.

The 16th Congressional District of Pennsylvania includes all of Lancaster County, plus parts of southwestern Chester County that adjoin the Maryland and Delaware borders, as well as a small slice of Berks County that reaches to Reading. Outside the regional hub of Lancaster, the 16th is mostly small-town territory, with numerous quaint and quirkily named villages, such as Bird-in-Hand, Blue Ball and Intercourse (the first two named for the posted logos of old pubs, the third for reasons that are obscure, but almost certainly not sexual in nature). Closer to Philadelphia, the district takes in suburbs, including West Chester and Kennett Square. During the 1990s, Reading and Berks County attracted a large number of Hispanics in search of jobs. The district is now the third-most Hispanic in the state, at 10%. Still, this remains a Republican district. In 2008, Republican presidential nominee John McCain won it 51%-48%. He lost in Chester and Berks, and led 55%-44% in Lancaster, which cast 73% of the votes.

The congressman from the 16th District is Joe Pitts, a Republican elected in 1996. Pitts was born in Kentucky, and spent time in the Philippines with his parents, where they served as religious missionaries. He joined the Air Force after college, and served three tours of duty, flying 116 B-52 combat missions in Vietnam. He returned to become a math and science teacher in Malvern in Chester County, and later owned a nursery near Kennett Square. He and his daughter have exhibited their artwork, everything from painting to sculpture and woodwork, at local galleries. In 1972, at age 33, he was elected to the Pennsylvania General Assembly. In 1989, he became chairman of the Appropriations Committee, and oversaw the restoration of the Pennsylvania Capitol. When Republican Rep. Bob Walker, one of the conservative reformers of the Newt Gingrich era in the House, cited the "Pennsylvania Dutch tradition" of not serving over 20 years, Pitts ran to succeed him. In the primary, he ran as a "true conservative," speaking out in favor of home schooling and against gambling. He raised the most money and won with 45%. The runner-up, a moderate Republican, received 26%. In the general election, Pitts easily defeated newspaper publisher James Blaine, a descendant of James G. Blaine, the "Plumed Knight" and Republican presidential nominee in 1884.

In the House, Pitts has a conservative record, though he sometimes is a centrist on foreign policy. He was an early advocate of the 2001 Bush tax cuts, and later was an avid booster of the president's failed plan in 2005 to introduce private savings accounts into the Social Security program. Pitts has been an outspoken advocate of increased energy production, including the construction of new oil refineries on closed military bases.

Pitts led the Pro-Life Caucus and headed the Republicans' "values action team" that worked with the Christian Coalition and other groups to promote a pro-family agenda. Before the bankruptcy bill was enacted in 2005, he played a key role in scuttling a provision, added to the legislation by Sen. Charles Schumer, D-N.Y., which would have made fines and criminal penalties for abortion protesters nondischargeable under bankruptcy protection. He was a chief proponent of legislation to ban human cloning. With his appreciation for both human rights and national defense, Pitts founded two diverse groups:

the Religious Prisoners' Congressional Task Force to plead for human rights around the world, and the Electronic Warfare Working Group, to encourage more congressional support for military technology. In 2008, he urged a boycott of the Olympics in Beijing unless China improved its human-rights record.

In 2006, Pitts had a tough re-election contest. Former corporate executive Lois Herr said that Bush went after Iraqi leader Saddam Hussein on "flimsy evidence," and she called for bringing home the troops from Iraq. But Pitts won 57%-40%. In 2008, he defeated a weakly-funded challenger, 56%-39%, comfortable enough, but his smallest vote share to date and a sign of shifting views in this once solidly Republican bastion.

SEVENTEENTH DISTRICT

Tim Holden (D)

Elected 1992, 9th term; b. March 5, 1957, Pottsville; home, St. Clair; U. of Richmond, 1976–78, Bloomsburg St. U., B.A. 1980; Catholic; married (Gwen).

Elected Office: Schuylkill Cnty. sheriff, 1985–92.

Professional Career: Real estate agent; Insurance broker, Holden Insurance Agency, 1980–85; Probation officer, 1980–85.

DC Office: 2417 RHOB, 20515, 202-225-5546; Fax: 202-226-0996; Web site: www.holden.house.gov.

State Offices: Harrisburg, 717-234-5904; Lebanon, 717-270-1395; Pottsville, 570-622-4212; Temple, 610-921-3502.

Committees: *Agriculture* (2nd of 28 D): Conservation, Credit, Energy & Research (Chmn); Livestock, Dairy & Poultry. *Transportation & Infrastructure* (13th of 44 D): Aviation; Highways & Transit.

Group Ratings

	ADA	ACLU	AFS	LCV	ITIC	NTU	COC	ACU	CFG	FRC
2008	85	82	100	85	60	18	61	16	8	35
2007	80	—	100	70	—	6	45	16	1	—

National Journal Ratings

	2007 LIB	—	2007 CONS		2008 LIB	—	2008 CONS
Economic	56%	—	44%		64%	—	35%
Social	53%	—	47%		51%	—	48%
Foreign	50%	—	49%		59%	—	37%
Composite	53%	—	47%		59%	—	41%

Key Votes of the 110th Congress

1. Increase minimum wage	Y	5. Share immigration data	Y	9.Withdraw troops 8/08	Y
2. Expand SCHIP	Y	6. Foreign aid abortion ban	Y	10. No operations in Iran	N
3. Raise CAFE standards	Y	7. Ban gay bias in workplace	Y	11. Free trade with Peru	N
4. Bail out financial markets	N	8. Repeal D.C. gun law	Y	12. Overhaul FISA	Y

Election Results

2008 general	Tim Holden (D)	192,699	(64%)	($1,096,079)
	Toni Gilhooley (R)	109,909	(36%)	($104,485)
2008 primary	Tim Holden (D)	unopposed		

Prior Winning Percentages: 2006 (65%); 2004 (59%); 2002 (51%); 2000 (66%); 1998 (61%); 1996 (59%); 1994 (57%); 1992 (52%)

Population		Race/Ethnicity		Work	
Pop. 2007:	658,375	White:	85.5%	Private:	78.6%
Change since 2000:	Up 1.8%	Black:	7.6%	Government:	15.3%
Urban:	68.6%	Hispanic:	4.3%	Self-employed:	5.9%
Rural:	31.4%	Asian:	1.4%	Blue collar:	27.6%
Area size:	2,378 sq. mi.	Native Am.:	0.1%	White collar:	56.7%
		Hawaiian:	0.0%	Khaki collar:	0.1%
Age		Two+ races:	1.0%	Other:	15.6%
Median age:	40.3 yrs.			Median income:	$48,888
More than 65 yrs:	15.4%	*Ancestry*		Median home value:	$129,100
Less than 18 yrs:	22.3%	German:	29.1%	Poverty:	9.6%
		Irish:	10.2%		
Education		Italian:	6.2%	**Military Veterans**	
H.S. grad:	84.6%			% of Pop:	12.3%
College grad:	19.7%				
Grad degree:	6.9%				

Through the center of Pennsylvania flows the Susquehanna, the longest river in the East if you include the Chesapeake Bay, which is actually the flooded lower Susquehanna Valley. Starting in Cooperstown, N.Y., emptying into the Chesapeake next to the antique town of Havre de Grace, Md., the Susquehanna is the one river strong enough to break through the Appalachian Mountain chains of central Pennsylvania. But few songs are written to celebrate the Susquehanna. It has not been named

<table>
<tr><td colspan="3">2008 Presidential Vote</td></tr>
<tr><td>McCain (R)</td><td>158,374</td><td>(51%)</td></tr>
<tr><td>Obama (D)</td><td>147,634</td><td>(48%)</td></tr>
<tr><td colspan="3">2004 Presidential Vote</td></tr>
<tr><td>Bush (R)</td><td>172,343</td><td>(58%)</td></tr>
<tr><td>Kerry (D)</td><td>124,141</td><td>(42%)</td></tr>
<tr><td colspan="3">Cook Partisan Voting Index:　R + 6</td></tr>
</table>

for a fever (Potomac), for a school of painting (Hudson) or economics (Charles), or for a state (Delaware, Connecticut, Ohio, Mississippi, Alabama, Illinois, Missouri, Colorado, Tennessee). And its dams are silting up and threatening environmental havoc on the tenuously recovering Chesapeake, unless the unwieldy grouping of states through which the Susquehanna runs can find a solution. Already, millions of fish and fish eggs are killed each year by pollution. In 2005, the conservation group American Rivers rated the Susquehanna the nation's "most endangered river," due mostly to sewer system discharge. Low river flows in recent droughts resulted in large fish kills.

The 17th Congressional District of Pennsylvania includes two distinct areas: the agricultural lands adjoining the Susquehanna River, and the industrial areas of Schuylkill and Berks counties. Forty percent of the district is centered on the state capital of Harrisburg. It includes Dauphin County, part of Perry County and Lebanon County. Harrisburg features a string of mansions-turned-lobbying headquarters gracefully lining the banks of the Susquehanna and boasts Pennsylvania's marvelously restored Capitol building—its dome is modeled after St. Peter's in Rome, its stairway on the Paris Opera. Nearby is Hershey, the town erected by chocolate magnate Milton S. Hershey as a carefully planned, utopian village for his factory workers and their families. The surrounding area, fed by a steady flow of tourists to the Hersheypark amusement park, has attracted top-flight hospitals and cultivated a prosperous air. (The U.S. House of Representatives held "civility retreats" here during the 1990s, but they lapsed due to insufficient interest). Directly south is Middletown, whose leafy, gridded streets and handsome homes give no hint that it is the location of the Three Mile Island nuclear plant, site in 1979 of the worst nuclear accident in American history.

The eastern half of the district has a grittier heritage. In Berks and Schuylkill counties, towns existed solely to mine rich veins of anthracite coal, the nation's primary energy source in the late 19th and early 20th centuries. These mountain towns were less orderly, filled with tough-talking miners and factory workers—the Pennsylvania that John O'Hara knew growing up and wrote about in the 1930s and 1940s. Although the big companies abandoned the mines long ago, some local entrepreneurs still go deep underground to blast their way into the anthracite. Pottsville is the home of Yuengling lager (known locally as "Vitamin Y"), and produced the Maroons, the team that may have won the 1925 National Football League championship—the league disputed the claim, to Pottsville's eternal chagrin—and whose ties to coal country are emblematic of the game's hardscrabble roots. With a disproportionately old population, Schuylkill County had 228,000 people in 1940 and 147,000 in 2007.

Politically, the 17th leans Republican. Harrisburg has been a Republican town from the days when the party seemed to conquer all in Pennsylvania. Republicans held the governorship for all but eight years from 1860 to 1934 and filled the Capitol with Republican patronage hacks. Lebanon County is even more solidly Republican. Schuylkill County, in contrast, has a Democratic heritage from its mining days, though its Democrats tend to take conservative stands on cultural issues. The district voted 58% for Republican President George W. Bush in 2004 and 51% for GOP presidential nominee John McCain in 2008.

The congressman from the 17th District is Tim Holden, a Democrat first elected from the old 6th District in 1992 and the winner of a 2002 battle between incumbents thrown together by redistricting. Holden comes from a political family from the coal mining hamlet of St. Clair. His great-grandfather was a coal miner who founded the forerunner to the United Mine Workers, and his father served four terms as Schuylkill County commissioner. Holden gained fame as a local football player, although tuberculosis cut short his college career. In 1985, at age 28, after selling insurance and real estate in the family business for five years, he was elected Schuylkill County sheriff. Holden's opponent in the 1992 race for an open U.S. House seat was the better-financed John Jones III, a lawyer. But Holden's regular guy appeal played well in culturally conservative and economically polarized Schuylkill County. He won 52%-48%.

Holden has a moderate voting record, though it is more conservative on cultural issues. He is one of the conservative Blue Dog Democrats and has consistently been near the center of the House. "The problems our country is facing need to be solved in a bipartisan manner," he said. "There're about 70 liberals and 70 ultraconservatives still in the House. They need to be left behind." He opposes abortion rights, but in 2007, he supported federal funding for embryonic-stem-cell research, which uses excess embryos from in vitro fertilizations.

On the Agriculture Committee, he is the No. 2-ranking Democrat and chairman of the Conservation, Credit, Energy and Research Subcommittee. On the farm bill enacted in 2008, he played a central role in doubling farmland preservation funding, which he called "extremely important in Pennsylvania." He also crafted provisions aimed at reducing farm runoff into the Chesapeake. On the energy issue, his philosophy is: "Drill everywhere," as he said in 2008, sounding like a Republican in calling for more energy production.

Holden also has gained influence as the senior Pennsylvanian on the Transportation and Infrastructure Committee. On the 2005 highway bill, he took credit for $10 million in local projects, far less than claimed by more influential or vulnerable members. But as earmarking has become controversial in recent years and criticized as wasteful, his earmarks have come under closer scrutiny in the press. In April 2009, the *Lebanon Daily News* reported that in the past year Holden got $3.2 million in earmarks for clients of the controversial PMA lobbying firm, which has close ties to the powerful Rep. John Murtha, the Defense Appropriations Subcommittee chairman, and has been a major contributor to Holden's campaigns.

After redistricting in 2001, Holden was thrown into the then newly created 17th District with Republican Rep. George Gekas. The Republican edge in the district favored Gekas, but Holden spent many hours knocking on doors in Dauphin and Lebanon County, while Gekas was less organized and slower to introduce himself to new voters. Holden won 51%-49%. In 2004, Republicans nominated Scott Paterno, a lawyer and the son of longtime Penn State football coach Joe Paterno. Holden won 59%-39%. Since then, Republicans have focused elsewhere.

EIGHTEENTH DISTRICT

Tim Murphy (R)

Elected 2002, 4th term; b. Sept. 11, 1952, Cleveland, OH; home, Upper St. Clair; Wheeling Jesuit U., B.S. 1974, Cleveland St. U., M.S. 1976, U. of Pittsburgh, Ph.D. 1979; Catholic; divorced; 1 child.

Elected Office: PA Senate, 1996–2002

Professional Career: Practicing psychologist, 1976–2002; author.

DC Office: 322 CHOB, 20515, 202-225-2301; Fax: 202-225-1844; Web site: murphy.house.gov.

State Offices: Greensburg, 724-850-7312; Mt. Lebanon, 412-344-5583.

Committees: *Energy & Commerce* (19th of 23 R): Commerce, Trade & Consumer Protections; Health.

Group Ratings

	ADA	ACLU	AFS	LCV	ITIC	NTU	COC	ACU	CFG	FRC
2008	60	18	57	31	43	39	81	48	32	100
2007	40	—	45	20	—	39	85	68	30	—

National Journal Ratings

	2007 LIB — 2007 CONS		2008 LIB — 2008 CONS	
Economic	41%	— 59%	42%	— 57%
Social	31%	— 67%	41%	— 58%
Foreign	39%	— 61%	41%	— 58%
Composite	37%	— 63%	42%	— 58%

Key Votes of the 110th Congress

1. Increase minimum wage	Y	5. Share immigration data	Y	9. Withdraw troops 8/08	N
2. Expand SCHIP	Y	6. Foreign aid abortion ban	Y	10. No operations in Iran	N
3. Raise CAFE standards	N	7. Ban gay bias in workplace	N	11. Free trade with Peru	N
4. Bail out financial markets	N	8. Repeal D.C. gun law	Y	12. Overhaul FISA	Y

Election Results

2008 general	Tim Murphy (R)	213,349	(64%)	($2,073,251)
	Steve O'Donnell (D)	119,661	(36%)	($536,308)
2008 primary	Tim Murphy (R)	unopposed		

Prior Winning Percentages: 2006 (58%); 2004 (63%); 2002 (60%)

Population		Race/Ethnicity		Work	
Pop. 2007:	652,404	White:	94.0%	Private:	84.6%
Change since 2000:	Up 0.9%	Black:	2.4%	Government:	9.7%
Urban:	84.1%	Hispanic:	0.9%	Self-employed:	5.5%
Rural:	15.9%	Asian:	1.7%	Blue collar:	18.5%
Area size:	1,437 sq. mi.	Native Am.:	0.1%	White collar:	66.6%
		Hawaiian:	0.0%	Khaki collar:	0.1%
Age		Two+ races:	0.8%	Other:	14.8%
Median age:	43.1 yrs.			Median income:	$53,930
More than 65 yrs:	17.7%	*Ancestry*		Median home value:	$132,400
Less than 18 yrs:	20.7%	German:	22.7%	Poverty:	6.9%
		Irish:	14.6%		
Education		Italian:	13.4%	**Military Veterans**	
H.S. grad:	92.0%			% of Pop:	12.1%
College grad:	32.5%				
Grad degree:	11.7%				

Pittsburgh was built on the unlikeliest terrain of any major U.S. city. Just about the only level places in the city or its suburbs are the bottomlands along the rivers. Everything else is hills that approach the magnitude of mountains. Only a propitious location, where the Allegheny and Monongahela rivers join to form the Ohio, and the confluence of economically valuable natural resources—coal from the mountains and iron ore from the Great Lakes—can explain why a large metropolitan area sprang up on

2008 Presidential Vote
McCain (R).............................187,911   (55%)
Obama (D) 151,182   (44%)

2004 Presidential Vote
Bush (R) 183,210   (54%)
Kerry (D)................................154,079   (46%)

Cook Partisan Voting Index: R + 6

such land. The great cities of California were built around and over mountains, but they are vast expanses of contiguous communities, most of them little distinguishable from the next. The cities and towns of greater Pittsburgh, in contrast, are discontinuous, separated from each other not just by miles but by altitude. So the region's high-income suburbs and its gritty factory towns are not concentrated in one quarter, but are scattered all around. This is long-settled country, with many more old towns than sparkling new suburbs. Since 2000, the population in the area has been declining, but with some increase in high-wage jobs to counter an ongoing loss of blue-collar jobs.

The 18th Congressional District of Pennsylvania covers an irregularly shaped swath of the southern part of the Pittsburgh metropolitan area and was designed by Republican redistricters in Harrisburg to maximize the GOP vote. It includes most of southern Allegheny County, most of Westmoreland County and most of Washington County. It stretches from the Pittsburgh city limit to the West Virginia border. It contains the Pittsburgh International Airport and the towns of Monroeville, Greensburg and Ligonier. The area is dotted with the vast estates of Mellons and other scions of Pittsburgh's industrial elite. The district's backbone is comprised of middle- to upper-middle-class bedroom suburbs, like Mount Lebanon and Upper St. Clair in Allegheny County and Penn Township and Greensburg in Westmoreland County. These areas lean Republican, but not overwhelmingly so. Although Democratic presidential candidate John Kerry's wife, Teresa Heinz Kerry, has an estate in Fox Chapel, the Democratic ticket did not do well here. Republican George W. Bush carried the district with 54% in 2004. Republican presidential nominee John McCain won the district with 55% in 2008.

The congressman from the 18th District is Tim Murphy, a Republican elected in 2002. He grew up in Cleveland in a family of 11 children. He graduated from Wheeling Jesuit University, got a Ph.D. from the University of Pittsburgh and became a child psychologist. He worked in several Pittsburgh area hospitals and was an adjunct faculty member in public health and pediatrics at the University of Pittsburgh. He became well-known locally as "Dr. Tim," offering advice in television appearances and on radio talk shows. He also co-authored the book, *The Angry Child: Regaining Control When Your Child is Out of Control*. (After getting elected to Congress, he co-authored another book titled, *Overcoming Passive-Aggression*, behavior that he sees on a regular basis on Capitol Hill.) In 1996, Murphy was elected to the state Senate, where he sponsored a new Patient Bill of Rights and increased funding for medical research. Redistricters drew the 18th District with Murphy in mind. The new district included the house of incumbent Democratic Rep. Frank Mascara, but he opted to run in the newly drawn 12th District. Murphy was unopposed in the Republican primary, and presented himself as an experienced and accomplished legislator who opposed abortion rights and supported gun ownership. He had extensive support from state and national Republicans and outspent Democratic nominee Jack Machek, a school district administrator, $894,000 to $126,000. Murphy won 60%-40%, an impressive showing in an open seat race.

In the House, Murphy quickly gained recognition as president of his freshman class. In 2005, he won a seat on the Energy and Commerce Committee, giving him an opportunity to focus on health care issues. He focused in particular on programs for military veterans with mental illness and on improving security for their medical records. In 2007, he backed the Democrats' plan to expand the State Children's Health Insurance Program, which he said had "a proven track record of helping families make sure their children lead healthy lives." He worked on legislation, enacted in 2008, to provide parity for mental health coverage in health insurance policies. In 2009, Murphy called for creation of a trust fund to pay physicians a few dollars for every patient that converts to an electronic personal health record. "Everybody has a stake in healthcare IT," he said.

Murphy has not been seriously challenged for re-election. In 2006, he escaped what likely would have been a competitive contest when former state Treasurer Barbara Hafer decided against a challenge. In 2008, consultant Beth Hafer, Barbara Hafer's daughter, was the favorite of Democratic leaders. But she was a disappointing candidate, and finished second in the Democratic primary. Businessman Steve O'Donnell, the nominee, got little traction against Murphy, who won 64%-36%.

NINETEENTH DISTRICT

Todd Platts (R)

Elected 2000, 5th term; b. March 5, 1962, York; home, York; Shippensburg U., B.S. 1984, Pepperdine U., J.D. 1991; Episcopalian; married (Leslie); 2 children.

Elected Office: PA House of Reps., 1992–2000.

Professional Career: Practicing atty, 1991–93.

DC Office: 2455 RHOB, 20515, 202-225-5836; Fax: 202-226-1000; Web site: www.house.gov/platts.

State Offices: Carlisle, 717-249-0190; Gettysburg, 717-338-1919; York, 717-600-1919.

Committees: *Armed Services* (25th of 25 R): Air & Land Forces; Oversight & Investigations. *Education & Labor* (8th of 19 R): Early Childhood, Elementary & Secondary Education; Healthy Families & Communities (RMM). *Transportation & Infrastructure* (12th of 30 R): Coast Guard & Maritime Transportation; Highways & Transit; Water Resources & Environment.

Group Ratings

	ADA	ACLU	AFS	LCV	ITIC	NTU	COC	ACU	CFG	FRC
2008	55	27	57	62	57	51	78	68	57	76
2007	45	—	27	55	—	46	70	64	34	—

National Journal Ratings

	2007 LIB	—	2007 CONS		2008 LIB	—	2008 CONS
Economic	42%	—	57%		40%	—	59%
Social	38%	—	60%		31%	—	62%
Foreign	32%	—	64%		29%	—	69%
Composite	39%	—	62%		35%	—	65%

Key Votes of the 110th Congress

1. Increase minimum wage	Y	5. Share immigration data	Y	9. Withdraw troops 8/08	N
2. Expand SCHIP	Y	6. Foreign aid abortion ban	Y	10. No operations in Iran	N
3. Raise CAFE standards	N	7. Ban gay bias in workplace	Y	11. Free trade with Peru	Y
4. Bail out financial markets	N	8. Repeal D.C. gun law	Y	12. Overhaul FISA	Y

Election Results

2008 general	Todd Platts (R)	218,862	(67%)	($192,495)
	Philip Avillo (D)	109,533	(33%)	($66,030)
2008 primary	Todd Platts (R)	unopposed		

Prior Winning Percentages: 2006 (64%); 2004 (91%); 2002 (91%); 2000 (73%)

Population		Race/Ethnicity		Work	
Pop. 2007:	698,262	White:	90.0%	Private:	82.0%
Change since 2000:	Up 8.0%	Black:	3.7%	Government:	12.3%
Urban:	71.4%	Hispanic:	3.7%	Self-employed:	5.5%
Rural:	28.6%	Asian:	1.4%	Blue collar:	26.6%
Area size:	1,666 sq. mi.	Native Am.:	0.1%	White collar:	58.5%
		Hawaiian:	0.0%	Khaki collar:	0.1%
Age		Two+ races:	1.0%	Other:	14.9%
Median age:	39.2 yrs.	*Ancestry*		Median income:	$54,506
More than 65 yrs:	14.1%	German:	32.4%	Median home value:	$161,400
Less than 18 yrs:	22.3%	Irish:	10.4%	Poverty:	7.7%
Education		English:	7.3%	**Military Veterans**	
H.S. grad:	86.5%			% of Pop:	12.4%
College grad:	24.3%				
Grad degree:	8.7%				

The Mason-Dixon Line, the historic boundary between Maryland and Pennsylvania, runs through some of the country's most pleasant rolling farmlands, west of the Susquehanna River and through the Appalachian Mountains. The area was home to the westernmost capital of the United States during the Revolutionary War: the small city of York, capital from September 1777 to June 1778. York is where the Continental Congress passed the Articles of Confederation, received word from Benjamin

2008 Presidential Vote
McCain (R)............................187,857   (56%)
Obama (D) 142,398   (43%)

2004 Presidential Vote
Bush (R) 198,192   (64%)
Kerry (D)...............................110,274   (36%)

Cook Partisan Voting Index: R + 12

Franklin in Paris that the French would help the colonies with money and ships, and issued the first proclamation calling for a national day of thanksgiving. A little more than four score years later, Robert E. Lee's Confederate troops crossed over this invisible line and were repelled in the Battle of Gettysburg in July 1863. Not much today suggests that this region was either a frontier or the object of bloody struggle. The green farmland seems peaceful, prosperous and mostly undisturbed by the current era's commercial trappings and stylistic excesses. This is where former President Dwight D. Eisenhower, of Pennsylvania Dutch stock, chose to quietly spend his retirement years.

The Mason-Dixon Line forms the southern boundary of the 19th Congressional District of Pennsylvania, which includes all of Adams and York counties and part of Cumberland County to the north—relatively fast-growing areas in slow-growing Pennsylvania. The 19th takes in the fruit belt of Adams County, the Harrisburg suburbs across the Susquehanna and part of the old town of Carlisle, with Dickinson College, the Carlisle Barracks, and the U.S. Army War College. Hanover, in York County, is one of the world's snack headquarters, home to Snyder's of Hanover, which makes one of every four pretzels sold in the U.S., as well as potato chip giant Utz. The district's biggest city is York, the site of Harley-Davidson's largest manufacturing plant, with about 2,500 employees. York is also home to the USA Weightlifting Hall of Fame at the York Barbell Company. Many of its residents commute less than an hour to work in Baltimore and a few hardy souls commute to jobs in Washington D.C. With an 8% population increase from 2000 to 2007, York has been one of the fastest-growing large counties in the Northeast. The city also has a growing Hispanic population, mainly Puerto Rican. In Gettysburg, many Hispanics work the abundant orchards, which has led local farmers to advocate for increased immigration. Politically, the 19th is heavily Republican. President George W. Bush won 64% of the vote here in 2004, and Republican nominee John McCain won 56% in 2008.

The congressman from the 19th District is Todd Platts, a Republican elected in 2000. Platts grew up in York, graduated from Shippensburg University and Pepperdine University School of Law. In 1992, at age 30, he was elected to the state House, where he served four terms. In 2000, he was the first to announce his candidacy after longtime Republican Rep. Bill Goodling, chairman of the House Education and the Workforce Committee, said that he would retire. Platts's chief primary opponents were state Rep. Al Masland, attorney Dick Stewart, who was endorsed by Goodling, and Charlie Gerow, head of the state Citizens Against Government Waste. The campaign motto for Platts, who refused contributions from political action committees and was outspent by his chief Republican rivals, was "Putting People First." Platts won with 33% of the vote to 29% for Masland and 19% for Stewart, rolling up huge margins in his home base of York County. In the general election, Platts won 73%-26%. He has been re-elected with only minor opposition.

In the House, Platts has a moderate voting record for a Republican. In January 2007, he was one of only three House Republicans who voted in favor of all six bills that new Democratic majority brought to the floor as part of their "first 100 hours" agenda. Also that year, he was the chief Republican co-sponsor of a successful bill to increase fuel-efficiency standards for cars and trucks. In 2009, he allied with Democrats on their ambitious initiative to reduce global warming. However, Platts also supports increased oil drilling and additional nuclear facilities as part of an overall policy to increase energy supplies.

When his party was in the majority, he chaired the Government Management, Finance and Accountability Subcommittee on the Government Reform Committee and took a special interest in oversight of federal agencies. He pushed legislation to require review of all government programs at least once every five years to evaluate their performance, and he chaired hearings where he demanded that the Homeland Security Department improve its accounting practices. He sponsored legislation to overturn a federal court ruling that he said created loopholes in the Whistleblower Protection Act. In 2007, in response to adverse court rulings, the House passed a bill that he helped to write to expand protections for national security officials.

In the minority, he is the ranking member of the Healthy Families and Communities Subcommittee on the Education and Labor Committee. He bucked most Republicans by opposing tax-paid vouchers for private school tuition for parents of children in underperforming schools.

Platts has not been afraid to challenge sacred cows in Congress. He sponsored, with Rep. Jim Matheson, D-Utah, a bill to repeal automatic annual pay raises for members of Congress. He supported "real lobbying reform," including an outside Office of Public Integrity to police the behavior of members of Congress. But in 2009, he abandoned a pledge not to accept earmarked spending for his district because, he said, it would be an unfair disadvantage for his constituents. Earmarks have come under increasing criticism as a waste of taxpayer money.

Platts may hold the title for the longest daily commute to Congress. He drives the roughly 100 miles from his home in York to Washington nearly every day that the House is in session.

★ RHODE ISLAND ★

Rhode Island and Providence Plantations, this tiny state with a mouthful of an official name, boasts as long and as turbulent a political history as any in the union. It was founded by Roger Williams as a refuge for religious dissenters, "the sewer of New England," as the orthodox Puritan Cotton Mather put it. It has been a successful trading community since the late 16th century and a leader in manufacturing since Samuel Slater replicated from memory an English water-powered cotton textile mill in Pawtucket in 1791. Rhode Island profited from slavery (two-thirds of America's slaves arrived from Africa on ships owned by Rhode Islanders) and war (the state boomed during the Civil War), and carried its tradition of tolerating just about anything into its politics. Rhode Island refused to pay its share for the Revolutionary War, declined to send delegates to the 1787 Constitutional Convention, and delayed joining the union until the other 12 states had, prompting George Washington to say, "Rhode Island still perseveres in that impolitic, unjust—and one might add without much impropriety—scandalous conduct, which seems to have marked all her public counsels of late." The new nation's first bank failure occurred here in 1809, when a bank capitalized at $45 issued $800,000 in bank notes. In the 1840s, conflict between hard-money merchants and soft-money farmers resulted in two state governments and a conflict known as Dorr's War, with the outcome determined when merchant Thomas Dorr's two ancient cannons failed to fire.

Then, in the 1930s, the state had something resembling a political revolution. Thousands of immigrants from French Canada, Ireland, and Italy came to Rhode Island to work in the textile mills, and this colony of dissident Protestants became the most heavily Catholic state in the nation. Yankee Republicans tried to appeal to Catholics by running French Canadians for office. But national events—Catholic Democrat Al Smith's presidential candidacy in 1928, when he carried Rhode Island, and Franklin Roosevelt's New Deal—moved the Catholics toward the Democrats. Then came the revolution: Although they had won only 20 of the 42 state Senate seats, the Democrats under Gov. Theodore Green refused to seat two Republicans in 1935. With the lieutenant governor's tiebreaker, they voted Democrats into the seats, and proceeded in 14 minutes to declare the state Supreme Court vacant, to abolish state boards that controlled Democratic cities, to increase the power of the governor, and to reorganize state government to purge Republicans. This ended the direct political control of Rhode Island's "Five Families"—the Browns, Metcalfs, Goddards, Lippitts, and Chafees—who owned or ran many of the textile mills, the Rhode Island Hospital Trust (long the largest bank), the Providence *Journal-Bulletin*, Brown University, the Rhode Island School of Design and the state Republican Party. Democrats have won most elections ever since with the lion's share of votes from Rhode Island's Catholic majority, starting with Green's election in 1936, at age 69. From 1940 to 1980, Democrats won every election for U.S. House seats. The state's Democratic percentages in presidential elections from 1968 to 2008 are rivaled only by Massachusetts'. Republicans have won when they've been able to capitalize on scandal or Democratic disarray, as governors Lincoln Almond and Donald Carcieri did in 1994 and 2002. But even the most durable Republican politician here, the late Gov. and Sen. John Chafee, lost elections as well as won them.

Rhode Island has gone through a long and often painful economic transformation, from blue collar to white collar, from textiles to high-tech. It suffered economic problems in the early 1990s, as the submarine factory and Navy base at Quonset Point shed thousands of jobs, and employment in costume jewelry, Rhode Island's major manufacturer, fell from 32,500 in 1977 to 6,300 in 2000. But Republican Gov. Lincoln Almond, elected in 1994 and 1998, persuaded the overwhelmingly Democratic Legislature to gradually cut income taxes and eliminate the car tax, and Providence Mayor Buddy Cianci promoted successful redevelopment in the state's capital and largest city. Its downtown was enlivened with new buildings such as the GTECH tower and events such as the SoundSession music festival and WaterFire, an art fair with 100 bonfires lit along the city's three rivers. After the Legislature passed a 25% tax rebate for moviemakers, Disney was given free rein to shoot *Underdog* film scenes in the Statehouse, and all 11 episodes of the *Brotherhood* series were shot in the state. Tourism became Rhode Island's second-largest industry and computer data processing a major part of the economy. The state's population, after hovering around 1 million for decades, started to grow again.

But all was not well. Cianci, caught up in scandal, was disgraced and imprisoned, and investigators honed in on state legislators. As in neighboring Connecticut and Massachusetts, economic inequality increased, with the state divided between a growing professional class and a blue-collar remnant that scraped along in an increasingly service economy. The population's makeup remains tilted toward the elderly, and taxes remain relatively high by national standards. Rhode Island has embraced green policies, such as requiring 16% of electricity to be generated by renewable sources by 2020, at some cost in the short term. Voters rejected a Narragansett Indian casino in West Warwick in 2006, but politicians continued to try to compete with Foxwoods in nearby Connecticut and with casinos proposed in Massachusetts. Legislators have grappled with whether same-sex couples married in Massachusetts can get a divorce after they have moved to Rhode Island. In the face of looming budget deficits, Republican Gov.

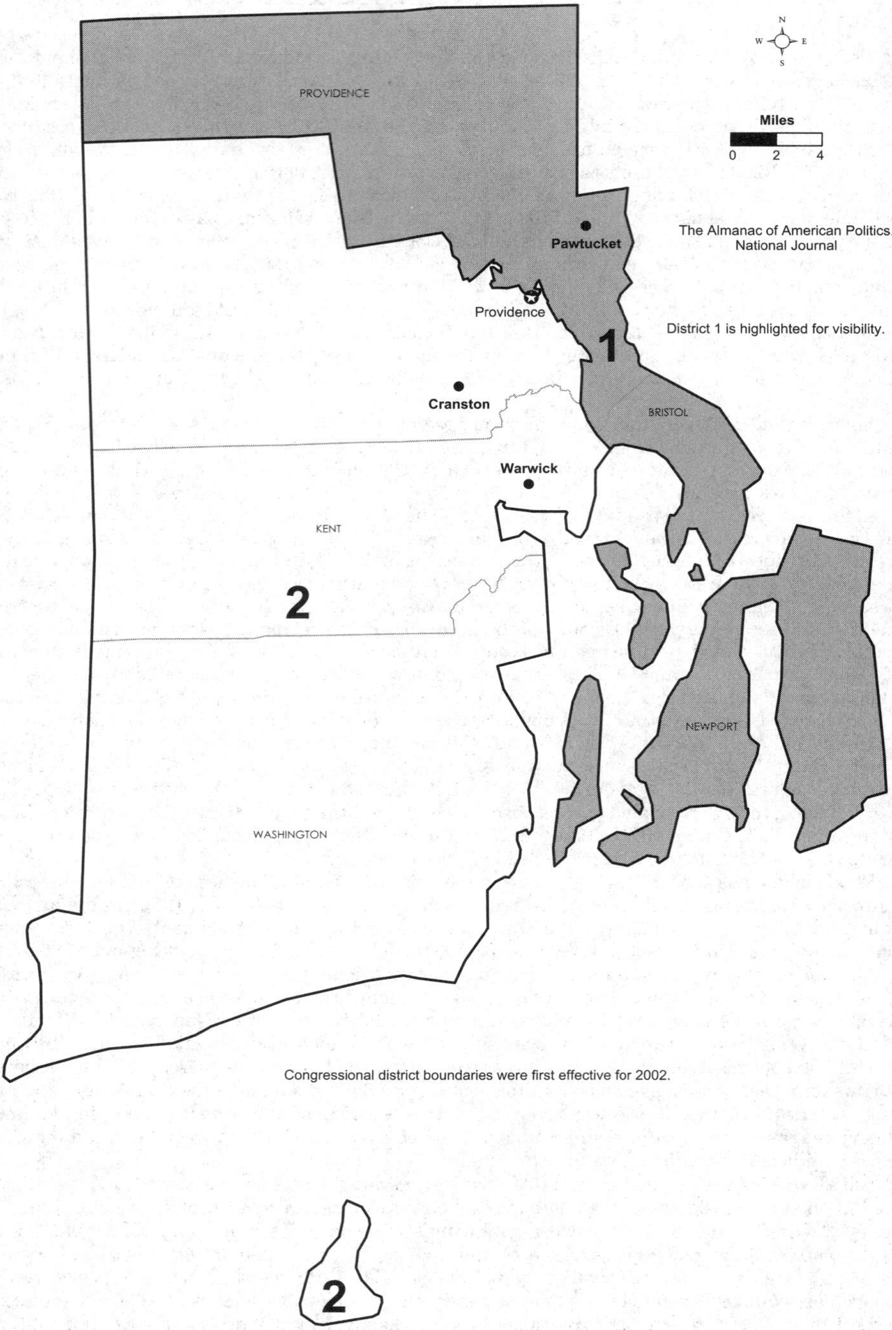
PROVIDENCE
N
W
E
S
Miles
0 2 4
Pawtucket
The Almanac of American Politics.
National Journal
Providence
1
District 1 is highlighted for visibility.
Cranston
BRISTOL
Warwick
KENT
2
NEWPORT
WASHINGTON
2

Congressional district boundaries were first effective for 2002.

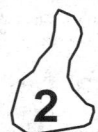

Population		Household Income		Work	
Pop. 2007:	1,062,065	Under $15k:	13.9%	Private:	80.4%
State rank:	43rd of 50	$15k to $50k:	32.7%	Government:	13.6%
Change since 2000:	Up 1.3%	$50k to $100k:	32.2%	Self-employed:	5.9%
Urban:	90.6%	$100k to $150k:	17.8%	Unemployment (3-yr. average):	4.1%
Rural:	9.4%	Over $150k:	3.4%	Poverty:	11.7%
Native of state:	59.4%	Median income:	$54,060	Blue collar:	21.0%
Not a citizen:	6.8%			White collar:	60.8%
Area size:	1,545 sq. mi.	**Home Value**		Khaki collar:	0.3%
		Under $100k:	2.4%	Other:	17.9%
Most populous cities		$100k to $300k:	50.9%		
1. Providence	170,220	$300k to $500k:	33.8%	**Age**	
2. Warwick	84,975	$500k to $1 mil:	11.3%	Median age:	38.3 yrs.
3. Cranston	82,397	Over $1 million:	1.7%	More than 65 yrs:	13.9%
4. Pawtucket	72,335	Median:	$289,400	Less than 18 yrs:	22.3%

Race/Ethnicity				Military Veterans		Registered Voters in 2008	
White:	79.0%	*Language*		% of Pop:	10.1%	D:	298,388 (42.6%)
Black:	4.7%	English:	79.5%	*Veterans by Period*		R:	76,651 (10.9%)
Hispanic:	10.9%	Spanish:	9.8%	WWII and before:	15.1%	Other:	326,268 (46.5%)
Asian:	2.7%	Asian:	2.0%	Korea:	14.4%	Voter turnout:	471,099
Native Am.:	0.4%	Other		Vietnam:	30.8%	Turnout as % of	
Hawaiian:	0.0%	European	8.1%	Gulf (pre-2001):	8.6%	voting age:	57.3%
Two+ races:	1.5%	**Education**		Gulf (post-2001):	7.0%	**General Assembly**	
Ancestry		H.S. grad:	82.7%	Peace time:	24.1%	Senate:	33 D 4 R 1 I
Irish:	15.1%	College grad:	29.4%			House:	69 D 6 R
Italian:	14.4%	Grad degree:	11.5%				
English:	9.6%						

Donald Carcieri in 2008 called for requiring proof of citizenship by hospitals and schools, while others urged reducing prison populations by releasing inmates early.

Politically, Rhode Island continues to be heavily Democratic, although not always so; Carcieri was re-elected 51%-49% in 2006, and the state has not elected a Democratic governor since 1992. Carcieri lost Providence and Pawtucket and some working-class suburbs, but carried just about every other city and town. Republican Sen. Lincoln Chafee, appointed to succeed his late father in 1999 and elected to a full term in 2000 by 57%-41%, compiled the most liberal record of any Republican senator, but he faced fierce opposition in 2006. Chafee defeated conservative Cranston Mayor Steven Laffey in the GOP primary by only 54%-46%, and then lost to Democratic Attorney General Sheldon Whitehouse by the same margin. (This is a small state: The two candidates' fathers were roommates at Yale.) Whitehouse won 72% in Providence, which had voted 63% for Chafee in the primary and had given him 44% of the vote six years before; his percentages declined similarly in other ethnic cities and by somewhat lesser margins in affluent suburbs. A Democratic trend was also observable in the 52%-48% approval of restoring felons' right to vote, which had been taken away by voters in 1986.

Presidential politics   Rhode Island is almost always one of the most Democratic states in presidential elections—over the last generation, the most Democratic, though just a little bit less so lately. It voted 61%-32% for Al Gore in 2000—his best state in the country—but gave John Kerry from neighboring Massachusetts a somewhat smaller margin of 59%-39% in 2004. In 2008, it voted 63%-35% for Barack Obama, his third best percentage in the nation, after his native Hawaii and liberal Vermont. Turnout was 469,000, well above the records of 437,000 in 2004 and 432,000 in 1980. Rhode Island's Catholic majority is heavily Democratic and, interestingly, favors abortion rights: In states where Catholics are beleaguered minorities they may stand together and strongly oppose abortion; here, where they're the strong majority and where the mostly Mediterranean Catholics traditionally don't pay strict attention to the mostly Irish priests, they come out against the church position.

For years Rhode Island held a presidential primary on the same day as Massachusetts, usually with the lowest turnout rate in the nation. In 2008, the state voted on March 4, the same day as Vermont, Ohio, and Texas. At that point, the Republican contest

2008 Presidential Vote
Obama (D)	296,571	(63%)
McCain (R)	165,391	(35%)

2008 Democratic Presidential Primary
Clinton (D)	108,949	(58%)
Obama (D)	75,316	(40%)

2008 Republican Presidential Primary
McCain (R)	17,480	(64%)
Huckabee (R)	5,847	(21%)
Paul (R)	1,777	(7%)

2004 Presidential Vote
Kerry (D)	259,760	(59%)
Bush (R)	169,046	(39%)

was effectively decided, although Mike Huckabee remained in the race and lost to John McCain here by a predictably large 64%-21%. But the Democratic race, after Barack Obama's string of victories in February, was very much alive, and both his campaign and that of Hillary Rodham Clinton's opened Rhode Island offices and sent in paid staff and recruited local volunteers. The economic divide seemed fairly apparent in the results. As in Massachusetts, Obama carried upscale towns and city neighborhoods, while Clinton ran much better in blue-collar areas that have not shared in the regional prosperity. She won the state by 58%-40%, and with her narrower victories in Ohio and Texas, could claim to have won the majority of the March 4 primaries. That outcome kept her in the race for three more months.

Congressional districting

111th Congress Lineup
2 D
110th Congress Lineup
2 D

Rhode Island legislators had a heck of a time redrawing the boundaries of their own districts in 2001 and 2002. Voters in 1994 adopted a constitutional amendment reducing the size of the state House after the 2000 census from 100 seats to 75 seats and the state Senate from 50 to 38 seats. Redrawing the state's two congressional districts was much easier. Rhode Island's two districts have remained pretty much the same since 1842, except for the period from 1912 to 1932 when the state had three districts. Providence is split, and both districts are overwhelmingly Democratic. For the 2002 redistricting, 14,000 people needed to be moved from the 2nd House District to the 1st House District. Democratic incumbents Patrick Kennedy and Jim Langevin agreed on a change in Providence that gave Kennedy his old state legislative district near Providence College. Rhode Island will not lose its second district in the apportionment following the 2010 census, and the boundaries of the two districts are likely to change little.

Governor

Donald Carcieri (R)

Elected 2002, term expires Jan. 2011, 2nd term; b. Dec. 16, 1942, East Greenwich; home, East Greenwich; Brown U., B.A. 1965; Catholic; married (Suzanne); 4 children.

Professional Career: High schl. teacher, 1965–71; Banker, Old Stone Bank, 1971–81; Director, Catholic Relief Services, Jamaica, 1981–83; CEO, Cookson America, 1983–97.

Office: The State House, Room 115, Providence, 2903, 401-222-2080; Fax: 401-222-8096; Web site: www.governor.state.ri.us.

Election Results

2006 general	Donald Carcieri (R)	197,306	(51%)
	Charles Fogarty (D)	190,686	(49%)
2006 primary	Donald Carcieri (R)	unopposed	

Prior Winning Percentages: 2002 (55%)

Donald Carcieri, elected governor of Rhode Island in 2002, grew up in East Greenwich, on Narragansett Bay, where his father was a teacher and coach at the town high school and worked in the summers harvesting quahogs, large clams found in the waters off the coast. East Greenwich today is one of the state's most affluent suburbs, but when Carcieri was growing up there in the 1950s, it was a more modest enclave of fishermen and farmers. Carcieri was class president and a top athlete in high school; he attended Brown University on scholarship and played varsity football and baseball. He taught high school math in Newport and then in Concord, Mass., before going to work for Old Stone Bank. Within 10 years, he was executive vice president. In 1981, he moved to Jamaica to head the Catholic Relief Service's West Indies operation, but two years later, returned to Rhode Island to join Cookson America, the U.S. branch of a London conglomerate that owned dozens of manufacturing, electronic, and precious metals companies around the world. He rose to become chief executive officer of Cookson America and a joint managing director of Cookson Group Worldwide. He moved Cookson America's headquarters to the former Providence train station, overlooking Burnside Park and the Statehouse. He retired from business in 1997, and in 2002, launched his political career by running for governor.

The incumbent, Republican Lincoln Almond, was ineligible for a third term. Three Democrats and two Republicans ran to succeed him; Carcieri was the only one without experience in public office, though he did serve as Rhode Island chairman for George W. Bush's 2000 presidential campaign. His primary opponent was James Bennett, former head of the Convention Center Authority and the owner of Mitkem, an environmental testing laboratory. Carcieri and Bennett mostly agreed on priorities—rein in the Legislature, cut spending increases, and promote economic development. Both avoided Rhode Island's public financing system and spent their own money on their campaigns—$600,000 for Carcieri and $275,000 for Bennett. Bennett spent much of his money on fierce negative ads, charging that under Carcieri's leadership Cookson's debt rose, layoffs increased, and Carcieri was given a $2.6 million golden handshake. But Carcieri won the September primary, 67%-33%.

Running again as the Democratic nominee was liberal Myrth York, who twice lost to Almond in 1994 and 1998. York's father had founded a successful chemical equipment company, and she managed the family's money. She also spent $2 million of her own money before the primary. The *Providence Journal's* post-primary poll showed York ahead 49%-35%, but she had led in early polls in 1994 and 1998, too. Their differing stances were apparent in a September debate. York said, "I have a knowledge of government and a knowledge of how to get things done in government. Government is there to provide opportunity for folks." Carcieri said, "I believe if real change is going to happen in the state, it's going to have to come from somebody who owes nothing to the system, somebody from outside." He pledged not to raise taxes in his first year; York said she didn't want to but wouldn't make a pledge. She also called for new prescription drug and education programs; Carcieri said his focus would be economic development.

In mid-October York ran a series of negative ads about Cookson. One said the company brokered a "tin mining deal" that ravaged an Amazon rain forest, and another said that it owned a plant in Philadelphia that released hazardous lead into a neighborhood. But the ads had little effect. Carcieri won 55%-45%. York won big in Providence but in the rest of the state carried only East Providence and the tiny textile mill town of Central Falls. Altogether, York spent $3.8 million of her own money, Carcieri $1.5 million of his.

Carcieri faced an overwhelmingly Democratic Legislature (32-6 in the Senate, 63-11-1 in the House) but posted early achievements. In 2003, he won praise for scheduling monthly office hours for average citizens to meet the governor for a 10-minute private visit. He was tested the same year when a nightclub fire in West Warwick killed 100 people and injured many others. In a state with only 1 million residents, nearly everyone knew someone affected by the tragedy. At a Warwick memorial service, Carcieri stood in the back of the church greeting mourners. His empathy, decisiveness, and calm resolve in the days after the fire won him much acclaim. In July, Carcieri signed the Comprehensive Fire Safety Act, requiring most nightclubs to install sprinklers, banning pyrotechnics from all but the largest venues, and eliminating a grandfather clause that exempted buildings constructed before the state fire code was written. State officials called the new fire regulations the toughest in the nation.

Carcieri launched a weekly deli lunch with legislators to get them to agree to send to the voters a measure strengthening the governor's appointment authority on commissions and boards. For more than three centuries, dating to the original colonial charter, the General Assembly had had wide-ranging powers, including the authority to appoint members to, and have legislators serve on, hundreds of boards and commissions that make state policy and control billions of dollars in state assets. The arrangement encouraged political patronage, cronyism, and a culture of behind-the-scenes deal-making, and after a decade of assorted scandals that brought down a state Supreme Court justice and sent former Gov. Edward DiPrete and Providence Mayor Buddy Cianci to prison, voters in 2004 passed the "separation of powers" referendum, 78%-22%.

The governor battled regularly with Democratic leaders on a stream of bills that often returned to the Legislature for override votes. Carcieri vetoed a bill that would have allowed home-based child care providers to unionize and bargain with the state. He vetoed a medical marijuana bill, but that decision was overridden. In the face of a likely override, Carcieri backed away from threats in 2006 to veto an increase in the hourly minimum wage to $7.40. He was also forced to back down from a plan to create a statewide system to evaluate teacher performance.

Like Almond, Carcieri also ran into resistance when it came time to limit spending. He vetoed the Legislature's budgets in 2003 and 2004, but was overridden both times, resulting in tax increases on hotel rooms, cellphone usage and cigarettes. He had more success in subsequent years in part because he worked more closely with Democrats, including House Speaker William Murphy. In 2006, the Legislature approved a $6.6 billion tax and spending plan that restrained overall spending increases to about 5% and limited property tax increases to 4% over six years.

Lt. Gov. Charles Fogarty, a Democrat barred by term limits from seeking a third term, challenged Carcieri in 2006. Fogarty was a career politician whose father was a state senator and whose uncle, the late Rep. John E. Fogarty, served in Congress for a quarter-century. Fogarty ran on access to affordable health care and on government reform, while Carcieri touted his attempts to control government spending. Some Democrats questioned the wisdom of Fogarty's focus on corruption because of Carcieri's already strong record of reform. On economic issues, Carcieri was more vulnerable. During a televised debate, Fogarty cited Rhode Island's high unemployment rate and pressed Carcieri on his failure to create 20,000 new private sector jobs as he had promised. "I think 15,000 is pretty good," Carcieri responded. "We are outperforming all of New England." Each candidate spent just over $2 million for the race. Fogarty benefited from the Democrats' solid voter turnout operation and from a strong Democratic current in the state. But he fell shy of victory, and Carcieri was re-elected, 51%-49%.

In his second term, Carcieri focused on illegal immigration in this heavily ethnic state, which has many recent legal migrants. Citing the failure of Congress to act, he said, "At the end of the day, the states and governors around the country are bearing the burden, and our citizens—hardworking citizens—are bearing the burden." In 2008, he required state agencies and vendors to review the immigration status of new workers. Raucous crowds protested outside Carcieri's office, and were forced away by police, although no one was arrested. Religious leaders in the state argued that the governor's policies were discriminatory and sparked fear among migrants. Although Carcieri cited public polling that favored his position, legislators were not moved. They rejected his plan to deny driver's licenses and workers' compensation to illegal immigrants.

The governor also struggled to reduce the largest budget deficit in state history, which he said in January 2008 left Rhode Island at "a tipping point" of financial disaster. His funding targets ranged from Head Start programs to health care subsidies for low-income adults. Some Democrats responded by seeking to raise taxes on the wealthy and to reverse the flat tax that had been enacted in 2006. The Legislature's continuing battles with the governor made the state seem increasingly dysfunctional, and Democrats focused on the prospect of electing in 2010 their first governor since 1990.

Senior Senator

Jack Reed (D)

Elected 1996, term expires 2014, 3rd term; b. Nov. 12, 1949, Providence; home, Jamestown; U.S. Military Acad., West Point, B.S. 1971, Harvard U., M.P.P. 1973, J.D. 1982; Catholic; married (Julia Hart); 1 child.

Military Career: Army, 1967–79; Army Reserves, 1979–91.

Elected Office: RI Senate, 1984–90; U.S. House of Reps., 1990–96.

Professional Career: Assoc. prof., U.S. Military Acad. at West Point, 1978–79; Practicing atty., 1982–90.

DC Office: 728 HSOB, 20510, 202-224-4642; Fax: 202-224-4680; Web site: reed.senate.gov.

State Offices: Cranston, 401-943-3100; Providence, 401-528-5200.

Committees: *Appropriations* (13th of 18 D): Agriculture, Rural Development, Food and Drug Administration & Related Agencies; Commerce, Justice, Science & Related Agencies; Energy & Water Development; Interior, Environment & Related Agencies; Labor, Health and Human Services, Education & Related Agencies; Military Construction, Veterans Affairs & Related Agencies. *Armed Services* (5th of 15 D): Emerging Threats & Capabilities (Chmn); Seapower; Strategic Forces. *Banking, Housing & Urban Affairs* (3rd of 13 D): Financial Institutions; Housing, Transportation & Community Development; Securities, Insurance & Investment (Chmn). *Health, Education, Labor & Pensions* (7th of 13 D).

Group Ratings

	ADA	ACLU	AFS	LCV	ITIC	NTU	COC	ACU	CFG	FRC
2008	95	93	100	100	80	11	50	4	8	0
2007	95	—	100	93	—	8	40	0	12	—

National Journal Ratings

	2007 LIB	—	2007 CONS		2008 LIB	—	2008 CONS
Economic	94%	—	0%		77%	—	13%
Social	84%	—	15%		91%	—	0%
Foreign	68%	—	30%		94%	—	0%
Composite	84%	—	17%		92%	—	9%

Key Votes of the 110th Congress

1. Raise CAFE standards	Y	5. Make English official language	N	9. Withdraw troops 3/08	Y
2. Expand SCHIP	Y	6. Path to citizenship	Y	10. Iran guard is terrorist group	Y
3. Cap greenhouse gases	Y	7. Fetus is unborn child	N	11. Increase missile defense $	N
4. Bail out financial markets	Y	8. Prosecute hate crimes	Y	12. Overhaul FISA	N

Election Results

2008 general	Jack Reed (D)	320,644	(73%)	($2,258,706)
	Robert Tingle (R)	116,174	(27%)	
2008 primary	Jack Reed (D)	48,038	(87%)	
	Christopher Young (D)	7,277	(13%)	

Prior Winning Percentages: 2002 (78%); 1996 (63%); 1994 House (68%); 1992 House (71%); 1990 House (59%)

Jack Reed, Rhode Island's senior senator, was elected to the House in 1990 and the Senate in 1996. He grew up in working-class Cranston, the second of three children of a school custodian and a housewife. Disappointed that she never got to go to college, Mary Reed prepared her children for success in school. She insisted on music and art classes for young Jack, beginning at age 5. But her son was fascinated by history and World War II as a child, and eventually decided he wanted to go to the U.S. Military Academy. At LaSalle Academy, a Catholic prep school in Providence, he played football, though he was small for the sport. He also ran track, was elected to the student council, and worked on the school newspaper. Reed was accepted at West Point, and then went on to serve in the 82nd Airborne as a paratrooper. He racked up other sterling academic credentials, including a master's degree from Harvard University's prestigious John F. Kennedy School of Government and a degree from Harvard Law School. Throughout his life, Reed has kept a spot in his heart for West Point. He taught there briefly in the late 1970s, serves on the academy's governing board and chose it as the site of his marriage to Julia Hart in April 2005.

In 1984, at age 35, Reed won public office for the first time, beating an incumbent in the primary for the state Senate, where he served six years. When Republican Claudine Schneider left the U.S. House to run against Sen. Claiborne Pell in 1990, Reed ran for her seat, overcoming several better-known candidates in the primary and winning the general election with 59%.

In 1995, when Pell announced his retirement after 36 years, Reed was ready to run for the Senate. He was easily nominated, and faced GOP state Treasurer Nancy Mayer in the general election. National Republicans spent nearly $1 million on ads attacking Reed as a liberal for opposing "workfare" and for supporting labor unions; these tactics did not hurt him in liberal, heavily unionized Rhode Island, and perhaps even helped him. Mayer spent $773,000; Reed, $2.7 million. His biography was his message: Reed launched his campaign in a public school conference room named for his late father, he stressed his bootstraps rise from a working-class background, and he called for education spending to help others, he said, experience the same success. That message and his pleasant, unassuming demeanor evidently touched a chord. Reed won 63%-35%.

Reed arrived as one of the few senators of his generation with military experience, and today he is one of the most respected authorities on defense and foreign affairs in Congress, though he is among the least well known of senators. Reed accompanied Democratic presidential candidate Barack Obama on his 2008 trip to Iraq and Afghanistan, and Obama considered him a potential running mate until Reed ruled himself out. Reed remained on the short list of possible Defense secretaries in an Obama administration until Secretary Robert Gates agreed to stay on. Reed has served on the Armed Services Committee since January 1999, and he got a waiver from the Democratic leadership to remain on the panel after securing a seat on another top committee, Appropriations, in 2007.

Reed supported Democratic President Clinton's bombing strikes in Afghanistan and Sudan in 1998, but four years later, he was a staunch opponent of Republican President Bush's decision to invade Iraq, joining the dozen Senate Democrats to vote against the 2002 war resolution. He later was one of the first prominent members of Congress to call for the resignation of Defense Secretary Donald Rumsfeld for his handling of the conflict. Reed felt that Rumsfeld grossly underestimated the strength of anti-American insurgents in Iraq and failed to send in adequate troops and equipment. Reed has traveled to the region a dozen times, often straying from the safe zones to talk with officers and soldiers on the front lines. In 2005, after his fifth trip to Iraq, he said: "My job is to be critical about what's going on and what needs to be improved. I think my criticism has been accurate, certainly in the operations in this region, in that we didn't organize ourselves for the appropriate occupation and stabilization" after the overthrow of Saddam Hussein.

In March 2006, Reed said it was time to "redeploy our forces as quickly as possible" to other parts of the Middle East. That year, he and Michigan Democratic Sen. Carl Levin sponsored a bill calling for a "phased redeployment" in six months, with no deadline for complete withdrawal; it also called for U.S. forces to transition to training Iraqi security forces. The Levin-Reed amendment lost 60-39. A more extreme alternative, Massachusetts Democrat John Kerry's amendment calling for withdrawal by June 2007, was defeated 86-13. In summer 2006, Reed said that Iraq had deteriorated into a "low-grade civil war," but pointed to gains in training Iraqis. In December 2006, he said the Iraq Study Group's report "may be the last chance to get it right" and noted that its recommendations were "strikingly similar" to the Levin-Reed amendment.

In September 2007, in giving the Democratic response to Bush's address to the nation on the success of the troop surge in Iraq, Reed criticized the adverse impact on the pursuit of the Al Qaeda terrorist network. "Democrats and Republicans in Congress and throughout the nation cannot and must not stand idly by while our interests throughout the world are undermined and our armed forces are stretched toward the breaking point." It was time, he added, to "redefine our mission in Iraq." With Levin, he continued to push for alternatives that would leave only a residual force in Iraq for counter-terrorism, protection of U.S. personnel, and logistics support for Iraqi security forces. But most Republicans were opposed, and Reed failed to gain the 60 votes required to force a final vote.

Reed has been out front in the bipartisan effort to permanently increase the size of the Army. In October 2003, the Senate voted 52-45 for his amendment to add 10,000 troops, but it was dropped in conference with the House. The following year, he and Nebraska Sen. Chuck Hagel, a Republican, called for an increase of 30,000 troops, and the Senate agreed to 20,000. In 2006, Reed worked with the GOP leadership to add $3.7 billion for more soldiers and marines in the budget, and sponsored an amendment to add $10 billion to replace damaged or destroyed equipment. His 2006 amendment to repeal the extension of the capital gains and dividend tax cuts and use the increased revenue for military equipment was defeated 53-44.

On most issues, Reed has a solidly liberal voting record. He has championed the Low-Income Home Energy Assistance Program popular with members of Congress from the Northeast. He called the Senate's action in November 2005 classifying LIHEAP funding as emergency spending a "terrible precedent," and sponsored an amendment to more than double spending from $2 billion to $5 billion. Reed fought Bush administration efforts to partially privatize Social Security, and he was the lead opponent of a bill to prevent victims from suing to hold gun manufacturers liable for crimes committed with their products. Reed voted against confirming conservative justices John Roberts and Samuel Alito to the Supreme Court. In 2008, during debate on legislation to address the financial crisis in the housing market, Reed pushed for expanding the affordable housing fund and said that federal regulators had been "too complacent" in overseeing the financial derivatives market.

An important issue for Reed back home is the immigration status of an estimated 10,000 Liberian refugees of civil war who have settled in Rhode Island. Reed favors giving them permanent immigrant status. He got such a provision into the immigration bill that passed the Senate in May 2006, but the measure died in the House. He has sponsored an annual bill allowing the Liberians to stay temporarily.

In Rhode Island politics, Reed has always been his own man, unentangled with local Democratic Party affairs. He was easily re-elected in 2002, getting 78% of the vote against a Foxwoods Resort Casino manager, who got just 22%. His 2008 election for a third term was never in doubt. This is a Senate seat whose members have had long tenures. Theodore Green, elected at age 69, served 24 years; Claiborne Pell, elected at 41, served 36 years. Reed was elected just before turning 47. For most of his life, Reed was a bachelor. He met Hart on a trip to Afghanistan, which she helped arrange as the Senate's coordinator of overseas travel. They married when Reed was 55, and Hart, considerably younger at 39, gave birth to a daughter, Emily, in January 2007.

Junior Senator

Sheldon Whitehouse (D)

Elected 2006, term expires 2012, 1st term; b. Oct. 20, 1955, New York City; home, Providence; Yale U., B.A. 1978, U. of VA, J.D. 1982; Protestant; married (Sandra); 2 children.

Elected Office: RI Atty. Gen., 1998–2002.

Professional Career: RI spec. asst. atty. gen., 1984–90; Legal counsel, Gov. Bruce Sundlun, 1991; Policy director, Gov. Bruce Sundlun, 1992; Director, RI Dept. of Business Regulation, 1992–1994; U.S. atty. for RI, 1994–1998; Practicing atty., 2003–2006.

DC Office: 502 HSOB, 20510, 202-224-2921; Fax: 202-228-6362; Web site: whitehouse.senate.gov.

State Offices: Providence, 401-453-5294.

Committees: *Aging (Special)* (8th of 13 D). *Budget* (11th of 13 D). *Environment & Public Works* (8th of 12 D). *Intelligence (Select)* (8th of 8 D). *Judiciary* (8th of 12 D): Administrative Oversight & the Courts (Chmn); Antitrust, Competition Policy & Consumer Rights; Constitution; Immigration, Refugees & Border Security.

Group Ratings

	ADA	ACLU	AFS	LCV	ITIC	NTU	COC	ACU	CFG	FRC
2008	90	79	100	100	80	10	50	8	8	0
2007	95	—	100	93	—	6	36	0	12	—

National Journal Ratings

	2007 LIB	—	2007 CONS		2008 LIB	—	2008 CONS
Economic	94%	—	0%		77%	—	13%
Social	88%	—	8%		79%	—	20%
Foreign	94%	—	2%		65%	—	6%
Composite	94%	—	6%		80%	—	20%

Key Votes of the 110th Congress

1. Raise CAFE standards	Y	5. Make English official language	N	9.Withdraw troops 3/08	Y
2. Expand SCHIP	Y	6. Path to citizenship	Y	10. Iran guard is terrorist group	Y
3. Cap greenhouse gases	Y	7. Fetus is unborn child	N	11. Increase missile defense $	N
4. Bail out financial markets	Y	8. Prosecute hate crimes	Y	12. Overhaul FISA	Y

Election Results

2006 general	Sheldon Whitehouse (D) 206,043	(54%)	($6,494,266)
	Lincoln Chafee (R) 178,950	(46%)	($5,381,488)
2006 primary	Sheldon Whitehouse (D) 69,290	(82%)	
	Christopher Young (D) 8,739	(10%)	
	Carl Sheeler (D) 6,755	(8%)	

The junior senator from Rhode Island is Sheldon Whitehouse, a Democrat elected in 2006. He is a wealthy descendant of Charles Crocker, one of California's "Big Four" men who built the Central Pacific Railroad, the eastbound section of railroad that connected with the Union Pacific line at Promontory Summit, Utah, to form the nation's first transcontinental railroad. His grandfather was a diplomat and so was his father, Charles Whitehouse, a World War II Marine Corps pilot who became U.S. ambassador to Laos and Thailand in the 1970s. Sheldon Whitehouse was born in New York City and spent his formative years overseas, including in Cambodia, South Africa, the Philippines, and Guinea; as a teenager, he taught English to Vietnamese children in Saigon. He attended the prestigious St. Paul's prep school before graduating from Yale University and the University of Virginia Law School. Whitehouse clerked for the West Virginia Supreme Court of Appeals in 1982–83, then moved to Rhode Island to take a job as assistant state attorney general. After the 1990 election of Democratic Gov. Bruce Sundlun, Whitehouse became Sundlun's legal counsel and policy director, working on the state's banking crisis and also doing a stint as the state's top business regulator.

In 1994, with support from family friend Democratic Sen. Claiborne Pell, he was appointed U.S. attorney for Rhode Island by President Clinton. In that role, Whitehouse launched an undercover investigation that resulted in the conviction of Providence Mayor Buddy Cianci for public corruption. Whitehouse also focused on environmental cleanup, leading an investigation that resulted in the largest fine in state history for an oil spill on Narragansett Bay. His wife, Sandra Thornton Whitehouse, is a marine biologist and environmental advocate.

Whitehouse ran for office for the first time in 1998, when he sought to become Rhode Island attorney general. In the three-way Democratic primary, his opponents portrayed him as an inexperienced, fox-hunting patrician trying to buy his way into public office. But Whitehouse was better known in the state than his opponents, and he secured the nomination. The general election against state Treasurer Nancy Mayer wasn't much easier. Mayer forced him to concede that he had tried drugs as a student and questioned whether he was tough enough for the job. Whitehouse told the *The Providence Journal*, "The book on me was, 'Smart kid, works hard, but, you know, has no common touch, can't relate to people, will be a disaster.' In fact, I got advice from some political types to run sort of a Rose Garden strategy: You know, 'Don't go out, don't let people see you, 'cause if they see you they're not going to like you. Just mail your résumé around, you know, and spend a lot of money on television.' " But the tide began to turn after Mayer ran highly negative ads on the drug issue that backfired in the absence of evidence that the incident was more than a short chapter from Whitehouse's distant past. He won the election, and went on to burnish his reputation for fighting corporate abusers. Whitehouse successfully sued to hold paint companies legally liable for toxic levels of lead in their products.

By 2002, Whitehouse was widely viewed as a contender for governor. He ran, but lost the Democratic primary by 926 votes to Myrth York, a wealthy liberal and a Federal Hill neighbor in Providence. She outspent Whitehouse by more than 2-to-1 in the primary, but went on to lose in the general election to Republican Donald Carcieri. Whitehouse also harbored ambitions for the U.S. Senate. He had considered running when Republican John Chafee announced in 1999 that he would not seek a fifth term, but decided against it. But when the Chafee seat came up again in 2006, Whitehouse was ready to make the race.

John Chafee, who had roomed with Whitehouse's father at Yale, died in office in October 1999. His son, Lincoln, was appointed to finish his term, then went on to win a full term in 2000 with 57% of the vote. A moderate Republican like his father, Lincoln Chafee often sided with the Democrats, and there was frequent speculation that he would switch parties. But the national Republican Party understood that he might be the only Republican in heavily Democratic Rhode Island who could hold the seat—he and his father were the only Republicans elected to the Senate from Rhode Island in the previous 70 years. Still, Chafee never had a firm hold on the seat. In 2006, he had to fight for renomination in the primary against Cranston Mayor Steve Laffey, a GOP fiscal conservative and a sharp-elbowed campaigner who was backed by the anti-tax Club for Growth. The National Republican Senatorial Committee under Sen. Elizabeth Dole of North Carolina vigorously defended Chafee, reasoning that he would be the stronger general election candidate; he won the September primary 54%-46%.

Whitehouse also looked to have a competitive primary in 2006, but he won easily after Rhode Island Secretary of State Matt Brown dropped out in April amid allegations of campaign finance violations. That gave Whitehouse a decided advantage over Chafee. The incumbent had little cash left after the bruising primary, while Whitehouse began the contest with more than $1 million. Chafee emphasized his willingness to work across party lines, but Whitehouse urged voters to vote their party preference, a problem for Chafee in a state where registered Democrats outnumber Republicans by more than 2-to-1. There was little daylight between the candidates on issues—both backed more federal support for embryonic-stem-cell research, abortion rights, and gun control—so Whitehouse hung the unpopular Bush administration and the national party around Chafee's neck, running ads with the tagline, "Finally, a Whitehouse in Washington you can trust."

Whitehouse won 54% to 46%. He took 72% of the vote in Providence, 66% in Pawtucket, 61% in East Providence, 64% in Woonsocket, and 77% in Central Falls—mill towns and gentrifiers. Chafee won 54% in Warwick, carried Kingston and Westerly's Washington County, and ran not much better than even in Newport and Bristol counties.

Whitehouse was one of eight new Democratic senators whose election gave control of the Senate to the Democrats in 2007. He immediately got seats on desirable committees: Environment and Public Works, Budget, Intelligence, and Judiciary, where he joked that he was the only WASP among the committee's mostly Catholic and Jewish Democrats. "This is the first time in my life I've brought diversity to a group," he quipped at one of his first committee meetings. On Judiciary, amid a scandal over suspected political firings of U.S. attorneys, Whitehouse joined criticisms of Attorney General Alberto Gonzales as partisan and disrespectful of prosecutorial autonomy. After Gonzales resigned under pressure, Whitehouse opposed the nomination of his successor, Michael Mukasey, for refusing to say whether a form of coercion called waterboarding was an illegal tactic against terrorism suspects. "America for centuries has been called a 'shining city on a hill.' We are a lamp to other nations," he said in challenging Mukasey's failure to take a stand. He also backed legislation to limit torture by intelligence agencies and their contractors.

In other areas, Whitehouse was more conciliatory with the Republicans. After a March 2007 visit to Iraq, he toned down his earlier criticism of the Bush administration and pointed to improved security in the country. He worked across the aisle with Sen. Tom Coburn, an Oklahoma Republican, to encourage stepped-up use of health information technology, including electronic prescriptions. On the environment panel, Whitehouse signed on to an ambitious bill to curb greenhouse gases that cause global warming.

In the presidential campaign, Whitehouse was an early backer of Democratic Sen. Hillary Rodham Clinton of New York, who easily won the Rhode Island primary.

FIRST DISTRICT

Patrick Kennedy (D)

Elected 1994, 8th term; b. July 14, 1967, Brighton, MA; home, Portsmouth; Providence Col., B.A. 1991; Catholic; single.

Elected Office: RI House of Reps., 1988–94.

DC Office: 407 CHOB, 20515, 202-225-4911; Fax: 202-225-3290; Web site: www.house.gov/patrickkennedy.

State Offices: Pawtucket, 401-729-5600.

Committees: *Appropriations* (15th of 37 D): Commerce, Justice, Science & Related Agencies; Labor, HHS, Education & Related Agencies; Military Construction, Veterans Affairs & Related Agencies. *Oversight & Government Reform* (15th of 24 D): Domestic Policy; National Security & Foreign Affairs.

Group Ratings

	ADA	ACLU	AFS	LCV	ITIC	NTU	COC	ACU	CFG	FRC
2008	100	100	100	77	86	6	59	0	0	0
2007	100	—	100	90	—	4	50	0	6	—

National Journal Ratings

	2007 LIB	—	2007 CONS		2008 LIB	—	2008 CONS
Economic	82%	—	0%		78%	—	20%
Social	89%	—	8%		82%	—	0%
Foreign	69%	—	29%		64%	—	36%
Composite	84%	—	16%		78%	—	22%

Key Votes of the 110th Congress

1. Increase minimum wage	Y	5. Share immigration data	N	9. Withdraw troops 8/08	Y
2. Expand SCHIP	Y	6. Foreign aid abortion ban	N	10. No operations in Iran	Y
3. Raise CAFE standards	Y	7. Ban gay bias in workplace	Y	11. Free trade with Peru	N
4. Bail out financial markets	Y	8. Repeal D.C. gun law	N	12. Overhaul FISA	N

Election Results

2008 general	Patrick Kennedy (D)	145,254	(69%)	($1,791,870)
	Jonathan Scott (R)	51,340	(24%)	($265)
	Kenneth Capalbo (I)	15,108	(7%)	
2008 primary	Patrick Kennedy (D)	unopposed		

Prior Winning Percentages: 2006 (69%); 2004 (64%); 2002 (60%); 2000 (67%); 1998 (67%); 1996 (69%); 1994 (54%)

Population		Race/Ethnicity		Work	
Pop. 2007:	527,865	White:	79.5%	Private:	81.3%
Change since 2000:	Up 0.7%	Black:	5.4%	Government:	12.8%
Urban:	95.5%	Hispanic:	9.8%	Self-employed:	5.7%
Rural:	4.5%	Asian:	2.2%	Blue collar:	21.3%
Area size:	565 sq. mi.	Native Am.:	0.3%	White collar:	60.8%
		Hawaiian:	0.0%	Khaki collar:	0.6%
Age		Two+ races:	1.7%	Other:	17.3%
Median age:	38.3 yrs.			Median income:	$52,102
More than 65 yrs:	14.7%	*Ancestry*		Median home value:	$298,500
Less than 18 yrs:	21.7%	Irish:	14.1%	Poverty:	12.4%
		Italian:	11.3%		
Education		French:	10.1%	**Military Veterans**	
H.S. grad:	81.1%			% of Pop:	9.9%
College grad:	29.7%				
Grad degree:	12.5%				

The 1st Congressional District is the eastern half of Rhode Island, divided from the state's only other congressional district by a boundary line that cuts through the state capital of Providence and then proceeds west and north to the Massachusetts-Connecticut border. It includes the eastern coast of Narragansett Bay and the small island chain off Rhode Island's coast. In recent years, once down-on-its-luck Providence has been revived, with a more accessible waterfront, active night life, and

2008 Presidential Vote
Obama (D) 148,176   (65%)
McCain (R)..............................75,806   (33%)

2004 Presidential Vote
Kerry (D)................................131,245   (62%)
Bush (R) 77,480   (36%)

Cook Partisan Voting Index: D + 13

restoration of neighborhoods around the state capitol. The district takes in much of the city, including the elite East Side and College Hill around Brown University. It also captures all of next-door Pawtucket, whose Slater Mill is known as the birthplace of the American Industrial Revolution. It is also home to Hasbro, the nation's second-largest toy company. The onetime textile-mill towns of the Blackstone Valley, Woonsocket and Central Falls, are also in the 1st, along with high-income Barrington and Bristol. To the south on the ocean is the old city of Newport, with its restored 18th-century houses and summer "cottages" that are more like mansions. Newport was once home to the America's Cup races and now hosts a famous jazz festival; it is also the site of the oldest synagogue in North America, where George Washington once told a congregation that the United States gives "to bigotry no sanction, to persecution no assistance." Ethnically, this district is the more French Canadian and the less Italian of Rhode Island's two congressional districts. Politically, it is strongly Democratic.

The representative from the 1st District is Patrick Kennedy, a Democrat first elected in 1994 and the son of Sen. Edward Kennedy, D-Mass. Patrick was born in 1967, during his father's fifth year in the Senate. His uncle John F. Kennedy was assassinated before Patrick was born. When Patrick was 2, his father's career was nearly ended by the scandal of Chappaquiddick. A young woman traveling with Sen. Kennedy in his car drowned after the car plunged off a bridge. Patrick grew up in McLean, Va., and had a somewhat troubled youth, spending time in a drug rehabilitation clinic in 1986. The next year, he enrolled in Providence College in Rhode Island at age 20, and almost immediately ran for public office. He beat longtime incumbent John Skeffington for a seat in the state House after Kennedy family members swarmed the tiny district to raise money for him. In 1991, his famous family again was a factor in his career, but not in a positive way. It was revealed that Patrick spent the Easter weekend in Palm Beach, Fla., with his father and cousin William Kennedy Smith, who was accused of raping a young woman during the trip. Smith was later acquitted. In 1994, when Republican U.S. Rep. Ron Machtley ran for governor, Kennedy decided to try for Machtley's seat. He had an attractive and energetic Republican opponent in Kevin Vigilante, a doctor who worked with handicapped orphans in Romania. But Kennedy had the advantages of party, money and the Kennedy name, and won 54%-46% in a Republican year.

In the House, Kennedy has a mostly liberal voting record with more-centrist views on national security issues. He has proven an excitable if not always eloquent debater. He has strongly supported gun control, an issue with family reverberations. He supported reauthorization of the assault weapons ban and, in 2003, criticized Democratic presidential candidate Howard Dean for his statements that new gun control laws should be left to the states. But on foreign policy, Kennedy has strongly opposed Fidel Castro; he voted for the 2000 bill that would have made 6-year-old refugee Elian Gonzalez a U.S. citizen and for keeping the travel ban on Cuba in 2003. Kennedy also voted for the 2002 Iraq war resolution, which his father opposed in the Senate. As the insurgency against U.S. forces grew, the younger Kennedy criticized President Bush's conduct of the war and said he had been deceived by the administration's statements on the presence of weapons of mass destruction in Iraq. He has voted several times for the "partial-birth" abortion ban, which abortion-rights forces opposed.

After easily winning re-election with 69% of the vote in 1996, Kennedy eyed a race for the Senate seat held by Republican John Chafee. He criticized Chafee sharply for several votes, but Chafee fought back gamely, returning often to the state, working hard on local projects, and his standing in the polls, never weak, slowly rose. Meanwhile, the harshness of Kennedy's attacks evidently grated; his job approval fell from 62% to 44% during the year. So Kennedy turned his focus to increasing his influence in the House. He struck up a friendship with Minority Leader Dick Gephardt and let it be known that he would support Gephardt for president against Al Gore in 2000. When Gephardt decided not to run, but rather to concentrate on helping Democrats win a House majority, he enlisted Kennedy as an ally. In November 1998, Gephardt named him chairman of the Democratic Congressional Campaign Committee, which helps elect Democrats to the House.

As DCCC chairman, Kennedy excelled not as a strategist but as a fundraiser. He traveled indefatigably around the country and made yeoman efforts to raise soft money, even while calling for campaign finance legislation that would outlaw the large, uncapped donations. As a result, the DCCC in 1999 and 2000 raised nearly $50 million in soft money, reaching parity with the National Republican Congressional Committee. The Republicans raised more hard money, but Kennedy vastly reduced the disadvantage his party labored under in the 1996 and 1998 elections. Sadly for Kennedy, Democrats were unsuccessful in their effort to achieve a net gain of six seats and a majority in the House.

Kennedy had spent only 40 days in the state while heading the DCCC. His standing with the folks at home was further eroded by a series of imbroglios. In March 2000, he shoved an airport security guard in Los Angeles, sending her backward and jostling the metal detector. A police complaint was filed, and during an informal hearing in May 2000, Kennedy apologized to the woman. It was also revealed that his insurance company had had to settle multiple damage claims made against Kennedy by owners of sailboats he had chartered. Kennedy won re-election with 67% of the vote, but his job-approval ratings in the district plummeted. In January 2001, his New Year's resolution seemed to be to make amends to his district. He successfully secured federal money for Rhode Island's military bases and for hospitals, schools and bridges. Kennedy joined Democratic Sen. Jack Reed in seeking to give permanent residence to the 10,000 Liberian refugees in Rhode Island, and in March 2006, he helped get the Appropriations Committee to vote for $50 million in extra aid for Liberia. No local cause seemed too small for Kennedy. He got $750,000 for the Norman Bird Sanctuary, $25,000 for computers at the Leon Matthieu Senior Center in Pawtucket and $4 million for the Blackstone River Bikeway. He sometimes presented the checks personally, and he was defiant as critics increasingly condemned such "earmarking" of federal funds for parochial projects. Handing a $150,000 check to the Smithfield police department, Kennedy said, "This is from me. This is one of those famous earmarks."

Kennedy, who has struggled through the years with manic depression, alcoholism and addiction to pain killers, made parity for mental health insurance coverage his signature national issue. In 2004, he co-sponsored with his father a bipartisan bill extending the 1996 parity law by eliminating unequal limits on numbers of inpatient days and outpatient days in insurance policies. But the dark cloud shadowing the Kennedy clan never seemed to permanently dissipate for Patrick. At 2:50 a.m. in May 2006, he drove his car into a security barrier outside the House office buildings. He told the Capitol police that he needed to vote, but the House had adjourned hours before. Kennedy said he had not been drinking but had become disoriented by prescription medicines he was taking. He checked himself into the Mayo Clinic for a one-month addiction treatment program. In June 2006, Kennedy pleaded guilty to driving under the influence of prescription medicines and was sentenced to one year of probation. This incident seems to have caused him no political problems in Rhode Island. A *Washington Post* reporter could find nary a constituent who said he was less likely to vote for him that year. One said, "Course not. You kidding me? Politicians drink like fish around here."

In the run-up to the 2006 election, some of his supporters even urged Kennedy to run against Lincoln Chafee, the son of John Chafee who'd been appointed to his father's seat after the elder Chafee died in office in 1999. But Kennedy declined to make the race, saying he wanted to keep working in the House and on the Appropriations Committee. He endorsed former Attorney General Sheldon Whitehouse, a Democrat who beat Chafee 54%-46%. With his father, Kennedy was an early and active supporter of Illinois Sen. Barack Obama for the 2008 Democratic presidential nomination. The following year brought further personal travails for the family. While Edward Kennedy fought for life against a malignant brain tumor, son Patrick in June 2009 again sought treatment at a rehab facility.

SECOND DISTRICT

Jim Langevin (D)

Elected 2000, 5th term; b. April 22, 1964, Warwick; home, Warwick; RI Col., B.A. 1990, Harvard U., M.P.A. 1994; Catholic; single.

Elected Office: RI House of Reps., 1988–94; RI sec. of state, 1994–2000.

DC Office: 109 CHOB, 20515, 202-225-2735; Fax: 202-225-5976; Web site: langevin.house.gov.

State Offices: Warwick, 401-732-9400.

Committees: *Armed Services* (14th of 36 D): Seapower & Expeditionary Forces; Strategic Forces; Terrorism, Unconventional Threats & Capabilities. *Budget* (19th of 24 D). *Intelligence (Select)* (9th of 13 D): Terrorism, Human Intelligence, Analysis & Counterintelligence; Technical & Tactical Intelligence.

Group Ratings

	ADA	ACLU	AFS	LCV	ITIC	NTU	COC	ACU	CFG	FRC
2008	100	82	100	92	86	7	61	0	4	5
2007	100	—	100	95	—	4	50	0	6	—

National Journal Ratings

	2007 LIB	—	2007 CONS		2008 LIB	—	2008 CONS
Economic	82%	—	0%		81%	—	15%
Social	77%	—	17%		75%	—	18%
Foreign	72%	—	27%		65%	—	32%
Composite	81%	—	19%		76%	—	24%

Key Votes of the 110th Congress

1. Increase minimum wage	Y	5. Share immigration data	N	9. Withdraw troops 8/08	Y
2. Expand SCHIP	Y	6. Foreign aid abortion ban	N	10. No operations in Iran	Y
3. Raise CAFE standards	Y	7. Ban gay bias in workplace	Y	11. Free trade with Peru	N
4. Bail out financial markets	Y	8. Repeal D.C. gun law	N	12. Overhaul FISA	Y

Election Results

2008 general	Jim Langevin (D)	158,416	(70%)	($679,026)
	Mark Zaccaria (R)	67,433	(30%)	($52,545)
2008 primary	Jim Langevin (D)	unopposed		

Prior Winning Percentages: 2006 (73%); 2004 (75%); 2002 (76%); 2000 (62%)

Population		Race/Ethnicity		Work	
Pop. 2007:	534,200	White:	78.6%	Private:	79.5%
Change since 2000:	Up 1.9%	Black:	4.1%	Government:	14.3%
Urban:	86.3%	Hispanic:	12.0%	Self-employed:	6.1%
Rural:	13.7%	Asian:	3.1%	Blue collar:	20.6%
Area size:	980 sq. mi.	Native Am.:	0.5%	White collar:	60.7%
Age		Hawaiian:	0.0%	Khaki collar:	0.1%
Median age:	38.3 yrs.	Two+ races:	1.3%	Other:	18.5%
More than 65 yrs:	13.0%	*Ancestry*		Median income:	$56,031
Less than 18 yrs:	22.9%	Italian:	17.4%	Median home value:	$281,600
Education		Irish:	16.1%	Poverty:	11.0%
H.S. grad:	84.2%	English:	10.4%	**Military Veterans**	
College grad:	29.1%			% of Pop:	10.4%
Grad degree:	10.5%				

The 2nd Congressional District is the western half of Rhode Island. Most of its population is concentrated in towns like working-class Cranston and more upscale Warwick, which, despite their British names, are inhabited mostly by people with Irish, Italian, French, and Portuguese surnames. The 2nd also includes the fastest-growing part of the state: South County, which is not an official place but the common name for Rhode Island south of East Greenwich. This area takes in the affluent suburbs

2008 Presidential Vote		
Obama (D)	148,394	(61%)
McCain (R)	89,586	(37%)
2004 Presidential Vote		
Kerry (D)	128,515	(57%)
Bush (R)	91,566	(41%)
Cook Partisan Voting Index:	D+9	

and beachfront communities along Narragansett Bay, the Kingston home of the University of Rhode Island, and the area around Westerly, where many residents work at the Electric Boat shipyards in Groton, Conn. The district also includes Rhode Island's rolling farmland, although there is not that much acreage, and the communities along the bay and the ocean, where many people still make their living building boats and catching fish. Although this remains a heavily Democratic district, George W. Bush cut the Democratic margin from 60%-33% in 2000 to 57%-41% in 2004. Democratic presidential nominee Barack Obama won the district with 61% in 2008.

The congressman from the 2nd District is Jim Langevin, a Democrat first elected in 2000. He grew up in Warwick and as a boy hoped to become an FBI agent. But in 1980, at age 16, when he was a police cadet in the Boy Scout Explorer program, he was shot by a police officer when a gun accidentally discharged. The bullet went through his upper back and throat and damaged the upper part of his spinal column; ever since, he has been a quadriplegic. Today, he is the first quadriplegic to serve in Congress. After the accident, Langevin received $2.2 million in a settlement with the city of Warwick, and although he disliked the attention it brought him, he says he became determined to do something meaningful with his life. He worked as an intern in the state House and for Democratic Sen. Claiborne Pell. In 1988, while still a student at Rhode Island College, he was elected to the state House of Representatives, where he styled himself as a reformer. After finishing his undergraduate degree, he went on to get a master's degree from the John F. Kennedy School of Government at Harvard. (Langevin's 1st District colleague, Rep. Patrick Kennedy, was also elected to the state House that year as a college student.) In 1994, Langevin was elected Rhode Island's secretary of state.

When Democratic Rep. Bob Weygand ran for the Senate in 2000, Langevin ran for his seat in the U.S. House. In a four-way contest for the Democratic nomination, Langevin's most strenuous opposition came from Kate Coyne-McCoy, the executive director of the Rhode Island Association of Social Workers who made an issue of Langevin's opposition to abortion rights. Although Langevin had support from many Democratic Party leaders and some unions, and won the party's endorsement at the April convention, Coyne-McCoy waged an aggressive campaign financed by unions, health care workers, and EMILY's List. "There's no such thing as being too liberal," Coyne-McCoy said. Langevin called her positions "unrealistic and extreme." He favored less stringent forms of gun control and said, "No one has to tell me how dangerous weapons can be." When Coyne-McCoy attacked him for opposing abortion rights, a position out of step with his party, Langevin responded, "Because of what happened to me, I became aware of how precious life is." He spoke often about the accident that paralyzed him. "Certainly, being disabled is part of who I am, but it doesn't define me." Langevin won the primary. His chief opposition in the general election came from Rodney Driver, nominee of the Conscience for Congress Party and a retired mathematics professor who spent $300,000 of his retirement savings on his campaign. Langevin won 62%-21%.

The House chamber in the U.S. Capitol was made wheelchair accessible for Langevin, with two of the fixed seats in the front removed to give him space to maneuver and to talk to colleagues. Later, at his urging, Speaker Nancy Pelosi agreed to more far-reaching structural changes to make all parts of the chamber, including the speaker's rostrum, accessible to the disabled.

Langevin has been liberal on economic issues and more centrist on cultural and foreign-policy issues, an apt reflection of his district's ethnic communities. In 2005, he was one of only three House Democrats from New England to join conservatives in the controversial case of Terri Schiavo, a severely brain-damaged Florida woman at the center of a court battle over removing her life-sustaining feeding tube. But he was back in the liberal fold on the issue of embryonic-stem-cell research, opposed by anti-abortion groups because it relies on surplus embryos from in vitro fertilization. Langevin took the view that the research might alleviate suffering from certain diseases and injuries. He protested President Bush's opposition to federal funding for such research by inviting Dana Reeve, the widow of actor and spinal repair research activist Christopher Reeve, to Bush's 2005 State of the Union address. In 2007, he opposed Bush's veto of the stem-cell-research bill and was criticized by the Roman Catholic bishop of Providence.

Langevin has sponsored several gun control bills, and he has called universal health care coverage his overriding priority. In 2008, he co-sponsored with Rep. Christopher Shays, R-Conn., a plan for national health care coverage for all Americans that would resemble the one provided to federal employees. An increase in the payroll tax would finance the program. "The reality is we can't wait another day" to overhaul the existing system, he said. In 2006, Langevin won passage of a law that established a respite program that aids caregivers of individuals with special needs. He introduced the bill in 2002 but had difficultly advancing it in the GOP-controlled Congress until he asked a Republican, Rep. Michael Ferguson of New Jersey, to become a co-sponsor.

In the 110th Congress (2007–08), Langevin chaired the Homeland Security subcommittee on emerging threats and cyber security, where he took a special interest in biological warfare and prepared a report to assist the next president in assessing the threat of cyber-terrorism. The House passed his resolution calling for greater awareness of computer security. On the Intelligence Committee, Langevin took a more conservative approach than many other Democrats by supporting the Bush administration's electronic surveillance program.

Langevin had the opportunity to run for Senate in 2006. One statewide poll in early 2005 showed him leading Republican Sen. Lincoln Chafee, and both state and national Democrats urged him to consider challenging Chafee. But abortion-rights groups objected to Langevin's candidacy. In March 2005, Langevin announced that he would not run for the Senate, though he did not rule out a later run for statewide office. Democrat Sheldon Whitehouse, the former state attorney general, challenged Chafee and won. Langevin decided to run again for his House seat in 2006. But it was not a clear shot at re-election.

Brown University political scientist Jennifer Lawless challenged Langevin in the primary. Lawless, who had recently moved to Rhode Island, drew support from national abortion-rights groups and ran an aggressive and negative campaign that hit Langevin hard on his abortion stance and the war in Iraq. Lawless and Langevin ran dueling television ads on abortion. Lawless's spot featured a doctor talking about rape, and cited 27 votes that Langevin cast "against a woman's right to choose." Langevin countered that he supported abortion rights in sexual assault cases. Lawless also accused Langevin of not mounting stronger opposition to the Iraq war and compared Langevin with Sen. Joe Lieberman of Connecticut, who lost his Democratic primary in August 2006 because of his support for the war. Langevin in December 2005 voted against a proposed timetable for withdrawing U.S. troops, but said he supported the redeployment of U.S. troops from Iraq. "The big difference between me and Joe Lieberman is that Joe Lieberman voted for the war and continued to defend it, and I voted against the war and have been a constant critic," Langevin told the *Providence Journal*. Langevin raised more than double what Lawless did, and wound up defeating her 62%-38% in the September primary. In the general election, Republicans failed to field a candidate in the district for the first time in 149 years.

★ SOUTH CAROLINA ★

South Carolina, at times beleaguered and under attack, stands proud but not untroubled, a state that has made much progress but still has some distance to go. Within living memory, South Carolina looked like an underdeveloped country. Aside from a relatively small pool of very wealthy people, it was among the poorest of states, with income levels less than half the national average and with high levels of illiteracy and disease. The state was founded by planters from Barbados and even today there are reminders of the West Indies—the semitropical climate, the lush foliage and trademark palmettos, and the billions in damage from hurricanes. South Carolina started off with a plantation economy built on the swampy Lowcountry below the Fall Line, where 18th and 19th century planters built rice paddies and cultivated exotic crops like indigo in the days before cotton was king. The great wealth of these Lowcountry planters was destroyed by the Civil War which they, more than any other Southerners, provoked. But their pride and way of life continued as did that of former slaves. As late as 1940, 43% of South Carolinians were black, most living in conditions inconceivable today. South Carolina's economic growth started only in the 1920s, with the low-wage textile industry. Mills were built in the Upstate region northwest of Columbia, hiring poor whites (never blacks) from the hardscrabble farms in the area. Politics remained a rough business, with harsh appeals to racial fear and economic envy, and with limited participation. In 1940, just 99,000 South Carolinians voted for president, 96% of them Democratic, the highest Democratic percentage in the nation. In the 1946 Democratic primary, the year Strom Thurmond was elected governor, only 271,000 people voted in a state of more than 2 million.

In the last half-century, this once underdeveloped state has joined the First World. Personal incomes have risen dramatically and are near the national average, and factory productivity rose 59%. Poverty fell sharply. Health standards are as good as those in the rest of the nation. Educational achievement still lags, though not nearly as much as before, with 80% of white and 65% of black adults classified as high school graduates. Homeownership is well above the national average. Back in the 1970s, much of South Carolina's economy depended on the military bases clustered around Charleston and on the big textile mills around Greenville and Spartanburg. Then South Carolina became the most aggressive state in the South in attracting new industry. It advertised its business climate, with the nation's lowest rates of unionization, its low taxes, its willingness to give tax breaks and a $300 to $1,500 job creation income tax credit. From 1960 to 1990, international investment in the state grew from $80 million to $16.4 trillion. It enticed French and German firms to set up major operations in the Piedmont and the Lowcountry, a process capped when BMW in 1992 built its first U.S. assembly plant in Spartanburg. Nearby are big Michelin and Fuji Photo plants. Vought Aircraft and Alenia Aeronautica's airplane plant in North Charleston is building aft parts of fuselages for Boeing's successful 787 Dreamliner. Hilton Head and the Grand Strand around Myrtle Beach bring in millions of tourists every year, along with thousands of new residents, many of them affluent retirees. In Columbia, the University of South Carolina has been building a big Innovista research area in Columbia's Congaree Vista. Many of South Carolina's military bases have long since been closed, and much of the textile work has migrated elsewhere. Lower-income workers have gravitated to the poultry industry, the state's No. 1 agricultural product. Economically and culturally, South Carolina has been part of the booming South Atlantic region from Maryland to Florida, filling up with new retirement condominiums, time shares (it ranks No.2 in the country in time shares), factories, office buildings, and giant shopping centers. It grew robustly for two decades, though not as rapidly as neighboring Georgia and North Carolina. From 2000 to 2008, its population increased 18%, with two-thirds of that from internal migration. But some of that growth proved to be a bubble, and by 2008, South Carolina was throttled by the national recession, with the highest unemployment in the South Atlantic.

As South Carolina's economy was transformed, the state slowly, sometimes grudgingly, overcame its heritage of slavery and racial segregation. Starting in the 1950s, fewer people were kept from voting by the poll tax, and turnout surged as South Carolina became competitive in the presidential elections of 1952, 1956 and 1960. Clemson University was peaceably desegregated during the governorship of Democrat Ernest Hollings (1959–62). Most South Carolina whites opposed integration, but not with the violence of their counterparts in Alabama and Mississippi. Then, the Civil Rights Act of 1964 and the Voting Rights Act of 1965 ended legal segregation of public accommodations and workplaces and brought blacks into the electorate. This changed the political balance. Republican Sen. Strom Thurmond, who staged a record-setting filibuster of the 1957 Civil Rights Act, started appointing black staffers and a black federal judge in the late 1960s and early 1970s. But politics still cleaves the electorate along racial lines. In 2008, South Carolina whites voted 73%-26% for Republican presidential nominee John McCain and blacks voted 96%-4% for Democratic nominee Barack Obama. For several years, South Carolina grappled with a controversy over the Confederate battle flag, flown over the state Capitol since 1962. Successive governors—Republican David Beasley and Democrat Jim Hodges—favored taking it down. The NAACP organized a boycott of the state. Finally in May 2000, the Legislature voted to fly the flag

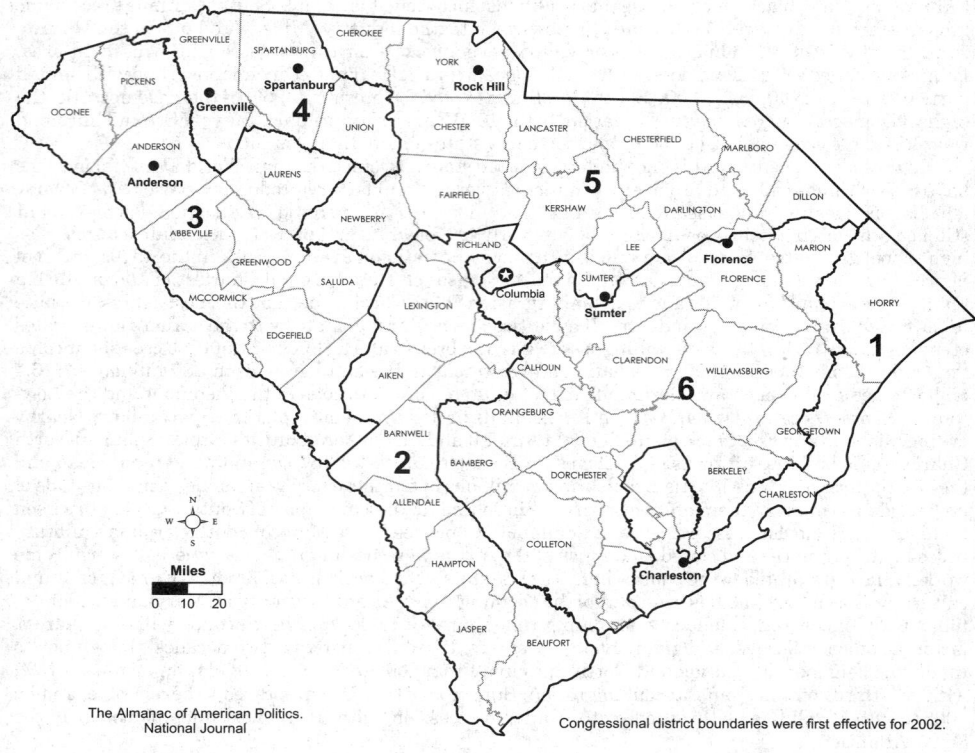

GREENVILLE
SPARTANBURG
CHEROKEE
PICKENS
YORK
OCONEE
● Greenville
Spartanburg
Rock Hill
4
ANDERSON
UNION
CHESTER
LANCASTER
CHESTERFIELD
MARLBORO
● Anderson
LAURENS
5
DARLINGTON
DILLON
FAIRFIELD
KERSHAW
3
ABBEVILLE
NEWBERRY
RICHLAND
LEE
● Florence
MARION
GREENWOOD
SALUDA
SUMTER
FLORENCE
MCCORMICK
LEXINGTON
☆ Columbia
HORRY
Sumter
EDGEFIELD
CALHOUN
CLARENDON
1
AIKEN
6
WILLIAMSBURG
BARNWELL
ORANGEBURG
GEORGETOWN
2
BAMBERG
DORCHESTER
BERKELEY
ALLENDALE
CHARLESTON
COLLETON
HAMPTON
Charleston
JASPER
BEAUFORT

N
W E
S

Miles
0 10 20

The Almanac of American Politics.
National Journal

Congressional district boundaries were first effective for 2002.

not from the Capitol, but from a 30-foot pole on the Capitol grounds, and a monument to African-American history was opened nearby. The state NAACP was still not satisfied, and continued the boycott.

Until the 1960s, South Carolina was an inward-looking state, with few people except military personnel moving in. That has changed as the economy has grown. Most of the newcomers are white, with conservative attitudes but less feeling for the state's ancient traditions. Only in the last few years has there been significant immigration. In 2008, South Carolina's population was 29% black, far below the near-majority of the 1940s, and 4% Hispanic. The fastest growth in recent years has been in coastal resort areas around Hilton Head and Myrtle Beach and in suburban counties outside Charleston and just south of Charlotte, N.C. This demographic change has moved South Carolina politically toward the Republicans. But that change might not have occurred without the efforts of two individuals. One was Thurmond, who had voted for Franklin D. Roosevelt at the 1932 Democratic National Convention, but who switched to the Republican Party in September 1964 and provided critical votes to nominate Richard Nixon at the 1968 Republican National Convention. South Carolina voted for Republican Barry Goldwater in 1964 and Nixon in 1968 and has only once voted for a Democrat since, Jimmy Carter in 1976, by a narrow margin. The other individual was Carroll Campbell, elected governor in 1986 and 1990, who with the aid of the late Lee Atwater built a Republican Party capable of electing statewide officials and majorities in the Legislature. In 1988, Campbell and Atwater, by then George H. W. Bush's campaign manager, set up the early Republican primary, on the Saturday before Super Tuesday, which enabled Bush to clinch the Republican nomination that year. It did the same for Republican Bob Dole in 1996 and, against John McCain's strong challenge, for Republican George W. Bush in 2000. In 1989, Campbell and Atwater seemed to be Thurmond's heirs. But Atwater died of a brain tumor at 39 in 1991 and Campbell died in 2005 at age 65.

South Carolina's other senator for years, Democrat Ernest Hollings, retired in 2004 after 38 years, 36 of them as a junior senator—a record. South Carolina politics now belongs to a new generation. In 2002, former U.S. Rep. Mark Sanford, at odds with many organization Republicans, beat Democratic Gov. Jim Hodges 53%-47%, and Rep. Lindsey Graham won the race to succeed Thurmond, 54%-44%. In 2004, President George W. Bush carried the state 58%-41%, Republican Rep. Jim DeMint beat Democrat Inez Tenenbaum for Hollings' Senate seat 54%-44%, and Republicans held their majority in the state Senate and gained one seat in the state House. Sanford was re-elected 55%-45% in 2006, and Republicans held onto their legislative majorities. The Republican tide ebbed a bit in 2008, when McCain carried the state by just 54%-45%. Graham was re-elected to the Senate comfortably and Republicans lost two seats in the state House. Sanford is term-limited in 2010, and was the subject of a sensational sex scandal in 2009.

Population		Household Income		Work	
Pop. 2007:	4,330,933	Under $15k:	16.5%	Private:	76.8%
State rank:	24th of 50	$15k to $50k:	40.9%	Government:	16.9%
Change since 2000:	Up 7.9%	$50k to $100k:	29.6%	Self-employed:	6.1%
Urban:	59.4%	$100k to $150k:	10.9%	Unemployment (3-yr. average):	4.7%
Rural:	40.6%	Over $150k:	2.2%	Poverty:	15.6%
Native of state:	60.8%	Median income:	$42,405	Blue collar:	26.9%
Not a citizen:	2.9%			White collar:	55.5%
Area size:	32,020 sq. mi.	**Home Value**		Khaki collar:	1.2%
		Under $100k:	39.8%	Other:	16.4%
Most populous cities		$100k to $300k:	47.6%		
1. Columbia	118,786	$300k to $500k:	8.0%	**Age**	
2. Charleston	110,866	$500k to $1 mil:	3.5%	Median age:	37.0 yrs.
3. North Charleston	84,491	Over $1 million:	1.2%	More than 65 yrs:	12.8%
4. Mount Pleasant	67,545	Median:	$122,600	Less than 18 yrs:	24.2%

Race/Ethnicity				Military Veterans		Registered Voters in 2008	
White:	65.3%	*Language*		% of Pop:	12.2%	No party registration	
Black:	28.5%	English:	94.1%	*Veterans by Period*		Voter turnout:	1,920,969
Hispanic:	3.6%	Spanish:	3.6%	WWII and before:	10.0%	Turnout as % of	
Asian:	1.1%	Asian:	0.7%	Korea:	9.9%	voting age:	56.3%
Native Am.:	0.3%	Other		Vietnam:	32.8%	**General Assembly**	
Hawaiian:	0.0%	European	1.4%	Gulf (pre-2001):	13.7%	Senate:	19 D 27 R
Two+ races:	1.1%	**Education**		Gulf (post-2001):	8.7%	House:	53 D 71 R
Ancestry		H.S. grad:	81.4%	Peace time:	24.9%		
USA:	10.9%	College grad:	22.8%				
German:	8.9%	Grad degree:	7.9%				
English:	8.4%						

Presidential politics　In presidential general elections, South Carolina has been reliably Republican for a long time. It was the only Deep South state to vote for Richard Nixon over George Wallace in 1968 and since then has voted Democratic only once, for Jimmy Carter in 1976. In the 2004 general election, Democratic vice presidential candidate John Edwards did return to his hometown, Seneca, S.C., but took care not to linger long.

The presidential primaries are another matter. South Carolina has been important, indeed decisive, in determining the Republican nomination since its 1988 primary, and, with an early spot on the calendar, played a major role in the Democratic race in 2008. Back in 1980, the state Republican chairman scheduled the South Carolina primary early, to help Ronald Reagan, and in 1987, GOP operative Lee Atwater craftily scheduled the Republican primary for the Saturday before Super Tuesday, a collection of mostly Southern primaries that Democrats hoped would move their party toward choosing a moderate Southerner. Instead, South Carolina moved Republicans toward choosing a

2008 Presidential Vote		
McCain (R)............................1,034,896	(54%)
Obama (D) 862,449	(45%)

2008 Democratic Presidential Primary		
Obama (D) 294,898	(55%)
Clinton (D).............................140,990	(26%)
Edwards (D).............................93,801	(18%)

2008 Republican Presidential Primary		
McCain (R).............................147,686	(33%)
Huckabee (R) 132,943	(30%)
Thompson (R) 69,651	(16%)
Romney (R) 68,142	(15%)

2004 Presidential Vote		
Bush (R)................................937,974	(58%)
Kerry (D)................................661,699	(41%)

moderate Southern Republican, George H.W. Bush of Texas, who won a 49%-21%-19% victory here over Bob Dole and Pat Robertson, a foretaste of the Southern sweep that clinched his nomination four days later. Democrats chose their delegates by caucus. A Democratic primary would have had an electorate about 50% African-American and would surely have produced a victory for civil rights leaders and South Carolina native Jesse Jackson, which would not have been helpful to the party in state elections. In 1992, Bush beat Pat Buchanan 67%-26%, squashing Buchanan's claims to Southern support. Democrats held a primary the same day, which Bill Clinton won with 63% of the vote. In 1996, former Gov. Carroll Campbell and Gov. David Beasley led a grass-roots campaign that gave Dole, after his disappointing showings elsewhere, an impressive 45%-29% victory over Buchanan. And in 2000 Campbell and Beasley, both by then ex-governors, supported George W. Bush, as he beat John McCain 53%-42%. Democrats chose their delegates by caucus in 1996 and 2000.

In 2004, Democrats held a primary on February 2, a week after New Hampshire, and attracted 292,000 voters, only about half of what Republicans attracted in 2000. Native son Edwards won 45% of the vote, more than John Kerry's 30%, but perhaps not the landslide he wanted. He had campaigned hard in South Carolina and spent little time in Oklahoma, which voted the same day; there he lost to Wesley Clark of Arkansas by 1,300 votes. That kept Clark in the race and gave Edwards a Southern rival who probably cost him some votes.

Presidential primaries in South Carolina are conducted by the state's two political parties, not by state government, and they can choose to hold them on different days. For 2008, the Republicans first chose February 2, the earliest date under the national party's rules and in the Atwater tradition held on a Saturday to set an example for the bunch of states voting the following Tuesday. But after Florida moved to schedule its primary on January 29, South Carolina Republicans responded by moving their primary to January 19 to protect the state's first-in-the-South status. They were careful to act in tandem with New Hampshire, which moved its date backward from January 22 to, finally, January 8. On the other side, the Democratic National Committee chose South Carolina as the only state allowed to hold a pre-February 5 primary, except of course for New Hampshire, and South Carolina Democrats picked January 26.

Candidates started coming into the state early. Sen. Lindsey Graham once again backed fellow Republican Sen. John McCain strongly. Republican Sen. Jim DeMint endorsed Mitt Romney, and Gov. Mark Sanford, to the consternation of the McCain camp, stayed neutral. On the Democratic side, the most coveted endorsement was that of Rep. James Clyburn, the House majority whip and an African-American who was an obvious force in a primary whose electorate was likely to be about 50% black. Candidates and surrogates thronged to his 16th annual fish fry in Columbia in April, where the crowd consumed 1,200 pounds of whiting, but Clyburn frustrated all sides by staying determinedly neutral right through the January 26 election.

McCain, wary of a repetition of unfounded charges that he fathered a black child that were spread anonymously against him in the 2000 campaign, did not flinch from returning, even when his campaign was at low ebb. Romney spent large sums and made frequent trips to the state. Mike Huckabee, fresh from his victory in the Iowa caucuses, looked forward to competing in another state with a large evangelical Protestant population and hoped to expand his appeal beyond that base. Fred Thompson, doubtful of his chances in earlier states, decided to stake his campaign on this seemingly friendly turf. Reporters continued to bring up the issue of the Confederate battle flag. McCain and Romney opposed the flying of the flag, while Huckabee said, "You don't like people from outside the state coming in and telling you what to do with your flag." McCain and Romney targeted the Lowcountry, Huckabee and Thompson the Upstate region and rural areas. South Carolina proved a turning point for each of the campaigns. Turnout was 446,000 people, down 22% from 2000.

Romney, having failed to win either Iowa or New Hampshire and apparently not catching on in the Lowcountry, flew to Nevada on the Thursday before the Saturday primary. He finished fourth, with 15% of the vote, and a few hours later won the Nevada caucuses, in which half the voters were Mormons like him. Thompson, for all his folksiness and experience, failed to break Huckabee's connection with religious conservatives, and finished third with 16%. After the results were in, he quietly left the race. At the top of the ballot, McCain finished ahead of Huckabee by only 33%-30%. Huckabee got 43% from evangelical Protestants, but few votes from everyone else. McCain carried the Lowcountry and the Columbia media market, beating Romney in affluent suburbs. But his percentage was lower than in the two-candidate 2000 primary. Had Thompson not been on the ballot, Huckabee would probably have won. But the same could be said of Romney, and there were more votes cast for McCain and Romney than for Huckabee and Thompson. In any case, this narrow victory not only kept McCain in the race but did much to make him the frontrunner, as he became after winning the Florida primary on January 29.

The Democrats had a three-candidate contest in South Carolina, their last in the primary season. Edwards, who was born in South Carolina, visited the state most frequently and assured voters he understood their plight. Obama visited also and hoped that African-American voters would support him. Hillary Rodham Clinton did not concede black votes and particularly targeted black women. This was the first contest with significant numbers of African-American voters, and observers watched the polls closely. At the outset, black voters in South Carolina seemed split about evenly between Obama and Clinton. But by mid-December, Obama started getting more support, and his victory in the Iowa caucuses convinced many skeptical blacks that whites would vote for him and therefore he had a serious chance to win. By early January, Obama appeared to be sweeping African-American voters. Former President Bill Clinton, campaigning for his wife, seemed desperate to turn things around. He remarked that Obama's claim to have strongly opposed the Iraq war from the beginning was "a fairy tale," and accused the Obama campaign of coercing voters in the Nevada caucus (held before South Carolina Democrats voted). Clyburn, while careful to stay neutral, criticized the former president, saying, "He needs to chill a little bit." The comment may have sent a signal to black voters that Clyburn leaned to Obama, who was also helped by the appearance of television personality Oprah Winfrey at a rally in Columbia.

Turnout in the Democratic primary on January 26 was 532,000 voters, 19% more than in the Republican contest, though still below Republican turnout in 2000. Obama won a crushing victory with 55% of the vote, winning 78% among blacks and a not inconsiderable 24% among whites. Obama carried all but two counties at opposite ends of the state. Hillary Clinton was second, with 26% of the vote. She won about 36% among whites and 19% among blacks, and she carried Horry County (the Grand Strand). Edwards was a poor third, with only 18% in the state where he was born. He carried his boyhood home of Oconee County and nothing else. He won about 40% among whites and virtually nothing among blacks. His third place finish in the one primary state that he'd won four years earlier ended Edwards's six-year career as a presidential candidate. Clinton, in contrast, was able to hold on, but with the knowledge that she was likely to lose the lion's share of African-American votes, and therefore every primary in which the electorate was heavily or majority black, from here on out. Had Obama not run, she probably would have swept black voters everywhere.

Few national political reporters returned to South Carolina after the January contests. While North Carolina was seriously contested in the fall and actually voted for Obama, and Georgia proved to be quite close indeed, McCain carried South Carolina by the comfortable but not huge spread of 54%-45%. Whites voted nearly 3-to-1 for McCain, including young whites. Blacks voted 96%-4% for Obama. Although the Obama campaign did not target South Carolina, many blacks were inspired to vote. First-time voters went 59%-40% for Obama. Whether this will permanently improve Democrats' position in the state is unclear; the exit poll showed party identification 41%-38% Republican.

Congressional districting

111th Congress Lineup	
4 R	2 D
110th Congress Lineup	
4 R	2 D

After the 2000 census, control of the South Carolina redistricting process was split between Democratic Gov. Jim Hodges and the Republican-controlled Legislature. In September 2001, the Legislature passed a plan with no major changes. It expanded the black-majority 6th District, which extends from Columbia to Charleston and includes much of the Lowcountry and Pee Dee area. Hodges vetoed the plan and Republicans failed to override. A three-judge federal court took over, and in March 2002 decided on a plan that smoothed out the lines considerably and reduced the black percentage in the 6th District to 57%.

South Carolina is expected to gain a seat from the 2010 census, though if the recession reduces growth, it might not. Republicans enter the 2010 election cycle with the governorship and substantial legislative majorities, and are likely to retain them. In addition, there may be pressure to create a second black-majority district, though that would require boundaries considerably more convoluted than the current plan. The state's highest-growth areas—metro Charleston and Hilton Head, the Grand Strand, the exurbs of metro Charlotte—tend to vote Republican.

Governor

Mark Sanford (R)

Elected 2002, term expires Jan. 2011, 2nd term; b. May 28, 1960, Ft. Lauderdale, FL; home, Charleston; Furman U., B.A. 1983; U. of VA, M.B.A. 1988; Episcopalian; married (Jenny); 4 children.

Elected Office: U.S. House of Reps., 1994–2000.

Professional Career: Real estate investor, 1988–92; Owner, Norton & Sanford real estate investment firm, 1992–2002.

Office: P.O. Box 12267, Columbia, 29211, 803-734-2100; Fax: 803-734-5167; Web site: scgovernor.com.

Election Results

2006 general	Mark Sanford (R)	601,868	(55%)
	Tommy Moore (D)	489,076	(45%)
2006 primary	Mark Sanford (R)	160,238	(65%)
	Oscar Lovelace (R)	87,043	(35%)

Prior Winning Percentages: 2002 (53%)

Republican Mark Sanford was elected governor of South Carolina in 2002 and re-elected in 2006. He was badly damaged by a 2009 scandal in which the married Sanford admitted abandoning his duties for several days to rendezvous with his lover in Argentina.

Sanford grew up in Fort Lauderdale, Fla., the son of a heart surgeon. The family spent summers and vacations on a 3,000-acre farm in Beaufort County, once known as Coosaw Plantation, and moved there permanently when Mark was 18. He graduated from high school in South Carolina and from Furman University in Greenville and the University of Virginia business school. He worked in real estate investment in New York, where he met his wife, Jenny, a Midwesterner. In 1992, he started a real estate investment firm in Charleston. He lives in the town of Sullivan's Island at the entrance to Charleston Harbor, and is perpetually tanned from windsurfing. In 1994, 1st District incumbent Rep. Arthur Ravenel ran for governor, and Sanford, with no political experience, ran for the U.S. House. His campaign was managed by his wife and financed by $100,000 of his own money. He campaigned as an outsider, and pledged to serve only three terms, to take no political action committee money, to vote for no tax increases and to refuse any salary increase until the federal budget was balanced. He finished second in the primary and then won the runoff 52%-48%. He carried the general election with 66% of the vote. In the House, Sanford voted consistently against spending increases and pork barrel spending, including projects for South Carolina.

After honoring his term-limit pledge, Sanford in 2002 was back in the state and launched a campaign for governor. Well-known and well-liked in Charleston but unknown in the rest of the state, he set about getting better acquainted. His opponent in the Republican primary was Lt. Gov. Bob Peeler, originally from Cherokee County east of Greenville-Spartanburg, who was traveling around the state in his trademark red pickup truck. Peeler had backed George W. Bush for president in 2000 and was supported by most of the state Republican establishment, although former Gov. Carroll Campbell endorsed Sanford. Attorney General Charlie Condon, who had won much publicity from his conservative stands on hot-button issues, also got into the primary contest. The three Republicans called for major changes in taxes and spending. Sanford proposed phasing out the income tax over 18 years and making up for fluctuations in revenues with a transition fund established by a sales tax on gas. He also called for government vouchers for private school tuition. Sanford raised more money and ran more ads than the other two. Peeler led in polls in the run-up to the June 11 primary, and many expected that Condon would cut into Sanford's Lowcountry base. Instead, Sanford finished first with 39% of the vote, just ahead of Peeler's 38%; Condon was far behind with 16%. Still, Sanford carried only 11 of 46 counties, and it was expected that more of the culturally conservative Condon's votes would go to Peeler in the June 25 runoff. But the race was not defined ideologically. Peeler criticized Sanford for votes on the breast cancer stamp, military housing and supporting military action; Sanford said these issues were taken out of context and were "negative." Sanford won 60%-40%.

In the general election, Sanford challenged Democratic Gov. Jim Hodges, who had upset Republican incumbent David Beasley in 1998. Hodges' chief plank was a lottery to pay for college scholarships, and a call for more funding for school construction and all-day kindergarten. Hodges also played a major role in getting the Legislature to vote in 2000 to take the Confederate flag off the dome of the Capitol and put it up on the grounds, which became controversial among people who favored prominent display of the flag. Hodges' biggest success was passage of his lottery bill in 2001. His job ratings were not particularly high, and Republicans were confident they could beat him in this largely Republican state.

In the campaign, Hodges played up his modest background and called Sanford a wealthy Charleston plantation owner from south Florida. But Hodges had embarrassments of his own. One of his ads attacked Sanford for having voted "against programs for disabled kids." But then it was revealed that Hodges had transferred $300,000 from a fund for emotionally disturbed children to the operating account for the governor's office. Hodges was also embarrassed by his failure to keep an oft-repeated promise to block the shipment of spent plutonium to the Savannah River Site for reprocessing. In 2002, a federal judge ordered Hodges not to block the shipment, and Hodges backed down on his promise to stand in the road in front of the convoy if necessary. Hodges had more money, but Sanford seemed to attract more positive attention. Dressed usually in khakis and a plaid shirt, he emphasized change and getting away from politics as usual. In November, Sanford won 53%-47%. Metro Charleston and the coast, which had voted for Hodges in 1998, this time went 55%-45% for Sanford, as did metro Columbia-Aiken. The Greenville area gave Sanford 60%. Hodges carried the rest of the state by only 55%-45%.

As governor, Sanford defied convention. He instituted an open-door policy that allowed citizens to line up for five-minute chats with the governor. Sanford wondered out loud whether he should quit the Air Force Reserve, which he joined in 2002 just prior to running for governor, lest he be called to active duty. He decided to stay in, and he was not called up, although he did spend two weeks in training.

He called on the Legislature for major changes: abolishing the elective offices of secretary of state, treasurer, comptroller, adjutant general, superintendent of education and agriculture commissioner, and putting their functions under the governor; putting the state universities, accustomed to lobbying for themselves, under a single board of regents; and enacting tax-paid private school vouchers for children in failing schools. Sanford managed to lower the drunken-driving blood alcohol threshold to .08, to win campaign finance changes that added more transparency and to bring the Division of Motor Vehicles directly under the governor's office. But he failed to enact any of his major initiatives. That was the beginning of his strained relationship with the Republican-controlled Legislature. South Carolina's governorship is constitutionally weak and the Legislature is relatively strong. Sanford struggled to work within these confines. After the failure of his plan in 2003 to swap a phaseout of the income tax for an increase in the cigarette tax, Sanford promised to visit districts of lawmakers from both parties who did not support the plan and he vetoed bills that were routinely signed in the past. He angered legislators by commissioning a poll to measure his personal popularity against theirs. In 2004, Sanford again pursued an ambitious agenda, calling for workers' compensation reform, an increase in the number of charter schools, and a 15% reduction in income taxes, offset by a 5-cent sales tax on lottery tickets and a 61-cent tax increase on a pack of cigarettes. The General Assembly, primarily the Senate, again balked at his proposals, and Sanford did little to persuade them. He issued 106 budget vetoes to cut spending and the House overrode 105 of them. He also vetoed an economic development bill offering tax incentives to biotech and medical research companies. Though he once supported the economic development initiative, he objected to various projects that legislators tacked onto the final bill. The Legislature overwhelmingly overrode his veto. He angered legislators in the final week of the five-month legislative session by sneaking two piglets into the State House to symbolize the legislative appetite for pork barrel spending. He said the pigs' names were "Pork" and "Barrel." The pigs defecated on the carpet. But the public, it turned out, loved the stunt.

In 2006, Sanford ended up vetoing the entire budget, rather than utilize his line-item veto power. Legislators were faced with the dilemma of either overriding the veto or shutting down state government. They chose to override the veto. *Time* magazine in November 2005 named Sanford one of the three worst governors in the nation, a stinging rebuke that listed as evidence Standard & Poor's lowering of South Carolina's bond rating, a 6.3% unemployment rate and the state's losing bid for a $500 million Airbus plant. Sanford dismissed the story as the product of a liberal magazine, and pointed to *National Review* article that had earlier described him as "one of the best new governors in the country." The libertarian Cato Institute had also given him high ratings for his fiscal record. But the *Time* story nonetheless provided fuel to his many critics on the eve of his 2006 re-election campaign.

Sanford drew opposition in the primary from physician Oscar Lovelace, who criticized Sanford's inability to get along with the Legislature. Sanford won 65%-35%, but there were troubling signs. He lost two counties, including the Republican stronghold of Lexington County where voters were angered over his veto of a bill that would have created a new heart surgery center there. More ominously, the underfunded Lovelace had won more than a third of the primary vote. Republican hostility to Sanford still ran high weeks after the primary. Republican state Sen. Jake Knotts of Lexington County sought to get on the November ballot as a petition candidate, a maneuver which, by splitting the Republican vote, might have led to a Democratic victory. But in mid-July he dropped his bid.

The Democratic nominee was state Sen. Tommy Moore of Aiken County, a veteran legislative dealmaker who touted his ability to bring people together. Sanford framed the race to the *The State* newspaper as a choice between his outsider approach and the state's business-as-usual legislative culture.

"I've not been a part of Columbia, and the way that things work around here. At times, that's been to my detriment." Moore called for increased economic development in rural areas and he focused on public education, although without much specificity. Sanford called for government restructuring, spending restraint, tax cuts and merit pay for teachers. Sanford raised over $8 million, compared to Moore's $3 million. On Election Day, Sanford won 55%-45%. Moore won in the Midlands and metro Columbia, but Sanford carried his Lowcountry base and won large margins in the Greenville and Spartanburg Upstate areas. He managed to win Lexington County 59%-41, but with a diminished share from 2002 when he won 66%.

This was not the kind of sweeping victory that draws notice outside a state's border, but Sanford's fiscal record was popular with some national conservatives and there was still mention of him as a possible presidential candidate in 2008. Sanford made no moves in that direction. Sanford continued to raise his national profile during his second term, appearing as a frequent guest on cable news channels, and rumors persisted that he was in the mix to be Republican presidential candidate John McCain's running mate. Then, during a July 2008 interview on CNN's "Late Edition," host Wolf Blitzer asked Sanford for distinctions between McCain and President George W. Bush on the economy. Sanford drew a blank for several seconds, before citing the North American Free Trade Agreement as a difference between the two. Blitzer pointed out Bush and McCain agreed on free trade. The clip of the Sanford's flub replayed for days, probably sinking Sanford's chances of joining the ticket. In 2009, he took over the chairmanship of the Republican Governors Association.

The 2007 budget session with legislators was no smoother than their past negotiations. Sanford proposed a $6.5 billion budget that allocated more money for schools but also included an increase in cigarette taxes and $205 million in income tax cuts. Notable were his $92 million cuts to state health and education research programs. More than a third of his budget was dedicated to paying down state debt. Both the state House and Senate drastically slashed the income tax breaks Sanford wanted, and essentially ignored Sanford's pleas for fiscal discipline, sending him a $7.4 billion budget full of money for local projects. Sanford sent back 243 vetoes against $167 million in spending, but the Legislature overturned all but 15 of them. They also overturned his veto of a program extending health insurance to 100,000 poor children. The governor had argued qualifying families should be required to shoulder more of the cost. Sanford had also pushed legislators to tackle immigration reform that year, although no consensus bill emerged. And the Legislature also killed Sanford's proposal to reorganize state government to make most cabinet-level offices appointed rather than elected.

Sanford's 2008 budget aimed to cut spending by $326 million while again cutting income taxes and raising cigarette taxes. He also called for adding 300 state prison guards and troopers, saving more land from development, expanding college scholarships and making kindergarten available to 4-year-olds. The Legislature this time upped his budget only slightly, to $7 billion, and Sanford issued only 69 vetoes. He again axed funding for children's health insurance, along with rejecting money for rural hospitals, hydrogen fuel research, teen pregnancy prevention and indigent defense aid. Lawmakers sustained only 13 of Sanford's vetoes, restoring funds for children's health insurance, drug and alcohol programs and funds for public defenders. Sanford charged lawmakers with passing an unbalanced budget and threatened to bring them back in session to deal with additional budget cuts. "It is an extreme problem," he told *The State*. "It might solicit a lawsuit." After Sanford asked state agency heads to prepare budget cuts, legislators complied. In 2008, Sanford also opposed a national directive from the Department of Homeland Security to comply with a national identification program, known as Real ID. Sanford wrote to DHS Secretary Michael Chertoff, calling the program expensive and unnecessary.

In early 2009, President Barack Obama's $787 billion economic stimulus bill presented Sanford with a perfect pulpit to preach against government spending. Sanford and conservative Sen. Jim DeMint became the ringleaders of economic conservatives who opposed boosting spending as a way to forestall a further slowdown in the recessionary economy. "I think it's a gut-check vote on sort of this moral issue of, at the end of the day, borrowing money and printing money to pay for (a) current dilemma, and handing the tab to the next generation . . . to your kids and grandkids, is wrong," he told *The State*. Sanford opposed any additional spending in the state, even as layoffs statewide mounted. When South Carolina registered the nation's third highest unemployment rate, Sanford begrudgingly agreed to apply for a $146 million federal loan to continue unemployment benefits, although he had maintained for weeks he would not. Members of his own party were aghast that Sanford might allow unemployment payments to expire. "I can't believe anybody would be this heartless, and create such a heartless act on these people," the Republican chairman of the Senate Finance Committee told *The New York Times*.

Sanford then hinted he would not accept federal stimulus funds. U.S. Rep. James Clyburn of South Carolina, the third-ranking House Democrat, inserted a provision into the stimulus bill allowing state legislators to accept federal aid if a governor fails to act within 45 days. State House and Senate leaders urged Sanford to accept the funds. But Sanford remained steadfast. As state legislators began to draft a budget around the anticipated share of the stimulus funds, Sanford announced in March 2009 that he would accept the money only if Obama allowed the state to use it to pay down debt. "Once that money runs out, South Carolina will be in a deeper hole than if it chose to deal with budget deficits now," Sanford wrote to lawmakers. State Democrats charged that Sanford's move was a political ploy to advance his own career, and the Obama administration denied Sanford's request.

As the deadline to accept the funds loomed, South Carolina's jobless rate rose to 10.4%, the second worst in the nation behind Michigan. Sanford asked the Obama White House if the state could use the money to preserve jobs for teachers, police and public employees along with debt reduction. His request was again denied. Meanwhile, South Carolina Attorney General Henry McMaster said he agreed with a Congressional Research Service report that cast doubt on whether the state Legislature could legally circumvent Sanford. Just hours before the deadline to accept the funds, Sanford became the last governor to request the money. But he said he would continue to try to use the funds for preserving education and law enforcement jobs. Sanford still controlled when the state tapped the funds, and he remained adamant that he would do so only if the Legislature agreed to pay down debt.

In their legislative session, lawmakers passed a budget forcing Sanford to accept the stimulus money, and Sanford promptly filed a federal lawsuit against the General Assembly claiming its mandate was unconstitutional. Petitions from two South Carolina students and the South Carolina Association of School Administrators made their way to the state Supreme Court in early June 2009, each arguing that the state's educational system was being harmed by Sanford's refusal to accept the federal funds. The court ruled unanimously that Sanford had to apply for the $700 million, finding that the General Assembly had the sole authority to appropriate funds. Sanford then agreed to drop his lawsuit and apply for the funds. In his application, Sanford wrote that Obama's stimulus bill was a "monumentally terrible idea."

In 2008, Sanford told *The State* he was considering a career outside of politics when his term ends in 2010, and he probably sealed that fate with a series of decisions he made in mid-2009. On June 22, a Monday, reports surfaced that Sanford had not been at work for several days. As legislators wondered where he was, and whether he had transferred power in his absence, their alarm gained credence when Sanford's wife, Jenny, told reporters she didn't know where her husband was, but that he was probably off working on a writing project. Sanford, the father of four young sons, also had missed Father's Day, on June 21. Then, Sanford's spokesman reported that the governor was in the mountains hiking the Appalachian Trail, leaving him unreachable, but that he would cut short his trip and return to work on Wednesday in response to the media attention his absence was generating.

On Wednesday morning, a reporter for *The State*, acting on a tip, staked out Atlanta's Hartsfield-Jackson Airport and confronted Sanford as he got off a flight from Argentina. Sanford admitted then that he had not been hiking, but had been in Buenos Aires. Back in Columbia that afternoon, Sanford divulged the details of his mysterious disappearance. At a rambling press conference, Sanford admitted that he been carrying on an extramarital affair with a woman from Argentina and that he had spent the previous several days with her. His unscripted comments were laced with childhood memories, apologies to his family, and biblical references. But he made clear he intended to remain as governor, although he did resign as chairman of the Republican Governors Association. Later in the day, *The State* published intimate email exchanges between Sanford's mistress, Maria Belen Chapur, and the governor. A few days later, Sanford gave an interview to the Associated Press in which he called Chapur his "soul mate." Becoming emotional several times, he told the Associated Press, "This was a whole lot more than a simple affair. . . . It's a love story, a forbidden one, a tragic one but a love story at the end of the day." He also admitted to having "crossed lines" with other women during his marriage but underscored he had not had sex with them.

More than half of the Republicans in the state Senate called for Sanford's resignation. Several members of the state's congressional delegation either publicly or privately urged him to step down as well. In July, the state Republican Party elected to censure Sanford rather than to call for his resignation. Sanford was determined to finish out his second term, and it appeared he would be able to survive the scandal. Officials determined that state funds were not used for the trip, although Sanford did reimburse the state $3,300 for his air fare for a 2008 trade mission to Buenos Aires, during which he saw Chapur. Also working in Sanford's favor was the fact that legislators were not eager to see him replaced by Republican Lt. Gov. André Bauer, who was known for unpredictable behavior himself. Thirdly, Jenny Sanford, who had gained great public sympathy during the scandal, issued a statement saying she would consider reconciling with the wayward governor.

Senior Senator

Lindsey Graham (R)

Elected 2002, term expires 2014, 2nd term; b. July 9, 1955, Central; home, Seneca; U. of SC, B.A. 1977, J.D. 1981; Baptist; single.

Military Career: Air Force, 1982–88; SC Air Natl. Guard, 1989–94 (Operation Desert Storm); Air Force Reserves, 1995–present.

Elected Office: SC House of Reps., 1992–94; U.S. House of Reps., 1994–2002.

Professional Career: U.S. Air Forces Europe Circuit Trial Counsel, 1984–88; Asst. Oconee Cnty. atty., 1988–92; Practicing atty., 1988–94; Judge advocate, McEntire Air Natl. Guard Base, 1989–94; Central SC city atty., 1990–94.

DC Office: 290 RSOB, 20510, 202-224-5972; Fax: 202-224-3808; Web site: lgraham.senate.gov.

State Offices: Columbia, 803-933-0112; Florence, 843-669-1505; Greenville, 864-250-1417; Mt. Pleasant, 843-849-3887; Pendleton, 864-646-4090; Rock Hill, 803-366-2828.

Committees: *Aging (Special)* (7th of 8 R). *Armed Services* (5th of 11 R): Emerging Threats & Capabilities; Personnel (RMM); Strategic Forces. *Budget* (9th of 10 R). *Homeland Security & Governmental Affairs* (6th of 7 R): Disaster Recovery (RMM); Oversight of Government Management, the Federal Workforce & the District of Columbia; State, Local & Private Sector Preparedness & Integration. *Judiciary* (5th of 7 R): Administrative Oversight & the Courts; Constitution; Crime & Drugs (RMM); Human Rights & the Law. *Veterans' Affairs* (5th of 5 R).

Group Ratings

	ADA	ACLU	AFS	LCV	ITIC	NTU	COC	ACU	CFG	FRC
2008	15	20	0	9	80	52	100	82	52	100
2007	20	—	0	7	—	80	100	88	80	—

National Journal Ratings

	2007 LIB	—	2007 CONS	2008 LIB	—	2008 CONS
Economic	18%	—	80%	13%	—	86%
Social	35%	—	64%	0%	—	79%
Foreign	13%	—	86%	21%	—	76%
Composite	23%	—	77%	16%	—	85%

Key Votes of the 110th Congress

1. Raise CAFE standards	Y	5. Make English official language	Y	9. Withdraw troops 3/08	*
2. Expand SCHIP	N	6. Path to citizenship	Y	10. Iran guard is terrorist group	Y
3. Cap greenhouse gases	*	7. Fetus is unborn child	Y	11. Increase missile defense $	Y
4. Bail out financial markets	Y	8. Prosecute hate crimes	N	12. Overhaul FISA	Y

Election Results

2008 general	Lindsey Graham (R)	1,076,534	(58%)	($4,463,619)
	Bob Conley (D)	790,621	(42%)	($15,202)
2008 primary	Lindsey Graham (R)	187,736	(67%)	
	Buddy Witherspoon (R)	93,125	(33%)	

Prior Winning Percentages: 2002 (54%); 2000 House (68%); 1998 House (100%); 1996 House (60%); 1994 House (60%)

Lindsey Graham, South Carolina's senior senator, was elected to the House in 1994 and to the Senate in 2002. Graham grew up in Pickens County, where his parents owned a tavern in the textile mill town of Central, S.C. Both his parents died young, while Graham was still attending the University of South Carolina, and he became his younger sister's legal guardian. He was the first in his family to graduate from college, and then received a law degree from the University of South Carolina. He was an Air Force prosecutor who worked on assignments overseas, including one case that led to major changes in the service's drug testing program for soldiers. In 1988, he returned home and practiced law in Seneca, the same town where former Democratic Sen. John Edwards grew up. In 1992, he was elected to the state House. Graham was called up to active duty and served stateside during the Gulf War, and he has been in the Air Force Reserves since 1995, as a senior instructor in the Air Force's JAG school and also as a reserve judge on the Air Force Court of Criminal Appeals.

In 1994, with the retirement of 20-year Democratic U.S. Rep. Butler Derrick, Graham ran for the House. Both parties had contested primaries, and Graham won the Republican primary without a runoff with 52% of the vote. In the general election, he faced state Sen. Jim Bryan. Graham called for term limits, supported more defense spending and opposed gays in the military. His attitude toward the Clinton administration and the Democratic leadership was unequivocal. He said, "I'm one less vote for an agenda that makes you want to throw up." Graham won 60%-40%, a smashing victory in a district represented only by Democrats since Reconstruction. In the House, Graham had a solidly conservative voting record but did not always support the Republican leadership. In the summer of 1997, he was among a small group of junior House members who plotted with some of the senior GOP to try to oust Speaker Newt Gingrich, R-Ga., who by then had lost the confidence of his Republican troops. But the attempt failed. In a Republican Conference meeting, when Majority Leader Dick Armey of Texas, one of the plotters, asserted that no member of the leadership was involved, Graham challenged that assertion as false.

As a member of the House Judiciary Committee, Graham played a major role in the 1998 impeachment of President Bill Clinton. In the Senate trial, Graham's folksy manner and clear description of Clinton's offenses— "Where I come from, a man who calls someone up at 2:30 in the morning is up to no good" —made him one of the most effective GOP impeachment managers. In 2000, Graham, by then an ally of Republican Sen. John McCain of Arizona, was one of McCain's staunchest supporters in his first bid for the presidency that year.

Republican Sen. Strom Thurmond, re-elected to his eighth term in 1996 one month before he turned 94, had promised not to run again in 2002. There had not been an open South Carolina Senate seat since 1941. (Both Thurmond and longtime Democratic Sen. Ernest Hollings won their seats by beating incumbent senators appointed to fill vacancies.) Yet in this now heavily Republican state, Graham had no opposition in the Republican primary. His work on impeachment and in the McCain campaign had made him well-known and popular statewide, and he was endorsed by three former governors and Thurmond. Democrats portrayed him as lacking in substance and recruited Alex Sanders, president of the College of Charleston, who had a colorful résumé. Sanders ran off as a teenager and joined the circus and was briefly a juggler and fire-eater. He served in the state Legislature for many years, and in 1985 was appointed to the state Court of Appeals. He was a gifted raconteur, charming and well-connected around the state.

Sanders was a solid fundraiser as well, eventually raising $4.2 million, below Graham's $5.8 million, but a considerable achievement for a candidate who was consistently behind in the polls. He supported the Bush tax cuts and military action in Iraq. But he opposed the death penalty, on religious grounds, and he opposed a constitutional amendment to allow criminalization of flag burning. Graham hammered him on the death penalty and the flag amendment but most of all tried to label him as a liberal, saying Sanders would advance the agenda of Sens. Hillary Rodham Clinton of New York and Edward Kennedy of Massachusetts. "My opponent is a nice guy, but he's getting Democratic support out the ying-yang," Graham said. Sanders struck back by emphasizing Graham's endorsement by New York Mayor Rudolph Giuliani: "He's an ultraliberal. His wife kicked him out and he moved in with two gay men and a Shih Tzu. Is that South Carolina values? I don't think so," he said. But Sanders was put on the defensive by his own comment that South Carolinians could prove they were not racists by voting for him. Trying to explain, he said, "When I said I would show America that we are not ignorant, racist, redneck Dixiecrats, I was referring to the false stereotype many people in the North have of us in South Carolina."

Graham won 54%-44% and took the place of a senator first elected in the year he was born. He has had a mostly conservative voting record but has disagreed with the Bush administration on important issues. He voted against the Medicare prescription drug bill in 2003 and called for ceilings on the program's cost. He voted against the Republican medical malpractice bill in 2003 and 2004, calling it "one of the worst pieces of legislation I have ever seen." But he supported the class action bill that passed in February 2005, and co-sponsored a bill requiring that the losing party pays the other side's legal fees in lawsuits between parties from different states. In 2005, he proposed a federal law shielding reporters from having to disclose their sources in court.

Despite his hard-right rhetoric, Graham proved adept at working across the aisle with Democrats, including Sen. Clinton, with whom he co-sponsored a bill to expand health care for reservists and National Guard troops. "If Senator Clinton is willing to come to the middle to provide better benefits for the military, I will get a car and drive her," he said. In 2005, he and New York Democrat Charles Schumer sponsored a bill to impose a 27.5% tariff on all Chinese goods until the Chinese government revalues its currency, then tied to the dollar. The Chinese devalued their currency by 2% and suggested that it would periodically be adjusted. Schumer and Graham continued to fight for further concessions from China. Graham's most prominent collaboration with Democrats was as part of the "Gang of 14," seven Democrats and seven Republicans who agreed in 2005 not to filibuster judicial nominees except in "extraordinary circumstances." He voted for Bush Supreme Court nominee John Roberts and supported the high court nomination of Samuel Alito, saying "There's nothing to suggest that Alito is anything but a solid conservative judge. He's probably one of the most qualified."

Graham was harder on the Bush administration over its increasingly bold techniques in terrorism investigations. He objected to surveillance of communications between al Qaeda suspects abroad and persons in the United States, saying in 2006, "When I voted for it, I never envisioned that I was giving to this president or any other president the ability to go around [the Foreign Intelligence Surveillance Act] carte blanche." He was also a critic of the policy of holding unlawful combatants in the military prison at Guantanamo Bay, Cuba, without offering them an array of rights. When the Bush administration proposed procedures for trying the detainees, Graham criticized them for not allowing detainees to see all the evidence against them and for defying Geneva Convention protections, although he agreed that such unlawful combatants were not entitled to full Geneva Convention protections. Working with Armed Services Chairman John Warner, R-Va., and his frequent ally McCain, Graham marshaled his expertise in military law and procedure to produce a bill allowing aggressive and classified interrogation techniques, defining what is a "grave breach" of the Geneva Conventions and establishing military tribunals allowing defendants to confront the evidence against them. The legislation, which passed as part of the 2006 defense spending bill, also prohibited habeas corpus suits by detainees and left up to the Annual Review Board at Guantanamo the amount of time enemy combatants could be held when they are acquitted.

Since his arrival in the Senate, Graham has been interested in solutions to the Social Security solvency issue. In 2003, he unveiled his own plan: 4% personal retirement accounts, with higher taxes for workers who do not choose them. The proposal was sharply criticized by some conservatives, but Graham persisted. He participated in private meetings with both Democratic and Republican senators, and he insisted that raising the payroll tax limit was necessary if a plan was to get Democratic support.

In 2006 and 2007, Graham supported the McCain-Kennedy and Kennedy-Kyl immigration bills, positions which got him in considerable trouble with conservatives who opposed giving illegal immigrants a process to achieve citizenship. Radio talk show host Rush Limbaugh belittled him as "Lindsey Grahamnesty" and the Greenville County Republican party voted to censure him. Graham's public comments suggesting that immigration bill opponents were "bigots" did not help his cause. He tried to rebound in late 2007 by including a $3 billion border-security amendment in a defense spending bill. It would fund 700 miles of fence along the U.S.-Mexico border and provide additional vehicle barriers and ground censors, but it was stripped from the final version of the bill by Senate Democrats. In December 2007 he joined with Sen. Evan Bayh to support the Indiana Democrat's legislation to impose higher penalties on people found smuggling illegal immigrants across the border, but the amendment never made it out of the Judiciary Committee.

Graham's support of the immigration bills and his opposition to the Bush administration on the treatment of unlawful combatants led to efforts to find a primary challenger for 2008. Anti-Graham sentiment eventually coalesced behind retired Lexington orthodontist Buddy Witherspoon, a conservative but a political novice. Witherspoon focused on Graham's immigration positions, running an ad with a voiceover of Mexican immigrants saying "Muchas gracias, Lindsey Graham!" His campaign slogan was: "Buddy Witherspoon—because Lindsey's too liberal for South Carolina." Graham largely ignored Witherspoon's candidacy, but did ridicule his opponent's claim that U.S. leaders were secretly creating a North American currency called the Amero with Mexico and Canada. The Witherspoon campaign reported less than $500,000, half of which had come from Witherspoon himself, compared to Graham's more than $8 million. The June primary wasn't even close. Graham won 2-to-1, getting 67% of the vote to Witherspoon's 33%. In the general election, Graham faced Bob Conley, a pilot from Myrtle Beach aligned with the Constitution Party who raised only $17,000. Graham easily won a second term, 58%-42%.

Without much of a threat to his own re-election bid, Graham in 2008 traveled the country with his close friend McCain, the Republican presidential nominee. McCain, Graham and Connecticut independent Sen. Joseph Lieberman formed a sort of bipartisan triumvirate on the campaign trail. Graham's support was likely helpful to McCain in the pivotal January 2008 South Carolina primary, in which McCain redeemed his 2000 loss by winning with 33% of the vote. The close alliance between Graham and McCain became more evident as the general election wore on. "There's nobody I trust more than Lindsey Graham," McCain told the *Myrtle Beach Sun-News*. Graham said of McCain, "If I make his day better by being someone he can talk to, confide in, have a good laugh with, I am honored to play that role. I enjoy his company." Graham was said to be among the members of McCain's inner circle urging him to tap Lieberman as his running mate. But McCain settled on Alaska then-Gov. Sarah Palin.

After McCain's loss, Graham echoed McCain's promise to provide bipartisan support for new Democratic President Barack Obama. He supported Obama's decision to close the U.S. military prison at Guantanamo Bay, and even defended Treasury secretary nominee Timothy Geithner after it was revealed Geithner had failed to pay back taxes. Although he had supported the Bush administration's Wall Street bailout legislation in 2008, Graham's centrist tendencies ceased when it came to Obama's $787 billion economic stimulus bill in January 2009. He said the legislation "created more government than jobs," and criticized Obama's outreach to Republican colleagues. When Republican Gov. Mark Sanford initially said he would refuse South Carolina's share of the federal stimulus money unless a portion of it could go to pay down state's debt, Graham said he believed Sanford should accept the money. But he disagreed with the strategy of House Democratic Whip James Clyburn of South Carolina, who called on the state Legislature to bypass Sanford to accept the funds. But on some economic matters, Graham was still the maverick bucking his party. In February 2009, he said he supported a limited nationalization of some banks and Obama's proposal to "stress-test" banks. "I'm not going to be the Herbert Hoover of 2009, saying 'Just let the free market work it out,'" he told the *Charlotte Observer*.

Junior Senator

Jim DeMint (R)

Elected 2004, term expires 2010, 1st term; b. Sept. 2, 1951, Greenville; home, Greenville; U. of TN, B.S. 1973, Clemson U., M.B.A. 1981; Presbyterian; married (Debbie); 4 children.

Elected Office: U.S. House of Reps., 1998–2004.

Professional Career: Sales rep., Scott Paper, 1973–75; Acct. rep., Henderson Advertising, 1975–81; V.P., Leslie Advertising, 1981–84; Pres., DeMint Marketing, 1983–98.

DC Office: 340 RSOB, 20510, 202-224-6121; Fax: 202-228-5143; Web site: demint.senate.gov.

State Offices: Charleston, 843-727-4525; Columbia, 803-771-6112; Greenville, 864-233-5366.

Committees: *Banking, Housing & Urban Affairs* (7th of 10 R): Economic Policy (RMM); Financial Institutions; Housing, Transportation & Community Development. *Commerce, Science & Transportation* (4th of 11 R): Aviation Operations, Safety & Security (RMM); Communications, Technology & the Internet; Competitiveness, Innovation & Export Promotion; Consumer Protection, Product Safety & Insurance; Surface Transportation & Merchant Marine Infrastructure, Safety & Security. *Foreign Relations* (5th of 8 R): African Affairs; European Affairs (RMM); International Development & Foreign Assistance, Economic Affairs & International Environmental Protection; International Operations & Organizations, Human Rights, Democracy & Global Women's Issues. *Joint Economic Committee* (2nd of 4 R).

Group Ratings

	ADA	ACLU	AFS	LCV	ITIC	NTU	COC	ACU	CFG	FRC
2008	0	15	0	9	25	96	57	100	100	100
2007	0	—	0	7	—	93	55	100	100	—

National Journal Ratings

	2007 LIB — 2007 CONS		2008 LIB — 2008 CONS	
Economic	10%	— 89%	4%	— 95%
Social	0%	— 91%	0%	— 79%
Foreign	0%	— 93%	0%	— 84%
Composite	6%	— 94%	8%	— 92%

Key Votes of the 110th Congress

1. Raise CAFE standards	N	5. Make English official language	Y	9. Withdraw troops 3/08	N
2. Expand SCHIP	N	6. Path to citizenship	N	10. Iran guard is terrorist group	Y
3. Cap greenhouse gases	*	7. Fetus is unborn child	Y	11. Increase missile defense $	Y
4. Bail out financial markets	N	8. Prosecute hate crimes	N	12. Overhaul FISA	Y

Election Results

2004 general	Jim DeMint (R)	857,167	(54%)	($9,036,086)
	Inez Tenenbaum (D)	704,384	(44%)	($6,265,786)

Prior Winning Percentages: 2002 House (69%); 2000 House (80%); 1998 House (58%)

South Carolina's junior senator is Jim DeMint, a Republican elected in 2004. DeMint was born in Greenville, where his father was stationed in the Air Force. When his parents divorced, his mother supported the family by establishing a dance school, the DeMint Academy of Dance and Decorum. He graduated from the University of Tennessee and Clemson University's business school, and returned to Greenville to work in his father-in-law's advertising business. In 1983, he founded DeMint Marketing, a research firm with businesses, schools, colleges and hospitals as clients. In 1992, he was hired by Republican Bob Inglis in his campaign for the 4th District House seat, helping Inglis hone his message using focus groups and advertising techniques. In 1998, when Inglis ran for the Senate, DeMint ran to succeed him. Like Inglis, he pledged to serve only three terms and take no political action committee money. He called for replacing the graduated income tax with a national sales tax or flat tax, for individual retirement accounts in Social Security, and for a "right-to-life" amendment to the Constitution. In the Republican primary, he faced state Sen. Mike Fair, a former University of South Carolina quarterback who was favored to win. On the first ballot, Fair led with 32%, to 23% for DeMint. In the runoff campaign, DeMint labeled Fair a "career politician," and upset him in the final balloting, 53%-47%. He won the general election 58%-40%.

In the House, DeMint was elected president of the GOP freshman class and joined other junior Republicans seeking to rein in spending by the appropriators. He resisted local pressures and was the only South Carolina House member to vote for normalizing trade relations with China, arguing that the best way to remedy human rights abuses was "to export our products and principles." DeMint's votes on trade provoked serious opposition in his textile-producing district. DeMint opposed President George W. Bush's centerpiece, "No Child Left Behind" education bill in 2001, and sought to replace that bill with one to create a state-based block-grant program for schools. Education and the Workforce Chairman John Boehner tried without success to get DeMint to back down, but Bush persuaded him to do so in a meeting in the Oval Office. On Social Security, he worked to advance the creation of individual investment accounts in the federally run program by getting 117 House members to sign a letter of support, and sponsored a legislation in 2003 to allow people under age 55 to set aside 3% to 8% of their Social Security withholding income in personal investment accounts. In 2002, former state Rep. Phil Bradley challenged him in the primary and had the support of textile titan Roger Milliken, long a financer of conservative and protectionist candidates. But DeMint defended his support for free trade as beneficial for international investment in the district and won 62%-38%.

In 2003, DeMint said that he would keep his promise to serve only three House terms and that he would run for Democrat Ernest Hollings' Senate seat in 2004. DeMint could not have been more different than the man he sought to replace. DeMint was from South Carolina's Upstate region while Hollings was a Charleston native with a Lowcountry political base. Hollings was one of the Senate's leading protectionists; DeMint was an unwavering free trader. Where Hollings served in a variety of elected offices over a political career that spanned more than a half-century, DeMint's public service began with his first House term. Commenting on South Carolina's increasingly Republican electorate, the retiring Hollings said, "It wouldn't be easy for anybody who's a Democrat in this state to get elected." There were three competitive challengers to DeMint in the Republican primary: former Gov. David Beasley, who lost his re-election bid in 1998, former state Attorney General Charlie Condon, and millionaire Charleston developer Thomas Ravenel.

Trade policy was consequential in the race. South Carolina had lost nearly 70,000 manufacturing jobs since 1999. DeMint and Ravenel ran as free traders, while Beasley and Condon took protectionist positions. DeMint was backed by the anti-tax Club for Growth, and Beasley's biggest contributors were Roger Milliken and other textile executives and political action committees. Beasley ran ads featuring an empty textile plant and that claimed DeMint advocated trade policies that had cost the state more than 50,000 jobs. A Condon ad singled out DeMint's vote to allow China into the World Trade Organization. DeMint responded with ads showing the BMW manufacturing plant near Greer and pointed to increased U.S. exports to China. Beasley led the primary with 37%, but did not get the 50% required to avoid a runoff. DeMint came in second with 26%, Ravenel had 25%, and Condon 9%. In the runoff, DeMint picked up endorsements from Ravenel and Condon and won support from Republican voters still unhappy with Beasley's policies as governor. He won 59%-41%.

DeMint's general election opponent was state schools Superintendent Inez Tenenbaum, a popular Democrat who had twice won statewide election. Tenenbaum ran on her record in education and the improving SAT scores of South Carolina high school students. Her signature outfits were red dresses and suits, and she campaigned around the state aboard the Red Dress Express, a recreational vehicle with an image of her on its sides. She picked up where the Republican contest left off, arguing that DeMint's House votes cost the state tens of thousands of jobs. She opposed the 2005 Central American Free Trade Agreement, which DeMint supported, and she was funded by textile interests. Tenenbaum also claimed that DeMint's advocacy of a national sales tax would result in a 95% tax hike on South Carolina residents. He ran radio and television ads accusing Democrats of misrepresenting his position. The Democratic Senatorial Campaign Committee spent $2.5 million through September for Tenenbaum. In October, the National Republican Senatorial Committee ran a $1.3 million ad campaign to shore up DeMint.

DeMint's campaign was also sidetracked by controversy over comments he made in a campaign debate, indicating that gay people should not be allowed to teach in public schools. "Folks teaching in schools need to represent our values," he said. But DeMint said he would not require teachers to admit whether or not they were gay. He also suggested that unwed pregnant women also should not teach in public schools. Overall, DeMint spent $9 million to Tenenbaum's $6.2 million. He won 54%-44%. DeMint lost Charleston County by 100 votes, but won big margins in his Upstate home turf: 63%-35% in Greenville County and 59%-38% in Spartanburg County. His election gave South Carolina two Republican senators for the first time since 1877.

DeMint is among the most conservative senators, according to *National Journal*'s ratings in 2007 and 2008. With fellow Republican Sen. Lindsey Graham of South Carolina, he called in 2005 for eliminating the income tax and replacing it with an 8.5% sales consumption tax plus a tax on business profits, although the proposal went nowhere. Unlike Graham, he voted against the Senate's immigration bill in 2007, labeling it "amnesty" for illegal aliens. His proposal to eliminate a provision that would have allowed undocumented workers to gain legal status and remain in the country indefinitely was defeated, but he ultimately played a role in the bill's demise. A reliable ally of the Pentagon and staunch supporter of the Iraq war, DeMint in a May 2007 speech in Spartanburg, said, "Al Qaeda knows that we've got a lot of wimps in Congress. I believe a lot of the casualties can be laid at the feet of all the talk in Congress about how we've got to get out, we've got to cut and run." He also suggested that Senate Majority Leader Harry Reid should be censured for declaring defeat in Iraq.

In 2007, as chairman of the Steering Committee, the informal group of Senate conservatives, DeMint joined Republican Sen. Tom Coburn of Oklahoma to limit earmarks in spending bills and to require increased disclosure of earmarks, the special provisions tucked into the appropriations bills by individual lawmakers. His opposition to pork barrel spending quickly became a signature issue. In the 2008 appropriations bills, he requested no earmarks for South Carolina and blocked 10,000 earmarks by others. In March 2008, DeMint proposed a one-year moratorium on earmarks, which won the support of all three then-presidential candidates—Republican John McCain and Democrats Barack Obama and Hillary Rodham Clinton—but ultimately failed 71-29. Among his successes was elimination of $25 million for spinach producers during a vote on the spending bill for Iraq. He also opposed an expansion of Bush's global AIDS program, telling Columbia's *The State* that "for us to attempt to buy friendship around the world by spending $50 billion is just completely irresponsible. There are enough worthy causes around the world to bankrupt us a hundred times over." The Senate rejected DeMint's proposals to cut the program.

In April 2008, DeMint published a book detailing his view on the decline of cultural conservatism, *Why We Whisper: Restoring Our Right to Say It's Wrong*. When Republican losses mounted in the November 2008 election, he told *The State*, "The election reflects a failure of Republicans to keep their conservative promises."

DeMint's outspoken opposition to even some of his party's positions have chafed with GOP leaders. He raises money only for conservative Republicans, not the party at large. DeMint frequently goes public with his concerns on party positions rather than deferring to leaders and committee chairmen. In 2007, he irked Democratic Sen. Byron Dorgan of North Dakota by showing up late for a committee meeting on reauthorization of the Consumer Product Safety Commission because he was on the floor trying to kill Dorgan's Indian health care bill. DeMint then proceeded to offer an amendment on prescription drug reimportation that was identical to one written by Dorgan and Maine Republican Sen. Olympia Snowe. Dorgan accused DeMint of a "stunning lack of courtesy." DeMint blamed the incident on staff miscommunication and said he thought he was supposed to offer the amendment. In July 2007, he forced a Saturday vote on a housing bill, infuriating Democrats and Republicans alike, but then didn't show up for the weekend session's votes. After the 2008 elections, DeMint proposed rules to impose term limits on party leadership positions, which lost overwhelmingly on the Senate floor. He accused leaders of trying to "humiliate" him.

His combative tactics probably cost him a cherished seat on the Senate Finance Committee, which he has sought to no avail. But both the criticism from the left and from within his own party have endeared DeMint to diehard champions of the conservative cause, particularly his outspoken opposition to both the 2008 government rescue of the financial services industry and to President Obama's $787 billion economic stimulus bill in 2009.

FIRST DISTRICT

Henry Brown (R)

Elected 2000, 5th term; b. Dec. 20, 1935, Bishopville; home, Hanahan; attended The Citadel; Baptist Col.; Baptist; married (Billye); 3 children.

Military Career: SC Natl. Guard, 1953–62.

Elected Office: Hanahan City Council, 1981–85; SC House of Reps., 1985–00.

Professional Career: V.P., Piggly Wiggly Carolina Co., 1958–85.

DC Office: 103 CHOB, 20515, 202-225-3176; Fax: 202-225-3407; Web site: brown.house.gov.

State Offices: Myrtle Beach, 843-445-6459; N. Charleston, 843-747-4175.

Committees: *Natural Resources* (6th of 20 R): Insular Affairs, Oceans & Wildlife (RMM); National Parks, Forests & Public Lands. *Transportation & Infrastructure* (10th of 30 R): Highways & Transit; Railroads, Pipelines & Hazardous Materials; Water Resources & Environment. *Veterans' Affairs* (4th of 11 R): Health (RMM).

Group Ratings

	ADA	ACLU	AFS	LCV	ITIC	NTU	COC	ACU	CFG	FRC
2008	20	18	14	8	71	56	94	83	63	100
2007	10	—	0	5	—	70	90	96	77	—

National Journal Ratings

	2007 LIB — 2007 CONS			2008 LIB — 2008 CONS	
Economic	25%	—	75%	25%	—	75%
Social	21%	—	75%	31%	—	62%
Foreign	0%	—	72%	29%	—	69%
Composite	21%	—	79%	30%	—	70%

Key Votes of the 110th Congress

1. Increase minimum wage	N	5. Share immigration data	Y	9. Withdraw troops 8/08	N
2. Expand SCHIP	N	6. Foreign aid abortion ban	Y	10. No operations in Iran	N
3. Raise CAFE standards	N	7. Ban gay bias in workplace	N	11. Free trade with Peru	Y
4. Bail out financial markets	Y	8. Repeal D.C. gun law	Y	12. Overhaul FISA	Y

Election Results

2008 general	Henry Brown (R)..	177,540	(52%)	($1,287,308)
	Linda Ketner (D)..	163,724	(48%)	($2,248,361)
2008 primary	Henry Brown (R)..	42,588	(70%)	
	Katherine Jenerette (R).....................................	11,488	(19%)	
	Paul Norris (R)...	6,718	(11%)	

Prior Winning Percentages: 2006 (60%); 2004 (88%); 2002 (89%); 2000 (60%)

Population		**Race/Ethnicity**		**Work**	
Pop. 2007:	780,300	White:	72.8%	Private:	75.0%
Change since 2000:	Up 16.7%	Black:	20.3%	Government:	17.9%
Urban:	78.4%	Hispanic:	3.6%	Self-employed:	6.9%
Rural:	21.6%	Asian:	1.6%	Blue collar:	21.8%
Area size:	3,419 sq. mi.	Native Am.:	0.3%	White collar:	59.5%
		Hawaiian:	0.0%	Khaki collar:	1.2%
Age		Two+ races:	1.2%	Other:	17.5%
Median age:	36.9 yrs.	*Ancestry*		Median income:	$48,022
More than 65 yrs:	12.8%	German:	10.8%	Median home value:	$180,200
Less than 18 yrs:	23.7%	USA:	10.2%	Poverty:	12.6%
Education		English:	9.7%		
H.S. grad:	88.0%			**Military Veterans**	
College grad:	28.1%			% of Pop:	15.2%
Grad degree:	9.4%				

Looking out across the harbor to Fort Sumter are the glorious mansions of the Battery, gazing on the same view that the hot-blooded young swells of Charleston did in April 1861 when they fired the shots that began the Civil War. Today, there are few more beautiful urban scenes in America than the pastel "single houses" of Charleston, built flush with the sidewalk, turning their shoulders to the streets, with open piazzas inside their iron gateways facing south to catch the breeze. Founded

2008 Presidential Vote		
McCain (R)............................	196,996	(56%)
Obama (D)	148,218	(42%)
2004 Presidential Vote		
Bush (R)................................	172,836	(61%)
Kerry (D)................................	109,790	(39%)
Cook Partisan Voting Index:	R + 10	

in 1670, Charleston was blessed with one of the finest harbors on the Atlantic, at the point where, Charlestonians like to say, the Ashley and Cooper rivers meet to form the Atlantic Ocean. It was one of the South's two leading cities through the Civil War. Cargoes of rice, indigo, cotton and slaves, crossed its docks, enriching the white planters and merchants who dominated the state's economic and political life. After the war, Charleston became an economic backwater, enabling the old buildings to survive. The loving restorations of recent years have made the center city look better than ever and attracted a considerable tourist trade.

Charleston's old society is descended from Barbados planters and French Huguenots, Sephardic Jews and the second sons of English gentry, and was once a leading force in American political life. The hotheads in the gallery disrupted the 1860 Democratic National Convention here so boisterously that it was adjourned and reconvened in Baltimore, while Southern Democrats split off and nominated their own candidate, enabling Abraham Lincoln to win with 38% of the popular vote. The history of black South Carolinians, memorialized in George Gershwin's *Porgy and Bess*, is noteworthy, but the tale of slavery, once hidden under a blanket of politeness, is only now emerging, as many, though not all, plantations near Charleston add programs on the history of slavery to tours once dominated by romantic tales of the old South.

Navy and Air Force bases once accounted for 20% of payrolls in metropolitan Charleston. Many of these bases are now closed, but a vibrant private economy with lots of small companies has emerged, most notably at the 1,600-acre Charleston Naval Base, where, thanks to concerted efforts by regional officials, thousands of new jobs have been created since the base closed in 1996. In 2007, the port handled goods worth more than $60 billion. It is the 16th busiest port in the nation; it's larger than Norfolk but not as big as Savannah. Ninety miles northeast, Myrtle Beach has witnessed a boom in retirees and vacationers. Myrtle Beach and the 60-mile Grand Strand, miles of beachfront and golf courses, attract 14 million tourists annually and the population of Horry County has grown 31% since 2000.

The 1st Congressional District of South Carolina stretches along the coast from south of Charleston to north of Myrtle Beach, and takes in Murrells Inlet, Pawleys Island and Litchfield Beach. It includes the heavily white Battery and the area west of the Ashley River but not the heavily African-American areas to the north and in North Charleston. But the 1st District is still relatively diverse, with a 20% black population. It also includes the burgeoning suburbs in Berkeley and Dorchester counties. Google in 2008 opened a $600 million data center in Berkeley, with an expected 200 new jobs. In addition to the dominant tourism industry, the chief sources of local jobs are the port, the military and farming. This is solidly Republican country. It voted 61% for George W. Bush in 2004 and 56% for John McCain in 2008. The conservatism of the Lowcountry—the term for South Carolina's coastal counties, including Charleston—is more economic and less cultural than the conservatism of the Upstate region of South Carolina. Many voters here favor environmental restrictions and efforts to curb sprawl.

The congressman from the 1st District is Henry Brown, a Republican elected in 2000. Brown grew up on a small farm in Cordesville in Berkeley County, worked at the Charleston Naval Shipyard as his father had, and then spent almost 30 years working for the Piggly Wiggly grocery chain, where he eventually became a vice president. In 1981, at age 45, Brown was elected to the City Council in Hanahan, north of North Charleston. In 1985, he was elected to the state House in a special election, and ultimately rose to chairman of the Ways and Means Committee, where he shepherded the largest tax cut in state history. When Republican Mark Sanford, first elected to the U.S. House in 1994, made clear he would keep his promise to serve only three terms, Brown and other Republicans started running for the seat after the 1998 election. Brown stressed issues of concern to the district's many senior citizens—property tax relief and shoring up the Social Security fund. To boost his name recognition, he distributed 20,000 "Oh! Henry" chocolate bars. Brown won endorsements from many legislators and from Christian conservatives. Buck Limehouse, his chief opponent and a Charleston developer, spent $790,000 to Brown's $315,000 and had the support of most party leaders. In the six-candidate primary Brown led 44%-34%. In the runoff, he won 55%-45%. In the anticlimactic general election, Brown won 60%-36%.

In the House, Brown has moved his conservative voting record toward the center of his party in recent years. He is the ranking member of the Insular Affairs, Oceans and Wildlife Subcommittee of the Natural Resources Committee, which allows him to oversee aquaculture programs at Fort Johnson, which was built in the harbor in 1704 and has become a prominent marine biology laboratory. Even in this coastal district, he was a big booster of off-shore drilling during a heated partisan debate over the issue in 2008. "Have you ever heard of a natural gas spill?" he said. In the event that military detainees were released from Guantanamo Bay in Cuba, he sought in 2008 to assure that they were not transferred to a Navy brig in Charleston.

Looking after the interests of his district, Brown brokered a deal to add a Veterans Affairs facility next to Medical University of South Carolina. He also helped to secure $81 million to connect Interstate 73 with Myrtle Beach. But he got some negative attention at home in 2004, when brush that he was burning on his property, with a permit, jumped to adjacent federal lands and burned 20 acres. When the U.S. Forest Service fined him, Brown threatened to retaliate with congressional action. He ultimately paid a $250 fine plus $4,700 in fire-fighting costs.

In 2008, Brown unexpectedly faced his first close re-election since he took office. His opponent, Democrat Linda Ketner, ran an aggressive campaign, including an ad that criticized his dealings with the Forest Service on his brush fire. She advocated an 18-month deadline for a troop withdrawal from Iraq, a reduction in carbon emissions, and increased reliance on renewable fuels. She spent $2.2 million, nearly half of it from her fortune as an heiress to the Food Lion supermarkets; Brown spent nearly $1.3 million. Ketner, who was running her first campaign, said that she is openly gay and had a female partner. Brown did not make an issue of her lifestyle, though he criticized her support of gay marriage as part of her "ultra-liberal record." He won 52%-48%. In Charleston County, which cast 37% of the total vote, Ketner led 54%-46%; Brown won the other four counties, including 57%-43% in Horry.

SECOND DISTRICT

Joe Wilson (R)

Elected Dec. 2001, 4th full term; b. July 31, 1947, Charleston; home, Springdale; Washington & Lee U., B.A., 1969, U. of S.C., J.D., 1972; Presbyterian; married (Roxanne); 4 children.

Military Career: Army Reserves, 1972–75; SC Natl. Guard, 1975–2003.

Elected Office: SC Senate, 1985–2001.

Professional Career: Practicing atty., 1972–2001.

DC Office: 212 CHOB, 20515, 202-225-2452; Fax: 202-225-2455; Web site: joewilson.house.gov.

State Offices: Beaufort, 843-521-2530; West Columbia, 803-939-0041.

Committees: *Armed Services* (8th of 25 R): Air & Land Forces; Military Personnel (RMM). *Education & Labor* (10th of 19 R): Health, Employment, Labor & Pensions; Workforce Protections. *Foreign Affairs* (11th of 19 R): Europe; Middle East & South Asia.

Group Ratings

	ADA	ACLU	AFS	LCV	ITIC	NTU	COC	ACU	CFG	FRC
2008	10	18	0	0	57	68	100	92	87	100
2007	10	—	9	0	—	85	65	96	87	—

National Journal Ratings

	2007 LIB	—	2007 CONS		2008 LIB	—	2008 CONS
Economic	9%	—	90%		12%	—	87%
Social	0%	—	91%		9%	—	85%
Foreign	0%	—	72%		21%	—	79%
Composite	9%	—	91%		15%	—	85%

Key Votes of the 110th Congress

1. Increase minimum wage	N	5. Share immigration data	Y	9. Withdraw troops 8/08	N
2. Expand SCHIP	N	6. Foreign aid abortion ban	Y	10. No operations in Iran	N
3. Raise CAFE standards	N	7. Ban gay bias in workplace	N	11. Free trade with Peru	Y
4. Bail out financial markets	Y	8. Repeal D.C. gun law	Y	12. Overhaul FISA	Y

Election Results

2008 general	Joe Wilson (R)	184,583	(54%)	($1,266,821)
	Rob Miller (D)	158,627	(46%)	($624,365)
2008 primary	Joe Wilson (R)	44,783	(85%)	
	Phil Black (R)	7,831	(15%)	

Prior Winning Percentages: 2006 (63%); 2004 (65%); 2002 (84%); 2001 (73%)

Population		Race/Ethnicity		Work	
Pop. 2007:	755,188	White:	65.2%	Private:	71.2%
Change since 2000:	Up 12.9%	Black:	27.0%	Government:	23.1%
Urban:	66.0%	Hispanic:	4.7%	Self-employed:	5.5%
Rural:	34.0%	Asian:	1.3%	Blue collar:	20.9%
Area size:	5,237 sq. mi.	Native Am.:	0.3%	White collar:	60.1%
Age		Hawaiian:	0.0%	Khaki collar:	4.5%
Median age:	36.6 yrs.	Two+ races:	1.3%	Other:	14.6%
More than 65 yrs:	12.1%	*Ancestry*		Median income:	$50,017
Less than 18 yrs:	24.8%	German:	11.5%	Median home value:	$144,700
Education		English:	10.0%	Poverty:	11.8%
H.S. grad:	87.3%	USA:	9.2%	**Military Veterans**	
College grad:	31.2%			% of Pop:	13.6%
Grad degree:	11.7%				

In 1786, soon after the Revolutionary War, the South Carolina Legislature decided to move the state capital away from the Charleston aristocracy and into the Upstate interior, away from a city named after a king to a new city named after a discoverer of America. So began Columbia. The State House was built on high ground above the Congaree River in a town of one-and-a-half story houses with first floor porticos, dormers and raised brick basements—"Columbia cottages." In 1865,

Gen. William Tecumseh Sherman's army burned almost everything here but the State House. Columbia recovered, but grew slowly, with state government and the university, the Army's Fort Jackson and local insurance companies providing steady employment. Manufacturing boomed in the 1970s and again in recent years, making Columbia a confident city and the state's largest. For a time, Columbia's politics was personified by Jimmy Byrnes, the Democrat who returned from top posts in Franklin D. Roosevelt's Washington to serve as governor and lament the *Brown v. Board of Education* decision in 1954. Since then, upwardly mobile South Carolinians, transplanted from underdeveloped rural areas to comfortable two-car-garage subdivisions, turned Republican, first in national elections and then at the state and local levels. The metro Columbia area has been mostly Republican. But African-American population, now 46% of the total in Columbia's Richland County, has helped Democrats carry it. Across the river, faster-growing Lexington County, which is 14% black, has remained heavily Republican.

The 2nd Congressional District of South Carolina includes most of metro Columbia, except for the African-American neighborhoods in northern and western Columbia and the southern and eastern parts of Richland County that are in the black-majority 6th District. It contains the city's affluent white neighborhoods and the spread-out towns of Richland and Lexington counties, with their shopping centers, churches and the Army's huge training center, Fort Jackson, where $1 billion in construction projects resulted from the 2005 base realignment. The district extends south, taking in Barnwell County, which includes half of the Savannah River Site, one of the nation's nuclear weapons manufacturing complexes and the location of a landfill for low-level nuclear waste. A massive clean-up of the landfill has been going on since the reactors were shut down in 1992, but plans are now underway for a $5 billion plant to convert weapons-grade plutonium for commercial use.

The district takes in horse farm country around Aiken and several lightly populated, low-income rural counties. The 2nd also includes fast-growing Beaufort County on the coast, with the old county seat of Beaufort, the carefully manicured developments of Hilton Head Island and the Marine Corps' Parris Island training base and air station. This part of the district distinctively blends old and new. Beaufort's wonderful mansions and evocative Spanish moss provided the backdrop for the prose of novelist Pat Conroy and the 1983 movie *The Big Chill*, while the posh condominium developments and golfing resorts around Hilton Head and the Sun City Hilton Head development helped drive up Beaufort County's population by 24% since 2000. On nearby St. Helena Island, slave-owners, hating the heat and mosquitoes, ran largely absentee operations, thus allowing Gullah culture—a fusion of English and African elements—to thrive. Republican President George W. Bush won 60% of the vote here in 2004, and GOP presidential nominee John McCain got 54% in 2008.

The congressman from the 2nd District is Joe Wilson, a Republican chosen in a 2001 special election. Wilson grew up in Charleston and graduated from Washington and Lee University and the University of South Carolina law school. He worked as aide to Rep. Floyd Spence, a Republican who represented the 2nd, and then for Republican Sen. Strom Thurmond. Wilson was the deputy general counsel at the U.S. Energy Department during the Reagan administration. He practiced law in West Columbia for 25 years and worked on many campaigns. In 1984, he was elected to the state Senate, where he chaired the Transportation Committee. All four of his sons have been Eagle Scouts and served in the military, two of them in Iraq. In 2001, when Spence died after more than 30 years in the House, Wilson became the frontrunner to replace his longtime friend and mentor and pledged to continue his focus on national defense. He won the Republican primary with 76% of the vote and defeated his Democratic opponent 73%-25%.

In the House, Wilson has had a mostly conservative voting record. Following in the footsteps of Spence, the longtime chairman of the House Armed Services Committee, Wilson secured a seat on the panel, where he has advocated a closer military relationship with India in the war on terrorism and supported President Bush in the Iraq war. During the 2004 presidential campaign, he demanded an apology from Democratic candidate John Kerry, who served in Vietnam, for criticizing the conduct of some soldiers in Vietnam in 1971 when he returned from the war. Former Sen. Max Cleland, D-Ga., who lost both his legs and an arm in Vietnam, dismissed Wilson as a "chicken hawk" who never went to war. In 2009, Wilson became the ranking Republican on the Military Personnel Subcommittee at Armed Services.

On trade, he joined most other Carolina Republicans in opposing expanded powers for the president to negotiate free trade deals, but Wilson voted for the Central America Free Trade Agreement in 2005. On the Education and Labor Committee, he won House passage of a bill to expand college loan forgiveness for math, science and special education teachers who work in impoverished areas. He has worked with

Democrats to make permanent the child adoption tax credit. In 2008, he waded into the controversy over congressional earmarks, which critics call wasteful spending, but refusing to request highway projects for his district until Congress sets uniform rules that remove political favoritism from the process.

　　To stay visible to constituents, Wilson makes an annual five-day bus tour across the district. In 2008, he faced his first serious challenge for re-election against Rob Miller, a retired Marine and an Iraq veteran. Without any help from national Democrats, Miller spent $624,365, half of what Wilson spent, and ran as a social conservative and critic of the Bush administration. He prevailed in Richland and four of the rural counties, but Wilson got 65% of the vote in Lexington to win overall 54%-46%.

THIRD DISTRICT

Gresham Barrett (R)

Elected 2002, 4th term; b. Feb. 14, 1961, Westminster; home, Westminster; The Citadel, B.S. 1983; Baptist; married (Natalie); 3 children.

Military Career: Army, 1983–87.

Elected Office: SC House of Reps., 1996–2002.

Professional Career: Furniture store owner, 1987–96.

DC Office: 439 CHOB, 20515, 202-225-5301; Fax: 202-225-3216; Web site: barrett.house.gov.

State Offices: Aiken, 803-649-5571; Anderson, 864-224-7401; Greenwood, 864-223-8251.

Committees: *Financial Services* (14th of 29 R): Capital Markets, Insurance & Government Sponsored Enterprises; Financial Institutions & Consumer Credit. *Foreign Affairs* (13th of 19 R): Europe; Middle East & South Asia; Terrorism, Nonproliferation & Trade.

Group Ratings

	ADA	ACLU	AFS	LCV	ITIC	NTU	COC	ACU	CFG	FRC
2008	5	18	0	8	60	82	94	96	91	100
2007	0	—	0	5	—	91	70	100	89	—

National Journal Ratings

	2007 LIB	—	2007 CONS		2008 LIB	—	2008 CONS
Economic	4%	—	95%		2%	—	98%
Social	0%	—	91%		0%	—	91%
Foreign	0%	—	72%		0%	—	95%
Composite	8%	—	92%		3%	—	97%

Key Votes of the 110th Congress

1. Increase minimum wage	N	5. Share immigration data	Y	9. Withdraw troops 8/08	N
2. Expand SCHIP	N	6. Foreign aid abortion ban	Y	10. No operations in Iran	N
3. Raise CAFE standards	N	7. Ban gay bias in workplace	N	11. Free trade with Peru	Y
4. Bail out financial markets	Y	8. Repeal D.C. gun law	Y	12. Overhaul FISA	Y

Election Results

2008 general	Gresham Barrett (R)	186,799	(65%)	($765,832)
	Jane Dyer (D)	101,724	(35%)	($82,865)
2008 primary	Gresham Barrett (R)	unopposed		

Prior Winning Percentages: 2006 (63%); 2004 (100%); 2002 (67%)

Population		Race/Ethnicity		Work	
Pop. 2007:	694,669	White:	75.0%	Private:	77.8%
Change since 2000:	Up 3.9%	Black:	19.9%	Government:	15.4%
Urban:	50.3%	Hispanic:	3.0%	Self-employed:	6.5%
Rural:	49.7%	Asian:	0.7%	Blue collar:	31.1%
Area size:	5,568 sq. mi.	Native Am.:	0.2%	White collar:	53.0%
		Hawaiian:	0.0%	Khaki collar:	0.0%
Age		Two+ races:	1.1%	Other:	15.9%
Median age:	38.0 yrs.			Median income:	$40,597
More than 65 yrs:	14.4%	**Ancestry**		Median home value:	$103,400
Less than 18 yrs:	23.2%	USA:	13.2%	Poverty:	15.7%
		Irish:	10.0%		
Education		German:	9.3%	**Military Veterans**	
H.S. grad:	78.6%			% of Pop:	11.4%
College grad:	19.4%				
Grad degree:	6.9%				

The Upstate in South Carolina is many days' travel by wagon from the Lowcountry plantations along the coast. It was first settled by Scots-Irish farmers, including the family of future Vice President John C. Calhoun, around the time of the Revolutionary War. The pioneers wanted to make big plantations of these forests, but the land was too hilly for the labor-intensive rice crops grown in the Lowcountry and sometimes too cold for cotton. So relatively few slaves were brought here, and the land became mostly small farms. Today, the racial and cultural tone of the Upstate shows traces of these roots. This is a mostly white part of the South, with a hell-of-a-fella tone to daily life and a tradition-minded slice of Middle America. Yet it is not untouched by change. Aiken, with its horsey trappings for polo and steeplechase, has long attracted affluent transplants. The nearby Savannah River Site—a 310-square-mile federal weapons plant complex that for four decades produced tritium and plutonium that fueled America's nuclear arsenal—employed generations of highly trained engineers. More than 12,000 were laid off when the plant closed in 1992, though many were hired for the clean-up of nuclear waste stored at the site. Plans are also underway for a new $5 billion plant to convert plutonium from nuclear warheads for use in commercial reactors. Today, Interstate 85—once the Main Street of America's textile belt—travels through a booming southeastern corridor that runs from Raleigh-Durham to Atlanta. Clemson University was founded here by Calhoun's son-in-law and is one of the state's two land-grant institutions.

2008 Presidential Vote		
McCain (R)	188,692	(64%)
Obama (D)	103,804	(35%)
2004 Presidential Vote		
Bush (R)	169,283	(66%)
Kerry (D)	86,947	(34%)
Cook Partisan Voting Index:	R + 17	

The 3rd Congressional District of South Carolina follows the Georgia border north from the Savannah River Site through the tree-harvesting country around McCormick County to mountains along the North Carolina border. The southern part of the 3rd has a few heavily African-American areas, like Edgefield County, where the late Sen. Strom Thurmond grew up and first won public office in the 1930s. The former segregationist retired in 2002 at age 100. Edgefield County has grown significantly as it became part of the metropolitan area around Aiken and Augusta, Ga. This part of South Carolina, ancestrally Democratic, began trending Republican in the 1950s as cultural issues became more important in this fervently religious region. The district has consistently voted Republican even when Democrats have won statewide elections. In 2008, Republican presidential candidate John McCain won 64% of the vote, his best showing in a South Carolina district.

The congressman from the 3rd District is Gresham Barrett, a Republican elected in 2002. Barrett grew up in Westminster in Oconee County and graduated from The Citadel in Charleston. After serving as an artillery captain in the First Cavalry Division at Fort Hood, he returned home to run his family's furniture store. In 1996, he was elected to the state House. In 2001, when Lindsey Graham, the first Republican to hold this seat since Reconstruction, started running for the Senate, Barrett became the frontrunner to succeed him. He opposed abortion rights, defended gun owner rights, called for a national missile defense system and new weapons technology as part of the effort to "hunt down scum like Osama bin Laden and wipe their kind from the face of the Earth." He told voters that government should operate more like his business. Government should work "like Barrett's Furniture, where you get service, you get simplicity and people are there to help you." With a superior grass-roots organization, he led the six-candidate primary with 43% of the vote. In the two-week runoff campaign, state Rep. Jim Klauber argued that Barrett would not be sufficiently tough in supporting a crackdown on illegal immigrants. Barrett insisted that military issues were paramount. He raised more money, won more endorsements and won the runoff 65%-35%. He won the general election 67%-31%.

In the House, Barrett had a solidly conservative voting record, especially on cultural issues, and is a member of the Republican Study Committee, a group of the most conservative members of the House. Ever the Citadel graduate (his father, brother and two nephews are also graduates), he is distinguished by his crisp, military bearing. "With his pressed suits and posture as perfect as the Washington Monument's, Gresham Barrett is perhaps Congress' most starched member," wrote *The State* newspaper. He was one of the 15 House Republicans who voted against both the Republican Medicare prescription drug deal in 2003 and the GOP leadership-backed omnibus appropriations bill in late 2003. He was the only lawmaker from South Carolina to vote against an extension of the Voting Rights Act, and he introduced the Public Prayer Protection Act to permit public officials to pray in public as they see fit.

On fiscal issues, Barrett has called for a Taxpayer Bill of Rights "to ensure that Washington will become more efficient and accountable to the taxpayers that pay for it." Seeking "fresh air and sunshine" for federal spending, he made public in 2008 his requests for local spending projects. The practice of earmarking money in the appropriations bills for individual districts had become controversial, with critics deriding it as a waste of taxpayer money. In January 2009, Barrett, citing the nation's economic recession, announced he would donate his yearly congressional pay raise to a local charity. Barrett won passage in the House of an amendment for the Energy Department to study the feasibility of commercial nuclear energy production at Savannah River.

This has been a safe district for Barrett. In March 2009, he announced his campaign for governor in 2010, when Republican Mark Sanford is term-limited. He said that he would emphasize economic development and his experience in "bringing people together." Several local office-holders were considering campaigns for the House seat, which likely will remain Republican.

FOURTH DISTRICT

Bob Inglis (R)

Elected 2004, 6th term; b. Oct. 11, 1959, Bluffton; home, Travelers Rest; Duke U., B.A. 1981, U. of VA Law Schl., J.D. 1984; Presbyterian; married (Mary Anne); 5 children.

Elected Office: U.S. House of Reps., 1992–98.

Professional Career: Practicing atty., 1984–92.

DC Office: 100 CHOB, 20515, 202-225-6030; Fax: 202-226-1177; Web site: inglis.house.gov.

State Offices: Greenville, 864-232-1141; Spartanburg, 864-582-6422; Union, 864-427-2205.

Committees: *Foreign Affairs* (18th of 19 R): Asia, the Pacific & the Global Environment; Europe; Middle East & South Asia. *Science & Technology* (11th of 17 R): Energy & Environment (RMM); Research & Science Education.

Group Ratings

	ADA	ACLU	AFS	LCV	ITIC	NTU	COC	ACU	CFG	FRC
2008	5	45	0	31	71	69	89	84	83	100
2007	5	—	0	25	—	84	80	88	82	—

National Journal Ratings

	2007 LIB	—	2007 CONS	2008 LIB	—	2008 CONS
Economic	29%	—	70%	30%	—	70%
Social	34%	—	66%	9%	—	85%
Foreign	40%	—	60%	41%	—	59%
Composite	35%	—	66%	28%	—	72%

Key Votes of the 110th Congress

1. Increase minimum wage	N	5. Share immigration data	Y	9. Withdraw troops 8/08	N
2. Expand SCHIP	N	6. Foreign aid abortion ban	Y	10. No operations in Iran	N
3. Raise CAFE standards	N	7. Ban gay bias in workplace	N	11. Free trade with Peru	Y
4. Bail out financial markets	Y	8. Repeal D.C. gun law	Y	12. Overhaul FISA	Y

Election Results

2008 general	Bob Inglis (R)	184,440	(60%)	($495,289)
	Paul Corden (D)	113,291	(37%)	($75,167)
	C. Faye Walters (Green)	7,332	(2%)	
2008 primary	Bob Inglis (R)	37,571	(67%)	
	Charles Jeter (R)	18,545	(33%)	

Prior Winning Percentages: 2006 (64%); 2004 (70%); 1996 (71%); 1994 (73%); 1992 (50%)

Population		Race/Ethnicity		Work	
Pop. 2007:	721,153	White:	72.0%	Private:	83.8%
Change since 2000:	Up 7.8%	Black:	19.7%	Government:	10.1%
Urban:	73.5%	Hispanic:	5.3%	Self-employed:	5.9%
Rural:	26.5%	Asian:	1.7%	Blue collar:	28.0%
Area size:	2,165 sq. mi.	Native Am.:	0.2%	White collar:	57.2%
		Hawaiian:	0.1%	Khaki collar:	0.1%
Age		Two+ races:	0.8%	Other:	14.7%
Median age:	37.4 yrs.			Median income:	$43,202
More than 65 yrs:	12.5%	*Ancestry*		Median home value:	$121,400
Less than 18 yrs:	24.3%	USA:	12.3%	Poverty:	13.7%
		Irish:	9.2%		
Education		English:	8.8%	**Military Veterans**	
H.S. grad:	80.4%			% of Pop:	10.5%
College grad:	23.8%				
Grad degree:	8.0%				

A century ago, Northern investors seeking sites for textile mills looked at the Upstate of South Carolina and found what was described then as "mild climate, abundant water power, proximity to the cotton fields and plenty of native labor already accustomed to a low standard of living." As mills fled New England, textile factories settled along the Southern Railway and Seaboard Coast Line tracks between Charlotte and Atlanta, especially in the Piedmont of South Carolina. The textile country might

2008 Presidential Vote		
McCain (R)	190,004	(60%)
Obama (D)	119,246	(38%)
2004 Presidential Vote		
Bush (R)	181,255	(65%)
Kerry (D)	94,760	(34%)
Cook Partisan Voting Index:	R + 15	

look bucolic, but Greenville, Spartanburg and the dozens of mill towns thick in the surrounding countryside became as industrial as Lancashire or the Ruhr, with mills rising up on what were once twisting woodland paths. In the days before child labor laws, factory work sometimes began at age 6, condemning workers to a life of illiteracy. Escapes to a brighter future, such as the brilliant but brief baseball career of West Greenville's "Shoeless" Joe Jackson, were rare.

Today, this same stretch of land along Interstate 85, which parallels the Southern Railway, remains one of the largest textile-producing areas in the United States, even though most mills have shut down and the others are not likely to survive. The state had 35,000 textile and apparel workers in 2008, but has lost more than 30,000 textile jobs since 2000, with closings accelerated by the end of the Multifiber Agreement in 2005. But there is much more to the local economy than textiles. Many former textile workers have taken jobs with the new companies that have moved to the area. So many other jobs have been created that the South Carolina Textile Manufacturers Alliance dropped "Textiles" from its name. Financial sweeteners, tax incentives, the absence of unions and solid infrastructure—airports, interstate highways and the busy port of Charleston—attracted an enormous BMW plant, although it laid off 700 workers in 2008 during the recession and worldwide auto slowdown. The region has the American headquarters of Michelin and a big Fuji Photo factory, among others. Greenville's revitalized downtown now boasts fancy hotels and restaurants, including Korean, Thai and Vietnamese cuisine—each catering to the new corporate manager class.

The 4th Congressional District of South Carolina includes all of Greenville and Spartanburg counties, plus much smaller Union County and a sliver of Laurens County. Greenville is the largest county in the state, and has grown 15% since 2000. Culturally, the 4th ranges from conservative to very conservative, with strong influence from Greenville's many evangelical and fundamentalist churches. Bob Jones University is here as well; it has dropped its longtime ban on interracial dating but students are still prohibited from smoking, drinking, dancing and wearing jeans or shorts to class. Here, the real political divide is between religious and economic conservatives. But large new subdivisions have sprouted between Greenville and Spartanburg, and newcomers have brought religious diversity. Greenville has growing populations not only of Catholics and Jews, but also Muslims, Buddhists, Hindus, Baha'is, and the only gay-oriented church within 60 miles. When President George W. Bush in 2008 gave the commencement address at Furman University in Greenville, several dozen people protested and more than 30 professors got permission not to attend because they objected to his policies. Still, this is a heavily Republican district, with the smallest African-American percentage in the state. In 2008, GOP presidential candidate John McCain won 60% of the vote in the district.

The congressman from the 4th District once again is Bob Inglis, who was elected in 2004 after having served from 1993 to 1999. He grew up in the Lowcountry, excelled at Duke University and the University of Virginia law school and moved to Greenville to practice commercial law. He ran for the U.S. House against a Democratic incumbent in 1992 and pledged to serve only three terms, to take no money from political action committees and to oppose pork barrel projects. He won 50%-48%. Inglis kept his promises. When Republicans won the House in 1994, he supported reforms, including one to apply all U.S. laws to Congress, which had exempted itself from many laws and regulations, and a ban on gifts and other perks to members. Inglis resisted joining the Washington culture and slept in his office on an air mattress. In 1998, he ran against Democratic Sen. Ernest Hollings and lost 53%-46%. He returned to Greenville to practice law, specializing in commercial real estate and corporations.

In 2004, Inglis traded places with Rep. Jim DeMint, his House successor, who honored his own term-limits pledge and was elected to the Senate as Hollings retired. Inglis again ran as a citizen-politician, saying he was "reinvigorated" by his time in private life. But this time, he refused to make another term limits pledge, which he likened to "unilateral disarmament." He suggested that the Capitol Hill culture had changed, so that the same strategies that made sense after Republicans captured the House majority, no longer were required. Ever the budget hawk, Inglis enlisted his wife as his top campaign aide, eschewed political consultants, ran his race out of his home and refused political action committee contributions. By getting an early start and raising large amounts of money, he scared off serious competition. He won 84% of the vote in the Republican primary and easily won the general election 70%-29% over funeral home executive Brandon Brown.

His voting record moved toward the center from the more conservative stances that he took in his first stint in the House. He opposed oil drilling in the Arctic National Wildlife Refuge and renewal of rules for warrantless electronic surveillance. He joined a congressional delegation to Antarctica, where scientific research convinced him of the risk of global warming. He is the ranking Republican on the Energy and Environment Subcommittee on the Science and Technology Committee, and has been outspoken about the need to reduce carbon emissions that cause global warming. He worked on legislation to promote alternative fuels, including the enactment in December 2007 of annual cash prices for hydrogen-based inventions. During his initial tenure, he told *The Greenville News*, "I just sort of reeked of sanctimony." No more, he pledged.

Inglis had an easy re-election in 2006. But his February 2007 support of the Democratic resolution opposing the military surge in Iraq, which he called "a vote of conscience," caused anger among many Republicans at home, including the chairman of the state party and a few county party leaders. When they encouraged potential primary challengers, Inglis responded by proposing "benchmarks" for success in Iraq. Charles Jeter, an Environmental Protection Agency regional official in the Reagan Administration, challenged Inglis and said that his environmental views made him the "Al Gore of the Republican Party." But Inglis won the primary over Jeter 67%-33%, and went on to win the general election 60%-37%. He faces another likely primary challenge in 2010.

FIFTH DISTRICT

John Spratt (D)

Elected 1982, 14th term; b. Nov. 1, 1942, Charlotte, NC; home, York; Davidson Col., A.B. 1964, Oxford U., M.A. 1966, Yale U., LL.B. 1969; Presbyterian; married (Jane Stacy); 3 children.

Military Career: Army Operations, U.S. Dept. of Defense, 1969–71.

Professional Career: Practicing atty., 1971–82; Pres., Bank of Ft. Mill, 1973–82; Pres., Spratt Insurance Agcy., 1973–82.

DC Office: 1401 LHOB, 20515, 202-225-5501; Fax: 202-225-0464; Web site: spratt.house.gov.

State Offices: Darlington, 843-393-3998; Rock Hill, 803-327-1114; Sumter, 803-773-3362.

Committees: *Armed Services* (2nd of 36 D): Air & Land Forces; Oversight & Investigations; Strategic Forces. *Budget* (Chmn of 24 D).

Group Ratings

	ADA	ACLU	AFS	LCV	ITIC	NTU	COC	ACU	CFG	FRC
2008	85	91	100	92	86	6	61	4	0	17
2007	95	—	100	85	—	5	55	4	1	—

National Journal Ratings

	2007 LIB	—	2007 CONS		2008 LIB	—	2008 CONS
Economic	77%	—	22%		71%	—	25%
Social	57%	—	43%		62%	—	34%
Foreign	56%	—	43%		65%	—	32%
Composite	64%	—	36%		68%	—	32%

Key Votes of the 110th Congress

1. Increase minimum wage	Y	5. Share immigration data	Y	9. Withdraw troops 8/08	Y
2. Expand SCHIP	Y	6. Foreign aid abortion ban	N	10. No operations in Iran	Y
3. Raise CAFE standards	Y	7. Ban gay bias in workplace	Y	11. Free trade with Peru	N
4. Bail out financial markets	Y	8. Repeal D.C. gun law	Y	12. Overhaul FISA	Y

Election Results

2008 general	John Spratt (D)	188,785	(62%)	($829,176)
	Albert Spencer (R)	113,282	(37%)	($9,590)
2008 primary	John Spratt (D)	unopposed		

Prior Winning Percentages: 2006 (57%); 2004 (63%); 2002 (86%); 2000 (59%); 1998 (58%); 1996 (54%); 1994 (52%); 1992 (61%); 1990 (100%); 1988 (70%); 1986 (100%); 1984 (92%); 1982 (68%)

Population		Race/Ethnicity		Work	
Pop. 2007:	720,254	White:	63.5%	Private:	79.2%
Change since 2000:	Up 7.7%	Black:	31.3%	Government:	14.9%
Urban:	46.7%	Hispanic:	2.8%	Self-employed:	5.7%
Rural:	53.3%	Asian:	0.7%	Blue collar:	32.1%
Area size:	7,141 sq. mi.	Native Am.:	0.5%	White collar:	51.6%
		Hawaiian:	0.0%	Khaki collar:	0.4%
Age		Two+ races:	1.1%	Other:	16.0%
Median age:	36.9 yrs.	*Ancestry*		Median income:	$39,353
More than 65 yrs:	12.4%	USA:	12.4%	Median home value:	$100,700
Less than 18 yrs:	25.1%	English:	7.5%	Poverty:	16.9%
		German:	7.4%	**Military Veterans**	
Education				% of Pop:	11.4%
H.S. grad:	76.4%				
College grad:	17.2%				
Grad degree:	5.8%				

Some of the fiercest battles of the Revolutionary War were fought in South Carolina's Upstate, on hilly lands just being settled by Scots-Irish farmers moving up from the Lowcountry or down the Virginia Piedmont valley. This was a country of violent passions and unclear lines. Carolinians have long argued over which side of the North and South Carolina boundary Andrew Jackson was born in 1767. Ever since, the fighting spirit and Calvinist faith of Upstate Carolinians have not wavered. This

2008 Presidential Vote

McCain (R)............................166,948   (53%)
Obama (D) 145,036   (46%)

2004 Presidential Vote

Bush (R) 143,001   (57%)
Kerry (D)...............................104,850   (42%)

Cook Partisan Voting Index: R + 7

"Olde English District" remains intensely religious and pro-military, but it is no longer impoverished. For many years, the dominant industry here was textiles, traditionally the first factory enterprise of industrializing countries, with low pay and poor working conditions. But the number of textile jobs has declined markedly since the 1980s, and small business prosperity more recently has been barreling down the interstates from Greenville-Spartanburg and Columbia and Charlotte to transform counties once dependent on tobacco fields and textile mills.

The 5th Congressional District of South Carolina consists of all or part of 14 counties, mostly in the Upstate and some in the Midlands. It includes Rock Hill-based York County, which grew 21% from 2000 to 2007 and is on the edge of the Charlotte, N.C., metro area. Just to the east is Lancaster County, where Del Webb's Sun City Carolina Lakes is building a retirement community of more than 3,400 new homes. Further east, the 5th includes Dillon County and Darlington, site of the Southern 500 stock car race every Labor Day. It also includes lowland tobacco country, including Marlboro and Chesterfield counties. Politically, this homeland of Andrew Jackson is ancestrally Democratic, but Republicans are now competitive if not dominant. The tobacco counties are heavily Democratic, but York County is trending Republican. President George W. Bush won 57% of the district's vote in 2004; GOP presidential nominee John McCain won 53% in 2008, including 58%-40% in York.

The congressman from the 5th District is John Spratt, a Democrat elected in 1982 and the chairman of the House Budget Committee. He comes from a prominent York County family and graduated from Davidson College, Oxford University and Yale Law School. He served two years in the Army, in the Operations Analysis Group in the office of the Pentagon comptroller. He first got involved in politics in Charles Ravenel's unsuccessful 1974 Democratic campaign for governor. In 1982, the 5th District incumbent announced his retirement a week before the filing deadline. Spratt quickly put together a campaign and won 38% in the primary, 55% in the runoff against a high-spending candidate, and 68% in the general election. A hastily improvised campaign led to a long political career. Today, Spratt is a widely respected member of Congress with a substantial role in shaping national legislation.

Spratt is the second-ranking Democrat on the Armed Services Committee. In the 1980s, he worked with Chairman Les Aspin, D-Wis., and, in his thick Carolina accent and with impressive knowledge of details, stitched together compromises on the MX missile, binary nerve gas weapons, the Strategic Defense Initiative, and the Savannah River Site. He kept military projects flowing through the House, when many members were looking to cut military spending. In the late 1990s, Spratt was the House Democrats' lead man for limits on missile defense. His amendment on the subject prevailed in February 1995 by 218-212, the first significant defeat of a Contract with America promise in the Republican House.

On the Iraq War resolution, Spratt played a key role for Democrats. In September 2002, House Minority Leader Dick Gephardt turned to Spratt and Rep. Ike Skelton of Missouri, the ranking Democrat on Armed Services, for help in drafting an alternative to the broad White House resolution authorizing the use of force. Spratt sought another round of weapons inspections and suggested removing a phrase authorizing any action to ensure peace and security in the region. The administration agreed to delete the phrase. When Gephardt went to the White House and agreed on a resolution, Spratt continued to prepare a Democratic alternative, working with Minority Whip Nancy Pelosi of California. He saw "no need to invoke preemptive intervention or to draw a tenuous connection between Iraq and Al Qaeda." His resolution authorized military action if the United Nations approved, and left room for the administration to seek another resolution from Congress if the U.N. did not approve. His alternative was defeated 270-155; Democrats favored it 147-60 but Republicans opposed it 210-8. Spratt then joined the majority voting for the resolution sponsored by the administration and Gephardt, which passed 296-133.

After the 2002 election, Gephardt stepped down, and Pelosi was elected minority leader. One of her first acts was to appoint Spratt assistant to the leader and name him her designee on budget issues. Spratt in turn agreed to be a team player, and Pelosi, as a liberal, could argue that Democratic budget policy was being driven by a member with a deserved reputation as a moderate.

Spratt has long been immersed in the budget process. He played a major role in putting together the May 1997 agreement between Democrats and the then new ruling majority Republicans to reach a balanced budget. It required, he said, "Some stiff, tough bargaining. As a matter of process, it was a major accomplishment." But the bipartisanship of that period did not continue, and Spratt was often in the position of offering Democratic budget alternatives that were routinely defeated on party lines. After the September 11 attacks, he issued a report predicting, accurately, that the budget surplus would disappear in 2002 and quite possibly for several years. In 2002, he called for negotiations like those that produced the 1997 budget agreement or the 1990 budget summit in which Bush's father agreed to break his promise and raise taxes. "He can take a page from his father's experience and hope it doesn't cost him what it cost his dad. But his dad did the right thing," Spratt said then. But the Republicans once again passed a budget resolution along party lines. Spratt blamed subsequent deficits on the 2001 Bush tax cuts but did not urge their repeal.

In 2005, Spratt complained that Congressional Budget Office forecasts of the deficit were unduly optimistic because they did not include all of the costs of fighting wars in Iraq and Afghanistan. The following year, as the majority Republicans continued to dominate the budget proceedings, he argued that while the administration's approach of restraining domestic discretionary spending and waiting for a surge in revenues might shrink deficits in the short term, it would be inadequate for long-range fiscal challenges. "This is not a cyclical deficit. It's a structural deficit built into our budget," he said.

After Democrats won majorities in both houses in 2006, he and Senate Budget Committee Chairman Kent Conrad, D-N.D., called for a more realistic statement of war costs in the administration's budget. He complained that the administration was counting on vastly increased revenues from the Alternative Minimum Tax, assuming that the 4.2 million taxpayers hit by the AMT, without the one-year patch that had become routine, would balloon to 23 million—concentrated in high-income, high-tax states which vote heavily Democratic. Then came the hard work, unnecessary when he was in the minority, of assembling 218 votes for the Democratic budget. "If you can't budget, you can't govern," Spratt is fond of saying. His Democratic budget resolution that passed the House in 2007 assumed that the middle-class would get relief from the AMT, which was designed to tax the wealthy but had been ensnaring an increasing number of middle-income taxpayers. It included the administration's estimate of the cost of the war in Iraq in 2009 at $50 billion. It assumed also that all the Bush tax cuts would stay in place until 2010 and then might disappear, prompting Republicans to label it the "biggest tax increase in American history." After an extended battle with the Senate, Spratt and other House Democrats in late 2007 abandoned their campaign to "pay for" relief from the AMT extension with tax hikes elsewhere.

In the largely uneventful 2008 budget debate, Spratt sought to focus attention on how the federal debt had increased while Bush was president from $5.7 trillion to the eventual $10.6 trillion when he left office. "Mr. Bush came into office with the biggest surpluses in history and will leave with the biggest deficits in history. That is the bottom line," he said. Spratt has opposed calls for an entitlement commission to come up with solutions to future shortages in Medicare, Medicaid and Social Security on the grounds that previous such efforts have had little or no effect.

Spratt played a vital role in the early months of the Obama administration. Pelosi's "maestro of the budget" sought a wider stage as he urged Obama to "get a quick start" and "keep his eye on the prize," which for Spratt was chiefly the domestic economy. He cooperated with other senior House Democrats to shape the contents of the $787 billion economic stimulus bill, which was enacted in February 2009. In the subsequent budget debate, Spratt worked with the Obama team as they sought to emphasize the positive aspects of reducing the budget deficit from a projected $1.2 trillion in 2010 to $523 billion in 2014, still higher than any in the nation's history. He was mostly successful in personally selling the budget to the conservative Blue Dog Democrats.

On other issues, Spratt has a moderate record. He voted for the North America Free Trade Agreement in 1993 but opposed the Central America Free Trade Agreement in 2005. He won an amendment in the 2006 defense bill providing free life insurance for all troops in combat. In early 2007, he was among the first Democrats who urged increased attention to Afghanistan, which he called "the forgotten war." In recent years, he won passage of a bill setting up a study of Revolutionary War sites in the Upstate of South Carolina to be included in a Southern Campaign of the Revolution Heritage Area. He also passed a bipartisan bill prohibiting the slaughter of horses for human consumption, whose markets for horse meat were primarily in France and Belgium.

Spratt has had two tough races, in 1994 and 1996, when he won by margins of 52%-48% and 54%-45%, respectively. From 1998 to 2004, he was re-elected by wide margins. In 2006, Republicans targeted Spratt, recruiting Rock Hill state Rep. Ralph Norman, a residential and commercial real estate developer. Vice President Dick Cheney, Republican Sens. Lindsey Graham and Jim DeMint, and Gov. Mark Sanford all campaigned for Norman. Spratt responded with an ad claiming Norman had been cited for hiring illegal immigrants. In mid-October, national Republicans, in trouble in races across the country and worried about protecting GOP incumbents, quit pouring money into Norman's campaign. Spratt outspent him nearly 2-to-1 and won 57%-43%, a solid margin, but the closest race he had encountered since 1996, despite the national Democratic trend. In 2008, Spratt was re-elected easily.

Apparently secure in his district and with Pelosi, Spratt is positioned to resume his attention to military issues and take over as Armed Services Committee chairman if Skelton retires, possibly after redistricting in 2012.

SIXTH DISTRICT

James Clyburn (D)

Elected 1992, 9th term; b. July 21, 1940, Sumter; home, Columbia; SC St. U., B.A. 1962; African Methodist Episcopal; married (Emily); 3 children.

Professional Career: Teacher, 1962–66; Dir., Charleston Neighborhood Youth Corps, 1966–68; Exec. dir., SC Comm. for Farm Workers, 1968–71; Asst., SC Gov. West, 1971–74; SC Human Affairs Comm., 1974–92.

DC Office: 2135 RHOB, 20515, 202-225-3315; Fax: 202-225-2313; Web site: clyburn.house.gov.

State Offices: Columbia, 803-799-1100; Florence, 843-622-1212; Santee, 803-854-4700.

Committees: *Majority Whip.*

Group Ratings

	ADA	ACLU	AFS	LCV	ITIC	NTU	COC	ACU	CFG	FRC
2008	95	91	100	92	100	4	56	0	0	0
2007	95	—	100	80	—	3	68	0	11	—

National Journal Ratings

	2007 LIB — 2007 CONS		2008 LIB — 2008 CONS	
Economic	82%	— 0%	85%	— 0%
Social	85%	— 13%	75%	— 18%
Foreign	65%	— 33%	65%	— 32%
Composite	81%	— 19%	79%	— 21%

Key Votes of the 110th Congress

1. Increase minimum wage	Y	5. Share immigration data	N	9. Withdraw troops 8/08	Y
2. Expand SCHIP	Y	6. Foreign aid abortion ban	N	10. No operations in Iran	Y
3. Raise CAFE standards	Y	7. Ban gay bias in workplace	Y	11. Free trade with Peru	Y
4. Bail out financial markets	Y	8. Repeal D.C. gun law	N	12. Overhaul FISA	Y

Election Results

2008 general	James Clyburn (D)..193,378	(67%)	($2,389,430)
	Nancy Harrelson (R)..93,059	(32%)	
2008 primary	James Clyburn (D).....................................unopposed		

Prior Winning Percentages: 2006 (64%); 2004 (67%); 2002 (67%); 2000 (72%); 1998 (73%); 1996 (69%); 1994 (64%); 1992 (65%)

Population		Race/Ethnicity		Work	
Pop. 2007:	659,369	White:	40.9%	Private:	74.7%
Change since 2000:	Down 1.4%	Black:	55.4%	Government:	19.1%
Urban:	48.0%	Hispanic:	1.8%	Self-employed:	6.0%
Rural:	52.0%	Asian:	0.7%	Blue collar:	30.7%
Area size:	8,490 sq. mi.	Native Am.:	0.3%	White collar:	48.6%
		Hawaiian:	0.0%	Khaki collar:	0.4%
Age		Two+ races:	0.9%	Other:	20.3%
Median age:	36.2 yrs.			Median income:	$32,125
More than 65 yrs:	12.6%	*Ancestry*		Median home value:	$87,000
Less than 18 yrs:	24.2%	USA:	7.7%	Poverty:	24.2%
		English:	5.2%		
Education		German:	5.1%	**Military Veterans**	
H.S. grad:	76.0%			% of Pop:	10.8%
College grad:	15.6%				
Grad degree:	5.1%				

South Carolina was first settled by planters from Barbados, bringing with them a tropical plantation economy, which they transferred to the not-quite-tropical climate of the Carolina coastal lowlands. The flat Lowcountry and the coastal islands are laced with sluggish rivers and swamps. The planters brought thousands of slaves from Africa, and Colonial South Carolina quickly became one of the richest parts of North America, with dazzling Georgian architecture in Charleston and classic

2008 Presidential Vote
Obama (D) 188,098   (64%)
McCain (R)............................102,387   (35%)

2004 Presidential Vote
Kerry (D)...............................151,061   (61%)
Bush (R) 97,248   (39%)

Cook Partisan Voting Index: D + 12

plantation gardens. The planters built great irrigation systems and grew rice and cotton and the dye-plant indigo, all heavily in demand in Britain and elsewhere. All this wealth, of course, was built on the slave labor of countless African-Americans. In colonial times, a majority of South Carolinians were slaves, as were a majority of lowlands residents when Fort Sumter was fired upon (although there were also many free blacks in Charleston, a few of whom owned slaves themselves). South Carolina's black heritage has left a lasting imprint on American culture. Gullah, a mixture of English, French and African dialects is still spoken on the sea islands, and Gullah customs survive—oyster roasts and sweet potato feasts at Christmas, handmade dolls and sweetgrass baskets. The poverty that was the almost universal lot of lowland blacks after the Civil War has eased only in the last generation, as development came to the coast and cultural isolation dissipated. But many African-Americans decided not to wait for progress. They abandoned South Carolina for opportunities in the North.

The 6th Congressional District of South Carolina, created in 1992 as a black-majority district, includes only a bit of the South Carolina coast, which is increasingly lined with affluent retirement and recreational communities. The district's boundaries take in the black central city neighborhoods of Charleston, North Charleston and Columbia, but leave out their affluent white areas, both urban and suburban, in the adjacent 1st and 2d Districts. The 6th includes Orangeburg, home of the historically black South Carolina State University, and Florence, at the center of the Pee Dee tobacco-growing country in eastern South Carolina. Orangeburg was the scene of a massacre in February 1968, when three black students were killed and 27 wounded by police while protesting a segregated bowling alley. The Pee Dee area has had substantial economic growth as a warehousing and distribution center: the QVC home shopping network opened a $75 million facility there in 2007. In Orangeburg, the Dubai-based Economic Zones World unveiled in late 2008 plans for an industrial and warehouse site that would create more than 3,000 jobs. Most of the cargo would arrive through the Charleston port. The 6th's population in 2007 was 55% African-American. In 2008, Democratic presidential nominee Barack Obama got 64% of the vote, carrying every county except for Florence. This was the only South Carolina district he won.

The congressman from the 6th District is James Clyburn, a Democrat elected in 1992 and the House majority whip, the third-ranking leadership position. He is also the highest ranking African-American in Congress. Clyburn grew up in Sumter, the son of a minister, and was educated at a private, all-black boarding school. As a young man, he joined the Student Nonviolent Coordinating Committee, which took its cues from the Rev. Martin Luther King's Southern Christian Leadership Conference. In 1960, he was one of seven people who organized the state's first sit-ins, at a five-and-dime store in the Orangeburg town square. He met his wife while in jail for three days. Clyburn worked as a teacher, as an employment counselor and in government antipoverty programs. In 1970, he ran for the South Carolina House and lost narrowly. Democratic Gov. John West appointed Clyburn as state Human Affairs commissioner and he served 18 years, under two Democratic and two Republican governors. He ran twice for secretary of state, in 1978 and 1986, losing narrowly. Then the new, black-majority 6th District was created. Clyburn ran for the seat, and in the Democratic primary, won 56% of the vote against four African-American opponents, all with serious claims for the nomination. Clyburn was better known, ran first or second in every part of the district, and piled up 88% of the vote in his home county of Sumter. Clyburn became the only black to represent South Carolina in Congress since George Washington Murray (a distant relative of his) left in 1897.

In the House, he established a moderate-to-liberal voting record, and in his early years, focused on local priorities. He also joined the moderate New Democrat Coalition at its 1997 inception, the only African-American House member to do so. When cigarette tax increases were proposed, he urged safeguards for tobacco farmers. The House twice passed his bill to create a Gullah/Geechee Heritage Corridor from northern Florida to North Carolina. On the Appropriations Committee from 1998 to 2006, he focused on securing federal funds to develop the corridor around Interstate 95, which passes through rural counties in the district that historically were dependent on tobacco and cotton.

He became chairman of the Congressional Black Caucus in 1999, and in that role Clyburn urged the Democratic National Committee to become more responsive to blacks. After the 2002 election, he ran for vice chairman of the Democratic Caucus and prevailed with 95 votes to 56 for New York Rep. Gregory Meeks and 53 for California Rep. Zoe Lofgren. He said the leadership needed to more reflect the party's diversity. In 2006, he was elected to move up to Democratic Caucus chairman, the No. 4 position in the party leadership, and later that year, was was chosen majority whip after Democrats won control of the House. Then-Rep. Rahm Emanuel of Illinois also wanted the job, and would have had to leapfrog over Clyburn to get it. But Emanuel backed down at the urging of Speaker Nancy Pelosi, who favored Clyburn for the post. Emanuel took Clyburn's spot as Democratic Caucus chairman in recognition of his work raising money and successfully recruiting challengers in the pivotal 2006 election as chairman of the Democratic Congressional Campaign Committee. Clyburn said, "I'm going to be leery of going away from seniority. African-Americans supported the seniority system and waited their turn. Now, we get nervous when people talk about changing the rules." He described his approach to leadership this way: "When it comes to working with the Democratic Caucus, I have to fish in a lot of ponds. I go fishing with the Blue Dogs. I go fishing with the New Dems. I go fishing with the Hispanics and I go fishing with the Asian Pacific Islanders, trying to cobble together the 218 votes I need. But a lot of times I have to be a hunter, and they tell me, even though I never hunt, they tell me that a good hunter knows how to work both sides of the ditch. I fish among my caucus, Democratic members, and I go hunting sometimes, among my Republican members."

Clyburn sought enhanced influence for his whip organization in crafting policy, a way of getting more points of view from across party factions into the process of drafting major legislation in the committees. In 2007, he held a series of "listening sessions" with Democrats to explore options for an immigration bill. He also coordinated the House's continuing response to the devastation caused by Hurricane Katrina, especially in the poor sections of Louisiana. With experience in dealing with hurricane damage in his home state, he led the Katrina Task Force, which made visits to the Gulf Coast and had regular meetings with local officials. He worked to waive the 10% matching requirement required for local communities seeking federal funds for disaster recovery. "I truly believe that if the demographics of the affected areas had been different, the response of the federal government would have been different," he said in a May 2007 speech in Baton Rouge.

Back home Clyburn has not faced serious opposition for re-election. He has been a player in the state's often pivotal Democratic presidential primary. African-Americans cast about half the votes in the primary, and Clyburn is the most prominent black politician in the state. In the 2004 presidential primary campaign, he first backed Rep. Dick Gephardt of Missouri, with whom he had worked in the House. But Gephardt withdrew after the Iowa caucuses, and Clyburn endorsed frontrunner John Kerry rather than South Carolina native John Edwards. Throughout 2007, his support was eagerly sought by Democratic contenders, who attended his annual Fish Fry in Columbia. Although he did not take sides in the January 2008 primary, he clashed with Hillary Rodham Clinton when she seemed to suggest that President Lyndon Johnson, in signing the Civil Rights Act of 1964, had a more important role than the Rev. King and other key civil rights figures at the time. "That bothered me a great deal," Clyburn told *The New York Times*. As the leader of an older generation of civil rights leaders, he was initially skeptical that Obama could win the presidential nomination. When Obama clinched it in June 2008, Clyburn told a radio interviewer that he went home to watch it alone on television "because what I was feeling was indescribable and I was afraid that I would not be able to control my emotions."

After the election, Clyburn got into an unusual conflict with Republican Gov. Mark Sanford, who said that he would not use all of the money available to South Carolina in the economic stimulus bill enacted in February 2009. He called the governor's action a "slap in the face" of the predominantly black constituents who would benefit. In April 2009, President Obama nominated Clyburn's daughter, Mignon Clyburn, for a seat on the Federal Communications Commission. Since 1998, she has been on the Public Service Commission in South Carolina.

★ SOUTH DAKOTA ★

One of the last great stretches of the American Wild West was the southern part of the Dakota Territory, admitted to the Union in 1889 as the state of South Dakota. For years, this land had been the home of the Oglala Sioux, one of the largest Native American tribes, who had built a buffalo hunting civilization by becoming masters of the horses the Spaniards had imported to North America 350 years earlier. It was the Sioux warrior chief Sitting Bull, buried on a bluff above the Missouri River, who destroyed Custer at Little Big Horn in 1876. Just a few years later, many of the remaining Oglala Sioux Indians in South Dakota were massacred at Wounded Knee in 1890. After half a century of disease and a decade of defeat fighting the westward advance of white settlement, the Sioux were a traumatized people, and still are today, living on reservations with proud traditions but in terrible poverty. Isolated from the mainstream economic marketplace, they are beset by high rates of crime, alcoholism and suicide, with life expectancy and disease rates akin to those of sub-Saharan Africa. On the Pine Ridge Reservation in Shannon County, unemployment is a staggering 85% and incomes average $3,700 a year. Incremental progress has been made over the years, at least in preserving the vestiges of the Sioux culture and staunching some of the decline in standards of living. Infant mortality has been reduced and the American Indian population has been growing rapidly. In 2007, the state added to school curricula units on the language and culture of the Lakota and other Indians. In 2004, 98 buffalo were rounded up on California's Catalina Island, the descendants of animals brought there to film a Western in the 1920s, and returned to the Lakota Reservation. Indians account for 8% of the population in South Dakota, more than in any other state except New Mexico and Alaska.

Once the Sioux were subdued and forced to surrender their territory, white settlement of South Dakota came fast, fueled by the gold strikes in the Black Hills beginning in 1876. Soon, the mountains swarmed with settlers. Deadwood became a city of 20,000 where Calamity Jane ruled the saloons and Wild Bill Hickok was shot in the back while holding two pair—aces and eights. Ranchers, knowing that the buffalo could not be contained by barbed wire fences, massacred them so thoroughly that when Teddy Roosevelt got to the Dakota Territory in 1884, he had a hard time finding one to shoot. It was not long before the railroad came through, and then permanent settlers, many of them German and Scandinavian immigrants recruited by the railroads. They built sodhouses, broke the land and set down roots.

Demographically, South Dakota has never entirely filled up. In the 25 years between statehood and World War I, the eastern third of the state, sectioned off Midwestern style into 640-acre square miles, was settled by farmers. But moving westward, before a traveler reaches the Missouri River in the middle of the state, green turns to brown, cultivation grows sparse and then stops. The West River plains are open grazing land, scarcely touched by the white men who were so eager to establish dominion over them a century ago. The land is punctuated, not by roads meeting every mile at precise angles, but by buttes, gullies and grasslands sweeping to the horizon with no sign of human habitation except the occasional missile silos that once pointed toward the Soviet Union. Far in the west, in Butte County, is the Geographic Center of the United States, designated as such after Alaska was admitted to the Union.

South Dakota's political patterns were fairly well set by the early 1900s. Its early settlers were mostly Midwesterners who brought their Republicanism with them. Voters here never had much use for the Non-Partisan League, which caught on in North Dakota, and there was never anything here comparable to the Farmer-Labor Party of Minnesota. But the nature of the farm economy—its dependence on the great railroads and milling companies, and on the vagaries of international markets—meant that South Dakota was subject to periodic farm revolts. It voted for Populists and William Jennings Bryan in the 1890s. It supported the early New Deal, and it revolted against the Eisenhower administration in the 1950s by electing a young Democratic congressman named George McGovern, then a professor at Dakota Wesleyan University in Mitchell. South Dakota shared the isolationist impulse of much of the Great Plains. McGovern's opposition to the Vietnam War in the late 1960s was not a liability here. In the mid-1970s, Democrats seemed on the verge of becoming the majority party.

Then South Dakota moved sharply to the Republicans, beginning with the administration of Republican Gov. Bill Janklow, elected in 1978 and 1982 and then again in 1994 and 1998. In 1979, Sioux Falls banker Thomas Reardon suggested that the state get rid of its usury law limiting interest rates; inflation was driving market rates over the usury limits and choking off credit to consumers. Janklow and the Legislature repealed the usury law and in 1981 passed laws enabling Citibank to move its credit card operations to Sioux Falls, where it could charge market interest rates—all in a state with no corporate or personal income taxes, and a community with a literate low-wage work force. The Citibank operation here has grown from 50 employees to 3,200, servicing some 118 million cardholders, replacing the meat-packer John Morrell as the biggest employer. Other banks and telemarketing followed. More than 15,000 people in the Sioux Falls area work in financial services.

All this has made South Dakota an unusually productive place economically. The state leads the nation in the percentage of young children in two-income families and has the highest rate of employed

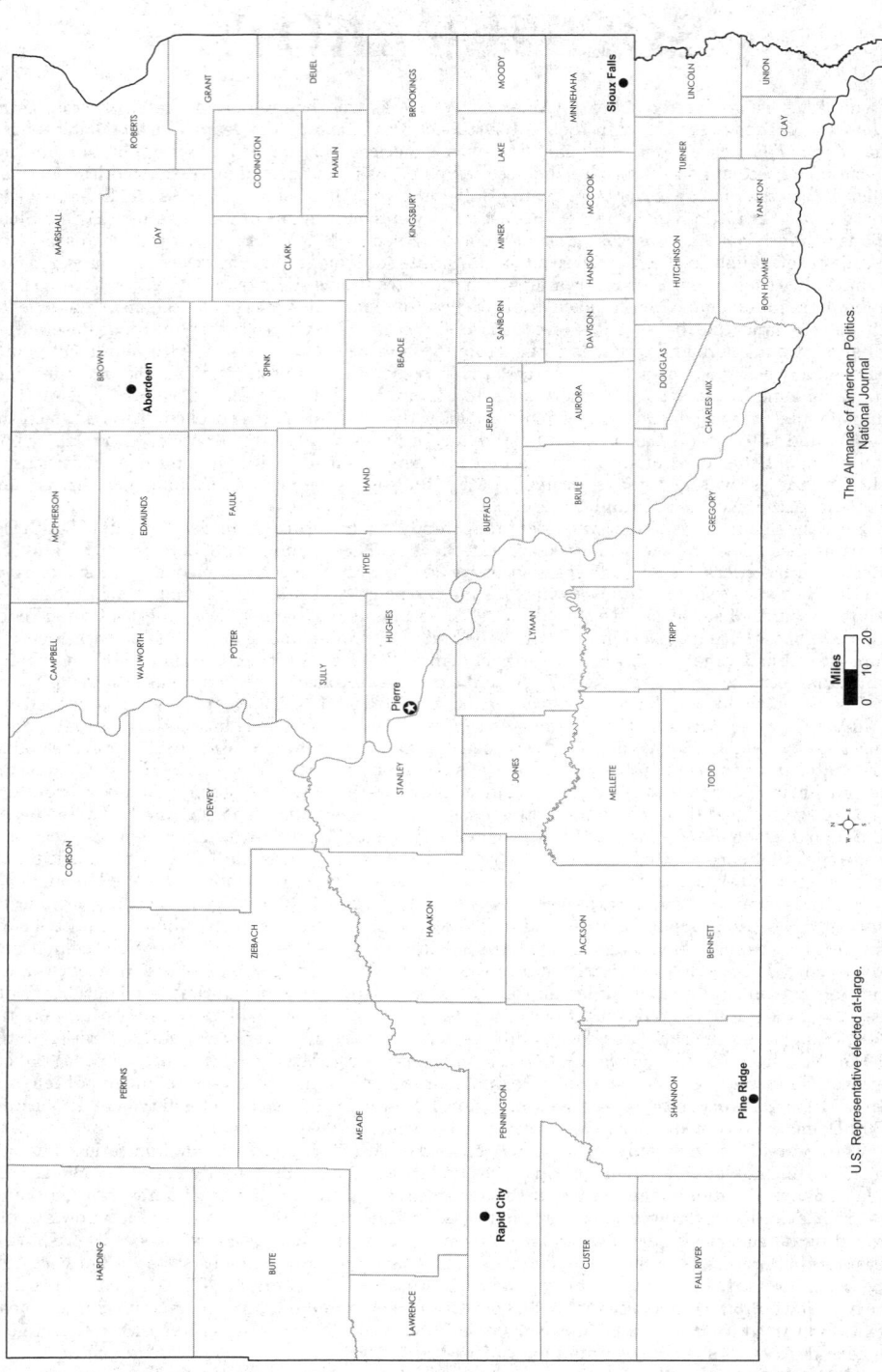

The Almanac of American Politics.
National Journal

Miles
0   10   20

U.S. Representative elected at-large.

seniors—a third of people age 65 to 74 are working. It ranks high in credit ratings, low in foreclosures, and high in repaying college loans. Even as some big employers disappeared—Gateway Computer moved to San Diego, IBP was bought by Tyson Foods, NorthWestern Energy went bankrupt—other jobs have been created, and the National Science Foundation picked the Homestake gold mine in the Black Hills as the site of a new physics lab. As the recession hit in 2007 and 2008, South Dakota was the only Midwestern state with population growth that exceeded the national average. It has relatively low wages, but also some of the nation's lowest unemployment and housing prices. Its residents and those in North Dakota spend less time commuting to work than Americans elsewhere. It leads the nation in percentage of home-based businesses. Some meatpacking plants have closed, but others are manned now by a largely Hispanic work force, recruited from the Southwest and beyond. Some 40 languages are spoken on the floor of the John Morrell plant in Sioux Falls.

South Dakota has long been thought of as a farm state, but farm counties have been losing population. In the 1990 census, 11% of the workforce was employed in farming, forestry or fishing, but by 2000, that figure had dropped to 8%. Ranching is also important, and there is still some mining here, but it is tapering off. One reason is increased productivity. South Dakota in 2008 had half as many dairy cows as it did in 1970 but produced more milk. As local meatpacking plants have closed, the state has promoted the production of luxury beef, with computer tracking of each cow to guarantee its provenance and freedom from disease. Wide open spaces leave room for initiatives like the attempt by American Sign Language advocates to set up a town for the deaf in McCook County. Economically and demographically, South Dakota is coming to resemble the Rocky Mountain states, with most people concentrated around a few prosperous and growing cities and towns, while vast acreage remains vacant, punctuated with infrequent ranches and resort areas. Lincoln County, just south of Sioux Falls, was the nation's seventh fastest-growing county from 2000 to 2008, and in 2008, Sioux Falls's Minnehaha County and Lincoln County together had 27% of the state's population. Politically, this growth has been a standoff between the parties. Democrats have benefited from growth and increased turnout on the reservations, while Republicans have benefited from growth in the Black Hills and the two parties have slugged it out in the Sioux Falls area.

In recent years, South Dakota has been the scene of heated partisan fights. Briefly, from June 2004 to January 2005, it had an all-Democratic congressional delegation—Senators Tom Daschle and Tim Johnson and Representative-at-Large Stephanie Herseth Sandlin—for only the second time in its history. (The other time was a period of five days in 1936–37.) Johnson held his seat in 2002 against a challenge by then Republican Rep. John Thune as a big turnout drive on the Pine Ridge Reservation enabled him to win by 524 votes. But in 2004, Thune came back and beat Daschle, then the Senate minority leader, by 4,508 votes. Herseth won the state's single House seat in a special election after Janklow resigned and has held it ever since. This is a state where voters traditionally have expected to meet and talk with their representatives in Congress, which has made Democrats more competitive in these races than they have been in presidential or state politics. Republicans have held the governorship since 1978 and have had wide margins in the state Legislature.

South Dakota also has been a major battleground in the abortion rights fight in recent years. The Legislature in February 2006 passed a law criminalizing abortion and providing no exceptions for rape and incest, the nation's most stringent abortion law. Republican Gov. Mike Rounds signed the bill, calling it a "full frontal attack" on *Roe v. Wade,* the Supreme Court decision legalizing most abortions. Ironically, anti-abortion advocates outside the state criticized the South Dakotans for fashioning a test case of *Roe* when it seemed obvious that the votes were lacking on the Supreme Court to overturn it. But the strongest opposition came from inside the state. Petitions began circulating to put the bill on the ballot in November. Democrats suddenly found they had many more legislative candidates than in previous years, and some Republicans opposed the bill as too restrictive and confrontational. It became an issue in Oglala Sioux politics as well. Cecelia Fire Thunder, the first woman elected tribal president, called for setting up an abortion clinic on the Pine Ridge Reservation, and was impeached and ousted from office in July 2006. Opponents of the abortion ban fared better. South Dakotans voted 56%-44% to repeal the law. The Legislature responded by passing a more restrained bill, banning abortion with exceptions for rape, incest and life and health of the mother. Abortion-rights supporters again put the issue on the ballot and voters repealed it 55%-45% in November 2008. These results must be counted as a major defeat for those who want to recriminalize abortion in the United States. Even in this culturally conservative state, people are against outlawing abortion. Still, the number of abortions in the state has been declining, and in June 2008, a federal appeals court upheld the state law requiring doctors to tell women that abortion ends a human life.

The abortion issue did not totally overturn the political order here. Rounds was re-elected 62%-36%, and voters did pass, though by a narrow margin, a constitutional amendment banning same-sex marriage and the establishment of domestic partnerships or civil unions. Democrats gained a few seats in the Legislature, but were far short of the majority. The trend held in 2008. Democrats made small gains in the House and lost one seat in the Senate. Members of the state's congressional delegation are popular. Democratic Sen. Johnson, after suffering a stroke in December 2006, made a slow but determined recovery and was re-elected by a wide margin in 2008. Republican Sen. Thune seemed headed to a similar

Population			Household Income		Work	
Pop. 2007:	788,241		Under $15k:	14.4%	Private:	73.0%
State rank:	46th of 50		$15k to $50k:	42.6%	Government:	16.3%
Change since 2000:	Up 4.4%		$50k to $100k:	31.8%	Self-employed:	10.1%
Urban:	52.4%		$100k to $150k:	9.3%	Unemployment (3-yr. average):	3.2%
Rural:	47.6%		Over $150k:	1.8%	Poverty:	13.3%
Native of state:	66.1%		Median income:	$43,586	Blue collar:	22.6%
Not a citizen:	1.3%				White collar:	58.9%
Area size:	77,116 sq. mi.		**Home Value**		Khaki collar:	0.2%
			Under $100k:	44.2%	Other:	18.3%
Most populous cities			$100k to $300k:	48.4%		
1. Sioux Falls	147,085		$300k to $500k:	5.2%	**Age**	
2. Rapid City	62,500		$500k to $1 mil:	1.7%	Median age:	37.1 yrs.
3. Aberdeen	23,459		Over $1 million:	0.5%	More than 65 yrs:	14.2%
4. Watertown	20,589		Median:	$110,900	Less than 18 yrs:	24.8%

Race/Ethnicity				Military Veterans		Registered Voters in 2008	
White:	86.5%	*Language*		% of Pop:	12.5%	D:	204,413 (38.5%)
Black:	0.9%	English:	93.6%	*Veterans by Period*		R:	241,528 (45.5%)
Hispanic:	2.1%	Spanish:	1.8%	WWII and before:	12.5%	Other:	84,521 (15.9%)
Asian:	0.8%	Asian:	0.6%	Korea:	14.4%	Voter turnout:	381,975
Native Am.:	8.0%	Other		Vietnam:	32.1%	Turnout as % of	
Hawaiian:	0.0%	European	2.2%	Gulf (pre-2001):	10.7%	voting age:	63.0%
Two+ races:	1.5%	**Education**		Gulf (post-2001):	8.7%	**Legislature**	
Ancestry		H.S. grad:	88.3%	Peace time:	21.4%	Senate:	14 D 20 R 1 I
German:	32.9%	College grad:	24.5%			House:	24 D 46 R
Norwegian:	11.4%	Grad degree:	7.0%				
Irish:	8.5%			**Cook Partisan Voting Index:** R+9			

victory in 2010, and Rep. Herseth Sandlin seemed sure of re-election unless she runs for the office her grandfather held in 1959–61, the governorship.

Presidential politics   South Dakota has voted Democratic for president just four times since statehood, in 1896, 1932, 1936 and 1964. But it was fairly close in five of the seven elections between 1972, when South Dakota's George McGovern was the Democratic nominee, and 1996, when Bill Clinton came within 3% of winning. In 2000, the environmental policies of Democratic nominee Al Gore were unpopular here, and Republican George W. Bush carried the state 60%-38%. Gore carried only Indians, a rising but small percentage of the electorate, and ran even among the elderly, but the percentage of voters who became Democrats during President Franklin D. Roosevelt's time was on the wane. In 2004, Bush once again carried the state 60%-38%, winning every county except those containing Indian reservations, where Democratic registration drives in 2002 and 2004 vastly increased turnout, and the University of South Dakota. In 2008, with no contest generating the interest that the Tom Daschle-John Thune Senate race had four years earlier, turnout was down 2%, contrary to the national trend. GOP nominee John McCain carried the state by just 53%-45%. Democrat Barack Obama won the Indian reservations plus several counties in the northeast and southeast, and he won Sioux Falls' Minnehaha County by 587 votes out of 80,000 cast.

2008 Presidential Vote
McCain (R)...........................203,054   (53%)
Obama (D) 170,924   (45%)

2008 Democratic Presidential Primary
Clinton (D)..............................54,128   (55%)
Obama (D) 43,669   (45%)

2008 Republican Presidential Primary
McCain (R)..............................42,788   (70%)
Paul (R)...................................10,072   (17%)
Huckabee (R) 4,328   (7%)

2004 Presidential Vote
Bush (R)................................232,584   (60%)
Kerry (D)...............................149,244   (38%)

In 1988, South Dakota switched its presidential primary from the traditional June date to February, just one week after New Hampshire. It proved to be a booster of Great Plains candidates who did not fare well elsewhere: Republican Bob Dole of Kansas in 1988 and 1996, Democrat Dick Gephardt of Missouri in 1988, Democrats Bob Kerrey of Nebraska and Tom Harkin of Iowa in 1992. But in 1996, it attracted few candidates, and the South Dakota Legislature decided to save $400,000 in election costs by reverting to a June primary. In January 2007, a move to hold the 2008 primary on February 5 was blocked by a 35-35 vote in the state House. As it turned out, there was a robust race for the Democratic nomination up through June 3, when South Dakota and Montana voted. Obama had long since won the endorsements of leading South Dakota Democrats—Johnson and former Senators Daschle and George McGovern. U.S. Rep. Stephanie Herseth Sandlin switched to Obama after her initial preference, John Edwards, dropped out. But Obama campaigned only briefly in South Dakota, while Hillary Rodham Clinton and husband Bill Clinton and daughter Chelsea Clinton crisscrossed the state in the two weeks before the primary. It paid off. Clinton won 55%-45%. She ran especially strong in the eastern counties and lost on the Indian reservations. It was her only victory north of the 42nd parallel and west of Indiana and Michigan, and raised the question of whether she might have won the nomination if more states in the region had held primaries rather than the caucuses in which the better-organized Obama campaign prevailed.

Governor

Mike Rounds (R)

Elected 2002, term expires Jan. 2011, 2nd term; b. Oct. 24, 1954, Huron; home, Pierre; SD St. U., B.S. 1977; Catholic; married (Jean); 4 children.

Elected Office: SD Senate, 1990–2000; Maj. ldr. 1995–2000.

Professional Career: Businessman, 1979–2002.

Office: 505 E. Capitol Ave., Pierre, 57501, 605-773-3212; Fax: 605-773-5844; Web site: www.state.sd.us/governor.

Election Results

2006 general	Mike Rounds (R)	206,990	(62%)
	Jack Billion (D)	121,226	(36%)
2006 primary	Mike Rounds (R)	unopposed	

Prior Winning Percentages: 2002 (57%)

Mike Rounds, a Republican, was elected governor of South Dakota in 2002. He grew up the eldest of 11 children in Pierre, the state's tiny capital. His father was director of the Office of Highway Safety and worked as a lobbyist for the petroleum industry. Rounds graduated from South Dakota State University, the first governor to do so. He worked as a partner in an insurance and real estate agency in Pierre. In 1990, he was elected to the state Senate, and in 1995 he became Senate majority leader. He was prevented by term limits from running for re-election in 2000. In December 2001, he announced he was running for governor. Rounds sought to replace the governor who had dominated state government for the past quarter-century, Republican Bill Janklow. A former state attorney general and governor from 1979 to 1982, Janklow ran for the U.S. Senate and lost in 1986. In 1994, he ran to get his old job as governor back, and defeated Gov. Walter Dale Miller in the Republican primary. He won the general election 55%-41% and four years later was re-elected 64%-33%.

In the Republican primary, Rounds faced two much more well-financed opponents, former Lt. Gov. Steve Kirby and Attorney General Mark Barnett. Rounds ran on property tax relief and opposition to an income tax and abortion rights. "No gimmicks, no grandstanding, just good government," was his slogan. He took some positions in opposition to popular viewpoints, and was credited with being straight with people. Rounds told a truckers' group that he might favor a higher gas tax if it would bring in significant federal money, and he was the only candidate in either party to oppose mandated use of ethanol fuel, despite the state's many ethanol plants and corn growers. He told the South Dakota Education Association that there were "very limited funds" for education spending increases. And he refused to pledge to oppose all tax increases.

Kirby and Barnett bitterly attacked each other on economic development and spent a lot of money on their campaigns. Kirby spent over $2.5 million and Barnett $1.75 million. Rounds spent just $147,000. But he had a strategy. "For the time being, I haven't minded being considered by the other two candidates as this fly buzzing away over in the corner," he said, and aimed his advertising "right between Kirby and Barnett." In a small state where voters expect to see candidates in person, candidate forums held in small towns can make a difference. While Kirby and Barnett attacked each other, Rounds always seemed to be smiling. In the June primary, Rounds won 44% of the vote, to 30% for Barnett and 26% for Kirby. It was a classic illustration of the rule in politics that it is not wise to launch a negative campaign in a multi-candidate race.

The Democratic nominee was Jim Abbott, a businessman who served in the Legislature, lost races for lieutenant governor in 1994 and the House in 1996 and was on leave as president of the University of South Dakota. This was a gentlemanly race between old friends. After the primary, Abbott said, "Mike Rounds is just a good guy. I really think the people of South Dakota like the idea of a positive message for the future." Abbott called for state-sponsored research for economic development and for higher education to partner with the private sector to create jobs. While negative ads were hitting the air in the hard-fought Senate race between Democratic incumbent Tim Johnson and Republican challenger John Thune, the dialogue in the governor's race was positive. Rounds led in polls from the primary on, and in November won 57%-42%.

After the election, Rounds went to work on the state budget problems. In December, Janklow had presented figures showing spending requests $54 million higher than projected revenue, with $90 million in the state reserve. In 2003, Rounds angered conservatives by proposing tax increases on cigarettes and alcoholic beverages and making more interstate phone calls subject to the sales tax. Though the Legislature failed to pass his proposed tax on alcohol, it ended up passing 19 of the 22 bills he proposed. He successfully cut the cost of prescription drugs for senior citizens and managed to increase state aid to school districts by $15 million. He also got a 2% pay raise for state workers, though it was 1% less than he sought. But the big news story that year was Janklow, who had by then become the state's at-large representative in the U.S. House. In August, Janklow, well-known for his aggressive driving, blew through a stop sign in his car and killed a motorcyclist. In December, a jury in his hometown of Flandreau convicted him of felony manslaughter. He announced his resignation from Congress the same day.

Janklow wasn't the only national story in 2004. A restrictive abortion bill, which passed both the House and Senate, would have banned almost all abortions in the state; the only exception was to save the life of the mother. The bill's sponsor acknowledged that the measure would be challenged in court but had hoped for it to eventually reach the U.S. Supreme Court, where it might be used to overturn the *Roe v. Wade* decision legalizing most abortions. Abortion rights advocates, as expected, harshly criticized the bill. But many abortion opponents also opposed it, convinced that it could not survive legal scrutiny and might have the unintended effect of spurring a decision that strengthened abortion rights. Rounds said he supported overturning *Roe* but he issued a "form veto," which suggests changes and clarification of some of the bill's provisions. The Senate rejected the revisions and the bill died.

In 2006, strong economic growth enabled Rounds to propose a $3.2 million budget with a $130 million increase in spending. He outlined an ambitious education initiative aimed at making South Dakota first in the nation in the percentage of students who go on to college, technical school or advanced training. But for a governor with high approval ratings and a Legislature controlled by his own party, Rounds ran into considerable resistance on some high-profile initiatives. Several of his 2010 education proposals foundered, including a requirement for mandatory kindergarten and an increase in the age of mandatory school attendance from 16 to 18. He called for raising the state's minimum wage from $5.15 per hour to $6, the first raise since 1997, but it died in committee. He took a tough stance and vetoed a bill that eased the penalty on high school students caught using drugs—under an existing law, students were suspended for a year from high school activities—but the House and Senate voted to override.

Abortion again dominated the headlines. In February 2006, the Legislature revisited the issue, passing a law criminalizing abortion and providing no exceptions for rape and incest—the nation's most stringent abortion law. Rounds signed the bill in March and called it a "full frontal attack" on *Roe v. Wade*. Ironically, anti-abortion forces outside the state criticized the South Dakotans for fashioning a test case of *Roe* when it seemed obvious that the votes were lacking on the Supreme Court to overturn it. But the strongest opposition came from inside the state. Petitions began circulating to put the bill on the ballot in November, and Democrats suddenly found they had many more legislative candidates than in previous years. Some Republicans opposed the bill as too restrictive and confrontational. There was an immediate affect on Rounds' poll ratings. For much of his time in office, his job approval ratings were at or above 70%, among the highest in the nation. In the aftermath of the bill signing, his approval rating dropped to 58% while his disapproval rating spiked from 23% to 38%.

Even so, Rounds was in a solid position for re-election. His opponent was Jack Billion, a former state legislator and a retired Sioux Falls surgeon. Rounds touted his work on economic development and education. Billion criticized the "rigid, no exception" abortion law. Rounds emphasized that the ban included an exception for the life of the mother and permitted the use of emergency contraception before a pregnancy is detected. The abortion law roiled state politics, but not Rounds' re-election. He held a steady lead in the polls throughout the campaign and won a landslide 62%-36% victory. Rounds carried all but four counties. As in 2002, his Democratic opponent carried Indian reservations and the area around the University of South Dakota in Vermillion. Opponents of the abortion ban prevailed as well. South Dakotans voted 56%-44% to repeal the abortion law. Democrats gained five seats in the state Senate but only one in the state House.

Rounds started his second term by calling for the creation of a pilot preschool program in Sioux Falls as part of his long-term goal to increase school retention. He won enactment of a bill to cut the tax on biodiesel fuel blends, which consist of diesel fuel and soybean or corn oil, by 2 cents per gallon. And in March 2009, Rounds signed legislation banning smoking in South Dakota restaurants and bars.

Like other governors around the country, Rounds faced potential budget shortfalls as the 2007 recession worsened. In early 2009, Rounds proposed cutting $46 million from the state budget, cuts that threatened a number of cherished programs, including the South Dakota School for the Deaf and the state fair. He and the Legislature agreed to use $71 million from the Obama administration's economic stimulus program to balance the 2009 budget. An additional $300 million of stimulus money was allocated for road construction, education and other state projects. The Legislature trimmed Rounds' proposed cuts to $37 million, and with the governor's approval, restored funding for the school for the deaf and the fair.

Senior Senator

Tim Johnson (D)

Elected 1996, term expires 2014, 3rd term; b. Dec. 28, 1946, Canton; home, Vermillion; U. of SD, B.A. 1969, M.A. 1970, J.D. 1975, MI St. U., 1970–71; Lutheran; married (Barbara); 3 children.

Elected Office: SD House of Reps., 1978–82; SD Senate, 1982–86; U.S. House of Reps., 1986–96.

Professional Career: Budget analyst, MI Senate, 1971–72; Practicing atty., 1975–85; Clay Cnty. dpty. atty., 1985.

DC Office: 136 HSOB, 20510, 202-224-5842; Fax: 202-228-5765; Web site: johnson.senate.gov.

State Offices: Aberdeen, 605-226-3440; Rapid City, 605-341-3990; Sioux Falls, 605-332-8896.

Committees: *Appropriations* (11th of 18 D): Agriculture, Rural Development, Food and Drug Administration & Related Agencies; Energy & Water Development; Interior, Environment & Related Agencies; Military Construction, Veterans Affairs & Related Agencies (Chmn); State, Foreign Operations & Related Programs; Transportation, Housing and Urban Development & Related Agencies. *Banking, Housing & Urban Affairs* (2nd of 13 D): Financial Institutions (Chmn); Securities, Insurance & Investment. *Energy & Natural Resources* (4th of 13 D): Public Lands & Forests; Water & Power. *Indian Affairs* (5th of 9 D).

Group Ratings

	ADA	ACLU	AFS	LCV	ITIC	NTU	COC	ACU	CFG	FRC
2008	80	50	100	91	75	21	75	12	27	22
2007	40	—	0	33	—	8	80	0	30	—

National Journal Ratings

	2007 LIB — 2007 CONS		2008 LIB — 2008 CONS	
Economic	*%	*%	55%	43%
Social	*%	*%	53%	46%
Foreign	49%	49%	56%	40%
Composite	*%	*%	56%	44%

Key Votes of the 110th Congress

1. Raise CAFE standards	*	5. Make English official language *	9. Withdraw troops 3/08	*
2. Expand SCHIP	*	6. Path to citizenship *	10. Iran guard is terrorist group	Y
3. Cap greenhouse gases	N	7. Fetus is unborn child *	11. Increase missile defense $	N
4. Bail out financial markets	N	8. Prosecute hate crimes Y	12. Overhaul FISA	Y

Election Results

2008 general	Tim Johnson (D)	237,889	(62%)	($4,712,283)
	Joel Dykstra (R)	142,784	(38%)	($905,366)
2008 primary	Tim Johnson (D)	unopposed		

Prior Winning Percentages: 2002 (50%); 1996 (51%); 1994 House (60%); 1994 House (60%); 1992 House (69%); 1990 House (68%); 1988 House (72%); 1986 House (59%)

Democrat Tim Johnson was elected to the Senate in 1996. He grew up in Canton, Flandreau and Vermillion in southeast South Dakota and went to the University of South Dakota, where he ultimately earned a law degree. Johnson served briefly in the Army, but was discharged because of a hearing problem. He opened a law practice in Vermillion, and then got increasingly involved in politics. He was elected to the state House in 1978, at age 31, and served four years. In 1982, he was elected to the state Senate for another four years. When Democratic U.S. Rep. Tom Daschle ran for the Senate in 1986, Johnson ran for the at-large House seat and won the general election 59%-41%. He was re-elected easily every two years. In the House, Johnson compiled a generally liberal voting record, though he sometimes voted for conservative fiscal proposals, such as the balanced budget amendment of the 1990s.

In 1996, Johnson challenged Republican Sen. Larry Pressler, then chairman of the influential Senate Commerce, Science and Transportation Committee. This was a high-spending, high-stakes race.

Pressler spent $5.1 million, and Johnson spent almost $3 million. The race was neck-and-neck for 15 months. Since South Dakota television is relatively inexpensive, that meant one barrage of ads after another, plus seven debates. Pressler attacked Johnson as too liberal, going back to a 1981 vote in the Legislature against workfare, the practice of requiring welfare recipients to work. Johnson attacked Pressler as a clone of Republican House Speaker Newt Gingrich of Georgia and a Medicare-cutter. Pressler spent much time in 1995 and 1996 on the telecommunications bill, a heavily lobbied and complex bill. He succeeded in passing the bill, a significant accomplishment. But back home, Johnson charged that phone and cable rates were going up because of Pressler's work. The final result was a 51%-49% Johnson victory.

Johnson's voting record has been toward the center of the Senate, though more liberal on foreign affairs issues. He seldom seeks or gets publicity as other senators do. "There are enough show horses in Washington to go around," he likes to say. By early 2001, it was apparent that Johnson would face a tough challenge in 2002. President George W. Bush talked popular Republican Rep. John Thune into running for the Senate. Senate Majority Leader Tom Daschle of South Dakota immediately made saving his friend and fellow home-state Democrat "the most important political effort for me" in 2002. Daschle helped Johnson get a seat on the Appropriations Committee, where he could secure federal money for South Dakota. And Johnson was careful to cast some moderate votes on big issues. (He did not tout the fact that a victory for him could have given the Republicans a Senate majority and demote Daschle to minority leader, making him a less powerful advocate for the state.) The two candidates spent record amounts for a South Dakota race—about $6 million each—and the national parties and independent expenditure groups on both sides spent much more. A week of TV ads cost only about $80,000 in South Dakota, as compared to about $1.5 million in Los Angeles. The ads started running in late 2001, and by November 2002 the average voter had seen more than 1,000 of them.

Thune was the more outgoing of the two, a candidate who loved shaking hands and seldom forgot a face. The reserved Johnson was nevertheless tenacious. Of all the seriously contested Democratic senators in 2002, Johnson ran the most conservative-sounding campaign. "Tim Johnson has strongly supported President Bush, the war against terrorism, his tax cut and his education reform," one ad said. Thune attacked him for voting against making the Bush tax cut permanent. Johnson replied that he supported eliminating the estate tax for family farmers and ranchers and family-owned businesses.

The biggest local issue was the drought that hit western South Dakota in 2002. Ranchers were selling off their herds for low prices, and business losses were estimated at $1.8 billion. Daschle and Johnson responded by sponsoring $5 billion in disaster aid for farmers and ranchers, arguing that if floods and tornadoes triggered disaster relief, then droughts should too. In mid-September, Agriculture Secretary Ann Veneman announced $750 million in aid for 30 states. Democrats grumbled that it was a pittance, but Daschle's bill was stalled in the Senate. On defense issues, Thune tried to make an issue of Johnson's opposition to the first Gulf War in 1991, but the impact was mitigated when Johnson announced he would vote for the pending resolution authorizing war in Iraq. He also noted that his son, Brooks Johnson, served with the 101st Airborne Division in Afghanistan in 2001 and 2002 and could be sent to Iraq.

The election turned out to be the closest in the nation that year. During most of election night, Thune was in the lead, but the last two precincts to be counted came in from Shannon County, which includes most of the Pine Ridge Indian Reservation. They put Johnson over the top by a margin of 524 votes. The county voted 92%-8% for Johnson. In the six main reservation counties, turnout was 11,275, up from 7,500 in 2000. These six counties voted 78%-21% for Johnson. In 43 of the other 60 counties, including the 10 largest, Johnson's percentage declined from 1996, when he won 51% statewide. Many Republicans urged Thune to contest the election, but he declined. Johnson had won two full terms in the Senate by the smallest combined popular vote margin, 9,103, of any senator since Republican George Malone of Nevada, elected by a combined margin of 7,970 in 1946 and 1952.

In his second term, Johnson, back in the minority again, worked hard on South Dakota issues. He helped get passed country-of-origin meat labeling and a bill to provide more funding for housing on Indian reservations. In 2006, he supported funding for improved access to affordable health care in rural communities, and in the 2005 energy bill he worked on increases for ethanol and other renewable fuels. South Dakota devotes more of its corn to ethanol than any other state. On other issues, he co-sponsored a bipartisan bill to overhaul regulation of the insurance industry, giving companies the option of federal or state regulation. And in March 2006, Johnson derided as "extreme and radical" a new South Dakota ban on most abortions.

After Daschle's strenuous efforts to save Johnson in 2002, he could not save himself two years later when Thune came back for a second run at the Senate. Shortly after Thune's stunning defeat of Daschle, Johnson convened a meeting of the new delegation with Thune and Democratic At Large Rep. Stephanie Herseth Sandlin to call a truce and to suggest they work together on South Dakota projects. The three joined forces successfully in saving Ellsworth Air Force Base in the base-closing review process of 2005.

With Democratic successes at the polls in 2006, Democrats gained a Senate majority and Johnson got the gavels of the Appropriations Subcommittee on Military Construction and Veterans Affairs, and the Banking Subcommittee on Financial Institutions. Then, on December 13, 2006, Johnson suffered a brain hemorrhage while working at the Capitol. Within hours, he had extensive brain surgery. With prospects of his survival unclear and the assumption that Republican Gov. Mike Rounds would appoint a Republican successor, speculation grew that Johnson's departure from the Senate could reverse the Democrats' expected assumption of majority control. Although Johnson survived the immediate crisis, it became clear that he would be absent from the Senate for at least several months. Veteran Senate observers recalled that Republican Sen. Karl Mundt, also of South Dakota, had a stroke in November 1969 and did not vote during the final three years of his Senate tenure. By March, Johnson's office released photographs of a smiling Johnson with his family. Amid the uncertainty and also out of respect for Johnson, Democratic senators assisted him in fundraising for his 2008 re-election and potential Republican rivals such as Rounds delayed their decisions. On September 5, 2007, Johnson returned to the Senate and made his first floor speech of the year. "My speech is not 100 percent," he said. "But my thoughts are clear and my mind is sharp."

Johnson has continued to suffer lingering health effects such as slurred speech and partial paralysis on his right side, but they have not impaired his ability to work. He successfully fought to include more than $87 million for South Dakota water projects in the 2009 appropriations bills. And, on the 2008 farm bill, Johnson won passage of a provision requiring meat products to carry country-of-origin labeling, which he had worked on for several years. In April 2009, Johnson broke with Democrats on the Senate Banking, Housing and Urban Affairs Committee and voted against legislation to bar credit card companies from engaging in practices such as charging interest on late fees. The credit card industry is one of South Dakota's biggest employers.

Johnson sought a third term in 2008, and was challenged by Republican State Rep. Joel Dykstra. He suggested that Johnson was not physically up to the rigors of service in the Senate and criticized his vote against a 2005 bill that would have increased oversight of mortgage lending practices, an issue with potential resonance during the housing foreclosure crisis of 2008. But neither line of attack struck a chord with voters, and Johnson trounced Dykstra 62%-38%. Exit polls showed that he won support from about a third of the voters who identified themselves as Republicans.

Junior Senator

John Thune (R)

Elected 2004, term expires 2010, 1st term; b. Jan. 7, 1961, Pierre; home, Sioux Falls; Biola U., B.A. 1983, U. of SD, M.B.A. 1984; Baptist; married (Kimberley); 2 children.

Elected Office: U.S. House of Reps., 1996–2002.

Professional Career: Legis. asst., U.S. Sen. James Abdnor, 1985–87; Special asst., U.S. Small Business Admin., 1987–89; Exec. dir., SD Republican Party, 1989–91; SD railroad dir., 1991–93; Exec. dir., SD Municipal League, 1993–96.

DC Office: 493 RSOB, 20510, 202-224-2321; Fax: 202-228-5429; Web site: thune.senate.gov.

State Offices: Aberdeen, 605-225-8823; Rapid City, 605-348-7551; Sioux Falls, 605-334-9596.

Committees: *Republican Conference Vice Chairman. Agriculture, Nutrition & Forestry* (8th of 9 R). *Armed Services* (6th of 11 R): Airland (RMM); Personnel; Readiness & Management Support. *Commerce, Science & Transportation* (5th of 11 R): Aviation Operations, Safety & Security; Communications, Technology & the Internet; Competitiveness, Innovation & Export Promotion; Consumer Protection, Product Safety & Insurance; Science & Space; Surface Transportation & Merchant Marine Infrastructure, Safety & Security (RMM). *Small Business & Entrepreneurship* (4th of 8 R).

Group Ratings

	ADA	ACLU	AFS	LCV	ITIC	NTU	COC	ACU	CFG	FRC
2008	10	14	11	18	100	61	100	84	82	100
2007	20	—	0	33	—	68	55	88	74	—

National Journal Ratings

	2007 LIB	—	2007 CONS	2008 LIB	—	2008 CONS
Economic	36%	—	63%	14%	—	84%
Social	0%	—	91%	0%	—	79%
Foreign	9%	—	87%	0%	—	84%
Composite	17%	—	83%	11%	—	89%

Key Votes of the 110th Congress

1. Raise CAFE standards	Y	5. Make English official language	Y	9. Withdraw troops 3/08	N
2. Expand SCHIP	N	6. Path to citizenship	N	10. Iran guard is terrorist group	Y
3. Cap greenhouse gases	N	7. Fetus is unborn child	Y	11. Increase missile defense $	Y
4. Bail out financial markets	Y	8. Prosecute hate crimes	N	12. Overhaul FISA	Y

Election Results

2004 general	John Thune (R) 197,848	(51%)	($14,666,225)
	Tom Daschle (D) 193,340	(49%)	($19,991,369)
2004 primary	John Thune (R) .... unopposed		

Prior Winning Percentages: 2000 House (73%); 1998 House (75%); 1996 House (58%)

The junior senator from South Dakota is John Thune, a Republican elected in 2004. He grew up in Murdo, on the dusty plains west of the Missouri River, where his father was a teacher and the family was Democratic. He went to college and business school at the University of South Dakota. As a high school freshman, he met U.S. Rep. Jim Abdnor, a Republican who spotted Thune at a grocery checkout counter and recalled that he had missed one of six free throws in the basketball game the previous night. They kept in touch, and Thune got a job on then-Sen. Abdnor's staff in Washington in 1985. He stayed until Abdnor lost the seat to Democrat Tom Daschle. Thune returned to South Dakota in 1989 and, at age 28, became executive director of the state Republican Party. In 1991, he became state railroad director under GOP Gov. George Mickelson, and in 1993 was the director of the state Municipal League. In 1996, Thune entered a race for the state's open at large seat in the U.S. House as an underdog. The favorite in the Republican primary was Lt. Gov. Carole Hillard. But Thune attracted the support of religious conservatives, and won the primary 59%-41%. In the general election, he faced Democrat Rick Weiland, a former state director for Daschle. Thune opposed all tax increases and promised to serve only three terms. He won 58%-37%. In the House, the conservative Thune was chosen as freshman class representative to the Republican leadership. He was re-elected 75%-25% in 1998, the largest vote margin ever for a statewide candidate in South Dakota.

At a White House dinner in April 2001, Republican President George W. Bush urged Thune to challenge Democratic Sen. Tim Johnson in 2002. By that time, Daschle had become quite powerful, and in June 2001, rose to majority leader, the top job in the Senate. Daschle pledged to do everything he could to protect his friend and home-state Democratic colleague Johnson and secured for Johnson a coveted seat on the Appropriations Committee, where he could bring home federal dollars for South Dakota. Thune argued that the state would be better off with a bipartisan Senate delegation, neglecting to mention that a victory for him would give control of the narrowly divided Senate to the Republicans and knock Daschle from his perch as majority leader and make him a less effective advocate for the state in Washington. Johnson even argued that he and Daschle made a uniquely powerful team. The two candidates spent a record amount for South Dakota—about $6 million each. The national parties and independent groups on both sides spent much more.

Johnson tried to hone an image as a conservative, and emphasized votes he had cast for Bush administration policies. Thune attacked him for voting against making the Bush tax cut permanent. On defense issues, Thune tried to make an issue of Johnson's opposition to the first Gulf War in 1991, but the impact was mitigated when Johnson announced he would vote for the pending resolution authorizing war in Iraq. He also noted that his son, Brooks Johnson, served with the 101st Airborne Division in Afghanistan in 2001 and 2002 and could be sent to Iraq, which he later was.

The election was the closest in the nation that year. During most of election night and into the morning, Thune led in the count. Then the last two precincts came in, from Shannon County, which includes most of the Pine Ridge Indian Reservation, and they put Johnson over the top, by a margin of 524 votes—in percentage terms, 50.1%-49.9%. In Shannon County, the vote was 92%-8% for Johnson. In the six main reservation counties, turnout was 11,275, up from 7,500 in 2000, and the six voted 78%-21% for Johnson. Many Republicans urged Thune to contest the election. But on November 13, he said: "The people of South Dakota have been subjected to one of the longest and most expensive campaigns in South Dakota history. I choose not to subject them to more."

Thune hung out a shingle as a lobbyist and consultant in Washington, biding his time until the next political opportunity came along. His old nemesis Daschle had been re-elected easily in 1992 and 1998, but against lightly funded opponents. The emergence of a narrowly divided Senate controlled by Democrats and a White House in Republican hands made Daschle one of the pivotal figures in American politics. Thune's favorable ratings remained high after his defeat, and early Republican polls showed Thune 1% to 2% ahead of Daschle—the same kind of dead heat in almost every poll taken during the Johnson-Thune race, and an encouraging sign for Thune. He also could count on the full-throttle support of the Bush White House to match Daschle's fundraising prowess. And Bush, who carried South Dakota 60%-38% in 2000, would be at the top of the ballot in 2004.

After Democrats lost control of the Senate in the 2002 election, Daschle returned as minority leader and stepped up his criticism of the Bush administration. On March 17, 2003, as Bush was to address the nation that evening announcing a final 48-hour ultimatum to Iraqi Leader Saddam Hussein, Daschle said, "I'm saddened that this president failed so miserably at diplomacy that we're now forced to war. Saddened that we have to give up one life because this president couldn't create the kind of diplomatic effort that was so critical for our country." Republicans chastised him for criticizing the president at an inappropriate time. And in January 2004, Thune announced that he would run against Daschle.

Thune sought to portray Daschle as the chief obstructionist to the Bush agenda in the Senate. To underscore the idea, Majority Leader Bill Frist broke with Senate tradition of party leaders refraining from campaigning against each other and traveled to South Dakota to stump for Thune. Daschle began running ads in the summer of 2003, arguing that a freshman senator could not hope to match his influence in Washington and the federal largesse he'd brought to South Dakota. It was the most expensive election of the year, as both national parties and numerous third-party interest groups poured millions of dollars into South Dakota. By the end, they had spent $35 million. Almost nothing was off-limits. The state Republican Party sent a mailer attacking the lobbying practices of Daschle's wife, Linda, an aviation industry lobbyist. The anti-tax group Club for Growth ran an ad called "Tom's House" that featured Daschle's $2 million house in a well-to-do Washington-area neighborhood. Another attack ad showed Daschle as a bobble-head doll, nodding in unison with bobble-head dolls of liberal Sens. Edward Kennedy of Massachusetts and Hillary Rodham Clinton of New York. Daschle aired an ad that featured him embracing Bush, which infuriated Republicans, while Thune boasted of his friendship with the then popular president. He contended that Daschle had put his party's interests ahead of the needs of the state. "He's not the same guy who put his suitcase in his station wagon and drove the family to Congress in 1978," Thune told *National Journal*. "He now is an inside-Washington, D.C., guy who lives in a multimillion-dollar mansion. The broader question is, who is more in touch with South Dakota?"

The closely fought race brought a huge turnout, up 23% from 2000 in a state with only modest growth. Thune won 51%-49%, marking the first defeat for a Senate party leader since Democrat Ernest McFarland of Arizona lost to Republican Barry Goldwater in 1952. The popular vote margin was 4,508—small, but more than eight times the margin by which Thune had lost to Johnson two years earlier. The contours of the vote were similar. Thune narrowly lost Sioux Falls's Minnehaha County, but won fast-growing Lincoln County by a bigger margin. He carried Mitchell, North Sioux City, Pierre and Rapid City's Pennington County and the Black Hills counties around it. He also increased his share of the vote significantly in the Pine Ridge and Rosebud Indian reservations, where his decision not to challenge the election outcome two years earlier may have earned him goodwill. Daschle won most of the counties in eastern South Dakota. Thune was celebrated by Republicans as a giant-killer. He became a talk-show favorite, a fundraising star and a celebrity among GOP freshmen.

Thune established a mostly conservative voting record in the Senate, especially on cultural issues, but he showed some independence. In May 2005, he suffered a setback when Ellsworth Air Force Base, with nearly 4,000 local jobs and one-half of the nation's B-1 bombers, landed on the base-closing list. He had said during the campaign that a Republican senator with good relations with the Bush administration could better look out for Ellsworth's interests. Thune turned the initial setback to his favor by showing his independence in taking on the Bush administration. The initial news was "like a death in the family," he recounted. "In Washington, you can't count on anybody else to fight your battles." With home-state colleagues Johnson and Democratic Rep. Stephanie Herseth Sandlin, he put aside the recent bitter partisanship at home, and made his case to the commission, the Pentagon, White House officials, and anybody else with clout about the high cost of closing Ellsworth. They generated a crowd of more than 10,000 and a pep-rally atmosphere when the base-closing commission held a hearing in Rapid City. The base survived. "It is a huge sense of relief," said Thune.

On other issues, Thune has been a leading critic of the Employment Free Choice Act, a bill sought by labor unions that would make it easier for workers to form unions. He voted against the 2005 Central American Free Trade Agreement and joined Democrats to increase veterans' health care funding. He helped to get the Senate to agree to an annual mandate of 8 billion gallons of ethanol production by 2012, and he voiced concern in March 2007 when Bush visited Brazil to promote ethanol in that nation. Republican Majority Leader Trent Lott of Mississippi tapped him as his chief deputy whip. In 2007, he helped author a section of the farm bill establishing a permanent disaster program to provide financial aid to farmers whose crops are harmed by natural disasters. He also successfully fought for the inclusion of a provision creating financial incentives for manufacturers that produce cellulosic ethanol from switchgrass, which is abundant in South Dakota. As gas prices climbed in the summer of 2008, Thune helped form a bipartisan group of senators with the goal of producing legislation to lower prices. The original group had 10 members, but its ranks swelled as gas prices became a pertinent campaign issue in the fall of 2008. The group pushed to allow more drilling off the coasts of some states, arousing national interest in the issue. Both houses of Congress allowed a ban on offshore drilling to expire in October 2008.

Thune was one of the first Senate Republicans to endorse Arizona Sen. John McCain's 2008 presidential campaign, and he was mentioned as a possible running mate after McCain won the party's nomination. Thune moved up the GOP leadership ladder in June 2009, when he became Republican Policy Committee chairman, putting him charge of generating the Republican position on issues. He replaced Nevada Sen. John Ensign after Ensign confessed to an extramarital affair with the wife of his chief of staff and stepped down from the leadership post.

Thune's legislative savvy, good looks and relative young age have made him an attractive spokesman for the Republicans on the Sunday morning talk shows. He is also one of the Senate's best basketball players, and he finished first among Senate runners in an annual charity three-mile run for lawmakers and the media in Washington.

Representative-At-Large

Stephanie Herseth Sandlin (D)

Elected June 2004, 3rd full term; b. Dec. 3, 1970, Aberdeen; home, Brookings; Georgetown U., B.A. 1993, M.A. 1996, J.D. 1997; Lutheran; married (Max Sandlin); 1 child.

Professional Career: Clerk, U.S. District Court, Judge Charles Kornmann 1998–99; Clerk, Judge Diana Gribbon Motz, U.S. Court of Appeals, 1999–2000; Practicing atty., 2000–01; Ex. dir., SD Farmers Union Foundation, 2003; Legal cnsl., South Dakota Made Store, 2003.

DC Office: 331 CHOB, 20515, 202-225-2801; Fax: 202-225-5823; Web site: hersethsandlin.house.gov.

State Offices: Aberdeen, 605-626-3440; Rapid City, 605-394-5280; Sioux Falls, 605-367-8371.

Committees: *Agriculture* (9th of 28 D): Conservation, Credit, Energy & Research; General Farm Commodities & Risk Management. *Natural Resources* (24th of 29 D): National Parks, Forests & Public Lands. *Veterans' Affairs* (5th of 18 D): Economic Opportunity (Chmn).

Group Ratings

	ADA	ACLU	AFS	LCV	ITIC	NTU	COC	ACU	CFG	FRC
2008	70	73	86	77	57	22	56	28	16	17
2007	90	—	91	70	—	6	65	12	12	—

National Journal Ratings

	2007 LIB	—	2007 CONS		2008 LIB	—	2008 CONS
Economic	56%	—	43%		47%	—	52%
Social	52%	—	47%		54%	—	42%
Foreign	52%	—	48%		50%	—	48%
Composite	54%	—	46%		52%	—	49%

Key Votes of the 110th Congress

1. Increase minimum wage	Y	5. Share immigration data	N	9. Withdraw troops 8/08	Y
2. Expand SCHIP	Y	6. Foreign aid abortion ban	N	10. No operations in Iran	N
3. Raise CAFE standards	Y	7. Ban gay bias in workplace	Y	11. Free trade with Peru	Y
4. Bail out financial markets	N	8. Repeal D.C. gun law	Y	12. Overhaul FISA	Y

Election Results

2008 general	Stephanie Herseth Sandlin (D)	256,041	(68%)	($1,568,461)
	Chris Lien (R)	122,966	(32%)	($606,781)
2008 primary	Stephanie Herseth Sandlin (D)	unopposed		

Prior Winning Percentages: 2006 (69%); 2004 (53%); 2004 special (51%)

South Dakota's lone member of the House is Stephanie Herseth Sandlin, a Democrat chosen in a June 2004 special election. Herseth Sandlin gave birth to her first child, Zachary Lars Sandlin, while in office in December 2008. The previous year, she married former House member Max Sandlin, who had served eight years as a Democrat from Texas before he became a victim of redistricting. Stephanie Herseth Sandlin grew up on a farm near Brookings in northeastern South Dakota, in a family with a fine political pedigree. Her grandfather, Ralph Herseth, was governor from 1958 to 1960. Her grandmother, Lorna Herseth, was secretary of state from 1972 to 1978. Her father, Lars Herseth, served in the Legislature from 1974 to 1986 and from 1988 to 1996. In 1986, he ran for governor and lost 52%-48%. In a state where voters expect to meet the candidates, the Herseths were well-liked and respected. Herseth Sandlin graduated from Georgetown University and its law school, interned with Democratic Sen. Tim Johnson, a college classmate of her father's, and then clerked for federal judges in South Dakota and

Maryland. She taught at Georgetown law school and worked for a law firm in Washington. She turned down invitations to run against Republican Attorney General Mark Barnett in 1998. In 2002, she decided to run for the U.S. House when Republican incumbent John Thune decided to run for the Senate.

As the House contest began, the clear favorite was former Gov. Bill Janklow, a Republican. Blunt and plain-spoken, Janklow pledged to be a "sledgehammer" in the House. In the June primary, he beat former Sen. Larry Pressler 55%-27%, while Herseth Sandlin beat Democrat Rick Weiland 58%-32%. She was in her own right a dynamic candidate, articulate and at ease around people. She also proved to be a great fundraiser. With help from the women's fundraising group EMILY's List, she raised $1.5 million, more than Janklow's $1.3 million. Herseth Sandlin, who was just 31 years old, argued that South Dakota had "a tradition of sending young passionate leaders to Congress," and cited Democrats Johnson and Tom Daschle, then the Senate majority leader, and Republicans Pressler and Thune, all first elected in their 30s. She avoided phrases that might be construed as "liberal," because, as she put it, "that's not a term that's respected here." When asked about abortion, she would typically say she wanted to make it "as rare as possible." When asked about gun control, she noted that she grew up on a farm in pheasant hunting country and saw no need for new restrictions on guns. Herseth Sandlin was respectful of Janklow. "When I made the decision to seek office, I never thought I would be running against Bill Janklow. He is larger than life, especially for people of my generation," she said, noting that when she was in high school, then-Gov. Janklow took time from his schedule to answer questions for a report she was writing. His campaign also stayed positive. When the National Republican Congressional Committee ran a television spot attacking Herseth Sandlin as a carpetbagger, Janklow insisted it be pulled.

The two candidates agreed on many local issues but they differed in their approaches to Iraq at a time Congress was debating whether to authorize going to war. Janklow said, "I'd love to have the support of our allies, but it's the American World Trade Center they flew the planes into. I'd love to have the support of our allies, but if we can't get the support of these people, then in this war they're not our allies, and we may have to go it alone." Herseth Sandlin said, "We are looking at putting our men and women in urban warfare, hand-to-hand combat on the streets of Baghdad. I view it as a sliding scale. To the extent that we have little support from allies, the need goes way up for congressional approval. With more allied support, the bar goes down a little for congressional approval." Janklow pulled ahead in the polls in October, and on Election Day, he won 53%-46%.

But Janklow's House career was cut short. In August 2003, he sped through a stop sign in his Cadillac and killed a motorcyclist in Moody County. He was indicted, tried, and in December 2003, convicted of felony manslaughter. He immediately announced that he would resign. Republican Gov. Mike Rounds declared that the vacancy would be filled in a special election in June 2004, the same day as South Dakota's primary. Herseth Sandlin, who was teaching at South Dakota State University and heading the South Dakota Farmers Union Foundation, was the obvious and unanimous choice for the House race for the Democrats. The Republican nominee was state Sen. Larry Diedrich, a corn, hog and soybean farmer who had headed the South Dakota and American Soybean Associations and served eight years in the Legislature.

Herseth Sandlin campaigned as a "fiscally conservative and ideologically moderate" candidate, calling for changes in the 2003 Medicare prescription drug bill and a ban on meatpacker ownership of livestock. She supported abortion rights, while Diedrich opposed abortion and criticized her for refusing to promise to vote for a constitutional amendment banning same-sex marriage. He also criticized her opposition to making the Bush-era tax cuts permanent and tried to focus attention on her lack of life experience. Herseth Sandlin, who was single then, said, "A lot of people today know women, or even have women in their family, who have postponed marriage and family-raising for professional reasons. Some of the stereotypes that were once out there are not so strong any more." Herseth Sandlin started off far ahead in the polls. But Diedrich campaigned hard and caught up by late May. Herseth Sandlin won 51%-49%, with a popular vote margin of just 3,005. Turnout in the heavily Republican Black Hills area was low, and Herseth Sandlin carried the Indian reservations by wide margins.

She had to run again in November 2004 to secure a new, two-year term, and Diedrich was again the Republican nominee. As in the special election contest, the candidates debated frequently and civilly. Herseth Sandlin even gave Diedrich credit for lobbying an Appropriations subcommittee chairman for a water project that helped the state. But negative notes were also struck. Diedrich and national Republicans attacked Herseth Sandlin for roll call votes against making various Bush-era tax cuts permanent. National Democrats ran ads criticizing Diedrich's votes as a legislator to increase taxes on gasoline, cell phones and hospitals and opposing abolition of the inheritance tax. At one debate Herseth Sandlin was asked how she would vote if the presidential election went to the House. "I represent South Dakota. And I'm going to put South Dakota first," she said. When Diedrich pressed further, she said, "I guess Larry is parsing my words. I would vote for George Bush for president." The race was overshadowed by the hot and even closer Senate race, in which Thune was making inroads in his challenge to Senate Democratic Leader Tom Daschle, a giant in South Dakota politics. While Daschle lost, Herseth Sandlin managed to widen her winning split to 53%-46%. In 2006, she finally had an easy contest, with a 69%-29% victory against Bruce Whalen, a member of the Oglala Sioux Tribe. Herseth Sandlin solidified her hold on the seat in 2008 with an impressive 68%-32% victory over Republican businessman Chris Lien, beating him in every county in the state.

In the House, Herseth Sandlin's voting record ranks her among the more conservative Democrats. She cosponsored a bill that restricts victims of a shooting from filing a lawsuit against gun manufacturers and dealers. She worked closely with Senators Johnson and Thune in their successful effort in 2005 to remove Ellsworth Air Force Base from the base-closing list. Herseth Sandlin became active in the Blue Dog Coalition of conservative Democrats, especially in their call for fiscal discipline, and was elected as the caucus' co-chair of administration in November 2008. She also co-chaired the Democrats' Rural Working Group and served on the Agriculture Committee, where she was an avid supporter of increased production of renewable fuels such as ethanol. On the 2008 farm bill, she pressed successfully to establish a permanent disaster fund.

When Democrats achieved a House majority in 2007, she got the chairmanship of the Veterans' Affairs Subcommittee on Economic Opportunity. In 2008, the House passed her bill granting veterans the right to a preliminary hearing when they are seeking to regain jobs lost during their deployments. House Speaker Nancy Pelosi tapped her for a seat on the speaker's Select Committee on Energy Independence and Global Warming—the only farm-state Democrat on the panel. Herseth Sandlin was also the only House Democrat in 2008 to vote against a bill clamping down on questionable practices by credit card companies, such as retroactive rate increases. The credit card industry is one of the largest employers in South Dakota.

Many Democrats see Herseth Sandlin as a future national star and a potential statewide candidate. A 2008 *New York Times* article compared her oratorical style favorably to President Barack Obama's.

★ TENNESSEE ★

Tennessee is a battleground state, with a fighting temperament since it was settled 200 years ago. It produced so many soldiers for Andrew Jackson's wars with Indians and the British that it came to be known as the Volunteer State. In the 1860s, Yankee troops swept down the Tennessee and Cumberland rivers on their way to Mississippi, traveling through Chattanooga's Lookout Mountain on their way to Atlanta and the sea. But Tennessee is a battleground with a certain civility: Both Confederate and Union generals paid respectful calls on the widow of President James K. Polk, who stayed carefully neutral, in her Nashville mansion. Tennessee also has been a cultural battleground for much of the 20th century. On one side were the Fugitives, writers like John Crowe Ransom and Allen Tate, who contributed to "I'll Take My Stand," a manifesto calling for retaining the South's rural economy and heritage. On the other side have been business leaders and politicians who have made Tennessee the fastest-growing state of the interior South. The state gave birth to the first supermarket (a Piggly Wiggly), the Holiday Inn, FedEx and Goo-Goo Clusters. Both influences remain strong in this elongated state, despite the long distance between its two ends: Johnson City in East Tennessee is closer to Dover, Del., than it is to Memphis, and Memphis is closer to Dallas, Texas than to Johnson City.

The state has also been a marshaling ground for the music traditions that have a large place in Americans' lives. East Tennessee is one of the original homes of bluegrass music and mountain fiddling, with string bands and vocal harmony. Knoxville's *Tennessee Barn Dance* has been broadcast since 1942. Gospel music has long been centered in Nashville, which is also the nation's leading center of religious publishing, the headquarters of Thomas Nelson, FaithWorks, Integrity Books and LifeWay's Broadman & Holman. Country music got its commercial start in Nashville, with broadcasts of the Grand Ole Opry from Ryman Auditorium in 1925. Nashville remains indisputably the capital of country music. The Mississippi lowlands around Memphis, which is economically and culturally the metropolis of the Mississippi Delta, gave birth to the blues in the years from 1890 to 1920, and the blues were in turn the inspiration for the jazz musicians of Beale Street in the 1920s and for Elvis Presley's rock 'n' roll in the 1950s and 1960s. Presley's Graceland mansion is now a major tourist destination.

Tennessee has long been a political battleground. Its political divisions have their roots in the Civil War, and many counties today still vote their 1860s loyalties, The Union counties, mainly in East Tennessee but also a scattering in the west, vote solidly Republican, while the Confederate counties in Middle and West Tennessee long voted heavily Democratic. Within the limits of these enduring party loyalties, political entrepreneurs have set the tone for the state. From the 1920s to 1948, Edward Crump, longtime mayor of Memphis, used his total control of Democratic primary votes there to elect governors and senators. (Crump, unlike other Southern Democrats, allowed blacks to vote, and they voted his way.) The Tennessee Valley Authority and the cheap electric power it generated provided an institutional base for reform liberal Democrats Estes Kefauver and Albert Gore Sr., who beat incumbents in primaries when they were elected to the Senate in 1948 and 1952, respectively. They were soon national figures, with reliable enough backing from Tennessee's yellow-dog Democratic majority to vote for civil rights bills and to refuse to sign the segregationist Southern Manifesto. Kefauver died in 1963 and Gore was defeated in 1970, but he lived to see his son twice elected vice president before his death in 1998. Tennessee has never had a large black population—17% today, half of whom live in and around Memphis—and the state was not riven by the racial animosity that divided so much of the South in the 1950s and 1960s, thanks in large part to the actions of its leading politicians but also thanks in part to the continuing hold of ancestral partisan preferences.

Today the political balance has changed, and Tennessee has become a mostly Republican state. Democrats' cultural liberalism moved rural voters in West and Middle Tennessee away from their ancestral loyalties, and the surging growth in the ring of counties around Nashville in the last two decades created a new voting bloc that is conservative on both economic and cultural issues. The first movement toward the Republicans occurred in the 1960s and 1970s, with the election of Republican Senators Howard Baker and Bill Brock in 1966 and 1970, and Republican Gov. Lamar Alexander in 1978. Then, as Georgia Democrat Jimmy Carter changed the image of the Democratic Party, Democrats rallied. Democrats Jim Sasser and Al Gore Jr. were elected to the Senate in 1976 and 1984, respectively, and Democrat Ned Ray McWherter was elected governor in 1986. This movement was still strong enough for the Clinton-Gore ticket to carry Tennessee 47%-42% in 1992. But the narrowness of the margin was a warning. In 1994, Tennessee turned against the Clinton administration and produced a kind of political revolution. Republican Fred Thompson, famous as a Watergate investigator and movie actor, won the remainder of Gore's Senate term by a landslide, Republican heart transplant surgeon Bill Frist beat Sasser, and Republican Don Sundquist was elected governor. Republicans won most of the votes for the U.S. House, gaining two seats and coming close in a third. The Republican trend was strong enough in 1996 that only after extraordinary efforts—Gore made 16 appearances here and the campaign pumped in money for late ads—was the Clinton-Gore ticket able to win by a narrow 48%-46%.

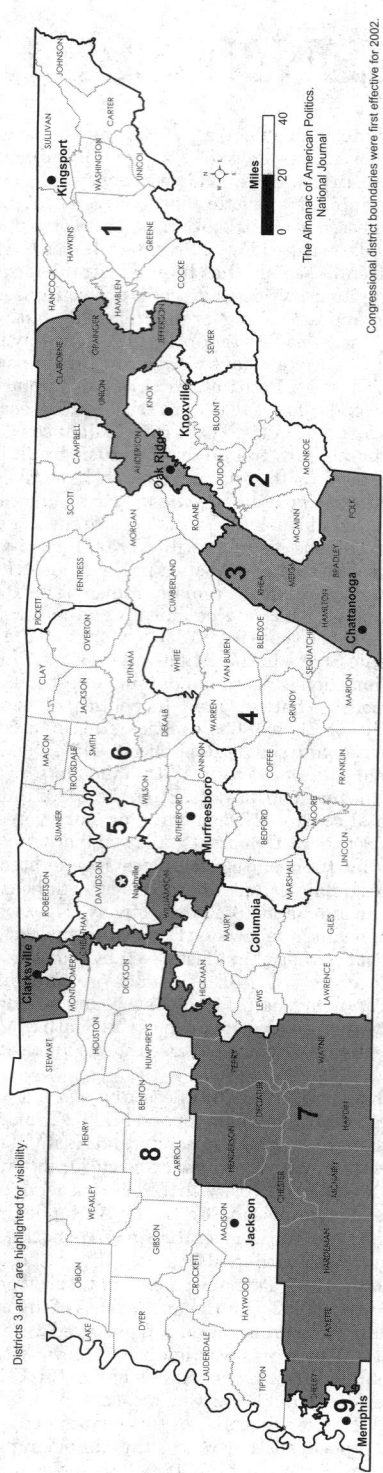

Districts 3 and 7 are highlighted for visibility.

The Almanac of American Politics,
National Journal

Congressional district boundaries were first effective for 2002.

In 2000, the tide was even stronger. Republican presidential candidate George W. Bush targeted the state early and worked it energetically. Headquartered in Nashville, the Gore campaign seemed to assume the state would come around in the end and campaigned hard here only in the last few days. Bush carried the state 51%-47% and Gore became only the fourth major party nominee to lose his home state in 85 years. (The others were South Dakota's George McGovern in 1972, Kansas' Alf Landon in 1936 and New Jersey's Woodrow Wilson in 1916.) The 2002 election saw some movement back to Tennessee Democrats. Former Nashville Mayor Phil Bredesen won the governorship 51%-48%. Tennessee has now alternated parties in the governor's office at eight-year intervals for a quarter-century. Democrats, aided by partisan redistricting, also picked up one congressional district and maintained control of the Legislature. But Republican Alexander, 20 years after he won his second election as governor, was elected to the U.S. Senate by 54%-44%. In 2004, Bush carried Tennessee by a solid 57%-43%, Republicans won the popular vote for the House, and for the first time since Reconstruction, voters elected a Republican majority in the state Senate. Even 2006, a Democratic year nationally, was mixed in Tennessee. Bredesen, after trimming the TennCare health insurance program, was re-elected 69%-30%, carrying all 95 counties. But Republican Bob Corker, after winning a bitter primary, was able to beat Democratic U.S. Rep. Harold Ford 51%-48%—this, despite an effective campaign by Ford, whose strong showing looks, in retrospect, as a harbinger of Democrat Barack Obama's national victory two years later. But not in Tennessee, which was part of the Jacksonian swath of America running along the Appalachians and to the southwest where Obama ran weakly both in the primaries and in the general election. In 2008, Republican presidential nominee John McCain carried Tennessee 57%-42%, Alexander was re-elected 65%-32%, and Republicans, to the surprise of almost everyone, won majorities in both houses of the Legislature for the first time since Reconstruction.

Tennessee has been expanding economically, but hasn't abandoned its cultural roots. If its economy lagged behind the nation's through much of the 20th century, its open climate for entrepreneurism enabled it to grow mightily over the last three decades. The expansion started in the early 1980s, when Alexander helped bring big auto plants to Middle Tennessee. The lack of strong unions and of bitter racial divisions—Tennessee was mostly untouched by the racial strife of the 1930s and the civil rights battles of the 1960s—attracted Japanese companies, which in turn attracted General Motors' Saturn division. In 2006, Nissan moved its American headquarters from the Los Angeles suburbs to Nashville, and in July 2008, Volkswagen chose Chattanooga as the site of one of its first American factories. In the past few years, as the Big Three auto companies' problems sank Michigan's economy, Tennessee's mostly Japanese auto companies thrived. There were 126,000 auto-related jobs in the state in 2008. Some of Tennessee's old industries have fallen behind. Apparel and textile factories have closed, and the tobacco harvest in 2006, after the federal tobacco buyout, was down 72% from its peak in 1982. But country music has continued to be popular and successful. And Nashville has become a major health care center. Growth has been particularly robust in the ring of counties around Nashville, which have been attracting significant Hispanic immigration. Tennessee's economy seemed to be faltering a bit in early 2008, as auto sales plummeted, and Bredesen ordered waves of state budget cuts. But the housing bubble here was relatively small and Tennessee's diversified economy seemed poised to fare better than some states.

During its years of growth, Tennessee state politics became, well, a battleground. Tennessee has been growing more than neighboring states in part because of its low taxes. It has no income tax and it ranks low on the list of state and local taxes as a percentage of per capita income. But in 1994, Gov. Ned McWherter created TennCare, an extension of Medicaid, and TennCare spending accelerated far above projections, from $2.5 billion in 1995 to $8 billion in 2004. Republican Gov. Sundquist, elected on a no-income-tax platform, nonetheless pressed unsuccessfully for an income tax. Democrat Bredesen, also elected on a no-income-tax platform, kept his promise and has scaled back TennCare significantly. In 2008, he started a new state health insurance program, which has cost less than projected. Partisan skirmishing in the Legislature has taken odd turns. In 2007, a Democrat defected and the state Senate elected a Republican speaker, who is also the lieutenant governor. In 2009, a Republican refused to support

Population		Household Income		Work	
Pop. 2007:	6,073,646	Under $15k:	17.0%	Private:	78.0%
State rank:	17th of 50	$15k to $50k:	41.1%	Government:	14.0%
Change since 2000:	Up 6.8%	$50k to $100k:	28.9%	Self-employed:	7.8%
Urban:	62.2%	$100k to $150k:	10.6%	Unemployment (3-yr. average):	4.6%
Rural:	37.8%	Over $150k:	2.4%	Poverty:	15.9%
Native of state:	62.4%	Median income:	$41,821	Blue collar:	27.3%
Not a citizen:	2.7%	**Home Value**		White collar:	56.4%
Area size:	42,143 sq. mi.	Under $100k:	38.6%	Khaki collar:	0.3%
Most populous cities		$100k to $300k:	51.0%	Other:	16.0%
1. Memphis	649,443	$300k to $500k:	7.3%	**Age**	
2. Nashville	586,214	$500k to $1 mil:	2.6%	Median age:	37.2 yrs.
3. Knoxville	177,362	Over $1 million:	0.6%	More than 65 yrs:	12.7%
4. Chattanooga	159,111	Median:	$122,500	Less than 18 yrs:	24.1%

Race/Ethnicity				
White:	77.4%	*Language*		
Black:	16.6%	English:	94.3%	
Hispanic:	3.3%	Spanish:	3.2%	
Asian:	1.3%	Asian:	0.9%	
Native Am.:	0.2%	Other		
Hawaiian:	0.0%	European	1.2%	
Two+ races:	1.1%	**Education**		
Ancestry		H.S. grad:	80.9%	
USA:	16.4%	College grad:	21.7%	
Irish:	9.6%	Grad degree:	7.6%	
English:	9.3%			

Military Veterans	
% of Pop:	11.1%
Veterans by Period	
WWII and before:	10.4%
Korea:	10.6%
Vietnam:	33.5%
Gulf (pre-2001):	12.4%
Gulf (post-2001):	6.6%
Peace time:	26.5%

Registered Voters in 2008	
No party registration	
Voter turnout:	2,599,749
Turnout as % of	
voting age:	54.9%
General Assembly	
Senate:	14 D 19 R
House:	49 D 49 R 1 I

his party's choice for House speaker, throwing control of the Legislature into turmoil. The battles reached across the state border. In 2008, the Legislature in drought-stricken Georgia passed a resolution declaring that the border with Tennessee had been incorrectly drawn by a surveyor in 1818 and demanded that it be redrawn a mile north. This would mean that part of the Tennessee River would be in Georgia, giving it a new water source. The resolution directed Georgia Gov. Sonny Perdue to negotiate a settlement with his Tennessee counterpart. Bredesen, his spokesman said, "has made it clear he has no intention of moving Tennessee's border, nor will he give away Tennessee's natural resources." The issue came up once before, in 1887 and, now as then, no actual fighting broke out.

Presidential politics   Tennessee is one of only two states—the other is Arkansas—that has given Republican presidential candidates increasing percentages of its votes in each of the last four elections. One reason is that Arkansas' Bill Clinton and Tennessee's Al Gore were running in 1992 and 1996 and ran unusually well for Democrats in their home states. But Gore's hometown status was not enough for him to carry the state—which would have made him president regardless of Florida's outcome—because of the unpopularity here of the cultural liberalism that won Clinton and Gore so many suburban votes in the nation's largest metropolitan areas. Further Republican gains, such as George W. Bush's 56.8% of the vote here in 2004 and John McCain's 56.9% in 2008, probably owe something to attitudes on foreign policy and war.

Tennessee's most famous son is President Andrew Jackson, and much of the state was settled by his fellow Scots-Irish, who were famously ready to fight to the death when their families or their country were threatened. (Jackson killed two men in

2008 Presidential Vote		
McCain (R)	1,479,178	(57%)
Obama (D)	1,087,437	(42%)
2008 Democratic Presidential Primary		
Clinton (D)	336,245	(54%)
Obama (D)	252,874	(40%)
2008 Republican Presidential Primary		
Huckabee (R)	190,904	(34%)
McCain (R)	176,091	(32%)
Romney (R)	130,632	(24%)
Paul (R)	31,026	(6%)
2004 Presidential Vote		
Bush (R)	1,384,375	(57%)
Kerry (D)	1,036,477	(43%)

duels after they said unkind things about his wife.) The Jacksonian belt, throughout the Appalachian chain and running west from Tennessee to Arkansas and Oklahoma, seemed repelled by the antiwar policies of Democratic nominees John Kerry in 2004 and Barack Obama in 2008, and perhaps particularly by Obama's generally conciliatory demeanor. Obama carried Memphis's Shelby County, which is about half African-American, and Nashville's Davidson County, but he won only four of the state's other 95 counties, each of them a declining-population rural area where Democratic loyalties go back to the Civil War. McCain carried whites 63%-34% and white evangelical Protestants (52% of the electorate) 75%-22%. As Bredesen said, Barack Obama's strategy of concentrating on target states "that produced our national win came at a real cost to Democrats here in Tennessee."

For several election seasons, Tennessee held its presidential primary on Super Tuesday (though Tennessee holds its state primaries on Thursdays, the only state to do so). But it was far from the biggest state to vote that day, and received little attention. In 2004, it voted earlier, on February 10, just two weeks after New Hampshire, and the only other primary that day was in Virginia. This was just a week after Democrat John Edwards had won in South Carolina and Democrat Wesley Clark had led Edwards and Kerry in a virtual three-way tie in Oklahoma. Both Edwards and Clark were from next-door states, but Kerry won with 41% to 27% for Edwards and 23% for Clark. Turnout was 369,000, far lower than the record Democratic primary turnout in 1988 of 576,000, when Gore was running. For 2008, Tennessee set its primary on Super Tuesday, February 5. But it did not see much campaigning. Democrat Hillary Rodham Clinton was well ahead in polls, and won a solid 54%-40%. Turnout was a record high, 625,000, and 25% of voters were African-American. Obama carried Shelby and Davidson counties, plus four small rural counties. Clinton carried the rest, getting as much as 86% in yellow-dog Democratic Grundy County.

On the Republican side, everyone assumed that Fred Thompson, who announced his candidacy in September 2007, would carry his home state. But he dropped out of the race after his weak showing in South Carolina, and the remaining candidates suddenly started putting Tennessee on their schedules. Mike Huckabee carried most of rural Tennessee and Shelby County as well and won with 34% of the vote. John McCain carried Knoxville and its suburbs and got his highest percentage in the county that includes Fort Campbell, for a total of 32%. Mitt Romney carried most of metro Nashville and got 24%.

Congressional districting

111th Congress Lineup	
5 D	4 R
110th Congress Lineup	
5 D	4 R

Tennessee's Democratic Legislature controlled redistricting after the 2000 census, since Republican Gov. Don Sundquist's veto could be overridden by majority votes in both houses. The plan provided critical votes to Democrat Lincoln Davis in the open Republican 4th district in 2002, and he has held the district since. It also strengthened Bart Gordon in the 6th district. It was not clear in early 2009 which party would control redistricting after the 2010 census, or whether either party would. Republicans currently have a 19-14 majority in the state Senate. They also have a narrow 50-49 majority in the state House, but the minority Democrats have an inordinate amount of power. They successfully maneuvered in early 2009 to elect their own candidate as speaker, Republican Kent Williams, who cooperated in the plot. Democrats banded together to vote for Williams for speaker, and then he cast the deciding vote for himself. Williams got no votes from fellow Republicans.

Governor

Phil Bredesen (D)

Elected 2002, term expires Jan. 2011, 2nd term; b. Nov. 21, 1943, Oceanport, NJ; home, Nashville; Harvard U., B.S. 1967; Presbyterian; married (Andrea Conte); 1 child.

Elected Office: Lexington, MA, City Cncl., 1972–73; Nashville mayor, 1991–99.

Professional Career: Founder, HealthAmerica Corp., 1980–86.

Office: State Capitol, Nashville, 37243, 615-741-2001; Fax: 615-532-9711; Web site: www.tn.gov/governor.

Election Results

2006 general	Phil Bredesen (D)	1,247,491	(69%)
	Jim Bryson (R)	540,853	(30%)
2006 primary	Phil Bredesen (D)	393,004	(89%)
	John Jay Hooker (D)	31,933	(7%)

Prior Winning Percentages: 2002 (51%)

Phil Bredesen is a Democrat who was elected governor of Tennessee in 2002 on his second try. Bredesen grew up far from Nashville, in Shortsville, N.Y., 30 miles southeast of Rochester. His parents were divorced and his mother worked as a bank teller; his grandmother lived with him and took in sewing for a living. He got a scholarship to Harvard University and graduated with a degree in physics. In 1967, he moved to Lexington, Mass., where he went to work for Itek, doing classified work that got him a draft deferment during the Vietnam War. He caught the political bug early. In 1968, he volunteered for Democratic presidential candidate Eugene McCarthy in New Hampshire. In 1970, he ran for the Massachusetts state Senate and lost to a longtime incumbent. In 1972 he won a seat on the Lexington Town Meeting. He went to work for Searle, a pharmaceutical firm, and moved to London, where he met his wife. She was recruited by Hospital Corporation of America, so he quit his job to follow her to Nashville in 1975. There he got a job with Hospital Affiliates International, negotiating management contracts with hospitals. He started his own business in 1980 with $50,000 cash and $250,000 in backing from local venture capitalists, operating from a computer in his den. Bredesen launched HealthAmerica, which began acquiring and operating health maintenance organizations across the country. When it went public in 1983, it ran 20 HMOs with 400,000 members. His backers decided to sell the firm to Maxicare in 1986; Bredesen's share of the sale was $47 million.

In 1987, he ran for mayor of Nashville, a particularly powerful position because the city includes all of Davidson County. Bredesen spent $2 million on his campaign but lost the primary. In 1991, he ran for mayor again and won with 71%. He had some spectacular successes. He lined up financing for a hockey arena and, later, a football stadium and brought the National Hockey League's Predators and National Football League's Tennessee Titans to Nashville. He enticed Dell to locate a facility in Nashville. The city boomed in the 1990s and gained 106,000 jobs. Once a regional center, Nashville now seemed to be a major national city.

Nashville is Tennessee's largest media market, covering almost all of Middle Tennessee, and a successful Nashville mayor is a natural candidate for statewide office. In 1994, Bredesen spent $6 million on a run for governor and won the Democratic nomination with 53% of the vote in a 10-candidate field. He did not campaign heavily in East and West Tennessee and lost to Republican Don Sundquist by 54%-45%. But in the years that followed, Bredesen had a more successful record than Sundquist. The state's expensive health care program, TennCare, had one of the nation's lowest revenue bases, with no state income tax. TennCare, established in 1994 with federal waivers, covered not only those eligible for Medicaid but others with relatively low incomes or who were uninsured; enrollment zoomed and costs increased. In his second term, Sundquist went back on a campaign promise and sought an income tax. Most Republicans opposed him, arguing that Tennessee's low taxes fostered its more robust economic growth as compared to neighboring states. Barraged by honking motorists and slogan-chanting anti-tax crusaders mobilized by radio talk show hosts, the Legislature refused to pass the tax hike.

Against this background Bredesen decided to run for governor again. He said that he opposed an income tax and argued that his experience managing health care systems would enable him to straighten out TennCare. He won the Democratic primary easily, but the favorite was Republican Rep. Van Hilleary, who based his campaign on opposition to an income tax. Hilleary charged that Bredesen was a rich Northerner who didn't really understand Tennessee. Bredesen undercut that by sitting down with folks over coffee and describing his youth in a small town. Unusual for a Democrat, he appeared on conservative talk radio shows and made a favorable impression. Much of Hilleary's campaign was based on the premise that Bredesen didn't really oppose an income tax, and pointing out that he had raised property taxes three times as mayor of Nashville. Bredesen focused more on fixing TennCare. "Everybody in the state of Tennessee knows somebody on TennCare they don't think should be on TennCare. It needs to be the bronze package, not the platinum package," he said.

Bredesen spent $3 million of his own money on his campaign, to counter, he said, money raised for Hilleary by President George W. Bush. This turned out to be the closest Tennessee governor's race since 1896. Bredesen won 51%-48%. This time he had campaigned across the state, raising money in small fundraisers, holding chili suppers in rural counties. He broke into the Republican base in East Tennessee, carrying Knoxville's Knox County, and holding Hilleary to a narrow lead in his own region. Bredesen carried Nashville solidly, had a big lead in Memphis and carried rural West Tennessee, often a swing area in Tennessee elections.

Facing a predicted $800 million budget shortfall, Bredesen got the Legislature to cut state spending 9% across the board in 2003 and to vote for a lottery to pay for college scholarships. He supported changes in workmen's compensation supported by businesses and opposed by trial lawyers. He got the Legislature to limit driver's licenses to citizens and aliens with permanent resident status. In 2004, he pushed through a $174 million education increase, raising teacher pay above the Southeastern average and starting voluntary pre-kindergarten.

But the big elephant remained in the room: TennCare. By early 2004, it consumed nearly one-third of the state budget and its 2005 cost was estimated to be $650 million over budget. In May 2004, the Legislature approved Bredesen's proposed changes. In November, Bredesen announced that he would abolish TennCare and move back to standard Medicaid, which would eliminate coverage for 430,000 people, one-third of beneficiaries. On January 10, 2005, he announced that all non-Medicaid-eligible adults would be removed from TennCare and that strict limits would be imposed on prescription drugs and doctor visits, with no appeals. By the end of the year, the state trimmed 191,000 people from the program and by 2006, the overhaul of TennCare had reduced the cost increase from $650 million to $115 million and resulted in budget surpluses. Bredesen sought to ease the pain of the cuts by using money saved from TennCare to establish a "safety net" of health clinics, indigent hospital care and prescription drug assistance for the mentally ill. Bredesen also used the savings to boost state education spending by $366 million, targeting pre-kindergarten initiatives.

The governor in 2006 also launched Cover Tennessee to fund health care for those with pre-existing medical conditions, uninsured children and working adults. Unlike TennCare, the new state program would not receive federal money, except to cover children, and would tap some of the TennCare savings to get the program started. Bredesen said he would consider a tobacco tax increase in the future, but not an income tax. Fixing the state's health care system, a preoccupation for much of his first term, became a personal cause for Bredesen that year. The governor had returned home to New York to watch his younger brother, an alcoholic, die of liver disease. Dean Bredesen, a vacuum cleaner salesman, had never asked his older brother, the multimillionaire former health care executive, for the $10,000 deposit that would have gotten him access to health care. Bredesen grieved publicly. He said he did not know if better care would have saved his brother but said the death gave him insight into what it is like to be an uninsured American.

Bredesen's administration has faced criticism on ethics matters, although the governor sought to address the issues before they became major distractions. He ordered a shake-up of hiring practices at the Tennessee Highway Patrol after the Nashville *Tennessean* ran a story in 2005 about political insiders who were given official-looking identification that some of them tried to use to get out of traffic violations and drunk driving arrests. An outside review found evidence of corruption and cronyism at the THP, and Bredesen backed reforms. In 2006, Bredesen called the state Legislature back in to session to write an ethics bill to limit cash contributions from lobbyists after the Federal Bureau of Investigation's Tennessee Waltz bribery investigation resulted in the arrests of five current and former state legislators.

Bredesen began his final term forced to reconcile a looming state financial crisis with his desire to expand both education and health care spending. In 2007, he proposed $343 million in additional money for schools, paid for by increasing the state's cigarette tax threefold. Bredesen's budget also included $55 million in job training and infrastructure improvement for companies to keep jobs in the state. Lawmakers kept Bredesen's wishes largely intact, particularly approving his education initiatives, giving $136 million to TennCare and $14 million to a new program providing health care for uninsured children. The state ended the year with a surplus.

But in 2008, as the national economy faltered, Bredesen's budget shrank from the previous year's. He proposed more education funding along with $29.3 million for job creation. But he also called for $129 million in spending cuts across government agencies and a voluntary buyout program aimed at encouraging 2,011 state workers to leave, reducing the workforce by 5 percent without layoffs. In 2009, Republicans controlled both the House and Senate for the first time since Reconstruction, and lawmakers began pushing bills to curb abortion rights and expand gun rights. Legislators passed a bill allowing people legally carrying guns to bring them into restaurants and bars where liquor is served. In May 2009, Bredesen vetoed the bill, only his sixth veto. "There are sensible rules to be applied to the exercise of [gun] rights. I believe this bill crossed that line," he said. In June, the House overrode his veto 69-27, with the Senate following the next day, 21-9. It was the first time a Bredesen veto had been overridden.

The New Republic ran a laudatory cover story about Bredesen in 2005. The following year, he was up for re-election. A strong fundraiser who also could spend his own millions, Bredesen ended up with weak Republican opposition in freshman state Sen. Jim Bryson, who ran negative television ads accusing Bredesen of not doing enough to crack down on illegal immigrants. Bredesen carried all 95 counties and won 69%-30%.

Bredesen was mentioned by some as a possible vice presidential candidate in 2008. As the Democratic primary became a dead heat between Barack Obama of Illinois and Hillary Rodham Clinton of New York over undecided superdelegates, Bredesen proposed a "mini convention" for superdelegates to decide their presidential pick. "We have an obligation as a party to try to find some way to bring closure to this thing and not let it tear us apart," Bredesen said on "Fox News Sunday." Bredesen himself remained neutral until after Obama secured the required delegates in June 2008. After Obama's first Health and Human Services Secretary nominee, former South Dakota Sen. Tom Daschle, was forced to withdraw because of tax problems, Bredesen was mentioned as a candidate. But some liberal advocacy groups such as MoveOn.org and Families USA objected to him, citing the TennCare cuts he made during his first term. The job went to Kansas Gov. Kathleen Sebelius.

Senior Senator

Lamar Alexander (R)

Elected 2002, term expires 2014, 2nd term; b. July 3, 1940, Maryville; home, Nashville; Vanderbilt U., B.A. 1962, N.Y.U., J.D. 1965; Presbyterian; married (Honey); 4 children.

Elected Office: TN governor, 1978–86.

Professional Career: Pres., Univ. of TN, 1988–91; U.S. Edu. Sect., 1991–93; Co-director, Empower America, 1994–95; Prof., Harvard U. JFK Schl. of Govt., 2001–02.

DC Office: 455 DSOB, 20510, 202-224-4944; Fax: 202-228-3398; Web site: alexander.senate.gov.

State Offices: Blountville, 423-325-6240; Chattanooga, 423-752-5337; Jackson, 731-423-9344; Knoxville, 865-545-4253; Memphis, 901-544-4224; Nashville, 615-736-5129.

Committees: *Republican Conference Chairman. Appropriations* (9th of 12 R): Commerce, Justice, Science & Related Agencies; Energy & Water Development; Financial Services & General Government; Interior, Environment & Related Agencies (RMM); Labor, Health and Human Services, Education & Related Agencies; Transportation, Housing and Urban Development & Related Agencies. *Budget* (10th of 10 R). *Environment & Public Works* (7th of 7 R). *Health, Education, Labor & Pensions* (3rd of 10 R). *Rules & Administration* (6th of 8 R).

Group Ratings

	ADA	ACLU	AFS	LCV	ITIC	NTU	COC	ACU	CFG	FRC
2008	25	23	0	18	100	50	75	72	58	88
2007	20	—	14	33	—	58	82	76	55	—

National Journal Ratings

	2007 LIB — 2007 CONS		2008 LIB — 2008 CONS	
Economic	30% —	68%	31% —	68%
Social	16% —	83%	0% —	79%
Foreign	28% —	70%	21% —	76%
Composite	26% —	75%	22% —	79%

Key Votes of the 110th Congress

1. Raise CAFE standards	Y	5. Make English official language	Y	9. Withdraw troops 3/08	N
2. Expand SCHIP	Y	6. Path to citizenship	N	10. Iran guard is terrorist group	Y
3. Cap greenhouse gases	N	7. Fetus is unborn child	Y	11. Increase missile defense $	Y
4. Bail out financial markets	Y	8. Prosecute hate crimes	N	12. Overhaul FISA	Y

Election Results

2008 general	Lamar Alexander (R)	1,579,477	(65%)	($4,571,728)
	Robert Tuke (D)	767,236	(32%)	($751,915)
2008 primary	Lamar Alexander (R)	unopposed		

Prior Winning Percentages: 2002 (54%)

Lamar Alexander, former governor of Tennessee and Education secretary, was elected to the Senate in 2002 and is the state's senior senator. Alexander grew up Maryville, in East Tennessee between Knoxville and the Smoky Mountains, the son of a principal and a teacher. He started piano lessons at age 4 and still plays. Like former President Bill Clinton, he was elected governor of Boys State, the high school summer leadership program run by the American Legion. He graduated from Vanderbilt University, where in the early 1960s he wrote editorials for the school newspaper *The Hustler* urging integration. He got a law degree from New York University, then clerked for Judge John Minor Wisdom of the Fifth Circuit federal appeals court. In 1966, he wrote Howard Baker, then the Republican candidate for Senate, and volunteered for his Senate campaign against Democrat Frank Clement. Instead, Baker gave him a job, establishing a critical connection in Alexander's career. After Baker won, Alexander went to work on his Washington staff. In 1969, on Baker's recommendation, Alexander got a job working for Republican President Richard Nixon's congressional liaison Bryce Harlow. On a trip back to Tennessee in 1970, he met Memphis dentist Winfield Dunn, who was running for governor. Alexander agreed to manage his campaign and Dunn became the first Republican elected governor in 50 years. Alexander decided that next time he would be the candidate, and in 1974, at age 34, he ran for governor. He ran a conventional campaign and in that Watergate year, he lost 55%-44% to Democratic U.S. Rep. Ray Blanton.

He ran again in 1978, but this time with a more colorful campaign strategy: Wearing a red plaid shirt, Alexander walked 1,000 miles across Tennessee. He won 56%-44%. After the election Blanton started issuing many pardons of criminals, who, it would turn out, were paying him bribes. The U.S. attorney urged that Alexander be sworn in three days early, and Democratic legislative leaders and the state's chief justice agreed. In a hurried ceremony, Alexander took the oath and announced that he was naming Fred Thompson, famous for his work as Baker's chief counsel in the Senate Watergate hearings, as a special prosecutor. As governor, Alexander got Nissan to build its first American plant in Rutherford County and General Motors to build its Saturn plant in Williamson County. The plants became the sparkplugs of rapid growth in the counties around Nashville. He was re-elected 60%-40% in 1982. After leaving office, he spent six months living in Australia, writing a book called *Six Months Off*. In 1988, he became president of the University of Tennessee and in 1991, he was appointed George H.W. Bush's Education secretary. In these years, he also reaped big profits from small investments: An option to buy the *Knoxville Journal* was sold to Gannett and yielded $620,000; an option given for his consultant work at Whittle Communications earned him $330,000. Alexander started a company called Corporate Child Care and is still part-owner.

The year 1994 turned out to be a good one for Tennessee Republicans. Thompson and Bill Frist were elected to the Senate and Don Sundquist was elected governor. Alexander probably could have won either office. But he was after bigger things; he was running for president. His 1996 campaign was keyed to the mood of 1994: He campaigned as an outsider, wore his red plaid shirt and called, as Baker often had, for citizen-politicians. Of members of Congress, he said, "Cut their pay and bring them home!" His bumper stickers said, "Lamar!" But he also had a sophisticated message, based on the idea that the nation needed more decentralized government. He had a superb fundraising organization that made Nashville one of the leading Republican money sources in the nation. He hired top-notch political consultants and good organizers in Iowa and New Hampshire. Alexander finished third in the Iowa caucuses, behind Kansas' Bob Dole and conservative commentator Pat Buchanan and ahead of magazine publisher Steve Forbes.

New Hampshire was his best chance for a breakthrough. Dole, the favorite, had been concentrating his fire on Buchanan. But five days before the primary, Dole began running ads attacking Alexander. This was shrewd strategy. Buchanan was likely to do well in New Hampshire, but probably could never be nominated. The candidate who finished second in New Hampshire would likely be his chief rival and Dole would easily win the nomination. So it turned out. Buchanan did win, with 27% of the vote, to 26% for Dole and 23% for Alexander.

In 1999, Alexander started running for president again. But the plaid shirt and the 1994-style themes failed to resonate. George W. Bush, with his celebrity and his fundraising, dominated the race, and Forbes' extensive, expensive campaigning in Iowa left little room for Alexander. His fundraising faltered and after his disappointing sixth-place finish in the August 1999 Ames, Iowa, straw poll, he dropped out and endorsed Bush. He didn't go to the 2000 Republican National Convention, though, he revealed later, he was interviewed by Dick Cheney as a possible vice presidential nominee. Critical of the frontloaded presidential primary calendar, Alexander in 2007 was a chief co-sponsor of legislation to implement a system of rotating regional primaries. "If professional football were presidential politics, SportsCenter would pick the Super Bowl teams after two pre-season games," he told *The Tennessean*.

Then, in March 2002, just 27 days before the filing deadline, Thompson announced that he would not run for re-election. He gave Alexander a heads-up on his decision, allowing Alexander to get his campaign underway shortly after Thompson made his announcement. He started with 93% name recognition in the state and 66% of voters had favorable feelings toward him. Republican U.S. Rep. Ed Bryant of suburban Memphis also got into the race even though some Republicans tried to talk him out of it. His campaign theme was that he was the real conservative in the race. But Alexander also campaigned as a conservative. On talk radio shows, he ran a series of "plain talk" ads taking conservative stands on taxes, the word "God" in the Pledge of Allegiance, charter schools and oil drilling in the Arctic National Wildlife Refuge. Bryant's ads called him "the one without the plaid shirt" and urged, "Don't be plaid. Be solid for Bryant." Alexander was endorsed on March 12 by Gov. Sundquist, unpopular with many of his fellow Republicans for his advocacy of a state income tax. Bryant noted that Alexander increased the sales and gasoline taxes when he was governor. But Alexander won 54%-43%.

In the general election, his opponent was U.S. Rep. Bob Clement, who started with good name identification. He had been elected a congressman from Nashville, the center of the state's largest media market, in 1988. Like Alexander, he had been a university president, of Cumberland University. Clement had a relatively moderate voting record, having supported the Bush tax cuts and the 2002 Iraq war resolution. But much of the campaign dialogue concerned their business investments. Clement said Alexander was a political insider who became wealthy through political connections. Alexander charged that Clement, while public service commissioner in the 1970s, served on the board of one of the banks of Jake Butcher, Alexander's 1978 opponent, whose banks imploded in scandal in the 1980s. Clement at first denied that he'd served on the board, and then said it was just an advisory board a decade before the scandal. Alexander said that Clement had voted 143 times to raise taxes and asserted Clement would be part of "that crowd" voting against President Bush.

Alexander won 54%-44%. He won 63% in his native (and ancestrally Republican) East Tennessee, which cast nearly 40% of the votes. Clement carried Nashville's Davidson County and rural counties in Middle Tennessee, but Alexander carried the fast-growing ring of suburban counties around Nashville and held Clement to 53% in his home area. In West Tennessee, Alexander made some inroads among Memphis blacks and carried the rural counties.

And so a politician who ran for governor at 34 became a senator at 62. On his office wall, he mounted not the usual array of framed photographs but a 27-foot authentic barn wall, with 40 antique items (a guitar made of matches, a banjo made from a fruitcake tin) on loan from the Museum of Appalachia in Norris, Tenn. As a former governor and cabinet secretary, he got a little seniority over other freshmen, and he joined his Tennessee colleague, Majority Leader Frist, on the Health, Education, Labor, and Pensions Committee. There he worked on successful bills to help states ensure special education teachers meet federal standards, to permit parents more choice in special education services, and to create summer academies for teachers and students to study American history. Another Alexander proposal was legislation creating $4,000 scholarships for private schools for students in failing public schools.

He differed with the Bush administration on the environment. He joined Delaware Democrat Tom Carper's bill that would limit emissions of carbon dioxide as well as other pollutants, and created a system of emissions trading, both of which the White House opposed. Air pollution had been high in Knoxville and threatening the tourism industry in the Smoky Mountains area. To counter the effects of a federal court ruling, he also pushed to restrict emissions from coal-fired power plants. For his ongoing support of the Great Smoky Mountains and its environmental quality, researchers in 2007 named a newly discovered bug in the park after Alexander, calling it the *lamaralexandrei*. Its checkerboard markings reminded them of Alexander's trademark red and black flannel shirts.

In the deliberations on the energy bill in 2005, Alexander proposed an amendment to give local governments a veto over wind power projects and to require environmental impact statements of such projects in offshore areas and within 20 miles of scenic areas and military bases. "At a time when America needs large amounts of low-cost reliable power, wind produces puny amounts of high-cost unreliable power," he said. He won passage of an amendment providing a 30% solar investment tax credit for homeowners. Alexander has continued to champion alternative energy, and even purchased a Toyota Prius with a special battery making the vehicle entirely electric.

He took more traditionally conservative positions on immigration. After the well-publicized singing of the national anthem in Spanish ("Nuestro Himno"), Alexander sponsored a successful resolution stating that the anthem and similar songs should be sung in English, and he supported a measure designating English as the national language. In 2008, he introduced a bill to protect employers from language-based anti-discrimination lawsuits.

With his Tennessee colleague Frist retiring, and Whip Mitch McConnell likely to replace him as Senate leader, Alexander started in summer 2005 to gather votes for the position of Republican whip. His likely opponent seemed to be Pennsylvania conservative Rick Santorum, and in mid-October 2006, when Santorum was trailing badly in polls for re-election in Pennsylvania, Alexander said he had enough support to win. He said he wouldn't run later for party leader: "I'm glad at this stage in my career to play second fiddle." Santorum lost, but six days after the election, Trent Lott, the former Senate majority leader from Mississippi, announced he was running. Alexander said he still had enough votes. But Lott won by a 25-24 secret ballot vote. "Senators, like most Americans, like a comeback. Trent proved he is a better vote counter," Alexander said.

As consolation, Alexander was awarded seats on the Appropriations and Environment and Public Works Committees in the 110th Congress (2007–08). He formed a Bipartisan Members Group with independent Joe Lieberman of Connecticut to meet at breakfast every Tuesday. On the Iraq War, he and Colorado Democratic Sen. Ken Salazar urged Bush to set goals for troop withdrawals. While opposed to a fixed end date, Alexander pushed for troops to transition into training Iraqi forces to defend themselves. He angered both sides in the debate because he didn't fit neatly into either camp. He told the *New York Times,* "We just can't keep shouting at one another. I think it is inexcusable for United States senators to be lecturing Baghdad about being in a political stalemate, yet we can't come up with a consensus ourselves."

When Lott resigned from the Senate in December 2007, Alexander again saw a chance to move up in the party ranks. With Conference Chairman Jon Kyl of Arizona expected to become minority whip, Alexander announced he would run for the vacant Conference chairman slot. North Carolina Sen. Richard Burr also declared his candidacy and began to pull some support from younger conservatives. But Alexander prevailed, winning on the secret ballot 31-16. As the party's chief spokesman, he turned his attention to courting independent voters. He set a moderate tone, hoping to chart the same path for fellow Republicans as he had for himself in the past year—work with Democrats to get Republican policies passed rather than simply attack Democratic ideas. One of his first tests was the debate over the 2008 economic stimulus bill. As Minority Leader McConnell worked to block a Democratic bill and force Majority Leader Harry Reid to accept a simple tax rebate bill, Alexander promoted the idea that the plan should be bipartisan while also trying to hold together a diverse party. "We have 49 senators with very different points of view," Alexander told the *Knoxville News-Sentinel.* "My job is not to make us all sing the same note. It's to make us sing at least in some harmony." After Republicans suffered more losses at the polls in November 2008, Alexander argued that his bipartisan approach was even more salient and also urged GOP leaders not to give up on African-American voters. "You have to make it clear that you want to earn the respect and support of Democrats and independents," he told the *Chattanooga Times Free Press.*

Alexander was up for re-election in 2008, but his path to a second term was relatively effortless. After more prominent Tennessee Democrats passed on the race, former state Democratic Chairman Robert Tuke got his party's nomination, but mustered only slightly more than $700,000 in fundraising compared to Alexander's $8.3 million. Tuke tried to paint Alexander as a Bush lackey, but the assertion did not ring true. Alexander prevailed 65%-32%, winning 94 of 95 counties.

Junior Senator

Bob Corker (R)

Elected 2006, term expires 2012, 1st term; b. Aug. 24, 1952, Orangeburg, SC; home, Chattanooga; U. of TN, B.S. 1974; Protestant; married (Elizabeth); 2 children.

Elected Office: Chattanooga mayor, 2001–05.

Professional Career: Owner, Bencor Corp., 1978–90; Commissioner, TN Dept. of Fin. and Admin., 1995–96; Owner, Corker Group, 1982–2006.

DC Office: 185 DSOB, 20510, 202-224-3344; Fax: 202-228-0566; Web site: corker.senate.gov.

State Offices: Blountville, 423-323-1252; Chattanooga, 423-756-2757; Jackson, 731-424-9655; Knoxville, 865-637-4180; Memphis, 901-683-1910; Nashville, 615-279-8125.

Committees: *Aging (Special)* (4th of 8 R). *Banking, Housing & Urban Affairs* (6th of 10 R): Financial Institutions; Securities, Insurance & Investment; Security & International Trade & Finance (RMM). *Energy & Natural Resources* (10th of 10 R): Energy; National Parks; Public Lands & Forests. *Foreign Relations* (2nd of 8 R): African Affairs; European Affairs; International Development & Foreign Assistance, Economic Affairs & International Environmental Protection (RMM); Near Eastern & South & Central Asian Affairs.

Group Ratings

	ADA	ACLU	AFS	LCV	ITIC	NTU	COC	ACU	CFG	FRC
2008	20	14	0	27	100	56	75	83	73	100
2007	20	—	14	27	—	63	82	83	61	—

National Journal Ratings

	2007 LIB	—	2007 CONS		2008 LIB	—	2008 CONS
Economic	32%	—	66%		24%	—	75%
Social	0%	—	91%		0%	—	79%
Foreign	34%	—	64%		31%	—	68%
Composite	24%	—	76%		22%	—	78%

Key Votes of the 110th Congress

1. Raise CAFE standards	Y	5. Make English official language	Y	9. Withdraw troops 3/08	N
2. Expand SCHIP	Y	6. Path to citizenship	N	10. Iran guard is terrorist group	Y
3. Cap greenhouse gases	N	7. Fetus is unborn child	Y	11. Increase missile defense $	N
4. Bail out financial markets	Y	8. Prosecute hate crimes	N	12. Overhaul FISA	Y

Election Results

2006 general	Bob Corker (R)	929,911	(51%)	($18,565,935)
	Harold Ford (D)	879,976	(48%)	($15,302,455)
2006 primary	Bob Corker (R)	231,541	(48%)	
	Ed Bryant (R)	161,189	(34%)	
	Van Hilleary (R)	83,078	(17%)	

Bob Corker, the only freshman Republican elected to the Senate in 2006, is the junior senator from Tennessee. He was born in South Carolina, grew up in Chattanooga and graduated from the University of Tennessee in 1974 with a degree in industrial management. Just a few years out of college, he started his own successful construction company, which he sold before he turned 40. Before that, Corker took a church mission trip to Haiti, which inspired him to help create Chattanooga Neighborhood Enterprise, a non-profit organization designed to get low-income families into affordable housing. In 1994, he ran for the Senate, finishing second in the Republican primary to Bill Frist, who went on to defeat Democratic incumbent Jim Sasser and rise to Senate majority leader. Fresh off that race, Republican Gov. Don Sundquist named him state finance commissioner, which gave Corker responsibility for state government spending. After 18 months, he returned to private business by purchasing two real estate and development companies in Chattanooga. In 2001, he won election as Chattanooga mayor, and in that job, got credit for a decline in crime and for the success of the city's revitalized waterfront.

Corker was not yet through his first term as mayor in October 2004 when he announced his bid for Senate in 2006 to succeed Frist, who stuck to his initial campaign promise to serve just two terms. By the end of the year, Corker had raised $2 million. Other Republicans joined the field, including two conservative former congressmen: Ed Bryant, who lost to Lamar Alexander in the 2002 Senate primary, and Van Hilleary, who lost to Democrat Phil Bredesen in the 2002 governor's race. The more moderate Corker drew on his personal wealth and spent $5 million alone in an effort to introduce himself to voters and defend against charges that he was insufficiently conservative. Bryant and Hilleary claimed he raised property taxes in Chattanooga and criticized his position on abortion, noting that he supported abortion rights during his 1994 Senate campaign. Corker responded by calling his opponents "ineffective career politicians" and talked about his background as a successful businessman and mayor. He said he was "wrong" on abortion in 1994 and now held a "pro-life" position, though, unlike Bryant and Hilleary, he would make exceptions in cases of rape and incest. Corker ended up winning by a comfortable margin as Bryant and Hilleary split the conservative vote. Corker carried nearly every county east of Nashville and a half-dozen west of it, winning 48% to Bryant's 34%; Hilleary finished third with 17%.

The Democratic nominee was U.S. Rep. Harold Ford of Memphis, who in the absence of serious primary opposition was able to conserve his resources for the general election. Youthful, ambitious and telegenic, Ford was an immensely attractive candidate. The son of former Democratic Rep. Harold Ford Sr., he was first elected to the House in 1996, just months after graduating from law school, and his record was sufficiently moderate to make him a competitive statewide candidate. The national media took great interest in the race. Ford was seeking to become the first African-American senator popularly elected in the South and from a state that had never before elected a black candidate to statewide office. For much of the general election campaign, it appeared Corker might defy Tennessee's recent Republican trend in national elections and lose a seat that was critical to the party's hopes of retaining its Senate majority.

Corker struggled to unify the party after the contentious primary and failed to gain traction in the two months following the August primary. Meanwhile, Ford ran a nearly flawless campaign. Corker's efforts to frame Ford as too liberal for Tennessee fell flat in the face of Ford's centrist positions on illegal immigration, the Iraq war, border security and gay marriage. Ford also put Corker on the defensive about his business dealings and his tenure as Chattanooga mayor.

The national media tended to view the race through a racial prism, but Ford faced two more daunting obstacles. The first was the state's political landscape. The last Democrat that Tennessee elected to the Senate was Al Gore in 1990, and Republican George W. Bush embarrassed Gore by defeating him 51%-47% on his home turf in 2000. Bush then widened his Tennessee margin in 2004 with a 57%-43 re-election victory. Then there was the Ford family. The scion of a Memphis political dynasty, Ford had to weather distractions caused by several family members, including his uncle, former state Sen. John Ford, who was indicted on federal corruption charges the day after Harold Ford filed to run for the Senate; John Ford later resigned from office. John Ford's sister—Harold's aunt—won the special election to replace him but she was ousted by the state Senate in April amid allegations of vote fraud. Meanwhile, in the racially-charged House race to succeed Harold Ford, his brother Jake unexpectedly ran as an independent candidate against white Jewish Democratic nominee Steve Cohen.

Heading into the final weeks of the campaign, the election appeared to be a dead heat. But Corker gained momentum after Republicans began zeroing in on Ford's personal story, characterizing it as a life of privilege. Ford went to preparatory school in Washington, graduated from an Ivy League university and attended law school in Michigan before taking over his father's seat in Congress. Corker's ads described his rise from a laborer who poured concrete. In late October, the Republican National Committee weighed in with a controversial ad featuring purported on-the-street interviews with regular people, all of whom had unpleasant things to say about Ford. But one individual, an attractive young, blonde and white woman, drew all the attention, claiming that she had "met Harold at the Playboy party," a reference to news stories that Ford had attended a Super Bowl party hosted by Playboy magazine. The commercial ended with the woman saying, "Harold, call me." Critics called the ad racial politicking. Republicans insisted it was about values. Corker's campaign asked television stations not to air the spot. Earlier, after Ford had run an ad filmed in a Memphis church, the National Republican Senatorial Committee responded with a commercial asking, "What kind of man parties with Playboy playmates in lingerie, then films political ads from a church pew?"

More votes were cast in this election, 1.8 million, than in two other high-profile state contests—the governor's race and an amendment to ban same-sex marriage, which passed 81%-19%. Corker won 51%-48%. Whites voted 59%-40% for Corker and African-Americans voted 95%-4% for Ford. Ford won 61%-38% in the Memphis area while Corker carried the Nashville area 50%-49%. Corker far outpaced Ford in East Tennessee, winning 58%-40%. Ford carried Middle and West Tennessee 52%-46%.

In the Senate, Corker tried to further separate himself from the NRSC ads. He introduced a bill to allow candidates to approve commercials and direct mail pieces from political parties before they are released to the public. While he was a reliable vote for Republicans on issues such as opposing embryonic-stem-cell and troop withdrawal timetables in Iraq, Corker broke with the party on some high-profile issues. He backed an energy bill to raise gas mileage standards for cars and trucks, which Republicans tried to kill. He also joined the bipartisan "Gang of 10" to promote a 2008 energy bill allowing offshore drilling while also emphasizing renewable energy sources. When he was criticized by Republicans who wanted to highlight the energy issue in the fall elections, Corker told the *Chattanooga Times Free Press,* "It's really, candidly, grotesque to watch that. Energy is a major issue, and I know there are many in my party that don't want to solve it."

In 2007, he voted for a Democratic bill to expand the State Children's Health Insurance Program, and also played a crucial role in negotiations to renew federal funding for the state's TennCare program for the poor and disabled. When the administration stalled on renewing the state's funding, he blocked confirmation of President George W. Bush's non-military nominees until the state got its money. Tennessee Democratic Gov. Bredesen praised Corker, telling reporters "We would not have nearly as good a deal today without Bob Corker laying down on the track the way that he did."

In January 2008, Corker, a former commissioner of finance for Tennessee, got a seat on the Banking Committee. That year, he was a key negotiator on the $700 billion government rescue of the financial services market. When the big three domestic auto makers sought a multi-billion-dollar bailout, Corker criticized auto executives who appeared before the committee, chiding their plans for securing government loans and waiting for mergers, and telling the head of Chrysler: "While this is happening, you're going to be going to spas and getting facials and hopefully finding someone to marry you." Corker offered then an alternative proposal that required retiring autoworkers to accept most of their benefits in stock rather than in cash, forced bondholders to accept a steep cut in the value of their bonds and required wages to be comparable to U.S. employees of foreign automakers, which generally pay their workers less than domestic manufacturers. His proposals angered autoworkers and unions, including many in Tennessee at GM's Spring Hill plant. Corker's work on the issue positioned him as a player on economic issues and as a bipartisan negotiator.

FIRST DISTRICT

Phil Roe (R)

Elected 2008, 1st term; b. July 21, 1945, Clarksville; home, Johnson City; Austin Peay St. U., B.S. 1967; U. of TN, M.D. 1970; Methodist; married (Pam); 3 children.

Military Career: Army, 1973–74.

Elected Office: Johnson City Commission, 2003–09, Vice mayor, 2005–07, Mayor, 2007–09.

Professional Career: Obstetrician/gynecologist, 1970–2008.

DC Office: 419 CHOB, 20515, 202-225-6356; Fax: 202-225-5714; Web site: roe.house.gov.

State Offices: Blountville, 423-354-0144; Morristown, 423-254-1400.

Committees: *Agriculture* (14th of 18 R): Livestock, Dairy & Poultry; Specialty Crops, Rural Development & Foreign Agriculture. *Education & Labor* (18th of 19 R): Health, Employment, Labor & Pensions; Healthy Families & Communities; Higher Education, Lifelong Learning & Competitiveness. *Veterans' Affairs* (11th of 11 R): Oversight & Investigations (RMM).

Group Ratings and Key Votes: Newly Elected

Election Results

2008 general	Phil Roe (R)	168,343	(72%)	($717,171)
	Rob Russell (D)	57,525	(25%)	($10,354)
2008 primary	Phil Roe (R)	25,993	(50%)	
	David Davis (R)	25,511	(49%)	

Population		Race/Ethnicity		Work	
Pop. 2007:	659,480	White:	93.7%	Private:	79.4%
Change since 2000:	Up 4.3%	Black:	2.2%	Government:	12.4%
Urban:	55.4%	Hispanic:	2.2%	Self-employed:	8.0%
Rural:	44.6%	Asian:	0.5%	Blue collar:	29.9%
Area size:	4,174 sq. mi.	Native Am.:	0.2%	White collar:	52.5%
Age		Hawaiian:	0.0%	Khaki collar:	0.1%
Median age:	40.0 yrs.	Two+ races:	1.1%	Other:	17.5%
More than 65 yrs:	15.5%	*Ancestry*		Median income:	$35,969
Less than 18 yrs:	21.4%	USA:	21.9%	Median home value:	$101,700
Education		German:	10.9%	Poverty:	17.6%
H.S. grad:	76.9%	Irish:	10.5%	**Military Veterans**	
College grad:	16.4%			% of Pop:	12.3%
Grad degree:	5.8%				

Between the corduroy-like ridges of the Appalachian chains, as they bend west and then south, the valley of Virginia extends far into northeastern Tennessee. The communities of this region are a hilly patchwork of industrial centers, small farms and federal land. The land rush immediately after the Revolutionary War populated the area. In tiny Jonesborough, the early settlers established the free state of Franklin in 1784, and many pioneer cabins, federal mansions and Greek Revival

2008 Presidential Vote		
McCain (R)	181,898	(70%)
Obama (D)	75,528	(29%)
2004 Presidential Vote		
Bush (R)	172,079	(68%)
Kerry (D)	79,507	(31%)
Cook Partisan Voting Index:	R + 21	

churches are lovingly preserved. It was the building of the railroads in the 1850s, however, that determined the winners and losers. Other Appalachian areas were cut off from the rest of America, with tracks running only to the coal mines. The small industrial cities that developed—Johnson City, Kingsport and Bristol, now collectively known as the Tri-Cities—were on the main lines of national commerce before the Civil War. As president, Abraham Lincoln talked about building a 150-mile railroad through these hills, partly as a political gesture to Union supporters. The Civil War had a different political effect here than in most of the South: Northeast Tennessee, the home of wartime Gov. and then Vice President Andrew Johnson, had few slaves, and with its connection to northern industry, was Union territory. It remains heavily Republican to this day.

The political continuity may be surprising because this area had decades of continuous economic growth and developed the sort of industrial economy that produced unions and Democrats in the North.

Its growth was helped by a skilled labor force, low electric power rates because of the Tennessee Valley Authority and good transportation routes (rail lines and now Interstate 81). Its small cities used to boast major paper and printing plants, but most of those industries are gone. One of the largest employers is Eastman Kodak in Kingsport. At one time, the company's plant in Sullivan County plant employed more than 6,000, but in April 2009, the recession took a toll and the facility announced it was laying off 200 people. There has been some economic growth in Sevier County near Knoxville, where Gatlinburg and Pigeon Forge (home of Dolly Parton's Dollywood theme park) have more than 10,000 hotel rooms at the entry point to the Great Smoky Mountains National Park, the nation's most-visited national park. The area surrounding the park suffers from heavy acid rain and ozone pollution from nearby power plants and factories. Jonesborough, Tennessee's oldest town, is home to the International Storytelling Center where every October more than 8,000 people gather to hear two dozen storytellers spin yarns at the National Storytelling Festival.

The 1st Congressional District takes in the far northeastern end of Tennessee, a district so heavily Republican that it has not elected a Democrat to the House for more than 100 years. Nonetheless, it has had turbulent politics on occasion. For almost 40 years, the seat was held by B. Carroll Reece (1921–61, with one four-year and one two-year hiatus), a fierce mountain politician who was Republican national chairman from 1946 to 1948. After Reece died in 1961, and his widow was elected to fill out his term, there was a hotly contested primary. The winner, Republican Jimmy Quillen, a bread-and-butter politician, homebuilder and former owner of the *Johnson City Times*, represented the district for the next 34 years, a record tenure for the Tennessee congressional delegation. True to its roots, the district gave GOP nominee John McCain his highest percentage in Tennessee, 70%, in 2008.

The new congressman from the 1st District is Phil Roe, a Republican elected in 2008. Roe grew up in Clarksville and attended a one-room schoolhouse with no running water. He went on to receive degrees from Austin Peay State University and a medical degree from the University of Tennessee. He served in the Army Medical Corps and then relocated to Johnson City, setting up practice as an obstetrician/gynecologist and delivering babies for 30 years. In 2003, the political bug bit Roe, and he ran successfully for the Johnson City Commission. Roe was chosen by commission members to be vice mayor in 2005 and mayor 2007. When five-term U.S. Rep. Bill Jenkins retired in 2006, Roe competed in a crowded GOP primary but finished fourth with 17% of the vote, behind health care business owner David Davis, who went on to win the seat in the general election.

In his first term in the House, Davis quickly gained a reputation as a combative partisan and was criticized in the local press for securing earmarks for companies with political action committees that contributed to his campaign. Roe decided to challenge Davis when he sought re-election in 2008, and embarked on a grass-roots campaign, personally visiting each county multiple times, talking to voters, stumping in restaurants and waving signs at busy intersections. In ads featuring an elderly grandmother trying to fill up her car with gas, Roe criticized Davis for accepting money from oil companies, attacks that resonated as gas prices spiked. Davis led in fundraising, pulling in $400,000 more than Roe and outspending his challenger 3-to-1. But two years after finishing fourth behind Davis in a crowded Republican field, Roe rebounded to narrowly upset the one-term Davis, becoming the first challenger in more than 40 years to defeat an incumbent representative in Tennessee.

Roe's challenge to Davis was barely on the national radar, and his win surprised Davis as well, leading to one of the more unusual escapades of the congressional election season. As vote tallies trickled in from precincts across the rural eastern Tennessee district, Davis refused to emerge from his hotel room to greet supporters. With the unofficial vote tally the next morning at roughly 500 votes in Roe's favor, Davis refused to concede, despite winning the 2006 primary by only 573 votes himself. Instead, Davis tried to raise doubt on the validity of the outcome, issuing a statement saying Democrats had conspired to throw the election by voting in the Republican primary. The charge gained little traction considering Tennessee has an open primary system that does not require registration by party. Davis conceded a week later. Roe's margin of victory was 482 votes. He won the district's two largest counties, Washington and Sullivan, while Davis was strong along the western edge of the district, winning Sevier and Hawkins counties. In November, Roe easily beat Democrat Robert Russell with 72% of the vote.

Roe's positions are similar to Davis', mirroring the conservative bent of the district. He's anti-abortion rights and pro-gun ownership. He opposes any form of amnesty for illegal immigrants. As a doctor, Roe says he is committed to reforming the medical insurance system, but opposes government-run health care. And he says his experience as a physician and as a mayor taught him the need for bipartisanship. "What we get separated on are the little issues that get all the noise," he said.

Roe was appointed to the Agriculture, Education and Labor and Veterans' Affairs committees. Davis said in March 2009 that he hadn't ruled out trying to get the seat back in 2010, and was continuing to push for a bill in the Tennessee Legislature to require voters to register by party for primaries.

SECOND DISTRICT

John Duncan (R)

Elected 1988, 11th full term; b. July 21, 1947, Lebanon; home, Knoxville; U. of TN, B.S. 1969, George Washington U., J.D. 1973; Presbyterian; married (Lynn); 4 children.

Military Career: Army Natl. Guard & Army Reserves, 1970–87.

Professional Career: Practicing atty., 1973–81; Knox Cnty. judge, 1981–88.

DC Office: 2207 RHOB, 20515, 202-225-5435; Fax: 202-225-6440; Web site: www.house.gov/duncan.

State Offices: Athens, 423-745-4671; Knoxville, 865-523-3772; Maryville, 865-984-5464.

Committees: *Natural Resources* (4th of 20 R): National Parks, Forests & Public Lands. *Oversight & Government Reform* (6th of 15 R): Government Management, Organization & Procurement; National Security & Foreign Affairs. *Transportation & Infrastructure* (5th of 30 R): Aviation; Highways & Transit (RMM); Water Resources & Environment.

Group Ratings

	ADA	ACLU	AFS	LCV	ITIC	NTU	COC	ACU	CFG	FRC
2008	15	18	0	8	14	87	72	84	87	100
2007	20	—	18	10	—	86	70	84	81	—

National Journal Ratings

	2007 LIB — 2007 CONS		2008 LIB — 2008 CONS	
Economic	14% —	86%	29% —	71%
Social	31% —	67%	16% —	82%
Foreign	46% —	54%	45% —	54%
Composite	31% —	69%	31% —	70%

Key Votes of the 110th Congress

1. Increase minimum wage	Y	5. Share immigration data	Y	9. Withdraw troops 8/08	N
2. Expand SCHIP	N	6. Foreign aid abortion ban	Y	10. No operations in Iran	Y
3. Raise CAFE standards	N	7. Ban gay bias in workplace	N	11. Free trade with Peru	N
4. Bail out financial markets	N	8. Repeal D.C. gun law	Y	12. Overhaul FISA	Y

Election Results

2008 general	John Duncan (R)	227,120	(78%)	($511,959)
	Bob Scott (D)	63,639	(22%)	
2008 primary	John Duncan (R)	unopposed		

Prior Winning Percentages: 2006 (78%); 2004 (79%); 2002 (79%); 2000 (89%); 1998 (89%); 1996 (71%); 1994 (90%); 1992 (72%); 1990 (81%); 1988 (57%); 1988 special elec. (56%)

Population		Race/Ethnicity		Work	
Pop. 2007:	695,313	White:	88.8%	Private:	79.2%
Change since 2000:	Up 10.0%	Black:	6.4%	Government:	13.5%
Urban:	71.4%	Hispanic:	2.1%	Self-employed:	7.1%
Rural:	28.6%	Asian:	1.2%	Blue collar:	23.2%
Area size:	2,492 sq. mi.	Native Am.:	0.2%	White collar:	60.7%
Age		Hawaiian:	0.0%	Khaki collar:	0.1%
Median age:	38.3 yrs.	Two+ races:	1.3%	Other:	16.0%
More than 65 yrs:	13.7%	*Ancestry*		Median income:	$44,232
Less than 18 yrs:	22.3%	USA:	16.0%	Median home value:	$135,000
Education		German:	11.7%	Poverty:	14.1%
H.S. grad:	83.5%	English:	10.9%	**Military Veterans**	
College grad:	25.9%			% of Pop:	11.5%
Grad degree:	9.4%				

Knoxville, the largest city in East Tennessee, is nestled between mountain ridges where the Holston and French Broad rivers join to form the Tennessee River. It was established not long after the first wave of pioneers came through the gaps and down the mountains of the Appalachian chain. During the Civil War, it was Union territory, and it has remained Republican in allegiance and progressive on civil rights ever since. But its Republican heritage is tempered by another tradition, that of the

2008 Presidential Vote		
McCain (R)	195,423	(64%)
Obama (D)	104,004	(34%)
2004 Presidential Vote		
Bush (R)	185,450	(64%)
Kerry (D)	100,032	(35%)
Cook Partisan Voting Index:	R + 16	

Tennessee Valley Authority. A venturesome program when created in the 1930s, it is now part of the fabric of life in East Tennessee, sometimes criticized as it has reached capacity to produce cheap hydroelectric power and began to rely more on expensive and sometimes poorly functioning nuclear power plants. The area's largest cash crop remains tobacco.

Both TVA and the region have undergone turbulent changes in recent years. In a competitive electricity market, and laboring under billions of dollars in debt mostly incurred in building its nuclear plants, TVA has cut its payroll sharply and held down rates. Heavy ozone pollution in Knoxville led the Environmental Protection Agency to impose growth limits. TVA spent several billion dollars to reduce pollution at its coal-fired power plants and the result has been marked improvement in recent years in local air quality due, in part, to TVA emission controls. Delay in construction of a national nuclear-waste repository at Yucca Mountain in Nevada has forced TVA to spend tens of millions of dollars for new storage pools.

Yet Knoxville has overcome setbacks and grown robustly without much notice in the national press. In 2006, it ranked ninth on *Expansion Management* magazine's list of the best cities for business expansion and relocation, with growth in construction and services. It was the headquarters of Goody's Family Clothing, the chain of primarily Southern and Midwestern stores that went bankrupt in 2009. And the University of Tennessee's football complex, Neyland Stadium, on fall Saturdays contains one of the nation's largest crowds—it qualifies as the state's 5th largest city during games—cheering on the Vols. The 1982 World's Fair site is the home of the Women's Basketball Hall of Fame. Women's basketball is nearly as popular as football here, and in 2009, Lady Vols' coach Pat Summitt became the only Division I coach, men's or women's, to win 1,000 career games. The city is also the home base of Instapundit.com, the popular blog of University of Tennessee law professor Glenn Reynolds.

The 2d Congressional District of Tennessee includes Knoxville and Knox County, plus four mountainous counties and part of another to the south. Most of its people live within the Knoxville metro area. Its less populated areas span the foothills of the Great Smoky Mountains. The district is heavily Republican; it has not elected a Democratic congressman since the Civil War. Knox County surprised many by giving a narrow plurality to Democratic Gov. Phil Bredesen in 2002, but Republican Van Hilleary carried the rest of the district by a wider margin. In 2006, Bredesen swept the county 71%-27%, as well as the district. In the 2008 presidential election, the area swung back to its Republican roots. GOP nominee John McCain won Knox County comfortably and the rest of the district with 64%.

The congressman from the 2d District is John (Jimmy) Duncan, a Republican first elected in 1988. His father, who was the senior Republican on the House Ways and Means Committee, represented the 2nd District from 1964 until his death in May 1988. Jimmy Duncan got a bachelor's degree in journalism at the University of Tennessee and a law degree from George Washington University. He practiced law and was a trial judge in the 1980s. When his father died, he won the seat despite a spirited challenge from Democrat Dudley Taylor, a scion of another prominent East Tennessee political family. Taylor attacked Duncan for his ties to scandal-tarred banker and Democratic politician Jake Butcher. But Duncan won with 57% in November. He has not been seriously challenged since then.

Duncan has been a frequent maverick on economic and foreign policy issues. He opposed normal trade relations with China and the Bush administration's No Child Left Behind education law that imposed mandatory testing on schools. In October 2002, he was one of six Republicans—and the only Tennessean—who voted against the use of force in Iraq. He argued that there was not sufficient proof that Iraqi Leader Saddam Hussein had weapons of mass destruction. A year later, he opposed the $87 billion spending bill for the war. "There is just no enthusiasm for this war," he said in August 2005. "It certainly is not going to help Republican candidates." In February 2007, he was one of 17 who voted to express disapproval of President Bush's troop "surge" strategy, and in May of that year, he was one of two House Republicans to vote against funding for Iraq military operations.

But his independence had its price. He was a candidate for the chairmanship of the Resources Committee in 2003, but Republican Speaker Dennis Hastert passed over him and five other senior Republicans to give the post to the more loyal Richard Pombo of California. Perhaps mindful of that setback, Duncan voted for Hastert's Medicare prescription drug bill in 2003. Then in 2006, he made a big push for the top Republican position on the Transportation and Infrastructure Committee. But he lost to John Mica of Florida, who was more junior but, once again, more of a party regular. In 2009, Duncan was named the ranking Republican on the committee's Subcommittee on Highways and Transit. In response to skyrocketing gas prices in summer 2008, Duncan became a supporter of drilling in the Arctic National Wildlife Refuge and of offshore drilling.

Duncan hasn't been shy about seeking funding for local projects, from resurfacing the Foothills Parkway in the Great Smoky Mountains National Park to a rail and trolley system for downtown Knoxville. Another of his legislative interests has been a bill to require the disclosure of contributions to presidential libraries, which the House passed in early 2009 by 388-31.

In Knoxville, Duncan's annual barbecue dinner draws as many as 5,000 people and reinforces his local popularity. Although he shows no signs of retiring, when Duncan does decide to leave Congress, his son, John Duncan III, is said to be interested in the seat.

THIRD DISTRICT

Zach Wamp (R)

Elected 1994, 8th term; b. Oct. 28, 1957, Fort Benning, GA; home, Chattanooga; U. of NC, 1976–77, 1979–80, U. of TN, 1978–79; Baptist; married (Kim); 2 children.

Professional Career: Regional sales super., 1981–82, Partner, Wamp Alliance Architectural Devel. Co., 1983–89; Real estate broker, 1989–94.

DC Office: 1436 LHOB, 20515, 202-225-3271; Fax: 202-225-3494; Web site: www.house.gov/wamp.

State Offices: Chattanooga, 423-756-2342; Oak Ridge, 865-576-1976.

Committees: *Appropriations* (8th of 23 R): Energy & Water Development; Military Construction, Veterans Affairs & Related Agencies (RMM).

Group Ratings

	ADA	ACLU	AFS	LCV	ITIC	NTU	COC	ACU	CFG	FRC
2008	15	27	0	15	71	72	100	96	79	100
2007	20	—	18	10	—	75	75	92	73	—

National Journal Ratings

	2007 LIB — 2007 CONS		2008 LIB — 2008 CONS	
Economic	24%	— 75%	26%	— 74%
Social	21%	— 75%	20%	— 74%
Foreign	0%	— 72%	22%	— 74%
Composite	21%	— 80%	24%	— 76%

Key Votes of the 110th Congress

1. Increase minimum wage	Y	5. Share immigration data	Y	9. Withdraw troops 8/08	N
2. Expand SCHIP	N	6. Foreign aid abortion ban	Y	10. No operations in Iran	N
3. Raise CAFE standards	N	7. Ban gay bias in workplace	N	11. Free trade with Peru	Y
4. Bail out financial markets	Y	8. Repeal D.C. gun law	Y	12. Overhaul FISA	Y

Election Results

2008 general	Zach Wamp (R)	184,964	(69%)	($1,440,107)
	Doug Vandagriff (D)	73,059	(27%)	
2008 primary	Zach Wamp (R)	31,782	(91%)	
	Teresa Sheppard (R)	3,125	(9%)	

Prior Winning Percentages: 2006 (66%); 2004 (65%); 2002 (65%); 2000 (64%); 1998 (66%); 1996 (56%); 1994 (52%)

Population		Race/Ethnicity		Work	
Pop. 2007:	668,749	White:	84.0%	Private:	78.6%
Change since 2000:	Up 5.8%	Black:	11.2%	Government:	13.5%
Urban:	64.2%	Hispanic:	2.3%	Self-employed:	7.5%
Rural:	35.8%	Asian:	1.1%	Blue collar:	28.5%
Area size:	3,597 sq. mi.	Native Am.:	0.3%	White collar:	56.0%
		Hawaiian:	0.0%	Khaki collar:	0.1%
Age		Two+ races:	0.9%	Other:	15.3%
Median age:	38.9 yrs.			Median income:	$40,538
More than 65 yrs:	14.3%	*Ancestry*		Median home value:	$120,700
Less than 18 yrs:	22.6%	USA:	19.5%	Poverty:	14.7%
		Irish:	10.0%		
Education		English:	9.6%	**Military Veterans**	
H.S. grad:	79.7%			% of Pop:	11.3%
College grad:	20.5%				
Grad degree:	7.4%				

Etching its way through the serrated ridges of East Tennessee, with some of the most vivid scenery in the Appalachian Mountain chain, is the river that gave Tennessee its name. From Knoxville, the river cuts through a ridge and then plunges down a long valley to the city of Chattanooga at the Georgia line. There it switches course again, winding around the tabletop Lookout Mountain and then moving into northern Alabama. At the base of the mountain, Chattanooga was just a village when it

2008 Presidential Vote		
McCain (R).............................174,696	(62%)
Obama (D) 103,767	(37%)
2004 Presidential Vote		
Bush (R)...................................163,612	(61%)
Kerry (D)................................102,390	(38%)
Cook Partisan Voting Index: R + 13		

was a Civil War battlefield. It then became the industrial "Dynamo of Dixie." Four decades ago, it was labeled America's most polluted city. But regional political leaders, prodded by influential and civic-minded remnants of its Industrial Age aristocracy, used creative measures, such as a locally built electric shuttle bus, to reduce pollution and to spruce up the city's scenic river banks. Reduction in ozone levels moved ahead of schedule. With big job cuts at the Tennessee Valley Authority, the region has pinned its hopes for growth more on the private sector, including a large food-service industry. The district is home to both the MoonPie and Little Debbie confectioners. Downtown Chattanooga is the home of the 12-story, well-visited Tennessee Aquarium. At Lookout Mountain, the popular century-old Incline Railway climbs at a 72.7% grade. Nearby are the 145-foot waterfall of Ruby Falls, as well as the rock formations and native gardens of Rock City. Grainger County, north of the Interstate 75 and Interstate 40 split, was the home of President Andrew Johnson and the South's first paper mill.

The 3rd Congressional District of Tennessee includes Chattanooga and runs northeasterly from the Tennessee-Georgia border to the Virginia border, making this one of three Tennessee districts that span the state from north to south. Most of the population is in Chattanooga and the counties around it. Chattanooga is the state's fourth largest city, but in recent years it has been challenging Knoxville for third place. The city is the fastest growing major city in Tennessee, adding more than 14,000 residents between 2000 and 2008. Volkswagen is building a $1 billion plant there, expected to add more than 10,000 jobs to the region.

The district's thin strip of land to the north includes Dayton, the "buckle of the Bible Belt" where John Scopes was tried for teaching evolution in 1925 and was defended by Clarence Darrow and prosecuted by William Jennings Bryan, events immortalized in the play *Inherit the Wind*. Farther north is Oak Ridge, which was secretly constructed in virgin Appalachian forest during World War II to house the nuclear facility that made uranium isotopes for the Hiroshima bomb and is now the Oak Ridge National Laboratory. For years, it did not appear on maps. Politically, this area was split historically, with Chattanooga voting Democratic and the mountain counties Republican. Today, it is solidly Republican, with none of its counties voting less than 57% for George W. Bush in 2004. In 2008, GOP presidential nominee John McCain won the district with a comfortable 62%.

The congressman from the 3rd District is Zach Wamp, a Republican first elected in 1994. Wamp (*WOMP*) left college before graduating to become a salesman for a local film company and a real estate developer in Chattanooga. Years later, he spoke about his heavy cocaine use during this period, including weeks in drug rehabilitation. In 1992, he ran for Congress against 20-year Democratic incumbent Marilyn Lloyd. She won by just 49%-47%, the closest margin of her career, and retired in 1994. Wamp ran again as a strong conservative. One of his proposals was to pay members of Congress the same as a lieutenant colonel and billet them in officer housing. Democrat Randy Button attacked Wamp on the character issue, and Wamp, like many Republicans that year, ran an ad showing his opponent's face morphing into Democratic President Bill Clinton's. Wamp won 52%-46%.

In 2008, he became the ranking member on the Subcommittee on Military Construction, Veterans Affairs and Related Agencies of the Appropriations Committee. In 2007, he authored legislation to name the new Capitol Visitor Center's main hall "Emancipation Hall" to honor slaves that originally built the Capitol building.

Wamp has a moderate-to-conservative record that is more conservative on social issues. He called himself "a heat-seeking missile on behalf of Tennessee and my district." He has won additional benefits for employees with work-related illnesses at Oak Ridge National Laboratory. His support for TVA, including opposition to attempts to sell off its non-hydro power plants, annoyed many conservatives. He has pushed hydrogen fuel cell technology, and on energy legislation, such as curbing oil speculation when it drives up prices at the pump, he's been unafraid to side with Democrats on some issues. He vocally supported campaign finance reform efforts in recent years, a stance that irritated the Republican leadership and prompted the National Right to Life Committee to run radio ads against him, even though he is opposed to abortion rights. But he tacked toward social conservatives by sponsoring a bill to permit local governments to post the Ten Commandments in public buildings, and he sought to restrict Internet access to pornography for children.

Wamp says he is one-sixteenth Cherokee, and he has taken an interest in the tribe, helping to deliver $1.3 million for an interpretive visitors' center and memorial wall at Cherokee Removal Memorial Park in Meigs County. Wamp's bills to add routes on the Trail of Tears National Historic Trail were passed by

Congress in 2006 and 2009. A fitness buff, Wamp runs 20 to 30 miles a week, and in 2007, proposed a provision for additional physical education in schools to fight childhood obesity.

Wamp has crusaded for political reforms, including an independent commission to supervise redistricting to take the heavy partisanship out of the process. But he has also toned down his rhetoric from the early days of the Republican majority in the mid-1990s, when he and other GOP newcomers blasted Congress as a haven for entrenched, out-of-touch insiders. He said when he first ran for the House, he would limit himself to 12 years, but has since broken that pledge. "My attitude toward the Congress has changed," Wamp told *The New York Times Magazine*. "We must realize public service is a great way of life. I came in with the attitude there were a bunch of thieves here. That's not true."

In 1996, he faced a spirited challenge from the second-place finisher in the 1994 Democratic primary. With Lloyd's endorsement, Wamp won 56%-43%. Since then, he has won easily. He considered running for the Senate in 2006, but deferred to Republican Chattanooga Mayor Bob Corker after Corker got an early start and quickly raised $2 million. Wamp announced his candidacy for Tennessee governor in January 2009. The race to replace Wamp is expected to be crowded, with the winner of the Republican primary likely to be headed to Washington.

FOURTH DISTRICT

Lincoln Davis (D)

Elected 2002, 4th term; b. Sept. 13, 1943, Pall Mall; home, Pall Mall; TN Tech. U., B.S. 1966; Baptist; married (Lynda); 3 children.

Elected Office: Byrdstown Mayor, 1978–82; TN House of Reps, 1980–84; TN Senate, 1996–2002.

Professional Career: Owner, Diversified Construction Co.

DC Office: 410 CHOB, 20515, 202-225-6831; Fax: 202-226-5172; Web site: www.house.gov/lincolndavis.

State Offices: Columbia, 931-490-8699; Jamestown, 931-879-2361; McMinnville, 931-473-7251; Rockwood, 865-354-3323.

Committees: *Appropriations* (36th of 37 D): Agriculture, Rural Development, FDA & Related Agencies; Energy & Water Development. *Science & Technology* (17th of 26 D): Energy & Environment; Investigations & Oversight.

Group Ratings

	ADA	ACLU	AFS	LCV	ITIC	NTU	COC	ACU	CFG	FRC
2008	80	45	100	85	86	16	61	12	9	82
2007	75	—	82	75	—	9	68	38	12	—

National Journal Ratings

	2007 LIB	—	2007 CONS	2008 LIB	—	2008 CONS
Economic	53%	—	47%	53%	—	46%
Social	48%	—	51%	50%	—	49%
Foreign	47%	—	53%	50%	—	48%
Composite	50%	—	51%	52%	—	48%

Key Votes of the 110th Congress

1. Increase minimum wage	Y	5. Share immigration data	Y	9. Withdraw troops 8/08	N
2. Expand SCHIP	Y	6. Foreign aid abortion ban	Y	10. No operations in Iran	Y
3. Raise CAFE standards	Y	7. Ban gay bias in workplace	N	11. Free trade with Peru	Y
4. Bail out financial markets	N	8. Repeal D.C. gun law	Y	12. Overhaul FISA	Y

Election Results

2008 general	Lincoln Davis (D)	146,776	(59%)	($1,074,524)
	Monty Lankford (R)	94,447	(38%)	($528,945)
2008 primary	Lincoln Davis (D)	30,487	(90%)	
	Bert Mason (D)	3,233	(10%)	

Prior Winning Percentages: 2006 (66%); 2004 (55%); 2002 (52%)

Population		Race/Ethnicity		Work	
Pop. 2007:	664,128	White:	91.8%	Private:	75.1%
Change since 2000:	Up 5.1%	Black:	3.9%	Government:	14.2%
Urban:	32.1%	Hispanic:	2.0%	Self-employed:	10.3%
Rural:	67.9%	Asian:	0.3%	Blue collar:	34.7%
Area size:	10,155 sq. mi.	Native Am.:	0.3%	White collar:	48.7%
		Hawaiian:	0.0%	Khaki collar:	0.1%
Age		Two+ races:	1.5%	Other:	16.5%
Median age:	39.1 yrs.			Median income:	$36,395
More than 65 yrs:	15.4%	*Ancestry*		Median home value:	$99,100
Less than 18 yrs:	23.1%	USA:	22.6%	Poverty:	17.4%
		Irish:	10.3%		
Education		English:	10.2%	**Military Veterans**	
H.S. grad:	75.5%			% of Pop:	11.4%
College grad:	13.2%				
Grad degree:	4.6%				

The invisible line between Civil War Republican and Civil War Democratic territory runs along the Cumberland Plateau, the westernmost swelling of the Appalachians, west of the valley where the Tennessee River runs south from Knoxville to Chattanooga. This is cave country. Under its green hills, Tennessee has 8,500 caves, more than any other state, with 15 species of bats and more than 100 species of rare insects. This invisible line separates the Tennessee Valley, which had few slaves and whose

2008 Presidential Vote		
McCain (R)	173,022	(64%)
Obama (D)	93,483	(35%)

2004 Presidential Vote		
Bush (R)	154,457	(58%)
Kerry (D)	109,802	(41%)

Cook Partisan Voting Index: R + 13

economic ties were with the North, from the rolling farmlands of middle Tennessee, first settled by Andrew Jackson in the 1790s and resolutely Democratic from 1829 when Jackson became the first president to call himself a Democrat. Sewanee is the pleasant home of the University of the South, and Bledsoe County, the pumpkin capital of the world. Columbia is the home of former President James K. Polk.

General Motors launched its Saturn brand in Spring Hill in 1990, igniting growth in the region. But when the erstwhile auto giant went bankrupt in 2009, it shut down the factory and furloughed most of its 2,700 employees. Decherd in Franklin County has a large Nissan engine assembly plant. Lynchburg in dry Moore County produces Jack Daniel's sour-mash whiskey, the nation's No. 2 spirit in overseas sales that has been distilled in Lynchburg for generations. It is every bit the idealized small town that the distillery's folksy, black-and-white advertisements make it out to be. Campbell County, where the construction of the Tennessee Valley Authority's Norris Dam once forced massive resettlements and low living standards, has rebounded as a retirement and tourist haven. Cattle are the district's No. 1 commodity.

The 4th Congressional District of Tennessee crosses the state for some 200 miles. It reaches almost to Virginia in the northeast and almost to Mississippi in the southwest, bordering both Kentucky and Alabama. It ranks as the fourth most rural district in the nation. Republican nominee John McCain won every county here in 2008, picking up 64% district-wide.

The congressman from the 4th District is Lincoln Davis, a Democrat elected in 2002. Davis grew up in Fentress County on his family farm, which was purchased from World War I hero Sgt. Alvin York, a 1920s and 1930s celebrity who was played by Gary Cooper in the 1941 movie *Sergeant York*. Davis started his own construction company, which builds homes and businesses, and develops land. He also has been a soil scientist, and farms cattle and tobacco. He began his political career in 1978 as the mayor of Byrdstown near the Kentucky border and was elected to the state House in 1980. In 1984, when Al Gore left the U.S. House to run for the Senate, Davis ran unsuccessfully for his House seat. In 2002, when Republican Rep. Van Hilleary ran for governor, Davis was the early favorite to replace him. He won support in the Democratic primary from national and local party leaders, organized labor, anti-abortion groups, and the National Rifle Association. But he had a difficult time against Democratic newcomer Fran Marcum, a wealthy businesswoman with backing from the women's fundraising group EMILY's List. She also spent $1.6 million of her own money. Her ads depicted Davis as a political retread, and tied him to the Legislature's unpopular handling of budget problems. But Davis won, 57%-43%.

In the general election, Janice Bowling, a Tullahoma alderwoman and self-described "pistol-packing Mama," attempted to seize on Gore's endorsement of Davis in the primary by asking voters to vote against Gore one more time. She campaigned in a white chenille dress, red boots and an American flag scarf. She was significantly outspent by Davis, who vowed not to let any opponent "out-gun me, out-pray me, or out-family me." In the words of *The Tennessean* newspaper, Davis combined a "folksy, slap-on-the-back attitude with the oratorical punch of a revival preacher." He won 52%-46%.

In the House, Davis fits near the center of the Democratic Caucus. He is a member of the Blue Dog Coalition of fiscally conservative Democrats and keeps his distance from most national Democrats, especially on cultural issues. He worked with other Democrats to promote their interest in "faith-based" issues when President Bush popularized the notion of religious organizations getting government support in his first term. When Republicans forced a vote on a gay-marriage ban, he sarcastically suggested that they also include bans on divorce and adultery to highlight the partisan debate.

After the 2008 election, he secured a coveted seat on the powerful Appropriations Committee. Before that, he focused on his work on the Financial Services Committee, where in 2007 he sponsored a bill to protect low-income renters whose homes had been sold or redeveloped. On energy issues in recent years, he has favored offshore drilling but says he doesn't believe it will solve all of the nation's energy problems. On foreign policy, Davis initially supported President George W. Bush on the war in Iraq but later supported withdrawing troops from the region and transitioning to a support mission.

In 2004, Bowling ran again but again received little party support. Davis emphasized his independence, and with endorsements from the Chamber of Commerce, National Right to Life and the NRA, he increased his victory margin to 55%-44%. In 2008, Davis was challenged by medical equipment company owner Monty Lankford. Lankford raised $529,000, though Davis passed him with $1 million, and tried unsuccessfully to tie Davis to national Democrats and their presidential nominee, Barack Obama. Even as McCain carried every county in the district, Lincoln won 59%-38%.

FIFTH DISTRICT

Jim Cooper (D)

Elected 2002, 10th term; b. June 19, 1954, Nashville; home, Nashville; U. of NC, B.A. 1975, Oxford U., B.A./M.A. 1977, Harvard U., J.D. 1980; Episcopalian; married (Martha); 3 children.

Elected Office: U.S. House of Reps., 1982–94.

Professional Career: Practicing atty., 1980–82; Investment banker, 1995–99; Founder and partner, investment bank, 1999–2002.

DC Office: 1536 LHOB, 20515, 202-225-4311; Fax: 202-226-1035; Web site: www.cooper.house.gov.

State Offices: Nashville, 615-736-5295.

Committees: *Armed Services* (16th of 36 D): Air & Land Forces; Oversight & Investigations; Terrorism, Unconventional Threats & Capabilities. *Oversight & Government Reform* (10th of 24 D): Domestic Policy; Government Management, Organization & Procurement.

Group Ratings

	ADA	ACLU	AFS	LCV	ITIC	NTU	COC	ACU	CFG	FRC
2008	60	73	71	100	100	26	72	20	38	17
2007	85	—	91	80	—	21	75	16	28	—

National Journal Ratings

	2007 LIB	—	2007 CONS		2008 LIB	—	2008 CONS
Economic	49%	—	51%		50%	—	49%
Social	62%	—	37%		54%	—	42%
Foreign	52%	—	47%		52%	—	46%
Composite	55%	—	45%		53%	—	47%

Key Votes of the 110th Congress

1. Increase minimum wage	Y	5. Share immigration data	Y	9. Withdraw troops 8/08	Y
2. Expand SCHIP	Y	6. Foreign aid abortion ban	N	10. No operations in Iran	Y
3. Raise CAFE standards	Y	7. Ban gay bias in workplace	Y	11. Free trade with Peru	Y
4. Bail out financial markets	Y	8. Repeal D.C. gun law	Y	12. Overhaul FISA	Y

Election Results

2008 general	Jim Cooper (D)	181,467	(66%)	($429,556)
	Gerard Donovan (R)	85,471	(31%)	($14,240)
2008 primary	Jim Cooper (D)	unopposed		

Prior Winning Percentages: 2006 (69%); 2004 (69%); 2002 (64%); 1992 (66%); 1990 (69%); 1988 (100%); 1986 (100%); 1984 (75%); 1982 (66%)

Population		Race/Ethnicity		Work	
Pop. 2007:	683,973	White:	64.8%	Private:	80.5%
Change since 2000:	Up 8.2%	Black:	24.8%	Government:	11.9%
Urban:	88.7%	Hispanic:	6.5%	Self-employed:	7.4%
Rural:	11.3%	Asian:	2.6%	Blue collar:	20.7%
Area size:	932 sq. mi.	Native Am.:	0.3%	White collar:	62.8%
Age		Hawaiian:	0.0%	Khaki collar:	0.1%
Median age:	35.9 yrs.	Two+ races:	0.8%	Other:	16.4%
More than 65 yrs:	10.8%	*Ancestry*		Median income:	$45,038
Less than 18 yrs:	23.8%	USA:	12.5%	Median home value:	$152,500
Education		German:	8.5%	Poverty:	14.3%
H.S. grad:	84.2%	English:	8.5%	**Military Veterans**	
College grad:	29.4%			% of Pop:	9.5%
Grad degree:	10.2%				

Nashville is the home of country music and is in almost every way the heart of Tennessee. It was one of the first American cities established west of the Appalachian Mountains. President Andrew Jackson built his Hermitage nearby above the banks of the Cumberland River, and his political home base has remained Democratic ever since. It was the capital of Tennessee early on, just as it was, and still is, the center of the state's political life and discourse, the so-called "Athens of the South," home to

2008 Presidential Vote		
Obama (D)	166,867	(56%)
McCain (R)	127,394	(43%)
2004 Presidential Vote		
Kerry (D)	140,874	(52%)
Bush (R)	129,455	(48%)
Cook Partisan Voting Index: D+3		

The Tennessean, a classically partisan Democratic newspaper, and the state's biggest television market. Nashville is proud of its universities: Christian liberal arts college Belmont University was the site of an October 2008 presidential debate between Democrat Barack Obama and Republican John McCain. With its columned Capitol and its Parthenon, Nashville is perhaps the greatest center of Greek revival architecture in America. It also produces more bibles than any other city in the world.

Country music, an art form that emerged from the hardscrabble, mountainous counties of East Tennessee, is a more than $2 billion-a-year business and one of the nation's dominant radio formats and creates local jobs with music publishers and recording studios. Run from a series of deceptively modest homes-turned-offices on what's called Music Row, the industry congregated in Nashville because local radio station WSM had a clear channel in the 1920s from which to beam its weekly "barn dances" throughout the South. The broadcasts later became known as the Grand Ole Opry, the longest continuously running radio show (since 1925). An expanded Country Music Hall of Fame and Museum opened as part of a downtown revitalization in recent years, and the city now offers good music of all sorts, sushi bars and a lively cafe scene.

For years, both the city's elite and its religious leaders resented the growing local influence of country music. The former looked down on the music's uneducated practitioners, while the latter cringed at the musicians' unwholesome endeavors. But all three groups made their peace in the 1970s, and since then, Nashville has become one of the South's boom cities—the fastest growing metropolitan area between the still-larger Atlanta and the Dallas-Fort Worth metropolis. Nashville is also a center of the for-profit health industry. An agreeable quality of life, plenty of non-union, high-skill labor, a central location, and absence of urban strife have all helped make Nashville the largest metropolitan area in the state, with suburban growth in all directions. Since 2000, 39% of Tennessee's growth has been centered in metro Nashville and the surrounding counties. The dominant cultural tone remains conservative, and fast-growing surrounding counties have become increasingly Republican, but Nashville and Davidson County remain Democratic bulwarks.

The 5th Congressional District of Tennessee includes most of Nashville-Davidson County, plus the bulk of suburban Wilson County to the east and Cheatham County to the west. The 5th is reliably Democratic in statewide elections. It has elected rather liberal Democrats to Congress, and was the home of 2000 Democratic presidential nominee Al Gore. He was a divinity student at Vanderbilt University and a reporter for *The Tennessean.* He and wife, Tipper, have a house in the elegant Belle Meade neighborhood. The 5th was one of only two districts in Tennessee to vote for Obama in 2008, 56%-43%.

The congressman from the 5th District is Jim Cooper, a Democrat elected in 2002. His father, Prentice Cooper, was governor for six years. Jim Cooper, educated at the University of North Carolina, Oxford and Harvard Law School, won the 4th District seat in 1982 by beating the bearer of another famous name, Republican Cissy Baker, the daughter of then-Senate Majority Leader Howard Baker. When he first took office at age 28, he was the youngest member of the U.S. House. Notable for his frankness, he spoke out against tobacco use and opposed the National Rifle Association in a state where both were popular. He participated actively in the "Group of Nine" Democrats on the Energy and Commerce Committee that produced a compromise between Michigan Democrat John Dingell, an ally of the auto industry, and

California Democrat Henry Waxman of California, who was pro-environmental regulation, on the Clean Air Act of 1990. When, years later, Waxman successfully challenged Dingell for the chairmanship of the influential Energy and Commerce Committee in 2009, Cooper was a key ally of Waxman's. In 1994, Cooper ran against Republican Fred Thompson for the Senate seat Gore vacated when he was elected vice president and lost.

Cooper then went to work as an investment banker in Nashville and as a teacher at Vanderbilt University's business school. In 2002, when Democratic U.S. Rep. Bob Clement jumped into a Senate race, Cooper joined a flurry of Democratic candidates for his seat. His toughest opponent was Davidson County Sheriff Gayle Ray, the first female sheriff in Tennessee, who had support from the national fundraising group EMILY's List. Ray attacked Cooper's voting record on women's health issues. An abortion-rights supporter, Cooper said that Ray's charges were inaccurate and ran positive ads showing his children describing what he does well—banjo playing, helping with homework, getting health care for senior citizens—and what he doesn't do well—cooking, playing basketball. The AFL-CIO and *The Tennessean* endorsed Ray. Cooper had support from the Sierra Club environmental group and several smaller newspapers, and raised twice as much money as Ray, including $700,000 of his own money. He won the primary with 47%. Ray got 23% in the seven-candidate field. Cooper won the general easily and has not been seriously challenged since.

Once back in the House, Cooper joined the Armed Services, Budget, and Government Reform committees and joined the Blue Dogs, a group of fiscally conservative Democrats, in seeking limits on spending earmarks and enforcement of pay-as-you-go rules that require tax cuts or spending increases to be offset elsewhere in the budget. Cooper also urged expanded powers for the president to veto specific items in the budget. A longtime proponent of increased government oversight, his bill to strengthen the independence of federal inspectors passed Congress and, despite a veto threat from President George W. Bush, became law in October 2008.

Still relatively young, Cooper seems to have abandoned his interest in statewide office and is focused on being a leader of the Blue Dogs and a consensus-builder within the national Democratic party. He has proposed closing tax loopholes and spending cuts. He was mentioned as candidate to head the White House budget office, but he fell out of favor with the Obama administration after an incident during Congress' work on the $787 billion economic stimulus bill in 2009. Cooper was one of 11 Democrats to vote against the initial version of the bill and told a Nashville radio station he had gotten "quiet encouragement" from the White House to oppose it because Obama disagreed with changes in the legislation made by the House Democratic leadership. The White House denied urging Cooper to vote against the leadership-backed bill. Cooper also took at shot at House Speaker Nancy Pelosi, saying, "We're just told how to vote. We are treated like mushrooms most of the time."

Cooper urged Obama to convene a "fiscal responsibility summit" to focus on entitlements, which the president did in February 2009, but Cooper was not invited to attend. The liberal *The Nation* magazine suggested Cooper is reprising his role as the "dissident in chief among House Democrats" that he once played during the Clinton health care talks in 1993.

SIXTH DISTRICT

Bart Gordon (D)

Elected 1984, 13th term; b. Jan. 24, 1949, Murfreesboro; home, Murfreesboro; Middle TN St. U., B.S. 1971, U. of TN, J.D. 1973; United Methodist; married (Leslie); 1 child.

Military Career: Army Reserves, 1971–72.

Professional Career: Practicing atty., 1974–84; Chmn., TN Dem. Party, 1981–83.

DC Office: 2306 RHOB, 20515, 202-225-4231; Fax: 202-225-6887; Web site: bart.house.gov.

State Offices: Cookeville, 931-528-5907; Gallatin, 615-451-5174; Murfreesboro, 615-896-1986.

Committees: *Energy & Commerce* (6th of 36 D): Commerce, Trade & Consumer Protections; Communications, Technology & the Internet; Health. *Science & Technology* (Chmn of 26 D).

Group Ratings

	ADA	ACLU	AFS	LCV	ITIC	NTU	COC	ACU	CFG	FRC
2008	80	64	100	85	100	6	67	4	1	23
2007	85	—	91	80	—	7	70	20	12	—

National Journal Ratings

	2007 LIB	—	2007 CONS	2008 LIB	—	2008 CONS
Economic	55%	—	45%	75%	—	24%
Social	51%	—	48%	53%	—	46%
Foreign	57%	—	43%	54%	—	46%
Composite	55%	—	46%	61%	—	39%

Key Votes of the 110th Congress

1. Increase minimum wage	Y	5. Share immigration data	Y	9. Withdraw troops 8/08	Y
2. Expand SCHIP	Y	6. Foreign aid abortion ban	N	10. No operations in Iran	Y
3. Raise CAFE standards	Y	7. Ban gay bias in workplace	N	11. Free trade with Peru	Y
4. Bail out financial markets	Y	8. Repeal D.C. gun law	Y	12. Overhaul FISA	Y

Election Results

2008 general	Bart Gordon (D)	194,264	(74%)	($1,123,083)
	Chris Baker (I)	66,764	(26%)	
2008 primary	Bart Gordon (D)	unopposed		

Prior Winning Percentages: 2006 (67%); 2004 (64%); 2002 (66%); 2000 (62%); 1998 (55%); 1996 (54%); 1994 (51%); 1992 (57%); 1990 (67%); 1988 (76%); 1986 (77%); 1984 (63%)

Population		Race/Ethnicity		Work	
Pop. 2007:	728,407	White:	85.8%	Private:	78.3%
Change since 2000:	Up 15.2%	Black:	7.3%	Government:	12.7%
Urban:	53.2%	Hispanic:	4.4%	Self-employed:	8.8%
Rural:	46.8%	Asian:	1.3%	Blue collar:	31.8%
Area size:	5,576 sq. mi.	Native Am.:	0.2%	White collar:	53.6%
Age		Hawaiian:	0.1%	Khaki collar:	0.1%
Median age:	35.3 yrs.	Two+ races:	0.9%	Other:	14.5%
More than 65 yrs:	11.0%	*Ancestry*		Median income:	$44,998
Less than 18 yrs:	25.0%	USA:	22.3%	Median home value:	$134,000
Education		Irish:	9.7%	Poverty:	14.1%
H.S. grad:	80.4%	English:	9.6%	**Military Veterans**	
College grad:	19.0%			% of Pop:	10.1%
Grad degree:	5.5%				

The rolling countryside of Middle Tennessee, west of the Cumberland Plateau and the last of the Appalachian Mountain chain, has been called "the dimple of the universe." This is hilly and fertile land, cut by deep, curvy rivers. The terrain here was never much suited for plantation crops. It has long been a land of small farmers and small county-seat towns, nestled amid what people here regard as some of the loveliest scenery on earth. Middle Tennessee has also been one of the heartlands of the

2008 Presidential Vote

McCain (R)	189,726	(62%)
Obama (D)	112,584	(37%)

2004 Presidential Vote

Bush (R)	167,372	(60%)
Kerry (D)	111,203	(40%)

Cook Partisan Voting Index: R+13

Democratic Party. It was the political home base of President Andrew Jackson and supported him nearly unanimously during the Civil War, and though it had very few slaves, it resisted the invading Union armies. For 140 years after Jackson, it voted solidly Democratic and elected as its representatives in Congress some of the luminaries of the national Democratic Party: James K. Polk (1825–39), speaker of the House and later president; Cordell Hull (1907–21, 1923–31), later senator and secretary of state; Albert Gore Sr. (1939–53), later senator; and Albert Gore Jr., (1977–85), later senator and vice president.

The 6th Congressional District includes 14 Middle Tennessee counties surrounding Nashville, plus the eastern half of Wilson County. The heritage here is old and rural, but economic growth has fanned out into the farmland from Nashville, evident in thousands of jobs created by Japanese companies and American startups, firms fleeing the North and entrepreneurs fleeing taxes. Nearby is Smyrna and its Nissan plant, which has the largest automobile production capacity in the nation and is the home of the Altima, the seventh best-selling car in the United States in 2008. Nissan plans to build and sell its first all-electric car there in 2010. In Rutherford County, Murfreesboro, which is the district's largest city, has grown from a crumbling town in the 1980s to a thriving community and the home of Middle Tennessee State University, the second-largest in the state. In 2008, *Business Week* magazine named Murfreesboro the fifth most affordable city in the nation for families. In the 1990s, its population grew 51%, and since 2000, it has grown 26%, an average rate of 5,000 new residents a year.

This is one of two fast-growing Tennessee congressional districts; the other is the neighboring 7th District. The new voters here are Republican, but Democrats in control of redistricting in 2002 removed rapidly growing Republican suburbs in Wilson and Williamson counties from the district. They added Robertson County north of Nashville, which is significantly less Republican. But that was not enough to halt Republican advances. Without the district's former House representative, Al Gore, on the Democratic ticket, Bush carried the 6th by 60%-40% in 2004. Republican presidential nominee John McCain won it 62%-37%, carrying every county except Jackson.

The congressman from the 6th District is Bart Gordon, a Democrat first elected in 1984 when Gore gave up his House seat to run for the Senate. Gordon grew up in Murfreesboro, and graduated from Middle Tennessee State University and the University of Tennessee law school. He practiced law and became Tennessee Democratic Party chairman in 1981. He's been in politics most of his life. In 1984, he ran a computerized fundraising operation and voter contact system, then a novelty in a district where a personal handshake from a candidate was the norm. He won a multi-candidate primary with 28% of the vote (Democrat Lincoln Davis, now the 4th District's congressman, was second with 22%) and won the general election 63%-37%.

In the House, Gordon has built a moderate record and used his insider skills to pass legislation and to build a close relationship with Democratic leaders. In 2007, he became chairman of the House Science and Technology Committee, Tennessee's first full committee chairman in 30 years. As chairman, he wants to get more federal funding for science education, and in his first year, he successfully pushed through legislation to strengthen math and science curricula. He has pushed for more technology to be incorporated into the health care industry. Earlier, as a member of the committee, he convened an advisory panel that urged broad efforts to strengthen the nation's scientific competitiveness. In 2008, Gordon won passage of his bill to modernize the nation's 911 emergency system to include Internet phone services and vehicle-based phones.

In the past, he voted for some Bush-era tax policies. Gordon supported making permanent the repeal of the marriage penalty and the estate tax, and was one of nine Democrats to support President George W. Bush's tax cuts in 2005. He opposed the 2005 Central American Trade Agreement, and sought to repeal tax breaks for companies that send jobs overseas. Gordon supported the use of force in Iraq in 2002. On other issues, he won enactment of his proposal for Federal Trade Commission oversight of the practices of sports agents representing student athletes. Gordon is also a Civil War buff who is interested in proposals to preserve the nation's military history.

With the population surge in metro Nashville and the unpopularity of the Clinton administration in the mid-1990s, Gordon struggled through a couple of re-election campaigns. In 1994, he was challenged by Steve Gill, a lawyer from heavily Republican Williamson County. Gordon spent $1.4 million, more than twice what Gill spent, and won just a slim victory, 51%-49%. In a 1996 rematch, Gordon won 54%-42%. Then, as the Democrats' point man in the 2002 redistricting, he drew new district lines that made the seat safe for him. In the four elections since, he won with at least 64% of the vote.

A notable accomplishment in the increasingly fit House: Gordon has been the fastest government official in the annual three-mile race for members of Congress, the media and the executive branch 19 consecutive times. At age 59 in 2008, his time was 18 minutes and 40 seconds.

SEVENTH DISTRICT

Marsha Blackburn (R)

Elected 2002, 4th term; b. June 6, 1952, Laurel, MS; home, Brentwood; MS St. U., B.S. 1973; Presbyterian; married (Chuck); 2 children.

Elected Office: TN Senate, 1998–2002.

Professional Career: Retail marketing consultant, 1973–98.

DC Office: 217 CHOB, 20515, 202-225-2811; Fax: 202-225-3004; Web site: blackburn.house.gov.

State Offices: Clarksville, 931-503-0391; Franklin, 615-591-5161; Memphis, 901-382-5811.

Committees: *Energy & Commerce* (21st of 23 R): Communications, Technology & the Internet; Health; Oversight & Investigations.

Group Ratings

	ADA	ACLU	AFS	LCV	ITIC	NTU	COC	ACU	CFG	FRC
2008	10	20	0	0	43	80	83	96	100	100
2007	5	—	0	5	—	90	72	100	98	—

National Journal Ratings

	2007 LIB	—	2007 CONS	2008 LIB	—	2008 CONS
Economic	5%	—	94%	6%	—	94%
Social	0%	—	91%	9%	—	85%
Foreign	0%	—	72%	22%	—	74%
Composite	8%	—	92%	14%	—	86%

Key Votes of the 110th Congress

1. Increase minimum wage	N	5. Share immigration data	Y	9. Withdraw troops 8/08	N
2. Expand SCHIP	N	6. Foreign aid abortion ban	Y	10. No operations in Iran	N
3. Raise CAFE standards	N	7. Ban gay bias in workplace	N	11. Free trade with Peru	Y
4. Bail out financial markets	N	8. Repeal D.C. gun law	Y	12. Overhaul FISA	Y

Election Results

2008 general	Marsha Blackburn (R)	217,332	(69%)	($1,558,273)
	Randy Morris (D)	99,549	(31%)	($5,152)
2008 primary	Marsha Blackburn (R)	30,997	(62%)	
	Tom Leatherwood (R)	19,025	(38%)	

Prior Winning Percentages: 2006 (66%); 2004 (100%); 2002 (71%)

Population		Race/Ethnicity		Work	
Pop. 2007:	726,337	White:	80.3%	Private:	74.9%
Change since 2000:	Up 14.9%	Black:	13.1%	Government:	16.7%
Urban:	61.0%	Hispanic:	2.9%	Self-employed:	8.1%
Rural:	39.0%	Asian:	2.2%	Blue collar:	20.8%
Area size:	6,349 sq. mi.	Native Am.:	0.2%	White collar:	64.0%
Age		Hawaiian:	0.1%	Khaki collar:	1.6%
Median age:	37.0 yrs.	Two+ races:	1.2%	Other:	13.6%
More than 65 yrs:	10.5%	*Ancestry*		Median income:	$60,360
Less than 18 yrs:	26.2%	Irish:	11.0%	Median home value:	$169,000
Education		English:	10.8%	Poverty:	9.6%
H.S. grad:	87.8%	German:	10.3%	**Military Veterans**	
College grad:	32.5%			% of Pop:	12.7%
Grad degree:	11.2%				

Rural Tennessee north of Mississippi is one of the most sparsely settled areas in the state. Along each side of the Tennessee River, as it flows north and widens out into Kentucky Lake amid heavy forests, are small rural communities. Many date to pre-Civil War days and have not grown much since. One of these is Waynesboro, where Davy Crockett delivered campaign speeches from the base of a huge natural stone double bridge overlooking the Buffalo River. Farther west is McNairy County,

2008 Presidential Vote

McCain (R)	233,645	(66%)
Obama (D)	119,046	(33%)

2004 Presidential Vote

Bush (R)	206,410	(66%)
Kerry (D)	104,792	(33%)

Cook Partisan Voting Index: R+18

where Sheriff Buford Pusser of *Walking Tall* fame carried his big stick and fought organized crime until his untimely death in a car crash 1974. In Fayette County, outside of Memphis, black sharecroppers in 1959 were removed from white-owned land and protested by creating a "tent city" that went on for a decade, the longest civil rights protest in the nation. This mostly empty land is bounded on two sides by large metropolitan areas, Nashville to the east and Memphis to the west. South of Nashville is booming Williamson County, which had more slaves than whites prior to the Civil War, was occupied by the Union Army for three years and was a scene of devastation. Though pockets of poverty linger, its bedroom communities of Franklin and Brentwood make it today the most affluent, highly educated and fastest-growing county in Tennessee. To the north, along the Cumberland River, is fast-growing Clarksville, with many well-restored 19th century homes, a large industrial park and the sprawling Fort Campbell army base, which is home to the 101st Airborne Division and has more than 20,000 military personnel just across the Kentucky border. In 2007, Clarksville was the country's 10th fastest-growing metropolitan area.

The 7th Congressional District of Tennessee spans this territory, packing in Republican voters from Montgomery County's seat of Clarksville, south through the western half of Cheatham County and most of Williamson County plus a bite of Nashville-Davidson. It rambles on west across the Tennessee River and south to the Mississippi border and finally to the east side of Memphis and Shelby County. On the map, this looks like a rural district. Demographically, it's mostly suburban. The 7th District grew by 15% between 2000 and 2007, making this the fastest-growing district in the state. Almost 40% of its votes are cast in metro Memphis and 30% in metro Nashville, mostly in the Republican stronghold of

Williamson County. Another 11% are cast in Montgomery County and only 21% are from the smaller rural counties. The 7th is solidly Republican. In 2004, while Democratic presidential nominee John Kerry won Nashville 55%-45%, Republican George W. Bush carried the four rapidly growing counties in the southern and eastern suburbs of Nashville by 91,000 votes (66%-33%), with 72% in Williamson. In 2008, GOP nominee John McCain won every county here except for Hardeman, losing it by only 694 votes. He won the district 66%-33%.

The congresswoman from the 7th District is Marsha Blackburn, a Republican elected in 2002. She grew up in a Farm Bureau family in Laurel, Miss., where her father sold oil-field production equipment. Her interest in gardening and canning won her a 4-H college scholarship at Mississippi State University, where she majored in merchandising and clothing. She helped pay her way through college by selling books door-to-door. She then became a sales manager with Southwestern Company, which sells educational materials, and moved to Williamson County. Her hilltop home is known as "Up Yonder," named by its former owner, Grand Ole Opry star Minnie Pearl. Blackburn became director of retail fashion for a Nashville department store and was appointed by Republican Gov. Don Sundquist as executive director of the Tennessee Film, Entertainment and Music Commission. In 1992, she was the Republican nominee who challenged Democrat Bart Gordon in the 6th District. She lost 57%-41%. Blackburn was elected in 1998 to the Tennessee Senate, where she became an outspoken opponent of Sundquist's proposed income tax. She was well known there for her appearances on conservative radio talk shows and for organizing rallies against the income tax.

When Republican Rep. Ed Bryant decided to run for the Senate, Blackburn sought to replace him. Seven candidates ran in the GOP primary, three of them familiar figures in the Memphis area. Blackburn was the only well-known candidate from the Nashville area. She benefited from $100,000 in advertising and another $90,000 in contributions by the national anti-tax group Club for Growth, and from attacks by the Shelby County candidates on one another. She ran as anti-abortion rights, pro-gun and pro-military. Blackburn won 40% to 20% for the runner-up, and went on to easily win in the general election.

In the House, Blackburn's voting record is among the most conservative. She has urged across-the-board cuts for non-defense discretionary spending, and she co-sponsored the bill to make sales taxes deductible in states that have no income tax; it was passed as part of the corporate tax bill. On the Energy and Commerce Committee, she urged renewal of the federal ban on Internet access taxes and sponsored a bill to reduce regulations on cable programming. A fervent advocate of the music industry central to her district, she has fought to protect intellectual property rights of artists against illegal music downloads. On energy issues, she supported a gas tax holiday in 2008 after prices at the pump spiked upward and she participated in the recess protest on the House floor after Democratic House Speaker Nancy Pelosi refused to allow a vote on opening up coastal areas to oil drilling.

In the immigration debate of recent years, Blackburn has been an outspoken advocate of securing the borders, including erection of a 700-mile fence along the Mexican border. She called for cutting federal funds to cities that don't enforce immigration laws and also pushed to ban banks from giving checking accounts or credit cards to illegal immigrants. A staunch supporter of the Iraq war, she criticized fellow Republicans who opposed President George W. Bush's troop "surge" strategy in January 2007. "Whose side are you on?" she said. "Are you on the side of freedom, or are you on the side of allowing the terrorists to get the upper hand?"

Blackburn was mentioned as a possible candidate for the Senate or governor in 2006. But once she won a seat on the powerful Energy and Commerce Committee, she had sufficient incentive to remain in the House. After the 2006 election, she was one of four candidates for chairman of the Republican Conference, but she was eliminated on the second ballot. Instead, she became communications chair for both the National Republican Congressional Committee and the conservative Republican Study Committee.

In 2008, she faced a primary challenge from Shelby County Register Tom Leatherwood, whose campaign gained ammunition when it was revealed Blackburn had misreported more than $440,000 on campaign finance disclosure forms dating to her first House campaign in 2002. Blackburn filed amended returns, but the watchdog group Citizens for Responsibility and Ethics in Washington filed a complaint with the Federal Election Commission. The underdog Leatherwood, hoping to cement West Tennessee support, also charged that Blackburn had used her campaign funds to help her family's businesses and that she hadn't been effective in Washington. But Blackburn easily won the primary, 62%-38%, carrying every county except Shelby. She won easily in November.

In the presidential contest that year, Blackburn initially endorsed Mitt Romney but went on to be a busy campaign surrogate for eventual nominee John McCain. She was a frequent defender of his sometimes controversial vice presidential nominee, Alaska Gov. Sarah Palin.

EIGHTH DISTRICT

John Tanner (D)

Elected 1988, 11th term; b. Sept. 22, 1944, Halls; home, Union City; U. of TN, B.S. 1966, J.D. 1968; Disciples of Christ; married (Betty Ann); 2 children.

Military Career: Navy, 1968–72; TN Natl. Guard, 1974–2000.

Elected Office: TN House of Reps., 1976–88.

Professional Career: Practicing atty., 1973–88; Business owner, Farmer

DC Office: 1226 LHOB, 20515, 202-225-4714; Fax: 202-225-1765; Web site: www.house.gov/tanner.

State Offices: Jackson, 731-423-4848; Millington, 901-873-5690; Union City, 731-885-7070.

Committees: *Chief Deputy Whip. Foreign Affairs* (15th of 28 D): Europe; Western Hemisphere. *Ways & Means* (7th of 26 D): Social Security (Chmn); Trade.

Group Ratings

	ADA	ACLU	AFS	LCV	ITIC	NTU	COC	ACU	CFG	FRC
2008	80	60	100	85	100	5	71	13	0	23
2007	80	—	82	70	—	12	65	21	14	—

National Journal Ratings

	2007 LIB	—	2007 CONS		2008 LIB	—	2008 CONS
Economic	49%	—	50%		52%	—	48%
Social	52%	—	48%		54%	—	46%
Foreign	48%	—	52%		50%	—	50%
Composite	50%	—	50%		52%	—	48%

Key Votes of the 110th Congress

1. Increase minimum wage	Y	5. Share immigration data	Y	9. Withdraw troops 8/08	Y
2. Expand SCHIP	Y	6. Foreign aid abortion ban	N	10. No operations in Iran	N
3. Raise CAFE standards	Y	7. Ban gay bias in workplace	N	11. Free trade with Peru	Y
4. Bail out financial markets	Y	8. Repeal D.C. gun law	Y	12. Overhaul FISA	Y

Election Results

2008 general	John Tanner (D)..unopposed	($923,820)
2008 primary	John Tanner (D)..unopposed	

Prior Winning Percentages: 2006 (73%); 2004 (74%); 2002 (70%); 2000 (72%); 1998 (100%); 1996 (67%); 1994 (64%); 1992 (84%); 1990 (100%); 1988 (62%)

Population		Race/Ethnicity		Work	
Pop. 2007:	645,147	White:	72.5%	Private:	76.0%
Change since 2000:	Up 2.1%	Black:	23.4%	Government:	16.6%
Urban:	47.0%	Hispanic:	2.1%	Self-employed:	7.2%
Rural:	53.0%	Asian:	0.5%	Blue collar:	33.6%
Area size:	8,528 sq. mi.	Native Am.:	0.4%	White collar:	48.8%
Age		Hawaiian:	0.0%	Khaki collar:	0.6%
Median age:	37.3 yrs.	Two+ races:	1.0%	Other:	17.0%
More than 65 yrs:	13.3%	*Ancestry*		Median income:	$36,891
Less than 18 yrs:	24.9%	USA:	15.3%	Median home value:	$92,000
Education		Irish:	10.1%	Poverty:	19.5%
H.S. grad:	78.5%	English:	7.4%	**Military Veterans**	
College grad:	14.4%			% of Pop:	11.9%
Grad degree:	5.1%				

West of Nashville and the lakes along the Tennessee River and north of Memphis, the rivers roll lazily through flat or gently rolling land that almost could be the northern end of Mississippi. Cotton and soybeans are the main crops, and they often are abundant. More African-Americans remain in rural areas here than in any other part of Tennessee, a reminder of its old plantation economy. The towns are small, edged in by farm fields. The river bottoms, often flooded, are heavily forested. Henning, the hometown of Alex Haley, is where he used to sit on his porch and listen to his aunts tell him stories about slave ships and the Civil War, which became his book *Roots*.

2008 Presidential Vote		
McCain (R)	146,739	(56%)
Obama (D)	112,243	(43%)
2004 Presidential Vote		
Bush (R)	131,524	(53%)
Kerry (D)	116,327	(47%)
Cook Partisan Voting Index:	R + 6	

The 8th Congressional District of Tennessee includes much of this West Tennessee farmland, from the lakes west to the Mississippi. Its largest city is Jackson, which Morgan Quinto Press ranked ninth on its annual list of the most dangerous American cities in 2006. Delta faucets and Toyota parts are manufactured in Jackson, and the district also includes the northern fringes of Memphis. Historically, this is Democratic country. Republicans haven't represented most of the counties that make up the 8th since the end of Reconstruction. The region trended Republican in national races in the 1960s and 1970s, then turned toward the Democrats with the help of some smart local politicians. One of them was Ned McWherter, Tennessee House speaker from 1973 to 1986, then governor for eight years. Recent movement has been back toward Republicans. Rural Carroll County is filled with small factories and is something of a bellwether in Tennessee politics, voting 50%-49% for Republican George W. Bush in 2000 and 56%-43% for him in 2004. In 2008, the county voted for John McCain by 3,475 votes. Overall, the district voted 51%-48% for Al Gore in 2000, switched to Bush 53%-47% in 2004, and then supported McCain 56%-43% in 2008.

The congressman from the 8th District is John Tanner, a Democrat first elected in 1988. Tanner, who is a cousin of McWherter, grew up in Obion County, and went to college and law school at the University of Tennessee. He served four years in the Navy, and then practiced law in Union City. He served in the Army National Guard, and retired as a colonel. In 1976, at age 32, he successfully ran for the Tennessee House, where he served 12 years. In 1988, when the incumbent retired, Tanner ran for Congress and won with a whopping 66% of the vote in a four-candidate primary. He got 62% in the general election.

Tanner's voting record puts him solidly in the middle of the Democratic House. He was a founder of the moderate-to-conservative Democratic coalition called the Blue Dogs, and now heads the group's political action committee. He has a seat on the powerful House Ways and Means Committee, where he has worked on tax issues, including elimination of estate taxes on family-owned farms and small businesses. When Democrat Bill Clinton was president, Tanner was a leading Democrat advocating elimination of the estate tax. President George W. Bush signed a bill eliminating it in 2010, though the changes will "sunset," reverting to the old rates the next year unless Congress acts. He has consistently supported free trade deals, including normalizing trade relations with China and the 2005 Central American Free Trade Agreement. His advocacy of free trade on Ways and Means has angered many Democrats and union allies.

In 1992, Tanner could have been a senator: McWherter was ready to appoint him to succeed Al Gore when Gore became vice president. But Tanner chose to stay in the House, where he has become a major force. Tanner helped to create the Blue Dogs' welfare proposal, which was the genesis for the welfare reform plan that Clinton signed in 1996. His modifications won the support of half the House's Democrats. That bipartisanship, as well as Tanner's support, later disappeared when House Republicans sought to extend the law with tougher requirements for eligibility.

In the Bush era, he was a harsh critic of Republican deficit policies, and offered alternatives to make their tax cuts revenue-neutral. He has sponsored a resolution to require a three-fifths vote in the House to pass any bill that would increase the federal deficit. When gas prices skyrocketed in recent years, Tanner and other moderate Democrats introduced legislation to lift the ban on domestic oil drilling while also encouraging alternative fuels and nuclear energy. As part of his non-partisan approach, he took up the cause of redistricting reform, which would switch control from state legislators to independent commissions. In 2007, he introduced the bill with 34 cosponsors.

As a member of the Foreign Affairs Committee, Tanner has been active in work involving NATO. In 2007, Speaker Nancy Pelosi appointed him to chair the U.S. delegation to the NATO Parliamentary Assembly, a gathering of legislative bodies from the 26 NATO member nations to discuss security and economic issues. In November 2008, the body elected Tanner parliamentarian of the group. He supported the war in Iraq, but got the House to pass his amendment requiring the Army to consider a shift to six-month deployments in order to improve soldier morale and ease the strain on their families. His bill to require the secretary of Defense to provide updates to Congress on redeployments passed the House 377-46, but stalled in the Senate.

In the 8th District, Tanner has been re-elected by wide margins. In 2000, the United Steelworkers backed his Democratic primary opponent because of Tanner's free trade support, but Tanner won the primary 87%-13%. He was unopposed in 2008.

NINTH DISTRICT

Steve Cohen (D)

Elected 2006, 2nd term; b. May 24, 1949, Memphis; home, Memphis; Vanderbilt U., B.A. 1971, U. of Memphis, J.D. 1973; Jewish; single.

Elected Office: Shelby Cnty. Comm., 1977–78, TN Senate, 1982–2006.

Professional Career: Practicing atty., 1974–2006.

DC Office: 1005 LHOB, 20515, 202-225-3265; Fax: 202-225-5663; Web site: cohen.house.gov.

State Offices: Memphis, 901-544-4131.

Committees: *Judiciary* (12th of 24 D): Commercial & Administrative Law (Chmn); Constitution, Civil Rights & Civil Liberties; Crime, Terrorism & Homeland Security. *Transportation & Infrastructure* (31st of 44 D): Aviation; Highways & Transit; Railroads, Pipelines & Hazardous Materials.

Group Ratings

	ADA	ACLU	AFS	LCV	ITIC	NTU	COC	ACU	CFG	FRC
2008	100	100	100	100	86	5	61	0	0	5
2007	100	—	100	95	—	3	50	0	6	—

National Journal Ratings

	2007 LIB	—	2007 CONS		2008 LIB	—	2008 CONS
Economic	61%	—	38%		67%	—	33%
Social	71%	—	28%		82%	—	0%
Foreign	94%	—	4%		70%	—	25%
Composite	76%	—	24%		77%	—	23%

Key Votes of the 110th Congress

1. Increase minimum wage	Y	5. Share immigration data	Y	9. Withdraw troops 8/08	Y
2. Expand SCHIP	Y	6. Foreign aid abortion ban	N	10. No operations in Iran	Y
3. Raise CAFE standards	Y	7. Ban gay bias in workplace	Y	11. Free trade with Peru	N
4. Bail out financial markets	Y	8. Repeal D.C. gun law	N	12. Overhaul FISA	N

Election Results

2008 general	Steve Cohen (D)	198,798	(88%)	($886,339)
	Jake Ford (I)	11,003	(5%)	
	Dewey Clark (I)	10,047	(4%)	
	Mary Wright (I)	6,434	(3%)	($47,715)
2008 primary	Steve Cohen (D)	50,306	(79%)	
	Nikki Tinker (D)	11,817	(19%)	

Prior Winning Percentages: 2006 (60%)

Population			Race/Ethnicity		Work	
Pop. 2007:	602,112		White:	29.3%	Private:	79.8%
Change since 2000:	Down 4.8%		Black:	62.8%	Government:	14.5%
Urban:	99.6%		Hispanic:	4.8%	Self-employed:	5.6%
Rural:	0.4%		Asian:	1.7%	Blue collar:	24.7%
Area size:	340 sq. mi.		Native Am.:	0.1%	White collar:	57.2%
			Hawaiian:	0.1%	Khaki collar:	0.1%
Age			Two+ races:	0.8%	Other:	18.0%
Median age:	33.7 yrs.		*Ancestry*		Median income:	$35,914
More than 65 yrs:	10.3%		USA:	5.5%	Median home value:	$96,200
Less than 18 yrs:	27.2%		English:	5.4%	Poverty:	23.4%
Education			Irish:	5.0%		
H.S. grad:	80.8%				**Military Veterans**	
College grad:	22.8%				% of Pop:	8.6%
Grad degree:	8.6%					

Memphis is the largest city in Tennessee, though its metropolitan area is second to Nashville. In the state's far southwestern corner, 500 miles from the Appalachian border with Virginia but only 20 miles from Mississippi's cotton fields and riverboat casinos, metropolitan Memphis has one of the highest percentages of African-Americans in the country, evidence of the city's economic heritage as a capital of the Cotton Kingdom. Big Mississippi planters used to come north to sell their crops in the court-

2008 Presidential Vote		
Obama (D)	199,915	(78%)
McCain (R)	56,635	(22%)
2004 Presidential Vote		
Kerry (D)	171,547	(70%)
Bush (R)	74,020	(30%)
Cook Partisan Voting Index:	D + 23	

yard of the Peabody Hotel, then make financial arrangements for the next growing season. According to tradition, ducks still famously march daily to the hotel's fountain for a dip.

The city's most celebrated tradition is the blues, a musical form worlds apart from Nashville's country music, which emerged from mountainous, mainly white Middle and East Tennessee. The Memphis sound originated from the self-taught musical stylings of poor, rural blacks in the Mississippi Delta. Throughout the first half of the 20th century, the most talented black musicians migrated north to Memphis and congregated downtown on Beale Street. The blues sound was later adapted by Elvis Presley, a poor white from rural Mississippi, in pivotal sessions in July 1954 at Sam Phillips' Sun Studio in Memphis—the birth of rock 'n' roll. In the early 1960s, Memphis once again became the crucible of a new sound, soul music, which emerged as a counterpoint to rock, its increasingly white-dominated cousin. For some years, Memphis tried to downplay its musical heritage. Much of Beale Street was razed and set on a misguided path toward urban renewal. But the city came to recognize its history as an asset. Graceland, Presley's garishly decorated mansion, attracts hordes of musical pilgrims from all over the world, and a Museum of American Soul Music opened in 2003 on the site of the Stax studio, demolished in 1989. Otis Redding, Isaac Hayes, the Staple Singers and Sam & Dave made their records at the Stax studio.

Geographically central, Memphis is the home of the first supermarket chain: the Piggly Wiggly, founded in 1916 (its symbol, Mr. Pig, has slimmed down since then). It also hosted the first Holiday Inn. The biggest employer by far is FedEx, operating out of the world's busiest cargo airport, although the company did announce layoffs in 2009. The airport pumps nearly $21 billion into the economy every year. Northwest Airlines had a domestic hub at Memphis, until it merged in 2008 with Delta Airlines. For some years, racial discord scarred the political life of Memphis. The Rev. Martin Luther King Jr. was assassinated there in 1968, and the site, the Lorraine Motel, has been converted into a civil rights museum. Even today, resurgent Beale Street is one of the few racially integrated spaces in the city, a division that holds equally true in voting. Blacks vote almost unanimously Democratic, and whites vote Republican by margins almost as great. Blacks narrowly outnumber whites in Shelby County. Many African-Americans have moved into the middle class, although Memphis continues to have the highest poverty rate in Tennessee. In recent years, Memphis has been losing population, shrinking by nearly 12,000 people between 2000 and 2006.

The 9th Congressional District of Tennessee consists of most of the city of Memphis, some of its suburban fringe and about 30 precincts in east Shelby County. The black-majority 9th remains the strongest Democratic district in the state and is essential to the success of Democrats running statewide. In 2008, Democratic presidential nominee Barack Obama greatly improved on Al Gore's 63% in 2000 and John Kerry's 70% in 2004 by winning 78% in the district in 2008.

The congressman from the 9th District is Steve Cohen, a Democrat elected in 2006. Cohen is a fourth-generation Memphian, the son of a psychiatrist. At age 5, Cohen was diagnosed with polio, an illness that would shift his focus from sports to politics. Cohen studied at Vanderbilt University and went on to law school at the University of Memphis. After graduation in 1973, he worked as a legal advisor for the Memphis Police Department and then started a law practice in 1978. He was elected to the Shelby County Commission and, in 1982, to a Memphis-based state Senate seat, where he served for the next 24 years. He became known as the father of the Tennessee State Lottery for his successful efforts in 2002 to pass a referendum repealing a lottery ban and for passing legislation that used the lottery revenue to fund college scholarships.

Cohen wanted to run for Congress in 1996 when 22-year Rep. Harold Ford announced his retirement, but he found his path to Washington blocked by the incumbent's 26-year-old son, an African-American who secured the seat. Cohen, who is white and Jewish, expressed frustration over the inexperienced Ford's strong performance in black precincts. But he got a second chance in 2006 when Ford ran unsuccessfully for Senate. As the only serious white contender among the 15 candidates who filed to run, Cohen faced considerable criticism from local black leaders, who publicly asserted that an African-American should represent the district. "For the first time in 30 years Memphis could be without African-American representation," Democratic candidate Ron Redwing's campaign told voters in an e-mail. Cohen's supporters charged that another primary foe paid for a push poll that asked, "Are you more likely to vote for a born-again Christian or a Jew?" Cohen quipped that his staunchly liberal record would make people mistake him for a black woman. The district's black leaders were unable to narrow the crowded field and the primary results splintered. Cohen won with 31%. Nikki Tinker, the former campaign manager for Ford Jr., finished second with 25%. The incumbent's cousin, Joe Ford Jr., finished third with 12%.

The Democratic primary is typically the only election that matters in this solidly Democratic district, but Cohen faced a challenge in November from yet another Ford—Jake Ford, the incumbent's younger brother, who ran as an independent candidate. Jake Ford was a high school dropout who had had a few scrapes with the law, but he had support from his father and other African-American leaders who opposed Cohen. He argued that he was in better sync with the community, noting that more than two-thirds of the primary vote went against Cohen. Cohen's critics also suggested that Cohen, who is single and supports same-sex marriage, is gay (he has said that he is not). He won the general election with 60%, ending the Ford family's 32-year hold on the district and becoming the only white member of Congress to represent a majority-black district. Cohen wanted to join the Congressional Black Caucus, but he backed off when CBC leaders made it clear he would not be allowed to join.

In his first term, Cohen worked to quickly secure his hold on the seat, knowing that he faced a near-certain primary challenge in 2008. Among his first moves was a resolution apologizing for slavery. While it seemed like a relatively harmless motion that easily passed the House on a voice vote, Cohen's office was slammed with constituent calls charging the measure was a political ploy. It was called up for a vote just days before the August 2008 primary. Cohen also succeeded in naming a Memphis federal building and post offices after prominent African-Americans.

Winning a plum seat on the Judiciary Committee, Cohen was unabashed in his questioning of Bush administration officials and succeeded in getting Federal Bureau of Investigation Director Robert Mueller to acknowledge that the agency's interrogation techniques, including use of water-boarding, a form of coercion that simulates drowning, "might not be appropriate." On the Transportation and Infrastructure Committee, he opposed a bill favored by Chairman James Oberstar of Minnesota that could have subjected FedEx to worker strikes. Cohen also made himself a fixture on C-SPAN, which covers floor proceedings. In 2008, he ranked 10th among House members for face time on C-SPAN.

When Cohen was up for re-election in 2008, his race was his biggest obstacle. African-American leaders in the district coalesced around Tinker, who had come in second to Cohen two years earlier and who was back to challenge him in the Democratic primary. "He's not black and he can't represent me," one minister told the Memphis *Commercial Appeal.* "I don't care how people try to dress up, it always comes down to race and he can't know what it's like to be black." A Tinker campaign ad charged that Cohen went into "our churches, clapping his hands and tapping his feet" but was the only congressman "who thought our kids shouldn't be allowed to pray in school." She got financial help from the Congressional Black Caucus and EMILY's list, the women's fundraising group. But prominent black leaders from outside the district, including Judiciary Chairman John Conyers of Michigan and Rep. Jesse Jackson Jr. of Illinois made radio ads for Cohen and donated to his campaign. He financially outraised Tinker by more than 2-to-1.

A week before the election, Tinker aired a television ad highlighting a vote Cohen had cast in 2005 while he served on a Memphis development board. He had voted against removing a statue of Nathan Bedford Forrest, an early Ku Klux Klan leader, from Forrest Park on the University of Tennessee Medical Center campus. The ad juxtaposed a photo of Cohen with a hooded Klansman. Cohen defended his vote, citing the complexities that would result from moving the statue from the park, which also included Forrest's grave, and he pointed out that several African-American leaders also opposed the relocation of the statue and grave. The August primary wasn't even close. Cohen crushed Tinker, 79%-19%. Cohen faced three independent candidates in November and won with 88% of the vote.

★ TEXAS ★

Texas is a nation-sized state, one of four states that had been independent republics earlier in their histories. (The others are California, Vermont and Hawaii.) It may come as no surprise that Texas stuck with its independent status the longest. Today, it is a state with an international image and international impact. The nation has voted for president 12 times since 1960. It elected Californians four times, and it elected Texans four times. These two largest states have put their stamp on national politics in our time, just as New York did up from 1900 to 1960, when it was the residence of five of the winners and eight of the losers in 15 elections. Texas has been the second-largest state in area since Alaska was admitted to the Union in 1959. It became the second-largest in population in 1994, when it passed New York. (California is the largest.) A formative strain in the state's history is that it is a society without an aristocratic past, a state not formed by plantation owners or plutocrats but by dirt farmers. Texas was founded by Southerners, particularly Tennesseans, who wanted to establish their own republic within the borders of Mexico, a republic with Anglo-Saxon freedoms and black slavery. They defended their dream to the death at the Alamo and to a bloody victory at San Jacinto. They entered the Union willingly in 1845 and left it enthusiastically in 1861. The Texas that emerged from the Civil War was still young and poor. Not until 1901 was oil discovered at Spindletop, setting Texas wildcatters on the road to riches.

Without the underpinnings and burdens of tradition, 20th century Texas produced fabulous wealth, generously rewarding success while being unforgiving of failure. It has respect for learning and style—think of its great universities and Neiman Marcus—and it revels in rough manners and western wear. Texans are prone to wild swings in fortune—think of Sam Houston and the wildcatters, or Lyndon B. Johnson and George W. Bush. As the 21st century began, Texans, for their history of slavery and segregation, proved open to immigrants and friendly with their Mexican neighbors. The North American Free Trade Agreement, the opening up of the border and the coming together of these two countries that are at such different economic levels and have such different cultures, was a project mainly of Texans of both political parties, of Republican President George H. W. Bush and Democratic Treasury Secretary Lloyd Bentsen, of Democratic Gov. Ann Richards and Republican Gov. George W. Bush. At the same time, Texas has become a high-technology powerhouse with some of the nation's most creative businesses. But its success is not just economic. There are elements of heroism—some mythical, some genuine—in Texas history that every elementary and high school student learns.

Texas started off as a marchland on the border of the Third World with an economy based on commodities, mainly cotton, and cotton's prices were in long-term decline. Its farmers felt like they were part of a colonial economy controlled by bankers and Wall Street financiers. After Spindletop, Texas became the nation's—and for a time the world's—leading producer of oil. But oil prices, too, fell in free markets and were propped up by politicians—the 1936 "hot oil" act that Democrat Sam Rayburn, as chairman of the House Commerce Committee, pushed through and the oil depletion allowance maintained for years by Rayburn when he was speaker, by Johnson, when he was Senate majority leader, and by Bentsen, when he was Senate Finance Committee chairman. These politicians also secured subsidies for cotton growers and contracts for defense plants and space facilities in World War II and through the Cold War years. Most Texas voters stayed Democratic up to 1970 because of Confederate memories, New Deal affections and the clout and competence of Texas Democratic officeholders.

But the state's economy grew more complex. By the 1970s, it was no longer dependent on raw commodities. The "awl bidness" here became less a matter of extracting oil than it was playing host to the greatest concentration of highly skilled specialists in extracting oil and natural gas in any part of the world. Also, beginning in the 1960s, Texas became a center for technology with the critical mass of knowledge and finances needed to produce firms like Texas Instruments and Dell Computer and a university infrastructure in the University of Texas and Texas A&M to match the highway system that ties the state together. The Dallas-Fort Worth Metroplex is rich with defense contractors and with erstwhile small firms that grew large with exports to Mexico. Houston is home to firms like Schlumberger, the global oil services company, to many of the high-tech spinoffs from the space program, and to the enormous Texas Medical Center. San Antonio, with the Air Force's prime hospital, has significant medical technology and biotech industries. Austin, as UT doubled its number of engineering professors, became a high-tech center vying for second place after California's Silicon Valley. Texas state courts, once a happy hunting ground for trial lawyers, have been transformed by changes in tort law passed by the Legislature in 1995 and 2003. Meanwhile, the federal court in Marshall, thanks to a fast discovery process and the willingness of juries to bring in big verdicts against patent violators, has become one of the nation's prime venues for patent cases. Texas' low taxes, and lack of a state income tax, helped attract corporate headquarters like American Airlines, GTE, J.C. Penney and Exxon Mobil. Oil is just a small part of the Texas economy now. As a result, Dallas-Fort Worth and Houston are ahead of old industrial centers like Detroit, Cleveland, Pittsburgh and St. Louis on the Top 10 list of metropolitan areas, and they are in the process of overtaking Philadelphia and San Francisco.

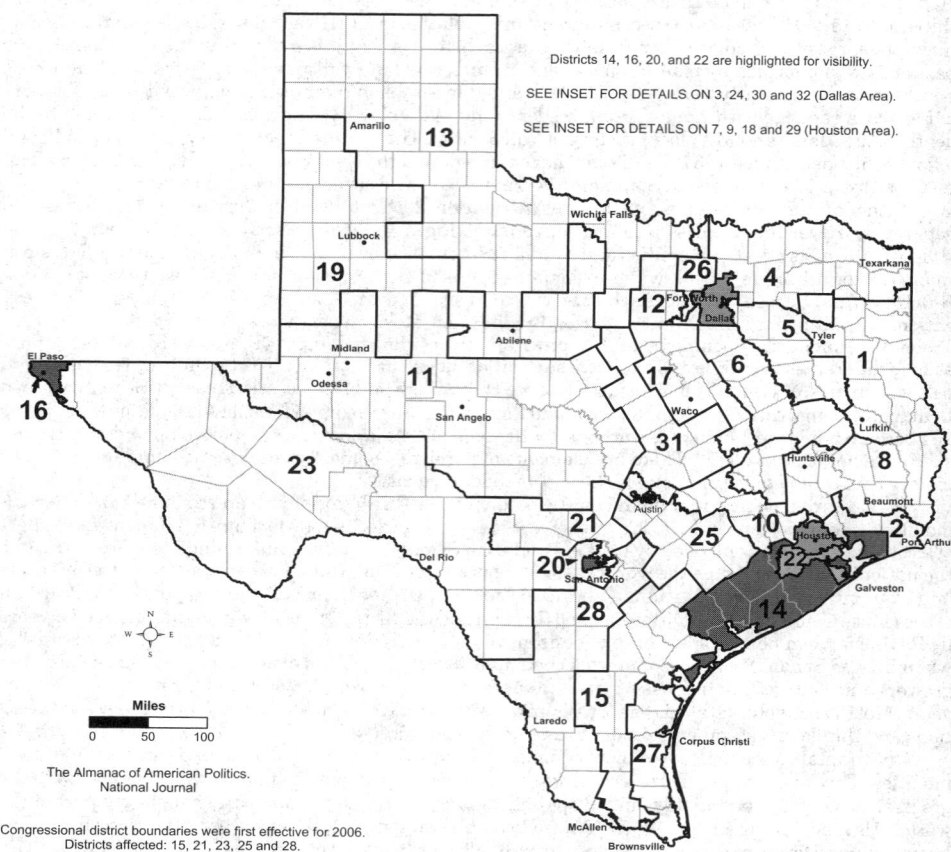

Districts 14, 16, 20, and 22 are highlighted for visibility.

SEE INSET FOR DETAILS ON 3, 24, 30 and 32 (Dallas Area).

SEE INSET FOR DETAILS ON 7, 9, 18 and 29 (Houston Area).

Miles
0   50   100

The Almanac of American Politics.
National Journal

Congressional district boundaries were first effective for 2006.
Districts affected: 15, 21, 23, 25 and 28.

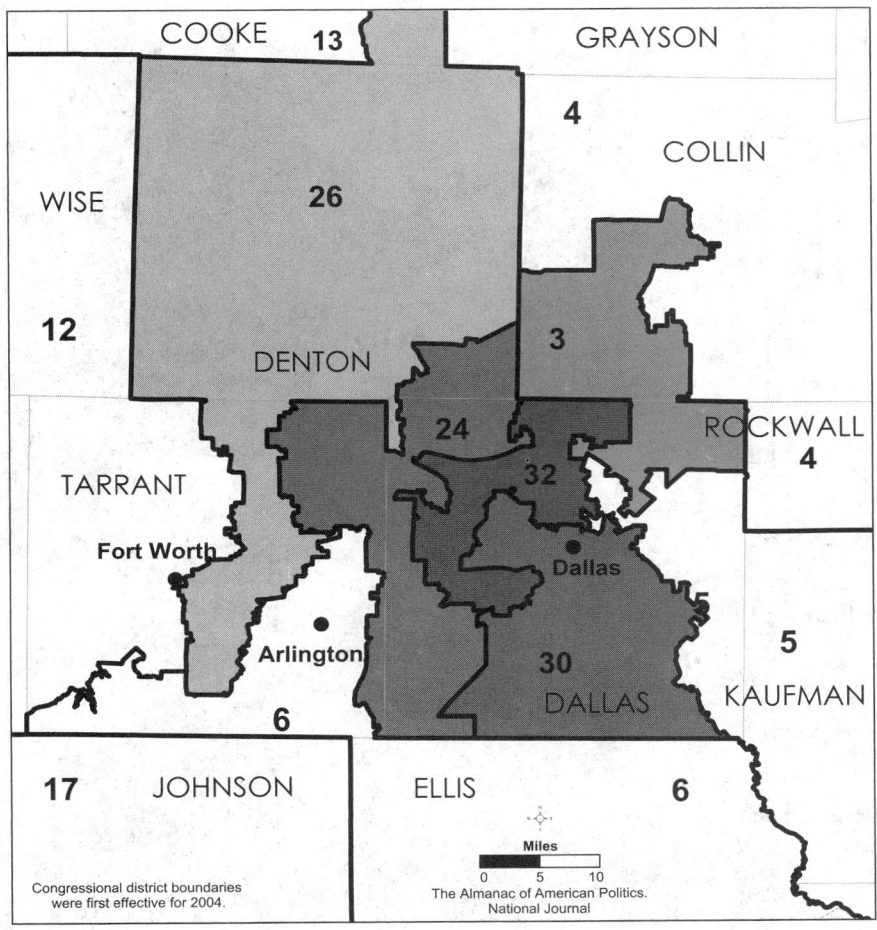

COOKE 13

GRAYSON

4

COLLIN

WISE

26

12

DENTON

3

24

ROCKWALL
4

32

TARRANT

Fort Worth

● **Dallas**

● **Arlington**

5

30

KAUFMAN

DALLAS

6

17 JOHNSON

ELLIS

6

Miles

0   5   10

Congressional district boundaries
were first effective for 2004.

The Almanac of American Politics.
National Journal

Texas surged ahead despite the crash of oil prices in the early 1980s and the savings and loan crisis in the late 1980s, the defense cuts of the early 1990s and the World Trade Organization ruling against cotton subsidies in 2005. Its economy quietly boomed during the first seven years of the new century and it was hit late and only lightly by the recession that started in late 2007. Low housing prices, tight lending practices and tough foreclosure laws meant that Texas did not have much of a housing bubble. Foreclosure rates in 2008 and early 2009 were well below the national average and far below those in California, Nevada, Arizona and Florida. Texas has developed a civic culture of adaptability and resilience, as it demonstrated by taking in thousands of Hurricane Katrina evacuees in 2005. Three years later, Houston weathered Hurricane Ike with orderly and timely evacuations and an absence of panic and looting. While other states pass laws requiring alternative energy sources in some distant year, Texas already produces more electricity from wind power than any other state, more than twice as much as California. In July 2008, regulators approved a $5 billion wind power transmission line project that will allow production to quadruple, enough for 3.7 million homes on a Texas-hot summer day.

Texas is proud of its history and requires a year of Texas history in its high schools. In 1845, when the Republic of Texas was annexed by the United States, New Englander Edward Everett Hale wrote a pamphlet entitled *"How to Conquer Texas Before It Conquers Us,"* calling for emigration from the North to dilute "an unprincipled population of adventurers." But the newcomers joining ancestral Texans—think of the Bushes—have done much to put the stamp of Texas on the whole of the United States. Texas' vast economy has outperformed the national average and most other large states. It has some of the lowest taxes in the country and some of the lowest welfare levels. Most spectacularly, Texas has an economy that has, seemingly effortlessly, generated a massive increase in jobs. Job growth has been about double the national average—Texas has 8% of the nation's population and generated 14% of

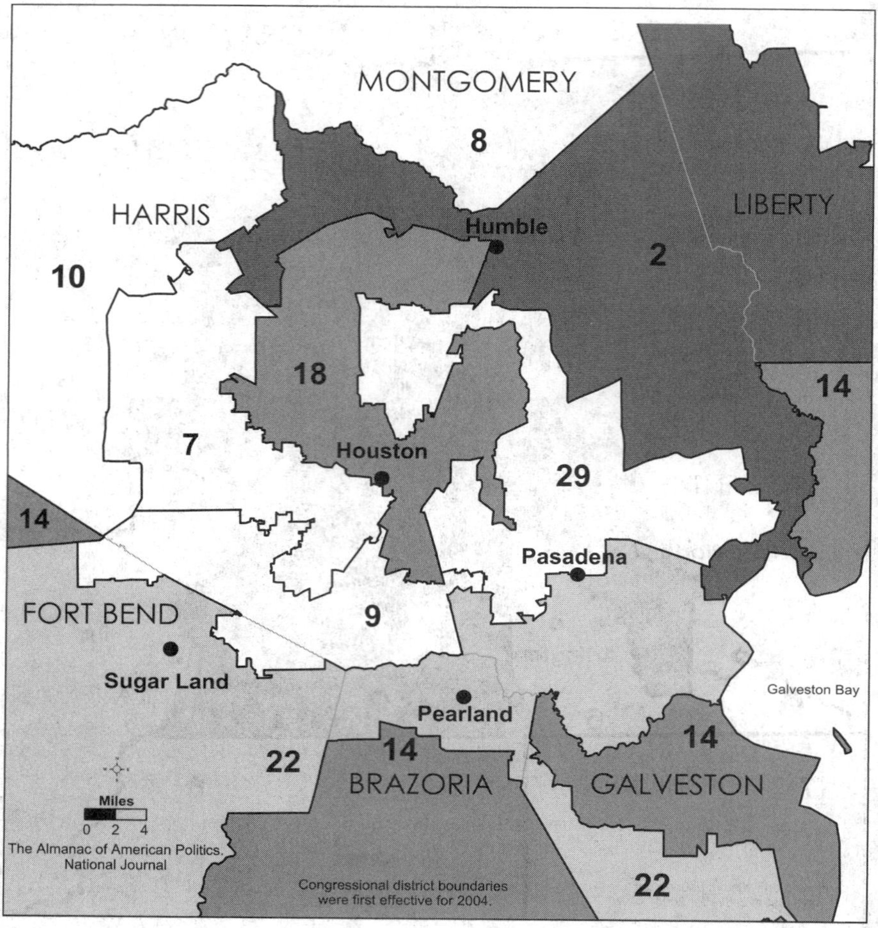
MONTGOMERY
8
HARRIS
10
Humble
LIBERTY
2
18
14
7
Houston
29
14
Pasadena
FORT BEND
9
Sugar Land
Galveston Bay
Pearland
14
14
22
BRAZORIA
GALVESTON
Miles
0 2 4
The Almanac of American Politics.
National Journal
Congressional district boundaries
were first effective for 2004.
22

the nation's job growth from 1999 to early 2008. Texas also exports more goods to other countries than any other state. Growth has been most rapid in the exurban counties at the edges of its big metropolitan areas; between 2000 and 2008, the population rose 55% in Collin County north of Dallas, 50% in Fort Bend County west of Houston, 58% in Williamson County north of Austin and 41% in Comal County northeast of San Antonio. Rural counties in West Texas, like so many in the Great Plains to the north, have been emptying out, but there has been steady growth in much of East Texas and rapid growth on the Lower Rio Grande, from Laredo to Brownsville. Growth has come almost equally from internal migration—a net 711,000 from 2000 to 2008—and immigration—851,000 during the same period.

Texas has surged in part because, in vivid contrast to that other onetime republic, California, it has nurtured and profited from its relationship with its southern neighbor, Mexico. California has been relatively indifferent to Mexico and even at times portrayed its southern neighbor as a burden, generating illegal aliens that California taxpayers must pay for. Texas has taken a different course. Its border with Mexico is longer, some 1,200 miles, and more often crossed. Southern Texas along the Rio Grande is a transition zone between two very different economies. Despite a history of racial segregation, Texas has shown a friendly face to Mexicans, while Mexican immigrants have been happy to become Texans. Fewer Latinos have crossed the border here to take advantage of welfare programs, which are much less generous in Texas than in California. Political leadership has made a difference. Gov. Bush, like Gov. Richards before him, journeyed often to Mexico and invited Mexican leaders to Texas, emphasizing the positive in public and leaving negative details to private negotiations. Republican Gov. Rick Perry, who prepared for his office by taking Spanish lessons, has followed the lead of Richards and Bush, and has opposed putting up a border fence on the Rio Grande. Nearly half of U.S. merchandise exports to Mexico are from Texas, significantly more than California. The NAFTA secretariat of labor is in Dallas, the North American Development Bank is headquartered in San Antonio, the Border Environmental Cooperation Commission is in Juarez, across the Rio Grande from El Paso, and the busiest truck crossing between the countries is the new World Trade Bridge near Laredo and Nuevo Laredo.

Politically, Texas is now a predominantly Republican state. George W. Bush carried it 59%-38% in 2000 and 61%-38% in 2004. In 2008, GOP nominee John McCain carried it by a lesser margin, 55%-44%, but still ran 9 points ahead of his national average in Texas. It was not always so. The Republican trend was a long time coming. One-party Democratic dominance ended in the 1960s, and for two decades Democrats had real competition, except in the cases of a few perennially popular figures like Bentsen, who was on the ballot in 1970, 1976, 1982 and 1988. Metro Dallas-Fort Worth and Houston were the first parts of Texas to go Republican, and Bentsen relied on Democratic strength in the Texas countryside to win. Now the pattern is the other way around. The counties containing Dallas and Houston, San Antonio and Austin are to varying degrees trending Democratic, mostly because of expanding Latino and African-American populations. Democratic nominee Barack Obama carried all four in 2008. Most of the fast-growing exurban counties around them are heavily Republican, but McCain carried metro Dallas with only 55% and Houston with only 54% of the vote, well below Bush's 62% in Dallas and 58% in Houston in 2004. McCain also carried metro San Antonio with 52% and lost metro Austin 58%-42%. The heavily Hispanic border counties, which voted 52%-48% for Democrat John Kerry in 2004, voted 65%-35% for Obama in 2008. The rest of Texas, some 203 rural and small urban counties, is now the state's Republican bastion, voting 68%-31% for McCain over Obama. But they are a declining demographic force, growing just 5% from 2000 to 2008, while metro Dallas grew 22%; metro Houston, 21%; metro San Antonio, 19%; metro Austin, 32%; and the border area, 13%.

Republicans now hold all 29 statewide elective offices, including the entire state Supreme Court. They have won every gubernatorial election but one since 1986 and every U.S. Senate election since 1990. But there are signs their dominance may be in peril. One is demographic: the seemingly inevitable increase in the percentage of Latino voters. From 1990 to 2008, more than half of Texas' population increase was accounted for by the increase in the number of Hispanics, and the Census Bureau estimates that the state population was 36% Hispanic at the end of that period. A slowdown in immigration may mean that percentage won't rise as rapidly as previously projected, but the number who are eligible to vote will grow nevertheless. The 2008 exit poll showed that just 20% of Texas voters were Hispanic (more than the 13% who were African-American but far less than the 63% who were white). But that percentage will undoubtedly increase, with considerable repercussions. If the electorate were 15 percentage points more Hispanic and 15 percentage points less white and each group split as they did in the 2008 presidential election, the result in Texas would have been a 50%-49% McCain victory. Bush and political strategist Karl Rove cultivated Hispanic voters with some success. Bush won 49% or 39% of their votes (depending on which exit poll you believe) in his 1998 re-election for governor and 42% and 49% in his presidential races in 2000 and 2004, respectively. Republican Sen. Kay Bailey Hutchison did about as well, 44%, in her 2006 race for re-election, but Perry got only 31% of Hispanics in the four-candidate 2006 race for governor. In 2008, McCain won 35% of Latino voters and GOP Sen. John Cornyn won 36%. In future elections, Republicans are going to have to do as well as Bush or Hutchison with Hispanic voters in order to carry Texas by anything more than narrow margins.

The other threat to Republican dominance is the fact that they have been visibly and sometimes controversially in control of the state for some time now, time enough to accumulate political baggage and to inspire creative campaigning by the opposition. The congressional redistricting plan that then-U.S. House Majority Leader Tom DeLay of Texas, state House Speaker Tom Craddick and Lt. Gov. David Dewhurst slammed through in October 2003 made Texas' House delegation more reflective of the party's popular vote majorities but also set in motion a chain of events that resulted in DeLay's resignation from the House under an ethics cloud. Craddick's heavy-handed leadership sparked a move for his ouster in 2007 and fueled Democratic gains in legislative races in three successive elections that reduced the Republicans' House majority to 76-74 and resulted in the election in 2009 of a new Republican speaker, Joe

Population		Household Income		Work	
Pop. 2007:	23,385,340	Under $15k:	14.6%	Private:	77.7%
State rank:	2nd of 50	$15k to $50k:	38.7%	Government:	14.7%
Change since 2000:	Up 12.2%	$50k to $100k:	29.2%	Self-employed:	7.4%
Urban:	79.9%	$100k to $150k:	14.1%	Unemployment (3-yr. average):	4.6%
Rural:	20.1%	Over $150k:	3.5%	Poverty:	16.9%
Native of state:	60.9%	Median income:	$46,248	Blue collar:	24.2%
Not a citizen:	11.0%	**Home Value**		White collar:	58.3%
Area size:	268,581 sq. mi.	Under $100k:	43.1%	Khaki collar:	0.5%
Most populous cities		$100k to $300k:	47.9%	Other:	17.0%
1. Houston	2,034,749	$300k to $500k:	6.1%	**Age**	
2. San Antonio	1,267,984	$500k to $1 mil:	2.2%	Median age:	33.1 yrs.
3. Dallas	1,187,603	Over $1 million:	0.6%	More than 65 yrs:	10.0%
4. Austin	725,306	Median:	$113,800	Less than 18 yrs:	27.7%

Race/Ethnicity					Military Veterans		Registered Voters in 2008	
White:	48.3%	*Language*			% of Pop:	9.7%	No party registration	
Black:	11.3%	English:	66.5%		*Veterans by Period*		Voter turnout:	8,077,795
Hispanic:	35.5%	Spanish:	28.9%		WWII and before:	10.3%	Turnout as % of	
Asian:	3.3%	Asian:	2.2%		Korea:	9.8%	voting age:	45.9%
Native Am.:	0.3%	Other			Vietnam:	32.9%	**Legislature**	
Hawaiian:	0.1%	European	1.9%		Gulf (pre-2001):	14.6%	Senate:	12 D 19 R
Two+ races:	1.0%	**Education**			Gulf (post-2001):	8.9%	House:	74 D 76 R
Ancestry		H.S. grad:	78.6%		Peace time:	23.6%		
German:	9.8%	College grad:	24.7%					
Irish:	7.1%	Grad degree:	8.1%					
English:	6.7%							

Straus, supported mostly by Democrats. Perry won re-election in 2006 against three opponents with only 39% of the vote and in early 2009, he and Hutchison were preparing to fight each other in the 2010 gubernatorial primary. Hutchison has said she will resign her Senate seat before that race, which would allow Perry to name a successor. But it would also trigger a special election, in which two Democrats with strong moderate records, Houston Mayor Bill White and former state Comptroller John Sharp, could be strong contenders. Texas politics, like the Texas economy, doesn't stand still.

Presidential politics   In 2008, Texas was, for the first time in 20 years, a pivotal state in presidential politics, more so in the two parties' nomination contests than in the general election, although the result there was notably closer than many people had anticipated. In 1988, Texas' presidential primary was moved to March, for Super Tuesday. Then, Democrats dominated the Legislature and far more Texans chose to vote in the Democratic than in the Republican primary. That year, 1.7 million voted in the Democratic primary, and Michael Dukakis led with 33% of the vote, Jesse Jackson got 25%, ahead of Al Gore, running as a Southern moderate, with 20%. Dukakis had support from urban liberals and Hispanics, Jackson from African-Americans, Gore from the dwindling number of rural and small-town yellow dog Democrats. Just over 1 million votes were cast on the Republican side, most of them for Texas' own George H. W. Bush. In 1992, turnout was lower in both parties' primaries. And in 1996, 2000 and 2004, both parties' nominations were determined by the time Texas voted.

2008 Presidential Vote		
McCain (R)	4,479,328	(55%)
Obama (D)	3,528,633	(44%)

2008 Democratic Presidential Primary		
Clinton (D)	1,462,734	(51%)
Obama (D)	1,362,476	(47%)

2008 Republican Presidential Primary		
McCain (R)	697,767	(51%)
Huckabee (R)	518,002	(38%)

2004 Presidential Vote		
Bush (R)	4,526,917	(61%)
Kerry (D)	2,832,704	(38%)

Not so in 2008. After Democrat Barack Obama in February won 14 straight primaries and 11 caucuses, Texas and Ohio, both voting on March 4, were must-wins for Democrat Hillary Rodham Clinton. On the Republican side, Mike Huckabee was still campaigning against John McCain. So Texas got a lot more attention than it would have if the Legislature had chosen to set the primary for Super Tuesday on February 5. Obama and Clinton debated and campaigned hard in Texas. Democratic turnout was nearly 2.9 million, more than triple the 839,000 who voted in 2004 and 70% above the peak in 1988. The primary was a closer contest than Ohio's. Clinton won by just 51%-47%. As in other states, Clinton carried women, older voters, downscale and rural whites and Latinos by wide margins. Obama carried men, younger voters, upscale and urban whites and blacks by wide margins. Clinton won 61% to 70% of the vote in San Antonio and border state Senate districts. (For some reason, Texas Democrats elect delegates by state Senate districts.) Obama won 73% in heavily African-American state Senate districts in Houston and Dallas. Rural districts, except for one which includes exurban Austin—Williamson County—voted for Clinton. Obama carried metro Dallas with 56%, metro Houston with 55%, and metro Austin with 60%. Clinton carried 18 Senate districts to Obama's 13, but Obama won more delegates overall because one-third of them were selected in caucuses held on primary night and more Obama voters apparently showed up.

Turnout on the Republican side was much lower; 1.3 million, less than half the Democratic turnout and only slightly above the 1.1 million Republicans who voted in the not seriously contested primary in 2000. McCain beat Huckabee 51%-38%. Huckabee carried only one U.S. House district, the 4th, which includes Texarkana, right on the border with his native Arkansas. Half the primary voters were white evangelical Protestants, and Huckabee won more than 40% of the vote in the northern more Baptist half of the state, including the Dallas-Fort Worth Metroplex. He won less than 40% in most parts of the state. McCain's biggest majorities were in the border areas and in the most upscale districts in Houston and Dallas.

In general elections, Texas has not voted Democratic since 1976, when it narrowly backed Jimmy Carter of Georgia. The best the Democratic ticket has done here since then was 43% in 1988, when Texas Democratic Sen. Lloyd Bentsen was on the ticket as Dukakis' running mate, and 44% in 1996, as Texas businessman Ross Perot split the opposition to Democratic nominee Bill Clinton and Republican nominee Bob Dole carried the state with 49% of the vote.

In 2008, Obama got 44%, which left him well behind McCain's 55%, but not so far behind as to banish Democrats' hopes that they may once again be competitive for what are expected to be Texas' 38 electoral votes in 2012. Obama carried the central city counties including Dallas, Houston, San Antonio and Austin, something no Democrat has done since Lyndon Johnson swept his home state in 1964. Republicans led in party identification by only 34%-33%, but conservatives outnumbered liberals 46%-15%. Whites voted 73%-26% for McCain. He also won 83% among white evangelical Protestants and 69% among white voters under 30. African-Americans voted 98%-2% for Obama. Hispanics voted 63%-35% for Obama. Hispanics and upscale white voters were the most likely to have switched from Bush in 2004 to Obama in 2008. As a result, the coalitions supporting each candidate were very different in hue. More than 80% of McCain's votes were cast by whites. A little more than one-third of Obama voters were whites with a little less than one-third black and about the same share Hispanic.

Congressional districting

111th Congress Lineup	
20 R	12 D
110th Congress Lineup	
19 R	13 D

Before 2001, redistricting in Texas had always been the prerogative of Democrats. For many years, it was not particularly partisan; there weren't enough Republicans to matter. By the 1990s, there were, and in 1991, the Democrats produced their masterpiece. Modified slightly by a 1996 court ruling, it clumped heavily Republican areas into hugely Republican districts, and then carved out, with convoluted lines, three new districts for Democrats. Starting in 1994, Republicans outpolled Democrats in House races and Anglo Democrats found themselves increasingly imperiled. Still, Democrats held a 17-13 majority in the delegation after the 2000 election.

Texas gained two new seats after the 2000 census, and Republicans like then-U.S. House Majority Whip Tom DeLay predicted that their party would pick up six to eight seats. But that didn't happen. The Legislature was unable to agree on a map in 2001, and a three-judge federal court in Tyler, with two Democratic judges and one Republican judge, later took control and came up with a plan that protected all the incumbents and created two new Republican districts. But in effect, the partisan Democratic plan of 1991 was given new life, with the Republicans given two new seats as a consolation prize. The result was, predictably, a 17-15 Democratic delegation.

In 2002, Republicans won big majorities in the Legislature, and DeLay, by then one of the most powerful people in the state, lost no time in urging the Legislature to pass a new plan. Senate Republicans balked. But DeLay continued to press newly installed Republican House Speaker Tom Craddick, a longtime ally. As the legislative session neared adjournment, the House Redistricting Committee approved a new map on May 6, 2003. The disciplined Republican majority ignored Democrats' protests. On the eve of the House's scheduled debate on the plan, 51 Democrats fled the state and secretly settled in a Holiday Inn in Ardmore, Okla. to prevent the Republicans from getting the two-thirds required for a quorum. The stunt attracted national attention. The state police were dispatched to track down the "Killer D's." Once their location was revealed, the Democrats insisted they would not return to Austin until after May 15, the final day the House could take up the bill in its regular session. The maneuver worked only temporarily. Republican Gov. Rick Perry convened a special session on June 30, and in late July, the House approved the redistricting plan and sent it to the Senate.

Once Republicans hammered out details of the plan, with lines drawn to satisfy Craddick and DeLay, the pro-Republican plan passed. Twenty-two of the 32 districts had voted Republican in statewide races, and two others came close to doing so. The 2003 plan also shuffled around counties, so that Democrats who had been representing districts carried by Bush suddenly found themselves running in unfamiliar territory. The drafters attempted to comply with the Voting Rights Act by drawing safe districts for Texas' two African-American and five Hispanic incumbent Democrats. The new map in fact added a third heavily black district, in the Houston area, and increased from seven to eight the number of districts with Hispanic majorities. But it pointedly made what Texans called WD-40s—white Democrats over 40—an endangered species. There were 15 of them in the Texas delegation who were elected in 1992, 11 in 2000, 10 in 2002 and only three in 2004.

On December 19, 2003, the Justice Department ruled the plan was in compliance with the Voting Rights Act. And a federal court, after Democrats sued, ruled that it was permissible to redistrict more than once in the 10 years between censuses. On January 6, 2004, the court approved the plan 2-1. In September of that year, three DeLay associates who pushed the redistricting plan were indicted by Austin District Attorney Ronnie Earle on campaign finance charges related to the 2002 state House elections. And in October, the U.S. Supreme Court ordered the three-judge court to reconsider the case in light of its decision in a redistricting case in Pennsylvania, in which the high court upheld a Republican plan as egregiously partisan as the Texas plan. In June 2005, the federal court again rejected the legal challenge.

But by then, an election under the new map had already been held and the new House members had taken office in 2004. George W. Bush carried Texas 61%-38%, and in the 32 House races, Republicans won 58% of the votes to Democrats' 39%. Five WD-40s were defeated. Only three survived: Chet Edwards of Waco and Lloyd Doggett and Gene Green in majority Hispanic districts. The Texas delegation, 17-15 Democratic under the old map, was 21-11 Republican under the new map. Nationally, Republicans gained three seats in the House, with the help of Texas, to bring their total to 232, the most won by Republicans in any biennial election since 1946.

In December 2005, the Supreme Court agreed to hear an appeal, and in June, the Court upheld the basic plan, rejecting 7-2 the charge that it was "an unconstitutional political gerrymander." But it also ruled, 5-4, that the fact that the 23rd District, held by Republican Henry Bonilla, had a population that was only 55% Hispanic violated the Voting Rights Act, and it suggested that the 25th District, stretching from Austin to the Rio Grande and 69% Hispanic (represented by Democrat Doggett), might also have to be redrawn. The three-judge district court adopted a new plan that gave a larger portion of San Antonio to the 23rd District and kept the 25th District within easy driving distance of Austin. Filing was reopened for the five altered districts with primaries to be held on Election Day and runoffs between the party nominees later in December.

The overall result was a victory for Republicans but with two offsetting losses. Democrat Nick Lampson, ousted in the 2nd District in 2004, came back and won in DeLay's old 22nd District despite its heavy Republican leanings. And Bonilla, running after the Republicans had lost the House, lost his 23rd District seat to Democrat Ciro Rodriguez. That left Republicans with a 19-13 majority in the delegation. In 2008, Republican Pete Olson beat Lampson, raising the Republican advantage to 20-12.

Texas is expected to gain four House seats from the reapportionment following the 2010 census, although demographers suggest it may gain only three if the recession slows population growth. Control of the redistricting process is uncertain. In early 2009, Republican Sen. Kay Bailey Hutchison was preparing to challenge Perry in the 2010 Republican primary, setting up what could be a bitter contest and possibly leaving an opening for a serious Democratic candidate. The Republicans' 19-12 advantage in the state Senate seems unlikely to be overturned. Democrats would have to win four of the nine Republican Senate seats up in 2010, and in only one did the Republican receive less than 69% of the vote in 2006. The state House is another matter. In 2008, Democrats reduced the Republican advantage there to 76-74, and Democrats provided most of the votes that enabled moderate Republican Joe Straus to oust six-year Republican Speaker Craddick in January 2009. The Texas Legislature traditionally has been less strictly partisan than those in most other states. Speakers and lieutenant governors routinely appoint House and Senate committee chairmen of the other party.

So, while it is possible that Republicans will have the absolute control over redistricting that they exercised in 2003, it is far from certain. Demographically, the most rapid growth in the state has been in exurban counties, almost all of them heavily Republican. But the prevailing interpretation of the Voting Rights Act will probably result in the creation of at least one more majority-Hispanic district and presumably a Democratic seat. All of this suggests that there may be only a minimal increase, and perhaps not any, in the current party split in the state's House delegation. But changing demographics and the changed political balance make it unlikely that the Democrats can hope to restore something like the 1991 plan.

Governor

Rick Perry (R)

Assumed office Dec. 2000, term expires Jan. 2011, 2nd full term; b. March 4, 1950, Paint Creek; home, Austin; Texas A&M U., B.S. 1972; United Methodist; married (Anita); 2 children.

Military Career: Air Force, 1972–77.

Elected Office: TX House of Reps., 1984–90; Comm., TX Dept. of Agriculture, 1990–98; Lt. gov., 1998–2000.

Professional Career: Farmer & rancher.

Office: State Capitol, P.O. Box 12428, Austin, 78711, 512-463-2000; Fax: 512-463-1849; Web site: www.governor.state.tx.us.

Election Results

2006 general	Rick Perry (R)	1,716,803	(39%)
	Chris Bell (D)	1,310,353	(30%)
	Carole Keeton Strayhorn (I)	797,577	(18%)
	Kinky Friedman (I)	546,869	(12%)
2006 primary	Rick Perry (R)	552,545	(84%)
	Larry Kilgore (R)	50,119	(8%)
	Rhett Smith (R)	30,225	(5%)

Prior Winning Percentages: 2002 (58%)

Republican Rick Perry succeeded George W. Bush as governor of Texas on December 21, 2000, and was elected to full four-year terms in 2002 and 2006. In December 2008, he became the longest-serving governor in Texas history.

Perry grew up on his family's farm in Paint Creek, in Haskell County, near where his great-great grandfather settled after fighting in the Civil War; he was elected to the Texas House in the 1890s. Perry's family owns a 10,000-acre ranch, and his father served 28 years as a county commissioner, as a Democrat, like pretty much everyone in those parts at that time. Rick Perry was an Eagle Scout and went to Texas A&M University to study to be a veterinarian. While working on a degree in animal science, he became a yell leader, or cheerleader, a coveted position at A&M. It was the late 1960s, a time of great student rebellions, but apparently not in College Station. Perry says he never saw a war protest. After college, he served five years in the Air Force, piloting C-130 transports. In 1977, he returned to work on the family ranch. In 1984, he was elected to the state House as a Democrat. He was part of a group called the Pit Bulls, who focused on trying to cut state agency budgets. In 1989, he was passed over for a leadership position by Democratic Speaker Gib Lewis and switched to the Republican Party. In 1990, he ran for agriculture commissioner against the colorful populist incumbent Jim Hightower. With the help of Karl Rove, then working as a consultant in Texas, Perry got the support of the Farm Bureau and won an upset victory with ads pointing out that Hightower had supported civil rights leader Jesse Jackson for president. In the increasingly Republican Texas, Perry was easily re-elected in 1994.

Four years later, when storied Democratic Lt. Gov. Bob Bullock retired, Perry ran for that office, which in Texas is a powerful position. The lieutenant governor presides over the state Senate, controls its proceedings, and appoints its committee members and chairmen. Governors and lieutenant governors are elected separately in Texas, and Bush and Perry ran separate campaigns in 1998. Interestingly, Perry had no Republican primary opposition for a post that obviously could lead directly to the governorship. His Democratic opponent was state Comptroller John Sharp, who Perry had known during college (Sharp had been student-body president at A&M when Perry was a yell leader). Perry's 50%-48% victory opened the way to the governor's office.

After Bush was elected president in 2000, Perry became the first Aggie governor of Texas. In 2002, when Perry had to run for the job, Democrats believed that he was vulnerable and gamely tried to put together a ticket. The chief organizer was Sharp, who decided to run for lieutenant governor again, not governor, and worked to get a gubernatorial candidate who could swell Democratic turnout among Latinos. His dream candidate was Tony Sanchez, chief shareholder of International Bank of Commerce and Sanchez Oil & Gas in Laredo, who was said to have a net worth of $600 million. Sanchez was no political naïf. In the early 1970s, he had worked for Lt. Gov. Ben Barnes, one of the state's canniest politicians. Sharp and former San Antonio Mayor Henry Cisneros persuaded Sanchez to run for governor. Sanchez spent $18 million on ads and beat former Attorney General Dan Morales in the Democratic primary 61%-33%. Meanwhile, in the April 2002 runoff, Democrats nominated for senator the business-friendly former mayor of Dallas, Ron Kirk, who is black. Sharp had his "Dream Team," which he hoped would drive Latino and African-American turnout while he appealed to Anglo voters.

Perry and Sanchez agreed on many issues, but much of the campaign consisted of vitriolic ads. Sanchez's theme was that Perry was beholden to campaign contributors and did their bidding. Perry hit Sanchez for not voting in some elections and for his business practices. In the fall, he ran a number of hard-hitting ads linking Sanchez to drug kingpins' money laundering. It was undisputed that some $25 million had been laundered through Tesoro Savings & Loan, a company Sanchez owned, in the early 1980s. Sanchez said that he had not known of the transactions and pointed out that no one at the S&L had been charged with a crime. Nevertheless, Perry's ads linked the money laundering to the 1985 murder of a Drug Enforcement Administration agent in Mexico. In one Perry ad, another DEA agent said, "We investigated the murder. The same drug dealers who killed Kiki laundered millions in drug money through Tony Sanchez's bank." Sanchez was outraged. He called Perry "by far the most disgusting human being I have ever known."

Election Night was a nightmare for the "Dream Team." Republicans won up and down the line. Perry beat Sanchez 58%-40%, although Sanchez had spent $67 million to Perry's $28 million. Kirk and Sharp, who led the Democratic ticket, both lost. The high Latino turnout that Democrats had hoped for did materialize, but only in the Rio Grande Valley. Turnout in Latino neighborhoods in Houston, Dallas and San Antonio was not up by much. Rather, the big increases in turnout were in the fast-growing, heavily Republican counties at the edge of metro areas. Republicans won big margins in the Legislature:

19-12 in the state Senate and 88-62 in the state House. The new Republican leaders of the Legislature were Lt. Gov. David Dewhurst in the Senate and Speaker Tom Craddick in the House—the first Republican speaker since 1871. Perry called his victory a mandate for restricting tort lawsuits, providing rate relief on homeowner insurance, changes in medical malpractice law, and government-paid vouchers for private school tuition.

Redistricting dominated the Texas political landscape in 2003. Early that year, U.S. House Majority Leader Tom DeLay urged the Legislature to pass a new congressional district map. Senate Republicans and Dewhurst were reluctant, but DeLay pressed longtime ally Craddick. As the legislative session neared adjournment, the House Redistricting Committee approved a new map that added five to seven new Republican seats and jeopardized each of the delegation's 10 Anglo Democrats, though it protected the five incumbent Latino Democrats and two African-Americans. On the eve of the House's scheduled May 12 debate, 51 Democrats fled the state and secretly settled at a Holiday Inn in Ardmore, Okla., to prevent the Republicans from getting the two-thirds required for a quorum. The spectacle attracted national attention, and the state police were dispatched to track down the "Killer D's." Once their location was revealed, the Democrats insisted they would not return to Austin until after May 15, the final day the House could take up the bill in its regular session. The maneuver worked, temporarily. But Perry convened a special session on June 30. After House Republicans passed their plan, the 30-day session deadlocked when senators abided by their traditional rule for two-thirds approval to debate legislation. Perry called a second 30-day session. When Republicans threatened to take action this time with a simple majority, 11 Senate Democrats fled to Albuquerque to prevent a quorum for legislative action or apprehension by state law-enforcement officers. With cheers from Democrats nationwide and growing anger from Republicans, they remained there for the month of August. When Perry indicated in early September that he would call a third special session, Democratic state Sen. John Whitmire effectively broke the deadlock by returning to his legislative duties. On October 9, DeLay's redistricting plan was passed by the Legislature.

School finance has long been a major issue in Texas government and politics. In 1993, Democratic Gov. Ann Richards and the Democratic Legislature passed a "Robin Hood" plan to distribute money from high-property-value school districts to poorer ones. By 2004, many school districts had reached their maximum taxing levels, voters were complaining about high property taxes, and others were saying the schools were starved for money. In 2004, Perry advanced legislation with property-tax reductions, more spending on schools and a $1 cigarette-tax increase. But it was fiercely criticized by Republican state Comptroller Carole Keeton Strayhorn and failed to pass. In September 2004, a state trial judge ruled that the school finance system was unconstitutional and gave the Legislature a year to come up with a solution; the state appealed directly to the Texas Supreme Court. In 2005, Perry declared school financing a "legislative emergency." The House and Senate came close to a deal but failed in the final hours of the session. Perry vetoed a $35 billion education bill in June 2005 and called a special session to consider the issue. A couple more special sessions failed to produce a solution. In November 2005, the state Supreme Court ruled the financing system unconstitutional, on the grounds that it amounted to a statewide property tax. In September, Perry appointed a commission headed by his old college friend and political foe Sharp. It recommended a plan that Perry brought before a special session in April 2006. The Senate passed a bill in May with a one-third property-tax cut, a $2,000 pay raise for teachers, a 4% spending increase, new math and science initiatives and a cigarette-tax increase. It also incorporated changes in business taxes and expanded the franchise tax to reach every significant business operation, with revenues to be used to finance property- tax reductions.

Perry next tackled Texas's traffic-choked roads. Interstate 35 from the Dallas-Fort Worth Metroplex on south has been pounded by trucks headed for the border at Laredo, the busiest crossing point for truck traffic between the United States and Mexico. Perry argued that the state's 20-cent gas tax was no longer adequate to build needed infrastructure, and in 2005, the Legislature authorized his Trans-Texas Corridor plan to build a network of toll highways, with freight and passenger-rail corridors and utility zones for water and gas pipelines and electric transmission lines, at a cost of $184 billion or more. The first segment of the Central Texas Turnpike bypassing Austin opened in September 2006. The plan was to build a highway corridor just east of and parallel to I-35. This sparked protests from local governments, landowners and others. Comptroller Strayhorn called it the "Trans-Texas Catastrophe." But Perry plunged ahead. Another problem was border enforcement. In 2006, Perry ordered video surveillance cameras placed on the border and sent large numbers of state troopers to protect Texans from Mexican drug cartels operating just south of the border. "Enforcing the border is the federal government's responsibility, but Texas will not wait for them to act," he said. He denounced proposals for a border fence and for taking away birthright citizenship.

Going into his 2006 re-election campaign, Perry had a job-approval rating of under 50%. Republican U.S. Sen. Kay Bailey Hutchison gave long thought to challenging him in the March 2006 primary, which she had also considered in 2002, but decided against it. Strayhorn decided to challenge him, saying memorably: "I am not a weak leadin', ethics ignorin', pointin'-the-finger-at-everyone blamin', special session callin', public school slashin', slush fund spendin', toll road buildin', special interest panderin', rainy day fund raidin', fee increasin', no property tax cuttin', promise breakin', do-nothin' Rick Perry phony conservative." She called for repealing Perry's business tax and called the property-tax reductions a "$23 billion hot check." Also entering the race was musician Kinky Friedman. "How hard could it be?" was his theme. "The far religious right and the politically correct left are holding the greatest state in the Union hostage. . . . Musicians can run this state better than politicians. We didn't put the train in the ditch. We'll work late at night. We won't work in the morning, though." Democrats had more difficulty coming up with a candidate. Finally Chris Bell, a one-term congressman from Houston who had been defeated as a result of the 2003 redistricting plan, stepped forward. Just before the filing deadline, Strayhorn said she would run as an independent rather than go up against Perry in the Republican primary. Early 2006 polls showed Perry running around 40% and his three opponents each receiving about half as many votes.

Despite a long and raucous campaign, that was pretty much how things turned out. In the March primary, 656,000 votes were cast on the Republican side and 509,000 on the Democratic side—a bit of a decline in Republican strength. In November, Perry received 39% of the vote, to 30% for Bell, 18% for Strayhorn and 12% for Friedman. Perry carried metro Dallas 41%-31%, Houston 38%-31%, and San Antonio 36%-28%. Bell carried metro Austin 39%-31% and the border counties 38%-33%. Whites voted 44%-24% for Perry, African-Americans 63%-16% for Bell. Hispanics, who cast 15% of the votes, voted 41%-31% for Bell. Republicans gained one seat in the state Senate, for a 20-11 margin, and lost seats in the state House, leaving their majority at 81-69.

In June 2007, with a booming economy and a budget surplus, Perry signed a $152 billion, two-year budget. It raised spending 12% and included $3 billion in bonds for cancer research, a health-insurance pool, a $146 million increase in college aid and a $100 million increase in funds for border security. The Legislature rejected his proposal to sell the state lottery to pay for health insurance and his property-tax changes. He vetoed an eminent domain bill—inspired by fears about the Trans-Texas Corridor and supported by the Texas Farm Bureau—that would have provided compensation for any diminished access to property. But he signed a bill limiting toll road construction to regional toll agencies—another swipe at the Trans-Texas Corridor. Perry opposed the border fence ordered by Congress. "We know how to deal with border security, and you don't do it by building a fence. You do it by putting boots on the ground," he said. However, he said a "strategic" fence might be useful in urban border areas.

On other issues, Perry signed a bill barring confiscation of guns in a state of emergency and, after the Virginia Tech University massacre of 32 students, supported repeal of the law prohibiting guns on campuses, saying, "It makes sense for Texans to be able to protect themselves from deranged individuals." He issued a widely criticized order requiring teenage girls to receive the HPV vaccine, which has shown promise in combating genital warts and cervical cancer.

In January 2009, the state government faced no budget deficit and had an $11.7 billion rainy day fund to draw on, though revenues were declining. Yet Perry faced some obstacles. In November 2008, Democrats had reduced the Republicans' majority in the state House to 76-74, and in January 2009, 11 "Anybody-but-Craddick" Republicans forced out conservative Speaker Craddick and installed, mostly with Democratic votes, a more-moderate Republican, Joe Straus. In January 2009, the Texas Department of Transportation officially abandoned the Trans-Texas Corridor project in the face of widespread opposition from landowners and suspicion of the foreign contractor, Cintra. Some of the roads would still be built, but not all of the 1,200-foot-wide corridor of toll roads, rail lines, pipelines and electrical transmission wires. Legislators also questioned Perry's 2005 mandate that at least 65% of school spending go to classroom instruction.

In December 2008, Perry, as head of the Republican Governors Association, came out against President-elect Obama's $787 billion economic stimulus bill. He said, "The message that the bailout sends is that you don't have to be responsible for your actions." He also said, "I believe that our federal government has become oppressive in its size, its intrusion into the lives of our citizens and its interference with the affairs of our state." In March, he opposed taking $555 million in stimulus money that required Texas to expand its unemployment-compensation program. Nonetheless, a bipartisan majority in the Senate voted to accept the $555 million and to change state law, and the House voted to tap the Texas Enterprise Fund for unemployment compensation if the state refused to take the federal money.

Perry also began to seek a national profile, promoting Texas's economic strengths and his own policies. "Our low taxes, controlled government spending and fair legal system give us a leg up on other states," he said, noting that Texas led the nation in exports and Fortune 500 company headquarters. Looking out at the rest of the nation suffering from recession, he said, "I can't imagine what Texas would look like if we had applied the same principles and the same decision-making in Texas that they're applying in Washington. Well, California." In February 2008, he published a book, *On My Honor: Why the American Values of the Boy Scouts Are Worth Fighting For*, which depicts the Boy Scouts as a bulwark against "nihilism" and "moral relativism."

Perry has made it clear he will seek another four-year term in 2010. He is likely to have competition for the GOP nomination from Hutchison. In late 2008, she had $8 million for a race, compared to Perry's $6.6 million. Texas law barred him from raising money until the end of the legislative session in June 2009. Hutchison criticized the Trans-Texas Corridor as Perry's "quest to cover our state with massive toll roads." She also attacked him for reducing the State Children's Health Insurance Program and called for more education funding. After Hutchison voted for the $700 billion government rescue of the financial services industry, Perry's campaign press secretary called her "Kay Bailout." Perry also burnished his conservative credentials by supporting a "Choose Life" license plate in the 2009 legislative session and a bill requiring women seeking an abortion to first view an ultrasound of their unborn child.

Senior Senator

Kay Bailey Hutchison (R)

Elected June 1993, term expires 2012, 3rd full term; b. July 22, 1943, Galveston; home, Dallas; U. of TX, B.A. 1962, J.D. 1967; Episcopalian; married (Ray); 2 children.

Elected Office: TX House of Reps., 1972–76; TX treasurer, 1990–93.

Professional Career: Political & legal corresp., KPRC–TV, 1967–70; Vice chmn., Natl. Transp. Safety Bd., 1976–78; V.P. & gen. cnsl., RepublicBank Corp., 1978–82; Owner, McCraw Candies, 1984–88.

DC Office: 284 RSOB, 20510, 202-224-5922; Fax: 202-224-0776; Web site: hutchison.senate.gov.

State Offices: Abilene, 325-676-2839; Austin, 512-916-5834; Dallas, 214-361-3500; Harlingen, 956-425-2253; Houston, 713-653-3456; San Antonio, 210-340-2885.

Committees: *Appropriations* (7th of 12 R): Commerce, Justice, Science & Related Agencies; Defense; Energy & Water Development; Labor, Health and Human Services, Education & Related Agencies; Military Construction, Veterans Affairs & Related Agencies (RMM); Transportation, Housing and Urban Development & Related Agencies. *Banking, Housing & Urban Affairs* (10th of 10 R): Financial Institutions; Housing, Transportation & Community Development. *Commerce, Science & Transportation* (RMM of 11 R). *Rules & Administration* (5th of 8 R).

Group Ratings

	ADA	ACLU	AFS	LCV	ITIC	NTU	COC	ACU	CFG	FRC
2008	20	14	0	18	100	54	100	76	70	88
2007	20	—	14	7	—	63	90	88	63	—

National Journal Ratings

	2007 LIB	—	2007 CONS		2008 LIB	—	2008 CONS
Economic	28%	—	70%		26%	—	72%
Social	26%	—	72%		21%	—	73%
Foreign	16%	—	79%		0%	—	84%
Composite	25%	—	75%		20%	—	80%

Key Votes of the 110th Congress

1. Raise CAFE standards	N	5. Make English official language	Y	9. Withdraw troops 3/08	N
2. Expand SCHIP	Y	6. Path to citizenship	N	10. Iran guard is terrorist group	Y
3. Cap greenhouse gases	N	7. Fetus is unborn child	Y	11. Increase missile defense $	Y
4. Bail out financial markets	Y	8. Prosecute hate crimes	N	12. Overhaul FISA	Y

Election Results

2006 general	Kay Bailey Hutchison (R)	2,661,789	(62%)	($5,734,146)
	Barbara Radnofsky (D)	1,555,202	(36%)	($1,432,107)
2006 primary	Kay Bailey Hutchison (R)	unopposed		

Prior Winning Percentages: 2000 (65%); 1994 (61%); 1993 (67%)

Kay Bailey Hutchison, the senior senator from Texas, is a Republican who first won her seat in a June 1993 special election. She has said she will leave the Senate in the fall of 2009 to run for governor. Hutchison is of old Texas stock, the great-great-granddaughter of Charles S. Taylor, a signer of the Texas Declaration of Independence. She grew up in LaMarque, near the refinery town of Texas City, a prom queen who went to college and then law school at the University of Texas. Unable to get a job in law in 1967, she worked for a Houston television station as a reporter. In 1972, she won a seat in the Texas Legislature, its first Republican woman. In 1976, she went to Washington for a top job at the National Transportation Safety Board. She married Ray Hutchison, moved to Dallas, went into banking and became a small-business owner in 1978. In 1982, she lost a race for the U.S. House race to Republican Steve Bartlett, later mayor of Dallas. But she stayed active in Republican politics and was elected state treasurer in 1990. This was a breakthrough year for state Republicans, who before that had not been successful in down-ballot statewide races. Hutchison began her political career when it was no advantage to be a woman and has been mocked by liberals for her tight-lipped good manners and by Washington conservatives as a "Texas pom-pom girl." Her response: "This is what I have faced all my life—the trivialization of me—which I have not ever let bother me. I have always been able to rise above the expectations." Indeed, she is a senator from the nation's second-largest state and one of only six senators in history to have been elected with more than 4 million votes. (The others: Democrats Barbara Boxer and Dianne Feinstein of California, Daniel Patrick Moynihan and Charles Schumer of New York, and Republican John Cornyn of Texas.)

Hutchison's next chance to run for Congress came in January 1993, when Democrat Lloyd Bentsen resigned his Senate seat after 22 years to become President Bill Clinton's Treasury secretary. Democratic Gov. Ann Richards appointed Bob Krueger, a two-term U.S. representative from Texas in the 1970s who was then the state railroad commissioner. Running against him in the May 1993 all-party primary were three Republicans: Hutchison and Reps. Joe Barton and Jack Fields. Krueger opposed the Clinton budget and tax plan, but Democrats were so unpopular in Texas then—Bill Clinton had a 73% negative job rating—that Krueger won only 29% of the total vote, just behind Hutchison, also with 29%. Barton and Fields won 14% each. Hutchison kept the focus on Clinton and won the June runoff by an astonishing 67%-33%. Three serious Democrats were running as she entered the race for the full term in 1994. The potentially strongest candidate, moderate U.S. Rep. Mike Andrews of Houston, was eliminated in the March primary. In the April runoff, former Attorney General Jim Mattox lost 54%-46% to Richard Fisher, a free-spending moderate who campaigned extensively in the border counties in Spanish. Hutchison cruised to a solid 61%-38% victory.

Hutchison has not had trouble being taken seriously by fellow Republicans in the Senate. She moved up quickly in the leadership, and in 2006, she was elected chairman of the Senate Republican Policy Committee, the No. 4 position in the leadership. The following year, she declined to run for the conference chairman, the No. 3 position. She is the ranking Republican on the influential Senate Commerce, Science and Transportation Committee. For a long time, she has had her eye on the Texas governorship. After several false starts, she made it plain that she would run even if Republican Gov. Rick Perry ran for re-election in 2010. In July 2009, she said she would step down from the Senate in the fall of 2009 to focus on her challenge to Perry and her quest for the governorship.

Hutchison is a conservative, but her positions contrast pointedly with Perry's on some issues, notably her support of embryonic-stem-cell research and of the proposal to expand the State Children's Health Insurance Program. By mid-2009, their contest was shaping up to be a spirited one. Hutchison picked a fight with Perry on an important state issue: whether to impose tolls on Texas's interstate highways. Perry has proposed a toll-financed "Trans-Texas Corridor" paralleling Interstate 35 from Laredo to Dallas-Fort Worth. Hutchinson called it a "quest to cover our state with massive toll roads." Perry's campaign press secretary dubbed Hutchison "Kay Bailout" for her support of the $700 billion government rescue of the financial-services industry in 2008.

Hutchison's electoral position has been strong. She was re-elected 65%-32% in 2000, carrying 237 of 254 counties, and 62%-36% in 2006, carrying 238 of the counties. She has run about even in the heavily Democratic border counties, and her losses in Austin's Travis County have been offset by her margins in suburban Williamson County just to the north. In late 2008, she began transferring money from her Senate campaign account to her state campaign account, and in January 2009, she had $8 million, more than Perry's $6.6 million. In 2006, Perry was re-elected with only 39% in a four-candidate race. Polls in early 2009 showed Hutchison leading him in the Republican primary.

In recent legislative battles, Hutchison withdrew her support of immigration legislation in 2007 after the Senate rejected 53-45 her so-called "touch back" amendment, which required illegal immigrants who wished to stay in the United States to return first to their countries of origin. Also in 2007, she backed the DREAM Act, which would allow high school graduates and military volunteers who had illegally immigrated as children with their parents to become citizens. She also called for 300,000 additional visas for high-skill workers and for more Border Patrol agents.

In 2008, Hutchison authored an amicus curiae brief in *District of Columbia v. Heller*, the Washington gun control case, which was signed by Vice President Dick Cheney and several senators and House members. The U.S. Supreme Court came down on her side, ruling that the Washington, D.C., handgun ban violated the Second Amendment. On another legal issue, she supported the Democrats' bill extending the statute of limitations on court cases involving gender pay discrimination, though she sought unsuccessfully to put a higher burden of proof on plaintiffs.

Hutchison rose to the top minority slot on the Commerce panel after the indictment of Republican Sen. Ted Stevens of Alaska in July 2008. Before that, she had been the senior Republican on the Aviation Subcommittee, where she sponsored a 2000 law strengthening airport security that was being put into effect on September 11. She also worked with Democratic Chairman Jay Rockefeller of West Virginia and strongly supported federalization of airport security. Also with Rockefeller, she sought to add funding for upgrading the air-traffic-control system to the 2009 economic stimulus bill. In 2006, she supported the pension bill that gave Delta and Northwest, which had gone through bankruptcy, more time to fund their pensions. She also worked to repeal the Wright amendment, which barred many interstate flights from Dallas's Love Field, the home base of Southwest, while minimizing harm to American Airlines, which was based at Dallas-Forth Worth Airport. Hutchison has been a longtime supporter of the Amtrak system and of Amtrak lines in Texas. In 2005, when Bush's budget cut Amtrak funding, she objected: "We need to either commit to a national railroad or abandon the pretense of one. National or nothing."

Having grown up near what is now the Johnson Space Center, Hutchison is also a strong supporter of the manned space program. Before the February 2003 *Columbia* shuttle disaster, she warned of underfunding. She hailed the June 2005 Commerce Committee decision to keep the space shuttle flying past 2010, until the first crew exploration vehicle can be launched, which is slated for 2015. Hutchison has suggested including China in the space station.

On foreign policy, Hutchison has been mostly supportive of the Bush administration. In October 2006, she said there was "chaos" in Iraq and suggested that more consideration should be given to dividing Iraq into semi-autonomous regions. When President George W. Bush announced plans to restore order with a "surge" in troop strength in January 2007, she said, "It is critical that the initiative be given a chance to succeed. I respect the president for admitting mistakes, correcting the course." On the Appropriations Committee, Hutchison has shepherded along the Military Housing Privatization Initiative, through which the government hires private firms to build military housing. In 2004, she helped get $1.4 billion for housing at San Antonio's Fort Sam Houston.

Over the past few years, she has also had a hand in tax policy. In 2006, she worked successfully on legislation allowing taxpayers in Texas and other states with no state income taxes to continue to be able to deduct state sales taxes. She supported the 2001 Bush tax cut and advanced her own version that included a homemakers' Individual Retirement Account. She also focused on repealing the tax code's marriage penalty, which forces some married taxpayers to pay more than they would if they filed separately.

Junior Senator

John Cornyn (R)

Elected 2002, term expires 2014, 2nd term; b. Feb. 2, 1952, Houston; home, San Antonio; Trinity U., B.A. 1973, St. Mary's Law Schl., J.D. 1977, U. of VA, L.L.M. 1995; Church of Christ; married (Sandy); 2 children.

Elected Office: San Antonio dist. ct. judge, 1984–90; TX Sup. Ct., 1990–97; TX atty. gen., 1998–2002.

Professional Career: Practicing atty., 1977–84.

DC Office: 517 HSOB, 20510, 202-224-2934; Fax: 202-228-2856; Web site: cornyn.senate.gov.

State Offices: Austin, 512-469-6034; Dallas, 972-239-1310; Harlingen, 956-423-0162; Houston, 713-572-3337; Lubbock, 806-472-7533; San Antonio, 210-224-7485; Tyler, 903-593-0902.

Committees: *NRSC Chairman. Budget* (8th of 10 R). *Finance* (10th of 10 R): Energy, Natural Resources & Infrastructure; Health Care; Taxation, IRS Oversight & Long-Term Growth. *Judiciary* (6th of 7 R): Antitrust, Competition Policy & Consumer Rights; Constitution; Human Rights & the Law; Immigration, Refugees & Border Security (RMM); Terrorism & Homeland Security.

Group Ratings

	ADA	ACLU	AFS	LCV	ITIC	NTU	COC	ACU	CFG	FRC
2008	20	14	0	18	100	56	100	79	74	88
2007	15	—	0	0	—	79	80	96	88	—

National Journal Ratings

	2007 LIB	—	2007 CONS		2008 LIB	—	2008 CONS
Economic	9%	—	90%		16%	—	83%
Social	13%	—	86%		0%	—	79%
Foreign	0%	—	93%		21%	—	76%
Composite	9%	—	91%		17%	—	84%

Key Votes of the 110th Congress

1. Raise CAFE standards	N	5. Make English official language	Y	9. Withdraw troops 3/08	N
2. Expand SCHIP	N	6. Path to citizenship	N	10. Iran guard is terrorist group	Y
3. Cap greenhouse gases	*	7. Fetus is unborn child	Y	11. Increase missile defense $	Y
4. Bail out financial markets	Y	8. Prosecute hate crimes	N	12. Overhaul FISA	Y

Election Results

2008 general	John Cornyn (R)	4,337,469	(55%)	($16,454,518)
	Richard Noriega (D)	3,389,365	(43%)	($4,157,553)
	Yvonne Schick (Lib)	185,241	(2%)	($7,370)
2008 primary	John Cornyn (R)	997,216	(81%)	
	Larry Kilgore (R)	226,649	(19%)	

Prior Winning Percentages: 2002 (55%)

John Cornyn, a Republican, was elected to the Senate in 2002. He was born in Houston and spent much of his childhood in San Antonio. His father was an oral pathologist in the Air Force stationed in Japan, where Cornyn went to high school. After his father retired from the service, the family settled in San Antonio. Cornyn graduated from Trinity University and St. Mary's University Law School, both in San Antonio, in the 1970s. He practiced law for five years with a firm that defended doctors and insurance companies in medical malpractice cases. In 1984, he ran for district court judge on the Republican ticket in Bexar County and, at age 32, upset a strong favorite in the race. In 1990, Cornyn was elected to the state Supreme Court. In 1995, he wrote a 5-4 decision upholding the "Robin Hood" school finance system, in which property-wealthy school districts had to send money to property-poor districts. In 1997, he resigned from the court to run for attorney general, defeating two better-known opponents in the Republican primary. In the general election, he faced a grizzled veteran of Texas politics, Jim Mattox, a populist Democrat, a former U.S. House member from Dallas, and the second-place finisher to Ann Richards in the 1990 runoff for Texas governor. Cornyn won 54%-44%, becoming the first Republican attorney general in Texas since Reconstruction. He argued two cases before the U. S. Supreme Court, including the Santa Fe Independent School District's defense of reading the Lord's Prayer at football games (the Court nixed it).

When Republican Sen. Phil Gramm announced that he would not seek re-election in 2002, Cornyn got into the contest to succeed him. He had no serious opposition in the primary. Democrats nominated Dallas Mayor Ron Kirk, the son of the first black mailman in Austin, a teacher, and former aide to Democratic Sen. Lloyd Bentsen. He had been elected mayor of Dallas in 1995, and four years later, he was re-elected by a wide margin. In the primary, he overcame challenges from former U.S. Rep. Ken Bentsen of Houston, the senator's nephew, and Victor Morales, a track coach from suburban Dallas. Morales finished just narrowly ahead of Kirk in the first round of balloting, and Bentsen was eliminated. In the four weeks before the runoff, Kirk was endorsed by Bentsen and Houston Mayor Lee Brown. In the lower-turnout runoff, he won 60%-40%.

In the general election, Cornyn ran as a supporter of President George W. Bush. He called for making Bush's 2001 tax cuts permanent, for extending the research and development tax credit, and for raising Texas's share of gas-tax funds from 90.5 cents to 95 cents of each dollar of gas-tax revenues. He supported government vouchers for private school tuition, individual investment accounts as part of Social Security and color-blind standards for college and university admissions. Kirk took an opposite stand on most of the issues but portrayed himself as a moderate Democrat who would support Bush on many issues. Republicans ran ads linking him to New York Sen. Hillary Rodham Clinton and liberal out-of-state contributors. Eventually he spent $8.9 million—almost as much as Cornyn's $9.5 million.

Kirk campaigned with a sense of humor and considerable charm, making fun of his bald pate and answering—mindful of Texas mores—when asked whether he owned a gun, "I have a wife and two little girls. You figure it out." But he made some mistakes. He opposed the nomination to a federal judgeship of Texas Supreme Court Justice Priscilla Owen, something Republicans seized on in ads. He refused to disclose his income tax returns, except for allowing reporters one peek at his 2001 return. When Cornyn came out for a bill in the Texas Legislature requiring district attorneys to seek the death penalty for killers of law enforcement officials (the Austin district attorney had not sought the death penalty for the killer of a Travis County sheriff's deputy), Kirk said Cornyn was acting like he was running for district attorney—and then had to apologize abjectly to a convention of law enforcement officials a few days later. Meanwhile, Cornyn met with the deputy's widow. In San Antonio in September, Kirk said that Cornyn might not support military action in Iraq if the military forces were not "disproportionately ethnic [and] disproportionately minority." He said he supported military action only if it met with international approval. Four days later he apologized and he endorsed the Iraq war resolution in October.

Texas Democrats called their ticket of Kirk for senator and Tony Sanchez for governor the "Dream Team" and hoped it would draw a large turnout of African-Americans and Hispanics. Meanwhile, Republicans quietly registered thousands of new voters in the heavily Republican and fast-growing suburban counties around Dallas-Fort Worth, Houston, San Antonio and Austin. Polls showed the race close in the spring. Democrats operated on the assumption that Kirk had to win 85% of blacks, 65% of Hispanics and 35% of whites to win. He clearly achieved the first and probably achieved the second of those goals, but failed by a solid margin to achieve the third. Cornyn won 55%-43%—almost the same numbers as in his race for attorney general in 1998 and a fair reflection of basic party identification in Texas in recent years. Kirk carried historically Republican Dallas County 50%-49%. But Cornyn carried the entire Dallas-Fort Worth Metroplex 58%-41%. Cornyn also won metro Houston 55%-43% and the combined San Antonio and Austin metro areas 51%-47%. The border went 69%-29% for Kirk, a 148,000-vote margin. But rural Texas, much larger, went 62%-37% for Cornyn, a 346,000-vote margin. Kirk may have increased black turnout in Dallas, and Sanchez clearly increased Hispanic turnout in Laredo. But turnout was also up, from 25% to 52%, in the fast-growing counties around Dallas-Fort Worth, Houston, San Antonio and Austin, where Cornyn ran strong. He won the seat that dates to Sam Houston, who won it shortly after Texas was annexed in 1845, and later was occupied by Democrat Lyndon B. Johnson and Republican John Tower. Cornyn is also the first Texas senator to come from San Antonio, once the state's largest city.

In 2009, Cornyn assumed a high-profile role in the Senate GOP leadership as the new chairman of the National Republican Senatorial Committee, which will raise money and recruit candidates for 2010 contests. His chief competitor for the post, Republican Norm Coleman of Republican, was eliminated by his failure to win his own re-election race in Minnesota. (After protracted vote counting, Democrat Al Franken was declared the winner in June 2009.) Cornyn said he planned to adopt the strategy of Sen. Charles Schumer of New York, who as the head of the Senate Democrats' campaign committee in the 2006 and 2008 election seasons recruited candidates who would appeal to electorates in states that had not necessarily been friendly to Democrats in recent presidential contests. Cornyn sought to recruit U.S. Rep. Mike Castle in Delaware, former Gov. George Pataki in New York and Gov. Charlie Crist in Florida. "I probably couldn't get elected in places like the Northeast," Cornyn said. "We're going to have to find, as I think Chuck Schumer did, good candidates who can win in those states."

Cornyn has been an active member of the Judiciary Committee. In 2003 and 2004, he chaired the Constitution Subcommittee and held hearings on continuity of government, hostility to religious expression in the public square and same-sex marriage. He proposed a constitutional amendment to give each house of Congress the authority to decide how vacancies would be filled if one-quarter or more of its members were killed or incapacitated, which got less than 50 votes. He was a lead sponsor of the amendment to ban same-sex marriage, which got less than 50 votes. He also supported amendments to expand the rights of crime victims and to overturn the Ninth Circuit decision banning the phrase "one nation under God" in the Pledge of Allegiance. He cosponsored the class-action and bankruptcy bills opposed by trial lawyers but passed by the Senate and signed by Bush in 2005.

Cornyn supported Bush's judicial nominees against Democrats who continually delayed and opposed the president's selections. In 2005, he stirred some controversy when he asked "whether there may be some connection between the perception in some quarters on some occasions where judges are making political decisions yet are unaccountable to the public, that it builds up and builds up and builds up to the point where some people engage in violence." A few months later, in March 2006, Supreme Court Justice Sandra Day O'Connor spoke out "against those who would strong-arm the judiciary. It takes a lot of degeneration before a country falls into dictatorship, but we should avoid these ends by avoiding these beginnings" —a remark many took as a criticism of Cornyn's statement. It was "hyperbole, to say the least," Cornyn said. "There's no danger of dictatorship while people feel free to express their views." He took a lead role in seeking to confirm Bush appellate court appointees and urged colleagues to change the Senate rules to stop the Democratic filibusters. He was initially critical of the "Gang of 14," a bipartisan group of senators who ultimately succeeded in hammering out a compromise on the explosive issue of changing Senate rules to stop filibusters. He later said, "In retrospect, I have to concede they actually broke the logjam that allowed us to get some very good people confirmed."

In a split with the Bush administration in 2007, he criticized Attorney General Alberto Gonzales for his handling of the firings of U.S. attorneys and in August 2007 told the *Austin American-Statesman,* "The rest of it is really a matter of how he handled the inquiry, and I just think he has not handled that well." On other issues as well, Cornyn sought areas of compromise with Democrats on the committee. With Democrat Patrick Leahy of Vermont, he moved to strengthen the Freedom of Information Act, proposing a bill that would penalize federal agencies and employees if they failed to respond to requests in a timely manner. A bill establishing a commission to consider changes in FOIA was approved unanimously by the Senate in 2005. The bill was passed in the Senate again in 2007 and later by the House. In 2009, he worked with Leahy to get more funding for public corruption investigations and prosecutions.

When he was the ranking Republican on the Senate Ethics Committee, Cornyn proposed in 2008 more stringent disclosure of members' mortgages, and Democratic Chairman Barbara Boxer concurred. Under their leadership, the committee admonished Republican Larry Craig of Idaho after he was arrested in a homosexual sex sting at a Minneapolis airport and Republican Pete Domenici of New Mexico for his role in the attorneys general firings.

Cornyn's hometown of San Antonio is only 150 miles from Mexico, and he has taken an interest in the immigration reform debate in recent years. He is also the ranking Republican on Judiciary's Subcommittee on Immigration, Refugees and Border Security. One of Cornyn's first successful bills reduced from three years to one the waiting period for citizenship for legal aliens serving in the armed forces. He has opposed military patrols of the border and the building of a fence along most of its length, which he says would disrupt life in South Texas. In 2006, he voted for the 700-mile border fence pushed by House Republicans, though he questioned whether it would be a "practical use" of federal money. In spring 2007, as Arizona Republican Jon Kyl negotiated an immigration bill with Massachusetts Democrat Edward Kennedy, Cornyn took some part in the negotiations but skipped an unveiling of the bill's terms in May. Arizona Republican John McCain angrily accused him of raising arcane legal issues to scuttle the bill. Cornyn said of the talks, "I didn't so much walk away as got chased away." His amendment to bar illegal immigrants convicted of identity theft from legalization processes was defeated 51-46. From then on, he opposed the larger immigration bill.

Cornyn supported the Bush administration on the war in Iraq, including the president's 2007 troop surge aimed at restoring order in Iraq. He said, "We know that if things spiral out of control in Iraq, that if we decide to precipitously leave Iraq and it becomes a failed state, or if it becomes a killing field for ethnic cleansing, that we will more likely have to return at even greater loss of blood and treasure."

Cornyn began his campaign for re-election in 2008 with poll numbers showing he wasn't as well-known or popular as his fellow Republican Sen. Kay Bailey Hutchison of Texas. But through the summer of 2007, the Democrats' attempts to attract a well-known challenger failed. The Democratic nominee was Houston state Rep. Rick Noriega, who had served with the Texas Army National Guard in Afghanistan. He set a goal of raising $10 million but ultimately was able to raise only $4 million to Cornyn's $17 million. Polls pretty consistently showed Cornyn ahead, though not by wide margins, and neither national party invested in the contest. Cornyn won 55%-43%, the same split as in 2002. He won 36% of the Hispanic vote, an improvement over 2002. He carried 223 of the state's 254 counties, running behind only in the Rio Grande Valley and in the counties with the central cities of Houston, Dallas, Austin and San Antonio. He carried the Dallas-Fort Worth Metroplex 55%-43% and metro Houston 52%-46%.

FIRST DISTRICT

Louie Gohmert (R)

Elected 2004, 3rd term; b. Aug. 18, 1953, Pittsburg; home, Tyler; TX A&M U., B.A. 1975, Baylor U. Law Schl., J.D. 1977; Baptist; married (Kathy); 3 children.

Military Career: Army, 1978–82.

Elected Office: Smith Cnty. Dist. Ct. judge, 1992–2002.

Professional Career: Practicing atty., 1982–92; Chief justice, TX 12th Ct. of Appeals, 2002–03.

DC Office: 511 CHOB, 20515; 202-225-3035; Fax: 202-226-1230; Web site: www.gohmert.house.gov.

State Offices: Longview, 903-236-8597; Lufkin, 936-632-3180; Marshall, 903-938-8386; Nacogdoches, 936-715-9514; Tyler, 903-561-6349.

Committees: *Judiciary* (11th of 16 R): Constitution, Civil Rights & Civil Liberties; Crime, Terrorism & Homeland Security (RMM). *Natural Resources* (8th of 20 R): Energy & Mineral Resources; National Parks, Forests & Public Lands. *Small Business* (6th of 12 R): Investigations & Oversight.

Group Ratings

	ADA	ACLU	AFS	LCV	ITIC	NTU	COC	ACU	CFG	FRC
2008	10	10	14	8	43	69	75	96	83	94
2007	10	—	10	0	—	81	80	100	83	—

National Journal Ratings

	2007 LIB	—	2007 CONS		2008 LIB	—	2008 CONS
Economic	15%	—	85%		19%	—	81%
Social	0%	—	91%		16%	—	84%
Foreign	0%	—	72%		19%	—	79%
Composite	11%	—	89%		18%	—	82%

Key Votes of the 110th Congress

1. Increase minimum wage	N	5. Share immigration data	Y	9. Withdraw troops 8/08	N
2. Expand SCHIP	N	6. Foreign aid abortion ban	Y	10. No operations in Iran	N
3. Raise CAFE standards	N	7. Ban gay bias in workplace	N	11. Free trade with Peru	Y
4. Bail out financial markets	N	8. Repeal D.C. gun law	Y	12. Overhaul FISA	*

Election Results

2008 general	Louie Gohmert (R)	189,012	(88%)	($834,732)
	Roger Owen (I)	26,814	(12%)	
2008 primary	Louie Gohmert (R)	unopposed		

Prior Winning Percentages: 2006 (68%); 2004 (61%)

Population		Race/Ethnicity		Work	
Pop. 2007:	685,144	White:	67.8%	Private:	78.9%
Change since 2000:	Up 5.1%	Black:	17.8%	Government:	12.8%
Urban:	50.9%	Hispanic:	12.3%	Self-employed:	8.0%
Rural:	49.1%	Asian:	0.7%	Blue collar:	29.8%
Area size:	8,916 sq. mi.	Native Am.:	0.4%	White collar:	52.4%
		Hawaiian:	0.0%	Khaki collar:	0.0%
Age		Two+ races:	1.0%	Other:	17.7%
Median age:	35.8 yrs.	*Ancestry*		Median income:	$39,332
More than 65 yrs:	14.3%	USA:	13.3%	Median home value:	$86,900
Less than 18 yrs:	25.2%	Irish:	10.1%	Poverty:	17.0%
Education		English:	9.2%	**Military Veterans**	
H.S. grad:	81.0%			% of Pop:	11.3%
College grad:	18.8%				
Grad degree:	6.2%				

The gently rolling land of East Texas was settled by Tennessee farmers in the years before the Civil War. It sits at the western edge of Scots-Irish America, a swath of land that starts in the Appalachian ridge and is inhabited by a combative, honor-bound and highly religious populace. A hundred years ago, this was one of the poorest parts of America, where farmers scratched a living off the land and hoped for good weather and good prices in the marketplace.

2008 Presidential Vote		
McCain (R)	184,560	(69%)
Obama (D)	81,749	(31%)
2004 Presidential Vote		
Bush (R)	178,409	(69%)
Kerry (D)	78,609	(31%)
Cook Partisan Voting Index:		R+21

When a peach blight in the early 20th century wiped out much of the local fruit industry, many farmers turned to growing roses, which proved ideally suited to the climate and soil of the area. By the 1940s, more than half the nation's rose bushes were grown within 10 miles of Tyler, which has become known for its annual Texas Rose Festival and the East Texas State Fair. Longview, which in the 1870s was the western terminus of the Southern Pacific Railroad, became a trading center for wagon trains and local cotton growers and timber cutters. In 1943, the Big Inch pipeline began sending millions of barrels of crude oil from the "Black Giant" oil field near Longview—the largest ever in the state—to the East for refining. Since then, the Longview area has become an industrial center for earth-moving equipment and chemicals. A giant U.S. Steel pipe plant has been a mainstay in the community since the 1950s, but in April 2009, the company idled the plant and fired most of its workforce. Marshall was the hometown of the late Lady Bird Johnson. The fields and woodlands around Nacogdoches—the oldest city in Texas—have the distinction as the site where debris from the Space Shuttle Columbia fell in February 2003. An organized search by 25,000 people recovered more than 84,000 pieces—38% of the shuttle.

The 1st Congressional District of Texas, covering the heart of East Texas, is made up of 12 counties, the most populous being Tyler's Smith County and Longview's Gregg County. East Texas is ancestrally Democratic, a region that responded to the populist rhetoric of presidential candidate William Jennings Bryan in the 1890s and President Franklin D. Roosevelt in the 1930s and 1940s. But Republicans began making inroads in Tyler and Longview in the 1950s and the GOP eventually gained dominance in the region. When Republican George H. W. Bush ran for the Senate against Democratic Sen. Lloyd Bentsen in 1970, East Texas was solidly Democratic. By the time Republican George W. Bush ran for reelection as governor in 1998, it was solidly Republican. Still, Democratic congressmen held onto the district until the 2003 redistricting, masterminded by former Republican House Majority Leader Tom DeLay of Texas to give the GOP a strong advantage in the state. Counties that knew their Democratic incumbent were removed, and replaced by heavily Republican Smith and Gregg counties. In 2008, Republican presidential candidate John McCain carried the district with 69% of the vote.

The congressman from the 1st District is Louie Gohmert, a Republican first elected in 2004. Gohmert *(GO-mert)* grew up in Mount Pleasant, and got an Army scholarship at Texas A&M University, where he was class president. He went on get a law degree from Baylor University, and then served as a captain in the Army. He practiced law in Tyler and spent a decade as a district court judge. Republican Gov. Rick Perry named him chief justice of the Texas Appellate Court in 2002. While on the bench, Gohmert earned a reputation as a tough law-and-order judge with a knack for attracting attention. In 1996, he ordered an HIV-positive convicted car thief, as a condition of probation, to notify future sexual partners of his HIV status and to obtain written consent from them before engaging in sexual activity. After the 2003 redistricting, Gohmert was one of six Republicans who got into the primary to challenge four-term Democratic Rep. Max Sandlin, who had a moderate voting record but was a close ally of liberal Democratic Minority Leader Nancy Pelosi. Gohmert led in the primary with 42% of the vote to 30% for lawyer John Graves. In the month-long runoff campaign, few differences separated the two conservatives. Gohmert prevailed 57%-43%. Graves carried nine of the 13 counties, but Gohmert won 77% of the vote in his home base of Smith County, where half the votes were cast.

In the general election, Gohmert linked Sandlin to the national Democratic Party and their 2004 presidential nominee, John Kerry. In one debate, Gohmert repeatedly asked Sandlin about his choice for president; Sandlin sidestepped the question. Gohmert frequently mentioned his strong support for President Bush and, unlike Sandlin, attended his party's national convention. Sandlin criticized Gohmert for his support from DeLay. The result wasn't close. Gohmert won 61%-38%, with 79% in Smith County and 64% in Gregg County.

In the House, Gohmert has a mostly conservative voting record. His legislative work has been mostly on the Judiciary Committee. When the House in 2006 considered a bill to extend the Voting Rights Act, which allows extensive federal oversight of elections in states with histories of minority vote suppression, Gohmert tried to amend it to apply to every state. He said Southern states were unfairly targeted in the enforcement of the law. Gohmert voted for the final version. In 2005, the House passed his bill to upgrade security measures in courthouses to protect judges, prosecutors and witnesses, and to add penalties for carrying weapons in a courthouse. On the Natural Resources Committee, his legislation to establish a memorial to the victims of the space shuttle *Columbia* was enacted as part of a public lands bill in 2008. In January 2009, he proposed a two-month national tax holiday as an alternative to the Democrats' economic stimulus bill.

Gohmert has been criticized for making comments of questionable judgment or taste. He drew fury from Jewish members of Congress when, during a 2007 debate on a bill prohibiting hiring discrimination in government-funded charitable organizations, he argued that religious groups should be allowed to hire employees of their own faith, otherwise Jewish organizations would be forced to hire Nazis. Later that year, he took, without asking, a sign in front of the office of Rep. Heath Shuler, D-N.C., that showed the size of the national debt. Gohmert said he needed the sign to make a point during a debate on the House floor. Shuler called him a "gutless" thief.

SECOND DISTRICT

Ted Poe (R)

Elected 2004, 3rd term; b. Sept. 10, 1948, Temple; home, Humble; Abilene Christian U., B.A. 1970, U. of Houston, J.D. 1973; Church of Christ; married (Carol).

Military Career: Air Force Reserve, 1970–76.

Elected Office: Harris Cnty. judge, 1981–2003.

Professional Career: Asst. dist. atty., 1973–81.

DC Office: 430 CHOB, 20515, 202-225-6565; Fax: 202-225-5547; Web site: poe.house.gov.

State Offices: Beaumont, 409-212-1997; Kingwood, 281-446-0242.

Committees: *Foreign Affairs* (17th of 19 R): Europe; International Organizations, Human Rights & Oversight; Terrorism, Nonproliferation & Trade. *Judiciary* (13th of 16 R): Crime, Terrorism & Homeland Security; Immigration, Citizenship, Border Security & International Law.

Group Ratings

	ADA	ACLU	AFS	LCV	ITIC	NTU	COC	ACU	CFG	FRC
2008	10	9	0	0	17	78	56	96	86	100
2007	5	—	18	5	—	79	72	96	85	—

National Journal Ratings

	2007 LIB	—	2007 CONS		2008 LIB	—	2008 CONS
Economic	26%	—	74%		12%	—	88%
Social	0%	—	91%		0%	—	91%
Foreign	31%	—	69%		19%	—	79%
Composite	21%	—	80%		12%	—	88%

Key Votes of the 110th Congress

1. Increase minimum wage	Y	5. Share immigration data	Y	9. Withdraw troops 8/08	N
2. Expand SCHIP	*	6. Foreign aid abortion ban	Y	10. No operations in Iran	N
3. Raise CAFE standards	N	7. Ban gay bias in workplace	N	11. Free trade with Peru	*
4. Bail out financial markets	N	8. Repeal D.C. gun law	Y	12. Overhaul FISA	Y

Election Results

2008 general	Ted Poe (R)	175,101	(89%)	($391,238)
	Craig Wolfe (Lib)	21,813	(11%)	
2008 primary	Ted Poe (R)	unopposed		

Prior Winning Percentages: 2006 (66%); 2004 (56%)

Population		Race/Ethnicity		Work	
Pop. 2007:	741,520	White:	57.2%	Private:	80.4%
Change since 2000:	Up 13.8%	Black:	20.6%	Government:	13.6%
Urban:	89.5%	Hispanic:	17.5%	Self-employed:	5.7%
Rural:	10.5%	Asian:	3.3%	Blue collar:	24.3%
Area size:	2,180 sq. mi.	Native Am.:	0.3%	White collar:	61.0%
Age		Hawaiian:	0.0%	Khaki collar:	0.1%
Median age:	35.7 yrs.	Two+ races:	0.8%	Other:	14.6%
More than 65 yrs:	10.1%	*Ancestry*		Median income:	$54,253
Less than 18 yrs:	26.9%	German:	10.0%	Median home value:	$115,800
Education		Irish:	7.6%	Poverty:	11.8%
H.S. grad:	83.8%	USA:	7.2%	**Military Veterans**	
College grad:	24.0%			% of Pop:	10.3%
Grad degree:	7.4%				

The spongy land of the Texas Gulf Coast, where French explorer Robert de La Salle and Spanish conquistador Bernardo de Galvez dreamed of thriving settlements, remained mostly unsettled until well into the 19th century. When oil was found at the Spindletop field near Beaumont in 1901, the area all around it boomed, first with oil exploration, then petroleum refining, and then petrochemical production. The rig workers and mechanical engineers they attracted have given a kind of permanent roughneck air to the region. But oil drilling has declined in this area. From 1994 to 2004, annual production in East Texas from the Red River to the Gulf of Mexico dropped from 90.5 million barrels to 43.5 million barrels. Hurricanes Gustav and Ike in 2008 shut down oil pipelines for months and toppled some platforms, but some local refineries have been expanding and adding jobs thanks to high oil prices.

2008 Presidential Vote		
McCain (R)	159,165	(60%)
Obama (D)	105,745	(40%)
2004 Presidential Vote		
Bush (R)	160,365	(63%)
Kerry (D)	92,842	(37%)
Cook Partisan Voting Index:	R + 13	

The 2nd Congressional District of Texas occupies much of this territory. Nearly 40% of its people live in and around the highly polluted "Golden Triangle" industrial area that includes Beaumont and Port Arthur. This is still very much oil country, and one of the few places in Texas where labor unions have any strength. The Humble oil field was once the largest in Texas and the local Humble Oil and Refining Company is now known as Exxon. Beaumont is the home of several trial lawyers who have become billionaires through asbestos and tobacco cases. Local juries are known for their willingness to bring in large verdicts against big corporations. Port Arthur was the home of 1960s blues and rock singer Janis Joplin. These cities increasingly are in the shadow of Houston, and the majority of the people in the district live in the city's north and east suburbs in Harris County, where oil is an important part of the local economy but hardly all of it. The district grew 14% from 2000 to 2007, largely because of minorities: The African-American population has increased to 21% and Hispanics are now 18% of the population of the district. In 2008, Republican presidential nominee John McCain got 60% of the vote in this district.

The congressman from the 2nd District is Ted Poe, a Republican first elected in 2004. A former prosecutor who served 22 years as a Houston-area district court judge, Poe became a publicity magnet and a judicial celebrity for meting out humiliating "Poe-tic justice" punishments to criminals. He required murderers to hang pictures of their victims in their prison cells and ordered drunken drivers and shoplifters to stand at the entrances to taverns and stores carrying signs publicizing their offenses. He also gained national recognition as a legal commentator on national television. In 2003, Poe stepped down as a judge to run for Congress. In a six-candidate Republican primary, Poe's high name recognition and bench experience helped him win with 61% of the vote.

In the general election, Poe faced incumbent Democratic Rep. Nick Lampson, who was running in largely unfamiliar territory due to the 2003 Republican-engineered redistricting of Texas. Lampson had a moderate voting record, a low-key style and was a big booster of NASA. At first it was not clear whether Poe would be able to capitalize on the favorable redistricting. National Republicans fretted about his fundraising and his seemingly complacent campaign. Lampson also outspent Poe nearly 2-to-1. But on Election Day, the new district's solid Republican bent was too much for the Democrat to overcome. Lampson led 68%-31% in Jefferson County, the area he had previously represented and where 36% of votes were cast. But Poe won 70%-28% in Harris County, where 58% of the votes were cast. Overall, Poe won 56%-43%.

In the House, Poe has had a relatively moderate voting record for a Republican from Texas. As a member of the Transportation and Infrastructure Committee in the 110th Congress (2007–08), he sought to reduce local noise from Houston's international airport, and worked to restore funding to maintain and dredge the Sabine-Neches Waterway in his district. He joined a bipartisan group that in 2007 passed a House amendment to block the Bush administration from easing requirements for foreign ownership of U.S. airlines.

After Hurricanes Katrina and Rita led to a large migration of refugees to Texas in 2005, Poe filed legislation to create a national registry of convicted child molesters who have been released from prison to make it easier to identify newcomers who were criminals. He also has been a leader of the Immigration Reform Caucus, where he sought tighter enforcement at the border with Mexico. He successfully lobbied President George W. Bush to commute the prison terms of two border agents who were convicted for wounding a drug smuggler. He joined Democrats and libertarian Republicans in 2005 to restrict access to library records under the USA Patriot Act.

He often ends speeches on the House floor with his trademark, "And that's just the way it is." But he has also drawn negative attention for some of his remarks. He was criticized for a floor speech in which he quoted Nathan Bedford Forest, an early Ku Klux Klan leader. Arguing for more money for U.S. troops in Iraq, Poe said, "Nathan Bedford Forest, successful Confederate general, said it best about winning and victory and the means to do so. He said, 'Get there firstest with the mostest.' Congress needs to send the generals the mostest."

Poe has not been seriously challenged for re-election.

THIRD DISTRICT

Sam Johnson (R)

Elected May 1991, 9th full term; b. Oct. 11, 1930, San Antonio; home, Dallas; S. Methodist U., B.B.A. 1951, George Washington U., M.S. 1974; Methodist; married (Shirley); 3 children.

Military Career: Air Force, 1950–79 (Korea & Vietnam).

Elected Office: TX House of Reps., 1984–91.

Professional Career: Home builder.

DC Office: 1211 LHOB, 20515, 202-225-4201; Fax: 202-225-1485; Web site: www.samjohnson.house.gov.

State Offices: Richardson, 972-470-0892.

Committees: *Ways & Means* (3rd of 15 R): Health; Social Security (RMM).

Group Ratings

	ADA	ACLU	AFS	LCV	ITIC	NTU	COC	ACU	CFG	FRC
2008	0	22	0	8	50	86	83	96	93	94
2007	0	—	0	5	—	89	79	100	94	—

National Journal Ratings

	2007 LIB	—	2007 CONS		2008 LIB	—	2008 CONS
Economic	8%	—	91%		15%	—	84%
Social	0%	—	91%		16%	—	82%
Foreign	0%	—	72%		0%	—	95%
Composite	9%	—	91%		12%	—	88%

Key Votes of the 110th Congress

1. Increase minimum wage	N	5. Share immigration data	Y	9. Withdraw troops 8/08	N
2. Expand SCHIP	N	6. Foreign aid abortion ban	Y	10. No operations in Iran	N
3. Raise CAFE standards	N	7. Ban gay bias in workplace	N	11. Free trade with Peru	Y
4. Bail out financial markets	N	8. Repeal D.C. gun law	Y	12. Overhaul FISA	Y

Election Results

2008 general	Sam Johnson (R)	170,742	(60%)	($1,569,813)
	Tom Daley (D)	108,693	(38%)	($73,653)
	Christopher Claytor (Lib)	6,348	(2%)	
2008 primary	Sam Johnson (R)	36,050	(87%)	
	Harry Pierce (R)	3,466	(8%)	

Prior Winning Percentages: 2006 (63%); 2004 (86%); 2002 (74%); 2000 (72%); 1998 (91%); 1996 (73%); 1994 (91%); 1992 (86%); 1991 (53%)

Population		Race/Ethnicity		Work	
Pop. 2007:	808,963	White:	55.9%	Private:	85.3%
Change since 2000:	Up 24.1%	Black:	10.9%	Government:	8.3%
Urban:	99.0%	Hispanic:	21.1%	Self-employed:	6.2%
Rural:	1.0%	Asian:	10.4%	Blue collar:	16.4%
Area size:	266 sq. mi.	Native Am.:	0.3%	White collar:	70.6%
		Hawaiian:	0.0%	Khaki collar:	0.0%
Age		Two+ races:	1.2%	Other:	13.0%
Median age:	32.9 yrs.			Median income:	$66,228
More than 65 yrs:	6.5%	*Ancestry*		Median home value:	$177,600
Less than 18 yrs:	28.6%	German:	11.0%	Poverty:	9.7%
		Irish:	7.9%		
Education		English:	7.7%	**Military Veterans**	
H.S. grad:	86.5%			% of Pop:	7.4%
College grad:	41.2%				
Grad degree:	13.6%				

North Dallas, the putative location of the 1980s television program "Dallas," conjures up a certain image of sudden affluence and insolent disdain for those who don't have it and of shady dealings and immoral trysts in an environment of outward embrace of traditional values. The caricature doesn't tell the whole story. Dallas got its start as a railroad junction and cotton-shipping center. In recent decades, it has been at the cutting edge of high-technology, and is the home of Texas Instruments,

2008 Presidential Vote		
McCain (R)	171,119	(57%)
Obama (D)	124,027	(42%)
2004 Presidential Vote		
Bush (R)	174,711	(67%)
Kerry (D)	86,718	(33%)
Cook Partisan Voting Index:	R + 14	

where an integrated circuit on a silicon chip was invented in 1958, and of Electronic Data Systems, the source of former independent presidential candidate Ross Perot's fortune. The high-tech, telecommunications and defense businesses are less robust than in the 1980s, but the Dallas-Fort Worth Metroplex continues to thrive. Growth has come from corporate headquarters relocated from less business-friendly precincts, from small businesses, and from companies making money trading with Mexico. Dallas is the nation's chief beneficiary of the North America Free Trade Agreement. Health care and universities have created many jobs.

Dallas's growth has extended far into the countryside. The home of the city's old elite may still be in the mansion-lined streets of Highland Park, only a few miles north of downtown, but Dallas's business and professional classes have moved farther in Dallas County and up into Collin County's scrub-covered hills. Back in 1960, Collin County was mostly rural, still part of the district that sent Democratic Speaker Sam Rayburn to the House. It had 41,000 people then, and actually lost population in the 1950s. Then the Dallas-Fort Worth Metroplex exploded. Collin County's population grew from 66,000 in 1970 to 730,000 in 2007. It is now the third-wealthiest and the seventh-largest county in Texas. The biggest city here is Plano, with 261,000 people. This former farming community is now the corporate headquarters of companies such as EDS, which was purchased by Hewlett-Packard in 2008, but remained in Plano, and also Dr. Pepper and J.C. Penney. This edge city is the state's ninth-largest site of mega-mansion subdivisions and the new face of successful Texas. The fastest growth is in the old county seat of McKinney; its population has more than doubled since 2000, to 121,000. Politically, Collin County has been very Republican, even more Republican than Dallas County ever was.

The 3rd Congressional District of Texas includes most of Collin County and centers on Plano. It also covers the northeastern corner of Dallas County, beyond the LBJ Freeway, including much of Rowlett and Garland. In 2008, Republican presidential candidate John McCain got 60% of the vote in the Collin County portion of the district, and he trailed Democratic candidate Barack Obama by 221 votes in Dallas County, which cast 27% of the total. Overall, McCain led 57%-42%, a big drop from President George W. Bush's 70%-30% win in 2000.

The congressman from the 3rd District is Sam Johnson, a Republican first elected in 1991. Johnson grew up in Dallas and graduated from Southern Methodist University and George Washington University. He was a director of the Air Force Fighter Weapons (Top Gun) School, and as a fighter pilot, flew 87 combat missions during the wars in Korea and Vietnam. After his F-4 was shot down over North Vietnam during his 25th mission, he was imprisoned from 1966 to 1973 in the "Hanoi Hilton," where he spent 42 months in solitary confinement. He weighed 120 pounds on his release, and was left with a slight stoop in his walk and a disfigured hand. On his return, Johnson started a homebuilding company and was elected to the Texas House in 1984. He was elected to Congress in a 1991 special election, after Republican Steve Bartlett resigned to become mayor of Dallas. Johnson ran second in the primary, behind former Peace Corps director Tom Pauken. In the runoff, he emphasized his war record and won 53%-47% over Pauken; he won without difficulty in the general election.

Johnson has one of the most conservative voting records in the House. He was a founder of the Conservative Action Team, now known as the Republican Study Committee, which has pressed Republican leaders to support goals ranging from a balanced budget amendment to shutting down the National Endowment for the Arts. His chief source of concern is taxation. Every two years, he offers a constitutional amendment to repeal the 16th Amendment, which authorized the federal income tax. On the Ways and Means Committee, where he is the third-most senior Republican, Johnson sponsored the successful repeal in 2000 of the earnings limit for Social Security recipients. He was a leading proponent of pension reform that was enacted in 2006, and in 2007 he introduced a bill to encourage small businesses to join forces to purchase health insurance at lower costs. In 2008, he introduced a bill to repeal the Internal Revenue Service's requirement that people keep detailed records of their business cellular phone use in order to claim them as tax deductions. That year, he sponsored a bill to increase tax deductions for electronic medical records equipment.

Johnson has also focused on military issues. He helped to enact the Military Family Tax Relief Act of 2003, which doubled the death benefit for families of active members of the military who pass away and also reduced taxes for those families. Johnson has been a defender of the F-22 fighter jet, partly produced at the Lockheed Martin plant in Fort Worth near his district. Johnson gained national attention in February 2007 when he spoke emotionally on the House floor against a plan by Democratic Speaker Nancy Pelosi to set a timetable to withdraw from Iraq. Invoking his memories of Vietnam, he said, "I know what it's like to be far from home and hear that your country and your Congress don't care about you. Our troops stand up for us every minute of every day. We must stand up for them in Congress." Even though he and McCain, who was also a Vietnam prisoner of war, shared a cell for 18 months, they have had a chilly political relationship. Johnson strongly backed Bush in the 2000 primaries, stating that McCain "cannot hold a candle to George Bush." And in 2008, he did not endorse McCain until late February, after McCain had wrapped up the nomination. During the 2004 presidential campaign, Johnson was an outspoken critic of John Kerry, whom he called "Hanoi John" on the House floor, a reference to Kerry's active opposition to the war once he returned from service in Vietnam.

In 2008, Johnson was reelected with 60% of the vote against a poorly financed foe. This was his smallest share of the vote since his first win. Both Johnson and Republican Rep. Ralph Hall of the adjacent 4th district will be in their 80s by the 2010 election, and changes in representation and district boundaries in the North Texas suburbs seem imminent.

FOURTH DISTRICT

Ralph Hall (R)

Elected 1980, 15th term; b. May 3, 1923, Fate; home, Rockwall; U. of TX, TX Christian U., S. Methodist U., LL.B. 1951; United Methodist; widowed; 3 children.

Military Career: Navy, 1942–45 (WWII).

Elected Office: Rockwall Cnty. judge, 1950–62; TX Senate, 1962–72.

Professional Career: Practicing atty., 1951–80; Pres. & CEO, TX Aluminum Corp., 1967–68; Spec. cnsl., Howmet Corp., 1970–74.

DC Office: 2405 RHOB, 20515, 202-225-6673; Fax: 202-225-3332; Web site: www.house.gov/ralphhall.

State Offices: McKinney, 214-726-9949; New Boston, 903-628-8309; Rockwall, 972-771-9118; Sherman, 903-892-1112; Sulphur Springs, 903-885-8138; Texarkana, 903-794-4445.

Committees: *Energy & Commerce* (2nd of 23 R): Energy & Environment; Health. *Science & Technology* (RMM of 17 R).

Group Ratings

	ADA	ACLU	AFS	LCV	ITIC	NTU	COC	ACU	CFG	FRC
2008	30	18	43	0	43	66	83	84	82	94
2007	10	—	0	0	—	74	90	96	83	—

National Journal Ratings

	2007 LIB	—	2007 CONS	2008 LIB	—	2008 CONS
Economic	26%	—	74%	32%	—	68%
Social	0%	—	91%	16%	—	82%
Foreign	38%	—	62%	0%	—	95%
Composite	23%	—	77%	17%	—	83%

Key Votes of the 110th Congress

1. Increase minimum wage	N	5. Share immigration data	Y	9. Withdraw troops 8/08	N
2. Expand SCHIP	N	6. Foreign aid abortion ban	Y	10. No operations in Iran	N
3. Raise CAFE standards	N	7. Ban gay bias in workplace	N	11. Free trade with Peru	Y
4. Bail out financial markets	N	8. Repeal D.C. gun law	Y	12. Overhaul FISA	Y

Election Results

2008 general	Ralph Hall (R)	206,906	(69%)	($939,674)
	Glenn Melancon (D)	88,067	(29%)	($83,243)
2008 primary	Ralph Hall (R)	41,764	(73%)	
	Kathy Seei (R)	5,835	(10%)	
	Gene Christensen (R)	5,492	(10%)	
	Kevin George (R)	2,965	(5%)	

Prior Winning Percentages: 2006 (64%); 2004 (68%); 2002 (58%); 2000 (60%); 1998 (58%); 1996 (64%); 1994 (59%); 1992 (58%); 1990 (100%); 1988 (66%); 1986 (72%); 1984 (58%); 1982 (74%); 1980 (52%)

Population		Race/Ethnicity		Work	
Pop. 2007:	770,849	White:	74.9%	Private:	77.5%
Change since 2000:	Up 18.3%	Black:	10.0%	Government:	14.7%
Urban:	49.6%	Hispanic:	11.3%	Self-employed:	7.5%
Rural:	50.4%	Asian:	1.6%	Blue collar:	25.4%
Area size:	9,839 sq. mi.	Native Am.:	0.7%	White collar:	57.8%
		Hawaiian:	0.1%	Khaki collar:	0.1%
Age		Two+ races:	1.5%	Other:	16.7%
Median age:	35.5 yrs.			Median income:	$48,804
More than 65 yrs:	12.4%	*Ancestry*		Median home value:	$107,900
Less than 18 yrs:	26.1%	German:	11.1%	Poverty:	12.7%
		Irish:	11.0%		
Education		USA:	9.6%	**Military Veterans**	
H.S. grad:	82.9%			% of Pop:	12.2%
College grad:	21.3%				
Grad degree:	6.5%				

The Red River Valley is hardscrabble farm country along an unnavigable river. First settled in the 1830s, in the days of the Texas Republic, many counties here reached their population peak around 1900, when a large extended farm family worked every 160 acres. It includes towns like Denison, which was the birthplace of Dwight Eisenhower and has become a manufacturing center, and Sherman, which was the site of a major race riot in 1930 when a black farm worker accused of rape was trap-

2008 Presidential Vote
McCain (R)	213,967	(69%)
Obama (D)	93,439	(30%)

2004 Presidential Vote
Bush (R)	192,926	(70%)
Kerry (D)	81,269	(30%)

Cook Partisan Voting Index: R + 21

ped in the courthouse after an angry white mob set it on fire. To the east is Texarkana, noteworthy because its neat grid streets cross the Texas-Arkansas state line, which is straddled by the city's downtown post office. This small city and its hinterland produced two presidential candidates in the 1990s: Ross Perot grew up in Texarkana, while Bill Clinton's boyhood home of Hope, Ark., is 30 miles east. This part of Texas sent Democrat Sam Rayburn to Congress in 1912. He was the powerful House speaker from 1940 until his death in 1961, except for two terms when Republicans had the majority. The Red River Valley was one of the strongest Democratic parts of the country, with a sentimental regard for Confederate veterans and a seething hatred of Wall Street bankers. This was Rayburn's politics, and he arguably was the most skillful lawmaker of the 20th century. He helped write the securities laws that for 75 years provided the basis for confidence in American securities markets. Today, Rayburn's politics has almost completely vanished from the area. The cause of the Confederacy has been left behind, populist suspicion of Wall Street has been replaced by active brokerage accounts and allegiance to the Democratic Party is a thing of the past.

The 4th Congressional District of Texas is the lineal descendant of the seat that Rayburn held, and still includes his hometown of Bonham in Fannin County, which houses a Rayburn museum. But it is quite a different district. In Rayburn's time it was a farm district, separate and distinct from citified Dallas. Today, it still has its farm counties, but they are only a short hop on the interstate from the Dallas-Fort Worth Metroplex, and nearly half the district's people live in the metropolitan area. The counties at the edge of the Metroplex, Collin and Rockwall, are among the fastest-growing in the country; with 71% growth from 2000 to 2007. Rockwall ranked third among the fastest-growing counties in the nation. The two counties are home now to upwardly-mobile families, far more trusting of free markets than of government regulation, and more than 2-to-1 are Republican. In 1940, the year Rayburn became speaker, his district voted 90% for Franklin D. Roosevelt. In 2008, the 4th District voted 69% for Republican presidential nominee John McCain.

The congressman from the 4th District is Ralph Hall, who was born in 1923 and first elected in 1980. He turned 86 in 2009 and is the oldest member of the House; he is also the dean of the Texas delegation in Congress. Hall grew up in Rockwall County, served in the Navy during World War II as a lieutenant and aircraft carrier pilot, and had a 30-year career in local politics and business before coming to Washington. He got his law degree from Southern Methodist University, was a county judge in the 1950s, and from 1962 to 1972, served in the Texas Senate. In 1980, he was elected to the House as a Democrat. His evolution to the Republican Party was a long time in gestation. He supported just about everything in the GOP's Contract with America policy agenda in 1995 and was one of only five House Democrats who voted to impeach President Bill Clinton. He voted for Bush administration policies on taxes, trade and foreign policy. (But Hall is not a pure free marketer. He voted against the North American Free Trade Agreement.) During the 2002 campaign, he promised to vote for Republican Speaker Dennis Hastert if his vote decided which party would control the House. And in January 2003, he voted "present" rather than vote for liberal Democrat Nancy Pelosi for speaker, because, he said, "she just don't think like we do."

Republicans restlessly waited for years for Hall to join them. When he failed to switch after the 2001 redistricting, local and national Republicans expressed interest in a serious challenge to Hall. But they backed off after Hall met with President George W. Bush at the White House and the president strongly opposed a challenge. In March 2003, Hall was the only Democrat to vote for the Republican budget, which barely passed. Bush called to thank him. "I didn't want him to have a setback in Washington, D.C., when he's working his heart out two oceans away to win a war," Hall said. The 2003 redistricting finally convinced Hall to change parties. With Republican candidates lined up to run against him, he switched parties on January 2, 2004, the final day for filing. He said that his Democratic Party affiliation was limiting his ability to get appropriations for his district. And so Hall moved from being the most conservative Democrat in the House to a relatively centrist Republican.

When he joined their side, Republicans rewarded him with the chairmanship of the Energy and Air Quality Subcommittee of the powerful Energy and Commerce Committee, an attractive perk for a Texan. Hall helped to enact the energy bill of 2005, and later fought Democratic proposals to raise taxes on oil companies. When Republicans lost the majority in 2007, Hall became the ranking Republican of a full committee, the Science and Technology Committee. He has collaborated with Chairman Bart Gordon, D-Tenn., on the $20 billion reauthorization of NASA programs in 2008 and on energy research and development.

Party-switching has played well at home. With support from Bush and then-Republican House Speaker Dennis Hastert, Hall won 77% against two opponents in the Republican primary in 2004 and went on to win in the general, 68%-30%, his largest margin in more than a decade. The *Dallas Morning News* was less impressed, urging Hall to retire. He has won the subsequent elections with over 60% of the vote. When Hall retires, his son, Rockwall County District Judge Brett Hall, a Republican, is said to be interested in running for the seat.

FIFTH DISTRICT

Jeb Hensarling (R)

Elected 2002, 4th term; b. May 29, 1957, Stephenville; home, Dallas; TX A&M U., B.A. 1979, U. of TX, J.D. 1982; Christian; married (Melissa); 2 children.

Professional Career: Practicing atty., 1982–84; TX dir., U.S. Sen. Phil Gramm, 1985–90; Exec. dir., NRSC, 1991–93; Communications exec., 1993–02.

DC Office: 129 CHOB, 20515, 202-225-3484; Fax: 202-226-4888; Web site: www.house.gov/hensarling/.

State Offices: Athens, 903-675-8288; Dallas, 214-349-9996.

Committees: *Budget* (4th of 15 R). *Financial Services* (12th of 29 R): Capital Markets, Insurance & Government Sponsored Enterprises; Financial Institutions & Consumer Credit (RMM).

Group Ratings

	ADA	ACLU	AFS	LCV	ITIC	NTU	COC	ACU	CFG	FRC
2008	5	9	0	8	57	91	78	100	100	100
2007	0	—	0	15	—	93	70	100	100	—

National Journal Ratings

	2007 LIB	—	2007 CONS	2008 LIB	—	2008 CONS
Economic	6%	—	94%	0%	—	98%
Social	0%	—	91%	0%	—	91%
Foreign	0%	—	72%	0%	—	95%
Composite	8%	—	92%	3%	—	97%

Key Votes of the 110th Congress

1. Increase minimum wage	N	5. Share immigration data	Y	9. Withdraw troops 8/08	N
2. Expand SCHIP	N	6. Foreign aid abortion ban	Y	10. No operations in Iran	N
3. Raise CAFE standards	N	7. Ban gay bias in workplace	N	11. Free trade with Peru	Y
4. Bail out financial markets	N	8. Repeal D.C. gun law	Y	12. Overhaul FISA	Y

Election Results

2008 general	Jeb Hensarling (R)..162,894	(84%)	($1,005,714)
	Ken Ashby (Lib) 31,967	(16%)	
2008 primary	Jeb Hensarling (R)....................................... unopposed		

Prior Winning Percentages: 2006 (62%); 2004 (64%); 2002 (58%)

Population		Race/Ethnicity		Work	
Pop. 2007:	704,518	White:	65.3%	Private:	78.6%
Change since 2000:	Up 8.1%	Black:	13.2%	Government:	13.5%
Urban:	67.7%	Hispanic:	18.2%	Self-employed:	7.7%
Rural:	32.3%	Asian:	1.8%	Blue collar:	26.5%
Area size:	5,609 sq. mi.	Native Am.:	0.5%	White collar:	57.3%
		Hawaiian:	0.1%	Khaki collar:	0.0%
Age		Two+ races:	0.8%	Other:	16.2%
Median age:	36.0 yrs.			Median income:	$46,453
More than 65 yrs:	12.1%	*Ancestry*		Median home value:	$110,200
Less than 18 yrs:	25.6%	USA:	11.9%	Poverty:	13.4%
		English:	8.6%		
Education		Irish:	8.6%	**Military Veterans**	
H.S. grad:	79.3%			% of Pop:	10.4%
College grad:	19.6%				
Grad degree:	5.9%				

Not all of Dallas is glitz and postmodern marble. East of downtown, on one of the three street grids that skew to each other, is an older Dallas with neighborhoods of old mansions, modest bungalows and shotgun houses. They extend past the old airport at Love Field, and past the State Fair Grounds and the Cotton Bowl in east Dallas. Some of this older section of Dallas is being renovated and rebuilt, with chic cafes and trendy stores. Other once middle-class neighborhoods are filling up with im-

2008 Presidential Vote

McCain (R)............................158,356	(63%)
Obama (D) 90,135	(36%)

2004 Presidential Vote

Bush (R).................................160,240	(67%)
Kerry (D).................................77,952	(33%)

Cook Partisan Voting Index: R + 17

migrants from Mexico and are once again noisy with children as they were in the 1950s when people moved here not from Mexico or Central America, but from the almost all-Anglo counties of north and central Texas. With the economic downturn and the scarcity of jobs, some of them are returning to Mexico.

The 5th Congressional District includes much of east and southeast Dallas County, including neighborhoods in east Dallas and suburban Mesquite, which has become a destination for immigrants moving up the economic ladder. It also covers a more upscale slice of Dallas inside the freeway, including parts of Lakewood and White Rock Lake, which was rescued by President Franklin Roosevelt's Civilian Conservation Corps during the New Deal. Nearly half of the district's population is in Dallas County. The 5th contains six counties in East Texas, the largest of which are Henderson and Kaufman, which are the next high-growth areas in the Metroplex. One of the booming small towns is Forney, which has become a destination for young families. Each of the outlying counties is more heavily Republican than the Dallas portion of the district. As rural areas have swung away from the Democrats, the district switched from being a battleground in the early 1990s to safely Republican. In 2008, GOP presidential nominee John McCain won 63% of the vote in the district and 53% in Dallas County.

The congressman from the 5th District is Jeb Hensarling, a Republican first elected in 2002. Hensarling grew up in Morris County in East Texas. He worked on his father's poultry farm near College Station as a teenager and decided that he did not want to be a farmer. In high school, he started a Republican club and began organizing political events. He graduated from Texas A&M University and went on to get a law degree from the University of Texas law school. After a short stint practicing law, he got a job on the staff of U.S. Sen. Phil Gramm, a Republican. Hensarling rose quickly through the ranks of Gramm's staff and was named the senator's 1990 campaign manager. When Gramm was chosen by fellow senators as chairman the National Republican Senatorial Committee, Gramm named Hensarling as his executive director. Hensarling later returned to Texas to become vice president of communications for Green Mountain Energy, a local utility, and was co-founder of Family Support Assurance, a firm that sought to modernize child support collections.

After the congressional redistricting in 2001, Republican Rep. Pete Sessions, who had represented the 5th District for the previous six years, decided to run in the new and more compact 32nd District on the north side of Dallas. Hensarling became the frontrunner for the Republican nomination in the 5th District. Like his mentor, Gramm, he listed cutting taxes as his top priority. Against four opponents, he won the nomination with 54% of the vote. For the general election, Democrats nominated Ron Chapman, a former Dallas County appellate judge who described himself as a loyal Democrat who could work with Republicans. Hensarling referred to his opponent as "Judge Softie" for his record on capital murder cases. The folksy Chapman emphasized his fiscal conservatism and deep local roots. He tried to paint Hensarling as too conservative and extreme for the district, but his message failed to take hold, especially as high-profile Republicans came through the district with endorsements, including President George W. Bush, Vice President Dick Cheney, and Gramm. Hensarling won 58%-40%, and has been re-elected easily since.

In the House, Hensarling has a solidly conservative voting record. He styled himself as a fiscal conservative in the mold of Gramm and has not been afraid to push Republican leaders to take more conservative positions, though he usually voted with them in the end when they didn't. He joined the Republican Study Committee, a group of the most conservative House members and took the lead in budget legislation. His efforts did not endear him to Republicans on the Appropriations Committee and others in the party establishment. He tried to influence Republican strategy without abandoning his own beliefs or stirring the pot with party leaders too much.

His dilemma was apparent in 2003 when he struggled over whether to vote for the Republicans' Medicare prescription drug bill, which many conservatives criticized for creating a costly new government entitlement but was strongly supported by Bush. Hensarling claimed credit for a modest cost-containment provision and waited until the final hours before deciding to vote for the bill. Later, he led an effort to identify cuts in spending to offset the huge costs resulting from Hurricane Katrina in 2005. On the Financial Services Committee in 2008, Hensarling was an outspoken opponent of the bill to rescue the financial services industry, which went against his free market principles. After the legislation passed, Hensarling was named to the House Republican slot on an oversight board to review how the money was spent. In 2009, he became the ranking Republican on the Financial Institutions and Consumer Credit Subcommittee.

An avid foe of campaign regulations on the grounds that many of them violate the right to free speech, he sought unsuccessfully to exempt bloggers from campaign finance rules in response to a court ruling making them subject to the rules. In 2006, he spearheaded a successful effort to repeal the Wright Amendment, which limited long-distance flights from Love Field in Dallas as a way of protecting the Dallas-Forth Worth Airport from competition from Love Field. The action was a major boost for Southwest Airlines, which uses Love Field for its flights into Dallas and Fort Worth.

In December 2006, Hensarling secured what for him was the dream job in the House—chairman of the ultra conservative Republican Study Committee, where he could be the "keeper of the conservative flame" as he put it. Also at that time, Hensarling managed the losing campaign of conservative Republican Mike Pence of Indiana in his bid against John Boehner of Ohio for the post of Republican leader. Boehner won, putting Hensarling on the wrong side of a major intraparty leadership contest.

In 2007, after Republicans lost their majority in the 2006 election, Hensarling said that Republicans needed to regain their commitment to limited government. "There is nothing quite like a two-by-four smacked across your head to get your attention," he said in January 2007. The next year, Hensarling, as RSC chairman, crafted a seven-point strategy for House Republicans that included a constitutional amendment to limit spending and a flat tax to replace the progressive income-tax system with graduate rates as income rises. The party embraced his platform, except for his call for a moratorium on spending earmarks in appropriations bills. After the 2008 election, Hensarling was named to head fundraising for the National Republican Congressional Committee, chaired by his Dallas-area conservative colleague Pete Sessions.

SIXTH DISTRICT

Joe Barton (R)

Elected 1984, 13th term; b. Sept. 15, 1949, Waco; home, Ennis; Texas A&M U., B.S. 1972, Purdue U., M.S. 1973; United Methodist; married (Terri); 4 children.

Professional Career: Asst. to V.P., Ennis Business Forms, 1973–81; White House Fellow, U.S. Dept. of Energy, 1981–82; Consultant, Atlantic Richfield Co., 1982–84.

DC Office: 2109 RHOB, 20515, 202-225-2002; Fax: 202-225-3052; Web site: joebarton.house.gov.

State Offices: Arlington, 817-543-1000; Crockett, 936-544-8488; Ennis, 972-875-8488.

Committees: *Energy & Commerce* (RMM of 23 R).

Group Ratings

	ADA	ACLU	AFS	LCV	ITIC	NTU	COC	ACU	CFG	FRC
2008	10	18	14	0	43	74	94	96	79	82
2007	10	—	0	0	—	80	85	96	85	—

National Journal Ratings

	2007 LIB — 2007 CONS		2008 LIB — 2008 CONS	
Economic	6%	93%	17%	83%
Social	21%	75%	9%	85%
Foreign	0%	72%	5%	93%
Composite	15%	86%	12%	88%

Key Votes of the 110th Congress

1. Increase minimum wage	N	5. Share immigration data	Y	9. Withdraw troops 8/08	N
2. Expand SCHIP	N	6. Foreign aid abortion ban	Y	10. No operations in Iran	N
3. Raise CAFE standards	N	7. Ban gay bias in workplace	N	11. Free trade with Peru	Y
4. Bail out financial markets	N	8. Repeal D.C. gun law	Y	12. Overhaul FISA	Y

Election Results

2008 general	Joe Barton (R)	174,008	(62%)	($1,934,766)
	Ludwig Otto (D)	99,919	(36%)	($29,634)
	Max Koch (Lib)	6,655	(2%)	
2008 primary	Joe Barton (R)	unopposed		

Prior Winning Percentages: 2006 (60%); 2004 (66%); 2002 (70%); 2000 (88%); 1998 (73%); 1996 (77%); 1994 (76%); 1992 (72%); 1990 (66%); 1988 (68%); 1986 (56%); 1984 (57%)

Population		Race/Ethnicity		Work	
Pop. 2007:	759,132	White:	57.7%	Private:	80.2%
Change since 2000:	Up 16.5%	Black:	15.4%	Government:	13.0%
Urban:	80.0%	Hispanic:	21.1%	Self-employed:	6.6%
Rural:	20.0%	Asian:	3.7%	Blue collar:	25.9%
Area size:	6,336 sq. mi.	Native Am.:	0.4%	White collar:	58.6%
Age		Hawaiian:	0.1%	Khaki collar:	0.0%
Median age:	33.1 yrs.	Two+ races:	1.4%	Other:	15.5%
More than 65 yrs:	9.1%	*Ancestry*		Median income:	$52,008
Less than 18 yrs:	28.0%	German:	9.7%	Median home value:	$122,800
Education		Irish:	8.4%	Poverty:	13.3%
H.S. grad:	82.7%	English:	7.6%	**Military Veterans**	
College grad:	23.9%			% of Pop:	10.5%
Grad degree:	6.9%				

The Dallas-Fort Worth Metroplex—a name even the locals use—has spread outward from its historic nodes in downtown Dallas and downtown Fort Worth. Although Dallas is the larger population center, much of the development has moved west, across the plains and the barely perceptible Balcones Escarpment, the geologist's boundary between green and grassy East Texas and brown, barren and hilly West. The plains have been filled in with subdivisions and shopping centers under

2008 Presidential Vote		
McCain (R)............................172,061	(60%)
Obama (D) 114,133	(40%)
2004 Presidential Vote		
Bush (R)...............................173,476	(66%)
Kerry (D)..............................87,454	(34%)
Cook Partisan Voting Index: R + 15		

the enormous Texas sky. Among the larger suburbs is Arlington, right between Dallas and Fort Worth and an easy highway commute to both cities. Its location has made it ideal as a site for regional attractions like Six Flags over Texas and the Ballpark in Arlington, commissioned by the former part-owner of the Texas Rangers, George W. Bush. In 2009, the Dallas Cowboys football team opened a new stadium in Arlington. The city's population of 371,000 in 2007 was 26% Hispanic, 17% African-American and 6% Asian. Arlington provides extra pay to police officers who can speak Spanish or Vietnamese. As Arlington has filled up, the big growth now is to the south in Mansfield, where the population increased 76% from 2000 to 2007, and in Crowley. Growth in the area has been so robust that Tarrant County, the third-largest county in Texas, was the 18th largest in the country in 2007.

The 6th Congressional District of Texas includes all of Arlington and the southern fringe of Fort Worth to the west. Two-thirds of its people live in Arlington and Tarrant County. Much of the rest are in Ellis County, directly south of Dallas County, which has grown 24% since 2000. The district includes all or part of six counties to the southeast, reaching most of the way to Houston. Politically, this territory was ancestrally Democratic for many years, but no longer. It twice voted for Republican native son George W. Bush with 66%, and it voted for Republican nominee John McCain in 2008 with 60% of the vote.

The congressman from the 6th District is Joe Barton, a Republican first elected in 1984. He is the ranking Republican on the House Energy and Commerce Committee and is a former chairman of the committee. Barton grew up in Ennis, in then-rural Ellis County. He graduated from Texas A&M and Purdue universities, worked as an oil company engineer and then was a White House Fellow. When Republican Rep. Phil Gramm ran successfully for the Senate in 1984, Barton ran for his 6th District House seat. Barton won the Republican runoff by only 10 votes, and he went on to win the general election with 57% of the vote. Although he remains a solid conservative, he sometimes strays to the center on cultural issues.

As the top Republican on the powerful Energy and Commerce Committee, Barton has had the unenviable duty in the last few years of leading the opposition against the panel's formidable chairman, Henry Waxman of California, and against a Democratically-controlled Congress. He was the party's lead spokesman against the sweeping climate change bill passed by the House in June 2009. The bill establishes a cap on greenhouse gas emissions scientists blame for global warming, aiming to reduce them by 80% from 2005 levels by 2050. Barton, who has long questioned the scientific underpinnings of global warming legislation, called it "a triumph of fear over good sense and science." In 2007 hearings discussing global warming, he told former Democratic Vice President Al Gore, who has led the push for curbs on greenhouse gas emissions for several years, "You're not just off a little. You're totally wrong."

Barton also has fought the Democrats' health care proposals tooth-and-nail, but often is outgunned by Waxman there as well. In 2007, he worked with President George W. Bush to keep Republican centrists from signing on to the Democrats' proposal to expand the State Children's Health Insurance Program. The bill passed in 2007 by margins too narrow to override Bush's veto. Democrats succeeded in passing a bill in 2009, which was signed into law by President Barack Obama. Also in 2009, he was the opposing voice on the committee when the Democrats unveiled a restricting of the nation's health care delivery system. But on some issues, Barton sought common ground with Waxman, as he had with Waxman's predecessor as chairman, Democrat John Dingell of Michigan. He worked with committee Democrats on a proposal to approve generic versions of biologic drugs following a 12-year period of exclusivity for the inventor to recoup costs. And he worked with Dingell and other Democrats for a consensus approach to improved electronic medical records.

In earlier years, Barton had enjoyed a fair degree of success in the majority on the committee. In 1995, he became chairman of the panel's Oversight and Investigation Subcommittee and used the platform to conduct extensive hearings of the nation's food and drug laws. The result was enactment, with bipartisan support, of significant modernization of the Food and Drug Administration, encouraging the agency to more quickly review innovative drugs and medical devices. In 1999, he became chairman of the Energy and Power Subcommittee with jurisdiction over energy legislation. He managed to reach agreement in 2001 with Dingell on higher fuel economy standards. Barton pressed for action on electricity regulation, but he retreated from requiring utilities to join regional transmission organizations and sought to encourage them to do so. His bill passed the House but died in the Senate.

In 2004, after full commerce chairman Billy Tauzin, R-La., stepped down, Barton was selected to succeed him—the only Texan other than former Democratic speaker Sam Rayburn to hold the post. He aroused some partisan ire when in September of that year he blocked committee Democrats' demand for information about Vice President Dick Cheney's 2001 energy task force. But he also worked successfully to win Democratic votes on some issues and to defend and expand the committee's jurisdiction. Telecommunications issues are a major responsibility of Energy and Commerce. In 2006, the House passed Barton's bill to make it easier for telephone companies to enter the broadband market, but influential Democrats opposed the measure, and it died in the Senate.

On the 2005 energy bill, Barton insisted on retaining provisions protecting manufacturers of MTBE, a fuel additive that was discovered to be polluting groundwater. The bill became hung up over that provision as some lawmakers fought to hold the manufacturers responsible for expensive cleanup projects. Barton ultimately agreed to drop it in order to get a bill that could pass both chambers. He also convinced other Republicans to keep a provision allowing oil drilling in the Arctic National Wildlife Refuge out of the bill in order to remove another stumbling block. With his help, the GOP majority was able to enact major energy legislation with $12 billion in incentives, an inventory of oil and natural gas reserves, and a one-month extension of daylight savings time. Also in 2005, the House narrowly passed Barton's bill to encourage the construction of new refineries, but it died in the Senate.

Energy and Commerce is a great platform for raising money for campaigns from deep-pocketed industries, and Barton raised much more money than he is ever likely to need to spend in his district. In 2004, he hosted a fundraiser for Republican Billy Tauzin III, who was running for his father's old seat, just as Tauzin had hosted a fundraiser for Barton's son when he ran for Congress (both sons lost). At home, Barton was criticized by Democrats for seeking in 2003 and 2004 to keep Ellis County outside the Environmental Protection Agency's Dallas region in applications of the stringent rules of the Clean Air Act. Ellis County is home to three cement producers and other companies whose political action committees and executives were big contributors to Barton's campaigns, and the county produces 40% of the industrial emissions in North Texas. Barton said there was no connection between the contributions and his action and argued that there was no scientific basis for Ellis County's inclusion. But in 2004 the EPA decided otherwise and that Ellis County must take steps to reduce air pollution.

One of Barton's early projects was trying to secure funding for the proposed Superconducting Super Collider, an enormous scientific laboratory that was to have been built in Waxahachie in Ellis County. But the House voted in 1993 to zero out the project. Another of his early causes was a proposed constitutional amendment requiring a two-thirds vote to raise taxes. When the House took up the issue in 1995, Barton managed to pull together 253 votes, though he fell short of the 290 votes needed. Nevertheless, Barton claimed progress after many states approved tax-limitation plans.

Barton has had some political disappointments. He ran for the Senate in 1993 after Democrat Lloyd Bentsen resigned to become President Bill Clinton's Treasury secretary. He finished third with just 14% of the vote in the all-party primary. In September 2001, when Gramm announced his retirement from the Senate, Barton considered running for his seat. But the Bush White House favored Texas Attorney General John Cornyn for the seat and Barton stepped aside. After the 2006 election, he made a bid for minority leader, but discovered that John Boehner, R-Ohio, had wrapped up sufficient votes to win. Barton withdrew after six days.

He has been re-elected easily in the 6th District. He suffered a heart attack in December 2005 but made a full recovery. Under House Republicans' term limit rules, he would be required to step down from the top post at Energy and Commerce after 2010. He is said to be interested in running for Republican Kay Bailey Hutchison's Senate seat when she runs for governor in 2010.

SEVENTH DISTRICT

John Culberson (R)

Elected 2000, 5th term; b. Aug. 24, 1956, Houston; home, Houston; Southern Methodist U., B.A. 1981, S. TX Col. of Law, J.D. 1988; Methodist; married (Belinda); 1 child.

Elected Office: TX House of Reps., 1986–2000, Maj. whip, 1999–2000.

Professional Career: Jim Culberson Advertising, 1981–85; Practicing atty., 1988–2000.

DC Office: 1514 LHOB, 20515, 202-225-2571; Fax: 202-225-4381; Web site: www.culberson.house.gov.

State Offices: Houston, 713-682-8828.

Committees: *Appropriations* (14th of 23 R): Commerce, Justice, Science & Related Agencies; Financial Services & General Government; Homeland Security.

Group Ratings

	ADA	ACLU	AFS	LCV	ITIC	NTU	COC	ACU	CFG	FRC
2008	5	18	14	0	71	83	88	100	95	100
2007	0	—	0	0	—	84	79	100	92	—

National Journal Ratings

	2007 LIB	—	2007 CONS		2008 LIB	—	2008 CONS
Economic	3%	—	97%		10%	—	90%
Social	0%	—	91%		20%	—	80%
Foreign	36%	—	63%		0%	—	95%
Composite	15%	—	85%		11%	—	89%

Key Votes of the 110th Congress

1. Increase minimum wage	N	5. Share immigration data	Y	9. Withdraw troops 8/08	N
2. Expand SCHIP	N	6. Foreign aid abortion ban	Y	10. No operations in Iran	*
3. Raise CAFE standards	N	7. Ban gay bias in workplace	N	11. Free trade with Peru	Y
4. Bail out financial markets	N	8. Repeal D.C. gun law	Y	12. Overhaul FISA	Y

Election Results

2008 general	John Culberson (R)	162,635	(56%)	($1,757,226)
	Michael Skelly (D)	123,242	(42%)	($3,080,655)
2008 primary	John Culberson (R)	unopposed		

Prior Winning Percentages: 2006 (59%); 2004 (64%); 2002 (89%); 2000 (74%)

Population		Race/Ethnicity		Work	
Pop. 2007:	759,409	White:	58.5%	Private:	82.2%
Change since 2000:	Up 16.5%	Black:	8.1%	Government:	8.9%
Urban:	99.7%	Hispanic:	23.4%	Self-employed:	8.6%
Rural:	0.3%	Asian:	8.3%	Blue collar:	13.5%
Area size:	198 sq. mi.	Native Am.:	0.2%	White collar:	74.3%
		Hawaiian:	0.0%	Khaki collar:	0.0%
Age		Two+ races:	1.2%	Other:	12.1%
Median age:	36.4 yrs.			Median income:	$65,630
More than 65 yrs:	9.5%	**Ancestry**		Median home value:	$186,300
Less than 18 yrs:	23.8%	German:	11.0%	Poverty:	9.5%
		English:	8.6%		
Education		Irish:	7.7%	**Military Veterans**	
H.S. grad:	90.2%			% of Pop:	7.9%
College grad:	48.4%				
Grad degree:	18.8%				

When George H.W. Bush moved from Midland in West Texas to Houston in 1960, he bought a house in Briarwood in what was then the western outskirts of the fast-growing city. He returned to Houston in 1993 after losing his re-election bid for the presidency and built a new house a mile from his old one, near lush Memorial Park. Briarwood is not far from the retail and commercial epicenter of Houston. The lavish Galleria, the fourth-largest mall in the United States, draws more than 24 million

2008 Presidential Vote

McCain (R)	173,162	(58%)
Obama (D)	121,472	(41%)

2004 Presidential Vote

Bush (R)	179,456	(64%)
Kerry (D)	99,422	(36%)

Cook Partisan Voting Index: R + 13

shoppers a year under its impressive glass atriums. Downtown Houston is sprouting residential apartments. Although the sale of high-priced homes fell in 2008, the economy of Houston is still relatively strong. Oil company revenues have been up and many businesses moved here from the New Orleans area following the devastation of Hurricane Katrina in 2005.

The 7th Congressional District of Texas is the lineal descendant of the House district that in 1966 elected Bush as the first Republican ever to represent Houston. It occupied far more territory then, half of Harris County. In successive redistrictings, its boundaries have been pared back, as the population of the west side of Houston has skyrocketed. Today, more than 1.5 million people live in an area where 350,000 lived when Bush was first elected. The 7th District touches the western edge of downtown Houston and includes most of the land between the Katy Freeway (Interstate 10) and Westheimer running straight west to Highway 6. To the south, it includes the affluent neighborhoods southwest of downtown Houston, Rice University and the Texas Medical Center, Belleaire, some small Buffalo Bayou towns and a swatch of Houston west of the 610 highway loop. Most of Houston's business and professional elite live within its boundaries: the partners of the big law firms, cutting-edge medical researchers, and society mavens. Since 2000, Hispanics have increased from 18% to 23% of the total population.

Back in the 1980s, the 7th District was one of the most Republican districts in the country, and it still is. But as with many precincts of the very elite, it did not take a liking to President George W. Bush's brand of Republicanism. Within these boundaries he won 69% of the vote in 2000 but dropped to 64% in 2004. As with other close-in Texas suburbs, local Republican fortunes continued to slide in 2008, although it was still a safe GOP district. It voted 58% for Republican presidential candidate John McCain.

The congressman from the 7th District is John Culberson, a Republican first elected in 2000. Culberson grew up in Houston, the son of the owner of an advertising agency. He graduated from Southern Methodist University and from South Texas College of Law and then worked as a civil defense attorney. In 1986, at age 29, Culberson won a seat in the Texas House, where he served for 14 years. In 2000, Republican Rep. Bill Archer, Bush's successor in the House, retired after being forced to give up the chairmanship of the Ways and Means Committee by Republican term limits. The frontrunners in the GOP primary were Culberson and Peter Wareing, a Houston merchant banker and son-in-law of Texas oilman Jack Blanton. Culberson led Wareing in the first round 38%-27%. Wareing spent nearly $4 million to Culberson's $650,000, but Culberson had an extensive grassroots campaign and won the runoff four weeks later 60%-40%. The general election was no contest in this GOP-dominant district.

Culberson calls himself a "Jeffersonian Republican" and is passionate about transferring power from the federal to local governments. He has a mostly conservative voting record. He opposes affirmative action, gun control, and abortion under most circumstances. Like his predecessor, Archer, he dreams of junking the current tax system and replacing it with a national sales tax. An amateur astronomer and self-proclaimed science buff, Culberson is an enthusiast for NASA and has an interest in nanotechnology research, which is a specialty at Rice. "My eyes are too bad and my feet too flat for me to be an astronaut," he told the *Houston Chronicle* with regret.

In the House, Culberson often goes his own way. He ruffled feathers as one of only two Texas Republicans to oppose the $400 billion Medicare expansion of 2003. Despite the pioneering research at medical centers in his district, he voted against embryonic stem cell research, which he said would encourage "production and harvesting of human embryos like a crop of corn, which is creepy and unacceptable." Culberson has a coveted spot on the Appropriations Committee, which he has used to secure money for projects in his district, including medical research, flood control projects and funds for the Houston Ship Channel. He has fought with Houston officials who wanted money for local light-rail projects, insisting that expanded highway capacity be included in any plan before helping to secure $1 billion for a proposal that included both highway and public transit projects. Culberson claimed credit for the highway expansion but in 2007 criticized local officials for the slow pace of construction of the light-rail train lines.

In 2008, Culberson faced his first well-financed Democratic challenger. Wind energy executive Michael Skelly spent nearly $3.1 million, including $1 million from his own pocket. Culberson spent a relatively modest $1.8 million, which left some Republicans worried about a possible upset. Skelly criticized Culberson's lack of support for alternative energy and for the space program, citing Culberson's call to reduce the bureaucracy at NASA, which employs about 20,000 people locally. Skelly also emphasized his support for a balanced budget. Culberson ran as a strong social and fiscal conservative, but he suffered from discontent in the Republican grassroots over perceived weak enforcement of immigration law and a spike in deficit spending during the Bush years. National Democrats placed the contest in their top-level "Red to Blue" program. Culberson won, 56%-42%—a warning sign of future challenges.

EIGHTH DISTRICT

Kevin Brady (R)

Elected 1996, 7th term; b. April 11, 1955, Vermillion, SD; home, The Woodlands, TX; U. of SD, B.S. 1990; Catholic; married (Cathy); 2 children.

Elected Office: TX House of Reps., 1990–96.

Professional Career: Exec., The Woodlands Chamber of Commerce, 1978–96.

DC Office: 301 CHOB, 20515, 202-225-4901; Fax: 202-225-5524; Web site: www.house.gov/brady.

State Offices: Conroe, 936-441-5700; Huntsville, 936-439-9542; Orange, 409-883-4197.

Committees: *Joint Economic Committee* (RMM of 4 R). *Ways & Means* (4th of 15 R): Social Security; Trade (RMM).

Group Ratings

	ADA	ACLU	AFS	LCV	ITIC	NTU	COC	ACU	CFG	FRC
2008	10	18	14	0	71	66	88	86	76	100
2007	5	—	0	0	—	80	75	100	90	—

National Journal Ratings

	2007 LIB	—	2007 CONS		2008 LIB	—	2008 CONS
Economic	7%	—	92%		8%	—	92%
Social	29%	—	71%		29%	—	71%
Foreign	30%	—	69%		0%	—	95%
Composite	22%	—	78%		13%	—	87%

Key Votes of the 110th Congress

1. Increase minimum wage	N	5. Share immigration data	*	9. Withdraw troops 8/08	N
2. Expand SCHIP	N	6. Foreign aid abortion ban	Y	10. No operations in Iran	N
3. Raise CAFE standards	N	7. Ban gay bias in workplace	N	11. Free trade with Peru	Y
4. Bail out financial markets	Y	8. Repeal D.C. gun law	*	12. Overhaul FISA	Y

Election Results

2008 general	Kevin Brady (R)	207,128	(73%)	($610,288)
	Kent Hargett (D)	70,758	(25%)	($2,928)
	Brian Stevens (Lib)	7,565	(3%)	
2008 primary	Kevin Brady (R)	unopposed		

Prior Winning Percentages: 2006 (67%); 2004 (69%); 2002 (93%); 2000 (92%); 1998 (93%); 1996 (59%)

Population		**Race/Ethnicity**		**Work**	
Pop. 2007:	759,496	White:	76.7%	Private:	77.8%
Change since 2000:	Up 16.6%	Black:	8.5%	Government:	14.2%
Urban:	49.6%	Hispanic:	12.2%	Self-employed:	7.8%
Rural:	50.4%	Asian:	1.1%	Blue collar:	27.1%
Area size:	8,415 sq. mi.	Native Am.:	0.5%	White collar:	56.2%
		Hawaiian:	0.0%	Khaki collar:	0.0%
Age		Two+ races:	0.9%	Other:	16.7%
Median age:	35.4 yrs.	*Ancestry*		Median income:	$48,430
More than 65 yrs:	11.8%	German:	12.3%	Median home value:	$104,900
Less than 18 yrs:	25.1%	Irish:	10.8%	Poverty:	14.2%
Education		English:	9.2%		
H.S. grad:	82.1%			**Military Veterans**	
College grad:	20.2%			% of Pop:	11.3%
Grad degree:	6.0%				

Montgomery County, to the north of Houston, was once fenceless cattle country, dotted with roadside stands and barbecues and unpainted farmhouses with water pooling on low swampy fields. In 1931, wildcatter George Strake struck oil near Conroe. Thousands of other wildcatters and roughnecks quickly joined in the boom, and this became one of the richest oil-producing areas in the nation. Active production continues today. The oil boom centered on Conroe was followed by a population boom. In

2008 Presidential Vote

McCain (R)	215,845	(72%)
Obama (D)	74,695	(26%)

2004 Presidential Vote

Bush (R)	194,696	(72%)
Kerry (D)	73,946	(28%)

Cook Partisan Voting Index: R + 25

1972, construction began on a planned community called The Woodlands, 30 miles north of Houston and 15 miles south of Conroe. Development of this new city has barreled along since then, with corporate parks, glistening steel condos, pristine golf courses, and a man-made waterway. Greater Houston has spread far out into this countryside, past the now mislabeled Farm-Market Route 1960, past The Woodlands and even past Conroe. Montgomery County had 49,000 people in 1970 and 413,000 in 2007. It is the seventh fastest-growing county in Texas. There were few signs of the recession that began in 2007 in this region of the country. Even with local devastation from Hurricane Ike in 2008, sales tax revenues increased 74%.

The 8th Congressional District includes all of Montgomery County, which contains slightly more than half of the district's people. The district extends east to the Sabine River on the Louisiana border, and takes in all of eight counties and parts of two others. It covers the Big Thicket National Preserve, a primeval swamp described as "America's Ark" because of its vast array of animals and plants. The district also includes the town of Huntsville, with one of Texas's oldest prisons, and the oil refinery town of Orange on the Sabine River, which is popular for bass fishing. It's gun-totin' territory as well. After the November 2008 election, local gun shop owners reported a big increase in automatic weapons sales from customers concerned about potential changes in gun laws under Democratic President Barack Obama. Redistricting changes in recent years have made the district less affluent and metropolitan, but it is still solidly Republican. President George W. Bush won 72% of the vote in the district in 2004. In 2008, Republican presidential nominee John McCain won 74% of the vote, his sixth-best district in the nation.

The congressman from the 8th District is Kevin Brady, a Republican first elected in 1996. Brady grew up and went to college in South Dakota, moved to Montgomery County in 1978 and headed The Woodlands Chamber of Commerce for 18 years. In 1990, he was elected to the Texas House. When Republican U.S. Rep. Jack Fields announced his retirement in 1995, Brady ran for the seat. His main opponent in the decisive Republican primary was Eugene Fontenot, a physician who said he wanted "to restore America to its Christian heritage." Brady was the choice of party regulars, while Fontenot was backed by religious conservatives. Fontenot attacked Brady for being one of two Republicans to vote against the state's concealed weapons law. Brady had opposed most gun control bills but not the concealed weapons bill. When he was 12 years old, his father, an attorney, was shot and killed while trying a case in a South Dakota courtroom. "I couldn't look Mom in the eye and vote for this," he told *The Houston Chronicle* after the vote. After Fontenot led Brady in the March primary, Brady won the April runoff by 53%-47%. After the U.S. Supreme Court in June ordered a redrawing of 13 districts, Brady led Fontenot 41%-39% in an all-party primary in November. Finally, in the December runoff, turnout was sharply down and Brady won 59%-41%.

In the House, Brady has compiled a conservative voting record, though a bit less so on foreign issues and has gained a reputation as more of a pragmatist than other Texas Republicans. Brady is also a deputy whip for the House Republican leadership.

He has focused on economic issues and has a coveted spot on the House Ways and Means Committee. Brady was a central figure in the successful effort in 2004 to make state and local sales taxes deductible in the seven states, including Texas, that have no personal income tax. He was also the chief House sponsor of the 2005 Central America Free Trade Agreement. After Republicans lost control of the House in 2007, he took on two prime committee assignments. He is the ranking Republican on the Trade Subcommittee at Ways and Means, where he has fought for more free trade agreements. He also is the ranking Republican on the Joint Economic Committee, which provides little opportunity for him to influence legislation but is a great soapbox for his views on budget issues. In September 2008, he was the only Houston-area member of the House in either party to vote for the government bailout of the financial services industry. "I don't give a flip about Wall Street. But as much as I detest this bill, doing nothing is worse," he said.

Brady has had no problem winning re-election.

NINTH DISTRICT

Al Green (D)

Elected 2004, 3rd term; b. Sept. 1, 1947, New Orleans, LA; home, Houston; TX Southern U., J.D. 1973; Baptist; single.

Elected Office: Harris Cnty. justice of the peace, 1977–2004.

Professional Career: Practicing atty., 1973–77; Pres., Houston NAACP, 1986–95.

DC Office: 236 CHOB, 20515, 202-225-7508; Fax: 202-225-2947; Web site: www.house.gov/algreen.

State Offices: Houston, 713-383-9234.

Committees: *Financial Services* (20th of 42 D): Domestic Monetary Policy & Technology; Financial Institutions & Consumer Credit; Housing & Community Opportunity. *Homeland Security* (16th of 20 D): Border, Maritime & Global Counterterrorism; Intelligence, Information Sharing & Terrorism Risk Assessment; Management, Investigations & Oversight.

Group Ratings

	ADA	ACLU	AFS	LCV	ITIC	NTU	COC	ACU	CFG	FRC
2008	100	91	100	85	86	10	67	4	0	5
2007	100	—	100	85	—	4	50	4	0	—

National Journal Ratings

	2007 LIB	—	2007 CONS		2008 LIB	—	2008 CONS
Economic	69%	—	28%		85%	—	0%
Social	92%	—	0%		72%	—	26%
Foreign	94%	—	4%		70%	—	25%
Composite	87%	—	13%		79%	—	21%

Key Votes of the 110th Congress

1. Increase minimum wage	Y	5. Share immigration data	N	9. Withdraw troops 8/08	Y
2. Expand SCHIP	Y	6. Foreign aid abortion ban	N	10. No operations in Iran	Y
3. Raise CAFE standards	Y	7. Ban gay bias in workplace	Y	11. Free trade with Peru	N
4. Bail out financial markets	Y	8. Repeal D.C. gun law	N	12. Overhaul FISA	Y

Election Results

2008 general	Al Green (D) 143,868	(94%)	($384,442)
	Brad Walters (Lib) 9,760	(6%)	
2008 primary	Al Green (D) .... unopposed		

Prior Winning Percentages: 2006 (100%); 2004 (72%)

Population		Race/Ethnicity		Work	
Pop. 2007:	687,481	White:	13.5%	Private:	81.9%
Change since 2000:	Up 5.5%	Black:	35.6%	Government:	10.6%
Urban:	99.8%	Hispanic:	40.4%	Self-employed:	7.4%
Rural:	0.2%	Asian:	9.4%	Blue collar:	27.0%
Area size:	154 sq. mi.	Native Am.:	0.2%	White collar:	49.9%
		Hawaiian:	0.1%	Khaki collar:	0.0%
Age		Two+ races:	0.6%	Other:	23.0%
Median age:	30.3 yrs.	*Ancestry*		Median income:	$35,652
More than 65 yrs:	6.3%	Subsaharan:	3.4%	Median home value:	$107,400
Less than 18 yrs:	29.3%	German:	2.7%	Poverty:	23.3%
		USA:	2.0%	**Military Veterans**	
Education				% of Pop:	5.0%
H.S. grad:	71.9%				
College grad:	21.7%				
Grad degree:	6.7%				

Spreading out in all directions from its historic center at Allen's Landing on Buffalo Bayou, Houston has become one of the great metropolises of North America. A half-century ago, the steaming flatlands south of Houston running down to the Gulf of Mexico did not seem a likely site for one of the world's most advanced civilizations. But they are today. Most of the scientific work in NASA's early years was done in Houston, and the first word spoken when man landed on the moon was "Houston."

2008 Presidential Vote

Obama (D) 137,619	(77%)
McCain (R)..............................40,240	(23%)

2004 Presidential Vote

Kerry (D)................................112,065	(70%)
Bush (R) 48,052	(30%)

Cook Partisan Voting Index: D + 22

It is the undisputed center of expertise in the oil business. In 2008, 70% of the city's economic growth came from the energy industry. Houston has also become a medical mecca, with the giant Texas Medical Center and its 13 hospitals leaving their mark on the health care statewide. And Houston has become one of the great surprise growth cities, creating thousands of small businesses, many owned by immigrants. This success is testimony to human, and Texas, creativity, and to the triumph of air conditioning, which facilitated the growth of what is now the fourth-largest city in the nation, with a population that grew by more than one-third from 1990 to 2007. After all, far fewer people would have moved here if they had to sweat through Houston's steamy five-month summer. The city's growth is expected to continue. In 2007, Houston unveiled a 30-year plan that projected an increase of 3.5 million people in the region.

The 9th Congressional District of Texas slices across the southern part of metropolitan Houston on the streets and freeways and waterways spreading out from the center of the city. It begins just southwest of where Interstate 45 crosses the I-610 Loop, continues west with a slight intrusion inside 610 near the Reliant Astrodome and Reliant Stadium, and then heads past Meadows Place and Mission Bend outside Beltway 8 toward the western end of Harris County. It includes two wedges of Fort Bend County, which form a crescent around the 22nd District.

The district includes many African-American neighborhoods, low-income and middle-income, in Harris and Fort Bend counties. Its population is 36% black, the third highest in any Texas district. It also includes many Asians, who form 9% of the total population, the highest percentage in Texas. Along Belleaire Boulevard is a Chinese-American community. Entrepreneurial Vietnamese boat people settled in the Alief neighborhood of southwest Houston on Bray's Bayou and have created quality schools, an Asian-oriented shopping mall and businesses that serve the largest Vietnamese community in the nation outside of California. And of course, there are many Hispanics, who made up 40% of the district's population in 2007, though many are not citizens or do not vote. Half of the district's population speaks a language other than English at home. The devastation of Katrina that emptied out New Orleans moved approximately 200,000 residents to Houston, and tens of thousands have remained. Overall this is a heavily Democratic district, which voted 77% for Democratic presidential candidate Barack Obama in 2008.

The congressman from the 9th District is Al Green, a Democrat first elected in 2004. Green grew up in New Orleans, attended college at Florida A&M University and graduated from Texas Southern University's law school, where he later taught. From 1986 to 1995, he was president of the Houston chapter of the NAACP. In 1977, he was elected justice of the peace and served 26 years. After new district boundaries were created in 2003, Green saw an opening to run for Congress. The representative from the old district that covered much of this area was Chris Bell, a white Democrat first elected in 2002. That year, he ran with liberal support and beat a more conservative black candidate. The primary against Green was a different matter. Green said that he wanted to fight racial profiling and discrimination in law enforcement, and used subtle racial references on the campaign trail, including his promise to bring "a mountain of soul" to the new district. He amassed an impressive roster of endorsements from prominent local and national black leaders. Bell responded by asking voters "not to focus on the color of my skin, but on the size of my heart." He spent more than $1 million on the primary, while Green spent less than half as much. Bell was endorsed by the AFL-CIO, Texas teachers, abortion rights groups and Democratic Minority Leader Nancy Pelosi. But he struggled as a white candidate running in a district where minorities constituted two-thirds of the electorate. And, a little more than half of the district was new to him.

As the primary neared, the racially charged atmosphere intensified. When state Democratic Chairman Charles Soechting endorsed Bell, Green said that it reminded him of "the double standards when African-Americans had to ride on the back of the bus and drink from colored-only water fountains." The Congressional Black Caucus was drawn into the campaign after California Rep. Maxine Waters hand-delivered a $5,000 check to Green from the caucus' political action committee and announced that nearly a dozen CBC members backed Green. Bell complained that caucus Chairman Elijah Cummings, D-Md., had earlier promised to support him. Although the caucus itself never made a formal endorsement, its role in the primary angered other Democratic members. In the end, it may not have mattered. Green won the primary in a landslide, 66%-31%. "It's been a divisive race and in some ways a rather ugly race," Bell said in conceding. Green faced no real opposition in the general election.

In the House, Green has had a relatively moderate voting record. On the Financial Services Committee, he has worked to eliminate housing practices that discriminated against minorities. He passed an amendment in the House in 2005 to add $7.7 million to fight housing discrimination. In 2008, he worked with then-Rep. Christopher Shays, R-Conn., on a plan to reduce the number of mortgage holders with unstable sub-prime loans, and he passed a bill in the House to expand housing assistance for low-income veterans. Green broke with most House Democrats by voting in 2006 to permit oil drilling in the Arctic National Wildlife Refuge, probably the smart vote in a Houston-based district that relies on oil profits. In March 2005, Green complained that he had been racially profiled after Houston airport security officials pulled him out of a line, questioned him and searched him.

He has been re-elected twice without Republican opposition.

TENTH DISTRICT

Michael McCaul (R)

Elected 2004, 3rd term; b. Jan. 14, 1962, Dallas; home, Austin; Trinity U., B.A. 1984, St. Mary's U., J.D. 1987; Catholic; married (Linda); 5 children.

Professional Career: Fed. prosecutor, 1990–99; Dep. atty. gen., 1999–2003; Chief, Western Div. of TX., U.S. Attys. Office, 2003–04.

DC Office: 131 CHOB, 20515, 202-225-2401; Fax: 202-225-5955; Web site: www.house.gov/mccaul.

State Offices: Austin, 512-473-2357; Brenham, 979-830-8497; Katy, 281-398-1247; Tomball, 281-255-8372.

Committees: *Foreign Affairs* (16th of 19 R): Middle East & South Asia; Western Hemisphere. *Homeland Security* (6th of 13 R): Border, Maritime & Global Counterterrorism; Emergency Communications, Preparedness & Response; Intelligence, Information Sharing & Terrorism Risk Assessment (RMM). *Science & Technology* (12th of 17 R): Space & Aeronautics.

Group Ratings

	ADA	ACLU	AFS	LCV	ITIC	NTU	COC	ACU	CFG	FRC
2008	25	18	14	8	86	68	89	96	84	100
2007	15	—	0	10	—	76	85	96	84	—

National Journal Ratings

	2007 LIB	—	2007 CONS		2008 LIB	—	2008 CONS
Economic	27%	—	72%		21%	—	79%
Social	9%	—	85%		20%	—	74%
Foreign	0%	—	72%		27%	—	72%
Composite	18%	—	82%		24%	—	76%

Key Votes of the 110th Congress

1. Increase minimum wage	N	5. Share immigration data	Y	9. Withdraw troops 8/08	N
2. Expand SCHIP	N	6. Foreign aid abortion ban	Y	10. No operations in Iran	*
3. Raise CAFE standards	N	7. Ban gay bias in workplace	N	11. Free trade with Peru	Y
4. Bail out financial markets	N	8. Repeal D.C. gun law	Y	12. Overhaul FISA	Y

Election Results

2008 general	Michael McCaul (R)	179,493	(54%)	($1,728,339)
	Larry Joe Doherty (D)	143,719	(43%)	($1,189,406)
	Matt Finkel (Lib)	9,871	(3%)	($14,673)
2008 primary	Michael McCaul (R)	unopposed		

Prior Winning Percentages: 2006 (55%); 2004 (79%)

Population		Race/Ethnicity		Work	
Pop. 2007:	857,383	White:	58.2%	Private:	78.0%
Change since 2000:	Up 31.6%	Black:	9.6%	Government:	14.2%
Urban:	80.8%	Hispanic:	25.1%	Self-employed:	7.5%
Rural:	19.2%	Asian:	5.4%	Blue collar:	19.8%
Area size:	3,846 sq. mi.	Native Am.:	0.3%	White collar:	66.0%
		Hawaiian:	0.0%	Khaki collar:	0.1%
Age		Two+ races:	1.2%	Other:	14.1%
Median age:	32.9 yrs.			Median income:	$60,872
More than 65 yrs:	7.4%	*Ancestry*		Median home value:	$150,700
Less than 18 yrs:	28.1%	German:	13.9%	Poverty:	10.3%
		Irish:	7.5%		
Education		English:	7.4%	**Military Veterans**	
H.S. grad:	86.3%			% of Pop:	8.8%
College grad:	34.8%				
Grad degree:	10.8%				

Two of Texas' major cities are named for leaders of the old Texas Republic, Sam Houston and Stephen Austin. They were not entirely attractive characters: Houston had episodes of alcoholic depression and Austin was a slaveholder who argued that Mexico infringed on Texas' liberty when it freed its slaves. But they were also men of courage and determination who built a distinctively American culture in what was then the northeast of Mexico. Today, the two metropolises named for them are quite dif-

2008 Presidential Vote

McCain (R)	187,496	(55%)
Obama (D)	150,713	(44%)

2004 Presidential Vote

Bush (R)	177,555	(62%)
Kerry (D)	109,287	(38%)

Cook Partisan Voting Index: R + 10

ferent in character. Houston is about commerce, the world capital of the oil business, an entrepreneurial hub spread out over the swampy, humid plains north of the Gulf of Mexico. Austin is the creature of the state government headquartered in the grand Capitol building and of the University of Texas with a huge endowment of land in West Texas that turned out to be full of oil.

The historic Austin is a liberal enclave in the heart of a conservative state. But the area around north Austin and its suburbs has taken on some of Houston's character in recent years despite the continuing popularity of "Keep Austin Weird" bumper stickers. North of the Capitol and the university, on land that was vacant when Lyndon Johnson celebrated his 87-vote victory in the 1948 Senate primary in the Driskill Hotel, an entrepreneurial Austin has taken shape. It embraces technology and the free market and spreads out over the hills into adjacent Williamson County. Curiously, there is no superhighway between Austin and Houston. To get from one to the other, one drives through rural counties with monuments and plaques recalling the days of the Texas Republic.

The 10th Congressional District of Texas connects the western edge of Houston with the northern precincts of Austin through a corridor of still mostly rural counties. It is split into three parts. Approximately 40% live in Austin and Travis County, where the district includes the northern third of Austin, with one tentacle reaching southwest beyond the city limits and another dropping south to Austin State Hospital. Another 40% are in the western edge of Houston's Harris County, a fast-growing area, with lots of young families, new subdivisions and sparkling megachurches. In between, are the six lightly populated rural counties. Overall, this has been a heavily Republican district—and the fastest-growing in the state, with an increase from 19% to 25% in its Hispanic population and an overall 32% population increase between 2000 and 2007. Republican President George W. Bush won the district with 62% in 2004. Republican candidate John McCain got 55% in 2008. Democratic candidate Barack Obama won the Travis County portion with 63%, while McCain got 68% in Harris County.

The congressman from the 10th District is Michael McCaul, a Republican first elected in 2004. He grew up in Dallas, studied business and history at Trinity University and went to law school at St. Mary's University, both in San Antonio. He worked as a federal prosecutor and then moved to Austin in 1999 to be a deputy to then-Attorney General John Cornyn in Austin. In 2002, he joined the U.S. attorney's office and was chief of the Terrorism and National Security Section for West Texas. McCaul was one of eight candidates in the Republican primary for the newly created congressional district in 2004. The top Republican contenders were McCaul, mortgage company owner Ben Streusand and former Judge John Devine. McCaul focused on his anti-terrorism work in the U.S. attorney's office. "I'm the only candidate that's had a top-secret security clearance," he said. "I won't have a learning curve." Streusand, based in Harris County, called for less government regulation and opposed the Bush administration's immigration proposals. Devine, who had refused to remove a Ten Commandments display from his Harris County courtroom, had the support of Christian conservatives and called for a crackdown on illegal immigration. In the primary, Streusand carried seven of the eight counties to finish with 28% of the vote, to 24% for McCaul and 21% for Devine.

In the runoff campaign, McCaul and Streusand agreed on most issues. In the absence of clear distinctions, they traded accusations about each other's background. McCaul criticized Streusand's past donations to Democratic candidates, while Streusand questioned McCaul's service in the Clinton administration Justice Department. McCaul used his connections—his father-in-law is Clear Channel Communications chairman and Bush family friend Lowry Mays—to collect major Republican endorsements, including from former President George H.W. Bush, Gov. Rick Perry and Sen. Kay Bailey Hutchison. He was also endorsed by his old boss, Sen. John Cornyn. McCaul won 63%-37% in a contest in a low-turnout event with only 24,000 votes. He carried every county except one, which he lost by seven votes. He faced no major-party opposition in the general election.

In the House, McCaul has a moderate-to-conservative voting record. He is on the Homeland Security Committee and is the ranking Republican on its Intelligence, Information Sharing and Terrorism Risk Assessment Subcommittee. As a freshman, he gained headlines with hearings that revealed more than $1 billion in fraud in Hurricane Katrina disaster relief. At the request of Republican leaders in 2006, he took the lead in a successful bill to increase the Federal Emergency Management Agency's tracking of payments to victims in order to reduce corruption. In 2007, he collaborated with Rep. Jim Langevin, D-R.I., on a commission to recommend steps to improve cyber-security. In 2008, he helped attach an amendment to an appropriations bill that prohibited sitting members of Congress from requesting money for projects named for them.

His re-election performances suggest he needs to work harder in this once-solidly GOP district. In 2006, against retired Navy Captain Ted Ankrum, an underfunded challenger, McCaul won 55%-40%. Hs challenger in 2008 was Larry Joe Doherty, a Houston lawyer who stars as a judge in a courtroom reality television show called "Texas Justice." Doherty raised $1.2 million while McCaul raised $1.7 million. Doherty characterized McCaul as voting most of the time for the Republican agenda, including cuts in Medicare. McCaul said that he is an "independent voice" and accused Doherty of supporting a health care plan that would lead to rationing. McCaul won 54%-43%. He could face another tough re-election challenge in 2010.

ELEVENTH DISTRICT

Mike Conaway (R)

Elected 2004, 3rd term; b. June 11, 1948, Borger; home, Midland; E. TX St. U., B.B.A. 1970; Baptist; married (Suzanne); 4 children.

Military Career: Army, 1970–72.

Elected Office: Midland Schl. Bd., 1985–88.

Professional Career: Tax mgr., Price Waterhouse & Co., 1972–80; CFO, Keith G. Graham, 1980–81; CFO, Lantern Petroleum Comp., 1981; CFO, Arbusto Energy Inc./Bush Exploration Comp., 1982–84; CFO, Spectrum 7 Energy Corp., 1984–86; CFO, United Bank, 1987–90; Sr. VP, TX Comm. Bank, 1990–92; Board member, TX Bd. of Pub. Accountancy, 1995–2002, Chmn., 1997–2002; Owner, K. Michael Conaway, CPA, 1993–2004.

DC Office: 1527 LHOB, 20515, 202-225-3605; Fax: 202-225-1783; Web site: www.conaway.house.gov.

State Offices: Brownwood, 325-646-1950; Llano, 325-247-2826; Midland, 432-687-2390; Odessa, 432-331-9667; San Angelo, 325-659-4010.

Committees: *Chief Deputy Minority Whip. Agriculture* (9th of 18 R): General Farm Commodities & Risk Management; Livestock, Dairy & Poultry; Rural Development, Biotechnology, Specialty Crops & Foreign Agriculture (RMM). *Armed Services* (17th of 25 R): Readiness; Terrorism, Unconventional Threats & Capabilities. *Intelligence (Select)* (8th of 9 R): Intelligence Community Management; Terrorism, Human Intelligence, Analysis & Counterintelligence. *Standards of Official Conduct* (3rd of 5 R):

Group Ratings

	ADA	ACLU	AFS	LCV	ITIC	NTU	COC	ACU	CFG	FRC
2008	5	18	0	0	43	71	89	92	77	100
2007	5	—	9	0	—	84	70	96	94	—

National Journal Ratings

	2007 LIB — 2007 CONS		2008 LIB — 2008 CONS	
Economic	3%	— 97%	3%	— 95%
Social	0%	— 91%	16%	— 82%
Foreign	0%	— 72%	5%	— 93%
Composite	7%	— 93%	9%	— 91%

Key Votes of the 110th Congress

1. Increase minimum wage	N	5. Share immigration data	Y	9. Withdraw troops 8/08	N
2. Expand SCHIP	N	6. Foreign aid abortion ban	Y	10. No operations in Iran	N
3. Raise CAFE standards	N	7. Ban gay bias in workplace	N	11. Free trade with Peru	Y
4. Bail out financial markets	Y	8. Repeal D.C. gun law	Y	12. Overhaul FISA	Y

Election Results

2008 general	Mike Conaway (R)	189,625	(88%)	($951,802)
	John Strohm (Lib)	25,051	(12%)	
2008 primary	Mike Conaway (R)	.... unopposed		

Prior Winning Percentages: 2006 (100%); 2004 (77%)

Population		Race/Ethnicity		Work	
Pop. 2007:	672,208	White:	60.8%	Private:	72.7%
Change since 2000:	Up 3.2%	Black:	3.7%	Government:	16.8%
Urban:	70.8%	Hispanic:	33.1%	Self-employed:	10.2%
Rural:	29.2%	Asian:	0.7%	Blue collar:	27.8%
Area size:	35,185 sq. mi.	Native Am.:	0.4%	White collar:	52.5%
		Hawaiian:	0.0%	Khaki collar:	0.7%
Age		Two+ races:	1.2%	Other:	19.1%
Median age:	36.6 yrs.			Median income:	$40,895
More than 65 yrs:	15.0%	*Ancestry*		Median home value:	$76,500
Less than 18 yrs:	25.6%	German:	12.4%	Poverty:	16.4%
		English:	9.4%		
Education		Irish:	9.1%	**Military Veterans**	
H.S. grad:	76.4%			% of Pop:	11.7%
College grad:	17.9%				
Grad degree:	5.0%				

More than 400 years ago, in the 1540s, the conquistador Francisco Coronado and his men rode their horses over the plains of the land they called the Llano Estacado, or "flat palisades," land that is now the plains of West Texas. They saw a vast empty land, gradually and imperceptibly rising in elevation to the west, with only scrub vegetation and small bands of Comanche Indians. What they did not see, lying far beneath the surface, was oil, discovered in the 1940s in large amounts in the

2008 Presidential Vote		
McCain (R)	185,350	(75%)
Obama (D)	58,323	(24%)

2004 Presidential Vote		
Bush (R)	188,929	(78%)
Kerry (D)	52,174	(22%)

Cook Partisan Voting Index: R + 28

Permian Basin. When oil was found, two tiny county seats 25 miles apart suddenly became small cities—Odessa, home of the roughneck oil well workers, and Midland, the more upscale town where oil entrepreneurs lived and started their own Petroleum Club. The Permian Basin boomed in the years just after World War II. In 1940, Ector and Midland counties had a population of 26,000. By 1960, they had grown to 159,000. Midland in the 1950s was an affluent town by west Texas standards, but hardly a luxurious town. Air conditioning had not yet become standard in homes or schools, and there were no mansions at the edge of town, just barren desert and oil derricks. George and Barbara Bush moved to the Permian Basin in 1948 in search of success in the oil industry and room for a growing family. They rented houses in Odessa before upgrading to a series of larger, but by no means grand, ranch houses in Midland.

Since then, growth has slowed, as new discoveries have grown fewer, but the area still yields about 80% of the state's oil and 30% of its gas. Midland's unemployment rate in 2008 was among the lowest in the nation following the oil-price boom, but the familiar boom-and-bust fears pervaded as the subsequent price drop quickly led to the closing of dozens of rigs. Republican President George W. Bush and his wife Laura, also from Midland, came here immediately after leaving Washington, D.C. in January 2009, and enjoyed a local reception as warm as their Washington departure was chilly.

The 11th Congressional District of Texas covers much of West Texas and encompasses 36 counties. The district sweeps 400 miles across much of the state, beginning in the hills of fast-growing Burnet County just north of Austin and Gillespie County, home to Democratic President Lyndon Johnson. To the west is oil-producing Loving County, on the New Mexico border. With 55 people in 2007, it was the least populous county the United States. Geographically the district is larger than 12 states; 54% of the population is in Midland, Ector and Tom Green (San Angelo) counties. None of the other counties have more than 39,000 people. The district's Hispanic population is 33% and poverty is a bit above the national average, but no longer as pervasive as when Lyndon Johnson was a kid.

Politically, West Texas in the 1940s was, like nearly every other part of Texas, almost totally Democratic. That began to change in the 1950s as Midland moved toward Republicans. Newcomers like the Bushes were an important part of this trend. The current 11th District is overwhelmingly Republican, and the first district in which Midland and Odessa have been dominant. In 2004, the 11th District cast 78% of its votes for Bush, his highest percent in the nation. In 2008, John McCain did almost as well. His 75% was his fifth-best district in the nation.

The congressman from the 11th District is Mike Conaway, a Republican first elected in 2004. Conaway grew up in Odessa and graduated from East Texas State University, before it became known as Texas A&M-Commerce. He worked as a certified public accountant for, among others, George W. Bush, and was chief financial officer in Arbusto/Bush Exploration during the 1980s. After Bush became governor, he named Conaway to the state Board of Public Accountancy, and Conaway later chaired the National Association of State Boards of Accountancy. In May 2003, he finished second in the all-party special primary election in the old 19th District, which included nearly half of the new 11th. In June, he lost by fewer than 600 votes in a hard-fought runoff with Republican Randy Neugebauer of Lubbock, who later won the seat.

After state Republicans pushed through a new redistricting plan that October, Conaway was the obvious frontrunner for this seat. Democratic Rep. Charles Stenholm, who represented much of the area in the old 17th District, decided to run against Neugebauer in the new 19th District. Conaway's Republican primary opponent was Bill Lester, a political science professor who campaigned against Bush's proposed guest worker program. Lester called for the militarization of the border with helicopter patrols to stop illegal immigration. Conaway, a supporter of the Bush immigration proposal, said that increased documentation would strengthen national security by separating "those who are seeking economic opportunity" from "those who would do us harm." Conaway won 75%- 25%, carrying 33 of the 36 counties and losing only in the eastern part of the district. In the general election, he won easily, 77%-22%.

Conaway has a solidly conservative voting record and wasn't shy about touting his relationship with Bush. "I believe I will be more effective if the president knows my first name than if he didn't," he told his hometown newspaper after he took office. Their relationship paid dividends for Bush. Conaway, who voted against the original $700 billion bailout of the financial services industry in October 2008, voted for the final version after Bush called him to urge his support. Conaway led opposition in 2008 to a bill to require radio stations to pay royalties for playing music, arguing that many small stations might not survive.

In 2007, Conaway, a certified public accountant, joined the executive committee of the National Republican Congressional Committee to take charge of auditing. He uncovered an internal fraud scheme by the committee's longtime treasurer, who had embezzled almost $1 million. In January 2009, he sought a seat on the powerful House Ways and Means Committee but was unsuccessful. However, as ranking Republican on the Agriculture specialty crops Subcommittee, he is well-positioned to advocate for local farmers. He has been re-elected without major-party opposition.

TWELFTH DISTRICT

Kay Granger (R)

Elected 1996, 7th term; b. Jan. 18, 1943, Greenville; home, Ft. Worth; TX Wesleyan Col., B.S. 1965; Methodist; divorced; 3 children.

Elected Office: Ft. Worth City Cncl., 1989–91; Ft. Worth mayor, 1991–96.

Professional Career: Teacher, 1965–78; Life Insurance agent, 1978–85; Chmn., Ft. Worth Zoning Comm., 1981–88; Founder & Pres., Kay Granger Insurance Co., Inc., 1985–present.

DC Office: 320 CHOB, 20515, 202-225-5071; Fax: 202-225-5683; Web site: kaygranger.house.gov.

State Offices: Ft. Worth, 817-338-0909.

Committees: *Appropriations* (12th of 23 R): Defense; State, Foreign Operations & Related Programs (RMM).

Group Ratings

	ADA	ACLU	AFS	LCV	ITIC	NTU	COC	ACU	CFG	FRC
2008	5	18	14	0	50	67	100	92	75	70
2007	10	—	0	0	—	79	79	92	91	—

National Journal Ratings

	2007 LIB	—	2007 CONS		2008 LIB	—	2008 CONS
Economic	13%	—	87%		14%	—	86%
Social	36%	—	63%		27%	—	71%
Foreign	36%	—	64%		12%	—	87%
Composite	29%	—	72%		18%	—	82%

Key Votes of the 110th Congress

1. Increase minimum wage	N	5. Share immigration data	Y	9. Withdraw troops 8/08	N
2. Expand SCHIP	N	6. Foreign aid abortion ban	Y	10. No operations in Iran	N
3. Raise CAFE standards	*	7. Ban gay bias in workplace	N	11. Free trade with Peru	Y
4. Bail out financial markets	Y	8. Repeal D.C. gun law	Y	12. Overhaul FISA	Y

Election Results

2008 general	Kay Granger (R)	181,662	(68%)	($1,452,977)
	Tracey Smith (D)	82,250	(31%)	($16,300)
2008 primary	Kay Granger (R)	unopposed		

Prior Winning Percentages: 2006 (67%); 2004 (72%); 2002 (92%); 2000 (63%); 1998 (62%); 1996 (58%)

Population		Race/Ethnicity		Work	
Pop. 2007:	752,348	White:	63.2%	Private:	81.6%
Change since 2000:	Up 15.5%	Black:	5.9%	Government:	11.5%
Urban:	82.8%	Hispanic:	26.5%	Self-employed:	6.7%
Rural:	17.2%	Asian:	2.8%	Blue collar:	27.0%
Area size:	2,217 sq. mi.	Native Am.:	0.4%	White collar:	57.5%
		Hawaiian:	0.0%	Khaki collar:	0.2%
Age		Two+ races:	1.0%	Other:	15.3%
Median age:	33.5 yrs.			Median income:	$51,216
More than 65 yrs:	9.5%	*Ancestry*		Median home value:	$111,600
Less than 18 yrs:	26.6%	German:	10.4%	Poverty:	12.9%
		USA:	9.1%		
Education		Irish:	8.6%	**Military Veterans**	
H.S. grad:	80.2%			% of Pop:	10.5%
College grad:	23.0%				
Grad degree:	7.2%				

Fort Worth, has a fair claim to being the quintessential mid-American city. It sits halfway across the continent, just west of the Balcones Escarpment that divides the dry treeless grazing lands of West Texas from the humid green croplands of East Texas, "where the West begins," as its 19th century boosters proclaimed, coining the slogan used by the city. This was the last stop for cattle drives before they returned to Kansas. It is Southern in heritage and Northern in its advanced post-

2008 Presidential Vote

McCain (R)	171,408	(63%)
Obama (D)	99,083	(36%)

2004 Presidential Vote

Bush (R)	162,192	(67%)
Kerry (D)	79,862	(33%)

Cook Partisan Voting Index: R + 16

industrial economy. It has the nation's longest row of Western wear shops and one of the nation's richest families, the Basses, whose steel skyscrapers dominate the skyline.

"Cowtown," as the city is sometimes called, is the 17th largest city in the nation, larger than Boston, Memphis and Baltimore. Fort Worth has a high-tech economy and has been an aviation center since the 1940s, though one hard hit by defense cuts. The big Lockheed Martin (formerly General Dynamics) plant produces numerous bombers and fighter planes for the armed forces. Next door is Carswell Air Force Base, the home of B-52 bombers for years, which was expanded after the base review of 2005. The assembly lines at Bell Helicopter Textron's nearby plant were rescued when the Texas delegation and others overruled the cancellation of the accident-prone V-22 Osprey. Since then, it won the contract for a new reconnaissance helicopter. *The New York Times* has called the city "an irresistible combination of cowboys and culture," in part because it has some of the nation's premier small museums, including the Amon Carter Museum of Western Art, the Kimbell Museum, the Museum of Modern Art and the Sid Richardson Museum. The city has Texas-sized watering holes and eateries, like Billy Bob's Texas, the world's largest honky-tonk, in the Stockyards. Culturally, it tends to be more conservative than large cities in the East. In December 2008, the local Episcopal diocese broke with the national church over the ordination of a gay bishop.

The 12th Congressional District of Texas includes two-thirds of Fort Worth and western suburban Tarrant County, as well as all of Parker and Wise counties to the west and northwest. Approximately 75% of the population is in Tarrant, which has grown an impressive 19% since 2000. The district includes northern and western city neighborhoods and the affluent southwest quarter beyond Texas Christian University, downtown and the Stockyards. Parker County was once windswept open land around the courthouse town of Weatherford, where former U.S. House Speaker Jim Wright, a Democrat, grew up and was first elected to the House in 1954. Today, it is sprouting subdivisions and it grew 23% from 2000 to 2007. Fort Worth and Tarrant County stayed Democratic in the 1950s when Dallas went Republican. With Dallas recently swinging back to Democrats, Fort Worth and Tarrant have remained Republican. The 12th District, which Wright represented until 1989, is now solidly Republican—67% of voters here backed Republican President George W. Bush in 2004 and 63% supported Republican candidate John McCain in 2008.

The congresswoman from the 12th District is Kay Granger, a Republican first elected in 1996. Granger grew up in Fort Worth, graduated from Texas Wesleyan College, and worked as a teacher in North Richland Hills. She raised three children and started her own insurance agency. In 1989, she was elected to the Fort Worth Council, and two years later, was elected as mayor. In 1995, when Rep. Pete Geren, a conservative Democrat who succeeded Wright, announced he would not seek re-election, both Republican and Democratic leaders tried to recruit Granger. She decided to run in the Republican primary. In a three-candidate race, she was attacked as a liberal, partly for her support of abortion rights. But she won with 69% of the vote. Her Democratic opponent was Hugh Parmer, a former Fort Worth mayor and the Democratic nominee against Republican Sen. Phil Gramm in 1990. Parmer attacked Republican cuts in Medicare and the stewardship of Republican House Speaker Newt Gingrich. Granger called for a balanced budget and tax cuts for business, and ran on her record as mayor. Granger won 58%-41%, a stunning victory in Wright's old district.

In the House, Granger's voting record has tended to be moderate on cultural issues and more conservative on economic issues. She became a favorite of Republican leaders, although she has split with them on issues such as the Food and Drug Administration's approval of the RU-486 abortion pill and her support for increasing federal funding for embryonic stem cell research. In 2007 and 2008, she was vice-chair of the Republican Conference, where she promoted issues such as retirement planning and reducing the influence of gangs. She stepped down after the 2008 election.

With a seat on the Appropriations Committee, Granger keeps a close eye on local Pentagon spending. She has worked to maintain production of Lockheed Martin planes that are produced in her district. In 2009, Granger became the ranking Republican on the Appropriations Committee's Subcommittee on State and Foreign Operations, where her experience with military spending and her interest in human rights are useful.

In response to criticism of the Wright Amendment, which protected Dallas/Fort Worth International Airport from competition from Dallas' Love Field, Granger worked to create a local regional airport authority to encourage cooperation between DFW and Love. In 2006, she joined others from the Metroplex in repealing the amendment.

Granger has produced some original initiatives. One of her legislative achievements was enactment of tax-free savings accounts for higher education expenses. In 2003, she and Rep. Sander Levin, D-Mich., proposed a national gynecological cancer detection program. In January 2005, she traveled to Iraq, where she and Rep. Ellen Tauscher, D-Calif., conducted a training session for women candidates in their election. In 2007, she helped to create the bipartisan Anti-Terror Caucus.

Granger has been re-elected by wide margins. She is the author of a book, *What's Right About America: Celebrating Our Nation's Values*, published in 2006.

THIRTEENTH DISTRICT

Mac Thornberry (R)

Elected 1994, 8th term; b. July 15, 1958, Clarendon; home, Clarendon; TX Tech. U., B.A. 1980, U. of TX Law Schl., J.D. 1983; Presbyterian; married (Sally); 2 children.

Professional Career: Legis. cnsl., U.S. Rep. Tom Loeffler, 1983–85; Chief of staff, U.S. Rep. Larry Combest, 1985–88; Dpty. asst. secy. of state for Legis. Affairs, 1988–89; Practicing atty., 1989–94; Rancher 1989–94.

DC Office: 2209 RHOB, 20515, 202-225-3706; Fax: 202-225-3486; Web site: www.house.gov/thornberry.

State Offices: Amarillo, 806-371-8844; Wichita Falls, 940-692-1700.

Committees: *Armed Services* (3rd of 25 R): Strategic Forces; Terrorism, Unconventional Threats & Capabilities. *Intelligence (Select)* (3rd of 9 R): Oversight & Investigations; Technical & Tactical Intelligence.

Group Ratings

	ADA	ACLU	AFS	LCV	ITIC	NTU	COC	ACU	CFG	FRC
2008	5	18	0	0	86	71	89	92	82	100
2007	5	—	0	0	—	81	85	100	89	—

National Journal Ratings

	2007 LIB — 2007 CONS		2008 LIB — 2008 CONS	
Economic	6%	93%	6%	93%
Social	0%	91%	9%	85%
Foreign	0%	72%	8%	89%
Composite	8%	92%	9%	91%

Key Votes of the 110th Congress

1. Increase minimum wage	N	5. Share immigration data	Y	9. Withdraw troops 8/08	N
2. Expand SCHIP	N	6. Foreign aid abortion ban	Y	10. No operations in Iran	N
3. Raise CAFE standards	N	7. Ban gay bias in workplace	N	11. Free trade with Peru	Y
4. Bail out financial markets	Y	8. Repeal D.C. gun law	Y	12. Overhaul FISA	Y

Election Results

2008 general	Mac Thornberry (R)	180,078	(78%)	($789,264)
	Roger Waun (D)	51,841	(22%)	($13,211)
2008 primary	Mac Thornberry (R)	unopposed		

Prior Winning Percentages: 2006 (74%); 2004 (92%); 2002 (79%); 2000 (68%); 1998 (68%); 1996 (67%); 1994 (55%)

Population		Race/Ethnicity		Work	
Pop. 2007:	652,282	White:	70.0%	Private:	71.9%
Change since 2000:	Up 0.1%	Black:	6.0%	Government:	19.1%
Urban:	69.9%	Hispanic:	20.5%	Self-employed:	8.7%
Rural:	30.1%	Asian:	1.3%	Blue collar:	27.9%
Area size:	40,403 sq. mi.	Native Am.:	0.6%	White collar:	51.3%
		Hawaiian:	0.0%	Khaki collar:	1.5%
Age		Two+ races:	1.4%	Other:	19.3%
Median age:	35.8 yrs.			Median income:	$40,384
More than 65 yrs:	13.7%	*Ancestry*		Median home value:	$75,900
Less than 18 yrs:	25.5%	German:	12.6%	Poverty:	15.6%
		Irish:	9.8%		
Education		USA:	8.7%	**Military Veterans**	
H.S. grad:	79.2%			% of Pop:	11.5%
College grad:	18.0%				
Grad degree:	5.4%				

The farther west one travels in Texas, the browner the land gets and the smaller the towns get, until you arrive at counties containing only a few hundred people each—plus quite a few more head of cattle. At that point, the land rises nearly 1,000 feet in elevation, up steep hillsides from the gullies along the rivers that for most of the year are just tiny trickles, to the tilted tableland that makes up the High Plains of West Texas. The winds here sweep down from the Rockies, the land is barren

2008 Presidential Vote

McCain (R)	181,456	(76%)
Obama (D)	53,837	(23%)

2004 Presidential Vote

Bush (R)	183,375	(78%)
Kerry (D)	52,431	(22%)

Cook Partisan Voting Index: R + 29

except where irrigated, often with the now dangerously depleted waters of the Ogallala Aquifer. The land alternates between grazing areas and cotton fields. But here and there in this demanding environment—sticky-hot in the summer, swept by north winds from Canada in winter, always threatened in "Tornado Alley"—comfortable cities have been built to house the people and businesses that bring forth some of the nation's most abundant oil, natural gas, helium and other elements from the earth.

The 13th Congressional District of Texas covers more than 40,000 square miles, from the New Mexico border to just north of Dallas, and it includes 42 counties and parts of two others. The population of this region has been either in decline or stagnant for nearly three decades. In the 1990s, the district registered a population increase of just 5%, the smallest gain of any Texas district. From 2000 to 2007, growth in the district was less than 1%. Around Wichita Falls is the agricultural land of the Red River Valley and one of Bell Helicopter's V-22 Osprey plants. Sheppard Air Force Base, a medical facility and pilot training center, was hit hard by cutbacks in the 2005 base review.

The area produces cotton and milo, a variety of sorghum, and is home to one of the nation's oldest cattle auctions. The area was long dominated by Texas Anglos, but Latinos lately have been moving here in large numbers to work in the fields or in crop processing. Today, the district is 21% Hispanic. Much of the High Plains economy is based on natural resources. The largest city here is Amarillo in the heart of cowboy country. It is the center of the largest natural gas development in the world, and is—not Chicago—the windiest city in the United States. Just outside town is the Pantex plant that secretly assembled the nation's thousands of nuclear warheads and was the epicenter of American defense in the Cold War. Its 16,000 acres have been used to dismantle some disarmed weapons and now maintain the remainder of the arsenal. Settled by Confederate veterans, the valley was heavily Democratic through the 1970s. The High Plains was for years more Republican. Both parts are now solidly Republican. The 78% that George W. Bush won here in 2004 was his third-best performance in the nation. GOP presidential nominee John McCain won 76.4% in 2008, his second-best district in the nation, behind Alabama's 6th District.

The congressman from the 13th District is Mac Thornberry, a Republican first elected in 1994. His great-great-grandfather, Amos Thornberry, a Union Army veteran and staunch Republican, moved to Clay County, just east of Wichita Falls, in the 1880s. A year after Amos died in 1925, his son bought the cattle ranch that Mac Thornberry, his brothers and father now run. From the window of his ranch house, writes *The Texas Techsan*, "as far as the eye can see is the Golden Spread of Texas for which this part of the state is named. There are no buildings, no roadways, no signs of life. Gaze out long enough and you begin to think you can actually see the curvature of the earth." After college and law school in Texas, Thornberry worked for Texas Republican Reps. Tom Loeffler and Larry Combest. He returned to practice law in West Texas, and in 1994, challenged Democratic Rep. Bill Sarpalius, whom he attacked for voting for President Bill Clinton's budget and tax package. He also profited from news stories that said Sarpalius failed to pay a company that moved him to Washington, and then accepted a fee for speaking at the company's convention in Las Vegas. Thornberry won 55%-45%.

In the House, Thornberry has compiled a solidly conservative voting record, though he has a pragmatic streak and is hardly the most ideological in the Texas delegation. His hard work on defense and homeland security issues has earned him a reputation as one of the brainiest and most accessible lawmakers on those issues. In March 2001, he sponsored a bill to create a homeland security agency and the next year, played a key role in the establishment of the new executive branch department.

In 2009, he took over as the ranking Republican on the Technical and Tactical Intelligence Subcommittee of the Permanent Select Committee on Intelligence. He earlier criticized delays in integrating computer networks and intelligence analysis into the new Homeland Security Department. On the Armed Services Committee, he has championed missile defense and called for better coordination of military space programs and on the Intelligence Committee he helped to enact new rules for the handling of terror suspects and detainees in 2006.

On domestic issues, Thornberry has pressed for repeal of the estate tax repeal and also tax credits to encourage production of oil in marginal wells. In 2008, he proposed a "No More Excuses" energy plan to develop several new sources of energy.

FOURTEENTH DISTRICT

Ron Paul (R)

Elected 1996, 10th full term; b. Aug. 20, 1935, Pittsburgh, PA; home, Surfside; Gettysburg Col., B.A. 1957, Duke U., M.D. 1961; Protestant; married (Carol); 5 children.

Military Career: Flight surgeon, Air Force, 1963–68.

Elected Office: U.S. House of Reps., 1976, 1978–84.

Professional Career: Practicing physician, 1968–96.

DC Office: 203 CHOB, 20515, 202-225-2831; Web site: www.house.gov/paul.

State Offices: Galveston, 409-766-7013; Lake Jackson, 979-285-0231; Victoria, 361-576-1231.

Committees: *Financial Services* (6th of 29 R): Domestic Monetary Policy & Technology (RMM); International Monetary Policy & Trade; Oversight & Investigations. *Foreign Affairs* (8th of 19 R): International Organizations, Human Rights & Oversight; Western Hemisphere. *Joint Economic Committee* (2nd of 4 R).

Group Ratings

	ADA	ACLU	AFS	LCV	ITIC	NTU	COC	ACU	CFG	FRC
2008	10	33	14	0	0	96	47	90	88	52
2007	15	—	10	15	—	91	47	77	80	—

National Journal Ratings

	2007 LIB	—	2007 CONS		2008 LIB	—	2008 CONS
Economic	20%	—	80%		8%	—	91%
Social	47%	—	52%		41%	—	58%
Foreign	52%	—	48%		42%	—	57%
Composite	40%	—	60%		31%	—	69%

Key Votes of the 110th Congress

1. Increase minimum wage	N	5. Share immigration data	*	9. Withdraw troops 8/08	N
2. Expand SCHIP	N	6. Foreign aid abortion ban	*	10. No operations in Iran	Y
3. Raise CAFE standards	*	7. Ban gay bias in workplace	*	11. Free trade with Peru	N
4. Bail out financial markets	N	8. Repeal D.C. gun law	Y	12. Overhaul FISA	*

Election Results

2008 general	Ron Paul (R).. unopposed	
2008 primary	Ron Paul (R)..37,777	(70%)
	Chris Peden (R)...15,859	(30%)

Prior Winning Percentages: 2006 (60%); 2004 (100%); 2002 (68%); 2000 (60%); 1998 (55%); 1996 (51%); 1982 (99%); 1980 (51%); 1978 (51%); 1976 (56%)

Population		Race/Ethnicity		Work	
Pop. 2007:	719,509	White:	59.2%	Private:	76.6%
Change since 2000:	Up 10.4%	Black:	9.3%	Government:	15.9%
Urban:	71.1%	Hispanic:	27.2%	Self-employed:	7.2%
Rural:	28.9%	Asian:	2.5%	Blue collar:	26.1%
Area size:	9,369 sq. mi.	Native Am.:	0.3%	White collar:	56.8%
		Hawaiian:	0.1%	Khaki collar:	0.1%
Age		Two+ races:	1.1%	Other:	17.0%
Median age:	35.9 yrs.	*Ancestry*		Median income:	$50,622
More than 65 yrs:	11.4%	German:	13.3%	Median home value:	$112,300
Less than 18 yrs:	26.8%	Irish:	9.3%	Poverty:	13.8%
Education		English:	6.9%		
H.S. grad:	81.3%			**Military Veterans**	
College grad:	22.1%			% of Pop:	10.8%
Grad degree:	6.8%				

Retreating east from the Alamo, the ragtag army led by Sam Houston passed over what would become, after their bloody and conclusive victory at San Jacinto, some of the prime cropland in the Republic and later the state of Texas. The hilly and river-crossed land between Houston and Austin, named after Texas' first two leaders, was settled early. The first capital of the Republic of Texas was in Brazoria County. The flat coastal plains, steamy and humid so much of the year, were settled later,

2008 Presidential Vote

McCain (R)............................177,370	(66%)
Obama (D) 88,532	(33%)

2004 Presidential Vote

Bush (R).................................169,480	(67%)
Kerry (D).................................82,792	(33%)

Cook Partisan Voting Index: R + 18

when the railroads came in. Rice is grown along the coast, with cotton and cattle production inland. The Gulf of Mexico coastline, though it has plenty of inlets, never had any important ports in the stretch between Houston and Corpus Christi until the discovery of oil here made it worthwhile to build channels to ship the oil out.

This is the land of the 14th Congressional District of Texas. With rural countryside and the cities of Victoria and El Campo, it runs along the Gulf coast between Corpus Christi and Port Arthur. Victoria is a rail hub that serves Gulf ports, and it also includes large industrial plants, such as DuPont, Union Carbide, Alcoa and BP Chemicals. Galveston, on a barrier island on the Gulf, was an immigrant port known as the Ellis Island of the West until a 1900 hurricane killed thousands. The city is now guarded by a 17-foot seawall and connected to the mainland by a hurricane-resistant bridge. In September 2008, Galveston feared a direct hit from Hurricane Ike, which would have been its first since 1900. Although the storm caused billions of dollars in damage and left thousands of people temporarily homeless, it veered north just before striking land and Galveston escaped the worst-case scenario. This district is mostly small-city Texas, but much of it now surrounds the suburban fringes of metropolitan Houston. The region is ancestrally Democratic, but it has trended Republican since the 1980s. The district voted 67% for Republican President George W. Bush in 2004 and 66% for Republican presidential nominee John McCain in 2008.

The congressman from the 14th District is Ron Paul, a Republican first elected to Congress more than three decades ago. He failed in his only attempt to win statewide office yet he gained celebrity status in 2008 in his second run for president.

Paul grew up on dairy farm in western Pennsylvania, and, with his four brothers, started helping out with the chores when he was still a boy. When he got older, he had a newspaper route, and then a job as a dairy truck driver. He was a track standout in high school, winning a state championship in the 220-yard dash his junior year. Paul was also student body president. He got a science degree from Gettysburg College in 1957 and a medical degree from Duke University. He served as an Air Force flight surgeon in the 1960s, and then moved with his wife, Carol, to Texas to practice obstetrics and gynecology in Brazoria County. Paul recalls that he was dismayed when Republican President Richard Nixon cut the connection between the dollar and gold in 1971, and led to him becoming increasingly interested in politics, although he continued to practice medicine. In 1976, he won a special election by defeating Democratic state Rep. Bob Gammage. But when the congressional seat came up in the general election seven months later, Gammage defeated Paul by less than 300 votes. Two years later, Paul won the seat back from Gammage. Paul ran for the Senate in 1984 and lost the Republican primary to U.S. Rep. Phil Gramm 73%-16%. (His House seat was won by a young legislator and exterminating company owner, Tom DeLay, a Republican who rose to become one of the most powerful members of Congress until an ethics scandal drove him from office.) In 1988, Paul ran for president as a Libertarian candidate, finishing a distant third with 432,000 votes, 0.47% of the total.

Paul reentered electoral politics after Democratic U.S. Rep. Greg Laughlin switched to the Republican Party in June 1995. Laughlin had a moderate voting record, and Republicans offered him a seat on the powerful House Ways and Means Committee to make the switch, and he did. Paul challenged him in 1996, raising money from a nationwide network of Libertarians, gold bugs and subscribers to the *Ron Paul Political Report*. Laughlin led in the primary with 43% of the vote, but Paul won the runoff 54%-46%. In the general election, Democrats ran Charles "Lefty" Morris, a former president of the state trial lawyers' association. With the slogan "Lefty is right," Morris hit Paul for favoring abolition of the minimum wage, repeal of federal anti-drug laws and anti-prostitution laws. Paul won 51%-48%.

In his first stint in the House, Paul had advanced some ideas that by the mid-1990s, when he was returning to Congress, had almost become mainstream: term limits and abolition of the income tax. Other Paul ideas remained outside the political norm. He endorsed a group that wanted to end all government funding of education, and he supported cutting $150 billion from the defense budget and returning to the gold standard. Paul practices what he preaches. He will not accept payment by Medicare or Medicaid, he wouldn't let his children accept federal student loans and he refuses his congressional pension. He has written several books.

With his Libertarian views, Paul's voting record has been anything but rock-solid Republican. *National Journal* ratings place him near the middle of the House. "Dr. No," as he is called, never votes for legislation that in his view is not expressly authorized by the Constitution. Frequently, his insistence on limited government made Paul the House's lone dissenter—against bills to require states to report on their progress in improving student achievement, to award Congressional Gold Medals to Rosa Parks and Pope John Paul II, to pass the USA Patriot Act after the September 11 attacks, and to spend money on homeland security. He favors relaxation of restrictions on illegal drugs, though he says that he has never even smoked a cigarette, and he filed a lawsuit challenging the 2002 McCain-Feingold campaign finance act as a violation of the First Amendment. After his district in September 2005 was rocked by Hurricane Rita, he voted against hurricane relief. And then, without explanation, he voted against the September 2008 appropriation bill that included $23 billion in disaster aid for victims of Hurricane Ike (though he joined President Bush's visit to Houston, where Bush promised federal aid after the storm).

Paul also opposed the constitutional ban on same-sex marriages, saying that the states should set such policy. He favors elimination of laws against gambling and guns, though he has rarely participated in either gambling or hunting. He deliberately delivers few spending bill earmarks to his district. Paul's isolationist views on foreign policy made his voting record on those issues indistinct from many liberal Democrats. He was the only Republican to vote "present" on the resolution expressing support for the military forces at the start of the war with Iraq. In June 2005, he cosponsored with Rep. Dennis Kucinich, D-Ohio, and others a resolution to withdraw from Iraq. In February 2007, he was one of 17 House Republicans who voted for the resolution opposing Bush's troop surge in Iraq. Paul envisions virtually no role for the U.S. government overseas—from military defense to international trade. He calls himself a "noninterventionist," not an isolationist. In a July 2003 speech in the House, which he called "Neo-Conned," he harshly attacked the Bush administration. "The so-called conservative revolution of the past two decades has given us massive growth in government size, spending and regulation," Paul said. His iconoclasm makes him probably the least dependable and persuadable Republican in the House and it explains why many liberals like him. And he does offer alternatives. He has been among the most prolific legislators, sponsoring dozens of bills and amendments each year. Typically, none pass.

Given his political isolation, his entry into the 2008 presidential campaign was not taken seriously. In March 2007, at age 71, he announced his candidacy for the Republican presidential nomination with the slogan, "The Taxpayers' Best Friend." Paul drew widespread attention, and the ire of former New York City Mayor Rudy Giuliani, when he suggested during a May 2007 Republican debate that interventionist American foreign policy led to September 11. "They attack us because we've been over there," he said. "We've been bombing Iraq for 10 years." Despite being dismissed by party professionals and most of the news media, Paul's campaign generated grass-roots interest and online support—sometimes with an appeal that appeared to extend beyond the candidate. His bloggers and other Internet backers sometimes flooded the dominant political websites. "Effective immediately, new users may not shill for Ron Paul in any way, shape, form or fashion," an editor for *www.redstate.com* wrote in October 2007. Paul raised $34 million, largely through the Internet, including a single-day fundraising record of $6 million in December 2007. He finished fifth in both the Iowa caucuses and the New Hampshire primary, though exit polls showed that he fared much better among young voters.

His well-organized and web-savvy supporters helped him to win many Internet polls, though that yielded scant impact on the official nominating contest. Nationwide, he received nearly 1.2 million Republican votes: 5.6% of the total cast. He won 12.3 % of the total caucus vote, running second in Louisiana, Montana and Nevada. Despite his plodding speeches and self-effacing style, his popularity continued even after his campaign sputtered. He got 16% in the Pennsylvania primary and he drew more than 1,000 people at a Louisville, Ky., rally after Republican candidate John McCain had wrapped up the nomination. In May 2008, his book *The Revolution: A Manifesto* was No. 1 on *The New York Times* best-seller list. Republican convention organizers refused to permit him to speak because he would not endorse McCain. So he sponsored his own events in Minneapolis-St. Paul, where the GOP convention was held, including a loud counter-rally for more than 10,000 in Minneapolis. Paul briefly considered a third-party run in the fall, but instead he urged support for other third-party candidates.

Back home, the national campaign raised speculation that the renewed attention to his views could weaken him in seeking to return to Congress. He was challenged by Chris Peden, a Friendswood city councilman who raised $268,000 and campaigned as a conventional Republican. He criticized Paul for failing to pass legislation or to vote with his party in Congress. On the day that McCain clinched the nomination and Paul received only 4.9% of his home-state vote in the presidential primary, he won the primary for re-election to the House 70%-30%. Democrats ran no challenger in November.

FIFTEENTH DISTRICT

Rubén Hinojosa (D)

Elected 1996, 7th term; b. Aug. 20, 1940, Mercedes; home, Mercedes; U. of TX, B.B.A. 1962, M.B.A. 1980; Catholic; married (Marty); 5 children.

Elected Office: TX Bd. of Educ., 1974–84.

Professional Career: Pres. & CEO, H&H Foods Inc., 1962–present.

DC Office: 2463 RHOB, 20515, 202-225-2531; Fax: 202-225-5688; Web site: www.house.gov/hinojosa.

State Offices: Beeville, 361-358-8400; Edinburg, 956-682-5545.

Committees: *Education & Labor* (7th of 29 D): Early Childhood, Elementary & Secondary Education; Higher Education, Lifelong Learning & Competitiveness (Chmn). *Financial Services* (13th of 42 D): Capital Markets, Insurance & Government Sponsored Enterprises; Financial Institutions & Consumer Credit.

Group Ratings

	ADA	ACLU	AFS	LCV	ITIC	NTU	COC	ACU	CFG	FRC
2008	80	88	100	85	100	9	59	9	4	5
2007	90	—	100	55	—	6	63	4	12	—

National Journal Ratings

	2007 LIB	—	2007 CONS	2008 LIB	—	2008 CONS
Economic	59%	—	41%	52%	—	47%
Social	71%	—	29%	72%	—	26%
Foreign	65%	—	35%	68%	—	31%
Composite	65%	—	35%	65%	—	35%

Key Votes of the 110th Congress

1. Increase minimum wage	Y	5. Share immigration data	N	9. Withdraw troops 8/08	Y
2. Expand SCHIP	Y	6. Foreign aid abortion ban	N	10. No operations in Iran	*
3. Raise CAFE standards	Y	7. Ban gay bias in workplace	Y	11. Free trade with Peru	Y
4. Bail out financial markets	Y	8. Repeal D.C. gun law	N	12. Overhaul FISA	Y

Election Results

2008 general	Rubén Hinojosa (D)	107,578	(66%)	($388,362)
	Eddie Zamora (R)	52,303	(32%)	($23,843)
	Gricha Raether (Lib)	3,827	(2%)	
2008 primary	Rubén Hinojosa (D)	.... unopposed		

Prior Winning Percentages: 2006 (62%); 2004 (58%); 2002 (100%); 2000 (88%); 1998 (58%); 1996 (62%)

Population		**Race/Ethnicity**		**Work**	
Pop. 2007:	731,723	White:	16.9%	Private:	69.7%
Change since 2000:	Up 12.3%	Black:	1.7%	Government:	20.2%
Urban:	82.1%	Hispanic:	80.0%	Self-employed:	9.7%
Rural:	17.9%	Asian:	0.7%	Blue collar:	21.8%
Area size:	10,849 sq. mi.	Native Am.:	0.2%	White collar:	53.4%
		Hawaiian:	0.0%	Khaki collar:	0.0%
Age		Two+ races:	0.4%	Other:	24.8%
Median age:	29.8 yrs.	*Ancestry*		Median income:	$30,181
More than 65 yrs:	11.2%	German:	5.4%	Median home value:	$65,000
Less than 18 yrs:	32.2%	Irish:	3.3%	Poverty:	33.7%
Education		English:	2.6%	**Military Veterans**	
H.S. grad:	64.2%			% of Pop:	7.5%
College grad:	14.5%				
Grad degree:	4.3%				

A century ago, there was little here but desert wilderness in the Lower Rio Grande Valley in South Texas. Only a handful of people lived anywhere near the shallow, sluggish Rio Grande. There was no Border Patrol because very few people wanted to venture across desert. Then came pioneers like Lloyd Bentsen Sr., father of the former senator and Treasury secretary, who arrived after World War I with $5 in his pocket and became one of the Valley's biggest landowners. Bentsen and others cleared the

2008 Presidential Vote		
Obama (D)	101,566	(60%)
McCain (R)	67,650	(40%)
2004 Presidential Vote		
Bush (R)	81,280	(51%)
Kerry (D)	77,011	(49%)
Cook Partisan Voting Index:	D + 3	

land and dug canals, hired Mexican and Mexican-American workers, and with irrigated water from the Rio Grande, planted citrus groves, cornfields and palm windbreaks, ran cattle and drilled for oil and gas. Along U.S. 83, north of the Rio Grande, these pioneers built a string of towns with Anglo names and storefronts. But most of the people here were Latino in culture and language. Wage levels higher than in Mexico, though low by U.S. standards, brought more Mexicans over the border.

The 15th Congressional District of Texas is one of three districts dividing up the Lower Rio Grande Valley. It has gone through four iterations in this decade alone. A court-drawn redistricting plan in August 2006 imposed modest changes, making the district more favorably Democratic and increasing its Hispanic population to 80%. The days are past when ranchers and oilmen wielded absolute political power here. There is instead a robust, mostly Hispanic, politics. Although the district reaches as far north as the rural area between Corpus Christi and San Antonio, about 70% of the district's residents live just north of the river in Hidalgo and Cameron counties, in or near the string of towns from McAllen to Harlingen. Reasonably priced real estate has helped make this the third-fastest growing metropolitan area in the nation. Hidalgo and Cameron counties' populations rose 70% from 1990 to 2007 from 644,000 to 1,098,000. The local infrastructure has barely kept up as subdivisions have replaced citrus groves. In the McAllen area, new suburbanites work just across the border as corporate managers in the low-wage "maquiladoras," or factories. There is great poverty here. Hidalgo County has the lowest median family income of any large county in the nation, and Cameron County doesn't fare much better. Increased border patrols, construction of a border fence and the recession that began in 2007 all took their toll on the local economy through the first half of 2009.

The congressman from the 15th District is Rubén Hinojosa, a Democrat first elected in 1996. Hinojosa (*Hee-no-HO-sa*) grew up in Mercedes, where his family owns H&H Foods, a company that produces Mexican foods and is one of the largest employers in the Valley. Hinojosa graduated from the University of Texas, then went into the family business and was active in civic affairs, primarily in education and regional development. He served on the state Board of Education and led an effort to create three regional magnet schools. After Democratic Rep. Kika de la Garza announced he would not seek re-election, Hinojosa decided to run. In the Democratic primary, he led Anglo lawyer Jim Selman 34%-33%. Selman questioned Hinojosa's Democratic credentials and said he profited from government contracts. Hinojosa emphasized his interest in improving educational opportunities and extending highways to the Lower Rio Grande Valley. Hinojosa took some moderate positions, calling for a reduction of the capital gains tax and investment tax credits for those making capital improvements. He won the runoff 52%-48% and easily won the general election.

Hinojosa has a moderate voting record among House Democrats, especially on economic issues. He has sought to protect benefits for legal immigrants, to promote the North American Free Trade Agreement and to demand that Mexico deliver on its agreement for water to South Texas farmers. He has a proclivity for holding out on votes to make last-minute legislative deals. He got Democratic President Bill Clinton to agree in principle to funding for the Cross-Border Institute for Regional Development in his district before voting for Clinton's initiative to normalize trade with China in 2000. He supported Republican President George W. Bush's proposal for broader authority to negotiate trade deals after he was promised a job-training project for his district.

But Hinojosa has struggled to advance in the House. Despite support in 2003 from the Texas delegation for a spot on the Ways and Means Committee, Hinojosa was passed over in favor of Texas Rep. Max Sandlin, an ally of Minority Whip Nancy Pelosi. In early 2005, Hinojosa made an unsuccessful bid for a leadership post when he ran for vice-chairman of the Democratic Caucus, but he abandoned his candidacy after two weeks due to lack of support. After Democrats regained control of the House in 2007, Hinojosa chaired the Higher Education, Life Long Learning and Competitiveness Subcommittee, where he focused on families traditionally left behind in American education.

After a series of easy election victories, Hinojosa had a scare in 2004, largely because of redistricting. His opponent, Republican Michael Thamm, received little national party support and spent only $50,000. Hinojosa spent $819,000 and reminded voters that he favored school prayer and opposed abortion. Thamm won the six most northern counties 60%-38%. But in Hidalgo County, which cast 37% of the vote, Hinojosa won 70%-29% to win 58%-41% overall. The 2006 court-ordered redistricting returned Hinojosa to firmer footing. It removed four of the six troublesome northern counties Hinojosa lost in 2004. He has not faced serious opposition since.

SIXTEENTH DISTRICT

Silvestre Reyes (D)

Elected 1996, 7th term; b. Nov. 10, 1944, Canutillo; home, El Paso; El Paso Commun. Col., A.A. 1977; Catholic; married (Carolina); 3 children.

Military Career: Army, 1966–68 (Vietnam).

Elected Office: Canutillo Schl. Board, 1968–70.

Professional Career: Border Patrol agent, 1969–95.

DC Office: 2433 RHOB, 20515, 202-225-4831; Fax: 202-225-2016; Web site: www.house.gov/reyes.

State Offices: El Paso, 915-534-4400.

Committees: *Armed Services* (6th of 36 D): Air & Land Forces; Readiness. *Intelligence (Select)* (Chmn. of 13 D).

Group Ratings

	ADA	ACLU	AFS	LCV	ITIC	NTU	COC	ACU	CFG	FRC
2008	70	82	100	85	100	8	67	8	0	5
2007	95	—	100	70	—	5	63	4	12	—

National Journal Ratings

	2007 LIB	—	2007 CONS	2008 LIB	—	2008 CONS
Economic	56%	—	44%	60%	—	39%
Social	70%	—	29%	62%	—	34%
Foreign	59%	—	41%	55%	—	43%
Composite	62%	—	38%	60%	—	40%

Key Votes of the 110th Congress

1. Increase minimum wage	Y	5. Share immigration data	N	9. Withdraw troops 8/08	Y
2. Expand SCHIP	Y	6. Foreign aid abortion ban	N	10. No operations in Iran	Y
3. Raise CAFE standards	Y	7. Ban gay bias in workplace	Y	11. Free trade with Peru	Y
4. Bail out financial markets	Y	8. Repeal D.C. gun law	Y	12. Overhaul FISA	Y

Election Results

2008 general	Silvestre Reyes (D)	130,375	(82%)	($1,034,725)
	Benjamin Mendoza (I)	16,348	(10%)	
	Mette Baker (Lib)	12,000	(8%)	
2008 primary	Silvestre Reyes (D)	75,058	(80%)	
	Jorge Artalejo (D)	18,274	(20%)	

Prior Winning Percentages: 2006 (79%); 2004 (68%); 2002 (100%); 2000 (68%); 1998 (88%); 1996 (71%)

Population		Race/Ethnicity		Work	
Pop. 2007:	693,085	White:	14.3%	Private:	70.0%
Change since 2000:	Up 6.4%	Black:	2.5%	Government:	22.6%
Urban:	98.3%	Hispanic:	80.9%	Self-employed:	7.2%
Rural:	1.7%	Asian:	1.1%	Blue collar:	23.0%
Area size:	582 sq. mi.	Native Am.:	0.3%	White collar:	55.9%
		Hawaiian:	0.1%	Khaki collar:	1.7%
Age		Two+ races:	0.6%	Other:	19.4%
Median age:	31.2 yrs.			Median income:	$33,721
More than 65 yrs:	10.6%	*Ancestry*		Median home value:	$88,400
Less than 18 yrs:	30.9%	German:	3.6%	Poverty:	27.8%
		USA:	3.6%		
Education		Irish:	2.6%	**Military Veterans**	
H.S. grad:	69.4%			% of Pop:	10.1%
College grad:	18.5%				
Grad degree:	6.2%				

El Paso, Texas, and Juarez, Mexico, face each other across the narrow Rio Grande, their tree-shaded streets spread out below the rough brown face of Comanche Peak. Downtown El Paso is only a few blocks from the bridge to Juarez. The two border cities are surrounded by hundreds of miles of some of North America's most rugged and desolate landscape. El Paso is closer to San Diego than to Houston, it's 600 miles from Dallas-Fort Worth, and it's in a different time zone from the rest of the state.

2008 Presidential Vote		
Obama (D)	118,219	(66%)
McCain (R)	60,306	(33%)
2004 Presidential Vote		
Kerry (D)	92,792	(56%)
Bush (R)	71,454	(44%)
Cook Partisan Voting Index:	D + 10	

Still, the region has grown significantly. In the 1950s, El Paso and Juarez each had a population of 140,000. In 2006, there were 736,000 people in El Paso County, about 80% of them Hispanic, and the Mexican census counted 1.2 million in metro Juarez. This is a bilingual, bicultural pair of cities, where most people have a Mexican heritage. El Paso is one of the lowest-wage and lowest-education locales in the United States, and the third-poorest county in the nation. Juarez, though struggling with drug cartel violence and crime that has caused some residents to flee, is one of the highest-wage cities in Mexico. Big companies have moved back-office jobs to El Paso. Cotton is the predominant local crop, and the city is known as a boot-making center. Maquiladora factories created a cross-border economy, bolstered by the North American Free Trade Agreement. The economy is not all based on low-skill labor, though much of it is. South of the border, there is a large General Motors technical center. Many factories on both sides of the border were shuttered during the recession that began in December 2007 and Juarez had lost 42,000 jobs by early 2009.

The 16th Congressional District of Texas is made up of 96% of El Paso County—the city itself, the suburban fringe, giant Fort Bliss to the north and rural housing settlements known as colonias, most without electricity and running water, spread out to the east and south. Fort Bliss was a big winner in the 2005 base closing review, with a $5 billion expansion and a net gain of nearly 30,000 soldiers. The district is overwhelmingly Democratic, though native son George W. Bush got 44% of the vote against Democrat John Kerry in the district in 2004. Republican presidential nominee John McCain got just 33% in 2008, with Democratic presidential nominee Barack Obama's winning easily with 66%.

The congressman from the 16th District is Silvestre Reyes, a Democrat first elected in 1996. He is the chairman of the House Intelligence Committee. Reyes grew up on a farm in Canutillo, five miles north of El Paso, the oldest of 10 children. He went to college in El Paso and Austin, then served in the Army in Vietnam, where he lost hearing in one ear during an enemy rocket attack. Once home, he "took as many civil service tests as I could, and the Border Patrol called" in 1969. He worked for the Immigration and Naturalization Service in four cities in Texas and Glynco, Ga., before returning to El Paso in 1993 as a chief border patrol agent. When he got there, he found that "people could basically cross the border at any time, wherever they wanted to." Reyes started "Operation Hold the Line," positioning 400 officers on the border instead of trying to intercept illegal aliens after they had already crossed into El Paso (amazingly enough, that had been firmly-rooted INS policy). Mexico complained about threats to its sovereignty, merchants worried about the loss of sales, homeowners fretted about finding domestic help, and border agents feared losing credit for apprehending aliens. But the innovative Reyes reduced the flow of illegal immigrants in the area by more than half. The move was almost universally popular north of the border and ultimately was accepted to the south.

With local name recognition at 65%, Reyes retired from the INS in November 1995 and ran for Congress. He talked of the need for integrity and common sense in Washington against a vulnerable Democratic incumbent, Rep. Ron Coleman, who had 673 overdrafts at the House bank during the scandal that revealed widespread abuses by members of their tax-subsidized banking privileges. Coleman had also been accused by Texas Attorney General Dan Morales, a Democrat, of trying to block the prosecution of a local developer. In December, Coleman announced he was retiring, and he and labor unions backed Jose Luis Sanchez, his legislative assistant, as his successor. Sanchez accused Reyes of being a Republican in disguise for backing a cut in capital gains taxes. Reyes hewed to his moderate platform, promising more high-technology jobs and more highways. He led in the primary 42%-28%, and despite a full court press by Sanchez and the unions in the runoff campaign, he won 51%-49%. He easily won the general election.

In the House, Reyes's voting record has been to the left of center. On the immigration issue, he opposed the Republican plan for placing a fence along the border as unconstitutional, impractical and "a waste of federal dollars," and said he preferred an increase in federal personnel and resources. In 2006, he praised President Bush's call for a guest-worker program. As violence increased in Mexico in 2009, Reyes discussed with Mexican leaders steps to decrease drug violence and to reduce gun smuggling from north of the border. He said that the permanent solution for the border is economic stabilization for Mexico and backed retraining for American workers displaced by NAFTA, which he said has been a great success overall.

Reyes moved into the national spotlight in December 2006, when Nancy Pelosi selected "Silver" to chair the Intelligence Committee, passing over Reps. Jane Harman, D-Calif., and Alcee Hastings, D-Fla. She cited his "impeccable national security credentials." As chairman, he got the U.S. Justice Department to turn over previously withheld documents from the surveillance program of the National Security Agency, and he voiced doubt about the "hyped" claims of the Bush administration that Iran was interfering in Iraq. In a February 2008 letter to Bush, Reyes warned against eavesdropping practices that might violate civil liberties. "We cannot allow ourselves to be scared into suspending the Constitution," he said. But Reyes mostly kept a low profile and sought bipartisanship and cooperation with the Bush administration where possible. He distanced himself from liberal Democrats who opposed renewal of the Foreign Intelligence Surveillance Act and he sought to avoid a confrontation with the White House over the controversial use of water boarding in terrorism investigations. Water boarding is a form of coercion that simulates drowning. When Obama took office in early 2009, Reyes recommended additional intelligence resources in Iraq and Afghanistan.

As a senior member on the Armed Services Committee, Reyes has been a supporter of the missile defense program. He worked to protect Fort Bliss from possible base closing, and he claimed credit when additional soldiers were stationed there. He opposed the use of force in Iraq and criticized the intelligence failures in Iraq in the months before the war, but he later called for a troop increase in Iraq to dismantle local militias stirring up conflict.

Reyes is a former chairman of the all-Democratic Hispanic Caucus. He unsuccessfully tried to convince Hispanic Republicans to join the group. At home, Reyes has not been seriously challenged for re-election.

SEVENTEENTH DISTRICT

Chet Edwards (D)

Elected 1990, 10th term; b. Nov. 24, 1951, Corpus Christi; home, Waco; TX A&M U., B.A. 1974, Harvard U., M.B.A. 1981; Methodist; married (Lea Ann); 2 children.

Elected Office: TX Senate, 1982–90.

Professional Career: Legis. & dist. dir., U.S. Rep. Olin Teague, 1975–77; Marketing rep., Trammell Crow Co., 1981–85; Pres., Edwards Communications, 1985–90.

DC Office: 2369 RHOB, 20515, 202-225-6105; Fax: 202-225-0350; Web site: edwards.house.gov.

State Offices: Cleburne, 817-645-4743; Bryan, 979-691-8797; Waco, 254-752-9600.

Committees: *Appropriations* (14th of 37 D): Energy & Water Development; Financial Services & General Government; Military Construction, Veterans Affairs & Related Agencies (Chmn). *Budget* (17th of 24 D).

Group Ratings

	ADA	ACLU	AFS	LCV	ITIC	NTU	COC	ACU	CFG	FRC
2008	80	73	100	77	100	6	67	8	0	23
2007	85	—	100	60	—	8	75	12	9	—

National Journal Ratings

	2007 LIB	—	2007 CONS	2008 LIB	—	2008 CONS
Economic	48%	—	51%	53%	—	47%
Social	55%	—	45%	62%	—	34%
Foreign	57%	—	42%	55%	—	43%
Composite	54%	—	46%	58%	—	42%

Key Votes of the 110th Congress

1. Increase minimum wage	Y	5. Share immigration data	N	9. Withdraw troops 8/08	Y
2. Expand SCHIP	Y	6. Foreign aid abortion ban	N	10. No operations in Iran	Y
3. Raise CAFE standards	Y	7. Ban gay bias in workplace	N	11. Free trade with Peru	Y
4. Bail out financial markets	Y	8. Repeal D.C. gun law	Y	12. Overhaul FISA	Y

Election Results

2008 general	Chet Edwards (D)	134,592	(53%)	($2,114,653)
	Rob Curnock (R)	115,581	(46%)	($109,335)
2008 primary	Chet Edwards (D)	unopposed		

Prior Winning Percentages: 2006 (58%); 2004 (51%); 2002 (52%); 2000 (55%); 1998 (82%); 1996 (57%); 1994 (59%); 1992 (67%); 1990 (53%)

Population		Race/Ethnicity		Work	
Pop. 2007:	712,215	White:	68.7%	Private:	74.2%
Change since 2000:	Up 9.3%	Black:	9.7%	Government:	18.1%
Urban:	64.2%	Hispanic:	18.0%	Self-employed:	7.4%
Rural:	35.8%	Asian:	1.7%	Blue collar:	26.4%
Area size:	7,808 sq. mi.	Native Am.:	0.5%	White collar:	55.1%
Age		Hawaiian:	0.1%	Khaki collar:	0.1%
Median age:	31.5 yrs.	Two+ races:	1.1%	Other:	18.3%
More than 65 yrs:	11.7%	*Ancestry*		Median income:	$41,305
Less than 18 yrs:	24.4%	German:	13.3%	Median home value:	$100,400
Education		English:	9.8%	Poverty:	19.3%
H.S. grad:	80.1%	Irish:	9.6%	**Military Veterans**	
College grad:	21.8%			% of Pop:	10.3%
Grad degree:	7.4%				

Waco, about midway between Dallas to Austin, is deep in the heart of Texas. In the late 19th century, Waco was one of the largest cotton markets in the world, a rip-roaring town with legalized prostitution. In 1870, it opened a suspension bridge across the Brazos River, then the largest single-span suspension bridge in the United States, and it became the main depot along the Chisholm Trail, which cattlemen used to drive their longhorns north to Kansas shipyards. In 1885, a Waco pharmacist

2008 Presidential Vote

McCain (R)	172,821	(67%)
Obama (D)	82,326	(32%)

2004 Presidential Vote

Bush (R)	172,355	(70%)
Kerry (D)	74,358	(30%)

Cook Partisan Voting Index: R + 20

concocted the first Dr. Pepper. Not far from Waco is Baylor University, the oldest college in Texas and the largest Baptist university in the world. (Waco was the site of the tragedy of February 1993, when agents of the Bureau of Alcohol, Tobacco and Firearms moved in on cult leader David Koresh's Branch Davidian compound. Koresh and many of his followers died in the ensuing fire.) In Waco's McLennan County is the tiny town of Crawford, with its Rainey Creek that traverses former President George W. Bush's 1,583-acre Prairie Chapel Ranch.

The 17th Congressional District of Texas includes all of nine counties and parts of three more but is centered on Waco, which has 30% of the district's population. To the north, are fast-growing Johnson, Hood and Somervell counties. This once-rural area is now part of exurban Forth Worth. The other population center in the district is Brazos County, whose largest city, College Station, is home to Texas A&M University. The school's agricultural and military tradition sets it apart from the University of Texas. It has a more conservative atmosphere, is the site of the George H.W. Bush Presidential Library, and Defense Secretary Robert Gates was its president until he left for Washington in December 2006. Even in the recession, the university-fueled growth in College Station kept the local economy strong. The political tradition in central Texas for more than a century was heavily Democratic. This area voted for Democrat Hubert Humphrey in 1968, while most of the rural South went for Dixiecrat George Wallace and Republican Richard Nixon. As recently as 1990, it voted Democratic for governor, supporting Waco native Ann Richards. But the district has followed most of Texas and become Republican. George W. Bush carried the area when running for governor in 1994 and 1998, and the district voted 68% for him for president in 2000 and 70% in 2004. It voted 67.1% for GOP presidential nominee John McCain in 2008, his second-strongest district represented in Congress by a Democrat. (The first was Mississippi's 4th District.)

The congressman from the 17th District is Chet Edwards, a Democrat first elected in 1990, and only the third congressman from the Waco-centered district since 1937. Edwards is one of those highly skilled and motivated Democrats who has made politics his life—and who helped keep the Texas Legislature and the U.S. House Democratic for so many years. He grew up in Corpus Christi and was a junior golf champion. Edwards played against future Masters winner Ben Crenshaw. "After playing in the same junior events he did, I realized the Lord had a different plan for me, and I'd better spend more time in the library," he has said. Edwards graduated from Texas A&M, where he studied economics under future Republican Sen. Phil Gramm, then a conservative Democrat and an economics professor. Edwards met Democratic Rep. Olin "Tiger" Teague while still in school, and Teague was impressed enough to hire him as his district director when Edwards graduated. In 1978, when Teague retired after 42 years in the House, Edwards ran for his seat at age 26. In the Democratic primary, Edwards wound up in third place but finished just 115 votes behind Gramm, who went on to win the seat. Edwards went off to Harvard University to get an M.B.A., returned to Texas and moved to Duncanville in southwest Dallas County. He ran for the state Senate in 1982, at age 31, and won. In 1990, when Democratic Rep. Marvin Leath retired, Edwards moved his residence to Waco and ran for the 11th District seat. He was unopposed in the Democratic primary and with strong support from Leath, secured a promise of an Armed Services Committee seat from then-Democratic House Speaker Thomas Foley. Edwards won 53%-47%.

In the House, Edwards eventually won a seat on Appropriations. With a voting record near the center of the House, Edwards has taken conservative stands on some, but by no means all issues. After Democrats lost their majority in 1994, Minority Leader Dick Gephardt asked Edwards to serve as one of four chief deputy whips. Edwards accepted but promptly voted for the Republicans' Contract with America's balanced budget amendment and line-item veto. He has voted for oil drilling in the Arctic National Wildlife Refuge and for the constitutional amendment to ban same-sex marriage. But he also toed the party line on issues that sometimes put him at odds with the conservative voters in his district. He supported a waiting period for sales at gun shows, opposed the repeal of the estate tax and voted against banning partial birth abortions.

In the years running up to the 2003 redistricting, Edwards won re-election in an increasingly Republican district by narrowing margins. When the Republican-drawn district lines were announced in October 2003, it was obvious he would face a serious challenge. The Republicans nominated state Rep. Arlene Wohlgemuth from Johnson County, an experienced and aggressive challenger. "I am proud that I will be receiving the vote of President George W. Bush," Wohlgemuth frequently proclaimed and featured President Bush prominently in her ads. She attacked Edwards for voting against the partial birth abortion ban. "This is a Republican district. It deserves to have a conservative Republican representing it," she said. Edwards responded aggressively, attacking his opponent as overly partisan: "While Mrs. Wohlgemuth is focusing on partisanship on every breath in this campaign, I find voters feel strongly, including Republicans, that we need less partisanship in Washington, not more." He repeatedly charged that a bill she sponsored in the Legislature had removed 147,000 children from the state children's health insurance program; she said the real number was 26,000. He argued that his seniority and his seat on the Appropriations Committee made him much better positioned to help the district, cited the projects he had funded, and pledged to keep the threatened Waco Veterans' Affairs hospital open. Edwards was one of six white male Democratic incumbents in Texas seriously threatened by the 2003 redistricting (a seventh retired), and he was the only one to win, by 51%-47%. In McLennan and Bosque counties, the only two counties in his old 11th District, he led 63%-36%, a big improvement over his 2002 showing there, and an impressive 30 percentage points ahead of John Kerry, the Democratic presidential nominee in 2004. In Johnson County and the two adjacent counties in the Dallas/Fort Worth media market, Wohlgemuth led 61%-37%, running 13 percentage points behind Bush.

Since the Democrats won control of the House in the 2006 elections, Edwards has chaired the Appropriations Military Construction, Veterans Affairs and Related Agencies Subcommittee. In 2007, he reacted cautiously to President Bush's troop surge. "I have serious concerns about the ability of a U.S. troop surge to solve the sectarian violence. But I think the Congress should be extremely careful before it stops the commander-in-chief from implementing the plan," he said. Edwards resisted fellow Appropriations subcommittee Chairman John Murtha's attempt to put readiness requirements into the 2007 war funding bill that would prevent scheduled troops from reaching Iraq, and Murtha's plan was stopped. On the Appropriations committee in 2007, Edwards helped pass a $10 billion increase for the VA, mostly for veterans' health care and benefits. Democratic House Speaker Nancy Pelosi has relied heavily on the politically savvy Edwards in reaching out to veterans' groups. The economic stimulus bill enacted in February 2009 included $8 million for construction projects at the Waco VA hospital.

Edwards' growing influence did not mean an end to Republican efforts to defeat him. In 2006, he faced wealthy Iraq war veteran Van Taylor. Edwards unleashed attacks on Taylor, pointing out that he had only recently moved into the district (although Edwards himself moved from Dallas County to Waco to run in 1990) and asking exactly how much Exxon Mobil stock Taylor owned. Taylor's disclosure forms said it was between $5 million and $25 million. Taylor spent $1 million of his own money. But in the more

Democratic climate of 2006, Edwards won by his widest margin in the decade, 58%-40%. In 2008, his GOP challenger, Robert Curnock, garnered little money or national attention, but he sought to turn to his advantage Edwards' support for Democratic presidential candidate Barack Obama. Edwards won 53%-46%. Curnock won Johnson County, but Edwards benefited from a 60%-39% lead in McLennan. In 2008, Pelosi enthusiastically encouraged Obama to place Edwards on his short list of potential vice presidents.

EIGHTEENTH DISTRICT

Sheila Jackson Lee (D)

Elected 1994, 8th term; b. Jan. 12, 1950, Queens, NY; home, Houston; Yale U., B.A. 1972, U. of VA Law Schl., J.D. 1975; Seventh Day Adventist; married (Elwyn); 2 children.

Elected Office: Houston City Cncl., 1990–94.

Professional Career: Practicing atty., 1975–77, 1978–87; Staff cnsl., U.S. House Select Assassinations Cmte., 1977–78; Houston assoc. municipal judge, 1987–90.

DC Office: 2160 RHOB, 20515, 202-225-3816; Fax: 202-225-3317; Web site: jacksonlee.house.gov.

State Offices: Acres Home, 713-691-4882; Fifth Ward, 713-227-7740; Heights, 713-861-4070; Houston, 713-691-4882; Houston, 713-655-0050.

Committees: *Foreign Affairs* (18th of 28 D): Africa & Global Health; Middle East & South Asia; Terrorism, Nonproliferation & Trade. *Homeland Security* (7th of 20 D): Border, Maritime & Global Counterterrorism; Transportation Security & Infrastructure Protection (Chmn). *Judiciary* (8th of 24 D): Constitution, Civil Rights & Civil Liberties; Courts & Competition Policy; Crime, Terrorism & Homeland Security; Immigration, Citizenship, Border Security & International Law.

Group Ratings

	ADA	ACLU	AFS	LCV	ITIC	NTU	COC	ACU	CFG	FRC
2008	100	100	100	77	86	12	59	4	0	11
2007	100	—	100	90	—	4	55	0	7	—

National Journal Ratings

	2007 LIB	—	2007 CONS		2008 LIB	—	2008 CONS
Economic	69%	—	28%		85%	—	0%
Social	77%	—	17%		82%	—	0%
Foreign	94%	—	4%		85%	—	8%
Composite	82%	—	18%		91%	—	9%

Key Votes of the 110th Congress

1. Increase minimum wage	Y	5. Share immigration data	N	9. Withdraw troops 8/08	Y
2. Expand SCHIP	Y	6. Foreign aid abortion ban	N	10. No operations in Iran	Y
3. Raise CAFE standards	Y	7. Ban gay bias in workplace	Y	11. Free trade with Peru	N
4. Bail out financial markets	Y	8. Repeal D.C. gun law	N	12. Overhaul FISA	N

Election Results

2008 general	Sheila Jackson Lee (D)	148,617	(77%)	($562,708)
	John Faulk (R)	39,095	(20%)	($59,213)
	Mike Taylor (Lib)	4,486	(2%)	
2008 primary	Sheila Jackson Lee (D)	unopposed		

Prior Winning Percentages: 2006 (77%); 2004 (89%); 2002 (77%); 2000 (76%); 1998 (90%); 1996 (77%); 1994 (73%)

Population		Race/Ethnicity		Work	
Pop. 2007:	674,592	White:	16.2%	Private:	82.8%
Change since 2000:	Up 3.5%	Black:	37.9%	Government:	11.1%
Urban:	99.9%	Hispanic:	41.8%	Self-employed:	6.0%
Rural:	0.1%	Asian:	3.2%	Blue collar:	32.5%
Area size:	228 sq. mi.	Native Am.:	0.1%	White collar:	48.2%
		Hawaiian:	0.0%	Khaki collar:	0.0%
Age		Two+ races:	0.6%	Other:	19.2%
Median age:	31.6 yrs.	*Ancestry*		Median income:	$35,049
More than 65 yrs:	8.2%	German:	3.6%	Median home value:	$100,700
Less than 18 yrs:	28.7%	English:	2.6%	Poverty:	25.5%
Education		USA:	2.5%	**Military Veterans**	
H.S. grad:	66.5%			% of Pop:	6.4%
College grad:	16.4%				
Grad degree:	5.9%				

Within its vast bounds, Houston contains income and wealth disparities as striking as any city in the United States, the product of an expanding city with dynamic economic growth, a high rate of immigration, and the absence of centralized planning. The contrast is most obvious at the edge of Houston's gleaming downtown. Just blocks from the Heritage Plaza, Pennzoil and Bank of America buildings, and the sports complexes for baseball's Astros and basketball's Rockets are slums where many African-

2008 Presidential Vote
Obama (D) 150,973   (77%)
McCain (R)..............................43,292   (22%)

2004 Presidential Vote
Kerry (D)................................125,155   (72%)
Bush (R) 48,753   (28%)

Cook Partisan Voting Index: D + 24

Americans and Mexican-Americans live in unpainted frame houses with cracks wide enough to let in Houston's humid, smoggy air. But the contrasts are less obvious as one moves outward from Houston's historic center.

Half a century ago, Houston had a Third World economy. It was a low-skill producer of basic commodities, where a few got rich and many lived near subsistence level. Since then, Houston has gained a high-tech economy offering myriad opportunities and a wider range of economic outcomes. It has also greatly expanded its international trade. The Port of Houston brought in 225 million tons of cargo in 2008, the second most of any port in the United States. Many of Houston's blacks and Hispanics have moved to comfortable middle-class neighborhoods. In 2007, Hispanics for the first time outnumbered Anglos in Harris County, which has grown 16% since 2000. While the city has diversified economically, oil is still king. The city was shielded in 2008 from the recession, with 70% of the city's economic growth that year coming from the energy industry, but the drop in oil prices in early 2009 reduced local jobs. The city also suffered from the September 2008 devastation of Hurricane Ike, though skillful management by local officials and a last-minute turn of the storm away from the city limited casualties.

The 18th Congressional District of Texas contains Houston's downtown and the African-American and Latino neighborhoods immediately south toward Loop 610. It has two spokes running out beyond Loop 610—one is northeast between the Eastex Freeway and Beaumont Highway and then south to near Jacinto City and Galena Park, and the other is northwest between the Northwest Freeway and Hempstead, then heads east to include George Bush Intercontinental Airport. African-Americans made up 38% of the district's population in 2007, a drop from previous years, while the Hispanic population continues to grow, increasing to 42%. This and the 30th District in Dallas are the two most heavily Democratic districts in Texas.

The congresswoman from the 18th District is Sheila Jackson Lee, a Democrat first elected in 1994. A native of Queens, N.Y., she was educated at Yale University and Virginia University's law school. She practiced law in Houston, where she was a local judge and won two terms as an at-large member of the Houston City Council. After a local term limits law took effect in 1994, she ran for Congress. The incumbent was Democratic Rep. Craig Washington, a talented but iconoclastic legislator who voted against funding for the space station, a source of many local jobs, and against the 1993 North American Free Trade Agreement, which was a boon to port traffic. Jackson Lee supported NAFTA and raised a lot of money from business interests that favored it as well. She won the primary, 63%-37%, and she prevailed in the general election. She has been re-elected easily since.

In the House, Jackson Lee has a liberal voting record, though she has leaned toward the center on economic issues. She is prolific in proposing bills and offering amendments on the floor. Typically, her measures call for studies on one topic or another, add small amounts to spending bills, or are non-controversial, such as one that called on Afghanistan to prohibit the use of children as soldiers. When Republicans controlled the House, her more substantive proposals—for example, in favor of NASA funding and abortion rights—were usually defeated. In the 110th Congress (2007–08), she reportedly made more House speeches than any other Democratic member. In *Washingtonian* magazine's annual poll of House staffers, Jackson Lee won best "Show Horse" every Congress since 2000, and she has routinely taken top honors in the poll's "Biggest Windbag" category. She also draws negative reviews for her treatment of her staff. She used to have an aide drive her one block to and from her Capitol Hill apartment daily, and she has required aides to drive her to late-night hair appointments.

Jackson Lee came into national prominence as an outspoken defender of Democratic President Bill Clinton during his impeachment in 1998. On the Judiciary Committee, she has faced conflicting desires from Latino constituents who favor more generous treatment of immigrants and African-American constituents who see immigrants as dangerous competition for jobs. She frequently takes the pro-immigrant side. She favors an increase in visas and access to permanent resident status. She has vigilantly pursued alleged racial injustices in local courts; she called the Houston-area judicial system "tarnished" in 2008 after a grand jury failed to convict a white man who killed two black men after they robbed his neighbor.

Jackson Lee has chaired the Homeland Security Subcommittee on the Transportation Security Committee and Infrastructure Protection, an assignment that suits the port city of Houston. In March 2009, she complained that the Transportation Security Administration was not moving fast enough to meet the August 2010 deadline for screening all cargo on passenger planes. She sponsored a bill to mandate wireless communications systems for flight attendants on commercial airplanes to replace telephones that she said were "from the Howard Hughes era."

Jackson Lee has been mindful to keep her name recognition in the district high, going so far as to have aides track constituents' deaths and then call their grieving families to ask if she can speak at their funerals. Her most famous eulogy came in July 2009, when Jermaine Jackson asked her to speak at his famous brother Michael Jackson's memorial service in Los Angeles. She delivered a rambling speech to the crowd of 20,000 who gathered for the pop star's funeral, speaking for more time than many of the stars there who knew Jackson personally. Jackson Lee caused some anger at home during the 2008 presidential primary when she remained a steadfast supporter of Democratic Sen. Hillary Rodham Clinton "in the spirit and the idea of opportunity for women." Supporters of Democratic candidate Barack Obama said they think she should have a primary challenger in 2010.

NINETEENTH DISTRICT

Randy Neugebauer (R)

Elected June 2003, 3rd full term; b. Dec. 24, 1949, Lubbock; home, Lubbock; TX Tech. U., B.B.A. 1972; Baptist; married (Dana); 2 children.

Elected Office: Lubbock City Cncl., 1992–98; Mayor pro tem, Lubbock, 1994–96.

Professional Career: Mgr., Sentry Property Mngt., 1972–75; Instructor, South Plains College, 1975–78; V.P., First National Bank, 1975–82; Pres., Prestige Homes, 1983–87; Pres., Lubbock Land Co., 1987-present.

DC Office: 1424 LHOB, 20515, 202-225-4005; Fax: 202-225-9615; Web site: randy.house.gov.

State Offices: Abilene, 325-675-9779; Big Spring, 432-264-0722; Lubbock, 806-763-1611.

Committees: *Agriculture* (8th of 18 R): Conservation, Credit, Energy & Research; Livestock, Dairy & Poultry (RMM). *Financial Services* (16th of 29 R): Capital Markets, Insurance & Government Sponsored Enterprises; Financial Institutions & Consumer Credit; Housing & Community Opportunity. *Science & Technology* (10th of 17 R): Energy & Environment; Research & Science Education.

Group Ratings

	ADA	ACLU	AFS	LCV	ITIC	NTU	COC	ACU	CFG	FRC
2008	5	18	0	0	57	78	82	96	88	100
2007	0	—	0	0	—	85	70	100	95	—

National Journal Ratings

	2007 LIB	—	2007 CONS		2008 LIB	—	2008 CONS
Economic	0%	—	97%		5%	—	94%
Social	0%	—	91%		15%	—	84%
Foreign	0%	—	72%		0%	—	95%
Composite	7%	—	93%		8%	—	92%

Key Votes of the 110th Congress

1. Increase minimum wage	N	5. Share immigration data	Y	9. Withdraw troops 8/08	N
2. Expand SCHIP	N	6. Foreign aid abortion ban	Y	10. No operations in Iran	N
3. Raise CAFE standards	N	7. Ban gay bias in workplace	N	11. Free trade with Peru	Y
4. Bail out financial markets	N	8. Repeal D.C. gun law	*	12. Overhaul FISA	Y

Election Results

2008 general	Randy Neugebauer (R)	168,501	(72%)	($1,052,072)
	Dwight Fullingim (D)	58,030	(25%)	($41,374)
	Richard Peterson (Lib)	6,080	(3%)	
2008 primary	Randy Neugebauer (R)	unopposed		

Prior Winning Percentages: 2006 (68%); 2004 (58%); 2003 (51%).

Population		Race/Ethnicity		Work	
Pop. 2007:	661,558	White:	60.5%	Private:	71.0%
Change since 2000:	Up 1.5%	Black:	5.3%	Government:	20.2%
Urban:	74.0%	Hispanic:	31.8%	Self-employed:	8.5%
Rural:	26.0%	Asian:	1.0%	Blue collar:	24.2%
Area size:	25,356 sq. mi.	Native Am.:	0.3%	White collar:	54.7%
		Hawaiian:	0.0%	Khaki collar:	0.5%
Age		Two+ races:	1.0%	Other:	20.6%
Median age:	33.3 yrs.			Median income:	$38,065
More than 65 yrs:	13.1%	*Ancestry*		Median home value:	$74,400
Less than 18 yrs:	26.0%	German:	11.2%	Poverty:	18.4%
		Irish:	8.8%		
Education		English:	7.8%	**Military Veterans**	
H.S. grad:	77.3%			% of Pop:	10.0%
College grad:	20.5%				
Grad degree:	6.4%				

Until water was discovered in the giant Ogallala Aquifer that lies under Lubbock and its environs, this was Indian country, then a land of Army forts and cattle ranches. When the water was tapped, well into the 20th century, what had been grazing land suddenly became cotton fields, with green crops grown in circles where the sprinklers reached, surrounded by parched land. Lubbock became a regional center, the home of Texas Tech University, and grew rapidly at mid-century. Lubbock County's population increased from 101,000 in 1950 to 156,000 in 1960. Since then, the regional economy has grown more slowly, as the aquifer seemed to be going dry. In 2007, Lubbock County's population reached 258,000 and populations of neighboring, much smaller, counties declined. Cotton growers have struggled with international competitors and adverse trade rulings, as well as pressure to reduce agricultural subsidies. However, wind power has become a source of energy, with hundreds of towers between Abilene and Sweetwater. This area has the most wind energy capacity in the nation. Lubbock also has made an outsized contribution to American popular culture. The city and nearby counties have produced a slew of fine musicians: Buddy Holly, Tanya Tucker, Jimmy Dean, Waylon Jennings, Mac Davis, Joe Ely, Roy Orbison and Don Williams. Lubbock native Natalie Maines and her band the Dixie Chicks took a lot of heat when she criticized Republican President George W. Bush in 2003, both locally and throughout the South. They responded by recording the song "Lubbock or Leave It."

2008 Presidential Vote		
McCain (R)	171,023	(72%)
Obama (D)	65,034	(27%)

2004 Presidential Vote		
Bush (R)	181,516	(77%)
Kerry (D)	52,800	(23%)

Cook Partisan Voting Index: R + 26

Lubbock is separated from the great metropolises of Texas by hundreds of miles of mostly, but not entirely, empty land. Nearly 200 miles southeast of Lubbock, over gully-ridden territory, are Abilene and the surrounding Big Country, with ranches specializing in Angora goats and sheep and exotic animals like ostriches, emus and aoudad sheep. There also are cotton fields and pecan trees and mesquite, and many oil wells, which yielded a temporary economic boom during the 2008 price-spike. Archer City, the boyhood and current home of novelist Larry McMurtry, was chronicled in *The Last Picture Show* and *Texasville*. Some of the nation's B-1 bombers are stationed at Dyess Air Force Base near Abilene.

The 19th Congressional District of Texas connects these two wide-open regions. The population of Lubbock and its surrounding area is about twice as large as the Abilene area population. The two areas combined account for about 60% of the district's population. As recently as 1978, these parts of West Texas were Democratic enough that in an open-seat election, they rejected the candidacy of a young Midland oilman named George W. Bush in favor of Lubbock Democrat Kent Hance. Today, they are heavily Republican. Bush received 77% of the votes for president in this district in 2004. Republican candidate John McCain won the district with 72% in 2008.

The congressman from the 19th District is Randy Neugebauer, a Republican who won the seat in a June 2003 special election. Neugebauer *(NAW-ga-bower)* graduated from Texas Tech, became a banker and then ran his own land-development company. From 1992 to 1998, he was a Lubbock city councilman. His chance for a House seat was prompted by the unexpected resignation, announced a week after the November 2002 election, of Republican Rep. Larry Combest. In the all-party primary, the four leading contenders to succeed Combest were all Republicans. They were Mike Conaway, a Midland accountant, plus three candidates from Lubbock: Neugebauer, state Rep. Carl Isett and former Lubbock Mayor David

Langston. Neugebauer was the biggest spender and emphasized his positions on national defense. He focused on his business connections to oil and farming and was helped because Isett—the only active office-holder—was tied down by legislative business in Austin. Langston, who previously won election as a Democrat, pitched himself as a Bush-like "compassionate conservative." Neugebauer finished first, with 821 more votes than Conaway. Neugebauer won in Lubbock while Conaway swept the Midland and Odessa areas. The runoff featured few differences on the issues, and regional patterns held firm. In the combined vote from Midland and Odessa areas, Conaway won 85% of the vote. In Lubbock County, which cast 47% of the vote, Neugebauer led 71%-29%. Overall, Neugebauer won 51%-49%.

He barely had a chance to get settled in the House before the Texas Legislature drew up a new plan for congressional districts in October 2003. The new lines placed the home of 13-term Democratic Rep. Charlie Stenholm in the new 13th District, but that district was almost entirely unfamiliar territory for him and heavily Republican to boot, so Stenholm decided to run in the 19th against Neugebauer. Stenholm was arguably the last conservative Democrat from Texas in the House. He and party-switching former Rep. Phil Gramm were leaders of the "Boll Weevils" backing Republican President Ronald Reagan's 1981 budget and tax cuts. Stenholm was also one of only five Democrats who voted to impeach Democratic President Bill Clinton in 1998. In their 2004 showdown, most of the advantages—the district's partisan tilt, the fact that Neugebauer had represented 58% of its residents and Stenholm only 31%—favored the Republican. Both candidates promised to protect farm subsidies. Stenholm emphasized his social conservatism, his dedication to West Texas constituent services, and his independence as a Democrat. He criticized Neugebauer's ads that suggested he supported abortion rights and sought to link Neugebauer with then-Majority Leader Tom DeLay of Texas, who was increasingly mired in an ethics scandal. The Texas Farm Bureau, which earlier honored Stenholm as "one of the giants of Texas agriculture," endorsed Neugebauer. He won 58%-40%, capturing 22 of the 27 counties. In Lubbock, Stenholm trailed 65%-33%. In his base of Abilene, which cast half as many votes as Lubbock, Stenholm led 50%-48%.

In the House, Neugebauer has been a reliable conservative, and he has seats on the Agriculture and Financial Services committees. In 2009, he was named the ranking Republican on the Livestock, Dairy, and Poultry Subcommittee. In 2004, the House passed his amendment to add $3 billion for drought assistance to farmers, which was offset by a reduction in payments for a farm conservation program. The measure was added to the disaster aid bill for hurricane victims that President Bush signed into law in October 2004. During debate in 2007 on the 2008 farm bill, he introduced amendments, knocked down by Democrats, to prevent indexing food stamps to inflation and to bar members of Congress from directing Environmental Quality Incentives Program funds to specific industries. He has defended farm subsidies for his district after the Environmental Working Group listed it as the nation's fourth-highest recipient of crop subsidies. On Financial Services, Neugebauer said in 2006 that post-Katrina reconstruction of public housing in New Orleans would be "the second worst disaster" in the city's history. With Rep. Melissa Bean, D-Ill., he passed an amendment to the housing rescue bill in 2008 that strengthened the regulations of the Fannie Mae and Freddie Mac mortgage giants.

Neugebauer easily won re-election in 2006 and 2008.

TWENTIETH DISTRICT

Charles Gonzalez (D)

Elected 1998, 6th term; b. May 5, 1945, San Antonio; home, San Antonio; U. of TX, B. A. 1969; St. Mary's Law Schl., J.D. 1972.; Catholic; divorced; 1 child.

Military Career: TX Air Natl. Guard, 1969–75.

Elected Office: Judge, San Antonio Municipal Court; Judge, Bexar Cnty. Court at Law, 1983–87; Judge, 57th State Judicial Dist. Court, 1988–97.

Professional Career: Elem. schl. teacher, 1969–71; Practicing atty., 1972–82.

DC Office: 303 CHOB, 20515, 202-225-3236; Fax: 202-225-1915; Web site: gonzalez.house.gov.

State Offices: San Antonio, 210-472-6195.

Committees: *Energy & Commerce* (17th of 36 D): Commerce, Trade & Consumer Protections; Energy & Environment; Health. *House Administration* (4th of 6 D): Elections. *Judiciary* (19th of 24 D): Courts & Competition Policy; Immigration, Citizenship, Border Security & International Law.

Group Ratings

	ADA	ACLU	AFS	LCV	ITIC	NTU	COC	ACU	CFG	FRC
2008	90	91	100	85	100	8	61	8	0	0
2007	95	—	100	85	—	6	60	4	12	—

National Journal Ratings

	2007 LIB	—	2007 CONS		2008 LIB	—	2008 CONS
Economic	53%	—	46%		55%	—	45%
Social	71%	—	28%		82%	—	0%
Foreign	63%	—	35%		59%	—	37%
Composite	63%	—	37%		69%	—	31%

Key Votes of the 110th Congress

1. Increase minimum wage	Y	5. Share immigration data	N	9. Withdraw troops 8/08	Y
2. Expand SCHIP	Y	6. Foreign aid abortion ban	N	10. No operations in Iran	Y
3. Raise CAFE standards	Y	7. Ban gay bias in workplace	Y	11. Free trade with Peru	Y
4. Bail out financial markets	Y	8. Repeal D.C. gun law	N	12. Overhaul FISA	N

Election Results

2008 general	Charles Gonzalez (D)	127,298	(72%)	($821,805)
	Robert Litoff (R)	44,585	(25%)	
	Michael Idrogo (Lib)	5,172	(3%)	
2008 primary	Charles Gonzalez (D)	unopposed		

Prior Winning Percentages: 2006 (87%); 2004 (65%); 2002 (100%); 2000 (88%); 1998 (63%)

Population		Race/Ethnicity		Work	
Pop. 2007:	674,203	White:	20.5%	Private:	77.1%
Change since 2000:	Up 3.5%	Black:	6.3%	Government:	17.3%
Urban:	99.8%	Hispanic:	69.8%	Self-employed:	5.3%
Rural:	0.2%	Asian:	1.7%	Blue collar:	22.6%
Area size:	184 sq. mi.	Native Am.:	0.4%	White collar:	53.2%
		Hawaiian:	0.1%	Khaki collar:	2.1%
Age		Two+ races:	1.0%	Other:	22.2%
Median age:	31.7 yrs.	*Ancestry*		Median income:	$35,956
More than 65 yrs:	10.4%	German:	6.4%	Median home value:	$81,600
Less than 18 yrs:	27.1%	Irish:	3.4%	Poverty:	22.0%
Education		USA:	3.2%	**Military Veterans**	
H.S. grad:	74.9%			% of Pop:	12.4%
College grad:	15.9%				
Grad degree:	5.5%				

San Antonio, with its antique past and Hispanic heritage, its military superstructure and its high-technology hopes, is unlike any other city in the United States. It is the home of the Alamo, preserved by the Daughters of the Republic of Texas, where Davy Crockett, Jim Bowie and 184 others were killed in 1836. (Crockett was a Tennessee congressman for three terms; if he had not lost his reelection in 1834, he presumably would not have left Tennessee for Texas.) Its Spanish architecture re-

2008 Presidential Vote

Obama (D)	115,739	(63%)
McCain (R)	64,886	(36%)

2004 Presidential Vote

Kerry (D)	96,539	(55%)
Bush (R)	78,757	(45%)

Cook Partisan Voting Index: D + 8

calls San Antonio's days as the most important town in Texas, when the state was part of Mexico, and contrasts with the 31-story Tower Life Building, which contrasts with the armadillo-like Alamodome. And its Paseo del Rio, the Riverwalk along the tiny San Antonio River that was redeveloped in the 1970s, also recalls an earlier era. The city includes old neighborhoods that evoke the Germans who were its chief Anglo citizens for many years.

For most of the 20th century, San Antonio's economy was built on the military. What the locals call "Military City, U.S.A." remains the home of Lackland Air Force Base, Fort Sam Houston and a giant military hospital. In 1995, President Bill Clinton bent the rules of the base-closing process to keep in San Antonio the thousands of jobs at Kelly Air Force Base, a move so resented that Congress blocked new rounds of base closings until 2005. Kelly was finally closed in 2001. In the 2005 base review, Fort Sam's renowned Brooke Army Medical Center was transformed into a regional military medical center, for a net gain of more than 4,000 jobs in the area. The local health industry, which includes the Texas Health Science Center, has been thriving and is the largest local employer. San Antonio has many military retirees and is the largest tourist center in Texas. The city also is the Union Pacific rail hub.

Since 2000, its population has grown 16%, and San Antonio has surpassed Dallas as Texas's second-largest city. However, its metropolitan-area population of 2.3 million is only about half the size of metro Houston and one-third the size of the Dallas–Fort Worth Metroplex. Its low education and income levels are partially due to the high levels of new immigrants in the city. Yet it has mostly avoided polarized politics and ethnic strife as it has progressed as a low-wage, high-tech center that has some links to, and sometimes competes with, nearby Austin.

The 20th Congressional District of Texas includes most of central San Antonio and its lower-income west side. (Affluent neighborhoods are in the 21st and 23rd districts.) The district is wholly contained within Bexar County. On the west it extends beyond Lackland Air Force Base toward the county line. The district is 70% Hispanic and is one of the state's seven Hispanic-majority districts. It is Democratic. Republican favorite-son candidate George W. Bush won 45% of the vote here in 2004. Republican presidential nominee John McCain got 36% in 2008.

The congressman from the 20th District is Charles Gonzalez, a Democrat first elected in 1998. He is one of eight children of former U.S. Rep. Henry Gonzalez, who held the seat for 37 years. Charles Gonzalez grew up in San Antonio, graduated from the University of Texas and St. Mary's University School of Law, and served in the Texas Air National Guard. He was an elementary school teacher, practiced law and served as a judge from 1983 to 1997. When his father announced his retirement, Charles Gonzalez was the front-runner for the seat, but the contest was more competitive than many had expected. Gonzalez campaigned as a consensus builder, emphasizing his background in negotiation and compromise. Symbolizing the economic transformation of San Antonio, he said he would work for the entire district, not simply its low-income groups. Taking a feistier tone was Maria Berriozabal, a former San Antonio City Council member, who called for more outspoken leadership. She displayed a picture of Henry Gonzalez in her campaign literature and claimed that she was more in his mold than was his son. Just before the March primary, Henry Gonzalez issued a brief statement endorsing his son, who wound up leading Berriozabal 44%-22%. In the April runoff campaign, he benefited from a fundraising advantage of more than 2-to-1 and mostly ignored his opponent. He won 62%-38% and went on to easily win the general election.

In the House, Gonzalez has a relatively moderate voting record, especially on economic issues. He has a seat on the influential Energy and Commerce Committee, and during the committee's debate on climate-change legislation in 2009, he advocated incentives for the nuclear-power industry. He backed a proposal to require satellite-television operators to end a practice that forced users to have two satellite dishes to receive channels in both English and Spanish. Gonzalez also has called for stiffer penalties on businesses that hire undocumented workers.

As a member of both the Democratic Caucus and the Hispanic Caucus—which his father had refused to join—Gonzalez has been a leading proponent of census sampling, which statistically estimates the number of members in a community for use in redistricting processes and generally increases population totals for immigrant communities. But he opposed Latino activists who wanted to create an additional Hispanic-majority district for Texas in the 2001 redistricting, arguing that because of low voter turnout among Hispanics, such a step would reduce the Democratic majorities in other districts, an argument corroborated by subsequent redistricting in the state. After Democrats gained the majority in the 2006 elections, he led the House Administration Committee review of the contested 2006 result in the 13th District of Florida, in which Democrat Christine Jennings lost by 369 votes; more than 18,000 ballots had not been recorded. The panel unanimously dismissed the case in February 2008, after concluding that voting machines had not malfunctioned.

In 2004, Gonzalez faced his first re-election challenge since taking office, and it had unusual personal overtones. Initially, his ex-wife, Becky Whetstone, a marriage and family therapist, said that she would run against him so that voters would have a choice and he would be "held accountable." But she failed to get the 500 signatures required to get on the ballot as an independent. In the general election, Gonzalez beat Republican Roger Scott 65%-32%.

Gonzalez was among the few Hispanics in Congress who endorsed Democratic Sen. Barack Obama of Illinois early in the presidential primaries. He said Obama brought "the wind of change."

TWENTY-FIRST DISTRICT

Lamar Smith (R)

Elected 1986, 12th term; b. Nov. 19, 1947, San Antonio; home, San Antonio; Yale U., B.A. 1969, S. Methodist U., J.D. 1975; Christian Scientist; married (Beth); 2 children.

Elected Office: TX House of Reps., 1980–82; Bexar Cnty. comm., 1982–85.

Professional Career: U.S. Small Business Admin., 1969–70; Business writer, *Christian Science Monitor*, 1970–72; Practicing atty., 1975–76.

DC Office: 2409 RHOB, 20515, 202-225-4236; Fax: 202-225-8628; Web site: lamarsmith.house.gov.

State Offices: Austin, 512-306-0439; Kerrville, 830-896-0154; San Antonio, 210-821-5024.

Committees: *Homeland Security* (2nd of 13 R). *Judiciary* (RMM of 16 R). *Science & Technology* (3rd of 17 R).

Group Ratings

	ADA	ACLU	AFS	LCV	ITIC	NTU	COC	ACU	CFG	FRC
2008	15	20	29	0	100	62	100	88	66	100
2007	15	—	9	0	—	76	84	88	83	—

National Journal Ratings

	2007 LIB — 2007 CONS		2008 LIB — 2008 CONS	
Economic	21% —	78%	22% —	77%
Social	21% —	75%	20% —	74%
Foreign	0% —	72%	12% —	88%
Composite	20% —	81%	19% —	81%

Key Votes of the 110th Congress

1. Increase minimum wage	Y	5. Share immigration data	Y	9. Withdraw troops 8/08	N
2. Expand SCHIP	N	6. Foreign aid abortion ban	Y	10. No operations in Iran	N
3. Raise CAFE standards	N	7. Ban gay bias in workplace	N	11. Free trade with Peru	Y
4. Bail out financial markets	Y	8. Repeal D.C. gun law	Y	12. Overhaul FISA	Y

Election Results

2008 general	Lamar Smith (R)	243,471	(80%)	($1,069,346)
	James Strohm (Lib)	60,879	(20%)	($3,353)
2008 primary	Lamar Smith (R)	unopposed		

Prior Winning Percentages: 2006 (60%); 2004 (61%); 2002 (73%); 2000 (76%); 1998 (91%); 1996 (76%); 1994 (90%); 1992 (72%); 1990 (75%); 1988 (93%); 1986 (61%)

Population		Race/Ethnicity		Work	
Pop. 2007:	770,645	White:	63.0%	Private:	74.3%
Change since 2000:	Up 18.3%	Black:	6.5%	Government:	16.2%
Urban:	81.0%	Hispanic:	25.8%	Self-employed:	9.3%
Rural:	19.0%	Asian:	3.1%	Blue collar:	14.7%
Area size:	5,181 sq. mi.	Native Am.:	0.3%	White collar:	70.4%
Age		Hawaiian:	0.0%	Khaki collar:	0.9%
Median age:	35.9 yrs.	Two+ races:	1.3%	Other:	14.0%
More than 65 yrs:	11.8%	*Ancestry*		Median income:	$58,564
Less than 18 yrs:	25.3%	German:	15.8%	Median home value:	$156,700
Education		English:	9.2%	Poverty:	10.2%
H.S. grad:	90.8%	Irish:	8.9%	**Military Veterans**	
College grad:	39.3%			% of Pop:	14.5%
Grad degree:	14.5%				

The Balcones Escarpment is a bulwark of cracked and weathered rock that crosses Texas diagonally from the Dallas–Fort Worth Metroplex southwest to Austin and San Antonio and all the way to the Rio Grande. It separates the flatlands of central Texas from the stony hills to the north and west. It is a boundary between cropland and grazing land, between acres rich with greenery and acres whose rolling brown hills blaze out in color when the wildflowers bloom in Texas's early spring, between

2008 Presidential Vote		
McCain (R)	215,006	(59%)
Obama (D)	148,477	(40%)

2004 Presidential Vote		
Bush (R)	212,196	(66%)
Kerry (D)	110,288	(34%)

Cook Partisan Voting Index: R + 14

places where the sky is hemmed in by trees and buildings and places where the sky seems to surround you. The Balcones Escarpment separates Dallas and Fort Worth; it runs through Austin and the western edge of San Antonio. But it is less familiar to Texans today than the highway that runs pretty much along the same line: Interstate 35. This is one of the most heavily traveled and congested interstates in America, thick with truck traffic in the populated stretches between the Metroplex and the Mexican border even as it passes through the lightly populated near-desert between San Antonio and Laredo. It is one of the great routes of commerce in America, or rather between the United States and Mexico.

I-35 connects Austin and San Antonio, two booming Texan cities with very different beginnings and different characters now. Austin is the creation of state government, with the pink marble Capitol and the sprawling University of Texas. But it has gone beyond its roots, becoming one of America's leading high-technology and entrepreneurial centers, with an office-building boom downtown and in the suburbs. San Antonio was the creation of Texas's Mexican settlers, a town with a Spanish accent and a heavily Latino population. It is proud of the Alamo and the Riverwalk, but it also has corporate headquarters, numerous lakes for water supply and recreation, and an array of military bases.

In the counties between these two cities and in the Hill Country to the west, is the Texas German country, originally settled by Germans fleeing the reaction against the failed revolutions of 1848. The Texas German country has always been a set of orderly communities in rip-roaring Texas, economically prosperous in a state that considered itself poor until it struck oil. It was anti-slavery and politically Republican in a state whose enthusiasm for the Democratic Party had roots in Confederate loyalties and populist rebellions. The Texas German heritage is still visible, and an antique German is sometimes heard on the streets in towns like New Braunfels, Boerne and Fredericksburg (there are about 10,000 speakers now, compared to 159,000 in the 1940s). These communities, with their neat houses, low cost of living and Hill Country ambience, attract new residents to new subdivisions and lakeside developments.

The 21st Congressional District of Texas includes much of this territory. About half of its people are in San Antonio and Bexar County. It includes the northeast corner of the city and county, Fort Sam Houston plus some north-side neighborhoods, with many houses being bought by rich Mexicans from Monterrey. This is mostly Anglo San Antonio, though 27% of the Bexar County residents in the district are Hispanic. About one-fourth of the residents are in Austin and Travis County, including the downtown University of Texas campus. This is the most Republican part of a Democratic county. The district includes all of New Braunfels and Comal County just northeast of San Antonio as well as several Hill Country counties to the west: Blanco County, where Lyndon Johnson was born, in Johnson City, and which was his legal residence when he was first elected to the House in 1937 (but only a sliver of the LBJ Ranch near Fredericksburg, just to the west); Kendall County, a fast-growing area north of San Antonio; Kerr County, the most populous part of the Hill Country, and two smaller counties to the south. The political heritage of the district is mixed. While Travis County was always Democratic and the Texas German country was Republican, San Antonio was mixed. Overall, the district is heavily Republican. It voted 59% for Republican presidential nominee John McCain in 2008.

The congressman from the 21st District is Lamar Smith, a Republican first elected in 1986. He is the ranking Republican on the House Judiciary Committee. Smith is from an old San Antonio and South Texas ranching family. Their Jim Wells County ranch has been in the family for four generations. Smith graduated from Texas Military Institute (now TMI, the Episcopal School of Texas), Yale University and Southern Methodist University's law school. He worked as a reporter for the *Christian Science Monitor* newspaper and as a lawyer in San Antonio. He was elected to the Texas House in 1980 and the Bexar County Commission in 1982. In 1986, when Republican U.S. Rep. Tom Loeffler ran for governor, Smith ran for the House seat. He won by beating two other San Antonio-based candidates in the primary and then winning the runoff 54%-46% against a religious conservative. His campaign was run by then little-known Texas political consultant Karl Rove.

In the House, Smith compiled a conservative voting record. When Republicans were in the majority, he chaired the Judiciary Committee's Immigration Subcommittee from 1995 to 2001. He is a strong believer in stronger action to stop illegal immigration and to reduce legal immigration. He opposed President George W. Bush's guest-worker proposal in 2004 and bipartisan proposals to provide a path to citizenship for illegal immigrants living in the United States. The guest-worker program, Smith said, "opens up every job in America" to low-wage competition. Like other House Republican leaders, he insisted that better border enforcement must be in place before new guest-worker programs or legalization policies were established. "It's hard to justify legislation that would reward millions of lawbreakers, attract more illegal immigrants and depress American workers' wages," Smith said. He hailed the 700-mile border-fence bill that passed in 2006, saying, "It is an important first step and shows that Republicans are serious about border security." His bill to split the Immigration and Naturalization Service into two agencies, one concentrating on law enforcement, the other on aid to immigrants, was passed as part of the homeland-security bill in 2002.

In 2001, Smith became chairman of what was then the Crime Subcommittee, where he focused on cybercrime and high-technology issues. He strongly supported the USA PATRIOT Act, the Bush administration's anti-terrorism law. He also worked with Republican Sen. John Cornyn of Texas and Democratic Sen. Patrick Leahy of Vermont on bipartisan changes to the Freedom of Information Act to make it easier and faster for the public to obtain government information. Smith's bill creating a 20-year sentence for fraudulently obtaining consumer and business phone records and distributing them over the Internet became law in January 2007. Three years earlier, he also succeeded in passing a bill allowing firms to sell software that could delete offensive passages from DVDs.

When Democrats took majority control of the House in 2007, Smith became the ranking Republican on the full Judiciary Committee. Despite deep partisan conflicts on the committee, he gets along with Democrats better than do many in his party and found common ground on bills to strengthen cyber security and intellectual-property enforcement. Smith worked with Rep. Zoe Lofgren, D-Calif., to increase visas for skilled workers. But he joined Republicans who opposed closing the terrorist-detention facility at Guantanamo Bay, Cuba.

Smith has been active on the Committee on Standards of Official Conduct, which polices the ethical behavior of fellow House members. In 2008, as a member of a special panel to determine whether the House required an outside body to police its ethics, he opposed the move.

Smith has been easily re-elected by wide margins.

TWENTY-SECOND DISTRICT

Pete Olson (R)

Elected 2008, 1st term; b. Dec. 9, 1962, Fort Lewis, WA; home, Sugar Land; Rice U., B.A. 1985; U of TX, J.D. 1988; Methodist; married (Nancy); 2 children.

Military Career: Navy, 1988–98, Naval Reserves, 1998–Present.

Professional Career: Naval officer; Staffer, U.S. Sen. Phil Gramm, U.S. Sen. John Cornyn.

DC Office: 514 CHOB, 20515, 202-225-5951; Fax: 202-225-5241; Web site: olson.house.gov.

State Offices: Clear Lake, 281-486-1095; Sugar Land, 281-494-2649.

Committees: *Homeland Security* (11th of 13 R): Emergency Communications, Preparedness & Response; Transportation Security & Infrastructure Protection. *Science & Technology* (17th of 17 R): Space & Aeronautics (RMM). *Transportation & Infrastructure* (30th of 30 R): Coast Guard & Maritime Transportation; Railroads, Pipelines & Hazardous Materials; Water Resources & Environment.

Group Ratings and Key Votes: Newly Elected

Election Results

2008 general	Pete Olson (R)	161,996	(52%)	($2,366,149)
	Nick Lampson (D)	140,160	(45%)	($2,385,202)
	John Wieder (Lib)	6,839	(2%)	($13,469)
2008 runoff	Pete Olson (R)	15,511	(69%)	
	Shelley Sekula-Gibbs (R)	7,125	(31%)	
2008 primary	Shelley Sekula-Gibbs (R)	16,697	(30%)	
	Pete Olson (R)	11,634	(21%)	
	John Manlove (R)	8,399	(15%)	
	Robert Talton (R)	8,169	(15%)	
	Dean Hrbacek (R)	5,864	(10%)	

Population		**Race/Ethnicity**		**Work**	
Pop. 2007:	816,085	White:	51.1%	Private:	79.7%
Change since 2000:	Up 25.2%	Black:	12.6%	Government:	14.3%
Urban:	94.6%	Hispanic:	24.3%	Self-employed:	5.8%
Rural:	5.4%	Asian:	10.2%	Blue collar:	19.3%
Area size:	1,002 sq. mi.	Native Am.:	0.3%	White collar:	67.5%
		Hawaiian:	0.1%	Khaki collar:	0.1%
Age		Two+ races:	1.0%	Other:	13.1%
Median age:	33.8 yrs.			Median income:	$68,140
More than 65 yrs:	7.5%	*Ancestry*		Median home value:	$147,500
Less than 18 yrs:	27.8%	German:	10.8%	Poverty:	9.2%
		Irish:	7.0%		
Education		English:	6.9%	**Military Veterans**	
H.S. grad:	86.5%			% of Pop:	8.7%
College grad:	33.5%				
Grad degree:	11.6%				

Those seeking the story of Houston's booming growth over the past dozen years would be well advised to drive out the Southwest Freeway for about 45 minutes, if the traffic is not too bad, to Sugar Land. There has been a big change from the sugar plantations that flourished here before the Civil War and from the locale of *The Sugarland Express,* a 1970s B-movie about a fugitive convict. In once-rural Fort Bend County, on the site of the old Imperial Sugar Mill, is an immaculately clean and fast

2008 Presidential Vote

McCain (R)	183,172	(58%)
Obama (D)	129,414	(41%)

2004 Presidential Vote

Bush (R)	177,378	(64%)
Kerry (D)	98,180	(36%)

Cook Partisan Voting Index: R + 13

growing privately planned city of nearly 80,000 people, with privatized water and other services. (There were 33,000 people here in 1990.) The entrepreneurial spirit is alive and well, with thousands of new and growing businesses, and so is a communitarian spirit, with dozens of churches and civic associations buzzing with activity. People welcome the new freeways and toll roads being built to link them with Houston's airports and other business nodes.

The image of suburbia has long been one of an all-white haven, but Sugar Land and Fort Bend County are welcoming to immigrants and minorities. Some 21% of the county population is African-American, 23% is Hispanic, and 14% is Asian. In 2003, a reporter from the *San Francisco Chronicle* came to Sugar Land, which was then represented by the powerful conservative Republican Tom DeLay, to see "the anti-San Francisco" and seemed charmed by a community that "welcomes immigrants, shopping centers and jogging paths." Sugar Land has elected Daniel Wong, from Macao, to the City Council, and Dinesh Shah, from India, served on the board of the Chamber of Commerce. People came from around the world to consecrate the huge new Hindu temple in 2007. This is 21st-century America.

The 22nd Congressional District of Texas covers more than two-thirds of Fort Bend County, including Sugar Land. It also includes one-quarter of Brazoria County, centering on fast-growing Pearland, just south of Houston, plus parts of Galveston County, including Santa Fe, La Marque and Hitchcock. Nearly one-half of its residents are in Harris County, which includes working-class Deer Park, Pasadena and LaPorte south of the Houston Ship Channel, and the more upscale Webster, Clear Lake and Taylor Lake Village surrounding the Johnson Space Center. Overall, the district's population is 51% white, 13% black, 24% Hispanic and 10% Asian. Politically, the 22nd District leans Republican. Native son George W. Bush won here 67%-33% in 2000, but his majority fell to 64%-36% in 2004. GOP nominee John McCain won the district in 2008 with 58% of the vote.

The new congressman from the 22nd district is Republican Pete Olson. Considering the Republican leanings of this district, which DeLay represented for more than two decades, Olson's victory over freshman Democratic Rep. Nick Lampson was hardly an upset. It was simply the district reverting to form, having elected Lampson two years earlier to register its anger at DeLay, who had become the symbol of influence peddling and political opportunism in the Republican majority in Congress.

The son of an Army veteran, Olson followed in his father's footsteps and entered the Navy on the same day he took the Texas bar exam. He served as a naval aviator, flew anti-submarine missions, and finished his military career as a liaison to the U.S. Senate. His next job was as a staff member for Republican Sen. Phil Gramm of Texas. After Gramm retired in 2002, Olson was the chief of staff to his successor, Republican Sen. John Cornyn.

In 2006, DeLay resigned his seat after being indicted in Texas on criminal campaign-finance charges, and several of his aides and lobbyists close to him came under investigation for influence peddling. Houston City Council member Shelley Sekula-Gibbs, a Republican, won a special election for the seat, served for several weeks, but then lost in the general election. A legal technicality kept her name off the ballot, however. Having to run as a write-in candidate hurt Sekula-Gibbs, as did the lingering taint of the DeLay scandal, and Lampson grabbed victory by a fairly narrow margin. Republicans targeted Lampson for defeat in 2008. Olson, who had been living in the suburbs of Washington, moved back to the district in 2007 and joined a crowded primary field that included Sekula-Gibbs and Sugar Land Mayor Dean Hrbacek. Sekula-Gibbs won the primary but failed to get the 50% share of the vote needed to avoid a runoff with second-place Olson. Republicans at the state and national levels regarded Sekula-Gibbs as a weak candidate and coalesced around Olson, who won the runoff with 69% of the vote.

In the general election campaign, Olson touted a conservative message. Lampson tried to tar Olson with DeLay's image, charging that Olson employed consultants who had previously worked for DeLay. Democratic leaders also came to his aid, saying that if re-elected, Lampson would chair the House subcommittee with jurisdiction over NASA, an important local employer. Lampson's response to Hurricane Ike in September won bipartisan praise as well. But in the end, all of this could not stop the district from returning to its GOP roots on Election Day. Olson won 52% to 45%.

In the House, Olson got a seat on the Transportation and Infrastructure Committee, a valuable assignment for any road-heavy district, which most Texas districts are. He encountered some health problems in his first term. In March 2009, he collapsed while lifting weights in the House gym. He was taken to George Washington University Hospital, where he underwent emergency surgery to install a pacemaker. He was expected to make a full recovery.

TWENTY-THIRD DISTRICT

Ciro Rodriguez (D)

Elected 2006, 5th full term; b. Dec. 9, 1946, Piedras Negras, Coah., Mexico; home, San Antonio; St. Mary's U., B.A. 1973, Our Lady of the Lake U., M.S.W., 1978; Catholic; married (Carolina); 1 child.

Elected Office: Harlandale Schl. Bd., 1975–87; TX House of Reps., 1986–97; U.S. House of Reps. 1997–2004.

Professional Career: Substance abuse counselor, 1971–74, 1978–80; Educ. consultant, 1980–87; Faculty, Our Lady of the Lake U., 1987–97; Founder, Rio Strategy Group, 2005.

DC Office: 2351 RHOB, 20515, 202-225-4511; Fax: 202-225-2237; Web site: rodriguez.house.gov.

State Offices: Del Rio, 830-774-5500; Eagle Pass, 830-757-8398; Fort Stockton, 432-336-3975; S. San Antonio, 210-922-1874; N. San Antonio, 210-561-9421.

Committees: *Appropriations* (35th of 37 D): Homeland Security; Legislative Branch; Transportation, HUD & Related Agencies. *Veterans' Affairs* (11th of 18 D): Disability Assistance & Memorial Affairs; Health.

Group Ratings

	ADA	ACLU	AFS	LCV	ITIC	NTU	COC	ACU	CFG	FRC
2008	80	73	100	77	71	22	61	24	16	11
2007	95	—	100	80	—	6	60	8	8	—

National Journal Ratings

	2007 LIB	—	2007 CONS		2008 LIB	—	2008 CONS
Economic	54%	—	46%		51%	—	49%
Social	65%	—	34%		54%	—	42%
Foreign	57%	—	42%		55%	—	43%
Composite	59%	—	41%		54%	—	46%

Key Votes of the 110th Congress

1. Increase minimum wage	Y	5. Share immigration data	N	9. Withdraw troops 8/08	Y
2. Expand SCHIP	Y	6. Foreign aid abortion ban	N	10. No operations in Iran	Y
3. Raise CAFE standards	Y	7. Ban gay bias in workplace	Y	11. Free trade with Peru	N
4. Bail out financial markets	N	8. Repeal D.C. gun law	Y	12. Overhaul FISA	Y

Election Results

2008 general	Ciro Rodriguez (D)	134,090	(56%)	($2,362,363)
	Lyle Larson (R)	100,799	(42%)	($813,774)
	Lani Connolly (Lib)	5,581	(2%)	
2008 primary	Ciro Rodriguez (D)	unopposed		

Prior Winning Percentages: 2006 (54%); 2002 (71%); 2000 (89%); 1998 (91%); 1997 (67%)

Population		Race/Ethnicity		Work	
Pop. 2007:	747,229	White:	29.0%	Private:	73.9%
Change since 2000:	Up 14.7%	Black:	3.0%	Government:	18.9%
Urban:	76.4%	Hispanic:	65.3%	Self-employed:	6.9%
Rural:	23.6%	Asian:	1.5%	Blue collar:	23.8%
Area size:	48,562 sq. mi.	Native Am.:	0.2%	White collar:	57.1%
		Hawaiian:	0.1%	Khaki collar:	0.4%
Age		Two+ races:	0.6%	Other:	18.7%
Median age:	32.7 yrs.			Median income:	$41,890
More than 65 yrs:	10.3%	*Ancestry*		Median home value:	$86,600
Less than 18 yrs:	30.7%	German:	8.3%	Poverty:	20.1%
		Irish:	4.6%		
Education		English:	4.2%	**Military Veterans**	
H.S. grad:	72.3%			% of Pop:	11.2%
College grad:	20.9%				
Grad degree:	7.5%				

The Mexican-American tradition in the part of South Texas radiating from San Antonio is anchored in two culturally conservative institutions, the Catholic Church and the United States military. Both are a major presence in San Antonio, just 150 miles north of the border, which for many years had the largest Mexican-American population of any American city and where Spanish has long been widely spoken. The church in San Antonio was led for years by liberal bishops; they also ran St. Mary's

2008 Presidential Vote
Obama (D) 124,936   (51%)
McCain (R)............................118,324   (48%)

2004 Presidential Vote
Bush (R) 120,672   (57%)
Kerry (D)................................90,057   (43%)

Cook Partisan Voting Index: R + 4

University, which educated many Hispanic politicians and leaders, including two longtime House Democratic committee chairmen, former Reps. Henry B. Gonzalez and Kika de la Garza, as well as Republican Sen. John Cornyn, who graduated from St. Mary's law school. Just as visible a presence in San Antonio are the Army and Air Force, with huge Fort Sam Houston, Lackland Air Force Base, and the Randolph Air Force Base, all in or near the city limits. In 2006, at the site of the former Brooks Air Force Base, Toyota opened a $1.2 billion plant to manufacture Tundra pickup trucks. About 55% of the nearly 2,000 workers are Hispanic. Mexican-Americans have long volunteered for military service in numbers higher than members of most other ethnic groups, and for many years Mexican-Americans in San Antonio worked in civilian jobs for the military service. San Antonio's Mexican-American community also has produced many politicians who are liberal on economic issues and civil rights but also are pro-military and at home with traditional religious and cultural values.

Although farmland has disappeared around San Antonio, some small towns remain, such as Castroville, where you can see 19th-century Alsatian architecture and where citizen groups have been fighting big development projects. Fifty or so miles west of San Antonio, the hills flatten out and become the parched uplands of West Texas. This is a borderland, just north of Mexico, where people are concentrated in tiny hamlets amid the empty ranchlands. Most residents are Latino. Once Indians were the threat on this frontier. Now the challenge is assimilation, and the threat is lack of water. The aquifers of West Texas are being drained, and state law still allows landowners to pump out as much water as they want. The Rio Grande, dried out by a dam in New Mexico, gets most of its water from the Rio Conchos in the Mexican state of Chihuahua. Mexico owes the United States hundreds of thousands of acre-feet under a 1944 treaty.

Big cities have sprung up on the border. But in the hundreds of miles between El Paso and Juarez, Chihuahua, which between them have about 2 million people, and Laredo and Nuevo Laredo, Tamaulipas, which between them have about 900,000, there are only a few border crossings and much wilderness. The mountains of Big Bend National Park rise above the Rio Grande, where in the clean air you can find dozens of species of birds and can see for 180 miles. Eccentrics have built an art colony in Marfa and stage a chili cook-off in Terlingua. Texas's frontier in many ways is thriving. Huge wind farms have flowered along the interstate in Crockett County. Unlike in California and Arizona, trade is actively conducted here, and local communities often have a binational "good neighbor" policy. But all this activity makes people thirsty. Private companies are buying ranchland so that they can pump water out to Texas's growing cities, and there is even some talk of building a pipeline from Hoover Dam in Nevada.

The 23rd Congressional District of Texas is geographically the largest in the state, larger than almost any state east of the Mississippi River. It stretches from the west side of San Antonio to the outskirts of El Paso, from Eagle Pass and Maverick County to the New Mexico border. About two-thirds of its population is in Bexar County. The August 2006 court-ordered redistricting added a large portion of the south side of Bexar County, which includes many Latinos. The district's Latino population is 65%. Many of the border counties are Democratic. With the changes, the district voted 57% for Republican President George W. Bush in 2004 compared to the 65% he would have received if the old boundaries had held up. In 2008, Democratic presidential nominee Barack Obama won the district 51%-48%, though GOP nominee John McCain won the Bexar County portion by about 300 votes.

The congressman from the 23rd District is Ciro Rodriguez, who was elected in 2006 and previously served three full terms in the old 28th District. Rodriguez grew up in San Antonio, was a social worker, teacher and educational consultant. He spent 12 years on the Harlandale school board, and in 1986, he was elected to the Texas House, where he had a liberal voting record. He started running for the U.S. House soon after Democratic Rep. Frank Tejeda, of the old 28th District, died of a brain tumor in January 1997. He got the critical endorsement of the San Antonio Central Labor Council, and House Democratic leaders promised him Tejeda's seat on the Armed Services Committee. His only serious competition for the seat came from San Antonio Councilman Juan Solis. Like Tejeda, Solis opposed abortion and gun control, and he called Rodriguez "a wild-eyed liberal." But in the March primary, Rodriguez led Solis 46%-27%, and he won the low-turnout runoff 67%-33%. In the House, he had the most liberal voting record of Texas's six Hispanic congressmen.

Then in 2004, Rodriguez lost the 28th District seat in a bitter contest with Henry Cuellar after the district was revamped to include half of Laredo's Webb County. When the ambitious Cuellar announced his decision to run, Rodriguez said he had a hard time believing that a friend and former legislative colleague for whom he had raised money in 2002 would run against him. In their five-month campaign, Cuellar campaigned more aggressively. He mobilized voters more effectively from his base in Laredo than Rodriguez did from his in San Antonio. After recounts and court reviews that took four months to resolve, Rodriguez lost by 203 votes. Their bitter conflict resumed in the 2006 primary for the 28th District. But without incumbency working for him, Rodriguez raised less money than Cuellar, and his campaign skills seemed stale. He lost again, this time by 53% to 40%. His political obituary appeared to be written.

But a court-ordered redistricting gave Rodriguez the unusual opportunity to run for a second time in 2006, against a new opponent and in a very different district. The contest was hardly a straight line to victory. The 23rd District's representative, Republican Henry Bonilla, first elected in 1992, was chairman of the Agriculture Appropriations Subcommittee and also served on the Defense Appropriations Subcommittee. He had earmarked money for many district projects. He also had had good relationships with President Bush. When the August redistricting added large sections of south San Antonio to the 23rd, Rodriguez became a logical challenger to Bonilla. But five other Democrats also entered the contest. In the Election Day all-party primary, the main question was whether Bonilla could get the 50% required to avoid a runoff. He fell just short, with 48.6%. Rodriguez was runner-up with 20%.

For the December runoff, Bonilla began with nearly $2 million in campaign funds, while Rodriguez had all but depleted his account. But Rodriguez had some factors in his favor, including the enthusiasm generated by Democrats taking control of the House that November. National Democrats thought Bonilla was vulnerable, and Rodriguez agreed to let them send in professionals to help run the campaign in place of his wife, Carolina, who in the past had run an old-fashioned volunteer effort. Rodriguez criticized Bonilla for voting in 2003 against a $1,500 bonus to soldiers serving in Iraq and Afghanistan. Bonilla said that Rodriguez showed "dangerous judgment" for opposing a law to allow the use of secret evidence in immigration hearings. In the closing days, with polls showing a tight contest, Bonilla ran an ad that depicted Rodriguez as a terrorist sympathizer. The Democratic Congressional Campaign Committee put nearly $1 million into the contest, and former President Bill Clinton made a last-minute campaign appearance in San Antonio. Rodriguez won 54%-46%. He took 56% in Bexar County, where his 5,700 vote lead was nearly the margin of his victory district-wide. Bonilla won 13 of the other 19 counties, but Rodriguez ran especially well around Eagle Pass and Big Bend, where Bonilla was hurt by his support for the GOP's bill creating a border fence.

Back in the House, Rodriguez sealed his remarkable comeback when House Democrats gave him a seat on the Appropriations Committee, which more senior Texas Democrats had been seeking. With his new constituency, his voting record shifted to the center, and his focus shifted to issues such as water rights, agriculture and the border. He said, "It's a totally different ball game. Although my basic values haven't changed, what changes is that I am responding to views of different constituents. I have a better appreciation of members who represent swing districts and how the leadership has to deal with those members." During the 2007 energy debate, Rodriguez helped pass an amendment to require utilities to produce 15% of their electricity from renewable energy sources by 2020.

Rodriguez faced a competitive re-election in 2008. Republican Bexar County Commissioner Lyle Larson said Rodriguez was part of the big spending problem in Washington. With a large increase in campaign funds, aided in part by his powerful position on Appropriations, Rodriguez emphasized his vote against the $700 billion government rescue of the financial-services industry in 2008. In an easier than expected victory, he won 56%-42%, including 52%-45% in Bexar County.

TWENTY-FOURTH DISTRICT

Kenny Marchant (R)

Elected 2004, 3rd term; b. Feb. 23, 1951, Bonham; home, Coppell; Southern Nazarene U., B.A. 1973, attended Nazarene Theol. Sem. 1975–76; Nazarene; married (Donna); 4 children.

Elected Office: Carrollton City Cncl., 1980–84; Mayor, 1984–86; TX House of Reps., 1986–2004.

Professional Career: Homebuilder, developer, 1975–2004.

DC Office: 227 CHOB, 20515, 202-225-6605; Fax: 202-225-0074; Web site: marchant.house.gov.

State Offices: Irving, 972-556-0162.

Committees: *Financial Services* (22nd of 29 R): Financial Institutions & Consumer Credit; Housing & Community Opportunity.

Group Ratings

	ADA	ACLU	AFS	LCV	ITIC	NTU	COC	ACU	CFG	FRC
2008	0	20	0	0	71	85	83	100	91	100
2007	10	—	9	5	—	83	78	96	87	

National Journal Ratings

	2007 LIB	—	2007 CONS	2008 LIB	—	2008 CONS
Economic	12%	—	87%	10%	—	90%
Social	21%	—	75%	0%	—	91%
Foreign	0%	—	72%	0%	—	95%
Composite	17%	—	84%	6%	—	94%

Key Votes of the 110th Congress

1. Increase minimum wage	Y	5. Share immigration data	Y	9. Withdraw troops 8/08	N
2. Expand SCHIP	N	6. Foreign aid abortion ban	Y	10. No operations in Iran	N
3. Raise CAFE standards	N	7. Ban gay bias in workplace	N	11. Free trade with Peru	Y
4. Bail out financial markets	N	8. Repeal D.C. gun law	Y	12. Overhaul FISA	Y

Election Results

2008 general	Kenny Marchant (R)..151,434	(56%)	($644,822)
	Tom Love (D)..111,089	(41%)	($21,990)
	David Casey (Lib) 7,972	(3%)	
2008 primary	Kenny Marchant (R) .... unopposed		

Prior Winning Percentages: 2006 (60%); 2004 (64%)

Population		Race/Ethnicity		Work	
Pop. 2007:	754,506	White:	52.9%	Private:	83.7%
Change since 2000:	Up 15.8%	Black:	11.9%	Government:	10.4%
Urban:	99.2%	Hispanic:	24.9%	Self-employed:	5.7%
Rural:	0.8%	Asian:	8.1%	Blue collar:	18.5%
Area size:	354 sq. mi.	Native Am.:	0.4%	White collar:	68.4%
		Hawaiian:	0.3%	Khaki collar:	0.0%
Age		Two+ races:	1.2%	Other:	13.0%
Median age:	33.5 yrs.	*Ancestry*		Median income:	$58,661
More than 65 yrs:	6.7%	German:	10.1%	Median home value:	$155,900
Less than 18 yrs:	28.2%	English:	8.3%	Poverty:	9.0%
Education		Irish:	7.7%		
H.S. grad:	86.9%			**Military Veterans**	
College grad:	36.5%			% of Pop:	8.7%
Grad degree:	10.9%				

The gigantic (larger than Manhattan Island) Dallas–Fort Worth International Airport, the third-busiest in the world, bisects the Metroplex and its two adjacent counties with its large terminals and the Texas-sized highway network that feeds them. DFW, as everyone calls it, also has been a focal point for the huge local development in both Dallas and Tarrant counties. "DFW is no longer solely an airport. DFW is our home," the *Fort Worth Star-Telegram* wrote. New cities, with as many people as Dallas and Fort Worth had in the 1950s—Grand Prairie and Irving—grew up around the airport during the next two decades in these once-impoverished lands. For years, DFW and its supporters fiercely opposed efforts to repeal the Wright Amendment, which limited the number of cities that can be reached on flights out of the old Love Field in Dallas. In 2006, a political consensus in Texas and in Washington resulted in it being repealed, partly at the behest of locally based airlines seeking to throw off its anticompetitive shackles in a rapidly changing transportation world.

2008 Presidential Vote		
McCain (R).............................153,758	(55%)
Obama (D) 124,128	(44%)
2004 Presidential Vote		
Bush (R)..................................161,864	(65%)
Kerry (D)..................................86,786	(35%)
Cook Partisan Voting Index: R + 11		

North of DFW are newer and more upscale suburbs: Grapevine and Southlake, with huge shopping malls and resort centers, in northeast Tarrant County. Across the International Parkway in northwest Dallas County are Coppell, Farmers Branch and Carrollton. To the north are the fast-growing suburbs and exurbs of Denton County. The Dallas–Fort Worth–Arlington Metropolitan Statistical Area has passed Philadelphia as the nation's fourth-largest MSA. It is 44% African-American, Asian or Hispanic, compared with 30% in the Philadelphia MSA. The MSA has grown 22% since 2000, compared with a rate of 5% or less in the other MSAs in the top five. The area's job growth from July 2007 to July 2008 was the highest in the nation.

The 24th Congressional District of Texas is based in this area and has three large spokes that reach out from DFW. The largest extends northeast through Dallas County and into Denton County, up to Route 121, including one-third of Irving and almost all of Farmers Branch, Coppell and Carrollton. To the west, another spoke reaches into Tarrant County out to Precinct Line Road and includes Grapevine, Bedford, Colleyville and Southlake. South of the airport it takes in Cedar Hill, part of Irving and almost all of Grand Prairie, where oil and gas drilling is common in residential neighborhoods. About half of the population is in Dallas County, a third is in Tarrant County and the rest is in Denton County. After its transformation by the 2003 redistricting, the new 24th District voted 65% for Bush in 2004 and 55% for GOP presidential nominee John McCain in 2008.

The congressman from the 24th District is Kenny Marchant, a Republican elected in 2004. He graduated from Southern Nazarene University. A local homebuilder and successful developer, Marchant served a quarter-century in elected offices before running for Congress, on the Carrollton City Council, as Carrollton mayor, and then in the state House. He also has been active in private humanitarian projects around the world. The Ken Marchant Foundation funds church loans, mission projects and scholarships. In contrast to other upwardly mobile Republicans in Austin, he enjoyed a reputation on both sides of the aisle as a levelheaded peacemaker. Despite serving in some of the Legislature's most partisan leadership posts, the mild-mannered and deeply religious Marchant managed to maintain a cool demeanor, even as his colleagues engaged in acrimonious battle. As *Texas Monthly* magazine wrote: "His role was that of the genial, kindly sheriff in a western who allows the cowboys to gamble, drink and fight—but when they show up at the jail, rope in hand, he stands on the steps and says, 'Boys, just go on home and cool off.' "

Marchant had been chairman and floor leader of the Texas House Republican caucus and served on the House Redistricting Committee during the bitter 2003 redistricting battle. Unsurprisingly, the redistricting plan couldn't have been more favorable to him. In their effort to draw a Dallas-area seat that former Democratic Caucus Chairman Martin Frost could not win, Republicans designed a district where Marchant could not lose. He denied that the new 24th was created specifically for him, but it incorporated nearly his entire state legislative district and was heavily Republican. He campaigned as "a proven leader for George W. Bush," a reference to his close legislative relationship with the former governor. Marchant drew no serious major-party opposition. In the primary, he defeated three other candidates with 73% of the vote and in the general election won 64%-34%.

In the House, Marchant has a solidly conservative voting record, though he does not have the hard rhetorical edge of a Tom DeLay, the controversial former GOP majority leader from Texas. As the only one of the five House Republicans elected as the result of DeLay's redistricting plan who had prior legislative experience, Marchant settled comfortably into Congress. He developed a fruitful relationship with Republican Leader John Boehner of Ohio, joining the Education and the Workforce Committee that Boehner chaired in 2005 and becoming one of the few Texans to back Boehner in his bid to become majority leader when Republicans still controlled the House.

Marchant's legislative priorities have been mostly parochial. As the only North Texas Republican on the Transportation Committee, he helped coordinate the eight-year phased repeal of the Wright Amendment. In January 2009, he unsuccessfully sought a seat on the House Ways and Means Committee, but he retained his seat on the Financial Services Committee. Since 2007, he has refused to request spending earmarks for his district. With the big amounts that Washington already is spending, "We felt we did not need to contribute to any more big spending," he told the *Fort Worth Star-Telegram* in April 2009. Earmarks, which exploded in number and size during the Republican majority, became controversial in recent years as budget hawks in both parties began to focus on them as wasteful, pork-barrel spending.

TWENTY-FIFTH DISTRICT

Lloyd Doggett (D)

Elected 1994, 8th term; b. Oct. 6, 1946, Austin; home, Austin; U. of TX, B.B.A. 1967, J.D. 1970; Methodist; married (Libby); 2 children.

Elected Office: TX Senate, 1972–84; TX Supreme Ct. justice, 1989–94.

Professional Career: Practicing atty., 1970–89; Adjunct prof., U. of TX Law Schl., 1989–94.

DC Office: 201 CHOB, 20515, 202-225-4865; Fax: 202-225-3073; Web site: www.house.gov/doggett.

State Offices: Austin, 512-916-5921.

Committees: *Budget* (5th of 24 D). *Ways & Means* (9th of 26 D): Health; Social Security; Trade.

Group Ratings

	ADA	ACLU	AFS	LCV	ITIC	NTU	COC	ACU	CFG	FRC
2008	90	100	100	92	83	18	50	8	9	5
2007	95	—	100	90	—	7	53	4	14	—

National Journal Ratings

	2007 LIB	—	2007 CONS		2008 LIB	—	2008 CONS
Economic	64%	—	34%		67%	—	32%
Social	71%	—	29%		67%	—	28%
Foreign	86%	—	11%		92%	—	0%
Composite	75%	—	26%		78%	—	22%

Key Votes of the 110th Congress

1. Increase minimum wage	Y	5. Share immigration data	N	9. Withdraw troops 8/08	Y
2. Expand SCHIP	Y	6. Foreign aid abortion ban	N	10. No operations in Iran	Y
3. Raise CAFE standards	Y	7. Ban gay bias in workplace	Y	11. Free trade with Peru	Y
4. Bail out financial markets	N	8. Repeal D.C. gun law	N	12. Overhaul FISA	N

Election Results

2008 general	Lloyd Doggett (D)...191,755	(66%)	($401,449)
	George Morovich (R) 88,693	(30%)	($64,134)
	Jim Stutsman (Lib)..10,848	(4%)	
2008 primary	Lloyd Doggett (D)................................... unopposed		

Prior Winning Percentages: 2006 (67%); 2004 (68%); 2002 (84%); 2000 (85%); 1998 (85%); 1996 (56%); 1994 (56%)

Population		Race/Ethnicity		Work	
Pop. 2007:	749,130	White:	51.0%	Private:	73.2%
Change since 2000:	Up 15.0%	Black:	8.6%	Government:	18.3%
Urban:	75.2%	Hispanic:	36.6%	Self-employed:	8.3%
Rural:	24.8%	Asian:	2.2%	Blue collar:	22.2%
Area size:	6,182 sq. mi.	Native Am.:	0.3%	White collar:	59.7%
		Hawaiian:	0.1%	Khaki collar:	0.1%
Age		Two+ races:	0.9%	Other:	18.0%
Median age:	31.7 yrs.	*Ancestry*		Median income:	$45,738
More than 65 yrs:	8.6%	German:	13.6%	Median home value:	$147,500
Less than 18 yrs:	25.1%	Irish:	7.9%	Poverty:	17.1%
Education		English:	7.2%	**Military Veterans**	
H.S. grad:	80.5%			% of Pop:	8.2%
College grad:	30.7%				
Grad degree:	10.2%				

Austin is the capital of the second-largest state in the United States and the site of the largest Capitol building, if not the most rambunctious state legislature in the country. It is one of many capitals with a first-rate university, but one of only two with its own musical tradition (Nashville is the other). Not long ago, Austin was laid-back and countrified. There had never been much commerce here, and state government provided much of the local employment. Its skies were untainted by industrial

2008 Presidential Vote

Obama (D) 176,935	(59%)
McCain (R).............................117,845	(39%)

2004 Presidential Vote

Kerry (D)................................140,063	(54%)
Bush (R) 120,715	(46%)

Cook Partisan Voting Index: D + 6

smoke, its landscape unpocked by oil rigs, and its downtown streets lined not with business offices but with buildings holding a few lobbyists and the antique Driskill Hotel. Its biggest industry was the University of Texas, with 50,000 students and an endowment of thousands of west Texas acres that turned out to sit on top of oil. The university has long had a distinguished faculty and some of the world's great scholarly collections, including the LBJ Presidential Library and its 35 million documents. The university has been a shelter for liberal intellectuals since the 1940s, and it helped spark Austin's high-technology boom in the 1980s and 1990s. Half a century ago, in Lyndon Johnson's time, Austin had a metropolitan population of 132,000. The compact Austin that was Johnson's headquarters in 1948, when the Duval County returns came in and gave him the 87-vote Senate victory that made his national career, is a very different Austin from the metropolitan center of 1.2 million that waited up in the rain to hear the results of the election of Texas native son George W. Bush in 2000.

Growth has also brought political change. For many years, Austin was the central focus of Texas's hardy but almost always outnumbered liberals, based in the university, state government and the *Texas Observer* magazine. They supported the New Deal and generous social programs and mocked the business lobbyists who called the shots when the "Leg" (pronounced *lej*) was in session. But as the Austin area grew, it became more conservative, especially as its private sector made up a larger share of the local economy. The techies who settled in the Silicon Hills from Austin's Travis County to once-rural Williamson County have tended to vote Republican. Some businesses cater to the old liberal bastions: the upscale organic-food chain, Whole Foods Market, is based in Austin. The city core and the university area are still Democratic, and Texas liberals still are potent in the media. But this is a state capital where Gov.

Bush could feel at home, perhaps more so than he did 30 years earlier when his application for admission was rejected by UT's law school. Bush lost Austin and Travis County 59%-41% when he first ran for governor in 1994, but he carried the county 60%-38% in 1998 when he ran for re-election and 47%-42% in 2000 when he ran for president (10% went for Green Party nominee Ralph Nader). In 2004, Austin's liberal community registered large numbers of new voters, and Bush lost Travis County 56%-42%, even as he increased his margin statewide. Democratic nominee Barack Obama carried Travis County with 64% of the vote.

The 25th Congressional District of Texas, a new seat created by the 2003 redistricting and revised significantly by a federal court in August 2006, encompasses nearly half of Travis County, including most of the east side of Austin and the city's heavily Latino and African-American neighborhoods. The increasingly settled Hispanic community includes many people moving toward the middle class. The Capitol and the UT campus are just outside the district, in the 21st, while the 10th District takes in most of the Republican northern part of the city and county. Seven rural counties that extend to the south and east now account for 40% of the 25th district. The largest of them are Hays and Bastrop, both of which are among the fastest-growing in the state, having increased more than 25% from 2000 to 2007. The district was 37% Hispanic and 9% African-American in 2007. In 2008, Democratic presidential candidate Barack Obama carried the district 59%-39%, taking a 71% share of the vote in Travis County, which cast 59% of the total vote. Republican nominee John McCain carried all the other seven counties, three of them by 2-to-1 or better.

The congressman from the 25th District is Lloyd Doggett, first elected in 1994 in the old 10th District. He is a liberal Democrat with a career that includes some notable twists. Doggett grew up in Austin, finished first in his class at the University of Texas and was student-body president in 1967. In 1972, at age 26, he was elected to the state Senate. In the 70s, as part of a large liberal bloc, he pushed for laws against job discrimination and cop-killer bullets and for generic drugs. He has long been a close ally of trial lawyers, the one strong institutional force supporting liberal Democrats in Texas. In the Legislature, he was one of the "Killer Bees" who hid out to prevent a quorum on changing the rules in the Democratic primary and filibustered—wearing sneakers—against what he called anti-consumer bills. In 1984, he ran for the U.S. Senate, narrowly edging out two House members to win the Democratic nomination. Then, despite the campaign help of crack Democratic consultant James Carville, Doggett lost the general election 59%-41% to party-switching U.S. Rep. Phil Gramm, a Democrat turned Republican. Doggett came back and was elected to the Texas Supreme Court in 1988. When Democratic U.S. Rep. Jake Pickle retired after 31 years, Doggett ran for his seat. He won the Democratic primary with token opposition and in the general election won by a solid 56%-40%.

In the House, Doggett's voting record puts him among the most-liberal Texans and near the center of all Democrats. In the days of the Republican majority, he was a frequent critic of House Speaker Newt Gingrich and a close ally of minority whips David Bonior of Michigan and Nancy Pelosi of California. (He backed Pelosi against fellow Texan Martin Frost in her race for minority leader.) In 1999, he gained a seat on the House Ways and Means Committee. Along with other Democrats, he voted against most of Bush's major tax bills and other initiatives. In 2002, he was a leader in opposing the resolution authorizing the use of force in Iraq. (Even he reported being surprised that 126 House Democrats voted against it.)

When Democrats took control of the House in 2007, Doggett set his priorities as eliminating tax shelters and loopholes and negotiating prescription-drug prices for Medicare. He also sought tax incentives for purchasers of plug-in hybrid electric cars. Often without the publicity of his earlier days in the minority, he had real impact on a number of issues. In May 2009, when President Obama announced his plan to reform international tax policy, he cited Doggett's input on proposals to crack down on overseas tax evasion.

Reflecting his district's environmental activism, Doggett was among the Ways and Means Democrats who asserted the panel's role in global-warming legislation, dominated by the House Energy and Commerce Committee. "In my view, the more the merrier," he said in 2008. He won House passage in September 2008 of a bill to create a "silver alert" modeled on the Texas program to track wandering senior citizens who may have Alzheimer's disease. He helped increase funds for UT in the Democratic economic-stimulus bill of 2009 and won a new tax credit for higher education.

Republicans were giddy in 2003 at the prospect that redistricting might end Doggett's congressional career. But he took up the challenge. As some other dislocated Texas Democrats took their fight to the courts, Doggett took his case to the voters of his new district. He started by working hard to get the support of elected officials and party activists along the border. "I chose to spend not a few hours here in the Valley in the month of December (2003), but a few weeks, to resume old friendships," he said in McAllen. Meanwhile, the best-known Hispanic challengers for a Democratic primary dropped out for various reasons. Doggett faced Leticia Hinojosa, a former district-court judge from McAllen. She called herself a "pragmatist" in contrast to the outspoken Doggett, and she claimed a closer identification with voters. "I'm Leticia Hinojosa, and I grew up poor in the Valley," she said in her radio ad. But Doggett's strong local base and relentless pursuit of new voters prevailed. He campaigned less against Hinojosa than against the redistricters. If he lost, Doggett told voters, "Tom DeLay will have won," a reference to the powerful GOP majority leaders from Texas who had orchestrated the remap. Doggett won the primary 64%-36%. He led 88%-12% in Travis County and held Hinojosa to a standoff in Hidalgo County.

  Although the primary effectively sealed his re-election, Doggett faced a spirited challenge in the 2004 general from Becky Armendariz Klein. She called herself a conservative "new voice with new ideas" and cited her experience as policy director for Gov. Bush and as chairwoman of the Texas Public Utility Commission. Klein raised more than $800,000 and criticized Doggett for failing to work across party lines. Doggett tweaked her for her bid for ethnic voters, saying she'd pulled out her "long forgotten maiden name" to run for the seat. He won 68%-31%, getting 79% in Travis County and 60% in Hidalgo County.

TWENTY-SIXTH DISTRICT

Michael Burgess (R)

Elected 2002, 4th term; b. Dec. 23, 1950, Rochester, MN; home, Lewisville; N. TX St. U., B.S. 1972, M.S. 1976, U. of TX Med. Schl., M.D. 1977, U. of TX Dallas, M.S. 2000; Episcopalian; married (Laura); 3 children.

Professional Career: Practicing obstetrician, 1981–2003.

DC Office: 229 CHOB, 20515, 202-225-7772; Fax: 202-225-2919; Web site: burgess.house.gov.

State Offices: Ft. Worth, 817-531-8454; Lewisville, 972-434-9700.

Committees: *Energy & Commerce* (20th of 23 R): Energy & Environment; Health; Oversight & Investigations. *Joint Economic Committee* (3rd of 4 R).

Group Ratings

	ADA	ACLU	AFS	LCV	ITIC	NTU	COC	ACU	CFG	FRC
2008	10	18	17	0	29	80	76	96	92	100
2007	10	—	0	0	—	77	74	100	78	—

National Journal Ratings

	2007 LIB	—	2007 CONS		2008 LIB	—	2008 CONS
Economic	17%	—	82%		20%	—	79%
Social	15%	—	84%		20%	—	74%
Foreign	28%	—	71%		7%	—	92%
Composite	21%	—	80%		17%	—	83%

Key Votes of the 110th Congress

1. Increase minimum wage	N	5. Share immigration data	Y	9. Withdraw troops 8/08	N
2. Expand SCHIP	N	6. Foreign aid abortion ban	Y	10. No operations in Iran	N
3. Raise CAFE standards	N	7. Ban gay bias in workplace	N	11. Free trade with Peru	N
4. Bail out financial markets	N	8. Repeal D.C. gun law	Y	12. Overhaul FISA	Y

Election Results

2008 general	Michael Burgess (R)	195,181	(60%)	($1,021,104)
	Ken Leach (D)	118,167	(36%)	($974)
	Stephanie Weiss (Lib)	11,028	(3%)	
2008 primary	Michael Burgess (R)	unopposed		

Prior Winning Percentages: 2006 (60%); 2004 (66%); 2002 (75%)

Population		Race/Ethnicity		Work	
Pop. 2007:	821,385	White:	62.4%	Private:	81.8%
Change since 2000:	Up 26.1%	Black:	13.2%	Government:	11.9%
Urban:	90.5%	Hispanic:	19.4%	Self-employed:	6.1%
Rural:	9.5%	Asian:	2.9%	Blue collar:	20.7%
Area size:	1,377 sq. mi.	Native Am.:	0.3%	White collar:	64.1%
Age		Hawaiian:	0.0%	Khaki collar:	0.1%
Median age:	32.6 yrs.	Two+ races:	1.7%	Other:	15.1%
More than 65 yrs:	7.6%	*Ancestry*		Median income:	$59,369
Less than 18 yrs:	28.7%	German:	12.4%	Median home value:	$145,400
Education		English:	9.0%	Poverty:	12.3%
H.S. grad:	85.5%	Irish:	8.8%	**Military Veterans**	
College grad:	30.0%			% of Pop:	10.0%
Grad degree:	8.5%				

Until the Texas Land and Immigration Company settled this portion of northeast Texas with a land grant from the Texas Congress in 1841, settlers were scarce and Indian raids were common. The area now known as Denton County takes its name from John Bunyan Denton, a Methodist pioneer preacher and lawyer killed in a skirmish with Indians. Today, this area on the northern edge of the Dallas-Fort Worth Metroplex is teeming with new arrivals, filled with young, well-educated, middle-

2008 Presidential Vote		
McCain (R)............................193,163	(58%)
Obama (D) 137,622	(41%)
2004 Presidential Vote		
Bush (R)...............................181,989	(65%)
Kerry (D)..............................99,633	(35%)
Cook Partisan Voting Index: R + 13		

class families. The University of North Texas, with nearly 35,000 students, is the fourth-largest in the state. The county's chief cities are Denton and Lewisville, Carrollton and Flower Mound, all north of the DFW Airport. And there is plenty of room for more growth along Interstates 35E and 35W. Truck manufacturer Peterbilt Motors Company in Denton is one of the largest private employers. Near Justin, in the southwest corner of Denton County, nearly 1 billion cubic feet of natural gas are produced daily. With sophisticated imaging and drilling technology, other natural-gas wells operate within 10 miles of downtown Fort Worth. In 1940, there were 33,000 people in Denton County, and they voted 88% Democratic for president. In 2008, there were 636,000 people in the county, and they voted Republican by 62% for John McCain.

The 26th Congressional District of Texas is at the heart of the northern expansion of the Dallas-Fort Worth Metroplex. It includes three-quarters of suburban and exurban Denton County, most of rural Cooke County on the Oklahoma border, and a large slice of urban Tarrant County dipping south of the DFW airport. The Tarrant County portion was designed in the 2003 redistricting to include Fort Worth's African-American neighborhoods, and it also takes in booming new subdivisions north of Fort Worth's downtown district and the Alliance Airport business parks, founded and operated by Ross Perot Jr. and employing more than 27,000 people. Since 2000, the district's population has grown 26%, the second-largest increase of any Texas district, behind only the 10th. Under the previous boundaries, Republican presidential candidate George W. Bush won 73%-27% in 2000. With the new boundaries, he won 65%-35% in 2004. GOP nominee John McCain won the district 58%-41% in 2008.

The congressman from the 26th District is Michael Burgess, a Republican first elected in 2002. He grew up in Denton County, the son of a physician, and graduated from the University of North Texas and the University of Texas Medical School in Houston. He trained at Parkland Hospital in Dallas and set up an obstetrics-gynecology practice in Lewisville. After 21 years in practice, Burgess decided to run for Congress, his first bid for elective office. When House Majority Leader Dick Armey announced in December 2001 that he would not run again, there was no doubt that he would be succeeded by a Republican. But almost no one expected that the winner would be political novice Burgess. The widespread expectation, in Texas and in Washington, was that the winner would be the majority leader's son, Scott Armey, a former Denton County judge. He made the networking rounds on Capitol Hill and among lobbyists. He was only 32, and it seemed likely he would be a congressman for many years to come.

In the primary, Armey outspent Burgess by more than 6-to-1. But turnout was light—only 25,000 people out of 456,000 voting-age residents took part. There were no Republican primary contests at the top of the ticket, and there didn't seem to be much suspense about the outcome. Armey won 45% of the vote, which was not enough to avoid a runoff. Burgess won 23%, just 91 votes ahead of the third-place finisher. Then, in the four-week runoff campaign, Burgess benefited from a series of hard-hitting articles in the *Dallas Morning News* about Scott Armey's record as a county judge. The paper reported that he had used his position to steer county jobs and contracts to close friends, including a $1.5 million transportation consulting contract. Burgess focused primarily on two issues—health care and taxes. A patients' rights advocate, he had helped to draft and pass the Texas Patients' Bill of Rights, and he vowed to do the same on a national level. His campaign was helped by the support of medical societies and local physicians who urged their patients to vote for him. Only 19,000 people turned out to vote in the April runoff, and Burgess won 55%-45%. Armey carried Collin and Tarrant counties but lost 60%-40% in Denton County, where he was known best. After the runoff, his formerly powerful father spoke bitterly of the *Morning News*'s "vicious unprofessionalism" and accused the paper of a vendetta against the Armey family. In the general election, Burgess won 75%-23% over a Democrat whose son he had delivered. He has been re-elected comfortably since, though with smaller margins since the 2003 redistricting.

In the House, Burgess has a reliably conservative voting record. He is best known for his work on health-care issues, especially since he joined the influential Energy and Commerce Committee, which has broad jurisdiction over the medical industry. In March 2009, he joined a bipartisan agreement to permit the Food and Drug Administration to approve generic versions of biologic drugs. He supported George W. Bush's call for limited federal funding of embryonic stem-cell research, and he played a role in enacting a measure to prepare the nation for a possible bird-flu epidemic. At home, he sought answers to the high infant-mortality rate in Tarrant County and looked into the cost to public hospitals of children born to illegal immigrants. As the only Texas Republican on the Transportation and Infrastructure Committee during his first term, Burgess worked to change the funding formula so that Texas "receives its fair share" of gas-tax revenues.

Burgess also has made some inroads into the GOP leadership. He served as vice chairman of the Republican Policy Committee, which hammers out the party's positions on issues. In 2008, he was presidential candidate McCain's point person on health-care policy and campaigned for him on that issue in 10 states. "We really just weren't developing [health-care principles] on our side of the House," he told the *Morning News*. "In a lot of ways, the McCain campaign was my salvation." After the election, he unsuccessfully challenged Michigan Rep. Thaddeus McCotter for chairman of the Republican Policy Committee.

TWENTY-SEVENTH DISTRICT

Solomon Ortiz (D)

Elected 1982, 14th term; b. June 3, 1937, Robstown; home, Corpus Christi; Del Mar Col., Natl. Sheriffs Training Inst., 1977; Methodist; divorced; 2 children.

Military Career: Army, 1960–62.

Elected Office: Nueces Cnty. constable, 1965–68, Commissioner, 1969–76, Sheriff, 1976–82.

DC Office: 2110 RHOB, 20515, 202-225-7742; Fax: 202-226-1134; Web site: ortiz.house.gov.

State Offices: Brownsville, 956-541-1242; Corpus Christi, 361-883-5868.

Committees: *Armed Services* (3rd of 36 D): Readiness (Chmn); Seapower & Expeditionary Forces. *Transportation & Infrastructure* (35th of 44 D): Aviation; Highways & Transit; Water Resources & Environment.

Group Ratings

	ADA	ACLU	AFS	LCV	ITIC	NTU	COC	ACU	CFG	FRC
2008	75	78	100	77	100	16	65	17	0	5
2007	80	—	100	35	—	5	71	10	13	—

National Journal Ratings

	2007 LIB	—	2007 CONS		2008 LIB	—	2008 CONS
Economic	55%	—	44%		52%	—	48%
Social	64%	—	36%		62%	—	38%
Foreign	56%	—	44%		54%	—	45%
Composite	59%	—	42%		56%	—	44%

Key Votes of the 110th Congress

1. Increase minimum wage	Y	5. Share immigration data	N	9. Withdraw troops 8/08	Y
2. Expand SCHIP	Y	6. Foreign aid abortion ban	*	10. No operations in Iran	Y
3. Raise CAFE standards	*	7. Ban gay bias in workplace	Y	11. Free trade with Peru	Y
4. Bail out financial markets	Y	8. Repeal D.C. gun law	Y	12. Overhaul FISA	Y

Election Results

2008 general	Solomon Ortiz (D)	104,864	(58%)	($719,709)
	William Vaden (R)	69,458	(38%)	
	Robert Powell (Lib)	6,629	(4%)	
2008 primary	Solomon Ortiz (D)	unopposed		

Prior Winning Percentages: 2006 (57%); 2004 (63%); 2002 (61%); 2000 (63%); 1998 (63%); 1996 (65%); 1994 (59%); 1992 (56%); 1990 (100%); 1988 (100%); 1986 (100%); 1984 (64%); 1982 (64%)

Population		Race/Ethnicity		Work	
Pop. 2007:	698,184	White:	24.8%	Private:	71.8%
Change since 2000:	Up 7.1%	Black:	2.3%	Government:	20.3%
Urban:	88.6%	Hispanic:	71.1%	Self-employed:	7.7%
Rural:	11.4%	Asian:	0.9%	Blue collar:	24.7%
Area size:	6,319 sq. mi.	Native Am.:	0.2%	White collar:	52.9%
		Hawaiian:	0.0%	Khaki collar:	0.6%
Age		Two+ races:	0.6%	Other:	21.7%
Median age:	31.3 yrs.			Median income:	$34,373
More than 65 yrs:	10.9%	*Ancestry*		Median home value:	$79,600
Less than 18 yrs:	30.7%	German:	6.0%	Poverty:	28.2%
		Irish:	4.1%		
Education		English:	3.5%	**Military Veterans**	
H.S. grad:	69.3%			% of Pop:	10.0%
College grad:	17.0%				
Grad degree:	5.8%				

Inland from the Laguna Madre in Kleberg County are the vast grazing and oil lands of the 825,000-acre—that's 1,289 square miles—King Ranch. This still seemingly vacant land between the Nueces River and the Rio Grande was the territory in contention during the Mexican-American War. The United States won that war and declared its sovereignty. Today most people here are of Mexican ancestry, some from families who have lived for generations on this side of the border, some recent

2008 Presidential Vote		
Obama (D)	97,830	(53%)
McCain (R)	84,366	(46%)
2004 Presidential Vote		
Bush (R)	99,087	(55%)
Kerry (D)	81,201	(45%)
Cook Partisan Voting Index:	R + 2	

immigrants. The culture here is *Tejano*, proudly American but with Mexican flair and vitality. (Adjacent to the King Ranch is the Armstrong Ranch, where in February 2006, Vice President Cheney accidentally shot a hunting partner.) Fronting the Gulf of Mexico is an altogether different bit of geography: the sand spit of Padre Island, an 80-mile barrier-reef island and national seashore, at the southern tip of which is a high-rise resort where college students throng for spring break.

The 27th Congressional District of Texas includes the land from Corpus Christi south to the Rio Grande. Its population is concentrated at the northern and southern ends of the district. In the north, Corpus Christi and surrounding Nueces County, with a 59% Hispanic population, is the southernmost natural port on Texas's Gulf Coast and the nation's sixth largest in trading volume. There are big petrochemical plants here, but along the bay front, there are also palm trees and recreational areas. At the southern end is Cameron County, which includes South Padre Island. The population is 86% Hispanic. In addition to tourism, construction is under way on the nation's largest offshore wind farm; more than 100 turbines will generate power for 100,000 homes.

The biggest city is Brownsville, on the Lower Rio Grande opposite Matamoros, Mexico, one of the major border crossings in Texas. The 1993 North American Free Trade Agreement has lifted the economy in parts of this area, and there has been a boom in commercial construction. But pockets of grinding poverty remain: Not far from the border is the *colonia* of Cameron Park, where people live in trailers or makeshift structures without water or sewage service, rated by the Census Bureau as one of the poorest places in the nation. At the Brownsville campus of the University of Texas in December 2007, there were protests over the completion of border fencing erected by the Homeland Security Department.

Politically, the 27th District is Democratic, but not as Democratic as one might expect from a 71% Hispanic district. In 2004, Texan George W. Bush carried it with 55% of the vote. In 2008, Democrat Barack Obama won it 53%-46%, with Cameron County providing more than the margin of victory.

The congressman from the 27th District is Solomon Ortiz, a Democrat and the only representative this district has had since its creation in the 1982 redistricting. He grew up inland from Corpus in the Canta Ranas (singing frogs) neighborhood of Robstown, which is known for its political activism. His father died when he was 14, leaving him the eldest of four children who scratched out a living as migrant farmworkers, sometimes working as far away as Colorado and Michigan. Ortiz worked as an Army investigator and translator, adding French to the Spanish he already spoke fluently. He took a correspondence course in police work and returned home to run for constable. In 1976, he was the first Hispanic elected Nueces County sheriff. In his first run for Congress, he got only 26% in the primary, but he made a propitious alliance with Democratic leaders in the Brownsville area and won the runoff with 52%. He has not been seriously challenged since.

Ortiz's voting record has leaned toward the conservative end of House Democrats. He is a sturdy internationalist, an enthusiastic supporter of NAFTA and of normalizing trade relations with China. During the immigration-reform debate in recent years, he expressed reservations about President George W. Bush's guest-worker program, saying it served corporate interests and adding that he preferred to focus on family reunification. He also opposed the Bush administration's "catch and release" program for illegal immigrants caught along the border, where there are insufficient detention centers.

As the chairman on the Readiness Subcommittee of the Armed Services Committee, Ortiz looked out for the large military installations in the Coastal Bend region around Corpus Christi and has adamantly opposed additional rounds of base closings. The Coastal Bend region was hit hard by the 2005 round of base closings: Naval Station Ingleside, which has supported the Navy's fleet of mine hunters and mine-sweepers, was closed, with a net loss of 7,000 civilian and military employees; Naval Air Station Corpus Christi was realigned, with a net loss of 1,000 jobs. Ortiz blamed "mixed signals" from members of the Corpus Christi community, including some who saw opportunities for development of the prime real estate. When the General Accounting Office reported in 2007 that the Pentagon had spent $10 billion more than expected on the 2005 round of base closings, Ortiz said it bolstered his long-held view that "the process was flawed and would not achieve the savings DOD (Department of Defense) boasted it would." Ortiz has sought without success to bring a Veterans Administration hospital to the valley, but he has been able to expand some clinics that serve his district's more than 100,000 veterans.

In recent years, Ortiz has also attracted a spate of negative publicity back home over ethics issues. In 2001, five months after the Port of Corpus Christi dedicated its new conference center in his name, the *San Antonio Express-News* reported that he got favored treatment when the port awarded a contract for security to a firm he owned even though it was not the low bidder. Ortiz defended the contract as awarded in open competition, but in 2003, he agreed to sell the business. In 2005, the *Los Angeles Times* reported that Ortiz and his top aide took a free trip to Asia after getting a courthouse named for the father of the lawyer who paid for the trip. Ortiz called it a coincidence.

Still, he remains strong politically. In 2000 and 2002, Ortiz's Republican opponent was former Brownsville Mayor Pat Ahumada, who tried to take advantage of the controversy over the port's contract with Ortiz. Ortiz won with over 60% of the vote each time. Ingleside Mayor Willie Vaden ran against him in the past three elections and lost each time, though he narrowed Ortiz's victory to 58%-38% in 2008. Ortiz reportedly is grooming his son, Solomon Ortiz Jr., to succeed him. His son represents Nueces County in the Texas House.

TWENTY-EIGHTH DISTRICT

Henry Cuellar (D)

Elected 2004, 3rd term; b. Sept. 19, 1955, Laredo; home, Laredo; Georgetown U., B.S. 1976, U. of TX, J.D. 1981, Ph.D. 1998, TX A&M U., M.A. 1982; Catholic; married (Imelda); 2 children.

Elected Office: TX House of Reps., 1986–2000; TX secy. of state, 2001.

Professional Career: Practicing atty., 1981–2004.

DC Office: 336 CHOB, 20515, 202-225-1640; Fax: 202-225-1641; Web site: www.house.gov/cuellar.

State Offices: Laredo, 956-725-0639; McAllen, 956-631-4826; Rio Grande City, 956-487-5603; San Antonio, 210-271-2851; Seguin, 830-401-0457.

Committees: *Agriculture* (10th of 28 D): Department Operations, Oversight, Nutrition & Forestry; Specialty Crops, Rural Development & Foreign Agriculture. *Homeland Security* (8th of 20 D): Border, Maritime & Global Counterterrorism; Emergency Communications, Preparedness & Response (Chmn). *Oversight & Government Reform* (18th of 24 D): Government Management, Organization & Procurement; National Security & Foreign Affairs.

Group Ratings

	ADA	ACLU	AFS	LCV	ITIC	NTU	COC	ACU	CFG	FRC
2008	80	64	86	77	100	14	72	12	12	29
2007	90	—	100	65	—	7	70	20	13	—

National Journal Ratings

	2007 LIB — 2007 CONS	2008 LIB — 2008 CONS
Economic	47% — 53%	50% — 50%
Social	56% — 44%	54% — 42%
Foreign	48% — 51%	50% — 50%
Composite	51% — 50%	52% — 48%

Key Votes of the 110th Congress

1. Increase minimum wage	Y	5. Share immigration data	Y	9. Withdraw troops 8/08	Y
2. Expand SCHIP	Y	6. Foreign aid abortion ban	N	10. No operations in Iran	N
3. Raise CAFE standards	Y	7. Ban gay bias in workplace	Y	11. Free trade with Peru	Y
4. Bail out financial markets	Y	8. Repeal D.C. gun law	Y	12. Overhaul FISA	Y

Election Results

2008 general	Henry Cuellar (D)	123,494	(69%)	($1,181,840)
	Jim Fish (R)	52,524	(29%)	($7,028)
	Ross Leone (Lib)	3,722	(2%)	
2008 primary	Henry Cuellar (D)	unopposed		

Prior Winning Percentages: 2006 (68%); 2004 (59%)

Population		Race/Ethnicity		Work	
Pop. 2007:	765,317	White:	18.9%	Private:	70.9%
Change since 2000:	Up 17.4%	Black:	1.3%	Government:	19.1%
Urban:	79.4%	Hispanic:	78.6%	Self-employed:	9.7%
Rural:	20.6%	Asian:	0.6%	Blue collar:	26.0%
Area size:	13,738 sq. mi.	Native Am.:	0.1%	White collar:	52.5%
		Hawaiian:	0.0%	Khaki collar:	0.2%
Age		Two+ races:	0.3%	Other:	21.2%
Median age:	28.9 yrs.			Median income:	$34,586
More than 65 yrs:	9.9%	*Ancestry*		Median home value:	$80,400
Less than 18 yrs:	33.6%	German:	6.8%	Poverty:	28.3%
		Irish:	3.2%		
Education		English:	2.6%	**Military Veterans**	
H.S. grad:	64.0%			% of Pop:	7.8%
College grad:	15.0%				
Grad degree:	4.5%				

Hard by the Mexican border is the place where singer Johnny Cash, in "Streets of Laredo," summoned up images of lonely cowboys on dusty streets outside a row of saloons in a tiny town. But this is not the Laredo of today. On the Rio Grande River 150 miles south of San Antonio, Laredo is the busiest border crossing for U.S.-Mexico trade. Some 14,000 trucks and 1,200 railcars cross its three bridges every day, with relatively light inspection of merchandise worth upward of $100 billion a year—more than that of all the other Mexican border crossings combined. (Frustrated law-enforcement agents contend that tons of cocaine slip through with the legitimate traffic, often hidden on commercial buses.) Laredo was America's second-fastest-growing city in the 1990s, with more warehouse space than San Antonio and Austin combined. Its old downtown streets, with their bargain stores, are filled with Mexicans who cross the border on foot; those with cars head up the freeway to the Wal-Mart. Incomes and housing prices in greater Laredo, pop. 237,000, are low by U.S. standards but far above those of Nuevo Laredo across the Rio Grande, and there is money to be made here. Laredo's Tony Sanchez, proprietor of a family oil-and-gas business and owner of International Bank of Commerce, became rich enough here to spend $60 million on his unsuccessful 2002 campaign for governor.

2008 Presidential Vote

Obama (D)	103,458	(56%)
McCain (R)	80,741	(44%)

2004 Presidential Vote

Bush (R)	90,730	(54%)
Kerry (D)	77,349	(46%)

Cook Partisan Voting Index: Even

The border country along the Rio Grande is in some ways a region all its own, a mixture of the United States and Mexico, where many people have roots on both sides of the border. As former Laredo Mayor Betty Flores has said, "The river for us is more like some street that we cross. It's really not a border." Laredo's Webb County had a 95% Hispanic population in 2007. Local fast-food restaurants feature enchiladas more often than hamburgers. Years ago, movements like La Raza Unida—which had its beginnings here in 1969 when Hispanic youngsters pushed to be allowed to elect high school cheerleaders in Crystal City—wanted the border country to become more like Mexico, with its union and party apparatchiks. More recently, Mexico, with its economic reforms and the North American Free Trade Agreement, has been trying to become more like the United States, and particularly like Texas, with its open markets and privatized companies and limited control by political or labor bosses. The region has its problems, including a high crime rate from the trade in illegal immigration and illegal drugs.

The 28th Congressional District of Texas is centered in Laredo and Webb County and extends in two directions. South along the Rio Grande, it crosses Starr County, one of the poorest counties in Texas and home of many blatant and wealthy drug smugglers. It reaches Mission in a slice of the southwest corner of Hidalgo County. These border counties make up more than two-thirds of the district. It also includes thinly settled ranch and oil-well country and a small piece of Bexar County. The redistricting plan imposed by a three-judge federal court in August 2006 made major changes in the district. Historically, the

28th was based in Bexar County, anchored by the Hispanic community on the south side of San Antonio, but those neighborhoods were needed to ensure a sufficient number of Hispanic voters in the 23rd District. Yet the 28th is still 79% Hispanic. Its per capita income of $14,500 is just 55% of the national average. In the 2008 presidential contest, Democrat Barack Obama won the district 56%-44%, quite a change from Republican George W. Bush's 54%-46% win with the same district boundaries in 2004.

The congressman from the 28th District is Henry Cuellar, a Democrat elected in 2004. Cuellar *(KWAY ar)* was the oldest of eight children of migrant workers who had only elementary school educations. He graduated from Georgetown University and the University of Texas law school, and he later got a Ph.D. in government from UT. From his base in Laredo, he served in the Texas House from 1986 to 2000, where he helped to author the Texas Grant college-aid program. In 2001, Republican Gov. Rick Perry appointed him secretary of State even though he is a Democrat. Cuellar resigned in 2002 to run against veteran Republican Rep. Henry Bonilla in the old 23rd District. He was helped when Bonilla said he didn't need Laredo to win. In response, the Webb County Republican chairman endorsed Cuellar. Cuellar attacked Bonilla for his votes against funding the State Children's Health Insurance Program, the Family and Medical Leave Act, and funding for Pell grants. He also accused Bonilla of being insufficiently Hispanic. Bonilla had the money advantage. Cuellar carried Webb County 84%-15%, but only when the Bexar County votes were counted a few days later was it clear that Bonilla had won 52%-47%.

Redistricting in 2003 strengthened Bonilla in the 23rd District, but it also gave Cuellar an opportunity to run in the 28th against incumbent Democratic Rep. Ciro Rodriguez of San Antonio, who had the most liberal voting record of Texas's Hispanic Democrats in Congress and was chairman of the Hispanic Caucus. When Cuellar announced he was running, Rodriguez said he had a hard time believing that a friend and former legislative colleague for whom he had raised money in 2002 would run against him. The ambitious Cuellar explained that primary bids like his were a common political occurrence in South Texas. Besides, he told a local reporter, "Nobody died and made him king. . . . Democrats run against Democrats all the time, and that's what it's all about." Rodriguez had little time to get acquainted with the new district, since the March primary took place just five months after passage of the map. He had the support of the Hispanic Caucus in Washington, but that delivered few votes in Texas. Cuellar criticized Rodriguez for voting against the GOP's 2003 Medicare prescription drug bill. Rodriguez said that Cuellar had sided with Republicans as secretary of State. The initial vote count showed Rodriguez ahead by 145 votes, but Cuellar demanded a recount. When officials in Zapata County, the border county just south of Webb, found 177 additional votes for Cuellar and none for Rodriguez, Cuellar was ahead by 203 votes. After a lawsuit, a second recount, and a state appellate court ruling in July, Cuellar was declared the Democratic nominee by 58 votes out of 49,000 cast. He went on to win in November 59%-39%. Later, in September 2007, the Federal Election Commission fined Cuellar $28,500 for failing to disclose a $200,000 bank loan in his 2004 campaign.

In the House, Cuellar's voting record is the most conservative of the Hispanic Democrats from Texas, putting him near the center of the House as a whole. He has kept his distance from Democratic leaders, voting for tax cuts and opposing a move to close tax loopholes for energy companies. He likes to tout the *Wall Street Journal's* description of him as "a pro-growth member (of Congress) in the John F. Kennedy mold."

On the Agriculture Committee, he backed the 2005 Central American Free Trade Agreement, which he called an opportunity for "real transformation and progress" in the region, and he was among the handful of House Democrats who supported the Bush administration's trade deal with Colombia. He backed sending drug-fighting aid to Mexico but disagreed with Republicans in their call for a fence along the border.

As the chairman of the Homeland Security Committee's Emergency Communications, Preparedness, and Response Subcommittee, Cuellar in July 2008 complained that Bush administration officials continued to "drag their feet" on a plan for national emergency-communications standards. And in early 2009, he sponsored a bill to improve law-enforcement coordination in border communities. He has emphasized a bipartisan approach and has shown a knack for getting legislation passed. With Republican help, he won passage of legislation to create a national gang-intelligence center at the Federal Bureau of Investigation and to toughen penalties on sex offenders who break the terms of their release.

In Cuellar's first re-election bid in 2006, Rodriguez was back to challenge him in the primary, but struggled to match him in fundraising, bringing in $750,000 to Cuellar's $1.1 million. Cuellar won the endorsement of the national anti-tax group Club for Growth, but it was of little political value in his district. Rodriguez said that Cuellar's votes in Washington had "sold out" the district. Cuellar said that voters were tired of the usual partisanship. The *San Antonio Express-News* endorsed Cuellar for his "independent non-partisan mindset" and said that his willingness to place the district ahead of his party was "refreshing." Cuellar won the primary comfortably this time, 53% to 40%. (With the court-ordered redistricting changes, Rodriguez had another opportunity later in the year, when he ran and won against Republican incumbent Henry Bonilla in the 23rd District.) In 2008, Cuellar easily won re-election.

TWENTY-NINTH DISTRICT

Gene Green (D)

Elected 1992, 9th term; b. Oct. 17, 1947, Houston; home, Houston; U. of Houston, B.A., 1971, Bates Col. of Law at U. of Houston, 1973–77; Methodist; married (Helen); 2 children.

Elected Office: TX House of Reps., 1972–84; TX Senate, 1985–92.

Professional Career: Practicing atty., 1977–92.

DC Office: 2372 RHOB, 20515, 202-225-1688; Fax: 202-225-9903; Web site: www.house.gov/green.

State Offices: Baytown, 281-420-0502; Houston, 713-330-0761; Houston, 281-999-5879.

Committees: *Energy & Commerce* (11th of 36 D): Commerce, Trade & Consumer Protections; Energy & Environment; Health; Oversight & Investigations. *Foreign Affairs* (16th of 28 D): Middle East & South Asia; Western Hemisphere.

Group Ratings

	ADA	ACLU	AFS	LCV	ITIC	NTU	COC	ACU	CFG	FRC
2008	80	82	100	85	71	20	59	26	12	5
2007	95	—	100	65	—	7	63	12	2	—

National Journal Ratings

	2007 LIB	—	2007 CONS		2008 LIB	—	2008 CONS
Economic	50%	—	50%		50%	—	49%
Social	61%	—	39%		53%	—	46%
Foreign	58%	—	41%		50%	—	48%
Composite	57%	—	44%		52%	—	48%

Key Votes of the 110th Congress

1. Increase minimum wage	Y	5. Share immigration data	N	9. Withdraw troops 8/08	Y
2. Expand SCHIP	Y	6. Foreign aid abortion ban	N	10. No operations in Iran	Y
3. Raise CAFE standards	N	7. Ban gay bias in workplace	Y	11. Free trade with Peru	N
4. Bail out financial markets	N	8. Repeal D.C. gun law	Y	12. Overhaul FISA	Y

Election Results

2008 general	Gene Green (D)	79,718	(75%)	($860,643)
	Eric Story (R)	25,512	(24%)	($13,200)
2008 primary	Gene Green (D)	unopposed		

Prior Winning Percentages: 2006 (74%); 2004 (94%); 2002 (95%); 2000 (73%); 1998 (93%); 1996 (68%); 1994 (73%); 1992 (65%)

Population		Race/Ethnicity		Work	
Pop. 2007:	674,183	White:	16.2%	Private:	84.6%
Change since 2000:	Up 3.5%	Black:	9.8%	Government:	8.7%
Urban:	99.4%	Hispanic:	71.8%	Self-employed:	6.3%
Rural:	0.6%	Asian:	1.5%	Blue collar:	46.7%
Area size:	249 sq. mi.	Native Am.:	0.2%	White collar:	35.2%
Age		Hawaiian:	0.0%	Khaki collar:	0.0%
Median age:	29.0 yrs.	Two+ races:	0.4%	Other:	18.0%
More than 65 yrs:	6.9%	*Ancestry*		Median income:	$34,828
Less than 18 yrs:	32.4%	USA:	3.4%	Median home value:	$84,600
Education		German:	2.9%	Poverty:	24.3%
H.S. grad:	53.8%	Irish:	2.7%	**Military Veterans**	
College grad:	6.7%			% of Pop:	5.2%
Grad degree:	1.8%				

"What built Houston," wrote John Gunther in *Inside U.S.A.* "was a combination of cotton, oil, and the ship canal." The cotton and oil were gifts of nature, though they required much human effort and ingenuity to produce in commercial quantities. The 54-mile Houston Ship Channel was almost totally man's creation. After the sand-spit port of Galveston was destroyed by a hurricane and tidal wave in 1900, Houston's elders decided to dredge out Buffalo Bayou and make their inland city a seaport.

2008 Presidential Vote		
Obama (D) 66,808	(62%)
McCain (R)..............................40,884	(38%)
2004 Presidential Vote		
Kerry (D)..................................59,897	(56%)
Bush (R) 47,734	(44%)
Cook Partisan Voting Index:	D + 8

When the channel officially opened in November 1914, a sluggish, 6-foot-deep creek had become a 40-foot-deep waterway that would turn Houston into one of the nation's biggest ports. Today, the channel is 45 feet deep and 530 feet wide. More than 8,000 ships a year come through with an estimated $150 billion in foreign trade. The port also is the site of the largest petrochemical complex in the nation. On its west side, Houston seems entirely a white-collar, office-bound city. But on the east and north, around the port and through the maze of refinery towers and pipelines, Houston remains blue-collar, a job magnet for Mexican-Americans and workers from the rural South and even Michigan and California.

The 29th Congressional District of Texas covers much of the Ship Channel area and working-class Houston. Included is much of Houston's Northside, between the Eastex and North Freeways almost to George Bush Intercontinental Airport. It takes in blue-collar neighborhoods in northeast Houston as well. Neighborhoods in this area ballooned in size as more than 200,000 Hurricane Katrina refugees temporarily or permanently relocated to Houston. From 2000 to 2007, the district's Hispanic population grew from 66% to 72%. Harris County has the second-largest Hispanic population in the U.S. (only Los Angeles County has more). This part of Houston has always been considered heavily Democratic, but in 2004 Republican President George W. Bush lost it by only 56%-44%. In 2008, Democratic nominee Barack Obama won it 62%-38%.

The congressman from the 29th District is Gene Green, a Democrat first elected in 1992. Green grew up in the largely Hispanic Lindale section of north Houston, worked as a printer's apprentice, and got business and law degrees from the University of Houston. He was elected to the state House in 1972, at age 25, and to the state Senate in a special election in 1985. He has been a friend to unions and trial lawyers in Austin and Washington, and an opponent of gun control, a politician whose natural political base is Texas's small, unionized blue-collar class. He is committed to constituent service—his office hosts an annual "Immunization Day" to provide free vaccines—and a compulsive campaigner, the kind who goes door-to-door and carries lawn signs and a hammer in his trunk. It's a good thing, for as an Anglo he probably never would have won the minority-majority district otherwise. In the 1992 primary, he faced Ben Reyes, a tempestuous Houston councilman who once protested official inaction on crime by demolishing a crack house. In the primary, Reyes led 34%-28%. But in the runoff, Green came out ahead by 180 votes out of 31,508 cast. Reyes went to court and charged that Republican voters had illegally crossed over to vote in the runoff. That got him a July re-runoff, but to no avail. This time, Green won with 52%. He went on to win the general election with 65% of the vote.

In the House, Green has a moderate voting record, especially for a member of a heavily minority urban district. After a spirited fight with other Texas Democrats in 1996, he won a seat on the influential Energy and Commerce Committee, where he, naturally, has focused on issues important to the oil industry. In 2008, he became chairman of the Environment and Hazardous Materials Subcommittee. But Democrat Henry Waxman of California eliminated the panel—and Green's chairmanship—soon after taking over as Energy and Commerce chairman in 2009. Green had been an ally of Michigan Democrat John Dingell in the pitched battle for control of the committee gavel in November 2008.

But Green has continued to be active legislatively on the panel. In May 2009, he got significant concessions for oil refineries in the climate-change bill the committee produced, which capped emissions at certain levels and created a system for companies to "trade" emissions limits. During the 2008 oil-price spike, he worked with Democratic leaders on an offshore-drilling bill that would allow coastal states to decide whether to permit drilling within 50 miles of the shoreline and would remove federal limits on drilling more than 100 miles away from shore. Green has had to strike a balance between the industry's desires and quality-of-life issues in the district. For example, he fought Republican proposals to encourage new oil refineries because the environmental exemptions could have jeopardized the clean-air program in Houston. In January 2007, he cast a "difficult" vote for the Democratic bill to cut subsidies for the oil industry.

On another issue, Green in 2009 took up the cause of local radio stations trying to preserve their long-standing exemption from paying royalties on the music they air. He persuaded more than 200 House members to sign on to a resolution opposing performance fees or royalties for local stations, which Green says will help small local stations to survive. He also successfully sponsored a bill to name the Department of Education building for President Lyndon Johnson.

Green has been re-elected easily and has had no significant primary challenges despite the fact that the 29th remains an inviting opportunity for an ambitious Hispanic politician. Perhaps anticipating such an event, Green organized a Spanish-language class for members of Congress.

THIRTIETH DISTRICT

Eddie Bernice Johnson (D)

Elected 1992, 9th term; b. Dec. 3, 1935, Waco; home, Dallas; St. Mary's at Notre Dame, B.A. 1955, TX Christian U., B.S. 1967, S. Methodist U., M.P.A. 1976; Baptist; divorced; 1 child.

Elected Office: TX House of Reps., 1972–1977; TX Senate, 1986–92.

Professional Career: Registered nurse; Regional dir., U.S. Dept. of HEW, 1977–80; Mgmt. consultant, Sammons Corp., 1979–81; Owner, Eddie Bernice Johnson & Assoc., 1981–present.

DC Office: 1511 LHOB, 20515, 202-225-8885; Fax: 202-226-1477; Web site: www.house.gov/ebjohnson.

State Offices: Dallas, 214-922-8885.

Committees: *Science & Technology* (3rd of 26 D): Energy & Environment; Research & Science Education. *Transportation & Infrastructure* (9th of 44 D): Aviation; Railroads, Pipelines & Hazardous Materials; Water Resources & Environment (Chmn).

Group Ratings

	ADA	ACLU	AFS	LCV	ITIC	NTU	COC	ACU	CFG	FRC
2008	100	100	100	92	67	5	56	0	0	5
2007	80	—	91	80	—	3	60	0	7	—

National Journal Ratings

	2007 LIB — 2007 CONS		2008 LIB — 2008 CONS	
Economic	60% —	40%	85% —	0%
Social	92% —	0%	82% —	0%
Foreign	77% —	23%	70% —	25%
Composite	78% —	22%	85% —	15%

Key Votes of the 110th Congress

1. Increase minimum wage	Y	5. Share immigration data	N	9. Withdraw troops 8/08	Y
2. Expand SCHIP	*	6. Foreign aid abortion ban	N	10. No operations in Iran	Y
3. Raise CAFE standards	Y	7. Ban gay bias in workplace	Y	11. Free trade with Peru	Y
4. Bail out financial markets	Y	8. Repeal D.C. gun law	N	12. Overhaul FISA	N

Election Results

2008 general	Eddie Bernice Johnson (D)	168,249	(82%)	($459,462)
	Fred Wood (R)	32,361	(16%)	
2008 primary	Eddie Bernice Johnson (D)	unopposed		

Prior Winning Percentages: 2006 (80%); 2004 (93%); 2002 (74%); 2000 (92%); 1998 (72%); 1996 (55%); 1994 (73%); 1992 (72%)

Population		Race/Ethnicity		Work	
Pop. 2007:	663,782	White:	17.3%	Private:	82.0%
Change since 2000:	Up 1.9%	Black:	39.1%	Government:	11.5%
Urban:	98.8%	Hispanic:	40.9%	Self-employed:	6.4%
Rural:	1.2%	Asian:	1.2%	Blue collar:	33.8%
Area size:	319 sq. mi.	Native Am.:	0.2%	White collar:	47.5%
		Hawaiian:	0.1%	Khaki collar:	0.1%
Age		Two+ races:	0.9%	Other:	18.5%
Median age:	31.8 yrs.	*Ancestry*		Median income:	$35,680
More than 65 yrs:	7.9%	German:	3.2%	Median home value:	$96,600
Less than 18 yrs:	28.4%	Irish:	2.8%	Poverty:	23.8%
		English:	2.7%		
Education				**Military Veterans**	
H.S. grad:	66.2%			% of Pop:	6.5%
College grad:	16.8%				
Grad degree:	5.8%				

Cotton was originally the major crop in northern Texas, and many of Dallas's first enterprising businessmen, after the railroad reached the Trinity River in the 1870s, were cotton brokers. Railroads made Dallas rich and helped it to grow. Geographically, Dallas is directly west of the Black Belt of Alabama and the Mississippi Delta, both heavy cotton-producing areas in the days before the boll weevil. Many blacks and whites came west on U.S. 80—and now Interstate 20—to the Dallas-Fort Worth

2008 Presidential Vote		
Obama (D)	170,826	(82%)
McCain (R)	37,465	(18%)
2004 Presidential Vote		
Kerry (D)	136,116	(75%)
Bush (R)	45,148	(25%)
Cook Partisan Voting Index:	D + 27	

Metroplex, now the largest metro area in the South. The south side of Dallas is predominately African-American. The Trinity River Corridor project, which has been discussed for decades and is estimated to cost $1.2 billion, is moving toward reality, with its ambitious plans for flood control, recreational facilities, and transportation improvements, including three new suspension bridges.

The 30th Congressional District of Texas, designed as the Dallas-Fort Worth Metroplex's black-majority district, includes most of the city's African-American neighborhoods. Its creation in 1991 was insisted on by the then-chairman of the Texas Senate's redistricting committee, and the result was one of the most grotesquely shaped districts in the country. Its center was south and east Dallas, but it had tentacles as complex as a DNA molecule. Since then, lawsuits and two more rounds of redistricting have smoothed out the lines and left this as the only Democratic district in the Metroplex. Today, the 30th District includes two compact geographic units centered in downtown Dallas. One consists of most of the south side of Dallas; the other runs northwest out Stemmons Freeway. In between is the "mixmaster," where three busy interstates—Interstates 30, 35E and 45—come together within a square mile, surrounding many of the prominent sites in Dallas.

The district's population was 41% black and 34% Hispanic in 2000 and now is 39% black and 41% Hispanic. The Hispanic population is mostly young and foreign-born, and 90% of the Latinos are from Mexico. Redistricting in 2011 likely will produce a Hispanic-majority district in the Dallas area. The growing influence of racial minorities in the city has been a major factor in the Democrats' recent capture of control of many Dallas County offices and seats in the Texas Legislature. In 2004, George W. Bush lost here 75%-25%, his worst performance in Texas. In 2008, Republican nominee John McCain lost 82%-18%, also his worst performance in the state.

The congresswoman from the 30th District is Eddie Bernice Johnson, first elected in 1992. She grew up in Texas, graduated from Texas Christian University with a nursing degree, and later got a master's degree in public administration at Southern Methodist University. She worked at St. Paul Hospital and was the chief psychiatric nurse at the Veterans Administration Hospital in Dallas. In 1972, she was elected to the Texas House, the first black woman elected to the Legislature from Dallas. She became a regional director of the old Health, Education and Welfare Department under Democratic President Jimmy Carter. She was elected to the Texas Senate in 1986. As the Senate's Redistricting Committee chairman in 1991, she was instrumental in creating the new 30th District. She won the Democratic primary with 92% of the vote and has not had effective opposition since.

In the House, Johnson has a mostly liberal voting record, but she has been attentive to business interests in Dallas. She has sharp political instincts. In the past, she has chaired the influential Congressional Black Caucus. And she supported Democrat Nancy Pelosi of California for minority leader over her former Metroplex colleague Rep. Martin Frost, with whom Johnson had a testy relationship, particularly on redistricting issues. Her support for Pelosi put her in good stead with the Democratic leadership when Pelosi rose to House speaker in 2007. Though Johnson once pledged to labor unions to oppose the North American Free Trade Agreement, she changed her mind and voted for it in 1993. Dallas probably exports more to Mexico than any other American city, and many jobs depend on those exports. Johnson also sided with business on normalizing trade relations with China.

On the Science Committee, Johnson shared credit for passing the Networking and Information Research and Development Act to double funding for information research. She also sought to double spending for the National Science Foundation. As a health-care professional, she has taken an interest in minority health issues.

On the Transportation and Infrastructure Committee, Johnson got a seat on the Aviation Subcommittee, of great importance to her district. The 30th District is close to the bustling Dallas-Fort Worth International Airport, and it includes three other airports: Love Field, Lancaster, and Dallas Executive. Although she initially had objections, which included concerns about additional air traffic, she eventually cooperated with Republicans from the Metroplex in repealing the Wright Amendment. Named for former Democratic House Speaker Jim Wright, a Democrat from Forth Worth, the amendment restricted air traffic out of Dallas's Love Field as a way of protecting the competitive position of the larger Dallas-Fort Worth Airport. Johnson helped broker the deal by encouraging more local coordination between the airports.

She is now the chairman of the panel's Water Resources and Environment Subcommittee. As her top local priority, she worked to secure funds for construction of the Interstate 30 suspension bridge over the Trinity River, and she continues to support Trinity River projects.

THIRTY-FIRST DISTRICT

John Carter (R)

Elected 2002, 4th term; b. Nov. 6, 1941, Houston; home, Round Rock; TX Tech. U., B.A. 1964, U. of TX, J.D. 1969; Christian; married (Erika); 4 children.

Elected Office: Dist. Ct. judge, 1982–2001.

Professional Career: Practicing atty., 1969–81.

DC Office: 409 CHOB, 20515, 202-225-3864; Fax: 202-225-5886; Web site: www.house.gov/carter/.

State Offices: Round Rock, 512-246-1600; Temple, 254-933-1392.

Committees: *Republican Conference Secretary. Appropriations* (18th of 23 R): Homeland Security; Military Construction, Veterans Affairs & Related Agencies; Transportation, HUD & Related Agencies.

Group Ratings

	ADA	ACLU	AFS	LCV	ITIC	NTU	COC	ACU	CFG	FRC
2008	5	20	0	0	40	79	94	96	87	100
2007	0	—	0	0	—	79	80	100	91	—

National Journal Ratings

	2007 LIB	—	2007 CONS		2008 LIB	—	2008 CONS
Economic	13%	—	87%		5%	—	95%
Social	0%	—	91%		9%	—	85%
Foreign	0%	—	72%		18%	—	81%
Composite	11%	—	90%		12%	—	88%

Key Votes of the 110th Congress

1. Increase minimum wage	N	5. Share immigration data	Y	9. Withdraw troops 8/08	N
2. Expand SCHIP	N	6. Foreign aid abortion ban	Y	10. No operations in Iran	N
3. Raise CAFE standards	N	7. Ban gay bias in workplace	N	11. Free trade with Peru	Y
4. Bail out financial markets	N	8. Repeal D.C. gun law	Y	12. Overhaul FISA	Y

Election Results

2008 general	John Carter (R)	175,563	(60%)	($1,053,850)
	Brian Ruiz (D)	106,559	(37%)	($23,020)
	Barry Cooper (Lib)	9,182	(3%)	
2008 primary	John Carter (R)	unopposed		

Prior Winning Percentages: 2006 (58%); 2004 (65%); 2002 (69%)

Population

Pop. 2007:	783,376
Change since 2000:	Up 20.2%
Urban:	77.9%
Rural:	22.1%
Area size:	7,194 sq. mi.

Age

Median age:	31.8 yrs.
More than 65 yrs:	9.2%
Less than 18 yrs:	29.2%

Education

H.S. grad:	87.4%
College grad:	27.5%
Grad degree:	8.3%

Race/Ethnicity

White:	63.0%
Black:	12.3%
Hispanic:	18.8%
Asian:	2.8%
Native Am.:	0.4%
Hawaiian:	0.2%
Two+ races:	2.3%

Ancestry

German:	14.7%
Irish:	8.2%
English:	8.0%

Work

Private:	67.4%
Government:	25.4%
Self-employed:	7.0%
Blue collar:	20.1%
White collar:	59.5%
Khaki collar:	5.6%
Other:	14.8%
Median income:	$52,927
Median home value:	$131,000
Poverty:	11.1%

Military Veterans

% of Pop:	14.9%

Williamson County, Texas, long a rural backwater, has become a major population and business center deep in the heart of Texas. Its population has virtually doubled in every recent decade. It was 77,000 in 1980, 140,000 in 1990, 250,000 in 2000, and 394,000 in 2008. Williamson County is just north of Austin, and much of this growth has been generated by the Austin area's high-technology boom. Hugely successful computer producer Dell is headquartered in Round Rock, with 18,000 local employees

and is still expanding. And more growth has been generated by Texas 130, a 49-mile 10-lane toll road that opened in 2008. Georgetown has become a popular retirement destination. Bell and Coryell counties, just north of Williamson County, are the site of Fort Hood, the largest U.S. military base in the world and the largest employer in Texas. The base is the only post in the United States capable of supporting two full armored divisions. It covers 218,000 acres—340 square miles. Toward the end of World War II, about 4,000 German prisoners of war were interned at Hood. Today, its mission is maintaining readiness for combat missions, including training Army Reservists in urban combat. East of Fort Hood is Temple, a rail center. Decades ago, the freight carried from its rail yards was mostly cotton. Now, it serves a variety of industries, including plastics manufacturers.

The 31st Congressional District of Texas, created in the 2001 redistricting and sharply altered in the 2003 Republican redistricting, is dominated by Williamson, Bell and Coryell counties, which account for 92% of its population. Historically this was solidly Democratic country, devoted to the party of the Confederacy and later, the New Deal, full of cotton farmers who distrusted Wall Street and railroads and who trusted politicians like Sam Rayburn and Lyndon Johnson and later Ann Richards and Lloyd Bentsen. But people in this district took a shine to George W. Bush's brand of Republicanism, first as governor and then as president. In 2004, he carried the district 67%-33%. In 2008, GOP nominee John McCain did not fare as well, getting 57% to 41% for Democratic nominee Barack Obama. Also that year, a Democrat based in Williamson County won a state legislative seat for the first time in more than a decade.

The congressman from the 31st District is John Carter, a Republican first elected in 2002. He grew up in Houston and graduated from Texas Tech University and the University of Texas law school. He practiced law in Williamson County and served as a municipal judge in Round Rock. He was appointed a district judge in 1981 by Republican Gov. Bill Clements and in 1982 stood for election. Judicial elections are partisan in Texas, and Carter was the first Republican judge elected in Williamson County. Carter became known as the father of the county Republican Party. In 2001, after a three-judge district court created a new Republican 31st District stretching from Williamson County to Houston, Carter retired from the bench and ran for Congress. The real contest in this district was among the eight candidates for the Republican nomination. Carter's main rivals were Peter Wareing, the son-in-law of Texas oilman Jack Blanton, and Brad Barton, son of U.S. Rep. Joe Barton of the 6th District. In the primary, Wareing led with 37% to 26% for Carter and 16% for Barton.

In the four-week runoff campaign, Carter attacked Wareing as a liberal in disguise, pointing to his campaign contributions to Democrats like U.S. Rep. Sheila Jackson Lee of Houston. When Wareing proposed that each candidate sign a "clean campaign pledge," Carter offered what he called a "homestead pledge" —a ploy to highlight his charge that Wareing was a Houston carpetbagger who had rented an apartment in the district for the sole purpose of running for the seat. Rep. Barton endorsed Carter as "the only true conservative in this race." Wareing outspent Carter more than 2-to-1, but Carter won 57%-43%. He got 78% of the vote in Williamson County, which cast 33% of the vote. Carter won the general election easily.

In the House, Carter has been a reliable conservative who has opposed abortion and supported voluntary prayer in schools. He was his freshman class's representative on the Republican Steering Committee, which makes committee assignments.

On the Judiciary Committee, he won passage of a bill to establish penalties for identity theft. He also won House passage of his Terrorist Penalties Enhancement Act. He objected to continuing the Voting Rights Act requirement that Texas get federal approval of changes in its voting laws, but he voted to extend the act. In 2005, with help from then Majority Leader Tom DeLay of Texas, Carter got a coveted seat on the Appropriations Committee. As a member of the Military Construction and Veterans Affairs Subcommittee, he was well positioned—with Democratic Chairman Chet Edwards of the neighboring 17th District—to defend the interests of Fort Hood. He criticized Republican conservatives who objected to the appropriators' heavy use of earmarking, the practice of funding projects for individual lawmakers' districts rather than on a merit system. In 2006, Carter was elected without opposition to the party leadership as secretary of the Republican Conference.

In 2006, Carter faced a challenge from Democrat Mary Beth Harrell, a lawyer in Killeen whose son served in Iraq and who advocated withdrawal from the conflict. Carter won, 58%-39%. In 2008, he won 60%-37% against a little-known Democrat.

THIRTY-SECOND DISTRICT

Pete Sessions (R)

Elected 1996, 7th term; b. March 22, 1955, Waco; home, Dallas; SW U., B.S. 1978; Methodist; married (Juanita); 2 children.

Professional Career: District mgr., SW Bell Telephone Co., 1978–93; V.P., public policy, Natl. Center for Policy Analysis, 1994–95.

DC Office: 2233 RHOB, 20515, 202-225-2231; Fax: 202-225-5878; Web site: sessions.house.gov.

State Offices: Dallas, 972-392-0505.

Committees: *NRCC Chairman. Rules* (3rd of 4 R): Rules & Organization of the House (RMM).

Group Ratings

	ADA	ACLU	AFS	LCV	ITIC	NTU	COC	ACU	CFG	FRC
2008	5	18	0	0	100	72	100	92	85	82
2007	10	—	0	0	—	82	94	96	89	—

National Journal Ratings

	2007 LIB — 2007 CONS		2008 LIB — 2008 CONS	
Economic	13%	— 87%	3%	— 95%
Social	19%	— 81%	9%	— 85%
Foreign	0%	— 72%	16%	— 83%
Composite	15%	— 85%	11%	— 89%

Key Votes of the 110th Congress

1. Increase minimum wage	N	5. Share immigration data	*	9. Withdraw troops 8/08	N
2. Expand SCHIP	N	6. Foreign aid abortion ban	Y	10. No operations in Iran	N
3. Raise CAFE standards	N	7. Ban gay bias in workplace	N	11. Free trade with Peru	Y
4. Bail out financial markets	Y	8. Repeal D.C. gun law	Y	12. Overhaul FISA	Y

Election Results

2008 general	Pete Sessions (R)	116,283	(57%)	($1,629,824)
	Eric Roberson (D)	82,406	(41%)	($110,003)
	Alex Bischoff (Lib)	4,421	(2%)	
2008 primary	Pete Sessions (R)	unopposed		

Prior Winning Percentages: 2006 (56%); 2004 (54%); 2002 (68%); 2000 (54%); 1998 (56%); 1996 (53%)

Population		Race/Ethnicity		Work	
Pop. 2007:	663,900	White:	44.3%	Private:	85.1%
Change since 2000:	Up 1.9%	Black:	7.9%	Government:	6.9%
Urban:	99.9%	Hispanic:	42.3%	Self-employed:	7.9%
Rural:	0.1%	Asian:	4.2%	Blue collar:	25.5%
Area size:	161 sq. mi.	Native Am.:	0.2%	White collar:	58.3%
Age		Hawaiian:	0.0%	Khaki collar:	0.0%
Median age:	33.4 yrs.	Two+ races:	0.8%	Other:	16.2%
More than 65 yrs:	10.0%	*Ancestry*		Median income:	$49,164
Less than 18 yrs:	26.0%	German:	7.7%	Median home value:	$170,400
Education		English:	7.6%	Poverty:	15.6%
H.S. grad:	74.9%	Irish:	6.4%	**Military Veterans**	
College grad:	36.0%			% of Pop:	7.0%
Grad degree:	13.1%				

North Dallas has long been the home of the city's elite, and indeed, of a good portion of the nation's elite. Early in the 20th century, the city's richest citizens started moving away from old neighborhoods adjacent to downtown and out past Turtle Creek to the area around the suburbs of Highland Park and University Park—the Park Cities. Dallas grew lustily from mid-century on, and beyond the Park Cities, miles of affluent neighborhoods were built, especially between the Central Expressway

2008 Presidential Vote		
McCain (R)	110,397	(53%)
Obama (D)	96,203	(46%)
2004 Presidential Vote		
Bush (R)	120,970	(60%)
Kerry (D)	81,846	(40%)
Cook Partisan Voting Index:	R+8	

and the Dallas North Tollway. Galleries and office complexes followed. Not all of North Dallas is like that. There is an entertainment and singles apartment corridor along Greenville Avenue, working-class neighborhoods here and there, and pockets of Latino neighborhoods near the freeways. But overall, the tone has been set by the Dallas elite. In the 1960s and 1970s, this was one of the most politically conservative parts of the country. People believed in free markets, personal responsibility and the Republican Party. Since 1992, North Dallas has moved, like elite parts of other big metropolitan areas, toward the Democrats. The number of affluent women voting Democratic on the abortion issue is much smaller than in affluent quadrants of New York and Los Angeles, but there are some. In the 1990s, both Republicans George W. Bush and Dick Cheney lived in North Dallas, in or near the Park Cities. Bush moved to Austin in January 1995 to become governor, and Cheney changed his residence back to Wyoming in July 2000 so that he could be nominated vice president. After eight years in the White House, George and Laura Bush returned to their Preston Hollow neighborhood, to an 8,500-square-foot home on an acre of land that's only a few miles from his planned presidential library at Southern Methodist University.

The 32nd Congressional District of Texas includes most of the area commonly thought of as North Dallas: the Park Cities and affluent North Dallas neighborhoods extending to the Dallas County line. The district also includes some affluent suburbs in Dallas County: parts of racially diverse Richardson northeast of the city and Addison to the northwest. The 2003 redistricting removed some suburban territory and added blue-collar and Democratic-tending Irving and the heavily Latino Oak Cliff neighborhoods south of the Trinity River, where Lee Harvey Oswald was captured inside the old Texas Theater on November 22, 1963, shortly after he killed President John F. Kennedy. Bush's vote declined here in 2004 to 60%, and the Republican vote dropped further in 2008, when John McCain got 53%, in part because of an increase in Democratic-voting Latino voters. (Redistricting and an influx of Latinos had raised the Hispanic percentage from 27% to 42% by 2007.) With the adjacent 30th District also heavily Hispanic, it's easy to envision redistricters after the 2010 census creating a new Hispanic district in this area. Texas is expected to gain three or four seats following the 2010 census.

The congressman from the 32nd District is Pete Sessions, a Republican first elected in 1996. He is the chairman of the National Republican Congressional Committee, the No. 4 leadership position in the House minority.

Sessions grew up in Waco, graduated from Southwestern University, then worked at Southwestern Bell in Dallas for 16 years. His father is William Sessions, a federal judge who served as director of the Federal Bureau of Investigation from 1987 to 1993. The vagaries of redistricting led Sessions to run for Congress in several different House districts. In 1991, he ran and finished sixth in the special election in the 3rd District, which then included much of North Dallas. In 1993, he resigned from the phone company to run against Democratic Rep. John Bryant in the 5th District, which included much of the east side of Dallas and several rural counties to the south. The district had been drawn to re-elect Bryant, a liberal Democrat. Sessions ran a vigorous campaign, making a two-day, 12-city tour of the district's rural portions with a livestock trailer full of horse manure and a sign saying, "The Clinton health care plan stinks worse than this trailer." Although he outspent Sessions 2-to-1 in 1994, Bryant won by just 50%-47%. Two years later, Bryant ran, unsuccessfully, for the Senate. Sessions ran again for the House seat and won the primary. In the general election, he faced John Pouland, a former regional General Services Administration director. Sessions charged that Pouland was a big-government liberal and would abandon U.S. military bases overseas. Pouland criticized Republican cuts in Medicare. Sessions won 53%-47%.

Sessions's voting record is among the most conservative in the House. In 1999, he got a seat on the leadership-run Rules Committee. He sponsored the constitutional amendment to require a two-thirds vote to raise taxes, was a leading advocate of the Republican proposal to stop the government from spending Social Security and Medicare surpluses, and called for scrapping the income-tax code. He is generally tightfisted but is apt to support government spending to help families with disabled children. Sessions and his wife have a son with Down syndrome.

In 2001, redistricting made the 5th District more Republican. But Sessions surprised state politicos by leaving the 5th to run in the newly created 32nd, which had no incumbent but included only 16% of his old district. He said he wanted to spend less time traveling around his district—the new 32nd was considerably more compact—and he thought the new district was more compatible with his pro-business philosophy; the 32nd certainly has a stronger fundraising base. Sessions had only token primary opposition and won the seat in 2002, 68%-30%.

In 2003, Republican Tom DeLay of Texas, the powerful majority leader in the U.S. House, persuaded the Republican-controlled Texas Legislature to draw the lines yet again. Although most Republicans were well served by the new lines, Sessions wound up in a somewhat less Republican district and with a re-election challenge from 13-term Democratic incumbent Martin Frost, whose 24th District had been shorn of its most Democratic precincts in the DeLay remap. Frost chose to run in the 32nd because of its large, Democrat-friendly Jewish population in the Park Cities. Frost also felt Sessions was too conservative for the new district. From the start, Sessions voiced confidence that he would win, though he braced for negative attacks. Frost focused on his own legislative accomplishments and his work on local issues to help the Dallas business community; he rarely mentioned 2004 Democratic presidential nominee John Kerry.

This was the most expensive House campaign of 2004. Sessions spent $4.5 million and Frost $4.8 million, and more still was spent by party committees and independent groups. The candidates hurled charges at each other, and tangential issues came into play. Frost criticized Sessions for a streaking incident in college. Sessions criticized Frost for scheduling a fundraiser with Peter Yarrow, the Peter, Paul and Mary singer who had been convicted of "taking indecent liberties" with a 14-year-old girl in 1969. Frost cited Sessions's vote against the establishment of new air-passenger security rules after the September 11 attacks and ran an ad with images of the World Trade Center in flames and the message "Protect America. Say No to Pete Sessions." Frost was endorsed by the *Dallas Morning News,* local police and firefighters groups, teachers' organizations, and the Sierra Club. Sessions had support from the national anti-tax group Club for Growth and the National Federation of Independent Business. Sessions won 54%-44%, capturing more than 80% of the vote in some Park Cities precincts; Frost failed to get the higher turnout he needed in Oak Cliff. Sessions has not had great difficulty getting re-elected since.

After his victory over Frost, Sessions sought to get on the House leadership track by running in 2006 for chairman of the National Republican Congressional Committee, which raises money for Republicans and recruits challengers in House races. But he lost to Republican Tom Cole of Oklahoma. After the 2008 election, Sessions succeeded in a second bid to head the NRCC. He had the strong support of Minority Leader John Boehner of Ohio—Sessions was among the few Texas Republicans who had backed Boehner for party leader against Roy Blunt of Missouri in 2006. Cole wanted a second term as NRCC chairman, but he carried the burden of the party's 21-seat loss in the November 2008 election.

Sessions had a rocky start as chairman. In a March 2009 special election for New York's 20th District, Jim Tedisco fell short of winning what had long been a Republican seat, despite several hundred thousand dollars from the NRCC. Sessions was lampooned by Democrats for his sometimes odd comments, including his statement that President Barack Obama was trying "to inflict damage and hardship on the free enterprise system, if not to kill it." Sessions set a challenging goal of gaining the 40 seats the party needs to recapture the majority in 2010, and he reorganized the committee to improve fundraising, communications and candidate recruitment.

★ UTAH ★

U tah is a triumph of man over nature, the creation of a productive and orderly civilization in a remote expanse of desert and mountain, arrayed around a desolate salt sea. Today's Utah and its ubiquitous Mormon Church have their roots in events that unfolded in upstate New York more than 170 years ago. There, Joseph Smith, a 14-year-old farmer, experienced a vision in which the angel Moroni appeared to him and told him where to unearth several golden tablets inscribed with hieroglyphic writings. With the aid of special spectacles, Smith translated the tablets and published them as the Book of Mormon in 1831. He later declared himself to be a prophet and founded the Church of Jesus Christ of Latter-day Saints. The Mormons, as they were called, attracted thousands of converts and created their own communities. Persecuted for their beliefs, they moved west to Ohio, Missouri and then Illinois. In 1844, the Mormon colony at Nauvoo, Ill., had some 15,000 members living under Smith's theocratic rule. It was there that Smith received a revelation sanctioning the practice of polygamy, which led to his death at the hands of a mob. After the murder, the new church president, Brigham Young, decided to move the faithful, "the saints," farther west into territory that was still part of Mexico and far beyond white settlement. Young led a well-organized march across the Great Plains and into the Rocky Mountains. In 1847, they stopped on the western slope of the Wasatch Range and, as Young gazed over the valley of the Great Salt Lake spread out below, he said, "This is the place."

The place was Utah. Young was governor of the territory for many years. It is the only state that has continued, to varying degrees, to live by the teachings of a church. The early pioneers laid out towns foursquare to the points of the compass with huge city blocks. They built sturdy houses and planted dozens of trees. Young's home still stands a block away from Temple Square, where the Salt Lake LDS Temple, closed to non-Mormons, stands in gleaming marble, topped by the golden angel Moroni and situated across from the oval Mormon Tabernacle, where its great choir sings. For 160 years, this "Zion" has attracted thousands of converts from the Midwest, the north of England and Scandinavia. The object of religious fear and prejudice, Utah was not granted statehood until 1896, after the church renounced polygamy. Utah has grown steadily since then, and remains heavily Mormon. Without the Mormons, Utah's inhospitable landscape would probably have remained as unpopulated as Nevada would have been without gambling.

The LDS Church remains distinctive in many ways. It cares deeply about its past. In caves in the mountains of Utah, the church preserves America's most complete genealogical records in its Family History Library and has made them available on the Internet. It tries to spread the faith: Young Mormons, 65,000 every year, spend missionary years in the United States and abroad. (An ancillary result is that Utah has one of the lowest rates of Army enlistment in the country.) The missionaries' experiences give Utah the biggest inventory of people with knowledge of obscure foreign languages of any state in the union, a nice commercial advantage, and one that prompted the National Security Agency to set up language analyst offices in Utah in 2006. The church prohibits the consumption of tobacco, alcohol and caffeine. It encourages hard work and large families. Mormons are healthier than the average American. They are also better educated, work longer hours and earn more money. In an individualist country, the church fosters communitarian attitudes. The LDS Church has no clergy, but members serve in positions for which they are chosen, conducting religious services but also keeping in touch with members and counseling them when they need help. The church also maintains its own social service organizations. While American mainline denominations have been losing members, the Mormon Church is growing. There were 2.9 million Mormons in 1970 and nearly 11 million in 2000, with more than half outside the United States and just 15% in Utah. This has been the fastest-growing church in the United States in recent decades and was the nation's fifth largest denomination in 2003.

Mormons and Utahns are heavily Republican today, but this was not always so. In the 19th century, Republicans led the fight to keep Utah out of the union and a Democrat, President Grover Cleveland, signed the statehood act. Before World War II, Utah saw itself as a colonial victim of East Coast bankers and financiers, and Mormons saw themselves as suffering religious discrimination and bigotry—all with some cause. Utah's income levels were well below the national average, its cost of living higher, and the prices paid for the things it produced seemed to be controlled elsewhere. In political terms, this perspective translated into a Democratic allegiance. In 1940, Utah was represented by staunch New Dealers in Congress and cast 62% of its votes for Franklin D. Roosevelt. Today, Utah sees itself as a busy generator of wealth, with a raft of successful businesses, a knack for high-tech innovation, and longer work weeks than the rest of the nation.

Utah achieves all this with cultural attitudes and demographic patterns that resemble the America of the 1950s. The state has the highest percentage of households headed by married couples, the highest fertility rate for non-Hispanic whites, the youngest median age of first marriage, and the lowest rate of birth to unmarried mothers. It has many more children per capita than any other state, and this can make its economic statistics misleading: Utah has a per capita income 17% below the national average

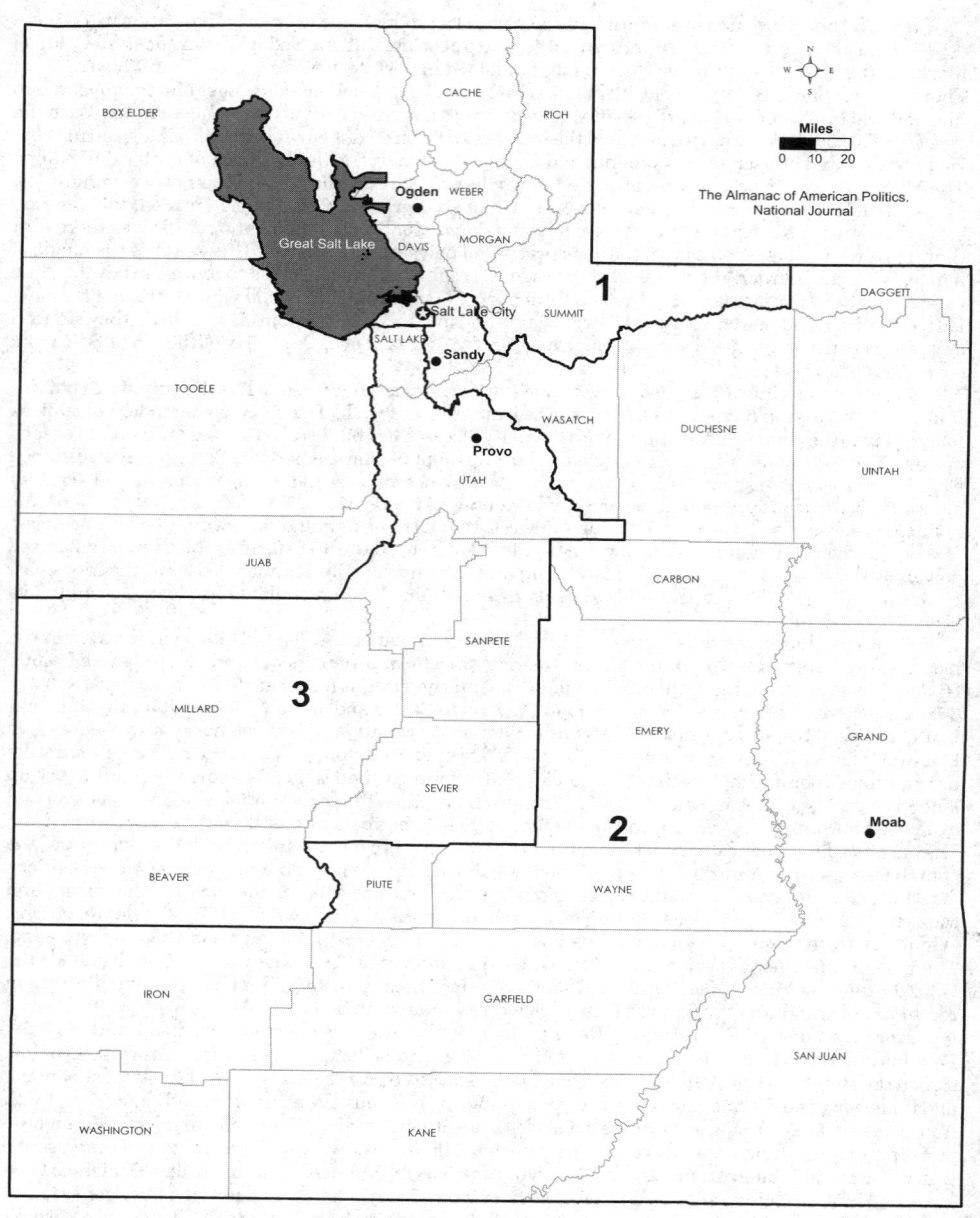

Congressional district boundaries were first effective for 2002.

(because all those kids aren't earning salaries), but a median household income 7% above the national average. It has the youngest population of any state, with the largest families and one of the longest life expectancies. It also has the highest rate of volunteerism. Some 62% of Utahns are Mormons, a percentage that has been declining but is still a solid majority. And pervading the cultural atmosphere of the state is the LDS Church. Its opposition to abortion is widely shared and it has always discouraged gambling. It is one of only two states (Hawaii is the other) with no form of gambling, although many Mormons are employed in the gaming industry across the state line in Las Vegas. Utah has been way ahead of the rest of the nation in discouraging the use of tobacco and has had restrictive liquor laws. Only in 2009 could you get a drink served at a bar without joining a private club, and then if beer is your preference, it will have a mere 3.2% alcohol by volume. Republican Gov. Jon Huntsman Jr. got the Legislature to make that change by arguing that the old restrictions hurt tourism. Polls show that nearly 80% of Mormons vote Republican, but church leaders make a point of stating that "principles compatible with the gospel may be found in the platforms of all political parties."

Between 2007 and 2008, Utah had the highest rate of population growth in the nation, in large part because migration into previously faster-growing Nevada and Arizona fell as the real estate market crashed, while most of Utah's population growth happens internally—all those kids. Utah, with a much smaller housing bubble, fell into recession later and less painfully, although state revenues tumbled sharply. Utah has also had substantial domestic inflow, especially from California, including Hispanics. The state population is now 11% Hispanic but just 1% African-American. This has helped to reduce the Mormon percentage in Utah, even as the church continues making new converts in other states and around the world. Interestingly, the Salt Lake City neighborhoods close to the church headquarters, with gracious old houses and a smaller street grid that attract academic and professional newcomers, have become the most heavily "gentile" (the Mormon term for non-Mormons) and politically liberal part of the state. Just as the Yankee hub of Boston filled up with Irish Catholic Democrats in the 1890s, so Salt Lake City has been getting secular liberal Democrats. Former Salt Lake City Mayor Rocky Anderson called President George W. Bush a "war criminal" and in 2004 the city voted 58% for Democratic presidential nominee John Kerry. In 2008, all of Salt Lake County went for Democrat Barack Obama, albeit by only 296 votes out of 367,000 cast, and Democrats won control of the county government and elected most of its state legislators. But Democrats won almost no legislative seats in the rest of the state and in Utah County, centered on Provo and Brigham Young University, which voted 78%-19% for Republican nominee John McCain. And while Salt Lake County grew by 14% from 2000 to 2008, Utah County grew by 44%. There has been even faster growth in Washington County, in the far southwest corner of the state just northeast of Las Vegas, where local Mormons have been highly critical of polygamists, like the prosecuted Warren Jeffs, living in communities on the Utah-Arizona line.

Politically, Utah has been generally the most Republican state since the 1980s. It does elect one Democratic congressman these days, Jim Matheson, who started off with the advantage of having a father

Population		Household Income		Work	
Pop. 2007:	2,576,626	Under $15k:	9.2%	Private:	78.5%
State rank:	34th of 50	$15k to $50k:	37.1%	Government:	15.8%
Change since 2000:	Up 15.4%	$50k to $100k:	36.2%	Self-employed:	5.4%
Urban:	85.6%	$100k to $150k:	14.9%	Unemployment (3-yr. average):	3.2%
Rural:	14.4%	Over $150k:	2.6%	Poverty:	10.3%
Native of state:	63.0%	Median income:	$53,324	Blue collar:	23.9%
Not a citizen:	5.5%			White collar:	60.9%
Area size:	84,899 sq. mi.	**Home Value**		Khaki collar:	0.2%
		Under $100k:	10.0%	Other:	15.0%
Most populous cities		$100k to $300k:	67.7%		
1. Salt Lake City	182,610	$300k to $500k:	16.2%	**Age**	
2. West Valley City	122,409	$500k to $1 mil:	5.1%	Median age:	28.3 yrs.
3. Provo	115,163	Over $1 million:	1.1%	More than 65 yrs:	8.7%
4. West Jordan	99,348	Median:	$189,700	Less than 18 yrs:	30.9%

Race/Ethnicity				Military Veterans		Registered Voters in 2008	
White:	82.8%	*Language*		% of Pop:	8.6%	No party registration	
Black:	0.9%	English:	86.1%	*Veterans by Period*		Voter turnout:	952,370
Hispanic:	11.1%	Spanish:	9.0%	WWII and before:	14.2%	Turnout as % of	
Asian:	1.9%	Asian:	2.0%	Korea:	12.6%	voting age:	50.5%
Native Am.:	1.1%	Other		Vietnam:	30.2%	**Legislature**	
Hawaiian:	0.7%	European	2.2%	Gulf (pre-2001):	11.9%	Senate:	8 D 21 R
Two+ races:	1.3%	**Education**		Gulf (post-2001):	9.2%	House:	22 D 53 R
Ancestry		H.S. grad:	90.0%	Peace time:	21.9%		
English:	21.6%	College grad:	28.2%				
German:	9.7%	Grad degree:	9.0%				
USA:	5.6%						

who was a well-remembered Democratic governor. But it has not elected a Democratic governor since Matheson's father, Scott, in 1980, or a Democratic senator since 1970. And it has not voted Democratic for president since 1964.

Presidential politics   Utah has been the most Republican state in six of the last nine presidential elections. As recently as 1960, Richard Nixon carried Utah with just 55% of the vote, but by 1972, he won re-election with 68%. Ronald Reagan won 73% here in 1980 and 75% in 1984. George H.W. Bush won 66% here in 1988 and son George W. Bush 67% in 2000 and 72% in 2004. In 1992, this was also the least Democratic state: third-party candidate Ross Perot finished ahead of Democratic nominee Bill Clinton, 27% to 25%. But in 2008, the movement toward Democrats in Salt Lake County and widespread enthusiasm for Democratic candidate Barack Obama—some 600 Young Democrats campaigned for him at Brigham Young, and the campaign opened an office in Washington County during the primary—left Republican John McCain carrying the state by just 63%-34%, behind his showings in Oklahoma and Wyoming. This was the best Democratic showing since Hubert Humphrey

2008 Presidential Vote		
McCain (R)	596,030	(63%)
Obama (D)	327,670	(34%)
2008 Democratic Presidential Primary		
Obama (D)	74,538	(57%)
Clinton (D)	51,333	(39%)
2008 Republican Presidential Primary		
Romney (R)	264,956	(89%)
McCain (R)	15,931	(5%)
2004 Presidential Vote		
Bush (R)	663,742	(72%)
Kerry (D)	241,199	(26%)

won 37% of the vote in 1968. Obama carried Salt Lake County, if only by 296 votes. In matrimony-minded Utah, there was no gender gap at all, and young voters went 62% for McCain. The best Obama age group was the 30- to 44-year-olds, Generation X, which gave McCain only a 52%-44% advantage. The exit poll showed Mormons voting 78%-19% for McCain, which suggests that "gentiles" actually voted for Obama.

Utah's attempts to become a force in presidential primaries have not been successful. Former Republican Gov. Mike Leavitt spent much time and effort promoting a Western regional primary for the Friday following the South-dominated Super Tuesday, March 10, 2000. But only Colorado and Wyoming (with a caucus, not a primary) adopted the date, and candidates paid less attention to Western issues than Leavitt had hoped. In 2004, Utah held a Democratic primary on February 24, but the Legislature would not pay for it, so the state Democratic Party footed the bill of $50,000; 35,000 people voted in a state of 2.3 million, and John Kerry beat John Edwards 55%-30%.

For the 2008 presidential contest, the Legislature decided to hold state-financed primaries on February 5, which turned out to be Super Tuesday, when many larger states voted. Nonetheless, Hillary Rodham Clinton and Obama ran television spots, perhaps the first Democratic presidential ads many native Utahns had ever seen. Chelsea Clinton and Michelle Obama came in to campaign. Some 131,000 Utahns voted in the Democratic primary, 57% for Obama and 39% for Clinton. There was little suspense on the Republican side. Mitt Romney, as a Mormon and as the savior of the 2002 Winter Olympics, won 89% of the vote, with a robust turnout of 296,000, far higher than the 91,000 in 2000. But it was not enough to salvage his candidacy.

Congressional districting   Utahns expected that the 2000 census would give Utah a fourth seat in the House of Representatives. But, under the formula used for reapportionment, Utah fell 857 residents short of getting a new district. Instead, North Carolina got an unexpected 13th seat. Utah sued, twice. The first lawsuit contended that if military personnel stationed abroad should be counted in their states of residence, so should Mormon missionaries, who also can be accurately tracked and matched with their home states. North Carolina had thousands of military personnel stationed abroad and only 107 attributable Mormon missionaries. Utah had fewer military personnel stationed abroad but 11,176 Mormon missionaries. In April 2001, a three-judge federal court threw out Utah's case and the U.S. Supreme Court later affirmed the ruling.

111th Congress Lineup	
2 R	1 D
110th Congress Lineup	
2 R	1 D

Utah's other lawsuit charged that the Census Bureau violated the Constitution's injunction that it conduct an "actual enumeration" of the population when it employed what statisticians call "hot-deck imputation," when census takers, after repeated failed efforts to contact residents of one housing unit, assume that it contains the same number of people in similar housing units nearby. Utah argued that this is "sampling," which, the Supreme Court ruled in another case, was prohibited for use in reapportionment. This argument did better in court. Utah lost by a 2-to-1 in a three-judge district court in 2001 and by 5-4 on the Supreme Court in June 2002. But the upshot was that North Carolina, not Utah, got the 435th House district in the 2000 reapportionment. Utah's Legislature drew new congressional district lines in September 2001. Aware that the state was suing for another district, it adopted both three- and four-district plans. Utah conducted its 2002 election with the three-district plan in place.

In 2006, Utah's quest for a fourth House seat got a boost with a bill by U.S. Rep. Tom Davis, R-Va., to award the District of Columbia a full voting member of the House. It balanced that obvious gain for the Democrats by awarding another seat, until the next reapportionment after the 2010 census, to the state entitled to the 436th district under the statutory formula, which is Utah. But how would the new member from Utah be elected? House Republicans insisted that the Utah Legislature draw up a plan with four congressional districts before the bill would be considered. The Utah legislature did so in December 2006, with a plan that allayed Democrats' fears and gave Jim Matheson, the only Democrat in the Utah congressional delegation, a much more Democratic district. But time was running out on the Republican Congress, and the D.C. bill never reached the floor.

With Democrats gaining solid majorities in both houses of Congress in 2008, it was widely expected that the D.C.-Utah bill would pass and be signed by President Obama. The Senate did pass it 61-37 in February 2009, but in March, House Republicans managed to attach to the bill an amendment repealing D.C.'s strict gun-control laws. Many Democrats from rural, pro-gun districts supported the move, but a large faction of Democrats who favor gun control opposed it, and House leaders shelved the bill.

Utah will likely gain a fourth district in the 2010 census, and it seems likely that the Republican Legislature—given Matheson's success in winning re-election in 2008 by nearly 2-to-1 in a district that voted 58% for McCain—will produce a redistricting plan with a solidly Democratic district for Matheson in 2012, plus three safely Republican districts. It also seems exceedingly unlikely that Utah, or any other solidly Republican state, will be in line, under the 2010 reapportionment, for the 436th House seat, in which case the Davis stratagem of balancing a new D.C. seat with one in Utah or another Republican state would not be feasible in the future.

Governor

Jon Huntsman (R)

Elected 2004, 2nd term; b. March 26, 1960, Palo Alto, CA; home, Salt Lake City; Attended U. of UT; U. of PA, B.A. 1987; Mormon; married (Mary Kaye).

Professional Career: Staff Asst., White House, 1982–83; Exec., Huntsman Corp., 1983–89; Dep. Asst. Sec. of Commerce, Trade Dev. Bureau, 1989–90; Dep. Asst. Sec. of Commerce for E. Asia & the Pacific, 1990–91; Amb. to Singapore, 1992–93; Pres., Huntsman Cancer Foundation, 1995–2001; U.S. trade amb., 2001–03; Chairman and CEO, Huntsman Family Holdings Co., 2003–04.

Office: Utah State Capitol Complex, 350 North State Street, Suite 200, PO Box 142220, Salt Lake City, 84114, 801-538-1000; Fax: 801-538-1528; Web site: www.utah.gov/governor.

Election Results

2008 general	Jon Huntsman (R)	734,049	(78%)
	Bob Springmeyer (D)	186,503	(20%)
	Dell Schanze (Lib)	24,820	(3%)
2008 primary	Jon Huntsman (R)	unopposed	

Since 2004, Utah's governor has been Republican Jon Huntsman Jr. But in 2009, President Barack Obama appointed Huntsman as the United States ambassador to China. At press time for *The Almanac of American Politics* in July 2009, Huntsman was awaiting what was expected to be a routine confirmation by the Senate. Utah Lt. Gov. Gary Herbert, a Republican, was expected to succeed him.

Herbert was born in American Fork, Utah, where his father owned a construction company. He studied engineering and accounting at Brigham Young University but left school before graduating and became a realtor. He ran for the Orem City Council in 1989, but lost the election by 32 votes. The next year, he was elected to the Utah County Commission and served as its chairman for 13 years. During his tenure, Utah County had one of the state's lowest certified tax rates. He entered the 1994 race to unseat Democratic U.S. Rep. Bill Orton in Utah's 3rd Congressional District but dropped out after struggling to raise money.

In 2003, Herbert left the Utah County Commission to run for governor. The field for the 2004 Republican primary was crowded with better known politicians such as former U.S. Rep. Jim Hansen, former Utah House Speaker Nolan Karras and Huntsman. Herbert cast himself as a "David" in a field of political "Goliaths." He stressed his rural roots and ties to local government. Unable to generate enough support for his own candidacy, Herbert accepted Huntsman's invitation to join his ticket as the nominee for lieutenant governor. At the time, Huntsman was perceived as lacking credibility in state politics and rural affairs, two areas in which Herbert was solid. Their ticket won with 58% of the vote.

As lieutenant governor, Herbert made it clear that he would not be content performing the ceremonial duties often associated with the office. Under Utah's Constitution, the lieutenant governor's sole official duty is overseeing the state Elections Office, but Huntsman expanded Herbert's responsibilities to include overseeing the state's public lands policies, transportation plans and homeland security operations. That gave Herbert more influence than his predecessors. He pushed for the creation of a Public Lands Policy Coordination Office to help manage the state's role in land management issues. He also oversaw the state Elections Office's transition from paper ballots to electronic voting and the transfer of candidate and lobbyist disclosure forms from paper to the Internet.

After Huntsman announced that he would accept the nomination to be ambassador to China, the conservative faction of Utah's Republican Party expressed excitement over Herbert, who is more conservative than Huntsman. But before taking office, Herbert said that he agreed with Huntsman on most issues and would not seek to implement major policy changes. His decision to follow the path blazed by the popular Huntsman may partially be motivated by the fact that he will face a special election in 2010, and his re-election is not a foregone conclusion. A poll conducted in May 2009 showed that only 42% of Utahns could identify Herbert as the state's lieutenant governor. Herbert may face competition in the 2010 Republican primary, and several potential challengers were eyeing the contest in 2009.

As governor of America's most conservative state, Huntsman blazed a moderate political path with highly successful results. He relaxed the state's notoriously strict liquor laws, entered Utah into multistate agreement to reduce greenhouse gas emissions and implemented a four-day work week for state employees in an effort to reduce energy costs. He visited China in October 2006 on a weeklong trade mission and impressed Chinese officials by speaking fluent Mandarin.

Huntsman was elected to a second term in 2008 by 78%-20%, the largest victory for a governor that election cycle. A few months into his second term, Huntsman shocked the Utah political establishment by coming out in favor of legalizing same-sex unions, a stark contrast to his 2004 campaign-year support of a proposed state constitutional amendment to ban same-sex marriage, ratified by Utah voters almost 2-to-1. Despite grumbling from the state's most conservative political factions, his approval ratings stood in the 80s around the time he announced he would step down as governor.

Senior Senator

Orrin Hatch (R)

Elected 1976, term expires 2012, 6th term; b. March 22, 1934, Pittsburgh, PA; home, Salt Lake City; Brigham Young U., B.S. 1959; U. of Pittsburgh, J.D. 1962; Mormon; married (Elaine); 6 children.

Professional Career: Practicing atty., 1962–76.

DC Office: 104 HSOB, 20510, 202-224-5251; Fax: 202-224-6331; Web site: hatch.senate.gov.

State Offices: Cedar City, 435-586-8435; Ogden, 801-625-5672; Provo, 801-375-7881; Salt Lake City, 801-524-4380; St. George, 435-634-1795.

Committees: *Aging (Special)* (5th of 6 R). *Finance* (2nd of 10 R): Energy, Natural Resources & Infrastructure; Health Care (RMM); Taxation, IRS Oversight & Long-Term Growth. *Health, Education, Labor & Pensions* (7th of 10 R): Children & Families; Employment & Workplace Safety. *Intelligence (Select)* (2nd of 7 R). *Joint Committee on Taxation* (2nd of 2 R). *Judiciary* (2nd of 7 R): Antitrust, Competition Policy & Consumer Rights (RMM); Crime & Drugs; Terrorism & Homeland Security.

Group Ratings

	ADA	ACLU	AFS	LCV	ITIC	NTU	COC	ACU	CFG	FRC
2008	10	21	11	18	80	56	100	80	69	88
2007	30	—	14	13	—	57	91	76	53	—

National Journal Ratings

	2007 LIB	—	2007 CONS		2008 LIB	—	2008 CONS
Economic	34%	—	64%		17%	—	81%
Social	30%	—	69%		30%	—	68%
Foreign	34%	—	64%		24%	—	71%
Composite	34%	—	67%		25%	—	75%

Key Votes of the 110th Congress

1. Raise CAFE standards	N	5. Make English official language	Y	9. Withdraw troops 3/08	N
2. Expand SCHIP	Y	6. Path to citizenship	N	10. Iran guard is terrorist group	Y
3. Cap greenhouse gases	N	7. Fetus is unborn child	Y	11. Increase missile defense $	Y
4. Bail out financial markets	Y	8. Prosecute hate crimes	N	12. Overhaul FISA	Y

Election Results

2006 general	Orrin Hatch (R)..	356,238	(63%)	($3,340,902)
	Pete Ashdown (D)	177,459	(31%)	($255,729)
	Scott Bradley (CNP)	21,526	(4%)	($24,526)
2006 primary	Orrin Hatch (R)...	unopposed		

Prior Winning Percentages: 2000 (66%); 1994 (69%); 1988 (67%); 1982 (58%); 1976 (54%)

Republican Orrin Hatch, Utah's senior senator, was first elected to the Senate in 1976. Hatch grew up in Pittsburgh, where his father was a metal lather. The family lost their home during the Depression, and lived for a time in a shelter made of salvaged wood and metal. They had no indoor plumbing. He worked his way through Brigham Young University as a janitor and a metal lather, like his father. He went on to get a law degree from the University of Pittsburgh, and practiced law there. He and his wife and their young family moved to Salt Lake City, and the newly minted lawyer got interested in politics. In 1976, he ran for the U.S. Senate; an endorsement from Republican presidential candidate Ronald Reagan helped him get attention and he ultimately won the GOP nomination. In the general, he upset three-term Democrat Frank Moss 54%-45%. His toughest re-election fight came in 1982, when he was opposed by Democratic Salt Lake City Mayor Ted Wilson. Hatch won 58%-41%.

Hatch's Senate career has been shaped by two impulses that are sometimes in tension with each other: a strong conservative philosophy and a sense of responsibility to pass legislation. He first attracted attention in a Senate dominated by Democrats when he successfully filibustered the AFL-CIO's labor law bill, which had been expected to pass. Then, in just four years, he became chairman of the Labor Committee after Republicans won a Senate majority in 1980. He remained a strong opponent of the striker replacement law sought by unions. On the Judiciary Committee, he fought abortion rights legislation and a civil rights bill that produced racial quotas and preferences. He also staunchly defended conservative Supreme Court nominees Robert Bork and Clarence Thomas. In 1995, Hatch became chairman of the Judiciary Committee, where he worked on limiting tort liability and regulatory law and managed the balanced budget amendment to one-vote defeats in 1995 and 1997. He also helped draft the 2001 USA Patriot Act, the Bush administration's centerpiece anti-terrorism law, and in 2004 defended it against attempts to eliminate some of its main provisions. "It seems to me that we should not make it any harder to go after suspected terrorists than after suspected drug dealers," Hatch said. During negotiations to reauthorize the Foreign Intelligence Surveillance Act, Hatch supported a provision to grant retroactive immunity to phone companies that had participated in the administration's warrantless wiretapping program. Hatch described the phone companies as "patriotic" in a speech on the Senate floor. The FISA reauthorization passed the Senate in 2008 with a retroactive immunity provision for the companies.

Hatch has taken some surprising and bipartisan positions. In 1997, he joined liberal Massachusetts Sen. Edward Kennedy in sponsoring a $24 billion program to get states to provide health insurance for children of low-income working parents who don't qualify for Medicaid. Despite his longstanding opposition to abortion, he has supported embryonic-stem-cell research and argued that life is created in the womb, "not in a petri dish." In 2004, he gained wide bipartisan support for setting up a trust fund to handle asbestos cases, but in 2005, when incoming Chairman and then-Republican Arlen Specter of Pennsylvania proposed a $140 billion trust fund, some businesses withdrew their support. In 2006, the Senate passed a measure Hatch sponsored with Illinois Democrat Dick Durbin that required reporting to the Food and Drug Administration bad side effects of dietary supplements and over-the-counter drugs. Hatch has expressed doubts about the use of mandatory minimum sentences in some drug cases and has interceded on behalf of a music producer arrested in the United Arab Emirates and a young Utahn who fled the country, both of whom he believes were treated unjustly. With then-Sen. Barack Obama, D-Ill., he got a provision in a tax bill to bar bankruptcy courts from preventing the carrying out of charitable and tithing pledges.

But Hatch has also defended to the hilt traditional Republican positions, sponsoring bills to restrict class action lawsuits and to set limits on medical malpractice cases. As chairman of the committee from June 2001 to January 2003 and as the ranking minority member, Hatch defended the Bush Justice Department and judicial nominees against Democrats' attacks, and took them to task for refusing to hold hearings on many appointees when they were in the majority. Hatch in 2007 staunchly defended embattled Attorney General Alberto Gonzales and Gonzales' role in the controversial firings of eight U.S. attorneys. Hatch stood out as one of Gonzales' sole defenders, saying the attacks were an attempt by Democrats to indirectly sully Bush's reputation. After the Supreme Judicial Court of Massachusetts ruled that its state constitution required legalization of same-sex marriages, Hatch proposed a constitutional amendment that would authorize states to refuse to recognize such marriages contracted in another state. After same-sex couples in Massachusetts started obtaining marriage licenses, Hatch supported the amendment sponsored by Colorado Republican Wayne Allard that would ban same-sex marriage altogether. Hatch has opposed federal gun control measures and in 2003 sponsored a bill to make it easier to carry handguns in the District of Columbia.

Another of his strong interests is the issue of protecting intellectual property in the face of technological advance. He supported the Digital Millennium Copyright Act of 1998 banning unlawful downloading of copyrighted music and movies and backed the record industry against the threat raised by Napster. In 2004, the Senate passed his bill, co-sponsored with Democrat Patrick Leahy of Vermont, to authorize the Justice Department to bring civil lawsuits as well as criminal actions for illegal downloading. In 2007, Hatch, with Leahy, co-sponsored bipartisan legislation revising patent law, but it stalled in committee. Leahy reintroduced the bill in 2009 and forged a compromise with Specter and Sen. Dianne Feinstein, D-Calif., to assure its passage in the Judiciary Committee. The compromise included changes that Hatch argued undermined the bill's ability to limit litigation costs and improve patent quality, two of the reasons he pushed for the patent bill in the first place. He ended up voting against the legislation, but it passed the Judiciary Committee 15-4.

Hatch's interest in these issues is not just theoretical. He has long written poetry and in 1995 began writing songs. He has since written about 300, some of which have been recorded by a Utah firm, including a 13-song album of Christmas music. Some of his songs have been recorded by singer Gladys Knight, a convert to the Mormon Church. His music has earned praise from Bono, the lead singer of the popular and politically-oriented rock band U2. In 2003, the two men met to discuss the AIDS crisis in Africa, and the singer suggested for Hatch the state name "Johnny Trapdoor." One of his songs was used in the movie *Ocean's 12*. In 2006, Hatch lobbied for the release of rapper John Forte, imprisoned five years earlier for possession of liquid cocaine. Forte, whom Hatch referred to as a genius in letters asking for his release, had his sentence commuted by President George W. Bush in December 2008.

Hatch and Utah colleague Bob Bennett for some time supported a permanent nuclear waste repository in Yucca Mountain, Nev., on the theory it was better to have the waste transported over Utah than deposited there. They worked together to prevent the Skull Valley Branch of the Goshute Indians' proposal to store radioactive waste on their reservation, and in 2005 helped to get a wilderness area provision in the defense bill which appeared to block railroad transport to the site.

Every senator, it sometimes seems, must run for president, and the time came for Hatch with the 2000 election. He conceded that it would take a "miracle" to win, but argued that he had more experience in federal office than the other candidates and could work with Democrats, and that he was not "beholden to the Republican establishment." In the Iowa caucuses in January 2000, he won only 1% of the vote, fewer than Republican John McCain, who did not campaign in the state. Two days later, he withdrew from the race and endorsed Bush. In the 2008 presidential primaries, Hatch endorsed fellow Mormon Mitt Romney of Massachusetts. At the American Society of Newspaper Editors convention, he spoke out against what he considered religious bigotry and negative discourse on the Mormon Church during the campaign season.

In 2000, Hatch won 66%-31% and became the first Utahn popularly elected five times to the Senate. The only other five-term senator in Utah history, Reed Smoot, who served from 1903 to 1933, was elected to his first term by the Legislature. In 2006, he won 63%-31% and after he was sworn into his sixth term became the longest-serving senator in Utah history.

Junior Senator

Robert Bennett (R)

Elected 1992, term expires 2010, 3rd term; b. Sept. 18, 1933, Salt Lake City; home, Salt Lake City; U. of UT, B.S. 1957; Mormon; married (Joyce); 6 children.

Military Career: Chaplain, Army Natl. Guard, 1957–60.

Professional Career: Staff aide, U.S. Rep. Sherm Lloyd, 1962; Staff aide, U.S. Sen. Wallace F. Bennett, 1963; Cong. liaison, U.S. Dept. of Transp., 1969–70; Pres., Robert Mullen P.R., 1970–74; P.R. dir., Summa Corp., 1974–78; Pres., Osmond Communications, 1978–79; Chmn., American Computers Corp., 1979–81; Pres., Microsonics Corp., 1981–84; CEO, Franklin Quest Co., 1984–91; Chmn., UT Educ. Strategic Plng. Comm., 1988.

DC Office: 431 DSOB, 20510, 202-224-5444; Fax: 202-228-1168; Web site: bennett.senate.gov.

State Offices: Cedar City, 435-865-1335; Ogden, 801-625-5676; Provo, 801-851-2525; Salt Lake City, 801-524-5933; St. George, 435-628-5514.

Committees: *Appropriations* (6th of 12 R): Agriculture, Rural Development, Food and Drug Administration & Related Agencies; Defense; Energy & Water Development (RMM); Interior, Environment & Related Agencies; State, Foreign Operations & Related Programs; Transportation, Housing and Urban Development & Related Agencies. *Banking, Housing & Urban Affairs* (2nd of 10 R): Financial Institutions; Housing, Transportation & Community Development; Securities, Insurance & Investment. *Energy & Natural Resources* (7th of 10 R): Energy; Public Lands & Forests; Water & Power. *Joint Economic Committee* (4th of 4 R). *Rules & Administration* (RMM of 8 R).

Group Ratings

	ADA	ACLU	AFS	LCV	ITIC	NTU	COC	ACU	CFG	FRC
2008	15	14	0	18	100	54	100	64	63	88
2007	15	—	0	7	—	66	100	75	77	—

National Journal Ratings

	2007 LIB	—	2007 CONS		2008 LIB	—	2008 CONS
Economic	16%	—	82%		33%	—	66%
Social	33%	—	66%		32%	—	66%
Foreign	27%	—	72%		35%	—	63%
Composite	26%	—	74%		34%	—	66%

Key Votes of the 110th Congress

1. Raise CAFE standards	N	5. Make English official language	Y	9. Withdraw troops 3/08	N
2. Expand SCHIP	N	6. Path to citizenship	Y	10. Iran guard is terrorist group	Y
3. Cap greenhouse gases	N	7. Fetus is unborn child	Y	11. Increase missile defense $	N
4. Bail out financial markets	Y	8. Prosecute hate crimes	N	12. Overhaul FISA	Y

Election Results

2004 general	Robert Bennett (R)	626,640	(69%)	($2,649,234)
	Paul Van Dam (D)	258,955	(28%)	($116,959)
2004 primary	Robert Bennett (R)	unopposed		

Prior Winning Percentages: 1998 (64%); 1992 (55%)

Bob Bennett, Utah's junior senator, is a Republican who was first elected in 1992. He grew up in Salt Lake City, the grandchild of a president of The Church of Jesus Christ of Latter-day Saints (Mormon Church). He was 17 when his father, Wallace Bennett, was elected in 1950 to the first of four terms in the Senate. He graduated from the University of Utah, worked as a congressional staffer, and then was the Transportation Department's chief lobbyist during the Nixon administration. He also headed the public relations firm that employed Watergate burglar Howard Hunt but was involved in no wrongdoing himself. Some Watergate buffs wrongly believed that Bennett was *Washington Post* reporter Bob Woodward's source known as "Deep Throat." Later, Bennett headed Microsonics, which makes audio discs for talking toys, and then became head of Franklin Quest, which produces the Franklin day planners and organizers, building the company from four to 700 employees and sales of $80 million a year. He sold his interest in the company in 1991 for a reported $25 million. He headed a commission that produced Utah's Strategic Plan for Education and wrote *Gaining Control*, a book about how to control your daily life.

In 1992, when Republican Jake Garn retired from the Senate, Bennett ran for the seat his father once held. He was not the only multi-millionaire in the race. The initial favorite was Republican Joseph Cannon, who had taken over the old Geneva Steel plant and made it profitable, and who spent $5 million of his own money. But Bennett spent $1.4 million of his own, effectively attacked Geneva's environmental record and won the primary 51%-49%. The Democratic nominee, U.S. Rep. Wayne Owens, was a familiar face, with a voting record that was moderate but evidently too liberal for Utah. Bennett won 55%-40%.

Bennett has had a moderate-to-conservative voting record and became the Republican chief deputy whip in 2003. A close advisor to GOP Leader Mitch McConnell of Kentucky, he gave up his deputy whip position to become McConnell's official counsel when McConnell became minority leader in 2007. This gave Bennett a seat at the leadership table. Their friendship began when Bennett joined McConnell to oppose fellow Utah Republican Orrin Hatch's constitutional amendment to bar desecration of the flag, out of First Amendment concerns. Later, for the same reason, they united in opposition to campaign finance reform. Bennett has gained another Senate insider post as ranking Republican on the Rules and Administration Committee. He also has an interest in high-tech issues, and chaired the special Senate committee that was responsible for steps to avoid problems in the year 2000 computer switch. He has embraced some new technology himself. In 2001, he became the first member of Congress to own a hybrid vehicle and in 2006, he pushed for tax breaks for purchasers of fuel-efficient vehicles. He has favored sales taxes on Internet transactions. In his mail order business, he said, he charged customers sales tax in every state and no one protested.

Despite generally supporting the Bush administration, in 2001 he voted against the president's centerpiece education bill, No Child Left Behind, which later became unpopular in Utah. As chairman of the

Joint Economic Committee, he called for rewriting the nation's tax laws, starting from scratch. During the debate over possible changes in Social Security in 2005, he advocated progressively cutting future benefits and establishing personal retirement accounts. "You can not solve the financial problems with personal accounts. But you can not solve the long-term demographic problem without personal accounts," he said. In 2006, he caused an uproar when he suggested that parts of Katrina-ravaged New Orleans not be rebuilt. "I'm happy to appropriate money to help people who are in trouble," he said. "Building a city 10 feet below sea level does not strike me as, inherently, basically a good idea." The New Orleans *Times-Picayune* editorialized against his "poor grasp of physics" and called him a "lunkhead." Four months later, he visited the city and concluded, "My instinct is to bulldoze [abandoned housing] and start over again." Bennett again displayed his knack for frank assessments after a trip to Afghanistan in 2007, when he noted that it might be necessary for U.S. troops to remain in the country for several decades.

Bennett has pressed for land exchanges between Utah and the federal government to eliminate the checkerboard pattern of land ownership that prevents Utah from producing revenue for education from mining on state lands. As a member of the Appropriations Committee and the ranking Republican on the Energy and Water Development Subcommittee, he is an aggressive advocate for federal funding for Utah. In recent years, he has secured $9 million for a 44-mile commuter rail project between Salt Lake City and Ogden and $4 million for statewide bus facilities. Citizens Against Government Waste has criticized Bennett for several projects, including $300,000 for a think tank started by former Republican Gov. Mike Leavitt, $1 million for an education initiative for Western Governors University, and $750,000 for the Range Creek ranch. Bennett has said that he is proud of the money that he directs to Utah in the face of the increasing controversy in recent years over so-called earmarks, which critics denounce as wasteful government spending. In the past, Bennett has refused to release the names of companies that would potentially benefit from earmarks he adds to appropriations bill, but in October 2008, he announced that he would begin to make the information available to the public.

In 2007, Bennett joined Sen. Ron Wyden, D-Ore., in introducing the bipartisan Healthy Americans Act, which seeks to eliminate the bond between health insurance and employment by giving Americans tax breaks to purchase insurance from a group of government-approved private companies. After reviewing the legislation, the Congressional Budget Office said the bill could be budget-neutral by 2014, meaning it would not run a deficit, and might even deliver budget surpluses in years to come. It has not been voted on, but could be in the mix of proposals as Congress tackles the health care issue, a priority of the Obama administration.

As the country's financial crisis worsened in the fall of 2008, Bennett emerged as a lead negotiator for Senate Republicans. He attended a series of meetings intended to craft legislation to give the U.S. Treasury Department the money and authority to purchase the troubled assets of financial institutions. After one such meeting, Bennett told reporters that Democrats and Republicans had brokered an agreement suitable to both parties, but after that agreement fell through, Republican leaders replaced Bennett with Senate Budget Committee ranking member Judd Gregg of New Hampshire. Gregg credited Bennett for his role in the negotiations after the Troubled Assets Relief Program passed both the Senate and the House in early October 2008.

When he was first elected, Bennett said he would serve for only two Senate terms. But in 1998, he said he would not rule out running again. He was re-elected 64%-33% that year. In 2004, his Democratic opponent was former Attorney General Paul Van Dam, who rode around the state with his wife on a tandem bicycle. Bennett's campaign put up a series of humorous billboards without using his name, but describing him in ways voters might recognize: "Big Heart. Big Ideas. Big Ears," read one. "Better Looking than Abraham Lincoln (Just Barely)," read another. He outspent Van Dam $2.6 million to $117,000 and won 69%-28%. Bennett's 2010 re-election campaign could be more difficult. His recent support of issues opposed by bedrock conservatives, such as the government rescue of the financial services industry, could make it difficult for him to withstand a primary challenge from a conservative.

FIRST DISTRICT

Rob Bishop (R)

Elected 2002, 4th term; b. July 13, 1951, Kaysville; home, Brigham City; U. of UT, B.A. 1974; Mormon; married (Jeralyn Hansen); 5 children.

Elected Office: UT House of Reps., 1978–94; Speaker, 1993–94.

Professional Career: H.S. teacher, 1974–2002; Chair, UT Rep. Party, 1997–2001.

DC Office: 123 CHOB, 20515, 202-225-0453; Fax: 202-225-5857; Web site: robbishop.house.gov.

State Offices: Ogden, 801-625-0107.

Committees: *Armed Services* (10th of 25 R): Air & Land Forces; Readiness. *Education & Labor* (13th of 19 R): Early Childhood, Elementary & Secondary Education. *Natural Resources* (9th of 20 R): National Parks, Forests & Public Lands (RMM).

Group Ratings

	ADA	ACLU	AFS	LCV	ITIC	NTU	COC	ACU	CFG	FRC
2008	0	18	17	0	40	79	81	100	86	94
2007	10	—	18	0	—	77	88	100	74	—

National Journal Ratings

	2007 LIB	—	2007 CONS		2008 LIB	—	2008 CONS
Economic	8%	—	92%		14%	—	85%
Social	19%	—	81%		9%	—	85%
Foreign	30%	—	70%		0%	—	95%
Composite	19%	—	81%		10%	—	90%

Key Votes of the 110th Congress

1. Increase minimum wage	N	5. Share immigration data	Y	9. Withdraw troops 8/08	N
2. Expand SCHIP	N	6. Foreign aid abortion ban	Y	10. No operations in Iran	*
3. Raise CAFE standards	N	7. Ban gay bias in workplace	N	11. Free trade with Peru	N
4. Bail out financial markets	N	8. Repeal D.C. gun law	Y	12. Overhaul FISA	Y

Election Results

2008 general	Rob Bishop (R)	196,799	(65%)	($325,769)
	Morgan Bowen (D)	92,469	(30%)	($24,587)
	Kirk Pearson (CNP)	7,397	(2%)	
	Joseph Buchman (Lib)	6,780	(2%)	
2008 primary	Rob Bishop (R)	unopposed		

Prior Winning Percentages: 2006 (63%); 2004 (68%); 2002 (61%)

Population		Race/Ethnicity		Work	
Pop. 2007:	842,432	White:	81.4%	Private:	75.1%
Change since 2000:	Up 13.2%	Black:	1.6%	Government:	19.9%
Urban:	88.7%	Hispanic:	12.8%	Self-employed:	4.8%
Rural:	11.3%	Asian:	1.7%	Blue collar:	25.2%
Area size:	22,700 sq. mi.	Native Am.:	0.6%	White collar:	58.8%
Age		Hawaiian:	0.5%	Khaki collar:	0.4%
Median age:	28.5 yrs.	Two+ races:	1.4%	Other:	15.5%
More than 65 yrs:	8.6%	**Ancestry**		Median income:	$53,652
Less than 18 yrs:	30.8%	English:	20.9%	Median home value:	$168,600
Education		German:	9.6%	Poverty:	10.2%
H.S. grad:	89.7%	USA:	8.6%	**Military Veterans**	
College grad:	27.4%			% of Pop:	10.2%
Grad degree:	8.6%				

In May 1869, a motley crowd of Irish and Chinese laborers, teamsters, engineers, train crews, officials and guests from Salt Lake City gathered at Promontory Summit, Utah, to watch the opening of the transcontinental railroad. The Union Pacific train was late and railroad tycoon Leland Stanford's raised hammer totally missed the golden spike, but an alert telegrapher mimicked the sound over the wire and a photographer recorded the scene for posterity: United at last were the civilized East and

2008 Presidential Vote

McCain (R)	197,433	(64%)
Obama (D)	103,737	(33%)

2004 Presidential Vote

Bush (R)	220,869	(73%)
Kerry (D)	75,728	(25%)

Cook Partisan Voting Index: R + 21

the mostly untamed West. In Salt Lake City, the center of the Mormon Church—and of Utah—is Temple Square, illuminated by 300,000 lights during Christmas week and nestled beneath the towering mountains that flank Salt Lake City. The Mormon Tabernacle, home of the famous choir, is here, as is the Salt Lake LDS Temple itself, crowned with the golden angel Moroni. This area has been the focal point of Utah since Mormon leader Brigham Young, looking down at this valley, said, "This is the place." Ironically, this part of Salt Lake City is the least Mormon and most cosmopolitan part of Utah, with the state university and businesses bringing in outsiders who, flouting Mormon strictures, keep purveyors of alcohol and caffeine in business. Salt Lake County voted 60% for George W. Bush in 2004, up from 55% in 2000, but Democratic presidential nominee Barack Obama narrowly carried the county by 296 votes in 2008.

The 1st Congressional District of Utah consists of the northern end of the state. It includes most of Salt Lake City's historic downtown, its distinctive Avenues District and the airport, but it takes in little of the fast-growing suburbia that stretches south of the city. More than half the people in the district live in the stretch of the Wasatch Front, between the mountains and Great Salt Lake, just north of Salt Lake City, in Davis and Weber counties. Davis County is suburban and fairly affluent. Ogden in Weber County is an old working-class railroad town, an industrial center that depends on nearby Hill Air Force Base, home of the advanced F-22A fighter jets.

Farther north in the Cache Valley is Logan, home of Utah State University. This is farming country and very heavily Mormon. Over the mountains to the east of Salt Lake City is Park City, the old mining town that is now a fashionable ski resort and home of actor Robert Redford's annual Sundance Film Festival. West of Salt Lake City is the desolate Bonneville Salt Flats, where land speed records have been set. This land of stark beauty, much of it federally owned, has been used roughly by man, as a repository for hazardous wastes at civilian and military dumps in Tooele County and as a place for military experimentation on the Dugway Proving Ground, where scientists test defenses against chemical and biological agents. New suburbs out Interstate 80 have made Tooele, where real estate remains affordable, one of the state's fastest growing counties. With continued delay in making Yucca Mountain in Nevada the nation's nuclear-waste repository, the Skull Valley temporary storage site, near Dugway, is looking less and less temporary. Politically this is a heavily Republican area, with patches of Democratic strength. The district's portions of Salt Lake County are trendy and working-class Democratic. Park City is on its way to becoming another Aspen, and is Democratic. The Cache Valley is very heavily Republican, though, and overall the district voted 73% for Republican George W. Bush in 2004 and 64% for Republican John McCain in 2008.

The congressman from the 1st District is Rob Bishop, a Republican first elected in 2002. He grew up in Davis County and graduated from the University of Utah. He became a high school history and government teacher in Box Elder County. In 1978, at age 27, he was elected to the state House. In 1993 and 1994, he was House speaker. He continued working as a teacher after leaving the Legislature, and also worked as a lobbyist for state Republicans and for the National Rifle Association. When the seat became open, both Bishop and former House Majority Leader Kevin Garn ran. As a former state party chair for four years, Bishop won 58% of the vote at the Republican nominating convention. With mostly similar conservative views, their chief difference was a contentious issue in Utah, the ongoing battle between banks and credit unions. The credit union lobby endorsed Bishop who, as a lobbyist in 1999, helped defeat legislation to curtail the credit unions' tax-exempt status. Garn, the wealthy chairman of a Layton bank, had the support of Utah bankers. The credit unions were the more valuable ally: They poured at least $100,000 in independent expenditures into an anti-Garn campaign, which helped even out the financial balance since Garn outspent Bishop by 4-to-1. Bishop won the primary 60%-40%. Democrats believed they had a chance in the general election with nominee Dave Thomas, a wealthy advertising executive and an anti-abortion Mormon bishop who presented himself as a fiscal conservative and "a regular guy" not tied to special interests. Bishop won more easily than expected, 61%-37%.

In the House, Bishop usually has been a reliable conservative vote. In 2005, Republican Speaker Dennis Hastert signaled that Bishop had favorably impressed party insiders by giving him a seat on the Rules Committee. But the Democratic takeover of the House in 2007 forced him from Rules. He moved to the committees on Armed Services, Education and Labor, and Natural Resources.

Bishop now is the ranking Republican at the National Parks, Forests and Public Lands Subcommittee—a useful assignment in a state where the federal government controls nearly two-thirds of the land. It also puts him in the middle of environment and energy issues. He unsuccessfully tried to block two bills sponsored by House Democrats who sought federal protection for rivers in the Northeast United States. As gas prices skyrocketed in the summer of 2008, Bishop introduced the Americans for American Energy Act, which would increase domestic energy production, including the construction of 10 refineries on public lands. Bishop consistently criticized Democrats for refusing to debate increased domestic oil production. He found more legislative success on home-state issues. He pushed a bill through the House to facilitate a land exchange between Bountiful City, Utah and the federal government. The bill would give the city ownership of a 40-acre rifle range that the city wants jurisdiction over.

On other local issues, Bishop in 2005 won enactment of his bill to block private disposal of nuclear waste on the Skull Valley Goshute Indian reservation and to convert the land to a wilderness area. He helped protect Hill Air Force Base from the base-closing review that year as well. He was criticized at home for supporting a change in federal law to permit Envirocare of Utah (now known as EnergySolutions) to dispose additional radioactive waste material from a bomb plant in Ohio. Envirocare, which was a client of his former lobbying firm, dropped the proposal after three months of controversy. Bishop later advocated recycling the waste.

Bishop has been comfortably re-elected every two years. Bishop's 2008 opponent repeatedly labeled him as a pawn of special interests, but the charge failed to resonate with voters, and Bishop won 65%-30%.

SECOND DISTRICT

Jim Matheson (D)

Elected 2000, 5th term; b. March 21, 1960, Salt Lake City; home, Salt Lake City; Harvard U., B.A. 1982, U.C.L.A., M.B.A. 1987; Mormon; married (Amy); 2 children.

Professional Career: Staff, Environmental Policy Inst., 1982–85; Project dev. mgr., Bonneville Pacific, 1987–91; Sr. assoc., Energy Strategies Inc., 1992–98; Founder & pres., The Matheson Group, 1998–99.

DC Office: 2434 RHOB, 20515, 202-225-3011; Fax: 202-225-5638; Web site: www.house.gov/matheson.

State Offices: Price, 435-636-3722; Salt Lake City, 801-486-1236; St. George, 435-627-0880.

Committees: *Energy & Commerce* (22nd of 36 D): Commerce, Trade & Consumer Protections; Energy & Environment; Health. *Science & Technology* (16th of 26 D): Energy & Environment.

Group Ratings

	ADA	ACLU	AFS	LCV	ITIC	NTU	COC	ACU	CFG	FRC
2008	55	64	57	77	86	40	78	36	39	17
2007	75	—	73	55	—	24	80	36	28	—

National Journal Ratings

	2007 LIB — 2007 CONS		2008 LIB — 2008 CONS	
Economic	46%	— 54%	46%	— 53%
Social	51%	— 48%	51%	— 49%
Foreign	50%	— 50%	48%	— 52%
Composite	49%	— 51%	49%	— 52%

Key Votes of the 110th Congress

1. Increase minimum wage	Y	5. Share immigration data	Y	9. Withdraw troops 8/08	N
2. Expand SCHIP	Y	6. Foreign aid abortion ban	N	10. No operations in Iran	Y
3. Raise CAFE standards	Y	7. Ban gay bias in workplace	Y	11. Free trade with Peru	Y
4. Bail out financial markets	N	8. Repeal D.C. gun law	Y	12. Overhaul FISA	Y

Election Results

2008 general	Jim Matheson (D)	220,666	(63%)	($1,389,004)
	Bill Dew (R)	120,083	(34%)	($632,101)
2008 primary	Jim Matheson (D)	unopposed		

Prior Winning Percentages: 2006 (59%); 2004 (55%); 2002 (49%); 2000 (56%)

Population		Race/Ethnicity		Work	
Pop. 2007:	842,890	White:	86.2%	Private:	78.5%
Change since 2000:	Up 13.2%	Black:	0.7%	Government:	14.6%
Urban:	84.9%	Hispanic:	7.4%	Self-employed:	6.6%
Rural:	15.1%	Asian:	2.0%	Blue collar:	20.5%
Area size:	46,034 sq. mi.	Native Am.:	2.1%	White collar:	64.3%
		Hawaiian:	0.3%	Khaki collar:	0.1%
Age		Two+ races:	1.2%	Other:	15.1%
Median age:	31.0 yrs.			Median income:	$52,510
More than 65 yrs:	11.4%	*Ancestry*		Median home value:	$225,200
Less than 18 yrs:	28.2%	English:	22.6%	Poverty:	9.8%
		German:	10.9%		
Education		Irish:	5.7%	**Military Veterans**	
H.S. grad:	91.2%			% of Pop:	8.9%
College grad:	31.7%				
Grad degree:	10.8%				

Demographically, Utah is an urban state. Geographically, it is not just rural but, over most of its acreage, scarcely inhabited. Three-quarters of its people live in the Wasatch Front, from Ogden south through Salt Lake City to Provo, between the Great Salt Lake and Utah Lake and the Wasatch Mountains. The scenery here has grandeur but is surpassed by the landscape of much of southern Utah, most of it preserved in five national parks, five national monuments and a national recreation

2008 Presidential Vote		
McCain (R)	202,534	(58%)
Obama (D)	138,790	(40%)
2004 Presidential Vote		
Bush (R)	227,668	(66%)
Kerry (D)	108,286	(31%)
Cook Partisan Voting Index:	R + 15	

area. The terrain of southern Utah ranges from the soaring cliffs of Zion National Park to the popsicle-like outcroppings of Bryce Canyon National Park to the red-walled river cuts of Canyonlands National Park to the surreal moonscape of Arches National Park. Monument Valley, on Navajo land in far southeastern Utah, has become familiar to Americans as the site of countless car commercials, and the land around Moab and Springdale is a tourist destination. Land is mostly owned by one agency or another of the federal government, and there have been bitter fights between locals dependent on mining and environmentalists who want to preserve scenery. (You can see evidence of old uranium mines in some of the national parks.) President Bill Clinton's campaign-year creation of the Grand Staircase-Escalante National Monument in 1996, in a ceremony across the border in Arizona, enraged many Utahns, since it effectively removed 1.7 million acres from mineral development, much of it land owned by the state that used the proceeds for schools. Years later, local groups battled over access to the lands. Areas adjoining Dead Horse Point State Park and Arches National Park have been eyed for possible oil and gas projects.

The 2nd Congressional District of Utah includes this vast region of the state, but the majority of its people live in Salt Lake County, east of a wobbling line between Interstate 15 and the often dry Jordan River. The area includes most of the affluent neighborhoods in Salt Lake City and the suburbs of South Salt Lake, Murray (an old smelter city settled by southern and central Europeans), Midvale, Sandy and Draper. In Washington County, St. George ranked as the second-fastest growing metro area in the nation from 2000 to 2008, with expensive homes and traffic jams and some spillover from Las Vegas. Half of the new residents came from elsewhere in Utah and many are retirees. Republican President George W. Bush won the district with 66% in 2004, and GOP presidential nominee John McCain carried it with 58% in 2008.

The congressman from the 2nd District is Jim Matheson, a Democrat first elected in 2000. Matheson grew up in Salt Lake City, graduated from Harvard University and interned on Capitol Hill for Democratic House Speaker Tip O'Neill. His father, Scott Matheson, was elected governor of Utah in 1976 and 1980. Jim Matheson worked for the Environmental Policy Institute and then earned an M.B.A. from the University of California at Los Angeles. He returned to Salt Lake City to join Bonneville Pacific, an energy development company, where he was a project development manager. He moved in 1992 to Energy Strategies, a consulting firm, where he was a senior associate. He served four years on the Salt Lake Public Utilities Board. In 1998, he started the Matheson Group to help businesses adapt to electricity deregulation, but he closed it a year later to run for the U.S. House in a district with turbulent politics. From 1992 to 2000, it elected two Democrats and two Republicans to Congress. In the 2000 Republican primary election, aides had to intervene to stop a fist fight between Republicans Merrill Cook, the incumbent and businessman Derek Smith. Smith won the primary and then ran against Matheson, who played down his party affiliation and criticized Democratic presidential candidate Al Gore's prescription drug plan. Smith denounced Clinton's creation of the Grand Staircase-Escalante National Monument, and charged that Matheson was trying to look like a Republican. Matheson was vastly outspent by Smith, but still won 56%-41%.

In the House, Matheson has a voting record that is among the most conservative of Democrats, and he has crossed party lines on many issues. He has been a leader of the fiscally conservative Blue Dog Democrats. He supported the Bush administration's 2001 tax cuts, the use of force in Iraq in 2002, and was one of 16 Democrats who voted for the GOP's Medicare prescription drug bill in 2003. But he voted against a constitutional amendment on flag burning, oil drilling in the Arctic National Wildlife Refuge and making the Bush tax cuts permanent.

During the 110th Congress (2007–08), he was the only member of Utah's congressional delegation to co-sponsor a bill to give the Nuclear Regulatory Commission authority to prevent foreign nuclear waste from being brought into the United States. The bill had direct implications for Utah. At the time, the Salt Lake City-based company EnergySolutions, formerly known as Envirocare, was seeking a license to import nuclear waste from Italy, which Matheson opposes. He reintroduced the legislation in 2009. Matheson also opposed the detonation of a 700-ton weapon at the Nevada Test Site. Though the explosive was non-nuclear, it would have created a mushroom cloud and possibly have stirred up radioactive particles in the area. The test was canceled. In the past, Matheson has called for mandatory environmental reviews before resumption of nuclear weapons testing in Nevada. Matheson's father died of cancer as the result of radioactive fallout from nuclear tests.

Over the years, Matheson has been a prime Republican target. In 2002, John Swallow, a three-term state legislator, emphasized his strong support for tax cuts and gun ownership rights, and reminded voters of Matheson's Democratic Party affiliation at every opportunity. Matheson reminded rural voters of his family's local connections and said that Swallow would harm public schools by giving tax money to parents to send their kids to private schools (the 2nd District has the lowest private school enrollment in the nation). Both national parties spent lavishly. Matheson won by 1,641 votes, 49.4%-48.7%, the narrowest victory for any House incumbent that year. Swallow won most of the rural counties by huge margins but lost 59%-39% in Salt Lake County, which cast 60% of the vote. In 2004, Swallow ran again and had support from the deep-pocketed anti-tax group Club for Growth. The House Republican campaign committee also spent nearly $1 million on the contest. Still, Matheson won 55%-43%. In 2006, he raised nearly $2 million and won against state Rep. LaVar Christensen, 59%-37%. Conventional wisdom says he cannot rest in this district, but Matheson's grip on the seat seems to grow stronger with time. He had his best winning percentage to date in 2008, 63% of the vote.

Matheson turned down calls that he run against Republican Sen. Orrin Hatch of Utah in 2006. Eager for him to stay in the House, Democratic leaders in 2007 gave him a seat on the influential Energy and Commerce Committee. His brother, Scott Matheson, ran for governor in 2004 and lost to Republican Jon Huntsman.

THIRD DISTRICT

Jason Chaffetz (R)

Elected 2008, 1st term; b. March 26, 1967, Los Gatos, CA; home, Alpine; Brigham Young U., B.A. 1989; Mormon; married (Julie); 3 children.

Professional Career: Spokesman & public relations, Nu Skin International; Chief of staff to Gov. Jon Huntsman, 2005–08.

DC Office: 1032 LHOB, 20515, 202-225-7751; Fax: 202-225-5629; Web site: chaffetz.house.gov.

State Offices: Provo, 801-851-2500; West Jordan, 801-282-5502.

Committees: *Judiciary* (14th of 16 R): Courts & Competition Policy; Immigration, Citizenship, Border Security & International Law. *Natural Resources* (17th of 20 R): Energy & Mineral Resources; Insular Affairs, Oceans & Wildlife. *Oversight & Government Reform* (14th of 15 R): Federal Workforce, Postal Service & the District of Columbia (RMM); Information Policy, Census & National Archives.

Group Ratings and Key Votes: Newly Elected

Election Results

2008 general	Jason Chaffetz (R)	187,035	(66%)	($409,628)
	Bennion Spencer (D)	80,626	(28%)	($41,601)
	Jim Noorlander (CNP)	17,408	(6%)	($6,160)
2008 primary	Jason Chaffetz (R)	28,618	(60%)	
	Chris Cannon (R)	19,255	(40%)	

Population		Race/Ethnicity		Work	
Pop. 2007:	891,304	White:	80.8%	Private:	82.0%
Change since 2000:	Up 19.7%	Black:	0.6%	Government:	13.0%
Urban:	91.2%	Hispanic:	13.2%	Self-employed:	4.8%
Rural:	8.8%	Asian:	2.0%	Blue collar:	25.7%
Area size:	16,165 sq. mi.	Native Am.:	0.6%	White collar:	59.7%
		Hawaiian:	1.4%	Khaki collar:	0.1%
Age		Two+ races:	1.4%	Other:	14.5%
Median age:	25.7 yrs.			Median income:	$53,832
More than 65 yrs:	6.3%	*Ancestry*		Median home value:	$183,000
Less than 18 yrs:	33.6%	English:	21.3%	Poverty:	10.8%
		German:	8.7%		
Education		Danish:	5.0%	**Military Veterans**	
H.S. grad:	89.1%			% of Pop:	6.7%
College grad:	25.2%				
Grad degree:	7.6%				

Part of the heartland of the Mormon Church in America is in a geographically isolated valley between 11,000-foot peaks of the Wasatch Range and the shores of Utah Lake. It is Provo, the home of Brigham Young University, an institution long known for the conservative views of its faculty, the old-fashioned moral standards it encourages and its welcoming of technological innovation. The Mormon commonwealth, after all, started off with a huge shortage of both labor and water, and its

2008 Presidential Vote		
McCain (R)............................196,063	(67%)
Obama (D) 85,143	(29%)
2004 Presidential Vote		
Bush (R)................................215,205	(77%)
Kerry (D)................................57,185	(20%)
Cook Partisan Voting Index: R + 26		

inhabitants were eager to use technology to compensate and prosper in this fearsome terrain. Provo produced Philo Farnsworth, the inventor of television, and Harvey Fletcher, inventor of the hearing aid. It has become one of America's high-tech centers, the home of Novell and hundreds of other computer-related firms. Overseas missionary work has bequeathed the area with unusual resources in foreign languages.

The 3rd Congressional District of Utah includes all or part of seven counties in central and western Utah. Many of them are remote. During World War II, Japanese-Americans were interned near Topaz in Millard County. The vast majority of its people live in Utah and Salt Lake counties. The 3rd includes the west side of Salt Lake City and the suburbs south of the city, including West Valley City (the state's second-largest city, home to many recent Mormon converts from Polynesia), West Jordan, South Jordan and Riverton. Kennecott, the old mining conglomerate that owns 90,000 acres in Salt Lake and Tooele counties, unloaded some of its landholdings to real estate developers, who have built many subdivisions and the unique Sunrise, a "walkable" community of 30,000 in South Jordan. The district includes almost all of Utah County, with Provo and the string of counties between high-jutting mountains and Utah Lake. Eagle Mountain and Saratoga Springs were created in the early 1990s and have grown rapidly. From 2000 to 2008, the youthful Provo was the third fastest-growing metro area in the nation. Politically, Utah County is heavily Republican; a 2005 study by the nonpartisan Bay Area Center for Voting Research rated Provo as the most conservative city in the United States. Republican President George W. Bush carried the district with 77% in 2004. Republican presidential nominee John McCain won the district with 67% of the vote in 2008.

The new congressman from the 3rd District is Jason Chaffetz, a Republican elected in 2008. Born in Los Gatos, Calif., Chaffetz grew up in Arizona and attended his senior year of high school in Colorado. His family's politics were Democratic, and they boasted one notable tie to the party: His father's first wife, Katharine Dickson, would later enter the national consciousness as "Kitty" while she stumped for votes with her second husband, 1988 Democratic presidential nominee Michael Dukakis. During college, Chaffetz was named an honorary co-chairman of the Dukakis campaign in Utah in 1988. Growing up, Chaffetz had a passion for soccer, but he switched to football when his high school discovered that he made a decent placekicker. He won an athletics scholarship to Brigham Young University, where he converted to Mormonism and began what he views in hindsight as a natural gravitation toward the political right. The lure of the GOP intensified when Chaffetz learned that Jon Huntsman, a prominent Republican businessman from Utah, had given millions of his fortune to cancer research; Chaffetz's mother died of cancer in 1995.

After college, Chaffetz worked in public relations, first as an executive for NuSkin Enterprises, a company selling skin care products, and then at a firm he started with his brother. In 2003, Chaffetz took a brief hiatus from work to volunteer for Republican Jon Huntsman Jr.'s gubernatorial campaign. When his campaign manager abruptly resigned, Huntsman asked Chaffetz, who had barely any political experience, to replace him. After the election, Chaffetz served for one year as the new governor's chief of staff.

Although his residence in Alpine sits just outside the 3rd District, Chaffetz sensed an opportunity in early 2007 as perennial discontent with incumbent Republican Rep. Chris Cannon simmered within the Republican ranks. (The Constitution requires only that House members live in the state they represent, not the district.) Chaffetz entered the race in October, at a steep disadvantage in both cash and name recognition. Chaffetz criticized Cannon's support of President Bush's proposal for a guest worker program and a path to citizenship for illegal immigrants, both deeply unpopular in this conservative district. He called for immediate deportation of all illegal immigrants and the construction of tent cities, ringed by barbed-wire fences, to detain those who had committed crimes while in the United States. Chaffetz also attacked the six-term incumbent's record, faulting Cannon for earmarking funds for special projects in the district and casting him as symptomatic of why Republicans lost their House majority in 2006. His staunchly conservative platform played well at the state Republican convention in May, where he came 10 votes short of the 60% needed to win the GOP nomination outright.

Bush and most of the state's Republican establishment endorsed Cannon, although Huntsman stayed neutral. Cannon attacked Chaffetz as an opportunist and raised more than $840,000 for the race. Chaffetz, by contrast, spent less than $200,000. In the low-turnout June contest, he stacked up big margins in the district's population centers in Salt Lake and Utah counties to win by a whopping 20 percentage points. Although Chaffetz came under fire nationally from some Japanese American interest groups for his advocacy of tent cities, the outcome of the general election in this crimson segment of Utah was never truly in doubt after the primary. Chaffetz won with 66%.

Chaffetz has no plans to relocate into the district he will represent, noting that Utah is on track to pick up another House seat after the 2010 census, and preliminary redistricting plans drawn up by the state Legislature would move Alpine into the 3rd District. But in early 2009, Chaffetz called a bill to give Utah a new fourth House seat unconstitutional on the grounds that it contained a provision to give the District of Columbia a voting House member.

In his first term, Chaffetz said that he would not seek or accept spending earmarks for his district, saying the practice encourages lawmakers to cut backroom deals to benefit their biggest political supporters.

★ VERMONT ★

Early America and contemporary America come together in Vermont. The state is a mixture of the 19th and 21st centuries—maple syrup and Ben & Jerry's ice cream, tiny clapboard villages and carefully zoned towns with unobtrusively signed outlet malls, covered bridges and civil unions. Not so long ago, Vermont seemed an entirely antique state, almost as carefully preserved as its Shelburne Museum, with its barn and jail, railroad station and blacksmith shop, covered bridge, and 37 buildings full of folk art. But in just a few decades, the state has been transformed by newcomers, who were attracted to its antique look but transformed Vermont's culture in their own image. The state may be tiny—the Legislature and Republican Gov. Jim Douglas sparred over the latter's proposal for a tax holiday priced at $2 million, a rounding error in most state budgets—but it can also be cosmopolitan. *The Simpsons Movie* premiered in Vermont's Springfield in July 2007 and *The Dark Knight*, in which Democratic Sen. Patrick Leahy had a cameo role, premiered in his home town of Montpelier in July 2008.

Vermont was first settled by flinty Yankees from Connecticut, and the state showed an independent streak from the beginning. After Ethan Allen's Green Mountain Boys repulsed the British in 1777, this was an independent republic for 14 years, claimed by New York and New Hampshire to no avail. Allen tried to persuade George Washington to make it a new state; several books argue that Vermont never voluntarily joined the United States, but in any case Vermont was admitted as the 14th state in 1791. The economy was almost entirely agricultural, as second sons and daughters from small New England farms struggled to scratch out livings from the rocky soil. Eventually, they quit that struggle and raised dairy cows instead, producing milk for the masses in New York City. Vermont developed commerce as well. With its legendary thriftiness, the state accumulated capital that, invested wisely, was used to build the solid stone office buildings and courthouses, the thick-timbered houses, and gold-topped state Capitol that have remained long after ramshackle wooden buildings of the early19th century have crumbled. Vermont made an economic asset of its maple trees and its quaintness. Beginning in the 1890s, the state government promoted it as a tourist destination and passed a law requiring Vermont maple syrup to be made from only local trees. But Vermont never developed labor-intensive industry, and so over the years it exported people and its population aged. From 1850 to the 1960s, as a result of continuous out-migration, Vermont's population hovered between 300,000 and 400,000. Today, 621,000 people live here, many of whom have no Vermont ancestry at all. Two presidents were born in Vermont, but both made their careers elsewhere—Chester Arthur in New York and Calvin Coolidge in Massachusetts. Two great foreign writers lived there for years—Rudyard Kipling and Aleksandr Solzhenitsyn.

Since the 1960s—perhaps the key date was 1963, when people first outnumbered cows—Vermont has changed rapidly. Its economy has boomed, led by leisure-time industries—ski resorts, summer homes—and high-tech companies in and around the Burlington area on the mostly undeveloped shores of glorious Lake Champlain. You can find big-box retailers in Williston but also ethnic diversity—Vietnamese, Bosnians, Koreans—in Winooski. Sheldon has the highest representation of native Vermonters, 83%, and tiny Buels Gore, a sliver of land left out when the first settlers drew town lines, had a population boom in the 1990s, when it grew from two residents to 12. Homegrown firms started by Baby-Boomer rebels—Ben & Jerry's, founded in 1978, is the archetype—have flourished. The newcomers cherished what novelist Paul Greenberg calls "maple's homespun image." Vermont's population growth from 390,000 in 1960 to well over 600,000 today hasn't come from random settlement. Next-door New Hampshire, trumpeting its low taxes and aversion to government, attracted right-leaning migrants from Massachusetts and elsewhere to settle spanking-new developments. Vermont, proclaiming its desire to preserve the environment and the past, attracted left-leaning migrants from New York and elsewhere who were willing to pay higher taxes and higher prices and submit to tough environmental restrictions for the privilege of living in a seemingly pristine setting. The state's greatest fans may be members of the 251 Club, the 4,000 people who have traveled to all 251 of Vermont's cities and towns.

Public policy played a part in the evolution of Vermont. Back in 1970, Republican Gov. Deane Davis (the last Vermont native to hold the job), facing a primary challenge, pushed through Act 250, a sweeping land-use law that helped give Vermont its environmental reputation. Housing developments and new ski resorts were required to meet 10 environmental criteria and get the approval of five different commissions, with opponents granted a right to appeal. Since then, Vermont has passed its own Clean Air Act that levies a tax on new cars that get less than 20 miles to the gallon. It bans billboards and rooftop air conditioning units. It passed Act 60, which attempted to equalize property taxes throughout the state, and Act 200, which provided state support for regional planning boards. It has a state land trust that buys development rights of farmland to stop the disappearance of family farms. Distressed by the demise of dairy farming—more than half of such farms have gone out of business since 1982—the state government loans money to help farmers buy water buffalo to produce mozzarella. There are now four Wal-Marts in the state, but two of them are in pre-existing buildings. And when Home Depot tried to build a store in one town, the locals insisted on a vegetation-covered roof on which cows could graze. Home Depot

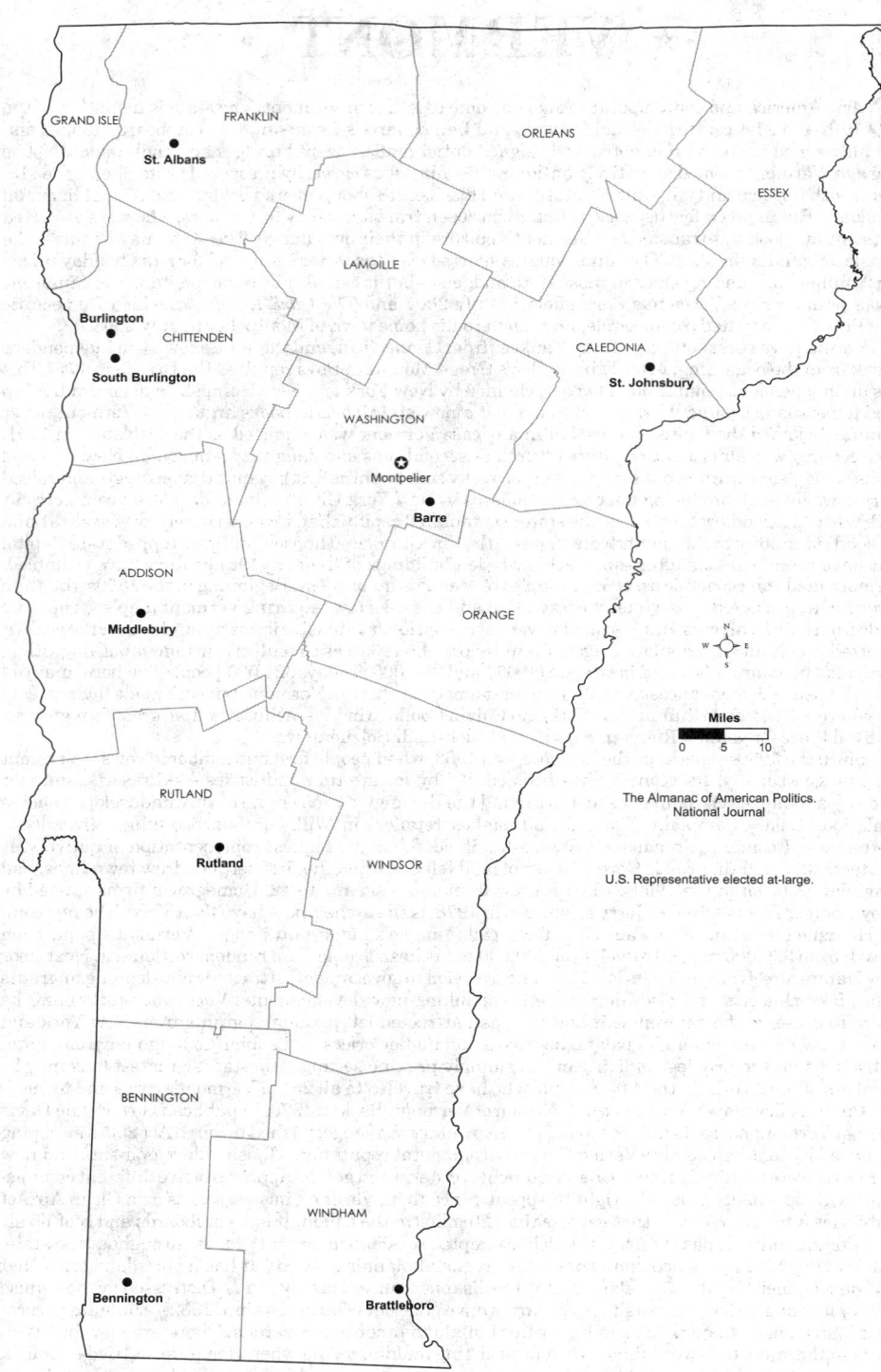

The Almanac of American Politics.
National Journal

U.S. Representative elected at-large.

passed on the idea. Some dairy farmers are processing their animals' solid waste, mixed with bacteria from their digestive systems, into methane fuel. The Grass Energy Collaborative is making fuel pellets from grass and corn; other farmers are making biodiesel fuel from canola beans, sunflower seeds, and flax. An organization called Rural Vermont is pressing for a certification process to allow farmers to sell more than the 50 quarts a day of raw unpasteurized milk that current law allows. But Vermont does not try to regulate everything. It is the one state with no gun control laws, and the state Senate voted for a task force to consider lowering the drinking age to 18.

As Vermont has changed culturally, it has also changed politically. In the 19th century, Yankee Vermont was the most Republican state in the nation; in 1936, Vermont and Maine were the only states to resist Franklin D. Roosevelt's landslide. For three decades thereafter, Vermont's Yankee Protestant Republicans outnumbered its French Canadian and Irish Catholic Democrats. But now, political issues slice Vermont along different lines—between liberal, highly educated newcomers, and conservative, less-educated old Vermonters. In the 2008 presidential election, Vermont was the second-most-Democratic state, after Barack Obama's native Hawaii. Its last Republican member of Congress, James Jeffords, became an independent in May 2001 and voted to make the Democrats the Senate majority party. In January 2003, former Gov. Howard Dean set off to run for president. By July his opposition to the Iraq War (and not his relatively moderate fiscal record in Vermont) made him the leading fundraiser and the front-runner for the Democratic nomination. Vermont, valuing tradition, had become the leader of America's Left.

One issue that made Dean attractive to leftist Democrats was civil unions. Ironically, it was one on which he had not taken the lead. In a lawsuit brought by three same-sex couples, the Vermont Supreme Court ruled that the Legislature had to pass a gay-marriage law or give same-sex couples the same rights under state law as married couples. In April 2000, the Legislature passed a law authorizing civil unions for same-sex couples, and Dean signed it out of sight of cameras. Opposition to civil unions was fierce and vocal, though seldom articulated in the state's liberal press. Groups were formed called Take Back Vermont and Who Would Have Thought, while backers of civil unions and other liberal policies formed a group called Move Vermont Forward. Republican gubernatorial candidate Ruth Dwyer vociferously opposed civil unions. Several pro-civil-union Republican legislators lost their seats in the September primary, and Republicans won control of the state House in November. But Dwyer lost, and Democrats held the state Senate. In subsequent years, the controversy has abated. Both major-party candidates for governor in 2002 opposed repeal. And the legalization of same-sex marriage in neighboring Massachusetts and Connecticut has made Vermont seem moderate by comparison.

Democrats have mostly prevailed since 2000. Vermont voted 51% Democratic for president in 2000, 59% in 2004, and 67% in 2008. Obama carried all but four of the state's 251 cities and towns, and those cast only 370 votes. Democratic Sen. Patrick Leahy has won re-election by very wide margins, and Bernie Sanders, an independent re-elected easily to the House every two years, was elected to Jeffords's Senate seat in 2006 by 65%-32%, while Democrat Peter Welch won the at-large House seat. Yet at the same time, Vermont may have become somewhat less liberal on economic issues. Job losses at IBM and slow economic growth in what had been the booming Burlington area prompted second-guessing of the costs associated with Act 200 and Act 60. In the 2002 election for governor, longtime Republican officeholder Jim Douglas beat Democratic Lt. Gov. Doug Racine, 45%-42%. Douglas's prime goal was revision of Act 200, and in 2004, the Democratic Senate and Republican House voted for major changes. But Vermont's cultural liberalism persisted. Douglas was proud of a law cleaning up Lake Champlain, and he let a medical marijuana bill become law without his signature. Republicans lost their majority in the state House in 2004. After the 2008 election, Democrats held a 95-48 majority there, plus a 23-7 edge in the state Senate—party breakdowns that look almost like Massachusetts. But as Rhode Island, and Connecticut have done for many years, Vermont has voted to keep its Republican governor. Douglas has been re-elected three times by solid margins. Vermont is one of only two states (New Hampshire is the other) that has two-year terms for governor.

Population		Household Income		Work	
Pop. 2007:	620,589	Under $15k:	12.3%	Private:	74.4%
State rank:	49th of 50	$15k to $50k:	38.2%	Government:	14.4%
Change since 2000:	Up 1.9%	$50k to $100k:	33.0%	Self-employed:	10.9%
Urban:	37.3%	$100k to $150k:	14.0%	Unemployment (3-yr. average):	3.5%
Rural:	62.7%	Over $150k:	2.4%	Poverty:	10.7%
Native of state:	52.5%	Median income:	$49,382	Blue collar:	21.2%
Not a citizen:	1.7%	**Home Value**		White collar:	61.0%
Area size:	9,614 sq. mi.	Under $100k:	15.8%	Khaki collar:	0.2%
Most populous cities		$100k to $300k:	62.4%	Other:	17.6%
1. Burlington	38,600	$300k to $500k:	16.0%	**Age**	
2. South Burlington	17,574	$500k to $1 mil:	4.8%	Median age:	40.4 yrs.
3. Rutland	16,742	Over $1 million:	1.1%	More than 65 yrs:	13.3%
4. Essex Junction	9,056	Median:	$191,500	Less than 18 yrs:	21.6%

Race/Ethnicity				Military Veterans		Registered Voters in 2008	
White:	95.4%	*Language*		% of Pop:	11.5%	No party registration	
Black:	0.6%	English:	94.7%	*Veterans by Period*		Voter turnout:	325,046
Hispanic:	1.3%	Spanish:	1.1%	WWII and before:	12.4%	Turnout as % of	
Asian:	1.1%	Asian:	0.6%	Korea:	11.8%	voting age:	66.0%
Native Am.:	0.3%	Other		Vietnam:	34.5%	**General Assembly**	
Hawaiian:	0.0%	European	3.5%	Gulf (pre-2001):	8.7%	Senate:	23 D 7 R
Two+ races:	1.3%	**Education**		Gulf (post-2001):	5.5%	House:	95 D 48 R 7 I
Ancestry		H.S. grad:	89.7%	Peace time:	27.1%		
English:	13.8%	College grad:	32.7%				
Irish:	13.2%	Grad degree:	12.7%				
French:	11.7%			**Cook Partisan Voting Index:** D+13			

Presidential politics

Vermont was the most Republican state in the 1936 presidential election, when Franklin Roosevelt's campaign manager had a good laugh updating an old adage to say, "As goes Maine, so goes Vermont." Times have changed. In 2004, Vermont was the third-most-Democratic state, after Massachusetts and Rhode Island, and in 2008, the second–most-Democratic, after Hawaii. Vermont has become solidly liberal on cultural and foreign issues and it is not very conservative on economics. The state seems downright hostile to conservative national Republicans. Ronald Reagan got his seventh-lowest percentage here in 1980, and in early 2007, some 29 town meetings voted to urge Congress to impeach President Bush. It is the only state that Bush did not visit as president.

The conflict between the old and the new Vermont is apparent in the exit polls. Back in 2000, people without college degrees voted 48%-46% for Bush, but Al Gore carried college graduates 51%-36%, and those with postgraduate degrees 62%-29%. By 2008, the percentage for Obama among those with no college degree was 61%-38%, the split among those with college degrees was 67%-29%, and among those with postgraduate degrees it was 80%-20%. The old divide between Protestants and Catholics has nearly vanished: Obama won 63% of Catholics and 58% of Protestants. But he did even better, 82%, among the 24% of voters who said they had no religion.

2008 Presidential Vote		
Obama (D)	219,262	(67%)
McCain (R)	98,974	(30%)

2008 Democratic Presidential Primary		
Obama (D)	91,901	(59%)
Clinton (D)	59,806	(39%)

2008 Republican Presidential Primary		
McCain (R)	28,417	(71%)
Huckabee (R)	5,698	(14%)
Paul (R)	2,635	(7%)

2004 Presidential Vote		
Kerry (D)	184,067	(59%)
Bush (R)	121,180	(39%)

The Vermont presidential primary, abolished for 1992, reappeared in 1996, but got little notice then and in 2000. Turnout in 2000 was light and tilted Republican because the Democratic race was over. In 2004, Vermont was naturally Dean's campaign headquarters, and though Dean was effectively eliminated by the time Vermont voted on March 2, Vermonters still came out in droves and gave him his only primary victory; turnout was 83,000 Democratic and 27,000 in the uncontested Republican primary. In 2008, Vermont voted on March 4, when the Democratic race was still raging. In the GOP contest, John McCain had only token opposition from Mike Huckabee; turnout was 155,000 Democratic and 40,000 Republican. Obama beat Hillary Rodham Clinton, 59%-39%, but Obama got three times as many votes and Clinton twice as many as John McCain did in winning the Republican primary, 71%-14%.

Governor

Jim Douglas (R)

Elected 2002, term expires Jan. 2011, 4th term; b. June 21, 1951, Springfield, MA; home, Middlebury; Middlebury Col., A.B. 1972; Congregationalist; married (Dorothy); 2 children.

Elected Office: VT House of Reps., 1972–79; Maj. ldr., 1977–79; VT secy. of st., 1980–92; VT treasurer, 1994–2002.

Office: 109 State St., Montpelier, 5609, 802-828-3333; Fax: 802-828-3339; Web site: www.vermont.gov/governor.

Election Results

2008 general	Jim Douglas (R)	170,492	(53%)
	Anthony Pullina (Prog)	69,791	(22%)
	Gaye Symington (D)	69,534	(22%)
2008 primary	Jim Douglas (R)	unopposed	

Prior Winning Percentages: 2006 (56%); 2004 (59%); 2002 (45%)

Republican Jim Douglas was elected governor of Vermont in 2002, an event put in motion 34 years earlier when he decided to attend Middlebury College. Douglas grew up in Longmeadow, Mass. He was a political junkie and a hardy Republican early on, passing out "AuH2O" stickers for Barry Goldwater in 1964, at age 13. In 1968, he enrolled at Middlebury and almost immediately decided to live in the town. His wife, Dorothy, is from Middlebury and they have lived there ever since. Douglas's college years were a time of campus protests against the Vietnam War, but he was unmoved by the liberal politics of the time. He organized a rally for Republican President Nixon in Middlebury in 1970. In 1972, the year he graduated, he ran for state representative from Middlebury and won. He was elected majority leader in 1977. Two years later, he lost a race for House speaker and became an aide to Republican Gov. Richard Snelling. In between sessions of the Legislature, Douglas worked as a radio announcer and became executive director of the local United Way. In 1980, he was elected secretary of state and served for 12 years. In 1992, he ran against Democratic Sen. Patrick Leahy and lost 54%-43%—the closest race Leahy has had since 1980. After working for the Porter Medical Center in Middlebury, Douglas in 1994 spotted an opening for state treasurer and was elected to the first of four terms. By the time he ran for governor, Douglas had been on the Vermont ballot every two years since 1972, and for most of that time, he had gotten up before 6 a.m. to commute over the Green Mountains to the tiny state capital of Montpelier.

His opening to seek the governorship came when Democratic Gov. Howard Dean announced in September 2001 that he would not run again. Dean had been returned to office every two years—Vermont and New Hampshire are the last two states with two-year gubernatorial terms—by advancing a number of innovative policies, which put him on the radar as a possible candidate for president in 2004. But there was discontent in Vermont with some of his policies, especially higher property taxes levied statewide to improve the schools, long delays in land development caused by environmental reviews, and, most of all, job losses and a rising sense that Vermont was developing an anti-business reputation. In his campaign against Democratic Lt. Gov. Douglas Racine, Douglas called for tax cuts and promised to "create a more business-friendly environment." His theme was, it's "time for a change" in a state that had had Democratic governors for 17 of the previous 18 years.

In the initial balloting, Douglas led Racine 45%-42%, with independent Con Hogan, the former director of state human services, receiving 10 %. Under Vermont law, if no candidate receives 50% of the vote, the governor is chosen by a combined vote of the two houses of the Legislature. Republicans entered the campaign with a large majority of legislative seats. Before the election, Racine had said he would not take his candidacy to the Legislature if he won less than 50%, while Douglas had said he would. Then, contrary to most expectations, Democrats made gains in the Legislature that year. But Racine kept his word, and Douglas became governor.

His great success as governor was getting the Legislature to pass in 2004 a bill revising the law that had slowed economic development. Five-member citizen approval boards were abolished and their powers given to a single Environmental Court; opponents of development were no longer given an automatic right to intervene; and developers were allowed to pay for storm-water runoff by offsetting reductions elsewhere. Yet, Douglas was unsuccessful in getting the Legislature to roll back property taxes.

Up for re-election in 2004, Douglas's opponent was Peter Clavelle, the longtime mayor of Burlington and a member of the Progressive Party. Clavelle's major issue was health care; he proposed to use the state's $90 million in Medicaid spending for a universal health care insurance policy for all citizens, and he asserted that it could be paid for with greater efficiencies. Douglas's response was: "I think most Vermonters are pretty skeptical of that." He favored incentives for private insurers, health savings accounts, and initiatives encouraging healthy lifestyles for children. Clavelle called for a statewide ban on smoking in bars, while Douglas preferred to leave the decision to localities. Douglas won handily, 59%-38%, carrying all but one county. However, Democrats that year increased their numbers in the state Senate and replaced a small Republican majority in the House with a large Democratic majority. Douglas's solid re-election performance made him the Republicans' best chance for capturing the seat of retiring Sen. James Jeffords in 2006, but he announced in May 2005 that he would not run.

Health care remained a major issue after the election. In 2005, the Legislature passed a sweeping plan providing near-universal coverage, paid for in part by a tax on payrolls of businesses that did not offer insurance; Douglas vetoed the measure. In 2006, the Legislature tried a more free-market-oriented approach, and Douglas signed it. Going into the 2006 election, Douglas's approval rating was above 60%. He ran on what he called his "Agenda of Affordability," which took aim at the increasingly high cost of living in Vermont, and highlighted what he called a Democratic willingness to raise taxes for more spending. His Democratic opponent, former state Sen. Scudder Parker, struggled to make headway until the fall. Parker criticized Douglas for not doing enough on renewable energy and consistently sought to tie him to President Bush, who had disapproval ratings over 70% in Vermont. "I'm not trying to say Jim equals George," Parker said. "What I am saying is that Jim has consistently supported Bush administration policies and those policies are coming home to have a direct impact on Vermont's budget, Vermont's quality of life." But voters judged Douglas as his own man, and he won, 56%-41%, again carrying all but one county.

In 2007, Douglas fought the Legislature's plan to overhaul campaign finance laws. He criticized contribution limits as too low and as unconstitutional, and the House sustained his veto by one vote. He voiced interest in decriminalization of marijuana, and allowed a bill to become law without his signature that gave farmers the right to grow industrial hemp. He backed federal immigration reform to help Vermont farmers secure sufficient migrant workers. And he advocated making Vermont a "global center" for environmental engineering.

In 2008, Douglas's Democratic opponent was former House Speaker Gaye Symington. Douglas ran on his record of bringing business to the state, reducing taxes, and creating jobs. Symington struggled from the start to find an issue that would work against Douglas, resorting ultimately to small-bore themes—one criticism was that the governor did not reimburse the state for some of his campaign travel expenses. The results were remarkably lopsided considering Symington's prominence. Douglas won with 53% to her 22%. Independent candidate Anthony Pollina, with the Progressive Party, got 22%.

Senior Senator

Patrick Leahy (D)

Elected 1974, term expires 2010, 6th term; b. March 31, 1940, Montpelier; home, Middlesex; St. Michael's Col., B.A. 1961, Georgetown U., J.D. 1964; Catholic; married (Marcelle); 3 children.

Elected Office: VT st. atty., Chittenden Cnty., 1966–74.

Professional Career: Practicing atty., 1964–74.

DC Office: 433 RSOB, 20510, 202-224-4242; Fax: 202-224-3479; Web site: leahy.senate.gov.

State Offices: Burlington, 802-863-2525; Montpelier, 802-229-0569.

Committees: *Agriculture, Nutrition & Forestry* (2nd of 12 D). *Appropriations* (3rd of 18 D): Commerce, Justice, Science & Related Agencies; Defense; Homeland Security; Interior, Environment & Related Agencies; State, Foreign Operations & Related Programs (Chmn); Transportation, Housing and Urban Development & Related Agencies. *Judiciary* (Chmn of 13 D): Immigration, Refugees & Border Security.

Group Ratings

	ADA	ACLU	AFS	LCV	ITIC	NTU	COC	ACU	CFG	FRC
2008	100	93	100	100	80	4	50	4	3	0
2007	95	—	100	80	—	7	36	0	7	—

National Journal Ratings

	2007 LIB — 2007 CONS		2008 LIB — 2008 CONS	
Economic	90%	6%	77%	13%
Social	88%	8%	80%	9%
Foreign	85%	8%	65%	6%
Composite	90%	10%	82%	18%

Key Votes of the 110th Congress

1. Raise CAFE standards	Y	5. Make English official language N	9. Withdraw troops 3/08	Y
2. Expand SCHIP	Y	6. Path to citizenship Y	10. Iran guard is terrorist group N
3. Cap greenhouse gases	Y	7. Fetus is unborn child N	11. Increase missile defense $ N
4. Bail out financial markets	Y	8. Prosecute hate crimes Y	12. Overhaul FISA N

Election Results

2004 general	Patrick Leahy (D)	216,972	(71%)	($1,531,833)
	Jack McMullen (R)	75,398	(25%)	($736,086)
2004 primary	Patrick Leahy (D)	27,459	(95%)	
	Craig Hill (D)	1,573	(5%)	

Prior Winning Percentages: 1998 (72%); 1992 (54%); 1986 (63%); 1980 (50%); 1974 (50%)

Patrick Leahy, Vermont's longest-serving senator, was first elected to the Senate in 1974. He has held public office for most of his adult life. He grew up in Burlington, went to law school at Georgetown University, then returned home to practice law. He was elected Chittenden County state's attorney in 1966, at age 26, and after eight years in that post he ran for the U.S. Senate at age 34. It was 1974, and Leahy had made a name for himself in the tiny state as the Burlington-area prosecutor who tried all major felony cases personally and who attacked the Big Oil companies during the 1970s energy crisis. He had a solid base in Democratic Burlington, together with the kind of quiet, thoughtful temperament that Yankee Vermonters like in their public officials. He outpolled Republican U.S. Rep. Richard Mallary by a narrow margin to win the Senate seat.

Over the years, Leahy has made his mark as chairman of the Judiciary Committee. He was formerly chairman of the Agriculture Committee, and he may chair the powerful Appropriations panel in the next few years, given his seniority. Judiciary handles many of the cultural issues—such as abortion and gun control—that have polarized the two parties and their constituencies, and the committee has been sharply divided at least since the hearings on the Supreme Court nomination of Judge Robert Bork in 1987. In the 1990s, when Republicans were in the majority, Leahy criticized them for holding up President Clinton's judicial appointments, and he stoutly defended Clinton during the impeachment proceedings in 1998 and 1999. When Leahy became chairman during the Democrats' 19 months in the majority in 2001 and 2003, he, in turn, held up the Republicans' judicial nominations. He led the rejection on party-line votes of two judicial nominees for the 5th Circuit and insisted that another nominee produce the memos he had written while working in the office of the solicitor general—an unprecedented demand. As ranking minority member of the committee in 2003–07, Leahy led filibusters against 10 Appeals Court nominees, tactics that the Republicans bitterly attacked. Leahy noted that the committee had approved the vast majority of appellate nominees and almost every trial court nominee, and argued that he had been fairer to President Bush's appointees than Republicans had been to Clinton's.

In 2005, Leahy led the minority's questioning of Bush's Supreme Court nominees John Roberts and Samuel Alito, both of whom were ultimately confirmed by the Senate. The liberal senator surprised many when he voted to approve the conservative Roberts. "I know this will not be popular with many of my constituency, and I understand that," Leahy said. "I came here to do what I thought was right, and as a Vermonter I can do nothing different." He also asked tough questions of Alito, and that time he voted no. He said, "This president is in the midst of a radical realignment of the powers of government and its intrusiveness into the private lives of Americans. This nomination is part of that plan."

Another major chapter in Leahy's tenure as chairman was handling legislation that grew out of the September 11 terrorist attacks. He and his staff worked with the Bush administration to hammer out the USA PATRIOT Act, the sweeping law that sparked a national debate over whether government investigators should be given broader powers at the expense of individual liberties. It was essentially the Senate version, not the House bill, that was enacted in October 2001. But Leahy fought the administration when it sought to expand police powers in the wake of the attacks. He opposed a proposal to allow the government to detain and deport immigrants suspected of terrorism without presenting evidence in court. In 2002, he said that the Justice Department should be required to disclose the number of U.S. citizens being spied on, the number of secret foreign-intelligence wiretaps that had become part of criminal proceedings, and the total number of persons targeted by foreign-intelligence surveillance warrants.

After the story broke on the Abu Ghraib prison scandal in 2004, Leahy sharply criticized the administration, and he strongly disagreed with Bush's declaration that the Geneva Conventions did not apply to unlawful combatants in Afghanistan. In 2005, Leahy objected to the government's surveillance of communications between suspected Al Qaeda terrorists abroad and people in the United States. As chairman in 2007, he made life difficult for Attorney General Alberto Gonzales by requesting an internal investigation of whether Gonzales had told the truth about the warrantless wiretapping program. Leahy subsequently placed Gonzales's successor, Michael Mukasey, on the spot with demands that he denounce the use of waterboarding, a harsh interrogation tactic that simulates drowning and that has been used on terrorism suspects.

Leahy is a gadgeteer and an amateur photographer. He is also an avid student of popular culture, and a huge fan of the *Batman* movies. (He appeared briefly in one of the films, with a speaking part. Leahy tells the Joker, "We're not intimidated by you thugs.") He can recite verses from Shakespeare and lyrics from the Grateful Dead rock band. In 1995, he became the second senator, after Democrat Edward Kennedy of Massachusetts, to set up a personal website, and in 2003, he was the first member of Congress with a blog. Titled "More From the Floor," the site is updated several times a day and informs readers about floor debates and roll-call votes. Leahy's fascination with gadgets helps to explain his interest in patent issues; on the committee, he has fought piracy and counterfeiting. He co-sponsored with Arizona Sen. Jon Kyl, a Republican, legislation making the theft of personal identification information a crime.

Another Leahy cause is the elimination of land mines. Since 1989, he has been crusading against the export and use of land mines, which are easy and cheap to implant yet difficult and expensive to remove. In many places, land mines continue to injure and kill civilians long after hostilities have ended. In 1994, Leahy persuaded the United Nations to unanimously call for the eventual elimination of land mines. On a similar issue, he co-sponsored in 2006 an amendment to ban the use of cluster bombs near civilian sites in Iraq and Afghanistan, but it was defeated 70-30. On other foreign-policy and defense issues, Leahy tends to the left as well. He has been an outspoken critic of the Iraq War. He was one of three senators to vote against authorization of missile defense in March 1999, and he has called for an end to the ban on travel to Cuba.

Leahy is one of the few members of the Agriculture Committee who is not from a state with heavily subsidized crops such as wheat, corn, soybeans, and cotton. As the ranking Democrat on the committee, he worked with Indiana Republican Richard Lugar in the 1990s to phase out the subsidy system. But after their success in passing the Freedom to Farm Act of 1996, crop prices fell, and lawmakers' resolve dissipated; Congress took to voting large annual subsidies in the form of emergency relief to farmers. The 2002 farm bill largely rolled back the 1996 act.

That is not to say that Leahy is not at times as parochial as the next senator. On Agriculture, he is a staunch defender of the interests of the 1,150 dairy farms in Vermont. With the other members of the Vermont and New Hampshire delegations, he pushed successfully in 2006 for a wilderness designation for 42,000 acres in the Green Mountain National Forest. And he helped defeat a Bush administration proposal for a study of a wall between the United States and Canada that would have included the Vermont border.

Leahy has had relatively easy re-election contests. His one close call was in 1980, when he narrowly survived that year's Republican sweep. He defeated Republican Stewart Ledbetter just 50%-49%. Six years later, he was completely rehabilitated politically. In 1986, he defeated popular Gov. Richard Snelling, 63%-35%. Leahy was an early supporter of Illinois Sen. Barack Obama in the 2008 Democratic presidential primaries and should have a reservoir of goodwill with the new administration.

Junior Senator

Bernie Sanders (I)

Elected 2006, term expires 2012, 1st term; b. Sept. 8, 1941, New York, NY; home, Burlington; Attended Brooklyn Col., U. of Chicago, B.A. 1964; Jewish; married (Jane O'Meara Sanders); 4 children.

Elected Office: Burlington mayor, 1981–89; U.S. House of Reps., 1990–2006.

Professional Career: Writer; Dir., Amer. People's Historical Soc., 1977–81; Lecturer, Harvard U., 1989; Prof., Hamilton Col., 1990

DC Office: 332 DSOB, 20510, 202-224-5141; Fax: 202-228-0776; Web site: sanders.senate.gov.

State Offices: Brattleboro, 802-254-8732; Burlington, 802-862-0697; St. Johnsbury, 802-748-9269.

Committees: *Budget* (10th of 13 D). *Energy & Natural Resources* (9th of 13 D): Energy; National Parks; Water & Power. *Environment & Public Works* (6th of 12 D). *Health, Education, Labor & Pensions* (8th of 13 D): Children & Families; Retirement & Aging. *Veterans' Affairs* (4th of 10 D).

Group Ratings

	ADA	ACLU	AFS	LCV	ITIC	NTU	COC	ACU	CFG	FRC
2008	100	93	100	100	60	18	38	8	13	0
2007	95	—	100	93	—	6	27	4	8	—

National Journal Ratings

	2007 LIB — 2007 CONS		2008 LIB — 2008 CONS	
Economic	90%	— 6%	77%	— 13%
Social	88%	— 8%	80%	— 9%
Foreign	98%	— 0%	65%	— 6%
Composite	94%	— 6%	82%	— 18%

Key Votes of the 110th Congress

1. Raise CAFE standards	Y	5. Make English official language	N	9. Withdraw troops 3/08	Y
2. Expand SCHIP	Y	6. Path to citizenship	N	10. Iran guard is terrorist group	N
3. Cap greenhouse gases	Y	7. Fetus is unborn child	N	11. Increase missile defense $	N
4. Bail out financial markets	N	8. Prosecute hate crimes	Y	12. Overhaul FISA	N

Election Results

2006 general	Bernie Sanders (I)	171,638	(65%)	($6,004,222)
	Richard Tarrant (R)	84,924	(32%)	($7,300,392)
2006 primary	Bernie Sanders (D)	35,954	(94%)	

Prior Winning Percentages: 2004 House (67%); 2002 House (64%); 2000 House (69%); 1998 House (63%); 1996 House (55%); 1994 House (50%); 1992 House (58%); 1990 House (56%)

Vermont's junior senator is Bernie Sanders, a Socialist elected as an independent in 2006 but treated as a Democrat in the Senate. Sanders grew up in the Flatbush section of Brooklyn, the son of a paint sales-man who had emigrated from Poland; his mother died when he was a teenager. He became involved in radical leftist politics at the University of Chicago, then came to Vermont as part of the hippie migration of 1968 and worked as a carpenter. Four years later, he ran in a special U.S. Senate election to replace Republican Winston Prouty, who died in office in 1971; Sanders won just 2% of the vote as the candidate of the socialist Liberty Union Party. He went on to lose four more statewide races until his rumpled, tieless, sincere persona finally won over the people of Burlington, who elected him mayor in 1981 by just 10 votes. In 1988, when Republican Rep. James Jeffords ran for the Senate, Sanders made a bid for the House but lost to Republican Peter Smith in a close, three-way race. Two years later, he ran again and reversed the result by capitalizing on Smith's support of the 1990 budget agreement and his vote to ban semiautomatic weapons. The National Rifle Association came out against Smith, and Sanders's opposi-tion to gun control helped him carry 227 of Vermont's 251 cities and towns, plus three gores and one grant, as unincorporated areas in Vermont are known. Sanders became only the third Socialist elected to the House, after Victor Berger of Milwaukee (1911–13, 1923–29) and Meyer London of Manhattan's Lower East Side (1915–23). His views haven't changed much since his first election.

In the House, where Sanders served as Vermont's single, at-large member, Democrats initially balked at accepting him in their caucus, but they granted him seniority as a Democrat when he arrived in 1991. He amassed a heavily liberal voting record and formed a Progressive Caucus with a somewhat quixotic agenda: progressive tax reform, a Canada-style single-payer health care system, a 50% cut in military spending, a national energy policy, and—a Vermont touch—support for family farms.

He was at times a practical and successful legislator, gaining Republican allies in targeting so-called corporate welfare—government benefits to well-heeled companies. With Republican Chris Smith of New Jersey, he passed an amendment barring spending for defense contractor mergers. In 2001, he proposed a $300 per person income-tax rebate. It quickly became Democratic Party policy, and Republicans, in assembling majorities for the Bush tax cuts, included it in diluted form—a $300 rebate for income-tax-paying adults. Sanders and the Democrats noted ruefully that Bush took credit for a tax-cutting proposal that was initially theirs. As much as any member of Congress, Sanders made the cost of prescription drugs a national issue. Since the 1980s, he has called for government programs to pay for prescription drugs, and he was the first member of Congress to lead bus trips to Canada to buy drugs there. He has denounced "the insatiable greed that consumes this runaway [pharmaceutical] industry."

On trade issues, Sanders is predictably on the far left. He has called for repeal of the North American Free Trade Agreement, which organized labor has long opposed, and for a moratorium on new free-trade pacts. He argues that workers in both the United States and foreign nations would be better off without them. On national security, Sanders has been a critic of the Bush administration's anti-terrorism policies, particularly those allowing government investigators to obtain records from libraries and bookstores. As Vermont's lone representative in the House, he was a leading backer of the dairy compact that propped up Northeast dairy prices. After the compact expired in 2001, his bill to establish a national dairy compact passed the House, but was killed in conference committee with the Senate after Midwestern dairy states objected.

All of this played well with Vermont voters, and by the late 1990s, Sanders began winning by large margins as Democratic candidates failed to gain support from the state party, if they filed to run against Sanders at all.

Sanders twice gave serious consideration to challenging Jeffords for his Senate seat. But in May 2001, Jeffords left the Republican Party, an event that gave Democrats a majority in the Senate for 19 months. Like Sanders in the House, Jeffords called himself an independent but caucused with the Demo-crats. In April 2005, Jeffords announced he would not run for another term in 2006. Sanders became the early front-runner and quickly amassed endorsements from top Vermont Democrats, including former Gov. Phil Hoff, Burlington Mayor Peter Clavelle, Senate President Pro Tempore Peter Welch, and House Speaker Gaye Symington. Ever the loner, Sanders said he would neither seek nor accept the Democratic nomination—but, with his consent, Democrats ran his name on the primary ballot anyway. In the Demo-cratic primary, he won 94% of the vote, though he formally declined the nomination and petitioned the state to list him on the general election ballot as an independent. Still, Howard Dean, chairman of the Democratic National Committee and a former Vermont governor, declared, "A victory for Bernie Sanders is a win for Democrats."

On the Republican side, Gov. Jim Douglas was considered the strongest Republican candidate, but he declined to run. Richard Tarrant, a multimillionaire businessman and former high school basketball star, became the nominee. His campaign was almost entirely self-funded: He spent $7.3 million of his own money, much of it on television commercials. His ads sought to portray Sanders as an ineffective radical who was soft on sexual predators and drug dealers. The strategy might have worked elsewhere but not in Vermont, where voters were well acquainted with Sanders and his iconoclastic ways. Despite the harsh attacks—or perhaps because of them—Tarrant was never able to close the gap in the polls. He outspent Sanders, but Sanders also proved to be well funded. He raised and spent over $6 million, many times more than ever before and enough to make this the costliest race in state history. Sanders won easily, 65%-32%.

He settled with surprising ease into the Senate's more structured ways, and he grew more sensitive to his reputation as a troublemaker. Democrat Patrick Leahy, the state's senior senator, told a Vermont reporter that other senators confided to him "what a pleasant surprise [Sanders] has turned out to be" with his willingness to forge legislative deals. With seats on committees that deal with energy and environment issues, Sanders worked for deep cuts in industrial pollution in the global-warming bill. He sought to promote new technology to reduce emissions in the automobile and energy industries. In 2007, the Senate passed his amendment to the energy bill to encourage universities to support energy-efficient projects. Sanders also resumed his opposition to international trade deals, blaming them for lowering domestic wages and shuttering U.S. factories.

Sanders remains a fervent opponent of the Iraq war, but none of his amendments to set a deadline for withdrawal were enacted. In another futile gesture, he delayed for weeks the confirmation of Jim Nussle as director of the White House Office of Management and Budget; Nussle, he said, "doesn't get the economic realities facing working people in our country." Over time, Sanders has become the very definition of "liberal" in Congress—Democratic Sen. Barack Obama of Illinois was chagrined to learn that he had amassed a more liberal voting record than Sanders in 2007, a fact that was used against him by some critics during his presidential campaign.

Representative-At-Large

Peter Welch (D)

Elected 2006, 2nd term; b. May 2, 1947, Springfield, MA; home, Hartland; Col. of the Holy Cross, A.B. 1969, U. of CA, J.D. 1973; Catholic; married (Margaret Cheney); 8 children.

Elected Office: VT Senate, 1980–88, 2001–2006; VT Senate min. ldr., 1982–84; VT Senate pres. pro tem, 1985–88, 2002–06.

Professional Career: Robert F. Kennedy fellow, 1969–70; Practicing atty., 1974–2006.

DC Office: 1404 LHOB, 20515, 202-225-4115; Fax: 202-225-6790; Web site: www.welch.house.gov.

State Offices: Burlington, 802-652-2450.

Committees: *Energy & Commerce* (36th of 36 D): Communications, Technology & the Internet; Energy & Environment; Oversight & Investigations. *Oversight & Government Reform* (21st of 24 D): Domestic Policy; National Security & Foreign Affairs. *Standards of Official Conduct* (5th of 5 D).

Group Ratings

	ADA	ACLU	AFS	LCV	ITIC	NTU	COC	ACU	CFG	FRC
2008	90	91	100	92	86	13	56	8	4	0
2007	95	—	100	95	—	5	55	0	6	—

National Journal Ratings

	2007 LIB — 2007 CONS		2008 LIB — 2008 CONS	
Economic	77%	— 23%	76%	— 24%
Social	89%	— 8%	59%	— 38%
Foreign	75%	— 24%	85%	— 8%
Composite	81%	— 19%	75%	— 25%

Key Votes of the 110th Congress

1. Increase minimum wage	Y	5. Share immigration data	N	9. Withdraw troops 8/08	Y
2. Expand SCHIP	Y	6. Foreign aid abortion ban	N	10. No operations in Iran	Y
3. Raise CAFE standards	Y	7. Ban gay bias in workplace	Y	11. Free trade with Peru	N
4. Bail out financial markets	Y	8. Repeal D.C. gun law	Y	12. Overhaul FISA	N

Election Results

2008 general	Peter Welch (Democrat/Republican)	248,203	(83%)	($58,128)
	Mike Bethel (I)	14,349	(5%)	
	Jerry Trudell (I)	10,818	(4%)	
	Thomas Hermann (I)	9,081	(3%)	
	Cris Ericson (I)	7,841	(3%)	
2008 primary	Peter Welch (D)	19,566	(88%)	
	Craig Hill (D)	2,635	(12%)	

Prior Winning Percentages: 2006 (53%)

Vermont's only House member is Peter Welch, a Democrat first elected in 2006. He grew up in Springfield, Mass., the son of a dentist, and graduated from Holy Cross College. The summer before his junior year, he worked for a Jesuit group that did community outreach in poor black neighborhoods in Chicago. While there, he was inspired by a speech by the Rev. Martin Luther King Jr., a leader of the growing civil-rights movement in the 1960s. After graduating from law school at the University of California, Berkeley, Welch backpacked down the Pan-American Highway to Santiago, Chile, went overland to Salvador and Brazil, then worked on a freighter that sailed to Portugal. After that, he was ready to settle down to practice law, and chose White River Junction, Vt. He married a professor at Dartmouth, just across the river, and became a stepfather to Joan Smith's five children. In 1980, Welch was elected as only the second Democrat to represent Windsor County in the state Senate—and the first since the Civil War. In 1982, he became Senate minority leader. In 1984, after Democrats won a majority in the Senate for the first time ever, he was elected Senate president pro tem. He focused on environment, education, and tax issues and helped establish the Housing and Land Conservation Trust, which worked to create affordable housing and to conserve farmland and forests. In 1988, when Republican Rep. James Jeffords ran for the Senate, Welch aimed for the U.S. House but lost the Democratic primary by 266 votes. In 1990, Welch ran for governor but lost 52%-46% to Republican Richard Snelling. For some years after that, Welch retired from political life. His wife, Joan, who had been his closest adviser and campaign manager, fought cancer for nine years, and Welch at times was her full-time caregiver. She died in 2004.

In 2001, Democratic Gov. Howard Dean appointed Welch to the state Senate to fill a vacancy in Windsor County. In 2003, he became president pro tem once again and focused on health care issues. He also helped negotiate a deal for the storage of spent nuclear fuel on the site of the Vermont Yankee nuclear power plant. In the spring of 2005, Sen. Jeffords announced he would not seek re-election in 2006. Socialist Rep. Bernie Sanders, after 15 years in the House, announced he would run for the Senate seat and attracted little opposition. So Welch decided to run once again for the U.S. House, this time for the seat that Sanders was giving up. He was supported by many Democratic leaders and, although other potential candidates canvassed for support, no one else ended up running, and Welch won the September 2006 primary unopposed. The winner of the Republican primary, by 71%-28%, was Martha Rainville, the commander of the Vermont National Guard, who had a sterling résumé. A Navy brat born on a base in Connecticut, she graduated from the University of Mississippi, enlisted in the Air Force in 1979, and, after four years of active duty, served in the Air National Guard. In 1997, she was chosen by the Legislature to serve as state Adjutant General, becoming the first woman to command a state's National Guard. Welch campaigned as an opponent of military action in Iraq from the start, and he condemned the "corrupt" Republicans in Washington. He supported a universal health care program and called for the resignation of Defense Secretary Donald Rumsfeld. Rainville said she would have voted for military action in Iraq in 2002 given what was known then, but she also criticized some of the Bush administration's decisions since. Both candidates favored access to abortion.

Both also pledged not to run negative campaigns, and this was probably the only seriously contested 2006 House race in the country without a single negative ad on the airwaves. But there was dispute. Welch called Rainville the "hand-picked" candidate of the by then unpopular national Republicans. Rainville countered that Vermont Republicans are "something very different," and insisted that "the party has a lot of room for diversity." Welch spent $1.7 million to Rainville's $1.1 million. But the House Republican campaign committee outspent its Democratic counterpart, $750,000 to $300,000. This was one of the few Democratic seats that Republicans thought they had a good chance of picking up. (Though technically not a Democrat, Sanders had caucused voted with the Democrats.) The contest was close in the polls throughout the summer, but by late September Welch began opening up a lead. Rainville was embarrassed when she was forced to fire a speechwriter in early October for plagiarizing from Democratic Sen. Hillary Rodham Clinton of New York. Welch won, 53%-45%.

In the House, Welch quickly became one of the most active and legislatively savvy members of the large freshman class, though he retained an understated and collegial style. He was one of four freshman Democrats to get a seat on the Rules Committee, an influential, leadership-run panel that establishes the procedures for any bill coming to the floor. With his legislative experience, he became a player on a range of issues. "It's like he has been here for years. He is connected in every way," an admiring Democratic leadership aide said. Welch took the lead in urging the Environmental Protection Agency to approve a waiver for California's stricter tailpipe-emissions standards. During debate on a higher-education bill, the House passed his amendment to require universities to report to Congress how they are using their endowment to reduce costs for middle-class families. He also won passage of his proposal to close a loophole that exempted overseas government contracts from federal reporting requirements. In 2009, he got a seat on the influential Energy and Commerce Committee.

At home, Welch secured his seat early and faced no serious re-election threat. Perhaps his most difficult challenge at home was a March 2007 protest outside his White River Junction office by anti-war activists who demanded the impeachment of Bush; they were arrested after failing to leave his office. Shortly after his first term ended, Welch remarried. In 2009, he tied the knot with state Rep. Margaret Cheney over recess. The couple held their reception at the Norwich Inn in Vermont, the setting for the 1980s television comedy series *Newhart*.

★ VIRGINIA ★

In Virginia, with a bustling economy and sometimes painful growth, traditions endure. Through 400 years of history, Virginians have honored, and sometimes have been transfixed by traditions going back to the American Revolution and earlier. For the last half-century, Virginia has been growing lustily. After World War II, its growth was mainly sparked by expanding employment in the federal government; in more recent years, the state has developed a vibrant private sector as well. But the first state in the nation to elect an African-American governor in some ways has still hewn to a course close to its roots. The first Virginia was a commonwealth ruled by a landed gentry that, in the words of historian David Hackett Fischer, was "elitist and libertarian." From the tobacco-growing counties then emerged in the 1770s a group of leaders—George Washington, George Mason, Patrick Henry, Thomas Jefferson, Richard Henry Lee, and James Madison—that in learning, wisdom and strength of character, equaled any such group from any similarly sized polity since Periclean Athens or republican Rome. They were slaveholders who insisted on liberty, armed men who insisted on the rule of law, and believers in racial inequality who set forth principles of equality that would in time form the basis of a non-racist society. The Virginia they led into the American Revolution was not only the most populous and the richest of the 13 colonies, but it also was the indispensable creator of the republic and the Constitution that has held together the world's greatest democracy.

After the Revolutionary War, control by the gentry continued even as Virginia was eclipsed in population and wealth by Pennsylvania and New York and, its tobacco fields all but exhausted, became a breeding ground for slaves. But Virginia had two more great heroes, Robert E. Lee and Stonewall Jackson, both of whom reluctantly and brilliantly fought for their state rather than the larger nation. Virginia's leadership class was impoverished and embittered by the Civil War, so much of which was fought on Virginia soil. Industrialization was haphazard. Railroads were constructed to ship cotton up from the South and coal east to the seaports. Textile mills were built in Southside towns and tobacco factories in Richmond. The giant Newport News Shipbuilding & Drydock Company was built by railroad magnate Collis Huntington. Politically, Virginia was ruled by local gentry who worshipped their revolutionary past and mourned their "Lost Cause" of the Confederacy. They were pessimists, looking not for economic growth but for stability, bent on maintaining Virginia's segregation and content with its second-class economy. County courthouse organizations became the political machine of Harry Byrd, who ran Virginia politics from 1925, when he was elected governor, until 1965, when he retired from the U.S. Senate. In national politics, this machine lost battles more often than Lee lost on the battlefield, and less gallantly. For years, the machine succeeded in keeping most vestiges of racial equality out of Virginia, to the point of closing public schools in the 1950s rather than obeying federal court desegregation orders.

This "massive resistance" collapsed in the late 1950s. Virginia's demographics were changing and its politics went through a quarter-century of flux. The government-employee-filled Northern Virginia suburbs of Washington D.C. and the industrial Tidewater region around Norfolk and Newport News, plus the enfranchisement of blacks, provided a political base for liberal Democrats. In the years since, Virginia has undergone a demographic revolution. In 1970, its major metropolitan areas, as then defined, included only a minority of the state's residents: Northern Virginia had just 12%, Tidewater 17%, and metro Richmond 10%. The rest of Virginia—rural, small town, small industrial and textile mill cities—had 61% of the state's population, and was solidly conservative. Most African-Americans didn't vote and the poll tax held down voting among whites. With less than half Virginia's population, West Virginia cast more votes in 1960. Nearly 40 years later, in 2008, Virginia's population was 67% larger. Northern Virginia had spread out into once rural counties, some of which were the nation's fastest growing exurbs in the 1990s and early 2000s, and accounted for 32% of the state's population. Tidewater, spreading out into swampy lands on either side of the James River, accounted for another 21%. Metropolitan Richmond expanded outward in every direction and accounted for 16% of the state's population. The traditional Virginia had shrunk, geographically and demographically. Left with the Northern Neck and the two Eastern Shore counties in the east and Southside Virginia, the Shenandoah Valley and the mountains of southwest Virginia, it accounted for only 31% of the state's population.

Growth and change produced unstable politics. In the 1970s, conservatives who left the Democratic Party and ran as independents or Republicans held Democrats at bay. In the 1980s, three moderate Democrats were elected governor—Charles Robb in 1981, Gerald Baliles in 1985, and Douglas Wilder in 1989—because they did not represent an attempt to impose a liberal agenda on an unwilling Virginia, and because they argued they could use government effectively to improve education and build the state's economy. Wilder's election was a national breakthrough, a successful attempt by an African-American politician to campaign and to govern on equal terms. His fiscal conservatism, which resulted in sharp spending cuts in the early 1990s, like his elegant manners and thick Richmond accent, echoed Virginia's elitist and libertarian tradition; his insistence on the rule of law helped him win election as Richmond's mayor in 2004.

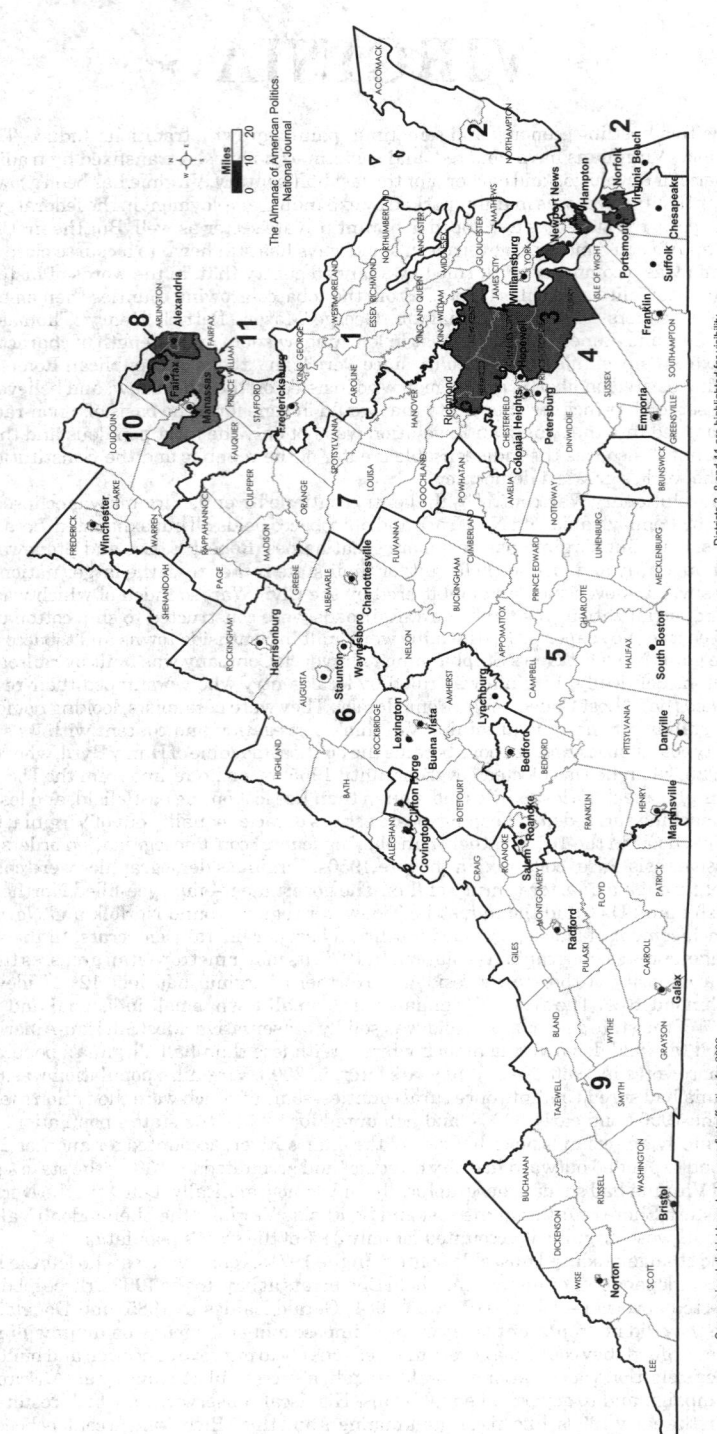

The Almanac of American Politics.
National Journal

Districts 3, 8 and 11 are highlighted for visibility.

Congressional district boundaries were first effective for 2002.

In the 1990s, Virginia developed ideological politics along party lines, and Republicans made historic strides by winning majorities with traditional party platforms. George Allen was elected governor by a wide margin in 1993 as a Republican who believed in lower taxes, traditional cultural values, longer prison terms, and teaching basic skills—he combined confrontational issue positions with a sunny temperament. In the 1997 contest for governor (Virginia is the last state which bars its governors from running for re-election, another tradition that endures), Republican James Gilmore made his centerpiece issue the phasing out of the property tax on automobiles, and won a 56%-43% victory over Democrat Don Beyer. Republicans for the first time swept the top three statewide offices. In 1999, Gilmore led Republicans to legislative majorities in both chambers for the first time ever.

But the first decade of the 2000s belonged to the Democrats. Republicans haven't won a contested race for senator or governor since 2000. The first Democratic winner was cell phone millionaire Mark Warner, who won the governorship in 2001 primarily due to an intensive 18-month campaign in rural Virginia, where he paid attention to the parts of the state not blessed by 1990s growth. Warner carried Northern Virginia and the Hampton Roads area only narrowly. But he also carried non-urban Virginia, which Republican presidential candidate George W. Bush had won 56%-41% the year before. Warner's big success was persuading the Legislature to raise taxes by a record amount in 2004. The Republican state Senate wanted to raise them even more, but a lot of arms had to be twisted to get the needed votes in the Republican House of Delegates. The key impetus for raising taxes was the demand for more roads and mass transit in Northern Virginia and Tidewater. As it turned out, revenues poured in and produced a big surplus. Warner left office with high ratings and, after considering a run for president in 2008, instead ran for Republican Sen. John Warner's open Senate seat and won in a landslide.

Warner's victory was the first of several Democratic breakthroughs, fueled in large part by changes in the Northern Virginia electorate. Great surges of Hispanic and Asian immigrants filled downscale neighborhoods inside the Capital Beltway, and singles apartment buildings went up in Arlington and Alexandria. Meanwhile, more conservative whites moved out to the exurbs. Young professionals moving into the suburbs, originally averse to higher taxes, embraced them as they languished for hours in rush hour traffic. And they were repelled by the Republicans' embrace of conservative rural values. Bush carried Northern Virginia in 2000, and then lost it four years later, 51%-48%; it was one of the few metropolitan areas in the nation where his vote fell off in 2004. In 2008, Northern Virginia passed a milestone in its transformation by voting 49%-47% for Democrat Barack Obama for president. This trend was presaged by the election of Democrat Tim Kaine as governor in 2005, over Republican Jerry Kilgore, whose deep mountain accent and hard-line conservative stands were a hard sell in Northern Virginia. Kaine won the area 58%-40% and carried exurban Loudoun and Prince William counties as well. He won statewide 52%-46%. In 2006, Republican Allen was expected to win re-election to the Senate easily, and even contemplated a presidential campaign. But Jim Webb, a Navy secretary in the Reagan administration but now a Democrat, campaigned against the Iraq war and carried Northern Virginia 57%-42%, on his way to a 50%-49% statewide win. In 2008, Obama's campaign did brilliant work registering African-American voters all over the state and new, young voters in Northern Virginia and in college towns. When Obama won the state in November, Kaine proclaimed, "Old Virginny is dead. We are a new and dynamic and exciting commonwealth."

But Virginia politics may be ready for another turn. Democratic turnout was low in special elections for the Legislature and Fairfax County offices in early 2009. Democrats had a tough, three-way gubernatorial primary in June, with state Sen. Creigh Deeds finally winning the nod to face Republican Bob McDonnell, elected attorney general by just 323 votes in 2005 over Deeds, who was the Democratic nominee. Their respective primary victories set up a rematch in November 2009, this time for governor. McDonnell deemphasized the crime and cultural issues he had worked on for years and ran as a jobs candidate at a time when Virginia was hit fairly hard by the national recession. Over the past 40 years, Virginia's tradition has been to switch parties about once every decade and, every time a new party has won the presidency starting in 1976, to elect a governor of the other party the following year.

Population		Household Income		Work	
Pop. 2007:	7,636,644	Under $15k:	10.9%	Private:	72.0%
State rank:	12th of 50	$15k to $50k:	32.1%	Government:	22.5%
Change since 2000:	Up 7.9%	$50k to $100k:	32.1%	Self-employed:	5.3%
Urban:	72.4%	$100k to $150k:	19.6%	Unemployment (3-yr. average):	3.3%
Rural:	27.6%	Over $150k:	5.4%	Poverty:	9.9%
Native of state:	50.6%	Median income:	$58,378	Blue collar:	20.3%
Not a citizen:	5.8%			White collar:	63.0%
Area size:	42,774 sq. mi.	**Home Value**		Khaki collar:	1.6%
		Under $100k:	16.6%	Other:	15.1%
Most populous cities		$100k to $300k:	42.1%		
1. Virginia Beach	436,903	$300k to $500k:	22.0%	**Age**	
2. Norfolk	237,309	$500k to $1 mil:	16.9%	Median age:	36.8 yrs.
3. Chesapeake	218,145	Over $1 million:	2.5%	More than 65 yrs:	11.6%
4. Arlington	201,798	Median:	$238,600	Less than 18 yrs:	23.9%

Race/Ethnicity				Military Veterans		Registered Voters in 2008	
White:	67.5%	*Language*		% of Pop:	13.2%	No party registration	
Black:	19.4%	English:	87.0%	*Veterans by Period*		Voter turnout:	3,723,260
Hispanic:	6.3%	Spanish:	5.8%	WWII and before:	8.1%	Turnout as % of	
Asian:	4.7%	Asian:	3.1%	Korea:	8.1%	voting age:	62.6%
Native Am.:	0.2%	Other		Vietnam:	28.9%	**General Assembly**	
Hawaiian:	0.1%	European	3.1%	Gulf (pre-2001):	17.7%	Senate:	21 D 19 R
Two+ races:	1.6%	**Education**		Gulf (post-2001):	15.0%	House of	
Ancestry		H.S. grad:	85.3%	Peace time:	22.1%	Delegates:	45 D 53 R 2 I
German:	11.0%	College grad:	32.9%				
English:	10.0%	Grad degree:	13.3%				
USA:	9.2%						

Presidential politics Long ignored in presidential politics, Virginia was a major battleground in 2008. In the first half of the 20th century, it was part of the solid Democratic South. From 1952 to 1960, it obeyed the "golden silence" of Democratic Sen. Harry Byrd and voted Republican. It voted narrowly for Democrat Lyndon Johnson for president in 1964, and then voted Republican in the next 10 elections. But over time the margins narrowed. Democrat Bill Clinton lost here by only 48%-46% in 1996. In 2000, George W. Bush won 52%-44%. In 2004, Democrats, heartened by Mark Warner's election as governor in 2001, targeted the state early. John Kerry spent $1 million in advertising in the spring and early summer. But in August, the polls showed Bush well ahead, and Virginia dropped off the target list. Bush lost Northern Virginia 51%-48% and his statewide margin was reduced to 54%-45%, just 3 percentage points above his national average.

2008 Presidential Vote
Obama (D) 1,959,532 (53%)
McCain (R)..........................1,725,005 (46%)

2008 Democratic Presidential Primary
Obama (D) 627,820 (64%)
Clinton (D) 349,766 (35%)

2008 Republican Presidential Primary
McCain (R)............................244,829 (50%)
Huckabee (R) 199,003 (41%)

2004 Presidential Vote
Bush (R) 1,716,959 (54%)
Kerry (D)..............................1,454,742 (45%)

In 2008, Democrat Barack Obama targeted Virginia from start to finish, with satisfying results. His organizing efforts for the February 12 primary gave him a head start. He won the primary 64%-35% over Hillary Rodham Clinton—one of his best showings in the nation. Still, Republicans had difficulty believing polls showing Obama leading throughout most of the summer and fall, but the polls proved accurate. He won the state 53%-46%, exactly at the national average, running 8 percentage points ahead of John Kerry's showing in 2004. Another way to look at it: Republican nominee John McCain got 8,000 more votes than Bush; Obama got 505,000 more votes than Kerry.

In Northern Virginia, the Obama campaign registered immigrants and young singles and carried the region 59%-40%. In Tidewater and metro Richmond, there was more emphasis on registering African-Americans, and turnout rose 19% and 20%, respectively, way ahead of population growth in those two areas. Obama ran 10 percentage points ahead of Kerry in Tidewater, winning 56%-43%, and 9 percentage points ahead of Kerry in metro Richmond, winning an area assumed to be staunchly Republican by 53%-47%. In the rest of the state, Obama ran only 5 percentage points ahead of Kerry. The county returns show sharp improvement in areas with many African-Americans. The Obama campaign opened offices and canvassed in counties where no one had ever seen a Democratic operation before. But that was not effective everywhere. In the Shenandoah Valley, where there are few blacks, he ran only slightly ahead of Kerry, and in southwest Virginia, where there are almost none, turnout was down and Obama's percentages were lower than Kerry's. The impact of Obama's organization was apparent from the exit poll showing that 22% of voters were contacted by his campaign compared to 10% contacted by McCain's. Obama did not triumph everywhere. He lost non-college whites 66%-32% and young whites 56%-42%. But white Democrats stuck with him 86%-14%. Quite clearly, the state that elected a black governor 19 years earlier was not averse to electing a black president.

Virginia has not had much of a tradition of presidential primaries, but that changed in 2008 as well. Virginia did hold presidential primaries on the original Super Tuesday in March 1988, when it voted for Republican George H. W. Bush and Democrat Jesse Jackson, but it then switched back to choosing delegates at state conventions. Republicans held a primary in 2000, in which George W. Bush beat McCain 53%-44%. In 2004, Virginia held its presidential primary in February in order to gain the attention of presidential candidates and the national media. But candidate Wesley Clark concentrated on Tennessee and John Edwards split his time between Tennessee and southwest Virginia. They may have thought that Kerry had an insuperable lead in Northern Virginia. As it turned out, Kerry carried every part of the state and won 52% of the vote, to 27% for Edwards and 9% for Clark.

For 2008, Virginia scheduled primaries for February 12, one week after Super Tuesday. Many people had expected both nominations to be settled by then, but the Democratic nomination was still very much in play and the Republican nomination, though pretty obviously headed to McCain, was still being contested. Obama showed his mettle in this contest, out-organizing the Clinton campaign and, with his big victories the same day in Maryland and the District of Columbia, generating an enthusiasm that proved to be contagious for the rest of the month. He went on to win 11 straight contests. Turnout was 986,000, more than double the 396,000 in 2004. Obama won 64%-35%, his biggest percentage in any primary but those in the District of Columbia (75%), Georgia (66%) and Illinois (65%). Obama carried Northern Virginia 61%-39%, running well in upscale areas as usual. But he also won over 70% of the vote in Tidewater and metro Richmond, reflecting a major effort at turning out black voters. He even prevailed, 54%-45%, in the rest of the state. Clinton carried only one of the 11 congressional districts, the "Fighting 9th" in southwest Virginia.

The Republican contest attracted less attention, and, significantly in a state with no party registration, only about half as many voters, 489,000. McCain beat Mike Huckabee 50%-41%. Most of McCain's margin came from Northern Virginia, where he won 60% of the votes. He got 49% in Tidewater, 52% in metro Richmond and only 41% in the rest of the state, as Huckabee carried almost everything west of the big metro areas. McCain's high mark was in Alexandria, just outside Washington, where he got 70% of the vote. Huckabee's was in Campbell County, just outside of Lynchburg and within hailing distance of the late Rev. Jerry Falwell's Liberty University, where he got 71% of the vote.

Congressional districting

111th Congress Lineup	
6 D	5 R
110th Congress Lineup	
8 R	3 D

Republicans won control of both houses of the Virginia Legislature in 1999 and, with Republican Jim Gilmore as governor, controlled the redistricting process in 2001 for the first time ever. Republican legislators promptly drew new lines, which made relatively minimal changes. They moved some black precincts from the 4th District to the 3rd and increased its black majority, while making the 4th more secure. They followed the wishes of the three Northern Virginia incumbents, two Republicans and one Democrat, who all strengthened themselves. They made the 9th District, held for many years by Democrat Rick Boucher, a little more Republican, but it would have been difficult to do otherwise without drawing a geographical monstrosity. Bobby Scott, of the black-majority 3rd District, raised questions about the 3rd and 4th District lines, but the U.S. Justice Department approved the plan.

In 2007 and again in 2009, the Republican-controlled House of Delegates rejected a proposal for a nonpartisan redistricting procedure. Democrats won a 21-19 majority in the state Senate in 2007, which has four-year terms. That should assure them of at least a veto on any redistricting plan, provided they can hold together. (They are split between metro and rural members.) Republicans won a 53-45 margin in the state House in 2007, with two independents. That could conceivably be overturned in 2009, although most Virginia House seats have not been seriously contested in recent years. So it is likely that neither party will be in control. Since Virginia is not expected to gain a House seat in the reapportionment following the 2010 census, the legislators and the new governor might opt to compromise on an incumbent-protection plan. But it's not clear who the incumbents will be. In 2008, Democrats captured the 2nd and 5th districts by narrow margins, and the 11th District by a wider margin. Republicans may have a chance to win one or more of these seats back in 2010. In any case, Virginia is one more example of how partisan redistricting can be unavailing over the course of an intercensal decade: Republicans devised this plan, but Democrats now hold six of the 11 seats.

Governor

Tim Kaine (D)

Elected 2005, term expires Jan. 2010, 1st term; b. Feb. 26, 1958, St. Paul, MN; home, Richmond; Univ. of MO, B.A. 1979, Harvard U., J.D. 1983; Catholic; married (Anne Holton); 3 children.

Elected Office: Richmond City Cncl., 1994–98; Mayor, 1998–2001; Lt. gov., 2001–05.

Professional Career: Practicing atty., 1983–2000.

Office: Patrick Henry Bldg., 3rd Floor, 1111 E. Broad St., Richmond, 23219, 804-786-2211; Fax: 804-371-6351; Web site: www.governor.virginia .gov.

Election Results

2005 general	Tim Kaine (D)	1,025,942	(52%)
	Jerry Kilgore (R)	912,327	(46%)
2005 primary	Tim Kaine (D)	unopposed	

Democrat Tim Kaine was elected governor of Virginia in 2005. He grew up in Overland Park, Kan., a suburb of Kansas City, where his father was an electrical engineer who opened a small manufacturing business and his mother taught home economics. He attended the University of Missouri, where he graduated in three years, then went on to Harvard Law School. Midway through, Kaine left to spend nine months teaching at a Jesuit mission in Honduras, then returned to complete his law degree in 1983. It was there that he met his wife, Anne Holton, the daughter of Linwood Holton, Virginia's first Republican governor in the 20th century. They settled in Richmond, where Kaine went into private practice as a civil rights attorney. In 1994, he defeated an incumbent to win a seat on the Richmond City Council, and four years later he was elected mayor. His record as mayor was closely scrutinized in 2001 when he ran for lieutenant governor. His opposition to the death penalty and support for gun restrictions and abortion rights led his conservative opponent to paint him as an extreme liberal. Kaine talked about setting aside political divisions, focused on quality of life issues and won a narrow 50%-48% victory.

Virginia's lieutenant governorship does not confer much responsibility, but it is an excellent platform for running for governor. Kaine immediately was assumed to be the Democratic Party's leading candidate for governor in 2005. Republicans also had a presumptive nominee: Jerry Kilgore, a conservative former prosecutor from southwest Virginia who was elected attorney general at the same time Kaine was elected lieutenant governor. Democratic Gov. Mark Warner, who was considering running for president, took an interest in electing his successor. In a mutually beneficial arrangement, he campaigned across the state with Kaine and raised money for him in the hopes of polishing his own legacy and proving himself as a serious national candidate with an ability to connect with red-state voters. Kaine, in turn, sought to tap into Warner's popularity. He frequently touted the accomplishments of the "Warner-Kaine administration" and framed his candidacy as an opportunity to continue Warner's policies.

Yet Kaine ran with a dramatically different strategy than the one Warner successfully employed in 2001. Warner had called himself a "fiscal conservative" and pledged not to raise the income or sales taxes. He opposed any new gun control laws and wooed the National Rifle Association, which remained neutral, quite a victory for a Democrat. He ran ads featuring old pickup trucks and bluegrass music, and he traveled to all parts of rural Virginia to build an urban-rural coalition. That approach was hardly practical for Kaine, a former big-city mayor who held positions well to the left of Kilgore. Instead, Kaine pitched a quality-of-life agenda designed to appeal to urban and suburban voters, one that emphasized tax relief for homeowners, a statewide pre-kindergarten initiative, a balanced approach to growth and new transportation solutions.

Kilgore took an opposite tack. He relied on hot-button issues like the death penalty and illegal immigration, dismissing Kaine as "too liberal for Virginia." In one tough ad, a man whose son and daughter-in-law were murdered criticized Kaine for opposing the death penalty for "the worst mass murderer in modern times." Unlike the last two Republicans to win the governorship, Kilgore had no signature proposal such as ending parole (George Allen in 1993) or eliminating the car tax (Jim Gilmore in 1997). He criticized Kaine's support for a controversial, Warner-backed $1.3 billion tax increase that passed in 2004. Kaine talked frequently about how his Catholic faith colored his positions, while Kilgore accused Kaine of a certain political convenience in opposing the death penalty and abortion on moral grounds while insisting that he would not seek to change the laws or to infringe on a woman's right to choose. "We can't trust Tim Kaine," concluded Kilgore ads.

Kaine won 52%-46%, a victory powered by large margins in suburban Northern Virginia where Kilgore's Appalachian twang may have seemed out of place. Kaine crushed Kilgore 60%-38% in suburban Fairfax County, the state's most populous. He won 74% in nearby Arlington County and 72% in the city of Alexandria. Kaine's focus on managing growth enabled him to carry six of the state's 10 fastest-growing counties, including two, Loudoun and Prince William, that have been among the fastest-growing in the nation. Kaine's victory in one of two governor's races that year was viewed by the national party as a harbinger for the 2006 midterm elections. Shortly after being sworn into office, he was asked to deliver the nationally-televised Democratic response to President George W. Bush's State of the Union address. In office, he faced Republican majorities in the state House and Senate and had some successes in his first year, which included legislation requiring rigorous teacher evaluations. But he was unable to deliver on his primary objective of finding a reliable source of transportation financing to relieve traffic congestion. Resistance from House Republicans led to rejection of his package of tax and fee increases. Kaine did not stand in the way of four executions of death row inmates, though he delayed the execution of a fifth after questions were raised about the inmate's mental capacity. He symbolically refused to sign a proposed constitutional amendment banning same-sex marriage that was approved by the General Assembly for placement on the November 2006 ballot.

Kaine's second year was dominated by two events in 2007: the mass shootings at Virginia Tech University and passage of a compromise $1 billion transportation package. Kaine was in Japan on an overseas trade mission at the time a deranged Virginia Tech student, armed to the teeth, opened fire on fellow students during classes, killing 32 before taking his own life. Kaine immediately flew back home and won praise for his handling of the tragedy. On the transportation package, Kaine managed to reach an agreement with the Republican House and Senate on the biggest transportation funding increase in two decades. Since Republicans would not agree to a significant statewide tax increase, the plan called for borrowing up to $3 billion over 10 years and giving taxing powers to regional authorities in the two traffic-choked big metro areas, Northern Virginia and Tidewater. But the plan was frustrated when the state Supreme Court ruled that the regional authorities couldn't raise taxes.

As part of his $78 billion, two-year budget in 2008, Kaine proposed $1.1 billion for transportation, with a penny sales tax increase in Northern Virginia and Tidewater. But House Republicans steadfastly resisted it. Kaine was frustrated too when the Federal Transit Administration in early 2008 seemed poised to refuse funding for extending Metrorail to Dulles Airport and Loudoun County. But in December 2008, the last full month of the Bush administration, the FTA reversed itself and approved $900 million in financing; the rest was to come from special taxing districts in the edge cities of Tysons Corner and Reston and increased tolls. Barred from considering tax increases by the Republican House, Kaine in 2008 and early 2009 cut spending and laid off employees to adjust for revenue shortfalls. He also used money from the state's rainy day fund. He had one success, when he and House Speaker William Howell reached agreement on a ban on smoking in bars and restaurants that passed in February 2009. He failed to get the Legislature to agree to require background checks on sales at gun shows, and to get approval for universal pre-kindergarten. He also angered some environmental groups when he voiced support for plans for a coal-burning electric power plant in Wise County in southwest Virginia.

Kaine had some political successes. Democrats won a 21-19 majority in the state Senate in the November 2007 elections. In February 2007, Kaine endorsed Democrat Barack Obama of Illinois for president, the first governor to do so outside of Obama's home state. He campaigned heavily for Obama in Virginia and helped him win one of his biggest primary victories there. He was regarded as a possibility for the vice presidential nomination. After the election, Obama named Kaine as chairman of the Democratic National Committee. In the first two months of 2009, he was preoccupied with Virginia's legislative session and the DNC raised less money than its Republican counterpart.

Virginia is the last state which bars its governors from running for re-election, so Kaine did not run again in 2009.

Senior Senator

Jim Webb (D)

Elected 2006, term expires 2012, 1st term; b. Feb. 9, 1946, St. Joseph, MO; home, Arlington; U.S. Naval Academy, B.S. 1968, Georgetown U., J.D. 1975; Christian; married (Hong Le); 6 children.

Military Career: Marine Corps, 1968–72 (Vietnam).

Professional Career: Writer/journalist; Counsel, U.S. House Cmte. on Veterans Affairs, 1977–81; Asst. sec. of defense for Reserve Affairs, 1984–87; U.S. Navy sect., 1987–88.

DC Office: 248 RSOB, 20510, 202-224-4024; Fax: 202-228-6363; Web site: webb.senate.gov.

State Offices: Arlington, 703-807-0581; Danville, 434-792-0976, Norton, 276-679-4925; Richmond, 804-771-2221; Roanoke, 540-772-4236; Virginia Beach, 757-518-1674.

Committees: *Armed Services* (10th of 15 D): Airland; Personnel; Seapower. *Foreign Relations* (8th of 11 D): African Affairs; East Asian & Pacific Affairs (Chmn); European Affairs; Western Hemisphere, Peace Corps & Global Narcotics Affairs. *Joint Economic Committee* (6th of 6 D). *Veterans' Affairs* (6th of 10 D).

Group Ratings

	ADA	ACLU	AFS	LCV	ITIC	NTU	COC	ACU	CFG	FRC
2008	95	57	100	91	100	3	63	8	3	0
2007	85	—	100	87	—	13	45	16	13	—

National Journal Ratings

	2007 LIB	—	2007 CONS		2008 LIB	—	2008 CONS
Economic	53%	—	44%		68%	—	30%
Social	66%	—	30%		60%	—	38%
Foreign	57%	—	41%		61%	—	38%
Composite	60%	—	40%		64%	—	36%

Key Votes of the 110th Congress

1. Raise CAFE standards	Y	5. Make English official language	Y	9. Withdraw troops 3/08	Y
2. Expand SCHIP	Y	6. Path to citizenship	N	10. Iran guard is terrorist group	N
3. Cap greenhouse gases	Y	7. Fetus is unborn child	N	11. Increase missile defense $	N
4. Bail out financial markets	Y	8. Prosecute hate crimes	Y	12. Overhaul FISA	Y

Election Results

2006 general	Jim Webb (D)	 1,175,606	(50%)	($8,559,590)
	George Allen (R)	 1,166,277	(49%)	($16,071,564)
2006 primary	Jim Webb (D)	 83,298	(53%)	
	Harris Miller (D)	 72,486	(47%)	

Democrat Jim Webb, Virginia's senior senator, was elected to the Senate in 2006. Of Scots-Irish descent, he is the son of an Air Force colonel who enlisted after Pearl Harbor. The family moved at least a dozen times when he was a child. He enrolled in the University of Southern California, then a year later in the U.S. Naval Academy. He was a reader who wanted to become a writer, but he was also a combative young man, and a boxing match in 1967 with future Iran-contra operative Oliver North at Annapolis became the subject of legend (North won). He graduated in 1968, and in 1969 went into combat in Vietnam as a Marine lieutenant. He commanded 170 men and earned the Navy Cross, a Silver Star and two Purple Hearts. He suffered wounds that left him with shrapnel in his body and a limp—and forced him to retire from active duty. He was one of the subjects of Robert Timberg's moving 1995 book, *The Nightingale's Song*. Webb entered Georgetown Law School in 1972 and was appalled by his antiwar schoolmates who he believed had shirked duty and then considered themselves morally superior because of their opposition to the war. He started writing, and his respected novel about Vietnam, *Fields of Fire*, was published in 1978. He has since written five other novels, a 2004 history-cum-memoir, *Born Fighting: How the Scots-Irish Shaped America*, and his 2008 memoir-cum-policy-book *Time to Fight: Reclaiming a Fair and Just America*.

In the years after *Fields of Fire*, Webb wrote movie scripts (he still has some options out) and many articles. In the process, he made some controversial public statements. He praised Confederate heroes, attacked feminists and Hollywood, academics and the news media. In 1979, he wrote an article for *Washingtonian* magazine criticizing the new policy on women in the military. "I have never met a woman, including the dozens of female midshipmen I encountered during my recent semester as a professor at the Naval Academy, whom I would trust to provide those men with combat leadership." Bancroft Hall, he wrote, "which houses 4,000 males and 300 females" was "a horny woman's dream." The Navy banned him from speaking at the academy. He helped lead the fights against Maya Lin's Vietnam War memorial and for an additional sculpture depicting soldiers. Disgusted with President Jimmy Carter's amnesty for draft law violators, he left the Democratic Party and became a Republican, and in 1980, supported Ronald Reagan for president. In interviews, he said he wouldn't walk across the street to see antiwar activist Jane Fonda and for 20 years he refused to shake the hand of Massachusetts Sen. John Kerry, another Vietnam War hero who criticized the war effort on his return from combat. In 1984, Webb won an Emmy for his coverage for PBS' NewsHour of the 1983 barracks bombing that killed 241 Marines in Lebanon. In 1987, President Reagan appointed him secretary of the Navy. He issued a directive that performance in combat be given greater weight in promotions, which was criticized by advocates of equality for women in the military. Webb publicly complained about budget cuts imposed by Congress, which angered Defense Secretary Frank Carlucci. Webb resigned in 1988, saying, "It's no secret that I'm not a person who wears a bridle well."

Nor did he wear a political label well. In the late 1980s and early 1990s, both major parties tried to recruit him to run for the Senate, but he turned them down. In 1994, he backed Democratic Sen. Charles Robb against his one-time sparring partner North, who lost the contest. In 2000, he backed Republican George Allen against Robb, arguing that Robb had not done enough oversight of his party's administration. He wrote an article in the *Wall Street Journal* in 2000 attacking racial quotas and preferences as "a permeating state-sponsored racism that is as odious as the Jim Crow laws it sought to countermand." Of Democratic President Bill Clinton he said, "Every time I see him salute a Marine, it infuriates me," and on another occasion, said, "ethical fraudulence . . . has characterized his entire political career." Once the Republicans were in power, he began thinking more like a Democrat. His research for *Born Fighting* convinced him that Scots-Irish people of modest means who willingly served in the military might better be served by the Democrats, and he foresaw a coalition of Scots-Irish and African-Americans. "You measure the health of a society not at its apex, but at its base," he said. In 2002, Webb opposed military action in Iraq, asserting that it would destabilize the region and mire the United States in a long occupation. His opposition continued even as his son dropped out of Penn State University to join the Marines. In the 2004 presidential contest, despite his feelings about Kerry, Webb supported him over George W. Bush. The "last straw for me" in this political odyssey was the response to Hurricane Katrina, he said, which reminded him how people of little means were treated.

So in 2006, Webb found himself running against Allen, whom he had supported six years before. Allen began the campaign on the list of possible Republican presidential candidates in 2008. He had served in the House, then ran for governor in 1993 and won 58%-41%. In 2000, he challenged Democratic Sen. Robb and won 52%-48%. It was widely assumed that he would win by a bigger margin in 2006. As the year went on, he made trips to Iowa and New Hampshire and on occasion told reporters that the job of senator was boring and that he preferred being an executive. In January 2006, the only visible Democratic candidate was Harris Miller, the head of the Information Technology Association of America. He had serious credentials, some financial backing and some moderate issue positions. But he was universally regarded as the underdog.

Webb was encouraged to run by Kerry and by Democratic Senatorial Campaign Committee Chairman Charles Schumer, D-N.Y., who had already recruited a candidate at odds with the liberal Democratic base, Bob Casey, Jr., in Pennsylvania, and saw in Webb a similar opportunity to cut into the conservative vote. Webb announced his candidacy on March 7, 2006, late in the season for such things. Noting that his son was being deployed to Iraq, he reiterated his opposition to military action there. "The invasion of Iraq was a double strategic blunder. First, it was a diversion from, not a response to, the war against international terrorism. Second, it has tied down our military in a costly occupation, fighting an insurgency that has strengthened not only the Shia population of Iraq, but also Iran itself." At the same time, he opposed a precipitous withdrawal. On cultural issues, he said, "My belief is that the power of government stops at the front door unless there is a compelling reason for it to come inside." He supported abortion rights; he said he wanted "to do better on rights for gays" and supported civil unions; and he argued that racial preferences should be limited to African-Americans, because of their unique heritage, and not accorded to women or other ethnic groups. He strongly opposed new gun control laws, noting that his father had given him his first gun when he was eight and that he had done the same with his son. He hired strategists with experience in Democratic campaigns appealing to culturally conservative voters.

They had their work cut for them. In the primary campaign, Miller outspent Webb 3-to-1. Prominent African-Americans, nettled by Webb's statements on racial preferences, supported Miller, as did women military veterans. Webb was not a natural candidate, reluctant to handshake his way across a room, stiff in his public speeches. "I don't wake up in the morning wanting to be a U.S. senator. I wake up every morning very concerned about the country." His prime asset turned out to be support from antiwar activists, especially bloggers, who argued that he was the only candidate who could beat Allen. Turnout was light in the June 13 primary, and Webb won 53%-47%. For a candidate who expressed scorn for Washington elites, he ran best in the Washington D.C. suburbs in Northern Virginia, which he carried 2-to-1. He also ran well in the western part of the state, carrying most counties just east of the Blue Ridge and in the Shenandoah Valley and the valleys to the south. Miller carried the Richmond area and just about everything south of Fredericksburg and east of Lynchburg, running especially strong in cities and counties with high black percentages.

Webb had no money left after the primary; Allen had $7.5 million—and ultimately outspent him 2-to-1. But money was not decisive. On August 11, Allen was speaking in Breaks, Va., in Dickenson County, near the Kentucky border. He pointed at S. R. Siddarth, a 20-year-old student of Indian descent, who had been following him around for the Webb campaign, taping everything he said. "This fellow over here," Allen said, "with the yellow shirt, Macaca or whatever his name is, he's with my opponent. . . Let's give a welcome to Macaca here. Welcome to America, and welcome to the real world of Virginia." In another era, such an incident would have remained unknown. But it became the center of the campaign, thanks to YouTube, which gave anyone with a computer ready access to the footage, and to the *Washington Post*, which ran several front-page stories on the incident. The subtext was that "macaca" was a racial epithet, evidence that Allen was a bigot. Allen's strange word choice came against the backdrop of an unflattering profile in the *New Republic* in 2006, which said Allen had hung a Confederate flag on his wall as a young lawyer and had used the "n-word" while a student. (Webb's response, when asked if he had ever used the word: "I don't think that there's anyone who grew up around the South that hasn't had the word pass through their lips at one time in their life.") Former schoolmates of Allen's countered this barrage of negative publicity by saying they had never heard Allen use such language or show bigotry in any way. At a September debate, Washington area television reporter Peggy Fox, a panelist, noted that "macaca" is a racial slur in Tunisia, where Allen's mother had grown up. She then asked Allen whether it was true, as had been reported by *The Forward*, that his mother's side of the family was Jewish. Allen replied that his religious background, or Webb's, didn't matter. Shortly afterward, Allen revealed that his mother had concealed her heritage for many years and only revealed it, tearfully, a month before.

Allen and his experienced campaign managers, Dick Wadhams and Chris LaCivita, had expected to run a campaign based on taxes and support of the military. Now they were on the defensive. Webb was running closely behind or even with Allen in the polls by September. At the end of the month, Allen ran an ad with quotes from Webb's 1979 *Washingtonian* article on women in the military and showing three female academy graduates criticizing Webb. He responded with an ad showing testimonials from military women. An Allen ad claimed that Webb wanted to raise taxes on married couples and families, costing the average Virginia family $2,000. Webb rebutted with an ad saying that Allen wanted to raise taxes on retirement savings, make college more expensive and give billions in tax cuts to oil companies. To charges that he was bigoted, Allen pointed to his pilgrimages to civil rights sites and to the work he had done to aid historically black colleges and universities. And Allen's campaign attacked Webb for the sexually racy passages in some of his novels.

This was one of the two closest Senate races in the nation, and the one which, when the result became clear two days after the election, gave the Senate majority to the Democrats. Webb won by 9,000 votes, 49.6%-49.2%. His victory was almost entirely due to Northern Virginia. Webb carried Hampton Roads 52%-46%, almost the same as Robb's 52%-48% there two years before. In the half of the state outside the two big metro areas, Allen won 55%-44%, down just slightly from his 56%-44% in 2000. Northern Virginia was a different story. Webb carried it 57%-42%. Robb's popular vote margin in the area had been 21,000. Webb's was 110,000, five times larger. The exit poll showed Webb with 42% of whites and 85% of blacks, the latter a bit low for a Democrat.

Webb's victory produced exultation among Democrats—and some curiosity as to what kind of Democratic senator he would be. Addressing the concerns, Webb said, "There are going to be times when I've got some strong ideas, but I'm not looking to simply be a renegade. I think people in the Democratic Party leadership have already begun to understand that I know how to work inside a structure." His attitude toward Bush was not friendly. When he attended a reception at the White House a few days after the election, Bush approached Webb and asked about his son in Iraq. "How's your boy?" Webb responded, "I'd like to get them out of Iraq, Mr. President." "That's not what I asked you," said the president. "How's your boy?" "That's between me and my boy, Mr. President," Webb starchily replied.

Webb was chosen by Democratic leaders to give the rebuttal to Bush's State of the Union speech in January 2007, and he gave a speech opposing Bush on Iraq and pointing to what he said was a widening difference between the rich and the poor. In January 2007, he introduced his new GI Bill of Rights, paying for four years of college tuition for veterans with three years of service. A modified version passed the Senate a little over a year later, then passed in the House and was signed into law in June 2008 as part of a military spending bill, a considerable achievement for a second-year senator.

Webb continued to speak out strongly against the Iraq war. In January 2007, he called Bush "a failed president." In April of that year, he sharply criticized Pentagon plans to extend troop tours in Iraq from 12 months to 15 months. With support from fellow Virginia Sen. John Warner, a Republican, Webb won passage of an amendment creating an independent commission to investigate wartime contracting in Iraq, and was angry when Bush refused to abide by it, saying it threatened executive authority.

Webb weighed in on other issues. Again with Warner, he co-sponsored bills giving technological grants to historically black colleges and universities and providing schools with many foreign students a one-year grace period for meeting the requirements of the 2001 No Child Left Behind act, which tied federal funding to student performance on tests. His amendment to the Senate's immigration bill to reduce the number of illegal immigrants eligible for eventual citizenship from 12 million to 4 million was opposed by the bill's sponsors and defeated 79-18. None of that got as much attention as a bizarre incident in March 2007, when Webb's top aide was arrested for attempting to carry a loaded handgun into a Senate office building. A month later, the charges were dropped. Webb later acknowledged that the gun was his and said that he often carried a gun to protect himself and his family.

Webb caused a minor stir in political circles when he gave the keynote speech at the October 2007 Jefferson-Jackson Day dinner in New Hampshire, an indication he may have aspirations that reach beyond the Senate.

Junior Senator

Mark Warner (D)

Elected 2008, term expires 2014, 1st term; b. Dec. 15, 1954, Indianapolis, IN; home, Alexandria; George Washington U., B.A. 1977; Harvard U., J.D. 1980; Presbyterian; married (Lisa Collis); 3 children.

Elected Office: VA gov., 2002–06.

Professional Career: Fundraiser, DNC, 1980–82; Venture capitalist, 1982–89; Mng. dir., Columbia Capital Corp., 1989–2001; Chairman, VA Democratic Party, 1993–95.

DC Office: 459A RSOB, 20510, 202-224-2023; Fax: 202-224-6296; Web site: warner.senate.gov.

State Offices: Abingdon, 276-628-8158; Norfolk, 757-441-3079; Richmond, 804-739-0247; Roanoke, 540-857-2676.

Committees: *Banking, Housing & Urban Affairs* (11th of 13 D): Housing, Transportation & Community Development; Securities, Insurance & Investment; Security & International Trade & Finance. *Budget* (12th of 13 D). *Commerce, Science & Transportation* (13th of 14 D): Aviation Operations, Safety & Security; Communications, Technology & the Internet; Competitiveness, Innovation & Export Promotion; Science & Space; Surface Transportation & Merchant Marine Infrastructure, Safety & Security. *Rules & Administration* (11th of 11 D).

Group Ratings and Key Votes: Newly Elected

Election Results

2008 general	Mark Warner (D)	2,369,327	(65%)	($12,515,479)
	James Gilmore (R)	1,228,830	(34%)	($2,420,635)
2008 primary	Mark Warner (D)	unopposed		

Prior Winning Percentages: 2001 governor (52%)

Democrat Mark Warner, a former Virginia governor, was elected U.S. senator in 2008. Warner grew up in Indianapolis and Connecticut. He graduated from George Washington University, the first college graduate in his family, and from Harvard Law School. Although he has emphasized his business experience in his campaigns, his first love seems to have been politics. After law school, he worked in fundraising for the Democratic National Committee and in 1989, managed Douglas Wilder's successful campaign to become Virginia's first African-American governor. His business success in fact grew out of his political contacts. While working for the DNC, Warner met Rep. Tom McMillen, a Maryland Democrat, who told him about the potential of cell phone markets just as the Reagan administration was about to award 1,500 free licenses for metropolitan markets. Warner cobbled together investor groups and packaged their applications in exchange for a fee and a 5% ownership stake if they received the licenses. The best known of these ventures was Nextel, and Warner quickly became a wealthy man. His net worth in 2008 was estimated at $200 million.

But politics was always on Warner's mind. From 1993 to 1995, he was the Virginia Democratic chairman. In 1996, he ran against Republican Sen. John Warner in what seemed a quixotic race: the senior Warner, elected narrowly in 1978, had won re-election in a landslide in 1984 and had no Democratic opponent in 1990. But the incumbent had antagonized conservatives by refusing to endorse Republican nominee Oliver North in his 1994 race against Democratic Sen. Charles Robb and by his liberal stands on some cultural issues. Mark Warner pitched his campaign not to his home turf in Northern Virginia but to the Shenandoah Valley and southwest Virginia, where North had done well. He carried southwest Virginia and lost the part of the state outside the three big metropolitan areas by only 51%-49%, a considerable achievement for a Democrat. But John Warner's strength among moderates enabled him to carry Northern Virginia 55%-45%, and to carry Tidewater and metropolitan Richmond with smaller majorities. The result was a 52%-47% win for John Warner, but certainly not an end to upstart Mark Warner's political career.

In the late 1990s, Mark Warner put millions of dollars into philanthropic efforts and set up four regional business investment funds in southwest Virginia, Southside Virginia, Richmond and Tidewater. By 1999, it was plain that he was going to run for governor in 2001, as an entrepreneur who could bring savvy business methods to government. He picked a good year. Incumbent Republican Gov. Jim Gilmore had succeeded in electing Republican majorities in both houses of the Legislature, but then battled with them over the budget. Gilmore wanted to fulfill his 1997 promise to cut the state's automobile tax, but revenues were coming in under projections. Republicans had a primary battle in 2001 between Lt. Gov. John Hager and former Attorney General Mark Earley. Earley won but had little money and no clear campaign strategy. Warner ultimately spent $5 million of his own money on the campaign, but used his fundraising skills to raise more in Virginia and around the nation.

Warner, who lives in a mansion in Old Town Alexandria, avoided being typed as an urban liberal. He called himself a fiscal conservative and pledged not to raise the income or sales taxes. Responding to complaints from traffic-choked Northern Virginia and Tidewater, he called for regional referenda on local sales tax increases for transportation. This pleased business interests and local legislators who feared congestion would stop growth and propitiated some tax opponents who felt they would get a chance to vote no. He opposed any new gun control laws and wooed the National Rifle Association, which remained neutral. He ran ads featuring old pickup trucks and bluegrass music, and he sponsored a NASCAR race truck. He traveled to all parts of rural Virginia, much as Wilder had in 1989, showing that he was in touch with everyday folks and reminding them of his investment funds and philanthropic initiatives. In October, Earley came out against the regional referenda, but this evidently hurt him with both sides. Businessmen and legislators were angry that he opposed transportation spending, while some tax opponents outside Northern Virginia feared it would make a statewide tax increase more likely. Earley ran ads on taxes and abortion, but Warner had inoculated himself on taxes and Earley's opposition to abortion put off some suburban Republicans.

Warner won, but not resoundingly, by 52%-47%, a reversal of the numbers in the 1996 Senate race. He carried all major regions of the state, albeit by narrow margins.

Once in office, Warner had to cope with an unpleasant fiscal situation. He got the Legislature to approve transportation tax referenda in Northern Virginia and Tidewater, but the House of Delegates rejected his education initiative in 2002. As the budget shortfall grew, Warner continued to rule out a tax increase, cut $858 million in spending and laid off 1,800 state employees. Meanwhile, in Northern Virginia and Tidewater, transportation tax increases were opposed by conservatives who argued that politicians would misuse the money and "smart growth" advocates who argued that more highways would mean more growth and traffic congestion. In November 2002, Northern Virginia rejected the tax increase 55%-45% and Tidewater rejected it 62%-38%. Warner said the results showed a "sobering" mistrust of politicians.

In November 2003, after the legislative elections and when Virginia seemed to be in danger of losing its AAA bond rating, Warner presented his new fiscal plan, a $1 billion tax increase, with increases in the income, sales and cigarette taxes and tax reductions for those with low incomes and in the car and food taxes. He argued that state government needed the revenue and that under his plan, 65% of Virginians would pay less. In early 2004, his plan was rejected by the heavily Republican House of Delegates, which increased taxes by just $520 million and provided few spending increases. But the state Senate passed a $3.8 billion tax increase, with $1.7 billion in new spending for schools and $1.6 billion for transportation. GOP Speaker William Howell was obdurate, but unable to hold his Republicans in line: 17 Republican delegates abandoned their anti-tax position and by April a conclusion was reached. The Senate agreed to a $1.3 billion tax increase, more than Warner had requested, and the House went along. Warner had gotten his program through a Republican Legislature.

By December 2004, the fiscal picture had changed. State government was facing a $1.2 billion surplus. Warner called for spending $32 million to offset state employees' health insurance premiums, $200 million more for Medicaid, $70 million to cover cost overruns in college construction, and $824 million in transportation spending. He also sought a larger national profile. He became chairman of the National Governors Association, urged Democratic presidential candidate John Kerry to target Virginia (which Kerry did, until August) and advised other Democrats around the country about how to win support in rural areas and among conservative voters on culture issues.

Warner had the satisfaction of seeing his lieutenant governor, Tim Kaine, win the 2005 gubernatorial election, though with a coalition more heavily tilted to Northern Virginia and away from the rural areas. Warner was viewed as a potential presidential candidate, as a Democrat who would appeal to moderates. But in October 2006, he announced he would not run, citing the impact a national campaign would have on his family. Then, when Sen. John Warner announced in August 2007 that he would retire from the Senate after five terms, Mark Warner announced he would run for the seat. He had no serious opposition for the Democratic nomination.

On the Republican side, Jim Gilmore, Warner's predecessor as governor, decided to make the race. Gilmore had briefly run for president and was widely considered the favorite for the GOP Senate nomination, and when the Virginia Republican Party announced that the nomination would be determined at a state party convention rather than in a primary, U.S. Rep. Tom Davis, a Northern Virginia Republican, who had been mulling a Senate race for many years, announced he would not run. But at the state Republicans' nominating convention in June 2008, Gilmore barely prevailed after being challenged from the right by Delegate Robert Marshall because of Gilmore's support for some abortion rights. He only narrowly secured the nomination.

It turned out not to be a seriously contested campaign. Warner led in polls by 20 percentage points or more throughout 2008. Warner raised $13.6 million while Gilmore raised just $2.8 million. John Warner declined to endorse Gilmore and spoke favorably of his 1996 opponent, Mark Warner. Mark Warner argued that Gilmore left him a bad fiscal hand when he took office in 2002 and that he had been able to turn things around. Warner won 65%-34%, losing only two counties in the Shenandoah Valley, two exurban Richmond counties and two small independent cities. He got 2.37 million votes, the only candidate in Virginia history to win more than 2 million votes. He won 69% of the votes in Northern Virginia, 68% in Tidewater, 64% in Richmond and 62% in the rest of the state, running far ahead of Democratic presidential nominee Barack Obama even as Obama was carrying the state by six points. For the first time since 1970, when Harry Byrd Jr. declared himself an independent, Virginia had two Democratic senators.

In the Senate, Warner was appointed to the Banking, Housing and Urban Affairs and Budget committees, along with the Commerce, Science and Technology and the Rules and Administration committees. He immediately began to fashion himself as a moderate, joining the Moderate Dems Working Group with other centrist Democratic senators. He also tried to secure a reputation for bipartisanship early. Warner not only inherited the same email and web addresses from his predecessor, but three of Republican Warner's key staff members stayed on to work for the new Democratic Warner, whom some of his staff humorously referred to as "Warner 2.0."

FIRST DISTRICT

Rob Wittman (R)

Elected Dec. 2007, 1st full term; b. Feb. 3, 1959, Washington, D.C.; home, Montross; VA Tech., B.S., 1981, U. of NC, M.S., 1990, VA Commonwealth U., Ph.D., 2002; Episcopalian; married (Kathryn); 2 children.

Elected Office: Montross Town Cncl., 1986–1996, Montross Mayor, 1992–1996, Westmoreland Cnt. Bd. of Supervisors, 1996–2005, VA House of Del., 2005–07.

Professional Career: Field dir., VA Health Dept.

DC Office: 1318 LHOB, 20515, 202-225-4261; Fax: 202-225-4382; Web site: wittman.house.gov.

State Offices: Fredericksburg, 540-548-1086; Tappahannock, 804-443-0668; Yorktown, 757-874-6687.

Committees: *Armed Services* (19th of 25 R): Oversight & Investigations (RMM); Readiness; Seapower & Expeditionary Forces. *Natural Resources* (13th of 20 R): Insular Affairs, Oceans & Wildlife; National Parks, Forests & Public Lands.

Group Ratings

	ADA	ACLU	AFS	LCV	ITIC	NTU	COC	ACU	CFG	FRC
2008	35	25	29	23	0	65	83	92	81	100
2007	—	—	—	—	—	—	—	100	—	—

National Journal Ratings

	2007 LIB	—	2007 CONS	2008 LIB	—	2008 CONS
Economic	*%	—	*%	29%	—	71%
Social	*%	—	*%	20%	—	74%
Foreign	*%	—	*%	29%	—	69%
Composite	*%	—	*%	27%	—	73%

Key Votes of the 110th Congress

1. Increase minimum wage	*	5. Share immigration data	*	9. Withdraw troops 8/08	*
2. Expand SCHIP	*	6. Foreign aid abortion ban	*	10. No operations in Iran	*
3. Raise CAFE standards	*	7. Ban gay bias in workplace	*	11. Free trade with Peru	*
4. Bail out financial markets	N	8. Repeal D.C. gun law	Y	12. Overhaul FISA	Y

Election Results

2008 general	Rob Wittman (R)	203,839	(57%)	($952,691)
	Bill Day (D)	150,432	(42%)	($218,889)
2008 primary	Rob Wittman (R)	unopposed		
2007 special	Rob Wittman (R)	42,772	(61%)	
	Philip Forgit (D)	26,282	(37%)	
	Lucky Narain (I)	1,253	(2%)	

Population		Race/Ethnicity		Work	
Pop. 2007:	740,901	White:	71.1%	Private:	67.0%
Change since 2000:	Up 15.1%	Black:	18.6%	Government:	27.8%
Urban:	64.0%	Hispanic:	5.1%	Self-employed:	5.1%
Rural:	36.0%	Asian:	2.4%	Blue collar:	20.7%
Area size:	4,612 sq. mi.	Native Am.:	0.3%	White collar:	61.0%
		Hawaiian:	0.1%	Khaki collar:	2.8%
Age		Two+ races:	2.2%	Other:	15.5%
Median age:	36.1 yrs.	*Ancestry*		Median income:	$63,665
More than 65 yrs:	11.5%	German:	12.3%	Median home value:	$285,100
Less than 18 yrs:	24.8%	English:	11.9%	Poverty:	6.7%
Education		Irish:	10.5%		
H.S. grad:	88.1%			**Military Veterans**	
College grad:	30.0%			% of Pop:	16.6%
Grad degree:	11.3%				

When the English first sailed up the estuaries that flow into the Chesapeake Bay, they were searching for gold, hoping to sail back soon with fortunes. But they couldn't help noticing that the spot where the James River feeds into the bay, now Hampton Roads, was a fine natural harbor, with calm, deep water and good anchorages. So some of them stayed and established communities that achieved not only the high craftsmanship of restored Williamsburg but also endured the pitiless hardship brought to life by the four-century story of Jamestown and other early settlements. Tidewater Virginia brought slavery to America and tobacco to the world, and slave-raised tobacco was the center of its economy in the colonial era and in the years afterward, when its most talented sons left its depleted soil for better opportunities elsewhere. Now, the economy and tone of life in Tidewater Virginia are set by the American military. More than six decades ago, as America faced world war, the Navy base at Norfolk and the shipbuilding centers in Newport News across Hampton Roads became the center of American naval might in the Atlantic. There were fewer than 370,000 people living then on both sides of Hampton Roads. Today there are more than 1.6 million—a population collected from all over the country, making this a metropolitan area that is not so much Southern in atmosphere as it is, in the manner of military bases abroad, national.

2008 Presidential Vote

McCain (R)	193,273	(51%)
Obama (D)	179,442	(48%)

2004 Presidential Vote

Bush (R)	188,417	(60%)
Kerry (D)	122,771	(39%)

Cook Partisan Voting Index: R + 7

The 1st Congressional District of Virginia contains much of this territory. The district ranges as far north from the Peninsula as rural Fauquier County, outside Washington, D.C., but the bulk of the population lives between the Potomac and James Rivers. Most of the major Hampton Roads military installations are in surrounding congressional districts, but the 1st remains steeped in military culture, and the Department of Defense and NASA continue to be significant employers. Historic Yorktown is adjacent to a Naval Weapons Station on the banks of the York River. To the north, in Caroline County, Fort A.P. Hill serves as a training site for active and reserve-component units. Not far from there is the Naval Surface Warfare Center in Dahlgren, located on the Potomac River, originally established as the Navy's main proving ground for large-caliber guns.

The 1st takes in all of 13 counties and parts of five others, including the cities of Fredericksburg and colonial Williamsburg, the Marine Corps Base at Quantico, and the Northern Neck between the Rappahannock and Potomac Rivers. Ancestrally, much of this area was Democratic. But with a large military population plus growing retirement communities, the 1st District is now reliably Republican in most elections.

The congressman from the 1st District is Rob Wittman, a Republican who won a special election in December 2007. He replaced Republican Jo Ann Davis, who died of breast cancer two months earlier. Wittman was born in Washington, D.C., and became a marine scientist. He also has a Ph.D. in public policy and administration from Virginia Commonwealth University. Wittman served for many years as an environmental health specialist in the Northern Neck and Peninsula regions, including as field director for the state's shellfish sanitation division. His first public office was a seat on the Montross Town Council, where he served for 10 years, including four as mayor. In 1995, he began a decade on the Westmoreland County Board of Supervisors. In 2005, he was elected to the Virginia House of Delegates.

Republicans chose their nominee to succeed Davis at a party convention five weeks after her death. Wittman's chief opponent was Paul Jost, a businessman and anti-tax activist who lost to Davis 35%-30% in 2000. The low-key Wittman cited his experience in public office and "the basics of good government." With help from several busloads of supporters, Jost led in the earlier balloting, which began with 11 candidates. The key moment came after five ballots, when Davis's widower, Chuck Davis, threw his support to Wittman, who became the compromise candidate.

Democrats nominated Philip Forgit, a school teacher and Navy reservist who won a Bronze Star for his service in Iraq. He described himself as a centrist and called for improved training to bring strategic change in Iraq. Wittman emphasized his conservative credentials, including his support for gun rights and opposition to abortion. He also touted the fact that House Minority Leader John Boehner had pledged to give him a seat on the Armed Services Committee. The Democratic Congressional Campaign Committee paid little attention to the contest in this heavily Republican district. Wittman won the low-turnout contest 61%-37%, carrying all 18 counties.

In the House, Wittman got a seat on Armed Services as promised, and also a seat on the Natural Resources Committee, another good fit for his district's issues. He bucked his party as one of 33 House Republicans to support creation of an office of congressional ethics, which for the first time would give an outside panel the power to investigate the misdeeds of lawmakers. On local issues, he helped to secure a Commerce Department declaration in September 2008 that the Chesapeake had become a "commercial fishery failure," which opened the door to economic aid to the bay's struggling watermen. He was elected to a full term with a smaller share of 57%-42%, but with five times as many votes as the special election.

SECOND DISTRICT

Glenn Nye (D)

Elected 2008, 1st term; b. Sept. 9, 1974, Philadelphia, PA; home, Norfolk; Georgetown U., B.A. 1996; Presbyterian; single.

Professional Career: U.S. State Dept. Foreign Service, 2001–03; Operations dir., USAID, 2003–07.

DC Office: 116 CHOB, 20515, 202-225-4215; Fax: 202-225-4218; Web site: nye.house.gov.

State Offices: Accomac, 757-789-5092; Virginia Beach, 757-326-6201.

Committees: *Armed Services* (28th of 36 D): Oversight & Investigations; Readiness; Seapower & Expeditionary Forces. *Small Business* (7th of 17 D): Contracting & Technology (Chmn); Finance & Tax. *Veterans' Affairs* (18th of 18 D): Health.

Group Ratings and Key Votes: Newly Elected

Election Results

2008 general	Glenn Nye (D)	141,857	(52%)	($1,334,146)
	Thelma Drake (R)	128,486	(47%)	($2,033,543)
2008 primary	Glenn Nye (D)	unopposed		

Population		Race/Ethnicity		Work	
Pop. 2007:	652,514	White:	64.9%	Private:	63.9%
Change since 2000:	Up 1.4%	Black:	21.9%	Government:	31.7%
Urban:	91.7%	Hispanic:	5.7%	Self-employed:	4.3%
Rural:	8.3%	Asian:	4.5%	Blue collar:	20.6%
Area size:	2,776 sq. mi.	Native Am.:	0.3%	White collar:	57.7%
		Hawaiian:	0.1%	Khaki collar:	6.2%
Age		Two+ races:	2.4%	Other:	15.5%
Median age:	34.2 yrs.	*Ancestry*		Median income:	$56,952
More than 65 yrs:	10.3%	German:	10.6%	Median home value:	$233,900
Less than 18 yrs:	25.1%	English:	9.6%	Poverty:	8.7%
Education		Irish:	9.4%	**Military Veterans**	
H.S. grad:	90.1%			% of Pop:	19.0%
College grad:	28.5%				
Grad degree:	9.9%				

The U.S. Navy Atlantic fleet berthed in its home port of Norfolk is one of the awe-inspiring sights in America, or anywhere. The aggregation of destructive power in the line of towering gray ships is probably greater than in any other single port in history. Several dozen ships are based here—aircraft carriers, cruisers, destroyers, large amphibious ships, submarines, supply and logistics ships—and many more aircraft. Norfolk has been a Navy port since 1801 and has long been recognized as one of the best

2008 Presidential Vote
Obama (D) 142,257   (51%)
McCain (R).............................136,725   (49%)

2004 Presidential Vote
Bush (R) 141,097   (58%)
Kerry (D)...............................101,576   (42%)

Cook Partisan Voting Index: R+5

natural harbors on the East Coast, one that never freezes, has a channel 50 feet deep and is within 750 miles of three-quarters of U.S. manufacturing capacity. The Norfolk Naval Station is now the world's largest naval station, situated on 4,300 acres on Sewell's Point, and the Hampton Roads region is the world's largest naval base, where residents are always within minutes of one naval installation or another. Once a small city, Norfolk is now a metropolitan area of 1.6 million people. The local Navy community— active duty and civilian personnel, dependents, retirees, and workers at the Newport News Shipbuilding & Drydock—is estimated at more than 300,000, and military spending pours some $11 billion annually into the local economy, including $1 billion in construction projects from 2004 to 2008. The Port of Hampton Roads is the third-busiest port on the East Coast, and its cargo volume has grown steadily since 2000.

Next-door Virginia Beach, once a sleepy beach resort, is the state's largest city, with 434,000 people. It began attracting tourists when rail service to Norfolk began in 1883. It is home to the headquarters of evangelist Pat Robertson's Christian Broadcasting Network, where the *700 Club* is produced. The city has a growing industrial base, including a large tool plant of the German-based Stihl company. But like Norfolk, Virginia Beach is infused with military culture. It is home to four military installations with 35,000 service and civilian employees and an annual payroll of over $1 billion. East Coast Navy SEAL teams are based in Virginia Beach; these elite commandos endure punishing military training and have taken on some of the military's most secretive and daring missions in Afghanistan and Iraq.

The 2nd Congressional District of Virginia includes all of Virginia Beach, plus small parts of Norfolk and Hampton, including the Norfolk Navy base and Langley Air Force Base and, on a spit of land in the bay, Fort Monroe, where Jefferson Davis was confined after the Civil War. It covers more than 100 miles of Atlantic Ocean coastline and stretches from Maryland's Eastern Shore to North Carolina. There are 110,000 active-duty military personnel in the larger metropolitan area. The district also includes a more placid area, the two Virginia counties of the Delmarva Peninsula, and Virginia's Eastern Shore, the site of the annual roundup of wild Chincoteague ponies. These rural counties with their fishing villages are two of the state's poorest. The overwhelming majority of the district's population is in Virginia Beach. The district leans Republican. George W. Bush carried it handily twice, but Democrat Barack Obama beat former Navy aviator John McCain here 51%-49% in 2008.

The new congressman from the 2nd District is Glenn Nye, a Democrat elected in 2008. He grew up in Norfolk, where his family has deep roots. He graduated from Georgetown University's School of Foreign Service and joined the State Department in 2001. His first assignment was in the former Yugoslav Republic of Macedonia, where civil conflict led the U.S. State Department to close the American embassy and evacuate its employees. Nye stayed behind and helped 26 Americans escape the country and negotiated the release of an American hostage held captive by insurgents. He later served in Singapore, where he worked on the U.S.-Singapore Free Trade Agreement. He also worked in Afghanistan on developing its constitutional convention and in Iraq on economic development and voter registration efforts.

Nye returned to his hometown of Norfolk, where he decided to challenge incumbent Republican Rep. Thelma Drake in the 2nd District. Two years earlier, Drake had fended off Democrat Phil Kellam by only 51%-48% and was vulnerable. Nye quickly raised $100,000, which impressed national Democrats, and they targeted the seat, hoping strong registration efforts by the Obama campaign and the strength of U.S. Senate candidate Mark Warner's campaign would tip the balance in Nye's favor. Still, Drake's strong base of support among military personnel made her a formidable candidate, and she outraised Nye by almost 2-to-1.

The candidates engaged in a mudslinging fest. Nye passed out literature hammering Drake for voting in May 2008 against an overhaul of the GI Bill that increased veterans' benefits; he neglected to mention that she voted for a revised version of the bill a month later. At a September debate, Drake claimed Nye broke the law by accepting a tax exemption on a house he co-owns in Washington, D.C., and she questioned whether Nye actually lived in the congressional district. A spokeswoman for the D.C. Office of Tax and Revenue found the tax exemption to be legal, and Nye maintained that his primary residence was in Norfolk.

The bickering took a humorous turn when Nye ridiculed Drake for suggesting that actress-turned-humanitarian Angelina Jolie address members of Congress about the situation in Iraq. Drake's campaign spokesman hit back by claiming Jolie's input was just as valuable as Nye's. The *Virginia-Pilot's* endorsement of Nye—it endorsed Drake in 2006—may have been indicative of the impending political shift. Nye won 52%-47%, running slightly ahead of Obama district-wide, but well behind Warner.

House Democratic leaders gave Nye a seat on the Armed Services Committee, where he can look after the district's military installations. He joined the Blue Dog Coalition, a group of fiscally-conservative Democrats. In one of his first legislative ventures, Nye was successful in adding a provision to the Democrats' $787 billion economic stimulus plan to create tax credits of up to $2,400 for businesses that hire unemployed veterans.

THIRD DISTRICT

Bobby Scott (D)

Elected 1992, 9th term; b. April 30, 1947, Washington, D.C.; home, Newport News; Harvard U., B.A. 1969, Boston Col., J.D. 1973; Episcopalian; single.

Military Career: Army Natl. Guard, 1970–73; Army Reserves, 1973–76.

Elected Office: VA House of Delegates, 1977–82; VA Senate, 1983–92.

Professional Career: Practicing atty., 1973–91.

DC Office: 1201 LHOB, 20515, 202-225-8351; Fax: 202-225-8354; Web site: www.house.gov/scott.

State Offices: Newport News, 757-380-1000; Richmond, 804-644-4845.

Committees: *Budget* (18th of 24 D). *Education & Labor* (5th of 29 D): Early Childhood, Elementary & Secondary Education; Healthy Families & Communities. *Judiciary* (5th of 24 D): Commercial & Administrative Law; Constitution, Civil Rights & Civil Liberties; Crime, Terrorism & Homeland Security (Chmn).

Group Ratings

	ADA	ACLU	AFS	LCV	ITIC	NTU	COC	ACU	CFG	FRC
2008	100	100	100	100	71	15	53	8	8	5
2007	100	—	100	90	—	3	50	4	6	—

National Journal Ratings

	2007 LIB — 2007 CONS		2008 LIB — 2008 CONS	
Economic	69%	— 28%	81%	— 15%
Social	92%	— 0%	82%	— 0%
Foreign	90%	— 8%	70%	— 25%
Composite	86%	— 14%	82%	— 18%

Key Votes of the 110th Congress

1. Increase minimum wage	Y	5. Share immigration data	N	9. Withdraw troops 8/08	Y
2. Expand SCHIP	Y	6. Foreign aid abortion ban	N	10. No operations in Iran	Y
3. Raise CAFE standards	Y	7. Ban gay bias in workplace	Y	11. Free trade with Peru	N
4. Bail out financial markets	N	8. Repeal D.C. gun law	N	12. Overhaul FISA	N

Election Results

2008 general	Bobby Scott (D)	239,911	(97%)	($506,728)
2008 primary	Bobby Scott (D)	unopposed		

Prior Winning Percentages: 2006 (96%); 2004 (69%); 2002 (96%); 2000 (100%); 1998 (76%); 1996 (82%); 1994 (79%); 1992 (79%)

Population		Race/Ethnicity		Work	
Pop. 2007:	654,581	White:	37.5%	Private:	70.7%
Change since 2000:	Up 1.7%	Black:	55.2%	Government:	25.1%
Urban:	92.2%	Hispanic:	3.3%	Self-employed:	4.1%
Rural:	7.8%	Asian:	1.5%	Blue collar:	25.5%
Area size:	1,306 sq. mi.	Native Am.:	0.4%	White collar:	53.5%
		Hawaiian:	0.1%	Khaki collar:	3.0%
Age		Two+ races:	1.8%	Other:	18.1%
Median age:	34.2 yrs.	*Ancestry*		Median income:	$40,444
More than 65 yrs:	11.6%	USA:	6.9%	Median home value:	$154,600
Less than 18 yrs:	25.7%	German:	6.7%	Poverty:	18.4%
Education		English:	6.3%	**Military Veterans**	
H.S. grad:	80.0%			% of Pop:	15.0%
College grad:	19.3%				
Grad degree:	6.8%				

The history of American slavery literally began along the tidal expanse of the James River. In 1607, the first English colonists chose one of the marshiest, least healthy spots along the broad river as the site of their settlement at Jamestown. Only a dozen years later, the first slave ship sailed up the James and offloaded its human cargo, giving birth to the biracial society of the American South. In the 21st century, the great plantation houses of the Tidewater, entire communities once adorned by the most

2008 Presidential Vote
Obama (D) 229,822 (76%)
McCain (R)...............................72,249 (24%)

2004 Presidential Vote
Kerry (D).................................158,561 (66%)
Bush (R) 79,302 (33%)

Cook Partisan Voting Index: D+20

impressive architecture of the day and attended by hundreds of slaves, still dot the banks of the James. Charles City County—the site of William Byrd II's Westover, Benjamin Harrison III's Berkeley, and John Carter's Shirley—also was the birthplace of two successive presidents, William Henry Harrison and John Tyler. The county's population continues to be heavily African-American. The demography of the plantation remains.

The 3rd Congressional District of Virginia is the descendant of a black-majority district formed in 1992, and redrawn three times since then. The district jumps back and forth across the James River to string together black precincts and communities in Norfolk, Hampton and Newport News. It moves upriver on the peninsula past Jamestown and Charles City County all the way to Richmond and eastern suburban Henrico County. It includes the Army's Fort Eustis and all of the majority-black city of Portsmouth, a Navy port and industrial town with a charming old section. The population of Hampton and Newport News has shrunk since 2000, while nearby areas have grown. In 2008, the final two container shipping companies in Newport News announced that they were moving operations to a new cargo terminal in Portsmouth. Politically, the 3rd is the most Democratic district in Virginia and the state's only black-majority district. Its economy depends heavily on the Newport News Shipbuilding & Drydock Company, the largest industrial employer in Virginia, now owned by Northrop Grumman. The ships loom larger than life over nearby neighborhoods. During the Cold War, Newport News built two of the largest tankers ever made in the western hemisphere. In addition to its *Nimitz* -class nuclear aircraft carriers and *Los Angeles* class nuclear attack submarines, the USS George H.W. Bush, the tenth and final *Nimitz* -class aircraft carrier, was commissioned in January 2009.

The congressman from the 3rd District is Bobby Scott, a Democrat first elected when the district was created in 1992. He grew up in Newport News, the son of a doctor, went to Harvard, where he was a classmate of Al Gore, and then to Boston College law school, where he preceded John Kerry, the former Democratic presidential nominee. He served in the National Guard and Army Reserves, and returned home to practice law. In 1977, he was elected to the Virginia House of Delegates, and in 1983, to the state Senate, representing a multi-racial district in a community where, because of the military tradition of integration, biracial politics came more naturally than in other places. In 1986, he ran a credible race for Congress and lost to Republican Herb Bateman, 56%-44%. In 1992, with his base on the peninsula, Scott won the crucial Democratic primary with 67% of the vote against two Richmond-based candidates. He is the only African-American member of Congress elected from Virginia since Reconstruction.

Scott has a solidly liberal voting record, with occasional exceptions on economic and defense issues, and he is one of the House's most outspoken civil libertarians. When bipartisan coalitions passed legislation to permit states to display the Ten Commandments in schools or government buildings, he raised First Amendment objections. After the September 11 attacks, he opposed the USA PATRIOT Act, the nation's tough new anti-terrorism law, arguing that it might promote racial profiling. He opposed the Iraq war resolution in 2002, and was an outspoken critic of the Bush administration's conduct of the war. Scott was one of three lawmakers to oppose condemnation of a federal court decision declaring unconstitutional the words "one nation under God" in the Pledge of Allegiance. "We ought to be standing up for unpopular decisions" and not voting for a resolution that "everyone knows is stupid, but it sounds popular," he said.

He is the chairman of the Judiciary Subcommittee on Crime, Terrorism and Homeland Security, where he conducts oversight of criminal laws with the goal of shifting the focus from enforcement to prevention. One of Scott's legislative successes was the bipartisan Death in Custody Act, which requires states to report deaths of arrestees and prisoners. With Rep. Randy Forbes, R-Va., Scott won enactment of a bill in October 2008 to strengthen treatment of mentally ill defendants. He also worked to build support for his Youth Promise Act for street gang prevention and for a bill to eliminate mandatory minimum sentences for cocaine. In May 2009, the Congressional Black Caucus urged President Barack Obama to select Scott to replace retiring Supreme Court Justice David Souter, although Obama ultimately settled on federal appellate Judge Sonia Sotomayor.

In 2007, he joined with then senators Obama of Illinois and Joe Biden of Delaware in pushing for compensation for black farmers who had been victims of government discrimination. Scott also has been the prime sponsor of the CBCs' alternative budget plan, which would phase out the Bush-era tax cuts for upper-income taxpayers to finance more spending on domestic programs. The House has routinely defeated the annual proposals, voting 126-292 in March 2008.

In 2004, Scott faced his first Republican challenger since 1996, Winsome Sears, a former Marine and the first black Republican woman in the House of Delegates. Sears criticized Scott as "radical" on national security, education, gay rights and abortion. Scott focused on his record and criticized Republican policies, including an "overextended" military. In this strongly Democratic district, he won 69%-31%. Since then, he has run unopposed.

FOURTH DISTRICT

Randy Forbes (R)

Elected June 2001, 4th full term; b. Feb. 17, 1952, Chesapeake; home, Chesapeake; Randolph-Macon Col., B.A. 1974, U. of VA, J.D. 1977; Baptist; married (Shirley); 4 children.

Elected Office: VA House of Del., 1989–97; VA Senate, 1997–2001.

Professional Career: Practicing atty., 1977–2001.

DC Office: 2438 RHOB, 20515, 202-225-6365; Fax: 202-226-1170; Web site: forbes.house.gov.

State Offices: Chesapeake, 757-382-0080; Colonial Heights, 804-526-4969; Emporia, 434-634-5575.

Committees: *Armed Services* (6th of 25 R): Readiness (RMM); Seapower & Expeditionary Forces. *Judiciary* (8th of 16 R): Commercial & Administrative Law; Crime, Terrorism & Homeland Security.

Group Ratings

	ADA	ACLU	AFS	LCV	ITIC	NTU	COC	ACU	CFG	FRC
2008	25	18	29	0	86	66	78	91	81	82
2007	20	—	9	5	—	70	79	92	74	—

National Journal Ratings

	2007 LIB	—	2007 CONS		2008 LIB	—	2008 CONS
Economic	27%	—	72%		30%	—	69%
Social	17%	—	81%		0%	—	91%
Foreign	0%	—	72%		22%	—	74%
Composite	20%	—	80%		20%	—	80%

Key Votes of the 110th Congress

1. Increase minimum wage	Y	5. Share immigration data	Y	9. Withdraw troops 8/08	N
2. Expand SCHIP	N	6. Foreign aid abortion ban	Y	10. No operations in Iran	N
3. Raise CAFE standards	N	7. Ban gay bias in workplace	N	11. Free trade with Peru	Y
4. Bail out financial markets	N	8. Repeal D.C. gun law	Y	12. Overhaul FISA	Y

Election Results

2008 general	Randy Forbes (R)	199,075	(60%)	($942,026)
	Andrea Miller (D)	135,041	(40%)	($37,670)
2008 primary	Randy Forbes (R)	unopposed		

Prior Winning Percentages: 2006 (76%); 2004 (64%); 2002 (98%); 2001 (52%)

Population		Race/Ethnicity		Work	
Pop. 2007:	711,914	White:	59.4%	Private:	71.2%
Change since 2000:	Up 10.6%	Black:	33.5%	Government:	24.6%
Urban:	70.9%	Hispanic:	3.5%	Self-employed:	4.1%
Rural:	29.1%	Asian:	1.7%	Blue collar:	25.0%
Area size:	4,575 sq. mi.	Native Am.:	0.4%	White collar:	57.8%
		Hawaiian:	0.1%	Khaki collar:	1.8%
Age		Two+ races:	1.4%	Other:	15.5%
Median age:	36.4 yrs.	*Ancestry*		Median income:	$56,933
More than 65 yrs:	10.5%	USA:	11.8%	Median home value:	$193,300
Less than 18 yrs:	25.1%	English:	9.7%	Poverty:	9.5%
Education		German:	8.1%	**Military Veterans**	
H.S. grad:	83.1%			% of Pop:	14.9%
College grad:	21.8%				
Grad degree:	7.7%				

The clash of arms resounds through much of the history of Tidewater Virginia. The region was the scene of the final victory of the Revolutionary War and saw bitter fighting more than 80 years later in the Civil War, as Union troops invested the battlements of the small industrial city of Petersburg, 25 miles south of Richmond. The Blackwater River was a prominent dividing line between Union and Confederate troops. Today, the Tidewater boasts one of the densest concentrations of military power in the

2008 Presidential Vote
Obama (D) 178,795   (50%)
McCain (R).............................173,358   (49%)

2004 Presidential Vote
Bush (R) 166,689   (57%)
Kerry (D)................................125,164   (43%)

Cook Partisan Voting Index: R+4

world. The Hampton Roads area has the nation's largest accumulation of Navy bases, while Fort Lee, the big Army base near Petersburg, will more than double in size by 2011, employing more than 14,000.

The 4th Congressional District of Virginia includes much of the Tidewater south of the James River. The district covers some of Richmond's suburbs but about half its people are in the Hampton Roads area, mostly in the fast-growing suburbs of Chesapeake and Suffolk. *Money* magazine named Chesapeake one of the best places to live in the country, with its quality schools, open local government and ample green space; it has attracted international investment and is close to passing Norfolk as the state's second largest city. Suffolk was the original home of the Planters Nut and Chocolate Company and the eastern edge of Virginia's Peanut Belt, though production has dropped markedly. Growth in Suffolk has centered on high-tech defense contracting firms. The district also takes in the flat lands of Southside Virginia fanning south from the James River. These were tobacco lands after the English first settled them in the 17th century. Today, they also produce Smithfield hams in an area that calls itself the "Ham Capital of the World." The Great Dismal Swamp, which crosses into North Carolina, is a breathtaking national wildlife preserve that features long hikes into marshy woodland and the shallow Lake Drummond; it was a sanctuary for runaway slaves. The district includes all of Petersburg and Hopewell, with its Honeywell plant and 18th century plantations.

The congressman from the 4th District is Randy Forbes, a Republican who won a June 2001 special election. Forbes grew up in Chesapeake, majored in government at Randolph-Macon College, and graduated from the University of Virginia law school. He started a law firm in Chesapeake that later merged with a larger Norfolk firm. His first job in politics was as an aide to the Democratic member of the House of Delegates from Chesapeake. When his boss retired in 1989, Forbes ran and won the seat as a Republican. Four years later, when Republicans were still in the minority, he became the party's floor leader. In 1997, he was elected to the state Senate. Forbes was a classmate and friend of Governors George Allen and Jim Gilmore in law school, and in 1996 Allen made him Republican State chairman. In that job, he helped engineer the historic Republican 1997 sweep of all three statewide offices.

When 10-term Democratic Rep. Norman Sisisky died after cancer surgery in 2001, national and state Republican leaders asked Forbes to run in the competitive seat. He was nominated at a party convention, and then got a break when the strongest Democrat, Sisisky's son, Mark, declined to run. Democrats chose state Sen. Louise Lucas of Portsmouth, an African-American who held a majority-black seat. Both national parties and their interest-group allies spent heavily on the race. Republicans attacked Lucas for opposing repeal of the sales tax on non-prescription drugs and for supporting a gasoline tax increase. Democrats criticized Forbes for his position on Social Security after Forbes said that he favored President George W. Bush's proposal to let younger workers invest some of their payroll taxes in individual investment accounts. Lucas carried Portsmouth 63%-37%. But Forbes won in more populous Chesapeake 61%-39% and in rural counties for an overall victory of 52%-48%.

In the House, the conservative Forbes is the new ranking Republican on the Readiness Subcommittee of the House Armed Services Committee, a plum post considering the military presence in his district. He generally backed the Bush administration on the war in Iraq, though in June 2006 he did call for a gradual withdrawal of troops by the end of that year if the Iraqi government wouldn't declare legal protections for U.S troops.

In the 110th Congress (2007–08), Forbes was the ranking Republican on the Crime, Terrorism and Homeland Security Subcommittee of the Judiciary Committee, where he pushed a "law and order" agenda to address drug trafficking, child pornography and gang violence. In 2006, the House passed his bill to make any illegal alien found to be a member of a criminal gang detainable, deportable and ineligible to receive political asylum or other benefits. On the committee, Forbes also cosponsored a constitutional amendment to ban same-sex marriages and supported an effort to force doctors to inform pregnant women that a fetus can feel pain during an abortion. He founded the Congressional Prayer Caucus, which has tried to halt the removal of references to God in public dialogue.

Forbes is also interested in energy issues. In 2008, he unveiled a "New Manhattan Project for Energy Independence," calling for cash awards for companies that meet certain goals such as designing a car that gets 70 miles per gallon of gasoline.

In 2008, Forbes was held to a 60%-40% re-election victory against poorly-funded Democrat Andrea Miller, a former regional director for MoveOn.org who benefited from the local strength of presidential nominee Barack Obama and Senate candidate Mark Warner.

FIFTH DISTRICT

Tom Perriello (D)

Elected 2008, 1st term; b. Oct. 9, 1974, Charlottesville; home, Ivy; Yale U., B.A. 1996, J.D. 2001; Catholic; single.

Professional Career: Yale Law Schl. teaching fellow, Sierra Leone, 2001–02; U. of Sierra Leone, Special advisor to the intl. prosecutor of Special Court for Sierra Leone, 2003–03; Consultant, Intl. Centre for Transitional Justice, 2003 (Kosovo), 2005 (Darfur) & 2007 (Afghanistan); Fellow, Century Foundation, Founding Partner, Res Publica, 2003–08

DC Office: 1520 LHOB, 20515, 202-225-4711; Fax: 202-225-5681; Web site: perriello.house.gov.

State Offices: Charlottesville, 434-293-9631; Danville, 434-791-2596; Farmville, 434-392-1997.

Committees: *Transportation & Infrastructure* (42nd of 44 D): Economic Development, Public Buildings & Emergency Management; Railroads, Pipelines & Hazardous Materials; Water Resources & Environment. *Veterans' Affairs* (9th of 18 D): Economic Opportunity; Health.

Group Ratings and Key Votes: Newly Elected

Election Results

2008 general	Tom Perriello (D)	158,810	(50%)	($1,822,148)
	Virgil Goode (R)	158,083	(50%)	($1,939,824)
2008 primary	Tom Perriello (D)	unopposed		

Population		Race/Ethnicity		Work	
Pop. 2007:	660,968	White:	72.1%	Private:	73.6%
Change since 2000:	Up 2.7%	Black:	22.8%	Government:	19.5%
Urban:	36.0%	Hispanic:	2.3%	Self-employed:	6.8%
Rural:	64.0%	Asian:	1.2%	Blue collar:	26.8%
Area size:	9,054 sq. mi.	Native Am.:	0.1%	White collar:	55.4%
Age		Hawaiian:	0.0%	Khaki collar:	0.2%
Median age:	39.6 yrs.	Two+ races:	1.1%	Other:	17.6%
More than 65 yrs:	15.4%	*Ancestry*		Median income:	$41,445
Less than 18 yrs:	21.3%	USA:	14.9%	Median home value:	$130,200
Education		English:	11.3%	Poverty:	14.4%
H.S. grad:	78.3%	German:	8.9%	**Military Veterans**	
College grad:	21.5%			% of Pop:	11.3%
Grad degree:	8.8%				

Southside Virginia is a geographic name that for years was shorthand for a state of mind. Located here is Appomattox Court House, in the serene little hamlet where Robert E. Lee surrendered to his one-time subordinate Ulysses S. Grant; and also Danville, where the tobacco auction originated in 1858. In Prince Edward County, Democratic Sen. Harry Byrd's massive resistance to a federal court desegregation order shut down public schools in 1957. The eastern counties are flat and humid—frontier

2008 Presidential Vote		
McCain (R)............................164,874	(51%)
Obama (D) 157,362	(48%)
2004 Presidential Vote		
Bush (R)................................158,568	(56%)
Kerry (D)..............................121,960	(43%)
Cook Partisan Voting Index:	R + 5	

in the late colonial period, plantation country by 1800, and now peanut fields and pine forests. Along U.S. 58 are the vestiges of Virginia's Tobacco Road, and in South Hill the Tobacco Farm Life Museum pays tribute to that heritage, though only one tobacco warehouse is still in business. To the west, into the Piedmont, the land gradually gets more hilly. There is a D-Day Memorial in Bedford, which lost more men per capita, 23 of its 35 soldiers, in the Normandy invasion than any other town in the nation. Nearby are the abandoned textile mills and furniture factories of Danville and Martinsville, with Virginia's highest unemployment. Their economy is on the rebound with an IKEA furniture factory, the nation's largest indoor fish farm called Blue Ridge Aquaculture, and biofuel and wind energy research centers financed by the state's tobacco settlement money.

Other new influences are taking root in Southside Virginia. Metro Richmond is reaching out and rural counties have sprouted subdivisions and shopping centers. Charlottesville, once a tiny town centered on Thomas Jefferson's lawn at the University of Virginia, and surrounding Albemarle County have attracted new residents to the college town atmosphere and the beauty of the rolling hills of the Piedmont. A half century ago, the politics of Southside were Democratic and segregationist, run by chain-smoking local bankers and courthouse lawyers. But they are long gone. UVA's Board of Visitors voted in 2007 to apologize for its treatment of slaves.

The 5th district of Virginia consists of much of Southside Virginia, west of metropolitan Richmond, and spreads out to the Blue Ridge Mountains. It includes all of liberal Charlottesville and Albemarle County and fast-growing Fluvanna County, but skirts around conservative Lynchburg. In recent decades, the district has mostly gone Republican. But Virginia's recent Democratic governors, Mark Warner and Tim Kaine, have energized Charlottesville and Albemarle County liberals, and Democrat Barack Obama's presidential campaign in 2008 registered thousands of Southside blacks. The 5th district was politically competitive in 2008 and produced one of the biggest upsets in congressional contests that year.

The new congressman from the 5th district is Tom Perriello (*PEAR-ee-ello*), a Democrat elected by a margin of 727 votes in 2008. He defeated veteran Republican Rep. Virgil Goode. Perriello was raised in Albemarle County, which houses the liberal college town of Charlottesville. He worked as a page for former Virginia state Delegate Mitchell Van Yahres, a Democrat, and as a legislative aide for former Democratic Rep. L.F. Payne. He earned a bachelor's degree and a law degree from Yale University. In 2001, Perriello worked as an advisor to prosecution lawyers at a special court for war criminals in the Republic of Sierra Leone. Perriello subsequently was as a national security consultant for several years, and his work took him to the war-torn regions of Kosovo, Darfur and Afghanistan. He has also helped found two faith-based non-profit organizations: Catholics in Alliance for the Common Good, which promotes social justice, and Res Publica, an advocacy group aimed at ending the conflict in Darfur. Returning to Charlottesville, he taught a course at the UVA Law School.

His decision to challenge Goode in 2008 was a formidable undertaking. The six-term incumbent had been reelected with 64% of the vote in 2004 and 59% in 2006. But Perriello got off to a fast start by raising just under $270,000. With help from national Democrats, he eventually raised $1.8 million, about the same as Goode and an indication he would have a fighting chance in this conservative-leaning district. Perriello campaigned on his religious convictions, running ads that claimed his non-profit work was his way of answering God's calling. He also attacked Goode, who won the seat in 1996 as a Democrat, as being unable to work across party lines and blamed Republican policies for the district's economic woes. He also criticized Goode for taking campaign contributions from the scandal-plagued defense contractor MZM as he was working to get $3.6 million in federal funds for the company to locate a military intelligence center in Danville.

Goode responded with negative ads of his own, one showing Perriello wearing a beard, with his face darkened, and referring to him as a "New York lawyer." Late in the campaign it was reported that Goode, a strong opponent of gay rights, had supported the filming in Danville of "Eden's Curve," which described homosexual relationships. Goode denied it, but his press secretary had a bit part in the film and after the story broke, he resigned from the staff.

Perriello won by 50.1%-49.9%, with huge majorities in Charlottesville and Albemarle County, large margins in heavily African-American Southside counties and a victory in fast-growing Fluvanna County. The Obama campaign's registration drive in Southside increased turnout sharply and helped Perriello trim Goode's margins in rural counties. The result was close enough to trigger a recount, but Perriello was declared the winner on December 17 by 727 votes.

Early in his first term, Perriello broke with the Democratic majority and voted against releasing the second $350 billion from the financial services industry bailout, calling for greater accountability before troubled firms received more federal money. In early 2009, he succeeded in adding to the Democrats' massive economic stimulus bill a provision to increase tax credits for college tuition and other higher education expenses. Then in April 2009, Perriello joined 19 other House Democrats in voting against President Obama's budget, saying it did not do enough to address deficits. He also signed onto a bill that would prevent lawmakers from accepting campaign contributions from people or businesses that benefit from the spending earmarks they insert into appropriations bills. Perriello posted his own earmark requests on his website and urged other members to do the same.

Perriello could well be a Republican target in 2010. The National Republican Congressional Campaign Committee aired a radio ad in the district criticizing him for voting against a proposal to investigate Democratic House Speaker Nancy Pelosi's claim that the Central Intelligence Agency failed to inform her about the use of water boarding, a form of coercion that simulates drowning.

SIXTH DISTRICT

Bob Goodlatte (R)

Elected 1992, 9th term; b. Sept. 22, 1952, Holyoke, MA; home, Roanoke; Bates Col., B.A. 1974, Washington & Lee Law Schl., J.D. 1977; Christian Scientist; married (Maryellen); 2 children.

Professional Career: Dist. dir., U.S. Rep. Caldwell Butler, 1977–79; Practicing atty., 1979–92.

DC Office: 2240 RHOB, 20515, 202-225-5431; Fax: 202-225-9681; Web site: www.house.gov/goodlatte.

State Offices: Harrisonburg, 540-432-2391; Lynchburg, 434-845-8306; Roanoke, 540-857-2672; Staunton, 540-885-3861.

Committees: *Agriculture* (2nd of 18 R): Conservation, Credit, Energy & Research (RMM); Livestock, Dairy & Poultry. *Judiciary* (5th of 16 R): Courts & Competition Policy; Crime, Terrorism & Homeland Security.

Group Ratings

	ADA	ACLU	AFS	LCV	ITIC	NTU	COC	ACU	CFG	FRC
2008	15	18	14	0	71	69	83	96	79	100
2007	15	—	27	0	—	78	75	92	73	—

National Journal Ratings

	2007 LIB — 2007 CONS		2008 LIB — 2008 CONS	
Economic	25%	— 74%	26%	— 73%
Social	0%	— 91%	9%	— 85%
Foreign	0%	— 72%	8%	— 89%
Composite	15%	— 85%	16%	— 84%

Key Votes of the 110th Congress

1. Increase minimum wage	Y	5. Share immigration data	Y	9. Withdraw troops 8/08	N
2. Expand SCHIP	N	6. Foreign aid abortion ban	Y	10. No operations in Iran	N
3. Raise CAFE standards	N	7. Ban gay bias in workplace	N	11. Free trade with Peru	Y
4. Bail out financial markets	N	8. Repeal D.C. gun law	Y	12. Overhaul FISA	Y

Election Results

2008 general	Bob Goodlatte (R)	192,350	(62%)	($1,996,993)
	Sam Rasoul (D)	114,367	(37%)	($382,473)
2008 primary	Bob Goodlatte (R)	unopposed		

Prior Winning Percentages: 2006 (75%); 2004 (97%); 2002 (97%); 2000 (100%); 1998 (69%); 1996 (67%); 1994 (100%); 1992 (60%)

Population		Race/Ethnicity		Work	
Pop. 2007:	672,728	White:	83.5%	Private:	80.0%
Change since 2000:	Up 4.5%	Black:	10.8%	Government:	13.9%
Urban:	64.7%	Hispanic:	2.9%	Self-employed:	5.9%
Rural:	35.3%	Asian:	1.3%	Blue collar:	27.0%
Area size:	5,664 sq. mi.	Native Am.:	0.2%	White collar:	56.8%
		Hawaiian:	0.1%	Khaki collar:	0.1%
Age		Two+ races:	1.1%	Other:	16.2%
Median age:	38.9 yrs.			Median income:	$44,664
More than 65 yrs:	15.5%	*Ancestry*		Median home value:	$152,400
Less than 18 yrs:	21.4%	USA:	17.0%	Poverty:	12.8%
		German:	13.9%		
Education		English:	10.4%	**Military Veterans**	
H.S. grad:	81.6%			% of Pop:	12.2%
College grad:	23.5%				
Grad degree:	8.2%				

The sturdy men and women who settled the Valley of Virginia west of the Blue Ridge were quite different from the "second sons" of the European aristocracy who cleared the marshy forests of the Tidewater and built Revolutionary grand plantations there. Even before the Revolutionary War, Scots and Scots-Irish, German Protestants and Mennonites and Moravians—members of religious communities and fiercely independent farmers—poured down the great Wagon Road from Pennsylvania to the valley.

2008 Presidential Vote
McCain (R) 182,573   (57%)
Obama (D) 134,212   (42%)

2004 Presidential Vote
Bush (R) 177,133   (63%)
Kerry (D) 100,561   (36%)

Cook Partisan Voting Index: R + 12

They were looking not for the flat, mahogany-brown land that eastern tobacco growers sought, but for land that could support wheat, corn, and hay—crops that could be rotated and that an individual farmer and his family could handle. That same independent spirit nurtured the growth of higher education here. In Lexington alone are Washington and Lee University, which Robert E. Lee headed, and the Virginia Military Institute, where Stonewall Jackson taught philosophy and artillery tactics and which did not admit women until 1996, when it was forced to by the U.S. Supreme Court. A trio of distinguished women's colleges are nearby: Mary Baldwin College at Staunton, Sweet Briar College at Sweet Briar, and Hollins University at Roanoke. Also nearby is the respected Randolph College, which is now co-ed. President Woodrow Wilson's birthplace is in Staunton. Industry flourished here more than in most of Virginia east of the Blue Ridge. In the 19th century, the Norfolk and Western Railway established its chief junction at Roanoke, and as the years passed the city became the headquarters of the railroad, now Norfolk Southern, and many other companies. The city has lost population since the 1980s, but recently benefited from downtown renovation and a new biomedical center. It has a way to go to catch up to more high-tech savvy regions of the country, though: The Roanoke-Lynchburg area ranked last among 79 U.S. markets for broadband use.

The 6th Congressional District of Virginia covers the heart of the Valley of Virginia, from Strasburg south to Roanoke, and it crosses over the Blue Ridge to take in Lynchburg, the home of Liberty University, a fundamentalist Baptist college. In recent decades, the ancestral conservatism of the region and the feisty politics of the mountain rebels have melded into a single conservative Republicanism, more populist than elitist in tone, as concerned with moral values as economic freedom, and prickly about interference from Washington or even from Richmond. In 2004, the 6th District voted 63% for Republican President George W. Bush, his highest percentage in a Virginia district. In 2008, GOP nominee John McCain easily defeated Democrat Barack Obama here, 57%-42%.

The congressman from the 6th District is Bob Goodlatte, a Republican first elected in 1992. Goodlatte grew up in Massachusetts, the son of a Friendly's ice cream store manager and a part-time retail clerk. He attended Bates College in Maine, where he was president of the College Republicans, and then went on to law school at Washington & Lee. After college, he got a job on the staff of Republican U.S. Rep. Caldwell Butler of Roanoke. Goodlatte practiced law in Roanoke and stayed active in politics. In 1992, when Democrat Jim Olin retired, Goodlatte was nominated by the Republican convention to run for the seat and won the general election 60%-40%.

Goodlatte has a conservative voting record, and is best known for his work on the House Agriculture Committee, which he chaired when Republicans were in the majority. The agriculture in his district, as he notes, is "free-market oriented: poultry, livestock, orchards. It gives me a pretty free hand to work with all the different regions of the country." In the minority, he worked closely with committee Chairman Collin Peterson, D-Minn., to enact the new farm bill in 2008, serving as the committee's informal liaison to the White House. He helped to broker a compromise on country-of-origin labeling of meat in the bill. In 2008, he joined 50 other House Republicans in urging the Environmental Protection Agency to reduce ethanol production requirements. "I support the development and use of alternative fuels. However, we cannot allow government mandates to pick winners and losers," he said. In 2004, he worked with other tobacco state lawmakers to successfully steer to passage the tobacco buyout program—specifically, the end of Depression-era quotas and price supports—while also blocking the Senate's attempt to make the buyout conditional on Food and Drug Administration regulation of tobacco. On another issue, he met major protests, including some at home, when he objected to a bill designed to stop the slaughter of horses. He argued that it would produce increased horse abuse and neglect, but the House passed the bill in 2006. Term limits imposed by Republican Conference rules forced him to give up his leadership position on the committee in 2009.

Goodlatte's other locus of activity is the Judiciary Committee. In 2003, he sponsored the House-passed bill to limit class-action lawsuits against tobacco companies, gun makers and other companies, and a separate bill to give federal courts jurisdiction over large class-action suits. In response to conservatives' complaints over federal court decisions that cite legal rulings of other nations, he sponsored a bill stating that judicial decisions should not be based on foreign precedents.

With 9th District Democrat Rick Boucher of Virginia, Goodlatte has been a House leader on technology issues and has chaired the GOP's High-Tech Working Group. He supports a permanent ban on Internet taxes, and failing to achieve that goal in 2007, he helped to broker an agreement for a four-year prohibition. Goodlatte sponsored the Communications Decency Act, allowing censorship of obscene material on the Internet, which was overturned by the Supreme Court. To combat spyware software that tracks users' activities and identifying information, he won House passage of his "I-SPY Prevention Act" to criminalize the installation of such software without the owner's approval. In 2009, Goodlatte co-sponsored a bill to require presidential candidates to make their birth certificates public. Detractors said the legislation's sole purpose was to feed unsubstantiated theories that Democratic President Barack Obama was not born in the United States and therefore not eligible to serve as president.

Goodlatte has been consistently reelected without difficulty, and encountered no problem when he abandoned in 2002 his pledge to serve no more than 12 years. In 2008, he faced businessman Sam Rasoul, who was 26 and Goodlatte's first Democratic challenger since 1998. Goodlatte won 62%-37%.

SEVENTH DISTRICT

Eric Cantor (R)

Elected 2000, 5th term; b. June 6, 1963, Richmond; home, Richmond; George Washington U., B.A. 1985, Col. of William & Mary, J.D. 1988, Columbia U., M.S., 1989; Jewish; married (Diana); 3 children.

Elected Office: VA House of Del., 1991–2000.

Professional Career: Practicing atty., 1990–2000.

DC Office: 329 CHOB, 20515, 202-225-2815; Fax: 202-225-0011; Web site: cantor.house.gov.

State Offices: Culpeper, 540-825-8960; Richmond, 804-747-4073.

Committees: *Minority Whip. Ways & Means (6th of 15 R).*

Group Ratings

	ADA	ACLU	AFS	LCV	ITIC	NTU	COC	ACU	CFG	FRC
2008	5	18	14	8	71	73	94	92	86	88
2007	0	—	0	5	—	87	80	100	95	—

National Journal Ratings

	2007 LIB	—	2007 CONS		2008 LIB	—	2008 CONS
Economic	4%	—	95%		9%	—	91%
Social	17%	—	81%		26%	—	73%
Foreign	0%	—	72%		8%	—	89%
Composite	12%	—	88%		15%	—	85%

Key Votes of the 110th Congress

1. Increase minimum wage	N	5. Share immigration data	Y	9. Withdraw troops 8/08	N
2. Expand SCHIP	N	6. Foreign aid abortion ban	Y	10. No operations in Iran	N
3. Raise CAFE standards	N	7. Ban gay bias in workplace	N	11. Free trade with Peru	Y
4. Bail out financial markets	Y	8. Repeal D.C. gun law	*	12. Overhaul FISA	Y

Election Results

2008 general	Eric Cantor (R)	233,531	(63%)	($3,823,907)
	Anita Hartke (D)	138,123	(37%)	($63,152)
2008 primary	Eric Cantor (R)	unopposed		

Prior Winning Percentages: 2006 (64%); 2004 (75%); 2002 (69%); 2000 (67%)

Population		Race/Ethnicity		Work	
Pop. 2007:	724,942	White:	74.9%	Private:	77.8%
Change since 2000:	Up 12.7%	Black:	16.8%	Government:	16.0%
Urban:	70.0%	Hispanic:	3.3%	Self-employed:	6.0%
Rural:	30.0%	Asian:	3.0%	Blue collar:	17.7%
Area size:	3,556 sq. mi.	Native Am.:	0.3%	White collar:	68.3%
		Hawaiian:	0.0%	Khaki collar:	0.1%
Age		Two+ races:	1.4%	Other:	13.9%
Median age:	37.8 yrs.	*Ancestry*		Median income:	$62,780
More than 65 yrs:	12.0%	English:	13.2%	Median home value:	$235,600
Less than 18 yrs:	23.8%	German:	12.0%	Poverty:	7.4%
Education		USA:	10.1%	**Military Veterans**	
H.S. grad:	87.4%			% of Pop:	11.1%
College grad:	36.1%				
Grad degree:	13.0%				

In the center of Virginia, on a hill in downtown Richmond above the James River, is Thomas Jefferson's Capitol, one of the first classical-style buildings in North America, chaste and simple in the Jefferson style. A mile or so west is Monument Avenue, Richmond's grand 140-foot-wide boulevard, punctuated by circles, each with a statue of a Confederate hero—Robert E. Lee (62 feet tall, dedicated Memorial Day 1890), Jeb Stuart, Jefferson Davis, Stonewall Jackson, and Matthew Fountain Maury,

2008 Presidential Vote
McCain (R)............................205,949   (53%)
Obama (D) 177,789   (46%)

2004 Presidential Vote
Bush (R) 204,273   (61%)
Kerry (D)................................128,166   (38%)

Cook Partisan Voting Index: R+9

"the Pathfinder of the Sea." Richmond itself is a monument to Jefferson and to the Confederacy. Its metropolitan area is only the third largest in the state, but it still sets the tone for Virginia. It is home to many of the state's great institutions—Dominion Resources, Main Street banks, big law firms, and the *Richmond Times-Dispatch*. Richmond's metro area has grown far past its city borders, covering almost all of suburban Henrico and Chesterfield counties and spreading into what was until recently countryside. For many years, Richmond was riven by racial differences. In the 1950s, Virginia's leaders gathered in Richmond and called for massive resistance to desegregation. When Richmond elected its first black-majority City Council in the 1970s, the outgoing Council deeded the statue of Lee to the state for fear it would be torn down. Now Richmond has come to a better place. African-Americans have been a majority in the city for two decades now, and in 1989 Virginia elected a black governor, Douglas Wilder, who grew up on Church Hill in a segregated neighborhood overlooking the Capitol. In 2005, Wilder made a triumphant return as mayor, elected by a biracial majority. When he stepped down in January 2009, the *Times-Dispatch* wrote that he had "spent his term trying to deliver his vision for an office he helped create—a strong mayor under a new form of government." A statue of Richmond-born African-American tennis champion Arthur Ashe has been added to Monument Avenue. Richmond has been thriving economically with banking, securities, and health care corporate offices and the Philip Morris headquarters. Politically, the city is solidly Democratic. Henrico, Chesterfield and the counties beyond are heavily Republican.

The 7th Congressional District of Virginia includes some city precincts and most of the area surrounding Richmond. The black precincts in the city and Henrico County are mostly in the black-majority 3rd District. The 7th District extends past President James Madison's home at Montpelier to fast-growing Spotsylvania and Culpeper counties and as far north as Rappahannock County and the Blue Ridge Mountains. Like many other affluent and growing areas, some of these locales have been struggling with illegal immigration. The 7th is 17% African-American and 80% of its votes are cast in metro Richmond. This is one of the two most Republican districts in Virginia. George W. Bush twice won 61% of the vote here. In 2008, GOP presidential nominee John McCain beat Barack Obama 53%-46%. (However, Obama took the Henrico County suburbs by 679 votes of 116,000 cast.)

The congressman from the 7th District is Eric Cantor, a Republican first elected in 2000 who has risen through the ranks to become the Republican whip, the second-ranking post in the House minority leadership. He grew up in Henrico County, graduated from George Washington University and from William and Mary's law school. He also got a master's degree in real estate from Columbia University, and practiced law in his family's real estate firm in Richmond. In 1991, he was elected to the first of five terms in Virginia's House of Delegates. In the Legislature, Cantor was a leading ally of business, sponsoring a bill to limit the liability of Philip Morris in a Florida court decree and opposing restrictions on telemarketers. When GOP Rep. Tom Bliley announced his retirement in 2000, after six years as chairman of the Energy and Commerce Committee, Cantor entered the race to succeed him. Cantor had interned for Bliley in college, served as Bliley's campaign chairman and had the backing of his political organization. Still, he faced a serious contest in the Republican primary from state Sen. Stephen Martin, who emphasized his humble background and had a solid base of social and religious conservatives. Their contest turned negative. Cantor attacked Martin for supporting a back-door pay raise for legislators, and

Martin questioned Cantor's business dealings. Cantor put on a substantial advertising campaign. Martin raised less than $200,000, a quarter of what Cantor spent in the primary. Cantor won the primary by only 263 votes. He got 74% of the vote in Henrico, while Martin got 77% in his Chesterfield County base. In the general election, Cantor won 67%-33%, assuming the seat that Madison once held.

In the House, Cantor has been reliably conservative in the Richmond tradition. His first bill provided a tax credit of $1,000 per child for parents of school-age children until they graduate from high school. He backed cuts in corporate taxes to spur economic growth, and in 2007 he opposed tax increases on hedge funds and private equity firms. Drawing a parallel between the 2008 energy crisis and the labor and transportation shortage during World War II, he said that Americans needed to "harken back" to those days of nationwide collaboration. He supported all forms of energy development to achieve energy independence by 2025. Cantor is the only Jewish House Republican. With his knowledge of the Middle East and his strong support for Israel, he chaired the Republican task force on terrorism and unconventional warfare, and he praised President George W. Bush as more committed to Israel than any other president. In 2007, Cantor warned that anti-Semitism—including "Holocaust denial" —was increasing around the world and was a danger "for all people."

But his more significant activity occurred outside the public spotlight as a member of the Republican leadership team. His efforts to assure support for Republican initiatives impressed House leaders and led to a meteoric rise to leadership. In December 2002, incoming Majority Whip Roy Blunt, R-Mo., named Cantor as his chief deputy whip, giving him a seat at the party's leadership table and handing him the often thankless task of tracking his colleagues' sentiments on pending legislation. Cantor also won a seat on the powerful Ways and Means Committee, where he was a booster of the 2003 Medicare prescription drug bill and is an active proponent of health savings accounts.

When Blunt ran against John Boehner of Ohio to replace Texan Tom DeLay as majority leader in early 2006, Cantor backed Blunt and built an aggressive campaign to replace him as whip if Blunt won the contest. But Blunt lost to Boehner and remained as whip. Cantor had pledged not to challenge Blunt for the whip's post and kept his word. Arguably, Cantor's decision served the interests of both men. Blunt remained in leadership for another two years, which prepared him to run for a Senate seat in Missouri in 2010, while Cantor earned additional chits in his continued move up the leadership ladder. He was also able to rebuild his relationship with Boehner after backing his opponent in the leadership contest. In 2007, Cantor became finance chairman of the National Republican Congressional Committee, a testament to his prodigious fundraising skills. Cantor raised more money for Republican candidates for the House than anyone else except for Boehner. With Reps. Paul Ryan, R-Wis., and Kevin McCarthy, R-Calif., Cantor created the Young Guns to identify and finance conservatives and "new blood" candidates for the House, in tandem with the NRCC.

Cantor's political rise was accompanied by his enthusiastic salesmanship for GOP presidential nominee John McCain during the 2008 campaign, when he was among McCain's most outspoken backers in Congress. He embraced McCain's centrist approach on issues such as global warming and immigration, and his more conservative views on national security. As chairman of the 2008 Victory Jewish Coalition, Cantor also was an aggressive fundraiser for McCain. Later, he was reported to be among McCain's finalists for vice president.

After the party's dismal showing in 2008 and Blunt's decision to step down as Republican whip, Cantor was selected to replace him without opposition. In January 2009, he moved quickly to establish his mark as a leader of the loyal opposition to President Obama's programs. With Boehner's encouragement, Cantor prepared an alternative to the Democrats' $787 billion economic stimulus plan, which he said would create twice as many jobs at half the cost. In part because of Cantor's efforts as whip, all House Republicans opposed Obama's stimulus plan when it came to a vote on the House floor. Also in 2009, Cantor, with Republican Sen. John Thune of South Dakota, led a Republican working group to focus on waste, fraud and abuse in the spending of the stimulus money. And he was among the first Republicans to voice specific doubts about Democratic proposals on the federal budget, reform of the financial services industry, and expanded health-care coverage.

Cantor also has been deeply involved in party efforts to rebrand itself after two consecutive disappointing elections in 2006 and 2008. Modeling himself after former Republican House Speaker Newt Gingrich of Georgia, who led his party to take control of the House in 1994, Cantor's aggressive style has earned him the enmity of House Democrats, who derisively dubbed him "Dr. No" and accused him of spoiling any hope for bipartisanship in Obama's first months. Unfazed, Cantor rallied his deputy whips to begin focusing on fundraising for the 2010 congressional elections. In May 2009, Cantor launched the National Council for a New America to spotlight Republican alternatives to Obama's proposals. The group's agenda rollout attracted McCain and possible 2012 hopefuls, including former Massachusetts Gov. Mitt Romney, Mississippi Gov. Haley Barbour and Louisiana Gov. Bobby Jindal. But the group's policy statements made no mention of social issues, leading social conservatives such as former Arkansas Gov. Mike Huckabee, another potential contender in 2012, to criticize their approach to expanding the Republican tent.

With his active media presence and beefed-up press staff, Cantor has increased his public profile and is a strong possibility for future statewide office. At home, Cantor has faced only nominal opposition since his 2000 election but has raised more than $13 million. In the 2008 election, he spent $3.8 million against Anita Hartke, the Culpeper County Democratic chairman who raised just $75,000 and was hoping for a Democratic surge. Cantor largely ignored her and won 63%-37%.

EIGHTH DISTRICT

Jim Moran (D)

Elected 1990, 10th term; b. May 16, 1945, Buffalo, NY; home, Alexandria; Col. of Holy Cross, B.A. 1967, attended City U. of NY, 1967–68, U. of Pittsburgh, M.P.A. 1970; Catholic; married (LuAnn); 4 children.

Elected Office: Alexandria City Cncl., 1979–82; Alexandria vice mayor, 1982–84, Alexandria mayor, 1985–90.

Professional Career: Budget analyst & auditor, U.S. Dept. of H.E.W., 1968–74; Fiscal policy spec., Library of Congress, 1974–76; Staff, U.S. Senate Approp. Cmte., 1976–80; Investment broker, 1980–88.

DC Office: 2239 RHOB, 20515, 202-225-4376; Fax: 202-225-0017; Web site: moran.house.gov.

State Offices: Alexandria, 703-971-4700.

Committees: *Appropriations* (10th of 37 D): Defense; Interior, Environment & Related Agencies; Labor, HHS, Education & Related Agencies.

Group Ratings

	ADA	ACLU	AFS	LCV	ITIC	NTU	COC	ACU	CFG	FRC
2008	95	100	100	100	100	7	61	0	8	5
2007	95	—	100	95	—	5	55	0	15	—

National Journal Ratings

	2007 LIB — 2007 CONS		2008 LIB — 2008 CONS	
Economic	67% —	31%	81% —	19%
Social	77% —	23%	67% —	28%
Foreign	85% —	14%	85% —	8%
Composite	77% —	23%	80% —	20%

Key Votes of the 110th Congress

1. Increase minimum wage	Y	5. Share immigration data	N	9. Withdraw troops 8/08	Y
2. Expand SCHIP	Y	6. Foreign aid abortion ban	N	10. No operations in Iran	Y
3. Raise CAFE standards	Y	7. Ban gay bias in workplace	Y	11. Free trade with Peru	Y
4. Bail out financial markets	Y	8. Repeal D.C. gun law	N	12. Overhaul FISA	N

Election Results

2008 general	Jim Moran (D)	222,986	(68%)	($1,207,945)
	Mark Ellmore (R)	97,425	(30%)	($65,940)
	J. Ron Fisher (IG)	6,829	(2%)	
2008 primary	Jim Moran (D)	11,792	(87%)	
	Matthew Famiglietti (D)	1,764	(13%)	

Prior Winning Percentages: 2006 (66%); 2004 (60%); 2002 (60%); 2000 (63%); 1998 (67%); 1996 (66%); 1994 (59%); 1992 (56%); 1990 (52%)

Population		Race/Ethnicity		Work	
Pop. 2007:	656,537	White:	58.5%	Private:	68.9%
Change since 2000:	Up 2.0%	Black:	13.2%	Government:	25.7%
Urban:	100.0%	Hispanic:	16.0%	Self-employed:	5.3%
Rural:	0.0%	Asian:	9.8%	Blue collar:	10.6%
Area size:	125 sq. mi.	Native Am.:	0.2%	White collar:	75.0%
Age		Hawaiian:	0.1%	Khaki collar:	1.1%
Median age:	37.7 yrs.	Two+ races:	1.7%	Other:	13.2%
More than 65 yrs:	9.7%	*Ancestry*		Median income:	$85,604
Less than 18 yrs:	20.3%	German:	10.6%	Median home value:	$515,300
Education		Irish:	9.7%	Poverty:	7.0%
H.S. grad:	90.1%	English:	8.9%	**Military Veterans**	
College grad:	59.2%			% of Pop:	10.7%
Grad degree:	29.3%				

More than 200 years ago, when George Washington trod the brick sidewalks of Alexandria on his way to market or court or church, it was the largest city in Northern Virginia, far larger than Georgetown, just up the Potomac River. The areas that are now Capitol Hill and downtown Washington, D.C., were hills above the river's mud flats. But Washington became the national capital, and as it grew, Northern Virginia seemed left behind. In 1846, the District of Columbia retroceded its land south of the Potomac—now Alexandria and Arlington—to Virginia because it seemed obvious that the federal government would never need it, and it was 97 years before the first federal building was built on the Virginia side—the Pentagon. President Franklin Roosevelt wondered out loud what they would do with all that space after the war. When the Pentagon was built, Alexandria and the rural countryside of Northern Virginia were represented in Congress by Judge Howard W. Smith, a Harry Byrd Democrat and later the House Rules Committee chairman, who saw as his mission the maintenance of the standards of George Washington, Thomas Jefferson and Robert E. Lee. Yet by the 1960s, the area was changing around him. New subdivision dwellers with white-collar jobs and lots of children wanted schools with good academic programs, not the segregated schoolhouses Judge Smith's friends were willing to finance. The new generation wanted freeways, parks and recreation facilities. As Smith's district was moved farther out into the countryside, two-party politics came to the suburbs. Now the onetime suburbs of Alexandria and Arlington are "edge cities," as author Joel Garreau put it. Arlington County has the seventh highest median income of any county in the nation and has a greater share of people with college degrees than any other county in the nation. Giant office developments sprang up from rail yards in Crystal City and from used car lots up-river in Rosslyn. Commuters find roads jammed, and there are plans to widen Interstate 66, which was built with just four lanes.

The 8th Congressional District of Virginia consists of all of Arlington County and the cities of Alexandria and Falls Church. It takes in two sections of Fairfax County: a stretch of land from Tysons Corner west to Reston, and several areas south of Alexandria's Old Town. It includes George Washington's Mount Vernon, lower-income Groveton, suburban Springfield and the more rural areas around Fort Belvoir. The district now is solidly Democratic.

The congressman from the 8th District is Democrat Jim Moran, elected in 1990. He was one of seven children in an Irish Catholic family in suburban Boston. His father was a professional boxer and Washington Redskins football player. Moran graduated from the College of the Holy Cross and got a master's degree from the University of Pittsburgh. He was elected to the Alexandria City Council in 1979 and became vice mayor in 1982. Then in 1984, the first of what would be many career controversies flared, and Morgan pleaded no contest to a conflict of interest charge and resigned from the Council. The charges were later dropped, and in 1985, Moran was elected mayor. In 1990, he ran for Congress against Republican incumbent Stanford Parris. It was a nasty race. Parris said Moran was a supporter of Iraqi Leader Saddam Hussein, and Moran responded that he wanted to "break [Parris's] nose," and called him "a deceitful, fatuous jerk." The major substantive issue was abortion rights; Moran ran an ad portraying Lady Liberty behind bars to demonstrate his "pro choice" position. With a big margin in Alexandria, he won 52%-45%.

In the House, Moran has styled himself as a moderate among Democrats. In 1997, he co-founded the New Democrat Coalition, made up of moderate Democrats to support alternatives to liberal policies. Unlike many liberals, Moran has supported free trade agreements, and, he is a strong ally of the high-tech industry. Concerned about young television audiences, Moran in April 2009 introduced a bill to ban advertisements for erectile dysfunction products from airing on commercial television between 6 a.m. and 10 p.m.

With a district chock full of federal employees, Moran watches out for their interests, and has sponsored a bill to create a public service academy. He is also an advocate for his district when it comes to earmarking, the practice of inserting special projects into appropriations bills to benefit lawmakers' constituencies. On the Defense Appropriations Subcommittee, he was among the top recipients of earmarks in the 2008 defense spending bill. But one of the downsides of earmarking in recent years has been the occasional scandals involving the beneficiaries. In 2009, it was reported that Moran received over $37,000 from the PMA lobbying firm and its employees during the 2008 election season, and that also in 2008, he secured a $1.6 million earmark for a PMA client. PMA is under federal investigation for possible improper campaign donations.

His short temper and edgy remarks sometimes land him in hot water. In 1995, he had a shoving match with California Republican Duke Cunningham on the House floor after Cunningham said that Moran had "turned his back on Desert Storm." At an antiwar forum in 2003, Moran's comments seemed to blame the pro-Israel lobby for the war in Iraq. "If it were not for the strong support of the Jewish community for this war with Iraq we would not be doing this," he said. "The leaders of the Jewish community are influential enough that they could change the direction of where this is going and I think they should."

2008 Presidential Vote
Obama (D)	234,203	(69%)
McCain (R)	100,234	(30%)

2004 Presidential Vote
Kerry (D)	189,525	(64%)
Bush (R)	104,298	(35%)

Cook Partisan Voting Index: D + 16

The furious reaction prompted Moran to apologize. In 2006, Moran, in backing fellow defense appropriator John Murtha of Pennsylvania in his unsuccessful bid for majority leader, accused fellow members of double-crossing Murtha in the secret balloting and said freshmen who had not voted for his friend would "screw themselves for the rest of their lives" and threatened unwanted committee assignments as punishment.

Moran's personal finances have raised problems as well. In 2000, the *Washington Post* reported that a pharmaceutical company lobbyist gave Moran a $25,000 loan on generous terms. Moran quickly agreed to repay the loan and suffered no apparent political damage. More trouble followed in 2002 with reports that he borrowed $50,000 from the founder of America Online, and that MBNA, the big credit card company, had given him a favorable rate on a mortgage.

In 2004, his primary opponent was Alexandria attorney Andrew Rosenberg, a political newcomer who criticized Moran's character and rhetoric. Moran cited his advocacy for his district and prevailed 59%-41%. He went on to win the general election easily and has had uneventful re-elections since.

NINTH DISTRICT

Rick Boucher (D)

Elected 1982, 14th term; b. Aug. 1, 1946, Abingdon; home, Abingdon; Roanoke Col., B.A. 1968, U. of VA, J.D. 1971; United Methodist; married (Amy Hauslohner).

Elected Office: VA Senate, 1975–1983.

Professional Career: Practicing atty., 1971–83.

DC Office: 2187 RHOB, 20515, 202-225-3861; Fax: 202-225-0442; Web site: www.boucher.house.gov.

State Offices: Abingdon, 540-628-1145; Big Stone Gap, 540-523-5450; Pulaski, 540-980-4310.

Committees: *Energy & Commerce* (4th of 36 D): Communications, Technology & the Internet (Chmn); Energy & Environment. *Judiciary* (3rd of 24 D): Courts & Competition Policy.

Group Ratings

	ADA	ACLU	AFS	LCV	ITIC	NTU	COC	ACU	CFG	FRC
2008	80	91	100	77	86	7	61	8	4	11
2007	95	—	100	75	—	5	65	8	6	—

National Journal Ratings

	2007 LIB	—	2007 CONS		2008 LIB	—	2008 CONS
Economic	54%	—	45%		55%	—	45%
Social	58%	—	42%		53%	—	46%
Foreign	62%	—	37%		55%	—	43%
Composite	58%	—	42%		55%	—	45%

Key Votes of the 110th Congress

1. Increase minimum wage	Y	5. Share immigration data	N	9. Withdraw troops 8/08	Y
2. Expand SCHIP	Y	6. Foreign aid abortion ban	N	10. No operations in Iran	Y
3. Raise CAFE standards	Y	7. Ban gay bias in workplace	Y	11. Free trade with Peru	N
4. Bail out financial markets	Y	8. Repeal D.C. gun law	Y	12. Overhaul FISA	Y

Election Results

2008 general	Rick Boucher (D)	207,306	(97%)	($1,153,918)
2008 primary	Rick Boucher (D)	unopposed		

Prior Winning Percentages: 2006 (68%); 2004 (59%); 2002 (66%); 2000 (70%); 1998 (61%); 1996 (65%); 1994 (59%); 1992 (63%); 1990 (97%); 1988 (63%); 1986 (99%); 1984 (52%); 1982 (50%)

Population		Race/Ethnicity		Work	
Pop. 2007:	639,759	White:	92.4%	Private:	74.6%
Change since 2000:	Down 0.6%	Black:	4.1%	Government:	19.2%
Urban:	34.1%	Hispanic:	1.3%	Self-employed:	6.0%
Rural:	65.9%	Asian:	1.0%	Blue collar:	30.6%
Area size:	8,838 sq. mi.	Native Am.:	0.1%	White collar:	51.8%
		Hawaiian:	0.0%	Khaki collar:	0.1%
Age		Two+ races:	0.9%	Other:	17.5%
Median age:	39.0 yrs.	*Ancestry*		Median income:	$34,506
More than 65 yrs:	15.4%	USA:	17.0%	Median home value:	$90,700
Less than 18 yrs:	19.5%	German:	11.3%	Poverty:	18.1%
Education		Irish:	10.0%	**Military Veterans**	
H.S. grad:	75.3%			% of Pop:	10.1%
College grad:	16.2%				
Grad degree:	6.0%				

As early as 1765, settlements were carved out of the great Valley of Virginia, which bends westward and south toward Tennessee and the Cumberland Gap. Most founders were of Scots-Irish lineage, and they moved to a mountainous area that developed almost apart from the rest of Virginia. The fiercely independent settlers were first farmers, later coal miners, as in West Virginia, which wasn't a separate state until 1863. Politically, this virtually all-white area opposed slavery and was skeptical, if

2008 Presidential Vote
McCain (R)............................160,430   (59%)
Obama (D) 108,220   (40%)

2004 Presidential Vote
Bush (R)................................153,868   (59%)
Kerry (D)...............................101,662   (39%)

Cook Partisan Voting Index: R + 11

not hostile, to the Confederacy. Out of the crucible of struggle between secessionists and unionists, Southwest Virginia developed a robust two-party politics after the Civil War, with both parties resembling their national counterparts more closely than in the rest of Virginia. It is a long way from here to plantation country—the state's extreme southwest corner is closer to the Mississippi River than to the Potomac River.

The 9th Congressional District covers all of southwest Virginia west of Roanoke. Over the years, the district became known as the "Fighting Ninth," because of its taste for raucous politics, which by and large were culturally conservative and economically populist. In recent decades, as development has moved down Interstate 81, it has become somewhat more like the rest of Virginia. With encouragement from state officials, businesses have created jobs at high-tech companies and telephone call centers. Agriculture has been thriving, especially with produce and dairy. Mountain counties farther west continue to depend on coal and to lose population. In 1990, mining employed 10,300 people and produced 46.5 million tons of coal; by 2008, the figures dropped by about half. The district voted narrowly for Democrat Bill Clinton twice, but voted by much wider margins for Republican George W. Bush in 2000 and 2004. In 2008, the district went 59%-40% for Republican nominee John McCain.

The congressman from the 9th District is Rick Boucher *(BOW-chur)*, a Democrat first elected in 1982. Boucher grew up in the antique town of Abingdon, went to Roanoke College and then to the University of Virginia Law School. He practiced law in Abingdon and was elected to the Virginia Senate in 1975, at age 29. Politics run in the family: His father was the Republican commonwealth's attorney in Washington County, while his mother was county Democratic chairwoman. His grandfather and great-grandfather were Democratic members of the state House of Delegates. In 1982, Boucher defeated veteran Republican Rep. William Wampler with big margins in coal counties along the Kentucky border. Boucher tends to vote with House Democrats, but he sometimes strays, especially on economic issues. Following the deadly shootings at Virginia Tech in his district in 2007, Boucher softened his opposition to gun control laws and in December 2007 helped to enact in a bill requiring states to report mental health court judgments to a federal data base that screens gun purchasers.

He has devoted much of his legislative time to technology issues and is the chairman of the Communications, Technology and the Internet Subcommittee of the influential Energy and Commerce Committee. Boucher sees new technologies, from satellite TV to the Internet, as a means for out-of-the-way places like the 9th to compete with urban areas on an equal commercial basis. In the late 1980s, he sponsored the Satellite Home Viewers Act, so viewers without over-the-air network reception could subscribe to satellite services carrying network channels: the beginning of the now-booming satellite television business. He helped write provisions in the 1996 Telecommunications Act to open competition in local telephone and cable TV markets. He worked with fellow Virginian Bob Goodlatte, a Republican on the Judiciary Committee, to update copyright laws for the digital age. He expressed concern that the recording industry's anti-piracy technology on CDs might override the consumer's ability to copy albums for personal use, as permitted by law, and he filed a bill to permit circumventing such technology in digital content for "fair use."

Boucher also plays an influential role on climate change and energy issues. He functions as the chief negotiator for moderate Democrats on the Energy and Commerce Committee. Boucher worked closely with then-Chairman John Dingell, D-Mich., to enact the 2007 energy bill, including on provisions for tougher fuel-efficiency standards for cars and trucks. (When Waxman successfully challenged Dingell for the chairmanship, Boucher strongly backed Dingell, saying, "Legislating with John Dingell is like playing baseball with Babe Ruth.") His faction refused to support a global warming bill until targeted goals for carbon emissions and renewable energy production were reduced, which got the attention of Chairman Henry Waxman of California. He and Waxman eventually reached a compromise on the sweeping climate change bill that passed the House 219-212 in June 2009. The bill establishes a cap on greenhouse gas emissions and aims to reduce them by 80% from 2005 levels by 2050. It offers some protections of the coal industry. Without the support of Boucher and other members his coal-state faction, Waxman would have had difficulty passing the bill, which was a top priority of the majority Democrats in 2009.

His committee posting helps him raise large sums of political money from industries the panel oversees, and he usually wins re-election comfortably. But he faced spirited opposition in 2004 from challenger Kevin Triplett, a former NASCAR executive with significant support from national Republicans. Triplett promised to do more to foster local economic development and criticized Boucher for voting in 2003 against $87 billion for the war in Iraq. Boucher won 59%-39%. In 2008, Boucher did not have a Republican challenger.

TENTH DISTRICT

Frank Wolf (R)

Elected 1980, 15th term; b. Jan. 30, 1939, Philadelphia, PA; home, Vienna; PA St. U., B.A. 1961, Georgetown U., LL.B. 1965; Presbyterian; married (Carolyn); 5 children.

Military Career: Army, 1962–63, Army Reserves 1963–67.

Professional Career: Legis. asst., U.S. Rep. Edward Biester, 1968–71; Asst., U.S. Interior Secy. Rogers Morton, 1971–74; Dep. asst. secy., U.S. Dept. of Interior, 1974–75; Practicing atty., 1975–80.

DC Office: 241 CHOB, 20515, 202-225-5136; Fax: 202-225-0437; Web site: wolf.house.gov.

State Offices: Herndon, 703-709-5800; Winchester, 540-667-0990.

Committees: *Appropriations* (4th of 23 R): Commerce, Justice, Science & Related Agencies (RMM); Transportation, HUD & Related Agencies.

Group Ratings

	ADA	ACLU	AFS	LCV	ITIC	NTU	COC	ACU	CFG	FRC
2008	30	18	43	31	100	52	94	79	58	100
2007	40	—	18	60	—	44	80	68	37	—

National Journal Ratings

	2007 LIB	—	2007 CONS	2008 LIB	—	2008 CONS
Economic	41%	—	58%	34%	—	66%
Social	36%	—	64%	20%	—	74%
Foreign	0%	—	72%	40%	—	59%
Composite	31%	—	70%	33%	—	68%

Key Votes of the 110th Congress

1. Increase minimum wage	Y	5. Share immigration data	Y	9. Withdraw troops 8/08	N
2. Expand SCHIP	Y	6. Foreign aid abortion ban	Y	10. No operations in Iran	N
3. Raise CAFE standards	N	7. Ban gay bias in workplace	N	11. Free trade with Peru	Y
4. Bail out financial markets	Y	8. Repeal D.C. gun law	Y	12. Overhaul FISA	Y

Election Results

2008 general	Frank Wolf (R)	223,140	(59%)	($2,053,375)
	Judy Feder (D)	147,357	(39%)	($2,206,307)
	Neeraj Nigam (I)	8,457	(2%)	($8,815)
2008 primary	Frank Wolf (R)	16,726	(92%)	
	Vern McKinley (R)	1,506	(8%)	

Prior Winning Percentages: 2006 (57%); 2004 (64%); 2002 (72%); 2000 (84%); 1998 (72%); 1996 (72%); 1994 (87%); 1992 (64%); 1990 (62%); 1988 (68%); 1986 (60%); 1984 (63%); 1982 (53%); 1980 (51%)

Population		Race/Ethnicity		Work	
Pop. 2007:	780,188	White:	69.3%	Private:	77.0%
Change since 2000:	Up 21.2%	Black:	7.5%	Government:	17.2%
Urban:	83.3%	Hispanic:	11.0%	Self-employed:	5.6%
Rural:	16.7%	Asian:	10.0%	Blue collar:	15.1%
Area size:	1,864 sq. mi.	Native Am.:	0.2%	White collar:	71.8%
		Hawaiian:	0.1%	Khaki collar:	0.4%
Age		Two+ races:	1.6%	Other:	12.8%
Median age:	35.1 yrs.			Median income:	$91,470
More than 65 yrs:	8.0%	*Ancestry*		Median home value:	$478,500
Less than 18 yrs:	27.8%	German:	13.4%	Poverty:	5.2%
		Irish:	10.9%		
Education		English:	10.2%	**Military Veterans**	
H.S. grad:	90.0%			% of Pop:	11.0%
College grad:	47.4%				
Grad degree:	19.5%				

When George Washington decided to place the new nation's capital on the Potomac just upriver from his estate at Mount Vernon, where the falls blocked navigation above the port of Georgetown, the area was buzzing with new settlers. The land above the fall line on the Virginia side of the river consisted of rolling green Piedmont and the fertile mountain-bound Shenandoah Valley. The settlers came up the great Wagon Road from Pennsylvania and traveled the Potomac and the runs (a Virginia word for

2008 Presidential Vote		
Obama (D)	205,964	(53%)
McCain (R)	179,337	(46%)

2004 Presidential Vote		
Bush (R)	182,210	(55%)
Kerry (D)	145,741	(44%)

Cook Partisan Voting Index: R + 2

small rivers) that feed the valley. During the Civil War, this was some of the most heavily contested land on the continent. The Piedmont, historian C. Vann Woodward wrote, "soaked up more of the blood, sweat and tears of American history than any other part of the country. It has bred more founding fathers, inspired more soaring hopes and ideals and witnessed more triumphs, failures, victories and lost causes than any other place in the country." After the Civil War, the region was quiet. The frontier was very far to the west, and on these lands farmers quietly raised hay and grazed cattle and kept horses and hounds for fox hunting. During World War II and immediately afterward, this was still open country. Gen. George Marshall, driving from his office in the Pentagon to the old house he bought in Leesburg 30 miles away, would pass a few gas stations and crossroads villages and hundreds of acres of farm fields.

If Marshall made the trip today, he would see something very different. Metropolitan Washington has consumed the countryside. There are still some horse farms in the Piedmont, long the first or second home of some of the richest people in America, but they are increasingly flanked by subdivisions that sprout up seemingly overnight. Fairfax County, by some measures the highest-income county in the nation, had 99,000 people in 1950 and passed the 1 million mark in 2002. The explosive growth for the last decade or so has been in Loudoun County, just past Dulles Airport, the fifth fastest-growing county in the United States from 2000 to 2008, increasing 71% from 170,000 people to 290,000 people. The Washington metro area now extends past Fairfax and Loudoun and over the Blue Ridge into the Shenandoah Valley.

In the 1950s and 1960s, the Northern Virginia suburbs of Washington were bedroom communities where most commuters headed into the District of Columbia for work and where one-third of them were employed by the federal government. But in the 1980s and 1990s, Northern Virginia became an employment center and focus of innovation on its own. The Dulles Access Road, which ran through rural-looking territory 20 years ago, is now lined with office buildings holding high-tech firms and entrepreneurial startups, defense contractors and "Beltway bandit" lobbying firms. There have been growing pains: traffic is mightily congested and Loudoun County voters have swung pro-growth proposals to anti-growth regulation. Loudoun is family country—41% of households have children under 18. Unemployment has been far lower than the national average in Northern Virginia, and Fairfax and Loudoun have alternated as the county with the highest median household incomes ($105,000 in 2007) among counties with populations of more than 250,000. Recent trends have caused some unease: AOL moved its headquarters from Dulles, Va., to New York in the first half of 2008, and Loudoun County had as many foreclosures as new housing permits that year. Immigrants have flocked in to work on construction sites. Gang graffiti and an uptick in more crime prompted Loudoun voters to pass an ordinance denying services to illegal immigrants.

The 10th Congressional District covers much of Northern Virginia. It starts inside the Capital Beltway and includes most of McLean, home of Washington's political and lawyer-lobbyist elite, from Democratic Sen. Bobby Kennedy's widow Ethel Kennedy to former Vice President Dick Cheney and his wife, Lynne Cheney. It goes beyond the Beltway to include woodsy Great Falls, Herndon and the Route 28 corridor around Dulles Airport. It includes all of Loudoun County, heavily built-up in the east with some still-rural areas west of Leesburg, and the northern half of Fauquier County, which has limited development and is still mostly horse farms. It includes three counties in the northern end of the Shenandoah Valley, the country around Front Royal and Winchester. In 2008, 32% of the district's votes were cast in Fairfax County, 36% in Loudoun County, 10% in Prince William and Manassas, and 17% in the Shenandoah Valley. The district was once reliably Republican; it voted for George W. Bush for president twice, by 56% in 2000 and by 55% in 2004. With the influx of immigrants and as a reaction against religious conservatives who have pursued bans on books and other controversial positions, Northern Virginia is becoming friendlier to the Democrats. The 10th district voted for Democratic Gov. Tim Kaine in 2005 and Sen. Jim Webb in 2006. And it voted 53%-46% for Democratic presidential nominee Barack Obama in 2008.

The congressman from the 10th District is Frank Wolf, a Republican first elected in 1980. Wolf grew up in Philadelphia, the son of a police officer. As a child, he developed a strong interest in American history and precociously consumed biographies of Thomas Jefferson and Abraham Lincoln. He majored in political science at Pennsylvania State University and went on to get a law degree from Georgetown University in Washington, D.C. He worked as an aide on Capitol Hill and was an Interior Department appointee in the Nixon and Ford administrations. In 1976, he ran for Congress and lost the Republican primary. In 1978, he won the nomination to run against Joseph Fisher, a liberal who had won the district (then not extending beyond Fairfax County) in 1974, and again lost, 53%-47%. In 1980, Wolf ran again and won 51%-49%.

Wolf started off his House career, in the suburban Washington manner, concentrating on issues affecting federal employees. With Democrat Steny Hoyer, who represents a suburban D.C. district in Maryland, he sponsored a bill in 2007 to increase the government contribution to federal employees' health insurance premiums. He has long promoted telecommuting for federal employees. With Rep. Maurice Hinchey, D-N.Y., he sought to repeal a 2005 law that allows high-voltage electric wire systems to be built even if states object. In June 2007, they lost on a 257-174 vote. Wolf helped set up a Northern Virginia gang task force in 2003 and has sought funding for it since. In 2008, Congress enacted his 175-mile Journey Through Hallowed Ground National Heritage Trail, which will run from Gettysburg to Charlottesville, passing six presidential houses, 13 national historic landmarks and many Revolutionary War and Civil War battlefields.

For many years he used his seat on the Transportation Appropriations Subcommittee to work on projects in his traffic-choked district. From 1995 to 2001, he was the committee's chairman. He opposed earmarking proposals for specific congressmen before that position became popular with budget reformers in recent years. And it put him at odds with the powerful chairman of the Transportation and Infrastructure Committee at the time, Republican Bud Shuster of Pennsylvania. In February 2007, the moratorium on earmarks that he and Rep. Jack Kingston, R-Ga., sponsored failed in a floor vote, 204-196. Wolf also used the subcommittee chairmanship to push to passage a national .08% blood alcohol limit for drunk driving. He has sought funding for a Metro rail link to Dulles Airport which, astonishingly, was not foreseen by the system's planners. In August 2008, the Federal Transportation Administration approved plans for the link, a major hurdle cleared for Wolf.

Wolf has been one of the House's leading crusaders for human rights and is co-chairman of the Congressional Human Rights Caucus. He traces his interest in the issue to a 1984 trip he took to Ethiopia with his best friend in Congress, liberal Ohio Rep. Tony Hall (1978–2002). The country was in the middle of a famine, and Wolf called his close-up view of the impact on the Ethiopian people "a life-changing experience." Since then, Wolf has been to El Salvador, Chechnya, the Sudan, Sierra Leone and other global trouble spots. In 1998, Wolf sponsored the law setting up a religious freedom office in the State Department and requiring annual reports on religious freedom throughout the world. With Democrat Nancy Pelosi of California, he led the annual efforts in the 1990s to withdraw normalized trade relations with China because of human right violations, citing China's acts of jailing dissidents, persecuting Tibetan Buddhists and aiming missiles at the United States. In March 2008, he sponsored a bill to prevent officials other than the president from attending the Olympics in Beijing and urged President George W. Bush not to attend. In June 2008, he and New Jersey Republican Chris Smith said that the Chinese had hacked into their office computers searching for casework information involving Chinese dissidents. When he and Smith tried to meet with dissidents' lawyers in China, the lawyers were arrested. In December 2008, he worked successfully to get $15 million set aside to thwart governments that erect Internet firewalls. Pelosi once called Wolf "an unmatched leader in his commitment to human rights."

Wolf has also been influential on policy toward Iraq. After his third visit to the country in September 2005, he called for "fresh eyes" to look at American policy there and suggested a bipartisan study group. He pressed this idea with Secretary of State Condoleezza Rice and Defense Secretary Donald Rumsfeld. The result was the influential Iraq Study Group, headed by former Secretary of State James Baker and former Indiana Democratic Rep. Lee Hamilton. When Bush ordered a troop surge to try to restore order in Iraq, rather than move toward withdrawal as the ISG recommended, Wolf sponsored a bill to implement its recommendations, but the Democratic leadership declined to bring it up. He did get the House to vote 355-69 in June 2007 to keep the ISG operating. In early 2007, Wolf pleaded with Rice to send an envoy to Syria after Syria threatened Israel. With Bob Aderholt, R-Ala., and Joe Pitts, R-Pa., Wolf then met with Syrian leaders in April 2007. Their meeting was not assailed by the administration like a similar session that House Speaker Pelosi conducted with Syrian leader Bashir Assad a short time later. In 2009,

Wolf became a vocal opponent of transferring detainees from Guantanamo Bay Detention Camp to prisons within the continental United States.

Wolf also has long been one of Congress's leading opponents of gambling and has unsuccessfully tried to stop the proliferation of Indian casinos.

He has generally been re-elected by wide margins, but the Democratic trend in Northern Virginia has produced well-financed challenges to him in the last three elections. In 2004, he faced Democrat James Socas, who made a fortune in high-tech boom, and spent $500,000 of his own money. Wolf spent $1.6 million and won 64%-36%. In 2006 and 2008, his opponent was Judy Feder, former dean of Georgetown's Public Policy Institute, who worked in the Clinton administration. She spent $1.5 million the first time and $2.2 million the second, attacking him for supporting the Bush administration and for GOP inaction on the health care crisis. Wolf kept pace with her spending and criticized her for backing the 1993 Clinton health care plan. He won 57%-41% in 2006. Two years later, despite Obama's success in boosting Democratic turnout in Northern Virginia, Wolf won, 59%-39%, carrying every county.

ELEVENTH DISTRICT

Gerald Connolly (D)

Elected 2008, 1st term; b. March 30, 1950, Boston, MA; home, Mantua; Maryknoll Col., B.A. 1971; Harvard U., M.A. 1979; Catholic; married (Cathy); 1 child.

Elected Office: Fairfax Cnty. Bd. of Supervisors, 1995–2008, Chmn., 2004–08.

Professional Career: Non-profit executive; U.S. Senate aide; Defense contractor.

DC Office: 327 CHOB, 20515, 202-225-1492; Fax: 202-225-3071; Web site: connolly.house.gov.

State Offices: Annandale, 703-256-3071; Prince William, 703-670-4989.

Committees: *Budget* (23rd of 24 D). *Foreign Affairs* (13th of 28 D): Middle East & South Asia; Terrorism, Nonproliferation & Trade. *Oversight & Government Reform* (11th of 24 D): Federal Workforce, Postal Service & the District of Columbia; Government Management, Organization & Procurement.

Group Ratings and Key Votes: Newly Elected

Election Results

2008 general	Gerald Connolly (D)	196,598	(55%)	($1,974,640)
	Keith Fimian (R)	154,758	(43%)	($2,010,087)
	Joseph Oddo (Green)	7,271	(2%)	
2008 primary	Gerald Connolly (D)	14,233	(58%)	
	Leslie Byrne (D)	8,196	(33%)	
	Douglas Denneny (D)	1,508	(6%)	

Population		Race/Ethnicity		Work	
Pop. 2007:	741,612	White:	59.0%	Private:	68.6%
Change since 2000:	Up 15.2%	Black:	11.0%	Government:	25.6%
Urban:	95.9%	Hispanic:	14.0%	Self-employed:	5.6%
Rural:	4.1%	Asian:	13.8%	Blue collar:	11.9%
Area size:	404 sq. mi.	Native Am.:	0.2%	White collar:	74.2%
Age		Hawaiian:	0.1%	Khaki collar:	1.3%
Median age:	37.2 yrs.	Two+ races:	1.7%	Other:	12.6%
More than 65 yrs:	8.6%	*Ancestry*		Median income:	$101,455
Less than 18 yrs:	26.3%	German:	11.6%	Median home value:	$517,600
Education		Irish:	10.0%	Poverty:	4.3%
H.S. grad:	92.2%	English:	8.8%	**Military Veterans**	
College grad:	52.1%			% of Pop:	13.4%
Grad degree:	23.2%				

When author and *Washington Post* reporter Joel Garreau coined the term "edge city" to describe the autonomous urban centers developing on the rims of some of the nation's largest metropolitan areas, his prime example was Tysons Corner, Va. Rising on a hill west of Washington, D.C., Tysons Corner was a back-country intersection 50 years ago. By the late 1980s, it was the largest concentration of office space to be found anywhere between Wash-

<table>
<tr><td colspan="3">2008 Presidential Vote</td></tr>
<tr><td>Obama (D)</td><td>211,466</td><td>(57%)</td></tr>
<tr><td>McCain (R)</td><td>156,003</td><td>(42%)</td></tr>
<tr><td colspan="3">2004 Presidential Vote</td></tr>
<tr><td>Bush (R)</td><td>161,104</td><td>(50%)</td></tr>
<tr><td>Kerry (D)</td><td>159,055</td><td>(49%)</td></tr>
<tr><td colspan="3">Cook Partisan Voting Index: D+2</td></tr>
</table>

ington and Atlanta, with a modern skyline and busy multi-lane avenues that served as arteries to the Capital Beltway. Fairfax County, which includes Tysons Corner, had been a typical postwar suburb. It had only 99,000 people in 1950, far fewer than Washington's 802,000, and less than the 197,000 people who lived in closer-in Arlington and Alexandria. But in the years that followed, the trickle moving into Fairfax became a gusher. In 2000, it had 991,000 people, nearly twice D.C.'s. 572,000 and three times the 318,000 population of Arlington and Alexandria. They were mostly affluent people. Fairfax County in 2000 had the highest median household income of any county over 250,000 population, with dazzlingly high percentages of residents with college degrees and two or more cars.

In the last decade, Fairfax County has changed. Just as Tysons Corner made it a major commercial center, so it has taken on other characteristics traditionally associated with a central city. Population growth has been slow since 2000; the county passed the 1 million mark in 2002 and stopped for the most part. Meanwhile, suburban Loudoun County vaulted ahead of Fairfax in median household income, and Prince William County has been growing at a fast clip, attracting the young families that Fairfax once did. Some communities have remained unchanged, like Clifton, which still resembles a quaint old Virginia village. But much has changed. Immigrants—Koreans and Vietnamese, Ethiopians and Afghans, Salvadorans and Mexicans—have put their stamp what once were mostly white, heavily Protestant neighborhoods.

The recession hit Fairfax with less force than much of America. Unemployment rose in 2008, but remained well below national levels. The federal government still provides a solid base for the local economy and the Federal Transportation Administration in August 2008 approved the nearly $5.2 billion extension of the Washington-area Metrorail system from Tysons Corner to Dulles Airport. Unlike Loudoun and Prince William counties, Fairfax has declined to pass ordinances denying services to illegal immigrants, but as construction and service jobs vanish, there is evidence of immigrant outflow from the area.

The 11th Congressional District of Virginia consists of much of Fairfax County and most of Prince William County. It straddles the Capital Beltway and includes Tysons Corner. Inside the Beltway is Annandale; beyond are Vienna, Fairfax, much of Springfield, Burke, Clifton, Centreville and part of Mount Vernon. In Prince William County, it includes Woodbridge and Dale City, areas with large Latino immigrant populations, and stretches west to Haymarket. This is a cosmopolitan district: it is 11% African-American, 14% Hispanic, and 14% Asian. Demographic change has produced political change. Immigrants have been voting more Democratic than the people they have replaced, and among non-immigrants, liberal attitudes on cultural issues moved voters against President George W. Bush and his Republicans and toward Democrats like Gov. Tim Kaine and Senators Jim Webb and Mark Warner. In recent presidential contests, the district voted 52%-45% for Bush in 2000 but only 50%-49% for him in 2004 and 57%-42% for Democratic nominee Barack Obama in 2008. The seat also fell into Democratic hands in the congressional election that year.

The new congressman from the 11th district is Gerald Connolly, a Democrat elected in 2008 to the open seat left by retiring Republican Rep. Tom Davis. Connolly grew up in the Boston area. He considered joining the priesthood, and studied for six years at a Catholic seminary. But his interest in public policy led him to Washington, D.C., after college, where in the 1970s he managed the American Freedom from Hunger Fund and the U.S. Committee on Refugees. He got a master's degree from Harvard and worked for a decade on the staff of the Senate Foreign Relations Committee, where he specialized in Middle Eastern affairs and foreign aid. In 1989, he left Capitol Hill to run the Washington office of Stanford Research Institute International, and then became vice president of the San Diego-based defense contractor SAIC. In 1995, Connolly won a seat on the Fairfax County Board of Supervisors, whose former chairman, Davis, had been elected to the 11th District seat in 1994. In 2003, Connolly was elected board chairman, putting him in charge of a large local government at a time of rapid growth. Transportation was a major preoccupation, and his biggest project was the Metrorail extension from Tysons Corner to Dulles. Connolly was attacked for backing an above-ground line rather than a more expensive tunnel.

In these battles, Connolly worked with Davis, who paid close attention to local issues as well as playing a major national role as the chairman of National Republican Congressional Committee in the 2000 and 2002 election seasons. But Davis, an expert on political demographics, could see that Northern Virginia was changing, a lesson that was driven home when his wife, Jeannemarie Devolites Davis, was defeated for re-election to the state Senate in November 2007. In January 2008, Davis announced he would not seek re-election. Connolly was obviously a prime candidate for the office. Also getting into the primary however was former U.S. Rep. Leslie Byrne, who was defeated in the 11th District in 1994 by Davis. She had the backing of the national women's fundraising group EMILY's List, but Connolly outpaced her in fundraising, in part because of his support from defense contractors. Both ran as solid liberals. Byrne said Connolly's contributions from defense contractors cast doubt on his opposition to the Iraq war. Byrne was endorsed by Democratic Sen. Webb, but Connolly was endorsed by Byrne's 2005 running mate when she ran for lieutenant governor, Democratic Gov. Tim Kaine. In a low turnout June primary—only 24,000 people voted—Connolly won by a solid 58%-33%.

The Republican nominee was Keith Fimian, a businessman and newcomer to Northern Virginia politics who self-financed much of his campaign. Democrats attacked Fimian as a conservative on cultural issues, in contrast to Davis' moderate record, and Fimian got little help from national Republicans. Connolly won by a solid 55%-43%. Connolly's victory, and that of 8th District incumbent Democratic Rep. Jim Moran, means that most of Northern Virginia is now represented by Boston natives with thick Massachusetts accents.

★ WASHINGTON ★

Washington state is national trendsetter. From Starbucks coffee to grunge music, from America's leading exporter, Boeing, to the world's leading software maker, Microsoft, to America's most visible dot-com, amazon.com, Washington has been on the cutting edge of innovation. What was for many years an odd far corner of America is in many ways today a model for the rest of the nation. An unusual environment and human creativity combined to produce these achievements. Seattle's cold, misty air and 225 overcast days a year stimulate the appetite for strong, aromatic coffee, and the shapeless blue jeans and sweatshirts worn year-round in this moist climate by professionals and teenagers alike created a trend made famous by Nirvana, Soundgarden and other grunge artists. Boeing's airframe business took off during World War II because the Pacific Northwest's abundant hydroelectric power made cheap aluminum possible, and the boom in air travel in the 1980s and 1990s kept Boeing's huge assembly lines humming. Microsoft, founded by the usually tie-less and tousle-haired Bill Gates and based in Redmond, across Lake Washington from Seattle, became one of America's great success stories as its software became embedded in the vast majority of the world's computers. With flannel shirts and umbrellas, blue-collar types (as if in a Raymond Carver story) as well as white-collar professionals relaxing on woodsy acreage, Washington set a tone for the late 1990s, a style plainly Middle American but with attitude, an ordinariness so hip it is no longer ordinary. Washington is a commonwealth of nearly 6.5 million people, advancing economically in spite of big setbacks in recent years and pleased to the point of smugness with its physical environment and lifestyle. Washington has had its woes, but has bounced back, displaying strengths that have proved to be more durable than fashion.

Washington is not much more than a century old. In the two decades after it became a state in 1889, it built a new civilization as transcontinental railroads reached the great ports of Puget Sound, the wheat-processing city of Spokane, and the orchard towns, fishing ports and lumber settlements. Shielded from the storms of the Pacific Ocean by the Olympic Mountains and the sound, Seattle quickly became a serious American city, a lusty town full of lumbermen and railroad workers. When gold was struck in the Klondike and in Alaska, Seattle became a metropolis of miners, prospectors and get-rich-quick operators, the site of the original "Skid Road," where logs were rolled downhill to the port (today it's part of gentrified Pioneer Square). In the years before World War I, thriving young Seattle's politics were turbulent, as class warfare pitted the Industrial Workers of the World (the IWW, or Wobblies) against city business and civic leaders. The businessmen, after some violence, prevailed. Adding to the area's distinctiveness was its large number of Scandinavian immigrants, with their favorable views of cooperative enterprises and government ownership.

Over time, Washington was transformed by a series of national decisions that set its course for decades. One was government development of hydroelectric power. The Columbia River and its tributary, the Snake River, falling thousands of feet in a relatively short distance, had far greater hydroelectric potential than any other American river system, and President Franklin D. Roosevelt, who grew up in another scenic river valley, was always interested in these aqueous projects. In 1937, Bonneville Dam was completed on the lower Columbia. In 1940, Grand Coulee Dam, the largest man-made structure in the world at the time and still the nation's single greatest producer of electricity, was opened where the Columbia cuts through the arid, surrealistically contoured plains of eastern Washington. Washington proved hospitable to the industrial-union movement of the 1930s and became one of the nation's most heavily unionized states. When war came, Washington's hydroelectric power—the cheapest electricity in the country—made it the natural site for huge aluminum-production plants, which required vast amounts of electricity. The Seattle area became the home not only of shipbuilders, but also of the biggest aircraft manufacturer in the country, Boeing, founded in 1916 by William Boeing in a converted shipyard on the Duwamish River. During the war, the Hanford plant on the Columbia was secretly one of the government's main nuclear-weapons manufacturing sites; after the war, it was open about that status. Cheap power, aluminum, aircraft, nuclear weapons and high unionized wages—these became Washington's economic foundations in the post-World War II years.

Today's Washington lives less off the brawn of hydroelectric power and rail and ship tonnage and more off the brains that made Boeing the world leader in aircraft and Microsoft the world leader in software. Yet there has been some trouble in this misty paradise. One turning point was December 1999, when Seattle hosted a meeting of the World Trade Organization. It was supposed to be an occasion for the city to shine in the international spotlight. But 50,000 demonstrators took control of the streets, smashing Starbucks windows and preventing leaders from President Bill Clinton on down from attending meetings. Seattle's police chief and mayor either did not or could not stop the violence, and the world's lasting image of Seattle was lawlessness and violence in the streets. That event was followed by the Mardi Gras riots in February 2001, and fed-up voters took charge. Mayor Paul Schell carried only 22% of the vote in the September 2001 primary, becoming the first Seattle mayor in 45 years to lose a re-election bid.

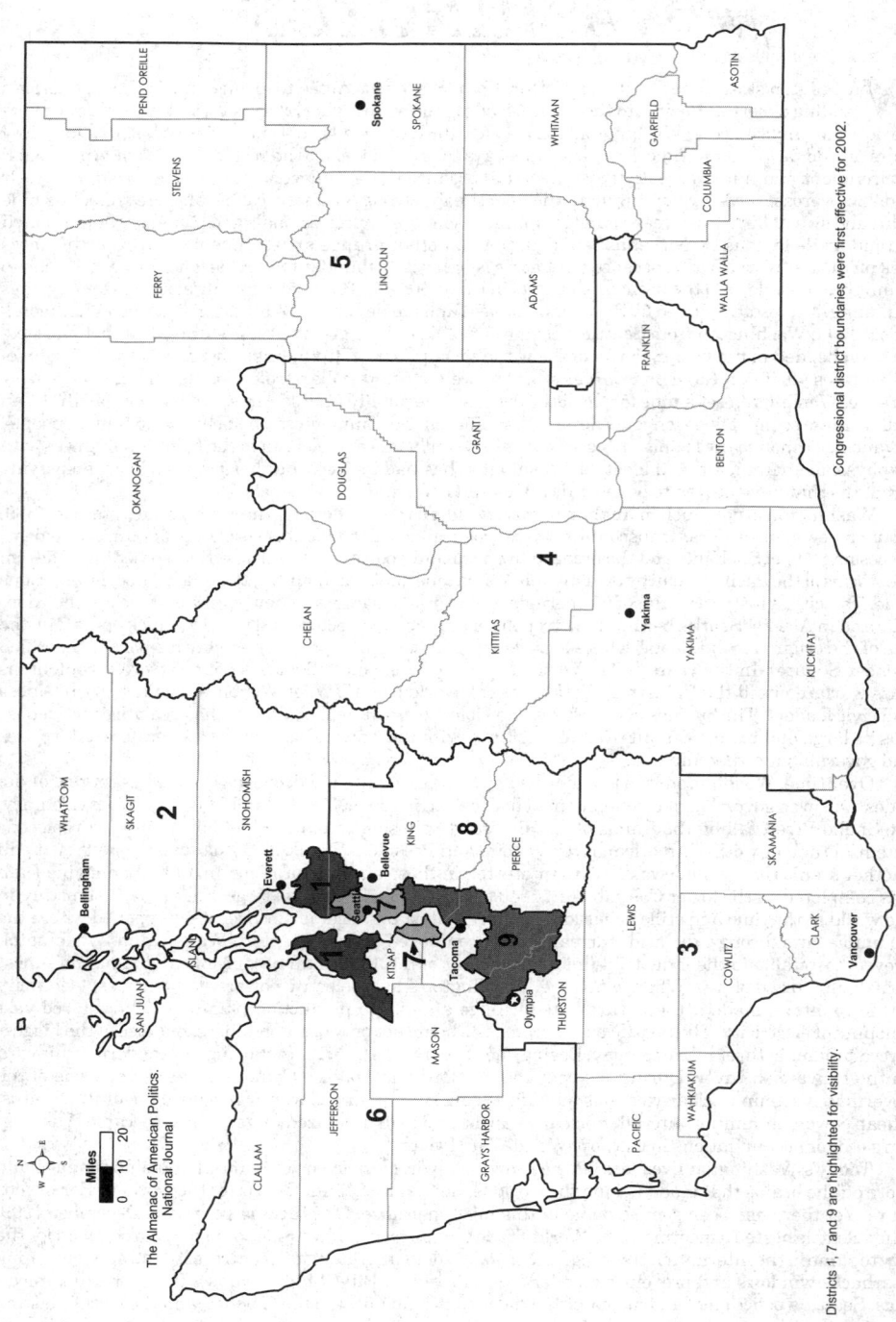

The Almanac of American Politics.
National Journal

Congressional district boundaries were first effective for 2002.

Districts 1, 7 and 9 are highlighted for visibility.

Washington also took a body blow from the dot-com bust. The high-tech industry boomed as businesses retooled to avoid Y2K problems, and then it suddenly became apparent that customers had all the technology they needed. The stock market started tanking in March 2000, and thousands of dot-com companies were taken down. Microsoft had been sued by the U.S. Justice Department's Antitrust Division in 1998. And in March 2001, Boeing's chairman announced that the firm's headquarters would move out of Seattle to Chicago. Then, after the September 11 attacks, the hard-hit airline industry cut back on orders. Boeing reduced its Seattle-area employment from 102,000 in 1997 to 62,000 in 2002. The company continued to suffer from the airline recession, competition from Airbus and congressional opposition to the proposal to lease KC-767 aerial refueling tankers, a proposal that failed amid revelations of corruption. Recovery from the recession was slow. For a couple of years, Washington's unemployment was the second highest in the nation, after Oregon's; the state lost 84,000 jobs between 2001 and 2003. Amid this turbulence, the fundamentals undergirding Washington's affluent lifestyle seemed threatened. Proposals by the Clinton administration to breach the dams on the Snake River threatened to reduce hydroelectric supply and to choke the agriculture of eastern Washington just as the court decision to protect the endangered spotted owl had largely shut down Washington's logging industry in the early 1990s. Light snowpacks and melting glaciers also threatened to reduce the supply of hydroelectric power even as demand from energy-starved California seemed likely to draw down the supply. For years, the Hanford Nuclear Reservation, which produced plutonium for the military, leaked radioactive waste, and it has been undergoing a multiyear cleanup costing billions of dollars annually.

All these problems may turn out to be no more than footnotes. Look at a map that shows elevation of mountains and density of population. On both sides of the Pacific, vast numbers of people are squeezed into small margins of level land between steeply rising volcanic mountains and the sea or tucked into nearby valleys. These islands of settlement are surrounded by vast wildernesses—desert and mountains, open sea and Arctic lands. Yet in the past three decades, the inhabitants of these pockets along the Pacific Rim have produced more economic growth than anywhere else in the world, and though there have been occasional slumps, the Pacific Rim has always come surging back. Boeing overcame the 767 scandal, and its 787 Dreamliner has clobbered Airbus's troubled A350 in advanced orders. However, the plane's inaugural flight has been delayed for almost two years, and concerns about its weight prompted Boeing to reduce the projected flight range for the first set of Dreamliners. Microsoft has survived the federal antitrust case, a huge fine from European Union antitrust authorities, Bill Gates's retirement and ventures into superphilanthropy. Its 35,000-employee Redmond campus may have produced a competitor for Google in Bing. Starbucks, once the fastest-growing retail business of all time, has had problems during the latest recession, as people have tended to curb their $3.50 caffè latte habits. But amazon.com has made big profits, while brick-and-mortar booksellers struggle. Hydroelectric power may have reached its capacity, but Washington ranks fifth among the states in wind power, and a state Supreme Court ruling has barred local governments from banning wind farms. The insurance firm Safeco was bought by Boston-based Liberty Mutual, and subprime lender Washington Mutual collapsed. But its bad loans were concentrated elsewhere, and Washington has had lower-than-average foreclosure rates.

Politically, Washington, with its Scandinavian and labor-union heritage, was in the 1930s one of the most Democratic northern states. Roosevelt's campaign manager, James Farley, used to refer to "the 47 states and the Soviet of Washington." Its mainstream Democrats—notably Warren Magnuson and Henry (Scoop) Jackson, who represented the state in Congress for a total of 87 years—believed in an active and compassionate federal government that built dams, aluminum plants and the Hanford Works at home and an internationalist, anti-Communist foreign policy abroad. Their political strength came out of a blue-collar base, augmented by the respect big business had for their political clout. Today, the fulcrum of the electorate has moved from blue collar to white collar, from economic class warfare to culture wars, with the balance favoring the Democrats. In presidential races, Washington has voted exclusively Democratic since 1988. Washington's governor and both of its senators are Democrats, and all are women. Democrats seem to have a secure hold on six of Washington's nine U.S. House seats. Four different Democrats have held the governorship since 1984, but the party almost lost it in 2004. The official count, after many shenanigans and legal challenges, declared Democrat Christine Gregoire the winner by 129 votes. And although Republicans lost control of the state Senate, they gained the attorney general's office. In 2006, the pendulum swung hard in favor of the Democrats. They nearly captured the 8th District U.S. House seat, which would have eliminated Republican representation west of the Cascades, and Democratic Sen. Maria Cantwell was re-elected by a solid 57%-40%, sweeping western Washington and carrying Spokane County in the east as well. Democrats increased their majorities from three to 15 in the state Senate and from 14 to 28 in the state House. Gregoire attributed these gains to the Democrats' moderation, their resolution of a water dispute in eastern Washington, passage of tax relief for farmers and timber sellers, a compromise settlement on unemployment insurance and tough penalties for sex offenders. She pressed for pay increases for teachers and other public employees, and Washington now has the nation's highest minimum wage. The balance seemed to remain steady in 2008. Gregoire was re-elected in a rematch with her 2004 opponent, Republican Dino Rossi, by a not-dazzling but not-ambiguous 53%-47%. Republicans held the 8th District House seat, and Republican Attorney General Rob McKenna was re-elected 59%-41%. In the state Legislature, Republicans gained one seat in the Senate and lost one seat in the House. And by a 58%-42% split, Washington voters approved an assisted-suicide law similar to Oregon's.

The political lines are fairly clear. The central city of Seattle is a liberal bastion, the upscale suburbs are trending Democratic, and while in the past, the old blue-collar lumber-country strongholds have soured on many Democrats, they've been tilting Democratic too. Seattle's King County, by far the most affluent county in the state, casts 30% of the state's votes, and it went 65% for Democratic presidential nominee John Kerry in 2004 and 70% for Democrat Barack Obama in 2008. Eastern Washington, the arid country east of the Cascades with much lower income levels, is generally Republican but casts only about 20% of the state's votes. The region went 59% for GOP President George W. Bush in 2004 and 54% for Republican nominee John McCain in 2008. Gov. Gregoire lost eastern Washington 60%-40% in 2008, but her 64%-36% advantage in King County would have elected her even if she had not carried the rest of western Washington, which cast half the state's votes, 52%-48%. Demographics may work in the Republicans' favor. King County had a population gain of only 8% between 2000 and 2008, while the heavily Republican Tri-Cities area (Benton and Franklin counties) gained 23%, as did marginal Clark County, north of Portland. (Washington has no income tax and Oregon no sales tax, so you can avoid both taxes by living in Clark County and shopping across the line in Oregon.) But Republican hopes may depend on changing their conservative approach. Rossi, Gregoire's opponent, combined fiscal conservatism with a feisty call for change in 2004 and 2008, but fell short. In his race for attorney general, the more moderate McKenna carried King County 54%-46% and won 60% in the rest of the west and 68% in the east.

A footnote on Washington's primaries: The state does not have party registration, and from 1935 to 2000, it allowed voters to choose candidates of various parties in its primaries: The top Democrat and top Republican in each constituency was deemed nominated, and the percentage of total votes won by incumbents in September primaries was often a harbinger of their performance in November general elections. But in 2000, the U.S. Supreme Court, in a 7-2 ruling, threw out a similar California primary system, and in 2003, a federal appeals court ruled Washington's system invalid. The Supreme Court's argument was that this arrangement violated the political parties' right to self-expression. In 2004, Washington voters passed Initiative 872, which allowed voters to select a candidate from either party, so that the two candidates with the most votes would move to the general election, regardless of party. In anticipation of the 2005 off-year primaries, both parties held nominating conventions to avoid application of 872, and in July 2005, a federal appeals court ruled the initiative invalid. That seemed to be the end of that, but in February 2007, the U.S. Supreme Court agreed to hear a case on the validity of 872, and in March 2008, it upheld the law in a 7-2 ruling. That decision came after the February presidential caucuses and primaries, but the August 2008 primary was run under 872. The result that some critics dreaded—two candidates of the same party facing off in the general election—occurred in only four of 124 state legislative races and in none of the nine congressional races.

Population			Household Income		Work	
Pop. 2007:		6,371,390	Under $15k:	11.5%	Private:	75.9%
State rank:		13th of 50	$15k to $50k:	34.7%	Government:	17.2%
Change since 2000:		Up 8.1%	$50k to $100k:	33.1%	Self-employed:	6.7%
Urban:		81.2%	$100k to $150k:	17.1%	Unemployment (3-yr. average):	4.3%
Rural:		18.8%	Over $150k:	3.6%	Poverty:	11.8%
Native of state:		47.1%	Median income:	$53,940	Blue collar:	20.9%
Not a citizen:		7.0%			White collar:	61.0%
Area size:		71,300 sq. mi.	**Home Value**		Khaki collar:	0.8%
			Under $100k:	9.6%	Other:	17.4%
Most populous cities			$100k to $300k:	47.7%		
1. Seattle		565,809	$300k to $500k:	27.4%	**Age**	
2. Spokane		205,559	$500k to $1 mil:	12.8%	Median age:	36.8 yrs.
3. Tacoma		193,920	Over $1 million:	2.5%	More than 65 yrs:	11.6%
4. Vancouver		158,944	Median:	$261,200	Less than 18 yrs:	23.9%

Race/Ethnicity				Military Veterans		Registered Voters in 2008	
White:	76.3%	*Language*		% of Pop:	13.0%	No party registration	
Black:	3.3%	English:	83.6%	*Veterans by Period*		Voter turnout:	3,036,878
Hispanic:	9.1%	Spanish:	7.1%	WWII and before:	10.5%	Turnout as % of	
Asian:	6.5%	Asian:	5.0%	Korea:	10.0%	voting age:	60.6%
Native Am.:	1.2%	Other		Vietnam:	34.5%	**Legislature**	
Hawaiian:	0.4%	European	3.5%	Gulf (pre-2001):	12.7%	Senate:	31 D 18 R
Two+ races:	2.9%	**Education**		Gulf (post-2001):	8.1%	House:	64 D 34 R
Ancestry		H.S. grad:	88.9%	Peace time:	24.1%		
German:	15.8%	College grad:	30.0%				
English:	9.7%	Grad degree:	10.6%				
Irish:	9.5%						

Presidential politics   For three decades, Washington was one of the most contrarian states in presidential politics, voting for Republican losers Richard Nixon in 1960 and Gerald Ford in 1976 and Democratic losers Hubert Humphrey in 1968 and Michael Dukakis in 1988. In the 1990s, it was more in sync with the nation, voting for Democrat Bill Clinton twice. Since then, it has moved significantly toward the Democrats, voting 50%-45% for Al Gore in 2000, 53%-46% for John Kerry in 2004 and 58%-40% for Barack Obama in 2008. In the first two contests, the winning margin and more came from just one of the state's nine congressional districts, the 7th District, which includes all of Seattle and close-in suburbs to the north and south in King County, where Democrats won more than 70% of the vote. In 2008, Obama carried the 7th district with 84% of the vote, but would have won without it. Voting behavior seems to be a function more of cultural values than of economic status. High-income voters were not much less likely than others to vote for Obama, and his support was greater among college

2008 Presidential Vote		
Obama (D)	1,750,848	(58%)
McCain (R)	1,229,216	(40%)

2008 Democratic Presidential Primary		
Obama (D)	354,112	(51%)
Clinton (D)	315,744	(46%)

2008 Republican Presidential Primary		
McCain (R)	262,304	(50%)
Huckabee (R)	127,657	(24%)
Romney (R)	86,140	(16%)
Paul (R)	40,539	(8%)

2004 Presidential Vote		
Kerry (D)	1,510,201	(53%)
Bush (R)	1,304,894	(46%)

graduates than non-graduates, and even greater among those with graduate degrees. Some 24% of voters were white evangelical Protestants, and they voted 70% for Republican nominee John McCain; 19% reported their religion as "other" or "none," and they voted 71% for Obama.

Washington switched from a caucus system to primaries in 1992, after conservative evangelical candidate Pat Robertson won among Republicans and civil rights leader Jesse Jackson finished a solid second among Democrats in 1988. But Democrats have never chosen to allocate delegates according to the results, preferring to use the results from party caucuses for that. In 2000, Democrat Bill Bradley, having lost in Iowa and New Hampshire and having no other states to contest for five weeks, came to Washington for the February 29 contest to no avail; Gore won the caucus by about 2-to-1. Republican George W. Bush beat McCain by a razor-thin margin in a primary that counted a little toward delegate selection. In 2004, Washington's Democrats held caucuses on February 7, and Kerry defeated Howard Dean, despite the huge crowds the bombastically liberal Dean had attracted in Seattle.

In early 2007, the parties were divided on what to do in 2008. Republicans, including Secretary of State Sam Reed, wanted to hold a primary on February 5 that would count toward electing delegates. Democrats were divided, with many favoring eliminating the primary. In June, a bipartisan panel of state lawmakers and party leaders came to agreement and voted unanimously to hold the primary on February 19, in hopes of being early enough to be relevant but not so early as to get lost amid the many states holding February 5 contests. But both parties also held caucuses on February 9. Republicans decided to allocate about half their delegates based on primary results; Democrats decided to use only caucus results to allocate delegates.

When Democrats caucused on the Saturday after Super Tuesday, Obama beat Hillary Rodham Clinton 68%-31%. He carried every county, getting 100% in tiny Garfield County, where only one person showed up to vote. In the primary 10 days later, Obama prevailed by a much narrower margin, 51%-46%, illustrating the huge advantage he and his organization had in caucus states. Turnout was 691,000; Obama ran strongest, 55.5%, in King County and barely won the rest of the state, running behind in more-downscale areas like Pierce County (Tacoma) and Clark County (Vancouver, across the Columbia from Portland, Ore.).

The Republican contests produced murkier results. In the February 9 caucus, McCain got 26% of the votes, Mike Huckabee 24% and Ron Paul 22%. All three, unlike the Democrats, campaigned in the 10 days before the February 19 primary, in which McCain won 50% of the votes, Huckabee 24%, Mitt Romney 16% and Paul 8%. McCain carried every county. Turnout was 530,000; McCain did better in King County and the rest of western Washington than in the eastern part of the state.

Congressional districting   In 1983, Washington voters approved a constitutional amendment that provided that congressional and legislative districts be drawn by a bipartisan commission; the lines can be changed by a two-thirds vote of the Legislature. If the commission is deadlocked, the issue goes to the state Supreme Court. In 1991, the commission created four districts that were pretty evenly divided between the parties. The one problem was that even minor alterations in the closely divided districts—the 1st, 2nd, 3rd and 9th—could turn out to be of partisan significance. But a decade later, the 2002 plan followed pretty closely the lines drawn in 1991. The Washington plan has been lauded by many for taking partisanship out of redistricting and for creating more districts that both parties can win. But

111th Congress Lineup	
6 D	3 R
110th Congress Lineup	
6 D	3 R

in Washington, where the commission is not bound by the mathematical requirements that in Iowa have resulted in districts not tailored to incumbents, incumbent protection has been the result.

Projections indicate there's a chance that Washington will gain a House seat in the reapportionment following the 2010 census. In that case, most or all of the new district will probably be west of the Cascades; the heavily Republican area east of the Cascades, which currently is carved into two districts, will be entitled to about 2.2 districts. If the state continues to have nine districts, there probably will not be major changes in the lines.

Governor

Christine Gregoire (D)

Elected 2004, term expires Jan. 2013, 2nd term; b. March 24, 1947, Adrian, MI; home, Olympia; U. of WA, B.A. 1969; Gonzaga U., J.D. 1977; Catholic; married (Mike); 2 children.

Elected Office: WA atty. gen., 1992–2004.

Professional Career: Dep. atty. gen., 1982–88; Dir., WA Dept. of Ecology, 1988–92.

Office: 416 14th Ave. SW, Suite 200, P.O. Box 40002, Olympia, 98504, 360-902-4111; Fax: 360-753-4110; Web site: www.governor.wa.gov.

Election Results

2008 general	Christine Gregoire (D)	1,598,738	(53%)
	Dino Rossi (R)	1,404,124	(47%)
2008 primary	Christine Gregoire (D)	696,306	(48%)
	Dino Rossi (R)	668,571	(46%)

Prior Winning Percentages: 2004 (49%)

Christine Gregoire is a Democrat elected governor in 2004 in the closest race in Washington history. Gregoire *(Greg-WHAR)* grew up on a small farm in Auburn, Washington, just south of Seattle. Her mother was a short-order cook who moved west to escape an abusive husband. She graduated from the University of Washington and, unable to find a teaching position, took a job as a clerk-typist for the state parole board. She worked as a welfare caseworker, attended law school at Gonzaga University in eastern Washington, then worked for Republican Sen. Slade Gorton in his Spokane office. There, she drew the attention of another Republican, Attorney General Ken Eikenberry, who hired her as a deputy attorney general in Olympia. In 1988, she was Democratic Gov. Booth Gardner's choice to head the Department of Ecology. Gregoire ran for attorney general in 1992, nationally a good year for women candidates but especially good in Washington state, where Democrat Patty Murray was elected to the Senate and Democrat Maria Cantwell to the House. Gregoire won the post and served three terms, getting national headlines in 1998 as the lead negotiator for the 46-state, $206 billion settlement with the tobacco industry.

With high name recognition from the tobacco settlement, Gregoire came to be viewed as a governor-in-waiting. When Democrat Gary Locke, elected governor in 1996 and 2000, announced in 2003 that he would not run for a third term, Gregoire became the front-runner to succeed him. She almost didn't run. She was diagnosed with an early form of breast cancer and had to have a mastectomy. She considered dropping out of the race, sought counsel from Democrats Janet Napolitano and Heidi Heitkamp, both former attorneys general and breast cancer survivors who had run for governor. (Napolitano won in Arizona in 2002; Heitkamp lost in North Dakota in 2000.) Gregoire decided to have the surgery, and she returned to the campaign trail a month later.

She had primary opposition from King County Executive Ron Sims, whose political base was in the state's most populous county and biggest media market. At the time, Washington was only slowly recovering from the recession and had the nation's second-highest unemployment rate. Jobs, education, taxes and the environment were the major issues in the campaign. But the campaign was also sidetracked by the issue of Gregoire's sorority at the University of Washington, which excluded African-Americans. She charged that the Sims campaign was behind the story. Sims, who would have been the state's first African-American governor, denied being the source. Local black leaders harshly criticized Gregoire, and she angrily defended her record on race issues and said that she had fought to eliminate the sorority's exclusionary policy. Voters didn't seem to hold it against her. She defeated Sims 66%-30%, carrying every county in the state, including Sims's base in Seattle's King County, 59%-38%.

Republicans nominated state Sen. Dino Rossi, a former Senate Ways and Means Committee chairman from the Seattle suburbs who billed himself as a "fiscal conservative with a social conscience." He has an admirable life story: The grandson of an Italian immigrant coal miner, he grew up in a family that endured financial hardship and the alcoholism of his mother, and he became a successful commercial real-estate investor. He campaigned as an agent of change in a state where Republicans had not won the governorship since John Spellman's victory in 1980. Business interests lined up with Rossi, who said he wanted to change the culture in Olympia to a "free-enterprise model" and who promised to create a cabinet-level office of regulatory reform. Gregoire, who ran as a fiscal moderate, received strong support from the state's largest labor unions. Rossi's opposition to abortion spurred abortion-rights groups to donate heavily to Gregoire's campaign and led Democrats to characterize him as a right-wing extremist—the same tactic that had worked against the previous two Republican nominees. As a youthful suburban legislator with four children who focused on economic rather than social issues, Rossi was not so easily caricatured. But by October, Gregoire had built a double-digit lead in most public polls, and national Republicans, who early in the campaign had had high hopes for the ticket of Bush, Senate nominee George Nethercutt and Rossi, began to write off the state as a lost cause. In the final weeks, Rossi's change theme gained traction against Gregoire, a cautious candidate who had spent nearly her entire career in government jobs.

Washington is one of just two states that allow absentee ballots to be postmarked as late as Election Day, so it took nearly three weeks for all the votes to be counted. The lead seesawed for days, and in the ensuing weeks, there were protests, legal challenges, allegations of ballot fraud and the intervention of national parties. On November 12, the state Democratic Party sued the King County Elections Department over its handling of provisional ballots, seeking the names of those whose ballots had been invalidated. Three days later, King County, the state's Democratic stronghold, discovered 10,000 uncounted ballots, and Gregoire took a 158-vote lead. Republicans sought a restraining order to stop the counting of provisional ballots, but a King County judge denied the request. On November 17, after all counties had reported their results, Rossi was the winner by just 261 votes out of 2.8 million cast.

Washington state law requires a machine recount if the margin of victory is under 2,000 votes and half of one percent. A machine recount began, and on November 24, Rossi was again the winner, this time by 42 votes. Rossi called on Gregoire to concede, but she refused. On November 29, he was certified as governor-elect. Gregoire still had another option. State election law allowed for a hand recount under such circumstances, provided that the party requesting it paid the cost. The state party said it would pay, but only in the counties where Gregoire stood to gain the most votes. Republicans were quick to condemn the idea, and Gregoire said she would concede the race unless the party could raise enough money for a full statewide recount.

With financial assistance from John Kerry's presidential campaign, MoveOn.org and the Democratic National Committee, the party raised the money for a $730,000 statewide hand recount. The vote counting slogged on through December. King County discovered 561 wrongly disqualified ballots on December 13. Then King County found even more uncounted ballots. Republicans filed suit in neighboring Pierce County, which they said was a fairer venue than King County, to prevent the counting of all the new found ballots. A Pierce County judge found in their favor and kept the votes out. Democrats appealed to the state Supreme Court, which unanimously ruled that the disputed ballots could be counted. The votes were enough to put Gregoire over the top. On December 30, 58 days after the election, she was declared governor-elect by 129 votes. She won 48.873% to Rossi's 48.868%.

In January, just days before Gregoire's inauguration, Rossi and the Republican Party filed a lawsuit in Chelan County Superior Court in central Washington asking that Gregoire's victory be nullified and a new election held, presenting evidence of allegedly improper votes. But the court upheld Gregoire's election, and Rossi decided not to appeal.

Working with solid Democratic majorities in both the House and Senate, Gregoire had an accomplished first year. In one of her first acts as governor, she created an election-reform task force, which eventually called for a statewide voter database, mandatory audits of local election systems by the Secretary of State and an earlier primary date. She signed a controversial labor-backed unemployment-insurance bill for seasonal workers, a mental-health-parity bill, and legislation requiring the state to adopt the same car-emissions standards used by California, which are stricter than the federal government's. She followed through on a campaign promise to create a $350 million Life Sciences Discovery Fund that would use tobacco-settlement money for biotechnology research. But the big news was passage of a contentious $8.5 billion transportation bill that paid for scores of highway and bridge projects with a 9.5-cent increase in the gas tax over four years. The measure generated considerable hostility, and it didn't take long for opponents to get enough signatures to place a repeal initiative on the November 2005 ballot. But the initiative—opposed by Gregoire, big business, and labor and environmental groups—lost 55%-45%, thanks in large part to Seattle's King County, where nearly half the money was to be spent on crumbling transportation infrastructure.

Yet despite these successes, Gregoire's job-approval ratings remained low at the end of her first year, a vestige of her tainted victory and a reflection of a style that was not inclined toward glad-handing and of a record marked by several tax increases. There was talk that Gregoire, who often came across as intense and stiff, needed a "makeover." Her press releases late in the year began to refer to her as "Chris."

In 2006, Gregoire helped pass a compromise medical-malpractice bill and signed off on a landmark agreement for water storage in eastern Washington. She also signed a gay-rights bill and a bill making

Washington the first state with an electronics-waste-recycling mandate. In 2007, she proposed a $30 billion budget, up $3 billion from her first two-year budget. There was significant criticism of spending increases on her watch, and she muted opposition by proposing a "rainy-day fund" to put aside 1% of revenues each year as a hedge against future hard times.

In 2008, Gregoire proposed a budget that put $1.2 billion of a projected $1.4 billion surplus in reserve but also increased spending by $237 million. The Legislature rejected her attempt to give Microsoft, Yahoo and other high-tech companies tax exemptions on equipment used at computer data centers. Lawmakers also rejected her attempt to establish random drunk-driving checkpoints throughout the state. Gregoire signed a law giving couples in domestic partnerships benefits such as guardianship and powers of attorney previously accorded only married couples. She also signed a law to reduce the state's greenhouse-gas emissions to 25% of 1990 levels by the year 2035.

Gregoire's approval ratings slowly went up. Meanwhile, Rossi wrote a book and traveled the state giving speeches, gearing up for a rematch in 2008.

The second Gregoire-Rossi contest was even more expensive and harder fought than the first match. Gregoire touted her accomplishments in office, blamed the state's economic downturn on Republican President George W. Bush, and painted Rossi as a social conservative out of touch with voters. Rossi criticized Gregoire's spending policies and emphasized the state's projected $3.2 billion deficit in coming years. He also opted to place the designation "prefers GOP" rather than "prefers Republican" next to his name on the final ballot. Democrats protested that Ross was trying to obscure his party affiliation and filed a lawsuit, but Rossi prevailed in court. In Washington's primary system, all candidates run on a single ballot, and the top two finishers advance. Gregoire beat Rossi, but only by 48%-46%.

In the campaign's final stretch, a poll conducted by the University of Washington showed that voters worried about the economy favored Gregoire by 16 percentage points. Democratic presidential nominee Barack Obama's popularity in Washington buoyed Gregoire's campaign, and she won, 53%-47%. Political observers said that a 7% increase in voter turnout aided Gregoire. Central Washington, typically viewed as Republican country, did not vote as strongly for Rossi as it had in 2004, and Gregoire improved her percentages throughout the state. The election ended up being the most expensive in state history. Gregoire and Rossi spent more than $12 million each, and outside groups spent a combined $20 million.

Gregoire started her second term by proposing a budget that reduced state spending by $3.6 billion. It eliminated pay raises for teachers and state employees and canceled plans to expand health care for children. Her budget did increase spending on projects relating to Puget Sound, one of her signature environmental issues, by more than $50 million.

Senior Senator

Patty Murray (D)

Elected 1992, term expires 2010, 3rd term; b. Oct. 11, 1950, Seattle; home, Seattle; WA St. U., B.A. 1972; Catholic; married (Rob); 2 children.

Elected Office: Shoreline Schl. Bd., 1985–89, Pres., 1985–86; WA Senate, 1988–92.

DC Office: 173 RSOB, 20510, 202-224-2621; Fax: 202-224-0238; Web site: murray.senate.gov.

State Offices: Bellevue, 425-462-4460; Everett, 425-259-6515; Seattle, 206-553-5545; Spokane, 509-624-9515; Tacoma, 253-572-3636; Vancouver, 360-696-7797; Yakima, 509-453-7462.

Committees: *Democratic Conference Secretary. Appropriations* (7th of 18 D): Defense; Energy & Water Development; Homeland Security; Labor, Health and Human Services, Education & Related Agencies; Military Construction, Veterans Affairs & Related Agencies; Transportation, Housing and Urban Development & Related Agencies (Chmn). *Budget* (2nd of 13 D). *Health, Education, Labor & Pensions* (6th of 13 D). *Rules & Administration* (8th of 11 D). *Veterans' Affairs* (3rd of 10 D).

Group Ratings

	ADA	ACLU	AFS	LCV	ITIC	NTU	COC	ACU	CFG	FRC
2008	95	92	100	91	100	3	63	0	3	0
2007	90	—	100	87	—	6	64	0	13	—

National Journal Ratings

	2007 LIB	—	2007 CONS	2008 LIB	—	2008 CONS
Economic	66%	—	30%	91%	—	0%
Social	94%	—	0%	80%	—	9%
Foreign	85%	—	8%	94%	—	0%
Composite	85%	—	16%	93%	—	7%

Key Votes of the 110th Congress

1. Raise CAFE standards	Y	5. Make English official language	N	9. Withdraw troops 3/08	Y
2. Expand SCHIP	Y	6. Path to citizenship	Y	10. Iran guard is terrorist group	Y
3. Cap greenhouse gases	Y	7. Fetus is unborn child	N	11. Increase missile defense $	N
4. Bail out financial markets	Y	8. Prosecute hate crimes	Y	12. Overhaul FISA	N

Election Results

2004 general	Patty Murray (D)	1,549,708	(55%)	($11,556,148)
	George Nethercutt (R)	1,204,584	(43%)	($7,726,296)
2004 primary	Patty Murray (D)	709,497	(92%)	
	Warren Hanson (D)	46,490	(6%)	

Prior Winning Percentages: 1998 (58%); 1992 (54%)

Patty Murray is the senior senator from Washington, first elected in 1992. Murray grew up in the Seattle suburb of Bothell, one of seven children of a disabled World War II veteran. She graduated from Washington State University in 1972, married and stayed home to raise her children. In 1980, she was in Olympia trying to save a parent-education class she was teaching at Shoreline Community College, which was the target of budget cuts. A state legislator told her gruffly, "You're just a mom in tennis shoes. You can't make a difference." As she said later, "Almost every woman I've ever met in politics got into it because she was mad about something." She won her fight over the parents' class, then ran for the Shoreline School District board. She eventually was chosen board president. In 1988, she challenged a Republican state senator, knocked on 17,000 doors and won the seat. Then in late 1991, Murray decided to run against U.S. Sen. Brock Adams, a Democrat who was under a cloud following charges of sexual harassment. He ultimately decided not to seek re-election.

Amid a crowd of better-known, conventional male politicians, Murray, with her flat, Midwestern-style accent and "mom in tennis shoes" line, attracted most of the attention. In the 1992 all-party primary, her main Democratic opponent was former U.S. Rep. Don Bonker, who had narrowly lost a Senate nomination in 1988. But Murray won 28% of the total vote to Bonker's 19%. She then sprinted to a big lead in polls against Republican U.S. Rep. Rod Chandler, winning 54%-46% in November.

In the Senate, Murray has had a largely liberal voting record. In her first years, she was criticized as too staff reliant, but she grew into the role of senator and eventually moved into leadership roles in the Senate Democratic Caucus. She won a seat on the Appropriations Committee and immersed herself in Washington state issues. She was one of the Senate's staunchest proponents of normal trade relations with China, a position strongly backed by Boeing. When Democrats gained their Senate majority in June 2001, Murray became chairman of the Transportation Appropriations Subcommittee. She delivered for the state, and then some: $190 million in projects, more than twice as much as in 2000. She has continued to deliver large sums for her state, earning appreciation from the folks at home, no doubt, but also a reputation as one of the Senate's worst pork-barrel spenders. The Washington watchdog group Taxpayers for Common Sense dubbed her the "Queen of Pork." Murray is unapologetic about using her Appropriations seat to steer funding to her state, arguing that lawmakers, not bureaucrats, should make funding decisions. "Earmarks are how those of us who live 2,500 miles from the nation's Capitol ensure projects critical to our state are funded," she said. In 2005, she defended Republican Sen. Ted Stevens of Alaska by threatening to drop targeted projects from her appropriations bill if Democrats supported an amendment to strip "pork" from spending bills.

Murray also has worked to remove restrictions on abortion and has prevailed in the Senate on legislation allowing abortions in military hospitals. With Democratic Sen. Hillary Rodham Clinton of New York, she waged a fight with the Bush administration over the approval of over-the-counter sales of the Plan B contraceptive. They threatened to put a hold on the president's nominee to head the Food and Drug Administration, then dropped the hold when the administration assured them the FDA would make a decision. When the FDA again postponed its decision, citing regulatory complications for sales to teenagers, they were incensed. "This is not only a broken promise to us, but another frightening example of politics trumping science at the FDA," Murray said. Murray and Clinton again threatened to hold up appointments at the FDA, and in 2006, the agency gave its approval to Plan B sales for women 18 years and older.

On defense issues, Murray voted in 2002 against using force in Iraq and has been a vociferous critic of the Bush administration's war policy, accusing the administration of failing to plan for the full cost of the war. In 2007, she managed the Senate floor debate on the Iraq War supplemental funding bill. Murray also is one of the Senate's most persistent advocates for veterans' funding. She has sponsored bills for more benefits for National Guard and Reserve troops called up to active duty and successfully fought for more health-care funding for veterans of the Iraq and Afghanistan wars. Republicans initially rejected her attempt to add $2 billion for veterans' health care, but relented and added $1.5 billion after it was revealed that the Veterans' Administration was using dated cost estimates and expected a shortfall. Conservative Sen. Rick Santorum of Pennsylvania conceded, "We were in error. Senator Murray was right." She also advocated specialized care for soldiers returning from Iraq with traumatic brain injuries, a common hazard for troops exposed to roadside bombings. And she and Republican Sen. Christopher (Kit) Bond of Missouri co-authored a provision in 2008 to provide $75 million for housing vouchers for homeless veterans.

Murray strongly backed the Air Force's controversial proposals to either lease or buy KC-767 aerial refueling tankers from Boeing. The European consortium Airbus wanted to bid on the contract, which Murray said would be "the outsourcing of our national defense." In March 2008, she said she was considering legislation that would require military equipment to be manufactured exclusively in the United States. On another issue of interest back home, Murray's longtime efforts to create a Wild Sky wilderness area near Washington's Skykomish River came to fruition in April 2008, when Congress passed her bill designating 106,000 acres as wilderness.

In the 2002 election, Murray chaired the Democratic Senatorial Campaign Committee, which put her in charge of recruiting candidates and raising money for the party. She nearly doubled the committee's fundraising, bringing in $158 million during the cycle, and her recruiting efforts were mostly successful. But the results were disappointing, to say the least. Democrats lost more seats than they won that year, and they lost their Senate majority. Still, Murray's efforts got high marks. In 2004, Democratic Leader Harry Reid appointed Murray assistant floor leader, and after Democrats won back the majority in 2006, her colleagues elected her Democratic Conference Secretary, the fourth-ranking position in the leadership.

Murray has won re-election twice by impressive margins. In 1998, she was challenged by U.S. Rep. Linda Smith, a Republican and a strong opponent of abortion and of free trade. Murray raised far more money than Smith and won 58%-42%. In 2004, she faced Republican George Nethercutt, another U.S. House member, who in 1994 earned a reputation as a giant killer by defeating Democratic House Speaker Tom Foley. But the former mom in tennis shoes had become a hardball fundraiser: An aide put out the word to lobbyists that the senator would regard contributions to Nethercutt as hostile, even if contributors gave to her too. Murray raised $11.5 million, much more than Nethercutt's $7.7 million.

Nethercutt campaigned vigorously, and big-name Republicans came in for him. He tried to put his own stamp on one of Murray's efforts to create the Wild Sky wilderness. He had never supported it, but in 2004, he had sponsored the bill in the House and persuaded the chairman of Resources at the time, Richard Pombo, R-Calif., who had bottled it up, to allow a vote on it. But Pombo insisted on eliminating 13,000 acres of low-level forest, and leaders of environmental groups strenuously objected. In September, Nethercutt ran an ad featuring Murray's controversial 2002 comments on Osama bin Laden's good works and speculating about bin Laden's popularity in some corners of the world. The *Seattle Times* denounced the ad, but Nethercutt responded, "I defy her to find a day-care center that Osama bin Laden has built." Yet the ad did not seem to move votes, and he remained well behind in the polls.

Murray also ran attack ads, charging that Nethercutt had missed House votes, characterizing him as an extreme conservative, and referring to his opposition to abortion by showing a woman being booked in jail on an abortion charge. On Election Day, Nethercutt reduced Murray's 1998 margin, but not by much. She won 55%-43%. It was almost as if the election had been held in two states: Nethercutt carried every county east of the Cascades, and Murray carried all but two counties to the west.

Only in her 50s, Murray is young enough to advance far up the chain on Appropriations. And she is well positioned to one day become the first woman to chair the Veterans' Affairs Committee.

Junior Senator

Maria Cantwell (D)

Elected 2000, term expires 2012, 2nd term; b. Oct. 13, 1958, Indianapolis, IN; home, Edmonds; Miami U. (OH), B.A. 1980; Catholic; single.

Elected Office: WA House of Reps., 1986–92; U.S. House of Reps., 1992–94.

Professional Career: Owner, Cantwell & Assoc. PR firm, 1985–91; Real-Networks, 1995–2000.

DC Office: 511 DSOB, 20510, 202-224-3441; Fax: 202-228-0514; Web site: cantwell.senate.gov.

State Offices: Everett, 425-303-0114; Richland, 509-946-8106; Seattle, 206-220-6400; Spokane, 509-353-2507; Tacoma, 253-572-2281; Vancouver, 360-696-7838.

Committees: *Commerce, Science & Transportation* (7th of 14 D): Aviation Operations, Safety & Security; Communications, Technology & the Internet; Oceans, Atmosphere, Fisheries & Coast Guard (Chmn); Surface Transportation & Merchant Marine Infrastructure, Safety & Security. *Energy & Natural Resources* (6th of 13 D): Energy (Chmn); Public Lands & Forests; Water & Power. *Finance* (10th of 13 D): Energy, Natural Resources & Infrastructure; Health Care; International Trade, Customs & Global Competitiveness; Taxation, IRS Oversight & Long-Term Growth. *Indian Affairs* (6th of 9 D). *Small Business & Entrepreneurship* (6th of 11 D).

Group Ratings

	ADA	ACLU	AFS	LCV	ITIC	NTU	COC	ACU	CFG	FRC
2008	100	93	89	100	80	18	50	12	17	0
2007	95	—	100	87	—	9	64	4	13	—

National Journal Ratings

	2007 LIB	—	2007 CONS	2008 LIB	—	2008 CONS
Economic	63%	—	35%	60%	—	39%
Social	92%	—	6%	80%	—	9%
Foreign	84%	—	15%	94%	—	0%
Composite	81%	—	20%	81%	—	19%

Key Votes of the 110th Congress

1. Raise CAFE standards	Y	5. Make English official language N	9. Withdraw troops 3/08	Y
2. Expand SCHIP	Y	6. Path to citizenship	Y	10. Iran guard is terrorist group	N
3. Cap greenhouse gases	Y	7. Fetus is unborn child	N	11. Increase missile defense $	N
4. Bail out financial markets	N	8. Prosecute hate crimes	Y	12. Overhaul FISA	N

Election Results

2006 general	Maria Cantwell (D)	1,184,659	(57%)	($14,013,932)
	Mike McGavick (R)	832,106	(40%)	($10,842,132)
2006 primary	Maria Cantwell (D)	570,677	(91%)	
	Hong Tran (D)	33,124	(5%)	

Prior Winning Percentages: 2000 (49%); 1992 House (55%)

Democrat Maria Cantwell is Washington's junior senator and was elected in 2000. Cantwell grew up in Indianapolis, where her father, Paul Cantwell, a construction worker, served as county commissioner, a city councilman and a state legislator. As a child, Cantwell observed politics firsthand as her father dispensed advice to the union members, laborers and politicians who stopped by to talk politics. During her father's stint as an aide to U.S. Rep. Andrew Jacobs, she awoke one morning to the distinctive Boston accent of Sen. Edward Kennedy of Massachusetts downstairs. Cantwell graduated from Miami University of Ohio in 1980, the first in her family to graduate from college. She worked in Ohio for television personality Jerry Springer's 1982 campaign for governor. (In 2003, when Springer was considering running for senator in Ohio, she said, "I think people will be surprised by his intellect. There's much more to him than his TV show.") Then she worked for Democratic Sen. Alan Cranston's presidential campaign, going to Seattle to set up a regional campaign office. The Cranston campaign went nowhere, but Cantwell loved the Pacific Northwest and decided to stay. She moved to Mountlake Terrace, a suburb in Snohomish County just north of Seattle, where she organized a coalition to build a new library. In 1986, at age 28, she was elected to the Washington state House.

In 1992 Cantwell ran for an open U.S. House seat and won a solid 55%-42% victory. In the House, she did not support President Bill Clinton's health-care plan, and she was a strong supporter of abortion rights and of stands backed by environmental advocacy groups. But she lost her 1994 bid for re-election to Republican Rich White, 52%-48%.

Back in the Seattle area, she joined a start-up firm called Progressive Networks in 1995. Five years later, it had become RealNetworks, a leader in Internet-based audio and visual software. In late 1999, her stock was worth about $40 million, and she decided to run against Republican Sen. Slade Gorton. Gorton, Microsoft's leading advocate on Capitol Hill, had an increasingly conservative record on environmental and economic issues. Cantwell was an answer to Democrats' prayers. Insurance Commissioner Deborah Senn, who also was running, was widely considered too liberal to win. The real difference was money. Cantwell, who liquidated more than $5 million in stock, spent freely, while Senn was on television only during the last two weeks before the September all-party primary. Cantwell won 37% of the total vote, to only 13% for Gorton, with 44% of the vote, was ahead but short of a majority.

Cantwell said she would spend "whatever it takes" to win in the general election. At the same time, she made her support of McCain-Feingold-type campaign-finance regulation a major issue and refused to take contributions from political action committees or large donations known as "soft money" from the Democratic Party (though it put $640,000 into the state before Cantwell won the primary). She charged that Gorton was beholden to special-interest contributors, singling out his late-night amendment to open a cyanide-leach gold mine in Okanogan County. Gorton called Cantwell an old-style liberal Democrat who would have government meddling in health care, education and local environmental issues. Cantwell highlighted her experience in the high-tech private sector. Overall, she spent $11.5 million, $10.3 million of it her own money, to Gorton's $6.4 million.

Gorton led on election night, but not by much. That year, 54% of the votes were cast absentee, and it took three weeks to count them all. The last two days' worth of absentee ballots from heavily Democratic King County put Cantwell over the top by 1,953. A mandated recount left the margin at 2,229 for Cantwell, out of 2.4 million cast, the closest Senate contest of 2000. Cantwell carried only five counties: King, Snohomish, Thurston, which includes the state capital of Olympia, and two small counties in the west. Gorton carried eastern Washington 61%-36%, a lot but not quite enough to win. Cantwell's victory created a tie in the Senate, until Vermont's James Jeffords became an independent in May 2001 and gave Democrats a razor-thin majority. This race was a big loss for the Republican Party.

In the 111th Congress (2009–10), Cantwell chairs the Senate Energy and Natural Resources' Energy Subcommittee. An energy bill passed by Congress in December 2008 contained a provision by Cantwell giving the Federal Trade Commission authority to fine companies or individuals that manipulate petroleum markets. She has an interest in environmental issues as well. She spearheaded an effort that removed an amendment inserted into a federal spending bill that she contended would hinder efforts to restore wild salmon populations in Northwest rivers. She has also advocated establishing an office within the Environmental Protection Agency to oversee efforts to clean up pollution in Puget Sound. She co-sponsored a bill to extend tax credits for wind, solar and other sources of renewable energy, which was included in the $700 billion bailout of the financial-services industry in 2008, although she voted against the final version of the bailout anyway.

In 2005, Cantwell waged a series of floor fights with then-Senate Commerce Chairman Ted Stevens over drilling in the Arctic National Wildlife Refuge that antagonized the powerful Alaska senator. Republicans narrowly rebuffed attempts by Cantwell in March and November to remove ANWR drilling from a budget bill. Stevens retaliated by introducing a bill that would expand oil-tanker traffic in the environmentally sensitive Puget Sound. Washington politicians of both parties protested the move, and a furor erupted when emails from BP were leaked that showed the oil giant, a Stevens contributor, had worked with Stevens for a year to open Puget Sound to more tankers that docked at BP's Cherry Point refinery. Cantwell did little to defuse the conflict. She sponsored a bill that would require more tugboats to escort tankers into Puget Sound and send the bill to oil companies. The final battle over ANWR came in December 2005, when Republicans attached an ANWR measure to a defense spending bill. Cantwell worked the phones to round up votes among moderate Republicans to thwart it. Of the 60 votes needed to cut off debate and go to final resolution of the bill, they got 56 votes. Stevens was incensed and suggested there would be political retribution: "I hope the senator from Washington likes my visits to Washington state, because I'm gonna visit there often," he said.

Cantwell also has a seat on the powerful Finance Committee, which she got in 2006. In July 2007, she was the only member of the committee to vote against legislation aimed at preventing currency manipulation by foreign countries, saying the legislation would be viewed as protectionist. In 2008, she secured passage, also in the financial-services bailout bill, of a measure to temporarily extend the deductibility of state sales taxes, a popular tax break in Washington. Cantwell had helped pass the original legislation in 2003 with Republican Sen. Kay Bailey Hutchison of Texas. It allows taxpayers to deduct state sales taxes as well as state income taxes on their federal income-tax forms; Washington, like Texas, has a sales tax but no income tax. In 2004, she tried to add to the corporate tax bill an extension of unemployment benefits. Republicans agreed to allow a vote on her amendment only if Democrats agreed to limit debate on the bill. Because of Senate rules, the amendment required 60 votes, but it got only 59.

A strong supporter of campaign-finance regulation, Cantwell had campaign-finance problems of her own. To fund her 2000 campaign, she had sold $5.6 million of her RealNetworks stock and had borrowed $3.8 million from a bank using the company's stock as collateral. That enabled her to run the last-minute ads that surely were essential to her victory. The Federal Election Commission ruled in January 2004 that she had violated the law by failing to disclose the terms of the loans, but it evidently saw the offense as minor because it took no action against her. Paying off the loans should have been easy; Cantwell's net worth at one point was around $40 million. But RealNetworks, like other high-tech firms, saw its stock price plummet, from $80 in spring 2000 to $6 in spring 2001. Suddenly she owed far more than the collateral was worth. She negotiated another loan that would come due December 2001, guaranteed by the DSCC. By the end of 2004, she had reduced the debt to $2.5 million. With $435,000 in cash, she was able to pay off the remaining $130,000 in bank loans.

Cantwell's narrow victory in 2000 placed her high on the Republicans target list for 2006. National Republicans recruited Mike McGavick, chairman and chief executive officer at Safeco insurance. He was a smart, successful businessman, with moderate positions, personal wealth and speaking ability. He also had political smarts, having managed Gorton's 1988 campaign and served as his chief of staff. But McGavick also acknowledged that he had been charged with drunken driving in 1993. Cantwell faced lingering discontent from liberals in the party for her 2002 vote in favor of the Iraq war resolution. But the earlier, well-publicized dustup with Stevens helped the reserved and cautious Cantwell, allowing her to show she could stand up to Stevens and the oil lobby in defense of Washington's environment. "Cantwell never had it so good until she had it so bad with Stevens," *Seattle Times* columnist Joni Balter wrote in January 2006. Stevens withdrew his tanker bill in March 2006, saying McGavick had persuaded him to pull the bill. When McGavick attended a fundraiser in April in Anchorage hosted by the Alaska delegation, the news made the front page of the *Seattle Times*.

McGavick poured $2.5 million of own money in race, but in the end he was still outspent $14 million to $10.8 million by Cantwell. In a Democratic year in a Democratic-leaning state, she won 57%-40%.

FIRST DISTRICT

Jay Inslee (D)

Elected 1998, 7th term; b. Feb. 9, 1951, Seattle; home, Bainbridge Island; Stanford U., 1969–70, U. of WA, B.A. 1973, Willamette U., J.D. 1976.; Christian; married (Trudi); 3 children.

Elected Office: WA House of Reps., 1988–92; U.S. House of Reps., 1992–94.

Professional Career: Practicing atty., 1976–92, 1995–96; Regional dir., U.S. Dept. of H.H.S., 1997–98.

DC Office: 403 CHOB, 20515, 202-225-6311; Fax: 202-226-1606; Web site: www.house.gov/inslee.

State Offices: Poulsbo, 360-598-2342; Shoreline, 206-361-0233.

Committees: *Energy & Commerce* (18th of 36 D): Communications, Technology & the Internet; Energy & Environment. *Natural Resources* (22nd of 29 D): National Parks, Forests & Public Lands; Water & Power.

Group Ratings

	ADA	ACLU	AFS	LCV	ITIC	NTU	COC	ACU	CFG	FRC
2008	90	100	100	100	83	22	61	12	11	5
2007	80	—	100	95	—	8	63	4	19	—

National Journal Ratings

	2007 LIB	—	2007 CONS		2008 LIB	—	2008 CONS
Economic	63%	—	36%		69%	—	29%
Social	83%	—	16%		82%	—	0%
Foreign	94%	—	4%		70%	—	25%
Composite	81%	—	19%		78%	—	22%

Key Votes of the 110th Congress

1. Increase minimum wage	Y	5. Share immigration data	N	9. Withdraw troops 8/08	Y
2. Expand SCHIP	Y	6. Foreign aid abortion ban	N	10. No operations in Iran	Y
3. Raise CAFE standards	Y	7. Ban gay bias in workplace	Y	11. Free trade with Peru	Y
4. Bail out financial markets	N	8. Repeal D.C. gun law	N	12. Overhaul FISA	N

Election Results

2008 general	Jay Inslee (D)	233,780	(68%)	($776,198)
	Larry Ishmael (R)	111,240	(32%)	($49,230)
2008 primary	Jay Inslee (D)	104,342	(66%)	
	Larry Ishmael (R)	52,700	(34%)	

Prior Winning Percentages: 2006 (68%); 2004 (62%); 2002 (56%); 2000 (55%); 1998 (50%); 1992 (51%)

Population		Race/Ethnicity		Work	
Pop. 2007:	708,265	White:	77.9%	Private:	78.1%
Change since 2000:	Up 8.1%	Black:	2.2%	Government:	15.0%
Urban:	95.4%	Hispanic:	5.7%	Self-employed:	6.8%
Rural:	4.6%	Asian:	9.8%	Blue collar:	16.6%
Area size:	616 sq. mi.	Native Am.:	0.6%	White collar:	69.0%
		Hawaiian:	0.2%	Khaki collar:	0.7%
Age		Two+ races:	3.4%	Other:	13.8%
Median age:	38.1 yrs.	*Ancestry*		Median income:	$69,072
More than 65 yrs:	10.3%	German:	15.1%	Median home value:	$369,400
Less than 18 yrs:	23.4%	English:	10.5%	Poverty:	6.4%
Education		Irish:	9.8%	**Military Veterans**	
H.S. grad:	93.5%			% of Pop:	12.0%
College grad:	39.6%				
Grad degree:	13.3%				

In the past 30 years, metropolitan Seattle grew to the north and to the east, as a wave of newcomers arrived seeking the area's distinctive blend of natural beauty, robust and creative economic expansion and freewheeling culture. In the process, some of the distinctiveness of the old Seattle was left behind. The fishy odor of its docks does not permeate new subdivisions built on vegetable fields and vineyards. The Scandinavian heritage of old neighborhoods like Ballard has been muted into a Pacific

2008 Presidential Vote		
Obama (D) 226,292	(63%)
McCain (R)............................130,104	(36%)
2004 Presidential Vote		
Kerry (D)...............................189,566	(56%)
Bush (R) 143,146	(42%)
Cook Partisan Voting Index:	D + 9	

Northwest blend. The heart of new Seattle is east of Lake Washington, in the edge city of Redmond. Here are the turquoise, pine-shaded, low-rise buildings of the Microsoft campus—a tranquil environment for a booming and boisterously aggressive company. With more than 40,000 employees in the Puget Sound area, the company in 2006 undertook a $1 billion expansion of its 300-acre Redmond campus, but then put major parts of the massive project on hold when the economy soured in 2008 and 2009. Still, Microsoft has fueled Redmond's transformation from a sleepy hamlet of 1,426 people in 1960 to a hip center of commerce with more than 49,000 people. Not far away, on the eastern shore of Lake Washington, are the homes and estates of the newly rich "Microsoft millionaires" who exercised company stock options before the economic bust.

The 1st Congressional District of Washington includes most of Redmond, many of the other suburbs east of Seattle, Shoreline in the northwest corner of King County, and Kirkland, where Google's research and development center came up with Google Maps. It also takes in Edmonds, Lynnwood, Mukilteo and biotech-heavy Bothell. Booming growth during the 1990s has been followed by some resistance to increased urbanization. Across Puget Sound, the 1st includes the northern tip of Kitsap County and Bainbridge Island, where residents commute by ferry to downtown Seattle, and the Trident Submarine Base in Bangor. Politically, this area has been torn by forces of roughly equal strength—cultural liberalism and economic conservatism—though the former seems predominant. Most Seattle area residents appreciate, and want to preserve, the region's unique natural aura: the evergreen smell of well-watered land and the regional style that is plainly American yet distinct. But it is impossible not to recognize the spectacular success of market economics in the 1st District.

The congressman from Washington's 1st Congressional District is Jay Inslee, a Democrat elected in 1998. Inslee grew up in north Seattle, the son of a high school biology teacher and football coach. He graduated from the University of Washington and Willamette School of Law. He moved to Selah, in Yakima County east of the Cascades, to practice law and served on the State Trial Lawyers board of directors. In 1988, at age 37, he was elected to the state House over a former Yakima mayor. In 1992, when 4th District Congressman Sid Morrison ran for governor, Inslee won the general election to succeed him 51%-49% over Doc Hastings, a conservative supported by the Christian Coalition. In the House, Inslee voted for the Clinton budget and tax increase and for a crime bill with a ban on assault weapons. In 1994, Hastings challenged Inslee and beat him, 53%-47%. After his defeat, Inslee moved to Bainbridge Island and practiced law in Seattle. In 1996, he ran for governor and finished fifth, with 10% of the total vote, in the all-party primary. He briefly served as regional director of the U.S. Health and Human Services Department.

In 1998, Inslee decided to run for Congress again, this time in the 1st District against Republican incumbent Rick White, an economic conservative with liberal votes on some cultural issues. Inslee attacked White for voting to reduce spending on education and the environment and for supporting electricity deregulation, claiming that White was "willing to sell our reasonably priced electricity to California." White painted Inslee as a carpetbagger. In the September all-party primary, White led 50%-44%. But by November, two issues changed the balance. One was White's divorce. Inslee ran ads claiming that White intended to spend 10 years in the House and then become a lobbyist, a charge his ex-wife had made in divorce papers. He also ran ads highlighting White's vote to impeach President Bill Clinton, which said: "Rick White and Newt Gingrich shouldn't be dragging us through this. Enough is enough." In the acrimony, the primary numbers were reversed in November, and Inslee won 50%-44%.

In the House, Inslee is a moderate-to-liberal Democrat and likes to focus on technology issues. He joined in protecting the privacy of consumer financial records, an issue important to Microsoft. When Congress passed the electronic signature bill, Inslee included an amendment to require that terms of consumer consent to receive electronic records be obvious and separate from other terms.

On the Energy and Commerce Committee, Inslee has focused on conservation and increasing renewable energy sources. As early as 2005, he had introduced bills to address global warming and reduce U.S. dependence on foreign oil. When Democrats took control of the House in 2007, Speaker Nancy Pelosi appointed him to her Select Committee on Energy Independence and Global Warming. He has advocated reducing greenhouse gas emissions to 20% of 1990 levels by 2020. And he supports a cap-and-trade system allowing companies to swap carbon emissions "credits," but he has argued that giving too many free emission credits to certain companies would essentially create windfall profits for them. A book Inslee coauthored about ending the United States' dependence on foreign oil was published in 2007. He sponsored a provision in a 2009 bill to give rebates to certain industries, such as steel and cement, which face tough competition from international companies. In another issue recently before the committee, Inslee supported legislation to nullify a decision by the Federal Communications Commission allowing media companies in the nation's 20 largest cities to own both a newspaper and a broadcast outlet.

In 2000, Inslee won his first re-election in the district 55%-43%. His margins expanded as local antipathy to President George W. Bush's policies increased. He gave serious thought to running again for governor in 2004, but decided against it. With the governor's office and both Senate seats in the hands of Democrats, his statewide ambitions are on hold for now.

SECOND DISTRICT

Rick Larsen (D)

Elected 2000, 5th term; b. June 15, 1965, Arlington; home, Lake Stevens; Pacific Lutheran U., B.A. 1987, U. of MN, M.P.A. 1990; Methodist; married (Tiia); 2 children.

Elected Office: Snohomish City Cncl., 1998–2000, Pres., 1999–2000.

Professional Career: Econ. dev. ofcl., Port of Everett, 1990–91; Dir., pub. affairs, WA St. Dental Assn., 1991–98.

DC Office: 108 CHOB, 20515, 202-225-2605; Fax: 202-252-6606; Web site: www.house.gov/larsen.

State Offices: Bellingham, 360-733-4500; Everett, 425-252-3188.

Committees: *Armed Services* (15th of 36 D): Seapower & Expeditionary Forces; Strategic Forces. *Budget* (20th of 24 D). *Transportation & Infrastructure* (15th of 44 D): Coast Guard & Maritime Transportation; Highways & Transit; Railroads, Pipelines & Hazardous Materials.

Group Ratings

	ADA	ACLU	AFS	LCV	ITIC	NTU	COC	ACU	CFG	FRC
2008	90	100	100	92	100	7	56	0	4	5
2007	95	—	100	80	—	4	65	0	12	—

National Journal Ratings

	2007 LIB	—	2007 CONS		2008 LIB	—	2008 CONS
Economic	61%	—	38%		63%	—	37%
Social	77%	—	17%		82%	—	0%
Foreign	68%	—	31%		65%	—	32%
Composite	70%	—	30%		74%	—	27%

Key Votes of the 110th Congress

1. Increase minimum wage	Y	5. Share immigration data	N	9. Withdraw troops 8/08	Y
2. Expand SCHIP	Y	6. Foreign aid abortion ban	N	10. No operations in Iran	Y
3. Raise CAFE standards	Y	7. Ban gay bias in workplace	Y	11. Free trade with Peru	Y
4. Bail out financial markets	Y	8. Repeal D.C. gun law	N	12. Overhaul FISA	N

Election Results

2008 general	Rick Larsen (D)	217,416	(62%)	($1,155,691)
	Rick Bart (R)	131,051	(38%)	($44,576)
2008 primary	Rick Larsen (D)	98,304	(54%)	
	Rick Bart (R)	68,189	(38%)	

Prior Winning Percentages: 2006 (64%); 2004 (64%); 2002 (50%); 2000 (50%)

Population		Race/Ethnicity		Work	
Pop. 2007:	724,891	White:	83.4%	Private:	74.3%
Change since 2000:	Up 10.7%	Black:	1.4%	Government:	17.9%
Urban:	69.4%	Hispanic:	7.4%	Self-employed:	7.6%
Rural:	30.6%	Asian:	3.8%	Blue collar:	26.1%
Area size:	7,976 sq. mi.	Native Am.:	1.6%	White collar:	54.5%
		Hawaiian:	0.2%	Khaki collar:	1.1%
Age		Two+ races:	2.1%	Other:	18.3%
Median age:	36.5 yrs.			Median income:	$52,706
More than 65 yrs:	12.1%	*Ancestry*		Median home value:	$276,600
Less than 18 yrs:	24.2%	German:	15.4%	Poverty:	11.5%
		English:	10.2%		
Education		Irish:	9.7%	**Military Veterans**	
H.S. grad:	88.9%			% of Pop:	13.8%
College grad:	24.8%				
Grad degree:	8.1%				

The 172 San Juan Islands, in the waters of Puget Sound at the far northwest corner of Washington, were the last part of the continental United States to be turned over to this country. These waters were great whaling grounds, and not until 1860 did the British relinquish them. Today, ferryboats ply the waters of the sound, connecting the islands to mainland Washington and to British Columbia, directly to the west. The publicly operated Washington State Ferries system has more than 26 million pas-

2008 Presidential Vote		
Obama (D)	202,452	(56%)
McCain (R)	152,074	(42%)
2004 Presidential Vote		
Kerry (D)	169,420	(51%)
Bush (R)	156,632	(47%)
Cook Partisan Voting Index:	D+3	

sengers annually. Whale-watching is popular not only with tourists, but also among scientists on both sides of the border. This is some of the most beautiful land and water of North America: the steely blue sound with green forested hills rising behind, shielded from the full force of Pacific rains by the Olympic Mountains, though still seldom dry. The little towns, on bits of level land between the water and the mountains, have the look of pristine New England villages or Midwestern historic towns but are better preserved. The stores are full of fresh produce and local seafood. The Seattle metropolitan area has marched north along the shore of Puget Sound, beyond the old lumber port and railroad terminus of Everett, with the huge Boeing plant where 747s, 777s and the new long-range twin-engine 787s are built. Sales of 787 Dreamliners have been especially strong. However, the plane's inaugural flight has been delayed for almost two years, and concerns about its weight prompted Boeing to reduce the projected flight range for the first set of Dreamliners. To the north of Seattle are Bellingham and Blaine (named for the House Speaker and 1884 presidential nominee), on the 49th parallel, with America's most attractively landscaped border crossing and the International Peace Arch, just south of British Columbia. Local studies have aroused fears that global warming combined with shifting ocean wind patterns will raise the water level of the sound higher than in most other areas. But for now, the region's deepwater ports, two days closer to Asia than Southern California ports, are booming with container cargo.

The 2nd Congressional District of Washington encompasses the San Juan Islands, including 45-mile-long Whidbey Island, and most of the margin of mainland along the sound and the huge Cascade Mountains, topped by snow-capped Mount Baker. The district has several military installations, including a relatively new, high-tech Navy base at Everett and a naval air station on Whidbey Island. The political tradition in most of the lumbering and fishing areas here is Democratic, while the rich agricultural areas, like the flower-bulb-growing Skagit Valley, are more Republican. Everett tends to be Democratic, some of the nearby new suburban towns Republican. Overall, this is a nearly evenly balanced district that tends to vote close to the state average. George W. Bush lost here 51%-47% in 2004. Democratic presidential nominee Barack Obama won the district 56%-42% in 2008.

The congressman from the 2nd District is Rick Larsen, a Democrat first elected in 2000. He grew up in Arlington, in Snohomish County, graduated from Pacific Lutheran University and got a master's degree at the University of Minnesota. He spent a year doing research on economic development for the Port of Everett. For six years, he was director of public affairs for the Washington State Dental Association. In 1998, he won a seat on the Snohomish County Council and later became its president. In 2000, Republican Jack Metcalf kept his promise to retire after three terms in Congress. The Democratic field was cleared for Larsen when a state legislator unpopular with labor leaders withdrew. The Republican field was cleared for conservative state Rep. John Koster when a moderate legislator failed to raise much money and dropped out. In the September all-party primary, Koster won 49%-46%. The general election became a battleground for political action committees and one of the premier contests in the nation. Anti–abortion rights groups and the National Rifle Association backed Koster, and unions and abortion rights groups fought for Larsen. Larsen said that the contest offered "a clear choice" on abortion, and he criticized Koster for referring to "our American holocaust." Larsen won 50%-46%, doing better than his primary performance in each major county.

In the House, Larsen joined the New Democrat Coalition and leans toward the center in his voting record. He voted for the Bush tax cuts in 2001. After voting against the Iraq war resolution in 2002, Larsen became a staunch supporter of the military effort. But the 2006 election results led him to oppose President George W. Bush's troop surge. "The president does not understand the meaning of the election in 2006," he said in January 2007. In July of that year, he joined Washington's five other Democratic House members in voting for a resolution to set a firm date for troop withdrawal.

Larsen co-chairs the U.S.-China Working Group, a bipartisan group of House members that seeks to build lasting diplomatic ties with China. In October 2007, he hosted a meeting with lawmakers and Treasury Secretary Henry Paulson that focused on the value of China's currency and on intellectual-property abuses by the Chinese.

For a long time Larsen worked to have 106,000 acres in the Mount Baker-Snoqualmie National Forest designated as wilderness; the House initially defeated his bill but finally passed it in 2008. The designation allows the land in Snohomish County to receive the highest level of federal protection. On other local issues, he has pushed to secure funds for upgraded border security at Bellingham and increased support for the Puget Sound ferries.

National Republicans made a play for the seat in 2006, raising money for retired Navy Capt. Doug Roulstone. But Roulstone turned out to be a weaker than expected candidate, and Larsen won 64%-36%. In 2008, Republicans recruited former Snohomish County Sheriff Rick Bart, but Bart entered the contest late, which hurt his ability to raise money. Larsen defeated him 62%-38%.

THIRD DISTRICT

Brian Baird (D)

Elected 1998, 6th term; b. March 7, 1956, Chama, NM; home, Vancouver; U. of UT, B.A. 1977, U. of WY, M.S. 1980, Ph.D. 1984; Protestant; married (Rachel); 2 children.

Professional Career: Prof., Pacific Lutheran U., 1986–98.

DC Office: 2350 RHOB, 20515, 202-225-3536; Fax: 202-225-3478; Web site: www.house.gov/baird.

State Offices: Olympia, 360-352-9768; Vancouver, 360-695-6292.

Committees: *Science & Technology* (6th of 26 D): Energy & Environment (Chmn); Research & Science Education. *Transportation & Infrastructure* (14th of 44 D): Coast Guard & Maritime Transportation; Highways & Transit; Water Resources & Environment.

Group Ratings

	ADA	ACLU	AFS	LCV	ITIC	NTU	COC	ACU	CFG	FRC
2008	80	90	100	100	100	7	50	4	9	5
2007	95	—	100	95	—	7	58	0	16	—

National Journal Ratings

	2007 LIB	—	2007 CONS		2008 LIB	—	2008 CONS
Economic	76%	—	23%		56%	—	43%
Social	64%	—	36%		62%	—	34%
Foreign	51%	—	49%		59%	—	37%
Composite	64%	—	36%		61%	—	40%

Key Votes of the 110th Congress

1. Increase minimum wage	Y	5. Share immigration data	Y	9. Withdraw troops 8/08	Y
2. Expand SCHIP	Y	6. Foreign aid abortion ban	N	10. No operations in Iran	*
3. Raise CAFE standards	*	7. Ban gay bias in workplace	Y	11. Free trade with Peru	Y
4. Bail out financial markets	Y	8. Repeal D.C. gun law	Y	12. Overhaul FISA	Y

Election Results

2008 general	Brian Baird (D)	216,701	(64%)	($926,288)
	Michael Delavar (R)	121,828	(36%)	($78,385)
2008 primary	Brian Baird (D)	83,409	(51%)	
	Michael Delavar (R)	32,372	(20%)	
	Christine Webb (R)	27,738	(17%)	
	Cheryl Crist (D)	21,356	(13%)	

Prior Winning Percentages: 2006 (63%); 2004 (62%); 2002 (62%); 2000 (56%); 1998 (55%)

Population		Race/Ethnicity		Work	
Pop. 2007:	743,037	White:	85.7%	Private:	75.6%
Change since 2000:	Up 13.5%	Black:	1.4%	Government:	17.2%
Urban:	70.9%	Hispanic:	5.9%	Self-employed:	7.0%
Rural:	29.1%	Asian:	3.2%	Blue collar:	24.7%
Area size:	7,961 sq. mi.	Native Am.:	0.7%	White collar:	58.0%
		Hawaiian:	0.2%	Khaki collar:	0.3%
Age		Two+ races:	2.7%	Other:	17.1%
Median age:	36.6 yrs.			Median income:	$52,012
More than 65 yrs:	11.9%	*Ancestry*		Median home value:	$227,800
Less than 18 yrs:	24.9%	German:	17.8%	Poverty:	11.6%
		English:	9.9%		
Education		Irish:	9.6%	**Military Veterans**	
H.S. grad:	89.3%			% of Pop:	13.7%
College grad:	23.7%				
Grad degree:	8.4%				

From the Pacific Ocean to the majestic row of active and inactive volcanoes, from Mount Rainier to Mount St. Helens, southwest Washington was long one of America's most productive lumber areas. The moist air and almost constant rains blown in from the Pacific keep the trees on the coast growing rapidly. Precipitation is heavy in the valleys just past the Coast Range, and the forests there are also fast growing. Then come the high mountains. The Cascades are a genuine divide, wringing almost all of

2008 Presidential Vote		
Obama (D)	188,888	(53%)
McCain (R)	158,774	(45%)
2004 Presidential Vote		
Bush (R)	164,643	(50%)
Kerry (D)	158,503	(48%)
Cook Partisan Voting Index:	Even	

the moisture out of the air and making the climate eastward for a thousand miles arid. Americans were reminded of the force of the volcanoes when Mount St. Helens, dormant for 123 years, erupted in 1980, killing 65 people, destroying its own peak and paving the land around it with lava. Americans had long been taught that the lower 48 states had no active volcanoes, but Mount St. Helens proved that wrong. Today, plants, animals and fish are surging back.

In 1805, explorers Meriwether Lewis and William Clark came down the Columbia River to a rainy and foggy winter by the ocean. For many years, this part of Washington was sparsely settled, with lumbermill and fishing-boat towns scattered between mountains and water. It was flannel-shirt country, Democratic since the New Deal days. In the early 1990s, its resource-based economy was threatened by the environmental movement, which restricted fishing practices and produced a court decision shutting down logging in old-growth forests to save spotted owl habitat. This roiled local politics and gave Republicans an opening. An important demographic shift has been the spread of two great metropolitan areas into these valleys. Clark County, across the Columbia from Portland, Ore., has filled up with new residents, eager to avoid Oregon's income tax but still make big purchases in Oregon free of sales tax. The county's population grew by 45% in the 1990s and by another 23% after 2000. Olympia, the increasingly trendy and fast-growing state capital, has added residents at a greater rate than the Seattle-Tacoma metro area in recent years. The region is one of America's great international trading areas, with big exports of logs and timber and imports arriving on the Puget Sound docks. The Columbia River Gorge features spectacular outdoor activities, including some of the finest windsurfing in the nation.

The 3rd Congressional District of Washington covers the southwestern corner of the state, between the ocean and the Cascades, from Olympia south to Vancouver. Economic growth and diversification and the coming of many new residents with no roots in the old industries have made the district politically marginal; George W. Bush won here with 48% of the vote in 2000 and 50% in 2004. Democratic presidential nominee Barack Obama won here with 53% of the vote in 2008.

The congressman from the 3rd District is Brian Baird, a Democrat first elected in 1998. Baird was born in northern New Mexico and grew up in western Colorado. He earned a Ph.D. in clinical psychology from the University of Wyoming and worked with veterans, brain-injured patients and families dealing with cancer, as well as with juvenile delinquents in prison and psychiatric hospitals. He wrote *The Internship and Practicum Handbook* to help interns in the social services professions and *Are We Having Fun Yet?* for couples and families on vacation. He moved to Washington in 1980 to complete work on a doctorate degree, and eventually he became a professor at Pacific Lutheran University in Tacoma. He ran for the U.S. House in 1996 against Republican Rep. Linda Smith, who had strong support from Christian conservatives. Baird got little national party help, but he led on Election Night until more than 40,000 absentee votes were counted; Smith won by just 887 votes, 50.2%-49.8%. Taking a leave from his job, Baird never stopped running. Two years later, Smith was running (unsuccessfully, it turned out) against Democratic Sen. Patty Murray, and Republicans nominated state Sen. Don Benton to run for her House seat. Benton called for a flat tax and protection of gun rights and property rights. Baird spent twice as much money as Benton and won 55%-45%.

In the House, Baird has a mostly moderate voting record. In the 111th Congress (2009–10), he became the chairman of the Science and Technology Committee's Energy and Environment subcommittee, which has an important role in shaping Democrats' climate-change agenda. Baird is particularly focused on ocean acidification, one of his personal interests. In the past, he has proposed incentives for owners of gas-electric hybrid cars, one of which he owns.

Baird voted against the use of force in Iraq in 2002, but in 2007 he returned from a visit there and said that progress was being made and that the Bush administration's troop surge strategy needed more time to work. His change of heart drew tough criticism at home and from his Democratic House colleagues. In February 2009, he visited the Gaza Strip with Rep. Keith Ellison, D-Minn., to view damage caused by an Israeli military offensive in the area. They were the first House members to visit Gaza since the Islamist movement Hamas won Palestinian Authority legislative elections in 2006.

Among Baird's legislative achievements was a bill to restore income-tax deductibility for state sales taxes, which he had promised to deliver in his first campaign for the House. With a big boost from the large Texas congressional delegation, a modified version was passed as part of the 2004 corporate-tax bill. Baird has since worked with Washington Democratic Sen. Maria Cantwell to make the deduction permanent. In 2008, Baird and Rep. John Tanner, D-Tenn., inserted a provision into the $700 billion bailout of the financial-services industry to require firms that receive bailout money to repay the government, through fees or a tax, if their investments fail to turn a profit in five years. In 2005, the House passed Baird's amendment to add $20 million to the fight against methamphetamine abuse. Also that year, he enacted a bill to protect a 20-mile stretch of the upper White Salmon River system.

Baird is interested in a variety of institutional issues affecting the U.S. House and gained national attention after the September 11 attacks by proposing a constitutional amendment providing that if one-fourth of House seats became vacant, governors would appoint successors within seven days from a list of replacements proposed by existing members. It was ultimately shelved by Congress. He has sought to tighten insider-trading restrictions on members of Congress and their aides. He has also advocated posting the text of bills on the Internet for 72 hours prior to a vote. And in 2006, he proposed making it harder for the House to waive the three-day waiting period between introducing legislation and voting on it; he wanted the rule to require a two-thirds majority rather than a simple majority.

Baird has been re-elected easily, even though Bush twice carried the district. In October 2008, he got some negative publicity when the television program *Inside Edition* aired a segment called "The Trip of a Lifetime on Your Dime" about a trip that he and other lawmakers took to the Galapagos Islands. Members of the group were caught on hidden cameras enjoying what was depicted as a luxury vacation financed by tax dollars. Baird defended the trip as a chance for House members to obtain first-hand knowledge about ocean acidification, El Niño and the spread of invasive species. There was no fallout for him electorally. In November, he defeated Republican nominee Michael Delavar with 64% of the vote.

FOURTH DISTRICT

Doc Hastings (R)

Elected 1994, 8th term; b. Feb. 7, 1941, Spokane; home, Pasco; Columbia Basin Col., 1959–61, Central Washington U., 1963–64; Protestant; married (Claire); 3 children.

Military Career: Army Reserves, 1964–69.

Elected Office: WA House of Reps., 1979–87.

Professional Career: Pres., Columbia Basin Paper & Supply, 1967–94.

DC Office: 1203 LHOB, 20515, 202-225-5816; Fax: 202-225-3251; Web site: www.house.gov/hastings.

State Offices: Pasco, 509-543-9396; Yakima, 509-452-3243.

Committees: *Natural Resources* (RMM of 20 R).

Group Ratings
	ADA	ACLU	AFS	LCV	ITIC	NTU	COC	ACU	CFG	FRC
2008	15	18	14	0	57	74	88	96	80	100
2007	10	—	0	5	—	76	74	100	79	—

National Journal Ratings
	2007 LIB	—	2007 CONS		2008 LIB	—	2008 CONS
Economic	17%	—	83%		12%	—	87%
Social	0%	—	91%		20%	—	74%
Foreign	28%	—	71%		5%	—	93%
Composite	17%	—	83%		14%	—	86%

Key Votes of the 110th Congress
1. Increase minimum wage	N	5. Share immigration data	Y	9. Withdraw troops 8/08	N
2. Expand SCHIP	N	6. Foreign aid abortion ban	Y	10. No operations in Iran	N
3. Raise CAFE standards	N	7. Ban gay bias in workplace	N	11. Free trade with Peru	N
4. Bail out financial markets	N	8. Repeal D.C. gun law	Y	12. Overhaul FISA	Y

Election Results
2008 general	Doc Hastings (R)	169,940	(63%)	($682,931)
	George Fearing (D)	99,430	(37%)	($291,784)
2008 primary	Doc Hastings (R)	93,241	(62%)	
	George Fearing (D)	49,841	(33%)	

Prior Winning Percentages: 2006 (60%); 2004 (63%); 2002 (67%); 2000 (61%); 1998 (69%); 1996 (53%); 1994 (53%)

Population		Race/Ethnicity		Work	
Pop. 2007:	713,860	White:	64.3%	Private:	76.6%
Change since 2000:	Up 9.0%	Black:	0.9%	Government:	16.8%
Urban:	70.5%	Hispanic:	29.8%	Self-employed:	6.4%
Rural:	29.5%	Asian:	1.5%	Blue collar:	23.4%
Area size:	19,430 sq. mi.	Native Am.:	1.8%	White collar:	50.6%
		Hawaiian:	0.1%	Khaki collar:	0.1%
Age		Two+ races:	1.4%	Other:	25.9%
Median age:	33.1 yrs.			Median income:	$43,379
More than 65 yrs:	11.5%	*Ancestry*		Median home value:	$148,800
Less than 18 yrs:	28.6%	German:	15.2%	Poverty:	17.6%
		English:	8.8%		
Education		Irish:	7.6%	**Military Veterans**	
H.S. grad:	77.0%			% of Pop:	11.0%
College grad:	19.0%				
Grad degree:	6.9%				

The rugged peaks of the Cascade Mountains divide Washington State into two starkly different climate zones and two almost as starkly different political cultures. West of the Cascades, Washington is moist, green and crammed with watery inlets. To the east, it is barren and brown, except where irrigation ditches channel the water of the Columbia River into thirsty valleys and where the mountain-top waters fall east, as they do above the apple orchards in the Yakima Valley. The federal govern-

2008 Presidential Vote
McCain (R)............................159,660   (58%)
Obama (D) 111,374   (40%)

2004 Presidential Vote
Bush (R) 160,310   (63%)
Kerry (D)................................90,083   (35%)

Cook Partisan Voting Index: R + 13

ment has been a presence east of the Cascades since the 1930s, when it began to build dams that provided cheap power and boosted economic development in this forbidding, often surreal, landscape. A giant bust of Franklin D. Roosevelt gazes from a bluff on the Columbia out over 550-foot-high Grand Coulee Dam, which Roosevelt initiated and which was one of his favorite projects. Other dams are strung like beads on the necklace of the Columbia most of the way downriver to Bonneville Dam near Portland, where the river breaks through the Cascades. In 1996, a 9,300-year-old skeleton was found on the banks of the Columbia River in Richland. It was named the Kennewick man and is one of the oldest skeletons ever found in North America.

The last undammed, undeveloped stretch of the upper Columbia River is near the 640-square-mile Hanford Nuclear Reservation, north of the Tri-Cities of Richland, Kennewick and Pasco. Hanford was built by the Army to manufacture plutonium for the Manhattan Project and was where the Nagasaki bomb was constructed. After the war, the Hanford Works became the primary producer of materials for America's nuclear weapons and eastern Washington's largest employer. Then in 1989, Hanford's plutonium plant, which produced two-thirds of the nation's plutonium, was shut down because of hazardous leaks and contaminated waste. The spent fuel was scheduled to be shipped to a permanent repository at Yucca Mountain in Nevada, but that project has been delayed by stiff resistance from Nevada politicians, leaving the future of Hanford's high-level waste in doubt. In 2004, voters approved a referendum to prohibit the Energy Department from sending more radioactive waste into Washington until the existing sites were cleaned up. In 2009, the ongoing clean-up effort received $2 billion from the federal economic-stimulus bill; but the final cost could approach $50 billion.

The 4th Congressional District of Washington covers much of the center of the state east of the Cascades, running from Grand Coulee and the Columbia River through the Hanford Works down to the Dalles Dam and the Columbia River Gorge. Thirty percent of the district's residents are Hispanic, many of them farm workers or the children of farm workers who have picked fruit for generations. Farmers in the Yakima Valley, which produces most of the nation's apples and many other crops, were enraged when environmentalists proposed breaching the Snake River dams upriver to save salmon. Lumber towns in the Cascades responded angrily when the logging business was hurt by efforts to preserve the spotted owl. In an area that was once narrowly split between the parties and that as recently as 1992 elected a Democrat to Congress, this has become the most Republican district in the state. The cultural liberalism of Seattle seems very far away.

The congressman from the 4th District is Doc Hastings, a Republican first elected in 1994. He became the ranking Republican on the House Natural Resources Committee in 2009. Hastings grew up in the Tri-Cities, went to college in Ellensburg and is one of the few members of Congress without a college degree. He got his nickname from a brother who could not pronounce his given name, Richard, when they were kids. Hastings served in the Army Reserves and for 27 years ran the Columbia Basin Paper and Supply Company in Pasco, where he was also president of the Chamber of Commerce. In 1979, he was elected to the state House, served as a Republican leader, then retired in 1987. In 1992, he won the Republican nomination for the U.S. House seat, but was beaten 51%-49% by Democrat Jay Inslee. In office, Inslee voted for the Clinton budget and tax package and for the crime bill with its gun-control provisions—big liabilities when ran for re-election in 1994 and faced Hastings again. In their second contest, Hastings won 53%-47%. Since then, Democrats have not seriously competed here.

In the House, Hastings has had a mostly conservative voting record. Until 2009, he had a seat on the leadership-run Rules Committee, and he has been a prominent behind-the-scenes player in the House GOP. Hastings is a friend and ally of House Minority Leader John Boehner of Ohio.

As chairman of the investigating subcommittee of the House Ethics Committee, he had the thankless task of reviewing the case against Ohio Democrat James Traficant, who was convicted of bribery in federal court in 2002. The panel voted unanimously to expel Traficant from the House, only the second such action since the Civil War. Hastings also was part of the unanimous, 10-member panel in 2004 that voted to admonish Majority Leader Tom DeLay of Texas three times, the mildest possible sanction. DeLay was accused of a host of infractions surrounding his close ties with lobbyists who wanted favors from him. In what was viewed as a ham-handed rebuke to the committee for even mildly punishing his ally DeLay, Republican Speaker Dennis Hastert removed Colorado's Joel Hefley as chairman and replaced him with Hastings.

The next year, Hastings was at the center of another dustup at the committee that did not reflect well on him or other Republicans. He supported the GOP leadership's change in House rules to make it harder to launch investigations of members. He also ousted the committee's top staff. When committee Democrats protested by refusing to attend committee meetings, Hastings and the Republicans agreed to restore the earlier rules. They redeemed themselves somewhat in 2006 with an aggressive review of what Republican leaders and their staffs knew about Florida Republican Mark Foley's sexually explicit emails to House pages, with Hastert and others testifying in the committee's pre-election probe. All of the testimony was behind closed doors, but the revelations became a black eye for House Republicans. In December 2006, following the election, the committee issued a unanimous report saying that no members or employees had violated House rules but that panel members were "disturbed" by the conduct of some of those involved who chose "to remain willfully ignorant of the potential consequences of former Representative Foley's conduct with respect to House pages."

When Republicans lost the House majority in 2007, Hastings objected to the Democrats' creation of an independent panel of House members to consider ethics complaints against other members, saying such a panel would interfere with the committee's work and bring about more partisan attacks. He was briefly embroiled in the 2007 scandal surrounding Attorney General Alberto Gonzales and the firing of several U.S. attorneys around the country. One of the fired attorneys, John McKay, alleged that in 2005, Hastings' chief of staff, Ed Cassidy, called him and asked about allegations of voter fraud in the 2004 Washington gubernatorial election, which had resulted in the election of a Democrat, Christine Gregoire. Hastings said he did not remember instructing Cassidy to contact McKay.

Hastings is a vocal defender of Washington's asparagus industry, and during the 110th Congress (2007–08), he voted against the United States-Peru Trade Promotion Agreement Implementation Act and an extension of the 1991 Andean Trade Preferences Act, both of which he said hurt Washington growers. Much of his time has been spent on issues surrounding the Hanford Nuclear Reservation. When President George W. Bush proposed cuts in the Energy Department budget, Hastings protected the Hanford cleanup program from reductions. Congress enacted his bill requiring the Interior Department to study preservation of the Manhattan Project's historic sites at Hanford as part of the national park system. Hastings says that his proudest legislative achievement was the 2003 passage of the Citizens' Soldier Act, which makes legal immigrants serving in the military eligible for citizenship after one year in uniform.

In 2006, Democratic challenger Richard Wright criticized Hastings for his handling of ethics issues, but Hastings won 60%-40%—not a bad performance in a rough year for Republicans.

FIFTH DISTRICT

Cathy McMorris Rodgers (R)

Elected 2004, 3rd term; b. May 22, 1969, Salem, OR; home, Deer Lake; Pensacola Christian Col., B.A. 1990, U. of WA, M.B.A. 2002; Christian; married (Brian Rodgers); 1 child.

Elected Office: WA House of Reps., 1994–2004; Min. ldr. 2002–04.

Professional Career: Owner-operator, Peachcrest Fruit Basket orchard, 1984–98; State legislative aide, 1990–94.

DC Office: 1323 LHOB, 20515, 202-225-2006; Fax: 202-225-3392; Web site: www.mcmorris.house.gov.

State Offices: Colville, 509-684-3481; Spokane, 509-353-2374; Walla Walla, 509-529-9358.

Committees: *Republican Conference Vice Chairwoman. Armed Services* (16th of 25 R): Air & Land Forces; Oversight & Investigations. *Education & Labor* (11th of 19 R): Early Childhood, Elementary & Secondary Education; Workforce Protections (RMM). *Natural Resources* (7th of 20 R): Water & Power (RMM).

Group Ratings

	ADA	ACLU	AFS	LCV	ITIC	NTU	COC	ACU	CFG	FRC
2008	20	29	29	0	71	65	89	92	78	88
2007	15	—	0	5	—	67	75	85	62	—

National Journal Ratings

	2007 LIB	—	2007 CONS	2008 LIB	—	2008 CONS
Economic	31%	—	69%	24%	—	76%
Social	19%	—	80%	20%	—	74%
Foreign	30%	—	70%	21%	—	79%
Composite	27%	—	73%	23%	—	77%

Key Votes of the 110th Congress

1. Increase minimum wage	N	5. Share immigration data	Y	9. Withdraw troops 8/08	N
2. Expand SCHIP	Y	6. Foreign aid abortion ban	Y	10. No operations in Iran	*
3. Raise CAFE standards	N	7. Ban gay bias in workplace	N	11. Free trade with Peru	N
4. Bail out financial markets	N	8. Repeal D.C. gun law	Y	12. Overhaul FISA	Y

Election Results

2008 general	Cathy McMorris Rodgers (R)	211,305	(65%)	($1,139,376)
	Mark Mays (D)	112,382	(35%)	($101,027)
2008 primary	Cathy McMorris Rodgers (R)	96,584	(56%)	
	Mark Mays (D)	34,251	(20%)	
	Barbara Lampert (D)	19,645	(11%)	
	Kurt Erickson (R)	12,155	(7%)	

Prior Winning Percentages: 2006 (56%); 2004 (60%)

Population

Pop. 2007:	690,203	**Race/Ethnicity**		**Work**	
Change since 2000:	Up 5.4%	White:	86.5%	Private:	73.6%
Urban:	71.9%	Black:	1.2%	Government:	18.8%
Rural:	28.1%	Hispanic:	5.3%	Self-employed:	7.3%
Area size:	23,166 sq. mi.	Asian:	2.2%	Blue collar:	19.9%
		Native Am.:	2.1%	White collar:	60.3%
Age		Hawaiian:	0.2%	Khaki collar:	0.3%
Median age:	36.4 yrs.	Two+ races:	2.5%	Other:	19.6%
More than 65 yrs:	13.3%	*Ancestry*		Median income:	$42,244
Less than 18 yrs:	23.1%	German:	20.5%	Median home value:	$158,000
Education		Irish:	11.2%	Poverty:	15.6%
H.S. grad:	89.7%	English:	10.2%	**Military Veterans**	
College grad:	25.4%			% of Pop:	14.3%
Grad degree:	9.3%				

Eastern Washington is a land of great rivers and bare parched land, where the Columbia, Spokane and Snake rivers wind among vast plateaus, bringing water from the Rockies to the desert. Spokane grew up at the falls of the Spokane River when the railroads first came through, and early in the 20th century, it became a major wheat, mining, electrical and railroad center. It celebrated with the 1974 World's Fair and Exposition on the downtown riverfront. Nearby are some of the most fascinating land-

2008 Presidential Vote		
McCain (R)	171,670	(52%)
Obama (D)	152,970	(46%)

2004 Presidential Vote		
Bush (R)	177,311	(57%)
Kerry (D)	127,162	(41%)

Cook Partisan Voting Index: R + 7

scapes in the United States: undulating yellow wheat fields on the rolling ridges of the Palouse, where the wheat-growing topsoil is 200 feet deep; bare-rock coulees rising above dammed-up lakes and barren desert; and the vast wilderness of Okanogan County, which has long been gold country. Construction of a new mine began in January 2008 after an agreement was reached with local conservation groups on water-quality monitoring. This is remote and inhospitable land. The summers can be blazing hot and the winters bitter cold. Many rivers run wild. But much of it has been tamed by man, and the water from the Grand Coulee and other dams irrigates some of the richest farmland in the country.

The 5th Congressional District of Washington covers the easternmost part of the state. Two-thirds of the people here live in greater Spokane, a city whose voting habits have grown apart from the Washington west of the Cascades, especially on natural resource issues. Several Spokane area politicians have called for creating a 51st state of Eastern Washington, with 60% of the current state's land and 22% of its population. Near the Oregon border is Walla Walla, long dependent on wheat and sweet onions but now attracting tourists with its budding wine industry. The political inclinations are Republican, but not as Republican as most of the nearby Rocky Mountain states. Spokane County voted for Democrat Bill Clinton in 1992 and 1996, but Republican George W. Bush won the county 56%-44% in 2004. In 2008, Republican presidential nominee John McCain carried the county 49%-48% and won the district 52%-46%.

The congresswoman from the 5th District is Cathy McMorris Rodgers, a Republican elected in 2004. She spent much of her childhood in northern British Columbia, graduated from Pensacola Christian College in Florida and got an MBA from the University of Washington. Her background suggests she is primed for the leadership track. While working in a family-owned orchard and fruit stand in Kettle Falls, she was appointed and later elected to the state House, where she served for 10 years and chaired the Commerce and Labor Committee. She eventually rose to minority leader, the first female House leader in state history. In 2004, George Nethercutt, who defeated Democratic House Speaker Tom Foley in 1994 to become the first person to defeat a House speaker since Charles Denison defeated Galusha Grow in 1862, ran for the Senate. McMorris Rodgers and two other Republicans filed to compete for his seat in the Republican primary. McMorris Rodgers was backed by the economic conservatives of the national Club for Growth. The three primary candidates agreed on most major issues. Each opposed abortion and favored a constitutional amendment banning same-sex marriage. Each supported tort law changes and making the Bush administration tax cuts permanent, and each criticized the Endangered Species Act. McMorris Rodgers won 50% of the vote in the primary to 27% for state Sen. Larry Sheahan and 23% for Spokane lawyer Shaun Cross.

The Democratic nominee, Don Barbieri, a wealthy businessman, had a geographical edge over McMorris Rodgers. He was from Spokane, while she was from rural northeastern Washington. Barbieri also had a heavy financial advantage. He had no primary opposition and was well funded going into the general. The National Republican Congressional Committee spent heavily on McMorris Rodgers's behalf, including airing an ad charging that Barbieri had put "profits before jobs" when his hotel-development company laid off workers following a merger. McMorris Rodgers highlighted her pro-business credentials and agricultural background as a farmer's daughter. That was enough to give her a comfortable victory, 60%-40%, another sign of how much has changed in Foley's old district, where these days Democrats rarely win anything. She carried every county.

In the House, McMorris Rodgers was elected the freshman representative to the Republican Steering Committee, which makes House committee assignments. She is now the ranking Republican on the Water and Power Subcommittee of the Natural Resources Committee.

McMorris Rodgers has had a mostly conservative voting record, but she is not a rubber stamp for the Republican Party. In 2007, she voted to expand the State Children's Health Insurance Plan, a move favored by Democrats but opposed by President George W. Bush. She has backed Bush's Iraq war policies, but she also criticized the administration on veterans' health care and on a delay in rules for country-of-origin meat labeling. In 2007, she introduced legislation that would impose federal penalties on registered sex offenders who access websites with the purpose of contacting children. During her first term, she won passage in the House a bill to increase the number of qualified teachers for advanced-placement courses.

In 2007, the Citizens for Responsibility and Ethics in Washington listed McMorris Rodgers as one of 96 lawmakers who had hired family members for their congressional campaigns in the last six years. The following year, she faced five opponents in the primary, including two who campaigned for support among the district's conservatives. McMorris Rodgers won the primary with 56% of the vote and then won the general election by defeating Democrat Mark Mays, the primary runner-up, 65%-35%.

That November, congressional Republicans suffered another drubbing at the hands of Democrats. Afterward, McMorris Rodgers was elected vice chairwoman of the Republican Conference. Her candidacy was backed by Minority Leader John Boehner of Ohio, who had befriended McMorris Rodgers in 2005, when the two served on the Education and Labor Committee. Her first task was to head a 10-member Select Committee on Earmark Reform with the goal of producing recommendations to reform the practice of individual lawmakers inserting special spending projects into appropriations bills. She pledged not to seek earmarks for her district for an entire year. By April 2009, the task force had not yet produced recommendations, and McMorris Rodgers submitted requests for 35 earmarks worth $120 million to the Appropriations Committee.

In April 2007, McMorris Rodgers and her husband had their first child, a boy, Cole McMorris Rodgers, who was born four weeks premature and was diagnosed with Down syndrome. Only eight women, all of them in the House, have given birth while serving in Congress, inclusive of McMorris Rodgers. She formed the Congressional Down Syndrome Caucus in the spring of 2008 to raise awareness about institutional barriers that individuals with Down syndrome face.

SIXTH DISTRICT

Norm Dicks (D)

Elected 1976, 17th term; b. Dec. 16, 1940, Bremerton; home, Belfair; U. of WA, B.A. 1963, J.D. 1968; Lutheran; married (Suzanne); 2 children.

Professional Career: Legis. asst., U.S. Sen. Warren Magnuson, 1968–73, A.A., 1973–76.

DC Office: 2467 RHOB, 20515, 202-225-5916; Fax: 202-226-1176; Web site: www.house.gov/dicks.

State Offices: Bremerton, 360-479-4011; Port Angeles, 360-452-3370; Tacoma, 253-593-6536.

Committees: *Appropriations* (3rd of 37 D): Defense; Interior, Environment & Related Agencies (Chmn); Military Construction, Veterans Affairs & Related Agencies.

Group Ratings

	ADA	ACLU	AFS	LCV	ITIC	NTU	COC	ACU	CFG	FRC
2008	90	91	100	92	86	6	67	0	0	11
2007	95	—	100	95	—	5	50	0	12	—

National Journal Ratings

	2007 LIB	—	2007 CONS		2008 LIB	—	2008 CONS
Economic	78%	—	18%		69%	—	31%
Social	68%	—	32%		75%	—	18%
Foreign	68%	—	31%		55%	—	43%
Composite	72%	—	28%		68%	—	32%

Key Votes of the 110th Congress

1. Increase minimum wage	Y	5. Share immigration data	N	9. Withdraw troops 8/08	Y
2. Expand SCHIP	Y	6. Foreign aid abortion ban	N	10. No operations in Iran	Y
3. Raise CAFE standards	Y	7. Ban gay bias in workplace	Y	11. Free trade with Peru	Y
4. Bail out financial markets	Y	8. Repeal D.C. gun law	N	12. Overhaul FISA	Y

Election Results

2008 general	Norm Dicks (D)	205,991	(67%)	($1,159,193)
	Doug Cloud (R)	102,081	(33%)	($18,408)
2008 primary	Norm Dicks (D)	96,862	(57%)	
	Doug Cloud (R)	51,300	(30%)	
	Paul Richmond (D)	14,983	(9%)	

Prior Winning Percentages: 2006 (71%); 2004 (69%); 2002 (64%); 2000 (65%); 1998 (68%); 1996 (66%); 1994 (58%); 1992 (64%); 1990 (61%); 1988 (68%); 1986 (71%); 1984 (66%); 1982 (63%); 1980 (54%); 1978 (61%); 1976 (74%)

Population		Race/Ethnicity		Work	
Pop. 2007:	680,098	White:	76.5%	Private:	70.4%
Change since 2000:	Up 3.8%	Black:	5.4%	Government:	22.3%
Urban:	78.8%	Hispanic:	6.2%	Self-employed:	7.0%
Rural:	21.2%	Asian:	4.9%	Blue collar:	23.9%
Area size:	8,592 sq. mi.	Native Am.:	2.0%	White collar:	54.8%
Age		Hawaiian:	0.8%	Khaki collar:	1.1%
Median age:	38.6 yrs.	Two+ races:	4.0%	Other:	20.2%
More than 65 yrs:	14.5%	*Ancestry*		Median income:	$45,753
Less than 18 yrs:	22.5%	German:	15.5%	Median home value:	$219,700
Education		Irish:	9.8%	Poverty:	13.9%
H.S. grad:	87.7%	English:	9.7%	**Military Veterans**	
College grad:	22.1%			% of Pop:	17.3%
Grad degree:	7.9%				

The rainiest part of the continental United States is its far northwest corner, where the Olympic Mountains of Washington thrust into the Pacific Ocean. The waters of the Pacific evaporate, condense and then mist or rain down on the hills and mountains that jut up from the ocean and Puget Sound. The mountains here are always green, the trees that line the inlets towering, and during heavy rainfalls, the rivers can rise six feet a day. This has long been lumbering and fishing country, where people start work

2008 Presidential Vote		
Obama (D)	182,789	(57%)
McCain (R)	128,883	(41%)
2004 Presidential Vote		
Kerry (D)	163,145	(53%)
Bush (R)	137,891	(45%)
Cook Partisan Voting Index:	D + 5	

at 6 a.m. and where the vagaries of nature and environmental laws—like the ban on old-growth logging to protect the habitat of the spotted owl—have strengthened a traditional surly independence and suspicion of authority. Still, respect for the beauty of nature endures, including at the 3,310-square-mile Olympic Coast National Marine Sanctuary, a vast underwater reserve. There are some fears that too much land is being bought up to build subdivisions and second homes.

The many inlets of Puget Sound, winding sinuously through mountains, are among America's most picturesque waterways and strategically among its most important. During World War II, shipyards were built to shelter much of the U.S. Navy's Pacific fleet, and during the Cold War, much of the nuclear submarine fleet was anchored at the giant Bremerton Navy base. The Tacoma Straits Bridge was built to replace a narrow span that, in a scene preserved on newsreel and still viewed by civil engineering students, started vibrating on the wrong harmonic in high winds and collapsed in 1940. On the other side is Tacoma, long the second-ranking city on Puget Sound, with its massive docks, former pulp mills, pleasant hilly residential neighborhoods and recently revived waterfront.

The 6th Congressional District of Washington includes the Olympic Peninsula, Bremerton, much of surrounding Kitsap County and most of Tacoma. Politically, the Olympic Peninsula and Bremerton are working-class Democratic. Tacoma also is traditionally Democratic. Seattle and King County were somewhat more Republican than Tacoma and Pierce County as late as the early 1980s, but now they are much more heavily Democratic. In 2004, the district voted 53%-45% for Democratic presidential candidate John Kerry, and in 2008, it voted 57%-41% for Democrat Barack Obama.

The congressman from the 6th District is Norm Dicks, a Democrat first elected in 1976. He is the chairman of the Interior and Environment Appropriations Subcommittee. Dicks grew up in Bremerton, the son of a shipyard worker. At the University of Washington, he was a 185-pound linebacker who was dubbed "Dizzy Dicks" and played in two Rose Bowls. After graduation from the university's law school, Dicks joined the staff of Democratic Sen. Warren Magnuson, one of the best senators of his time. The job put Dicks on a political fast track. When 6th District Rep. Floyd Hicks, a Democrat, left Congress to accept a judgeship, Dicks got his chance to jump from staffer to member. He ran a hard-charging campaign and prevailed in a four-candidate primary, then cruised to a 74%-26% general-election victory. Unlike Magnuson, who took advantage of an early opportunity to run for the Senate while in his 30s, Dicks stayed in the House. He signaled his intentions early on, with the unusual feat of winning a seat on the Appropriations Committee in his first term, over a fellow Democratic freshman named Al Gore. In his second term, he got a seat on the Defense Subcommittee, of vital interest to the 6th District and to the country's military. Although Dicks ultimately rose to chairman of the Interior and Environment subcommittee in 2007, Dicks has remained quite active on the Defense panel.

Dicks has a moderate voting record and has been considered more supportive of military spending and an interventionist foreign policy than most House Democrats, in the tradition of noted former Washington Sen. Henry (Scoop) Jackson. He has often quoted Jackson saying, "I'm not a hawk or a dove. I just don't want my country to be a pigeon." During the post-Cold War downsizing of the Pentagon, he worked with Gore and Armed Services Chairman Les Aspin of Wisconsin in support of the MX missile, successfully looked out for cuts in the budget for the F-117 Stealth aircraft and pushed for expanded production of the B-2 Stealth bomber. He was vindicated when the B-2 was used in the bombing of Serbia and Kosovo in 1999, Afghanistan in 2001 and Iraq in 2003, delivering weapons with pinpoint accuracy and sometimes flying halfway around the world to do so. In the 1980s, Dicks helped Texas Rep. Charlie Wilson covertly send money and equipment to Afghans who were trying to repel invading Soviets. (Wilson's swashbuckling involvement in Afghanistan was chronicled in a book and a 2007 movie, *Charlie Wilson's War*.)

Dicks voted for the Iraq war resolution in 2002 and rounded up support for it among Democrats. In 2005, he said he'd been misled by the Bush administration's claims of Iraqi weapons of mass destruction and regretted his past support. Unlike Defense Subcommittee Chairman John Murtha of Pennsylvania, he did not favor withdrawing U.S. troops on a six-month timetable. But he was angry about Republican attacks on Murtha, with whom he has served on the subcommittee since 1979. He voted for a nonbinding resolution calling for withdrawal and for a war supplemental appropriation with a timetable, but he voted against a version of the spending bill demanding immediate withdrawal.

Dicks certainly does not neglect the 6th District's military facilities. The Bremerton Naval Shipyard, by far the largest employer in Kitsap County, is also the largest naval shore facility in the Pacific Northwest. The 2005 base-closing procedure moved two nuclear subs from Groton, Conn., to Bremerton, in line with the nation's increasingly Pacific Rim-oriented military stationing. The base-closing round also increased personnel at Fort Lewis near Tacoma, Bremerton Naval Station and Whidbey Island Naval Air Station. Dicks worked hard to promote a $23 billion, 10-year lease of up to 100 Boeing 767s to replace aging KC-135 tankers. Opponents, notably Sen. John McCain, R-Ariz., argued that it would be cheaper in the long run to design a new tanker. The deal came undone after the criminal convictions of a top Boeing official and the Air Force's top procurement officer on bribery charges. Dicks said, "Misconduct blew the deal. It is painful. It would have been the greatest thing I had done." He has consistently supported the acquisition of more C-17 transports than the Pentagon has requested. He has been harshly critical of the Army's record on procurement of the Future Combat System, and he opposed former Defense Secretary Donald Rumsfeld's proposed changes in collective-bargaining and union agreements.

But Dicks' close ties to the defense-contracting establishment have also caused him some problems. In 2009, the Federal Bureau of Investigation began investigating his relationship with the PMA group, a defense lobbying firm under federal investigation for possible improper campaign donations. Since 2003, Dicks has received $84,000 from donors with ties to PMA, and he supported nine spending earmarks worth $20 million that benefited PMA clients. During that time period, only three other members of Congress received more money from donors linked to PMA.

Dicks's first year as chairman of the Interior-Environment Subcommittee on Appropriations put him at odds with Bush administration, which tried to compel him to eliminate almost $1 billion from the subcommittee's appropriations bill in 2007. Dicks criticized the White House for refusing to negotiate spending proposals, but he also expressed displeasure with Democratic Senate Majority Leader Harry Reid for deciding to cut billions of dollars from appropriation bills in order to ensure their passage. As an Appropriations subcommittee chairman, and so a member of the powerful "College of Cardinals," Dicks relishes the collegiality and relative bipartisanship of Appropriations. Over the years, he has helped Washington communities win federal contracts and funding, sending $1.2 billion to lumber-mill towns when logging in old-growth forests was banned in the campaign to save the spotted owl, passing timber-salvage riders to keep mills going, and finding federal dollars for maintaining salmon runs in dammed rivers. He helped get funding for the multi-billion-dollar Hanford Reservation cleanup, for light rail in Tacoma, and for revitalizing the city's once-grimy waterfront. He hammered out a deal with the Skokomish tribe and a Bellingham seafood company to end the dumping of salmon carcasses into Hood Canal, which suffered from algae overgrowth. He wants to designate Hood Canal as critical habitat for orcas and other whales. He fought to get $36 million to reopen Mount Rainier National Park in May 2007; it had closed after suffering severe storm damage in November 2006. In 2008, he objected to the Bush administration's attempt to end a ban on bringing loaded weapons into national parks.

Dicks has supported free-trade agreements and was one of the few House Democrats to vote for the Central American Free Trade Agreement in 2005. He was a strong supporter of normalizing trade relations with China. One-quarter of U.S. exports to China go through Washington ports. In the early 1980s, Dicks took the lead in restoring Export-Import Bank loan authority—Boeing is America's biggest exporter and biggest user of the loans—when the Reagan administration wanted to cut it, and he led a campaign that switched 80 House votes overnight.

Dicks had something of a close election in 1980, but he has been re-elected by wide margins ever since.

SEVENTH DISTRICT

Jim McDermott (D)

Elected 1988, 11th term; b. Dec. 28, 1936, Chicago, IL; home, Seattle; Wheaton Col., B.S. 1958, U. of IL, M.D. 1963; Episcopalian; married (Therese Hansen); 2 children.

Military Career: U.S. Navy Medical Corps., 1968–70.

Elected Office: WA House of Reps., 1970–72; WA Senate, 1974–87.

Professional Career: Asst. prof., U. of WA, Practicing psychiatrist, 1970–83; Medical officer, U.S. Foreign Svc., Zaire, 1987–88.

DC Office: 1035 LHOB, 20515, 202-225-3106; Fax: 202-225-6197; Web site: www.house.gov/mcdermott.

State Offices: Seattle, 206-553-7170.

Committees: *Ways & Means* (4th of 26 D): Income Security & Family Support (Chmn); Trade.

Group Ratings

	ADA	ACLU	AFS	LCV	ITIC	NTU	COC	ACU	CFG	FRC
2008	95	100	100	92	60	19	50	8	15	5
2007	85	—	100	95	—	9	50	4	17	—

National Journal Ratings

	2007 LIB	—	2007 CONS	2008 LIB	—	2008 CONS
Economic	73%	—	27%	81%	—	15%
Social	92%	—	0%	67%	—	28%
Foreign	81%	—	16%	85%	—	8%
Composite	84%	—	16%	80%	—	20%

Key Votes of the 110th Congress

1. Increase minimum wage	Y	5. Share immigration data	N	9. Withdraw troops 8/08	Y
2. Expand SCHIP	Y	6. Foreign aid abortion ban	N	10. No operations in Iran	Y
3. Raise CAFE standards	Y	7. Ban gay bias in workplace	Y	11. Free trade with Peru	Y
4. Bail out financial markets	N	8. Repeal D.C. gun law	N	12. Overhaul FISA	N

Election Results

2008 general	Jim McDermott (D)	291,963	(84%)	($1,033,233)
	Steve Beren (R)	57,054	(16%)	($32,473)
2008 primary	Jim McDermott (D)	95,344	(74%)	
	Steve Beren (R)	19,307	(15%)	
	Donovan Rivers (D)	6,685	(5%)	

Prior Winning Percentages: 2006 (79%); 2004 (81%); 2002 (74%); 2000 (73%); 1998 (88%); 1996 (81%); 1994 (75%); 1992 (78%); 1990 (72%); 1988 (76%)

Population		Race/Ethnicity		Work	
Pop. 2007:	650,935	White:	66.8%	Private:	77.5%
Change since 2000:	Down 0.6%	Black:	7.7%	Government:	15.1%
Urban:	98.5%	Hispanic:	7.3%	Self-employed:	7.3%
Rural:	1.5%	Asian:	13.4%	Blue collar:	13.3%
Area size:	246 sq. mi.	Native Am.:	0.7%	White collar:	71.1%
		Hawaiian:	0.5%	Khaki collar:	0.1%
Age		Two+ races:	3.5%	Other:	15.6%
Median age:	38.0 yrs.	*Ancestry*		Median income:	$56,172
More than 65 yrs:	11.0%	German:	12.5%	Median home value:	$417,500
Less than 18 yrs:	16.5%	English:	9.3%	Poverty:	12.8%
Education		Irish:	9.1%		
H.S. grad:	90.3%			**Military Veterans**	
College grad:	49.4%			% of Pop:	8.4%
Grad degree:	19.4%				

Seattle rises from the Puget Sound harbor of Elliott Bay on steep hills once covered with 300-foot-high Douglas firs. Behind the hills and buildings on a clear day, you can see from almost anywhere the nimbus of Mount Rainier. On the picturesque waterfront, below gleaming high-rises, is Pike Place Market, where you can get fresh salmon and Dungeness crabs. Nearby is Pioneer Square, where stores and warehouses from the turn of the 20th century have been restored. Yesler Way was Ameri-

2008 Presidential Vote

Obama (D)	308,226	(84%)
McCain (R)	55,200	(15%)

2004 Presidential Vote

Kerry (D)	288,161	(79%)
Bush (R)	70,167	(19%)

Cook Partisan Voting Index: D+31

ca's original Skid Road—literally a path for skidding newly cut logs to transportation terminals—and it still has some homeless people. Seattle's upper class, like San Francisco's, continues to be anchored in downtown, with its upscale stores and busy sidewalks. Seattle first broke into the national consciousness with the 1897 Klondike gold strike and has been a major American city since around 1910. It hosted its own World's Fair in 1962. In the 1990s, its combination of economic growth and creativity plus its physical beauty and distinctive style made it a national trendsetter. Seattle has some old ethnic neighborhoods, like the once heavily Scandinavian Ballard, which has been moving toward boutiques and nightspots, and the countercultural Capitol Hill, where shoppers jam busy stores, galleries and clubs. But it also has a new ethnic mix, with thousands of Asian immigrants. The dominant tone is set by highly educated, affluent, single professionals, who have made the Victorian houses overlooking the harbor and the 1940s houses in Capitol Hill among the nation's highest-priced residential real estate. There are still blue-collar workers on the south side of the city and in the valleys. Factories, warehouses and railroad yards are concentrated on a flat plain near Puget Sound and south of downtown. Boeing, long based in Seattle, is America's biggest exporter, but Seattle has had other exports, such as Nordstrom department stores with their famously attentive service and fashionable goods. Seattle also is the headquarters, in an old industrial district, of Starbucks coffee, which now has more than 13,000 stores.

Seattle ranks as one of the nation's most desirable, and liberal, cities. But it has suffered some black eyes in the past decade. In 1999, a World Trade Organization meeting turned into the "Battle in Seattle" after anti-globalism protests were hijacked by anarchists, sending riot police into the streets with tear gas. The city cancelled its millennium celebration at the Space Needle because of a terrorist threat. Then, a federal judge ruled that Microsoft was a monopoly. And in perhaps the toughest economic blow, Boeing announced in 2001 that it was relocating its corporate headquarters to Chicago. The airplane-manufacturing giant also began experimenting with sending some of its work offshore and contracting out work to build parts of its new 787 Dreamliner. The move did not go over well in labor union-friendly Seattle, prompting a strike by the company's Machinist union in 2009.

Three other local icons hit hard times at the end of the decade. Starbucks not only ceased its rapid expansion, it closed stores and laid off baristas. The city's professional basketball team, the SuperSonics, moved to Oklahoma City after Starbucks owner Howard Schultz sold the team to a group of Oklahoma businessmen who broke a promise to keep the team in the Northwest. And in March 2009, Seattle's oldest running newspaper, the *Seattle Post-Intelligencer*, stopped its printing presses and began publishing exclusively online, leaving *The Seattle Times* as the city's only daily newspaper. But Seattle's economic foundation remains strong. Amazon is expanding into a huge new campus south of Lake Union, and Microsoft founder Bill Gates' decision to turn his attention to global health philanthropy has made Seattle the Davos of health care, drawing experts in malaria, tuberculosis, AIDS and other global scourges. And the city's new professional soccer team, The Sounders FC, is drawing as many fans as the departed basketball team did.

The 7th Congressional District of Washington includes nearly all of the city of Seattle, some industrial suburban fringe to the south, a white-collar suburban fringe to the north, and artsy, bucolic Vashon Island in Puget Sound. Seattle is one of the whitest major cities in the nation, so this district—13% Asian, 8% black and 7% Hispanic—is the closest thing to a minority district in the Seattle area. It shares more with San Francisco than hills and scenery. It is heavily populated by singles, gays, young professionals and elderly pensioners. It has one of the nation's lowest percentages of married couples and children. A generation ago, Seattle was roughly split between the parties. Today, it is heavily Democratic. John Kerry carried the district 79%-19% in 2004, and Barack Obama won it 84%-15% in 2008.

The congressman from the 7th District is Jim McDermott, first elected in 1988. McDermott grew up in the Chicago suburb of Downers Grove, one of three boys, and was the first in his family to attend college. His father, a fundamentalist Christian, ministered in a church run out of the garage. McDermott graduated from conservative Christian Wheaton College, the alma mater of the Rev. Billy Graham. He went on to get a medical degree from the University of Illinois and did the last two years of his psychiatric residency at the University of Washington. He fell in love with the area and decided to make it his home. But first, with the Vietnam War under way, McDermott volunteered for a stint in the Navy as a psychiatrist. The experience left him adamantly opposed to the war, and when he returned to Seattle, he got involved in politics. In 1970, while he was operating his medical practice, he was elected to the state House, and in 1974, he was elected to the state Senate. He ran for governor three times and lost every time. In 1987, he retired from the Legislature and went to Zaire (now the Democratic Republic of the Congo) as a medical officer in the Foreign Service. When the House seat opened in 1988, he returned to Seattle and won easily, beating Norm Rice 38%-29% in the primary and taking 76% in the general. He is the only psychiatrist in the House.

In his early years in the House, McDermott rose quickly in influence. Democratic leader Tom Foley of Washington state tapped him for influential assignments. His great cause has been health care, but he has shared the frustration many have felt in dealing with the issue. He has long backed a single-payer, Canadian-style national health-insurance program. In August 1994, as the Clinton health-care plan was failing and Democratic leaders were scrambling to come up with an alternative, McDermott urged Congress to abandon all health-care bills for the year. He evidently expected a more favorable political environment after the election; like many, he was surprised by the results. After Republicans took majority control of the House, he said: "A lot of people around here have never been in the minority. I have. I know what to do: Attack."

He kept his word. He was harshly critical of the Bush administration on a number of fronts, especially the war in Iraq. In September 2002, with a congressional delegation in Baghdad, McDermott said in a statement broadcast on ABC's *This Week* that Bush was willing to "mislead the American people"; he also said that he found Iraqi Leader Saddam Hussein more credible than Bush. This sparked harsh criticism from Republicans and dismay from those Democrats who felt his comments had gone too far. "He combined the judgment of Neville Chamberlain before World War II and Jane Fonda in Hanoi," Texas Democrat Chet Edwards told the *New York Times*. (In 2008, it was revealed that McDermott's trip to Iraq was financed by Muthanna Al-Hanooti, an Iraqi activist who'd been indicted in 2008 on charges of being a spy for Saddam.) McDermott continued to be a harsh critic of the war, arguing that President George W. Bush had failed to make the case for military action. In a 2007 floor speech he said, "In less than one generation we have done what we vowed never to do again. We allowed a president to stampede the nation into a hopeless war, not because we had to, but because he wanted to."

McDermott is upfront about his legislative interests, which tend not to include the parochial matters and pork-barrel spending that consume some of his congressional colleagues. He has promoted health issues overseas; he founded and chaired the Congressional Task Force on International HIV/AIDS. He also sponsored a measure that at first seemed quixotic but was enacted in 2000: The African Growth and Opportunity Act, which reduced import quotas and tariffs on African goods and included investment funds.

With the Democrats' return to the majority in 2007, legislative life for McDermott became considerably more enjoyable. A longtime ally of House Speaker Nancy Pelosi, he again had a friendly ear in high places. In the opening days of the 110th Congress (2007–08), he helped shape the House-passed bill to rescind some tax breaks for oil companies. As a senior member of the House Ways and Means Committee, he chairs the Income Security and Family Support Subcommittee. In 2008, McDermott was the lead sponsor of two bills that extended unemployment benefits for American workers. He also shepherded to enactment legislation aimed at improving foster-care programs through initiatives such as allowing children to remain in foster care until age 21. He tends to reach for broad legislative fixes to entrenched social problems, even though Congress moves at best slowly and incrementally. The first hearing he held as subcommittee chairman was on solutions to poverty. He has continued to advocate for a universal health-care system guaranteeing every American coverage, and he thinks "wage insurance" should be provided to laid-off workers.

McDermott stirred controversy in 2004 when he omitted the words "under God" as he led the House in its daily Pledge of Allegiance to the flag. After leaders of both parties criticized him, he replied that his omission had not been deliberate and that the fallout "ain't fun." In 2007, he was attacked by conservatives for voting against a House resolution recognizing the importance of Christmas. They noted that he had previously voted for resolutions recognizing the Islamic holy month of Ramadan.

Until recently, McDermott was bogged down in a years-long partisan battle with House Republicans stemming from an incident when he was ranking minority member on the Ethics Committee, during its consideration in 1997 of charges against Republican Speaker Newt Gingrich. In that highly charged political atmosphere, a Florida couple, both Democratic activists, happened to tape from a police scanner a cell-phone conversation between Ohio Republican John Boehner and other GOP leaders. They gave the tape to McDermott. A few days later, excerpts from it appeared in the *New York Times* and the *Atlanta Journal-Constitution*. Boehner sued McDermott in federal court for invasion of privacy, and the case lingered in the courts for years. McDermott approached Boehner in 2002—they had not spoken in the 12 years they served together—and sought to settle the case. He agreed to one of Boehner's demands, that he apologize to the House, but would not agree to the other two: admit that he was wrong and make a contribution to charity. In 2004, the judge found McDermott guilty of violating the federal wiretapping law and ordered him to pay $60,000 in damages and $500,000 in attorneys' fees. McDermott appealed the ruling. But the court case took yet another turn against him in 2007, when the divided D.C. Circuit Court concluded that House rules on confidentiality barred him from disclosing the contents of the tape. The judges ordered payment of the damages to Boehner. McDermott claimed the ruling infringed on his free-speech rights and took his case to the Supreme Court, which refused to hear it. In April 2008, a federal judge ordered McDermott to pay Boehner over $1.2 million in legal fees.

His outspokenness has not hurt McDermott in Seattle, where he regularly wins re-election with more than 70% of the vote. He considered running against Republican Sen. Slade Gorton in 2000, but backed away soon after he underwent open-heart surgery, saying he didn't want to raise the $8 million that would be required. Democrat Maria Cantwell defeated Gorton to capture the seat.

EIGHTH DISTRICT

Dave Reichert (R)

Elected 2004, 3rd term; b. Aug. 29, 1950, Detroit Lakes, MN; home, Auburn; Concordia Lutheran Col., A.A. 1970; Lutheran; married (Julie); 3 children.

Military Career: Air Force Reserve, 1971–76.

Elected Office: King Cnty. Sheriff, 1997–2004.

Professional Career: King Cnty. police officer, 1972–1997.

DC Office: 1730 LHOB, 20515, 202-225-7761; Fax: 202-225-4282; Web site: reichert.house.gov.

State Offices: Mercer Island, 206-275-3438.

Committees: *Ways & Means* (12th of 15 R): Oversight; Social Security; Trade.

Group Ratings

	ADA	ACLU	AFS	LCV	ITIC	NTU	COC	ACU	CFG	FRC
2008	60	36	71	69	80	52	78	56	53	52
2007	40	—	18	85	—	33	85	48	35	—

National Journal Ratings

	2007 LIB	—	2007 CONS		2008 LIB	—	2008 CONS
Economic	46%	—	54%		41%	—	58%
Social	45%	—	55%		44%	—	56%
Foreign	0%	—	72%		35%	—	62%
Composite	35%	—	65%		41%	—	59%

Key Votes of the 110th Congress

1. Increase minimum wage	Y	5. Share immigration data	N	9. Withdraw troops 8/08	N
2. Expand SCHIP	Y	6. Foreign aid abortion ban	Y	10. No operations in Iran	N
3. Raise CAFE standards	Y	7. Ban gay bias in workplace	Y	11. Free trade with Peru	Y
4. Bail out financial markets	N	8. Repeal D.C. gun law	Y	12. Overhaul FISA	Y

Election Results

2008 general	Dave Reichert (R)...	191,568	(53%)	($2,852,514)
	Darcy Burner (D)	171,358	(47%)	($4,462,884)
2008 primary	David Reichert (R)	74,140	(49%)	
	Darcy Burner (D)	68,010	(45%)	

Prior Winning Percentages: 2006 (51%); 2004 (52%)

Population		Race/Ethnicity		Work	
Pop. 2007:	760,915	White:	76.2%	Private:	81.2%
Change since 2000:	Up 16.2%	Black:	2.8%	Government:	12.4%
Urban:	87.6%	Hispanic:	5.4%	Self-employed:	6.2%
Rural:	12.4%	Asian:	11.4%	Blue collar:	17.6%
Area size:	2,621 sq. mi.	Native Am.:	0.6%	White collar:	69.8%
		Hawaiian:	0.3%	Khaki collar:	0.2%
Age		Two+ races:	2.9%	Other:	12.4%
Median age:	37.4 yrs.	*Ancestry*		Median income:	$78,367
More than 65 yrs:	9.1%	German:	15.1%	Median home value:	$375,600
Less than 18 yrs:	26.7%	English:	10.0%	Poverty:	6.3%
Education		Irish:	9.2%	**Military Veterans**	
H.S. grad:	93.4%			% of Pop:	11.0%
College grad:	40.7%				
Grad degree:	13.9%				

The land east of Seattle's Lake Washington half a century ago was quiet countryside. Orchards and vineyards flourished in the rich, moist soil just below the rise of the Cascades Mountains, while farms and broad pasturelands spread toward 14,410-foot Mount Rainier like a living green quilt. But as Seattle has grown over the years, people have crossed the pontoon bridge across Mercer Island to Bellevue and have made this area one of the most vibrant parts of metropolitan Seattle. With

2008 Presidential Vote

Obama (D) 211,045	(57%)
McCain (R)............................155,936	(42%)

2004 Presidential Vote

Kerry (D)................................177,601	(51%)
Bush (R) 168,291	(48%)

Cook Partisan Voting Index: D + 3

121,000 people, almost a quarter of them of Asian descent, and enough office space to make it an edge city, Bellevue has grown out of the shadow of Seattle. Its tallest skyscraper has hit the city's 450-foot height limit, a departure from the strip malls and parking lots that defined downtown a quarter century ago. While downtown Seattle specialized in banks and law firms and trading companies, Bellevue and other communities in Overlake specialized in high-tech start-ups. Redmond is the headquarters of Microsoft, and dozens of other firms here help make it one of America's leading high-tech centers.

The 8th Congressional District of Washington takes in most of the eastern edge of metro Seattle. It includes most of Bellevue, Mercer Island and the affluent suburbs on Lake Washington—Medina, Clyde Hill, Yarrow Point, Hunts Point, Beaux Arts. It includes Bill Gates' $60 million, 66,000-square-foot high-tech home with its trampoline room, video walls that can be electronically programmed with art from the world's great museums, and a garage large enough to hold 30 cars. According to the King County Assessor's office, annual property taxes on the house exceed $1 million. The 8th also includes the suburbs to the south in King and Pierce counties. It goes east to the crest of the Cascades Mountains and encompasses all of Mount Rainier and one of the nation's last inland old-growth rain forests. This is the most affluent district in Washington, rivaled only by the 1st District in suburban Seattle. Politically, it is a swing district. In 2004, Democratic nominee John Kerry won it 51% to 48%, and in 2008, Democrat Barack Obama won it 57%-42%.

The congressman from the 8th District is Dave Reichert, a Republican elected in 2004. Reichert was born in Detroit Lakes, Minn., but his family moved to the Seattle area a year later. He graduated from Concordia Lutheran College in Portland and then joined the Air Force Reserves. He worked for 32 years in the King County sheriff's office and was elected sheriff in 1997. He was a national leader on gun-crime reduction and methamphetamine prevention. During the riots that accompanied the 1999 international trade meeting in Seattle, he criticized city leaders and the police force for inadequate preparation. He gained national attention for his prominent role in capturing Gary Ridgway, the "Green River Killer" who had terrorized the Seattle area with a two-decade murder spree that left 48 women dead. After Ridgway's capture in 2001, Reichert was featured on national television shows and in documentaries, and he published a book about the experience, *Chasing the Devil: My Twenty-Year Quest to Capture the Green River Killer*.

When Republican Rep. Jennifer Dunn announced that she was retiring after 12 years in the House, Republicans actively recruited Reichert to run. He defeated three opponents in the September Republican primary, winning the nomination with 43% of the vote. The leading Democrat was Dave Ross, a longtime Seattle radio talk-show host who stayed on the air until July. He won the September primary with 48% of the vote.

In the general election, Reichert argued that local law-enforcement agencies should receive more money and equipment for homeland security. Sounding like a talk-show host, Ross said that he wanted to be the eyes and ears of the public, checking "into what's going on, who's making the trades, where the money is going and whether it's being wisely spent." The national parties stormed in, spending well over $5 million and organizing visits by prominent leaders. Each candidate tried to portray the other as lacking in public-policy experience and holding views too extreme for the swing district. Both Seattle newspapers, with strong liberal traditions, endorsed Ross for his greater familiarity with issues and suggested that Reichert was too conservative for the district. But Reichert won 52%-47%.

When Reichert arrived in the House, Republicans were in the majority. He backed New York Rep. Peter King's bid to chair the Homeland Security Committee and was rewarded by King with the chairmanship of the Emergency Preparedness Subcommittee, making him the only freshman in his class to chair a subcommittee. He won enactment of a bill that established standards for interoperable communications. He also established his independence from the GOP, a sound political move given his politically divided district. He voted to override President George W. Bush's veto of the stem-cell-research bill and voted against allowing drilling in the Arctic National Wildlife Refuge.

In the 110th Congress (2007-08), Reichert took liberal positions on many environmental issues. He supported tougher fuel-economy standards for cars and trucks and advocated expanding the Alpine Lakes Wilderness area in the Cascade Mountains. His positions earned him praise from the pro-environmental-protection League of Conservation Voters. He also sponsored a successful bill to fund programs fostering intelligence sharing with state and local governments.

National Democrats targeted Reichert when he was up for re-election the first time in 2006. The Democratic Congressional Campaign Committee ran radio ads against him a full 18 months before Election Day. In a competitive district where dissatisfaction with Bush would likely be a major liability, Reichert was unapologetic about inviting him to the district: "I know it's controversial to have the president come to the northwest part of the United States. I don't care. He's the president." Former Microsoft executive Darcy Burner, a political novice, was the Democratic nominee. She called Reichert a "Bush Republican" and "Rubber Stamp Reichert." The candidates each spent $3 million, and together, the national parties poured in more than $4 million. Reichert won 51%-49%.

In 2008, Burner was back for a rematch. She outraised Reichert $4.3 million to $3 million, but he won 53%-47%. During the campaign, he had asked House Republicans to give him a seat on the Appropriations Committee to help guarantee his re-election. He was instead named to the powerful House Ways and Means Committee in early 2009.

NINTH DISTRICT

Adam Smith (D)

Elected 1996, 7th term; b. June 15, 1965, Washington, DC; home, Tacoma; Fordham U., B.A. 1987, U. of WA, J.D. 1990; Christian; married (Sara); 2 children.

Elected Office: WA Senate, 1990–96.

Professional Career: Practicing atty., 1991–92; City prosecutor, 1992–95.

DC Office: 2402 RHOB, 20515, 202-225-8901; Fax: 202-225-5893; Web site: www.house.gov/adamsmith.

State Offices: Tacoma, 253-593-6600.

Committees: *Armed Services* (8th of 36 D): Air & Land Forces; Terrorism, Unconventional Threats & Capabilities (Chmn). *Intelligence (Select)* (12th of 13 D): Technical & Tactical Intelligence; Terrorism, Human Intelligence, Analysis & Counterintelligence.

Group Ratings

	ADA	ACLU	AFS	LCV	ITIC	NTU	COC	ACU	CFG	FRC
2008	85	91	100	92	100	16	67	4	11	5
2007	95	—	100	90	—	8	65	0	16	—

National Journal Ratings

	2007 LIB	—	2007 CONS		2008 LIB	—	2008 CONS
Economic	64%	—	34%		65%	—	35%
Social	63%	—	37%		75%	—	18%
Foreign	73%	—	27%		70%	—	25%
Composite	67%	—	33%		72%	—	28%

Key Votes of the 110th Congress

1. Increase minimum wage	Y	5. Share immigration data	Y	9. Withdraw troops 8/08	Y
2. Expand SCHIP	Y	6. Foreign aid abortion ban	N	10. No operations in Iran	Y
3. Raise CAFE standards	Y	7. Ban gay bias in workplace	Y	11. Free trade with Peru	Y
4. Bail out financial markets	Y	8. Repeal D.C. gun law	N	12. Overhaul FISA	Y

Election Results

2008 general	Adam Smith (D)	176,295	(65%)	($612,066)
	James Postma (R)	93,080	(35%)	($12,421)
2008 primary	Adam Smith (D)	81,503	(65%)	
	James Postma (R)	44,472	(35%)	

Prior Winning Percentages: 2006 (66%); 2004 (63%); 2002 (59%); 2000 (62%); 1998 (65%); 1996 (50%)

Population		Race/Ethnicity		Work	
Pop. 2007:	699,186	White:	68.7%	Private:	74.1%
Change since 2000:	Up 6.8%	Black:	7.2%	Government:	20.9%
Urban:	95.0%	Hispanic:	9.2%	Self-employed:	4.9%
Rural:	5.0%	Asian:	8.7%	Blue collar:	24.1%
Area size:	691 sq. mi.	Native Am.:	1.0%	White collar:	56.5%
Age		Hawaiian:	1.3%	Khaki collar:	3.0%
Median age:	36.1 yrs.	Two+ races:	3.6%	Other:	16.5%
More than 65 yrs:	10.8%	*Ancestry*		Median income:	$53,442
Less than 18 yrs:	24.7%	German:	15.0%	Median home value:	$254,800
Education		Irish:	9.1%	Poverty:	11.6%
H.S. grad:	89.0%	English:	8.3%	**Military Veterans**	
College grad:	23.3%			% of Pop:	15.5%
Grad degree:	7.4%				

The misty shores of Puget Sound have seen some of America's most vibrant economic growth over the past two decades. It has spread south and west from Seattle, over the suburban territory to the outskirts of the once-industrial city of Tacoma. The subdivisions along the sound, which have some of the loveliest views in America, tend to be high-income. But much of greater Seattle's prime industrial territory lies between the ridges that run north and south inland. Weyerhaeuser, the world's largest private owner of softwood timber, has its headquarters in Federal Way. Boeing is a major presence in Renton, on the south end of Lake Washington. Its aircraft and electronic-components plants have made it America's No. 1 exporter for many years. Renton, which gained renown as the home of 1960s guitarist Jimi Hendrix, manufactures 737s, the best-selling commercial jet in history. A host of smaller factories cluster near the rail lines that run from Minneapolis-St. Paul across the Great Plains to Puget Sound.

2008 Presidential Vote		
Obama (D)	166,812	(58%)
McCain (R)	116,915	(41%)

2004 Presidential Vote		
Kerry (D)	146,494	(53%)
Bush (R)	126,428	(46%)

Cook Partisan Voting Index: D+5

The 9th Congressional District of Washington covers much of this area. It includes Sea-Tac Airport, Burien and Renton, not far south of Seattle, as well as Kent, Des Moines, most of Auburn and Federal Way, farther south in King County. It includes the container port of Tacoma, though most of the rest of that city is in the 6th District. In surrounding Pierce County (the nation's largest producer of rhubarb), it takes in Edgewood and Puyallup, plus Fort Lewis, the largest Army base in the West, and McChord Air Force Base, home of the C-17. It also includes a part of Thurston County outside the state capital, Olympia, including the Nisqually National Wildlife Refuge, an important transit point for migratory birds. The district was created after the 1990 census and politically was almost perfectly balanced in the mid-1990s. It elected a Democratic representative in 1992, a Republican in 1994 and a Democrat in 1996. But as the Seattle region trended toward the Democrats, the district has done likewise.

The congressman from the 9th District is Adam Smith, a Democrat first elected in 1996. He grew up in the Sea-Tac area. His father, a baggage handler for United Airlines who was active in the Machinists Union, died when Smith was 17. The family went on welfare. Smith worked his way through Fordham University driving trucks for UPS, then went to the University of Washington Law School. He worked as a lawyer, then as a Seattle prosecutor, handling drunk-driving and domestic-abuse cases. In 1990, at age 25, he was elected to the state Senate, beating an incumbent Republican by canvassing the district door-to-door. In 1995, he decided to run against first-term U.S. Rep. Randy Tate, a Republican. The two had similar backgrounds. They were born in the same year to families of modest means, were first elected to office at young ages and were firm believers in grassroots campaigning. But Tate was a religious conservative and a strong supporter of Republican House Speaker Newt Gingrich, while Smith campaigned as a moderate Democrat, supporting the death penalty and tougher penalties for criminals. He attacked Tate for supporting Gingrich on 96% of House votes and for backing cuts in Medicare. Tate attacked Smith for his opposition to assigning youthful offenders to adult courts and prisons and for voting for Democratic Gov. Mike Lowry's $1.2 billion tax increase in 1993. This was one of the closest races in the country. In the September all-party primary, Smith led 49%-48%. In November, he won 50%-47%.

In the House, Smith got a seat on the Armed Services Committee, a useful assignment back home, and joined the New Democrat Coalition. He established a moderate voting record and showed a willingness to take on established interests within his party. He voted against government-paid vouchers for private school tuition. He voted to authorize military action in Iraq and sought to improve compensation and other quality-of-life benefits for military personnel. In 2004, he was one of four Democrats who opposed a provision in the USA PATRIOT Act to bar law enforcement access to library and bookstore records. In 2007, he called on the administration to change its strategy in Iraq, but he also criticized liberal activists for pressuring Democrats to end the war. When Democrats took control of the House in 2007, Smith became chairman of the Subcommittee on Terrorism and Unconventional Threats and Capabilities, which he called the "tip of the spear" in the war on terrorism.

Smith's independence has worked well for him back home. He has won re-election easily, and Republicans have quit targeting this district. In the 2004 presidential campaign, he was one of the first congressional supporters of Democratic presidential candidate John Kerry and chaired his campaign in Washington. In 2008, he was an early supporter of Democrat Barack Obama for president and chaired Obama's Washington state campaign. Smith briefly explored the possibility of taking a job with the Obama administration, but in February 2009, he announced that he would keep his seat in the House. He earned a seat on the House Permanent Select Committee on Intelligence, further bolstering his legislative credentials on military operations and foreign affairs.

★ WEST VIRGINIA ★

Almost heaven—that's what the song says about West Virginia. And there's something to it, at least in the minds of West Virginians who have never lost their sense of hope or their affection for the hills and mountains that make this the most unhorizontal state in the nation. Democratic Sen. Robert Byrd, working in a shipyard in Baltimore in 1944, painted a landscape of the mountains he was forced to leave behind (lithographs of it can be found on eBay). But West Virginia has had more than its share of tragedy and heartbreak. It was first settled by Scots-Irish immigrants, fresh from internecine fighting in the British Isles and determined to stake out homesteads where they could do as they like. The state slogan is *Montani semper liberi:* Mountain people are always free. It was born out of the tragedy of the Civil War, when 55 mountain counties with few slaves seceded from Virginia, and were declared a state in 1863. It has made its living most of the years since from that cruelest of minerals, coal. West Virginia is laced with coal. There are coal seams in 53 of its 55 counties and production even today, after many mines have closed, in 26 counties. Coal kept the sons of large mountaineer families here for much of the 20th century, men who would otherwise have left for big cities. Coal brought immigrants in, a few from odd corners of Europe, but more from adjacent areas of the South where the local farming economies were stagnant as West Virginia's coal economy was booming. Fifty years ago, coal and local rock salt and brines brought the large concentration of chemical plants to the Kanawha Valley around Charleston. Steel mills and glass factories were established in the panhandle and in the Monongahela River valley, not far south of Pittsburgh.

But for many years, coal did not build a reliable economy. When America was beleaguered abroad, demand for coal increased and energy prices rose, and West Virginia boomed, during World War II (the state reached its all-time population peak of 2 million in 1950) and during the oil shocks of the 1970s. Coal changed the state's politics too. West Virginia's heritage from the Civil War days was Republican, though some counties tilted toward the Confederacy and the Democrats. The United Mine Workers organized most of the West Virginia mines by 1902, and there were bloody strikes in 1912–13 and 1920–21. Under the UMW's John L. Lewis, the coal country shifted toward the New Deal Democrats, and West Virginia for more than half a century was one of the most Democratic states, deserting the national ticket only in Republican landslide years (1956, 1972, 1984) until George W. Bush carried it in 2000. Its Legislature has been controlled by Democrats since 1930. But neither Democratic administrations nor the pensions and medical benefits the UMW negotiated for retired miners were able to provide the economic growth to keep thousands of West Virginians from leaving their mountains to find work elsewhere. As miners were replaced by strip-mining machines, coal tonnage went way up but coal mine employment dropped from 22% of the state's work force in 1950 to 10% in 1980 and to only 4% in the late 1990s. Coal mines employed 126,000 West Virginians in 1948 and 13,500 in 2002. The state's population, 2 million in 1950, fell to 1.8 million in 2000—the largest decrease over that period, absolutely and in percentage terms, of any state. Of the state's 55 counties, 39 had fewer people in 2007 than they did in 1950. The only big population increases over that half-century have been in the eastern panhandle, the university town of Morgantown and several Ohio River counties below Charleston and around Parkersburg. In the 2000 census, West Virginia ranked 50th among states in household income, 50th in median value of housing (but first in percentage of home ownership), 48th in percentage of adults with a high school diploma and second in percentage living in poverty. It has attracted few immigrants over the last two generations. Its population is only 3% black and 1% Hispanic (the latter the lowest of any state). In any case, the West Virginians who remained have a strong attachment to this unique state, where the accent sounds Southern and the early 20th century factories and houses look Northern, where the landscape is rural and the economy is industrial.

In the past two decades, however, West Virginia's aging population has finally built a steadier and at least slowly growing economy. The outflow of young people over the decades has left the state with the nation's third oldest population—the median age is older than Florida's—and it is the only state with more deaths than births. But the number of jobs rose during most of the 1990s and 2000s, even as the number of manufacturing and underground mining jobs decreased. Unemployment has been below the national average much of the time. If West Virginia did not have a housing boom, except in a few eastern panhandle counties, it also did not have a housing bust in 2007 and 2008. And the demand for coal, despite the talk about alternative energy sources, has been robust. Government has played a role. Under Democratic Gov. Joe Manchin, the state has had budget surpluses with revenues that consistently exceed projections—something few other states can claim. In his more than 50 years on the Appropriations Committee, Byrd has exceeded his career goal of channeling $1 billion of federal projects into West Virginia. Forest products are replacing coal in rural counties, health care is growing and telemarketing is growing as well. West Virginia has finally completed its interstate highway network and, in the computer age, it is no longer isolated.

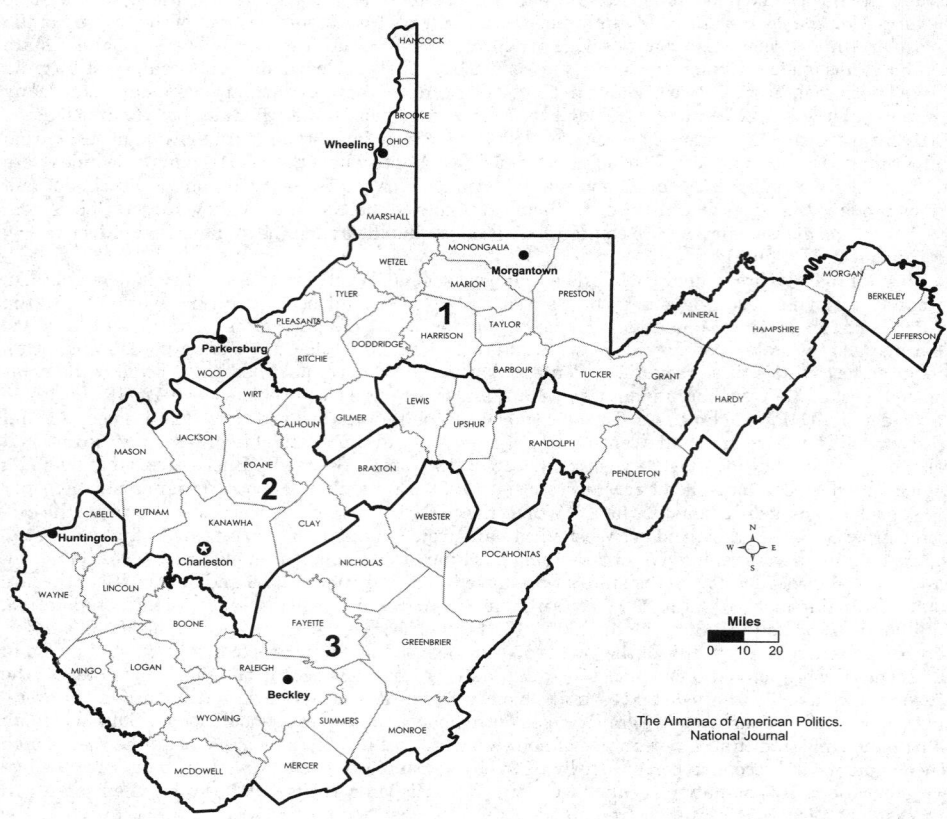

The Almanac of American Politics.
National Journal

Congressional district boundaries were first effective for 2002.

One factor that has sustained West Virginia's economy and reshaped its political attitudes has been the mountaintop mining of coal. Far fewer miners are needed for this work than in underground mining, but the pay is good and the jobs are far safer. The jobs are also highly valued in counties that have half the population they had 50 years ago. Mountaintop mining also has kept West Virginia competitive with the number No. 1 coal state, Wyoming, which has only surface mining. In October 1999, a federal judge ruled that mountaintop mining violates federal environmental laws. Byrd tried to overturn the decision in an appropriations bill, but was blocked by President Bill Clinton. The issue became important—arguably crucial—in the 2000 presidential race. Clinton opposed a ban but backed stricter regulation of the practice. Democratic presidential nominee Al Gore was caught in the middle between environmentalists who supported it and West Virginia's then all-Democratic congressional delegation that opposed it. Republican candidate George W. Bush, spotting an opening, came out in favor of mountaintop mining and called for increased federal support of clean coal technology. Bush's support of coal and his opposition to gun control enabled him to carry West Virginia 52%-46%, a stunning upset in a state that had not voted for a Republican in an open presidential race since 1928. Its five electoral votes were crucial: Without them, it would not have mattered who won Florida. The environmental stands that helped Gore in large East and West Coast states proved fatal to his candidacy in West Virginia.

In April 2001, the federal court decision was reversed by the Fourth Circuit Court of Appeals. The appellate court ruled that West Virginia's mining restrictions superseded federal standards. But Bush continued to push Congress to spend billions of dollars on clean coal technology and backed import quotas to help the steel industry, still a major coal user. All this helped Bush in the 2004 election. Massachusetts Sen. John Kerry, the Democratic nominee, had voted against Byrd's amendment to save mountaintop mining and for air pollution control bills that would have cut coal usage by as much as 40%. West Virginia slipped off both candidates' target lists, and Bush ended up winning 46 of 55 counties on his way to a 56%-43% victory. Republicans also won surprise victories in races for secretary of state and the state Supreme Court. In 2008, polls suggested West Virginia might be in play if the Democratic nominee were Hillary Rodham Clinton, who won the primary here by a more than 2-to-1 ratio. But Democrat Barack Obama had little appeal anywhere in the Appalachian chain, from western Pennsylvania southwest to Tennessee. Republican John McCain won West Virginia 56%-43%, the same margin as Bush's, carrying 48 of 55 counties, even though in party identification Democrats led Republicans 48%-34%. Republicans just missed winning races for attorney general and a Court of Appeals seat.

Population		Household Income		Work	
Pop. 2007:	1,808,787	Under $15k:	20.0%	Private:	76.0%
State rank:	37th of 50	$15k to $50k:	44.2%	Government:	18.2%
Change since 2000:	Up 0.0%	$50k to $100k:	26.7%	Self-employed:	5.6%
Urban:	46.4%	$100k to $150k:	7.8%	Unemployment (3-yr. average):	3.8%
Rural:	53.6%	Over $150k:	1.4%	Poverty:	17.7%
Native of state:	72.0%	Median income:	$36,088	Blue collar:	27.6%
Not a citizen:	0.6%	**Home Value**		White collar:	54.2%
Area size:	24,230 sq. mi.	Under $100k:	56.6%	Khaki collar:	0.1%
Most populous cities		$100k to $300k:	37.2%	Other:	18.1%
1. Charleston	51,295	$300k to $500k:	4.7%	**Age**	
2. Huntington	48,988	$500k to $1 mil:	1.2%	Median age:	40.3 yrs.
3. Parkersburg	31,551	Over $1 million:	0.3%	More than 65 yrs:	15.4%
4. Wheeling	29,307	Median:	$89,500	Less than 18 yrs:	21.5%

Race/Ethnicity				Military Veterans		Registered Voters in 2008	
White:	93.7%	*Language*		% of Pop:	12.3%	D:	675,305 (55.7%)
Black:	3.4%	English:	97.6%	*Veterans by Period*		R:	353,437 (29.2%)
Hispanic:	1.0%	Spanish:	1.1%	WWII and before:	13.0%	Other:	183,375 (15.1%)
Asian:	0.6%	Asian:	0.4%	Korea:	12.9%	Voter turnout:	713,451
Native Am.:	0.2%	Other		Vietnam:	33.6%	Turnout as % of	
Hawaiian:	0.0%	European	0.8%	Gulf (pre-2001):	10.4%	voting age:	50.0%
Two+ races:	1.1%	**Education**		Gulf (post-2001):	5.9%	**Legislature**	
Ancestry		H.S. grad:	81.0%	Peace time:	24.2%	Senate:	28 D 6 R
German:	16.2%	College grad:	16.9%			House of Del.:	71 D 29 R
USA:	12.3%	Grad degree:	6.6%				
Irish:	12.1%						

Presidential politics West Virginia has voted Republican in the last three consecutive presidential elections. Before that, the last times it did so were in 1920, 1924 and 1928, and it was then very much in line with the national trend. Not so in 2000, 2004 and 2008, when it has voted significantly more Republican than the national average. This divergence can be explained by two factors: culture and coal. West Virginians tend to be more religious and tradition-minded than Americans generally, more supportive of gun ownership, and more skeptical of environmental regulation that affects the economy. That leads to the issue of coal. At a time when national Democrats are bent on reducing carbon emissions to curb global warming, West Virginia has an economy that is growing enough to sustain an aging population and that depends heavily on coal. Political reporters were puzzled when Republican candidate George W. Bush targeted West Virginia in his 2000 campaign; between 1928 and 2000, the only Republican nominees it voted for were incumbents headed for landslide victories—

2008 Presidential Vote		
McCain (R)	397,466	(56%)
Obama (D)	303,857	(43%)

2008 Democratic Presidential Primary		
Clinton (D)	240,890	(67%)
Obama (D)	92,736	(26%)
Edwards (D)	26,284	(7%)

2008 Republican Presidential Primary		
McCain (R)	90,469	(76%)
Huckabee (R)	12,310	(10%)
Paul (R)	5,969	(5%)

2004 Presidential Vote		
Bush (R)	423,778	(56%)
Kerry (D)	326,541	(43%)

Dwight Eisenhower in 1956, Richard Nixon in 1972, and Ronald Reagan in 1984. But Bush's support of mountaintop mining and his promotion of clean coal technology enabled him to beat Democrat Al Gore here 52%-46% in 2000 and John Kerry 56%-43% in 2004. It also helped that about half of West Virginia voters are white evangelical Protestants and about 70% are gun owners.

In 2008, the result in West Virginia was not in doubt once Barack Obama clinched the Democratic nomination. Obama visited the state only twice during the primary season and not at all after clinching the nomination. Turnout was 713,000, down 6% from 2004, though well above the levels from 1988 to 2000 and far below the all-time high, 873,000 in 1952, the year Byrd was first elected to Congress. Republican John McCain beat Obama 56%-43%, and Obama carried only seven counties. McCain ran well ahead of Bush in the southern coal counties and well behind in the fast-growing eastern panhandle, some of it now officially part of the Washington D.C. metro area. McCain carried both the young and the elderly, and ran best among Generation X (ages 30 to 44). Obama carried union members by only 54%-43% and lost white evangelical Protestants 66%-34%. Thirty-two percent of voters who supported Clinton in the primary voted for McCain, one of the largest defection rates in the country.

West Virginia's presidential primary, held in May, has not attracted much attention since 1960, when Democrat John F. Kennedy took on Hubert Humphrey and beat him with 61% of the vote, proving that a Catholic could carry a virtually all-Protestant state. For 2008, West Virginia Republicans chose delegates in a party convention on Super Tuesday on February 5. Thanks to some last-minute switches by McCain supporters, Mike Huckabee beat Mitt Romney 52%-47%, a result that was broadcast in the early afternoon Eastern time, which may have hurt Romney in some of the other contests held that day. Republicans also voted in the May 13 primary, two months after Huckabee's withdrawal. Turnout was 117,000 voters, a little more than in 2004 and 2000 and well under the levels of 1980–88. McCain got 76% of the vote.

The Democratic contest was not an epic battle as in 1960, but it was hard fought nonetheless by Hillary Rodham Clinton and her former-president husband, who campaigned extensively in the state and hoped for a win that would, for once, provide her with a significant delegate edge. Obama, by contrast, appeared in the state only twice. Turnout was a robust 356,000, well over the levels in the three previous primaries, though less than in 1984, 1976 and 1972. Clinton won 67%-26%, her biggest victory except for Arkansas, and carried every county. The results were close only in Jefferson County, in the far end of the eastern panhandle. "We all know from the Bible, faith can move mountains," Clinton said on Election Night. "My friends, the faith of the Mountain State has moved me."

Congressional districting West Virginia's three congressional districts, created after the state lost one House seat in the 1990 Census, were not significantly altered in redistricting after the 2000 census. The process was dominated by Democrats and the sole Republican, Shelley Moore Capito, who won an open seat narrowly in 2000, could have been harmed by a partisan redrawing of the lines. But one or both of the state's two Democratic incumbents might also have been weakened, if not for the general election, then in a possible primary. Most state legislators, preoccupied with redrawing their own districts, were content to please all three congressional incumbents. In 2001, the Legislature, with one dissenting vote, removed Gilmer County from the 2nd District and placed it in the 1st, and removed Nicholas County from the 2nd and placed it in the 3rd. Both are Democratic counties that had no significant impact on the 2002 election results.

111th Congress Lineup	
2 D	1 R

110th Congress Lineup	
2 D	1 R

Projections based on 2000–08 population growth indicate that West Virginia will not lose a district in the reapportionment following the 2010 census. Democrats will control the redistricting process, but no one expects that they will try to manipulate the lines in any major way to defeat Capito.

Governor

Joe Manchin (D)

Elected 2004, term expires Jan. 2013, 2nd term; b. Aug. 24, 1947, Farmington; home, Marion County; WV U., B.S. 1970; Catholic; married (Gayle); 3 children.

Elected Office: WV House, 1982–84; WV Senate 1986–96; WV sec. of state, 2000–04.

Professional Career: Co-owner, Manchin's Carpet and Tile, 1968–82; Owner, Enersystems, 1989–2000.

Office: 1900 Kanawha Blvd. E., Charleston, 25305, 888-438-2731; Fax: 304-558-2722; Web site: www.wvgov.org.

Election Results

2008 general	Joe Manchin (D)	492,697	(70%)
	Russ Weeks (R)	181,612	(26%)
	Jesse Johnson (MP)	31,486	(4%)
2008 primary	Joe Manchin (D)	264,775	(75%)
	Melvin Kessler (D)	90,074	(25%)

Prior Winning Percentages: 2004 (64%)

Democrat Joe Manchin, elected governor of West Virginia in 2004 and re-elected in 2008, comes from a family involved in politics for many years. Manchin grew up in Farmington, a few miles up Buffalo Creek from the industrial city of Fairmont on the Monongahela River. He remembers working in his grandfather's grocery store, and later, in his father's carpet and furniture store. He took a semester off from college to help his father rebuild the store after a fire. His grandfather and father were elected mayor of Farmington. His uncle, A. James Manchin, was elected to the West Virginia House of Delegates and, statewide, as secretary of state and state treasurer. After graduating from West Virginia University, Joe Manchin went to work in the carpet and furniture business, helping to send his four siblings to college. Then he started a coal brokerage company and eventually moved to Fairmont. In 1982, at age 35, Manchin was elected to the House of Delegates, and in 1986, to the state Senate. After 10 years in the state Senate, Manchin ran for governor. The Democratic primary was a rip-roaring contest between Manchin and legislator Charlotte Pritt, who had the support of organized labor. She attacked Manchin as the business candidate, and unions opposed him because of his votes on workmen's compensation bills. Pritt beat Manchin in the 11-candidate primary 40%-32%. He declined to support her in the general election and attacked her in October. She lost to 74-year-old Republican Cecil Underwood.

Manchin returned to Fairmont and seemed out of politics. But in 2000, when 86-year-old Secretary of State Ken Hechler ran for the U.S. House, Manchin ran to succeed him. So did Pritt. This time, Manchin beat her in the primary 51%-29%. He worked with Republican U.S. attorneys to prevent vote fraud and was one of the few secretaries of state to comply with the federal requirement of a statewide voter registry. In May 2003, he announced he was challenging Democratic Governor Bob Wise in the 2004 primary. That seemed a daunting task. Wise had already raised $1.2 million. But timing is everything in politics. Later that month, Wise announced that he had had an extramarital affair and would not seek re-election. In quick time, eight Democrats and 10 Republicans joined the race.

This time, Manchin worked successfully to get support from both unions and business and could not be easily tagged "the candidate of big business." His stands on cultural issues were impeccably conservative: against abortion, gun control, and same-sex marriage. He emphasized economic issues, calling for a concentrated state effort to spur economic development. Manchin's best financed opponent was former state Sen. Lloyd Jackson. Another was Charleston lawyer Jim Lees. Jackson ran tough negative ads against Manchin, but they apparently didn't have much impact. Manchin won with 53% of the vote to 27% for Jackson and 14% for Lees. In the Republican primary, Monty Warner, a retired Army colonel and Monongalia County developer, won with 23% of the vote.

Manchin and Warner were old friends, and pledged to run a positive campaign; they mostly did. But the advantage was all with Manchin. He had far more money, and his implicitly low-tax platform undercut Warner's tax-cut, stop-lawsuit-abuse theme. Warner wasn't invited to appear on stage with President George W. Bush during many of his frequent appearances in West Virginia, and Manchin's business support, plus the formation of a Republicans for Manchin group that included top Bush backers, helped convince the usually Republican *Charleston Daily Mail* to endorse him. The business community concentrated on an ultimately successful attempt to defeat Democratic state Supreme Court Justice Warren McGraw. Republicans also made gains in state legislative races—a dividend, perhaps, of Bush's 56%-43% victory in the state. But Manchin won by a wider 64%-34%, carrying 52 of 55 counties.

Manchin had been in office for just a year when he gained national renown as the public face of desperate attempts to rescue 13 trapped coal miners after the January 2, 2006 explosion at the Sago Mine in central West Virginia. Manchin, whose uncle was killed in a 1968 accident that claimed 78 lives, arrived at the Sago mine within hours of the accident to offer comfort to the families and act as their main conduit of information. During the two-day ordeal, the governor appeared frequently at news conferences and gave numerous televised news interviews. But he also made an astounding mistake, announcing "the miracle of all miracles," that 12 of the miners had survived when in fact they had died, an error understandably devastating for the grief-stricken families. The blunder could have been career-ending. But in fact, Manchin's standing skyrocketed in the polls, largely due to his sincerity and tirelessness but also in small part because West Virginia Republicans decided that the mining accident was a line that they would not cross. Asked by *USA Today* to comment on Manchin's performance, the state Republican Party chairman said, "There's nothing political about this crisis. The governor represents the state, and we're all united in the heartache that we're all experiencing."

On January 26, Manchin signed into law a package of mine safety improvements, including wireless emergency communication devices, tracking devices and extra air supplies, plus a $100,000 penalty for mine operators that fail to report mine fires and explosions to a central hotline within 15 minutes. After two other deadly mining accidents in the state, Manchin in early February ordered safety inspections at all West Virginia mines. In April 2007, Manchin signed new coal safety laws mandating certain ventilation practices and giving the state authority to temporarily shut down mines with safety violations.

Manchin has achieved legislative success on other issues. In April 2006, he signed into law eight bills designed to improve state health care, including a new mental health commission, a low-income health care plan providing basic care at clinics around the state, and a catastrophic health care insurance program. He also signed legislation restricting city governments in taking property in eminent domain cases. Increased coal mining and video lottery revenue helped boost state tax revenues, which Manchin persuaded the Legislature to use to pay down the state's portion of debt it owes to state employee pension funds. Manchin also proposed a law increasing penalties for sex offenders. The bill died in the regular session after Senate Republicans added strict mandatory sentencing language. After legislators met in a special June session and approved a compromise bill, Manchin signed it. During a second special session in November 2006, legislators delivered to Manchin a series of tax cuts, including a cut in the food tax and a reduction of business franchise and corporate income taxes. Manchin enjoyed high approval ratings as Democrats headed into the 2006 elections, and he proved to be a popular draw for Democratic candidates. In a bid to shift control of the House of Delegates to Republicans, coal executive Don Blankenship pumped more than $2 million into state delegate races. Democrats ended up improving their majority in the state House by four seats, giving them a 72-28 advantage.

In January 2007, Manchin pledged to raise teachers' pay 2.5%, with a minimum of $30,000 a year. The Legislature raised that to 3.5%. State government revenues rolled ahead of projections, and in March, Manchin signed a $10 billon budget. He called for hauling away abandoned cars, saying, "People will not pay to come see a garbage dump. They want what we have in West Virginia, the quality of life. They can work here and raise a family." After objections to his new welcome sign slogan, "Open for Business," he promoted an Internet poll pitting it against the 1975–91 state slogan, "Wild, Wonderful," and got 49,000 responses, with the old slogan prevailing in the vote. Also in 2007, Manchin hailed the groundbreaking of a new coal-fired electric power plant in Monongalia County, the first new facility since 1993.

In 2008, with the state again in good fiscal shape, the Legislature increased the teachers' pay raise to 4.5% and left in place the scheduled cut in the corporate tax from 8.75% to 6.5%. As the recession began to affect state budgets in 2008, Manchin said, "Our revenues are still exceeding our projections, which is strong in a volatile market. Like every other state, we won't escape financial losses from this shakeout. But we're in good shape to handle it." He also expressed disapproval of the federal government's rescue of Wall Street firms, telling Fox News, "I come from a little West Virginia community. I never got rewarded for bad performance. I never got a bonus if I lost your money. . . . How, all of a sudden, can that work in the financial community? Who allowed that to happen? It's not hard to figure out what went wrong. They took the regulations off and allowed people to make money in any way." In 2009, Manchin was focused on proposals for boosting student achievement and allowing local officials to develop jobs programs on mined land.

He did not have serious competition for re-election in 2008. He spent $1 million by October while his Republican opponent borrowed $10,000. In November, he won 70%-26%, the largest ever margin of victory for a West Virginia governor unless you count the unanimous margins for Republican Arthur Boreman in two elections during the Civil War. His popularity has sparked discussions about his political future beyond the governor's office. He would presumably be a strong candidate for the Senate if one of the state's two seats opens up.

Senior Senator

Robert Byrd (D)

Elected 1958, term expires 2012, 9th term; b. Nov. 20, 1917, North Wilkesboro, NC; home, Sophia; American U., J.D. 1963, Marshall U., B.A. 1994; Baptist; widowed; 4 children.

Elected Office: WV House of Delegates, 1946–50; WV Senate, 1950–52; U.S. House of Reps., 1952–58; U.S. Senate majority whip, 1971–76, Majority ldr., 1977–80, 1987–88, Minority ldr., 1981–86.

DC Office: 311 HSOB, 20510, 202-224-3954; Fax: 202-228-0002; Web site: byrd.senate.gov.

State Offices: Charleston, 304-342-5855; Martinsburg, 304-264-4626.

Committees: *Appropriations* (2nd of 18 D): Defense; Energy & Water Development; Homeland Security (Chmn); Interior, Environment & Related Agencies; Military Construction, Veterans Affairs & Related Agencies; Transportation, Housing and Urban Development & Related Agencies. *Armed Services* (3rd of 15 D): Emerging Threats & Capabilities; Readiness & Management Support; Strategic Forces. *Budget* (5th of 13 D). *Rules & Administration* (3rd of 11 D).

Group Ratings

	ADA	ACLU	AFS	LCV	ITIC	NTU	COC	ACU	CFG	FRC
2008	55	86	100	73	80	9	57	0	10	22
2007	80	—	86	73	—	7	40	8	7	—

National Journal Ratings

	2007 LIB	—	2007 CONS		2008 LIB	—	2008 CONS
Economic	51%	—	47%		66%	—	33%
Social	52%	—	47%		69%	—	30%
Foreign	85%	—	8%		94%	—	0%
Composite	64%	—	36%		78%	—	22%

Key Votes of the 110th Congress

1. Raise CAFE standards	Y	5. Make English official language	Y	9. Withdraw troops 3/08	Y
2. Expand SCHIP	Y	6. Path to citizenship	N	10. Iran guard is terrorist group	N
3. Cap greenhouse gases	*	7. Fetus is unborn child	N	11. Increase missile defense $	N
4. Bail out financial markets	Y	8. Prosecute hate crimes	Y	12. Overhaul FISA	N

Election Results

2006 general	Robert Byrd (D)	296,276	(64%)	($4,944,546)
	John Raese (R)	155,043	(34%)	($3,147,967)
2006 primary	Robert Byrd (D)	159,154	(86%)	
	Billy Hendricks (D)	26,609	(14%)	

Prior Winning Percentages: 2000 (78%); 1994 (69%); 1988 (65%); 1982 (69%); 1976 (100%); 1970 (78%); 1964 (68%); 1958 (59%); 1956 House (57%); 1954 House (63%); 1952 House (56%)

Robert Byrd, the longest-serving member of the U.S. Senate in history, may come closer to the kind of senator the founding fathers had in mind than any other. He comes from the humblest of beginnings, and when first elected to the Senate, as part of the large and talented Democratic class of 1958, he was scarcely noticed. Now, he is the only member of that class still in Congress. He is also the Senate president pro tempore, thus third in line for the presidency. On June 12, 2006, Byrd became the longest-serving senator in history (a milestone made bittersweet by the fact that it was the birthday of his wife of nearly 69 years, Erma Byrd, who had died in March of that year). When he cast his 17,000th vote in March 2004, Democratic Sen. Edward Kennedy of Massachusetts noted, "Every time Bob casts a vote, he sets a new record. It is not fair, though, that he counts the votes he cast in the Roman Senate too, but we love him anyway and we never stop learning from him." By the end of the 110th Congress in late 2008, he had cast well over 18,000 votes.

Byrd grew up desperately poor. "I lived in a house without electricity," he once recalled. "No running water, no telephone, little wooden outhouse." The son of a coal miner in southern West Virginia, Byrd was a toddler when his mother died. His father gave the boy to an aunt and uncle to raise, Titus and Vlurma Byrd. As a young man, Byrd worked as a welder in wartime shipyards and a meat cutter in a coal company town. When he won his seat in the state House of Delegates in 1946, he campaigned in every hollow, playing his fiddle and, as he later said, joining the Ku Klux Klan to better fit in with his constituents. He later said that he quickly regretted the decision and quit. But the episode haunted him his entire career. Byrd worked hard in the Legislature, and went on to win a U.S. House seat in 1952. Six years later, when he was 40 years old, he was elected to the Senate, even though the United Mine Workers initially opposed him and the coal companies never supported him.

In the Senate, he became a supporter of Democratic Majority Leader Lyndon B. Johnson and in return got a seat on the powerful Appropriations Committee. He backed Hubert Humphrey against John F. Kennedy in the 1960 West Virginia Democratic presidential primary not because he shared Humphrey's liberal politics—Byrd's voting record then was as conservative as any Southerner's and he opposed the Civil Rights Act of 1964—but because Johnson wanted to stop Kennedy. In his early years, he took care to master the Senate's arcane rules. As he said in 2002, "Nobody has ever used the rules of the Senate more than I have." In the 1960s, Byrd's career took what in retrospect was a helpful detour. In 1965, he became assistant majority whip, an unimportant position then. In 1971, Sen. Edward Kennedy neglected his duties as majority whip after the accident at Chappaquiddick, when he drove his car off a bridge, killing a young woman riding with him. Byrd quietly lined up support and, with the deathbed vote of Democratic Sen. Richard Russell of Georgia, ousted Kennedy from his leadership position and took over as whip. Byrd performed ably in the role, managing Senate business and accommodating colleagues' needs. When Majority Leader Mike Mansfield retired in 1976, Byrd easily won the top job. All the while, Byrd's popularity grew at home. In 1970, he won 78% of the vote, becoming the first West Virginian in history to carry all 55 counties in the state. Byrd did not like being majority leader. Contrary to most people's assumptions, he considered the job to have little power. Senate rules requiring unanimous consent or a supermajority to get anything done allow a minority of senators or even an individual senator to block progress on legislation. Byrd was aware that his power came from meeting other senators' needs. He did not have a national agenda of his own, though his voting record became notably less conservative as time went on. In 1987, with Democrats back in the majority after six years out of power, Byrd established some legislative priorities and then announced he would leave the post after the 1988 election.

In 1989, Byrd got the position he really wanted—chairman of the Appropriations Committee. For the next 20 years, he was either the chairman or ranking minority member of the panel, which controls the government's purse strings. "I want to be West Virginia's billion dollar industry," he said in 1990, and he went on to succeed handsomely. Citizens Against Government Waste, a watchdog group and a Byrd critic, reported in 2006 that West Virginia had gotten nearly $3 billion in federal projects since 1991, and that 33 of them were named for Byrd, including the Robert C. Byrd Highway, the Robert C. Byrd Health Sciences Center, the Robert C. Byrd Center for Legislative Studies, the Robert C. Byrd Hilltop Office Complex and the Robert C. Byrd Hardwood Technologies Center. Clarksburg got a Federal Bureau of Investigation office, Parkersburg got U.S. Treasury and Internal Revenue Service offices, the town of Harper's Ferry got a Fish and Wildlife Training Center, Martinsburg got a Bureau of Alcohol, Tobacco and Firearms office and Wheeling got a NASA research center. Byrd likes to boast that when he was in the House of Delegates in 1947, West Virginia had just four miles of divided, four-lane highway. Today, it has 1,087 miles.

But a string of recent congressional scandals involving appropriations earmarks aroused public concerns about the proliferation of earmarks, and Byrd has come under increasing pressure to restrict them. In 2007, he announced new rules requiring that sponsors of earmarks be identified in documents accompanying the spending bills and that they certify that they or their spouses would not benefit financially from them. Byrd himself continues to be a robust earmarker, inserting $123 million in projects for his state in the 2008–2009 omnibus appropriations bill alone, more than any other senator. The projects included $12 million for construction at Bluestone Lake and $5 million for a DNA laboratory at Marshall University. "An earmark may be pork to some political chatterbox on television, but to many communities in West Virginia and other states, earmarks are economic lifelines," Byrd said in 2008. "Earmarks may fund a road that has fallen into dangerous disrepair or a bridge that is on the verge of collapse. An earmark addresses economic needs that many times fall between the cracks of the Washington bureaucracy. When that happens, the people I represent cannot call some unelected bureaucrat in the White House budget office or a Cabinet secretary. They call me! . . . and (I) will not ever apologize for my efforts on behalf of the good people I represent."

In 2007, Byrd stood like Cato in the Roman Senate against the latest proposal to pass the line-item veto, which would give the president the power to selectively disapprove of individual items in appropriations bills. "I will stand back here and let my bones crumble under me, until I no longer have any breath in me," Byrd said, with his typical oratorical flourish. "Such a process is a lethal, lethal, lethal aggrandizement of the chief executive's role in the legislative process. Lethal. Deadly. . . . It is a gross, gross, colossal distortion of the congressional power of the purse. It is a dangerous, dangerous proposition, a wolf in the sheep's clothing of fiscal responsibility." Similarly, when Republican Majority Leader Bill Frist threatened to change the filibuster rule in the confirmation fight over Supreme Court nominee Samuel Alito, Byrd reacted furiously, even though he ended up voting to confirm Alito.

Byrd's positions are not just parochial, but are the product of serious study of the Constitution and of history. He keeps a copy of the Constitution in his left breast pocket. With the assistance of Senate historian Richard Baker, he wrote *The Senate 1789–1989*, a two-volume history, plus two volumes of classic speeches and statistics. The collection is based on impressive research, gracefully written, full of arresting anecdotes and sound insights, and it surpassed any previous work on the subject. Byrd earned a law degree while serving in the Senate, collecting his diploma from President Kennedy at the 1963 American University commencement where Kennedy delivered his most important foreign policy speech. In 1994, Byrd was awarded his bachelor's degree summa cum laude by Marshall University, which he had attended for one semester 43 years before before running out of money. He earned As in all eight courses he took. Byrd is devoutly self-educated as well. He systematically reads the classics, and takes to quoting Shakespeare, Thucydides or Cato the Younger in debates on the budget or the line-item veto. But Byrd is also capable of having a little fun. He played a Confederate general in the film *Gods and Generals* in 2001.

Byrd turned 91 in November 2008 and has been in frail health for the last few years. He was away from the Senate for nearly two months in the first part of 2009 with multiple infections and other problems that required a six-week hospital stay. He returned to work in late July 2009 with the aid of a wheelchair and an attendant. He also was hospitalized after a fall in March 2008. "My only adversity is age," Byrd has said. "I will continue to do this work until this old body just gives out and drops." His sporadic absences from the Senate prompted quiet discussion among Democratic colleagues about urging him to give up his cherished gavel at Appropriations. Byrd at first resisted, but then gave in. Three days after the November 2008 election, he issued a statement saying: "I have been privileged to be a member of the Senate Appropriations Committee for 50 years and to have chaired the committee for 10 years, during a time of enormous change in our great country, both culturally and politically. A new day has dawned in Washington, and that is a good thing. For my part, I believe it is time for a new day at the top of the Senate Appropriations Committee." The job went to next-in-line Sen. Daniel Inouye, a Hawaii Democrat, age 84.

Byrd's relations with several administrations have been strained. Republican President George W. Bush went out of his way to shake Byrd's hand at his first speech to a joint session of Congress. But Byrd staunchly opposed the new president's centerpiece legislation, the 2001 tax cut, as "sheer madness," arguing that it was based on inevitably untrustworthy economic forecasts and complaining that it would cut off funds for appropriators. Byrd's insistence on maintaining what he regards as the Senate's constitutional prerogatives, and his distaste for Bush administration policies, led him to embark on two crusades in 2002 that probably contributed to the Democrats' loss of their Senate majority in November that year. One was his opposition to the bill setting up the Department of Homeland Security. He insisted that the biggest reorganization of the federal government since the creation of the Department of Defense required more scrutiny, and he opposed giving the president authority to shift money between agencies without permission from congressional appropriators. In his persistent speeches, he never used the word filibuster, but that's what he did. After the election, Democrats realized it was in their political interest to pass the bill, and a motion to limit debate passed 65-29.

Byrd's other crusade was against military action in Iraq. In September 2002, he accused Bush of political motivation, saying, "All of a sudden the president was dropping in the polls, and the domestic situation was such that the administration was appearing to be much like the emperor who had no clothes. All of a sudden, Bam! All of this war talk—the war fervor, the drums of war, the bugles of war, the clouds of war, this war hysteria—has blown in like a hurricane. And what has that done to the president's polls? Seventy percent." In October, Byrd threatened to delay action on the Iraq war resolution by insisting on votes on individual clauses. He was foiled when Connecticut Sen. Joe Lieberman and Democratic Leader Tom Daschle of South Dakota made a wording change that caused his motion to be ruled out of order. His attempt to filibuster lost and the Senate passed the resolution 77-23.

He was not particularly fond of Democratic President Bill Clinton either, but Byrd's distaste for the Bush administration was acute. "I've never seen an administration so discourteous, so arrogant toward the legislative branch as this one is. I've been here 51 years, so why shouldn't I speak out?" He opposed the Bush energy bill, even though it included money for clean coal research helpful to West Virginia. He attended the Democratic National Convention in 2004, his first since 1988, to plug his just-published book *Losing America: Confronting a Reckless and Arrogant Presidency*. In 2008, Byrd, the former Klansman, finally found a modern president he liked in Democrat Barack Obama. He had endorsed Obama in advance of the West Virginia primary, calling the Illinois Democrat "a shining young statesman, who possesses the personal temperament and courage necessary to extricate our country from this costly misadventure in Iraq, and to lead our nation at this challenging time in history."

West Virginia has had only three U.S. senators in 50 years—since 1958, which saw the election of both Byrd and Jennings Randolph, who retired in 1984, 52 years after he first entered Congress. Sen. Jay Rockefeller, also a Democrat, was elected to Randolph's seat in 1984. Byrd was elected to a ninth term in 2006. Republicans, noting that George W. Bush had carried the state twice and that Byrd would turn 89 two weeks after the election, hoped for a strong opponent but could not persuade a top candidate to run against Byrd. Finally, in January 2006 a candidate stepped forward, John Raese, a businessman from Morgantown who ran against Rockefeller in 1984 and lost by only 52%-48%. But Raese was hardly of a mind to run a tough campaign against Byrd, who was a friend of his father, Dyke Raese, a former basketball coach at West Virginia University. Raese recalled, "My dad would come down and say, 'Guess who called me on my birthday?' I'd say, 'I'll take three guesses. Two of them don't count. It was Robert

Byrd.'" Raese's campaign message was: "I'm running for U.S. Senate, not against Senator Byrd. I have a lot of different ideas, not that his are right or wrong. Mine might be better." Byrd won 64%-34%. At a spirited rally at the end of an earlier successful re-election campaign, Byrd said, "West Virginia has always had four friends: God Almighty, Sears Roebuck, Carter's Liver Pills and Robert C. Byrd."

Junior Senator

Jay Rockefeller (D)

Elected 1984, term expires 2014, 5th term; b. June 18, 1937, New York, NY; home, Charleston; Harvard U., B.A. 1961, Intl. Christian U., Tokyo, Japan, 1957–60; Presbyterian; married (Sharon); 4 children.

Elected Office: WV House of Delegates, 1966–68; WV secy. of state, 1968–72; WV gov., 1976–84.

Professional Career: Natl. Advisory Cncl., Peace Corps, 1961; Asst., Peace Corps Dir. Sargent Shriver, 1962–63; VISTA worker, 1964–66; Pres., WV Wesleyan Col., 1973–75.

DC Office: 531 HSOB, 20510, 202-224-6472; Fax: 202-224-7665; Web site: rockefeller.senate.gov.

State Offices: Beckley, 304-253-9704; Charleston, 304-347-5372; Fairmont, 304-367-0122; Martinsburg, 304-262-9285.

Committees: *Commerce, Science & Transportation* (Chmn of 14 D). *Finance* (2nd of 13 D): Health Care (Chmn); International Trade, Customs & Global Competitiveness; Social Security, Pensions & Family Policy; Taxation, IRS Oversight & Long-Term Growth. *Intelligence (Select)* (2nd of 8 D). *Joint Committee on Taxation* (2nd of 3 D). *Veterans' Affairs* (2nd of 10 D).

Group Ratings

	ADA	ACLU	AFS	LCV	ITIC	NTU	COC	ACU	CFG	FRC
2008	85	57	100	91	100	3	63	0	3	0
2007	85	—	100	73	—	5	45	8	6	—

National Journal Ratings

	2007 LIB	—	2007 CONS		2008 LIB	—	2008 CONS
Economic	65%	—	34%		76%	—	23%
Social	66%	—	30%		56%	—	43%
Foreign	72%	—	27%		65%	—	6%
Composite	69%	—	31%		71%	—	29%

Key Votes of the 110th Congress

1. Raise CAFE standards	Y	5. Make English official language	N	9. Withdraw troops 3/08	Y
2. Expand SCHIP	Y	6. Path to citizenship	N	10. Iran guard is terrorist group	Y
3. Cap greenhouse gases	Y	7. Fetus is unborn child	N	11. Increase missile defense $	N
4. Bail out financial markets	Y	8. Prosecute hate crimes	Y	12. Overhaul FISA	Y

Election Results

2008 general	Jay Rockefeller (D)	447,560	(64%)	($4,820,379)
	Jay Wolfe (R)	254,629	(36%)	($123,720)
2008 primary	Jay Rockefeller (D)	271,425	(77%)	
	Sheirl Fletcher (D)	50,173	(14%)	
	Billy Hendricks (D)	29,707	(8%)	

Prior Winning Percentages: 2002 (63%); 1996 (77%); 1990 (68%); 1984 (52%)

Jay Rockefeller is a Democrat and junior senator from West Virginia. After the 2008 election, Rockefeller gave up the chairmanship of the Senate Intelligence Committee to take the gavel of the Commerce, Science and Transportation Committee.

Rockefeller's full name, John D. Rockefeller IV, has a familiar ring to those who remember his great-grandfather as the oil billionaire who was America's richest man, and his grandfather as the heir who had more than enough money to build New York's Rockefeller Center, restore Colonial Williamsburg, and found the Museum of Modern Art during the Depression of the 1930s. Jay Rockefeller's father and uncles were men of impressive achievement in different fields. Father John D. Rockefeller III was the head of the family's philanthropic efforts and founder of the Asia Society. Uncle David Rockefeller was the head of Chase Manhattan Bank. Two uncles became governors—Nelson, governor of New York for 15 years and a man of great building projects and fitful presidential ambitions; and Winthrop, who moved to impoverished and out-of-the-way Arkansas and served four years as a reform governor when the state needed it most. At various points in his life, Jay Rockefeller has followed the example of each, with emphases and achievements of his own.

John D. Rockefeller IV grew up in New York, graduated from Harvard, and lived and studied in Japan for three years (evidence of his father's Asiaphilia). He worked for a year in Washington D.C. running the early Peace Corps program in the Philippines. Then, like so many of the elite of those years, he turned his attention from abroad to home, and in 1964 went to the impoverished hill country of West Virginia to work as a VISTA volunteer in Emmons on the Big Coal River. "Although I went to Emmons to help that community," he has reminisced. "They helped me much more. My experience in Emmons set the course for the rest of my life." He moved on, more quickly than his uncles Nelson and Winthrop, to electoral politics. He was elected to the state House of Delegates from Kanawha County in 1966 and as West Virginia secretary of state in 1968. Rockefeller then had the chastening experience of losing a 1972 race for governor to Republican Arch Moore. He served three years as president of West Virginia Wesleyan College in Buckhannon, and became more practical, dropping his opposition to strip mining. He was not shy about spending his own millions—his net worth was estimated at $200 million in 2006—and was elected governor in 1976 and re-elected in 1980. In 1984, he ran for the U.S. Senate and beat Republican businessman John Raese by just 52%-48% after spending $12 million.

In his first years in the Senate, Rockefeller deferred to fellow West Virginia Democrat Robert Byrd and compiled a liberal voting record, somewhat inclined toward free trade because of his experience in East Asia. He began to concentrate on health care. With a seat on the Finance Committee, he got a place on the Pepper Commission on long-term health care. As chairman, he got majorities on the commission to back long-term care for all Americans regardless of age and universal medical insurance coverage. But getting others to agree was harder. He was motivated in part by anger at his mother's treatment during a long terminal illness—an experience that would be much worse for people of ordinary incomes, he thought—and he worked to increase the number of general practitioners, especially in states like West Virginia and Arkansas. As he was working on health issues, Rockefeller in 1991 gave serious consideration to running for president. He was 54, an age at which his uncle, Nelson, was about to make his second attempt at running, and when he had developed expertise on an issue that seemed likely to be a major domestic priority.

After he decided against running, he warmly endorsed Democrat Bill Clinton and applauded his emphasis on health care. When the Clinton health care bill crashed and burned in September 1994, Rockefeller still wanted system-wide health care reform but recognized that it could not pass, so he worked for incremental changes. He opposed the Republicans' Medicare prescription drug bill in 2003 and later called it a "national disaster." One of his biggest legislative achievements was a 1992 law, passed over furious opposition from Western coal states, that forced union and non-union coal companies and "reachback" companies that had gone out of the coal business to pay for the exploding cost of the United Mine Workers' health care trust funds; he has worked ever since to continue funding of this program for retired miners and their widows. In 2007, as chairman of the Senate Finance Committee's subcommittee on health, he was at the fore of Democratic efforts to expand the State Children's Health Insurance Program.

Steel has been a preoccupation of Rockefeller for a long time. He helped Weirton Steel become employee-owned in 1984. In the late 1990s, he called for aid to steel makers in the face of what he regarded as a flood of subsidized steel imports, arguing that workers and companies that have "played by the book" should get government help to allow them to continue in their jobs and their homes. In 2002, he called for 40% tariffs for four years on steel imports. The Bush administration in 2002 imposed a 24% tariff in the second year and 18% in the third. Rockefeller complained loudly when the administration made exceptions and then dropped the quotas.

In 2003, Rockefeller became vice chairman of the Intelligence Committee. That July, he argued that National Security Adviser Condoleezza Rice, and not just Central Intelligence Agency Director George Tenet, should be blamed for the "16 words" about British intelligence in Africa in President George W. Bush's 2003 State of the Union address. But at the same time, he was criticized by some Democrats for not being a partisan "team player" and for not countering Republican Chairman Pat Roberts' opposition to a far-ranging investigation of intelligence before the September 11 attacks and of intelligence on Iraq. In June 2003, when Democratic Sen. John Kerry of Massachusetts said Bush had "lied" about intelligence, Rockefeller said, "The senator is running for president. And I think that Pat Roberts and I make a distinction between people who are running for president and therefore need to capture attention and what we on the Intelligence Committee have to do." Roberts decided to hold hearings and in October 2003, he agreed with Rockefeller to include witnesses from the State and Defense departments as well as from the CIA. But the bipartisan working relationship between the two was not to last.

On November 4, a memo by Democratic committee staffers became public; it recommended that Democrats "pull the majority along" in extracting damaging disclosures from officials and then "pull the trigger" in 2004 to use the material to discredit Bush. Rockefeller said he never passed the memo along but declined to apologize for it, and approached Roberts with a letter promising not to let partisan motives affect the hearings. Roberts was not mollified. On November 12, he cancelled the committee's weekly assessment meeting and the next day wrote in *The Washington Post*, "The Democrats planned to undermine the integrity of the committee by conducting a partisan attack, which threatens to destroy the credibility of an institution that has served the U.S. Senate and the nation well for nearly 30 years. I oppose them, and I make no apologies." Rockefeller responded, "One has to confront the very real possibility that this whole war was predetermined, so that the intelligence had to fit with the policymaking plans. So the Republicans just pounce on this little, pathetic stolen memo as the perfect opportunity to cover up whether there was White House manipulation of intelligence or whether there was [a] predetermined plan for war." In March 2004, Rockefeller, who had voted for the Iraq war resolution, said, "If I had known then what I know now, I would have voted against it. . . . The decision got made before there was a whole bunch of intelligence. I think the intelligence was shaped. And I think the interpretation of the intelligence was shaped."

In December 2005, after *The New York Times* revealed National Security Agency surveillance of communications between terrorist suspects abroad and persons in the United States, and that Rockefeller had been informed of the program several years before, Rockefeller charged that administration officials were misstating the facts and that they never offered him the opportunity to approve or disapprove of the program. In February 2006, he suggested that the *Times'* story resulted from leaks by administration officials, though they had tried to persuade the *Times* not to publish the story. Rockefeller protested vigorously that month when Chairman Roberts adjourned a committee meeting after Democrats demanded an inquiry into the NSA surveillance program.

After Democrats won majority control of the Senate, Rockefeller in 2007 ascended to the chairmanship of Intelligence. Roberts rotated off the committee and the new vice chairman was Republican Christopher (Kit) Bond of Missouri. He said that he and Bond would pursue a more bipartisan course, and that staffers would be shared without a partisan divide. He proposed an agency-by-agency review of the law centralizing control in the Director of National Intelligence. Closed hearings in January 2007 focused on recommendations made by the Iraq Study Group. Rockefeller agreed to accept Bond's suggestions that it investigate shortcomings in human intelligence and radical Islamist ideology. He called for a separate warrant on every wiretap of a person in the United States and questioned whether the CIA should be running a secret prison network. In October 2007, he produced a compromise on the issue of immunity for telecommunications companies who cooperated in the government's secret surveillance of people in the United States. It provided that the companies be able to assert as a defense that they were told by the administration that the surveillance was legal.

On other issues, Rockefeller co-sponsored, with Byrd and Democratic Rep. Nick Rahall of West Virginia, a constitutional amendment to allow voluntary prayer in schools. He and Republican Mike DeWine of Ohio passed a bill in 2006 requiring labels on new cars showing their crash-worthiness. He and Mississippi Republican Trent Lott backed a $25 surcharge on airline tickets and business aircraft flights to finance an updated air traffic control system in 2007. He also co-sponsored a bill to require cell phone companies to disclose charges more clearly and to eliminate or reduce early termination fees.

Rockefeller has been in strong shape politically—strong enough that since 1984 he has not self-financed any of his campaigns and has still been re-elected by handsome margins. In 2008, he ran for a fifth term. That year, he got some negative attention with comments about presidential candidate John McCain's activities in the Vietnam War. He charged that McCain had sent laser-guided missiles down on Vietnam from 35,000 feet, and asserted: "He was long gone when they hit. What happened when they get to the ground? He doesn't know. That's unkind, because that's fighting for your nation and that's honorable. But you have to care about the lives of people. McCain never got into those issues." But McCain piloted fighters, not bombers, and Rockefeller quickly admitted, "I made an inaccurate and wrong analogy, and I have extended my sincere apology to him." None of this caused Rockefeller any problems in November. He spent $5.9 million to his Republican opponent's $123,000 and won 64%-36%, carrying 52 of 55 counties.

FIRST DISTRICT

Alan Mollohan (D)

Elected 1982, 14th term; b. May 14, 1943, Fairmont; home, Fairmont; Col. of William & Mary, A.B. 1966, WVU., J.D. 1970; Baptist; married (Barbara); 5 children.

Military Career: Army, 1970, Army Reserves, 1970–83.

Professional Career: Practicing atty., 1970–82.

DC Office: 2302 RHOB, 20515, 202-225-4172; Fax: 202-225-7564; Web site: www.house.gov/mollohan.

State Offices: Clarksburg, 304-623-4422; Morgantown, 304-292-3019; Parkersburg, 304-428-0493; Wheeling, 304-232-5390.

Committees: *Appropriations* (4th of 37 D): Commerce, Justice, Science & Related Agencies (Chmn); Homeland Security; Interior, Environment & Related Agencies.

Group Ratings

	ADA	ACLU	AFS	LCV	ITIC	NTU	COC	ACU	CFG	FRC
2008	85	100	100	92	57	6	59	4	0	52
2007	95	—	100	55	—	6	55	17	1	—

National Journal Ratings

	2007 LIB	—	2007 CONS		2008 LIB	—	2008 CONS
Economic	51%	—	48%		71%	—	25%
Social	59%	—	41%		75%	—	18%
Foreign	59%	—	40%		59%	—	37%
Composite	57%	—	43%		71%	—	29%

Key Votes of the 110th Congress

1. Increase minimum wage	Y	5. Share immigration data	N	9. Withdraw troops 8/08	Y
2. Expand SCHIP	Y	6. Foreign aid abortion ban	Y	10. No operations in Iran	Y
3. Raise CAFE standards	Y	7. Ban gay bias in workplace	Y	11. Free trade with Peru	N
4. Bail out financial markets	Y	8. Repeal D.C. gun law	Y	12. Overhaul FISA	N

Election Results

2008 general	Alan Mollohan (D)..	unopposed
2008 primary	Alan Mollohan (D)..	unopposed

Prior Winning Percentages: 2006 (64%); 2004 (68%); 2002 (100%); 2000 (88%); 1998 (85%); 1996 (100%); 1994 (70%); 1992 (100%); 1990 (67%); 1988 (75%); 1986 (100%); 1984 (54%); 1982 (53%)

Population		Race/Ethnicity		Work	
Pop. 2007:	595,910	White:	95.0%	Private:	76.8%
Change since 2000:	Down 1.1%	Black:	1.9%	Government:	17.5%
Urban:	53.7%	Hispanic:	0.9%	Self-employed:	5.3%
Rural:	46.3%	Asian:	0.8%	Blue collar:	26.8%
Area size:	6,344 sq. mi.	Native Am.:	0.1%	White collar:	54.1%
		Hawaiian:	0.1%	Khaki collar:	0.1%
Age		Two+ races:	1.1%	Other:	19.0%
Median age:	40.2 yrs.			Median income:	$35,743
More than 65 yrs:	15.8%	*Ancestry*		Median home value:	$87,900
Less than 18 yrs:	20.5%	German:	19.8%	Poverty:	18.0%
		Irish:	13.3%		
Education		USA:	10.5%	**Military Veterans**	
H.S. grad:	84.5%			% of Pop:	12.4%
College grad:	18.3%				
Grad degree:	7.6%				

The northern part of West Virginia is in many ways an extension of the Pittsburgh metropolitan area. People here are Steelers and Pirates fans, they drink Iron City and Rolling Rock beer, they watch Pittsburgh television, and they live in the crevasses between hills cut by the Monongahela and Ohio Rivers, on terrain that seems to forbid industrial and urban development. Yet this has been one of America's prime industrial areas. Northern West Virginia is part of the same coal-and-steel economy

2008 Presidential Vote		
McCain (R)	140,421	(57%)
Obama (D)	102,826	(42%)

2004 Presidential Vote		
Bush (R)	150,052	(58%)
Kerry (D)	107,904	(42%)

Cook Partisan Voting Index: R+9

that made Pittsburgh one of the nation's largest cities and filled the narrow bottomlands along the rivers with steel and glass factories, foundries and coal yards. These industries have been declining, and they have become far less labor-intensive. Since 1980, the 12,000 mining jobs in this part of the state have dropped by more than two-thirds, with comparable fall-offs in manufacturing. The Weirton tin and steel mill, which employed 14,000 in the mid-1970s and was the subject of an employee buyout at one point, was down to fewer than 1,000 workers in 2008. Service jobs have replaced some of these losses. West Virginia's largest employer now is Wal-Mart, and the government has brought in thousands more jobs, compliments of the powerful Senate appropriator Robert Byrd, the West Virginia Democrat. One of the largest employers in Harrison County is the U.S. Department of Justice.

The 1st Congressional District of West Virginia includes the northern third of the state and borders Maryland, Ohio and Pennsylvania. On the panhandle along the Ohio River is Victorian Wheeling, once one of the richest cities in the country with its steel and glass companies. There is Weirton, named for Ernest T. Weir, the anti-union Pittsburgh industrialist who transformed it from a farming community to a steel town in the early 1900s. South of Pittsburgh on the Monongahela River are Morgantown, site of West Virginia University and white-water rafting, as well as Fairmont and Clarksburg. To the west, the district includes three lonely mountain counties—Doddridge, Ritchie and Tyler—that were never heavily industrialized and have remained firmly Republican since the Civil War. Doddridge was the only one of West Virginia's 55 counties to vote against Byrd for re-election in 2006. West of these, on the Ohio River, is the former oil-refining and shipping center of Parkersburg, which has become a plastics and manufacturing hub. From 2000 to 2007, the district lost 1% of its population; Morgantown gained 7%, while Wheeling and Parkersburg dropped 9% and 10%, respectively. For most of the 20th century, much of this territory was solidly Democratic. But dissatisfaction with the Clinton-Gore policies on coal mining and the environment helped Republican George W. Bush carry the district twice. And in 2008, GOP nominee John McCain won all of the 20 counties except for the two based in Morgantown and Fairmont. He carried the district 57%-42%.

The congressman from the 1st District is Alan Mollohan, a Democrat first elected in 1982. His father, Robert Mollohan, was elected to Congress in 1952 and 1954, ran for governor and lost in 1956, and then won back the House seat a dozen years later when his Republican successor, Arch Moore, was elected governor. Alan Mollohan was born in Fairmont while his father served as superintendent of the State Industrial School for Boys. He grew up in West Virginia and Washington, D.C., and graduated from William and Mary and West Virginia University's law school. He was working in Washington as a lawyer for Consolidated Coal, among other clients, when his father retired in 1982. He returned home and promptly won the seat. His one major challenge came in the 1992 primary, when he was redistricted into a district with another incumbent, Democrat Harley Staggers Jr., also the son of a congressman and an ally of the National Rifle Association. Mollohan, who had represented more of the new district than Staggers, won 62%-38%.

Mollohan's voting record has become increasingly centrist, and he has concentrated on bringing projects to the district while keeping a low profile on Capitol Hill. He got a seat on the Appropriations Committee in 1986 and today is chairman of the Commerce, Justice, Science, and Related Agencies Subcommittee. On Appropriations, many members earmark projects for their districts, a practice that became increasingly common—and controversial, as budget hawks in both parties have zeroed in on earmarks as wasteful spending. Mollohan's earmarks in particular have come under scrutiny and caused him increasing discomfort politically.

He long has had a strategy of encouraging the creation of non-profit organizations, many led by former staffers and close friends, through which he has funneled money into northern West Virginia. The watchdog group Citizens Against Government Waste reported that Mollohan brought $480 million to the district between 1995 and 2006, more than half of it going to those five nonprofits: the Institute for Scientific Research, the West Virginia High Technology Consortium Foundation, the Vandalia Heritage Foundation, the MountainMade Foundation and the Canaan Valley Institute. Mollohan argues that these nonprofits have created thousands of jobs in West Virginia, including high-tech jobs for 200 firms along the Interstate 79 corridor from Morgantown to Weston.

But in April 2006, the conservative National Legal and Policy Center charged that Mollohan had failed to disclose all of his assets and issued a 500-page report that listed some 250 alleged misrepresentations and omissions. As amplified in a *Wall Street Journal* article, Mollohan had made real estate investments with nonprofit officials who were former staffers or contributors that boosted his assets from $565,000 in 2000 to at least $6 million in 2004. The newspaper also reported that Mollohan bought a farm on the Cheat River in Tucker County with the head of a defense contracting firm that had obtained a contract funded by a Mollohan earmark. Mollohan said the two were old friends. In June 2006, Mollohan filed a revised personal disclosure statement, correcting 19 "unintentional" errors. Federal prosecutors began investigating his finances, the *Journal* reported. But Mollohan said that he had not been questioned and that he had profited from rapidly rising real estate properties in Washington and in North Carolina. In April 2006, under pressure from Minority Leader Nancy Pelosi, he resigned as ranking minority member on the Committee on Standards of Official Conduct, which enforces House ethics rules.

Mollohan had served on the panel during some of its most difficult days in the Republican majority. In 2004, the bipartisan committee unanimously voted to admonish—the weakest rebuke possible—House Majority Leader Tom DeLay for offenses related to his close ties to lobbyists who wanted favors from him. Although Mollohan kept his customary low profile, he faced a no-win situation. Republicans complained he was sharing sensitive information with Democratic leaders, and Democrats were unhappy that DeLay had not been more harshly punished. Along with Republican Chairman Joel Hefley of Colorado, Mollohan defended the committee's work and criticized "erroneous" press reports. Then, GOP Speaker Dennis Hastert, angry that DeLay had been admonished at all, dumped Hefley as chairman and replaced him with a presumably more compliant Republican chairman, Doc Hastings of Washington state. Republican leaders also tried to change the ethics rules in the aftermath of the DeLay case to make it harder to open an investigation against a member. Mollohan resisted, and the committee largely ceased to function until the GOP leaders backed off and reverted to the old, more stringent rules.

On national issues, Mollohan voted against the war in Iraq and strongly opposed the initial Bush tax cuts. He supported Bush's steel import restrictions in 2002 as a vital step against unfair competition from foreign steelmakers, but he protested when the administration subsequently granted a series of waivers in response to pressure from domestic steel users complaining about price increases. He has fought successfully to continue loan guarantees for steel companies, which has helped to keep Weirton Steel alive despite its financial troubles. In 2007, he opposed a program backed by the Bush administration to allow trucks from Mexican companies to operate in the United States.

Mollohan generally has had easy re-election contests. In 2004, against his first Republican opponent since 1994, he won 68% of the vote. In 2006, after the *Wall Street Journal* story broke and Mollohan resigned from the ethics committee, national Republicans made a major effort on behalf of the Republican candidate, Wheeling Delegate Chris Wakim. But Wakim was hurt by charges that he had overstated his military record, claiming to be a disabled Gulf War veteran when he served stateside. Mollohan won 64%-36%, carrying all but Grant County and Doddridge County. Despite attacks from national Republicans in 2007 focused on his earmarks and personal finances, Mollohan was unopposed in 2008.

SECOND DISTRICT

Shelley Moore Capito (R)

Elected 2000, 5th term; b. Nov. 26, 1953, Glen Dale; home, Charleston; Duke U., B.S. 1975, U. of VA, M.Ed. 1976; Presbyterian; married (Charles); 3 children.

Elected Office: WV House of Del., 1996–2000.

Professional Career: Career counselor, WV State Col., 1976–78; Dir., Educ. Info. Center, WV Board of Regents, 1978–81.

DC Office: 2443 RHOB, 20515, 202-225-2711; Fax: 202-225-7856; Web site: capito.house.gov.

State Offices: Charleston, 304-925-5964; Martinsburg, 304-264-8810.

Committees: *Financial Services* (11th of 29 R): Capital Markets, Insurance & Government Sponsored Enterprises; Financial Institutions & Consumer Credit; Housing & Community Opportunity (RMM). *Transportation & Infrastructure* (16th of 30 R): Aviation; Economic Development, Public Buildings & Emergency Management; Highways & Transit.

Group Ratings

	ADA	ACLU	AFS	LCV	ITIC	NTU	COC	ACU	CFG	FRC
2008	60	18	57	38	86	41	78	48	36	70
2007	35	—	36	20	—	40	90	56	42	—

National Journal Ratings

	2007 LIB	—	2007 CONS		2008 LIB	—	2008 CONS
Economic	42%	—	57%		43%	—	57%
Social	38%	—	62%		31%	—	62%
Foreign	32%	—	64%		40%	—	60%
Composite	38%	—	62%		39%	—	61%

Key Votes of the 110th Congress

1. Increase minimum wage	Y	5. Share immigration data	Y	9. Withdraw troops 8/08	N
2. Expand SCHIP	Y	6. Foreign aid abortion ban	Y	10. No operations in Iran	N
3. Raise CAFE standards	N	7. Ban gay bias in workplace	N	11. Free trade with Peru	Y
4. Bail out financial markets	N	8. Repeal D.C. gun law	Y	12. Overhaul FISA	Y

Election Results

2008 general	Shelley Moore Capito (R)	147,334	(57%)	($2,283,316)
	Anne Barth (D)	110,819	(43%)	($1,182,701)
2008 primary	Shelley Moore Capito (R)	unopposed		

Prior Winning Percentages: 2006 (57%); 2004 (57%); 2002 (60%); 2000 (48%)

Population		Race/Ethnicity		Work	
Pop. 2007:	627,371	White:	92.5%	Private:	73.9%
Change since 2000:	Up 4.2%	Black:	4.0%	Government:	19.5%
Urban:	46.2%	Hispanic:	1.4%	Self-employed:	6.3%
Rural:	53.8%	Asian:	0.6%	Blue collar:	28.1%
Area size:	8,512 sq. mi.	Native Am.:	0.1%	White collar:	55.5%
		Hawaiian:	0.0%	Khaki collar:	0.2%
Age		Two+ races:	1.4%	Other:	16.2%
Median age:	39.9 yrs.			Median income:	$40,825
More than 65 yrs:	14.6%	*Ancestry*		Median home value:	$110,500
Less than 18 yrs:	22.7%	German:	16.8%	Poverty:	14.6%
		USA:	12.7%		
Education		English:	10.5%	**Military Veterans**	
H.S. grad:	82.5%			% of Pop:	12.7%
College grad:	18.7%				
Grad degree:	7.1%				

Not all of West Virginia has been coal country, and not all of its hills are scarred with strip mining wounds or piled with tailings. It's true that for miles you can see gentle hills and rugged mountains, stands of green trees and vistas stretching to far horizons. Yet over another hill you may find, amid scenery primeval and rural, sudden evidence of industrialization: a pulp mill or charcoal factory in a clearing scraped out of the forest; a small factory town, built close to a river in a cleft bordered with

2008 Presidential Vote
McCain (R)............................142,112   (55%)
Obama (D) 113,853   (44%)

2004 Presidential Vote
Bush (R).................................151,019   (57%)
Kerry (D)................................112,418   (42%)

Cook Partisan Voting Index: R + 8

hills, its houses built in the same 1910s style as in the factory suburbs of Pittsburgh; the entrance to an underground coal mine or a mountaintop blasted open to allow surface mining. Large parts of this naturally beautiful state look as verdant and unchanged as they must have when George Washington was speculating in land here or when John Brown was launching his assault on the federal arsenal at Harper's Ferry in 1859.

The 2nd Congressional District of West Virginia is a central slice of the state, a belt of land from Berkeley Springs and Harper's Ferry in the Washington exurbs all the way west to the Ohio River town of Point Pleasant, where the Kanawha River flows into the Ohio. The district includes the few fast-growing parts of West Virginia: the eastern panhandle counties, which are part of the Washington, D.C., metro area, and chemical-producing Putnam County, where Toyota built an engine plant. The major urban center is Charleston, where on the banks of the Kanawha rises West Virginia's Capitol, built in 1932 and designed by Cass Gilbert with a dome higher than the U.S. Capitol and a chandelier with 10,000 pieces of cut glass. Charleston, with its two partisan newspapers, the Democratic *The Charleston Gazette* and the Republican *Charleston Daily Mail*, is the center of the state's political culture. It also is a major industrial center, with coal in the hills all around and, downriver from the Capitol, huge petrochemical plants that convert coal tar into everyday products.

In the 1940s, the area produced all the nation's Lucite, polyethylenes and nylon, as well as much of its artificial rubber and antifreeze. Today, the state boasts it is home to more polymer producers than any other place on the planet; the chemical industry makes products used in the manufacturing of cosmetics, detergents, shampoo, rubber, paints and coatings, fire retardants and agricultural products. Charleston is also West Virginia's professional center, with a few downtown skyscrapers and some affluent residential districts. But like much of the state, Kanawha County has continued to lose population, about 9,000 people since the 2000 census. County school enrollment has dropped nearly in half since the 1950s. Politically, this is an ancestrally Democratic district now trending Republican. Berkeley County, which has grown 34% in population since 2000 to become the second-largest county in the state, votes like a Republican exurb. GOP presidential nominee John McCain in 2008 won the district 55%-44%.

The congresswoman from the 2nd District is Shelley Moore Capito, a Republican first elected in 2000. She grew up in northern West Virginia and in the Washington, D.C., area, when her father, Arch Moore, served in the House from 1957 to 1969. He was elected governor in 1968 and 1972, and then again in 1984. He later was convicted and served three years in jail for fraud and extortion. Shelley Moore Capito graduated from Duke University and the University of Virginia, and is the first Cherry Blossom Princess elected to Congress. She worked for two years as a career counselor at West Virginia State College, and then was director of the state's Educational Information Center from 1978 to 1981. She served two terms in the West Virginia House of Delegates. Her opportunity to follow in her father's footsteps came when Democratic Rep. Bob Wise ran for governor in 2000. She benefited from a divisive Democratic primary that was won by Jim Humphreys, a former state senator and a lawyer who made a fortune in asbestos litigation and spent $3 million of his own money to win the Democratic nomination. Capito, who supported abortion rights, started as the underdog but Humphreys, who spent another $6 million in the general election, proved to be a poor candidate. One of the few beneficiaries of Republican presidential candidate George W. Bush's coattails that year, she won 48%-46%, with big margins in the eastern pan-handle counties.

In the House, Capito has received special attention from Republican leaders because of her precarious district. She was one of the few House Republicans to get a free pass to vote against the president's position on free trade bills. After Democrats took control of Congress in 2007, Capito voted for five of the Democratic "Six for '06" agenda items, voting only against requiring the government to negotiate with drug companies under the Medicare prescription drug program. As the ranking Republican on the Housing and Community Opportunity Subcommittee at Financial Services, she worked in recent years with Democrats on bipartisan proposals to reduce home foreclosures. But Capito is a firm Bush ally on the Iraq war.

After a deadly accident at the Sago mine in 2006, Capito joined the West Virginia delegation in supporting legislation to improve mine safety by requiring that coal miners be given communications and tracking equipment and two-hour reserves of oxygen. After the Senate passed the bill, she persuaded House Republican leaders to schedule it for the floor, and Bush signed the bill into law in 2006. She joined the Select Committee on Energy Independence and Global Warming in 2009 to, as she put it, "bring a coal-state perspective." She was a leading supporter of mandates to produce coal-to-liquids fuel. Her work on coal issues has earned her admirers in strange quarters. The United Mine Workers endorsed Capito in her 2004 re-election bid after praising her for blocking a Labor Department bid to weaken regulations on coal dust, and for legislation to protect medical benefits for retired miners, including 15,000 in West Virginia.

At home, Capito has settled comfortably into her seat. In 2002, Democrats gave her a big break by again nominating Humphreys, who won another expensive primary and then ran an even more ineffective campaign than the one two years earlier. Capito won 60%-40%. In 2004, her Democratic opponent was former television anchorman Erik Wells, but national Democrats abandoned interest in the district. In 2006, she had a well-funded opponent in attorney Mike Callaghan, a former state Democratic Party chairman. In a year when Bush was a drag for many Republicans, Capito was unafraid to align herself with Bush on issues like energy policy. Capito outspent her opponent by nearly 4-to-1 and won 57%-43%. In 2008, longtime Byrd aide Anne Barth was her Democratic challenger and raised $1.2 million, including support from the United Mine Workers, EMILY's List and the National Organization for Women. She criticized Capito for her support of "big oil," while Capito cited Barth's backing from "anti-coal" politicians in Washington. Capito won, again by 57%-43%.

THIRD DISTRICT

Nick Rahall (D)

Elected 1976, 17th term; b. May 20, 1949, Beckley; home, Beckley; Duke U., B.A. 1971; Presbyterian; married (Melinda); 3 children.

Professional Career: Civil Air Patrol, 1977–88; Staff asst., U.S. Sen. Robert Byrd, 1971–74; Bd. of Dir., Rahall Communications Corp. 1974–76; Pres., Mountaineer Tour & Travel Agency, 1974–76; Pres., WV Broadcasting Corp. 1980–2001.

DC Office: 2307 RHOB, 20515, 202-225-3452; Fax: 202-225-9061; Web site: www.rahall.house.gov.

State Offices: Beckley, 304-252-5000; Bluefield, 304-325-6222; Huntington, 304-522-6425; Logan, 304-752-4934.

Committees: *Natural Resources* (Chmn of 29 D). *Transportation & Infrastructure* (2nd of 44 D): Aviation; Highways & Transit; Railroads, Pipelines & Hazardous Materials.

Group Ratings

	ADA	ACLU	AFS	LCV	ITIC	NTU	COC	ACU	CFG	FRC
2008	85	91	100	85	43	11	67	8	9	70
2007	85	—	100	75	—	7	60	16	9	—

National Journal Ratings

	2007 LIB	—	2007 CONS		2008 LIB	—	2008 CONS
Economic	59%	—	41%		56%	—	43%
Social	56%	—	44%		54%	—	42%
Foreign	68%	—	31%		85%	—	8%
Composite	61%	—	39%		67%	—	33%

Key Votes of the 110th Congress

1. Increase minimum wage	Y	5. Share immigration data	N	9. Withdraw troops 8/08	Y
2. Expand SCHIP	Y	6. Foreign aid abortion ban	Y	10. No operations in Iran	Y
3. Raise CAFE standards	Y	7. Ban gay bias in workplace	N	11. Free trade with Peru	N
4. Bail out financial markets	Y	8. Repeal D.C. gun law	Y	12. Overhaul FISA	Y

Election Results

2008 general	Nick Rahall (D)	133,522	(67%)	($592,264)
	Marty Gearheart (R)	66,005	(33%)	
2008 primary	Nick Rahall (D)	unopposed		

Prior Winning Percentages: 2006 (69%); 2004 (65%); 2002 (70%); 2000 (91%); 1998 (87%); 1996 (100%); 1994 (64%); 1992 (66%); 1990 (52%); 1988 (61%); 1986 (71%); 1984 (67%); 1982 (81%); 1980 (77%); 1978 (100%); 1976 (46%)

Population		Race/Ethnicity		Work	
Pop. 2007:	585,506	White:	93.7%	Private:	77.6%
Change since 2000:	Down 3.0%	Black:	4.1%	Government:	17.2%
Urban:	38.4%	Hispanic:	0.7%	Self-employed:	4.9%
Rural:	61.6%	Asian:	0.5%	Blue collar:	27.9%
Area size:	9,375 sq. mi.	Native Am.:	0.2%	White collar:	52.7%
		Hawaiian:	0.0%	Khaki collar:	0.1%
Age		Two+ races:	0.8%	Other:	19.3%
Median age:	40.9 yrs.			Median income:	$31,734
More than 65 yrs:	15.8%	*Ancestry*		Median home value:	$75,500
Less than 18 yrs:	21.1%	USA:	13.9%	Poverty:	20.6%
		Irish:	12.5%		
Education		German:	11.6%	**Military Veterans**	
H.S. grad:	76.0%			% of Pop:	11.6%
College grad:	13.5%				
Grad degree:	5.1%				

Early in the 20th century, the coal fields of southern West Virginia were one of America's boom areas. Into rural farmland and hollows, inhabited by the same families that settled these mountains 100 years before, came coal company lawyers with mineral rights' leases to sign, coal company engineers to design and sink the mineshafts, and men from other mountain counties, as well as Europe, to work the mines. Company houses were built, company stores were stocked with goods as the

2008 Presidential Vote

McCain (R)	114,933	(56%)
Obama (D)	87,178	(42%)

2004 Presidential Vote

Bush (R)	122,707	(53%)
Kerry (D)	106,219	(46%)

Cook Partisan Voting Index: R+6

company dictated, and company paymasters kept close tabs on the finances of every employee. These conditions bred dull discontent, which was ignited into the fire of industrial unionism by the tongue of John L. Lewis, president of the United Mine Workers, who organized most of the mines in the 1930s. Lewis was not only a militant unionist, but also an isolationist, and during and after World War II, he called out his coal miners on strikes, to the fury of Democratic Presidents Franklin Roosevelt and Harry Truman. The national war effort and postwar economic recovery were threatened by these labor stoppages involving some 300,000 workers, centered in back corners of the country like southern West Virginia.

All that is history now. Coal is no longer central to the U.S. economy and there are only a few thousand coal miners left in southern West Virginia, and many are not UMW members anymore. Most of the old underground mines have been abandoned, leaving behind mineshafts and piles of tailings—and lives that were snuffed out by cave-ins or simple carelessness in America's deadliest industry. Manufacturing jobs in the area, which had been predominantly in the chemical industry, also have been reduced by more than half since 1980. The region has still not hit bottom: Of seven counties in the nation with more than 20,000 residents that suffered a 10% population loss or greater in the 1990s, four of them—Logan, McDowell, Mingo and Wyoming—were in southern West Virginia. All four have continued to decline in population since 2000. In September 2008, a faint hope of recovery through "clean coal" technology was snuffed out when the U.S. Energy Department cancelled the Bush administration's proposed $215 million clean-coal project in Greenbrier County after deciding it was unlikely to succeed.

The 3rd Congressional District of West Virginia includes most of the mountainous coal country in the southern part of the state that for years was heavily Democratic. But the coal mining counties now make up less than half of the district. About a quarter of the population is in and around the industrial city of Huntington on the Ohio River, which includes Marshall University. Another quarter is to the east, in Beckley and the farming uplands. (Also located there is the Greenbrier Hotel resort, where the government built a massive secret fallout shelter, code-named "Project Greek Island," to house the entire U.S.

Congress in the event of nuclear war). The population of the 3rd District in 2007 was 585,000, down significantly over the last half-century. The district has shifted to Republicans in the past decade. In 2000, Democratic presidential nominee Al Gore won the district 51%-47%. In 2008, Republican John McCain won it 56%-42%.

The congressman from the 3rd District is Nick Rahall, a Democrat first elected in 1976. He was 27 years old at the time and the youngest member of the 95th Congress. Today he is the chairman of the House Natural Resources Committee. He comes from the thin economic upper crust of the coal country. His family owned radio and television stations in Beckley and in St. Petersburg, Fla. He graduated from Duke University, worked on Democratic Sen. Robert Byrd's staff and then in the family's businesses. In 1976, when Democratic Rep. Ken Hechler ran for governor, Rahall ran for the House and won a five-candidate Democratic primary with 37% of the vote. Hechler, after losing the primary to Jay Rockefeller, returned to the district and ran as a write-in. Rahall spent $236,000 of his own money on his campaign—an enormous sum in those days—and beat Hechler 46%-37%. Rahall got seats on the Interior and Public Works committees in his first term, fine assignments for a young member from a rural district with low incomes and poor roads. In addition to being the chairman of the renamed Natural Resources Committee, he is now the No. 2 Democrat on the renamed Transportation and Infrastructure Committee.

Rahall predictably has worked over the years to help the coal industry and coal miners. He was the chief House sponsor of the law requiring union and non-union coal operators to bail out the United Mine Workers health care funds and he has continued to secure federal funds for retired mineworkers. He and Byrd passed an amendment to the Export-Import Bank reauthorization forbidding financing of foreign mining ventures. In 2006, after the Sago mine disaster in Upshur County, he and Rep. Shelley Moore Capito, R-W.Va., co-sponsored legislation requiring companies to have updated mine emergency response plans, wireless two-way communication and electronic tracking systems. It quickly passed both houses and became law. From 1993 to 2001, he was chairman and ranking minority member on the Surface Transportation subcommittee, where he established the Rahall Transportation Institute, a consortium of five colleges at Marshall University and obtained $90 million for the Heartland Corridor, the old Norfolk Southern route through southern West Virginia connected to the Port of Virginia.

Environmental groups were disappointed when Rahall in 2001 became ranking Democrat on the Resources Committee because he had shown little support for their views. But, while he promotes the use of coal, he has by no means been a reliable supporter of measures sought by oil companies. He has opposed oil drilling in the Arctic National Wildlife Refuge and he has favored expanding wilderness areas in the West. In 2004, he received the Wilderness Society's Ansel Adams award for being "forceful, energetic and wise in preventing special interests from exploiting places that Americans hold dear."

In the majority, Rahall's agenda included increasing the royalties that oil and gas companies pay to the federal government for rights to deepwater exploration and overhauling the Mining Law of 1872. His chief focus in the 2007 energy bill was to require hard-rock miners to pay royalties for mining on federal lands. According to Rahall, coal mines and oil and gas producers have been paying royalties for decades, while miners of gold, silver and other hard-rock minerals have gotten away without making payments. Critics said that the proposed 8% royalty would destroy the industry. The House passed the bill 244-166, but Senate Republicans blocked it from being included in the energy bill.

Rahall also had limited success with his proposal to slow oil and gas development on federal lands. In 2008, he worked with House Speaker Nancy Pelosi to mandate that oil companies with leases on 68 million acres of federal land "use it or lose it." But Democrats did not make a serious effort to pass his proposal. In early 2009, he prepared a plan to increase oil and gas royalties on federal lands by 50%, and to reduce lease periods from to 10 to five years.

Rahall's family roots are in Lebanon, and he is often in the small minority of members voicing support for Arab causes and voting against Israel. In 2002, he opposed military action in Iraq, saying, "I feel the Iraqis want to give peace a chance."

Since his first election in 1976, Rahall has dropped below 61% of the vote only once, and he has not been seriously challenged in 20 years.

★ WISCONSIN ★

Wisconsin, tucked off north of the main east-west routes across the country, was at the beginning of the 20th century—and again at the century's end—one of America's premier "laboratories of reform," in Justice Louis Brandeis's phrase, a state originating new public policies, observing whether or not they worked, and serving as an example for other states. Wisconsin's reputation for innovative public policy was established during the Progressive era that began around 1900 and owes its development to an extraordinary governor, Robert La Follette Sr., and the state's German heritage. Wisconsin was settled first by New England Yankees, and then by waves of immigrants from Germany and Scandinavia. The German language is seldom heard now, but the once plainly German beer brands and today's microbrews now seem quintessentially American. In the late 19th and early 20th centuries, Germans were among America's most numerous immigrants, and until the 1890s probably the most distinct. They implanted, on the rolling dairy land of Wisconsin and the orderly streets of Milwaukee, their separate religions, often retaining their language and maintaining old customs, from country weddings to beer drinking—a source of friction in temperance-minded America—to eating bratwurst. Wisconsin still has an orderliness and steadiness that owes something to its Germanic heritage, evident in its excellence in precision manufacturing, its low crime rates, its respect for higher learning and its hold on its people—the state ranks number five in the percentage of people born there who are still living there. In the 2000 census, 30% of Wisconsin residents reported being of German descent.

Politically, the Germans were not monolithic. Their origins were diverse and they were spread too widely across the nation. But where they were concentrated, there was a distinctive politics, basically American, but with echoes of progressive ideas then popular in German-speaking countries in Europe. Nowhere was the politics of German-Americans more apparent than in Wisconsin. This is one of the two states that gave birth to the Republican Party in 1854 (the other is Michigan), and Germans, then arriving in America in vast numbers, heavily favored it. They abhorred slavery and welcomed the free lands Republicans delivered in the Homestead Act, the free education promised by setting up land grant colleges, and the transportation routes constructed by subsidized railroad builders. Then came the Progressive movement of La Follette, elected governor of Wisconsin in 1900. Up to that time a conventional Republican politician, La Follette completely revamped the state government before going to the U.S. Senate in 1906. At a time when Germany was the world's leader in graduate education and the application of science to government, La Follette had professors from the University of Wisconsin help develop the state workmen's compensation system and income tax. The Progressive movement favored rational use of government to improve the lot of ordinary citizens, an idea borrowed partly from German liberals and adopted by the New Dealers a generation later. All these programs were an attempt to bring bureaucratic rationality—Germanic systematization—to the seemingly disordered America of free markets and multiple cultures, gigantic fortunes and vast open spaces.

La Follette became a national figure. He tried to run for president in 1912 as a Progressive, but was shoved aside by Theodore Roosevelt. He did run in 1924 on his Progressive ticket and won 18% of the vote, the best third-candidate showing between 1912 and 1992. He ran strongest in the northern tier of states from Wisconsin west and along the West Coast, the same area of strength of later liberals like George McGovern of South Dakota, Walter Mondale of Minnesota, and Michael Dukakis and John Kerry, both of Massachusetts. After La Follette died in 1925, his sons carried on his tradition, progressive at home and isolationist abroad. Robert La Follette Jr., served 22 years in the Senate; Philip La Follette was elected governor in 1930, 1934 and 1936. Philip created his own Progressive Party in 1934, with ominous overtones: a "Cross in Circle" symbol his critics called a circumcised swastika, huge rally-like parades reminiscent of some in Europe at the time and a call for the governor to propose all legislation. But Philip lost in 1938 and did not run again, and Robert Jr. ran for re-election in 1946 as a Republican but lost the primary to Joseph McCarthy. McCarthy's charges that Communists were influencing American foreign policy fed on the inarticulate convictions of many in Wisconsin and elsewhere that the United States should have been fighting Russia as well as Germany in World War II. McCarthy's national prominence made Wisconsin seem like a Republican state. But he won by narrow margins, and the La Follette Progressive tradition was taken up by liberal Democrats like Sens. William Proxmire and Gaylord Nelson and Gov. Patrick Lucey. Like most liberals of their era, these progressives saw Washington rather than Madison as the main site of their laboratory of reform. Wisconsin, a mostly Republican state in the mostly Democratic years from 1944 to 1964, became a mostly Democratic state in the mostly Republican years from 1968 to 1988.

Wisconsin's economy likewise has been an outgrowth of its immigrant heritage. Its high-skill, precision manufacturing economy jumped into gear in the late 1980s, and helped lead the nation's export boom of the 1990s. Yet much of the political focus remained on the dwindling number of dairy farmers. Wisconsin ranks No. 2 in milk production and No. 1 in cheese production. But thanks to improved productivity, the number of dairy farms has declined from 105,000 in 1960 to 45,000 in 1980 to 21,000 in 2000. For

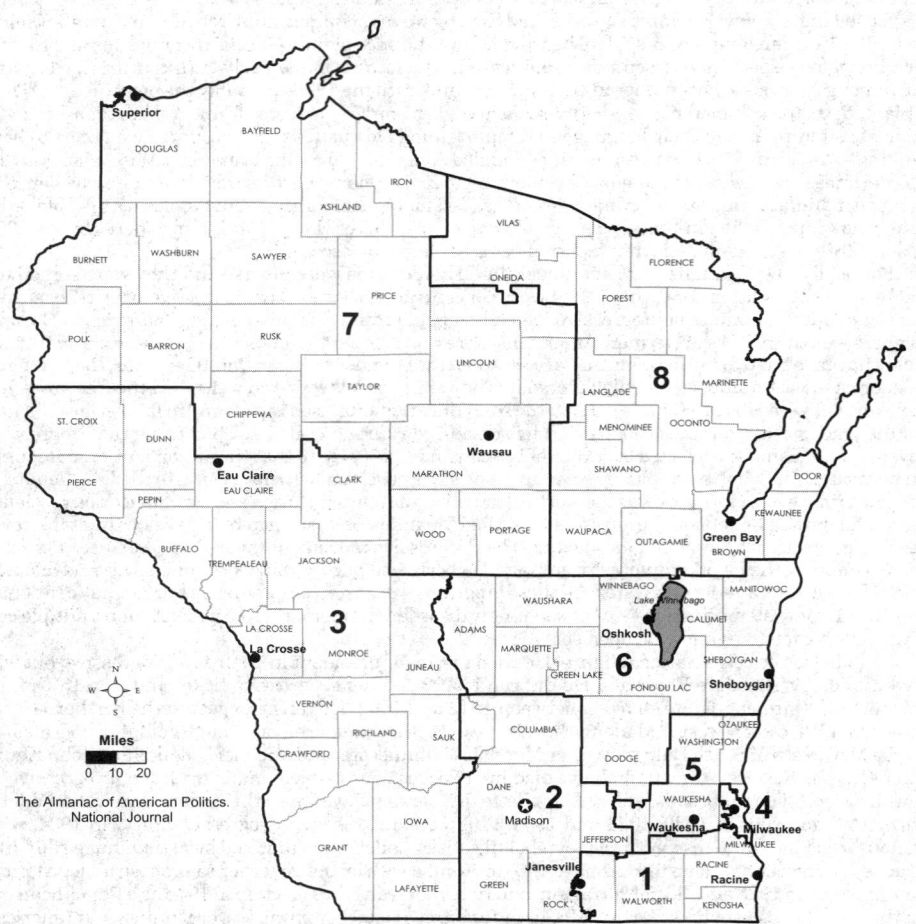

Congressional district boundaries were first effective for 2002.

years, the federal milk price-fixing system was biased against Wisconsin, with prices higher the farther a farm is from Eau Claire. The Milk Income Loss Contract program, adopted in 2002, is biased toward Wisconsin, with a limit on individual payments that works against big dairy farms in California. (California is threatening to overtake Wisconsin as the nation's leading cheese producer. Will Wisconsin continue to put the words "America's dairy land" on its license plates?)

In the 1990s, Wisconsin was a laboratory for reforms of a different nature. The motivating force was another Republican governor, Tommy Thompson, who beat a liberal Democrat in 1986. He cut taxes, sponsored a school choice program, and passed a series of welfare reforms—the nation's most thoroughgoing—that dramatically cut caseloads. Across the nation, other governors and leaders of the Republican Congress watched Wisconsin's experiment with interest. It's a fair question whether the 1996 overhaul of federal welfare policy would have passed without Wisconsin's example to give its backers confidence. Since Thompson left to be become President George W. Bush's Health and Human Services Secretary in 2001, Wisconsin has moved back toward the Democrats. It was a target state in the 2000 and 2004 presidential races, when Democrat Al Gore carried it 47.8%-47.6% and then John Kerry won it 49.7%-49.3%. In 2008, it gave a resounding 56%-42% majority to Illinois Democrat Barack Obama. Starting in 1992, it has elected only Democratic senators, though sometimes by narrow margins, and Democrats have a 5-3 edge in its U.S. House delegation. In 2002, Wisconsin replaced Thompson's successor as governor, Scott McCallum, with Democrat Jim Doyle, who won less than 50% of the vote. Also that year, Republicans won solid majorities in the state Senate and Assembly, but then in 2006, Democrats captured the Senate and in 2008, the Assembly. Economic distress played some role in these results. Wisconsin's steady workers were dismayed by the closing of a General Motors sports utility vehicle plant in Janesville, and unemployment has soared in Racine and Green Bay.

Wisconsin has a political pattern the opposite of most other Great Lakes states, where the biggest metro areas are Democratic and the countryside Republican. The three suburban counties around Milwaukee voted more than 60% for Republican presidential nominee John McCain in 2008, and metro Milwaukee delivered a smaller Obama percentage than the rest of the state. The western Wisconsin counties along the Mississippi River—whose scenic beauty rivals that of the Rhine—have moved heavily toward the Democrats, and so in 2008 did the heavily Catholic Fox River Valley around Green Bay, Appleton and Oshkosh. And while Thompson's welfare program was aimed primarily at Milwaukee, Doyle has come up with policies—increased tax credits for farmers, certification of organic farms—with appeal in rural areas.

The 2010 election will indicate whether these trends are lasting. Doyle is not term-limited and Democratic Sen. Russ Feingold, who has won three terms by narrow margins, is up again. But there are a few crosscurrents. In April 2008, voters ousted a Doyle appointee on the Supreme Court in favor of a northern Wisconsin judge who campaigned on a pro-business, tough-on-crime platform. They also voted to restrict the governor's veto. Previously, Wisconsin governors could veto specific words in a bill passed by the Legis-

Population			Household Income		Work	
Pop. 2007:	5,571,593		Under $15k:	11.8%	Private:	81.5%
State rank:	20th of 50		$15k to $50k:	37.9%	Government:	12.1%
Change since 2000:	Up 3.9%		$50k to $100k:	34.7%	Self-employed:	6.1%
Urban:	67.1%		$100k to $150k:	13.2%	Unemployment (3-yr. average):	4.0%
Rural:	32.9%		Over $150k:	2.4%	Poverty:	10.8%
Native of state:	72.1%		Median income:	$50,309	Blue collar:	26.4%
Not a citizen:	2.5%		**Home Value**		White collar:	57.1%
Area size:	65,498 sq. mi.		Under $100k:	19.7%	Khaki collar:	0.1%
Most populous cities			$100k to $300k:	66.2%	Other:	16.5%
1. Milwaukee	584,007		$300k to $500k:	10.4%	**Age**	
2. Madison	219,843		$500k to $1 mil:	3.1%	Median age:	37.7 yrs.
3. Green Bay	98,476		Over $1 million:	0.6%	More than 65 yrs:	13.1%
4. Kenosha	96,653		Median:	$162,000	Less than 18 yrs:	23.8%

Race/Ethnicity				Military Veterans		Registered Voters in 2008	
White:	85.6%	*Language*		% of Pop:	10.7%	No party registration	
Black:	5.9%	English:	91.9%	*Veterans by Period*		Voter turnout:	2,983,417
Hispanic:	4.7%	Spanish:	4.2%	WWII and before:	13.4%	Turnout as % of	
Asian:	2.0%	Asian:	1.3%	Korea:	12.7%	voting age:	69.2%
Native Am.:	0.8%	Other		Vietnam:	31.9%	**Legislature**	
Hawaiian:	0.0%	European	2.3%	Gulf (pre-2001):	9.3%	Senate:	18 D 15 R
Two+ races:	1.0%	**Education**		Gulf (post-2001):	5.1%	Assembly:	52 D 46 R 1 I
Ancestry		H.S. grad:	88.5%	Peace time:	27.5%		
German:	32.7%	College grad:	25.1%				
Irish:	8.6%	Grad degree:	8.3%				
Polish:	7.2%						

lature; Thompson actually crossed off letters within words to create new ones, and Doyle in 2005 diverted millions of transportation dollars to schools by crossing out some words. By 71%-29%, voters imposed some limits, though analysts say the veto power here remains stronger than in any other state.

Presidential politics   Wisconsin has voted Democratic in the last six presidential elections, starting in 1988. But sometimes the margin has been exceedingly narrow. Al Gore carried Wisconsin by only 5,708 votes in 2000, John Kerry by only 11,384 in 2004. In both elections, the state was inundated by ads and lawn signs by both campaigns, and was especially heavily contested in 2004. Kerry stumbled when he came to Green Bay and referred to "Lambert Field" —it's Lambeau Field, as any Cheesehead can tell you. But Kerry perhaps atoned by abjuring the Northeast Dairy Compact. In both these races some historic patterns were reversed. Bush carried metro Milwaukee, which casts about one-third of the state's votes, while Gore and Kerry carried many historically Republican or marginal counties in western Wisconsin. Indeed, this was the only rural part of the country where Gore and Kerry carried large numbers of counties and ran ahead of Democratic norms.

2008 Presidential Vote		
Obama (D) 1,677,211	(56%)
McCain (R)........................1,262,393	(42%)
2008 Democratic Presidential Primary		
Obama (D) 646,851	(58%)
Clinton (D).............................453,954	(41%)
2008 Republican Presidential Primary		
McCain (R)..............................224,755	(55%)
Huckabee (R) 151,707	(37%)
2004 Presidential Vote		
Kerry (D)..............................1,489,504	(50%)
Bush (R) 1,478,120	(49%)

Then in 2008, Wisconsin fell off the target list. Although polls tightened after the Republican National Convention and there was speculation that vice presidential nominee Sarah Palin might attract votes in the rural North, it became apparent by early October that Illinois Democrat Barack Obama was far ahead. He ended up winning 56%-42%, carrying 59 of the 72 counties. Republican John McCain carried only one of the eight congressional districts, in the steadily Republican Milwaukee suburbs, and he barely won in the state's fastest-growing county, St. Croix, just east of St. Paul, Minn. Obama made especially large gains over previous Democrats in the Fox River Valley and in the rural southwestern counties.

Wisconsin once had one of the nation's most influential presidential primaries. It knocked Wendell Willkie out of the race in 1944, helped John F. Kennedy establish his lead over Hubert Humphrey in 1960, prompted Lyndon B. Johnson to withdraw as Eugene McCarthy was about to beat him here in 1968, gave George McGovern his first victory in 1972 and chose "New Democrat" Gary Hart over Minnesota neighbor Walter Mondale in 1984. After that, Wisconsin's primary, even after it was moved from April to March, tended to be ignored. So in 2003, the Legislature moved the date up another month, to February 17, 2004, the only primary held that day. Wisconsin saw heavier campaigning than it had in years, at least for a few days. It may have proved crucial. Kerry led John Edwards 40%-34%, with Howard Dean in third place with only 18%. Dean went back to Vermont and ended his campaign, while Edwards failed to get the momentum a victory here might have given him. Wisconsin does not have party registration and few people bothered to vote in the uncontested Republican primary.

Wisconsin scheduled its 2008 primary on February 19. A week earlier, Obama swept the primaries in Maryland, Virginia and the District of Columbia. Democratic Gov. Jim Doyle campaigned actively for Obama and he was endorsed by longtime U.S. Rep. David Obey, the dean of the Wisconsin congressional delegation. Obama outspent Hillary Rodham Clinton on television 5-to-1, and he won a smashing 58%-41% victory, demonstrating, as he did in the Iowa caucuses, that he could prevail among a mostly white electorate. He carried all eight congressional districts and lost only 10 counties, mostly at the edge of the state and presumably out of range of most television stations. Clinton got the votes of 50% of women, but Obama got the votes of 67% of men. He won 68% of the vote in Dane County, home to the University of Wisconsin at Madison and 64% in Milwaukee County, with its large black population. Turnout topped 1 million, far above that in recent years, though just slightly below the turnout in 1972, when McGovern's 30% of the vote beat George Wallace's 22% and Hubert Humphrey's 21%.

There was less action on the Republican side. McCain had serious opposition only from Mike Huckabee, who was far behind in delegates, and the two campaigns together spent about as much money on ads as Clinton did, which is to say that each spent about one-tenth the amount that Obama did. Turnout was 410,000, below that of the primaries in 1968, 1976, 1992, 1996 and 2000, and less than half the turnout in 1980. McCain beat Huckabee 55%-37%. Huckabee did well enough in the central and western parts of the state to carry the 3rd and 7th congressional districts. McCain ran best in the Milwaukee suburbs. On Election Night, he was able to say, "Thank you, Wisconsin, for bringing us to the point where even a superstitious military aviator can claim with confidence and humility that I will be our party's nominee for president of the United States."

Congressional districting

111th Congress Lineup	
5 D	3 R
110th Congress Lineup	
5 D	3 R

Wisconsin lost a congressional district in the 2000 census. Ordinarily that would trigger a fierce battle between a Republican governor and Assembly and Democratic state Senate. But in May 2001, 5th District Democrat Tom Barrett announced he was running for governor. His north Milwaukee district had lost population and was easy to eliminate. The result was a consensus plan, approved by the congressional House delegation, passed by both houses of the Legislature and signed by the governor in March 2002. This is one state that produced a plan with regularly shaped districts with obvious communities of interest. It was also a plan that enabled all eight incumbents running to win re-election easily.

Wisconsin is not expected to lose a House seat in the reapportionment following the 2010 census. Democrats now hold the governorship and have majorities in the state Senate and Assembly, for the first time since Republican Tommy Thompson unseated Democratic incumbent Tony Earl in 1986. If they hold on in the 2010 election, they will have control of redistricting. But growth has been relatively even throughout the state, Democrats have a 5-3 edge in the U.S. House delegation, the heavily Republican Milwaukee suburbs will inevitably dominate one seat and the other two Republican congressman, Tom Petri and Paul Ryan, have been running well ahead of party lines. So it does not seem that there will be politically significant changes resulting from any redistricting plan.

Governor

James Doyle (D)

Elected 2002, term expires Jan. 2011, 2nd term; b. Nov. 23, 1945, Washington, DC; home, Maple Bluff; Attended Stanford U. 1963–66, U. of WI, B.A. 1967, Harvard U., J.D. 1972; Catholic; married (Jessica); 2 children.

Elected Office: Dane Cnty. D.A., 1976–82; WI atty. gen. 1990–02.

Professional Career: Peace Corps, Tunisia, 1967–69; Atty., Navajo Indian Reservation (Chinle, AZ), 1972–75; Practicing atty., 1982–90.

Office: 115 E. State Capitol, Madison, 53702, 608-266-1212; Fax: 608-267-8983; Web site: www.wisgov.state.wi.us.

Election Results

2006 general	James Doyle (D)	1,139,115	(53%)
	Mark Green (R)	979,427	(45%)
2006 primary	James Doyle (D)	unopposed	

Prior Winning Percentages: 2002 (45%)

James Doyle, a Democrat, was elected governor of Wisconsin in 2002. He grew up in Madison in a political family. His parents were part of a group of Madison liberals in the 1950s and 1960s who backed Sen. Gaylord Nelson, Sen. William Proxmire, Gov. Pat Lucey, and Gov. John Reynolds. Doyle's mother was elected to the Wisconsin Assembly in 1948, the second woman to have the distinction and the fourth generation of her family (the Bachhubers) to serve in the Legislature. His father ran for governor in 1954 and lost the primary to Proxmire; in 1967, he became a federal judge and for years was the only judge in the Western District of Wisconsin. Jim Doyle was a star basketball player and top student in high school, went to Stanford University for three years and then graduated from the University of Wisconsin. With his wife, a niece of former Defense Secretary Melvin Laird, he spent two years in the Peace Corps in Tunisia. Back in the United States, the couple marched in Washington to protest the Vietnam War. Doyle graduated from Harvard Law School, then worked for three years as a lawyer on the Navajo Reservation in Arizona.

He returned to Madison in 1975 and the following year, ran against and beat Dane County District Attorney Humphrey Lynch, a Democrat. Doyle served for six years, then went into private practice in Madison. In 1990, he ran for attorney general and defeated the incumbent Republican. His most publicized accomplishment was the state's $6 billion tobacco settlement, but he was criticized for paying the state's lawyers $847 million in fees for the case. Ed Garvey, a Democrat who had run for governor, sued and got the fee blocked.

Republican Tommy Thompson, long the dominant figure in state politics and the author of the changes in welfare laws that became a model for the nation, left Madison in January 2001 after 14 years as governor to become President George W. Bush's secretary of Health and Human Services. When

Lt. Gov. Scott McCallum took over, he was faced with more serious budget problems than Thompson had faced in many years and proposed cuts of $1 billion in aid to local governments over three years. The move was unpopular, and McCallum's job rating fell to about 35% in spring 2002. Four Democrats lined up to run against him, including Doyle, who was endorsed by Nelson, former Gov. Martin Schreiber and Lucey, who had managed his father's campaign for governor. Doyle started off much better known than his two major Democratic rivals, U.S. Rep. Tom Barrett of Milwaukee and Dane County Executive Kathleen Falk. The Democratic candidates avoided negative campaigning; their ads were mostly positive. Doyle's showed his two grown sons, who are adopted and of African-American descent, praising him. He won the September primary.

Doyle came out of primary night swinging at McCallum. "He's living proof that not all on-the-job training programs are successful," he said. He promised to cut $1 billion from the budget by reducing the number of state employees and attacked McCallum for spending the state's entire tobacco settlement on balancing a single year's budget. McCallum, who emerged from the primary with three times as much money as Doyle, ran an ad showing a messy desk and spilled coffee and attacked Doyle for missing deadlines while doing the state's legal business. McCallum said he would balance the budget through revenue growth and said Doyle had promised teachers' unions and other groups programs that would cost $2.7 billion on top of an anticipated $2.8 billion shortfall. Into the fray stepped a third candidate, Libertarian nominee and Tomah, Wis., Mayor Ed Thompson, Tommy Thompson's brother. In public polls Doyle held a slight lead, McCallum never seemed to rise above his lackluster job ratings, and Thompson ran in the high single digits. In November, Doyle beat McCallum 45%-41%, with 10% going to Ed Thompson. Doyle's narrow win was accompanied by Republican gains in legislative races. Republicans won control of the state Senate 18-15 and enlarged their Assembly majority to 58-41.

In office, Doyle faced a $3.2 billion deficit, but working with Republican legislators, he was able to balance the budget without increasing sales, income or corporate taxes. A tax on job creation was eliminated, and a single-tax formula based on corporate sales established. So was a sales-tax exemption for the cost of energy used in manufacturing. Doyle declared that taxes as a percentage of income were the lowest they'd been in Wisconsin in 34 years. In December 2004, he cut state employment by 1,500, a little below his goal. He also sought to increase Wisconsin's trade with China, Japan and Mexico.

Wisconsin's governor has broad and quirky veto powers, collectively known as the "Frankenstein veto" because the governor can stitch together major alterations in bills by striking particular words and phrases. Doyle regularly used the power against a Republican Legislature eager to advance its agenda. He vetoed 54 bills in his first session and 47 in the 2005–2006 session. He twice vetoed bills allowing residents to carry concealed weapons and was just one vote away from being overridden. He vetoed three times a bill requiring voters to show a photo ID, arguing that senior citizens often have a hard time producing identification. But he signed the Real ID bill, which requires those applying for driver's licenses to show proof of local residency. And he supported a bill to raise the cap on enrollment in Milwaukee's school-choice program and another to cap noneconomic damages in medical malpractice cases at $750,000.

In January 2005, facing a two-year projected deficit of $1.6 billion, Doyle again came out against a tax increase and proposed increasing school aid while holding down property-tax increases. Republicans wanted a freeze on school spending. Doyle threatened to veto the entire two-year $54 billion budget that Republicans had approved because it gave him less than half of the additional $938 million he had sought for school spending. Instead he made creative use of his line-item veto authority to bring the bill more closely in line with his priorities. He made 139 separate changes that redirected $360 million in other funding to boost school spending by $861 million while still placing limits on property-tax increases.

Despite his successes with a Legislature controlled by the opposition, Doyle was unable to move his approval ratings above 50%. That seemed to leave him vulnerable in 2006 to a challenge by U.S. Rep. Mark Green, who had traveled the state stumping for Assembly candidates in 2004 and began the governor's race by transferring $1.3 million from his federal account. Green ran on an anti-tax platform and said he would limit state spending. Doyle portrayed himself as a problem solver who had cleaned up the problems created by Republican administrations. An energetic supporter of the University of Wisconsin's pioneering embryonic-stem-cell research, Doyle made Green's votes against such research a central line of attack. Actor Michael J. Fox, afflicted with Parkinson's disease, appeared in an ad for Doyle just before Election Day.

Republicans tried reminding voters about the state procurement official who had been found guilty of steering travel contracts to Doyle contributors (she was later exonerated) and about Doyle appointees who had approved the sale of a nuclear power plant the same month the plant's owners donated to Doyle's campaign. But Green ran into his own fundraising conflicts when the state elections board ordered him to return nearly $470,000 from out-of-state political action committees that he had transferred from his federal campaign account. The Republican Legislature placed same-sex marriage and death-penalty initiatives on the November ballot, raising the prospect of increased conservative voter turnout. But Doyle won 53%-45%, becoming the first Democratic governor in over 30 years to win re-election in Wisconsin. Democrats also won four seats in the state Senate to claim an 18-15 majority and picked up eight seats in the Assembly to narrow the Republican majority to a 52-47 margin.

In 2007, Doyle achieved one of his central goals when the Legislature agreed to expand the BadgerCare Plus health-care program to cover all of the state's uninsured children. It also went along with his proposals to increase the state cigarette tax by $1 per pack and to add millions of dollars in new funding for schools, universities and student financial aid. Still, Doyle had some setbacks. The 2007 budget was passed in October, four months late and barely in time to avoid a statewide government shutdown. Doyle ended up compromising with Assembly Republicans and accepted a reduction in his cigarette tax from $1.25 to $1 a pack. He also jettisoned his proposals to place new taxes on oil companies and on hospitals. The budget still came in $892 million too high. Doyle promised to balance it by using his Frankenstein veto but promised to refrain from using that power as much as he had on previous budgets. Doyle had also pushed a statewide ban on smoking in restaurants, bars and other businesses. The Legislature did not pass it during that session, although it was adopted two years later, in May 2009.

The 2008 elections proved beneficial for Doyle. Democrats took over the state Assembly, gaining a 52-46 margin of control, and kept a majority in the Senate. An early supporter of President Barack Obama's candidacy in 2008, Doyle was rumored to be a contender for a Cabinet position, but no offer came. He was a vocal supporter of Obama's $787 million economic-stimulus bill, which passed in February 2009, and was one of a group of six Democratic governors who successfully pushed to have the bill include funds for state education and health-care programs in addition to the money for infrastructure.

Shortly after the election, it became clear that the state faced a projected three-year budget shortfall of more than $5 billion. In February 2009, Doyle called for a bill to raise taxes by $1.7 billion over three years, with a planned 10% increase in business taxes by 2011 and with a revised version of his hospital tax. The bill passed both houses of the Legislature just three days after he released his proposals, with every Republican in opposition and nearly every Democrat in support. Then in May, revised revenue estimates showed the budget shortfall to be closer to $6.5 billion. Doyle found himself making more unpopular decisions. He told state legislators they had to either back his proposal to lay off 1,100 state workers and furlough many others or propose their own tax hikes. He called for additional taxes on cigarettes and for an overhaul of the welfare system that would loosen some of the restrictions on access that Gov. Thompson had instituted in the early 1990s.

In 2009, Doyle also met with Republican Minnesota Gov. Tim Pawlenty to work out a pooling of resources that would help both states meet their budget shortfalls. The two governors agreed to a series of small plans that would save each state approximately $10 million. This is not the first time the two states have worked together on "Minnesconsin" projects. They already have reciprocity agreements for in-state college tuition. Doyle's other proposed initiatives included the creation of domestic-partnership benefits for same-sex couples and a requirement that health-insurance companies cover autism treatments. That June, Doyle signed into law a bill requiring equal pay for women. He has been coy about running for re-election in 2010, but most observers expect him to do so. Milwaukee County Executive Scott Walker, a Republican, announced his candidacy for governor in 2009.

Senior Senator

Herb Kohl (D)

Elected 1988, term expires 2012, 4th term; b. Feb. 7, 1935, Milwaukee; home, Milwaukee; U. of WI, B.A. 1956, Harvard U., M.B.A. 1958; Jewish; single.

Military Career: Army Reserves, 1958–64.

Professional Career: Businessman; Pres., Kohl Corp., 1970–79; Chmn., WI Dem. Party, 1975–77; Pres., Herbert Kohl Investments, 1979–88; Owner, Milwaukee Bucks pro basketball team, 1985–present.

DC Office: 330 HSOB, 20510, 202-224-5653; Fax: 202-224-9787; Web site: kohl.senate.gov.

State Offices: Appleton, 920-738-1640; Eau Claire, 715-832-8424; LaCrosse, 608-796-0045; Madison, 608-264-5338; Milwaukee, 414-297-4451.

Committees: *Aging (Special)* (Chmn of 13 D). *Appropriations* (6th of 18 D): Agriculture, Rural Development, Food and Drug Administration & Related Agencies (Chmn); Commerce, Justice, Science & Related Agencies; Defense; Interior, Environment & Related Agencies; Labor, Health and Human Services, Education & Related Agencies; Transportation, Housing and Urban Development & Related Agencies. *Banking, Housing & Urban Affairs* (10th of 13 D): Financial Institutions; Housing, Transportation & Community Development; Security & International Trade & Finance. *Judiciary* (2nd of 12 D): Antitrust, Competition Policy & Consumer Rights (Chmn); Crime & Drugs; Terrorism & Homeland Security.

Group Ratings

	ADA	ACLU	AFS	LCV	ITIC	NTU	COC	ACU	CFG	FRC
2008	95	64	100	100	100	5	63	4	7	0
2007	95	—	100	93	—	7	45	0	14	—

National Journal Ratings

	2007 LIB	—	2007 CONS		2008 LIB	—	2008 CONS
Economic	72%	—	23%		77%	—	13%
Social	81%	—	16%		65%	—	33%
Foreign	74%	—	24%		94%	—	0%
Composite	77%	—	23%		82%	—	18%

Key Votes of the 110th Congress

1. Raise CAFE standards	Y	5. Make English official language	N	9. Withdraw troops 3/08	Y
2. Expand SCHIP	Y	6. Path to citizenship	Y	10. Iran guard is terrorist group	Y
3. Cap greenhouse gases	Y	7. Fetus is unborn child	N	11. Increase missile defense $	N
4. Bail out financial markets	Y	8. Prosecute hate crimes	Y	12. Overhaul FISA	Y

Election Results

2006 general	Herb Kohl (D)..1,439,214	(67%)	($6,347,126)
	Robert Lorge (R)...630,299	(29%)	($176,987)
2006 primary	Herb Kohl (D)...308,178	(86%)	
	Ben Masel (D) 51,245	(14%)	

Prior Winning Percentages: 2000 (62%); 1994 (58%); 1988 (52%)

Herb Kohl, Wisconsin's senior senator, is a Democrat elected in 1988. He grew up in Milwaukee, where his parents had opened a food store after emigrating from Russia and Poland in the 1920s. Kohl got degrees from the University of Wisconsin and Harvard Business School, then returned home and with his brothers, developed the family business into a department chain, which became the wildly successful Kohl's department stores. They sold the business in 1975, and Kohl followed his love of sports into a new business venture. In a city smarting because of sports franchises with lousy records that were eager to move elsewhere, Kohl spent $18 million to buy the Milwaukee Bucks basketball team to keep it from leaving. His efforts to make the team respectable lost him money for several years, but he should turn a nice profit if he decides to sell the team—it was valued at $264 million by *Forbes* magazine in 2007. He has remained an active owner, involved in personnel decisions and pushing for a new stadium. Kohl is one of the richest members of Congress. He personally funds the Herb Kohl Educational Foundation, which has given millions of dollars in scholarships and grants to Wisconsin students, teachers and schools. He donated $25 million to the University of Wisconsin for the Kohl Center arena, which opened in 1998.

Throughout his long career in business, Kohl was in Democratic politics as a contributor, and in the mid-70s, he was chairman of the Wisconsin Democratic Party. When Democratic Sen. William Proxmire retired in 1988, Kohl decided to run for the Senate. He spent his own money liberally, running an extensive ad campaign with the theme "Nobody's senator but yours." He won 47% of the vote in the primary to 38% for former Gov. Tony Earl. In the general election campaign, against moderate Republican state Sen. Susan Engeleiter, Kohl stressed his support of defense cuts—popular in dovish Wisconsin—and for requiring businesses to provide health insurance. Engeleiter stressed her environmental stands, her legislative experience and her status as a wife and mother. This turned out to be one of the closest Senate races in the country that year, with Kohl winning 52%-48% after spending $7 million of his own money.

Kohl is an earnest man of transparent good will, seemingly little guile and a natural tendency toward bipartisanship. In the Senate, he once told the Milwaukee *Journal Sentinel*, "there's too much of the I-I-I-I, me-me-me-me, and these are my needs and you have to do them and you have to take care of me. When I see that in other people, I think it's a weakness." His voting record has been moderate to liberal. Kohl wrote the 1990 law banning guns in schools that was overturned by the U.S. Supreme Court in 1995. He was one of 12 Democratic senators who voted for the Bush tax cut in 2001, but he opposed the Bush tax cut in 2003. In October 2002, he voted for the Iraq war resolution but later called the administration's handling of the war "mistake after mistake after mistake." However, he resisted Democratic proposals for a specific timetable for withdrawing troops. In 2009, Kohl helped form the Moderate Dems Working Group, a coalition of 15 Democratic senators who, as Kohl put it, "still believe we need to be fiscally responsible and have a dialogue with amenable people of the other party." That March, he voiced concerns about President Barack Obama's 2009 budget, saying "deficits do matter." Also that year, he voted against a procedural move that would have allowed a simple majority of senators to pass legislation creating an emissions-trading system among polluting industries as a way of limiting greenhouse-gas emissions.

Kohl and former Republican Sen. Mike DeWine of Ohio ran the Antitrust Subcommittee of the Judiciary Committee on a bipartisan basis in both the Clinton and Bush years. Together, they stopped several proposed megamergers: the proposed AT&T-SBC merger in 1997, the proposed American Airlines–British Airways merger in 1998 and the U.S. Airways–United Airlines merger in 2001. In 2005, they co-sponsored a bill to allow the Justice Department to seek wiretaps on antitrust violators. As chairman of the subcommittee, beginning in 2007, Kohl introduced legislation that would repeal antitrust exemptions for the railroad industry, although the bill was dropped after Bush threatened to veto it. In 2009, Kohl worked with Republican ranking member Orrin Hatch of Utah to revise the bill, which passed without opposition in the committee after rail-industry lobbyists accidentally emailed committee members their internal deliberations on how to kill the legislation. On the full committee, Kohl supported the nomination of John Roberts in 2005 to be chief justice of the Supreme Court, but in 2006, he opposed Samuel Alito's appointment to the court.

Kohl, who chairs the Appropriations Committee's agriculture subcommittee, has fought with uncharacteristic fierceness to change what he considers the unfair treatment of Wisconsin dairy farmers. Since 1937, the Agriculture Department has fixed national milk prices using a formula that allows higher prices the farther a farmer is from Eau Claire, Wis. This increases prices to consumers, creates an oversupply of milk, and reduces dairy prices in the upper Midwest. Further aggravating the problem is the Northeast Dairy Compact, set up in the 1980s, which allows New England states to set even higher prices. During the debate on the 1996 Freedom to Farm Act, Kohl persuaded the Senate to vote 50-46 to end the Northeast Dairy Compact, but in conference it was extended to 1999, and the agriculture secretary was ordered to set new milk-marketing rules by then.

In October 1999, New England senators inserted into an appropriations bill a two-year extension of the compact and rejected then-Agriculture Secretary Dan Glickman's new rules. Kohl was outraged and filibustered the bill. He was forced to desist but got verbal promises from leaders of both parties that the issue would be revisited. In 2001, he got 41 senators to sign a letter opposing the Northeast Dairy Compact, enough to threaten a filibuster if the issue was brought up, and on September 30, the compact expired. To take its place, Kohl helped pass in 2002 the Milk Loss Income Contract program, which pays dairy farmers if market prices fall. In its first three years, it provided $2 billion to dairy farmers nationally, and $413 million of that to Wisconsin farmers. In 2005, he and Republican Norm Coleman of Minnesota pushed for renewal of MILC, and he was pleased when the administration budget continued the program, though with a 5% funding decrease. He voted for the 2008 farm bill because it had provisions that would help Wisconsin's dairy farmers, including the extension of MILC and increased payment levels for farmers.

On another subcommittee issue, Kohl consistently has pushed for higher funding for the Food and Drug Administration. In 2007, he made sure the FDA received a $1.8 billion budget for fiscal 2008, about $186 million more than it had received the previous year. In 2008, he pushed for another increase, of $375 million.

After Democrats won the majority in 2007, Kohl became chairman of the Special Committee on Aging, which he has used as a platform to advocate for a change in the law allowing the government to use its buying power to negotiate lower prescription-drug prices. Kohl also introduced a bill that encourages businesses to retain employees beyond their retirement age. In May 2007, he worked with other Wisconsin lawmakers to add funding for Wisconsin's SeniorCare program to an Iraq war spending bill, circumventing a plan to end the program and move senior citizens to the national Medicare plan. The following year, he introduced legislation with Republican Sen. Charles Grassley of Iowa to increase regulation of nursing homes.

Kohl has been re-elected easily, with the help of his personal fortune. He spent $6.5 million of his own money on his campaign in 1994 and $5 million in 2000. His ability to self-finance has deterred many well-known Republicans from running against him. Former Republican Gov. Tommy Thompson flirted with the possibility in 2006 but declined. Republicans eventually nominated attorney Robert Gerald Lorge, a perennial candidate. Kohl spent more than $6 million on his re-election and sailed to a fourth term with 67% of the vote. If he completes his fourth term, he will be tied for Wisconsin's second-longest-serving senator, still far short of Proxmire's 31-year tenure.

Junior Senator

Russell Feingold (D)

Elected 1992, term expires 2010, 3rd term; b. March 2, 1953, Janesville; home, Middleton; U. of WI, B.A. 1975, Rhodes Scholar, Oxford U., 1977, Harvard U., J.D. 1979; Jewish; divorced; 2 children.

Elected Office: WI Senate, 1982–92.

Professional Career: Practicing atty., 1979–83; Prof., Beloit Col., 1985–93.

DC Office: 506 HSOB, 20510, 202-224-5323; Fax: 202-224-2725; Web site: feingold.senate.gov.

State Offices: Green Bay, 920-465-7508; LaCrosse, 608-782-5585; Middleton, 608-828-1200; Milwaukee, 414-276-7282; Wausau, 715-848-5660.

Committees: *Budget* (4th of 13 D). *Foreign Relations* (3rd of 11 D): African Affairs (Chmn); East Asian & Pacific Affairs; International Operations & Organizations, Democracy & Global Women's Issues; Near Eastern & South & Central Asian Affairs. *Intelligence (Select)* (6th of 8 D). *Judiciary* (4th of 12 D): Administrative Oversight & the Courts; Constitution (Chmn); Crime & Drugs; Human Rights & the Law.

Group Ratings

	ADA	ACLU	AFS	LCV	ITIC	NTU	COC	ACU	CFG	FRC
2008	100	93	100	100	60	21	38	24	20	0
2007	95	—	100	93	—	12	18	4	3	—

National Journal Ratings

	2007 LIB	—	2007 CONS		2008 LIB	—	2008 CONS
Economic	79%	—	13%		58%	—	40%
Social	94%	—	0%		80%	—	9%
Foreign	76%	—	23%		48%	—	47%
Composite	86%	—	15%		65%	—	35%

Key Votes of the 110th Congress

1. Raise CAFE standards	Y	5. Make English official language	N	9. Withdraw troops 3/08	Y
2. Expand SCHIP	Y	6. Path to citizenship	Y	10. Iran guard is terrorist group	N
3. Cap greenhouse gases	Y	7. Fetus is unborn child	N	11. Increase missile defense $	N
4. Bail out financial markets	N	8. Prosecute hate crimes	Y	12. Overhaul FISA	N

Election Results

2004 general	Russell Feingold (D)	1,632,697	(55%)	($9,239,908)
	Tim Michels (R)	1,301,183	(44%)	($5,542,087)
2004 primary	Russell Feingold (D)	unopposed		

Prior Winning Percentages: 1998 (51%); 1992 (53%)

Russ Feingold, Wisconsin's junior senator, is a Democrat first elected to the Senate in 1992. He grew up in Janesville, where his father and Republican Rep. Paul Ryan's father practiced law in the same building. Politics was in his blood. His father, Leon Feingold, ran for district attorney as a Progressive and practiced law in Janesville for 45 years. He once lost an election to the county board by one vote. His uncle, Louis Binstock, was a prominent Chicago rabbi involved in the civil rights movement. In the second grade, Feingold cast the only vote in his class for Democrat John F. Kennedy and decided he wanted to be president, although he also said he would settle for senator. He did his undergraduate work at the University of Wisconsin, where his father had gotten his law degree, and was a Rhodes Scholar. He got his law degree from Harvard, then moved to Middleton, a Madison suburb. In 1982, at age 29, he beat an 83-year-old veteran state senator by 31 votes. Feingold has a flair for publicity, for political-reform issues and for novel arguments. His signature issue in the Legislature was a ban on bovine growth hormones.

In 1992, Feingold decided to run for the Senate seat held by Bob Kasten, a free-market Republican conservative who had won by narrow margins in 1980 and 1986. In the Democratic primary, while Milwaukee businessman Joseph Checota and U.S. Rep. Jim Moody battered each other with negative ads, Feingold ran clever, humorous spots. One showed Elvis Presley alive and endorsing Feingold; another showed Feingold at home, opening up a closet and saying, "No skeletons." He also had detailed position papers, including an 82-point plan for reducing the deficit. As primary day neared, Checota apologized for his ads and asked voters to vote for Feingold if they didn't vote for him. Already ahead in the polls, Feingold zoomed to an astonishing 70% win in the three-way race. He also bounced way ahead of Kasten, who ran his own Elvis ads attacking Feingold on issues. Feingold in turn attacked Kasten's negativity and avoided engaging on specifics. The race narrowed, but Feingold won 53%-46%.

In the Senate, Feingold has had a liberal record on cultural and foreign issues and a somewhat more moderate record on economics. He attacked many spending programs and did not respond in lockstep with other Democrats to the scandals of the Clinton era. For instance, in 1997, he called for an independent counsel to look into the Clinton-Gore fundraising operations. And in 1999, he was the only Democrat to vote against West Virginia Sen. Robert Byrd's motion to dismiss impeachment charges against Clinton.

Calling the campaign-finance system "legalized bribery," Feingold took on the issue, joining with Republican Sen. John McCain of Arizona. Out of this collaboration came the various versions of McCain-Feingold campaign-finance bills, which were filibustered multiple times in 1996 and 1998. In October 1999 McCain-Feingold was again beaten, but in June 2000, the two senators pushed through a bill requiring disclosure by Section 527 fundraising committees. McCain's presidential campaign and his threat to bring up the issue at every turn forced then-Republican Senate Majority Leader Trent Lott, R-Miss., to schedule two weeks of debate in March 2001. This time McCain and Feingold prevailed. They beat by 60-40 an amendment from Nebraska Sen. Chuck Hagel calling for lesser changes, and the bill passed 59-41 in April. In July, it was about to come up for a vote when the Republican leadership pulled it from the calendar. After energy giant Enron went bankrupt, pressure mounted. The House version's advocates got 218 signatures on a discharge petition, and the bill was brought to the floor and passed. The Senate passed a final version in March 2002. President George W. Bush expressed doubts about the constitutionality of some provisions but signed it anyway, without ceremony and without inviting McCain or Feingold to the White House. The argument switched to the courts. In May 2003, a deeply divided three-judge federal court issued 1,700 pages of opinions, upholding some of the provisions of McCain-Feingold but not others. That December, the U.S. Supreme Court upheld most sections of the law.

The campaign-finance act had an impact, though not the expected one, on the 2004 elections. The parties were able to raise large sums anyway, much of it over the Internet and from 527 organizations not covered by the act. Feingold and McCain asked the Federal Election Commission to rule that the act covered 527s, but it declined to do so. In January 2005, they and their House co-sponsors, Republican Chris Shays of Connecticut and Democrat Marty Meehan of Massachusetts, introduced a bill to require 527s to register as political committees and to use only regulated campaign donations for advertisements that mentioned federal candidates. That produced some interesting responses: Left-leaning organizations like the Sierra Club and the League for Conservation Voters opposed it, while other liberal organizations questioned whether 501(c) charitable organizations would be covered. Senate Rules Committee Chairman Lott announced that he was all for it and would shepherd it through his committee, but prominent members of both parties objected to the bill, and it was never brought to a vote. Next, Feingold crusaded against the Senate's unique practice of requiring the filing of campaign-finance reports on paper, rather than electronically as the House does, making them more accessible to the public. In March 2007, the Rules Committee approved an electronic-filing bill sponsored by Feingold and Republican Sen. Thad Cochran of Mississippi, but even though the bill had 47 co-sponsors, Majority Leader Harry Reid never brought it up for a vote.

Feingold and McCain have maintained a close relationship. McCain once referred to Feingold as his "philosophical soul mate" on reform issues. During the 2008 presidential campaign, Feingold endorsed Democratic candidate Barack Obama of Illinois because of his policy positions, but he regularly complimented McCain for his personal integrity. He called McCain "very original" and a "maverick by nature," although that October, he criticized McCain for "seeming to look the other way as his campaign employs certain tactics . . . intended to appeal to the fears of some Americans," a reference to McCain's failure to rebuke supporters at rallies when they shouted "treason," "terrorist," and "kill him" when Obama's name was mentioned. After the election, Feingold and McCain renewed their partnership, working together on a bill to give the president power to cut spending earmarks from appropriations bills.

Feingold has pursued other ethics issues. He was one of the crusaders against lobbyists' gifts to lawmakers and against members using for personal travel the frequent-flier miles they earned on business trips. In 2007, he worked with Obama on successful legislation and rules changes that limited gifts, meals and travel paid for by lobbyists and required senators to disclose the spending earmarks they slip into appropriations bills.

Feingold also has tried to ban cost-of-living adjustments to congressional pay and refuses to accept his own pay raises. In November 2002, he lost one such amendment 58-36. He took another shot in 2009. After Republican Sen. David Vitter of Louisiana attempted to amend an unrelated bill to include repeal of the COLA, Reid allowed Feingold to have a vote on a stand-alone repeal bill. It passed the Senate unanimously (no senator was likely to vote publicly in favor of a cost-of-living increase), but as Reid anticipated, the House declined to take up the bill, and it died. Members of Congress got their pay increases.

In 2001, Feingold offered amendments to limit the greatly expanded law-enforcement powers created by the USA PATRIOT Act. He wanted to limit secret searches, computer surveillance and roving wiretaps. But then-Majority Leader Tom Daschle had all the amendments tabled, and Feingold cast the sole vote against the larger bill. In December 2005, he filibustered the renewal of the PATRIOT Act, but Republican leaders were ultimately able to pass the bill.

Casting sole votes is not unusual for Feingold. In 2002, he was the only Democrat on the Budget Committee to join Republicans in voting for five-year caps on spending. He fought to apply pay-as-you-go rules to the budget, requiring that all spending increases or tax cuts be compensated for by corresponding spending cuts or tax increases. The Senate agreed to the rules in 2003 and 2004, which resulted in deadlock on the budget resolution, since the Republican House wouldn't accept the pay-go rules for taxes. He was also one of three senators to vote against the annual defense bill for 2008 because it did not include a timetable for the drawdown of troops in Iraq.

Feingold has staked out some original positions on the Judiciary Committee. He has called for repeal of all federal death-penalty statutes. He was one of eight Democrats who voted to confirm John Ashcroft as attorney general in Bush's first term, arguing that a president should be given great deference in Executive Branch appointments. But he hasn't been consistent on that score, voting against the confirmation of Alberto Gonzales as attorney general in Bush's second term. And in February 2009, after indicted Democratic Gov. Rod Blagojevich of Illinois appointed Roland Burris to the Senate despite an ongoing pay-to-play scandal, Feingold called for a constitutional amendment barring the appointment of senators by governors. The amendment had cosponsors from both parties but didn't go anywhere.

On foreign policy, Feingold was one of three Democratic senators to vote in March 1999 against air strikes in Serbia and Kosovo, and in October 2002, he voted against the Iraq war resolution. In August

2005, he was the first senator to propose a timetable for withdrawing troops from Iraq. In 2006 and 2007, he pushed a resolution to censure Bush for the secret surveillance of communications between Al Qaeda suspects abroad and people in the United States, although his effort got very little support. When Democrats won a Senate majority in 2007, he held a hearing on exercising Congress's constitutional power to end a war. Throughout 2007 and 2008, he pushed to cut off funding for the war and to set specific timetables for troop withdrawals. One of them would have barred federal funds from being spent on the Iraq War after June 2008, but it was defeated 28-68. Reid agreed to hold a vote on another of Feingold's bills restricting war funding, but security improvements in the region made Republicans confident they could win the debate, and Reid pulled the bill from the floor, infuriating Feingold.

In 1998, Feingold faced a strong Republican opponent in U.S. Rep. Mark Neumann, a conservative elected in 1994. They agreed to limit their campaign spending—Feingold to $3.8 million, Neumann to $4.7 million (he actually spent $4.4 million)—and to limit contributions from political action committees. By fall, Feingold's lead of 10% had melted away, and the race was about even. Neumann ran humorous ads attacking Feingold for sending dollars to Russia to study monkeys in space and for voting for a study of cow flatulence; the ad showed smock-clad scientists out in a field trying to isolate samples of cow gas. In one of the nation's closest Senate races, Feingold won 51%-48%.

In 2001, Feingold talked occasionally about running for president, and that fall, he made a campaign speaking tour. He ultimately decided against a run. He was next up for re-election to the Senate in 2004, when his Republican challenger was Tim Michels, a Waukesha County businessman who had served 12 years as an Army Airborne Ranger. This time, Feingold decided not to be outspent. By August, he had raised $9 million, and he started running his characteristically humorous ads nonstop in June, knowing that Wisconsin would be inundated with presidential advertising in the summer and fall. Michels argued that Feingold had spent too much time on campaign-finance legislation and not enough on health care and job creation, and he attacked Feingold for his vote against the PATRIOT Act. But Michels did not make much headway. Feingold's message that he was an independent vote and a candid voice seemed to resonate. That fall, national Republicans dropped plans to spend $1.2 million on ads against Feingold. He won by a solid 55%-44%.

After the election, Feingold once again showed interest in running for president, making appearances in Florida and New Hampshire and raising $2 million. He had a clear political profile to present: an opponent of the Iraq War from the beginning and the only vote against the PATRIOT Act. But he received only a tepid response and decided against making the race in 2008.

FIRST DISTRICT

Paul Ryan (R)

Elected 1998, 6th term; b. Jan. 29, 1970, Janesville; home, Janesville; Miami U. of OH, B.A., 1992; Catholic; married (Janna); 3 children.

Professional Career: Aide, U.S. Sen. Bob Kasten, 1992; Advisor & speechwriter, Empower America, 1993–95; Legis. dir., U.S. Sen. Sam Brownback, 1995–97; Mktg. consultant., Ryan Inc. Central, 1997–98.

DC Office: 1113 LHOB, 20515, 202-225-3031; Fax: 202-225-3393; Web site: www.house.gov/ryan.

State Offices: Janesville, 608-752-4050; Kenosha, 262-654-1901; Racine, 262-637-0510.

Committees: *Budget* (RMM of 15 R). *Ways & Means* (5th of 15 R): Health; Oversight.

Group Ratings

	ADA	ACLU	AFS	LCV	ITIC	NTU	COC	ACU	CFG	FRC
2008	15	18	0	8	71	71	83	84	79	94
2007	15	—	9	25	—	85	75	96	94	—

National Journal Ratings

	2007 LIB	—	2007 CONS	2008 LIB	—	2008 CONS
Economic	17%	—	83%	16%	—	84%
Social	29%	—	69%	9%	—	85%
Foreign	0%	—	72%	8%	—	89%
Composite	20%	—	80%	13%	—	88%

Key Votes of the 110th Congress

1. Increase minimum wage	N	5. Share immigration data	Y	9. Withdraw troops 8/08	N
2. Expand SCHIP	N	6. Foreign aid abortion ban	Y	10. No operations in Iran	N
3. Raise CAFE standards	N	7. Ban gay bias in workplace	Y	11. Free trade with Peru	Y
4. Bail out financial markets	Y	8. Repeal D.C. gun law	Y	12. Overhaul FISA	Y

Election Results

2008 general	Paul Ryan (R)	231,009	(64%)	($2,251,389)
	Marge Krupp (D)	125,268	(35%)	($143,292)
2008 primary	Paul Ryan (R)	unopposed		

Prior Winning Percentages: 2006 (63%); 2004 (65%); 2002 (67%); 2000 (67%); 1998 (57%)

Population		Race/Ethnicity		Work	
Pop. 2007:	717,402	White:	85.0%	Private:	85.0%
Change since 2000:	Up 7.0%	Black:	5.0%	Government:	10.5%
Urban:	84.4%	Hispanic:	7.2%	Self-employed:	4.4%
Rural:	15.6%	Asian:	1.3%	Blue collar:	27.1%
Area size:	1,724 sq. mi.	Native Am.:	0.3%	White collar:	57.8%
		Hawaiian:	0.0%	Khaki collar:	0.1%
Age		Two+ races:	1.0%	Other:	15.1%
Median age:	38.3 yrs.	*Ancestry*		Median income:	$56,144
More than 65 yrs:	12.5%	German:	28.9%	Median home value:	$183,600
Less than 18 yrs:	25.0%	Polish:	9.5%	Poverty:	8.6%
Education		Irish:	9.2%	**Military Veterans**	
H.S. grad:	88.3%			% of Pop:	11.4%
College grad:	24.1%				
Grad degree:	7.8%				

With its rolling hills, blanketed by snow during most of the winter, gloriously green under blue skies in summer, the southern tier of Wisconsin, from Lake Michigan to the Rock River Valley, is some of America's prime industrial country. Settled by Yankee and German farmers 170 years ago, it was once primarily dairy land. By the early 20th century, the steady habits and high skills of the local dairy farmers had made them a good labor pool for factories. There are still major plants here, includ-

2008 Presidential Vote

Obama (D)	191,901	(51%)
McCain (R)	177,162	(47%)

2004 Presidential Vote

Bush (R)	197,970	(54%)
Kerry (D)	170,371	(46%)

Cook Partisan Voting Index: R + 2

ing the operations center for S. C. Johnson Wax in Racine, with its Frank Lloyd Wright–designed tower. But the recent collapse of the domestic auto industry had a powerful impact on the local economy. In 2008, General Motors closed its Janesville plant, laying off 2,500 workers, and the following year, Chrysler announced that it would shutter its Kenosha plant and lay off 850. Unemployment in Rock County, which includes Janesville, jumped from 4.8% in October 2007 to 13.5% in March 2009.

Kenosha, once primarily a factory town, has undergone a bit of a transformation, with some of the old smokestacks and shipyards along its lakefront replaced with museums, a marina, restaurants and boutiques that attract weekending Chicagoans and Chicago-based businesses. Other towns in the area have tried to follow suit, offering tax breaks and other enticements to lure Chicago businesses north. Most of this region is becoming metropolitan, part of the almost continuously suburban zone where metro Milwaukee melds into metro Chicago. But there are still some thriving old lake resorts, most notably Lake Geneva, a favorite of wealthy Chicagoans. In nearby Williams Bay is the University of Chicago's historic Yerkes Observatory, long one of the nation's largest astronomy research centers and often referred to as the birthplace of modern astrophysics.

This is the 1st Congressional District of Wisconsin. It runs from Lake Michigan west to Janesville in Rock County and encompasses all of Racine and Kenosha counties on Lake Michigan as well as parts of Walworth County, including Lake Geneva. It also takes in the southern Milwaukee County suburbs of Oak Creek and Greenfield and the southern tier of townships in suburban Waukesha County, including New Berlin. Generally, it tilts Republican, and Waukesha and Walworth counties are heavily Republican. In this presidential battleground state, the district voted 54% for Republican George W. Bush in 2004 but broke narrowly for Democrat Barack Obama in 2008, 51%-47%.

The congressman from the 1st District is Paul Ryan, a Republican elected in 1998 at age 28. He is the ranking Republican on the House Budget Committee. Ryan grew up in Janesville, where in 1884 his great-grandfather started a family construction firm, now run by his cousins. His father and Democratic Sen. Russ Feingold's father had law offices in the same building. Ryan got started in politics early, as a staffer for Republican Sen. Bob Kasten while attending college at Miami University in Ohio. He planned to apply to the University of Chicago and eventually become an economist, but says he "just kept getting really interesting jobs" in politics. Ryan worked as a speechwriter for Republican Rep. Jack Kemp of New York and for the think tank of conservative pundit William Bennett, Empower America, and he was legislative director for Republican Sen. Sam Brownback of Kansas. Ryan returned to the 1st District to run for the House when GOP Rep. Mark Neumann ran for the Senate in 1998 (Neumann lost to Feingold). Ryan won the Republican primary with 81% of the vote. Democrats nominated Kenosha County official Lydia Spottswood, who had lost to Neumann in 1996. Ryan campaigned against tax increases and in favor of gun ownership rights. This was a strenuously contested election, one of the Democrats' top 10 priorities in the nation. Spottswood spent $1.33 million, and Ryan spent $1.24 million. However, the results were not close. Ryan won 57%-43%.

In the House, Ryan has become a mainstream Republican who occasionally bucks his party and who takes centrist positions on foreign policy and some social issues. In 2007, he voted for a bill to prohibit employment discrimination on the basis of sexual orientation and later said he supported the bill because he has friends "who didn't choose to be gay . . . they were just created that way." He said he "took a lot of crap" for the vote from social conservatives.

One of the most effective communicators among Republican fiscal conservatives, Ryan has pressed for the line-item veto and changes in the federal budget process to impose more spending discipline. He has also pressed the appropriations committees to cut spending, to no avail. On the Ways and Means Committee, he advocates business tax cuts to spur economic growth and was an ally of the conservative anti-tax group Club for Growth in criticizing President Bush's tax cuts as too modest. He pushed for increased competition in Medicare plans and for the creation of health savings accounts. Ryan was an eager proponent of Bush's plan to add personal retirement accounts to the Social Security program. In 2005, with Republican Sen. John Sununu of New Hampshire, he sponsored a plan to create payroll-tax-funded private retirement accounts that would be financed largely through spending cuts and new revenues predicted to result from the accounts. He complained that threatened retribution from Democratic leaders made it difficult for him to secure Democratic supporters.

In 2005, early in Bush's second term, Ryan was offered the job of White House budget director but turned it down to remain in Congress. Two years later, he became the top Republican on the Budget Committee, vaulting over 12 more-senior Republicans on the committee. "We lost our brand as the party of fiscal responsibility, and we've got to get it back," Ryan said after his selection. "It's important that we give voters a very clear choice on fiscal policy." That year, he wrote an alternative budget blueprint that would have trimmed discretionary and entitlement spending and extended all expiring tax cuts, aiming for a balanced budget in 2012. It lost 160-268, which was no surprise in the Democratically controlled House, but he also lost 40 Republican votes.

In late 2008, Ryan helped to almost derail negotiations on a $700 billion bailout of the financial-services industry when he and other fiscal conservatives introduced an alternative plan to the one backed by Treasury Secretary Henry Paulson and Democratic leaders. Eventually, the Democrats included some of his provisions, and he supported the compromise bill. He also voted for the 2008 government bailout of the domestic auto industry, citing "mounting hardships" in his district after two auto factories were shuttered.

Following the Democratic victories in the 2008 election, a *Wall Street Journal* editorial called for Ryan to challenge Minority Leader John Boehner of Ohio, arguing that Ryan's "economic knowledge and youthful energy make him the best choice to pull his party in a more promising direction." Some Republican House members encouraged the move as well, but Ryan decided against a challenge. He was the keynote speaker at the 2009 Conservative Political Action Conference, the largest nationwide gathering of conservatives. He also helped write the Republicans' alternate plan to Obama's first budget, along with Boehner, Republican Study Committee Chairman Mike Pence of Indiana, and Minority Whip Eric Cantor of Virginia, a close ally of Ryan's. Ryan and Cantor pushed to include more details about how the Republicans would control spending and trim the deficit, but Boehner disagreed, and he prevailed; the plan was criticized in the press for lacking detail, and the effort was scrapped. In March 2009, Ryan introduced a bill with Republican Sen. John McCain of Arizona and Feingold, a friend of Ryan's despite their philosophical differences, to give the president the power to trim spending earmarks from appropriations bills.

Ryan is considerably more conservative than the balance of his district. As he told the *Milwaukee Journal Sentinel* in April 2009, "A lot of guys get to vote how they want, then go home and go fishing. . . . I've got to vote and then go home and explain what I did and why I did it." Still, Ryan is secure in the seat, having cruised to re-election in 2008 with 64% of the vote, besting McCain's performance in the district by 17 points. National conservatives have held up his political success as an example for Republicans across the nation. Ryan says he is "not looking to become some famous conservative movement leader" and would rather be "a policy leader," perhaps chairman of Ways and Means if Republicans retake control of the House. Ryan has often been mentioned as a potential candidate for the Senate, and he has expressed an interest in running if Democratic Sen. Herb Kohl retires in 2012.

An avid sportsman, Ryan co-chairs the Congressional Sportsmen's Caucus, the largest bipartisan caucus in the House. He enjoys fishing (walleye and muskie) and hunting, particularly bow hunting, and has been known to send emails from his BlackBerry while waiting in the brush for deer to appear.

SECOND DISTRICT

Tammy Baldwin (D)

Elected 1998, 6th term; b. Feb. 11, 1962, Madison; home, Madison; Smith Col., A.B. 1984; U. of WI Law Schl., J.D. 1989; No religious affiliation; partner (Lauren Azar).

Elected Office: Dane Cnty. Bd. of Supervisors, 1986–94; WI Assembly, 1992–98.

Professional Career: Practicing atty, 1989–92.

DC Office: 2446 RHOB, 20515, 202-225-2906; Fax: 202-225-6942; Web site: www.tammybaldwin.house.gov.

State Offices: Beloit, 608-362-2800; Madison, 608-258-9800.

Committees: *Energy & Commerce* (19th of 36 D): Energy & Environment; Health. *Judiciary* (18th of 24 D): Constitution, Civil Rights & Civil Liberties.

Group Ratings

	ADA	ACLU	AFS	LCV	ITIC	NTU	COC	ACU	CFG	FRC
2008	100	100	100	100	86	7	56	0	0	0
2007	100	—	100	100	—	5	45	0	6	—

National Journal Ratings

	2007 LIB	—	2007 CONS		2008 LIB	—	2008 CONS
Economic	82%	—	0%		85%	—	0%
Social	92%	—	0%		82%	—	0%
Foreign	96%	—	0%		85%	—	8%
Composite	95%	—	5%		91%	—	9%

Key Votes of the 110th Congress

1. Increase minimum wage	Y	5. Share immigration data	N	9. Withdraw troops 8/08	Y
2. Expand SCHIP	Y	6. Foreign aid abortion ban	N	10. No operations in Iran	Y
3. Raise CAFE standards	Y	7. Ban gay bias in workplace	Y	11. Free trade with Peru	N
4. Bail out financial markets	Y	8. Repeal D.C. gun law	N	12. Overhaul FISA	N

Election Results

2008 general	Tammy Baldwin (D)	277,914	(69%)	($1,159,588)
	Peter Theron (R)	122,513	(31%)	($27,213)
2008 primary	Tammy Baldwin (D)	18,414	(99%)	

Prior Winning Percentages: 2006 (63%); 2004 (63%); 2002 (66%); 2000 (51%); 1998 (53%)

Population		Race/Ethnicity		Work	
Pop. 2007:	722,652	White:	86.9%	Private:	75.3%
Change since 2000:	Up 7.8%	Black:	3.7%	Government:	19.0%
Urban:	75.6%	Hispanic:	4.5%	Self-employed:	5.6%
Rural:	24.4%	Asian:	3.0%	Blue collar:	19.8%
Area size:	3,602 sq. mi.	Native Am.:	0.3%	White collar:	65.0%
		Hawaiian:	0.0%	Khaki collar:	0.1%
Age		Two+ races:	1.4%	Other:	15.1%
Median age:	35.8 yrs.			Median income:	$55,192
More than 65 yrs:	11.0%	*Ancestry*		Median home value:	$197,000
Less than 18 yrs:	22.3%	German:	30.4%	Poverty:	10.2%
		Irish:	10.3%		
Education		Norwegian:	9.4%	**Military Veterans**	
H.S. grad:	91.7%			% of Pop:	9.2%
College grad:	35.8%				
Grad degree:	13.7%				

On a narrow isthmus between Lakes Mendota and Monona is the center of Madison and in many ways the center of Wisconsin. The state Capitol rises at one end of State Street, and at the other end is the main campus of the University of Wisconsin, in a beautiful, park like setting above Lake Mendota. For most of the 20th century, Wisconsin politics was dominated by the Madison-based La Follettes and their liberal Democratic successors. University faculty were devoted to former governor and senator

2008 Presidential Vote	
Obama (D) 286,089	(69%)
McCain (R)...........................123,495	(30%)
2004 Presidential Vote	
Kerry (D).............................250,151	(62%)
Bush (R).............................151,024	(37%)
Cook Partisan Voting Index: D + 15	

Bob La Follette's "Wisconsin idea" of an apolitical bureaucracy and to his Wisconsin Tax Commission and workmen's compensation law—both firsts in the nation. Madison spawned an activist and sometimes violent student movement during the Vietnam War. A graduate student was killed in a laboratory by a bomb set off by a protester. In recent years the liberal campus opposed the welfare-reform and school-choice laws enacted while Republican Tommy Thompson was governor, and it was not entirely happy with the centrist policies of his Democratic successor, Jim Doyle. A steady debate goes on here between the very liberal Madison *Capital Times* and its more conservative rival, the *Wisconsin State Journal*; the two newspapers practice the kind of competitive journalism now seen in only a few other major cities and state capitals. This is an urban capital in the midst of farmland; the Dane County farmers' market is the largest in the nation.

Madison is the center of Wisconsin's 2nd Congressional District, which is roughly equal parts urban, suburban and rural. It includes surrounding Dane County and dairy and alfalfa country to the north and south, as well as several rural dairy counties that have traditionally been Republican. It takes in the birthplace of the Ringling Brothers Circus in Baraboo, and the Swiss-settled town of New Glarus, known statewide for the New Glarus Brewing Company and its Fat Squirrel and Spotted Cow beers. Prairie du Sac, to the north of Madison, is home to the corporate headquarters of the rapidly expanding Culver's fast-food chain, famous for its quintessentially Wisconsin butter burgers, with an optional side of fried cheese curds. The Wisconsin Dells, and its giant water park, has long been a family vacation destination for city dwellers.

Median family income in Madison is nearly twice the level in Milwaukee, with its shrinking job base. Local industry, rooted in the university and the state government, has proved to be recession resistant; the growth industries include health care (Madison is home to American Family Insurance) and biotechnology start-ups tied to the university. In the early 1990s, rural Dane County was open to Republicans like Thompson. But even the rural areas have become bluer as Madison-area liberals move to the countryside. The 2nd is now a very Democratic district. Democratic presidential nominee John Kerry carried it 62%-37% in 2004, and Democrat Barack Obama won it 69%-30% in 2008.

The congresswoman from the 2nd District is Tammy Baldwin, a Democrat elected in 1998 and the first woman to represent Wisconsin in Congress. Baldwin grew up in Madison, where she was raised by her mother, a University of Wisconsin student when Tammy was born, and her maternal grandparents, a UW biochemist and the theater department's head costume designer. She graduated first in her class at Madison West High School and went on to Smith College and UW law school. In 1986, at age 24 and still in law school, she was elected to the Dane County Board of Supervisors. In 1992, she was elected to the Wisconsin Assembly, winning a heavily Democratic Madison seat. Six years later, when moderate Republican Scott Klug honored his promise to serve only four terms in the U.S. House, Baldwin got into the race, along with three other Democrats and six Republicans. As a woman who favored abortion rights, she was supported by EMILY's List, which helped raise about one-quarter of her $1.5 million campaign chest. As an openly gay woman, Baldwin had enthusiastic support from national gay and lesbian organizations, which also helped her raise money. With 86% of Democratic primary votes cast in Dane County, Baldwin won with 37% of the vote.

Republicans nominated former state Insurance Commissioner Jo Musser. Baldwin roused the enthusiasm of Madison liberals in a way not seen in years. She called for a single-payer health-insurance system and suggested that Musser was captive to insurance companies. Musser, a nurse who had founded the Madison Employers Health Care Alliance, argued that a single-payer system would reduce choices and create long waiting periods for elective surgery. Both sides were well financed. Dane County went 57%-42% for Baldwin, and she won the district 53%-47%. Having come out as a lesbian during her college years, Baldwin became the first openly homosexual non-incumbent to win a seat in the House. Democrat Barney Frank of Massachusetts, the other openly gay member of the House, revealed his sexual orientation after serving several terms. The vast majority of voters, Baldwin has said, care more about her positions on issues that affect their lives than about her sexual orientation.

True to her Madison constituents, she has a strongly liberal voting record, though she prefers to be called a progressive. Her driving issue is guaranteed health care for all Americans. She sponsored the Health Security for All Americans Act to guarantee universal coverage. With a seat on the Energy and Commerce Committee and on its Health Subcommittee, she has been a leader in urging additional federal support for embryonic-stem-cell research, some of which has been done at UW. With Republican cosponsors, she introduced a bill to encourage flexibility in how the states cover the uninsured. In 2007, the House passed her bill to expand breast and cervical-cancer screening for poor and uninsured women.

Baldwin has been a leader of the opposition to a proposed constitutional amendment to bar same-sex marriages. She joined a bipartisan initiative to bar workplace discrimination against gays, reinserting a previously dropped provision in the bill to include transsexuals. The provision threatened the bill's passage, and she eventually agreed to drop it. She also sought to broaden the definition of hate crimes to include people targeted because of gender, sexual orientation or disability. In 2008, she and Frank created the House Lesbian, Gay, Bisexual and Transgender Equality Caucus, starting with 52 members. Baldwin has faced discrimination, even as a member of Congress. In 2008, the Pentagon initially barred her life partner from traveling with her on a military flight to Europe, citing a rule that allowed only congressional spouses on such trips. Baldwin's partner was allowed on the plane only after Democratic House Speaker Nancy Pelosi intervened.

Baldwin was a staunch supporter of Hillary Clinton in the 2008 Democratic primary, standing by Clinton until she dropped out of the race even though Baldwin's district had backed Obama overwhelmingly in the primary. After gay-rights groups criticized Obama for his choice of evangelical Pastor Rick Warren of the Saddleback Church to deliver the invocation at his inauguration, Obama named Baldwin one of 16 honorary co-chairs of the ceremony.

Baldwin has been an outspoken opponent of the Iraq War, and she was one of only 13 House members to vote against the defense budget for fiscal 2008. She signed on as a cosponsor of Ohio Democrat Dennis Kucinich's 2007 resolution to impeach former Vice President Dick Cheney for "deceptive actions leading up to the Iraq war, the revelation of the identity of a covert agent for political retaliation, and the illegal wiretapping of American citizens." In 2008, Baldwin sponsored a bill that would end the railroad industry's exemption from antitrust law. She has many farmers and paper manufacturers in her district who rely on shipping and have been hurt by what she calls the "antiquated railroad antitrust exemption that has allowed for skyrocketing prices and declining service for rail shippers." The bill passed the Judiciary Committee by a voice vote despite strong industry opposition but was never put to a vote by the full House. *National Journal* ranked her as one of the most liberal House members in 2008.

In 2000, in her first re-election campaign, Baldwin faced Republican John Sharpless, whose ads in UW newspapers called him "our professor, our congressman, our voice." He accused Baldwin of accomplishing little, ignoring farmers and raising most of her campaign money out of state. Baldwin won by only 51%-49%, a smaller margin than her first House election and a reversal of the usual pattern. Since then, she has secured the seat with victories of 63% or more. In 2008, she beat computer programmer Scott Theron 69%-31%.

THIRD DISTRICT

Ron Kind (D)

Elected 1996, 7th term; b. March 16, 1963, La Crosse; home, La Crosse; Harvard U., B.A. 1985, London Schl. of Econ., 1986, U. of MN, J.D. 1990; Lutheran; married (Tawni); 2 children.

Professional Career: Practicing atty., 1990–92; Asst. st. prosecutor, La Crosse Cnty., 1992–96.

DC Office: 1406 LHOB, 20515, 202-225-5506; Fax: 202-225-5739; Web site: www.house.gov/kind.

State Offices: Eau Claire, 715-831-9214; La Crosse, 608-782-2558.

Committees: *Natural Resources* (20th of 29 D): Insular Affairs, Oceans & Wildlife; National Parks, Forests & Public Lands. *Ways & Means* (14th of 26 D): Health; Oversight; Social Security.

Group Ratings

	ADA	ACLU	AFS	LCV	ITIC	NTU	COC	ACU	CFG	FRC
2008	80	91	100	100	100	16	72	8	10	5
2007	90	—	100	95	—	8	60	12	16	—

National Journal Ratings

	2007 LIB	—	2007 CONS		2008 LIB	—	2008 CONS
Economic	60%	—	40%		54%	—	45%
Social	66%	—	33%		62%	—	34%
Foreign	63%	—	35%		70%	—	25%
Composite	64%	—	37%		64%	—	36%

Key Votes of the 110th Congress

1. Increase minimum wage	Y	5. Share immigration data	Y	9. Withdraw troops 8/08	Y
2. Expand SCHIP	Y	6. Foreign aid abortion ban	N	10. No operations in Iran	Y
3. Raise CAFE standards	Y	7. Ban gay bias in workplace	Y	11. Free trade with Peru	Y
4. Bail out financial markets	Y	8. Repeal D.C. gun law	Y	12. Overhaul FISA	Y

Election Results

2008 general	Ron Kind (D)	225,208	(63%)	($916,105)
	Paul Stark (R)	122,760	(34%)	($59,942)
	Kevin Barrett (Lib)	8,236	(2%)	
2008 primary	Ron Kind (D)	unopposed		

Prior Winning Percentages: 2006 (65%); 2004 (56%); 2002 (63%); 2000 (64%); 1998 (71%); 1996 (52%)

Population		Race/Ethnicity		Work	
Pop. 2007:	704,479	White:	95.2%	Private:	77.6%
Change since 2000:	Up 5.1%	Black:	0.8%	Government:	13.1%
Urban:	43.1%	Hispanic:	1.3%	Self-employed:	8.8%
Rural:	56.9%	Asian:	1.4%	Blue collar:	27.8%
Area size:	13,849 sq. mi.	Native Am.:	0.6%	White collar:	53.9%
Age		Hawaiian:	0.0%	Khaki collar:	0.1%
Median age:	36.7 yrs.	Two+ races:	0.7%	Other:	18.1%
More than 65 yrs:	13.3%	*Ancestry*		Median income:	$47,801
Less than 18 yrs:	23.3%	German:	34.1%	Median home value:	$142,400
Education		Norwegian:	14.2%	Poverty:	11.3%
H.S. grad:	89.0%	Irish:	9.4%	**Military Veterans**	
College grad:	22.5%			% of Pop:	11.0%
Grad degree:	7.1%				

On the rolling land of western Wisconsin, in the knobby hills just east of the Mississippi River, is some of the most beautiful river landscape in the country. This is where author Laura Ingalls Wilder's family built their little house in the big woods in the 1870s, before the first railroad came steaming up the narrow floodplain alongside the Mississippi River. Today, it is hard to imagine the big woods. The trees have long since been cut down, and the hillsides are covered with grass grazed by placid

2008 Presidential Vote		
Obama (D)	213,211	(58%)
McCain (R)	150,618	(41%)
2004 Presidential Vote		
Kerry (D)	192,297	(51%)
Bush (R)	178,367	(48%)
Cook Partisan Voting Index:	D+4	

dairy cattle. Where the pioneers tried to scratch out diversified crops, later generations of farmers created America's premier dairy region, producing milk, butter and especially cheese. Some Amish communities from Pennsylvania have relocated here in recent years because land is cheaper. But since 1980, the area has been in flux. More than half of family dairy farmers have gone out of business. Cows have become more productive, and demand for milk has decreased. Wisconsin has also had trouble competing against the European Common Market's subsidized cheese and butter, and more recently, with products from California's large-scale agribusiness. But other businesses have done better; Dodgeville, in Iowa County (which is not on the Iowa border), is the headquarters of Lands' End, the catalog retailer that was sold to Sears Roebuck. In the 1980s, many communities here lost population, but there has been growth since 1990. The most rapid growth in the state has been in commuter-oriented St. Croix County, part of the Minneapolis-St. Paul metro area.

The 3rd Congressional District of Wisconsin follows the Mississippi from the border with Illinois north to St. Croix County, just east of St. Paul, covering the western edge of the state. The district's two largest cities are Eau Claire, home to home-improvement giant Menards, and La Crosse. This is the nation's No. 2 dairy district, with 6,000 dairy farms, but it is very different in character from the No. 1 district, California's 21st, which has more dairy cows concentrated on just 400 farms. It was settled largely by German and Scandinavian immigrants, and it once consistently voted for Wisconsin's La Follette progressives. More recently, the district has leaned Democratic. Western Wisconsin was the one segment of rural America where Democratic presidential nominees Al Gore and John Kerry ran even with historic Democratic percentages, which was vital to the narrow victory that each won in this state. It produced solid victories for other Democrats, including Gov. Jim Doyle in 2002 and 2006 and Sen. Russ Feingold in 2004. Democratic presidential nominee Barack Obama carried the district 58%-41%, winning in every county except St. Croix.

The congressman from the 3rd District is Ron Kind, a Democrat elected in 1996. He grew up in a large family in La Crosse, the son of a telephone repairman and a secretary in the local schools. He went to Harvard University on a scholarship and played quarterback. He worked as a summer intern for Democratic Sen. William Proxmire, doing research for Proxmire's Golden Fleece awards pointing out wasteful government spending. Kind attended the London School of Economics and the University of Minnesota's law school, practiced law in a large firm in Milwaukee, then returned home to La Crosse to work as an assistant prosecutor on rape and sexual-abuse cases. Kind started running for Congress soon after moderate Republican Steve Gunderson announced in 1994 that he would not seek re-election. Former state Sen. Jim Harsdorf won the Republican primary and made a hard-edged case for a balanced budget and for Republican Gov. Tommy Thompson's "Wisconsin Works" welfare-reform program. Kind presented his own balanced-budget proposal and urged reform of the campaign-finance system. Kind won, 52%-48%.

In the House, Kind has compiled a moderate voting record. With dairy farming prominent in his district, he is vitally interested in issues affecting farmers. In 2007, he joined with conservative deficit hawks and suburban and urban Democrats in an attempt to add provisions to the farm bill that would have changed federal policy for agricultural subsidies and provided more funds for land conservation and school nutrition. "For too long, we've had large taxpayer subsidies going to a few very large farming entities to the disadvantage of family farmers," Kind said. "It ultimately distorts the marketplace and distorts trade policy, which also hurts agriculture." Although his district receives more farm subsidies than most others, he said that the vast majority of producers he represents don't get huge agriculture subsidies because they're not large agribusinesses. Kind won 200 votes for similar provisions in the 2002 farm bill, including support from then-Minority Whip Nancy Pelosi, but this time around, the Democratic leadership was worried about angering farmers' groups in rural swing districts and refused to allow a vote by the full House. The plan died in committee. Kind voted against the final version of the farm bill, calling it a "nightmare." He said that congressional negotiators "managed to avoid every opportunity to reform wasteful, outdated subsidies while piling on additional layers of unnecessary spending."

Kind is a co-founder of the Upper Mississippi River Congressional Task Force. His own home is on the river and was flooded in 2001. With members from Illinois and Iowa, he got the House to pass a bill to establish a water-quality monitoring network in the Upper Mississippi River Basin. As co-chairman of the centrist New Democrat Coalition, he said he wanted to expand access to broadband in rural areas and make his area "the Silicon Valley of agricultural research." On foreign policy, Kind voted for the use of force in Iraq in 2002, for which he was criticized by liberals back home. Like many other lawmakers, he has since become critical of Bush-era policies in Iraq. He and Republican Paul Ryan of Wisconsin co-chair the Congressional Sportsmen's Caucus, a group of pro-conservation hunters who make up the largest bipartisan caucus in the House.

In 2004, Kind had his first credible challenger, Republican state Sen. Dale Schultz, a moderate in the Wisconsin Legislature for more than two decades. Schultz ran with an unlikely Republican theme, criticizing Kind as a free trader who had sent jobs overseas. Kind affirmed his support for trade agreements, but he criticized the Bush administration for its failure to enforce their labor and environmental protection terms. Schultz backed Bush's handling of the war and promised to do more for agriculture, while Kind called for more support for education. Kind won, 56%-43%. He did not have a serious challenger in 2008 and won with 63% of the vote.

FOURTH DISTRICT

Gwen Moore (D)

Elected 2004, 3rd term; b. April 18, 1951, Racine; home, Milwaukee; Marquette U., B.A. 1978; Baptist; single; 3 children.

Elected Office: WI Assembly, 1989–92; WI Senate, 1992–2004; Senate pres. pro tem, 1997–98.

Professional Career: Housing and urban dev. specialist, 1985–89.

DC Office: 1239 LHOB, 20515, 202-225-4572; Fax: 202-225-8135; Web site: www.house.gov/gwenmoore.

State Offices: Milwaukee, 414-297-1140.

Committees: *Budget* (22nd of 24 D). *Financial Services* (23rd of 42 D): Capital Markets, Insurance & Government Sponsored Enterprises; International Monetary Policy & Trade; Oversight & Investigations.

Group Ratings

	ADA	ACLU	AFS	LCV	ITIC	NTU	COC	ACU	CFG	FRC
2008	95	100	100	100	57	16	50	4	7	5
2007	95	—	100	95	—	5	53	0	7	—

National Journal Ratings

	2007 LIB	—	2007 CONS		2008 LIB	—	2008 CONS
Economic	82%	—	0%		80%	—	19%
Social	92%	—	0%		82%	—	0%
Foreign	96%	—	0%		85%	—	8%
Composite	95%	—	5%		87%	—	13%

Key Votes of the 110th Congress

1. Increase minimum wage	Y	5. Share immigration data	N	9. Withdraw troops 8/08	Y
2. Expand SCHIP	Y	6. Foreign aid abortion ban	N	10. No operations in Iran	Y
3. Raise CAFE standards	Y	7. Ban gay bias in workplace	Y	11. Free trade with Peru	*
4. Bail out financial markets	Y	8. Repeal D.C. gun law	N	12. Overhaul FISA	N

Election Results

2008 general	Gwen Moore (D)	222,728	(88%)	($559,761)
	Michael LaForest (I)	29,282	(12%)	
2008 primary	Gwen Moore (D)	18,342	(96%)	

Prior Winning Percentages: 2006 (71%); 2004 (70%)

Population		Race/Ethnicity		Work	
Pop. 2007:	660,493	White:	45.8%	Private:	84.0%
Change since 2000:	Down 1.5%	Black:	34.2%	Government:	12.3%
Urban:	100.0%	Hispanic:	14.5%	Self-employed:	3.6%
Rural:	0.0%	Asian:	3.1%	Blue collar:	25.7%
Area size:	113 sq. mi.	Native Am.:	0.7%	White collar:	53.4%
		Hawaiian:	0.1%	Khaki collar:	0.0%
Age		Two+ races:	1.4%	Other:	20.9%
Median age:	32.8 yrs.	*Ancestry*		Median income:	$36,116
More than 65 yrs:	9.9%	German:	18.9%	Median home value:	$137,300
Less than 18 yrs:	27.9%	Polish:	8.7%	Poverty:	23.6%
Education		Irish:	5.7%	**Military Veterans**	
H.S. grad:	80.2%			% of Pop:	8.3%
College grad:	19.3%				
Grad degree:	6.3%				

Milwaukee is America's most German city, with an ethnic heritage noticeable not just in the names of its beers and its old German restaurants but in the solidness of its houses and the orderliness of its streets. Until World War I made this German character seem un-American, German was spoken on the streets and read in city newspapers, German beer was produced in dozens of breweries, and German cultural traditions lived on in churches, union halls and parlors. The world's largest four-sided

2008 Presidential Vote
Obama (D)	234,468	(75%)
McCain (R)	73,447	(24%)

2004 Presidential Vote
Kerry (D)	219,636	(70%)
Bush (R)	94,090	(30%)

Cook Partisan Voting Index: D + 22

clock, nearly twice the size of London's Big Ben, rises above the Allen-Bradley factory, looking out over the industrial city. It is an apt symbol, a piece of precision engineering in this high-skill manufacturing town, with its skyline of smokestacks and church steeples—the closest thing in America to the German factory cities Milwaukee's early immigrants once knew well. The city has led the nation in beer brewing, industrial control equipment, mining gear, cranes and independent foundries. Harley-Davidson began manufacturing on the West Side a century ago. The city had large and efficiently run factories that paid good wages to highly-skilled and well-disciplined workers.

But like other Rust Belt cities, Milwaukee has lost its share of plants over the past three decades. It hemorrhaged population in the 1990s, though it has finally stopped shrinking, thanks in part to a rapidly expanding Hispanic population, which grew to more than 85,000 in 2007. For the most part, the city has embraced its Latinos. A chorizo sausage now competes against the bratwurst, Polish sausage and Italian sausage mascots during the famous Sausage Race at Milwaukee Brewers baseball games, and plush chorizo dolls outsell the other mascots at stadium stores. Many Latinos have settled in the old immigrant neighborhoods of the city's south side. The west side and north side are home to many of the city's African-American neighborhoods, such as Sherman Park and Bronzeville, home to America's Black Holocaust Museum. Though some neighborhoods are beset by crime and drug use, most of Milwaukee is solid, and parts of it are making a comeback, with redevelopment projects near Marquette University, in the historic Third Ward, and along Lake Michigan and the Milwaukee River.

The 4th Congressional District of Wisconsin covers the entire city of Milwaukee and a few of its working-class suburbs—St. Francis, Cudahy and South Milwaukee on Lake Michigan, West Milwaukee, and part of West Allis.

The congresswoman from the 4th District is Gwen Moore, a Democrat elected in 2004 and Wisconsin's first African-American member of Congress. Moore was born in Racine, the eighth of nine children, and raised on the north side of Milwaukee. As an 18-year-old college freshman, she became a single mother who relied on welfare to help support her daughter. She graduated from Marquette University and worked as a housing and urban development specialist. Moore said she got active in politics when a rent-to-own center repossessed her washer and dryer even though she had paid three times their value in exorbitant interest rates. She led an effort to establish a community credit union. She was elected to the state House in 1988 and to the state Senate in 1992, making her the state's first black woman senator.

In 2003, when 4th District Democrat Gerald Kleczka announced that he was retiring after 20 years, Moore became the early front-runner, but she had serious competition in the September 2004 Democratic primary from two political veterans, state Sen. Tim Carpenter and former state party Chairman Matt Flynn, both white. The candidates agreed on most issues: All three supported abortion rights, focused on jobs and economic concerns, and called for eliminating the Bush administration's tax cuts for people with incomes exceeding $200,000 a year. In the absence of significant ideological clashes, the fallout from Milwaukee's mayoral primary earlier that year played a role. The nonpartisan election had pitted former Rep. Tom Barrett, who is white, against acting Mayor Marvin Pratt, who wanted to become the city's first black elected mayor. Barrett won, but the vote divided along racial lines and caused hard feelings in the black community.

Moore took advantage of the energized black voter base, and she leveraged financial support from national women's organizations, teachers' unions and other liberal groups. Flynn had chaired Democratic presidential candidate John Kerry's campaign in Wisconsin, was endorsed by Kleczka, and boasted that he had backed Pratt for mayor. But he was damaged politically by his work as general counsel for the local Roman Catholic archdiocese in a priest sex-abuse scandal. Carpenter was the only openly gay member of the Senate and had the support of national gay-rights groups. Moore won 64% of the vote to 25% for Flynn and 10% for Carpenter. Flynn won the five aldermanic districts and 49% of the vote on the south side, but Moore won about 80% of the vote north of Interstate 94. In the general election, Republican Gerald Boyle tried to win over Democrats disaffected with Moore. But he got no national money, and Moore won, 70%-28%.

Some of the luster of Moore's victory was diminished in January 2005, when her 25-year-old son was one of five Kerry campaign employees charged with slashing the tires of more than 20 vans rented by Republicans to drive voters and monitors to the polls on Election Day. Her son was sentenced to four months in jail for misdemeanor property damage.

Moore has a solidly liberal voting record. She sponsored a bill to provide funding to help low-income workers buy cars to increase their access to better jobs. In 2005, the House incorporated provisions of her SHIELD Act into the reauthorization of the Violence Against Women Act that would protect the identity of domestic-violence victims who receive homeless assistance. As a member of the "Out of Iraq" caucus, Moore considered voting against the 2007 war funding bill, but at the urging of Appropriations Chairman David Obey, D-Wis., she voted for it as well as for a timetable for withdrawing U.S. troops.

Moore has developed an interest in foreign relations and defense but has said she wants to focus on a few issues or "you have little or no credibility, because you're just all over the place." In 2006, she was arrested along with other members of the Congressional Black Caucus at the Sudanese Embassy, where they were protesting genocide in Darfur. She was one of only five House members to vote against a resolution expressing congressional support for Israel during its 2008 military actions in the Gaza Strip. She called Israel a "strong ally" but expressed concern about civilian Palestinian deaths and called for renewed diplomatic efforts in the region. In November 2008, she was elected vice chairwoman of the Congressional Caucus for Women's Issues, a group comprised of women serving in the House. And she was the first representative from Wisconsin to endorse Democratic presidential candidate Barack Obama.

Moore, who said she is learning Spanish to help her reach out to the Hispanic population on Milwaukee's south side, appears well established in her district and was re-elected with 88% of the vote in 2008.

FIFTH DISTRICT

Jim Sensenbrenner (R)

Elected 1978, 16th term; b. June 14, 1943, Chicago, IL; home, Menomonee Falls; Stanford U., A.B. 1965, U. of WI, J.D. 1968; Episcopalian; married (Cheryl); 2 children.

Elected Office: WI Assembly, 1968–74; WI Senate, 1974–78.

Professional Career: Practicing atty., 1968–69; Staff asst., U.S. Rep. Arthur Younger, 1965.

DC Office: 2449 RHOB, 20515, 202-225-5101; Fax: 202-225-3190; Web site: www.house.gov/sensenbrenner.

State Offices: Brookfield, 262-784-1111.

Committees: *Judiciary* (2nd of 16 R): Constitution, Civil Rights & Civil Liberties (RMM); Courts & Competition Policy. *Science & Technology* (2nd of 17 R): Space & Aeronautics.

Group Ratings

	ADA	ACLU	AFS	LCV	ITIC	NTU	COC	ACU	CFG	FRC
2008	10	18	0	8	57	87	67	96	91	100
2007	0	—	0	20	—	91	75	96	91	—

National Journal Ratings

	2007 LIB	—	2007 CONS		2008 LIB	—	2008 CONS
Economic	11%	—	88%		18%	—	81%
Social	9%	—	85%		0%	—	91%
Foreign	40%	—	60%		31%	—	67%
Composite	21%	—	79%		18%	—	82%

Key Votes of the 110th Congress

1. Increase minimum wage	N	5. Share immigration data	Y	9. Withdraw troops 8/08	N
2. Expand SCHIP	N	6. Foreign aid abortion ban	Y	10. No operations in Iran	N
3. Raise CAFE standards	N	7. Ban gay bias in workplace	N	11. Free trade with Peru	Y
4. Bail out financial markets	N	8. Repeal D.C. gun law	Y	12. Overhaul FISA	Y

Election Results

2008 general	Jim Sensenbrenner (R)	275,271	(80%)	($567,709)
	Robert Raymond (I)	69,715	(20%)	
2008 primary	Jim Sensenbrenner (R)	47,144	(78%)	
	Jim Burkee (R)	13,078	(22%)	

Prior Winning Percentages: 2006 (62%); 2004 (67%); 2002 (87%); 2000 (74%); 1998 (91%); 1996 (74%); 1994 (100%); 1992 (70%); 1990 (100%); 1988 (75%); 1986 (78%); 1984 (73%); 1982 (100%); 1980 (78%); 1978 (61%)

Population		Race/Ethnicity		Work	
Pop. 2007:	702,236	White:	91.6%	Private:	85.6%
Change since 2000:	Up 4.7%	Black:	2.1%	Government:	9.0%
Urban:	84.9%	Hispanic:	2.9%	Self-employed:	5.3%
Rural:	15.1%	Asian:	2.1%	Blue collar:	19.4%
Area size:	1,301 sq. mi.	Native Am.:	0.2%	White collar:	68.5%
Age		Hawaiian:	0.0%	Khaki collar:	0.0%
Median age:	40.9 yrs.	Two+ races:	1.0%	Other:	12.1%
More than 65 yrs:	14.2%	*Ancestry*		Median income:	$66,889
Less than 18 yrs:	23.5%	German:	36.8%	Median home value:	$232,600
Education		Irish:	10.0%	Poverty:	4.9%
H.S. grad:	93.2%	Polish:	8.6%	**Military Veterans**	
College grad:	38.4%			% of Pop:	10.1%
Grad degree:	13.4%				

For decades, the orderly, heavily German-American factory city of Milwaukee has been spreading slowly, mostly west and north, into Wisconsin dairy country. There are high-income enclaves here, like close-in Elm Grove and exurban Oconomowoc, halfway to Madison and tucked in around numerous lakes. There is office development in Brookfield, and subdivisions spread out in Mequon and Menomonee Falls and farther, reaching small towns with roots in the

2008 Presidential Vote		
McCain (R)	243,597	(58%)
Obama (D)	174,174	(41%)
2004 Presidential Vote		
Bush (R)	265,537	(63%)
Kerry (D)	151,968	(36%)
Cook Partisan Voting Index:	R+12	

19th century. This is comfortable but not fancy territory, and the economy is still based heavily on skilled manufacturing. Not far from Milwaukee are Port Washington, with Allen-Edmonds shoes; West Bend, with West Bend kitchen appliances; and Pewaukee, with Harken sailboat hardware. Closer to Milwaukee are tonier, liberal suburbs along Lake Michigan, many with sizeable Jewish populations—Shorewood, Whitefish Bay, and Fox Point. In April 2006, Shorewood and Whitefish Bay voters approved referenda calling for the withdrawal of U.S. troops from Iraq.

The 5th Congressional District of Wisconsin includes most of the western, northwestern and northern suburbs of Milwaukee. Among them are the close-in lakefront suburbs in Milwaukee County and the suburbs in Ozaukee County north of Milwaukee and in Washington County to the west. It also takes in most of the Milwaukee County suburbs of Wauwatosa and West Allis, most of the northern three tiers of townships in Waukesha County just to the west, and a part of Jefferson County farther west. Farmland in Ozaukee and Washington counties has dropped by one-third since the 1970s. This is by far the most Republican district in the state. It voted 62% and 63% for George W. Bush in 2000 and 2004, respectively. And it voted 58% for GOP nominee John McCain in 2008. It was the only district in Wisconsin that he carried.

The congressman from the 5th District is Jim Sensenbrenner, a Republican first elected in 1978. Sensenbrenner grew up in the Milwaukee area, with strong Wisconsin roots. His great-grandfather was a founder of Kimberly-Clark who invented the sanitary napkin, and Sensenbrenner is an heir to the paper and cellulose fortune. He reports a net worth of over $10 million, and on top of that, he won $250,000 in the District of Columbia lottery after buying two tickets while picking up some beer for an office party at a Capitol Hill liquor store. He graduated from Stanford University and the University of Wisconsin law school and has spent most of his adult life in politics. He served briefly as a staffer in the U.S. House, then was elected to the Wisconsin Assembly in 1968 and to the Wisconsin Senate in 1974. When Republican Rep. Bob Kasten ran for governor, Sensenbrenner ran in this district and won the Republican primary by 589 votes.

Sensenbrenner has a rough and often partisan edge, but his voting record has leaned toward the center, and he prides himself on his legislative skills. He has long been a stickler on ethics and was one of the first to urge that Congress apply to itself the same laws it imposes on the rest of the country. In 2001, when Republicans were still in power, he became chairman of the Judiciary Committee. He sought to protect the committee's jurisdiction from raids by other House committees, notably Energy and Commerce. And he was proud of enacting the first congressional authorization of the Department of Justice in many years, citing the vital role that it gave his committee in improving oversight of the department. "I am a hawk on oversight," he said. "I don't back down because the president is in my party." After the September 11 attacks, he pressed for a thorough congressional review of Attorney General John Ashcroft's proposal for beefed-up law-enforcement investigative powers. Concerned about possible violations of civil liberties, he insisted on a sunset provision for the 2001 USA PATRIOT Act that would let it expire in four years.

Sensenbrenner had decided by 2005 that his concerns about civil liberties infringements in the PATRIOT Act had been addressed, and pushed to make most of the law permanent. Some questionable parliamentary maneuvering during one of his hearings on renewal led Democrats to file an unusual resolution condemning Sensenbrenner for alleged abuse of power. The House rejected the resolution on a party-line vote, and Sensenbrenner refused demands for an apology. After a difficult conference committee with the Senate, he won an extension of the PATRIOT Act for the Bush administration. But Sensenbrenner had differences with Attorney General Alberto Gonzalez over the scope of the domestic surveillance program and demanded steps to protect "the freedoms we cherish."

Sensenbrenner worked steadily for years to pass some major bills. One of them was the bankruptcy bill, which passed in 2005 after being held up for years by a Democratic provision preventing abortion protesters from filing for bankruptcy to avoid fines and damages if convicted of violence against abortion clinics. Sensenbrenner has backed limitations in tort law on class-action, medical-malpractice, and asbestos-liability suits and has sought to increase penalties for frivolous lawsuits. But he has not always followed the party line. In 2003, he said he saw no need to amend the Constitution to ban same-sex marriages. In 2004, after the Massachusetts Supreme Judicial Court ruled that such marriages were allowed by the state's constitution, the Republican leadership bypassed the committee and brought their amendment to the floor directly, but it fell well short of the required two-thirds majority vote.

Another of Sensenbrenner's major efforts was immigration. In 2004, he successfully added to the intelligence reorganization bill provisions setting national standards for driver's licenses; among other things, they denied licenses to illegal immigrants, prohibited the use of Mexican *matricula consular* cards for identification, tightened standards for asylum, and overrode state laws and regulations blocking border barriers. When Sensenbrenner objected to the conference report with the Senate, GOP Speaker Dennis Hastert promised that the immigration provisions would come to the floor in 2005. That year, the House approved Sensenbrenner's immigration bill 261-161, and it became law. After the House later passed additional measures to penalize illegal aliens, Sensenbrenner criticized the Senate-passed immigration bill as "amnesty" and said that President George W. Bush had failed to address conservative demands to toughen border enforcement. The two chambers never agreed on a comprehensive bill.

In 2006, Sensenbrenner spearheaded the 25-year extension of the Voting Rights Act. He had led negotiations on the 1982 renewal of the bill as well. He counts among his most cherished keepsakes the pens used by President Ronald Reagan and by President Bush to sign the two reauthorizations. In September 2006, Sensenbrenner won House passage of the bill for presidential authority to conduct warrantless surveillance, but it died in the Senate.

The House Republicans' six-year term limit for senior committee members forced Sensenbrenner to give up the Judiciary gavel in January 2007. In March, Minority Leader John Boehner of Ohio named Sensenbrenner the ranking Republican on the Select Committee on Energy Independence and Global Warming. A global-warming skeptic, Sensenbrenner had voted against the creation of the panel, saying it was nothing more than a publicity stunt, but he promised to participate in the debate. In 2008, he sponsored a bill to bolster research and development of hybrid-fuel utility and delivery trucks.

Sensenbrenner has been re-elected easily every two years. In 2008, he faced an odd "tag-team" when two political-science professors decided to run against him, one in the Republican primary and one in the general election as a Democrat. The two planned to make joint appearances, share a campaign website and even share fundraising, but the Democrat backed out of the race. Sensenbrenner easily bested his Republican challenger, 78%-22%, but the race put enough of a scare into him that he skipped the Republican National Convention in Minnesota to campaign at home. He easily beat an independent candidate in the general election.

SIXTH DISTRICT

Tom Petri (R)

Elected April 1979, 15th full term; b. May 28, 1940, Marinette; home, Fond du Lac; Harvard U., B.A. 1962, J.D. 1965; Lutheran; married (Anne); 1 child.

Elected Office: WI Senate, 1972–79.

Professional Career: Peace Corps, Somalia, 1966–67; Law clerk, Fed. Judge James Doyle, 1965–66; White House aide, 1969; Practicing atty., 1970–79.

DC Office: 2462 RHOB, 20515, 202-225-2476; Fax: 202-225-2356; Web site: www.house.gov/petri.

State Offices: Fond du Lac, 920-922-1180; Oshkosh, 920-231-6333.

Committees: *Education & Labor* (2nd of 19 R): Early Childhood, Elementary & Secondary Education. *Transportation & Infrastructure* (3rd of 30 R): Aviation (RMM); Highways & Transit; Railroads, Pipelines & Hazardous Materials.

Group Ratings

	ADA	ACLU	AFS	LCV	ITIC	NTU	COC	ACU	CFG	FRC
2008	40	27	14	38	57	72	72	80	79	100
2007	30	—	27	50	—	70	85	72	54	—

National Journal Ratings

	2007 LIB	—	2007 CONS		2008 LIB	—	2008 CONS
Economic	37%	—	63%		36%	—	64%
Social	27%	—	72%		20%	—	74%
Foreign	44%	—	55%		38%	—	61%
Composite	36%	—	64%		33%	—	68%

Key Votes of the 110th Congress

1. Increase minimum wage	Y	5. Share immigration data	Y	9. Withdraw troops 8/08	N
2. Expand SCHIP	Y	6. Foreign aid abortion ban	Y	10. No operations in Iran	N
3. Raise CAFE standards	N	7. Ban gay bias in workplace	N	11. Free trade with Peru	Y
4. Bail out financial markets	N	8. Repeal D.C. gun law	Y	12. Overhaul FISA	Y

Election Results

2008 general	Tom Petri (R) 221,875	(64%)	($1,271,787)
	Roger Kittelson (D) 126,090	(36%)	($17,207)
2008 primary	Tom Petri (R) .... unopposed		

Prior Winning Percentages: 2006 (100%); 2004 (67%); 2002 (100%); 2000 (65%); 1998 (93%); 1996 (73%); 1994 (100%); 1992 (53%); 1990 (100%); 1988 (74%); 1986 (97%); 1984 (76%); 1982 (65%); 1980 (59%); 1979 (50%)

Population		Race/Ethnicity		Work	
Pop. 2007:	687,107	White:	92.7%	Private:	83.4%
Change since 2000:	Up 2.5%	Black:	1.3%	Government:	10.7%
Urban:	60.7%	Hispanic:	3.1%	Self-employed:	5.7%
Rural:	39.3%	Asian:	1.6%	Blue collar:	32.5%
Area size:	5,816 sq. mi.	Native Am.:	0.4%	White collar:	50.2%
Age		Hawaiian:	0.0%	Khaki collar:	0.1%
Median age:	38.8 yrs.	Two+ races:	0.8%	Other:	17.2%
More than 65 yrs:	14.2%	*Ancestry*		Median income:	$49,370
Less than 18 yrs:	22.6%	German:	43.0%	Median home value:	$138,100
Education		Irish:	7.9%	Poverty:	8.4%
H.S. grad:	87.5%	Polish:	6.1%	**Military Veterans**	
College grad:	18.9%			% of Pop:	11.4%
Grad degree:	5.6%				

Central Wisconsin is solid country, a producer of basic commodities—milk, butter and cheese, Kleenex, Mercury outboard motors, and military trucks. This is where the rolling hills and prairies of southern Wisconsin begin to give way to the pine and hardwood forests and glacial lakes of the North Woods. Settled first by Yankee Protestants, it was one of the birthplaces of the Republican Party in February 1854, when a group of Whigs, Free Soilers and Democrats met in a small white schoolhouse in

2008 Presidential Vote

Obama (D) 181,198	(50%)
McCain (R).............................176,871	(49%)

2004 Presidential Vote

Bush (R).................................208,931	(56%)
Kerry (D)................................157,212	(43%)

Cook Partisan Voting Index: R+4

Ripon, Wis., and proclaimed themselves Republicans. (A similar gathering took place in Jackson, Mich., which also claims to be the birthplace of the party.) The party grew rapidly, winning a near majority in the U.S. House in that year's elections. The 1850s brought the first surge of German migration into the United States, and central Wisconsin was a favorite destination. They built the dairy farms and factory towns that seemed steadfastly prosperous, and they developed a manufacturing economy. The German influence is still felt. Sheboygan is the Bratwurst Capital of the World, though these days it's also home to more than 4,400 Asians, mostly Hmong, and 5,200 Hispanics. Fond du Lac County was the testing ground for former Republican Gov. Tommy Thompson's welfare-reform program. The county's welfare rolls, never high, fell to zero after the program began in 1994.

The 6th Congressional District is a slice of central Wisconsin from Lake Michigan to the Wisconsin River. In the 2000 census, it had the highest percentage of residents of German ancestry, 39%, in the nation. It includes Sheboygan and Manitowoc on Lake Michigan, Oshkosh and Fond du Lac on Lake Winnebago in the Fox River Valley, and the towns of Menasha and Kimberly, just outside Appleton. It also takes in five rural counties to the west and south. Oshkosh, the largest city in the district, is no longer the place where children's clothing maker OshKosh B'Gosh manufactures its products. But it is home to the Oshkosh Corporation, which employs more than 14,000 people worldwide and produces everything from dump trucks to military vehicles. Politically, this had been Republican territory since that first meeting in Ripon, but its GOP leanings have waned as the national party has become increasingly dominated by Southern conservatives. In 2008, the district voted narrowly for Democratic presidential nominee Barack Obama, 50%-49%. Traditionally, it has elected moderate Republicans who have come up with thoughtful and original policies. One was the late William Steiger, first elected to Congress in 1966, who hired a University of Wisconsin graduate student named Dick Cheney. Steiger's chief monuments were the all-volunteer military, the creation of the Occupational Safety and Health Administration, and one of the first efforts to cut capital-gains tax rates.

The congressman from the 6th District is Tom Petri (*PEE try*), a Republican first elected in the 1979 contest to succeed Steiger. Petri had spent his early years in Puerto Rico, where his father, a Navy pilot, was stationed. Petri's father died in World War II. His family moved to Fond du Lac, where, as a teenager, Petri was the host of a popular Wisconsin radio show called "Teen Time." Petri got both his undergraduate and law degrees from Harvard University, then was a Peace Corps volunteer in Somalia. In 1972, at age 32, he was elected to the state Senate. Two years later, he was the Republican nominee running against Democratic Sen. Gaylord Nelson. He walked across the state campaigning, but lost 62%-36%. When he ran for the House in 1979, Petri beat Republican Tommy Thompson, then a state legislator, in the primary 35%-19%; he won the special election with 50%.

Petri has a centrist voting record in the House. He long supported the Earned Income Tax Credit, a policy most closely associated with Democrats that guarantees a tax credit to low-wage earners. During the Clinton era, Petri called for expanding the EITC with a $1,000 tax credit per child. Congress adopted a similar plan, although it went along with President Bill Clinton's proposal for a $500 per child credit. Later, Petri focused on alleviating what he called the poverty trap: As low-income households increase their earnings, they become ineligible for the EITC and other federal benefits. In 2004, Petri joined the bipartisan call for a $500 grant to all newborn children, to be held in an investment account and used after age 18 for an education or a first home.

After the 2000 elections, Petri hoped to become chairman of the Education and the Workforce Committee—he was the most senior Republican on the committee—but his party's leadership passed over him and installed the fourth-most-senior Republican, John Boehner of Ohio, who went on to become the majority leader. Petri decried the "purge of moderate Republicans," and afterward, his voting record became even more moderate. Working with California Democrat George Miller in 2005, he sponsored a $1,000 increase in Pell college grants, to $5,050 a year. The same year, Petri was one of 12 House Republicans to vote against a proposed constitutional amendment to ban flag desecration, and in February 2007, he was one of 17 Republicans to oppose President George W. Bush's troop surge in Iraq. Also that year, Petri supported Democratic efforts to expand the State Children's Health Insurance Program and the Democrats' energy bill, which called for limits on greenhouse-gas emissions. In early 2008, while other Republicans were attacking Democrats for a year of a "do-nothing Congress," Petri was more generous, describing the past year to the *Sheboygan* as "more of a getting-oriented Congress."

From 1995 to 2006, Petri was chairman of the Highways and Transit Subcommittee—a key subcommittee of Transportation and Infrastructure—and he played a major role in highway and other transportation bills. In 2005, he argued for increases in transportation spending. In the subcommittee and the full committee, he pushed for a $375 billion bill, funded by a 5-cent gas-tax increase. He also pressed for ending the 5.2-cent lower tax on ethanol. One reason for the high spending was the need to propitiate donor states—those that got back less than 100% of their gas-tax revenues (they wanted at least 95 cents on the dollar)—and the states that got back more than they kicked in but objected to any cuts. Also stuffed in the bill were expensive special projects for individual members' districts. The Bush administration threatened to veto any tax increase, and Congress finally passed a $286 billion bill. Included were projects for Petri's district: $25 million for Sheboygan to link local centers with bicycle and pedestrian paths and $10 million to replace the Wisconsin Street Bridge in Oshkosh.

In 2006, after Democrats won control of the House, Petri was the most-senior member of the full Transportation and Infrastructure Committee and hoped to assume the ranking Republican slot. Once again, the leadership passed him over, this time for the more-partisan John Mica of Florida. "Maybe I'm missing something," Petri told the *Milwaukee Journal Sentinel*. "Sometimes I think you can be more effective by working with people." He became ranking Republican on the Aviation Subcommittee. Despite his setbacks in Washington, Petri has been re-elected easily and was among the few Republicans who ran without opposition in 2006. In 2008, Petri won with 64% of the vote, outperforming GOP nominee John McCain by 15 percentage points in the district.

SEVENTH DISTRICT

David Obey (D)

Elected April 1969, 20th full term; b. Oct. 3, 1938, Okmulgee, OK; home, Wausau; U. of WI, B.S. 1960, M.A., 1962; Catholic; married (Joan); 2 children.

Elected Office: WI Assembly, 1962–69.

Professional Career: Asst., family-run supper club & motel, 1962–68.

DC Office: 2314 RHOB, 20515, 202-225-3365; Web site: www.obey.house.gov.

State Offices: Superior, 715-398-4426; Wausau, 715-842-5606.

Committees: *Appropriations* (Chmn of 37 D): Labor, HHS, Education & Related Agencies (Chmn).

Group Ratings

	ADA	ACLU	AFS	LCV	ITIC	NTU	COC	ACU	CFG	FRC
2008	95	100	100	100	86	6	56	0	0	17
2007	100	—	100	90	—	3	50	0	6	—

National Journal Ratings

	2007 LIB	—	2007 CONS		2008 LIB	—	2008 CONS
Economic	82%	—	0%		81%	—	15%
Social	62%	—	37%		82%	—	0%
Foreign	86%	—	11%		92%	—	0%
Composite	80%	—	20%		90%	—	10%

Key Votes of the 110th Congress

1. Increase minimum wage	Y	5. Share immigration data	Y
2. Expand SCHIP	Y	6. Foreign aid abortion ban	N
3. Raise CAFE standards	Y	7. Ban gay bias in workplace	Y
4. Bail out financial markets	Y	8. Repeal D.C. gun law	*

9. Withdraw troops 8/08	Y
10. No operations in Iran	Y
11. Free trade with Peru	N
12. Overhaul FISA	N

Election Results

2008 general	David Obey (D)	212,666	(61%)	($1,560,229)
	Dan Mielke (R)	136,938	(39%)	($92,501)
2008 primary	David Obey (D)	25,100	(99%)	

Prior Winning Percentages: 2006 (62%); 2004 (86%); 2002 (64%); 2000 (63%); 1998 (61%); 1996 (57%); 1994 (54%); 1992 (64%); 1990 (62%); 1988 (62%); 1986 (62%); 1984 (61%); 1982 (68%); 1980 (65%); 1978 (62%); 1976 (73%); 1974 (71%); 1972 (63%); 1970 (68%); 1969 (52%)

Population		Race/Ethnicity		Work	
Pop. 2007:	681,238	White:	94.5%	Private:	79.4%
Change since 2000:	Up 1.6%	Black:	0.5%	Government:	11.8%
Urban:	42.0%	Hispanic:	1.1%	Self-employed:	8.4%
Rural:	58.0%	Asian:	1.6%	Blue collar:	30.8%
Area size:	19,391 sq. mi.	Native Am.:	1.4%	White collar:	51.5%
		Hawaiian:	0.0%	Khaki collar:	0.1%
Age		Two+ races:	0.9%	Other:	17.7%
Median age:	40.1 yrs.	*Ancestry*		Median income:	$45,409
More than 65 yrs:	15.6%	German:	33.6%	Median home value:	$127,400
Less than 18 yrs:	22.6%	Polish:	9.6%	Poverty:	10.3%
		Norwegian:	7.8%	**Military Veterans**	
Education				% of Pop:	12.2%
H.S. grad:	87.7%				
College grad:	18.6%				
Grad degree:	5.9%				

In the late 19th century, thousands of migrants traveled the rail lines radiating northwest from Chicago and Milwaukee to settle the northern reaches of Wisconsin, the most thickly settled land this far north in the United States and east of the Mississippi. What attracted them was not cropland—there are no industrial-size wheat farms as in the Red River Valley of North Dakota—but trees, iron and cows. This was one of America's largest virgin timberlands, and the river towns are still dotted

2008 Presidential Vote

Obama (D)	200,562	(56%)
McCain (R)	152,507	(42%)

2004 Presidential Vote

Kerry (D)	185,076	(50%)
Bush (R)	179,963	(49%)

Cook Partisan Voting Index: D + 3

with paper mills. Farther north, iron brought Finns and Italians to the port of Superior, Wis., next to Duluth, Minn., and to smaller towns on the chilly lake, like Bayfield near the Apostle Islands. The cleared forest lands became dairy farms. Dairy cattle, properly cared for, thrive in these northern uplands, and the sons of Wisconsin dairymen, many of them immigrants from Germany and Norway, moved their dairy herds even farther north towards Canada. Small cities grew, and some became home to big enterprises. Wausau has paper mills, Wisconsin Rapids has Stora Enso paper, and Stevens Point has Sentry Insurance; these three cities have continued to generate new businesses and jobs and have retained a highly skilled workforce. But the number of dairy farmers in the region is in sharp decline; some farmers have turned to potatoes, vegetables, cranberries and even ginseng. Wausau, which the 1980 census found to be the most ethnically homogeneous city in the nation, now has a sizeable immigrant community. Many Hmong refugees moved there in the 1980s, and as of 2007, 9% of the city's population was Asian.

This area makes up Wisconsin's 7th Congressional District, which stretches from Stevens Point in the south to Lake Superior in the north. The politics of northern Wisconsin and the 7th District have a rough-hewn quality, a lumberjack-populist flavor. Ancestrally Republican, the area favored the progressivism of the La Follettes. Today, the Superior and Stevens Point areas are heavily Democratic, though Wausau's Marathon County and many of the smaller counties have leaned Republican. The district was closely divided in the 2000 and 2004 presidential elections. Democrat Al Gore carried it 47.5%-46.8%, Democrat John Kerry 50.1%-48.7%. In 2008, Democratic nominee Barack Obama beat John McCain here 56%-42%, winning 18 of the 20 counties in the district.

The congressman from the 7th District is David Obey, a Democrat first elected in April 1969 and now the powerful chairman of the House Appropriations Committee. He is the third-most-senior member of the House and one of the most capable and strongly motivated legislators on either side of the aisle. And he certainly is among the most colorful when he's worked up over an issue, which is fairly frequently. Obey grew up in Wausau, where his father worked in a roofing factory. As a kid, he was expelled from Catholic school after punching a nun who had hit him. He started his young adulthood as a Republican but was turned off by the anticommunism scare tactics of Sen. Joe McCarthy of Wisconsin in the 1950s. He switched his support from Dwight Eisenhower to Adlai Stevenson. Obey graduated from the University of Wisconsin, studied Soviet politics for three years in graduate school, and in 1962, when he was 24 and before he'd finished his master's degree, was elected to the Wisconsin Assembly. When Melvin Laird resigned his House seat to become President Richard Nixon's Defense secretary, Obey won an upset victory in the April 1969 special election to succeed him.

Even as he has moved to the top of the seniority ladder, Obey has retained his eagerness to fight for what he believes in and continues to display abundant energy and leadership on a host of fronts. He is prickly and does not suffer fools gladly, though he can leaven his impact on others with humor. He has had his disappointments. He lost the Budget Committee chairmanship to Oklahoma's Jim Jones in 1980 by 121-116. In 1984, he wanted to become Democratic Caucus chairman, but backed off when it became clear that Missouri's Dick Gephardt had the votes. Even so, Obey became an informal leader of liberal Democrats. He supported House Speaker Nancy Pelosi's rise in the leadership, despite some friction with other Pelosi supporters, including California's George Miller and Pennsylvania's John Murtha.

Obey was inspired in politics by older New Deal Democrats and by the liberals who led the charge against the Vietnam War. He remains a true believer in traditional liberalism, in Keynesian economics and in economic redistribution. He thinks that government should provide economic security, create jobs and build infrastructure through public investment, that it should control health-care costs and guarantee coverage and a choice of providers. During the years when Democrat Bill Clinton was president, he vocally opposed the North American Free Trade Agreement. When the president backed away from universal health-care coverage in 1994, Obey said "then I will walk away from the Clinton health care plan" and supported his real preference, a single-payer system. He was one of Clinton's harshest critics when the president accepted the congressional Republican majority's goal of a balanced budget within seven years. Obey also breaks with Democratic orthodoxy on abortion, having voted for limits on the procedure, though he says he is not for abolishing abortion rights. When former La Crosse Archbishop Raymond Burke admonished Catholic officeholders who hadn't sought to outlaw abortion, Obey wrote in the Jesuit publication *America*, "While I detest abortion and agree with Catholic teaching that in most instances it is morally wrong, I decline to force my views into laws that, if adopted, would be unenforceable and would tear this society apart." As a representative of a district chock-full of North Woods hunters, he also opposes gun control.

Obey is above all an appropriator and takes some justifiable pride in his skill at this work. He first got his seat on Appropriations in August 1969, when he was just 30. He became chairman in March 1994, after the death of William Natcher of Kentucky. He was the youngest person to hold the post since James Good of Iowa did in 1919, and he won the job over the more-senior Neal Smith of Iowa. Smith had the support of the "cardinals," as the powerful Appropriations subcommittee chairmen are known, but Obey had more support from non-committee liberals and less-senior members. He won the vote in the Democratic Caucus 152-106. Obey showed a determination to get things done on time—which is not always how appropriating works. For years, much of his work was on the Foreign Operations Subcommittee, which he chaired from 1985 to 1995. This panel handles small sums of money but deals with some sensitive issues, and it was often rocked by disputes over aid to the Nicaraguan Contras, the pace of negotiations in the Middle East, and the treatment of the liberated nations of Eastern Europe. Obey has not always gotten his way, but in each case he tried to move appropriations bills forward in an orderly manner. He passed separate foreign-operations appropriation bills nine out of 10 years, something that had been accomplished only twice in 10 years by his predecessors. Similarly, when Obey became chairman of the full committee in 1994, all 13 appropriations bills were signed into law prior to the beginning of the new fiscal year, the first time in 47 years that that had happened.

Unlike most other committees, Appropriations runs on bipartisanship. There may be partisan votes on alternative bills, but the subcommittees and the full committee tend to come to consensus on how to spend the amounts they are allocated by the budget resolution. During the 12 years of Republican control of the House, Obey worked relatively amicably with Chairman Bob Livingston of Louisiana from 1995 to 1999 and with Chairman Bill Young of Florida from 1999 to 2005. His relationship with Republican Jerry Lewis of California, who was the chairman from 2005 to 2007 and is now the ranking minority member, is not as warm. When Lewis reduced the number of subcommittees from 13 to 10 in 2005, Obey complained that Democrats had been frozen out of the process: "The result of this is you have not seen power this centralized since the days of Czar Cannon." In June 2008, as gas prices were skyrocketing, Lewis and other Republicans pushed to reopen the issue of lifting the ban on offshore drilling. When Obey and other Democrats refused to allow hearings on the topic, Lewis took them by surprise, attempting to steer an Appropriations meeting scheduled to discuss other issues to a vote on drilling. Obey exploded and halted all work on appropriations bills for the rest of the session. Lewis sent an olive branch in July, offering to drop the issue, but Obey wouldn't budge. Without appropriations bills, the House had to adopt a special resolution to keep money flowing to the government for the rest of the year.

Obey is not one of the appropriators notorious for lavishing earmarks on their districts, though he has supported some. In 2007, he attached funding for Wisconsin's SeniorCare prescription-drug program to an Iraq War spending bill after federal officials decided to end the program and move senior citizens to the national Medicare plan. The maneuver saved the state program.

The practice of earmarking funds became vastly more common during the years when Republicans held a majority in the House, and as an appropriator who did relatively little earmarking in support of his own district's projects, Obey wasn't averse to reforming the process. After he and Democratic Sen. Robert Byrd of West Virginia took over the Appropriations committees in their respective chambers, they announced that they would not allow any earmarks to go into effect in 2007. "The best way to get people's attention that there needs to be serious reform is to say there won't be any earmarks," Obey said. "We have to build in some protection for when some idiot goes too far and fouls the nest. The problem is not earmarking. The problem is the abuse of earmarking." The following year, he threatened to do away with earmarks completely if the minority party decided to "demagogue" the issue. In the resulting uproar, Republicans stalled progress on appropriations bills on the House floor for three days. Obey and party leaders eventually brokered a compromise that let the first two appropriations bills go forward without earmarks but allowed earmarks to be added up front to later bills. Republicans also agreed to let bills proceed in a timely fashion.

Obey has stirred controversy on other issues as well. In 2006, he called President George W. Bush's budget "wrongheaded and embarrassing" and said the administration had "the most fiscally irresponsible people to ever occupy the White House." He was especially critical of the freeze on Pell grants. In October 2007, he suggested a temporary tax to cover Bush's request for $145 billion in supplemental spending for Iraq. Republicans ridiculed the plan, and the Democratic leadership, wary of any proposal that reminded the public of the "tax-and-spend" label, immediately shot down the idea. In early 2009, Pelosi put Obey in charge of designing the $787 billion economic-stimulus bill sought by the Obama administration. Obey told the *Washington Post* in January 2009 that he favored an even bigger stimulus bill, but added, "This is my honest effort to find the equilibrium where a majority of people in the place can feel comfortable with what we have done." He guided the bill to passage in the House in February.

Obey voted against the Iraq war resolution in October 2002 and was harshly critical of the Bush administration's actions in Iraq. In 2003, he called on Defense Secretary Donald Rumsfeld to resign. In 2007, he was tasked with constructing a supplemental appropriations bill for Iraq with timetables for withdrawal. In the halls of the Rayburn House Office Building, he was approached by antiwar activist Tina Richards, who said he should immediately curtail war funding. "Do you see a magic wand in my pocket? We don't have the votes for it," he said in a caustic, six-minute exchange with Richards captured by a cell-phone camera and posted on the YouTube website. He charged that "idiot liberals" didn't understand the bill and said, "We're trying to use the supplemental to end the war." When details of the plan were leaked to the press, Obey announced that he had deliberately fed false information to different committee members in order to "see who the hell was leaking that information" and to keep those members from being invited to future meetings. Obey claimed that he had identified two leakers, but never said who they were.

Obey faced a balancing act with the bill: He had to keep sufficient numbers of liberals in the Out of Iraq Caucus satisfied but also keep conservative Blue Dog Democrats on board. When Democrats cheered Obey as he arrived on the House floor to discuss the bill, he yelled in frustration, "I don't want your applause! I want your damned votes!" Obey managed to cobble together a bill that added benchmarks for progress in the war and a timetable for troop withdrawal, but fully funded the war through 2008. His compromise kept defections low enough for the bill to pass the House, albeit by just six votes. Seven Blue Dog Democrats and seven liberal Democrats voted no, but two moderate Republicans voted yes.

Almost always combative toward Republicans, Obey doesn't kowtow to members of his own party. Shortly after Obama's election as president, Obey derisively referred to him as a "crown prince." He only reluctantly backed Obama's plans to send more troops to Afghanistan and added a provision to a war spending bill requiring the administration to report in 2010 on progress toward stability and security in Afghanistan and Pakistan. He also cut $80 million from the bill that would have gone to close the Guantanamo Bay detainee camp because, he said, Obama's plan was not well developed. He added, "While I don't mind defending a concrete program, I'm not much interested in wasting my energy defending a theoretical program."

Obey has been re-elected by wide margins, except in 1994, when he won 54%-46%. He has said he plans to run at least through 2010, before the next round of redistricting.

EIGHTH DISTRICT

Steve Kagen (D)

Elected 2006, 2nd term; b. Dec. 12, 1950, Appleton; home, Appleton; U. of WI, B.S. 1972, M.D. 1976; Jewish; married (Gayle); 4 children.

Professional Career: Practicing allergist, 1979–2007; Founder, Kagen Allergy Clinics, 1981; Asst. clinical prof., Medical Col. of WI, 1983–2007; Allergy consultant, CNN, 1985–92.

DC Office: 1232 LHOB, 20515, 202-225-5665; Fax: 202-225-5729; Web site: kagen.house.gov.

State Offices: Appleton, 920-380-0061; Green Bay, 920-437-1954.

Committees: *Agriculture* (14th of 28 D): Department Operations, Oversight, Nutrition & Forestry; Livestock, Dairy & Poultry. *Transportation & Infrastructure* (30th of 44 D): Coast Guard & Maritime Transportation; Highways & Transit; Water Resources & Environment.

Group Ratings

	ADA	ACLU	AFS	LCV	ITIC	NTU	COC	ACU	CFG	FRC
2008	90	100	100	92	71	20	50	16	16	5
2007	95	—	91	90	—	7	50	4	7	—

National Journal Ratings

	2007 LIB — 2007 CONS		2008 LIB — 2008 CONS	
Economic	78%	— 18%	66%	— 34%
Social	57%	— 42%	52%	— 47%
Foreign	73%	— 26%	78%	— 17%
Composite	70%	— 30%	66%	— 34%

Key Votes of the 110th Congress

1. Increase minimum wage	Y	5. Share immigration data	N	9. Withdraw troops 8/08	Y
2. Expand SCHIP	Y	6. Foreign aid abortion ban	N	10. No operations in Iran	Y
3. Raise CAFE standards	Y	7. Ban gay bias in workplace	Y	11. Free trade with Peru	N
4. Bail out financial markets	N	8. Repeal D.C. gun law	Y	12. Overhaul FISA	N

Election Results

2008 general	Steve Kagen (D)	193,662	(54%)	($2,218,166)
	John Gard (R)	164,621	(46%)	($1,597,322)
2008 primary	Steve Kagen (D)	unopposed		

Prior Winning Percentages: 2006 (51%)

Population

Pop. 2007:	695,986
Change since 2000:	Up 3.8%
Urban:	56.0%
Rural:	44.0%
Area size:	10,118 sq. mi.

Age

Median age:	38.9 yrs.
More than 65 yrs:	14.0%
Less than 18 yrs:	23.6%

Education

H.S. grad:	88.9%
College grad:	21.8%
Grad degree:	6.4%

Race/Ethnicity

White:	90.8%
Black:	0.9%
Hispanic:	3.1%
Asian:	1.6%
Native Am.:	2.5%
Hawaiian:	0.0%
Two+ races:	1.0%

Ancestry

German:	33.6%
Irish:	7.6%
Polish:	7.6%

Work

Private:	82.9%
Government:	10.2%
Self-employed:	6.7%
Blue collar:	28.8%
White collar:	53.9%
Khaki collar:	0.0%
Other:	17.2%
Median income:	$48,866
Median home value:	$145,600
Poverty:	9.9%

Military Veterans

% of Pop:	11.7%

In 1673, the French Catholic missionary and explorer Jacques Marquette sailed from the open waters of Lake Michigan into what is now Green Bay. He had hoped to find the Northwest Passage to the Pacific. He actually found the Fox River, which leads to Lake Winnebago and, after a not-too-difficult portage, the Wisconsin River, which flows into the Mississippi. Green Bay and the Fox River Valley remained mostly wilderness and Indian country for more than 150 years. But once

2008 Presidential Vote		
Obama (D) 195,608	(54%)
McCain (R)............................164,696	(45%)
2004 Presidential Vote		
Bush (R) 202,238	(55%)
Kerry (D)...............................162,793	(44%)
Cook Partisan Voting Index: R + 2		

settled by Europeans, they became, as Father Marquette would have liked, one of the most heavily Catholic parts of the United States. The area has thrived economically, with paper mills, a busy port and high-skill manufacturing in Green Bay and Appleton in the Fox River Valley. While paper products have long been an economic mainstay, the industry has experienced some instability. Low water levels in Lake Michigan in 2007 and 2008 hurt Green Bay's port traffic, and the recession that began in December 2007 further hampered shipping and also lowered demand for the region's timber.

No reference to Green Bay is complete without a mention of professional football's Packers, owned by 110,000 shareholding Wisconsinites and unlikely ever to move. Under the team's charter, if the Packers were ever sold, the proceeds would go to the local Sullivan-Wallen American Legion Post 11 "for the purposes of erecting a proper soldier's memorial." The city, by far the smallest to have a National Football League franchise, has earned the nickname Titletown for the Packers' numerous championships. Thirty miles south is Appleton, which has produced a number of famous, and infamous, Americans—novelist Edna Ferber, escape artist Harry Houdini and demagogue Sen. Joseph McCarthy, the central figure in the Red Scare of the 1950s. Both Green Bay and Appleton are growing, thanks in part to booming Hispanic populations. Green Bay's Latino community has increased from approximately 1,000 people in 1990 to nearly 10,000 today; the city is now more than 10% Hispanic.

The 8th Congressional District of Wisconsin includes Green Bay and the Fox River Valley south to Appleton. It also includes the inland dairy counties and the North Woods, which has hundreds of pine-ringed lakes where city dwellers from Chicago and Milwaukee keep summer homes. The Door County peninsula, which juts out into Lake Michigan, is another popular summer destination that is closer to the big population centers and as a consequence is more upscale, with art galleries, boutiques and restaurants. Politically, this has often been malleable territory and is one of the must-win regions in this traditional swing state. Republican presidential nominee George W. Bush won 52% of the vote here in 2000 and 55% in 2004, but Democrat Barack Obama carried the district with 54% of the vote in 2008.

The congressman from the 8th District is Steve Kagen, a Democrat first elected in 2006. A native of Appleton, Kagen was a competitive speed skater in his youth. He earned a medical degree from the University of Wisconsin and founded Kagen Allergy Clinics in the Fox River Valley. His clinics—one is in Green Bay, another in Appleton—made him wealthy. He also taught at the Medical College of Wisconsin and was an allergy expert for CNN. His father, dermatologist Marvin Kagen, a contemporary and friend of former senators Gaylord Nelson and William Proxmire, ran unsuccessfully for Congress in 1966. Steve Kagen's chance to run for the same seat came when four-term Republican Mark Green announced that he would run for governor. Kagen entered the campaign in August 2005, running on a universal-health-care platform he called "No Patient Left Behind," which included a national insurance risk pool, a deductible limited to 3% of a household's federal taxable income, and government-sponsored coverage for the poor.

Kagen became the Democratic nominee by beating two formidable candidates. Former Brown County Executive Nancy Nusbaum had wide name recognition and the backing of the women's fundraising group EMILY's List, while business consultant Jamie Wall had the support of prominent Democratic Rep. David Obey, from the neighboring 7th district. The National Republican Congressional Committee saw Kagen as a threat because of his outsider image, his ability to self-fund and his health-care expertise, and it ran ads during the primary calling him "Dr. Millionaire." The ploy failed. Kagen carried 12 of the district's 15 counties and won 48% to Wall's 29% and Nusbaum's 24%.

Republicans nominated John Gard, Wisconsin's Assembly Speaker, who won early support from state and national party leaders and easily turned back primary opposition from state Rep. Terri McCormick. Democrats used a March fundraising visit by Vice President Dick Cheney to attack Gard as a "rubber stamp" for the increasingly unpopular Bush administration, and Gard's nearly two decades in the Assembly made it difficult to sidestep criticism that he was a "career politician." Kagen told the Appleton *Post-Crescent*, "I'm an outsider in an outsider year. I'm not a professional politician. I'm the only candidate in this race, on both sides of the aisle, who hasn't been involved in government. I've never been part of the problem. I've been solving problems as a doctor."

Kagen's political inexperience wasn't always an asset. He had to apologize in late October for saying he was on "Injun time" as a way of explaining his tardiness for a meeting on an Indian reservation. Republicans used the comment as evidence that he was ill prepared to serve in Congress, although it drew few condemnations from tribal leaders. Republicans claimed Kagen would support higher taxes and amnesty for illegal immigrants. In the final weeks of the campaign, one Kagen ad called Gard "the most corrupt politician in Madison," though it offered no evidence to back up that claim. Kagen spent $3.2 million on the race, $2.6 million of it his own money, while Gard spent $2.8 million—making it the most expensive House race in Wisconsin history. In a tough political environment for Republican candidates, Kagen won by fewer than 6,000 votes, 51%-49%.

After the election, Kagen said he was mindful that Republicans would work to make him a "one-timer," but he nevertheless covered himself in controversy. Apparently unaware that an editor for an alternative monthly newspaper, the *Scene*, was present, Kagen bragged to local peace activists that he had, during a chance encounter with Bush political advisor Karl Rove in a White House bathroom, told Rove: "You recognize me? My name's Dr. Multimillionaire and I kicked your ass." Kagen also claimed to have insulted Bush by intentionally greeting First Lady Laura Bush by her mother-in-law's name, Barbara Bush. The White House denied Kagen's story, and Kagen apologized in a letter to constituents, but not before newspaper editorialists questioned his judgment.

In the House, Kagen established a moderate voting record, with more-conservative positions on gun-ownership rights and immigration. In 2007, he co-sponsored the Secure America with Verification and Enforcement Act, which sought increased border controls and heightened enforcement of existing immigration laws. In May 2008, Kagen sponsored a bill to label the Organization of Petroleum Exporting Countries an illegal cartel. It quickly passed the House but was ignored by the Senate. Kagen supports renegotiating the North American Free Trade Agreement and co-sponsored legislation in 2008 to end a program created under NAFTA that allows Mexican truckers to drive in the United States. A provision similar to Kagen's was added to a 2009 spending bill, leading to $2.4 billion in retaliatory tariffs from Mexico, including one that targeted the carbonless-paper manufacturers in Kagen's district. As one of the few Democratic physicians in the House, Kagen has a unique opportunity to influence the health-care policy that was kicked off by the Obama administration in 2009.

As expected, Kagen was a top Republican target in 2008. Gard ran again, accusing Kagen of being soft on illegal immigration and weak on the economy. Both sides spent considerably less than they had two years earlier, with Kagen outspending Gard $2.2 million to $1.6 million. The National Rifle Association endorsed Kagen, a plus for him in the hunter-heavy North Woods. He beat Gard by a wider margin this time, 54%-46%. Republican presidential nominee John McCain's weak performance and Democrat Barack Obama's heavy spending in the region likely helped Kagen, whose county-by-county totals mirrored Obama's.

Kagen has kept his skills as an allergist and doctor sharp since being elected. In May 2008, he came to the aid of a woman who had fainted during a flight to Minneapolis, then helped the paramedics treat her once the flight touched down.

★ WYOMING ★

W yoming is "the land of the cowboy," as the *WPA Guide* said more than 60 years ago. "Its mountains, plains, and valleys are essentially livestock country. A cowboy astride a bucking bronco greets the visitor from enameled license plates, from newspapers, magazines and painted signs." The cowboy is still on the license plates, and Wyoming remains the most western of states in spirit—largely unsettled, the least populous state, a thin veneer of civilization stretched over a forbidding and beautiful land. But it is more than the land of the cowboy now. It is the land of the oil and gas worker, of the coal mine operator, and of the tourism operator.

Today, Wyoming's economy depends not on cowboys and cattle but on mining and minerals. The state boomed with oil prospectors during the energy price surge of the 1970s, but was hit hard by steep drops in oil prices in the early 1980s and again in the late 1990s. As oil exploration slumped, the production of other minerals surged. The 1970 Clean Air Act put a premium on Wyoming's low-sulfur coal, and it is now the No. 1 coal state, producing one-third of the nation's coal, more than West Virginia and Kentucky combined. In the Powder River Basin 30-story high machines blast away the topsoil and scoop out coal. It is then hauled away by 65 trains a day by the Burlington Northern and Union Pacific. Wyoming is also the nation's seventh-largest oil producer and its second largest natural gas producer. It is also the top producer of the mineral bentonite, which is used in oil drilling and cosmetics, and it has the world's largest reserve of trona, which is used in making glass and baking soda. Much of the natural gas is coal-bed methane, mixed with water next to coal seams. Only in 1989 did engineers figure out how to separate the natural gas from the water. Now 200-foot drilling rigs are sinking wells as deep as 25,000 feet, and production has jumped enormously since 2000. These are capital-intensive industries that produce relatively few jobs for highly educated young people. But they have a major impact in this small state, and nearly 10% of its jobs are in mining, the highest percentage in the nation, compared to only 4% in manufacturing, one of the lowest percentages in the nation. Everything seems to be coming together for Wyoming: high oil and gas prices, continued demand for coal, rising beef prices, rapidly rising revenues from tourists. The American Legislative Exchange Council rated Wyoming as the No. 3 state for economic performance in 2009.

Wyoming's second industry is tourism. Yellowstone National Park continues to draw millions of people, and Jackson Hole, just to the south of the park, has become one of America's elite resort areas year-round. The Jackson Hole airport is the state's busiest and the only one that accommodates jets. There has been growth as well in the scenic and pastoral country on the eastern slope of the Big Horn Mountains around Buffalo and Sheridan. The third industry is agriculture. Wyoming is second in the nation in wool production and third in sheep inventory. It also produces hay, sugar beets, barley, pinto beans and beef cattle. This mix of tourism and agriculture sometimes leads to a cultural clash. The movie *Brokeback Mountain*, about gay sheep herders, premiered in Jackson Hole in December 2005, but played to mostly empty houses in the rest of the state. The juxtaposition of civilization and wilderness also raises some difficult policy issues. For years, the state has run feeding grounds for elk near Jackson Hole, and the herd has grown to tens of thousands. Environmental groups, worried about the spread of chronic wasting disease, want the feeding stopped, though thousands of elk induced over generations to depend on the feeding grounds will die. Local ranchers want it continued, to keep the elk away from their cattle, especially in winter. The grizzly bear, once endangered and protected in Yellowstone park, have now increased in number and have been removed from the endangered list. Environmental groups filed suit to prevent the delisting of the grizzly bear, but Democratic Gov. Dave Freudenthal, responding to ranchers worried about livestock, said the issue should be fought out not in federal court but in the states most affected, including Wyoming. Meanwhile, as utilities try to buy easements to build electric transmission lines to deliver wind power to consumers in California and elsewhere, Wyoming ranchers are forming wind associations to assure that they will have some say in this development.

Reliance on high-tech mineral extraction and high-end tourism may seem a contradiction of Wyoming's Old West heritage. But the state has always depended on new technology to tame age-old nature. After the open-range era, cattle ranches were made possible only by the barbed wire that could fence in roaming herds, and the steam locomotives that could carry cattle to markets in the East. This 19th-century high technology was brought to Wyoming by large capitalist operators, some of them onetime Texas cowhands or second sons of English landed gentry, who started the first big operations after the Civil War. And of course, mining depends on intricate machinery and responsiveness to markets that reward innovation and penalize stasis. At the same time, Wyoming still is a kind of frontier. It was, until recently, one of the few states with more men than women, which was one reason that Wyoming, when it was still a territory in 1869, was the first to give women the vote. (The exception: New Jersey allowed women with property to vote between 1776 and 1807, but there weren't many women with property.) Wyoming's amazing landscape has long elicited national notice. It is home to the first national park, Yellowstone,

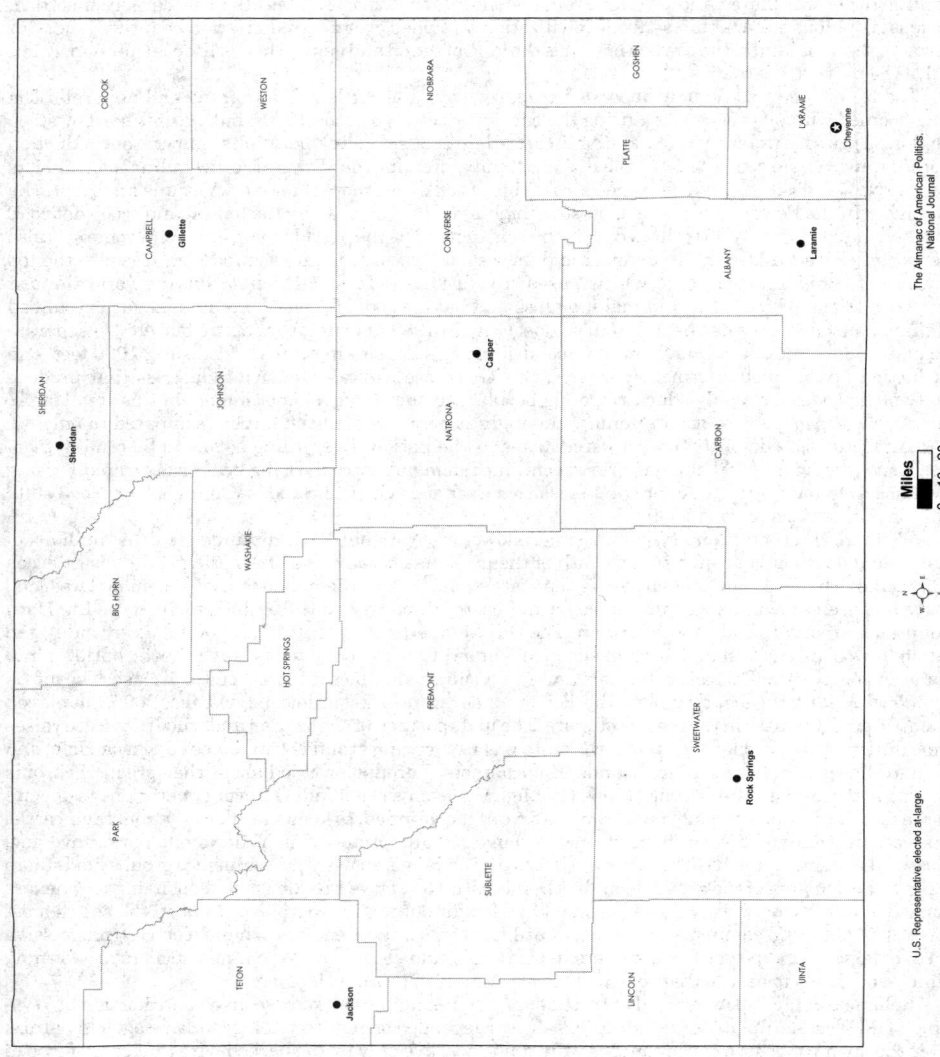

The Almanac of American Politics.
National Journal

Miles

0 10 20

U.S. Representative elected at-large.

which was established in 1872. It has the first national forest, designated in 1891 by President Benjamin Harrison, and the first national monument, Devils Tower, in 1906.

The settled part of Wyoming consists of medium-sized towns, which are the state's largest cities, and settlements tucked among sheep and cattle ranches, and sugar beet and malting barley farms. It is a small state for sure, a single community really, where people remember who played what position, when and how well, and for what high school football team. (Former Republican Vice President Dick Cheney and *Almanac* founding co-author Grant Ujifusa remember playing against each other when they were in high school in Natrona and Washakie counties.) The locals set the tone of life in Wyoming.

There was once a sharp economic and regional split reflected in its partisan politics. The big economic interests—cattle ranchers, organized in the Wyoming Stock Growers' Association, and the Union Pacific Railroad management—favored the Republicans, as did the wildcatters, independent producers and oil company geologists. The main Democratic constituency was the Union Pacific Railroad workers who built the first transcontinental line across southern Wyoming in the 1860s. (Cheyenne was established because it was the midpoint between the UP's operations in Omaha and Ogden, Utah.) The southern tier of counties, from Cheyenne through Laramie to Evanston, once voted Democratic. But now the Democrats are strongest in Teton County, the home of Jackson Hole, which voted nearly 2-to-1 for Democratic presidential nominee Barack Obama in 2008, and in Albany County, home of Laramie and the University of Wyoming, the only other county Obama carried. All other counties gave Republican John McCain between 59% (Cheyenne's Laramie County) and 81% (coal-mining Crook County) of their votes. Wyoming hasn't elected a Democrat to the Senate since 1970 or to the House since 1976, though it has had mostly Democratic governors over that time. How to explain that anomaly? In a small state with not much more than half a million people—the nation's smallest population congressional district—Wyoming voters expect to talk person-to-person with their governors, senators and congressmen every so often. Personal campaigning is important, and it enabled Democrats Ed Herschler, Mike Sullivan and Dave Freudenthal to win six of the last eight races for governor. Party tends to trump personality when it comes to federal office.

Population		Household Income		Work	
Pop. 2007:	514,044	Under $15k:	10.5%	Private:	71.4%
State rank:	50th of 50	$15k to $50k:	39.5%	Government:	20.1%
Change since 2000:	Up 4.1%	$50k to $100k:	34.3%	Self-employed:	8.1%
Urban:	64.5%	$100k to $150k:	13.5%	Unemployment (3-yr. average):	2.9%
Rural:	35.5%	Over $150k:	2.2%	Poverty:	8.9%
Native of state:	42.1%	Median income:	$50,009	Blue collar:	28.1%
Not a citizen:	1.7%	**Home Value**		White collar:	53.2%
Area size:	97,814 sq. mi.	Under $100k:	27.2%	Khaki collar:	0.5%
Most populous cities		$100k to $300k:	58.5%	Other:	18.2%
1. Cheyenne	55,199	$300k to $500k:	8.5%	**Age**	
2. Casper	53,043	$500k to $1 mil:	4.1%	Median age:	37.3 yrs.
3. Laramie	27,136	Over $1 million:	1.8%	More than 65 yrs:	12.2%
4. Gillette	23,765	Median:	$150,500	Less than 18 yrs:	24.0%

Race/Ethnicity				Military Veterans		Registered Voters in 2008	
White:	87.7%	*Language*		% of Pop:	13.8%	D:	65,640 (26.8%)
Black:	0.7%	English:	93.6%	*Veterans by Period*		R:	150,504 (61.5%)
Hispanic:	7.2%	Spanish:	4.1%	WWII and before:	10.7%	Other:	28,674 (11.7%)
Asian:	0.8%	Asian:	0.5%	Korea:	10.9%	Voter turnout:	254,658
Native Am.:	2.0%	Other		Vietnam:	35.4%	Turnout as % of	
Hawaiian:	0.0%	European	1.3%	Gulf (pre-2001):	10.7%	voting age:	63.0%
Two+ races:	1.6%	**Education**		Gulf (post-2001):	8.9%	**Legislature**	
Ancestry		H.S. grad:	90.5%	Peace time:	23.4%	Senate:	7 D 23 R
German:	21.8%	College grad:	23.1%			House:	18 D 41 R 1 V
English:	12.0%	Grad degree:	7.6%				
Irish:	11.0%			**Cook Partisan Voting Index:** R+20			

Presidential politics   Wyoming is one of the least likely states in the nation to be seriously contested in presidential general elections. It is too Republican, too remote and has only three electoral votes.
Candidates have seldom visited, except when Che-
ney visited his home in Jackson. This was Republican presidential candidate George W. Bush's best
state in 2000, when he carried it 69%-28%, and it
was his second best state in 2004, when he carried
it 69%-29%. It was Republican nominee John
McCain's No. 2 state in 2008; he won it with 65% of
the vote. It was Democrat Barack Obama's 50th; he
got just 33% of the vote. This is a counterintuitive
state in which Democrats tend to do better with the elite and Republicans with ordinary folks. Obama
carried the richest county in the state, Jackson Hole's Teton County, and he won Albany County, which
includes Laramie and the University of Wyoming. McCain won the votes of just 53% of college graduates,
but he won 78% of those who did not graduate from college.

2008 Presidential Vote		
McCain (R)	164,958	(65%)
Obama (D)	82,868	(33%)
2004 Presidential Vote		
Bush (R)	167,629	(69%)
Kerry (D)	70,776	(29%)

Wyoming has typically held presidential caucuses in early March, with no significant impact on the
presidential nominating process. In early 2007, Wyoming Republicans pledged to caucus on the same
date as the New Hampshire Republican primary. With New Hampshire Secretary of State Bill Gardner
holding his cards close until December (New Hampshire law gives him sole authority to set the date of
its presidential primary), Wyoming Republicans blinked, and decided in August 2007 to hold their caucuses on January 5, which turned out to be two days after the Iowa caucuses and three days before the
New Hampshire primary. The date was against party rules and cost the state half of its 28 delegates, but
state party leaders evidently decided it was a minimal price to pay.

As in most other Republican caucus states, Mitt Romney's well-organized campaign dominated here.
Romney, his wife, Ann, and sons Josh and Craig campaigned in Wyoming. In county conventions, Romney
won 13 delegates, to four for Fred Thompson, two for Duncan Hunter, one for McCain and four for "uncommitted." (Each county got one delegate, except for Cheyenne's Laramie County, which got two.) In retrospect, it was a high water mark for the Thompson and Hunter campaigns. Wyoming Republicans in characteristic fashion assembled early in the morning and made quick work of it. The Albany County
chairwoman made sure that the caucus was over by 10 a.m. because she had a funeral to attend.

Wyoming Democrats held their caucuses on March 8, a date on which most observers thought the
nomination would be determined. Not so. Obama's brilliant February, with 11 straight primary and caucus wins, was followed by Hillary Rodham Clinton's victories in Ohio and Texas on March 4. Obama,
anticipating a prolonged campaign, opened a Cheyenne office in mid-February and ran television ads.
The Clinton campaign, caught short-funded, sent in former President Bill Clinton and daughter Chelsea
and ran radio spots. The Wyoming media wrote stories about state Democrats being energized, and
Obama half filled the University of Wyoming's Arena-Auditorium in Laramie. But Democratic Gov.
Dave Freudenthal declined to support either candidate. And of the 59,000 registered Democrats, only
8,753 showed up at 23 county caucuses. Obama won 61%-38%, thanks in large part to big percentages
in affluent Jackson Hole's Teton County (80%) and in the University of Wyoming's Albany County (74%).
Clinton carried the Democrats' historical base, the Union Pacific railroad worker counties of Carbon and
Sweetwater that cover most of the southern half of the state. Comparison of these results with those in
adjacent states that had a primary, such as South Dakota, or both primaries and caucuses, such as
Nebraska and Idaho, suggests that an Obama-Clinton Wyoming primary would have been closer than
the caucus results.

Governor

Dave Freudenthal (D)

Elected 2002, term expires Jan. 2011, 2nd term; b. Oct. 12, 1950, Thermopolis; home, Cheyenne; Amherst Col., B.A. 1973, U. of WY, J.D. 1980; Episcopalian; married (Nancy); 4 children.

Professional Career: Practicing atty. 1980–94; U.S. atty. for WY, 1994–2001

Office: State Capitol, West 24th St., Cheyenne, 82002, 307-777-7434; Fax: 307-632-3909; Web site: governor.wy.gov.

Election Results

2006 general	Dave Freudenthal (D)	135,516	(70%)
	Ray Hunkins (R)	58,100	(30%)
2006 primary	Dave Freudenthal (D)	26,550	(90%)
	Al Hamburg (D)	3,062	(10%)

Prior Winning Percentages: 2002 (50%)

Dave Freudenthal, a Democrat, was elected governor of Wyoming in 2002. He grew up on a farm north of Thermopolis, the seventh of eight children. Freudenthal (*FREE-den-thal*) graduated from Amherst College and then returned to Wyoming to work for the state Department of Economic Planning and Development. Democratic Gov. Ed Herschler appointed him state planning coordinator in 1975. Freudenthal went to University of Wyoming Law School, graduating in 1980. He practiced law in Cheyenne, while remaining active in politics, serving from 1981 to 1985 as the Wyoming Democratic chairman. In 1994, he was appointed U.S. attorney for Wyoming and stayed in that position until 2001, when he began planning his campaign for governor. The incumbent, Republican Jim Geringer, was ineligible to run for a third term. Five Republicans and four Democrats got into the race, and focused on economic development. Freudenthal's chief competitor in the Democratic primary was Paul Hickey, son of former Democratic Gov. Joseph Hickey. In the August primary, Freudenthal beat Hickey 54%-37%. The winner in the Republican primary was state House Speaker Eli Bebout.

The two nominees had similar positions on many issues. They favored the death penalty, opposed gun control laws and a state income tax. Bebout liked to point out that Freudenthal, as a U.S. Attorney, was an appointee of Democratic President Bill Clinton, who was not very popular in the conservative state. But his business interests caused him some problems. The *Casper Star-Tribune* reported that he had not repaid a $468,000 loan given to him in 1983 by a company on whose board he served. Freudenthal won 50%-48%, including 59%-39% in the five counties in the southern end of the state, the traditionally Democratic Union Pacific counties.

In Freudenthal's first term, the state was in remarkably good fiscal position. Increases in land values due to mining activity had produced surges in state revenue and a budget surplus. Higher natural gas and oil prices gave the state projected surpluses of more than $1 billion in 2004 and 2005, and nearly to $2 billion in 2006. While most other states struggled with deficits, the only issue in Wyoming was how much to put into savings and how much to spend. Some of the surplus was socked away in a Permanent Mineral Trust Fund, which produced interest earnings to pay state operating costs and to keep taxes low. Some school districts in mineral-rich regions were collecting so much from high mineral prices and production that it skewed the state's attempts to equalize school funding. Under a constitutional amendment, these districts were allowed to keep some of the excess money, rather than send it to the state for redistribution to less wealthy districts. Freudenthal supported a constitutional amendment abolishing the limit on redistribution of property tax revenues, but it failed.

In 2005, Freudenthal proposed $293 million of additional spending, and got the Republican-controlled Legislature to agree to a $30 million wildlife trust (although he'd originally sought $70 million). He was also able to fund raises for teachers, a college scholarship endowment, a University of Wyoming library complex, and new four-lane highways. Fueled by booming natural gas prices, the state entered 2006 with yet another massive surplus, and Freudenthal proposed $772 million in new spending for tax cuts, a pay hike for state employees, school construction, highways, water projects, scholarships, and home heating assistance. He also proposed boosting the state's "rainy day" fund to $500 million with the surplus revenues. The Legislature approved a 2-year budget that funded many of the governor's priorities, but opted to put only $183 million in the reserve fund and an extra $200 million into the Permanent

Mineral Trust Fund. The budget also spent more than $2.2 billion on education funding and school construction and included a two-year repeal of grocery taxes.

Freudenthal also signed a suicide prevention bill that year. Wyoming has the highest rate in the country, about double the 11 per 100,000 national rate. The governor's approval ratings remained high—67% in 2005. One of the rare low points for him in his first term was some criticism from environmentalists unhappy with several of his appointments, including one that put a mining executive in charge of the Department of Environmental Quality.

Freudenthal showed sensitivity on some environmental issues, but was mindful of the importance of natural resources to the Wyoming economy. He opposed a move in Congress in 2005 to lift restrictions on winter drilling on federal lands designed to protect wildlife and resisted a Forest Service plan to auction off 20,000 acres of Bridger-Teton National Forest for oil and gas development until conservation objections were resolved. He also was on the front lines of several longstanding water disputes with Wyoming's neighbors. In 2006, he signed an agreement with Nebraska and Colorado over use of water from the Platte River that balanced the needs of water use and endangered species protection. Freudenthal and Republican Gov. Arnold Schwarzenegger of California also signed a memorandum of understanding in 2006 that would tap federal funding to develop "clean coal" power plants in Wyoming that would generate electricity for power-hungry California and be transmitted via a new multi-billion dollar Frontier Line transmission project.

Freudenthal entered his 2006 re-election campaign in a strong position. His Republican opposition was rancher and attorney Ray Hunkins, who had run unsuccessfully for the Republican nomination in 2002. Hunkins accused the governor of an ineffective fight against methamphetamine use and for failing to plan for the lean times by diversifying the economy. Freudenthal's campaign mailed out an 11-page "Report to the Citizens of Wyoming" detailing his success and praising the Republican Legislature for working with him. State Republican Chairman Drake Hill angered members of both parties when he conducted opposition research on Freudenthal and funded a negative radio ad that portrayed the governor as living a lavish lifestyle and using a state-financed "party plane." The plane, which Freudenthal had not in fact traveled on, was actually used by the state to conduct aerial surveying work, and the issue reinforced Freudenthal's attempt to portray himself as above partisan politics. He campaigned as "Gov. Dave" and a *Star-Tribune* poll showed him with a 33-point lead in the final weeks of the campaign. The poll proved only slightly inaccurate. Freudenthal won a second term 70%-30%.

In 2006 and 2007, declining natural gas prices reduced projected budget surpluses, but the state was still in good shape fiscally. In 2007, the Legislature approved a $470 million supplemental spending bill, which included $100 million for highway construction, and permanent repeal of the grocery tax. Freudenthal also signed bills that increased fees for hunting and fishing licenses by 20%, an open container law prohibiting alcohol consumption in moving vehicles, and property tax relief for combat veterans.

Heading into the 2008 session, Freudenthal was feeling more cautious as gas revenue continued to decline. He asked for only minor increases in spending, except for a splurge on education. He proposed $1.8 billion for K-through-12 education, up about $500 million from his last budget. The Legislature passed his $8 billion budget with only minor revisions. He also signed a bill extending property tax refunds for low-income residents, but criticized the Legislature for not doing more to alleviate property taxes. After the nation's mortgage bubble burst in 2008, he asked the Legislature to revive a homestead property tax exemption to give homeowners "short-term relief," saving them between $185 and $290 annually on their mortgage bills. But his proposal failed to pass.

By early 2009, Wyoming was feeling the recession like every other state, only perhaps not quite as badly. Money for discretionary spending was down by two-thirds, and Freudenthal ordered state agencies to plan for budget cuts of 5% to 10%. Still, in March 2009, legislators approved $164 million in new spending, with the largest appropriation, $69 million, going to build a complex in Cheyenne for new public health, environmental quality and criminal investigation laboratories.

Freudenthal is technically term-limited in 2010, but the popular Democrat could feasibly seek an unprecedented third term. A state law passed in the 1980s to limit governors to two terms and a voter-approved referendum in 1992 limited the terms of state officeholders. But in 2004, a lawsuit brought by two term-limited state legislators resulted in a court ruling that an amendment to the state constitution would be required to enforce the limits. Although that decision didn't apply to the state's chief executive, legal analysts believe that if Freudenthal challenged the constitutionality of his own term limits, he would win. He has been mum about his own intentions. If he does run, he would likely be re-elected. Otherwise, Republicans sense a pickup opportunity in a state where Republican presidential nominee John McCain won with 65% of the vote.

Senior Senator

Michael Enzi (R)

Elected 1996, term expires 2014, 3rd term; b. Feb. 1, 1944, Bremerton, WA; home, Gillette; George Washington U., B.S. 1966, Denver U., M.B.A. 1968; Presbyterian; married (Diana); 3 children.

Military Career: WY Natl. Guard, 1967–73.

Elected Office: Gillette mayor, 1975–82; WY House of Reps., 1986–90; WY Senate, 1990–96.

Professional Career: Owner, NZ Shoes, 1969–95; Dir. & chmn., First WY Bank of Gillette, 1978–88; Accounting mgr. & computer programmer, Dunbar Well Service, 1985–97; Educ. Comm. of States, 1989–93; Dir., Black Hills Corp., 1992–96; Western Interstate Comm. for Higher Educ., 1995–96.

DC Office: 379-A RSOB, 20510, 202-224-3424; Fax: 202-228-0359; Web site: enzi.senate.gov.

State Offices: Casper, 307-261-6572; Cheyenne, 307-772-2477; Cody, 307-527-9444; Gillette, 307-682-6268; Jackson, 307-739-9507.

Committees: *Budget* (3rd of 10 R). *Finance* (9th of 10 R): Energy, Natural Resources & Infrastructure; Health Care; Taxation, IRS Oversight & Long-Term Growth. *Health, Education, Labor & Pensions* (RMM of 10 R). *Small Business & Entrepreneurship* (5th of 8 R).

Group Ratings

	ADA	ACLU	AFS	LCV	ITIC	NTU	COC	ACU	CFG	FRC
2008	5	21	0	18	60	80	75	96	95	100
2007	10	—	0	13	—	86	55	96	85	—

National Journal Ratings

	2007 LIB	—	2007 CONS		2008 LIB	—	2008 CONS
Economic	7%	—	91%		0%	—	96%
Social	0%	—	91%		0%	—	79%
Foreign	14%	—	84%		0%	—	84%
Composite	9%	—	91%		7%	—	93%

Key Votes of the 110th Congress

1. Raise CAFE standards	N	5. Make English official language	Y	9. Withdraw troops 3/08	N
2. Expand SCHIP	N	6. Path to citizenship	N	10. Iran guard is terrorist group	Y
3. Cap greenhouse gases	N	7. Fetus is unborn child	Y	11. Increase missile defense $	Y
4. Bail out financial markets	N	8. Prosecute hate crimes	N	12. Overhaul FISA	Y

Election Results

2008 general	Michael Enzi (R)	189,046	(76%)	($1,247,841)
	Chris Rothfuss (D)	60,631	(24%)	($27,258)
2008 primary	Michael Enzi (R)	unopposed		

Prior Winning Percentages: 2002 (73%); 1996 (54%)

Michael Enzi, the senior senator from Wyoming, was elected in 1996. He is the ranking Republican on the Health, Education, Labor and Pensions Committee. Enzi grew up in Thermopolis and Sheridan, the son of a shoe salesman. He earned degrees in accounting and retail marketing, moved to Gillette and became an accountant for an oil well servicing company. He and his wife, Diana, started a small business, NZ Shoes. In the 1970s, at a Jaycees meeting, Enzi met Republican Sen. Alan Simpson, who was impressed by his volunteerism and suggested he run for public office. In 1975, Enzi was elected mayor of Gillette, the center of Wyoming's coal belt and its fastest-growing town. He was mayor for eight years. In 1986, he was elected to the Wyoming state House and in 1990 to the state Senate. After Simpson announced his retirement in December 1995, Enzi was one of nine Republicans and two Democrats who ran for the seat. With support from a grass-roots network of conservatives, Enzi finished first in a straw poll at the May 1996 Republican state convention. In second place was John Barrasso, an orthopedic surgeon from Casper who had statewide name recognition as a television commentator on health issues. Their chief difference was on abortion rights. Enzi opposed abortion rights, and Barrasso did not. Barrasso also had more money, but Enzi won 32%-30%. The Democratic nominee was former Secretary of State Kathy Karpan, who opposed gun control and abortion. But she had the liabilities of having supported the presidential candidacies of Bill Clinton, who was unpopular in conservative Wyoming, and Bruce Babbitt, who was unpopular in Wyoming as Clinton's Interior secretary. Enzi led in polls throughout the campaign and won 54%-42%.

Enzi started off in the Senate by attempting to bring technology to the tradition-bound Senate chamber. He lobbied colleagues for permission to bring his laptop on the floor, but the Rules Committee voted 6-1 to continue a ban on electronic devices on the floor.

In 2002, his sixth year in the Senate, Enzi was still little known nationally, but he played a key role on a major piece of legislation. The issue was corporate accountability, and as the only accountant in the Senate, Enzi could claim special expertise. Enzi opposed a move by Securities and Exchange Commission Chairman Arthur Levitt to bar accounting firms from doing auditing and consulting work for the same corporation. After the Enron bankruptcy in December 2001 raised questions about accounting, Enzi still urged caution and said he feared overregulation. Banking Chairman Paul Sarbanes, D-Md., introduced a bill that did not go as far as Levitt's proposal, but included an accounting board independent of the SEC with power to set rules, investigate, punish violations and conduct regular inspections of accounting firms' work. Enzi worked closely with lobbyists for the big accounting firms but also held negotiations with Sarbanes, who was eager to have a bipartisan bill. In June, Enzi and Sarbanes negotiated a compromise. They agreed that two of the four members of the board be accountants, that the board could adopt rules favored by the accounting industry and that the board would not be financed by accountants. Disciplinary proceedings would be confidential. Enzi led six of the 10 committee Republicans in voting for the Sarbanes bill. The Senate later passed the bill without a single no vote. It became known as the Sarbanes-Oxley corporate accounting law (after House Republican Michael Oxley of Ohio, who pushed it through the House).

In early 2005, when Republicans still controlled the Senate, Enzi became chairman of the Health, Education, Labor and Pensions Committee, where he earned a reputation as a hard worker who was knowledgeable about the details of legislation and took into account the views of those affected. He also did not always follow the lead of the Bush administration. His unassuming manner helped him manage the egos on a panel featuring four former chairmen of the committee (Republicans Judd Gregg of New Hampshire and Orrin Hatch of Utah, and Democrats James Jeffords of Vermont and Edward Kennedy of Massachusetts) and seven senators who had run for president or were planning to in 2008. He put together the reauthorization of the Carl Perkins vocational and technical education bill, which passed the Senate 99-0 and was enacted in August 2005. Enzi also won passage of renewed versions of a major jobs training bill and the higher education law. He sided with ranking minority member Kennedy in opposing a White House proposal to encourage more use of government vouchers for private school tuition in the recovery following Hurricane Katrina in 2005. Working with leaders of the Senate Finance Committee, he also participated in the protracted negotiations with the House on pension reform. "Promises made will be promises kept by limiting when benefits may be increased," he said when Congress completed action in 2006. On an issue of special interest back home, Enzi helped to enact a bill to expedite the clean-up of abandoned coal mines. In the closing days of the Republican majority, he helped to resolve conflicts over the funding formula to renew domestic AIDS programs.

When Democrats took control in of the Senate in 2007, Enzi became the ranking member on the HELP Committee, taking a backseat to Kennedy, the new chairman. Despite his ideological differences with the liberal Kennedy, he forged a productive and largely bipartisan working relationship with him. The two established what they call the 80-20 principle: reach broad agreement on 80% of an issue and leave out the 20% where no agreement can be found. The two successfully pushed through the committee a bill requiring insurance companies to treat mental illness the same as other ailments in coverage decisions. And they agreed on reauthorization of Head Start early education programs and on renewal of college programs. Still, talks on reauthorization of No Child Left Behind, the Bush-era law tying federal education funding to performance, stalled in both 2007 and 2008 and efforts continued into 2009. They also disagreed on Kennedy's bill requiring employers to provide workers with paid sick leave, with Enzi arguing the rule would have an adverse effect on employee health benefits. The bill stalled. On Wyoming issues, Enzi successfully opposed a change in the 2008 spending bill that decreased the amount of mineral royalties the state would receive.

In the 111th Congress (2009–10), Enzi has remained a firm backer of health care reform through collaboration between the public and private sectors, and he was a key GOP negotiator in the Obama administration's early efforts to get a health care bill through Congress. His own 10-point health care proposal called for tax credits for buying health care, assistance to help small businesses provide coverage for their employees and requirements for the states to reduce the cost of medical malpractice insurance. He also has been a vocal advocate for increased implementation of health information technology, such electronic health records. Although a bill failed in the 110th Congress (2007–08), he worked successfully to get funds for health IT into the January 2009 economic stimulus bill.

Enzi briefly considered retirement after being passed over twice for appointment to the Finance Committee. In 2007, Enzi had lobbied for a vacancy but GOP Senate leaders gave it to the less-senior John Ensign of Nevada as reward for his work leading the National Republican Senatorial Committee. He tried again when a second vacancy opened in late 2007, but the spot instead went to New Hampshire Sen. John Sununu, who also had less seniority but was facing a difficult re-election in 2008. "That was a really down time in my life," Enzi told the Associated Press. Sununu lost in 2008, and Enzi finally got his appointment to the powerful Finance panel. "An accountant working on tax issues, now here is finally something in Washington that makes sense," Enzi said. Among his first acts on the committee was to vote against Treasury Secretary Timothy Geithner's nomination, citing Geithner's unpaid back taxes.

Enzi did not have serious opposition in 2002. He won the Republican primary 86%-14% and the general election 73%-27%. The death of Craig Thomas in June 2007 set up an unusual situation in which each Wyoming senator faced election in November 2008. Democrats tried to recruit popular Gov. Dave Freudenthal to run against Enzi, but to no avail. He cruised to a third term 76-24%.

Junior Senator

John Barrasso (R)

Appointed June 2007, term expires 2012, 1st full term; b. July 21, 1952, Reading, PA; home, Casper; Georgetown U., B.A. 1974, M.D. 1978; Presbyterian; married (Bobbi); 3 children.

Elected Office: WY Senate, 2002–07.

Professional Career: Orthopedic surgeon 1983–2007; RNC Committeeman, 1992–96; Chief of staff, WY Medical Center, 2003–05.

DC Office: 307 DSOB, 20510, 202-224-6441; Fax: 202-224-1724; Web site: barrasso.senate.gov.

State Offices: Casper, 307-261-6413; Cheyenne, 307-772-2451; Riverton, 307-856-6642; Rock Springs, 307-362-5012; Sheridan, 307-672-6456.

Committees: *Energy & Natural Resources* (3rd of 10 R): Energy; National Parks; Public Lands & Forests (RMM). *Environment & Public Works* (4th of 7 R). *Foreign Relations* (6th of 8 R): East Asian & Pacific Affairs; International Operations & Organizations, Democracy & Global Women's Issues; Near Eastern & South & Central Asian Affairs; Western Hemisphere, Peace Corps & Global Narcotics Affairs (RMM). *Indian Affairs* (VChmn of 6 R).

Group Ratings

	ADA	ACLU	AFS	LCV	ITIC	NTU	COC	ACU	CFG	FRC
2008	5	17	0	18	50	81	75	96	95	100
2007	10	—	0	33	—	76	75	100	80	—

National Journal Ratings

	2007 LIB — 2007 CONS		2008 LIB — 2008 CONS	
Economic	*% —	*%	0% —	96%
Social	0% —	91%	0% —	79%
Foreign	16% —	79%	0% —	84%
Composite	*% —	*%	7% —	93%

Key Votes of the 110th Congress

1. Raise CAFE standards	*	5. Make English official language	*	9. Withdraw troops 3/08	*
2. Expand SCHIP	N	6. Path to citizenship	N	10. Iran guard is terrorist group	Y
3. Cap greenhouse gases	N	7. Fetus is unborn child	Y	11. Increase missile defense $	Y
4. Bail out financial markets	N	8. Prosecute hate crimes	N	12. Overhaul FISA	Y

Election Results

2008 general	John Barrasso (R)	183,063	(73%)	($1,981,441)
	Nick Carter (D)	66,202	(27%)	($273,688)
2008 primary	John Barrasso (R)	unopposed		

Republican John Barrasso, the junior senator from Wyoming, was appointed in June 2007 after Republican Sen. Craig Thomas died of leukemia. Barrasso was then elected in November 2008 to fill the remaining four years of Craig's unexpired term.

Barrasso *(bah-RAH-soh)* and grew up in Reading, Penn., the son of a World War II veteran who made a living as a cement finisher and who took his family to Washington every four years for the president's inauguration. John Barrasso got his undergraduate and medical degrees from Georgetown University, then moved to Wyoming in the 1980s and set up practice as an orthopedic surgeon in Casper. Barrasso quickly made his name in local Republican politics, serving as a Republican national committeeman and state party treasurer. He also was a local radio and television personality, dispensing practical medical advice on news programs and in public service announcements. He also hosted the annual Jerry Lewis telethon for muscular dystrophy.

In 1996, he ran for the U.S. Senate when Republican Alan Simpson retired. He faced then-state Sen. Mike Enzi in a crowded GOP primary where the abortion issue played a key role. Running as a moderate,

Barrasso favored abortion rights and had opposed a 1994 constitutional amendment to ban most abortions. Enzi, who had support from social conservatives, opposed abortion rights and narrowly edged Barrasso 32% to 30%. The two then joined forces for the general election, with Barrasso serving as Enzi's finance chairman in the fall.

In 2002, Barrasso won election to the state Senate, where he worked on health care issues and chaired the Transportation, Highways and Military Affairs Committee. He sponsored a bill to increase the criminal penalty for killing a pregnant woman, but Democratic Gov. Dave Freudenthal vetoed it. He occasionally crossed the political aisle to join with Democrats, backing a bill to exempt food from the state sales tax and supporting a ban on smoking in public buildings. He also sponsored a law enabling physicians to talk freely with patients about medical complications, without the risk that the conversations would be used against them in a lawsuit.

After Thomas died on June 4, 2007, the state Republican Central Committee had 15 days to select three candidates to fill the vacancy, from which the governor was required to pick the successor under Wyoming law. That triggered a scramble by 31 candidates who applied for consideration. They conducted a week-long beauty pageant among the 71 members of the party committee. The roster of applicants included state Rep. Colin Simpson, the son of former U.S. Sen. Simpson, and numerous state legislators, attorneys, ranchers, and other professionals. Barrasso emphasized his strong conservative credentials, saying in a statement to the committee, "I believe in limited government, lower taxes, less spending, traditional family values, local control, and a strong national defense." He noted he had an "A" rating from the National Rifle Association and had voted for prayer in public schools, opposed gay marriage and sponsored legislation "to protect the sanctity of life."

At a June 19 meeting, the Republican committee named three finalists: Barrasso, Cynthia Lummis, who served 14 years in the Legislature and two terms as state treasurer, and Tom Sansonetti, who had been Thomas' chief of staff and an assistant attorney general in the Bush administration. Freudenthal met the three candidates in private interviews. Barrasso's competitors had drawbacks: Lummis reportedly was not on good terms with the governor, and Sansonetti had been a lobbyist for mining, energy and ranching interests at a time lobbyists were unpopular with the public after a series of bribery and influence-peddling scandals involving lobbyists and members of Congress. By contrast, Barrasso had worked with the governor on health care issues in the Legislature. In announcing his selection of Barrasso on June 22, Freudenthal said, "While I don't intend to indulge the speculation on why I made this decision, I will say that I hope I made the right choice."

In the Senate, Barrasso was appointed to the Energy and Natural Resources Committee, where Wyoming has had a senator continuously since 1899. He also joined the Foreign Relations, Environment and Public Works and the Indian Affairs committees. Barrasso quickly became involved on issues of energy and public lands. In 2008, he opposed legislation by Virginia Democrat John Warner and Connecticut independent Joe Lieberman on climate change, which sought to reduce greenhouse gas emissions by 70% by 2050. Barrasso said the bill would harm Wyoming's coal industry, and he sought amendments to increase funding for states to implement the new standards and also to allow more types of coal to qualify for program incentives, benefiting Wyoming coal plants. On a bill to ban the exportation of elemental mercury, Barrasso got an exemption for mercury found in coal, again to protect the state's coal industry.

Continuing work on an issue that was dear to Thomas' heart, Barrasso pushed for more protection of Wyoming wilderness and wildlife. He proposed legislation to protect undeveloped areas of the Wyoming range from oil and gas development and to preserve 387 miles around the Snake River. Barrasso also supported removing gray wolves from the Endangered Species List because of the danger they pose to livestock. He told the Associated Press, "This is a Wyoming concern that requires a Wyoming solution. It does not require interference from Washington." The U.S. Fish and Wildlife Service eventually removed gray wolves from the list. Against the wishes of the Bush administration, Barrasso and Democratic Sen. Jon Tester of Montana sponsored a bill to give livestock owners federal compensation after their animals are killed by wolves. Barrasso's protections for Wyoming lands around the Snake River and wolf compensation bill became law as part of a larger land management bill in March 2009.

On national issues, Barrasso's voting record has been in line with conservative Republicans. *National Journal*'s 2008 vote ratings put him in a four-way tie as the most conservative member of the Senate. He opposed both the 2008 government rescue of financial services firms and President Barack Obama's $787 billion economic stimulus bill in early 2009. Although he opposed the Democratic proposal to extend the State Children's Health Insurance Program, he successfully included a provision in the bill to benefit rural doctors and hospitals. Among his first bills was a proposal to withhold 10% of highway funds from states that issue driver's licenses to illegal immigrants.

In 2008, Barrasso was unopposed in the Republican primary, and his eventual Democratic challenger was Gillette attorney Nick Carter, a political newcomer. Barrasso stressed his many years in public service in Wyoming and highlighted his early successes in the Senate. Carter tried to tie Barrasso to national Republicans and corporate special interests, but the assertions didn't stick. Barrasso vastly outspent Carter, with $2 million compared to Carter's $273,000. Barraso won easily 73%-27%, carrying every county. He faces re-election in 2012.

Representative-At-Large

Cynthia Lummis (R)

Elected 2008, 1st term; b. Sept. 10, 1954, Cheyenne; home, Cheyenne; U. of WY, B.S. 1976, B.S. 1978; J.D. 1985; Lutheran; married (Alvin Wiederspahn); 1 child.

Elected Office: WY House of Reps., 1979–83, 1985–93; WY Senate, 1994–95; WY treasurer 1998–2006.

Professional Career: WY Supreme Court law clerk, 1985–86; Wiederspahn, Lummis & Liepas, P.C., 1986–96; Lummis Livestock Co. LLC, 1976–present.

DC Office: 1004 LHOB, 20510, 202-225-2311; Fax: 202-225-3057; Web site: lummis.house.gov.

State Offices: Casper, 307-261-6595; Cheyenne, 307-772-2595; Rock Springs, 307-362-4095; Sheridan, 307-673-4608.

Committees: *Agriculture* (18th of 18 R): Department Operations, Oversight, Nutrition & Forestry; Horticulture & Organic Agriculture. *Budget* (12th of 15 R). *Natural Resources* (18th of 20 R): Energy & Mineral Resources; National Parks, Forests & Public Lands.

Group Ratings and Key Votes: Newly Elected

Election Results

2008 general	Cynthia Lummis (R)	131,244	(53%)	($1,517,018)
	Gary Trauner (D)	106,758	(43%)	($1,716,008)
	W. David Herbert (Lib)	11,030	(4%)	
2008 primary	Cynthia Lummis (R)	33,149	(46%)	
	Mark Gordon (R)	26,827	(37%)	
	Bill Winney (R)	8,537	(12%)	

Wyoming, the nation's least populous state, has elected one representative-at-large since it was admitted to the Union in 1890. The new congresswoman from Wyoming is Cynthia Lummis, a Republican who succeeded GOP Rep. Barbara Cubin in 2009.

Lummis *(LUM iss)* grew up on her family's ranch in Cheyenne. She earned two bachelor's degrees and a law degree at the University of Wyoming. When she won a seat in the state House of Representatives at age 24, Lummis became the youngest woman ever elected to the Wyoming Legislature. She chaired the Revenue Committee and helped revise the state's taxation of the mining industry, which is the state's chief source of revenue. She served in the state Senate from 1994 to 1995, and went on to become state treasurer in 1998. In that office, she diversified the state's investment portfolio—at the time it contained large investments in mortgage giants Fannie Mae and Freddie Mac—to include various equities totaling $8.5 billion. According to Lummis, the move helped Wyoming weather the recent economic downturn spurred by a credit crisis in the home mortgage market.

In 2007, the Wyoming Republican party placed Lummis on a list of three potential candidates to succeed Sen. Craig Thomas, a Republican who died of leukemia in June of that year. Under Wyoming state law, if a senator leaves office prematurely, his political party must nominate three possible replacements. The governor then chooses a successor from those candidates. Lummis' name was submitted along with state Sen. John Barrasso and ex-Justice Department attorney Tom Sansonetti. Lummis' poor relationship with Freudenthal made her a dark horse candidate. It was reported that during a private meeting in 2002, Freudenthal threatened her by saying, "Don't ever cross me or your head will be in your lap before you even know I've drawn my knife." Lummis verified this report, and Freudenthal did not deny it. Freudenthal selected Barrasso for the Senate seat, but Lummis says the experience encouraged her to seek federal office. She announced her candidacy for the state's at-large seat in the U.S. House, which came open in 2008 when Cubin retired from Congress.

In the Republican primary, Lummis faced rancher Mark Gordon, who invested $1 million of his own money and outspent Lummis by 4-to-1. The candidates' similar political views made the race a reflection on leadership. Gordon ran as a political outsider, but Lummis criticized him for supporting Democratic presidential nominee John Kerry in 2004 and Democrat Gary Trauner in his 2006 race against Cubin. Lummis won with 46% of the vote to Gordon's 37%.

In the general election, Lummis faced Trauner, a businessman who came out of nowhere in 2006 and used a well-financed grassroots campaign to nearly unseat Cubin. The Democratic Congressional Campaign Committee put Trauner on their top priority "Red to Blue" list, but his chances of winning in a heavily Republican state diminished with the prospect of having to face a candidate other than Cubin, whose poor roll call attendance and penchant for outlandish comments had weakened her politically. Lummis ran as a staunch conservative, pledging to oppose new taxes and calling for making the Bush administration tax cuts permanent. Trauner claimed that Lummis would threaten the stability of the country's Social Security system by investing money from the program in unstable capital markets, which she denied. Several October polls showed the candidates in a statistical dead heat, but the numbers proved to be misleading. Lummis won 53%-43% with Libertarian candidate David Herbert getting 4% of the vote.

In the House, Lummis joined the Republican Study Committee, a group of the most conservative members of the House. As a new member of the Budget Committee, Lummis called for reform of spending earmarks and promised that she would not request them for her state. Appropriations earmarks have come under fire in recent years as wasteful spending. Lummis criticized President Barack Obama for signing an omnibus appropriations bill containing thousands of earmarks. "I ran for Congress to end this type of self-serving legislation," Lummis said. "The president promised to change the process. He promised he would not sign bills containing earmarks. Yet, it is apparent that promise was merely lip service during an election year."

She also co-sponsored a successful bill with other Wyoming members of Congress. It allows gun owners to carry concealed weapons in national parks, and was signed into law by Obama as part of credit card-holders consumer protection bill.

THE INSULAR
★ TERRITORIES ★

PUERTO RICO

Puerto Rico has a unique history. For four centuries, from Columbus' landing in 1493 until the Spanish-American War of 1898, Puerto Rico was a Spanish colony, and for three centuries the port of San Juan was the gathering place for its annual convoy of gold and silver from the Americas to Spain. Today, with nearly 4 million people (more than Oregon or Connecticut), it is the largest American territory. Sixty years ago, it was "the poorhouse of the Caribbean," heavily populated, and devoted almost entirely to sugar and coffee cultivation. Now, Puerto Rico has a recognizably First World economy, although it has lagged other Latin America powerhouses in recent years. The island's economy contracted from 2006 to 2008 as unemployment rose to 12%. Puerto Ricans of all political stripes rejoiced at the Supreme Court nomination in June 2009 of Judge Sonia Sotomayor, whose parents were born in Puerto Rico and who has long proclaimed her pride in her Puerto Rican heritage.

Puerto Rico has elected a resident commissioner to Congress since 1900, the only member of Congress with a four-year term, and its residents have been American citizens since 1917. But it didn't elect its own governor until 1948. From the 1940s until the early 1960s, Puerto Rico was transformed by Gov. Luis Muñoz Marin and his Popular Democratic Party. Muñoz initiated "Operation Bootstrap" to lure businesses to Puerto Rico with promises of low-wage labor and government-built factories and tax exemptions. Muñoz also developed Puerto Rico's commonwealth form of government—in Spanish, Estado Libre Asociado (ELA): Free Associated State—approved by referendum in 1952. Under ELA, Puerto Rico is part of the United States for purposes of international trade, foreign policy and war, but has its own laws, taxes and representative government. It is not subject to federal income taxes and is not eligible for all federal benefits, though some have been approved by Congress. Puerto Rico has also developed its own political parties: Muñoz's Popular Democrats (the Spanish acronym is PPD), the New Progressives (PNP) who favor statehood, and two small Independence parties.

The commonwealth solution, by its own terms, was open to amendment, and ever since Muñoz retired in 1964, the central issue in Puerto Rico's politics has been status: Should the island continue or modify ELA, should it seek statehood, or should it seek independence? For many years, there was gradual movement toward statehood. In the July 1967 referendum, conducted when the Popular Democrats were in power, Puerto Ricans voted for ELA over statehood 60%-39%. In the November 1993 referendum, conducted with PNP Gov. Pedro Rosselló in office, the vote was 48% for ELA, 46% for statehood. In March 1998, the U.S. House voted 209-208 for a referendum setting terms for statehood. This was a project of Speaker Newt Gingrich, R-Ga., who hoped to attract Hispanic votes, and of Natural Resources Committee Chairman Don Young, R-Alaska, who saw in statehood backers' demands echoes of Alaska's fight for statehood. But the bill went nowhere in the U.S. Senate. Rosselló ordered a referendum on his terms, which were unlikely to be accepted in Congress, in December 1998; 47% voted for statehood and 50% for "none of the above," the option favored by the PPD. Independence has low levels of support (4% in 2008), primarily from university students.

More recently, the action on status has moved from the island to the mainland. In December 2005, a White House task force, originally set up during President Bill Clinton's administration, finally reported. It recommended a two-step referendum, with Puerto Ricans both on the island and on the mainland first voting on whether to consider a change in the current ELA status, and then, if they favored a change, choosing between statehood and independence. A bill incorporating this recommendation was sponsored by Rep. Jose Serrano, D-N.Y., and then-Resident Commissioner Luis Fortuño of the PNP in 2006. The approach was criticized by Gov. Aníbal Acevedo, who argued that the two-step approach would frustrate the wishes of the majorities or pluralities that had voted for ELA in previous referenda and would produce a verdict for an option, statehood, which clearly lacked majority support. Acevedo called for "enhanced commonwealth," under which Puerto Rico could set its own foreign and trade policies and opt out of federal law as negotiated with Congress. To advance this, Rep. Nydia Velazquez, D-N.Y., sponsored a bill in 2007 authorizing a constitutional convention on the island in which delegates could decide on status and define Puerto Rico's relationship with the mainland.

In October 2007, the Natural Resources Committee unanimously approved a bill requiring a referendum by the end of 2009 on whether Puerto Rico should maintain its current status, with an amendment by Velasquez declaring that if the result was negative, then Congress would recognize the Puerto Rico government's "inherent authority" to decide between holding a constitutional convention or holding a second referendum on status. But the bill never came to the floor. In December 2007, the Bush administration issued a report arguing that Puerto Rico had only three options—statehood, remaining a territory or independence—and that Acevedo's "new commonwealth" was unconstitutional.

There may be action on this issue in the near future. The PNP won a sweeping victory in the November 2008 elections. Fortuño was elected governor, and Pedro Pierluisi was elected to represent Puerto Rico in Washington. President Barack Obama in a letter to Fortuño pledged to "enable the question of Puerto Rico's status to be resolved" in his first term. When it was read at Fortuño's inauguration it got a standing ovation. In May 2009, Pierluisi and Serrano introduced a bill similar to Fortuño's. The bill had 147 co-sponsors from both parties. If it passes the House and Senate, there is little doubt that Fortuño and the PNP-controlled Puerto Rico Senate would authorize a second referendum and that statehood could prevail.

A vote for statehood would raise the question whether Congress would accept Puerto Rico as a state under the terms and conditions advocated by the PNP (Spanish as an official language, for example, and continuation of Puerto Rico's eligibility under certain welfare laws). As for mainland politicians, Democrats and many Republicans assume that as a state Puerto Rico would be solidly Democratic, with five or six House members, though Fortuño, a Republican, and Senate President Kenneth McClintock, a statehood backer and Democrat, argue that it would actually lean Republican. McClintock points out that in the 1950s, almost everyone assumed that Hawaii would be Republican and Alaska Democratic, when it has turned out to be the other way around. Over the last century, Congress has admitted new states only when there has been a widespread consensus for statehood.

As the debate over status has gone on, Puerto Rico's economy has been evolving, and not entirely in a positive direction. In the 1990s, Gov. Pedro Rosselló moved Puerto Rico away from big government, selling off the government-owned Navieras shipping line, telephone company and hospitals. Gov. Calderon moved a bit in the other direction in 2002, with a program investing $1 billion in the 700 poorest communities in the island, in infrastructure, education and health care programs. But none of this has spurred enough private sector growth. Puerto Rico has some of the lowest male work force participation in the world. Crime rates are much higher than on the mainland, and there is a new movement of bilingual professionals—nurses, policemen, doctors, teachers—from the island to mainland locations where fluency in Spanish is an asset. The Census Bureau estimates net outmigration of only 41,000—about 1% of the population—from 2000 to 2008.

The 2008 election seems to have broken a partisan deadlock in Puerto Rico, which had seen its leaders elected by razor-thin margins in recent years. The PNP won big in 2008. Fortuño won in the governor's race by eight percentage points, a large margin, and Pedro Pierluisi won the resident commissioner's race by a similar vote. The PNP won in all eight Senate districts and in 31 of the 40 House of Representatives districts. Upon taking office, Fortuño announced that he hoped to cut government payrolls by attrition. Soon, however, he was announcing substantial layoffs, even as the government faced a $3.2 billion budget shortfall on a $9.5 billion budget.

One of the complaints of Puerto Rico's New Progressives is that it cannot vote for president, despite efforts by PNP politicians over the years to change this. Puerto Rico does send delegates to the two mainland parties' national conventions. Since Puerto Rico's Democratic delegates in the past have voted as a bloc, while Democratic rules require most other states' delegates to be split proportionately, in a divided Democratic convention (if there ever is one again) Puerto Rico theoretically has more leverage than all but a half dozen or so states.

For 2008, Puerto Rico Democrats planned to select delegates in caucuses on June 7, four days after the last scheduled primary. But after the March 4 primaries, when it became apparent that the contest between Illinois Sen. Barack Obama and New York Sen. Hillary Rodham Clinton would likely continue until the last primaries, the PPD, allied with the national Democratic Party, decided to hold a primary on June 1, two days before the last primaries in Montana and South Dakota. Even though Clinton consistently led in the polls, many Puerto Rico politicians of both parties endorsed Obama, including the PNP's Pierluisi and PPD Gov. Acevedo. Obama avoided taking a stance on the status issue. Clinton, many of whose constituents in New York have roots in Puerto Rico, got fewer major endorsements but campaigned heavily around the island, while Obama concentrated on Montana and South Dakota.

Clinton won a solid 68%-32% victory, winning 38 delegates to Obama's 17. But this was far too few to overcome Obama's delegate lead, and her hopes of coming out ahead in the popular vote were frustrated by the low turnout. Puerto Rico had 2.4 million registered voters, but only 384,000 voted in the June Democratic primary. Still, the Democratic turnout dwarfed Republican participation: only 208 people participated in the GOP's caucus.

Governor   Luis Fortuño, a member of the New Progressive Party (PNP), was elected governor of Puerto Rico in 2008. Fortuño grew up in San Juan and graduated from Georgetown University and the University of Virginia law school. He practiced corporate law at a San Juan law firm until Gov. Pedro Rosselló appointed him executive director of the Puerto Rico Tourism Company in 1993. In 1994, he became Puerto Rico's first Economic Development and Commerce secretary. In 1996, he returned to private practice. Like some but not all members of the PNP, he identifies with the mainland Republican Party. In 2001, he became Puerto Rico's Republican National Committeeman, and in 2004 he won an election to become Puerto Rico's resident commissioner, the island's representative in Congress.

Puerto Ricans tend to vote along strict party lines, and the results in 2004 were very close. Fortuño won 48.5%-48.0%, outperforming his party's candidate for governor (who narrowly lost) by only 0.5%.

That made Fortuño the first Republican to represent Puerto Rico in the House since 1904. This was also the first time Puerto Rico has elected a split ticket, sharply divided on the key issue of Puerto Rico's status. The pro-statehood Fortuño frequently quarreled with the Popular Democratic Party's (PPD) Gov. Aníbal Acevedo Vila, who supports the island's current commonwealth status. Fortuño co-sponsored a bill with Rep. Jose Serrano, D-N.Y., based on the December 2005 White House task force recommendation for a two-step referendum, the first vote on whether to retain the current status, the second, if it is rejected, to choose between independence and statehood. He opposed New York Democratic Rep. Nydia Velazquez's bill for a constitutional convention in Puerto Rico, which was more likely to lead to Acevedo's choice of "enhanced commonwealth," arguing that Acevedo's proposal that Puerto Rico set its own foreign and trade policies was unrealistic. "Three administrations have told you what you are proposing is unconstitutional. What part of no don't you understand?" But to get unanimous approval for his bill in the Natural Resources Committee in October 2007, Fortuño agreed to compromise between his bill and Velazquez's. The bill never reached the floor.

In February 2007 Fortuño announced he would challenge Acevedo in 2008's gubernatorial election. Acevedo was in a difficult position. He had been elected by just 48.4%-48.2% after a lengthy court battle, and he had fought with a PNP-controlled Senate and House about how to best deal with Puerto Rico's declining employment and severe fiscal problems. Their fights had resulted in a government shutdown in 2006. In March 2008, Acevedo was indicted on 19 counts of using campaign funds for personal expenses and accepting family trips as far afield as China and $37,000 worth of clothing. He proclaimed his innocence and allies accused the prosecution of harboring political motivations. He was acquitted in March 2009, but the trial severely damaged his re-election chances. Fortuño won his election 53%-41%, the biggest victory in a Puerto Rico gubernatorial election since 1964.

Resident Commissioner

Pedro Pierluisi (D)

Elected 2008, 1st term; b. April 26, 1959, San Juan; home, San Juan; Tulane U., B.A. 1981; George Washington U., J.D. 1984; Catholic; married (Maria-Elena Carrion); 4 children.

Elected Office: PR atty. gen., 1993–96

Professional Career: Practicing atty., 1997–2007

DC Office: 1218 LHOB, 20515, 202-225-2615; Fax: 202-225-2154; Web site: pierluisi.house.gov.

State Offices: Old San Juan, 787-723-6333.

Committees: *Education & Labor* (27th of 29 D): Early Childhood, Elementary & Secondary Education; Higher Education, Lifelong Learning & Competitiveness. *Judiciary* (14th of 24 D): Crime, Terrorism & Homeland Security; Immigration, Citizenship, Border Security & International Law. *Natural Resources* (29th of 29 D): Insular Affairs, Oceans & Wildlife; National Parks, Forests & Public Lands.

Pedro Pierluisi, a member of the New Progressive Party (PNP) who caucuses with the Democrats in Washington, was elected Puerto Rico's resident commissioner in November 2008. Pierluisi grew up in San Juan, the son of former Puerto Rico Housing Secretary Jorge Pierluisi. Pedro Pierluisi graduated from Tulane University and George Washington Law School in the early 1980s and served as an aide to Resident Commissioner Baltasar Corrada of the PNP. He practiced law for six years in Washington. In 1993, Gov. Pedro Rosselló of the PNP appointed him attorney general of Puerto Rico. He argued two constitutional cases before the Puerto Rico Supreme Court and got Puerto Rico designated as a High Intensity Drug Trafficking Area. He left Rosselló's scandal-plagued administration in 1996 and practiced law in Puerto Rico.

In February 2007, the PNP's Luis Fortuño, then the resident commissioner, announced he was running for governor. Three months later, Pierluisi decided to run for resident commissioner. Although the two have different mainland party affiliations (Fortuño is a Republican), they both are strong backers of statehood for Puerto Rico, and ran on a united ticket. Pierluisi spent $1.5 million, while his PPD opponent Alfred Salazar spent only $529,000. Pierluisi won by 53%-42%, an almost identical result as Fortuño's victory, and carried 71 of Puerto Rico's 78 municipalities. This was basically a straight-ticket election, the biggest win for the PNP ever and the biggest win for either party in Puerto Rico since 1964.

In the House, Pierluisi caucuses with the Democrats and has seats on the Education and Labor, Judiciary and Natural Resources Committees. He has the largest office budget of any House member, including Speaker Nancy Pelosi, D-Calif., because he represents by far the largest constituency, with nearly 4 million people compared to the average congressional district's 700,000. In March 2009, Pierluisi and Del. Madeleine Bordallo, D-Guam, co-sponsored a bill to provide military retirees, dependents and survivors in Puerto Rico and Guam with more robust health insurance. In May 2009, he introduced a bill on Puerto Rico status, similar to a bill introduced by Fortuño in 2007 that passed in committee but never received a floor vote. It calls for a referendum on maintaining Puerto Rico's current status and, if the vote is negative, authorizes the government of Puerto Rico to hold a referendum to choose between common-wealth, statehood or independence.

VIRGIN ISLANDS

The United States' other insular territory in the Caribbean is the Virgin Islands, a very different sort of place from Puerto Rico, and the only place under the U.S. flag where people drive on the left. It is much smaller, with a resident population of only 110,000, mainly on the three islands of St. Thomas, St. John and St. Croix, purchased by the United States from Denmark in 1917. They were settled by Dutch and Danes and had a polyglot colonial society with one of the oldest Jewish communities in the Western Hemisphere. The islands' most famous son is Alexander Hamilton, who grew up on St. Croix. The Virgin Islands have lived primarily off tourism and refineries. The Hovensa refinery on St. Croix, half-owned by the Venezuelan government, is the largest refinery in the Western Hemisphere and one of the ten largest in the world. These industries have produced high incomes for a few employees but have not pro-vided the basis for a steady economy. Tourism, hurt by hurricanes in the 1990s, was up sharply in 2004, when cruise ships returned to St. Croix after a two-year hiatus because of high crime. But Hurricane Omar's indirect hit in October 2008 and the global economic recession that began in 2007 badly hurt tourism. Still, St. Thomas remains the No. 1 cruise ship port in the world, with nearly 400 ships coming in each year.

Investment businesses are attracted to the Virgin Islands by tax breaks established by Congress and the Virgin Islands government. Individuals and businesses that qualify under the Economic Develop-ment Authority pay a maximum of 3.5% in income tax, which has yielded revenues of about $100 million a year to the island government. To qualify, taxpayers must live and do business in the Virgin Islands. Since 2004, Congress has been gradually tightening restrictions on who can claim residency, and the Internal Revenue Service has been increasingly performing audits of those who abuse the tax loophole. This has cost the island tens of millions.

This loss of revenue is a serious problem. The Virgin Islands government has been running structural deficits estimated at between $50 million and $100 million out of a budget of about $600 million. Another problem is the crushing burden of a $1 billion bond debt, which requires $45 million in debt service. One-third of workers on the islands are employed by government, which has been teetering on the brink of financial collapse.

Salvation may come through rum. In October 2008, House Ways and Means Chairman Charles Rangel, D-N.Y., put into a the $700 billion bailout of the financial services industry a renewal of the Carib-bean rum rebate which sends $13.25 of the $13.50 per gallon federal excise tax on rum back to the produc-ing territory. And in July 2008, Diageo announced that it would move its Captain Morgan production from Puerto Rico to the Virgin Islands in return for a $250 million bond to finance the distillery.

The U.S. Virgin Islands plays a small role in the presidential selection process. It held a Democratic presidential primary on February 9, 2008, in which Illinois Sen. Barack Obama beat New York Sen. Hillary Rodham Clinton 90%-8% (the actual vote count was 1,772 to 149) and got all three pledged dele-gates. Republicans held a tiny caucus in a local restaurant that April, after Sen. John McCain had already locked up the nomination; all delegates chosen supported him. The U.S. Virgin Islands played a role in electing Michael Steele as Republican National Committee chairman in February 2009. The 15 delegates from the territories all backed Steele, who said he would pay close attention to them, and they gave him his margin of victory.

Governor   John deJongh, a Democrat, has been governor of the Virgin Islands since 2006. DeJongh (*dee YOUNG*) grew up in St. Thomas and in Detroit and attended Antioch College. He returned to St. Thomas, worked on the Tri-Island Development Council's historic redevelopment projects, then ran all consumer banking for Chase Bank in the U.S. and British Virgin Islands and St. Maarten. From 1987 to 1990, he was commissioner of finance and headed the U.S. Virgin Islands Public Finance Authority. From 1990 to 1992, he was executive assistant to Democratic Gov. Alexander Farrelly. For the next dozen years, he worked in the private sector in the Virgin Islands, including a stint as president of the chamber of commerce.

In 2002, deJongh ran for governor as an independent and finished second to incumbent Democratic Gov. Charles Turnbull, nearly forcing Turnbull into a runoff. Turnbull was term-limited in 2006, after eight years dealing with the Virgin Islands' massive financial problems. This was a close race. On the first ballot, deJongh was just two votes short of winning the required absolute majority. In a runoff, he defeated Republican Kenneth Mapp 57%-43%. To try to help cover the government's large deficit, de-Jongh sought in 2007 to revamp residential property taxes. The resulting bill eliminated the territory's single tax rate that had been used on all property since 1936 and established four property classes with a different tax rate for each. The new system was expected to increase property tax revenues, but lawsuits against the law were still pending in early 2009.

Delegate

Donna Christensen (D)

Elected 1996, 7th term; b. Sept. 19, 1945, Teaneck, NJ; home, St. Croix; St. Mary's Col., B.S. 1966, George Washington U., M.D. 1970; Moravian; married (Christian); 6 children.

Professional Career: Practicing physician, 1975–97; Territorial Asst., Commissioner of Health, 1988–94; Acting Commissioner of Health, 1994–95.

DC Office: 1510 LHOB, 20515, 202-225-1790; Fax: 202-225-5517; Web site: donnachristensen.house.gov.

State Offices: St. Croix, 340-778-5900; St. Thomas, 340-774-4408.

Committees: *Energy & Commerce* (28th of 36 D): Communications, Technology & the Internet; Health; Oversight & Investigations. *Natural Resources* (18th of 29 D): Insular Affairs, Oceans & Wildlife; National Parks, Forests & Public Lands.

The delegate from the Virgin Islands is Donna Christensen, a Democrat first elected in 1996. Christensen is from an old St. Croix family. Her father was Virgin Islands Chief District Court Judge Almeric Christian. She graduated from St. Mary's College and George Washington Medical School, then practiced medicine for more than 20 years in the Virgin Islands. She was elected a Democratic national committeewoman in 1984 and ran for delegate in 1994, losing to Victor Frazer, a Republican who ran as an independent. In 1996, she ran again. Christensen led Frazer 38%-34% on November 5, and won in a runoff, 52%-48%. It was a regional race: Christensen won 69% on St. Croix, Frazer 64% on St. Thomas and St. John. In the House, Christensen has forged alliances with the Congressional Black Caucus, and she is the first female physician to serve in Congress.

The Virgin Islands have been heavily dependent on a tax loophole that allows people from other parts of the United States to claim residency there and pay lower income taxes. In 2006, Christensen pressed for passage of a bill to recognize as Virgin Islands residents investors who spend 122 days there over three years, rather than the Treasury's requirement of 183 days in one year. In 2007, she called the Internal Revenue Service's audits that extended back many years "unfair" and "intrusive." She supported a provision that was also backed by Ways and Means Chairman Charles Rangel, D-N.Y., that limited their audits to the preceding three years. In April 2006, Christensen passed a measure creating a border patrol unit for the Virgin Islands.

In 2007 and 2008, Christensen served as chairman of the Insular Affairs Subcommittee of the Natural Resources Committee. She worked not only on Virgin Islands issues, but also on those involving other territories. She took interest in Puerto Rico's fight for revised status, and with Natural Resources Chairman Nick Rahall, D-W.Va., she co-sponsored the successful bill to provide stable immigration and minimum wage rules for the Commonwealth of the Northern Marianas Islands and to grant the CNMI a non-voting delegate in the House of Representatives.

In 2008, she got a seat on the powerful Energy and Commerce Committee. This made her the first territorial delegate ever to have a spot on one of the five "A-list" committees. She had to give up the chairmanship of Insular Affairs. In 2008, after easily dispatching her old rival Frazer in the primary, she ran unopposed in the general election.

GUAM

Some 7,800 miles west of Los Angeles and 3,800 miles west of Hawaii, 17 hours of flying time from Washington, D.C., is Guam, where America's day begins. Guam lies west of the International Date Line, and people there are in the early hours of Tuesday when the rest of us are well into Monday afternoon. The Interior Department came to Guam to see whether there were Y2K problems, as the clock struck midnight, January 1, 2000, while it was 9 a.m., December 31, 1999 in Washington. Geographically, it is in the center of the Mariana Islands, but Guam is legally separate. While the Northern Marianas were administered by the United States as a United Nations trust territory until they became the Commonwealth of the Northern Marianas (CNMI) in 1978, Guam was ruled by Navy captains from 1898 to 1949, except for 32 months of Japanese occupation during World War II. In 1950, the Guam Organic Act made Guamanians U.S. citizens. Guam's first civilian governor, Carlton Skinner, who as a captain integrated the crew of his Navy ship in 1943, established the University of Guam and wrote its constitution. Guam elects its local government, GovGuam, but Congress still retains final power over the territory. It gave Guam a non-voting delegate to the House in 1972.

Guam, as the *Washington Post's* Blaine Harden put it, "marries the beauty of Bali with the banality of Kmart." It is 36 miles long by four to nine miles wide, with 178,000 people. Thirty-seven percent are Chamorro (descendants of the original islanders) or from elsewhere in Micronesia, 26% are Filipino, 11% other Pacific Islander, 6% other Asian, 7% white and 12% other or "mixed"; 85% of Guamanians are Catholic. The Catholic Church helped defeat a proposal for casino gambling 61%-39% in 2004, despite the competition for tourists. Proposals for slot machines in race tracks in 2006 and 2008 also failed. Guam is tropical, but not an easy environment. In August 1993, it lived through an earthquake rated at 8.2 on the Richter scale, comparable to San Francisco's in 1906. In December 2002, Supertyphoon Pongsona, with winds up to 184 miles per hour, caused hundreds of millions in damage. And Guam suffers from an invasive species, the semi-poisonous brown tree snake, which has killed off nearly all of the island's bird population and severely disrupted the island's ecosystem. The 10-foot long snakes climb up electric poles and cut off the current and have been known to attack infants. Their population peaked in the 1980s, but no one knows how to get rid of them.

Economically, Guam depends on tourism and service businesses, but most of all on the U.S. military. Bases occupy one-third of the land, and 60% of income comes from the federal government, which has produced a per capita gross domestic product higher than in any other Pacific islands except Hawaii. The ups and downs of military deployments have a strong impact on Guam's economy. The drawdown in the 20 years after the Vietnam War, from 30,000 personnel to 5,000 in the late 1980s, resulted in plummeting housing values and high unemployment. Guam, 3,700 miles closer to Asia than Hawaii, is valuable strategically, especially in light of events such as the September 11 attacks, popular protests in South Korea and Japan against the U.S. military presence there, the threats of the North Korean government, and the need to supply operations in South Asia.

By 2005, military spending here was nearly double the levels of the mid-1990s. The Navy spent $30 million dredging Apra Harbor and repairing World War II-era wharves; $500 million was spent on construction at Andersen Air Force Base. Guam is a good site for training. The Marines rent typhoon-damaged structures for urban warfare exercises and the southern jungles are good for rural warfare training. In October 2005, the United States and Japan agreed that 8,000 Marines would be relocated from Okinawa to Guam by 2012. They would more than double the military presence, and make Guam the strategic "tip of the spear" in the Pacific, as Rear Admiral John Bird put it. Japan agreed to provide $6 billion for the transfer, but the United States will have to spend billions more. Guam's population is expected to swell by 40,000, straining already near-capacity water and wastewater systems. "No American community can shoulder the challenges of a 30% increase in population," Gov. Felix Camacho said in May 2008. GovGuam, which has been borrowing money to meet current expenses, is seeking $2 billion to $3 billion from the federal government to pay for infrastructure and other costs.

For much of the 1990s, Guam sought a change in status, to give the Guam government control over immigration. Chamorros said they want to block others from coming in, establishing citizenship and making them a minority. Another motive was to bring in guest workers as the surrounding Commonwealth of the Northern Marianas Islands had done with its exemption from federal immigration laws. This push went nowhere for years, and in 2007, Congress stripped the CNMI of its exemption as well. This led to demands from both Guam and the CNMI, which had been attracting Chinese tourists to its gambling parlors, for a waiver to the visa requirements for Chinese and Russian tourists.

Guam votes for Democrats more often than Republicans, but politics here are a family matter. Gov. Camacho's father was also governor; his former lieutenant governor, Kaleo Moylan, is the son of the elder Camacho's lieutenant governor. Del. Madeleine Bordallo, wife of former Democratic Gov. Ricardo Bordallo, won the 2002 Democratic nomination by beating Judith Won Pat, daughter of former Del. Antonio Borja Won Pat. In 2006, there were two primary contests for governor, on the Republican side between Camacho and Moylan, whom he had dumped from the ticket; on the Democratic side between former Del. Richard Underwood and former Gov. Carl Gutierrez, whose wife Underwood had bested in the 2002 primary.

Guam, of course, does not cast any electoral votes for president, but has a part in presidential politics. It elects delegates to party national conventions—6 for Republican President George W. Bush and 6 for Democrat John Kerry in 2004. In 2008, Guam Democrats scheduled a primary on May 3, when the Democratic contest was still raging and the winds of political war wafted clear across the Pacific. Hillary Rodham Clinton and Barack Obama both ran television ads. Former President Bill Clinton called in to a morning Guam radio show, while Obama opened an office in the capital of Hagatna, with three paid staffers. Obama stressed his Hawaiian roots and ties to the Pacific islands. Clinton called for a presidential vote for Guam and supported some of Del. Bordallo's proposed legislation. The final result was closer than anywhere else: Obama won 2,264 votes to Clinton's 2,257. That meant, under Democrats' proportional representation delegate allocation rules, that they split evenly Guam's four delegate votes. Guam

Republicans held a convention on March 8, after John McCain clinched the Republican nomination. All nine delegates supported him. In its November election, Guam conducts a straw poll for president, and has voted for the winner every time since 1984. In 2000 George W. Bush beat Al Gore 52%-47%; in 2004, after the big military buildup, Bush beat John Kerry 65%-35%. Barack Obama beat John McCain 62%-37% in 2008.

Governor   Felix Camacho, a Republican, was elected governor of Guam in 2002. Camacho grew up in Guam and attended Catholic schools. His father, Carlos Camacho, was appointed governor in 1969 and elected to a single term in 1970. Felix Camacho graduated from Marquette University in Milwaukee and returned to Guam and worked for Pacific Financial Corporation and IBM. In 1988, Republican Gov. Joseph Ada appointed Camacho deputy chief of the Public Utility Agency and director of the Civil Service Commission. In 1992, Camacho was elected to the Guam Legislature, where he became assistant majority leader.

In 2002, Camacho ran for governor, beating Guam Legislature Speaker Tony Unpingco in the Republican primary, 54%-46%. He faced Democratic U.S. Del. Robert Underwood in the general election and won 55%-45%. But Democrats won a 9-6 majority in the Legislature.

In September 2004, Camacho vetoed the Legislature's $447 million budget, saying it would overspend revenue by $50 million, and the Legislature partially overrode his veto. He also helped arrange the privatization of the Guam Telephone Authority, sold for $150 million in December 2004 to TeleGuam Holdings. In 2006, Camacho declined to challenge a court ruling requiring millions in delinquent cost-of-living payments to GovGuam retirees. Not surprisingly, in September 2006 the Pacific Command said GovGuam was a "financial mess" because of its reluctance to lay off public employees and because of "borrowing in financial markets to pay employees."

Camacho also fought with his lieutenant governor, Kaleo Moylan, and in December 2005, announced that he would choose a different running mate for his re-election bid. Moylan decided to challenge him in the Republican primary, but Camacho prevailed by 63%-36%. In the general election, Camacho once again faced Underwood. The election got ugly: Camacho was attacked for having worked with disgraced Republican lobbyist Jack Abramoff, whose emails showed contempt for Chamorros, the island's largest indigenous group. Meanwhile, Underwood accused Camacho of spreading charges that Underwood was anti-Filipino. Camacho won narrowly 50%-48%.

GovGuam's fiscal problems continued, and Camacho again fought with the Democratic majority in the Legislature. The most controversial issue of his second term was garbage. After GovGuam failed to comply with a judge's order to clean up the Ordot dump, it was ordered in early 2009 to pay a fine of nearly $1 million per week. This put an additional burden on a government already strapped for cash.

Camacho is not eligible to run for a third term in 2010.

Delegate

Madeleine Bordallo (D)

Elected 2002, 4th term; b. May 31, 1933, Graceville, MN; home, Tamuning; St. Mary's Col. 1952, St. Katherine's Col., A.A. 1953; Catholic; widowed; 1 child.

Elected Office: GU Senate, 1981–82, 1986–94; GU Lt. Gov., 1994–2002.

DC Office: 427 CHOB, 20515, 202-225-1188; Fax: 202-226-0341; Web site: www.house.gov/bordallo.

State Offices: Hagatna, 671-477-4272.

Committees: *Armed Services* (18th of 36 D): Military Personnel; Readiness. *Natural Resources* (9th of 29 D): Insular Affairs, Oceans & Wildlife (Chmn); National Parks, Forests & Public Lands.

Madeleine Bordallo, a Democrat, was elected delegate from Guam in 2002. She grew up in Minnesota and, after age 14, on Guam. She studied vocal music at St. Katherine's College in St. Paul and worked for a few Guam radio stations. Madeleine Bordallo became Guam's Democratic National Committeewoman in 1964 and has held that position ever since (she is the most senior member of the Democratic National Committee). Her husband, Ricardo Bordallo, was elected governor in 1974, defeated for re-election in 1978, then elected governor again in 1982. Madeleine Bordallo ran for the Guam Legislature and was first elected in 1980. On Feb. 1, 1990, Ricardo Bordallo, facing a prison term for bribery, chained himself to the statue of Chief Quipuha and shot himself in the head, dying later that day. Madeleine Bordallo was a candidate for governor that year, and lost 57%-43% to incumbent Republican Joseph Ada. In 1994, she was elected lieutenant governor and was re-elected in 1998.

In 2002, when Del. Robert Underwood decided to run for governor, Bordallo ran for delegate. In the primary she faced Judith Won Pat, daughter of Guam's first delegate, Antonio Borja Won Pat. In this contest between longtime friends, Bordallo won 59%-41%. In the general election, she once again faced Ada. This time, Bordallo won by 65%-35%.

Bordallo got a seat on the Armed Services Committee and proceeded to lobby her colleagues for more military deployments in Guam. The 2004 defense reauthorization included $90 million in military construction for Guam. It also included $250,000 for Bordallo's invasive species pilot project; Guam has been plagued by the voracious and repulsive brown tree snake, which has wiped out most of the island's native birds. In 2003, she got a bill signed into law giving Guam and other insular areas the same access to guaranteed loans as the 50 states. She sought $157 million of debt relief for Guam but her request was denied by the Bush administration. Working closely with her mentor, Hawaii Democratic Sen. Daniel Inouye, she successfully got $30 million annual compact aid for 20 years, to be divided among Guam, Hawaii, the Northern Mariana Islands and American Samoa. In 2005, she secured passage of a bill designating Guam as a Historically Underutilized Business Zone, which gave small businesses preferred treatment in federal contracting.

Bordallo, like other Guam delegates before her, has sought reparations for Guamanians for human rights abuses suffered during Japan's occupation during World War II, even though the 1951 treaty between the U.S. and Japan absolved Japan of any claims. In May 2007, the House approved her bill for reparations for Guamanians who suffered during the occupation. It died in the Senate after Sen. Jim DeMint, R-S.C., objected to it. In 2009, Bordallo became chairman of the Natural Resources Committee's Insular Affairs Subcommittee and continued to lobby members of both parties for the bill. Also that year, she held oversight hearings on implementation of the 2008 law imposing federal immigration law on the Northern Mariana Islands. She called for a waiver of the cap on temporary work visas for foreign workers and a waiver of visa requirements for Chinese tourists to both Guam and the Northern Marianas.

Bordallo has not had major party opposition since her first election in 2002.

NORTHERN MARIANA ISLANDS

The Commonwealth of the Northern Mariana Islands, in American hands since 1944, gained representation in Congress for the first time in January 2009. This is a chain of approximately 15 islands, only five inhabited, running north and south from Guam in the Western Pacific. The northern islands are volcanic, the southern islands are limestone and are fringed with coral reefs. They are much closer to mainland Asia than the U.S. mainland, and sit some 7,800 miles southwest of Los Angeles and 3,800 miles west of Hawaii. Typhoons are common from August to November.

The Northern Marianas were first peopled by Micronesians three millennia ago and were visited by Magellan in 1521. Spanish Jesuits arrived in 1668, and the islands were a possession of Spain until the Spanish-American War in 1898. In the treaty that followed, Guam was acquired by the United States, but the Northern Marianas were sold to Germany in 1899. They were seized by Japan in 1914 soon after they entered World War I, and The League of Nations gave Japan legal claim to them in 1920. They were occupied by U.S. forces in 1944. The Enola Gay took off in August 1945 from Tinian, on its mission to drop the atomic bomb on Hiroshima. In 1945, the Northern Marianas were put in the custody of the new U.N. Security Council, and in 1947, they were declared part of the U.S. Trust Territory of the Pacific Islands. While the other islands in time opted for independence, the Northern Marianas took a different course.

In 1972, negotiations began on territorial status. In 1975, the Islanders voted to approve a Covenant with the United States creating the Commonwealth of the Northern Mariana Islands (CNMI), which went into effect in March 1976. Under its terms, the CNMI was not subject to federal immigration or labor laws and not obliged to pay U.S. taxes, but it deferred entirely to the United States in foreign and military affairs. Foreign investors were limited to a 49% share of businesses or property, and land could be owned only by "persons of Northern Marianas descent." The CNMI government started operating after the 1977 elections. CNMI citizens did not automatically become U.S. citizens until 1986.

These arrangements were of little interest to Americans on the mainland. The Northern Marianas in the early 1970s had only 12,000 people, about 90% of them on Saipan. There were no modern runways and only one rickety flight a day from Guam. The U.S. government discouraged development in the islands after World War II because the CIA operated a covert training base on half of Saipan until 1962. The private sector economy at that time consisted of some farming and 55 businesses with 673 employees. But the CNMI government began to make decisions which transformed the Northern Marianas. In the mid-1980s, with the current governor, Benigno Fitial, playing an important role as speaker, the CNMI opened up its economy to foreign investment and wrote its immigration laws to permit a huge influx of guest workers. This resulted in heavy investment in garment factories that imported guest workers, mostly female, from low-wage countries like the Philippines, China and Vietnam. Products made here could be labeled "Made in U.S.A." and imported into the United States without being subject to textile import quotas. By the mid-1990s, there were some 34 garment factories, employing 17,000 guest workers. In addition, after a 1986 trade agreement between the U.S. and Japan reduced the value of the dollar against the yen, Japanese investors began building tourist destinations, with many low-wage jobs for guest workers.

The result was a population boom. The 2000 census counted 69,000 people in the Northern Marianas. More than 90% of the people were on Saipan. The population was 32% Chamorro (the original inhabitants) or other Micronesian, 56% Asian, 2% white and 10% other and mixed. The people were a multilingual mix: 24% spoke Philippine languages, 23% Chinese, 22% Chamorro, 11% English, 10% other Pacific languages. Only 44% were U.S. citizens; 54% were women, thanks to the large number of female guest workers; the islands' female-to-male ratio is the highest in the world. The booming garment industry and tourism business were hailed by some free-market conservatives as a triumph of free enterprise. Then U.S. House Majority Leader Tom DeLay, R-Texas, working with later disgraced lobbyist Jack Abramoff, was a strong booster of the CNMI's arrangements, particularly its exemption from federal immigration laws and the federal minimum wage. Others, including U.S. Rep. George Miller, D-Calif., and other Democrats, as well as some conservatives, were appalled at the exploitation of the mostly female Chinese and Filipina guest workers, who were often forced to work dangerously long hours in sweat shops to pay off $7,000 in recruiting fees needed to get such jobs. Many were forced into prostitution by unmonitored recruiters. They had no legal recourse, they could not become U.S. citizens, and they were subject to summary deportation. Members of Congress who wanted reform responded by trying to deny the "Made in U.S.A." label to clothing manufactured in the CNMI. Alaska Republican Frank Murkowski got the Senate to vote unanimously to do so in 1995 and 2000. Rep. Bob Franks, R-N.J., got more than half of his colleagues to co-sponsor a House version, but DeLay kept the bill from coming to a vote.

Two outside developments transformed the situation. In January 2005, a treaty that had set quotas on textile imports into the U.S. expired. Suddenly the CNMI's exemption from those quotas became irrelevant, and Saipan was subject to lower-wage competition from Vietnam, Cambodia and China. Within two months, seven garment factories closed, and four more did so in 2006. Then, in October 2005, Japan Airlines cancelled its daily flights to Saipan after nearly 30 years of direct service. Japanese investors sold three hotels, a golf course and shopping center. Tourism, which had employed half the workforce, nosedived. "The CNMI now faces an economic crisis so dire that the U.S. possession's short-term future appears at best bleak," wrote *Pacific Magazine* in December 2005.

The increase in the federal minimum wage that passed in January 2007 included a gradual increase in the hourly minimum wage for the CNMI from $3.05 to $7.25 by 2014. This further destroyed the business model of the garment factories, which claimed they could not survive an hourly wage above $4. By July 2007, 19 of the original 34 factories had closed, and by January 2009, they were all vacant. The House voted in December 2007 to bring the CNMI under federal immigration law. The Senate followed suit in April 2008, and the bill was signed in May. This will phase out the current guest worker program by 2017, replacing it with a federally monitored temporary worker program that will provide worker protections, end sweat shop conditions, and seek to eliminate the CNMI's burgeoning sex industry. Most CNMI politicians opposed the bill, but had little power to stop it. The bill also gave the CNMI its first ever delegate in Congress, partially as a response to island politicians' arguments that they had needed Abramoff because they had no other voice in Washington.

The CNMI does not vote for president and plays less of a role in presidential politics than the other four territories represented in Congress. On February 23, 2008, all nine of its delegates to the Republican National Convention "decided to vote as a team for McCain." The national Democratic Party does not recognize the CNMI Democratic Party. The successful candidate for delegate in 2008, Gregorio Kilili Sablan, said he was a Democrat but ran as an independent because the Democratic Party "is not organized." In February 2009, the three Republican Party delegates joined 12 colleagues from the territories in casting the decisive votes for Michael Steele as Republican National Chairman.

Governor   Benigno Fitial was elected governor of the CNMI in November 2005 as a candidate of the Covenant Party. He is the first governor of Carolinian descent; the Carolinians immigrated to the Northern Marianas from Micronesia about a century ago. He grew up on Saipan and graduated from the University of Guam. He was elected to the first CNMI Legislature in 1977 and served for the majority of the years since, and had much to do with fashioning the CNMI immigration and property laws which led to the vast growth in the garment and tourism industries in the 1980s and 1990s. He was also an active participant in the Bank of Saipan, Tan Holdings and various insurance, travel and home improvement companies. Long a Republican, he was head of the islands' 2000 campaign for George W. Bush and says he was a "good friend" of disgraced lobbyist Jack Abramoff, who took members of Congress on junkets to the islands. He decided to run for governor in 2005 under the label of the Covenant Party. It was an exceedingly close race. Fitial won by only 99 votes.

Fitial opposes the imposition of federal immigration law on the CNMI, and in September 2008, he filed a lawsuit challenging it on the grounds that it violated the covenant agreed to by the Marianas and the United States in 1976, which allowed the commonwealth to pass its own labor laws. After Homeland Security Secretary Janet Napolitano agreed to delay implementation of federalized immigration from

May 2009 to November 2009, he called for a further delay, and he pressed Congress to grant visa waivers for Chinese and Russian tourists without which, he said, the CNMI would face "economic genocide." During his May 2009 State of the Commonwealth Address, he said, "Over the past three years, the commonwealth essentially faced the perfect financial storm."

Delegate

Gregorio Kilili Camacho Sablan (D)

Elected 2008, 1st term; b. Jan. 19, 1955, Saipan; home, Saipan; Attended U. of Guam, 1972; Attended Armstrong U., 1973–74; Attended U. of HI-Manoa, 1989–90; Catholic; married (Andrea); 6 children.

Military Career: Army Reserves, 1982–87.

Elected Office: Northern Marianas Commonwealth Legislature, 1982–86.

Professional Career: Governor's deputy chief admin. officer, CNMI government, 1980–81; Spec. asst. for mgmt. & budget, CNMI government, 1994–95; Exec. dir., Commonwealth Election Commission, 1999–2008.

DC Office: 423 CHOB, 20515, 202-225-2646; Fax: 202-225-2649; Web site: sablan.house.gov.

State Offices: Saipan, 670-323-2647.

Committees: *Education & Labor* (28th of 29 D): Early Childhood, Elementary & Secondary Education; Workforce Protections. *Natural Resources* (12th of 29 D): Energy & Mineral Resources; Insular Affairs, Oceans & Wildlife.

The first delegate to the U.S. House of Representatives from the Commonwealth of the Northern Mariana Islands is Gregorio Kilili Camacho Sablan, elected in November 2008. He grew up in Saipan in an extended family much involved in politics. His grandfather was the first elected mayor of Saipan, and his uncle was the city's longest serving mayor. At age 11, he moved to the Federated States of Micronesia and attended boarding school, the only ethnic Chamorro there. He attended the University of Guam and the University of California at Berkeley, but did not get a degree. He went to work for Republican Gov. Carlos Camacho, the CNMI's first elected governor, and then was elected to serve in the Legislature from 1982 to 1986. Sablan was on the Washington staff of Sen. Daniel Inouye, D-Hawaii, who has long taken a close interest in the Pacific territories, and served for 18 months. When he returned to Saipan, Sablan was special assistant for management and budget for Democratic Gov. Froilan Tenorio and special assistant for Republican Gov. Pedro Tenorio. Later, he was appointed executive director of the Commonwealth Election Commission and won praise for his conduct of CNMI's closely contested election in 2006.

After Congress voted in April 2008 to give the CNMI a non-voting delegate in Congress for the first time, Sablan ran for the office with eight others. Two of them spent large sums—large for the CNMI, at least—on their campaigns. Retired Judge Juan Tudela Lizama spent $52,000 and seven-year CNMI Washington representative Pete A. Tenorio, a Republican, spent $37,000. Sablan ran as an independent rather than as a Democrat because, he said, the local Democratic Party was "not organized," spent only $15,000 and relied on grass-roots campaigning. He was endorsed by the Filipino-American group CREAM, a group that claims 1,200 registered voters as members. Of 10,161 votes cast, Sablan received 2,474, edging his nearest competition, Tenorio, by 357 votes.

In the House, Sablan's first bill was to convey to the CNMI submerged lands within three miles of the islands, which would reverse a 2005 Ninth Circuit Appellate Court decision. His bill got the support of Insular Affairs Subcommittee Chairman, Del. Madeleine Bordallo, D-Guam, and the ranking Republican, Rep. Jeff Flake of Arizona. In March 2009, Sablan called for a 180-day delay in implementing federal immigration law in the CNMI, and later that month, Homeland Security Secretary Janet Napolitano agreed to the delay.

AMERICAN SAMOA

American Samoa, the only American territory south of the Equator, has been little influenced by Western settlers and remains almost as Polynesian today as it was when the United States took possession of it in 1900 at the request of tribal chiefs. These seven hot, rainy islands are 2,300 miles southwest of Hawaii, 1,600 miles northeast of New Zealand, and have a land area slightly larger than the District of Columbia. American Samoa has 65,000 people, 90% of them on the island of Tutuila, 92% of them pacific islanders, mostly Christian (50% Congregationalist, 20% Catholic). They are U.S. nationals but not U.S. citizens; they can serve in the American military, but not as officers. An estimated 50,000 Samoans live on the

U.S. mainland and 20,000 on Hawaii, including Honolulu Mayor Mufi Hannemann. The islands' population has doubled in the last 20 years, and fear that outsiders will change the culture has prompted some demands for stricter immigration standards. American Samoa is an unincorporated territory that has been administered by the Interior Department since 1951. Minimum wages have been set for industries by the Department of Labor. American Samoa elects a governor and a two-house Legislature known as the Fono. It is a bilingual society and government. Government is mostly conducted in English, Fono proceedings are in Samoan, and court sessions are conducted in English with each sentence then translated into Samoan.

The market economy has not made much progress here. American Samoa lives primarily off the federal government, which contributes about 60% of its government revenues plus varying amounts for construction. The islands received $759 per capita from the 2009 economic stimulus bill. Most private industry revolves around two big StarKist and Chicken of the Sea tuna canneries, which employ 5,150 workers and provide one-third of all U.S. canned tuna. Another 4,000 people work for the American Samoan government, most at $7.99 an hour. Residents are eligible for food stamps and welfare. Local agriculture is minimal and sheltered (the territorial government in 2000 wanted to quadruple tariffs on bananas and taro). The bedrock of the local economy is the territorial government. Congressional Democrats initially excluded American Samoa from their 2007 minimum wage increase, although Guam and the Commonwealth of the Northern Marianas Islands were included. This was done at the request of American Samoa Del. Democrat Eni Faleomavaega, who cited lower-wage competition from Thailand and Vietnam. After House Republicans attacked the Democrats for being hypocritical, however, Democrats provided that the minimum wage in American Samoa would rise to $7.25 an hour by 2014. Partially because of the increased minimum wage levels, Chicken of the Sea announced in May 2009 that it would close its Samoa packing plant, exacerbating the problems facing the local economy. StarKist has threatened to leave as well.

The cold words of an official report summarize American Samoa's difficulty in finding alternatives to the tuna canneries. "Attempts by the government to develop a larger and broader economy are restrained by Samoa's remote location, its limited transportation and its devastating hurricanes. Tourism is a promising developing sector." But not terribly promising, at least yet. Togiola (surnames come first in Samoan) would like to have controls over immigration, and says he hopes to develop "controlled tourism in a way that won't affect our fragile environment."

If American Samoans are proud Samoans, they are also proud Americans. On April 17, 2000, they celebrated the 100th anniversary of the American takeover, with a 60-foot American flag raised on Sogelau Hill where the flag was first raised on the island. There was traditional singing and dancing and a long boat race in Pago Pago Harbor. And Samoans have become devoted to one staple of American life: football. The island has six high school football teams and a 5,000-seat stadium where just about everyone comes to cheer. The style of play is aggressive, with lots of body contact. A dozen mainland college coaches take the 15-hour twice-weekly flights to American Samoa to scout players and schools offer them SAT preparatory classes; more than 10% receive football scholarships and 41 players of Samoan descent were listed on NFL rosters in 2007.

American Samoa does not cast electoral votes for president, but it does send delegates to the parties' national conventions. In 2004, Massachusetts Sen. John Kerry got 2.5 votes at the Democratic National Convention divided between five delegates and Ohio Rep. Dennis Kucinich got the remaining half-vote from the sixth delegate. The week before, President George W. Bush won all six Republican delegates. In 2008, Sen. Hillary Rodham Clinton, D-N.Y., edged out Sen. Barack Obama, D-Ill., receiving two convention votes split among four delegates, while Obama got one vote and two delegates. Sen. John McCain of Arizona swept the Republican caucus, receiving all nine delegates.

American Samoa also plays some role in national party politics. Democratic National Chairman Howard Dean, fulfilling his promise to visit every state and territory during his tenure as head of the DNC, visited American Samoa in January 2009 and remained publicly cheerful when the Obama transition team snubbed him by announcing that Virginia Gov. Tim Kaine would be his successor and then holding introduction ceremonies without inviting Dean. In February 2009, the Republican territorial chairman and national committeeman and committeewoman were part of a 15-member bloc from the five territories who provided the critical votes in the election of Michael Steele as Republican National Chairman.

Governor   Democrat Togiola T.A. Tulafono was sworn in as American Samoa's governor on April, 7, 2003, after the sudden death of Gov. Tauese Sunia on March 26. Togiola grew up in American Samoa. He graduated from the Honolulu Police Academy and worked as a policeman for a year. After attending college and law school on the mainland, he returned to American Samoa, where he practiced law for 20 years and served as a judge and a senator. Togiola was elected lieutenant governor in 1996 and served under Tauese until his death.

As governor in 2004, Togiola sponsored a statute criminalizing human trafficking, to complement the federal statute under which a Korean garment factory operator was prosecuted in 2001. Also in 2004 he expressed concern that all the 200 Army reservists in American Samoa would be called to active duty at the same time, and asked the Army to modify the policy to allow for partial deployments. In December 2004, 56 were deployed, including his daughter Olita Tulafono. In 2005, Togiola called for controls on immigration from Samoa. He has also drawn notice for his attempt to get a new airline to serve American Samoa. Only Hawaiian Airlines serves American Samoa, with four flights weekly between Pago Pago and Honolulu, and it receives a federal subsidy under the Essential Air Services program to do so. Togiola has charged that the airline charges too much and frequently reschedules flights at great inconvenience to passengers. Togiola issued an executive order ending service, but that was overturned by the U.S. Department of Transportation.

In the 2008 election, Togiola won 41% of the votes in the first round to 31% for Utu Abe Malae and 27% for Afoa Leulumoega Lufu, even though Togiola's lieutenant governor was facing federal corruption charges. In the runoff he beat Malae by a 56%-44% margin.

In 2008 and 2009, Togiola opposed the six-month incremental increases in the minimum wage voted by Congress. Also in 2008 he complained to Sen. Daniel Inouye, D-Hawaii, and other congressional leaders about Delegate Eni Faleomavaega's amendment to the Coast Guard Authorization Bill allowing Taiwan-built tuna vessels to sail under the U.S. flag. He argued that this would allow foreign boats to encroach on Samoan business. In 2009 he blamed the provision for costing American Samoa its Chicken of the Sea packing plant because it allowed the company to process the tuna in Vietnam and can it in Georgia.

Delegate

Eni F.H. Faleomavaega (D)

Elected 1988, 11th term; b. Aug. 15, 1943, Vailoatai; home, Pago Pago; Brigham Young U., B.A. 1966, U. of Houston, J.D. 1972, U. of CA, LL.M. 1973; Mormon; married (Hinanui); 5 children.

Military Career: Army, 1966–69 (Vietnam).

Elected Office: AS Lt. Gov., 1984–89.

Professional Career: A.A., U.S. Del. from AS, 1973–75; Cnsl., U.S. House Interior Cmte., 1975–81; AS Dpty. Atty. Gen., 1981–84.

DC Office: 2422 RHOB, 20515, 202-225-8577; Fax: 202-225-8757; Web site: www.house.gov/faleomavaega.

State Offices: Pago Pago, 684-633-1372.

Committees: *Foreign Affairs* (3rd of 28 D): Asia, the Pacific & the Global Environment (Chmn); Western Hemisphere. *Natural Resources* (3rd of 29 D): Energy & Mineral Resources; Insular Affairs, Oceans & Wildlife.

American Samoa has elected a delegate to Congress since 1980. Del. Eni F. H. Faleomavaega is a Democrat first elected in 1988. He went to high school in Hawaii, to Brigham Young University, and then to law school in Houston and Berkeley. He served in Vietnam in the Army. In the 1970s, he worked on the Natural Resources Insular Subcommittee staff and for Utah Democrat Gunn McKay. In 1981, he became deputy attorney general of American Samoa, and in 1985 lieutenant governor. In 1987 he was a crew member on the Hawaiian-Polynesian canoe Hokule'a which sailed from Tahiti to Hawaii, a reprise of the epic Polynesian voyages of the first millennium A.D. He is one of four Mormon Democrats in Congress (the others are Sens. Harry Reid of Nevada and Tom Udall of New Mexico and Rep. Jim Matheson of Utah) and Faleomavaega has campaigned in Utah among Samoans living or studying there.

Faleomavaega (he uses his last name, rather than the first name used to refer to Samoan chiefs) serves on the Natural Resources Committee, where he has been ranking minority member on various subcommittees. In January 2007, he became the chairman of the Subcommittee on Asia, the Pacific and the Global Environment on the Foreign Affairs Committee. He has taken a particular interest in the independence movement in Indonesia's West Papua, where his relatives were Christian missionaries in the late 1800s. The Indonesian government denied him entry to West Papua in July 2007, on the grounds that it would stimulate demonstrations and violence, but that December, Indonesian President Susilo Bambang Yudhoyono allowed him limited, closely monitored access to the island. Faleomavaega complained to Yudhoyono about his travel restrictions and told him that Indonesia "has done such a lousy job in the treatment of West Papuans, you might as well give them their independence."

For several years, Faleomavaega pressed for a bill to exempt interest on American Samoa bonds from state and local taxes—the same treatment given bonds issued by Puerto Rico, Guam and the Virgin Islands—and it was signed into law in 2004. He has also worked successfully for favorable tax treatment for tuna canneries. In 2007, Faleomavaega urged his fellow Democrats not to include American Samoa in their minimum wage increase. "The truth is that the global tuna industry is so competitive that it is no longer possible for the federal government to demand mainland minimum wage rates for American

Samoa without causing the collapse of our economy and making us welfare wards of the federal government."

In April 2008, he secured an amendment to the Coast Guard appropriation allowing Taiwan-built tuna vessels to sail under the U.S. flag on the grounds that the fishing fleet is old and no U.S. shipyards will build tuna vessels. "No fish means no canneries, and no canneries means no jobs." This was sharply opposed by Democratic Gov. Togiola Tulafono, as well as by Aumua Amata Coleman, his Republican opponent in every election since 2000, and fought in Washington by her husband, lobbyist Fred Radewagen, on the grounds it would encroach on Samoan businesses. In February 2009, when there was talk that StarKist and Chicken of the Sea would close their American Samoa canneries because of scheduled wage increases, Faleomavaega met in Washington with Togiola and Commonwealth of the Northern Marianas Governor Benigno Fitial and they agreed to seek a postponement of the increases. Faleomavaega has sought a comprehensive review of the policy by the Department of Labor, which is tasked with administering the minimum wage in the territory.

In 2008, Faleomavaega once again faced Coleman, who usually presents a strong challenge. This time he beat her by a more comfortable margin, 60%-35%.

LEADERSHIP

The 111th Congress
2009-2010

U.S. Senate

58D, 40R, 2I

Democrats

Senate Majority Leader..............................	Harry Reid (NV)
President Pro Tempore.................................	Robert Byrd (WV)
Senate Assistant Majority Leader and Whip........	Richard Durbin (IL)
Senate Democratic Conference Vice Chairman.....	Charles Schumer (NY)
Senate Democratic Conference Secretary............	Patty Murray (WA)
Senate Democratic Policy Committee Chairman....	Byron Dorgan (ND)
Democratic Senatorial Campaign Committee Chairman...	Robert Menendez (NJ)
Senate Democratic Steering and Outreach Committee Chairwoman............................	Debbie Stabenow (MI)

Republicans

Senate Minority Leader...............................	Mitch McConnell (KY)
Senate Assistant Minority Leader and Whip........	Jon Kyl (AZ)
Senate Republican Conference Chairman...........	Lamar Alexander (TN)
Senate Republican Conference Vice Chairman......	Lisa Murkowski (AK)
Senate Republican Policy Committee Chairman....	John Thune (SD)
National Republican Senatorial Committee Chairman...	John Cornyn (TX)

U.S. House of Representatives

256D, 179R

Democrats

House Speaker...	Nancy Pelosi (CA-8)
Majority Leader.......................................	Steny Hoyer (MD-5)
Majority Whip..	James Clyburn (SC-6)
House Democratic Caucus Chairman...............	John Larson (CT-1)
House Democratic Caucus Vice Chairman..........	Xavier Becerra (CA-31)
Democratic Congressional Campaign Committee Chairman...	Chris Van Hollen (MD-8)
Democratic Steering Committee Co-Chair..........	Rosa DeLauro (CT-3)
Democratic Steering Committee Co-Chair..........	George Miller (CA-7)
Senior Chief Deputy Whip...........................	John Lewis (GA-5)
Chief Deputy Whip...................................	G.K. Butterfield (NC-1)
Chief Deputy Whip...................................	Joseph Crowley (NY-7)
Chief Deputy Whip...................................	Diana DeGette (CO-1)
Chief Deputy Whip...................................	Ed Pastor (AZ-4)
Chief Deputy Whip...................................	Jan Schakowsky (IL-9)
Chief Deputy Whip...................................	John Tanner (TN-8)

Chief Deputy Whip.. Debbie Wasserman Schultz
                                                              (FL-20)
Chief Deputy Whip.. Maxine Waters (CA-35)

Republicans

House Minority Leader................................ John Boehner (OH-8)
House Minority Whip................................... Eric Cantor (VA-7)
House Chief Deputy Minority Whip................. Kevin McCarthy (CA-22)
House Republican Conference Chairman........... Mike Pence (IN-6)
House Republican Policy Committee Chairman.... Thaddeus McCotter (MI-11)
House Republican Conference Vice
     Chairwoman... Cathy McMorris Rodgers (WA-5)
House Republican Conference Secretary............ John Carter (TX-31)
National Republican Congressional Committee
     Chairman... Pete Sessions (TX-32)

Party breakdowns as of August 1, 2009.

SENATE SENIORITY

This list of senators in order of their seniority is from the U.S. Senate secretary.

Democrats

Member (State)	Start of Service	Member (State)	Start of Service
Robert Byrd (WV)	January 3, 1959	Evan Bayh (IN)	January 3, 1999
Edward Kennedy (MA)	November 7, 1962	Bill Nelson (FL)	January 3, 2001
Daniel Inouye (HI)	January 3, 1963	Thomas Carper (DE)	January 3, 2001
Patrick Leahy (VT)	January 3, 1975	Debbie Stabenow (MI)	January 3, 2001
Max Baucus (MT)	December 15, 1978	Maria Cantwell (WA)	January 3, 2001
Carl Levin (MI)	January 3, 1979	Ben Nelson (NE)	January 3, 2001
Christopher Dodd (CT)	January 3, 1981	Frank Lautenberg (NJ)	January 3, 2003[1]
Arlen Specter (PA)	January 3, 1981	Mark Pryor (AR)	January 3, 2003
Jeff Bingaman (NM)	January 3, 1983	Robert Menendez (NJ)	January 18, 2006
John Kerry (MA)	January 2, 1985	Ben Cardin (MD)	January 3, 2007
Tom Harkin (IA)	January 3, 1985	Sherrod Brown (OH)	January 3, 2007
Jay Rockefeller (WV)	January 15, 1985	Bob Casey (PA)	January 3, 2007
Barbara Mikulski (MD)	January 3, 1987	Jim Webb (VA)	January 3, 2007
Harry Reid (NV)	January 3, 1987	Claire McCaskill (MO)	January 3, 2007
Kent Conrad (ND)	January 3, 1987	Amy Klobuchar (MN)	January 3, 2007
Herb Kohl (WI)	January 3, 1989	Sheldon Whitehouse (RI)	January 3, 2007
Daniel Akaka (HI)	May 16, 1990	Jon Tester (MT)	January 3, 2007
Dianne Feinstein (CA)	November 10, 1992	Mark Udall (CO)	January 3, 2009
Byron Dorgan (ND)	December 15, 1992	Tom Udall (NM)	January 3, 2009
Barbara Boxer (CA)	January 3, 1993	Jeanne Shaheen (NH)	January 3, 2009
Patty Murray (WA)	January 3, 1993	Mark Warner (VA)	January 3, 2009
Russell Feingold (WI)	January 3, 1993	Kay Hagan (NC)	January 3, 2009
Ron Wyden (OR)	February 6, 1996	Jeff Merkley (OR)	January 3, 2009
Richard Durbin (IL)	January 3, 1997	Mark Begich (AK)	January 3, 2009
Tim Johnson (SD)	January 3, 1997	Roland Burris (IL)	January 12, 2009
Jack Reed (RI)	January 3, 1997	Ted Kaufman (DE)	January 15, 2009
Mary Landrieu (LA)	January 3, 1997	Michael Bennet (CO)	January 21, 2009
Charles Schumer (NY)	January 3, 1999	Kirsten Gillibrand (NY)	January 26, 2009
Blanche Lincoln (AR)	January 3, 1999	Al Franken (MN)	July 7, 2009

Republicans

Member (State)	Start of Service	Member (State)	Start of Service
Richard Lugar (IN)	January 3, 1977	Mike Crapo (ID)	January 3, 1999
Orrin Hatch (UT)	January 3, 1977	George Voinovich (OH)	January 3, 1999
Thad Cochran (MS)	December 27, 1978	John Ensign (NV)	January 3, 2001
Charles Grassley (IA)	January 3, 1981	Lisa Murkowski (AK)	December 20, 2002
Mitch McConnell (KY)	January 3, 1985	Saxby Chambliss (GA)	January 3, 2003
Richard Shelby (AL)	January 3, 1987	Lindsey Graham (SC)	January 3, 2003
John McCain (AZ)	January 3, 1987	Lamar Alexander (TN)	January 3, 2003
Christopher "Kit" Bond (MO)	January 3, 1987	John Cornyn (TX)	December 2, 2002
Judd Gregg (NH)	January 3, 1993	Richard Burr (NC)	January 3, 2005
Robert Bennett (UT)	January 3, 1993	Jim DeMint (SC)	January 3, 2005
Kay Bailey Hutchison (TX)	June 14, 1993	Tom Coburn (OK)	January 3, 2005
James Inhofe (OK)	November 17, 1994	John Thune (SD)	January 3, 2005
Olympia Snowe (ME)	January 3, 1995	Johnny Isakson (GA)	January 3, 2005
Jon Kyl (AZ)	January 3, 1995	David Vitter (LA)	January 3, 2005
Sam Brownback (KS)	November 7, 1996	Mel Martinez (FL)	January 3, 2005
Pat Roberts (KS)	January 3, 1997	Bob Corker (TN)	January 3, 2007
Jeff Sessions (AL)	January 3, 1997	John Barrasso (WY)	June 22, 2007
Susan Collins (ME)	January 3, 1997	Roger Wicker (MS)	December 31, 2007
Michael Enzi (WY)	January 3, 1997	Mike Johanns (NE)	January 3, 2009
Jim Bunning (KY)	January 3, 1999	James Risch (ID)	January 3, 2009

[1] First served 1982-2001.

Independents

Member (State)	Start of Service	Member (State)	Start of Service
Joe Lieberman (CT)	January 3, 1989	Bernie Sanders (VT)	January 3, 2007

HOUSE SENIORITY

House Democrats base seniority on length of time in office. Democratic members who return after previous House service are given seniority over others elected at that time, but do not receive full credit for their previous stint. Start of service dates were provided by the U.S. House clerk.

Democrats

Member (State)	Start of Service	Member (State)	Start of Service
John Dingell (MI)	December 13, 1955	Robert Andrews (NJ)	November 6, 1990
John Conyers (MI)	January 3, 1965	Neil Abercrombie (HI)	January 3, 1991[1]
David Obey (WI)	April 1, 1969	Rosa DeLauro (CT)	January 3, 1991
Charles Rangel (NY)	January 3, 1971	Chet Edwards (TX)	January 3, 1991
Pete Stark (CA)	January 3, 1973	Jim Moran (VA)	January 3, 1991
John Murtha (PA)	February 5, 1974	Collin Peterson (MN)	January 3, 1991
George Miller (CA)	January 3, 1975	Maxine Waters (CA)	January 3, 1991
James Oberstar (MN)	January 3, 1975	John Olver (MA)	June 4, 1991
Henry Waxman (CA)	January 3, 1975	Ed Pastor (AZ)	September 24, 1991
Edward Markey (MA)	November 2, 1976	Jerrold Nadler (NY)	November 4, 1992
Norm Dicks (WA)	January 3, 1977	Xavier Becerra (CA)	January 3, 1993
Dale Kildee (MI)	January 3, 1977	Sanford Bishop (GA)	January 3, 1993
Nick Rahall (WV)	January 3, 1977	Corrine Brown (FL)	January 3, 1993
Ike Skelton (MO)	January 3, 1977	James Clyburn (SC)	January 3, 1993
Barney Frank (MA)	January 3, 1981	Anna Eshoo (CA)	January 3, 1993
Steny Hoyer (MD)	May 19, 1981	Bob Filner (CA)	January 3, 1993
Howard Berman (CA)	January 3, 1983	Gene Green (TX)	January 3, 1993
Rick Boucher (VA)	January 3, 1983	Luis Gutierrez (IL)	January 3, 1993
Marcy Kaptur (OH)	January 3, 1983	Alcee Hastings (FL)	January 3, 1993
Sander Levin (MI)	January 3, 1983	Maurice Hinchey (NY)	January 3, 1993
Alan Mollohan (WV)	January 3, 1983	Tim Holden (PA)	January 3, 1993
Solomon Ortiz (TX)	January 3, 1983	Eddie Bernice Johnson (TX)	January 3, 1993
John Spratt (SC)	January 3, 1983	Carolyn Maloney (NY)	January 3, 1993
Edolphus Towns (NY)	January 3, 1983	Earl Pomeroy (ND)	January 3, 1993
Gary Ackerman (NY)	March 1, 1983	Lucille Roybal-Allard (CA)	January 3, 1993
Bart Gordon (TN)	January 3, 1985	Bobby Rush (IL)	January 3, 1993
Paul Kanjorski (PA)	January 3, 1985	Bobby Scott (VA)	January 3, 1993
Peter Visclosky (IN)	January 3, 1985	Bart Stupak (MI)	January 3, 1993
Peter DeFazio (OR)	January 3, 1987	Nydia Velázquez (NY)	January 3, 1993
John Lewis (GA)	January 3, 1987	Melvin Watt (NC)	January 3, 1993
Louise Slaughter (NY)	January 3, 1987	Lynn Woolsey (CA)	January 3, 1993
Nancy Pelosi (CA)	June 2, 1987	Bennie Thompson (MS)	April 13, 1993
Jerry Costello (IL)	August 9, 1988	Sam Farr (CA)	June 8, 1993
Frank Pallone (NJ)	November 8, 1988	Lloyd Doggett (TX)	January 3, 1995
Eliot Engel (NY)	January 3, 1989	Mike Doyle (PA)	January 3, 1995
Nita Lowey (NY)	January 3, 1989	Chaka Fattah (PA)	January 3, 1995
Jim McDermott (WA)	January 3, 1989	Sheila Jackson Lee (TX)	January 3, 1995
Richard Neal (MA)	January 3, 1989	Patrick Kennedy (RI)	January 3, 1995
Donald Payne (NJ)	January 3, 1989	Zoe Lofgren (CA)	January 3, 1995
John Tanner (TN)	January 3, 1989	Jesse Jackson Jr. (IL)	December 12, 1995
Gene Taylor (MS)	October 17, 1989	Elijah Cummings (MD)	April 16, 1996
José Serrano (NY)	March 20, 1990	Earl Blumenauer (OR)	May 21, 1996

[1] Also served Sep. 1986-Jan. 1987

Member (State)	Start of Service	Member (State)	Start of Service
David Price (NC)	January 3, 1997[2]	Dennis Cardoza (CA)	January 3, 2003
Marion Berry (AR)	January 3, 1997	Artur Davis (AL)	January 3, 2003
Leonard Boswell (IA)	January 3, 1997	Lincoln Davis (TN)	January 3, 2003
Allen Boyd (FL)	January 3, 1997	Raúl Grijalva (AZ)	January 3, 2003
Danny Davis (IL)	January 3, 1997	Jim Marshall (GA)	January 3, 2003
Diana DeGette (CO)	January 3, 1997	Kendrick Meek (FL)	January 3, 2003
Bill Delahunt (MA)	January 3, 1997	Michael Michaud (ME)	January 3, 2003
Bob Etheridge (NC)	January 3, 1997	Brad Miller (NC)	January 3, 2003
Rubén Hinojosa (TX)	January 3, 1997	Dutch Ruppersberger (MD)	January 3, 2003
Carolyn Cheeks		Tim Ryan (OH)	January 3, 2003
Kilpatrick (MI)	January 3, 1997	Linda Sánchez (CA)	January 3, 2003
Ron Kind (WI)	January 3, 1997	David Scott (GA)	January 3, 2003
Dennis Kucinich (OH)	January 3, 1997	Chris Van Hollen (MD)	January 3, 2003
Carolyn McCarthy (NY)	January 3, 1997	Ben Chandler (KY)	February 17, 2004
Jim McGovern (MA)	January 3, 1997	Stephanie Herseth	
Mike McIntyre (NC)	January 3, 1997	Sandlin (SD)	June 1, 2004
Bill Pascrell (NJ)	January 3, 1997	G.K. Butterfield (NC)	July 20, 2004
Silvestre Reyes (TX)	January 3, 1997	John Barrow (GA)	January 3, 2005
Steven Rothman (NJ)	January 3, 1997	Melissa Bean (IL)	January 3, 2005
Loretta Sanchez (CA)	January 3, 1997	Dan Boren (OK)	January 3, 2005
Brad Sherman (CA)	January 3, 1997	Russ Carnahan (MO)	January 3, 2005
Adam Smith (WA)	January 3, 1997	Emanuel Cleaver (MO)	January 3, 2005
Vic Snyder (AR)	January 3, 1997	Jim Costa (CA)	January 3, 2005
John Tierney (MA)	January 3, 1997	Henry Cuellar (TX)	January 3, 2005
Robert Wexler (FL)	January 3, 1997	Al Green (TX)	January 3, 2005
Gregory Meeks (NY)	February 3, 1998	Brian Higgins (NY)	January 3, 2005
Lois Capps (CA)	March 10, 1998	Dan Lipinski (IL)	January 3, 2005
Barbara Lee (CA)	April 7, 1998	Charlie Melancon (LA)	January 3, 2005
Robert Brady (PA)	May 19, 1998	Gwen Moore (WI)	January 3, 2005
Jay Inslee (WA)	January 3, 1999[3]	John Salazar (CO)	January 3, 2005
Brian Baird (WA)	January 3, 1999	Allyson Schwartz (PA)	January 3, 2005
Tammy Baldwin (WI)	January 3, 1999	Debbie Wasserman	
Shelley Berkley (NV)	January 3, 1999	Schultz (FL)	January 3, 2005
Michael Capuano (MA)	January 3, 1999	Doris Matsui (CA)	March 8, 2005
Joseph Crowley (NY)	January 3, 1999	Albio Sires (NJ)	November 13, 2006
Charles Gonzalez (TX)	January 3, 1999	Ciro Rodriguez (TX)	January 4, 2007[6]
Rush Holt (NJ)	January 3, 1999	Baron Hill (IN)	January 4, 2007[7]
John Larson (CT)	January 3, 1999	Jason Altmire (PA)	January 4, 2007
Dennis Moore (KS)	January 3, 1999	Michael Arcuri (NY)	January 4, 2007
Grace Napolitano (CA)	January 3, 1999	Bruce Braley (IA)	January 4, 2007
Jan Schakowsky (IL)	January 3, 1999	Christopher Carney (PA)	January 4, 2007
Mike Thompson (CA)	January 3, 1999	Kathy Castor (FL)	January 4, 2007
Anthony Weiner (NY)	January 3, 1999	Yvette Clarke (NY)	January 4, 2007
David Wu (OR)	January 3, 1999	Steve Cohen (TN)	January 4, 2007
Joe Baca (CA)	November 17, 1999	Joe Courtney (CT)	January 4, 2007
Jane Harman (CA)	January 3, 2001[4]	Joe Donnelly (IN)	January 4, 2007
William Lacy Clay (MO)	January 3, 2001	Keith Ellison (MN)	January 4, 2007
Susan Davis (CA)	January 3, 2001	Brad Ellsworth (IN)	January 4, 2007
Mike Honda (CA)	January 3, 2001	Gabrielle Giffords (AZ)	January 4, 2007
Steve Israel (NY)	January 3, 2001	John Hall (NY)	January 4, 2007
Jim Langevin (RI)	January 3, 2001	Phil Hare (IL)	January 4, 2007
Rick Larsen (WA)	January 3, 2001	Dean Heller (NV)	January 4, 2007
Jim Matheson (UT)	January 3, 2001	Mazie Hirono (HI)	January 4, 2007
Betty McCollum (MN)	January 3, 2001	Paul Hodes (NH)	January 4, 2007
Mike Ross (AR)	January 3, 2001	Hank Johnson (GA)	January 4, 2007
Adam Schiff (CA)	January 3, 2001	Steve Kagen (WI)	January 4, 2007
Diane Watson (CA)	June 5, 2001	Ron Klein (FL)	January 4, 2007
Stephen Lynch (MA)	October 16, 2001	Dave Loebsack (IA)	January 4, 2007
Jim Cooper (TN)	January 3, 2003[5]	Jerry McNerney (CA)	January 4, 2007
Tim Bishop (NY)	January 3, 2003	Harry Mitchell (AZ)	January 4, 2007

---

[2] Also served 1987-1995
[3] Also served 1993-1995
[4] Also served 1993-1999
[5] Also served 1983-1995
[6] Also served 1997-2005
[7] Also served 1999-2005

Member (State)	Start of Service	Member (State)	Start of Service
Chris Murphy (CT)	January 4, 2007	Martin Heinrich (NM)	January 6, 2009
Patrick Murphy (PA)	January 4, 2007	Jim Himes (CT)	January 6, 2009
Ed Perlmutter (CO)	January 4, 2007	Mary Jo Kilroy (OH)	January 6, 2009
John Sarbanes (MD)	January 4, 2007	Ann Kirkpatrick (AZ)	January 6, 2009
Joe Sestak (PA)	January 4, 2007	Larry Kissell (NC)	January 6, 2009
Carol Shea-Porter (NH)	January 4, 2007	Suzanne Kosmas (FL)	January 6, 2009
Heath Shuler (NC)	January 4, 2007	Frank Kratovil (MD)	January 6, 2009
Zack Space (OH)	January 4, 2007	Ben Ray Luján (NM)	January 6, 2009
Betty Sutton (OH)	January 4, 2007	Dan Maffei (NY)	January 6, 2009
Tim Walz (MN)	January 4, 2007	Betsy Markey (CO)	January 6, 2009
Peter Welch (VT)	January 4, 2007	Eric Massa (NY)	January 6, 2009
Charlie Wilson (OH)	January 4, 2007	Michael McMahon (NY)	January 6, 2009
John Yarmuth (KY)	January 4, 2007	Walt Minnick (ID)	January 6, 2009
Laura Richardson (CA)	September 4, 2007	Glenn Nye (VA)	January 6, 2009
Niki Tsongas (MA)	October 18, 2007	Tom Perriello (VA)	January 6, 2009
Bill Foster (IL)	March 11, 2008	Gary Peters (MI)	January 6, 2009
André Carson (IN)	March 13, 2008	Chellie Pingree (ME)	January 6, 2009
Jackie Speier (CA)	April 10, 2008	Jared Polis (CO)	January 6, 2009
Travis Childers (MS)	May 20, 2008	Mark Schauer (MI)	January 6, 2009
Donna Edwards (MD)	June 19, 2008	Kurt Schrader (OR)	January 6, 2009
Marcia Fudge (OH)	November 19, 2008	Harry Teague (NM)	January 6, 2009
John Adler (NJ)	January 6, 2009	Dina Titus (NV)	January 6, 2009
Bobby Bright (AL)	January 6, 2009	Paul Tonko (NY)	January 6, 2009
John Boccieri (OH)	January 6, 2009	Mike Quigley (IL)	April 21, 2009
Gerald Connolly (VA)	January 6, 2009	Scott Murphy (NY)	April 29, 2009
Kathy Dahlkemper (PA)	January 6, 2009		
Steve Driehaus (OH)	January 6, 2009		
Alan Grayson (FL)	January 6, 2009		
Parker Griffith (AL)	January 6, 2009		
Debbie Halvorson (IL)	January 6, 2009		

Republicans

House Republicans base seniority on length of time in office. Members who return after previous House service are usually allowed to claim most of their earlier service for seniority purposes, although final decisions are made by the Republican leadership. Start of service dates were provided by the U.S. House clerk.

Member (State)	Start of Service	Member (State)	Start of Service
Bill Young (FL)	January 3, 1971	Dave Camp (MI)	January 3, 1991
Don Young (AK)	March 6, 1973	Sam Johnson (TX)	May 18, 1991
Jerry Lewis (CA)	January 3, 1979	Spencer Bachus (AL)	January 3, 1993
Jim Sensenbrenner (WI)	January 3, 1979	Roscoe Bartlett (MD)	January 3, 1993
Tom Petri (WI)	April 3, 1979	Steve Buyer (IN)	January 3, 1993
David Dreier (CA)	January 3, 1981	Ken Calvert (CA)	January 3, 1993
Ralph Hall (TX)	January 3, 1981	Michael Castle (DE)	January 3, 1993
Harold Rogers (KY)	January 3, 1981	Nathan Deal (GA)	January 3, 1993
Chris Smith (NJ)	January 3, 1981	Lincoln Diaz-Balart (FL)	January 3, 1993
Frank Wolf (VA)	January 3, 1981	Bob Goodlatte (VA)	January 3, 1993
Dan Burton (IN)	January 3, 1983	Pete Hoekstra (MI)	January 3, 1993
Joe Barton (TX)	January 3, 1985	Peter King (NY)	January 3, 1993
Howard Coble (NC)	January 3, 1985	Jack Kingston (GA)	January 3, 1993
Elton Gallegly (CA)	January 3, 1987	John Linder (GA)	January 3, 1993
Wally Herger (CA)	January 3, 1987	John McHugh (NY)	January 3, 1993
Lamar Smith (TX)	January 3, 1987	Buck McKeon (CA)	January 3, 1993
Fred Upton (MI)	January 3, 1987	Don Manzullo (IL)	January 3, 1993
John Duncan (TN)	November 8, 1988	John Mica (FL)	January 3, 1993
Dana Rohrabacher (CA)	January 3, 1989	Ed Royce (CA)	January 3, 1993
Cliff Stearns (FL)	January 3, 1989	Vernon Ehlers (MI)	December 7, 1993
Ileana Ros-Lehtinen (FL)	August 29, 1989	Frank Lucas (OK)	May 10, 1994
Ron Paul (TX)	January 3, 1997[8]	Rodney Frelinghuysen (NJ)	January 3, 1995
John Boehner (OH)	January 3, 1991	Doc Hastings (WA)	January 3, 1995

[8] Also served 1976-1977; 1979-1985

Member (State)	Start of Service	Member (State)	Start of Service
Walter Jones (NC)	January 3, 1995	Jim Gerlach (PA)	January 3, 2003
Tom Latham (IA)	January 3, 1995	Phil Gingrey (GA)	January 3, 2003
Steven LaTourette (OH)	January 3, 1995	Jeb Hensarling (TX)	January 3, 2003
Frank LoBiondo (NJ)	January 3, 1995	Steve King (IA)	January 3, 2003
Dan Lungren (CA)	January 3, 2005[9]	John Kline (MN)	January 3, 2003
Sue Myrick (NC)	January 3, 1995	Thaddeus McCotter (MI)	January 3, 2003
George Radanovich (CA)	January 3, 1995	Candice Miller (MI)	January 3, 2003
John Shadegg (AZ)	January 3, 1995	Tim Murphy (PA)	January 3, 2003
Mark Souder (IN)	January 3, 1995	Devin Nunes (CA)	January 3, 2003
Mac Thornberry (TX)	January 3, 1995	Mike Rogers (AL)	January 3, 2003
Todd Tiahrt (KS)	January 3, 1995	Mike Turner (OH)	January 3, 2003
Zach Wamp (TN)	January 3, 1995	Randy Neugebauer (TX)	June 3, 2003
Ed Whitfield (KY)	January 3, 1995	Charles Boustany (LA)	January 3, 2005
Jo Ann Emerson (MD)	November 5, 1996	Mike Conaway (TX)	January 3, 2005
Robert Aderholt (AL)	January 3, 1997	Geoff Davis (KY)	January 3, 2005
Roy Blunt (MO)	January 3, 1997	Charlie Dent (PA)	January 3, 2005
Kevin Brady (TX)	January 3, 1997	Jeff Fortenberry (NE)	January 3, 2005
Kay Granger (TX)	January 3, 1997	Virginia Foxx (NC)	January 3, 2005
Jerry Moran (KS)	January 3, 1997	Louie Gohmert (TX)	January 3, 2005
Joe Pitts (PA)	January 3, 1997	Michael McCaul (TX)	January 3, 2005
Pete Sessions (TX)	January 3, 1997	Patrick McHenry (NC)	January 3, 2005
John Shimkus (IL)	January 3, 1997	Cathy McMorris	
Mary Bono Mack (CA)	April 7, 1998	Rodgers (WA)	January 3, 2005
Judy Biggert (IL)	January 3, 1999	Connie Mack (FL)	January 3, 2005
Bob Inglis (SC)	January 3, 2005[10]	Kenny Marchant (TX)	January 3, 2005
Gary Miller (CA)	January 3, 1999	Ted Poe (TX)	January 3, 2005
Paul Ryan (WI)	January 3, 1999	Tom Price (GA)	January 3, 2005
Mike Simpson (ID)	January 3, 1999	Dave Reichert (WA)	January 3, 2005
Lee Terry (NE)	January 3, 1999	Lynn Westmoreland (GA)	January 3, 2005
Greg Walden (OR)	January 3, 1999	Jean Schmidt (OH)	August 2, 2005
Brian Bilbray (CA)	June 6, 2006[11]	John Campbell (CA)	December 7, 2005
Todd Akin (MO)	January 3, 2001	Michele Bachmann (MN)	January 4, 2007
Henry Brown (SC)	January 3, 2001	Gus Bilirakis (FL)	January 4, 2007
Eric Cantor (VA)	January 3, 2001	Vern Buchanan (FL)	January 4, 2007
Shelley Moore Capito (WV)	January 3, 2001	Mary Fallin (OK)	January 4, 2007
Ander Crenshaw (FL)	January 3, 2001	Jim Jordan (OH)	January 4, 2007
John Culberson (TX)	January 3, 2001	Doug Lamborn (CO)	January 4, 2007
Jeff Flake (AZ)	January 3, 2001	Kevin McCarthy (CA)	January 4, 2007
Sam Graves (MO)	January 3, 2001	Peter Roskam (IL)	January 4, 2007
Darrell Issa (CA)	January 3, 2001	Adrian Smith (NE)	January 4, 2007
Tim Johnson (IL)	January 3, 2001	Paul Broun (GA)	July 25, 2007
Mark Kirk (IL)	January 3, 2001	Bob Latta (OH)	December 13, 2007
Mike Pence (IN)	January 3, 2001	Rob Wittman (VA)	December 13, 2007
Todd Platts (PA)	January 3, 2001	Steve Scalise (LA)	May 7, 2008
Adam Putnam (FL)	January 3, 2001	Steve Austria (OH)	January 6, 2009
Denny Rehberg (MT)	January 3, 2001	Joseph Cao (LA)	January 6, 2009
Mike Rogers (MI)	January 3, 2001	Bill Cassidy (LA)	January 6, 2009
Pat Tiberi (OH)	January 3, 2001	Jason Chaffetz (UT)	January 6, 2009
Bill Shuster (PA)	May 15, 2001	Mike Coffman (CO)	January 6, 2009
Randy Forbes (VA)	June 19, 2001	John Fleming (LA)	January 6, 2009
Jeff Miller (FL)	October 16, 2001	Brett Guthrie (KY)	January 6, 2009
John Boozman (AR)	November 20, 2001	Gregg Harper (MS)	January 6, 2009
Joe Wilson (SC)	December 18, 2001	Duncan D. Hunter (CA)	January 6, 2009
John Sullivan (OK)	February 27, 2002	Lynn Jenkins (KS)	January 6, 2009
Rodney Alexander (LA)	January 3, 2003	Leonard Lance (NJ)	January 6, 2009
Gresham Barrett (SC)	January 3, 2003	Chris Lee (NY)	January 6, 2009
Rob Bishop (UT)	January 3, 2003	Blaine Luetkemeyer (MO)	January 6, 2009
Marsha Blackburn (TN)	January 3, 2003	Cynthia Lummis (WY)	January 6, 2009
Jo Bonner (AL)	January 3, 2003	Tom McClintock (CA)	January 6, 2009
Ginny Brown-Waite (FL)	January 3, 2003	Pete Olson (TX)	January 6, 2009
Michael Burgess (TX)	January 3, 2003	Erik Paulsen (MN)	January 6, 2009
John Carter (TX)	January 3, 2003	Bill Posey (FL)	January 6, 2009
Tom Cole (OK)	January 3, 2003	Phil Roe (TN)	January 6, 2009
Mario Diaz-Balart (FL)	January 3, 2003	Tom Rooney (FL)	January 6, 2009
Trent Franks (AZ)	January 3, 2003	Aaron Schock (IL)	January 6, 2009
Scott Garrett (NJ)	January 3, 2003	Glenn Thompson (PA)	January 6, 2009

[9] Also served 1979-1989
[10] Also served 1993-1999
[11] Also served 1995-2001

CONGRESSIONAL CLASS OF 2008

Senators

Mark Begich.............. D-Alaska	Kay Hagan................. D-N.C.
Michael Bennet............D-Colo.	Jeanne Shaheen........... D-N.H.
Mark Udall.................D-Colo.	Tom Udall................. D-N.M.
Ted Kaufman............. D-Del.	Kirsten Gillibrand.........D-N.Y.
James Risch................R-Idaho	Mike Johanns..............R-Neb.
Roland Burris.............D-Ill.	Jeff Merkley................D-Ore.
Al Franken................ D-Minn.	Mark Warner............. D-Va.
Roger Wicker............. R-Miss.	

Representatives

Bobby Bright...............D-Ala.	Erik Paulsen.............. R-Minn.
Parker Griffith.............D-Ala.	Travis Childers............ D-Miss.
Ann Kirkpatrick........... D-Ariz.	Gregg Harper............. R-Miss.
Judy Chu................... D-Calif.	Blaine Luetkemeyer...... R-Mo.
Duncan D. Hunter........ R-Calif.	Larry Kissell...............D-N.C.
Tom McClintock........... R-Calif.	John Adler................. D-N.J.
Jackie Speier...............D-Calif.	Leonard Lance.............R-N.J.
Mike Coffman..............R-Colo.	Martin Heinrich........... D-N.M.
Betsy Markey.............. D-Colo.	Ben Ray Luján.............D-N.M.
Jared Polis................. D-Colo.	Harry Teague............. D-N.M.
Jim Himes..................D-Conn.	Chris Lee................. R-N.Y.
Alan Grayson............. D-Fla.	Dan Maffei............... D-N.Y.
Suzanne Kosmas.......... D-Fla.	Eric Massa................. D-N.Y.
Bill Posey...................R-Fla.	Michael McMahon.........D-N.Y.
Tom Rooney...............R-Fla.	Scott Murphy............. D-N.Y.
Walt Minnick............. D-Idaho	Paul Tonko................. D-N.Y.
Bill Foster..................D-Ill.	Dina Titus.................D-Nev.
Debbie Halvorson......... D-Ill.	Steve Austria............. R-Ohio
Mike Quigley...............D-Ill.	John Boccieri..............D-Ohio
Aaron Schock............. R-Ill.	Steve Driehaus........... D-Ohio
André Carson............. D-Ind.	Marcia Fudge............. D-Ohio
Lynn Jenkins.............. R-Kan.	Mary Jo Kilroy............D-Ohio
Brett Guthrie.............. R-Ky.	Kurt Schrader............. D-Ore.
Joseph Cao................. R-La.	Kathy Dahlkemper........D-Pa.
Bill Cassidy................ R-La.	Glenn Thompson.......... R-Pa.
John Fleming.............. R-La.	Phil Roe....................R-Tenn.
Steve Scalise............... R-La.	Pete Olson.................R-Texas
Chellie Pingree............ D-Maine	Jason Chaffetz.............R-Utah
Donna Edwards........... D-Md.	Gerald Connolly........... D-Va.
Frank Kratovil.............D-Md.	Glenn Nye.................D-Va.
Gary Peters................ D-Mich.	Tom Perriello............. D-Va.
Mark Schauer..............D-Mich.	Cynthia Lummis.......... R-Wyo.

MINORITIES IN CONGRESS

African-American

Senate (1 D)

Roland Burris (D-Ill.)

House (41 D)

Artur Davis (D-Ala.)
Barbara Lee (D-Calif.)
Laura Richardson (D-Calif.)
Maxine Waters (D-Calif.)
Diane Watson (D-Calif.)
Del. Eleanor Holmes Norton (D-D.C.)
Corrine Brown (D-Fla.)
Alcee Hastings (D-Fla.)
Kendrick Meek (D-Fla.)
Sanford Bishop (D-Ga.)
Hank Johnson (D-Ga.)
John Lewis (D-Ga.)
David Scott (D-Ga.)
Danny Davis (D-Ill.)
Jesse Jackson, Jr. (D-Ill.)
Bobby Rush (D-Ill.)
André Carson (D-Ind.)
Elijah Cummings (D-Md.)
Donna Edwards (D-Md.)
John Conyers (D-Mich.)
Carolyn Cheeks Kilpatrick (D-Mich.)

Keith Ellison (D-Minn.)
Bennie Thompson (D-Miss.)
William Lacy Clay (D-Mo.)
Emanuel Cleaver (D-Mo.)
G.K. Butterfield (D-N.C.)
Melvin Watt (D-N.C.)
Donald Payne (D-N.J.)
Yvette Clarke (D-N.Y.)
Gregory Meeks (D-N.Y.)
Charles Rangel (D-N.Y.)
Edolphus Towns (D-N.Y.)
Marcia Fudge (D-Ohio)
Chaka Fattah (D-Pa.)
James Clyburn (D-S.C.)
Al Green (D-Texas)
Sheila Jackson Lee (D-Texas)
Eddie Bernice Johnson (D-Texas)
Del. Donna Christensen (D-V.I.)
Bobby Scott (D-Va.)
Gwen Moore (D-Wis.)

Hispanic

Senate (1 D, 1 R)

Mel Martinez (R-Fla.)

Robert Menendez (D-N.J.)

House (21D, 3R)

Raúl Grijalva (D-Ariz.)
Ed Pastor (D-Ariz.)
Joe Baca (D-Calif.)
Xavier Becerra (D-Calif.)
Grace Napolitano (D-Calif.)
Lucille Roybal-Allard (D-Calif.)
Linda Sánchez (D-Calif.)
Loretta Sanchez (D-Calif.)
John Salazar (D-Colo.)
Lincoln Diaz-Balart (R-Fla.)

Mario Diaz-Balart (R-Fla.)
Ileana Ros-Lehtinen (R-Fla.)
Luis Gutierrez (D-Ill.)
Albio Sires (D-N.J.)
Ben Ray Luján (D-N.M.)
José Serrano (D-N.Y.)
Nydia Velázquez (D-N.Y.)
Res. Cmmsr. Pedro Pierluisi (D-P.R.)
Henry Cuellar (D-Texas)
Charles Gonzalez (D-Texas)

Rubén Hinojosa (D-Texas)
Solomon Ortiz (D-Texas)

Silvestre Reyes (D-Texas)
Ciro Rodriguez (D-Texas)

Asian

Senate (2 D)

Daniel Akaka (D-Hawaii)

Daniel Inouye (D-Hawaii)

House (7 D, 2 R)

Del. Eni F.H. Faleomavaega
  (D-Am. Samoa)
Judy Chu (D-Calif.)
Mike Honda (D-Calif.)
Doris Matsui (D-Calif.)
Mazie Hirono (D-Hawaii)

Joseph Cao (R-La.)
Del. Gregorio Kilili Camacho Sablan
  (D-CNMI)
Steve Austria (R-Ohio)
David Wu (D-Ore.)

American Indian

House (1 R)

Tom Cole (R-Okla.)

Minority Governors

Bobby Jindal (Indian) (R-La.)
Deval Patrick (African-American)
  (D-Mass.)

Bill Richardson (Hispanic) (D-N.M.)
David Paterson (African-American)
  (D-N.Y.)

WOMEN IN CONGRESS

Senate (13 D, 4 R)

Lisa Murkowski (R-Alaska)
Blanche Lincoln (D-Ark.)
Barbara Boxer (D-Calif.)
Dianne Feinstein (D-Calif.)
Mary Landrieu (D-La.)
Susan Collins (R-Maine)
Olympia Snowe (R-Maine)
Barbara Mikulski (D-Md.)
Debbie Stabenow (D-Mich.)

Amy Klobuchar (D-Minn.)
Claire McCaskill (D-Mo.)
Kay Hagan (D-N.C.)
Jeanne Shaheen (D-N.H.)
Kirsten Gillibrand (D-N.Y.)
Kay Bailey Hutchison (R-Texas)
Maria Cantwell (D-Wash.)
Patty Murray (D-Wash.)

House (59 D, 17 R)

Gabrielle Giffords (D-Ariz.)
Ann Kirkpatrick (D-Ariz.)
Mary Bono Mack (R-Calif.)
Lois Capps (D-Calif.)
Judy Chu (D-Calif.)
Susan Davis (D-Calif.)
Anna Eshoo (D-Calif.)
Jane Harman (D-Calif.)
Barbara Lee (D-Calif.)
Zoe Lofgren (D-Calif.)
Doris Matsui (D-Calif.)
Grace Napolitano (D-Calif.)
Nancy Pelosi (D-Calif.)
Laura Richardson (D-Calif.)
Lucille Roybal-Allard (D-Calif.)
Linda Sánchez (D-Calif.)
Loretta Sanchez (D-Calif.)
Jackie Speier (D-Calif.)
Maxine Waters (D-Calif.)
Diane Watson (D-Calif.)
Lynn Woolsey (D-Calif.)
Betsy Markey (D-Colo.)
Diana DeGette (D-Colo.)
Rosa DeLauro (D-Conn.)
Del. Eleanor Holmes Norton (D-D.C.)
Corrine Brown (D-Fla.)
Ginny Brown-Waite (R-Fla.)
Kathy Castor (D-Fla.)
Suzanne Kosmas (D-Fla.)
Ileana Ros-Lehtinen (R-Fla.)
Debbie Wasserman Schultz (D-Fla.)
Del. Madeleine Bordallo (D-Guam)
Mazie Hirono (D-Hawaii)
Melissa Bean (D-Ill.)

Judy Biggert (R-Ill.)
Debbie Halvorson (D-Ill.)
Jan Schakowsky (D-Ill.)
Lynn Jenkins (R-Kan.)
Chellie Pingree (D-Maine)
Niki Tsongas (D-Mass.)
Donna Edwards (D-Md.)
Carolyn Cheeks Kilpatrick (D-Mich.)
Candice Miller (R-Mich.)
Michele Bachmann (R-Minn.)
Betty McCollum (D-Minn.)
Jo Ann Emerson (R-Mo.)
Virginia Foxx (R-N.C.)
Sue Myrick (R-N.C.)
Carol Shea-Porter (D-N.H.)
Yvette Clarke (D-N.Y.)
Nita Lowey (D-N.Y.)
Carolyn Maloney (D-N.Y.)
Carolyn McCarthy (D-N.Y.)
Louise Slaughter (D-N.Y.)
Nydia Velázquez (D-N.Y.)
Shelley Berkley (D-Nev.)
Dina Titus (D-Nev.)
Marcia Fudge (D-Ohio)
Marcy Kaptur (D-Ohio)
Mary Jo Kilroy (D-Ohio)
Jean Schmidt (R-Ohio)
Betty Sutton (D-Ohio)
Mary Fallin (R-Okla.)
Kathy Dahlkemper (D-Pa.)
Allyson Schwartz (D-Pa.)
Stephanie Herseth Sandlin (D-S.D.)
Marsha Blackburn (R-Tenn.)
Kay Granger (R-Texas)

Sheila Jackson Lee (D-Texas)
Eddie Bernice Johnson (D-Texas)
Del. Donna Christensen (D-V.I.)
Shelley Moore Capito (R-W.Va.)

Cathy McMorris Rodgers (R-Wash.)
Tammy Baldwin (D-Wis.)
Gwen Moore (D-Wis.)
Cynthia Lummis (R-Wyo.)

Women Who Are Governors (3 D, 3 R)

Jan Brewer (R-Ariz.)
M. Jodi Rell (R-Conn.)
Linda Lingle (R-Hawaii)

Jennifer Granholm (D-Mich.)
Bev Perdue (D-N.C.)
Christine Gregoire (D-Wash.)

CONGRESSIONAL FACTIONS

Blue Dog Coalition

The coalition is a group of fiscally moderate to conservative House Democrats.

Bobby Bright (AL-02)
Parker Griffith (AL-05)
Marion Berry (AR-01)
Mike Ross (AR-04)
Harry Mitchell (AZ-05)
Gabrielle Giffords (AZ-08)
Mike Thompson (CA-01)
Dennis Cardoza (CA-18)
Jim Costa (CA-20)
Adam Schiff (CA-29)
Jane Harman (CA-36)
Joe Baca (CA-43)
Loretta Sanchez (CA-47)
John Salazar (CO-03)
Allen Boyd (FL-02)
Sanford Bishop (GA-02)
Jim Marshall (GA-08)
John Barrow (GA-12)

David Scott (GA-13)
Leonard Boswell (IA-03)
Walt Minnick (ID-01)
Joe Donnelly (IN-02)
Brad Ellsworth (IN-08)
Baron Hill (IN-09)
Dennis Moore (KS-03)
Ben Chandler (KY-06)
Charlie Melancon (LA-03)
Frank Kratovil (MD-01)
Michael Michaud (ME-02)
Collin Peterson (MN-07)
Travis Childers (MS-01)
Gene Taylor (MS-04)
Mike McIntyre (NC-07)
Heath Shuler (NC-11)
Earl Pomeroy (ND-AL)
Michael Arcuri (NY-24)

Charlie Wilson (OH-06)
Zack Space (OH-18)
Dan Boren (OK-02)
Kathy Dahlkemper (PA-03)
Jason Altmire (PA-04)
Patrick Murphy (PA-08)
Chris Carney (PA-10)
Tim Holden (PA-17)
Stephanie Herseth Sandlin
  (SD-AL)
Lincoln Davis (TN-04)
Jim Cooper (TN-05)
Bart Gordon (TN-06)
John Tanner (TN-08)
Henry Cuellar (TX-28)
Jim Matheson (UT-02)
Glenn Nye (VA-02)

Congressional Black Caucus

The CBC is a group of black lawmakers who focus on issues affecting African-Americans.

Artur Davis (AL-07)
Barbara Lee (CA-09)
Diane Watson (CA-33)
Maxine Waters (CA-35)
Laura Richardson (CA-37)
Corrine Brown (FL-03)
Kendrick Meek (FL-17)
Alcee Hastings (FL-23)
Sanford Bishop (GA-02)
Hank Johnson (GA-04)
John Lewis (GA-05)
David Scott (GA-13)
Bobby Rush (IL-01)
Jesse Jackson Jr. (IL-02)

Danny Davis (IL-07)
André Carson (IN-07)
Donna Edwards (MD-04)
Elijah Cummings (MD-07)
Carolyn Cheeks Kilpatrick
  (MI-13)
John Conyers (MI-14)
Keith Ellison (MN-05)
William Lacy Clay (MO-01)
Emanuel Cleaver (MO-05)
Bennie Thompson (MS-02)
G.K. Butterfield (NC-01)
Melvin Watt (NC-12)
Donald Payne (NJ-10)

Gregory Meeks (NY-06)
Edolphus Towns (NY-10)
Yvette Clarke (NY-11)
Charles Rangel (NY-15)
Marcia Fudge (OH-11)
Chaka Fattah (PA-02)
James Clyburn (SC-06)
Al Green (TX-09)
Sheila Jackson Lee (TX-18)
Eddie Bernice Johnson (TX-30)
Bobby Scott (VA-03)
Gwen Moore (WI-04)

Congressional Hispanic Caucus

The caucus consists of Latino members of Congress who focus on issues affecting Hispanics.

Ed Pastor (AZ-04)
Raúl Grijalva (AZ-07)
Dennis Cardoza (CA-18)
Jim Costa (CA-20)
Xavier Becerra (CA-31)
Lucille Roybal-Allard (CA-34)
Grace Napolitano (CA-38)

Linda Sánchez (CA-39)
Joe Baca (CA-43)
John Salazar (CO-03)
Luis Gutierrez (IL-04)
Albio Sires (NJ-13)
Ben Ray Luján (NM-03)
Nydia Velázquez (NY-12)

José Serrano (NY-16)
Rubén Hinojosa (TX-15)
Silvestre Reyes (TX-16)
Charles Gonzalez (TX-20)
Ciro Rodriguez (TX-23)
Solomon Ortiz (TX-27)
Henry Cuellar (TX-28)

Republican Main Street Partnership

This group includes House members, senators and governors who advance centrist ideas within the GOP.

David Dreier (CA-26)
Jerry Lewis (CA-41)
Ken Calvert (CA-44)
Mary Bono Mack (CA-45)
Brian Bilbray (CA-50)
Michael Castle (DE-AL)
Ginny Brown-Waite (FL-05)
Lincoln Diaz-Balart (FL-21)
Mario Diaz-Balart (FL-25)
Mark Kirk (IL-10)
Judy Biggert (IL-13)
Tim Johnson (IL-15)
Lynn Jenkins (KS-02)

Ed Whitfield (KY-01)
Roscoe Bartlett (MD-06)
Vernon Ehlers (MI-03)
Dave Camp (MI-04)
Fred Upton (MI-06)
Candice Miller (MI-10)
Thaddeus McCotter (MI-11)
Jo Ann Emerson (MO-08)
Lee Terry (NE-02)
Frank LoBiondo (NJ-02)
Leonard Lance (NJ-07)
Rodney Frelinghuysen (NJ-11)
Michael Turner (OH-03)

Steve Austria (OH-07)
Pat Tiberi (OH-12)
Steven LaTourette (OH-14)
Greg Walden (OR-02)
Jim Gerlach (PA-06)
Charlie Dent (PA-15)
Tim Murphy (PA-18)
Todd Platts (PA-19)
Frank Wolf (VA-10)
Dave Reichert (WA-08)
Tom Petri (WI-06)
Shelley Moore Capito (WV-02)

Republican Study Committee

The RSC advocates conservative positions within the House GOP.

Jo Bonner (AL-01)
Robert Aderholt (AL-04)
Spencer Bachus (AL-06)
John Boozman (AR-03)
Trent Franks (AZ-02)
John Shadegg (AZ-03)
Jeff Flake (AZ-06)
Wally Herger (CA-02)
Dan Lungren (CA-03)
Tom McClintock (CA-04)
George Radanovich (CA-19)
Buck McKeon (CA-25)
Ed Royce (CA-40)
Gary Miller (CA-42)
John Campbell (CA-48)
Darrell Issa (CA-49)
Brian Bilbray (CA-50)
Duncan D. Hunter (CA-52)
Doug Lamborn (CO-05)
Mike Coffman (CO-06)
Jeff Miller (FL-01)
Cliff Stearns (FL-06)
Gus Bilirakis (FL-09)
Vern Buchanan (FL-13)
Connie Mack (FL-14)
Bill Posey (FL-15)
Tom Rooney (FL-16)
Jack Kingston (GA-01)
Lynn Westmoreland (GA-03)
Tom Price (GA-06)
John Linder (GA-07)
Nathan Deal (GA-09)
Paul Broun (GA-10)
Phil Gingrey (GA-11)
Steve King (IA-05)
Peter Roskam (IL-06)
Donald Manzullo (IL-16)

Aaron Schock (IL-18)
John Shimkus (IL-19)
Mark Souder (IN-03)
Dan Burton (IN-05)
Mike Pence (IN-06)
Jerry Moran (KS-01)
Todd Tiahrt (KS-04)
Brett Guthrie (KY-02)
Geoff Davis (KY-04)
Steve Scalise (LA-01)
John Fleming (LA-04)
Rodney Alexander (LA-05)
William Cassidy (LA-06)
Roscoe Bartlett (MD-06)
Peter Hoekstra (MI-02)
Dave Camp (MI-04)
Thaddeus McCotter (MI-11)
John Kline (MN-02)
Michele Bachmann (MN-06)
Todd Akin (MO-02)
Sam Graves (MO-06)
Blaine Luetkemeyer (MO-09)
Gregg Harper (MS-03)
Denny Rehberg (MT-AL)
Virginia Foxx (NC-05)
Sue Myrick (NC-09)
Patrick McHenry (NC-10)
Jeff Fortenberry (NE-01)
Scott Garrett (NJ-05)
Chris Lee (NY-26)
Jean Schmidt (OH-02)
Mike Turner (OH-03)
Jim Jordan (OH-04)
Bob Latta (OH-05)
Steve Austria (OH-07)
John Sullivan (OK-01)
Frank Lucas (OK-03)

Tom Cole (OK-04)
Mary Fallin (OK-05)
Glenn Thompson (PA-05)
Joe Pitts (PA-16)
Henry Brown (SC-01)
Joe Wilson (SC-02)
Gresham Barrett (SC-03)
Bob Inglis (SC-04)
Phil Roe (TN-01)
Zach Wamp (TN-03)
Marsha Blackburn (TN-07)
Louie Gohmert (TX-01)
Ted Poe (TX-02)
Sam Johnson (TX-03)
Jeb Hensarling (TX-05)
Joe Barton (TX-06)
John Culberson (TX-07)
Kevin Brady (TX-08)
Michael McCaul (TX-10)
Mike Conaway (TX-11)
Mac Thornberry (TX-13)
Randy Neugebauer (TX-19)
Lamar Smith (TX-21)
Pete Olson (TX-22)
Kenny Marchant (TX-24)
Michael Burgess (TX-26)
John Carter (TX-31)
Pete Sessions (TX-32)
Rob Bishop (UT-01)
Jason Chaffetz (UT-03)
Rob Wittman (VA-01)
Randy Forbes (VA-04)
Bob Goodlatte (VA-06)
Eric Cantor (VA-07)
Cathy McMorris Rodgers (WA-05)
Paul Ryan (WI-01)
Cynthia Lummis (WY-AL)

Progressive Caucus

The caucus advocates liberal ideas within the Democratic Party.

Ed Pastor (AZ-04)
Raúl Grijalva (AZ-07)
Lynn Woolsey (CA-06)
George Miller (CA-07)
Barbara Lee (CA-09)
Pete Stark (CA-13)
Mike Honda (CA-15)
Sam Farr (CA-17)
Henry Waxman (CA-30)
Xavier Becerra (CA-31)
Judy Chu (CA-32)
Diane Watson (CA-33)
Lucille Roybal-Allard (CA-34)
Maxine Waters (CA-35)
Laura Richardson (CA-37)
Linda Sánchez (CA-39)
Bob Filner (CA-51)
Jared Polis (CO-02)
Rosa DeLauro (CT-03)
Corrine Brown (FL-03)
Alan Grayson (FL-08)
Robert Wexler (FL-19)
Alcee Hastings (FL-23)
Hank Johnson (GA-04)
John Lewis (GA-05)
Neil Abercrombie (HI-01)
Mazie Hirono (HI-02)

Dave Loebsack (IA-02)
Bobby Rush (IL-01)
Jesse Jackson Jr. (IL-02)
Luis Gutierrez (IL-04)
Danny Davis (IL-07)
Jan Schakowsky (IL-09)
Phil Hare (IL-17)
André Carson (IN-07)
John Olver (MA-01)
Jim McGovern (MA-03)
Barney Frank (MA-04)
John Tierney (MA-06)
Edward Markey (MA-07)
Michael Capuano (MA-08)
Donna Edwards (MD-04)
Elijah Cummings (MD-07)
Chellie Pingree (ME-01)
Carolyn Cheeks Kilpatrick (MI-13)
John Conyers (MI-14)
Keith Ellison (MN-05)
William Lacy Clay (MO-01)
Emanuel Cleaver (MO-05)
Bennie Thompson (MS-02)
Melvin Watt (NC-12)
Frank Pallone (NJ-06)
Donald Payne (NJ-10)

Ben Ray Luján (NM-03)
Jerrold Nadler (NY-08)
Yvette Clarke (NY-11)
Nydia Velázquez (NY-12)
Carolyn Maloney (NY-14)
Charles Rangel (NY-15)
José Serrano (NY-16)
John Hall (NY-19)
Maurice Hinchey (NY-22)
Louise Slaughter (NY-28)
Eric Massa (NY-29)
Marcy Kaptur (OH-09)
Dennis Kucinich (OH-10)
Marcia Fudge (OH-11)
Earl Blumenauer (OR-03)
Peter DeFazio (OR-04)
Robert Brady (PA-01)
Chaka Fattah (PA-02)
Steve Cohen (TN-09)
Sheila Jackson Lee (TX-18)
Eddie Bernice Johnson (TX-30)
Jim Moran (VA-08)
Peter Welch (VT-AL)
Jim McDermott (WA-07)
Tammy Baldwin (WI-02)
Gwen Moore (WI-04)

Tuesday Group

This is a caucus of moderate House Republicans.

Mary Bono Mack (CA-45)
Michael Castle (DE-AL)
Ginny Brown-Waite (FL-05)
Mark Kirk (IL-10)
Judy Biggert (IL-13)
Tim Johnson (IL-15)
Aaron Schock (IL-18)
Lynn Jenkins (KS-02)
Ed Whitfield (KY-01)
Joseph Cao (LA-02)
Roscoe Bartlett (MD-06)

Vernon Ehlers (MI-03)
Fred Upton (MI-06)
Candice Miller (MI-10)
Thaddeus McCotter (MI-11)
Jo Ann Emerson (MO-08)
Jeff Fortenberry (NE-01)
Frank LoBiondo (NJ-02)
Leonard Lance (NJ-07)
Rodney Frelinghuysen (NJ-11)
Chris Lee (NY-26)
Pat Tiberi (OH-12)

Steven LaTourette (OH-14)
Greg Walden (OR-02)
Jim Gerlach (PA-06)
Charlie Dent (PA-15)
Tim Murphy (PA-18)
Todd Platts (PA-19)
Michael Burgess (TX-26)
Cathy McMorris Rodgers (WA-05)
Dave Reichert (WA-08)
Tom Petri (WI-06)
Shelley Moore Capito (WV-02)

FORMER HOUSE MEMBERS IN THE SENATE

	In House	Elected to Senate
Richard Shelby, R-Ala.	1978-86	1996
John McCain, R-Ariz.	1982-86	1986
Jon Kyl, R-Ariz.	1986-94	1994
Blanche Lincoln, D-Ark.	1992-96	1998
Barbara Boxer, D-Calif.	1982-92	1992
Mark Udall, D-Colo.	1998-2008	2008
Christopher Dodd, D-Conn.	1974-80	1980
Thomas Carper, D-Del.	1982-92	2000
Bill Nelson, D-Fla.	1978-90	2000
Saxby Chambliss, R-Ga.	1994-2002	2002
Johnny Isakson, R-Ga.	1999-2004	2004
Daniel Inouye, D-Hawaii	1959-62	1962
Daniel Akaka, D-Hawaii	1976-90	1990*
Mike Crapo, R-Idaho	1992-98	1998
Richard Durbin, D-Ill.	1982-96	1996
Charles Grassley, R-Iowa	1974-80	1980
Tom Harkin, D-Iowa	1974-84	1984
Sam Brownback, R-Kansas	1994-96	1996
Pat Roberts, R-Kansas	1980-96	1996
Jim Bunning, R-Ky.	1986-98	1998
David Vitter, R-La.	1999-2004	2004
Olympia Snowe, R-Maine	1978-94	1994
Barbara Mikulski, D-Md.	1976-86	1986
Ben Cardin, D-Md.	1986-2006	2006
Debbie Stabenow, D-Mich.	1996-2000	2000
Thad Cochran, R-Miss.	1972-78	1988
Roger Wicker, R-Miss.	1994-2008	2007*
Max Baucus, D-Mont.	1974-78	1978
Harry Reid, D-Nev.	1982-86	1986
John Ensign, R-Nev.	1994-98	2000
Judd Gregg, R-N.H.	1980-88	1992
Robert Menendez, D-N.J.	1992-2006	2006*
Tom Udall, D-N.M.	1998-2008	2008
Kirsten Gillibrand, D-N.Y.	2006-09	2009*
Charles Schumer, D-N.Y.	1980-1998	1998
Richard Burr, R-N.C.	1994-2004	2004
Byron Dorgan, D-N.D.	1980-92	1992
Sherrod Brown, D-Ohio	1992-2006	2006
James Inhofe, R-Okla.	1986-94	1994
Tom Coburn, R-Okla.	1994-2000	2004
Ron Wyden, D-Ore.	1980-96	1996
Jack Reed, D-R.I.	1990-96	1996
Lindsey Graham, R-S.C.	1994-2002	2002
Jim DeMint, R-S.C.	1998-2004	2004
Tim Johnson, D-S.D.	1986-96	1996
John Thune, R-S.D.	1996-2002	2004
Bernie Sanders, I-Vt.	1990-2006	2006
Maria Cantwell, D-Wash.	1992-94	2000
Robert Byrd, D-W.Va.	1952-58	1958

*Appointed to Senate

FORMER GOVERNORS IN CONGRESS

	Governor	Elected to Congress
Sen. Lamar Alexander, R-Tenn.	1979-86	2002
Sen. Evan Bayh, D-Ind.	1989-96	1998
Sen. Christopher "Kit" Bond, R-Mo.	1973-76; 1981-84	1986
Sen. Thomas Carper, D-Del.	1993-2000	2000
Rep. Mike Castle, R-Del.	1985-92	1992
Sen. Mike Johanns, R-Neb.	1999-2004	2008
Sen. Judd Gregg, R-N.H.	1989-92	1992
Sen. Ben Nelson, D-Neb.	1991-98	2000
Sen. James Risch, R-Idaho	2006	2008
Sen. Jay Rockefeller, D-W.V.	1977-84	1984
Sen. Jeanne Shaheen, D-N.H.	1997-2002	2008
Sen. George Voinovich, R-Ohio	1991-98	1998
Sen. Mark Warner, D-Va.	2002-05	2008

FORMER MEMBERS WHO ARE GOVERNORS

Bob Riley, R-Ala.	U.S. House, 1996-2002
C.L. "Butch" Otter, R-Idaho	U.S. House, 2000-06
Bobby Jindal, R-La.	U.S. House, 2004-08
John Baldacci, D-Maine	U.S. House, 1994-2002
John Corzine, D-N.J.	U.S. Senate, 2000-05
Bill Richardson, D-N.M.	U.S. House, 1982-97
Jim Gibbons, R-Nev.	U.S. House, 1996-2006
Ted Strickland, D-Ohio	U.S. House, 1992-94, 1996-2006
Mark Sanford, R-S.C.	U.S. House, 1994-2000.

MEMBERS AND GOVERNORS WHO SWITCHED PARTIES

Senate	State	Old Party	New Party	Year Switched
Mike Johanns	Neb.	D	R	1988
Joseph Lieberman	Conn.	D	I	2007
Richard Shelby	Ala.	D	R	1994
Arlen Specter	Pa.	R	D	2009

House	State	Old Party	New Party	Year Switched
Rodney Alexander	La.	D	R	2004
Nathan Deal	Ga.	D	R	1995
Ralph Hall	Texas	D	R	2004
Walter Jones	N.C.	D	R	1993
Albio Sires	N.J.	I	D	1998

Governor	State	Old Party	New Party	Year Switched
Rick Perry	Texas	D	R	1989
Mark Parkinson	Kan.	R	D	2006

MILITARY SERVICE

This is a list of members of Congress and governors who have served in the United States Army, Navy, Air Force or Coast Guard. It includes members and governors who have served in the National Guard or the Reserves.

Senate (11 R, 14 D)

Daniel Akaka	D-Hawaii	Army Corps of Engineers, 1945-47
Robert Bennett	R-Utah	Chaplain, Army Natl. Guard, 1957-60
Jeff Bingaman	D-N.M.	Army Res., 1968-74
Thomas Carper	D-Del.	Navy, 1968-73; Naval Res., 1973-91
Thad Cochran	R-Miss.	Navy, 1959-61
Christopher Dodd	D-Conn.	Army Res., 1969-75
Michael Enzi	R-Wyo.	Wyo. Natl. Guard, 1967-73
Lindsey Graham	R-S.C.	Air Force, 1982-88; S.C. Air Natl. Guard, 1989-94; Air Force Res., 1995-present
Tom Harkin	D-Iowa	Navy, 1962-67; Naval Res., 1969-72
James Inhofe	R-Okla.	Army, 1957-58
Daniel Inouye	D-Hawaii	Army, 1943-47
Johnny Isakson	R-Ga.	Ga. Air Natl. Guard, 1966-72
Edward Kennedy	D-Mass.	Army, 1951-53
John Kerry	D-Mass.	Navy, 1966-70; Naval Res. 1970-78
Herb Kohl	D-Wis.	Army Res., 1958-64
Frank Lautenberg	D-N.J.	Army Signal Corps, 1942-46
Richard Lugar	R-Ind.	Navy, 1957-60
John McCain	R-Ariz.	Navy, 1958-80
Bill Nelson	D-Fla.	Army, 1968-70; Army Res., 1965-71
Jack Reed	D-R.I.	Army, 1967-79; Army Res., 1979-91
Pat Roberts	R-Kan.	Marines, 1958-62
Jeff Sessions	R-Ala.	Army Res., 1973-86
Arlen Specter	D-Pa.	Air Force, 1951-53
Jim Webb	D-Va.	Marines, 1968-72
Roger Wicker	R-Miss.	Air Force, 1976-80; Air Force Reserve, 1980-present

House (48 R, 48 D)

Todd Akin	R-Mo.	Army Res., 1972-80
Rodney Alexander	R-La.	Air Force Res., 1965-71
Joe Baca	D-Calif.	Army, 1966-68
Spencer Bachus	R-Ala.	Natl. Guard, 1969-71
Gresham Barrett	R-S.C.	Army, 1983-87
Sanford Bishop	D-Ga.	Army, 1970-71
John Boccieri	D-Ohio	Air Force Res., 1994-present
John Boehner	R-Ohio	Navy, 1969
Leonard Boswell	D-Iowa	Army, 1956-76
Allen Boyd	D-Fla.	Army, 1969-71
Paul Broun	R-Ga.	Marine Res., 1964-67; Naval Res., 1967-73; Ga. Air Natl. Guard, 1972-73; Air Force Res., 1973-88
Henry Brown	R-S.C.	S.C. Natl. Guard, 1953-62
Vern Buchanan	R-Fla.	Mich. Air Natl. Guard, 1970-76
Dan Burton	R-Ind.	Army, 1956-57; Army Res., 1957-62
G.K. Butterfield	D-N.C.	Army, 1968-70
Steve Buyer	R-Ind.	Army, 1984-87, 1990-91; Army Res., 1980-84, 1987-present
Christopher Carney	D-Pa.	Naval Res., 1995-present

Howard Coble	R-N.C.	Coast Guard, 1952-56, 1977-78; Coast Guard Res., 1960-81
Mike Coffman	R-Colo.	Army, 1972-79; Marines, 1979-94, 2005-06
Mike Conaway	R-Texas	Army, 1970-72
John Conyers	D-Mich.	Natl. Guard, 1948-50; Army, 1950-54; Army Res., 1954-57
Geoff Davis	R-Ky.	Army, 1976-87
Nathan Deal	R-Ga.	Army, 1966-68
Peter DeFazio	D-Ore.	Air Force, 1967-71
Bill Delahunt	D-Mass.	Coast Guard, 1963; Coast Guard Res., 1963-71
John Dingell	D-Mich.	Army, 1944-46
John Duncan	R-Tenn.	Army Natl. Guard & Army Res., 1970-87
Bob Etheridge	D-N.C.	Army, 1965-67
Eni F.H. Faleomavaega	D-Am. Samoa	Army, 1966-69
John Fleming	R-La.	Navy, 1976-82
Rodney Frelinghuysen	R-N.J.	Army, 1969-71
Louie Gohmert	R-Texas	Army, 1978-82
Charles Gonzalez	D-Texas	Texas Air Natl. Guard, 1969-75
Bart Gordon	D-Tenn.	Army Res., 1971-72
Parker Griffith	D-Ala.	Va. Army Res., 1970-73
Brett Guthrie	R-Ky.	Army, 1987-2001
Ralph Hall	R-Texas	Navy, 1942-45
Phil Hare	D-Ill.	Army Res., 1969-75
Doc Hastings	R-Wash.	Army Res., 1964-69
Maurice Hinchey	D-N.Y.	Navy, 1956-59
Duncan Hunter	R-Calif.	Marines, 2002-05; Marine Res., 2005-present
Darrell Issa	R-Calif.	Army, 1970-72, 1976-80
Sam Johnson	R-Texas	Air Force, 1950-79
Walter Jones	R-N.C.	N.C. Natl. Guard, 1967-71
Paul Kanjorski	D-Pa.	Army Res., 1960-61
Peter King	R-N.Y.	Army Natl. Guard, 1968-73
Mark Kirk	R-Ill.	U.S. Naval Res., 1989-present
John Kline	R-Minn.	Marines, 1969-94
John Linder	R-Ga.	Air Force, 1967-69
Edward Markey	D-Mass.	Army Res., 1968-73
Jim Marshall	D-Ga.	Army, 1968-70
Eric Massa	D-N.Y.	Navy, 1977-2001
Jim McDermott	D-Wash.	U.S. Navy Medical Corps, 1968-70
Gary Miller	R-Calif.	Army, 1967
Walt Minnick	D-Idaho	Army, 1970-72
Alan Mollohan	D-W.Va.	Army, 1970; Army Res., 1970-83
Dennis Moore	D-Kan.	Army, 1970; Army Res., 1971-73
Patrick Murphy	D-Pa.	Army, 1996-2004; Army Res., 2004-present
John Murtha	D-Pa.	Marines, 1952-55, 1966-67; Marine Res., 1955-66, 1967-90
Pete Olson	R-Texas	Navy, 1988-98; Naval Res., 1998-present
Solomon Ortiz	D-Texas	Army, 1960-62
Bill Pascrell	D-N.J.	Army, 1961; Army Res., 1962-67
Ron Paul	R-Texas	Flight surgeon, Air Force, 1963-68
Gary Peters	D-Mich.	Naval Res., 1993-2005
Collin Peterson	D-Minn.	Army Natl. Guard, 1963-69
Joe Pitts	R-Pa.	Air Force, 1963-69
Ted Poe	R-Texas	Air Force Res., 1970-76
Charles Rangel	D-N.Y.	Army, 1948-52
Dave Reichert	R-Wash.	Air Force Res., 1971-76
Silvestre Reyes	D-Texas	Army, 966-68
Phil Roe	R-Tenn.	Army, 1973-74

Harold Rogers	R-Ky.	Army Natl. Guard, 1957-64
Mike Rogers	R-Mich.	Army, 1985-88
Tom Rooney	R-Fla.	Army JAG, 2000-04; Army Res., 2004-07
Bobby Rush	D-Ill.	Army, 1963-68
Del. Gregorio Kilili Camacho Sablan	D-C.N.M.I.	Army, 1981-86
John Salazar	D-Colo.	Army Criminal Investigations Unit, 1973-76
Bobby Scott	D-Va.	Army Natl. Guard, 1970-73; Army Res., 1973-76
José Serrano	D-N.Y.	Army Medical Corps, 1964-66
Joe Sestak	D-Pa.	Navy, 1974-2005
John Shadegg	R-Ariz.	Air Natl. Guard, 1969-75
John Shimkus	R-Ill.	Army, 1980-85; Army Res., 1985-2008
Vic Snyder	D-Ark.	Marines, 1967-69
John Spratt	D-S.C.	Army Operations, U.S. Dept. of Defense, 1969-71
Pete Stark	D-Calif.	Air Force, 1955-57
Cliff Stearns	R-Fla.	Air Force, 1963-67
John Tanner	D-Tenn.	Navy, 1968-72; Tenn. Natl. Guard, 1974-2000
Gene Taylor	D-Miss.	Coast Guard Res., 1971-84
Mike Thompson	D-Calif.	Army, 1969-73
Edolphus Towns	D-N.Y.	Army, 1956-58
Tim Walz	D-Minn.	Army Natl. Guard, 1981-2005
Ed Whitfield	R-Ky.	Army Res., 1967-73
Joe Wilson	R-S.C.	Army Res., 1972-75; S.C. Natl. Guard, 1975-2003
Frank Wolf	R-Va.	Army, 1962-63; Army Res., 1963-67
Bill Young	R-Fla.	Army Natl. Guard, 1948-57
Don Young	R-Alaska	Army, 1955-57

Governors (6R, 5D)

Mike Beebe	D-Ark.	Army Res., 1968-74
Steve Beshear	D-Ky.	Army Res., 1969-75
Jon Corzine	D-N.J.	Marine Res., 1969-75
Jim Gibbons	R-Nev.	Air Force, 1967-71; Nev. Air Natl. Guard, 1975-96
Dave Heineman	R-Neb.	Army Ranger, 1970-75
Ted Kulongski	D-Ore.	Marines, 1959-63
C.L. "Butch" Otter	R-Idaho	Idaho Natl. Guard, 1967-73
Sonny Perdue	R-Ga.	Air Force, 1971-74
Rick Perry	R-Texas	Air Force, 1972-77
Ed Rendell	D-Pa.	Army Res., 1968-74
Arnold Schwarzenegger	R-Calif.	Austrian Army, 1965-66

NATIONAL JOURNAL VOTE RATINGS

Most Liberal, Most Conservative

These are the members at the far ends of the ideological spectrum, based on *National Journal*'s 2008 vote ratings. Scores are a composite of ratings of economic, social and foreign policy votes. Members marked with an asterisk were no longer in Congress as of July 29, 2009.

Senate

Most Liberal			Liberal Score
1st		Patty Murray, D-Wash............................	92.7
2nd		Jack Reed, D-R.I.	91.5
3rd		Barbara Boxer, D-Calif............................	90.2
4th		Frank Lautenberg, D-N.J........................	88.3
5th		Jeff Bingaman, D-N.M....	88.2
6th		Daniel Akaka, D-Hawaii...........................	86.8
7th	(tie)	Ben Cardin, D-Md..................................	85.7
		Richard Durbin, D-Ill.............................	85.7
		Charles Schumer, D-N.Y..........................	85.7
10th		Joe Biden, D-Del.*...............................	84.8
11th		Debbie Stabenow, D-Mich........................	83.2
12th		Christopher Dodd, D-Conn.......................	82.8
13th	(tie)	Patrick Leahy, D-Vt..............................	82.3
		Bernie Sanders, I-Vt.............................	82.3
15th	(tie)	Hillary Rodham Clinton, D-N.Y.*...............	82.2
		Robert Menendez, D-N.J.........................	82.2

Most Conservative			Conservative Score
1st	(tie)	John Barrasso, R-Wyo............................	93.2
		John Ensign, R-Nev...............................	93.2
		Michael Enzi, R-Wyo..............................	93.2
		Jon Kyl, R-Ariz....................................	93.2
5th		Jim DeMint, R-S.C................................	92.3
6th		Tom Coburn, R-Okla..............................	92
7th		Wayne Allard, R-Colo.*..........................	91.3
8th		James Inhofe, R-Okla............................	90.7
9th		Jim Bunning, R-Ky................................	90.3
10th		David Vitter, R-La................................	90
11th		John Thune, R-S.D................................	88.8
12th		Richard Burr, R-N.C..............................	88.2
13th	(tie)	Christopher "Kit" Bond, R-Mo....................	85.3
		Mitch McConnell, R-Ky...........................	85.3
15th		Lindsey Graham, R-S.C...........................	84.5

House

Most Liberal			Liberal Score
1st	(tie)	Robert Brady, D-Pa...............................	93.2
		Raúl Grijalva, D-Ariz.............................	93.2
		Betty McCollum, D-Minn.........................	93.2
		George Miller, D-Calif............................	93.2
		Grace Napolitano, D-Calif........................	93.2
		John Olver, D-Mass...............................	93.2
		Linda Sánchez, D-Calif...........................	93.2

Most Liberal   **Liberal Score**

		Louise Slaughter, D-N.Y	93.2
		Hilda Solis, D-Calif.*	93.2
		Jackie Speier, D-Calif	93.2
		John Tierney, D-Mass	93.2
		Nydia Velázquez, D-N.Y	93.2
13th	(tie)	Tammy Baldwin, D-Wis	90.7
		Keith Ellison, D-Minn	90.7
		Barney Frank, D-Mass	90.7
		Mike Honda, D-Calif	90.7
		Jesse Jackson Jr., D-Ill	90.7
		Sheila Jackson Lee, D-Texas	90.7
		Jim McGovern, D-Mass	90.7
		Richard Neal, D-Mass	90.7
21st	(tie)	Edward Markey, D-Mass	90
		David Obey, D-Wis	90
		Lucille Roybal-Allard, D-Calif	90
24th		Bill Delahunt, D-Mass	89.5
25th	(tie)	John Larson, D-Conn	89.2
		Charles Rangel, D-N.Y	89.2

Most Conservative   **Conservative Score**

1st	(tie)	Paul Broun, R-Ga	97.3
		Trent Franks, R-Ariz	97.3
		Jeb Hensarling, R-Texas	97.3
4th		Gresham Barrett, R-S.C	97
5th		Todd Akin, R-Mo	96.8
6th	(tie)	Virginia Foxx, R-N.C	96.3
		Doug Lamborn, R-Colo	96.3
		Jeff Miller, R-Fla	96.3
9th		Steve King, R-Iowa	95.8
10th		John Shadegg, R-Ariz	95.7
11th		Tom Price, R-Ga	95.5
12th		Ed Royce, R-Calif	95
13th	(tie)	Phil Gingrey, R-Ga	94.7
		Bill Sali, R-Idaho*	94.7
15th		Kenny Marchant, R-Texas	94.3
16th	(tie)	John Boehner, R-Ohio	93.7
		Chris Cannon, R-Utah*	93.7
18th		Mike Pence, R-Ind	92.7
19th		Randy Neugebauer, R-Texas	92.2
20th		Roy Blunt, R-Mo	92
21st		Adrian Smith, R-Neb	91.8
22nd		Wally Herger, R-Calif	91.5
23rd		Patrick McHenry, R-N.C	91.2
24th	(tie)	Mike Conaway, R-Texas	91
		George Radanovich, R-Calif	91

The Centrists

These are the members at the ideological center of the Senate and the House in 2008, according to *National Journal*'s 2008 vote ratings. The members with composite scores closest to 50 are at the exact center of each chamber. Members marked with an asterisk were no longer in Congress as of July 29, 2009.

Senate

	Liberal Score	Conservative Score
Robert Bennett, R-Utah	34.2	65.8
John Sununu, R-N.H.*	34.2	65.8
Thad Cochran, R-Miss.	34.3	65.7
Mel Martinez, R-Fla.	37.5	62.5
Richard Lugar, R-Ind.	38.2	61.8
George Voinovich, R-Ohio	38.7	61.3
Norm Coleman, R-Minn.*	39	61
Elizabeth Dole, R-N.C.*	39.2	60.8
Chuck Hagel, R-Neb.*	40.2	59.8
John Warner, R-Va.*	40.2	59.8
Ted Stevens, R-Alaska*	41	59
Lisa Murkowski, R-Alaska	42.2	57.8
Arlen Specter, R-Pa.	44.8	55.2
Gordon Smith, R-Ore.*	45.7	54.3
Evan Bayh, D-Ind.	47.3	52.7
Susan Collins, R-Maine	49	51
Ben Nelson, D-Neb.	49.8	50.2
Mary Landrieu, D-La.	50.7	49.3
Olympia Snowe, R-Maine	50.8	49.2
Claire McCaskill, D-Mo.	51.8	48.2
Tim Johnson, D-S.D.	55.8	44.2
Mark Pryor, D-Ark.	56.8	43.2
Joe Lieberman, I-Conn.	59.3	40.7
Thomas Carper, D-Del.	62.2	37.8
Jon Tester, D-Mont.	63	37
Jim Webb, D-Va.	63.8	36.2
Kent Conrad, D-N.D.	64.7	35.3
Russell Feingold, D-Wis.	65	35
Amy Klobuchar, D-Minn.	65	35
Blanche Lincoln, D-Ark.	65.5	34.5

House

	Liberal Score	Conservative Score
Chip Pickering, R-Miss.*	34.3	65.7
Randy Kuhl, R-N.Y.*	34.7	65.3
Walter Jones, R-N.C.	35	65
Todd Platts, R-Pa.	35	65
Tom Davis, R-Va.*	35.2	64.8
Mary Bono Mack, R-Calif.	35.3	64.7
Jerry Weller, R-Ill.*	35.3	64.7
Robin Hayes, R-N.C.*	35.7	64.3
Judy Biggert, R-Ill.	35.8	64.2
Ralph Regula, R-Ohio*	35.8	64.2
Michael Ferguson, R-N.J.*	36.2	63.8
John McHugh, R-N.Y.	36.2	63.8
Candice Miller, R-Mich.	36.2	63.8
Joe Knollenberg, R-Mich.*	36.7	63.3

	Liberal Score	Conservative Score
Don Young, R-Alaska	36.7	63.3
David Hobson, R-Ohio*	37	63
Vern Buchanan, R-Fla.	38	62
Steven LaTourette, R-Ohio	38.3	61.7
Jeff Fortenberry, R-Neb.	38.8	61.2
Shelley Moore Capito, R-W.Va.	39.2	60.8
Peter King, R-N.Y.	39.7	60.3
Frank LoBiondo, R-N.J.	40	60
Fred Upton, R-Mich.	40	60
Charlie Dent, R-Pa.	40.2	59.8
Vernon Ehlers, R-Mich.	40.2	59.8
Phil English, R-Pa.*	40.5	59.5
Dave Reichert, R-Wash.	40.7	59.3
Ray LaHood, R-Ill.*	40.8	59.2
Mario Diaz-Balart, R-Fla.	41.3	58.7
Jo Ann Emerson, R-Mo.	41.3	58.7
James Walsh, R-N.Y.*	41.3	58.7
Tim Johnson, R-Ill.	41.7	58.3
Lincoln Diaz-Balart, R-Fla.	41.8	58.2
Tim Murphy, R-Pa.	41.8	58.2
Jim Gerlach, R-Pa.	42	58
Mark Kirk, R-Ill.	42.2	57.8
Jon Porter, R-Nev.*	42.7	57.3
Nick Lampson, D-Texas*	43.8	56.2
Jim Ramstad, R-Minn.*	44.2	55.8
Jim Marshall, D-Ga.	45	55
Michael Castle, R-Del.	45.3	54.7
Ileana Ros-Lehtinen, R-Fla.	45.3	54.7
Dan Boren, D-Okla.	47.2	52.8
Christopher Shays, R-Conn.*	47.2	52.8
Chris Smith, R-N.J.	47.3	52.7
Brad Ellsworth, D-Ind.	47.8	52.2
John Barrow, D-Ga.	48.2	51.8
Joe Donnelly, D-Ind.	48.2	51.8
Don Cazayoux, D-La.*	48.3	51.7
Jim Matheson, D-Utah	48.5	51.5
Melissa Bean, D-Ill.	49.5	50.5
Jason Altmire, D-Pa.	50	50
Christopher Carney, D-Pa.	50.3	49.7
Wayne Gilchrest, R-Md.*	50.5	49.5
Gene Taylor, D-Miss.	51	49
Baron Hill, D-Ind.	51.3	48.7
Heath Shuler, D-N.C.	51.3	48.7
Stephanie Herseth Sandlin, D-S.D.	51.5	48.5
Lincoln Davis, D-Tenn.	51.7	48.3
Gene Green, D-Texas	51.7	48.3
Tim Mahoney, D-Fla.*	51.7	48.3
Henry Cuellar, D-Texas	52	48
Collin Peterson, D-Minn.	52	48
John Tanner, D-Tenn.	52	48
Gabrielle Giffords, D-Ariz.	52.3	47.7
Charlie Melancon, D-La.	52.3	47.7
Mike McIntyre, D-N.C.	52.7	47.3
Harry Mitchell, D-Ariz.	52.7	47.3
Jim Costa, D-Calif.	52.8	47.2
Jim Cooper, D-Tenn.	53.2	46.8

	Liberal Score	Conservative Score
Mark Udall, D-Colo.*	53.8	46.2
Zack Space, D-Ohio	54	46
Allen Boyd, D-Fla.	54.3	45.7
Ciro Rodriguez, D-Texas	54.3	45.7
Rick Boucher, D-Va.	54.8	45.2
Ben Chandler, D-Ky.	55	45
Artur Davis, D-Ala.	55	45
Jerry McNerney, D-Calif.	55.2	44.8
Bill Foster, D-Ill.	55.5	44.5
Solomon Ortiz, D-Texas	56.2	43.8
Mike Ross, D-Ark.	56.3	43.7
Bud Cramer, D-Ala.*	56.5	43.5
Charlie Wilson, D-Ohio	56.7	43.3
John Salazar, D-Colo.	56.8	43.2
Nancy Boyda, D-Kan.*	57	43
Dennis Kucinich, D-Ohio	57.5	42.5
Patrick Murphy, D-Pa.	57.5	42.5
Chet Edwards, D-Texas	57.7	42.3
Michael Arcuri, D-N.Y.	57.8	42.2
Paul Kanjorski, D-Pa.	58.3	41.7
Dennis Cardoza, D-Calif.	58.8	41.2
Tim Holden, D-Pa.	59	41
Shelley Berkley, D-Nev.	59.3	40.7
Marion Berry, D-Ark.	59.5	40.5
Ed Perlmutter, D-Colo.	59.7	40.3
Ron Klein, D-Fla.	59.8	40.2
Silvestre Reyes, D-Texas	60.2	39.8
Brian Baird, D-Wash.	60.5	39.5
Tim Walz, D-Minn.	60.5	39.5
Bart Gordon, D-Tenn.	61	39
Dennis Moore, D-Kan.	61.2	38.8
Earl Pomeroy, D-N.D.	61.8	38.2
Loretta Sanchez, D-Calif.	62	38
Chris Murphy, D-Conn.	62.3	37.7
Ike Skelton, D-Mo.	62.8	37.2
Vic Snyder, D-Ark.	62.8	37.2
John Murtha, D-Pa.	63.2	36.8
Ron Kind, D-Wis.	63.7	36.3
Joe Baca, D-Calif.	64.7	35.3
Rubén Hinojosa, D-Texas	64.7	35.3
Paul Hodes, D-N.H.	65.2	34.8
Peter DeFazio, D-Ore.	65.5	34.5

DISTRICT DEMOGRAPHICS

African-American

Districts with highest percentages of African-Americans

District	%	Member
IL-2	67.4	Jackson (D)
MS-2	65.4	Thompson (D)
IL-1	63.7	Rush (D)
AL-7	63.6	Davis (D)
TN-9	62.8	Cohen (D)
MI-14	61.1	Conyers (D)
NY-10	60.5	Towns (D)
LA-2	59.5	Cao (R)
PA-2	59.3	Fattah (D)
MI-13	58.9	Kilpatrick (D)

Hispanic

Districts with highest percentages of Hispanics

District	%	Member
TX-16	80.9	Reyes (D)
TX-15	80	Hinojosa (D)
CA-34	79.5	Roybal-Allard (D)
TX-28	78.6	Cuellar (D)
CA-38	74.1	Napolitano (D)
IL-4	73.8	Gutierrez (D)
FL-21	73.1	Diaz-Balart, L. (R)
TX-29	71.8	Green (D)
TX-27	71.1	Ortiz (D)
TX-20	69.8	Gonzalez (D)

Asian

Districts with highest percentages of Asians

District	%	Member
HI-1	52.5	Abercrombie (D)
CA-13	34.7	Stark (D)
CA-15	33.6	Honda (D)
CA-12	32.5	Speier (D)
NY-5	28.9	Ackerman (D)
CA-8	28.9	Pelosi (D)
CA-16	27.5	Lofgren (D)
CA-29	26.4	Schiff (D)
HI-2	25.6	Hirono (D)
CA-32	20.3	Chu (D)

American Indian

Districts with highest percentages of American Indians

District	%	Member
AZ-1	20.2	Kirkpatrick (D)
NM-3	17.2	Luján (D)
OK-2	14.5	Boren (D)
AK-AL	13.1	Young (R)
SD-AL	8	Herseth Sandlin (D)
NC-7	7.8	McIntyre (D)
MT-AL	5.9	Rehberg (R)
OK-3	5.3	Lucas (R)
NM-2	5.3	Teague (D)
OK-4	5	Cole (R)

Youngest

Disticts with lowest median age

District	Median Age	Member
UT-3	25.7	Chaffetz (R)
CA-20	27.6	Costa (D)
CA-43	27.9	Baca (D)
AZ-4	28	Pastor (D)
UT-1	28.5	Bishop (R)
NY-16	28.8	Serrano (D)
TX-28	28.9	Cuellar (D)
TX-29	29	Green (D)
CA-47	29.4	Sanchez, Lor. (D)
IL-4	29.4	Gutierrez (D)

Oldest

Districts with highest median age

District	Median Age	Member
FL-13	46.5	Buchanan (R)
FL-10	45.5	Young (R)
FL-19	45.5	Wexler (D)
FL-14	44.8	Mack (R)
FL-22	44.7	Klein (D)
FL-16	43.5	Rooney (R)
PA-18	43.1	Murphy (R)
FL-5	43	Brown-Waite (R)
PA-4	42.6	Altmire (D)
MA-10	42.3	Delahunt (D)

Wealthiest

Districts with highest median household income

District	Median Income	Member
VA-11	$101,455	Connolly (D)
NJ-11	$94,562	Frelinghuysen (R)
VA-10	$91,470	Wolf (R)
CA-14	$90,905	Eshoo (D)
NJ-7	$90,502	Lance (R)
NJ-5	$87,505	Garrett (R)
NY-3	$87,066	King (R)
CA-42	$87,051	Miller (R)
NJ-12	$86,316	Holt (D)
NY-2	$85,847	Israel (D)

Poorest

Districts with highest percentage of people in poverty

District	%	Member
NY-16	40	Serrano (D)
TX-15	33.7	Hinojosa (D)
MI-13	30.6	Kilpatrick (D)
PA-1	30.1	Brady (D)
CA-20	29.2	Costa (D)
MS-2	28.7	Thompson (D)
TX-28	28.3	Cuellar (D)
TX-27	28.2	Ortiz (D)
TX-16	27.8	Reyes (D)
NY-15	27.2	Rangel (D)

Most Educated

Districts with highest percentage of post-graduate degrees

District	%	Member
MD-8	29.8	Van Hollen (D)
VA-8	29.3	Moran (D)
NY-14	28.1	Maloney (D)
CA-14	27.9	Eshoo (D)
NY-8	25.5	Nadler (D)
DC-AL	25	Norton (D)
NY-18	24.2	Lowey (D)
CA-30	24.1	Waxman (D)
VA-11	23.2	Connolly (D)
MA-8	22	Capuano (D)

Least Educated

Districts with lowest percentage of high school graduates

District	%	Member
TX-29	53.8	Green (D)
CA-34	54.4	Roybal-Allard (D)
CA-20	55.1	Costa (D)
CA-47	56.1	Sanchez, Lor. (D)
NY-16	57.9	Serrano (D)
CA-31	58.8	Becerra (D)
IL-4	60.9	Gutierrez (D)
AZ-4	62.6	Pastor (D)
TX-28	64	Cuellar (D)
TX-15	64.2	Hinojosa (D)

Government Workers

Districts with highest percentage of government employees

District	%	Member
VA-2	31.7	Nye (D)
MD-5	30.6	Hoyer (D)
NC-3	30.2	Jones (R)
FL-2	28.6	Boyd (D)
AK-AL	28.4	Young (R)
VA-1	27.8	Wittman (R)
HI-1	27.6	Abercrombie (D)
DC-AL	27.3	Norton (D)
MD-4	27.1	Edwards (D)
VA-8	25.7	Moran (D)

Veterans

Districts with highest percentage of military veterans

District	%	Member
FL-1	19.4	Miller (R)
VA-2	19	Nye (D)
CO-5	17.8	Lamborn (R)
WA-6	17.3	Dicks (D)
AZ-8	17	Giffords (D)
FL-5	16.7	Brown-Waite (R)
VA-1	16.6	Wittman (R)
FL-6	16.5	Stearns (R)
AZ-2	16	Franks (R)
FL-15	15.6	Posey (R)

SENATE SEATS

2010 ELECTION

Democrats (18)	Previous %	Republicans (18)	Previous %
Evan Bayh (Ind.)	62%	Robert Bennett (Utah)	69%
Michael Bennet (Colo.)	Appointed	Christopher "Kit" Bond[1](Mo.)	56%
Barbara Boxer (Calif.)	58%	Sam Brownback[1](Kan.)	69%
Roland Burris[1] (Ill.)	Appointed	Jim Bunning[1](Ky.)	51%
Christopher Dodd (Conn.)	66%	Richard Burr (N.C.)	52%
Byron Dorgan (N.D.)	68%	Tom Coburn (Okla.)	53%
Russell Feingold (Wis.)	55%	Mike Crapo (Idaho)	99%
Kirsten Gillibrand[2] (N.Y.)	Appointed	Jim DeMint (S.C.)	54%
Daniel Inouye (Hawaii)	76%	Charles Grassley (Iowa)	70%
Ted Kaufman[1](Del.)	Appointed	Judd Gregg[1](N.H.)	66%
Patrick Leahy (Vt.)	71%	Johnny Isakson (Ga.)	58%
Blanche Lincoln (Ark.)	56%	Mel Martinez[1](Fla.)	49%
Barbara Mikulski (Md.)	65%	John McCain (Ariz.)	77%
Patty Murray (Wash.)	55%	Lisa Murkowski (Alaska)	49%
Harry Reid (Nev.)	61%	Richard Shelby (Ala.)	68%
Charles Schumer (N.Y.)	71%	John Thune (S.D.)	51%
Arlen Specter[3] (Penn.)	53%	David Vitter (La.)	51%
Ron Wyden (Ore.)	63%	George Voinovich[1](Ohio)	64%

2012 ELECTION

Democrats (21)	Previous %	Republicans (9)	Previous %
Daniel Akaka (Hawaii)	61%	John Barrasso (Wy.)	73%
Jeff Bingaman (N.M.)	71%	Bob Corker (Tenn.)	51%
Sherrod Brown (Ohio)	56%	John Ensign (Nev.)	55%
Robert Byrd (W.Va.)	64%	Orrin Hatch (Utah)	63%
Maria Cantwell (Wash.)	57%	Kay Bailey	
Ben Cardin (Md.)	54%	Hutchison[4] (Texas)	62%
Bob Casey (Penn.)	59%	Jon Kyl (Ariz.)	53%
Kent Conrad (N.D.)	69%	Richard Lugar (Ind.)	87%
Dianne Feinstein (Calif.)	59%	Olympia Snowe (Maine)	74%
Kirsten Gillibrand[2] (N.Y.)	Appointed	Roger Wicker (Miss.)	55%
Edward Kennedy (Mass.)	69%		
Amy Klobuchar (Minn.)	58%	**Independents (2)**	**Previous %**
Herb Kohl (Wis.)	67%	Joe Lieberman (Conn.)	50%
Claire McCaskill (Mo.)	50%	Bernie Sanders (Vt.)	65%
Robert Menendez (N.J.)	53%		
Ben Nelson (Neb.)	64%		
Bill Nelson (Fla.)	60%		
Debbie Stabenow (Mich.)	57%		
Jon Tester (Mont.)	49%		
Jim Webb (Va.)	50%		
Sheldon Whitehouse (R.I.)	54%		

[1]Will not seek reelection in 2010.

[2]If elected in 2010 to serve out the remainder of Hillary Rodham Clinton's term, Gillibrand would have to run again in 2012 to keep the seat.

[3]Elected as a Republican.

[4]Hutchison has said she will resign in 2009.

GOVERNORSHIPS

2009, 2 States

New Jersey	(D)	**Virginia**	**(D)**

2010, 37 States

Alabama	**(R)**	Nebraska	(R)
Alaska	(R)	Nevada	(R)
Arizona	(R)	New Hampshire*	(D)
Arkansas	(D)	**New Mexico**	**(D)**
California	**(R)**	New York	(D)
Colorado	(D)	Ohio	(D)
Connecticut	(R)	**Oklahoma**	**(D)**
Florida	**(R)**	**Oregon**	**(D)**
Georgia	**(R)**	**Pennsylvania**	**(D)**
Hawaii	**(R)**	**Rhode Island**	**(R)**
Idaho	(R)	**South Carolina**	**(R)**
Illinois	(D)	**South Dakota**	**(R)**
Iowa	(D)	**Tennessee**	**(D)**
Kansas	**(D)**	Texas	(R)
Maine	**(D)**	Utah	(R)
Maryland	(D)	Vermont*	(R)
Massachusetts	(D)	Wisconsin	(D)
Michigan	**(D)**	**Wyoming**	**(D)**
Minnesota	(R)		

2011, 3 States

Kentucky	(D)	**Mississippi**	**(R)**
Louisiana	(R)		

2012, 11 States

Delaware	(D)	North Dakota	(R)
Indiana	**(R)**	**Utah**	**(R)**
Missouri	(D)	Vermont*	(R)
Montana	**(D)**	Washington	(D)
New Hampshire*	(D)	**West Virginia**	**(D)**
North Carolina	(D)		

Partisan breakdown of governorships at press time: 28 Democrats, 22 Republicans.
*New Hampshire and Vermont have two-year terms. All other states have four-year terms.
Boldface indicates governors who are term-limited or are not seeking re-election.

FILING DEADLINES

STATE	CONGRSSIONAL FILING DEADLINE	CONGRESSIONAL PRIMARY DATE	RUNOFF DATE	ELECTION DIVISION PHONE NUMBER
Alabama	April 2, 2010	June 1, 2010	July 13, 2010	334-242-7210
Alaska	June 1, 2010	August 24, 2010		907-465-4611
Arizona	May 26, 2010	August 24, 2010		602-542-8683
Arkansas	March 8, 2010	May 18, 2010	June 8, 2010	501-682-1010
California	March 12, 2010	June 8, 2010		916-657-2166
Colorado	TBD	August 10, 2010		303-894-2200
Connecticut	May 25, 2010	August 10, 2010		860-509-6100
Delaware	TBD	September 14, 2010		302-739-4277
Florida	April 30, 2010	August 24, 2010		850-245-6200
Georgia	April 30, 2010	July 20, 2010	August 10, 2010	404-656-2871
Hawaii	July 20, 2010	September 18, 2010		808-453-8683
Idaho	March 19, 2010	May 25, 2010		208-334-2852
Illinois	November 2, 2009	February 2, 2010		217-782-4141
Indiana	February 19, 2010	May 4, 2010		317-232-3939
Iowa	March 19, 2010	June 8, 2010		515-281-0145
Kansas	June 10, 2010	August 3, 2010		785-296-4561
Kentucky	January 26, 2010	May 18, 2010		502-564-3490
Louisiana	July 9, 2010	August 28, 2010	October 2, 2010	225-922-0900
Maine	March 15, 2010	June 8, 2010		207-624-7736
Maryland	July 5, 2010	September 14, 2010		410-269-2840
Massachusetts	June 1, 2010	September 14, 2010		617-727-2828
Michigan	May 11, 2010	August 3, 2010		517-373-2540
Minnesota	July 20, 2010	September 14, 2010		651-215-1440
Mississippi	March 1, 2010	June 1, 2010	June 22, 2010	601-359-6359
Missouri	March 30, 2010	August 3, 2010		573-751-2301
Montana	March 15, 2010	June 8, 2010		406-444-4732
Nebraska	March 1, 2010	May 11, 2010		402-471-2555
Nevada	March 12, 2010	June 8, 2010		775-684-5705
New Hampshire	June 11, 2010	September 14, 2010		603-271-3242
New Jersey	April 12, 2010	June 8, 2010		609-292-3760
New Mexico	TBD	TBD		505-827-3600
New York	TBD	September 14, 2010		518-473-5086
North Carolina	February 26, 2010	May 4, 2010	June 22, 2010	919-733-7173
North Dakota	April 9, 2010	June 8, 2010		701-328-4146
Ohio	February 18, 2010	May 4, 2010		614-466-2585
Oklahoma	June 9, 2010	July 27, 2010	August 24, 2010	405-521-2391
Oregon	March 9, 2010	May 18, 2010		503-986-1518
Pennylvania	March 9, 2010	May 18, 2010		717-787-5280
Rhode Island	June 30, 2010	September 14, 2010		401-222-2345
South Carolina	March 30, 2010	June 8, 2010	June 22, 2010	803-734-9060
South Dakota	March 30, 2010	June 8, 2010	June 29, 2010	605-773-3537
Tennessee	April 1, 2010	August 5, 2010		615-741-7956
Texas	January 4, 2010	March 2, 2010	April 13, 2010	800-252-8683
Utah	March 19, 2010	June 22, 2010		801-538-1041
Vermont	July 19, 2010	September 14, 2010		800-439-8683
Virginia	April 9, 2010	June 8, 2010		804-864-8901
Washington	June 11, 2010	August 17, 2010		360-902-4180
West Virginia	January 30, 2010	May 11, 2010		304-558-6000
Wisconsin	July 13, 2010	September 14, 2010		608-266-8005
Wyoming	May 28, 2010	August 17, 2010		307-777-7186

TBD: To be determined

Compiled from information provided by state election offices; all dates and deadlines as of July 28, 2009.

CLOSEST CONGRESSIONAL ELECTIONS

These are the elections that had the smallest margins of victory in 2008, based on statistics from the research firm Polidata.

Senate

State	Winner	Loser	Vote Difference	% Difference
Minn.	Al Franken (D)	Norm Coleman (R)	312	0.01
Alaska	Mark Begich (D)	Ted Stevens (R)	3,953	1.25
Ore.	Jeff Merkley (D)	Gordon Smith (R)	59,233	3.35
Ky.	Mitch McConnell (R)	Bruce Lunsford (D)	106,811	5.94
N.H.	Jeanne Shaheen (D)	John Sununu (R)	44,035	6.34
La.	Mary Landrieu (D)	John Kennedy (R)	121,121	6.39
N.C.	Kay Hagan (D)	Elizabeth Dole (R)	361,801	8.47
Miss.	Roger Wicker (R)	Ronnie Musgrove (D)	123,345	9.92

House

District	Winner	Loser	Vote Difference	% Difference
VA-5	Tom Perriello (D)	Virgil Goode (R)	727	0.23
LA-4	John Fleming (R)	Paul Carmouche (D)	350	0.38
NY-20*	Scott Murphy (D)	Jim Tedisco (R)	726	0.45
CA-4	Tom McClintock (R)	Charlie Brown (D)	1,800	0.48
AL-2	Bobby Bright (D)	Jay Love (R)	1,790	0.62
OH-15	Mary Jo Kilroy (D)	Steve Stivers (R)	3,212	0.76
MD-1	Frank Kratovil (D)	Andy Harris (R)	2,852	0.79
ID-1	Walt Minnick (D)	Bill Sali (R)	4,211	1.22
NY-29	Eric Massa (D)	Randy Kuhl (R)	5,330	1.93
MI-7	Mark Schauer (D)	Tim Walberg (R)	7,432	2.31
CA-44	Ken Calvert (R)	Bill Hedrick (D)	6,047	2.38
PA-3	Kathy Dahlkemper (D)	Phil English (R)	7,089	2.48
MO-9	Blaine Luetkemeyer (R)	Judy Baker (D)	8,075	2.50
LA-2	Joseph Cao (R)	William Jefferson (D)	1,814	2.71
MN-6	Michele Bachmann (R)	Elwyn Tinklenberg (D)	12,031	2.98
AL-5	Parker Griffith (D)	Wayne Parker (R)	9,328	3.06
PA-11	Paul Kanjorski (D)	Lou Barletta (R)	9,228	3.26
CT-4	Jim Himes (D)	Christopher Shays (R)	11,621	3.76
NE-2	Lee Terry (R)	Jim Esch (D)	10,572	3.86
NY-24	Michael Arcuri (D)	Richard Hanna (R)	9,919	3.94

*March 2009 special election

CAMPAIGN FINANCE

Here are the congressional candidates who raised and spent the most money on their races in 2007 and 2008.

Senate

Most Raised			Most Spent		
Candidate	Money Raised	Won/ Lost	Candidate	Money Spent	Won/ Lost
Al Franken (DFL-MN)	$22,502,124	W	Mitch McConnell (R-KY)	$21,306,296	W
Norm Coleman (R-MN)	$19,298,843	L	Al Franken (DFL-MN)	$21,066,834	W
Mitch McConnell (R-KY)	$18,681,961	W	Norm Coleman (R-MN)	$19,011,108	L
Elizabeth Dole (R-NC)	$17,268,326	L	Elizabeth Dole (R-NC)	$17,468,134	L
John Kerry (D-MA)	$16,116,152	W	John Cornyn (R-TX)	$16,454,518	W
Saxby Chambliss (R-GA)	$13,969,329	W	Saxby Chambliss (R-GA)	$15,692,294	W
John Cornyn (R-TX)	$13,727,473	W	Mark Udall (D-CO)	$12,987,562	W
Mark Warner (D-VA)	$13,663,049	W	Mark Warner (D-VA)	$12,515,479	W
Mark Udall (D-CO)	$11,787,048	W	John Kerry (D-MA)	$12,279,425	W
Bruce Lunsford (D-KY)	$10,883,172	L	Gordon Smith (R-OR)	$11,372,481	L
Gordon Smith (R-OR)	$9,254,837	L	Bruce Lunsford (D-KY)	$10,801,203	L
Mary Landrieu (D-LA)	$9,210,825	W	Mary Landrieu (D-LA)	$10,146,669	W
Kay Hagan (D-NC)	$8,965,412	W	Kay Hagan (D-NC)	$8,953,274	W
Max Baucus (D-MT)	$8,433,751	W	Jeanne Shaheen (D-NH)	$8,225,580	W
Carl Levin (D-MI)	$8,276,479	W	Max Baucus (D-MT)	$8,164,703	W
Jeanne Shaheen (D-NH)	$8,239,025	W	Frank Lautenberg (D-NJ)	$8,135,752	W
Richard Durbin (D-IL)	$8,116,764	W	Richard Durbin (D-IL)	$8,016,455	W
Susan Collins (R-ME)	$7,593,350	W	John Sununu (R-NH)	$8,010,010	L
Jim Martin (D-GA)	$7,490,201	L	Tom Udall (D-NM)	$7,841,887	W
Tom Udall (D-NM)	$7,447,684	W	Susan Collins (R-ME)	$7,765,295	W

House

Most Raised			Most Spent		
Candidate	Money Raised	Won/ Lost	Candidate	Money Spent	Won/ Lost
Jared Polis (D-CO)	$7,353,034	W	Jared Polis (D-CO)	$7,323,502	W
Sandy Treadwell (R-NY)	$7,043,425	L	Sandy Treadwell (R-NY)	$7,038,552	L
Mark Kirk (R-IL)	$5,456,604	W	Mark Kirk (R-IL)	$5,449,409	W
Deborah Honeycutt (R-GA)	$5,356,722	L	John Boehner (R-OH)	$5,342,022	W
John Boehner (R-OH)	$5,161,922	W	Deborah Honeycutt (R-GA)	$5,204,670	L
Charles Rangel (D-NY)	$5,093,239	W	Jim Oberweis (R-IL)	$5,084,489	L
Jim Oberweis (R-IL)	$5,091,510	L	Bill Foster (D-IL)	$5,047,815	W
Bill Foster (D-IL)	$5,061,265	W	Kirsten Gillibrand (D-NY)	$4,489,391	W
Ron Paul (R-TX)	$5,014,283	W	Darcy Burner (D-WA)	$4,462,884	L
Kirsten Gillibrand (D-NY)*	$4,649,651	W	Vern Buchanan (R-FL)	$4,345,554	W
Darcy Burner (D-WA)	$4,450,646	L	Charles Rangel (D-NY)	$4,209,400	W
Vern Buchanan (R-FL)	$4,434,205	W	Joe Knollenberg (R-MI)	$4,135,864	L
Eric Cantor (R-VA)	$3,990,894	W	Patrick Murphy (D-PA)	$3,917,416	W
Patrick Murphy (D-PA)	$3,964,703	W	Jim Himes (D-CT)	$3,909,937	W
Ron Klein (D-FL)	$3,955,503	W	Christopher Shays (R-CT)	$3,828,300	L
Jim Himes (D-CT)	$3,940,028	W	Eric Cantor (R-VA)	$3,823,907	W
Joe Sestak (D-PA)	$3,889,073	W	Robin Hayes (R-NC)	$3,808,201	L
Joe Knollenberg (R-MI)	$3,790,742	L	John Murtha (D-PA)	$3,656,397	W
Christopher Shays (R-CT)	$3,774,740	L	Dan Seals (D-IL)	$3,566,123	L
Robin Hayes (R-NC)	$3,768,678	L	Michele Bachmann (R-MN)	$3,565,248	W

Left seat after election because of appointment to Senate

Donor Zip Codes To Major Party Candidates For
2007-08 Election Cycle

Zip code analysis is based on research by The Center for Responsive Politics (opensecrets.org), as of July 13, 2009. The following list includes only major party donors.

Zip Code	Location	Total Amount	D %	R %
10021	New York, NY	$21,124,010	72%	28%
10022	New York, NY	$14,288,638	71%	29%
10024	New York, NY	$11,349,195	86%	14%
10023	New York, NY	$10,761,805	84%	16%
10028	New York, NY	$10,559,795	73%	27%
10128	New York, NY	$10,257,972	80%	20%
90210	Beverly Hills, CA	$8,874,815	65%	35%
10019	New York, NY	$8,714,364	75%	25%
20007	Washington, DC	$8,603,437	79%	21%
20016	Washington, DC	$8,244,958	78%	22%
20815	Chevy Chase, MD	$8,080,421	81%	19%
20854	Potomac, MD	$7,922,367	64%	36%
60614	Chicago, IL	$7,788,140	83%	17%
20008	Washington, DC	$7,509,609	84%	16%
22101	McLean, VA	$7,362,457	48%	52%
90049	Los Angeles, CA	$7,347,039	77%	23%
60611	Chicago, IL	$7,270,828	70%	30%
06831	Greenwich, CT	$6,466,117	57%	43%
60093	Winnetka, IL	$6,373,487	59%	41%
06830	Greenwich, CT	$6,311,038	52%	48%
10003	New York, NY	$6,140,910	92%	8%
33480	Palm Beach, FL	$6,032,833	38%	62%
10011	New York, NY	$5,899,154	91%	9%
75205	Dallas, TX	$5,662,066	30%	70%
10017	New York, NY	$5,162,713	73%	27%

SENATE COMMITTEES

AGING (SPECIAL)
G31 Dirksen
aging.senate.gov
202-224-5364
Majority (D 13): Kohl (WI), Chmn; Wyden (OR), Lincoln (AR), Bayh (IN), Nelson (FL), Casey (PA), McCaskill (MO), Whitehouse (RI), Udall (CO), Gillibrand (NY), Bennet (CO), Franken (MN), Specter (PA)
Minority (R 7): Martinez (FL), RMM; Shelby (AL), Collins (ME), Corker (TN), Hatch (UT), Brownback (KS), Graham (SC)

AGRICULTURE, NUTRITION & FORESTRY
328A Russell
agriculture.senate.gov
202-224-2035
Majority (D 12): Harkin (IA), Chmn; Leahy (VT), Conrad (ND), Baucus (MT), Lincoln (AR), Stabenow (MI), Nelson (NE), Brown (OH), Casey (PA), Klobuchar (MN), Bennet (CO), Gillibrand (NY)
Minority (R 9): Chambliss (GA), RMM; Lugar (IN), Cochran (MS), McConnell (KY), Roberts (KS), Johanns (NE), Grassley (IA), Thune (SD), Cornyn (TX)

SUBCOMMITTEES

RURAL REVITALIZATION, CONSERVATION, FORESTRY & CREDIT
Majority (D 6): Lincoln, Chmn; Leahy, Stabenow, Nelson, Casey, Bennet
Minority (R 5): Cornyn, RMM; Cochran, McConnell, Grassley, Thune

ENERGY, SCIENCE & TECHNOLOGY
Majority (D 7): Stabenow, Chmn; Conrad, Nelson, Brown, Klobuchar, Bennet, Gillibrand
Minority (R 6): Thune, RMM; Lugar, Roberts, Johanns, Grassley, Cornyn

DOMETIC & FOREIGN MARKETING, INSPECTION, & PLANT & ANIMAL HEALTH
Majority (D 5): Gillibrand, Chmn; Conrad, Baucus, Nelson, Klobuchar
Minority (R 4): Johanns, RMM; Lugar, McConnell, Roberts

PRODUCTION, INCOME PROTECTION & PRICE SUPPORT
Majority (D 6): Casey, Chmn; Leahy, Conrad, Baucus, Lincoln, Brown
Minority (R 5): Roberts, RMM; Cochran, Johanns, Grassley, Thune

HUNGER, NUTRITION & FAMILY FARMS
Majority (D 9): Brown, Chmn; Leahy, Baucus, Lincoln, Stabenow, Casey, Klobuchar, Bennet, Gillibrand
Minority (R 4): Lugar, RMM; Cochran, McConnell, Cornyn

APPROPRIATIONS
S-128 The Capitol
appropriations.senate.gov
202-224-7363
Majority (D 18): Inouye (HI), Chmn; Byrd (WV), Leahy (VT), Harkin (IA), Mikulski (MD), Kohl (WI), Murray (WA), Dorgan (ND), Feinstein (CA), Durbin (IL), Johnson (SD), Landrieu (LA), Reed (RI), Lautenberg (NJ), Nelson (NE), Pryor (AR), Tester (MT), Specter (PA)
Minority (R 12): Cochran (MS), RMM; Bond (MO), McConnell (KY), Shelby (AL), Gregg (NH), Bennett (UT), Hutchison (TX), Brownback (KS), Alexander (TN), Collins (ME), Voinovich (OH), Murkowski (AK)

SUBCOMMITTEES

AGRICULTURE, RURAL DEVELOPMENT, FOOD AND DRUG ADMINISTRATION & RELATED AGENCIES
Majority (D 10): Kohl, Chmn; Harkin, Dorgan, Feinstein, Durbin, Johnson, Nelson, Reed, Pryor, Specter
Minority (R 6): Brownback, RMM; Bennett, Cochran, Bond, McConnell, Collins

COMMERCE, JUSTICE, SCIENCE & RELATED AGENCIES
Majority (D 10): Mikulski, Chmn; Inouye, Leahy, Kohl, Dorgan, Feinstein, Reed, Lautenberg, Nelson, Pryor
Minority (R 7): Shelby, RMM; Gregg, McConnell, Hutchison, Alexander, Voinovich, Murkowski

DEFENSE
Majority (D 11): Inouye, Chmn; Byrd, Leahy, Harkin, Dorgan, Durbin, Feinstein, Mikulski, Kohl, Murray, Specter
Minority (R 8): Cochran, RMM; Bond, McConnell, Shelby, Gregg, Hutchison, Bennett, Brownback

ENERGY & WATER DEVELOPMENT
Majority (D 10): Dorgan, Chmn; Byrd, Murray, Feinstein, Johnson, Landrieu, Reed, Lautenberg, Harkin, Tester
Minority (R 8): Bennett, RMM; Cochran, McConnell, Bond, Hutchison, Shelby, Alexander, Voinovich

FINANCIAL SERVICES & GENERAL GOVERNMENT
Majority (D 5): Durbin, Chmn; Landrieu, Lautenberg, Nelson, Tester
Minority (R 3): Collins, RMM; Bond, Alexander

HOMELAND SECURITY
Majority (D 9): Byrd, Chmn; Inouye, Leahy,
Mikulski, Murray, Landrieu, Lautenberg, Tester,
Specter
Minority (R 6): Voinovich, RMM; Cochran, Gregg,
Shelby, Brownback, Murkowski

**INTERIOR, ENVIRONMENT & RELATED
AGENCIES**
Majority (D 10): Feinstein, Chmn; Byrd, Leahy,
Dorgan, Mikulski, Kohl, Johnson, Reed, Nelson,
Tester
Minority (R 6): Alexander, RMM; Cochran,
Bennett, Gregg, Murkowski, Collins

**LABOR, HEALTH AND HUMAN SERVICES,
EDUCATION & RELATED AGENCIES**
Majority (D 9): Harkin, Chmn; Inouye, Kohl,
Murray, Landrieu, Durbin, Reed, Pryor, Specter
Minority (R 5): Cochran, RMM; Gregg, Hutchison,
Shelby, Alexander

LEGISLATIVE BRANCH
Majority (D 3): Nelson, Chmn; Pryor, Tester
Minority (R 1): Murkowski, RMM

**MILITARY CONSTRUCTION, VETERANS
AFFAIRS & RELATED AGENCIES**
Majority (D 8): Johnson, Chmn; Inouye, Landrieu,
Byrd, Murray, Reed, Nelson, Pryor
Minority (R 5): Hutchison, RMM; Brownback,
McConnell, Collins, Murkowski

**STATE, FOREIGN OPERATIONS & RELATED
PROGRAMS**
Majority (D 9): Leahy, Chmn; Inouye, Harkin,
Mikulski, Durbin, Johnson, Landrieu,
Lautenberg, Specter
Minority (R 6): Gregg, RMM; McConnell, Bennett,
Bond, Brownback, Voinovich

**TRANSPORTATION, HOUSING AND URBAN
DEVELOPMENT & RELATED AGENCIES**
Majority (D 12): Murray, Chmn; Byrd, Mikulski,
Kohl, Durbin, Dorgan, Leahy, Harkin, Feinstein,
Johnson, Lautenberg, Specter
Minority (R 8): Bond, RMM; Shelby, Bennett,
Hutchison, Brownback, Alexander, Collins,
Voinovich

ARMED SERVICES
armed-services.senate.gov

228 Russell
202-224-3871

Majority (D 15): Levin (MI), Chmn; Kennedy (MA), Byrd (WV), Lieberman (CT), Reed (RI), Akaka (HI), Nelson
(FL), Nelson (NE), Bayh (IN), Webb (VA), McCaskill (MO), Udall (CO), Hagan (NC), Begich (AK), Burris (IL)
Minority (R 11): McCain (AZ), RMM; Inhofe (OK), Sessions (AL), Chambliss (GA), Graham (SC), Thune (SD),
Martinez (FL), Wicker (MS), Burr (NC), Vitter (LA), Collins (ME)

SUBCOMMITTEES

AIRLAND
Majority (D 7): Lieberman, Chmn; Bayh, Webb,
McCaskill, Hagan, Begich, Burris
Minority (R 5): Thune, RMM; Inhofe, Sessions,
Chambliss, Burr

EMERGING THREATS & CAPABILITIES
Majority (D 7): Reed, Chmn; Kennedy, Byrd,
Nelson (FL), Nelson (NE), Bayh, Udall
Minority (R 5): Wicker, RMM; Graham, Martinez,
Burr, Collins

PERSONNEL
Majority (D 9): Nelson (NE), Chmn; Kennedy,
Lieberman, Akaka, Webb, McCaskill, Hagan,
Begich, Burris
Minority (R 7): Graham, RMM; Chambliss, Thune,
Martinez, Wicker, Vitter, Collins

READINESS & MANAGEMENT SUPPORT
Majority (D 6): Bayh, Chmn; Byrd, Akaka,
McCaskill, Udall, Burris
Minority (R 4): Burr, RMM; Inhofe, Chambliss,
Thune

SEAPOWER
Majority (D 7): Kennedy, Chmn; Lieberman, Reed,
Akaka, Nelson (FL), Webb, Hagan
Minority (R 5): Martinez, RMM; Sessions, Wicker,
Vitter, Collins

STRATEGIC FORCES
Majority (D 6): Nelson (FL), Chmn; Byrd, Reed,
Nelson (NE), Udall, Begich
Minority (R 4): Vitter, RMM; Sessions, Inhofe,
Graham

BANKING, HOUSING & URBAN AFFAIRS
banking.senate.gov

534 Dirksen
202-224-7391

Majority (D 13): Dodd (CT), Chmn; Johnson (SD), Reed (RI), Schumer (NY), Bayh (IN), Menendez (NJ), Akaka
(HI), Brown (OH), Tester (MT), Kohl (WI), Warner (VA), Merkley (OR), Bennet (CO)
Minority (R 10): Shelby (AL), RMM; Bennett (UT), Bunning (KY), Crapo (ID), Martinez (FL), Corker (TN),
DeMint (SC), Vitter (LA), Johanns (NE), Hutchison (TX)

SUBCOMMITTEES

ECONOMIC POLICY
Majority (D 4): Brown, Chmn; Tester, Merkley,
Dodd
Minority (R 1): DeMint, RMM

FINANCIAL INSTITUTIONS
Majority (D 10): Johnson, Chmn; Reed, Schumer,
Bayh, Menendez, Akaka, Tester, Kohl, Merkley,
Bennet
Minority (R 7): Crapo, RMM; Bennett, Hutchison,
Bunning, Martinez, Corker, DeMint

**HOUSING, TRANSPORTATION &
COMMUNITY DEVELOPMENT**
Majority (D 10): Menendez, Chmn; Johnson, Reed,
Schumer, Akaka, Brown, Tester, Kohl, Warner,
Merkley
Minority (R 8): Vitter, RMM; Johnson, Hutchison,
Bennett, Johanns, Crapo, Martinez, DeMint

SECURITIES, INSURANCE & INVESTMENT
Majority (D 10): Reed, Chmn; Johnson, Schumer, Bayh, Menendez, Akaka, Brown, Warner, Bennet, Dodd
Minority (R 7): Bunning, RMM; Martinez, Bennett, Crapo, Vitter, Johanns, Corker

SECURITY & INTERNATIONAL TRADE & FINANCE
Majority (D 5): Bayh, Chmn; Kohl, Warner, Bennet, Dodd
Minority (R 2): Corker, RMM; Johanns

BUDGET
budget.senate.gov
624 Dirksen
202-224-0642
Majority (D 13): Conrad (ND), Chmn; Murray (WA), Wyden (OR), Feingold (WI), Byrd (WV), Nelson (FL), Stabenow (MI), Menendez (NJ), Cardin (MD), Sanders (VT), Whitehouse (RI), Warner (VA), Merkley (OR)
Minority (R 10): Gregg (NH), RMM; Grassley (IA), Enzi (WY), Sessions (AL), Bunning (KY), Crapo (ID), Ensign (NV), Cornyn (TX), Graham (SC), Alexander (TN)

COMMERCE, SCIENCE & TRANSPORTATION
commerce.senate.gov
508 Dirksen
202-224-5115
Majority (D 14): Rockefeller (WV), Chmn; Inouye (HI), Kerry (MA), Dorgan (ND), Boxer (CA), Nelson (FL), Cantwell (WA), Lautenberg (NJ), Pryor (AR), McCaskill (MO), Klobuchar (MN), Udall (NM), Warner (VA), Begich (AK)
Minority (R 11): Hutchison (TX), RMM; Snowe (ME), Ensign (NV), DeMint (SC), Thune (SD), Wicker (MS), Isakson (GA), Vitter (LA), Brownback (KS), Martinez (FL), Johanns (NE)

SUBCOMMITTEES

AVIATION OPERATIONS, SAFETY & SECURITY
Majority (D 12): Dorgan, Chmn; Inouye, Kerry, Boxer, Nelson, Cantwell, Lautenberg, Pryor, McCaskill, Klobuchar, Warner, Begich
Minority (R 10): DeMint, RMM; Snowe, Ensign, Thune, Wicker, Isakson, Vitter, Brownback, Martinez, Johanns

COMMUNICATIONS, TECHNOLOGY & THE INTERNET
Majority (D 12): Kerry, Chmn; Inouye, Dorgan, Nelson, Cantwell, Lautenberg, Pryor, McCaskill, Klobuchar, Udall, Warner, Begich
Minority (R 10): Ensign, RMM; Snowe, DeMint, Thune, Wicker, Isakson, Vitter, Brownback, Martinez, Johanns

COMPETITIVENESS, INNOVATION & EXPORT PROMOTION
Majority (D 7): Klobuchar, Chmn; Kerry, Dorgan, McCaskill, Udall, Warner, Begich
Minority (R 6): Martinez, RMM; Ensign, DeMint, Thune, Brownback, Johanns

CONSUMER PROTECTION, PRODUCT SAFETY & INSURANCE
Majority (D 7): Pryor, Chmn; Dorgan, Boxer, Nelson, McCaskill, Klobuchar, Udall
Minority (R 6): Wicker, RMM; Snowe, DeMint, Thune, Isakson, Vitter

OCEANS, ATMOSPHERE, FISHERIES & COAST GUARD
Majority (D 6): Cantwell, Chmn; Inouye, Kerry, Boxer, Lautenberg, Begich
Minority (R 5): Snowe, RMM; Wicker, Isakson, Vitter, Martinez

SCIENCE & SPACE
Majority (D 7): Nelson, Chmn; Inouye, Kerry, Boxer, Pryor, Udall, Warner
Minority (R 6): Vitter, RMM; Snowe, Ensign, Thune, Isakson, Johanns

SURFACE TRANSPORTATION & MERCHANT MARINE INFRASTRUCTURE, SAFETY & SECURITY
Majority (D 10): Lautenberg, Chmn; Inouye, Kerry, Dorgan, Boxer, Cantwell, Pryor, Udall, Warner, Begich
Minority (R 9): Thune, RMM; Snowe, Ensign, DeMint, Wicker, Isakson, Vitter, Brownback, Johanns

ENERGY & NATURAL RESOURCES
energy.senate.gov
304 Dirksen
202-224-4971
Majority (D 13): Bingaman (NM), Chmn; Dorgan (ND), Wyden (OR), Johnson (SD), Landrieu (LA), Cantwell (WA), Menendez (NJ), Lincoln (AR), Sanders (VT), Bayh (IN), Stabenow (MI), Udall (CO), Shaheen (NH)
Minority (R 10): Murkowski (AK), RMM; Burr (NC), Barrasso (WY), Brownback (KS), Risch (ID), McCain (AZ), Bennett (UT), Bunning (KY), Sessions (AL), Corker (TN)

SUBCOMMITTEES

ENERGY
Majority (D 10): Cantwell, Chmn; Dorgan, Wyden, Landrieu, Menendez, Sanders, Bayh, Stabenow, Udall, Shaheen
Minority (R 8): Risch, RMM; Burr, Barrasso, Brownback, Bennett, Bunning, Sessions, Corker

NATIONAL PARKS
Majority (D 8): Udall, Chmn; Dorgan, Landrieu, Menendez, Lincoln, Sanders, Bayh, Stabenow
Minority (R 6): Burr, RMM; Barrasso, Brownback, McCain, Bunning, Corker

PUBLIC LANDS & FORESTS
Majority (D 8): Wyden, Chmn; Johnson, Landrieu,
    Cantwell, Menendez, Lincoln, Udall, Shaheen
Minority (R 6): Barrasso, RMM; Risch, McCain,
    Bennett, Sessions, Corker

WATER & POWER
Majority (D 8): Stabenow, Chmn; Dorgan, Johnson,
    Cantwell, Lincoln, Sanders, Bayh, Shaheen
Minority (R 6): Brownback, RMM; Risch, McCain,
    Bennett, Bunning, Sessions

ENVIRONMENT & PUBLIC WORKS
epw.senate.gov

410 Dirksen
202-224-8832

Majority (D 12): Boxer (CA), Chmn; Baucus (MT), Carper (DE), Lautenberg (NJ), Cardin (MD), Sanders (VT),
    Klobuchar (MN), Whitehouse (RI), Udall (NM), Merkley (OR), Gillibrand (NY), Specter (PA)
Minority (R 7): Inhofe (OK), RMM; Voinovich (OH), Vitter (LA), Barrasso (WY), Crapo (ID), Bond (MO),
    Alexander (TN)

SUBCOMMITTEES

CHILDREN'S HEALTH
Majority (D 4): Klobuchar, Chmn; Udall, Merkley,
    Specter
Minority (R 2): Alexander, RMM; Vitter

CLEAN AIR & NUCLEAR SAFETY
Majority (D 5): Carper, Chmn; Baucus, Cardin,
    Sanders, Merkley
Minority (R 3): Vitter, RMM; Voinovich, Bond

GREEN JOBS & THE NEW ECONOMY
Majority (D 3): Sanders, Chmn; Carper, Gillibrand
Minority (R 2): Bond, RMM; Voinovich

OVERSIGHT
Majority (D 3): Whitehouse, Chmn; Udall,
    Gillibrand
Minority (R 2): Barrasso, RMM; Vitter

SUPERFUND, TOXICS & ENVIRONMENTAL HEALTH
Majority (D 6): Lautenberg, Chmn; Baucus,
    Klobuchar, Whitehouse, Gillibrand, Specter
Minority (R 3): Inhofe, RMM; Crapo, Bond

TRANSPORTATION & INFRASTRUCTURE
Majority (D 7): Baucus, Chmn; Carper,
    Lautenberg, Cardin, Sanders, Klobuchar, Specter
Minority (R 4): Voinovich, RMM; Vitter, Barrasso,
    Crapo

WATER & WILDLIFE
Majority (D 5): Cardin, Chmn; Lautenberg,
    Whitehouse, Udall, Merkley
Minority (R 3): Crapo, RMM; Barrasso, Alexander

ETHICS (SELECT)
ethics.senate.gov

220 Hart
202-224-2981

Majority (D 3): Boxer (CA), Chmn; Pryor (AR), Brown (OH)
Minority (R 3): Isakson (GA), RMM; Roberts (KS), Risch (ID)

FINANCE
finance.senate.gov

219 Dirksen
202-224-4515

Majority (D 13): Baucus (MT), Chmn; Rockefeller (WV), Conrad (ND), Bingaman (NM), Kerry (MA), Lincoln
    (AR), Wyden (OR), Schumer (NY), Stabenow (MI), Cantwell (WA), Nelson (FL), Menendez (NJ), Carper (DE)
Minority (R 10): Grassley (IA), RMM; Hatch (UT), Snowe (ME), Kyl (AZ), Bunning (KY), Crapo (ID), Roberts
    (KS), Ensign (NV), Enzi (WY), Cornyn (TX)

SUBCOMMITTEES

ENERGY, NATURAL RESOURCES & INFRASTRUCTURE
Majority (D 8): Bingaman, Chmn; Conrad, Kerry,
    Lincoln, Stabenow, Cantwell, Nelson, Carper
Minority (R 5): Bunning, RMM; Crapo, Cornyn,
    Hatch, Enzi

HEALTH CARE
Majority (D 11): Rockefeller, Chmn; Bingaman,
    Kerry, Lincoln, Wyden, Schumer, Stabenow,
    Cantwell, Nelson, Menendez, Carper
Minority (R 8): Hatch, RMM; Snowe, Ensign, Enzi,
    Cornyn, Kyl, Bunning, Crapo

INTERNATIONAL TRADE, CUSTOMS & GLOBAL COMPETITIVENESS
Majority (D 7): Wyden, Chmn; Rockefeller,
    Bingaman, Kerry, Stabenow, Cantwell,
    Menendez
Minority (R 4): Crapo, RMM; Snowe, Bunning,
    Roberts

SOCIAL SECURITY, PENSIONS & FAMILY POLICY
Majority (D 5): Lincoln, Chmn; Rockefeller,
    Conrad, Schumer, Nelson
Minority (R 3): Roberts, RMM; Kyl, Ensign

TAXATION, IRS OVERSIGHT & LONG-TERM GROWTH
Majority (D 9): Conrad, Chmn; Baucus, Rockefeller,
    Wyden, Schumer, Stabenow, Cantwell,
    Menendez, Carper
Minority (R 7): Kyl, RMM; Hatch, Snowe, Roberts,
    Ensign, Enzi, Cornyn

FOREIGN RELATIONS
foreign.senate.gov

446 Dirksen
202-224-4651

Majority (D 11): Kerry (MA), Chmn; Dodd (CT), Feingold (WI), Boxer (CA), Menendez (NJ), Cardin (MD), Casey (PA), Webb (VA), Shaheen (NH), Kaufman (DE), Gillibrand (NY)
Minority (R 7): Lugar (IN), RMM; Corker (TN), Isakson (GA), Risch (ID), DeMint (SC), Barrasso (WY), Wicker (MS)

SUBCOMMITTEES

AFRICAN AFFAIRS
Majority (D 5): Feingold, Chmn; Cardin, Webb, Kaufman, Shaheen
Minority (R 4): Isakson, RMM; DeMint, Corker, Risch

EAST ASIAN & PACIFIC AFFAIRS
Majority (D 6): Webb, Chmn; Dodd, Feingold, Boxer, Casey, Gillibrand
Minority (R 3): Isakson, RMM; Barrasso, Wicker

EUROPEAN AFFAIRS
Majority (D 6): Shaheen, Chmn; Dodd, Menendez, Casey, Webb, Kaufman
Minority (R 4): DeMint, RMM; Risch, Corker, Wicker

INTERNATIONAL DEVELOPMENT & FOREIGN ASSISTANCE, ECONOMIC AFFAIRS & INTERNATIONAL ENVIRONMENTAL PROTECTION
Majority (D 6): Menendez, Chmn; Boxer, Cardin, Casey, Shaheen, Gillibrand
Minority (R 3): Corker, RMM; Wicker, DeMint

INTERNATIONAL OPERATIONS & ORGANIZATIONS, DEMOCRACY & GLOBAL WOMEN'S ISSUES
Majority (D 6): Boxer, Chmn; Feingold, Menendez, Kaufman, Shaheen, Gillibrand
Minority (R 3): Wicker, RMM; DeMint, Barrasso

NEAR EASTERN & SOUTH & CENTRAL ASIAN AFFAIRS
Majority (D 6): Casey, Chmn; Dodd, Feingold, Boxer, Cardin, Kaufman
Minority (R 4): Risch, RMM; Corker, Barrasso, Isakson

WESTERN HEMISPHERE, PEACE CORPS & GLOBAL NARCOTICS AFFAIRS
Majority (D 5): Dodd, Chmn; Menendez, Cardin, Webb, Gillibrand
Minority (R 3): Barrasso, RMM; Isakson, Risch

HEALTH, EDUCATION, LABOR & PENSIONS
help.senate.gov

428 Dirksen
202-224-5375

Majority (D 13): Kennedy (MA), Chmn; Dodd (CT), Harkin (IA), Mikulski (MD), Bingaman (NM), Murray (WA), Reed (RI), Sanders (VT), Brown (OH), Casey (PA), Hagan (NC), Merkley (OR), Franken (MN)
Minority (R 10): Enzi (WY), RMM; Gregg (NH), Alexander (TN), Burr (NC), Isakson (GA), McCain (AZ), Hatch (UT), Murkowski (AK), Coburn (OK), Roberts (KS)

SUBCOMMITTEES

CHILDREN & FAMILIES
Majority (D 9): Dodd, Chmn; Bingaman, Murray, Reed, Sanders, Brown, Casey, Hagan, Merkley
Minority (R 7): Alexander, RMM; Gregg, McCain, Hatch, Murkowski, Coburn, Roberts

EMPLOYMENT & WORKPLACE SAFETY
Majority (D 8): Murray, Chmn; Dodd, Harkin, Mikulski, Brown, Hagan, Merkley, Franken
Minority (R 6): Isakson, RMM; Gregg, Burr, McCain, Hatch, Murkowski

RETIREMENT & AGING
Majority (D 7): Mikulski, Chmn; Harkin, Bingaman, Reed, Sanders, Casey, Franken
Minority (R 5): Burr, RMM; Gregg, Alexander, Isakson, Coburn

HOMELAND SECURITY & GOVERNMENTAL AFFAIRS
hsgac.senate.gov

340 Dirksen
202-224-2627

Majority (D 10): Lieberman (CT), Chmn; Levin (MI), Akaka (HI), Carper (DE), Pryor (AR), Landrieu (LA), McCaskill (MO), Tester (MT), Burris (IL), Bennet (CO)
Minority (R 6): Collins (ME), RMM; Coburn (OK), McCain (AZ), Voinovich (OH), Ensign (NV), Graham (SC)

SUBCOMMITTEES

CONTRACTING OVERSIGHT
Majority (D 5): McCaskill, Chmn; Levin, Carper, Pryor, Tester
Minority (R 3): Collins, RMM; Coburn, McCain

DISASTER RECOVERY
Majority (D 3): Landrieu, Chmn; McCaskill, Burris
Minority (R 1): Graham, RMM

FEDERAL FINANCIAL MANAGEMENT, GOVERNMENT INFORMATION, FEDERAL SERVICES & INTERNATIONAL SECURITY
Majority (D 6): Carper, Chmn; Levin, Akaka, Pryor, McCaskill, Burris
Minority (R 4): McCain, RMM; Coburn, Voinovich, Ensign

INVESTIGATIONS (PERMANENT)
Majority (D 6): Levin, Chmn; Carper, Pryor, McCaskill, Tester, Bennet
Minority (R 4): Coburn, RMM; Collins, McCain, Ensign

OVERSIGHT OF GOVERNMENT MANAGEMENT, THE FEDERAL WORKFORCE & THE DISTRICT OF COLUMBIA
Majority (D 5): Akaka, Chmn; Levin, Landrieu, Burris, Bennet
Minority (R 2): Voinovich, RMM; Graham

STATE, LOCAL & PRIVATE SECTOR PREPAREDNESS & INTEGRATION
Majority (D 5): Pryor, Chmn; Akaka, Landrieu, Tester, Bennet
Minority (R 3): Ensign, RMM; Voinovich, Graham

INDIAN AFFAIRS
838 Hart
indian.senate.gov
202-224-2251
Majority (D 9): Dorgan (ND), Chmn; Inouye (HI), Conrad (ND), Akaka (HI), Johnson (SD), Cantwell (WA), Tester (MT), Udall (NM), Franken (MN)
Minority (R 6): Barrasso (WY), RMM; McCain (AZ), Murkowski (AK), Coburn (OK), Crapo (ID), Johanns (NE)

INTELLIGENCE (SELECT)
211 Hart
intelligence.senate.gov
202-224-1700
Majority (D 8): Feinstein (CA), Chmn; Rockefeller (WV), Wyden (OR), Bayh (IN), Mikulski (MD), Feingold (WI), Nelson (FL), Whitehouse (RI)
Minority (R 7): Bond (MO), RMM; Hatch (UT), Snowe (ME), Chambliss (GA), Burr (NC), Coburn (OK), Risch (ID)

JUDICIARY
224 Dirksen
judiciary.senate.gov
202-224-7703
Majority (D 12): Leahy (VT), Chmn; Kohl (WI), Feinstein (CA), Feingold (WI), Schumer (NY), Durbin (IL), Cardin (MD), Whitehouse (RI), Klobuchar (MN), Kaufman (DE), Specter (PA), Franken (MN)
Minority (R 7): Sessions (AL), RMM; Hatch (UT), Grassley (IA), Kyl (AZ), Graham (SC), Cornyn (TX), Coburn (OK)

SUBCOMMITTEES

ADMINISTRATIVE OVERSIGHT & THE COURTS
Majority (D 6): Whitehouse, Chmn; Feinstein, Feingold, Schumer, Cardin, Kaufman
Minority (R 4): Sessions, RMM; Grassley, Kyl, Graham

ANTITRUST, COMPETITION POLICY & CONSUMER RIGHTS
Majority (D 6): Kohl, Chmn; Schumer, Whitehouse, Klobuchar, Kaufman, Specter
Minority (R 3): Hatch, RMM; Grassley, Cornyn

CONSTITUTION
Majority (D 6): Feingold, Chmn; Feinstein, Durbin, Cardin, Whitehouse, Specter
Minority (R 4): Coburn, RMM; Kyl, Graham, Cornyn

CRIME & DRUGS
Majority (D 9): Specter, Chmn; Kohl, Feinstein, Feingold, Schumer, Durbin, Cardin, Klobuchar, Kaufman
Minority (R 5): Graham, RMM; Hatch, Grassley, Sessions, Coburn

HUMAN RIGHTS & THE LAW
Majority (D 5): Durbin, Chmn; Feingold, Cardin, Kaufman, Specter
Minority (R 3): Coburn, RMM; Graham, Cornyn

IMMIGRATION, REFUGEES & BORDER SECURITY
Majority (D 5): Schumer, Chmn; Leahy, Feinstein, Durbin, Whitehouse
Minority (R 4): Cornyn, RMM; Grassley, Kyl, Sessions

TERRORISM & HOMELAND SECURITY
Majority (D 6): Cardin, Chmn; Kohl, Feinstein, Schumer, Durbin, Kaufman
Minority (R 5): Kyl, RMM; Hatch, Sessions, Cornyn, Coburn

RULES & ADMINISTRATION
305 Russell
rules.senate.gov
202-224-6352
Majority (D 11): Schumer (NY), Chmn; Byrd (WV), Inouye (HI), Dodd (CT), Feinstein (CA), Durbin (IL), Nelson (NE), Murray (WA), Pryor (AR), Udall (NM), Warner (VA)
Minority (R 8): Bennett (UT), RMM; McConnell (KY), Cochran (MS), Hutchison (TX), Chambliss (GA), Alexander (TN), Ensign (NV), Roberts (KS)

SMALL BUSINESS & ENTREPRENEURSHIP

428A Russell
sbc.senate.gov
202-224-5175

Majority (D 11): Landrieu (LA), Chmn; Kerry (MA), Levin (MI), Harkin (IA), Lieberman (CT), Cantwell (WA), Bayh (IN), Pryor (AR), Cardin (MD), Shaheen (NH), Hagan (NC)

Minority (R 7): Snowe (ME), RMM; Bond (MO), Vitter (LA), Thune (SD), Enzi (WY), Isakson (GA), Wicker (MS)

VETERANS' AFFAIRS

412 Russell
veterans.senate.gov
202-224-9126

Majority (D 10): Akaka (HI), Chmn; Rockefeller (WV), Murray (WA), Sanders (VT), Brown (OH), Webb (VA), Tester (MT), Begich (AK), Burris (IL), Specter (PA)

Minority (R 5): Burr (NC), RMM; Isakson (GA), Wicker (MS), Johanns (NE), Graham (SC)

HOUSE COMMITTEES

AGRICULTURE
agriculture.house.gov

1301 Longworth
202-225-2171

Majority (D 28): Peterson (MN), Chmn; Holden (PA), McIntyre (NC), Boswell (IA), Baca (CA), Cardoza (CA), Scott (GA), Marshall (GA), Herseth Sandlin (SD), Cuellar (TX), Costa (CA), Ellsworth (IN), Walz (MN), Kagen (WI), Schrader (OR), Halvorson (IL), Dahlkemper (PA), Massa (NY), Bright (AL), Markey (CO), Kratovil (MD), Schauer (MI), Kissell (NC), Boccieri (OH), Murphy (NY), Pomeroy (ND), Childers (MS), Minnick (ID)
Minority (R 18): Lucas (OK), RMM; Goodlatte (VA), Moran (KS), Johnson (IL), Graves (MO), Rogers (AL), King (IA), Neugebauer (TX), Conaway (TX), Fortenberry (NE), Schmidt (OH), Smith (NE), Latta (OH), Roe (TN), Luetkemeyer (MO), Thompson (PA), Cassidy (LA), Lummis (WY)

SUBCOMMITTEES

CONSERVATION, CREDIT, ENERGY & RESEARCH
Majority (D 18): Holden, Chmn; Herseth Sandlin, Halvorson, Dahlkemper, Markey, Schauer, Kissell, Boccieri, McIntyre, Costa, Ellsworth, Walz, Massa, Bright, Kratovil, Murphy, Minnick, Pomeroy
Minority (R 12): Goodlatte, RMM; Moran, Graves, Rogers, King, Neugebauer, Schmidt, Smith, Latta, Luetkemeyer, Thompson, Cassidy

DEPARTMENT OPERATIONS, OVERSIGHT, NUTRITION & FORESTRY
Majority (D 6): Baca, Chmn; Cuellar, Kagen, Schrader, Dahlkemper, Childers
Minority (R 4): Fortenberry, RMM; King, Schmidt, Lummis

GENERAL FARM COMMODITIES & RISK MANAGEMENT
Majority (D 11): Boswell, Chmn; Marshall, Ellsworth, Walz, Schrader, Herseth Sandlin, Markey, Kissell, Halvorson, Pomeroy, Childers
Minority (R 7): Moran, RMM; Johnson, Graves, King, Conaway, Latta, Luetkemeyer

HORTICULTURE & ORGANIC AGRICULTURE
Majority (D 6): Cardoza, Chmn; Massa, Costa, Schrader, Kratovil, Murphy
Minority (R 4): Schmidt, RMM; Moran, Johnson, Lummis

LIVESTOCK, DAIRY & POULTRY
Majority (D 11): Scott, Chmn; Costa, Kagen, Kratovil, Holden, Boswell, Baca, Cardoza, Markey, Murphy, Minnick
Minority (R 7): Neugebauer, RMM; Goodlatte, Rogers, King, Conaway, Smith, Roe

SPECIALTY CROPS, RURAL DEVELOPMENT & FOREIGN AGRICULTURE
Majority (D 6): McIntyre, Chmn; Bright, Marshall, Cuellar, Kissell, Minnick
Minority (R 4): Conaway, RMM; Roe, Thompson, Cassidy

APPROPRIATIONS
appropriations.house.gov

H-218 Capitol
202-225-2771

Majority (D 37): Obey (WI), Chmn; Murtha (PA), Dicks (WA), Mollohan (WV), Kaptur (OH), Visclosky (IN), Lowey (NY), Serrano (NY), DeLauro (CT), Moran (VA), Olver (MA), Pastor (AZ), Price (NC), Edwards (TX), Kennedy (RI), Hinchey (NY), Roybal-Allard (CA), Farr (CA), Jackson (IL), Kilpatrick (MI), Boyd (FL), Fattah (PA), Rothman (NJ), Bishop (GA), Berry (AR), Lee (CA), Schiff (CA), Honda (CA), McCollum (MN), Israel (NY), Ryan (OH), Ruppersberger (MD), Chandler (KY), Wasserman Schultz (FL), Rodriguez (TX), Davis (TN), Salazar (CO)
Minority (R 23): Lewis (CA), RMM; Young (FL), Rogers (KY), Wolf (VA), Kingston (GA), Frelinghuysen (NJ), Tiahrt (KS), Wamp (TN), Latham (IA), Aderholt (AL), Emerson (MO), Granger (TX), Simpson (ID), Culberson (TX), Kirk (IL), Crenshaw (FL), Rehberg (MT), Carter (TX), Alexander (LA), Calvert (CA), Bonner (AL), LaTourette (OH), Cole (OK)

SUBCOMMITTEES

AGRICULTURE, RURAL DEVELOPMENT, FDA & RELATED AGENCIES
Majority (D 8): DeLauro, Chmn; Farr, Boyd, Bishop, Davis, Kaptur, Hinchey, Jackson
Minority (R 4): Kingston, RMM; Latham, Emerson, Alexander

COMMERCE, JUSTICE, SCIENCE & RELATED AGENCIES
Majority (D 8): Mollohan, Chmn; Kennedy, Fattah, Schiff, Honda, Ruppersberger, Visclosky, Serrano
Minority (R 4): Wolf, RMM; Culberson, Aderholt, Bonner

DEFENSE
Majority (D 10): Murtha, Chmn; Dicks, Visclosky, Moran, Kaptur, Boyd, Rothman, Bishop, Hinchey, Kilpatrick
Minority (R 6): Young, RMM; Frelinghuysen, Tiahrt, Kingston, Granger, Rogers

ENERGY & WATER DEVELOPMENT
Majority (D 10): Visclosky, Chmn; Edwards, Pastor, Berry, Fattah, Israel, Ryan, Olver, Davis, Salazar
Minority (R 6): Frelinghuysen, RMM; Wamp, Simpson, Rehberg, Calvert, Alexander

FINANCIAL SERVICES & GENERAL GOVERNMENT
Majority (D 8): Serrano, Chmn; Wasserman Schultz, DeLauro, Edwards, Boyd, Fattah, Lee, Schiff
Minority (R 4): Emerson, RMM; Culberson, Kirk, Crenshaw

HOMELAND SECURITY
Majority (D 9): Price, Chmn; Serrano, Rodriguez, Ruppersberger, Mollohan, Lowey, Roybal-Allard, Farr, Rothman
Minority (R 5): Rogers, RMM; Carter, Culberson, Kirk, Calvert

INTERIOR, ENVIRONMENT & RELATED AGENCIES
Majority (D 8): Dicks, Chmn; Moran, Mollohan, Chandler, Hinchey, Olver, Pastor, Price
Minority (R 4): Simpson, RMM; Calvert, LaTourette, Cole

LABOR, HHS, EDUCATION & RELATED AGENCIES
Majority (D 11): Obey, Chmn; Lowey, DeLauro, Jackson, Kennedy, Roybal-Allard, Lee, Honda, McCollum, Ryan, Moran
Minority (R 5): Tiahrt, RMM; Rehberg, Alexander, Bonner, Cole

LEGISLATIVE BRANCH
Majority (D 6): Wasserman Schultz, Chmn; Honda, McCollum, Ryan, Ruppersberger, Rodriguez
Minority (R 3): Aderholt, RMM; LaTourette, Cole

MILITARY CONSTRUCTION, VETERANS AFFAIRS & RELATED AGENCIES
Majority (D 8): Edwards, Chmn; Farr, Salazar, Dicks, Kennedy, Bishop, Berry, Israel
Minority (R 4): Wamp, RMM; Crenshaw, Young, Carter

SELECT INTELLIGENCE OVERSIGHT PANEL
Majority (D 8): Holt, Chmn; Obey, Murtha, Reyes, Dicks, Lowey, Schiff, Israel
Minority (R 5): Calvert, RMM; Lewis, Young, Hoekstra, Frelinghuysen

STATE, FOREIGN OPERATIONS & RELATED PROGRAMS
Majority (D 8): Lowey, Chmn; Jackson, Schiff, Israel, Chandler, Rothman, Lee, McCollum
Minority (R 4): Granger, RMM; Kirk, Crenshaw, Rehberg

TRANSPORTATION, HUD & RELATED AGENCIES
Majority (D 8): Olver, Chmn; Pastor, Rodriguez, Kaptur, Price, Roybal-Allard, Berry, Kilpatrick
Minority (R 4): Latham, RMM; Wolf, Carter, LaTourette

ARMED SERVICES
armedservices.house.gov

2120 Rayburn
202-225-4151

Majority (D 36): Skelton (MO), Chmn; Spratt (SC), Ortiz (TX), Taylor (MS), Abercrombie (HI), Reyes (TX), Snyder (AR), Smith (WA), Loretta Sanchez (CA), McIntyre (NC), Brady (PA), Andrews (NJ), Davis (CA), Langevin (RI), Larsen (WA), Cooper (TN), Marshall (GA), Bordallo (GU), Ellsworth (IN), Patrick Murphy (PA), Johnson (GA), Shea-Porter (NH), Courtney (CT), Loebsack (IA), Sestak (PA), Giffords (AZ), Tsongas (MA), Nye (VA), Pingree (ME), Kissell (NC), Heinrich (NM), Kratovil (MD), Massa (NY), Bright (AL), Murphy (NY), Boren (OK)
Minority (R 25): McKeon (CA), RMM; Bartlett (MD), Thornberry (TX), Jones (NC), Akin (MO), Forbes (VA), Miller (FL), Wilson (SC), LoBiondo (NJ), Bishop (UT), Turner (OH), Kline (MN), Rogers (AL), Franks (AZ), Shuster (PA), McMorris Rodgers (WA), Conaway (TX), Lamborn (CO), Wittman (VA), Fallin (OK), Hunter (CA), Fleming (LA), Coffman (CO), Rooney (FL), Platts (PA)

SUBCOMMITTEES

AIR & LAND FORCES
Majority (D 16): Abercrombie, Chmn; Spratt, Reyes, Smith, McIntyre, Brady, Cooper, Marshall, Sestak, Giffords, Tsongas, Kissell, Kratovil, Massa, Bright, Boren
Minority (R 13): Bartlett, RMM; McMorris Rodgers, Fallin, Hunter, Fleming, Coffman, Akin, Miller, Wilson, LoBiondo, Bishop, Turner, Platts

DEFENSE ACQUISITION REFORM
Majority (D 4): Andrews, Chmn; Cooper, Ellsworth, Sestak
Minority (R 3): Conaway, RMM; Hunter, Coffman

MILITARY PERSONNEL
Majority (D 9): Davis, Chmn; Snyder, Sanchez, Bordallo, Murphy (PA), Johnson, Shea-Porter, Loebsack, Tsongas
Minority (R 6): Wilson, RMM; Jones, Kline, Rooney, Fallin, Fleming

OVERSIGHT & INVESTIGATIONS
Majority (D 8): Snyder, Chmn; Spratt, Sanchez, Davis, Cooper, Sestak, Nye, Pingree
Minority (R 7): Wittman, RMM; Jones, Rogers, Franks, McMorris Rodgers, Lamborn, Platts

READINESS
Majority (D 17): Ortiz, Chmn; Taylor, Abercrombie, Reyes, Marshall, Bordallo, Johnson, Shea-Porter, Courtney, Loebsack, Giffords, Nye, Kissell, Heinrich, Kratovil, Bright, Boren
Minority (R 12): Forbes, RMM; Bishop, Rogers, Franks, Shuster, Conaway, Lamborn, Wittman, Fallin, Fleming, LoBiondo, Turner

SEAPOWER & EXPEDITIONARY FORCES
Majority (D 10): Taylor, Chmn; Ortiz, Langevin, Larsen, Ellsworth, Courtney, Sestak, Nye, Pingree, Massa
Minority (R 7): Akin, RMM; Wittman, Bartlett, Forbes, Hunter, Coffman, Rooney

STRATEGIC FORCES
Majority (D 7): Langevin, Chmn; Spratt, Sanchez, Andrews, Larsen, Heinrich, Murphy (NY)
Minority (R 5): Turner, RMM; Thornberry, Franks, Lamborn, Rogers

TERRORISM, UNCONVENTIONAL THREATS & CAPABILITIES
Majority (D 10): Smith, Chmn; McIntyre, Andrews, Langevin, Cooper, Marshall, Ellsworth, Murphy (PA), Bright, Murphy (NY)
Minority (R 7): Miller, RMM; LoBiondo, Kline, Shuster, Conaway, Rooney, Thornberry

BUDGET
budget.house.gov

207 Cannon
202-226-7200

Majority (D 24): Spratt (SC), Chmn; Schwartz (PA), Kaptur (OH), Becerra (CA), Doggett (TX), Blumenauer (OR), Berry (AR), Boyd (FL), McGovern (MA), Tsongas (MA), Etheridge (NC), McCollum (MN), Melancon (LA), Yarmuth (KY), Andrews (NJ), DeLauro (CT), Edwards (TX), Scott (VA), Langevin (RI), Larsen (WA), Bishop (NY), Moore (WI), Connolly (VA), Schrader (OR)

Minority (R 15): Ryan (WI), RMM; Hensarling (TX), Garrett (NJ), Mario Diaz-Balart (FL), Simpson (ID), McHenry (NC), Mack (FL), Campbell (CA), Jordan (OH), Lummis (WY), Austria (OH), Aderholt (AL), Nunes (CA), Harper (MS), Latta (OH)

EDUCATION & LABOR
edlabor.house.gov

2181 Rayburn
202-225-3725

Majority (D 29): George Miller (CA), Chmn; Kildee (MI), Payne (NJ), Andrews (NJ), Scott (VA), Woolsey (CA), Hinojosa (TX), McCarthy (NY), Tierney (MA), Kucinich (OH), Wu (OR), Holt (NJ), Davis (CA), Grijalva (AZ), Bishop (NY), Sestak (PA), Loebsack (IA), Hirono (HI), Altmire (PA), Hare (IL), Clarke (NY), Courtney (CT), Shea-Porter (NH), Fudge (OH), Polis (CO), Tonko (NY), Pierluisi (PR), Sablan (MP), Titus (NV)

Minority (R 19): Kline (MN), RMM; Petri (WI), McKeon (CA), Hoekstra (MI), Castle (DE), Souder (IN), Ehlers (MI), Biggert (IL), Platts (PA), Wilson (SC), McMorris Rodgers (WA), Price (GA), Bishop (UT), Guthrie (KY), Cassidy (LA), McClintock (CA), Hunter (CA), Roe (TN), Thompson (PA)

SUBCOMMITTEES

EARLY CHILDHOOD, ELEMENTARY & SECONDARY EDUCATION

Majority (D 17): Kildee, Chmn; Payne, Scott, Holt, Davis, Grijalva, Sestak, Loebsack, Hirono, Polis, Pierluisi, Sablan, Woolsey, Hinojosa, Kucinich, Altmire, Titus

Minority (R 12): Castle, RMM; Petri, Hoekstra, Souder, Ehlers, Biggert, Platts, McMorris Rodgers, Bishop, Cassidy, McClintock, Hunter

HEALTH, EMPLOYMENT, LABOR & PENSIONS

Majority (D 13): Andrews, Chmn; Wu, Hare, Tierney, Kucinich, Fudge, Kildee, McCarthy, Holt, Sestak, Loebsack, Clarke, Courtney

Minority (R 8): Price, RMM; Kline, McKeon, Wilson, Guthrie, McClintock, Hunter, Roe

HEALTHY FAMILIES & COMMUNITIES

Majority (D 7): McCarthy, Chmn; Clarke, Scott, Shea-Porter, Tonko, Polis, Miller

Minority (R 5): Platts, RMM; McKeon, Guthrie, Roe, Thompson

HIGHER EDUCATION, LIFELONG LEARNING & COMPETITIVENESS

Majority (D 14): Hinojosa, Chmn; Bishop, Altmire, Courtney, Tonko, Titus, Andrews, Tierney, Wu, Davis, Hirono, Fudge, Polis, Pierluisi

Minority (R 9): Guthrie, RMM; Kline, Castle, Souder, Ehlers, Biggert, Cassidy, Roe, Thompson

WORKFORCE PROTECTIONS

Majority (D 7): Woolsey, Chmn; Shea-Porter, Payne, Grijalva, Bishop, Hare, Sablan

Minority (R 4): McMorris Rodgers, RMM; Hoekstra, Wilson, Price

ENERGY & COMMERCE
energycommerce.house.gov

2125 Rayburn
202-225-2927

Majority (D 36): Waxman (CA), Chmn; Dingell (MI), Markey (MA), Boucher (VA), Pallone (NJ), Gordon (TN), Rush (IL), Eshoo (CA), Stupak (MI), Engel (NY), Gene Green (TX), DeGette (CO), Capps (CA), Doyle (PA), Harman (CA), Schakowsky (IL), Gonzalez (TX), Inslee (WA), Baldwin (WI), Ross (AR), Weiner (NY), Matheson (UT), Butterfield (NC), Melancon (LA), Barrow (GA), Hill (IN), Matsui (CA), Christensen (VI), Castor (FL), Sarbanes (MD), Murphy (CT), Space (OH), McNerney (CA), Sutton (OH), Braley (IA), Welch (VT)

Minority (R 23): Barton (TX), RMM; Hall (TX), Upton (MI), Stearns (FL), Deal (GA), Whitfield (KY), Shimkus (IL), Shadegg (AZ), Blunt (MO), Buyer (IN), Radanovich (CA), Pitts (PA), Bono Mack (CA), Walden (OR), Terry (NE), Rogers (MI), Myrick (NC), Sullivan (OK), Tim Murphy (PA), Burgess (TX), Blackburn (TN), Gingrey (GA), Scalise (LA)

SUBCOMMITTEES

COMMERCE, TRADE & CONSUMER PROTECTION

Majority (D 18): Rush, Chmn; Schakowsky, Sarbanes, Sutton, Pallone, Gordon, Stupak, Green, Gonzalez, Weiner, Matheson, Butterfield, Barrow, Matsui, Castor, Space, Braley, DeGette

Minority (R 11): Radanovich, RMM; Stearns, Whitfield, Pitts, Bono Mack, Terry, Myrick, Sullivan, Murphy, Gingrey, Scalise

COMMUNICATIONS, TECHNOLOGY & THE INTERNET

Majority (D 21): Boucher, Chmn; Markey, Gordon, Rush, Eshoo, Stupak, DeGette, Doyle, Inslee, Weiner, Butterfield, Melancon, Hill, Matsui, Christensen, Castor, Murphy, Space, McNerney, Welch, Dingell

Minority (R 13): Stearns, RMM; Upton, Deal, Shimkus, Shadegg, Blunt, Buyer, Radanovich, Bono Mack, Walden, Terry, Rogers, Blackburn

ENERGY & ENVIRONMENT

Majority (D 21): Markey, Chmn; Doyle, Inslee, Butterfield, Melancon, Hill, Matsui, McNerney, Welch, Dingell, Boucher, Pallone, Engel, Green, Capps, Harman, Gonzalez, Baldwin, Ross, Matheson, Barrow

Minority (R 13): Upton, RMM; Hall, Stearns, Whitfield, Shimkus, Shadegg, Blunt, Pitts, Bono Mack, Walden, Sullivan, Burgess, Scalise

HEALTH

Majority (D 23): Pallone, Chmn; Dingell, Gordon, Eshoo, Engel, Green, DeGette, Capps, Schakowsky, Baldwin, Ross, Weiner, Matheson, Harman, Gonzalez, Barrow, Christensen, Castor, Sarbanes, Murphy, Space, Sutton, Braley

Minority (R 14): Deal, RMM; Hall, Whitfield, Shimkus, Shadegg, Blunt, Buyer, Pitts, Rogers, Myrick, Murphy, Burgess, Blackburn, Gingrey

OVERSIGHT & INVESTIGATIONS

Majority (D 11): Stupak, Chmn; Braley, Markey, DeGette, Doyle, Schakowsky, Ross, Christensen, Welch, Green, Sutton

Minority (R 7): Walden, RMM; Deal, Radanovich, Sullivan, Burgess, Blackburn, Gingrey

ENERGY INDEPENDENCE & GLOBAL WARMING (SELECT)

B243 Longworth
globalwarming.house.gov
202-225-4012

Majority (D 9): Markey (MA), Chmn; Blumenauer (OR), Inslee (WA), Larson (CT), Herseth Sandlin (SD), Cleaver (MO), Hall (NY), Salazar (CO), Speier (CA)

Minority (R 6): Sensenbrenner (WI), RMM; Shadegg (AZ), Miller (MI), Sullivan (OK), Blackburn (TN), Capito (WV)

FINANCIAL SERVICES

2129 Rayburn
financialservices.house.gov
202-225-4247

Majority (D 42): Frank (MA), Chmn; Kanjorski (PA), Waters (CA), Maloney (NY), Gutierrez (IL), Velázquez (NY), Watt (NC), Ackerman (NY), Sherman (CA), Meeks (NY), Moore (KS), Capuano (MA), Hinojosa (TX), Clay (MO), McCarthy (NY), Baca (CA), Lynch (MA), Miller (NC), Scott (GA), Al Green (TX), Cleaver (MO), Bean (IL), Moore (WI), Hodes (NH), Ellison (MN), Klein (FL), Wilson (OH), Perlmutter (CO), Donnelly (IN), Foster (IL), Carson (IN), Speier (CA), Childers (MS), Minnick (ID), Adler (NJ), Kilroy (OH), Driehaus (OH), Kosmas (FL), Grayson (FL), Himes (CT), Peters (MI), Maffei (NY)

Minority (R 29): Bachus (AL), RMM; Castle (DE), King (NY), Royce (CA), Lucas (OK), Paul (TX), Manzullo (IL), Jones (NC), Biggert (IL), Gary Miller (CA), Capito (WV), Hensarling (TX), Garrett (NJ), Barrett (SC), Gerlach (PA), Neugebauer (TX), Price (GA), McHenry (NC), Campbell (CA), Putnam (FL), Bachmann (MN), Marchant (TX), McCotter (MI), McCarthy (CA), Posey (FL), Jenkins (KS), Lee (NY), Paulsen (MN), Lance (NJ)

SUBCOMMITTEES

CAPITAL MARKETS, INSURANCE & GOVERNMENT SPONSORED ENTERPRISES

Majority (D 30): Kanjorski, Chmn; Ackerman, Sherman, Capuano, Hinojosa, McCarthy, Baca, Lynch, Miller, Scott, Velázquez, Maloney, Bean, Moore (WI), Hodes, Klein, Perlmutter, Donnelly, Carson, Speier, Childers, Wilson, Foster, Minnick, Adler, Kilroy, Kosmas, Grayson, Himes, Peters

Minority (R 20): Garrett, RMM; Price, Castle, King, Lucas, Manzullo, Royce, Biggert, Capito, Hensarling, Putnam, Barrett, Gerlach, Campbell, Bachmann, McCotter, Neugebauer, McCarthy, Posey, Jenkins

DOMESTIC MONETARY POLICY & TECHNOLOGY

Majority (D 10): Watt, Chmn; Maloney, Meeks, Clay, Sherman, Green, Cleaver, Ellison, Adler, Kosmas

Minority (R 7): Paul, RMM; Castle, Lucas, Gerlach, Price, Posey, Lance

FINANCIAL INSTITUTIONS & CONSUMER CREDIT

Majority (D 27): Gutierrez, Chmn; Maloney, Watt, Ackerman, Sherman, Moore (KS), Kanjorski, Waters, Hinojosa, McCarthy, Baca, Green, Clay, Miller, Scott, Cleaver, Bean, Hodes, Ellison, Klein, Wilson, Meeks, Foster, Perlmutter, Speier, Childers, Minnick

Minority (R 18): Hensarling, RMM; Barrett, Castle, King, Royce, Jones, Capito, Garrett, Gerlach, Neugebauer, Price, McHenry, Campbell, McCarthy, Marchant, Lee, Paulsen, Lance

HOUSING & COMMUNITY OPPORTUNITY

Majority (D 15): Waters, Chmn; Velázquez, Lynch, Cleaver, Green, Clay, Ellison, Donnelly, Capuano, Kanjorski, Gutierrez, Driehaus, Kilroy, Himes, Maffei

Minority (R 10): Capito, RMM; McCotter, Biggert, Miller, Neugebauer, Jones, Putnam, Marchant, Jenkins, Lee

INTERNATIONAL MONETARY POLICY & TRADE

Majority (D 9): Meeks, Chmn; Gutierrez, Waters, Watt, Moore (WI), Carson, Driehaus, Peters, Maffei

Minority (R 6): Miller, RMM; Royce, Paul, Manzullo, Bachmann, Paulsen

OVERSIGHT & INVESTIGATIONS
Majority (D 9): Moore (KS), Chmn; Lynch, Klein,
Speier, Moore (WI), Adler, Kilroy, Driehaus,
Grayson

Minority (R 6): Biggert, RMM; McHenry, Paul,
Bachmann, Lee, Paulsen

FOREIGN AFFAIRS
foreignaffairs.house.gov

2170 Rayburn
202-225-5021

Majority (D 28): Berman (CA), Chmn; Ackerman (NY), Faleomavaega (AS), Payne (NJ), Sherman (CA), Wexler
(FL), Engel (NY), Delahunt (MA), Meeks (NY), Watson (CA), Carnahan (MO), Sires (NJ), Connolly (VA),
McMahon (NY), Tanner (TN), Gene Green (TX), Woolsey (CA), Jackson Lee (TX), Lee (CA), Berkley (NV),
Crowley (NY), Ross (AR), Miller (NC), Scott (GA), Costa (CA), Ellison (MN), Giffords (AZ), Klein (FL)
Minority (R 19): Ros-Lehtinen (FL), RMM; Smith (NJ), Burton (IN), Gallegly (CA), Rohrabacher (CA), Manzullo
(IL), Royce (CA), Paul (TX), Flake (AZ), Pence (IN), Wilson (SC), Boozman (AR), Barrett (SC), Mack (FL),
Fortenberry (NE), McCaul (TX), Poe (TX), Inglis (SC), Bilirakis (FL)

SUBCOMMITTEES

AFRICA & GLOBAL HEALTH
Majority (D 7): Payne, Chmn; Watson, Lee, Miller,
Meeks, Jackson Lee, Woolsey
Minority (R 4): Smith, RMM; Flake, Boozman,
Fortenberry

**ASIA, THE PACIFIC & THE GLOBAL
ENVIRONMENT**
Majority (D 7): Faleomavaega, Chmn; Ackerman,
Watson, Ross, Sherman, Engel, Meeks
Minority (R 5): Manzullo, RMM; Inglis,
Rohrabacher, Royce, Flake

EUROPE
Majority (D 9): Wexler, Chmn; Tanner, Delahunt,
Sires, McMahon, Berkley, Miller, Scott, Costa
Minority (R 7): Gallegly, RMM; Bilirakis, Wilson,
Poe, Boozman, Inglis, Barrett

**INTERNATIONAL ORGANIZATIONS, HUMAN
RIGHTS & OVERSIGHT**
Majority (D 5): Delahunt, Chmn; Carnahan,
Ellison, Payne, Wexler
Minority (R 3): Rohrabacher, RMM; Paul, Poe

MIDDLE EAST & SOUTH ASIA
Majority (D 14): Ackerman, Chmn; Carnahan,
Jackson Lee, Berkley, Crowley, Ross, Costa,
Ellison, Klein, Sherman, Wexler, Engel,
Connolly, Green
Minority (R 9): Burton, RMM; Wilson, Barrett,
Fortenberry, McCaul, Inglis, Bilirakis,
Rohrabacher, Royce

TERRORISM, NONPROLIFERATION & TRADE
Majority (D 7): Sherman, Chmn; Connolly, Scott,
Watson, McMahon, Jackson Lee, Klein
Minority (R 5): Royce, RMM; Poe, Manzullo,
Boozman, Barrett

WESTERN HEMISPHERE
Majority (D 11): Engel, Chmn; Meeks, Sires,
Green, Giffords, Faleomavaega, Payne, Tanner,
Lee, Crowley, Klein
Minority (R 8): Mack, RMM; McCaul, Smith,
Burton, Gallegly, Paul, Fortenberry, Bilirakis

HOMELAND SECURITY
homeland.house.gov

176 Ford HOB
202-226-2616

Majority (D 20): Thompson (MS), Chmn; Loretta Sanchez (CA), Harman (CA), DeFazio (OR), Norton (DC),
Lofgren (CA), Jackson Lee (TX), Cuellar (TX), Carney (PA), Clarke (NY), Richardson (CA), Kirkpatrick (AZ),
Luján (NM), Pascrell (NJ), Cleaver (MO), Al Green (TX), Himes (CT), Kilroy (OH), Massa (NY), Titus (NV)
Minority (R 13): King (NY), RMM; Smith (TX), Souder (IN), Lungren (CA), Rogers (AL), McCaul (TX), Dent
(PA), Bilirakis (FL), Broun (GA), Miller (MI), Olson (TX), Cao (LA), Austria (OH)

SUBCOMMITTEES

**BORDER, MARITIME & GLOBAL
COUNTERTERRORISM**
Majority (D 9): Sanchez, Chmn; Harman, Lofgren,
Jackson Lee, Cuellar, Kirkpatrick, Pascrell,
Green, Massa
Minority (R 5): Souder, RMM; McCaul, Bilirakis,
Rogers, Miller

**EMERGENCY COMMUNICATIONS,
PREPAREDNESS & RESPONSE**
Majority (D 6): Cuellar, Chmn; Norton, Richardson,
Pascrell, Cleaver, Titus
Minority (R 4): Rogers, RMM; Olson, Cao, McCaul

**EMERGING THREATS, CYBERSECURITY &
SCIENCE AND TECHNOLOGY**
Majority (D 5): Clarke, Chmn; Sanchez,
Richardson, Luján, Kilroy
Minority (R 3): Lungren, RMM; Broun, Austria

**INTELLIGENCE, INFORMATION SHARING &
TERRORISM RISK ASSESSMENT**
Majority (D 6): Harman, Chmn; Carney, Clarke,
Kirkpatrick, Green, Himes
Minority (R 4): McCaul, RMM; Dent, Broun,
Souder

**MANAGEMENT, INVESTIGATIONS &
OVERSIGHT**
Majority (D 5): Carney, Chmn; DeFazio, Pascrell,
Green, Kilroy
Minority (R 3): Bilirakis, RMM; Cao, Lungren

**TRANSPORTATION SECURITY &
INFRASTRUCTURE PROTECTION**
Majority (D 9): Jackson Lee, Chmn; DeFazio,
Norton, Kirkpatrick, Luján, Cleaver, Himes,
Massa, Titus
Minority (R 5): Dent, RMM; Lungren, Olson,
Miller, Austria

HOUSE ADMINISTRATION
cha.house.gov

1309 Longworth
202-225-2061

Majority (D 6): Brady (PA), Chmn; Lofgren (CA), Capuano (MA), Gonzalez (TX), Davis (CA), Davis (AL)
Minority (R 3): Lungren (CA), RMM; McCarthy (CA), Harper (MS)

SUBCOMMITTEES

CAPITOL SECURITY
Majority (D 2): Capuano, Chmn; Brady
Minority (R 1): Lungren, RMM

ELECTIONS
Majority (D 4): Lofgren, Chmn; Gonzalez, Davis (CA), Davis (AL)

INTELLIGENCE (PERMANENT SELECT)
intelligence.house.gov

HVC-304 Capitol
202-225-7690

Majority (D 13): Reyes (TX), Chmn; Hastings (FL), Eshoo (CA), Holt (NJ), Ruppersberger (MD), Tierney (MA), Thompson (CA), Schakowsky (IL), Langevin (RI), Patrick Murphy (PA), Schiff (CA), Smith (WA), Boren (OK)
Minority (R 9): Hoekstra (MI), RMM; Gallegly (CA), Thornberry (TX), Rogers (MI), Myrick (NC), Blunt (MO), Miller (FL), Conaway (TX), King (NY)

SUBCOMMITTEES

INTELLIGENCE COMMUNITY MANAGEMENT
Majority (D 5): Eshoo, Chmn; Holt, Hastings, Schakowsky, Murphy
Minority (R 3): Myrick, RMM; Blunt, Conaway

OVERSIGHT & INVESTIGATIONS
Majority (D 7): Schakowsky, Chmn; Tierney, Murphy, Ruppersberger, Thompson, Schiff, Boren
Minority (R 5): Miller, RMM; Thornberry, Rogers, Blunt, King

TERRORISM, HUMAN INTELLIGENCE, ANALYSIS & COUNTERINTELLIGENCE
Majority (D 7): Thompson, Chmn; Hastings, Ruppersberger, Langevin, Schiff, Smith, Boren
Minority (R 5): Rogers, RMM; Gallegly, Myrick, Miller, Conaway

TECHNICAL & TACTICAL INTELLIGENCE
Majority (D 6): Ruppersberger, Chmn; Holt, Langevin, Murphy, Schiff, Smith
Minority (R 4): Thornberry, RMM; Rogers, Miller, King

JUDICIARY
judiciary.house.gov

2138 Rayburn
202-225-3951

Majority (D 24): Conyers (MI), Chmn; Berman (CA), Boucher (VA), Nadler (NY), Scott (VA), Watt (NC), Lofgren (CA), Jackson Lee (TX), Waters (CA), Delahunt (MA), Wexler (FL), Cohen (TN), Johnson (GA), Pierluisi (PR), Quigley (IL), Gutierrez (IL), Sherman (CA), Baldwin (WI), Gonzalez (TX), Weiner (NY), Schiff (CA), Linda Sánchez (CA), Wasserman Schultz (FL), Maffei (NY)
Minority (R 16): Smith (TX), RMM; Sensenbrenner (WI), Coble (NC), Gallegly (CA), Goodlatte (VA), Lungren (CA), Issa (CA), Forbes (VA), King (IA), Franks (AZ), Gohmert (TX), Jordan (OH), Poe (TX), Chaffetz (UT), Rooney (FL), Harper (MS)

SUBCOMMITTEES

COMMERCIAL & ADMINISTRATIVE LAW
Majority (D 9): Cohen, Chmn; Delahunt, Watt, Sherman, Maffei, Lofgren, Johnson, Scott, Conyers
Minority (R 6): Franks, RMM; Jordan, Coble, Issa, Forbes, King

CONSTITUTION, CIVIL RIGHTS & CIVIL LIBERTIES
Majority (D 10): Nadler, Chmn; Watt, Scott, Delahunt, Johnson, Baldwin, Conyers, Cohen, Sherman, Jackson Lee
Minority (R 6): Sensenbrenner, RMM; Rooney, King, Franks, Gohmert, Jordan

COURTS & COMPETITION POLICY
Majority (D 9): Johnson, Chmn; Conyers, Boucher, Wexler, Gonzalez, Jackson Lee, Watt, Sherman, Quigley
Minority (R 6): Coble, RMM; Chaffetz, Sensenbrenner, Goodlatte, Issa, Harper

CRIME, TERRORISM & HOMELAND SECURITY
Majority (D 10): Scott, Chmn; Pierluisi, Nadler, Lofgren, Jackson Lee, Waters, Cohen, Weiner, Wasserman Schultz, Quigley
Minority (R 6): Gohmert, RMM; Poe, Goodlatte, Lungren, Forbes, Rooney

IMMIGRATION, CITIZENSHIP, BORDER SECURITY & INTERNATIONAL LAW
Majority (D 10): Lofgren, Chmn; Berman, Jackson Lee, Waters, Pierluisi, Gutierrez, Sánchez, Weiner, Gonzalez, Delahunt
Minority (R 6): King, RMM; Harper, Gallegly, Lungren, Poe, Chaffetz

TASK FORCE ON JUDICIAL IMPEACHMENT
Majority (D 7): Schiff, Chmn; Jackson Lee, Delahunt, Cohen, Johnson, Gonzalez, Pierluisi
Minority (R 5): Goodlatte, Chmn; Lungren, Forbes, Gohmert, Sensenbrenner

NATURAL RESOURCES
resourcescommittee.house.gov

1324 Longworth
202-225-6065

Majority (D 29): Rahall (WV), Chmn; Kildee (MI), Faleomavaega (AS), Abercrombie (HI), Pallone (NJ), Napolitano (CA), Holt (NJ), Grijalva (AZ), Bordallo (GU), Costa (CA), Boren (OK), Sablan (MP), Heinrich (NM), George Miller (CA), Markey (MA), DeFazio (OR), Hinchey (NY), Christensen (VI), DeGette (CO), Kind (WI), Capps (CA), Inslee (WA), Baca (CA), Herseth Sandlin (SD), Sarbanes (MD), Shea-Porter (NH), Tsongas (MA), Kratovil (MD), Pierluisi (PR)

Minority (R 20): Hastings (WA), RMM; Young (AK), Gallegly (CA), Duncan (TN), Flake (AZ), Brown (SC), McMorris Rodgers (WA), Gohmert (TX), Bishop (UT), Shuster (PA), Lamborn (CO), Smith (NE), Wittman (VA), Broun (GA), Fleming (LA), Coffman (CO), Chaffetz (UT), Lummis (WY), McClintock (CA), Cassidy (LA)

SUBCOMMITTEES

ENERGY & MINERAL RESOURCES
Majority (D 10): Costa, Chmn; Faleomavaega, Holt, Boren, Sablan, Heinrich, Markey, Hinchey, Sarbanes, Tsongas
Minority (R 6): Lamborn, RMM; Young, Gohmert, Fleming, Chaffetz, Lummis

INSULAR AFFAIRS, OCEANS & WILDLIFE
Majority (D 13): Bordallo, Chmn; Kildee, Faleomavaega, Abercrombie, Pallone, Sablan, Christensen, DeGette, Kind, Capps, Shea-Porter, Kratovil, Pierluisi
Minority (R 8): Brown, RMM; Young, Flake, Lamborn, Wittman, Fleming, Chaffetz, Cassidy

NATIONAL PARKS, FORESTS & PUBLIC LANDS
Majority (D 20): Grijalva, Chmn; Kildee, Abercrombie, Napolitano, Holt, Bordallo, Boren, Heinrich, DeFazio, Hinchey, Christensen, DeGette, Kind, Capps, Inslee, Herseth Sandlin, Sarbanes, Shea-Porter, Tsongas, Pierluisi
Minority (R 13): Bishop, RMM; Young, Gallegly, Duncan, Flake, Brown, Gohmert, Shuster, Wittman, Broun, Coffman, Lummis, McClintock

WATER & POWER
Majority (D 7): Napolitano, Chmn; Miller, Grijalva, Costa, DeFazio, Inslee, Baca
Minority (R 4): McClintock, RMM; McMorris Rodgers, Smith, Coffman

OVERSIGHT & GOVERNMENT REFORM
oversight.house.gov

2157 Rayburn
202-225-5051

Majority (D 24): Towns (NY), Chmn; Kanjorski (PA), Maloney (NY), Cummings (MD), Kucinich (OH), Tierney (MA), Clay (MO), Watson (CA), Lynch (MA), Cooper (TN), Connolly (VA), Quigley (IL), Kaptur (OH), Norton (DC), Kennedy (RI), Davis (IL), Van Hollen (MD), Cuellar (TX), Hodes (NH), Murphy (CT), Welch (VT), Foster (IL), Speier (CA), Driehaus (OH)

Minority (R 15): Issa (CA), RMM; Burton (IN), McHugh (NY), Mica (FL), Souder (IN), Duncan (TN), Turner (OH), Westmoreland (GA), McHenry (NC), Bilbray (CA), Jordan (OH), Flake (AZ), Fortenberry (NE), Chaffetz (UT), Schock (IL)

SUBCOMMITTEES

DOMESTIC POLICY
Majority (D 9): Kucinich, Chmn; Cummings, Tierney, Watson, Cooper, Kennedy, Welch, Foster, Kaptur
Minority (R 6): Jordan, RMM; Souder, Burton, Turner, Fortenberry, Schock

FEDERAL WORKFORCE, POSTAL SERVICE & THE DISTRICT OF COLUMBIA
Majority (D 7): Lynch, Chmn; Norton, Davis, Cummings, Kucinich, Clay, Connolly
Minority (R 4): Chaffetz, RMM; McHugh, Souder, Bilbray

GOVERNMENT MANAGEMENT, ORGANIZATION & PROCUREMENT
Majority (D 9): Watson, Chmn; Kanjorski, Cooper, Connolly, Cuellar, Speier, Hodes, Murphy, Quigley
Minority (R 4): Bilbray, RMM; Schock, Duncan, Flake

INFORMATION POLICY, CENSUS & NATIONAL ARCHIVES
Majority (D 7): Clay, Chmn; Kanjorski, Maloney, Norton, Davis, Driehaus, Watson
Minority (R 4): McHenry, RMM; Westmoreland, Mica, Chaffetz

NATIONAL SECURITY & FOREIGN AFFAIRS
Majority (D 12): Tierney, Chmn; Maloney, Kennedy, Van Hollen, Hodes, Murphy, Welch, Foster, Driehaus, Lynch, Cuellar, Kucinich
Minority (R 9): Flake, RMM; Burton, Mica, Duncan, Turner, Westmoreland, McHenry, Jordan, Fortenberry

RULES

H-312 Capitol
202-225-9091
www.rules.house.gov

Majority (D 9): Slaughter (NY), Chmn; McGovern (MA), Hastings (FL), Matsui (CA), Cardoza (CA), Arcuri (NY), Perlmutter (CO), Pingree (ME), Polis (CO)
Minority (R 4): Dreier (CA), RMM; Lincoln Diaz-Balart (FL), Sessions (TX), Foxx (NC)

SUBCOMMITTEES

LEGISLATIVE & BUDGET PROCESS
Majority (D 5): Hastings, Chmn; Cardoza, Pingree, Polis, Slaughter
Minority (R 2): Diaz-Balart, RMM; Dreier

RULES & ORGANIZATION OF THE HOUSE
Majority (D 5): McGovern, Chmn; Matsui, Arcuri, Perlmutter, Slaughter
Minority (R 2): Sessions, RMM; Foxx

SCIENCE & TECHNOLOGY

2321 Rayburn
202-225-6375
science.house.gov

Majority (D 26): Gordon (TN), Chmn; Costello (IL), Bernice Johnson (TX), Woolsey (CA), Wu (OR), Baird (WA), Miller (NC), Lipinski (IL), Giffords (AZ), Edwards (MD), Fudge (OH), Luján (NM), Tonko (NY), Griffith (AL), Rothman (NJ), Matheson (UT), Davis (TN), Chandler (KY), Carnahan (MO), Hill (IN), Mitchell (AZ), Wilson (OH), Dahlkemper (PA), Grayson (FL), Kosmas (FL), Peters (MI)
Minority (R 17): Hall (TX), RMM; Sensenbrenner (WI), Smith (TX), Rohrabacher (CA), Bartlett (MD), Ehlers (MI), Lucas (OK), Biggert (IL), Akin (MO), Neugebauer (TX), Inglis (SC), McCaul (TX), Mario Diaz-Balart (FL), Bilbray (CA), Smith (NE), Broun (GA), Olson (TX)

SUBCOMMITTEES

ENERGY & ENVIRONMENT
Majority (D 12): Baird, Chmn; Tonko; Costello, Woolsey, Edwards, Luján, Johnson, Lipinski, Giffords, Matheson, Davis, Chandler
Minority (R 7): Inglis, RMM; Bartlett, Ehlers, Biggert, Akin, Neugebauer, Diaz-Balart

INVESTIGATIONS & OVERSIGHT
Majority (D 6): Miller, Chmn; Dahlkemper; Rothman, Davis, Wilson, Grayson
Minority (R 2): Broun, RMM; Bilbray

RESEARCH & SCIENCE EDUCATION
Majority (D 7): Lipinski, Chmn; Fudge; Johnson, Baird, Griffith, Tonko, Carnahan
Minority (R 4): Ehlers, RMM; Neugebauer, Bilbray, Inglis

SPACE & AERONAUTICS
Majority (D 10): Giffords, Chmn; Edwards; Fudge, Griffith, Wu, Rothman, Hill, Wilson, Grayson, Kosmas
Minority (R 5): Olson, RMM; Sensenbrenner, Rohrabacher, Lucas, McCaul

TECHNOLOGY & INNOVATION
Majority (D 7): Wu, Chmn; Luján; Edwards, Tonko, Lipinski, Mitchell, Peters
Minority (R 4): Smith (NE), RMM; Biggert, Akin, Broun

SMALL BUSINESS

2361 Rayburn
202-225-4038
www.house.gov/smbiz

Majority (D 17): Velázquez (NY), Chmn; Moore (KS), Shuler (NC), Dahlkemper (PA), Schrader (OR), Kirkpatrick (AZ), Nye (VA), Michaud (ME), Bean (IL), Lipinski (IL), Altmire (PA), Clarke (NY), Ellsworth (IN), Sestak (PA), Bright (AL), Griffith (AL), Halvorson (IL)
Minority (R 12): Graves (MO), RMM; Bartlett (MD), Akin (MO), King (IA), Westmoreland (GA), Gohmert (TX), Fallin (OK), Buchanan (FL), Luetkemeyer (MO), Schock (IL), Thompson (PA), Coffman (CO)

SUBCOMMITTEES

CONTRACTING & TECHNOLOGY
Majority (D 8): Nye, Chmn; Clarke, Ellsworth, Schrader, Halvorson, Bean, Sestak, Griffith
Minority (R 5): Schock, RMM; Bartlett, Akin, Fallin, Thompson

FINANCE & TAX
Majority (D 8): Schrader, Chmn; Moore, Kirkpatrick, Bean, Sestak, Halvorson, Nye, Michaud
Minority (R 5): Buchanan, RMM; King, Akin, Luetkemeyer, Coffman

INVESTIGATIONS & OVERSIGHT
Majority (D 4): Altmire, Chmn; Shuler, Ellsworth, Griffith
Minority (R 2): Fallin, RMM; Gohmert

REGULATIONS & HEALTHCARE
Majority (D 7): Dahlkemper, Chmn; Lipinski, Griffith, Bean, Altmire, Sestak, Bright
Minority (R 5): Westmoreland, RMM; King, Buchanan, Thompson, Coffman

RURAL DEVELOPMENT, ENTREPRENEURSHIP & TRADE
Majority (D 6): Shuler, Chmn; Michaud, Bright, Dahlkemper, Kirkpatrick, Clarke
Minority (R 4): Luetkemeyer, RMM; King, Schock, Thompson

STANDARDS OF OFFICIAL CONDUCT
ethics.house.gov
HT-2 Capitol
202-225-7103
Majority (D 5): Lofgren (CA), Chmn; Chandler (KY), Butterfield (NC), Castor (FL), Welch (VT)
Minority (R 5): Bonner (AL), RMM; Barrett (SC), Conaway (TX), Dent (PA), Harper (MS)

TRANSPORTATION & INFRASTRUCTURE
transportation.house.gov
2165 Rayburn
202-225-4472
Majority (D 44): Oberstar (MN), Chmn; Rahall (WV), DeFazio (OR), Costello (IL), Norton (DC), Nadler (NY), Brown (FL), Filner (CA), Bernice Johnson (TX), Taylor (MS), Cummings (MD), Boswell (IA), Holden (PA), Baird (WA), Larsen (WA), Capuano (MA), Bishop (NY), Michaud (ME), Carnahan (MO), Napolitano (CA), Lipinski (IL), Hirono (HI), Altmire (PA), Walz (MN), Shuler (NC), Arcuri (NY), Mitchell (AZ), Carney (PA), Hall (NY), Kagen (WI), Cohen (TN), Richardson (CA), Sires (NJ), Edwards (MD), Ortiz (TX), Hare (IL), Boccieri (OH), Schauer (MI), Markey (CO), Griffith (AL), McMahon (NY), Perriello (VA), Titus (NV), Teague (NM)
Minority (R 30): Mica (FL), RMM; Young (AK), Petri (WI), Coble (NC), Duncan (TN), Ehlers (MI), LoBiondo (NJ), Moran (KS), Gary Miller (CA), Brown (SC), Johnson (IL), Platts (PA), Graves (MO), Shuster (PA), Boozman (AR), Capito (WV), Gerlach (PA), Mario Diaz-Balart (FL), Dent (PA), Mack (FL), Westmoreland (GA), Schmidt (OH), Miller (MI), Fallin (OK), Buchanan (FL), Latta (OH), Guthrie (KY), Cao (LA), Schock (IL), Olson (TX)

SUBCOMMITTEES

AVIATION
Majority (D 24): Costello, Chmn; Carnahan, Griffith, McMahon, DeFazio, Norton, Filner, Johnson, Boswell, Holden, Capuano, Lipinski, Hirono, Mitchell, Hall, Cohen, Richardson, Boccieri, Rahall, Brown, Cummings, Altmire, Ortiz, Schauer
Minority (R 17): Petri, RMM; Coble, Duncan, Ehlers, LoBiondo, Moran, Graves, Boozman, Capito, Gerlach, Dent, Mack, Westmoreland, Schmidt, Fallin, Buchanan, Guthrie

COAST GUARD & MARITIME TRANSPORTATION
Majority (D 9): Cummings, Chmn; Brown, Larsen, Taylor, Baird, Bishop, Kagen, McMahon, Richardson
Minority (R 6): LoBiondo, RMM; Young, Coble, Ehlers, Platts, Olson

ECONOMIC DEVELOPMENT, PUBLIC BUILDINGS & EMERGENCY MANAGEMENT
Majority (D 11): Norton, Chmn; Markey, Michaud, Shuler, Griffith, Carnahan, Walz, Arcuri, Carney, Edwards, Perriello
Minority (R 7): Diaz-Balart, RMM; Johnson, Graves, Capito, Fallin, Guthrie, Cao

HIGHWAYS & TRANSIT
Majority (D 31): DeFazio, Chmn; Rahall, Nadler, Filner, Holden, Baird, Capuano, Bishop, Michaud, Napolitano, Lipinski, Hirono, Altmire, Walz, Shuler, Arcuri, Mitchell, Carney, Cohen, Richardson, Sires, Edwards, Taylor, Boswell, Larsen, Hall, Kagen, Ortiz, Hare, Boccieri, Schauer
Minority (R 22): Duncan, RMM; Young, Petri, Coble, Moran, Miller (CA), Brown, Johnson, Platts, Shuster, Boozman, Capito, Gerlach, Diaz-Balart, Dent, Mack, Schmidt, Miller (MI), Fallin, Buchanan, Latta, Schock

RAILROADS, PIPELINES & HAZARDOUS MATERIALS
Majority (D 26): Brown, Chmn; Titus, Teague, Rahall, Nadler, Cummings, Napolitano, Altmire, Walz, Arcuri, Carney, Sires, Schauer, Markey, McMahon, Perriello, DeFazio, Costello, Filner, Johnson, Boswell, Larsen, Michaud, Lipinski, Cohen, Richardson
Minority (R 18): Shuster, RMM; Petri, Moran, Miller (CA), Brown, Johnson, Graves, Gerlach, Dent, Westmoreland, Schmidt, Miller (MI), Buchanan, Latta, Guthrie, Schock, Cao, Olson

WATER RESOURCES & ENVIRONMENT
Majority (D 22): Johnson, Chmn; Perriello, Costello, Taylor, Baird, Bishop, Carnahan, Kagen, Edwards, Ortiz, Hare, Titus, Teague, Norton, Capuano, Napolitano, Hirono, Mitchell, Hall, Griffith, Filner, Brown
Minority (R 16): Boozman, RMM; Young, Duncan, Ehlers, LoBiondo, Miller (CA), Brown, Platts, Shuster, Diaz-Balart, Mack, Westmoreland, Miller (MI), Latta, Cao, Olson

VETERANS' AFFAIRS

335 Cannon
202-225-9756

veterans.house.gov
Majority (D 18): Filner (CA), Chmn; Brown (FL), Snyder (AR), Michaud (ME), Herseth Sandlin (SD), Mitchell (AZ), Hall (NY), Halvorson (IL), Perriello (VA), Teague (NM), Rodriguez (TX), Donnelly (IN), McNerney (CA), Space (OH), Walz (MN), Adler (NJ), Kirkpatrick (AZ), Nye (VA)
Minority (R 11): Buyer (IN), RMM; Stearns (FL), Moran (KS), Brown (SC), Miller (FL), Boozman (AR), Bilbray (CA), Lamborn (CO), Bilirakis (FL), Buchanan (FL), Roe (TN)

SUBCOMMITTEES

DISABILITY ASSISTANCE & MEMORIAL AFFAIRS
Majority (D 5): Hall, Chmn; Halvorson, Donnelly, Rodriguez, Kirkpatrick
Minority (R 3): Lamborn, RMM; Miller, Bilbray

ECONOMIC OPPORTUNITY
Majority (D 5): Herseth Sandlin, Chmn; Perriello, Adler, Kirkpatrick, Teague
Minority (R 3): Boozman, RMM; Moran, Bilirakis

HEALTH
Majority (D 10): Michaud, Chmn; Brown, Snyder, Teague, Rodriguez, Donnelly, McNerney, Nye, Halvorson, Perriello
Minority (R 6): Brown, RMM; Stearns, Moran, Boozman, Bilirakis, Buchanan

OVERSIGHT & INVESTIGATIONS
Majority (D 5): Mitchell, Chmn; Space, Walz, Adler, Hall
Minority (R 3): Roe, RMM; Stearns, Bilbray

WAYS & MEANS

1102 Longworth
202-225-3625

waysandmeans.house.gov
Majority (D 26): Rangel (NY), Chmn; Stark (CA), Levin (MI), McDermott (WA), Lewis (GA), Neal (MA), Tanner (TN), Becerra (CA), Doggett (TX), Pomeroy (ND), Thompson (CA), Larson (CT), Blumenauer (OR), Kind (WI), Pascrell (NJ), Crowley (NY), Van Hollen (MD), Meek (FL), Schwartz (PA), Davis (AL), Davis (IL), Etheridge (NC), Linda Sánchez (CA), Higgins (NY), Yarmuth (KY)
Minority (R 15): Camp (MI), RMM; Herger (CA), Sam Johnson (TX), Brady (TX), Ryan (WI), Cantor (VA), Linder (GA), Nunes (CA), Tiberi (OH), Brown-Waite (FL), Davis (KY), Reichert (WA), Boustany (LA), Heller (NV), Roskam (IL)

SUBCOMMITTEES

HEALTH
Majority (D 9): Stark, Chmn; Doggett, Thompson, Becerra, Pomeroy, Kind, Blumenauer, Pascrell, Berkley
Minority (R 5): Herger, RMM; Johnson, Ryan, Nunes, Brown-Waite

INCOME SECURITY & FAMILY SUPPORT
Majority (D 9): McDermott, Chmn; Stark, Davis (AL), Lewis, Berkley, Van Hollen, Meek, Levin, Davis (IL)
Minority (R 5): Linder, RMM; Boustany, Heller, Roskam, Tiberi

OVERSIGHT
Majority (D 9): Lewis, Chmn; Becerra, Kind, Pascrell, Larson, Davis (AL), Davis (IL), Etheridge, Higgins
Minority (R 5): Boustany, RMM; Reichert, Roskam, Ryan, Linder

SELECT REVENUE MEASURES
Majority (D 9): Neal, Chmn; Thompson, Larson, Schwartz, Blumenauer, Crowley, Meek, Higgins, Yarmuth
Minority (R 5): Tiberi, RMM; Linder, Heller, Roskam, Davis

SOCIAL SECURITY
Majority (D 9): Tanner, Chmn; Pomeroy, Schwartz, Becerra, Doggett, Kind, Crowley, Sánchez, Yarmuth
Minority (R 5): Johnson, RMM; Brady, Tiberi, Brown-Waite, Reichert

TRADE
Majority (D 9): Levin, Chmn; Tanner, Van Hollen, McDermott, Neal, Doggett, Pomeroy, Etheridge, Sánchez
Minority (R 5): Brady, RMM; Davis, Reichert, Herger, Nunes

JOINT COMMITTEES

JOINT COMMITTEE ON TAXATION
www.jct.gov
1015 Longworth
202-225-3621
House (5): Rangel (NY), Chmn; Stark (CA), Levin (MI), Camp (MI), Herger (CA)
Senate (5): Baucus (MT), V Chmn; Rockefeller (WV), Conrad (ND), Grassley (IA), RMM; Hatch (UT)

JOINT ECONOMIC COMMITTEE
jec.senate.gov
G-01 Dirksen
202-224-5171
House (10): Maloney (NY), Chmn; Hinchey (NY), Hill (IN), Loretta Sanchez (CA), Cummings (MD), Snyder (AR), Brady (TX), RMM; Paul (TX), Burgess (TX), Campbell (CA)
Senate (10): Schumer (NY), V Chmn; Kennedy (MA), Bingaman (NM), Klobuchar (MN), Casey (PA), Webb (VA), Brownback (KS), RMM; DeMint (SC), Risch (ID), Bennett (UT)

INDEX

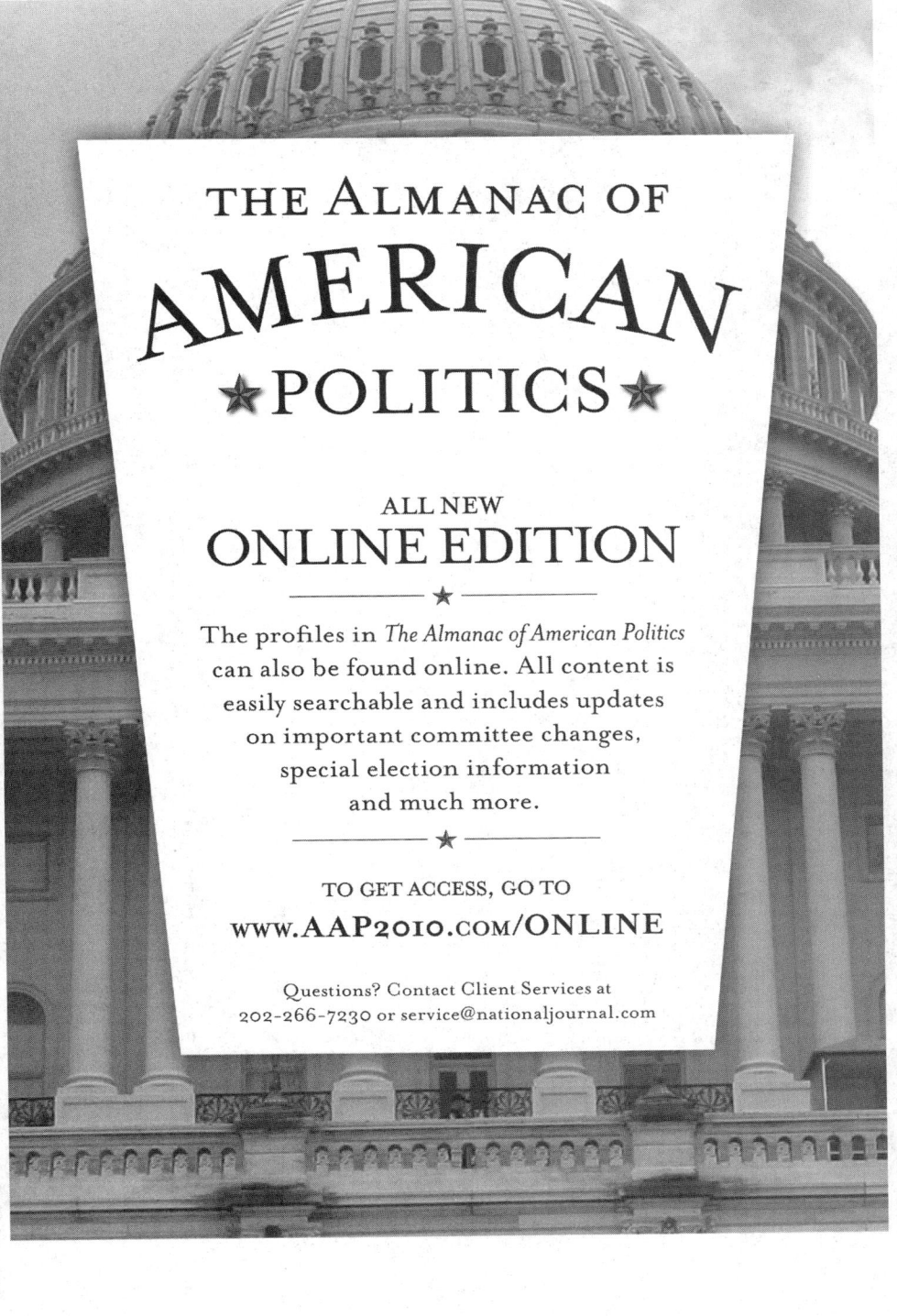

THE AUTHORS

Michael Barone is the senior political analyst for the *Washington Examiner* and a Fox News Channel contributor. He is also a resident fellow at the American Enterprise Institute. The *Chicago Tribune* says, "Michael Barone is to politics what statistician-writer Bill James is to baseball, a mix of historian, social observer, and numbers cruncher who illuminates his subject with perspective and a touch of irreverence." His most recent book is *Our First Revolution: The Remarkable British Upheaval That Inspired America's Founding Fathers*, published by Random House in 2007.

Richard E. Cohen has written about Congress and national politics for *National Journal* magazine in Washington, D.C., since 1977. He is a past winner of the annual Everett McKinley Dirksen Award for distinguished reporting on Congress. Cohen has also written several books about Congress, including *Rostenkowski: The Pursuit of Power and the End of the Old Politics*, published in 1999, and *Changing Course in Washington: Clinton and the New Congress*, published in 1994.

THE PUBLISHER

Since 1969, National Journal Group has provided "insight for insiders" through nonpartisan publications that cover the power players in Congress, the executive branch, the lobbying world, and beyond.

This 2010 edition of *The Almanac of American Politics* marks the fourteenth volume to be published by National Journal Group.

In addition to the *Almanac*, National Journal Group properties include *National Journal*, *CongressDaily*, *The Hotline* and *NationalJournal.com*.

Washington, D.C.

600 New Hampshire Ave., NW, Washington, DC 20037 Telephone (202) 739-8400